The Form Book ®

FLAT ANNUAL FOR 2011

THE OFFICIAL FORM BOOK

ALL THE 2010 RETURNS

Complete record of Flat Racing
from 1 January to 31 December 2010

Raceform

Associated Raceform products

The Form Book, is updated weekly. Subscribers receive a b·der, together with all the early racing. Weekly sections and a nev index are threaded into the binder to keep it up to date.

The data contained in The Form Book Flat Annual · 2011 is available in paper form or on computer disk. The ·sk service, Raceform Interactive, contains the same data as Race·m, The Form Book, and operates on any PC within a 'Windows' ·ironment. The database is designed to allow access to the inforr·on in a number of different ways, and is extremely quick and eas· use.

Publis·d in 2011 by Raceform Ltd
Comptc· Newbury, Berkshire, RG20 6NL

A catalogue record for this book is available from the British Library,

ISBN 978-1-906820-62-6

Printed and bound in the UK by Polestar Wheatons, Exeter

Full details of all Raceform services and publications are available from:

Raceform Ltd, Compton, Newbury, Berkshire RG20 6NL
Tel: 01933 304858 • Fax: 01933 270300
Email: rfsubscription@racingpost.co.uk
www.racingpost.com

Cover photo: Stable companions Dick Turpin (left) and Canford Cliffs contest a close finish to the Bathwick Tyres Greenham Stakes at Newbury (April 2010)
© Edward Whitaker/Racing Post

CONTENTS

Editor: Graham Dench

Head of Analysis Team: Ashley Rumney

Race Analysts & Notebook Writers:
Gavin Beech, Dave Bellingham, Mark Brown, Steffan Edwards,
Walter Glynn, Jeremy Grayson, Niall Hannity, David Lawrence,
Richard Lowther, Lee McKenzie, Tim Mitchell,
Dave Moon, Graeme North, Sandra Noble, David Orton,
Ashley Rumney, Anthony Rushmer, Andrew Sheret,
Steve Taylor, David Toft, Ron Wood, Richard Young.

Production: Ashley Rumney & Richard Lowther

The Official Scale of Weight, Age & Distance (Flat)

The following scale should only be used in conjunction with the Official ratings published in this book. Use of any other scale will introduce errors into calculations. The allowances are expressed as the number of pounds that is deemed the average horse in each group falls short of maturity at different dates and distances.

Dist		Jan		Feb		Mar		Apr		May		Jun		Jul		Aug		Sep		Oct		Nov		Dec	
(fur)	Age	1-15	16-31	1-14	15-28	1-15	16-31	1-15	16-30	1-15	16-31	1-15	16-30	1-15	16-31	1-15	16-31	1-15	16-30	1-15	16-31	1-15	16-30	1-15	16-31
5	2	-	-	-	-	-	47	44	41	38	36	34	32	30	28	26	24	22	20	19	18	17	17	16	16
	3	15	15	14	14	13	12	11	10	9	8	7	6	5	4	3	2	1	1	-	-	-	-	-	-
6	2	-	-	-	-	-	-	-	-	44	41	38	36	33	31	28	26	24	22	21	20	19	18	17	17
	3	16	16	15	15	14	13	12	11	10	9	8	7	6	5	4	3	2	2	1	1	-	-	-	-
7	2	-	-	-	-	-	-	-	-	-	-	-	-	38	35	32	30	27	25	23	22	21	20	19	19
	3	18	18	17	17	16	15	14	13	12	11	10	9	8	7	6	5	4	3	2	2	1	1	-	-
8	2	-	-	-	-	-	-	-	-	-	-	-	-	-	-	37	34	31	28	26	24	23	22	21	20
	3	20	20	19	19	18	17	15	14	13	12	11	10	9	8	7	6	5	4	3	3	2	2	1	1
9	3	22	22	21	21	20	19	17	15	14	13	12	11	10	9	8	7	6	5	4	4	3	3	2	2
	4	1	1	-	-	-	-	-	-	-	-	-	-	-	-	-	-	-	-	-	-	-	-	-	-
10	3	23	23	22	22	21	20	19	17	15	14	13	12	11	10	9	8	7	6	5	5	4	4	3	3
	4	2	2	1	1	-	-	-	-	-	-	-	-	-	-	-	-	-	-	-	-	-	-	-	-
11	3	24	24	23	23	22	21	20	19	17	15	14	13	12	11	10	9	8	7	6	6	5	5	4	4
	4	3	3	2	2	1	1	-	-	-	-	-	-	-	-	-	-	-	-	-	-	-	-	-	-
12	3	25	25	24	24	23	22	21	20	19	17	15	14	13	12	11	10	9	8	7	7	6	6	5	5
	4	4	4	3	3	2	2	1	1	-	-	-	-	-	-	-	-	-	-	-	-	-	-	-	-
13	3	26	26	25	25	24	23	22	21	20	19	17	15	14	13	12	11	10	9	8	8	7	7	6	6
	4	5	5	4	4	3	3	2	1	-	-	-	-	-	-	-	-	-	-	-	-	-	-	-	-
14	3	27	27	26	26	25	24	23	22	21	20	19	17	15	14	13	12	11	10	9	9	8	8	7	7
	4	6	6	5	5	4	4	3	2	1	-	-	-	-	-	-	-	-	-	-	-	-	-	-	-
15	3	28	28	27	27	26	25	24	23	22	21	20	19	17	15	14	13	12	11	10	9	8	8	7	7
	4	6	6	5	5	4	4	3	3	2	1	-	-	-	-	-	-	-	-	-	-	-	-	-	-
16	3	29	29	28	28	27	26	25	24	23	22	21	20	19	17	15	14	13	12	11	10	9	9	8	8
	4	7	7	6	6	5	5	4	4	3	2	1	-	-	-	-	-	-	-	-	-	-	-	-	-
18	3	31	31	30	30	29	28	27	26	25	24	23	22	21	20	18	16	14	13	12	11	10	10	9	9
	4	8	8	7	7	6	6	5	5	4	3	2	1	-	-	-	-	-	-	-	-	-	-	-	-
20	3	33	33	32	32	31	30	29	28	27	26	25	24	23	22	20	18	16	14	13	12	11	11	10	10
	4	9	9	8	8	7	7	6	6	5	4	3	2	1	-	-	-	-	-	-	-	-	-	-	-

The Form Book

Welcome to the 2011 edition of *The Form Book,* comprising the complete year's results from 2010.

Race details contain Racing Post Ratings assessing the merit of each individual performance, speed figures for every horse that clocks a worthwhile time, weight-for-age allowances, stall positions for every race and the starting price percentage, in addition to the traditional features.

Race Focus comments are printed below each race along with official explanations and notebook comments for all British races of Class 3 and above, all two-year-old races and foreign races. The comments provide an analysis of the winning performance and, where applicable, explain possible reasons for improvement or attempt to explain why any horse failed to run to its best. More importantly, our team will also indicate the conditions under which horses are likely to be seen to best advantage.

The official record

THE FORM BOOK records comprehensive race details of every domestic race, every major European Group race and every foreign event in which a British-trained runner participated. In the **NOTEBOOK** section, extended interpretation is provided for all runners worthy of a mention, including all placed horses and all favourites. Generally speaking, the higher the class of race, the greater the number of runners noted.

MEETING BACK REFERENCE NUMBER is the Raceform number of the last meeting run at the track and is shown to the left of the course name. Abandoned meetings are signified by a dagger.

THE GOING, The Official going, shown at the head of each meeting, is recorded as follows: Turf: Hard; Firm; Good to firm; Good; Good to soft; Soft; Heavy. All-Weather: Fast; Standard to fast; Standard; Standard to slow; Slow. There may be variations for non-British meetings

Where appropriate, a note is included indicating track bias and any differences to the official going indicated by race times.

THE WEATHER is shown below to th e date for selected meetings.

THE WIND is given as a strength and direction at the Winning Post, classified as follows:
Strength: gale; v.str; str; fresh; mod; slt; almost nil; nil.
Direction: (half) against; (half) bhd; (half) across from or towards stands.

VISIBILITY is good unless otherwise stated.

RACE NUMBERS for Foreign races carry the suffix 'a' in the race header and in the index.

RACE TITLE is the name of the race as shown in the Racing Calendar.

COMPETITIVE RACING CLASSIFICATIONS are shown on a scale from Class 1 to Class 7. All Pattern races are Class 1.

THE RACE DISTANCE is given for all races, and is accompanied by (s) for races run on straight courses and (r) for courses where there is a round track of comparable distance. On All-Weather courses (F) for Fibresand or (P) for Polytrack indicates the nature of the artificial surface on which the race is run.

OFFICIAL RACE TIME as published in the Racing Calendar is followed in parentheses by the time when the race actually started. This is followed by the race class, age restrictions, handicap restrictions and the official rating of the top weight.

PRIZE MONEY shows penalty values down to sixth place (where applicable).

THE POSITION OF THE STARTING STALLS is shown against each race, in the form of: High (H), Centre (C) or Low (L). If one stands at the start facing towards the finish, the stalls are numbered from left to right. If the stalls are placed adjacent to the left rail they are described as low, if against the right rail they are described as high. Otherwise they are central.

IN THE RACE RESULT, the figures to the far left of each horse (under FORM) show the most recent form figures. The figure in bold is the finishing position in this race as detailed below.

1...40 - finishing positions first to fortieth; **b** - brought down; **c** - carried out; **f** - fell; **p** - pulled up; **r** - refused; **ro** - ran out; **s** - slipped up; **u** - unseated rider; **v** - void race.

THE OFFICIAL DISTANCES between the horses are shown on the left-hand side immediately after their position at the finish.

NUMBER OF DAYS SINCE PREVIOUS RUN is the superscript figure immediately following the horse name and suffix.

PREVIOUS RACEFORM RACE NUMBER is the boxed figure to the right of the horse's name.

THE HORSE'S AGE is shown immediately before the weight carried.

WEIGHTS shown are actual weights carried.

OFFICIAL RATING is the figure in bold type directly after the horse's name in the race result. This figure indicates the Official BHB rating, at entry, after the following adjustments had been made:
(i) Overweight carried by the rider.
(ii) The number of pounds out of the handicap (if applicable).
(iii) Penalties incurred after the publication of the weights.
However, no adjustments have been made for:
(i) Weight-for-age.
(ii) Riders' claims.

HEADGEAR is shown immediately befoe the jockey's name and in parentheses and expressed as: **b** (blinkers); **v** (visor); **h** (hood); **e** (eyeshield); **c** (eyecover); **p** (sheepskin cheekpieces).

THE JOCKEY is shown for every runner followed, in superscript, by apprentice allowances in parentheses.

APPRENTICE ALLOWANCES The holders of apprentice jockeys' licences under the provisions of Rule 60(iii) are permitted to claim the following allowances in Flat races:
7lb until they have won 20 Flat races run under the Rules of any recognised Turf Authority; thereafter 5lb until they have won 50 such Flat races; thereafter 3lb until they have won 95 such Flat races. These allowances can be claimed in the Flat races set out below, with the exception of races confined to apprentice jockeys:
(a) All handicap handicaps other than those Rated stakes which are classified as listed races.
(b) All selling and claiming races.
(b) All weight-for-age races classified 3, 4, 5, 6 and 7.

THE DRAW for places at the start is shown after each jockey's name.

RACING POST RATINGS, which record the level of performance attained in this race for each horse, appear in the end column after each horse. These are the work of handicappers Simon Turner, Sam Walker and Paul Curtis, who head a dedicated team dealing with Flat races for Raceform and sister publication, the *Racing Post*.

THE TRAINER is shown for every runner.

COMMENT-IN-RUNNING is shown for each horse in an abbreviated form. Details of abbreviations appear later in this section.

STARTING PRICES appear below the jockey in the race result. The favourite indicator appears to the right of the Starting Price; 1 for the favourite, 2 for the second-favourite and 3 for third-favourite. Joint favourites share the same number.

RACE TIMES in Great Britain are official times which are electronically recorded and shown to 100th of a second. Figures in parentheses following the time show the number of seconds faster or slower than the Raceform Median Time for the course and distance.

RACEFORM MEDIAN TIMES are compiled from all races run over the course and distance in the preceding five years. Times equal to the median are shown as (0.00). Times under the median are preceded by minus, for instance, 1.8 seconds under the median would be shown (-1.8). Record times are displayed either referring to the juvenile record (1.2 under 2y best) or to the overall record (1.2 under best).

GOING CORRECTION appears against each race to allow for changing conditions of the ground. It is shown to a hundredth of a second and indicates the adjustment per furlong against the median time. The going based on the going correction is shown in parentheses and is recorded in the following stages:
Turf: HD (Hard); F (Firm); GF (Good to firm); G (Good); GS (Good to soft); S (Soft); HVY (Heavy). All-Weather: FST (Fast); SF (Standard to fast); STD (Standard); SS (Standard to slow); SLW (Slow)

WEIGHT-FOR-AGE allowances are given where applicable for mixed-age races.

STARTING PRICE PERCENTAGE follows the going correction and weight-for-age details, and gives the total SP percentage of all runners that competed. It precedes the number of runners taking part in the race.

SELLING DETAILS (where applicable) and details of any claim are given. Friendly claims are not detailed.

SPEED RATINGS appear below the race time and going correction. They are the work of time expert Dave Bellingham and differ from conventional ratings systems in that they are an expression of a horse's ability in terms of lengths-per-mile, as opposed to pounds in weight. They are not directly comparable with BHB and Racing Post ratings.

The ratings take no account of the effect of weight, either historically or on the day, and this component is left completely to the user's discretion. What is shown is a speed rating represented in its purest form, rather than one that has been altered for weight using a mathematical formula that treats all types of horses as if they were the same.

A comparison of the rating achieved with the 'par' figure for the grade of race - the rating that should be achievable by an average winner in that class of race- will both provide an at-a-glance indication of whether or not a race was truly run and also highlight the value of the form from a time perspective.

In theory, if a horse has a best speed figure five points superior to another and both run to their best form in a race over a mile, the first horse should beat the second by five lengths. In a race run over two miles, the margin should be ten lengths and so on.

Before the speed figures can be calculated, it is necessary to establish a set of standard or median times for every distance at every track, and this is done by averaging the times of all winners over a particular trip going back several years. No speed ratings are produced when insufficient races have been run over a distance for a reliable median time to be calculated.

Once a meeting has taken place, a raw unadjusted speed rating is calculated for each winner by calculating how many lengths per mile the winning time was faster or slower than the median for the trip. A difference of 0.2 of a second equals one length. The raw speed ratings of all winners on the card are then compared to the 'par' figure for the class of race. The difference between the 'raw' speed rating and the 'par' figure for each race is then noted, and both the fastest and slowest races are discarded before the rest are averaged to produce the going allowance or track variant. This figure gives an idea as to how much the elements, of which the going is one, have affected the final times of each race.

The figure representing the going allowance is then used to adjust the raw speed figures and produce the final ratings, which represent how fast the winners would have run on a perfectly good surface with no external influences, including the weather. The ratings for beaten horses are worked out by taking the number of lengths they were behind the winner, adjusting that to take into account the distance of the race, and deducting that figure from the winner's rating. The reader is left with a rating which provides an instant impression of the value of a time performance.

The speed 'pars' below act as benchmark with which to compare the speed figures earned by each horse in each race. A horse that has already exceeded the 'par' for the class he is about to run in, is of special interest, especially if he has done it more than once, as are horses that have consistently earned higher figures than their rivals.

Class 1 Group One	117
Class 1 Group Two	115
Class 1 Group Three	113
Class 1 Listed	111
Class 2	109
Class 3	107
Class 4	105
Class 5	103
Class 6	101
Class 7	97

Allowances need to be made for younger horses and for fillies. These allowances are as follows.

MONTH	2yo	3yo
Jan / Feb	n/a	-6
Mar / Apr	-11	-5
May / Jun	-10	-4
Jul / Aug	-9	-3
Sep / Oct	-8	-2
Nov / Dec	-7	-1
Races contested by fillies only		-3

Allowances are cumulative. For example, using a combination of the above pars and allowances, the par figure for the Epsom Oaks would be 110. The Group One par is 117, then deduct 4 because the race is confined to three year olds and run in June, then subtract another 3 because the race is confined to fillies.

TOTE prices include £1 stake. Exacta dividends are shown in parentheses. The Computer Straight Forecast dividend is preceded by the letters CSF, Computer Tricast is preceded by CT and Tote Trio dividend is preceded by the word Trio. Jackpot, Placepot and Quadpot details appear at the end of the meeting to which they refer.

OWNER is followed by the breeder's name and the trainer's location.

STEWARDS' ENQUIRIES are included with the result, and any suspensions and/or fines incurred. Objections by jockeys and officials are included, where relevant.

HISTORICAL FOCUS details occasional points of historical significance.

FOCUS The Focus section has been enhanced to help readers distinguish good races from bad races and reliable form from unreliable form, by drawing together the opinions of handicapper, time expert and paddock watcher and interpreting their views in a punter-friendly manner.

NOTEBOOK horses marked with the diamond symbol are those deemed by our racereaders especially worthy of note in future races.

OFFICIAL EXPLANATIONS, where the horse is deemed to have run well above or below expectations

Abbreviations and their meanings

Paddock comments

gd sort - well made, above average on looks
h.d.w - has done well, improved in looks
wl grwn - well grown, has filled to its frame
lengthy - longer than average for its height
tall - tall
rangy - lengthy and tall but in proportion.
cl cpld - close coupled
scope - scope for physical development
str - strong, powerful looking
w'like - workmanlike, ordinary in looks
lt-f - light-framed, not much substance
cmpt - compact
neat - smallish, well put together
leggy - long legs compared with body
angular - unfurnished behind the saddle, not filled to frame
unf - unfurnished in the midriff, not filled to frame
narrow - not as wide as side appearance would suggest
small - lacks any physical scope
nt grwn - not grown
lw - looked fit and well
bkwd - backward in condition
t - tubed
swtg - sweating
b (off fore or nr fore) - bandaged in front
b.hind (off or nr) - bandaged behind

At the start

stdd s - jockey purposely reins back the horse
dwlt - missed the break and left for a short time
s.s - slow to start, left longer than a horse that dwelt
s.v.s - started very slowly
s.i.s - started on terms but took time to get going
ref to r - either does not jump off, or travels a few yards and then stops
rel to r - tries to pull itself up in mid-race
w.r.s - whipped round start

Position in the race

led - in lead on its own
disp ld - upsides the leader

w ldr - almost upsides the leader
w ldrs - in a line of three or more disputing the lead
prom - on the heels of the leaders, in the front third of the field
trckd ldr(s) - just in behind the leaders giving impression that it could lead if asked
chsd ldr - horse in second place
chsd clr ldrs - horse heads main body of field behind two clear leaders
chsd ldrs - horse is in the first four or five but making more of an effort to stay close to the pace than if it were tracking the leaders.
clsd - closed
in tch - close enough to have a chance
hdwy - making ground on the leader
gd hdwy - making ground quickly on the leader, could be a deliberate move
sme hdwy - making some ground but no real impact on the race
w.w - waited with
stdy hdwy - gradually making ground
ev ch - upsides the leaders when the race starts in earnest
rr - at the back of main group but not detached
bhd - detached from the main body of runners
hld up - restrained as a deliberate tactical move
nt rcvr - lost all chance after interference, mistake etc.
wknd - stride shortened as it began to tire
lost tch - had been in the main body but a gap appeared as it tired
lost pl - remains in main body of runners but lost several positions quickly

Riding

effrt - short-lived effort
pushed along - received urgings with hands only, jockey not using legs
rdn - received urgings from saddle, including use of whip
hrd rdn - received maximum assistance from the saddle including use of whip
drvn - received forceful urgings, jockey putting in a lot of effort and using whip
hrd drvn - jockey very animated, plenty of kicking, pushing and reminders

Finishing comments

jst failed - closing rapidly on the winner and probably would have led a stride after the line
r.o - jockey's efforts usually involved to produce an increase in pace without finding an appreciable turn of speed
r.o wl - jockey's efforts usually involved to produce an obvious increase in pace without finding an appreciable turn of speed
unable qckn - not visibly tiring but does not possess a sufficient change of pace
one pce - not tiring but does not find a turn of speed, from a position further out than unable qckn
nt r.o. - did not consent to respond to pressure
styd on - going on well towards the end, utilising stamina
nvr able to chal - unable to produce sufficient to reach a challenging position
nvr nr to chal - in the opinion of the racereader, the horse was never in a suitable position to challenge.
nrst fin - nearer to the winner in distance beaten than at any time since the race had begun in earnest
nvr nrr - nearer to the winner position-wise than at any time since the race had begun in earnest
rallied - responded to pressure to come back with a chance having lost its place
no ex - unable to sustain its run
bttr for r - likely to improve for the run and experience
rn green - inclined to wander and falter through inexperience
too much to do - left with too much leeway to make up

Winning comments

v.easily - a great deal in hand
easily - plenty in hand
comf - something in hand, always holding the others
pushed out - kept up to its work with hands and heels without jockey resorting to whip or kicking along and wins fairly comfortably
rdn out - pushed and kicked out to the line, with the whip employed
drvn out - pushed and kicked out to the line, with considerable effort and the whip employed
all out - nothing to spare, could not have found any more
jst hld on - holding on to a rapidly diminishing lead, could not have found any more if passed
unchal - must either make all or a majority of the running and not be challenged from an early stage

Complete list of abbreviations

a - always
gng - going
qckn - quicken
a.p - always prominent
gp - group
r - race
abt - about
grad - gradually
racd - raced
appr - approaching
grnd - ground
rch - reach
awrdd - awarded
hd - head
rcvr - recover
b.b.v - broke blood-vessel
hdd - headed
rdn - ridden
b.d - brought down
hdwy - headway
rdr - rider
bdly - badly
hld - held
reard - reared
bef - before
hmpd - hampered
ref - refused
bhd - behind
imp - impression
rn - ran
bk - back
ins - inside
rnd - round
blkd - baulked
j.b - jumped badly
r.o - ran on
blnd - blundered
j.w - jumped well
rr - rear
bmpd - bumped

jnd - joined
rspnse - response
bnd - bend
jst - just
rt - right
btn- beaten
kpt - kept
s - start
bttr - better
l - length
sddle - saddle
c - came
ld - lead
shkn - shaken
ch - chance
ldr - leader
slt - slight
chal - challenged
lft - left
sme - some
chse - chase
m - mile
sn - soon
chsd - chased
m.n.s - made no show
spd- speed
chsng - chasing
mde - made
st - straight
circ - circuit
mod - moderate
stmbld - stumbled
cl - close
mid div - mid division
stdd - steadied
clr - clear
mstke - mistake
stdy - steady
clsd - closed
n.d - never dangerous
strly - strongly
comf - comfortably
n.g.t - not go through
styd - stayed
cpld - coupled
n.m.r - not much room
styng - staying
crse - course
nk - neck
s.u - slipped up
ct - caught
no ex - no extra
swtchd - switched
def - definite
nr - near
swvd - swerved
dismntd - dismounted
nrr - nearer
tk - took
disp - disputed
nrst fin - nearest finish
t.k.h - took keen hold
dist - distance
nt - not
t.o - tailed off
div - division
nvr - never
tch - touch
drvn - driven
one pce - one pace
thrght - throughout
dwlt - dwelt
out - from finish
trbld - troubled
edgd - edged
outpcd - outpaced
trckd - tracked
effrt - effort
p.u - pulled up
u.p - under pressure
ent - entering
pce - pace
u.str.p- under strong pressure
ev ch - every chance
pckd - pecked
w - with
ex - extra
pl - place
w.r.s - whipped round start
f - furlong
plcd - placed
wd - wide
fin - finished
plld - pulled
whn - when
fnd - found
press - pressure
wknd - weakened
fnl - final
prog - progress
wl - well
fr - from
prom - prominent
wnr - winner
gd - good
qckly - quickly
wnt - went
w.w - waited with
1/2-wy - halfway

Racing Post Ratings

Racing Post Ratings for each horse are shown in the right hand column, headed RPR, and indicate the actual level of performance attained in that race. The figure in the back index represents the BEST public form that Raceform's Handicappers still believe the horse capable of reproducing.

To use the ratings constructively in determining those horses best-in in future events, the following procedure should be followed:

(i) In races where all runners are the same age and are set to carry the same weight, no calculations are necessary. The horse with the highest rating is best-in.

(ii) In races where all runners are the same age but are set to carry different weights, add one point to the Raceform Rating for every pound less than 10 stone to be carried; deduct one point for every pound more than 10 stone.

For example,

Horse	Age & wt	Adjustment from 10st	Base rating	Adjusted rating
Treclare	3-10-1	-1	78	77
Buchan	3-9-13	+1	80	81
Paper Money	3-9-7	+7	71	78
Archaic	3-8-11	+17	60	77

Therefore Buchan is top-rated (best-in)

(iii) In races concerning horses of different ages the procedure in (ii) should again be followed, but reference must also be made to the Official Scale of Weight-For-Age.

For example,

12 furlongs, July 20th

Horse	Age & wt	Adjustment from 10st	Base rating	Adjusted rating	W-F-A deduct	Final rating
Orpheus	5-10-0	0	90	90	Nil	90
Lemonora	4-9-9	+5	88	88	Nil	88
Tamar	3-9-4	+10	85	95	-12	83
Craigangower	4-8-7	+21	73	94	Nil	94

Therefore Craigangower is top-rated (best-in)

(A 3-y-o is deemed 12lb less mature than a 4-y-o or older horse on 20th July over 12f. Therefore, the deduction of 12 points is necessary.)

The following symbols are used in conjunction with the ratings:

++: almost certain to prove better

+: likely to prove better

d: disappointing (has run well below best recently)

?: form hard to evaluate

t: tentative rating based on race-time rating may prove unreliable

Weight adjusted ratings for every race are published daily in Raceform Private Handicap and our new service Raceform Private handicap ONLINE (www.raceform.co.uk).

For subscription terms please contact the Subscription Department on 01933 304858.

Effect of the draw

(R.H.) denotes right-hand and (L.H.) left-hand courses.

* Draw biases shown below apply to straight-course races unless otherwise stipulated.

** Most races, outside Festival meetings, are now restricted to 20 runners, which means it's now particularly worth looking at the stalls position, as many courses can accommodate more than that number.

ASCOT (R-H) - Following extensive redevelopment there have been some pretty exaggerated draw biases. Watering often seems to be the deciding factor and far too much has been applied on more than one occasion.

STALLS: Usually go up the stands' side (low).

BIASES: One side or other was often favoured last season but the middle can also ride best, and biases remain very hard to predict.

SPLITS: Are common in big-field handicaps and occasionally will occur on soft ground in round-course races, when some head for the outside rail (covered by trees).

AYR (L-H) - Throughout the 90s high numbers were massively favoured in the Gold and Silver Cups but things have become less clear-cut since. Traditionally the centre of the course has ridden slower here but the strip is nothing like the disadvantage it once was.

STALLS: Usually go up the stands' side (high) in sprints, but occasionally go on the other side. It isn't uncommon for jockeys to switch from the far side to race down the centre or even come right across to the stands' rail.

BIASES: There's ultimately not a lot between the two sides in big fields now.

SPLITS: Are becoming more common, having only usually occurred in the Silver and Gold Cups in the past.

BATH (L-H) - The draw is of less importance than the pace at which races are run. In big fields, runners drawn low are often inclined to go off too fast to hold a rail position (the course turns left most of the way, including one major kink) and this can see hold-up horses drawn wide coming through late. Conversely, in smaller fields containing little pace, up front and on the inside is often the place to be.

STALLS: Always go on the inside (low).

SPLITS: Fields almost always stick together, but soft ground can see a split, with the outside rail (high) then favoured.

BEVERLEY (R-H) - A high draw used to be essential on good to soft or faster ground over 5f and also on the round course, particularly in races of 7f100y and 1m100y. However, things were far less clear cut last year, presumably down to watering. The course management experimented with moving stalls to the stands' side over 5f in 2002 (unsuccessfully, as it led to a huge low bias) and haven't done so since.

STALLS: Go on the inside (high) at all distances.

BIASES: High numbers are traditionally best on good to soft or faster ground but watering looked to play a big part last year.

SPLITS: Splits are rare and only likely over 5f on soft ground.

BRIGHTON (L-H) - Much depends on the going and time of year. On good to soft or slower ground runners often head for the outside rail, while in late season it's usually just a case of whichever jockey finds the least cut-up strip of ground. Otherwise, low-drawn prominent-racers tend to hold sway in fast-ground sprints, with double figures always facing an uphill task over 5f59y.

STALLS: Always go on the inside (low) in sprints.

SPLITS: These occur frequently, as jockeys look for a fresh strip on ground that seems to churn up easily.

CARLISLE (R-H) - Runners racing with the pace and hardest against the inside rail (high) do well in big fields on decent ground. This is largely down to the fact that the Flat course and NH course are one and the same, and that those racing nearest the fence are running where the hurdle wings were positioned, while those wider out are on the raced-on surface. On soft ground, the bias swings completely, with runners racing widest (low) and grabbing the stands' rail in the straight favoured at all distances.

STALLS: Normally go on the inside (high) but can go down the middle in sprints (usually on slow ground).

BIASES: High numbers are best in fast-ground sprints, but look to back low numbers on soft/heavy ground.

SPLITS: Rarely will two groups form but, on easy ground, runners often spread out.

CATTERICK (L-H) - When the ground is testing, the stands' rail is definitely the place to be, which suits high numbers in 5f races and high-drawn prominent-racers at all other distances. However, when the ground is good to firm or faster, horses drawn on the inside (low) often hold the edge, and there have been several meetings over the last few seasons in which those racing prominently hardest against the inside rail have dominated (over all distances).

STALLS: Go on the inside (low) at all distances these days (they often used to go on the outer over 5f212y).

BIASES: Low numbers are best in sprints on fast ground (particularly watered firm going) but the stands' rail (high) rides faster under slower conditions.

SPLITS: Are common over 5f on easy ground.

CHEPSTOW (L-H) - High numbers enjoyed a massive advantage in straight-course races in 2000 and the course management duly took steps to eradicate the faster strip, using the same 'earthquake' machine as had been employed at Goodwood in the late 90s. This has led to little in the way of a draw bias since.

STALLS: Always go stands' side (high) on the straight course.

BIASES: Have become hard to predict in recent times.

SPLITS: Are common and jockeys drawn low often head far side.

CHESTER (L-H) - It's well known that low numbers are favoured at all distances here, even in the 2m2f Chester Cup, and the bias is factored into the prices these days. That said sprints (and in particular handicaps) are still playable, as it often pays to stick to a runner drawn 1-3.

STALLS: Go on the inside (low) at all distances bar 1m2f75y and 2m2f117y (same starting point) when they go on the outside. Certain starters ask for the stalls to come off the inside rail slightly in sprints.

BIASES: Low numbers are favoured at all distances. Soft ground seems to accentuate the bias until a few races have been staged, when a higher draw becomes less of a disadvantage as the ground on the inside becomes chewed up.

DONCASTER (L-H) - There's been very little between the two sides since the course reopened. Jockeys now tend to swerve the stands' rail (high) on good or slower ground, instead preferring to head for the centre.

STALLS: Can go either side but tend to go up the stands' side (high) when possible.

BIASES: Runners down the centre are usually worst off. The longer the trip on the straight course the better chance the far side (low) has against the stands' side in big fields.

EPSOM (L-H) - When the going is on the soft side, jockeys tack over to the stands' side for the better ground (this strip rides quicker in such conditions as the course cambers away from the stands' rail). In 5f races, the stalls are invariably placed on the stands' side, so when the going is soft the majority of the runners are on the best ground from the outset. Prominent-racers drawn low in round-course races are able to take the shortest route around Tattenham Corner, and on faster ground have a decisive edge over 6f, 7f and 1m114y. Over 5f, high numbers used to hold quite an advantage, but the bias is not so great on fast going these days.

STALLS: Always go on the outside (high) over 5f and 6f (races over the latter trip start on a chute) and inside (low) at other distances, bar 1m4f10y (centre).

BIASES: Low-drawn prominent racers are favoured at between 6f and 1m114y.

SPLITS: Good to soft ground often leads to a few trying the stands'-side route.

FFOS LAS (L-H) - So far the evidence suggests there is no clear bias in races on the straight track, despite the stalls being placed on the stands' side. On the round course high numbers are slightly favoured.

STALLS Usually go up the stands' side (high)on the straight course.

BIASES High numbers appear to have a slight advantage, particlarly in races beyond a mile.

SPLITS As fields are not often big, splits are rare.

FOLKESTONE (R-H) - Prior to 1998, Folkestone was never thought to have much in the way of a bias, but nowadays the draw is often crucial on the straight course (up to 7f). On very soft ground, the far rail (high) rides faster than the stands' rail. However, on good to soft or faster ground runners tend to stay up the near side now (the ambulance used to go this side of the far rail but now goes the other side of the fence) and those racing on the pace hardest against the fence often enjoy a major advantage.

STALLS: Usually go up the stands' side (low) on the straight track, but occasionally down the centre.

BIASES: High numbers are favoured over 6f and 7f, and also over the minimum trip when 14 or more line up. However, very low numbers have a good record in smaller fields over 5f. Front-runners are well worth considering at all distances.

SPLITS: Often occur.

GOODWOOD (R-H) & (L-H) - The course management took steps to end the major high bias seen in the Stewards' Cup throughout the late 90s by breaking up the ground by machine in 1998. This led to the stands' side (low) dominating the race in 1999 before the far side gradually took over again.

STALLS: Invariably go on the stands' side (low).

BIASES: High numbers are best at between 7f-1m1f and the faster the ground the more pronounced the bias (keep an eye out for the rail on the home turn being moved during Glorious week, usually after the Thursday).

SPLITS: Although fields tend not to break into groups in most sprints, runners often spread out to about two-thirds of the way across in fields of around 20.

HAMILTON (R-H) - Extensive drainage work was carried out in the winter of 2002 in a bid to level up the two sides of the track but, after encouraging early results, the natural bias in favour of high numbers (far side) kicked in again. This can be altered by watering on faster going, though, and low numbers were definitely favoured under such conditions in 2008. Things were less clear cut last year, however, and jockeys more often than not headed for the centre. High numbers are best over 1m65y, thanks to runners encountering a tight right-handed loop soon after the start.

STALLS: It's not uncommon for the ground to become too soft for the use of stalls, but otherwise they go either side.

BIASES: High draws are best in soft/heavy-ground sprints, but the bias becomes middle to high otherwise (often switching to low on watered fast ground). Front-runners do particularly well at all distances.

SPLITS: Rarely happen now.

HAYDOCK (L-H) - High numbers used to enjoy a major advantage in soft-ground sprints and there were signs last year that this bias has returned. Otherwise, runners usually head for the centre these days, the draw rarely making much of a difference.

STALLS: Usually go down the centre in the straight.

KEMPTON All-Weather (R-H) - High numbers are best over 5f and preferable over 6f, while those drawn very low over 7f often have a bit to do. Otherwise, pace of races counts for a lot and this is one of the fairest courses around in that respect.

LEICESTER (R-H) - There was a four-year spell between 1998 and 2001 when the centre-to-far-side strip (middle to high) enjoyed a decisive advantage over the stands' rail, jockeys eventually choosing to avoid the near side. However, that's changed recently, with very low numbers more than holding their own.

STALLS: Invariably go up the stands' side (low).

SPLITS: Still occur occasionally.

LINGFIELD Turf (L-H) - Following a less predictable spell, the stands' rail (high) has taken over again in the past couple of years. The one factor that can have a massive effect on the draw is heavy rainfall on to firm ground. Presumably because of the undulating nature of the track and the fact that the far rail on the straight course is towards the bottom of a slope where it joins the round course, rainfall seems to make the middle and far side ride a deal slower. In these conditions, the top three or four stalls have a massive edge.

STALLS: Go up the stands' side (high) at between 5f and 7f and down the middle over 7f140y.

BIASES: High numbers favoured unless ground is genuinely soft.

SPLITS: It's unusual to see two distinct groups, but runners often fan out centre to stands' side in big fields.

LINGFIELD All-Weather (L-H) - There is little bias over most trips, but it is an advantage to be drawn low over 6f and 1m2f, with both starts being situated very close to the first bend. A low to middle draw is preferable over 5f, even with a safety limit of just ten, though the very inside stall has a poor recent record. No horse managed to win from stall 1 over that trip in 2004, which suggests the ground right against the inside rail is slower than elsewhere.

STALLS: Go against the outside rail (high) over 5f and 1m, but against the inside rail (low) for all other distances.

SPLITS: Fields never split but runners usually come wide off the home turn.

MUSSELBURGH (R-H) - The bias in favour of low numbers over 5f isn't as pronounced as many believe, apart from on soft ground, while the bias in favour of high numbers at 7f and 1m isn't that big.

STALLS: Usually go up the stands' side (low) over 5f nowadays, but they can be rotated.

SPLITS: Look out for runners drawn very high in big-field 5f races on fast ground, as they occasionally go right to the far rail.

NEWBURY (L-H) - There's basically little between the two sides these days, apart from on soft ground, in which case the stands' rail (high) is definitely the place to be. When the ground is testing it's not uncommon to see runners race wide down the back straight and down the side at between 1m3f56y and 2m (particularly over 1m5f61y). In such circumstances, a high draw becomes an advantage.

STALLS: Can go anywhere for straight-course races.

SPLITS: Are pretty rare.

NEWCASTLE (L-H) - It used to be a case of high numbers best at up to and including 7f on good or firmer, and low numbers having the advantage when the ground is good to soft or softer. However, now things depend largely on the positioning of the stands' rail. If the course is at its widest high numbers are almost always best off, while if the rail is further in things are less clear cut.

STALLS: Invariably go on the stands' side (high) and are only switched to the inside under exceptional circumstances.

SPLITS: Two groups are usually formed when 14+ go to post, and often when 8-13 line up.

NEWMARKET July Course (R-H) - The major draw biases seen under the former Clerk of the Course have become a thing of the past and now only the occasional meeting will be affected. The course is permanently divided into two halves by a rail (the Racing Post now carry information regarding which side is to be used) and, as a rule of thumb, the two outside rails (stands' rail when they're on the stands'-side half, far rail when they're on the far-side half) ride faster than the dividing rail.

Stands'-side half - On fast ground (particularly watered) very high numbers are often favoured at up to 1m, when there's a narrow strip hard against the fence that rides quicker. However, on good to soft or slower ground, runners racing in the centre are favoured.

Far-side half - There's rarely much in the draw, apart from on slow ground, when the far side (low) rides faster.

STALLS: Can go either side on either half of the track.

SPLITS: Runners just about tend to form two groups in capacity fields, but are more likely to run to their draw here than at tracks such as Newcastle.

NEWMARKET Rowley Mile (R-H) - Similarly to the July Course, the draw seems to have been evened out since the Clerk of the Course change, although it's still generally a case of the further away from the stands' rail (low) the better.

STALLS: Can go anywhere and are rotated.

BIASES: High numbers have dominated the 2m2f Cesarewitch in recent years, the logic being that those on the inside can be switched off early, while low numbers have to work to get into position before the sole right-handed turn.

SPLIT: It's not unusual for jockeys to come stands' side on slow ground in round-course races.

NOTTINGHAM (L-H) - Biases are far harder to predict now on the both the inner (spring/autumn) and outer (summer) course.

STALLS: Tend to go on the stands' side (high) unless the ground is very soft.

SPLITS: Fields usually split in sprints when 14+ line up.

PONTEFRACT (L-H) - Low numbers have always been considered best here for the same reason as at Chester, in that the course has several distinct left-hand turns with a short home straight, and it's always worth considering low-drawn front-runners on fast going. Drainage work was carried out in the late 90s to try and eradicate the outside-rail bias on slow ground, and this worked immediately afterwards, but during the last few seasons there have been definite signs that it's now riding much faster when it's bottomless.

STALLS: Go on the inside (low) unless the ground is very soft, when they're switched to the outside rail.

SPLITS: Although it's uncommon to see distinct groups, high numbers usually race wide these days on soft/heavy ground.

REDCAR (L-H) - It's not unusual to see big fields throughout the season but the draw rarely makes a difference.

STALLS: Go towards the stands' side (high).

SPLITS: Splits are unusual.

RIPON (R-H) - The draw is often the sole deciding factor in big-field sprints and watering plays a major part. As a general rule, low numbers are best when the ground is good to firm or faster, while the far side is always best on softer going but, ultimately, the best guide these days is the most recent meeting.

STALLS: Go on the stands' side (low) apart from under exceptional circumstances.

BIASES: Front-runners (particularly from high draws over 1m) have an excellent record and any horse trying to make ground from behind and out wide is always facing a tough task.

SPLITS: Fields tend to stay together in races of 12 or fewer, but a split is near guaranteed when 15 or more line up. Look for 'draw' jockeys who might chance going far side in fields of 13-14.

SALISBURY (R-H) - For most of last year those racing against the inside rail (high) on fast ground looked worst off if anything (centre often best), which is the opposite of how things have been in the past. Presumably this was down to watering. On slower ground jockeys invariably head towards the stands' rail (good to soft seems to be the cut-off point) and whoever grabs the fence in front can prove hard to pass.

STALLS: Go on the far side (high) unless the ground is soft, when they're often moved to the near side.

BIASES: Low numbers are always best on soft/heavy ground.

SPLITS: Fields only tend to divide on good to soft ground; otherwise they converge towards either rail, dependent on going.

SANDOWN (R-H) - On the 5f chute, when the going is on the soft side and the stalls are on the far side (high), high numbers enjoy a decisive advantage. On the rare occasions that the stalls are placed on the stands' side, low numbers enjoy a slight advantage when all the runners stay towards the stands' rail, but when a few break off and go to the far side high numbers comfortably hold the upper hand again. High numbers enjoy a decent advantage in double-figure fields over 7f and 1m on good going or faster, but jockeys invariably head for the stands' side on slow ground.

STALLS: Usually go far side (high) over 5f, as the course is more level that side.

SPLITS: It's unusual for runners to split over 5f, with capacity fields rare and jockeys all inclined to head for the far rail.

SOUTHWELL All-Weather (L-H) - Over most trips on the round track it is preferable to be drawn away from the extreme inside or outside. The exceptions are over 6f and 1m3f, which both start close to the first bend (better to be drawn low to middle). At most meetings the centre of the track rides faster than either rail, although that can change in extreme weather when power-harrowing can even out the bias. A low to middle draw is preferable over 5f.

STALLS: Are placed next to the inside rail (low), except over 5f when they go next to the stands' rail (high).

SPLITS: Fields don't split into groups as such, but can fan out and take varied routes once into the home straight. Even in big fields over the straight 5f, the runners basically stick to their draw and race straight from start to finish.

THIRSK (L-H) - This used to be the biggest draw course in the country, back in the days of the old watering system (which was badly affected by the wind) but, while biases still often show up, they're not as predictable as used to be the case. Field sizes, watering and going always have to be taken into account when 12 or more line up (11 or fewer runners and it's rare to see anything bar one group up the stands' rail, with high numbers best). Otherwise, either rail can enjoy the edge on watered fast ground (the one place not to be under any circumstances is down the middle). Low-drawn prominent-racers are well worth considering whatever the distance on the round course.

STALLS: Always go up the stands' side (high).

BIASES: High numbers are best in sprints when 11 or fewer line up, but it's hard to know which side is likely to do best in bigger fields on fast ground. The far (inside) rail is always best on slow going (the softer the ground, the greater the advantage).

SPLITS: Runners invariably stay towards the stands' side in sprints containing 12 or fewer runners (unless the ground is soft) and frequently when 13-14 line up. Any more and it becomes long odds-on two groups.

WARWICK (L-H) - Low numbers are no longer favoured, whatever the ground, and jockeys rarely if ever stick to the inside rail now. Presumably this is down to watering (hold-up runners are not as badly off as they used to be).

STALLS: Always go on the inside (low).

WINDSOR (Fig. 8) - The bias in favour of high numbers on fast ground is nothing like as predictable as it used to be, presumably because of watering. On slower ground, jockeys head centre to far side, and right over to the far rail (low) on genuine soft/heavy.

STALLS: Can be positioned anywhere for sprints.

BIASES: High-drawn prominent-racers are often favoured in fast-ground sprints, and also over 1m67y. On good to soft going, there's rarely much between the two sides, but it's a case of nearer to the far rail (low) the better on bad ground.

SPLITS: Splits only tend to occur on good to soft ground, and even then it's rare to see two defined groups.

WOLVERHAMPTON All-Weather (L-H) - A low draw is a big advantage over 5f20y and 5f216y, and low to middle is preferable over 7f32y. Beyond that it doesn't seem to matter, although it's never a good idea to race too wide on the home bend, as those that do rarely seem to make up the lost ground.

STALLS: Are placed against the outside rail (high) over 7f32y and against the inside (low) at all other distances.

YARMOUTH (L-H) - High numbers enjoyed a major advantage for much of the 90s, but this was put an end to by the course switching from pop-up sprinklers (which were affected by the off-shore breeze) to a Briggs Boom in '99. These days a bias will appear occasionally but it's hard to predict, and runners often head for the centre whatever the going.

STALLS: Go one side or the other.

SPLITS: It's common to see groups form, often including one down the centre, in big fields.

YORK (L-H) - The draw is nothing like as unpredictable in sprints as many believe, although things are never quite as clear cut in September/October as earlier in the season. Essentially, on good or faster ground, the faster strip is to be found centre to far side, which means in capacity fields, the place to be is stall 6-12, while in fields of 12-14 runners drawn low are favoured (the course is only wide enough to house 20 runners). On soft/heavy ground, the stands' side (high) becomes the place to be.

STALLS: Can go anywhere.

BIASES: Prominent-racers drawn down the centre are favoured in fast-ground sprints, but high numbers take over on genuine soft/heavy ground.

SPLITS: Defined groups are rare.

Key to racereaders' initials

WG ....Walter Glynn	JN ....Jonathan Neesom	JR ....Joe Rowntree
RL ....Richard Lowther	DO ....Darren Owen	AS ....Andrew Sheret
LM....................Lee McKenzie	SP ....Steve Payne	ST ....Steve Taylor
TM ....Tim Mitchell	CR ....Colin Roberts	RY ....Richard Young

SOUTHWELL (L-H)

Friday, January 1

OFFICIAL GOING: Standard to slow

Wind: Nil Weather: Fine and sunny, but cold

1 HAPPY NEW YEAR APPRENTICE MEDIAN AUCTION MAIDEN STKS — 1m 3f (F)

12:25 (12:25) (Class 6) 4-6-Y-O **£1,774** (£523; £262) **Stalls** Low

Form RPR

035- **1** **Mehendi (IRE)**[68] [6769] 4-8-8 61 DeclanCannon(5) 5 67
(B Ellison) *hld up: rdn over 3f out: hdwy u.p and hung lft over 1f out: nt clr run and swtchd lft ins fnl f: styd on wl to ld nr fin* **9/4**[1]

3- **2** *1 3/4* **Look Officer (USA)**[23] [7694] 4-8-5 65 (v1) RossAtkinson(3) 3 59
(Tom Dascombe) *sn chsng ldr: led over 3f out: rdn clr and hung lft over 2f out: hung rt and wkng whn hdd nr fin* **3/1**[2]

432- **3** *3* **Dovedon Angel**[16] [7765] 4-8-8 51 WilliamCarson 7 54
(Miss Gay Kelleway) *led after 1f: rdn and hdd over 3f out: sn outpcd: rallied over 1f out: styd on same pce ins fnl f* **4/1**

0- **4** *1* **Lady Champagne**[25] [7671] 4-8-3 0 TobyAtkinson(5) 6 52
(Miss J Feilden) *hld up: hdwy over 5f out: outpcd over 3f out: rallied over 1f out: styd on* **40/1**

006- **5** *1 1/2* **Time To Play**[23] [7687] 5-9-2 53 RussKennemore 4 55
(T T Clement) *chsd ldrs: rdn over 3f out: outpcd sn after: rallied over 1f out: wknd ins fnl f* **14/1**

4- **6** *33* **Danderek**[16] [7765] 4-8-6 0 LeeTopliss(7) 2 —
(R A Fahey) *hld up: plld hrd: rdn 4f out: sn wknd: t.o* **7/2**[3]

- **7** *21* **Daraqala (FR)**[48] 4-8-8 55 KellyHarrison 1 —
(Paul Murphy) *led 1f: chsd ldrs: rdn and wknd over 3f out* **40/1**

2m 34.92s (6.92) **Going Correction** +0.45s/f (Slow)
WFA 4 from 5yo 3lb 7 Ran SP% **109.5**
Speed ratings: **92,90,88,87,86 62,47**
toteswinger:1&2:£2.50, 2&3:£2.20, 1&3:£1.90 CSF £8.38 TOTE £3.70: £1.80, £2.30; EX 14.60.
Owner Koo's Racing Club **Bred** Ballymacoll Stud Farm Ltd **Trained** Norton, N Yorks

FOCUS
The surface was described as on the slow side of standard and that translated to very testing. This maiden produced an unusual finish for the track, with the leader getting tired and stopping in front, and the winner staying on from well back to grab the spoils, having touched 1000 on Betfair for £6.

2 BET FA CUP - BETDAQ H'CAP — 5f (F)

1:00 (1:00) (Class 2) (0-100,97) 4-Y-O+ **£10,361** (£3,083; £1,540; £769) **Stalls** High

Form RPR

052- **1** **Rebel Duke (IRE)**[3] [7866] 6-8-8 86 BarryMcHugh(5) 6 103
(Ollie Pears) *hmpd s: sn trcking ldrs: led wl over 1f out: drvn clr ins fnl f: hung lft towards fin* **3/1**[2]

121- **2** *2 1/2* **Nickel Silver**[17] [7758] 5-9-1 88 (v) TomEaves 1 96+
(B Smart) *sn chsng ldr: rdn and ev ch over 1f out: edgd rt and styd on same pce ins fnl f* **9/2**[3]

3/1- **3** *nk* **Fitz Flyer (IRE)**[3] [7866] 4-9-10 97 6ex PhillipMakin 8 104
(D H Brown) *hmpd s: in rr: hdwy u.p over 1f out: nt rch ldrs* **6/1**

023- **4** *1 3/4* **Equuleus Pictor**[3] [7866] 6-8-6 86 DeclanCannon(7) 4 87
(J L Spearing) *led: rdn and hdd wl over 1f out: no ex fnl f* **6/1**

066- **5** *2* **Canadian Danehill (IRE)**[3] [7866] 8-9-1 88 (p) GrahamGibbons 3 81
(R M H Cowell) *chsd ldrs: sn pushed along: outpcd over 3f out: n.d after* **25/1**

111- **6** *2* **Lesley's Choice**[24] [7676] 4-9-4 91 (v) FrankieMcDonald 5 77
(R Curtis) *wnt rt s: chsd ldrs: rdn 3f out: wknd over 1f out* **11/4**[1]

320- **7** *1 1/4* **Colorus (IRE)**[3] [7866] 7-8-1 77 (p) KellyHarrison(3) 7 59
(W J H Ratcliffe) *hmpd s: sn pushed along in rr: rdn 1/2-way: no ch whn hung lft and eased ins fnl f* **16/1**

035- **8** *3 3/4* **Pawan (IRE)**[3] [7866] 10-8-5 83 ow3 (b) AnnStokell(5) 2 51
(Miss A Stokell) *s.i.s: outpcd* **16/1**

59.97 secs (0.27) **Going Correction** +0.30s/f (Slow) 8 Ran SP% **114.0**
Speed ratings (Par 109): **109,105,104,101,98 95,93,87**
toteswinger:1&2:£2.00, 2&3:£5.00, 1&3:£4.80 CSF £16.86 CT £75.44 TOTE £3.90: £1.40, £1.60, £2.40; EX 19.10 Trifecta £68.00 Pool: £514.42 - 5.59 winning units.
Owner Ian Bishop **Bred** Rathbarry Stud **Trained** Norton, N Yorks

FOCUS
A valuable and competitive handicap featuring a number of front-runners, and predictably it was run at a brisk gallop. Six of these met in a similar race here three days earlier, won by Fitz Flyer.

NOTEBOOK
Rebel Duke(IRE) sat just off the pace, travelled strongly throughout and quickened right away in the closing stages for an emphatic success. Beaten by the narrowest of margins by Fitz Flyer over C&D three days earlier, he had no trouble reversing that form on 6lb better terms, and he can now expect a bit of a hike in the weights. There's a similar race for him back here on March 18, while connections are also considering taking a chance in conditions company on turf early in the campaign, providing the ground is on the soft side. (op 7-2)
Nickel Silver, 7lb higher than when successful over the C&D last time, showed good pace towards the centre of the track and did little wrong. He simply bumped into a better handicapped rival. (op 4-1)
Fitz Flyer(IRE), drawn highest of all, stayed on strongly up the stands' rail but the 6lb penalty he picked up for winning three days earlier (from five of today's rivals) just found him out. (op 11-2 tchd 13-2)
Equuleus Pictor, who remains above his last winning mark, showed his usual early pace but he could have done with not being harried for the lead. (op 11-2 tchd 5-1)
Canadian Danehill(IRE) struggled to keep up with the strong gallop and remains below his best. (tchd 22-1)
Lesley's Choice likes to be up there, but she failed in trying to match the pace of the leading trio and paid the price, weakening right out inside the last 2f. (op 7-2)
Pawan(IRE) Official explanation: jockey said gelding was never travelling

3 BETDAQ THE BETTING EXCHANGE H'CAP — 1m 6f (F)

1:35 (1:35) (Class 5) (0-75,72) 4-Y-O+ **£2,331** (£693; £346; £173) **Stalls** Low

Form RPR

021- **1** **Dart**[10] [7842] 6-9-3 61 6ex RobertWinston 5 72
(Mrs S Lamyman) *chsd ldrs: wnt 2nd over 4f out: rdn to ld over 1f out: styd on u.p* **1/2**[1]

100- **2** *3 1/2* **My Friend Fritz**[228] [2129] 10-9-10 68 ChrisCatlin 2 74
(P W Hiatt) *led: pushed along over 3f out: rdn and hdd over 1f out: no ex ins fnl f* **16/1**

014- **3** *6* **Ibrox (IRE)**[20] [7724] 5-10-0 72 (p) GrahamGibbons 6 70
(A D Brown) *hld up: pushed along 1/2-way: rdn to go mod 4th over 3f out: wnt 3rd wl ins fnl f: nvr on terms* **6/1**[3]

324- **4** *nk* **Baltimore Patriot (IRE)**[32] [7594] 7-9-3 61 TonyCulhane 3 58
(R Curtis) *prom: pushed along over 4f out: rdn to go 3rd over 3f out: no imp: lost 3rd wl ins fnl f* **4/1**[2]

550- **5** *21* **Victory Quest (IRE)**[3] [7867] 10-9-9 67 (v) AndrewMullen 1 35
(Mrs S Lamyman) *chsd ldr tl rdn over 4f out: wknd over 3f out: t.o* **25/1**

53/ **6** *1/2* **Mirpour (IRE)**[425] [3980] 11-8-8 55 (t) KellyHarrison(3) 4 22
(Paul Murphy) *sn pushed along in rr: rdn 7f out: sn bhd: t.o* **40/1**

3m 15.35s (7.05) **Going Correction** +0.45s/f (Slow) 6 Ran SP% **113.1**
Speed ratings (Par 103): **97,95,91,91,79 79**
toteswinger:1&2:£2.40, 2&3:£4.60, 1&3:£1.40 CSF £10.99 TOTE £1.70: £1.10, £1.90; EX 6.50.
Owner Mrs S Lamyman **Bred** St Clare Hall Stud **Trained** Ruckland, Lincs

FOCUS
Quite a test in the conditions and, with Victory Quest harrying My Friend Fritz up front, the pace was a decent one.
Ibrox(IRE) Official explanation: jockey said gelding was never travelling

4 BET WORLD DARTS - BETDAQ H'CAP — 6f (F)

2:05 (2:05) (Class 5) (0-75,71) 3-Y-O **£2,456** (£725; £362) **Stalls** Low

Form RPR

360- **1** **Love Delta (USA)**[16] [7763] 3-9-4 71 JoeFanning 1 83+
(M Johnston) *sn led: hdd over 3f out: led again 2f out: sn rdn and edgd rt: hung rt ins fnl f: styd on wl* **5/2**[2]

13- **2** *1 3/4* **Sweet Child O'Mine**[6] [7844] 3-8-11 69 BillyCray(5) 4 75
(R C Guest) *w wnr tl led over 3f out: hdd 2f out: sn rdn: edgd lft 1f out: styd on same pce* **7/2**[3]

061- **3** *1 1/2* **Flow Chart (IRE)**[5] [7849] 3-9-2 69 6ex (b) PhillipMakin 5 71
(T D Barron) *trckd ldrs: rdn over 1f out: no ex ins fnl f* **1/1**[1]

500- **4** *16* **Mr Smithson (IRE)**[95] [6345] 3-8-5 58 ChrisCatlin 2 8
(B Ellison) *s.s: sn pushed along in rr: hdwy over 3f out: wknd 2f out: eased fnl f* **10/1**

1m 19.0s (2.50) **Going Correction** +0.45s/f (Slow) 4 Ran SP% **109.9**
Speed ratings (Par 97): **101,98,96,75**
CSF £10.99 TOTE £3.20; EX 13.60.
Owner Crone Stud Farms Ltd **Bred** Palides Investments N V Inc & Hair 'Em Corporation **Trained** Middleham Moor, N Yorks

5 NEW YEAR AT SOUTHWELL GOLF CLUB (S) STKS — 1m (F)

2:40 (2:40) (Class 6) 3-Y-O **£1,774** (£523; £262) **Stalls** Low

Form RPR

1 **Mororless** 3-8-0 0 DeclanCannon(7) 5 64
(A J McCabe) *s.s: sn pushed along in rr: hdwy over 3f out: styd on u.p to ld wl ins fnl f* **14/1**

331- **2** *1 3/4* **Inside Track (IRE)**[15] [7781] 3-9-4 72 (b) TonyCulhane 3 71
(P T Midgley) *led early: stdd to trck ldr: led over 2f out: sn rdn: whip broke over 1f out: hdd wl ins fnl f: styd on same pce: rdr threw remains of whip away nr fin* **1/1**[1]

040- **3** *6* **Hubble Space**[15] [7788] 3-8-7 60 (p) JimmyQuinn 2 46
(M Botti) *sn led: rdn and hdd whn rdr had whip knocked out of his hands over 1f out: wknd ins fnl f* **6/1**[3]

442- **4** *8* **City Gossip (IRE)**[15] [7781] 3-8-4 62 MartinLane(3) 7 28
(M G Quinlan) *prom: pushed along over 3f out: rdn over 2f out: sn wknd* **5/2**[2]

000- **5** *nk* **Heligoland**[32] [7597] 3-8-7 52 LukeMorris 6 27
(A G Newcombe) *prom: rdn 1/2-way: wknd over 3f out* **14/1**

000- **6** *9* **Twoellies**[15] [7788] 3-8-7 42 ChrisCatlin 4 6
(Ollie Pears) *chsd ldrs: hmpd and lost pl over 5f out: rdn and wknd wl over 3f out* **25/1**

005- **7** *17* **Develop U**[29] [7616] 3-8-9 48 JackDean(3) 1 —
(W G M Turner) *chsd ldrs: sn rdn along: lost pl 6f out: wknd 1/2-way: t.o* **33/1**

1m 48.69s (4.99) **Going Correction** +0.45s/f (Slow) 7 Ran SP% **113.0**
Speed ratings (Par 95): **93,91,85,77,76 67,50**
totewinger:1&2:£4.50, 2&3:£1.70, 1&3:£4.60 CSF £28.05 TOTE £13.50: £6.60, £1.10; EX 37.30.There was no bid for the winner.
Owner A J McCabe **Bred** M R M Bloodstock **Trained** Averham Park, Notts

FOCUS
A moderate seller.

6 PLAY GOLF BEFORE RACING AT SOUTHWELL H'CAP — 1m (F)

3:15 (3:15) (Class 2) (0-100,95) 4-Y-O+ **£10,361** (£3,083; £1,540; £769) **Stalls** Low

Form RPR

1 **Reve De Nuit (USA)**[80] 4-8-4 88 DeclanCannon(7) 5 102
(A J McCabe) *a.p: chsd ldr over 3f out: rdn to ld over 1f out: styd on u.p* **8/1**

423- **2** *3 1/2* **Nightjar (USA)**[10] [7837] 5-9-4 95 NeilCallan 8 101
(K A Ryan) *sn led: rdn and hdd over 1f out: styd on same pce* **7/2**[2]

012- **3** *2 1/2* **Miss Glitters (IRE)**[17] [7759] 5-8-5 82 JimmyQuinn 6 82
(H Morrison) *prom: hung lft and outpcd over 4f out: hdwy over 3f out: rdn over 2f out: styd on same pce appr fnl f* **5/2**[1]

545- **4** *5* **Faithful Ruler (USA)**[15] [7789] 6-8-8 85 TomEaves 4 74
(R A Fahey) *chsd ldrs: rdn over 2f out: wknd over 1f out* **11/2**

521- **5** *1* **Mcconnell (USA)**[15] [7782] 5-8-6 83 ChrisCatlin 2 69
(P Butler) *broke wl and led early: stdd and lost pl sn after: drvn along 1/2-way: hdwy u.p over 1f out: wknd fnl f* **4/1**[3]

100- **6** *7* **Stand Guard**[12] [7827] 6-8-7 89 AndrewHeffernan(5) 7 59
(P Howling) *sn outpcd: drvn along 1/2-way: wknd over 2f out* **17/2**

250- **7** *33* **Flores Sea (USA)**[5] [7854] 6-8-4 81 oh6 (b) JoeFanning 3 —
(T D Barron) *dwlt: hdwy to chse ldr over 6f out tl rdn and wknd over 3f out* **20/1**

1m 44.26s (0.56) **Going Correction** +0.45s/f (Slow) 7 Ran SP% **112.6**
Speed ratings (Par 109): **115,111,109,104,103 96,63**
toteswinger:1&2:£5.60, 2&3:£2.00, 1&3:£4.20 CSF £34.84 CT £89.91 TOTE £8.90: £2.60, £1.90; EX 32.50 Trifecta £92.20 Pool: £615.63 - 4.94 winning units.
Owner Jaber Ali Alsabah **Bred** Ecurie Du Haras De Meautry **Trained** Averham Park, Notts

FOCUS
Despite the top-weight weighing in 5lb below the ceiling for the race, this was a decent handicap.

NOTEBOOK
Reve De Nuit(USA), formerly trained in France, changed hands in November for 19,000euros and was debuting for Alan McCabe. The colt had galloped at the track so there was reason to expect that he would act on the surface, and on some of his French form, for example his second at Deauville on Polytrack back in July when given an RPR of 100, he looked well handicapped off a mark of 88. He showed that to be very much the case and, as this was his first start for 80 days, there's every chance this son of Giant's Causeway will come on for it. His trainer holds him in some regard and has one eye on the Winter Derby later in the year. (op 10-1)

Nightjar(USA), all the better for his return from a two-month break, remains on a pretty stiff mark but he put up a great effort here against a well-handicapped rival over a trip that stretches his stamina a touch. A similarly forceful ride back over 7f could see him back in the winner's enclosure. (tchd 3-1)
Miss Glitters(IRE), only 2lb higher for a sound second over this C&D last time, had every chance turning into the straight but was simply not good enough. This was a higher class of race than she normally competes in. (op 9-4 tchd 11-4)
Faithful Ruler(USA) remains 4lb above his last winning mark and this slow going was probably never going to see him at his best. (op 9-2)
Mcconnell(USA) likes it here, but he only won a claimer last time and this was far more competitive. (op 5-1 tchd 11-2)
Stand Guard, who is more of a Polytrack horse, was being pushed along and was struggling to go the pace from an early stage. (op 10-1)

7 SOUTHWELL-RACECOURSE.CO.UK H'CAP — 1m (F)
3:45 (3:45) (Class 6) (0-55,55) 4-Y-0+ £1,774 (£523; £131; £131) Stalls Low

Form RPR

060- **1** **Camerooney**[5] 7855 7-8-4 48 .... WilliamCarson(3) 2 61
(B Ellison) *mde all: rdn fr over 3f out: jnd over 1f out: styd on gamely u.p* **14/1**

430- **2** *nk* **Special Cuvee**[13] 7818 4-9-0 55 ....(v) PhillipMakin 4 67
(A B Haynes) *s.i.s: hld up: hdwy u.p over 2f out: edgd lft over 1f out: ev ch ins fnl f: r.o* **7/1**

455- **3** *7* **Bajan Pride**[15] 7784 6-8-7 55 .... FrazerWilliams(7) 7 51
(R A Fahey) *mid-div: hdwy over 2f out: sn rdn: styd on same pce appr fnl f* **9/2**[2]

0U0- **3** *dht* **Very Well Red**[15] 7784 7-8-13 54 .... ChrisCatlin 12 50
(P W Hiatt) *a.p: rdn to chse wnr over 2f out: sn ev ch: wknd ins fnl f* **11/1**

666- **5** *½* **Bicksta**[15] 7780 4-8-6 47 .... FrankieMcDonald 9 42
(P T Midgley) *chsd wnr: rdn over 2f out: wknd fnl f* **20/1**

250- **6** *1 ¼* **Louisiade (IRE)**[5] 7855 9-8-0 46 oh1 ....(p) BillyCray(5) 13 38
(R C Guest) *broke wl: stdd and lost pl sn after: hld up: rdn over 2f out: nt trble ldrs* **20/1**

251- **7** *nk* **Kielty's Folly**[13] 7814 6-8-12 53 .... TonyCulhane 11 44
(B P J Baugh) *chsd ldrs: rdn over 2f out: wknd fnl f* **4/1**[1]

004- **8** *1* **Jenny's Pride (IRE)**[14] 7796 4-8-9 50 .... DavidProbert 3 39
(John A Harris) *prom: rdn over 3f out: hung lft and wknd over 1f out* **11/1**

402- **9** *¾* **Fairplaytomyself**[13] 7814 5-8-3 51 ow5 .... TobyAtkinson(7) 10 38
(P W Hiatt) *s.i.s: sn pushed along in rr: n.d* **5/1**[3]

600- **10** *3* **Kannon**[14] 7795 5-7-12 46 oh1 .... DeclanCannon(7) 14 26
(A J McCabe) *prom: rdn over 3f out: wknd over 1f out* **12/1**

006- **11** *½* **Isabella's Fancy**[119] 5634 5-8-5 46 oh1 ....(b) LukeMorris 5 25
(A G Newcombe) *mid-div: rdn over 3f out: wknd over 1f out* **25/1**

500- **12** *11* **Cause For Applause (IRE)**[20] 7726 4-8-8 49 ....(v) JimmyQuinn 1 3
(R Craggs) *prom: rdn 1/2-way: wknd over 3f out* **16/1**

0/6- **13** *23* **Baby Is Here (IRE)**[43] 7455 4-8-5 46 oh1 .... AndrewMullen 6 —
(D J S Ffrench Davis) *mid-div: sn drvn along: lost pl 5f out: bhd fr 1/2-way: t.o* **50/1**

1m 46.11s (2.41) **Going Correction** +0.45s/f (Slow) **13** Ran SP% **119.6**
Speed ratings (Par 101): **105,104,97,97,97 95,95,94,93,90 90,79,56**TRIFECTA: C/S/B Part won. £234.00. Pool: £632.69 - 0.84 winning units. Pool of £50.61 cf to Lingfield January 2nd; C/S/V £150.00 - 1.56 winning units.TOTESWINGER: BP&SP £3.00, BP&CM £8.20, SP&CM £27.30, VWR&CM £14.70. Place 6 £66.24, Place 5 £48.56. CSF £104.01 CT TOTE £9.60: 4.50,2.40,1.10,2.20 Owner Mrs J Stapleton: Bred, Miss D Hill, Trained, Norton.
■ Stewards' Enquiry : William Carson seven-day ban: excessive use of the whip (January 15-21)

FOCUS
A very ordinary handicap.
Fairplaytomyself Official explanation: jockey said mare finished lame behind
T/Plt: £110.70 to a £1 stake. Pool: £74,664.55. 491.95 winning tickets. T/Qpdt: £42.60 to a £1 stake. Pool: £7,506.80. 130.25 winning tickets. CR

LINGFIELD (L-H)
Saturday, January 2

OFFICIAL GOING: Standard
Wind: Medium, across Weather: Bright and cold

8 BET TEST MATCH CRICKET - BETDAQ H'CAP (DIV I) — 6f (P)
12:35 (12:36) (Class 6) (0-58,58) 4-Y-0+ £1,706 (£503; £252) Stalls Low

Form RPR

006- **1** **Tanley**[14] 7815 5-8-8 48 .... JimmyQuinn 8 56
(J F Coupland) *restless in stalls: fly-jmpd leaving stalls: chsd ldrs: nt clr run 2f out: swtchd lft wl over 1f out: drvn over 1f out: led fnl 100yds: styd on* **9/1**

160- **2** *½* **Spoof Master (IRE)**[11] 7839 6-9-1 55 ....(t) LiamKeniry 7 62
(C R Dore) *chsd ldr: rdn ent fnl 2f: hrd drvn to ld 1f out: hdd fnl 100yds: no ex* **12/1**

206- **3** *½* **Golden Prospect**[5] 7861 6-9-4 58 ....(v[1]) PaulFitzsimons 4 63
(Miss J R Tooth) *hld up wl bhd: rdn and hdwy wl over 1f out: kpt on wl u.p fnl f: nt rch ldrs* **13/2**[3]

500- **4** *hd* **Dream Express (IRE)**[22] 7716 5-9-3 57 .... HayleyTurner 2 61
(P Howling) *stmbld leaving stalls: hld up bhd: stl last over 2f out: hdwy and nt clr run 2f out: sn swtchd rt: effrt but hanging rt over 1f out: awkward hd carriage but kpt on wl fnl f: nt rch ldrs* **9/2**[1]

200- **5** *¾* **Waterloo Dock**[24] 7691 5-9-3 57 .... MartinDwyer 3 59
(M Quinn) *sn pushed along in midfield: rdn and outpcd over 3f out: hdwy on inner over 1f out: chsd ldrs ins fnl f: no ex fnl 75yds* **9/2**[1]

502- **6** *1 ½* **Equinity**[3] 7879 4-8-7 47 ....(t) FergusSweeney 6 44
(J Pearce) *taken down early: trckd ldrs: swtchd rt wl over 1f out: sn rdn and fnd little: wknd ins fnl f* **13/2**[3]

004- **7** *nse* **Oxbridge**[37] 7533 5-8-6 46 ....(b[1]) LukeMorris 11 43
(J M Bradley) *swtchd lft after s: bhd: rdn ent fnl 2f: no hdwy tl r.o wl ins fnl f: nt rch ldrs* **25/1**

000- **8** *2 ¼* **Music Box Express**[14] 7819 6-8-12 57 ....(v[1]) MatthewDavies(5) 10 47
(George Baker) *sn chsng ldrs: rdn ent fnl 2f: wknd u.p 1f out* **5/1**[2]

000- **9** *nse* **Mandhooma**[15] 7795 4-9-2 56 .... PaulDoe 1 46
(P W Hiatt) *led at fast gallop: rdn wl over 1f out: hdd 1f out: fdd ins fnl f* **14/1**

006- **10** *3 ½* **Sunshine Ellie**[22] 7714 4-8-6 46 oh1 .... DavidProbert 9 24
(D Shaw) *racd in midfield: rdn and outpcd over 3f out: bhd fr over 1f out* **66/1**

200- **11** *17* **Crystal B Good (USA)**[2] 7890 4-9-4 58 .... RobertWinston 5 —
(J R Best) *hmpd s and s.i.s: sn rdn along towards rr: bhd fr 1/2-way: lost tch 2f out: eased ins fnl f* **20/1**

1m 11.18s (-0.72) **Going Correction** +0.025s/f (Slow) **11** Ran SP% **114.2**
Speed ratings (Par 101): **105,104,103,103,102 100,100,97,97,92 69**
toteswingers: 1&2 £14.70, 1&3 £14.50, 2&3 £16.70 CSF £105.91 CT £749.38 TOTE £8.80: £2.40, £4.00, £2.50; EX 92.70.
Owner J F Coupland **Bred** Mrs J A Moffatt And Brian T Clark **Trained** East Ravendale, Lincs
■ Stewards' Enquiry : Fergus Sweeney one-day ban: careless riding (Jan 16)

FOCUS
This was an extra meeting added due to the number of abandonments caused by bad weather. This moderate but competitive sprint handicap was run at a good gallop from the off and, although the first two were in the leading group throughout, they were being closed down by the strong-finishing hold-up horses at the finish.

9 BET FA CUP - BETDAQ MAIDEN STKS — 7f (P)
1:05 (1:05) (Class 5) 3-Y-0+ £2,590 (£770; £385; £192) Stalls Low

Form RPR

530- **1** **Tiradito (USA)**[13] 7824 3-8-9 74 .... MartinDwyer 6 68+
(M Botti) *trckd ldng trio: hdwy to press ldr ent fnl 2f: led wl over 1f out: clr 1f out: pushed out: comf* **1/1**[1]

06- **2** *3* **Abhar (USA)**[35] 7571 3-8-9 0 .... RobertWinston 2 60
(J R Best) *t.k.h: trckd ldng pair: swtchd rt off of rail and rdn 2f out: unable qck over 1f out: chsd clr wnr ins fnl f: no imp* **3/1**[2]

404- **3** *1 ¼* **Ant Music (IRE)**[15] 7804 3-8-9 63 ....(b[1]) LiamKeniry 7 57
(J S Moore) *sn led: rdn and hrd pressed ent fnl 2f: sn hdd: nt pce of wnr over 1f out: lost 2nd ins fnl f* **7/1**[3]

4 *¾* **Oceans Edge** 4-9-13 0 .... StephenCraine 1 59
(J R Boyle) *s.i.s: in tch in midfield on inner: rdn over 1f out: unable qck and edgd rt ins fnl f: kpt on fnl 100yds* **20/1**

000- **5** *shd* **Belle Park**[26] 7661 3-8-4 55 .... JamieMackay 8 49
(Karen George) *s.i.s: in tch in rr: rdn and hdwy on inner over 1f out: kpt on but nvr gng pce to threaten wnr* **66/1**

0- **6** *3* **Royal Torbo (ISR)**[15] 7800 3-8-4 0 .... MatthewDavies(5) 3 46
(George Baker) *t.k.h: hld up in tch: wd and dropped to rr bnd ent fnl 2f: n.d after* **33/1**

030- **7** *1 ½* **Emma Jean Lass (IRE)**[6] 7849 3-7-13 65 .... AndrewHeffernan(5) 5 37
(P D Evans) *in tch towards rr: sltly hmpd and pushed along 5f out: struggling u.p 2f out: n.d after* **7/1**[3]

06- **8** *3* **Gibraltar Lass (USA)**[35] 7582 3-8-4 0 .... LukeMorris 4 29
(H J Collingridge) *chsd ldr tl jst over 2f out: sn lost pl and no ch fr over 1f out* **25/1**

1m 24.83s (0.03) **Going Correction** +0.025s/f (Slow)
WFA 3 from 4yo 18lb **8** Ran SP% **113.0**
Speed ratings (Par 103): **100,96,95,94,94 90,89,85**
toteswingers: 1&2 £1.80, 1&3 £2.60, 2&3 £4.60 CSF £3.79 TOTE £2.00: £1.10, £1.30, £1.60; EX 5.30.
Owner El Catorce **Bred** F J F M Llc **Trained** Newmarket, Suffolk

FOCUS
A maiden that didn't take much winning.

10 BET MULTIPLES - BETDAQ H'CAP — 7f (P)
1:35 (1:35) (Class 6) (0-56,55) 4-Y-0+ £2,047 (£604; £302) Stalls Low

Form RPR

162- **1** **Tamino (IRE)**[3] 7880 7-9-0 51 .... JimmyQuinn 8 62
(P Howling) *mde all: rdn over 1f out: kpt on u.p fnl f: unchal* **5/2**[1]

022- **2** *2* **Party In The Park**[19] 7754 5-8-13 55 .... MatthewDavies(5) 4 61
(J R Boyle) *in tch: disp 2nd fr 3f out tl chsd wnr u.p over 1f out: no imp fnl f* **3/1**[2]

000- **3** *nk* **Josiah Bartlett (IRE)**[3] 7877 4-8-11 48 ....(p) HayleyTurner 2 53
(Ian Williams) *in tch in midfield: chsd ldng trio and drvn wl over 1f out: wnt 3rd ins fnl f: nvr threatened wnr* **4/1**[3]

004- **4** *2* **Black Draft**[17] 7770 8-8-4 46 ow1 .... SophieDoyle(5) 11 45
(B Forsey) *taken down early: chsd wnr tl over 1f out: wknd ins fnl f* **33/1**

004- **5** *nk* **Strategic Mover (USA)**[12] 7834 5-9-1 55 ....(vt) RobertLButler(3) 3 54
(P Butler) *hld up in tch in rr: rdn and effrt jst over 2f out: styd on u.p fnl f: nvr threatened ldrs* **20/1**

400- **6** *nk* **Divine White**[4] 7869 7-8-8 45 .... LukeMorris 10 43
(G P Enright) *in tch in midfield on outer: rdn and no prog 2f out: no ch w wnr after: plugged on* **66/1**

425- **7** *hd* **Greystoke Prince**[17] 7774 5-8-9 53 ....(t) CarolineKelly(7) 7 50
(P S McEntee) *awkward leaving stalls: t.k.h in midfield: v wd and lost pl bnd 2f out: kpt on ins fnl f: n.d* **15/2**

000- **8** *1 ¼* **Know No Fear**[17] 7768 5-8-11 55 .... AmyScott(7) 5 49
(A J Lidderdale) *rrd as stalls opened and v.s.a: wl bhd: sme hdwy on inner fnl f: nvr on terms* **10/1**

430- **9** *8* **Makshoof (IRE)**[17] 7774 6-9-4 55 ....(p) JimCrowley 6 27
(I W McInnes) *a towards rr: lost tch 2f out: wl btn and eased ins fnl f: sddle slipped* **16/1**

140- **10** *4* **Admirals Way**[275] 1080 5-9-4 55 .... RobertWinston 9 16
(C N Kellett) *t.k.h: chsd ldrs ldrs tl rdn and lost pl wl over 2f out: wl bhd and eased ins fnl f* **20/1**

600- **11** *3 ½* **Mickys Mate**[247] 1628 5-8-8 45 .... DavidProbert 1 —
(S A Harris) *in tch tl rdn and wknd qckly over 2f out: wl bhd and eased ins fnl f* **100/1**

1m 24.77s (-0.03) **Going Correction** +0.025s/f (Slow) **11** Ran SP% **115.3**
Speed ratings (Par 101): **101,98,98,96,95 95,95,93,84,80 76**
toteswingers: 1&2 £2.40, 1&3 £3.40, 2&3 £5.40 CSF £9.18 CT £28.64 TOTE £3.30: £1.30, £1.30, £1.70; EX 12.60.
Owner Paul Howling **Bred** Century Bloodstock **Trained** Newmarket, Suffolk

FOCUS
This ordinary handicap was run only fractionally faster than the preceding maiden.
Makshoof(IRE) Official explanation: jockey said saddle slipped
Mickys Mate Official explanation: jockey said gelding ran too free

11 BETDAQ THE BETTING EXCHANGE H'CAP — 1m (P)
2:10 (2:10) (Class 6) (0-68,68) 4-Y-0+ £2,047 (£604; £302) Stalls High

Form RPR

111- **1** **Wunder Strike (USA)**[20] 7742 4-8-12 62 ....(p) StephenCraine 12 73+
(J R Boyle) *broke wl and led early: sn stdd to trck ldng pair: wnt 2nd gng wl 2f out: pushed into ld ins fnl f: comf* **2/1**[1]

550- **2** *½* **Goodbye Cash (IRE)**[7] 7845 6-8-7 57 .... PaulDoe 8 65
(P D Evans) *taken down early: t.k.h: chsd ldr over 7f out: led over 2f out: sn rdn: hdd ins fnl f: kpt on same pce* **14/1**

006- 3 nk **Lopinot (IRE)**[34] 7587 7-8-7 57..............(v) FergusSweeney 4 64
(M R Bosley) *hld up in last trio: hdwy over 2f out: drvn and r.o wl fnl f: gng on fin but nvr gng pce to rch ldrs* **8/1**

144- 4 1 ¾ **Fine Ruler (IRE)**[34] 7586 6-8-9 59 ow1.............. LiamKeniry 9 62
(M R Bosley) *stdd s: hld up in last trio: rdn and hdwy over 1f out: styd on wl fnl f: nvr trbld ldrs* **9/1**

204- 5 ¾ **Fly By Nelly**[12] 7829 4-8-11 61.............. SteveDrowne 6 63+
(H Morrison) *in tch in midfield: jostled and lost pl jst over 2f out: hmpd and dropped to rr wl over 1f out: rallied u.p fnl f: nvr able to chal ldrs* **14/1**

040- 6 hd **Ivory Lace**[35] 7575 9-9-3 67.............. JimCrowley 2 68
(S Woodman) *stdd s: hld up in rr: hdwy and swtchd ins ent fnl f: r.o but nvr threatened ldrs* **25/1**

600- 7 1 **Wavertree Warrior (IRE)**[114] 5791 8-8-13 63.............. LukeMorris 5 62
(N P Littmoden) *chsd ldrs: rdn wl over 2f out: disputing 3rd and unable qck u.p over 1f out: wknd ins fnl f* **16/1**

246- 8 1 **Ymir**[24] 7693 4-8-7 57.............. DavidProbert 3 54
(M J Attwater) *in tch on inner: effrt to dispute 3rd over 1f out: unable qck u.p ent fnl f: wknd qckly ins fnl f* **8/1**

402- 9 2 ¼ **Dr Wintringham (IRE)**[34] 7591 4-8-11 61.............. JerryO'Dwyer 7 52
(Karen George) *in tch on outer: rdn and unable qck bnd 2f out: no ch fr over 1f out* **9/2[2]**

206- 10 9 **Whotsit (IRE)**[106] 6052 4-8-7 60..............(b) MartinLane(3) 11 27
(Miss Amy Weaver) *sn led: rdn and hdd over 2f out: wknd over 1f out: wl bhd and eased ins fnl f: fin 11th, plcd 10th* **20/1**

000- D 1 ½ **Take The Micky**[17] 7769 4-9-4 68.............. IanMongan 10 56
(C F Wall) *s.i.s: t.k.h: sn in tch in midfield: rdn and wknd over 1f out: eased whn no ch ins fnl f: b.b.v: fin 10th, disq. prohibited substance* **7/1[3]**

1m 37.06s (-1.14) **Going Correction** +0.025s/f (Slow) 11 Ran SP% **124.1**
Speed ratings (Par 101): **106,105,105,103,102 102,101,100,98,87 96**
toteswingers: 1&2 £10.50, 1&3 £11.40, 2&3 £42.00 CSF £35.93 CT £203.68 TOTE £3.80: £1.60, £4.90, £2.40; EX 59.70 Trifecta £475.00 Pool: £31,867.65 - 49.64 winning units..
Owner Mrs B Powell B Walsh P Hughes C Murphy **Bred** Mike Abraham **Trained** Epsom, Surrey

FOCUS
Another success for an in-form horse.
Take The Micky Official explanation: jockey said gelding bled from the nose

12 BETDAQ.CO.UK H'CAP 1m 2f (P)
2:40 (2:40) (Class 5) (0-70,70) 4-Y-0+ **£2,590** (£770; £385; £192) **Stalls** Low

Form RPR

161- 1 **Chalice Welcome**[24] 7695 7-9-4 70.............. HayleyTurner 10 78
(N B King) *dwlt: chsd ldr 9f out tl led 2f out: drvn ent fnl f: narrowly hdd fnl 75yds: rallied gamely u.p to ld again on post* **7/2[1]**

000- 2 nse **Alfie Tupper (IRE)**[26] 7664 7-8-4 61.............. MatthewDavies(5) 2 69
(J R Boyle) *chsd ldr for 1f: styd handy: effrt to chal over 1f out: hld hd awkwardly but rdn to ld fnl 75yds: hdd on post* **6/1**

350- 3 ¾ **Formidable Guest**[19] 7752 6-8-13 65.............. FergusSweeney 8 71
(J Pearce) *hld up in tch in rr: hdwy on inner jst over 2f out: swtchd rt and rdn over 1f out: r.o to go 3rd wl ins fnl f: nt rch ldrs* **11/1**

513- 4 1 ½ **Marmooq**[23] 7699 7-8-12 64.............. LukeMorris 6 67
(M J Attwater) *t.k.h: hld up in tch in last trio: hdwy on outer 3f out: rdn and outpcd bnd 2f out: rallied u.p fnl f: nt rch ldrs* **5/1[3]**

/00- 5 shd **Meydan Dubai (IRE)**[23] 7699 5-8-10 65.............. MarcHalford(3) 9 68
(J R Best) *hld up in tch in rr: n.m.r ent fnl 2f: plld to outer and rdn over 1f out: styd on fnl f: nt gng pce to rch ldrs* **16/1**

342- 6 hd **Hector Spectre (IRE)**[3] 7881 4-8-5 64..............(v) AndrewHeffernan(5) 3 66
(P D Evans) *chsd ldrs: effrt and ev ch 2f out: wanting to edge lft and nt pce of ldng pair ent fnl f: wknd fnl 100yds* **9/2[2]**

200- 7 4 ½ **Vinces**[17] 7777 6-8-13 65.............. DavidProbert 4 58
(T D McCarthy) *sn led: pushed along and qcknd gallop 4f out: rdn wl over 2f out: hdd 2f out: wknd ent fnl f* **15/2**

1- 8 5 **Woolfall Sovereign (IRE)**[19] 7753 4-8-11 65.............. StevieDonohoe 5 48
(G G Margarson) *in tch: dropped towards rr but stl in tch 5f out: rdn whn sltly hmpd and stmbld bnd 2f out: n.d after* **5/1[3]**

2m 6.93s (0.33) **Going Correction** +0.025s/f (Slow)
WFA 4 from 5yo+ 2lb 8 Ran SP% **114.0**
Speed ratings (Par 103): **99,98,98,97,97 96,93,89**
toteswingers: 1&2 £5.50, 1&3 £7.90, 2&3 £8.50 CSF £24.53 CT £206.72 TOTE £4.10: £1.60, £2.10, £3.60; EX 27.10 Trifecta £622.35 Part won. Pool: £622.35 - 0.50 winning units..
Owner The Dyball Partnership **Bred** The Dyball Partnership **Trained** Newmarket, Suffolk

FOCUS
A modest handicap run at a steady early gallop.
Woolfall Sovereign(IRE) Official explanation: trainer had no explanation for the poor form shown

13 BETDAQ ON 0870 178 1221 H'CAP 1m 4f (P)
3:15 (3:18) (Class 6) (0-60,58) 4-Y-0+ **£2,047** (£604; £302) **Stalls** Low

Form RPR

301- 1 **Winning Show**[17] 7767 6-9-0 54..............(t) LiamKeniry 1 59
(C Gordon) *in tch in midfield: effrt to chse ldng pair on inner over 1f out: rdn to ld fnl 100yds: wnt rt last strides* **9/1**

050- 2 ½ **Star Choice**[24] 7695 5-9-4 58.............. FergusSweeney 5 62
(J Pearce) *chsd ldr tl rdn to ld jst over 2f out: drvn ent fnl f: hdd and no ex fnl 100yds: hld whn sltly hmpd last strides* **7/2[2]**

042- 3 ½ **Little Richard (IRE)**[7] 7847 11-9-2 56..............(p) AdamKirby 2 59
(M Wellings) *chsd ldrs: rdn and switching out rt wl over 1f out: kpt on u.p fnl f: nvr quite gng pce to rch ldng pair* **4/1[3]**

402- 4 1 ¼ **Achromatic**[19] 7755 4-8-11 55..............(v) RobertWinston 10 56
(W R Swinburn) *stdd and dropped in bhd: gd hdwy on outer 3f out: edgd lft bnd 2f out: ev ch and rdn wl over 1f out tl ins fnl f: wknd fnl 100yds* **8/1**

004- 5 ¾ **Kickahead (USA)**[24] 7688 8-8-11 51..............(t) StevieDonohoe 7 51
(Ian Williams) *t.k.h: hld up in tch in midfield: effrt whn hmpd bnd 2f out: plld to outer and rdn wl over 1f out: wanting to hang lft u.p: kpt on but nvr able to chal* **3/1[1]**

006- 6 1 ¾ **Free Falling**[11] 7842 4-8-1 45..............(tp) JimmyQuinn 4 42?
(A J Lidderdale) *led at stdy gallop: qcknd pce wl over 3f out: rdn and hdd jst over 2f out: wknd ent fnl f* **40/1**

000- 7 hd **Bet Noir (IRE)**[47] 1210 5-8-5 45.............. HayleyTurner 8 42?
(A W Carroll) *hld up in tch towards rr: rdn whn sltly hmpd bnd 2f out: hdwy towards inner u.p ent fnl f: nvr threatened ldrs* **12/1**

250- 8 ¾ **Primera Rossa**[92] 6446 4-8-3 47..............(p) LukeMorris 6 43
(J S Moore) *in tch: rdn wl over 3f out: edgd out rt bnd 2f out: nt clr run and sltly hmpd wl over 1f out: no prog after* **16/1**

001- 9 1 ½ **Binnion Bay (IRE)**[26] 7660 9-8-11 54..............(b) MarcHalford(3) 3 47
(J J Bridger) *stdd s: t.k.h: hld up in tch in rr: rdn and effrt on inner wl over 1f out: no prog* **16/1**

000- 10 19 **Rock Art (IRE)**[25] 7677 4-8-8 52..............(p) JamieMackay 9 15
(Karen George) *t.k.h: in tch on outer tl rdn and lost pl qckly 3f out: wl bhd fnl 2f* **40/1**

2m 34.33s (1.33) **Going Correction** +0.025s/f (Slow)
WFA 4 from 5yo+ 4lb 10 Ran SP% **112.7**
Speed ratings (Par 101): **96,95,95,94,94 92,92,92,91,78**
toteswingers: 1&2 £9.70, 1&3 £9.40, 2&3 £5.00 CSF £39.13 CT £145.89 TOTE £13.20: £3.00, £1.80, £1.60; EX 39.20.
Owner Roger Alwen **Bred** Sir Gordon Brunton **Trained** Morestead, Hants

FOCUS
There was a slow gallop on early in this ordinary handicap and it developed into something of a half-mile sprint.
Achromatic Official explanation: jockey said gelding hung left on the bend
Rock Art(IRE) Official explanation: jockey said filly hung right

14 BET TEST MATCH CRICKET - BETDAQ H'CAP (DIV II) 6f (P)
3:45 (3:47) (Class 6) (0-58,58) 4-Y-0+ **£1,706** (£503; £252) **Stalls** Low

Form RPR

403- 1 **Peopleton Brook**[3] 7879 8-9-4 58..............(t) SteveDrowne 10 67
(B G Powell) *stdd after s: hld up in last trio: str run u.p on outer 1f out: r.o wl to ld wl ins fnl f* **13/2**

260- 2 ¾ **Bollywood Style**[22] 7716 5-9-2 56.............. RobertWinston 2 63
(J R Best) *in tch: swtchd out off of rail 2f out: rdn and wnt between horses to ld fnl 150yds: hdd and no ex wl ins fnl f* **15/2**

260- 3 1 **The Geester**[14] 7807 6-9-4 58..............(p) FergusSweeney 8 61
(Stef Higgins) *chsd ldrs on outer: ev ch jst over 2f out: drvn over 1f out: kpt on same pce fnl f* **5/1[2]**

421- 4 nk **Only A Game (IRE)**[17] 7771 5-9-3 57..............(tp) AdamKirby 4 64+
(I W McInnes) *stdd after s: hld up in tch in rr: hdwy towards inner over 1f out: nt clr run ent fnl f tl swtchd rt fnl 100yds: r.o but nvr able to chal* **7/4[1]**

045- 5 nk **Tenancy (IRE)**[4] 7869 6-8-6 46..............(p) DavidProbert 9 47
(S A Harris) *led: rdn and hrd pressed 2f out: kpt on wl tl hdd fnl 150yds: wknd fnl 75yds* **11/1**

300- 6 1 ½ **Muktasb (USA)**[194] 3227 9-9-3 57..............(v) JimCrowley 6 54
(D Shaw) *s.i.s: bhd: rdn and hdwy jst over 1f out: r.o wl ins fnl f: nvr trbld ldrs* **25/1**

006- 7 ½ **Brazilian Brush (IRE)**[25] 7680 5-8-6 46 oh1..............(tp) LukeMorris 1 41
(J M Bradley) *chsd ldr: ev ch and rdn 2f out: wknd jst ins fnl f* **25/1**

360- 8 ½ **Commandingpresence (USA)**[17] 7771 4-8-4 47..... MarcHalford(3) 11 40
(J J Bridger) *in tch: rdn and effrt ent fnl 2f: drvn and one pce fr over 1f out: hld whn nt clr run ins fnl f* **25/1**

300- 9 2 **Spring Bridge (IRE)**[101] 6206 4-8-9 49 oh1 ow3........(p) SamHitchcott 5 36
(Mrs L C Jewell) *in tch on inner: rdn jst over 2f out: wknd u.p jst over 1f out* **100/1**

35- 10 3 ¼ **Acrosstheuniverse (USA)**[85] 6641 4-9-3 57.............. MartinDwyer 3 34
(J R Gask) *t.k.h: in tch: rdn wl over 2f out: wknd 2f out* **11/2[3]**

000- 11 1 ¼ **Jeannie (IRE)**[77] 6857 4-8-10 50.............. StevieDonohoe 7 23
(N P Littmoden) *in tch in midfield: rdn over 2f out: bhd wl over 1f out* **25/1**

1m 11.38s (-0.52) **Going Correction** +0.025s/f (Slow) 11 Ran SP% **118.2**
Speed ratings (Par 101): **104,103,101,101,100 98,98,97,94,90 88**
toteswingers: 1&2 £7.00, 1&3 £4.00, 2&3 £6.50 CSF £51.18 CT £270.24 TOTE £6.40: £1.90, £2.70, £2.00; EX 40.70 Place 6: £59.88, Place 5: £8.36..
Owner G S Thompson & P Banfield **Bred** Lower Hill Farm Stud **Trained** Upper Lambourn, Berks

FOCUS
Another good finish in this second division of the sprint handicap.
Only A Game(IRE) ◆ Official explanation: jockey said gelding was denied a clear run
T/Jkpt: Part won. £27,050.40 to a £1 stake. Pool: £38,099.26. 0.50 winning tickets. T/Plt: £43.40 to a £1 stake. Pool: £124,894.56. 2,099.68 winning tickets. T/Qpdt: £6.20 to a £1 stake. Pool: £11,308.40. 1,345.44 winning tickets. SP

[1]SOUTHWELL (L-H)
Saturday, January 2

OFFICIAL GOING: Standard to slow
Wind: Light half behind Weather: Overcast and cold

15 DOREEN FRIZZLE AMATEUR RIDERS' H'CAP 2m (F)
12:25 (12:25) (Class 6) (0-65,65) 4-Y-0+ **£1,714** (£527; £263) **Stalls** Low

Form RPR

550- 1 **William's Way**[186] 1966 8-10-9 **65**.............. MrCMartin(5) 14 79+
(I A Wood) *t.k.h: hld up in rr: gd hdwy to trck ldrs over 6f out: cl up over 3f out: led wl over 2f out: sn clr: easily* **15/2[3]**

0/3- 2 7 **Spring Breeze**[49] 3760 9-9-13 **53**.............. TomDavid(3) 11 55
(J J Quinn) *in tch: pushed along 1/2-way: rdn along and lost pl 6f out: drvn over 3f out: styd on u.p fnl 2f: tk 2nd nr line* **5/4[1]**

1/0- 3 shd **Mujamead**[207] 112 6-10-5 **63**.............. MissCBoxall(7) 4 64
(G A Ham) *chsd ldrs: rdn along and sltly outpcd over 4f out: kpt on to chse wnr wl over 1f out: sn one pce: lost 2nd nr line* **16/1**

/00- 4 10 **Cumbrian Knight (IRE)**[45] 301 12-10-4 **58**.......... MissRJefferson(3) 8 47
(J M Jefferson) *dwlt: sn trcking ldrs: effrt to ld over 4f out: rdn along and hdd over 3f out: grad wknd* **14/1**

005- 5 nk **Russian Invader (IRE)**[11] 7840 6-10-4 **55**..............(be) MrSDobson 12 44
(R C Guest) *in tch on outer: hdwy 1/2-way: led over 3f out: rdn and hdd wl over 2f out: sn drvn and wknd fnl 2f* **11/1**

204- 6 ¾ **Ramvaswani (IRE)**[2] 627 7-9-9 **53** ow4..............(p) MrMMarris(7) 7 41
(N B King) *midfield: on inner: swtchd outside and hdwy after 6f: chsd ldrs 1/2-way: rdn along over 4f out: drvn and one pce fr 3f out* **7/1[2]**

0/0- 7 ¾ **Treeko (IRE)**[46] 5438 5-10-1 **59**.............. MrATBrook(7) 6 46
(P A Kirby) *in tch: effrt to chse ldrs 6f out: rdn along 4f out: sn outpcd* **50/1**

0/0- 8 8 **Global Strategy**[199] 459 7-10-9 **65**.............. MrJSherwood(5) 5 43
(O Sherwood) *dwlt: sn trcking ldrs: cl up 1/2-way: led over 6f out: rdn and hdd over 4f out: sn wknd* **25/1**

336/ 9 29 **Delorain (IRE)**[527] 1925 7-9-3 **47** oh1 ow1..............(vt) MissCScott(7) 3 —
(W B Stone) *chsd ldrs on inner: rdn along and lost pl after 6f: bhd fr 1/2-way* **100/1**

610- 10 18 **K'Gari (USA)**[28] 7649 4-9-7 **58** ow8..............(b) MrJohnWilley(7) 13 —
(B Ellison) *led: rdn along and hdd over 6f out: sn wknd and bhd fnl 3f* **17/2**

126- **11** 2½ **Ingenue**[30] 7415 4-9-11 **60**...(b) MrJBanks(5) 1 —
(P Howling) *chsd ldr: pushed along over 6f out: sn rdn and wknd: bhd fnl 3f* **20/1**

3m 59.74s (14.24) **Going Correction** +0.50s/f (Slow)
WFA 4 from 5yo+ 7lb **11** Ran SP% **111.7**
Speed ratings (Par 101): **84,80,80,75,75 74,74,70,56,47 45**
toteswingers: 1&2 £3.90, 1&3 £19.90, 2&3 £7.90 CSF £15.77 CT £143.17 TOTE £10.60: £2.40, £1.10, £3.90; EX 21.30 TRIFECTA Not won..
Owner Neardown Stables **Bred** Lewis Caterers **Trained** Upper Lambourn, Berks
■ Stewards' Enquiry : Mr John Willey three-day ban: used whip when out of contention (tbn)

FOCUS
This very moderate handicap for amateurs was run at a steady pace, but even so very few got home.

16 MEMBERSHIP AT SOUTHWELL GOLF CLUB H'CAP 7f (F)
12:55 (12:55) (Class 4) (0-85,81) 4-Y-0+ **£4,209** (£1,252; £625; £312) **Stalls** Low

Form RPR

205- **1** **Follow The Flag (IRE)**[14] 7811 6-8-6 **76**...(p) DeclanCannon(7) 4 87
(A J McCabe) *trckd ldrs: hdwy 3f out: rdn to chse ldr over 1f out: edgd rt and drvn to chal ins fnl f: styd on wl to ld last 75yds* **16/1**

363- **2** ¾ **Elusive Fame (USA)**[6] 7854 4-8-9 **72**...(b) JoeFanning 8 81
(M Johnston) *cl up: led wl over 2f out: rdn over 1f out: edgd rt and drvn ins fnl f: hdd and no ex last 75yds* **5/1**[3]

025- **3** 2¾ **Tamasou (IRE)**[18] 7759 5-9-1 **78**... ShaneKelly 7 80
(A J McCabe) *trckd ldrs on outer: hdwy 3f out: rdn to chse ldng pair over 1f out: swtchd lft and drvn ins fnl f: one pce* **11/2**

142- **4** 4 **Jonnie Skull (IRE)**[15] 7797 4-8-4 **67**...(vt) ChrisCatlin 5 58
(P S McEntee) *cl up: led briefly 3f out: sn rdn and hdd wl over 2f out: drvn and wknd over 1f out* **14/1**

1/0- **5** 6 **Prohibition (IRE)**[30] 7620 4-9-0 **80**... WilliamCarson(3) 6 55
(W J Haggas) *trckd ldrs: effrt 3f out: sn rdn and btn 2f out* **7/2**[1]

052- **6** hd **Dig Deep (IRE)**[39] 7506 8-8-12 **75**... PhillipMakin 2 49
(J J Quinn) *hld up in tch: swtchd outside and effrt wl over 2f out: sn rdn and no hdwy* **8/1**

201- **7** 3 **Caprio (IRE)**[36] 7558 5-9-4 **81**... NickyMackay 1 47
(J R Boyle) *chsd ldrs on inner: rdn along over 3f out: drvn over 2f out and sn btn* **7/1**

204- **8** 4 **Hits Only Jude (IRE)**[18] 7759 7-8-13 **76**... DavidNolan 3 31
(D Carroll) *led: rdn along 1/2-way: hdd 3f out and sn wknd* **4/1**[2]

1m 32.57s (2.27) **Going Correction** +0.50s/f (Slow) **8** Ran SP% **110.4**
Speed ratings (Par 105): **107,106,103,98,91 91,87,83**
toteswingers: 1&2 £9.10, 1&3 £11.30, 2&3 £4.50 CSF £87.27 CT £480.30 TOTE £17.30: £4.50, £2.50, £2.50; EX 96.80 TRIFECTA Not won..
Owner S Gillen **Bred** Martin Francis **Trained** Averham Park, Notts

FOCUS
Run in driving snow, this was just a fair race for the grade. It proved difficult to make up ground from off the pace.
Hits Only Jude(IRE) Official explanation: jockey said gelding hung left

17 BOOK TICKETS AT SOUTHWELL-RACECOURSE.CO.UK CLAIMING STKS 6f (F)
1:25 (1:26) (Class 6) 3-Y-0 **£1,774** (£523; £262) **Stalls** Low

Form RPR

433- **1** **Anjomarba (IRE)**[14] 7805 3-8-3 71...(p) WilliamCarson(3) 3 63
(W G M Turner) *chsd ldrs: rdn along and sltly outpcd over 2f out: drvn over 1f out: styd on gamely ins fnl f to ld nr fin* **6/1**

303- **2** ½ **Tamarind Hill (IRE)**[6] 7850 3-8-1 67...(b) DeclanCannon(7) 7 63
(A J McCabe) *chsd ldrs: hdwy 2f out: rdn to ld ent fnl f: sn edgd lft: hdd and nt qckn nr fin* **13/2**

510- **3** 2¾ **Clear Ice (IRE)**[14] 7805 3-9-0 73... AndrewMullen 2 61
(D Nicholls) *cl up: led over 3f out: rdn 2f out: drvn and hdd ent fnl f: kpt on same pce* **7/2**[2]

202- **4** 1¼ **Star Promise**[6] 7850 3-8-4 76... JoeFanning 5 47
(T D Barron) *in tch: effrt to chse ldrs wl over 2f out: drvn and no imp fr wl over 1f out* **13/8**[1]

040- **5** ¾ **Baby Judge (IRE)**[15] 7791 3-8-6 48 ow1... DavidKenny(7) 8 53?
(M C Chapman) *s.i.s and bhd: rdn and sme hdwy 2f out: nvr nr ldrs* **100/1**

324- **6** 4½ **Olympic Ceremony**[28] 7636 3-8-12 71... TonyHamilton 6 38
(R A Fahey) *led: rdn along and hdd over 3f out: drvn over 2f out: grad wknd* **11/2**[3]

316- **7** 1¾ **Silver Linnet (IRE)**[6] 7849 3-8-10 70... ChrisCatlin 1 30
(M G Quinlan) *hld up in tch on inner: hdwy over 2f out: sn rdn and btn* **16/1**

1m 20.65s (4.15) **Going Correction** +0.50s/f (Slow) **7** Ran SP% **110.2**
Speed ratings (Par 95): **92,91,87,86,85 79,76**
toteswingers: 1&2 £4.00, 1&3 £3.70, 2&3 £6.20 CSF £40.50 TOTE £7.30: £2.00, £4.00; EX 29.30 Trifecta £198.60 Pool: £749.07 - 2.79 winning units..
Owner Marbary Partnership **Bred** Tally-Ho Stud **Trained** Sigwells, Somerset
■ Stewards' Enquiry : William Carson two-day ban: used whip with excessive frequency (Jan 22-23)

FOCUS
Modest claiming form.

18 BET WORLD DARTS - BETDAQ MAIDEN STKS 1m 4f (F)
2:00 (2:01) (Class 5) 4-Y-0+ **£2,456** (£725; £362) **Stalls** Low

Form RPR

020- **1** **Stormy Summer**[11] 7842 5-9-0 64...(b) TobyAtkinson(7) 7 68+
(R W Price) *hld up towards rr: stdy hdwy 1/2-way: trckd ldrs 4f out: led 2f out and sn clr: rdn and kpt on wl fnl f* **3/1**[1]

364- **2** 2¼ **All Guns Firing (IRE)**[16] 7780 4-9-3 70... DavidNolan 11 62
(D Carroll) *led: rdn along over 3f out: drvn and hdd 2f out: kpt on same pce* **4/1**[3]

000/ **3** 8 **Arisea (IRE)**[208] 4195 7-9-2 0...(t) J-PGuillambert 6 45
(Paul Murphy) *in rr and rdn along 1/2-way: hdwy over 3f out: styd on u.p fr 2f out: tk 3rd nr line* **9/1**

4 nse **Haka Dancer (USA)**[36] 7-9-7 0... LeeVickers 10 50
(P A Kirby) *prom: rdn along 4f out: drvn wl over 2f out and grad wknd fr wl over 1f out* **7/1**

520- **5** 6 **Oke Bay**[11] 7840 4-8-12 54...(b[1]) RichardKingscote 8 35
(R M Beckett) *chsd ldrs: hdwy to chse ldr over 4f out: rdn along over 3f out: sn drvn and wknd* **7/1**

325- **6** 16 **Mister Frosty (IRE)**[6] 7851 4-9-3 52... SaleemGolam 3 14
(G Prodromou) *chsd ldrs on inner: rdn along over 4f out: sn outpcd* **7/2**[2]

500- **7** 15 **Owls FC (IRE)**[16] 7780 4-8-12 37...(b[1]) AmirQuinn 1 —
(M C Chapman) *sn outpcd and a bhd* **250/1**

00/ **8** 8 **All About Jack**[20] 7608 6-9-7 0...(p) FrankieMcDonald 4 —
(G A Ham) *prom: rdn along 1/2-way: sn lost pl and bhd fnl 3f* **250/1**

U0- **9** 3 **Gospel Spirit**[13] 7826 5-9-7 0... ShaneKelly 9 —
(J R Jenkins) *in tch: hdwy to chse ldrs 1/2-way: sn rdn along and wknd 4f out* **50/1**

10 11 **Distant Florin**[32] 5-9-2 0...(t) DaneO'Neill 2 —
(M E Rimmer) *s.i.s: sn rdn along and a bhd* **16/1**

650- **11** 28 **Aven Mac (IRE)**[31] 7272 4-8-12 42...(p) ChrisCatlin 5 —
(N Bycroft) *sn outpcd and a bhd* **33/1**

2m 48.42s (7.42) **Going Correction** +0.50s/f (Slow)
WFA 4 from 5yo+ 4lb **11** Ran SP% **113.8**
Speed ratings (Par 103): **95,93,88,88,84 73,63,58,56,48 30**
toteswingers: 1&2 £4.10, 1&3 £8.40, 2&3 £9.70 CSF £14.44 TOTE £4.30: £1.40, £1.50, £2.90; EX 18.40 Trifecta £76.30 Pool: £625.19 - 6.06 winning units..
Owner Michael C Whatley **Bred** Deerfield Farm **Trained** Newmarket, Suffolk

FOCUS
A very weak maiden.

19 BET FA CUP - BETDAQ CLAIMING STKS 1m (F)
2:30 (2:30) (Class 6) 4-Y-0+ **£1,774** (£523; £262) **Stalls** Low

Form RPR

264- **1** **Miss Bootylishes**[18] 7762 5-8-9 64... AmyBaker(5) 5 76
(A B Haynes) *cl up: led 2f out: sn rdn and edgd lft over 1f out: drvn ins fnl f: jst hld on* **13/2**

321- **2** hd **Clear Sailing**[29] 7631 7-8-11 65...(p) TonyHamilton 1 73
(Ollie Pears) *trckd ldrs on inner: hdwy 3f out: swtchd rt and rdn to chse wnr wl over 1f out: drvn and styd on ins fnl f: jst failed* **3/1**[1]

246- **3** 2¼ **Moonlight Man**[6] 7854 9-8-12 74...(tp) BarryMcHugh(5) 2 73
(C R Dore) *in rr: hdwy on outer 2f out: sn rdn and kpt on u.p ins fnl f: nrst fin* **17/2**

024- **4** 1¾ **Transmission (IRE)**[6] 7855 5-8-13 66... PhillipMakin 4 65
(B Smart) *cl up: led over 3f out: rdn and hdd over 2f out: sn drvn and grad wknd* **7/2**[2]

66-5 **5** 5 **Bicksta**[1] 7 4-8-2 47... FrankieMcDonald 8 43
(P T Midgley) *prom on outer: effrt to chse ldng pair over 2f out: sn rdn and wknd* **22/1**

111- **6** 12 **What's Up Doc (IRE)**[71] 4450 9-9-1 72... DaneO'Neill 9 28
(Mrs Lawney Hill) *led: rdn along and hdd over 3f out: sn wknd* **4/1**[3]

004- **7** 1¼ **Northern Tour**[14] 7817 4-9-5 67...(t) JoeFanning 7 29
(P F I Cole) *s.i.s: hdwy and in tch over 3f out: sn rdn and wknd* **17/2**

0/5- **8** nk **Back To Paris (IRE)**[14] 7817 8-8-4 68... KellyHarrison(3) 6 17
(Paul Murphy) *a towards rr* **16/1**

200- **9** 40 **Michael Collins (IRE)**[51] 7349 4-8-11 51...(p) KevinGhunowa 3 —
(G J Smith) *cl up: rdn along and wknd 1/2-way: sn bhd* **100/1**

1m 47.19s (3.49) **Going Correction** +0.50s/f (Slow) **9** Ran SP% **112.8**
Speed ratings (Par 101): **102,101,99,97,92 80,79,79,—**
toteswingers: 1&2 £8.40, 1&3 £14.40, 2&3 £8.20 CSF £25.64 TOTE £8.60: £2.70, £1.50, £2.10; EX 32.40 Trifecta £264.40 Pool: £604.01 - 1.14 winning units..Clear Sailing was claimed by Mr J Babb for £6,000.
Owner Mrs H Adams & Miss C Berry **Bred** T P Young And D Hanson **Trained** Limpley Stoke, Bath

FOCUS
A very ordinary claimer, and moderate form.

20 BETDAQ.CO.UK H'CAP 6f (F)
3:05 (3:06) (Class 5) (0-70,70) 4-Y-0+ **£2,456** (£725; £362) **Stalls** Low

Form RPR

556- **1** **Charles Parnell (IRE)**[21] 7729 7-8-9 **64**... MichaelStainton(3) 4 78+
(S P Griffiths) *in tch: hdwy over 2f out: effrt and nt clr run over 1f out: sn swtchd rt and rdn: str run ins fnl f to ld last 40yds* **6/1**[3]

342- **2** 1 **Onceaponatime (IRE)**[4] 7870 5-9-2 **68**... AlanMunro 3 76
(M D Squance) *in tch: smooth hdwy on inner over 2f out: qckand to ld 1 1/2f out: rdn and edgd over 1f out: drvn ins fnl f: hdd and nt qckn last 40yds* **11/4**[1]

431- **3** shd **Whitbarrow (IRE)**[18] 7762 11-8-13 **68**...(b) JamesMillman(3) 6 76
(B R Millman) *prom: hdwy 2f out: rdn to chse wnr ins fnl f: sn drvn and ev ch tl nt qckn towards fin* **17/2**

004- **4** ¾ **Not My Choice (IRE)**[36] 7555 5-8-10 **62**...(t) GregFairley 11 67
(J Balding) *prom on outer: effrt 3f out: rdn to ld over 2f out: hdd 1 1/2f out and sn drvn: one pce ins fnl f* **20/1**

000- **5** shd **Premier Lad**[13] 7828 4-9-0 **66**... PhillipMakin 10 71
(T D Barron) *hld up in rr: gd hdwy on outer over 2f out: sn rdn and styd on ins fnl f: nrst fin* **11/2**[2]

062- **6** 4½ **Gracie's Gift (IRE)**[14] 7815 8-8-0 **57**... BillyCray(5) 8 48
(R C Guest) *in rr tl styd on fnl 2f: nvr nr ldrs* **12/1**

405- **7** nk **Loose Caboose (IRE)**[6] 7852 5-8-13 **65**...(be) AndrewMullen 2 55
(A J McCabe) *wnt rt s: cl up: rdn over 2f out: drvn and hld whn n.m.r over 1f out: wknd* **18/1**

402- **8** 1¼ **First Order**[14] 7819 9-8-6 **63**...(v) AnnStokell(5) 12 49
(Miss A Stokell) *a towards rr* **28/1**

101- **9** ½ **Ponting (IRE)**[15] 7795 4-8-10 **62**... TonyCulhane 7 46
(P T Midgley) *chsd ldrs: rdn along over 2f out: sn drvn and no imp* **15/2**

100- **10** ½ **Cape Of Storms**[15] 7795 7-8-6 **63** ow1...(b) BarryMcHugh(5) 1 45
(R Brotherton) *trckd ldrs on inner: hdwy over 2f out: sn rdn and wknd over 1f out* **33/1**

200- **11** ½ **Dancing Wave**[11] 7838 4-7-12 **57**... MissRachelKing(7) 14 38
(M C Chapman) *in tch on wd outside: rdn along 3f out and sn wknd* **80/1**

203- **12** ¾ **Chosen One (IRE)**[20] 7738 5-8-10 **62**... TonyHamilton 5 40
(B Smart) *sn led: rdn along and hdd over 2f out: sn drvn and wknd* **14/1**

321- **13** ½ **Sherjawy (IRE)**[12] 7835 6-8-4 **56**...(p) ChrisCatlin 9 33
(Miss Z C Davison) *a towards rr* **12/1**

1m 18.28s (1.78) **Going Correction** +0.50s/f (Slow) **13** Ran SP% **118.3**
Speed ratings (Par 103): **108,106,106,105,105 99,99,97,96,96 95,94,93**
toteswingers: 1&2 £6.50, 1&3 £11.90, 2&3 £5.40 CSF £21.70 CT £143.31 TOTE £8.20: £2.60, £1.70, £2.40; EX 22.10 Trifecta £458.30 Pool: £706.15 - 1.14 winning units..
Owner J N Griffiths **Bred** R And Mrs R Hodgins **Trained** Easingwold, N Yorks
■ Stewards' Enquiry : Andrew Mullen two-day ban: used whip on the shoulder in the forehand position and without giving mare time to respond (Jan 16-17)

FOCUS
A modest but competitive handicap.

21 PLAY GOLF AT SOUTHWELL GOLF CLUB H'CAP 7f (F)
3:35 (3:35) (Class 6) (0-60,60) 4-Y-0+ **£1,774** (£523; £262) **Stalls** Low

Form RPR

554- **1** **Dontuwishitwereso**[4] 7869 4-8-6 **48**...(b[1]) LiamJones 7 62
(P W D'Arcy) *dwlt and rdn along to chse ldrs after 1f: hdwy wl over 2f out: rdn to ld over 1f out: drvn clr ins fnl f: styd on wl* **13/2**[3]

420- **2** 3 1/4 **Mocha Java**[7] 7845 7-8-12 **59**....(p) RossAtkinson(5) 4 64
(Matthew Salaman) *a.p: effrt 2f out: sn rdn and ev ch tl drvn and one pce jst ins fnl f* **9/1**

010- **3** 2 **Headache**[15] 7796 5-9-0 **56**....(bt) DaneO'Neill 5 56
(B W Duke) *cl up: led 1/2-way: rdn over 2f out: drvn and hdd over 1f out: wknd ins fnl f* **6/1[2]**

334- **4** 3/4 **Luisa Tetrazzini (IRE)**[15] 7797 4-8-10 **57**.... MarkCoumbe(5) 11 55
(John A Harris) *cl up: effrt over 2f out: sn rdn and ev ch tl drvn and one pce appr fnl f* **20/1**

050- **5** 3/4 **Royal Crest**[79] 6804 4-8-12 **54**.... JoeFanning 10 50
(A Crook) *chsd ldrs: rdn along wl over 2f out: drvn over 1f out and no imp* **14/1**

005- **6** shd **Kheskianto (IRE)**[15] 7797 4-8-7 **56** ow1.... DavidKenny(7) 3 52
(M C Chapman) *midfield: hdwy 3f out: rdn to chse ldrs wl over 1f out: sn drvn and no imp appr fnl f* **50/1**

431- **7** 4 1/2 **King Of Rhythm (IRE)**[15] 7796 7-9-1 **57**....(b) DavidNolan 9 40
(D Carroll) *towards rr: hdwy over 2f out and sn rdn: drvn wl over 1f out and no imp* **2/1[1]**

400- **8** 5 **Megalo Maniac**[12] 7834 7-8-1 **50**.... MarzenaJeziorek(7) 13 20
(R A Fahey) *a in rr* **12/1**

040- **9** 1 3/4 **Tri Chara (IRE)**[25] 7680 6-9-1 **57**....(p) TonyCulhane 6 22
(R Hollinshead) *led: hdd 1/2-way and sn rdn along: drvn over 2f out and grad wknd* **6/1[2]**

006- **10** 2 1/4 **If You Knew Suzy**[6] 7853 5-8-13 **58**.... KellyHarrison(3) 12 17
(R E Barr) *chsd ldrs on outer: rdn along 3f out: sn wknd* **50/1**

500- **11** 1 3/4 **Romantic Verse**[14] 7815 5-8-7 **52**.... MichaelStainton(3) 8 6
(R A Harris) *a towards rr* **33/1**

430- **12** 14 **One Cool Dream**[78] 6824 4-9-3 **59**.... ChrisCatlin 1 —
(P W Hiatt) *chsd ldrs on inner: rdn along bef 1/2-way and sn wknd* **16/1**

000- **13** 2 1/2 **Desert Mile (IRE)**[18] 7762 7-8-13 **60**.... BarryMcHugh(5) 14 —
(Ollie Pears) *swtchd lft s: a bhd* **25/1**

1m 32.56s (2.26) **Going Correction** +0.50s/f (Slow) **13** Ran SP% **121.0**
Speed ratings (Par 101): **107,103,101,100,99 99,94,88,86,83 81,65,62**
toteswingers: 1&2 £13.70, 1&3 £6.90, 2&3 £7.90 CSF £61.16 CT £374.19 TOTE £8.70: £2.60, £2.40, £2.20; EX 80.70 Trifecta £471.00 Part won. Pool: £636.50 - 0.82 winning units. Place 6: £190.98, Place 5: £130.06..
Owner The Redesdalers **Bred** David John Brown **Trained** Newmarket, Suffolk

FOCUS
A very moderate handicap, but it was competitive enough.
Desert Mile(IRE) Official explanation: jockey said mare lost its action
T/Plt: £99.10 to a £1 stake. Pool: £108,163.90. 796.69 winning tickets. T/Qpdt: £24.20 to a £1 stake. Pool: £8,877.56. 271.10 winning tickets. JR

KEMPTON (A.W) (R-H)
Sunday, January 3

OFFICIAL GOING: Standard
Wind: Moderate behind Weather: Overcast

22 BET FA CUP - BETDAQ CLAIMING STKS 1m (P)
2:05 (2:05) (Class 5) 3-Y-O **£2,456** (£725; £362) **Stalls** High

Form RPR
226- **1** **Master Of Dance (IRE)**[25] 7685 3-9-4 81.... PatrickHills(3) 1 73
(R Hannon) *in rr but in tch: hdwy 2f out: rdn to ld jst ins fnl f: sn edgd lft: drvn out* **4/9[1]**

00- **2** 1 1/2 **Brenda Duke**[67] 7120 3-8-3 0.... FrankieMcDonald 5 52
(J G Portman) *trckd ldr tl over 4f out: styd cl 3rd: rdn to chse ldr over 2f out: str chal over 1f out: styd on fnl f but nt pce of wnr* **33/1**

021- **3** 3/4 **Lily Lily**[16] 7792 3-8-13 62....(b) NeilCallan 4 60
(K McAuliffe) *sn led: rdn over 2f out: hdd jst ins fnl f: styd on one pce* **4/1[2]**

545- **4** 8 **Underworld Dandy**[27] 7669 3-8-11 60.... MartinDwyer 2 40
(R T Phillips) *in rr: rdn: hung lft and wknd over 2f out* **9/1[3]**

306- **5** 1/2 **Indigo Ink**[25] 7690 3-8-2 55 ow1.... HayleyTurner 3 29
(Miss Amy Weaver) *chsd ldr over 4f out tl over 2f out: wknd qckly over 1f out* **12/1**

1m 41.02s (1.22) **Going Correction** 0.0s/f (Stan) **5** Ran SP% **109.9**
Speed ratings (Par 97): **93,91,90,82,82**
CSF £16.98 TOTE £1.50: £1.20, £8.40; EX 27.90.Master Of Dance claimed by J. G. Given for £18,000.
Owner P D Merritt **Bred** Mick McGinn **Trained** East Everleigh, Wilts

FOCUS
Not a bad pace considering there were only five runners, but this was a modest claimer in which the eventual winner had comfortably the best chance on adjusted BHA ratings and he probably didn't need to run to his best.

23 BET WORLD DARTS - BETDAQ H'CAP 1m (P)
2:35 (2:35) (Class 5) (0-75,75) 4-Y-O+ **£2,590** (£770; £385; £192) **Stalls** High

Form RPR
014- **1** **Hereford Boy**[13] 7830 6-8-10 **67**....(p) RobertHavlin 2 76
(D K Ivory) *hld up in rr and stl bhd 2f out: rapid hdwy on outside over 1f out to ld fnl 110yds: won gng away* **12/1**

030- **2** 1 **Prince Of Thebes (IRE)**[14] 7823 9-8-13 **70**.... PaulDoe 4 76
(M J Attwater) *trckd ldr: led 2f out: sn rdn: kpt narrow advantage tl hdd and outpcd fnl 110yds* **12/1**

121- **3** hd **Istiqdaam**[23] 7715 5-9-3 **74**....(b) PhillipMakin 1 80
(M W Easterby) *s.i.s: t.k.h in rr: hdwy on outer fr 2f out: styd on wl fnl f to press for 2nd cl home but no ch w wnr* **4/1[1]**

310- **4** nk **Dinner Date**[25] 7684 8-9-0 **71**.... LiamKeniry 3 76
(T Keddy) *chsd ldrs: rdn 2f out: ev ch 1f out: styd on same pce fnl 110yds* **7/1[3]**

002- **5** 3/4 **Mister Green (FR)**[27] 7664 4-9-4 **75**.... NeilCallan 7 79
(K McAuliffe) *t.k.h: chsd ldrs: rdn 2f out: styd on fnl f but nvr gng pce to chal* **4/1[1]**

210- **6** 1/2 **Perfect Class**[139] 5099 4-8-13 **70**.... EddieAhern 6 72
(C G Cox) *chsd ldrs: rdn and ev ch appr fnl f: wknd ins fnl f* **15/2**

012- **7** 3 1/2 **Hilbre Court (USA)**[7] 7854 5-9-3 **74**....(p) TonyCulhane 5 68
(B P J Baugh) *chsd ldrs: rdn 2f out: wknd fnl f* **6/1[2]**

600- **8** shd **Sapphire Prince (USA)**[21] 7742 4-8-5 **62**.... HayleyTurner 8 56
(J R Best) *in rr: rdn and sme prog over 2f out: kpt on same pce fnl f* **25/1**

650- **9** 2 1/2 **Carlitos Spirit (IRE)**[102] 6212 6-8-13 **70**.... AdamKirby 10 58
(I W McInnes) *led tl hdd 2f out: wknd rapidly 1f out* **10/1**

006- **10** 3 **Weald Park (USA)**[50] 7393 4-9-4 **75**.... DaneO'Neill 9 57
(R Hannon) *a in rr* **10/1**

1m 39.64s (-0.16) **Going Correction** 0.0s/f (Stan) **10** Ran SP% **116.0**
Speed ratings (Par 103): **100,99,98,98,97 97,93,93,91,88**
toteswingers: 1&2 £23.30, 1&3 £6.20, 2&3 £12.20 CSF £145.81 CT £531.22 TOTE £12.40: £4.00, £4.00, £2.00; EX 98.40.
Owner Recycled Products Limited **Bred** Mrs L R Burrage **Trained** Radlett, Herts

FOCUS
Quite a competitive handicap for the grade with several in-form horses in opposition, but a fair gallop saw quite a few of the runners racing a bit too keenly for their own good early on and the winner deserves extra credit for coming from the rear.
Carlitos Spirit(IRE) Official explanation: jockey said gelding hung right

24 BETDAQ THE BETTING EXCHANGE MAIDEN STKS 6f (P)
3:05 (3:06) (Class 5) 3-Y-O **£2,590** (£770; £385; £192) **Stalls** High

Form RPR
0- **1** **Avenuesnalleyways (IRE)**[132] 5311 3-9-3 0.... JimCrowley 1 73
(R M Beckett) *chsd ldrs: drvn along over 2f out str run fr over 1f out to ld ins fnl f: styd on strly* **11/4[2]**

04- **2** 1 3/4 **Singingintherain (IRE)**[18] 7772 3-8-12 0.... NeilCallan 3 63
(T G Mills) *disp ld tl led after 2f: drvn clr over 2f out: hdd ins fnl f and kpt on same pce* **9/2[3]**

03- **3** 1/2 **Tatawor (IRE)**[155] 4537 3-8-12 0.... MatthewDavies(5) 6 66
(J R Boyle) *chsd ldrs: drvn along over 2f out: styd on wl fnl f but nvr gng pce to chal* **5/2[1]**

66- **4** 3/4 **Mint Whip (IRE)**[55] 7317 3-8-12 0.... DaneO'Neill 9 59
(R Hannon) *despited ld 2f: styd chsd ldrs: rdn over 2f out: one pce fnl f* **11/2**

\- **5** 1/2 **Mary's Pet** 3-8-12 0.... ShaneKelly 7 57
(J Akehurst) *in rr: sme hdwy whn checked over 2f out: drvn and kpt on fnl f but nvr any threat* **16/1**

00- **6** 2 3/4 **Maxijack (IRE)**[3] 7885 3-9-3 0.... StephenCraine 10 53?
(G Brown) *disp ld 2f: styd chsng ldrs tl wknd ins fnl f* **100/1**

000- **7** 3/4 **Private Olley**[154] 4568 3-9-3 0.... AdamKirby 8 51
(J Akehurst) *towards rr: pushed along over 2f out: kpt on fnl f but nvr a threat* **20/1**

0- **8** 1 1/4 **Sweet Avon**[35] 7585 3-8-12 0.... HayleyTurner 5 42
(Matthew Salaman) *s.i.s: outpcd most of way* **12/1**

9 2 **Captain Tony (IRE)** 3-9-3 0.... LiamKeniry 4 40
(Matthew Salaman) *slowly away: outpcd* **16/1**

1m 13.42s (0.32) **Going Correction** 0.0s/f (Stan) **9** Ran SP% **114.0**
Speed ratings (Par 97): **97,94,94,93,92 88,87,86,83**
toteswingers: 1&2 £3.50, 1&3 £2.80, 2&3 £1.70 CSF £15.40 TOTE £3.30: £1.40, £1.10, £2.50; EX 12.20.
Owner Tony Perkins & James D Cameron **Bred** P G Lyons **Trained** Whitsbury, Hants
■ Stewards' Enquiry : Jim Crowley three-day ban: careless riding (Jan 17-19)

FOCUS
An ordinary maiden for the time of year and one that wasn't run at much of a gallop either with the complete outsider in the thick of things until that last furlong.

25 BETDAQ.CO.UK H'CAP 1m 4f (P)
3:35 (3:35) (Class 4) (0-85,85) 4-Y-O+ **£4,209** (£1,252; £625; £312) **Stalls** Centre

Form RPR
101- **1** **Tripitaka**[32] 7612 4-9-3 **84**.... NeilCallan 9 94
(M A Jarvis) *mde virtually all: hung bdly lft ins fnl 2f: styd on strly fnl f* **4/1[1]**

042- **2** 2 **Paktolos (FR)**[15] 7811 7-9-0 **82**....(p) MarkCoumbe(5) 1 88
(John A Harris) *in rr tl rapid prog 6f out: chsd wnr over 3f out: crossed by wnr and sltly hmpd ins fnl 2f: rallied to regain 2nd cl home but no imp on wnr* **6/1[3]**

201- **3** hd **Dreamwalk (IRE)**[13] 6454 4-8-11 **78**....(v) JimCrowley 3 84
(R Curtis) *in tch tl stdd in rr 5f out: rdn and hdwy over 2f out: styd on to chse wnr fnl f: no imp and lost 2nd cl home* **14/1**

436- **4** 3 1/4 **Evident Pride (USA)**[15] 7811 7-9-5 **82**.... LiamKeniry 6 83
(B R Johnson) *in rr tl gd hdwy over 2f out: pressed ldrs on far rail over 1f out: wknd ins fnl f* **8/1**

411- **5** 1 3/4 **Free Tussy (ARG)**[43] 7475 6-9-2 **79**....(bt) FergusSweeney 11 77
(G L Moore) *mid-div: outpcd 5f out: hdwy and hung lft 2f out: styd on wl fnl f but nt rch ldrs* **9/2[2]**

606- **6** 1 1/4 **Croix Rouge (USA)**[18] 7766 8-8-1 **71** oh14.... KierenFox(7) 10 67
(R J Smith) *in rr: rdn and hdwy over 2f out: styd on same pce fnl f* **100/1**

020- **7** 1 **Buddy Holly**[83] 6724 5-9-5 **82**.... AdamKirby 13 76
(Pat Eddery) *chsd ldrs: rdn and ev ch over 1f out: wknd ins fnl f* **16/1**

160- **8** 1 3/4 **War Of The Roses (IRE)**[267] 1215 7-9-4 **81**.... PhillipMakin 12 73
(R Brotherton) *in tch: chsd ldrs over 3f out: rdn over 2f out: wknd fnl f* **18/1**

050/ **9** 1 1/4 **Alaghiraar (IRE)**[64] 6186 6-8-9 **72**....(p) AlanMunro 5 62
(Miss E C Lavelle) *chsd ldrs: rdn over 2f out: wknd qckly fnl f* **25/1**

641- **10** 2 3/4 **King Supreme (IRE)**[63] 7201 5-8-12 **75**....(b) DaneO'Neill 8 60
(R Hannon) *chsd ldrs: rdn over 2f out: wknd 1f out* **8/1**

622- **11** 1 1/2 **Maslak (IRE)**[18] 7777 6-8-12 **75**.... ChrisCatlin 2 58
(P W Hiatt) *chsd ldrs: rdn 3f out: wknd ins fnl 2f* **12/1**

350- **12** nk **Awatuki (IRE)**[18] 7775 7-8-7 **73** ow2.... RobertLButler(3) 4 55
(J R Boyle) *slowly away: a towards rr* **50/1**

365- **13** 1 **Dakiyah (IRE)**[35] 7589 6-9-8 **85**....(p) IanMongan 7 66
(Mrs L J Mongan) *in rr: rdn into mid-div 4f out: wknd 3f out* **13/2**

2m 32.07s (-2.43) **Going Correction** 0.0s/f (Stan)
WFA 4 from 5yo+ 4lb **13** Ran SP% **120.3**
Speed ratings (Par 105): **108,106,106,104,103 102,101,100,99,97 96,96,96**
toteswingers: 1&2 £8.30, 1&3 £10.10, 2&3 £26.80 CSF £27.64 CT £312.62 TOTE £3.90: £1.20, £3.00, £3.80; EX 46.60 TRIFECTA Not won..
Owner The Tripitaka Partnership **Bred** Genesis Green Stud Ltd **Trained** Newmarket, Suffolk
■ Stewards' Enquiry : Neil Callan two-day ban: careless riding (Jan 17-18)

FOCUS
Plenty of runners, but not many that could be fancied seriously and it turned into something of a tactical affair.
Free Tussy(ARG) Official explanation: jockey said gelding lost a shoe

26 BET TEST MATCH CRICKET - BETDAQ H'CAP 6f (P)
4:05 (4:06) (Class 4) (0-85,82) 4-Y-O+ **£4,209** (£1,252; £625; £312) **Stalls** High

Form RPR
021- **1** **Tiddliwinks**[25] 7692 4-9-4 **82**.... NeilCallan 5 97+
(K A Ryan) *trckd ldrs: led ins fnl 2f: shkn up and hung lft fnl f: readily* **5/2[1]**

601- **2** 1 3/4 **Perfect Act**[14] 7828 5-9-0 **78**.... AdamKirby 6 84
(C G Cox) *hld up in tch: trcking ldrs: rdn and styd on fr over 1f out: kpt on ins fnl f to take 2nd cl home but no ch w wnr* **5/2[1]**

663- **3** *nk* **Dvinsky (USA)**[4] 7875 9-8-8 **72**....(b) JimmyQuinn 1 77
(P Howling) *chsd ldr: rdn to chse wnr over 1f out: no ch ins fnl f and lost 2nd cl home* **6/1**[3]
004- **4** *1 1/2* **Timeteam (IRE)**[25] 7692 4-9-3 **81**.... DavidProbert 7 82
(A Bailey) *sn drvn to ld: hdd ins fnl 2f: lost 2nd over 1f out: wknd fnl 150yds* **4/1**[2]
030- **5** *shd* **Little Pete (IRE)**[24] 7702 5-9-4 **82**.... LiamKeniry 3 82
(I W McInnes) *hld up in rr: sme hdwy over 1f out: one pce ins fnl f* **9/1**
001- **6** *1 1/4* **Cawdor (IRE)**[80] 6798 4-9-1 **79**.... DaneO'Neill 2 75
(Mrs L Stubbs) *chsd ldrs: rdn 3f out: wknd over 1f out* **12/1**
000- **7** *1/2* **Mogok Ruby**[24] 7702 6-8-9 **73**.... AlanMunro 4 68
(L Montague Hall) *a outpcd* **20/1**

1m 11.63s (-1.47) **Going Correction** 0.0s/f (Stan) 7 Ran SP% **113.9**
Speed ratings (Par 105): **109,106,106,104,104 102,101**
toteswingers: 1&2 £1.70, 1&3 £3.90, 2&3 £3.60 CSF £8.67 CT £32.00 TOTE £3.60: £1.60, £2.10; EX 8.50.
Owner Guy Reed **Bred** Guy Reed **Trained** Hambleton, N Yorks
FOCUS
Two withdrawals rather took some of the gloss of this handicap, but it was a well-run affair in which the two with the best credentials finished first and second and the winner looks worth following.

27 BET MULTIPLES - BETDAQ H'CAP 7f (P)
4:35 (4:35) (Class 5) (0-70,67) 4-Y-0+ **£2,590** (£770; £385; £192) **Stalls** High

Form RPR
133- **1** **Nacho Libre**[22] 7735 5-8-13 **62**....(b) GrahamGibbons 9 77
(M W Easterby) *led 1f: styd trcking ldrs: led again ins fnl 2f: styd on u.p whn chal jst ins fnl f: asserted and in command fnl 100yds* **5/2**[1]
012- **2** *2 1/2* **Valentino Swing (IRE)**[3] 7890 7-8-7 **59**.... JackDean(3) 6 67
(Miss T Spearing) *in tch: hdwy on ins over 2f out: drvn so chal 1f out: outpcd by wnr 100yds* **13/2**[3]
50-2 **3** *1* **Goodbye Cash (IRE)**[1] 11 6-8-8 **57**.... PaulDoe 5 62
(P D Evans) *led after 1f: rdn and hdd ins fnl 2f: kpt on same pce u.p fnl f* **5/1**[2]
000- **4** *shd* **Hip Hip Hooray**[81] 6780 4-8-11 **60**.... RobertHavlin 2 65
(L A Dace) *hld up in rr: hdwy on ins over 2f out: chsd ldrs u.p appr fnl f: sn one pce* **25/1**
062- **5** *nk* **Espy**[27] 7673 5-9-4 **67**.... LiamKeniry 4 71
(I W McInnes) *chsd ldrs: rdn 2f out: styd wl there tl no ex ins fnl f* **12/1**
0- **6** *1 1/2* **The Mouse Carroll (IRE)**[13] 7830 6-8-13 **62**.... FrankieMcDonald 7 62
(B R Johnson) *in rr tl hdwy over 1f out: kpt on fnl f but nvr a threat* **33/1**
344- **7** *hd* **Resplendent Nova**[4] 7876 8-9-4 **67**.... JimmyQuinn 3 67
(P Howling) *chsd ldrs: rdn 2f out: wknd fnl f* **5/2**[1]
600- **8** *1* **Expensive Problem**[83] 6726 7-8-11 **67**.... KierenFox(7) 8 64
(R J Smith) *s.i.s: in rr and wd bnd 3f out: nvr in contention* **16/1**
346- **9** *5* **Melt (IRE)**[245] 1710 5-8-9 **58**.... HayleyTurner 1 41
(R Hannon) *in rr: rdn: hung rt and little rspnse wl over 2f out* **12/1**

1m 25.79s (-0.21) **Going Correction** 0.0s/f (Stan) 9 Ran SP% **115.2**
Speed ratings (Par 103): **101,98,97,96,96 94,94,93,87**
toteswingers: 1&2 £4.00, 1&3 £4.20, 2&3 £8.30 CSF £19.46 CT £75.77 TOTE £3.40: £1.70, £1.70, £2.00; EX 17.80 Place 6: £13.82 Place 5: £29.94.
Owner Tri Nations Racing Syndicate **Bred** Lostford Manor Stud **Trained** Sheriff Hutton, N Yorks
FOCUS
Enough in-form horses in opposition to think this was quite a competitive finale and it was a race that ended up being run at a stronger pace than seemed likely beforehand given the number of hold-up horses in the field.
T/Plt: £15.70 to a £1 stake. Pool: £87,611.65. 4,060.84 winning tickets. T/Qpdt: £5.40 to a £1 stake. Pool: £6,779.26. 915.58 winning tickets. ST

28 - (Foreign Racing) - See Raceform Interactive

WOLVERHAMPTON (A.W) (L-H)
Monday, January 4

OFFICIAL GOING: Standard
Wind: Almost nil Weather: Sunny and cold

29 BET WORLD DARTS - BETDAQ APPRENTICE H'CAP 1m 141y(P)
1:55 (1:55) (Class 5) (0-75,75) 4-Y-0+ **£2,456** (£725; £362) **Stalls** Low

Form RPR
322- **1** **Bawaardi (IRE)**[16] 7812 4-9-0 **75**.... LeeTopliss(5) 3 86+
(R A Fahey) *hld up in tch: led over 2f out: rdn and edgd lft over 1f out: drvn out* **9/4**[1]
441- **2** *1/2* **Quick Release (IRE)**[16] 7812 5-9-6 **75**.... MartinLane 5 83
(D M Simcock) *hld up: hdwy over 2f out: rdn wl over 1f out: chsd wnr fnl f: kpt on* **5/2**[2]
000- **3** *2* **Aflaam (IRE)**[25] 7699 5-8-10 **65**.... AndrewHeffernan 1 68
(R A Harris) *a.p: rdn over 2f out: swtchd rt jst over 1f out: kpt on to take 3rd wl ins fnl f* **8/1**
250- **4** *1* **Nora Mae (IRE)**[22] 7741 4-9-2 **75**.... TobyAtkinson(3) 2 76
(S Kirk) *chsd ldr tl wl over 2f out: sn rdn: one pce fnl 2f* **18/1**
215- **5** *1 1/4* **Ella Woodcock (IRE)**[17] 7798 6-8-9 **67**.... KierenFox(3) 9 65
(E J Alston) *hld up and bhd: pushed along over 2f out: c wd st: nvr trbld ldrs* **7/1**[3]
013- **6** *3/4* **Justcallmehandsome**[16] 7812 8-9-2 **74**....(v) BillyCray(3) 7 70
(D J S Ffrench Davis) *led: hdd over 2f out: rdn wl over 1f out: wknd fnl f* **12/1**
001- **7** *nse* **Forward Feline (IRE)**[23] 7729 4-8-8 **64**.... AshleyMorgan 8 60
(B Palling) *hld up and bhd: c wd st: rdn wl over 1f out: n.d* **16/1**
453- **8** *shd* **Pride Of Nation (IRE)**[7] 7858 8-8-11 **66**....(p) JamieJones 4 62
(A J McCabe) *hld up in tch: pushed along over 2f out: rdn and wknd wl over 1f out* **12/1**

1m 50.8s (0.30) **Going Correction** +0.10s/f (Slow)
WFA 4 from 5yo+ 1lb 8 Ran SP% **109.5**
Speed ratings (Par 103): **102,101,99,98,97 97,97,96**
toteswinger:1&2:£1.80, 2&3:£5.60, 1&3:£4.30 CSF £7.26 CT £31.80 TOTE £2.60: £1.30, £1.70, £2.00; EX 7.40 Trifecta £61.50 Pool: £631.89 - 7.60 winning units.
Owner The Matthewman One Partnership **Bred** Millsec Limited **Trained** Musley Bank, N Yorks
FOCUS
Reportedly the coldest night at the course since Polytrack replaced Fibresand and the surface was power-harrowed in the morning to a depth of 4 inches before being reinstated. An ordinary handicap in which the gallop was steady and the winner edged towards the inside rail in the straight. The front pair ran similar races to their recent meeting over C/D, with the third running to his latest.

30 SPONSOR A RACE BY CALLING 01902 390000 (S) STKS 5f 216y(P)
2:30 (2:30) (Class 6) 4-Y-0+ **£1,774** (£523; £262) **Stalls** Low

Form RPR
446- **1** **Interchoice Star**[7] 7858 5-8-11 53....(p) ChrisCatlin 7 62
(R Hollinshead) *w ldr: led wl over 1f out: hrd rdn fnl f: r.o* **11/4**[2]
030- **2** *1* **Well Of Echoes**[5] 7880 4-8-6 49....(tp) AndrewMullen 9 54
(A J McCabe) *w ldrs: led over 4f out: rdn and hdd wl over 1f out: nt qckn ins fnl f* **7/2**[3]
005- **3** *2 1/2* **Peninsular War**[14] 7829 4-8-11 64.... TonyHamilton 1 51
(R A Fahey) *hld up in tch: wnt 3rd and rdn wl over 1f out: one pce: b.b.v* **11/10**[1]
430- **4** *1 1/2* **Ride A White Swan**[23] 7727 5-8-8 46.... MartinLane(3) 4 46
(D Shaw) *s.i.s: hld up in rr: pushed along wl over 1f out: rdn and kpt on same pce ins fnl f* **20/1**
305- **5** *2 3/4* **Gower**[13] 7839 6-8-9 44....(p) JohnCavanagh(7) 2 42
(R J Price) *hld up in tch: rdn over 2f out: wknd wl over 1f out* **16/1**
006- **6** *13* **Desert Dust**[13] 7839 7-8-11 43.... StevieDonohoe 5 —
(H J Collingridge) *led over 1f: w ldrs tl rdn and wknd 2f out* **22/1**

1m 14.7s (-0.30) **Going Correction** +0.10s/f (Slow) 6 Ran SP% **111.5**
Speed ratings (Par 101): **106,104,101,99,95 78**
toteswinger:1&2:£2.10, 2&3:£2.00, 1&3:£1.70 CSF £12.55 TOTE £4.10: £2.20, £1.70; EX 11.50 Trifecta £32.40 Pool: £754.67 - 17.20 winning units.There was no bid for the winner.
Owner John P Evitt **Bred** M P Bishop **Trained** Upper Longdon, Staffs
■ Stewards' Enquiry : Stevie Donohoe one-day ban: careless riding
FOCUS
A weak race, even by selling standards, and one that took less winning than seemed likely with the market leader disappointing. The pace was sound and the field came down the centre in the straight. A length personal best from the winner.
Peninsular War Official explanation: vet said gelding had bled from the nose

31 WOLVERHAMPTON HOSPITALITY - A PLEASURE MAIDEN STKS 1m 141y(P)
3:05 (3:05) (Class 5) 3-Y-0+ **£2,456** (£725; £362) **Stalls** Low

Form RPR
3- **1** **High Constable**[30] 7644 3-8-5 0.... MartinDwyer 7 89+
(R Charlton) *hld up in tch: chsd clr ldr over 4f out: led over 1f out: sn shkn up: comf* **4/6**[1]
4- **2** *3 1/2* **Greyfriarschorista**[153] 4618 3-8-5 0.... JoeFanning 8 77
(M Johnston) *sn led: clr over 6f out: rdn and hdd over 1f out: one pce* **11/2**[3]
3 *5* **Beyond (IRE)** 3-8-5 0.... ChrisCatlin 2 65+
(J Noseda) *s.i.s: hld up towards rr: pushed along over 3f out: styd on to take 3rd ins fnl f: no ch w ldng pair* **4/1**[2]
/45- **4** *3 3/4* **Giant Strides**[356] 144 4-9-2 60.... RichardEvans(5) 5 56
(P D Evans) *hld up in mid-div: wnt modest 3rd wl over 1f out: sn pushed along: no imp: lost 3rd ins fnl f* **66/1**
55- **5** *2 1/2* **Silken Sands (IRE)**[15] 7826 4-9-7 0.... AdamKirby 4 50
(C G Cox) *led early: chsd ldr tl over 4f out: rdn over 3f out: wknd over 2f out* **12/1**
6 *29* **Boxer Shorts** 4-9-12 0.... GregFairley 9 —
(M Mullineaux) *a towards rr: rdn over 3f out: sn struggling* **150/1**
7 *hd* **Big Eric** 3-8-0 0.... AndrewHeffernan(5) 3 —
(P D Evans) *dwlt: a in rr: rdn over 3f out: sn lost tch* **66/1**
0- **8** *11* **Barony (IRE)**[7] 7863 4-9-7 0.... JamesSullivan(5) 1 —
(Lee Smyth, Ire) *prom: lost pl 5f out: lost tch fnl 3f* **200/1**

1m 49.9s (-0.60) **Going Correction** +0.10s/f (Slow)
WFA 3 from 4yo 22lb 8 Ran SP% **107.2**
Speed ratings (Par 103): **106,102,98,95,92 67,66,57**
toteswinger:1&2:£2.10, 2&3:£2.60, 1&3:£1.80 CSF £4.02 TOTE £1.70: £1.10, £1.30, £1.30; EX 4.60 Trifecta £10.40 Pool: £1276.54 - 90.06 winning units.
Owner The Queen **Bred** The Queen **Trained** Beckhampton, Wilts
FOCUS
An uncompetitive maiden run at a reasonable gallop in which the first two had the race to themselves from some way out. The winner raced centre to far side in the straight. Tricky form to pin down but the time was quicker than the thre older-horse handicaps and a fairly positive view has been taken of the form.

32 HOTEL & CONFERENCING AT WOLVERHAMPTON CLAIMING STKS 1m 4f 50y(P)
3:35 (3:35) (Class 6) 4-Y-0+ **£1,774** (£523; £262) **Stalls** Low

Form RPR
063- **1** **Royal Rainbow**[21] 7750 6-8-13 45.... ChrisCatlin 5 57
(P W Hiatt) *hld up in tch: wnt 2nd over 2f out: rdn wl over 1f out: r.o u.p to ld nr fin* **8/1**[3]
622- **2** *nk* **Fujin Dancer (FR)**[19] 7776 5-9-4 68.... NeilCallan 3 62
(K A Ryan) *set stdy pce: qcknd over 2f out: 3 l clr whn rdn jst over 1f out: ct nr fin* **1/1**[1]
216- **3** *3* **Bee Stinger**[19] 7776 8-8-13 65.... DaneO'Neill 8 52
(P R Hedger) *hld up: stdy prog over 5f out: pushed along 3f out: rdn wl over 1f out: one pce* **15/8**[2]
/02- **4** *4* **Blackstone Vegas**[92] 2627 4-8-13 62.... MartinLane(3) 6 52
(D Shaw) *hld up and bhd: pushed along on outside over 2f out: c wd st: rdn wl over 1f out: sn hung lft: tk 4th wl ins fnl f: n.d* **33/1**
450- **5** *1 1/2* **Mrs Slocombe (IRE)**[32] 5063 4-7-12 50.... MissRachelKing(7) 1 39
(Mrs N S Evans) *t.k.h: chsd ldr tl over 2f out: rdn and wknd over 1f out* **66/1**
26- **6** *3* **Naxox (FR)**[23] 7724 9-9-0 68.... MatthewDavies(5) 4 44
(George Baker) *hld up and bhd: pushed along 3f out: struggling whn rdn over 1f out* **20/1**
000/ **7** *10* **Solarias Quest**[635] 153 8-9-1 70.... ShaneKelly 2 24
(W M Brisbourne) *hld up: pushed along over 2f out: struggling whn rdn over 1f out* **12/1**

2m 43.84s (2.74) **Going Correction** +0.10s/f (Slow)
WFA 4 from 5yo+ 4lb 7 Ran SP% **112.8**
Speed ratings (Par 101): **94,93,91,89,88 86,79**
toteswinger:1&2:£2.50, 2&3:£1.90, 1&3:£3.20 CSF £16.17 TOTE £12.10: £3.80, £1.80; EX 21.10 Trifecta £61.50 Pool: £918.17 - 11.04 winning units.
Owner Clive Roberts **Bred** T G And B B Mills **Trained** Hook Norton, Oxon

FOCUS
A modest claimer and a steady gallop means this bare form may not be entirely reliable. The winner came down the centre in the straight and stepped up on recent efforts.

33 BET TEST MATCH CRICKET - BETDAQ H'CAP — 1m 1f 103y(P)
4:05 (4:05) (Class 5) (0-75,75) 3-Y-O — £2,456 (£725; £362) Stalls Low

Form — RPR

001- **1** **Danger Mulally**[26] 7685 3-9-1 **72**....(t) DavidProbert 4 — 72
(A M Balding) *sn led: hung bdly rt wl over 1f out: rdn fnl f: hld on* **3/1**[3]

1- **2** *hd* **Brooklands Bay (IRE)**[79] 6858 3-9-4 **75**.... JimmyQuinn 6 — 75
(J R Weymes) *hld up and bhd: hdwy and missed trble wl over 1f out: sn chsng wnr: rdn and ev ch wl ins fnl f: kpt on* **10/1**

551- **3** *2 ½* **If I Were A Boy (IRE)**[16] 7816 3-8-11 **73**....(p) LeeNewnes(5) 1 — 69+
(S Kirk) *v awkward and s.s: hdwy 5f out: rdn and ev ch over 2f out: hmpd wl over 1f out: rdn and hung rt ins fnl f: kpt on same pce* **9/4**[1]

112- **4** *1 ¼* **Mary Helen**[23] 7731 3-8-7 **64** ow1.... ShaneKelly 5 — 58+
(W M Brisbourne) *hld up in tch: pushed along over 2f out: carried rt wl over 1f out: rdn whn carried sltly rt ins fnl f: one pce* **11/4**[2]

005- **5** *1 ¼* **A P Ling**[31] 7630 3-8-4 **61** oh8.... SaleemGolam 7 — 50
(C N Kellett) *sn chsng ldr: pushed along and lost 2nd over 2f out: rdn whn hmpd wl over 1f out: n.d after* **80/1**

004- **6** *½* **Second Brook (IRE)**[23] 7722 3-8-4 **61** oh6.... HayleyTurner 3 — 49
(R Hollinshead) *hld up: lost pl over 5f out: sn bhd: struggling whn pushed along over 2f out: n.d after* **16/1**

405- **7** *2 ¼* **Jazz Age (IRE)**[19] 7764 3-8-10 **67**.... ChrisCatlin 2 — 50
(J A Glover) *led early: prom tl pushed along and wknd over 3f out* **7/1**

2m 8.51s (6.81) **Going Correction** +0.10s/f (Slow) — **7** Ran SP% **111.1**
Speed ratings (Par 97): **73,72,70,69,68 67,65**
toteswinger:1&2:£3.70, 2&3:£3.60, 1&3:£2.20 CSF £30.09 TOTE £4.20: £2.20, £3.70; EX 19.20.
Owner John Dwyer **Bred** D Robb **Trained** Kingsclere, Hants
■ Stewards' Enquiry : Lee Newnes caution: careless riding

FOCUS
A couple of unexposed sorts in an ordinary handicap but another slowly run race and form to tread carefully with. The winner came down the centre in the straight but hung right and inconvenienced the third and fourth. The fifth and sixth were out of the weights and not beaten far.

34 ENJOY THE LUCKY 7 GROUP OFFER H'CAP (DIV I) — 1m 141y(P)
4:35 (4:35) (Class 6) (0-60,60) 4-Y-0+ — £1,433 (£423; £211) Stalls Low

Form — RPR

041- **1** **Shake On It**[17] 7802 6-8-10 **56**.... JamieJones(5) 1 — 64+
(M R Hoad) *hld up in mid-div: smooth hdwy over 2f out: chal on bit wl over 1f out: rdn to ld cl home* **3/1**[1]

634- **2** *hd* **Mackintosh (IRE)**[7] 7857 4-8-3 **52**....(b) KierenFox(7) 5 — 60
(Patrick Morris) *s.i.s: hld up in rr: swtchd rt to outside over 2f out: c wd st: hdwy wl over 1f out: sn rdn: and edgd lft: chal ins fnl f: r.o* **9/2**[2]

305- **3** *nk* **Spinning Ridge (IRE)**[7] 7856 5-9-5 **60**.... TonyCulhane 8 — 67
(R A Harris) *hld up towards rr: hdwy 3f out: rdn to ld over 1f out: hdd cl home* **8/1**

600- **4** *1* **Alfredtheordinary**[30] 7650 5-9-2 **57**.... SamHitchcott 11 — 62
(M R Channon) *hld up towards rr: pushed along and hdwy over 2f out: rdn over 1f out: nt qckn ins fnl f* **11/1**

600- **5** *1 ¼* **Inside Story (IRE)**[7] 7856 8-9-3 **58**....(b) LiamKeniry 3 — 60+
(C R Dore) *hld up towards rr: nt clr run over 2f out: hdwy on ins wl over 1f out: rdn and one pce fnl f* **17/2**

400- **6** *nk* **National Monument (IRE)**[100] 6288 4-9-4 **60**.... ShaneKelly 6 — 61
(J A Osborne) *hld up in mid-div: pushed along over 2f out: swtchd rt over 1f out: rdn and kpt on same pce fnl f* **14/1**

160- **7** *1 ¼* **Mighty Mover (IRE)**[35] 7600 8-8-13 **54**.... DavidProbert 7 — 52
(B Palling) *prom: pushed along over 2f out: btn wl over 1f out* **7/1**

054- **8** *2 ½* **Dark Ranger**[22] 7742 4-9-2 **58**.... RobertHavlin 2 — 51
(T J Pitt) *prom: wkng whn nt clr run on ins wl over 2f out* **11/2**[3]

05-6 **9** *1 ½* **Kheskianto (IRE)**[2] 21 4-8-6 **55**.... DavidKenny(7) 4 — 44
(M C Chapman) *chsd ldr: led 2f out: rdn and hdd over 1f out: sn wknd* **33/1**

005- **10** *1 ½* **Turn To Dreams**[16] 7818 4-8-1 **48**....(v) AndrewHeffernan(5) 10 — 34
(P D Evans) *led: rdn and hdd 2f out: wknd over 1f out* **25/1**

000- **11** *19* **Valentine Bay**[19] 7270 4-8-5 **47** oh1 ow1.... GregFairley 9 — —
(M Mullineaux) *stdd s: hld up in rr: pushed along and struggling 3f out: sn lost tch* **150/1**

1m 51.16s (0.66) **Going Correction** +0.10s/f (Slow)
WFA 4 from 5yo+ 1lb — **11** Ran SP% **115.2**
Speed ratings (Par 101): **101,100,100,99,98 98,97,94,93,92 75**
toteswinger:1&2:£3.70, 2&3:£7.10, 1&3:£4.50 CSF £15.42 CT £98.70 TOTE £3.30: £1.20, £2.00, £2.70; EX 20.70 Trifecta £75.20 Pool: £823.88 - 8.10 winning units.
Owner Mrs L Bangs **Bred** Car Colston Hall Stud **Trained** Lewes, E Sussex

FOCUS
A moderate handicap in which the gallop was only fair and the winner raced towards the inside rail in the straight. It was the slowest of the four C/D times and the form is a bit muddling, rated around the third.
Dark Ranger Official explanation: jockey said gelding was denied a clear run

35 BETDAQ ON 0870 178 1221 H'CAP — 7f 32y(P)
5:05 (5:07) (Class 5) (0-75,75) 3-Y-O — £2,456 (£725; £362) Stalls High

Form — RPR

111- **1** **Lisahane Bog**[29] 7654 3-9-0 **71**....(p) DaneO'Neill 1 — 73
(P R Hedger) *s.i.s: hld up in rr: pushed along over 3f out: rdn and hdwy on ins over 1f out: led wl ins fnl f: drvn out* **10/3**[2]

240- **2** *hd* **Ramamara (IRE)**[15] 7824 3-8-10 **72**.... AndrewHeffernan(5) 4 — 73
(P D Evans) *hld up: pushed along over 2f out: rdn and swtchd rt jst over 1f out: r.o u.p ins fnl f: tk 2nd nr fin* **33/1**

254- **3** *hd* **Push Me (IRE)**[17] 7791 3-8-7 **64**.... ShaneKelly 7 — 64
(A J McCabe) *hld up and bhd: pushed along over 2f out: rdn over 1f out: r.o u.p ins fnl f: tk 3rd last strides* **8/1**

611- **4** *hd* **Blue Lyric**[33] 7611 3-9-4 **75**.... NeilCallan 5 — 75
(L M Cumani) *a.p: led 1f out: sn edgd lft: rdn and hdd wl ins fnl f: kpt on* **6/5**[1]

045- **5** *2 ½* **Layla's Lad (USA)**[17] 7791 3-8-6 **63**.... JoeFanning 2 — 56
(R A Fahey) *chsd ldr: pushed along and ev ch whn carried lft jst ins fnl f: no ex towards fin* **14/1**

043- **6** *1 ¼* **Sternlight (IRE)**[97] 6364 3-9-3 **74**.... GrahamGibbons 3 — 66+
(E S McMahon) *hld up in tch: wnt 2nd briefly 2f out: rdn whn hmpd ins fnl f: one pce* **9/1**

052- **7** *3 ¼* **Itsthursdayalready**[9] 7846 3-9-3 **74**.... J-PGuillambert 6 — 55
(J G Given) *led: rdn and hdd 1f out: wknd ins fnl f* **4/1**[3]

1m 30.34s (0.74) **Going Correction** +0.10s/f (Slow) — **7** Ran SP% **119.3**
Speed ratings (Par 97): **99,98,98,98,95 94,90**
toteswinger:1&2:£11.30, 2&3:£18.60, 1&3:£4.60 CSF £93.43 TOTE £4.60: £1.90, £7.70; EX 94.20.
Owner P C F Racing Ltd **Bred** J J Whelan **Trained** Dogmersfield, Hampshire

FOCUS
A fair handicap featuring a couple of in-form and progressive sorts. The gallop was only moderate and the first four finished in a heap, so it is hard to rate thr form much higher. The winner raced just off the inside rail in the straight.

36 ENJOY THE LUCKY 7 GROUP OFFER H'CAP (DIV II) — 1m 141y(P)
5:35 (5:35) (Class 6) (0-60,60) 4-Y-0+ — £1,433 (£423; £211) Stalls Low

Form — RPR

000- **1** **Chia (IRE)**[7] 7856 7-9-3 **58**....(p) DaneO'Neill 2 — 65
(D Haydn Jones) *hld up in rr: pushed along and c wd st: hdwy over 1f out: sn rdn and edgd lft: led wl ins fnl f: r.o* **7/2**[3]

000- **2** *¾* **The Graig**[21] 7755 6-8-12 **53**....(t) JerryO'Dwyer 8 — 59
(J R Holt) *hld up in mid-div: hdwy over 2f out: ev ch ins fnl f: rdn and kpt on* **16/1**

122- **3** *hd* **Join Up**[7] 7856 4-8-5 **52**.... RossAtkinson(5) 9 — 58+
(W M Brisbourne) *hld up towards rr: nt clr run 2f out: rdn and hdwy 1f out: sn edgd lft: r.o to take 3rd post* **2/1**[1]

303- **4** *nse* **Kirstys Lad**[16] 7814 8-8-5 **46**.... GregFairley 10 — 51
(M Mullineaux) *sn w ldr: led over 2f out: rdn over 1f out: hdd wl ins fnl f* **6/1**

016- **5** *nk* **Tallest Peak (USA)**[17] 7802 5-9-2 **57**....(b) AdamKirby 6 — 61
(M G Quinlan) *hld up in mid-div: n.m.r over 2f out: swtchd lft and hdwy on ins wl over 1f out: rdn and nt qckn ins fnl f* **10/3**[2]

000- **6** *1 ½* **Colonel Sherman (USA)**[13] 7840 5-8-13 **54**.... LeeVickers 3 — 55
(P A Kirby) *a.p: rdn jst over 1f out: one pce ins fnl f* **40/1**

366- **7** *6* **Jord (IRE)**[17] 7795 6-9-5 **60**.... ChrisCatlin 1 — 47
(J A Glover) *led: hdd over 2f out: rdn and wknd over 1f out* **11/1**

600- **8** *1* **Obe Brave**[7] 7860 7-8-11 **57**.... JamesSullivan(5) 5 — 42
(Lee Smyth, Ire) *hld up towards rr: rdn wl over 1f out: no rspnse* **20/1**

165- **9** *10* **Pacific Bay (IRE)**[18] 6701 4-9-2 **58**.... StephenCraine 4 — 20
(D McCain Jnr) *prom: bmpd over 2f out: sn n.m.r: rdn and wknd wl over 1f out* **25/1**

1m 50.78s (0.28) **Going Correction** +0.10s/f (Slow)
WFA 4 from 5yo+ 1lb — **9** Ran SP% **118.2**
Speed ratings (Par 101): **102,101,101,101,100 99,94,93,84**
toteswinger:1&2:£11.60, 2&3:£7.50, 1&3:£3.10 CSF £56.18 CT £142.62 TOTE £3.60: £1.80, £3.40, £1.30; EX 54.20 Trifecta £223.50 Pool: £887.97 - 2.94 winning units. Place 6 £30.88, Place 5 £23.19.
Owner Mrs E M Haydn Jones **Bred** Shane Moroney **Trained** Efail Isaf, Rhondda C Taff

FOCUS
Division two of a moderate handicap. The pace was only fair and the winner came down the centre in the straight. The time was slightly quicker than the first division and the form seems fairly straightforward with the third and fourth performing to their marks.
T/Jkpt: Not won. T/Plt: £28.30 to a £1 stake. Pool: £143,656.62. 3,697.47 winning tickets. T/Qpdt: £6.40 to a £1 stake. Pool: £11,915.36. 1,372.56 winning tickets. KH

[15] SOUTHWELL (L-H)
Tuesday, January 5

OFFICIAL GOING: Standard to slow
Wind: Virtually nil Weather: Snow showers

37 BET CARLING CUP - BETDAQ CLAIMING STKS — 6f (F)
12:40 (12:40) (Class 6) 4-Y-0+ — £1,774 (£523; £262) Stalls Low

Form — RPR

110- **1** **Stonecrabstomorrow (IRE)**[222] 2402 7-8-2 73(b) MarzenaJeziorek(7) 5 — 65
(R A Fahey) *cl up: effrt over 2f out: rdn to ld wl over 1f out: kpt on ins fnl f* **15/8**[2]

020- **2** *nk* **Mango Music**[28] 7679 7-8-10 59.... ShaneKelly 1 — 65
(M Quinn) *led: pushed along 1/2-way: rdn 2f out: sn hdd: drvn and kpt on fnl f* **15/2**

430- **3** *4* **Rosie Says No**[9] 7852 5-7-9 60....(p) RichardRowe(7) 2 — 44
(A J McCabe) *chsd ldng pair: rdn along wl over 2f out: drvn wl over 1f out and kpt on one pce* **6/1**[3]

001- **4** *nk* **Machinist (IRE)**[234] 2093 10-9-7 93.... AndrewMullen 4 — 62
(D Nicholls) *chsd ldrs: rdn along 1/2-way: drvn over 2f out and sn btn* **4/5**[1]

1m 18.81s (2.31) **Going Correction** +0.325s/f (Slow) — **4** Ran SP% **116.4**
Speed ratings (Par 101): **97,96,91,90**
CSF £14.41 TOTE £3.10; EX 12.60.
Owner R A Fahey **Bred** P Dillon **Trained** Musley Bank, N Yorks
■ A first winner for Polish-born Marzena Jeziorek.

FOCUS
This was a very moderate claimer in which the two market leaders were returning from lengthy layoffs. The form is rated around the runner-up. The winning time was 4.51 seconds outside standard, suggesting the track was again riding slow.

38 BET IN RUNNING - BETDAQ MAIDEN FILLIES' STKS — 6f (F)
1:10 (1:10) (Class 5) 3-Y-0+ — £2,456 (£725; £362) Stalls Low

Form — RPR

502- **1** **Ambrogina**[18] 7792 3-8-8 61....(p) JimmyQuinn 5 — 66
(M Botti) *chsd ldrs: rdn along and outpcd 1/2-way: hdwy and swtchd rt 2f out: chal and edgd lft over 1f out: drvn ins fnl f: rdr dropped whip last 50yds: kpt on to ld nr line* **7/4**[1]

302- **2** *nse* **Freddie's Girl (USA)**[20] 7772 3-8-8 67.... ChrisCatlin 6 — 66
(Stef Higgins) *cl up: rdn to ld wl over 1f out: drvn ent fnl f: hdd and no ex nr line* **9/4**[2]

424- **3** *5* **Cross Section (USA)**[16] 7826 4-9-10 60....(b[1]) ShaneKelly 8 — 54
(E F Vaughan) *chsd ldrs: swtchd rt and rdn over 2f out: sn drvn and no imp* **5/1**[3]

065- **4** *1 ¼* **Lindy Hop (IRE)**[8] 7863 4-9-10 58....(p) PhillipMakin 4 — 50
(K A Ryan) *led: rdn along 1/2-way: drvn and hdd wl over 1f out: grad wknd* **11/1**

304- **5** *¾* **Montego Breeze**[9] 7853 4-9-10 0.... RobertWinston 2 — 48
(John A Harris) *a towards rr* **16/1**

046- **6** *1 ½* **Hold The Star**[8] 7863 4-9-5 55.... AnnStokell(5) 3 — 43
(Miss A Stokell) *chsd ldng pair on inner: rdn along over 2f out: wknd wl over 1f out* **40/1**

34-4 **7** 3/4 **Luisa Tetrazzini (IRE)**[3] [21] 4-9-5 57...................... MarkCoumbe(5) 7 40+
(John A Harris) *rrd s and s.i.s: hdwy on outer 1/2-way: sn rdn and wknd 2f out* **15/2**

1m 18.47s (1.97) **Going Correction** +0.325s/f (Slow)
WFA 3 from 4yo 16lb **7** Ran SP% **112.2**
Speed ratings (Par 100): **99,98,92,90,89 87,86**
toteswinger:1&2:£2.30, 2&3:£3.10, 1&3:£3.10 CSF £5.63 TOTE £2.50: £1.10, £2.20; EX 4.30 Trifecta £9.90 Pool: £304.24 - 22.57 winning units.
Owner Immobiliare Casa Paola SRL **Bred** Newsells Park Stud Limited **Trained** Newmarket, Suffolk

FOCUS
An older-horse fillies' maiden which is about as bad as it gets, and this lot had managed to avoid winning after 47 attempts between them. The form is best rated around the front pair. The winning time was 0.34 seconds faster than the claimer.
Luisa Tetrazzini(IRE) Official explanation: jockey said filly reared at the gates and was slowly away

39 BETDAQ.CO.UK (S) STKS 7f (F)
1:40 (1:40) (Class 6) 3-Y-O+ **£1,774** (£523; £262) **Stalls** Low

Form RPR

622- **1** **Elusive Warrior (USA)**[21] [7762] 7-9-9 62........................(p) ShaneKelly 2 63+
(A J McCabe) *mde all: rdn along over 2f out: drvn and edgd rt over 1f out: kpt on* **8/11**[1]

431- **2** 1 3/4 **Obe Gold**[6] [7879] 8-10-0 66.. J-PGuillambert 5 63
(P Howling) *dwlt and in rr: pushed along 1/2-way: rdn over 2f out: styd on ins fnl f: nt rch wnr* **4/1**[3]

005- **3** 2 1/2 **Tango Step (IRE)**[24] [7723] 10-9-9 40.................................. DavidNolan 4 52?
(D Carroll) *trckd ldr: hdwy to chse wnr wl over 1f out: sn rdn and wknd ent fnl f* **50/1**

420- **4** 1/2 **Boss Hog**[71] [7051] 5-9-9 56.. TonyCulhane 1 50
(P T Midgley) *trckd ldrs on inner: sme hdwy 2f out: tenderly rdn and wknd ent fnl f* **10/3**[2]

/62- **5** 8 **Cleveland**[319] [619] 8-9-6 60.. RussKennemore(3) 3 29
(R Hollinshead) *cl up: rdn along over 2f out: sn drvn and wknd wl over 1f out* **10/1**

/00- **6** 1 1/2 **Favouring (IRE)**[162] [4372] 8-9-2 38...................................(b) DavidKenny(7) 6 25
(M C Chapman) *a in rr: outpcd fr wl over 2f out* **100/1**

1m 32.07s (1.77) **Going Correction** +0.325s/f (Slow) **6** Ran SP% **113.0**
Speed ratings (Par 101): **102,100,97,96,87 85**
toteswinger:1&2:£1.60, 2&3:£6.40, 1&3:£4.00 CSF £4.17 TOTE £1.80: £1.20, £1.90; EX 3.40.There was no bid for the winner.
Owner Mrs M J McCabe **Bred** Steve Peskoff **Trained** Averham Park, Notts

FOCUS
A very ordinary seller and effectively a four-horse race according to the market. The form is best rated around the winner.
Obe Gold Official explanation: jockey said gelding jumped awkwardly and was slowly away
Cleveland Official explanation: jockey said gelding hung right throughout

40 BOOK ON LINE AT SOUTHWELL-RACECOURSE.CO.UK H'CAP 1m (F)
2:10 (2:10) (Class 5) (0-70,70) 4-Y-O+ **£2,456** (£725; £362) **Stalls** Low

Form RPR

316- **1** **Hit The Switch**[9] [7855] 4-8-2 59...............................(p) JamesSullivan(5) 3 69
(Patrick Morris) *towards rr and pushed along over 4f out: hdwy on outer 2f out: rdn to ld and hung sharply lft over 1f out: kpt on* **3/1**[2]

255- **2** 1 3/4 **Borasco (USA)**[17] [7813] 5-8-12 64.................................... PhillipMakin 7 70
(T D Barron) *trckd ldrs: hdwy 3f out: rdn to chal 2f out and ev ch whn bmpd over 1f out: kpt on same pce ins fnl f* **5/2**[1]

100- **3** 2 1/2 **General Tufto**[9] [7854] 5-8-10 67...................................(b) PaulPickard(5) 2 67
(C Smith) *chsd ldrs on inner: hdwy 3f out: rdn over 2f out: drvn over 1f out and sn one pce* **15/2**

260- **4** 1/2 **Vogarth**[17] [7813] 6-8-1 60..(b) MissRachelKing(7) 5 59
(M C Chapman) *cl up: rdn to ld 2f out: drvn and hdd whn sltly hmpd over 1f out: kpt on same pce* **16/1**

604- **5** 4 1/2 **West End Lad**[19] [7783] 7-9-1 67...(b) DaneO'Neill 4 56
(S R Bowring) *led: rdn along 3f out: drvn and hdd 2f out: sn wknd* **4/1**[3]

000- **6** 5 **Amber Moon**[182] [3717] 5-8-6 63 oh4 ow7...........................(b) AnnStokell(5) 1 40
(Miss A Stokell) *chsd ldrs: rdn along bef 1/2-way: sn outpcd and bhd* **50/1**

6- **7** 20 **Scrupulous**[33] [7620] 4-9-4 70.. RichardKingscote 6 1
(Tom Dascombe) *chsd ldrs on outer: rdn along and hung bdly rt to stands' rail over 2f out: sn wknd and eased* **9/2**

1m 45.45s (1.75) **Going Correction** +0.325s/f (Slow) **7** Ran SP% **111.4**
Speed ratings (Par 103): **104,102,99,99,94 89,69**
toteswinger:1&2:£2.50, 2&3:£4.40, 1&3:£3.60 CSF £10.33 CT £47.07 TOTE £4.30: £1.90, £1.90; EX 12.00 Trifecta £42.90 Pool: £514.93 - 8.87 winning units.
Owner Rob Lloyd Racing Limited **Bred** Mrs M T Dawson **Trained** Tarporley, Cheshire

FOCUS
An ordinary handicap. The winner is rated back to his best, with the second to her recent best.
Amber Moon Official explanation: jcokey said mare hung right
Scrupulous Official explanation: jockey said filly hung badly right throughout

41 PLAY GOLF AT SOUTHWELL GOLF CLUB H'CAP 1m 6f (F)
2:40 (2:41) (Class 6) (0-60,66) 4-Y-O+ **£1,774** (£523; £262) **Stalls** Low

Form RPR

521- **1** **Russian Music (USA)**[22] [7751] 5-9-4 54...................... StevieDonohoe 1 66+
(Ian Williams) *trckd ldrs: hdwy on inner 3f out: rdn to ld over 1f out: clr ins fnl f* **5/1**[3]

21-1 **2** 2 1/4 **Dart**[4] [3] 6-10-2 66 6ex... RobertWinston 10 73
(Mrs S Lamyman) *trckd ldrs: hdwy 4f out: rdn 2f out: drvn over 1f out: chsd wnr ins fnl f: no imp* **9/4**[1]

230- **3** 1 1/4 **Sonny Sam (IRE)**[34] [2018] 5-9-3 53.................................. TonyHamilton 8 58
(R A Fahey) *cl up: led over 4f out: rdn along 3f out: drvn and hdd over 1f out: kpt on same pce* **20/1**

002- **4** 3 **Bright Sparky (GER)**[10] [7751] 7-8-7 48................(bt) JamesSullivan(5) 9 49
(M W Easterby) *in tch: rdn along 4f out: drvn over 2f out: kpt on appr fnl f: nrst fin* **10/1**

004- **5** 1 1/4 **Muntami (IRE)**[25] [7642] 9-8-10 46 oh1.........................(p) HayleyTurner 12 45
(John A Harris) *hld up: hdwy and in tch 1/2-way: chsd ldrs over 4f out: rdn along 3f out: plugged on same pce fnl 2f* **20/1**

253- **6** 1 1/4 **Aleron (IRE)**[24] [5554] 12-9-0 50.....................................(p) PhillipMakin 13 47
(J J Quinn) *prom: effrt 4f out: cl up 3f out: sn rdn and ev ch tl drvn and wknd 2f out* **8/1**

014- **7** 3 3/4 **Stagecoach Emerald**[31] [7635] 8-8-7 50.....................(p) TobyAtkinson(7) 5 42
(R W Price) *in rr: sme hdwy over 3f out: rdn along over 2f out: nvr nr ldrs* **5/1**[3]

034- **8** 1/2 **Summer Affair (IRE)**[23] [7495] 5-9-2 57.................... MatthewDavies(5) 3 48
(B I Case) *hld up: a towards rr* **28/1**

533- **9** 8 **Dawn Storm (IRE)**[14] [7842] 5-8-12 48..............................(b) AdamKirby 4 28
(J L Spearing) *in tch on inner: rdn along over 4f out: sn wknd* **7/2**[2]

440- **10** 1 1/2 **Veronicas Boy**[34] [5011] 4-8-9 51.. ChrisCatlin 2 29
(G M Moore) *led: rdn along and hdd over 4f out: sn wknd* **14/1**

602- **F** **Seaquel**[23] [7740] 4-8-4 53.. GillianDawson(7) 7 —
(A B Haynes) *trckd ldrs whn stmbld and fell after 1 1/2f* **16/1**

3m 13.63s (5.33) **Going Correction** +0.325s/f (Slow)
WFA 4 from 5yo+ 6lb **11** Ran SP% **132.0**
Speed ratings (Par 101): **97,95,95,93,92 91,89,89,84,84** —
toteswinger:1&2:£3.90, 2&3:£11.60, 1&3:£22.10 CSF £18.45 CT £229.07 TOTE £7.90: £2.40, £1.60, £7.30; EX 21.20 Trifecta £317.30 Pool: 694.67- 1.62 winning units.
Owner D & Js Boys Racing Club **Bred** Denis O'Flynn **Trained** Portway, Worcs

FOCUS
A modest handicap, but quite a competitive one and a decent test of stamina on this deep surface. There was a very nasty incident after a couple of furlongs when Seaquel crashed to the ground, badly hampering Summer Affair and to a lesser extent Stagecoach Emerald. The race is rated around the runner-up, with improved form from the winner.
Summer Affair(IRE) Official explanation: jockey said gelding suffered interference in running
Dawn Storm(IRE) Official explanation: jockey said gelding stopped quickly

42 HOSPITALITY AT SOUTHWELL RACECOURSE H'CAP 1m 4f (F)
3:10 (3:11) (Class 6) (0-65,65) 4-Y-O+ **£1,774** (£523; £262) **Stalls** Low

Form RPR

613- **1** **Dream In Blue**[9] [7851] 5-9-7 65..(p) DaneO'Neill 7 73
(J A Glover) *in tch: pushed along over 3f out: rdn over 2f out: drvn wl over 1f out: styd on u.p ins fnl f to ld nr fin* **13/2**

022- **2** hd **Silken Promise (USA)**[20] [7766] 4-8-9 57...................(p) RobertWinston 2 64
(W R Swinburn) *mde most: rdn clr 3f out: drvn over 1f out: hdd and no ex nr fin* **13/2**

454- **3** 3/4 **Charging Indian (IRE)**[18] [7794] 4-9-3 65..................(b[1]) TonyCulhane 11 71
(P T Midgley) *hld up in rr: tk clsr order 4f out: gd hdwy on inner 3f out: chsd clr ldr over 2f out and sn rdn: drvn and ev ch ins fnl f: no ex last 100yds* **12/1**

050- **4** 8 **Brave Mave**[42] [7505] 5-9-5 63.. ShaneKelly 10 56
(Jane Chapple-Hyam) *hld up towards rr: effrt and sme hdwy 4f out: rdn along 3f out: sn drvn and plugged on same pce fnl 2f* **8/1**

053- **5** 3 1/4 **Eightdaysaweek**[18] [7794] 4-8-4 55................................(p) MartinLane(3) 4 43
(A J McCabe) *hld up in rr: gd hdwy 4f out: trckd ldrs 3f out: sn rdn and btn over 2f out* **6/1**[3]

045- **6** 7 **Crimson Mitre**[19] [7779] 5-9-7 65.. LukeMorris 5 42
(J Jay) *chsd ldrs: rdn along 4f out: drvn 3f out and sn wknd* **7/1**

443- **7** 1 1/4 **Greenbelt**[34] [7093] 9-8-8 52.. HayleyTurner 1 27
(G M Moore) *trckd ldrs on inner: rdn along 4f out: drvn over 3f out and sn wknd* **5/1**[2]

/46- **8** 9 **Nayessence**[25] [7080] 4-8-4 52....................................(vt[1]) AndrewMullen 8 12
(M W Easterby) *t.k.h: cl up: rdn along over 4f out and sn wknd* **40/1**

122- **P** **Moonshine Creek**[19] [7779] 8-9-6 64.................................. ChrisCatlin 9 —
(P W Hiatt) *trckd ldrs tl p.u 1/2-way: lame* **11/4**[1]

2m 42.67s (1.67) **Going Correction** +0.325s/f (Slow)
WFA 4 from 5yo+ 4lb **9** Ran SP% **118.0**
Speed ratings (Par 101): **107,106,106,101,98 94,93,87,**—
toteswinger:1&2:£5.30, 2&3:£8.50, 1&3:£10.10 CSF £49.33 CT £501.04 TOTE £9.40: £2.90, £2.10, £3.70; EX 57.90 Trifecta £463.60 Part won. Pool: £626.59 - 0.45 winning units..
Owner Paul J Dixon & Brian Morton **Bred** Shutford Stud **Trained** Babworth, Notts

FOCUS
A modest handicap. It was run at a sound pace and the form looks straightforward. A clear personal best from the winner.

43 SOUTHWELL GOLF CLUB H'CAP 6f (F)
3:40 (3:42) (Class 6) (0-60,60) 3-Y-O **£1,774** (£523; £262) **Stalls** Low

Form RPR

512- **1** **The Love Guru**[9] [7849] 3-8-13 60.............................(b) MatthewDavies(5) 6 68
(J R Boyle) *bmpd s: led after 1f: rdn 2f out: drvn ent fnl f: hld on gamely* **6/4**[1]

022- **2** shd **Knightfire (IRE)**[18] [7791] 3-9-1 57.. AdamKirby 8 65
(W R Swinburn) *wnt lft s: chsd ldrs: hdwy 1/2-way: rdn to chal wl over 1f out: sn hung rt: drvn and ev ch ent fnl f tl nt qckn nr fin* **6/4**[1]

40-5 **3** 2 **Baby Judge (IRE)**[3] [17] 3-7-13 48.............................. MissRachelKing(7) 7 49
(M C Chapman) *in rr: hdwy over 2f out: swtchd lft and rdn over 1f out: styd on to chse ldng pair ins fnl f: kpt on* **11/1**[2]

062- **4** 2 3/4 **Clayton Flick (IRE)**[21] [7756] 3-8-7 54.................................. AmyBaker(5) 4 46
(A B Haynes) *t.k.h: in tch: hdwy on outer to chse ldrs over 2f out: sn rdn and kpt on same pce* **12/1**[3]

054- **5** 2 1/4 **Lady Brickhouse**[9] [7849] 3-8-4 46.. LukeMorris 2 31
(M D Squance) *chsd ldrs on inner: rdn along 3f out: drvn over 2f out and grad wknd* **14/1**

646- **6** nk **Charlottesometimes (USA)**[162] [4379] 3-8-7 52............ MartinLane(3) 3 36
(D M Simcock) *chsd ldrs: rdn along 1/2-way: sn wknd* **20/1**

030- **7** 1 3/4 **Lets Move It**[6] [7871] 3-8-8 50.......................................(v) HayleyTurner 1 29
(D Shaw) *led 1f: cl up tl rdn along 1/2-way and sn wknd* **33/1**

1m 18.11s (1.61) **Going Correction** +0.325s/f (Slow) **7** Ran SP% **110.4**
Speed ratings (Par 95): **102,101,99,95,92 92,89**
toteswinger:1&2:£1.40, 2&3:£4.20, 1&3:£4.00 CSF £3.37 CT £12.61 TOTE £2.40: £1.60, £1.30; EX 3.90 Trifecta £28.10 Pool: £1173.65 - 30.83 winning units. Place 6 £67.22, Place 5 £15.34..
Owner M Khan X2 **Bred** Ambersham Stud **Trained** Epsom, Surrey

FOCUS
A modest 3-y-o sprint handicap run at a solid pace and not many ever got into it. It was the quickest of the C/D races and the front pair progressed again. Probably reasonable form for the grade.
T/Jkpt: £5,651.10 to a £1 stake. Pool: £31,837.28. 4.00 winning tickets. T/Plt: £40.70 to a £1 stake. Pool: £113,278.94. 2,028.77 winning tickets. T/Qpdt: £7.80 to a £1 stake. Pool: £12,828.58. 1,204.60 winning tickets. JR

[22]KEMPTON (A.W) (R-H)
Wednesday, January 6
44 Meeting Abandoned - Roads around track unsafe

[8]LINGFIELD (L-H)
Wednesday, January 6
51 Meeting Abandoned - Roads around track unsafe

[22]KEMPTON (A.W) (R-H)

Thursday, January 7

58 Meeting Abandoned - No available ambulance cover

[8]LINGFIELD (L-H)

Thursday, January 7

65 Meeting Abandoned - No available ambulance cover

Mixed meeting - last three races under jumps rules.

[37]SOUTHWELL (L-H)

Thursday, January 7

OFFICIAL GOING: Slow

Wind: Fresh, half-behind Weather: Bright but bitterly cold

69 BET WORLD DARTS - BETDAQ H'CAP (DIV I) 6f (F)

12:10 (12:10) (Class 6) (0-52,54) 4-Y-0+ **£1,433** (£423; £211) **Stalls** Low

Form RPR

06-0 **1** **Brazilian Brush (IRE)**[5] 14 5-8-6 **46** oh1..................(bt[1]) LukeMorris 3 60
(J M Bradley) *trckd ldr on inner: hdwy to ld 2f out: sn rdn and wl clr ent fnl f: eased towards fin* **18/1**

05-3 **2** *10* **Tango Step (IRE)**[2] 39 10-7-13 **46** oh1......................... NeilFarley[(7)] 1 28
(D Carroll) *trckd ldrs: hdwy on inner over 2f out: rdn wl over 1f out: sn one pce* **8/1**[3]

001- **3** *shd* **Angle Of Attack (IRE)**[9] 7869 5-9-0 **54** 6ex............(v) GrahamGibbons 6 36
(A D Brown) *led: rdn along 1/2-way: hdd 2f out: sn drvn and one pce* **6/4**[1]

003- **4** *hd* **Divertimenti (IRE)**[16] 7839 6-8-12 **52**............................(b) PhillipMakin 5 33
(S R Bowring) *dwlt: sn in tch: hdwy over 2f out and sn rdn: drvn over 1f out: kpt on ins fnl f: nrst fin* **2/1**[2]

000- **5** *3 1/2* **Fulford**[30] 7680 5-8-6 **46** oh1.. JoeFanning 9 16
(M Brittain) *in rr: rdn along and hdwy on wd outside wl over 1f out: kpt on ins fnl f: nvr nr ldrs* **14/1**

000- **6** *3 3/4* **Gracie's Games**[19] 7814 4-8-3 **46** oh1......................... KellyHarrison[(3)] 7 4
(R J Price) *sn outpcd a in rr* **33/1**

600- **7** *nk* **Top Flight Splash**[26] 7727 4-8-7 **50**.......................(v) AndreaAtzeni[(3)] 11 7
(Mrs G S Rees) *chsd ldrs: hdwy and cl up 1/2-way: sn rdn and wknd over 2f out* **11/1**

006- **8** *4* **Bertbrand**[26] 7727 5-8-7 **52**.......................................(b) BarryMcHugh[(5)] 8 —
(I W McInnes) *cl up: rdn along wl over 2f out: sn drvn and wknd* **14/1**

1m 19.66s (3.16) **Going Correction** +0.70s/f (Slow) **8** Ran SP% **114.3**

Speed ratings (Par 101): **106,92,92,92,87 82,82,76**

toteswingers: 1&2 £12.70, 1&3 £6.00, 2&3 £2.80. CSF £151.66 CT £349.05 TOTE £19.70: £4.00, £1.80, £1.10; EX 150.80 Trifecta £220.40 Part won. Pool £297.91 - 0.10 winning units..

Owner J M Bradley **Bred** Mrs T Mahon **Trained** Sedbury, Gloucs

FOCUS

With the temperature dropping to -4C overnight the track had to be worked continuously and the surface definitely rode slow. A modest 46-54 sprint handicap but a shock wide-margin winner. He is rated somewhere near his old form, but this was not an easy race to rate.

Fulford Official explanation: trainer said gelding did not act on the deep surface

70 BET WORLD DARTS - BETDAQ H'CAP (DIV II) 6f (F)

12:40 (12:40) (Class 6) (0-52,52) 4-Y-0+ **£1,433** (£423; £211) **Stalls** Low

Form RPR

000- **1** **Jul's Lad (IRE)**[21] 7784 4-8-12 **52**....................................(b) DavidNolan 2 63
(D Carroll) *dwlt and pushed along in rr: hdwy 1/2-way: chsd ldrs 2f out: swtchd rt and rdn to chal whn bmpd sltly ent fnl f: styd on wl to ld last 100yds* **12/1**[3]

642- **2** *1 1/2* **Tag Team (IRE)**[9] 7869 9-8-8 **48**....................................(p) DavidProbert 6 54
(John A Harris) *led: rdn 2f out: drvn and edgd rt ent fnl f: hdd and no ex last 100yds* **11/4**[1]

602- **3** *1 1/4* **Hart Of Gold**[8] 7877 6-8-5 **50**.............................(p) AndrewHeffernan[(5)] 10 52
(R A Harris) *in tch: hdwy on outer over 2f out and sn rdn: drvn and ch tl edgd lft and one pce ins fnl f* **5/1**[2]

544- **4** *1/2* **Nabeeda**[27] 7710 5-8-12 **52**.. RobertWinston 3 53
(M Brittain) *trckd ldrs: hdwy 1/2-way: rdn 2f out and ev ch tl drvn appr fnl f and grad wknd* **11/4**[1]

023- **5** *3* **Tadlil**[9] 7869 8-8-8 **48**...(v) LukeMorris 5 39
(J M Bradley) *chsd ldrs: hdwy over 2f out and sn cl up: rdn wl over 1f out and sn wknd* **5/1**[2]

00-0 **6** *2* **Mickys Mate**[5] 10 5-7-13 **46** oh1............................... NathanAlison[(7)] 8 31
(S A Harris) *cl up: rdn along 1/2-way: grad wknd fnl 2f* **100/1**

406- **7** *1/2* **All You Need (IRE)**[48] 7460 6-8-11 **51**.............................(e[1]) ChrisCatlin 4 34
(R Hollinshead) *a towards rr* **12/1**[3]

05-5 **8** *15* **Gower**[3] 30 6-8-3 **46** oh1...(tp) KellyHarrison[(3)] 7 —
(R J Price) *rrd s and s.i.s: a bhd* **14/1**

000- **9** *2 1/2* **Ronnie Howe**[16] 7838 6-8-6 **46** oh1..............................(bt) JimmyQuinn 9 —
(S R Bowring) *prom: rdn along wl over 2f out: sn wknd* **25/1**

1m 20.17s (3.67) **Going Correction** +0.70s/f (Slow) **9** Ran SP% **113.6**

Speed ratings (Par 101): **103,101,99,98,94 92,91,71,68**

toteswingers: 1&2 £8.80, 1&3 £10.70, 2&3 £4.40. CSF £44.39 CT £191.52 TOTE £15.80: £3.50, £1.50, £1.20; EX 54.20 Trifecta £244.20 Part won. Pool £330.03 - 0.10 winning units..

Owner T & J Tuohy **Bred** E O'Leary **Trained** Sledmere, E Yorks

FOCUS

Part two was a 46-52 affair and the time was half a second slower than the opener, although the pace looked strong. The form is rated around the runner-up.

Nabeeda Official explanation: trainer said gelding struggled on the slow surface

71 BETDAQ.CO.UK H'CAP 6f (F)

1:10 (1:10) (Class 4) (0-85,88) 4-Y-0+ **£4,209** (£1,252; £625; £312) **Stalls** Low

Form RPR

301- **1** **Harlech Castle**[9] 7870 5-9-3 **81** 6ex...........................(b) StephenCraine 3 89
(J R Boyle) *stmbld sltly s: cl up: led over 3f out: pushed along 2f out: rdn ent fnl f: edgd lft and hld on wl towards fin* **5/2**[2]

42-2 **2** *nk* **Onceaponatime (IRE)**[5] 20 5-8-4 **68**.............................. LukeMorris 1 75
(M D Squance) *trckd ldng pair on inner: hdwy to chse wnr 2f out: rdn to chal over 1f out: drvn and ev ch ins fnl f tl no ex towards fin* **9/4**[1]

141- **3** *1 1/2* **Autumn Blades (IRE)**[7] 7891 5-9-10 **88** 6ex................(p) DavidProbert 5 90
(A Bailey) *trckd ldrs: hdwy over 2f out: chsd ldng pair over 1f out: sn rdn: edgd lft and one pce ins fnl f* **13/2**

020- **4** *10* **Xpres Maite**[23] 7759 7-9-1 **79**..(p) PhillipMakin 2 49
(S R Bowring) *wnt rt s: led: pushed along and hdd over 3f out: rdn along wl over 2f out and sn wknd* **4/1**[3]

024- **5** *4* **Resplendent Alpha**[18] 7828 6-8-8 **72**.............................. JimmyQuinn 4 29
(P Howling) *chsd ldrs: rdn along wl over 2f out and sn btn* **12/1**

061- **6** *2 3/4* **Green Park (IRE)**[33] 7646 7-8-12 **76**..............................(b) DavidNolan 6 25
(D Carroll) *in tch: rdn along and sme hdwy over 2f out: sn rdn and no imp* **12/1**

030- **7** *31* **Burnwynd Boy**[109] 6135 5-9-1 **79**.................................... SteveDrowne 7 —
(J A McShane) *sn outpcd and bhd fr 1/2-way* **25/1**

1m 18.54s (2.04) **Going Correction** +0.70s/f (Slow) **7** Ran SP% **111.9**

Speed ratings (Par 105): **114,113,111,98,92 89,47**

toteswingers: 1&2 £2.20, 1&3 £5.20, 2&3 £2.40. CSF £8.16 TOTE £3.70: £2.10, £1.70; EX 10.50.

Owner Elite Racing Club **Bred** Elite Racing Club **Trained** Epsom, Surrey

FOCUS

A tight 68-88 handicap but the first three finished a long way clear. It was sound run and the form is fair for the grade and looks sound.

Burnwynd Boy Official explanation: jockey said the gelding moved poorly throughout

72 BETDAQEXTRA.COM CLAIMING STKS 7f (F)

1:40 (1:40) (Class 6) 3-Y-O **£1,774** (£523; £262) **Stalls** Low

Form RPR

335- **1** **Miss Taken (IRE)**[9] 7868 3-7-7 47..................................(b) NeilFarley[(7)] 5 55
(D Carroll) *cl up on outer: led over 2f out: pushed clr ent fnl f: kpt on* **11/1**[3]

131- **2** *1 1/2* **Lord Victor**[9] 7868 3-8-9 64.. ShaneKelly 4 59
(A J McCabe) *cl up: led 1/2-way: rdn along and hdd over 2f out: drvn over 1f out: kpt on u.p ins fnl f* **1/4**[1]

653- **3** *3* **Angie's Nap (USA)**[9] 7868 3-7-11 63........................(p) AndreaAtzeni[(3)] 2 42
(P S McEntee) *led: hdd 1/2-way and sn rdn along: drvn 2f out and kpt on same pce* **5/1**[2]

50- **4** *16* **Last Of The Ravens**[9] 7864 3-8-1 0...................... AndrewHeffernan[(5)] 1 5
(J F Coupland) *s.i.s: a outpcd and bhd* **80/1**

1m 36.6s (6.30) **Going Correction** +0.70s/f (Slow) **4** Ran SP% **106.2**

Speed ratings (Par 95): **92,90,86,68**

CSF £14.71 TOTE £8.20; EX 16.70.

Owner K & D Racing Partnership **Bred** Ceka Ireland Limited **Trained** Sledmere, E Yorks

■ Neil Farley's first winner.

FOCUS

The Fibresand surface was officially changed to slow ahead of this seemingly one-sided claimer. With the favourite disappointing this is not form to be confident about. It has been rated around the winner.

Lord Victor Official explanation: jockey said cold was unsuited by the slow going

73 SOUTHWELL-RACECOURSE.CO.UK RATING RELATED MAIDEN STKS 1m (F)

2:10 (2:10) (Class 6) 3-Y-O+ **£1,774** (£523; £262) **Stalls** Low

Form RPR

650- **1** **Cosimo de Medici**[25] 7736 3-8-8 65 ow1........................ SteveDrowne 5 73
(H Morrison) *trckd ldng pair on outer: rdn along over 3f out: wd st: drvn and hdwy over 1f out: edgd lft ent fnl f: sn led and kpt on strly* **5/2**[3]

032- **2** *4 1/2* **Gold Party**[9] 7865 3-8-7 62..(t) RobertWinston 1 61
(K McAuliffe) *cl up: led after 1f: rdn along 2f out: drvn over 1f out: edgd lft and hdd ins fnl f: one pce* **7/4**[1]

233- **3** *1/2* **Tobrata**[24] 7753 4-9-6 63.. JohnCavanagh[(7)] 3 64
(M Brittain) *trckd ldrs on inner: hdwy to chse ldr over 2f out: rdn and ev ch over 1f out: drvn and wknd ent fnl f* **8/1**

343- **4** *23* **Honest Broker (IRE)**[26] 7722 3-8-7 60..........................(b[1]) JoeFanning 6 5
(M Johnston) *led 1f: cl up tl rdn along 3f out and sn wknd* **9/4**[2]

000- **5** *7* **Spiders Tern**[38] 7596 5-9-13 30.. LukeMorris 4 —
(J M Bradley) *dwlt: a in rr* **200/1**

1m 49.14s (5.44) **Going Correction** +0.70s/f (Slow)

WFA 3 from 4yo+ 20lb **5** Ran SP% **107.3**

Speed ratings (Par 101): **100,95,95,72,65**

toteswingers: 1&2 £4.70. CSF £6.89 TOTE £3.20: £1.80, £1.50; EX 10.10.

Owner Bevan, Doyle & Lawrence **Bred** Shortgrove Manor Stud **Trained** East Ilsley, Berks

FOCUS

A 0-65 rating related maiden race. It was steadily run and the form is not the most solid. Improvement from the winner, but the runner-up was 8lb off his latest figure.

Cosimo de Medici Official explanation: trainer said, regarding the apparent improvement in form, that the gelding had strengthened up and was better suited by the step up to a mile today

74 HAPPY 58TH BIRTHDAY RICHARD ARCHER H'CAP 5f (F)

2:40 (2:40) (Class 4) (0-85,84) 4-Y-O+ **£4,209** (£1,252; £625; £312) **Stalls** High

Form RPR

300- **1** **Argentine (IRE)**[26] 7735 6-8-9 **75** ow3.........................(b) SteveDrowne 6 84
(J A McShane) *cl up: effrt on stands' rail 1/2-way: led 2f out: rdn over 1f out: kpt on u.p ins fnl f* **3/1**[2]

35-0 **2** *3/4* **Pawan (IRE)**[6] 2 10-8-9 **80**..(p) AnnStokell[(5)] 1 86
(Miss A Stokell) *dwlt and wnt lft s: sn chsng ldrs: hdwy on outer 1/2-way: rdn wl over 1f out and sn ev ch: kpt on ins fnl f* **15/2**

302- **3** *nk* **The Tatling (IRE)**[8] 7872 13-9-0 **80**............................... LukeMorris 4 85
(J M Bradley) *hld up in tch: hdwy 2f out: rdn over 1f out: drvn and kpt on ins fnl f* **11/4**[1]

016- **4** *1* **Wotashirtfull (IRE)**[126] 5592 5-9-4 **84**.......................(p) StephenCraine 2 86
(J R Boyle) *led: rdn along 1/2-way: hdd 2f out: drvn and wknd over 1f out* **7/2**[3]

040- **5** *7* **Spiritofthewest (IRE)**[23] 7759 4-8-4 **70** oh1................(p) DavidProbert 7 46
(D H Brown) *a towards rr* **4/1**

423- **6** *1 1/4* **Garstang**[90] 6632 7-8-11 **77**..(b) ChrisCatlin 3 49
(J Balding) *chsd ldrs: rdn along 1/2-way: wknd wl over 1f out* **12/1**

61.10 secs (1.40) **Going Correction** +0.425s/f (Slow) **6** Ran SP% **113.3**

Speed ratings (Par 105): **105,103,103,101,90 88**

toteswingers: 1&2 £4.40, 1&3 £2.80, 2&3 £3.70. CSF £25.03 TOTE £3.70: £1.80, £3.30; EX 24.20.

Owner Mrs Carol Auld **Bred** Tony Hirschfeld & L K Piggott **Trained** Chapelton, S Lanarks

FOCUS

A competitive 70-84 sprint handicap. Straightforward form which makes sense at face value.

Spiritofthewest(IRE) Official explanation: jockey said the gelding was never travelling

75 SOUTHWELL-RACECOURSE.CO.UK H'CAP 1m (F)

3:10 (3:10) (Class 6) (0-60,65) 4-Y-0+ **£1,774** (£523; £262) **Stalls** Low

Form RPR

413- **1** **Bestowed**[10] 7856 5-8-11 **58**....(v) AndrewHeffernan(5) 2 68+
(P D Evans) *plld hrd early: chsd ldrs on inner: hdwy over 3f out: rdn to ld wl over 1f out: drvn ent fnl f and kpt on* **7/2**[3]

000- **2** 1 ½ **Silca Meydan**[24] 7755 4-8-7 **49**.... ShaneKelly 1 56
(R J Price) *cl up: rdn along and sltly outpcd 2f out: drvn over 1f out: styd on ins fnl f: nt rch wnr* **22/1**

002- **3** 1 ¼ **Trans Sonic**[11] 7855 7-8-11 **58**.... BarryMcHugh(5) 5 62
(J Hetherton) *dwlt: in tch: pushed along over 3f out: rdn over 2f out: kpt on u.p appr fnl f: nrst fin* **9/4**[2]

16-5 **4** 1 **Tallest Peak (USA)**[3] 36 5-9-1 **57**....(b) JamieSpencer 9 58
(M G Quinlan) *led: rdn along over 2f out: hdd wl over 1f out: drvn and wknd appr fnl f* **2/1**[1]

000- **5** 4 **Anduril**[20] 7802 9-7-11 **46**.... NeilFarley(7) 4 38
(D Carroll) *chsd ldrs on outer: rdn along 3f out: drvn 2f out and grad wknd* **16/1**

200- **6** 8 **King Of Legend (IRE)**[47] 7475 6-8-13 **60**.... TobyAtkinson(5) 8 34
(D Morris) *chsd ldrs: rdn along 1/2-way: sn wknd* **12/1**

504- **7** 11 **Plenilune (IRE)**[21] 7784 5-8-8 **50**....(v1) JoeFanning 7 —
(M Brittain) *dwlt: t.k.h and sn chsng ldrs: rdn along over 3f out: wknd over 2f out* **7/1**

1m 49.56s (5.86) **Going Correction** +0.70s/f (Slow) **7 Ran SP% 116.7**
Speed ratings (Par 101): **98,96,95,94,90 82,71**
toteswingers: 1&2 £6.10, 1&3 £2.80, 2&3 £10.00. CSF £71.26 CT £210.23 TOTE £5.00: £2.10, £5.60; EX 62.20 Trifecta £134.80 Pool £756.28 - 4.15 winning units..
Owner Diamond Racing Ltd **Bred** Mrs A M Jenkins And E D Kessly **Trained** Pandy, Monmouths

FOCUS
A modest 46-60 handicap. The pace was not that strong yet they came home well strung out. It is hard to be confident about the form but the winner is probably worth a bit of extra credit.

76 MEMBERSHIP AT SOUTHWELL GOLF CLUB APPRENTICE H'CAP 1m 4f (F)

3:40 (3:40) (Class 5) (0-70,70) 4-Y-0+ **£2,456** (£725; £362) **Stalls** Low

Form RPR

0/0- **1** **Dan Buoy (FR)**[38] 7598 7-8-11 **58**....(p) RossAtkinson 7 64
(R C Guest) *mde all: pushed along 3f out: rdn 2f out: jnd and drvn over 1f out: hld on gamely towards fin* **20/1**

05-5 **2** shd **Russian Invader (IRE)**[5] 15 6-8-6 **56** oh1....(be) TobyAtkinson(3) 6 62
(R C Guest) *stdd s and hld up in tch: hdwy over 3f out: rdn along 2f out: drvn over 1f out: styd on to chal ins fnl f: jst failed* **6/1**

123- **3** 1 ¾ **Onemoreandstay**[21] 7779 5-9-6 **67**....(p) AshleyMorgan 2 70
(M D Squance) *hld up in tch: hdwy on bit on inner 3f out: sn cl up and ev ch over 1f out: sn rdn and one pce ins fnl f* **3/1**[2]

021- **4** 2 **Lava Steps (USA)**[26] 7725 4-9-5 **70**.... PaulPickard 4 70
(P T Midgley) *t.k.h: trckd ldr: effrt on inner 3f out: rdn along 2f out: drvn and wknd appr fnl f* **5/4**[1]

200/ **5** ½ **Nawow**[60] 6079 10-9-2 **68**....(p) MissRachelKing(5) 5 67
(M G Hazell) *trckd ldr: effrt over 3f out and sn rdn: drvn 2f out and grad wknd appr fnl f* **12/1**

321- **6** nk **Boundless Prospect (USA)**[21] 7779 11-9-9 **70**.... AndrewHeffernan 3 69
(P D Evans) *trckd ldrs on inner: rdn along over 3f out and sn wknd* **5/1**[3]

2m 53.15s (12.15) **Going Correction** +0.70s/f (Slow)
WFA 4 from 5yo+ 4lb **6 Ran SP% 112.9**
Speed ratings (Par 103): **87,86,85,84,84 83**
toteswingers: 1&2 £6.60, 1&3 £5.00, 2&3 £3.40. CSF £129.41 TOTE £16.00: £4.70, £3.20; EX 57.30 Place 6 £257.67, Place 5 £150.95..
Owner Bamboozelem **Bred** London Thoroughbred Services **Trained** Stainforth, S Yorks
■ Stewards' Enquiry : Toby Atkinson one day ban: used whip with excessive frequency (Jan 21)

FOCUS
A modest 56-70 apprentice handicap run at a very steady pace to past halfway. As a result there is a bit of doubt over the form, with a surprise winner making all from his stablemate who was 5lb wrong.

T/Jkpt: Not won. T/Plt: £684.30 to a £1 stake. Pool: £101,440.06. 108.21 winning tickets. T/Qpdt: £230.30 to a £1 stake. Pool: £11,455.30. 36.80 winning tickets. JR

8 LINGFIELD (L-H)

Friday, January 8

OFFICIAL GOING: Standard

Wind: Light, against Weather: Overcast becoming fine, track surrounds covered with snow

77 BET NFL - BETDAQ H'CAP (DIV I) 5f (P)

12:30 (12:31) (Class 6) (0-65,65) 4-Y-0+ **£1,433** (£423; £211) **Stalls** High

Form RPR

404- **1** **Silver Prelude**[30] 7682 9-9-0 **64**....(t) WilliamCarson(3) 3 74
(S C Williams) *trckd ldr: shkn up to ld jst ins fnl f: styd on wl and sn in command* **7/2**[1]

006- **2** 1 ¾ **Ten Down**[20] 7807 5-8-8 **55**.... MartinDwyer 6 59
(M Quinn) *led: rdn and hdd jst ins fnl f: one pce* **9/2**[3]

044- **3** 1 ¾ **Bluebok**[33] 7657 9-8-7 **57**....(bt) JackDean(3) 8 55
(J M Bradley) *in tch: pushed along fr 1/2-way: plugged on to take 3rd 1f out: no imp on ldng pair* **13/2**

000- **4** hd **Steel City Boy (IRE)**[20] 7807 7-8-10 **57**.... JimCrowley 7 54
(D Shaw) *hld up in last: brought wd and stl last jst over 1f out: styd on fnl f: nrly snatched 3rd* **13/2**

303- **5** 1 ¼ **Style Award**[63] 7280 5-8-13 **60**....(p) RichardKingscote 2 52
(W J H Ratcliffe) *trckd ldng pair and racd on inner: nt qckn over 1f out: wknd fnl f* **4/1**[2]

606- **6** ¾ **Meikle Barfil**[30] 7689 8-8-4 **51** oh4....(p) DavidProbert 10 41
(J M Bradley) *racd wd: chsd ldrs: rdn 2f out: fdd over 1f out* **25/1**

614- **7** ¾ **Thoughtsofstardom**[17] 7838 7-9-1 **62**.... ChrisCatlin 9 49
(P S McEntee) *chsd ldrs: pushed along 2f out: grad wknd* **9/2**[3]

58.15 secs (-0.65) **Going Correction** +0.05s/f (Slow) **7 Ran SP% 109.1**
Speed ratings (Par 101): **107,104,101,101,99 97,96**
toteswinger:1&2:£3.20, 2&3:£4.80, 1&3:£4.00 CSF £17.52 CT £86.00 TOTE £5.30: £2.30, £3.40; EX 19.20 Trifecta £86.00 Pool £174.41 - 1.50 winning units..
Owner Mrs A Shone **Bred** Bearstone Stud **Trained** Newmarket, Suffolk

FOCUS
An ordinary sprint handicap. It paid to race handily despite a strong early pace. The form is sound, rated around the front pair.

78 TRY BETDAQ FOR AN EXCHANGE H'CAP 6f (P)

1:00 (1:01) (Class 6) (0-65,65) 4-Y-0+ **£1,774** (£523; £262) **Stalls** Low

Form RPR

306- **1** **Imperial House**[34] 7645 4-9-3 **64**....(b) StephenCraine 2 73
(R A Harris) *trckd ldng trio gng wl: effrt to chal 1f out w hd at awkward angle: drvn ahd wl ins fnl f: hld on* **10/1**

0/3- **2** shd **Double Bill (USA)**[11] 7861 6-8-13 **60**.... JosedeSouza 7 68
(P F I Cole) *t.k.h: sn trckd ldr: effrt on outer to ld narrowly 1f out: hdd wl ins fnl f: styd on: jst hld* **5/1**[3]

521- **3** ¾ **Divine Force**[38] 7602 4-9-2 **63**.... SimonWhitworth 6 69+
(M Wigham) *reluctant to go nr stalls: s.s: t.k.h and hld up in 7th: prog and nt clr run 1f out: wnt 3rd ins fnl f: nvr able to chal* **6/4**[1]

430- **4** ½ **Kyle (IRE)**[10] 7870 6-9-2 **63**.... FergusSweeney 10 67
(C R Dore) *hld up in 6th: shkn up and nt qckn over 1f out: styd on wl last 150yds: nrst fin* **6/1**

052- **5** 1 ¼ **Lord Deevert**[38] 7606 5-8-12 **62**....(p) JackDean(3) 9 62
(W G M Turner) *led at modest: pce: qcknd over 2f out: hdd and fdd 1f out* **9/2**[2]

000- **6** nse **Trip Switch**[8] 7890 4-8-13 **60**.... SaleemGolam 12 60
(G Prodromou) *s.i.s: hld up in last: pushed along over 2f out: stl last whn reminders 150yds out: r.o fnl 100yds* **40/1**

03-1 **7** ½ **Peopleton Brook**[6] 14 8-9-3 **64** 6ex....(t) SteveDrowne 3 63
(B G Powell) *wl away but sn restrained bhd ldng pair: tried to chal jst over 1f out: wknd rapidly last 150yds* **10/1**

406- **8** nk **Musical Script (USA)**[19] 7828 7-9-4 **65**....(b) ChrisCatlin 1 63
(Mouse Hamilton-Fairley) *t.k.h: hld up in 5th: effrt on inner over 1f out: wknd rapidly ins fnl f* **7/1**

1m 12.41s (0.51) **Going Correction** +0.05s/f (Slow) **8 Ran SP% 122.3**
Speed ratings (Par 101): **98,97,96,96,94 94,93,93**
toteswinger:1&2:£20.40, 2&3:£1.90, 1&3:£10.10 CSF £63.20 CT £120.51 TOTE £10.10: £4.40, £2.20, £1.10; EX 113.40 Trifecta £199.00 Part won. Pool £268.99 - 0.10 winning units..
Owner Mrs Ruth M Serrell **Bred** Imperial & Mike Channon Bloodstock Ltd **Trained** Earlswood, Monmouths

FOCUS
A moderate handicap which saw a tight four-way finish. It was run at a muddling pace and the form is not the most solid, but it has been rated at face value.

79 BET NFL - BETDAQ H'CAP (DIV II) 5f (P)

1:30 (1:31) (Class 6) (0-65,65) 4-Y-0+ **£1,433** (£423; £211) **Stalls** High

Form RPR

646- **1** **Raimond Ridge (IRE)**[20] 7808 4-8-7 **61**.... MatthewCosham(7) 9 69+
(J Jay) *v s.i.s: hld up in last pair: prog on wd outside over 1f out: pushed into ld last 150yds: styd on wl* **8/1**

304- **2** 1 **Kheley (IRE)**[26] 7738 4-9-2 **63**.... DaneO'Neill 4 67
(W M Brisbourne) *sn led: hdd over 3f out: chal and upsides 1f out: nt qckn last 150yds* **8/1**

224- **3** ½ **Decider (USA)**[20] 7807 7-9-3 **64**....(p) ChrisCatlin 3 66
(R A Harris) *plld hrd: led over 3f out: hdd and no ex last 150yds* **7/2**[2]

350- **4** ½ **Nawaaff**[23] 7771 5-8-4 **51** oh5.... HayleyTurner 7 51
(M Quinn) *chsd ldng trio: rdn and cl enough jst over 1f out: nt qckn* **16/1**

531- **5** ¾ **Fromsong (IRE)**[20] 7807 12-9-4 **65**....(p) MartinDwyer 5 63+
(D K Ivory) *v awkward s and lost several l: in last pair tl effrt on inner over 1f out: fdd ins fnl f* **3/1**[1]

266- **6** ½ **Namir (IRE)**[58] 7329 8-8-11 **58**....(vt) JimCrowley 6 54+
(H J Evans) *t.k.h: hld up in 5th: pushed along whn nt clr run jst over 1f out and again ins fnl f whn snatched up: nt rcvr: fin w plenty lft* **9/2**[3]

232- **7** ¾ **Jolly Ranch**[33] 7651 4-8-6 **56**.... MartinLane(3) 2 49
(A G Newcombe) *ldng trio: upsides jst over 1f out: wknd ins fnl f* **9/2**[3]

59.70 secs (0.90) **Going Correction** +0.05s/f (Slow) **7 Ran SP% 111.7**
Speed ratings (Par 101): **94,92,91,90,89 88,87**
toteswinger:1&2:£5.40, 2&3:£2.90, 1&3:£5.80 CSF £64.78 CT £260.53 TOTE £10.20: £5.80, £4.20; EX 82.50 TRIFECTA Not won..
Owner David Fremel **Bred** Myles And Mrs Joan Doyle **Trained**
■ Matthew Cosham's first winner.
■ Stewards' Enquiry : Chris Catlin one-day ban: careless riding (Jan 22)
Dane O'Neill caution: used whip down shoulder in the forehand position.

FOCUS
This second division of the sprint saw a messy start and the form is worth treating with a degree of caution. The time was over 1.5sec slower than division 1. The winner could go in again but this is not form to be confident about.

Fromsong(IRE) Official explanation: jockey said gelding stumbled leaving stalls
Namir(IRE) Official explanation: jockey said gelding was denied a clear run

80 MARRIOTT HOTEL OPENING SPRING 2010 (S) STKS 1m 4f (P)

2:00 (2:01) (Class 6) 4-Y-0+ **£1,774** (£523; £262) **Stalls** Low

Form RPR

500- **1** **Classic Blue (IRE)**[12] 7855 6-8-12 52....(v1) StevieDonohoe 4 58
(Ian Williams) *t.k.h: hld up in tch: 5th and gng easily over 3f out: prog over 2f out to ld wl over 1f out: edgd lft but kpt on wl* **8/1**

020- **2** 1 ¾ **Sunset Boulevard (IRE)**[179] 3923 7-9-3 55.... ChrisCatlin 2 60
(Miss Tor Sturgis) *trckd ldng pair on inner: effrt 2f out: wnt 2nd over 1f out: kpt on but nvr able to chal* **4/5**[1]

545- **3** 1 ¾ **Nyetimber (USA)**[28] 7712 4-8-13 56.... SteveDrowne 5 57
(J A Osborne) *led: rdn and hdd wl over 1f out: one pce fnl f* **11/2**[3]

360- **4** 10 **Cactus King**[216] 2708 7-9-3 65....(p) IanMongan 6 41
(P M Phelan) *plld hrd: hld up tl prog to trck ldr 1/2-way: stmbld sn after: tried to chal over 2f out: sn wknd rapidly* **7/2**[2]

5 5 **Randomer**[613] 7-9-0 0.... RobertLButler(3) 1 33
(P Butler) *dwlt: hld up in last pair: lost tch and rdn over 3f out: sn wl bhd* **25/1**

604- **6** 23 **Kamanja (UAE)**[9] 7881 4-8-8 46.... JoeFanning 3 —
(M J Attwater) *plld hrd: trckd ldr to 1/2-way: wknd rapidly 3f out: t.o* **9/1**

2m 35.49s (2.49) **Going Correction** +0.05s/f (Slow)
WFA 4 from 6yo+ 4lb **6 Ran SP% 118.1**
Speed ratings (Par 101): **93,91,90,84,80 65**
toteswinger:1&2:£6.60, 2&3:£2.20, 1&3:£5.80 CSF £15.99 TOTE £8.30: £4.60, £1.30; EX 21.70.There was no bid for the winner.
Owner Boston R S Ian Bennett **Bred** Michael Conlon **Trained** Portway, Worcs

The Form Book, Raceform Ltd, Compton, RG20 6NL

FOCUS
A weak and slowly run seller which didn't take much winning. Classic Blue showed her first form this year.

81 LINGFIELDPARK.CO.UK H'CAP 1m 4f (P)
2:30 (2:30) (Class 2) (0-100,97) 4-Y-0+ **£10,361** (£3,083; £1,540; £769) **Stalls** Low

Form RPR
024- **1** **Mister New York (USA)**[20] 7811 5-8-10 **85**..................(b) JimCrowley 7 95+
(Noel T Chance) *hld up in last: swift move on outer over 2f out to ld wl over 1f out: 3 l clr ins fnl f: in n.d after* **8/1**
623- **2** 2 **Waldvogel (IRE)**[22] 7789 6-9-8 **97**........................ DaneO'Neill 6 102
(L M Cumani) *hld up in 5th: trckd ldrs gng easily over 2f out: outpcd wl over 1f out: drvn on inner and styd on to take 2nd nr fin* **11/4**[1]
011- **3** shd **Mildoura (FR)**[20] 7811 5-8-13 **88**........................ IanMongan 3 93
(Mrs L J Mongan) *trckd ldr: rdn to ld over 2f out: hdd and outpcd wl over 1f out: no ch w wnr fnl f: lost 2nd nr fin* **11/2**
414- **4** 3/4 **Full Toss**[10] 7867 4-8-12 **91**........................ J-PGuillambert 4 95
(P D Evans) *hld up in 6th: pushed along over 2f out: sn outpcd: styd on ins fnl f* **12/1**
023- **5** 3/4 **Dance The Star (USA)**[28] 7720 5-8-10 **88**.................. MartinLane(3) 2 91
(D M Simcock) *trckd ldng pair on inner: nt qckn over 2f out then outpcd: n.d over 1f out* **3/1**[2]
216- **6** 1 1/2 **Bound By Honour (SAF)**[22] 7789 7-9-7 **96**.............(b) StephenCraine 9 96
(G L Moore) *trckd ldng pair on outer: nt qckn and lost pl 2f out: one pce u.p* **8/1**
/45- **7** 9 **Luberon**[34] 7640 7-9-2 **91**........................ JoeFanning 8 77
(M Johnston) *led at decent pce: hdd over 2f out: losing pl rapidly whn squeezed for room wl over 1f out: wknd* **5/1**[3]

2m 29.11s (-3.89) **Going Correction** +0.05s/f (Slow) course record
WFA 4 from 5yo+ 4lb 7 Ran SP% **113.6**
Speed ratings (Par 109): **114,112,112,112,111 110,104**
toteswinger:1&2:£3.40, 2&3:£3.70, 1&3:£7.80 CSF £29.89 CT £132.07 TOTE £7.10: £2.90, £1.70; EX 30.10 Trifecta £84.30 Pool £506.95 - 4.45 winning units..
Owner Chance, Talbot & Taylor **Bred** J S McDonald **Trained** Upper Lambourn, Berks

FOCUS
A good and competitive handicap, run at a sound enough pace. A personal best from the winner with the next three close to their recent marks.

NOTEBOOK
Mister New York(USA) got back to winning ways in great fashion. Ridden out the back early on, he crept into things with 4f to run and, once brought wide of runners at the top of the home straight, shot clear when asked. The way the race was run proved right up his street and he is clearly still improving. However, the handicapper will now hike him up and a switch to hurdling, whenever the ground thaws out, is very likely to be on his agenda. (op 7-1)
Waldvogel(IRE), back down from 1m6f, travelled nicely into contention yet lacked anything like the finishing speed of the winner. He has now been placed on his last three outings, but doesn't look ungenuine and this track was probably sharper than he cares for. (op 3-1 tchd 5-2)
Mildoura(FR) readily beat today's winner off a 4lb lower mark over C&D last time out, but she got very much the run of things that day. Despite that form being well and truly reversed, this was still another sound effort from her. (op 6-1 tchd 9-2)
Full Toss won a claimer when with Richard Hannon on his last visit to the track and, despite this being a drop back in trip, he still had stamina to truly prove. He was the first to crack on the far side, but to his credit he stayed on again down the home straight and clearly got the distance. (op 9-1)
Dance The Star(USA), a winner over C&D on his only previous run here, proved one paced when it mattered and was below his previous level. (op 4-1)
Bound By Honour(SAF) failed to see out the step up in trip, despite having won over the distance when trained in South Africa, and should get closer again back over 1m2f. (tchd 10-1)
Luberon had his own way out in front, but proved a bit keen and was a sitting duck off the home bend. (op 9-2 tchd 15-2)

82 BET MULTIPLES - BETDAQ MEDIAN AUCTION MAIDEN STKS 1m 4f (P)
3:00 (3:00) (Class 5) 4-6-Y-O **£2,456** (£725; £362) **Stalls** Low

Form RPR
203- **1** **Moscow Oznick**[22] 7790 5-9-7 58........................(p) DavidProbert 1 68
(D Donovan) *confidently rdn: hld up and mostly in 5th: prog 2f out on inner: rdn to ld ins fnl f: styd on wl* **3/1**[2]
4- **2** 1 1/4 **On Terms (USA)**[30] 7694 4-8-12 0........................ HayleyTurner 3 61
(S Dow) *trckd ldr after 2f: led 3f out on outer and tried to kick on: hdd and one pce ins fnl f* **4/1**[3]
/03- **3** 2 **Big Nige (IRE)**[9] 7882 4-9-3 64........................ SaleemGolam 4 63
(J Pearce) *trckd ldr 2f: cl up after: wnt 2nd again jst over 2f out: chal jst over 1f out: rdn and fnd nil* **9/4**[1]
050- **4** 7 **Set Em Up Mo**[9] 7882 4-8-5 49........................(v) KierenFox(7) 2 47
(M J Attwater) *led to 3f out: wknd 2f out* **50/1**
/65- **5** hd **Mayta Capac (USA)**[30] 7694 4-9-3 55........................ MartinDwyer 8 51
(D M Simcock) *trckd ldng trio: rdn 3f out: wknd 2f out* **17/2**
200- **6** 3/4 **Very Distinguished**[11] 7856 4-8-12 54........................ DaneO'Neill 5 45
(S Kirk) *hld up in 6th: rdn and wknd over 2f out* **8/1**
7 7 **Swell Fellow**[61] 5-9-7 0........................ J-PGuillambert 7 39
(P D Evans) *dwlt: hld up in 7th: rdn 3f out: wknd 2f out* **14/1**
8 49 **Bellaetta** 4-8-12 0........................ ChrisCatlin 6 —
(Miss Amy Weaver) *rn green and sn last: lost tch 1/2-way: wl t.o* **12/1**

2m 32.71s (-0.29) **Going Correction** +0.05s/f (Slow)
WFA 4 from 5yo 4lb 8 Ran SP% **113.7**
Speed ratings: **102,101,99,95,95 94,89,57**
toteswinger:1&2:£3.20, 2&3:£4.00, 1&3:£4.00 CSF £15.29 TOTE £4.50: £1.60, £1.80, £1.10; EX 17.50 Trifecta £30.20 Pool £483.03 - 11.80 winning units..
Owner W P Flynn **Bred** Llety Stud **Trained** Newmarket, Suffolk

FOCUS
A very moderate maiden althe time was reasonable. The favourite disappointed and the race is best rated around the winner.

83 VIEW OUR 2010 FIXTURES AT LINGFIELDPARK.CO.UK H'CAP 1m 2f (P)
3:30 (3:31) (Class 6) (0-65,65) 4-Y-0+ **£1,774** (£523; £262) **Stalls** Low

Form RPR
0/- **1** **Sedgwick**[644] 1188 8-9-3 **62**........................ StevieDonohoe 5 70
(Ian Williams) *hld up wl in rr: gd run through on inner fr 2f out to cl on ldrs 1f out: drvn ahd ins fnl f: jst hld on* **10/1**
00-2 **2** nse **Alfie Tupper (IRE)**[6] 12 7-9-2 **61**........................ DaneO'Neill 1 69
(J R Boyle) *trckd ldng pair: gng strly over 2f out: effrt over 1f out to chal fnl f: pressed wnr nr fin but nvr looked like getting past* **2/1**[1]
/00- **3** shd **Maximus Aurelius (IRE)**[91] 6640 5-9-6 **65**..................(t) ChrisCatlin 12 73
(J Jay) *t.k.h: sn trckd ldr: led and kicked on over 2f out: hdd ins fnl f: styd on but hld nr fin* **14/1**
00-0 **4** 1 1/4 **Vinces**[6] 12 6-9-6 **65**........................ HayleyTurner 2 70
(T D McCarthy) *hld up in tch: trckd ldrs gng easily over 2f out: cl enough over 1f out but nt qckn: kpt on* **16/1**
001- **5** 3/4 **Atacama Sunrise**[23] 7776 4-9-4 **65**........................ SaleemGolam 6 69
(J Pearce) *hld up in rr: gng wl enough in last trio over 2f out: let wnr through on inner sn after: prog over 1f out: one pce fnl f* **13/2**[3]
13-4 **6** 1 3/4 **Marmooq**[6] 12 7-9-5 **64**........................ LukeMorris 11 64
(M J Attwater) *wl in tch: chsd ldrs over 4f out: rdn in 5th over 2f out: sn outpcd* **11/2**[2]
000- **7** 3/4 **Naheell**[32] 7664 4-9-4 **65**........................ AmirQuinn 3 64
(G Prodromou) *trckd ldng pair: drvn 2f out: sn outpcd: fdd* **25/1**
503- **8** 1 1/2 **Dream Huntress**[30] 7693 4-9-0 **61**........................ SteveDrowne 9 57
(J W Hills) *hld up and sn last: wl off the pce whn reminders fr over 1f out: nvr nr ldrs* **14/1**
050- **9** 2 3/4 **Woolston Ferry (IRE)**[51] 7432 4-9-2 **63**........................ FergusSweeney 7 53
(David Pinder) *mostly in rr: rdn and no prog over 2f out: btn after* **20/1**
004- **10** 2 1/2 **Pachakutek (USA)**[21] 7803 4-9-2 **63**........................ MartinDwyer 4 48
(L M Cumani) *mostly in midfield: drvn wl over 2f out: steadily wknd* **7/1**
546- **11** 1 1/2 **Venir Rouge**[13] 7847 6-8-12 **62**........................(p) LeeNewnes(5) 10 44
(Matthew Salaman) *racd wd: reminders fr 6f out and nvr gng wl after: wl in rr and btn 2f out* **10/1**
510/ **12** 3/4 **Grit (IRE)**[473] 6162 5-9-6 **65**........................ StephenCraine 13 46
(B G Powell) *wl away fr wd draw: led to over 2f out: wknd rapidly* **22/1**

2m 5.48s (-1.12) **Going Correction** +0.05s/f (Slow)
WFA 4 from 5yo+ 2lb 12 Ran SP% **124.9**
Speed ratings (Par 101): **106,105,105,104,104 102,102,101,98,96 95,95**
toteswinger:1&2:£9.80, 2&3:£13.40, 1&3:£36.30 CSF £31.09 CT £302.73 TOTE £9.80: £3.00, £1.70, £5.40; EX 56.70 Trifecta £446.50 Part won. Pool £603.38 - 0.30 winning units..
Owner A L R Morton **Bred** G And Mrs Middlebrook **Trained** Portway, Worcs

FOCUS
This was a tight handicap with only 4lb covering the field. There was an uneven pace on and the first three, who came clear, fought out a blanket finish. The form was sound judged around the second and fourth.

84 LINGFIELDPARK.CO.UK APPRENTICE H'CAP 1m (P)
4:00 (4:00) (Class 5) (0-75,75) 4-Y-0+ **£2,456** (£725; £362) **Stalls** High

Form RPR
30-2 **1** **Prince Of Thebes (IRE)**[5] 23 9-9-0 **70**........................ KierenFox 1 81
(M J Attwater) *mde all: drew away fr over 2f out: rdn out fnl f: unchal* **9/4**[2]
064- **2** 3 1/2 **Dajen**[48] 7479 4-8-3 **62**........................ JosephineBruning(3) 5 65
(D M Simcock) *hld up in last pair: off the pce 1/2-way: prog on inner over 2f out: wnt 2nd over 1f out: no ch w wnr* **13/2**[3]
00-0 **3** 2 **Expensive Problem**[5] 27 7-8-8 **67**........................ RyanPowell(3) 4 65
(R J Smith) *s.s: hld up in last: off the pce 1/2-way: prog on wd outside 2f out: kpt on to take 3rd ins fnl f* **25/1**
11-1 **4** 1 1/2 **Wunder Strike (USA)**[6] 11 4-8-7 **68** 6ex.............(p) NathanAlison(5) 2 62
(J R Boyle) *t.k.h: mostly chsd wnr: pushed along and lft bhd fr over 2f out: lost 2nd over 1f out: fdd* **7/4**[1]
13-6 **5** nse **Justcallmehandsome**[4] 29 8-9-1 **74**........................(v) SoniaEaton(3) 3 68
(D J S Ffrench Davis) *t.k.h: hld up and sn in last trio: off the pce 1/2-way: pushed along and no real prog fnl 2f* **12/1**
660- **6** 3/4 **Grey Boy (GER)**[26] 7741 9-8-5 **68**........................ GeorgeDowning(7) 7 60
(A W Carroll) *sn chsd ldng trio: no imp over 2f out: lost pl and wd bnd sn after: no ch over 1f out* **20/1**
50-4 **7** 5 **Nora Mae (IRE)**[4] 29 4-9-5 **75**........................ TobyAtkinson 6 55
(S Kirk) *t.k.h: disp 2nd pl tl rdn and wknd rapidly jst over 2f out* **7/1**

1m 37.77s (-0.43) **Going Correction** +0.05s/f (Slow) 7 Ran SP% **109.3**
Speed ratings (Par 103): **104,100,98,97,96 96,91**
toteswinger:1&2:£3.50, 2&3:£13.70, 1&3:£11.60 CSF £15.54 TOTE £3.20: £1.30, £3.70; EX 19.70 Place 6 £122.13, Place 5 £57.55.
Owner Canisbay Bloodstock **Bred** Mrs A Rothschild & London Thoroughbred Services L **Trained** Epsom, Surrey

FOCUS
A tactical affair in which the winner dominated. He appeared to return to his best, but he was allowed an easy lead and the favourite disappointed. The form is rated around him and the runner-up.
T/Plt: £78.60 to a £1 stake. Pool: £83,824.65. 778.45 winning tickets. T/Qpdt: £47.60 to a £1 stake. Pool: £8,029.20. 124.70 winning tickets. JN

[69]SOUTHWELL (L-H)
Friday, January 8

OFFICIAL GOING: Slow
Wind: Light against Weather: Fine, but cold

85 HOSPITALITY AT SOUTHWELL RACECOURSE RATING RELATED MAIDEN STKS 6f (F)
1:15 (1:15) (Class 5) 3-Y-0+ **£2,590** (£770; £385; £192) **Stalls** Low

Form RPR
322- **1** **Master Leon**[27] 7721 3-8-11 70........................(v) PhillipMakin 1 75
(B Smart) *mde virtually all: rdn over 1f out: styd on wl* **1/1**[1]
032- **2** 3 1/2 **Boy The Bell**[28] 7708 3-8-11 68........................ ShaneKelly 6 63
(J A Osborne) *chsd wnr tl rdn 2f out: styd on same pce: wnt 2nd again on line* **85/40**[2]
03-2 **3** hd **Tamarind Hill (IRE)**[6] 17 3-8-6 68........................(b) DeclanCannon(5) 3 62
(A J McCabe) *a.p: rdn to chse wnr 2f out: no ex ins fnl f: lost 2nd on line* **9/2**[3]
46-6 **4** 6 **Hold The Star**[3] 38 4-9-5 53........................ AnnStokell(5) 2 44
(Miss A Stokell) *s.i.s: sn pushed along in rr: outpcd fr 1/2-way* **33/1**
355- **5** 12 **Future Regime (IRE)**[13] 7843 3-8-3 56........................ JamesSullivan(5) 5 —
(Patrick Morris) *sn pushed along in rr: rdn over 3f out: wknd 1/2-way* **16/1**

1m 20.44s (3.94) **Going Correction** +0.675s/f (Slow)
WFA 3 from 4yo 16lb 5 Ran SP% **109.0**
Speed ratings (Par 103): **100,95,95,87,71**
toteswinger:1&2:£1.60 CSF £3.27 TOTE £2.00: £1.10, £1.10; EX 3.40.
Owner Alan Zheng **Bred** Ms R A Myatt **Trained** Hambleton, N Yorks

FOCUS
The jockeys involved in the first agreed that the ground was not riding as slow as it had been the day before. This was a very ordinary maiden, but the form makes sense and looks sound at its fairly lowly level. A small personal best from the winner.

86 MEMBERSHIP AT SOUTHWELL GOLF CLUB H'CAP — 7f (F)
1:45 (1:45) (Class 6) (0-60,60) 4-Y-O+ — **£2,729** (£806; £403) **Stalls** Low

Form — RPR

20-2 **1** **Mocha Java**[6] 21 7-8-12 59....(p) RossAtkinson(5) 1 — 66
(Matthew Salaman) *chsd ldr: rdn 1/2-way: styd on u.p to ld over 1f out: hung rt ins fnl f: kpt on* **5/1**[3]

050- **2** *2 1/2* **Artesium**[9] 7877 4-8-1 48....(v1) JamesSullivan(5) 3 — 48
(Patrick Morris) *chsd ldrs: rdn 1/2-way: styd on same pce fnl f: wnt 2nd nr fin* **11/1**

60-4 **3** *1/2* **Vogarth**[3] 40 6-8-11 60....(b) DavidKenny(7) 6 — 59
(M C Chapman) *sn led: rdn over 2f out: hdd over 1f out: no ex ins fnl f* **17/2**

54-1 **4** *8* **Dontuwishitwereso**[6] 21 4-8-13 55....(b) TonyCulhane 5 — 32
(P W D'Arcy) *s.i.s: sn drvn along in rr: mod prog u.p to go 4th over 1f out: nvr on terms* **6/4**[1]

305- **5** *18* **Manana Manana**[12] 7853 4-9-4 60....(b) AdamKirby 2 — —
(J Balding) *s.i.s: sn rdn along in rr: lost tch 1/2-way: t.o* **16/1**

62-6 **6** *46* **Gracie's Gift (IRE)**[6] 20 8-9-1 57.... RobertWinston 7 — —
(R C Guest) *chsd ldrs: rdn over 4f out: wknd sn after 1/2-way: eased fnl 2f: t.o* **5/2**[2]

1m 34.87s (4.57) **Going Correction** +0.675s/f (Slow) — **6** Ran SP% **110.0**
Speed ratings (Par 101): **100,97,96,87,66 14**
toteswinger:1&2:£7.30, 2&3:£10.00, 1&3:£4.70 CSF £50.99 CT £423.93 TOTE £4.60: £1.60, £3.80; EX 40.30.
Owner R H Brookes **Bred** A H And C E Robinson Partnership **Trained** Upper Lambourn, Berks

FOCUS
A low-grade handicap in which only three were ever involved. Weak form, with the favourite disappointing, and t is doubtful if the winner had to improve.
Gracie's Gift(IRE) Official explanation: jockey said gelding lost its action

87 BOOK ONLINE AT SOUTHWELL-RACECOURSE.CO.UK CLAIMING STKS — 1m (F)
2:15 (2:15) (Class 6) 4-Y-O+ — **£2,047** (£604; £302) **Stalls** Low

Form — RPR

24-4 **1** **Transmission (IRE)**[6] 19 5-8-13 65.... PhillipMakin 3 — 75
(B Smart) *chsd ldrs: led 3f out: sn rdn: hung lft ins fnl f: styd on dourly* **9/2**

30-2 **2** *1* **Special Cuvee**[7] 7 4-8-7 60....(v) RobertHavlin 7 — 67
(A B Haynes) *s.i.s: hld up: hdwy over 3f out: rdn to chse wnr over 1f out: edgd lft ins fnl f: sn ev ch: unable qck towards fin* **5/2**[1]

000- **3** *7* **Tidal Force (USA)**[35] 7627 4-8-2 60....(p) DeclanCannon(5) 1 — 51
(A J McCabe) *led: hdd 3f out: sn rdn: wknd fnl f* **18/1**

222- **4** *1 3/4* **Lost Soldier Three (IRE)**[24] 7760 9-9-9 72....(p) AndrewMullen 4 — 63
(D Nicholls) *s.i.s: hld up: drvn along over 3f out: styd on to go 4th ins fnl f: nvr on terms* **13/2**

140- **5** *3 1/4* **Royal Dignitary (USA)**[107] 6217 10-9-9 79.... AdrianNicholls 9 — 55
(D Nicholls) *chsd ldrs: rdn over 3f out: wknd over 1f out* **4/1**[3]

422- **6** *2 1/2* **Ten Pole Tudor**[11] 7858 5-8-10 60....(p) MarkCoumbe(5) 2 — 41
(John A Harris) *hld up: last and drvn along 1/2-way: nvr on terms* **12/1**

46-3 **7** *8* **Moonlight Man**[6] 19 9-8-8 70....(tp) BarryMcHugh(5) 8 — 21
(C R Dore) *chsd ldrs: rdn over 3f out: sn wknd* **11/4**[2]

00-6 **8** *1 3/4* **Favouring (IRE)**[3] 39 8-8-0 38....(b) MissRachelKing(7) 5 — 11
(M C Chapman) *prom: rdn 1/2-way: wknd over 3f out* **125/1**

1m 47.47s (3.77) **Going Correction** +0.675s/f (Slow) — **8** Ran SP% **120.5**
Speed ratings (Par 101): **108,107,100,98,95 92,84,82**
totswinger:1&2:£4.60, 2&3:£13.60, 1&3:£9.50 CSF £17.19 TOTE £6.70: £1.70, £1.40, £4.00; EX 18.90.
Owner M Barber **Bred** M J Halligan **Trained** Hambleton, N Yorks

FOCUS
An ordinary claimer. The first two finished clear and were the only ones to give their running on this slow surface.
Moonlight Man Official explanation: trainer had no explanation for the poor form shown

88 SOUTHWELL GOLF CLUB H'CAP — 1m (F)
2:45 (2:46) (Class 6) (0-55,54) 4-Y-O+ — **£2,729** (£806; £403) **Stalls** Low

Form — RPR

030- **1** **Positivity**[10] 7869 4-8-13 49....(p) PhillipMakin 1 — 57
(B Smart) *chsd ldrs: led over 3f out: rdn and edgd rt over 1f out: styd on* **6/1**[3]

000- **2** *1 3/4* **Highland River**[12] 7855 4-9-4 54.... ShaneKelly 8 — 58
(A Sadik) *chsd ldr: led over 4f out: rdn and hdd over 3f out: chsd wnr thereafter: hung lft ins fnl f: styd on same pce* **4/1**[1]

00-0 **3** *3 1/2* **Kannon**[7] 7 5-8-4 45....(p) DeclanCannon(5) 6 — 41
(A J McCabe) *s.i.s: sn pushed along in rr: hdwy over 3f out: rdn over 2f out: no ex fnl f* **11/2**[2]

400- **4** *1 1/4* **Sairaam (IRE)**[11] 7856 4-8-7 48.... PaulPickard(5) 7 — 41
(C Smith) *sn pushed along in rr: hdwy 5f out: rdn over 3f out: styd on same pce appr fnl f* **13/2**

00-6 **5** *4 1/2* **Amber Moon**[3] 40 5-8-11 52....(b) AnnStokell(5) 3 — 35
(Miss A Stokell) *prom: rdn and lost pl 5f out: last and struggling 1/2-way: n.d after* **14/1**

50-6 **6** *1/2* **Louisiade (IRE)**[7] 7 9-8-4 45....(p) RossAtkinson(5) 2 — 27
(R C Guest) *chsd ldrs: rdn over 3f out: wknd 2f out* **11/2**[2]

650- **7** *34* **Bella Fighetta**[35] 7629 4-8-9 45....(p) TonyHamilton 5 — —
(Ollie Pears) *sn led: hdd over 4f out: rdn and wknd over 3f out: t.o* **25/1**

1m 49.11s (5.41) **Going Correction** +0.675s/f (Slow) — **7** Ran SP% **88.9**
Speed ratings (Par 101): **99,97,93,92,88 87,53**
toteswinger:1&2:£3.80, 2&3:£2.80, 1&3:£4.40 CSF £17.87 CT £59.67 TOTE £4.80: £2.90, £1.80; EX 19.00.
Owner Mrs F Denniff **Bred** Mrs Fiona Denniff **Trained** Hambleton, N Yorks

FOCUS
A very moderate handicap that was weakened further when Hint Of Honey broke out under the front of the stalls and was withdrawn (7/2F, deduct 20p in the £ under R4). There was little solid recent form to go on and the race is rated around the winner.
Highland River Official explanation: trainer said gelding lost its left-hind shoe

89 SOUTHWELL-RACECOURSE.CO.UK (S) STKS — 6f (F)
3:15 (3:15) (Class 6) 4-Y-O+ — **£2,047** (£604; £302) **Stalls** Low

Form — RPR

31-2 **1** **Obe Gold**[3] 39 8-9-4 66.... RobertWinston 2 — 72+
(P Howling) *s.i.s: pushed along in last pl ealry: hdwy to chse ldr over 2f out: sn rdn: led 1f out: styd on wl u.p* **5/6**[1]

000- **2** *4 1/2* **Whatyouwoodwishfor (USA)**[20] 7813 4-8-12 60.... TonyHamilton 3 — 50
(R A Fahey) *chsd clr ldr tl rdn over 2f out: styd on same pce: wnt 2nd cl home* **14/1**

000- **3** *nk* **Truly Divine**[9] 7880 5-8-5 46....(v) RyanClark(7) 5 — 49
(C A Dwyer) *edgd lft s and sn led: clr over 4f out: rdn and edgd lft over 1f out: sn hdd and no ex* **33/1**

030- **4** *4* **Verinco**[24] 7762 4-8-12 57....(p) PhillipMakin 4 — 36
(B Smart) *hld up in tch: racd keenly: outpcd over 4f out: hdwy u.p and hung lft over 1f out: nt trble ldrs* **7/1**

30-3 **5** *3 1/2* **Rosie Says No**[3] 37 5-8-13 59....(v1) AdamKirby 1 — 26
(A J McCabe) *prom: lost pl over 4f out: sn rdn: wknd 1/2-way* **5/1**[2]

60-2 **6** *1/2* **Spoof Master (IRE)**[6] 8 6-8-13 56....(t) DeclanCannon(5) 6 — 29
(C R Dore) *chsd ldrs: rdn over 3f out: wknd over 2f out* **6/1**[3]

1m 19.91s (3.41) **Going Correction** +0.675s/f (Slow) — **6** Ran SP% **107.6**
Speed ratings (Par 101): **104,98,97,92,87 86**
toteswinger:1&2 £2.80, 2&3 £10.20, 1&3 £7.80 CSF £12.56 TOTE £2.00: £1.30, £4.30; EX 11.80.There was no bid for the winner.
Owner Paul Howling **Bred** Mrs M Mason **Trained** Newmarket, Suffolk

FOCUS
An uncompetitive seller in which Truly Divine was soon half a dozen lengths clear of the other five. It is doubtful if the winner had to improve on his recent best.

90 SOUTHWELL H'CAP — 1m 4f (F)
3:45 (3:45) (Class 7) (0-50,50) 4-Y-O+ — **£1,706** (£503; £252) **Stalls** Low

Form — RPR

306- **1** **Dontpaytheferryman (USA)**[30] 6770 5-8-9 46....(e1) DeclanCannon(5) 8 — 55
(B Ellison) *hld up: hdwy over 8f out: led 5f out: rdn clr over 3f out: hung lft over 1f out: styd on: eased nr fin* **11/8**[1]

000- **2** *4* **Cragganmore Creek**[38] 7608 7-8-10 45.... KellyHarrison(3) 2 — 48
(D Morris) *a.p: rdn to chse wnr over 3f out: hung lft over 1f out: no imp* **12/1**

534- **3** *nk* **Hassadin**[22] 5123 4-8-4 45.... AmyBaker(5) 9 — 48
(A B Haynes) *sn pushed along in rr: hdwy over 3f out: kpt on: nt rch ldrs* **15/2**[3]

000- **4** *1* **Black Falcon (IRE)**[31] 7677 10-8-11 48.... MarkCoumbe(5) 3 — 49
(John A Harris) *s.i.s: hld up: hdwy over 3f out: hung lft fr over 1f out: nt rch ldrs* **9/1**

404- **5** *3 1/2* **Satindra (IRE)**[47] 385 6-8-13 45....(tp) PhillipMakin 4 — 40
(C R Dore) *prom: swtchd rt 5f out: rdn over 3f out: wknd over 1f out* **15/2**[3]

240- **6** *6* **Fongoli**[52] 4470 4-9-0 50....(b1) RobertWinston 1 — 36
(B G Powell) *drvn along early: sn chsng ldr: rdn over 3f out: wknd 2f out* **9/2**[2]

00/- **7** *26* **Gouranga**[26] 7775 7-8-6 45....(b) JakePayne(7) 10 — —
(A W Carroll) *s.i.s: sn pushed along in rr: bhd fnl 8f: t.o* **20/1**

000/ **8** *27* **Heroic Lad**[21] 4707 5-8-8 47....(t) DavidKenny(7) 11 — —
(A B Haynes) *sn led: hdd 5f out: sn rdn and wknd: t.o* **50/1**

00- **9** *45* **Firsaan (IRE)**[45] 7504 4-8-9 50....(v1) PaulPickard(5) 6 — —
(J R Norton) *mid-div: dropped in rr 8f out: sn bhd: t.o* **25/1**

2m 50.1s (9.10) **Going Correction** +0.675s/f (Slow)
WFA 4 from 5yo+ 4lb — **9** Ran SP% **112.1**
Speed ratings (Par 97): **96,93,93,92,90 86,68,50,20**
toteswinger:1&2:£6.60, 2&3:£7.70, 1&3:£4.70 CSF £18.44 CT £91.03 TOTE £2.60: £1.40, £2.70, £2.00; EX 19.10 Place 6 £68.1, Place 5 £59.87 .
Owner Koo's Racing Club **Bred** Rojan Farms **Trained** Norton, N Yorks

FOCUS
A very moderate handicap which was further weakened by five non-runners. They went a fair pace considering the sound surface and the form seems sound enough. The winner did not need match his previous Flat best.
Black Falcon(IRE) Official explanation: jockey said gelding hung left-handed throughout
T/Jkpt: £9,833.30 to a £1 stake. Pool: £20,774.58. 1.50 winning tickets. T/Plt: £39.50 to a £1 stake. Pool: £96,943.26. 1,787.90 winning tickets. T/Qpdt: £7.10 to a £1 stake. Pool: £8,743.36. 909.92 winning tickets. CR

[29]WOLVERHAMPTON (A.W) (L-H)
Friday, January 8

91 Meeting Abandoned - Snow

[22]KEMPTON (A.W) (R-H)
Saturday, January 9

OFFICIAL GOING: Standard
Wind: fresh, half against Weather: very cold, dry

98 WILLIAMHILL.COM/BONUS25 MAIDEN STKS — 1m 2f (P)
12:55 (12:55) (Class 5) 4-Y-O+ — **£2,590** (£770; £288; £288) **Stalls** High

Form — RPR

/00- **1** **Gheed (IRE)**[20] 7826 5-8-7 0....(t) RyanClark(7) 5 — 61+
(K A Morgan) *t.k.h: stdd after s: hld up in last pair: hdwy on outer 3f out: rdn over 1f out: kpt on wl fnl 100yds to ld last strides* **28/1**

2 *hd* **Jan Mayen** 4-8-12 0.... TomQueally 1 — 60
(M Johnston) *awkward leaving stalls: sn rcvrd to press ldr: ev ch and rdn wl over 1f out: kpt on fnl f: wnt 2nd last stride* **7/2**[3]

443- **3** *shd* **Freedom Fire (IRE)**[13] 6720 4-9-3 63.... FergusSweeney 3 — 65
(G L Moore) *trckd ldrs: pushed along and effrt jst over 2f out: ev ch over 1f out: rdn ent fnl f: nt qckn fnl 150yds* **2/1**[1]

05- **3** *dht* **Mutajaaser (USA)**[33] 7671 5-9-5 0.... JimmyQuinn 9 — 65
(K A Morgan) *t.k.h: led: rdn 2f out: kpt on gamely to hold narrow advantage tl hdd and lost 2 pls last strides* **3/1**[2]

4/0- **5** *1/2* **Boogie Dancer**[140] 115 6-9-0 52.... DaneO'Neill 7 — 59
(H S Howe) *hld up in tch in last trio: rdn and effrt wl over 1f out: styd on steadily u.p fnl f: nt quite rch ldrs* **10/1**

043- **6** *2* **Major Lawrence (IRE)**[12] 7863 4-9-3 66....(v1) ShaneKelly 4 — 60
(J Noseda) *t.k.h early: trckd ldrs: rdn and nt qckn over 2f out: one pce and hld whn swtchd rt ins fnl f* **5/1**

00- **7** *25* **Sir Tom**[20] 7826 5-9-2 0.... MarcHalford(3) 8 — 10
(J J Bridger) *in tch in midfield tl rdn and btn over 2f out: t.o fnl f* **66/1**

The Form Book, Raceform Ltd, Compton, RG20 6NL

40/ 8 42 **Our Jane**[24] 919 5-9-0 0 .... JackMitchell 6 —
(R A Teal) *s.i.s: in tch in last trio: rdn 5f out: lost tch 3f out: t.o and eased fr over 1f out* **25/1**

2m 10.47s (2.47) **Going Correction** +0.25s/f (Slow)
WFA 4 from 5yo+ 2lb 8 Ran SP% **115.1**
Speed ratings (Par 103): **100,99,99,99,99 97,77,44**
PL: FF £0.50, MJ £0.60. toteswinger: GH&JM:£11.20, MJ&JM:£1.30, MJ&GH:£4.60, FF&JM:£1.00, FF&GH:£4.70 CSF £123.10 TOTE £34.30: £6.20, £1.50; EX 205.80.
Owner P Doughty **Bred** Shadwell Estate Company Limited **Trained** Newmarket, Suffolk

FOCUS
The highest-rated runner with an official rating in this maiden had a mark of 66, so it was a modest contest. The early pace was not strong and a sprint developed up the home straight, which resulted in five horses crossing the line in union.

99 WILLIAMHILL.COM - BEST ODDS GUARANTEED H'CAP (DIV I) 1m 2f (P)
1:25 (1:25) (Class 6) (0-52,57) 4-Y-O+ **£1,706** (£503; £252) **Stalls** High

Form RPR
064- 1 **Lyrical Intent**[21] 7814 4-8-8 46 .... JimmyQuinn 7 54
(P Howling) *hld up in midfield: hdwy on outer over 3f out: rdn to ld over 1f out: edgd rt but styd on wl fnl f* **5/2**[1]
600- 2 1 ½ **Mid Wicket (USA)**[26] 7755 4-9-0 52 .... DaneO'Neill 4 57
(Mouse Hamilton-Fairley) *hld up in last pair: rdn and hdwy over 2f out: chsd ldng pair ins fnl f: kpt on to go 2nd on post* **8/1**
600- 3 nse **Womaniser (IRE)**[33] 7662 6-9-2 52 ....(b) SaleemGolam 10 57
(T Keddy) *t.k.h: chsd ldrs: swtchd arnd wkng rival 4f out: swtchd lft and rdn wl over 1f out: chsd wnr and drvn ent fnl f: one pce after: lost 2nd on post* **15/2**
504- 4 2 ½ **Sir Haydn**[24] 7766 10-8-4 47 ....(v) DannyBrock[(7)] 9 47
(J R Jenkins) *stdd and hmpd sn after s: bhd and niggled along early: hdwy and pushed along over 2f out: kpt on steadily to go 4th ins fnl f: nvr trbld ldrs* **5/1**[2]
005- 5 2 ¾ **Fitzwarren**[33] 7666 9-8-10 46 oh1 ....(tp) ShaneKelly 2 40
(A D Brown) *dwlt: chsd ldr after 1f tl led 4f out: drvn and hdd over 1f out: wknd ent fnl f* **13/2**
05-0 6 1 ¼ **Turn To Dreams**[5] 34 4-8-7 48 ....(v) WilliamCarson[(3)] 5 40
(P D Evans) *led for 1f: chsd ldrs after: rdn over 2f out: wknd u.p over 1f out* **7/1**
005- 7 26 **Foxtrot Bravo (IRE)**[34] 7652 4-9-0 52 ....(p) SteveDrowne 1 —
(Miss S L Davison) *in tch in last trio: pushed along and nt gng wl fr 6f out: reminder 5f out: lost tch over 2f out: t.o* **11/2**[3]
000- 8 27 **Tuning Fork**[199] 3269 10-8-3 46 oh1 ....(e) KierenFox[(7)] 13 —
(M J Attwater) *led after 1f tl hdd and rdn 4f out: sn dropped out: t.o and eased fr wl over 1f out* **22/1**

2m 9.90s (1.90) **Going Correction** +0.25s/f (Slow)
WFA 4 from 5yo+ 2lb 8 Ran SP% **113.7**
Speed ratings (Par 101): **102,100,100,98,96 95,74,53**
toteswinger:1&2:£6.80, 2&3:£8.90, 1&3:£5.60 CSF £22.99 CT £130.43 TOTE £3.10: £1.80, £3.00, £3.00; EX 24.50.
Owner Ajaz Ahmed **Bred** Mrs S France **Trained** Newmarket, Suffolk

FOCUS
This was the first of two divisions of a moderate 1m2f handicap. The early pace was steady.

100 WILLIAMHILL.COM - BEST ODDS GUARANTEED H'CAP (DIV II) 1m 2f (P)
1:55 (1:56) (Class 6) (0-52,52) 4-Y-O+ **£1,706** (£503; £252) **Stalls** High

Form RPR
004- 1 **Litenup (IRE)**[10] 7882 4-9-0 52 ....(t) WandersonD'Avila 4 59
(A J Lidderdale) *mde all: rdn and qcknd 2f out: styd on wl fnl f* **8/1**
000- 2 1 ½ **Space Pirate**[39] 4667 5-8-10 46 oh1 ....(b) SaleemGolam 8 50+
(J Pearce) *s.i.s and rdn along early: bhd: stl plenty to do and rdn jst over 2f out: hdwy towards inner over 1f out: r.o strly fnl f to go 2nd nr fin: nvr gng to rch wnr* **33/1**
235- 3 nk **Dobravany (IRE)**[41] 3552 6-8-13 49 ....(v) JimmyQuinn 12 52
(K A Morgan) *in tch in midfield: rdn and effrt over 2f out: hdwy towards inner over 1f out: chsd wnr jst ins fnl f: no imp fnl 150yds: lost 2nd nr fin* **8/1**
043- 4 1 ¾ **Playful Asset (IRE)**[9] 7888 4-9-0 52 .... TonyCulhane 7 52
(P Howling) *chsd ldrs: rdn wl over 2f out: chsd wnr and drvn over 1f out tl ins jst fnl f f: kpt on same pce* **6/1**[3]
000- 5 3 ¾ **Sufficient Warning**[52] 7433 6-8-4 47 .... KierenFox[(7)] 3 39
(R J Smith) *chsd ldr after over 8f out tl over 1f out: hung rt and wknd jst over 1f out* **25/1**
200- 6 ½ **Piper's Song (IRE)**[49] 7490 7-9-2 52 .... ShaneKelly 11 43
(Patrick Morris) *hld up in tch towards rr: rdn and effrt jst over 2f out: no prog over 1f out* **9/2**[1]
060- 7 nk **Magic Amigo**[173] 4158 9-8-3 46 oh1 .... DannyBrock[(7)] 1 37
(J R Jenkins) *in tch tl lost pl and dropped to rr over 4f out: n.d after: styd on past btn horse fnl f* **33/1**
045- 8 ½ **Mr Deal**[33] 7660 4-8-12 50 .... TomQueally 2 40
(Eve Johnson Houghton) *s.i.s: t.k.h: hld up in tch towards rr: hdwy over 3f out: rdn and hanging rt wl over 1f out: no prog and wl hld fnl f* **5/1**[2]
0/0- 9 nk **Little Firecracker**[40] 537 5-8-10 46 oh1 ....(p) StevieDonohoe 9 35
(N B King) *s.i.s: a towards rr: rdn over 2f out: kpt on but nvr threatened ldrs* **10/1**
400- 10 4 **Imperium**[31] 7688 9-9-1 51 .... JimCrowley 6 32
(Jean-Rene Auvray) *t.k.h: in tch: chsd ldng pair over 2f out tl 2f out: sn wknd* **15/2**
000- 11 2 ¾ **Hatch A Plan (IRE)**[24] 7767 9-9-2 52 .... ChrisCatlin 5 28
(Mouse Hamilton-Fairley) *t.k.h: hld up in tch towards rr: rdn and no prog 2f out* **8/1**
060- 12 2 ¼ **Play Up Pompey**[132] 5473 8-8-7 46 oh1 .... MarcHalford[(3)] 10 17
(J J Bridger) *t.k.h: chsd wnr tl over 8f out: chsd ldrs after tl wknd u.p 3f out: wl bhd fnl f* **16/1**

2m 11.0s (3.00) **Going Correction** +0.25s/f (Slow)
WFA 4 from 5yo+ 2lb 12 Ran SP% **118.9**
Speed ratings (Par 101): **98,96,96,95,92 91,91,91,90,87 85,83**
toteswinger:1&2:£82.40, 2&3:£56.20, 1&3:£18.50 CSF £250.96 CT £2166.97 TOTE £14.30: £4.00, £16.40, £1.90; EX 459.50.
Owner A C Entertainment Technologies Ltd **Bred** Rathasker Stud **Trained** Eastbury, Berks

FOCUS
The second division of the 1m2f handicap was run in the slowest time of all three races over the distance. It also proved what can happen if a jockey gets the fractions right in front.
Sufficient Warning Official explanation: jockey said gelding hung right
Little Firecracker Official explanation: jockey said gelding was slowly away

101 WILLIAM HILL 0800 44 40 40 BET NOW! FILLIES' H'CAP 1m (P)
2:25 (2:25) (Class 5) (0-70,66) 4-Y-O+ **£2,590** (£770; £385; £192) **Stalls** High

Form RPR
0-23 1 **Goodbye Cash (IRE)**[6] 27 6-8-9 59 .... AndrewHeffernan[(5)] 5 66
(P D Evans) *racd keenly: led after 1f: mde rest: rdn and hung lft 2f out: kpt edging lft u.p: hld on gamely ins fnl f* **11/4**[1]
366- 2 nk **Support Fund (IRE)**[33] 7664 6-9-7 66 .... ShaneKelly 1 72
(Eve Johnson Houghton) *bhd and sn niggled along: swtchd rt wl over 1f out: gd hdwy to press wnr ins fnl f: nt qckn and hld fnl 75yds* **4/1**[2]
04-5 3 1 ¾ **Fly By Nelly**[7] 11 4-9-1 60 .... SteveDrowne 4 62
(H Morrison) *broke wl but sn stdd to trck ldrs: rdn and effrt over 2f out: chalng whn carried lft 2f out: chsd wnr over 1f out tl jst ins fnl f: one pce fnl 150yds* **11/4**[1]
000- 4 nk **Safaseef (IRE)**[24] 7770 5-8-2 47 oh2 ....(v) JimmyQuinn 3 49
(K A Morgan) *hld up in last trio: hdwy over 2f out: chsd ldrs and rdn jst over 1f out: no ex ins fnl f* **20/1**
556- 5 2 ½ **Lucky Score (IRE)**[19] 7829 4-9-0 59 ....(p) ChrisCatlin 2 55
(Mouse Hamilton-Fairley) *sn pushed up to chse ldrs: wnt 2nd over 4f out: chalng whn carried lft 2f out: wknd ent fnl f* **11/2**[3]
444- 6 4 ½ **Chatanoogachoochoo**[23] 7790 5-8-8 58 .... RossAtkinson[(5)] 7 43
(M Hill) *racd in midfield: rdn and effrt wl over 2f out: edgd rt and no prog over 1f out* **11/2**[3]
06-0 7 10 **Sunshine Ellie**[7] 8 4-8-5 50 oh2 ow3 .... SaleemGolam 6 12
(D Shaw) *hld up in last pair: rdn and wknd over 2f out: sn bhd* **50/1**
400- 8 11 **Intimar (IRE)**[24] 7765 4-8-2 47 oh2 .... LukeMorris 8 —
(R J Smith) *led for 1f: chsd wnr after tl over 4f out: wknd u.p over 2f out: wl bhd and eased ins fnl f* **33/1**

1m 40.73s (0.93) **Going Correction** +0.25s/f (Slow) 8 Ran SP% **113.8**
Speed ratings (Par 100): **105,104,102,102,100 95,85,74**
toteswinger:1&2:£2.40, 2&3:£2.60, 1&3:£2.60 CSF £13.66 CT £32.15 TOTE £3.80: £1.40, £1.20, £1.60; EX 15.40 Trifecta £35.20 Pool £352.80 - 7.40 winning units..
Owner Mrs I M Folkes **Bred** Mrs A C Peters **Trained** Pandy, Monmouths

FOCUS
A modest handicap.

102 2FOR1DOGS.COM - GO GREYHOUND RACING FOR £1 H'CAP 6f (P)
2:55 (2:56) (Class 4) (0-85,88) 4-Y-O+ **£4,533** (£1,348; £674; £336) **Stalls** High

Form RPR
21-1 1 **Tiddliwinks**[6] 26 4-9-5 88 6ex .... AmyRyan[(5)] 5 103+
(K A Ryan) *stdd and dropped in bhd after s: hdwy and swtchd ins ent fnl 2f: qcknd to ld over 1f out: clr fnl f: comf* **10/11**[1]
022- 2 2 **Vhujon (IRE)**[10] 7875 5-8-12 81 .... AndrewHeffernan[(5)] 1 87
(P D Evans) *s.i.s: sn t.k.h and hld up in tch in rr: rdn and effrt on outer 2f out: kpt on u.p fnl f to go 2nd towards fin: no ch w wnr* **13/2**
400- 3 ¾ **Ray Of Joy**[10] 7875 4-9-2 80 .... FergusSweeney 4 84
(J R Jenkins) *in tch: rdn and effrt ent fnl 2f: kpt on u.p to chse clr wnr fnl 100yds: lost 2nd towards fin* **12/1**
63-3 4 shd **Dvinsky (USA)**[6] 26 9-8-8 72 ....(b) JimmyQuinn 7 76
(P Howling) *led: rdn ent fnl 2f: hdd over 1f out: no ch w wnr fnl f: lost 2 pls fnl 100yds* **6/1**[3]
260- 5 2 **Milne Bay (IRE)**[92] 6642 5-8-0 71 ....(t) LauraPike[(7)] 2 68
(D M Simcock) *chsd ldr after 1f: rdn and unable qck 2f out: wknd over 1f out* **22/1**
101- 6 1 ¾ **Lujeanie**[10] 7875 4-9-3 81 ....(p) JimCrowley 6 73
(D K Ivory) *t.k.h: chsd ldr for 1f: chsd ldrs after: ev ch and rdn 2f out: wknd over 1f out* **11/4**[2]
000- 7 2 ½ **Gone Hunting**[10] 7875 4-9-3 81 ....(t) SaleemGolam 8 65
(J Pearce) *in tch: rdn over 2f out: wknd ent fnl 2f* **33/1**

1m 12.63s (-0.47) **Going Correction** +0.25s/f (Slow) 7 Ran SP% **121.7**
Speed ratings (Par 105): **113,110,109,109,106 104,100**
toteswinger:1&2:£2.60, 2&3:£7.30, 1&3:£5.10 CSF £8.74 CT £48.73 TOTE £2.10: £1.80, £3.90; EX 7.90 Trifecta £44.30 Pool £431.03 - 7.20 winning units..
Owner Guy Reed **Bred** Guy Reed **Trained** Hambleton, N Yorks

FOCUS
A fair sprint that saw short-price favourite Tiddliwinks readily complete the hat-trick.
Lujeanie Official explanation: jockey said gelding ran too freely

103 WILLIAMHILL.COM - BET IN PLAY NOW! H'CAP 6f (P)
3:25 (3:32) (Class 6) (0-52,52) 4-Y-O+ **£2,047** (£604; £302) **Stalls** High

Form RPR
00-0 1 **Know No Fear**[7] 10 5-9-2 52 ....(p) TomQueally 8 63
(A J Lidderdale) *stdd after s: hld up in rr: rdn ent fnl 2f: str run u.p fnl f to ld fnl 50yds* **9/2**[2]
06-1 2 nk **Tanley**[7] 8 5-9-1 51 .... TonyCulhane 10 61
(J F Coupland) *in tch: hdwy to ld over 1f out: rdn ent fnl f: hdd and no ex fnl 50yds* **2/1**[1]
066- 3 1 ¼ **Sonhador**[9] 7889 4-9-0 50 .... SaleemGolam 12 56
(G Prodromou) *t.k.h: chsd ldrs: ev ch u.p wl over 1f out: no ex ins fnl f* **7/1**[3]
344- 4 shd **Reigning Monarch (USA)**[30] 7703 7-8-13 49 ....(p) SamHitchcott 4 55
(Miss Z C Davison) *sn pushed up to ld: hrd pressed and rdn 2f out: hdd over 1f out: one pce fnl f* **10/1**
040- 5 1 ¼ **Davids Mark**[19] 7835 10-8-13 49 .... SimonWhitworth 6 51
(J R Jenkins) *in tch in rr: pushed along over 3f out: wd bnd 3f out: kpt on ins fnl f: nvr gng pce to rch ldrs* **9/2**[2]
230- 6 1 ¼ **Rocket Ruby**[9] 7889 4-9-2 52 .... DaneO'Neill 9 50
(D Shaw) *taken down early: s.i.s: in tch in rr: rdn and effrt on inner over 2f out: no hdwy over 1f out* **8/1**
050- 7 ½ **Cheshire Rose**[56] 7397 5-9-0 50 ....(p) JimmyQuinn 1 46
(A M Hales) *sn chsng ldr: ev ch u.p 2f out: wknd ent fnl f* **16/1**
60-0 8 2 **Commandingpresence (USA)**[7] 14 4-8-7 46 oh1.. MarcHalford[(3)] 3 36
(J J Bridger) *chsd ldrs tl wknd u.p jst over 2f out* **20/1**

1m 14.33s (1.23) **Going Correction** +0.25s/f (Slow) 8 Ran SP% **113.0**
Speed ratings (Par 101): **101,100,98,98,97 95,94,92**
toteswinger:1&2:£3.60, 2&3:£4.10, 1&3:£8.00 CSF £13.58 CT £60.28 TOTE £7.10: £2.90, £1.02, £3.60; EX 18.70 Trifecta £63.10 Pool £606.33 - 7.10 winning units..
Owner Kachina Racing **Bred** B Bargh **Trained** Eastbury, Berks

FOCUS
This was a moderate handicap.

104 WILLIAM HILL TELEPHONE BETTING - OPEN 24/7 H'CAP 7f (P)

3:55 (3:58) (Class 6) (0-60,59) 3-Y-O £2,047 (£604; £302) Stalls High

Form RPR

500- 1 **Feel The Magic (IRE)**[9] 7884 3-8-4 45..........(b[1]) NickyMackay 9 47
(S Kirk) *broke wl and led briefly: chsd ldr tl 4f out and again 2f out: drvn over 1f out: led ins fnl f: styd on* 6/1

231- 2 ½ **Bookiesindex Girl (IRE)**[9] 7887 3-9-0 55.......... ShaneKelly 5 56
(J R Jenkins) *bmpd s: t.k.h: sn rcvrd to ld: rdn and hung lft 2f out: hdd ins fnl f: kpt on same pce u.p* 11/10[1]

600- 3 ½ **Hathaway (IRE)**[22] 7799 3-8-10 51.......... LukeMorris 7 51
(W M Brisbourne) *in tch in midfield: rdn along and unable qck over 3f out: hdwy u.p and edgd rt over 1f out: styd on steadily fnl f* 8/1

404- 4 1 ¼ **Exceed Power**[30] 6938 3-8-8 52..........(t) MartinLane(3) 2 48+
(D M Simcock) *hld up in tch in last pair: hdwy and rdn jst over 2f out: chsd ldng pair over 1f out: no imp fnl f: lost 3rd fnl 100yds* 7/2[3]

005- 5 ¾ **Novillero**[45] 7513 3-8-4 45.......... FrankieMcDonald 6 42+
(J C Fox) *wnt rt and awkward leaving stalls: bhd: rdn over 3f out: nt clr run over 2f out tl swtchd ins ent fnl 2f: keeping on whn nt clr run again and swtchd lft over 1f out: hung lft one pce after* 3/1[2]

000- 6 2 ¼ **Dolly Will Do**[131] 5498 3-8-6 47 ow2.......... SaleemGolam 4 35
(N P Mulholland) *mounted on crse: chsd ldrs tl wnt 2nd 4f out tl 2f out: wknd u.p over 1f out* 25/1

030- 7 14 **Fareham Town**[22] 7799 3-9-0 55.......... DaneO'Neill 3 5
(S Kirk) *t.k.h: hld up in tch tl wknd u.p ent fnl 2f: wl btn and eased ins fnl f* 12/1

1m 28.64s (2.64) **Going Correction** +0.25s/f (Slow) 7 Ran SP% 131.8
Speed ratings (Par 95): **94,93,92,91,90 88,72**
toteswinger:1&2:£3.10, 2&3:£4.90, 1&3:£10.10 CSF £15.48 CT £62.53 TOTE £11.50: £6.10, £1.10; EX 18.60 Trifecta £63.70 Pool £637.15 - 7.40 winning units. Place 6 £29.18, Place 5 £24.39.
Owner I A N Wight **Bred** Frank & Martin O'Donnell **Trained** Upper Lambourn, Berks

FOCUS
A moderate contest.
Feel The Magic(IRE) Official explanation: trainer's rep said, regarding apparent improvement in form, that the filly had benefited from the first-time blinkers.
Novillero ◆ Official explanation: jockey said bit slipped through colt's mouth
T/Jkpt: Not won. T/Plt: £77.00 to a £1 stake. Pool: £134,813.62. 1,276.62 winning tickets. T/Qpdt: £27.60 to a £1 stake. Pool: £11,871.32. 317.75 winning tickets. SP

[77]LINGFIELD (L-H)

Saturday, January 9

OFFICIAL GOING: Standard
Wind: Moderate, half against Weather: Near freezing, overcast, snow from race 5

105 BET ALL WEATHER RACING - BETDAQ CLASSIFIED CLAIMING STKS 1m 2f (P)

12:35 (12:35) (Class 6) 4-Y-0+ £1,774 (£523; £262) Stalls Low

Form RPR

21-2 1 **Clear Sailing**[7] 19 7-8-6 65..........(p) PaulDoe 3 71
(P D Evans) *mde all: rdn over 1f out: hld on gamely fnl f* 13/8[1]

040- 2 nk **Magnitude**[31] 7695 5-8-3 61..........(bt) NickyMackay 4 67
(M E Rimmer) *chsd ldng pair: rdn to go 2nd over 2f out: chal fnl f: jst hld* 16/1

142- 3 3 ½ **Sir George (IRE)**[12] 7861 5-7-13 65.......... AndrewHeffernan(5) 9 61
(P D Evans) *hld up in rr: hdwy on outer 3f out: wd st: one pce* 10/3[2]

304- 4 3 ½ **The Dial House**[24] 7776 4-8-4 65..........(t) DavidProbert 1 56
(J A Osborne) *s.i.s: hld up in last pair: effrt on rail over 2f out: hrd rdn and wknd over 1f out* 4/1[3]

045- 5 1 ½ **Ladies Dancing**[22] 7794 4-8-4 65.......... FrankieMcDonald 7 53
(J A Osborne) *trckd wnr tl over 2f out: sn outpcd: disputing 5th and btn whn bmpd ent st* 9/1

503- 6 2 ½ **Hold The Bucks (USA)**[99] 6439 4-8-4 65..........(p) LukeMorris 5 48
(J S Moore) *in tch in 4th: rdn 3f out: hung lft and wknd ent st* 7/1

2m 5.22s (-1.38) **Going Correction** +0.025s/f (Slow)
WFA 4 from 5yo+ 2lb 6 Ran SP% 109.6
Speed ratings (Par 101): **106,105,102,100,98 96**
.Sir George was claimed by Ollie Pears for £6,000\n\x\x
Owner Diamond Racing Ltd **Bred** Juddmonte Farms Ltd **Trained** Pandy, Monmouths

FOCUS
A moderate affair. There was a fair pace on and the first pair came well clear in a tight finish.

106 BET MULTIPLES - BETDAQ MAIDEN STKS 1m 2f (P)

1:05 (1:05) (Class 5) 3-Y-O £2,456 (£725; £362) Stalls Low

Form RPR

02- 1 **Lovers Causeway (USA)**[14] 7844 3-9-3.......... JoeFanning 1 81+
(M Johnston) *mde all: rdn over 1f out: hld on wl fnl f* 5/2[2]

40- 2 ¾ **Banks And Braes**[89] 6736 3-9-3 73.......... RichardHughes 3 78
(R Hannon) *trckd wnr tl over 3f out: drvn to regain 2nd over 1f out: kpt on fnl f: a hld* 9/1

04- 3 ½ **Septemberintherain**[56] 7390 3-9-3.......... NeilCallan 4 77
(T G Mills) *chsd ldrs on outer: wnt 2nd over 3f out tl over 1f out: styd on again nr fin* 5/4[1]

05- 4 8 **Brave Enough (USA)**[12] 7859 3-9-3.......... LiamKeniry 6 61
(M A Magnusson) *in tch in 5th: hrd rdn 3f out: sn outpcd* 5/1[3]

04- 5 2 **Yorksters Prince (IRE)**[14] 7844 3-9-3.......... DavidProbert 8 57
(M G Quinlan) *towards rr: rdn over 3f out: nt pce to chal* 33/1

0- 6 3 ¼ **Mushagak (IRE)**[36] 7622 3-8-12.......... HayleyTurner 2 46
(E A L Dunlop) *chsd ldrs tl wknd over 2f out* 14/1

7 6 **Beat Route** 3-9-3.......... LukeMorris 7 39
(M J Attwater) *rn green and sn bhd: hung rt and wd 1st turn: rdn 3f out: nvr nr ldrs* 40/1

0- 8 1 ½ **Colonel Henry**[24] 7763 3-9-3.......... PaulDoe 5 36
(S Dow) *mid-div: rdn over 3f out: sn bhd* 100/1

00- 9 12 **Hovering Hawk (IRE)**[30] 7700 3-8-12.......... MichaelHills 9 7
(B W Hills) *a in last pair: rdn and no ch fnl 3f* 50/1

2m 6.09s (-0.51) **Going Correction** +0.025s/f (Slow) 9 Ran SP% 114.7
Speed ratings (Par 97): **103,102,102,95,94 91,86,85,75**
toteswinger:1&2:£4.70, 2&3:£3.20, 1&3:£1.10 CSF £24.17 TOTE £3.40: £1.20, £2.40, £1.10; EX 19.00 Trifecta £20.60 Pool £377.64 - 13.52 winning units..
Owner Crone Stud Farms Ltd **Bred** Skara Glen Stables **Trained** Middleham Moor, N Yorks
■ Stewards' Enquiry : Michael Hills one-day ban: used whip when out of contention (Jan 23)

FOCUS
A fair maiden for the time of year run at a reasonable pace.
Beat Route Official explanation: jockey said colt ran green

107 BET PREMIER LEAGUE FOOTBALL - BETDAQ H'CAP 1m (P)

1:35 (1:35) (Class 4) (0-85,79) 3-Y-O £4,435 (£1,309; £655) Stalls High

Form RPR

31- 1 **Prince Of Sorrento**[30] 7700 3-9-2 74.......... J-PGuillambert 4 75+
(J Akehurst) *hld up in 4th: effrt on outer whn carried wd ent st: slt ld ins fnl f: jnd 100yds out: drvn to get on top nr fin* 2/1[1]

362- 2 ½ **Transfixed (IRE)**[10] 7878 3-9-2 79.......... RichardEvans(5) 5 79
(P D Evans) *pressed ldr: carried wd ent st: shkn up and n.m.r fr 1f out: disp ld 100yds out: nt qckn nr fin* 5/1[3]

143- 3 ¾ **Exceedthewildman**[21] 7806 3-9-2 74..........(p) RichardHughes 2 72
(J S Moore) *led: rdn 2f out: rn wd ent st: hdd ins fnl f: one pce fnl 50yds* 2/1[1]

051- 4 1 ¾ **Cuthbert (IRE)**[9] 7885 3-9-0 72.......... JoeFanning 1 68
(W Jarvis) *hld up in 3rd: rdn 3f out: chal on inner over 1f out: no ex fnl 75yds* 3/1[2]

1m 38.37s (0.17) **Going Correction** +0.025s/f (Slow) 4 Ran SP% 108.3
Speed ratings (Par 99): **100,99,98,97**
CSF £11.30 TOTE £2.90; EX 7.20.
Owner Mrs Pam Akhurst **Bred** Mrs P Akhurst **Trained** Epsom, Surrey

FOCUS
This was a tight little handicap and, due to a tactical pace, all four of the runners were still in a line at the furlong pole. The form should be treated with a little caution, but the right horse probably still emerged on top.

108 BETDAQ THE BETTING EXCHANGE "SUPER 7" H'CAP (QUALIFIER) 7f (P)

2:10 (2:11) (Class 2) (0-100,105) 4-Y-O+ £10,361 (£3,083; £1,540; £769) Stalls Low

Form RPR

410- 1 **Elna Bright**[20] 7827 5-8-8 90.......... LiamKeniry 12 99
(B R Johnson) *hld up towards rr: gd hdwy and squeezed through on rail 1f out: r.o to ld fnl 50yds* 8/1

333- 2 hd **Atlantic Story (USA)**[105] 6283 8-9-9 105..........(bt) JamieSpencer 6 113
(M W Easterby) *trckd ldrs gng wl: edgd lft and rdn to ld 1f out: hdd and nt qckn fnl 50yds* 6/1[1]

200- 3 shd **The Scorching Wind (IRE)**[20] 7827 4-8-4 86 oh1....(t) NickyMackay 13 94
(S C Williams) *in tch disputing 5th: wd and lost pl bnd into st: swtchd ins and edgd lft: r.o wl fnl f* 9/1

500- 4 ¾ **Carcinetto (IRE)**[24] 7768 8-8-10 92.......... PaulDoe 14 98
(P D Evans) *bhd: forced wd ent st: gd hdwy fr over 1f out: nrst fin* 33/1

421- 5 ¾ **Fathsta (IRE)**[30] 7702 5-8-3 88.......... MartinLane(3) 11 92
(D M Simcock) *hld up in midfield: nt clr run ent st: shkn up and r.o fnl f* 15/2[3]

211- 6 1 ¼ **Imprimis Tagula (IRE)**[12] 7862 6-8-11 98..........(v) LeeNewnes(5) 5 99
(A Bailey) *led: rdn 2f out: hdd 1f out: no ex* 8/1

310- 7 ¾ **Wigram's Turn (USA)**[52] 7431 5-8-7 89.......... DavidProbert 8 88
(A M Balding) *dwlt and bmpd s: bhd: rdn 3f out: nt clr run and swtchd wd ins fnl f: gng on at fin* 10/1

303- 8 1 **Ceremonial Jade (UAE)**[24] 7768 7-9-9 105..........(t) JerryO'Dwyer 2 101
(M Botti) *dwlt: sn in tch disputing 5th: rdn to chse ldrs whn n.m.r over 1f out: no ex fnl f* 6/1[1]

314- 9 nse **Benandonner (USA)**[20] 7827 7-8-7 89.......... MartinDwyer 1 88+
(Mike Murphy) *pckd s: sn prom: disputing cl 3rd whn bdly squeezed 1f out: nt rcvr* 14/1

222- 10 hd **Ebraam (USA)**[12] 7862 7-9-3 99..........(t) RobertWinston 3 96+
(S Curran) *s.i.s: sn in midfield: pushed along 1/2-way: no imp whn n.m.r jst ins fnl f: eased* 12/1

564- 11 1 ½ **Flowing Cape (IRE)**[12] 7862 5-8-8 90..........(t) HayleyTurner 10 89+
(R Hollinshead) *towards rr: sme hdwy in midfield whn hmpd and snatched up jst ins fnl f* 16/1

244- 12 ½ **Eisteddfod**[18] 7837 9-9-5 101.......... EddieAhern 7 91+
(P F I Cole) *blindfold removed late: wnt rt and s.i.s: hld up towards rr: modest effrt on rail ent st: sn wknd* 25/1

420- 13 1 ¾ **Nezami (IRE)**[20] 7827 5-8-4 89.......... AndreaAtzeni(3) 9 74
(J Akehurst) *chsd ldr: chal 2f out: brushed by rival: edgd rt and wknd over 1f out* 7/1[2]

1m 23.57s (-1.23) **Going Correction** +0.025s/f (Slow) 13 Ran SP% 121.2
Speed ratings (Par 109): **108,107,107,106,105 104,103,102,102,102 100,99,97**
toteswinger:1&2:£14.50, 2&3:£8.00, 1&3:£26.50 CSF £56.24 CT £465.26 TOTE £10.20: £4.10, £2.20, £2.70; EX 84.00 TRIFECTA Pool £16,023.448 - 11.95 winning units..
Owner Peter Crate **Bred** D R Tucker **Trained** Ashtead, Surrey
■ Stewards' Enquiry : Jerry O'Dwyer two-day ban: careless riding (Jan 23-24)
Nicky Mackay four-day ban: careless riding (Jan 23-26)

FOCUS
This was a decent, competitive handicap, but it was a rough race, with a few of these finding trouble, despite the pace appearing strong.

NOTEBOOK
Elna Bright, well beaten after racing wide throughout from a poor draw at Kempton on his previous, was dropped in from an unfavourable stall this time. Having made good headway on the bridle around the final bend, he barged his way through against the inside rail just over a furlong out and just found enough. This was a career-best performance. (op 9-1 tchd 10-1)
Atlantic Story(USA) ◆ ran close to the pick of his form in defeat but still gave the impression he's capable of even better. Having travelled as well as anything for most of the way, just off the leaders, he didn't find as much as had looked likely after being brought wide when coming under pressure over a furlong out, edging left late on. Perhaps he hit the front a bit soon, plus he had been off for 105 days, so might have needed this fitness-wise. Whatever the case, though, despite having won at as far as 1m, he was being campaigned over sprint distances when last seen, and the impression this time was that he's a horse with more speed than stamina these days, so he'll be interesting if dropped back in trip. (op 9-1 tchd 10-1)
The Scorching Wind(IRE) ◆, given a poor ride at Kempton on his return from a break, ran much better this time, from 1lb out of the handicap, despite not getting the run of things. He came wide into the straight, before switching back inside, and ran on well to post a very useful effort in defeat. This progressive colt looks one to be interested in over the coming weeks. (op 8-1 tchd 10-1)
Carcinetto(IRE) did well to finish so close considering she came extremely wide into the straight. (op 40-1 tchd 50-1)
Fathsta(IRE), 5lb higher than when winning over 6f at Kempton on his previous start, didn't enjoy the clearest of runs in the straight but couldn't be described as unlucky. Still, this was a solid effort and he remains competitive. (op 7-1 tchd 11-2)
Imprimis Tagula(IRE), the winner of four of his last five starts, was up a further 6lb and it was a bit of a surprise to see him return to front-running tactics for his toughest task yet. After going off quickly, he could offer little resistance in the straight, but still performed creditably.

Wigram's Turn(USA), returning from 52 days off, had to be niggled along a fair way out and looked hard work, only really getting going when the race was as good as over, and having to switch late on made little difference. It would be no surprise to see headgear given another try. (op 16-1)
Ceremonial Jade(UAE), tucked away towards the inside after missing the break a touch, failed to pick up in the straight, even allowing for being a little short of room, and wasn't at his best on this return to handicap company. (tchd 13-2 in places)
Benandonner(USA) was still in contention, but perhaps more of a candidate for a place than the win, when badly hampered over 1f out. (op 16-1)
Ebraam(USA), a bit keen early on, was held when badly squeezed for room inside the final furlong, but that exaggerated the margin of defeat. (op 10-1)
Flowing Cape(IRE), who has yet to discover his best form this winter, had to be snatched up when staying on inside the final furlong, after which his apprentice stopped riding, and he would have been at least a couple of lengths closer with a clear run.
Eisteddfod had the blindfold removed late and started awkwardly. Left with a lot to do in the straight, he didn't get the best of runs through and looked to cross the line with something left.
Official explanation: jockey said gelding was denied a clear run (op 16-1)

109 BETDAQ.CO.UK CONDITIONS STKS 1m (P)
2:40 (2:40) (Class 3) 4-Y-0+ **£6,799** (£2,023; £1,011; £505) **Stalls** High

Form RPR
214- **1** **Beauchamp Viceroy**[49] 7489 6-9-0 92..........(b) EddieAhern 3 108
(G A Butler) *trckd ldr: led 2f out: rdn clr over 1f out: readily* **3/1**[3]
162- **2** 2 3/4 **Aeroplane**[20] 7827 7-8-11 102 ow2..........(p) RichardEvans(5) 5 104
(P D Evans) *hld up in 4th: wnt 3rd over 2f out: rdn to chse wnr jst ins fnl f: a comf hld* **7/4**[2]
505- **3** 2 **Plum Pudding (IRE)**[21] 7809 7-9-4 105.......... RichardHughes 2 101
(R Hannon) *led tl 2f out: no ex over 1f out* **13/8**[1]
000- **4** 3 **Samarinda (USA)**[36] 7626 7-9-0 92.......... JerryO'Dwyer 4 91
(Mrs P Sly) *stdd s: hld up in 3rd: outpcd fnl 2f* **11/1**

1m 36.92s (-1.28) **Going Correction** +0.025s/f (Slow) **4** Ran SP% **107.8**
Speed ratings (Par 107): **107,104,102,99**
CSF £8.52 TOTE £4.50; EX 8.40.
Owner Erik Penser **Bred** E Penser **Trained** Newmarket, Suffolk

FOCUS
A good conditions event but a tactical affair.

NOTEBOOK
Beauchamp Viceroy, well backed, justified the handicapper's decision to raise him 10lb for his effort in Listed company here last month and he ran out a convincing winner. Content to let old rival Plum Pudding set the tempo, he moved up to that rival nearing the 3f pole. He produced an immediate turn of foot when asked to quicken turning into the home straight, and that move proved to be a winning one as he came right away inside the final furlong. This trip is his optimum and it should rate a career-best effort, but this Polytrack specialist now faces another rise in the handicap, so a return to Listed company is probable. (op 9-2)
Aeroplane seemed to have a deal in his favour, other than the 2lb overweight, but he could have done with a stronger overall pace and simply found the winner getting first run on him. He's not an easy ride, though, and it is still unlikely he would have won even if things had been more in his favour. (op 11-8)
Plum Pudding(IRE) was a disappointment. He finished well behind the winner in Listed company here on his penultimate outing, but was back to his optimum distance and was returned to his favoured position at the head of affairs through the first half of the race. He got caught out when Beauchamp Viceroy quickened for home and the manner in which he finished suggests he would benefit from a break. (tchd 11-8 and 15-8)
Samarinda(USA) came into this struggling for form and was never seriously involved after a tardy start. (op 12-1)

110 BETDAQ ON 0870 178 1221 H'CAP 7f (P)
3:10 (3:10) (Class 5) (0-70,70) 4-Y-0+ **£2,456** (£725; £362) **Stalls** Low

Form RPR
102- **1** **Rubenstar (IRE)**[12] 7860 7-9-1 67.......... StephenCraine 5 74
(Patrick Morris) *hld up in midfield gng wl: hdwy on bit over 1f out: shkn up and r.o fnl f: got up on line* **4/1**[2]
202- **2** nse **Shaded Edge**[9] 7891 6-9-4 70.......... MartinDwyer 6 77
(D W P Arbuthnot) *prom: led over 1f out: hrd rdn and kpt on fnl f: jst ct* **4/1**[2]
200- **3** 1 **Elusive Ronnie (IRE)**[9] 7890 4-8-7 59 ow2..........(b) JackMitchell 9 63
(R A Teal) *mid-div: rdn over 3f out: hdwy over 1f out: pressed ldrs ins fnl f: nt qckn fnl 50yds* **25/1**
165- **4** 1/2 **Billberry**[19] 7832 5-9-2 68..........(t) JamieSpencer 4 71
(S C Williams) *bhd: rdn and hdwy over 1f out: styd on wl fnl f* **11/4**[1]
060- **5** 1 1/2 **Learo Dochais (USA)**[9] 7891 4-9-2 68..........(b[1]) NeilCallan 7 67
(M A Jarvis) *led tl over 1f out: wknd fnl f* **10/1**
041- **6** 1/2 **Lord Fidelio (IRE)**[38] 7610 4-9-0 66.......... LiamKeniry 1 66+
(A M Balding) *in tch in 5th: n.m.r on rail and lost pl appr st: rallied over 1f out: hrd rdn and no ex fnl f* **5/1**[3]
206- **7** 1/2 **Great Bounder (CAN)**[12] 7860 4-7-13 56.......... AmyBaker(5) 3 52
(A B Haynes) *s.s: bhd: rdn 2f out: n.d* **16/1**
46-0 **8** 1 **Melt (IRE)**[6] 27 5-8-6 58..........(b) HayleyTurner 8 51
(R Hannon) *chsd ldr: rdn 2f out: wknd over 1f out* **16/1**
406- **9** 1/2 **Durgan**[19] 7833 4-9-3 69.......... RobertWinston 2 61
(Mrs L C Jewell) *chsd ldrs: rdn over 2f out: wknd over 1f out* **20/1**

1m 25.64s (0.84) **Going Correction** +0.025s/f (Slow) **9** Ran SP% **112.8**
Speed ratings (Par 103): **96,95,94,94,92 91,91,90,89**
toteswinger:1&2:£2.80, 2&3:£28.50, 1&3:£13.90 CSF £19.83 CT £348.15 TOTE £4.80: £1.80, £1.50, £4.40; EX 20.10 Trifecta £307.80 Pool £852.72 - 2.05 winning units..
Owner L Walsh **Bred** Schwindibode Ag **Trained** Tarporley, Cheshire

FOCUS
A modest handicap run at a fair price. The weather was horrid, with a strong wind and some snow not making things easy for the horses and jockeys.
Great Bounder(CAN) Official explanation: jockey said gelding was slowly away

111 BET AFRICAN NATIONS CUP - BETDAQ H'CAP 5f (P)
3:40 (3:40) (Class 5) (0-70,69) 3-Y-O **£2,456** (£725; £362) **Stalls** High

Form RPR
263- **1** **Boogie Waltzer**[26] 7748 3-8-2 56.......... AndreaAtzeni(3) 7 65
(S C Williams) *w ldr: led over 2f out: pushed out: comf* **10/1**
332- **2** 2 **Athwaab**[10] 7871 3-9-3 68.......... JamieSpencer 2 70
(M G Quinlan) *chsd ldrs: kpt on to take 2nd ins fnl f: nt pce of wnr* **4/1**[3]
211- **3** 3/4 **Wanchai Whisper**[10] 7871 3-9-4 69.......... PaulDoe 3 68
(P D Evans) *chsd ldrs: wnt 2nd over 1f out tl ins fnl f: one pce* **5/2**[2]
001- **4** 1 3/4 **Billie Jean**[23] 7778 3-8-13 64.......... MichaelHills 6 57
(B W Hills) *sn pushed along in 5th: no imp fnl 2f* **9/4**[1]
643- **5** 3 3/4 **Kings Of Leo**[10] 7871 3-8-12 68.......... MatthewDavies(5) 1 48
(J R Boyle) *led tl over 2f out: wknd over 1f out* **7/1**
500- **6** 1 1/4 **Annia Galeria (IRE)**[117] 5950 3-8-1 55 oh1.......... KellyHarrison(3) 5 30
(C A Dwyer) *s.s: a bhd* **33/1**
336- **7** nse **Blue Neptune**[10] 7871 3-8-11 62.......... MartinDwyer 4 37
(W R Muir) *v.s.a: a bhd* **8/1**

60.36 secs (1.56) **Going Correction** +0.025s/f (Slow) **7** Ran SP% **115.0**
Speed ratings (Par 97): **88,84,83,80,74 72,72**
toteswinger:1&2:£9.30, 2&3:£1.70, 1&3:£6.90 CSF £49.90 TOTE £15.60: £6.00, £2.10; EX 60.60 Place 6 £169.61, Place 5 £84.20.
Owner Michael Edwards and John Parsons **Bred** Michael Edwards And John Parsons **Trained** Newmarket, Suffolk

FOCUS
A reasonable 3-y-o sprint handicap for the grade on paper, but another race run in a mix of strong wind and snow, and few were ever seriously involved.
Annia Galeria(IRE) Official explanation: jockey said filly slipped leaving stalls
Blue Neptune Official explanation: jockey said colt slipped leaving stalls
T/Plt: £546.50 to a £1 stake. Pool: £125,777.15. 167.99 winning tickets. T/Qpdt: £144.60 to a £1 stake. Pool: £11,289.30. 57.75 winning tickets. LM

85 SOUTHWELL (L-H)
Sunday, January 10

OFFICIAL GOING: Slow
Wind: Fresh across Weather: Snowing

112 BOOK TICKETS ONLINE APPRENTICE H'CAP 5f (F)
1:20 (1:20) (Class 6) (0-55,55) 4-Y-0+ **£1,774** (£523; £262) **Stalls** High

Form RPR
000- **1** **Lujiana**[44] 7561 5-8-5 48.......... JohnCavanagh(3) 2 62
(M Brittain) *chsd ldrs: led 1/2-way: rdn over 1f out: styd on* **25/1**
6-01 **2** 2 **Brazilian Brush (IRE)**[3] 69 5-8-8 51 6ex..........(bt) RyanClark(3) 7 58
(J M Bradley) *chsd ldrs: rdn over 1f out: styd on same pce ins fnl f* **9/4**[1]
154- **3** hd **Best One**[10] 7889 6-9-1 55..........(b) DeclanCannon 9 61
(R A Harris) *s.i.s: hdwy and hung lft 1/2-way: sn rdn: styd on same pce ins fnl f* **8/1**
00-3 **4** 1 **Truly Divine**[2] 89 5-8-3 46..........(v) MatthewLawson(3) 1 48
(C A Dwyer) *s.i.s: hdwy to ld over 3f out: hdd 1/2-way: sn rdn: no ex fnl f* **5/1**[2]
522- **5** 3/4 **Grand Palace (IRE)**[10] 7889 7-8-12 55..........(v) DavidKenny(3) 4 55
(H J Evans) *chsd ldrs: shkn up 1/2-way: styd on same pce appr fnl f* **5/1**[2]
45-5 **6** 2 1/4 **Tenancy (IRE)**[8] 14 6-8-1 46 oh1..........(b) NathanAlison(5) 6 38
(S A Harris) *led: hdd over 3f out: rdn 1/2-way: wknd fnl f* **12/1**
242- **7** 5 **Head To Head (IRE)**[30] 7709 6-8-10 50..........(vt[1]) BillyCray 3 24
(A D Brown) *in tch and sn pushed along: outpcd over 3f out: n.d after* **8/1**
631- **8** 2 **Mr Funshine**[19] 7838 5-8-8 51.......... LeeTopliss(3) 8 17
(D Shaw) *sn pushed along: a in rr* **11/2**[3]
000- **9** 10 **Take That**[68] 7219 5-8-1 46 oh1.......... NoraLooby(5) 5 —
(S P Griffiths) *hld up: wknd 1/2-way* **150/1**

61.57 secs (1.87) **Going Correction** +0.40s/f (Slow) **9** Ran SP% **113.9**
Speed ratings (Par 101): **101,97,97,95,94 91,83,79,63**
toteswingers: 1&2 £11.30, 1&3 £22.90, 2&3 £7.00. CSF £80.26 CT £512.78 TOTE £27.40: £3.00, £1.60, £2.70; EX 113.40 Trifecta £536.00 Part won. Pool: £724.34 - 0.10 winning units..
Owner Mel Brittain **Bred** Bearstone Stud **Trained** Warthill, N Yorks

FOCUS
Conditions looked particularly unpleasant for this opening sprint handicap, the snow being accompanied by a slight cross-wind in the straight.

113 SOUTHWELL-RACECOURSE.CO.UK (S) STKS 1m 3f (F)
1:50 (1:50) (Class 6) 4-Y-0+ **£1,774** (£523; £262) **Stalls** Low

Form RPR
00-4 **1** **Black Falcon (IRE)**[2] 90 10-9-3 48.......... RobertWinston 6 61
(John A Harris) *chsd ldrs: led over 3f out: rdn and hung lft over 2f out: hdd over 1f out: hung rt ins fnl f: styd on u.p to ld towards fin* **13/2**
00-5 **2** nk **Inside Story (IRE)**[6] 34 8-9-3 57..........(b) LiamKeniry 8 60
(C R Dore) *hld up in tch: trckd wnr 3f out: led over 1f out: sn rdn: hung lft ins fnl f: hdd and nt qckn towards fin* **4/1**[2]
/20- **3** 8 **Jazrawy**[19] 7840 8-9-3 56.......... ShaneKelly 5 47
(A J McCabe) *hld up: hdwy over 3f out: rdn and hung lft 2f out: styd on same pce* **9/2**[3]
030- **4** 2 **Bromhead (USA)**[30] 7094 4-9-0 55..........(t) JerryO'Dwyer 1 43
(Mrs C A Dunnett) *chsd ldrs: rdn over 2f out: sn wknd* **18/1**
236- **5** 4 1/2 **Via Mia**[38] 7615 4-8-4 68.......... MatthewDavies(5) 10 31
(George Baker) *hld up: hdwy over 3f out: rdn over 2f out: sn wknd* **2/1**[1]
046- **6** 7 **Nawamees (IRE)**[40] 7549 12-8-10 54..........(p) KevinLundie(7) 2 24
(P D Evans) *sn outpcd: in rr whn nt clr run over 3f out: nvr on terms* **15/2**
06-0 **7** 8 **If You Knew Suzy**[8] 21 5-8-12 55.......... TonyHamilton 3 5
(R E Barr) *led 1f: chsd ldr tl led wl over 3f out: sn rdn and hdd: wknd over 2f out: t.o* **20/1**
8 3 1/4 **Maree Prince (IRE)**[13] 5527 9-8-12 0.......... BarryMcHugh(5) 7 5
(Ferdy Murphy) *s.s: outpcd: latched on to main bunch leaving bk st: wknd sn after: t.o* **16/1**
000- **9** 11 **Intavac Boy**[29] 7733 9-9-0 39..........(p) MichaelStainton(3) 11 —
(S P Griffiths) *led after 1f: rdn: hdd & wknd wl over 3f out: t.o* **66/1**
050- **10** 20 **Govenor Eliott (IRE)**[33] 7681 5-9-3 49.......... PhillipMakin 4 —
(A J Lockwood) *chsd ldrs: rdn over 4f out: wknd over 3f out: t.o* **33/1**

2m 32.65s (4.65) **Going Correction** +0.375s/f (Slow)
WFA 4 from 5yo+ 3lb **10** Ran SP% **117.0**
Speed ratings (Par 101): **98,97,91,90,87 82,76,73,65,51**
toteswingers: 1&2 £5.10, 1&3 £6.70, 2&3 £5.40. CSF £32.26 TOTE £7.70: £2.50, £1.30, £1.80; EX 26.40 Trifecta £51.10 Pool: £824.547 - 11.92 winning units..No bid for the winner.
Owner Mrs A E Harris **Bred** Gainsborough Stud Management Ltd **Trained** Eastwell, Leics

FOCUS
The front pair drew clear in this seller.

114 TONY HADFIELD 80TH BIRTHDAY H'CAP 1m 3f (F)
2:20 (2:20) (Class 6) (0-65,68) 4-Y-0+ **£1,774** (£523; £262) **Stalls** Low

Form RPR
3-2 **1** **Look Officer (USA)**[9] 1 4-9-1 62..........(b) RichardKingscote 3 70
(Tom Dascombe) *hld up: pushed along over 3f out: hdwy u.p to ld over 1f out: cajoled along and styd on wl: eased towards fin* **15/2**
/0-1 **2** 3 3/4 **Dan Buoy (FR)**[3] 76 7-8-9 58..........(p) RossAtkinson(5) 4 60
(R C Guest) *trckd ldr: racd keenly: rdn and hung lft fr over 2f out: styd on same pce fnl f* **4/1**[2]
13-1 **3** 2 **Dream In Blue**[5] 42 5-9-5 68 6ex..........(p) AndrewHeffernan(5) 2 66
(J A Glover) *trckd ldrs: racd keenly: rdn over 3f out: no ex fnl f* **15/8**[1]
20-1 **4** 1 3/4 **Stormy Summer**[8] 18 5-9-5 68..........(b) TobyAtkinson(5) 7 63
(R W Price) *s.i.s: hld up: hdwy over 3f out: sn rdn: hung lft and wknd fnl f* **6/1**

050- **5** *1* **Jebel Tara**[141] 4431 5-9-6 **64**....................................(t) GrahamGibbons 1 58
(A D Brown) led: rdn over 2f out: hdd over 1f out: wknd ins fnl f **16/1**

265- **6** *3 ½* **Princess Flame (GER)**[24] 7036 8-9-3 **61**.................... RobertWinston 5 49
(B G Powell) chsd ldrs: rdn over 3f out: wknd over 1f out **9/2**[3]

060- **7** *2 ¼* **Silver Hotspur**[14] 7854 6-9-6 **64**... LiamKeniry 6 48
(C R Dore) s.s: hdwy to latch on to bk of main gp over 9f out: plld hrd: rdn: hung lft and wknd wl over 1f out **20/1**

2m 34.38s (6.38) **Going Correction** +0.375s/f (Slow)
WFA 4 from 5yo+ 3lb **7** Ran SP% **109.7**
Speed ratings (Par 101): **91,88,86,85,84 82,80**
toteswingers: 1&2 £5.40, 1&3 £2.60, 2&3 £3.80. CSF £34.22 CT £72.71 TOTE £6.10: £2.30, £2.70; EX 20.90 Trifecta £138.30 Pool: £807.49 - 4.32 winning units..
Owner Grant Thornton Racing Club **Bred** Thomas J Carroll **Trained** Malpas, Cheshire

FOCUS
A low-grade handicap run in a really slow time.
Silver Hotspur Official explanation: jockey said gelding ran too free

115 MEMBERSHIP OF SOUTHWELL GOLF CLUB H'CAP 7f (F)
2:50 (2:50) (Class 4) (0-85,80) 4-Y-O+ **£4,209** (£1,252; £625; £312) **Stalls** Low

Form RPR

010- **1** **Snow Bay**[19] 7837 4-9-3 **79**... PhillipMakin 1 87
(B Smart) chsd ldrs tl led over 4f out: rdn over 2f out: hdd over 1f out: rallied to ld wl ins fnl f **5/1**[2]

240- **2** *shd* **Bel Cantor**[26] 7758 7-8-12 **77**... KellyHarrison(3) 7 85
(W J H Ratcliffe) led: hdd over 4f out: chsd wnr tl rdn to ld over 1f out: edgd lft and hdd wl ins fnl f **20/1**

05-1 **3** *¾* **Follow The Flag (IRE)**[8] 16 6-8-13 **80**..............(p) DeclanCannon(5) 5 86+
(A J McCabe) s.s: last and pushed along: hdwy u.p fr over 1f out: hung lft ins fnl f: r.o: nt rch ldrs **5/1**[2]

/0-5 **4** *¾* **Prohibition (IRE)**[8] 16 4-8-10 **75**............................ WilliamCarson(3) 4 79
(W J Haggas) mid-div: hdwy u.p 2f out: styd on: nt rch ldrs **7/1**

42-4 **5** *1 ½* **Jonnie Skull (IRE)**[8] 16 4-8-0 **67**....................(vt) AndrewHeffernan(5) 6 67
(P S McEntee) trckd ldrs: racd keenly: rdn over 2f out: no ex fnl f **16/1**

63-2 **6** *3 ¼* **Elusive Fame (USA)**[8] 16 4-8-12 **74**..........................(b) JoeFanning 3 65
(M Johnston) trckd ldrs: plld hrd: rdn over 2f out: sn wknd **9/4**[1]

364- **7** *5* **Ravi River (IRE)**[11] 7883 6-8-13 **75**............................ J-PGuillambert 8 52
(P D Evans) mid-div: drvn along 1/2-way: wknd 2f out **11/2**[3]

423- **8** *12* **Mozayada (USA)**[24] 7783 6-8-13 **75**............................ RobertWinston 2 20
(M Brittain) prom: rdn 1/2-way: wknd 2f out **13/2**

1m 31.55s (1.25) **Going Correction** +0.375s/f (Slow) **8** Ran SP% **116.0**
Speed ratings (Par 105): **107,106,106,105,103 99,94,80**
toteswingers: 1&2 £20.50, 1&3 £4.20, 2&3 £8.50. CSF £95.10 CT £530.49 TOTE £6.10: £1.90, £4.40, £1.60; EX 74.80 Trifecta £544.90 Pool: £1,031.02 - 1.40 winning units..
Owner Pinnacle Bahamian Bounty Partnership **Bred** West Dereham Abbey Stud **Trained** Hambleton, N Yorks

FOCUS
A fair handicap, but the first two dominated pretty much throughout.
Elusive Fame(USA) Official explanation: trainer had no explanation for the poor form shown

116 BOOK CONFERENCING AT SOUTHWELL RACECOURSE H'CAP 6f (F)
3:20 (3:20) (Class 6) (0-55,56) 4-Y-O+ **£1,774** (£523; £262) **Stalls** Low

Form RPR

526- **1** **Zeffirelli**[23] 7796 5-8-12 **55**.. AndreaAtzeni(3) 9 63
(M Quinn) chsd ldrs: rdn over 2f out: hung lft and led ins fnl f: styd on **5/2**[1]

030- **2** *½* **Cheery Cat (USA)**[31] 7703 6-8-4 **51** ow1....................(p) DavidKenny(7) 7 58
(J Balding) chsd ldr: rdn to ld over 1f out: hdd ins fnl f: styd on **13/2**

0-06 **3** *6* **Mickys Mate**[3] 70 5-7-13 **46** oh1.............................. NathanAlison(7) 6 33
(S A Harris) led: rdn and hdd over 1f out: wknd ins fnl f **40/1**

334- **4** *1 ¼* **Kinigi (IRE)**[20] 7835 4-8-10 **55**....................(p) AndrewHeffernan(5) 3 38
(R A Harris) hmpd s: in rr and nt clr run over 4f out: rdn over 2f out: nvr on terms **7/2**[3]

303- **5** *4 ½* **Outer Hebrides**[40] 7602 9-8-13 **53**..................................(v) LukeMorris 8 22
(J M Bradley) prom: rdn over 3f out: wknd over 2f out **11/4**[2]

563- **6** *2* **Golden Dixie (USA)**[20] 7834 11-8-13 **53**........................ TonyCulhane 1 16
(R A Harris) hmpd s: in rr: hdwy over 3f out: rdn and wknd over 2f out **17/2**

060- **7** *6* **Mintoe**[170] 4279 4-9-1 **55**...(p) RobertWinston 4 —
(J O'Reilly) wnt lft s: sn pushed along in rr: wknd over 3f out **11/1**

1m 18.53s (2.03) **Going Correction** +0.375s/f (Slow) **7** Ran SP% **112.1**
Speed ratings (Par 101): **101,100,92,90,84 82,74**
toteswingers: 1&2 £5.20, 1&3 £4.50, 2&3 £14.20. CSF £18.35 CT £501.28 TOTE £3.80: £2.20, £2.70; EX 21.70 Trifecta £301.40 Pool: £1,181.53 - 2.90 winning units..
Owner A G MacLennan **Bred** J Spearing And Kate Ive **Trained** Newmarket, Suffolk

FOCUS
A really moderate handicap.
Outer Hebrides Official explanation: trainer said gelding was unsuited by the slow Fibresand.
Golden Dixie(USA) Official explanation: jockey said gelding was hampered at start
Mintoe Official explanation: jockey said gelding jumped awkwardly and saddle slipped

117 PLAY GOLF BEFORE RACING AT SOUTHWELL H'CAP 6f (F)
3:50 (3:50) (Class 4) (0-85,85) 3-Y-O **£4,209** (£1,252; £625; £312) **Stalls** Low

Form RPR

60-1 **1** **Love Delta (USA)**[9] 4 3-8-12 **76**.................................... JoeFanning 4 88+
(M Johnston) led: hdd over 4f out: shkn up to ld over 1f out: r.o wl: eased towards fin **4/6**[1]

020- **2** *1 ¼* **Coolree Star (IRE)**[37] 7625 3-8-13 **77**.......................... RobertWinston 1 82
(J A Glover) chsd wnr: led over 4f out: rdn and hdd over 1f out: styd on same pce fnl f **9/1**

021- **3** *3 ¼* **Maldon Prom (IRE)**[24] 7786 3-8-7 **74**.......................... AndreaAtzeni(3) 2 69
(C A Dwyer) awkward leaving stalls and rdr lost iron: in rr and pushed along: hdwy over 2f out: sn rdn: wknd ins fnl f **11/4**[2]

414- **4** *2 ¼* **Italian Tom (IRE)**[23] 7793 3-9-2 **80**.................................. TonyCulhane 6 67
(R A Harris) chsd ldrs: rdn over 2f out: wknd fnl f **7/1**[3]

1m 17.66s (1.16) **Going Correction** +0.375s/f (Slow) **4** Ran SP% **109.2**
Speed ratings (Par 99): **107,105,101,98**
toteswingers: 1&2 £5.40. CSF £7.08 TOTE £1.60; EX 7.20 Place 6: £140.31 Place 5: £59.28.
Owner Crone Stud Farms Ltd **Bred** Palides Investments N V Inc & Hair 'Em Corporation **Trained** Middleham Moor, N Yorks

FOCUS
Only four runners for this fair 3-y-o handicap.
T/Jkpt: Not won. T/Plt: £210.90 to a £1 stake. Pool: £165,253.14. 571.99 winning tickets. T/Qpdt: £39.20 to a £1 stake. Pool: £14,980.03. 282.43 winning tickets. CR

[98]KEMPTON (A.W) (R-H)
Monday, January 11

OFFICIAL GOING: Standard
Wind: Almost nil Weather: Overcast, cold

118 WILLIAMHILL.COM/BONUS 25 H'CAP 1m 2f (P)
2:15 (2:16) (Class 6) (0-60,59) 3-Y-O **£2,047** (£604; £302) **Stalls** High

Form RPR

006- **1** **Keenes Royale**[68] 7244 3-9-0 55......................................(t) JimCrowley 5 62
(R M Beckett) t.k.h early: a in ldng trio: wl plcd whn pce lifted 4f out: rdn to ld over 1f out: r.o and sn clr **3/1**[1]

432- **2** *2 ¾* **Captain Cool (IRE)**[11] 7887 3-8-10 51............................... EddieAhern 7 52
(R Hannon) hld up in 5th: pushed along over 3f out: prog over 1f out: wnt 2nd ins fnl f: styd on but wnr already clr **7/2**[2]

064- **3** *1 ¾* **Jennerous Blue**[42] 7597 3-8-11 52...................................... LukeMorris 6 50
(D K Ivory) hld up in 7th: pushed along 6f out and again whn pce lifted 4f out: struggling tl styd on fnl f to take 3rd nr fin **3/1**[1]

025- **4** *1 ¼* **Land Of Plenty (IRE)**[30] 7731 3-8-4 45............................ JimmyQuinn 8 40
(E A L Dunlop) trckd ldng pair: drvn over 3f out: nt qckn and struggling 2f out: plugged on **8/1**[3]

000- **5** *½* **Cordiality**[37] 7638 3-9-2 57.. NeilCallan 3 51
(P G Murphy) led at mod pce to 4f out: drvn over 2f out: lost 2nd wl over 1f out and sn outpcd **10/1**

000- **6** *½* **Joe Rua (USA)**[33] 7685 3-8-4 48.. MarcHalford(3) 1 41
(J Ryan) hld up in 6th: rdn whn pce lifted 4f out: struggling after **25/1**

005- **7** *½* **Anchorage Boy (USA)**[159] 4666 3-9-4 59......................... LiamKeniry 2 51
(Miss Amy Weaver) hld up in last: in trble whn pce lifted 4f out: effrt on inner 2f out: no prog fnl f **14/1**

550- **8** *1 ½* **Kyoatee Kilt**[11] 7887 3-9-0 55... TomQueally 4 44
(P F I Cole) t.k.h: hld up in 4th tl quick move to ld 4f out and injected pce: hdd over 1f out: wknd rapidly **8/1**[3]

2m 10.58s (2.58) **Going Correction** +0.075s/f (Slow) **8** Ran SP% **114.0**
Speed ratings (Par 95): **92,89,88,87,87 86,86,85**
toteswingers: 1&2 £4.20, 1&3 £3.90, 2&3 £1.90 CSF £13.58 CT £32.94 TOTE £4.30: £1.40, £1.40, £1.30; EX 14.80.
Owner Mrs R J Jacobs **Bred** Newsells Park Stud Limited **Trained** Whitsbury, Hants

FOCUS
This opening 3-y-o event was in all but name a maiden handicap. However, it was still an interesting affair for the class with three having their first outing outside of maiden company and a couple of other potential improvers in attendance. The form is limited but sound enough.
Cordiality Official explanation: vet said gelding had been struck into

119 WILLIAMHILL.COM/BEST ODDS GUARANTEED H'CAP 5f (P)
2:45 (2:46) (Class 5) (0-75,74) 4-Y-O+ **£2,590** (£770; £385; £192) **Stalls** High

Form RPR

14-0 **1** **Thoughtsofstardom**[3] 77 7-8-6 62................................ DavidProbert 4 72
(P S McEntee) mde all: drvn abt 2 l clr over 1f out: styd on fnl f: unchal **14/1**

31-5 **2** *1 ¼* **Fromsong (IRE)**[3] 79 12-8-9 65.................................(p) EddieAhern 10 71
(D K Ivory) trckd ldng quartet: effrt over 1f out: styd on to take 2nd 150yds out: no imp on wnr **6/1**[3]

010- **3** *nk* **Lord Of The Reins (IRE)**[12] 7872 6-9-4 74..................... TomQueally 9 78+
(J G Given) pushed along in last after 2f: gd prog jst over 1f out: nt clr run briefly 150yds out: r.o to take 3rd nr fin **4/1**[1]

522- **4** *nk* **Lithaam (IRE)**[23] 7807 6-8-7 70.................................(p) RyanClark(7) 7 73
(J M Bradley) mostly chsd wnr: rdn and no imp over 1f out: one pce and lost 2 pls ins fnl f **4/1**[1]

102- **5** *½* **Fantasy Fighter (IRE)**[30] 7735 5-8-5 61.......................... JimmyQuinn 1 63+
(J J Quinn) dwlt: mostly in last pair tl prog jst over 1f out: kpt on but nt pce to threaten **8/1**

065- **6** *2 ¼* **Chjimes (IRE)**[12] 7872 6-9-4 74... LiamKeniry 3 67
(C R Dore) hld up in 7th: quite wd bnd 2f out: sn rdn and nt qckn: n.d after **7/1**

410- **7** *1 ¼* **The Wee Chief (IRE)**[29] 7738 4-8-13 69......................... RichardSmith 2 58
(J C Fox) racd wd in 6th: lost grnd bnd 2f out: struggling after **10/1**

434- **8** *hd* **Littlemisssunshine (IRE)**[12] 7872 5-8-12 68..................(p) LukeMorris 8 56
(J S Moore) ssn chsd ldng trio: rdn and nt qckn wl over 1f out: wknd fnl f **5/1**[2]

040- **9** *shd* **Especially Special (IRE)**[23] 7808 4-8-4 60 oh2....... FrankieMcDonald 6 48
(Peter Grayson) chsd ldng pair: drvn wl over 1f out: wknd rapidly fnl f: dismntd after fin **40/1**

59.81 secs (-0.69) **Going Correction** +0.075s/f (Slow) **9** Ran SP% **112.8**
Speed ratings (Par 103): **108,106,105,105,104 100,98,98,98**
toteswingers: 1&2 £15.60, 1&3 £13.90, 2&3 £5.90 CSF £92.91 CT £403.57 TOTE £16.20: £5.40, £1.70, £1.20; EX 45.80.
Owner Eventmaker Racehorses **Bred** B Bargh **Trained** Newmarket, Suffolk

FOCUS
A wide-open looking sprint handicap. The winner, who was allowed an easy lead, is rated to the best view of his recent form.
Lord Of The Reins(IRE) Official explanation: jockey said gelding had been denied a clear run

120 WILLIAM HILL 0800 44 40 40 BET NOW! H'CAP (DIV I) 1m 4f (P)
3:15 (3:15) (Class 6) (0-65,65) 4-Y-O+ **£1,706** (£503; £252) **Stalls** Centre

Form RPR

405- **1** **Slick Mover (IRE)**[31] 7112 5-8-10 55............................... DavidProbert 9 65
(B G Powell) trckd ldrs: effrt to ld over 2f out: rdn and styd on wl fr over 1f out: in command fnl f **12/1**

242- **2** *1 ¾* **Taste The Wine (IRE)**[21] 7831 4-9-2 65.............................. LukeMorris 10 72
(J S Moore) restless in stalls: t.k.h early: hld up in midfield: prog over 3f out: chsd wnr jst over 2f out: nt qckn over 1f out and readily hld after **11/4**[1]

311- **3** *¾* **Kames Park (IRE)**[16] 7847 8-9-4 63.................................. JimCrowley 1 69
(R C Guest) dwlt: dropped in fr wd draw and hld up last: prog and taken v wd bnd over 3f out: wnt 3rd and clsd on ldng pair over 1f out: nt qckn fnl f **13/2**[3]

024- **4** *1 ½* **No Wonga**[29] 7222 5-8-10 60................................. AndrewHeffernan(5) 6 64
(P D Evans) rousted along early to rch midfield: effrt and drvn over 2f out: plugged on same pce fr over 1f out **4/1**[2]

06-6 **5** *½* **Croix Rouge (USA)**[8] 25 8-8-5 57.................................... KierenFox(7) 3 60
(R J Smith) hld up in last trio: prog over 3f out: cl enough over 2f out: sn rdn and fnd nil: one pce after **13/2**[3]

000- **6** ¾ **Jordan's Light (USA)**^{12} [7425] 7-8-9 54 PaulDoe 11 56
(P D Evans) *t.k.h: hld up in last trio: switched to ins rail and prog over 2f out: no imp on ldrs over 1f out* **7/1**

506- **7** 11 **Ibbetson (USA)**^{41} [6547] 5-9-4 63 LiamKeniry 7 47
(Mrs A M Thorpe) *sn led: rdn and hdd over 2f out: wknd* **20/1**

000- **8** 2¼ **Majd Aljazeera**^{124} [5775] 4-8-2 51 (t) FrankieMcDonald 13 31
(Mrs A M Thorpe) *t.k.h: trckd ldr over 4f: styd prom tl wknd wl over 2f out* **50/1**

224- **9** 15 **Golden Games (IRE)**^{145} [5152] 4-9-0 63 IanMongan 2 19
(D C O'Brien) *hld up in 6th tl swift move to press ldr over 7f out: wknd rapidly wl over 2f out: t.o* **20/1**

330/ **10** 4½ **Dream Esteem**^{528} [4607] 5-9-1 60 NeilCallan 12 9
(D E Pipe) *t.k.h: trckd ldrs tl wknd rapidly over 3f out: t.o* **13/2^{3}**

2m 35.87s (1.37) **Going Correction** +0.075s/f (Slow)
WFA 4 from 5yo+ 4lb 10 Ran SP% **118.3**
Speed ratings (Par 101): **98,96,96,95,95 94,87,85,75,72**
toteswingers: 1&2 £11.00, 1&3 £12.60, 2&3 £2.10 CSF £44.88 CT £242.40 TOTE £19.60: £5.70, £1.10, £1.20; EX 66.30.
Owner R Stanley **Bred** Wiji Bloodstock And Leo Powell **Trained** Upper Lambourn, Berks

FOCUS
This moderate handicap was run at a steady pace, but the form still looks sound enough. The winner is rated up 8lb.

121 WILLIAM HILL 0800 44 40 40 BET NOW! H'CAP (DIV II) 1m 4f (P)
3:45 (3:50) (Class 6) (0-65,65) 4-Y-O+ **£1,706** (£503; £252) **Stalls** Centre

Form RPR

53/ **1** **Gargano (IRE)**^{45} [7568] 5-9-2 61 NeilCallan 6 73
(M Johnston) *trckd ldr 5f: styd cl up: eased lft and effrt over 2f out: rdn to ld wl over 1f out: r.o wl* **4/1^{1}**

01-1 **2** ½ **Winning Show**^{9} [13] 6-8-13 58 (t) LiamKeniry 10 69+
(C Gordon) *t.k.h: hld up in last trio: looking for room 3f out: gd prog over 2f out: wnt 2nd ins fnl f and clsd on wnr: r.o but a jst hld* **8/1**

221- **3** 2¾ **Starburst**^{25} [7790] 5-9-6 65 DavidProbert 9 72
(A M Balding) *blindfold stl on whn stalls opened and slowest away: hld up in rr: prog on outer over 2f out: wnt 2nd briefly 1f out: outpcd fnl f* **4/1^{1}**

356- **4** 1¼ **Supernoverre (IRE)**^{38} [7214] 4-8-2 58 KierenFox$^{(7)}$ 8 63
(P Howling) *t.k.h: hld up in tch: stmbld after 2f: prog over 2f out: chsd wnr briefly jst over 1f out: sn outpcd* **6/1^{2}**

060/ **5** 1½ **Pearl (IRE)**^{37} [6421] 6-8-6 51 oh4 (p) JimmyQuinn 3 53
(Mrs A M Thorpe) *wl in tch: pushed along over 3f out: effrt over 2f out and chsng ldrs: one pce after* **50/1**

244- **6** nk **Ardmaddy (IRE)**^{12} [7873] 6-8-10 55 (b) JimCrowley 13 57
(G L Moore) *t.k.h: hld up on inner: lost pl after 4f: dropped to last pair 4f out: effrt on inner over 2f out: no imp over 1f out* **8/1**

606- **7** 2¼ **Hammer**^{113} [1892] 5-8-13 58 (t) StephenCraine 4 56
(Mrs A M Thorpe) *prom: wnt 2nd 7f out: upsides over 2f out to wl over 1f out: wknd tamely* **33/1**

50-2 **8** 1 **Star Choice**^{9} [13] 5-9-0 59 TomQueally 2 56
(J Pearce) *trckd ldrs: cl up but drvn 3f out: stl chsng over 1f out: wknd* **14/1**

203- **9** ¾ **Karky Schultz (GER)**^{12} [4156] 5-9-1 60 LukeMorris 7 56
(J M P Eustace) *dwlt: hld up in rr and racd on outer: effrt wl over 2f out: no prog and btn over 1f out: wandering after* **13/2^{3}**

546- **10** 2¾ **Wabbraan (USA)**^{25} [7785] 5-8-6 56 AmyBaker$^{(5)}$ 5 47
(M Hill) *mde most to wl over 1f out: wknd rapidly* **20/1**

120- **11** 1¾ **Little Sark (IRE)**^{61} [7336] 5-8-12 57 PaulDoe 11 45
(P D Evans) *chsd ldrs: rdn in midfield 4f out: effrt u.p over 2f out: wknd rapidly over 1f out* **7/1**

003- **12** 2¾ **Graylyn Ruby (FR)**^{90} [6758] 5-9-4 63 EddieAhern 1 47
(R Dickin) *hld up in rr: effrt on outer 3f out: squeezed out over 2f out: no ch after* **12/1**

2m 36.71s (2.21) **Going Correction** +0.075s/f (Slow)
WFA 4 from 5yo+ 4lb 12 Ran SP% **126.4**
Speed ratings (Par 101): **95,94,92,92,91 90,89,88,88,86 85,83**
toteswingers: 1&2 £9.60, 1&3 £4.70, 2&3 £6.10 CSF £38.58 CT £142.68 TOTE £5.10: £1.40, £3.30, £2.00; EX 45.10.
Owner F Towey **Bred** Frank Towey **Trained** Middleham Moor, N Yorks

FOCUS
The second division of the 1m4f handicap and a wide-open heat. The time was slower than division one and the form has a muddling look to it. The winner is rated to his old British form.
Starburst Official explanation: jockey said mare missed the break
Supernoverre(IRE) Official explanation: jockey said gelding had been struck into

122 2FOR1DOGS.COM - GO GREYHOUND RACING FOR £1 CLASSIFIED CLAIMING STKS 6f (P)
4:15 (4:18) (Class 5) 3-Y-O **£2,590** (£770; £385; £192) **Stalls** High

Form RPR

553- **1** **Marjolly (IRE)**^{27} [7757] 3-8-4 56 (p) JimmyQuinn 5 66
(M Botti) *stdd s: hld up last: prog on inner as rest of field edgd to centre fr 2f out: pushed into ld over 1f out: readily* **11/2**

426- **2** 2 **Maoi Chinn Tire (IRE)**^{38} [7625] 3-9-0 66 (p) LiamKeniry 8 70
(J S Moore) *plld hrd early: restrained bhd ldrs: effrt but nt qckn 2f out: kpt on to take 2nd ins fnl f* **9/2^{3}**

453- **3** ½ **Major Maximus**^{12} [7874] 3-8-7 66 (v^{1}) MatthewDavies$^{(5)}$ 6 66
(George Baker) *trckd ldrs: effrt over 2f out: upsides and edgd lft over 1f out: nt qckn* **12/1**

254- **4** 1½ **Mind The Monarch**^{11} [7884] 3-8-2 57 (p) NickyMackay 7 52
(R A Teal) *hld up in 6th: rdn over 2f out: kpt on same pce: nt pce to threaten* **11/1**

40-2 **5** nk **Ramamara (IRE)**^{7} [35] 3-8-5 70 AndrewHeffernan$^{(5)}$ 1 59
(P D Evans) *racd freely: led: hung lft fr over 2f out: hdd & wknd over 1f out* **13/8^{1}**

022- **6** nk **Avow (USA)**^{107} [6292] 3-8-10 66 (b) LukeMorris 3 58
(J S Moore) *prom: rdn to chal and upsides over 1f out: edgd lft and wknd* **4/1^{2}**

42-4 **7** 3 **City Gossip (IRE)**^{10} [5] 3-8-2 62 DavidProbert 2 40
(M G Quinlan) *sn chsd ldr: trying to chal whn carried lft over 2f out: nt qckn after: wknd fnl f* **16/1**

1m 13.23s (0.13) **Going Correction** +0.075s/f (Slow) 7 Ran SP% **113.6**
Speed ratings (Par 97): **102,99,98,96,96 95,91**
toteswingers: 1&2 £4.90, 2&3 £6.20, 1&3 not won. CSF £29.74 TOTE £8.10: £4.60, £4.10; EX 34.40.Marjolly was claimed by G. Baker for £5,000.
Owner Giuliano Manfredini **Bred** Peter McCutcheon **Trained** Newmarket, Suffolk

FOCUS
A very ordinary 3-y-o claimer, run at a sound pace. The form horses were not at their best and the race is rated around the runner-up.

123 WILLIAMHILL.COM - BET IN PLAY NOW H'CAP 7f (P)
4:45 (4:47) (Class 5) (0-75,74) 4-Y-O+ **£2,590** (£770; £385; £192) **Stalls** High

Form RPR

41-6 **1** **Lord Fidelio (IRE)**^{2} [110] 4-8-10 66 LiamKeniry 3 75+
(A M Balding) *hld up in 3rd: effrt to cl on ldr over 1f out: drvn ahd last 100yds: styd on wl* **4/1^{2}**

531- **2** nk **Defector (IRE)**^{12} [7876] 4-9-4 74 NeilCallan 1 82
(W R Muir) *t.k.h: trckd ldr: pushed into ld over 1f out: sn hrd pressed: hdd and hld last 100yds* **2/1^{1}**

10-4 **3** ¾ **Dinner Date**^{8} [23] 8-8-10 71 RossAtkinson$^{(5)}$ 2 77
(T Keddy) *dwlt: hld up in 4th: effrt on outer over 2f out: drvn to chal jst over 1f out: nt qckn and hld fnl f* **11/1**

420- **4** ½ **Rondeau (GR)**^{21} [7830] 5-9-2 72 JimCrowley 8 77+
(P R Chamings) *dwlt: tk fierce hold early: hld up in last: effrt on outer over 2f out: clsd on ldrs over 1f out: nt qckn fnl f* **4/1^{2}**

635- **5** ¾ **I Confess**^{21} [7830] 5-9-1 71 (v) PaulDoe 5 74
(P D Evans) *allowed easy ld: tried to kick on over 2f out: hdd over 1f out: grad fdd* **5/1^{3}**

44-0 **6** hd **Resplendent Nova**^{8} [27] 8-8-11 67 JimmyQuinn 4 69
(P Howling) *hld up in 5th: effrt on inner jst over 2f out: sn rdn and no prog* **7/1**

1m 27.34s (1.34) **Going Correction** +0.075s/f (Slow) 6 Ran SP% **110.8**
Speed ratings (Par 103): **95,94,93,93,92 92**
toteswingers: 1&2 £1.30, 1&3 £3.60, 2&3 £4.30 CSF £12.12 CT £74.15 TOTE £6.60: £5.70, £1.10; EX 12.10.
Owner J B Munz **Bred** G S A Bloodstock Ptl Ltd **Trained** Kingsclere, Hants

FOCUS
Despite the withdrawals this was still a tight handicap. It was run at an uneven pace and the field were fairly closely covered at the finish, so the form is worth treating with a little caution. It has been rated around the second and third.

124 WILLIAM HILL TELEPHONE BETTING - OPEN 24/7 H'CAP 1m (P)
5:15 (5:16) (Class 6) (0-55,55) 4-Y-O+ **£2,047** (£604; £302) **Stalls** High

Form RPR

U0-3 **1** **Very Well Red**^{10} [7] 7-9-2 53 LukeMorris 1 63
(P W Hiatt) *wl away fr wd draw: trckd ldng pair: cruising 3f out: quick move to ld 2f out: rdn and styd on strly: v readily* **14/1**

22-2 **2** 1½ **Party In The Park**^{9} [10] 5-8-13 55 MatthewDavies$^{(5)}$ 4 62
(J R Boyle) *hld up in midfield: prog over 2f out gng wl: chsd wnr over 1f out: styd on wl but no imp* **9/2^{2}**

22-3 **3** 1½ **Join Up**^{7} [36] 4-8-11 53 RossAtkinson$^{(5)}$ 5 57
(W M Brisbourne) *t.k.h: hld up in midfield: cl enough but nt qckn 2f out: styd on again fnl f to snatch 3rd last stride* **6/1**

004- **4** hd **Guildenstern (IRE)**^{14} [7861] 8-9-4 55 JimmyQuinn 13 58
(P Howling) *hld up in rr: rdn and prog fr 2f out: chsd ldng pair ins fnl f but no ch: lost 3rd last stride* **11/1**

01-0 **5** ½ **Binnion Bay (IRE)**^{9} [13] 9-8-13 53 (b) MarcHalford$^{(3)}$ 11 55
(J J Bridger) *slowest away: shoved along in rr and nvr gng wl: styd on u.p fnl 2f: nrst fin* **33/1**

023- **6** 3¾ **Cavalry Guard (USA)**^{12} [7880] 6-8-10 52 (b) AmyBaker$^{(5)}$ 7 45
(T D McCarthy) *led to 2f out: nt qckn: wknd fnl f* **16/1**

450- **7** ¾ **Flying Gazebo (IRE)**^{33} [7687] 4-9-1 52 LiamKeniry 10 44
(J S Moore) *snatched up on inner after 1f and dropped to midfield: in tch u.p 2f out: wknd jst over 1f out* **33/1**

060- **8** 1¼ **Spent**^{21} [2807] 5-8-13 50 EddieAhern 14 39
(Mrs A M Thorpe) *mostly chsd ldr to over 2f out: wknd jst over 1f out* **5/1^{3}**

25-0 **9** hd **Greystoke Prince**^{9} [10] 5-9-1 52 (t) TomQueally 12 40
(P S McEntee) *t.k.h early: trckd ldrs: rdn and nt qckn over 2f out: wknd rapidly jst over 1f out* **4/1^{1}**

066- **10** ¾ **Darfour**^{38} [5941] 6-9-1 52 JimCrowley 8 39
(M Hill) *hld up and last after 2f: shkn up over 2f out: no ch whn nt clr run jst over 1f out on inner* **9/1**

360- **11** 4 **Stark Contrast (USA)**^{14} [7856] 6-8-5 49 MissRachelKing$^{(7)}$ 6 26
(M D I Usher) *racd wd: hld up in rr: struggling on wd outside over 2f out: sn no ch* **28/1**

000- **12** 3¾ **Western Roots**^{26} [7776] 9-9-0 54 (p) RobertLButler$^{(3)}$ 2 23
(P Butler) *prom on outer: u.p and losing pl over 2f out: sn bhd* **66/1**

250- **13** ¾ **Yakama (IRE)**^{31} [7716] 5-9-3 54 DavidProbert 3 21
(Mrs C A Dunnett) *racd wd: prog fr rr into midfield over 3f out: rdn and wknd over 2f out* **16/1**

1m 39.34s (-0.46) **Going Correction** +0.075s/f (Slow) 13 Ran SP% **116.7**
Speed ratings (Par 101): **105,103,102,101,101 97,96,95,95,94 90,86,86**
toteswingers: 1&2 £12.40, 1&3 £3.90, 2&3 £9.00 CSF £72.30 CT £342.17 TOTE £24.00: £5.60, £1.10, £2.40; EX 48.00 Place 6: £52.02 Place 5: £41.13 .
Owner Phil Kelly **Bred** Butts Enterprises Limited **Trained** Hook Norton, Oxon

FOCUS
A moderate handicap, run at a fair pace. The form is rated around the second, with the winner back to her Polytrack best.
T/Jkpt: Not won. T/Plt: £145.00 to a £1 stake. Pool: £104,004.29. 523.26 winning tickets. T/Qpdt: £56.40 to a £1 stake. Pool: £7,960.41. 104.40 winning tickets. JN

29WOLVERHAMPTON (A.W) (L-H)
Monday, January 11

OFFICIAL GOING: Standard
Wind: Nil Weather: Overcast and cold

125 BET AFRICAN NATIONS CUP - BETDAQ FILLIES' H'CAP 5f 216y(P)
1:30 (1:31) (Class 5) (0-70,69) 4-Y-O+ **£2,456** (£725; £362) **Stalls** Low

Form RPR

061- **1** **Diapason (IRE)**^{14} [7861] 4-9-4 69 RichardKingscote 5 79+
(Tom Dascombe) *t.k.h early: in tch: wnt 2nd over 2f out: shkn up to ld jst ins fnl f: comf* **4/5^{1}**

04-2 **2** 2¼ **Kheley (IRE)**^{3} [79] 4-8-7 63 DeanHeslop$^{(5)}$ 4 66
(W M Brisbourne) *sn chsng ldr: led 3f out: rdn over 1f out: hdd jst ins fnl f: sn btn* **5/1^{2}**

510- **3** 2¾ **Leading Edge (IRE)**^{22} [7828] 5-9-1 66 TonyCulhane 1 60
(M R Channon) *hld up in rr: pushed along over 3f out: nt clr run wl over 2f out: kpt on to take 3rd wl ins fnl f: no ch w ldng pair* **8/1**

05-0 **4** 1 **Loose Caboose (IRE)**^{9} [20] 5-8-11 62 (p) RobertWinston 3 53
(A J McCabe) *sn led: hung rt and hdd 3f out: wknd wl over 1f out* **13/2^{3}**

000- **5** ½ **White Shift (IRE)**[29] 7738 4-9-0 **65** .... HayleyTurner 2 54
(P Howling) *led early: prom: rdn over 2f out: wknd over 1f out* **10/1**

550- **6** 2¼ **Berrymead**[20] 7839 5-8-6 **62** oh7 ow7 .... AnnStokell(5) 6 44
(Miss A Stokell) *hld up: pushed along 4f out: rdn and bhd wl over 1f out* **66/1**

1m 14.84s (-0.16) **Going Correction** +0.10s/f (Slow) **6** Ran SP% **107.3**
Speed ratings (Par 100): **105,102,98,97,96 93**
toteswingers: 1&2 £2.10, 1&3 £2.40, 2&3 £2.00 CSF £4.54 TOTE £1.60: £1.10, £1.90; EX 4.60.
Owner John Brown **Bred** Miss Alice Fitzgerald **Trained** Malpas, Cheshire

FOCUS
A weak fillies' handicap. The form is rated around the second and there might be more to come from the winner.
Loose Caboose(IRE) Official explanation: jockey said mare hung right-handed on first bend

126 PARADE RESTAURANT (S) STKS 1m 141y(P)
2:00 (2:00) (Class 6) 4-Y-0+ **£1,774** (£523; £262) **Stalls** Low

Form RPR

651- **1** **Heathyards Junior**[35] 7671 4-9-3 **69** .... GrahamGibbons 5 63+
(R Hollinshead) *hld up: hdwy and wnt 2nd over 3f out: led jst over 2f out: hung rt fr over 1f out: rdn ins fnl f: comf* **8/11**[1]

22-6 **2** 2¼ **Ten Pole Tudor**[3] 87 5-9-4 **60** .... (p) MarkCoumbe(5) 1 63
(John A Harris) *s.i.s: prog on outside over 3f out: ev ch over 2f out: rdn wl over 1f out: one pce fnl f* **9/2**[2]

05-0 **3** 2½ **Foxtrot Bravo (IRE)**[2] 99 4-8-12 **52** .... (p) RichardKingscote 3 47
(Miss S L Davison) *led: hdd 7f out: prom: ev ch over 2f out: sn rdn: one pce* **12/1**[3]

04-0 **4** 3¼ **Northern Tour**[9] 19 4-9-8 **62** .... (tp) JoeFanning 2 50
(P F I Cole) *chsd ldr 7f out tl pushed along over 3f out: rdn 2f out: wknd ins fnl f* **9/2**[2]

53-0 **5** 1 **Pride Of Nation (IRE)**[7] 29 8-10-3 **62** .... (p) NoraLooby(7) 4 62
(A J McCabe) *prom: led 7f out: clr over 5f out: pushed along and hdd jst over 2f out: wknd wl over 1f out* **14/1**

1m 52.57s (2.07) **Going Correction** +0.10s/f (Slow)
WFA 4 from 5yo+ 1lb **5** Ran SP% **108.6**
Speed ratings (Par 101): **94,92,89,86,86**
CSF £4.19 TOTE £1.60: £1.10, £1.60; EX 3.10.Ten Pole Tudor was claimed by R. A. Harris for £6000. The winner was sold to S Gillen for 7,000gns.
Owner L A Morgan **Bred** L A Morgan **Trained** Upper Longdon, Staffs

FOCUS
A weak seller in which the winner did not have to match his maiden win.

127 BET MASTERS SNOOKER - BETDAQ H'CAP 7f 32y(P)
2:30 (2:31) (Class 6) (0-65,63) 3-Y-0 **£1,774** (£523; £262) **Stalls** High

Form RPR

1 **The Glamour Cat (IRE)**[52] 7468 3-9-0 **62** .... AndreaAtzeni(3) 4 77+
(M Botti) *hld up: smooth hdwy over 2f out: led over 1f out: rdn and qcknd clr ins fnl f: easily* **13/2**[3]

051- **2** 4½ **Miami Gator (IRE)**[11] 7884 3-9-3 **62** .... AndrewElliott 6 65
(J R Weymes) *a.p: rdn wl over 1f out: chsd wnr fnl f: no imp* **9/2**[2]

100- **3** 3¼ **Vilnius**[11] 7884 3-9-0 **59** .... TonyCulhane 8 53
(M R Channon) *hld up towards rr: pushed along and hdwy 2f out: rdn and kpt on one pce fnl f: tk 3rd last strides* **20/1**

046- **4** hd **Pomeroy**[24] 7800 3-9-4 **63** .... RichardKingscote 1 57
(Tom Dascombe) *led: rdn and hdd over 1f out: wknd ins fnl f* **2/1**[1]

046- **5** ¾ **Scintillating (IRE)**[31] 7706 3-8-1 **49** oh3 .... KellyHarrison(3) 7 41
(R Hollinshead) *hld up in rr: pushed along wl over 1f out: swtchd rt ins fnl f: n.d* **40/1**

060- **6** hd **Bertie Buckle (IRE)**[29] 7736 3-8-12 **57** .... HayleyTurner 10 48
(J R Gask) *hld up: pushed along over 2f out: rdn over 1f out: no hdwy fnl f* **14/1**

006- **7** 4½ **Sixties Rock**[24] 7791 3-8-11 **56** .... StevieDonohoe 5 35
(J A Glover) *s.i.s: hld up in rr: pushed along 3f out: prog wl over 1f out: rdn and wknd fnl f* **15/2**

064- **8** 6 **Nabrina (IRE)**[27] 7757 3-7-12 **50** .... NoraLooby(7) 2 21
(M Brittain) *w ldr: rdn over 2f out: wknd wl over 1f out: eased ins fnl f* **16/1**

065- **9** 2¼ **Darling Buds**[24] 7799 3-8-13 **58** .... TomEaves 9 15
(K A Ryan) *s.i.s: hld up in rr: pushed along wl over 2f out: rdn and struggling wl over 1f out* **16/1**

036- **10** 14 **Infinity World**[24] 7799 3-9-0 **59** .... FrannyNorton 3 —
(G R Oldroyd) *prom tl wknd wl over 1f out: eased fnl f* **7/1**

1m 29.47s (-0.13) **Going Correction** +0.10s/f (Slow) **10** Ran SP% **114.7**
Speed ratings (Par 95): **104,98,95,94,94 93,88,81,79,63**
toteswingers: 1&2 £7.30, 1&3 £14.80, 2&3 £6.20 CSF £35.25 CT £554.11 TOTE £7.60: £2.90, £1.20, £3.80; EX 40.60 Trifecta £269.70 Pool: £371.86 - 1.02 winning units..
Owner Christopher McHale **Bred** Stephanie Hanly **Trained** Newmarket, Suffolk

FOCUS
Not a bad race for the grade, and the time was the quickest of three 7f races on the card. The form is rated around the runner-up and the winner can rate higher.
The Glamour Cat(IRE) ◆ Official explanation: trainer,s rep said, regarding apparent improvement in form, that this was the filly's first run for the trainer.
Infinity World Official explanation: jockey said filly never travelled

128 HOTEL & CONFERENCING AT WOLVERHAMPTON MAIDEN STKS 7f 32y(P)
3:00 (3:01) (Class 5) 3-Y-0 **£2,456** (£725; £362) **Stalls** High

Form RPR

1 **Burghley** 3-9-3 0 .... HayleyTurner 3 78+
(M L W Bell) *sn led: edgd rt ins fnl f: comf* **7/2**[2]

4- **2** 2½ **Duellist**[13] 7864 3-9-3 0 .... JoeFanning 12 70
(M Johnston) *hld up in tch: pushed along and chsd wnr over 2f out: rdn wl over 1f out: no imp ins fnl f* **3/1**[1]

3- **3** nk **Paintball (IRE)**[13] 7864 3-9-0 0 .... AndreaAtzeni(3) 2 69
(W R Muir) *a.p: pushed along and sltly outpcd over 3f out: rallied over 2f out: rdn wl over 1f out: one pce fnl f* **9/2**[3]

6- **4** hd **Sunrise Lyric (IRE)**[125] 5752 3-8-12 0 .... TomEaves 9 64
(P F I Cole) *hld up in mid-div: hdwy over 2f out: rdn and one pce fnl f* **16/1**

0- **5** 9 **Que Belle (IRE)**[24] 7792 3-8-12 0 .... RichardKingscote 5 39
(Tom Dascombe) *hld up in rr: pushed along over 3f out: sn struggling: styd on ins fnl f: nvr nr ldrs* **40/1**

3- **6** 1½ **Brave Decision**[14] 7859 3-9-3 0 .... RobertWinston 11 40
(A J McCabe) *t.k.h: prom: pushed along and chsd ldr over 3f out tl over 2f out: wknd wl over 1f out* **5/1**

7 nk **Miereveld** 3-9-3 0 .... StevieDonohoe 10 39
(Sir Mark Prescott) *dwlt: in rr: pushed along over 3f out: sn struggling* **25/1**

0- **8** ½ **Your Lad**[26] 7764 3-9-3 0 .... JackMitchell 6 38
(C F Wall) *s.i.s: in rr: pushed along 3f out: sn struggling* **25/1**

54- **9** 2 **American Agent (USA)**[16] 7843 3-9-3 0 .... JosedeSouza 4 33
(P F I Cole) *hld up in mid-div: wknd 3f out* **8/1**

0- **10** ¾ **Seek The Cash (USA)**[26] 7773 3-9-3 0 .... FrannyNorton 1 31
(M Quinn) *led early: chsd ldr tl over 3f out: pushed along and wknd over 2f out* **10/1**

0- **11** 7 **Bibiana Bay**[24] 7799 3-8-12 0 .... JerryO'Dwyer 7 7
(B I Case) *hld up in mid-div: pushed along and bhd fnl 3f* **100/1**

1m 29.61s (0.01) **Going Correction** +0.10s/f (Slow) **11** Ran SP% **119.3**
Speed ratings (Par 97): **103,100,99,99,89 87,87,86,84,83 75**
toteswingers: 1&2 £5.00, 1&3 £5.70, 2&3 £5.30 CSF £14.23 TOTE £4.60: £1.80, £1.60, £2.20; EX 23.70 Trifecta £81.70 Pool: £579.69 - 5.25 winning units..
Owner Sheikh Marwan Al Maktoum **Bred** Darley **Trained** Newmarket, Suffolk

FOCUS
This looked a fair maiden for the time of year on paper, and the time was just 0.14 seconds slower than the earlier 3-y-o handicap won by The Glamour Cat, who was rated only 62 but looks promising. The form choice diappointed in sixth and the winner is better than the bare form.

129 DINE IN HORIZONS APPRENTICE H'CAP 7f 32y(P)
3:30 (3:30) (Class 6) (0-65,65) 4-Y-0+ **£1,774** (£523; £262) **Stalls** High

Form RPR

21-3 **1** **Divine Force**[3] 78 4-8-12 **63** .... TobyAtkinson(5) 3 73+
(M Wigham) *hld up towards rr: hdwy over 2f out: c wd st: rdn over 1f out: edgd lft and led ins fnl f: r.o* **15/8**[1]

042- **2** 1¼ **Smalljohn**[33] 7691 4-8-9 **62** .... (v) AdamCarter(7) 6 66
(B Smart) *led: rdn and hdd ins fnl f: nt qckn* **11/2**[3]

66-0 **3** shd **Jord (IRE)**[7] 36 6-8-7 **60** .... JonathanHinch(7) 10 63
(J A Glover) *t.k.h: sn chsng ldr: chal wl over 1f out: rdn and nt qckn ins fnl f* **25/1**

500- **4** 1½ **Carmenero (GER)**[30] 7735 7-9-0 **60** .... WilliamCarson 5 59
(C R Dore) *hld up in mid-div: prog over 2f out: rdn and hung lft over 1f out: one pce ins fnl f* **11/1**

100- **5** ½ **Star Strider**[14] 7861 6-8-13 **62** .... KylieManser(3) 2 60
(T Keddy) *s.i.s: hld up in rr: pushed along and r.o ins fnl f: nvr nrr* **14/1**

30-2 **6** 1¼ **Well Of Echoes**[7] 30 4-8-3 **52** oh3 ow1 .... (tp) MartinLane(3) 8 47
(A J McCabe) *s.i.s: t.k.h: stdy prog over 5f out: rdn wl over 1f out: wknd wl ins fnl f* **9/1**

511- **7** 1½ **Just Jimmy (IRE)**[14] 7860 5-9-0 **63** .... RichardEvans(3) 7 54
(P D Evans) *prom: pushed along over 2f out: rdn and wknd over 1f out* **5/1**[2]

000- **8** ½ **Golden Penny**[25] 7782 5-9-5 **65** .... KellyHarrison 9 54
(M Dods) *hld up in rr: pushed along over 2f out: no rspnse* **22/1**

300- **9** 7 **A Big Sky Brewing (USA)**[30] 7729 6-9-0 **63** .... (b) DeanHeslop(3) 4 33
(T D Barron) *prom: n.m.r on ins over 3f out: sn lost pl* **6/1**

1m 29.88s (0.28) **Going Correction** +0.10s/f (Slow) **9** Ran SP% **114.3**
Speed ratings (Par 101): **102,100,100,98,98 96,95,94,86**
toteswingers: 1&2 £3.40, 1&3 £15.90, 2&3 £34.70 CSF £12.00 CT £190.76 TOTE £2.70: £1.10, £2.40, £6.90; EX 14.80 Trifecta £103.90 Pool: £501.27 - 3.57 winning units..
Owner R J Lorenz **Bred** Capt J H Wilson **Trained** Newmarket, Suffolk

FOCUS
A modest apprentice handicap run at a steady pace, resulting in a comparatively slow time. The winner is capable of better.
Star Strider Official explanation: jockey said gelding hung badly right-handed
A Big Sky Brewing(USA) Official explanation: jockey said gelding suffered interference in running

130 SPONSOR A RACE BY CALLING 01902 390000 H'CAP 1m 4f 50y(P)
4:00 (4:01) (Class 6) (0-52,52) 4-Y-0+ **£1,774** (£523; £262) **Stalls** Low

Form RPR

344- **1** **Fantasy Ride**[11] 7888 8-8-13 **51** .... SaleemGolam 9 59
(J Pearce) *hld up in tch: led jst over 2f out: rdn over 1f out: jst hld on* **7/1**[3]

0/4- **2** shd **Crimson Flame (IRE)**[14] 7858 7-8-10 **48** .... RobertWinston 11 56
(S Curran) *hld up and bhd: smooth prog 3f out: rdn wl over 1f out: sn edgd lft: r.o towards fin: jst failed* **20/1**

125- **3** 2¾ **Barbirolli**[16] 7847 8-8-9 **52** .... PaulPickard(5) 4 55
(W B Stone) *s.i.s: hld up in rr: stdy hdwy on outside 3f out: sn pushed along: rdn over 1f out: styd on u.p to take 3rd last strides* **18/1**

32-3 **4** nk **Dovedon Angel**[10] 1 4-8-9 **51** .... JerryO'Dwyer 2 54
(Miss Gay Kelleway) *t.k.h in tch: rdn and one pce ins fnl f* **10/1**

04-5 **5** ½ **Kickahead (USA)**[9] 13 8-8-12 **50** .... (t) StevieDonohoe 7 52
(Ian Williams) *t.k.h: a.p: led jst over 3f out tl jst over 2f out: rdn wl over 1f out: no ex ins fnl f* **2/1**[1]

400- **6** 1 **Bubses Boy**[26] 7392 4-8-10 **52** .... HayleyTurner 8 53
(P Howling) *led after 1f: hdd jst over 3f out: wknd 2f out* **18/1**

63-1 **7** 2½ **Royal Rainbow**[7] 32 6-8-10 **51** 6ex .... WilliamCarson 10 48
(P W Hiatt) *hld up in tch: ev ch over 2f out: rdn and wknd wl over 1f out* **5/2**[2]

000- **8** 3¾ **Sir Sandicliffe (IRE)**[28] 7751 6-8-9 **52** .... DeanHeslop(5) 1 43
(W M Brisbourne) *s.i.s: hld up in rr: pushed along over 3f out: rdn and struggling wl over 1f out* **9/1**

250- **9** 6 **Kochanski (IRE)**[45] 5838 4-8-9 **51** .... (t) JoeFanning 3 32
(J R Weymes) *led 1f: prom tl pushed along and wknd wl over 2f out* **18/1**

00- **10** 2¼ **Riverside**[34] 7678 5-8-5 **50** ow3 .... JohnCavanagh(7) 6 27
(M Brittain) *hld up towards rr: rdn and struggling 4f out* **50/1**

2m 44.5s (3.40) **Going Correction** +0.10s/f (Slow)
WFA 4 from 5yo+ 4lb **10** Ran SP% **116.0**
Speed ratings (Par 101): **92,91,90,89,89 88,87,84,80,79**
toteswingers: 1&2 £16.90, 1&3 £11.00, 2&3 £43.60 CSF £134.61 CT £2397.11 TOTE £7.10: £1.60, £6.90, £3.70; EX 125.50 TRIFECTA Not won..
Owner Mrs Jennifer Marsh **Bred** A J Holder **Trained** Newmarket, Suffolk
■ City Stable was withdrawn on vet's advice (11/2, deduct 15p in the £ under R4.)
■ Stewards' Enquiry : Robert Winston caution: used whip with excessive frequency

FOCUS
A moderate handicap and a steady pace resulted in quite a few of these racing keenly. The winner is the best guide to the form.

131 BET MULTIPLES - BETDAQ H'CAP 1m 1f 103y(P)
4:30 (4:31) (Class 6) (0-58,62) 4-Y-0+ **£1,774** (£523; £262) **Stalls** Low

Form RPR

502- **1** **Grey Command (USA)**[31] 7719 5-8-12 **52** .... RobertWinston 6 60
(M Brittain) *led 1f: chsd ldr: rdn to chal jst over 2f out: led ins fnl f: r.o* **9/2**[1]

41-1 **2** 1 **Shake On It**[7] 34 6-9-3 **62** 6ex .... JamieJones(5) 10 68
(M R Hoad) *hld up in rr: nt clr run wl over 1f out: sn swtchd lft and hdwy on ins: ev ch wl ins fnl f: kpt on* **8/1**[2]

00-4 **3** nk **Alfredtheordinary**[7] 34 5-9-3 **57** .... TonyCulhane 12 62
(M R Channon) *hld up in mid-div: stdy prog on outside 3f out: rdn wl over 1f out: kpt on u.p towards fin* **11/1**

100- **4** *hd* **Royal Society**[14] 7856 4-9-0 **55** GrahamGibbons 7 60
(R A Farrant) *hld up in tch: pushed along wl over 1f out: n.m.r ins fnl f: kpt on* **14/1**

043- **5** *shd* **Ryker (IRE)**[26] 7765 4-9-2 **57** HayleyTurner 13 62
(J W Hills) *hld up towards rr: hdwy wl over 1f out: rdn and nt qckn towards fin* **10/1**

03-4 **6** *½* **Kirstys Lad**[7] 36 8-8-3 **46** KellyHarrison(3) 9 50
(M Mullineaux) *led after 1f: rdn jst over 2f out: hdd ins fnl f: no ex* **8/1**[2]

144- **7** *1* **Head First**[14] 7856 4-9-0 **55** JoeFanning 1 56
(W Jarvis) *a.p: rdn 2f out: one pce ins fnl f* **9/2**[1]

02-4 **8** *nk* **Achromatic**[9] 13 4-9-0 **55** (p) AdamKirby 3 56
(W R Swinburn) *hld up towards rr: hdwy on ins over 2f out: sn pushed along: rdn 1f out: fdd wl ins fnl f* **9/1**[3]

026- **9** *½* **Libre**[14] 7857 10-8-8 **48** RichardKingscote 8 48
(F Jordan) *t.k.h: prom: rdn 2f out: fdd wl ins fnl f* **12/1**

010- **10** *4* **Climate (IRE)**[14] 7857 11-8-12 **57** (p) RichardEvans(5) 11 48
(P D Evans) *hld up in rr: pushed along over 2f out: struggling whn rdn jst over 1f out* **20/1**

400- **11** *hd* **Spring Fashion (IRE)**[33] 7687 4-8-9 **50** (p) JerryO'Dwyer 2 41
(M Botti) *hld up in tch: wkng whn n.m.r on ins over 2f out* **10/1**

300- **12** *5* **Lady Longcroft**[14] 7857 5-9-2 **56** SaleemGolam 4 36
(J Pearce) *bhd fnl 3f* **33/1**

2m 3.13s (1.43) **Going Correction** +0.10s/f (Slow)
WFA 4 from 5yo+ 1lb 12 Ran SP% 117.2
Speed ratings (Par 101): **97,96,95,95,95 95,94,93,93,89 89,85**
toteswingers: 1&2 £6.30, 1&3 £12.20, 2&3 £7.80 CSF £39.23 CT £375.79 TOTE £6.70: £2.30, £2.20, £4.00; EX 46.70 Trifecta £243.20 Pool: £499.72 - 1.52 winning units. Place 6: £48.20 Place 5: £41.33 .
Owner Mel Brittain **Bred** Darley **Trained** Warthill, N Yorks

FOCUS
A moderate but competitive handicap.
T/Plt: £58.30 to a £1 stake. Pool: £84,694.52. 1,059.12 winning tickets. T/Qpdt: £33.00 to a £1 stake. Pool: £6,308.37. 141.40 winning tickets. KH

105 LINGFIELD (L-H)
Tuesday, January 12

OFFICIAL GOING: Standard
Wind: very modest, behind Weather: cloudy, cold

132 LINGFIELD.CO.UK H'CAP 5f (P)
1:35 (1:36) (Class 6) (0-60,57) 4-Y-0+ **£2,047** (£604; £302) **Stalls** High

Form RPR

30-6 **1** **Rocket Ruby**[3] 103 4-8-13 52 NeilCallan 2 61
(D Shaw) *taken down early: mde all: rdn and qcknd clr over 1f out: in n.d fnl f: comf* **11/2**

00-4 **2** *2¾* **Steel City Boy (IRE)**[4] 77 7-9-4 57 JimCrowley 4 56+
(D Shaw) *taken down early: rrd as stalls opened and s.i.s: hld up in last pair: n.m.r over 1f out: swtchd rt and hdwy jst ins fnl f: r.o wl to go 2nd nr fin: no ch w wnr* **10/3**[2]

44-3 **3** *nk* **Bluebok**[4] 77 9-9-1 57 (bt) JackDean(3) 5 55
(J M Bradley) *chsd ldng trio: rdn and effrt ent fnl 2f: chsd clr wnr 1f out: no imp after: lost 2nd nr fin* **7/2**[3]

54-3 **4** *1¾* **Best One**[2] 112 6-9-2 55 (b) StephenCraine 8 47
(R A Harris) *dwlt: sn in midfield: rdn ent fnl 2f: squeezed through and hdwy over 1f out: no imp on wnr fnl f* **3/1**[1]

600- **5** *hd* **Magic Glade**[199] 3386 11-8-6 45 FrankieMcDonald 7 36
(Peter Grayson) *taken down early: s.i.s: hld up in last pair: nt clr run over 1f out tl ins fnl f: nvr able to chal* **66/1**

061- **6** *½* **Greek Secret**[12] 7889 7-9-3 56 (b) TonyCulhane 9 45
(J O'Reilly) *taken down early: hld up in tch in midfield on outer: rdn over 1f out: fnd nil and wl hld fnl f* **11/1**

001- **7** *3½* **Triskaidekaphobia**[37] 7657 7-8-11 50 (t) WandersonD'Avila 6 27
(Miss J R Tooth) *taken down early: pressed wnr: rdn 2f out: nt pce of wnr over 1f out: lost 2nd 1f out: wknd fnl f* **11/1**

000- **8** *1¼* **The Magic Of Rio**[75] 7136 4-9-2 55 AdamKirby 3 27
(Peter Grayson) *in tch in midfield on inner: rdn and unable qck over 1f out: wl btn fnl f* **20/1**

600- **9** *2* **Stoneacre Pat (IRE)**[37] 7657 5-8-7 46 ow1 (b) LiamKeniry 1 11
(Peter Grayson) *t.k.h: chsd ldng pair: rdn and struggling 2f out: wkng edgd rt and barging match over 1f out: wl btn fnl f* **33/1**

58.96 secs (0.16) **Going Correction** 0.0s/f (Stan) 9 Ran SP% 111.5
Speed ratings (Par 101): **98,93,93,90,90 89,83,81,78**
toteswinger:1&2:£5.60, 2&3:£4.60, 1&3:£5.40 CSF £22.86 CT £70.71 TOTE £6.80: £1.90, £1.20, £1.50; EX 27.50.
Owner Mrs Lyndsey Shaw **Bred** Brig Abdulla Mohammed Abdulla **Trained** Sproxton, Leics

FOCUS
A low-grade sprint handicap. Difficult form to assess, but front runners seemed favoured through the card so the race has been rated a bit negatively.
Steel City Boy(IRE) Official explanation: jockey said gelding was slowly away and reared leaving stalls
Magic Glade Official explanation: jockey said gelding was slowly away and denied a clear run
Stoneacre Pat(IRE) Official explanation: jockey said horse hung right in straight

133 MARRIOTT HOTEL OPENING SPRING 2010 CLAIMING STKS 1m 2f (P)
2:05 (2:05) (Class 5) 3-Y-0 **£2,590** (£770; £385; £192) **Stalls** Low

Form RPR

111- **1** **Glen Lass**[13] 7874 3-8-11 64 (b) SaleemGolam 4 57
(J Pearce) *in tch in midfield: rdn to chse ldng trio over 2f out: swtchd rt over 1f out: r.o u.p to ld towards fin* **6/4**[1]

12-4 **2** *½* **Mary Helen**[8] 33 3-8-13 63 EddieAhern 6 58
(W M Brisbourne) *in tch: chsd ldng pair 3f out: sn rdn: drvn to chse ldr jst over 1f out: kpt on u.p to ld fnl 75yds: hdd and no ex towards fin* **2/1**[2]

046- **3** *1* **The Great Husk (IRE)**[34] 7683 3-8-11 50 LiamKeniry 3 54
(J S Moore) *t.k.h early: chsd ldr over 8f out: rdn over 2f out: led wl over 1f out edgd lft u.p: hdd and one pce fnl 75yds* **50/1**

540- **4** *2¼* **Aegean Destiny**[26] 7788 3-8-6 52 HayleyTurner 7 45
(R A Harris) *racd in last trio: effrt u.p over 2f out: kpt on steadily u.p fnl f but nvr gng pce to chal ldrs* **20/1**

40- **5** *1¾* **Premium Charge**[31] 7731 3-8-12 0 DavidProbert 8 47
(C A Dwyer) *plld hrd: sn led: rdn and hdd wl over 1f out: wknd ent fnl f* **22/1**

0- **6** *1¾* **Magic Spirit**[39] 7622 3-8-11 0 LukeMorris 2 43
(J S Moore) *dwlt: sn pushed along towards rr: struggling u.p over 2f out: no ch whn edgd rt ins fnl f* **9/1**

005- **7** *1½* **During The War (USA)**[46] 7552 3-9-2 65 JerryO'Dwyer 5 45
(C A Dwyer) *s.i.s: a bhd: rdn and no prog over 2f out: wl btn over 1f out* **33/1**

21-3 **8** *81* **Lily Lily**[9] 22 3-9-2 62 (v[1]) NeilCallan 1 —
(K McAuliffe) *chsd ldng pair tl rdn ent fnl 3f: dropped to rr jst over 2f out: virtually p.u fr wl over 1f out: t.o* **8/1**[3]

2m 6.80s (0.20) **Going Correction** 0.0s/f (Stan) 8 Ran SP% 108.5
Speed ratings (Par 97): **99,98,97,96,94 93,92,27**
toteswinger:1&2:£1.20, 2&3:£12.60, 1&3:£9.80 CSF £3.97 TOTE £2.40: £1.10, £1.10, £12.20; EX 4.60.Aegean Destiny was claimed by David Penman for £5,000
Owner Ian Bishop **Bred** Limestone And Tara Studs **Trained** Newmarket, Suffolk

FOCUS
A low-grade affair. It is doubtful if the front pair were at their best, with the third and fifth the more likely guides.
The Great Husk(IRE) Official explanation: jockey said gelding hung left in straight
Premium Charge Official explanation: jockey said gelding ran too freely
During The War(USA) Official explanation: jockey said gelding never travelled
Lily Lily Official explanation: jockey said filly never travelled

134 VIEW OUR 2010 FIXTURES AT LINGFIELD.CO.UK H'CAP 1m (P)
2:35 (2:35) (Class 6) (0-60,59) 3-Y-0 **£2,047** (£604; £302) **Stalls** High

Form RPR

006- **1** **Ostentation**[46] 7551 3-9-1 56 NeilCallan 4 66+
(M Johnston) *led tl over 5f out: pressed ldr after untl led again ent fnl 3f: rdn clr over 1f out: kpt on wl* **2/1**[1]

000- **2** *1¼* **Rock A Doodle Doo (IRE)**[92] 6737 3-9-0 55 JimCrowley 5 62+
(W Jarvis) *in tch in midfield tl shuffled bk to last 4f out: hdwy on outer ent fnl 2f: r.o to chse clr wnr ins fnl f: gng on strly at fin but nvr gng to rch wnr* **6/1**[3]

046- **3** *2¾* **D'Urberville**[12] 7884 3-9-3 58 EddieAhern 7 59
(J R Jenkins) *t.k.h: chsd ldrs: rdn to chse wnr but outpcd wl over 1f out: kpt on same pce after: lost 2nd ins fnl f* **7/1**

052- **4** *1¼* **Rightcar**[12] 7884 3-8-13 54 LiamKeniry 9 52
(Peter Grayson) *stdd and dropped in bhd after s: switching to outer and n.m.r briefly over 2f out: swtchd lft and drvn over 1f out: kpt on same pce fnl f* **8/1**

00-3 **5** *nk* **Hathaway (IRE)**[3] 104 3-8-10 51 LukeMorris 8 48
(W M Brisbourne) *t.k.h: in tch in midfield: rdn to chse ldrs over 2f out: hung rt and outpcd bnd 2f out: one pce u.p and wl hld after* **9/2**[2]

066- **6** *2* **Bella Charlie (IRE)**[14] 7864 3-9-4 59 (p) AdamKirby 6 52
(M G Quinlan) *t.k.h: hld up in tch in last pair: gd hdwy on outer to chse ldr 3f out: hanging rt and outpcd bnd 2f out: sn wknd* **12/1**

440- **7** *3½* **Tenga Venga**[14] 7865 3-9-0 55 JamieSpencer 3 40
(P S McEntee) *t.k.h: pressed ldr tl led over 5f out: hdd ent fnl 3f: hung rt u.p bnd 2f out: wknd wl over 1f out* **14/1**

000- **8** *2* **Campaigner**[97] 6586 3-8-9 50 HayleyTurner 1 30
(J W Hills) *dwlt: sn t.k.h and chsng ldrs: losing pl and n.m.r jst over 2f out: no ch wl over 1f out* **33/1**

505- **9** *2½* **Holkham**[117] 6026 3-8-12 53 J-PGuillambert 2 27
(N P Littmoden) *t.k.h: chsd ldrs tl lost pl u.p over 2f out: bhd fr wl over 1f out* **16/1**

1m 39.26s (1.06) **Going Correction** 0.0s/f (Stan) 9 Ran SP% 112.6
Speed ratings (Par 95): **94,92,90,88,88 86,82,80,78**
toteswinger:1&2:£2.20, 2&3:£10.70, 1&3:£2.60 CSF £13.59 CT £68.23 TOTE £3.00: £1.10, £2.20, £2.40; EX 14.70.
Owner Sheikh Hamdan Bin Mohammed Al Maktoum **Bred** Wellsummers Stud **Trained** Middleham Moor, N Yorks

FOCUS
This moderate 3-y-o handicap was dominated from the outset by Ostentation, with little getting into it from the rear. The winner is arguably worth more than the bare form.
Ostentation Official explanation: trainer's rep had no explanation for the apparent improvement in form
Bella Charlie(IRE) Official explanation: jockey said colt ran too freely

135 ASHURST WOOD H'CAP 7f (P)
3:05 (3:05) (Class 6) (0-58,58) 4-Y-0+ **£2,047** (£604; £302) **Stalls** Low

Form RPR

353- **1** **Art Market (CAN)**[52] 7479 7-9-3 57 (p) JamieSpencer 13 72
(Miss Jo Crowley) *sn led and crossed over to rail: stdd gallop over 3f out: rdn and qcknd clr wl over 1f out: in n.d after: eased towards fin* **4/1**[1]

064- **2** *6* **Dicey Affair**[13] 7877 4-8-7 47 (t) LiamKeniry 9 46
(G L Moore) *hld up towards rr: hdwy ent fnl 2f: swtchd rt and drvn 1f out: styd on u.p to go 2nd towards fin: no ch w wnr* **14/1**

001- **3** *nk* **Bold Rose**[12] 7880 4-8-12 57 (p) LeeNewnes(5) 8 55
(M D I Usher) *s.i.s: bhd: hdwy on outer jst over 2f out: r.o wl fnl f to snatch 3rd on post: no ch w wnr* **20/1**

02-3 **4** *shd* **Hart Of Gold**[5] 70 6-8-13 53 (p) StephenCraine 11 51
(R A Harris) *t.k.h: chsd wnr tl n.m.r over 5f out: rdn to chse clr wnr again 2f out: no imp after: lost 2 pls nr fin* **9/2**[2]

06-0 **5** *½* **Whotsit (IRE)**[10] 11 4-8-11 58 (b) LauraPike(7) 3 54
(Miss Amy Weaver) *chsd ldrs: sltly hmpd over 5f out: rdn and unable qck jst over 2f out: plugged on same pce after* **14/1**

103- **6** *2* **Dynamo Dave (USA)**[13] 7877 5-8-2 49 (b) MissRachelKing(7) 2 40
(M D I Usher) *hld up towards rr: rdn and effrt over 1f out: styd on fnl f: n.d* **11/1**

456- **7** *1* **Imperial Skylight**[13] 7880 4-8-11 51 (v) TonyCulhane 10 39
(M R Channon) *hld up in last trio: rdn and no prog ent fnl 2f: styd on fnl f: n.d* **9/1**

00-4 **8** *½* **Dream Express (IRE)**[10] 8 5-9-3 57 HayleyTurner 7 44
(P Howling) *taken down early: stdd s: plld hrd and hld up in rr: swtchd ins and sme hdwy ent fnl f: n.d* **6/1**[3]

000/ **9** *hd* **Contented (IRE)**[506] 5315 8-8-1 48 (tp) RyanPowell(7) 14 34
(Mrs L C Jewell) *chsd wnr over 5f out tl outpcd u.p ent fnl 2f: wknd over 1f out* **40/1**

06-3 **10** *1¾* **Golden Prospect**[10] 8 6-9-4 58 (v) EddieAhern 4 40
(Miss J R Tooth) *in tch in midfield: rdn and btn 2f out: wl btn fnl f* **13/2**

62-1 **11** *2* **Tamino (IRE)**[10] 10 7-8-8 55 JulieCumine(7) 1 31
(P Howling) *t.k.h: chsd ldrs tl bdly hmpd and hit rail over 5f out: midfield after tl wknd 2f out* **7/1**

1m 24.32s (-0.48) **Going Correction** 0.0s/f (Stan) 11 Ran SP% 117.2
Speed ratings (Par 101): **102,95,94,94,94 91,90,90,89,87 85**
toteswinger:1&2:£14.80, 2&3:£53.90, 1&3:£10.70 CSF £60.69 CT £1004.54 TOTE £4.60: £1.90, £3.20, £6.90; EX 76.00.
Owner Mrs Liz Nelson **Bred** William Graham **Trained** Whitcombe, Dorset
■ Stewards' Enquiry : Jamie Spencer six-day ban: careless riding (Jan 26-31)

FOCUS
This had looked a competitive handicap but Art Market made most for an easy win. It is hard to take the form at face value so the race has been rated on the negative side.

136 MARSH GREEN H'CAP — 7f (P)
3:35 (3:35) (Class 4) (0-85,74) 3-Y-O £4,533 (£1,348; £674; £336) Stalls Low

Form RPR
213- 1 **Admiral Cochrane (IRE)**[23] 7824 3-9-3 70 JimCrowley 6 76+
(W Jarvis) *t.k.h: chsd ldng pair: rdn to chal wl over 1f out: led ent fnl f: r.o wl* 4/1[3]
41- 2 1 1/4 **Capricornus (USA)**[15] 7859 3-9-4 71 NeilCallan 3 74
(M Johnston) *in tch: shkn up over 2f out: rdn and wnt between horses jst ins fnl f: chsd wnr fnl 100yds: no imp after* 5/4[1]
021- 3 nk **Fazza**[12] 7886 3-9-3 70 DavidProbert 4 72+
(D W P Arbuthnot) *t.k.h: hld up in tch: rdn ent fnl 2f: hdwy u.p ins fnl f: r.o to go 3rd wl ins fnl f: nt rch ldrs* 3/1[2]
43-3 4 1 1/4 **Exceedthewildman**[3] 107 3-9-7 74 (p) LukeMorris 1 73
(J S Moore) *s.i.s: bhd: reminder 5f out: rdn and effrt on inner over 1f out: nt clr run and hmpd ins fnl f: swtchd rt and r.o fnl 100yds: nvr able to chal* 10/1
212- 5 1/2 **Kirsty's Boy (IRE)**[13] 7874 3-9-7 74 LiamKeniry 2 71
(J S Moore) *led tl over 5f out: rdn and clsd on ldr over 2f out: ev ch and drvn over 1f out: wknd ins fnl f* 25/1
32-2 6 1 1/2 **Gold Party**[5] 73 3-9-2 69 (bt[1]) JamieSpencer 5 62
(K McAuliffe) *awkward leaving stalls and s.i.s: dashed up to ld over 5f out: sn clr: rdn 2f out: hdd and edgd lft ent fnl f: wknd jst ins fnl f: last and eased towards fin* 6/1

1m 25.09s (0.29) **Going Correction** 0.0s/f (Stan) 6 Ran SP% 116.7
Speed ratings (Par 99): **98,96,96,94,94 92**
toteswinger:1&2:£4.00, 2&3:£1.50, 1&3:£3.00 CSF £9.97 TOTE £5.90: £1.30, £1.40; EX 13.00.
Owner Dr J Walker **Bred** E Landi **Trained** Newmarket, Suffolk

FOCUS
A tight little handicap. It was steadily run but looks a fair race of its type. The winner took another step forward.

137 FOREST ROW H'CAP — 6f (P)
4:05 (4:06) (Class 6) (0-60,60) 4-Y-O+ £1,325 (£1,325; £302) Stalls Low

Form RPR
60-3 1 **The Geester**[10] 14 6-9-2 58 AdamKirby 4 66
(Stef Higgins) *chsd clr ldng pair: rdn and clsd on ldrs over 2f out: drvn to ld over 1f out: hdd narrowly fnl 100yds: rallied to join ldr on post* 7/1
00-3 1 dht **Elusive Ronnie (IRE)**[3] 110 4-9-1 57 (b) JackMitchell 3 65
(R A Teal) *stdd s: wl bhd in last pair: rdn and hdwy over 2f out: drvn to chse ldr jst ins fnl f: led narrowly fnl 100yds: jnd on post* 7/2[2]
21-0 3 1 **Sherjawy (IRE)**[10] 20 6-8-9 56 (p) RossAtkinson(5) 6 61
(Miss Z C Davison) *racd off the pce in midfield: rdn over 2f out: kpt on u.p to go 3rd wl ins fnl f* 16/1
000- 4 3/4 **Diddums**[12] 7890 4-9-1 57 JamieSpencer 5 59
(P S McEntee) *racd off the pce in midfield: hdwy over 2f out: rdn over 1f out: chsd ldng pair 1f out: kpt on same pce ins fnl f* 9/2[3]
304- 5 nk **Don Pele (IRE)**[12] 7890 8-9-4 60 (p) StephenCraine 9 61+
(R A Harris) *awkward leaving stalls: off the pce towards rr: hdwy 2f out: nt clr run ent fnl f tl ins fnl f: kpt on towards fin but nvr able to chal* 11/1
511- 6 1 1/2 **Maggie Kate**[130] 5629 5-8-11 53 (b) NeilCallan 10 50
(R Ingram) *swtchd lft after s: racd off the pce in midfield: rdn over 1f out: kpt on ins fnl f but nvr gng pce to threaten ldrs* 14/1
000/ 7 shd **Castleburg**[447] 6910 4-8-11 60 HarryBentley(7) 2 56
(G L Moore) *s.i.s: hld up wl bhd: effrt on inner and rdn over 1f out: kpt on but nvr trbld ldrs* 33/1
506- 8 4 1/2 **Wreningham**[59] 7397 5-8-12 57 (e[1]) WilliamCarson(3) 11 39
(S C Williams) *racd v freely: sn clr w ldr: hdd over 1f out: sn fdd* 10/3[1]
006- 9 nk **Hatman Jack (IRE)**[12] 7890 4-9-1 57 (p) EddieAhern 8 38
(B G Powell) *led narrowly and sn clr w rival: hdd over 1f out: sn fdd* 8/1
000- 10 1 1/4 **Monte Cassino (IRE)**[22] 7834 5-8-10 52 TonyCulhane 7 29
(J O'Reilly) *s.i.s: a bhd* 33/1

1m 11.6s (-0.30) **Going Correction** 0.0s/f (Stan) 10 Ran SP% 113.9
Speed ratings (Par 101): **102,102,100,99,99 97,97,91,90,89**TOTE WIN: The Geester £4.10, Elusive Ronnie £1.90 PL: TG £2.40, ER £1.60, SJ £5.60. EX: TG/ER £10.70 ER/TG £13.40 CSF: TG/ER £15.46 ER/TG £13.40. TC: TG/ER/SJ £187.32, ER/TG/SJ £169.04. toteswinger: TG&ER: £3.80, TG&SJ: £11.40, ER&SJ: £4.70. Pla27 Owner.
Owner R J Ryan **Bred** The Ginger Group **Trained** Ashtead, Surrey

FOCUS
A wide-open handicap and the first two couldn't be split. It was about the only strong run race on the card and the form looks straightforward.
Don Pele(IRE) Official explanation: jockey said gelding was denied a clear run
T/Jkpt: £4,420.10 to a £1 stake. Pool: £71,593.90. 11.50 winning tickets. T/Plt: £45.60 to a £1 stake. Pool: £101,983.04. 1,631.11 winning tickets. T/Qpdt: £16.90 to a £1 stake. Pool: £8,100.48. 353.60 winning tickets. SP

112 SOUTHWELL (L-H)
Tuesday, January 12

OFFICIAL GOING: Slow

Wind: Light against Weather: Ovecast and dry

138 BET AFRICAN NATIONS CUP - BETDAQ (S) STKS — 5f (F)
12:50 (12:51) (Class 6) 4-Y-O+ £1,774 (£523; £262) Stalls High

Form RPR
400- 1 **Where's Reiley (USA)**[24] 7815 4-8-9 62 DeanHeslop(5) 5 71
(T D Barron) *blind removed late and s.i.s: in rr and swtchd lft after 1f: hdwy on wd outside 2f out: rdn to ld and edgd rt ent fnl f: styd on strly* 15/2
060- 2 1 3/4 **Monte Major (IRE)**[52] 7484 9-8-7 58 (v) SeanPalmer(7) 7 65
(D Shaw) *chsd ldrs: rdn along and outpcd 1/2-way: hdwy u.p over 1f out: sn drvn and edgd lft ins fnl f: kpt on* 33/1
050- 3 3/4 **Stash**[36] 7673 4-9-0 64 (t) GrahamGibbons 6 62
(R Hollinshead) *led: rdn along wl over 1f out: drvn and hdd jst ins fnl f: kpt on same pce* 7/2[2]
555- 4 nk **Bo McGinty (IRE)**[14] 7870 9-9-0 64 (v) TonyHamilton 3 63+
(R A Fahey) *prom: rdn along and outpcd 1/2-way: hdwy over 1f out: styng on whn nt clr run ent and again ins fnl f: nrst fin* 5/2[1]
003- 5 1 **Tartatartufata**[16] 7852 8-8-9 65 (v) JoeFanning 8 52
(J G Given) *chsd ldrs: pushed along and cl up 1/2-way: rdn to chal wl over 1f out and ev ch tl drvn: edgd lft and wknd ent fnl f* 15/2
304- 6 1 1/4 **Godfrey Street**[16] 7852 7-8-11 63 (b) KellyHarrison(3) 2 53
(A G Newcombe) *chsd ldrs: pushed along and outpcd bef 1/2-way: hdwy on outer 2f out: sn rdn and ev ch tl edgd rt and wknd appr fnl f* 8/1
012- 7 shd **Buy On The Red**[24] 7808 9-9-5 68 (b) AndrewMullen 1 57
(D Nicholls) *wnt lft s: sn chsng ldrs: cl up 1/2-way: rdn along 2f out and wkng whn n.m.r over 1f out* 6/1[3]
00-0 8 3/4 **Music Box Express**[10] 8 6-8-9 55 (v) MatthewDavies(5) 4 50
(George Baker) *cl up: rdn along over 2f out and sn wknd* 18/1

61.40 secs (1.70) **Going Correction** +0.375s/f (Slow) 8 Ran SP% 107.9
Speed ratings (Par 101): **101,98,97,96,94 92,92,91**
toteswinger:1&2:£28.90, 2&3:£15.00, 1&3:£5.80 CSF £180.80 TOTE £11.90: £2.90, £4.90, £1.20; EX 237.40 TRIFECTA Not won..There was no bid for the winner
Owner Dovebrace Ltd Air-Conditioning-Projects **Bred** Overrbook Farm **Trained** Maunby, N Yorks

FOCUS
A competitive seller, and with most of these wanting to race up the middle, it was a rough enough race. The form is rated around the winner.
Bo McGinty(IRE) Official explanation: jockey said gelding was denied a clear run
Tartatartufata Official explanation: jockey said mare hung left from halfway

139 BET MASTERS SNOOKER - BETDAQ H'CAP — 1m 4f (F)
1:20 (1:20) (Class 6) (0-60,60) 4-Y-O+ £1,774 (£523; £262) Stalls Low

Form RPR
43-0 1 **Greenbelt**[7] 42 9-9-4 52 TomEaves 11 61
(G M Moore) *trckd ldr: led 4f out: rdn along over 2f out: drvn over 1f out: hld on gamely ins fnl f* 20/1
501- 2 hd **Tyrana (GER)**[27] 7766 7-9-8 56 StevieDonohoe 5 65
(Ian Williams) *trckd ldrs: hdwy 3f out: rdn to chse wnr 2f out: drvn over 1f out: kpt on u.p ins fnl f: jst hld* 11/4[1]
5-52 3 1 **Russian Invader (IRE)**[5] 76 6-8-12 51 (be) TobyAtkinson(5) 6 58
(R C Guest) *hld up towards rr: hdwy 4f out: rdn to chse ldrs over 2f out: drvn over 1f out: kpt on ins fnl f: nrst fin* 4/1[2]
/53- 4 3/4 **Law Of The Jungle (IRE)**[15] 7857 4-9-8 60 (b[1]) RichardKingscote 8 66
(Tom Dascombe) *trckd ldrs: effrt to chse wnr 3f out and sn rdn: drvn wl over 1f out: edgd lft and kpt on same pce ins fnl f* 15/2[3]
332- 5 2 3/4 **Jackie Kiely**[21] 7840 9-9-4 52 (tp) PhillipMakin 2 53
(R Brotherton) *rn in snatches: hld up in midfield: pushed along over 5f out: rdn and outpcd 4f out: swtchd wd over 2f out and sn drvn: kpt on appr fnl f: nt rch ldrs* 11/4[1]
555- 6 7 **Noah Jameel**[15] 7857 8-9-2 53 KellyHarrison(3) 10 43
(A G Newcombe) *in rr: hdwy 4f out: rdn over 2f out: plodded on: nvr nr ldrs* 14/1
250/ 7 15 **Cream Of Esteem**[37] 5837 8-8-11 45 (b[1]) GrahamGibbons 9 11
(R Johnson) *ld: rdn along and hdd 4f out: drvn 3f out and sn wknd* 250/1
250- 8 13 **Carragold**[31] 7732 4-9-2 54 RobertWinston 3 —
(M Brittain) *prom: rdn along over 4f out and sn wknd* 12/1
504- 9 3 1/2 **Gulf Of Aqaba (USA)**[176] 4139 4-9-8 60 JoeFanning 7 —
(D E Pipe) *dwlt: a towards rr* 14/1
0- 10 50 **King Fernando**[208] 3068 7-9-2 50 (b) AndrewElliott 1 —
(P Beaumont) *midfield and rdn along after 1f: sn lost pl and bhd: t.o fnl 4f* 100/1

2m 43.83s (2.83) **Going Correction** +0.175s/f (Slow)
WFA 4 from 6yo+ 4lb 10 Ran SP% 112.3
Speed ratings (Par 101): **97,96,96,95,93 89,79,70,68,34**
toteswinger:1&2:£13.10, 2&3:£4.90, 1&3:£11.60 CSF £71.68 CT £271.28 TOTE £19.40: £3.90, £1.90, £1.60; EX 127.40 Trifecta £361.00 Pool: £570.86 - 1.17 winning units..
Owner Mrs A Roddis **Bred** Juddmonte Farms **Trained** Middleham Moor, N Yorks

FOCUS
A reasonable handicap for such a lowly grade. The surprise winner is rated to last year's best.
Greenbelt Official explanation: trainer's rep said, regarding apparent improvement in form, had no explanation regarding poor run last time, but added that the gelding appeared to appreciate being ridden with more daylight.
Carragold Official explanation: trainer said colt had been unable to act on the deep surface and failed to stay 1m 4f

140 BETDAQ ON 0870 178 1221 H'CAP — 2m (F)
1:50 (1:50) (Class 6) (0-60,60) 4-Y-O+ £1,774 (£523; £262) Stalls Low

Form RPR
21-1 1 **Russian Music (USA)**[7] 41 5-9-13 60 6ex StevieDonohoe 10 76+
(Ian Williams) *hld up in rr: smooth hdwy 4f out: led on bit over 2f out: pushed clr ent fnl f* 1/1[1]
/3-2 2 6 **Spring Breeze**[10] 15 9-9-4 51 (p) GrahamGibbons 8 59+
(J J Quinn) *led: rdn along 3f out: hdd over 2f out and sn drvn: ev ch tl outpcd ent fnl f* 3/1[2]
260- 3 1 1/4 **Pagan Starprincess**[38] 6767 6-9-8 55 TomEaves 6 57
(G M Moore) *trckd ldrs: pushed along 5f out: rdn 3f out: drvn wl over 1f out: kpt on same pce* 4/1[3]
134/ 4 3 **Sparkling Montjeu (IRE)**[26] 7688 5-9-1 53 MatthewDavies(5) 5 51
(George Baker) *trckd ldng pair: hdwy to chse ldr 1/2-way: cl up 4f out: rdn along 3f out: drvn over 2f out and grad wknd* 22/1
015- 5 18 **Dazzling Begum**[21] 7842 5-9-5 52 RobertWinston 1 29
(J Pearce) *chsd ldrs: rdn along over 3f out: drvn over 2f out and sn wknd* 20/1
50-0 6 26 **Primera Rossa**[10] 13 4-8-6 46 (p) FrannyNorton 7 —
(J S Moore) *hld up in tch: effrt over 4f out: rdn along over 3f out and sn wknd* 33/1
054- 7 45 **Brandy Butter**[51] 6935 4-8-13 53 (vt) JoeFanning 2 —
(D E Pipe) *cl up: rdn along over 6f out: sn wknd and bhd: t.o fnl 3f* 33/1

3m 47.49s (1.99) **Going Correction** +0.175s/f (Slow)
WFA 4 from 5yo+ 7lb 7 Ran SP% 110.0
Speed ratings (Par 101): **102,99,98,96,87 74,52**
toteswinger:1&2:£1.50, 2&3:£2.50, 1&3:£2.20 CSF £3.67 CT £6.57 TOTE £2.10: £1.20, £2.50; EX 5.20 Trifecta £11.70 Pool: £569.06 - 35.84 winning units..
Owner D & Js Boys Racing Club **Bred** Denis O'Flynn **Trained** Portway, Worcs

FOCUS
A moderate staying handicap. A clear personal best from the winner, and sound enough form.

141 PLAY GOLF AT SOUTHWELL GOLF CLUB H'CAP — 6f (F)
2:20 (2:20) (Class 5) (0-70,70) 3-Y-O £2,456 (£725; £362) Stalls Low

Form RPR
656- 1 **Novay Essjay (IRE)**[105] 6354 3-9-1 67 AndrewMullen 4 71
(D Nicholls) *mde all: rdn along 2f out: drvn over 1f out: edgd rt and kpt on gamely ins fnl f* 10/1
61-3 2 3/4 **Flow Chart (IRE)**[11] 4 3-9-4 70 (b) PhillipMakin 6 72
(T D Barron) *trckd ldrs on outer: hdwy over 2f out and sn rdn: drvn over 1f out: kpt on ins fnl f* 2/1[1]

061- 3 nk **Two Kisses (IRE)**[25] 7799 3-8-13 **65** StevieDonohoe 1 66
(B G Powell) *trckd ldrs on inner: pushed along 2f out: hdwy over 1f out: drvn and kpt on ins fnl f: nrst fin* **6/1**[3]

121- 4 ½ **Tealing**[25] 7791 3-9-1 **67** JoeFanning 5 68+
(R C Guest) *t.k.h: cl up: rdn along 2f out: drvn and every ch over 1f out: edgd lft and hld whn n.m.r and hit in face by wnr's whip ins fnl f: swtchd lft and one pce* **11/4**[2]

331- 5 2 ¼ **Exearti**[14] 7864 3-9-2 **68** RobertWinston 3 60
(A J McCabe) *t.k.h: trckd ldrs: hdwy over 2f out: sn rdn to chal and ev ch tl drvn ent fnl f and sn wknd* **11/4**[2]

1m 18.36s (1.86) **Going Correction** +0.175s/f (Slow) 5 Ran SP% **110.0**
Speed ratings (Par 97): **94,93,92,91,88**
toteswinger: 1&2:£10.50 CSF £30.23 TOTE £11.10: £6.50, £1.80; EX 32.10.
Owner Middleham Park Racing XXXI **Bred** Camogue Stud Ltd **Trained** Sessay, N Yorks

FOCUS
A modest but competitive sprint handicap. The form looks sound enough.

142 FREEBETS.CO.UK FREE BETS H'CAP 7f (F)
2:50 (2:50) (Class 6) (0-52,52) 4-Y-0+ **£1,774** (£523; £262) **Stalls** Low

Form RPR

6-55 1 **Bicksta**[10] 19 4-8-1 **46** (p) PaulPickard(5) 4 54
(P T Midgley) *towards rr: rdn along 1/2-way: hdwy u.p 2f out: drvn over 1f out: styd on ent fnl f to ld last 100yds: sn clr* **8/1**

000- 2 3 ¾ **Mr Fantozzi (IRE)**[16] 7855 5-8-9 **52** (bt) AndreaAtzeni(3) 6 50
(D Donovan) *cl up: rdn 2f out: sn drvn and ev ch tl one pce ins fnl f* **4/1**[2]

00-0 3 1 ¼ **Megalo Maniac**[10] 21 7-8-1 **48** (v) MarzenaJeziorek(7) 9 43
(R A Fahey) *mde most: rdn along wl over 2f out: edgd rt ent fnl f: hdd & wknd fnl 100yds* **11/1**

44-4 4 ¾ **Nabeeda**[5] 70 5-8-5 **52** JohnCavanagh(7) 7 44
(M Brittain) *t.k.h: chsd ldng pair: effrt wl over 2f out and sn rdn: drvn over 1f out and sn one pce* **5/1**[3]

/00- 5 8 **Eyesore**[25] 7796 4-7-13 **46** oh1 NathanAlison(7) 8 17
(S A Harris) *chsd ldrs on outer: rdn along 3f out: wknd over 2f out* **40/1**

001- 6 8 **Hard Ball**[31] 7727 4-8-11 **51** (v) FrannyNorton 2 —
(M Quinn) *towards rr: rdn along 3f out: nvr a factor* **15/8**[1]

303- 7 16 **Mojeerr**[25] 7796 4-8-10 **50** (p) RobertWinston 1 —
(A J McCabe) *sn rdn along and a bhd* **4/1**[2]

1m 31.08s (0.78) **Going Correction** +0.175s/f (Slow) 7 Ran SP% **113.3**
Speed ratings (Par 101): **102,97,96,95,86 77,58**
toteswinger:1&2:£5.90, 2&3:£6.90, 1&3:£7.90 CSF £38.98 CT £352.89 TOTE £8.10: £4.60, £2.30; EX 36.00 Trifecta £221.70 Pool: £808.94 - 2.70 winning units..
Owner R Wardlaw **Bred** The National Stud **Trained** Westow, N Yorks
■ Stewards' Enquiry : Nathan Alison £140 fine - failed to pass stands before going to the start

FOCUS
A weak handicap run at a good pace. The winner is rated back to her best but the form may not be the most solid.
Hard Ball Official explanation: trainer said gelding resented the kickback

143 BELVOIR LETTINGS MAIDEN STKS 1m (F)
3:20 (3:21) (Class 5) 3-Y-0+ **£2,456** (£725; £362) **Stalls** Low

Form RPR

044- 1 **Ming Master (FR)**[27] 7763 3-8-8 72 JoeFanning 1 83+
(W J Haggas) *sn led: pushed clr wl over 1f out: easily* **13/8**[1]

2 10 **Market Puzzle (IRE)**[100] 6515 3-8-8 68 GrahamGibbons 4 53
(W M Brisbourne) *cl up: rdn along wl over 2f out: drvn wl over 1f out: hung lft ent fnl f and one pce* **14/1**

00- 3 nk **Red Valerian Two (IRE)**[67] 7266 3-8-3 0 PaulPickard(5) 3 52
(P T Midgley) *in rr: pushed along and green 1/2-way: hdwy 2f out and sn rdn: drvn and sltly hmpd ent fnl f: kpt on same pce* **100/1**

5/5- 4 1 ¾ **Dream Win**[274] 1255 4-10-0 0 TomEaves 6 52
(B Ellison) *cl up on outer: effrt wl over 2f out and sn rdn: drvn wl over 1f out and kpt on same pce* **3/1**[3]

5 3 ½ **Albertus Pictor** 3-8-8 0 StevieDonohoe 2 40
(Sir Mark Prescott) *lost many l s: bhd tl sme late hdwy* **7/4**[2]

0- 6 2 **Luminosa**[45] 7580 3-8-0 0 AndreaAtzeni(3) 5 31
(D Donovan) *chsd ldrs: rdn along 3f out: sn wknd* **40/1**

1m 44.15s (0.45) **Going Correction** +0.175s/f (Slow)
WFA 3 from 4yo 20lb 6 Ran SP% **109.6**
Speed ratings (Par 103): **104,94,93,91,88 86**
toteswinger:1&2:£3.60, 2&3:£13.80, 1&3:£13.10 CSF £22.48 TOTE £2.40: £1.20, £4.30; EX 11.90.
Owner Lok Ho Ting **Bred** Brook Stud Ltd **Trained** Newmarket, Suffolk

FOCUS
An uncompetitive maiden in which the runner-up surely ran below his official rating of 68. There were plenty of doubts over what the winner beat, but he impressed all the same.
Albertus Pictor Official explanation: jockey said gelding missed the break

144 SOUTHWELL RACECOURSE FOR CONFERENCES H'CAP 7f (F)
3:50 (3:50) (Class 5) (0-70,70) 4-Y-0+ **£2,456** (£725; £362) **Stalls** Low

Form RPR

22-1 1 **Elusive Warrior (USA)**[7] 39 7-9-2 **68** 6ex (p) RobertWinston 2 77
(A J McCabe) *mde all: rdn along over 2f out: drvn over 1f out: kpt on wl u.p ins fnl f* **9/1**

31-3 2 1 ¼ **Whitbarrow (IRE)**[10] 20 11-9-0 **69** (b) JamesMillman(3) 3 75
(B R Millman) *cl up: effrt over 2f out: sn rdn and ev ch: drvn ins fnl f and kpt on same pce* **6/1**[3]

00-5 3 nse **Premier Lad**[10] 20 4-8-13 **65** PhillipMakin 10 71+
(T D Barron) *t.k.h early: hld up: hdwy over 2f out: rdn to chse ldng pair over 1f out: drvn ins fnl f: kpt on towards fin* **5/2**[1]

136- 4 3 ½ **Kipchak (IRE)**[13] 7876 5-8-13 **70** (p) BarryMcHugh(5) 1 66
(C R Dore) *chsd ldng pair on inner: rdn along over 2f out: drvn wl over 1f out and grad wknd* **11/2**[2]

0-43 5 1 ¼ **Vogarth**[4] 86 6-8-5 **60** (b) AndreaAtzeni(3) 9 53
(M C Chapman) *hld up: hdwy over 2f out and sn rdn: drvn to chse ldrs over 1f out: sn no imp* **12/1**

044- 6 ¾ **By Command**[83] 6940 5-8-3 **60** AmyRyan(5) 7 51
(K A Ryan) *towards rr: sme hdwy on inner fnl 2f: nvr a factor* **11/2**[2]

325- 7 ½ **Hypnotic Gaze (IRE)**[163] 4562 4-9-0 **66** (p) JoeFanning 6 56
(J Mackie) *a towards rr* **20/1**

20-4 8 2 **Boss Hog**[7] 39 5-8-1 **58** ow2 PaulPickard(5) 5 42
(P T Midgley) *chsd ldrs: rdn along wl over 2f out: drvn wl over 1f out and sn wknd* **8/1**

320- 9 ½ **Madison Belle**[14] 7870 4-9-1 **70** MartinLane(3) 8 53
(J R Weymes) *in tch: rdn along 3f out: sn wknd* **20/1**

123- 10 1 **Solis**[238] 2154 4-8-10 **62** GrahamGibbons 4 42
(J J Quinn) *chsd ldrs: rdn along 3f out: sn wknd* **12/1**

1m 30.34s (0.04) **Going Correction** +0.175s/f (Slow) 10 Ran SP% **119.6**
Speed ratings (Par 103): **106,104,104,100,99 98,97,95,94,93**
toteswinger:1&2:£4.10, 2&3:£6.30, 1&3:£9.30 CSF £63.82 CT £179.64 TOTE £8.30: £2.50, £2.00, £1.80; EX 26.70 Trifecta £63.80 Pool: £763.17 - 8.85 winning units. Place 6 £108.27, Place 5 £27.85.
Owner Mrs M J McCabe **Bred** Steve Peskoff **Trained** Averham Park, Notts

FOCUS
A modest handicap run in a time 0.74 seconds quicker than earlier 46-52 contest. Fair form for the grade, with the runner-up the best guide.
T/Plt: £323.30 to a £1 stake. Pool: £87,157.53. 196.78 winning tickets. T/Qpdt: £99.30 to a £1 stake. Pool: £8,323.80. 62.00 winning tickets. JR

[118]KEMPTON (A.W) (R-H)
Wednesday, January 13

OFFICIAL GOING: Standard
Wind: Almost nil Weather: Very overcast

145 KEMPTON.CO.UK H'CAP 7f (P)
4:15 (4:16) (Class 7) (0-50,50) 4-Y-0+ **£1,364** (£403; £201) **Stalls** High

Form RPR

046- 1 **Ejeed (USA)**[24] 7826 5-8-12 **50** (p) RossAtkinson(5) 10 60+
(Miss Z C Davison) *trckd ldrs: rdn over 1f out and trapped bhd rivals ent fnl f: gap appeared and r.o to ld last strides* **4/1**[1]

30-4 2 ½ **Ride A White Swan**[9] 30 5-8-10 **46** MartinLane(3) 12 55
(D Shaw) *t.k.h: hld up in midfield: prog on inner over 2f out: drvn ahd ins fnl f: hdd last strides* **15/2**[3]

005- 3 hd **Clever Omneya (USA)**[35] 7686 4-8-12 **45** StephenCraine 3 53
(J R Jenkins) *led: jnd 1/2-way: kpt on u.p over 2f out: hdd and one pce ins fnl f* **16/1**

0-66 4 1 ¼ **Louisiade (IRE)**[5] 88 9-8-7 **45** (p) BillyCray(5) 5 50
(R C Guest) *restless stalls: t.k.h: pressed ldr: upsides fr 1/2-way: hanging over 2f out: nt qckn over 1f out: hld after* **8/1**

040- 5 2 ½ **King's Miracle (IRE)**[24] 7826 4-9-1 **48** LiamKeniry 8 46
(J R Gask) *s.s: hld up in last: prog on inner to take 5th wl over 1f out: no imp on ldrs after* **11/2**[2]

23-5 6 2 **Tadlil**[6] 70 8-9-1 **48** (v) DavidProbert 11 41
(J M Bradley) *s.s: hld up in last pair: rdn and effrt over 2f out: no imp on ldrs over 1f out: lame* **4/1**[1]

050- 7 2 **Boundless Applause**[28] 7774 4-8-5 **45** MatthewCosham(7) 9 33
(I A Wood) *hld up in rr: outpcd by ldrs over 2f out: nvr on terms after* **9/1**

300- 8 8 **Flamestone**[203] 3269 6-9-0 **47** StevieDonohoe 2 13
(A E Price) *t.k.h: racd wd: chsd ldrs to 3f out: sn lost pl u.p* **14/1**

650- 9 1 **Grizedale (IRE)**[137] 5429 11-9-1 **48** PaulDoe 4 11
(M J Attwater) *dwlt: t.k.h: trckd ldrs: rdn and wknd over 2f out* **8/1**

000/ 10 1 ¼ **Clearing Sky (IRE)**[840] 5730 9-8-5 **45** NathanAlison(7) 6 5
(J R Boyle) *t.k.h: prom to 1/2-way: sn lost pl and btn* **22/1**

1m 27.31s (1.31) **Going Correction** -0.025s/f (Stan) 10 Ran SP% **116.3**
Speed ratings (Par 97): **91,90,90,88,85 83,81,72,71,69**
toteswingers: 1&2 £5.40, 1&3 £24.30, 2&3 £24.40 CSF £34.08 CT £443.34 TOTE £3.60: £1.50, £2.30, £5.20; EX 32.80.
Owner Mrs J Irvine **Bred** Shadwell Farm LLC **Trained** Hammerwood, E Sussex

FOCUS
Despite 6cm of snow overnight and during the morning, the track was cleared and the meeting passed a third inspection at 11am. A low-grade handicap to kick things off, and it was run at a steady early gallop. The form is not the most solid, with the first three appearing to have improved.
King's Miracle(IRE) Official explanation: jockey said filly missed the break
Tadlil Official explanation: vet said gelding finished lame
Grizedale(IRE) Official explanation: vet said gelding lost a shoe

146 BISTRO AT THE PANORAMIC BAR & RESTAURANT H'CAP 6f (P)
4:45 (4:45) (Class 7) (0-50,51) 4-Y-0+ **£1,364** (£403; £201) **Stalls** High

Form RPR

405- 1 **Diane's Choice**[14] 7880 7-9-3 **50** (b) DavidProbert 9 60
(Miss Gay Kelleway) *dwlt: settled in last pair: rdn and prog fr jst over 2f out: clsd on ldrs over 1f out: led ins fnl f: kpt on* **9/2**[2]

02-6 2 ¾ **Equinity**[11] 8 4-9-2 **49** (t) SaleemGolam 8 57
(J Pearce) *prom: chsd ldr wl over 2f out: disp ld and hung lft wl over 1f out: hdd and one pce ins fnl f* **10/1**

04-4 3 shd **Black Draft**[11] 10 8-8-7 **45** SophieDoyle(5) 10 52
(B Forsey) *hld up towards rr: prog wl over 2f out: disp ld over 1f out: hdd and nt qckn ins fnl f* **17/2**

0-00 4 1 ½ **Commandingpresence (USA)**[4] 103 4-8-9 **45** MarcHalford(3) 6 47
(J J Bridger) *led: hung lft over 2f out: hdd over 1f out: one pce* **16/1**

44-4 5 hd **Reigning Monarch (USA)**[4] 103 7-8-11 **49** (p) RossAtkinson(5) 3 51
(Miss Z C Davison) *chsd ldrs: rdn fr 1/2-way: nt qckn on outer over 2f out: plugged on same pce after* **5/1**[3]

04-0 6 2 ½ **Oxbridge**[11] 8 5-8-9 **45** (b) JackDean(3) 5 39
(J M Bradley) *chsd ldrs: rdn bef 1/2-way: one pce after: fdd fnl f* **12/1**

00-0 7 1 ¾ **Spring Bridge (IRE)**[11] 14 4-8-12 **45** (p) LiamKeniry 4 33
(Mrs L C Jewell) *nvr beyond midfield: dropped to last pair and struggling 2f out: n.d after* **40/1**

230- 8 nk **Place The Duchess**[15] 7869 4-8-8 **48** (t) NathanAlison(7) 2 35
(A J Lidderdale) *t.k.h: pressed ldr to wl over 2f out: sn lost pl and btn* **10/1**

-012 9 nk **Brazilian Brush (IRE)**[3] 112 5-8-11 **51** 6ex (bt) RyanClark(7) 11 37
(J M Bradley) *chsd ldrs: u.p and no prog over 2f out: wknd over 1f out* **9/4**[1]

300- 10 1 ¼ **Miss Jabba (IRE)**[38] 7653 4-8-12 **45** JimmyQuinn 12 27
(Miss J Feilden) *mostly in last: struggling over 2f out* **16/1**

1m 13.2s (0.10) **Going Correction** -0.025s/f (Stan) 10 Ran SP% **116.2**
Speed ratings (Par 97): **98,97,96,94,94 91,88,88,88,86**
toteswingers: 1&2 £7.80, 1&3 £7.40, 2&3 £12.80 CSF £48.76 CT £370.52 TOTE £5.90: £2.00, £3.20, £2.80; EX 43.90.
Owner The Dark Side, Gay Kelleway **Bred** Green Pastures Farm **Trained** Exning, Suffolk
■ Stewards' Enquiry : Saleem Golam caution: used whip above shoulder height

FOCUS
There was a good gallop on here and the winner came from well off the pace. Weak form, rated around the winner.
Commandingpresence(USA) Official explanation: jockey said filly hung left

Spring Bridge(IRE) Official explanation: jockey said gelding hung left

147 DIGIBET MAIDEN STKS 6f (P)
5:15 (5:16) (Class 5) 3-Y-0+ £2,590 (£770; £385; £192) Stalls High

Form RPR
0- 1 **Best Trip (IRE)**67 7288 3-8-11 0 FrannyNorton 7 72+
(R C Guest) *racd keenly: mde all at decent pce: pushed along and clr over 1f out: unchal* 14/1
042- 2 2 1/2 **Torres Del Paine**31 7736 3-8-11 71 LiamKeniry 1 64
(J C Fox) *hld up in 5th: prog to chse wnr 2f out: sn drvn and no imp* 5/2[2]
0- 3 2 1/4 **Apache Moon**38 963 4-9-13 0 KevinGhunowa 5 61
(R Curtis) *chsd wnr: rdn 1/2-way: lost 2nd 2f out: one pce after* 80/1
4 1 1/4 **Merals Choice** 3-8-6 0 NickyMackay 6 48
(J R Boyle) *mostly in last pair: rdn and struggling over 2f out: modest late prog* 8/1
626- 5 1 1/4 **Avon Castle**13 7886 3-8-6 64 JimmyQuinn 4 44
(G L Moore) *t.k.h: hld up in tch: nt qckn over 2f out: wl btn over 1f out* 11/2[3]
03-3 6 3 **Tatawor (IRE)**10 24 3-8-6 0 MatthewDavies(5) 2 39
(J R Boyle) *chsd ldng pair: wd bnd 3f out: u.p sn after: wknd 2f out* 6/4[1]
7 10 **Neville's Cross (IRE)** 3-8-11 0 StephenCraine 3 7
(J R Boyle) *dwlt: a last: wknd over 2f out: t.o* 16/1

1m 12.59s (-0.51) **Going Correction** -0.025s/f (Stan)
WFA 3 from 4yo 16lb 7 Ran SP% **108.9**
Speed ratings (Par 103): **102,98,95,94,92 88,75**
toteswingers: 1&2 £5.50, 1&3 £16.80, 2&3 £17.10 CSF £44.51 TOTE £16.00: £7.20, £1.50; EX 57.80.
Owner P J Duffen & P Brown **Bred** Limetree Stud **Trained** Stainforth, S Yorks

FOCUS
A very modest maiden run in a time 0.61 seconds quicker than the 50-rated Diane's Choice, carrying 9st3lb, recorded earlier on the card. The fifth and sixth disappointed and the race has been rated around the time and the runner-up.

148 DIGIBET.COM CLAIMING STKS 1m 4f (P)
5:45 (5:47) (Class 6) 4-Y-0+ £2,047 (£604; £302) Stalls Centre

Form RPR
143- 1 **Wicked Daze (IRE)**34 7701 7-9-7 85 NeilCallan 5 81
(K A Ryan) *mde all: drew clr wl over 2f out: drvn and kpt on fr over 1f out* 11/8[1]
315- 2 1 1/4 **Satwa Gold (USA)**42 7612 4-9-2 75 HayleyTurner 9 78
(E A L Dunlop) *hld up in last trio: prog on outer over 3f out: wnt 2nd wl over 1f out: styd on but nvr able to bridge the gap* 15/2[3]
250- 3 1 1/2 **Quince (IRE)**28 7777 7-9-0 65 (v) SaleemGolam 2 70
(J Pearce) *settled in midfield: prog on inner fr 3f out: wnt 3rd over 1f out: styd on same pce* 16/1
063- 4 2 1/2 **Such Optimism**22 7841 4-8-7 82 RichardKingscote 12 63
(R M Beckett) *chsd ldrs: pushed along 4f out: effrt over 2f out: kpt on to take 4th ins fnl f: n.d* 3/1[2]
304- 5 1 **Mustajed**29 7761 9-8-13 72 JamesMillman(3) 8 66
(B R Millman) *dwlt: hld up in last: plenty to do whn effrt over 2f out: plugged on one pce: no ch* 12/1
0/0- 6 nk **Pocket Too**16 7785 7-9-2 73 (p) RobertWinston 4 66
(Matthew Salaman) *prom: pushed along 4f out: outpcd over 2f out: grad fdd* 8/1
000- 7 8 **Cossack Prince**24 7823 5-9-2 67 IanMongan 7 53
(Mrs L J Mongan) *chsd wnr: lft bhd u.str.p fr 3f out: wknd wl over 1f out* 16/1
6- 8 6 **Ouste (FR)**59 541 8-8-11 43 JimmyQuinn 3 39
(Mrs A M Thorpe) *dwlt: hld up in last trio: nvr a factor* 50/1
000/ 9 1 **Pugilist**18 6721 8-8-12 56 StevieDonohoe 11 38
(K C Bailey) *a in rr: rdn 5f out: bhd over 2f out* 66/1
06-0 10 shd **Ibbetson (USA)**2 120 5-9-0 63 LiamKeniry 1 40
(Mrs A M Thorpe) *nvr beyond midfield: wknd 3f out: sn bhd* 40/1
/00- 11 62 **Blow Hole (USA)**86 4083 5-9-0 70 EddieAhern 10 —
(Mrs A M Thorpe) *prom tl wknd rapidly 4f out: t.o* 40/1

2m 33.22s (-1.28) **Going Correction** -0.025s/f (Stan)
WFA 4 from 5yo+ 4lb 11 Ran SP% **117.8**
Speed ratings (Par 101): **103,102,101,99,98 98,93,89,88,88 47**
toteswingers: 1&2 £2.40, 1&3 £8.50, 2&3 £9.70 CSF £12.37 TOTE £1.90: £1.10, £1.40, £6.40; EX 14.80.
Owner Dr Marwan Koukash **Bred** Bloomsbury Stud **Trained** Hambleton, N Yorks

FOCUS
A fair claimer although the main form rival to the winner was not at his best. The third is the best guide.

149 DIGIBET CASINO H'CAP 7f (P)
6:15 (6:15) (Class 5) (0-70,76) 3-Y-O £2,590 (£770; £385; £192) Stalls High

Form RPR
13-1 1 **Admiral Cochrane (IRE)**1 136 3-9-10 76 6ex JoeFanning 4 88+
(W Jarvis) *trckd ldr: led over 1f out: edgd rt after: drew clr fnl f* 1/1[1]
350- 2 3 3/4 **Volatilis (IRE)**132 5589 3-8-9 61 HayleyTurner 3 57
(J W Hills) *t.k.h: led: rdn and hdd over 1f out: hld whn hmpd and checked sn after: jst hld on for 2nd* 20/1
045- 3 nk **Rathbawn Girl (IRE)**15 7864 3-8-12 64 JimmyQuinn 6 59+
(Miss J Feilden) *hld up in last pair: hemmed in over 2f out: prog wl over 1f out: wnt 3rd ins fnl f: clsng on runner-up fin* 14/1
045- 4 nk **St Ignatius**34 7700 3-8-13 65 JimCrowley 7 59
(R M Beckett) *hld up last: prog to chse ldng pair 2f out: kpt on same pce: lost 3rd ins fnl f* 7/2[2]
223- 5 2 1/4 **Prince Yarraman (IRE)**15 7865 3-9-0 66 EddieAhern 5 54
(J A Osborne) *chsd ldrs: hrd rdn to go 3rd briefly over 2f out: nt qckn and wl btn whn rdr dropped whip jst over 1f out* 9/2[3]
300- 6 19 **May Chorus (IRE)**24 7824 3-8-8 60 NickyMackay 2 —
(J R Boyle) *dwlt: sn chsd ldng pair: wknd over 2f out: t.o* 12/1

1m 26.56s (0.56) **Going Correction** -0.025s/f (Stan) 6 Ran SP% **109.5**
Speed ratings (Par 97): **95,90,90,90,87 65**
toteswingers: 1&2 £5.60, 1&3 £3.50, 2&3 £6.70 CSF £21.67 CT £160.04 TOTE £1.70: £1.10, £15.40; EX 20.20.
Owner Dr J Walker **Bred** E Landi **Trained** Newmarket, Suffolk
■ Stewards' Enquiry : Joe Fanning one-day ban: careless riding (Jan 27)

FOCUS
An uncompetitive handicap and probably not a race to be too positive about. The front pair were always 1-2 and the winner appeared to improve by 10lb on his win the previous day.

May Chorus(IRE) Official explanation: jockey said filly had no more to give

150 BISTRO PRICES FROM £37 H'CAP 7f (P)
6:45 (6:45) (Class 4) (0-85,85) 4-Y-0+ £4,209 (£1,252; £625; £312) Stalls High

Form RPR
345- 1 **Indian Skipper (IRE)**22 7837 5-8-10 82 (be) BillyCray(5) 4 88
(R C Guest) *hld up in last pair: brought v wd in st: prog 2f out: styd on wl fnl f to ld post* 16/1
135- 2 shd **Bravo Echo**24 7827 4-9-4 85 DavidProbert 5 91
(M J Attwater) *t.k.h: pressed ldr: led wl over 2f out: sn drvn: narrowly hdd 1f out: upsides nr fin: jst pipped* 5/2[1]
165- 3 shd **Carnivore**23 7833 8-8-10 77 JimCrowley 2 83
(T D Barron) *hld up in 5th: prog over 2f out: rdn to ld narrowly 1f out: hdd last strides* 7/1[3]
112- 4 2 **Seek The Fair Land**23 7833 4-9-0 84 WilliamCarson(3) 1 84
(J R Boyle) *racd wd thrght: chsd ldng pair: rdn and nt qckn over 2f out: one pce after* 5/2[1]
313- 5 1 1/2 **My Best Bet**28 7769 4-9-0 81 AdamKirby 3 77
(Stef Higgins) *hld up in 6th: nt clr run over 2f out: prog over 1f out: one pce after* 5/1[2]
/40- 6 2 1/2 **Vintage (IRE)**23 7832 6-8-11 78 IanMongan 8 68
(J Akehurst) *plld hrd: hld up in 4th: nt qckn 2f out: grad wknd* 8/1
263- 7 nk **Desert Dreamer (IRE)**13 7891 9-8-12 79 PaulDoe 7 68
(P D Evans) *hld up in last pair: rdn and effrt on inner over 2f out: no prog over 1f out: wknd* 12/1
140- 8 17 **Simple Rhythm**87 6877 4-8-4 78 RyanPowell(7) 6 21
(J Ryan) *led to wl over 2f out: wknd rapidly over 1f out: t.o* 25/1

1m 24.69s (-1.31) **Going Correction** -0.025s/f (Stan) 8 Ran SP% **114.8**
Speed ratings (Par 105): **106,105,105,103,101 98,98,79**
toteswingers: 1&2 £9.70, 1&3 £13.40, 2&3 £7.50 CSF £56.45 CT £315.79 TOTE £19.80: £5.50, £1.10, £3.50; EX 59.80.
Owner Future Racing (Notts) Limited **Bred** Calley House Syndicate **Trained** Stainforth, S Yorks
■ Stewards' Enquiry : David Probert two-day ban: used whip with excessive frequency (Jan 27-28)

FOCUS
A fair handicap and unsurprisingly easily the quickest of the three 7f races on the card. Pretty straightforward form.

151 MIX BUSINESS WITH TWILIGHT RACING H'CAP 1m (P)
7:15 (7:17) (Class 4) (0-80,78) 4-Y-0+ £4,209 (£1,252; £625; £312) Stalls High

Form RPR
530- 1 **Totally Focussed (IRE)**14 7883 5-9-3 77 HayleyTurner 1 85
(S Dow) *stdd s and 3 l bhd leaving stalls: crossed fr wd draw and hld up in last trio: prog on inner 3f out: led over 1f out: drvn and jst hld on* 5/1[3]
464- 2 nk **Sunshine Always (IRE)**13 7891 4-9-3 77 JimCrowley 6 84+
(T D McCarthy) *hld up in last trio: gng easily but stl there over 2f out: only 9th over 1f out: rapid prog to go 2nd and cl on wnr fin: too much to do* 12/1
25-3 3 3/4 **Tamasou (IRE)**11 16 5-9-3 77 RobertWinston 13 83
(A J McCabe) *trckd ldng pair: rdn to go 2nd over 2f out to over 1f out: styd on u.p: a hld* 15/2
504- 4 nk **Hurakan (IRE)**24 7823 4-8-8 73 (v[1]) AndrewHeffernan(5) 2 78
(P D Evans) *rushed up to chse ldr after 1f: rdn and lost pl over 2f out: rallied u.p jst over 1f out: styng on nr fin* 12/1
22-1 5 2 1/4 **Bawaardi (IRE)**9 29 4-8-8 75 LeeTopliss(7) 9 75
(R A Fahey) *hld up in midfield: rdn over 2f out: sme prog over 1f out: one pce and no hdwy fnl f* 4/1[1]
126- 6 nk **Ensnare**40 7633 5-9-0 74 StevieDonohoe 14 73
(Ian Williams) *led: drvn over 2f out: hdd & wknd over 1f out* 9/2[2]
100- 7 3/4 **Final Verse**14 7883 7-9-4 78 (e) LiamKeniry 10 75
(Matthew Salaman) *trckd ldrs: rdn and nt qckn 2f out: one pce and no imp after* 12/1
042- 8 1/2 **Hallingdal (UAE)**24 7823 5-8-11 74 MarcHalford(3) 12 73+
(J J Bridger) *sn hld up in midfield: effrt on inner and hrd rdn over 2f out: rchd 4th over 1f out: wl hld in 6th whn nowhere to go and heavily eased last 50yds* 14/1
134- 9 1 **Red Suede Shoes**28 7769 4-9-0 77 (p) JamesMillman(3) 7 71
(B R Millman) *racd wd thrght: hld up in rr: prog rnd outside of field bnd 4f out: no hdwy over 2f out: sn btn* 15/2
600- 10 1/2 **Grand Honour (IRE)**14 7876 4-8-6 66 PaulDoe 5 59
(P Howling) *hld up in last trio: shuffled along over 2f out: nvr nr ldrs* 66/1
503- 11 3/4 **Laafet**32 7734 5-8-12 72 JimmyQuinn 8 63
(K A Morgan) *prom 5f: wknd* 12/1
146- 12 5 **Spiritual Art**14 7883 4-9-0 74 (p) EddieAhern 11 53
(L A Dace) *a towards rr: rdn and wd in st: sn wknd* 16/1

1m 38.98s (-0.82) **Going Correction** -0.025s/f (Stan) 12 Ran SP% **123.2**
Speed ratings (Par 105): **103,102,101,101,99 99,98,97,96,96 95,90**
toteswingers: 1&2 £18.40, 1&3 £10.00, 2&3 £5.80 CSF £66.66 CT £465.49 TOTE £6.30: £2.80, £5.50, £4.40; EX 81.20 Place 6: £119.85 Place 5: £47.06.
Owner The St Cloud Partnership **Bred** Fintan Doran **Trained** Epsom, Surrey

FOCUS
A really competitive handicap run at a good pace. A fair race for the grade, and sound form.
Laafet Official explanation: jockey sasid gelding ran too freely
T/Jkpt: Not won. T/Plt: £155.60 to a £1 stake. Pool: £100,038.75. 469.32 winning tickets. T/Qpdt: £26.40 to a £1 stake. Pool: £9,504.48. 265.57 winning tickets. JN

132 LINGFIELD (L-H)
Wednesday, January 13
152 Meeting Abandoned - Snow

132 LINGFIELD (L-H)
Thursday, January 14
OFFICIAL GOING: Standard
Wind: Almost nil Weather: Very overcast, Foggy from Race 2 onwards

159 STAR RACING MEDIAN AUCTION MAIDEN FILLIES' STKS 7f (P)
1:30 (1:31) (Class 6) 3-5-Y-O £2,047 (£604; £302) Stalls Low

Form RPR
520- 1 **Kinky Afro (IRE)**103 6481 3-8-4 70 ow1 RossAtkinson(5) 1 65+
(J S Moore) *hld up: pushed along over 2f out: prog over 1f out: r.o to ld last 150yds: hrd rdn and hld on* 5/2[2]

63- **2** ½ **Red Yarn**[14] 7885 3-8-8 0 ShaneKelly 5 65
(G L Moore) *t.k.h early: hld up in 4th: rdn wl over 1f out: r.o to take 2nd last 100yds: clsng on wnr fin* **3/1**[3]

43- **3** 2½ **Perfect Secret**[24] 7829 4-9-12 0 LiamKeniry 3 62
(A M Balding) *trckd ldr: gng strly 2f out: led briefly wl over 1f out: sn rdn and fnd nil* **5/4**[1]

30-0 **4** nk **Emma Jean Lass (IRE)**[12] 9 3-8-8 60 (v[1]) PaulDoe 2 57
(P D Evans) *t.k.h early: chsd ldng pair: rdn on inner to ld over 1f out: hdd & wknd last 150yds* **20/1**

0- **5** 18 **Miss Polly Plum**[29] 7772 3-8-8 0 JerryO'Dwyer 4 8
(C A Dwyer) *led to wl over 1f out: wknd rapidly: t.o* **25/1**

1m 26.04s (1.24) **Going Correction** +0.025s/f (Slow)
WFA 3 from 4yo 18lb **5** Ran SP% **106.6**
Speed ratings (Par 98): **93,92,89,89,68**
toteswinger: 1&2:£3.80 CSF £9.58 TOTE £3.50: £1.40, £1.70; EX 8.30.
Owner Phil Cunningham **Bred** S Couldrige **Trained** Upper Lambourn, Berks

FOCUS
Fog made visibility very limited on certain parts of the track, with the runners only tending to come into view around 5f out, turning into the straight, and again inside the final furlong. They went a steady gallop in this opening contest and the form is muddling. The winner did not need to match her 2yo level.

160 OPEN A STAR RACING ACCOUNT 08000 521 321 H'CAP 1m (P)
2:00 (2:01) (Class 7) (0-50,50) 4-Y-0+ **£1,364** (£403; £201) **Stalls** High

Form RPR

050- **1** **Musashi (IRE)**[45] 7549 5-9-2 50 (b) IanMongan 11 61
(Mrs L J Mongan) *in rr 5f out and tl effrt 2f out: str run fnl f to ld last 100yds: sn clr* **9/2**[1]

050- **2** 2¼ **Copper King**[57] 7438 6-9-1 49 LiamKeniry 7 55
(Miss Tor Sturgis) *prom: rdn to dispute 3rd over 2f out: effrt on inner over 1f out: upsides ins fnl f: sn outpcd* **6/1**[2]

-664 **3** ½ **Louisiade (IRE)**[1] 145 9-8-6 45 (p) BillyCray(5) 1 50
(R C Guest) *mde most: hdd and outpcd last 100yds* **9/2**[1]

630- **4** 1½ **Inquisitress**[15] 7880 6-8-12 49 MarcHalford(3) 4 51
(J J Bridger) *mostly in midfield: 5th and pushed along over 2f out: kpt on ins fnl f* **7/1**[3]

365- **5** nk **Sweet Virginia (USA)**[286] 1106 4-8-13 47 (v[1]) AndrewElliott 6 48
(J R Weymes) *pressed ldr to jst over 1f out: wknd last 100yds* **12/1**

004- **6** nk **Easy Wonder (GER)**[15] 7880 5-8-4 45 (b) MatthewCosham(7) 9 45
(I A Wood) *wl in rr: effrt on outer 2f out: kpt on fnl f: n.d* **11/1**

60-0 **7** nse **Play Up Pompey**[5] 100 8-8-11 45 JerryO'Dwyer 10 45
(J J Bridger) *mostly last: stl there over 2f out: styd on fnl f: nrst fin* **10/1**

055- **8** 1 **Rainiers Girl**[39] 7653 4-8-5 46 KierenFox(7) 3 44
(R A Teal) *nvr bttr than midfield: struggling in rr over 2f out* **15/2**

000- **9** 3 **Supplementary (IRE)**[38] 7666 8-8-8 49 RichardRowe(7) 8 40
(M J Coombe) *chsng ldrs 5f out: wkng u.p over 2f out* **33/1**

410- **10** shd **Riviera Red (IRE)**[74] 7197 10-8-13 47 (v) FrannyNorton 5 38
(L Montague Hall) *prom: rdn to dispute 3rd over 2f out: wknd rapidly over 1f out: eased nr fin* **10/1**

1m 37.44s (-0.76) **Going Correction** +0.025s/f (Slow) **10** Ran SP% **112.1**
Speed ratings (Par 97): **104,101,101,99,99 99,99,98,95,95**
toteswinger:1&2:£6.50, 2&3:£6.90, 1&3:£5.50 CSF £29.64 CT £128.92 TOTE £5.00: £1.60, £2.80, £1.90; EX 36.00.
Owner Mrs P J Sheen **Bred** Corduff Stud & J Corcorcan **Trained** Epsom, Surrey

FOCUS
The runners weren't in view for much of this contest, with the fog appearing to have thickened. This was a weak handicap. The form is rated around the second and third, the winner taking advantage of a falling mark.

161 STAR RACING - BOOKMAKERS OF DISTINCTION MEDIAN AUCTION MAIDEN STKS 1m (P)
2:30 (2:31) (Class 6) 3-5-Y-0 **£2,047** (£604; £302) **Stalls** High

Form RPR

305/ **1** **Noble Jack (IRE)**[456] 6737 4-10-0 77 LiamKeniry 3 67
(G L Moore) *chsng ldng pair 5f out: disputing 3rd and drvn 2f out: led ins fnl f: styd on* **1/1**[1]

2 1 **Takajan (IRE)**[121] 6084 3-8-8 76 RichardKingscote 7 60
(S Kirk) *5th 5f out: rdn on wd outside 2f out: styd on to take 2nd wl ins fnl f* **7/2**[3]

060- **3** ½ **New Den**[16] 7865 3-8-8 59 NickyMackay 1 59
(J R Boyle) *cl 2nd 5f out: led and drvn 2f out: hdd and one pce ins fnl f* **16/1**

4 ¾ **Peadar Miguel** 3-8-8 0 JerryO'Dwyer 2 57
(M G Quinlan) *cl 4th 5f out and 2f out where gng wl: effrt over 1f out: nt qckn* **3/1**[2]

4 **5** nk **Oceans Edge**[12] 9 4-10-0 0 StephenCraine 4 60
(J R Boyle) *last 5f out and 2f out where looking for room: keeping on same pce last 100yds* **11/1**

00- **6** 17 **Lunaticus**[24] 7829 4-9-2 0 KierenFox(7) 6 15
(M J Attwater) *narrow ld 5f out: stl cl 2nd 2f out: wknd rapidly: t.o* **100/1**

1m 38.53s (0.33) **Going Correction** +0.025s/f (Slow)
WFA 3 from 4yo 20lb **6** Ran SP% **112.4**
Speed ratings (Par 101): **99,98,97,96,96 79**
toteswinger:1&2:£1.50, 2&3:£6.40, 1&3:£4.00 CSF £4.87 TOTE £1.80: £1.50, £1.30; EX 4.50.
Owner M K George **Bred** Team Hogdala **Trained** Lower Beeding, W Sussex

FOCUS
Visibility continued to worsen. This was just a low-grade maiden but the first two set a fair standard. With the pace steady neither of the front pair were close to their best.

162 FRIENDLY AND PERSONAL SERVICE AT STAR RACING H'CAP 1m 2f (P)
3:00 (3:01) (Class 5) (0-70,68) 4-Y-0+ **£2,590** (£770; £385; £192) **Stalls** Low

Form RPR

50-3 **1** **Formidable Guest**[12] 12 6-9-6 67 SaleemGolam 9 73
(J Pearce) *hld up: in rr 1/2-way: impr into 2nd 2f out: in ld ins fnl f: jst hld on* **11/2**[3]

445- **2** hd **Carr Hall (IRE)**[14] 7888 7-8-6 53 oh3 RichardKingscote 5 59
(B G Powell) *hld up: effrt on wd outside to dispute 5th 2f out: r.o to take 2nd ins fnl f: jst failed* **6/1**

0-04 **3** ¾ **Vinces**[6] 83 6-9-2 63 HayleyTurner 7 68
(T D McCarthy) *hld up: effrt on outer and disputing 5th 2f out: styng on fnl f: jst outpcd* **9/2**[1]

00-0 **4** 1¼ **Naheell**[6] 83 4-9-2 65 AmirQuinn 6 67
(G Prodromou) *trcking ldr 1/2-way: in ld over 2f out: hdd and wkng ins fnl f* **16/1**

251- **5** 1½ **Pyrus Time (IRE)**[36] 7694 4-9-5 68 LiamKeniry 1 67
(J S Moore) *hld up: disputing 5th and urged along 2f out: no prog* **13/2**

42-6 **6** 3 **Hector Spectre (IRE)**[12] 12 4-9-1 64 (p) PaulDoe 4 57
(P D Evans) *chsd ldrs: drvn to dispute 2nd 2f out: wkng fnl f* **15/2**

503- **7** 6 **Coral Shores**[40] 7641 5-8-13 60 (v) JimCrowley 2 41
(P W Hiatt) *ldng early and at 1/2-way: detached in 8th and wkng 2f out* **16/1**

8 2 **Chaninbar (FR)**[15] 7-9-1 62 FrannyNorton 8 39
(M F Harris) *led to post: a in rr: rdn in 8th 1/2-way: detached in last 2f out* **5/1**[2]

3-46 **9** 19 **Marmooq**[6] 83 7-9-3 64 IanMongan 3 3
(M J Attwater) *mostly chsng ldng pair: stl 4th 2f out: wknd rapidly: lame* **9/1**

2m 5.13s (-1.47) **Going Correction** +0.025s/f (Slow)
WFA 4 from 5yo+ 2lb **9** Ran SP% **111.4**
Speed ratings (Par 103): **106,105,105,104,103 100,95,94,79**
toteswinger:1&2:£5.80, 2&3:£4.60, 1&3:£5.10 CSF £36.38 CT £155.55 TOTE £6.40: £1.80, £2.30, £1.60; EX 35.70.
Owner Macniler Racing Partnership **Bred** Kingwood Bloodstock **Trained** Newmarket, Suffolk

FOCUS
Visibility was poor again in this moderate handicap. Straightforward form, the winner rated back to her best.

163 STAR RACING CREDIT AND DEBIT ACCOUNTS CONDITIONS STKS 6f (P)
3:30 (3:30) (Class 3) 4-Y-0+ **£7,123** (£2,119; £1,059; £529) **Stalls** Low

Form RPR

015- **1** **Arganil (USA)**[54] 7488 5-9-2 108 NeilCallan 4 73+
(K A Ryan) *trckd ldr: rdn and wd bnd 2f out: led over 1f out: drvn out: jst hld on* **4/11**[1]

62-2 **2** hd **Aeroplane**[5] 109 7-8-11 102 (p) RichardEvans(5) 2 72+
(P D Evans) *hld up last: gng wl 2f out: effrt on inner sn after: urged along to press wnr last 100yds: jst failed* **3/1**[2]

45-1 **3** 1¼ **Indian Skipper (IRE)**[1] 150 5-8-11 82 (be) BillyCray(5) 3 68+
(R C Guest) *hld up in 3rd: rdn and carried wd bnd 2f out: kpt on same pce* **12/1**[3]

1-03 **4** 1 **Sherjawy (IRE)**[2] 137 6-8-11 56 RossAtkinson(5) 5 65
(Miss Z C Davison) *led: rdn over 2f out: hdd and outpcd over 1f out* **100/1**

1m 11.48s (-0.42) **Going Correction** +0.025s/f (Slow) **4** Ran SP% **107.0**
Speed ratings (Par 107): **103,102,101,99**
CSF £1.68 TOTE £1.30; EX 1.60.
Owner The Big Moment **Bred** The Big Moment **Trained** Hambleton, N Yorks

FOCUS
A good conditions race, but the pace was steady and the form is muddling, limited by the fourth.

NOTEBOOK
Arganil(USA), only fifth when favourite for a Listed race at the course in November, had just the one rival to worry about on ratings, but didn't win in the manner his odds entitled him to. He is probably best at 5f, though, and can show himself better than the bare form. He is likely to head for the Dubai Carnival. (op 2-5 tchd 4-9 and 1-2 in a place)
Aeroplane has been doing all his running over 7f and 1m of late, but he has always had a touch of class and really made the winner earn his victory. He may well have won in another couple of strides and can pick up a race when stepped back up in trip and down in grade. (op 11-4 tchd 10-3)
Indian Skipper(IRE), a winner at Kempton the previous day, had plenty to find with the front pair at the weights and ran about as well as could have been expected. (op 11-1 tchd 10-1)
Sherjawy(IRE), rated just 56, had no chance against these at the weights and did well to finish as close as he did, though there is no doubting he was flattered having made the running. (op 150-1)

164 MONEY BACK IF BEAT A SHORT HEAD H'CAP 2m (P)
4:00 (4:01) (Class 6) (0-65,65) 4-Y-0+ **£2,047** (£604; £302) **Stalls** Low

Form RPR

160- **1** **Purely By Chance**[31] 7750 5-8-13 50 (b) SaleemGolam 6 58
(J Pearce) *trckd ldng pair after 6f: rdn to ld 2f out: styd on* **12/1**

450- **2** 2 **Honorable Endeavor**[40] 7635 4-8-9 53 LiamKeniry 7 58
(E F Vaughan) *hld up towards rr: stl more in front than bhd 2f out: gd prog after: tk 2nd nr fin* **10/1**

003/ **3** hd **Hampton Court**[32] 1205 5-9-6 57 IanMongan 3 62
(J W Mullins) *prom: rdn in 5th 2f out: styd on ins fnl f* **40/1**

140- **4** nk **Prince Charlemagne (IRE)**[28] 7785 7-10-0 65 StephenCraine 12 70
(G L Moore) *hld up in last quartet: drvn on outer and stl in rr 2f out: styd on after: nrst fin* **7/2**[1]

256- **5** 1½ **Acropolis (IRE)**[14] 7888 9-9-4 55 VinceSlattery 8 58
(B G Powell) *mostly in midfield: in rr of main gp 2f out and u.p: styd on fnl f* **9/1**[3]

000- **6** 1 **Yonder**[46] 5802 6-9-11 65 (t) PatrickHills(3) 1 67
(H Morrison) *hld up in midfield on inner: rdn and stl in midfield 2f out: kpt on* **16/1**

006- **7** nk **Empire Seeker (USA)**[136] 4538 5-8-10 47 (t) PaulDoe 10 48
(Mrs H S Main) *racd wd: hld up in rr: drvn on wd outside 2f out: no prog fnl f* **33/1**

4/6- **8** ½ **Sarando**[33] 126 5-9-13 64 (t) RichardKingscote 5 65
(P R Webber) *led 6f: styd prom: upsides 2f out: wknd* **16/1**

061/ **9** ¾ **Kentmere (IRE)**[42] 3304 9-10-0 65 HayleyTurner 2 65
(P R Webber) *prom: drvn and stl disputing 3rd 2f out: wknd* **20/1**

003- **10** ½ **Spiritonthemount (USA)**[15] 7873 5-8-10 52 (b) TobyAtkinson(5) 13 51
(P W Hiatt) *hld up in last quartet: drvn on wd outside and effrt 2f out: no prog after* **12/1**

240- **11** ½ **Lady Pilot**[66] 6188 8-9-11 65 RobertLButler(3) 11 64
(Jim Best) *hld up in last quartet: rdn and struggling in midfield on inner 2f out: wknd* **16/1**

430- **12** 1½ **Kristallo (GER)**[42] 3788 5-9-7 58 FrannyNorton 9 55
(P R Webber) *led after 6f: drvn and hdd 2f out: wknd rapidly* **11/1**

263- **13** ¾ **Tribe**[33] 3986 8-9-10 61 JimCrowley 4 57
(P R Webber) *hld up and mostly last: no ch 2f out* **8/1**[2]

335- **14** 9 **Colourful Move**[31] 7750 5-8-12 49 (t) NeilCallan 14 34
(P G Murphy) *t.k.h in midfield: rdn and wkng rapidly 2f out* **7/2**[1]

3m 25.33s (-0.37) **Going Correction** +0.025s/f (Slow)
WFA 4 from 5yo+ 7lb **14** Ran SP% **126.2**
Speed ratings (Par 101): **101,100,99,99,99 98,98,98,97,97 97,96,96,91**
toteswinger:1&2:£22.10, 2&3:£99.70, 1&3:£59.00 CSF £130.66 CT £4654.28 TOTE £16.60: £4.20, £3.20, £7.50; EX 195.70 Place 6 £74.39, Place 5 £27.69.
Owner Lady Green **Bred** Lady Jennifer Green **Trained** Newmarket, Suffolk

FOCUS
They appeared to go no more than a steady gallop, but the runners didn't emerge from the gloom until deep inside the final furlong. Muddling form.
T/Plt: £134.80 to a £1 stake. Pool: £74,841.68. 405.05 winning tickets. T/Qpdt: £43.70 to a £1 stake. Pool: £6,122.21. 103.65 winning tickets. JN

[138]SOUTHWELL (L-H)
Thursday, January 14

OFFICIAL GOING: Slow
Wind: Virtually nil Weather: Dull but dry

165 BET TEST MATCH CRICKET - BETDAQ APPRENTICE CLASSIFIED CLAIMING STKS 5f (F)
12:50 (12:50) (Class 6) 4-Y-O+ £1,774 (£523; £262) Stalls High

Form RPR
60-2 1 **Monte Major (IRE)**[2] 138 9-8-3 58 (v) MartinLane(3) 4 67
(D Shaw) *cl up: rdn to ld over 1f out: drvn ins fnl f: edgd lft and kpt on wl towards fin* **8/1**
55-4 2 ½ **Bo McGinty (IRE)**[2] 138 9-8-3 64 ow1 (v) LeeTopliss(5) 3 67
(R A Fahey) *trckd ldrs: hdwy 1/2-way: rdn and cl up over 1f out: ev ch tl drvn and nt qckn nr fin* **5/2**[2]
060- 3 2½ **Cornus**[27] 7795 8-8-9 65 (be) DavidProbert 2 59
(J A Glover) *in tch on outer: hdwy 1/2-way: rdn and ev ch over 1f out: edgd rt and kpt on same pce ins fnl f* **14/1**
212- 4 hd **Grudge**[18] 7852 5-8-9 66 (e) WilliamCarson 6 58
(Ollie Pears) *led: rdn 2f out: hdd over 1f out: sn edgd rt and wknd ins fnl f* **2/1**[1]
006- 5 2¾ **Ingleby Star (IRE)**[30] 7758 5-8-4 68 (p) PaulPickard(3) 5 47
(N Wilson) *chsd ldrs: rdn along wl over 1f out: drvn and n.m.r appr fnl f: sn wknd* **4/1**[3]
000- 6 5 **Guto**[47] 7577 7-9-0 69 KellyHarrison 9 36
(W J H Ratcliffe) *chsd ldrs: rdn along over 2f out: wknd wl over 1f out* **10/1**

60.50 secs (0.80) **Going Correction** +0.05s/f (Slow) 6 Ran SP% **108.8**
Speed ratings (Par 101): **95,94,90,89,85 77**
toteswinger:1&2:£4.40, 2&3:£4.80, 1&3:£8.80 CSF £26.50 TOTE £7.70: £3.20, £1.90; EX 27.50 Trifecta £81.00 Pool: £389.78 - 3.56 winning units..
Owner Derek Shaw **Bred** B Kennedy **Trained** Sproxton, Leics

FOCUS
A weak event. The winner, who confirmed form with the runner-up from two days earlier, is probably the best guide.
Ingleby Star(IRE) Official explanation: jockey said gelding was denied a clear run

166 BET IN RUNNING - BETDAQ MAIDEN STKS 1m 3f (F)
1:20 (1:21) (Class 5) 4-Y-O+ £2,456 (£725; £362) Stalls Low

Form RPR
340- 1 **Ask The Oracle**[38] 7665 4-9-3 62 RobertWinston 8 68
(H Morrison) *led 3f: cl up: effrt over 2f out and sn rdn: drvn over 1f out: kpt on u.p to ld ins fnl f: drvn out* **15/8**[1]
55- 2 ¾ **Dubai Creek (IRE)**[29] 6673 4-9-3 0 PaulHanagan 4 67
(D McCain Jnr) *trckd ldrs: hdwy 4f out: rdn to chse ldng pair over 2f out: drvn over 1f out: kpt on u.p ins fnl f* **7/1**
333- 3 1 **Laureldeans Best (IRE)**[40] 7648 4-8-12 65 TonyHamilton 10 60
(R A Fahey) *cl up: led after 3f: rdn along over 2f out: marginal ld and drvn over 1f out: hdd and no ex ins fnl f* **11/2**[3]
63- 4 8 **Sure Fire (GER)**[33] 7725 5-9-6 0 TomQueally 9 51
(B J Curley) *chsd ldrs: rdn along and outpcd 4f out: drvn and kpt on fnl 2f* **9/2**[2]
5 shd **Railway Park (IRE)**[34] 6-9-6 0 (v[1]) PaddyAspell 1 51
(J S Wainwright) *in tch: hdwy to chse ldrs 1/2-way: rdn along over 3f out: drvn over 2f out and plugged on same pce* **80/1**
4 6 1¾ **Haka Dancer (USA)**[12] 18 7-9-6 0 LeeVickers 3 48
(P A Kirby) *chsd ldrs: rdn along 4f out and sn outpcd: swtchd markedly rt to wd outside 2f out: plugged on* **14/1**
- 7 2 **Try Cat** 4-8-12 0 StevieDonohoe 7 40
(Sir Mark Prescott) *dwlt: a in rr* **7/1**
8 1½ **Miss Ghena (USA)**[48] 7563 4-8-12 55 DavidNolan 5 37
(D Carroll) *hld up towards rr: hdwy 1/2-way: chsd ldrs 4f out: rdn along over 3f out: sn drvn and wknd* **14/1**
0/6- 9 38 **Oniz Tiptoes (IRE)**[34] 4806 9-9-1 43 (v) BarryMcHugh(5) 2 —
(J S Wainwright) *chsd ldrs: rdn along 1/2-way: sn lost pl and bhd* **28/1**

2m 30.77s (2.77) **Going Correction** -0.025s/f (Stan)
WFA 4 from 5yo+ 3lb 9 Ran SP% **111.4**
Speed ratings (Par 103): **88,87,86,80,80 79,78,77,49**
toteswinger:1&2:£5.30, 2&3:£7.80, 1&3:£3.10 CSF £14.61 TOTE £2.40: £1.10, £2.60, £1.70; EX 14.30 Trifecta £93.30 Pool: £539.70 - 4.28 winning units..
Owner Exors of the Late Miss B Swire **Bred** Miss B Swire **Trained** East Ilsley, Berks

FOCUS
A modest maiden, run at a fair pace. The winner is probably the best guide to the form.

167 BETDAQ POKER H'CAP 5f (F)
1:50 (1:51) (Class 6) (0-60,62) 3-Y-O £1,774 (£523; £262) Stalls High

Form RPR
63-1 1 **Boogie Waltzer**[5] 111 3-9-6 62 6ex WilliamCarson(3) 2 70+
(S C Williams) *trckd ldrs: hdwy wl over 1f out: sn rdn: drvn and styd on ins fnl f to ld nr line* **9/4**[1]
54-5 2 ½ **Lady Brickhouse**[9] 43 3-8-2 46 PaulPickard(5) 3 52
(M D Squance) *sltly hmpd s and sn swtchd lft to outer: hdwy 1/2-way: led 1 1/2f out: sn rdn and edgd lft: drvn and hung bdly lft ins fnl f: hdd and no ex nr line* **7/1**
002- 3 nk **Turf Time**[28] 7778 3-8-9 48 RobertWinston 5 53
(J A Glover) *chsd ldrs: rdn wl over 1f out: drvn and kpt on ins fnl f* **4/1**[3]
30-0 4 1¼ **Lets Move It**[9] 43 3-8-7 46 (v) DavidProbert 4 46
(D Shaw) *wnt lft s: led to 1/2-way: cl up: rdn wl over 1f out and grad wknd ins fnl f* **25/1**
634- 5 1½ **Caol Ila (IRE)**[28] 7778 3-9-3 56 TomQueally 1 51
(J G Given) *cl up: led 1/2-way: rdn and hdd 1 1/2f out: wknd ins fnl f* **8/1**
055- 6 2¼ **Lairy (IRE)**[30] 7757 3-8-6 45 (v[1]) JamieMackay 6 32
(M F Harris) *a towards rr* **16/1**
204- 7 3½ **Gower Sophia**[31] 7748 3-8-11 57 (v) JohnCavanagh(7) 7 31
(M Brittain) *cl up: rdn along 2f out: sn drvn and wknd* **14/1**
602- 8 5 **Ya Boy Sir (IRE)**[30] 7757 3-9-0 53 JimmyQuinn 8 9
(N Wilson) *sn one pce and bhd fr 1/2-way* **10/3**[2]

61.15 secs (1.45) **Going Correction** +0.05s/f (Slow) 8 Ran SP% **113.9**
Speed ratings (Par 95): **90,89,88,86,84 80,75,67**
toteswinger:1&2:£5.80, 2&3:£7.50, 1&3:£3.30 CSF £18.53 CT £58.80 TOTE £3.10: £1.10, £2.70, £2.00; EX 22.10 Trifecta £70.40 Pool: £672.97 - 7.07 winning units..
Owner Michael Edwards and John Parsons **Bred** Michael Edwards And John Parsons **Trained** Newmarket, Suffolk
■ Stewards' Enquiry : Paul Pickard one-day ban: used whip in incorrect place (Jan 28)
David Probert caution: used whip with excessive frequency.

FOCUS
A poor 3yo sprint ,but probably reasonable form for the grade. The winner is perhaps a bit better than the bare form suggests.

168 BOOK TICKETS ON LINE AT SOUTHWELL-RACECOURSE.CO.UK (S) STKS 7f (F)
2:20 (2:20) (Class 6) 3-Y-O £1,774 (£523; £262) Stalls Low

Form RPR
31-2 1 **Inside Track (IRE)**[13] 5 3-9-4 72 (b) TonyCulhane 6 71
(P T Midgley) *led: rdn along and hdd wl over 1f out: hmpd and swtchd rt over 1f out: sn drvn and styd on ins fnl f to ld nr line* **9/4**[2]
212- 2 nk **Bubbly Bellini (IRE)**[16] 7868 3-8-13 75 (p) MatthewDavies(5) 2 70+
(George Baker) *trckd ldrs: hdwy and cl up 3f out: led wl over 1f out: rdn and hung bdly lft over 1f out: drvn ins fnl f: hdd nr line* **11/8**[1]
3-23 3 2¾ **Tamarind Hill (IRE)**[6] 85 3-8-7 68 (b) DeclanCannon(5) 4 57
(A J McCabe) *trckd ldrs: hdwy to chse ldng pair 3f out and sn rdn: drvn over 1f out and kpt on same pce* **10/3**[3]
62-4 4 3½ **Clayton Flick (IRE)**[9] 43 3-8-12 54 PaulHanagan 3 47
(A B Haynes) *in tch: hdwy to chse ldrs 3f out: rdn over 2f out and no imp* **20/1**
40-3 5 3½ **Hubble Space**[13] 5 3-8-7 58 (p) JimmyQuinn 5 33
(M Botti) *in tch: sn rdn along and outpcd fr 1/2-way* **9/1**
000- 6 38 **Petit Belle**[48] 7556 3-8-7 25 DavidProbert 1 —
(N P Littmoden) *cl up on inner: rdn along bef 1/2-way: sn wknd and bhd* **100/1**

1m 31.59s (1.29) **Going Correction** -0.025s/f (Stan) 6 Ran SP% **111.7**
Speed ratings (Par 95): **91,90,87,83,79 36**
toteswinger:1&2:£1.70, 2&3:£1.90, 1&3:£1.80 CSF £5.67 TOTE £3.70: £2.10, £1.10; EX 6.40.There was no bid for the winner
Owner P T Midgley **Bred** Round Hill Stud **Trained** Westow, N Yorks

FOCUS
Another weak event in which winner would have been second had the runner-up not hung fire. The winner looks the best guide to the form.

169 WIN WHATEVER THE RESULT WITH BET ANGEL H'CAP 1m (F)
2:50 (2:50) (Class 5) (0-70,69) 4-Y-O+ £2,456 (£725; £362) Stalls Low

Form RPR
60-1 1 **Camerooney**[13] 7 7-7-13 55 oh1 DeclanCannon(5) 2 64
(B Ellison) *mde all: rdn over 2f out: drvn and edgd rt ent fnl f: kep on gamely* **9/2**[2]
64-1 2 ¾ **Miss Bootylishes**[12] 19 5-8-13 69 AmyBaker(5) 8 76
(A B Haynes) *prom: hdwy and cl up over 2f out: rdn wl over 1f out: n.m.r and swtchd lft ent fnl f: sn drvn and kpt on* **5/1**[3]
133- 3 shd **Vertigo On Course (IRE)**[78] 7113 5-8-9 60 PaulHanagan 7 67
(R A Fahey) *hld up in tch: hdwy over 2f out: rdn to chse ldrs over 1f out: drvn ins fnl f and kpt on: nrst fin* **5/1**[3]
00-3 4 3½ **General Tufto**[9] 40 5-8-9 65 (b) PaulPickard(5) 5 64
(C Smith) *dwlt and in rr: hdwy on outer 3f out: rdn along 2f out: drvn to chse ldrs over 1f out: kpt on same pce* **7/1**
55-3 5 ¾ **Bajan Pride**[13] 7 6-7-11 55 oh1 (v) TimothyAyres(7) 4 52
(R A Fahey) *trckd ldrs: hdwy 3f out: rdn 2f out and ch tl drvn and wknd appr fnl f* **9/1**
0-22 6 1 **Special Cuvee**[6] 87 4-8-9 60 (b[1]) StevieDonohoe 3 55
(A B Haynes) *dwlt: a in rr* **7/2**[1]
33-3 7 3 **Tobrata**[7] 73 4-8-12 63 RobertWinston 6 51
(M Brittain) *prom: rdn along wl over 2f out: drvn wl over 1f out: grad wknd* **9/1**
500- 8 2 **Miss Christophene (IRE)**[125] 5329 4-9-3 68 AndrewMullen 1 51
(Mrs S Lamyman) *dwlt: sn chsng ldrs on inner: rdn along 3f out: wknd 2f out* **18/1**

1m 42.87s (-0.83) **Going Correction** -0.025s/f (Stan) 8 Ran SP% **111.5**
Speed ratings (Par 103): **103,102,102,98,97 96,93,91**
toteswinger:1&2:£5.00, 2&3:£3.90, 1&3:£5.90 CSF £25.76 CT £113.11 TOTE £5.90: £1.30, £2.40, £1.90; EX 30.20 Trifecta £114.60 Pool: £389.00 - 2.51 winning units..
Owner Mrs Jean Stapleton **Bred** Miss Dianne Hill **Trained** Norton, N Yorks

FOCUS
An open handicap, run at a fair pace. Ordinary but sound form.

170 FREEBETS.CO.UK FREE BETS H'CAP 7f (F)
3:20 (3:20) (Class 5) (0-75,71) 4-Y-O+ £2,456 (£725; £362) Stalls Low

Form RPR
4-41 1 **Transmission (IRE)**[6] 87 5-9-5 71 6ex JoeFanning 5 80
(B Smart) *trckd ldrs: hdwy over 2f out: led wl over 1f out: rdn clr ent fnl f: kpt on strly* **3/1**[2]
1-32 2 4½ **Whitbarrow (IRE)**[2] 144 11-9-0 69 (b) JamesMillman(3) 6 66
(B R Millman) *chsd ldrs on outer: hdwy 2f out: rdn and edgd lft over 1f out: kpt on u.p fnl f* **10/3**[3]
2-45 3 hd **Jonnie Skull (IRE)**[4] 115 4-9-1 67 (vt) RobertWinston 4 63
(P S McEntee) *cl up: led 1/2-way: rdn over 2f out: hdd wl over 1f out: sn drvn and one pce* **7/1**
0-53 4 1 **Premier Lad**[2] 144 4-8-13 65 PhillipMakin 3 59
(T D Barron) *led to 1/2-way: rdn and cl up tl drvn wl over 1f out and sn btn* **6/4**[1]
00-3 5 5 **Tidal Force (USA)**[6] 87 4-8-3 60 (p) DeclanCannon(5) 1 40
(A J McCabe) *chsd ldrs: rdn along 3f out: wknd over 2f out* **25/1**
20-0 6 12 **Madison Belle**[2] 144 4-8-13 70 BarryMcHugh(5) 2 18
(J R Weymes) *a in rr: outpcd and bhd fr over 2f out* **20/1**

1m 29.25s (-1.05) **Going Correction** -0.025s/f (Stan) 6 Ran SP% **109.2**
Speed ratings (Par 103): **105,99,99,98,92 79**
toteswinger:1&2:£2.00, 2&3:£3.60, 1&3:£2.70 CSF £12.56 TOTE £3.50: £1.50, £2.40; EX 12.50.
Owner M Barber **Bred** M J Halligan **Trained** Hambleton, N Yorks

FOCUS
A modest handicap in which all six of the runners had appeared at Southwell within the previous six days. The winner produced a clear personal bdest and there seemed no fluke.
Whitbarrow(IRE) Official explanation: jockey said gelding was slowly away

171 SOUTHWELL-RACECOURSE.CO.UK H'CAP 6f (F)
3:50 (3:50) (Class 6) (0-65,65) 4-Y-O+ £1,774 (£523; £262) Stalls Low

Form RPR
01-0 1 **Ponting (IRE)**[12] 20 4-8-10 62 PaulPickard(5) 5 72
(P T Midgley) *mde all: rdn and edgd lft wl over 1f out: drvn and hung lft ent fnl f: kpt on wl* **11/2**
04-4 2 1¼ **Not My Choice (IRE)**[12] 20 5-9-0 61 (t) TomQueally 6 67
(J Balding) *trckd ldng pair: hdwy to chse wnr over 2f out: rdn wl over 1f out: drvn and ch ent fnl f: no imp last 100yds* **9/4**[1]

005- **3** 3 1/4 **Elijah Pepper (USA)**[33] 7735 5-9-1 **62**.................. PhillipMakin 7 58
(T D Barron) *in tch: hdwy on outer 1/2-way: rdn along over 2f out: sn drvn and no imp appr fnl f* **7/2**[2]
506- **4** 2 **Restless Genius (IRE)**[16] 7870 5-8-10 **62**............(e[1]) BarryMcHugh[(5)] 4 51
(B Ellison) *in tch: hdwy 1/2-way: rdn to chse ldrs over 2f out: sn drvn and btn over 1f out* **4/1**[3]
5-60 **5** 4 **Kheskianto (IRE)**[10] 34 4-8-7 **54**.................. DavidProbert 3 30
(M C Chapman) *sltly hmpd s: a in rr* **25/1**
000- **6** 3/4 **He's A Humbug (IRE)**[40] 7643 6-9-4 **65**.................. TonyCulhane 1 39
(J O'Reilly) *in tch: hdwy to chse ldrs 1/2-way: sn rdn along and wknd over 2f out* **14/1**
20-2 **7** *hd* **Mango Music**[9] 37 7-8-12 **59**.................. StevieDonohoe 2 32
(M Quinn) *chsd wnr on inner: rdn along 1/2-way: drvn wl over 2f out and sn wknd* **6/1**

1m 15.73s (-0.77) **Going Correction** -0.025s/f (Stan) **7** Ran SP% **113.2**
Speed ratings (Par 101): **104,102,98,95,90 89,88**
toteswinger:1&2:£3.40, 2&3:£2.70, 1&3:£4.60 CSF £17.92 TOTE £8.10: £3.00, £1.80; EX 21.70 Place 6 £25.37, Place 5 £10.06.
Owner A Taylor Jnr **Bred** John McEnery **Trained** Westow, N Yorks

FOCUS
A moderate handicap, run at a solid pace set by the winner. He is rated back to his best and the form seems sound enough.
T/Plt: £33.10 to a £1 stake. Pool: £70,745.74. 1,559.53 winning tickets. T/Qpdt: £5.60 to a £1 stake. Pool: £6,332.81. 832.30 winning tickets. JR

125 WOLVERHAMPTON (A.W) (L-H)

Thursday, January 14

OFFICIAL GOING: Standard
Wind: Nil Weather: Misty becoming foggy for 6.40 and 7.10

172 BET AFRICAN NATIONS CUP - BETDAQ H'CAP 5f 20y(P)

4:10 (4:10) (Class 4) (0-85,85) 4-Y-0+ **£4,415** (£1,321; £660; £330; £164) **Stalls** Low

Form RPR
140- **1** **Rocket Rob (IRE)**[124] 5871 4-8-13 **83**.................. AndreaAtzeni[(3)] 7 92
(M Botti) *hld up in mid-div: hdwy 2f out: rdn to ld 1f out: drvn out* **4/1**[2]
021- **2** *hd* **Excellent Show**[15] 7872 4-9-0 **81**.................. TomEaves 5 89
(B Smart) *led early: w ldr: led 2f out: edgd rt over 1f out: sn rdn and hdd: r.o* **7/2**[1]
000- **3** 1 1/4 **Peak District (IRE)**[16] 7866 6-9-4 **85**.................. JamieSpencer 11 89
(K A Ryan) *swtchd lft sn after s: hld up in rr: hdwy whn swtchd rt 1f out: hrd rdn and kpt on towards fin* **8/1**[3]
61-6 **4** 1 1/4 **Green Park (IRE)**[7] 71 7-8-2 **76**..................(b) NeilFarley[(7)] 2 75
(D Carroll) *hld up towards rr: hdwy on ins wl over 1f out: rdn and one pce ins fnl f* **14/1**
00-1 **5** 1/2 **Argentine (IRE)**[7] 74 6-8-11 **78** 6ex..................(b) J-PGuillambert 4 75
(J A McShane) *hld up in tch: rdn over 1f out: one pce* **8/1**[3]
66-5 **6** 1/2 **Canadian Danehill (IRE)**[13] 2 8-9-4 **85**.........(p) GrahamGibbons 10 80
(R M H Cowell) *hld up towards rr: rdn over 1f out: nvr trbld ldrs* **20/1**
123- **7** 2 1/2 **Perlachy**[41] 7634 6-8-1 **71** 0h5..................(v) KellyHarrison[(3)] 9 57
(J R Holt) *hld up in tch: pushed along over 2f out: c wd st: rdn over 1f out: wknd ins fnl f* **16/1**
23-6 **8** *shd* **Garstang**[7] 74 7-8-10 **77**..................(b) JackMitchell 3 63
(J Balding) *prom: ev ch over 1f out: rdn and wknd ins fnl f* **11/1**
604- **9** 8 **Stolt (IRE)**[30] 7758 6-8-13 **80**..................(p) EddieAhern 1 37
(N Wilson) *sn led: hdd 2f out: rdn and wknd wl over 1f out: eased ins fnl f* **4/1**[2]

61.28 secs (-1.02) **Going Correction** +0.075s/f (Slow) **9** Ran SP% **110.1**
Speed ratings (Par 105): **111,110,108,106,105 105,101,100,88**
toteswinger:1&2:£3.50, 2&3:£4.50, 1&3:£8.20 CSF £16.97 CT £97.82 TOTE £4.60: £2.20, £1.60, £1.90; EX 13.70.
Owner Bill Hinge, J Searchfield & N Callaghan **Bred** Mrs Marita Rogers **Trained** Newmarket, Suffolk

FOCUS
A competitive handicap run at a sound gallop. The first three all have something to recommend them and this promises to be solid form, with the first two progressive.

173 HOTEL & CONFERENCING AT WOLVERHAMPTON H'CAP 1m 5f 194y(P)

4:40 (4:41) (Class 5) (0-70,67) 4-Y-0+ **£2,729** (£806; £403) **Stalls** Low

Form RPR
123- **1** **Leyte Gulf (USA)**[37] 7675 7-9-6 **64**.................. AdamKirby 5 72+
(C C Bealby) *hld up: rdn and hdwy over 1f out: led ins fnl f: rdn out* **11/4**[1]
310- **2** 3/4 **Calculating (IRE)**[16] 7867 6-9-4 **67**.................. LeeNewnes[(5)] 6 72
(M D I Usher) *a.p: rdn over 2f out: led jst over 1f out: hdd ins fnl f: nt qckn* **13/2**
3/5- **3** 1 1/4 **Accompanist**[28] 7785 7-9-3 **66**..................(p) AndrewHeffernan[(5)] 4 69+
(T G McCourt, Ire) *hld up in tch: rdn 2f out: nt clr run briefly jst over 1f out: nt clr run and swtchd rt ins fnl f: styd on to take 3rd cl home* **9/1**
431- **4** *hd* **Elite Land**[40] 6102 7-9-2 **65**.................. AmyRyan[(5)] 3 68
(B Ellison) *hld up towards rr: pushed along over 2f out: swtchd rt wl over 1f out: styd on u.p wl ins fnl f* **4/1**[3]
0/0- **5** *nse* **Estate**[35] 7701 8-9-9 **67**.................. JamieSpencer 8 70
(D E Pipe) *stdd s: hld up in rr: pushed along over 2f out: rdn and hdwy over 1f out: styd on one pce ins fnl f* **11/1**
334- **6** 3/4 **Zuwaar**[30] 7760 5-9-9 **67**..................(tp) EddieAhern 2 69
(Ian Williams) *sn led: rdn and edgd rt whn hdd jst over 1f out: one pce* **7/2**[2]
7 9 **Heredias (GER)**[29] 4-8-11 **66**..................(v[1]) MatthewDavies[(5)] 9 55
(George Baker) *led early: chsd ldr: rdn over 2f out: wknd wl over 1f out* **20/1**

3m 12.53s (6.53) **Going Correction** +0.075s/f (Slow)
WFA 4 from 5yo+ 6lb **7** Ran SP% **105.3**
Speed ratings (Par 103): **84,83,82,82,82 82,77**
toteswinger:1&2:£2.70, 2&3:£5.90, 1&3:£4.70 CSF £17.47 CT £108.20 TOTE £3.50: £1.70, £2.50; EX 17.90.
Owner Robert Jenkinson **Bred** Paradigm Thoroughbred Inc **Trained** Barrowby, Lincs

FOCUS
A modest handicap lacking strength in depth. The stop-start gallop placed the emphasis more on finishing speed than stamina and the form is not the most solid, although the winner looked value for a bit further.

174 SPONSOR A RACE BY CALLING 01902 390000 H'CAP 1m 1f 103y(P)

5:10 (5:10) (Class 5) (0-75,75) 4-Y-0+ **£2,729** (£806; £403) **Stalls** Low

Form RPR
311- **1** **Chosen Forever**[17] 7857 5-8-10 **65**.................. JimmyQuinn 4 76+
(G R Oldroyd) *a.p: led wl over 1f out: drvn out* **2/1**[1]
604- **2** 1 1/4 **Boo**[63] 7127 8-9-0 **69**..................(v) EddieAhern 7 74
(J W Unett) *hld up in mid-div: c wd st: rdn and hdwy over 1f out: r.o to take 2nd ins fnl f: nt trble wnr* **33/1**
010- **3** 1/2 **Doubnov (FR)**[26] 7811 7-9-3 **72**..................(p) JamieSpencer 5 76
(Ian Williams) *dwlt: hld up in rr: c v wd st: rdn and hdwy over 1f out: r.o ins fnl f* **8/1**
236- **4** 2 1/2 **Resplendent Ace (IRE)**[18] 7851 6-9-3 **72**.................. AdamKirby 3 73+
(P Howling) *hld up towards rr: nt clr run and swtchd rt jst over 1f out: styd on ins fnl f* **12/1**
054- **5** 1 **Supercast (IRE)**[19] 7848 7-8-13 **71**..................(v[1]) WilliamCarson[(3)] 9 68
(N J Vaughan) *hld up in mid-div: hdwy on outside over 3f out: rdn over 2f out: edgd lft jst over 1f out: one pce ins fnl f* **8/1**
300- **6** 1 **Life's Challenge (USA)**[29] 7769 4-9-5 **75**.................. J-PGuillambert 8 72+
(M Johnston) *hld up in tch: pushed along over 3f out: rdn jst over 2f out: wkng whn nt clr run 1f out* **16/1**
22-2 **7** *shd* **Fujin Dancer (FR)**[10] 32 5-8-8 **68**.................. AmyRyan[(5)] 2 62
(K A Ryan) *chsd ldr: rdn over 2f out: wknd ins fnl f* **4/1**[2]
006- **8** *nse* **La Columbina**[28] 7779 5-8-10 **65**.................. FrankieMcDonald 6 59
(H J Evans) *hld up in mid-div: nt clr run on ins over 2f out: no hdwy fnl f* **125/1**
540- **9** 3/4 **Bomber Brown (IRE)**[96] 6680 4-9-4 **74**.................. JackMitchell 1 67
(P W Chapple-Hyam) *led: rdn and hdd wl over 1f out: wknd ins fnl f* **11/2**[3]
12-0 **10** 8 **Hilbre Court (USA)**[11] 23 5-9-5 **74**..................(p) GrahamGibbons 10 50
(B P J Baugh) *prom tl pushed along and wknd over 2f out* **12/1**

2m 0.94s (-0.76) **Going Correction** +0.075s/f (Slow)
WFA 4 from 5yo+ 1lb **10** Ran SP% **115.9**
Speed ratings (Par 103): **106,104,104,102,101 100,100,100,99,92**
toteswinger:1&2:£8.40, 2&3:£19.20, 1&3:£5.60 CSF £79.35 CT £448.74 TOTE £2.60: £1.50, £4.70, £2.10; EX 69.80.
Owner R C Bond **Bred** R C Bond **Trained** Brawby, N Yorks

FOCUS
A fair handicap which like the previous race was also run at something of a stop-start gallop, with the pace steadying down the far side. However, the time was reasonable and the runner-up sets the level.
Life's Challenge(USA) Official explanation: jockey said filly was denied a clear run

175 BET MASTERS SNOOKER - BETDAQ CONDITIONS STKS 1m 141y(P)

5:40 (5:40) (Class 2) 4-Y-0+
£10,592 (£3,172; £1,586; £793; £396; £198) **Stalls** Low

Form RPR
036- **1** **Philatelist (USA)**[35] 7704 6-9-0 **96**..................(v) JoeFanning 1 99
(M A Jarvis) *chsd ldr tl over 5f out: regained 2nd jst over 2f out: led jst over 1f out: pushed out* **6/1**
401- **2** 3 1/4 **Splinter Cell (USA)**[28] 7789 4-8-13 **94**.................. AndreaAtzeni 5 92
(M Botti) *hld up in rr: c wd st: rdn and hdwy over 1f out: hung lft fnl f: tk 2nd towards fin: no ch w wnr* **10/3**[2]
200- **3** 1/2 **Balcarce Nov (ARG)**[90] 6812 5-9-0 **105**.................. JamieSpencer 4 91
(T P Tate) *hld up and bhd: hdwy wl over 1f out: rdn and one pce ins fnl f* **7/4**[1]
1 **4** 1 1/4 **Reve De Nuit (USA)**[13] 6 4-9-4 **95**.................. DeclanCannon 6 93
(A J McCabe) *hld up: pushed along over 2f out: rdn wl over 1f out: no imp whn nt clr run and swtchd rt wl ins fnl f* **4/1**[3]
/16- **5** *nse* **Alsahil (USA)**[29] 7769 4-9-2 **80**.................. PaulHanagan 3 91?
(Micky Hammond) *sn led: rdn and hdd jst over 1f out: wknd wl ins fnl f* **33/1**
020- **6** *shd* **Noble Citizen (USA)**[110] 6270 5-9-0 **98**..................(be) MartinLane 2 88
(D M Simcock) *led early: prom: chsd ldr over 5f out tl jst over 2f out: wknd over 1f out* **8/1**

1m 50.55s (0.05) **Going Correction** +0.075s/f (Slow)
WFA 4 from 5yo+ 1lb **6** Ran SP% **107.8**
Speed ratings (Par 109): **102,99,98,97,97 97**
toteswinger:1&2:£4.20, 2&3:£2.70, 1&3:£2.60 CSF £23.92 TOTE £4.70: £2.10, £1.90; EX 19.60.
Owner Gary A Tanaka **Bred** Darley **Trained** Newmarket, Suffolk

FOCUS
A useful conditions event confined to horses that have not won a Pattern race since the end of 2008, but it turned into an unsatisfactory affair run at a muddling pace and with a couple of the supposed big guns underperforming, the form looks worth treating with caution.

NOTEBOOK
Philatelist(USA) hadn't been at his best in the second half of last year, but his win in a decent handicap at Kempton last March was one of the most impressive on the Polytrack last year and neither the drop back in trip or steady gallop fazed him as he stretched clear under hand riding to win easily. Something like the Lincoln Trial back here or the Rosebery Handicap at Kempton in the spring might be on his agenda, though connections might also be tempted by a crack the Winter Derby given the ease of this win. (op 5-1)
Splinter Cell(USA) had been progressing well and ran creditably again down in trip while never really having the opportunity to show what he could do having been held up at the rear. Back at 1m2f, or maybe even further, he can win another useful handicap. (op 11-4 tchd 7-2)
Balcarce Nov(ARG) had an outstanding chance at these weights but looked rather laboured in making his effort and has to be rated disappointing as the runner-up came from a similar position. An AW winner in Argentina, his action suggests that Fibresand will suit him better if ever a suitable opportunity arises. (op 11-4)
Reve De Nuit(USA) was another disappointment after his impressive Southwell win, but this race was run at a much slower tempo and he found it an insufficient test. (op 11-4)
Alsahil(USA) might well be flattered having been allowed to set a steady gallop to the home straight, and a rise in his mark as a consequence will make life tough back in handicaps. (op 28-1)
Noble Citizen(USA) has shown his best form when raced regularly but wasn't discredited back from a break at a trip beyond his best, though never a factor once the pace increased. (op 10-1)

176 STAY AT THE WOLVERHAMPTON HOLIDAY INN (S) STKS 1m 1f 103y(P)

6:10 (6:11) (Class 6) 4-Y-0+ **£1,774** (£523; £262) **Stalls** Low

Form RPR
123- **1** **Theocritus (USA)**[121] 5963 5-8-13 **76**.................. JamieSpencer 8 80
(D M Simcock) *hld up and bhd: pushed along and hdwy over 2f out: led wl over 1f out: sn hung lft: rdn clr ins fnl f: r.o wl* **4/1**[2]

262- **2** 4 ½ **New Star (UAE)**[285] 1133 6-8-13 76 ShaneKelly 4 71
(W M Brisbourne) *a.p: pushed along wl over 2f out: rdn and chsd wnr jst over 1f out: sn btn* **5/1**[3]

/46- **3** 1 ¾ **Painted Sky**[26] 7817 7-8-13 64 PaulHanagan 6 67
(R A Fahey) *chsd ldr after 1f: rdn and ev ch wl over 1f out: one pce fnl f* **18/1**

622- **4** ½ **Ahlawy (IRE)**[147] 5186 7-8-10 88 (bt) AndreaAtzeni(3) 9 66
(F Sheridan) *led after 1f: sn edgd lft: rdn and hdd wl over 1f out: one pce fnl f* **8/13**[1]

000- **5** 3 ½ **Old Romney**[50] 7524 6-8-13 63 J-PGuillambert 3 59
(P Howling) *hld up and bhd: pushed along 3f out: short-lived effrt 2f out* **40/1**

4- **6** 4 ½ **Spring Hawk (IRE)**[27] 7798 4-8-5 55 ow1 WilliamCarson(3) 5 45
(T G McCourt, Ire) *led 1f: hmpd 8f out: lost pl over 3f out: rdn and bhd fnl 2f* **20/1**

2m 1.81s (0.11) **Going Correction** +0.075s/f (Slow)
WFA 4 from 5yo+ 1lb **6** Ran SP% **111.1**
Speed ratings (Par 101): **102,98,96,96,92 88**
.The winner was bought in for 10,000gns. Ahlawy was the subject of a friendly claim of £6,000.
Owner Dr Marwan Koukash **Bred** Allen E Paulson Living Trust **Trained** Newmarket, Suffolk
■ Stewards' Enquiry : Andrea Atzeni three-day ban: careless riding (Jan 28-30)

FOCUS
An uncompetitive seller run at a modest gallop. The winner is rated to last year's turf form with the third to his recent best.

177 BET NFL - BETDAQ H'CAP 5f 216y(P)
6:40 (6:41) (Class 3) (0-95,92) 4-Y-0+ **£6,623** (£1,982; £991; £495; £246) **Stalls** Low

Form RPR

334- **1** **Tourist**[16] 7866 5-8-8 **82** JimmyQuinn 10 91
(D Shaw) *hld up: hdwy over 1f out: rdn ins fnl f: r.o to ld cl home* **14/1**

64-0 **2** ½ **Flowing Cape (IRE)**[5] 108 5-8-11 **90** (t) PaulPickard(5) 8 97
(R Hollinshead) *w ldr over 3f out: led over 1f out: hdd cl home* **7/1**

003- **3** *nk* **Orpsie Boy (IRE)**[101] 6540 7-9-0 **88** GrahamGibbons 5 94
(N P Littmoden) *hld up: pushed along 2f out: rdn over 1f out: r.o wl towards fin* **12/1**

22-2 **4** *nk* **Vhujon (IRE)**[5] 102 5-8-7 **81** PaulHanagan 1 86
(P D Evans) *hld up: hdwy on ins wl over 1f out: sn rdn: kpt on ins fnl f* **7/1**

003- **5** ¾ **Shifting Star (IRE)**[56] 7454 5-9-4 **92** (t) AdamKirby 3 95
(W R Swinburn) *a.p: rdn over 1f out: nt qckn ins fnl f* **9/2**[2]

115- **6** ½ **Earlsmedic**[17] 7862 5-8-13 **90** (e) WilliamCarson(3) 2 91
(S C Williams) *in ld over 3f out: rdn and hdd over 1f out: no ex wl ins fnl f* **13/2**

21-5 **7** ½ **Fathsta (IRE)**[5] 108 5-9-0 **88** EddieAhern 6 88
(D M Simcock) *a.p: rdn wl over 1f out: one pce* **2/1**[1]

314- **8** 1 ¼ **Orpenindeed (IRE)**[59] 7414 7-8-12 **89** (p) AndreaAtzeni(3) 4 85
(M Botti) *hld up in tch: rdn 2f out: fdd fnl f* **6/1**[3]

000- **9** 4 **My Gacho (IRE)**[23] 7837 8-9-1 **89** (v) J-PGuillambert 9 72
(M Johnston) *hld up and bhd: pushed along over 2f out: sn struggling* **33/1**

1m 14.49s (-0.51) **Going Correction** +0.075s/f (Slow) **9** Ran SP% **121.4**
Speed ratings (Par 107): **106,105,104,104,103 102,102,100,95**
toteswinger:1&2:£10.20, 2&3:£16.10, 1&3:£16.40 CSF £113.38 CT £1243.41 TOTE £14.00: £3.10, £2.70, £4.90; EX 130.20.
Owner M Shirley **Bred** Juddmonte Farms Ltd **Trained** Sproxton, Leics

FOCUS
A useful handicap but visibility had deteriorated significantly by this time, and though two that had been held up dominated the finish, the pace didn't appeared to be breakneck when the runners finally emerged from the fog. The form looks sound rated around the runner-up and fourth.

NOTEBOOK
Tourist is one of the most improved sprinters of the winter and he confirmed his promising Southwell effort at an inadequate 5f by returning to winning ways back at what might now be his optimum trip, coming with a sustained run after a patient ride. He's worth keeping on-side in this sort of grade in his current mood, not least back here where he is rarely out of the frame. (op 16-1)
Flowing Cape(IRE) goes well here and gave it a good go from the front after seeing off his fellow pace setter. He's bubbling under nicely and can get back to winning ways soon. (op 8-1)
Orpsie Boy(IRE) ran his best race for a long time. He ought to be more than capable of winning off his current mark and a return to form for his stable would increase confidence next time. (op 10-1)
Vhujon(IRE) was typically doing his best work late and clearly isn't handicapped out of things right now. (op 6-1)
Shifting Star(IRE) again left the impression that he has more to give on AW, possibly at 7f. (op 11-2)
Earlsmedic isn't the most straightforward and might not have appreciated being taken on for the lead. He's on a good mark though for when things fall more his way, and he shouldn't be written off. (op 5-1)
Fathsta(IRE) was well placed turning for home but had taken a wider course than most and wasn't able to find any extra. He's better than this and this run might be best ignored. (op 3-1 tchd 10-3)
Orpenindeed(IRE) ran below par for little apparent reason. (op 7-1)
My Gacho(IRE) has won at 6f on Fibresand but was never comfortable and really needs at least 7f on Polytrack. Official explanation: jockey said gelding reared up in stalls

178 HORIZONS RESTAURANT - THE PLACE TO DINE H'CAP 5f 20y(P)
7:10 (7:13) (Class 7) (0-50,50) 4-Y-0+ **£1,774** (£523; £262) **Stalls** Low

Form RPR

42-0 **1** **Head To Head (IRE)**[4] 112 6-8-13 **50** (bt) JimmyQuinn 6 61
(A D Brown) *in ld over 3f out: hrd rdn ins fnl f: all out* **6/1**

566- **2** *nse* **Admiral Bond (IRE)**[23] 7838 5-8-11 **48** (p) TomEaves 1 59
(G R Oldroyd) *mid-div: pushed along over 3f out: hdwy on ins 2f out: rdn and chal wl ins fnl f: r.o* **9/2**[3]

050- **3** 1 **Albero Di Giuda (IRE)**[15] 7877 5-8-10 **50** (t) AndreaAtzeni(3) 3 57
(F Sheridan) *a.p: chsd ldr 2f out tl rdn over 1f out: kpt on ins fnl f* **4/1**[2]

543- **4** *shd* **Cocktail Party (IRE)**[35] 7703 4-8-12 **49** (t) EddieAhern 2 56
(J W Hills) *hld up and bhd: hdwy over 1f out: rdn and kpt on ins fnl f* **3/1**[1]

06-6 **5** ¾ **Meikle Barfil**[6] 77 8-8-7 **47** (bt) JackDean(3) 8 51
(J M Bradley) *hld up in mid-div: swtchd rt 3f out: rdn and kpt on towards fin* **20/1**

000- **6** *nk* **Triumphant Welcome**[16] 7869 5-8-10 **47** (p) J-PGuillambert 4 50
(H J Evans) *in tch: pushed along over 3f out: rdn and nt qckn ins fnl f* **8/1**

050- **7** ½ **El Potro**[16] 7869 8-8-8 **45** NickyMackay 10 46
(J R Holt) *prom: c wd st: rdn wl over 1f out: one pce fnl f* **14/1**

300- **8** 2 **Taboor (IRE)**[79] 7100 12-8-8 **45** GrahamGibbons 13 39
(R M H Cowell) *bhd: pushed along over 3f out: c wd st: nvr trbld ldrs* **33/1**

01-0 **9** 7 **Triskaidekaphobia**[2] 132 7-8-13 **50** (t) PaulFitzsimons 9 19
(Miss J R Tooth) *w ldr over 3f out: rdn and wknd wl over 1f out* **12/1**

400- **10** 2 ¼ **North South Divide (IRE)**[15] 7877 6-8-3 **45** (b) AmyRyan(5) 5 6
(K A Ryan) *sn outpcd* **8/1**

006- **11** 1 **Gleaming Spirit (IRE)**[44] 7605 6-8-11 **48** (v) AndrewMullen 11 5
(Peter Grayson) *bhd: struggling 2f out* **40/1**

62.45 secs (0.15) **Going Correction** +0.075s/f (Slow) **11** Ran SP% **124.2**
Speed ratings (Par 97): **101,100,99,99,97 97,96,93,82,78 77**
toteswinger:1&2:£6.00, 2&3:£4.90, 1&3:£7.70 CSF £34.56 CT £127.72 TOTE £7.80: £2.10, £2.50, £1.90; EX 36.70 Place 6 £476.93, Place 5 £281.01.
Owner Mrs M Doherty **Bred** Sean Connolly **Trained** Yedingham, N Yorks

FOCUS
Low-level stuff but a good gallop on with several front runners in opposition and there didn't appear to be any obvious hard-luck stories. The form looks straightforward with the third and fourth close to recent marks.
T/Jkpt: Not won. T/Plt: £303.20 to a £1 stake. Pool: £91,140.72. 219.37 winning tickets. T/Qpdt: £75.40 to a £1 stake. Pool: £9,833.80. 96.50 winning tickets. KH

[159]LINGFIELD (L-H)
Friday, January 15

OFFICIAL GOING: Standard
Wind: Light, behind Weather: Overcast

179 GOLF AND RACING MAIDEN STKS 1m 4f (P)
1:10 (1:10) (Class 5) 4-Y-0+ **£2,456** (£725; £362) **Stalls** Low

Form RPR

1 **Buxted (IRE)** 4-9-3 0 JoeFanning 3 81+
(T G Mills) *trckd ldr: led wl over 3f out: pushed along briefly to draw clr 2f out: cantered rt away fnl f* **5/2**[2]

4/6- **2** 9 **Cozy Tiger (USA)**[352] 310 5-9-7 65 StevieDonohoe 1 61
(W J Musson) *t.k.h: hld up in last pair: stl keen over 4f out and stl in last pair over 2f out: pushed along and prog over 1f out: wnt 2nd last 150yds: no ch w wnr but styd on steadily* **13/2**[3]

622- **3** 1 ¼ **Alhaque (USA)**[106] 6417 4-9-3 75 TomQueally 6 59
(G L Moore) *hld up in 5th: pushed along on inner 3f out: laboured prog to take 2nd jst over 1f out tl last 150yds: no ch* **8/11**[1]

04- **4** *hd* **Dovedon Earl**[47] 7590 4-9-3 0 LiamKeniry 7 59
(T Keddy) *hld up in 6th: prog to dispute 2nd over 3f out to 1f out: no ex* **20/1**

5 5 **Peinture De Guerre (FR)**[38] 7-9-7 55 (t) AmirQuinn 4 51
(G L Moore) *t.k.h early: trckd ldng pair: chsd wnr over 3f out: rdn and lft bhd over 2f out: wknd over 1f out* **20/1**

6 ¾ **Happy Fleet**[29] 7-9-2 0 JimCrowley 5 45
(R Curtis) *hld up in last pair: brief effrt on outer over 3f out: wknd 2f out* **50/1**

7 3 **Jolly Cooper**[28] 7-9-2 0 ShaneKelly 2 40
(Mike Murphy) *t.k.h: trckd ldng trio to over 3f out: wknd over 2f out* **50/1**

8 20 **Allperksonice**[75] 7-9-2 0 DavidProbert 8 8
(Mark Gillard) *led to wl over 3f out: wknd rapidly: t.o* **40/1**

2m 33.48s (0.48) **Going Correction** -0.05s/f (Stan)
WFA 4 from 5yo+ 4lb **8** Ran SP% **115.7**
Speed ratings (Par 103): **96,90,89,89,85 85,83,69**
toteswinger:1&2:£2.00, 2&3:£2.20, 1&3:£1.60 CSF £17.09 TOTE £3.90: £1.40, £1.40, £1.02; EX 18.10 Trifecta £45.80 Pool: £633.43 - 10.23 winning units..
Owner Buxted Partnership **Bred** Ronan Burns **Trained** Headley, Surrey

FOCUS
An uncompetitive maiden and one weakened further with the below-par performance of the favourite, but the winner created a most favourable impression on his debut and looks potentially very useful. The gallop was a modest one and the winner came down the centre in the straight.

180 BET AFRICAN NATIONS CUP - BETDAQ MAIDEN STKS 7f (P)
1:40 (1:44) (Class 5) 3-Y-0+ **£2,456** (£725; £362) **Stalls** Low

Form RPR

234- **1** **Fivefold (USA)**[37] 7685 3-8-9 76 J-PGuillambert 7 74
(J Akehurst) *t.k.h: w ldr: led 4f out: hrd pressed and drvn over 1f out: jst lasted* **13/8**[1]

5- **2** *shd* **Monterosso**[63] 7376 3-8-9 0 JoeFanning 11 74
(M Johnston) *led 3f: pressed wnr after: nrly upsides fr over 1f out: nt qckn and jst hld* **5/2**[2]

00- **3** *hd* **Purple Gallery (IRE)**[30] 7773 3-8-9 0 AndrewElliott 9 73
(J S Moore) *chsd ldng pair: pushed along fr 1/2-way: no imp in 4th over 1f out: edgd rt but styd on wl fnl f: gaining at fin* **20/1**

00- **4** *nse* **Darshonin**[104] 6478 3-8-9 0 (v[1]) ShaneKelly 4 73
(J Noseda) *settled in midfield: outpcd over 2f out: rdn wl over 1f out: styd on wl fnl f: gaining at fin* **11/1**

4- **4** *dht* **Minortransgression (USA)**[27] 7806 3-8-9 0 LiamKeniry 12 73
(G L Moore) *green in preliminaries: settled in midfield: outpcd over 2f out: effrt wl over 1f out on wd outside: rn green but styd on wl: gaining at fin* **5/1**[3]

02-2 **6** ¾ **Freddie's Girl (USA)**[10] 38 3-8-4 67 HayleyTurner 3 66
(Stef Higgins) *chsd ldng pair: drvn and cl enough on inner jst over 1f out: one pce and lost 3 pls nr fin* **6/1**

7 3 ½ **Ceto** 3-8-4 0 DavidProbert 6 57
(P S McEntee) *s.s: t.k.h early: hld up in last trio: outpcd over 2f out: pushed along and no prog after* **100/1**

-5 **8** 1 **Mary's Pet**[12] 24 3-8-4 0 SimonWhitworth 2 54
(J Akehurst) *settled in last trio: shuffled along on inner and nvr nr ldrs fnl 2f* **33/1**

0- **9** 11 **Southern Breeze**[50] 7537 3-8-10 0 ow1 StevieDonohoe 10 30
(S Kirk) *a in last trio: wknd 2f out: t.o* **100/1**

1m 24.24s (-0.56) **Going Correction** -0.05s/f (Stan)
WFA 3 from 4yo 18lb **9** Ran SP% **115.6**
Speed ratings (Par 103): **101,100,100,100,100 99,95,94,82**
toteswinger:1&2:£2.50, 2&3:£12.10, 1&3:£7.00 CSF £5.65 TOTE £2.30: £1.10, £1.30, £5.30; EX 7.60 Trifecta £329.70 Pool: £592.69 - 1.33 winning units..
Owner A D Spence **Bred** Calming Syndicate **Trained** Epsom, Surrey

FOCUS
No more than a fair maiden in which the gallop was an ordinary one and the first five virtually finished in a line. The form looks ordinary but sound enough and the winner raced towards the centre in the straight.

181 BET AUSTRALIAN OPEN TENNIS - BETDAQ (S) STKS 7f (P)
2:10 (2:10) (Class 6) 4-Y-0+ **£1,774** (£523; £262) **Stalls** Low

Form RPR

-231 **1** **Goodbye Cash (IRE)**[6] 101 6-8-10 59 PaulDoe 2 65
(P D Evans) *mde all: hrd pressed and rdn over 2f out: grabbed l ld over 1f out: jst hld on* **15/8**[1]

52-5 **2** *hd* **Lord Deevert**[7] 78 5-8-7 62 .... JackDean(3) 1 64
(W G M Turner) *cl up: dropped to last and rdn over 2f out: rallied on outer over 1f out: wnt 2nd ins fnl f: clsd on wnr fin* **6/1**

1-21 **3** *3/4* **Obe Gold**[7] 89 8-9-1 66 .... J-PGuillambert 4 67
(P Howling) *cl up: chal wnr 2f out: nt qckn over 1f out: lost 2nd ins fnl f: one pce* **3/1**[3]

203- **4** *5* **Geezers Colours**[20] 7845 5-8-10 71 .... (v[1]) AndrewElliott 3 49
(J R Weymes) *t.k.h early: sn trckd wnr: pushed along 1/2-way: lost pl 2f out: wknd over 1f out* **2/1**[2]

1m 24.62s (-0.18) **Going Correction** -0.05s/f (Stan) 4 Ran SP% **107.4**
Speed ratings (Par 101): **99,98,97,92**
CSF £11.73 TOTE £2.90; EX 9.80.There was no bid for the winner
Owner Mrs I M Folkes **Bred** Mrs A C Peters **Trained** Pandy, Monmouths

FOCUS
A modest seller in which the market leader disappointed. The gallop was a moderate one and the winner raced just off the inside rail in the straight. She is probably the best guide but the form is not solid.
Geezers Colours Official explanation: jockey said gelding ran too free in first time visor

182 LINGFIELD PARK FOURBALL H'CAP 1m 4f (P)
2:40 (2:40) (Class 5) (0-70,70) 4-Y-O+ **£2,456** (£725; £362) **Stalls** Low

Form RPR

20-2 **1** **Sunset Boulevard (IRE)**[7] 80 7-8-6 55 .... DavidProbert 8 65
(Miss Tor Sturgis) *stdd s: hld up in last pair: prog on outer over 2f out: rdn to ld jst over 1f out: styd on wl* **4/1**[2]

552/ **2** *1 3/4* **Stumped**[66] 5098 7-9-0 63 .... JimCrowley 6 70
(H S Howe) *hld up in 4th: prog to chse ldr over 2f out: drvn to ld briefly over 1f out: readily hld by wnr fnl f* **8/1**

202- **3** *6* **Chanrossa (IRE)**[16] 7882 4-8-8 61 .... (p) HayleyTurner 1 58
(E A L Dunlop) *led 3f: led 5f out: drvn and hdd over 1f out: wknd* **5/1**[3]

015- **4** *1* **Calzaghe (IRE)**[35] 1537 6-9-3 69 .... (b[1]) RobertLButler(3) 4 65
(Jim Best) *led after 3f to 5f out: rdn 4f out: lost pl and btn over 2f out: last over 1f out: plugged on fnl f* **7/1**

100- **5** *1 1/4* **Choral Festival**[25] 7831 4-9-0 70 .... MarcHalford(3) 5 64
(J J Bridger) *trckd ldng pair: cl up on inner over 2f out: grad wknd fnl 2f* **25/1**

1-12 **6** *4* **Winning Show**[4] 121 6-8-9 58 .... (t) LiamKeniry 7 45
(C Gordon) *hld up in last pair on inner: already pushed along whn trapped bhd rivals over 2f out: sn btn* **5/4**[1]

2m 31.04s (-1.96) **Going Correction** -0.05s/f (Stan)
WFA 4 from 6yo+ 4lb 6 Ran SP% **108.6**
Speed ratings (Par 103): **104,102,98,98,97 94**
toteswinger:1&2:£3.40, 2&3:£4.30, 1&3:£3.50 CSF £31.60 CT £143.08 TOTE £4.60: £2.00, £4.00; EX 47.00 Trifecta £236.10 Pool: £520.14 - 1.63 winning units..
Owner Miss Tor Sturgis **Bred** A J Martin **Trained** Lambourn, Berks

FOCUS
Mainly exposed performers in a modest handicap and a race that took less winning than seemed likely with the market leader performing well below his recent best. The gallop was on the steady side and the winner came down the centre in the straight. The form is best rated around the first two.
Winning Show Official explanation: jockey said gelding never travelled

183 GOLF AT LINGFIELD PARK H'CAP 1m 2f (P)
3:10 (3:10) (Class 4) (0-85,71) 3-Y-O **£4,209** (£1,252; £625; £312) **Stalls** Low

Form RPR

50-1 **1** **Cosimo de Medici**[8] 73 3-9-7 71 6ex .... PatrickHills(3) 4 84
(H Morrison) *w ldr: led 3f out and sn qcknd clr: rdn and drew further away fr over 1f out* **9/4**[1]

2-42 **2** *8* **Mary Helen**[3] 133 3-9-2 63 .... ShaneKelly 3 60
(W M Brisbourne) *s.s: in tch in last pair: outpcd over 2f out: effrt on outer sn after: won battle for remote 2nd* **10/3**[2]

033- **3** *1 1/4* **Kathindi (IRE)**[15] 7886 3-9-7 68 .... LiamKeniry 1 63
(J S Moore) *sn restrained bhd ldng pair: urged along 4f out: outpcd over 2f out: disp modest 2nd 2f out tl ins fnl f* **10/3**[2]

32-2 **4** *1/2* **Captain Cool (IRE)**[4] 118 3-8-4 51 .... (p) DavidProbert 2 45
(R Hannon) *disp ld to 3f out: sn outpcd by wnr: dropped to last jst over 1f out* **9/4**[1]

2m 6.55s (-0.05) **Going Correction** -0.05s/f (Stan) 4 Ran SP% **107.7**
Speed ratings (Par 99): **98,91,90,90**
CSF £9.54 TOTE £2.10; EX 6.70.
Owner Bevan, Doyle & Lawrence **Bred** Shortgrove Manor Stud **Trained** East Ilsley, Berks

FOCUS
What looked a fairly open race on paper was turned into a procession by the progressive winner, who raced against the inside rail in the straight. The form is rated through the runner-up to his latest course form.

184 BET MASTERS SNOOKER - BETDAQ H'CAP 1m 2f (P)
3:40 (3:41) (Class 6) (0-55,58) 4-Y-O+ **£1,774** (£523; £262) **Stalls** Low

Form RPR

530- **1** **Turkish Sultan (IRE)**[35] 7718 7-8-6 46 oh1 .... (p) NickyMackay 11 52
(J M Bradley) *hld up bhd clr ldrs: clsd fr over 3f out: wnt 2nd over 2f out: drvn ahd 1f out: hld on* **25/1**

005- **2** *nk* **Turner's Touch**[40] 7658 8-7-13 46 oh1 .... (b) HarryBentley(7) 3 51
(G L Moore) *s.s: hld up in last trio: stl wl in rr 2f out: gd prog on wd outside over 1f out: jnd wnr ins fnl f: cajoled along and ref to overtake* **10/1**

25-6 **3** *1/2* **Mister Frosty (IRE)**[13] 18 4-8-3 52 .... CharlotteKerton(7) 8 56
(G Prodromou) *pressed ldr: led over 3f out: urged along and hdd 1f out: kpt on nr fin* **20/1**

00-3 **4** *3/4* **Womaniser (IRE)**[6] 99 6-8-12 52 .... (b) LiamKeniry 9 55
(T Keddy) *trckd ldng pair: cl enough 2f out: hrd rdn over 1f out: no rspnse and lost pl: kpt on again fnl f* **8/1**

665- **5** *shd* **Our Kes (IRE)**[30] 7766 8-9-1 55 .... TomQueally 6 57
(P Howling) *hld up towards rr and off the pce: gd prog on outer over 2f out to chse ldrs: kpt on same pce fr over 1f out* **8/1**

00-2 **6** *3/4* **Mid Wicket (USA)**[6] 99 4-8-10 52 .... (p) JimCrowley 5 53
(Mouse Hamilton-Fairley) *hld up in midfield: gng easily 3f out: effrt 2f out: hrd rdn and fnd nil over 1f out* **5/1**[1]

1-05 **7** *3/4* **Binnion Bay (IRE)**[4] 124 9-8-10 53 .... (b) MarcHalford(3) 7 55+
(J J Bridger) *s.i.s: wl in rr: stl there over 2f out and rdn: prog wl over 1f out: rchd 7th ins fnl f but nt clr run after* **14/1**

/0-5 **8** *2 1/4* **Boogie Dancer**[6] 98 6-8-12 52 .... HayleyTurner 13 47
(H S Howe) *awkward s: nvr beyond midfield: rdn and no prog 3f out* **14/1**

060/ **9** *1/2* **Topflight Wildbird**[20] 6258 7-8-6 46 .... (p) JoeFanning 4 40
(Mrs L Wadham) *hld up bhd clr ldrs: tried to cl 4f out: rdn over 3f out: lost pl over 2f out: wl hld whn short of room on inner over 1f out* **11/2**[2]

014- **10** *3/4* **Jiggalong**[24] 7840 4-8-11 53 .... PaulDoe 2 45
(Jim Best) *dwlt: a in rr: rdn and no prog 3f out* **16/1**

000- **11** *2* **Nicky Nutjob (GER)**[34] 4156 4-8-4 46 oh1 .... (b) AndrewElliott 1 34
(J Pearce) *s.s: mostly last: detached 4f out: modest late prog* **8/1**

04-1 **12** *3/4* **Litenup (IRE)**[6] 100 4-9-2 58 6ex .... (t) WandersonD'Avila 12 45
(A J Lidderdale) *led at generous pce: hdd over 3f out: wknd 2f out* **7/1**[3]

044- **13** *3 1/2* **Too Grand**[297] 945 5-9-1 55 .... DavidProbert 10 35
(J J Bridger) *settled off the pce in midfield: struggling whn n.m.r over 2f out: wknd* **33/1**

2m 5.76s (-0.84) **Going Correction** -0.05s/f (Stan)
WFA 4 from 5yo+ 2lb 13 Ran SP% **117.7**
Speed ratings (Par 101): **101,100,100,99,99 99,98,96,96,95 94,93,90**
toteswinger:1&2:£48.10, 2&3:£43.40, 1&3:£38.60 CSF £249.28 CT £5041.04 TOTE £25.70: £7.90, £4.00, £6.70; EX 160.80 TRIFECTA Not won..
Owner Miss Diane Hill **Bred** Lady Legard & Sir Tatton Sykes **Trained** Sedbury, Gloucs

FOCUS
Mainly exposed or disappointing sorts in a very moderate handicap. The pace was only fair and the winner edged into the centre in the closing stages.

185 MARRIOTT PLAY AND STAY H'CAP 5f (P)
4:10 (4:12) (Class 6) (0-65,68) 4-Y-O+ **£1,774** (£523; £262) **Stalls** High

Form RPR

0-42 **1** **Steel City Boy (IRE)**[3] 132 7-8-10 57 .... JimCrowley 5 65
(D Shaw) *taken down early: trckd ldrs on outer: drvn to cl over 1f out: styd on to gain narrow ld last 75yds* **5/2**[1]

051- **2** *nk* **Handsome Cross (IRE)**[15] 7890 9-9-1 62 .... (v) PaulDoe 4 69
(W J Musson) *hld up in 7th early: prog fr 2f out: nt clr run jst over 1f out: rdn to join ldr ins fnl f: jst outpcd* **10/1**

660- **3** *shd* **Figaro Flyer (IRE)**[33] 7739 7-9-4 65 .... TomQueally 2 72
(P Howling) *trckd ldng pair after 1f: clsd to chal over 1f out: narrow ld jst ins fnl f: sn jnd: hrd rdn and hdd last 75yds* **9/1**

66-6 **4** *1/2* **Namir (IRE)**[7] 79 8-8-11 58 .... (vt) HayleyTurner 10 63
(H J Evans) *taken down early: dropped in fr wd draw and hld up in last pair: prog on inner fr 2f out: hrd rdn and nrly upsides ins fnl f: nt qckn* **6/1**

325- **5** *1 1/4* **Monsieur Reynard**[40] 7651 5-8-7 57 .... JackDean(3) 6 58
(J M Bradley) *hld up in last trio: promising hdwy over 1f out to chse ldrs: one pce fnl f* **14/1**

005- **6** *1 1/4* **Cape Royal**[27] 7808 10-8-6 60 .... (bt) RyanClark(7) 1 56
(J M Bradley) *led at frntic pce: hdd & wknd jst ins fnl f* **10/1**

06-2 **7** *1 1/4* **Ten Down**[7] 77 5-8-8 55 .... JoeFanning 3 47
(M Quinn) *w ldr at v str pce tl wknd ent fnl f* **5/1**[2]

4-01 **8** *nk* **Thoughtsofstardom**[4] 119 7-9-7 68 6ex .... DavidProbert 9 59
(P S McEntee) *chsd ldrs: disp 5th and in tch 2f out: nt qckn over 1f out: sn lost pl and btn* **11/2**[3]

300- **9** *3/4* **Agnes Love**[51] 7518 4-8-5 59 .... KierenFox(7) 8 47
(J Akehurst) *chsd ldng pair 1f: sn lost pl and pushed along: struggling fr 2f out* **25/1**

044- **10** *1 1/2* **Sweet Applause (IRE)**[60] 7411 4-8-8 62 .... CharlotteKerton(7) 7 45
(G Prodromou) *hld up in last pair: wd bnd 2f out: nudged along and nvr on terms* **33/1**

58.17 secs (-0.63) **Going Correction** -0.05s/f (Stan) 10 Ran SP% **116.5**
Speed ratings (Par 101): **103,102,102,101,99 97,95,95,93,91**
toteswinger:1&2:£6.60, 2&3:£7.80, 1&3:£7.30 CSF £29.02 CT £196.57 TOTE £3.40: £1.30, £3.30, £3.30; EX 36.10 TRIFECTA Pool: £843.95 - 3.60 winning units. Place 6 £440.94, Place 5 £416.83.
Owner J Medley **Bred** Mrs A B McDonnell **Trained** Sproxton, Leics

FOCUS
A modest handicap run at a decent gallop and the form looks straightforward rated through the third. The winner raced in the centre in the straight.
T/Plt: £876.60 to a £1 stake. Pool: £80,041.99. 66.65 winning tickets. T/Qpdt: £604.90 to a £1 stake. Pool: £4,986.65. 6.10 winning tickets. JN

[165] SOUTHWELL (L-H)
Friday, January 15

OFFICIAL GOING: Slow
Wind: light 1/2 against Weather: rain then overcast and cold

186 FREEZY MONEY AT VICTORCHANDLER.COM MAIDEN STKS 2m (F)
1:15 (1:26) (Class 5) 4-Y-O+ **£2,590** (£770; £385; £192) **Stalls** Low

Form RPR

300- **1** **Venture Capitalist**[18] 7863 4-8-12 55 .... (b[1]) BarryMcHugh(5) 8 54
(B Ellison) *hld up towards rr: hdwy on outer 6f out: sn chsng ldrs: styd on to ld towards fin* **12/1**

00/3 **2** *nk* **Arisea (IRE)**[13] 18 7-9-5 50 .... (t) DavidNolan 11 48
(Paul Murphy) *hld up in rr: hdwy 9f out: chsng ldrs over 4f out: narrow ld over 2f out: hdd and no ex towards fin* **8/1**

400- **3** *1/2* **Mymateeric**[19] 7025 4-9-3 47 .... SaleemGolam 10 53
(J Pearce) *mid-div: hdwy 9f out: chsng ldrs over 4f out: upsides ins fnl f: kpt on same pce* **5/1**[3]

035/ **4** *shd* **Hope Road**[191] 6124 6-9-10 70 .... PhillipMakin 3 53
(A B Haynes) *trckd ldrs: t.k.h: upsides ins fnl f: no ex* **9/4**[2]

000- **5** *1 1/4* **Flannel (IRE)**[32] 5011 4-9-3 51 .... (v[1]) AdamKirby 4 51
(J R Fanshawe) *hld up towards rr: hdwy on far side 3f out: chsng ldrs 1f out: fdd towards fin* **15/2**

36/0 **6** *1 3/4* **Delorain (IRE)**[13] 15 7-9-10 40 .... (vt) JerryO'Dwyer 1 49
(W B Stone) *led: hdd 3f out: one pce fnl f* **66/1**

00-0 **7** *19* **Owls FC (IRE)**[13] 18 4-8-7 27 .... (b) DeclanCannon(5) 9 21
(M C Chapman) *reluctant to load: in rr: sn pushed along: bhd fnl 4f* **200/1**

33-0 **8** *nk* **Dawn Storm (IRE)**[10] 41 5-9-10 48 .... (b) RobertWinston 6 26
(J L Spearing) *trckd ldrs: led 3f out: sn hdd: wknd 2f out: eased fnl f* **2/1**[1]

0/-0 **9** *6* **Gouranga**[7] 90 7-9-5 42 .... (b) MattieBatchelor 2 14
(A W Carroll) *s.i.s: sn chsng ldrs: pushed along 7f out: lost pl over 3f out* **40/1**

10 *14* **Ringsend Rose (IRE)**[34] 7-9-5 0 .... LeeVickers 5 —
(A Sadik) *sn chsng ldrs: lost pl over 4f out: sn bhd* **150/1**

11 *4* **Kinkeel (IRE)**[33] 11-9-3 0 .... JakePayne(7) 7 —
(A W Carroll) *hld up towards rr: drvn 6f out: lost pl over 4f out: sn bhd* **50/1**

3m 43.38s (-2.12) **Going Correction** -0.10s/f (Stan)
WFA 4 from 5yo+ 7lb 11 Ran SP% **118.4**
Speed ratings (Par 103): **101,100,100,100,99 99,89,89,86,79 77**
toteswinger:1&2:£18.30, 2&3:£6.80, 1&3:£10.20 CSF £103.33 TOTE £9.70: £5.30, £3.50, £2.60; EX 76.60.
Owner Brian Ellison & Kristian Strangeway **Bred** Meon Valley Stud **Trained** Norton, N Yorks

FOCUS
This marathon maiden was run at an average gallop and there was a very tight finish between the first four. Very weak form, rated around the principals.

187 STAY WARM AT VICTOR CHANDLER CASINO CLAIMING STKS 6f (F)
1:45 (1:57) (Class 6) 4-Y-0+ £2,388 (£705; £352) Stalls Low

Form RPR
231- 1 **Total Impact**[19] 7852 7-9-5 76 RobertWinston 7 80
(C R Dore) *hld up: smooth hdwy to trck ldrs over 2f out: styd on u.p to ld last 75yds* **9/4**[1]
10-1 2 ¾ **Stonecrabstomorrow (IRE)**[10] 37 7-8-6 73..(b) MarzenaJeziorek[(7)] 2 71
(R A Fahey) *s.s: hdwy to trck ldrs over 4f out: led over 2f out: edgd lft fnl f: hdd and no ex last 75yds* **9/4**[1]
460- 3 2 ¼ **Kings Ace (IRE)**[27] 7817 4-8-2 53 (vt) MatthewDavies[(5)] 6 58
(A P Jarvis) *hld up: hdwy to chse ldrs over 2f out: kpt on same pce fnl f* **8/1**
0-21 4 3 ¼ **Mocha Java**[7] 86 7-8-4 59 (p) RossAtkinson[(5)] 5 50
(Matthew Salaman) *chsd ldrs: wknd over 1f out* **7/2**[2]
0-60 5 1 ½ **Favouring (IRE)**[7] 87 8-8-2 38 (v) DeclanCannon[(5)] 4 43
(M C Chapman) *drvn to sn chse ldrs: wknd over 1f out* **150/1**
660- 6 1 ½ **Flash McGahon (IRE)**[31] 7758 6-9-9 78 (b) AndrewMullen 8 54
(D Nicholls) *chsd ldrs on outside: drvn and outpcd over 2f out: lost pl over 1f out* **15/2**[3]
600- 7 4 **Conjecture**[139] 5443 8-8-11 55 JackMitchell 3 29
(R Bastiman) *led tl over 4f out: wknd 2f out* **33/1**
000- 8 13 **Owed**[172] 4372 8-9-2 47 (tp) TanyaRedden[(7)] 1 —
(R Bastiman) *dwlt: t.k.h: hdwy on ins to ld over 4f out: hdd over 2f out: wknd and eased over 1f out* **100/1**

1m 15.64s (-0.86) **Going Correction** -0.10s/f (Stan) 8 Ran SP% **111.2**
Speed ratings (Par 101): **101,100,97,92,90 88,83,66**
Stonecrabstomorrow was claimed by John Harris for £7000.
Owner Chris Marsh **Bred** C A Cyzer **Trained** Cowbit, Lincs

FOCUS
The two market leaders duly fought out the finish in this claimer and it was greater experience in the saddle that won the day. Ordinary form, the winner close to his recent best.

188 VICTOR CHANDLER LIVE CASINO ALWAYS OPEN H'CAP 1m (F)
2:15 (2:25) (Class 5) (0-70,67) 3-Y-O £2,729 (£806; £403) Stalls Low

Form RPR
1-30 1 **Lily Lily**[3] 133 3-9-2 62 (b) RobertWinston 1 65
(K McAuliffe) *led: qcknd 3f out: kpt on wl u.str.p fnl 2f: forged clr ins fnl f* **4/1**[3]
1 2 2 ¼ **Mororless**[14] 5 3-8-13 64 DeclanCannon[(5)] 4 62
(A J McCabe) *trckd ldrs: drvn 3f out: outpcd over 1f out: styd on wl to take 2nd ins fnl f* **9/4**[2]
21-4 3 1 **Tealing**[3] 141 3-9-2 67 BillyCray[(5)] 3 63
(R C Guest) *stdd s: hdwy to trck ldrs 4f out: effrt over 2f out: upsides over 1f out: kpt on same pce* **5/4**[1]
0-53 4 3 ¾ **Baby Judge (IRE)**[10] 43 3-8-3 52 AndreaAtzeni[(3)] 2 39
(M C Chapman) *trckd wnr: rdn 3f out: wknd fnl f* **7/1**

1m 44.48s (0.78) **Going Correction** -0.10s/f (Stan) 4 Ran SP% **107.7**
Speed ratings (Par 97): **92,89,88,85**
CSF £12.84 TOTE £4.50; EX 7.30.
Owner K W J McAuliffe **Bred** Dr Celia Marr **Trained** Fernham, Oxon

FOCUS
A tricky looking little 3-y-o handicap with the winner rated to previous C&D form.

189 VICTORCHANDLER.COM MEDIAN AUCTION MAIDEN STKS 7f (F)
2:45 (2:55) (Class 6) 3-5-Y-O £2,388 (£705; £352) Stalls Low

Form RPR
3-3 1 **Paintball (IRE)**[4] 128 3-8-5 0 AndreaAtzeni[(3)] 5 73+
(W R Muir) *trckd ldrs: effrt on outer over 2f out: styd on to ld jst ins fnl f: forged clr: v readily* **8/11**[1]
22- 2 3 ¾ **Midnight Strider (IRE)**[18] 7863 4-9-12 0 RichardKingscote 6 67
(Tom Dascombe) *trckd ldrs: led over 1f out: hdd and no ex jst ins fnl f* **11/4**[2]
6/6- 3 ¾ **Bravalto**[34] 7730 4-9-12 60 TomEaves 2 65
(B Smart) *trckd ldrs: shkn up over 4f out: outpcd 3f out: hdwy over 1f out: hung lft: kpt on same pce* **14/1**[3]
065- 4 3 ¾ **Quiet Mountain (IRE)**[32] 7753 5-9-7 0 BarryMcHugh[(5)] 1 55
(Ollie Pears) *trckd ldrs: led on bit 3f out: hdd over 1f out: sn wknd* **16/1**
00-6 5 8 **Gracie's Games**[8] 69 4-9-7 45 RobertWinston 4 28
(R J Price) *led tl 3f out: lost pl over 1f out* **66/1**
6 3 ¼ **Maigold Rose** 3-8-3 0 JimmyQuinn 3 15
(J R Weymes) *s.s: last and hung rt bnd over 4f out: styd far side: bhd fnl 2f* **33/1**
5- 7 5 **Kingston Folly**[39] 7663 3-8-3 0 AmyBaker[(5)] 7 11
(A B Haynes) *gave problems in stalls: s.i.s: sn chsng ldrs: lost pl wl over 1f out* **14/1**[3]

1m 28.8s (-1.50) **Going Correction** -0.10s/f (Stan)
WFA 3 from 4yo+ 18lb 7 Ran SP% **108.2**
Speed ratings (Par 101): **104,99,98,94,85 81,76**
toteswinger:1&2:£1.10, 2&3:£4.70, 1&3:£3.50 CSF £2.43 TOTE £1.80: £1.10, £1.80; EX 2.90.
Owner Mrs J M Muir **Bred** James Waldron **Trained** Lambourn, Berks

FOCUS
A weakish maiden but the winner stepped up again and the second sets the level rated to his previous form.

190 VICTOR CHANDLER & NOTTINGHAM FOREST CLAIMING STKS 1m 6f (F)
3:15 (3:25) (Class 6) 4-Y-O+ £2,388 (£705; £352) Stalls Low

Form RPR
21-6 1 **Boundless Prospect (USA)**[8] 76 11-8-10 70.. AndrewHeffernan[(5)] 2 71
(P D Evans) *hld up: effrt 5f out: styd on fnl f: led nr fin* **4/1**[3]
/40- 2 hd **Chocolate Caramel (USA)**[17] 7867 8-9-7 73 PaulHanagan 5 77
(R A Fahey) *trckd ldr: led after 4f: narrowly hdd over 2f out: hung lft and regained ld over 1f out: hdd nr fin* **9/2**
226- 3 nk **Dunaskin (IRE)**[17] 7867 10-9-2 76 (e) JohnCavanagh[(7)] 1 78
(B Ellison) *hdwy over 7f out: sn chsng ldrs: slt ld over 2f out: hdd over 1f out: styd on again towards fin* **3/1**[2]
002- 4 1 ¾ **Little Carmela**[32] 7750 6-8-10 56 (v) SaleemGolam 7 63
(S C Williams) *rn in snatches: drvn bnd after 4f: sn chsng ldrs: rdn over 4f out: rallied over 1f out: kpt on one pce* **9/4**[1]
00- 5 2 ¾ **Zaffeu**[249] 1936 9-8-13 57 VinceSlattery 6 62
(A G Juckes) *s.i.s: sn pushed along to chse ldrs: one pce fnl 2f* **11/1**
02-F 6 41 **Seaquel**[10] 41 4-8-0 52 AmyBaker[(5)] 4 3
(A B Haynes) *led 4f: drvn over 5f out: sn lost pl: t.o and eased 2f out: virtually p.u* **12/1**
000- 7 30 **Matinee Idol**[37] 603 7-8-4 28 (b) DeclanCannon[(5)] 3 —
(Mrs S Lamyman) *led 4f: reminders and lost pl 7f out: t.o 5f out: virtually p.u 3f out: eventually completed* **150/1**

3m 7.06s (-1.24) **Going Correction** -0.10s/f (Stan)
WFA 4 from 6yo+ 6lb 7 Ran SP% **110.6**
Speed ratings (Par 101): **99,98,98,97,96 72,55**
toteswinger:1&2:£3.80, 2&3:£3.10, 1&3:£3.00 CSF £20.69 TOTE £5.20: £2.40, £2.10; EX 20.50.
Owner Diamond Racing Ltd **Bred** Mrs Edgar Scott Jr & Mrs Lawrence Macelree **Trained** Pandy, Monmouths

FOCUS
Not a bad staying claimer, run at a sound gallop. The form makes sense at face value through the third and fourth.

191 PLAY NEVER STOPS AT VICTOR CHANDLER POKER H'CAP 7f (F)
3:45 (3:55) (Class 4) (0-80,77) 4-Y-O+ £4,776 (£1,410; £705) Stalls Low

Form RPR
021- 1 **Striker Torres (IRE)**[27] 7813 4-8-7 66 (v) TomEaves 6 80
(B Smart) *t.k.h: led tl over 4f out: led over 2f out: hung lft and drew clr fnl f* **5/2**[2]
2-11 2 4 ½ **Elusive Warrior (USA)**[3] 144 7-8-10 74 12ex (p) DeclanCannon[(5)] 4 76
(A J McCabe) *trckd ldr: led over 4f out: hdd over 2f out: edgd rt ins fnl f: wl btn and eased towards fin* **9/4**[1]
001- 3 4 ½ **Moojeh (IRE)**[25] 7830 4-9-2 75 JerryO'Dwyer 7 64
(M Botti) *in tch: effrt and wnt modest 3rd over 2f out: one pce* **4/1**
565/ 4 1 ¼ **Sacrilege**[36] 6528 5-8-12 76 (b) MarkCoumbe[(5)] 2 62
(M C Chapman) *rel to r: sn detached in last and reminders: kpt on fnl f* **18/1**
340- 5 39 **Ocean Transit (IRE)**[25] 7287 5-9-4 77 RobertWinston 5 —
(R J Price) *chsd ldng pair: sn drvn along: reminders over 3f out: lost pl over 2f out: sn bhd and eased: virtually p.u* **10/3**[3]

1m 27.58s (-2.72) **Going Correction** -0.10s/f (Stan) 5 Ran SP% **107.7**
Speed ratings (Par 105): **111,105,100,99,54**
toteswinger: 1&2: £3.80 CSF £8.10 TOTE £2.90: £1.80, £1.40; EX 7.60 Place 6 £142.24, Place 5 £39.65.
Owner R C Bond **Bred** T Stack & Lynchbages Ltd **Trained** Hambleton, N Yorks

FOCUS
A moderate handicap, but it was still an interesting heat with three last-time-out winners in attendance. It was run at a solid pace and the first two dominated, and they set the standard.
T/Plt: £77.20 to a £1 stake. Pool: £73,570.19. 695.25 winning tickets. T/Qpdt: £19.50 to a £1 stake. Pool: £5,912.14. 224.12 winning tickets. WG

[172]WOLVERHAMPTON (A.W) (L-H)
Friday, January 15

OFFICIAL GOING: Standard
Wind: Light half behind Weather: Fine

192 TRY BETDAQ FOR AN EXCHANGE H'CAP 5f 216y(P)
4:20 (4:21) (Class 4) (0-80,77) 4-Y-O+ £4,533 (£1,348; £674; £336) Stalls Low

Form RPR
2-22 1 **Onceaponatime (IRE)**[8] 71 5-8-11 **70** LukeMorris 6 81
(M D Squance) *hld up towards rr: hdwy on ins over 2f out: led on bit over 1f out: sn rdn: jst hld on* **9/4**[1]
631- 2 hd **Weet A Surprise**[70] 7273 5-9-0 **73** (v) GrahamGibbons 12 84
(J W Unett) *broke wl: sn lost pl and bhd: pushed along over 2f out: rdn and hdwy over 1f out: r.o wl u.p ins fnl f: jst failed* **20/1**
046- 3 1 ¾ **Fazbee (IRE)**[33] 7739 4-8-9 **68** (b[1]) TonyCulhane 4 73
(P W D'Arcy) *s.i.s: hld up in rr: pushed along over 2f out: swtchd rt over 1f out: rdn and r.o wl ins fnl f: nrst fin* **9/1**
553- 4 1 ¾ **Kersivay**[48] 7577 4-8-12 **71** (p) FrannyNorton 8 70
(Ollie Pears) *a.p: pushed along over 2f out: rdn jst over 1f out: one pce ins fnl f* **13/2**[2]
3-34 5 hd **Dvinsky (USA)**[6] 102 9-8-13 **72** (b) IanMongan 11 71
(P Howling) *a.p: pushed along over 2f out: rdn wl over 1f out: one pce ins fnl f* **18/1**
304- 6 1 ½ **Misaro (GER)**[25] 7832 9-9-1 **74** (b) PhillipMakin 1 68
(R A Harris) *w ldr: led over 2f out: rdn and hdd over 1f out: wknd ins fnl f* **16/1**
2/0- 7 ¾ **Bosun Breese**[60] 7414 5-8-13 **77** DeanHeslop[(5)] 5 69
(T D Barron) *plld hrd in mid-div: n.m.r and lost pl over 3f out: sn bhd: rdn wl over 1f out: sme late prog* **40/1**
022- 8 1 ¼ **Billy Red**[40] 7656 6-9-4 **77** (b) StephenCraine 9 65
(J R Jenkins) *led: hdd over 2f out: rdn wl over 1f out: wknd fnl f* **16/1**
333- 9 nk **Sanjay's Choice (IRE)**[51] 7528 4-8-12 **71** ow1 (p) AdamKirby 2 58
(T G McCourt, Ire) *hld up in tch on ins: pushed along and wknd ins fnl f* **10/1**
612- 9 dht **Apache Ridge (IRE)**[235] 2336 4-8-11 **70** NeilCallan 10 57
(K A Ryan) *s.i.s: hmpd sn after s: stdy prog over 3f out: nt clr run over 2f out tl wl over 1f out: sn pushed along and btn* **8/1**[3]
035- 11 2 **Methaaly (IRE)**[16] 7875 7-9-3 **76** (be) EddieAhern 3 56
(M Mullineaux) *hld up towards rr on ins: nt clr run briefly over 2f out: n.d after* **12/1**
40-2 12 1 ½ **Bel Cantor**[5] 115 7-9-1 **77** KellyHarrison[(3)] 13 52
(W J H Ratcliffe) *hld up in mid-div on outside: pushed along over 2f out: c wd st: wknd wl over 1f out* **10/1**

1m 14.49s (-0.51) **Going Correction** +0.05s/f (Slow) 12 Ran SP% **115.3**
Speed ratings (Par 105): **105,104,102,100,99 97,96,95,94,94 92,90**
toteswinger:1&2:£13.20, 2&3:£38.20, 1&3:£8.60 CSF £52.30 CT £351.43 TOTE £2.90: £1.30, £4.80, £3.20; EX 58.20.
Owner M D Squance **Bred** Dermot O'Rourke **Trained** Newmarket, Suffolk
■ Stewards' Enquiry : Stephen Craine one day: not riding to draw (Jan 29)

FOCUS
A decent sprint handicap run at a solid pace. The winner's best effort since his early 3yo days.

193 COLIN RIDSDALE 50TH BIRTHDAY CELEBRATION H'CAP (DIV I) 5f 216y(P)
4:50 (4:51) (Class 6) (0-55,59) 4-Y-O+ £1,433 (£423; £211) Stalls Low

Form RPR
00- 1 **Bishopbriggs (USA)**[16] 7880 5-8-11 **52** AdamKirby 10 65
(M G Quinlan) *mde all: rdn 1f out: drvn out* **7/2**[1]
040- 2 2 **Miss Firefly**[30] 7771 5-8-12 **53** JamieSpencer 2 60
(R J Hodges) *a.p: pressed wnr gng wl over 1f out: rdn and nt qckn ins fnl f* **13/2**

010- **3** 1¾ **Carnival Dream**[48] 7579 5-8-13 **54**............................ GrahamGibbons 8 55
(H A McWilliams) *hld up in mid-div: rdn and hdwy over 1f out: kpt on to take 3rd towards fin* **20/1**

00-6 **4** ½ **Muktasb (USA)**[13] 14 9-9-0 **55**......................(v) NeilCallan 1 54
(D Shaw) *hld up in mid-div on ins: pushed along and hdwy wl over 1f out: rdn and one pce fnl f* **7/2**[1]

46-1 **5** nk **Interchoice Star**[11] 30 5-8-11 **59** 6ex...................(p) DavidKenny(7) 13 57
(R Hollinshead) *a.p: wnt 2nd briefly 2f out: rdn over 1f out: no ex ins fnl f* **9/2**[2]

00-0 **6** 1 **Obe Brave**[11] 36 7-9-0 **55**............................ TonyHamilton 6 50
(Lee Smyth, Ire) *hld up and bhd: pushed along 2f out: kpt on fnl f: n.d* **14/1**

0-26 **7** 4½ **Well Of Echoes**[4] 129 4-8-7 **48**.........................(tp) AndrewMullen 12 29
(A J McCabe) *pushed along and sn prom: ev ch over 2f out: rdn and wknd over 1f out* **5/1**[3]

050- **8** nk **Vanadium**[47] 7592 8-8-5 **53**..........................(tp) AmyScott(7) 7 33
(A J Lidderdale) *hld up and bhd: pushed along over 2f out: sn struggling* **11/1**

40-0 **9** 10 **Admirals Way**[13] 10 5-8-7 **53**........................ LeeNewnes(5) 9 —
(C N Kellett) *prom tl wknd over 2f out* **33/1**

023- **10** 3¼ **Nimmy's Special**[141] 5362 4-8-6 **50**................... KellyHarrison(3) 4 —
(M Mullineaux) *s.i.s: outpcd* **25/1**

1m 15.1s (0.10) **Going Correction** +0.05s/f (Slow) **10** Ran SP% **119.2**
Speed ratings (Par 101): **101,98,96,95,94 93,87,87,73,69**
toteswinger:1&2:£8.60, 2&3:£13.20, 1&3:£14.50 CSF £26.67 CT £411.27 TOTE £4.70: £1.10, £2.20, £6.30; EX 30.50.
Owner Maurice Kirby **Bred** Sycamore Hall Farm Llc **Trained** Newmarket, Suffolk
■ Stewards' Enquiry : Adam Kirby caution: used whip without giving gelding time to respond

FOCUS
An ordinary handicap. The pace was not particularly strong and not many got into it from behind. The winner posted a good effort for the grade, and the form is rated around the second and third.

194 BETDAQ ON 0870 178 1221 H'CAP 7f 32y(P)
5:20 (5:21) (Class 6) (0-60,60) 4-Y-O+ **£1,774** (£523; £262) **Stalls** High

Form RPR

00-4 **1** **Carmenero (GER)**[4] 129 7-9-4 **60**.......................... EddieAhern 8 74
(C R Dore) *hld up towards rr: stdy prog 3f out: rdn to ld wl over 1f out: clr fnl f: eased towards fin* **8/1**[3]

400- **2** 6 **Angaric (IRE)**[38] 7679 7-8-8 **57**........................ AdamCarter(7) 12 55
(B Smart) *hld up in mid-div: pushed along over 2f out: rdn and hdwy over 1f out: wnt 2nd ins fnl f: no ch w wnr* **25/1**

000- **3** ½ **Sendreni (FR)**[46] 7596 6-9-4 **60**...................... StephenCraine 4 56
(M Wigham) *hld up in tch on ins: swtchd rt ent st: rdn over 1f out: one pce* **10/1**

000- **4** ¾ **Royal Envoy (IRE)**[52] 7506 7-9-1 **60**................ MichaelStainton(3) 7 54
(P Howling) *hld up towards rr: c v wd st: pushed along and hdwy over 1f out: one pce fnl f* **25/1**

5 nse **Sir Mozart (IRE)**[49] 7565 7-9-4 **60**...................... JamieSpencer 10 54
(A J Martin, Ire) *s.i.s: sn swtchd lft: hld up in rr: pushed along and hdwy whn swtchd lft over 1f out: sn rdn: one pce* **13/8**[1]

404- **6** 1¼ **Haasem (USA)**[18] 7860 7-9-3 **59**.........................(v) JimmyQuinn 9 50
(J R Jenkins) *hld up towards rr: hdwy on ins wl over 1f out: no further prog fnl f* **14/1**

6-03 **7** nk **Jord (IRE)**[4] 129 6-8-11 **60**........................ JonathanHinch(7) 6 50
(J A Glover) *broke wl: hld up in mid-div: stmbld over 3f out: bhd fnl 2f* **8/1**[3]

65-4 **8** 2¾ **Lindy Hop (IRE)**[10] 38 4-9-1 **57**............................ NeilCallan 3 40
(K A Ryan) *prom: led briefly wl over 1f out: sn rdn: wknd ins fnl f* **14/1**

31-0 **9** ½ **King Of Rhythm (IRE)**[13] 21 7-9-1 **57**....................(b) DavidNolan 5 38
(D Carroll) *hld up in mid-div on ins: pushed along 3f out: rdn and wknd over 1f out* **11/1**

6-54 **10** 3½ **Tallest Peak (USA)**[8] 75 5-9-1 **57**......................(p) AdamKirby 2 29
(M G Quinlan) *led: hdd over 3f out: rdn and wknd over 2f out* **5/1**[2]

24-3 **11** 6 **Cross Section (USA)**[10] 38 4-9-4 **60**...................... IanMongan 1 16
(E F Vaughan) *w ldr: led over 3f out tl wl over 1f out: sn wknd* **12/1**

1m 29.2s (-0.40) **Going Correction** +0.05s/f (Slow) **11** Ran SP% **123.1**
Speed ratings (Par 101): **104,97,96,95,95 94,93,90,90,86 79**
toteswinger:1&2:£37.10, 2&3:£31.50, 1&3:£25.50 CSF £196.40 CT £2050.08 TOTE £12.60: £3.70, £7.60, £4.70; EX 198.00.
Owner Andrew Page **Bred** Graf And Grafin Von Stauffenberg **Trained** Cowbit, Lincs

FOCUS
A modest handicap. The winner was apparently back to his best but the form is misleading.

195 COLIN RIDSDALE 50TH BIRTHDAY CELEBRATION H'CAP (DIV II) 5f 216y(P)
5:50 (5:52) (Class 6) (0-55,60) 4-Y-O+ **£1,433** (£423; £211) **Stalls** Low

Form RPR

305- **1** **Radiator Rooney (IRE)**[15] 7889 7-9-0 **55**...............(b) StephenCraine 12 66
(Patrick Morris) *hld up towards rr: stdy hdwy over 2f out: rdn to ld ins fnl f: r.o wl* **10/1**

06-0 **2** 2¼ **All You Need (IRE)**[8] 70 6-8-4 **52** ow1.................(vp) DavidKenny(7) 2 56
(R Hollinshead) *hld up in tch: pushed along and wnt 2nd wl ins fnl f: nt trble wnr* **20/1**

0-01 **3** shd **Know No Fear**[6] 103 5-8-10 **58** 6ex...............................(p) HollyHall(7) 3 62+
(A J Lidderdale) *s.i.s: hld up in rr: c v wd st: rdn wl over 1f out: gd late hdwy: nrst fin* **6/1**[3]

40-0 **4** ¾ **Tri Chara (IRE)**[13] 21 6-9-0 **55**.............................(tp) GrahamGibbons 8 56
(R Hollinshead) *hld up in tch: rdn over 1f out: one pce ins fnl f* **6/1**[3]

00-0 **5** ½ **Monte Cassino (IRE)**[3] 137 5-9-0 **60** ow8........... JamesO'Reilly(5) 11 60
(J O'Reilly) *a.p: led wl over 1f out: sn edgd lft: hdd ins fnl f: no ex* **22/1**

2-34 **6** nse **Hart Of Gold**[3] 135 6-8-12 **53**.................................(p) PhillipMakin 4 53
(R A Harris) *led early: prom: rdn wl over 1f out: one pce fnl f* **3/1**[2]

30-0 **7** ½ **Makshoof (IRE)**[13] 10 6-8-12 **53**..............................(p) NeilCallan 7 51
(I W McInnes) *hld up towards rr: rdn over 1f out: nvr nr to chal* **14/1**

356- **8** hd **Pipers Piping (IRE)**[100] 6587 4-8-10 **54**................ MichaelStainton(3) 5 51
(P Howling) *hld up towards rr: nt clr run on ins ins fnl f: sn swtchd rt: nvr able to chal* **12/1**

6-12 **9** shd **Tanley**[6] 103 5-8-10 **51**.. TonyCulhane 9 48
(J F Coupland) *hld up in mid-div: pushed along and wknd wl over 1f out* **5/2**[1]

60- **10** 1½ **Almatlaie (USA)**[125] 5882 4-8-9 **50** ow1.......................... EddieAhern 13 42
(J W Unett) *sn led: rdn and hdd wl over 1f out: eased whn btn ins fnl f* **40/1**

300- **11** 2½ **Mister Incredible**[255] 1781 7-8-6 **47**..............................(v) LukeMorris 1 31
(J M Bradley) *hld up in tch on ins: rdn over 1f out: one pce whn n.m.r and eased ins fnl f* **25/1**

1m 15.21s (0.21) **Going Correction** +0.05s/f (Slow) **11** Ran SP% **121.0**
Speed ratings (Par 101): **100,97,96,95,95 95,94,94,94,92 88**
toteswinger:1&2:£32.00, 2&3:£28.20, 1&3:£13.50 CSF £198.00 CT £1336.83 TOTE £10.20: £3.20, £6.50, £3.50; EX 126.90.
Owner Bellflower Racing Limited **Bred** Barry Lyons **Trained** Tarporley, Cheshire

FOCUS
A low-grade handicap run at a strong pace. The winner is rated back to something like his best.

196 STAY AT THE WOLVERHAMPTON HOLIDAY INN CLAIMING STKS 1m 141y(P)
6:20 (6:22) (Class 5) 4-Y-O+ **£2,729** (£806) **Stalls** Low

Form RPR

435- **1** **Soccerjackpot (USA)**[58] 7431 6-9-6 93.......................... AdamKirby 1 83+
(C G Cox) *mde all: hung lft wl over 1f out: comf* **1/6**[1]

540- **2** 2½ **Bolodenka (IRE)**[20] 7848 8-9-4 78.............................(t) TonyHamilton 3 75
(R A Fahey) *trckd wnr: swtchd rt wl over 1f out: sn rdn and btn* **5/1**[2]

1m 52.72s (2.22) **Going Correction** +0.05s/f (Slow) **2** Ran SP% **102.4**
Speed ratings (Par 103): **92,89**
TOTE £1.10.Soccerjackpot was claimed by Alan Jones for £17,000.
Owner sportaracing.com & George Houghton **Bred** Gary Chervenell **Trained** Lambourn, Berks

FOCUS
A claimer that was weakened by three withdrawals. The winner was left with a simple task on these terms.

197 BET PREMIER LEAGUE FOOTBALL - BETDAQ H'CAP 1m 141y(P)
6:50 (6:50) (Class 3) (0-90,89) 4-Y-O+ **£6,938** (£2,076; £1,038; £519; £258) **Stalls** Low

Form RPR

0- **1** **Winter Fever (SAF)**[26] 7827 6-9-1 **85**.............................. LukeMorris 9 93+
(J M P Eustace) *hld up in mid-div: rdn and hdwy 1f out: r.o to ld towards fin* **28/1**

41-2 **2** ¾ **Quick Release (IRE)**[11] 29 5-8-2 **75**.......................... MartinLane(3) 3 82
(D M Simcock) *a.p: led wl over 1f out: sn rdn: edgd rt ins fnl f: hdd and no ex towards fin* **5/1**[2]

340- **3** nk **Just Bond (IRE)**[20] 7848 8-9-0 **84**................................... JimmyQuinn 8 90
(G R Oldroyd) *led early: a.p: hrd rdn and nt qckn ins fnl f* **18/1**

415- **4** 1¼ **Plush**[20] 7848 7-8-7 **82**.. RossAtkinson(5) 4 85
(Tom Dascombe) *stdd and s.s: hld up in rr: pushed along and hdwy over 1f out: rdn and swtchd lft wl ins fnl f: nt qckn* **5/1**[2]

561- **5** nk **African Cheetah**[39] 7672 4-8-5 **76**.............................. FrannyNorton 13 78
(R Hollinshead) *sn swtchd lft: towards rr: pushed along over 3f out: rdn and hdwy 1f out: kpt on* **6/1**[3]

001- **6** nk **Scamperdale**[20] 7848 8-9-2 **86**... TonyCulhane 5 88
(B P J Baugh) *hld up towards rr: pushed along over 2f out: rdn ins fnl f: nvr nr to chal* **14/1**

300- **7** nk **Cobo Bay**[69] 7294 5-9-0 **89**...(b) AmyRyan(5) 6 90
(K A Ryan) *sn led: hdd wl over 1f out: sn rdn: fdd wl ins fnl f* **7/1**

103- **8** ½ **Iron Out (USA)**[20] 7848 4-8-11 **82**............................ RobertWinston 11 82
(R Hollinshead) *a.p: rdn over 2f out: one pce fnl f* **14/1**

00-6 **9** ½ **Stand Guard**[14] 6 6-8-12 **87**............................... AndrewHeffernan(5) 12 86
(P Howling) *hld up in mid-div: pushed along over 3f out: c wd st: rdn and wknd wl over 1f out* **14/1**

001- **10** 5 **Red Somerset (USA)**[20] 7845 7-8-11 **81**...................... JamieSpencer 2 68
(R J Hodges) *hld up in mid-div: nt clr run on ins over 2f out: rdn over 1f out: eased whn btn ins fnl f* **8/1**

021- **11** 4 **Inheritor (IRE)**[34] 7734 4-9-0 **85**.. TomEaves 10 63
(B Smart) *chsd ldr tl pushed along 2f out: rdn and wknd over 1f out* **4/1**[1]

1m 48.86s (-1.64) **Going Correction** +0.05s/f (Slow)
WFA 4 from 5yo+ 1lb **11** Ran SP% **119.9**
Speed ratings (Par 107): **109,108,108,106,106 106,106,105,105,100 97**
toteswinger:1&2:£37.10, 2&3:£18.50, 1&3:£41.10 CSF £166.24 CT £2676.61 TOTE £36.90: £10.30, £2.60, £4.00; EX 217.20.
Owner Rupert Plersch **Bred** Scott Bros **Trained** Newmarket, Suffolk

FOCUS
A competitive handicap. The pace was strong and there was an exciting finish. Sound form, the second and third setting the standard.

NOTEBOOK
Winter Fever(SAF) had to be switched out wide turning for home but showed a resilient attitude to overhaul the leader in the closing stages and spring a surprise on his second run for a new yard. He cut little ice in handicaps in Dubai early last year but was a Listed winner in South Africa and is still relatively lightly raced. He will not go up much for this win and should be capable of further success at this trip and a bit further. (op 25-1 tchd 33-1)
Quick Release(IRE) travelled well for a long way and looked the likely winner entering the final furlong but he drifted right and was just outgunned. He has proved very consistent since returning from 11 months off last summer and should continue to go well. (tchd 9-2 and 11-2)
Just Bond(IRE) has found life tougher since his mark re-entered the 80s but the likeable veteran put in a valiant bid here and may be able to add to his eight previous wins at this track. (op 16-1)
Plush was last turning into the straight and could never get to grips with the leaders. He has won five of his last nine starts at this track but has gone up 27lb since joining his current yard and the handicapper may have his measure. (tchd 7-1)
African Cheetah had a tough draw and did not get the clearest of runs but put in a fair effort up in grade in his bid to defy a 4lb rise for making a successful debut for new connections in a steadily run C&D handicap last month. (op 7-1 tchd 15-2 and 11-2)
Scamperdale was never a factor but finished powerfully from well off the pace over a trip that is on the sharp side for him these days. (tchd 16-1)
Inheritor(IRE) justified favouritism off 3lb lower over C&D last month but dropped away tamely after tracking the pace here and was reported to have raced too freely. Official explanation: trainer's rep said gelding ran too freely (op 9-2 tchd 5-1)

198 GREAT OFFERS AT WOLVERHAMPTON-RACECOURSE.CO.UK H'CAP 1m 5f 194y(P)
7:20 (7:21) (Class 6) (0-60,60) 4-Y-O+ **£1,774** (£523; £262) **Stalls** Low

Form RPR

4-55 **1** **Kickahead (USA)**[4] 130 8-9-0 **50**............................(t) StevieDonohoe 10 62
(Ian Williams) *hld up in rr: stdy hdwy over 3f out: pushed along over 2f out: rdn and hung lft whn led jst ins fnl f: styd on wl* **6/1**[2]

130- **2** 4 **Aaman (IRE)**[115] 6188 4-8-13 **55**.................................. JamieSpencer 4 61+
(E F Vaughan) *racd keenly: prom: led after 3f: rdn wl over 1f out: hdd jst ins fnl f: one pce* **15/2**

56-4 **3** hd **Supernoverre (IRE)**[4] 121 4-9-2 **58**................................ IanMongan 9 64
(P Howling) *hld up: stdy prog 4f out: chsd ldr 2f out: sn rdn: lost 2nd over 1f out: one pce* **3/1**[1]

00-0 **4** nk **Sir Sandicliffe (IRE)**[4] 130 6-9-2 **52**.............................. EddieAhern 7 58
(W M Brisbourne) *s.i.s: hld up towards rr: stdy hdwy over 3f out: pushed along over 2f out: rdn wl over 1f out: one pce fnl f* **14/1**

34-0 **5** 3¾ **Summer Affair (IRE)**10 41 5-9-2 **57**.................... MatthewDavies(5) 8 57
(B I Case) *hld up in mid-div: hdwy over 3f out: rdn over 2f out: wknd over 1f out* **12/1**

160- **6** *shd* **Nakoma (IRE)**29 7785 8-9-5 **60**.................................. DeclanCannon(5) 3 60
(B Ellison) *s.i.s: sn in tch: chsd ldr jst over 3f out tl hrd rdn 2f out: wknd over 1f out* **7/1**3

06-5 **7** 3½ **Time To Play**14 1 5-9-3 **53**.. AdamKirby 2 48
(T T Clement) *hld up in mid-div: lost pl 3f out: n.d after* **25/1**

500- **8** *nk* **Bold Adventure**29 7785 6-9-5 **55**.................................. TonyCulhane 12 50
(W J Musson) *hld up in rr: pushed along 3f out: sn struggling* **14/1**

000- **9** ½ **Mesbaah (IRE)**39 7085 6-9-5 **55**.................................. TonyHamilton 13 49
(R A Fahey) *hld up in rr: pushed along and struggling over 2f out* **12/1**

040/ **10** *9* **Bret Maverick (IRE)**67 6835 6-8-12 **48**..................(p) GrahamGibbons 5 30
(B P J Baugh) *led 3f: chsd ldr tl jst over 3f out: wknd qckly* **18/1**

/66- **11** *11* **Command Marshal (FR)**16 7873 7-9-10 **60**............... StephenCraine 1 26
(M J Scudamore) *prom tl wknd qckly over 3f out* **33/1**

341- **12** *21* **Squirtle (IRE)**32 7750 7-9-3 **53**.. LukeMorris 11 —
(W M Brisbourne) *towards rr: reminder over 7f out: rdn over 3f out: sn struggling* **7/1**3

3m 4.81s (-1.19) **Going Correction** +0.05s/f (Slow)
WFA 4 from 5yo+ 6lb **12** Ran SP% **116.8**
Speed ratings (Par 101): **105,102,102,102,100 100,98,98,97,92 86,74**
toteswinger:1&2:£7.50, 2&3:£7.00, 1&3:£6.00 CSF £49.80 CT £162.23 TOTE £8.90: £2.50, £1.90, £1.70; EX 49.60.
Owner Churchill Office Solutions Limited **Bred** Wertheimer Et Frere **Trained** Portway, Worcs

FOCUS
A weak handicap, but the pace was sound and three of the first four in the betting filled the first three places, so the form could prove reliable. The winner is rated in line with his old British Flat form.
Time To Play Official explanation: jockey said gelding hung left in the straight

199 DINE IN THE HORIZONS RESTAURANT H'CAP 1m 4f 50y(P)
7:50 (7:54) (Class 7) (0-50,50) 4-Y-0+ **£1,364** (£403; £201) **Stalls** Low

Form RPR
603- **1** **Fine Tolerance**40 7658 4-8-10 **49**.................................... DavidProbert 5 57
(Miss S L Davison) *hld up towards rr: hdwy over 3f out: rdn to ld jst over 1f out: r.o* **9/2**2

/4-2 **2** ¾ **Crimson Flame (IRE)**4 130 7-8-13 **48**.................... RobertWinston 11 54
(S Curran) *hld up in mid-div: stdy prog 3f out: wnt 2nd ins fnl f: rdn and nt qckn* **6/4**1

540- **3** 1¼ **Red Wine**41 7642 11-9-1 **50**... PhillipMakin 4 54
(J A Glover) *t.k.h in rr: hdwy over 1f out: rdn and r.o to take 3rd nr fin* **11/2**3

630- **4** *hd* **John Potts**18 7857 5-8-12 **47**.. TonyCulhane 2 51
(B P J Baugh) *hld up towards rr: stdy hdwy over 2f out: rdn and squeezed through 1f out: nt qckn towards fin* **8/1**

000- **5** ½ **Wacato King (IRE)**32 7755 4-8-6 **50**...................(t) AndrewHeffernan(5) 9 53
(R A Farrant) *rn wout tongue strap: hld up in tch on ins: pushed along 2f out: rdn and ev ch 1f out: nt qckn* **25/1**

00-5 **6** 1¼ **Anduril**8 75 9-8-4 **46**.. NeilFarley(7) 6 47
(D Carroll) *hld up in mid-div: nt clr run on ins wl over 1f out: plld out jst over 1f out: nvr able to chal* **22/1**

566- **7** 1¾ **Stravita**24 7840 6-9-1 **50**..(p) GrahamGibbons 8 48
(R Hollinshead) *led: clr after 2f tl 6f out: rdn and hdd over 2f out: wknd ins fnl f* **6/1**

0/0- **8** 2¾ **Take It There**36 6208 8-9-0 **49**.......................................(t) JamieSpencer 1 43
(A J Lidderdale) *t.k.h: prom: led over 2f out: rdn wl over 1f out: sn hdd: eased whn btn ins fnl f* **11/1**

0/0- **9** *23* **Viscaya (IRE)**361 215 5-8-12 **47**...................................(v1) LukeMorris 7 4
(N J Vaughan) *s.s: t.k.h in rr: rdn wl over 2f out: sn struggling* **33/1**

050- **10** 3¼ **Helpmeronda**18 7857 4-8-6 **50**.................................. RossAtkinson(5) 12 2
(W M Brisbourne) *chsd ldr tl pushed along over 3f out: wknd wl over 2f out* **40/1**

2m 43.62s (2.52) **Going Correction** +0.05s/f (Slow)
WFA 4 from 5yo+ 4lb **10** Ran SP% **120.9**
Speed ratings (Par 97): **93,92,91,91,91 90,89,87,72,69**
toteswinger:1&2:£3.30, 2&3:£4.90, 1&3:£9.50 CSF £11.67 CT £39.38 TOTE £6.60: £2.70, £1.50, £1.40; EX 17.90 Place 6 £614.53, Place 5 £281.00.
Owner Calne Engineering Ltd **Bred** Edward J G Young **Trained** Beckhampton, Wilts

FOCUS
A poor handicap in which most of the runners had finished well beaten on their previous start. It was steadily run and the form is far from convincing.
T/Jkpt: Not won. T/Plt: £2,359.50 to a £1 stake. Pool: £108,281.76. 33.50 winning tickets. T/Qpdt: £283.40 to a £1 stake. Pool: £12,256.58. 32.00 winning tickets. KH

179 LINGFIELD (L-H)
Saturday, January 16

OFFICIAL GOING: Standard
Wind: medium, behind Weather: dull, rain at times

200 TRY BETDAQ FOR AN EXCHANGE CLAIMING STKS 1m 2f (P)
1:00 (1:00) (Class 6) 4-Y-0+ **£1,774** (£523; £262) **Stalls** Low

Form RPR
1-21 **1** **Clear Sailing**7 105 7-8-11 67.. PaulDoe 8 75
(P D Evans) *mounted on crse: taken down early: pressed ldr: clr of field over 3f out: led gng wl over 2f out: rdn and flashed tail 1f out: kpt on* **1/1**1

500- **2** 1¼ **Cupid's Glory**51 7539 8-8-11 75.. LiamKeniry 7 73
(G L Moore) *s.i.s: t.k.h: hld up in last pair: hdwy on outer 3f out: rdn to chse wnr wl over 1f out: hung lft fr over 1f out: a hld after* **12/1**

0/5- **3** *6* **Kindlelight Blue (IRE)**304 873 6-9-5 73.................... J-PGuillambert 3 69
(N P Littmoden) *bustled along leaving stalls: racd in last trio: outpcd over 3f out: rdn and no prog over 2f out: plugged on u.p fnl f to go modest 3rd fnl 75yds: nvr trbld ldrs* **8/1**3

50-0 **4** *nk* **Awatuki (IRE)**13 25 7-8-5 68... NickyMackay 6 54
(J R Boyle) *stdd s: hld up in last pair: pushed along 4f out: rdn and no prog over 2f out: plugged on u.p fnl f: nvr trbld ldrs* **17/2**

03-6 **5** 1¼ **Hold The Bucks (USA)**7 105 4-8-9 64...........................(p) LukeMorris 5 57
(J S Moore) *chsd ldrs: pushed along over 7f out: rdn and outpcd by ldng pair over 3f out: rallied ent fnl 2f: wknd and wl btn over 1f out: lost 2 pls ins fnl f* **14/1**

003- **6** *4* **Laurie Grove (IRE)**17 7881 4-9-9 77.................................. JoeFanning 1 63
(T G Mills) *broke wl: led: clr w wnr over 3f out: hdd and rdn over 2f out: wknd wl over 1f out: wl btn fnl f* **9/2**2

100- **7** *9* **Head Down**17 7883 4-9-5 74.. JimmyQuinn 4 41
(Mrs L C Jewell) *chsd ldrs: rdn over 4f out: wknd u.p over 2f out: wl bhd fr over 1f out* **25/1**

2m 4.03s (-2.57) **Going Correction** -0.025s/f (Stan)
WFA 4 from 5yo+ 2lb **7** Ran SP% **108.0**
Speed ratings (Par 101): **109,108,103,102,101 98,91**
toteswingers: 1&2 £4.30, 1&3 £1.90, 2&3 £19.10 CSF £12.56 TOTE £1.90: £1.10, £4.70; EX 13.90 Trifecta £49.30 Pool: £385.17 - 5.78 winning units..
Owner Diamond Racing Ltd **Bred** Juddmonte Farms Ltd **Trained** Pandy, Monmouths

FOCUS
Not a bad claimer judged on official ratings, as the lowest-rated runner had a mark of 64, but most of these struggle to win these days.

201 BET PREMIER LEAGUE FOOTBALL - BETDAQ MAIDEN STKS 6f (P)
1:35 (1:36) (Class 5) 3-Y-O **£2,456** (£725; £362) **Stalls** Low

Form RPR
53-3 **1** **Major Maximus**5 122 3-8-12 66.........................(b1) MatthewDavies(5) 1 69
(George Baker) *racd freely: mde all: sn clr: rdn over 1f out: kpt on: unchal* **6/4**2

0-0 **2** 3¾ **Sweet Avon**13 24 3-8-12 0... EddieAhern 3 52
(Matthew Salaman) *chsd wnr thrght: rdn ent fnl 2f: kpt on same pce u.p fnl f* **6/1**3

3 *13* **Understory (USA)** 3-9-3 0... JoeFanning 4 15
(M Johnston) *s.i.s: rn green and sn rdn along in poor last: wnt 3rd wl over 1f out: nvr on terms* **11/10**1

- **4** *8* **Rightcar Joan (IRE)** 3-8-12 0... LiamKeniry 5 —
(Peter Grayson) *stdd s: t.k.h: a wl bhd in last pair: rdn and no prog 1/2-way: t.o* **33/1**

1m 12.1s (0.20) **Going Correction** -0.025s/f (Stan) **4** Ran SP% **104.8**
Speed ratings (Par 97): **97,92,74,64**
CSF £9.12 TOTE £2.30; EX 5.70.
Owner Mrs C E S Baker **Bred** Mrs S M Roy **Trained** Moreton Morrell, Warwicks

FOCUS
A poor maiden that took little winning.

202 BET AFRICAN NATIONS CUP - BETDAQ H'CAP 1m 2f (P)
2:10 (2:12) (Class 5) (0-70,70) 4-Y-0+ **£2,456** (£725; £362) **Stalls** Low

Form RPR
363- **1** **Jeer (IRE)**31 7777 6-9-6 **70**..(bt) JamieSpencer 1 77
(M W Easterby) *t.k.h: chsd ldrs: effrt to chse ldr ent fnl 2f: rdn to ld over 1f out: hld on wl fnl f* **5/1**3

322- **2** *hd* **Charlie Smirke (USA)**27 7826 4-8-8 **60**............................. LiamKeniry 4 67
(G L Moore) *t.k.h: hld up in midfield: hdwy to chse ldrs and rdn ent fnl 2f: str chal fnl 150yds: kpt on but a jst hld* **13/2**

115- **3** ¾ **Bosamcliff (IRE)**16 7641 5-8-12 **67**........................... RichardEvans(5) 5 72+
(P D Evans) *s.i.s: bhd: nudged along 4f out: hdwy on outer ent fnl f: r.o wl to snatch 3rd last strides: nt rch ldrs* **18/1**

01-5 **4** *nk* **Atacama Sunrise**8 83 4-8-13 **65**................................. SaleemGolam 9 70
(J Pearce) *hld up in tch: hdwy to chse ldrs 2f out: swtchd rt over 1f out: pressed ldrs but n.m.r thrght fnl f: one pce and hld whn nt clr run and eased nr fin: lost 3rd last strides* **4/1**2

100- **5** 1¼ **Whodunit (UAE)**17 7876 6-8-6 **56**..................................(b) LukeMorris 8 58
(P W Hiatt) *sn led: rdn and pressed ent fnl 2f: hdd over 1f out: wknd fnl 75yds* **33/1**

033- **6** 1¼ **Society Venue**34 6760 5-9-6 **70**... JimCrowley 10 70
(M J Scudamore) *chsd ldr tl ent fnl 2f: keeping on same pce u.p whn nt clr run ent fnl f: wknd ins fnl f* **15/2**

223- **7** *hd* **Bavarica**33 7752 8-8-10 **67**.. AdamBeschizza(7) 2 66
(Miss J Feilden) *jostling match w rival sn after s: hld up in last trio: effrt and nt clr run towards inner over 1f out: swtchd rt ent fnl f: rn but nvr able to chal* **9/1**

0-22 **8** 1¼ **Alfie Tupper (IRE)**8 83 7-8-13 **63**...........................(p) StephenCraine 3 60
(J R Boyle) *hld up in tch on inner: n.m.r bnd ent fnl 2f: rdn and nt qckn over 1f out: no prog after* **7/2**1

105- **9** 2½ **Rapid City**31 7776 7-9-4 **68**... PaulDoe 11 60
(P D Evans) *plld hrd: hld up in last trio tl hdwy on outer to chse ldrs over 5f out: wknd u.p wl over 1f out* **10/1**

106- **10** ¾ **Alqaahir (USA)**40 7672 8-9-6 **70**..................................... JimmyQuinn 6 60
(P Burgoyne) *t.k.h: hld up in tch towards rr: rdn and effrt wl over 1f out: carried rt and no prog ent fnl f* **16/1**

036- **11** *2* **Maybe I Will (IRE)**230 2518 5-9-2 **66**.............................. HayleyTurner 7 52
(S Dow) *chsd ldng trio tl lost pl and rdn over 2f out: n.d fnl 2f* **28/1**

2m 5.17s (-1.43) **Going Correction** -0.025s/f (Stan)
WFA 4 from 5yo+ 2lb **11** Ran SP% **120.6**
Speed ratings (Par 103): **104,103,103,103,102 101,100,99,97,97 95**
toteswingers: 1&2 £12.30, 1&3 £26.20, 2&3 £23.20 CSF £38.65 CT £552.27 TOTE £5.80: £2.00, £2.50, £6.00; EX 49.30 Trifecta £265.10 Part won. Pool: £358.37 - 0.44 winning units..
Owner Mrs Jean Turpin **Bred** Floors Farming And Side Hill Stud **Trained** Sheriff Hutton, N Yorks
■ Stewards' Enquiry : Adam Beschizza three-day ban: careless riding (Jan 30-Feb 1); caution: entered wrong stall.
Luke Morris caution: careless riding.

FOCUS
A competitive handicap but it was run in a time 1.14sec slower than the claimer earlier on the card.
Rapid City Official explanation: jockey said gelding ran too free

203 BETDAQ.CO.UK H'CAP 1m (P)
2:40 (2:41) (Class 4) (0-85,80) 3-Y-O **£4,209** (£1,252; £625; £312) **Stalls** High

Form RPR
3-34 **1** **Exceedthewildman**4 136 3-8-7 **73**..............................(p) KierenFox(7) 2 77
(J S Moore) *dwlt: in tch in last: rdn and hdwy on outer 2f out: led ent fnl f: r.o wl* **6/1**

11-1 **2** ½ **Lisahane Bog**12 35 3-9-1 **74**...(p) JimCrowley 1 77+
(P R Hedger) *t.k.h: chsd ldrs: rdn and effrt 2f out: hdwy between horses ent fnl f: chsd wnr ins fnl f: kpt on u.p but a hld* **10/3**2

303- **3** 1¾ **Epic (IRE)**29 7804 3-9-0 **73**.. JoeFanning 4 72+
(M Johnston) *t.k.h: w ldr: ev ch and rdn 2f out: edgd rt and led narrowly over 1f out: hdd ent fnl f: one pce ins fnl 150yds* **11/1**

31-1 **4** *1* **Prince Of Sorrento**7 107 3-9-3 **76**............................. J-PGuillambert 5 72
(J Akehurst) *t.k.h: hld up wl in tch: rdn and carried rt over 1f out: nt clr run and lost pl ent fnl f: sn swtchd rt: kpt on same pce after* **11/10**1

62-2 **5** *5* **Transfixed (IRE)**7 107 3-9-2 **80**................................. RichardEvans(5) 3 64
(P D Evans) *t.k.h: led: rdn 2f out: hdd over 1f out: wknd fnl f* **11/2**3

1m 39.15s (0.95) **Going Correction** -0.025s/f (Stan) **5** Ran SP% **108.7**
Speed ratings (Par 99): **94,93,91,90,85**
CSF £24.80 TOTE £5.70: £2.70, £1.90; EX 22.00.
Owner E Moore & J S Moore **Bred** Horizon Bloodstock Limited **Trained** Upper Lambourn, Berks

FOCUS
They went no gallop here and the race developed into a sprint from the turn in. As a result the form should be treated with caution.
Prince Of Sorrento Official explanation: jockey said colt was denied a clear run

204 BETDAQ THE BETTING EXCHANGE CONDITIONS STKS (QUALIFIER) 7f (P)
3:10 (3:11) (Class 3) 4-Y-0+ **£6,799** (£2,023; £1,011; £505) **Stalls** Low

Form RPR
33-2 **1** **Atlantic Story (USA)**[7] 108 8-9-0 108........................(bt) JamieSpencer 4 101+
(M W Easterby) *broke wl: sn stdd and hld up in 3rd: clsd gng wl jst over 2f out: shkn up to ld jst ins fnl f: in command after: comf* **1/2**[1]
2-22 **2** *1* **Aeroplane**[2] 163 7-8-9 102........................(p) RichardEvans(5) 3 98
(P D Evans) *hld up off the pce in last: clsd jst over 2f out: plld out jst over 1f out: rdn to chse wnr ins fnl f: no imp and comfortbly hld after* **7/2**[2]
00-4 **3** *3/4* **Carcinetto (IRE)**[7] 108 8-9-2 92........................ PaulDoe 1 98
(P D Evans) *sn clr w ldr: rdn and ev ch over 2f out: led wl over 1f out: hdd jst ins fnl f: one pce after* **14/1**
44-0 **4** *4 1/2* **Eisteddfod**[7] 108 9-9-5 101........................(b) EddieAhern 2 89
(P F I Cole) *led and sn clr w rival: rdn 2f out: sn hdd: wknd jst ins fnl f* **17/2**[3]

1m 23.58s (-1.22) **Going Correction** -0.025s/f (Stan) **4** Ran SP% **106.1**
Speed ratings (Par 107): **105,103,103,97**
CSF £2.38 TOTE £1.60; EX 2.10.
Owner G Smith (Worcestershire) **Bred** Arthur I Appleton **Trained** Sheriff Hutton, N Yorks

FOCUS
This looked like fairly easy pickings for Atlantic Story, and so it proved, with the front two ensuring a proper gallop and setting it up for him and Aeroplane.

NOTEBOOK
Atlantic Story(USA) had the race run to suit and, with the runner-up having few leadership qualities, it was plain sailing for Spencer in the straight, as he had no trouble at all holding that rival off inside the last. A smart performer on this surface, this was Atlantic Story's sixth win from 11 starts at this particular track. (tchd 8-15)
Aeroplane is picking up a few quid for his connections by placing in these conditions events, but he remains hard to win with against decent opposition. His best chance of success will be if dropped back into a claimer where he'll be in a position to win without coming off the bridle. (op 4-1 tchd 3-1)
Carcinetto(IRE) was 15lb worse off at the weights with Atlantic Story compared with when with when finishing a length behind Mick Easterby's gelding in a handicap here last time. In the circumstances she didn't run at all badly. (op 16-1 tchd 12-1)
Eisteddfod tried to make all but he could have done without Carcinetto pestering him as the result was that the pair just set it up for their two more patiently ridden rivals. (op 7-1 tchd 12-1)

205 BETDAQ ON 0870 178 1221 H'CAP 1m 2f (P)
3:40 (3:41) (Class 2) (0-100,100) 4-Y-0+ **£10,361** (£3,083; £1,540; £769) **Stalls** Low

Form RPR
144- **1** **Bridge Of Gold (USA)**[205] 3298 4-9-6 **100**........................ PaulHanagan 3 109
(M A Magnusson) *chsd ldng trio: hdwy to join ldrs over 2f out: rdn to ld and wanting to edge lft over 1f out: hdd ins fnl f: sn led again: r.o wl* **6/1**[3]
406- **2** *1/2* **Baylini**[49] 7574 6-8-10 **88**........................ HayleyTurner 8 96
(Ms J S Doyle) *stdd s: hld up towards rr: hdwy 3f out: chsd ldng trio and rdn wl over 1f out: rdn to ld ins fnl f: sn hdd and unable qck towards fin* **14/1**
P22- **3** *nk* **Mafeking (UAE)**[31] 7775 6-8-7 **85**........................ AndrewElliott 10 92
(M R Hoad) *sn chsng ldr: led 3f out: rdn ent fnl 2f: hdd over 1f out: stl ev ch but unable qck u.p fnl f* **4/1**[2]
14-4 **4** *1/2* **Full Toss**[8] 81 4-8-10 **90**........................ J-PGuillambert 7 96
(P D Evans) *t.k.h early: hld up in tch: hdwy to trck ldrs over 2f out: chal on inner over 1f out: ev ch 1f out: unable qck fnl f* **7/2**[1]
016- **5** *1 3/4* **Rock Ascot (URU)**[74] 7226 6-9-3 **95**........................(b) LiamKeniry 5 98
(G L Moore) *hld up in tch towards rr: pushed along and effrt over 2f out: chsng ldrs and hung lft u.p over 1f out: kpt on fnl f: nvr threatened ldrs* **20/1**
645- **6** *hd* **Vainglory (USA)**[90] 6876 6-8-3 **84**........................ MartinLane(3) 9 87
(D M Simcock) *t.k.h: in tch in midfield: effrt to chse ldrs and rdn ent fnl 2f: outpcd u.p over 1f out: kpt on again ins fnl f* **7/1**
006- **7** *7* **European Dream (IRE)**[62] 7245 7-8-10 **88**........................(p) JimCrowley 11 77
(R C Guest) *hld up in last trio: rdn and no prog over 2f out: nvr trbld ldrs* **10/1**
000- **8** *3/4* **Bureaucrat**[36] 4988 8-8-6 **84** oh1........................(p) FrannyNorton 6 71
(M F Harris) *sn rdn along in last: struggling over 4f out: modest hdwy fnl f: n.d* **25/1**
650- **9** *nk* **Puzzlemaster**[18] 6996 4-8-4 **84**........................ JimmyQuinn 1 70
(H Morrison) *in tch in midfield: rdn and struggling over 2f out: wl btn fnl f* **8/1**
45-0 **10** *3 1/4* **Luberon**[8] 81 7-8-10 **88**........................ JoeFanning 4 68
(M Johnston) *led: hdd 3f out: rdn over 2f out: wknd qckly 2f out: wl btn over 1f out* **8/1**
620- **11** *4 1/2* **John Terry (IRE)**[231] 2475 7-8-12 **90**........................ NeilCallan 2 61
(Mrs A J Perrett) *chsd ldrs: rdn wl over 2f out: shuffled bk and lost pl over 2f out: no ch after* **12/1**

2m 2.72s (-3.88) **Going Correction** -0.025s/f (Stan)
WFA 4 from 6yo+ 2lb **11** Ran SP% **123.3**
Speed ratings (Par 109): **114,113,113,112,111 111,105,105,104,102 98**
toteswingers: 1&2 £16.50, 1&3 £5.30, 2&3 £14.50 CSF £91.18 CT £384.67 TOTE £6.80: £2.90, £2.50, £2.30; EX 44.60 Trifecta £483.20 Part won. Pool: £358.37 - 0.44 winning units..
Owner Eastwind Racing Ltd And Martha Trussell **Bred** Hopewell Investments LLC **Trained** Upper Lambourn, Berks

FOCUS
A decent handicap run at a sound gallop and won by the least exposed runner in the line-up. Unsurprisingly it was by some margin the quickest of the three races run over the C&D.

NOTEBOOK
Bridge Of Gold(USA) didn't run well on his last start at Kempton in June and he had a virus soon afterwards, but he'd looked a smart performer in the making in his previous two starts and has always been well regarded. Upped 2f in distance here on his handicap debut, he was never to far off the pace and showed great determination when challenged on both sides inside the final furlong. He won snugly in the end, looks better than the bare form suggests and, while nominated for Dubai, may well now head to the US for the Grade 1 Santa Anita Handicap on March 6 instead. (op 5-1 tchd 9-2)
Baylini, whose losing run stretches back two years, came with a great run down the outside but found that the unexposed winner had a little left in the locker. She likes to run on late off a good gallop, and has conditions to suit here. (op 16-1)
Mafeking(UAE), who had not been held up at all by the recent bad weather according to his trainer, put up another fine effort in defeat. He deserves to find a race, but another little rise in the weights won't help in that regard. (op 9-2)
Full Toss, who nipped through on the inside turning into the straight, didn't go down without a real fight. He stays further than this and the decent gallop suited him, but he will surely be suited by a return to 1m4f. (op 5-1tchd 11-2 in a place)
Rock Ascot(URU) ran no sort of race at Kempton in November when last seen, but he won on his only previous start here, and this was far more encouraging. He's entitled to come on for the outing. (op 14-1)
Vainglory(USA), returning from a three-month break, is another entitled to come on for the run. He might need a little assistance from the handicapper, though, as he's still 1lb higher than when a narrow winner at Leicester back in the summer. (op 9-1)

206 BET MULTIPLES - BETDAQ MEDIAN AUCTION MAIDEN STKS 1m (P)
4:10 (4:11) (Class 5) 3-Y-0 **£2,456** (£725; £362) **Stalls** High

Form RPR
4-2 **1** **Greyfriarschorista**[12] 31 3-9-3 0........................ JoeFanning 4 82+
(M Johnston) *racd keenly: mde all: pushed clr over 1f out: v easily* **4/6**[1]
2 *5* **Into Wain (USA)** 3-9-3 0........................ JamieSpencer 3 67+
(D M Simcock) *hld up in tch in midfield: hdwy to chse ldng trio over 2f out: carried rt and sltly hmpd wl over 1f out: no ch w wnr after: pushed along and kpt on to go 2nd ins fnl f* **2/1**[2]
05- **3** *1* **Tilsworth Glenboy**[51] 7538 3-9-3 0........................ EddieAhern 6 65
(J R Jenkins) *t.k.h early: chsd ldr tl over 2f out: chsd wnr again and rdn wl over 1f out: sn hung bdly rt and btn: lost 2nd ins fnl f* **12/1**[3]
06- **4** *3 1/2* **Baggsy (IRE)**[66] 7326 3-8-12 0........................ AmirQuinn 7 52
(Miss J Feilden) *chsd ldng pair: rdn to chse wnr over 2f out tl wl over 1f out: sn carried rt and sltly hmpd: wl btn after* **25/1**
5 *3 3/4* **Pascalina** 3-8-12 0........................ J-PGuillambert 8 43
(J Akehurst) *s.i.s: a last trio: lost tch jst over 2f out* **25/1**
- **6** *3 1/2* **Madame Bonaparte (IRE)** 3-8-5 0........................ JosephineBruning(7) 1 34
(P L Gilligan) *racd in midfield: rdn jst over 2f out: wknd 2f out* **66/1**
0 **7** *1/2* **Big Eric**[12] 31 3-8-12 0........................ RichardEvans(5) 2 38
(P D Evans) *s.i.s: a in rr: rdn and lost tch over 2f out* **66/1**

1m 39.84s (1.64) **Going Correction** -0.025s/f (Stan) **7** Ran SP% **111.7**
Speed ratings (Par 97): **90,85,84,80,76 73,72**
toteswingers: 1&2 £1.60, 1&3 £2.90, 2&3 £4.00 CSF £2.01 TOTE £1.70: £1.10, £1.40; EX 2.40 Trifecta £10.20 Pool: £1,281.18 - 92.27 winning units. Place 6: £116.25 Place 5: £74.46 .
Owner Greyfriars UK Ltd **Bred** Castlemartin Stud And Skymarc Farm **Trained** Middleham Moor, N Yorks

FOCUS
An ordinary maiden and a penalty kick for the winner.
Tilsworth Glenboy Official explanation: jockey said colt hung right in straight
T/Plt: £135.00 to a £1 stake. Pool: £79,820.73. 431.59 winning tickets. T/Qpdt: £26.30 to a £1 stake. Pool: £6,323.35. 177.56 winning tickets. SP

CAGNES-SUR-MER
Saturday, January 16
OFFICIAL GOING: Standard

207a PRIX DE GARAVAN (CLAIMER) (ALL-WEATHER) 6f 110y
1:50 (1:54) 4-Y-0+ **£6,637** (£2,655; £1,991; £1,327; £664)

RPR
1 **Ceodora (GER)**[98] 5-9-2........................ DominiqueBoeuf 74
(W Baltromei, Germany)
2 *1 1/2* **Bonnie Prince Blue**[66] 7337 7-9-7........................ IoritzMendizabal 75
(D Nicholls) *prom: cl 2nd and pushed along st: rdn to ld over 1 1/2f out: r.o tl hdd 100yds out: styd on* **6/1**[1]
3 *1 1/2* **Derison (USA)**[79] 8-9-7........................(b) StephanePasquier 70
(P Monfort, France)
4 *3/4* **Wunderkind (GER)**[114] 5-9-5........................(b) 66
(P Chatelain, France)
5 *3/4* **Magic Sport (FR)**[74] 5-9-5........................ 64
(Mme C Barande-Barbe, France)
6 *shd* **Normanne (GER)** 5-8-11........................ 56
(G Martin, Austria)
7 *1/2* **Laokoon (GER)**[68] 5-9-4........................(b) 61
(Mario Hofer, Germany)
8 *2 1/2* **Butterfly Flip (FR)**[160] 6-8-11........................(p) 47
(J-P Perruchot, France)
9 *1* **Natal Lad (IRE)**[44] 5-9-7........................ 54
(N Bertran De Balanda, France)
10 *2 1/2* **Assam (GER)**[310] 8-9-1........................(b) 41
(Carmen Bocskai, Switzerland)
0 **Am Brose (USA)**[450] 11-8-11........................(b) —
(J-M Capitte, France)
0 **Grebe Huppe (FR)**[74] 5-9-2........................ —
(F Chappet, France)
0 **Palea (GER)**[210] 4-9-4........................ —
(S Jesus, France)
0 **Blu Basic (IRE)** 4-9-4........................(b) —
(M Planard, France)
F **Antigone (FR)**[74] 5-8-11........................ —
(K Borgel, France)

1m 17.61s (77.61) **15** Ran SP% **14.3**
PARI-MUTUEL (Including 1 Euro stake): WIN 21.30; PL 5.70, 2.90, 2.70;DF 56.30.
Owner Stall Australia **Bred** P Kusmin **Trained** Germany

192 WOLVERHAMPTON (A.W) (L-H)
Sunday, January 17
OFFICIAL GOING: Standard
Wind: Fresh, behind becoming lighter. Weather: Fine

208 ENJOY THE LUCKY 7 GROUP OFFER MAIDEN STKS 5f 20y(P)
1:55 (1:55) (Class 5) 3-Y-0+ **£2,456** (£725; £362) **Stalls** Low

Form RPR
033- **1** **Texas Queen**[22] 7843 3-8-7 70........................ JoeFanning 1 71
(M R Channon) *chsd ldrs: led 1f out: shkn up: edgd rt and styd on wl* **5/2**[2]
2- **2** *2* **American Light**[37] 7714 4-9-10 67........................ MartinLane(3) 7 75
(D M Simcock) *chsd ldrs: rdn to ld and hung lft over 1f out: hdd 1f out: hung rt and styd on same pce ins fnl f* **15/8**[1]
502- **3** *3 3/4* **Il Forno**[103] 6556 3-8-12 70........................ TonyHamilton 6 56
(D Nicholls) *hmpd s: hld up: hdwy over 1f out: styd on same pce fnl f* **3/1**[3]

- **4** *1* **Slap And Tickle (IRE)** 4-9-5 0 AndreaAtzeni(3) 3 53
(S C Williams) *hld up: swtchd lft and hdwy over 1f out: styd on same pce fnl f* **4/1**
006- **5** *2 ½* **True Red (IRE)**[31] 7778 3-8-0 52 MissRachelKing(7) 8 38
(Mrs N S Evans) *chsd ldr: rdn and ev ch wl over 1f out: wknd fnl f* **40/1**
00- **6** *11* **Riggs (IRE)**[73] 7254 4-9-13 0 (b) SaleemGolam 5 9
(Peter Grayson) *wnt rt s: hld up: rdn over 2f out: sn wknd* **100/1**
065- **7** *3 ¾* **Chenin (IRE)**[135] 5645 4-9-8 40 FrankieMcDonald 4 —
(Peter Grayson) *led: rdn and hdd over 1f out: sn wknd* **100/1**

61.83 secs (-0.47) **Going Correction** +0.025s/f (Slow)
WFA 3 from 4yo+ 15lb 7 Ran SP% **112.8**
Speed ratings (Par 103): **104,100,94,93,89 71,65**
toteswingers: 1&2 £2.10, 1&3 £2.30, 2&3 £2.10. CSF £7.39 TOTE £3.00: £1.30, £1.80; EX 7.80 Trifecta £15.10 Pool £371.76 - 18.10 winning units..
Owner M Channon **Bred** Rabbah Bloodstock Limited **Trained** West Ilsley, Berks

FOCUS
A modest maiden run at a strong pace. The two market leaders pulled clear of the rest.

209 PARADE RESTAURANT (S) STKS 5f 20y(P)
2:30 (2:30) (Class 6) 3-Y-O £1,774 (£523; £262) Stalls Low

Form RPR
01- **1** **Magenta Strait**[34] 7749 3-8-13 68 PaulPickard(5) 5 60
(R Hollinshead) *hld up: hdwy over 1f out: rdn and hung lft ins fnl f: r.o to ld post* **4/1**[2]
11-3 **2** *nk* **Wanchai Whisper**[8] 111 3-9-4 69 PaulDoe 6 59
(P D Evans) *stdd s: hld up: racd keenly: hdwy over 1f out: rdn to ld wl ins fnl f: hdd post* **8/11**[1]
36-0 **3** *nse* **Blue Neptune**[8] 111 3-9-6 62 AndreaAtzeni(3) 7 64
(W R Muir) *led: clr whn hung rt over 1f out: rdn: hung lft and hdd wl ins fnl f* **9/1**
00- **4** *4 ½* **Young George**[51] 7556 3-9-0 0 KellyHarrison(3) 1 42
(C W Fairhurst) *plld hrd and prom: rdn and hung lft over 1f out: wknd fnl f* **14/1**
336- **5** *¾* **Zelos Dream (IRE)**[37] 7713 3-9-4 62 LukeMorris 2 40
(R A Harris) *prom: rdn over 1f out: wknd fnl f* **11/2**[3]
000- **6** *3 ¼* **Rightcar Marian**[22] 7843 3-8-12 40 (b[1]) FrankieMcDonald 3 22
(Peter Grayson) *dwlt: hdwy over 3f out: rdn and wknd over 1f out* **125/1**
500- **7** *4 ½* **Daphne Du Maurier (IRE)**[125] 5942 3-8-12 35 GrahamGibbons 8 6
(E S McMahon) *chsd ldr: rdn 2f out: sn wknd* **100/1**

63.18 secs (0.88) **Going Correction** +0.025s/f (Slow) 7 Ran SP% **111.7**
Speed ratings (Par 95): **93,92,92,85,84 78,71**
toteswingers: 1&2 £1.80, 1&3 £2.70, 2&3 £2.00. CSF £6.91 TOTE £4.90: £1.80, £1.10; EX 7.60 Trifecta £30.10 Pool £627.93 - 15.43 winning units..The winner was bought in for 4,250gns.
Owner M Johnson **Bred** R Hollinshead And M Johnson **Trained** Upper Longdon, Staffs

FOCUS
An ordinary seller that produced a thrilling finish, and a second consecutive win for a lightly raced and improving type.

210 BET AUSTRALIAN OPEN TENNIS - BETDAQ APPRENTICE H'CAP 1m 4f 50y(P)
3:05 (3:05) (Class 6) (0-60,65) 4-Y-O+ £2,047 (£604; £302) Stalls Low

Form RPR
420- **1** **Mekong Miss**[26] 7840 4-8-10 56 MatthewCosham(5) 8 63
(J Jay) *a.p: chsd ldr over 6f out: led 4f out: pushed clr 2f out: sn edgd rt: styd on* **18/1**
4-6 **2** *½* **Spring Hawk (IRE)**[3] 176 4-8-11 55 KierenFox(3) 9 61
(T G McCourt, Ire) *chsd ldrs: rdn over 2f out: chsd wnr and hung lft ins fnl f: r.o* **14/1**
03-1 **3** *½* **Moscow Oznick**[9] 82 5-9-11 65 (p) DeclanCannon(3) 1 70
(D Donovan) *hld up: hdwy and hung lft over 1f out: r.o: nt rch ldrs* **11/2**[3]
24-4 **4** *¾* **No Wonga**[6] 120 5-9-9 60 RichardEvans 5 64+
(P D Evans) *hld up: rdn over 2f out: hdwy over 1f out: r.o: nt rch ldrs* **11/2**[3]
30-3 **5** *¾* **Sonny Sam (IRE)**[12] 41 5-8-10 52 LeeTopliss(5) 2 55
(R A Fahey) *a.p: chsd wnr over 2f out: rdn over 1f out: styd on same pce fnl f* **7/2**[1]
/54- **6** *½* **Covert Mission**[38] 7085 7-9-3 54 (p) AndrewHeffernan 12 56
(P D Evans) *hld up: rdn over 2f out: hdwy over 1f out: nvr nrr* **10/1**
53-4 **7** *nk* **Law Of The Jungle (IRE)**[5] 139 4-9-5 60 (p) RossAtkinson 11 62+
(Tom Dascombe) *hld up: racd keenly in last pl: rdn over 1f out: r.o ins fnl f: nvr nrr* **5/1**[2]
00-2 **8** *2 ½* **Highland River**[9] 88 4-8-13 54 AshleyMorgan 4 52
(A Sadik) *led 8f: chsd wnr tl rdn over 2f out: eased whn btn ins fnl f* **20/1**
054- **9** *1 ¼* **Duneen Dream (USA)**[34] 7751 5-8-4 46 MissRachelKing(5) 10 42
(Mrs N S Evans) *hld up: hdwy 5f out: rdn over 2f out: wknd over 1f out* **14/1**
25-3 **10** *nse* **Barbirolli**[6] 130 8-9-1 52 PaulPickard 6 48
(W B Stone) *hld up: rdn and nt clr run over 1f out: n.d* **8/1**
060- **11** *2 ¾* **Wizard Of Us**[56] 5732 10-8-4 46 oh1 AlexEdwards(5) 3 37
(M Mullineaux) *chsd ldr tl over 6f out: remained handy tl rdn and wknd over 2f out* **66/1**
60- **12** *4 ½* **Terminate (GER)**[81] 7113 8-9-5 56 (bt) DeanHeslop 7 40
(A Berry) *hld up: rdn and wknd over 2f out* **50/1**

2m 42.51s (1.41) **Going Correction** +0.025s/f (Slow)
WFA 4 from 5yo+ 4lb 12 Ran SP% **116.7**
Speed ratings (Par 101): **96,95,95,94,94 94,93,92,91,91 89,86**
toteswingers: 1&2 £57.00, 1&3 £26.40, 2&3 £15.20. CSF £240.94 CT £1576.87 TOTE £28.50: £6.40, £4.10, £2.40; EX 231.80 TRIFECTA Not won..
Owner Mrs J Martin & K Snell **Bred** Pollards Stables **Trained**

FOCUS
A low-grade handicap run at just a fair pace. The hold-up horses struggled to land a serious blow.

211 DINE IN THE HORIZONS RESTAURANT H'CAP 1m 141y(P)
3:40 (3:40) (Class 7) (0-50,50) 4-Y-O+ £1,774 (£523; £262) Stalls Low

Form RPR
004- **1** **King's Jester (IRE)**[29] 7818 8-8-7 50 (b) BarryMcHugh(5) 12 59
(Lee Smyth, Ire) *hld up in tch: led 2f out: hung lft ins fnl f: drvn out* **9/1**[3]
3-46 **2** *1 ¼* **Kirstys Lad**[6] 131 8-8-6 47 KellyHarrison(3) 13 53
(M Mullineaux) *hld up: hdwy over 2f out: rdn over 1f out: r.o: wnt 2nd nr fin* **4/1**[1]
26-0 **3** *nk* **Libre**[6] 131 10-8-10 48 JoeFanning 1 53
(F Jordan) *trckd ldrs: rdn over 1f out: r.o* **4/1**[1]
330- **4** *½* **Hi Spec (IRE)**[37] 7719 7-8-5 46 (p) AndreaAtzeni(3) 11 50
(Miss M E Rowland) *hld up: hdwy over 1f out: edgd lft ins fnl f: r.o* **11/1**
50-5 **5** *1* **Mrs Slocombe (IRE)**[13] 32 4-8-8 47 (t) DavidProbert 10 49
(Mrs N S Evans) *sn drvn along in rr: r.o ins fnl f: nvr trbld ldrs* **16/1**
400- **6** *¾* **Viking Awake (IRE)**[118] 6175 4-8-10 49 (t) RichardKingscote 9 49
(J W Unett) *hld up: r.o ins fnl f: nvr nrr* **12/1**
000- **7** *hd* **Le Reve Royal**[29] 7814 4-8-8 47 ow2 GrahamGibbons 4 47
(G R Oldroyd) *chsd ldr: rdn to ld briefly over 2f out: sn hdd: no ex fnl f* **22/1**
040- **8** *hd* **Son Of Monsieur**[29] 7818 4-8-9 48 JimmyQuinn 6 47
(G R Oldroyd) *hld up: hdwy over 2f out: rdn over 1f out: styd on same pce fnl f* **5/1**[2]
60-0 **9** *hd* **Stark Contrast (USA)**[6] 124 6-8-4 49 MissRachelKing(7) 7 48
(M D I Usher) *hld up: hdwy over 1f out: styd on: nt trble ldrs* **22/1**
656- **10** *2* **Always The Sun**[42] 7652 4-8-11 50 (p) StevieDonohoe 8 44
(P Leech) *mid-div: rdn over 3f out: sn lost pl: n.d after* **10/1**
060/ **11** *4* **Kims Rose (IRE)**[775] 7024 7-8-9 47 ow2 KevinGhunowa 5 32
(J L Flint) *chsd ldrs: rdn over 2f out: wknd over 1f out* **28/1**
600- **12** *4 ½* **Red Current**[31] 7787 6-8-10 48 (b) LukeMorris 3 23
(R A Harris) *prom: rdn over 2f out: wknd over 1f out* **16/1**
000- **13** *1 ¼* **Amber Ridge**[27] 5179 5-8-11 49 TonyCulhane 2 21
(B P J Baugh) *led: rdn and hdd over 2f out: wknd fnl f* **25/1**

1m 51.29s (0.79) **Going Correction** +0.025s/f (Slow)
WFA 4 from 5yo+ 1lb 13 Ran SP% **119.5**
Speed ratings (Par 97): **97,95,95,95,94 93,93,93,93,91 87,83,82**
toteswingers: 1&2 £6.90, 1&3 £5.90, 2&3 £5.00. CSF £42.64 CT £177.06 TOTE £9.70: £2.60, £1.60, £2.20; EX 43.80 Trifecta £68.10 Pool £547.68 - 5.95 winning units..
Owner Pircan Partnership **Bred** Gainsborough Stud Management Ltd **Trained** Dungannon, Co Tyrone

FOCUS
A poor handicap. Only one of the runners managed a win last year. The pace was fairly steady.
Hi Spec(IRE) Official explanation: jockey said gelding hung right

212 BET MASTERS SNOOKER - BETDAQ H'CAP 5f 20y(P)
4:10 (4:10) (Class 2) (0-100,102) 4-Y-O+
£10,592 (£3,172; £1,586; £793; £396; £198) Stalls Low

Form RPR
003- **1** **Matsunosuke**[20] 7862 8-9-6 102 TonyCulhane 2 111
(A B Coogan) *hld up: hdwy over 1f out: rdn to ld ins fnl f: r.o* **9/2**[2]
526- **2** *½* **Ivory Silk**[46] 7613 5-8-4 86 oh1 (b) LukeMorris 9 93
(J R Gask) *dwlt: hld up: hdwy over 1f out: sn rdn: r.o* **11/1**
21-2 **3** *½* **Nickel Silver**[16] 2 5-8-7 89 (v) TomEaves 6 94+
(B Smart) *led: rdn over 1f out: edgd rt and hdd ins fnl f: styd on* **4/1**[1]
22-0 **4** *½* **Ebraam (USA)**[8] 108 7-8-12 99 (t) DeclanCannon(5) 3 102
(S Curran) *pushed along early: sn mid-div: rdn 1/2-way: hdwy over 1f out: edgd lft ins fnl f: r.o* **5/1**[3]
15-6 **5** *1 ¼* **Earlsmedic**[3] 177 5-8-5 90 (e) AndreaAtzeni(3) 5 89
(S C Williams) *chsd ldrs: rdn over 1f out: styd on same pce fnl f* **4/1**[1]
6-56 **6** *½* **Canadian Danehill (IRE)**[3] 172 8-8-4 86 oh1 (p) FrannyNorton 4 83
(R M H Cowell) *chsd ldrs: rdn 1/2-way: no ex fnl f* **20/1**
00-3 **7** *1 ¾* **Peak District (IRE)**[3] 172 6-8-4 86 oh1 JimmyQuinn 7 77+
(K A Ryan) *trckd ldrs: stl gng wl enough whn n.m.r and lost pl over 1f out: n.d after* **9/2**[2]
600- **8** *½* **Hoh Hoh Hoh**[113] 6283 8-8-12 94 StevieDonohoe 1 83
(R J Price) *s.i.s: a in rr* **16/1**
001- **9** *2* **Glamorous Spirit (IRE)**[47] 7605 4-8-5 87 JoeFanning 8 69
(R A Harris) *chsd ldr tl rdn and edgd rt over 1f out: wknd fnl f* **25/1**

61.05 secs (-1.25) **Going Correction** +0.025s/f (Slow) 9 Ran SP% **115.9**
Speed ratings (Par 109): **111,110,109,108,106 105,103,102,99**
toteswingers: 1&2 £9.50, 1&3 £4.10, 2&3 £7.90. CSF £52.85 CT £215.80 TOTE £6.50: £1.90, £4.00, £1.60; EX 59.10 Trifecta £311.30 Pool £1,026.52 - 2.44 winning units..
Owner A B Coogan **Bred** R Coogan **Trained** Soham, Cambs

FOCUS
A hot handicap run at a good pace.

NOTEBOOK
Matsunosuke signalled his wellbeing with a close third off 1lb lower over 6f here last month. He got the strong pace he needs back at 5f and did the job in good style under a confident ride. The likeable veteran won four handicaps and a Listed race in December-February last year and will now head to Dubai in pursuit of a 15th career win. (op 4-1 tchd 5-1)
Ivory Silk put in a good effort with blinkers reapplied back from a short break. She can look a bit short of tactical speed and needs a strong pace but is a feisty campaigner at this level and has a record of 1322 over this C&D. (op 9-1)
Nickel Silver did really well to hang in there after dictating the decent pace. He has proved a revelation with five wins in headgear in the last 12 months and is still managing to be strongly competitive despite rising 29lb up the weights. (tchd 9-2)
Ebraam(USA), not at his best over 7f last time, bounced back with a good effort back at 5f, despite being forced wide. He is a generally reliable sprinter who deserves respect in these strong handicaps, but he has never won above a mark of 93 and has managed just two wins in his last 36 starts. (op 8-1)
Earlsmedic put in another respectable effort but seems to have reached a stalemate with the handicapper since completing a quick-fire double at Kempton in November. (op 5-1)
Canadian Danehill(IRE) was never really involved. The 16-time winner has dropped 6lb below his last winning mark but has found it tough to live with the early pace in competitive handicaps in the last six months. (tchd 22-1)
Peak District(IRE) was forced very wide and denied a run at a crucial stage early in the straight. He could be worth another chance next time. Official explanation: jockey said gelding was denied a clear run (tchd 5-1)

213 BET AFRICAN NATIONS CUP - BETDAQ H'CAP 7f 32y(P)
4:40 (4:40) (Class 6) (0-60,59) 3-Y-O £1,774 (£523; £262) Stalls High

Form RPR
440- **1** **Marosh (FR)**[188] 3925 3-9-3 58 GrahamGibbons 2 67+
(R M H Cowell) *led 6f out: rdn and edgd rt over 1f out: styd on wl* **4/1**[2]
05-5 **2** *2 ½* **Novillero**[8] 104 3-8-4 45 LukeMorris 7 46
(J C Fox) *hld up: hdwy 1/2-way: rdn to chse wnr over 1f out: styd on same pce ins fnl f* **15/8**[1]
600- **3** *1 ¼* **Teeraha (IRE)**[102] 6590 3-8-1 45 AndreaAtzeni(3) 5 43
(Miss M E Rowland) *hld up in tch: rdn over 1f out: edgd lft and styd on same pce ins fnl f* **80/1**
00-3 **4** *2 ½* **Vilnius**[6] 127 3-9-4 59 TonyCulhane 8 50
(M R Channon) *hld up: rdn over 2f out: edgd lft and styd on ins fnl f: n.d* **4/1**[2]
46-5 **5** *½* **Scintillating (IRE)**[6] 127 3-8-2 46 KellyHarrison(3) 3 36
(R Hollinshead) *prom: racd keenly: rdn over 1f out: no ex fnl f* **12/1**[3]
46-6 **6** *¾* **Charlottesometimes (USA)**[12] 43 3-8-5 49 MartinLane(3) 10 37
(D M Simcock) *s.i.s: in rr and rdn over 2f out: nvr on terms* **20/1**
30-0 **7** *½* **Fareham Town**[8] 104 3-8-12 53 DavidProbert 1 39
(S Kirk) *s.i.s: hld up: hdwy over 1f out: styd on same pce fnl f* **33/1**
00-1 **8** *1* **Feel The Magic (IRE)**[8] 104 3-8-7 48 (b) NickyMackay 6 32
(S Kirk) *led 1f: chsd wnr: rdn and ev ch 2f out: wknd fnl f* **4/1**[2]

65-0 **9** *6* **Darling Buds**[6] 127 3-9-3 **58**....(b[1]) TomEaves 4 25
(K A Ryan) *chsd ldrs: rdn and hung lft fr over 2f out: wknd fnl f* **33/1**

1m 30.71s (1.11) **Going Correction** +0.025s/f (Slow) **9** Ran SP% **114.4**
Speed ratings (Par 95): **94,91,89,86,86 85,84,83,76**
toteswingers: 1&2 £3.90, 1&3 £18.80, 2&3 £19.40. CSF £11.42 CT £501.77 TOTE £6.20: £1.50, £1.50, £10.70; EX 15.90 Trifecta £435.50 Pool £1,012.26 - 1.72 winning units. Place 6 £30.62, Place 5 £21.11..
Owner Le Deauville Racers **Bred** Earl Haras Du Camp Benard **Trained** Six Mile Bottom, Cambs

FOCUS
A weak handicap, run at a stop-start gallop.
Feel The Magic(IRE) Official explanation: jockey said filly had no more to give
Darling Buds Official explanation: jockey said filly hung badly left
T/Plt: £36.60 to a £1 stake. Pool: £86,672.59. 1,727.95 winning tickets. T/Qpdt: £25.80 to a £1 stake. Pool: £6,212.00. 178.17 winning tickets. CR

208 WOLVERHAMPTON (A.W) (L-H)
Monday, January 18

OFFICIAL GOING: Standard
Wind: Light behind Weather: Cloudy

214 WOLVERHAMPTON-RACECOURSE.CO.UK CLAIMING STKS 7f 32y(P)
2:20 (2:20) (Class 6) 4-Y-0+ **£1,774** (£523; £262) **Stalls** High

Form RPR
01-0 **1** **Caprio (IRE)**[16] 16 5-9-5 81.... JoeFanning 3 81
(J R Boyle) *a.p: pushed along over 2f out: led jst over 1f out: rdn out* **9/4**[1]
302- **2** *1/2* **Bahamian Kid**[23] 7845 5-9-1 69....(v) AdamKirby 2 76
(R Hollinshead) *hld up: hdwy over 1f out: chsd wnr ins fnl f: rdn and nt qckn* **11/4**[2]
00-0 **3** *3 1/2* **Gone Hunting**[9] 102 4-8-13 77....(t) SaleemGolam 5 65
(J Pearce) *led early: a.p: rdn 2f out: one pce fnl f* **11/2**
63-0 **4** *hd* **Desert Dreamer (IRE)**[5] 150 9-8-10 79.... RichardEvans(5) 6 66
(P D Evans) *hld up: pushed along wl over 2f out: sn struggling: rdn and kpt on ins fnl f: n.d* **7/2**[3]
33-0 **5** *5* **Sanjay's Choice (IRE)**[3] 192 4-8-11 70....(v[1]) ShaneKelly 4 49
(T G McCourt, Ire) *sn led: 3 l clr 2f out: rdn and hdd jst over 1f out: wknd ins fnl f* **6/1**

1m 29.12s (-0.48) **Going Correction** +0.05s/f (Slow) **5** Ran SP% **109.3**
Speed ratings (Par 101): **104,103,99,99,93**
CSF £8.55 TOTE £2.80: £1.50, £1.50; EX 7.40.
Owner M Khan X2 **Bred** P Rabbitte **Trained** Epsom, Surrey

FOCUS
A reasonable claimer run at a good pace, courtesy of Sanjay's Choice, who ultimately dropped away. The form is best rated through the runner-up and the winner did not need to be at his best.

215 BET AUSTRALIAN OPEN TENNIS - BETDAQ H'CAP 5f 216y(P)
2:50 (2:51) (Class 6) (0-55,55) 3-Y-0 **£1,774** (£523; £262) **Stalls** Low

Form RPR
02-3 **1** **Turf Time**[4] 167 3-8-6 **47**.... ChrisCatlin 2 52
(J A Glover) *s.i.s: t.k.h: sn swtchd rt to outside: hdwy to ld over 4f out: drvn out ins fnl f* **10/3**[1]
4-52 **2** *1/2* **Lady Brickhouse**[4] 167 3-8-5 **46** oh1.... LukeMorris 8 49
(M D Squance) *hld up in mid-div: hdwy over 1f out: hrd rdn and r.o ins fnl f: tk 2nd cl home* **9/2**[2]
04-4 **3** *nk* **Exceed Power**[9] 104 3-8-6 **50**....(t) MartinLane(3) 1 52
(D M Simcock) *s.i.s: hld up in mid-div on ins: hdwy over 1f out: chsd wnr ins fnl f: nt qckn and lost 2nd cl home* **11/2**[3]
52-4 **4** *1 1/2* **Rightcar**[6] 134 3-8-13 **54**.... AdamKirby 9 51
(Peter Grayson) *s.i.s: sn swtchd lft and carried rt: hld up in rr: hdwy whn swtchd rt ins fnl f: rdn and kpt on* **7/1**
000- **5** *2 1/4* **Duke Of Rainford**[32] 7778 3-8-9 **50**.... TonyCulhane 7 40
(M Herrington) *t.k.h in tch: ev ch over 2f out: pushed along over 1f out: wknd wl ins fnl f* **28/1**
056- **6** *1/2* **Princess Shamal**[33] 7772 3-9-0 **55**.... ShaneKelly 10 49+
(J R Jenkins) *hld up and bhd: swtchd lft ins fnl f: n.d* **14/1**
443- **7** *hd* **Moonlight Serenade**[18] 7887 3-8-11 **55**....(p) JackDean(3) 4 43
(W G M Turner) *prom: rdn over 1f out: wknd ins fnl f* **6/1**
360- **8** *4* **Raine Supreme**[35] 7749 3-8-13 **54**.... GrahamGibbons 3 29
(E S McMahon) *led over 1f: prom: pushed along over 1f out: wknd fnl f* **12/1**
606- **9** *shd* **Graceandgratitude**[39] 7698 3-8-9 **53**.... AndreaAtzeni(3) 5 28
(S C Williams) *hld up in tch: rdn and wknd wl over 1f out* **9/1**
000- **10** *shd* **Seeking Rio**[21] 7859 3-7-12 **46**.... MatthewCosham(7) 6 20
(R J Hodges) *hld up in rr: rdn and struggling wl over 1f out* **20/1**

1m 16.48s (1.48) **Going Correction** +0.05s/f (Slow) **10** Ran SP% **116.0**
Speed ratings (Par 95): **92,91,90,88,85 85,85,79,79,79**
toteswingers: 1&2 £3.10, 1&3 £3.20, 2&3 £6.40 CSF £17.88 CT £81.52 TOTE £3.30: £1.40, £1.70, £2.70; EX 15.60 Trifecta £60.70 Pool: £208.38 - 2.54 winning units..
Owner Sexy Six Partnership **Bred** Mrs Yvette Dixon **Trained** Babworth, Notts

FOCUS
The form of this moderate handicap needs treating with caution, as the early pace was unusually steady for a sprint. The form does make some sense though.

216 SPONSOR A RACE BY CALLING 01902 390000 H'CAP 1m 1f 103y(P)
3:20 (3:20) (Class 6) (0-60,59) 3-Y-0 **£1,774** (£523; £262) **Stalls** Low

Form RPR
00-2 **1** **Rock A Doodle Doo (IRE)**[6] 134 3-9-0 **55**.... J-PGuillambert 10 68+
(W Jarvis) *hld up: pushed along over 3f out: hdwy on outside over 2f out: edgd lft and led ins fnl f: readily* **6/5**[1]
504- **2** *2 1/2* **Vittachi**[32] 7788 3-8-9 **50**....(b) GrahamGibbons 5 58
(J D Bethell) *n.m.r s: sn prom: ev ch over 2f out: sn pushed along: rdn and kpt on same pce ins fnl f* **16/1**
46-3 **3** *1/2* **The Great Husk (IRE)**[6] 133 3-8-9 **50**.... LiamKeniry 6 57
(J S Moore) *led after 1f: rdn over 1f out: hdd ins fnl f: no ex* **9/2**[2]
304- **4** *4 1/2* **She's My Rock (IRE)**[18] 7887 3-8-11 **52**.... DavidProbert 1 50
(S Kirk) *led 1f: prom: rdn over 2f out: wknd over 1f out* **10/1**
002- **5** *1* **Pie Poudre**[32] 7788 3-9-2 **57**.... TomEaves 7 52
(R Brotherton) *s.i.s: hld up and bhd: sme prog on outside wl over 1f out: sn rdn and hung lft: no further prog* **12/1**
6-55 **6** *2 1/2* **Scintillating (IRE)**[1] 213 3-8-5 **46**.... ChrisCatlin 8 36
(R Hollinshead) *a in rr* **22/1**
60-3 **7** *1 1/2* **New Den**[4] 161 3-9-4 **59**.... StephenCraine 2 46
(J R Boyle) *t.k.h early: prom: stdd into mid-div: over 7f out: rdn over 3f out: sn bhd* **7/1**[3]
500- **8** *2 1/4* **Always Dixie (IRE)**[18] 7887 3-9-1 **56**.... JoeFanning 9 38
(M Johnston) *jnd ldr 8f out: wknd wl over 1f out* **16/1**
00-5 **9** *1 1/4* **Heligoland**[17] 5 3-8-6 **47**.... LukeMorris 3 27
(A G Newcombe) *t.k.h: prom: rdn over 3f out: wknd 2f out* **33/1**
050- **10** *6* **Concorde Kiss (USA)**[20] 7865 3-8-9 **50**.... FergusSweeney 4 17
(S Kirk) *hld up and bhd: pushed along over 2f out: struggling whn rdn wl over 1f out* **25/1**

2m 1.75s (0.05) **Going Correction** +0.05s/f (Slow) **10** Ran SP% **115.8**
Speed ratings (Par 95): **101,98,98,94,93 91,89,87,86,81**
toteswingers: 1&2 £5.20, 1&3 £2.50, 2&3 £7.10 CSF £22.80 CT £69.57 TOTE £2.40: £1.10, £4.60, £1.70; EX 28.20 Trifecta £42.10 Pool: £355.70- 6.24 winning units..
Owner The Doodle Doo Partnership **Bred** Mrs A S O'Brien And Lars Pearson **Trained** Newmarket, Suffolk

FOCUS
An uncompetitive handicap in which few of these really stayed, but it was truly run and the form looks fair for the grade, with the winner likely to improve further. He was value for perhaps twice the winning margin.

217 WOLVERHAMPTON HOSPITALITY - A PLEASURE CLAIMING STKS 1m 141y(P)
3:50 (3:50) (Class 6) 3-Y-0 **£1,774** (£523; £262) **Stalls** Low

Form RPR
133- **1** **Tuscan King**[32] 7788 3-8-13 63.... J-PGuillambert 1 65
(P D Evans) *led early: prom: wnt 2nd over 3f out: led wl over 1f out: rdn and edgd rt 1f out: bmpd wl ins fnl f: r.o* **8/11**[1]
0-6 **2** *1* **Magic Spirit**[6] 133 3-8-4 0....(p) LukeMorris 5 54
(J S Moore) *hld up: pushed along over 3f out: hdwy over 2f out: sn rdn: chalng whn hung bdly rt ins fnl f: nt qckn towards fin* **10/1**
40-5 **3** *3 3/4* **Premium Charge**[6] 133 3-8-5 0.... DavidProbert 4 50+
(C A Dwyer) *t.k.h: sn w ldr: led 7f out: hdd wl over 1f out: sn rdn: cl 3rd whn bdly hmpd wl ins fnl f: nt rcvr* **4/1**[2]
646- **4** *1 1/4* **Creevy (IRE)**[32] 7788 3-7-9 48.... AndreaAtzeni(3) 3 36
(S Kirk) *hld up: rdn whn n.m.r on ins briefly 3f out: n.d after* **9/2**[3]
05-0 **5** *19* **Holkham**[6] 134 3-8-9 53....(p) ChrisCatlin 2 4
(N P Littmoden) *sn led: hdd 7f out: chsd ldr tl over 3f out: pushed along and wknd wl over 2f out* **40/1**

1m 51.01s (0.51) **Going Correction** +0.05s/f (Slow) **5** Ran SP% **107.6**
Speed ratings (Par 95): **99,98,94,93,76**
CSF £8.34 TOTE £1.90: £1.10, £3.30; EX 4.00.
Owner J L Guillambert **Bred** Horizon Bloodstock Limited **Trained** Pandy, Monmouths
■ Stewards' Enquiry : Luke Morris three-day ban: careless riding (Feb 1-3)

FOCUS
A weak claimer run at a good pace. The winner probably stepped up a bit on his latest efforts.

218 BET IN RUNNING - BETDAQ H'CAP 1m 141y(P)
4:20 (4:20) (Class 5) (0-75,70) 3-Y-0 **£2,456** (£725; £362) **Stalls** Low

Form RPR
031- **1** **Thundering Home**[20] 7865 3-9-4 **70**.... HayleyTurner 1 77+
(E A L Dunlop) *hld up in tch: pushed along 2f out: led ins fnl f: sn rdn and edgd lft: r.o* **11/8**[1]
613- **2** *1 1/4* **House Red (IRE)**[67] 7359 3-9-3 **69**.... RobertWinston 4 73
(B W Hills) *led early: w ldr: led wl over 2f out: hung rt fr wl over 1f out: rdn and hdd ins fnl f: kpt on one pce* **11/8**[1]
004- **3** *2 1/4* **South African Gold (USA)**[21] 7859 3-9-1 **67**.... LukeMorris 3 66
(J M P Eustace) *hld up in tch: wnt 2nd 2f out: rdn and ev ch whn edgd lft 1f out: one pce* **6/1**[2]
05-0 **4** *3 3/4* **Jazz Age (IRE)**[14] 33 3-8-10 **62**....(b) ChrisCatlin 2 52
(J A Glover) *sn led: hdd wl over 2f out: rdn wl over 1f out: wknd ins fnl f* **9/1**[3]

1m 52.11s (1.61) **Going Correction** +0.05s/f (Slow) **4** Ran SP% **108.5**
Speed ratings (Par 97): **94,92,90,87**
CSF £3.49 TOTE £2.40; EX 3.10.
Owner Salem Suhail **Bred** Rabbah Bloodstock Limited **Trained** Newmarket, Suffolk

FOCUS
A disappointing turnout numerically, and it was slowly run. Muddling form, but the winner is capable of better.

219 STAY AT THE WOLVERHAMPTON HOLIDAY INN MAIDEN STKS 1m 1f 103y(P)
4:50 (4:52) (Class 5) 3-Y-0 **£2,456** (£725; £362) **Stalls** Low

Form RPR
002- **1** **Reallymissgreeley (USA)**[81] 7140 3-8-12 73....(p) TomEaves 2 57
(K A Ryan) *hld up in tch: rdn and sltly outpcd over 2f out: swtchd rt over 1f out: r.o to ld cl home* **6/5**[2]
0-6 **2** *nk* **Royal Torbo (ISR)**[16] 9 3-8-12 0.... MatthewDavies(5) 4 61
(George Baker) *sn led: rdn jst over 1f out: hdd cl home* **16/1**[3]
6- **3** *4 1/2* **Sternian**[20] 7865 3-8-5 0.... LauraPike(7) 3 47
(M E Rimmer) *sn w ldr: ev ch 2f out: rdn and wknd ins fnl f* **40/1**
4 *15* **Le Volcan D'Or (USA)** 3-9-3 0.... JoeFanning 1 20
(M Johnston) *led early: hld up in tch: pushed along and wknd wl over 2f out* **8/11**[1]

2m 3.83s (2.13) **Going Correction** +0.05s/f (Slow) **4** Ran SP% **111.7**
Speed ratings (Par 97): **92,91,87,74**
CSF £15.20 TOTE £2.10; EX 6.80.
Owner Mrs T Marnane **Bred** Edward A Cox Jr **Trained** Hambleton, N Yorks

FOCUS
A moderate maiden in which the favourite failed to run any sort of race, and the time was 2.08 seconds slower than the 55-rated Rock A Doodle Doo recorded in an earlier nursery. Dubious form, but the race has been rated fairly negatively.
Le Volcan D'Or(USA) Official explanation: jockey said colt ran green

220 BET MULTIPLES - BETDAQ H'CAP 1m 4f 50y(P)
5:20 (5:20) (Class 5) (0-75,75) 4-Y-0+ **£2,456** (£725; £362) **Stalls** Low

Form RPR
/5-3 **1** **Accompanist**[4] 173 7-8-6 **66**....(p) AndrewHeffernan(5) 7 73
(T G McCourt, Ire) *hld up in mid-div: pushed along 3f out: hdwy wl over 1f out: rdn to ld wl ins fnl f: r.o* **4/1**[2]
61-1 **2** *3/4* **Chalice Welcome**[16] 12 7-9-4 **73**.... HayleyTurner 9 79
(N B King) *hld up: hdwy 8f out: led over 1f out: rdn and hdd wl ins fnl f* **7/2**[1]
3-21 **3** *nk* **Look Officer (USA)**[8] 114 4-8-9 **68** 6ex....(b) RichardKingscote 6 74
(Tom Dascombe) *hld up in rr: hdwy on outside over 2f out: hrd rdn and edgd rt wl over 1f out: edgd lft ins fnl f: sn ev ch: nt qckn towards fin* **7/2**[1]
/10- **4** *1/2* **Ahmedy (IRE)**[86] 7020 7-9-4 **73**.... GrahamGibbons 2 78
(J J Quinn) *t.k.h: prom: wnt 2nd 7f out: led 2f out: hdd over 1f out: sn rdn: ev ch wl ins fnl f: no ex* **17/2**

301- **5** 1 1/4 **I'm In The Pink (FR)**[39] 7248 6-9-1 **75** .... RichardEvans(5) 4 78
(P D Evans) *stdd s: hld up in rr: rdn over 3f out: hdwy on ins over 1f out: one pce ins fnl f* **14/1**

040/ **6** 1/2 **Prince Sabaah (IRE)**[319] 6974 6-9-5 **74** .... (t) TonyCulhane 5 76
(Miss Venetia Williams) *hld up in tch: pushed along over 3f out: outpcd over 2f out: sme late prog* **12/1**

00/0 **7** 3 3/4 **Solarias Quest**[14] 32 8-8-10 **65** .... ShaneKelly 3 61
(W M Brisbourne) *hld up in mid-div: wknd over 2f out* **33/1**

526- **8** 2 **Into The Light**[186] 4021 5-8-13 **68** .... RobertWinston 8 61
(E S McMahon) *chsd ldr: led after 2f: hdd 2f out: sn rdn: wknd 1f out* **10/1**

665- **9** 1 **Dzesmin (POL)**[207] 3313 8-8-11 **66** .... PaulHanagan 1 57
(R A Fahey) *led 2f out: chsd ldr to 7f out: prom: pushed along over 2f out: wknd wl over 1f out* **11/2**[3]

2m 40.97s (-0.13) **Going Correction** +0.05s/f (Slow)
WFA 4 from 5yo+ 4lb **9** Ran SP% **116.7**
Speed ratings (Par 103): **102,101,101,100,100 99,97,95,95**
toteswingers: 1&2 £4.40, 1&3 £4.10, 2&3 £3.50 CSF £18.66 CT £53.55 TOTE £5.80: £1.70, £1.40, £1.40; EX 19.00 Trifecta £61.40 Pool: £722.75 - 8.71 winning units. Place 6: £14.10 Place 5: £10.68.
Owner Mrs P McCourt **Bred** Cheveley Park Stud **Trained** Stamullen, Co Meath

FOCUS
A modest but competitive handicap run at a steady pace. The form seems sound enough.
T/Plt: £14.90 to a £1 stake. Pool: £58,440.51. 2,862.47 winning tickets. T/Qpdt: £7.90 to a £1 stake. Pool: £3,916.18. 364.26 winning tickets. KH

207 CAGNES-SUR-MER
Monday, January 18

OFFICIAL GOING: Standard

221a PRIX DES BOUCHES DU LOUP (CLAIMER) (ALL-WEATHER) 1m 4f
2:55 (2:55) 4-Y-0+ **£6,637** (£2,655; £1,991; £1,327; £664)

RPR

1 **Almaguer**[98] 8-9-6 .... MorganGallene —
(M Boutin, France)

2 1 1/2 **Sham Risk (FR)**[272] 6-9-9 .... BriceRaballand —
(J Morin, France)

3 nk **Nummenor (FR)**[96] 13-9-9 .... (b) YoannRousset —
(Y Fertillet, France)

4 2 **Lost Soldier Three (IRE)**[10] 87 9-9-9 .... (p) RomainPerruchot —
(D Nicholls) *towards rr on outside: 10th 1/2-way: pushed along and stdy hdwy ent st: wnt 4th fnl strides: nvr in chalng position* **3/1**[1]

5 nk **Cartesio (USA)**[305] 6-9-2 .... (b) —
(J-M Lefebvre, France)

6 2 **Shin Kan Sen (FR)**[1375] 7-9-6 .... —
(P Khozian, France)

7 snk **Silver Virago (FR)**[96] 6-9-2 .... —
(P Costes, France)

8 9 **Shahdawar (FR)**[1072] 437 7-9-5 .... (p) —
(M Pimbonnet, France)

9 nk **Zaisan (FR)**[121] 4-8-11 .... —
(Mme L Audon, France)

10 1 **Golconde Mine (IRE)**[243] 8-8-13 .... —
(J Van Handenhove, France)

0 **Telmunireema (FR)**[96] 5-9-5 .... —
(J-P Perruchot, France)

0 **Alleesky (FR)** 8-9-2 .... (b) —
(W J Cargeeg, France)

0 **Del Mar (FR)** 4-8-11 .... —
(Y Fouin, France)

2m 31.61s (151.61)
WFA 4 from 5yo+ 4lb **13** Ran SP% **25.0**
PARI-MUTUEL (Including 1 Euro stake): WIN 4.10; PL 1.60, 2.30, 2.50;DF 12.20.
Owner Olivier Fernandez **Bred** Chevington Stud **Trained** France

214 WOLVERHAMPTON (A.W) (L-H)
Tuesday, January 19

OFFICIAL GOING: Standard changing to standard to fast after race 2 (2.50)
Wind: Almost nil Weather: Overcast

222 BET CARLING CUP - BETDAQ H'CAP 5f 20y(P)
2:20 (2:21) (Class 5) (0-75,74) 3-Y-O **£2,729** (£806; £403) **Stalls** Low

Form RPR

000- **1** **Lewyn**[67] 7372 3-8-13 **68** .... FergusSweeney 3 75
(K A Ryan) *a.p: rdn to ld wl ins fnl f: r.o* **5/1**

014- **2** 1/2 **R Woody**[20] 7871 3-9-4 **73** .... LiamKeniry 2 78
(Mrs L C Jewell) *wnt rt s: led over 1f: a.p: led wl over 1f out: rdn and edgd rt 1f out: hdd wl ins fnl f* **11/4**[2]

32-2 **3** 2 1/2 **Athwaab**[10] 111 3-9-0 **69** .... JamieSpencer 4 65
(M G Quinlan) *hld up in rr: hdwy on ins wl over 1f out: rdn fnl f: one pce* **7/4**[1]

040- **4** 1 1/2 **Mrs Boss**[116] 6241 3-9-0 **72** .... JamesMillman(3) 7 63
(B R Millman) *chsd ldr wl over 3f out: led 2f out: hdd wl over 1f out: sn rdn: one pce* **9/1**

341- **5** 2 **Point To Prove**[45] 7636 3-8-8 **63** .... LukeMorris 1 47
(J Balding) *hld up: rdn and edgd lft over 1f out: sn btn* **9/2**[3]

16-0 **6** 6 **Silver Linnet (IRE)**[17] 17 3-8-10 **65** .... JerryO'Dwyer 6 27
(M G Quinlan) *s.i.s: sn rcvrd: led wl over 3f out to 2f out: rdn and wknd wl over 1f out* **25/1**

61.72 secs (-0.58) **Going Correction** 0.0s/f (Stan) **6** Ran SP% **111.7**
Speed ratings (Par 97): **104,103,99,96,93 84**
toteswinger:1&2:£2.50, 2&3:£1.60, 1&3:£2.80 CSF £18.88 TOTE £5.70: £2.70, £1.90; EX 18.40.
Owner N Cable & M Smith **Bred** Mrs S J Walker **Trained** Hambleton, N Yorks

FOCUS
A modest sprint handicap contested by mainly exposed sorts. The winner was back to her best and the second turned around Kempton form with the favourite.

223 BET ASIAN H'CAPS - BETDAQ HANDICAP 5f 216y(P)
2:50 (2:52) (Class 5) (0-75,75) 4-Y-0+ **£2,729** (£806; £403) **Stalls** Low

Form RPR

1-31 **1** **Divine Force**[8] 129 4-8-6 **63** .... SimonWhitworth 10 79
(M Wigham) *hld up in mid-div: hdwy 2f out: led ins fnl f: drvn out* **4/1**[1]

31-2 **2** 1 **Weet A Surprise**[4] 192 5-8-9 **73** .... (v) AlexEdwards(7) 13 86
(J W Unett) *hld up in mid-div: hdwy over 1f out: r.o to take 2nd ins fnl f: nt trble wnr* **9/2**[2]

050- **3** 1 1/4 **Fen Spirit (IRE)**[29] 7832 4-9-3 **74** .... (b[1]) RobertHavlin 5 83
(J H M Gosden) *sn led: rdn over 1f out: hdd ins fnl f: no ex* **16/1**

063- **4** 2 **Loyal Royal (IRE)**[20] 7876 7-8-5 **62** .... (b) LukeMorris 1 65
(J M Bradley) *hld up in rr: hdwy on ins wl over 1f out: sn rdn: kpt on one pce ins fnl f* **16/1**

101- **5** 1 **Sarah's Art (IRE)**[38] 7735 7-9-4 **75** .... (t) AdamKirby 9 74
(Stef Higgins) *hld up in rr: pushed along wl over 1f out: rdn and kpt on fnl f: nt rch ldrs* **6/1**

30-4 **6** 3/4 **Kyle (IRE)**[11] 78 6-8-5 **62** .... DavidProbert 6 59
(C R Dore) *hld up in mid-div: rdn wl over 1f out: no real prog* **8/1**

500- **7** nk **Brierty (IRE)**[32] 7801 4-9-4 **75** .... DavidNolan 12 71
(D Carroll) *prom: rdn wl over 1f out: fdd ins fnl f* **20/1**

06-1 **8** 3/4 **Imperial House**[11] 78 4-8-10 **67** .... (b) StephenCraine 3 61
(R A Harris) *hld up in mid-div: pushed along and swtchd lft over 1f out: nvr trbld ldrs* **17/2**

435- **9** 1 1/4 **Light Sleeper**[48] 7610 4-9-1 **72** .... JamieSpencer 2 62
(P W Chapple-Hyam) *chsd ldrs: lost pl 4f out: pushed along over 2f out: c wd st: rdn wl over 1f out: no rspnse* **5/1**[3]

000- **10** 3/4 **Westwood**[30] 7828 5-8-8 **65** .... NickyMackay 11 52
(D Haydn Jones) *prom: chsd ldr over 4f out tl rdn jst over 1f out: eased whn btn wl ins fnl f* **12/1**

026- **11** 5 **Titus Gent**[43] 7673 5-8-10 **67** .... ChrisCatlin 7 38
(R A Harris) *led early: prom tl wknd wl over 2f out* **20/1**

10- **12** 2 1/2 **Norse Warrior (USA)**[20] 7872 4-8-12 **69** .... (v) LiamKeniry 4 32
(Peter Grayson) *pushed along over 3f out: a in rr* **50/1**

500- **13** 10 **Came Back (IRE)**[267] 1565 7-8-11 **73** .... AnnStokell(5) 8 —
(Miss A Stokell) *t.k.h: prom: pushed along over 2f out: wknd wl over 1f out: eased ins fnl f* **100/1**

1m 13.73s (-1.27) **Going Correction** 0.0s/f (Stan) **13** Ran SP% **122.7**
Speed ratings (Par 103): **108,106,105,102,101 100,99,98,96,95 89,85,72**
toteswinger:1&2:£3.70, 2&3:£25.30, 1&3:£18.70 CSF £21.46 CT £276.70 TOTE £4.50: £1.80, £1.90, £5.80; EX 17.50 Trifecta £308.30 winning units.
Owner R J Lorenz **Bred** Capt J H Wilson **Trained** Newmarket, Suffolk

FOCUS
A decent race for the grade and the form looks good for the level. The front pair were both 4lb well in.
Light Sleeper Official explanation: jockey said colt hung right-handed
Came Back(IRE) Official explanation: jockey said gelding ran too freely

224 BET IN RUNNING - BETDAQ H'CAP 1m 5f 194y(P)
3:20 (3:21) (Class 4) (0-85,85) 4-Y-0+ **£4,415** (£1,321; £660; £330; £164) **Stalls** Low

Form RPR

42-2 **1** **Paktolos (FR)**[16] 25 7-9-5 **84** .... (p) MarkCoumbe(5) 1 93
(John A Harris) *hld up in rr: stdy prog over 3f out: led wl over 1f out: rdn ins fnl f: comf* **3/1**[2]

10-2 **2** 3 1/2 **Calculating (IRE)**[5] 173 6-8-6 **66** .... DavidProbert 2 70
(M D I Usher) *hld up: hdwy 2f out: rdn over 1f out: wnt 2nd ins fnl f: no ch w wnr* **15/8**[1]

520/ **3** 1 1/2 **Rock 'N' Roller (FR)**[78] 6606 6-8-12 **72** .... FergusSweeney 4 74
(G L Moore) *led early: a.p: pushed along over 2f out: rdn and sltly outpcd wl over 1f out: styd on to take 3rd wl ins fnl f* **16/1**

221/ **4** 1 **Just Rob**[312] 5202 5-9-10 **84** .... StevieDonohoe 3 85
(Ian Williams) *hld up: stdy hdwy over 3f out: led 2f out: sn hdd and rdn: no ex ins fnl f* **11/2**

105- **5** 2 **Bushy Dell (IRE)**[21] 7867 5-8-1 **66** .... AmyBaker(5) 5 64
(Miss J Feilden) *sn led: hdd over 8f out: prom: pushed along over 2f out: hld whn nt clr run on ins and swtchd rt 1f out* **7/2**[3]

155- **6** 3/4 **Amanda Carter**[43] 7018 6-9-4 **85** .... LeeTopliss(7) 6 82
(R A Fahey) *t.k.h: prom: led over 8f out to 2f out: sn rdn: edgd lft jst over 1f out: wknd ins fnl f* **12/1**

3m 10.58s (4.58) **Going Correction** 0.0s/f (Stan) **6** Ran SP% **111.0**
Speed ratings (Par 105): **86,84,83,82,81 81**
toteswinger:1&2:£1.20, 2&3:£5.70, 1&3:£6.10 CSF £8.84 TOTE £4.80: £2.30, £1.40; EX 12.80.
Owner Martin Hignett **Bred** Stilvi Compania **Trained** Eastwell, Leics
■ Stewards' Enquiry : Lee Topliss One-day ban: careless riding (Feb 2)

FOCUS
A fair staying handicap, but the pace was steady, resulting in a slow time. The form is probably not solid but has been rated at face value for now.

225 WOLVERHAMPTON HOSPITALITY - A PLEASURE FILLIES' H'CAP 7f 32y(P)
3:50 (3:50) (Class 5) (0-75,75) 4-Y-0+ **£2,729** (£806; £403) **Stalls** High

Form RPR

113- **1** **Spinning Bailiwick**[30] 7828 4-9-4 **74** .... GeorgeBaker 8 83+
(G L Moore) *hld up and bhd: hdwy wl over 1f out: sn rdn: r.o to ld wl ins fnl f* **4/1**[2]

045- **2** 1 **Fine Silk (USA)**[144] 5394 4-8-5 **64** .... AndreaAtzeni(3) 7 70
(M G Quinlan) *led: rdn wl over 1f out: hdd wl ins fnl f* **33/1**

61-1 **3** 1 1/4 **Diapason (IRE)**[8] 125 4-9-5 **75** 6ex .... RichardKingscote 6 78
(Tom Dascombe) *hld up and bhd: hdwy on ins over 2f out: chal wl over 1f out: sn rdn: nt qckn ins fnl f* **4/5**[1]

2311 **4** 1 3/4 **Goodbye Cash (IRE)**[4] 181 6-8-7 **68** 6ex .... AndrewHeffernan(5) 1 66
(P D Evans) *chsd ldr: ev ch wl over 2f out: rdn and lost 2nd wl over 1f out: one pce fnl f* **6/1**[3]

01-3 **5** 2 1/4 **Bold Rose**[7] 135 4-8-4 **60** oh3 .... (p) DavidProbert 4 52
(M D I Usher) *hld up in tch: hung rt and rdn bnd over 2f out: lost pl and rn wd st: n.d after* **14/1**

/12- **6** 3 1/4 **Desert Bump**[346] 441 4-9-2 **72** .... JamieSpencer 3 55
(E F Vaughan) *hld up in tch: pushed along and wknd wl over 1f out* **9/1**

1m 29.72s (0.12) **Going Correction** 0.0s/f (Stan) **6** Ran SP% **109.4**
Speed ratings (Par 100): **99,97,96,94,91 88**
toteswinger:1&2:£8.40, 2&3:£3.90, 1&3:£1.90 CSF £87.76 CT £184.41 TOTE £3.40: £1.80, £5.80; EX 74.00 Trifecta £221.00 Part won. Pool: £355.70- 6.24 winning units..
Owner Dr Ian R Shenkin **Bred** Mrs M Shenkin **Trained** Lower Beeding, W Sussex

 The Form Book, Raceform Ltd, Compton, RG20 6NL

FOCUS
A modest fillies' handicap run at an ordinary pace. The winner continues on the upgrade but the favourite was a bit disappointing.
Bold Rose Official explanation: jockey said filly hung right-handed

226 ENJOY THE LUCKY 7 GROUP OFFER MAIDEN STKS 1m 141y(P)
4:20 (4:21) (Class 5) 3-Y-O+ £2,456 (£725; £362) Stalls Low

Form RPR
1 **Quarante Deux (USA)** 4-9-13 0.................(t) NickyMackay 3 72+
(G A Butler) *a.p: led wl over 1f out: rdn and hld on ins fnl f* 9/2[3]
33- 2 *hd* **Riviera Chic (USA)**[31] 7816 3-8-1 0.................(b[1]) DavidProbert 2 62
(R M Beckett) *a.p: rdn 2f out: ev ch ins fnl f: r.o* 3/1[2]
43-6 3 *1 ¾* **Major Lawrence (IRE)**[10] 98 4-9-13 63.................(v) ShaneKelly 1 68
(J Noseda) *led: hdd wl over 1f out: rdn fnl f: no ex towards fin* 9/1
2 4 *5* **Jan Mayen**[10] 98 4-9-8 0.................JoeFanning 7 51
(M Johnston) *sn chsng ldr: ev ch whn hung rt bnd over 2f out: sn rdn: wknd fnl f* 5/4[1]
5 *1* **Summer Sunrise** 3-7-12 0.................(t) AndreaAtzeni(3) 4 44
(M Botti) *s.i.s: hld up: rdn jst over 2f out: btn whn rn green over 1f out* 13/2
0- 6 *5* **Kiss 'n Tell**[159] 4955 4-9-8 0.................GeorgeBaker 6 38
(G L Moore) *hld up: pushed along wl over 2f out: sn struggling* 33/1
45-4 7 *2 ¼* **Giant Strides**[15] 31 4-9-3 57.................RichardEvans(5) 5 33
(P D Evans) *hld up: pushed along 4f out: short-lived effrt on outside over 2f out* 28/1

1m 50.6s (0.10) **Going Correction** 0.0s/f (Stan)
WFA 3 from 4yo 22lb 7 Ran SP% **117.3**
Speed ratings (Par 103): **99,98,97,92,91 87,85**
toteswinger:1&2:£2.90, 2&3:£2.20, 1&3:£4.10 CSF £19.19 TOTE £5.30: £2.60, £1.60; EX 21.70.
Owner C McFadden **Bred** March Thoroughbreds **Trained** Newmarket, Suffolk

FOCUS
An interesting maiden, although the third-placed finisher came into this with an official rating of just 63. Ordinary form, rated around him and the runner-up.

227 THE BLACK COUNTRY'S ONLY RACECOURSE H'CAP 1m 1f 103y(P)
4:50 (4:51) (Class 7) (0-50,51) 4-Y-O+ £1,774 (£523; £262) Stalls Low

Form RPR
64-1 1 **Lyrical Intent**[10] 99 4-8-11 49.................JimmyQuinn 11 59+
(P Howling) *hld up in mid-div: pushed along and hdwy over 2f out: rdn to ld towards fin* 7/2[2]
-462 2 *½* **Kirstys Lad**[2] 211 8-8-7 47.................KellyHarrison(3) 4 56
(M Mullineaux) *hld up in tch: pushed along 3f out: swtchd rt ent st: rdn to ld ins fnl f: hdd towards fin* 2/1[1]
/55- 3 *3 ½* **Roundthetwist (IRE)**[307] 872 5-8-7 47.................(v) MartinLane(3) 9 49
(J R Weymes) *chsd ldr: rdn to ld over 1f out: hdd ins fnl f: one pce* 33/1
354- 4 *2 ¼* **Desert Fairy**[32] 7802 4-8-11 49.................TomEaves 3 46
(J W Unett) *a.p: pushed along over 3f out: rdn and outpcd over 2f out: kpt on to take 4th post* 8/1
640- 5 *nse* **Meml**[71] 7318 4-8-9 47.................AndrewElliott 1 44
(J D Bethell) *led: rdn and hdd over 1f out: wknd ins fnl f* 20/1
00-4 6 *1* **Sairaam (IRE)**[11] 88 4-8-6 47.................AndreaAtzeni(3) 7 42
(C Smith) *hld up in mid-div: pushed along over 2f out: rdn wl over 1f out: no hdwy* 11/2[3]
000- 7 *1 ¼* **Solo Choice**[63] 7425 4-8-10 48.................(b) LiamKeniry 6 40
(I W McInnes) *hld up in mid-div: pushed along over 2f out: bhd whn rdn and swtchd lft jst over 1f out* 40/1
R05- 8 *1 ½* **Kirkie (USA)**[32] 7802 5-8-11 48.................(b) LukeMorris 13 37
(T J Pitt) *hld up towards rr: rdn wl over 1f out: no rspnse* 20/1
30-1 9 *nse* **Turkish Sultan (IRE)**[4] 184 7-9-0 51 6ex.................(p) NickyMackay 12 40
(J M Bradley) *hld up towards rr: pushed along on ins over 2f out: no rspnse* 6/1
/0-0 10 *11* **Viscaya (IRE)**[4] 199 5-8-5 47.................AndrewHeffernan(5) 2 13
(N J Vaughan) *dwlt: in rr: rdn jst over 3f out: sn struggling* 40/1

2m 1.49s (-0.21) **Going Correction** 0.0s/f (Stan)
WFA 4 from 5yo+ 1lb 10 Ran SP% **113.7**
Speed ratings (Par 97): **100,99,96,94,94 93,92,91,91,81**
toteswinger:1&2:£3.00, 2&3:£19.40, 1&3:£21.90 CSF £9.86 CT £185.33 TOTE £4.20: £1.60, £1.10, £6.40; EX 10.80 Trifecta £343.70 Pool: £576.09- 1.24 winning units. Place 6 £109.29, Place 5 £45.03..
Owner Ajaz Ahmed **Bred** Mrs S France **Trained** Newmarket, Suffolk

FOCUS
A moderate handicap run at a reasonable pace although nothing really got into it from the rear. A small personal best from the winner at face value.
T/Plt: £194.00 to a £1 stake. Pool: £69,689.19. 262.22 winning tickets. T/Qpdt: £47.00 to a £1 stake. Pool: £5,077.50. 79.90 winning tickets. KH

[145] KEMPTON (A.W) (R-H)
Wednesday, January 20

OFFICIAL GOING: Standard
Wind: Light, against Weather: Steady rain first 2 races; dry remainder

228 BOOK NOW FOR RACING POST CHASE DAY H'CAP 1m 4f (P)
4:30 (4:30) (Class 7) (0-50,55) 4-Y-O+ £1,364 (£403; £201) Stalls High

Form RPR
43-4 1 **Playful Asset (IRE)**[11] 100 4-8-13 50.................PaulDoe 4 57
(P Howling) *stdd s: hld up in rr on outer: wd bnd 3f out: prog fr 2f out: drvn to ld last 150yds: kpt on* 9/2[2]
03-1 2 *nk* **Fine Tolerance**[5] 199 4-8-13 55 6ex.................BarryMcHugh(5) 10 62
(Miss S L Davison) *stdd s: hld up in last trio on outer: wdst of all bnd 3f out: gd prog over 1f out: styd on to take 2nd nr fin: nt rch wnr* 7/1[3]
040/ 3 *½* **Kadouchski (FR)**[25] 6228 6-9-0 47.................RobertHavlin 14 53
(John Berry) *trckd ldrs on inner: prog to ld 2f out: drvn and hdd last 150yds: one pce* 10/1
306- 4 *nk* **Ocean Of Peace (FR)**[90] 6966 7-8-12 45.................FergusSweeney 7 50+
(M R Bosley) *hld up in last trio: stl there 2f out: gd prog and pushed along over 1f out: r.o to press ldrs last 100yds: nt qckn* 15/2
530/ 5 *¾* **Go On Ahead (IRE)**[388] 7806 10-9-1 48.................LukeMorris 13 52
(M J Coombe) *disp ld: advantage 3f out to 2f out: nt qckn over 1f out: kpt on same pce fnl f* 33/1
4-22 6 *nk* **Crimson Flame (IRE)**[5] 199 7-9-1 48.................RobertWinston 8 52
(S Curran) *hld up in midfield: looking for room fr wl over 2f out: prog to dispute 2nd over 1f out: nt qckn after: wknd fnl 75yds* 7/2[1]
350- 7 *1 ¼* **Midnight Bay**[20] 7888 4-8-7 49.................AndrewHeffernan(5) 9 51
(P D Evans) *t.k.h in midfield: looking for room and rdn over 2f out: prog to press ldrs over 1f out: wknd ins fnl f* 14/1
560- 8 *hd* **Inn For The Dancer**[155] 4263 8-8-11 47.................PatrickHills(3) 3 48
(J C Fox) *s.v.s and reminder: mostly last: effrt and swtchd 2f out: kpt on same pce: n.d* 20/1
00-2 9 *1* **Cragganmore Creek**[12] 90 7-8-9 45.................(v) KellyHarrison(3) 2 45
(D Morris) *racd on outer: pressed ldng pair: lost pl qckly 2f out: one pce fnl f* 25/1
060- 10 *2 ½* **Berrynarbor**[45] 7658 5-8-12 45.................DaneO'Neill 12 41
(A G Newcombe) *dwlt: lost pl after 4f and wl in rr: looking for room and rdn over 2f out: prog and clenough on inner over 1f out: wknd* 20/1
00-5 11 *hd* **Wacato King (IRE)**[5] 199 4-8-13 50.................LiamKeniry 5 45
(R A Farrant) *cl up: pressed ldrs over 1f out: sn wknd* 8/1
000/ 12 *1* **Sarah's Boy**[553] 4085 5-8-12 45.................ChrisCatlin 1 39
(D E Pipe) *s.i.s: pushed up and disp ld to 3f out: sn wknd* 33/1
210- F **Altos Reales**[29] 7840 6-9-2 49.................StephenCraine 6 —
(M J Scudamore) *racd on outer in midfield: rdn over 3f out: losing pl whn stmbld and fell over 1f out* 8/1

2m 35.95s (1.45) **Going Correction** -0.025s/f (Stan)
WFA 4 from 5yo+ 4lb 13 Ran SP% **121.9**
Speed ratings (Par 97): **94,93,93,93,92 92,91,91,90,89 89,88,—**
toteswingers: 1&2 £5.20, 1&3 £14.90, 2&3 £13.70 CSF £34.07 CT £303.91 TOTE £5.30: £2.00, £2.70, £5.20; EX 28.00.
Owner Joe Cole **Bred** P Murray And Eugene Blaney **Trained** Newmarket, Suffolk

FOCUS
A bottom-drawer handicap. The first six were closely covered at the finish and this is low-grade, muddling form. It has been rated around the winner to her recent best.

229 BISTRO IN PANORAMIC BAR & RESTAURANT H'CAP 1m (P)
5:00 (5:00) (Class 7) (0-50,56) 4-Y-O+ £1,364 (£403; £201) Stalls High

Form RPR
430- 1 **Prince Valentine**[21] 7880 9-8-6 46.................(p) HarryBentley(7) 12 56
(G L Moore) *cl up: effrt to ld 2f out: urged along and hrd pressed after: hld on wl* 12/1
/06- 2 *hd* **Stanley Rigby**[149] 5322 4-9-0 47.................JackMitchell 8 56+
(C F Wall) *towards rr: pushed along over 3f out: prog into midfield 2f out: drvn and picked up fnl f: r.o to take 2nd: jst failed* 11/2[2]
50-1 3 *hd* **Musashi (IRE)**[6] 160 5-9-9 56 6ex.................(b) IanMongan 4 65+
(Mrs L J Mongan) *dwlt: hld up in last pair: urged along and prog 2f out: clsng whn checked and swtchd lft jst over 1f out: r.o last 100yds: post c too sn* 7/4[1]
30-4 4 *2* **Inquisitress**[6] 160 6-8-13 49.................MarcHalford(3) 13 53
(J J Bridger) *hld up towards rr: prog over 2f out: drvn to press wnr ent fnl f: fnd little and fdd last 100yds* 10/1[3]
00-0 5 *¾* **Imperium**[11] 100 9-9-2 49.................(p) JimCrowley 3 52+
(Jean-Rene Auvray) *stdd s: hld up in last: prog over 1f out: rdn and r.o ins fnl f: hopeless task* 16/1
306- 6 *¾* **Djalalabad (FR)**[34] 7787 6-9-2 49.................(tp) RobertWinston 7 50
(Mrs C A Dunnett) *hld up in midfield: trapped on inner and hmpd over 2f out: prog to press wnr over 1f out tl ent fnl f: wknd* 10/1[3]
0-65 7 *¾* **Amber Moon**[12] 88 5-8-10 48.................(b) AnnStokell(5) 11 47
(Miss A Stokell) *t.k.h in midfield: lost pl and bmpd along in rr 2f out: sme late prog* 66/1
000- 8 *½* **Obvious**[33] 7796 4-9-2 49.................(p) AmirQuinn 14 47
(Miss J Feilden) *t.k.h bhd ldrs: effrt to chal 2f out: wknd jst over 1f out* 25/1
000/ 9 *2* **Global Guest**[584] 5602 6-9-0 50.................PatrickHills(3) 2 43
(S Curran) *hld up in rr: pushed along over 3f out: struggling and no prog over 2f out* 11/2[2]
5-03 10 *¾* **Foxtrot Bravo (IRE)**[9] 126 4-9-3 50.................DavidProbert 10 42
(Miss S L Davison) *led: edgd lft and hdd 2f out: sn wknd* 20/1
000- 11 *¾* **Michael Laskey**[32] 7818 4-8-13 49.................JamesMillman(3) 1 39
(B R Millman) *nvr beyond midfield: hanging and fnd nil on outer over 2f out: steadily wknd* 16/1
40-5 12 *12* **King's Miracle (IRE)**[7] 145 4-9-1 48.................LiamKeniry 6 10
(J R Gask) *t.k.h: pressed ldr to over 2f out: wknd rapidly: t.o* 16/1
00-5 13 *1 ½* **Sufficient Warning**[11] 100 6-8-6 46.................(b) KierenFox(7) 5 5
(R J Smith) *pressed ldng pair tl wknd rapidly over 2f out: t.o* 14/1

1m 40.1s (0.30) **Going Correction** -0.025s/f (Stan) 13 Ran SP% **127.4**
Speed ratings (Par 97): **97,96,96,94,93 93,92,91,89,89 88,76,74**
toteswingers: 1&2 £14.90, 1&3 £5.10, 2&3 £10.60 CSF £80.52 CT £184.10 TOTE £19.90: £5.00, £2.90, £1.50; EX 189.00.
Owner D R Hunnisett **Bred** Mrs E Y Hunnisett **Trained** Lower Beeding, W Sussex
■ Harry Bentley's first winner.

FOCUS
Another very weak affair and the slowest of the three C/D races. The form looks pretty sound overall with the fourth a fair guide.
Global Guest Official explanation: jockey said gelding had a breathing problem

230 DIGIBET CLAIMING STKS 1m (P)
5:30 (5:30) (Class 6) 4-Y-O+ £2,047 (£604; £302) Stalls High

Form RPR
000- 1 **Ilie Nastase (FR)**[32] 7821 6-9-7 80.................JamieSpencer 5 90
(D M Simcock) *mde all and racd wl away fr rail: stetched on over 2f out: single reminder 1f out: unchal* 15/8[1]
010- 2 *1 ¼* **Scartozz**[125] 6030 8-8-11 84.................(p) AndreaAtzeni(3) 4 80
(M Botti) *chsd wnr: rdn and nt qckn 2f out: plugged on fnl f: nvr able to chal* 9/4[2]
364- 3 *2 ¼* **Dichoh**[44] 7664 7-9-4 74.................(v) GeorgeBaker 6 79
(M Madgwick) *hld up in 3rd: rdn and nt qckn 2f out: n.d after* 7/1
64-0 4 *nk* **Ravi River (IRE)**[10] 115 6-8-9 75.................J-PGuillambert 1 69
(P D Evans) *hld up in 4th: rdn and struggling over 2f out: plugged on ins fnl f* 9/2[3]
66-2 5 *4* **Support Fund (IRE)**[11] 101 6-8-8 68.................(p) ShaneKelly 2 59
(Eve Johnson Houghton) *hld up in last: rdn and no prog over 2f out: wknd fnl f* 8/1

1m 39.52s (-0.28) **Going Correction** -0.025s/f (Stan) 5 Ran SP% **107.3**
Speed ratings (Par 101): **100,98,96,96,92**
toteswinger: 1&2 £3.30 CSF £6.01 TOTE £3.20: £3.60, £1.10; EX 6.50.
Owner Dr Marwan Koukash **Bred** Deln Limited **Trained** Newmarket, Suffolk

FOCUS
A fair claimer in which the winner made all in a very tactical affair. The order hardly chaned in the straight and this is not form to get behind, although it makes sense at face value.

231 DIGIBET.COM H'CAP 1m (P)
6:00 (6:03) (Class 3) (0-90,90) 4-Y-0+
£6,542 (£1,959; £979; £490; £244; £122) **Stalls** High

Form RPR
413- **1** **Audemar (IRE)**[98] 6773 4-8-13 **85** JamieSpencer 12 94+
(E F Vaughan) *t.k.h early: retrained in midfield after 3f: rdn and prog jst over 2f out: wnt 2nd jst ins fnl f: hrd rdn and r.o to ld last strides* **3/1**[1]
522- **2** *hd* **Den's Gift (IRE)**[21] 7883 6-8-12 **84** (b) AdamKirby 7 93
(C G Cox) *led at gd pce: fought on wl fr 2f out: collared last strides* **4/1**[2]
005- **3** *1 ¼* **Gallantry**[21] 7883 8-8-5 **77** oh2 ow1 SaleemGolam 9 83
(P Howling) *sn trckd ldng pair: drvn to chse ldr over 2f out tl ent fnl f: one pce after* **20/1**
260- **4** *1* **Cry Alot Boy**[35] 7775 7-8-4 **76** JimmyQuinn 13 80+
(K A Morgan) *stdd s: plld hrd and hld up in detached last: prog on inner over 2f out: drvn and styd on to take 4th ins fnl f: no ch* **25/1**
620- **5** *1* **Councellor (FR)**[222] 2883 8-9-4 **90** (t) TomQueally 2 92
(Stef Higgins) *chsd ldrs: in tch and drvn 2f out: steadily outpcd after* **25/1**
243/ **6** *½* **Hazzard County (USA)**[517] 5207 6-8-9 **84** AndreaAtzeni(3) 8 84+
(D M Simcock) *hld up in last trio: pushed along 2f out: stl 10th 1f out: styd on steadily after: nvr nr ldrs* **7/1**
056- **7** *1* **Grand Vizier (IRE)**[31] 7827 6-9-2 **88** GeorgeBaker 10 86
(C F Wall) *hld up towards rr: rdn and struggling over 2f out: sme modest late prog* **5/1**[3]
235- **8** *¾* **Bennelong**[35] 7769 4-7-13 **76** (p) AndrewHeffernan(5) 5 72
(G L Moore) *t.k.h: hld up but trckd ldrs 1/2-way: effrt and in tch 2f out: wknd jst over 1f out* **11/1**
21-5 **9** *½* **Mcconnell (USA)**[19] 6 5-8-8 **83** RobertLButler(3) 14 78
(P Butler) *hld up in rr: shkn up briefly over 2f out: pushed along in midfield over 1f out: nvr nr ldrs* **33/1**
004- **10** *1 ¼* **Kinsya**[35] 6695 7-8-5 **77** MartinDwyer 3 69
(M H Tompkins) *settled wl in rr: pushed along over 3f out: no prog and btn over 2f out* **10/1**
P20- **11** *1* **Brouhaha**[34] 7789 6-8-8 **85** RossAtkinson(5) 6 75
(Tom Dascombe) *mostly chsd ldr to over 2f out: sn wknd u.p* **16/1**
541- **12** *6* **L'Hirondelle (IRE)**[30] 7833 6-8-13 **85** PaulDoe 1 61
(M J Attwater) *racd wd: hld up in midfield: effrt over 2f out: sn wknd rapidly* **11/1**
436- **13** *nk* **Street Devil (USA)**[67] 2263 5-8-4 **76** oh1 (b[1]) FrankieMcDonald 11 52
(R Curtis) *plld hrd: hld up towards rr: wknd over 2f out* **50/1**

1m 38.44s (-1.36) **Going Correction** -0.025s/f (Stan) **13** Ran SP% **123.2**
Speed ratings (Par 107): **105,104,103,102,101 101,100,99,98,97 96,90,90**
toteswingers: 1&2 £4.10, 1&3 £43.10, 2&3 £14.80 CSF £13.99 CT £212.27 TOTE £4.10: £1.10, £2.00, £9.30; EX 20.00.
Owner Gute Freunde Partnership **Bred** Mrs Amanda Brudenell And Mr & Mrs R A **Trained** Newmarket, Suffolk

FOCUS
A good, competitive handicap run at a fair pace, although the first three were always prominent. The form is rated around the placed horses.

NOTEBOOK
Audemar(IRE) ◆ got up in the dying strides under a strong ride from the bang in-form Jamie Spencer. He was taken back after taking a keen hold and hugged the inside rail. He was given a smack nearing the 2f pole and responded positively, but ultimately took an age to master the runner-up. This was his first run for 98 days and he should improve for it, so it wouldn't be surprising to see him defy a likely higher mark. (op 4-1 tchd 9-2)
Den's Gift(IRE) was allowed an uncontested early lead which he relishes. He really stuck his head down throughout the home straight and only got mugged near the finish. The handicapper has him where he wants him and he has now finished second on his last three runs, but there is little wrong with his attitude. (tchd 9-2)
Gallantry ◆ was 3lb wrong due to being 2lb out of the handicap and his rider putting up 1lb overweight. He was still undeniably well treated on his previous best efforts, though, and finished fourth in this race last year from a 10lb higher mark. He got a lovely trip through the race and held every chance, but the first pair proved too strong. A drop down in grade could well see him back to winning ways in the coming weeks as he is evidently now back in good heart.
Cry Alot Boy was the only one to make any significant ground up from out the back and would have surely been closer had he not fluffed the start, but that has become something of a trend with him. This was also plenty sharp enough for him and he is another that could be found another winning turn soon. (op 20-1)
Councellor(FR) turned in a respectable return to action, but still looks high enough in the weights in this sphere.
Hazzard County(USA) was having his first outing since August 2008, but hails from the yard that took the preceding race and this event last year. He came in for support as he has gone well fresh before and ran well, but really shaped as though it was needed. (op 9-1 tchd 10-1)
Grand Vizier(IRE) is rarely far away here and looked set to improve on his latest run, but he was disappointingly one-paced in the home straight. (op 9-2)
Street Devil(USA) Official explanation: jockey said gelding ran too freely

232 DIGIBET CASINO H'CAP 2m (P)
6:30 (6:35) (Class 4) (0-85,85) 4-Y-0+ **£4,209** (£1,252; £625; £312) **Stalls** High

Form RPR
/60- **1** **Alsadaa (USA)**[81] 5802 7-9-5 **76** IanMongan 3 91
(Mrs L J Mongan) *racd wl away fr ins rail: mde all and allowed clr ld: kicked on 3f out: rdn out and gng further away fin* **10/1**
3/3- **2** *8* **L'Homme De Nuit (GER)**[47] 7255 6-8-11 **68** (p) FergusSweeney 5 73
(G L Moore) *heavily restrained s: hld up in 4th: prog to chse wnr 5f out: rdn and no imp over 1f out* **10/3**[2]
012- **3** *2 ½* **Moonbeam Dancer (USA)**[41] 7701 4-8-7 **71** NickyMackay 6 73
(D M Simcock) *v reluctant to enter stalls: hld up in 5th: prog to go 3rd 3f out: rdn and no imp over 2f out* **7/2**[3]
1-11 **4** *12* **Russian Music (USA)**[8] 140 5-8-9 **64** 6ex StevieDonohoe 7 54
(Ian Williams) *chsd ldng pair to 5f out: pushed along 4f out: wl btn 4th over 2f out* **7/4**[1]
/00- **5** *5* **Prairie Spirit (FR)**[293] 585 6-10-0 **85** DaneO'Neill 1 67
(C E Longsdon) *chsd clr wnr to 5f out: nt striding out wl and sn dropped to rr: wl btn 5th over 2f out* **66/1**
001- **6** *2 ¼* **Dani's Girl (IRE)**[21] 7873 7-9-4 **82** KierenFox(7) 2 61
(P M Phelan) *stdd s: keen early: hld up in last: effrt on outer 4f out: v wd bnd 3f out: bhd after* **10/3**[2]

3m 30.1s **Going Correction** -0.025s/f (Stan)
WFA 4 from 5yo+ 7lb **6** Ran SP% **115.3**
Speed ratings (Par 105): **99,95,93,87,85 84**
toteswingers: 1&2 £1.90, 1&3 £6.30, 2&3 £2.60 CSF £44.23 TOTE £15.20: £7.60, £1.10; EX 50.30.
Owner Mrs P J Sheen **Bred** Shadwell Farm LLC **Trained** Epsom, Surrey

FOCUS
A modest staying handicap. The winner was gifted the race from the front and the form is rated around him, but the form is suspect.

233 TRY OUR BISTRO MENU H'CAP 6f (P)
7:00 (7:04) (Class 5) (0-70,72) 3-Y-0 **£2,590** (£770; £385; £192) **Stalls** High

Form RPR
00-0 **1** **Private Olley**[17] 24 3-8-9 **57** ChrisCatlin 3 63
(J Akehurst) *trckd ldr: pushed into narrow ld wl over 1f out: drvn to assert fnl f* **33/1**
22-6 **2** *1 ¾* **Avow (USA)**[9] 122 3-8-11 **66** (b) KierenFox(7) 5 67
(J S Moore) *led: rdn and narrowly hdd wl over 1f out: pressed wnr tl no ex fnl f* **8/1**
26-2 **3** *½* **Maoi Chinn Tire (IRE)**[9] 122 3-9-4 **66** (p) LiamKeniry 2 65
(J S Moore) *trckd ldrs: rdn and nt qckn over 2f out: wnt 3rd ins fnl f: kpt on but n.d to wnr* **7/1**
3-31 **4** *½* **Major Maximus**[4] 201 3-9-5 **72** 6ex (b) MatthewDavies(5) 10 69
(George Baker) *t.k.h: hld up in last quartet: rdn over 2f out: prog over 1f out: styd on same pce fnl f: n.d* **5/1**[2]
305- **5** *½* **Val C**[128] 5950 3-9-2 **64** JerryO'Dwyer 11 60
(M Botti) *blindfold off as stalls opened: hld up in midfield: effrt over 2f out: sn rdn and one pce* **4/1**[1]
444- **6** *shd* **Starwatch**[31] 7824 3-8-8 **59** MarcHalford(3) 8 54
(J J Bridger) *chsd ldng pair to over 2f out: hrd rdn and fdd* **6/1**[3]
45-5 **7** *nk* **Layla's Lad (USA)**[16] 35 3-8-13 **61** (b[1]) PaulHanagan 7 56
(R A Fahey) *awkward s: reminder in last pair after 1f: no prog tl styd on fnl f* **7/1**
04-2 **8** *¾* **Singingintherain (IRE)**[17] 24 3-9-4 **66** JoeFanning 4 58
(T G Mills) *trckd ldrs: wnt 3rd over 2f out: sn shkn up and nt qckn: wknd rapidly last 150yds* **10/1**
035- **9** *1 ¾* **La Toya J (IRE)**[20] 7885 3-8-13 **61** DaneO'Neill 9 48
(R Curtis) *awkward s: detached in last early w jockey looking down: nvr a factor* **14/1**
555- **10** *2 ½* **Notte Di Note (IRE)**[72] 7317 3-8-11 **62** AndreaAtzeni(3) 1 41
(L M Cumani) *a in rr: rdn and struggling bef 1/2-way: no ch over 2f out* **8/1**

1m 12.98s (-0.12) **Going Correction** -0.025s/f (Stan) **10** Ran SP% **116.9**
Speed ratings (Par 97): **99,96,96,95,94 94,94,93,90,87**
toteswingers: 1&2 £1.90, 1&3 £6.30, 2&3 £2.60 CSF £277.52 CT £2079.75 TOTE £46.60: £12.20, £2.80, £1.20; EX 1157.10.
Owner David S M Caplin **Bred** Bearstone Stud **Trained** Epsom, Surrey

FOCUS
A modest 3-y-o handicap, run at an average pace. The front pair were always 1-2 and the form is rated around the second and third, with improvement from the winner.

234 KEMPTON.CO.UK H'CAP (DIV I) 7f (P)
7:30 (7:31) (Class 6) (0-55,56) 4-Y-0+ **£1,706** (£503; £252) **Stalls** High

Form RPR
46-1 **1** **Ejeed (USA)**[7] 145 5-8-10 **56** 6ex (p) RossAtkinson(5) 13 69
(Miss Z C Davison) *trckd ldng pair: prog on inner to ld over 1f out: rdn out and wl in command fnl f* **10/3**[1]
01-3 **2** *2 ¾* **Angle Of Attack (IRE)**[13] 69 5-9-0 **55** (v) GrahamGibbons 9 61
(A D Brown) *trckd ldr: chal 2f out: chsd wnr over 1f out: sn lft bhd: clung on for 2nd* **8/1**
04-6 **3** *nk* **Easy Wonder (GER)**[6] 160 5-8-5 **46** oh1 (b) MartinDwyer 11 51
(I A Wood) *trckd ldrs on inner: effrt over 2f out: wnt 3rd over 1f out: kpt on same pce* **16/1**
23-6 **4** *nk* **Cavalry Guard (USA)**[9] 124 6-8-6 **52** (b) AmyBaker(5) 5 56
(T D McCarthy) *racd on outer: hld up in midfield: effrt 2f out: urged along and styd on same pce fnl f* **10/1**
-346 **5** *½* **Hart Of Gold**[5] 195 6-8-12 **53** (b) StephenCraine 6 56
(R A Harris) *trckd ldrs: gng strly over 2f out: rdn and no rspnse over 1f out: one pce after* **6/1**[2]
04-4 **6** *½* **Guildenstern (IRE)**[9] 124 8-9-0 **55** IanMongan 3 56
(P Howling) *hld up in last trio: prog over 2f out: chsd ldrs over 1f out: kpt on same pce after* **13/2**[3]
040- **7** *hd* **Wicklewood**[34] 7787 4-8-7 **48** (b) SaleemGolam 7 49
(Mrs C A Dunnett) *racd wd in midfield: nt qckn and no prog over 2f out: plugged on* **25/1**
366- **8** *1 ½* **Bahkov (IRE)**[58] 6251 4-8-11 **52** RichardKingscote 4 49
(Andrew Turnell) *reminder in last trio after 1f: rdn 2f out: modest late prog: nvr a factor* **10/1**
50-0 **9** *2 ¼* **Grizedale (IRE)**[7] 145 11-8-0 **48** (tp) KierenFox(7) 1 39
(M J Attwater) *hld up in last trio: wd bnd 3f out: nvr a factor* **25/1**
0-00 **10** *½* **Music Box Express**[8] 138 6-8-9 **55** (b) MatthewDavies(5) 14 44
(George Baker) *led at decent pce: clr 1/2-way: hdd & wknd rapidly over 1f out* **20/1**
00-4 **11** *nse* **Safaseef (IRE)**[11] 101 5-8-5 **46** oh1 (v) JimmyQuinn 10 35
(K A Morgan) *s.i.s: a towards rr: u.p and struggling over 2f out* **8/1**
250- **12** *1 ¾* **Clerical (USA)**[49] 7614 4-8-12 **53** JimCrowley 8 38
(R M H Cowell) *a towards rr: struggling and no prog over 2f out* **9/1**
/00- **13** *11* **Igotim**[230] 2630 4-8-5 **46** oh1 LukeMorris 12 1
(P Burgoyne) *s.i.s: sn in midfield: wknd u.p over 2f out: t.o* **50/1**

1m 25.79s (-0.21) **Going Correction** -0.025s/f (Stan) **13** Ran SP% **121.4**
Speed ratings (Par 101): **100,96,96,96,95 95,94,93,90,89 89,87,75**
toteswingers: 1&2 £46.10, 1&3 £21.90, 2&3 £15.80 CSF £28.92 CT £385.14 TOTE £3.30: £1.30, £2.40, £2.90; EX 32.00.
Owner Mrs J Irvine **Bred** Shadwell Farm LLC **Trained** Hammerwood, E Sussex

FOCUS
A weak handicap where those racing handily proved at an advantage again. The form seems sound enough.

235 KEMPTON.CO.UK H'CAP (DIV II) 7f (P)
8:00 (8:01) (Class 6) (0-55,56) 4-Y-0+ **£1,706** (£503; £252) **Stalls** High

Form RPR
504- **1** **Munich (IRE)**[177] 4389 6-9-0 **55** (p) DaneO'Neill 4 71
(R Curtis) *dwlt: sn in 7th: gd prog on inner jst over 2f out: rdn to ld over 1f out: drew away fnl f: decisively* **3/1**[1]
463- **2** *3 ¾* **Towy Boy (IRE)**[94] 6880 5-8-11 **52** (v) JimCrowley 5 57
(I A Wood) *trckd ldng trio: rdn 2f out: prog to go 2nd jst over 1f out and looked threatening: ducked in bhd and fnd nil: stl clr 2nd best* **9/1**
4-45 **3** *1 ½* **Reigning Monarch (USA)**[7] 146 7-8-4 **50** ow2 (p) RossAtkinson(5) 1 51
(Miss Z C Davison) *dropped in fr wdst draw and hld up last: prog wl over 1f out: r.o fnl f to snatch 3rd last strides* **14/1**

34-4 **4** *hd* **Kinigi (IRE)**[10] 116 4-8-9 **55** (p) AndrewHeffernan(5) 12 55
(R A Harris) *chsd ldrs: hrd rdn fr 2f out: chsd clr ldng pair ins fnl f: no imp: lost 3rd last strides* **9/1**

6-64 **5** *1 3/4* **Hold The Star**[12] 85 4-8-7 **53** ow1 AnnStokell(5) 7 49
(Miss A Stokell) *racd wd in 6th: lost pl 2f out: bmpd along and kpt on ins fnl f* **40/1**

05-1 **6** *1/2* **Diane's Choice**[7] 146 7-9-1 **56** 6ex (b) DavidProbert 2 50
(Miss Gay Kelleway) *hld up in 8th: nt qckn and no prog 2f out: kpt on fnl f: n.d* **10/1**

406- **7** *hd* **Sovereignty (JPN)**[30] 7834 8-8-13 **54** MartinDwyer 6 48
(D K Ivory) *trckd ldr: pushed up to chal 2f out: shkn up and wknd over 1f out: eased* **13/2**[3]

2-10 **8** *3/4* **Tamino (IRE)**[8] 135 7-9-0 **55** JimmyQuinn 10 47
(P Howling) *led at fair pce to over 1f out: wknd* **4/1**[2]

030- **9** *2* **Metropolitan Chief**[35] 7770 6-8-5 **46** oh1 LukeMorris 9 32
(P Burgoyne) *dwlt: a in rr: rdn and no prog over 2f out* **20/1**

0/0- **10** *1 3/4* **Macademy Royal (USA)**[56] 7521 7-7-12 **46** oh1 (t) LindseyWhite(7) 11 28
(Miss N A Lloyd-Beavis) *dwlt: a in rr: urged along and no prog over 2f out* **50/1**

00/ **11** *1 1/4* **Wetherby Place (IRE)**[54] 7563 4-8-11 **52** NickyMackay 3 30
(M Wigham) *a in rr: struggling and no prog wl over 2f out* **8/1**

11-6 **12** *1/2* **Maggie Kate**[8] 137 5-8-12 **53** (b) RobertHavlin 8 30
(R Ingram) *chsd ldng pair tl wknd wl over 1f out* **16/1**

1m 25.26s (-0.74) **Going Correction** -0.025s/f (Stan) 12 Ran SP% **120.2**
Speed ratings (Par 101): **103,98,97,96,94 94,93,93,90,88 87,86**
toteswingers: 1&2 £13.70, 1&3 £16.60, 2&3 £23.90 CSF £30.66 CT £336.48 TOTE £4.50: £1.80, £2.20, £5.40; EX 42.30 Place 6 £194.86, Place 5 £72.84.
Owner R P Behan **Bred** Frank Dunne **Trained** Lambourn, Berks

FOCUS
The second division of the 7f handicap and another poor affair. It was quicker than division I and the form looks solid for the grade, rated around the runner-up.
T/Plt: £1,253.10 to a £1 stake. Pool: £74,501.16. 43.40 winning tickets. T/Qpdt: £154.30 to a £1 stake. Pool: £8,408.06. 40.30 winning tickets. JN

200 LINGFIELD (L-H)
Wednesday, January 20

OFFICIAL GOING: Standard
Wind: nil Weather: snowing

236 TRY BETDAQ FOR AN EXCHANGE MEDIAN AUCTION MAIDEN STKS 7f (P)
12:50 (12:51) (Class 6) 3-Y-0 **£2,047** (£604; £302) **Stalls** Low

Form RPR

1 **Nubar Boy**[117] 6259 3-9-3 78 (t) RichardKingscote 4 73
(Tom Dascombe) *s.i.s: in tch: shkn up and hdwy 2f out: rdn to ld ins fnl f: r.o wl* **7/4**[2]

5- **2** *1 1/4* **Neduardo**[60] 7477 3-9-3 0 TomQueally 7 69
(P W Chapple-Hyam) *chsd ldr: rdn ent fnl 2f: ev ch ins fnl f tl unable qck fnl 75yds* **6/1**

232- **3** *2 3/4* **Until The Man (IRE)**[20] 7886 3-9-3 65 (p) PaulDoe 5 62+
(R Ingram) *led: rdn over 1f out: drvn and hdd ins fnl f: fdd towards fin* **11/8**[1]

504- **4** *1/2* **Captain Bluebird (IRE)**[171] 4564 3-9-3 63 JimmyQuinn 3 61
(D Donovan) *rrd s and s.i.s: hld up in last pair: drvn over 1f out: kpt on but nvr gng pce to trble ldrs* **4/1**[3]

00- **5** *8* **Suzybee**[31] 7825 3-8-13 0 ow1 IanMongan 2 35
(M R Hoad) *wnt rt s: chsd ldng pair: rdn jst over 2f out: wknd over 1f out* **100/1**

0- **6** *8* **All Right Now**[23] 7859 3-9-3 0 LiamKeniry 1 17
(S Kirk) *s.i.s: sn bustled along in last: lost tch 2f out* **33/1**

1m 24.51s (-0.29) **Going Correction** +0.025s/f (Slow) 6 Ran SP% **116.7**
Speed ratings (Par 95): **102,100,97,96,87 78**
toteswingers: 1&2 £3.00, 1&3 £1.40, 2&3 £2.30 CSF £13.33 TOTE £3.40: £1.10, £3.80; EX 14.30.
Owner Phil Slater **Bred** Low Ground Stud **Trained** Malpas, Cheshire

FOCUS
A modest maiden run at a reasonable pace. The winner was probably near to the level of his best form in Ireland.
Captain Bluebird(IRE) Official explanation: jockey said colt was slowly away

237 MARRIOTT PLAY & STAY CLAIMING STKS 2m (P)
1:20 (1:20) (Class 6) 4-Y-0+ **£1,774** (£523; £262) **Stalls** Low

Form RPR

43-1 **1** **Wicked Daze (IRE)**[7] 148 7-9-12 85 JamieSpencer 7 82+
(K A Ryan) *chsd ldr tl led 11f out: mde rest: c centre st: nudged clr over 1f out: nt extended* **1/4**[1]

245- **2** *4* **Alrafid (IRE)**[75] 393 11-9-2 63 (b) GeorgeBaker 5 60
(G L Moore) *stdd s: hld up in last pair: hdwy to chse wnr over 2f out: rdn and no ch w wnr fr over 1f out* **11/1**[3]

56-5 **3** *3/4* **Acropolis (IRE)**[6] 164 9-9-2 55 VinceSlattery 3 59
(B G Powell) *hld up in last pair: swtchd out off rail over 2f out: rdn to chal 2nd over 1f out: fnd virtually nil u.p: no ch w wnr* **9/1**[2]

235- **4** *1* **Leulahleulahlay**[21] 7873 4-8-10 72 (p) ShaneKelly 2 59
(Evan Williams) *chsd ldrs: wnt 2nd 6f out: rdn 3f out: outpcd wl over 1f out: plugged on same pce after* **12/1**

0-06 **5** *21* **Primera Rossa**[8] 140 4-8-4 46 (p) LukeMorris 6 28
(J S Moore) *in tch: rdn to ldng pair 5f out tl 3f out: sn lost tch* **33/1**

5 **6** *20* **Randomer**[12] 80 7-9-1 0 RobertLButler(3) 4 11
(P Butler) *led tl 11f out: chsd ldr tl 6f out: dropped to last over 4f out: sn lost tch: t.o* **100/1**

3m 27.58s (1.88) **Going Correction** +0.025s/f (Slow)
WFA 4 from 7yo+ 7lb 6 Ran SP% **110.0**
Speed ratings (Par 101): **96,94,93,93,82 72**
.Wicked Daze was claimed by K McGarrity for £15,000.\n\x\x
Owner Dr Marwan Koukash **Bred** Bloomsbury Stud **Trained** Hambleton, N Yorks

FOCUS
A weak and uncompetitive claimer run at a steady pace.

238 BET CARLING CUP - BETDAQ MAIDEN FILLIES' STKS 1m (P)
1:55 (1:57) (Class 5) 3-Y-0+ **£2,456** (£725; £362) **Stalls** High

Form RPR

553- **1** **Pastel Blue (IRE)**[146] 5369 3-8-7 71 HayleyTurner 3 69+
(M L W Bell) *broke wl: t.k.h: mde all: set stdy gallop tl rdn and qcknd clr 2f out: in n.d after: easily* **6/4**[1]

00/0 **2** *3 3/4* **Castleburg**[8] 137 4-9-13 60 GeorgeBaker 6 65
(G L Moore) *t.k.h: hld up in tch: hdwy on inner jst over 2f out: swtchd rt wl over 1f out: drvn ent fnl f: chsd wnr ins fnl f: no imp* **16/1**

3 *1* **Palmilla (IRE)** 3-8-7 0 MartinDwyer 1 58
(L M Cumani) *dwlt and nudged along early: chsd wnr after 1f tl over 4f out: rdn to chse clr wnr again wl over 1f out: no imp and lost 2nd ins fnl f* **5/1**[3]

0- **4** *4* **Celestial Girl**[23] 7859 3-8-7 0 JimmyQuinn 5 49
(H Morrison) *in tch on outer: rdn and unable qck 2f out: btn and hung lft over 1f out: wnt modest 4th nr fin* **3/1**[2]

5 *nk* **Realta** 4-9-13 0 NickyMackay 4 53
(G A Butler) *t.k.h: chsd ldrs wnt 2nd over 4f out tl wl over 1f out: wknd over 1f out* **10/1**

0-5 **6** *3* **Que Belle (IRE)**[9] 128 3-8-7 0 RichardKingscote 7 41
(Tom Dascombe) *s.i.s: a in rr: reminder over 4f out: rdn and struggling wl over 2f out* **9/1**

0- **7** *2* **Chateau Zara**[88] 7024 3-8-7 0 LukeMorris 2 37
(C G Cox) *t.k.h: chsd wnr for 1f: in tch after tl rdn and wknd over 2f out* **20/1**

1m 39.25s (1.05) **Going Correction** +0.025s/f (Slow)
WFA 3 from 4yo 20lb 7 Ran SP% **111.4**
Speed ratings (Par 100): **95,91,90,86,85 82,80**
toteswingers: 1&2 £5.50, 1&3 £2.70, 2&3 £10.20 CSF £25.98 TOTE £2.10: £1.60, £8.60; EX 20.20.
Owner Sheikh Marwan Al Maktoum **Bred** Darley **Trained** Newmarket, Suffolk

FOCUS
A weak fillies' maiden run at a steady pace. It is doubtful if the easy winner had to improve.

239 BETDAQ.CO.UK H'CAP 1m 2f (P)
2:30 (2:31) (Class 4) (0-85,85) 4-Y-0+ **£4,209** (£1,252; £625; £312) **Stalls** Low

Form RPR

02-5 **1** **Mister Green (FR)**[17] 23 4-8-7 **74** (b) JoeFanning 12 85
(K McAuliffe) *stdd s: hld up in rr: gd hdwy on outer over 2f out: rdn to ld 1f out: sn clr: comfoetably* **8/1**

306- **2** *2* **December Draw (IRE)**[42] 7684 4-8-13 **80** ShaneKelly 2 87+
(W J Knight) *t.k.h: led tl over 8f out: hld up in tch after: shuffled bk and lost pl jst over 2f out: swtchd rt over 1f out: r.o wl to go 2nd fnl 75yds: no ch w wnr* **16/1**

412- **3** *1 1/4* **Confidentiality (IRE)**[25] 7848 6-9-6 **85** NickyMackay 9 90
(M Wigham) *t.k.h: hld up in tch: rdn to chse ldrs 2f out: chsd clr wnr ins fnl f: no imp and lost 2nd fnl 75yds* **3/1**[1]

04-4 **4** *nk* **Hurakan (IRE)**[7] 151 4-8-1 **73** (v) AndrewHeffernan(5) 13 77
(P D Evans) *t.k.h: chsd ldrs tl wnt 2nd over 7f out tl 5f out: chsd ldr again over 2f out tl rdn to ld wl over 1f out: hdd 1f out: one pce after* **11/2**[3]

230- **5** *1 1/4* **Indy Driver**[25] 7848 5-8-13 **78** (p) FrannyNorton 6 79
(Matthew Salaman) *wl in tch: rdn and effrt on inner over 1f out: no prog and wl hld fnl f* **14/1**

400/ **6** *nk* **Palomar (USA)**[24] 5548 8-9-1 **80** TomQueally 14 81
(N G Richards) *sn niggled along in rr: rdn 4f out: hdwy on outer over 2f out: styd on wl ins fnl f: nvr trbld ldrs* **14/1**

562- **7** *3/4* **Basra (IRE)**[50] 7607 7-9-0 **79** JamieSpencer 1 78+
(Miss Jo Crowley) *stdd after s: hld up in rr: nt clr run on inner and shuffled bk over 2f out: switching out rt and rdn wl over 1f out: styd on fnl f: nvr trbld ldrs* **5/1**[2]

336- **8** *1 1/4* **Prince Picasso**[35] 7775 7-8-8 **73** (t) PaulHanagan 10 70
(R A Fahey) *t.k.h: chsd ldr tl led over 8f out tl hdd 5f out: chsd ldr after tl over 2f out tl rdn to ld wl over 1f out: wknd u.p over 1f out* **10/1**

031- **9** *1 3/4* **Rocky's Pride (IRE)**[21] 7881 4-8-10 **77** RichardKingscote 7 70
(A B Haynes) *chsd ldrs: rdn and unable qck jst over 2f out: wknd over 1f out* **11/1**

305- **10** *1* **Suzi Spends (IRE)**[35] 7775 5-9-0 **79** JimmyQuinn 3 70+
(H J Collingridge) *in tch on inner: stmbld and lost pl 8f out: towards rr after: nt clr run and switching out rt over 1f out: nvr able to chal* **9/1**

041- **11** *1* **Young Dottie**[44] 7664 4-8-0 **74** KierenFox(7) 4 63+
(P M Phelan) *hld up in midfield: hmpd and sddle slipped 8f out: swtchd to outer and hdwy to ld 5f out: rdn and hdd wl over 1f out: sn wknd* **8/1**

0/0- **12** *1 1/2* **Outofoil (IRE)**[240] 2329 4-8-10 **77** JimCrowley 5 63
(R M Beckett) *hld up towards rr: rdn and struggling over 2f out: bhd fnl 2f* **20/1**

51- **13** *7* **Halling Gal**[215] 3100 4-8-10 **77** RobertWinston 11 49
(Evan Williams) *hld up towards rr: rdn and struggling over 2f out: bhd fnl 2f* **25/1**

2m 6.13s (-0.47) **Going Correction** +0.025s/f (Slow)
WFA 4 from 5yo+ 2lb 13 Ran SP% **134.5**
Speed ratings (Par 105): **102,100,99,99,98 97,97,96,94,94 93,92,86**
toteswingers: 1&2 £36.80, 1&3 £11.10, 2&3 £20.50 CSF £145.88 CT £489.41 TOTE £10.60: £3.60, £6.10, £1.80; EX 221.60 TRIFECTA Not won..
Owner K W J McAuliffe **Bred** Gainsborough Stud Management Ltd **Trained** Fernham, Oxon

FOCUS
This race was run in driving snow. A fair handicap run at a steady pace. The winner stepped up on recent efforts.
Confidentiality(IRE) Official explanation: jockey said mare was denied a clear run
Basra(IRE) Official explanation: jockey said mare was denied a clear run
Young Dottie Official explanation: jockey said saddle slipped

240 BOB LUCCHESI IS NOW 60 H'CAP 1m 2f (P)
3:05 (3:06) (Class 5) (0-75,79) 3-Y-0 **£2,456** (£725; £362) **Stalls** Low

Form RPR

02-1 **1** **Lovers Causeway (USA)**[11] 106 3-9-4 **75** JoeFanning 2 83+
(M Johnston) *led: jnd and rdn ent fnl 2f: narrowly hdd over 1f out: led again ins fnl f: styd on wl* **1/1**[1]

-341 **2** *3/4* **Exceedthewildman**[4] 203 3-9-1 **79** 6ex (p) KierenFox(7) 4 85
(J S Moore) *stdd after s: hld up in last: hdwy on outer 3f out: jnd wnr and rdn jst over 2f out: led narrowly over 1f out: hdd ins fnl f: kpt on same pce after* **9/2**[3]

04-3 **3** *5* **Septemberintherain**[11] 106 3-9-1 **72** TomQueally 1 68
(T G Mills) *racd in 3rd tl dropped to last and rdn 3f out: outpcd by ldng pair over 2f out: wl btn fnl 2f: wnt 3rd nr fin* **7/4**[2]

2-26 **4** *nk* **Gold Party**[8] 136 3-8-10 **67** (t) RobertWinston 3 62
(K McAuliffe) *t.k.h: chsd wnr tl over 2f out: sn rdn and outpcd by ldng pair: no ch w ldng pair fnl 2f: lost 3rd nr fin* **14/1**

2m 6.80s (0.20) **Going Correction** +0.025s/f (Slow) 4 Ran SP% **111.2**
Speed ratings (Par 97): **100,99,95,95**
CSF £6.00 TOTE £2.00; EX 5.00.
Owner Crone Stud Farms Ltd **Bred** Skara Glen Stables **Trained** Middleham Moor, N Yorks

FOCUS
A poor turnout numerically for this fair handicap. The winner confirmed maiden form with the disappointing third.
Septemberintherain Official explanation: jockey said colt never travelled

241 MARRIOTT HOTEL OPENING SPRING 2010 H'CAP 5f (P)
3:40 (3:41) (Class 5) (0-75,74) 4-Y-0+ £2,456 (£725; £362) Stalls High

Form RPR
251- **1** **Brynfa Boy**[40] 7714 4-8-8 **64** .... TonyCulhane 6 77+
(P W D'Arcy) *taken down early: in tch in rr: rdn and hdwy over 1f out: led ins fnl f: r.o wl* **5/2**[1]

1-52 **2** 1 ¼ **Fromsong (IRE)**[9] 119 12-8-9 **65** .... (p) MartinDwyer 1 73
(D K Ivory) *taken down early: chsd ldng pair: rdn and clsd 2f out ev ch over 1f out: led ins fnl f: sn hdd: kpt on same after* **11/2**[3]

140- **3** 1 ¼ **Master Lightfoot**[31] 7828 4-9-3 **73** .... AdamKirby 4 77+
(W R Swinburn) *in tch towards rr: looking for run and n.m.r over 1f out: swtchd lft 1f out: r.o to go 3rd towards fin* **5/1**[2]

200- **4** ½ **Even Bolder**[45] 7656 7-8-10 **73** .... KierenFox(7) 7 75
(E A Wheeler) *chsd ldrs: rdn and clsd 2f out: ev ch over 1f out: led jst ins fnl f: sn hdd: wknd fnl 75yds* **13/2**

34-0 **5** 1 ¼ **Littlemisssunshine (IRE)**[9] 119 5-8-7 **68** .... (p) RossAtkinson(5) 5 65
(J S Moore) *bhd: hdwy on inner over 1f out: drvn and kpt on same pce fnl f* **16/1**

210- **6** ¾ **Edith's Boy (IRE)**[32] 7808 4-8-13 **69** .... HayleyTurner 9 64
(S Dow) *s.i.s: racd on outer: bhd tl hdwy into midfield 1/2-way: no prog fr over 1f out* **7/1**

04-1 **7** 1 **Silver Prelude**[12] 77 9-8-6 **69** .... (t) RyanClark(7) 10 60
(S C Williams) *chsd ldr tl led over 3f out: rdn over 1f out: hdd jst ins fnl f: sn wknd* **13/2**

6-20 **8** shd **Ten Down**[5] 185 5-8-4 **60** oh5 .... FrannyNorton 3 51
(M Quinn) *led tl over 3f out: chsd ldr tl tl over 1f out: wkng whn short of room and eased ent fnl f: no ch after* **10/1**

000- **9** ½ **Woodcote (IRE)**[40] 7709 8-8-5 **61** oh15 ow1 .... (v) SaleemGolam 2 50
(Peter Grayson) *s.i.s: sn rcvrd and in midfield: rdn and unable qck jst over 2f out: wknd over 1f out* **66/1**

58.01 secs (-0.79) **Going Correction** +0.025s/f (Slow) 9 Ran SP% **116.3**
Speed ratings (Par 103): **107,105,103,102,100 99,97,97,96**
toteswingers: 1&2 £4.90, 1&3 £5.20, 2&3 £6.00 CSF £16.45 CT £64.49 TOTE £3.60: £1.80, £2.30, £2.00; EX 19.90 Trifecta £155.20 Pool of £570.83 - 2.72 winning units..
Owner The Golf Oil Partnership **Bred** David And Mrs Vicki Fleet **Trained** Newmarket, Suffolk

FOCUS
A modest but competitive sprint handicap run at a strong pace. The winner is progressve and the form is rated around the runner-up.

242 LINGFIELD PARK FOURBALL APPRENTICE H'CAP 6f (P)
4:10 (4:15) (Class 6) (0-60,60) 4-Y-0+ £1,774 (£523; £262) Stalls Low

Form RPR
-013 **1** **Know No Fear**[5] 195 5-8-11 **55** .... (p) HollyHall(3) 3 63
(A J Lidderdale) *restless in stalls: hld up in tch in midfield: switching out rt jst over 2f out: pushed along and effrt over 1f out: r.o wl to ld nr fin* **11/4**[2]

-034 **2** ½ **Sherjawy (IRE)**[6] 163 6-8-12 **56** .... RichardRowe(3) 9 62
(Miss Z C Davison) *led: rdn and hdd over 1f out: kpt on wl u.p to ld again fnl 50yds: hdd and no ex nr fin* **6/1**[3]

00-0 **3** nk **Agnes Love**[5] 185 4-9-4 **59** .... DeclanCannon 10 64
(J Akehurst) *chsd ldr tl rdn to ld over 1f out: drvn fnl f: hdd and no ex fnl 50yds* **10/1**

04-5 **4** 1 **Don Pele (IRE)**[8] 137 8-9-2 **60** .... (p) ShaneRyan(3) 7 62
(R A Harris) *t.k.h: chsd ldrs: looking for run on inner over 1f out: drvn ent fnl f: r.o same pce after* **15/8**[1]

00/0 **5** ½ **Contented (IRE)**[8] 135 8-8-7 **48** .... (tp) AmyScott 11 49
(Mrs L C Jewell) *hld up in rr: hdwy on outer wl over 1f out: rdn ent fnl f: styd on fnl f but nt pce to rch ldrs* **14/1**

00-2 **6** hd **Whatyouwoodwishfor (USA)**[12] 89 4-8-11 **55** .... (b[1]) LeeTopliss(3) 8 55
(R A Fahey) *dwlt: sn bustled along to chse ldrs: rdn and unable qck ent fnl 2f: drvn and one pce ins fnl f* **9/1**

00-5 **7** ¾ **Waterloo Dock**[18] 8 5-8-10 **56** .... MatthewCosham(5) 4 54
(M Quinn) *chsd ldrs: rdn along whn nt clr run and sltly hmpd bnd jst over 2f out: swtchd out rt over 1f out: styd on same pce fnl f* **7/1**

000- **8** 1 ½ **Fortezza**[161] 4913 4-8-8 **52** .... NannaHansen(3) 1 45
(C F Wall) *in rr: detached last and lost tch 3f out: no prog tl hdwy jst over 1f out: rdn and r.o strly ins fnl f: nvr trbld ldrs* **20/1**

/00- **9** nk **Proud Linus (USA)**[51] 7595 5-9-2 **60** .... (t) RyanPowell(3) 6 52
(J Ryan) *taken down early: t.k.h: stdd s: hld up in rr: hdwy towards inner over 1f out: no imp and btn whn hmpd ins fnl f* **33/1**

63-6 **10** nse **Golden Dixie (USA)**[10] 116 11-8-7 **53** .... JakePayne(5) 5 45
(R A Harris) *a towards rr: rdn and no prog fr jst over 2f out* **20/1**

00-0 **11** shd **Jeannie (IRE)**[18] 14 4-8-2 **46** oh1 .... RyanClark(3) 12 37
(N P Littmoden) *racd in midfield on outer: rdn and struggling jst over 2f out: wknd wl over 1f out* **33/1**

1m 11.82s (-0.08) **Going Correction** +0.025s/f (Slow) 11 Ran SP% **129.4**
Speed ratings (Par 101): **101,100,99,98,97 97,96,94,94,94 94**
toteswingers: 1&2 £4.10, 1&3 £9.40, 2&3 £15.20 CSF £21.16 CT £156.78 TOTE £3.50: £1.60, £2.00, £3.70; EX 14.10 Trifecta £118.60 Pool: £445.85 - 2.78 winning units. Place 6: £23.41 Place 5 £7.18.
Owner Kachina Racing **Bred** B Bargh **Trained** Eastbury, Berks
■ Stewards' Enquiry : Nanna Hansen ten-day ban: breach of Rule (B) 59.4 (Feb 3-12)

FOCUS
Moderate but straightforward form. The winner probably only had to match his Kempton win two runs back.
Waterloo Dock Official explanation: jockey said gelding suffered interference in running
Fortezza ◆ Official explanation: jockey said, regarding running and riding, that her instructions were to obtain the best early position and make the best her way home, adding that, on reflection, she should have ridden more positively in the middle of the race and made greater efforts to keep the filly in touch, feeling that if she had done so she may have obtained a better position.
Proud Linus(USA) Official explanation: jockey said gelding was slowly awau
T/Plt: £29.50 to a £1 stake. Pool: £60,255.27. 1,486.18 winning tickets. T/Qpdt: £8.30 to a £1 stake. Pool: £5,357.63. 476.38 winning tickets. SP

[186]SOUTHWELL (L-H)
Thursday, January 21

OFFICIAL GOING: Standard to slow changing to standard after race 2 (1.50)
Wind: Virtually nil Weather: Overcast and dry

243 BET FA CUP - BETDAQ H'CAP 5f (F)
1:20 (1:20) (Class 6) (0-60,64) 4-Y-0+ £2,047 (£604; £302) Stalls High

Form RPR
00-1 **1** **Lujiana**[11] 112 5-8-6 **48** .... JoeFanning 5 61+
(M Brittain) *cl up: led after 1f: jnd and rdn wl over 1f out: styd on strly ins fnl f* **5/2**[1]

460- **2** 2 **Dickie Le Davoir**[44] 7681 6-8-12 **54** .... (be) J-PGuillambert 6 60
(R C Guest) *towards rr and rdn along after 1f: hdwy on outer 2f out: sn rdn and styd on ins fnl f: nrst fin* **9/1**

00-0 **3** shd **Cape Of Storms**[19] 20 7-9-4 **60** .... (b) TomEaves 7 66
(R Brotherton) *chsd ldrs: hdwy 1/2-way: rdn to chal over 1f out and ev ch tl drvn and one pce ins fnl f* **16/1**

00-0 **4** 1 **Ronnie Howe**[14] 70 6-8-4 **46** oh1 .... (b) JimmyQuinn 1 48
(S R Bowring) *t.k.h: trckd ldrs: effrt wl over 1f out: sn rdn and one pce* **12/1**

0-31 **5** 2 ¼ **The Geester**[9] 137 6-9-8 **64** 6ex .... AdamKirby 4 58
(Stef Higgins) *trckd ldrs: effrt and edgd rt wl over 1f out: sn rdn and btn* **7/2**[2]

563- **6** 1 **Handsinthemist (IRE)**[41] 7709 5-8-2 **49** .... PaulPickard(5) 2 39
(P T Midgley) *cl up: effrt 2f out and sn rdn: drvn over 1f out and sn wknd* **4/1**[3]

31-0 **7** 2 ¼ **Mr Funshine**[11] 112 5-8-9 **51** .... HayleyTurner 10 33
(D Shaw) *towards rr: rdn along 1/2-way: nvr a factor* **16/1**

326- **8** 6 **Metal Guru**[25] 7852 6-9-3 **59** .... (p) ChrisCatlin 8 20
(R Hollinshead) *led 1f: prom tl rdn along over 2f out and sn wknd* **10/1**

U00- **9** 4 **Egyptian Lord**[30] 7838 7-8-6 **48** oh1 ow2 .... (b) SaleemGolam 9 —
(Peter Grayson) *dwlt: a in rr* **50/1**

59.49 secs (-0.21) **Going Correction** 0.0s/f (Stan) 9 Ran SP% **111.3**
Speed ratings (Par 101): **101,97,97,96,92 90,87,77,71**
toteswinger:1&2:£5.00, 2&3:£17.40, 1&3:£9.00 CSF £24.50 CT £283.36 TOTE £2.50: £1.30, £2.90, £4.50; EX 22.90 Trifecta £391.60 Part won. Pool of £529.23 - 0.43 winning units..
Owner Mel Brittain **Bred** Bearstone Stud **Trained** Warthill, N Yorks
■ Stewards' Enquiry : Tom Eaves one-day ban: used whip above shoulder height (Feb 4)
J-P Guillambert one-day ban: careless riding (Feb 4)

FOCUS
A modest sprint handicap and, as usual over this straight 5f, all the action took place down the centre of the track. Straightforward form, the winner not needing to improve on her recent win.

244 BET ASIAN H'CAPS - BETDAQ HANDICAP 1m 3f (F)
1:50 (1:50) (Class 6) (0-60,60) 4-Y-0+ £2,047 (£604; £151; £151) Stalls Low

Form RPR
0-20 **1** **Highland River**[4] 210 4-8-12 **54** .... LeeVickers 9 61
(A Sadik) *prom: pushed along over 4f out: rdn along and lost pl over 3f out: drvn and hdwy wl over 1f out: styd on ins fnl f to ld last 50yds* **20/1**

22-2 **2** ½ **Silken Promise (USA)**[16] 42 4-9-4 **60** .... (p) AdamKirby 1 66
(W R Swinburn) *in tch: hdwy to trck ldrs 4f out: chal 2f out: rdn to ld ent fnl f: sn drvn: hdd and no ex last 50yds* **4/1**[1]

3-01 **3** ¾ **Greenbelt**[9] 139 9-9-3 **56** 6ex .... TomEaves 6 61
(G M Moore) *trckd ldrs: hdwy 1/2-way: cl up 4f out: rdn along 3f out: drvn wl over 1f out: kpt on* **11/2**[2]

-523 **3** dht **Russian Invader (IRE)**[9] 139 6-9-4 **57** .... (be) J-PGuillambert 10 62
(R C Guest) *dwlt and towards rr: hdwy 4f out: rdn along to chse ldrs 2f out: sn drvn and kpt on ins fnl f* **4/1**[1]

245- **5** ½ **Royal Bet (IRE)**[113] 6371 4-8-10 **52** .... HayleyTurner 8 56
(M L W Bell) *led: pushed along 3f out: rdn 2f out: drvn and hdd fnl f: one pce* **4/1**[1]

0-52 **6** ½ **Inside Story (IRE)**[11] 113 8-9-4 **57** .... (b) LiamKeniry 3 60
(C R Dore) *hld up in tch: hdwy to chse ldrs over 4f out: rdn along over 2f out: drvn and one pce appr fnl f* **14/1**

00-6 **7** 1 ¾ **National Monument (IRE)**[17] 34 4-9-2 **58** .... ShaneKelly 13 58
(J A Osborne) *midfield: hdwy on wd outside over 3f out: rdn over 2f out: drvn and kpt on appr fnl f: nrst fin* **11/1**[3]

03-0 **8** 3 **Coral Shores**[7] 162 5-9-7 **60** .... (v) ChrisCatlin 12 55
(P W Hiatt) *cl up: rdn along 3f out and grad wknd* **18/1**

/00- **9** 7 **April The Second**[30] 7840 6-8-7 **46** .... JimmyQuinn 4 29
(R J Price) *dwlt: a towards rr* **66/1**

0-41 **10** 6 **Black Falcon (IRE)**[11] 113 10-9-0 **53** 6ex .... PaulHanagan 5 26
(John A Harris) *chsd ldrs: rdn along 5f out: sn wknd* **11/1**[3]

206/ **11** 4 ½ **Mandalay Prince**[581] 3160 6-9-2 **55** .... TonyCulhane 11 20
(W J Musson) *a towards rr* **12/1**

0-0 **12** 4 ½ **King Fernando**[9] 139 7-8-11 **50** .... (p) AndrewElliott 14 8
(P Beaumont) *a in rr: t.o fnl 4f* **100/1**

2m 25.97s (-2.03) **Going Correction** -0.125s/f (Stan)
WFA 4 from 5yo+ 3lb 12 Ran SP% **118.9**
Speed ratings (Par 101): **102,101,101,101,100 100,99,96,91,87 84,80**
Place: Greenbelt £1.20, Russian Invader £0.80. Tricast: HR, SP, RI: £199.22; HR, SP, GB: £258.84. toteswinger: SP&RI: £1.40, SP&GB: £2.60, SP&HR: £22.40, RI&HR: £11.60, GB&HR: £15.20. CSF £98.05 TOTE £31.00: £7.20, £1.40; EX 229.80 TRIFECTA Not won..
Owner A Sadik **Bred** John Wotherspoon **Trained** Wolverley, Worcs

FOCUS
They went a very decent pace in this moderate handicap and it became a war of attrition at the business end. Solid form.
Black Falcon(IRE) Official explanation: jockey said gelding hung badly left-handed throughout

245 VIC LEER 60 YEARS SUPPORTING CHELSEA F.C. H'CAP 1m (F)
2:20 (2:22) (Class 4) (0-80,80) 4-Y-0+ £5,180 (£1,541; £770; £384) Stalls Low

Form RPR
631- **1** **Ours (IRE)**[25] 7854 7-8-12 **79** .... (p) BarryMcHugh(5) 8 90
(John A Harris) *in rr: hdwy on outer 3f out: rdn to chse ldrs wl over 1f out: styd on ins fnl f to ld last 75yds* **12/1**

3-26 **2** 1 **Elusive Fame (USA)**[11] 115 4-8-12 **74** .... (b) JoeFanning 10 82
(M Johnston) *cl up on outer: led wl over 2f out: rdn over 1f out: drvn ins fnl f: hdd and no ex last 75yds* **17/2**

/25- **3** 1 ¾ **Im Ova Ere Dad (IRE)**[248] 2144 7-9-2 **78** .... DaneO'Neill 11 82+
(D E Cantillon) *dwlt: sn in tch: hdwy over 3f out: rdn to chse ldr wl over 1f out: sn drvn and one pce* **6/1**[3]

The Form Book, Raceform Ltd, Compton, RG20 6NL

0-34 **4** *1* **General Tufto**[7] 169 5-8-1 **66** oh1 ....(b) AndreaAtzeni(3) 6 68
(C Smith) *in tch: hdwy 3f out: rdn along to chse ldrs wl over 1f out: drvn and one pce appr fnl f* **20/1**

5-13 **5** *2 ½* **Follow The Flag (IRE)**[11] 115 6-8-13 **80** ....(p) DeclanCannon(5) 12 76
(A J McCabe) *dwlt and in rr: hdwy over 3f out: rdn along to chse ldrs wl over 1f out: sn drvn and no imp fnl f* **6/1**[3]

2-00 **6** *½* **Hilbre Court (USA)**[7] 174 5-8-12 **74** ....(p) GrahamGibbons 9 69
(B P J Baugh) *led 2f: chsd ldrs: rdn along over 3f out: sn one pce* **16/1**

-411 **7** *3* **Transmission (IRE)**[7] 170 5-8-12 **74** 6ex .... TomEaves 4 62
(B Smart) *trckd ldrs: hdwy 3f out: sn rdn and btn wl over 1f out* **11/4**[1]

336- **8** *9* **River Ardeche**[47] 7640 5-8-11 **78** .... PatrickDonaghy(5) 1 46
(P C Haslam) *cl up on inner: rdn along 3f out and sn wknd* **50/1**

0-54 **9** *3 ½* **Prohibition (IRE)**[11] 115 4-8-13 **75** .... TonyCulhane 2 34
(W J Haggas) *cl up: led after 2f: rdn along 3f out: hdd over 2f out and sn wknd* **13/2**

21-3 **10** *11* **Istiqdaam**[18] 23 5-8-13 **75** ....(b) PhillipMakin 5 9
(M W Easterby) *midfield: rdn along 1/2-way: sn wknd* **5/1**[2]

300- **11** *13* **Orpen Wide (IRE)**[104] 6645 8-9-1 **77** ....(b) ChrisCatlin 7 —
(M C Chapman) *a in rr: bhd fr 1/2-way* **33/1**

1m 40.41s (-3.29) **Going Correction** -0.125s/f (Stan) 11 Ran SP% **119.0**
Speed ratings (Par 105): **111,110,108,107,104 104,101,92,88,77 64**
toteswinger:1&2:£14.10, 2&3:£11.80, 1&3:£16.50 CSF £109.23 CT £682.80 TOTE £14.60: £3.40, £3.10, £2.70; EX 159.40 Trifecta £418.40 Pool of £605.09 - 1.07 winning units.
Owner Peter Smith P C Coaches Limited **Bred** David John Brown **Trained** Eastwell, Leics

FOCUS
A decent handicap, run at a strong pace, with four horses disputing the lead in the early stages. Solid form, rated around the runner-up.
Transmission(IRE) Official explanation: jockey said gelding had no more to give
Istiqdaam Official explanation: trainer said gelding was unsuited by the Fibresand surface
Orpen Wide(IRE) Official explanation: jockey said gelding moved poorly throughout

246 BET MULTIPLES - BETDAQ MAIDEN STKS 1m 4f (F)
2:50 (2:51) (Class 5) 4-Y-O+ **£3,070** (£906; £453) **Stalls** Low

Form RPR

/6-2 **1** **Cozy Tiger (USA)**[6] 179 5-9-7 65 .... TonyCulhane 1 64
(W J Musson) *hld up in rr: stdy hdwy 1/2-way: trckd ldrs 4f out: effrt to chal over 2f out: rdn to ld over 1f out: styd on strly ins fnl f* **13/2**[3]

55-2 **2** *3 ¼* **Dubai Creek (IRE)**[7] 166 4-9-3 0 .... PaulHanagan 7 59
(D McCain Jnr) *dwlt and sn pushed along to chse ldng pair: cl up after 3f: led over 4f out: rdn along 3f out: drvn and hdd over 1f out: kpt on same pce* **5/4**[1]

00-5 **3** *¾* **Flannel (IRE)**[6] 186 4-9-3 51 ....(v) AdamKirby 3 58
(J R Fanshawe) *trckd ldrs: smooth hdwy 4f out: effrt over 2f out: sn rdn and ev ch tl drvn: edgd lft and one pce fr over 1f out* **13/2**[3]

46 **4** *3 ½* **Haka Dancer (USA)**[7] 166 7-9-7 0 .... JimmyQuinn 2 52
(P A Kirby) *in rr: hdwy 4f out: rdn along 3f out: drvn and kpt on same pce fnl 2f* **28/1**

64-2 **5** *15* **All Guns Firing (IRE)**[19] 18 4-9-3 65 .... DavidNolan 4 28
(D Carroll) *chsd ldrs on inner: rdn along and outpcd over 4f out: sme hdwy u.p 3f out: nvr a factor* **3/1**[2]

-0 **6** *10* **Try Cat**[7] 166 4-8-12 0 .... StevieDonohoe 8 7
(Sir Mark Prescott) *sn led: rdn along and hdd over 4f out: wknd over 3f out* **16/1**

5- **7** *29* **Ta Aleem**[155] 5151 4-8-12 0 .... HayleyTurner 6 —
(B G Powell) *prom: rdn along 1/2-way: sn lost pl and bhd fnl 3f* **20/1**

2m 38.95s (-2.05) **Going Correction** -0.125s/f (Stan)
WFA 4 from 5yo+ 4lb 7 Ran SP% **110.2**
Speed ratings (Par 103): **101,98,98,96,86 79,60**
toteswinger:1&2:£3.30, 2&3:£3.90, 1&3:£3.90 CSF £13.99 TOTE £6.50: £2.40, £1.50; EX 12.60 Trifecta £53.80 Pool of £968.04 - 13.30 winning units.
Owner McHugh & Partners **Bred** Alan S Kline Et Al **Trained** Newmarket, Suffolk
■ Stewards' Enquiry : David Nolan one-day ban: used whip when out of contention (Feb 4)

FOCUS
A poor maiden, but run at a fair pace and they finished well spread out. With the runner-up disappointing the winner probably didn't have to improve.

247 FREEBETS.CO.UK FREE BETS H'CAP 7f (F)
3:20 (3:20) (Class 5) (0-70,67) 3-Y-O **£3,139** (£926; £463) **Stalls** Low

Form RPR

002- **1** **Seamster**[54] 7580 3-9-4 **67** .... JoeFanning 6 73
(M Johnston) *mde all: rdn along over 2f out: drvn over 1f out: styd on gamely ins fnl f* **9/4**[3]

22-2 **2** *1 ¼* **Knightfire (IRE)**[16] 43 3-8-12 **61** .... ShaneKelly 5 64
(W R Swinburn) *trckd ldng pair: hdwy to chse wnr 1/2-way: rdn to chal wl over 1f out and ev ch tl drvn and one pce ins fnl f* **6/4**[1]

02-1 **3** *1 ¾* **Ambrogina**[16] 38 3-9-4 **67** ....(p) JimmyQuinn 4 65
(M Botti) *trckd wnr: effrt on inner wl over 2f out: sn rdn: drvn and one pce appr fnl f* **85/40**[2]

500- **4** *5* **Alphacino**[52] 7597 3-8-8 **62** .... PatrickDonaghy(5) 3 47
(P C Haslam) *trckd ldng pair: hdwy on outer 1/2-way: rdn and cl up over 2f out: sn drvn and wknd wl over 1f out* **12/1**

1m 32.41s (2.11) **Going Correction** -0.125s/f (Stan) 4 Ran SP% **110.5**
Speed ratings (Par 97): **82,80,78,72**
toteswinger:1&2:£3.00 CSF £6.16 TOTE £3.50; EX 6.50.
Owner Sheikh Hamdan Bin Mohammed Al Maktoum **Bred** D G Hardisty Bloodstock **Trained** Middleham Moor, N Yorks

FOCUS
A race affected by the two non-runners, resulting in a tactical event. The winner made all and the form is rated at face value.

248 TRY.BETANGEL.COM ALL WEATHER "HANDS AND HEELS" APPRENTICE SERIES H'CAP 1m (F)
3:50 (3:50) (Class 6) (0-55,60) 4-Y-O+ **£2,047** (£604; £302) **Stalls** Low

Form RPR

5-35 **1** **Bajan Pride**[7] 169 6-8-13 **54** ....(v) LeeTopliss 4 63
(R A Fahey) *trckd ldrs: hdwy and swtchd lft to inner over 2f out: rdn to ld over 1f out: clr ins fnl f and kpt on wl* **7/2**[3]

06-0 **2** *3 ½* **Great Bounder (CAN)**[12] 110 4-9-0 **55** .... RyanClark 1 56
(A B Haynes) *s.i.s and bhd: hdwy on outer and in tch over 4f out: rdn along over 2f out: styd on u.p ins fnl f: tk 2nd towards fin* **2/1**[1]

0-11 **3** *½* **Camerooney**[7] 169 7-9-0 **60** 6ex .... MatthewCosham(5) 2 60
(B Ellison) *led 2f: cl up on inner tl led again over 2f out and sn rdn: hdd over 1f out: kpt on same pce* **3/1**[2]

30-1 **4** *1 ¾* **Positivity**[13] 88 4-8-9 **53** ....(p) AdamCarter(3) 7 49
(B Smart) *dwlt: hdwy to ld after 2f: pushed along and hdd over 2f out: sn rdn and wknd over 1f out* **4/1**

0-03 **5** *½* **Kannon**[13] 88 5-8-5 **46** oh1 ....(p) MatthewLawson 6 41
(A J McCabe) *prom on outer: pushed along 3f out: rdn 2f out and grad wknd* **20/1**

050/ **6** *10* **Edin Burgher (FR)**[701] 621 9-7-12 **46** oh1 .... JessicaSteven(7) 3 18
(T T Clement) *cl up: rdn along over 3f out and sn wknd* **66/1**

046- **7** *32* **New Couture (IRE)**[22] 7882 4-8-11 **52** .... DavidKenny 5 —
(P W Chapple-Hyam) *towards rr and sn pushed along: outpcd after 3f and sn bhd* **9/1**

1m 42.34s (-1.36) **Going Correction** -0.125s/f (Stan) 7 Ran SP% **116.8**
Speed ratings (Par 101): **101,97,97,95,94 84,52**
toteswinger:1&2:£3.80, 2&3:£2.70, 1&3:£2.70 CSF £11.38 TOTE £5.10: £2.30, £2.10; EX 17.30 Place 6 £159.43, Place 5 £66.73..
Owner R A Fahey **Bred** Plantation Stud **Trained** Musley Bank, N Yorks

FOCUS
A modest "hands and heels" apprentice handicap, though the pace seemed reasonable enough. The winner turned around recent form with the third.
New Couture(IRE) Official explanation: jockey said filly would not face kickback
T/Jkpt: Not won. T/Plt: £145.60 to a £1 stake. Pool: £75,186.30. 376.83 winning tickets. T/Qpdt: £42.20 to a £1 stake. Pool: £5,756.54. 100.73 winning tickets. JR

222 WOLVERHAMPTON (A.W) (L-H)
Thursday, January 21

OFFICIAL GOING: Standard
Wind: Almost nil Weather: Fine

249 DINE IN THE HORIZONS RESTAURANT H'CAP 7f 32y(P)
4:20 (4:21) (Class 7) (0-50,50) 4-Y-O+ **£1,364** (£403; £201) **Stalls** Low

Form RPR

00-0 **1** **Top Flight Splash**[14] 69 4-8-10 **48** ....(v) MartinDwyer 7 55
(Mrs G S Rees) *mde all: drvn out and hld on ins fnl f* **14/1**

60-0 **2** *nk* **Almatlaie (USA)**[6] 195 4-8-11 **49** .... FergusSweeney 4 55+
(J W Unett) *hld up in rr: hdwy over 1f out: rdn to take 2nd wl ins fnl f: r.o* **22/1**

6-02 **3** *½* **All You Need (IRE)**[6] 195 6-8-11 **49** ....(p) JerryO'Dwyer 10 53
(R Hollinshead) *hld up in mid-div: hdwy 2f out: sn pushed along: rdn ins fnl f: nt qckn cl home* **11/4**[1]

640- **4** *1 ¼* **Battimoore (IRE)**[35] 7787 4-8-11 **49** .... LiamKeniry 6 50
(I W McInnes) *hld up in mid-div: rdn fnl f: r.o towards fin* **20/1**

040- **5** *hd* **See That Girl**[82] 7176 4-8-11 **49** .... JimCrowley 1 49
(B Smart) *s.s: hld up in rr: c wd st: rdn and hdwy over 1f out: one pce ins fnl f* **14/1**

005- **6** *1* **Qualitas**[97] 6831 4-8-12 **50** .... GrahamGibbons 11 48
(M W Easterby) *chsd wnr: rdn jst over 2f out: lost 2nd over 1f out: one pce* **7/1**

06-6 **7** *nk* **Djalalabad (FR)**[1] 229 6-8-11 **49** ....(tp) SteveDrowne 8 46
(Mrs C A Dunnett) *hld up in tch: pushed along wl over 1f out: rdn fnl f: fdd towards fin* **9/2**[2]

03-0 **8** *¾* **Mojeerr**[9] 142 4-8-7 **50** ....(p) DeclanCannon(5) 2 45
(A J McCabe) *hld up in mid-div on ins: lost pl wl over 3f out: sn pushed along: rdn and prog on ins over 1f out: no imp fnl f* **9/1**

03-6 **9** *nk* **Dynamo Dave (USA)**[9] 135 5-8-4 **49** ....(v) MissRachelKing(7) 5 43
(M D I Usher) *hld up and bhd: swtchd lft ins fnl f: n.d* **8/1**

40-0 **10** *hd* **Wicklewood**[1] 234 4-8-10 **48** ....(b) FrannyNorton 3 42
(Mrs C A Dunnett) *prom on ins: pushed along over 3f out: wknd ins fnl f* **6/1**[3]

06-0 **11** *nk* **Bertbrand**[14] 69 5-8-12 **50** .... GregFairley 9 43
(I W McInnes) *hld up and bhd: rdn over 1f out: no rspnse* **20/1**

00-0 **12** *11* **Romantic Verse**[19] 21 5-8-9 **50** ....(v[1]) MichaelStainton(3) 12 13
(R A Harris) *t.k.h: prom: rdn over 2f out: wknd wl over 1f out* **33/1**

1m 31.03s (1.43) **Going Correction** +0.075s/f (Slow) 12 Ran SP% **122.9**
Speed ratings (Par 97): **94,93,93,91,91 90,89,89,88,88 88,75**
toteswinger:1&2:£75.40, 2&3:£20.70, 1&3:£14.50 CSF £298.20 CT £1123.12 TOTE £17.70: £4.50, £9.60, £1.50; EX 530.90.
Owner P Bamford **Bred** Dandy's Farm **Trained** Sollom, Lancs
■ A winner for Geraldine Rees on her final day as a trainer. It was also her first winner since July.

FOCUS
A weak contest and not form to be too positive about, but at least a couple of the beaten runners suggested they can do better. They seemed to go an even pace
See That Girl ◆ Official explanation: jockey said filly missed the break
Dynamo Dave(USA) Official explanation: jockey said gelding was denied a clear run

250 BETDAQ ON 0870 178 1221 H'CAP 5f 216y(P)
4:50 (4:51) (Class 4) (0-85,81) 4-Y-O+ **£4,533** (£1,348; £674; £336) **Stalls** Low

Form RPR

22-0 **1** **Billy Red**[6] 192 6-9-0 **77** ....(b) FergusSweeney 2 88
(J R Jenkins) *mde all: edgd rt and rdn over 1f out: drvn out* **11/1**

21-2 **2** *2 ½* **Excellent Show**[7] 172 4-9-4 **81** .... TomEaves 3 84
(B Smart) *a.p: pushed along over 2f out: chsd wnr over 1f out: sn rdn: no imp* **5/2**[2]

0-20 **3** *¾* **Bel Cantor**[6] 192 7-8-11 **77** .... KellyHarrison(3) 5 78
(W J H Ratcliffe) *chsd wnr: pushed along over 2f out: lost 2nd over 1f out: sn rdn: kpt on same pce* **12/1**

2-24 **4** *hd* **Vhujon (IRE)**[7] 177 5-8-13 **81** .... RichardEvans(5) 8 81
(P D Evans) *hld up: hdwy 2f out: rdn and kpt on one pce fnl f* **5/1**[3]

-221 **5** *2* **Onceaponatime (IRE)**[6] 192 5-8-13 **76** 6ex .... LukeMorris 4 70
(M D Squance) *hld up and bhd: rdn wl over 1f out: nvr trbld ldrs* **2/1**[1]

1-64 **6** *1 ¾* **Green Park (IRE)**[7] 172 7-8-6 **76** ....(b) NeilFarley(7) 7 64
(D Carroll) *s.i.s: hld up in rr: c wd st: rdn jst over 1f out: no rspnse* **20/1**

30-5 **7** *¾* **Little Pete (IRE)**[18] 26 5-9-3 **80** ....(p) LiamKeniry 1 66
(I W McInnes) *hld up: pushed along 4f out: bhd fnl 2f* **16/1**

006- **8** *½* **Princess Valerina**[22] 7875 6-9-0 **77** .... FrankieMcDonald 6 61
(D Haydn Jones) *s.i.s: pushed along 3f out: a in rr* **14/1**

1m 14.52s (-0.48) **Going Correction** +0.075s/f (Slow) 8 Ran SP% **111.9**
Speed ratings (Par 105): **106,102,101,101,98 96,95,94**
toteswinger:1&2:£6.60, 2&3:£6.00, 1&3:£8.90 CSF £37.14 CT £337.47 TOTE £15.50: £3.10, £1.40, £2.70; EX 41.80.
Owner Mrs Irene Hampson **Bred** D R Tucker **Trained** Royston, Herts

FOCUS
A race dominated by the front-runners and those out the back early never featured. The winner made all and recorded a personal best, but it is hard to know how literally to take the form.
Vhujon(IRE) Official explanation: jockey said gelding hung right throughout

Onceaponatime(IRE) Official explanation: trainer said gelding lost its right-fore shoe

251 WOLVERHAMPTON-RACECOURSE.CO.UK (S) STKS 5f 216y(P)
5:20 (5:20) (Class 6) 4-Y-0+ £1,774 (£523; £262) Stalls Low

Form RPR
6-15 1 **Interchoice Star**[6] [193] 5-9-3 55....(p) JerryO'Dwyer 7 71
(R Hollinshead) *hld up: hdwy over 1f out: rdn to ld wl ins fnl f: r.o* 15/2[3]
-213 2 ½ **Obe Gold**[6] [181] 8-9-3 66.... J-PGuillambert 6 69
(P Howling) *led early: a.p: pushed along wl over 2f out: rdn to ld ins fnl f: sn hdd: nt qckn* 2/1[2]
2-62 3 4½ **Equinity**[8] [146] 4-8-7 49....(t) SaleemGolam 5 45
(J Pearce) *sn chsng ldr: led over 2f out: rdn and hdd ins fnl f: wknd* 16/1
000- 4 ½ **River Kirov (IRE)**[45] [7662] 7-9-3 77.... SteveDrowne 3 53
(M Wigham) *hld up: hdwy over 2f out: rdn wl over 1f out: ev ch ent fnl f: wknd* 11/8[1]
614- 5 nk **Charlie Delta**[22] [7879] 7-9-3 61....(b) LukeMorris 1 52
(R A Harris) *prom tl rdn and wknd wl over 1f out* 12/1
500- 6 ½ **Great Knight (IRE)**[41] [5225] 5-8-12 54.... JamieSpencer 4 45
(John Joseph Hanlon, Ire) *hld up and bhd: pushed along and c wd st: sn struggling* 20/1
0-26 7 nk **Spoof Master (IRE)**[13] [89] 6-9-3 56.... LiamKeniry 2 49
(C R Dore) *sn led: hdd over 2f out: rdn and wknd wl over 1f out* 33/1
1m 14.77s (-0.23) **Going Correction** +0.075s/f (Slow) 7 Ran SP% **108.5**
Speed ratings (Par 101): **104,103,97,96,96 95,95**
toteswinger:1&2:£2.40, 2&3:£5.20, 1&3:£3.90 CSF £20.59 TOTE £9.50: £3.50, £1.50; EX 24.90.There was no bid for the winner.
Owner John P Evitt **Bred** M P Bishop **Trained** Upper Longdon, Staffs

FOCUS
A moderate seller but the pace was good, resulting in a time only 0.25 seconds slower than 77-rated Billy Red recorded in the earlier 71-85 handicap. The form is rated at face value, with the winner up 9lb.

252 BET AUSTRALIAN OPEN TENNIS - BETDAQ H'CAP 1m 4f 50y(P)
5:50 (5:50) (Class 3) (0-95,90) 4-Y-0+ £6,938 (£2,076; £1,038; £519; £258) Stalls Low

Form RPR
23-5 1 **Dance The Star (USA)**[13] [81] 5-9-7 87.... JamieSpencer 8 97
(D M Simcock) *stdd s: hld up in rr: gd hdwy on outside to ld 2f out: rdn fnl f: r.o wl* 3/1[1]
326- 2 3½ **Coeur De Lionne (IRE)**[41] [7720] 6-9-5 85.... HayleyTurner 1 89
(E A L Dunlop) *led 1f: chsd ldr: ev ch 2f out: rdn and one pce ins fnl f* 9/1
/26- 3 2¼ **Silk Hall (UAE)**[54] [2283] 5-9-3 83.... TomQueally 9 83
(A King) *a.p: rdn and btn over 1f out* 10/1
4-44 4 ¾ **Full Toss**[5] [205] 4-9-1 90.... AndrewHeffernan(5) 2 89
(P D Evans) *t.k.h in tch: pushed along over 2f out: rdn and btn over 1f out* 3/1[1]
640/ 5 ½ **Premier Dane (IRE)**[62] [4359] 8-9-0 80.... TomEaves 3 78
(N G Richards) *hld up in tch: pushed along over 3f out: wknd wl over 1f out* 20/1
211- 6 ½ **Blue Nymph**[95] [6875] 4-9-0 84.... GrahamGibbons 5 82
(J J Quinn) *hld up and bhd: short-lived effrt 2f out* 9/2[2]
06-2 7 8 **Baylini**[5] [205] 6-9-8 88.... AdamKirby 4 73
(Ms J S Doyle) *hld up and bhd: swtchd rt over 2f out: c wd st: rdn and struggling over 1f out* 11/2[3]
112- 8 10 **Worth A King'S**[50] [6636] 4-9-2 86....(b¹) PaulHanagan 10 55
(D McCain Jnr) *led after 1f: pushed along and hdd 2f out: sn wknd and eased* 12/1
2m 39.92s (-1.18) **Going Correction** +0.075s/f (Slow)
WFA 4 from 5yo+ 4lb 8 Ran SP% **115.1**
Speed ratings (Par 107): **106,103,102,101,101 101,95,89**
toteswinger:1&2:£4.10, 2&3:£6.50, 1&3:£9.00 CSF £31.31 CT £239.51 TOTE £3.70: £1.40, £3.20, £2.60; EX 28.80.
Owner Sultan Ali **Bred** B M Kelley And B P Walden **Trained** Newmarket, Suffolk

FOCUS
Probably not that strong a race for the grade and the pace was modest. The form may not be too solid but is rated at something like face value.

NOTEBOOK
Dance The Star(USA) circled the field rounding the final bend, going from last to first. He kept up the gallop in the straight to gain a long overdue success, his first since October 2008. He had been unlucky on more than one occasion since that last victory, and was in danger of not getting things go his way once again, as the steady pace was no use to a horse who doesn't possess a significant change of pace at the end of his races. But Jamie Spencer did the right thing by getting first run on his rivals, rather than allowing them to get away, and the colt stayed on dourly. The nature of these Polytrack venues means he won't always get the race run to suit, but he's very useful when things do go his way. (op 11-4 tchd 5-2)
Coeur De Lionne(IRE)'s rider looked to get caught out by Spencer's move and that allowed the winner first run. He was nicely enough positioned, but was still on the bridle when Dance The Star swept by with significantly more momentum, and he wasn't able to peg that rival back. (op 10-1)
Silk Hall(UAE), a decent hurdler, shaped reasonably well on his return to the Flat. He could build on this if kept to the level. (op 12-1)
Full Toss currently looks a bit high in the weights. (op 4-1)
Premier Dane(IRE), another useful jumps performer, was well held on his first Flat outing since 2006, but he didn't run badly. This first start in two months should put him right, be it for another run on the all-weather, or a return to jumping. (tchd 18-1)
Blue Nymph, a 68,000gns purchase out of Ralph Beckett's yard since she was last seen in October, offered little. She had won her last two starts, firstly over this trip on Polytrack at Kempton, and then over 1m6f on Fibresand, but she was well held this time off a 4lb higher mark. Perhaps the run was needed. (tchd 4-1)
Worth A King'S was reported to have hung right. Official explanation: jockey said gelding hung left (op 9-1)

253 CALL 01902 390000 TO SPONSOR A RACE MEDIAN AUCTION MAIDEN STKS 5f 216y(P)
6:20 (6:21) (Class 5) 3-5-Y-0 £2,456 (£725; £362) Stalls Low

Form RPR
43-6 1 **Sternlight (IRE)**[17] [35] 3-8-10 72....(v¹) JamieSpencer 6 79
(E S McMahon) *t.k.h: a.p: shkn up to ld wl over 1f out: clr fnl f: easily* 11/10[1]
03- 2 7 **Sparking**[49] [7618] 3-8-5 0.... JimmyQuinn 5 52
(Mrs G S Rees) *hld up in tch: pushed along over 2f out: rdn over 1f out: wnt 2nd ins fnl f: no ch w wnr* 13/2[3]
32-2 3 2 **Boy The Bell**[13] [85] 3-8-10 68.... ShaneKelly 4 50
(J A Osborne) *s.i.s: racd keenly: hdwy 4f out: pushed along and ev ch 2f out: rdn and one pce fnl f* 2/1[2]
4- 4 ¾ **Blades Harmony**[30] [7836] 3-8-10 0.... GrahamGibbons 7 48
(E S McMahon) *s.i.s: hdwy to ld over 4f out: pushed along and hdd wl over 1f out: wknd ins fnl f* 12/1
5 nk **Army Of Stars (IRE)** 4-9-12 0.... ChrisCatlin 3 51
(J A Osborne) *s.i.s: pushed along wl over 1f out: n.d* 20/1
6 3 **Wirral Way** 4-9-9 0....(t) AndreaAtzeni(3) 1 41
(F Sheridan) *hld up: sn bhd: pushed along over 2f out: sn struggling* 25/1
450- 7 2 **Shirley High**[41] [7714] 4-9-7 46.... J-PGuillambert 2 30
(P Howling) *led over 1f: prom: rdn over 1f out: wknd ins fnl f* 100/1
1m 15.94s (0.94) **Going Correction** +0.075s/f (Slow)
WFA 3 from 4yo 16lb 7 Ran SP% **111.6**
Speed ratings (Par 103): **96,86,84,83,82 78,75**
toteswinger:1&2:£2.00, 2&3:£1.50, 1&3:£1.30 CSF £8.47 TOTE £1.90: £1.10, £2.50; EX 8.50.
Owner J C Fretwell **Bred** Fin A Co S R L **Trained** Lichfield, Staffs

FOCUS
A weak maiden run at a steady pace, but a useful-looking winner. It is doubtful how literally this form should be taken.

254 GREAT OFFERS AT WOLVERHAMPTON-RACECOURSE.CO.UK H'CAP 1m 4f 50y(P)
6:50 (6:50) (Class 6) (0-65,63) 3-Y-0 £1,774 (£523; £262) Stalls Low

Form RPR
06-1 1 **Keenes Royale**[10] [118] 3-9-5 61 6ex....(t) JimCrowley 5 72+
(R M Beckett) *hld up in tch: wnt 2nd over 2f out: rdn to ld ins fnl f: r.o wl* 11/8[1]
6-33 2 2 **The Great Husk (IRE)**[3] [216] 3-8-8 50.... LiamKeniry 6 58
(J S Moore) *set stdy pce: qcknd over 2f out: hrd rdn and hdd ins fnl f: nt qckn* 4/1[2]
04-2 3 3¾ **Vittachi**[3] [216] 3-8-8 50....(b) GrahamGibbons 3 52
(J D Bethell) *hld up in tch: pushed along jst over 2f out: rdn over 1f out: one pce* 9/2[3]
25-4 4 ½ **Land Of Plenty (IRE)**[10] [118] 3-8-3 45.... JimmyQuinn 4 46
(E A L Dunlop) *prom: outpcd 2f out: hrd rdn over 1f out: no imp* 25/1
64-3 5 1¼ **Jennerous Blue**[10] [118] 3-8-10 52.... MartinDwyer 7 51
(D K Ivory) *hld up: pushed along 4f out: bhd fnl 3f* 8/1
04-6 6 1¾ **Second Brook (IRE)**[17] [33] 3-8-13 55.... AdamKirby 8 51
(R Hollinshead) *sn chsng ldr: reminder over 4f out: rdn and lost 2nd over 2f out: wknd wl over 1f out* 14/1
600- 7 1¾ **Port Hill**[172] [4557] 3-8-6 53.... PaulPickard(5) 2 46
(W M Brisbourne) *hld up in rr: sme prog over 5f out: pushed along 3f out: sn wknd* 33/1
-422 8 6 **Mary Helen**[6] [183] 3-9-7 63.... ShaneKelly 1 47
(W M Brisbourne) *hld up: pushed along over 2f out: rdn and struggling wl over 1f out* 8/1
2m 43.9s (2.80) **Going Correction** +0.075s/f (Slow) 8 Ran SP% **116.0**
Speed ratings (Par 95): **93,91,89,88,88 86,85,81**
toteswinger:1&2:£2.90, 2&3:£3.00, 1&3:£3.70 CSF £7.09 CT £19.32 TOTE £2.70: £1.50, £1.60, £1.80; EX 13.30.
Owner Mrs R J Jacobs **Bred** Newsells Park Stud Limited **Trained** Whitsbury, Hants

FOCUS
A stamina test for these young horses and the form is only modest. The winner is progressive though and may have more to offer.
Second Brook(IRE) Official explanation: jockey said bit pulled through

255 BET IN RUNNING - BETDAQ H'CAP 1m 1f 103y(P)
7:20 (7:20) (Class 5) (0-75,75) 4-Y-0+ £2,729 (£806; £403) Stalls Low

Form RPR
243- 1 **Thunderstruck**[32] [7823] 5-9-5 74....(p) ChrisCatlin 8 87
(J A Glover) *chsd ldr: led over 3f out: rdn wl over 1f out: hld on wl u.p ins fnl f* 9/4[1]
11-1 2 nk **Chosen Forever**[7] [174] 5-9-2 71 6ex.... JimmyQuinn 2 83+
(G R Oldroyd) *a.p: nt clr run wl over 2f out: chal over 1f out: hrd rdn wl ins fnl f: kpt on* 11/4[2]
512- 3 5 **Bolanderi (USA)**[131] [5869] 5-8-12 74.... AlexEdwards(7) 12 76
(Andrew Turnell) *wnt lft s: hld up in rr: hdwy on outside over 3f out: chsd wnr over 2f out tl rdn wl over 1f out: wknd ins fnl f* 25/1
33/ 4 1¼ **Houston Dynimo (IRE)**[60] [5371] 5-9-1 70.... TomEaves 10 69
(N G Richards) *a.p: pushed along over 2f out: rdn wl over 1f out: wknd ins fnl f* 25/1
/60- 5 1¼ **Taaresh (IRE)**[32] [7823] 5-8-12 70.... AndreaAtzeni(3) 1 67
(K A Morgan) *hld up in tch: nt clr run briefly over 2f out: swtchd rt ent st: rdn and wknd wl over 1f out* 40/1
04-2 6 1½ **Boo**[7] [174] 8-9-0 69....(v) FergusSweeney 5 62
(J W Unett) *hld up in rr: rdn over 3f out: short-lived effrt over 2f out* 9/1
400- 7 2¼ **Whooshka (USA)**[90] [6996] 4-9-5 75.... JamieSpencer 3 64
(P W Chapple-Hyam) *hld up towards rr: pushed along over 2f out: c v wd st: no ch whn hung lft jst over 1f out* 11/1
51-1 8 1½ **Heathyards Junior**[10] [126] 4-9-0 75 6ex.... DeclanCannon(5) 7 61
(A J McCabe) *hld up in tch: rdn and wknd wl over 1f out* 16/1
33-1 9 8 **Nacho Libre**[18] [27] 5-9-2 71....(b) GrahamGibbons 11 40
(M W Easterby) *n.m.r s: sn swtchd lft: hld up in rr: pushed along and no ch fnl 3f* 15/2[3]
360- 10 ½ **Mullitovermaurice**[34] [7798] 4-8-7 63.... HayleyTurner 9 31
(J G Given) *hld up: hdwy 4f out: wkng whn hmpd wl over 1f out* 25/1
6-30 11 2¼ **Moonlight Man**[13] [87] 9-8-12 67....(t) LiamKeniry 4 30
(C R Dore) *led: hdd over 3f out: wknd qckly over 2f out* 50/1
530- P **Castle Myth (USA)**[24] [7857] 4-8-4 60 oh1....(bt) PaulHanagan 6 —
(B Ellison) *a in rr: lost action and p.u over 4f out* 12/1
2m 0.31s (-1.39) **Going Correction** +0.075s/f (Slow)
WFA 4 from 5yo+ 1lb 12 Ran SP% **117.0**
Speed ratings (Par 103): **109,108,104,103,102 100,98,97,90,89 87,—**
toteswinger:1&2:£2.40, 2&3:£13.90, 1&3:£16.70 CSF £7.58 CT £118.92 TOTE £3.00: £1.30, £1.30, £6.70; EX 11.10 Place 6 £59.95, Place 5 £23.39.
Owner Paul J Dixon **Bred** Mrs Yvette Dixon **Trained** Babworth, Notts
■ Stewards' Enquiry : Andrea Atzeni three-day ban: careless riding (Feb 4-6)

FOCUS
A modest handicap in which they seemed to go an even pace. The first pair pulled clear and have been rated as posting personal bests.
Nacho Libre Official explanation: jockey said gelding ran flat
Castle Myth(USA) Official explanation: jockey said gelding lost its action but returned sound
T/Plt: £119.70 to a £1 stake. Pool: £78,000.31. 475.67 winning tickets. T/Qpdt: £16.90 to a £1 stake. Pool: £10,564.19. 461.82 winning tickets. KH

236 LINGFIELD (L-H)

Friday, January 22

OFFICIAL GOING: Standard

Wind: Fresh, behind Weather: Overcast, drizzly

256 LINGFIELDPARK.CO.UK H'CAP (DIV I) 1m (P)

12:30 (12:35) (Class 6) (0-65,65) 4-Y-0+ £1,433 (£423; £211) Stalls High

Form RPR

00-3 1 **Aflaam (IRE)**18 29 5-8-12 64 AndrewHeffernan(5) 5 72
(R A Harris) *led after 1f and maintained stdy pce tl 1/2-way: drvn wl over 1f out: hrd pressed fnl f: battled on wl* 8/1

625- 2 ½ **Eastern Gift**25 7860 5-9-4 65 (p) SimonWhitworth 1 72
(Miss Gay Kelleway) *stdd s: hld up in rr: smooth prog 2f out: nt clr run over 1f out: squeezed through on inner to press wnr fnl f: outbattled* 10/1

00-0 3 shd **Wavertree Warrior (IRE)**20 11 8-8-13 60 (b) LukeMorris 2 67
(N P Littmoden) *trckd ldng trio: rdn over 2f out: effrt on outer to chal fnl f: styd on but a hld* 20/1

06-3 4 2½ **Lopinot (IRE)**20 11 7-8-12 59 (v) FergusSweeney 3 60
(M R Bosley) *t.k.h: hld up in midfield: gng strly 2f out: hanging and fnd nil over 1f out: kpt on to take 4th nr fin* 11/1

2-22 5 hd **Party In The Park**11 124 5-8-3 55 MatthewDavies(5) 4 56
(J R Boyle) *trckd ldr after 1f: rdn to chal on inner 2f out to 1f out: wknd ins fnl f* 7/2[2]

045- 6 nk **Confide In Me**54 7586 6-8-9 56 (tp) J-PGuillambert 9 56
(J Akehurst) *t.k.h: led 1f: restrained into 3rd: rdn over 2f out: fdd over 1f out* 10/1

123- 7 hd **Holyfield Warrior (IRE)**31 7840 6-8-5 59 KierenFox(7) 7 58
(R J Smith) *chsd ldrs: rdn over 2f out: nt qckn and wl hld fr over 1f out* 9/4[1]

00-4 8 hd **Hip Hip Hooray**19 27 4-9-0 61 JimCrowley 8 60
(L A Dace) *hld up in last trio: stl there 2f out: rdn on wd outside over 1f out: no prog* 14/1

0-6 9 2 **The Mouse Carroll (IRE)**19 27 6-8-13 60 FrankieMcDonald 6 54
(B R Johnson) *stdd s: hld up in last: pushed along 1/2-way: one pce and no prog* 33/1

003- 10 nk **Bob Stock (IRE)**48 7650 4-9-1 62 TonyCulhane 11 55
(W J Musson) *hld up in last pair: pushed along 1/2-way: one pce and no prog* 7/1[3]

1m 38.88s (0.68) **Going Correction** 0.0s/f (Stan) 10 Ran SP% **117.5**
Speed ratings (Par 101): **96,95,95,92,92 92,92,92,90,89**
toteswingers: 1&2 £12.40, 1&3 £33.10, 2&3 £30.00 CSF £85.70 CT £1547.55 TOTE £11.20: £3.20, £3.80, £4.60; EX 97.80 TRIFECTA Not won..
Owner The Circle Bloodstock I Limited **Bred** Shadwell Estate Company Limited **Trained** Earlswood, Monmouths

FOCUS
Division one of this modest handicap. They went no pace, the winner making most, and the form is muddling. That said, the time, on a rain-slickened track, was not too bad, albeit slower than division II.
Lopinot(IRE) Official explanation: jockey said gelding hung left in straight
Party In The Park Official explanation: jockey said gelding hung right
Bob Stock(IRE) Official explanation: jockey said gelding hung right

257 BETDAQ POKER MAIDEN STKS 5f (P)

1:00 (1:06) (Class 5) 3-Y-O £2,456 (£725; £362) Stalls High

Form RPR

2-26 1 **Freddie's Girl (USA)**7 180 3-9-0 67 ow2 AdamKirby 6 66
(Stef Higgins) *mde all: stdy pce to 1/2-way: rdn 2 l clr fnl f: unchal* 4/1[3]

5- 2 1½ **Blue Zephyr**293 1119 3-9-3 0 MartinDwyer 1 64+
(W R Muir) *hld up in last: pushed along on inner over 2f out: prog against rail over 1f out: one reminder fnl f: styd on to take 2nd nr fin* 2/1[2]

40-4 3 hd **Mrs Boss**3 222 3-8-10 72 ow1 JamesMillman(3) 2 59
(B R Millman) *trckd wnr 1f: mostly 3rd after: shkn up over 1f out: pushed along to dispute 2nd fnl f: nvr cl enough to chal* 13/8[1]

400- 4 nk **Papageno**70 7365 3-9-3 60 JimCrowley 4 62
(J R Jenkins) *pushed up on outer to chse wnr after 1f: rdn and nt qckn wl over 1f out: lost 2 pls wl ins fnl f* 16/1

0-0 5 2½ **Seek The Cash (USA)**11 128 3-9-3 0 FrannyNorton 5 53
(M Quinn) *awkwards s: sn in tch: rdn 2f out: fdd over 1f out* 12/1

00-6 6 2 **Maxijack (IRE)**19 24 3-9-3 59 StephenCraine 3 46
(G Brown) *dropped to last 1/2-way: sn struggling* 33/1

59.32 secs (0.52) **Going Correction** 0.0s/f (Stan) 6 Ran SP% **107.9**
Speed ratings (Par 97): **95,92,92,91,87 84**
toteswingers: 1&2 £1.60, 1&3 £1.10, 2&3 £1.70 CSF £11.44 TOTE £4.20: £1.20, £1.40; EX 10.10.
Owner Mrs Anne & Fred Cowley **Bred** Respite Farm Inc **Trained** Lambourn, Berks

FOCUS
A weak maiden, and like the opener the winner was allowed the run of things up front. The favourite disappointed and the form is rated around the winner and fourth.
Seek The Cash(USA) Official explanation: jockey said colt missed the break

258 GOLF AT LINGFIELD PARK CLAIMING STKS 6f (P)

1:30 (1:35) (Class 6) 4-Y-0+ £1,774 (£523; £262) Stalls Low

Form RPR

3-10 1 **Peopleton Brook**14 78 8-8-10 62 (t) SteveDrowne 2 70
(B G Powell) *hld up in 5th: pushed along over 2f out: effrt on wd outside over 1f out: r.o fnl f to ld last strides* 25/1

31-1 2 nk **Total Impact**7 187 7-9-0 76 RobertWinston 5 73
(C R Dore) *trckd ldr: gng easily 2f out: asked to ld 1f out but limited rspnse and only narrow advantage: hrd rdn fnl f: hdd last strides* 11/10[1]

535- 3 shd **Sir Edwin Landseer (USA)**23 7879 10-8-2 74 (be) HarryBentley(7) 6 68
(G L Moore) *hld up in 4th: pushed along over 2f out: effrt on outer over 1f out: urged along and clsd on ldr: nt qckn nr fin* 10/1

04-6 4 ½ **Misaro (GER)**7 192 9-8-13 74 (v) StephenCraine 3 70
(R A Harris) *racd freely: led: modest pce early: drvn 2f out: narrowly hdd 1f out: kpt on but lost 2 pls nr fin* 11/4[2]

2-52 5 1¼ **Lord Deevert**7 181 5-8-9 62 (p) JackDean(3) 1 65
(W G M Turner) *chsd ldng pair: rdn over 2f out and nt qckn: lost pl fnl f* 7/1[3]

04-4 6 6 **Timeteam (IRE)**19 26 4-8-6 80 CharlotteKerton(7) 4 47
(G Prodromou) *lft abt 10 l s: lost more grnd despite modest early pce: stl t.o 1f out: fin full of running* 8/1

1m 12.21s (0.31) **Going Correction** 0.0s/f (Stan) 6 Ran SP% **110.8**
Speed ratings (Par 101): **97,96,96,95,94 86**
toteswingers: 1&2 £2.90, 1&3 £10.40, 2&3 £3.90 CSF £52.52 TOTE £30.00: £4.80, £1.40; EX 53.20.Timeteam was claimed by Mr P. D. Evans for £9,000.
Owner G S Thompson & P Banfield **Bred** Lower Hill Farm Stud **Trained** Upper Lambourn, Berks

FOCUS
No more than a fair claimer. Again the pace did not look all that strong. Minor improvement from the winner, with the next three all below par.

259 MARRIOTT HOTEL OPENING SPRING 2010 H'CAP 7f (P)

2:00 (2:06) (Class 5) (0-75,75) 4-Y-0+ £2,456 (£725; £362) Stalls Low

Form RPR

-311 1 **Divine Force**3 223 4-8-12 69 6ex SimonWhitworth 9 84+
(M Wigham) *hld up in last pair: impressive prog on wd outside over 1f out: led ins fnl f: idled but in no real danger nr fin* 7/4[1]

1- 2 ¾ **Celtic Sovereign (IRE)**32 7829 4-9-2 73 JerryO'Dwyer 3 84
(M G Quinlan) *hld up in last pair: looking for room on inner over 2f out: gd prog to chal 1f out: r.o but readily hld by wnr* 3/1[2]

02-1 3 3 **Rubenstar (IRE)**13 110 7-9-0 71 StephenCraine 8 74
(Patrick Morris) *hld up in rr: cruising 2f out: prog and cl up over 1f out: sn rdn and nt qckn: styd on but easily outpcd by ldng pair* 9/1

3-65 4 1½ **Justcallmehandsome**14 84 8-8-8 72 (v) KatiaScallan(7) 5 71
(D J S Ffrench Davis) *led: drew 2 l clr over 1f out: hdd & wknd ins fnl f* 50/1

02-2 5 2¼ **Shaded Edge**13 110 6-9-1 72 HayleyTurner 7 65
(D W P Arbuthnot) *reminder in rr 4f out: drvn wl over 2f out: nvr a factor: passed wkng rivals nr fin* 14/1

31-2 6 hd **Defector (IRE)**11 123 4-9-3 74 MartinDwyer 6 66
(W R Muir) *mostly chsd ldr: shkn up and nt qckn over 1f out: sn lost pl and eased* 15/2[3]

314- 7 1¾ **Trade Centre**27 7845 5-9-0 71 (p) LukeMorris 4 59
(R A Harris) *prom: rdn over 2f out: wknd jst over 1f out* 8/1

005- 8 nk **Fandango Boy**46 7672 9-9-2 73 StevieDonohoe 1 60
(Ian Williams) *chsd ldrs: rdn over 2f out: wknd jst over 1f out* 25/1

46-0 9 7 **Spiritual Art**9 151 4-9-3 74 (p) PaulDoe 10 42
(L A Dace) *racd wd: in tch: rdn and wknd over 2f out: t.o* 25/1

000- R **Grand Vista**177 4423 6-9-4 75 GeorgeBaker 2 —
(G L Moore) *ref to r* 25/1

1m 23.7s (-1.10) **Going Correction** 0.0s/f (Stan) 10 Ran SP% **114.4**
Speed ratings (Par 103): **106,105,101,100,97 97,95,94,86,—**
toteswingers: 1&2 £3.40, 1&3 £2.50, 2&3 £9.60 CSF £6.31 CT £35.48 TOTE £2.80: £1.10, £1.90, £2.00; EX 9.20 Trifecta £26.10 Pool: £582.76 - 16.51 winning units..
Owner R J Lorenz **Bred** Capt J H Wilson **Trained** Newmarket, Suffolk

FOCUS
A competitive handicap in which just 6lb separated the runners, and good form for the grade. The pace was sound and the first three home all came from the rear. The time was just 0.7 seconds outside the standard. Another improved run from the winner, who was value for a bit extra.
Shaded Edge Official explanation: jockey said gelding hung right
Defector(IRE) Official explanation: jockey said gelding ran flat and hung left
Grand Vista Official explanation: jockey said gelding refused to race

260 BET NFL - BETDAQ (S) STKS 1m 4f (P)

2:35 (2:35) (Class 6) 4-6-Y-O £1,774 (£523; £262) Stalls Low

Form RPR

15-2 1 **Satwa Gold (USA)**9 148 4-9-4 75 HayleyTurner 4 72+
(E A L Dunlop) *hld up last: clsd on ldrs 2f out: pushed along briefly over 1f out: coasted past rivals ins fnl f* 4/5[1]

34-6 2 1¼ **Zuwaar**8 173 5-9-3 67 (tp) JimCrowley 1 61
(Ian Williams) *led: set modest pce tl kicked on 3f out: narrowly hdd over 1f out: kpt on u.p: no match for wnr* 11/4[2]

03-3 3 nk **Big Nige (IRE)**14 82 4-8-13 63 SaleemGolam 2 61
(J Pearce) *trckd ldr: t.k.h after 4f: pushed up to chal 2f out: narrow ld over 1f out: hdd and nt qckn ins fnl f* 9/2[3]

0-34 4 1¾ **Womaniser (IRE)**7 184 6-9-3 52 (b) AdamKirby 3 58
(T Keddy) *hld up in 4th: pushed along over 2f out whn cl enough: nt qckn over 1f out: one pce* 14/1

500- 5 9 **Whiterocks**135 5775 4-8-10 49 RobertLButler(3) 5 44
(Miss Sheena West) *disp 2nd pl tl 4f out: wknd u.p 3f out* 150/1

2m 35.73s (2.73) **Going Correction** 0.0s/f (Stan)
WFA 4 from 5yo+ 4lb 5 Ran SP% **107.7**
Speed ratings: **90,89,88,87,81**
CSF £3.07 TOTE £1.70: £1.40, £1.30; EX 2.80.The winner was sold to Steff Liddiard for 15,800gns. Zuwaar was claimed by Mr P. Butler for £6,000.
Owner The Lamprell Partnership **Bred** B P Walden, L Taylor Et Al **Trained** Newmarket, Suffolk

FOCUS
An uncompetitive seller run at a steady pace. It was not a bad standard for the grade but this is essentially weak form, rated around the fourth.

261 BET FA CUP - BETDAQ H'CAP 1m 2f (P)

3:10 (3:11) (Class 6) (0-65,65) 4-Y-0+ £1,774 (£523; £262) Stalls Low

Form RPR

-043 1 **Vinces**8 162 6-9-6 65 HayleyTurner 10 72
(T D McCarthy) *hld up in 8th: stl only 7th and looking for room ent fnl f: str burst last 100yds to ld post* 7/1

43-3 2 shd **Freedom Fire (IRE)**13 98 4-9-1 62 GeorgeBaker 7 69
(G L Moore) *trckd ldrs: poised to chal 2f out gng strly: drvn fnl f: narrow ld last 75yds: hdd post* 4/1[1]

0-04 3 nse **Naheell**8 162 4-8-9 63 CharlotteKerton(7) 14 70
(G Prodromou) *racd wd in midfield: cajoled along fr 1/2-way: cl up 2f out: bmpd along and r.o to chal ins fnl f: upsides nr fin: nt qckn* 12/1

1-54 4 ½ **Atacama Sunrise**6 202 4-9-4 65 SaleemGolam 5 71
(J Pearce) *trckd ldng pair: rdn 2f out: effrt on inner to ld ent fnl f: hdd and outpcd last 75yds* 5/1[2]

600- 5 ¾ **City Stable (IRE)**183 4235 5-8-7 52 SimonWhitworth 4 56+
(M Wigham) *hld up in last pair: eased towards outer over 2f out: stl only 11th whn swtchd bk ins and rdn jst over 1f out: rapid prog against rail fnl f: edgd rt and nt clr run nr fin: hopeless task* 8/1

/56- 6 ¾ **Flighty Fellow (IRE)**35 7803 10-8-12 57 (v) VinceSlattery 13 60
(B G Powell) *s.s: wl in rr: effrt over 2f out: nt qckn and no prog over 1f out: styd on again last 150yds* 66/1

606- 7 nk **Siena Star (IRE)**43 7699 12-9-2 61 AdamKirby 9 63
(Stef Higgins) *trckd ldng pair: rdn to chal on outer and upsides 2f out: to 1f out: fdd* 10/1

/24- 8 ½ **Slew Charm (FR)**79 493 8-8-12 57....................(t) RichardKingscote 11 58
(Noel T Chance) *wl in rr: rdn over 3f out and struggling: no prog tl styd on fnl f: nrst fin* **33/1**

002- 9 ½ **New World Order (IRE)**69 7403 6-9-4+ 63....................(t) IanMongan 1 63
(R Curtis) *led at fair pce: jnd over 2f out: hdd over 1f out: wknd fnl f* **5/1**2

001- 10 nse **Make Amends (IRE)**25 7856 5-9-2 61.............................. JimCrowley 8 61
(R J Hodges) *trckd ldr: chal over 2f out: narrow ld over 1f out: hdd & wknd ent fnl f* **16/1**

302- 11 1 ½ **Guiseppe Verdi (USA)**25 7857 6-9-1 60................(p) FergusSweeney 3 61+
(Miss Tor Sturgis) *hld up in midfield: rdn wl over 2f out: lost pl and btn jst over 1f out* **13/2**3

-050 12 nk **Binnion Bay (IRE)**7 184 9-8-5 53.......................... MarcHalford(3) 12 49
(J J Bridger) *hld up in last pair: rdn and no prog 3f out: btn after: plugged on* **22/1**

00-1 13 9 **Chia (IRE)**18 36 7-9-2 61..(p) DaneO'Neill 2 39
(D Haydn Jones) *led to post and mounted at s: s.i.s: a towards rr: rdn over 3f out: sn wknd: t.o* **14/1**

2m 5.05s (-1.55) **Going Correction** 0.0s/f (Stan)
WFA 4 from 5yo+ 2lb 13 Ran SP% **128.4**
Speed ratings (Par 101): **106,105,105,105,104 104,104,103,103,103 102,101,94**
toteswingers: 1&2 £10.60, 1&3 £17.30, 2&3 £14.50 CSF £37.35 CT £350.02 TOTE £6.80: £2.50, £1.80, £5.40; EX 37.90 Trifecta £341.30 Part won. Pool:£461.30 - 0.20 winning units..
Owner Eastwell Manor Racing Ltd **Bred** Gestut Fahrhof **Trained** Godstone, Surrey

FOCUS
A blanket finish to this open handicap, which was run at a fair pace. Straightforward form.

262 LINGFIELDPARK.CO.UK H'CAP (DIV II) 1m (P)
3:45 (3:45) (Class 6) (0-65,65) 4-Y-O+ £1,433 (£423; £211) Stalls High

Form RPR

0-03 1 **Expensive Problem**14 84 7-8-11 65........................... KierenFox(7) 8 74
(R J Smith) *hld up in last: stl disputing last 2f out and plenty to do: rdn and rapid prog on wd outside over 1f out: r.o wl to ld last strides* **14/1**

22-2 2 ½ **Charlie Smirke (USA)**6 202 4-8-13 60.......................... ShaneKelly 2 68
(G L Moore) *trckd ldng pair: smooth prog on inner to ld over 2f out: rdn and looked in command over 1f out: edgd rt fnl f: hdd last strides* **9/4**1

040- 3 1 ¾ **Sadeek**32 7830 6-9-3 64.. RobertWinston 4 68
(B Smart) *t.k.h: chsd ldrs: rdn over 4f out to hold pl: stl chsng u.p 2f out: kpt on to take 3rd nr fin* **8/1**

421- 4 ½ **Sotik Star (IRE)**154 5229 7-9-2 63..............................(p) JimmyQuinn 3 66
(K A Morgan) *s.s: sn in tch in midfield: prog on inner to go 3rd over 2f out: nt qckn over 1f out: one pce after* **11/1**

05-3 5 2 **Spinning Ridge (IRE)**18 34 5-9-1 62....................(p) StephenCraine 6 60
(R A Harris) *hld up towards rr: gng bttr than most 2f out: pushed along and sme prog over 1f out: rdn and one pce fnl f* **12/1**

0-31 6 1 ¼ **Very Well Red**11 124 7-8-12 59 6ex............................ LukeMorris 1 54
(P W Hiatt) *racd freely: led: hdd over 2f out: wknd jst over 1f out* **13/2**3

44-0 7 1 ½ **Too Grand**7 184 5-8-5 55.................................... MarcHalford(3) 7 47
(J J Bridger) *a towards rr: u.p over 3f out: plugged on but nvr on terms* **66/1**

000- 8 ¾ **Straight And Level (CAN)**54 7586 5-9-0 61.................. DaneO'Neill 5 51
(Miss Jo Crowley) *chsd ldr: rdn 1/2-way: wknd over 2f out* **20/1**

222- 9 1 ¾ **King's Icon (IRE)**133 5842 5-8-7 59.................. TobyAtkinson(5) 9 45
(M Wigham) *chsd ldrs: rdn over 2f out: sn wknd* **4/1**2

44-4 10 3 **Fine Ruler (IRE)**20 11 6-8-11 58.............................. JimCrowley 10 37
(M R Bosley) *dropped in fr wd draw: hld up in last trio: rdn 3f out: no prog* **8/1**

10-0 11 3 ¾ **Riviera Red (IRE)**8 160 10-8-5 52 oh4 ow1...........(v) SaleemGolam 11 23
(L Montague Hall) *dropped in fr wd draw: hld up in last trio: rdn 1/2-way: struggling after* **80/1**

1m 37.38s (-0.82) **Going Correction** 0.0s/f (Stan) 11 Ran SP% **116.5**
Speed ratings (Par 101): **104,103,101,101,99 98,96,95,94,91 87**
toteswingers: 1&2 £6.90, 1&3 £15.80, 2&3 £4.80 CSF £44.80 CT £284.20 TOTE £16.90: £4.00, £1.60, £2.80; EX 59.50 Trifecta £419.40 Part won. Pool: £566.70 - 0.40 winning units.
Owner F Willson **Bred** T J Cooper **Trained** Epsom, Surrey

FOCUS
An ordinary handicap, but the faster of the two divisions by 1.50 seconds. The form seems to make sense at face value, with the second, third and fourth close to their marks.
King's Icon(IRE) Official explanation: jockey said gelding ran too freely

263 LINGFIELD PARK SPORTING MEMBERSHIP H'CAP 2m (P)
4:15 (4:21) (Class 6) (0-65,65) 4-Y-O+ £1,774 (£523; £262) Stalls Low

Form RPR

40-4 1 **Prince Charlemagne (IRE)**8 164 7-10-0 65.............. GeorgeBaker 7 75+
(G L Moore) *restless in stalls: hld up in last pair: smooth prog over 3f out: led over 1f out: sn clr: easily* **3/1**2

334- 2 3 ¼ **Valkyrie (IRE)**72 7324 4-8-2 46 oh1.............................. LukeMorris 5 49
(N P Littmoden) *hld up in rr: rdn and gd prog fr 5f out: led 2f out: hdd and outpcd over 1f out* **20/1**

40-0 3 nk **Lady Pilot**8 164 8-9-11 65.................................. RobertLButler(3) 3 67
(Jim Best) *hld up towards rr: prog on inner over 2f out: lft bhd whn r unfolded sn after: rdn over 1f out: styd on to take 3rd ins fnl f* **33/1**

100- 4 1 ¼ **Coda Agency**140 5642 7-9-12 63.................................. JimCrowley 9 64
(D W P Arbuthnot) *hld up in midfield: effrt to chse ldrs over 2f out: outpcd wl over 1f out* **10/1**

336- 5 ½ **Where's Susie**44 7695 5-9-8 59.................................. AdamKirby 14 59
(M Madgwick) *racd wd in midfield: rdn 5f out: prog after to chse ldrs over 2f out: outpcd sn after* **7/1**

60-1 6 ¾ **Purely By Chance**8 164 5-9-5 56 6ex...............(b) SaleemGolam 10 55
(J Pearce) *prom: chsd ldr 4f out to over 2f out: fdd* **13/2**3

3-10 7 1 **Royal Rainbow**11 130 6-9-4 55.................................. DaneO'Neill 12 53
(P W Hiatt) *t.k.h in midfield: outpcd 3f out: effrt u.p over 2f out: no prog after* **16/1**

563- 8 2 ¼ **Mountain Forest (GER)**40 7740 4-8-2 46 oh1.............. JimmyQuinn 2 41
(H Morrison) *led after 3f to 2f out: wknd rapidly* **9/1**

/62- 9 ½ **Isle De Maurice**45 7608 8-9-5 56......................(b) FergusSweeney 11 51
(G L Moore) *nvr beyond midfield: rdn 5f out: struggling 3f out* **11/4**1

300- 10 1 ¼ **Sahara Sunshine**19 4744 5-9-8 59..............................(t) IanMongan 6 52
(Mrs L J Mongan) *dwlt: hld up in last: rdn over 4f out: effrt on wd outside into midfield over 2f out: sn wknd* **40/1**

000- 11 3 ¾ **Trempari**52 7608 7-8-11 48.......................................(b) TonyCulhane 8 37
(Mike Murphy) *led 2f: chsd ldr after 3f to 4f out: sn wknd u.p* **33/1**

100/ 12 8 **Tavalu (USA)**57 5913 8-9-6 62............................(b) MatthewDavies(5) 1 41
(G A Ham) *t.k.h: hld up in tch: wknd over 4f out* **100/1**

06-6 13 9 **Free Falling**20 13 4-7-10 47 oh1 ow1................(tp) NathanAlison(7) 13 15
(A J Lidderdale) *led after 2f tl after 3f: wknd 4f out* **40/1**

/0-3 14 12 **Mujamead**20 15 6-9-11 62.. FrankieMcDonald 4 16
(G A Ham) *in tch: rdn 6f out: sn dropped to rr: t.o* **33/1**

3m 22.98s (-2.72) **Going Correction** 0.0s/f (Stan)
WFA 4 from 5yo+ 7lb 14 Ran SP% **121.9**
Speed ratings (Par 101): **106,104,104,103,103 102,102,101,101,100 98,94,90,84**
toteswingers: 1&2 £12.80, 1&3 £25.40, 2&3 £59.50 CSF £68.89 CT £1703.16 TOTE £3.90: £1.70, £4.80, £7.80; EX 80.20 Trifecta £297.90 Pool: £744.99 - 1.85 winning units. Place 6: £76.51 Place 5: £8.87.
Owner A Grinter **Bred** Michael O'Mahony **Trained** Lower Beeding, W Sussex

FOCUS
A moderate staying handicap that was run at a good pace following an early dawdle, and the principals came from the rear. Sound enough form.
T/Plt: £182.50 to a £1 stake. Pool: £68,121.01. 272.44 winning tickets. T/Qpdt: £8.50 to a £1 stake. Pool: £8,375.36. 721.42 winning tickets. JN

249 WOLVERHAMPTON (A.W) (L-H)
Friday, January 22

OFFICIAL GOING: Standard
Wind: Light across. Weather: Fine.

264 WOLVERHAMPTON-RACECOURSE.CO.UK H'CAP 5f 216y(P)
4:35 (4:36) (Class 7) (0-50,50) 4-Y-O+ £1,364 (£403; £201) Stalls Low

Form RPR

50-3 1 **Albero Di Giuda (IRE)**8 178 5-8-9 50....................(t) AndreaAtzeni(3) 6 58
(F Sheridan) *led early: a.p: rdn over 1f out: r.o to ld nr fin* **9/2**3

42-2 2 hd **Tag Team (IRE)**15 70 9-8-10 48.........................(p) JamieSpencer 10 56
(John A Harris) *sn w ldr: rdn to ld ins fnl f: hdd nr fin* **9/4**1

50-6 3 1 ½ **Berrymead**11 125 5-8-6 49 ow1.................................. AnnStokell(5) 9 52
(Miss A Stokell) *hld up in rr: rdn wl over 1f out: r.o u.p ins fnl f: tk 3rd cl home* **25/1**

00-0 4 nk **Mister Incredible**7 195 7-8-9 47..............................(b) DavidProbert 11 49
(J M Bradley) *hld up in mid-div: pushed along over 2f out: rdn and hdwy over 1f out: kpt on ins fnl f* **25/1**

244- 5 nk **Royal Acclamation (IRE)**211 3296 5-8-6 49............(v) PaulPickard(5) 1 50
(H J Evans) *sn led: rdn over 1f out: hdd ins fnl f: no ex* **9/2**3

50-0 6 ¾ **El Potro**8 178 8-8-7 45.. NickyMackay 13 44
(J R Holt) *hld up in rr: hdwy on ins over 1f out: one pce ins fnl f* **20/1**

-023 7 ¾ **All You Need (IRE)**1 249 6-8-4 49..........................(v) DavidKenny(7) 7 45
(R Hollinshead) *hld up towards rr: pushed along and hdwy 2f out: one pce fnl f* **4/1**2

500- 8 1 **Monsieur Harvey**242 2343 4-8-7 45.............................. TomEaves 3 38
(B Smart) *prom: rdn wl over 1f out: wknd ins fnl f* **14/1**

5-32 9 1 ½ **Tango Step (IRE)**15 69 10-8-2 47.............................. NeilFarley(7) 5 35
(D Carroll) *hld up in mid-div on ins: rdn wl over 1f out: wknd fnl f* **16/1**

0-65 10 2 ½ **Gracie's Games**7 189 4-8-4 45..............................(t) MartinLane(3) 8 25
(R J Price) *a towards rr* **33/1**

1m 15.32s (0.32) **Going Correction** 0.0s/f (Stan) 10 Ran SP% **115.1**
Speed ratings (Par 97): **97,96,94,94,93 92,91,90,88,85**
toteswingers: 1&2 £2.90, 1&3 £15.60, 2&3 £10.70 CSF £14.05 CT £224.71 TOTE £4.60: £2.00, £1.50, £4.80; EX 15.80.
Owner Jon Owen **Bred** Fattoria Di Marcianella Di Razza Del Pian Del Lago **Trained** Averham Park, Notts

FOCUS
A low-grade sprint in which the pace held up well. Straightforward form.

265 STAY AT THE WOLVERHAMPTON HOLIDAY INN H'CAP 5f 20y(P)
5:05 (5:05) (Class 6) (0-55,53) 3-Y-O £1,774 (£523; £262) Stalls Low

Form RPR

00-5 1 **Duke Of Rainford**4 215 3-8-11 50.............................. JamieSpencer 6 56
(M Herrington) *swtchd lft to ins sn after s: hld up towards rr: hdwy over 2f out: swtchd rt ent st: rdn to ld ins fnl f: r.o* **3/1**2

4-43 2 ¾ **Exceed Power**4 215 3-8-8 50.................................. MartinLane(3) 7 53
(D M Simcock) *hld up in rr: hdwy wl over 1f out: sn rdn: r.o to take 2nd cl home* **4/1**3

2-31 3 ½ **Turf Time**4 215 3-8-9 53 6ex.............................. BarryMcHugh(5) 5 55
(J A Glover) *chsd ldr: rdn over 1f out: ev ch ins fnl f: nt qckn* **13/8**1

005- 4 ½ **Pavement Games**79 7242 3-8-7 46.............................. FrannyNorton 1 46
(R C Guest) *a.p on ins: rdn and ev ch jst ins fnl f: nt qckn* **7/1**

06-0 5 3 **Graceandgratitude**4 215 3-8-7 53.............................. RyanClark(7) 9 42
(S C Williams) *hld up in mid-div: rdn wl over 1f out: no hdwy fnl f* **33/1**

00-6 6 nk **Annia Galeria (IRE)**13 111 3-8-13 52.......................... DavidProbert 3 40
(C A Dwyer) *led: rdn wl over 1f out: hdd ins fnl f: wknd* **28/1**

00-6 7 1 **Dolly Will Do**13 104 3-8-3 45............................ KellyHarrison(3) 4 29
(N P Mulholland) *broke wl: sn stdd to rr: pushed along over 2f out: struggling whn rdn jst over 1f out* **50/1**

005- 8 nk **Sandy Toes**168 4738 3-8-3 45............................ AndreaAtzeni(3) 10 28
(J A Glover) *hld up towards rr: rdn on outside over 2f out: c v wd st: nvr nr ldrs* **22/1**

0-00 9 3 ½ **Fareham Town**5 213 3-9-0 53.................................. LiamKeniry 8 24
(S Kirk) *prom tl pushed along and wknd 2f out* **20/1**

62.99 secs (0.69) **Going Correction** 0.0s/f (Stan) 9 Ran SP% **113.1**
Speed ratings (Par 95): **94,92,92,91,86 85,84,83,78**
toteswingers: 1&2 £3.00, 1&3 £1.80, 2&3 £2.30 CSF £13.84 CT £24.61 TOTE £4.40: £1.60, £1.10, £1.20; EX 17.90.
Owner P Ringer **Bred** Worksop Manor Stud **Trained** Cold Kirby, N Yorks
■ A first winner for trainer Michael Herrington, a former jump jockey.

FOCUS
There was a good gallop on here and the first two came from off the pace. The winner reversed latest 6f running with the second and third.

266 BETDAQ THE BETTING EXCHANGE CONDITIONS STKS 1m 1f 103y(P)
5:35 (5:35) (Class 3) 4-Y-O+ £6,938 (£2,076; £1,038; £519; £258) Stalls Low

Form RPR

24-1 1 **Mister New York (USA)**14 81 5-9-0 91......................(b) JoeFanning 6 99
(Noel T Chance) *hld up towards rr: pushed along over 3f out: hdwy and squeezed through wl over 1f out: rdn to ld wl ins fnl f: r.o* **4/1**3

244- 2 nk **Blue Bajan (IRE)**55 6854 8-9-0 107.............................. PaulHanagan 5 98
(Andrew Turnell) *hld up: hdwy over 2f out: rdn to ld 1f out: hdd wl ins fnl f* **5/2**1

-444 3 2 ½ **Full Toss**1 252 4-8-8 90.................................. AndrewHeffernan(5) 1 93
(P D Evans) *led 1f: chsd ldr: rdn to ld jst over 2f out: hdd 1f out: no ex wl ins fnl f* **15/2**

156- **4** *nk* **Snow Dancer (IRE)**[27] [7848] 6-8-4 74........................ JamesSullivan(5) 3 87
(H A McWilliams) *hld up: hdwy on ins over 2f out: rdn and ev ch 1f out: no ex wl ins fnl f* **66/1**

-222 **5** *2* **Aeroplane**[6] [204] 7-9-0 102...(p) JamieSpencer 4 88
(P D Evans) *hld up in rr: hdwy wl over 1f out: swtchd lft jst ins fnl f: one pce* **7/2**[2]

14 **6** *4* **Reve De Nuit (USA)**[8] [175] 4-8-12 95...................... DeclanCannon(5) 8 83
(A J McCabe) *prom tl rdn and wknd 2f out* **7/2**[2]

03-0 **7** *hd* **Iron Out (USA)**[7] [197] 4-8-8 82...................................... PaulPickard(5) 2 79
(R Hollinshead) *prom: ev ch over 2f out: rdn and wknd over 1f out* **20/1**

000- **8** *2 ½* **It's Dubai Dolly**[76] [7291] 4-8-10 77........................... WandersonD'Avila 7 71
(A J Lidderdale) *led after 1f: hdd jst over 2f: rdn and wknd wl over 1f out* **50/1**

2m 0.28s (-1.42) **Going Correction** 0.0s/f (Stan)
WFA 4 from 5yo+ 1lb **8** Ran SP% **113.0**
Speed ratings (Par 107): **106,105,103,103,101 97,97,95**
toteswingers: 1&2 £2.30, 1&3 £6.80, 2&3 £6.20 CSF £14.03 TOTE £5.50: £1.40, £1.10, £2.50; EX 19.20.
Owner Chance, Talbot & Taylor **Bred** J S McDonald **Trained** Upper Lambourn, Berks

FOCUS
An interesting conditions race run at a decent gallop. The proximity of the fourth casts some doubt over the form, and it is doubtful if the winner improved as much a a literal reading of his beating of the second and third may suggest.

NOTEBOOK
Mister New York(USA)'s last two wins came over 1m4f, so the strong pace suited. He got involved in some scrimmaging early in the straight but was braver than most and battled his way through and predictably finished his race strongly. A very useful performer on this surface, his trainer is hoping the gelding might get an invite to run in Dubai.
Blue Bajan(IRE), running here because the ground is currently against him over hurdles, is another more effective over further these days. He too was suited by the decent gallop, though, and ran well in defeat, although it has to be noted that he'd have been 16lb worse off at the weights with the winner had this been a handicap. (op 11-4 tchd 3-1)
Full Toss, making a quick reappearance after finishing fourth in a handicap here the previous day, had a good draw and saved ground on the inside before easing to the centre of the track up the straight. His rider never gave up and it was a fine effort in defeat. (op 11-1)
Snow Dancer(IRE) had no business finishing as close as she did on the ratings, but she's a consistent sort who likes it round here and, like the third, she was given a ride that maximised her chance of placing.
Aeroplane had been ridden to success by Jamie Spencer in a couple of claimers last year but the same jockey had been beaten on him seven times in better company prior to that. As usual the horse travelled well into the straight, but he went for the same gap as the winner and, once asked to battle, couldn't raise the white flag quick enough. He keeps picking up money for his connections in these races without winning, so despite his lack of bottle perhaps there's little incentive for the time being to drop him back into a claimer. (op 11-4)
Reve De Nuit(USA) is much probably more at home on Fibresand, but he was still given little chance the way he was ridden here, as he raced a minimum of three wide all the way round. (tchd 4-1)

267 WOLVERHAMPTON - THE BLACK COUNTRY'S ONLY RACECOURSE MAIDEN STKS 7f 32y(P)
6:05 (6:06) (Class 5) 3-Y-O+ **£2,456** (£725; £362) **Stalls** High

Form RPR
4-2 **1** **Duellist**[11] [128] 3-8-9 0.. JoeFanning 8 78+
(M Johnston) *chsd ldr after 1f: led jst over 2f out: clr 1f out: easily* **1/5**[1]

0- **2** *6* **Belles Beau**[35] [7800] 3-8-7 0 ow3................................ GrahamGibbons 3 53
(R Hollinshead) *prom: n.m.r and lost pl after 1f: bhd whn rdn wl over 2f out: hdwy over 1f out: r.o to take 2nd last strides: no ch w wnr* **20/1**

0- **3** *hd* **Adam De Beaulieu (USA)**[48] [7637] 3-8-9 0.....................(t) GregFairley 2 54
(P C Haslam) *hung lft thrght: a.p on ins: rdn and one pce fnl f* **20/1**

0- **4** *shd* **Cross The Boss (IRE)**[91] [6991] 3-8-4 0................(t) PatrickDonaghy(5) 7 54
(P C Haslam) *hld up in rr: hdwy on outside over 3f out: rdn wl over 1f out: one pce* **50/1**

5 *¾* **Zephyron (IRE)** 3-8-9 0.. JerryO'Dwyer 5 52
(J R Holt) *a.p: rdn 2f out: one pce* **28/1**

0 **6** *5* **Miereveld**[11] [128] 3-8-9 0.. StevieDonohoe 1 38
(Sir Mark Prescott) *hld up and bhd: pushed along over 2f out: struggling over 1f out* **10/1**[3]

0- **7** *3 ¼* **Wings Of Kintyre (IRE)**[137] [5731] 6-9-3 0................(p) MarkCoumbe(5) 6 30
(A Berry) *led: hdd jst over 2f out: rdn wl over 1f out: wknd fnl f* **100/1**

8 *11* **Spirited Lady (IRE)** 3-8-4 0.. PaulHanagan 4 —
(R A Fahey) *hld up and bhd: pushed along and lost tch over 2f out* **8/1**[2]

1m 30.46s (0.86) **Going Correction** 0.0s/f (Stan)
WFA 3 from 6yo 18lb **8** Ran SP% **119.5**
Speed ratings (Par 103): **95,88,87,87,86 81,77,64**
toteswingers: 1&2 £1.80, 1&3 £3.00, 2&3 £28.30 CSF £10.93 TOTE £1.20: £1.02, £2.80, £2.80; EX 7.10.
Owner Sheikh Hamdan Bin Mohammed Al Maktoum **Bred** Darley **Trained** Middleham Moor, N Yorks

FOCUS
A weak and uncompetitive maiden run in a slow time. The winner had little to beat but this will not do his mark for handicaps any harm.
Spirited Lady(IRE) Official explanation: jockey said filly hung badly left from 4f out

268 TRY BETDAQ FOR AN EXCHANGE H'CAP 7f 32y(P)
6:35 (6:38) (Class 4) (0-85,80) 3-Y-O **£4,533** (£1,348; £674; £336) **Stalls** High

Form RPR
51-4 **1** **Cuthbert (IRE)**[13] [107] 3-8-12 71.................................... PaulHanagan 1 78
(W Jarvis) *sn led: rdn whn strly pressed ins fnl f: r.o* **10/1**

22-1 **2** *¾* **Master Leon**[14] [85] 3-9-2 75...(v) TomEaves 2 80
(B Smart) *a.p: rdn over 1f out: chal ins fnl f: no ex cl home* **6/1**[3]

30-1 **3** *hd* **Tiradito (USA)**[20] [9] 3-9-1 74.. MartinDwyer 6 78
(M Botti) *hld up last: rdn over 2f out: hdwy on ins wl over 1f out: ev ch ins fnl f: nt qckn cl home* **7/2**[2]

41-2 **4** *3 ½* **Capricornus (USA)**[10] [136] 3-8-12 71................................ JoeFanning 3 66
(M Johnston) *led early: chsd ldr tl rdn 2f out: wknd over 1f out* **4/6**[1]

2-25 **5** *½* **Transfixed (IRE)**[6] [203] 3-9-2 80............................ AndrewHeffernan(5) 5 73
(P D Evans) *hld up in tch: hrd rdn over 2f out: wknd wl over 1f out* **14/1**

1m 28.59s (-1.01) **Going Correction** 0.0s/f (Stan) **5** Ran SP% **112.3**
Speed ratings (Par 99): **105,104,103,99,99**
toteswingers: 1&2 £13.80 CSF £62.97 TOTE £8.40: £2.00, £4.90; EX 55.90.
Owner The Square Mile Syndicate **Bred** Gerard Callanan **Trained** Newmarket, Suffolk
■ Playboy Blues was withdrawn on vet's advice (7/2, deduct 20p in the £ under R4). New market formed.

FOCUS
The favourite disappointed but this still looked a good race for the grade. The time was fast for a 3yo.

269 BETDAQ ON 0870 178 1221 H'CAP (DIV I) 7f 32y(P)
7:05 (7:05) (Class 6) (0-60,66) 4-Y-O+ **£1,433** (£423; £211) **Stalls** High

Form RPR
10-3 **1** **Headache**[20] [21] 5-8-13 55..(bt) DavidProbert 6 63
(B W Duke) *a.p: led wl over 2f out: hrd rdn over 1f out: jst hld on* **7/2**[2]

0-41 **2** *nse* **Carmenero (GER)**[7] [194] 7-9-10 66 6ex............................ LiamKeniry 8 74
(C R Dore) *hld up towards rr: pushed along over 2f out: rdn and hdwy on outside over 1f out: r.o ins fnl f: jst failed* **2/1**[1]

050- **3** *¾* **Silidan**[71] [7349] 7-8-10 52.. PaulHanagan 10 58
(Miss M E Rowland) *hld up towards rr: hdwy wl over 1f out: rdn and kpt on ins fnl f* **40/1**

/60- **4** *1 ¾* **Kladester (USA)**[251] [2091] 4-9-4 60...................................... TomEaves 11 61
(M Herrington) *s.i.s: hld up in rr: pushed along and hdwy 1f out: nt qckn ins fnl f* **50/1**

000- **5** *nk* **Misterisland (IRE)**[25] [7858] 5-8-4 46 oh1.......................... NickyMackay 4 46
(M Mullineaux) *a.p: pushed along 3f out: rdn over 1f out: kpt on same pce ins fnl f* **50/1**

00-3 **6** *1 ¼* **Josiah Bartlett (IRE)**[20] [10] 4-8-3 48......................(t) AndreaAtzeni(3) 5 45
(Ian Williams) *s.i.s: hld up towards rr: hdwy over 2f out: rdn wl over 1f out: swtchd lft jst ins fnl f: one pce* **7/1**[3]

6643 **7** *nk* **Louisiade (IRE)**[8] [160] 9-8-4 46 oh1..............................(p) FrannyNorton 3 42
(R C Guest) *sn led: hdd wl over 2f out: rdn wl over 1f out: fdd towards fin* **11/1**

-030 **8** *1* **Jord (IRE)**[7] [194] 6-9-2 58.. GregFairley 9 52
(J A Glover) *led early: hld up in tch: rdn 2f out: sn wknd* **14/1**

10-3 **9** *nk* **Carnival Dream**[7] [193] 5-8-12 54.................................. GrahamGibbons 7 47
(H A McWilliams) *hld up in mid-div: lost pl 4f out: no hdwy fnl 2f* **25/1**

00-2 **10** *½* **Angaric (IRE)**[7] [194] 7-8-8 57.. AdamCarter(7) 1 48
(B Smart) *rdn jst over 2f out: wknd ins fnl f* **15/2**

031- **11** *1 ¼* **Signora Frasi (IRE)**[93] [6945] 5-8-7 56............................ DavidKenny(7) 2 44
(A G Newcombe) *prom: rdn and wkng whn hmpd ins fnl f* **8/1**

1m 29.52s (-0.08) **Going Correction** 0.0s/f (Stan) **11** Ran SP% **116.1**
Speed ratings (Par 101): **100,99,99,97,96 95,94,93,93,92 91**
toteswingers: 1&2 £2.70, 1&3 £28.10, 2&3 £18.50 CSF £10.43 CT £228.72 TOTE £3.80: £2.20, £1.30, £8.50; EX 13.30.
Owner Brendan W Duke Racing **Bred** Bearstone Stud **Trained** Lambourn, Berks
■ Stewards' Enquiry : Andrea Atzeni two-day ban: careless riding (Feb 7-8)

FOCUS
A moderate affair run a shade slower than division 1. The winner ran a small personal best.
Misterisland(IRE) Official explanation: jockey said horse ran too free

270 BETDAQ ON 0870 178 1221 H'CAP (DIV II) 7f 32y(P)
7:35 (7:35) (Class 6) (0-60,60) 4-Y-O+ **£1,433** (£423; £211) **Stalls** High

Form RPR
104- **1** **Straight Face (IRE)**[41] [7726] 6-8-13 55......................(b) J-PGuillambert 8 69
(P D Evans) *hld up in mid-div: hdwy on outside 3f out: c wd st: led wl over 1f out: drvn clr ins fnl f: r.o wl* **4/1**[2]

01-6 **2** *4* **Hard Ball**[10] [142] 4-8-9 51...(v) FrannyNorton 2 54
(M Quinn) *led early: hld up in tch: led wl over 1f out: sn rdn and hdd: one pce ins fnl f* **11/2**

2-66 **3** *hd* **Gracie's Gift (IRE)**[14] [86] 8-9-1 57................................ DavidProbert 3 60
(R C Guest) *hld up in mid-div: rdn 3f out: hdwy whn nt clr run and swtchd rt 2f out: one pce ins fnl f* **9/2**[3]

00-6 **4** *2 ½* **Great Knight (IRE)**[1] [251] 5-8-12 54............................. JamieSpencer 4 50
(John Joseph Hanlon, Ire) *hld up and bhd: stdy hdwy on ins over 2f out: rdn jst over 1f out: one pce* **15/2**

4-40 **5** *1 ½* **Luisa Tetrazzini (IRE)**[17] [38] 4-8-9 56 ow1........... MarkCoumbe(5) 10 51
(John A Harris) *hdwy on outside to chse ldr over 5f out: ev ch 3f out: n.m.r briefly 2f out: sn rdn and wknd* **16/1**

6-30 **6** *hd* **Golden Prospect**[10] [135] 6-9-2 58............................(v) PaulFitzsimons 5 49
(Miss J R Tooth) *hld up and bhd: rdn 3f out: c wd st: nvr trbld ldrs* **8/1**

6-00 **7** *1 ½* **Melt (IRE)**[13] [110] 5-9-0 56.......................................(b) GrahamGibbons 7 43
(M W Easterby) *s.i.s: hld up in rr: pushed along wl over 2f out: rdn and short-lived effrt wl over 1f out* **8/1**

000- **8** *¾* **Avonlini**[141] [5614] 4-8-1 46 oh1...................................... KellyHarrison(3) 6 31
(B P J Baugh) *prom: ev ch wl over 1f out: rdn and wknd fnl f* **40/1**

00-3 **9** *3* **Sendreni (FR)**[7] [194] 6-9-4 60.....................................(p) NickyMackay 9 37
(M Wigham) *sn led: rdn and hdd wl over 1f out: sn wknd: eased ins fnl f* **3/1**[1]

000- **10** *3* **Chicamia**[39] [7753] 6-8-5 47 oh1 ow1..............................(be) GregFairley 1 16
(M Mullineaux) *rdn along sn after s: prom tl wknd over 3f out* **50/1**

1m 29.43s (-0.17) **Going Correction** 0.0s/f (Stan) **10** Ran SP% **122.8**
Speed ratings (Par 101): **100,95,95,92,90 90,88,87,84,80**
toteswingers: 1&2 £7.00, 1&3 £6.10, 2&3 £8.10 CSF £28.01 CT £108.32 TOTE £5.30: £2.30, £1.70, £1.80; EX 34.30.
Owner J L Guillambert **Bred** P J Towell **Trained** Pandy, Monmouths

FOCUS
Marginally the quicker of the two divisions. A return to form from the winner on his first start for a new yard.
Sendreni(FR) Official explanation: trainer had no explanation for the poor form shown

271 SPONSOR A RACE BY CALLING 01902 390000 H'CAP 5f 20y(P)
8:05 (8:05) (Class 7) (0-50,56) 4-Y-O+ **£1,364** (£403; £201) **Stalls** Low

Form RPR
6-65 **1** **Meikle Barfil**[8] [178] 8-8-9 47..(bt) NickyMackay 5 57
(J M Bradley) *chsd ldrs: wnt 2nd wl over 1f out: rdn to ld jst ins fnl f: drvn out* **16/1**

66-2 **2** *2 ¼* **Admiral Bond (IRE)**[8] [178] 5-8-10 48................................(p) TomEaves 4 50
(G R Oldroyd) *mid-div: pushed along over 3f out: hdwy on ins 2f out: rdn over 1f out: r.o to take 2nd cl home: nt trble wnr* **15/8**[1]

0-34 **3** *nk* **Truly Divine**[12] [112] 5-8-8 46..(v) DavidProbert 6 47
(C A Dwyer) *led: rdn and hdd jst ins fnl f: no ex and lost 2nd cl home* **6/1**[3]

43-4 **4** *1 ¼* **Cocktail Party (IRE)**[8] [178] 4-8-11 49..........................(t) JamieSpencer 7 46+
(J W Hills) *hld up in rr: hdwy fnl f: nvr nrr* **7/2**[2]

50-4 **5** *nse* **Nawaaff**[14] [79] 5-8-10 48.. FrannyNorton 3 44
(M Quinn) *s.i.s: hld up towards rr: hdwy over 1f out: rdn and kpt on same pce fnl f* **6/1**[3]

50-0 **6** *1 ½* **Cheshire Rose**[13] [103] 5-8-10 48....................................(p) JoeFanning 12 39
(A M Hales) *chsd ldrs: pushed along wl over 2f out: rdn and wknd over 1f out* **14/1**

06-0 **7** *1 ¼* **Gleaming Spirit (IRE)**[8] [178] 6-8-10 48..........................(v) LiamKeniry 8 34
(Peter Grayson) *w ldr tl rdn wl over 1f out: wknd fnl f* **80/1**

00-0 **8** ½ **Taboor (IRE)**[8] 178 12-8-7 **45** GrahamGibbons 10 30
(R M H Cowell) *s.i.s: pushed along over 2f out: c wd st: nvr nr ldrs* **33/1**
1-00 **9** *shd* **Triskaidekaphobia**[8] 178 7-8-12 **50** (t) PaulFitzsimons 9 34
(Miss J R Tooth) *mid-div: pushed along and wknd wl over 1f out* **25/1**
00-5 **10** 2 ¼ **Magic Glade**[10] 132 11-8-4 **45** AndreaAtzeni(3) 2 21
(Peter Grayson) *towards rr: rdn over 1f out: no reponse* **22/1**
30-0 **11** 2 **Place The Duchess**[9] 146 4-8-10 **48** (t) MartinDwyer 1 17
(A J Lidderdale) *towards rr: pushed along 3f out: no rspnse* **11/1**
065- **12** 3 ¾ **Sir Loin**[63] 7460 9-8-4 **45** ow2 (v) RossAtkinson(5) 11 2
(P Burgoyne) *prom: hung rt fr over 2f out: c wd st: wknd wl over 1f out* **33/1**

62.19 secs (-0.11) **Going Correction** 0.0s/f (Stan) **12** Ran SP% **121.8**
Speed ratings (Par 97): **100,96,95,93,93 91,89,88,88,84 81,75**
toteswingers: 1&2 £10.50, 1&3 £16.60, 2&3 £3.90 CSF £45.60 CT £216.71 TOTE £17.80: £4.80, £1.20, £2.40; EX 65.40 Place 6: £39.91 Place 5: £21.05.
Owner J M Bradley **Bred** Mrs Henry Keswick **Trained** Sedbury, Gloucs

FOCUS
Fast and furious stuff in which few got involved. The winner reversed latest C/D form with the second and fourth, posting his best effort in more than three years on the face of things.
Cocktail Party(IRE) Official explanation: jockey said filly was in season
Sir Loin Official explanation: jockey said gelding hung right
T/Plt: £47.90 to a £1 stake. Pool: £102,667.50. 1,563.56 winning tickets. T/Qpdt: £29.00 to a £1 stake. Pool: £9,084.64. 231.40 winning tickets. KH

221 CAGNES-SUR-MER
Friday, January 22

OFFICIAL GOING: Standard

272a PRIX DE CLAIREFONTIANE (ALL-WEATHER) 1m (F)
1:35 (1:35) 4-Y-0+ **£11,062** (£4,425; £3,319; £2,212; £1,106)

RPR
1 **All Ways To Rome (FR)**[55] 6-8-11 (b) FabriceVeron 80
(H-A Pantall, France)
2 *nk* **Garnica (FR)**[76] 7294 7-8-11 IoritzMendizabal 79
(D Nicholls) *racd in 6th: swtchd outside 2f out: wnt 2nd over 1f out: kpt on: nt rch wnr* **17/10**[1]
3 2 **Royal Power (IRE)**[117] 6312 7-8-11 DominiqueBoeuf 75
(D Nicholls) *in rr: last st: styd on down outside fnl 2f to take 3rd fnl 50yds* **12/1**[2]
4 ¾ **Heart Attack (FR)**[180] 4-8-11 73
(G Martin, Austria)
5 1 ½ **Zieto (FR)**[171] 6-9-2 (b) 75
(J-M Capitte, France)
6 1 **Outer Continent (IRE)**[96] 5-9-6 (b) 76
(X Nakkachdji, France)
7 ¾ **Tigron (USA)**[295] 9-9-5 (b) 74
(Mme C Barande-Barbe, France)
8 1 **Johanan (FR)**[64] 7458 4-9-6 72
(F-X De Chevigny, France)
9 2 ½ **Panichop (FR)**[92] 5-9-6 66
(J-M Capitte, France)
10 7 **Menestrol (FR)**[261] 8-8-11 41
(D Prod'Homme, France)

1m 36.61s (96.61) **10** Ran SP% **44.7**
PARI-MUTUEL (Including 1 Euro stake): WIN 7.20; PL 2.00, 1.50, 3.00;DF 11.20.
Owner Jean-Francois Gribomont **Bred** Mme Pascale Menard & Pierre Talvard **Trained** France

273a PRIX DES FIGIERS (CLAIMER) (ALL-WEATHER) 1m (F)
3:10 (3:13) 5-Y-0+ **£6,637** (£2,655; £1,991; £1,327; £664)

RPR
1 **Jack Junior (USA)**[111] 6495 6-9-1 Francois-XavierBertras 59
(D Nicholls) *prom on outside: 2nd 1/2-way: 3rd and pushed along st: led over 1 1/2f out: r.o wl: pushed out (claimed for 10:500euro - £9:292)* **71/10**[1]
2 1 **Indian City (FR)**[171] 6-9-12 (b) XavierBergeron 68
(J-M Capitte, France)
3 *shd* **Vestris (IRE)**[34] 7822 5-10-0 YoannRousset 70
(Y Fertillet, France)
4 1 **Torronto (FR)**[50] 7-9-7 (p) 60
(P Monfort, France)
5 *shd* **Royal Dignitary (USA)**[14] 87 10-9-1 IoritzMendizabal 54
(D Nicholls) *led: drvn 2f out: hdd over 1 1/2f out: no ex fnl f* **71/10**[1]
6 1 **Carimo (IRE)**[74] 6-9-12 (p) 63
(W Walton, France)
7 1 **Hiram (FR)**[50] 5-9-4 53
(S Cerulis, France)
8 2 ½ **Sprint Car (FR)**[96] 6-9-4 47
(J-L Gay, France)
9 *nse* **Noblement (GER)**[218] 5-0 57
(Mario Hofer, Germany)
10 *hd* **Manaba (GER)**[73] 5-9-4 (p) 46
(W Baltromei, Germany)
0 **Added Attraction (FR)**[19] 28 6-8-11 —
(R Laplanche, France)
0 **Shalamara (FR)**[50] 5-9-7 —
(P Demercastel, France)
0 **Fantasy King (FR)**[166] 5-9-11 (p) —
(P Demercastel, France)
0 **Daudet (GER)**[96] 6-8-11 —
(H Blume, Germany)
0 **Go Directa (GER)**[277] 7-9-7 (b) —
(Y Fertillet, France)
0 **Austria (GER)**[73] 5-8-11 —
(R Crepon, France)
0 **Fabulous Fong (IRE)** 5-8-11 (p) —
(S Labate, France)
0 **Betfair Lady (ITY)** 5-8-8 —
(M Manili, Italy)

1m 37.07s (97.07) **18** Ran SP% **24.7**
PARI-MUTUEL: WIN 8.10 (coupeld with Royal Dignitary); PL 9.00, 14.20,6.90; DF 684.50.
Owner Mrs Jackie Love & D Nicholls **Bred** Marablue Farm **Trained** Sessay, N Yorks

256 LINGFIELD (L-H)
Saturday, January 23

OFFICIAL GOING: Standard
Wind: very modest, against Weather: overcast

274 GOLF AT LINGFIELD PARK MAIDEN STKS 1m (P)
12:35 (12:36) (Class 5) 3-Y-0 **£2,456** (£725; £362) **Stalls High**

Form RPR
5-2 **1** **Monterosso**[8] 180 3-9-3 0 JoeFanning 6 79+
(M Johnston) *chsd ldr tl led 3f out: rdn clr 1f out: styd on strly* **13/8**[1]
00-4 **2** 3 ¼ **Darshonin**[8] 180 3-9-3 72 (v) ShaneKelly 10 72
(J Noseda) *chsd ldng pair: wnt 2nd over 2f out tl over 1f out: nt qckn u.p jst over 1f out: regained 2nd nr fin* **7/2**[3]
4-4 **3** *hd* **Minortransgression (USA)**[8] 180 3-9-3 0 GeorgeBaker 9 71
(G L Moore) *t.k.h: hld up in tch: hdwy to press ldrs 2f out: chsd wnr and nt qckn u.p jst over 1f out: lost 2nd nr fin* **2/1**[2]
402- **4** ¾ **Christmas Coming**[38] 7773 3-9-3 65 DaneO'Neill 7 69
(D R C Elsworth) *in tch: hdwy to chse ldng trio ent fnl 2f: outpcd u.p over 1f out: wl hld fnl f* **10/1**
5 4 ½ **Blues Forever (IRE)** 3-9-3 0 PaulHanagan 2 59
(P D Evans) *dwlt: in tch towards rr: sme hdwy over 2f out one pce u.p ent fnl 2f: no ch after* **25/1**
6 2 ¾ **Mental Reservation (USA)** 3-9-3 0 AdamKirby 1 53
(M G Quinlan) *s.i.s: hld up in last trio: hdwy into midfield over 2f out: outpcd wl over 1f out: wl hld after* **40/1**
0-0 **7** 11 **Colonel Henry**[14] 106 3-9-3 0 PaulDoe 5 27
(S Dow) *a in last trio: lost tch over 2f out* **100/1**
0-6 **8** 5 **Luminosa**[11] 143 3-8-9 0 AndreaAtzeni(3) 4 11
(D Donovan) *led tl 3f out wknd qckly ent fnl 2f: wl bhd fnl f* **100/1**
9 1 ¾ **Hazita** 3-8-12 0 LukeMorris 8 7
(J R Gask) *s.i.s: rn green and sn pushed along in rr: wl bhd fnl 2f* **40/1**
00- **10** 1 ¼ **Scarlet Ridge**[47] 7663 3-8-12 0 JackMitchell 3 4
(D K Ivory) *chsd ldrs tl struggling u.p 3f out: wl bhd fnl 2f* **100/1**

1m 38.05s (-0.15) **Going Correction** -0.025s/f (Stan) **10** Ran SP% **114.4**
Speed ratings (Par 97): **99,95,95,94,90 87,76,71,69,68**
toteswingers: 1&2 £2.00, 1&3 £1.80, 2&3 £2.40 CSF £7.31 TOTE £2.60: £1.10, £1.60, £1.50; EX 8.70 Trifecta £14.40 Pool: £481.79 - 24.60 winning units..
Owner Sheikh Hamdan Bin Mohammed Al Maktoum **Bred** Darley **Trained** Middleham Moor, N Yorks

FOCUS
The front three were closely matched on recent 7f course form but the winner made significantly more improvement than the next two home. The second and third look the best guides to the level.
Mental Reservation(USA) Official explanation: jockey said gelding hung left from 2 1/2f out
Colonel Henry Official explanation: jockey said, regarding running and riding, that his orders were to sit in mid-division and make his best way home, adding that the gelding was green on its previous runs, that it had hung both ways and did not go forward in latter stages.

275 LINGFIELD PARK FOURBALL H'CAP 6f (P)
1:05 (1:06) (Class 5) (0-75,72) 4-Y-0+ **£2,331** (£693; £346; £173) **Stalls Low**

Form RPR
46-3 **1** **Fazbee (IRE)**[8] 192 4-9-0 **68** (b) TonyCulhane 3 77
(P W D'Arcy) *hld up towards rr: n.m.r after 1f out: gd hdwy ent fnl f: rdn to ld ins fnl f: r.o wl* **6/1**[2]
20-4 **2** ½ **Rondeau (GR)**[12] 123 5-9-4 **72** JimCrowley 12 79+
(P R Chamings) *stdd and swtchd lft after s: hld up in rr: gd hdwy on outer ent fnl f: r.o wl to go 2nd wl ins fnl f: nt rch wnr* **7/2**[1]
065- **3** ½ **Secret Witness**[36] 7795 4-9-2 **70** (b) StephenCraine 6 76
(R A Harris) *t.k.h: hld up in tch in rr: hdwy over 1f out: r.o u.p fnl f: wnt 3rd wl ins fnl f: no imp towards fin* **7/1**[3]
500- **4** ½ **Peter's Gift (IRE)**[117] 6348 4-9-2 **70** JamieSpencer 9 74
(K A Ryan) *chsd ldr: drvn to ld jst over 1f out: hdd ins fnl f: no ex and lost 2 pls wl ins fnl f* **16/1**
65-6 **5** 1 **Chjimes (IRE)**[12] 119 6-9-4 **72** LiamKeniry 2 73
(C R Dore) *dwlt: sn bustled along to get in tch: chsd ldng pair and drvn ent fnl f: one pce ins fnl f* **10/1**
35-5 **6** *nse* **I Confess**[12] 123 5-9-2 **70** (v) PaulDoe 4 71
(P D Evans) *led: pressed and rdn jst over 2f out: hdd jst over 1f out: sn drvn: wknd fnl 75yds* **6/1**[2]
050- **7** *shd* **Suhayl Star (IRE)**[50] 7627 6-8-8 **62** LukeMorris 5 62
(P Burgoyne) *in tch: rdn wl over 1f out: kpt on same pce fnl f* **12/1**
230- **8** *nse* **Tejime**[27] 7853 4-9-4 **72** RobertHavlin 10 72+
(J H M Gosden) *t.k.h: in tch on outer: rdn and unable qck over 1f out: kpt on same pce fnl f* **7/1**[3]
24-5 **9** 2 **Resplendent Alpha**[16] 71 6-9-3 **71** JimmyQuinn 7 65+
(P Howling) *stdd s: hld up in tch towards rr: effrt and rdn jst over 1f out: nvr able to chal* **10/1**
06- **10** 1 ¾ **Highland Harvest**[73] 7327 6-8-13 **67** SteveDrowne 11 55
(Jamie Poulton) *chsd ldrs: rdn 2f out: struggling and btn whn short of room jst ins fnl f: nt pushed after* **18/1**
300- **11** ½ **Moral Duty (USA)**[145] 5502 5-8-8 **62** SaleemGolam 8 49
(W G M Turner) *a bhd: rdn over 4f out: nvr trbld ldrs* **40/1**
02-0 **12** 3 ½ **First Order**[21] 20 9-8-6 **65** ow2 (v) AnnStokell(5) 1 40
(Miss A Stokell) *chsd ldrs tl rdn and wknd wl over 1f out: bhd fnl f* **40/1**

1m 11.7s (-0.20) **Going Correction** -0.025s/f (Stan) **12** Ran SP% **117.7**
Speed ratings (Par 103): **100,99,98,98,96 96,96,96,93,91 90,86**
toteswingers: 1&2 £3.90, 1&3 £12.00, 2&3 £10.30 CSF £26.98 CT £152.63 TOTE £6.80: £2.60, £1.40, £2.20; EX 23.90 TRIFECTA Not won..
Owner Tony Burlton **Bred** Stuart McPhee Bloodstock & Morton Bstock **Trained** Newmarket, Suffolk

FOCUS
A modest but competitive sprint handicap. The winner was back to her autumn level with the second close to form.
Tejime ◆ Official explanation: jockey said gelding ran too freely
Resplendent Alpha Official explanation: jockey said gelding was denied a clear run

276 LINGFIELDPARK.CO.UK (S) STKS 6f (P)
1:40 (1:40) (Class 6) 3-Y-0 **£1,774** (£523; £262) **Stalls Low**

Form RPR
12-2 **1** **Bubbly Bellini (IRE)**[9] 168 3-8-12 74 (p) MatthewDavies(5) 9 76
(George Baker) *hld up in tch in last pl: gd hdwy towards inner over 1f out: rdn to chal 1f out: led fnl 100yds: r.o wl* **9/4**[1]
33-1 **2** ¾ **Anjomarba (IRE)**[21] 17 3-8-9 67 (p) JackDean(3) 6 69
(W G M Turner) *chsd ldr tl rdn to ld ent fnl 2f: drvn and pressed 1f out: hdd fnl 100yds: no ex* **10/1**

6-23 **3** *1* **Maoi Chinn Tire (IRE)**[3] 233 3-8-12 66........................(p) LiamKeniry 2 65
(J S Moore) *jostled s and over 5f out: chsd ldng pair: rdn to chse ldr over 1f out tl 1f out: kpt on same pce u.p fnl f* **5/2**[2]

3-36 **4** *2 ¾* **Tatawor (IRE)**[10] 147 3-8-12 70..............................(b[1]) DaneO'Neill 1 57
(J R Boyle) *t.k.h: hld up in tch in last pair: effrt ent fnl 2f: wnt modest 4th ins fnl f: kpt on but nvr able to chal* **10/1**

415- **5** *2* **Miss Lesley**[24] 7871 3-8-7 71..................................(b) MarkCoumbe(5) 5 50
(D K Ivory) *in tch: hmpd and lost pl wl over 4f out: effrt u.p on outer bnd 2f out: no prog and wl hld fr over 1f out* **6/1**[3]

36-5 **6** *6* **Zelos Dream (IRE)**[6] 209 3-8-12 62..............................(p) LukeMorris 4 31
(R A Harris) *wnt lft s: led: rdn and hdd ent fnl 2f: wknd qckly over 1f out* **33/1**

54-0 **7** *1 ½* **American Agent (USA)**[12] 128 3-8-12 59..............(b[1]) JamieSpencer 7 26
(P F I Cole) *chsd ldrs: rdn ent fnl 2f: btn wl over 1f out and sn wl bhd* **8/1**

050- **8** *2* **Wigan Lane**[70] 7389 3-8-12 58.. PaulDoe 8 20
(P Howling) *in tch on outer: hung lft and dropped to rr jst over 2f out: wl bhd over 1f out* **33/1**

0-04 **9** *hd* **Emma Jean Lass (IRE)**[9] 159 3-8-2 60...........(v) AndrewHeffernan(5) 3 14
(P D Evans) *sltly hmpd s: sn pushed along and cl up whn hmpd again over 5f out: in tch after tl wknd u.p ent fnl 2f* **16/1**

1m 12.01s (0.11) **Going Correction** -0.025s/f (Stan) 9 Ran SP% **114.7**
Speed ratings (Par 95): **98,97,95,92,89 81,79,76,76**
toteswingers: 1&2 £3.80, 1&3 £2.20, 2&3 £4.70 CSF £25.53 TOTE £3.40: £1.20, £3.10, £1.20; EX 21.20 Trifecta £25.60 Pool: £548.82 - 15.81 winning units..The winner was bought in for 5,200gns.
Owner Mrs C E S Baker **Bred** J P Hand **Trained** Moreton Morrell, Warwicks
■ Stewards' Enquiry : Jack Dean one-day ban: used whip with excessive frequency (Feb 6)
Luke Morris two-day ban: careless riding (Feb 6-7)

FOCUS
A decent 3-y-o seller run at a strong pace. The winner is rated back to his best.

277 THIRD "SHAREN BLAQUIERE - CELEBRATE A LIFE" H'CAP 5f (P)
2:15 (2:15) (Class 4) (0-85,80) 3-Y-O **£4,209** (£1,252; £625; £312) **Stalls** High

Form RPR
51- **1** **Clifton Bridge**[28] 7843 3-9-6 79.. JimCrowley 4 82
(R M Beckett) *chsd ldrs: swtchd rt over 1f out: r.o wl u.p fnl f to ld last stride* **11/4**[2]

14-2 **2** *shd* **R Woody**[4] 222 3-9-0 73.. SteveDrowne 1 76
(Mrs L C Jewell) *w ldrs tl over 3f out: rdn and effrt on inner over 1f out: drvn to ld wl ins fnl f: hdd last stride* **2/1**[1]

2-23 **3** *nk* **Athwaab**[4] 222 3-8-5 69.. TobyAtkinson(5) 3 71+
(M G Quinlan) *stdd after s: sn nudged along in last: hdwy 2f out: nt clr run and swtchd rt ins fnl f: r.o strly fnl 100yds: nt quite rch ldng pair* **13/2**

321- **4** *hd* **Lucky Mellor**[36] 7793 3-9-2 80...................................(b) MarkCoumbe(5) 2 81
(D K Ivory) *w ldrs tl le dover 3f out: drvn over 1f out: hdd wl ins fnl f: wnt rt and lost 2 pls nr fin* **7/1**

631- **5** *½* **Sakile**[63] 7485 3-9-4 77.. JamieSpencer 6 76
(P W Chapple-Hyam) *led narrowly tl over 3f out: chsd ldr after: drvn and unable qck over 1f out: one pce and lost 3 pls fnl 100yds* **5/1**[3]

320- **6** *6* **Six Wives**[24] 7871 3-8-12 71...(p) ChrisCatlin 5 49
(J A Glover) *dwlt: in tch on outer: rdn over 1f out: sn btn* **16/1**

59.27 secs (0.47) **Going Correction** -0.025s/f (Stan) 6 Ran SP% **108.4**
Speed ratings (Par 99): **95,94,94,94,93 83**
toteswingers: 1&2 £1.40, 1&3 £4.50, 2&3 £3.20 CSF £8.03 TOTE £4.10: £2.00, £1.20; EX 9.60.
Owner Landmark Racing Limited **Bred** D K Ivory **Trained** Whitsbury, Hants

FOCUS
There was a bunch finish, but the pace was strong and the form looks sound enough. The third may have been unlucky.

278 VIEW OUR 2010 FIXTURES AT LINGFIELDPARK.CO.UK H'CAP 1m (P)
2:45 (2:48) (Class 2) (0-100,100) 4-Y-O+ **£10,361** (£3,083; £1,540; £769) **Stalls** High

Form RPR
41-3 **1** **Autumn Blades (IRE)**[16] 71 5-8-5 87.......................(p) DavidProbert 7 97
(A Bailey) *in tch in midfield: hdwy to join ldrs: led and hung lft wl over 1f out: racd awkwardly but hld on to ld narrowly u.p fnl f* **5/1**[3]

14-0 **2** *shd* **Benandonner (USA)**[14] 108 7-8-3 88.......................... AndreaAtzeni(3) 4 98
(Mike Murphy) *chsd ldng pair: rdn to ld over 2f out: hdd over 1f out: kpt on gamely u.p fnl f: pressed wnr cl home: jst hld* **11/2**

2225 **3** *1 ½* **Aeroplane**[1] 266 7-8-13 100....................................(p) RichardEvans(5) 6 107
(P D Evans) *stdd after s: hld up in last pair: hdwy to chse ldrs 2f out: wnt 3rd and rdn ins fnl f: fnd nil and no imp after* **7/2**[2]

623- **4** *1 ½* **Everymanforhimself (IRE)**[63] 7486 6-8-11 93..........(v) JamieSpencer 2 96
(K A Ryan) *racd in midfield: hdwy to chse ldrs over 1f out: edging lft whn n.m.r and swtchd rt jst over 1f out: one pce fnl f* **5/2**[1]

00-0 **5** *¾* **My Gacho (IRE)**[9] 177 8-8-5 87.....................................(v) JoeFanning 1 88
(M Johnston) *dwlt and bustled along early and rcvrd to ld after 1f: rdn and hdd over 2f out: wknd u.p 1f out* **20/1**

0-43 **6** *2 ½* **Carcinetto (IRE)**[7] 204 8-8-11 93.. PaulDoe 3 89
(P D Evans) *led for 1f: chsd ldr after tl hmpd and lost pl over 2f out: rdn and unable qck over 1f out: wknd fnl f* **17/2**

000- **7** *1 ¼* **Unbreak My Heart (IRE)**[126] 6093 5-8-6 88.................. PaulHanagan 5 81+
(R A Fahey) *chsd ldrs: dropped to rr and hmpd over 2f out: rdn and no prog wl over 1f out* **5/1**[3]

1m 36.15s (-2.05) **Going Correction** -0.025s/f (Stan) course record 7 Ran SP% **114.8**
Speed ratings (Par 109): **109,108,107,105,105 102,101**
toteswingers: 1&2 £5.20, 1&3 £2.70, 2&3 £3.50 CSF £32.40 TOTE £5.50: £2.40, £3.10; EX 31.20.
Owner John Stocker **Bred** Dr D Crone & P Lafarge & P Johnston **Trained** Newmarket, Suffolk

FOCUS
Not that strong a race for the grade and it was a bit muddling, but another personal best from the winner. The second and third were close to their recent Kempton running.

NOTEBOOK
Autumn Blades(IRE) is a difficult ride and had gained all his previous six wins over 7f, so he looked to be in front plenty soon enough when taking over early in the straight, but despite carrying his head at an awkward angle as usual, he just did enough. He'll never really appeal as one to follow, but in fairness, this was probably his best performance to date. He was due to take his chance at Kempton the following the day, and his connections also plan to run him in one of the Super7 Challenge qualifiers. (op 9-2)
Benandonner(USA) ran much better than when badly hampered in a good race over 7f around here on his previous start and was just held. He's still very useful when things go his way. (op 6-1)
Aeroplane, well beaten over further at Wolverhampton the previous day, travelled strongly as usual but found little once coming under pressure around a furlong out. (op 5-1)
Everymanforhimself(IRE), trying 1m for the first time, was a bit keen early on and failed to pick up in the straight. He didn't get the clearest of runs late on, but looked held at the time. Official explanation: jockey said gelding hung left (op 9-4 tchd 11-4 and 3-1 in a place)
My Gacho(IRE) has yet to rediscover his best form since returning from a break.
Carcinetto(IRE), who has yet to run to her best over this trip, was under pressure when squeezed up between rivals before the turn into the straight and never recovered after losing her place. (op 8-1 tchd 15-2 and 9-1)
Unbreak My Heart(IRE) has won when fresh, but he was well held on this occasion after 126 days off. Trying Polytrack for the first time, he lost his place when short of room over 2f out and was never seen with a chance. (op 6-1 tchd 7-1)

279 MARRIOTT HOTEL & COUNTRY CLUB H'CAP 1m 2f (P)
3:20 (3:20) (Class 6) (0-65,65) 3-Y-O **£1,774** (£523; £262) **Stalls** Low

Form RPR
0-21 **1** **Rock A Doodle Doo (IRE)**[5] 216 3-9-5 65 6ex.......... J-PGuillambert 4 76+
(W Jarvis) *racd in midfield: rdn and chsd clr ldr wl over 3f out: clsd gng wl over 2f out: pushed ahd over 1f out: clr fnl f: easily* **2/5**[1]

216- **2** *3 ¾* **Bubbly Braveheart (IRE)**[42] 7731 3-9-4 64..............(p) RobertWinston 5 67
(A Bailey) *t.k.h: led: clr 7f out: pressed and rdn ent fnl 2f: hdd over 1f out: no ch w wnr fnl f but kpt on for clr 2nd* **9/2**[2]

000- **3** *2 ¼* **Astronomer's Dream**[80] 7235 3-9-3 63.............................. LiamKeniry 2 62
(E F Vaughan) *hld up towards rr: rdn and clsd on ldrs over 2f out: outpcd wl over 1f out: wnt modest 3rd 1f out: plugged on but no ch w ldng pair* **16/1**

05-0 **4** *2 ½* **Anchorage Boy (USA)**[12] 118 3-8-11 57.....................(v[1]) ChrisCatlin 7 51
(Miss Amy Weaver) *s.i.s: sn rdn up to chse ldrs: u.p 4f out: drvn and outpcd ent fnl 2f: no ch w ldrs after* **25/1**

46-4 **5** *nk* **Creevy (IRE)**[5] 217 3-8-4 50 oh2....................................... DavidProbert 3 43
(S Kirk) *hld up in last: hdwy and in tch over 2f out: rdn and btn 2f out* **14/1**[3]

05-5 **6** *nk* **A P Ling**[19] 33 3-8-9 55.. SaleemGolam 6 47
(C N Kellett) *hld up in last trio: pushed along briefly 5f out: hdwy to press ldng pair ent fnl 2f: drvn and wknd over 1f out* **33/1**

50-0 **7** *33* **Concorde Kiss (USA)**[5] 216 3-8-4 50............................ JimmyQuinn 1 —
(S Kirk) *chsd ldr tl wl over 3f out: sn dropped out and bhd: t.o over 1f out* **66/1**

2m 6.73s (0.13) **Going Correction** -0.025s/f (Stan) 7 Ran SP% **110.4**
Speed ratings (Par 95): **98,95,93,91,90 90,64**
toteswingers: 1&2 £1.10, 1&3 £3.40, 2&3 £3.60 CSF £2.21 TOTE £1.40: £1.10, £1.60; EX 2.00.
Owner The Doodle Doo Partnership **Bred** Mrs A S O'Brien And Lars Pearson **Trained** Newmarket, Suffolk

FOCUS
Quite simply, Rock A Doodle Doo is better than this level and totally outclassed some really moderate rivals, value for around 6l. He is likely to do better still. The standard is set around the next three home.

280 MARRIOTT PLAY & STAY H'CAP 1m 4f (P)
3:55 (3:55) (Class 5) (0-70,69) 4-Y-O+ **£2,456** (£725; £362) **Stalls** Low

Form RPR
53/1 **1** **Gargano (IRE)**[12] 121 5-9-4 65.. JoeFanning 5 74
(M Johnston) *mde all: rdn and forged 2 l clr over 1f out: hrd pressed fnl 100yds: hld on wl* **11/8**[1]

160- **2** *nse* **Red Hot Desert**[34] 7823 4-9-1 66.. AdamKirby 7 75
(W R Swinburn) *stdd after s: hld up in last pair: gd hdwy towards inner over 1f out: chsd wnr ins fnl f: str chal fnl 100yds: jst hld* **16/1**

3-13 **3** *1 ¼* **Moscow Oznick**[6] 210 5-9-4 65...................................(p) DavidProbert 9 72
(D Donovan) *stdd s: t.k.h: hld in last: hdwy over 1f out: r.o wl fnl f: nvr gng to rch ldng pair* **9/1**

0-21 **4** *2 ¼* **Sunset Boulevard (IRE)**[8] 182 7-9-0 61.................. FergusSweeney 3 64
(Miss Tor Sturgis) *hld up in tch in midfield: hdwy over 2f out: chsd ldng pair and unable qck u.p wl over 1f out: plugged on same pce fnl f* **8/1**

355- **5** *nse* **Sushitan (GER)**[120] 6258 5-9-7 68................................... GeorgeBaker 2 71
(G L Moore) *chsd wnr: rdn and unable qck wl over 1f out: lost 2nd jst ins fnl f: wknd* **9/1**

42-2 **6** *nk* **Taste The Wine (IRE)**[12] 120 4-8-8 66......................... KierenFox(7) 11 69
(J S Moore) *chsd ldng pair: rdn over 2f out: outpcd u.p wl over 1f out: no ch w ldrs fnl f* **17/2**

15-3 **7** *½* **Bosamcliff (IRE)**[7] 202 5-9-2 68................................. RichardEvans(5) 4 70
(P D Evans) *hld up in midfield: rdn on outer 3f out: no prog: switching lft and kpt on same pce fnl f* **15/2**[3]

314- **8** *3 ¼* **Bramalea**[41] 6498 5-9-4 65.. DaneO'Neill 1 62
(B W Duke) *taken down early: t.k.h: hld up wl in tch: rdn and struggling 2f out: wl btn fnl f* **33/1**

001- **9** *2 ¾* **Shannersburg (IRE)**[23] 7888 5-9-5 66........................(bt) ChrisCatlin 8 58
(D E Pipe) *stdd s: t.k.h: hld up in last trio: pushed along and struggling over 2f out: wl btn over 1f out* **7/1**[2]

2m 32.8s (-0.20) **Going Correction** -0.025s/f (Stan)
WFA 4 from 5yo+ 4lb 9 Ran SP% **116.8**
Speed ratings (Par 103): **99,98,98,96,96 96,96,93,92**
toteswingers: 1&2 £8.30, 1&3 £4.40, 2&3 £18.80 CSF £27.22 CT £152.10 TOTE £1.90: £1.50, £4.10, £2.50; EX 27.60 Trifecta £202.10 Pool: £726.72 - 2.66 winning units. Place 6 £12.10, Place 5 £11.31.
Owner F Towey **Bred** Frank Towey **Trained** Middleham Moor, N Yorks

FOCUS
A modest handicap run at an ordinary pace. The winner confirmed his Kempton improvement with another slight personal best and the second was back to form.
T/Plt: £16.60 to a £1 stake. Pool: £53,437.29. 2,337.25 winning tickets. T/Qpdt: £8.00 to a £1 stake. Pool: £3,876.91. 357.30 winning tickets. SP

272 CAGNES-SUR-MER
Saturday, January 23

OFFICIAL GOING: Very soft

281a PRIX DE GAND (CLAIMER) 1m 2f 165y
1:50 (1:52) 5-Y-O+ **£6,637** (£2,655; £1,991; £1,327; £664)

RPR
1 **Lost Soldier Three (IRE)**[5] 221 9-9-1 .... IoritzMendizabal 68
(D Nicholls) *racd in 2nd tl led under 6f out: rdn clr 2f out: easily* **13/5**[1]

2 *3* **Beringoer (FR)**[90] 7-9-4 .... GuillaumeMillet 65
(T Larriviere, France)

3 *1* **La Maddalena (FR)**[71] 5-9-4 .... StephanePasquier 63
(F-X De Chevigny, France)

4 *1 ½* **Wellango (GER)**[826] 10-8-11 53
(J-L Gay, France)

5 *1 ½* **Lovely Lips**[312] 5-8-8 47
(C Scandella, France)

6 1 1/2 **Sledmere (FR)**[36] 8-9-1 ....(b) 52
(P Monfort, France)
7 1/2 **Bring It Back (FR)**[679] 6-9-7 57
(Y Fertillet, France)
8 1 **Sham Risk (FR)**[5] 221 6-9-1 49
(J Morin, France)
9 1 **Asserdoun (FR)**[74] 10-9-5 51
(R Crepon, France)
10 2 1/2 **Shahdawar (FR)**[5] 221 7-9-4 45
(M Pimbonnet, France)
0 **Cosmoledo (FR)**[596] 10-8-11 .... —
(C Biancheri, France)
0 **Unirossa (FR)**[596] 6-8-11 .... —
(J-C Sarais, France)
0 **Riobamba D'Ho (FR)**[624] 1979 5-9-1 ....(b) —
(T Larriviere, France)
0 **Corneille (FR)**[74] 5-8-11 .... —
(J-L Gay, France)
0 **Pablo Quercus (FR)**[101] 5-8-11 .... —
(A Lyon, France)
0 **Vaccaria (GER)**[101] 5-8-11 .... —
(Mme C Jung, France)
0 **Simply Gold (FR)**[205] 5-9-5 ....(b) —
(J-M Capitte, France)
0 **Oa Sanrix (FR)** 6-8-11 .... —
(J-C Sarais, France)

2m 30.26s (150.26) **18** Ran SP% **27.8**
(including 1 Euro stake): WIN 3.60; PL 2.00, 18.70, 5.20; DF 88.10.
Owner Eamon Maher **Bred** Darley **Trained** Sessay, N Yorks

[228]KEMPTON (A.W) (R-H)

Sunday, January 24

OFFICIAL GOING: Standard
Wind: Almost nil Weather: Overcast

282 BETDAQ.CO.UK H'CAP — 1m 3f (P)
2:00 (2:01) (Class 5) (0-70,70) 4-Y-0+ **£2,590** (£770; £385; £192) **Stalls** High

Form RPR
061- 1 **Franco Is My Name**[71] 7392 4-9-0 **66** .... DaneO'Neill 2 76
(P R Hedger) *hld up towards rr: rdn and hdwy over 2f out: sn chsng clr ldr: styd on to ld ins fnl f: rdn out* **7/2**[1]
404- 2 1 3/4 **Eseej (USA)**[28] 7851 5-9-7 **70** .... ChrisCatlin 7 77
(P W Hiatt) *sn led: wnt 6 l clr over 2f out: hdd and no ex ins fnl f* **16/1**
11-3 3 shd **Kames Park (IRE)**[13] 120 8-9-0 **63** .... JimCrowley 1 69
(R C Guest) *stdd s: hld up in rr gng wl: hdwy on outer 2f out: chsd ldrs over 1f out: styd on same pce fnl f* **10/1**[3]
6-65 4 1/2 **Croix Rouge (USA)**[13] 120 8-8-7 **56** .... HayleyTurner 13 62
(R J Smith) *in tch: n.m.r over 2f out: rdn and styd on appr fnl f: nvr nrr* **16/1**
0-31 5 nk **Formidable Guest**[10] 162 6-9-7 **70** .... SaleemGolam 3 75+
(J Pearce) *hld up in rr of midfield: n.m.r and hdwy 2f out: one pce fnl f* **10/1**[3]
006- 6 3 **Regional Counsel**[62] 5780 6-9-4 **70** .... MartinLane(3) 10 70
(A M Hales) *mid-div: hmpd after 1f: rdn over 2f out: styd on fnl f* **33/1**
455- 7 nk **Divinatore**[45] 7699 4-8-8 **60** .... PaulHanagan 14 59
(D Haydn Jones) *prom: sltly lost pl and pushed along after 3f: no hdwy fnl 3f* **17/2**[2]
03-0 8 nk **Graylyn Ruby (FR)**[13] 121 5-8-12 **61** .... LukeMorris 5 60
(R Dickin) *sn chsng ldr: rdn 5f out: wknd 2f out* **20/1**
04-4 9 1 1/4 **The Dial House**[15] 105 4-8-11 **63** ....(t) ShaneKelly 12 59
(J A Osborne) *in tch: hmpd and dropped to midfield after 3f: effrt over 2f out: sn btn* **33/1**
312- 10 hd **Resentful Angel**[45] 7699 5-9-0 **68** .... TobyAtkinson(5) 6 64
(Pat Eddery) *prom tl wknd ins fnl 2f* **7/2**[1]
301- 11 3 1/2 **Champagne Fizz (IRE)**[39] 7765 4-8-1 **59** .... AndreaAtzeni(3) 8 46
(Miss Jo Crowley) *in tch on outer: rdn over 2f out: sn outpcd* **16/1**
005- 12 1/2 **Shanafarahan (IRE)**[43] 7732 5-8-9 **58** .... JimmyQuinn 11 47
(K A Morgan) *towards rr: n.m.r bnd after 2f: rdn 3f out: n.d* **11/1**
516/ 13 2 1/2 **Catholic Hill (USA)**[57] 6868 5-8-7 **56** .... GrahamGibbons 4 40
(C J Mann) *chsd ldr tl hrd rdn and wknd 2f out* **11/1**
042/ 14 1 1/2 **Angels Quest**[519] 5291 5-8-7 **56** oh1 .... FergusSweeney 9 38
(A W Carroll) *a bhd* **25/1**

2m 19.52s (-2.38) **Going Correction** -0.05s/f (Stan)
WFA 4 from 5yo+ 3lb **14** Ran SP% **122.0**
Speed ratings (Par 103): **106,104,104,104,104 101,101,101,100,100 97,97,95,94**
toteswingers:1&2:£23.00, 2&3:£20.70, 1&3:£10.00 CSF £64.55 CT £521.65 TOTE £5.00: £1.80, £6.10, £3.20; EX 85.80.
Owner P C F Racing Ltd **Bred** J J Whelan **Trained** Dogmersfield, Hampshire

FOCUS
Quite a competitive handicap but it featured a host of horses who like to be held up in their races, which is why Eseej, who was allowed an easy lead, had the field so well strung out turning for home. Straightforward form at face value.
Shanafarahan(IRE) Official explanation: jockey said gelding suffered interference on first bend

283 BET AFRICAN NATIONS CUP - BETDAQ CLASSIFIED CLAIMING STKS — 1m (P)
2:30 (2:31) (Class 6) 3-Y-0 **£2,047** (£604; £302) **Stalls** High

Form RPR
024- 1 **Ana Moutabahi**[37] 7800 3-9-4 66 ....(p) AdamKirby 4 67
(C G Cox) *mde virtually all: set gd pce: drvn and jnd by runner-up over 1f out: hld on gamely and got jst on top cl home* **5/1**[3]
04-3 2 hd **Ant Music (IRE)**[22] 9 3-8-5 63 ....(b) RossAtkinson(5) 9 59
(J S Moore) *prom: drvn to join wnr over 1f out: disp ld and kpt on wl: nt qckn fnl strides* **8/1**
33-1 3 1/2 **Tuscan King**[6] 217 3-9-0 63 ....(b) J-PGuillambert 8 62+
(P D Evans) *mid-div: rdn to chse ldrs over 1f out: nt clr run on far rail and swtchd lft ins fnl f: r.o: clsng at fin* **15/8**[1]
050- 4 1 1/4 **Delta Sky (IRE)**[24] 7884 3-8-12 58 .... HayleyTurner 6 57
(Miss Amy Weaver) *towards rr: hrd rdn and hdwy over 1f out: styd on fnl f* **33/1**
23-5 5 1 **Prince Yarraman (IRE)**[11] 149 3-8-10 64 .... ShaneKelly 10 53
(J A Osborne) *patiently rdn in rr: shkn up and sme hdwy over 1f out: rdn and styd on same pce fnl f* **7/2**[2]
00-2 6 1/2 **Brenda Duke**[21] 22 3-8-4 57 .... FrankieMcDonald 5 46
(J G Portman) *t.k.h: in tch: chsd ldrs 3f out: no ex over 1f out* **11/1**
45-4 7 1 3/4 **Underworld Dandy**[21] 22 3-8-8 58 ow1 ....(b[1]) WilliamCarson(3) 3 49
(R T Phillips) *chsd ldrs tl wknd 2f out* **25/1**
12 8 2 **Mororless**[9] 188 3-8-9 64 .... DeclanCannon(5) 1 47
(A J McCabe) *chsd ldr: rdn 3f out: wknd 2f out* **7/1**
05-0 9 1 1/2 **During The War (USA)**[12] 133 3-8-12 60 ....(v[1]) JimmyQuinn 7 41
(C A Dwyer) *a in rr: rdn 3f out: n.d after* **20/1**

1m 40.83s (1.03) **Going Correction** -0.05s/f (Stan) **9** Ran SP% **117.2**
Speed ratings (Par 95): **92,91,91,90,89 88,86,84,83**
Ana Moutabahi was claimed by P. D. Evans for £12,000.
Owner H E Sheikh Sultan Bin Khalifa Al Nahyan **Bred** Sultan Bin Khalifa Al Nahyan **Trained** Lambourn, Berks
■ Stewards' Enquiry : Adam Kirby one-day ban: failed to ride to draw (Feb 7)

FOCUS
An ordinary claimer. The first two were 1-2 and the form seems pretty sound.

284 BET AUSTRALIAN OPEN TENNIS - BETDAQ FILLIES' H'CAP — 1m (P)
3:00 (3:00) (Class 5) (0-75,74) 4-Y-0+ **£2,590** (£770; £385; £192) **Stalls** High

Form RPR
000- 1 **Toolentidhaar (USA)**[137] 5780 6-8-11 **67** .... ChrisCatlin 6 72
(Andrew Turnell) *chsd ldng pair: rdn and clsd 2f out: slt ld 1f out: drvn out* **33/1**
0-40 2 1/2 **Hip Hip Hooray**[2] 256 4-8-5 **61** .... FrannyNorton 8 65
(L A Dace) *hld up in rr: gd hdwy to press ldrs over 1f out: hrd rdn: kpt on* **16/1**
3114 3 3/4 **Goodbye Cash (IRE)**[5] 225 6-8-7 **63** .... PaulDoe 3 65
(P D Evans) *chsd clr ldr: led jst ins fnl 2f: hdd 1f out: kpt on u.p* **8/1**[3]
23-0 4 hd **Bavarica**[8] 202 8-8-3 **66** .... AdamBeschizza(7) 7 68
(Miss J Feilden) *hld up in rr: shkn up and hdwy over 1f out: nrst fin* **8/1**[3]
10-6 5 shd **Perfect Class**[21] 23 4-8-13 **69** .... LukeMorris 1 70
(C G Cox) *towards rr: rdn and hdwy over 1f out: styd on same pce fnl f* **8/1**[3]
33-3 6 1/2 **Vertigo On Course (IRE)**[10] 169 5-8-5 **61** .... PaulHanagan 5 61+
(R A Fahey) *mid-div: rn v wd and dropped towards rr bnd over 3f out: rallied and styd on wl fnl f* **5/2**[1]
41-0 7 1 3/4 **Young Dottie**[4] 239 4-9-4 **74** .... IanMongan 10 70
(P M Phelan) *towards rr: hdwy on inner to chse ldrs 2f out: wknd jst over 1f out* **3/1**[2]
0-40 8 2 3/4 **Nora Mae (IRE)**[16] 84 4-9-3 **73** .... LiamKeniry 9 63
(S Kirk) *mid-div: rdn and n.m.r 2f out: wknd over 1f out* **22/1**
350- 9 9 **Izzi Mill (USA)**[104] 6738 4-8-6 **67** ....(p) DeclanCannon(5) 4 36
(A J McCabe) *led at str pce: 5 l clr 1/2-way: hdd & wknd qckly jst ins fnl 2f* **20/1**
136- 10 4 **Farleigh**[164] 4956 4-9-3 **73** .... DavidProbert 2 33
(A M Balding) *in tch in 4th tl rdn and wknd over 3f out: sn bhd* **8/1**[3]

1m 38.53s (-1.27) **Going Correction** -0.05s/f (Stan) **10** Ran SP% **115.9**
Speed ratings (Par 100): **104,103,102,102,102 101,100,97,88,84**
toteswingers:1&2:£54.20, 2&3:£12.90, 1&3:£38.20 CSF £467.80 CT £4698.04 TOTE £33.40: £15.30, £4.80, £2.20; EX 250.00.
Owner Griffiths Gifts Limited **Bred** Shadwell Farm LLC **Trained** Broad Hinton, Wilts
■ Stewards' Enquiry : Chris Catlin one-day ban: failed to ride to draw (Feb 7)
Declan Cannon one-day ban: failed to ride to draw (Feb 7)

FOCUS
Hard to know what to make of this form as the winner was a 33-1 chance who had been badly out of sorts when last seen in September, and they finished in a heap but the time was strong, much quicker than the previous claimer and not bad at all for the grade. The form seems sound enough.

285 BET FA CUP - BETDAQ H'CAP — 7f (P)
3:35 (3:35) (Class 5) (0-70,70) 4-Y-0+ **£2,590** (£770; £385; £192) **Stalls** High

Form RPR
656- 1 **Ocean Legend (IRE)**[51] 7631 5-8-13 **65** .... AdamKirby 7 75
(A W Carroll) *prom: rdn to ld 2f out: drvn out* **12/1**
530- 2 1 1/2 **Kensington (IRE)**[25] 7876 9-8-10 **67** .... DeclanCannon(5) 8 73
(A J McCabe) *prom: rdn 2f out: kpt on to take 2nd ins fnl f* **20/1**
0131 3 1/2 **Know No Fear**[4] 242 5-7-12 **57** ....(p) AmyScott(7) 9 62
(A J Lidderdale) *stdd s: hld up in midfield: n.m.r on rail bnd 4f out: rdn and styd on fnl 2f* **9/2**[2]
06-0 4 3/4 **Durgan**[15] 110 4-8-13 **65** .... SteveDrowne 3 68
(Mrs L C Jewell) *hld up 2nd last: rdn and hdwy 2f out: styd on same pce fnl f* **33/1**
046/ 5 shd **Unlimited**[518] 5315 8-8-8 **60** .... FergusSweeney 6 63
(A W Carroll) *led tl 2f out: no ex over 1f out* **25/1**
64-2 6 1/2 **Dajen**[16] 84 4-8-7 **62** .... MartinLane(3) 1 63
(D M Simcock) *towards rr on outer: effrt in centre 2f out: nt pce to chal* **5/1**[3]
4-06 7 1/2 **Resplendent Nova**[13] 123 8-9-0 **66** .... JimmyQuinn 10 66
(P Howling) *s.i.s: bhd: mod effrt on ins 2f out: nt trble ldrs* **7/1**
343- 8 nk **Just Timmy Marcus**[27] 7860 4-8-13 **65** ....(v[1]) TonyCulhane 2 64
(B P J Baugh) *towards rr: rdn and no imp fnl 2f* **13/2**
1-61 9 1 1/4 **Lord Fidelio (IRE)**[13] 123 4-9-4 **70** ....(p) LiamKeniry 5 66
(A M Balding) *chsd ldrs tl hrd rdn and wknd over 1f out* **9/4**[1]
50-0 10 8 **Carlitos Spirit (IRE)**[21] 23 6-8-13 **68** .... JamesMillman(3) 4 42
(I W McInnes) *chsd ldrs tl rdn and wknd qckly 3f out* **16/1**

1m 25.2s (-0.80) **Going Correction** -0.05s/f (Stan) **10** Ran SP% **116.6**
Speed ratings (Par 103): **102,100,99,98,98 98,97,97,95,86**
toteswingers:1&2:£31.50, 2&3:£15.40, 1&3:£10.70 CSF £224.91 CT £916.63 TOTE £16.30: £4.30, £4.60, £3.40; EX 229.70.
Owner Ocean Trailers Ltd **Bred** Mark Commins **Trained** Cropthorne, Worcs

FOCUS
A modest handicap. The first two were always prominent but the form looks sound enough.
Know No Fear Official explanation: jockey said gelding suffered interference in running
Carlitos Spirit(IRE) Official explanation: jockey said gelding hung badly right-handed throughout

286 BET MULTIPLES - BETDAQ H'CAP — 7f (P)
4:05 (4:07) (Class 3) (0-90,93) 4-Y-0+
£6,542 (£1,959; £979; £490; £244; £122) **Stalls** High

Form RPR
1-31 1 **Autumn Blades (IRE)**[1] 278 5-9-9 **93** 6ex ....(p) FrannyNorton 4 100
(A Bailey) *reluctant to load: hld up in midfield: hdwy 2f out: drvn to ld ins fnl f: hld on wl* **7/1**[2]
10-0 2 hd **Wigram's Turn (USA)**[15] 108 5-9-4 **88** ....(v) DavidProbert 7 95
(A M Balding) *towards rr on outer: drvn along over 2f out: hdwy to press wnr fnl f: hrd rdn: kpt on wl* **8/1**[3]

0/0- **3** ¾ **Seasider**[219] 3091 5-8-10 **83** .... MartinLane(3) 5 88
(D M Simcock) *towards rr: rdn and r.o fnl 2f: nrst fin* **25/1**

343- **4** *nse* **Jake The Snake (IRE)**[177] 4502 9-8-3 **78** .... AmyBaker(5) 10 84+
(A W Carroll) *s.s: hld up in rr: swtchd lft over 2f out: squeezed through and gd hdwy fnl f: gng on wl at fin* **8/1**[3]

01-0 **5** *hd* **Red Somerset (USA)**[9] 197 7-8-7 **77** .... (b[1]) JimmyQuinn 2 81
(R J Hodges) *in tch in 5th: rdn to chse ldrs over 1f out: nt qckn ins fnl f* **16/1**

-244 **6** *nk* **Vhujon (IRE)**[3] 250 5-8-11 **81** .... (p) PaulDoe 1 84
(P D Evans) *bhd: rdn and styd on wl fr over 1f out: nvr nrr* **10/1**

616- **7** *1* **Esprit De Midas**[50] 7639 4-9-4 **88** .... FergusSweeney 8 88
(K A Ryan) *led: rdn over 2f out: hdd and no ex ins fnl f* **16/1**

5-33 **8** ¾ **Tamasou (IRE)**[11] 151 5-8-7 **77** .... HayleyTurner 3 75
(A J McCabe) *prom: rdn over 2f out: wknd over 1f out* **12/1**

033- **9** *shd* **Glow Star (SAF)**[51] 7626 6-9-3 **87** .... (b) GeorgeBaker 9 85
(G L Moore) *mid-div: rdn and no hdwy fnl 2f* **5/1**[1]

40-6 **10** *1 ¼* **Vintage (IRE)**[11] 150 6-8-6 **76** .... ChrisCatlin 11 71
(J Akehurst) *t.k.h: prom tl wknd 1f out* **33/1**

12-4 **11** *shd* **Seek The Fair Land**[11] 150 4-8-10 **83** .... WilliamCarson(3) 6 78+
(J R Boyle) *trckd ldrs: promising effrt whn bdly hmpd and snatched up over 1f out: no room after and nt rcvr: eased* **5/1**[1]

03-3 **12** *nk* **Orpsie Boy (IRE)**[10] 177 7-9-4 **88** .... GrahamGibbons 13 82+
(N P Littmoden) *in tch in 6th: effrt 2f out: n.m.r and wknd over 1f out* **17/2**

5-13 **13** *2 ½* **Indian Skipper (IRE)**[10] 163 5-9-0 **84** .... (be) JimCrowley 12 71+
(R C Guest) *hld up towards rr: promising effrt whn nowhere to go on far rail fr 2f out: nt rcvr: eased* **10/1**

1m 25.53s (-0.47) **Going Correction** -0.05s/f (Stan) **13** Ran SP% **123.0**
Speed ratings (Par 107): **100,99,98,98,98 98,97,96,96,94 94,94,91**
toteswingers:1&2:£12.60, 2&3:£37.10, 1&3:£30.90 CSF £64.05 CT £1350.19 TOTE £9.30: £2.90, £2.70, £11.60; EX 91.00 TRIFECTA Not won..

Owner John Stocker **Bred** Dr D Crone & P Lafarge & P Johnston **Trained** Newmarket, Suffolk

■ Stewards' Enquiry : William Carson one-day ban: careless riding (Feb 7)

FOCUS

A good quality competitive handicap but lots of trouble in running up the inside in the straight. Decent form for the grade, and sound enough.

NOTEBOOK

Autumn Blades(IRE), who won at Lingfield 24 hours earlier, stormed down the middle of the track and fought on gamely to repel the sustained late challenge of Wigram's Turn. He has not been straightforward in the past but he found plenty in front here and appears to be a reformed character nowadays. This was his fourth win in his last six outings and the handicapper can't be too harsh on him given the margin of victory. (op 10-1)

Wigram's Turn(USA) came from well off the pace to make a bold bid and he showed the benefit of his return to action at Lingfield earlier in the month.

Seasider, who hasn't been seen since June, finished strongly from off the pace on his first start for David Simcock and he is a lightly-raced sort this yard could do well with, especially if he can build on this. (op 18-1 tchd 16-1)

Jake The Snake(IRE), also back from a break, attracted support in the market beforehand and was still last approaching the final furlong but he flashed home down the middle of the track and shaped with plenty of promise. (op 14-1)

Red Somerset(USA) didn't improve for first-time blinkers and finds this kind of company is probably a bit too hot nowadays. (op 22-1 tchd 25-1)

Glow Star(SAF) Official explanation: jockey said gelding hung right-handed

Seek The Fair Land ◆, the track record holder, got no sort of run in the straight this time and this is best forgotten. (op 9-2 tchd 11-2)

Orpsie Boy(IRE) was another denied a clear run when trying to pick up. (op 8-1 tchd 15-2)

Indian Skipper(IRE) ◆ also had little room in the straight and couldn't show his best. He can be given another chance. Official explanation: jockey said gelding was denied a clear run (op 12-1)

287 TRY BETDAQ FOR AN EXCHANGE H'CAP 6f (P)
4:35 (4:35) (Class 5) (0-70,70) 4-Y-0+ **£2,590** (£770; £385; £192) **Stalls** High

Form RPR

201- **1** **Sutton Veny (IRE)**[42] 7739 4-9-4 **70** .... AdamKirby 2 82
(J R Gask) *mde all: hrd rdn over 1f out: drvn clr fnl f* **10/1**

/3-2 **2** *1 ¾* **Double Bill (USA)**[16] 78 6-8-10 **62** .... JosedeSouza 7 68
(P F I Cole) *in tch in 6th: hdwy to press wnr 2f out: nt qckn fnl f* **12/1**

23-0 **3** *2 ½* **Perlachy**[10] 172 6-8-11 **66** .... (v) KellyHarrison(3) 8 64
(J R Holt) *chsd ldrs: outpcd over 2f out: kpt on to take mod 3rd over 1f out* **8/1**

102- **4** ¾ **Another Try (IRE)**[36] 7813 5-8-9 **66** .... MatthewDavies(5) 1 62
(A P Jarvis) *dwlt: t.k.h: sn in midfield: racd wd and dropped to rr on bnd hding into st: rdn and styd on appr fnl f* **15/2**

12-0 **5** *hd* **Apache Ridge (IRE)**[9] 192 4-9-4 **70** .... ChrisCatlin 4 65
(K A Ryan) *prom: rdn over 2f out: sn outpcd* **8/1**

26-0 **6** ½ **Titus Gent**[5] 223 5-9-1 **67** .... LukeMorris 5 60
(R A Harris) *mid-div: drvn along over 2f out: styd on same pce* **20/1**

63-4 **7** *1 ¾* **Loyal Royal (IRE)**[5] 223 7-8-7 **62** .... (b) JackDean(3) 11 50
(J M Bradley) *plld hrd in 5th: rdn and outpcd fnl 2f* **7/1**[3]

000- **8** *nk* **Speedy Guru**[42] 7738 4-9-2 **68** .... DaneO'Neill 6 55
(H Candy) *hld up in rr: hdwy and in tch 2f out: wknd over 1f out* **22/1**

12-2 **9** *1 ¼* **Valentino Swing (IRE)**[21] 27 7-8-11 **63** .... HayleyTurner 12 56+
(Miss T Spearing) *towards rr: mod effrt over 2f out: no imp in midfield whn n.m.r ins fnl f* **4/1**[1]

00-0 **10** *2 ¾* **Westwood**[5] 223 5-8-13 **65** .... PaulHanagan 10 39
(D Haydn Jones) *chsd wnr tl over 2f out: sn wknd* **14/1**

60-5 **11** *3 ¾* **Milne Bay (IRE)**[15] 102 5-8-10 **69** .... (t) LauraPike(7) 9 31
(D M Simcock) *dwlt: a bhd* **9/2**[2]

1m 12.09s (-1.01) **Going Correction** -0.05s/f (Stan) **11** Ran SP% **117.2**
Speed ratings (Par 103): **104,101,98,97,97 96,94,93,92,88 83**
toteswingers:1&2:£8.10, 2&3:£12.50, 1&3:£9.70 CSF £123.46 CT £1028.11 TOTE £7.90: £2.50, £2.30, £2.70; EX 57.00 Place 6 £2985.76, Place 5 £1084.65.

Owner The Sutton Veny Syndicate **Bred** Rathbarry Stud **Trained** Sutton Veny, Wilts

FOCUS

There looked to be quite a few pace angles here so it was somewhat surprising that Sutton Veny was allowed the lead to herself. She improved again but the form has not been rated as positively as it could have been as pace held up well through the card.

Loyal Royal(IRE) Official explanation: jockey said gelding ran too free

Valentino Swing(IRE) Official explanation: jockey said gelding was denied a clear run

T/Jkpt: Not won. T/Plt: £602.00 to a £1 stake. Pool: £71,911.92. 87.19 winning tickets. T/Qpdt: £226.50 to a £1 stake. Pool: £5,050.69. 16.50 winning tickets. LM

[264]WOLVERHAMPTON (A.W) (L-H)
Monday, January 25

OFFICIAL GOING: Standard
Wind: Almost nil Weather: Overcast

288 BET AUSTRALIAN OPEN TENNIS - BETDAQ H'CAP 7f 32y(P)
1:45 (1:45) (Class 6) (0-60,64) 3-Y-O **£1,774** (£523; £262) **Stalls** High

Form RPR

40-1 **1** **Marosh (FR)**[8] 213 3-9-10 **64** 6ex .... GrahamGibbons 1 73
(R M H Cowell) *led 1f: a.p: wnt 2nd over 3f out: rdn to ld wl over 1f out: sn edgd lft: r.o wl* **11/10**[1]

0-53 **2** *2 ¾* **Premium Charge**[7] 217 3-8-9 **52** .... AndreaAtzeni(3) 8 53
(C A Dwyer) *t.k.h: led after 1f: rdn and hdd wl over 1f out: one pce fnl f* **13/2**[2]

000- **3** *1 ¾* **Rufus Roughcut**[90] 7098 3-8-5 **45** .... (t) DavidProbert 4 42
(S C Williams) *hld up and bhd: rdn and hdwy over 1f out: kpt on to take 3rd ins fnl f* **20/1**

06-0 **4** ¾ **Sixties Rock**[14] 127 3-9-0 **54** .... ChrisCatlin 9 48
(J A Glover) *hld up in tch: pushed along over 2f out: rdn wl over 1f out: one pce* **11/1**

5 ¾ **Gemma's Delight (IRE)**[59] 7562 3-9-4 **58** .... JoeFanning 2 50
(Noel Lawlor, Ire) *s.i.s: hld up in rr: pushed along and prog wl over 1f out: no imp fnl f* **7/1**[3]

0-35 **6** *2 ¼* **Hathaway (IRE)**[13] 134 3-8-12 **52** .... ShaneKelly 3 38
(W M Brisbourne) *prom: pushed along over 3f out: wknd wl over 1f out* **10/1**

340- **7** *1 ¼* **Better Be Blue (IRE)**[62] 7501 3-8-8 **55** .... KierenFox(7) 6 38
(A W Carroll) *a bhd* **28/1**

2-44 **8** *8* **Clayton Flick (IRE)**[11] 168 3-8-9 **54** .... AmyBaker(5) 5 15
(A B Haynes) *chsd ldr after 1f tl over 3f out: pushed along over 2f out: wknd wl over 1f out* **14/1**

0-10 **F** **Feel The Magic (IRE)**[8] 213 3-8-1 **48** .... (b) MatthewCosham(7) 7 —
(S Kirk) *towards rr: clipped heels and fell wl over 2f out* **20/1**

1m 30.44s (0.84) **Going Correction** +0.225s/f (Slow) **9** Ran SP% **110.5**
Speed ratings (Par 95): **104,100,98,98,97 94,93,84,—**
toteswingers:1&2:£2.40, 2&3:£18.70, 1&3:£8.50 CSF £7.48 CT £81.46 TOTE £1.60: £1.10, £2.20, £5.00; EX 7.00 Trifecta £50.30 Pool: £581.34 - 8.54 winning units..

Owner Le Deauville Racers **Bred** Earl Haras Du Camp Benard **Trained** Six Mile Bottom, Cambs

■ Stewards' Enquiry : Andrea Atzeni two-day ban: careless riding (Feb 9-10)

FOCUS

A really moderate 3-y-o handicap. The form makes sense at face value with the winner building on his latest C/D win.

Gemma's Delight(IRE) Official explanation: jockey said filly reared on leaving stalls

289 WOLVERHAMPTON RACECOURSE - ALL CONFERENCING NEEDS MET (S) STKS 1m 141y(P)
2:20 (2:20) (Class 6) 4-Y-O+ **£1,774** (£523; £262) **Stalls** Low

Form RPR

42-3 **1** **Sir George (IRE)**[16] 105 5-9-0 65 .... BarryMcHugh(5) 2 65
(Ollie Pears) *set stdy pce: qcknd 3f out: rdn and hld on towards fin* **6/5**[1]

630/ **2** *hd* **Kathleen Kennet**[53] 6908 10-8-2 43 .... KierenFox(7) 3 55
(M R Bosley) *hld up in tch: pushed along over 2f out: rdn fnl f: r.o towards fin* **66/1**

50-0 **3** *2* **Woolston Ferry (IRE)**[17] 83 4-8-13 60 .... (p) FergusSweeney 7 55
(David Pinder) *chsd wnr: ev ch over 2f out: rdn wl over 1f out: nt qckn ins fnl f* **4/1**[3]

/41- **4** *1* **Alf Tupper**[128] 6128 7-9-0 67 .... RobertWinston 5 53
(Adrian McGuinness, Ire) *s.i.s: sn prom: rdn over 2f out: one pce ins fnl f* **7/2**[2]

00-5 **5** *2* **Old Romney**[11] 176 6-9-0 60 .... J-PGuillambert 8 48
(P Howling) *hld up: pushed along 3f out: sn btn* **8/1**

000- **6** ¾ **James Pollard (IRE)**[74] 6208 5-9-0 52 .... StephenCraine 4 46
(B J Llewellyn) *hld up in rr: pushed along and struggling wl over 2f out: n.d after* **50/1**

260- **7** *hd* **Mountain Pass (USA)**[208] 3501 8-9-0 52 .... (p) DavidProbert 6 46
(B J Llewellyn) *hld up in rr: rdn and struggling wl over 1f out: n.d after* **12/1**

000- **8** *17* **La Diosa (IRE)**[114] 6497 4-8-8 51 .... ChrisCatlin 1 2
(Mrs S Lamyman) *hld up: pushed along over 3f out: struggling 2f out* **25/1**

1m 53.84s (3.34) **Going Correction** +0.225s/f (Slow)
WFA 4 from 5yo+ 1lb **8** Ran SP% **113.8**
Speed ratings (Par 101): **94,93,92,91,89 88,88,73**
toteswingers:1&2:£8.50, 2&3:£20.90, 1&3:£1.90 CSF £109.37 TOTE £2.10: £1.20, £4.70, £1.60; EX 41.40 Trifecta £409.70 Part won. Pool: £553.71 - 0.88 winning units..There was no bid for the winner.

Owner Ian Bishop **Bred** Bernard Colclough **Trained** Norton, N Yorks

FOCUS

A weak seller run at a steady pace and the time was by far the slowest of three races over the trip. The winner is rated in line with his recent best but the form is far from solid.

290 ENJOY THE LUCKY 7 GROUP OFFER H'CAP (DIV I) 1m 141y(P)
2:55 (2:55) (Class 6) (0-55,55) 4-Y-O+ **£1,433** (£423; £105; £105) **Stalls** Low

Form RPR

366- **1** **The City Kid (IRE)**[26] 7877 7-8-10 **51** .... SaleemGolam 10 57
(G D Blake) *hld up in rr: pushed along over 2f out: hdwy whn nt clr run and swtchd lft wl over 1f out: rdn to ld ins fnl f: drvn out* **6/1**[3]

200- **2** ¾ **Marjury Daw (IRE)**[56] 7600 4-8-12 **54** .... J-PGuillambert 2 58
(J G Given) *hld up in tch on ins: pushed along whn n.m.r over 1f out: rdn to take 2nd wl ins fnl f: kpt on* **17/2**

/00- **3** *1* **Northgate Lodge (USA)**[45] 7718 5-8-5 **46** oh1 .... JoeFanning 1 48
(M Brittain) *led: rdn wl over 1f out: hdd ins fnl f: nt qckn* **12/1**

626- **3** *dht* **Fitzolini**[42] 7755 4-8-13 **55** .... (p) JimmyQuinn 8 57
(A D Brown) *a.p: wnt 2nd 5f out: chal 2f out: rdn and nt qckn ins fnl f* **7/2**[2]

51-0 **5** ¾ **Kielty's Folly**[24] 7 6-8-12 **53** .... TonyCulhane 6 53
(B P J Baugh) *hld up towards rr: stdy hdwy over 2f out: c wd st: rdn and one pce ins fnl f* **3/1**[1]

10-0 **6** *nk* **Climate (IRE)**[14] 131 11-9-0 **55** .... (p) PaulDoe 11 55
(P D Evans) *hld up in rr: pushed along over 2f out: hdwy on ins wl over 1f out: sn rdn: no ex wl ins fnl f* **15/2**

002- **7** ½ **Boy Dancer (IRE)**[62] 7499 7-8-5 **46** oh1 .... (p) ChrisCatlin 7 44
(J J Quinn) *hld up towards rr: pushed along over 2f out: c wd st: rdn over 1f out: nvr nrr* **9/1**

600- 8 nk **Arch Event**[28] 7863 5-8-5 46 oh1 ....(v[1]) LukeMorris 3 44
(A W Carroll) hld up in mid-div: pushed along over 3f out: hdwy over 2f out: rdn wl over 1f out: wknd ins fnl f 66/1

650- 9 3 1/2 **Freya's Flight (IRE)**[29] 7853 4-8-12 54 .... TomEaves 9 44
(K A Ryan) hld up in mid-div: hdwy over 4f out: pushed along over 2f out: rdn wl over 1f out: sn wknd 8/1

0 10 3/4 **Miss Ghena (USA)**[11] 166 4-8-9 51 ....(v[1]) GrahamGibbons 4 39
(D Carroll) chsd ldr to 5f out: rdn whn bmpd jst over 1f out: wknd fnl f 14/1

1m 51.57s (1.07) **Going Correction** +0.225s/f (Slow)
WFA 4 from 5yo+ 1lb 10 Ran SP% 120.8
Speed ratings (Par 101): **104,103,102,102,101 101,101,100,97,97**Place: Northgate Lodge: £2.20 , Fitzolini: £0.70 . Tricast: Tck - Md - Nl: £309.57 , Tck - Md - Fl: £107.36 . Toteswingers: Fl&Md: £4.40, Tck&Fl: £3.40, Md&Tck £12.30, Md&Nl £8.90, Tck&Nl: £10.40. CSF £58.26 TOTE £8.40: £2.40, 3.40, NL£2.20, F£0.70 EX £72.30 Owner Luke McGarrigle: Bred, T B And Mrs T B Russell, Trained, Wendover, Bucks

■ Stewards' Enquiry : Saleem Golam two-day ban: careless riding (Feb 8-9)

FOCUS
A very moderate handicap run in a time 0.16 seconds slower than the second division. The form is rated around the winner. A first winner in Britain for South African trainer Gavin Blake.

291 NAME A RACE TO ENHANCE YOUR BRAND MAIDEN STKS 1m 1f 103y(P)
3:30 (3:30) (Class 5) 4-Y-0+ £2,456 (£725; £362) Stalls Low

Form RPR

5- 1 **Zerzura**[26] 7882 4-9-3 0 .... TomQueally 7 76+
(H R A Cecil) sn led: pushed clr over 1f out: edgd lft and rdn ins fnl f: r.o 10/3[2]

025- 2 1/2 **Capeability (IRE)**[53] 7620 4-9-3 70 .... ChrisCatlin 6 72
(M R Channon) hld up in tch: pushed along wl over 1f out: rdn to take 2nd wl ins fnl f: nt rch wnr 9/4[1]

402- 3 1/2 **Peace Corps**[45] 3279 4-9-3 71 ....(v) AdamKirby 9 71
(J R Fanshawe) chsd wnr to 5f out: regained 2nd 3f out: sn rdn: lost 2nd wl ins fnl f: kpt on 9/2[3]

55- 4 3 1/4 **Mydy Easy (USA)**[111] 6573 4-9-3 0 .... JackMitchell 1 64
(P W Chapple-Hyam) hld up towards rr: rdn and c wd st: kpt on same pce fnl f: n.d 12/1

624- 5 4 1/2 **Barbarian**[28] 7863 4-9-3 61 ....(v) GrahamGibbons 2 55
(A D Brown) led early: prom: pushed along over 3f out: rdn and wknd wl over 1f out 8/1

43-5 6 3 3/4 **Ryker (IRE)**[14] 131 4-9-3 57 .... HayleyTurner 5 47
(J W Hills) hld up towards rr: pushed along over 2f out: sn struggling 13/2

0/0- 7 7 **Fiveonthreeforjd**[44] 7723 5-9-1 0 .... KellyHarrison(3) 4 32
(W J H Ratcliffe) t.k.h early in rr: no ch fnl 2f 66/1

0- 8 39 **Melting Bob (USA)**[36] 7826 4-8-12 0 .... ShaneKelly 3 —
(Dr J D Scargill) hld up in tch: chsd wnr 5f out tl pushed along 3f out: sn wknd: t.o 7/1

2m 3.07s (1.37) **Going Correction** +0.225s/f (Slow)
WFA 4 from 5yo 1lb 8 Ran SP% 118.2
Speed ratings (Par 103): **102,101,101,98,94 90,84,50**
toteswingers:1&2:£3.10, 2&3:£2.60, 1&3:£4.40 CSF £11.73 TOTE £4.40: £1.10, £1.40, £2.00; EX 14.20 Trifecta £50.30 Pool: £308.66 - 4.54 winning units..
Owner Robert Brown & Partners **Bred** Mrs James Wigan **Trained** Newmarket, Suffolk

FOCUS
The time wasn't bad - 1.09 seconds quicker than a later handicap won by the 64-rated Hannicean - but this was an ordinary maiden and the runner-up is probably the best guide to the form. The winner looked a bit better than the bare form.
Melting Bob(USA) Official explanation: jockey said bit pulled through filly's mouth

292 BET IN RUNNING - BETDAQ H'CAP 7f 32y(P)
4:05 (4:06) (Class 4) (0-80,80) 4-Y-0+ £4,209 (£1,252; £625; £312) Stalls High

Form RPR

210- 1 **Steel Stockholder**[44] 7729 4-8-4 66 oh1 .... JimmyQuinn 1 74
(M Brittain) a.p: pushed along 2f out: rdn to ld 1f out: sn edgd rt: drvn out 12/1

505- 2 1 1/4 **Ektimaal**[35] 7832 7-9-4 80 .... PaulHanagan 6 85
(E A L Dunlop) led: hdd 1f out: sn rdn: nt qckn wl ins fnl f 5/1[3]

2-13 3 nk **Rubenstar (IRE)**[3] 259 7-8-9 71 .... StephenCraine 4 75+
(Patrick Morris) hld up: smooth hdwy over 2f out: swtchd lft wl ins fnl f: rdn and nt qckn 4/1[2]

0-50 4 1 1/4 **Little Pete (IRE)**[4] 250 5-9-4 80 .... AdamKirby 3 81
(I W McInnes) hld up: prog wl over 1f out: rdn and one pce fnl f 12/1

166- 5 1/2 **Hellbender (IRE)**[53] 7617 4-9-1 77 .... DavidProbert 2 76+
(S Kirk) hld up in rr: rdn and edgd rt over 1f out: nvr nrr 5/1[3]

65-3 6 nk **Carnivore**[12] 150 8-9-2 78 .... JimCrowley 7 76
(T D Barron) hld up in tch: wnt 2nd over 3f out: rdn over 1f out: one pce 7/2[1]

/02- 7 2 1/2 **Monsieur Fillioux (USA)**[35] 7830 4-8-13 75 .... HayleyTurner 5 67
(J R Fanshawe) hld up in rr: pushed along over 2f out: no rspnse 7/2[1]

00-0 8 13 **Orpen Wide (IRE)**[4] 245 8-8-8 77 ....(b) DavidKenny(7) 8 34
(M C Chapman) hld up in tch: wknd wl over 2f out 50/1

1m 29.9s (0.30) **Going Correction** +0.225s/f (Slow) 8 Ran SP% 115.1
Speed ratings (Par 105): **107,105,105,103,103 102,100,85**
toteswingers:1&2:£8.00, 2&3:£8.10, 1&3:£4.50 CSF £71.07 CT £289.55 TOTE £15.30: £3.30, £2.20, £1.50; EX 66.20 Trifecta £487.70 Part won. Pool: £659.121 - 0.74 winning units..
Owner Mel Brittain **Bred** Mrs Joan M Langmead **Trained** Warthill, N Yorks

FOCUS
A fair handicap, but another steadily run race with the first two always prominent. The form has been rated at face value.
Little Pete(IRE) Official explanation: jockey said gelding hung badly right-handed from 3f out

293 DINE IN THE HORIZONS RESTAURANT H'CAP 1m 5f 194y(P)
4:40 (4:41) (Class 5) (0-70,69) 4-Y-0+ £2,456 (£725; £362) Stalls Low

Form RPR

322- 1 **Augustus John (IRE)**[39] 7785 7-9-4 65 .... TomEaves 3 73
(R Brotherton) hld up: hdwy 5f out: led 4f out to 2f out: sn rdn: rallied to ld wl ins fnl f: styd on 4/1[2]

23-1 2 1 1/4 **Leyte Gulf (USA)**[11] 173 7-9-6 67 .... DaneO'Neill 4 73+
(C C Bealby) s.i.s: hld up: smooth prog on ins over 2f out: led jst over 1f out: sn rdn: hdd wl ins fnl f: no ex 7/4[1]

50-3 3 3/4 **Quince (IRE)**[12] 148 7-9-4 65 ....(v) SaleemGolam 7 70
(J Pearce) hld up and bhd: pushed along 3f out: hdwy over 1f out: styd on u.p to take 3rd wl ins fnl f: nt rch ldng pair 8/1

630- 4 3/4 **Weybridge Light**[46] 7701 5-9-1 62 .... FergusSweeney 5 66
(M R Bosley) set slow pce: hdd after 4f: chsd ldr: led over 5f out to 4f out: pushed along over 3f out: styd on same pce fnl f 6/1[3]

/0-5 5 1 **Estate**[11] 173 8-9-5 66 .... ChrisCatlin 2 69
(D E Pipe) sn stdd towards rr: pushed along over 2f out: rdn and sme prog on ins wl over 1f out: one pce fnl f 9/1

004- 6 nk **Paint The Town Red**[66] 7461 5-8-10 57 .... JackMitchell 1 59
(H J Collingridge) prom: led after 4f tl over 5f out: led 2f out: sn rdn: hdd jst over 1f out: wknd ins fnl f 13/2

42-3 7 hd **Little Richard (IRE)**[23] 13 11-8-9 56 ....(p) LiamJones 8 58
(M Wellings) prom: pushed along over 2f out: rdn over 1f out: one pce 14/1

415/ 8 6 **Tannenberg (IRE)**[1334] 2176 9-9-3 69 .... AndrewHeffernan(5) 6 62
(A W Carroll) hld up in rr: pushed along over 3f out: struggling 2f out 12/1

3m 18.45s (12.45) **Going Correction** +0.225s/f (Slow) 8 Ran SP% 119.5
Speed ratings (Par 103): **73,72,71,71,70 70,70,67**
toteswingers:1&2:£13.30, 2&3:£6.30, 1&3:£8.10 CSF £12.02 CT £54.41 TOTE £5.10: £1.60, £1.80, £2.10; EX 11.00 Trifecta £78.80 Pool: £652.80 - 6.13 winning units..
Owner Arthur Clayton **Bred** Rizerie Syndicate **Trained** Elmley Castle, Worcs

FOCUS
They went a very steady pace until the final half mile, resulting in a time over 18 seconds above standard, and this is form to treat with caution.

294 BET MULTIPLES - BETDAQ H'CAP 1m 1f 103y(P)
5:10 (5:10) (Class 5) (0-75,75) 4-Y-0+ £2,456 (£725; £362) Stalls Low

Form RPR

000- 1 **Hannicean**[70] 7416 6-8-9 64 .... StevieDonohoe 3 72
(Ian Williams) hld up in mid-div: hdwy over 1f out: rdn to ld last stride 12/1

06-0 2 shd **Alqaahir (USA)**[9] 202 8-8-13 68 .... TomQueally 2 76
(P Burgoyne) hld up in tch on ins: plld out ent st: led ins fnl f: hdd last stride 7/1

62-2 3 2 **New Star (UAE)**[11] 176 6-9-5 74 .... ShaneKelly 10 78
(W M Brisbourne) a.p: slt ld over 2f out: hdd wl over 1f out: rdn and one pce ins fnl f 7/2[1]

166- 4 1 **King Of Connacht**[28] 7856 7-8-5 60 oh2 ....(v) LiamJones 8 62
(M Wellings) hld up in rr: c v wd st: rdn and r.o ins fnl f: edgd lft: tk 4th nr fin 8/1

230- 5 hd **Bid For Glory**[108] 6640 6-8-13 68 ....(v) JimmyQuinn 9 69
(H J Collingridge) hld up in rr: effrt on ins wl over 1f out: rdn and kpt on towards fin: n.d 13/2[3]

63-4 6 shd **Such Optimism**[12] 148 4-9-5 75 .... JimCrowley 1 76
(R M Beckett) led: hung rt and hdd over 2f out: rdn to ld wl over 1f out: hdd ins fnl f: wknd 9/2[2]

10/0 7 1/2 **Grit (IRE)**[17] 83 5-8-8 63 .... DavidProbert 6 63
(B G Powell) hld up towards rr: pushed along and prog over 2f out: rdn and wknd wl over 1f out 14/1

320- 8 1 3/4 **New Beginning (IRE)**[271] 1615 6-8-11 66 .... RobertWinston 5 62
(Mrs S Lamyman) chsd ldr: pushed along and ev ch over 2f out: wknd wl over 1f out 20/1

360- 9 1 **All About You (IRE)**[60] 7534 4-9-4 74 .... J-PGuillambert 7 68
(P Howling) hld up in mid-div: pushed along over 2f out: wknd wl over 1f out 16/1

4- 10 10 **Monreale (GER)**[82] 7248 6-9-1 70 .... ChrisCatlin 4 43
(D E Pipe) hld up towards rr: pushed along over 2f out: sn struggling 8/1

2m 4.16s (2.46) **Going Correction** +0.225s/f (Slow)
WFA 4 from 5yo+ 1lb 10 Ran SP% 113.5
Speed ratings (Par 103): **98,97,96,95,95 94,94,92,92,83**
toteswingers:1&2:£23.00, 2&3:£9.00, 1&3:£12.90 CSF £90.85 CT £358.17 TOTE £19.10: £4.90, £2.50, £1.30; EX 160.50 Trifecta £309.00 Pool: £517.801 - 1.24 winning units..
Owner Ian Williams **Bred** Derek R Price **Trained** Portway, Worcs

FOCUS
A fair handicap, but the pace was just steady through the early stages and time was 1.09 seconds slower than the earlier 4-y-o-plus maiden won by Zerzura. The race has been rated at face value but it might pay not to take the form too literally.

295 ENJOY THE LUCKY 7 GROUP OFFER H'CAP (DIV II) 1m 141y(P)
5:40 (5:40) (Class 6) (0-55,55) 4-Y-0+ £1,433 (£423; £211) Stalls Low

Form RPR

44-0 1 **Head First**[14] 131 4-8-13 54 .... DavidProbert 9 64
(W Jarvis) hld up towards rr: hdwy over 2f out: rdn to ld over 1f out: drvn out 3/1[2]

6-02 2 2 **Great Bounder (CAN)**[4] 248 4-9-0 55 .... TomQueally 6 60
(A B Haynes) a.p: wnt 2nd over 6f out: led wl over 2f out: rdn and hdd over 1f out: nt qckn 11/4[1]

05-5 3 1 1/4 **Fitzwarren**[16] 99 9-8-5 45 ....(tp) JimmyQuinn 1 47
(A D Brown) hld up: hdwy over 1f out: rdn and one pce ins fnl f 16/1

500- 4 1 **Naledi**[214] 3322 6-8-0 45 .... AndrewHeffernan(5) 3 45
(R J Price) hld up: pushed along over 3f out: rdn and hdwy over 1f out: one pce ins fnl f 40/1

2-33 5 2 3/4 **Join Up**[14] 124 4-8-7 53 .... RossAtkinson(5) 10 47
(W M Brisbourne) hld up: pushed along and hdwy on outside over 2f out: c wd st: rdn and edgd lft over 1f out: wknd ins fnl f 11/4[1]

00-2 6 shd **The Graig**[21] 36 6-9-0 54 ....(t) JerryO'Dwyer 11 47
(J R Holt) hld up: hdwy on outside over 6f out: chsd ldr 2f out: sn rdn: lost 2nd over 1f out: wknd ins fnl f 7/1[3]

00-0 7 1 3/4 **Bet Noir (IRE)**[23] 13 5-8-5 45 .... LukeMorris 2 34
(A W Carroll) led early: prom on ins rdn and wknd 2f out 20/1

/00- 8 1 3/4 **Sofonisba**[252] 2143 4-8-7 51 .... AndreaAtzeni(3) 7 36
(M Botti) hld up in tch: pushed along over 2f out: wknd over 1f out 16/1

000- 9 4 1/2 **Mays Louise**[228] 2843 6-8-5 45 .... LiamJones 8 20
(B P J Baugh) a in rr 40/1

0-00 10 4 1/2 **Admirals Way**[10] 193 5-8-10 50 .... ChrisCatlin 5 15
(C N Kellett) sn led: hdd wl over 2f out: wknd wl over 1f out 33/1

1m 51.41s (0.91) **Going Correction** +0.225s/f (Slow)
WFA 4 from 5yo+ 1lb 10 Ran SP% 115.2
Speed ratings (Par 101): **104,102,101,100,97 97,96,94,90,86**
toteswingers:1&2:£4.10, 2&3:£9.80, 1&3:£8.30 CSF £11.06 CT £110.33 TOTE £3.80: £1.80, £2.00, £4.80; EX 12.60 Trifecta £106.60 Pool: £625.35 - 4.34 winning units. Place 6 £19.96, Place 5 £14.03.
Owner Mrs Jo Reffo **Bred** Amethyst Stud **Trained** Newmarket, Suffolk

FOCUS
This moderate handicap was run in a time slightly quicker than the first division but the pace was still pretty steady. Ordinary form for the grade but the winner may do better.
T/Jkpt: £67,397.30 to a £1 stake. Pool: £142,388.84. 1.50 winning tickets. T/Plt: £14.80 to a £1 stake. Pool: £59,522.28. 2,927.43 winning tickets. T/Qpdt: £9.70 to a £1 stake. Pool: £4,635.46. 351.00 winning tickets. KH

243 SOUTHWELL (L-H)

Tuesday, January 26

OFFICIAL GOING: Standard

Wind: Light half against Weather: Overcast and dry

296 BETDAQ ON 0870 178 1221 H'CAP 6f (F)

1:20 (1:21) (Class 6) (0-55,55) 4-Y-0+ £1,774 (£523; £262) Stalls Low

Form				RPR
0-26	1		**Whatyouwoodwishfor (USA)**[6] 242 4-9-0 **55**..........(b) PaulHanagan 5 (R A Fahey) *mde all: rdn along 2f out: drvn over 1f out: kpt on strly ins fnl f* **14/1**	67
103-	2	1	**Fuzzy Cat**[36] 7835 4-8-7 **53**.......... DeanHeslop(5) 4 (T D Barron) *wnt rt s: trckd ldrs: swtchd rt and effrt 2f out: rdn to chse wnr over 1f out: sn drvn and kpt on same pce ins fnl f* **11/4**[1]	62
00-5	3	¾	**Fulford**[19] 69 5-8-5 **46** oh1.......... JimmyQuinn 10 (M Brittain) *in tch: hdwy to chse ldrs 2f out and sn rdn: drvn and kpt on ins fnl f: nrst fin* **20/1**	53+
30-2	4	hd	**Cheery Cat (USA)**[16] 116 6-8-4 **52**..........(p) DavidKenny(7) 8 (J Balding) *prom: rdn along 2f out: drvn and one pce ent fnl f* **11/1**	58
1-62	5	¾	**Hard Ball**[4] 270 4-8-10 **51**..........(v) FrannyNorton 7 (M Quinn) *prom: rdn along and ev ch 2f out: sn drvn and one pce appr fnl f* **11/2**[2]	55
340-	6	2	**Dualagi**[97] 6933 6-8-8 **54**.......... BarryMcHugh(5) 12 (M R Bosley) *in rr: hdwy 2f out: sn rdn and styd on appr fnl f: nrst fin* **14/1**	51
4-44	7	nk	**Kinigi (IRE)**[6] 235 4-8-8 **54**..........(p) AndrewHeffernan(5) 6 (R A Harris) *midfield: hdwy and in tch over 2f out: sn rdn and no imp* **7/1**[3]	50
60-2	8	4 ½	**Dickie Le Davoir**[5] 243 6-8-8 **54**..........(be) BillyCray(5) 1 (R C Guest) *dwlt and in rr tl sme late hdwy* **7/1**[3]	36
-063	9	¾	**Mickys Mate**[16] 116 5-7-12 **46** oh1.......... NathanAlison(7) 3 (S A Harris) *midfield: hung lft and hmpd bnd after 2f: bhd after* **40/1**	25
0120	10	1 ½	**Brazilian Brush (IRE)**[13] 146 5-9-0 **55**..........(bt) LukeMorris 11 (J M Bradley) *chsd ldrs on outer: rdn along 1/2-way: sn edgd lft and wknd* **10/1**	30
500-	11	2 ½	**Sirjosh**[147] 5549 4-8-7 **51**.......... AndreaAtzeni(3) 13 (D Donovan) *a towards rr* **22/1**	18
-320	12	½	**Tango Step (IRE)**[4] 264 10-7-13 **47**.......... NeilFarley(7) 2 (D Carroll) *midfield on inner whn hmpd bnd after 2f: no ch after* **40/1**	12
256/	13	18	**Mister Beano (IRE)**[761] 7245 5-9-0 **55**.......... RobertWinston 9 (R J Price) *dwlt: a bhd* **25/1**	—

1m 15.48s (-1.02) **Going Correction** -0.175s/f (Stan) 13 Ran SP% **115.6**

Speed ratings (Par 101): **99,97,96,96,95 92,92,86,85,83 80,79,55**

toteswingers: 1&2 £6.30, 1&3 £39.10, 2&3 £16.60 CSF £47.52 CT £809.75 TOTE £16.30: £4.00, £1.40, £5.20; EX 55.60 TRIFECTA Not won..

Owner Mel Roberts & Ms Nicola Meese 1 **Bred** Manganaro Llc **Trained** Musley Bank, N Yorks

■ Stewards' Enquiry : Nathan Alison caution: careless riding

FOCUS

A couple of the jockeys felt the surface was riding fast. Just a moderate sprint handicap in which it proved difficult to make up ground. Whatyouwoodwishfor, who returned to form, was the first of five winners on the card to make all.

Tango Step(IRE) Official explanation: jockey said gelding suffered interference in running

297 BACK AND LAY AT BETDAQ (S) STKS 7f (F)

1:50 (1:52) (Class 6) 4-Y-0+ £1,774 (£523; £262) Stalls Low

Form				RPR
0-06	1		**Madison Belle**[12] 170 4-8-6 65.......... MartinLane(3) 9 (J R Weymes) *mde all: rdn 2f out: drvn ent fnl f: kpt on gamely* **9/2**[3]	57
60-3	2	¾	**Kings Ace (IRE)**[11] 187 4-8-9 55..........(vt) BillyCray(5) 3 (A Berry) *t.k.h early: hld up in tch: hdwy wl over 2f out: swtchd lftn and rdn to chse wnr over 1f out: drvn and kpt on ins fnl f* **6/1**	60
051-	3	nk	**Convince (USA)**[45] 7726 9-9-0 59..........(p) RossAtkinson(5) 10 (J L Flint) *chsd ldrs on outer: hung lft on home turn and sn rdn: drvn over 1f out: kpt on ins fnl f* **11/4**[1]	64
0-40	4	3 ¼	**Boss Hog**[14] 144 5-9-0 55.......... TonyCulhane 7 (P T Midgley) *trckd wnr: effrt over 2f out: rdn along wl over 1f out: drvn and wknd appr fnl f* **3/1**[2]	50
103/	5	hd	**Miss Xu Xia**[390] 5 4-8-9 54..........(p) JimmyQuinn 8 (G R Oldroyd) *midfield: hdwy to chse ldrs over 2f out: drvn wl over 1f out: kpt on same pce* **16/1**	45
0-46	6	¾	**Sairaam (IRE)**[7] 227 4-8-6 47.......... AndreaAtzeni(3) 4 (C Smith) *midfield on inner: swtchd rt and hdwy 2f out: sn rdn and kpt on appr fnl f: nt rch ldrs* **10/1**	43
-605	7	5	**Favouring (IRE)**[11] 187 8-8-9 45..........(v) DeclanCannon(5) 6 (M C Chapman) *nvr nr ldrs* **66/1**	34
060-	8	8	**Electric Warrior (IRE)**[29] 7858 7-8-9 58..........(p) BarryMcHugh(5) 2 (C R Dore) *chsd ldrs: rdn along 3f out: sn wknd* **13/2**	13
00-0	9	4	**Owed**[11] 187 8-9-4 45 ow11..........(tp) TanyaRedden(7) 1 (R Bastiman) *prom on inner: rdn along 1/2-way: sn wknd* **100/1**	13
3/0-	10	¾	**Lady Kingston**[305] 982 4-8-9 0.......... AndrewElliott 5 (J R Weymes) *a in rr* **66/1**	—

1m 29.11s (-1.19) **Going Correction** -0.175s/f (Stan) 10 Ran SP% **116.4**

Speed ratings (Par 101): **99,98,97,94,93 93,87,78,73,72**

toteswingers: 1&2 £6.60, 1&3 £5.50, 2&3 £3.90 CSF £31.59 TOTE £5.50: £1.80, £1.90, £1.40; EX 45.30 Trifecta £189.10 Pool: £360.33 - 1.41 winning units..The winner was bought in for 3,250gns.

Owner Mrs Elaine M Burke **Bred** Paul Sweeting **Trained** Middleham Moor, N Yorks

FOCUS

An ordinary seller, and just as in the opener, the winner made just about all. Sound form, the winner not needing to match her recent handicap efforts.

298 BETDAQ POKER H'CAP 1m (F)

2:20 (2:20) (Class 6) (0-65,65) 4-Y-0+ £1,774 (£523; £262) Stalls Low

Form				RPR
-344	1		**General Tufto**[5] 245 5-9-0 **64**..........(b) AndreaAtzeni(3) 1 (C Smith) *in tch: hdwy on outer 3df out: rdn to chal over 1f out: edgd lft ins fnl f: styd on to ld last 50yds* **9/1**	73
25-0	2	hd	**Hypnotic Gaze (IRE)**[14] 144 4-9-4 **65**..........(p) JoeFanning 2 (J Mackie) *in tch: hdwy over 3f out: rdn to ld wl over 1f out: drvn ent fnl f: sn edgd lft: hdd and no ex last 50yds* **7/1**[3]	74
13-1	3	3 ¾	**Bestowed**[19] 75 5-8-10 **62**..........(v) AndrewHeffernan(5) 6 (P D Evans) *chsd ldrs: hdwy to ld 3f out: rdn over 2f out: hdd and drvn wl over 1f out: kpt on same pce appr fnl f* **11/4**[2]	62
2-62	4	2 ¾	**Ten Pole Tudor**[15] 126 5-8-11 **58**..........(p) LiamJones 4 (R A Harris) *led: rdn along 1/2-way: hdd 3f out: drvn over 2f out and grad wknd* **33/1**	52
04-5	5	½	**West End Lad**[21] 40 7-9-4 **65**.......... RobertWinston 3 (S R Bowring) *chsd ldrs on inner: rdn along wl over 2f out: drvn wl over 1f out: sn one pce* **25/1**	57
40-2	6	2 ¾	**Magnitude**[17] 105 5-9-2 **63**.......... ChrisCatlin 10 (C C Bealby) *bhd tl sme late hdwy* **8/1**	49
16-1	7	¾	**Hit The Switch**[21] 40 4-8-12 **64**..........(p) JamesSullivan(5) 5 (Patrick Morris) *in rr: rdn along over 4f out: nvr a factor* **8/1**	48
005-	8	8	**Provost**[30] 7855 6-8-11 **58**.......... PhillipMakin 9 (M W Easterby) *sn rdn along and a towards rr: fin 8th, subs disq.* **2/1**[1]	24
-435	9	1 ½	**Vogarth**[14] 144 6-8-7 **59**..........(v) DeclanCannon(5) 8 (M C Chapman) *cl up: rdn along over 3f out and sn wknd* **22/1**	22
035-	10	10	**Noble Attitude**[178] 4531 4-8-12 **59**.......... FrannyNorton 7 (M Quinn) *chsd ldrs on outer: rdn along after 3f: sn lost pl and bhd* **50/1**	—

1m 41.11s (-2.59) **Going Correction** -0.175s/f (Stan) 10 Ran SP% **117.8**

Speed ratings (Par 101): **105,104,101,98,97 95,94,86,84,74**

toteswingers: 1&2 £10.60, 1&3 £5.80, 2&3 £6.30 CSF £68.11 CT £227.93 TOTE £11.80: £2.60, £2.50, £1.10; EX 107.80 Trifecta £472.90 Part won. Pool: £639.14 - 0.44 winning units..

Owner Phil Martin & Trev Sleath **Bred** Hascombe And Valiant Studs **Trained** Temple Bruer, Lincs

FOCUS

A modest handicap. The pace looked a bit overstrong but the form is rated at face value with the front pair back to their best marks.

Provost Official explanation: jockey said gelding never travelled

299 PLAY GOLF AT SOUTHWELL GOLF CLUB H'CAP 6f (F)

2:50 (2:51) (Class 2) (0-100,100) 4-Y-0+ £10,361 (£3,083; £1,540; £769) Stalls Low

Form				RPR
34-1	1		**Tourist**[12] 177 5-8-4 **86** oh1.......... JimmyQuinn 6 (D Shaw) *hld up towards rr: smooth hdwy to trck ldrs 1/2-way: rdn to ld over 1f out: kpt on strly u.p ins fnl f* **6/1**	97+
11-6	2	1 ½	**Imprimis Tagula (IRE)**[17] 108 6-9-2 **98**..........(v) RobertWinston 9 (A Bailey) *chsd ldrs: hdwy on outer over 2f out: rdn and ev ch appr last: sn drvn and edgd lft: kpt on same pce* **11/4**[1]	104
23-2	3	1	**Nightjar (USA)**[25] 6 5-8-13 **95**..........(b[1]) TomEaves 8 (K A Ryan) *in tch: hdwy to chse ldrs over 2f out: rdn and n.m.r over 1f out: swtchd rt ins fnl f and kpt on wl towards fin* **11/2**[3]	98+
-203	4	nk	**Bel Cantor**[5] 250 7-8-1 **86** oh7..........(p) KellyHarrison(3) 3 (W J H Ratcliffe) *cl up: led 1/2-way: rdn along 2f out: drvn and hdd over 1f out: wknd ins fnl f* **18/1**	88
000-	5	5	**Luscivious**[119] 6359 6-8-6 **88**..........(p) ChrisCatlin 7 (J A Glover) *prom: rdn along 3f out: drvn and grad wknd fnl 2f* **33/1**	74
4-02	6	3	**Flowing Cape (IRE)**[12] 177 5-8-4 **91**..........(t) PaulPickard(5) 2 (R Hollinshead) *cl up: rdn along wl over 2f out: sn drvn and wknd* **11/1**	67
122-	7	2 ½	**Ingleby Arch (USA)**[35] 7837 7-8-11 **93**.......... PhillipMakin 4 (T D Barron) *in tch: pushed along 1/2-way: sn rdn and wknd over 2f out* **10/3**[2]	61
2253	8	2	**Aeroplane**[3] 278 7-9-4 **100**..........(p) PaulDoe 5 (P D Evans) *sn rdn along and a in rr* **11/2**[3]	62
000-	9	½	**Smokey Ryder**[29] 7862 4-8-8 **90**.......... KevinGhunowa 1 (R A Harris) *slt ld on inner: rdn along and hdd 1/2-way: sn wknd* **50/1**	50

1m 14.11s (-2.39) **Going Correction** -0.175s/f (Stan) 9 Ran SP% **113.3**

Speed ratings (Par 109): **108,106,104,104,97 93,90,87,86**

toteswingers: 1&2 £5.70, 2&3 £5.60, 1&3 not won. CSF £22.39 CT £95.19 TOTE £6.20: £2.20, £1.60, £2.10; EX 24.10 Trifecta £143.80 Pool: £802.76 - 4.13 winning units..

Owner M Shirley **Bred** Juddmonte Farms Ltd **Trained** Sproxton, Leics

FOCUS

A cracking sprint handicap. A clear personal best from Tourist, and solid form apart from the proximity of the fourth.

NOTEBOOK

Tourist ◆ is now unbeaten in three races over 6f, and this success proved his effectiveness on Fibresand in no uncertain terms. Racing off a career-high mark, having been raised 4lb for his recent Wolverhampton win, he was always cruising in behind the leaders and found plenty in the straight. He's progressing into a very useful type. (op 8-1)

Imprimis Tagula(IRE) ◆ ran a massive race in defeat considering he was stuck at least five-wide throughout, with stall nine proving a real handicap. He might even have won granted a better trip, considering how much ground he conceded, and he can now be described as a smart performer. If he continues to progress, it won't be long before his connections can consider chasing decent prize money abroad. (op 3-1tchd 10-3 in a place)

Nightjar(USA) ◆ was an interesting contender with blinkers on for the first time, but he didn't enjoy the clearest of runs in the straight and got going too late after having to be switched wide late on. He never looked totally at ease under pressure, perhaps not facing the kickback, but the impression was that he will be worth another try in blinkers back over another furlong. (op 9-2)

Bel Cantor, with cheekpieces back on, ran a big race from 7lb out of the handicap. He's useful on his day and doesn't look flattered. (op 16-1 tchd 20-1)

Luscivious's trainer felt that he might need it after four months off, so he ran creditably in the circumstances. (op 28-1)

Flowing Cape(IRE) had been well beaten on his two previous tries on Fibresand, albeit without the tongue-tie he wears now, and it seems this surface isn't for him. (op 8-1)

Ingleby Arch(USA) was struggling from a long way out, but he's worth keeping in mind. If the handicapper eases him 3lb, he will be eligible for a 76-90 back over C&D in February, a race he's won for the last two years. (tchd 7-2)

Aeroplane didn't seem to take to Fibresand, but then this was his sixth run of the month and his third start in five days. Official explanation: jockey said horse was unsuited by the Fibresand (op 7-1)

300 FREEBETS.CO.UK FREE BETS H'CAP 1m 4f (F)

3:20 (3:20) (Class 4) (0-85,84) 4-Y-0+ £4,209 (£1,252; £625; £312) Stalls Low

Form				RPR
111-	1		**Shadows Lengthen**[46] 7712 4-9-1 **84**..........(b) JamesSullivan(5) 1 (M W Easterby) *t.k.h early: mde all: qcknd over 3f out: pushed along over 1f out: styd on strly ins fnl f: comf* **11/4**[1]	96+
343-	2	3 ¼	**Kingsdale Orion (IRE)**[143] 5671 6-8-9 **74**.......... BarryMcHugh(5) 4 (B Ellison) *hld up in tch: hdwy over 3f out: rdn along and sltly outpcd wl over 1f out: sn drvn and kpt on ins fnl f* **7/1**	80
612-	3	1	**Profit's Reality (IRE)**[35] 7841 8-9-8 **82**.......... LukeMorris 2 (M J Attwater) *trckd ldng pair hdwy on outer to chse wnr over 2f out and sn rdn: drvn over 1f out: kpt on same pce ins fnl f* **5/1**[2]	86
01-5	4	hd	**I'm In The Pink (FR)**[8] 220 6-9-1 **75**.......... PaulHanagan 3 (P D Evans) *trckd ldng pair: effrt 4f out: rdn along over 2f out: drvn wl over 1f out: kpt on same pce* **13/2**	79
501-	5	½	**Trachonitis (IRE)**[30] 7851 6-9-3 **77**.......... ShaneKelly 5 (J R Jenkins) *hld up in rr: swtchd ins and hdwy over 2f out: rdn wl over 1f out: drvn and one pce ent fnl f* **6/1**[3]	80

00-2 6 5 **My Friend Fritz**[25] 3 10-8-8 **68** ChrisCatlin 6 63
(P W Hiatt) *trckd wnr: effrt and cl up 4f out: rdn along 3f out: drvn over 2f out and sn wknd* **11/4**[1]

2m 38.74s (-2.26) **Going Correction** -0.175s/f (Stan)
WFA 4 from 6yo+ 4lb **6** Ran SP% **110.1**
Speed ratings (Par 105): **100,97,97,97,96 93**
toteswingers: 1&2 £4.30, 1&3 £2.20, 2&3 £4.10 CSF £21.31 TOTE £3.10: £1.50, £2.80; EX 22.20.
Owner T A F Frost **Bred** London Thoroughbred Services Ltd **Trained** Sheriff Hutton, N Yorks

FOCUS
This looked a fair race for the grade. Another clear best from the winner, and although he made all on a card that favoured front runners the form has been rated at face value.

301 WIN WHATEVER THE RESULT WITH BET ANGEL MAIDEN STKS 6f (F)
3:50 (3:50) (Class 5) 3-Y-0+ **£2,456** (£725; £362) **Stalls** Low

Form RPR
230- 1 **Ghazwah**[88] 7145 3-8-6 72 PaulHanagan 1 78
(R A Fahey) *mde all: rdn along wl over 2f out: kpt on u.p ins fnl f* **8/11**[1]
2- 2 2 ¼ **Bandstand**[30] 7853 4-9-13 0 TomEaves 4 80
(B Smart) *t.k.h: trckd ldrs: hdwy over 2f out and sn chsng wnr: rdn and hung lft ent fnl f: sn one pce* **9/4**[2]
0- 3 7 **Turning Circle**[50] 7671 4-9-6 0 JohnCavanagh(7) 6 58
(M Brittain) *t.k.h: cl up on outer: rdn to chse wnr over 2f out: drvn wl over 1f out and wknd appr fnl f* **25/1**
4 1 ¼ **Fine And Dandie (IRE)** 3-8-11 0 AndrewMullen 2 50
(D Nicholls) *t.k.h early: chsd ldrs: rdn along on inner wl over 2f out: sn one pce* **10/1**[3]
0-3 5 1 **Apache Moon**[13] 147 4-9-13 0 TonyCulhane 5 50
(R Curtis) *chsd wnr: rdn along and hung lft over 2f out: sn wknd* **16/1**
000- 6 3 ¼ **Cruise Control**[123] 6255 4-9-13 42 RobertWinston 3 40
(R J Price) *a in rr* **150/1**
00- 7 3 **Isle Of Ellis (IRE)**[285] 1312 3-8-11 0 ChrisCatlin 7 26
(J A Glover) *a towards rr* **80/1**

1m 14.89s (-1.61) **Going Correction** -0.175s/f (Stan)
WFA 3 from 4yo 16lb **7** Ran SP% **109.4**
Speed ratings (Par 103): **103,100,90,89,87 83,79**
toteswingers: 1&2 £1.80, 1&3 £4.80, 2&3 £5.10 CSF £2.22 TOTE £1.80: £1.20, £2.20; EX 3.10.
Owner Dr Marwan Koukash **Bred** Shadwell Estate Company Limited **Trained** Musley Bank, N Yorks

FOCUS
A weak, uncompetitive maiden but the time compared favourably with earlier handicaps. The first two finished clear and the winner ran somewhere near her 2yo form.

302 MORE JUMP RACING AT SOUTHWELL IN 2010 H'CAP 1m (F)
4:20 (4:20) (Class 6) (0-60,58) 3-Y-0 **£1,774** (£523; £262) **Stalls** Low

Form RPR
551- 1 **Wedding Dream**[45] 7722 3-9-4 **58** FrannyNorton 5 66+
(K A Ryan) *cl up: led after 1f: rdn clr over 1f out: styd on wl* **11/4**[2]
46-3 2 2 ¾ **D'Urberville**[14] 134 3-9-3 **57** ShaneKelly 6 57
(J R Jenkins) *hld up in tch: hdwy on outer to chse ldng pair 2f out: sn rdn: drvn ent fnl f: kpt on to take 2nd on line* **2/1**[1]
040- 3 nk **Temple Fair (USA)**[97] 6931 3-9-3 **57** JoeFanning 2 56
(M Johnston) *trckd ldrs: hdwy to chse wnr over 2f out: rdn along wl over 1f out: drvn and no imp appr fnl f* **4/1**[3]
005- 4 4 ½ **Little Meadow (IRE)**[39] 7792 3-8-13 **53** JimmyQuinn 8 42
(Miss J Feilden) *chsd ldrs: rdn along over 2f out: drvn and edgd lft wl over 1f out: sn one pce* **11/1**
666- 5 1 ¾ **Penderyn**[39] 7792 3-8-2 **45** KellyHarrison(3) 4 30
(C Smith) *chsd ldrs on inner: rdn along wl over 2f out: sn one pce* **12/1**
00-3 6 1 ¾ **Red Valerian Two (IRE)**[14] 143 3-9-1 **55** TonyCulhane 3 36
(P T Midgley) *a in rr: sme late hdwy* **6/1**
500- 7 18 **Lady Cavendish (IRE)**[66] 7474 3-8-7 **54** (p) NatashaEaton(7) 1 —
(A Bailey) *a in rr: bhd fnl 2f* **33/1**
550- 8 1 ¼ **Lord's Seat**[76] 7335 3-8-2 **47** BillyCray(5) 7 —
(A Berry) *led 1f: cl up tl rdn along 3f out and sn wknd: bhd whn heavily eased and virtually p.u fnl f* **25/1**

1m 42.9s (-0.80) **Going Correction** -0.175s/f (Stan) **8** Ran SP% **117.1**
Speed ratings (Par 95): **97,94,93,89,87 85,67,66**
toteswingers: 1&2 £1.90, 1&3 £3.90, 2&3 £3.20 CSF £8.93 CT £21.35 TOTE £3.90: £1.30, £1.30, £1.70; EX 7.70 Trifecta £20.00 Pool: £741.67 - 27.37 winning units. Place 6: £30.30 Place 5: £11.48 .
Owner J H Henderson **Bred** Lofts Hall Stud **Trained** Hambleton, N Yorks

FOCUS
A weak 3-y-o handicap and another all-the-way winner. It was probably no fluke though.
Lord's Seat Official explanation: jockey said gelding hung left-handed
T/Plt: £46.40 to a £1 stake. Pool: £62,778.92. 986.38 winning tickets. T/Qpdt: £9.40 to a £1 stake. Pool: £4,975.82. 390.56 winning tickets. JR

281 CAGNES-SUR-MER
Tuesday, January 26

OFFICIAL GOING: Standard

303a PRIX DU COL DE BRAUS (CLAIMER) (ALL-WEATHER) 6f 110y
2:40 (2:45) 4-Y-0+ **£6,637** (£2,655; £1,991; £1,327; £664)

RPR
1 **Bonnie Prince Blue**[10] 207 7-9-4 IoritzMendizabal 81
(D Nicholls) *broke wl: settled disputing 5th on outside: 6th st: led 1f out: r.o wl* **7/2**[1]
2 ¾ **Derison (USA)**[10] 207 8-9-7 (b) StephanePasquier 82
(P Monfort, France)
3 1 **Flower**[23] 28 5-9-9 (p) Francois-XavierBertras 81
(F Rohaut, France)
4 nse **Laokoon (GER)**[10] 207 5-9-4 76
(Mario Hofer, Germany)
5 nse **Ceodora (GER)**[10] 207 5-9-2 74
(J-P Perruchot, France)
6 1 **Wunderkind (GER)**[10] 207 5-9-5 (b) 74
(P Chatelain, France)
7 snk **Palea (GER)**[10] 207 4-9-1 70
(S Jesus, France)
8 nse **Am Brose (USA)**[10] 207 11-8-11 (b) 66
(J-M Capitte, France)
9 1 **La Rogerais (FR)**[84] 5-9-2 68
(T Doumen, France)
10 nk **Lanfranc (FR)**[938] 7-9-5 70
(M Gentile, France)
0 **Isander (USA)**[825] 6433 5-9-1 —
(F Chappet, France)
0 **Salut Adrien (FR)**[74] 7385 4-8-11 —
(Robert Collet, France)
0 **Tiberina (IRE)**[77] 5-9-4 —
(R Le Gal, France)
0 **Sweet Effie (USA)**[153] 5351 4-8-11 —
(K Borgel, France)
0 **Butterfly Flip (FR)**[10] 207 6-9-4 —
(J-P Perruchot, France)

1m 18.41s (78.41) **15** Ran SP% **22.2**
PARI-MUTUEL (Including 1 Euro stake): WIN 4.50; PL 1.70, 2.00, 2.80;DF 9.20.
Owner Middleham Park Racing XVII **Bred** George Joseph Hicks **Trained** Sessay, N Yorks

304a PRIX DE LA CRU (ALL-WEATHER) 6f 110y
3:40 (3:46) 4-Y-0+ **£11,062** (£4,425; £3,319; £2,212; £1,106)

RPR
1 **Parfum Des Dieux**[112] 6579 5-9-4 IoritzMendizabal 91
(J-C Rouget, France)
2 1 **Cadeau For Maggi**[86] 7216 5-9-6 FabriceVeron 90
(H-A Pantall, France)
3 nk **Zizany (IRE)**[521] 7-8-11 SebastienMaillot 80
(Robert Collet, France)
4 snk **Staraco (FR)**[83] 6-8-11 80
(Rod Collet, France)
5 1 **Kerno (IRE)**[89] 6-8-11 (p) 77
(P Monfort, France)
6 nse **Voie De Printemps (FR)**[78] 4-8-11 77
(D Smaga, France)
7 ½ **Film Set (USA)**[38] 7820 4-8-11 75
(F Vermeulen, France)
8 ¾ **Pink Candie (FR)**[48] 7696 4-8-12 74
(Mlle V Dissaux, France)
9 2 **Alhamark (IRE)**[325] 7-8-11 67
(F Foresi, France)
10 1 ½ **Marny (GER)**[23] 28 5-8-8 60
(H Blume, Germany)
0 **Green Pride**[54] 7-8-11 —
(G Martin, Austria)
0 **Garnica (FR)**[4] 272 7-8-11 Francois-XavierBertras —
(D Nicholls) *sn pressing ldr on ins: 2nd st: ev ch 2f out: sn rdn and wknd: fin 14th* **23/10**[1]
0 **Jane Blue (FR)**[157] 5-9-4 —
(W Walton, France)
0 **Kentish Dream**[254] 4-8-11 —
(F Chappet, France)
0 **Maggi Fong**[123] 4-8-8 —
(H-A Pantall, France)
0 **Hamilcar Barca (FR)** 4-8-11 —
(G Collet, France)

1m 17.03s (77.03) **16** Ran SP% **30.3**
PARI-MUTUEL: WIN 9.40; PL 3.80, 6.30, 8.10; DF 51.20.
Owner E Gann **Bred** Haras Des Capucines **Trained** Pau, France

282 KEMPTON (A.W) (R-H)
Wednesday, January 27

OFFICIAL GOING: Standard
Wind: Virtually nil Weather: cold

305 KEMPTON.CO.UK CLAIMING STKS 1m 2f (P)
4:40 (4:40) (Class 6) 3-Y-O **£2,047** (£604; £302) **Stalls** High

Form RPR
33-3 1 **Kathindi (IRE)**[12] 183 3-8-6 67 RossAtkinson(5) 1 62
(J S Moore) *led after 2f on modest pce: drvn over 2f out: hld on wl thrght fnl f* **5/2**[2]
0-62 2 hd **Magic Spirit**[9] 217 3-8-3 0 (p) LukeMorris 2 54
(J S Moore) *sn led: hdd and dropped bk to cl 2nd off modest pce: rdn over 2f out: styd on u.p to cl on wnr thrght fnl f but a hld* **8/1**
11-1 3 1 **Glen Lass**[15] 133 3-8-8 64 (b) SaleemGolam 6 57
(J Pearce) *chsd ldrs off modest pce: rdn over 2f out: styd on u.p thrght fnl f but a hld by ldng duo* **11/10**[1]
00-3 4 3 ½ **Rufus Roughcut**[2] 288 3-8-3 41 (t) WilliamCarson(3) 4 48
(S C Williams) *in rr but in tch off modest pce: rdn over 2f out: modest prog fnl f* **6/1**[3]
000- 5 ¾ **Whip Up (IRE)**[247] 2319 3-8-6 0 FrankieMcDonald 7 47
(J G Portman) *chsd ldrs and plld hrd of modest pce: rdn 2f out: sn btn* **80/1**
6-66 6 1 ½ **Charlottesometimes (USA)**[10] 213 3-8-1 49 NickyMackay 5 39
(D M Simcock) *a in rr off modest pce: rdn over 2f out and no rspnse: hung lft ins fnl f* **16/1**

2m 14.24s (6.24) **Going Correction** -0.05s/f (Stan) **6** Ran SP% **108.7**
Speed ratings (Par 95): **73,72,72,69,68 67**
toteswingers: 1&2 £2.10, 1&3 £1.20, 2&3 £2.00 CSF £20.36 TOTE £3.20: £1.20, £3.30; EX 21.30.
Owner John Wells **Bred** Pat Galavan **Trained** Upper Lambourn, Berks

FOCUS
Unwise to get carried away with this form as they went no gallop whatsoever. Muddling form, and it's doubtful if the winner had to match his best form here to hold off his stablemate.
Whip Up(IRE) Official explanation: jockey said gelding hung left-handed

306 CONGRATULATIONS ON 25 YEARS SERVICE MICHAEL H'CAP 5f (P)
5:10 (5:10) (Class 5) (0-70,70) 4-Y-0+ **£2,590** (£770; £385; £192) **Stalls** High

Form RPR
-010 1 **Thoughtsofstardom**[12] 185 7-9-0 **66** ChrisCatlin 5 74
(P S McEntee) *mde virtually all: drvn along 2f out: hrd rdn ins fnl f: hld on wl* **10/1**
51-2 2 ½ **Handsome Cross (IRE)**[12] 185 9-8-12 **64** (v) StevieDonohoe 4 72+
(W J Musson) *hld up in rr: hdwy and nt clr run fr over 1f out: swtchd lft of heels of horses jst ins fnl f: sn balanced and str run fnl 75yds: fin strly to take 2nd cl home: nt quite get up* **3/1**[2]

05-6 **3** *nk* **Cape Royal**[12] 185 10-8-6 **58**....................(bt) KevinGhunowa 1 63
(J M Bradley) *chsd wnr: rdn 2f out: styd on wl fnl f but a jst hld: lost 2nd cl home* **16/1**

200- **4** *nk* **Bookiesindex Boy**[49] 7682 6-8-13 **65**....................(b) StephenCraine 6 69
(J R Jenkins) *trckd ldrs: travelling smooth over 1f out: sn shkn up: styd on thrght fnl f but nvr quite gng pce to chal* **14/1**

22-4 **5** *½* **Lithaam (IRE)**[16] 119 6-9-4 **70**....................(p) NickyMackay 9 72
(J M Bradley) *chsd ldrs: disp 2nd tl rdr over 1f out: one pce ins fnl f* **4/1**[3]

-522 **6** *½* **Fromsong (IRE)**[7] 241 12-8-13 **65**....................(p) MartinDwyer 8 65+
(D K Ivory) *hld up in tch: nt clr run appr last and thrght fnl f: fin on bit* **11/4**[1]

24-3 **7** *nk* **Decider (USA)**[19] 79 7-8-11 **63**....................(p) LukeMorris 3 62
(R A Harris) *in rr: rdn and wd into st: nvr gng pce to rch ldrs* **8/1**

4-22 **8** *3 ¼* **Kheley (IRE)**[16] 125 4-8-11 **63**.................... LiamJones 2 50
(W M Brisbourne) *in rr: rdn and wd into st: a outpcd* **10/1**

59.85 secs (-0.65) **Going Correction** -0.05s/f (Stan) **8** Ran SP% **113.5**
Speed ratings (Par 103): **103,102,101,101,100 99,99,93**
toteswingers: 1&2 £5.80, 1&3 £34.30, 2&3 £13.60 CSF £39.58 CT £484.78 TOTE £14.40: £4.20, £2.90, £7.90; EX 53.40.
Owner Eventmaker Racehorses **Bred** B Bargh **Trained** Newmarket, Suffolk

FOCUS
Luck in running played a big part here and the runner-up was arguably unlucky. The third is the best guide to the form.
Fromsong(IRE) Official explanation: jockey said gelding was denied a clear run
Decider(USA) Official explanation: jockey said gelding was denied a clear run

307 DIGIBET H'CAP 5f (P)
5:40 (5:40) (Class 3) (0-90,89) 4-Y-0+
£6,542 (£1,959; £979; £490; £244; £122) **Stalls** High

Form RPR

1-23 **1** **Nickel Silver**[10] 212 5-9-4 **89**....................(v) TomEaves 4 97
(B Smart) *trckd ldr: rdn over 1f out: styd on u.p to ld fnl 100yds: kpt on strly* **7/2**[2]

40-1 **2** *¾* **Rocket Rob (IRE)**[13] 172 4-8-11 **85**.................... AndreaAtzeni(3) 6 90
(M Botti) *trckd ldrs: drvn along ins fnl 2f: r.o strly fnl f to take 2nd last strides but a hld by drvn out wnr* **15/8**[1]

01-0 **3** *shd* **Glamorous Spirit (IRE)**[10] 212 4-9-2 **87**.................... ChrisCatlin 5 92
(R A Harris) *led: rdn ins fnl 2f: hdd fnl 100yds: lost 2nd last strides* **16/1**

21- **4** *nk* **Absa Lutte (IRE)**[45] 7738 7-7-13 **75** oh1....................(t) JamesSullivan(5) 1 79
(Patrick Morris) *hld up towards rr: pushed along: hdwy over 1f out: kpt on ins fnl f and r.o cl to home: but a hld* **8/1**

5-65 **5** *½* **Earlsmedic**[10] 212 5-8-11 **89**....................(e) RyanClark(7) 7 91
(S C Williams) *trckd ldrs: pushed along over 1f out and n.m.r ins fnl f: one pce nr fin* **13/2**

10-3 **6** *shd* **Lord Of The Reins (IRE)**[16] 119 6-8-4 **75** oh1.................... JimmyQuinn 8 77
(J G Given) *in tch: rdn 1f out: kpt on ins fnl f: but nvr quite on terms* **11/2**[3]

02-3 **7** *1 ¼* **The Tatling (IRE)**[20] 74 13-8-7 **81**.................... JackDean(3) 3 78
(J M Bradley) *s.i.s: sn pushed along and nvr gng pce to get on terms* **16/1**

413- **8** *1 ½* **Step It Up (IRE)**[97] 6972 6-8-5 **76**.................... NickyMackay 2 68
(J R Boyle) *outpcd* **16/1**

58.95 secs (-1.55) **Going Correction** -0.05s/f (Stan) **8** Ran SP% **114.5**
Speed ratings (Par 107): **110,108,108,108,107 107,105,102**
toteswingers: 1&2 £1.10, 1&3 £14.00, 2&3 £9.20 CSF £10.49 CT £88.97 TOTE £3.40: £1.10, £2.00, £6.50; EX 11.10.
Owner M Barber **Bred** Mrs Sheila White **Trained** Hambleton, N Yorks

FOCUS
This was run at a scorching pace and in a record time. Solid form.

NOTEBOOK
Nickel Silver, who chased the pace in second, proved too strong in the finish to continue his excellent run of form, and that of his stable. This has to be something near a career best effort and this sharp 5f track suits him perfectly. (op 4-1)
Rocket Rob(IRE) stayed on from off the pace to snatch second but couldn't get to the winner. He ideally wants a stiffer track like Wolverhampton and remains one to be interested in. (op 13-8 tchd 2-1)
Glamorous Spirit(IRE) took off like a scalded cat from the gates and helped set up a new course record time of 58.95 seconds, one hundredth of a second faster than her own previous record. Just pipped for second, she did well to reach a place given how hard she'd gone through the first three furlongs and Chris Catlin was never able to get in a breather. She is well suited by this track and she can win one of these if conserving a little more energy for the finish. (op 20-1 tchd 14-1)
Absa Lutte(IRE) travelled well out wide and might well have needed this after 45 days off the track, so this was very encouraging. (op 7-1)
Earlsmedic ◆ kept on up the inside and is one to be very interested in back up to his optimum 6f trip. (op 8-1)
The Tatling(IRE) Official explanation: jockey said gelding missed the break

308 DIGIBET CASINO MAIDEN STKS 1m 3f (P)
6:10 (6:12) (Class 5) 3-Y-0+
£2,729 (£806; £403) **Stalls** High

Form RPR

1 **Cairnsmore**[456] 4-9-11 0.................... GregFairley 7 93+
(M Johnston) *trckd ldr: led ins fnl 4f: c clr fr over 2f out: easily* **4/7**[1]

2 *5* **Fix The Rib (IRE)**[31] 7-10-0 0.................... GeorgeBaker 3 76
(G L Moore) *s.i.s tl stdy hdwy fr 5f out: wnt 2nd appr fnl 2f: nvr any ch w wnr but kpt on for clr 2nd* **7/2**[2]

6 **3** *7* **Happy Fleet**[12] 179 7-9-9 0.................... DaneO'Neill 9 59
(R Curtis) *in rr: rdn over 3f out: styd on to take modest 3rd ins fnl f* **66/1**

4 *½* **Onegin (SAF)**[263] 4-9-0 0.................... MartinLane(3) 5 55
(D M Simcock) *in rr tl hdwy and drvn 3f out: styd on for modest 4th ins fnl f* **25/1**

00-3 **5** *1* **Astronomer's Dream**[4] 279 3-7-13 63.................... NickyMackay 2 53
(E F Vaughan) *chsd ldrs tl rdn and outpcd over 3f out: nvr any threat after* **8/1**[3]

05-3 **6** *½* **Mutajaaser (USA)**[18] 98 5-10-0 62.................... JimmyQuinn 6 61
(K A Morgan) *chsd ldrs: rdn fr 4f out: n.m.r and wknd over 2f out* **10/1**

7 *7* **Rubaa (IRE)**[14] 4-9-11 0.................... LiamKeniry 4 49
(C C Bealby) *slowly away: bhd and nvr on terms* **66/1**

U0-0 **8** *1* **Gospel Spirit**[25] 18 5-9-7 0.................... DannyBrock(7) 1 47
(J R Jenkins) *led tl hdd ins fnl 4f: wknd qckly ins fnl 2f* **100/1**

06- **9** *20* **Blue Celeste**[49] 7694 4-9-6 0.................... SteveDrowne 8 8
(R T Phillips) *in tch: rdn and wknd over 4f out* **80/1**

2m 19.44s (-2.46) **Going Correction** -0.05s/f (Stan)
WFA 3 from 4yo 24lb 4 from 5yo+ 3lb **9** Ran SP% **115.1**
Speed ratings (Par 103): **106,102,97,96,96 95,90,90,75**
toteswingers: 1&2 £1.10, 1&3 £16.80, 2&3 £58.80 CSF £2.70 TOTE £1.70: £1.10, £1.20, £17.80; EX 3.70.
Owner Sheikh Hamdan Bin Mohammed Al Maktoum **Bred** Darley **Trained** Middleham Moor, N Yorks

■ Stewards' Enquiry : Danny Brock one-day ban: used whip when out of contention (Feb 10)

FOCUS
There may not have been much strength in depth here, but the two market leaders were both fascinating propositions.

309 DIGIBET.COM H'CAP 1m 4f (P)
6:40 (6:44) (Class 6) (0-65,65) 4-Y-0+
£2,047 (£604; £302) **Stalls** Centre

Form RPR

05-1 **1** **Slick Mover (IRE)**[16] 120 5-9-4 **61**.................... SteveDrowne 4 69
(B G Powell) *trckd ldrs: drvn and styd on wl appr fnl f: r.o strly to ld cl home* **7/1**

44-6 **2** *hd* **Ardmaddy (IRE)**[16] 121 6-8-10 **53**....................(b) FergusSweeney 3 60
(G L Moore) *chsd ldrs: drvn to chal over 1f out: led fnl 120yds: hdd and no ex cl home* **8/1**

45-5 **3** *nk* **Ladies Dancing**[18] 105 4-9-1 **62**....................(b[1]) TomQueally 9 69
(J A Osborne) *in rr: rdn and hdwy fr 3f out: nt clr run over 2f out: swtchd lft and hdwy over 1f out to press ldrs wl ins fnl f: no ex cl home* **25/1**

-654 **4** *3* **Croix Rouge (USA)**[3] 282 8-8-13 **56**.................... HayleyTurner 12 58
(R J Smith) *chsd ldrs: rdn 2f out: one pce fnl f* **11/2**[2]

00-5 **5** *shd* **Choral Festival**[12] 182 4-9-1 **65**.................... MarcHalford(3) 13 67
(J J Bridger) *chsd ldr tl led appr fnl 2f: hdd & wknd fnl 120yds* **33/1**

6-43 **6** *1 ¼* **Supernoverre (IRE)**[12] 198 4-8-11 **58**.................... IanMongan 11 58+
(P Howling) *hld up towards rr: hdwy on outside over 2f out: kpt on ins fnl f but nvr a threat* **9/2**[1]

-043 **7** *nk* **Naheell**[5] 261 4-8-10 **64**.................... CharlotteKerton(7) 7 64
(G Prodromou) *in rr: t.k.h: hdwy on outside over 2f out: nt rch ldrs* **8/1**

00-6 **8** *½* **Jordan's Light (USA)**[16] 120 7-8-11 **54**.................... PaulDoe 10 53+
(P D Evans) *in rr: rdn fr 3f out: kpt on fnl f but nvr on terms* **14/1**

5233 **9** *1 ½* **Russian Invader (IRE)**[6] 244 6-8-6 **54**....................(be) BillyCray(5) 6 50
(R C Guest) *s.i.s: in rr: drvn and styd on fr over 2f out: nvr rchd ldrs* **7/1**

002- **10** *3 ¾* **Under Fire (IRE)**[42] 7767 7-8-11 **54**.................... StephenCraine 1 44
(A W Carroll) *sn led: t.k.h: rdn and hdd appr fnl 2f: sn wknd* **16/1**

0/00 **11** *2 ¼* **Solarias Quest**[9] 220 8-9-8 **65**.................... ShaneKelly 2 52
(W M Brisbourne) *in tch: hdwy 4f out: nvr rchd ldrs and wknd over 2f out* **40/1**

505- **12** *1 ½* **Sudden Impulse**[226] 2975 9-9-0 **57**.................... StevieDonohoe 5 41
(A D Brown) *in tch 9f* **16/1**

406- **13** *4 ½* **Stellar Cause (USA)**[44] 6248 4-8-13 **60**.................... DaneO'Neill 14 37
(R Curtis) *chsd ldrs tl wknd over 2f out* **33/1**

00-1 **14** *2* **Gheed (IRE)**[18] 98 5-9-2 **59**....................(t) JimmyQuinn 8 33
(K A Morgan) *nvr bttr then mid-div: bhd fnl 4f* **13/2**[3]

2m 35.27s (0.77) **Going Correction** -0.05s/f (Stan)
WFA 4 from 5yo+ 4lb **14** Ran SP% **124.7**
Speed ratings (Par 101): **95,94,94,92,92 91,91,91,90,87 86,85,82,80**
toteswingers: 1&2 £14.00, 1&3 £14.70, 2&3 £26.30 CSF £62.39 CT £1356.50 TOTE £5.90: £1.60, £3.50, £8.40; EX 67.40.
Owner R Stanley **Bred** Wiji Bloodstock And Leo Powell **Trained** Upper Lambourn, Berks
■ Stewards' Enquiry : Stevie Donohoe one-day ban: failed to keep straight from draw (Feb 10)

FOCUS
Low-grade handicap form and the pace wasn't overly strong. The form looks sound amongst the principals with the winner up 4lb.
Supernoverre(IRE) Official explanation: jockey said gelding was hampered after the start
Russian Invader(IRE) Official explanation: jockey said gelding never travelled
Gheed(IRE) Official explanation: jockey said mare was in season

310 JOAN AYRES' 93RD BIRTHDAY CELEBRATION TODAY H'CAP 6f (P)
7:10 (7:13) (Class 4) (0-85,82) 3-Y-0
£4,209 (£1,252; £625; £312) **Stalls** High

Form RPR

0-11 **1** **Love Delta (USA)**[17] 117 3-9-7 **82**.................... GregFairley 3 85+
(M Johnston) *chsd ldrs: rdn 2f out: led jst ins fnl f: styd on strly nr fin: readily* **2/1**[1]

14-4 **2** *¾* **Italian Tom (IRE)**[17] 117 3-9-4 **79**.................... LukeMorris 2 80
(R A Harris) *hld up in tch: rdn and hdwy over 1f out: styd on whn bmpd wl ins fnl f: tk 2nd last strides* **16/1**

20-2 **3** *nse* **Coolree Star (IRE)**[17] 117 3-9-3 **78**.................... ChrisCatlin 5 79
(J A Glover) *led: rdn and hdd wl over 1f out: styd wl there: edgd rt wl ins fnl f: rallied to take 3rd last strides* **4/1**[3]

66-4 **4** *nk* **Mint Whip (IRE)**[24] 24 3-8-2 **63**.................... HayleyTurner 4 63
(R Hannon) *chsd ldrs: led wl over 1f out: hdd jst ins fnl f: one pce and relagated to cl 4th last strides* **8/1**

-255 **5** *5* **Transfixed (IRE)**[5] 268 3-9-0 **80**.................... RichardEvans(5) 1 64
(P D Evans) *t.k.h: rdn towards outside 3f out and sn outpcd* **16/1**

2-1 **6** *3 ¼* **The Love Guru**[22] 43 3-8-4 **65**....................(b) NickyMackay 7 38
(J R Boyle) *chsd ldrs: rdn and ev ch wl over 1f out: wknd qckly* **7/2**[2]

1-43 **7** *1* **Tealing**[12] 188 3-8-0 **66**.................... BillyCray(5) 6 36
(R C Guest) *s.i.s: outpcd* **5/1**

1m 13.15s (0.05) **Going Correction** -0.05s/f (Stan) **7** Ran SP% **115.1**
Speed ratings (Par 99): **97,96,95,95,88 84,83**
toteswingers: 1&2 £7.90, 1&3 £1.50, 2&3 £4.30 CSF £36.04 TOTE £1.70: £1.02, £8.30; EX 40.50.
Owner Crone Stud Farms Ltd **Bred** Palides Investments N V Inc & Hair 'Em Corporation **Trained** Middleham Moor, N Yorks

FOCUS
Quite a competitive little handicap. The progressive winner did not need to repeat his latest Southwell form and the runner-up ran as well as ever.
The Love Guru Official explanation: jockey said gelding had no more to give

311 BOOK NOW FOR RACING POST CHASE DAY H'CAP 1m (P)
7:40 (7:40) (Class 4) (0-85,75) 3-Y-0
£4,209 (£1,252; £625; £312) **Stalls** High

Form RPR

4-21 **1** **Greyfriarschorista**[11] 206 3-9-2 **72**.................... GregFairley 2 98
(M Johnston) *mde all and sn in control: pushed steadily clr fnl 3f: unchal* **7/4**[1]

1-12 **2** *15* **Lisahane Bog**[11] 203 3-9-5 **75**....................(p) DaneO'Neill 4 67
(P R Hedger) *slowly away: sn mod 3rd: rdn over 3f out: chsdwnr fr 1f out: nvr any ch* **5/2**[2]

21-3 **3** *3 ¼* **Fazza**[15] 136 3-9-2 **72**.................... MartinDwyer 3 56
(D W P Arbuthnot) *chsd easy wnr and nvr any ch: lost 2nd and wknd into 3rd over 1f out* **5/1**[3]

1 **4** *4* **The Glamour Cat (IRE)**[16] 127 3-9-1 **74**.................... AndreaAtzeni(3) 1 49
(M Botti) *stdd s: rdn 3f out: little rspnse and a last* **5/2**[2]

1m 38.62s (-1.18) **Going Correction** -0.05s/f (Stan) **4** Ran SP% **110.2**
Speed ratings (Par 99): **103,88,84,80**
CSF £6.47 TOTE £2.70; EX 7.00 Place 6: £173.31 Place 5: £58.48.
Owner Greyfriars UK Ltd **Bred** Castlemartin Stud And Skymarc Farm **Trained** Middleham Moor, N Yorks

T/Plt: £214.70 to a £1 stake. Pool: £59,487.30. 202.26 winning tickets. T/Qpdt: £8.30 to a £1 stake. Pool: £10,109.64. 894.14 winning tickets. ST

[274]LINGFIELD (L-H)
Wednesday, January 27

OFFICIAL GOING: Standard
Wind: medium, half behind Weather: overcast, cold

312 BET AFRICAN NATIONS CUP - BETDAQ H'CAP 6f (P)
1:30 (1:30) (Class 6) (0-65,68) 4-Y-0+ **£1,774** (£523; £262) **Stalls** Low

Form RPR
542- **1** **Hollow Jo**[27] 7890 10-9-1 **62**.....................................(v) FergusSweeney 10 69+
(J R Jenkins) *hld up towards rr: hdwy jst over 2f out: rdn and r.o wl ins fnl f to ld on post* **12/1**
-120 **2** *nse* **Tanley**[12] 195 5-8-5 **52**.. JimmyQuinn 11 59
(J F Coupland) *stdd and swtchd lft after s: bhd: gd hdwy towards inner over 1f out: drvn to ld ins fnl f: hdd on post* **7/1[3]**
-315 **3** *3/4* **The Geester**[6] 243 6-9-0 **61** ow1.. AdamKirby 2 65
(Stef Higgins) *racd keenly: chsd ldrs: rdn and unable qck over 1f out: styd on again to chse ldr ins fnl f tl fnl 50yds: kpt on* **11/4[1]**
-101 **4** *3/4* **Peopleton Brook**[5] 258 8-9-7 **68** 6ex..........................(t) SteveDrowne 4 70+
(B G Powell) *t.k.h: hld up towards rr: nt clr run and swtchd rt wl over 1f out: r.o wl ins fnl f: nt rch ldrs* **10/1**
405- **5** *hd* **Amber Sunset**[30] 7861 4-9-0 **61**.. LukeMorris 8 62
(J Jay) *in tch in midfield: hdwy u.p ent fnl f: r.o but nt quite pce to rch ldrs* **14/1**
005- **6** *hd* **Love You Louis**[45] 7738 4-9-4 **65**.. ShaneKelly 5 66
(J R Jenkins) *t.k.h: chsd ldrs: rdn and unable qck wl over 1f out: styd on again ins fnl f: nt pce to chal ldrs* **11/2[2]**
0-31 **7** *hd* **Elusive Ronnie (IRE)**[15] 137 4-8-12 **59**.......................(b) JackMitchell 9 59
(R A Teal) *sn outpcd in rr: hdwy on inner over 1f out: r.o fnl f: nvr trbld ldrs* **7/1[3]**
00-5 **8** *1/2* **White Shift (IRE)**[16] 125 4-9-1 **62**.. PaulDoe 7 61
(P Howling) *sn bustled up to press ldr: ev ch and rdn wl over 1f out tl wknd ins fnl f* **20/1**
540- **9** *1* **Smirfys Systems**[30] 7860 11-9-1 **62**.............................. StevieDonohoe 3 57
(Mrs D J Sanderson) *led: rdn over 1f out: hrd drvn and hdd ins fnl f: wknd fnl 75yds* **12/1**
00-6 **10** *1* **Trip Switch**[19] 78 4-8-4 **58**.................................... CharlotteKerton[(7)] 12 50
(G Prodromou) *sn detached in last: styd on fnl f: nvr trbld ldrs* **20/1**
22-5 **11** *hd* **Grand Palace (IRE)**[17] 112 7-8-8 **55**..........................(v) HayleyTurner 1 46
(H J Evans) *in tch in midfield: rdn 1/2-way: no prog u.p fr over 1f out* **11/1**
623- **12** *hd* **Bold Diva**[254] 2134 5-8-7 **54**..(v) ChrisCatlin 6 45
(A W Carroll) *a towards rr: rdn and no prog fnl 2f* **16/1**

1m 11.37s (-0.53) **Going Correction** +0.05s/f (Slow) **12** Ran SP% **121.9**
Speed ratings (Par 101): **105,104,103,102,102 102,102,101,100,98 98,98**
toteswingers: 1&2 £12.90, 1&3 £3.90, 2&3 £6.50 CSF £96.33 CT £304.86 TOTE £7.80: £2.90, £2.60, £1.50; EX 74.20 Trifecta £250.30 Part won. Pool: £338.30 - 0.20 winning units..
Owner Mrs Wendy Jenkins **Bred** K J Reddington **Trained** Royston, Herts
■ Stewards' Enquiry : Charlotte Kerton ten-day ban: in breach of Rule (b)59.4 (Feb 10-19)

FOCUS
Quite a competitive handicap run at a solid pace and sound form. The runner-up and fourth are rated close to recent marks.
The Geester Official explanation: jockey said gelding lost a front shoe
Trip Switch Official explanation: jockey said, regarding running and riding, her instructions were to drop in from a wide draw and make her move turning into the straight. The trainer confirmed these were the instructions, adding the gelding could not go the early pace and needs further and had been disadvantaged by its wide draw

313 MARRIOTT HOTEL OPENING SPRING 2010 MAIDEN STKS 6f (P)
2:00 (2:00) (Class 5) 3-Y-0 **£2,456** (£725; £362) **Stalls** Low

Form RPR
02-3 **1** **Il Forno**[10] 208 3-9-3 70.. SteveDrowne 7 69
(D Nicholls) *led for 1f: chsd ldr after tl rdn to ld 1f out: styd on wl u.p fnl f* **9/4[2]**
0 **2** *1 1/4* **Ceto**[12] 180 3-8-12 0.. ChrisCatlin 4 60+
(P S McEntee) *s.i.s: in tch in last: rdn and hdwy ent fnl f: r.o to chse wnr fnl 100yds: no imp towards fin* **14/1**
250- **3** *nk* **Posy Fossil (USA)**[75] 7363 3-8-9 62.......................... WilliamCarson[(3)] 6 59
(S C Williams) *wl in tch on outer: rdn an dunable qck over 1f out: styd on again u.p ins fnl f* **11/2[3]**
0 **4** *nk* **Neville's Cross (IRE)**[14] 147 3-9-3 0.......................... StephenCraine 5 63
(J R Boyle) *dwlt: in tch in last trio: swtchd lft and hdwy ent fnl f: pressing for 2nd ins fnl f: kpt on* **66/1**
50- **5** *1/2* **Super Yellow**[75] 7376 3-9-3 0.. ShaneKelly 8 61
(J A Osborne) *steaded after s: hld up wl in tch: rdn and sltly outpcd wl over 1f out: kpt on again ins fnl f* **25/1**
-364 **6** *nse* **Tatawor (IRE)**[4] 276 3-9-3 70..(b) DaneO'Neill 3 61
(J R Boyle) *chsd ldrs: rdn and ev ch jst over 1f out: edgd rt u.p jst ins fnl f: btn and edgd lft fnl 75yds* **13/2**
7 *1* **Dreamacha** 3-8-5 0.. RyanClark[(7)] 2 53
(S C Williams) *chsd ldrs: outpcd and rdn 2f out: keeping on same pce whn n.m.r ins fnl f* **14/1**
6-4 **8** *nk* **Sunrise Lyric (IRE)**[16] 128 3-8-12 0.. GregFairley 1 52
(P F I Cole) *dwlt: sn pushed along and hdwy to ld after 1f: rdn over 1f out: hdd 1f out: wknd ins fnl f* **7/4[1]**

1m 12.88s (0.98) **Going Correction** +0.05s/f (Slow) **8** Ran SP% **114.5**
Speed ratings (Par 97): **95,93,92,92,91 91,90,90**
toteswingers: 1&2 £5.90, 1&3 £3.50, 2&3 £9.60 CSF £33.34 TOTE £3.00: £1.10, £4.60, £2.10; EX 38.70 Trifecta £114.20 Pool: £885.05 - 5.73 winning units..
Owner Dr Marwan Koukash **Bred** C J Murfitt **Trained** Sessay, N Yorks

FOCUS
They didn't go much pace early in this modest maiden and the winning time was 1.51sec slower than the earlier handicap. The form looks weak and muddling.

314 TRY BETDAQ FOR AN EXCHANGE CLAIMING STKS 1m 4f (P)
2:30 (2:31) (Class 6) 4-Y-0+ **£1,774** (£523; £262) **Stalls** Low

Form RPR
-211 **1** **Clear Sailing**[11] 200 7-9-3 72.. PaulDoe 2 76+
(P D Evans) *taken down early: hld up in tch: hdwy to chse ldr over 3f out: led over 2f out: edgd rt wl over 1f out: pushed clr over 1f out: easily* **11/10[1]**
23-1 **2** *2* **Theocritus (USA)**[13] 176 5-9-13 76.. GeorgeBaker 1 82
(D M Simcock) *stdd s: hld up in last pair: hdwy to chse wnr and rdn 2f out: drvn and swtchd lft 1f out: easily hld after* **9/4[2]**
0-04 **3** *8* **Awatuki (IRE)**[11] 200 7-8-9 64.. NickyMackay 3 51
(J R Boyle) *chsd ldrs: rdn over 2f out: outpcd and no ch w ldng pair over 1f out* **4/1[3]**
-344 **4** *2 1/4* **Womaniser (IRE)**[5] 260 6-8-11 52..(t) LiamKeniry 8 49
(T Keddy) *hld in tch in last pair: rdn and struggling over 2f out: no ch fnl 2f: wnt modest 4th ins fnl f* **12/1**
0/0- **5** *5* **Six Of Clubs**[8] 5987 4-8-6 0..(b[1]) WilliamCarson[(3)] 5 43
(W G M Turner) *chsd ldr tl led over 3f out: rdn and hdd over 2f out: wl btn over 1f out* **100/1**
30-4 **6** *10* **Bromhead (USA)**[9] 113 4-8-6 52 ow1..........................(tp) GregFairley 4 24
(Mrs C A Dunnett) *led tl rdn and hdd over 3f out: sn dropped out: wl bhd fnl 2f* **20/1**

2m 31.51s (-1.49) **Going Correction** +0.05s/f (Slow)
WFA 4 from 5yo+ 4lb **6** Ran SP% **111.8**
Speed ratings (Par 101): **106,104,99,97,94 87**
.Clear Sailing was claimed by P Leech for £9000. Theocritus was claimed by C Bjorling for £14000.\n\x\x
Owner Diamond Racing Ltd **Bred** Juddmonte Farms Ltd **Trained** Pandy, Monmouths

FOCUS
A fair claimer with the winner in line with recent form and the runner-up to last year's turf form.

315 BET ASIAN H'CAPS - BETDAQ HANDICAP 1m (P)
3:00 (3:10) (Class 5) (0-75,75) 4-Y-0+ **£2,456** (£725; £362) **Stalls** High

Form RPR
14-1 **1** **Hereford Boy**[24] 23 6-9-1 **72**..(p) AdamKirby 3 77
(D K Ivory) *broke wl: sn stdd and hld up in last pair: pushed along and effrt jst over 1f out: led ins fnl f: pushed out* **3/1[1]**
05-0 **2** *nk* **Rapid City**[11] 202 7-8-9 **66**.. PaulDoe 2 71
(P D Evans) *stdd s: hld up in tch in last: hdwy on outer over 2f out: kpt on wl ins fnl f: wnt 2nd nr fin* **4/1[3]**
235- **3** *nk* **El Libertador (USA)**[69] 7456 4-8-11 **68**.. LiamKeniry 1 72
(E A Wheeler) *in tch: effrt to press ldrs wl over 1f out: rdn to ld jst over 1f out: hdd ins fnl f: unable qck and lost 2nd nr fin* **4/1[3]**
05-3 **4** *1 1/2* **Gallantry**[7] 231 8-9-3 **74**.. SaleemGolam 4 75
(P Howling) *in tch: rdn and effrt over 1f out: n.m.r and swtchd rt ent fnl f: kpt on same pce ins fnl f* **3/1[1]**
0-21 **5** *1* **Prince Of Thebes (IRE)**[19] 84 9-8-11 **75**.......................... KierenFox[(7)] 5 73
(M J Attwater) *led at stdy gallop: hdd narrowly and rdn 2f out: wknd ins fnl f* **7/2[2]**
-654 **6** *nk* **Justcallmehandsome**[5] 259 8-8-10 **72**..........................(v) BillyCray[(5)] 6 70
(D J S Ffrench Davis) *chsd ldr tl rdn to ld narrowly ent fnl 2f: hdd jst over 1f out: wknd ins fnl f* **14/1**

1m 38.06s (-0.14) **Going Correction** +0.05s/f (Slow) **6** Ran SP% **118.9**
Speed ratings (Par 103): **102,101,101,99,98 98**
toteswingers: 1&2 £5.00, 1&3 £2.00, 2&3 £4.90 CSF £16.43 TOTE £3.10: £1.70, £2.70; EX 18.50.
Owner Recycled Products Limited **Bred** Mrs L R Burrage **Trained** Radlett, Herts

FOCUS
A competitive little heat, but the pace wasn't overly strong, with Prince Of Thebes slowing it down once in front, and it developed into a bit of a sprint from the turn in. The form is a bit muddling but is probably best rated at face value.
El Libertador(USA) Official explanation: jockey said gelding hung right

316 LINGFIELD PARK FOURBALL MEDIAN AUCTION MAIDEN STKS 1m 4f (P)
3:30 (3:37) (Class 5) 4-6-Y-0 **£2,456** (£725; £362) **Stalls** Low

Form RPR
3-32 **1** **Freedom Fire (IRE)**[5] 261 4-9-3 62.. GeorgeBaker 1 56+
(G L Moore) *hld up in tch: smooth hdwy to ld gng wl ent fnl 2f: pushed clr over 1f out: rdn and a doing enough ins fnl f* **11/10[1]**
4-2 **2** *1 1/4* **On Terms (USA)**[19] 82 4-8-12 0.. HayleyTurner 7 49
(S Dow) *s.i.s: hld up towards rr: hdwy and rdn over 2f out: kpt on u.p to chse wnr ins fnl f: no imp fnl 100yds* **5/2[2]**
6-0 **3** *1 1/2* **Always The Sun**[10] 211 4-8-12 50.. GregFairley 8 47
(P Leech) *hld up towards rr: rdn and hdwy on outer over 2f out: pressed ldrs u.p wl over 1f out: kpt on same pce after* **25/1**
3-40 **4** *nk* **Law Of The Jungle (IRE)**[10] 210 4-8-12 60....(p) RichardKingscote 11 46
(Tom Dascombe) *chsd ldrs: rdn over 2f out: ev ch u.p 2f out: nt pce of wnr over 1f out: kpt on same pce and lost 2 pls ins fnl f* **11/2[3]**
046/ **5** *nk* **Nelson Vettori**[539] 4735 6-9-7 44.. SteveDrowne 2 51
(C E Longsdon) *in tch in last trio: rdn over 2f out: hdwy over 1f out: styd on steadily fnl f: nvr gng pce to rch wnr* **33/1**
6 *1* **Two Oclock John** 4-9-3 0.. JackMitchell 3 49+
(H J Collingridge) *s.i.s: sn niggled along in last: stl last over 2f out: hdwy over 1f out: styd on ins fnl f: nvr trbld ldrs* **66/1**
00-3 **7** *3/4* **Mymateeric**[12] 186 4-9-3 52.. ChrisCatlin 6 48
(J Pearce) *chsd ldrs: 2nd tl over 5f out: rdn and unable qck jst over 2f out: one pce and wl hld fr over 1f out* **11/1**
-06 **8** *2* **Try Cat**[6] 246 4-8-12 0.. StevieDonohoe 5 40
(Sir Mark Prescott) *t.k.h in midfield: rdn and lost pl 5f out: racd awkwardly and struggling over 2f out* **50/1**
04-4 **9** *shd* **Dovedon Earl**[12] 179 4-9-3 58.. LiamKeniry 9 45
(T Keddy) *chsd ldrs on outer: wnt 2nd over 5f out tl over 2f out: wknd u.p over 1f out* **16/1**
50-4 **10** *5* **Set Em Up Mo**[19] 82 4-8-5 45..(v) KierenFox[(7)] 10 32
(M J Attwater) *chsd ldr tl led 10f out: rdn and hdd ent fnl 2f: wknd qckly over 1f out* **66/1**
006/ **11** *nk* **Abfabfong (IRE)**[27] 2719 5-9-7 43.. StephenCraine 4 36
(M R Bosley) *led for 2f: chsd ldr after tl 8f out: lost pl and rdn 5f out: bhd fnl 2f* **50/1**

2m 33.19s (0.19) **Going Correction** +0.05s/f (Slow)
WFA 4 from 5yo+ 4lb **11** Ran SP% **119.5**
Speed ratings: **101,100,99,98,98 98,97,96,96,92 92**
toteswingers: 1&2 £1.90, 1&3 £11.80, 2&3 £14.30 CSF £3.74 TOTE £2.10: £1.10, £1.70, £7.40; EX 4.50 Trifecta £66.30 Pool: £627.32 - 7.00 winning units..
Owner The Horse Players Two **Bred** Ennistown Stud **Trained** Lower Beeding, W Sussex

FOCUS
A moderate maiden and muddling form with the principals below their best.

Dovedon Earl Official explanation: jockey said gelding hung left

317 LINGFIELD PARK GOLF CLUB H'CAP — 7f (P)

4:00 (4:02) (Class 5) (0-70,67) 4-Y-0+ — **£2,456** (£725; £362) **Stalls** Low

Form				RPR
65-4	**1**		**Billberry**[18] [110] 5-9-4 **67**....(t) AdamKirby 3 (S C Williams) *in tch: swtchd ins and rdn over 1f out: led 1f out: drvn ins fnl f: kpt on* **13/8**[1]	74+
0-50	**2**	*nk*	**Waterloo Dock**[7] [242] 5-8-7 **56**.... GregFairley 5 (M Quinn) *t.k.h: w ldr: rdn wl over 1f out: led jst over 1f out: sn hdd and nt gng pce of wnr: rallied fnl 75yds: kpt on* **16/1**	62
0-46	**3**	*nk*	**Kyle (IRE)**[8] [223] 6-8-13 **62**.... LiamKeniry 6 (C R Dore) *hld up in tch in last trio: rdn and hdwy 1f out: r.o wl ins fnl f: nt quite rch ldng pair* **13/2**	67
00-0	**4**	*hd*	**Grand Honour (IRE)**[14] [151] 4-9-0 **63**.... IanMongan 8 (P Howling) *steaded s: hld up in tch in rr: plld wd and hdwy ent fnl f: r.o wl: nt quite rch ldrs* **20/1**	68
1143	**5**	*1 ¾*	**Goodbye Cash (IRE)**[3] [284] 6-9-0 **63**.... PaulDoe 1 (P D Evans) *taken down early: t.k.h: hld up in tch: rdn over 2f out: kpt on same pce u.p fr over 1f out* **6/1**[3]	63
45-2	**6**	*¾*	**Fine Silk (USA)**[8] [225] 4-8-12 **64**.... AndreaAtzeni[(3)] 7 (M G Quinlan) *led: rdn wl over 1f out: hedaed jst over 1f out: wknd ins fnl f* **11/4**[2]	62
-453	**7**	*nse*	**Jonnie Skull (IRE)**[13] [170] 4-9-4 **67**....(vt) FergusSweeney 4 (P S McEntee) *t.k.h: chsd ldrs: rdn and wknd over 1f out* **9/1**	65
60-6	**8**	*shd*	**Grey Boy (GER)**[19] [84] 9-8-9 **65**.... GeorgeDowning[(7)] 2 (A W Carroll) *v.s.a: sn rcvrd and in tch in last trio after 1f: rdn over 1f out: kpt on but nvr gng pce to trble ldrs* **16/1**	62

1m 24.87s (0.07) **Going Correction** +0.05s/f (Slow) — **8** Ran SP% **118.9**

Speed ratings (Par 103): **101,100,100,100,98 97,97,97**

toteswingers: 1&2 £8.60, 1&3 £3.60, 2&3 £16.00 CSF £31.95 CT £143.27 TOTE £2.70: £1.50, £4.00, £1.80; EX 40.60 Trifecta £157.60 Pool: £370.58 - 1.74 winning units..

Owner Essex Racing Club (Billberry) **Bred** G Deacon **Trained** Newmarket, Suffolk

FOCUS

Just a modest handicap with the winner not needing to run to his best and the placed horses close to their marks.

318 GOLF AT LINGFIELD PARK APPRENTICE H'CAP — 7f (P)

4:30 (4:32) (Class 6) (0-60,61) 4-Y-0+ — **£1,774** (£523; £262) **Stalls** Low

Form				RPR
0-31	**1**		**Headache**[5] [269] 5-9-6 **61** 6ex....(bt) MatthewLawson 13 (B W Duke) *w ldr: led over 2f out: pressed thrght fnl f: hld on gamely u.p* **7/2**[1]	73
04-1	**2**	*nk*	**Straight Face (IRE)**[5] [270] 6-8-13 **61** 6ex....(b) KevinLundie[(7)] 5 (P D Evans) *chsd ldrs: wnt 2nd 2f out: pressed wnr thrght fnl f: kpt on but a jst hld* **4/1**[2]	72
0/02	**3**	*2*	**Castleburg**[7] [238] 4-8-12 **58**.... HarryBentley[(5)] 11 (G L Moore) *hld up in rr: hdwy on outer over 2f out: rdn and hung lft over 1f out: kpt on to go 3rd ins fnl f: nvr gng pce to rch ldng pair* **9/2**[3]	64
013-	**4**	*¾*	**Batchworth Blaise**[49] [7691] 7-8-12 **53**.... RichardRowe 1 (E A Wheeler) *stdd s: hld up towards rr: hdwy to chse ldrs over 2f out: nt enough room over 1f out: kpt on same pce fnl f* **20/1**	57
60-2	**5**	*½*	**Bollywood Style**[25] [14] 5-9-3 **58**.... ShaneRyan 4 (J R Best) *chsd ldng pair: rdn and unable qck wl over 1f out: no imp fnl f* **6/1**	61
4-53	**6**	*1 ¼*	**Fly By Nelly**[18] [101] 4-9-4 **59**.... DavidKenny 10 (H Morrison) *in tch in midfield: pushed along on outer over 2f out: styd on same pce u.p fnl f* **7/1**	58
000-	**7**	*hd*	**Rony Dony (IRE)**[129] [5124] 6-8-0 **48** oh1 ow2.... AdamBeschizza[(7)] 12 (M E Rimmer) *bhd: rdn and hdwy on inner wl over 1f out: no imp fnl f* **66/1**	47
6-05	**8**	*nk*	**Whotsit (IRE)**[15] [135] 4-9-2 **57**....(b) LauraPike 9 (Miss Amy Weaver) *towards rr: rdn and hdwy into midfield jst over 2f out: no imp fnl f* **15/2**	55
3-60	**9**	*¾*	**Dynamo Dave (USA)**[6] [249] 5-8-3 **49**....(b) MissRachelKing[(5)] 2 (M D I Usher) *chsd ldrs tl lost pl over 2f out: no imp fr wl over 1f out* **20/1**	45
050-	**10**	*12*	**Torquemada (IRE)**[63] [7517] 9-8-2 **46**....(tp) JakePayne[(3)] 7 (M J Attwater) *stdd s: hld up in rr: hdwy and in tch over 2f out: rdn and sn btn wl over 1f out* **33/1**	9
00-0	**11**	*3 ½*	**Proud Linus (USA)**[7] [242] 5-9-5 **60**....(t) RyanPowell 8 (J Ryan) *taken down early and led to post: racd freely: led and clr w rival: hdd over 2f out: wknd qckly wl over 1f out: wl bhd fnl f* **25/1**	14

1m 24.83s (0.03) **Going Correction** +0.05s/f (Slow) — **11** Ran SP% **116.8**

Speed ratings (Par 101): **101,100,98,97,96 95,95,94,94,80 76**

toteswingers: 1&2 £4.20, 1&3 £5.10, 2&3 £7.80 CSF £16.07 CT £64.87 TOTE £3.30: £1.60, £1.80, £1.60; EX 13.30 Trifecta £49.50 Pool: £432.89 - 6.46 winning units. Place 6: £19.00 Place 5: £8.98 .

Owner Brendan W Duke Racing **Bred** Bearstone Stud **Trained** Lambourn, Berks

■ Stewards' Enquiry : Ryan Powell caution: used whip when out of contention

FOCUS

A moderate affair for apprentice riders but the form looks pretty good for the grade, with the third, fourth and fifth to recent form.

Torquemada(IRE) Official explanation: trainer said gelding had a breathing problem

T/Plt: £44.80 to a £1 stake. Pool: £55,356.68. 900.68 winning tickets. T/Qpdt: £7.30 to a £1 stake. Pool: £4,899.03. 496.20 winning tickets. SP

305 KEMPTON (A.W) (R-H)

Thursday, January 28

OFFICIAL GOING: Standard

Wind: Moderate across, away from stands Weather: Overcast

319 BET AFRICAN NATIONS CUP - BETDAQ H'CAP — 6f (P)

4:55 (4:55) (Class 7) (0-50,50) 4-Y-0+ — **£1,364** (£403; £201) **Stalls** High

Form				RPR
-623	**1**		**Equinity**[7] [251] 4-9-3 **50**....(t) SaleemGolam 3 (J Pearce) *dropped in fr wd draw and hld up: sn in midfield: prog over 2f out: led over 1f out: rdn clr* **7/1**[3]	61
-004	**2**	*2*	**Commandingpresence (USA)**[15] [146] 4-8-5 **45**.... KierenFox[(7)] 11 (J J Bridger) *chsd ldrs: effrt 2f out: styd on to take 2nd ins fnl f: no imp on wnr* **10/1**	49
40-5	**3**	*¾*	**Davids Mark**[19] [103] 10-9-1 **48**....(p) SimonWhitworth 7 (J R Jenkins) *hld up in last trio: prog 2f out: rdn and styd on to take 3rd last 100yds: nvr able to chal* **9/2**[2]	50
000-	**4**	*¾*	**Jessica Wigmo**[180] [4533] 7-9-3 **50**.... AdamKirby 4 (A W Carroll) *dwlt: dropped ins fr wd draw and hld up last: sme prog 2f out: nt clr run and swtchd lft over 1f out: styd on fnl f: nvr rchd ldrs* **11/1**	50+
65-0	**5**	*1 ¼*	**Sir Loin**[6] [271] 9-8-7 **45**....(v) RossAtkinson[(5)] 9 (P Burgoyne) *t.k.h: pressed ldr: upsides over 1f out: wknd ins fnl f* **25/1**	41
0-00	**6**	*½*	**Place The Duchess**[6] [271] 4-9-0 **47**....(bt[1]) TomQueally 5 (A J Lidderdale) *t.k.h: hld up in rr: looking for room over 2f out: rdn and nt qckn over 1f out: one pce after* **16/1**	41
550-	**7**	*nk*	**Tightrope (IRE)**[43] [7774] 4-8-12 **45**....(b) MartinDwyer 10 (T D McCarthy) *led to over 1f out: sort of room on inner after and grad lost pl* **16/1**	38
66-3	**8**	*¾*	**Sonhador**[19] [103] 4-9-3 **50**.... LiamJones 12 (G Prodromou) *pressed ldng pair on inner: looking for room over 2f out: wknd tamely over 1f out* **5/2**[1]	41
0/05	**9**	*1 ½*	**Contented (IRE)**[8] [242] 8-9-1 **48**....(tp) SteveDrowne 2 (Mrs L C Jewell) *racd wd: struggling in rr by 1/2-way: sn btn* **10/1**	34
00-6	**10**	*½*	**Divine White**[26] [10] 7-8-12 **45**.... DaneO'Neill 6 (G P Enright) *chsd ldrs: rdn wl over 2f out: wknd wl over 1f out* **20/1**	29
0630	**11**	*5*	**Mickys Mate**[2] [296] 5-8-7 **45**.... DeanHeslop[(5)] 8 (S A Harris) *racd wd: chsd ldrs: lost pl by 1/2-way: sn wknd and bhd* **7/1**[3]	13

1m 13.17s (0.07) **Going Correction** +0.075s/f (Slow) — **11** Ran SP% **118.6**

Speed ratings (Par 97): **102,99,98,97,95 95,94,93,91,90 84**

toteswingers: 1&2 £14.50, 1&3 £12.00, 2&3 £5.00 CSF £75.79 CT £360.01 TOTE £10.80: £4.10, £5.60, £3.20; EX 101.50.

Owner Killarney Glen **Bred** Whitwell Bloodstock **Trained** Newmarket, Suffolk

■ Stewards' Enquiry : Ross Atkinson caution: careless riding

FOCUS

A decent pace set the race up for the hold-up horses. The winner confirmed a couple of recent apparently improved efforts and the form is rated around the runner-up.

Sir Loin Official explanation: jockey said gelding hung right

Tightrope(IRE) Official explanation: jockey said gelding suffered interference

320 BET SUPER LEAGUE - BETDAQ H'CAP — 7f (P)

5:25 (5:25) (Class 7) (0-50,50) 4-Y-0+ — **£1,364** (£403; £201) **Stalls** High

Form				RPR
05-3	**1**		**Clever Omneya (USA)**[15] [145] 4-8-12 **45**.... TomQueally 12 (J R Jenkins) *trckd ldng pair: wnt 2nd wl over 2f out: drvn ahd over 1f out: narrow advantage after but a holding on* **6/1**[3]	53
56-0	**2**	*½*	**Imperial Skylight**[16] [135] 4-9-2 **49**.... ChrisCatlin 8 (M R Channon) *led: drvn and hdd over 1f out: pressed wnr after but a hld* **8/1**	56
30-4	**3**	*½*	**Hi Spec (IRE)**[11] [211] 7-8-13 **46**....(p) JimmyQuinn 11 (Miss M E Rowland) *t.k.h: hld up in midfield: prog towards inner 2f out: pressed ldng pair fnl f: nt qckn* **7/1**	52
0-00	**4**	*½*	**Grizedale (IRE)**[8] [234] 11-8-8 **48**....(tp) KierenFox[(7)] 13 (M J Attwater) *t.k.h: hld up in abt 6th: nt qckn 2f out: kpt on fnl f: nvr able to chal* **20/1**	52
-453	**5**	*shd*	**Reigning Monarch (USA)**[8] [235] 7-9-1 **48**.... SamHitchcott 1 (Miss Z C Davison) *dropped in fr wd draw: t.k.h and hld up in last trio: prog over 2f out: rdn to go 4th 1f out: nt qckn after* **9/2**[1]	52+
64-2	**6**	*1 ¼*	**Dicey Affair**[16] [135] 4-9-0 **47**....(t) FergusSweeney 7 (G L Moore) *trckd ldng trio: rdn and nt qckn 2f out: stl cl enough 1f out: wknd last 100yds* **11/2**[2]	48
4-63	**7**	*1*	**Easy Wonder (GER)**[8] [234] 5-8-12 **45**....(b) MartinDwyer 9 (I A Wood) *hld up in abt 5th: pushed along and lost pl over 2f out: no prog over 1f out: plugged on* **10/1**	43
6-60	**8**	*½*	**Djalalabad (FR)**[7] [249] 6-9-2 **49**....(tp) HayleyTurner 14 (Mrs C A Dunnett) *t.k.h: hld up in midfield: effrt on inner over 2f out: no imp over 1f out: wknd fnl f* **11/2**[2]	46
30-0	**9**	*1 ¾*	**Metropolitan Chief**[8] [235] 6-8-12 **45**.... SteveDrowne 3 (P Burgoyne) *tk fierce hold and racd wd: struggling over 2f out: n.d after* **25/1**	37
6-00	**10**	*½*	**Bertbrand**[7] [249] 5-9-3 **50**....(v[1]) LiamKeniry 4 (I W McInnes) *dropped in fr wd draw: t.k.h and hld up in last pair: shkn up and effrt over 2f out: sn no prog* **33/1**	41
00-6	**11**	*¾*	**Triumphant Welcome**[14] [178] 5-8-13 **46**.... DaneO'Neill 5 (H J Evans) *t.k.h: hld up in midfield on outer: no prog over 2f out: wknd* **16/1**	35
40-4	**12**	*nk*	**Battimoore (IRE)**[7] [249] 4-9-2 **49**.... AdamKirby 2 (I W McInnes) *dropped in fr wd draw: t.k.h and hld up in last pair: hrd rdn and effrt over 2f out: sn no prog* **25/1**	37
000-	**13**	*2*	**Vanatina (IRE)**[268] [1781] 6-9-0 **47**.... LiamJones 10 (W M Brisbourne) *chsd ldr to wl over 2f out: sn wknd* **33/1**	29
0/0-	**14**	*9*	**Zazous**[270] [1710] 9-9-0 **50**.... MarcHalford[(3)] 6 (J J Bridger) *s.i.s: t.k.h: hld up in rr: brought wd in st: sn wknd: t.o* **50/1**	8

1m 27.3s (1.30) **Going Correction** +0.075s/f (Slow) — **14** Ran SP% **122.1**

Speed ratings (Par 97): **95,94,93,93,93 91,90,90,88,87 86,86,83,73**

toteswingers: 1&2 £12.40, 1&3 £8.00, 2&3 £20.30 CSF £49.73 CT £351.96 TOTE £6.70: £2.10, £3.90, £1.90; EX 50.60.

Owner Sheik Ahmad Yousuf Al Sabah **Bred** Lantern Hill Farm Llc **Trained** Royston, Herts

FOCUS

Just a medium gallop, and by the time the hold-up horses started to stay on it was just too late. The winner built on her recent win and the next two give the form a bit of substance.

Vanatina(IRE) Official explanation: jockey said mare finished lame on its off foreleg

321 BETDAQ THE BETTING EXCHANGE MEDIAN AUCTION MAIDEN STKS — 7f (P)

5:55 (5:56) (Class 5) 3-5-Y-0 — **£2,590** (£770; £385; £192) **Stalls** High

Form				RPR
03-	**1**		**Highland Bridge**[71] [7429] 3-8-8 0.... MartinDwyer 4 (D R C Elsworth) *chsd ldr: rdn to dispute ld over 2f out to over 1f out: styd on to ld again ins fnl f: drvn out* **14/1**	63
0-	**2**	*¾*	**Sunley Spinalonga**[43] [7772] 3-7-12 0.... DeclanCannon[(5)] 11 (D R C Elsworth) *s.i.s: wl in rr: rdn and prog on inner over 2f out: clsd to chal 1f out: chsd wnr ins fnl f: a hld* **20/1**	56
3-63	**3**	*shd*	**Major Lawrence (IRE)**[9] [226] 4-9-12 63....(v) ShaneKelly 1 (J Noseda) *hld up in last trio: shkn up over 2f out: prog over 1f out w hd to one side: clsd on ldrs fnl f but nvr really chal* **6/1**[3]	66
4	**4**	*¾*	**Merals Choice**[15] [147] 3-8-3 0.... NickyMackay 10 (J R Boyle) *t.k.h: trckd ldng pair: rdn to dispute ld over 2f out to over 1f out: nt qckn u.p* **20/1**	54
-50	**5**	*hd*	**Mary's Pet**[13] [180] 3-8-3 0.... SimonWhitworth 8 (J Akehurst) *trckd ldrs: fnd room and prog to ld over 1f out: pushed along w no recrse to whip: hdd and fdd ins fnl f* **25/1**	53

5-2 **6** 3/4 **Neduardo**[8] [236] 3-8-8 0 .... JackMitchell 3 56
(P W Chapple-Hyam) *trckd ldrs on outer: rdn and nt qckn 2f out: one pce after and no imp fnl f* **5/4**[1]

43-3 **7** *hd* **Perfect Secret**[14] [159] 4-9-7 62 .... LiamKeniry 7 56
(A M Balding) *hld up towards rr: prog over 2f out: hrd rdn and cl enough 1f out: nt qckn* **15/2**

8 *nk* **Premier League** 3-8-8 0 .... JimmyQuinn 9 55
(P Howling) *s.i.s: hld up last: gng strly and looking for room over 2f out: swtchd to inner wl over 1f out and promising prog: shkn up and cl enough ent fnl f: fdd: nt disgracd* **66/1**

45 **9** 1/2 **Oceans Edge**[14] [161] 4-9-12 0 .... StephenCraine 6 59+
(J R Boyle) *hld up in last pair: shkn up over 2f out: promising hdwy over 1f out to latch on to bk of tightly gped field: no prog after* **33/1**

10 5 **Coxwain (IRE)** 3-8-8 0 .... JoeFanning 12 40+
(M Johnston) *s.i.s: hld up in midfield on inner: losing pl whn hmpd over 1f out: wknd* **5/2**[2]

00-6 **11** *dist* **Lunaticus**[14] [161] 4-9-0 25 .... (p) KierenFox(7) 5 —
(M J Attwater) *blasted off in front: hdd & wknd rapidly over 2f out: t.o* **100/1**

1m 26.62s (0.62) **Going Correction** +0.075s/f (Slow)
WFA 3 from 4yo 18lb 11 Ran SP% **124.5**
Speed ratings (Par 103): **99,98,98,97,96 96,95,95,94,89 54**
toteswingers: 1&2 £37.10, 1&3 £7.40, 2&3 £21.40 CSF £262.10 TOTE £22.00: £3.40, £6.00, £1.60; EX 155.80.

Owner J Wotherspoon **Bred** John Wotherspoon **Trained** Newmarket, Suffolk

■ Stewards' Enquiry : Liam Keniry one-day ban: careless riding (Feb 11)

FOCUS
They went a routine gallop and finished in a heap, so the form looks muddling. It is probably best viewed around the third.

Coxwain(IRE) Official explanation: jockey said colt hung left

322 BETDAQEXTRA.COM H'CAP 2m (P)
6:25 (6:25) (Class 5) (0-75,70) 4-Y-0+ **£2,590** (£770; £385; £192) **Stalls** High

Form RPR

30-0 **1** **Kristallo (GER)**[14] [164] 5-9-0 **56** .... DaneO'Neill 2 62
(P R Webber) *hld up in last: prog on outer 4f out: hdwy again to go 2nd jst over 2f out: jnd ldr wl over 1f out: narrow ld fnl f: drvn out* **9/2**[3]

24-4 **2** 1/2 **Baltimore Patriot (IRE)**[27] [3] 7-9-3 **59** .... FrankieMcDonald 8 64
(R Curtis) *hld up in last trio: dropped to last and outpcd 4f out: wd bnd 3f out: prog u.p after: wnt 3rd over 1f out: styd on to take 2nd last stride* **7/2**[2]

61/0 **3** *hd* **Kentmere (IRE)**[14] [164] 9-9-7 **63** .... HayleyTurner 3 68
(P R Webber) *trckd ldr: led over 3f out: drvn over 2f out: jnd wl over 1f out: narrowly hdd fnl f: kpt on but lost 2nd last stride* **14/1**

241- **4** 1 3/4 **M'Lady Rousseur (IRE)**[96] [7025] 4-8-10 **59** .... LiamKeniry 7 62
(C C Bealby) *hld up in last trio: pushed along and effrt over 3f out: trying to cl whn nt clr run and swtchd lft 2f out: sn rdn and nt qckn: plugged on* **3/1**[1]

00/0 **5** 3/4 **Pugilist**[15] [148] 8-8-10 **52** .... JoeFanning 5 54
(K C Bailey) *trckd ldrs: rdn to go 3rd 2f out: no imp: fdd fnl f* **25/1**

336/ **6** 8 **Dune Raider (USA)**[60] [5744] 9-9-9 **65** .... IanMongan 6 57
(P D Evans) *pushed up to chse ldng pair: rdn and lost pl rapidly over 4f out: sn last and no ch* **9/1**

03-0 **7** *shd* **Spiritonthemount (USA)**[14] [164] 5-8-6 **51** oh1 ....(b) WilliamCarson(3) 1 43
(P W Hiatt) *racd wd: hld up: prog over 4f out and sing taking t.k.h: wknd rapidly 2f out* **13/2**

/0-6 **8** 3 1/2 **Pocket Too**[15] [148] 7-9-9 **70** .... (p) LeeNewnes(5) 4 58
(Matthew Salaman) *led to over 3f out: wknd rapidly 2f out* **6/1**

3m 32.61s (2.51) **Going Correction** +0.075s/f (Slow)
WFA 4 from 5yo+ 7lb 8 Ran SP% **113.5**
Speed ratings (Par 103): **96,95,95,94,94 90,90,88**
toteswingers: 1&2 £5.70, 1&3 £16.60, 2&3 £11.10 CSF £20.32 CT £200.70 TOTE £5.10: £2.50, £2.00, £2.80; EX 26.80.

Owner Iain Russell Watters **Bred** Gestut Hof Ittlingen **Trained** Mollington, Oxon

■ Stewards' Enquiry : Frankie McDonald one-day ban: used whip with excessive frequency (Feb 11)

FOCUS
The pace was steady and the form may not be all that solid. The winner did not need to match last year's turf form.

Pocket Too Official explanation: jockey said gelding hung left

323 BET IN RUNNING - BETDAQ H'CAP 1m 4f (P)
6:55 (6:56) (Class 5) (0-75,73) 4-Y-0+ **£2,590** (£770; £385; £192) **Stalls** Centre

Form RPR

0- **1** **Oxford City (IRE)**[30] [7823] 6-9-1 **66** .... (t) LukeMorris 4 76
(P M Phelan) *hld up in 4th: pushed along 4f out: prog on inner to chal over 1f out whn jockey dropped whip: urged along to ld narrowly ent fnl f: hld on* **10/1**[3]

131- **2** *hd* **Quinsman**[38] [7831] 4-9-2 **71** .... LiamKeniry 3 81
(J S Moore) *trckd ldr: rdn to ld over 1f out: narrowly hdd u.p ent fnl f: pressed wnr after: nt qckn* **2/1**[1]

04-2 **3** 3 1/2 **Eseej (USA)**[4] [282] 5-9-5 **70** .... ChrisCatlin 5 75
(P W Hiatt) *led: set gd pce after 4f: drvn and hdd over 1f out: hld whn tightened up ent fnl f* **2/1**[1]

10-3 **4** 1 1/2 **Doubnov (FR)**[14] [174] 7-9-8 **73** .... (p) ShaneKelly 1 75
(Ian Williams) *s.s: sn trckd ldng pair: shkn up over 2f out: fnd nil* **9/2**[2]

36-4 **5** 6 **Resplendent Ace (IRE)**[14] [174] 6-9-5 **70** .... IanMongan 6 62
(P Howling) *hld up in last: drvn and no rspnse wl over 2f out* **9/2**[2]

2m 35.29s (0.79) **Going Correction** +0.075s/f (Slow)
WFA 4 from 5yo+ 4lb 5 Ran SP% **112.1**
Speed ratings (Par 103): **100,99,97,96,92**
toteswingers: 1&2 £9.40, 1&3 not won, 2&3 not won. CSF £30.80 TOTE £11.40: £3.70, £1.10; EX 56.30.

Owner Mrs Norah Kennedy & Miss Alison Jones **Bred** John McLoughlin **Trained** Epsom, Surrey

■ Stewards' Enquiry : Liam Keniry three-day ban: two for careless riding (Feb 12-13); one for excessive use of the whip (Feb 14)

FOCUS
For the second time in four days, Eseej ensured a decent gallop but merely set the race up for the pair who contested the finish. Muddling form with the winner's best effort since he was a 3yo.

Resplendent Ace(IRE) Official explanation: jockey said gelding ran flat

324 BETDAQ ON 0870 178 1221 H'CAP 1m (P)
7:25 (7:25) (Class 3) (0-95,93) 4-Y-0+
£6,542 (£1,959; £979; £490; £244; £122) **Stalls** High

Form RPR

45-6 **1** **Vainglory (USA)**[12] [205] 6-8-8 **83** .... MartinDwyer 3 93
(D M Simcock) *chsd ldrs: rdn over 2f out: prog to ld jst over 1f out: r.o wl and sn clr* **3/1**[2]

20-5 **2** 2 **Councellor (FR)**[8] [231] 8-9-1 **90** .... (t) TomQueally 7 95
(Stef Higgins) *snatched up sn after s: pushed up in midfield after 2f: effrt over 2f out: drvn and styd on to go 2nd last 100yds: no ch w wnr* **7/1**

-436 **3** 1 **Carcinetto (IRE)**[5] [278] 8-8-13 **93** .... RichardEvans(5) 9 96
(P D Evans) *hld up: last 1/2-way: effrt on inner over 2f out: rdn and kpt on fr over 1f out to take 3rd nr fin* **20/1**

41-0 **4** 1/2 **L'Hirondelle (IRE)**[8] [231] 6-8-10 **85** .... PaulDoe 4 87
(M J Attwater) *t.k.h: trckd ldr: chal fr 1/2-way: upsides jst over 1f out: chsd wnr after tl wknd fnl 100yds* **14/1**

/ **5** 1/2 **Mesa Marauder**[61] 6-9-1 **90** .... (p) JimmyQuinn 1 91
(M Botti) *s.i.s: mostly in last pair: drvn and prog on outer 2f out: tried to cl on ldrs 1f out: effrt petered out* **8/1**

22-2 **6** 1/2 **Den's Gift (IRE)**[8] [231] 6-8-9 **84** .... (b) LukeMorris 5 84
(C G Cox) *led: pestered for ld fr 1/2-way: shkn up 2f out: hdd & wknd jst over 1f out* **2/1**[1]

0-60 **7** 3 1/2 **Stand Guard**[13] [197] 6-8-6 **86** .... AndrewHeffernan(5) 2 78
(P Howling) *racd wd in midfield: hrd rdn wl over 2f out: sn btn* **12/1**

10-1 **8** 1 1/2 **Snow Bay**[18] [115] 4-8-7 **82** .... JoeFanning 6 70
(B Smart) *t.k.h: trckd ldrs tl wknd 2f out* **6/1**[3]

1m 38.12s (-1.68) **Going Correction** +0.075s/f (Slow) 8 Ran SP% **115.4**
Speed ratings (Par 107): **111,109,108,107,107 106,103,101**
toteswingers: 1&2 £6.70, 1&3 £9.40, 2&3 £9.50 CSF £24.52 CT £358.19 TOTE £5.00: £1.70, £2.50, £5.30; EX 45.40.

Owner DXB Bloodstock Ltd **Bred** Darley **Trained** Newmarket, Suffolk

FOCUS
Although the pace was modest for the first 3f, Den's Gift then stepped it up and the better quality of this field ensured that the time was a decent one in relation to the others. The winner's best effort since last summer with sound form among the placed horses.

NOTEBOOK
Vainglory(USA), back down to his last winning mark and with a recent pipe-opener behind him, put the race beyond doubt with a strong finishing effort. He has won over further and any trip up to 1m2f should be within his capabilities. (op 9-2)

Councellor(FR) has returned from a break in good form. He has never won off this mark so it was a gallant effort, and he will be particularly dangerous if the handicapper drops him 1-2lb. (op 6-1)

Carcinetto(IRE) has never won at 1m, so a return to 7f should not be an inconvenience, but she stayed on in a style which suggests she can yet make her mark at this distance. (tchd 16-1)

L'Hirondelle(IRE) has been on a stiff mark since winning here last month. That was over 7f, but he has won at 1m1f so the extra weight is probably the problem. (op 12-1)

Mesa Marauder, three times a winner in France (twice on soft ground), was making his British debut. He ran respectably after an awkward start and should improve as he acclimatises. (tchd 13-2)

Den's Gift(IRE) deserves to win more often than he does, but again he just set it up for his rivals. (op 9-4 tchd 5-2)

Snow Bay Official explanation: jockey said colt ran too free

325 BETDAQ THE BETTING EXCHANGE H'CAP 6f (P)
7:55 (7:55) (Class 5) (0-70,70) 4-Y-0+ **£2,590** (£770; £385; £96; £96) **Stalls** High

Form RPR

203- **1** **Jack Rackham**[46] [7739] 6-9-3 **69** .... (v) TomEaves 5 77
(B Smart) *trckd ldr: rdn 2f out: narrow ld jst over 1f out: kpt on wl to assert ins fnl f* **5/1**[2]

0-20 **2** 3/4 **Dickie Le Davoir**[2] [296] 6-8-0 **57** oh2 ow1 .... (v) BillyCray(5) 9 62+
(R C Guest) *dwlt: hld up in last: prog jst over 2f out: rdn and styd on fr over 1f out: tk 2nd last stride* **8/1**

-345 **3** *shd* **Dvinsky (USA)**[13] [192] 9-9-4 **70** .... (b) JimmyQuinn 4 75
(P Howling) *led: rdn over 2f out: narrowly hdd jst over 1f out: kpt on wl but hld after: lost 2nd last stride* **4/1**[1]

42-1 **4** *nk* **Hollow Jo**[1] [312] 10-9-2 **68** 6ex .... (v) FergusSweeney 2 72
(J R Jenkins) *hld up in 6th: rdn and nt qckn 2f out: styd on fnl f to cl on ldrs fin* **4/1**[1]

06-0 **4** *dht* **Highland Harvest**[5] [275] 6-9-1 **67** .... SteveDrowne 3 71
(Jamie Poulton) *t.k.h: trckd ldng trio: effrt on outer 2f out: cl enough to chal 1f out: nt qckn after* **10/1**

0342 **6** 1 1/2 **Sherjawy (IRE)**[8] [242] 6-8-6 **58** ow2 .... SamHitchcott 7 57
(Miss Z C Davison) *trckd ldng pair: effrt on inner 2f out: nrly upsides ent fnl f: wknd last 150yds* **11/2**[3]

10-0 **7** 1 1/4 **The Wee Chief (IRE)**[17] [119] 4-9-1 **67** .... RichardSmith 10 62
(J C Fox) *plld hrd: hld up in 7th: rdn 2f out: clsd on ldrs 1f out: wknd ins fnl f* **10/1**

00-4 **8** 1/2 **Diddums**[16] [137] 4-8-4 **56** oh1 .... ChrisCatlin 6 50
(P S McEntee) *plld hrd: hld up bhd ldrs: lost pl and btn wl over 1f out* **9/1**

-310 **9** 2 1/2 **Elusive Ronnie (IRE)**[1] [312] 4-8-7 **59** .... (b) JackMitchell 1 45
(R A Teal) *dwlt: a in last pair: u.p 1/2-way: lost tch 2f out* **14/1**

1m 12.74s (-0.36) **Going Correction** +0.075s/f (Slow) 9 Ran SP% **118.0**
Speed ratings (Par 103): **105,104,103,103,103 101,99,99,95**
toteswingers: 1&2 £10.50, 1&3 £4.90, 2&3 £8.50 CSF £45.54 CT £178.35 TOTE £7.20: £2.20, £4.40, £2.00; EX 46.80 Place 6: £474.64 Place 5: £196.55 .

Owner Mrs F Denniff **Bred** A S Denniff **Trained** Hambleton, N Yorks

FOCUS
A competitive if moderate sprint but the time was ordinary. The third is the most solid guide.

T/Plt: £2,920.40 to a £1 stake. Pool: £67,210.12. 16.80 winning tickets. T/Qpdt: £220.50 to a £1 stake. Pool: £9,271.07. 31.10 winning tickets. JN

The Form Book, Raceform Ltd, Compton, RG20 6NL

[296]SOUTHWELL (L-H)

Thursday, January 28

OFFICIAL GOING: Standard

Wind: Moderate, behind. Weather: Overcast but fine.

326 BET AUSTRALIAN OPEN TENNIS-BETDAQ MEDIAN AUCTION MAIDEN STKS — 1m (F)

1:35 (1:35) (Class 6) 3-5-Y-O — **£1,774** (£523; £262) **Stalls** Low

Form — RPR

1 **Reverend Green (IRE)**[15] 4-9-12 0 .... PhillipMakin 7 — 76+
(K A Ryan) *sn trcking ldrs: wnt 2nd over 3f out: sn drvn: styd on to ld last 100yds* **8/11**[1]

2 2 1 ¼ **Takajan (IRE)**[14] [161] 3-8-6 73 .... LiamKeniry 3 — 69
(S Kirk) *led: rdn 2f out: worn down ins fnl f* **15/8**[2]

335- 3 12 **Davana**[40] [7814] 4-9-4 47 .... (p) KellyHarrison(3) 2 — 41
(W J H Ratcliffe) *chsd ldrs: drvn over 3f out: tk modest 3rd 2f out* **16/1**

04-5 4 5 **Montego Breeze**[23] [38] 4-9-7 50 .... RobertWinston 1 — 30
(John A Harris) *w ldrs: outpcd over 3f out: sn wknd* **20/1**

5 nse **Kitty Koo (IRE)** 3-8-1 0 .... LukeMorris 4 — 24
(J Jay) *s.i.s: nvr nr ldrs* **14/1**[3]

000- 6 4 ½ **Candilejas**[71] [7433] 4-9-7 52 .... TonyCulhane 8 — 19
(R Curtis) *in rr on outside: lost pl over 3f out* **20/1**

0 7 3 ¾ **Swell Fellow**[20] [82] 5-9-7 0 .... (v1) AndrewHeffernan(5) 6 — 15
(P D Evans) *s.i.s: t.k.h: lost pl over 3f out* **33/1**

00- 8 7 **Paint By Numbers**[39] [7825] 3-8-6 0 .... PaulHanagan 5 — —
(J A Glover) *chsd ldrs: lost pl over 3f out* **66/1**

0/ 9 46 **Turnham Green**[407] [7699] 4-9-9 0 .... PatrickHills(3) 9 — —
(S Curran) *sn outpcd and detached in last: t.o 4f out* **100/1**

1m 41.48s (-2.22) **Going Correction** -0.20s/f (Stan)
WFA 3 from 4yo+ 20lb — **9** Ran SP% **120.2**
Speed ratings (Par 101): **103,101,89,84,84 80,76,69,23**
toteswingers: 1&2 £1.20, 1&3 £2.80, 2&3 £2.50. CSF £2.22 TOTE £1.90: £1.10, £1.10, £2.80; EX 2.10 Trifecta £10.20 Pool: £470.80 - 33.89 winning units..
Owner Mrs J Ryan **Bred** Rathbarry Stud **Trained** Hambleton, N Yorks

FOCUS
There did not seem to be much strength in depth in this ordinary auction maiden. It was run at a decent pace and the two market leaders pulled a long way clear of the rest. A nice start to his Flat career from the winner.

327 TRY BET ANGEL AT TRY.BETANGEL.COM CLAIMING STKS — 1m 3f (F)

2:10 (2:10) (Class 5) 4-Y-O+ — **£2,331** (£693; £346; £173) **Stalls** Low

Form — RPR

560- 1 **Friends Hope**[44] [7761] 9-8-4 67 .... (b1) FrankieMcDonald 4 — 68
(R Curtis) *dwlt: hld up in tch: hdwy to trck ldrs over 3f out: shkn up on outer: qcknd and led over 1f out: drvn out* **14/1**

1-61 2 2 **Boundless Prospect (USA)**[13] [190] 11-8-4 68.. AndrewHeffernan(5) 3 — 70
(P D Evans) *hld up in tch: wnt prom 6f out: drvn 4f out: kpt on fnl 2f: tk 2nd towards fin* **2/1**[2]

26-3 3 nse **Dunaskin (IRE)**[13] [190] 10-8-10 75 .... (be1) BarryMcHugh(5) 1 — 76
(B Ellison) *trckd ldr: t.k.h: effrt 3f out: sn rdn: styd on same pce appr fnl f* **5/4**[1]

503- 4 3 ½ **My Mate Mal**[44] [7761] 6-8-3 61 ow1 .... LeeTopliss(7) 5 — 65
(B Ellison) *set modest pce: qcknd 4f out: styd far side: hdd over 1f out: wknd ins fnl f* **9/2**[3]

434/ 5 6 **Ivestar (IRE)**[118] [1753] 5-8-8 68 .... (t) PatrickDonaghy(5) 6 — 58?
(P C Haslam) *hld up in tch: hdwy on outside to trck ldrs over 5f out: drvn 3f out: sn wl outpcd* **25/1**

6 28 **Plum Mac**[320] 6-8-8 0 ow2 .... AndrewElliott 2 — 5
(N Bycroft) *trckd ldng pair: t.k.h: lost pl over 4f out: sn bhd: t.o* **125/1**

2m 27.85s (-0.15) **Going Correction** -0.20s/f (Stan) — **6** Ran SP% **107.3**
Speed ratings (Par 103): **92,90,90,87,83 63**
toteswingers: 1&2 £3.40, 1&3 £2.10, 2&3 £1.30. CSF £38.74 TOTE £16.60: £5.40, £1.60; EX 54.70.
Owner Mrs Joanna Hughes **Bred** Huish Bloodstock **Trained** Lambourn, Berks

FOCUS
A fairly competitive claimer, four of the runners holding official ratings between 67 and 75. The pace was steady and they were very tightly grouped in the early stages. The form is a bit muddling and the winner did not need to get back to her old form.

328 PLAY GOLF BEFORE RACING AT SOUTHWELL (S) STKS — 6f (F)

2:45 (2:46) (Class 6) 4-Y-O+ — **£1,774** (£523; £262) **Stalls** Low

Form — RPR

2132 1 **Obe Gold**[7] [251] 8-9-4 66 .... J-PGuillambert 2 — 71
(P Howling) *sn struggling towards rr: outpcd and lost pl over 4f out: hdwy on ins over 2f out: styd on wl to ld nr fin* **11/10**[1]

-000 2 1 **Music Box Express**[8] [234] 6-8-7 54 .... (v) MatthewDavies(5) 6 — 62
(George Baker) *led: sent clr over 3f out: hdd wl ins fnl f* **25/1**

60-3 3 nk **Cornus**[14] [165] 8-8-12 62 .... (be) FrederikTylicki 1 — 61
(J A Glover) *chsd ldrs: wnt 2nd over 3f out: upsides ins fnl f: no ex* **7/1**[3]

30-P 4 2 ¼ **Castle Myth (USA)**[7] [255] 4-8-13 59 .... (b) BarryMcHugh(5) 4 — 60
(B Ellison) *sn detached in last: hdwy on outer over 2f out: nt rch ldrs* **14/1**

4-54 5 2 ½ **Don Pele (IRE)**[8] [242] 8-8-12 59 .... (p) LukeMorris 7 — 46
(R A Harris) *sn chsng ldrs: lost pl 2f out* **7/2**[2]

140- 6 2 ¼ **Bentley**[29] [7876] 6-9-4 59 .... RobertWinston 3 — 44
(J G Given) *chsd ldrs: wknd 2f out* **8/1**

0-32 7 1 ¼ **Kings Ace (IRE)**[2] [297] 4-8-7 55 .... (vt) BillyCray(5) 5 — 34
(A Berry) *in tch: outpcd over 3f out: lost pl over 2f out* **11/1**

1m 15.03s (-1.47) **Going Correction** -0.20s/f (Stan) — **7** Ran SP% **112.3**
Speed ratings (Par 101): **101,99,99,96,92 89,88**
toteswingers: 1&2 £11.90, 1&3 £2.30, 2&3 £18.70. CSF £31.32 TOTE £1.80: £1.50, £5.80; EX 33.90.There was no bid for the winner.
Owner Paul Howling **Bred** Mrs M Mason **Trained** Newmarket, Suffolk

FOCUS
An ordinary seller run at a good pace. The form is rated around the winer, the only runner with solid recent form.

329 FREEBETS.CO.UK FREE BETS H'CAP — 6f (F)

3:20 (3:20) (Class 6) (0-60,60) 3-Y-O — **£1,683** (£501; £250; £125) **Stalls** Low

Form — RPR

31-2 1 **Bookiesindex Girl (IRE)**[19] [104] 3-9-1 57 .... RobertWinston 4 — 66
(J R Jenkins) *hmpd s: sn w ldr: led 3f out: sn rdn: styd on to forge clr fnl f* **10/11**[1]

60-6 2 3 ¾ **Bertie Buckle (IRE)**[17] [127] 3-8-13 55 .... LukeMorris 1 — 52
(J R Gask) *swvd rt s: led: hdd 3f out: kpt on same pce fnl f* **5/2**[2]

046- 3 1 ¾ **Taper Jean Girl (IRE)**[44] [7756] 3-8-11 53 .... AndrewElliott 2 — 44
(Mrs R A Carr) *carried rt s: chsd ldrs: outpcd 2f out: styd on ins fnl f* **15/2**

05-0 4 2 ¾ **Sandy Toes**[6] [265] 3-8-4 46 oh1 .... PaulHanagan 6 — 28
(J A Glover) *chsd ldrs: outpcd over 2f out: kpt on fnl f* **13/2**[3]

5-05 5 3 **Holkham**[10] [217] 3-8-2 51 ow1 .... RyanClark(7) 3 — 24
(N P Littmoden) *hmpd s: detached in last: hdwy over 3f out: kpt on fnl 2f: nvr a factor* **25/1**

50-4 6 2 **Last Of The Ravens**[21] [72] 3-8-4 46 oh1 .... AndrewMullen 5 — 12
(J F Coupland) *swvd lft s: chsd ldrs: drvn over 3f out: lost pl 2f out* **100/1**

1m 16.36s (-0.14) **Going Correction** -0.20s/f (Stan) — **6** Ran SP% **110.9**
Speed ratings (Par 95): **92,87,84,81,77 74**
toteswingers: 1&2 £1.40, 1&3 £1.30, 2&3 £2.50. CSF £3.27 TOTE £1.70: £1.10, £1.60; EX 4.10.
Owner Bookmakers Index Ltd **Bred** Michael Woodlock And Seamus Kennedy **Trained** Royston, Herts

FOCUS
A low-grade handicap, and four of the runners had finished tailed off on their previous start. The form has been taken at face value but may be overrated.

330 BETDAQ.CO.UK H'CAP — 1m 3f (F)

3:50 (3:50) (Class 5) (0-70,69) 4-Y-O+ — **£2,331** (£693; £346; £173) **Stalls** Low

Form — RPR

54-3 1 **Charging Indian (IRE)**[23] [42] 4-9-3 67 .... (b) TonyCulhane 4 — 75
(P T Midgley) *trckd ldrs: t.k.h: led over 2f out: hrd rdn and edgd lft fnl f: all out* **5/2**[2]

5-30 2 nk **Bosamcliff (IRE)**[5] [280] 5-9-2 68 .... RichardEvans(5) 1 — 76
(P D Evans) *led early: trckd ldrs: edgd rt and chsd wnr 1f out: no ex nr fin* **15/2**

33-3 3 4 **Laureldeans Best (IRE)**[14] [166] 4-8-5 62 .... LeeTopliss(7) 2 — 63
(R A Fahey) *hld up in rr: hdwy on ins over 4f out: w ldrs 3f out: kpt on same pce appr fnl f* **14/1**

421- 4 ¾ **Shifting Gold (IRE)**[64] [5733] 4-9-5 69 .... (b) PhillipMakin 5 — 69
(K A Ryan) *sn led: hdd over 2f out: one pce* **14/1**

004- 5 2 ½ **Criterion**[32] [7854] 5-9-2 63 .... StevieDonohoe 7 — 58
(Ian Williams) *mid-div: reminders 7f out: outpcd and hung lft over 2f out: kpt on fnl f* **7/4**[1]

-201 6 1 **Highland River**[7] [244] 4-8-7 60 6ex .... RobertLButler(3) 8 — 54
(A Sadik) *w ldr: rdn 3f out: one pce* **7/1**[3]

312- 7 12 **Strikemaster (IRE)**[124] [4470] 4-9-1 65 .... TomEaves 6 — 38
(B Ellison) *hld up in rr: hdwy on outside over 5f out: drvn 3f out: sn lost pl and bhd* **12/1**

8 16 **Uncle Bunge (IRE)**[123] [5848] 4-8-9 59 .... AndrewMullen 3 — 5
(L Corcoran) *dwlt: in rr: hdwy to chse ldrs over 3f out: sn lost pl and bhd* **20/1**

2m 25.17s (-2.83) **Going Correction** -0.20s/f (Stan)
WFA 4 from 5yo 3lb — **8** Ran SP% **115.0**
Speed ratings (Par 103): **102,101,98,98,96 95,87,75**
toteswingers: 1&2 £5.20, 1&3 £7.60, 2&3 £8.80. CSF £21.79 CT £217.56 TOTE £4.10: £1.40, £2.30, £3.40; EX 18.00 Trifecta £136.60 Pool: £349.13 - 1.89 winning units..
Owner David Mann **Bred** Samac Ltd **Trained** Westow, N Yorks

■ Stewards' Enquiry : Richard Evans one-day ban: used whip down the shoulder in forehand position (Feb 11)

FOCUS
An ordinary but competitive handicap, involving two last-time-out winners and three others who were placed on their previous start. The pace was fair and the first two finished clear of the rest. The winner built on his return to form latest.
Criterion Official explanation: trainer had no explanation for the poor form shown

331 BET IN RUNNING-BETDAQ APPRENTICE H'CAP — 1m 6f (F)

4:20 (4:22) (Class 6) (0-55,55) 4-Y-O+ — **£1,683** (£501; £250; £125) **Stalls** Low

Form — RPR

30-2 1 **Aaman (IRE)**[13] [198] 4-9-0 55 .... RyanClark 11 — 81+
(E F Vaughan) *trckd ldrs: led over 8f out: shot wl clr over 1f out: canter* **2/1**[1]

65-5 2 16 **Mayta Capac (USA)**[20] [82] 4-8-11 52 .... LauraPike 3 — 53
(D M Simcock) *trckd ldrs: wnt 2nd on ins over 2f out: kpt on same pce* **33/1**

354- 3 nk **They All Laughed**[37] [7842] 7-9-4 53 .... (p) JohnCavanagh 14 — 54
(Mrs Marjorie Fife) *in rr: hdwy 5f out: styd on fnl 2f: jst hld for 2nd* **9/2**[3]

000- 4 4 ½ **Desert Hawk**[52] [7670] 9-8-4 46 oh1 .... JulieCumine(7) 13 — 40
(P Howling) *in rr: hdwy over 4f out: kpt on fnl 2f: nvr nrr* **100/1**

34/4 5 1 ¼ **Sparkling Montjeu (IRE)**[16] [140] 5-8-13 51 .... NathanAlison(3) 12 — 44
(George Baker) *in rr: kpt on fnl 3f: nvr a factor* **10/1**

06-1 6 ½ **Dontpaytheferryman (USA)**[20] [90] 5-9-5 54 .... (e) LeeTopliss 4 — 46
(B Ellison) *hld up in mid-div: hdwy to chse wnr 7f out: wknd fnl 2f* **11/4**[2]

40-3 7 nk **Red Wine**[13] [199] 11-8-8 50 .... JonathanHinch(7) 6 — 41
(J A Glover) *in rr: hdwy over 5f out: kpt on: nvr on terms* **14/1**

0/32 8 2 **Arisea (IRE)**[13] [186] 7-8-9 49 .... (t) NeilFarley(5) 9 — 38
(Paul Murphy) *in rr: sme hdwy over 3f out: nvr on terms* **14/1**

000/ 9 1 **Bansha (IRE)**[456] [7079] 4-8-4 50 .... NatashaEaton(5) 2 — 37
(A Bailey) *trckd ldrs: drvn over 4f out: wknd fnl 3f* **125/1**

000/ 10 21 **Stolen Light (IRE)**[44] [7042] 9-9-6 55 .... (b) GarryWhillans 8 — 13
(A Crook) *trckd ldrs: lost pl 4f out: sn bhd* **100/1**

20-3 11 9 **Jazrawy**[18] [113] 8-9-5 54 .... MatthewLawson 7 — —
(A J McCabe) *led: hdd over 8f out: lost pl 4f out: sn wl bhd* **20/1**

300- 12 ½ **Waterloo Corner**[51] [4944] 8-8-12 50 .... AdamCarter(3) 1 — —
(R Craggs) *rrd in stalls and s.v.s: a wl bhd* **28/1**

/4P- 13 dist **Nothing Is Forever (IRE)**[38] [449] 6-8-10 52 .... KevinLundie(7) 10 — —
(L Corcoran) *prom: lost pl 7f out: sn bhd: hopelessly t.o 3f out* **33/1**

3m 4.23s (-4.07) **Going Correction** -0.20s/f (Stan)
WFA 4 from 5yo+ 6lb — **13** Ran SP% **117.5**
Speed ratings (Par 101): **103,93,93,91,90 90,89,88,88,76 71,70,—**
toteswingers: 1&2 £14.90, 1&3 £3.10, 2&3 £22.50. CSF £83.38 CT £277.49 TOTE £2.80: £1.50, £6.40, £2.00; EX 71.30 Trifecta £316.80 Pool: £449.54 - 1.05 winning units. Place 6 £20.62, Place 5 £18.50.
Owner Mohammed Rashid **Bred** Darley **Trained** Newmarket, Suffolk

FOCUS
A very modest apprentice handicap. The pace was decent and they were well strung out around the final bend. The winner impressed and produced a big step up, with the next two to their marks.
T/Plt: £18.40 to a £1 stake. Pool: £52,490.50. 2,079.11 winning tickets. T/Qpdt: £8.70 to a £1 stake. Pool: £4,503.98. 382.65 winning tickets. WG

303 CAGNES-SUR-MER

Thursday, January 28

OFFICIAL GOING: Standard

332a PRIX DES ROMARINS (CLAIMER) (ALL-WEATHER) 1m 4f

2:20 (2:23) 5-Y-0+ **£6,637** (£2,655; £1,991; £1,327; £664)

RPR

1 **Lost Soldier Three (IRE)**[5] 281 9-9-9 (p) IoritzMendizabal 65
(D Nicholls) *disp 2nd: pressed ldr over 2f out: styd on to ld fnl 50yds* **31/10**[1]

2 *hd* **Supsonic**[88] 7-9-2 (p) ThierryThulliez 57
(R Le Gal, France)

3 *3/4* **Adostern (GER)**[245] 6-9-2 FabienLefebvre 56
(P Lacroix, France)

4 *nk* **Kipling (FR)**[41] 6-9-11 65
(Rod Collet, France)

5 *nk* **Almaguer**[10] 221 8-9-7 60
(M Boutin, France)

6 *1* **Schomir (FR)**[126] 7-9-1 52
(J Van Handenhove, France)

7 *nk* **Nummenor (FR)**[10] 221 13-9-1 (b) 52
(Y Fertillet, France)

8 *nk* **Fantasy King (FR)**[6] 273 5-9-8 58
(P Demercastel, France)

9 *1* **Stolen (FR)**[514] 9-8-11 46
(M Boutin, France)

10 *3* **Tintaglia (FR)**[929] 8-8-8 38
(J-M Capitte, France)

0 **Cat Chat (FR)**[2135] 10-8-11 —
(P Azzopardi, France)

0 **Golconde Mine (IRE)**[10] 221 8-8-8 (p) —
(J Van Handenhove, France)

0 **Willow Weep For Me (FR)**[228] 7-9-8 —
(J-M Lefebvre, France)

0 **Juquehy (FR)**[76] 5-9-1 —
(P Chatelain, France)

0 **Telmunireema (FR)**[10] 221 5-9-1 —
(J-P Perruchot, France)

2m 35.95s (155.95) **15** Ran SP% **24.4**

PARI-MUTUEL (including 1 Euro stake): WIN 4.10; PL 2.10, 6.70, 5.50;DF 57.40.

Owner Eamon Maher **Bred** Darley **Trained** Sessay, N Yorks

MEYDAN (L-H)

Thursday, January 28

OFFICIAL GOING: Standard

333a UAE 1000 GUINEAS TRIAL SPONSORED BY DAYJUR, SHADWELL FARM (CONDITIONS RACE) (FILLIES) (TAPETA) 7f

2:44 (2:45) 3-Y-0

£18,518 (£6,172; £3,086; £1,543; £925; £617)

RPR

1 **Raihana (AUS)**[187] 4-9-4 90 ChristopheSoumillon 13 105+
(M F De Kock, South Africa) *mid-div: smooth prog to ld 2 1/2f out: easily* **11/4**[1]

2 *3 1/4* **Waasemah (KSA)**[20] 3-8-8 95 TedDurcan 12 92
(B Al Subaie, Saudi Arabia) *trckd ldrs: wd 3f out: swtchd to rail 2f out: r.o wl* **8/1**

3 *1* **Silver Grey (IRE)**[111] 6656 3-8-8 97 (p) RobertHavlin 8 89
(R Ingram) *trckd ldng gp: ev ch 1 1/2f out: r.o wl* **9/1**

4 *4 3/4* **Talenta (BRZ)**[214] 4-9-11 100 WBlandi 3 88
(A Cintra Pereira, Brazil) *mid-div: nt clr run over 1f out: only 8th whn swtchd rt ins fnl f: r.o wl* **11/2**[3]

5 *1 3/4* **Jodi (ARG)**[20] 4-9-4 KShea 6 76
(M F De Kock, South Africa) *trckd ldrs: ev ch 2 1/2f out: wknd fnl f* **33/1**

6 *3/4* **Diamond Laura**[124] 6292 3-8-8 83 TadhgO'Shea 9 69
(Doug Watson, UAE) *mid-div: hrd rdn 2 1/2f out: r.o at one pce* **22/1**

7 *4* **Dawnbreak (USA)**[107] 6756 3-8-8 85 FrankieDettori 11 59
(Saeed Bin Suroor) *mid-div: gng wl 2 1/2f out: one pce fnl 1 1/2f* **4/1**[2]

8 *1/2* **Angelica Z (ARG)**[13] 4-9-4 (p) RoystonFfrench 2 62
(A Al Raihe, UAE) *a mid-div* **100/1**

9 *5 1/4* **Absolute Music (USA)**[86] 7230 3-8-8 104 RichardMullen 4 43
(R M H Cowell) *trckd ldrs: ev ch 3f out: one pce fnl 1 1/2f* **6/1**

10 *4* **Muntherah (KSA)**[34] 3-8-8 98 AJaen 5 32
(B Al Subaie, Saudi Arabia) *mid-div early: short of room whn trying to stay on 2f out: bdly hmpd 1 1/2f out: nt rcvr* **13/2**

11 *2 3/4* **Surprise Result (USA)**[13] 3-8-8 LJurado 10 25
(R Bouresly, Kuwait) *a in rr* **150/1**

12 *3 1/4* **Sensational Day (USA)**[20] 3-8-8 PatDobbs 1 16
(Doug Watson, UAE) *slowly away: racd in rr: nvr able to chal* **100/1**

13 *2* **Any Day (IRE)**[13] 3-8-8 68 AhmedAjtebi 7 11
(M Ramadan, UAE) *wl away: sn led: hdd 2 1/2f out: wknd qckly* **100/1**

1m 26.63s (86.63)
WFA 3 from 4yo 18lb **13** Ran SP% **121.7**

Owner Sheikh Mohammed Bin Khalifa Al Maktoum **Bred** Sheikh Mohammed Bin Khalifa Al Maktoum **Trained** South Africa

■ A new era for racing in Dubai with the opening of Meydan, the replacement for the carnival's original venue Nad Al Sheba.

FOCUS

A high draw was not the anticipated disadvantage, with the first two emerging from double-figure stalls and enjoying a clear run after going wide, whilst many of those towards the inside got in each other's way at the top of the straight. The first four finishers in this UAE 1,000 Guineas trial all look at least very useful.

NOTEBOOK

Raihana(AUS) ◆, a 7f maiden winner in South Africa when last seen in July, came into this with a tall reputation. She apparently couldn't contest any of the juvenile features last year owing to sore shins, but Mike de Kock said, judged on her homework, she was "always a cut above" his champion 2-y-o filly, and he had even mentioned the UAE Derby as a possible target. As it turned out, her trainer's bullishness was fully justified, with this likeable individual posting a comfortable success on her Dubai debut. She raced wide throughout, including into the straight, but that enabled her to enjoy a continuous run and she produced a nice change of pace when asked for her effort. It remains to be seen how much stronger the competition will be in the Guineas itself, but she'll surely go there with a big chance, with the trip unlikely to be a problem.

Waasemah(KSA), who won her maiden by more than 10l in a quick time in her native Saudi Arabia, and followed up in a better race over the same C&D, ran a game race in defeat. This daughter of 2005 Dubai World Cup runner-up Dynever was no match at all for the winner, but showed a good attitude to hold on for second, having looked sure to lose that position to Silver Grey.

Silver Grey(IRE), a tough and progressive sort on turf last year, who was last seen finishing second in a 1m Group 3 in France, travelled as well as anything but didn't see her race out. Perhaps this first run in 111 days was needed.

Talenta(BRZ) ◆, conceding weight all round owing to Southern Hemisphere breeding and the penalty incurred for her Group 1 success in Brazil when last seen in June, is better than she showed. Held up towards the inside after a slow start, she had little room for much of the straight, before running on well when finally able to be switched late on. The Guineas trip will suit her. (op 6-1)

Jodi(ARG), the winner's stablemate, had no excuses.

Diamond Laura was officially rated only 75 on the all-weather in Britain, when trained by Ruth Carr. She ran respectably but her proximity holds down the form.

Dawnbreak(USA) didn't improve as expected for the return to synthetics. That one was keen to post, and in the race itself, and looks unlikely to progress.

Absolute Music(USA), runner-up in a French Group 3 over 7f when last seen in November, never travelled and looked held when short of room over a furlong out. (op 7-1)

Muntherah(KSA) ◆ is much better than she was able to show. A stable companion of the runner-up who, like that one, was unbeaten in two starts in Saudi Arabia, she was seriously hampered on two occasions when trying to pick up in the straight. (op 6-1)

334a INTADAB SPONSORED BY SHADWELL FARM (H'CAP) (TAPETA) 1m 1f 110y

3:20 (3:22) (90-105,102) 3-Y-0+

£40,740 (£13,580; £6,790; £3,395; £2,037; £1,358)

RPR

1 **Lizard's Desire (SAF)**[215] 5-9-1 100 ChristopheSoumillon 1 109
(M F De Kock, South Africa) *led early: trckd ldrs after 3f: rdn to ld 1 1/2f out: r.o wl* **9/4**[1]

2 *2 1/2* **King Of Rome (IRE)**[6] 5-9-3 102 KShea 9 105+
(M F De Kock, South Africa) *hld up: chsd ldrs 2 1/2f out: r.o wl fnl 1 1/2f: nrst fin* **14/1**

3 *1/2* **Jaroslaw (SAF)**[40] 7810 7-9-1 100 WilliamBuick 14 102
(D M Simcock) *settled in rr: nvr able to chal: r.o wl fnl 1 1/2f: nrst fin* **20/1**

4 *shd* **Imvula (AUS)**[229] 6-9-0 99 FrankieDettori 5 101+
(Saeed Bin Suroor) *mid-div: trckd ldrs: ev ch 2 1/2f out: one pce fnl 1 1/2f* **6/1**[2]

5 *1/2* **Tartan Gigha (IRE)**[117] 6480 5-8-11 97 RyanMoore 13 97+
(M Johnston) *towards rr: styd on out wd fnl 2f* **10/1**

6 *1 1/4* **Emerald Wilderness (IRE)**[165] 4315 6-9-2 101 RichardMullen 11 99
(R M H Cowell) *hld up: nvr able to chal: r.o wl fnl 2f* **16/1**

7 *1 3/4* **Bennie Blue (SAF)**[6] 8-8-10 96 (bt) RoystonFfrench 2 90
(A Al Raihe, UAE) *cl up: led after 3f: kicked clr 3f out: hdd 1 1/2f out: wknd fnl 110yds* **33/1**

8 *3/4* **Proponent (IRE)**[119] 6429 6-8-13 98 (t) KierenFallon 3 91
(R Charlton) *mid-div: chal ldrs 2f out: wknd fnl f* **7/1**[3]

9 *3/4* **Clasp**[53] 8-8-9 95 (vt) TadhgO'Shea 7 86
(Doug Watson, UAE) *mid-div: smooth prog 3f out: ev ch 1 1/2f out: wknd fnl 110yds* **16/1**

10 *3 1/2* **Stock Market (USA)**[48] 5-8-9 95 (t) WRamos 6 78
(N Al Mandeel, Saudi Arabia) *settled in rr: nvr able to chal: r.o fnl 2f* **25/1**

11 *4 1/2* **Takhir (IRE)**[75] 7406 4-8-8 95 AStarke 12 70
(P Schiergen, Germany) *nvr able to chal* **10/1**

12 *3 1/4* **Good Again**[115] 6535 4-8-8 95 TedDurcan 10 63
(G A Butler) *taken to rail s: settled in rr: nvr able to chal* **10/1**

13 *hd* **Beauchamp Xerxes**[68] 7489 4-9-0 100 PJSmullen 4 69
(G A Butler) *taken to rail s: settled in rr: nvr nr to chal: eased fnl f* **16/1**

14 *1* **Tasteyville (USA)**[13] 7-9-0 99 RichardHills 8 64
(E Charpy, UAE) *trckd ldrs: rdn 3f out: sn wknd* **16/1**

2m 2.35s (122.35)
WFA 4 from 5yo+ 1lb **14** Ran SP% **126.6**

Owner Sheikh Mohammed Bin Khalifa Al Maktoum **Bred** A J Boshoff **Trained** South Africa

FOCUS

Mainly exposed sorts for this handicap but a good race nonetheless. The pace was just steady for much of the way. Having saddled the first winner, Mike De Kock was responsible for the one-two this time.

NOTEBOOK

Lizard's Desire(SAF), a Grade 3 scorer over 1m4f in South Africa, enjoyed a lovely trip throughout under the excellent Christophe Soumillon, who has quickly got to grips with this new track. Having led early from a favourable draw, this gelding then got a lead down the back straight, before making the most of a dream passage against the rail in the straight to win convincingly. Plenty went his way, but he can probably defy a rise. (op 5-2)

King Of Rome(IRE) was spot on after a recent spin on the dirt over 6f at Jebel Ali and showed his first worthwhile form for some time. He didn't enjoy as good a trip as the winner, and was no match for that rival, but he finished well towards the outside in the straight. A return to slightly further should suit.

Jaroslaw(SAF) shaped as though worth a try over this trip when winning a falsely run race over 1m on Polytrack last time, and it now looks as if he wants even further. Last early after being dropped in from his wide draw, he took a while to pick up in the straight, before finishing well, and he should have no trouble getting 1m2f. (op 16-1)

Imvula(AUS), essentially just a handicapper in Australia, travelled nicely for much of the way but didn't see his race out and might want dropping back to 1m. (op 5-1 tchd 11-2)

Tartan Gigha(IRE), 7lb higher than when runner-up in last season's Cambridgeshire, was wide for much of the way from stall 13, but finished his race quite well and gave the impression there will be more to come. He should win a race this carnival.

Emerald Wilderness(IRE), a faller on his chasing debut when last seen in August, just lacked the speed of some of these on his debut for new connections. This ought to have helped his confidence and there might be more to come back over slightly further.

Proponent(IRE), 6lb higher than when winning over 1m at Newmarket in October, was off the turf for the first time and didn't do enough.

Good Again, 4lb above the mark she won off at Pontefract when last seen, was trying this trip for the first time and offered nothing.

Beauchamp Xerxes failed to pick up after racing keenly.

335a DUMAANI SPONSORED BY SHADWELL FARM (H'CAP) (TAPETA) 1m 3f

4:05 (4:05) (90-105,105) 3-Y-O+

£40,740 (£13,580; £6,790; £3,395; £2,037; £1,358)

RPR

1 **Drunken Sailor (IRE)**[131] 6106 5-8-11 97 ....(b) KierenFallen 5 103+
(L M Cumani) *mid-div: smooth prog to ld 1 1/2f out: edgd rt: r.o wl* **5/1**[2]

2 2 ¼ **Monte Alto (IRE)**[13] 6-8-11 97 ....(t) RichardHills 3 98
(A Al Raihe, UAE) *in rr of mid-div: nt clr run fr 3f out tl swtchd rt 1 1/2f out: r.o wl but a hld* **22/1**

3 7 ¼ **Lindner (GER)**[474] 6664 5-8-13 98 .... AhmedAjtebi 9 88
(Saeed Bin Suroor) *in rr of mid-div: r.o wl fnl 1 1/2f: nrst fin* **14/1**

4 ½ **Petrovsky**[130] 6138 4-8-7 95 .... RoystonFfrench 13 85
(A Al Raihe, UAE) *mid-div: ev ch 2 1/2f out: nt qckn fnl 2f* **11/1**[3]

5 2 ½ **Kaolak (USA)**[117] 6480 4-8-7 95 ....(v) DaraghO'Donohoe 14 84
(J Ryan) *sn led: clr 3 1/2f out: hdd 1 1/2f out* **25/1**

6 2 ¼ **Bab Al Salam (USA)**[86] 7226 4-9-0 101 .... FrankieDettori 7 87
(Saeed Bin Suroor) *mid-div: impr to trck ldrs over 2f out: nt qckn fnl 1 1/2f* **6/5**[1]

7 ¾ **Colony (IRE)**[13] 5-8-7 99 ....(b) AntiocoMurgia(7) 11 80
(M Al Subouse, UAE) *mid-div: rdn 3f out: sn btn* **40/1**

8 1 ¼ **Mulaqat**[20] 7-9-4 104 .... WilliamBuick 6 82
(D Selvaratnam, UAE) *s.i.s: settled in rr: nvr able to chal* **25/1**

9 ¾ **Rohaani (USA)**[13] 8-8-9 95 .... TadhgO'Shea 2 73
(Doug Watson, UAE) *nvr bttr than mid-div* **33/1**

10 1 ½ **Alcomo (BRZ)**[117] 6574 7-9-3 102 ....(t) WBlandi 4 79
(A Cintra Pereira, Brazil) *settled in rr: nvr nr to chal* **16/1**

11 1 ¼ **Princess Taylor**[60] 7589 6-8-13 98 ....(t) PJSmullen 8 74
(D K Weld, Ire) *a mid-div* **14/1**

12 ½ **Lion Sands**[13] 6-9-5 105 .... CSanchez 1 78
(A bin Huzaim, UAE) *trckd ldrs tl rdn and outpcd 2 1/2f out* **40/1**

13 ½ **Distinctive Image (USA)**[171] 4840 5-8-9 95 .... RyanMoore 10 65
(G A Butler) *racd in last: mde no imp* **11/1**[3]

14 30 **Noisy Silence (IRE)**[13] 6-9-2 101 .... RichardThomas 12 72
(A Manuel, UAE) *trckd ldrs: rdn 3f out: wknd and eased fnl f* **14/1**

2m 20.49s (140.49)
WFA 4 from 5yo+ 3lb **14 Ran SP% 124.5**

Owner Samanda Racing **Bred** Cyril Kiernan **Trained** Newmarket, Suffolk

FOCUS
A good handicap run at a fair pace.

NOTEBOOK
Drunken Sailor(IRE) ◆, only 3lb higher than when runner-up in a decent Newbury handicap (won by Presvis last year) on his final start for Paul Flynn, created a fine impression. He found himself in front sooner than ideal, but there wasn't much Fallon could do about it, such was the enthusiasm with which this gelding had travelled, and in any case he was always holding the runner-up, despite edging right. It's true Monte Alto didn't enjoy the clearest of runs, but the winner appeared to have something left and looks better than this level. His cruising speed and ability to quicken are likely to see him make good progress this carnival, and we know he goes on turf, too.
Monte Alto(IRE) did well to finish so close, and so far clear of the remainder, having continually found trouble around the turn into the straight, but he wasn't unlucky. A repeat of this sort of form should see him land a similar race.
Lindner(GER), an ex-German gelding, ran a nice race after 474 days away from the track on his first start for Godolphin. He lacked the sharpness, and possibly the speed of the front two, but kept on well and is entitled to come on a good deal for this.
Petrovsky ◆, formerly trained by Mark Johnston, ran creditably after 130 days off. He's just a one-paced galloper, and duly found a few too quick in the straight, but kept on well, very much giving the impression he'll benefit from a step up in trip. This was only his ninth start, so there could be more to come, and he'll be interesting if allowed to take his chance in the 1m6f handicap (for horses rated 95 and above) on the turf on February 4. (op 10-1)
Kaolak(USA), who set a fair pace, ran respectably after 117 days off but failed to prove his stamina.
Bab Al Salam(USA) had won five of his previous six starts, including 3-3 on Polytrack, but was one of the disappointments of the race. Running off a mark 6lb higher than for his latest victory, and trying a furlong further than before, he seemed to travel well but found disappointingly little and may appreciate a drop in trip. (op 5-4)
Distinctive Image(USA), 13lb higher than when bolting up on Fibresand on his final start for Reg Hollinshead, was given a lot to do and never featured.

336a KAYRAWAN SPONSORED BY SHADWELL FARM (H'CAP) (TAPETA) 6f

4:50 (4:50) (95-110,110) 3-Y-O+

£44,444 (£14,814; £7,407; £3,703; £2,222; £1,481)

RPR

1 **Sir Gerry (USA)**[43] 7768 5-9-1 105 .... TedDurcan 11 105
(J R Best) *settled in rr: last 2f out: r.o strly out wd fnl 1 1/2f: led cl home* **25/1**

2 ½ **Musaalem (USA)**[117] 6487 6-9-2 106 .... RichardHills 5 104
(Doug Watson, UAE) *bdly hmpd s: racd in rr: t.k.h: hdwy but nt clr run 2f out: led fnl f: hdd cl home* **8/1**

3 ½ **Prince Tamino**[321] 7-9-0 104 ....(t) RoystonFfrench 1 100
(A Al Raihe, UAE) *trckd ldr: ev ch 2f out: one pce fnl f* **33/1**

4 ½ **Good Control (AUS)**[41] 5-8-13 102 .... MNunes 8 98
(Pat Lee, Macau) *t.k.h: trckd ldr for 3f: one pce fnl 2f* **7/1**[3]

5 1 ¼ **Frosty Secret (USA)**[321] 6-8-11 101 .... KShea 10 92
(M F De Kock, South Africa) *trckd ldrs: rdn 2 1/2f out: nt qckn* **9/1**

6 ½ **Prohibit**[124] 6282 5-8-13 102 .... RichardMullen 4 92
(R M H Cowell) *in rr of mid-div: n.m.r 2f out: stl looking for a gap whn bdly squeezed ins fnl f: nt rcvr* **11/2**[2]

7 ½ **Prince Shaun (IRE)**[32] 5-8-11 101 ....(t) TadhgO'Shea 12 89
(Doug Watson, UAE) *settled in rr: mid-div 2 1/2f out: one pce fnl f* **33/1**

8 ½ **Star Crowned (USA)**[342] 641 7-9-5 109 ....(t) LJurado 7 95
(R Bouresly, Kuwait) *sn led: hdd 1f out: one pce* **11/1**

9 1 ¼ **Aichi (AUS)**[280] 5-9-6 110 ....(b) FrankieDettori 3 92
(Saeed Bin Suroor) *nvr bttr than mid-div: one pce whn no room fnl f* **9/4**[1]

10 2 **Axiom**[124] 6270 6-9-1 105 .... KierenFallon 2 81
(L M Cumani) *mid-div: beginning to pick up whn denied clr run ins fnl f: lost all momentum and eased* **11/2**[2]

11 ½ **Rileyskeepingfaith**[460] 6979 4-8-13 102 .... AlanMunro 9 77
(M R Channon) *in tch: hdwy and ev ch over 1 1/2f: one pce whn bdly hmpd ins fnl f* **25/1**

U **Desuetude (AUS)**[257] 5-9-5 109 ....(b) AhmedAjtebi 6 —
(Saeed Bin Suroor) *wnt lft leaving stalls and uns rdr* **12/1**

1m 13.56s (73.56) **12 Ran SP% 124.7**

Owner Mrs Gerry Galligan **Bred** Dr Catherine Wills **Trained** Hucking, Kent

FOCUS
Further evidence that a wide draw is no bad thing at all over a short trip on the Tapeta course, with the winner coming from stall 11, while several of his rivals found trouble towards the inside. The pace was solid but they finished in something of a heap.

NOTEBOOK
Sir Gerry(USA) had won only once since landing the 2007 Gimcrack, but he showed himself on a good mark for this first-ever venture into handicap company, picking up well out widest to pass all of his rivals in the straight. This form needs treating with some caution, but he's obviously taken well to racing in Dubai.
Musaalem(USA), who was 5-11 for William Haggas (all on turf), ran a cracker on his UAE debut. He was badly hampered on leaving the stalls by Desuetude, but he soon recovered and raced keenly under a hold-up ride. He had to wait for a gap towards the inside in the straight, but was out in enough time to briefly hit the front, before being pegged back by a rival with more momentum.
Prince Tamino, like the runner-up, had to wait for a gap towards the inside rail in the straight, but he wasn't unlucky. This was a solid effort after 321 days off, especially as he was keen early. (op 28-1)
Good Control(AUS), a regular winner in Macau, did really well to finish so close considering he was very keen for much of the way. He clearly needs a strong pace and it's a shame there are no 5f races at the carnival this year. (op 15-2)
Frosty Secret(USA) ran a big race after a layoff of 321 days and is entitled to be better for the outing. (op 10-1)
Prohibit, sold out of John Gosden's yard for 85,000gns after running a close second at Haydock off a mark of 97, was blocked in his run at a crucial stage in the straight and is better than he was able to show. (op 6-1)
Star Crowned(USA) has a fine record when fresh and had apparently been laid out for this race, but he faded after going off quickly, failing to prove himself on the surface. (10-1)
Aichi(AUS), a Group 3 and more recently Listed winner in Australia who was debuting for Godolphin after 280 days off, was short of room at a vital stage and can do better. (op 5-2)
Axiom, back after four months off, was one of several denied a clear run and can be given another chance.
Rileyskeepingfaith ◆, gelded since he was last seen in October 2008, ran better than his finishing position suggests. He possibly didn't handle the bend all that well (first try left-handed), but ran nicely for a long way, before getting tired, and then being badly hampered inside the final furlong, which exaggerated the margin of defeat.

337a MUSTANFAR SPONSORED BY SHADWELL FARM (H'CAP) (TAPETA) 1m 2f

5:35 (5:35) (100-110,110) 3-Y-O+

£64,814 (£21,604; £10,802; £5,401; £3,240; £2,160)

RPR

1 **Whispering Gallery**[162] 5170 4-8-10 107 .... FrankieDettori 7 115+
(Saeed Bin Suroor) *sn led: rdn clr 2f out: comf* **6/4**[1]

2 3 ½ **Halicarnassus (IRE)**[96] 7031 6-9-1 110 .... AlanMunro 6 111
(M R Channon) *trckd ldr: ev ch 2f out: r.o wl* **16/1**

3 ¾ **Sopranist**[182] 4455 4-8-6 102 .... TedDurcan 4 103
(Saeed Bin Suroor) *mid-div: r.o wl fnl 1 1/2f but a hld* **5/1**[2]

4 3 ½ **We'll Come**[118] 6448 6-8-13 108 .... JRosales 1 101
(A bin Huzaim, UAE) *s.i.s: settled in rr: stl last 2f out: nt clr run 1 1/2f out: r.o fnl f: nvr nrr* **20/1**

5 ¼ **Eddie Jock (IRE)**[13] 6-8-9 105 .... RichardMullen 2 96
(S Seemar, UAE) *mid-div: in rr 4f out: gng okay whn n.m.r over 2f out: one pce whn denied clr run 1 1/2f out* **16/1**

6 ¼ **Red Rock Canyon (IRE)**[150] 5539 6-8-7 102 ....(t) KShea 5 94
(M F De Kock, South Africa) *a mid-div: gng wl over 2f out: one pce fnl 1 1/2f* **12/1**

7 1 ½ **Art Of War (SAF)**[306] 1008 6-8-9 105 .... ChristopheSoumillon 3 93
(M F De Kock, South Africa) *nvr bttr than mid-div* **13/2**[3]

8 1 ¼ **Merchant Marine (USA)**[13] 6-8-7 102 .... RichardHills 8 88
(Doug Watson, UAE) *settled in rr: sme prog 2f out: one pce fnl 2f* **33/1**

9 1 ¾ **Topclas (FR)**[137] 5930 4-8-10 107 .... WJSupple 11 90
(M bin Shafya, UAE) *mid-div: rdn 3 1/2f out: nvr nr to chal* **8/1**

10 ¼ **With Interest**[350] 527 7-8-10 106 ....(t) RoystonFfrench 10 87
(A Al Raihe, UAE) *trckd ldr tl 2 1/2f out: sn rdn and btn* **25/1**

11 17 **Khor Dubai (IRE)**[71] 7431 4-8-7 104 ....(v) CSanchez 9 52
(A bin Huzaim, UAE) *settled in rr: plld hrd and moved to 2nd over 4f out: wknd 2f out* **16/1**

2m 6.05s (126.05)
WFA 4 from 6yo+ 2lb **11 Ran SP% 118.0**

Owner Godolphin **Bred** Darley **Trained** Newmarket, Suffolk

FOCUS
The pace was steady, with the winner allowed a surprisingly soft lead. It proved difficult to make up ground.

NOTEBOOK
Whispering Gallery ◆ made the most of the easy time he enjoyed up front to record a comfortable success. He was 3-4 when trained by Mark Johnston, and with his latest success having come over 1m4f (off a mark of 99), he was always going to be hard to peg back considering how the race unfolded. It's true plenty went his way, but he's a classy gelding who may eventually be up to contesting Group races.
Halicarnassus(IRE), appearing at his third carnival, was always well positioned and ran a fine race under top weight behind the improving winner.
Sopranist, the winner's stablemate, was progressing for John Gosden when last seen in July and fared best of those to race off the pace. He looks well worth a try over 1m4f.
We'll Come, having his first start since leaving Michael Jarvis, was set a lot to do on and was blocked in his run when trying to stay on, so he might be capable of better.
Eddie Jock(IRE) travelled well, but couldn't pick up off the modest tempo and would have preferred a stronger pace.
Red Rock Canyon(IRE) ◆, formerly with Aidan O'Brien, shaped as though he can do better. So often used as a pacemaker for his former connections, he was held up this time and travelled just about as well as anything, looking like a horse with rediscovered confidence. However, with the leaders not coming back to him, he was unable to land a telling blow. He had apparently pleased Mike de Kock in a recent trial and is one to keep in mind when a stronger pace is likely.
Art Of War(SAF) was short of room against the inside rail turning into the straight, but he was under pressure at the time and didn't look unlucky.

338a AL MAKTOUM CHALLENGE R1 SPONSORED BY INVASOR, SHADWELL FARM (GROUP 3) (TAPETA) 1m

6:20 (6:21) 3-Y-O+

£74,074 (£24,691; £12,345; £6,172; £3,703; £2,469)

RPR

1 **Gloria De Campeao (BRZ)**[173] 4809 7-9-0 120 .... TJPereira 11 117
(P Bary, France) *prom or disputing ld early: cl 3rd 2f out: r.o gamely to ld ins fnl f* **12/1**

2 ½ **Forgotten Voice (IRE)**[103] 6850 5-9-0 113 .... RyanMoore 7 116+
(J Noseda) *wl bhd early: stl in rr whn rdn 2 1/2f out: r.o strly: nrst fin* **7/1**[2]

3 2¾ **Consul General**[97] 6-9-0 110 .... KierenFallon 2 110
(N Al Mandeel, Saudi Arabia) *trckd ldrs: rdn to chal 1 1/2f out: r.o wl* **25/1**

4 2¼ **Midshipman (USA)**[82] 7309 4-9-0 113 ....(vt) FrankieDettori 14 105
(Saeed Bin Suroor) *wl away: racd freely w pce: led over 2f out: jnd on both sides over 1f out: hdd ins fnl f: wknd clsng stages* **6/4**[1]

5 nse **Premio Loco (USA)**[123] 6323 6-9-0 116 .... GeorgeBaker 12 104
(C F Wall) *trckd ldrs: nt qckn fnl 1 1/2f* **15/2**[3]

6 1¼ **Without A Prayer (IRE)**[60] 7588 5-9-0 112 .... JimCrowley 8 102
(R M Beckett) *a mid-div* **7/1**[2]

7 ½ **Lovelace**[161] 5200 6-9-0 108 .... RichardHills 5 100
(M Johnston) *s.i.s: hld up towards ins: nt clr run towards ins over 2f out: kpt on one pce in the st* **16/1**

8 2¾ **Otaared**[20] 5-9-0 105 ....(t) WilliamBuick 3 94
(D Selvaratnam, UAE) *settled in rr: rdn 3f out: nvr able to chal* **16/1**

9 2½ **Hunting Tower (SAF)**[329] 770 8-9-0 112 .... ChristopheSoumillon 10 88
(M F De Kock, South Africa) *nvr bttr than mid-div* **14/1**

10 6½ **Al Samha (USA)**[300] 5-9-0 106 .... WRamos 4 73
(J Barton, Saudi Arabia) *nvr bttr than mid-div* **40/1**

11 3½ **Ocean's Minstrel**[180] 4521 4-9-0 102 .... JerryO'Dwyer 1 65
(J Ryan) *disp ld tl 3f out: wknd* **50/1**

12 nse **Philario (IRE)**[225] 3014 5-9-0 105 .... PJSmullen 6 65
(P D Deegan, Ire) *nvr bttr than mid-div* **50/1**

13 3¼ **Tam Lin**[172] 7-9-0 110 .... WJSupple 13 58
(M bin Shafya, UAE) *nvr bttr than mid-div* **33/1**

14 26 **My Indy (ARG)**[306] 1013 6-9-0 115 .... TedDurcan 9 —
(Saeed Bin Suroor) *trckd ldrs tl 3f out: sn wknd* **88/1**

1m 38.48s (98.48) **14** Ran SP% **117.2**

Owner Estrela Energia Stables **Bred** Haras Santarem **Trained** Chantilly, France

FOCUS

This has traditionally been the weakest of the three rounds of Al Maktoum Challenge, but while that may well prove to be the case once again, this year's race was a decent contest, certainly more competitive than usual. The pace was good.

NOTEBOOK

Gloria De Campeao(BRZ) deserves plenty of credit, for not only did his trainer expect him to come on for the run, he was racing over a trip short of his best. Having raced handily throughout, he looked in trouble when under strong pressure around the final bend, but he kept responding to gradually draw away from his rivals, and ultimately just had enough in hand to hold off the fast-finishing runner-up. Formerly trained in Brazil, he was a regular on the dirt at the last two carnivals, but while he managed to win on that surface, he proved to be a revelation back on the grass last year when defeating Presvis in a Singapore Group 1, and it seems grass, as well as synthetics, suit him best now. He's always looked short of top class, but while he's still a little way off that level, he certainly has to be taken more seriously these days. Presumably he'll now take his chance in the next two rounds, when the longer trip will suit, leading up to the World Cup, a race in which he finished eighth in 2008, and a distant second last year (both on dirt).

Forgotten Voice(IRE) ran a mighty race in second considering his trainer felt he might need the run, having taken longer than anticipated to get over a gelding operation, and also been held up by the cold weather back in Britain. He lacked the required race-sharpness to get a worthwhile position, having to be niggled on leaving the stalls, but once in the straight he finished really strongly to pass all bar one of his rivals. Last year's Hunt Cup winner is 3-3 on Polytrack, and this surface clearly suited, but while he can be expected to come on for the race, things will get tougher now. The second round of this series is now the obvious target, but he'll probably face better company and, despite the visual impression here, he's not sure to be suited by the trip of just under 1m2f. (op 15-2)

Consul General, formerly with Dermot Weld, is a regular winner in Saudi Arabia these days and ran a fine race after three months off. He looked one of the likelier winners when produced with every chance by Fallon at the top of the straight, but he didn't quite see his race out.

Midshipman(USA), the 2008 Breeders' Cup Juvenile winner and last year's Dirt Mile third (both on synthetics) was disappointing, especially as he had been the subject of positive reports from his trainer. He was basically too free and had little left late on after making a brief effort early in the straight. Perhaps headgear lights him up a bit too much these days, and he is entitled to come on for the run. (op 7-4)

Premio Loco(USA) might have been expected to perform a little better, for all that he didn't run badly. This dual German Group 2 winner is fully effective on Polytrack, but he failed to produce his usual change of pace, and perhaps either this surface didn't suit, or he just needed the run after four months off.

Without A Prayer(IRE), a recent Listed winner on Polytrack, ran well but wasn't quite up to the level.

Lovelace, expected to need the run by his trainer, was held up towards the inside after starting slowly and was unsurprisingly denied a clear run turning into the straight. He didn't run too badly all things considered, but is a hard horse to call right these days. (tchd 15-2)

My Indy(ARG) had won this race last year, as well as the second leg of the challenge, but he failed to prove himself as good on synthetics as he is on dirt. (op 15-2)

339a DAAHER SPONSORED BY SHADWELL FARM (H'CAP) (TAPETA) 7f

7:05 (7:06) (90-105,105) 3-Y-0+

£40,740 (£13,580; £6,790; £3,395; £2,037; £1,358)

RPR

1 **Leahurst (IRE)**[147] 5615 4-9-3 102 .... RyanMoore 5 109
(J Noseda) *trckd ldr: t.k.h: led 1 1/2f: r.o wl* **11/8**[1]

2 2½ **Aranel (IRE)**[86] 7232 4-9-1 100 .... JulienGrosjean 4 100
(M Delcher-Sanchez, Spain) *mid-div: impr to trck ldrs gng wl over 2f out: r.o wl but a hld* **33/1**

3 hd **Swop (IRE)**[117] 6480 7-9-3 102 .... KierenFallon 13 101+
(L M Cumani) *in rr of mid-div: swtchd rt 2f out and then swtchd bk ins over 1f out: r.o wl: nrst fin* **9/1**

4 1½ **Green Coast (IRE)**[20] 7-9-3 102 .... TadhgO'Shea 7 97
(Doug Watson, UAE) *broke awkwardly: racd in mid-div: r.o fnl 1 1/2f* **16/1**

5 1¼ **Mutheeb (USA)**[202] 3818 5-9-4 104 .... RichardHills 9 95
(M Al Muhairi, UAE) *t.k.h out wd in mid-div: kpt on one pce fnl 2f* **7/1**[3]

6 1¼ **Warsaw (IRE)**[6] 5-9-4 104 ....(b) ChristopheSoumillon 8 92
(M F De Kock, South Africa) *a mid-div* **14/1**

7 ¾ **Lucky Find (SAF)**[306] 1008 7-9-5 105 .... KShea 14 91
(M F De Kock, South Africa) *nvr bttr than mid-div* **25/1**

8 ¼ **Sirocco Breeze**[91] 7133 5-9-4 104 .... FrankieDettori 6 89
(Saeed Bin Suroor) *plld hrd early: trckd ldrs and ev ch 2f out: wknd fnl f* **11/4**[2]

9 1½ **Jaasoos (IRE)**[32] 6-9-3 102 .... WilliamBuick 10 84
(D Selvaratnam, UAE) *racd in rr: nvr nr to chal* **25/1**

10 ½ **Halkin (USA)**[83] 8-9-1 100 .... PatDobbs 11 81
(F Nass, Bahrain) *settled in rr: nvr nr to chal* **50/1**

11 5 **Snow Runner (ARG)**[53] 7-9-1 100 ....(t) TedDurcan 12 67
(Vanja Sandrup, Sweden) *towards rr: sme late prog: nvr in contention* **50/1**

12 1¼ **Rocks Off (ARG)**[6] 5-9-4 104 .... KLatham 1 67
(M F De Kock, South Africa) *rdn to ld s: hdd 2f out: wknd* **40/1**

13 ¾ **Seachantach (USA)**[145] 5687 4-8-11 99 .... MartinLane[(3)] 3 61
(D M Simcock) *trckd ldr tl 2 1/2f out: rdn and wknd* **33/1**

14 6¼ **Cafe Racer (IRE)**[41] 4-9-1 100 ....(t) WJSupple 2 45
(M bin Shafya, UAE) *trckd ldr on rail: wknd fnl 1 1/2f* **33/1**

1m 24.8s (84.80) **14** Ran SP% **126.7**

PLACEPOT £739.20. Pool £8,557.15 - 8.45 winning tickets. QUADPOT £456.10 Pool £616.46 - 1.00 winning tickets..

Owner Mrs Susan Roy **Bred** D & B Egan **Trained** Newmarket, Suffolk

FOCUS

A good handicap.

NOTEBOOK

Leahurst(IRE) ◆ is a lightly raced gelding with real potential. He was defying a 13lb rise for his easy Wolverhampton success back in September and is now 3-5 lifetime, as well as 3-3 on a synthetic surface. He was a bit keen early on, but managed to get a lead and didn't require maximum assistance from his jockey to win decisively. He's a classy individual and it will be a surprise if he doesn't follow up in handicap company before trying something better.

Aranel(IRE), a regular winner in Spain but exposed when tacking stronger company in Britain and France, ran a nice race in defeat. He obviously had no chance with the above-average winner, but travelled nicely in his own right, before keeping on, and might find a race in the coming weeks.

Swop(IRE) ◆, a winner on the turf over 7l/2f off a mark of 100 at last year's carnival, is a bit better than he showed as he didn't enjoy the clearest of runs when trying to pick up from off the pace and had to be switched on a couple of occasions. He has little in hand at the weights, but it wouldn't surprise to see him pick up one of these when faced with more exposed rivals.

Green Coast(IRE), a dual winner on dirt, proved himself on Tapeta with a solid effort.

Mutheeb(USA), third in the Bunbury Cup for Godolphin when last seen in July, raced a bit keenly out a little wide but kept on in the straight. He's lightly raced and open to improvement.

Warsaw(IRE) ◆ has won over this trip on dirt, but he's always looked a sprinter and shaped as though he will capable of better if dropped back to 6f next time.

Lucky Find(SAF), who had officially been off for 306 days but contested a recent trial, kept on after being set a lot to do.

Sirocco Breeze, having only his fourth start (has apparently had a problem with his hooves), is a naturally free-going type and his refusal to settle cost him his chance. He looked a decent colt in the making when scoring over this trip on Polytrack off a mark of 93 last season, but he can't get away with pulling hard in this sort of company and now looks the time to drop him back to 6f. His breeding certainly suggests that will suit - by Green Desert and a half-brother to winning sprinter Caustic Wit - and he remains interesting, albeit not one for maximum confidence until proving himself.

312 LINGFIELD (L-H)

Friday, January 29

OFFICIAL GOING: Standard

Wind: Against, strong races 1-4; becoming light. Weather: Cloudy with showers becoming bright by race 4

340 LINGFIELD PARK SPORTING MEMBERSHIP MAIDEN STKS 1m 2f (P)

1:05 (1:05) (Class 5) 3-Y-O **£2,456** (£725; £362) **Stalls** Low

Form RPR

3 **1** **Beyond (IRE)**[25] 31 3-9-3 0 .... GeorgeBaker 1 61+
(J Noseda) *str: trckd ldrs on inner: pushed along over 2f out: prog to take 2nd over 1f out: rdn to ld last 150yds: won gng away* **4/7**[1]

-332 **2** 2 **The Great Husk (IRE)**[8] 254 3-9-3 58 .... LiamKeniry 8 57
(J S Moore) *led at mod pce: qcknd over 2f out: hdd and one pce last 150yds* **14/1**

- **3** ¾ **Brave Talk** 3-9-3 0 .... DavidProbert 3 56
(S Kirk) *w'like: leggy: s.s: mostly in last pair and nt gng wl early: effrt over 2f out: hanging lft but styd on to take 3rd ins fnl f* **50/1**

0 **4** 1 **Beat Route**[20] 106 3-8-12 0 .... JemmaMarshall[(5)] 6 54
(M J Attwater) *chsd ldr to 6f out: lost pl: effrt 2f out: kpt on fnl f: n.d* **100/1**

06- **5** hd **Sansili**[76] 7388 3-9-3 0 .... RobertWinston 7 53
(Pat Eddery) *bit bkwd: prom on outer: chsd ldr 6f out to over 1f out: wknd* **6/1**[3]

6 1 **Abergavenny** 3-9-3 0 .... JoeFanning 2 55+
(M Johnston) *unf: settled in rr: last 4f out: effrt on inner to dispute 4th whn nowhere to go and snatched up over 2f out: dropped to last again: plugging on to dispute 4th whn hmpd ins fnl f* **3/1**[2]

00- **7** ¾ **Steely Bird**[100] 6931 3-9-3 0 .... RobertHavlin 5 50
(Miss Jo Crowley) *towards rr: rdn on outer over 2f out: hanging and wknd over 1f out* **100/1**

6-3 **8** 2 **Sternian**[11] 219 3-8-5 0 .... LauraPike[(7)] 4 41
(M E Rimmer) *racd wd in rr: wknd wl over 1f out* **66/1**

2m 10.61s (4.01) **Going Correction** +0.20s/f (Slow) **8** Ran SP% **115.0**

Speed ratings (Par 97): **91,89,88,88,87 87,86,84**

toteswingers: 1&2 £2.20, 1&3 £6.00, 2&3 £11.30 CSF £11.14 TOTE £1.50: £1.10, £1.70, £7.20; EX 7.60 Trifecta £58.30 Pool: £379.86 - 4.82 winning units..

Owner The Honorable Earle I Mack **Bred** Pat Fullam **Trained** Newmarket, Suffolk

FOCUS

An uncompetitive maiden in which only a couple mattered according to the market. They went no pace for much of the way and things didn't quicken appreciably until over 2f from home.

Brave Talk ◆ Official explanation: jockey said gelding ran green

Abergavenny ◆ Official explanation: jockey said colt suffered interference in running

341 GOLF AT LINGFIELD PARK H'CAP 1m 2f (P)

1:40 (1:40) (Class 4) (0-85,85) 4-Y-0+ **£4,209** (£1,252; £625; £312) **Stalls** Low

Form RPR

43-1 **1** **Thunderstruck**[8] 255 5-9-1 80 6ex ....(p) ChrisCatlin 8 90
(J A Glover) *led: rdn and pressed over 2f out: wd bnd sn after: hung rt and hdd 1f out: rallied and bmpd rival: led again nr fin* **11/4**[2]

2-51 **2** nk **Mister Green (FR)**[9] 239 4-8-13 80 6ex ....(b) JoeFanning 2 89
(K McAuliffe) *hld up in last: effrt on outer whn carried wd bnd 2f out: rapid prog to ld 1f out: drvn and bmpd rival ins fnl f: hdd nr fin* **2/1**[1]

342- **3** 3 **Can Can Star**[48] 7734 7-9-4 83 .... AdamKirby 7 86
(A W Carroll) *hld up in 6th: prog over 2f out: carried wd bnd sn after: effrt over 1f out: cl up but hld whn hmpd ent fnl f: kpt on* **10/1**

11-5 **4** 1½ **Free Tussy (ARG)**[26] 25 6-9-2 81 ow2 ....(bt) GeorgeBaker 5 81
(G L Moore) *lw: hld up bhd ldng trio: gng strly 3f out: wnt 2nd 2f out: nt qckn over 1f out: fdd* **7/1**

36-4 **5** 1½ **Evident Pride (USA)**[26] 25 7-9-3 82 .... LiamKeniry 4 79
(B R Johnson) *b.hind: settled in 5th: pushed along over 4f out: effrt u.p 2f out: no prog fnl f* **13/2**[3]

05-0 **6** 2½ **Suzi Spends (IRE)**[9] 239 5-9-0 79 .... JackMitchell 3 71
(H J Collingridge) *chsd wnr to 2f out: wknd over 1f out* **14/1**

The Form Book, Raceform Ltd, Compton, RG20 6NL

045- **7** *shd* **Valmari (IRE)**[132] 6113 7-8-13 **85**........................ CharlotteKerton(7) 6 77
(G Prodromou) *t.k.h: racd wd: cl up: lost pl 4f out: last over 2f out: no ch after* **50/1**

60-0 **8** *2 ½* **War Of The Roses (IRE)**[26] 25 7-9-1 **80**........................ TomEaves 1 67
(R Brotherton) *trckd ldrs on inner: rdn over 2f out: wknd rapidly over 1f out* **11/1**

2m 7.18s (0.58) **Going Correction** +0.20s/f (Slow)
WFA 4 from 5yo+ 2lb **8** Ran SP% **111.9**
Speed ratings (Par 105): **105,104,102,101,99 97,97,95**
toteswingers: 1&2 £1.80, 1&3 £4.00, 2&3 £3.80 CSF £8.24 CT £43.57 TOTE £3.60: £1.30, £1.30, £2.70; EX 8.60 Trifecta £44.00 Pool: £251.18 - 4.22 winning units..
Owner Paul J Dixon **Bred** Mrs Yvette Dixon **Trained** Babworth, Notts

FOCUS
A fair handicap, but again the early pace was moderate even though the winning time was 3.43 seconds faster than the slowly run opening maiden.
Valmari(IRE) Official explanation: jockey said the mare hung right on the final bend

342 LINGFIELDPARK.CO.UK CLASSIFIED CLAIMING STKS 7f (P)
2:15 (2:15) (Class 6) 4-Y-O+ **£1,774** (£523; £262) **Stalls** Low

Form RPR

36-4 **1** **Kipchak (IRE)**[17] 144 5-8-8 69........................(p) ShaneKelly 6 72
(C R Dore) *lw: mde all at fast pce and sn clr: hrd rdn over 1f out: nrly jnd nr fin: hld on wl* **13/8**[1]

64-3 **2** *hd* **Dichoh**[9] 230 7-9-4 74........................(v) AdamKirby 5 81
(M Madgwick) *stdd s: hld up in last: reminders over 4f out: prog 3f out and travelling bttr: wnt 3rd 2f out: clsd to chse wnr 1f out: nrly upsides nr fin: nt qckn* **10/3**[2]

-525 **3** *3 ½* **Lord Deevert**[7] 258 5-8-0 62........................ LukeMorris 2 54
(W G M Turner) *chsd wnr: drvn 2f out: tried to cl but lost 2nd 1f out: fdd* **5/1**

-214 **4** *6* **Mocha Java**[14] 187 7-7-12 64........................(p) AdrianMcCarthy 4 36
(Matthew Salaman) *chsd ldng pair: rdn 3f out: lost 3rd 2f out: no ch over 1f out* **10/1**

52-6 **5** *13* **Dig Deep (IRE)**[27] 16 8-8-8 75........................ TomEaves 3 11
(J J Quinn) *chsd ldng trio tl wknd rapidly 3f out: sn t.o* **7/2**[3]

00-0 **6** *6* **Rony Dony (IRE)**[2] 318 6-7-12 35........................ JamieMackay 1 —
(M E Rimmer) *s.i.s: nvr gng wl and sn pushed along: wknd 3f out: t.o* **40/1**

1m 24.38s (-0.42) **Going Correction** +0.20s/f (Slow) **6** Ran SP% **111.6**
Speed ratings (Par 101): **110,109,105,98,84 77**
toteswingers: 1&2 £1.70, 1&3 £2.70, 2&3 £3.40 CSF £7.20 TOTE £2.50: £1.50, £1.90; EX 7.20.
Owner Liam Breslin **Bred** Miss Mary Davidson & Mrs Steffi Von Schilcher **Trained** Cowbit, Lincs

FOCUS
A moderate claimer, but there was no hanging about.
Mocha Java Official explanation: jockey said gelding hung right on the bend
Dig Deep(IRE) Official explanation: trainer's representative said that the gelding was unsuited by the track

343 BETDAQ THE BETTING EXCHANGE CLAIMING STKS 5f (P)
2:50 (2:50) (Class 6) 3-Y-O **£1,774** (£523; £262) **Stalls** High

Form RPR

1-32 **1** **Wanchai Whisper**[12] 209 3-7-10 69........................ AndrewHeffernan(5) 1 57+
(P D Evans) *stdd s: hld up last and off the pce: stl plenty to do 2f out: nt clr run over 1f out and swtchd: prog to go 2nd ins fnl f: hrd rdn and r.o to ld last strides* **8/11**[1]

6-03 **2** *hd* **Blue Neptune**[12] 209 3-8-5 62........................ MartinDwyer 5 60
(W R Muir) *led: drvn over 1f out: kpt on fnl f: hdd last strides* **6/1**[3]

0-66 **3** *¾* **Annia Galeria (IRE)**[7] 265 3-8-0 52........................ DavidProbert 2 52
(C A Dwyer) *trckd ldr to 1/2-way: restrained: rdn to go 2nd again over 1f out to ins fnl f: no ex* **40/1**

2-62 **4** *shd* **Avow (USA)**[9] 233 3-8-0 66........................(b) KierenFox(7) 3 59
(J S Moore) *settled off the pce: pushed along after 2f: dropped to last over 1f out: styd on against rail fnl f: nt rch ldrs* **2/1**[2]

205- **5** *2 ¾* **Out The Ring (IRE)**[46] 7748 3-8-10 59........................(b[1]) LukeMorris 4 52
(Miss Gay Kelleway) *hld up: rushed up to chse ldr 1/2-way: rdn and wknd over 1f out* **25/1**

61.16 secs (2.36) **Going Correction** +0.20s/f (Slow) **5** Ran SP% **111.8**
Speed ratings (Par 95): **89,88,87,87,82**
CSF £6.00 TOTE £1.80: £1.20, £2.00; EX 5.70.Wanchai Whisper was claimed by K Strangeway for £6000.
Owner M & R Refurbishments Ltd **Bred** Mike Smith **Trained** Pandy, Monmouths

FOCUS
A moderate claimer and not very competitive according to the market, but only a little over a length covered the front four at the line.

344 BETDAQEXTRA.COM H'CAP 5f (P)
3:25 (3:25) (Class 6) (0-62,60) 4-Y-O+ **£1,774** (£523; £262) **Stalls** High

Form RPR

404- **1** **After The Show**[41] 7808 9-8-11 **57**........................ MartinDwyer 7 66
(Rae Guest) *hld up in last trio: pushed along 1/2-way: checked sltly wl over 1f out: prog on outer after: drvn and styd on wl fnl f to ld last stride* **8/1**

3426 **2** *shd* **Sherjawy (IRE)**[1] 325 6-8-10 **56**........................ SamHitchcott 9 65
(Miss Z C Davison) *racd wd: chsd ldrs: rdn to cl over 1f out: led last 150yds: styd on: hdd fnl stride* **4/1**[2]

6-64 **3** *1 ¼* **Namir (IRE)**[14] 185 8-8-12 **58**........................(vt) HayleyTurner 4 62
(H J Evans) *walked to post: hld up but sn in midfield: trckd ldrs over 1f out: rdn and limited rspnse fnl f: tk 3rd cl home* **4/1**[2]

633- **4** *½* **Shakespeare's Son**[29] 7889 5-8-6 **52**........................ LukeMorris 5 54
(H J Evans) *hld up in last trio: looking for room fr 2f out: decent burst 1f out to chse ldrs: kpt on same pce last 100yds* **8/1**

-200 **5** *hd* **Ten Down**[9] 241 5-8-6 **55**........................ WilliamCarson(3) 3 57
(M Quinn) *trckd ldr on inner: chal over 1f out: upsides ent fnl f: sn wknd* **7/2**[1]

44-0 **6** *1 ¾* **Sweet Applause (IRE)**[14] 185 4-8-7 **60**........................ CharlotteKerton(7) 2 55
(G Prodromou) *trckd ldr: chal over 1f out: upsides ent fnl f: bmpd along and wknd* **33/1**

000- **7** *nk* **Fasliyanne (IRE)**[38] 7838 4-8-11 **57**........................(b) ChrisCatlin 8 51
(K A Ryan) *lw: led: hdd & wknd last 150yds* **20/1**

06-0 **8** *nse* **Hatman Jack (IRE)**[17] 137 4-8-9 **55**........................ StevieDonohoe 6 49
(B G Powell) *sn in last trio: a struggling to go the pce: nvr a factor* **7/1**[3]

2-01 **9** *1 ¾* **Head To Head (IRE)**[15] 178 6-8-7 **53**........................(bt) JoeFanning 1 41
(A D Brown) *chsd ldrs on inner: rdn 1/2-way: brief effrt over 1f out: sn wknd* **10/1**

59.48 secs (0.68) **Going Correction** +0.20s/f (Slow) **9** Ran SP% **113.7**
Speed ratings (Par 101): **102,101,99,99,98 95,95,95,92**
toteswingers: 1&2 £6.60, 1&3 £5.50, 2&3 £3.80 CSF £39.39 CT £148.41 TOTE £8.60: £2.60, £1.90, £1.70; EX 48.10 Trifecta £60.20 Pool: £345.770 - 4.25 winning units..
Owner Miss L Thompson **Bred** Michael Ng **Trained** Newmarket, Suffolk

FOCUS
A wide open sprint according to the market, but with several confirmed front-runners in opposition a strong pace was a near-certainty.
Head To Head(IRE) Official explanation: jockey said that the gelding was denied a clear run

345 MARRIOTT HOTEL OPENING SPRING 2010 H'CAP 5f (P)
4:00 (4:04) (Class 4) (0-85,83) 4-Y-O+ **£4,209** (£1,252; £625; £312) **Stalls** High

Form RPR

00-4 **1** **Even Bolder**[9] 241 7-8-1 **73**........................ KierenFox(7) 8 82
(E A Wheeler) *hld up and sn last: prog on wd outside over 1f out: rdn and r.o fnl f to ld last 75yds* **13/2**

40-3 **2** *nk* **Master Lightfoot**[9] 241 4-8-8 **73**........................ ChrisCatlin 7 81
(W R Swinburn) *wl in tch: wnt 3rd 3f out: effrt on outer over 1f out: led jst ins fnl f: hrd rdn and hdd last 75yds* **2/1**[1]

140- **3** *1 ¼* **Incomparable**[112] 6647 5-9-1 **80**........................(p) FrederikTylicki 3 83
(J A Glover) *trckd ldr: upsides over 1f out tl jst ins fnl f: fdd* **9/2**[3]

2-01 **4** *½* **Billy Red**[8] 250 6-9-4 **83** 6ex........................(b) FergusSweeney 4 85
(J R Jenkins) *lw: racd wd: led: hrd pressed over 1f out: hdd and fdd jst ins fnl f* **4/1**[2]

/01- **5** *1* **Anne Of Kiev (IRE)**[56] 7634 5-8-13 **78**........................(t) LukeMorris 6 76
(J R Gask) *s.i.s: hld up in tch: tried to cl on ldrs over 1f out: swtchd towards inner ent fnl f: no prog* **9/2**[3]

3-60 **6** *5* **Garstang**[15] 172 7-8-10 **75**........................(b) HayleyTurner 5 55
(J Balding) *b: s.s: t.k.h: hld up in tch: wknd tamely over 1f out* **8/1**

40-0 **7** *7* **Simple Rhythm**[16] 150 4-8-3 **75**........................ RyanPowell(7) 2 30
(J Ryan) *chsd ldng pair 2f: lost pl and n.m.r: sn last and struggling* **33/1**

58.53 secs (-0.27) **Going Correction** +0.20s/f (Slow) **7** Ran SP% **117.1**
Speed ratings (Par 105): **110,109,107,106,105 97,85**
toteswingers: 1&2 £4.80, 1&3 £6.00, 2&3 £3.10 CSF £20.76 CT £65.94 TOTE £8.70: £4.60, £1.80; EX 25.60 Trifecta £237.70 Pool: £465.83 - 1.45 winning units..
Owner Astrod TA Austin Stroud & Co **Bred** Raffin Bloodstock **Trained** Whitchurch-on-Thames, Oxon

FOCUS
A better-quality sprint handicap and the winning time was almost a second faster than the preceding Class 6 event.
Garstang Official explanation: jockey said gelding ran too free

346 BET AUSTRALIAN OPEN TENNIS - BETDAQ H'CAP 7f (P)
4:30 (4:31) (Class 6) (0-60,60) 3-Y-O **£1,774** (£523; £262) **Stalls** Low

Form RPR

606- **1** **Orsett Lad (USA)**[29] 7887 3-9-1 **57**........................ SteveDrowne 3 62+
(J R Best) *hld up in last trio: prog towards inner fr 2f out and most of field swung wd: wnt 2nd ins fnl f: rdn to ld last 75yds* **7/2**[2]

00-6 **2** *nk* **May Chorus (IRE)**[16] 149 3-9-0 **56**........................ JoeFanning 1 60
(J R Boyle) *disp ld at modest pce: qcknd over 2f out: def advantage jst ins fnl f on inner: hdd and hld last 75yds* **12/1**

0-02 **3** *2* **Sweet Avon**[13] 201 3-8-11 **53**........................ ShaneKelly 8 52
(Matthew Salaman) *disp ld at modest pce: qcknd over 2f out: stl upsides ent fnl f: one pce after* **5/1**[3]

466- **4** *½* **Yawary**[137] 5934 3-9-4 **60**........................ ChrisCatlin 4 57
(C E Brittain) *t.k.h: trckd ldng pair: cl up and rdn 2f out: nt qckn over 1f out: one pce after* **5/1**[3]

5-52 **5** *hd* **Novillero**[12] 213 3-8-4 **46** oh1........................ LukeMorris 6 43
(J C Fox) *plld hrd: hld up bhd ldng pair: cl enough and rdn 2f out: nt qckn over 1f out* **15/8**[1]

43-0 **6** *½* **Moonlight Serenade**[11] 215 3-8-11 **56**........................(p) WilliamCarson(3) 7 52
(W G M Turner) *hld up in tch: effrt 2f out: hanging and fnd nil on outer over 1f out* **11/1**

50-0 **7** *¾* **Wigan Lane**[6] 276 3-9-2 **58**........................ J-PGuillambert 5 52
(P Howling) *wl away but sn restrained into last: outpcd fr 2f out: drvn and no ch after* **20/1**

66-6 **8** *6* **Bella Charlie (IRE)**[17] 134 3-9-1 **57**........................(p) VinceSlattery 2 34
(M G Quinlan) *t.k.h: hld up and racd wd: effrt whn wd bnd 2f out and hanging: wknd* **16/1**

1m 27.36s (2.56) **Going Correction** +0.20s/f (Slow) **8** Ran SP% **117.0**
Speed ratings (Par 95): **93,92,90,89,89 89,88,81**
toteswingers: 1&2 £8.10, 1&3 £4.00, 2&3 £9.10 CSF £45.18 CT £212.60 TOTE £5.10: £1.70, £4.20, £1.90; EX 42.90 Trifecta £304.70 Part won. Pool: £411.86 - 086 winning units. Place 6: £12.21 Place 5: £7.81.
Owner Bob Malt **Bred** Harold J Plumley **Trained** Hucking, Kent

FOCUS
A poor race and a muddling affair. Only one of these had had tasted success before and the form amounts to little.
T/Plt: £12.70 to a £1 stake. Pool: £52,724.47. 3,007.05 winning tickets. T/Qpdt: £8.30 to a £1 stake. Pool: £3,474.53. 307.20 winning tickets. JN

288 WOLVERHAMPTON (A.W) (L-H)
Friday, January 29

OFFICIAL GOING: Standard
Wind: Fresh across Weather: Fine

347 DINE IN THE HORIZONS RESTAURANT H'CAP 1m 141y(P)
4:40 (4:40) (Class 7) (0-50,55) 4-Y-O+ **£1,364** (£403; £201) **Stalls** Low

Form RPR

4-11 **1** **Lyrical Intent**[10] 227 4-9-2 **55** 6ex........................ JimmyQuinn 3 63
(P Howling) *chsd ldrs: led over 1f out: sn rdn: styd on u.p* **5/4**[1]

6-03 **2** *1 ¼* **Libre**[12] 211 10-8-9 **47**........................ RichardKingscote 11 52+
(F Jordan) *hld up: hdwy over 1f out: r.o to go 2nd nr fin: nt trble wnr* **5/1**[2]

3-00 **3** *shd* **Mojeerr**[8] 249 4-8-11 **50**........................(v[1]) RobertWinston 1 55
(A J McCabe) *s.i.s: hld up: hdwy over 1f out: styd on* **12/1**

00-6 **4** *nk* **Viking Awake (IRE)**[12] 211 4-8-10 **49**........................(t) GrahamGibbons 12 53
(J W Unett) *hld up in tch: rdn over 1f out: styd on* **8/1**[3]

-650 **5** *¾* **Amber Moon**[9] 229 5-8-7 **50** ow2........................(b) AnnStokell(5) 9 52
(Miss A Stokell) *chsd ldrs: pushed along to ld over 2f out: hdd over 1f out: kpt on* **33/1**

0-10 **6** *1 ¼* **Turkish Sultan (IRE)**[10] 227 7-8-11 **49**......................(p) NickyMackay 2 48
(J M Bradley) *mid-div: pushed along 1/2-way: hdwy over 2f out: sn rdn: styd on same pce fnl f* **11/1**

500- **7** *shd* **Machinate (USA)**[106] 5465 8-8-9 **47**.................................... LiamJones 7 46
(W M Brisbourne) *hld up: hdwy over 2f out: rdn over 1f out: one pce fnl f* **50/1**

003- **8** *7* **Alseraaj (USA)**[300] 1122 5-8-12 **50**............................(bt[1]) PaulHanagan 8 33
(Ian Williams) *s.i.s: pushed along early in rr: hdwy over 2f out: rdn and wknd over 1f out* **10/1**

50-0 **9** *1 ¼* **Vanadium**[14] 193 8-8-5 **50**...(t) AmyScott(7) 13 30
(A J Lidderdale) *stdd s: hld up and bhd: n.d* **20/1**

0-00 **9** *dht* **Stark Contrast (USA)**[12] 211 6-8-2 **47**.............(e[1]) MissRachelKing(7) 4 27
(M D I Usher) *prom: rdn over 2f out: wknd sn after* **22/1**

00-0 **11** *8* **Amber Ridge**[12] 211 5-8-6 **49**....................................... PaulPickard(5) 5 11
(B P J Baugh) *led: rdn and hdd over 2f out: wknd over 1f out* **40/1**

/00- **12** *1 ¼* **Complete Frontline (GER)**[255] 2155 5-8-11 **49**............ AndrewElliott 6 8
(J R Weymes) *chsd ldr tl rdn over 2f out: edgd lft and wknd over 1f out* **33/1**

1m 52.68s (2.18) **Going Correction** +0.225s/f (Slow)
WFA 4 from 5yo+ 1lb 12 Ran SP% **116.7**
Speed ratings (Par 97): **99,97,97,97,96 95,95,89,88,88 81,80**
toteswingers: 1&2 £1.80, 1&3 £6.00, 2&3 £7.40 CSF £6.25 CT £52.30 TOTE £2.10: £1.02, £2.10, £4.20; EX 6.60.
Owner Ajaz Ahmed **Bred** Mrs S France **Trained** Newmarket, Suffolk

FOCUS
A very weak opener that lacked strength in depth, very much as the one-sided betting suggested, but it was run at a decent clip and the was no obvious hard luck story in what was a very slow-motion finish.
Amber Moon Official explanation: jockey said mare hung right
Turkish Sultan(IRE) Official explanation: jockey said gelding hung right
Amber Ridge Official explanation: trainer said gelding returned distressed

348 HOTEL & CONFERENCING AT WOLVERHAMPTON CLASSIFIED CLAIMING STKS 1m 141y(P)
5:10 (5:10) (Class 5) 4-Y-0+ **£2,456** (£725; £362) **Stalls** Low

Form RPR

243- **1** **Networker**[42] 7798 7-8-6 63.. PaulHanagan 9 67
(P J McBride) *mde virtually all: stdd 6f out: qcknd 3f out: rdn over 1f out: hung lft fnl f: all out* **11/2**[3]

2-31 **2** *nk* **Sir George (IRE)**[4] 289 5-8-7 65................................... FrannyNorton 2 67
(Ollie Pears) *sn trcking wnr and pulling hrd: rdn over 1f out: r.o* **7/2**[2]

1-12 **3** *2 ½* **Shake On It**[18] 131 6-8-11 63 ow1........................... JamieJones(5) 3 71
(M R Hoad) *hld up: plld hrd: hdwy over 3f out: rdn over 1f out: edgd lft and styd on same pce fnl f* **8/1**

36-5 **4** *3 ¼* **Via Mia**[19] 113 4-8-2 67 ow1..................................(p) MatthewDavies(5) 4 55
(George Baker) *hld up: rdn over 3f out: nvr nrr* **8/1**

051- **5** *¾* **Daniel Thomas (IRE)**[32] 7858 8-8-3 70.........................(v) RyanClark(7) 5 55+
(Mrs A L M King) *s.i.s: hld up: rdn over 1f out: no ch whn hmpd ins fnl f* **11/4**[1]

11-0 **6** *¾* **Just Jimmy (IRE)**[18] 129 5-8-6 63.. PaulDoe 6 50+
(P D Evans) *hld up: plld hrd: hdwy u.p over 2f out: wknd over 1f out: hmpd ins fnl f* **13/2**

41-4 **7** *hd* **Alf Tupper**[4] 289 7-8-1 67.. JamesSullivan(5) 8 49
(Adrian McGuinness, Ire) *hld up in tch: plld hrd: rdn over 2f out: wkng whn hung lft fr over 1f out* **14/1**

51-3 **8** *½* **Convince (USA)**[3] 297 9-8-0 59.....................................(p) BillyCray(5) 1 47
(J L Flint) *chsd ldrs: rdn over 2f out: sn wknd: no ch whn hmpd ins fnl f* **20/1**

1m 52.69s (2.19) **Going Correction** +0.225s/f (Slow)
WFA 4 from 5yo+ 1lb 8 Ran SP% **111.3**
Speed ratings (Par 103): **99,98,96,93,92 92,92,91**
toteswingers: 1&2 £4.10, 1&3 £4.80, 2&3 £3.20 CSF £23.66 TOTE £7.90: £1.60, £1.20, £2.50; EX 26.50.
Owner P J McBride **Bred** T S And Mrs M E Child **Trained** Newmarket, Suffolk

FOCUS
A tight claimer at the weights on official ratings, but it was anything but as the race panned out with the eventual winner able to set a very steady pace and some of those in behind ruining their chance either by pulling too hard or being set too much to do. The form looks unreliable.
Just Jimmy(IRE) Official explanation: jockey said gelding suffered interference in running
Alf Tupper Official explanation: jockey said gelding hung left

349 ENJOY THE LUCKY 7 GROUP OFFER CLAIMING STKS 5f 20y(P)
5:40 (5:40) (Class 6) 4-Y-0+ **£1,774** (£523; £262) **Stalls** Low

Form RPR

1-12 **1** **Total Impact**[7] 258 7-9-1 78.. RobertWinston 2 82
(C R Dore) *broke wl and led early: stdd to trck ldrs: shkn up to ld ins fnl f: rdn: hung lft and r.o wl* **5/4**[1]

442- **2** *2* **Desperate Dan**[64] 7535 9-8-12 72....................................(v) TomQueally 1 72
(A B Haynes) *hld up: hdwy over 1f out: sn rdn: styd on same pce ins fnl f* **5/1**[3]

-220 **3** *nk* **Kheley (IRE)**[2] 306 4-8-8 63.. LiamJones 6 67
(W M Brisbourne) *sn led: hdd over 3f out: led again 2f out: sn rdn: hdd: edgd lft and no ex ins fnl f* **12/1**

12-4 **4** *hd* **Grudge**[15] 165 5-8-12 65...(e) FrannyNorton 4 70
(Ollie Pears) *s.i.s: hld up: hdwy over 1f out: sn rdn: r.o* **4/1**[2]

20-0 **5** *4* **Colorus (IRE)**[28] 2 7-8-10 75......................................(p) PaulPickard(5) 7 59
(W J H Ratcliffe) *chsd ldrs: led over 3f out: rdn and hdd 2f out: wknd fnl f* **4/1**[2]

040- **6** *6* **Tournedos (IRE)**[111] 6670 8-8-12 77..............................(p) AndrewElliott 3 34
(Mrs R A Carr) *chsd ldrs: rdn 1/2-way: wknd over 1f out* **10/1**

000- **7** *½* **Latin Connection (IRE)**[32] 7863 4-8-6 44............(b[1]) JamesSullivan(5) 5 31
(Lee Smyth, Ire) *sn pushed along in rr: rdn 1/2-way: sn lost tch* **100/1**

62.32 secs (0.02) **Going Correction** +0.225s/f (Slow) 7 Ran SP% **118.9**
Speed ratings (Par 101): **108,104,104,104,97 88,87**
toteswingers: 1&2 £2.30, 1&3 £4.10, 2&3 £6.70 CSF £8.68 TOTE £2.60: £1.30, £2.20; EX 6.50.
Owner Chris Marsh **Bred** C A Cyzer **Trained** Cowbit, Lincs

FOCUS
An uncompetitive claimer that readily went the way of the best horse at the weights in a race that was run at no more than a fair pace.

350 BET SUPER LEAGUE - BETDAQ H'CAP 5f 216y(P)
6:10 (6:10) (Class 4) (0-85,84) 4-Y-0+ **£4,533** (£1,348; £674; £336) **Stalls** Low

Form RPR

020- **1** **Bajan Tryst (USA)**[141] 5799 4-9-3 **83**................................ PaulHanagan 1 97
(K A Ryan) *mde all: qcknd clr over 2f out: rdn out* **3/1**[1]

-130 **2** *4* **Indian Skipper (IRE)**[5] 286 5-8-13 **84**..........................(be) BillyCray(5) 3 85
(R C Guest) *in rr: pushed along over 4f out: hdwy over 1f out: hung lft and chsd wnr fnl f: no imp* **3/1**[1]

50-3 **3** *3 ¾* **Fen Spirit (IRE)**[10] 223 4-8-8 **74**.....................................(p) RobertHavlin 2 63
(J H M Gosden) *chsd wnr: outpcd over 2f out: rdn and no rspnse over 1f out* **10/3**[2]

00-3 **4** *2 ¼* **Ray Of Joy**[20] 102 4-8-13 **79**.. JimmyQuinn 5 61
(J R Jenkins) *hld up: pushed along 1/2-way: sn outpcd* **7/2**[3]

5-02 **5** *4 ½* **Pawan (IRE)**[22] 74 10-8-10 **81**................................(p) AnnStokell(5) 4 48
(Miss A Stokell) *chsd ldrs: lost pl 4f out: wknd wl over 2f out* **12/1**

600- **6** *9* **Classic Descent**[100] 6944 5-8-13 **79**................................ AndrewElliott 6 18
(Mrs R A Carr) *s.i.s: hdwy 4f out: rdn and wknd over 2f out* **14/1**

1m 15.2s (0.20) **Going Correction** +0.225s/f (Slow) 6 Ran SP% **109.7**
Speed ratings (Par 105): **107,101,96,93,87 75**
toteswingers: 1&2 £2.50, 2&3 £1.70, 1&3 not won. CSF £11.65 TOTE £4.50: £2.90, £2.50; EX 12.80.
Owner Mrs Margaret Forsyth & Mrs R G Hillen **Bred** William Patterson & James Glenn **Trained** Hambleton, N Yorks

FOCUS
A weakish race for the grade with just a handful of runners and a race that the sole front runner and eventual winner was able to dominate much as looked likely beforehand, gradually increasing what was initially a steady pace. The form has a dubious look to it.

351 BET PREMIER LEAGUE FOOTBALL - BETDAQ H'CAP 5f 216y(P)
6:40 (6:41) (Class 6) (0-60,61) 4-Y-0+ **£1,774** (£523; £262) **Stalls** Low

Form RPR

00-1 **1** **Bishopbriggs (USA)**[14] 193 5-9-2 **58**.................................. AdamKirby 12 70+
(M G Quinlan) *drvn along to ld: hrd rdn fr over 1f out: all out* **5/1**[2]

611- **2** *hd* **Welcome Approach**[41] 7815 7-9-3 **59**............................... JimmyQuinn 9 70
(J R Weymes) *hld up: rdn and r.o wl ins fnl f: jst failed* **11/1**

21-4 **3** *2 ¼* **Only A Game (IRE)**[27] 14 5-9-1 **57**..........................(tp) DaneO'Neill 10 61
(I W McInnes) *hld up in tch: rdn to chse wnr fnl f: styng on same pce whn lost 2nd fnl 50yds* **7/1**[3]

300- **4** *1 ¼* **Captain Kallis (IRE)**[147] 5632 4-9-2 **58**.................. FrankieMcDonald 11 58
(D J S Ffrench Davis) *a.p: chsd wnr over 2f out: rdn over 1f out: no ex ins fnl f* **66/1**

1313 **5** *1* **Know No Fear**[5] 285 5-8-8 **57**.......................................(p) AmyScott(7) 5 54
(A J Lidderdale) *hld up: hdwy u.p over 1f out: nt rch ldrs* **7/1**[3]

/00- **6** *¾* **Doctor Hilary**[53] 7673 8-9-4 **60**..................................(v) RobertHavlin 13 55
(A B Haynes) *mid-div: rdn over 2f out: hdwy u.p over 1f out: nt trble ldrs* **40/1**

05-1 **7** *½* **Radiator Rooney (IRE)**[14] 195 7-9-4 **60**.....................(b) GeorgeBaker 1 53
(Patrick Morris) *hld up in tch: rdn and hung rt over 1f out: wknd ins fnl f* **5/1**[2]

00-1 **8** *shd* **Jul's Lad (IRE)**[22] 70 4-9-0 **56**..(b) DavidNolan 3 49
(D Carroll) *mid-div: rdn over 2f out: no imp whn hung lft over 1f out* **16/1**

4-33 **9** *1 ¼* **Bluebok**[17] 132 9-9-1 **57**..(bt) NickyMackay 6 46
(J M Bradley) *chsd ldrs: rdn over 1f out: wknd fnl f* **20/1**

00-4 **10** *2* **Royal Envoy (IRE)**[14] 194 7-8-13 **58**..................... MichaelStainton(3) 7 40
(P Howling) *s.s: a in rr* **20/1**

450- **11** *13* **Trick Or Two**[292] 1232 4-9-4 **60**....................................... AndrewElliott 2 —
(Mrs R A Carr) *chsd ldrs: rdn over 3f out: wknd over 2f out* **50/1**

-151 **12** *8* **Interchoice Star**[8] 251 5-9-5 **61** 6ex..............................(p) TomQueally 8 —
(R Hollinshead) *mid-div: sn pushed along: rdn and wknd over 2f out* **11/4**[1]

1m 15.47s (0.47) **Going Correction** +0.225s/f (Slow) 12 Ran SP% **114.6**
Speed ratings (Par 101): **105,104,101,100,98 97,97,96,95,92 75,64**
toteswingers: 1&2 £8.00, 1&3 £8.80, 2&3 £12.80 CSF £53.02 CT £384.33 TOTE £6.70: £2.30, £3.40, £2.50; EX 40.10.
Owner Maurice Kirby **Bred** Sycamore Hall Farm Llc **Trained** Newmarket, Suffolk
■ Stewards' Enquiry : Adam Kirby two-day ban: used whip with excessive frequency without giving gelding time to respond (Feb 12-13)

FOCUS
Competitive fare for the grade with five last-time-out winners in opposition and a race run at a strong pace that favoured neither those held up nor ridden prominently. There was no trouble in running to speak of and the form ought to stand up.
Interchoice Star Official explanation: jockey said gelding never travelled; vet said gelding was found to have a fibrillating heart

352 BET MULTIPLES - BETDAQ H'CAP 2m 119y(P)
7:10 (7:11) (Class 4) (0-85,83) 4-Y-0+ **£4,533** (£1,348; £674; £336) **Stalls** Low

Form RPR

1- **1** **Sheshali (IRE)**[88] 4480 6-10-0 **83**.................................... GeorgeBaker 7 91+
(Evan Williams) *a.p: chsd wnr 12f out: rdn over 2f out: styd on u.p to ld post* **5/1**

0-22 **2** *hd* **Calculating (IRE)**[10] 224 6-8-8 **68**................................. LeeNewnes(5) 3 76
(M D I Usher) *led after 1f: set stdy pce: qcknd over 4f out: rdn over 1f out: hdd post* **7/2**[2]

0/3- **3** *5* **Hydrant**[43] 7780 4-8-6 **68**... AndrewElliott 6 70
(P Salmon) *led 1f: chsd wnr to 12f out: remained handy: rdn over 2f out: no ex fnl f* **33/1**

01-3 **4** *nse* **Dreamwalk (IRE)**[26] 25 4-9-4 **80**.................................(v) DaneO'Neill 4 82
(R Curtis) *hld up in tch: rdn over 3f out: styd on same pce appr fnl f* **9/4**[1]

63-1 **5** *2 ¾* **Jeer (IRE)**[13] 202 6-8-13 **73**..................................(bt) JamesSullivan(5) 5 72+
(M W Easterby) *hld up: plld hrd: rdn over 2f out: wknd over 1f out* **9/1**

403- **6** *1 ½* **Tropical Blue**[43] 7785 4-8-12 **74**..................................... PaulHanagan 1 71
(Jennie Candlish) *hld up in last pl: rdn over 2f out: wknd over 1f out* **9/2**[3]

405- **7** *14* **Right Option (IRE)**[104] 5903 6-9-7 **76**........................ KevinGhunowa 2 56
(J L Flint) *chsd ldrs: rdn over 4f out: wknd 3f out* **17/2**

3m 51.77s (9.97) **Going Correction** +0.225s/f (Slow)
WFA 4 from 6yo 7lb 7 Ran SP% **111.3**
Speed ratings (Par 105): **85,84,82,82,81 80,73**
toteswingers: 1&2 £2.70, 1&3 £22.90, 2&3 £15.60 CSF £21.52 TOTE £5.40: £2.50, £2.00; EX 19.60.
Owner Edwards, Swinnerton, Babb, Howell **Bred** His Highness The Aga Khan's Studs S C **Trained** Llancarfan, Vale Of Glamorgan

The Form Book, Raceform Ltd, Compton, RG20 6NL

FOCUS
A uncompetitive handicap for the grade with more than half the field suspect in the stamina department, but in the event it turned into a steadily-run tactical affair where race position was the overriding factor and significantly the first two were always in those positions throughout. The form looks dubious.

353 GREAT OFFERS AT WOLVERHAMPTON-RACECOURSE.CO.UK H'CAP (DIV I) 1m 1f 103y(P)
7:40 (7:41) (Class 6) (0-55,56) 4-Y-O+ **£1,433** (£423; £211) **Stalls** Low

Form				RPR
4622	1		**Kirstys Lad**[10] 227 8-8-2 **46** KellyHarrison(3) 4 (M Mullineaux) *chsd ldrs: rdn to ld and hung lft over 1f out: styd on* **10/3**[1]	57
436-	2	3/4	**Zero Cool (USA)**[275] 1604 6-9-1 **56** ow1 (p) GeorgeBaker 6 (G L Moore) *led 1f: chsd ldrs: rdn and ev ch whn hmpd over 1f out: styd on same pce ins fnl f* **5/1**[2]	65
-335	3	2 1/4	**Join Up**[4] 295 4-8-6 **53** RossAtkinson(5) 2 (W M Brisbourne) *hld up in tch: rdn over 2f out: r.o ins fnl f: nt rch ldrs* **11/2**[3]	58
35-3	4	1/2	**Dobravany (IRE)**[20] 100 6-8-8 **49** (v) JimmyQuinn 11 (K A Morgan) *s.i.s: hld up: hdwy over 1f out: r.o: nrst fin* **20/1**	53
45-5	5	hd	**Royal Bet (IRE)**[8] 244 4-8-10 **52** PaulHanagan 8 (M L W Bell) *led over 8f out: rdn and hdd over 2f out: no ex ins fnl f* **5/1**[2]	55
04-1	6	1 1/4	**King's Jester (IRE)**[12] 211 8-8-10 **56** 6ex (b) BarryMcHugh(5) 13 (Lee Smyth, Ire) *hld up in tch: led over 2f out: rdn and hdd over 1f out: no ex ins fnl f* **12/1**	57
-526	7	1 1/2	**Inside Story (IRE)**[8] 244 8-9-0 **55** (b) LiamKeniry 5 (C R Dore) *s.i.s: sn pushed along in rr: rdn over 2f out: edgd rt over 1f out: nrst fin* **8/1**	52
006-	8	3 1/4	**Bobering**[49] 7719 10-8-0 **46** oh1 PaulPickard(5) 9 (B P J Baugh) *hld up: pushed along over 1f out: nvr nr ldrs* **40/1**	37
5/0-	9	5	**Itcanbedone Again (IRE)**[57] 4861 11-8-2 **50** ow2 AlexEdwards(7) 10 (J W Unett) *prom: chsd ldr over 6f out to over 3f out: rdn and wknd 2f out* **80/1**	30
0-00	10	2 1/4	**Wicklewood**[8] 249 4-8-6 **48** (b) SaleemGolam 1 (Mrs C A Dunnett) *s.i.s: sn pushed along and a in rr:* **50/1**	23
0-06	11	2 1/4	**Climate (IRE)**[4] 290 11-9-0 **55** (v) PaulDoe 12 (P D Evans) *hld up: rdn over 3f out: wknd 2f out* **16/1**	26
66-0	12	nk	**Bahkov (IRE)**[9] 234 4-8-10 **52** RichardKingscote 7 (Andrew Turnell) *hld up: rdn over 3f out: wknd over 2f out* **16/1**	22
0-55	13	5	**Mrs Slocombe (IRE)**[12] 211 4-8-5 **47** FrankieMcDonald 3 (Mrs N S Evans) *prom: rdn over 4f out: wknd 3f out* **16/1**	7

2m 3.61s (1.91) **Going Correction** +0.225s/f (Slow)
WFA 4 from 6yo+ 1lb **13** Ran SP% **118.6**
Speed ratings (Par 101): **100,99,97,96,96 95,94,91,86,84 82,82,78**
toteswingers: 1&2 £5.50, 1&3 £6.40, 2&3 £8.70 CSF £18.52 CT £90.50 TOTE £4.20: £1.50, £2.10, £2.70; EX 25.50.
Owner S A Pritchard **Bred** T S And Mrs Wallace **Trained** Alpraham, Cheshire

FOCUS
A modest handicap but the winner had been in good form lately, the runner-up had been given a chance by the handicapper and a couple of the others had something to recommend them, so all in all reasonably competitive and a race that should turn out to be reliable. The pace seemed fair.

354 GREAT OFFERS AT WOLVERHAMPTON-RACECOURSE.CO.UK H'CAP (DIV II) 1m 1f 103y(P)
8:10 (8:11) (Class 6) (0-55,56) 4-Y-O+ **£1,433** (£423; £211) **Stalls** Low

Form				RPR
02-1	1		**Grey Command (USA)**[18] 131 5-9-0 **55** RobertWinston 12 (M Brittain) *mde all: rdn over 1f out: r.o* **9/4**[1]	67
000-	2	2 1/2	**Barodine**[46] 7750 7-7-7 **48** JimmyQuinn 3 (R J Hodges) *hld up: nt clr run over 2f out: hdwy over 1f out: r.o wl to go 2nd towards fin: nt rch wnr* **7/1**[3]	55+
00-4	3	1	**Royal Society**[18] 131 4-8-13 **55** GrahamGibbons 8 (R A Farrant) *sn chsng wnr: rdn over 2f out: styd on same pce fnl f: lost 2nd towards fin* **15/2**	60
-351	4	1 3/4	**Bajan Pride**[8] 248 6-8-4 **52** (v) LeeTopliss(5) 6 (R A Fahey) *prom: rdn and outpcd over 2f out: styd on fnl f* **9/2**[2]	53
0-26	5	2	**Mid Wicket (USA)**[14] 184 4-8-10 **52** (p) LiamKeniry 2 (Mouse Hamilton-Fairley) *chsd ldrs: rdn over 2f out: wknd fnl f* **8/1**	49
54-4	6	1 3/4	**Desert Fairy**[10] 227 4-8-7 **49** DavidProbert 7 (J W Unett) *hld up: racd keenly: rdn over 2f out: n.d* **14/1**	42
3-41	7	1 1/4	**Playful Asset (IRE)**[9] 228 4-9-0 **56** 6ex PaulDoe 13 (P Howling) *s.i.s: hld up: rdn over 1f out: nvr nrr* **14/1**	47
300-	8	4 1/2	**Jobekani (IRE)**[41] 7818 4-8-9 **51** (p) TomEaves 9 (Mrs L Williamson) *mid-div: hmpd after 1f: rdn over 3f out: wknd over 2f out* **33/1**	32
1-00	9	2 1/4	**King Of Rhythm (IRE)**[14] 194 7-9-0 **55** DavidNolan 10 (D Carroll) *chsd ldrs: rdn over 2f out: wknd over 1f out* **16/1**	32
50-0	10	6	**Helpmeronda**[14] 199 4-7-13 **46** oh1 AndrewHeffernan(5) 1 (W M Brisbourne) *prom: racd keenly early on: rdn over 3f out: sn wknd* **80/1**	10
0/0-	11	3 3/4	**Immaculate Red**[44] 7766 7-7-12 **46** oh1 MissRachelKing(7) 11 (C Roberts) *hld up: a in rr: wknd 4f out* **100/1**	2
00-2	12	30	**Space Pirate**[20] 100 5-8-5 **46** (b) SaleemGolam 4 (J Pearce) *s.i.s and sn drvn along: rdn 1/2-way: sn wknd: t.o* **14/1**	—

2m 5.19s (3.49) **Going Correction** +0.225s/f (Slow)
WFA 4 from 5yo+ 1lb **12** Ran SP% **115.4**
Speed ratings (Par 101): **93,90,89,88,86 85,83,79,77,72 69,42**
toteswingers: 1&2 £4.20, 1&3 £3.70, 2&3 £11.90 CSF £17.29 CT £101.25 TOTE £2.80: £1.60, £2.60, £2.30; EX 19.80 Place 6: £57.86 Place 5: £42.54.
Owner Mel Brittain **Bred** Darley **Trained** Warthill, N Yorks

FOCUS
Less strength in depth than the first division and run in a much slower time as well on account of a very steady early gallop that played right into the hands of the eventual winner. Once again the form might not be entirely reliable.
T/Plt: £45.00 to a £1 stake. Pool: £79,706.27. 1,290.89 winning tickets. T/Qpdt: £12.60 to a £1 stake. Pool: £10,797.50. 631.00 winning tickets. CR

[340] LINGFIELD (L-H)
Saturday, January 30

OFFICIAL GOING: Standard
Wind: medium, half against Weather: bright, cold

355 LINGFIELD PARK FOURBALL MAIDEN STKS 1m 4f (P)
1:05 (1:05) (Class 5) 4-Y-O+ **£2,456** (£725; £362) **Stalls** Low

Form				RPR
	1		**Kindlelight Sun (JPN)** 4-9-3 0 J-PGuillambert 2 (N P Littmoden) *hld up in tch in last trio: hdwy to chse ldrs over 2f out: rdn over 1f out: r.o wl to ld ins fnl f: sn in command: comf* **12/1**	71+
	2	1 1/2	**Cashpoint**[43] 5-9-7 0 LiamKeniry 9 (A Middleton) *in tch in midfield: hdwy to join ldr over 2f out: led narrowly ent fnl 2f: drvn over 1f out: hdd and nt pce of wnr ins fnl f* **20/1**	66
55-5	3	1 3/4	**Sushitan (GER)**[7] 280 5-9-7 67 GeorgeBaker 1 (G L Moore) *chsd ldrs: led 3f out: hdd narrowly and rdn ent fnl 2f: stl ev ch and drvn over 1f out: wknd ins fnl f* **7/4**[1]	64
342-	4	3/4	**French Hollow**[56] 7648 5-9-7 70 RobertWinston 3 (T J Fitzgerald) *t.k.h: hld up in tch towards rr: hdwy and rdn along over 2f out: chsd ldng pair and nt qckn u.p wl over 1f out: plugged on same pce fnl f* **7/4**[1]	62
00-0	5	nk	**Nicky Nutjob (GER)**[15] 184 4-9-3 43 SaleemGolam 5 (J Pearce) *in tch: chsd ldrs and drvn ent fnl 2f: one pce fr over 1f out* **33/1**	62
0-	6	1/2	**Zafranagar (IRE)**[57] 7221 5-9-0 73 GeorgeDowning(7) 8 (A W Carroll) *t.k.h: chsd ldr tl 6f out: styd chsng ldrs: edgd lft and one pce fr wl over 1f out* **9/1**[3]	61
0-53	7	16	**Flannel (IRE)**[9] 246 4-9-3 55 (v) AdamKirby 7 (J R Fanshawe) *sn pushed up to ld: hdd and rdn 3f out: sn dropped out and wl btn fnl 2f* **13/2**[2]	36
0	8	2 1/4	**Jolly Cooper**[15] 179 7-9-2 0 ShaneKelly 4 (Mike Murphy) *hld up in tch: hdwy on outer to chse ldr 6f out tl 3f out: sn wknd: wl btn fnl 2f* **150/1**	27
	9	26	**Juniper Prince** 4-9-3 0 DaneO'Neill 10 (G P Enright) *s.i.s: in tch in rr: rdn and lost tch 3f out: t.o fr wl over 1f out* **100/1**	—
0-4	10	26	**Lady Champagne**[29] 1 4-8-7 0 TobyAtkinson(5) 6 (Miss J Feilden) *chsd ldrs tl lost pl and towards rr and rdn 4f out: sn lost tch: t.o fnl 2f* **25/1**	—

2m 34.66s (1.66) **Going Correction** +0.075s/f (Slow)
WFA 4 from 5yo+ 4lb **10** Ran SP% **117.0**
Speed ratings (Par 103): **97,96,94,94,94 93,83,81,64,46**
toteswingers: 1&2 £14.20, 1&3 £6.20, 2&3 £5.70 CSF £215.18 TOTE £15.70: £3.10, £3.40, £1.20; EX 87.40 TRIFECTA Not won..
Owner Kindlelight Ltd **Bred** Taihei Stud Farm Co Ltd **Trained** Newmarket, Suffolk

FOCUS
A modest event. The four at the head of the market disappointed to varying degrees and the race is held down by the proximity of the 43-rated fifth. The gallop was steady and the winner came down the centre in the straight.

356 CYPRIUM RESTAURANT AT MARRIOTT LINGFIELD MAIDEN STKS 1m (P)
1:40 (1:40) (Class 5) 3-Y-O+ **£2,456** (£725; £362) **Stalls** High

Form				RPR
00-3	1		**Purple Gallery (IRE)**[15] 180 3-8-7 72 (p) HayleyTurner 10 (J S Moore) *chsd ldr tl led over 3f out: hung bdly rt sn after: v wd bnd and hdd wl over 1f out: racd on stands' rail in st: drvn ins fnl f: r.o to ld again nr towards fin* **5/2**[2]	75+
0-42	2	1/2	**Darshonin**[7] 274 3-8-7 72 (v) ShaneKelly 3 (J Noseda) *dwlt: sn rcvrd to chse ldrs: sltly hmpd and chsd wnr wl over 2f out: lft in ld wl over 1f out: hrd drvn ent fnl f: hdd towards fin* **1/1**[1]	74
5	3	7	**Pascalina**[14] 206 3-8-2 0 JimmyQuinn 4 (J Akehurst) *s.i.s: hld up in tch towards rr: hdwy over 2f out: rdn and disputing 3rd over 1f out: wl outpcd by ldng pair fnl f* **50/1**	52
6-04	4	nk	**Durgan**[6] 285 4-9-13 65 SteveDrowne 5 (Mrs L C Jewell) *stdd after s: t.k.h: hld up in tch towards rr: hdwy over 2f out: disputing 3rd and rdn over 1f out: wl outpcd by ldng pair fnl f* **13/2**[3]	61
0-6	5	4	**Kiss 'n Tell**[11] 226 4-9-8 0 GeorgeBaker 1 (G L Moore) *in tch in midfield on inner: rdn and n.m.r over 2f out: n.d fr over 1f out* **40/1**	47
0-	6	nk	**Yourgolftravel Com**[233] 2862 5-9-8 0 TobyAtkinson(5) 7 (M Wigham) *t.k.h: chsd ldrs: wnt 3rd and sltly hmpd wl over 2f out: rdn and wknd over 1f out* **40/1**	51
	7	1 1/4	**Rosewood Lad** 3-8-7 0 LukeMorris 11 (J S Moore) *s.i.s: in tch in rr: rdn over 4f out: wknd u.p 2f out: wl bhd fnl f* **50/1**	43
	8	2 3/4	**Hopefull Blue (IRE)** 4-9-8 0 IanMongan 6 (J W Mullins) *t.k.h: hld up in tch in rr: rdn over 2f out: sn struggling: wl btn fnl 2f* **33/1**	37
4-	9	6	**Owen Jones (USA)**[110] 6741 4-9-10 0 WilliamCarson(3) 8 (P W Hiatt) *t.k.h: chsd ldrs tl wknd qckly wl over 1f out: wl btn and eased fnl f* **12/1**	27
0-	10	19	**Pete's Passion**[203] 3876 4-9-8 0 PaulHanagan 9 (R A Fahey) *t.k.h: led tl over 3f out: wknd qckly over 2f out: t.o and eased fnl f* **20/1**	—

1m 38.43s (0.23) **Going Correction** +0.075s/f (Slow)
WFA 3 from 4yo+ 20lb **10** Ran SP% **116.1**
Speed ratings (Par 103): **101,100,93,93,89 88,87,84,78,59**
toteswingers: 1&2 £1.90, 1&3 £12.30, 2&3 £11.90 CSF £4.99 TOTE £3.70: £1.50, £1.10, £6.20; EX 5.50 Trifecta £76.80 Pool: £505.82 - 4.87 winning units..
Owner The Chicken On A Chain Partnership **Bred** Fergus Cousins **Trained** Upper Lambourn, Berks
■ Stewards' Enquiry : William Carson one-day ban: failed to ride to draw (Feb 13)

FOCUS
Not a competitive race and one in which the two market leaders pulled clear in the straight. The gallop was on the steady side and the winner hung to the stands' rail in the straight.

357 MARRIOTT HOTEL OPENING SPRING 2010 H'CAP 6f (P)
2:15 (2:15) (Class 5) (0-70,70) 3-Y-O **£2,456** (£725; £362) **Stalls** Low

Form				RPR
46-4	1		**Pomeroy**[19] 127 3-8-9 **61** (bt[1]) RichardKingscote 2 (Tom Dascombe) *chsd ldng pair: effrt and rdn over 1f out: chsd ldr ent fnl f: drvn to ld fnl 100yds: kpt on* **11/4**[2]	65

-261 **2** *nk* **Freddie's Girl (USA)**[8] 257 3-9-1 **67** .... AdamKirby 1 70
(Stef Higgins) *led: rdn 2 l clr over 1f out: drvn and hdd fnl 100yds: kpt on gamely towards fin* **3/1**[3]

56-1 **3** *¾* **Novay Essjay (IRE)**[18] 141 3-9-4 **70** .... AndrewMullen 4 71
(D Nicholls) *chsd ldr: rdn and unable qck wl over 1f out: kpt on u.p ins fnl f* **13/8**[1]

54-4 **4** *1* **Mind The Monarch**[19] 122 3-8-5 **57** ....(p) LukeMorris 5 55
(R A Teal) *chsd ldng: edgd lft and one pce u.p fr over 1f out* **9/1**

500- **5** *2 ¼* **Bell's Ocean (USA)**[103] 6905 3-8-13 **65** .... StevieDonohoe 3 56
(J Ryan) *a last and sn niggled along: nvr gng pce to trble ldrs* **9/1**

1m 12.16s (0.26) **Going Correction** +0.075s/f (Slow) **5** Ran SP% **109.8**
Speed ratings (Par 97): **101,100,99,98,95**
CSF £11.18 TOTE £3.50: £1.80, £1.50; EX 9.30.
Owner South Wind Racing 2 & Partner **Bred** P J L Wright **Trained** Malpas, Cheshire

FOCUS
A modest handicap run at a reasonable pace throughout. The principals came down the centre in the straight.

358 SUPER 7 H'CAP (QUALIFIER) 7f (P)
2:45 (2:48) (Class 2) (0-100,99) 4-Y-O+ **£10,361** (£3,083; £1,540; £769) **Stalls** Low

Form RPR

00-3 **1** **The Scorching Wind (IRE)**[21] 108 4-8-5 **89** ....(t) WilliamCarson(3) 7 98
(S C Williams) *chsd ldrs: hdwy to join ldrs 2f out: carried rt wl over 1f out: hrd drvn ins fnl f: led fnl 50yds: r.o wl* **13/2**

35-2 **2** *hd* **Bravo Echo**[17] 150 4-8-5 **86** .... LukeMorris 9 94
(M J Attwater) *led for 1f: w ldr after tl led again over 2f out: edgd rt wl over 1f out: kpt on wl u.p tl hdd and no ex fnl 50yds* **11/2**[3]

-311 **3** *1 ¾* **Autumn Blades (IRE)**[6] 286 5-9-1 **96** 6ex..........(p) DavidProbert 5 100
(A Bailey) *awkward s and s.i.s: hld up in rr: hdwy on outer over 2f out: chsd ldrs and rdn over 1f out: kpt on same pce fnl f* **8/1**

1-11 **4** *1 ½* **Tiddliwinks**[21] 102 4-9-1 **96** .... PaulHanagan 6 96
(K A Ryan) *hld up in tch towards rr: looking for run and edging out rt over 2f out: swtchd rt and rdn over 1f out: edgd lft and no imp ins fnl f* **2/1**[1]

112- **5** *1* **Mr Willis**[44] 7789 4-8-10 **91** .... SteveDrowne 8 88
(J R Best) *in tch in last trio: rdn over 1f out: hdwy ent fnl f: kpt on but nvr gng pce to trble ldrs* **9/2**[2]

2U0- **6** *2 ¼* **Cyflymder (IRE)**[84] 7294 4-9-2 **97** .... RichardHughes 10 88
(R Hannon) *chsd ldrs: ev ch jst over 2f out: unable qck and rdn wl over 1f out: btn ent fnl f* **20/1**

2-04 **7** *4* **Ebraam (USA)**[13] 212 7-8-13 **99** ....(t) DeclanCannon(5) 2 79
(S Curran) *dwlt: sn bustled up to chse ldrs: rdn and racd awkwardly bnd 2f out: wknd over 1f out* **33/1**

1-62 **8** *½* **Imprimis Tagula (IRE)**[4] 299 6-9-3 **98** ....(v) RobertWinston 4 77
(A Bailey) *t.k.h: chsd ldrs tl drvn and wknd over 1f out: wl btn fnl f* **13/2**

/0-3 **9** *8* **Seasider**[6] 286 5-8-4 **85** oh2 .... NickyMackay 3 42
(D M Simcock) *sn prom: led 6f out tl over 2f out: wknd qckly 2f out and sn bhd* **11/1**

1m 22.92s (-1.88) **Going Correction** +0.075s/f (Slow) course record **9** Ran SP% **120.7**
Speed ratings (Par 109): **113,112,110,109,107 105,100,100,91**
toteswingers: 1&2 £12.60, 1&3 £12.60, 2&3 £9.10 CSF £44.10 CT £299.38 TOTE £10.00: £2.70, £1.90, £2.50; EX 57.70 Trifecta £221.70 Pool: £919.89 - 3.07 winning units..
Owner Chris Watkins And David N Reynolds **Bred** Mark Commins **Trained** Newmarket, Suffolk

FOCUS
A good-quality handicap and leg three of a series that has its final on Winter Derby day. Several in-form types but a race run at just an ordinary gallop. The majority raced in the centre in the straight.

NOTEBOOK
The Scorching Wind(IRE) ◆ had a better chance than the betting suggested and he fully confirmed his previous course and distance form from a poor draw when registering a career-best. He has a high cruising speed, a good attitude, will now go straight to the final and he should remain competitive after reassessment. (op 6-1 tchd 8-1)
Bravo Echo ◆ has bags of physical presence and, although he had the run of the race, he posted his best effort from this career-high mark and returned to this grade. He won't be inconvenienced by the return to 1m and he appeals strongly as the type to win races for this yard. (op 8-1)
Autumn Blades(IRE) is in the form of his life at present and, although he isn't the most straightforward, ran well from this 3lb higher mark given he was dropped out in a race run at just an ordinary gallop. A stronger pace over this trip would have suited and he should continue to run well in this type of event. (op 15-2 tchd 7-1)
Tiddliwinks has quickly made up into a very useful sort over 6f but, although a course and distance winner, didn't build on his latest run from this 8lb higher mark back up in trip and in a race run at this tempo. He wanted to hang left under pressure and, although this signalled the end of his improvement, things didn't really go his way and he will be worth another chance returned to sprinting. (op 11-4 tchd 3-1)
Mr Willis, who has reportedly missed work due to the weather, has a fine strike-rate at this course and he turned in another creditable effort returned to the track, though very much shaping as though this trip is a bare minimum for him these days. The return to 1m will suit and he isn't one to write off yet. (op 5-1 tchd 11-2)
Cyflymder(IRE) notched three consecutive wins from the front on turf last summer and shaped as though retaining a good chunk of his ability on this all-weather debut and first run since early November. However he looks to have very little margin for error from this mark. (op 16-1)
Ebraam(USA), who has little margin for error from his current mark, has still to prove he is as effective over this trip as over sprint distances. (op 28-1 tchd 25-1)
Seasider Official explanation: jockey said gelding lost its action final bend

359 BREATHE SPA AT MARRIOTT LINGFIELD H'CAP 1m (P)
3:20 (3:21) (Class 4) (0-85,85) 4-Y-O+ **£4,209** (£1,252; £625; £312) **Stalls** High

Form RPR

244- **1** **Thunderball**[79] 7360 4-8-11 **78** .... ChrisCatlin 6 86
(J A Glover) *restless stalls: broke wl but sn stdd to chse ldng pair: rdn and ev ch wl over 1f out: led narrowly over 1f out: kpt on wl fnl f* **7/2**[2]

000- **2** *½* **Salient**[85] 7271 6-8-10 **77** .... PaulDoe 3 84
(M J Attwater) *chsd ldr tl over 2f out: rdn and effrt on inner wl over 1f out: ev ch 1f out: kpt on wl but a jst hld fnl f* **16/1**

00-1 **3** *¾* **Ilie Nastase (FR)**[10] 230 6-9-4 **85** .... GeorgeBaker 8 90
(D M Simcock) *led: rdn and pressed 2f out: hdd over 1f out: one pce fnl f* **2/1**[1]

1-05 **4** *nk* **Red Somerset (USA)**[6] 286 7-8-10 **77** ....(b) JimmyQuinn 2 81
(R J Hodges) *in tch: hdwy on inner over 1f out: chsd ldrs and drvn ins fnl f: no imp fnl 100yds* **4/1**[3]

064- **5** *1* **Officer In Command (USA)**[156] 5366 4-8-4 **76** .... RossAtkinson(5) 7 78
(J S Moore) *hld up in tch: hdwy to chse ldrs on outer jst over 2f out: one pce u.p fr over 1f out* **13/2**

400- **6** *¾* **Alfresco**[60] 7603 6-8-10 **77** ....(b) RobertWinston 4 77
(J R Best) *stdd after s: t.k.h: hld up in last: rdn and effrt over 1f out: no prog and nvr trbld ldrs* **12/1**

05/1 **7** *½* **Noble Jack (IRE)**[16] 161 4-8-10 **77** .... LiamKeniry 1 76
(G L Moore) *s.i.s: hld up in tch: rdn and effrt 2f out: btn ent fnl f* **7/1**

1m 37.77s (-0.43) **Going Correction** +0.075s/f (Slow) **7** Ran SP% **115.0**
Speed ratings (Par 105): **105,104,103,103,102 101,101**
toteswingers: 1&2 £6.30, 1&3 £2.80, 2&3 £8.40 CSF £54.42 CT £139.83 TOTE £5.00: £2.80, £6.50; EX 59.80 Trifecta £263.10 Pool: £533.36 - 1.50 winning units..
Owner Paul J Dixon & Brian Morton **Bred** Mrs Yvette Dixon **Trained** Babworth, Notts

FOCUS
Mainly exposed sorts in a fair handicap but not much pace on and the whole field finished in a bit of a heap. The winner raced in the centre in the straight.

360 LINGFIELDPARK.CO.UK H'CAP 1m 2f (P)
3:55 (3:55) (Class 2) (0-100,106) 4-Y-O+ **£10,361** (£3,083; £1,540; £769) **Stalls** Low

Form RPR

6-20 **1** **Baylini**[9] 252 6-8-9 **89** .... HayleyTurner 1 94
(Ms J S Doyle) *hld up in tch on inner: hdwy over 1f out: rdn ins fnl f: r.o to ld on post* **13/2**

632- **2** *nse* **Suits Me**[42] 7809 7-9-12 **106** .... SteveDrowne 3 111
(T P Tate) *led: qcknd 2f out: hrd pressed and rdn over 1f out: hdd and edgd lft ins fnl f: kpt on wl towards fin* **9/2**[2]

12-3 **3** *shd* **Confidentiality (IRE)**[10] 239 6-8-6 **86** oh1 .... NickyMackay 4 91
(M Wigham) *chsd ldng pair: rdn and ev ch jst over 1f out: hrd drvn and led narrowly ins fnl f: hdd and lost 2 pls last stride* **7/1**

0-1 **4** *nk* **Winter Fever (SAF)**[15] 197 6-8-9 **89** .... LukeMorris 7 93
(J M P Eustace) *wl in tch in midfield: rdn and unable qck over 1f out: rallied ins fnl f: gng on fin: nt quite rch ldrs* **6/1**

22-3 **5** *hd* **Mafeking (UAE)**[14] 205 6-8-6 **86** .... ChrisCatlin 5 90
(M R Hoad) *chsd ldr: rdn and sltly outpcd over 1f out: kpt on again u.p fnl 100yds* **4/1**[1]

4443 **6** *nk* **Full Toss**[8] 266 4-8-8 **90** .... PaulHanagan 8 93+
(P D Evans) *hld up in tch in last pair: hdwy on outer over 2f out: wd bnd wl over 1f out: r.o strly fnl 100yds: nt rch ldrs* **5/1**[3]

43/6 **7** *¾* **Hazzard County (USA)**[10] 231 6-8-6 **86** oh2 .... LiamJones 2 90+
(D M Simcock) *hld up in tch in last pair: hdwy towards inner over 1f out: disputing 3rd and running on w wnr whn nt clr run wl ins fnl f: eased and lost 3 pls after* **14/1**

602- **8** *1* **The Cayterers**[63] 7574 8-8-7 **92** .... AndrewHeffernan(5) 9 92+
(A W Carroll) *dwlt: hld up in tch in last trio: nt clr run over 1f out: stl last ins fnl f: r.o strly towards fin: nvr able to chal* **8/1**

00-4 **9** *¾* **Samarinda (USA)**[21] 109 7-8-10 **90** .... StephenCraine 10 88
(Mrs P Sly) *broke wl: steadied and hld up in tch: rdn and effrt 2f out: kpt on same pce fr over 1f out* **28/1**

300- **10** *2* **Raptor (GER)**[156] 5363 7-8-12 **92** .... RobertWinston 6 86
(M E Rimmer) *t.k.h: chsd ldng trio: rdn and outpcd whn nt clr run over 1f out: n.d fnl f* **50/1**

2m 5.79s (-0.81) **Going Correction** +0.075s/f (Slow)
WFA 4 from 6yo+ 2lb **10** Ran SP% **118.2**
Speed ratings (Par 109): **106,105,105,105,105 105,104,103,103,101**
toteswingers: 1&2 £7.90, 1&3 £11.50, 2&3 £4.50 CSF £36.39 CT £214.50 TOTE £7.50: £2.60, £1.90, £2.50; EX 30.00 Trifecta £210.50 Pool: £822.26 - 2.89 winning units..
Owner Mrs R S Doyle **Bred** Templeton Stud **Trained**
■ Stewards' Enquiry : Nicky Mackay four-day ban: used whip with excessive frequency without giving mare time to respond (Feb 13-16)

FOCUS
Mainly exposed sorts in a decent-quality handicap in which the first six virtually finished in a line. The gallop was just a moderate one and the winner raced towards the far rail in the straight.

NOTEBOOK
Baylini hadn't been at her best over 1m4f on her previous start but proved suited by the return to this track and trip and she responded well to break a two-year losing run. She won't be going up much for this and she should continue to run well over this course and distance. (tchd 6-1 and 7-1)
Suits Me is a smart sort who had just been touched off in Listed company on his previous start and he both ran up to his best and showed a fine attitude returned to a handicap. He's best when able to dominate and should continue to run well in the better all-weather races around this trip on Polytrack. (tchd 5-1)
Confidentiality(IRE), a prolific winner on Polytrack, is another that is high enough in the weights but she had the run of the race against the inside rail and ran as well as she has all winter in this good-quality event. She's capable of winning one of these away from progressive or well-handicapped types. (op 8-1)
Winter Fever(SAF), 4lb higher than his Wolverhampton win, showed himself equally effective over this longer trip and ran up to his best. He may be capable of a bit better for current connections. (tchd 11-2 and 13-2)
Mafeking(UAE) is a reliable yardstick who had the run of the race and seemed to give it his best shot once again. Like several of these, he's high enough in the weights but should continue to give a good account. (op 11-2 tchd 6-1)
Full Toss ◆ extended his run of creditable efforts for his in-form yard and shaped better than the bare form as he was forced to go widest of all in the straight. He is equally effective on Fibresand and can win again for this yard. (op 9-2 tchd 11-2)
Hazzard County(USA) ◆, having his second quick run after a lengthy break, is better than the bare form. He was in the process of showing improved form on this first run over this trip when running out of room in the closing stages and can make amends. Official explanation: jockey said gelding suffered interference in running (tchd 12-1)
The Cayterers looks the type that needs things to drop right but he caught the eye with his finishing effort after having plenty to do turning for home. He'll be of more interest when a better overall gallop looks likely. (op 9-1)

361 MARRIOTT PLAY & STAY H'CAP 1m 2f (P)
4:25 (4:26) (Class 5) (0-70,70) 4-Y-O+ **£2,456** (£725; £362) **Stalls** Low

Form RPR

12-0 **1** **Resentful Angel**[6] 282 5-9-4 **68** .... RobertWinston 8 76+
(Pat Eddery) *stdd s: hld up in tch in last: hdwy on outer 2f out: sltly hmpd 1f out: str run to ld ins fnl f: r.o wl* **9/4**[1]

01-0 **2** *1* **Make Amends (IRE)**[8] 261 5-8-10 **60** .... JimmyQuinn 7 68+
(R J Hodges) *hld up in tch in last pair: hdwy over 1f out: running on whn hmpd jst ins fnl f: rallied to chse wnr wl ins fnl f: unable to rch wnr* **25/1**

46-3 **3** *1* **Painted Sky**[16] 176 7-9-0 **64** .... PaulHanagan 3 68
(R A Fahey) *led: rdn wl over 1f out: hung rt ent fnl f: hdd ins fnl f: one pce after* **10/1**

00-3 **4** *½* **Maximus Aurelius (IRE)**[22] 83 5-9-3 **67** ....(t) ChrisCatlin 5 70
(J Jay) *t.k.h: chsd ldr: ev ch and rdn wl over 1f out: short of room and hmpd 1f out: styd on one pce after* **10/1**

-031 **5** *¾* **Expensive Problem**[8] 262 7-9-6 **70** .... RichardHughes 4 72
(R J Smith) *hld up in tch: effrt over 1f out: rdn and no imp ins fnl f* **4/1**[3]

54-0 **6** *nk* **Dark Ranger**[26] 34 4-8-5 **57** ....(b[1]) LukeMorris 9 59+
(T J Pitt) *wl in tch: rdn and keeping on one pce whn hmpd 1f out: no threat to ldrs after* **11/1**

The Form Book, Raceform Ltd, Compton, RG20 6NL

0431 7 2 3/4 **Vinces**[8] 261 6-9-3 67 HayleyTurner 2 62
(T D McCarthy) *chsd ldrs: rdn and effrt over 1f out: wknd ins fnl f* **7/2**[2]
00-5 8 1 **Meydan Dubai (IRE)**[28] 12 5-8-12 65 MarcHalford(3) 1 58
(J R Best) *t.k.h early: hld up in tch towards rr: effrt on inner over 1f out: wknd ins fnl f* **16/1**
363- 9 1 1/4 **Apotheosis**[126] 6288 5-9-1 65 LiamKeniry 6 56
(C R Dore) *chsd ldrs: rdn 2f out: wkng whn short of room and swtchd lft 1f out: n.d after* **10/1**

2m 7.09s (0.49) **Going Correction** +0.075s/f (Slow)
WFA 4 from 5yo+ 2lb **9** Ran SP% **118.3**
Speed ratings (Par 103): **101,100,99,99,98 98,95,95,94**
toteswingers: 1&2 £21.10, 1&3 £3.50, 2&3 £21.70 CSF £65.09 CT £485.70 TOTE £3.50: £1.20, £6.40, £2.70; EX 87.20 TRIFECTA Not won. Place 6: £153.82 Place 5: £65.17.
Owner P J J Eddery, Mrs John Magnier, M Tabor **Bred** Patrick Eddery Ltd **Trained** Nether Winchendon, Bucks

FOCUS
A modest handicap in which the pace was only moderate. The winner came down the centre in the straight.
Painted Sky Official explanation: jockey said gelding hung right
Dark Ranger Official explanation: vet said gelding lost a shoe
Vinces Official explanation: trainer said gelding was struck into
T/Plt: £212.30 to a £1 stake. Pool: £77,328.27. 265.89 winning tickets. T/Qpdt: £50.90 to a £1 stake. Pool: £6,600.49. 95.94 winning tickets. SP

[319]KEMPTON (A.W) (R-H)
Sunday, January 31

OFFICIAL GOING: Standard
Wind: Light, across Weather: Fine but cloudy

362 BET MULTIPLES - BETDAQ MEDIAN AUCTION MAIDEN STKS 5f (P)
2:25 (2:26) (Class 6) 3-5-Y-O £2,047 (£604; £302) Stalls High

Form RPR
053- 1 **The Strig**[64] 7571 3-8-7 69 WilliamCarson(3) 2 77+
(S C Williams) *mde all: pushed along and in command over 1f out: nvr seriously threatened* **11/10**[1]
2 1 **Dominium (USA)** 3-8-10 0 LukeMorris 6 71
(J R Gask) *dwlt: in last pair tl effrt on inner 2f out: chsd wnr over 1f out: shkn up and grad clsd fnl f: nvr able to chal* **10/1**[2]
5-2 3 3 **Blue Zephyr**[9] 257 3-8-10 0 MartinDwyer 5 60
(W R Muir) *trblesme coming out on to the crse: cl up: rdn to chse wnr 1/2-way to over 1f out: fdd* **11/10**[1]
0-66 4 3 1/4 **Maxijack (IRE)**[9] 257 3-8-10 56 StephenCraine 3 48
(G Brown) *hld up in last pair: outpcd fr 2f out: nudged along and no prog over 1f out: fdd* **33/1**
0 5 3 1/2 **Captain Tony (IRE)**[28] 24 3-8-10 0 LiamKeniry 1 35
(Matthew Salaman) *chsd wnr to 1/2-way: wd bnd 2f out and sn wknd* **33/1**[3]

60.58 secs (0.08) **Going Correction** -0.025s/f (Stan)
WFA 3 from 4yo 15lb **5** Ran SP% **110.2**
Speed ratings (Par 101): **98,96,91,86,80**
toteswingers: 1&2 £5.30 CSF £13.42 TOTE £2.20: £1.90, £1.50; EX 12.20.
Owner Brian Piper & David Cobill **Bred** Old Mill Stud **Trained** Newmarket, Suffolk

FOCUS
A moderate maiden.

363 BETDAQ POKER H'CAP 5f (P)
2:55 (2:55) (Class 5) (0-75,75) 3-Y-O £2,590 (£770; £385; £192) Stalls High

Form RPR
33-1 1 **Texas Queen**[14] 208 3-8-13 70 JoeFanning 1 75
(M R Channon) *t.k.h: hld up in last: shkn up on outer over 1f out: r.o fnl f to ld last 75yds* **5/2**[2]
3-11 2 1/2 **Boogie Waltzer**[17] 167 3-8-5 65 WilliamCarson(3) 5 68
(S C Williams) *chsd ldr: rdn over 1f out: grad clsd fnl f but outpcd by wnr last 75yds* **13/8**[1]
4-22 3 hd **R Woody**[8] 277 3-9-4 75 SteveDrowne 6 77
(Mrs L C Jewell) *led at mod pce: kicked on over 1f out: hdd last 75yds: lost 2nd on post* **13/8**[1]
00-4 4 1 1/2 **Papageno**[9] 257 3-8-8 65 JimmyQuinn 4 62
(J R Jenkins) *t.k.h: trckd ldng pair: rdn and cl enough over 1f out: one pce* **10/1**[3]

60.97 secs (0.47) **Going Correction** -0.025s/f (Stan) **4** Ran SP% **113.9**
Speed ratings (Par 97): **95,94,93,91**
toteswingers: 1&2 £8.10 CSF £7.34 TOTE £3.30; EX 8.10.
Owner M Channon **Bred** Rabbah Bloodstock Limited **Trained** West Ilsley, Berks
■ Stewards' Enquiry : Steve Drowne one-day ban: used whip in incorrect place (Feb 14)

FOCUS
A tight little handicap, run at an average pace.

364 TRY BETDAQ FOR AN EXCHANGE CLASSIFIED CLAIMING STKS 6f (P)
3:25 (3:25) (Class 6) 4-Y-O+ £2,047 (£604; £302) Stalls High

Form RPR
3453 1 **Dvinsky (USA)**[3] 325 9-8-13 70 (b) JimmyQuinn 5 76
(P Howling) *trckd ldng pair: chal on inner 2f out: rdn to gain narrow ld ins fnl f: styd on wl* **11/8**[1]
4-64 2 1/2 **Misaro (GER)**[9] 258 9-8-9 72 (b) LukeMorris 3 70
(R A Harris) *led: hrd pressed fr over 2f out: hdd ins fnl f: kpt on wl but a hld* **11/4**[3]
220- 3 3 1/2 **Irish Music (IRE)**[43] 7819 5-8-4 61 MatthewDavies(5) 1 59
(A P Jarvis) *trckd ldr: upsides over 2f out: rdn and fnd nil over 1f out: fdd fnl f* **12/1**
10-0 4 2 3/4 **Norse Warrior (USA)**[12] 223 4-9-0 65 (v) DaneO'Neill 4 55
(Peter Grayson) *mostly in 4th: rdn and no rspnse 2f out: wl btn after* **20/1**
0-12 5 4 **Stonecrabstomorrow (IRE)**[16] 187 7-8-8 70 (b) MarkCoumbe(5) 2 42
(John A Harris) *mostly in last: pushed along on outer bef 1/2-way: struggling wl over 2f out: sn bhd* **5/2**[2]

1m 12.48s (-0.62) **Going Correction** -0.025s/f (Stan) **5** Ran SP% **109.8**
Speed ratings (Par 101): **103,102,97,94,88**
toteswingers: 1&2 £6.70 CSF £5.43 TOTE £2.20: £2.10, £3.60; EX 6.70.
Owner Richard Berenson **Bred** Eclipse Bloodstock & Tipperary Bloodstock **Trained** Newmarket, Suffolk
■ Stewards' Enquiry : Luke Morris two-day ban: used whip above shoulder height (Feb 14-15)

FOCUS
An ordinary claimer, run at a fair pace.

Stonecrabstomorrow(IRE) Official explanation: jockey said gelding never travelled

365 BETDAQ.CO.UK CONDITIONS STKS 6f (P)
3:55 (3:55) (Class 2) 4-Y-O+ £9,969 (£2,985; £1,492; £747; £372) Stalls High

Form RPR
10-1 1 **Elna Bright**[22] 108 5-9-5 94 LiamKeniry 5 99+
(B R Johnson) *chsd ldr to over 2f out: styd cl up: rdn over 1f out: urged along and r.o fnl f to ld last 50yds* **11/4**[1]
14-0 2 nk **Orpenindeed (IRE)**[17] 177 7-9-0 88 (p) AndreaAtzeni 4 93
(M Botti) *led: set v modest pce: kicked on over 2f out: looked set to hold on fnl f: worn down last 50yds* **7/2**[3]
1302 3 2 **Indian Skipper (IRE)**[2] 350 5-9-0 84 (be) BillyCray 3 87
(R C Guest) *lft abt 6 l s: t.k.h and easily ct up as rest of field dawdled: prog to chse ldr over 2f out to 1f out: one pce* **8/1**
1-50 4 1 1/2 **Fathsta (IRE)**[17] 177 5-9-0 87 JimCrowley 1 82
(D M Simcock) *t.k.h: hld up bhd ldng pair: lost pl over 2f out: shkn up and nt qckn as pce lifted: wl btn after* **11/4**[1]
2530 5 shd **Aeroplane**[5] 299 7-9-1 100 ow1 (b1) GeorgeBaker 2 83
(P D Evans) *hld up in last: rdn and no rspnse whn pce lifted over 2f out: no prog after* **3/1**[2]

1m 15.3s (2.20) **Going Correction** -0.025s/f (Stan) **5** Ran SP% **111.7**
Speed ratings (Par 109): **84,83,80,78,78**
toteswingers: 1&2 £14.00 CSF £12.71 TOTE £4.10: £1.40, £2.50; EX 14.00.
Owner Peter Crate **Bred** D R Tucker **Trained** Ashtead, Surrey
■ Stewards' Enquiry : Billy Cray two-day ban: used whip in incorrect place (Feb 14-15)

FOCUS
Another tricky little conditions race that had no guaranteed pacemaker, so the pace was a muddling one until it quickened up over 2f out

NOTEBOOK
Elna Bright sat just off the leader before staying on well to hit the front inside the final furlong. He has been in good heart for new connections and had to defy a 5lb penalty and drop back in distance to collect here. This was a good effort as he would have appreciated a stronger gallop. (op 5-2 tchd 3-1)
Orpenindeed(IRE) was given a soft lead and set the steady pace. He did not surrender the lead lightly and kept battling throughout the final furlong when hard pressed, but he was just outstayed by the winner. (op 9-2)
Indian Skipper(IRE) completely missed the break but was able to recover because of the steady pace. He moved through to help increase the tempo over 2f out but could only keep on at the same pace. (tchd 9-1)
Fathsta(IRE) had solid claims and was close enough turning in but, was undone by the steady early pace and could not land a blow. (op 3-1 tchd 5-2)
Aeroplane was being tried in first-time blinkers but they did not appear to help this enigmatic character. He has the ability to get his head in front but was probably done no favours by the steady pace. (op 5-2 and 10-3 in a place)

366 BETDAQ.CO.UK H'CAP 7f (P)
4:25 (4:25) (Class 5) (0-75,75) 3-Y-O £2,590 (£770; £385; £192) Stalls High

Form RPR
146- 1 **Highland Quaich**[42] 7824 3-9-2 73 DaneO'Neill 1 84+
(D R C Elsworth) *dropped in fr wd draw: hld up in last pair: nt clr run over 2f out and swtchd towards outer: nt clr run again briefly over 1f out: prog and drvn after: r.o to ld last 75yds: won gng away* **11/4**[2]
415- 2 1 **Khanivorous**[53] 7685 3-9-4 75 StephenCraine 2 80
(J R Boyle) *trckd ldng pair: rdn wl over 2f out: prog u.p to ld jst over 1f out: hdd and outpcd last 75yds* **7/1**
11-4 3 1 **Blue Lyric**[27] 35 3-9-4 75 MartinDwyer 6 78
(L M Cumani) *hld up in 5th: rdn and prog fr over 2f out: tried to chal over 1f out: one pce fnl f* **13/8**[1]
1-41 4 2 1/4 **Cuthbert (IRE)**[9] 268 3-9-3 74 JimCrowley 3 71+
(W Jarvis) *drvn fr s: led narrowly: hdd & wknd jst over 1f out* **4/1**[3]
305- 5 1 **Craicattack (IRE)**[36] 7846 3-9-4 75 LiamKeniry 7 69
(J S Moore) *chsd ldng pair: rdn to dispute 2nd 2f out: fdd u.p over 1f out* **20/1**
52-0 6 2 1/2 **Itsthursdayalready**[27] 35 3-9-3 74 J-PGuillambert 4 61
(J G Given) *t.k.h: hld up in last: brief effrt on wd outside over 2f out: sn wknd* **12/1**
065- 7 4 1/2 **Egyptology (IRE)**[74] 7430 3-8-8 65 JoeFanning 5 40
(M Johnston) *w ldr and seemingly gng wl tl wknd rapidly over 2f out* **6/1**

1m 25.53s (-0.47) **Going Correction** -0.025s/f (Stan) **7** Ran SP% **124.0**
Speed ratings (Par 97): **101,99,98,96,95 92,87**
toteswingers: 1&2 £4.90, 1&3 £2.90, 2&3 £4.30 CSF £24.61 TOTE £3.90: £2.10, £3.30; EX 27.40.
Owner J Wotherspoon **Bred** John Wotherspoon **Trained** Newmarket, Suffolk

FOCUS
Another tight handicap won by a progressive 3-y-o.

367 BET IN RUNNING - BETDAQ APPRENTICE H'CAP 1m (P)
4:55 (4:55) (Class 5) (0-70,71) 4-Y-O+ £2,590 (£770; £385; £192) Stalls High

Form RPR
01- 1 **Erinjay (IRE)**[42] 7826 4-9-5 70 TobyAtkinson 5 83
(M Wigham) *nt wl away: settled in 10th: swtchd to inner and gd prog over 2f out: clsd on ldrs over 1f out: drvn and hung lft fnl f: r.o to ld last 50yds* **2/1**[1]
56-1 2 3/4 **Ocean Legend (IRE)**[7] 285 5-9-6 71 6ex DeclanCannon 4 82
(A W Carroll) *towards rr: prog on outer fr over 2f out: rdn to ld jst over 1f out: styd on but hdd last 50yds* **9/2**[2]
0-31 3 3 1/4 **Aflaam (IRE)**[9] 256 5-8-12 68 JakePayne(5) 8 72
(R A Harris) *settled towards rr: nt pick up over 2f out and sn wl off the pce: urged along and r.o fr over 1f out: snatched 3rd last stride* **8/1**
6-02 4 nse **Alqaahir (USA)**[6] 294 8-9-3 68 CharlesEddery 11 72
(P Burgoyne) *t.k.h: trckd ldng pair: chsd ldr over 2f out to over 1f out: clsd enough ent fnl f: wknd last 150yds: lost 3rd on post* **7/1**
126- 5 2 3/4 **Teen Ager (FR)**[226] 3104 6-8-9 63 RyanClark(3) 12 60
(P Burgoyne) *t.k.h: led after 2f: at least 3 l clr over 3f out: hdd & wknd jst over 1f out* **14/1**
-316 6 2 **Very Well Red**[9] 262 7-8-8 59 KierenFox 13 52
(P W Hiatt) *chsd ldrs: rdn to dispute 2nd over 2f out: nt qckn sn after: grad wknd* **13/2**[3]
13-4 7 2 1/4 **Batchworth Blaise**[4] 318 7-8-2 56 oh3 RichardRowe(3) 3 44
(E A Wheeler) *s.s: hld up in last pair: prog on inner over 2f out: rchd midfield but nvr nr ldrs: no hdwy over 1f out* **25/1**
0-60 8 3 3/4 **Grey Boy (GER)**[4] 317 9-8-7 65 GeorgeDowning(7) 1 44
(A W Carroll) *sn chsd ldrs on outer: rdn over 3f out: wknd over 2f out* **16/1**
4530 9 3/4 **Jonnie Skull (IRE)**[4] 317 4-8-9 67 (vt) LeonnaMayor(7) 9 44
(P S McEntee) *led 2f: chsd ldr to over 2f out: wknd* **20/1**

530- **10** 2 **Stateside (CAN)**[147] 5698 5-8-8 **62**.................... LeeTopliss(3) 7 35
(R A Fahey) *s.s: mostly in last pair: rdn 1/2-way: nvr a factor* **10/1**
100- **11** 13 **Prince Rossi (IRE)**[205] 3800 6-8-9 **60**....................(v) BillyCray 2 —
(A E Price) *chsd ldrs: rdn towards outer over 3f out: wknd over 2f out: t.o* **16/1**
0-50 **12** 4 ½ **Sufficient Warning**[11] 229 6-8-2 **56** oh11.................... RyanPowell(3) 10 —
(R J Smith) *dropped to last over 3f out: sn t.o* **40/1**
1m 38.46s (-1.34) **Going Correction** -0.025s/f (Stan) **12** Ran SP% **127.0**
Speed ratings (Par 103): **105,104,101,100,98 96,93,90,89,87 74,69**
toteswingers: 1&2 £4.40, 1&3 £6.80, 2&3 £8.90 CSF £11.07 CT £65.10 TOTE £3.10: £1.50, £1.90, £3.20; EX 14.60 Place 6: £109.50 Place 5: £57.12.
Owner Seyhan Osman & Robert Kibble **Bred** Bill Benson **Trained** Newmarket, Suffolk
■ Stewards' Enquiry : Declan Cannon four-day ban: used whip with excessive frequency (Feb 14-17)

FOCUS
A moderate, but competitive enough handicap for apprentice riders.
T/Plt: £349.70 to a £1 stake. Pool: £69,156.32. 144.35 winning tickets. T/Qpdt: £36.10 to a £1 stake. Pool: £5,972.23. 122.13 winning tickets. JN

347 WOLVERHAMPTON (A.W) (L-H)

Monday, February 1

OFFICIAL GOING: Standard
Wind: Light, half-behind Weather: Sunny

368 FREE HORSE RACING TIPS @ BIGTIPS.CO.UK AMATEUR RIDERS' H'CAP (DIV I) 5f 216y(P)

2:05 (2:05) (Class 6) (0-55,55) 4-Y-O+ **£1,384** (£425; £212) **Stalls** Low

Form RPR
40-2 **1** **Miss Firefly**[17] 193 5-10-6 **54**....................(p) MrPPrince(7) 2 63
(R J Hodges) *hld up in mid-div on ins: swtchd rt ent st: hdwy over 1f out: rdn to ld nr fin* **5/1**[2]
-100 **2** nk **Tamino (IRE)**[12] 235 7-10-8 **54**.................... MrJPFeatherstone(5) 8 62
(P Howling) *led: rdn 1f out: hdd nr fin* **6/1**[3]
0-00 **3** nk **Metropolitan Chief**[4] 320 6-9-12 **46** oh1.................... MrPhilipThomas(7) 1 53
(P Burgoyne) *s.i.s: hld up in rr: pushed along and hdwy on ins wl over 1f out: kpt on ins fnl f* **25/1**
63-2 **4** ½ **Towy Boy (IRE)**[12] 235 5-10-6 **52**....................(v) MrCMartin(5) 9 58
(I A Wood) *hld up in tch: rdn wl over 1f out: ev ch ins fnl f: nt qckn* **11/4**[1]
00-0 **5** 2 ¾ **Sirjosh**[6] 296 4-10-3 **51**.................... MrESullivan(7) 13 48+
(D Donovan) *hld up in mid-div: c wd st: rdn over 1f out: edgd lft and kpt on ins fnl f: nvr trbld ldrs* **40/1**
3-44 **6** 1 **Cocktail Party (IRE)**[10] 271 4-10-3 **49**....................(v[1]) MissJCWilliams(5) 11 43
(J W Unett) *chsd ldr: ev ch over 2f out: rdn wl over 1f out: wknd ins fnl f* **8/1**
5-50 **7** hd **Gower**[25] 70 6-10-2 **46** oh1....................(p) MrMPrice(3) 3 39
(R J Price) *prom: pushed along wl over 1f out: rdn and wknd ins fnl f* **20/1**
1200 **8** 1 ¾ **Brazilian Brush (IRE)**[6] 296 5-10-9 **55**....................(bt) MissSBradley(5) 12 43
(J M Bradley) *hld up towards rr: rdn wl over 1f out: sn edgd lft: n.d* **14/1**
00-0 **9** shd **Conjecture**[17] 187 8-10-4 **50**.................... MissRBastiman(5) 7 37
(R Bastiman) *hld up in tch: wknd 2f out* **14/1**
500- **10** nk **Affirmatively**[194] 4204 5-9-12 **46** oh1....................(vt[1]) MissSPPearce(7) 4 32
(A W Carroll) *s.i.s: hld up towards rr: pushed along and sme prog wl over 1f out: wknd ins fnl f* **40/1**
03-5 **11** nse **Outer Hebrides**[22] 116 9-10-4 **52**....................(v) MissHDavies(7) 6 38
(J M Bradley) *hld up in tch: rdn over 2f out: sn wknd* **9/1**
660- **12** 7 **Commander Wish**[57] 7651 7-10-7 **48**....................(p) MrSDobson 5 12
(Lucinda Featherstone) *s.i.s: c wd st: a in rr* **6/1**[3]
1m 16.69s (1.69) **Going Correction** +0.20s/f (Slow) **12** Ran SP% **119.8**
Speed ratings (Par 101): **96,95,95,94,90 89,89,86,86,86 86,77**
toteswingers: 1&2 £12.70, 1&3 £19.40, 2&3 £36.50 CSF £34.07 CT £697.83 TOTE £6.80: £2.00, £2.20, £6.40; EX 47.50 TRIFECTA Not won..
Owner R J Hodges **Bred** Jeremy Gompertz **Trained** Charlton Mackrell, Somerset
■ A first winner for jockey Philip Prince.

FOCUS
A moderate amateur riders' contest run in a time 0.62 seconds quicker than the second division. Straightforward form for the grade.

369 FREE HORSE RACING TIPS @ BIGTIPS.CO.UK AMATEUR RIDERS' H'CAP (DIV II) 5f 216y(P)

2:40 (2:40) (Class 6) (0-55,55) 4-Y-O+ **£1,384** (£425; £212) **Stalls** Low

Form RPR
0-31 **1** **Albero Di Giuda (IRE)**[10] 264 5-10-5 **53**....................(t) MrMOwen(7) 1 64
(F Sheridan) *t.k.h: a.p: rdn to ld over 1f out: r.o* **6/1**
4-44 **2** 1 ¼ **Nabeeda**[20] 142 5-10-10 **51**.................... MrSDobson 13 58
(M Brittain) *w ldrs: ev ch over 2f out: rdn wl over 1f out: kpt on one pce ins fnl f* **9/2**[2]
04-5 **3** ¾ **Strategic Mover (USA)**[30] 10 5-10-8 **54**....................(vt) MissMBryant(5) 10 59
(P Butler) *hld up in mid-div: c wd st: rdn and hdwy over 1f out: edgd lft ins fnl f: nt qckn* **12/1**
00-5 **4** 1 ¾ **Misterisland (IRE)**[10] 269 5-10-0 **46** oh1.................... MissMMullineaux(5) 8 45
(M Mullineaux) *sn outpcd and bhd: gd late hdwy: fin wl* **14/1**
-651 **5** nse **Meikle Barfil**[10] 271 8-10-6 **52**....................(bt) MissSBradley(5) 6 51
(J M Bradley) *hld up in tch: rdn and carried sltly lft jst ins fnl f: one pce* **17/2**
25-5 **6** ½ **Monsieur Reynard**[17] 185 5-10-7 **55**.................... MissHDavies(7) 4 53
(J M Bradley) *w ldr: led over 3f out tl over 1f out: fdd wl ins fnl f* **5/1**[3]
56-0 **7** 1 ¼ **Pipers Piping (IRE)**[17] 195 4-10-6 **52**.................... MrJBanks(5) 5 46+
(P Howling) *s.s: sn wl in rr: nvr nrr* **4/1**[1]
050- **8** hd **Town House**[97] 7100 8-10-0 **46** oh1.................... MissAWallace(5) 11 39
(B P J Baugh) *hld up in mid-div: effrt wl over 1f out: sn rdn: fdd wl ins fnl f* **50/1**
002- **9** nk **Neo's Mate (IRE)**[46] 7787 4-10-2 **50**.................... MissACraven(7) 3 42
(Paul Green) *plld hrd: rdr sn lost stirrup iron: a bhd* **8/1**
50-0 **10** 3 ¼ **Boundless Applause**[19] 145 4-10-0 **46** oh1.................... MrCMartin(5) 2 28
(I A Wood) *outpcd* **10/1**
000/ **11** 4 ½ **African Blues**[650] 1533 7-9-12 **46** oh1.................... MrGOliver(7) 12 13
(D J S Ffrench Davis) *led over 2f: rdn and wknd wl over 1f out* **50/1**
1m 17.31s (2.31) **Going Correction** +0.20s/f (Slow) **11** Ran SP% **118.1**
Speed ratings (Par 101): **92,90,89,87,86 86,84,84,83,79 73**
toteswingers: 1&2 £4.00, 1&3 £14.30, 2&3 £12.70 CSF £33.33 CT £321.70 TOTE £6.80: £1.80, £1.70, £4.50; EX 22.20 Trifecta £252.50 Part won. Pool: £341.25 - 0.86 winning units..
Owner Jon Owen **Bred** Fattoria Di Marcianella Di Razza Del Pian Del Lago **Trained** Averham Park, Notts
■ A first winner for jockey Michael Owen on his first ride in public.
■ Stewards' Enquiry : Mr J Banks 10-day ban: failed to obtain best possible placing (tba)

FOCUS
The time was 0.62 seconds slower than the first division. The form looks straightforward enough with a British best from the winner. Well Of Echoes was withdrawn (7/1, arrived at start without the declared cheekpieces). Deduct 10p in the £ under R4, new market formed.
Pipers Piping(IRE) ◆ Official explanation: jockey said, regarding running and riding, that his orders were to drop the gelding out and bring it home through horses in the home straight, adding that he had not been prepared when the stalls opened and was left, with hindsight he thought he should have made more effort in back straight and get back on terms.
Neo's Mate(IRE) ◆ Official explanation: jockey said she lost her stirrup iron immediately after start

370 GREAT OFFERS AT WOLVERHAMPTON-RACECOURSE.CO.UK CLAIMING STKS 5f 216y(P)

3:15 (3:15) (Class 6) 3-Y-O **£1,774** (£523; £262) **Stalls** Low

Form RPR
3-12 **1** **Anjomarba (IRE)**[9] 276 3-8-2 67....................(p) DavidProbert 3 61
(W G M Turner) *led early: w ldr: rdn over 2f out: c wd st: led wl over 1f out: rdn out* **3/1**[2]
31-5 **2** 2 **Sakile**[9] 277 3-8-8 77.................... JackMitchell 5 60
(P W Chapple-Hyam) *hld up: hdwy over 2f out: rdn over 1f out: kpt on same pce ins fnl f* **7/2**[3]
1-32 **3** 1 **Flow Chart (IRE)**[20] 141 3-8-13 71....................(b) PhillipMakin 2 62
(T D Barron) *sn led: hdd wl over 1f out: sn rdn: no ex ins fnl f* **9/2**
306- **4** ½ **Arken Lad**[93] 7175 3-8-9 65....................(e) JimmyQuinn 4 57
(D Donovan) *prom: rdn and lost pl over 2f out: kpt on ins fnl f* **40/1**
45-4 **5** ½ **St Ignatius**[19] 149 3-8-9 64....................(b[1]) JohnFahy(7) 7 62
(R M Beckett) *hld up: pushed along over 2f out: rdn wl over 1f out: kpt on towards fin* **10/1**
01-1 **6** 2 ½ **Magenta Strait**[15] 209 3-8-0 68.................... PaulPickard(5) 1 43
(R Hollinshead) *prom on ins: ev ch wl over 1f out: sn rdn: wknd ins fnl f* **5/2**[1]
31-5 **7** 1 ¼ **Exearti**[20] 141 3-8-13 68.................... DeclanCannon(5) 6 52
(A J McCabe) *s.i.s: sn rcvrd and t.k.h in tch: pushed along and wknd 2f out* **22/1**
1m 16.26s (1.26) **Going Correction** +0.20s/f (Slow) **7** Ran SP% **109.9**
Speed ratings (Par 95): **99,96,95,94,93 90,88**
toteswingers: 1&2 £2.60, 1&3 £3.20, 2&3 £3.40 CSF £12.76 TOTE £3.70: £1.80, £2.60; EX 13.00.
Owner Marbary Partnership **Bred** Tally-Ho Stud **Trained** Sigwells, Somerset

FOCUS
A reasonable claimer but it's doubtful the winner had to improve, with the next two probably not at their best. Not a race to view too positively.

371 BACK & LAY AT BETDAQ H'CAP 1m 1f 103y(P)

3:50 (3:50) (Class 5) (0-70,66) 3-Y-O **£2,729** (£806; £403) **Stalls** Low

Form RPR
33-2 **1** **Riviera Chic (USA)**[13] 226 3-8-13 **61**....................(b) JimCrowley 2 73
(R M Beckett) *a.p: rdn to ld 1f out: drvn clr ins fnl f: r.o wl* **15/8**[1]
3322 **2** 6 **The Great Husk (IRE)**[3] 340 3-8-8 **56**.................... LiamKeniry 6 55
(J S Moore) *chsd ldr: rdn to ld wl over 1f out: hdd 1f out: one pce* **11/4**[2]
3-13 **3** 1 **Tuscan King**[8] 283 3-9-3 **65**....................(bt) J-PGuillambert 1 62
(P D Evans) *dwlt: hld up: pushed along over 2f out: rdn and hdwy on ins over 1f out: kpt on ins fnl f* **9/2**[3]
634- **4** 1 ¼ **Claddagh**[34] 7865 3-9-0 **62**.................... JoeFanning 3 56
(M Johnston) *led: rdn and hdd wl over 1f out: one pce fnl f* **5/1**
2 **5** shd **Market Puzzle (IRE)**[20] 143 3-9-0 **62**.................... ShaneKelly 4 56
(W M Brisbourne) *hld up: pushed along over 3f out: hdwy over 2f out: sn rdn: wknd over 1f out* **33/1**
04-4 **6** 14 **Captain Bluebird (IRE)**[12] 236 3-9-2 **64**.................... JimmyQuinn 7 29
(D Donovan) *stdd s: sn swtchd lft: hld up in rr: rdn and struggling jst over 3f out* **8/1**
-301 **7** 9 **Lily Lily**[17] 188 3-9-4 **66**....................(b) RobertWinston 5 12
(K McAuliffe) *hld up in tch: rdn 3f out: wknd over 2f out* **18/1**
2m 3.08s (1.38) **Going Correction** +0.20s/f (Slow) **7** Ran SP% **115.6**
Speed ratings (Par 97): **101,95,94,93,93 81,73**
toteswingers: 1&2 £2.40, 1&3 £2.70, 2&3 £2.80 CSF £7.42 TOTE £3.60: £1.90, £1.80; EX 10.20.
Owner Trevor C Stewart **Bred** Albert Bell And Phun Llc **Trained** Whitsbury, Hants

FOCUS
While this was a low-grade 3-y-o handicap, it was also a very tight affair on paper and several looked potential improvers. As expected there was a solid pace on and the form looks reliable rated through the consistent runner-up and the third. Improvement from the winner.

372 HOTEL & CONFERENCING AT WOLVERHAMPTON (S) STKS 1m 141y(P)

4:20 (4:21) (Class 6) 3-Y-O **£1,774** (£523; £262) **Stalls** Low

Form RPR
0-0 **1** **Your Lad**[21] 128 3-8-12 0.................... JackMitchell 5 58
(C F Wall) *hld up in rr: c wd st: rdn and hdwy on stands' rail fnl f: led cl home* **13/2**
400- **2** hd **Always De One**[63] 7597 3-8-7 59.................... JoeFanning 8 53
(M Johnston) *hld up in mid-div: pushed along over 2f out: pushed v wd st: hdwy wl over 1f out: rdn and ev ch wl ins fnl f: r.o* **7/1**
-440 **3** ½ **Clayton Flick (IRE)**[7] 288 3-8-12 54.................... StevieDonohoe 3 57
(A B Haynes) *s.i.s: hld up and bhd: hdwy 2f out: rdn to ld jst ins fnl f: hdd cl home* **16/1**
6-45 **4** 2 ½ **Creevy (IRE)**[9] 279 3-8-7 44....................(b[1]) DavidProbert 6 46
(S Kirk) *a.p: rn wd ent st: rdn to ld over 1f out: hdd jst ins fnl f: no ex towards fin* **11/2**[3]
0-26 **5** hd **Brenda Duke**[8] 283 3-8-7 57.................... FrankieMcDonald 7 46
(J G Portman) *hld up in mid-div: hdwy on ins over 2f out: rdn jst over 1f out: ev ch ins fnl f: one pce* **9/2**[2]
410- **6** 1 ½ **Tiger Hawk (USA)**[45] 7791 3-8-13 65....................(b) RichardEvans(5) 4 53
(P D Evans) *w ldr: led jst over 2f out: rdn and hdd over 1f out: wknd ins fnl f* **9/2**[2]
-556 **7** ½ **Scintillating (IRE)**[14] 216 3-8-7 42....................(p) ChrisCatlin 9 41
(R Hollinshead) *prom: pushed along over 2f out: wknd wl over 1f out* **12/1**
8 4 **Moors Gorse** 3-8-8 0 ow1.................... GrahamGibbons 2 33
(R Hollinshead) *led: rdn and hdd jst over 2f out: wknd ins fnl f* **4/1**[1]
0-56 **9** 2 ¼ **Que Belle (IRE)**[12] 238 3-8-7 48....................(v[1]) RichardSmith 10 27
(Tom Dascombe) *dwlt: hld up in rr: rdn over 2f out: sn struggling* **20/1**
0- **10** 16 **Makarthy**[49] 7749 3-8-7 0.................... JamesSullivan(5) 1 —
(H A McWilliams) *hld up in mid-div: pushed along and wknd over 3f out* **100/1**
1m 53.52s (3.02) **Going Correction** +0.20s/f (Slow) **10** Ran SP% **116.9**
Speed ratings (Par 95): **94,93,93,91,90 89,89,85,83,69**
toteswingers: 1&2 £12.40, 1&3 £16.30, 2&3 £18.50 CSF £51.61 TOTE £8.40: £2.50, £3.00, £4.90; EX 78.90 Trifecta £551.50 Part won. Pool: £745.29 - 0.20 winning units..There was no bid for the winner. Always De One was claimed by Miss J. Feilden for £6,000.

The Form Book, Raceform Ltd, Compton, RG20 6NL

Owner Des Thurlby **Bred** Haydock Park Stud **Trained** Newmarket, Suffolk

FOCUS

A moderate but competitive seller. The first two are possibly better than the bare form, which is not rock solid.

Brenda Duke Official explanation: jockey said filly hung right in home straight

373 BET CIS FOOTBALL - BETDAQ H'CAP 7f 32y(P)

4:50 (4:51) (Class 5) (0-70,70) 4-Y-O+ £2,729 (£806; £403) Stalls High

Form RPR

42-2 **1** **Smalljohn**[21] 129 4-8-10 **62**....(v) TomEaves 5 73
(B Smart) *sn led: clr whn rdn over 1f out: drvn out* **7/1**

0F2- **2** 2 ¾ **Seldom (IRE)**[52] 7716 4-8-12 **64**.... JimmyQuinn 1 68
(M Brittain) *led early: chsd wnr: rdn 2f out: no imp* **11/2**[3]

01-0 **3** ½ **Forward Feline (IRE)**[28] 29 4-8-12 **64**.... DavidProbert 6 66
(B Palling) *hld up in rr: nt clr run and swtchd lft over 1f out: r.o ins fnl f: tk 3rd cl home* **16/1**

0-04 **4** nk **Grand Honour (IRE)**[5] 317 4-8-11 **63**.... PaulDoe 8 64
(P Howling) *hld up and bhd: hdwy 2f out: c wd st: rdn jst over 1f out: sn edgd lft: one pce* **8/1**

3-05 **5** nk **Pride Of Nation (IRE)**[21] 126 8-8-9 **61**....(p) GrahamGibbons 4 62
(A J McCabe) *s.i.s: hld up in rr: nt clr run and swtchd rt jst over 2f out: hdwy 1f out: styng on whn nt clr run and swtchd lft towards fin* **25/1**

1-06 **6** ¾ **Just Jimmy (IRE)**[3] 348 5-8-11 **63**.... PaulHanagan 2 62
(P D Evans) *hld up in mid-div: pushed along and hdwy on ins 2f out: rdn over 1f out: one pce* **18/1**

53-4 **7** ½ **Kersivay**[17] 192 4-8-13 **70**.... BarryMcHugh(5) 3 67
(Ollie Pears) *hld up in mid-div: pushed along over 2f out: hdwy whn n.m.r over 1f out: no further prog* **10/3**[1]

43-0 **8** ¾ **Just Timmy Marcus**[8] 285 4-8-13 **65**....(v) TonyCulhane 7 60
(B P J Baugh) *s.i.s: hld up in rr: c v wd st: pushed along wl over 1f out: n.d* **16/1**

4-12 **9** ½ **Straight Face (IRE)**[5] 318 6-8-11 **63**....(b) J-PGuillambert 11 59
(P D Evans) *wnt rt s: hld up in tch: pushed along over 2f out: rdn wl over 1f out: eased whn btn wl ins fnl f* **4/1**[2]

30-2 **10** 1 ¾ **Kensington (IRE)**[8] 285 9-8-10 **67**.... DeclanCannon(5) 10 56
(A J McCabe) *hld up in tch: rdn wl over 1f out: wknd fnl f* **14/1**

-412 **11** 2 ¼ **Carmenero (GER)**[10] 269 7-9-4 **70**.... LiamKeniry 9 53
(C R Dore) *prom: nt clr run jst over 2f out: wknd wl over 1f out* **12/1**

100- **12** 25 **Whisky Jack**[101] 7000 4-9-1 **67**.... MartinDwyer 12 —
(W R Muir) *bmpd s: hdwy over 5f out: rdn over 2f out: wknd wl over 1f out: eased whn no ch fnl f* **40/1**

1m 30.04s (0.44) **Going Correction** +0.20s/f (Slow) 12 Ran SP% **119.7**

Speed ratings (Par 103): **105,101,101,100,100 99,99,98,97,95 93,64**

toteswingers: 1&2 £6.20, 1&3 £24.70, 2&3 £21.00 CSF £45.79 CT £613.46 TOTE £8.00: £2.40, £2.10, £5.30; EX 50.50 Trifecta £589.90 Part won. Pool: £797.27 - 0.10 winning units..

Owner B Smart **Bred** W H R John And Partners **Trained** Hambleton, N Yorks

FOCUS

A modest handicap. The winner made all and the race has been rated around him.

374 SPONSOR A RACE BY CALLING 01902 390000 MAIDEN STKS 7f 32y(P)

5:20 (5:21) (Class 5) 3-Y-O £2,456 (£725; £362) Stalls High

Form RPR

1 **Hacienda (IRE)** 3-9-3 0.... JoeFanning 1 91+
(M Johnston) *a.p: led over 1f out: clr fnl f: easily* **15/2**[3]

0-3 **2** 7 **Adam De Beaulieu (USA)**[10] 267 3-9-3 0....(t) GregFairley 8 64
(P C Haslam) *chsd ldr: led 2f out: rdn whn hung lft and hdd over 1f out: sn btn* **33/1**

0- **3** 2 ¼ **Penrod Ballantyne (IRE)**[111] 6754 3-9-3 0.... MartinDwyer 12 58
(B J Meehan) *prom: rdn over 2f out: wknd wl over 1f out* **5/2**[2]

4 ½ **Blues Music (IRE)** 3-9-3 0.... RobertWinston 6 57+
(B W Hills) *s.i.s: hld up in rr: styd on fr over 1f out: nvr nrr* **8/1**

0-4 **5** 3 ¼ **Cross The Boss (IRE)**[10] 267 3-8-12 0....(t) PatrickDonaghy(5) 11 48
(P C Haslam) *hld up in mid-div: pushed along and wknd over 2f out* **50/1**

032- **6** nse **Mnasikia (USA)**[35] 7859 3-8-12 64.... DaneO'Neill 5 43
(L M Cumani) *led: hdd 2f out: rdn and wknd over 1f out* **7/4**[1]

5 **7** 9 **Blues Forever (IRE)**[9] 274 3-9-3 0.... PaulHanagan 4 23
(P D Evans) *a bhd* **9/1**

6 **8** ¾ **Mental Reservation (USA)**[9] 274 3-9-3 0.... JerryO'Dwyer 10 21
(M G Quinlan) *hld up in tch: pushed along and wknd over 2f out* **16/1**

06 **9** 5 **Miereveld**[10] 267 3-9-3 0.... StevieDonohoe 3 8
(Sir Mark Prescott) *sn towards rr* **100/1**

0- **10** 1 ½ **Minimusic**[72] 7491 3-8-12 0.... DavidProbert 7 —
(B Palling) *a towards rr* **100/1**

-4 **11** 17 **Rightcar Joan (IRE)**[16] 201 3-8-12 0.... LiamKeniry 9 —
(Peter Grayson) *hld up in mid-div: pushed along over 3f out: wknd wl over 2f out: eased over 1f out* **150/1**

12 25 **Miss Reprieve** 3-8-12 0.... ChrisCatlin 2 —
(Miss S L Davison) *dwlt: sn t.o* **100/1**

1m 30.65s (1.05) **Going Correction** +0.20s/f (Slow) 12 Ran SP% **113.2**

Speed ratings (Par 97): **102,94,91,90,87 87,76,75,70,68 49,20**

toteswingers: 1&2 £14.60, 1&3 £4.50, 2&3 £20.90 CSF £224.59 TOTE £8.60: £2.80, £6.70, £1.30; EX 108.40 Trifecta £530.30 Parrt won. Pool: £716.73 - 0.20 winning units..

Owner Sheikh Hamdan Bin Mohammed Al Maktoum **Bred** Yeomanstown Stud **Trained** Middleham Moor, N Yorks

FOCUS

An interesting maiden. It didn't look a strong race on paper but the winner looks well above average. The form is rated around the third.

Mnasikia(USA) Official explanation: jockey said filly lost its action

375 BETDAQ THE BETTING EXCHANGE FILLIES' H'CAP 1m 4f 50y(P)

5:50 (5:50) (Class 5) (0-75,74) 4-Y-O+ £2,729 (£806; £403) Stalls Low

Form RPR

-315 **1** **Formidable Guest**[8] 282 6-9-1 **70**.... SaleemGolam 4 79
(J Pearce) *hld up last: stdy prog on ins over 3f out: led wl over 1f out: sn edgd rt: rdn ins fnl f: r.o* **3/1**[2]

451- **2** 2 ¼ **Crazy Chris**[68] 7512 5-9-5 **74**.... DavidProbert 1 79
(B Palling) *hld up in tch: chal 2f out: rdn wl over 1f out: no imp* **5/4**[1]

05-5 **3** 1 ¾ **Bushy Dell (IRE)**[13] 224 5-8-5 **65**.... AmyBaker(5) 3 68
(Miss J Feilden) *chsd ldr: led wl over 2f out tl wl over 1f out: sn rdn: one pce* **9/2**[3]

-213 **4** 13 **Look Officer (USA)**[14] 220 4-8-11 **69**....(b) RichardSmith 2 58
(Tom Dascombe) *led: hdd wl over 2f out: sn rdn: wknd wl over 1f out* **3/1**[2]

2m 45.15s (4.05) **Going Correction** +0.20s/f (Slow)

WFA 4 from 5yo+ 3lb 4 Ran SP% **112.6**

Speed ratings (Par 100): **94,92,91,82**

CSF £7.53 TOTE £3.00; EX 7.40 Place 6 £337.44, Place 5 £125.00.

Owner Macniler Racing Partnership **Bred** Kingwood Bloodstock **Trained** Newmarket, Suffolk

FOCUS

An ordinary fillies' handicap and a time over nine second above the standard suggests the pace was just modest. The winner looks better than ever but the form is not entirely solid.

T/Jkpt: £26,672.10 to a £1 stake. Pool: £75,132.83. 2.00 winning tickets. T/Plt: £446.40 to a £1 stake. Pool: £172,756.95. 282.45 winning tickets. T/Qpdt: £51.70 to a £1 stake. Pool: £16,145.02. 230.82 winning tickets. KH

[326] SOUTHWELL (L-H)

Tuesday, February 2

OFFICIAL GOING: Standard to slow

Wind: Light behind Weather: Overcast

376 BETDAQ ON 0870 178 1221 AMATEUR RIDERS' H'CAP 1m 6f (F)

1:30 (1:30) (Class 6) (0-65,65) 4-Y-O+ £1,714 (£527; £263) Stalls Low

Form RPR

0-21 **1** **Aaman (IRE)**[5] 331 4-9-13 **55**.... MissSBrotherton 2 77+
(E F Vaughan) *trckd ldr: smooth hdwy to ld 3f out: clr fnl 2f: unchal* **1/4**[1]

012- **2** 12 **Merrion Tiger (IRE)**[42] 7842 5-10-2 **60**.... MrMEnnis(7) 3 65
(A G Foster) *trckd ldrs: hdwy 4f out: chsd wnr 3f out and sn rdn: wknd wl over 1f out and plugged on same pce* **8/1**[3]

6-60 **3** 6 **Free Falling**[11] 263 4-9-1 **46** oh1....(vt[1]) MissZoeLilly(3) 1 43
(A J Lidderdale) *dwlt: reminders and sn led: pushed along 4f out: sn rdn and hdd 3f out: drvn 2f out and sn one pce: hung rt ent fnl f: kpt on* **150/1**

0-30 **4** 7 **Mymateeric**[6] 316 4-9-11 **53** ow1.... MrSDobson 8 40
(J Pearce) *hld up towards rr: hdwy 1/2-way: rdn along to chse ldrs over 3f out: sn drvn and n.d* **33/1**

63-0 **5** ¾ **Mountain Forest (GER)**[11] 263 4-8-11 **46** oh1.... MissNDumelow(7) 4 32
(H Morrison) *in rr: sme hdwy 3f out: plugged on: nvr a factor* **33/1**

0-03 **6** 1 **Lady Pilot**[11] 263 8-10-11 **65**.... MrJoshuaMoore(3) 7 50
(Jim Best) *hld up in rr: sme hdwy 4f out: sn rdn along and nvr a factor* **7/1**[2]

00/5 **7** 13 **Nawow**[26] 76 10-11-0 **65**....(p) MissEJJones 10 31
(M G Hazell) *chsd ldng pair: rdn along 4f out: sn wknd* **25/1**

333- **8** 24 **Front Rank (IRE)**[58] 6768 10-9-10 **52**.... MissECSayer(5) 5 —
(Mrs Dianne Sayer) *in tch: pushed along and lost pl after 5f: bhd over 4f out: t.o fnl 3f* **25/1**

/0-0 **9** 53 **Global Strategy**[31] 15 7-10-4 **60**.... MrJSherwood(5) 6 —
(O Sherwood) *a in rr: rdn along 1/2-way: sn bhd and t.o fnl 3f* **33/1**

3m 9.80s (1.50) **Going Correction** +0.075s/f (Slow)

WFA 4 from 5yo+ 5lb 9 Ran SP% **120.8**

Speed ratings (Par 101): **98,91,87,83,83 82,75,61,31**

toteswingers: 1&2 £2.10, 1&3 £14.60, 2&3 £37.70 CSF £2.90 CT £140.92 TOTE £1.40: £1.10, £1.90, £12.00; EX 4.60 Trifecta £141.50 Pool: £633.16 - 3.31 winning units..

Owner Mohammed Rashid **Bred** Darley **Trained** Newmarket, Suffolk

■ Stewards' Enquiry : Miss N Dumelow ten-day ban: breach of Rule (B) 59.4 (tbn)

FOCUS

A one-sided amateur riders' handicap which saw another bloodless win for Aaman, who was 20lb well in but looks worth his new mark. The runner-up was probably close to form.

Mountain Forest(GER) ◆ Official explanation: jockey said, regarding running and riding, that her orders wre to ride the gelding as she found it and obtain the best possible placing, adding that she had got very tired in closing stages and pushed it out as much as she could; trainer's rep said he was satisfied with the ride as it was her first attempt.

377 BET CIS FOOTBALL-BETDAQ (S) STKS 1m 4f (F)

2:00 (2:00) (Class 6) 4-Y-O+ £1,774 (£523; £262) Stalls Low

Form RPR

03-4 **1** **My Mate Mal**[5] 327 6-8-9 61.... BarryMcHugh(5) 2 66
(B Ellison) *mde all: rdn clr wl over 2f out: drvn and kpt on ins fnl f* **7/2**[2]

0-30 **2** 3 ½ **Jazrawy**[5] 331 8-8-9 54.... DeclanCannon(5) 1 60
(A J McCabe) *a.p: chsd wnr over 3f out and sn rdn: drvn wl over 1f out: kpt on ins fnl f* **14/1**

5260 **3** 7 **Inside Story (IRE)**[4] 353 8-9-0 54....(b) LiamKeniry 5 49
(C R Dore) *in tch: hdwy to chse ldrs over 4f out: rdn over 3f out: drvn and kpt on same pce fnl 2f* **7/1**[3]

3-13 **4** 3 ¼ **Dream In Blue**[23] 114 5-9-5 67....(p) ChrisCatlin 3 49
(J A Glover) *trckd ldng pair: effrt and cl up over 4f out: sn rdn: drvn and n.m.r 3f out and sn btn* **5/6**[1]

-410 **5** 13 **Black Falcon (IRE)**[12] 244 10-9-5 54.... RobertWinston 7 28
(John A Harris) *chsd ldrs: rdn along 4f out: drvn and wknd 3f out* **14/1**

-404 **6** 1 ¼ **Boss Hog**[7] 297 5-8-9 55.... PaulPickard(5) 6 21
(P T Midgley) *hld up: a in rr* **16/1**

00- **7** 38 **Soul Murmur (IRE)**[112] 6755 5-9-0 65....(t[1]) StephenCraine 8 —
(F Sheridan) *a in rr: wl bhd fnl 4f* **25/1**

2m 42.57s (1.57) **Going Correction** +0.075s/f (Slow) 7 Ran SP% **112.3**

Speed ratings (Par 101): **97,94,90,87,79 78,53**

toteswingers: 1&2 £6.30, 1&3 £2.50, 2&3 £6.40 CSF £46.68 TOTE £3.80: £1.80, £4.60; EX 43.40 Trifecta £433.60 Part won. Pool: £586.08 - 0.54 winning units..There was no bid for winner.

Owner Koo's Racing Club **Bred** Mrs A M Mallinson **Trained** Norton, N Yorks

■ Stewards' Enquiry : Barry McHugh two-day ban: used whip with excessive frequency (Feb 16-17)

FOCUS

A weak seller and not form to dwell on, with the favourite turning in a poor effort. The first two ran similar races here in December (race 7761) when well beaten by today's favourite.

Black Falcon(IRE) Official explanation: jockey said gelding hung left throughout

378 TRY BETDAQ FOR AN EXCHANGE H'CAP 6f (F)

2:30 (2:33) (Class 6) (0-65,65) 4-Y-O+ £1,774 (£523; £262) Stalls Low

Form RPR

062- **1** **Young Gladiator (IRE)**[82] 7348 5-9-1 **62**....(b) FrederikTylicki 4 73+
(Julie Camacho) *in tch on inner: pushed along and sltly outpcd wl over 2f out: sn rdn: kpt on to chal over 1f out: drvn and edgd rt ent fnl f: sn led and kpt on wl* **8/1**

0-00 **2** 1 ¼ **Westwood**[9] 287 5-9-1 **62**.... DaneO'Neill 6 69
(D Haydn Jones) *led: rdn over 2f out: drvn and hdd over 1f out: kpt on u.p to ld again ent fnl f: sn hdd and kpt on same pce* **6/1**[3]

4-42 **3** ½ **Not My Choice (IRE)**[19] 171 5-9-1 **62**....(tp) GregFairley 1 67
(J Balding) *cl up on inner: effrt over 2f out: sn rdn and ev ch tl drvn and one pce ins fnl f* **7/2**[1]

03-0 **4** 1 **Chosen One (IRE)**[31] 20 5-9-0 **61**....(p) TomEaves 8 63
(B Smart) *cl up: effrt over 2f out: rdn to ld over 1f out: hdd ent fnl f and kpt on same pce* **10/1**

00-1 **5** nk **Where's Reiley (USA)**[21] 138 4-8-13 **65**.... DeanHeslop(5) 3 66+
(T D Barron) *in rr and pushed along 1/2-way: hdwy on wd outside 2f out: sn rdn and kpt on ins fnl f: nrst fin* **9/2**[2]

65-4 **6** *1* **Quiet Mountain (IRE)**[18] [189] 5-8-5 **57** .... BarryMcHugh(5) 5 55
(Ollie Pears) *towards rr: effrt and pushed along over 2f out: rdn and swtchd lft wl over 1f out: kpt on ins fnl f* **10/1**

26-1 **7** *hd* **Zeffirelli**[23] [116] 5-8-8 **58** .... AndreaAtzeni(3) 10 55
(M Quinn) *chsd ldrs on outer: hdwy over 2f out and sn ev ch tl rdn and wknd appr fnl f* **9/2**[2]

400- **8** *1 ½* **Riflessione**[36] [7861] 4-9-2 **63** ....(b) ChrisCatlin 7 56
(R A Harris) *chsd ldrs: rdn along over 2f out: sn drvn and wknd* **22/1**

002- **9** *4 ½* **King's Sabre**[46] [7796] 4-8-1 **53** ....(be) BillyCray(5) 2 31
(R C Guest) *dwlt: a towards rr* **16/1**

/5-4 **10** *3 ½* **Dream Win**[21] [143] 4-8-13 **60** .... TonyHamilton 9 27
(B Ellison) *a toward rr* **25/1**

1m 17.58s (1.08) **Going Correction** +0.075s/f (Slow) **10** Ran SP% **116.2**
Speed ratings (Par 101): **95,93,92,91,90 89,89,87,81,76**
toteswingers: 1&2 £9.50, 1&3 £3.90, 2&3 £6.50 CSF £55.22 CT £204.78 TOTE £8.60: £2.70, £2.80, £1.60; EX 61.00 Trifecta £464.40 Pool: £ - winning units..
Owner Barrett,Hope,Postill,Adamson,Wainwright **Bred** Edmond And Richard Kent **Trained** Norton, N Yorks

FOCUS
An open sprint handicap that produced the slowest winning time of all the three races on the card over the trip. Sound form with the winner posting a personal best.

379 SOUTHWELL-RACECOURSE.CO.UK CLAIMING STKS 6f (F)
3:00 (3:00) (Class 6) 4-Y-0+ **£1,774** (£523; £262) **Stalls** Low

Form RPR

0-P4 **1** **Castle Myth (USA)**[5] [328] 4-8-4 58 ....(be) BarryMcHugh(5) 3 67
(B Ellison) *towards rr and pushed along 1/2-way: rdn and hdwy wl over 1f out: swtchd rt ent fnl f: drvn and styd on strly to ld last 100yds* **6/1**[3]

255- **2** *2* **Spin Again (IRE)**[176] [4845] 5-9-3 60 .... AdrianNicholls 6 68
(D Nicholls) *chsd ldng pair: hdwy 1/2-way: led wl over 1f out: rdn and hung rt appr fnl f: sn drvn: hdd and nt qckn fnl 100yds* **10/1**

4350 **3** *3 ¾* **Vogarth**[7] [298] 6-8-2 59 ....(b) DeclanCannon(5) 7 46
(M C Chapman) *in tch on outer: hdwy over 2f out: sn rdn and kpt on ins fnl f* **25/1**

-322 **4** *1* **Whitbarrow (IRE)**[19] [170] 11-9-0 69 ....(b) JamesMillman(3) 4 53
(B R Millman) *chsd ldrs: rdn along over 2f out: drvn wl over 1f out and sn one pce* **11/8**[1]

-125 **5** *1 ¼* **Stonecrabstomorrow (IRE)**[2] [364] 7-8-10 70 ....(b) MarkCoumbe(5) 2 47
(John A Harris) *in rr and rdn along 1/2-way: nvr nr ldrs* **5/1**[2]

0002 **6** *2 ¼* **Music Box Express**[5] [328] 6-8-3 53 ow1 ....(b) MatthewDavies(5) 5 33
(George Baker) *cl up: led after 2f: rdn along 2f out: sn hdd & wknd* **6/1**[3]

2-65 **7** *1 ¾* **Dig Deep (IRE)**[4] [342] 8-9-3 75 ....(b¹) TomEaves 1 36
(J J Quinn) *led 2f: cl up on inner: rdn along wl over 2f out: wknd wl over 1f out* **9/1**

1m 16.68s (0.18) **Going Correction** +0.075s/f (Slow) **7** Ran SP% **110.3**
Speed ratings (Par 101): **101,98,93,92,90 87,85**
toteswingers: 1&2 £9.30, 1&3 £15.70, 2&3 £13.90 CSF £57.19 TOTE £7.00: £3.00, £5.00; EX 58.40.
Owner Locketts Legends **Bred** Mr & Mrs Gerald J Stautberg **Trained** Norton, N Yorks
■ Stewards' Enquiry : Barry McHugh one-day ban: used whip with excessive frequency (Feb 18)

FOCUS
A moderate claimer run at a strong pace until it collapsed in the straight. The winner is the best guide to the form.
Whitbarrow(IRE) Official explanation: jockey said gelding ran flat
Stonecrabstomorrow(IRE) Official explanation: jockey said gelding never travelled

380 TWO FEBRUARY JUMPS MEETINGS AT SOUTHWELL H'CAP 6f (F)
3:30 (3:30) (Class 5) (0-75,75) 4-Y-0+ **£2,456** (£725; £362) **Stalls** Low

Form RPR

1- **1** **Poet's Place (USA)**[37] [7853] 5-9-4 **75** .... PhillipMakin 4 99+
(T D Barron) *trckd ldrs: smooth hdwy 1/2-way: led on bit wl over 1f out: sn qcknd clr: impressive* **10/11**[1]

56-1 **2** *4* **Charles Parnell (IRE)**[31] [20] 7-8-8 **68** .... MichaelStainton(3) 5 74
(S P Griffiths) *hld up: hdwy over 2f out and sn rdn: styd on to chse wnr ent fnl f: sn no imp* **9/2**[3]

003- **3** *1 ¼* **Gentle Guru**[35] [7870] 6-8-9 **66** .... RobertHavlin 6 68
(R T Phillips) *in rr: hdwy on outer wl over 2f out: sn rdn and kpt on appr fnl f: nrst fin* **12/1**

1-01 **4** *2 ¼* **Ponting (IRE)**[19] [171] 4-8-5 **67** .... PaulPickard(5) 7 62
(P T Midgley) *cl up: rdn to ld wl over 2f out: drvn and hdd wl over 1f out: wknd over 1f out* **10/3**[2]

00-6 **5** *1 ¼* **Guto**[19] [165] 7-8-7 **67** .... KellyHarrison(3) 2 58
(W J H Ratcliffe) *t.k.h: chsd ldng pair on inner: rdn along 1/2-way: drvn 2f out and sn btn* **40/1**

350- **6** *10* **Calmdownmate (IRE)**[49] [7758] 5-8-13 **70** .... AndrewElliott 1 29
(Mrs R A Carr) *in tch on outer: rdn along wl 1/2-way and sn wknd* **16/1**

00-0 **7** *11* **Came Back (IRE)**[14] [223] 7-8-9 **71** ow1 .... AnnStokell(5) 3 —
(Miss A Stokell) *t.k.h: led and set str pce: rdn 1/2-way: sn hdd & wknd* **66/1**

1m 16.5s **Going Correction** +0.075s/f (Slow) **7** Ran SP% **111.2**
Speed ratings (Par 103): **103,97,96,93,91 78,63**
toteswingers: 1&2 £2.30, 1&3 £2.90, 2&3 £3.10 CSF £5.03 TOTE £1.80: £1.40, £2.30; EX 5.00.
Owner Mrs Elaine Russell **Bred** Burning Daylight Farms **Trained** Maunby, N Yorks
■ Stewards' Enquiry : Paul Pickard one-day ban: careless riding (Feb 16)

FOCUS
All bar one of the runners had previously won at the course, although this wasn't a strong race. As expected this was run at a brisk early pace. The winner looks smart and is rated value for 6l.
Came Back(IRE) Official explanation: jockey said gelding ran too free

381 MEMBERSHIP OF SOUTHWELL GOLF CLUB MAIDEN STKS 1m (F)
4:00 (4:01) (Class 5) 3-Y-0 **£2,456** (£725; £362) **Stalls** Low

Form RPR

00- **1** **First Post (IRE)**[101] [7029] 3-9-3 0 .... DaneO'Neill 5 77
(D Haydn Jones) *cl up on outer: effrt to chse ldr 2f out: sn rdn and edgd lft over 1f out: drvn and styd on ent fnl f to ld last 100yds* **50/1**

45- **2** *1 ½* **Calculus Affair (IRE)**[33] [7886] 3-9-3 0 .... ShaneKelly 3 73
(J Noseda) *led: pushed clr 2f out: rdn over 1f out: drvn ins fnl f: hdd and one pce last 100yds* **5/2**[2]

3 *5* **Ancient Times (USA)** 3-9-3 0 .... JoeFanning 6 62+
(M Johnston) *trckd ldrs: pushed along and outpcd 1/2-way: rdn and hdwy to chse ldrs 2f out: sn drvn and no imp* **6/4**[1]

0-4 **4** *½* **Celestial Girl**[13] [238] 3-8-12 0 .... RobertWinston 4 56
(H Morrison) *cl up: rdn along over 2f out: grad wknd* **9/2**[3]

0-62 **5** *16* **Royal Torbo (ISR)**[15] [219] 3-8-12 66 .... MatthewDavies(5) 1 24
(George Baker) *sn pushed along and in tch tl rdn over 3f out and sn wknd* **12/1**

6 *2 ¾* **Balcombe (FR)** 3-9-3 0 .... PhillipMakin 2 18
(T P Tate) *dwlt: sn trcking ldrs: rdn along over 3f out and sn wknd* **5/1**

1m 43.62s (-0.08) **Going Correction** +0.075s/f (Slow) **6** Ran SP% **113.1**
Speed ratings (Par 97): **103,101,96,96,80 77**
toteswingers: 1&2 £7.00, 1&3 £1.80, 2&3 £7.10 CSF £173.23 TOTE £47.80: £6.10, £1.90; EX 122.80.
Owner Llewelyn, Runeckles **Bred** D Llewelyn & J Runeckles **Trained** Efail Isaf, Rhondda C Taff

FOCUS
This looked an interesting, and potentially fair maiden for the track beforehand, but there was an unexpected winner. With little form to go on this has been rated in line with the decent time.

382 FREE SOFTWARE AT FREE.BETANGEL.COM H'CAP 1m (F)
4:30 (4:30) (Class 5) (0-75,73) 3-Y-0 **£2,456** (£725; £362) **Stalls** Low

Form RPR

06-1 **1** **Ostentation**[21] [134] 3-8-10 **65** .... JoeFanning 4 78+
(M Johnston) *prom: chsd ldr fr 1/2-way: rdn to ld wl over 1f out: clr whn edgd lft appr fnl f: styd on wl* **5/2**[2]

13-2 **2** *4* **House Red (IRE)**[15] [218] 3-9-2 **71** ....(b¹) RobertWinston 6 74
(B W Hills) *led: pushed along and jnd 3f out: rdn and hdd wl over 1f out: sn drvn and kpt on same pce* **4/1**[3]

232- **3** *6* **Barlaman (USA)**[110] [6802] 3-9-2 **71** .... ChrisCatlin 1 61
(C E Brittain) *t.k.h: hld up in rr: hdwy over 3f out: rdn to chse ldng pair over 2f out: sn drvn and no imp* **10/1**

3-31 **4** *2* **Paintball (IRE)**[18] [189] 3-9-1 **73** .... AndreaAtzeni(3) 5 58
(W R Muir) *chsd ldrs on outer: rdn along 1/2-way: wd st: drvn and btn 2f out* **2/1**[1]

120 **5** *2 ¾* **Mororless**[9] [283] 3-8-4 **64** .... DeclanCannon(5) 7 43
(A J McCabe) *towards rr: pushed along over 3f out and sn outpcd* **22/1**

51-1 **6** *nk* **Wedding Dream**[7] [302] 3-8-4 **64** 6ex .... AmyRyan(5) 2 42
(K A Ryan) *chsd wnr on inner: rdn along over 3f out: drvn and wknd over 2f out* **4/1**[3]

1m 43.15s (-0.55) **Going Correction** +0.075s/f (Slow) **6** Ran SP% **115.3**
Speed ratings (Par 97): **105,101,95,93,90 89**
toteswingers: 1&2 £3.20, 1&3 £3.70, 2&3 £4.30 CSF £13.37 TOTE £4.30: £2.10, £2.20; EX 17.90 Place 6: £205.74 Place 5: £178.21.
Owner Sheikh Hamdan Bin Mohammed Al Maktoum **Bred** Wellsummers Stud **Trained** Middleham Moor, N Yorks

FOCUS
This looked a reasonable race for the grade, but they were strung out behind the winner who is on the upgrade. The form is rated around the runner-up.
T/Plt: £727.90 to a £1 stake. Pool: £82,290.70. 82.52 winning tickets. T/Qpdt: £312.00 to a £1 stake. Pool: £7,227.29. 17.14 winning tickets. JR

362 KEMPTON (A.W) (R-H)
Wednesday, February 3

OFFICIAL GOING: Standard
Wind: Brisk behind Weather: Dark

383 BOOK NOW FOR RACING POST CHASE DAY H'CAP 1m 2f (P)
5:00 (5:01) (Class 5) (0-75,75) 4-Y-0+ **£2,590** (£770; £385; £192) **Stalls** High

Form RPR

00-2 **1** **Cupid's Glory**[18] [200] 8-9-2 **72** .... LiamKeniry 2 80+
(G L Moore) *in rr: rdn and hdwy 2f out: str run to ld jst ins fnl f: kpt on wl* **7/1**

345- **2** *1 ¼* **Benedict Spirit (IRE)**[58] [7668] 5-8-11 **72** .... RichardEvans(5) 5 77
(P D Evans) *chsd ldr: rdn 2f out: led over 1f out: hdd jst ins fnl f: styd on same pce* **7/1**

331- **3** *½* **Dream Of Fortune (IRE)**[45] [7823] 6-8-12 **73** ....(t) JamieJones(5) 6 77+
(M G Quinlan) *s.i.s: hld up in rr: hdwy on ins fr 2f out: drvn to chse ldng duo ins fnl f: nt qckn nr fin* **4/1**[1]

60-5 **4** *¾* **Taaresh (IRE)**[13] [255] 5-8-4 **67** .... RyanClark(7) 1 70
(K A Morgan) *in tch: rdn and hdwy on outer fr 2f out: chsd ldrs 1f out: nt qckn u.p ins fnl f* **11/1**

00-6 **5** *¾* **Life's Challenge (USA)**[20] [174] 4-9-1 **72** .... JoeFanning 9 73
(M Johnston) *led: rdn over 2f out: hdd over 1f out: wknd fnl 110yds* **7/1**

-402 **6** *shd* **Hip Hip Hooray**[10] [284] 4-8-4 **61** oh1 .... FrannyNorton 8 62
(L A Dace) *chsd ldrs: pushed along over 2f out: styd on same pce ins fnl f* **12/1**

6544 **7** *2* **Croix Rouge (USA)**[7] [309] 8-8-5 **61** oh5 .... HayleyTurner 3 58
(R J Smith) *in rr: drvn along over 2f out: nvr gng pce to rch ldrs* **9/1**

006- **8** *nse* **Folio (IRE)**[240] [2773] 10-9-5 **75** .... TonyCulhane 7 72
(W J Musson) *a towards rr* **20/1**

002- **9** *nk* **Bull Market (IRE)**[74] [7490] 7-8-13 **69** .... StevieDonohoe 10 65
(M S Tuck) *t.k.h: in tch: tl wknd fr 2f out* **6/1**[3]

40-3 **10** *2 ¾* **Sadeek**[12] [262] 6-8-8 **64** .... TomEaves 4 55
(B Smart) *chsd ldrs tl wknd wl over 1f out* **11/2**[2]

2m 8.77s (0.77) **Going Correction** 0.0s/f (Stan)
WFA 4 from 5yo+ 1lb **10** Ran SP% **118.0**
Speed ratings (Par 103): **96,95,94,94,93 93,91,91,91,89**
toteswingers: 1&2 £15.40, 1&3 £7.50, 2&3 £5.10 CSF £55.97 CT £225.27 TOTE £11.00: £3.10, £3.20, £1.50; EX 122.10.
Owner K Johnson, K Jessup **Bred** Cheveley Park Stud Ltd **Trained** Lower Beeding, W Sussex

FOCUS
A fair handicap. The pace was steady and they were tightly grouped in the early stages. The time was five seconds above standard. The runner-up is probably the best guide to the form.
Bull Market(IRE) Official explanation: jockey said, regarding running and riding, that his orders were to jump out and get a good position and make the best of his way home, adding that he got shuffled back further than he wanted early on in a steady pace, the gelding got outpaced as they quickened around the final bend and was short of room before staying on one pace final 2f; vet said gelding was found to be slightly lame on right hind.

384 BISTRO IN THE PANORAMIC BAR & RESTAURANT H'CAP 5f (P)
5:30 (5:30) (Class 4) (0-85,85) 4-Y-0+ **£4,209** (£1,252; £625; £312) **Stalls** High

Form RPR

21-4 **1** **Absa Lutte (IRE)**[7] [307] 7-8-2 **74** ....(t) JamesSullivan(5) 9 85
(Patrick Morris) *trckd ldrs: led appr fnl f: drvn 2 l clr ins fnl f: jst hld on* **5/2**[1]

210- **2** *nk* **Zegna (IRE)**[35] [7875] 4-8-9 **76** .... TomEaves 8 86+
(B Smart) *n.m.r after s: in tch: hdwy over 1f out: str run to go 2nd ins fnl f: clsng on wnr nr fin: nt quite get up* **6/1**

4-46 **3** *1 ¼* **Timeteam (IRE)**[12] [258] 4-8-10 **82** ow2 .... RichardEvans(5) 6 87
(P D Evans) *in rr: hdwy on ins over 1f out: chsd ldrs ins fnl f: no imp* **20/1**

1-03 **4** *shd* **Glamorous Spirit (IRE)**[7] [307] 4-9-4 **85** .... ChrisCatlin 3 90
(R A Harris) *led after 1f: hdd appr fnl f: kpt on same pce ins fnl f* **9/2**[3]

The Form Book, Raceform Ltd, Compton, RG20 6NL

0-30 **5** ½ **Peak District (IRE)**[17] 212 6-8-13 **85**.......... AmyRyan(5) 7 88
(K A Ryan) *led 1f: chsd ldrs: rdn and styd on same pce fnl f* **11/4**[2]

0-36 **6** 1¼ **Lord Of The Reins (IRE)**[7] 307 6-8-7 **74**.......... JimmyQuinn 1 73
(J G Given) *in rr: sme prog fnl f but nvr gng pce to rch ldrs* **10/1**

2-30 **7** 3¾ **The Tatling (IRE)**[7] 307 13-8-13 **80**.......... RobertWinston 4 65
(J M Bradley) *chsd ldrs to 1/2-way* **14/1**

0101 **8** 4½ **Thoughtsofstardom**[7] 306 7-8-0 **72** 6ex.......... DeclanCannon(5) 2 41
(P S McEntee) *chsd ldrs 3f* **16/1**

58.92 secs (-1.58) **Going Correction** 0.0s/f (Stan) **8** Ran SP% **114.1**
Speed ratings (Par 105): **112,111,109,109,108 106,100,93**
toteswingers: 1&2 £3.90, 1&3 £8.50, 2&3 £21.90 CSF £17.92 CT £240.63 TOTE £3.80: £1.50, £1.90, £5.10; EX 17.50.
Owner D & D Coatings Ltd **Bred** Ian Amond **Trained** Tarporley, Cheshire

FOCUS
A decent sprint handicap run at a furious pace. The time was almost a second under standard and was a new course record. Personal bests from both the first two.

385 DIGIBET MEDIAN AUCTION MAIDEN STKS 1m (P)
6:00 (6:00) (Class 5) 3-5-Y-0 **£2,590** (£770; £385; £192) **Stalls** High

Form RPR

05- **1** **Ginger Jack**[126] 6382 3-8-9 0.......... JoeFanning 5 77+
(M Johnston) *chsd ldr: drvn to ld 2f out: c readily clr fnl f* **13/2**

2-22 **2** 2½ **Charlie Smirke (USA)**[12] 262 4-10-0 63.......... GeorgeBaker 3 72
(G L Moore) *chsd ldrs: rdn to go 2nd fnl f but no imp on wnr* **5/1**[3]

0/ **3** 1¼ **Roshina (IRE)**[115] 6709 4-9-9 70.......... IanMongan 4 64
(Miss Jo Crowley) *chsd ldrs: rdn and one pce over 2f out: styd on again ins fnl f but nvr a threat* **9/1**

-633 **4** ¾ **Major Lawrence (IRE)**[6] 321 4-10-0 63..........(v) ShaneKelly 10 67
(J Noseda) *sn led: hdd 2f out: lost 2nd 1f out and sn one pce* **8/1**

22 **5** ½ **Takajan (IRE)**[6] 326 3-8-9 73.......... DavidProbert 9 61
(S Kirk) *chsd ldrs: rdn over 2f out: wknd ins fnl f* **3/1**[2]

6 3 **Myplacelater** 3-7-13 0.......... DeclanCannon(5) 12 49+
(D R C Elsworth) *s.i.s: in rr: hdwy on outside over 2f out: styd on fr over 1f out but nvr gng pce to rch ldrs* **33/1**

7 1 **Corres (IRE)** 3-8-9 0.......... HayleyTurner 11 51+
(D R C Elsworth) *in rr: rdn 3f out: kpt on fr over 1f out but nvr gng pce to rch ldrs* **11/4**[1]

8 2 **Mack's Sister** 3-8-4 0.......... JimmyQuinn 1 42
(D K Ivory) *t.k.h early: mid-div: pushed along 3f out and nvr gng pce to get into contention* **50/1**

9 2 **Killing Moon (USA)** 3-8-9 0.......... FrannyNorton 2 42
(K A Ryan) *s.i.s: in rr: hdwy on outside and in tch over 2f out: sn rdn: hung rt over 1f out and wknd qckly* **25/1**

10 1¾ **Zafeen's Pearl** 3-8-4 0.......... ChrisCatlin 13 33
(D K Ivory) *nvr gng pce to get into contention* **50/1**

3-6 **11** nk **Brave Decision**[23] 128 3-8-10 0 ow1.......... StevieDonohoe 7 38
(A J McCabe) *in tch 1/2-way: wknd ins fnl 3f* **25/1**

12 1¾ **Swindlers Lass (IRE)** 3-8-4 0.......... AdrianMcCarthy 8 28
(Mark Gillard) *a towards rr* **66/1**

1m 40.2s (0.40) **Going Correction** 0.0s/f (Stan) **12** Ran SP% **118.8**
WFA 3 from 4yo 19lb
Speed ratings (Par 103): **98,95,94,93,93 90,89,87,85,83 82,81**
toteswingers: 1&2 £9.90, 1&3 £16.80, 2&3 £8.70 CSF £36.88 TOTE £8.40: £3.00, £2.30, £3.30; EX 34.10.
Owner Sheikh Hamdan Bin Mohammed Al Maktoum **Bred** Darley **Trained** Middleham Moor, N Yorks

FOCUS
An ordinary maiden run at a steady pace. Not many got into it but the winner was quite impressive and most of the main form contenders were in a bunch behind him, so the form could work out. The winner was value for 4l.
Myplacelater Official explanation: jockey said filly ran green
Killing Moon(USA) Official explanation: jockey said colt ran green and hung right in straight

386 DIGIBET.COM H'CAP 1m 4f (P)
6:30 (6:30) (Class 4) (0-85,80) 3-Y-0 **£4,209** (£1,252) **Stalls** Centre

Form RPR

3412 **1** **Exceedthewildman**[14] 240 3-8-12 **80**..........(p) KierenFox(7) 3 80
(J S Moore) *nvr far off ldr: shkn up over 2f out: rdn over 1f out: str run on rails ins fnl f to ld fnl 20yds* **10/11**[1]

01-1 **2** hd **Danger Mulally**[30] 33 3-9-2 **77**..........(t) DavidProbert 2 77
(A M Balding) *led and t.k.h 4f: shkn up 2f out: rdn appr fnl f: hdd and nt qckn fnl 20yds* **10/11**[1]

2m 43.33s (8.83) **Going Correction** 0.0s/f (Stan) **2** Ran SP% **104.8**
Speed ratings (Par 99): **70,69**
TOTE £1.90.
Owner E Moore & J S Moore **Bred** Horizon Bloodstock Limited **Trained** Upper Lambourn, Berks
■ Stewards' Enquiry : Kieren Fox five-day ban: excessive use of whip (Feb 17 to 21).

FOCUS
This was weakened by the withdrawal of the likely favourite Lovers Causeway, but it was still an intriguing tactical duel, and a tight battle between two improving rivals tackling this trip for the first time. The race is rated around the winner.

387 DIGIBET CASINO H'CAP 6f (P)
7:00 (7:01) (Class 6) (0-55,54) 3-Y-0 **£2,047** (£604; £302) **Stalls** High

Form RPR

2-44 **1** **Rightcar**[16] 215 3-8-13 **53**.......... RobertWinston 7 57
(Peter Grayson) *chsd ldrs: rdn to ld ins fnl f: drvn out* **15/2**

-313 **2** 1 **Turf Time**[12] 265 3-8-13 **53**.......... ChrisCatlin 8 54
(J A Glover) *sn led: rdn over 2f out: hdd ins fnl f: kpt on same pce* **7/2**[1]

0-60 **3** ½ **Dolly Will Do**[12] 265 3-8-2 **45**.......... KellyHarrison(3) 5 44
(N P Mulholland) *in rr tl hdwy over 2f out: sn n.m.r: styd on to chse ldng duo ins fnl f: no ex fnl 100yds* **40/1**

05-4 **4** ½ **Pavement Games**[12] 265 3-8-1 **46**.......... BillyCray(5) 1 44
(R C Guest) *hld up in rr: hdwy on outside fr over 2f out: styd on wl fnl f but nvr gng pce to rch ldrs* **6/1**[3]

000- **5** 2¾ **Ba Jetstream**[53] 7722 3-8-7 **47**.......... JoeFanning 9 36
(F Jordan) *chsd ldrs: rdn 2f out: wknd ins fnl f* **25/1**

-522 **6** 2¾ **Lady Brickhouse**[16] 215 3-8-3 **48**.......... PaulPickard(5) 2 28
(M D Squance) *in rr: pushed along over 2f out: nvr gng pce to get into contention* **5/1**[2]

050- **7** nk **Joan's Legacy**[100] 7050 3-8-13 **53**.......... RichardSmith 10 32
(J C Fox) *in rr tl gd hdwy on ins to chse ldrs over 2f out: rdn and wl on terms over 1f out: wknd ins fnl f* **11/1**

0-34 **8** 2 **Rufus Roughcut**[7] 305 3-8-3 **46** ow1..........(t) WilliamCarson(3) 3 19
(S C Williams) *chsd ldrs: hung rt and wknd over 2f out* **6/1**[3]

56-6 **9** 2½ **Princess Shamal**[16] 215 3-8-13 **53**.......... ShaneKelly 4 18
(J R Jenkins) *a outpcd* **8/1**

000- **10** 1¼ **Mactrac**[34] 7884 3-9-0 **54**.......... DaneO'Neill 6 15
(R Hannon) *chsd ldr: rdn wl over 2f out and sn btn* **9/1**

1m 13.13s (0.03) **Going Correction** 0.0s/f (Stan) **10** Ran SP% **115.0**
Speed ratings (Par 95): **99,97,97,96,92 89,88,85,82,80**
toteswingers: 1&2 £7.70, 1&3 £43.50, 2&3 £25.40 CSF £33.42 CT £987.70 TOTE £9.60: £2.60, £1.10, £8.50; EX 43.60.
Owner S Kamis & PGRC Ltd **Bred** J M Beever **Trained** Formby, Lancs

FOCUS
A modest handicap run at a fair tempo. Improvement from the winner to reverse Wolverhampton form with the second, but the proximity of the third devalues the form.
Lady Brickhouse Official explanation: jockey said filly hung left

388 TRY THE BISTRO IN THE PANORAMIC RESTAURANT H'CAP 7f (P)
7:30 (7:30) (Class 7) (0-50,51) 4-Y-0+ **£1,364** (£403; £201) **Stalls** High

Form RPR

50-2 **1** **Copper King**[20] 160 6-9-2 **49**.......... LiamKeniry 7 60
(Miss Tor Sturgis) *hld up towards rr but in tch: gd hdwy fr 2f out: str run fnl f to ld fnl 100yds: drvn out* **11/1**

00-4 **2** 1¼ **Jessica Wigmo**[6] 319 7-9-3 **50**.......... ShaneKelly 14 58
(A W Carroll) *hld up towards rr: stdy hdwy over 2f out: swtchd rt over 1f out: and sn qckn to ld: rdn ins fnl f: hdd and outpcd fnl 100yds* **11/2**[2]

0-36 **3** hd **Josiah Bartlett (IRE)**[12] 269 4-9-0 **47**.......... HayleyTurner 2 54
(Ian Williams) *in rr: stl plenty to do whn hdwy on outside 2f out: str run ins fnl f to take 3rd cl home and clsng for 2nd but no ch w wnr* **10/1**

5-31 **4** 1½ **Clever Omneya (USA)**[6] 320 4-9-4 **51** 6ex.......... TomQueally 4 54
(J R Jenkins) *chsd ldrs: drvn to chal 2f out: outpcd fnl 110yds* **5/1**[1]

6-02 **5** hd **Imperial Skylight**[6] 320 4-9-2 **49**..........(v) ChrisCatlin 12 51
(M R Channon) *chsd ldrs: slt ld 2f out: hdd appr fnl f: sn outpcd* **11/2**[2]

-004 **6** 1½ **Grizedale (IRE)**[6] 320 11-8-7 **47**..........(tp) KierenFox(7) 11 45
(M J Attwater) *towards rr but in tch: rdn over 2f out: styd on thrght fnl f but nvr gng pce to rch ldrs* **14/1**

4535 **7** ¾ **Reigning Monarch (USA)**[6] 320 7-9-1 **48**..........(p) SamHitchcott 13 44
(Miss Z C Davison) *in tch: hdwy on ins to chse ldrs over 2f out: stl wl there 1f out: wknd ins fnl f* **5/1**[1]

0-40 **8** ¾ **Battimoore (IRE)**[6] 320 4-8-11 **49**..........(b[1]) AndrewHeffernan(5) 5 43
(I W McInnes) *s.i.s: in rr tl hdwy over 2f out: nvr rchd ldrs and wknd over 1f out* **33/1**

000- **9** 4½ **Montmartre (USA)**[111] 6787 4-9-3 **50**..........(b[1]) FergusSweeney 9 32
(David Pinder) *sn slt ld: rdn and hdd 2f out: sn wknd* **8/1**[3]

0-00 **10** 9 **Vanadium**[5] 347 8-8-12 **50**..........(vt[1]) JemmaMarshall(5) 10 8
(A J Lidderdale) *a outpcd* **25/1**

0/0- **11** 1 **Saunton Sands**[234] 2950 4-9-3 **50**.......... DaneO'Neill 1 5
(A G Newcombe) *outpcd most of way* **40/1**

-000 **12** 4 **Admirals Way**[9] 295 5-8-12 **50**..........(b[1]) MarkCoumbe(5) 3 —
(C N Kellett) *pressed ldr over 4f: sn wknd* **40/1**

40-5 **13** nk **See That Girl**[13] 249 4-9-2 **49**.......... TomEaves 8 —
(B Smart) *chsd ldrs over 4f* **11/2**[2]

1m 25.67s (-0.33) **Going Correction** 0.0s/f (Stan) **13** Ran SP% **126.4**
Speed ratings (Par 97): **101,99,99,97,97 95,94,93,88,78 77,72,72**
toteswingers: 1&2 £17.80, 1&3 £10.50, 2&3 £11.70 CSF £72.61 CT £665.79 TOTE £13.00: £3.90, £2.80, £3.80; EX 76.20.
Owner Paul Reason **Bred** Miss A V Hill **Trained** Lambourn, Berks
■ Stewards' Enquiry : Chris Catlin one-day ban: used whip without giving gelding time to respond (Feb 17)

FOCUS
A low-grade handicap. The pace was strong and there was an exciting finish. Solid form for the grade.
Admirals Way Official explanation: jockey said gelding ran too free

389 BOOK KEMPTON TICKETS ON 0844 579 3008 H'CAP 1m (P)
8:00 (8:00) (Class 7) (0-50,50) 4-Y-0+ **£1,364** (£403; £201) **Stalls** High

Form RPR

0-43 **1** **Hi Spec (IRE)**[6] 320 7-8-13 **46**..........(p) JimmyQuinn 12 55
(Miss M E Rowland) *in rr tl gd hdwy on ins 3f out: chsd ldr wl over 1f out: drvn to ld fnl 110yds: styd on strly* **9/1**

020/ **2** 1½ **King Canute (IRE)**[490] 6374 6-9-3 **50**.......... JoeFanning 4 55
(D Morris) *sn led: rdn 2f out: kpt advantage tl hdd and one pce fnl 110yds* **4/1**[2]

60- **3** 1¾ **Granakey (IRE)**[68] 7555 7-9-0 **47**.......... StevieDonohoe 13 48
(Ian Williams) *chsd ldrs: rdn and chsd ldng duo wl over 1f out: kpt on same pce ins fnl f* **4/1**[2]

0-44 **4** 2¾ **Inquisitress**[14] 229 6-8-12 **48**.......... MarcHalford(3) 6 43
(J J Bridger) *in rr: hdwy over 2f out: rdn: hung rt and styd on fr over 1f out: nvr gng pce to rch ldrs* **16/1**

06-2 **5** ¾ **Stanley Rigby**[14] 229 4-9-2 **49**.......... JackMitchell 11 42+
(C F Wall) *hld up in rr: rdn and hdwy ins fnl 2f: styd on wl fnl f but nvr a threat* **9/4**[1]

-600 **6** 1¼ **Djalalabad (FR)**[6] 320 6-9-0 **47**..........(tp) TomQueally 9 37
(Mrs C A Dunnett) *mid-div: rdn and hdwy over 2f out: nvr gng pce to get into contention* **20/1**

30/2 **7** 1¾ **Kathleen Kennet**[9] 289 10-8-5 **45**.......... KierenFox(7) 5 31
(M R Bosley) *in rr tl hdwy on outside to chse ldrs ins fnl 3f: rdn: hung lft and wknd 2f out* **14/1**

00-0 **8** 1½ **Arch Event**[9] 290 5-8-7 **45**..........(v) DeclanCannon(5) 8 27
(A W Carroll) *chsd ldrs tl wknd u.p over 2f out* **50/1**

30-1 **9** 1 **Prince Valentine**[14] 229 9-9-2 **49**..........(p) GeorgeBaker 1 29
(G L Moore) *in tch: pushed along and effrt over 2f out: nvr rchd ldrs and wknd sn after* **8/1**[3]

600- **10** 2 **Doctor Of Music (IRE)**[134] 6184 4-9-3 **50**.......... TomEaves 14 25
(B Smart) *alwys outpcd* **14/1**

-650 **11** 4½ **Gracie's Games**[12] 264 4-8-7 **45**..........(t) AndrewHeffernan(5) 10 9
(R J Price) *chsd ldrs: rdn 3f out: wknd ins fnl 3f* **50/1**

0-40 **12** 3¾ **Safaseef (IRE)**[14] 234 5-8-5 **45**.......... RyanClark(7) 2 —
(K A Morgan) *chsd ldrs 5f* **25/1**

00-0 **13** 26 **Tuning Fork**[25] 99 10-8-7 **45**.......... JemmaMarshall(5) 3 —
(M J Attwater) *chsd ldrs 5f: wknd qckly over 2f out* **66/1**

1m 39.5s (-0.30) **Going Correction** 0.0s/f (Stan) **13** Ran SP% **125.1**
Speed ratings (Par 97): **101,99,97,95,94 93,91,89,88,86 82,78,52**
toteswingers: 1&2 £9.80, 1&3 £10.20, 2&3 £6.50 CSF £45.30 CT £179.25 TOTE £8.90: £2.70, £1.80, £2.20; EX 61.40 Place 6: £254.88 Place 5: £123.76.
Owner Miss M E Rowland **Bred** Mrs Marita Rogers **Trained** Lower Blidworth, Notts

FOCUS
An ordinary handicap. The first three finished clear of the rest and a massive gamble was just foiled. There is a chance that this was fair form for the grade.
Kathleen Kennet Official explanation: jockey said mare hung left

T/Plt: £107.50 to a £1 stake. Pool: £80,640.56. 547.33 winning tickets. T/Qpdt: £28.90 to a £1 stake. Pool: £8,808.19. 225.32 winning tickets. ST

[355]LINGFIELD (L-H)

Wednesday, February 3

OFFICIAL GOING: Standard

Wind: modest, half behind Weather: overcast

390 BREATHE SPA AT MARRIOTT LINGFIELD H'CAP (DIV I) 1m 2f (P)

12:40 (12:40) (Class 6) (0-60,60) 4-Y-O+ £1,433 (£423; £211) Stalls Low

Form RPR

02-3 **1** **Chanrossa (IRE)**[19] 182 4-9-5 **60**..............(p) JimCrowley 9 68+
(E A L Dunlop) *chsd ldr tl led over 2f out: rdn and qckng 2 l clr over 1f out: drvn and a doing enough fnl f* **10/3**[1]

0-43 **2** ¾ **Alfredtheordinary**[23] 131 5-9-3 **57**.............. SamHitchcott 11 64
(M R Channon) *t.k.h: in tch on outer: hdwy to chse wnr over 2f out: ev ch and rdn 2f out: nt qckn w wnr over 1f out: rallied u.p 1f out: a hld fnl 100yds* **9/2**[3]

056- **3** 1 ¾ **Geoffdaw**[31] 4732 5-8-8 **51**.............. RobertLButler(3) 6 54
(Miss Sheena West) *chsd ldrs: rdn and unable qck over 2f out: kpt on u.p fnl f to snatch 3rd nr fin: nvr gng pce to threaten ldng pair* **8/1**

16/0 **4** hd **Catholic Hill (USA)**[10] 282 5-9-2 **56**..............(b[1]) SteveDrowne 2 59
(C J Mann) *t.k.h: chsd ldng pair: nt qckn u.p wl over 1f out: plugged on same pce fnl f: lost 3rd nr fin* **12/1**

5-63 **5** ½ **Mister Frosty (IRE)**[19] 184 4-8-5 **53**.............. CharlotteKerton(7) 4 55
(G Prodromou) *wl in tch in midfield: pushed along on inner over 2f out: one pce and nt threaten ldrs fr over 1f out* **7/1**

506- **6** 1 ¼ **Kings Topic (USA)**[61] 7623 10-9-1 **60**..............(p) AmyBaker(5) 3 59
(A B Haynes) *s.i.s and sn pushed along in rr: nt clr run wl over 1f out: styd on fnl f: nvr trbld ldrs* **16/1**

-630 **7** ½ **Easy Wonder (GER)**[6] 320 5-8-6 **46** oh1..............(b) HayleyTurner 7 44
(I A Wood) *stdd s: t.k.h: hld up wl in tch in rr: rdn and effrt over 1f out: one pce and no prog after* **11/1**

06-0 **8** ½ **Siena Star (IRE)**[12] 261 12-9-5 **59**.............. TomQueally 1 56
(Stef Higgins) *led tl hdd and rdn over 2f out: wknd u.p over 1f out* **7/2**[2]

5 **9** 4 **Peinture De Guerre (FR)**[19] 179 7-9-1 **55**..............(t) GeorgeBaker 8 44
(G L Moore) *dwlt: wl in tch in last trio: hdwy on outer over 4f out: wknd wl over 1f out* **12/1**

000- **10** 1 ¼ **Jaq's Sister**[63] 7609 4-8-6 **47**.............. JimmyQuinn 5 34
(M Blanshard) *in tch in midfield: rdn and struggling ent fnl 2f: wl btn fnl f* **33/1**

2m 7.21s (0.61) **Going Correction** +0.05s/f (Slow)
WFA 4 from 5yo+ 1lb **10** Ran SP% **119.6**
Speed ratings (Par 101): **99,98,97,96,96 95,95,94,91,90**
toteswingers: 1&2 £2.60, 1&3 £8.40, 2&3 £7.20 CSF £19.13 CT £113.37 TOTE £4.10: £1.40, £2.40, £1.50; EX 13.50 Trifecta £50.40 Pool: £295.29 - 4.33 winning units..
Owner St Albans Bloodstock LLP **Bred** P Syndicate **Trained** Newmarket, Suffolk

FOCUS
The early pace wasn't hot and it paid to race fairly prominently. The time was 1.85secs slower than the second division. The form seems sound enough but the winner is worth a bit more than the bare figures.
Catholic Hill(USA) Official explanation: jockey said gelding hung left
Mister Frosty(IRE) Official explanation: jockey said gelding was denied a clear run

391 BET CIS CUP FOOTBALL - BETDAQ (S) STKS 6f (P)

1:10 (1:10) (Class 6) 4-Y-O+ £1,774 (£523; £262) Stalls Low

Form RPR

1321 **1** **Obe Gold**[6] 328 8-9-7 65.............. J-PGuillambert 3 73
(P Howling) *led: sn hdd: trckd ldrs after: effrt and rdn on inner wl over 1f out: ev ch ent fnl f: led fnl 75yds: r.o wl* **3/1**[1]

62-5 **2** nk **Espy**[31] 27 5-9-2 67.............. LiamKeniry 4 67
(I W McInnes) *t.k.h: chsd ldrs: rdn to chal ent fnl 2f: led over 1f out: hrd pressed and drvn 1f out: hdd and no ex fnl 75yds* **4/1**[3]

650- **3** ½ **Romantic Queen**[64] 7602 4-8-6 58..............(t) MatthewDavies(5) 1 61
(George Baker) *t.k.h: hld up wl in tch in last trio: nt clr run wl over 1f out tl swtchd rt ent fnl f: r.o to chse ldng pair ins fnl f: gng on fin* **12/1**

6231 **4** 2 ¼ **Equinity**[5] 319 4-9-2 50..............(t) SaleemGolam 8 59
(J Pearce) *taken down early: stdd and hmpd sn after s: t.k.h: hld up wl in tch: hdwy to chse ldrs 2f out: wknd ins fnl f* **5/1**

1014 **5** nk **Peopleton Brook**[7] 312 8-9-7 63..............(t) SteveDrowne 2 63+
(B G Powell) *t.k.h: hld up wl in tch in last trio: nt clr run wl over 1f out: swtchd rt over 1f out: r.o ins fnl f: nvr able to chal* **9/2**

6-06 **6** nk **Titus Gent**[10] 287 5-9-7 65..............(p) ChrisCatlin 5 62
(R A Harris) *wnt rt s: sn rcvrd and led: rdn and hdd over 1f out: wknd ins fnl f* **7/2**[2]

0-00 **7** 1 ¾ **Spring Bridge (IRE)**[21] 146 4-8-13 43..............(tp) MarcHalford(3) 9 51?
(Mrs L C Jewell) *racd keenly: w ldr: ev ch and rdn ent fnl 2f: wknd 1f out* **100/1**

1m 13.22s (1.32) **Going Correction** +0.05s/f (Slow) **7** Ran SP% **110.8**
Speed ratings (Par 101): **93,92,91,88,88 88,85**
Tote Swingers: 1&2 £2.50, 1&3 £7.90, 2&3 £10.10 CSF £14.26 TOTE £3.50: £1.60, £2.50; EX 13.10 Trifecta £91.50 Pool: £526.00 - 4.25 winning units..There was no bid for the winner.
Owner Paul Howling **Bred** Mrs M Mason **Trained** Newmarket, Suffolk
■ Stewards' Enquiry : Liam Keniry one-day ban: used whip with excessive frequency (Feb 17)

FOCUS
Quite a competitive seller based on adjusted ratings, but another race run at a fairly sedate pace. Muddling form, best judged around the winner to his recent best.
Romantic Queen Official explanation: jockey said filly was denied a clear run

392 MARRIOTT HOTEL OPENING SPRING 2010 MAIDEN STKS 6f (P)

1:40 (1:42) (Class 5) 3-Y-O+ £2,456 (£725; £362) Stalls Low

Form RPR

5- **1** **Arry's Orse**[166] 5234 3-8-11 0.............. TomEaves 4 89+
(B Smart) *racd off the pce in midfield: pushed along over 3f out: hdwy over 2f out: led ins fnl f: sn clr: readily* **5/6**[1]

2 4 **Pippbrook Ministar** 3-8-6 0.............. HayleyTurner 8 65+
(J R Boyle) *rn green and sn rdn along wl in rr: stl last whn hung bdly rt and v wd bnd 2f out: r.o strly u.p ins fnl f to snatch 2nd nr fin: no ch w wnr* **33/1**

5-26 **3** ½ **Fine Silk (USA)**[7] 317 4-9-7 67.............. NeilCallan 1 67
(M G Quinlan) *led at fast gallop: rdn wl over 1f out: hdd ins fnl f: sn no ch w wnr: lost 2nd nr fin* **8/1**

30-0 **4** 3 ½ **Tejime**[11] 275 4-9-12 70.............. NickyMackay 9 61
(J H M Gosden) *w ldr and clr of rivals: rdn and ev ch wl over 1f out tl wknd ins fnl f* **9/2**[2]

334- **5** nk **My Mandy (IRE)**[106] 6913 3-8-6 66.............. LiamJones 2 51
(R A Harris) *awkward s: chsd ldng trio tl wnt 3rd over 3f out: rdn over 2f out: no prog fnl 2f* **20/1**

02 **6** 1 ¼ **Ceto**[7] 313 3-8-6 0.............. ChrisCatlin 5 47
(P S McEntee) *sn wl outpcd in rr: pushed along over 3f out: kpt on u.p fnl f: nvr trbld ldrs* **10/1**

7 1 **Just Say Please** 3-8-6 0.............. JimmyQuinn 6 44
(D K Ivory) *v.s.a and swtchd lft after s: a bhd* **50/1**

8 1 **Edition** 3-8-11 0.............. LiamKeniry 7 45
(J R Gask) *sn rdn along in last trio: nvr trbld ldrs* **33/1**

-4 **9** nse **Slap And Tickle (IRE)**[17] 208 4-9-4 0.............. AndreaAtzeni(3) 3 44
(S C Williams) *chsd clr ldng pair tl over 3f out: wknd u.p wl over 1f out* **7/1**[3]

1m 11.36s (-0.54) **Going Correction** +0.05s/f (Slow)
WFA 3 from 4yo 15lb **9** Ran SP% **118.0**
Speed ratings (Par 103): **105,99,99,94,93 92,90,89,89**
toteswingers: 1&2 £10.10, 1&3 £2.90, 2&3 £26.10 CSF £44.69 TOTE £1.90: £1.02, £6.50, £2.70; EX 38.00 Trifecta £356.90 Pool: £631.90 - 1.31 winning units..
Owner Harry Redknapp **Bred** Genesis Green Stud Ltd **Trained** Hambleton, N Yorks

FOCUS
An uncompetitive maiden, but they went a good gallop. The impressive winner was value for extra and the form is rated around the third.
Pippbrook Ministar ◆ Official explanation: jockey said filly hung right on bend

393 BET MULTIPLES - BETDAQ H'CAP 7f (P)

2:15 (2:16) (Class 5) (0-75,75) 4-Y-O+ £2,456 (£725; £362) Stalls Low

Form RPR

01-5 **1** **Sarah's Art (IRE)**[15] 223 7-9-4 **75**..............(t) TomQueally 11 84
(Stef Higgins) *stdd and dropped in bhd after s: rdn and hdwy on outer over 1f out: chal ins fnl f: led fnl 100yds: r.o wl* **9/1**

000- **2** nk **Cut And Thrust (IRE)**[44] 7830 4-8-13 **70**..............(p) ChrisCatlin 9 78
(M Wellings) *stdd after s: hld up towards rr: hdwy on outer over 1f out: led ins fnl f: sn hdd: r.o wl but a jst hld* **16/1**

5-56 **3** 2 ½ **I Confess**[11] 275 5-8-6 **68**..............(b) AndrewHeffernan(5) 2 69
(P D Evans) *led: rdn ent fnl 2f: hrd drvn and edgd lft 1f out: hdd ins fnl f: nt pce of ldrs after: kpt on* **6/1**[3]

0-42 **4** nse **Rondeau (GR)**[11] 275 5-9-2 **73**.............. JimCrowley 1 74
(P R Chamings) *hld up in tch in midfield: swtchd ins and effrt on inner over 1f out: pressed ldr and drvn 1f out: nt pce of ldng pair fnl 150yds* **7/2**[2]

065- **5** ½ **Trafalgar Square**[64] 7603 8-9-4 **75**.............. GeorgeBaker 8 75
(M J Attwater) *hld up in rr: effrt over 1f out: swtchd rt jst ins fnl f: r.o towards fin: nt rch ldrs* **6/1**[3]

0/ **6** ¾ **Lady Kent (IRE)**[88] 7299 4-8-13 **70**.............. StephenCraine 5 68
(J R Boyle) *in tch: nt clr run over 1f out tl swtchd rt jst ins fnl f: r.o fnl 100yds: nt able to chal* **9/1**

21-1 **7** nk **Striker Torres (IRE)**[19] 191 4-9-1 **72**..............(v) TomEaves 10 69
(B Smart) *chsd ldrs: hdwy on outer to chse ldng pair over 2f out: outpcd u.p over 1f out: one pce fnl f* **11/4**[1]

3-10 **8** 1 ¾ **Nacho Libre**[13] 255 5-8-9 **71**..............(b) JamesSullivan(5) 6 63
(M W Easterby) *s.i.s: a in rr: n.d* **12/1**

200- **9** 1 ¾ **Bobs Dreamflight**[70] 7516 4-8-11 **73**.............. MarkCoumbe(5) 7 60
(D K Ivory) *w ldr: rdn and ev ch jst over 2f out: wknd over 1f out* **50/1**

644- **10** ¾ **Hypnotist (UAE)**[103] 6997 4-9-0 **71**..............(p) NeilCallan 4 56
(C E Brittain) *dwlt: sn bustled up to chse ldrs: rdn and chse ldr over 1f out tl 1f out: wknd fnl f* **10/1**

1m 23.86s (-0.94) **Going Correction** +0.05s/f (Slow) **10** Ran SP% **122.1**
Speed ratings (Par 103): **107,106,103,103,103 102,101,99,97,97**
toteswingers: 1&2 £19.50, 1&3 £7.50, 2&3 £20.10 CSF £148.53 CT £961.46 TOTE £7.70: £2.30, £4.70, £2.20; EX 183.80 TRIFECTA Not won..
Owner ownaracehorse.co.uk (Shefford) **Bred** Newtownbarry House Stud **Trained** Lambourn, Berks
■ Kyle was withdrawn on vet's advice (11/1, deduct 5p in the £ under R4). New market formed.

FOCUS
They went quite quick here and the race was set up for a closer. The winner matched his Wolverhampton win two starts back and the second is rated back to his best.

394 BETDAQ.CO.UK H'CAP 1m (P)

2:50 (2:50) (Class 4) (0-80,80) 4-Y-O+ £4,209 (£1,252; £625; £312) Stalls High

Form RPR

460- **1** **Gaily Noble (IRE)**[50] 7759 4-8-10 **77**.............. AmyBaker(5) 12 86
(A B Haynes) *broke wl and led early: chsd ldng pair: hdwy to chal 2f out: nudged ahd over 1f out: r.o wl fnl f* **20/1**

4-11 **2** 1 ¼ **Hereford Boy**[7] 315 6-9-2 **78** 6ex..............(p) RobertHavlin 3 84
(D K Ivory) *hld up in last trio: hmpd 5f out: hdwy over 1f out: r.o wl to chse wnr ins fnl f: no imp fnl 100yds* **9/1**

054- **3** 1 ¾ **Hawaana (IRE)**[56] 7684 5-9-4 **80**.............. SteveDrowne 11 82+
(Miss Gay Kelleway) *stdd after s: hld up in rr: bdly hmpd 5f out: hdwy ent fnl f: r.o wl ins fnl f to snatch 3rd last stride: nvr threatened ldng pair* **9/1**

5-34 **4** shd **Gallantry**[7] 315 8-9-1 **77**.............. GeorgeBaker 4 79
(P Howling) *chsd ldng trio: effrt u.p wl over 1f out: disp 2nd and drvn 1f out: kpt on same pce after* **8/1**[3]

30-1 **5** ½ **Totally Focussed (IRE)**[21] 151 5-9-4 **80**.............. HayleyTurner 5 81
(S Dow) *hld up in tch in midfield: rdn and unable qck over 1f out: styd on same pce fnl f* **11/2**[2]

-215 **6** nse **Prince Of Thebes (IRE)**[7] 315 9-8-13 **75**.............. PaulDoe 2 76
(M J Attwater) *sn chsng ldr: led ent fnl 2f: hrd drvn and hdd over 1f out: one pce ins fnl f* **12/1**

64-2 **7** ½ **Sunshine Always (IRE)**[21] 151 4-9-3 **79**.............. JimCrowley 9 78
(T D McCarthy) *hld up towards rr: hmpd 5f out: effrt and rdn on outer over 1f out: styd on fnl f: nvr trbld ldrs* **3/1**[1]

004- **8** 2 **Herschel (IRE)**[222] 2850 4-8-11 **73**.............. AmirQuinn 10 68
(G L Moore) *stdd s: hld up in rr: nvr trbld ldrs* **25/1**

1-30 **9** hd **Istiqdaam**[13] 245 5-8-8 **75**..............(b) JamesSullivan(5) 7 69
(M W Easterby) *sn led: rdn and hdd ent fnl 2f: wknd over 1f out: wl hld fnl f* **9/1**

34-0 **10** ¾ **Red Suede Shoes**[21] 151 4-8-12 **77**..............(p) JamesMillman(3) 1 70
(B R Millman) *in tch in midfield: rdn over 2f out: hdwy u.p on inner over 1f out: wknd 1f out: eased towards fin* **11/1**

04-0 **11** 1 **Kinsya**[14] 231 7-8-7 **74**.............. AshleyMorgan(5) 6 64
(M H Tompkins) *in tch in midfield: lost pl and towards rr jst over 2f out: nt clr run wl over 1f out: no ch after* **16/1**

30-5 **P** **Indy Driver**[14] 239 5-9-0 **76**........(p) FrannyNorton 8 —
(Matthew Salaman) *chsd ldrs tl stmbld and lost action 5f out: immediately p.u and dismntd* **8/1**[3]

1m 37.11s (-1.09) **Going Correction** +0.05s/f (Slow) **12** Ran SP% **123.1**
Speed ratings (Par 105): **107,105,104,103,103 103,102,100,100,99 98,—**
toteswingers: 1&2 £29.70, 1&3 £46.60, 2&3 £16.60 CSF £196.80 CT £1784.78 TOTE £20.20: £7.00, £1.90, £3.80; EX 138.70 Trifecta £369.10 Part won. Pool: £498.84 - 0.44 winning units..
Owner Athos Racing **Bred** Garry Chong **Trained** Limpley Stoke, Bath

FOCUS
A competitive handicap but the pace was not all that strong. The first two are rated back to their best with the hampered third 3lb off.
Hawaana(IRE) Official explanation: jockey said gelding suffered interference in running
Sunshine Always(IRE) Official explanation: jockey said gelding suffered interference in running
Kinsya Official explanation: jockey said gelding suffered interference in running

395 WE LOVE OUR NEW ZEALAND LAMB LEG STKS (H'CAP) 1m 5f (P)
3:25 (3:25) (Class 5) (0-75,74) 4-Y-0+ **£2,456** (£725; £362) **Stalls** Low

Form RPR
31-2 **1** **Quinsman**[6] 323 4-9-3 **71**........ LiamKeniry 4 82+
(J S Moore) *chsd ldng pair: clsd over 2f out: rdn to ld 2f out: hrd drvn and hdd jst ins fnl f: rallied gamely to ld again fnl 75yds: r.o wl* **6/4**[1]
010- **2** *nk* **Admirable Duque (IRE)**[74] 7476 4-8-12 **71**........(p) BillyCray(5) 6 81
(D J S Ffrench Davis) *stdd s: hld up in rr: hdwy on outer over 2f out: ev ch and rdn 2f out: led jst ins fnl f tl hdd and no ex fnl 75yds* **12/1**
5-21 **3** ¾ **Satwa Gold (USA)**[12] 260 4-9-6 **74**........ HayleyTurner 1 83
(Stef Higgins) *hld up in midfield: swtchd rt arnd wkng rival 2f out: chsd ldng pair and drvn ent fnl f: kpt on same pce fnl 150yds* **3/1**[2]
36-0 **4** 7 **Prince Picasso**[14] 239 7-8-13 **70**........(t) LeeTopliss(7) 5 69
(R A Fahey) *hld up in last pair: clsd and in tch over 2f out: rdn and fnd little over 1f out: wl hld fnl f* **5/1**[3]
40/6 **5** 1½ **Prince Sabaah (IRE)**[16] 220 6-9-8 **72**........(tp) TonyCulhane 2 68
(Miss Venetia Williams) *led for 1f: chsd ldr after tl led again jst over 2f out: sn hdd: wknd ent fnl f* **8/1**
0-50 **6** 1½ **Meydan Dubai (IRE)**[4] 361 5-8-12 **65**........ MarcHalford(3) 8 59
(J R Best) *hld up in rr: rdn and effrt wl over 1f out: no prog and wl hld fnl f* **14/1**
-043 **7** 7 **Awatuki (IRE)**[7] 314 7-8-11 **64**........(b¹) RobertLButler(3) 3 48
(J R Boyle) *dwlt: sn pushed up to ld after 1f: hdd and rdn jst over 2f out: wknd 2f out: wl btn fnl f* **22/1**

2m 46.6s (0.60) **Going Correction** +0.05s/f (Slow)
WFA 4 from 5yo+ 4lb **7** Ran SP% **111.5**
Speed ratings (Par 103): **100,99,99,95,94 93,88**
toteswingers: 1&2 £5.20, 1&3 £1.50, 2&3 £6.50 CSF £19.93 CT £47.04 TOTE £2.40: £1.40, £6.00; EX 20.80 Trifecta £63.90 Pool: £676.01 - 7.82 winning units..
Owner Donald M Kerr **Bred** Mr & Mrs G Middlebrook **Trained** Upper Lambourn, Berks

FOCUS
There was a fair pace on early, but they were well bunched turning into the straight and the race developed into a bit of a sprint. The form is a bit muddling and it is doubtful if the winner had to match his previous Kempton effort.
Admirable Duque(IRE) Official explanation: jockey said gelding ran too free early

396 BREATHE SPA AT MARRIOTT LINGFIELD H'CAP (DIV II) 1m 2f (P)
4:00 (4:00) (Class 6) (0-60,60) 4-Y-0+ **£1,433** (£423; £211) **Stalls** Low

Form RPR
36-2 **1** **Zero Cool (USA)**[5] 353 6-9-1 **55**........(p) GeorgeBaker 2 65
(G L Moore) *chsd clr ldr: clsd and pressed ldr ent fnl 2f: rdn to ld ent fnl f: drvn ins fnl f: a jst gng to hold on* **9/4**[1]
2 *nk* **Spruce (USA)**[200] 4-9-5 **60**........ JimmyQuinn 6 70
(Miss J Feilden) *chsd ldng pair: rdn and clsd jst over 2f out: drvn jst over 1f out: styd on u.p ins fnl f: pressed wnr cl home: nvr quite getting there* **9/4**[1]
00-5 **3** ¾ **Whodunit (UAE)**[18] 202 6-9-0 **54**........(b) ChrisCatlin 3 62
(P W Hiatt) *led: clr over 8f out: reduced advantage over 2f out: rdn 2f out: hdd ent fnl f: kpt on same pce after* **9/1**[3]
66-4 **4** 6 **King Of Connacht**[9] 294 7-9-4 **58**........(v) NeilCallan 5 54
(M Wellings) *stdd after s: hld up wl off pce in rr: hdwy over 2f out: rdn wl over 1f out: kpt on but nvr gng pce to threaten ldrs* **7/1**[2]
55-6 **5** ¾ **Noah Jameel**[22] 139 8-8-12 **52**........ FergusSweeney 7 47
(A G Newcombe) *hld up off pce in midfield: effrt to chse clr ldng trio over 2f out: no imp after* **16/1**
321- **6** 1 **Why Nee Amy**[77] 7426 4-8-11 **57**........ KylieManser(5) 8 50
(T Keddy) *hld up wl off pce in last pair: sltly hmpd over 2f out: sme hdwy 2f out: nvr trbld ldrs* **9/1**[3]
55-0 **7** 4½ **Rainiers Girl**[20] 160 4-8-5 **46** oh1........ DavidProbert 9 30
(R A Teal) *racd off the pce in midfield: rdn and racd awkwardly over 3f out: wl btn fnl 2f* **20/1**
0-55 **8** 2¼ **Old Romney**[9] 289 6-9-6 **60**........ J-PGuillambert 10 39
(P Howling) *stdd and dropped in bhd after s: nvr a factor* **16/1**
003- **9** 1¾ **Bertie Smalls**[232] 3005 4-8-6 **52**........ AshleyMorgan(5) 4 28
(M H Tompkins) *racd off the pce in midfield: lost pl and bhd over 2f out: n.d* **25/1**
060- **10** 6 **Bridge Of Fermoy (IRE)**[16] 6917 5-8-1 **46** oh1.....(b) DeclanCannon(5) 1 10
(D C O'Brien) *chsd ldng trio: rdn and struggling wl over 2f out: wl bhd fnl 2f* **33/1**

2m 5.36s (-1.24) **Going Correction** +0.05s/f (Slow)
WFA 4 from 5yo+ 1lb **10** Ran SP% **117.4**
Speed ratings (Par 101): **106,105,105,100,99 98,95,93,92,87**
toteswingers: 1&2 £3.10, 1&3 £6.40, 2&3 £5.80 CSF £6.49 CT £37.06 TOTE £3.70: £1.40, £1.50, £2.40; EX 9.30 Trifecta £47.60 Pool: £756.57 - 11.76 winning units..
Owner Dedman Properties **Bred** Robert N Clay & River Bend Farm **Trained** Lower Beeding, W Sussex

FOCUS
They went a decent gallop, thanks to Whodunit, and very few got into the race. The time was 1.85secs quicker than the first division. Straightforward form, with the winner close to his latest.

397 MARRIOTT PLAY AND STAY APPRENTICE H'CAP 1m (P)
4:35 (4:35) (Class 6) (0-60,60) 4-Y-0+ **£1,774** (£523; £262) **Stalls** High

Form RPR
300- **1** **Stanley Goodspeed**[36] 7870 7-8-13 **59**........(t) KierenFox(5) 7 70
(J W Hills) *t.k.h: hld up in tch in midfield: hdwy u.p on outer over 1f out: led fnl 100yds: r.o wl* **7/1**[3]
6-34 **2** 1 **Lopinot (IRE)**[12] 256 7-9-1 **59**........(v) AndrewHeffernan(3) 4 68
(M R Bosley) *t.k.h: hld up in midfield: swtchd off of rail ent fnl 2f: hrd rdn and edgd lft ent fnl f: ev ch ins fnl f: kpt edging lft no ex towards fin* **7/1**[3]
00/0 **3** 1½ **Wetherby Place (IRE)**[14] 235 4-8-6 **52**........ TobyAtkinson(5) 9 57
(M Wigham) *t.k.h: hld up in rr: rdn and effrt over 1f out: r.o wl ins fnl f: snatched 3rd on post* **14/1**
-225 **4** *nse* **Party In The Park**[12] 256 5-8-11 **55**........ MatthewDavies(3) 11 60
(J R Boyle) *chsd ldr: rdn and ev ch wl over 1f out: led jst ins fnl f: sn hdd and one pce after: n.m.r nr fin: lost 3rd on post* **3/1**[1]
06-0 **5** ½ **Sovereignty (JPN)**[14] 235 8-8-12 **53**........ AndreaAtzeni 10 57
(D K Ivory) *t.k.h: in tch in midfield: hdwy on outer to ld 4f out: hrd pressed and rdn 2f out: hdd 1f out: no ex ins fnl f* **8/1**
00-5 **6** *nk* **Star Strider**[23] 129 6-9-2 **60**........ KylieManser(3) 3 63
(T Keddy) *s.i.s: t.k.h: hld up in midfield: hdwy over 3f out: jnd ldr over 2f out: rdn wl over 1f out: led 1f out: sn hdd and one pce after* **12/1**
34-2 **7** *nk* **Mackintosh (IRE)**[30] 34 4-8-12 **53**........(b) PatrickHills 6 56
(Patrick Morris) *chsd ldrs: rdn and effrt on inner over 1f: drvn ent fnl f: wknd fnl 150yds* **7/2**[2]
500- **8** 1¼ **Our Day Will Come**[254] 2321 4-9-4 **59**........ DavidProbert 8 59
(B Palling) *chsd ldrs: rdn and unable qck ent fnl 2f: one pce and wl hld fnl f* **14/1**
50-0 **9** ½ **Clerical (USA)**[14] 234 4-8-10 **51**........(p) JackMitchell 5 49
(R M H Cowell) *in tch towards rr: rdn and no real prog fr wl over 1f out* **16/1**
1-35 **10** 4½ **Bold Rose**[15] 225 4-8-11 **57**........(p) BillyCray(5) 2 45
(M D I Usher) *s.i.s: a bhd* **16/1**
00-0 **11** 4½ **Moral Duty (USA)**[11] 275 5-9-4 **59**........ WilliamCarson 1 36
(W G M Turner) *led tl 4f out: chsd ldr tl over 2f out: wknd qckly u.p over 1f out* **25/1**

1m 39.8s (1.60) **Going Correction** +0.05s/f (Slow) **11** Ran SP% **120.0**
Speed ratings (Par 101): **94,93,91,91,90 90,90,89,88,84 79**
toteswingers: 1&2 £12.30, 1&3 £24.60, 2&3 £15.60 CSF £56.57 CT £691.42 TOTE £8.90: £2.70, £1.90, £6.00; EX 69.40 TRIFECTA Not won. Place 6: £ 215.00 Place 5: £119.46.
Owner R J Tufft **Bred** Burton Agnes Stud Co Ltd **Trained** Upper Lambourn, Berks

FOCUS
A moderate handicap run at a steady early pace, but the race got going plenty soon enough running down the hill, and the first three came from off the pace. Modest form which makes some sense.
Sovereignty(JPN) Official explanation: jockey said gelding ran too freely
Star Strider Official explanation: jockey said gelding hung right
Mackintosh(IRE) Official explanation: jockey said gelding ran flat
Bold Rose Official explanation: jockey said filly was denied a clear run
T/Jkpt: Not won. T/Plt: £196.90 to a £1 stake. Pool: £65,036.71. 241.04 winning tickets. T/Qpdt: £86.70 to a £1 stake. Pool: £6,575.17. 56.07 winning tickets. SP

[376] SOUTHWELL (L-H)
Thursday, February 4

OFFICIAL GOING: Standard
Wind: Light against Weather: Overcast

398 BET IN RUNNING - BETDAQ FILLIES' H'CAP 7f (F)
2:00 (2:01) (Class 5) (0-70,70) 4-Y-0+ **£2,593** (£765; £383) **Stalls** Low

Form RPR
55-2 **1** **Borasco (USA)**[30] 40 5-8-12 **64**........ PhillipMakin 7 72
(T D Barron) *trckd ldrs on outer: effrt 2f out: rdn and hdwy over 1f out: drvn and edgd lft ins fnl f: styd on to ld last 50yds* **11/4**[2]
00-4 **2** ¾ **Peter's Gift (IRE)**[12] 275 4-9-4 **70**........ NeilCallan 4 76
(K A Ryan) *trckd ldrs: hdwy to ld 2f out: rdn over 1f out: drvn and edgd lft ins fnl f: hdd and no ex last 50yds* **7/2**[3]
4-12 **3** 1¼ **Miss Bootylishes**[21] 169 5-8-13 **70**........ AmyBaker(5) 5 73
(A B Haynes) *hld up in rr: hdwy on inner over 2f out: rdn to chse ldrs over 1f out: drvn and ch ins fnl f: kpt on same pce towards fin* **5/2**[1]
/62- **4** 1¼ **Lilly Grove**[104] 7004 5-8-7 **59**........ JimmyQuinn 3 59
(G A Swinbank) *trckd ldrs: hdwy over 2f out: rdn to chse ldr wl over 1f out: drvn and ev ch wknd ins fnl f* **5/1**
50-0 **5** 2¼ **Izzi Mill (USA)**[11] 284 4-8-10 **67**........(p) DeclanCannon(5) 2 61
(A J McCabe) *led: rdn along 3f out: hdd 2f out: sn drvn and wknd over 1f out* **16/1**
500- **6** 6 **Bookiebasher Babe (IRE)**[116] 6703 5-9-3 **69**........ FrannyNorton 1 46
(M Quinn) *sn pushed along on inner and towards rr: hdwy 3f out: rdn over 2f out and nvr nr ldrs* **11/1**
50-0 **7** 29 **Freya's Flight (IRE)**[10] 290 4-8-4 **56** oh2........ ChrisCatlin 6 —
(K A Ryan) *prom: rdn along 1/2-way: sn wknd* **33/1**

1m 29.46s (-0.84) **Going Correction** 0.0s/f (Stan) **7** Ran SP% **111.3**
Speed ratings (Par 100): **104,103,101,100,97 90,57**
toteswinger:1&2:£2.60, 2&3:£1.90, 1&3:£1.80 CSF £12.08 TOTE £3.50: £1.90, £2.00; EX 15.70.
Owner Mrs Christine Barron **Bred** Kidder, Cole & J K & Linda Griggs **Trained** Maunby, N Yorks

FOCUS
An ordinary fillies' handicap. The form is rated around the winner and third.

399 BET SIX NATIONS RUGBY - BETDAQ MEDIAN AUCTION MAIDEN STKS 7f (F)
2:30 (2:31) (Class 6) 3-5-Y-0 **£2,047** (£604; £302) **Stalls** Low

Form RPR
4-32 **1** **Ant Music (IRE)**[11] 283 3-8-9 63........(b) LiamKeniry 5 64
(J S Moore) *set stdy pce: qcknd over 2f out: rdn over 1f out: drvn ins fnl f and kpt on wl towards fin* **7/1**[3]
0-3 **2** 1¼ **Turning Circle**[9] 301 4-9-5 0........ JohnCavanagh(7) 2 66
(M Brittain) *hld up in rr: swtchd outside and hdwy 1/2-way: chsd ldng pair wl over 1f out: rdn to chse wnr ent fnl f: edgd lft and ev ch tl no ex towards fin* **20/1**
2- **3** 3¾ **Golden Tiger**[44] 7836 3-8-12 0 ow3........ PhillipMakin 1 54
(T P Tate) *chsd wnr: rdn along over 2f out: sn drvn and btn wl over 1f out* **4/5**[1]
5- **4** ¾ **Your Gifted (IRE)**[127] 6402 3-7-13 64........ JamesSullivan(3) 3 43
(Patrick Morris) *stdd s: sn trcking ldrs: effrt to chse wnr 2f out: sn rdn and kpt on same pce appr fnl f* **8/1**
00- **5** 8 **Erfaan (USA)**[211] 3750 3-8-9 0........ PaulHanagan 4 27
(Julie Camacho) *t.k.h: trckd ldrs: pushed along wl over 2f out: sn wknd and eased fnl f* **11/4**[2]

1m 30.39s (0.09) **Going Correction** 0.0s/f (Stan)
WFA 3 from 4yo 17lb **5** Ran SP% **110.6**
Speed ratings (Par 101): **99,97,93,92,83**
toteswinger:1&2:£16.00 CSF £93.89 TOTE £6.50: £1.70, £4.90; EX 31.10.
Owner Phil Cunningham **Bred** E O'Gorman **Trained** Upper Lambourn, Berks

FOCUS
A weak maiden and the winning time was nearly a second slower than the fillies' handicap. The winner probably got back to something like his early juvenile level, but it is hard to be certain.

400 BETDAQ POKER H'CAP 1m 3f (F)
3:00 (3:00) (Class 5) (0-70,71) 4-Y-0+ £2,661 (£785; £393) Stalls Low

Form RPR
4-31 1 **Charging Indian (IRE)**[7] 330 4-9-7 71 6ex................(b) TonyCulhane 2 79
(P T Midgley) *hld up towards rr: hdwy 1/2-way: trckd ldr over 3f out: slt ld 2f out and sn rdn: drvn ent fnl f: sn hung lft and kpt on wl towards fin* 9/2[2]
-302 2 1 1/4 **Bosamcliff (IRE)**[7] 330 5-9-0 67................................ RichardEvans(5) 1 73
(P D Evans) *hld up in tch: hdwy 4f out: cl up over 2f out: rdn wl over 1f out and ev ch tl drvn and no ex wl ins fnl f* 11/2[3]
3441 3 4 1/2 **General Tufto**[9] 298 5-9-5 70 6ex............................(b) KellyHarrison(3) 5 68
(C Smith) *hld up in rr: hdwy on outer over 3f out: rdn 2f out: drvn and kpt on same pce appr fnl f* 17/2
60-0 4 2 1/4 **Mullitovermaurice**[14] 255 4-8-10 60........................... RobertWinston 4 55
(J G Given) *chsd ldrs: rdn along over 3f out: drvn over 2f out: sn wknd* 25/1
55-0 5 1/2 **Divinatore**[11] 282 4-8-10 60..(p) PaulHanagan 3 54
(D Haydn Jones) *led 1f: prom tl rdn along 4f out and sn wknd* 9/1
3/11 6 3 1/2 **Gargano (IRE)**[12] 280 5-9-6 68.. NeilCallan 6 56
(M Johnston) *led after 1f: clr over 6f out: rdn along 3f out: hdd and drvn 2f out: sn wknd* 10/11[1]

2m 27.45s (-0.55) **Going Correction** 0.0s/f (Stan)
WFA 4 from 5yo 2lb 6 Ran SP% 110.3
Speed ratings (Par 103): **102,101,97,96,95 93**
toteswinger:1&2:£2.00, 2&3:£4.80, 1&3:£3.70 CSF £27.46 TOTE £3.70: £1.80, £2.40; EX 20.20.
Owner David Mann **Bred** Samac Ltd **Trained** Westow, N Yorks

FOCUS
A fair handicap, and half the field were last-time-out winners, but with the favourite disappointing it perhaps did not take that much winning. The front pair pulled clear and it proved almost a carbon copy of the C&D handicap seven days earlier in which Charging Indian had a neck to spare over Bosamcliff.
Gargano(IRE) Official explanation: trainer had no explanation for the poor form shown

401 MEMBERSHIP OF SOUTHWELL GOLF CLUB H'CAP 1m 6f (F)
3:30 (3:30) (Class 4) (0-85,90) 4-Y-0+ £4,533 (£1,348; £674; £336) Stalls Low

Form RPR
50-5 1 **Victory Quest (IRE)**[34] 3 10-8-12 65...................(v) RobertWinston 4 72
(Mrs S Lamyman) *trckd ldrs: pushed along over 5f out: lost pl and rr 3f out: swtchd rt and rdn wl over 1f out: sn drvn on outer and styd on strly ins fnl f to ld nr fin* 22/1
-222 2 hd **Calculating (IRE)**[6] 352 6-8-10 68.............................. LeeNewnes(5) 3 74
(M D I Usher) *trckd ldrs: hdwy 5f out and sn cl up: effrt wl over 2f out and sn rdn: kpt on to ld 1f out: sn drvn: hdd and no ex nr line* 7/2[2]
11-1 3 1/2 **Shadows Lengthen**[9] 300 4-9-13 90 6ex.............(b) JamesSullivan(5) 1 96
(M W Easterby) *t.k.h: led after 1f: pushed along wl over 2f out: rdn wl over 1f out: drvn and jst hdd 1f out: kpt on gamely tl no ex nr fin* 5/6[1]
35-1 4 3 **Mehendi (IRE)**[34] 1 4-8-2 65................................. DeclanCannon(5) 7 66
(B Ellison) *hld up in rr: hdwy over 5f out: rdn to chse ldrs 3f out: sn drvn and outpcd wl over 1f out: kpt on u.p ins fnl f* 4/1[3]
-013 5 7 **Greenbelt**[14] 244 9-8-7 60 oh5.. PaulHanagan 2 60
(G M Moore) *led 1f: styd prom: rdn along over 3f out: drvn over 2f out and grad wknd* 10/1

3m 7.40s (-0.90) **Going Correction** 0.0s/f (Stan)
WFA 4 from 6yo+ 5lb 5 Ran SP% 110.2
Speed ratings (Par 105): **102,101,101,99,99**
toteswinger:1&2:£8.20 CSF £93.14 TOTE £21.10: £2.90, £1.80; EX 61.70 Trifecta £101.80 Pool: £395.20 - 2.87 winning units..
Owner Mrs S Lamyman **Bred** Miss Veronica Henley **Trained** Ruckland, Lincs

FOCUS
A contest weakened by the three non-runners, but despite the small field the race produced a thrilling finish. The winner produced his best run for about a year, and the favourite probably ran to somewhere near form.

402 SOUTHWELL-RACECOURSE.CO.UK H'CAP 5f (F)
4:00 (4:01) (Class 6) (0-60,60) 4-Y-0+ £2,047 (£604; £302) Stalls High

Form RPR
06-4 1 **Restless Genius (IRE)**[21] 171 5-8-12 59.............. BarryMcHugh(5) 13 71+
(B Ellison) *towards rr: gd hdwy 2f out: rdn over 1f out: str run appr fnl f: led last 75yds: readily* 7/1[2]
000- 2 1 1/4 **The Cuckoo**[92] 7241 4-8-8 50.. FrannyNorton 1 57
(M Quinn) *chsd ldrs: hdwy at 1/2-way: swtchd rt and rdn to ld over 1f out: drvn ins fnl f: hdd and nt qckn last 75yds* 25/1
5-63 3 1 1/4 **Cape Royal**[8] 306 10-9-2 58.......................................(bt) KevinGhunowa 3 61
(J M Bradley) *led: rdn along and hdd 2f out: drvn over 1f out: kpt on u.p ins fnl f* 7/1[2]
-343 4 1/2 **Truly Divine**[13] 271 5-8-4 46 oh1...............................(v) DavidProbert 14 47
(C A Dwyer) *cl up: led 2f out: rdn and hdd over 1f out: drvn and wknd ins fnl f* 14/1
0-11 5 2 **Lujiana**[14] 243 5-8-12 54... RobertWinston 5 48
(M Brittain) *chsd ldrs: rdn along 2f out: drvn over 1f out and sn one pce* 7/4[1]
03-5 6 1 3/4 **Tartatartufata**[23] 138 8-9-4 60...................................(v) LukeMorris 11 48
(J G Given) *towards rr: swtchd lft and moved to far rail: hdwy 2f out: rdn and kpt on appr fnl f: nvr nr ldrs* 18/1
04-6 7 nk **Godfrey Street**[23] 138 7-9-4 60...(p) NeilCallan 6 46
(A G Newcombe) *midfield: rdn along over 2f out: nt rch ldrs* 10/1
63-6 8 3/4 **Handsinthemist (IRE)**[14] 243 5-8-1 48...................(p) PaulPickard(5) 2 32
(P T Midgley) *towards rr: rdn along over 2f out: sme late hdwy* 8/1[3]
0-03 9 1 **Cape Of Storms**[14] 243 7-9-4 60...............................(b) PhillipMakin 12 40
(R Brotherton) *chsd ldrs: rdn along 2f out: sn edgd rt and wknd over 1f out* 12/1
0-06 10 3/4 **Cheshire Rose**[13] 271 5-8-5 47...................................(p) PaulHanagan 4 24
(A M Hales) *a towards rr* 12/1
03-4 11 nse **Divertimenti (IRE)**[28] 69 6-8-10 52...........................(b) GregFairley 10 29
(S R Bowring) *dwlt: a in rr* 16/1
0-04 12 2 **Ronnie Howe**[14] 243 6-8-4 46 oh1...................................(b) LiamJones 7 16
(S R Bowring) *prom: rdn along 2f out: sn edgd rt and wknd* 20/1
00-0 13 4 **Egyptian Lord**[14] 243 7-8-4 46 oh1.......................(b) FrankieMcDonald 9 2
(Peter Grayson) *a in rr* 100/1
00-6 14 10 **Riggs (IRE)**[18] 208 4-8-4 46 oh1.....................................(b) AndrewMullen 8 —
(Peter Grayson) *a in rr* 100/1

59.84 secs (0.14) **Going Correction** +0.075s/f (Slow) 14 Ran SP% 125.4
Speed ratings (Par 101): **101,99,97,96,93 90,89,88,86,85 85,82,76,60**
toteswinger:1&2:£51.90, 2&3:£44.70, 1&3:£9.10 CSF £182.45 CT £1318.03 TOTE £8.90: £2.50, £9.20, £2.10; EX 103.50 TRIFECTA Not won..
Owner Koo's Racing Club **Bred** Sunland Holdings Sc **Trained** Norton, N Yorks

FOCUS
A modest sprint handicap with 11 of the 14 runners sporting at least one type of headgear, but a competitive contest nonetheless. The principals all ended up in the middle of the track crossing the line, but the bias towards low draws wasn't as pronounced as usual with the first four starting from stalls 13, 1, 3 and 14. Fairly sound form with the winner running to a similar level to his one previous C/D start.
Lujiana Official explanation: jockey said mare never travelled
Tartatartufata Official explanation: jockey said mare missed the break
Riggs(IRE) Official explanation: jockey said colt hung left throughout

403 PLAY GOLF BEFORE RACING AT SOUTHWELL H'CAP 6f (F)
4:30 (4:31) (Class 7) (0-50,51) 4-Y-0+ £2,047 (£604; £302) Stalls Low

Form RPR
0-53 1 **Fulford**[9] 296 5-8-7 45.. FrannyNorton 10 59
(M Brittain) *hld up towards rr: smooth hdwy over 2f out: chal over 1f out: rdn to ld ent fnl f: sn clr* 7/4[1]
2-22 2 3 1/4 **Tag Team (IRE)**[13] 264 9-8-12 50...........................(p) RobertWinston 1 54
(John A Harris) *led: rdn 2f out: drvn and hdd ent fnl f: kpt on same pce* 3/1[2]
-000 3 1 1/4 **Bertbrand**[7] 320 5-8-10 48...(v) LiamKeniry 5 48
(I W McInnes) *cl up: effrt 2f out: sn rdn and ev ch tl drvn and wknd ent fnl f* 16/1
0-04 4 1/2 **Mister Incredible**[13] 264 7-8-9 47...................................(b) LukeMorris 6 45
(J M Bradley) *trckd ldrs: hdwy over 2f out: rdn wl over 1f out: kpt on same pce appr fnl f* 6/1[3]
000- 5 1 **Willent**[169] 5145 4-8-7 45.. PaulHanagan 7 40
(Julie Camacho) *chsd ldrs: rdn along over 2f out and grad wknd* 11/1
0-00 6 2 **Owed**[9] 297 8-8-7 45..(tp) GregFairley 8 34
(R Bastiman) *cl up: rdn along wl over 2f out: drvn wl over 1f out and sn wknd* 33/1
050- 7 1 3/4 **Redwater River**[154] 5601 6-8-7 50.................................(b) DeanHeslop(5) 9 33
(Mrs R A Carr) *dwlt: a bhd* 20/1
0/0- 8 4 **Steel Mask (IRE)**[55] 7709 5-8-6 51 ow4..................(t) JohnCavanagh(7) 4 21
(M Brittain) *rrd at s and slowly away: a bhd and hung bdly rt home turn* 12/1
50-2 9 hd **Artesium**[27] 86 4-8-5 48..(b[1]) JamesSullivan(5) 2 18
(Patrick Morris) *chsd ldrs on inner: rdn along over 2f out and grad wknd* 13/2

1m 15.94s (-0.56) **Going Correction** 0.0s/f (Stan) 9 Ran SP% 118.6
Speed ratings (Par 97): **103,98,97,96,95 92,90,84,84**
toteswinger:1&2:£2.70, 2&3:£12.00, 1&3:£10.10 CSF £7.17 CT £62.81 TOTE £2.60: £1.50, £1.10, £3.90; EX 9.30 Trifecta £81.30 Pool: £602.57 - 5.48 winning units. Place 6: £1,346.34, Place 5: £695.96.
Owner Mel Brittain **Bred** D Simpson **Trained** Warthill, N Yorks

FOCUS
A very poor race with recent winning form extremely thin on the ground.
T/Plt: £139.60 to a £1 stake. Pool: £61,810.43 - 323.22 winning units. T/Qpdt: £17.40 to a £1 stake. Pool: £5,750.76 - 244.14 winning units. JR

[368] WOLVERHAMPTON (A.W) (L-H)
Thursday, February 4

OFFICIAL GOING: Standard
Wind: Almost nil Weather: Fine

404 HOTEL & CONFERENCING AT WOLVERHAMPTON APPRENTICE H'CAP 5f 216y(P)
4:50 (4:51) (Class 5) (0-70,70) 4-Y-0+ £2,590 (£770; £385; £192) Stalls Low

Form RPR
065- 1 **Wyatt Earp (IRE)**[157] 5516 9-9-4 69..............................(p) TobyAtkinson 1 79
(P Salmon) *mde all: pushed along 2f out: rdn fnl f: r.o* 8/1
65-3 2 1/2 **Secret Witness**[12] 275 4-9-2 70.................................(b) ShaneRyan(3) 2 79
(R A Harris) *sn prom: chsd wnr over 2f out: rdn and ev ch jst ins fnl f: kpt on* 7/2[1]
0-64 3 2 3/4 **Muktasb (USA)**[20] 193 9-8-0 56 oh2...........................(v) SeanPalmer(5) 3 56
(D Shaw) *hld up in tch: one pce fnl 2f* 16/1
-202 4 1/2 **Dickie Le Davoir**[7] 325 6-8-5 56 oh2..................................(v) BillyCray 8 54
(R C Guest) *s.i.s: in rr: pushed along over 2f out: c v wd st: rdn and r.o ins fnl f: nvr nrr* 15/2
11-2 5 1 1/2 **Welcome Approach**[6] 351 7-8-5 59...................................... DavidKenny(3) 6 53
(J R Weymes) *hld up in mid-div: c wd st: rdn wl over 1f out: no hdwy* 4/1[2]
02-5 6 nse **Fantasy Fighter (IRE)**[24] 119 5-8-10 61............................ KierenFox 9 54
(J J Quinn) *hld up in rr: prog wl over 1f out: no imp fnl f* 5/1[3]
46-1 7 1 1/2 **Raimond Ridge (IRE)**[27] 79 4-8-9 65.............. MatthewCosham(5) 5 54
(J Jay) *s.i.s: hld up in rr on ins: hdwy wl over 1f out: rdn and wknd ins fnl f* 5/1[3]
3135 8 4 1/2 **Know No Fear**[6] 351 5-8-6 58 ow2...................................(p) HollyHall(3) 4 34
(A J Lidderdale) *t.k.h: prom: rdn 2f out: wknd wl over 1f out* 12/1
0-30 9 2 **Carnival Dream**[13] 269 5-8-2 56 oh4................................. LeeTopliss(3) 7 24
(H A McWilliams) *prom tl rdn and wknd 2f out* 25/1

1m 15.27s (0.27) **Going Correction** +0.10s/f (Slow) 9 Ran SP% 115.9
Speed ratings (Par 103): **102,101,97,97,95 94,92,86,84**
toteswinger:1&2:£6.10, 2&3:£3.10, 1&3:£5.70 CSF £36.29 CT £361.66 TOTE £11.10: £3.70, £1.60, £4.70; EX 22.10.
Owner Los Bandidos Racing **Bred** J W Parker And Keith Wills **Trained** Kirk Deighton, West Yorks
■ The first winner as a trainer for former jump jockey Peter Salmon.

FOCUS
A tight opener made more difficult by the probable lack of pace due to several of these being faulty from the stalls. The front pair were always 1-2 and the first three finished in draw order. The winner rather had the run of things.

405 BET SIX NATIONS RUGBY - BETDAQ H'CAP 1m 141y(P)
5:20 (5:20) (Class 4) (0-85,85) 4-Y-0+ £4,209 (£1,252; £625; £312) Stalls Low

Form RPR
-054 1 **Red Somerset (USA)**[5] 359 7-8-10 77........................(b) JimmyQuinn 10 87
(R J Hodges) *hld up in mid-div: hdwy over 3f out: chsd ldr wl over 2f out: led ins fnl f: drvn out* 9/2[2]

36-0 **2** 1 3/4 **River Ardeche**[14] 245 5-8-4 **76**............................(t) PatrickDonaghy[(5)] 7 82
(P C Haslam) *led: pushed along wl over 1f out: hdd ins fnl f: rdn and nt qckn* **16/1**

1-01 **3** 2 1/4 **Caprio (IRE)**[17] 214 5-9-0 **81**.. NickyMackay 9 82+
(J R Boyle) *hld up towards rr: pushed along and hdwy over 2f out: rdn wl over 1f out: sn edgd lft: one pce ins fnl f* **7/1**[3]

40-3 **4** 2 1/2 **Just Bond (IRE)**[20] 197 8-9-4 **85**.................................... PJMcDonald 8 80
(G R Oldroyd) *a.p: pushed along and wknd over 1f out* **9/2**[2]

6546 **5** 5 **Justcallmehandsome**[8] 315 8-7-13 **71**.......................(v) BillyCray[(5)] 2 55
(D J S Ffrench Davis) *nrly uns rdr and s.s: hld up in rr: prog on outside 5f out: pushed along over 2f out: wknd wl over 1f out* **8/1**

-135 **6** 2 1/2 **Follow The Flag (IRE)**[14] 245 6-8-13 **80**...............(p) GrahamGibbons 3 58
(A J McCabe) *hld up towards rr: pushed along over 3f out: no rspnse* **4/1**[1]

05-0 **7** shd **Fandango Boy**[13] 259 9-8-5 **72**.................................... SaleemGolam 5 50
(Ian Williams) *hld up in tch: pushed along over 3f out: wkng whn nt clr run on ins wl over 2f out* **18/1**

0-05 **8** 2 **My Gacho (IRE)**[12] 278 8-9-3 **84**....................................(v) JoeFanning 1 57
(M Johnston) *chsd ldr tl wl over 2f out: sn wknd* **9/2**[2]

3/4- **9** shd **Arabian Flame (IRE)**[35] 1355 4-8-1 **75**.........................(b[1]) CPHoban[(7)] 6 48
(Seamus Fahey, Ire) *hld up in mid-div: pushed along over 2f out: rdn and wknd wl over 1f out* **25/1**

1m 50.21s (-0.29) **Going Correction** +0.10s/f (Slow) 9 Ran SP% **113.1**
Speed ratings (Par 105): **105,103,101,99,94 92,92,90,90**
toteswinger:1&2:£19.00, 2&3:£24.00, 1&3:£7.00 CSF £70.95 CT £493.35 TOTE £4.70: £2.10, £5.40, £1.90; EX 91.00.
Owner R J Hodges **Bred** Haras D'Etreham **Trained** Charlton Mackrell, Somerset

FOCUS
Not a strong race for the grade. The winner was up 6l on recent efforts but may not have had to improve that much. The runer-up enjoyed a pretty easy lead.
Justcallmehandsome Official explanation: jockey said gelding stumbled leaving stalls

406 BETDAQ POKER H'CAP 7f 32y(P)
5:50 (5:51) (Class 4) (0-85,82) 3-Y-O **£4,533** (£1,348; £674; £336) **Stalls** High

Form RPR

-211 **1** **Greyfriarschorista**[8] 311 3-9-3 **78** 6ex............................ JoeFanning 2 95+
(M Johnston) *mde all: clr wl over 1f out: v easily* **2/7**[1]

221- **2** 8 **Robust Wish (USA)**[68] 7580 3-9-6 **81**..............................(b) ShaneKelly 5 72
(B J Meehan) *s.i.s: hld up: hdwy over 2f out: rdn and wnt 2nd over 1f out: no ch w wnr* **4/1**[2]

2555 **3** nk **Transfixed (IRE)**[8] 310 3-8-12 **78**............................ AndrewHeffernan[(5)] 1 68
(P D Evans) *a.p: rdn and one pce fnl 2f* **25/1**

-233 **4** 2 1/2 **Tamarind Hill (IRE)**[21] 168 3-8-1 **67**...................(v[1]) DeclanCannon[(5)] 4 50
(A J McCabe) *hld up: pushed along over 3f out: struggling whn rdn wl over 1f out* **20/1**[3]

403- **5** 2 1/4 **Tukitinyasok (IRE)**[55] 7717 3-9-3 **78**............................ TonyHamilton 6 55
(R F Fisher) *prom tl pushed along and wknd wl over 1f out* **28/1**

1m 29.6s **Going Correction** +0.10s/f (Slow) 5 Ran SP% **109.8**
Speed ratings (Par 99): **104,94,94,91,89**
toteswinger:1&2:£1.70 CSF £1.62 TOTE £1.40: £1.10, £1.50; EX 1.60.
Owner Greyfriars UK Ltd **Bred** Castlemartin Stud And Skymarc Farm **Trained** Middleham Moor, N Yorks

FOCUS
The winner, who was a stone well in, confirmed himself much improved with a very easy win, again recording a good time. There was little depth to this race.

407 GREAT OFFERS ONLINE AT WOLVERHAMPTON-RACECOURSE.CO.UK H'CAP 1m 1f 103y(P)
6:20 (6:20) (Class 7) (0-50,55) 4-Y-O+ **£1,706** (£503; £252) **Stalls** Low

Form RPR

00-2 **1** **Barodine**[6] 354 7-8-12 **48**.. JimmyQuinn 9 61
(R J Hodges) *s.i.s: hld up towards rr: stdy prog over 3f out: chsd ldr over 1f out: rdn to ld wl ins fnl f: drvn out* **9/2**[2]

50-0 **2** 3 **Midnight Bay**[15] 228 4-8-12 **48**.. HayleyTurner 5 55
(P D Evans) *hld up in tch: led jst over 2f out: rdn over 1f out: hdd wl ins fnl f: nt qckn* **16/1**

6221 **3** 5 **Kirstys Lad**[6] 353 8-9-2 **55** 6ex.................................... KellyHarrison[(3)] 7 52
(M Mullineaux) *hld up in mid-div: pushed along and hdwy over 2f out: rdn wl over 1f out: kpt on one pce: tk 3rd last strides* **11/2**[3]

360- **4** hd **My Mirasol**[349] 623 6-9-0 **50**..(p) ChrisCatlin 2 46
(D E Cantillon) *led 2f: w ldr: led over 3f out tl jst over 2f out: wknd wl over 1f out* **12/1**

/00- **5** 1 1/4 **Querido (GER)**[96] 7174 6-9-0 **50**.................................... StephenCraine 1 43
(M Wigham) *prom: chal gng wl over 2f out: sn pushed along: rdn and wknd over 1f out* **9/4**[1]

400- **6** 3/4 **Lytham (IRE)**[145] 5888 9-9-0 **50**.................................... FergusSweeney 8 42
(A W Carroll) *hld up towards rr: pushed along over 2f out: rdn and styd on fr over 1f out: n.d* **13/2**

-032 **7** 1 1/2 **Libre**[6] 347 10-8-13 **49**.. JoeFanning 13 38
(F Jordan) *hld up towards rr: hmpd over 3f out: sn pushed along: sme prog 2f out: nvr nr ldrs* **10/1**

500- **8** 3 **Royal Premium**[64] 6411 4-8-13 **49**................................ DarrenMoffatt 3 31
(James Moffatt) *hld up in mid-div: pushed along over 3f out: rdn and wknd wl over 1f out* **22/1**

606- **9** 1/2 **Flaming Blaze**[82] 3541 4-8-7 **48**...........................(tp) PatrickDonaghy[(5)] 4 29
(P C Haslam) *s.i.s: in rr: pushed along over 3f out: sn struggling* **20/1**

0-50 **10** 2 1/4 **Wacato King (IRE)**[15] 228 4-8-7 **48**.................... AndrewHeffernan[(5)] 11 25
(R A Farrant) *prom: rdn and wknd wl over 2f out* **33/1**

000- **11** 9 **Magic Queen (IRE)**[92] 7240 4-8-9 **50**....................(t) MatthewDavies[(5)] 6 8
(A P Jarvis) *hld up in mid-div: pushed along whn n.m.r on ins over 3f out: sn bhd* **80/1**

2-34 **12** 9 **Dovedon Angel**[24] 130 4-9-0 **50**................................(p) SteveDrowne 12 —
(Miss Gay Kelleway) *sn w ldr: led after 2f tl over 3f out: wknd wl over 2f out* **12/1**

2m 3.02s (1.32) **Going Correction** +0.10s/f (Slow) 12 Ran SP% **121.3**
Speed ratings (Par 97): **98,95,90,90,89 88,87,84,84,82 74,66**
toteswinger:1&2:£24.50, 2&3:£12.20, 1&3:£6.20 CSF £72.52 CT £413.47 TOTE £7.70: £2.10, £4.80, £2.30; EX 51.50.
Owner The Gardens Entertainments Ltd **Bred** Mrs A M Jenkins And E D Kessly **Trained** Charlton Mackrell, Somerset

FOCUS
The first two finished clear. The winner is rated back to his best and the runner-up to his recent best in this bottom-grade handicap.
Querido(GER) Official explanation: trainer said gelding scoped poorly
Flaming Blaze Official explanation: jockey said gelding never travelled

408 BET IN RUNNING - BETDAQ CONDITIONS STKS 1m 1f 103y(P)
6:50 (6:50) (Class 3) 4-Y-O+ **£6,938** (£2,076; £1,038; £519; £258) **Stalls** Low

Form RPR

4436 **1** **Full Toss**[5] 360 4-8-9 **90**.. AndrewHeffernan[(5)] 2 96
(P D Evans) *led early: chsd ldr: rdn to ld over 1f out: drvn out* **2/1**[1]

56-4 **2** 1 1/4 **Snow Dancer (IRE)**[13] 266 6-8-4 **80**............................ JamesSullivan[(5)] 6 88
(H A McWilliams) *hmpd s: hld up in rr: hdwy over 1f out: r.o to take 2nd towards fin: nt rch wnr* **16/1**

00-0 **3** 1 1/2 **Cobo Bay**[20] 197 5-8-9 **88**...(b) AmyRyan[(5)] 3 90
(K A Ryan) *wnt rt s: sn led: rdn and hdd over 1f out: no ex ins fnl f* **9/2**[3]

31-1 **4** 2 1/4 **Ours (IRE)**[14] 245 7-8-9 **85**.......................................(p) BarryMcHugh[(5)] 5 85
(John A Harris) *hmpd s: hld up: pushed along over 2f out: hung lft fr over 1f out: nvr trbld ldrs* **13/2**

01-6 **5** 3/4 **Scamperdale**[20] 197 8-9-0 **86**.. TonyCulhane 1 83
(B P J Baugh) *hld up: hdwy on ins over 2f out: sn pushed along: rdn and fdd ins fnl f* **12/1**

16-5 **6** 4 1/2 **Rock Ascot (URU)**[19] 205 6-9-0 **94**.............................(b) GeorgeBaker 7 74
(G L Moore) *hld up: stdy hdwy over 3f out: rdn and wknd wl over 1f out* **9/4**[2]

2m 1.00s (-0.70) **Going Correction** +0.10s/f (Slow) 6 Ran SP% **109.2**
Speed ratings (Par 107): **107,105,104,102,101 97**
toteswinger:1&2:£6.40, 2&3:£6.40, 1&3:£2.70 CSF £29.85 TOTE £3.30: £1.40, £4.70; EX 28.90.
Owner Mrs Sally Edwards **Bred** The Queen **Trained** Pandy, Monmouths
■ Stewards' Enquiry : Andrew Heffernan caution: used whip with excessive frequency.

FOCUS
A muddling conditions race in which the winner ran to form and the runner-up seemed to confirm the improvement of her latest run, also against today's winner.

NOTEBOOK
Full Toss won his second race since being claimed for £12,000 after winning at Lingfield in December over slightly further than this and although his only subsequent win in eight outings came over 1m3f on the slower Southwell surface, this looks more suitable. Racing off a 4lb higher mark here, he stayed on strongly enough but he has been beaten on his last three starts off a 1lb higher mark than this, so the handicapper knows just how to tweak him. (op 9-4)
Snow Dancer(IRE), last successful off 10lb lower here in November, produced an improved effort in defeat on a direct line through the winner, who had finished a neck ahead of her 13 days previously and was 7lb better off here. Snow Dancer also had to come from off the pace after meeting trouble at the start, so a praisworthy effort all round. (op 20-1 tchd 22-1)
Cobo Bay caused problems by veering right at the start but overcame the deviation then couldn't last home despite the small field size looking statistically in his favour. (op 4-1)
Ours(IRE) got a bump at the start but that was no excuse, more the 6lb rise for winning last time which puts him on a career high. (op 7-1)
Scamperdale remains on a career-high mark and was always struggling when the pace quickened. (op 11-1)
Rock Ascot(URU) ran very flat and was eased. Official explanation: trainer had no explanation for the poor form shown (tchd 5-2)

409 ENJOY LUCKY 7 GROUP OFFER H'CAP 2m 119y(P)
7:20 (7:21) (Class 6) (0-60,61) 4-Y-O+ **£2,047** (£604; £302) **Stalls** Low

Form RPR

432- **1** **Sinbad The Sailor**[105] 6969 5-9-4 **58**....................(v) MatthewDavies[(5)] 2 73
(George Baker) *a.p: wnt 2nd over 7f out: led over 3f out: clr whn rdn wl over 1f out: styd on wl* **12/1**

0-04 **2** 4 1/2 **Sir Sandicliffe (IRE)**[20] 198 6-8-9 **51**............................ KierenFox[(7)] 3 61
(W M Brisbourne) *s.i.s: hld up in rr: stdy hdwy over 4f out: rdn to chse wnr wl over 1f out: hung lft ent fnl f: no imp* **14/1**

4-42 **3** 9 **Baltimore Patriot (IRE)**[7] 322 7-9-10 **59**...................... TonyCulhane 5 58
(R Curtis) *hld up in tch: pushed along to chse wnr wl over 2f out: rdn and lost 2nd wl over 1f out: sn wknd* **13/2**[3]

0-35 **4** 5 **Sonny Sam (IRE)**[18] 210 5-9-1 **50**............................ FrederikTylicki 6 43
(R A Fahey) *hld up in mid-div: hdwy wl over 2f out: sn rdn: wknd wl over 1f out* **6/1**[2]

/0-0 **5** 1 3/4 **Treeko (IRE)**[33] 15 5-9-6 **55**...(p) LeeVickers 10 46
(P A Kirby) *hld up in mid-div: pushed along and wknd 3f out* **40/1**

160- **6** 7 **Market Watcher (USA)**[39] 7578 9-8-13 **55**...................... CPHoban[(7)] 8 38
(Seamus Fahey, Ire) *hld up in tch: rdn over 3f out: wknd wl over 2f out* **33/1**

-211 **7** 2 1/2 **Aaman (IRE)**[2] 376 4-9-6 **61** 6ex.. LiamKeniry 9 41
(E F Vaughan) *sn chsng ldr: led after 4f tl over 3f out: rdn and wknd over 2f out* **8/11**[1]

02-4 **8** 1 1/2 **Blackstone Vegas**[31] 32 4-8-9 **57**............................ SeanPalmer[(7)] 12 35
(D Shaw) *hld up towards rr: struggling over 3f out* **66/1**

6/0- **9** 3 1/2 **Foreign King (USA)**[76] 59 6-9-4 **53**................................ ChrisCatlin 4 27
(J W Mullins) *led 4f: chsd ldr tl over 7f out: wknd wl over 3f out* **33/1**

4- **10** 2 1/2 **Academy Gigsnreels (USA)**[49] 7779 5-9-8 **57**.............. DaneO'Neill 13 28
(Seamus Fahey, Ire) *a in rr* **33/1**

000- **11** 23 **Vertueux (FR)**[49] 7124 5-9-5 **54**.......................................(v[1]) LukeMorris 1 —
(A W Carroll) *prom: pushed along 9f out: rdn over 5f out: sn wknd: t.o fnl 3f* **40/1**

12 23 **Soprano (GER)**[11] 8-9-9 **58**..(p) GeorgeBaker 11 —
(Jonjo O'Neill) *a in rr: t.o fnl 5f* **28/1**

3m 42.92s (1.12) **Going Correction** +0.10s/f (Slow)
WFA 4 from 5yo+ 6lb 12 Ran SP% **118.5**
Speed ratings (Par 101): **101,98,94,92,91 88,87,86,84,83 72,61**
toteswinger:1&2:£19.00, 2&3:£10.00, 1&3:£4.70 CSF £154.20 CT £1195.36 TOTE £13.40: £2.40, £2.90, £2.40; EX 112.70.
Owner Sir Alex Ferguson **Bred** Sir Eric Parker **Trained** Moreton Morrell, Warwicks

FOCUS
A well run handicap. The well-in favourite was unable to match his recent Southwell runs but this is probably still sound form overall, rated around the runner-up. The first two finished clear.
Aaman(IRE) Official explanation: trainer rep said run may have come too soon
Vertueux(FR) Official explanation: jockey said gelding clipped heels with a circuit to run
Soprano(GER) Official explanation: trainer had no explanation for the poor form shown

410 RINGSIDE CONFERENCE SUITE, 700 THEATRE STYLE H'CAP (DIV I) 1m 4f 50y(P)
7:50 (7:50) (Class 6) (0-55,55) 4-Y-O+ **£1,706** (£503; £252) **Stalls** Low

Form RPR

0/2- **1** **Shandelight (IRE)**[59] 7670 6-8-6 **50**............................ BarryMcHugh[(5)] 1 63+
(Julie Camacho) *hld up in tch: wnt 2nd 4f out: rdn jst over 1f out: led wl ins fnl f: r.o* **9/2**[2]

00-6 **2** 1 **Colonel Sherman (USA)**[31] 36 5-9-0 **53**............................ LeeVickers 3 65
(P A Kirby) *plld hrd: led: clr over 7f out: rdn and hdd wl ins fnl f: no ex* **11/4**[1]

30-4 **3** *6* **John Potts**[20] 199 5-8-10 **49** ow2 .... TonyCulhane 11 51
(B P J Baugh) *hld up in mid-div: hdwy over 3f out: pushed along wl over 1f out: rdn and wknd ins fnl f* **25/1**

/10- **4** *3 ½* **Muncaster Castle (IRE)**[350] 608 6-8-12 **51** .... TonyHamilton 7 47
(R F Fisher) *sn chsng ldr: lost 2nd 4f out: sn wknd* **40/1**

452/ **5** *½* **Trysting Grove (IRE)**[531] 5232 9-8-8 **52** .... AshleyMorgan(5) 6 48
(E G Bevan) *s.i.s: hld up in rr: hdwy on outside over 1f out: c wd st: wknd wl over 1f out* **14/1**

65-5 **6** *1 ½* **Our Kes (IRE)**[20] 184 8-9-2 **55** .... RobertWinston 9 48
(P Howling) *hld up in mid-div: hdwy 4f out: rdn and wknd 2f out* **5/1**[3]

05-2 **7** *2* **Turner's Touch**[20] 184 8-8-2 **48** ....(b) HarryBentley(7) 10 38
(G L Moore) *s.s: sn swtchd lft: hld up in rr: hdwy 4f out: wknd 2f out* **8/1**

505- **8** *nse* **Key Of Fortune (IRE)**[185] 4593 4-8-7 **49** .... JoeFanning 4 39
(Jennie Candlish) *hld up in mid-div: pushed along and wknd 3f out* **14/1**

06/0 **9** *3 ¾* **Mandalay Prince**[14] 244 6-9-0 **53** .... StevieDonohoe 8 37
(W J Musson) *s.i.s: a in rr* **40/1**

6-03 **10** *6* **Always The Sun**[8] 316 4-7-13 **48** .... RyanPowell(7) 2 22
(P Leech) *prom tl wknd 4f out* **9/1**

-060 **11** *10* **Climate (IRE)**[6] 353 11-9-2 **55** ....(p) GeorgeBaker 12 13
(P D Evans) *hld up in tch: pushed along and wknd 3f out* **33/1**

40-0 **12** *14* **Son Of Monsieur**[18] 211 4-8-4 **46** .... JimmyQuinn 5 —
(G R Oldroyd) *hld up in tch: lost pl 4f out: rdn and bhd fnl 3f* **14/1**

2m 43.42s (2.32) **Going Correction** +0.10s/f (Slow)
WFA 4 from 5yo+ 3lb **12** Ran SP% **114.3**
Speed ratings (Par 101): **96,95,91,89,88 87,86,86,83,79 73,63**
toteswinger:1&2:£5.00, 2&3:£23.50, 1&3:£12.70 CSF £15.93 CT £269.09 TOTE £6.40: £2.00, £2.00, £3.90; EX 19.30.
Owner Bolingbroke, Andrew, Jordan, Thompson **Bred** Limestone And Tara Studs **Trained** Norton, N Yorks

FOCUS
A pretty weak race but the winner is rated back to her best. The first two finished clear.
Son Of Monsieur Official explanation: jockey said gelding moved poorly throughout

411 RINGSIDE CONFERENCE SUITE, 700 THEATRE STYLE H'CAP (DIV II) 1m 4f 50y(P)
8:20 (8:20) (Class 6) (0-55,55) 4-Y-0+ **£1,706** (£503; £252) **Stalls** Low

Form RPR

15-5 **1** **Dazzling Begum**[23] 140 5-8-11 **50** .... RobertHavlin 7 56
(J Pearce) *hld up in tch: led wl over 1f out: rdn and edgd rt ins fnl f: r.o* **11/2**[2]

34-2 **2** *nk* **Valkyrie (IRE)**[13] 263 4-8-4 **46** .... LukeMorris 9 52
(N P Littmoden) *hld up in tch: wnt 2nd over 3f out: led jst over 2f out: rdn and hdd wl over 1f out: carried rt ins fnl f: r.o* **4/1**[1]

54-3 **3** *½* **They All Laughed**[7] 331 7-9-0 **53** ....(p) PJMcDonald 12 58
(Mrs Marjorie Fife) *hld up towards rr: rdn 3f out: c wd st: hdwy over 1f out: r.o to take 3rd cl home* **6/1**[3]

346- **4** *¾* **Lisbon Lion (IRE)**[51] 7085 5-9-0 **53** .... DarrenMoffatt 10 57
(James Moffatt) *hld up in rr: hdwy over 2f out: rdn and carried rt ins fnl f: kpt on* **50/1**

00-0 **5** *1* **Solo Choice**[16] 227 4-8-5 **47** .... SaleemGolam 4 49
(I W McInnes) *hld up in mid-div: pushed along 3f out: hdwy 1f out: rdn and kpt on same pce* **40/1**

464 **6** *2 ¼* **Haka Dancer (USA)**[14] 246 7-8-13 **52** ....(b[1]) LeeVickers 8 51
(P A Kirby) *hld up towards rr: hdwy 3f out: rdn and btn over 1f out* **6/1**[3]

600- **7** *2 ¾* **Lough Beg (IRE)**[133] 1463 7-9-0 **53** ....(t) DaneO'Neill 2 47
(Miss Tor Sturgis) *hld up in mid-div: pushed along and hdwy on ins whn nt clr run briefly 2f out: rdn over 1f out: eased whn btn towards fin* **11/1**

356- **8** *8* **Diktatorship (IRE)**[52] 7750 7-8-7 **46** .... JoeFanning 5 27
(Jennie Candlish) *w ldr: led 6f out: rdn and hdd jst over 2f out: wknd over 1f out* **10/1**

00-6 **9** *nse* **Bubses Boy**[24] 130 4-8-5 **50** .... MichaelStainton(3) 1 31
(P Howling) *t.k.h: led: hdd 6f out: rdn and wknd wl over 3f out* **16/1**

055- **10** *8* **Corrib (IRE)**[48] 7803 7-8-7 **46** .... DavidProbert 3 15
(B Palling) *hld up in mid-div: pushed along and hdwy 3f out: rdn and wknd 2f out* **20/1**

431- **11** *3 ½* **Through The Forest (USA)**[48] 7794 4-8-12 **54** .... ChrisCatlin 11 17
(W R Swinburn) *prom tl wknd wl over 2f out* **4/1**[1]

56-6 **12** *2* **Flighty Fellow (IRE)**[13] 261 10-9-2 **55** ....(v) VinceSlattery 6 15
(B G Powell) *hld up towards rr: rdn 3f out: struggling 2f out* **22/1**

2m 42.7s (1.60) **Going Correction** +0.10s/f (Slow)
WFA 4 from 5yo+ 3lb **12** Ran SP% **120.8**
Speed ratings (Par 101): **98,97,97,96,96 94,92,87,87,82 79,78**
toteswinger:1&2:£3.90, 2&3:£4.90, 1&3:£7.30 CSF £27.21 CT £140.29 TOTE £7.60: £2.20, £2.50, £2.20; EX 37.30 Place 6: £230.75, Place 5: £77.88.
Owner Macniler Racing Partnership **Bred** Ian Bryant **Trained** Newmarket, Suffolk
■ Stewards' Enquiry : Robert Havlin caution: careless riding.

FOCUS
A weak handicap with the many of the field struggling to regain threads of form. The winner is rated to the level of his December win.
T/Plt: £418.50 to a £1 stake. Pool: £77,803.47. 135.71 winning tickets. T/Qpdt: £22.30 to a £1 stake. Pool: £10,986.23. 363.00 winning tickets. KH

[333]MEYDAN (L-H)
Thursday, February 4
OFFICIAL GOING: All-weather - standard; turf course - good to firm
The Tapeta track was riding slow according to Richard Hills.

412a DUBAL INTERNATIONAL CASTHOUSE TROPHY (H'CAP) (TAPETA) 1m
2:35 (2:36) (90-105,105) 3-Y-0+
£40,740 (£13,580; £6,790; £3,395; £2,037; £1,358)

RPR

1 **Al Arab (BRZ)**[131] 5-9-2 100 .... WBlandi 2 106+
(A Cintra Pereira, Brazil) *mid-div: chsd ldrs over 2 1/2f out: led 2f out: comf* **11/1**

2 *4 ¼* **Swift Gift**[131] 6270 5-9-0 98 .... TedDurcan 12 94
(B J Meehan) *mid-div: r.o wl ins fnl 1 1/2f: no ch w wnr* **7/2**[2]

3 *2 ¾* **Sovereign Remedy (USA)**[101] 7060 4-9-4 102 .... FrankieDettori 6 92
(Saeed Bin Suroor) *wl away: hld up in mid-div: chsd ldrs 2f out: one pce ins fnl f* **10/3**[1]

4 *¼* **Abbashiva (GER)**[200] 4129 5-9-5 104 ....(t) ChristopheSoumillon 4 92
(T Mundry, Germany) *trckd ldrs: ev ch 2f out: nt qckn* **16/1**

5 *½* **Balcarce Nov (ARG)**[21] 175 5-9-5 104 .... JamieSpencer 7 91
(T P Tate) *in rr of mid-div: hdwy and styd on fnl f: nrst fin* **7/1**[3]

6 *hd* **Commander Cave (USA)**[27] 5-9-2 100 ....(t) PJSmullen 5 87
(E Charpy, UAE) *hld up on rail in mid-div: chsd ldrs 2 1/2f out: one pce ins fnl f* **25/1**

7 *1* **Ocean's Minstrel**[7] 338 4-9-4 102 .... AlanMunro 3 87
(J Ryan) *trckd ldrs: ev ch 1 1/2f out: nt qckn* **33/1**

8 *3 ¼* **Ceremonial Jade (UAE)**[26] 108 7-9-6 105 ....(t) KierenFallon 10 82
(M Botti) *a in mid-div* **7/1**[3]

9 *1 ½* **King Jock (USA)**[123] 6530 9-8-13 97 .... RichardThomas 14 71
(A Manuel, UAE) *settled in rr: nvr able to chal* **18/1**

10 *½* **Masaalek**[32] 5-9-1 99 ....(v) RichardHills 1 72
(Doug Watson, UAE) *mid-div: chsd ldrs 2f out: one pce fnl f* **20/1**

11 *4 ½* **Born To Be King (USA)**[32] 4-9-0 98 ....(t) DaraghO'Donohoe 11 61
(D Selvaratnam, UAE) *rrd s: bhd: n.d* **40/1**

12 *1 ¾* **World Ruler**[20] 5-9-2 100 .... PatDobbs 8 59
(Doug Watson, UAE) *nvr bttr than mid-div* **16/1**

13 *1 ¾* **Liberation (IRE)**[96] 7185 4-9-4 102 .... AhmedAjtebi 9 57
(Saeed Bin Suroor) *nvr bttr than mid-div* **10/1**

14 *1 ½* **Taqdeyr**[6] 5-9-4 102 .... CSanchez 13 53
(A bin Huzaim, UAE) *sn led: clr 3 1/2f out: hdd 2f out: wknd* **16/1**

1m 39.7s (99.70) **14** Ran SP% **124.6**

Owner Haras Figueira Do Lago **Bred** Haras Figueira Do Lago **Trained** Brazil

FOCUS
They went a strong pace and this looks strong carnival form. That said a number of these were out of form going into the race.

NOTEBOOK
Al Arab(BRZ), a Group 3 winner and more recently a Listed winner in Brazil, showed himself to be well handicapped on his UAE debut, picking up smartly for a convincing success, having been well placed. Horses from Brazil don't always progress in Dubai, but this one must have a good chance of defying a rise if going the right way.
Swift Gift ◆ had raced exclusively over 7f on his 14 previous starts, but he stayed this trip well. The winner very much got first run on him, but he kept on nicely and this was a pleasing return from over four months off. He should be well up to winning at this year's carnival, especially considering he's versatile as regards trip and surface. (op 4-1)
Sovereign Remedy(USA) looked smart when winning a decent Fibresand handicap last October, but he's yet to prove himself fully effective on other surfaces. This was a solid effort, but still short of his peak form.
Abbashiva(GER), a German Group 3 winner in 2008, found little in the straight and possibly paid for having over-raced close to a strong pace.
Balcarce Nov(ARG) was set a lot to do and was switched out wide with his challenge entering the straight, but even allowing for that, he failed to pick up as well as one might have hoped.
Commander Cave(USA) has been lightly raced since switching to the UAE but he showed he retains plenty of ability. (op 20-1)
Ceremonial Jade(UAE) usually races over shorter these days and, although he managed a win and a second from his only two previous tries over this trip, he made no impression this time under top weight. (op 15-2)
Taqdeyr will surely be suited by a return to shorter.

413a DUBAL INTERNATIONAL BILLET TROPHY (H'CAP) (TAPETA) 7f
3:10 (3:14) (95-110,108) 3-Y-0+
£44,444 (£14,814; £7,407; £3,703; £2,222; £1,481)

RPR

1 **Mutheeb (USA)**[7] 339 5-9-1 104 .... RichardHills 1 111
(M Al Muhairi, UAE) *trckd ldrs: smooth prog to ld 1 1/2f out: easily* **6/1**[2]

2 *5* **Stoic (IRE)**[133] 6229 4-8-8 97 .... RyanMoore 13 93+
(J Noseda) *settled in rr: r.o wl fnl 1 1/2f: nrest at fin* **6/5**[1]

3 *1 ¾* **Gallagher**[173] 5024 4-9-4 107 .... JamieSpencer 5 96
(B J Meehan) *settled in mid-div: chsd wnr 2f out: r.o same pce* **11/1**

4 *¾* **Al Khaleej (IRE)**[180] 4796 6-8-11 100 .... TedDurcan 7 87
(E A L Dunlop) *s.i.s: in rr of mid-div: r.o fnl 2f* **18/1**

5 *¼* **Lovelace**[7] 338 6-9-5 108 .... KierenFallon 9 94
(M Johnston) *a in mid-div* **8/1**[3]

6 *¼* **Proclaim**[131] 6270 4-8-6 95 .... AhmedAjtebi 3 80
(Saeed Bin Suroor) *sn led: rdn 2 1/2f out: hdd 1 1/2f out: r.o same pce* **9/1**

7 *1 ¼* **Across The Rhine (USA)**[104] 7010 4-8-10 99 .... PJSmullen 2 81
(A Manuel, UAE) *settled in mid-div: rdn 3 1/2f out: kpt on same pce* **16/1**

8 *¼* **Khor Dubai (IRE)**[7] 337 4-9-1 104 .... CSanchez 14 85
(A bin Huzaim, UAE) *racd in rr: sn rdn: r.o fnl 2f* **25/1**

9 *3 ¾* **Aamaaq**[27] 7-8-6 95 ....(b) TadhgO'Shea 4 66
(A Al Raihe, UAE) *trckd ldr tl 2 1/2f out: wknd* **33/1**

10 *½* **Warsaw (IRE)**[7] 339 5-9-0 102 ....(b) ChristopheSoumillon 8 73
(M F De Kock, South Africa) *nvr bttr than mid-div* **16/1**

11 *3 ½* **Capricorn Run (USA)**[50] 7768 7-8-11 100 ....(v) JamesDoyle 11 60
(A J McCabe) *mid-div: rdn 3f out: wknd* **33/1**

12 *½* **Seachantach (USA)**[7] 339 4-8-6 98 ....(t) MartinLane(3) 6 57
(D M Simcock) *nvr bttr than mid-div* **50/1**

13 *2 ¼* **Fares (IRE)**[48] 6-8-6 95 ....(v) PatDobbs 10 48
(Doug Watson, UAE) *nvr able to chal* **40/1**

14 *9 ¼* **Skywards**[328] 8-8-6 95 ....(t) DavidBadel 12 23
(E Charpy, UAE) *nvr able to chal* **40/1**

1m 26.18s (86.18) **14** Ran SP% **122.8**

Owner Hamdan Al Maktoum **Bred** Jayeff B Stables **Trained** UAE

FOCUS
A good handicap that should produce carnival winners. The pace seemed decent enough.

NOTEBOOK
Mutheeb(USA) ◆ raced too keenly with little cover when well behind the smart-looking Leahurst from stall nine over C&D the previous week, but he was better placed this time, tracking the leaders from the off, and extended well in the straight to draw nicely clear of his rivals. It needs pointing out that he's flattered by the manner of his success, with the runner-up unlucky not to finish much closer, but he's a relatively lightly raced colt with the scope to go on improving and he should be competitive off higher ratings. (op 8-1)
Stoic(IRE) ◆, a progressive type who had been gelded since completing a hat-trick of wins over 1m, the last of which came off a 7lb lower mark, was left with too much to do after Ryan Moore elected to drop him out towards the rear from his wide draw, and his chance was further compromised when he had his path blocked early in the straight until around a furlong out by Lovelace. The manner in which he finished his race, without being given a hard time, was most encouraging and, granted a better trip next time, he should be well up to gaining compensation, especially if stepped back up in trip. (op 11-10)
Gallagher didn't look badly treated off a mark of 107 for his first start in a handicap, but he had been off for nearly six months and ran like a horse in need of the run.
Al Khaleej(IRE), returning from a six-month break, was a bit keen tucked away towards the inside early on and didn't look totally comfortable around the turn. In the circumstances, this was a decent effort and there might be a bit more to come.

Lovelace seemed unsuited by the drop back in trip and couldn't build on recent promise. He has become difficult to get right.
Proclaim went without any headgear (has worn blinkers and a visor) on first run since leaving Mark Johnston and found a few too strong after setting a decent pace. (op 15-2)
Across The Rhine(USA) had been raised 9lb for winning a Dundalk handicap in October, but that form didn't really work out.
Warsaw(IRE) ◆ again shaped as though he'll do better back over shorter, racing keenly through the early stages before fading late on. (op 14-1)

414a UAE 2000 GUINEAS TRIAL SPONSORED BY DUBAL INTERNATIONAL (CONDITIONS RACE) (TAPETA) 7f

3:45 (3:49) 3-Y-O

£18,518 (£6,172; £3,086; £1,543; £925; £617)

RPR

1 **Musir (AUS)**[215] 4-9-11 108 ChristopheSoumillon 1 109
(M F De Kock, South Africa) *mid-div: smooth prog to ld 1 1/2f out: r.o wl* **13/8**[1]
2 ¼ **Frozen Power (IRE)**[108] 6898 3-8-8 105 FrankieDettori 10 98
(Saeed Bin Suroor) *mid-div: chsd ldrs 2f out: r.o wl: nrest at fin* **9/2**[2]
3 1 ¼ **Oroveso (BRZ)**[124] 6505 4-9-4 96 TJPereira 6 98
(P Bary, France) *trckd ldrs: disp ld: led 2f out to 1 1/2f out: one pce fnl 110yds* **33/1**
4 ¾ **Solid Choice (AUS)**[194] 4-9-4 102 KShea 8 96
(M F De Kock, South Africa) *mid-div: chsd ldrs 2f out: nt qckn fnl f* **7/1**[3]
5 1 ½ **Black Snowflake (USA)**[108] 6898 3-8-8 97 AhmedAjtebi 2 89
(Saeed Bin Suroor) *mid-div: r.o fnl 1 1/2f* **20/1**
6 1 ¾ **Jardim (BRZ)**[138] 4-9-6 102 WBlandi 5 89
(A Cintra Pereira, Brazil) *disp ld: rdn to ld 2f out: hdd ins fnl f* **16/1**
7 2 ¼ **Mr. Crazy Boy (ARG)**[250] 4-9-8 98 RyanMoore 9 85
(M F De Kock, South Africa) *racd in rr: r.o fnl 1 1/2f: n.d* **12/1**
8 ¼ **Coeur Loyal (CHI)**[299] 4-9-6 95 TedDurcan 7 82
(Saeed Bin Suroor) *nvr able to chal* **10/1**
9 2 **Rock Jock (IRE)**[109] 6883 3-8-8 99 PJSmullen 13 72
(A Manuel, UAE) *nvr bttr than mid-div* **33/1**
10 ¾ **El Amarillista (ARG)**[279] 4-9-4 102 (t) OlivierPeslier 11 73
(J Barton, Saudi Arabia) *a mid-div* **12/1**
11 4 ¼ **Olympic Danz (BRZ)**[89] 4-9-4 98 RichardMullen 3 62
(A Cintra Pereira, Brazil) *s.i.s: trckd ldrs for 4f: wknd* **28/1**
12 1 ½ **Astonishment (IRE)**[108] 6898 3-8-8 95 KierenFallon 4 54
(F Nass, Bahrain) *disp ld tl 2f out: wknd* **33/1**
13 ½ **Percusionist (ARG)**[381] 4-9-4 98 MickaelBarzalona 12 56
(Saeed Bin Suroor) *sn rdn in rr: nvr able to chal* **20/1**
14 5 ¼ **Lamh Albasser (USA)**[117] 6663 3-8-8 97 JRosales 14 39
(A bin Huzaim, UAE) *trckd ldrs tl 2f out: wknd* **40/1**

1m 26.95s (86.95)
WFA 3 from 4yo 17lb 14 Ran SP% **123.4**

Owner Sheikh Mohammed Bin Khalifa Al Maktoum **Bred** Sh Mohd Bin Khalifa Al Maktoum **Trained** South Africa

FOCUS
This is the first time that this contest has been named as a trial, but the equivalent event was won by the subsequent UAE 2,000 Guineas winner in four of the last five years. The race has also produced the winner of the UAE Derby for the last three seasons. This year's race looked a strong contest, with loads of Graded/Group form on offer from around the world, and there was a potentially high-class winner. The early pace seemed surprisingly modest.

NOTEBOOK
Musir(AUS), last year's champion juvenile in South Africa, produced a really smart effort under the penalty he picked up for his Grade 1 success. He seemed to start awkwardly, and his jockey reported afterwards that the colt was trying to go out to his left, with there being no rail on his inside for a short period after a few yards. However, once this son of Redoute's Choice was covered up in about mid-division, he travelled strongly and was still on the bridle, going best, early in the straight. He didn't exactly sprint clear when coming under pressure over a furlong out, but he kept finding extra as the runner-up attempted to close the gap near the line, and in any case, not only was he carrying a big weight, but the steady early gallop was hardly conducive to an explosive change of pace. Unsurprisingly, the winner will now be aimed at the UAE Triple Crown series, where he'll probably face stiffer competition, and have his stamina for 1m-plus to prove, but at least he won't have a penalty to contend with in the Guineas or Derby.
Frozen Power(IRE), who was said by Saeed Bin Suroor to have improved physically since last year, was always being held by the winner. He'll be worthy of his place in the Triple Crown, but that said, it will be surprising if Godolphin don't have better horses for that series.
Oroveso(BRZ), Grade 1-placed over 1m in Brazil but last seen finishing down the field in a Group 2 at Longchamp on Arc weekend, was always nicely positioned and ran on to the line. This was a decent effort.
Solid Choice(AUS) actually defeated Musir in a conditions event last year but was considered immature and couldn't confirm that form in Grade 1 company. He ran creditably this time, but couldn't take advantage of the handy weight concession he received from the favourite.
Black Snowflake(USA) ran okay but simply didn't look quite good enough for this sort of company.
Jardim(BRZ), whose four wins in Brazil include a Grade 3 success, wasn't given a hard time once held and gave the impression he would come on for the run.
Mr. Crazy Boy(ARG) was outpaced for most of the way.
Coeur Loyal(CHI) had been off since winning a Grade 3 in Chile in April 2009 and lacked sharpness.

415a DUBAL INTERNATIONAL POTLINE TROPHY (H'CAP) (TAPETA) 1m 1f 110y

4:19 (4:22) (95-110,108) 3-Y-O+

£44,444 (£14,814; £7,407; £3,703; £2,222; £1,481)

RPR

1 **Mr Brock (SAF)**[82] 7408 7-9-3 106 KShea 8 111+
(M F De Kock, South Africa) *trckd ldrs: smooth prog to ld 1f out: r.o wl* **6/1**
2 3 ¾ **Tartan Gigha (IRE)**[7] 334 5-8-8 97 RyanMoore 1 94
(M Johnston) *mid-div on rail: led briefly 1 1/2f out: nt qckn fnl 110yrds* **5/2**[1]
3 1 ¼ **Walzertraum (USA)**[124] 6500 5-9-4 107 (p) OlivierPeslier 7 101
(Manfred Hofer, Germany) *mid-div: r.o wl fnl 2f* **11/1**
4 4 ¾ **Pascal (USA)**[27] 5-8-6 95 (t) TadhgO'Shea 5 80
(E Charpy, UAE) *settled in rr: r.o fnl 1 1/2f* **33/1**
5 ¾ **Soy Libriano (ARG)**[313] 1009 5-9-2 105 (t) AhmedAjtebi 11 88+
(Saeed Bin Suroor) *in rr of mid-div: r.o wl fnl 2f* **9/2**[2]
6 ¾ **Lucky Ray (ARG)**[20] 7-8-7 96 (vt) PatDobbs 9 78
(Doug Watson, UAE) *ld: hdd 1 1/2f out: kpt on one pce* **12/1**
7 ¼ **Royal Prince**[55] 9-8-6 95 DaraghO'Donohoe 4 76
(Doug Watson, UAE) *settled in rr: n.m.r in mid-div 1 1/2f out: nt rcvr* **33/1**
8 1 ¼ **Book Of Music (IRE)**[46] 7-8-11 100 (b) RichardMullen 6 79
(S Seemar, UAE) *a in mid-div* **16/1**
9 1 **Bermuda Rye (IRE)**[39] 5-8-6 95 (bt) RoystonFfrench 2 72
(A Al Raihe, UAE) *in rr of mid-div: n.d* **16/1**
10 1 ¼ **War Monger (USA)**[27] 6-9-5 108 RichardHills 10 82
(Doug Watson, UAE) *trckd ldr tl 3f out: wknd* **11/1**
11 shd **Aspectus (IRE)**[116] 6718 7-9-5 108 KierenFallon 3 82
(J A Osborne) *in rr of mid-div: nvr able to chal* **5/1**[3]

2m 1.58s (121.58) 11 Ran SP% **119.7**

Owner Mme Serge Seenyen **Bred** Mrs B D Oppenheimer **Trained** South Africa

FOCUS
Mainly exposed types for this handicap, and the pace was steady, so probably not strong form.

NOTEBOOK
Mr Brock(SAF), back with Mike de Kock after a spell in France, was always handy and picked up well in the straight to take this in good style, clearly relishing the synthetic surface. A rise in the weights should stop him following up. (op 11/2)
Tartan Gigha(IRE) might have preferred a stronger pace, but that's no real excuse seeing as he was never too far away. He's vulnerable off this sort of mark. (op 11/4)
Walzertraum(USA) ran respectably after three months off, without shaping as though about to win. (op 12/1)
Pascal(USA) got going too late and probably would have preferred a stronger pace.
Soy Libriano(ARG), who won a weak renewal of the middle leg of the UAE Triple Crown last year, was making his debut for Godolphin and had to prove himself on the surface. He looked set to finish up well beaten when dropping out to a detached last leaving the back straight, but he finally responded to pressure in the closing stages and finished really strongly. This was an odd performance, but something to build on nonetheless.
Royal Prince ◆ is significantly better than he showed and would surely have finished in the first four with a clear run. (op 28/1)
Aspectus(IRE), a multiple Group-race winner at 1m-1m3f when trained in Germany, was sold to these connections for 70,000gns since last seen in October, but he showed little.

416a DUBAL INTERNATIONAL INNOVATION TROPHY (H'CAP) (TAPETA) 6f

5:05 (5:05) (95-110,109) 3-Y-O+

£44,444 (£14,814; £7,407; £3,703; £2,222; £1,481)

RPR

1 **Global City (IRE)**[82] 7394 4-8-7 97 (t) TedDurcan 8 100+
(Saeed Bin Suroor) *in rr of mid-div: r.o wl fnl 1 1/2f: led last stride* **7/2**[1]
2 nse **Montpellier (IRE)**[13] 7-9-0 104 (t) RoystonFfrench 11 107
(A Al Raihe, UAE) *trckd ldr: led 1f out: hdd last stride* **11/1**
3 2 ¼ **Thor's Echo (USA)**[558] 8-8-11 101 (bt) WayneSmith 10 97
(S Seemar, UAE) *trckd ldr: ev ch 1 1/2f out: nt qckn fnl 110yds* **16/1**
4 nse **Sir Gerry (USA)**[7] 336 5-9-5 109 KierenFallon 1 105
(J R Best) *mid-div: chsd ldrs 1f out: r.o wl* **9/2**[2]
5 1 ¾ **Alo Pura**[20] 6-8-10 100 (e) FrankieDettori 3 90+
(D Selvaratnam, UAE) *racd in last: r.o wl fnl 2f: nvr able to chal* **8/1**
6 2 ½ **Awinnersgame (IRE)**[117] 6661 4-8-13 102 RyanMoore 6 85
(J Noseda) *sn rdn in rr: nvr able to chal* **6/1**[3]
7 shd **Mac Gille Eoin**[138] 6091 6-8-10 100 JimCrowley 4 82
(J Gallagher) *sn led on rail: hrd rdn 2f out: hdd & wknd 1f out* **14/1**
8 ¾ **Terrific Challenge (USA)**[48] 8-8-6 96 (vt) RichardMullen 7 75
(S Seemar, UAE) *s.i.s: mid-div: rdn 2 1/2f out: one pce* **12/1**
9 ¼ **Alsadeek (IRE)**[48] 5-8-7 97 PatDobbs 2 76
(Doug Watson, UAE) *mid-div on rail: nvr able to chal* **8/1**
10 ¼ **Classic Blade (IRE)**[13] 4-9-1 105 TadhgO'Shea 9 83
(Doug Watson, UAE) *trckd ldrs tl 3 1/2f out: sn wknd* **8/1**
11 5 ¾ **Iguazu Falls (USA)**[109] 5-8-6 96 (t) WJSupple 5 55
(M bin Shafya, UAE) *nvr able to chal* **25/1**

1m 13.48s (73.48) 11 Ran SP% **120.4**

Owner Godolphin **Bred** Mrs Monica Hackett **Trained** Newmarket, Suffolk

FOCUS
A decent enough sprint handicap run at a strong pace.

NOTEBOOK
Global City(IRE), 2-2 on Polytrack, including when landing a conditions event when last seen in November, didn't look badly treated for this return to handicap company, and so it proved, but only just. He came under pressure when hitting a flat spot over 2f out, and looked unlikely to even be placed at that stage, but once balanced in the straight, he picked up really well to record an unlikely success. He may now need stepping up to 7f, but unless he improves for that trip, a rise in the weights will probably find him out.
Montpellier(IRE)'s last two victories have been gained on dirt, but he has won on a synthetic surface and he came agonisingly close on this occasion. Having been ridden prominently from his wide draw, he picked up well in the straight to go clear, only to tire in the final strides.
Thor's Echo(USA), the 2006 Breeders' Cup Sprint winner, had been off since July 2008. He ran a fine race in defeat, keeping on after racing in a handy position from the off, and clearly retains plenty of ability.
Sir Gerry(USA) came from last when successful off a 4lb lower mark over C&D the previous week, but a lower draw this time meant he was ridden more prominently. He seemed to run his race, but was held off his new rating.
Alo Pura, a winner on turf when trained in Britain but whose last four wins have been gained on dirt, was set plenty to do and got going too late.
Awinnersgame(IRE), returning from nearly four months off, appeared to struggle to go the early pace and got going too late. It seems he'll benefit from a return to turf and/or 7f.
Mac Gille Eoin couldn't sustain his run after setting a quick pace on this return from 138 days off.

417a AL RASHIDIYA SPONSORED BY DUBAL INTERNATIONAL (GROUP 3) (TURF) 1m 1f

5:40 (5:41) 3-Y-O+

£74,074 (£24,691; £12,345; £6,172; £3,703; £2,469)

RPR

1 **Alexandros**[53] 7746 5-8-13 115 FrankieDettori 3 117+
(Saeed Bin Suroor) *trckd ldrs: smooth prog to ld 1 1/2f out: r.o wl: easily* **7/4**[1]
2 3 ½ **Crowded House**[243] 2705 4-8-13 118 JamieSpencer 5 109+
(B J Meehan) *settled in rr: nvr nr to chal: r.o wl fnl 2f: nrst fin* **7/2**[2]
3 ½ **Tam Lin**[7] 338 7-8-13 110 (t) WJSupple 8 108
(M bin Shafya, UAE) *trckd ldr: ev ch 2f out: nt qckn* **20/1**
4 ½ **Black Eagle (IRE)**[48] 4-8-13 95 CSandoval 1 107
(A bin Huzaim, UAE) *mid-div: chsd ldrs 2f out: nt qckn fnl 1f* **66/1**
5 1 ¼ **Kalahari Gold (IRE)**[39] 5-8-13 109 TadhgO'Shea 4 104
(Doug Watson, UAE) *a in mid-div* **14/1**
6 3 ½ **Front House (IRE)**[313] 1012 5-8-11 112 (e) KShea 7 95
(M F De Kock, South Africa) *set modest gallop: hdd 2f out: wknd* **13/2**
7 ½ **Naval Officer (USA)**[313] 1009 4-8-13 108 (t) OlivierPeslier 9 96
(J Barton, Saudi Arabia) *mid-div: rdn 3 1/2f out: sn btn* **14/1**

8 ¾ **Frozen Fire (GER)**[194] 4298 5-8-13 113...........(t) ChristopheSoumillon 6 94
(M F De Kock, South Africa) *settled in rr: nvr able to chal* 5/1[3]

9 ¾ **Oiseau De Feu (USA)**[124] 6503 4-9-1 117......................(t) RichardHills 2 94
(E Charpy, UAE) *t.k.h in rr: nvr able to chal* 6/1

1m 51.74s (111.74) 9 Ran SP% **122.5**

Owner Godolphin **Bred** Darley **Trained** Newmarket, Suffolk

■ The first race to be staged in public on the Meydan turf course.

FOCUS

They went just a steady pace early on and the bare form is limited by the proximity of Tam Lin and Black Eagle, but the front two are better than this level.

NOTEBOOK

Alexandros won comfortably on his first start since being outclassed in the Hong Kong Mile. Having travelled best of all, he quickened when asked in the straight, despite edging left, and was eased in the final few strides. The Group 2 Jebel Hatta back over this C&D on Super Thursday (March 4) is the obvious aim, ahead of his main target, which is the Duty Free (third last year).

Crowded House ◆ looked top class in the 2008 Racing Post Trophy but failed to reach that level last year and had been off since finishing sixth in the Derby. He was set a lot to do by Jamie Spencer, but one got the impression from listening to the rider beforehand that this run was probably going to be needed ahead of bigger targets, and anyway the horse was keen early and needed to be settled. He had no chance with the winner in the straight, such were their respective positions, but the manner in which this colt finished his race was most encouraging, and he should build on this, especially off a stronger pace. It will be fascinating to see whether he is pointed towards the Duty Free, or the Dubai World Cup. If it's the latter, the 33-1 generally available could look big.

Tam Lin showed he's still capable of smart form, stepping up significantly on his effort on Tapeta the previous week, but he's surely flattered by the bare result.

Black Eagle(IRE) progressed with each of his four runs when with Godolphin, but he showed nothing on his debut for this yard on the dirt in December and had plenty to find at this level. The switch in surface obviously suited, however, and he seems to still be on the upgrade.

Kalahari Gold(IRE) travelled well but found only the one pace for pressure and has not progressed as expected.

Front House(IRE), tried in eye-shields, had been off for 313 days and was racing over an inadequate trip. She was allowed an easy lead, but offered little in the straight and should be suited by a return to 1m4f, with the Dubai City Of Gold, a race she won last year, on Super Thursday looking the obvious aim. (op 6/1)

Naval Officer(USA), like Front House having his first start since last year's World Cup meeting, promised to be suited by the return to turf, but he was well beaten.

Frozen Fire(GER), the 2008 Irish Derby winner, had a tongue-tie on for his first start since leaving Aidan O'Brien, but offered no encouragement. It's true the trip was shorter than ideal, but he made no progress for pressure and it was noticeable that Soumillon was still pushing him along for a few yards after the line.

Oiseau De Feu(USA) had no easy task under the penalty he picked up for winning a Group 3, and his stamina was unproven, but even so, this was a disappointing first start for his new trainer. (op 7/1)

418a DUBAL INTERNATIONAL TROPHY (H'CAP) (TURF) 1m 6f

6:15 (6:15) (95-109,108) 3-Y-0+

£55,555 (£18,518; £9,259; £4,629; £2,777; £1,851)

RPR

1 **Age Of Reason (UAE)**[92] 7237 5-9-3 106..................... FrankieDettori 4 107+
(Saeed Bin Suroor) *s.i.s: mid-div: swtchd wd 2f out: r.o wl: led at the line* 7/2[1]

2 *shd* **Titurel (GER)**[124] 6500 5-9-0 102.................................... KierenFallon 12 104
(Manfred Hofer, Germany) *mid-div: t.k.h: ev ch fnl 1 1/2f: nt qckn cl home* 15/2

3 *shd* **Mojave Moon**[105] 6978 4-8-13 106..............................(v) AhmedAjtebi 11 108
(Saeed Bin Suroor) *racd in last: chsd ldrs 2f out: led 110yds out: hdd on line* 12/1

4 *1 ¾* **Sabotage (UAE)**[166] 5248 4-8-7 100................................... TedDurcan 6 99
(Saeed Bin Suroor) *mid-div: chsd ldrs 3f out: r.o fnl f* 5/1[2]

5 *shd* **Topclas (FR)**[7] 337 4-9-0 107... WJSupple 13 106
(M bin Shafya, UAE) *in rr of mid-div: chsd ldrs 3f out: led 1 1/2f out: wknd fnl 110yds* 20/1

6 *¼* **Pompeyano (IRE)**[20] 5-9-1 104....................................(t) RichardMullen 5 102
(S Seemar, UAE) *racd in rr: r.o fnl 1 1/2f: nrst fin* 16/1

7 *shd* **Montaff**[134] 6202 4-8-9 102.. AlanMunro 10 101
(M R Channon) *racd in rr: r.o fnl 1 1/2f: nvr nr to chal* 22/1

8 *2 ½* **Quai D'Orsay**[117] 6662 4-8-5 98.............................. MickaelBarzalona 14 93
(Saeed Bin Suroor) *trckd ldr: rdn 3f out: r.o one pce* 16/1

9 *7* **Weald**[20] 5-8-9 98.. PatDobbs 8 82
(Doug Watson, UAE) *mid-div: nvr able to chal* 33/1

10 *1 ¼* **Estrela Anki (BRZ)**[124] 6506 5-8-10 99................................ TJPereira 2 82
(P Bary, France) *in rr of mid-div: n.d* 20/1

11 *2 ¼* **Record Breaker (IRE)**[117] 6662 6-8-13 101.................(b) RichardHills 9 81
(M Johnston) *racd in rr: nvr able to chal* 7/1[3]

12 *1 ¾* **Red Rock Canyon (IRE)**[7] 337 6-8-11 100....(t) ChristopheSoumillon 1 77
(M F De Kock, South Africa) *trckd ldng duo tl 3f out: wknd* 7/1[3]

13 *¾* **Galactic Star**[343] 699 7-9-5 108...........................(t) RoystonFfrench 7 84
(A Al Raihe, UAE) *nvr bttr than mid-div* 14/1

14 *41* **Rohaani (USA)**[7] 335 8-8-6 95.. TadhgO'Shea 3 70
(Doug Watson, UAE) *sn led: rdn 2 1/2f out: wknd* 40/1

2m 58.59s (178.59)

WFA 4 from 5yo+ 5lb 14 Ran SP% **121.0**

Owner Godolphin **Bred** Darley **Trained** Newmarket, Suffolk

FOCUS

The runner-up and third in this race last year went on to finish first and second respectively in the DRC Gold Cup, a 2m contest which this season will be run on February 25. There was a bunch finish to this year's race, but the pace had been fair and the form looks reasonable enough.

NOTEBOOK

Age Of Reason(UAE) was unproven over this trip but needed every yard of it. This was a smart performance off a mark of 106 and it should set him up nicely for a crack at the DRC Gold Cup, with the extra couple of furlongs unlikely to trouble him.

Titurel(GER) proved suited by the trip and was just denied on his return from four months off.

Mojave Moon ran a big race on his first start since leaving Andre Fabre, only just losing out. It remains to be seen whether he can progress past this sort of mark, however.

Sabotage(UAE), having his first outing since leaving Mark Johnston, didn't seem to enjoy the clearest of runs in the straight, albeit his jockey never really had to stop riding, and gave the impression he will be capable of better.

Topclas(FR), trying his furthest trip to date, stepped up significantly on the form he showed on the Tapeta the previous week.

Pompeyano(IRE) ◆ is just a one-paced galloper and he was given too much to do. He finished strongly and could go well at a price in the DRC Gold Cup, with the longer trip almost sure to suit.

Montaff kept on at the one pace from a fair way back and offered some encouragement.

Red Rock Canyon(IRE) failed to build on the encouragement of his recent Tapeta outing. Perhaps he was unsuited by the step back up in trip.

419a DUBAL INTERNATIONAL DX TECHNOLOGY TROPHY (H'CAP) (TAPETA) 1m 2f

6:49 (6:50) (90-105,105) 3-Y-0+

£40,740 (£13,580; £6,790; £3,395; £2,037; £1,358)

RPR

1 **King Of Rome (IRE)**[7] 334 5-9-3 102....................................... KShea 4 106+
(M F De Kock, South Africa) *mid-div on rail: smooth prog 2f out: led 1f out: comf* 7/4[1]

2 *1 ½* **Hot Six (BRZ)**[123] 6526 5-9-5 105.. TJPereira 1 102
(P Bary, France) *mid-div: rdn to chse ldrs 3f out: ev ch 1f out: nt qckn* 10/1

3 *¼* **Antinori (IRE)**[138] 6106 4-8-9 96....................................(v) AhmedAjtebi 3 93+
(Saeed Bin Suroor) *in rr of mid-div: r.o wl fnl 2f: nrst fin* 8/1[3]

4 *hd* **Dr Faustus (IRE)**[25] 5-8-9 95.......................................(t) TadhgO'Shea 12 91
(Doug Watson, UAE) *mid-div on rail: r.o wl fnl 1 1/2f: nt qckn fnl 110yds* 16/1

5 *6 ¼* **Cadre (IRE)**[131] 6270 5-8-9 95..................................... FrankieDettori 10 79
(Saeed Bin Suroor) *settled last: r.o fnl 1 1/2f: nvr able to chal* 6/1[2]

6 *1 ¼* **Salute Him (IRE)**[124] 6480 7-9-4 104............................ JamieSpencer 9 85
(A J Martin, Ire) *in rr of mid-div: nvr able to chal* 8/1[3]

7 *2 ¾* **Dancourt (IRE)**[180] 4781 4-7-13 93.......................... AntiocoMurgia(7) 5 69
(Saeed Bin Suroor) *sn led: clr 7f out whn rdn: wknd 1 1/2f out* 8/1[3]

8 *hd* **Singing Poet (IRE)**[20] 9-8-9 95......................................(bt) RyanMoore 11 70
(E Charpy, UAE) *led main gp tl rdn 3f out* 22/1

9 *4 ¾* **Captain Webb**[350] 616 5-8-13 98..(t) PJSmullen 8 65
(E Charpy, UAE) *nvr bttr than mid-div* 16/1

10 *11* **Bennie Blue (SAF)**[7] 334 8-8-9 95........................(bt) RoystonFfrench 6 39
(A Al Raihe, UAE) *nvr bttr than mid-div* 25/1

11 *4* **Team Victory (BRZ)**[25] 6-8-7 93..............................(bt) RichardMullen 7 29
(S Seemar, UAE) *trckd ldrs tl 3f out* 50/1

12 *24* **Ask The Butler**[488] 6476 6-9-3 102.................................... RichardHills 2 —
(M Al Muhairi, UAE) *in rr of mid-div: n.d* 14/1

2m 7.42s (127.42)

WFA 4 from 5yo+ 1lb 12 Ran SP% **121.7**

PLACEPOT £14.80. Pool £9,842.45 - 483.10 winning tickets. QUADPOT £15.30 Pool £330 - 16.10 winning tickets..

Owner Sheikh Mohammed Bin Khalifa Al Maktoum **Bred** The Amizette Partnership **Trained** South Africa

FOCUS

A good handicap, but despite Dancourt setting a strong pace and building up a lead of around 10l before folding, few got involved.

NOTEBOOK

King Of Rome(IRE) ◆ finished second over the same C&D the previous week, but he didn't exactly get the run of things that day, racing well off the pace and wide for much of the way, and he enjoyed a better trip this time. Having travelled well in about mid-division, it was clear he was going to win once he had found a narrow gap between rivals early in the straight. This one-time high-class performer has got his confidence back and should defy a rise. (op 15/8)

Hot Six(BRZ), who was reported by his trainer pre-carnival to be fitter than Gloria De Campeao, ran well on this significant drop in grade. There were no excuses. (op 9/1)

Antinori(IRE), tried in a visor for the first time (replacing cheekpieces) on his first start since leaving Walter Swinburn, ran with credit, and while it remains to be seen whether he's totally straightforward, he may yet be capable of better.

Dr Faustus(IRE) ran well but he hasn't won for a long time.

Cadre(IRE), who was trying his furthest trip to date on first start since leaving John Gosden, kept on from a long way back but was never competitive and it's hard to know whether he stayed, although he is bred for the trip.

Salute Him(IRE) couldn't get involved after being dropped out at the start, and he can be given another chance.

Dancourt(IRE), having his first start since being sold for 40,000gns, went off too fast.

[390]LINGFIELD (L-H)

Friday, February 5

OFFICIAL GOING: Standard

Wind: Fresh, behind Weather: Fine

420 LINGFIELD PARK SPORTING MEMBERSHIP (S) H'CAP 2m (P)

1:15 (1:15) (Class 6) (0-60,60) 4-Y-0+ **£1,774** (£523; £262) **Stalls** Low

Form RPR

62-0 1 **Isle De Maurice**[14] 263 8-9-4 **55**..................................(b) GeorgeBaker 8 65
(G L Moore) *hld up in abt 8th: n.m.r on inner 5f out: taken wd and effrt in 7th 2f out: gd prog on outer to ld jst over 1f out: sn rdn wl clr* 11/4[1]

040/ 2 *4 ½* **Poppy Gregg**[82] 5269 5-8-4 **46** oh1................................(v[1]) AmyBaker(5) 7 51
(Dr J R J Naylor) *dwlt: hld up in last: rapid prog on outer fr over 3f out to join ldrs over 2f out: tried to chal over 1f out: chsd wnr fnl f: one pce* 50/1

35-0 3 *1 ¾* **Colourful Move**[22] 164 5-8-11 **48**...............................(t) RobertHavlin 11 51
(P G Murphy) *w ldr for 3f: styd prom: trckd ldrs and poised to chal 2f out: effrt over 1f out: sn outpcd: kpt on to take 3rd nr fin* 8/1

6-53 4 *¾* **Acropolis (IRE)**[16] 237 9-9-4 **55**.. NeilCallan 9 57
(A W Carroll) *hld up in abt 9th: clsd on ldrs fr over 3f out: rdn to ld briefly over 1f out: sn totally outpcd* 4/1[2]

000- 5 *2 ¼* **Broughtons Point**[60] 7660 4-8-3 **46** oh1.......................... JamieMackay 2 45
(W J Musson) *hld up in last trio: effrt on inner over 3f out: nt clr run over 2f out: 8th and rdn over 1f out: kpt on: nvr on terms* 33/1

44-1 6 *1* **Fantasy Ride**[25] 130 8-9-3 **54**... SaleemGolam 4 52
(J Pearce) *mostly trckd ldrs: gng wl enough on inner whn n.m.r over 2f out: effrt over 1f out: sn wknd* 13/2[3]

-100 7 *2 ¼* **Royal Rainbow**[14] 263 6-9-2 **53**.. ChrisCatlin 3 48
(P W Hiatt) *trckd ldrs: prog 5f out: led 3f out: hdd & wknd over 1f out* 7/1

50-4 8 *1 ¾* **Brave Mave**[31] 42 5-9-9 **60**..(p) ShaneKelly 10 53
(Jane Chapple-Hyam) *hld up in last trio: effrt over 2f out but already wl outpcd: n.d* 12/1

00-5 9 *3 ¾* **Whiterocks**[14] 260 4-8-4 **47**......................................(p) DavidProbert 5 35
(Miss Sheena West) *hld up in midfield: rapid prog on outer to ld 1/2-way: drvn and hdd 3f out: wknd wl over 1f out* 40/1

4/45 10 *10* **Sparkling Montjeu (IRE)**[8] 331 5-8-9 **51**............. MatthewDavies(5) 1 27
(George Baker) *mde most to 1/2-way: sn reminders: chsd ldr tl over 4f out: wknd rapidly* 8/1

40-6 11 *hd* **Fongoli**[17] 90 4-8-3 **46**..(v) LukeMorris 12 22
(B G Powell) *chsd ldrs on outer: u.p 5f out: sn wknd* 16/1

0/0- **12** *7* **Ruling Reef**[67] [566] 8-8-9 **46** oh1 FergusSweeney 6 14
(M R Bosley) *trckd ldr after 3f tl 1/2-way: wknd 6f out: t.o* **66/1**

3m 23.36s (-2.34) **Going Correction** 0.0s/f (Stan)
WFA 4 from 5yo+ 6lb **12** Ran SP% **117.1**
Speed ratings (Par 101): **105,102,101,101,100 99,98,97,96,91 90,87**
toteswingers: 1&2 £18.10, 1&3 £15.30, 2&3 £18.10 CSF £165.52 CT £1000.58 TOTE £3.00: £1.50, £11.10, £3.30; EX 107.80 TRIFECTA Not won..There was no bid for the winner.
Owner Ms J Lambert **Bred** Hascombe And Valiant Studs **Trained** Lower Beeding, W Sussex

FOCUS
A very moderate selling handicap and a repeat of the winner's penultimate form was sufficient. The pace was ordinary until quickening up around halfway.

421 BET PREMIER LEAGUE FOOTBALL - BETDAQ MAIDEN STKS 1m 2f (P)
1:45 (1:46) (Class 5) 3-Y-O+ **£2,456** (£725; £362) **Stalls** Low

Form RPR

6 **1** **Abergavenny**[7] [340] 3-8-5 0 GregFairley 7 64+
(M Johnston) *pressed ldr: chal fr 3f out: rdn to ld narrowly jst over 1f out: grad asserted last 100yds* **4/5**[1]

024- **2** *3/4* **Monaco Dream (IRE)**[232] [3056] 4-9-7 73 JimCrowley 2 61
(W Jarvis) *trckd ldng pair: effrt to chal over 2f out: upsides over 1f out: nt qckn u.p: kpt on* **15/8**[2]

0/0- **3** *1/2* **Sinchiroka (FR)**[58] [7694] 4-9-12 0 GeorgeBaker 3 65
(R J Smith) *led: rdn hrd pressed fr 3f out: narrowly hdd jst over 1f out: kpt on tl no ex last 100yds* **25/1**

4 *1/2* **Frameit (IRE)** 3-8-5 0 LukeMorris 5 60
(J S Moore) *dwlt: rn green but in tch: rdn over 3f out: kpt on u.p fnl 2f: nvr quite able to chal* **9/1**[3]

0- **5** *2 1/4* **Shame The Devil (IRE)**[259] [2229] 5-9-13 0 FergusSweeney 1 60?
(H J Evans) *sn trckd ldrs: rdn in 4th 2f out: fdd fnl f* **33/1**

60- **6** *3* **Lastroseofsummer (IRE)**[62] [7648] 4-9-7 0 ChrisCatlin 6 49
(Rae Guest) *hld up in last trio: urged along and nt on terms fr 4f out: plugged on* **16/1**

0-0 **7** *3 1/2* **Southern Breeze**[21] [180] 3-8-5 0 (t) SaleemGolam 8 43
(S Kirk) *stdd s: hld up: rdn and no prog fr 3f out* **50/1**

0- **8** *2* **Puitin**[47] [7826] 5-9-13 0 LiamKeniry 9 43
(M Madgwick) *in tch in rr: pushed along over 3f out: wknd 2f out* **50/1**

9 *34* **Mrs Onc**[57] 7-9-8 0 DavidProbert 4 —
(A J Chamberlain) *s.v.s: a last: t.o over 3f out* **66/1**

2m 8.40s (1.80) **Going Correction** 0.0s/f (Stan)
WFA 3 from 4yo 22lb 4 from 5yo+ 1lb **9** Ran SP% **118.4**
Speed ratings (Par 103): **92,91,91,90,88 86,83,82,54**
toteswingers: 1&2 £1.80, 1&3 £6.50, 2&3 £1.10 CSF £2.43 TOTE £1.70: £1.10, £1.10, £4.30; EX 2.60 Trifecta £18.70 Pool: £759.50 - 29.99 winning units..
Owner Sheikh Hamdan Bin Mohammed Al Maktoum **Bred** Mrs J Gittins **Trained** Middleham Moor, N Yorks

FOCUS
A very weak maiden for the track, with only one of these having previously shown any real ability. The early pace was very modest which suited those that raced prominently, but with little covering the first four at the line the form is moderate. The winenr is capable of better.
Mrs Onc Official explanation: jockey said mare missed the break and never travelled

422 BET SIX NATIONS RUGBY - BETDAQ H'CAP 1m 2f (P)
2:20 (2:22) (Class 6) (0-65,65) 3-Y-O **£1,774** (£523; £262) **Stalls** Low

Form RPR

16-2 **1** **Bubbly Braveheart (IRE)**[13] [279] 3-9-4 **65** RobertWinston 4 68
(A Bailey) *t.k.h: hld up bhd ldrs: wnt 4th 2f out: chal and n.m.r over 1f out: narrow ld ent fnl f: drvn to assert last 100yds* **5/2**[1]

0-30 **2** *1* **New Den**[18] [216] 3-8-13 **60** (v[1]) NickyMackay 2 61
(J R Boyle) *led: rdn over 2f out: narrowly hdd ent fnl f: kpt on wl tl no ex last 100yds* **20/1**

646- **3** *2* **Fair Nella**[172] [5096] 3-9-1 **62** FrankieMcDonald 11 59
(J G Portman) *dwlt: t.k.h: hld up in rr: prog on outer over 3f out to join ldng pair 2f out: wd bnd sn after and lost grnd: hanging over 1f out: kpt on* **14/1**

1-13 **4** *hd* **Glen Lass**[9] [305] 3-9-3 **64** (b) SaleemGolam 8 61
(J Pearce) *hld up in rr: rdn and effrt 3f out: in tch in midfield 2f out: kpt on u.p fnl f* **5/1**[2]

561- **5** *2 1/4* **Whipperway (IRE)**[76] [7482] 3-8-8 **58** ow3 RobertLButler[(3)] 6 50
(Miss Sheena West) *trckd ldrs: prog to go 2nd over 3f out: chal over 2f out: upsides over 1f out: sn wknd* **12/1**

-622 **6** *2 1/2* **Magic Spirit**[9] [305] 3-8-8 **55** (p) LukeMorris 7 42
(J S Moore) *towards rr: rdn and effrt over 3f out: tried to cl on ldrs u.str.p over 1f out: wknd rapidly fnl f* **10/1**

04-5 **7** *1 1/2* **Yorksters Prince (IRE)**[27] [106] 3-8-9 **56** DavidProbert 3 40
(M G Quinlan) *awkward s: hld up in midfield: lost pl 4f out and dropped to rr: shkn up over 2f out: hanging and nt qckn over 1f out* **5/1**[2]

005- **8** *2 1/4* **Barastar**[211] [3767] 3-9-2 **63** StephenCraine 1 43
(J R Boyle) *trckd ldrs on inner: cl enough over 2f out: rdn and fnd nil over 1f out: wknd rapidly fnl f* **14/1**

5-40 **9** *1/2* **Underworld Dandy**[12] [283] 3-8-8 **58** (b) WilliamCarson[(3)] 5 37
(R T Phillips) *hld up in last: rdn and no prog 3f out: no ch after* **33/1**

000- **10** *1/2* **The Mighty Mod (USA)**[109] [6901] 3-8-7 **54** GregFairley 9 32
(M Johnston) *pressed ldr to wl over 4f out: lost pl rapidly and last 3f out: looked like being t.o 2f out: plugged on* **6/1**[3]

-454 **11** *4 1/2* **Creevy (IRE)**[4] [372] 3-8-4 **51** oh6 (b) ChrisCatlin 10 20
(S Kirk) *t.k.h: prom: chsd ldr wl over 4f out to over 3f out: sn wknd rapidly* **25/1**

2m 7.20s (0.60) **Going Correction** 0.0s/f (Stan) **11** Ran SP% **117.9**
Speed ratings (Par 95): **97,96,94,94,92 90,89,87,87,86 83**
toteswingers: 1&2 £24.40, 1&3 £14.40, 2&3 £21.80 CSF £60.85 CT £597.60 TOTE £4.70: £1.02, £6.30, £11.70; EX 85.40 TRIFECTA Not won..
Owner The Champagne Club **Bred** Albert Conneally **Trained** Newmarket, Suffolk

FOCUS
A weak 3-y-o handicap run at a modest pace and the winning time was 1.2 seconds faster than the maiden. Fairly sound form, the winner close to his recent level.
Yorksters Prince(IRE) Official explanation: jockey said gelding reared leaving stalls

423 MARRIOTT HOTEL OPENING SPRING 2010 H'CAP 6f (P)
2:55 (2:55) (Class 6) (0-52,52) 4-Y-O+ **£1,774** (£523; £262) **Stalls** Low

Form RPR

100- **1** **Cwmni**[154] [5633] 4-8-11 **51** DavidProbert 6 58
(B Palling) *wl plcd in chsng gp: coaxed along to cl on ldrs over 1f out: rdn and r.o wl last 150yds to ld nr fin* **25/1**

3465 **2** *nk* **Hart Of Gold**[16] [234] 6-8-12 **52** (b) LiamJones 4 58
(R A Harris) *led at str pce: clr after 2f: kpt on wl whn rdn fr 2f out: hdd nr fin* **11/2**[3]

33-4 **3** *1 1/2* **Shakespeare's Son**[7] [344] 5-8-12 **52** JimCrowley 11 53
(H J Evans) *stdd s: hld up in last pair: taken to wd outside over 2f out: hrd rdn and gd prog over 1f out: disp 2nd 150yds out: nt qckn after* **7/2**[1]

0-05 **4** *1/2* **Sirjosh**[4] [368] 4-8-11 **51** GregFairley 8 51
(D Donovan) *hld up in last trio: prog between rivals over 1f out: kpt on same pce fnl f: tk 4th last strides* **5/1**[2]

1-60 **5** *nk* **Maggie Kate**[16] [235] 5-8-12 **52** (b) RobertHavlin 1 51
(R Ingram) *hld up towards rr on inner: prog fr 1/2-way: chsd ldr over 1f out: sn drvn and no imp: fdd ins fnl f* **16/1**

0-00 **6** *2 1/4* **Makshoof (IRE)**[21] [195] 6-8-12 **52** (p) NeilCallan 12 43
(I W McInnes) *towards rr on outer: rdn over 2f out: nt qckn and outpcd over 1f out: plugged on* **10/1**

0-00 **7** *2* **Conjecture**[4] [368] 8-8-10 **50** (v) JackMitchell 7 35
(R Bastiman) *stdd s: hld up in last pair: effrt against ins rail fr 2f out: no prog fnl f* **14/1**

0-45 **8** *shd* **Nawaaff**[14] [271] 5-8-8 **48** FrannyNorton 10 33
(M Quinn) *racd wd: chsd clr ldrs: u.p over 2f out: no prog over 1f out: wknd* **12/1**

036- **9** *1/2* **Stormburst (IRE)**[38] [7869] 6-8-7 **47** AdrianMcCarthy 5 30
(A J Chamberlain) *chsd ldrs: rdn 1/2-way: wknd over 1f out* **16/1**

6-30 **10** *3 1/4* **Sonhador**[8] [319] 4-8-7 **50** WilliamCarson[(3)] 3 23
(G Prodromou) *chsd clr ldr: drvn fr 1/2-way: wknd rapidly over 1f out* **8/1**

4-26 **11** *4* **Dicey Affair**[8] [320] 4-8-7 **47** (bt[1]) LiamKeniry 2 7
(G L Moore) *chsd ldng pair tl wknd rapidly 2f out* **13/2**

1m 11.81s (-0.09) **Going Correction** 0.0s/f (Stan) **11** Ran SP% **117.8**
Speed ratings (Par 101): **100,99,97,96,96 93,90,90,90,85 80**
toteswingers: 1&2 £19.80, 1&3 £6.50, 2&3 £3.60 CSF £157.66 CT £622.45 TOTE £20.60: £10.50, £1.30, £2.00; EX 247.60 TRIFECTA Not won..
Owner Flying Eight Partnership **Bred** Exors Of The Late Mrs M M Palling **Trained** Tredodridge, Vale Of Glamorgan

■ Stewards' Enquiry : Liam Jones three-day ban: careless riding (Feb 19-21)

FOCUS
A moderate if competitive sprint handicap and the pace was decent. Sound form among the placed horses.

424 BETDAQ ON 0870 178 1221 CLAIMING STKS 7f (P)
3:30 (3:31) (Class 6) 3-Y-O **£1,774** (£523; £262) **Stalls** Low

Form RPR

12-5 **1** **Kirsty's Boy (IRE)**[24] [136] 3-8-11 72 LiamKeniry 1 68
(J S Moore) *led after 2f: mde rest: hrd pressed 2f out: drvn to gain def advantage over 1f out: edgd rt but hld on wl* **7/2**[2]

4-43 **2** *1/2* **Minortransgression (USA)**[13] [274] 3-9-4 72 FergusSweeney 3 74+
(G L Moore) *hld up: rdn in 5th 3f out and nt on terms: no prog tl r.o wl fnl f: snatched 2nd on post* **4/1**[3]

-121 **3** *hd* **Anjomarba (IRE)**[4] [370] 3-8-3 67 (p) WilliamCarson[(3)] 2 61
(W G M Turner) *t.k.h: hld up in tch: rdn to dispute 3rd over 2f out: nt qckn over 1f out: kpt on ins fnl f* **11/4**[1]

5553 **4** *nse* **Transfixed (IRE)**[1] [406] 3-8-10 78 PaulDoe 6 65
(P D Evans) *trckd wnr over 4f out: rdn and upsides 2f out: nt qckn over 1f out: tried to cl last 100yds but lost 2 pls fnl stride* **5/1**

-314 **5** *3 1/4* **Major Maximus**[16] [233] 3-8-3 70 (b) MatthewDavies[(5)] 4 54
(George Baker) *dwlt: plld hrd: cl up on inner: rdn over 2f out: nt qckn over 1f out: wknd ins fnl f* **7/2**[2]

00- **6** *69* **Cockney Colonel (USA)**[200] [4153] 3-8-13 0 ChrisCatlin 5 —
(E J Creighton) *bolted to post: led 2f: wknd rapidly and sn t.o* **66/1**

1m 25.62s (0.82) **Going Correction** 0.0s/f (Stan) **6** Ran SP% **109.3**
Speed ratings (Par 95): **95,94,94,94,90 11**
toteswingers: 1&2 £2.00, 1&3 £3.40, 2&3 £2.20 CSF £16.66 TOTE £3.40: £1.50, £2.70; EX 10.30.
Owner F J Stephens **Bred** Edmond Kent **Trained** Upper Lambourn, Berks

FOCUS
A modest claimer, run at an ordinary pace, and little to split the front four at the line. The form is rated around the winner but is a little muddling.
Cockney Colonel(USA) Official explanation: jockey said gelding bolted to post

425 GOLF AND RACING H'CAP 6f (P)
4:05 (4:05) (Class 6) (0-65,65) 3-Y-O **£1,774** (£523; £262) **Stalls** Low

Form RPR

-233 **1** **Maoi Chinn Tire (IRE)**[13] [276] 3-9-4 **65** (p) LiamKeniry 2 72
(J S Moore) *mde all: hrd rdn fr over 1f out: kpt on wl enough* **5/1**[3]

0-62 **2** *1* **May Chorus (IRE)**[7] [346] 3-8-4 **56** MatthewDavies[(5)] 3 60
(J R Boyle) *trckd ldrs on inner: cl up fr 1/2-way: effrt against far rail over 1f out: wnt 2nd fnl f: a hld* **11/2**

0-01 **3** *nse* **Private Olley**[16] [233] 3-9-1 **62** ChrisCatlin 4 65
(J Akehurst) *free to post: chsd wnr: drvn 2f out: nt qckn over 1f out: lost 2nd fnl f: kpt on nr fin* **4/1**[2]

50-2 **4** *1/2* **Volatilis (IRE)**[23] [149] 3-9-0 **61** SteveDrowne 5 63
(J W Hills) *hld up: rdn and effrt over 2f out: chsd ldrs over 1f out: kpt on but nvr able to chal* **6/1**

6-06 **5** *2 1/4* **Silver Linnet (IRE)**[17] [222] 3-8-13 **60** (b) JerryO'Dwyer 6 55
(M G Quinlan) *stdd s: keen early and sn trckd ldrs: cl enough 2f out: wknd fnl f* **25/1**

06-4 **6** *1/2* **Arken Lad**[4] [370] 3-9-4 **65** (e) RobertWinston 9 58
(D Donovan) *hld up in last: rdn over 2f out: wd into st: no real prog after* **13/2**

32-3 **7** *1/2* **Until The Man (IRE)**[16] [236] 3-9-4 **65** (p) PaulDoe 8 56
(R Ingram) *chsd ldrs on outer: u.p to hold pl over 2f out: wl btn over 1f out* **7/2**[1]

26-5 **8** *1 1/2* **Avon Castle**[23] [147] 3-8-13 **60** FergusSweeney 7 47
(G L Moore) *stdd s: hld up in rr: rdn and no prog over 2f out* **16/1**

1m 11.83s (-0.07) **Going Correction** 0.0s/f (Stan) **8** Ran SP% **111.6**
Speed ratings (Par 95): **100,98,98,97,94 94,93,91**
toteswingers: 1&2 £4.90, 1&3 £4.60, 2&3 £7.20 CSF £30.86 CT £109.02 TOTE £6.10: £3.10, £1.60, £1.40; EX 25.30 Trifecta £84.10 Pool: £383.01 - 3.37 winning units..
Owner W Adams & J S Moore **Bred** Mrs E Thompson **Trained** Upper Lambourn, Berks

FOCUS
A very modest handicap, but the winning time was only fractionally slower than the earlier older-horse handicap over the same trip. Those that raced handily were at an advantage and few ever got into it. The winner is rated in line with the best view of his earlier form.

Volatilis(IRE) Official explanation: jockey said colt hung left

426 LINGFIELD PARK FOURBALL AMATEUR RIDERS' H'CAP 1m 4f (P)
4:40 (4:41) (Class 5) (0-70,72) 4-Y-O+ **£2,373** (£730; £365) **Stalls** Low

Form RPR
3-04 **1** **Bavarica**[12] 284 8-10-7 **66**............ MrRBirkett(3) 9 78
(Miss J Feilden) *trckd ldng pair 4f: styd handly: effrt on inner over 2f out: rdn to ld over 1f out: kpt gng wl and a holding on* **10/1**
0-20 **2** *nk* **Star Choice**[25] 121 5-10-2 **58**............ MrSWalker 4 69
(J Pearce) *trckd ldrs: prog to ld wl over 2f out: hdd over 1f out: hrd rdn and styd on fnl f: a jst hld* **4/1**[2]
510- **3** *3 ¼* **Prince Golan (IRE)**[60] 7668 6-9-13 **58**............ MrMPrice(3) 10 64
(R J Price) *racd wd: hld up in tch: prog on outer to press ldrs over 2f out: nt qckn wl over 1f out: wnt 3rd fnl f: outpcd* **28/1**
24-0 **4** *1 ¾* **Slew Charm (FR)**[14] 261 8-10-0 **56**............(t) MissEJJones 5 59
(Noel T Chance) *hld up in 10th: sme prog fr over 3f out: chsd ldrs over 2f out: outpcd wl over 1f out* **8/1**[3]
0-1 **4** *dht* **Oxford City (IRE)**[8] 323 6-10-13 **72** 6ex............(t) MrJoshuaMoore(3) 2 75
(P M Phelan) *hld up in midfield: trckd ldrs on inner fr 3f out: rdn and one pce fnl 2f* **4/1**[2]
215- **6** *shd* **Sagunt (GER)**[122] 6566 7-10-7 **68**............ MissLCGriffiths(5) 6 71+
(S Curran) *hld up in last trio: stl only 12th over 2f out and swtchd to inner: sme prog and swtchd rt 1f out: fnlly rdn and r.o: hopeless task* **8/1**[3]
310- **7** *3* **Strong Storm (USA)**[79] 7428 4-10-1 **63**............(p) MrJohnEnnis(3) 11 61
(H J Collingridge) *hld up in last trio: rapid prog on wd outside 3f out: lost plenty of grnd bnd 2f out: hanging over 1f out: fdd* **25/1**
46-6 **8** *1 ¾* **Nawamees (IRE)**[26] 113 12-9-7 **56** oh4............(p) MissHJones(7) 1 51
(P D Evans) *mde most to wl over 2f out: stl pressing on inner over 1f out: sn wknd* **40/1**
04-5 **9** *1* **Mustajed**[23] 148 9-10-9 **70**............ MrPMillman(5) 13 64
(B R Millman) *trckd ldrs: pushed along and losing pl whn squeezed out over 2f out: no ch after* **10/1**
3-65 **10** *¾* **Hold The Bucks (USA)**[20] 200 4-9-12 **62**............(p) MrFFairchild(5) 8 55
(J S Moore) *prom: prog to join ldr 4f out: wknd rapidly over 1f out* **28/1**
-214 **11** *3 ¾* **Sunset Boulevard (IRE)**[13] 280 7-10-4 **60**............ MissSBrotherton 3 47
(Miss Tor Sturgis) *settled towards rr: effrt over 3f out: in tch whn n.m.r over 2f out: sn wknd tamely* **10/3**[1]
000- **12** *1 ¼* **Captain Imperial (IRE)**[67] 7594 4-9-8 **58**............ MissRBastiman(5) 7 43
(R Bastiman) *blindfold off v late and slowly away: virtually a last: lost tch 3f out* **66/1**
4-62 **13** *1 ¼* **Zuwaar**[14] 260 5-10-2 **63**............(tp) MissMBryant(5) 12 46
(P Butler) *chsd ldr to 4f out: wknd rapidly 3f out* **16/1**

2m 33.38s (0.38) **Going Correction** 0.0s/f (Stan)
WFA 4 from 5yo+ 3lb **13** Ran SP% **124.0**
Speed ratings (Par 103): **98,97,95,94,94 94,92,91,90,90 87,86,85**
toteswingers: 1&2 £9.90, 1&3 £84.50, 2&3 £60.50 CSF £49.59 CT £1125.61 TOTE £10.70: £3.60, £2.00, £10.10; EX 74.20 TRIFECTA Not won. Place 6: £60.84 Place 5: £26.35.
Owner Miss J Feilden **Bred** Juddmonte Farms **Trained** Exning, Suffolk
■ Stewards' Enquiry : Mr M Price two-day ban: careless riding (tba)

FOCUS
An ordinary amateurs' event and the early pace was moderate. Fairly sound form with slight improvement from the winner.
T/Jkpt: Part won. £29,968.20 to a £1 stake. Pool: £42,208.80. 0.50 winning tickets. T/Plt: £54.80 to a £1 stake. Pool: £71,983.12. 958.71 winning tickets. T/Qpdt: £23.10 to a £1 stake. Pool: £5,560.51. 177.88 winning tickets. JN

404 WOLVERHAMPTON (A.W) (L-H)
Friday, February 5

OFFICIAL GOING: Standard
Wind: Almost nil Weather: Fine

427 DINE IN THE HORIZONS RESTAURANT APPRENTICE H'CAP 1m 1f 103y(P)
5:05 (5:05) (Class 6) (0-65,62) 4-Y-O+ **£1,774** (£523; £262) **Stalls** Low

Form RPR
2-11 **1** **Grey Command (USA)**[7] 354 5-9-4 **61** 6ex............ JohnCavanagh 4 73
(M Brittain) *mde all: qcknd clr 2f out: rdn wl over 1f out: r.o wl* **11/10**[1]
0-03 **2** *3 ¼* **Wavertree Warrior (IRE)**[14] 256 8-9-5 **62**............(b) RyanClark 6 67
(N P Littmoden) *prom: chsd wnr over 6f out: rdn wl over 1f out: no imp* **11/2**[2]
3 *1* **Rouvres Girl (IRE)**[52] 7568 5-8-5 **53**............(bt) CPHoban(5) 7 56
(Seamus Fahey, Ire) *hld up in tch: rdn wl over 1f out: one pce* **25/1**
22-0 **4** *½* **King's Icon (IRE)**[14] 262 5-9-2 **59**............(p) DavidKenny 1 61+
(M Wigham) *hld up and bhd: hdwy whn nt clr run over 1f out: kpt on ins fnl f* **11/2**[2]
/00- **5** *½* **Saving Grace**[53] 7754 4-8-7 **50**............ MatthewLawson 3 51
(E J Alston) *chsd wnr 3f: in tch: rdn over 2f out: one pce fnl f* **25/1**
4-20 **6** *½* **Mackintosh (IRE)**[2] 397 4-8-5 **53**............(b) MatthewCosham(5) 5 53
(Patrick Morris) *hld up and bhd: hdwy over 2f out: hung lft fr over 1f out: one pce* **11/2**[2]
161- **7** *2* **Coolnaharan (IRE)**[56] 7718 10-9-3 **60**............(p) LeeTopliss 2 56
(Lee Smyth, Ire) *stdd s: hld up in rr: rdn and short-lived effrt on outside over 2f out* **9/1**[3]

2m 4.65s (2.95) **Going Correction** +0.125s/f (Slow) **7** Ran SP% **111.5**
Speed ratings (Par 101): **91,88,87,86,86 85,84**
toteswingers: 1&2 £2.60, 1&3 £7.00, 2&3 £12.40 CSF £7.10 TOTE £1.90: £1.50, £2.50; EX 6.70.

Owner Mel Brittain **Bred** Darley **Trained** Warthill, N Yorks

FOCUS
No more than a modest handicap featuring only one recent winner. The gallop was only steady and those held up were at a disadvantage. The winner made all and came down the centre in the straight. The form is rated around the runner-up.
Coolnaharan(IRE) Official explanation: jockey said gelding suffered a knock behind

428 BET MULTIPLES - BETDAQ H'CAP 1m 1f 103y(P)
5:35 (5:35) (Class 4) (0-85,86) 3-Y-O **£4,533** (£1,348; £674; £336) **Stalls** Low

Form RPR
140- **1** **Whippers Love (IRE)**[105] 6993 3-9-6 **80**............ JoeFanning 3 85
(M Johnston) *chsd ldr: chal wl over 1f out: rdn to ld ins fnl f: r.o* **9/4**[2]
31-1 **2** *¾* **Thundering Home**[18] 218 3-9-1 **75**............ PaulHanagan 2 78
(E A L Dunlop) *a.p: led wl over 1f out: hdd and rdn ins fnl f: nt qckn* **6/4**[1]
610- **3** *3 ¾* **Miss Starlight**[79] 7434 3-9-7 **81**............ DaneO'Neill 1 76
(P J McBride) *led: rdn and hdd wl over 1f out: wknd ins fnl f* **13/2**
1-2 **4** *4* **Brooklands Bay (IRE)**[32] 33 3-9-5 **79**............ JimmyQuinn 5 66
(J R Weymes) *hld up last: pushed along over 3f out: sn struggling* **4/1**[3]

2m 2.99s (1.29) **Going Correction** +0.125s/f (Slow) **4** Ran SP% **104.1**
Speed ratings (Par 99): **99,98,95,91**
CSF £5.56 TOTE £2.90; EX 5.80.
Owner Crone Stud Farms Ltd **Bred** Jim McCormack **Trained** Middleham Moor, N Yorks

FOCUS
A couple of potential improvers but just a steady pace to the straight. The winner edged centre to far side in the closing stages. The form seems sound enough.

429 SPONSOR A RACE BY CALLING 01902 390000 CLAIMING STKS 1m 1f 103y(P)
6:05 (6:05) (Class 5) 4-Y-O+ **£2,914** (£867; £433; £216) **Stalls** Low

Form RPR
321- **1** **Shakalaka (IRE)**[37] 7882 4-9-5 79............(be) GeorgeBaker 4 82
(G L Moore) *hld up towards rr: hdwy wl over 1f out: rdn to ld wl ins fnl f: flashed tail cl home: r.o* **2/1**[1]
22-4 **2** *1 ½* **Ahlawy (IRE)**[22] 176 7-8-3 85............(bt) KierenFox(7) 1 70
(F Sheridan) *hld up and bhd: hdwy on outside 3f out: led jst over 2f out: rdn wl over 1f out: hdd wl ins fnl f: nt qckn* **9/4**[2]
140- **3** *¾* **Watchmaker**[86] 2039 7-8-6 70............ JoeFanning 5 64
(Miss Tor Sturgis) *hld up in tch: chal gng wl over 2f out: rdn and ev ch 1f out: no ex wl ins fnl f* **11/1**
150- **4** *½* **Farncombe (IRE)**[60] 7665 4-7-11 62............ AndrewHeffernan(5) 2 59
(R A Harris) *broke wl: plld hrd early: stdd and in tch over 7f out: rdn over 1f out: kpt on same pce ins fnl f* **20/1**
3-33 **5** *3* **Big Nige (IRE)**[14] 260 4-8-4 61............ SaleemGolam 3 55
(J Pearce) *plld hrd early: led 1f: prom: pushed along over 1f out: rdn and wknd ins fnl f* **7/2**[3]
4-0 **6** *¾* **Academy Gigsnreels (USA)**[1] 409 5-8-2 57............ CPHoban(7) 6 58
(Seamus Fahey, Ire) *hld up in rr: rdn over 1f out: nvr nr ldrs* **40/1**
06-0 **7** *14* **Weald Park (USA)**[33] 23 4-8-11 70............ DaneO'Neill 7 31
(R Hannon) *prom: chsd ldr 8f out: led over 3f out tl jst over 2f out: sn hung bdly lft: wknd wl over 1f out* **14/1**
000- **8** *6* **Days Of Thunder (IRE)**[48] 7817 5-8-6 30............ SamHitchcott 9 13
(B R Summers) *led after 1f tl over 3f out: wknd over 2f out* **100/1**
463- **9** *25* **Navajo Nation (IRE)**[71] 6549 4-8-4 65 ow1............ AshleyMorgan(5) 8 —
(W G M Turner) *hld up towards rr: short-lived effrt on outside 3f out* **28/1**

2m 2.36s (0.66) **Going Correction** +0.125s/f (Slow) **9** Ran SP% **113.0**
Speed ratings (Par 103): **102,100,100,99,96 96,83,78,56**
toteswingers: 1&2 £2.80, 1&3 £5.60, 2&3 £2.40 CSF £6.28 TOTE £2.40: £1.40, £1.30, £2.00; EX 7.20.
Owner Graham Gillespie **Bred** Swordlestown Stud **Trained** Lower Beeding, W Sussex
■ Stewards' Enquiry : Kieren Fox caution: careless riding; one-day ban: used whip with excessive frequency (Feb 19)

FOCUS
A wide range of ability on show but another race on the card run at just an ordinary gallop and it saw several pulling hard early. The winner ended up against the inside rail. Not many came here with soid recent profiles and it is doubtful how much the winner had to improve.
Weald Park(USA) Official explanation: jockey said gelding hung left-handed throughout

430 BET SIX NATIONS RUGBY - BETDAQ H'CAP 1m 1f 103y(P)
6:35 (6:36) (Class 4) (0-80,77) 4-Y-O+ **£4,533** (£1,348; £674; £336) **Stalls** Low

Form RPR
1-12 **1** **Chosen Forever**[15] 255 5-9-4 **77**............ JimmyQuinn 7 89+
(G R Oldroyd) *hld up: hdwy over 1f out: led ins fnl f: rdn out* **9/2**[2]
1-33 **2** *2 ¼* **Kames Park (IRE)**[12] 282 8-7-13 **63**............ BillyCray(5) 3 70
(R C Guest) *s.i.s: hld up in rr: stdy hdwy on outside over 2f out: c wd st: rdn and edgd lft ins fnl f: nt trble wnr* **16/1**
45-2 **3** *1 ¼* **Benedict Spirit (IRE)**[2] 383 5-8-9 **73** ow1............ RichardEvans(5) 8 77
(P D Evans) *chsd ldr: led over 3f out: rdn and hdd over 1f out: one pce ins fnl f* **10/1**
01-1 **4** *shd* **Erinjay (IRE)**[5] 367 4-8-6 **70**............ TobyAtkinson(5) 1 74
(M Wigham) *prom: rdn to ld over 1f out: hdd ins fnl f: no ex* **4/5**[1]
54-5 **5** *¾* **Supercast (IRE)**[22] 174 7-8-11 **70**............(t) LukeMorris 6 73
(N J Vaughan) *prom: chsd ldr over 2f out tl rdn wl over 1f out: one pce fnl f* **28/1**
/4-0 **6** *24* **Arabian Flame (IRE)**[1] 405 4-8-9 **75**............(b) CPHoban(7) 4 27
(Seamus Fahey, Ire) *led: hdd over 3f out: wkng whn lost action on ins over 2f out: sn lost tch* **50/1**
61-5 **P** **African Cheetah**[21] 197 4-9-3 **76**............ AdamKirby 2 —
(R Hollinshead) *p.u lame 7f out* **11/2**[3]

2m 1.03s (-0.67) **Going Correction** +0.125s/f (Slow) **7** Ran SP% **109.5**
Speed ratings (Par 105): **107,105,103,103,103 81,—**
toteswingers: 1&2 £4.60, 1&3 £5.80, 2&3 £10.40 CSF £62.36 CT £624.00 TOTE £4.80: £1.90, £6.20; EX 28.30.
Owner R C Bond **Bred** R C Bond **Trained** Brawby, N Yorks

FOCUS
A fair handicap but one that took less winning than seemed likely with the market leader disappointing and the third favourite pulling up early on. The gallop was an ordinary one but the time was the quickest of the four C/D races. The winner came down the centre in the straight and continued his recent progress, with the next two close to form.
African Cheetah Official explanation: trainer said colt returned lame

431 ENJOY THE LUCKY 7 GROUP OFFER H'CAP 5f 20y(P)
7:05 (7:05) (Class 5) (0-75,80) 4-Y-O+ **£2,729** (£806; £403) **Stalls** Low

Form RPR
3-03 **1** **Perlachy**[12] 287 6-8-7 **66**............(v) KellyHarrison(3) 1 75
(J R Holt) *bhd: pushed along over 2f out: hdwy on ins over 1f out: rdn to ld jst ins fnl f: edgd rt towards fin: r.o* **9/2**[3]
1-22 **2** *nk* **Handsome Cross (IRE)**[9] 306 9-8-8 **64**............(v) StevieDonohoe 9 72
(W J Musson) *mid-div: hdwy on ins over 2f out: ev ch 1f out: rdn and r.o* **7/2**[1]
00-0 **3** *½* **Brierty (IRE)**[17] 223 4-9-3 **73**............ DavidNolan 11 79
(D Carroll) *mid-div: pushed along 3f out: c wd st: hdwy 1f out: rdn and r.o ins fnl f* **25/1**
60-3 **4** *¾* **Figaro Flyer (IRE)**[21] 185 7-8-10 **66**............ J-PGuillambert 8 69+
(P Howling) *in rr: c v wd st: rdn and r.o ins fnl f: nrst fin* **8/1**
02-2 **4** *dht* **Bahamian Kid**[18] 214 5-9-2 **72**............(v) AdamKirby 10 75
(R Hollinshead) *hld up in rr: pushed along over 2f out: hdwy over 1f out: rdn and kpt on ins fnl f* **10/1**
5-42 **6** *nk* **Bo McGinty (IRE)**[22] 165 9-8-6 **62**............(b) PaulHanagan 3 64
(R A Fahey) *led 1f: ev ch 2f out: rdn over 1f out: no ex wl ins fnl f* **7/1**
050- **7** *¾* **La Capriosa**[94] 7223 4-8-10 **66**............ FrederikTylicki 2 66
(J A Glover) *w ldrs: led 2f out: rdn over 1f out: hdd jst ins fnl f: fdd towards fin* **16/1**

The Form Book, Raceform Ltd, Compton, RG20 6NL

0-41 **8** 1 1/2 **Even Bolder**[7] 345 7-9-1 **78** 6ex .... KierenFox(7) 5 72
(E A Wheeler) *hld up in mid-div: pushed along whn nt clr run wl over 1f out: n.d after* **4/1**[2]
300- **9** nk **Spic 'n Span**[118] 6669 5-8-6 **62** .... (b) JoeFanning 4 55
(R A Harris) *n.m.r s: t.k.h: sn prom: pushed along over 1f out: wknd ins fnl f* **12/1**
300- **10** 4 1/2 **Lucky Art (USA)**[73] 7506 4-8-9 **65** .... AndrewElliott 7 42
(Mrs R A Carr) *led after 1f: hdd 2f out: rdn and wknd over 1f out* **25/1**

61.90 secs (-0.40) **Going Correction** +0.125s/f (Slow) **10** Ran SP% **114.4**
Speed ratings (Par 103): **108,107,106,105,105 105,103,101,100,93**
toteswingers: 1&2 £7.50, 1&3 £16.00, 2&3 £24.20 CSF £20.19 CT £352.25 TOTE £4.20: £1.60, £2.50, £7.70; EX 28.20.
Owner Mrs N Macauley **Bred** J James **Trained** Peckleton, Leics
■ Stewards' Enquiry : Kelly Harrison three-day ban: used whip with excessive frequency without giving gelding time to respond (Feb 19-21)

FOCUS
A fair handicap and the first truly run race of the evening. The winner raced just off the inside rail in the straight. Solid form for the grade.

432 BET NFL SUPERBOWL - BETDAQ H'CAP 5f 216y(P)
7:35 (7:35) (Class 4) (0-85,83) 4-Y-0+ **£4,209** (£1,252; £625; £312) **Stalls** Low

Form RPR
640- **1** **Sir Nod**[149] 5768 8-8-6 **71** .... PaulHanagan 8 80
(Julie Camacho) *sn chsng ldr: led over 2f out tl wl over 1f out: sn rdn: rallied to ld last stride* **5/1**[3]
1-22 **2** nse **Weet A Surprise**[17] 223 5-8-5 **77** .... (v) AlexEdwards(7) 5 86
(J W Unett) *hld up in tch on ins: led wl over 1f out: sn rdn: hdd last stride* **4/1**[2]
3111 **3** hd **Divine Force**[14] 259 4-8-12 **77** .... SimonWhitworth 2 85+
(M Wigham) *hld up: c wd st: rdn and hdwy over 1f out: edgd lft ins fnl f: r.o* **9/4**[1]
2215 **4** 1 1/4 **Onceaponatime (IRE)**[15] 250 5-8-10 **75** .... LukeMorris 1 79
(M D Squance) *hld up: hdwy on ins 2f out: rdn over 1f out: ev ch ins fnl f: no ex towards fin* **6/1**
-566 **5** 1 1/2 **Canadian Danehill (IRE)**[19] 212 8-9-4 **83** .... (p) GrahamGibbons 4 82
(R M H Cowell) *led: hdd over 2f out: rdn and btn jst over 1f out* **12/1**
000- **6** 1/2 **Klynch**[126] 6458 4-8-13 **78** .... (b) AndrewElliott 3 76
(Mrs R A Carr) *outpcd in rr: rdn and kpt on fr over 1f out: n.d* **50/1**
06-0 **7** nk **Princess Valerina**[15] 250 6-8-9 **74** .... FrankieMcDonald 9 71
(D Haydn Jones) *s.i.s: rdn and swtchd lft over 1f out: nvr nr ldrs* **16/1**
13-1 **8** nk **Spinning Bailiwick**[17] 225 4-9-1 **80** .... GeorgeBaker 7 76
(G L Moore) *hld up in tch: pushed along and wknd wl over 1f out* **6/1**
000- **9** 8 **Albertine Rose**[186] 4601 4-8-13 **78** .... ShaneKelly 6 48
(E J Alston) *t.k.h in tch: wknd wl over 1f out* **25/1**

1m 14.49s (-0.51) **Going Correction** +0.125s/f (Slow) **9** Ran SP% **115.4**
Speed ratings (Par 105): **108,107,107,106,104 103,102,102,91**
toteswingers: 1&2 £6.80, 1&3 £3.80, 2&3 £3.20 CSF £25.31 CT £57.18 TOTE £7.00: £1.80, £1.90, £1.20; EX 22.60.
Owner Brian Nordan **Bred** B Nordan And Mrs S Camacho **Trained** Norton, N Yorks

FOCUS
A fair handicap but one in which the gallop was not overly strong. Solid form. The winner raced towards the centre in the straight.
Princess Valerina Official explanation: jockey said mare missed the break, trainer said, on return home, that mare had bled from the nose

433 GREAT OFFERS AT WOLVERHAMPTON-RACECOURSE.CO.UK MEDIAN AUCTION MAIDEN STKS 1m 141y(P)
8:05 (8:05) (Class 5) 3-5-Y-0 **£2,456** (£725; £362) **Stalls** Low

Form RPR
2 **1** **Into Wain (USA)**[20] 206 3-8-7 0 .... NickyMackay 1 65+
(D M Simcock) *hld up in tch: rdn wl over 1f out: led ins fnl f: r.o* **10/11**[1]
4-6 **2** 1/2 **Danderek**[35] 1 4-10-0 0 .... PaulHanagan 4 68
(R A Fahey) *a.p: rdn over 1f out: kpt on towards fin* **25/1**
3222 **3** 1 1/4 **The Great Husk (IRE)**[4] 371 3-8-0 56 .... KierenFox(7) 3 61
(J S Moore) *led: rdn wl over 1f out: hdd ins fnl f: no ex towards fin* **3/1**[2]
26- **4** 4 1/2 **Spice Fair**[36] 7885 3-8-7 0 .... LukeMorris 2 50
(M D I Usher) *chsd ldr tl pushed along 2f out: sn wknd* **9/1**
00-6 **5** 1/2 **Cruise Control**[10] 301 4-9-9 42 .... AndrewHeffernan(5) 5 54
(R J Price) *hld up: rdn and effrt wl over 1f out: wknd fnl f* **100/1**
00-0 **6** 19 **Jobekani (IRE)**[7] 354 4-10-0 51 .... (b[1]) StevieDonohoe 7 10
(Mrs L Williamson) *hld up: pushed along over 2f out: sn bhd* **33/1**
0 **P** **Premier League**[8] 321 3-8-7 0 .... JimmyQuinn 6 —
(P Howling) *s.i.s: bhd tl p.u lame 3f out* **7/1**[3]

1m 52.01s (1.51) **Going Correction** +0.125s/f (Slow)
WFA 3 from 4yo 21lb **7** Ran SP% **107.7**
Speed ratings (Par 103): **98,97,96,92,92 75,—**
toteswingers: 1&2 £7.70, 1&3 £1.10, 2&3 £7.50 CSF £24.99 TOTE £1.80: £1.60, £2.50; EX 21.80 Place 6: £65.10 Place 5: £48.07 .
Owner Ahmad Al Shaikh **Bred** Don M Robinson **Trained** Newmarket, Suffolk

FOCUS
A modest maiden in which the 56-rated third is a reliable yardstick but the 42-rated fifth finished close enough. The pace was a moderate one and the winner raced just off the inside rail in the straight. It is doubtful if he had to improve on his debut effort.
Spice Fair Official explanation: jockey said gelding hung both ways throughout
Premier League Official explanation: jockey said gelding pulled up lame
T/Plt: £66.40 to a £1 stake. Pool: £90,440.50. 993.45 winning tickets. T/Qpdt: £7.00 to a £1 stake. Pool: £10,701.24. 1,119.88 winning tickets. KH

412 MEYDAN (L-H)
Friday, February 5
OFFICIAL GOING: All-weather - standard; turf course - good to firm

434a JAGUAR XF TROPHY (H'CAP) (TAPETA) 6f
2:40 (2:40) (90-105,105) 3-Y-0+
£40,740 (£13,580; £6,790; £3,395; £2,037; £1,358)

RPR
1 **So Shiny (ARG)**[105] 5-9-1 100 .... (t) OlivierPeslier 11 103
(J Barton, Saudi Arabia) *trckd ldrs: rdn 2 1/2f out: r.o to ld 55yds out* **14/1**
2 1/2 **Oasis Star (IND)**[54] 6-9-5 105 .... YSrinath 4 107+
(C Katrak, India) *trckd ldrs on rail: swtchd wd 3f out: r.o wl fnl f: nrst fin* **9/4**[1]
3 1/4 **Frosty Secret (USA)**[8] 336 6-9-2 101 .... KShea 10 102
(M F De Kock, South Africa) *sn led: rdn 2f out: hdd ins fnl 55yds: styd on* **8/1**
4 1 1/2 **Prohibit**[8] 336 5-9-3 102 .... RichardMullen 9 98
(R M H Cowell) *mid-div: r.o wl fnl 2 1/2f: nrst fin* **7/1**[3]
5 hd **Sol De Angra (BRZ)**[188] 5-9-5 105 .... TJPereira 7 99
(A Cintra Pereira, Brazil) *a in mid-div* **7/1**[3]
6 1 3/4 **Five Star Junior (USA)**[39] 7862 4-8-13 98 .... KierenFallon 6 88
(Mrs L Stubbs) *a in mid-div* **14/1**
7 1 **Instant Recall (IRE)**[329] 9-9-5 105 .... (v) WayneSmith 8 91
(M Al Muhairi, UAE) *trckd ldrs: rdn and one pce 2f out* **20/1**
8 1/4 **Calrissian (GER)**[125] 6503 6-9-5 105 .... (t) PJSmullen 2 90+
(Fredrik Reuterskiold, Sweden) *in rr of mid-div: nvr able to chal* **16/1**
9 2 3/4 **Judd Street**[153] 5657 8-9-4 104 .... (v) RyanMoore 5 80+
(Eve Johnson Houghton) *nvr bttr than mid-div* **11/1**
10 7 1/2 **Matsunosuke**[19] 212 8-9-5 105 .... TedDurcan 1 57+
(A B Coogan) *a in rr* **6/1**[2]
11 3 1/4 **Cafe Racer (IRE)**[8] 339 4-9-1 100 .... (t) WJSupple 3 43+
(M bin Shafya, UAE) *nvr nr to chal* **50/1**
12 3/4 **Mannjal (USA)**[14] 8-9-5 105 .... (t) WilliamBuick 12 44+
(D Selvaratnam, UAE) *s.i.s: nvr able to chal* **10/1**

1m 12.97s (72.97) **12** Ran SP% **124.5**
CSF: £47.85 Tricast: £290.11.
Owner Prince Sultan Mohammed Saud Al Kabeer **Bred** La Quebrada **Trained** Saudi Arabia

FOCUS
A fascinating sprint handicap and the time was good, being almost identical to the later conditions contest won by the 110-rated Force Freeze, who carried 1lb less than the winner of this race.

NOTEBOOK
So Shiny(ARG), who won last year's UAE 1,000 Guineas over 1m on the dirt, proved herself equally effective under these vastly different conditions on her return from over three months off. She's clearly versatile and should be competitive off higher ratings.
Oasis Star(IND), a prolific winner in India, where she landed a couple of Group 1s, ran well on her UAE debut, but her lack of fluency around the bend into the straight arguably cost her the race. She was nicely enough placed early on, but lost ground when not appearing to handle the turn, before running on strongly once balanced. Perhaps she'll learn from this experience and it's clear she's not badly treated. (op 3-1)
Frosty Secret(USA) was allowed to dominate but simply couldn't sustain his challenge.
Prohibit, off the same mark as when unlucky not to go close over C&D the previous week, again didn't have things go his way, racing further back than ideal before not enjoying the clearest of runs in the straight, albeit his jockey never had to stop riding. It seems he needs everything to drop right to win off this sort of rating.
Sol De Angra(BRZ), a Grade 1 winner over 5f in Brazil, made some ground from off the pace but his run was flattening out near the line and he looked a suspect stayer, although he had been off for over six months. (op 6-1)
Five Star Junior(USA) was a bit keen and threatened only briefly to get involved in the straight.
Judd Street was never seen with a chance after a slow start. (op 10-1)
Matsunosuke couldn't get competitive off a 3lb higher rating than when winning over 5f on Polytrack last time. (op 11-2)

435a AL TAYER MOTORS TROPHY (H'CAP) (TAPETA) 1m 2f
3:15 (3:15) (95-120,120) 3-Y-0+ **£55,555** (£18,518; £9,259)

RPR
1 **Allybar (IRE)**[139] 6132 4-8-7 108 .... AhmedAjtebi 1 116+
(Saeed Bin Suroor) *trckd ldr: rdn 3f out: led 2f out: r.o* **3/1**[2]
2 7 1/2 **Presvis**[54] 7747 6-9-6 120 .... KierenFallon 4 113
(L M Cumani) *t.k.h in last: rdn 3f out: r.o one pce* **2/7**[1]
3 5 1/4 **Zulu Chief (USA)**[142] 5995 5-8-5 97 .... PDevlin 3 88
(M F De Kock, South Africa) *set stdy gallop: qckd 4f out: hdd 2f out* **14/1**[3]

2m 14.37s (134.37)
WFA 4 from 5yo+ 1lb **3** Ran SP% **109.4**
CSF: £4.61.
Owner Godolphin **Bred** Wertheimer Et Frere **Trained** Newmarket, Suffolk

FOCUS
A surprisingly poor turnout numerically for this valuable handicap, and it was an unsatisfactory contest with Zulu Chief setting a steady pace until the tempo increased leaving the back straight.

NOTEBOOK
Allybar(IRE), having his first start since leaving Carlos Laffon-Parias in France, where he won a 1m2f Listed race on soft ground last year, was not fancied by his connections according to Simon Crisford, and what he actually achieved is open to question. This was clearly a promising start, though. (op 5-2)
Presvis had been keen in rear early on, having missed the break, and failed to make any impression on the Godolphin runner, who had a 2l head start once in line for the finish and extended the advantage. Being a horse whose main asset in the past has been his turn of foot, he was clearly unsuited by the way the race unfolded, and it was also possible he didn't act on the surface, not least considering he was below form on Polytrack on his only previous try on a synthetic track. In truth, though, the potent change of pace that saw him progress from a handicapper to a Group 1 winner in 2009 has been missing since he returned from his summer break, and when labouring into third behind Vision D'Etat in the Hong Kong Cup last time, he looked in need of a step up to 1m4f, a trip that his trainer indicated some time ago would probably be required eventually. This performance seemed to confirm that view, and the Sheema Classic, back on the turf, will probably be his best option, with the Dubai City Of Gold on Super Thursday (March 4) the obvious prep. (op 2-5)
Zulu Chief(USA) had managed only one previous outing since joining this yard, finishing last of five in 1m Listed race at Sandown 142 days previously, and looks nothing like the racehorse his breeding (half-brother to Hawk Wing) suggested. (op 12-1)

436a FORD EDGE TROPHY (H'CAP) (TAPETA) 1m 3f
3:50 (3:50) (95-110,109) 3-Y-0+
£44,444 (£14,814; £7,407; £3,703; £2,222; £1,481)

RPR
1 **Anmar (USA)**[86] 7323 4-9-1 106 .... AhmedAjtebi 3 110+
(Saeed Bin Suroor) *settled in last: swtchd wd 2 1/2f out: r.o v wl fnl 1 1/2f: led cl home* **3/1**[1]
2 1 3/4 **Emirates Champion**[105] 6986 4-8-5 96 .... (t) TedDurcan 9 97
(Saeed Bin Suroor) *trckd ldrs: chsd ldr 2f out: ev ch 1f out: r.o wl* **3/1**[1]
3 1/2 **Monte Alto (IRE)**[8] 335 6-8-11 100 .... (t) TadhgO'Shea 11 100
(A Al Raihe, UAE) *settled in rr: mid-div 5f out: chsd ldrs 2 1/2f out: led 1 1/2f out: hdd cl home* **6/1**[2]
4 3 1/4 **Mashaahed**[21] 7-9-3 106 .... (t) RichardHills 5 101
(E Charpy, UAE) *mid-div on rail: swtchd wd 3f out: r.o one pce fnl 1 1/2f* **7/1**[3]
5 1/2 **Northern Glory**[97] 7-9-4 107 .... KKerekes 1 101
(W Figge, Germany) *sn led: set stdy pce: qckd 3 1/2f out: hdd 2f out: wknd* **25/1**

6 1 1/2 **Petrovsky**[8] 335 4-8-5 95 (t) RoystonFfrench 7 87
(A Al Raihe, UAE) *wl away: trckd ldr tl 2f out: sn rdn and wknd* **10/1**
7 4 **Merchant Marine (USA)**[8] 337 6-8-11 100 WilliamBuick 4 84
(Doug Watson, UAE) *trckd ldr tl 3 1/2f out: sn btn* **33/1**
8 3/4 **Fiery Lad (IRE)**[126] 6467 5-9-6 109 KierenFallon 8 92
(L M Cumani) *settled in rr: nvr able to chal* **6/1**[2]
9 3/4 **Dynamic Saint (USA)**[21] 7-8-8 97 (e) PatDobbs 6 79
(Doug Watson, UAE) *trckd ldrs: mid-div 4 1/2f out: nvr able to chal* **20/1**
10 2 1/4 **Raise Your Heart (IRE)**[82] 7077 7-9-4 107 PJSmullen 10 85
(Ms Joanna Morgan, Ire) *settled in rr: nvr able to chal* **9/1**

2m 21.68s (141.68)
WFA 4 from 5yo+ 2lb **10** Ran SP% **121.7**
CSF: £11.57 Tricast: £52.43.
Owner Godolphin **Bred** Shadwell Farm LLC **Trained** Newmarket, Suffolk

FOCUS
A decent handicap and there was a very smart winner. The pace was steady.

NOTEBOOK
Anmar(USA) ◆ looked to win despite the tactics used, having been held up last in a steadily run race. He was still out the back at the top of the straight, with around 5l to find, and the runner-up and third-placed finisher both made their moves before him, but once switched into the clear this Rahy colt displayed a fine change of pace, getting up to record a victory that looked unlikely 2f out but that was ultimately gained a shade comfortably. This looked a particularly noteworthy performance from Anmar, who went without the visor he had fitted when winning a Polytrack conditions race on his only start of 2009, and he's very much one to keep on side.
Emirates Champion ◆, 11lb higher than when bolting up in a 1m2f handicap on turf last October, coped with the surface (won his maiden on Polytrack) and ran a good race, nipping through against the inside rail in the straight to claim Monte Alto, only to be picked off near the line. This half-brother to Lend A Hand should be tough to beat next time.
Monte Alto(IRE), 3lb higher than when a good second over 1m2f on this surface the previous week, looked the likeliest winner for much of the straight, but he had raced wide with little cover for a lot of the way and did little once in front, losing two places after edging left near the line. (op 5-1)
Mashaahed, a Listed winner on the dirt at Jebel Ali last month, ran a creditable race under these different conditions.
Northern Glory posted a respectable effort after three months off on this first try away from turf. There could be a little better to come back over further on the grass.
Petrovsky needs more ground and, ideally, turf.
Fiery Lad(IRE) was well below form on his first start since leaving Ger Lyons.
Raise Your Heart(IRE), a Listed winner on his last start on the level in October, failed to pick up after racing wide without cover down the back straight. (op 11-1)

437a LAND ROVER TROPHY (CONDITIONS RACE) (TAPETA) 6f
4:35 (4:35) 3-Y-0+

£40,740 (£13,580; £6,790; £3,395; £2,037; £1,358)

RPR
1 **Force Freeze (USA)**[314] 1010 5-9-0 110 (t) TadhgO'Shea 7 109
(Doug Watson, UAE) *trckd ldrs: rdn 2 1/2f out: led 1/2f out: r.o wl* **11/4**[2]
2 1 1/2 **Star Crowned (USA)**[8] 336 7-8-11 109 LJurado 8 101
(R Bouresly, Kuwait) *wl away: sn led: hdd 1/2f out: r.o* **6/1**
3 shd **Asset (IRE)**[111] 6848 7-9-0 110 (b) FrankieDettori 1 104
(Saeed Bin Suroor) *settled in rr: smooth prog 2f out: n.m.r 2 1/2f out: r.o wl* **7/4**[1]
4 1/4 **Prince Tamino**[8] 336 7-8-11 104 (t) RoystonFfrench 3 100
(A Al Raihe, UAE) *mid-div: rdn 3 1/2f out: r.o wl* **6/1**
5 3 **League Champion (USA)**[322] 7-9-3 97 DaraghO'Donohoe 6 96
(R Bouresly, Kuwait) *chsd ldrs: ev ch 2f out: one pce fnl f* **66/1**
6 hd **Desuetude (AUS)**[8] 336 5-8-11 109 (b) AhmedAjtebi 4 90
(Saeed Bin Suroor) *a in mid-div* **5/1**[3]
7 5 **Upton Grey (IRE)**[21] 5-8-11 90 (p) KLatham 5 74
(M Gharib, UAE) *v.s.a: sn rdn in rr* **50/1**
8 5 1/4 **Absent Pleasure (USA)**[33] 4-8-11 94 (t) PatDobbs 2 57
(Doug Watson, UAE) *settled in rr: nvr able to chal* **33/1**

1m 12.96s (72.96) **8** Ran SP% **114.7**
CSF: £19.41.
Owner Sheikh Rashid bin Humaid Al Nuaimi **Bred** Dixiana Stables Inc **Trained** United Arab Emirates

FOCUS
A competitive enough conditions contest but all of these are pretty exposed and the form looks no more than smart. The time was almost identical to the earlier handicap won by the 100-rated So Shiny, a filly carrying 1lb more than the winner of this.

NOTEBOOK
Force Freeze(USA), last seen finishing fifth in the Golden Shaheen at the 2009 World Cup meeting, proved himself fully effective on synthetics with a gutsy win, gradually getting the better of the early leader, having been prominent from the off. The Group 3 Mahab Al Shimaal on Super Thursday (March 4) is the target, and while it remains to be seen whether he'll be quite good enough, he is entitled to come on for this run. (tchd 5-2)
Star Crowned(USA) was able to dominate and he reversed recent C&D form with Prince Tamino on 5lb better terms, but he still found one too strong. This is probably about as good as he is these days.
Asset(IRE) is a difficult ride and he never really looked likely to pick up sufficiently. He had to be switched around Star Crowned late on, but was not unlucky.
Prince Tamino, third in a C&D handicap off a mark of 104 the previous week, had a little bit to find at these weights.
League Champion(USA), the runner-up's stable companion, ran well considering he had loads to do at the weights and had been off for 322 days.
Desuetude(AUS) didn't pick up after racing keenly.

438a JAGUAR XJ TROPHY (H'CAP) (TAPETA) 7f
5:10 (5:10) (95-115,115) 3-Y-0+

£55,555 (£18,518; £9,259; £4,629; £2,777; £1,851)

RPR
1 **Barbecue Eddie (USA)**[28] 6-8-5 95 (b) WJSupple 6 106
(Doug Watson, UAE) *v wl away: clr after 1f: r.o wl* **25/1**
2 2 1/4 **Imbongi (SAF)**[209] 3841 6-9-6 115 ChristopheSoumillon 8 115
(M F De Kock, South Africa) *mid-div: chsd wnr 2 1/2f out: r.o wl: no ch w wnr* **3/1**[2]
3 2 **Munaddam (USA)**[344] 700 8-9-3 111 RichardHills 5 107
(E Charpy, UAE) *mid-div: r.o wl fnl 2f* **12/1**
4 1/4 **Summit Surge (IRE)**[271] 1913 6-9-5 113 KierenFallon 4 108
(L M Cumani) *mid-div: r.o fnl 2 1/2f* **11/4**[1]
5 3/4 **Wonder Lawn (SAF)**[208] 7-8-5 97 (b) DaraghO'Donohoe 7 92
(M F De Kock, South Africa) *led main gp: rdn 3f out: nt qckn* **20/1**
6 nse **Noble Citizen (USA)**[22] 175 5-8-5 95 (be) RichardMullen 12 92
(D M Simcock) *nvr bttr than mid-div* **16/1**
7 2 1/2 **Stubbs Art (IRE)**[188] 4543 5-8-5 98 TedDurcan 1 85
(M F De Kock, South Africa) *a in rr* **11/1**
8 1 **Ans Bach**[33] 7-8-5 96 (e) WilliamBuick 3 83
(D Selvaratnam, UAE) *in rr of mid-div: nvr able to chal* **16/1**
9 3/4 **Aqmaar**[28] 6-8-5 95 DavidBadel 2 81
(E Charpy, UAE) *s.i.s: nvr able to chal* **25/1**
10 1 1/4 **West Side Bernie (USA)**[279] 1688 4-9-4 112 FrankieDettori 11 90
(Saeed Bin Suroor) *nvr bttr than mid-div* **4/1**[3]
11 11 **Tasdeer (USA)**[56] 5-8-5 95 WayneSmith 9 48
(Doug Watson, UAE) *nvr able to chal* **33/1**
12 dist **Derbaas (USA)**[116] 6732 4-8-8 102 TadhgO'Shea 10 —
(A Al Raihe, UAE) *sn u.p* **16/1**

1m 26.03s (86.03) **12** Ran SP% **120.7**
CSF: £97.29 Tricast: £992.04.
Owner Hamdan Al Maktoum **Bred** Margaret Addis **Trained** United Arab Emirates

FOCUS
Form to treat with caution as the winner was allowed an incredibly easy lead. In addition a lot of these were coming off lengthy breaks.

NOTEBOOK
Barbecue Eddie(USA), quickly into his stride, soon found himself two-plus lengths in front, with none of his rivals being asked to challenge for the lead, and while he was a bit keen, he was getting away with setting no more than an ordinary gallop. Once in the straight, he never looked like being pegged back and duly stayed on well to record his first success since winning on a synthetic track in the US in 2008. It will be a surprise if things fall as kindly again this carnival.
Imbongi(SAF) ran a fine race on his first start since last July considering he was conceding weight all round and had no chance with the winner given the way the race panned out. (op 7-2)
Munaddam(USA) posted an encouraging effort on his first start for the best part of a year.
Summit Surge(IRE), a handicap winner on the turf off a mark of 109 at last year's carnival, was doing his best work in the closing stages on this first run since winning a Group 3 at Leopardstown in May. This was a pleasing enough debut for Luca Cumani and he can surely do better off a stronger pace, especially back over 1m. (op 5-2)
Wonder Lawn(SAF) was the only runner to try and keep tabs on the winner and as such looks flattered, although he had been off for 208 days. (op 18-1)
Noble Citizen(USA) was totally unsuited by the way the race unfolded but finished reasonably well. (op 14-1)
West Side Bernie(USA), a Grade 3 winner on Polytrack as a juvenile who was last seen finishing down the field in the Kentucky Derby, showed nothing on his debut for Godolphin.

439a CAPE VERDI SPONSORED BY AL TAYER MOTORS (F&M) (GROUP 3) (TURF) 1m
5:45 (5:45) 3-Y-0+

£74,074 (£24,691; £12,345; £6,172; £3,703; £2,469)

RPR
1 **Soneva (USA)**[125] 6503 4-9-0 111 ChristopheSoumillon 4 110
(M Botti) *mid-div: rdn to chse ldrs 2f out: r.o to ld cl home* **13/2**[3]
2 1/4 **Aspectoflove (IRE)**[110] 6884 4-8-11 102 FrankieDettori 2 106+
(Saeed Bin Suroor) *mid-div: veered rt 2f out: r.o wl once clr* **5/1**[2]
3 1 1/4 **Synergy (FR)**[86] 7347 5-9-0 105 OlivierPeslier 11 106
(Y Durepaire, Spain) *sn led: rdn clr 1 1/2f out: r.o wl: hdd 55yds out* **16/1**
4 1/4 **Cheyrac (FR)**[93] 7249 4-8-11 105 GregoryBenoist 6 103
(X Nakkachdji, France) *trckd ldr: ev ch 2f out: one pce* **20/1**
5 shd **Purple Sage (IRE)**[344] 701 4-8-11 95 KierenFallon 5 102
(F Nass, Bahrain) *slowly away: racd in rr: r.o fnl 1 1/2f: nvr able to chal* **33/1**
6 1 1/4 **Zirconeum (SAF)**[216] 5-9-3 107 KShea 10 105
(M F De Kock, South Africa) *in rr of mid-div: hmpd 2f out: nvr able to chal* **10/11**[1]
7 3/4 **Fourpenny Lane**[84] 7380 5-8-11 102 PJSmullen 9 98
(Ms Joanna Morgan, Ire) *nvr able to chal* **16/1**
8 1 1/4 **Indiana Gal (IRE)**[90] 7300 5-8-11 99 (p) TedDurcan 8 95
(Patrick Martin, Ire) *racd in rr: prog to mid-div: hmpd 2f out: n.d after* **16/1**
9 hd **Yana (IND)**[103] 6-8-11 100 (bt) RyanMoore 7 94
(B Chenoy, India) *mid-div: bdly hmpd 2f out* **16/1**
10 2 1/4 **Vattene (IRE)**[89] 7312 5-8-11 100 UmbertoRispoli 1 89
(M Gasparini, Italy) *trckd ldng pair: one pce fnl 1 1/2f* **33/1**
11 3/4 **Ahla Wasahl**[99] 7132 4-8-11 104 WilliamBuick 3 87
(D M Simcock) *in rr of mid-div: nvr able to chal* **11/1**

1m 38.4s (98.40) **11** Ran SP% **124.9**
CSF: £40.81.
Owner Arno Curty **Bred** Mineola Farm II Limited Partnership, D R Houchi **Trained** Newmarket, Suffolk

FOCUS
The second year this race has been run as a Group 3 and it was a good, competitive contest, certainly worthy of its status. The pace seemed fair, but with the going fast, it wasn't easy to make up significant amounts of ground. The time was 1.15 seconds slower than the later handicap won the 116-rated Snaafy.

NOTEBOOK
Soneva(USA), on her debut for a trainer who's going places, proved good enough to defy the penalty she incurred for last season's French Group 3 success. This win owes plenty to a fine ride from Christophe Soumillon, who had her well placed throughout, and she didn't look to have much in hand at all. As such, the obvious theory is that she'll struggle to see out the extra furlong in the Balanchine, her next intended target, when she will again be penalised, and her breeding offers little encouragement in the stamina department. (op 6-1)
Aspectoflove(IRE), a Listed winner over this trip at Naas on her final start for John Oxx last October, caused some trouble when switching into the clear around 2f out, but she had a clear shot herself from that stage and only just failed to get up; a fine effort considering others struggled get involved from the rear. Although by Danetime, whose stamina index is just 6.7f, there's plenty of stamina on the dam's side of her pedigree and she certainly ran as though she will get the extra furlong in the Blanchine. (op 9-2)
Synergy(FR) was allowed to dominate on a quick track, but even so, this was still a noteworthy performance considering her two most notable wins in France last year, a Listed contest and then a Group 3, had been gained over 1m3f on softish ground. (tchd 14-1)
Cheyrac(FR), a Listed winner on testing ground in France last year, was always well positioned and had her chance. (op 16-1)
Purple Sage(IRE) flashed her tail around the turn into the straight, but she ran on well from a long way back in the straight, suggesting further will suit.
Zirconeum(SAF), last seen finishing second in the prestigious Grade 1 Durban July in South Africa, is highly regarded, with her trainer saying he thought she could be his best filly since his Dubai Duty Free winner Ipe Tombe. However, Mike De Kock did stress beforehand that the filly might need the run, having suffered a slight setback, and that, combined with having to concede weight all round (Grade 1 penalty) over a trip short of her best, seemed to find her out. She was bumped around 2f from the finish, but already had a lot of ground to make up at that stage and, despite keeping on, she couldn't get on terms. There should be no excuses in the Balanchine, when she'll be race-fit and be suited by the extra furlong, and that will be the time to judge her. (op 11-8)
Fourpenny Lane ran a similar race to Zirconeum in that she had a lot to do when bumped around 2f out and never looked like getting seriously involved.

Yana(IND), a regular winner in India who won a 1m7f Grade 1 there in October, was bumped around 2f out and didn't have the pace to threaten. (op 14-1)

440a RANGE ROVER TROPHY (H'CAP) (TURF) — 1m
6:20 (6:20) (100-116,116) 3-Y-0+

£64,814 (£21,604; £10,802; £5,401; £3,240; £2,160)

			RPR
1		**Snaafy (USA)**[314] 1013 6-9-6 116 (v) RichardHills 11 (M Al Muhairi, UAE) *trckd ldrs: gng wl 2f out: led 1 1/2f out: r.o wl* **16/1**	117
2	1 ¼	**Yasoodd**[40] 7-8-6 101 (e) WilliamBuick 7 (D Selvaratnam, UAE) *mid-div: chsd wnr 1 1/2f out: r.o wl: no ch w wnr* **33/1**	100
3	¾	**Secrecy**[97] 7185 4-9-1 110 FrankieDettori 9 (Saeed Bin Suroor) *mid-div: chsd ldrs 2 1/2f out: one pce fnl 2f* **1/1**[1]	107
4	1 ½	**Calming Influence (IRE)**[344] 697 5-8-9 105 AhmedAjtebi 3 (Saeed Bin Suroor) *trckd ldrs: ev ch 2 1/2f out: one pce* **16/1**	98
5	3	**Cat Junior (USA)**[125] 6503 5-9-4 113 (t) JamieSpencer 2 (B J Meehan) *in rr of mid-div: r.o wl fnl 2 1/2f* **7/1**[2]	100
6	¾	**Emirates Gold (IRE)**[12] 7-8-7 102 (t) PJSmullen 8 (E Charpy, UAE) *s.i.s: nvr nr to chal* **20/1**	87
7	9 ½	**Dunelight (IRE)**[51] 7768 7-9-0 109 (v) KierenFallon 6 (C G Cox) *trckd ldrs: ev ch 2f out: wknd fnl 2f* **10/1**[3]	72
8	3	**Echoes Rock (GER)**[337] 771 7-8-10 106 (t) TadhgO'Shea 10 (Doug Watson, UAE) *disp tl 2f out: sn wknd* **33/1**	61
9	½	**Hunting Tower (SAF)**[8] 338 8-9-3 112 ChristopheSoumillon 5 (M F De Kock, South Africa) *a in mid-div* **10/1**[3]	67
10	13	**Poet**[145] 5924 5-9-6 116 DaraghO'Donohoe 4 (R Simpson, UAE) *racd in rr: nvr nr to chal* **11/1**	40
11	1	**Master Of Arts (USA)**[329] 4269 5-8-5 100 RoystonFfrench 12 (M Johnston) *chsd ldrs tl 2 1/2f out: wknd* **12/1**	23
12	1	**Olympic Election (BRZ)**[187] 5-8-6 101 WBlandi 1 (R Solanes, Brazil) *nvr bttr than mid-div* **16/1**	22

1m 37.25s (97.25) **12** Ran SP% **125.0**
CSF: £479.85 Tricast: £1017.46.
Owner Hamdan Al Maktoum **Bred** Shadwell Farm LLC **Trained** UAE

FOCUS
A high-class handicap run in a time 1.15 seconds quicker than Soneva, carrying 6lb less, recorded in the earlier fillies' Group 3.

NOTEBOOK
Snaafy(USA) ◆ was taking a significant drop in grade having finished seventh in 2009 World Cup when last seen. He has made tremendous progress on the dirt in recent years (his first Dubai success was gained off a rating of just 84) and he's clearly capable of continuing on the upward curve on turf, with this undoubtedly a career-best performance. It would be no surprise to see the winner kept to the grass now for the Al Fahidi Fort, or maybe the Zabeel Mile seeing as he could avoid a penalty in that contest, ahead of the Duty Free (should he continue to improve), but whatever the case, he has plenty of options, with Tapeta likely to suit as well.
Yasoodd, appearing at his fourth carnival but still looking for his first victory at the meeting, and indeed his first win since scoring in Ireland in 2006, followed the winner through but simply found that one too strong. (op 25-1)
Secrecy's jockey looked confident at the top of the straight, but this gelding, who was 8lb higher than when winning at Newmarket last October, had plenty of ground to make up and could never quite get there. It's possible the going was a bit too quick. (op 6-5)
Calming Influence(IRE) was plenty keen enough early on and did well to finish so close after 344 days off. (op 14-1)
Cat Junior(USA) was hampered after a few furlongs, which didn't help his chance, but even so he was set an awful lot to do and, in the circumstances, he finished about as close as could have been expected. This was his first start for four months and he should be capable of better.
Dunelight(IRE) was produced with every chance but his finishing effort was tame.
Hunting Tower(SAF)'s below-par run can be excused as he was bumped about a bit when short of room after a couple of furlongs or so, and was then denied a clear run when trying to stay on in the straight. (op 9-1)

441a FORD MUSTANG TROPHY (H'CAP) (TAPETA) — 1m 1f 110y
6:55 (6:55) (90-105,105) 3-Y-0+

£40,740 (£13,580; £6,790; £3,395; £2,037; £1,358)

			RPR
1		**Kal Barg**[49] 5-8-10 96 WilliamBuick 5 (D Selvaratnam, UAE) *in rr of mid-div: r.o wl fnl 1 1/2f: led cl home* **16/1**	99
2	1 ¼	**Espiritu (FR)**[118] 6665 4-9-2 102 (p) FrankieDettori 11 (Saeed Bin Suroor) *settled rr: r.o wl fnl f: nrst fin* **3/1**[1]	103
3	½	**Mister Fasliyev (IRE)**[28] 8-8-7 93 (bt) TadhgO'Shea 8 (E Charpy, UAE) *settled in rr: wd 3f out: r.o to ld 1 1/2f out: hdd fnl 55 yds* **33/1**	92
4	5 ½	**Hello Morning (FR)**[28] 5-8-9 95 RichardHills 6 (E Charpy, UAE) *sn led: hdd 1 1/2f out: kpt on same pce* **14/1**	83
5	hd	**Swinging Sixties (IRE)**[490] 6445 5-8-8 94 WayneSmith 12 (M Al Muhairi, UAE) *t.k.h in mid-div: disp 5f out: led 2f out: hdd 1 1/2f out: wknd fnl 55yds* **7/1**[3]	81
6	1 ¼	**Art Of War (SAF)**[8] 337 6-9-5 105 KShea 4 (M F De Kock, South Africa) *a in mid-div* **10/1**	90
7	½	**Keep Discovering (IRE)**[33] 5-8-7 93 (t) PJSmullen 1 (E Charpy, UAE) *wl away: a in mid-div* **28/1**	77
8	3 ¼	**Beauchamp Viceroy**[27] 109 6-9-4 104 (b) RyanMoore 7 (G A Butler) *trckd ldrs: one pce fnl 2 1/2f* **12/1**	81
9	1 ¼	**Rockette (FR)**[33] 28 5-8-9 95 KierenFallon 10 (E J O'Neill, France) *nvr bttr than mid-div* **10/3**[2]	70
10	¼	**Atila Sher Danon (GER)**[64] 4-8-11 98 AlanMunro 2 (W Hickst, Germany) *nvr able to chal* **16/1**	72
11	18	**Rocks Off (ARG)**[8] 339 5-9-3 102 ChristopheSoumillon 3 (M F De Kock, South Africa) *nvr able to chal* **8/1**	40
12	3 ¾	**Kaolak (USA)**[8] 335 4-8-8 95 (v) DaraghO'Donohoe 13 (J Ryan) *rdn to ld after 2 1/2f: hrd rdn 4f out: wknd fnl 1 1/2f* **14/1**	24
13	62	**Great Hawk (USA)**[678] 1077 7-9-1 100 (v) TedDurcan 9 (F Nass, Bahrain) *trckd ldrs tl 5f out: wknd* **33/1**	—

1m 59.13s (119.13) **13** Ran SP% **122.9**
CSF: £64.48 Tricast: £16.21.2 Placepot: £80.20. Pool of £12,642 - 115.05 winning units.
Quadpot: £15.00. Pool of £782 - 38.50 winning units..
Owner Sheikh Ahmed Al Maktoum **Bred** Mrs C G Gardiner **Trained** United Arab Emirates

FOCUS
A weak handicap for the grade run at an even pace.

NOTEBOOK
Kal Barg clearly benefited from a recent outing on the dirt at Jebel Ali and was a decisive winner after being produced wide, from well off the pace, with his challenge. His rider felt he won with a bit in hand, so he should be competitive off higher marks, but he'll probably face stiffer competition in future.
Espiritu(FR), 5lb higher than when narrowly beaten over 1m2f on turf for Jeremy Noseda last October, is a difficult ride and ran on just too late, having been produced with his run between rivals. (op 9-4)
Mister Fasliyev(IRE), produced wide with his challenge, briefly looked likely to end a losing run stretching back to 2007, but he couldn't sustain his run.
Hello Morning(FR) could only find the one pace for pressure.
Swinging Sixties(IRE) ◆, having his first start since winning a Newmarket handicap off a mark of 93 in October 2008, only tired late on after racing keenly through the early stages and there should be better to come, provided he stands training. (op 8-1)
Art Of War(SAF) travelled well but didn't get the best of runs when trying to pick up and made no impression. He was by no means unlucky, but can be given another chance. (op 12-1)
Keep Discovering(IRE), a bit keen early on, was keeping on when denied a clear run in the straight and is better than he showed.
Beauchamp Viceroy was produced with every chance but found little and is better suited by trips of around 1m.
Rockette(FR), a Listed winner over 1m at Deauville in January, seemed to travel okay but failed to pick up. (op 4-1)

420 LINGFIELD (L-H)
Saturday, February 6

OFFICIAL GOING: Standard
Wind: Half against; moderate, races 1-3, light remainder Weather: Becoming fine

442 LINGFIELDPARK.CO.UK APPRENTICE H'CAP — 7f (P)
1:25 (1:25) (Class 6) (0-65,66) 4-Y-0+ **£1,774** (£523; £262) **Stalls** Low

Form				RPR
00-1	1		**Stanley Goodspeed**[3] 397 7-9-2 65 6ex (t) KierenFox[(3)] 5 (J W Hills) *t.k.h: hld up in last trio: prog on wd outside 2f out: hanging over 1f out and stl only 7th: str run fnl f to ld last strides* **9/2**[1]	74+
056-	2	hd	**War And Peace (IRE)**[60] 7679 6-8-10 63 (e[1]) LewisWalsh[(7)] 10 (Jane Chapple-Hyam) *racd on outer: trckd ldrs: effrt 2f out: pushed along to ld ins fnl f: hdd last strides* **9/1**	71
0-25	3	¾	**Bollywood Style**[10] 318 5-8-7 58 RyanPowell[(5)] 6 (J R Best) *trckd ldrs: effrt towards outer 2f out: rdn to ld 1f out: sn hdd: kpt on* **13/2**[3]	64
311	4	¾	**Headache**[10] 318 5-9-1 66 (bt) MatthewLawson[(5)] 4 (B W Duke) *trckd clr ldr: rdn to cl and ld narrowly 2f out: hdd 1f out: one pce u.p* **5/1**[2]	70
-600	5	1 ¾	**Grey Boy (GER)**[6] 367 9-8-9 62 GeorgeDowning[(7)] 13 (A W Carroll) *hld up off the pce in midfield: urged along and effrt in 6th 2f out: kpt on but nvr gng pce to threaten* **20/1**	61
000-	6	½	**Count Ceprano (IRE)**[115] 5998 6-8-8 57 DeclanCannon[(3)] 12 (C R Dore) *hld up in last pair: stl there 2f out: rdn and r.o wl last 150yds: gaining at fin* **16/1**	55+
1435	7	¾	**Goodbye Cash (IRE)**[10] 317 6-9-3 63 AndrewHeffernan 3 (P D Evans) *chsd ldrs: rdn and cl enough towards inner 2f out: no imp over 1f out: fdd* **12/1**	59
040-	8	nse	**Ever Cheerful**[61] 7662 9-9-1 61 (p) AmyBaker 7 (A B Haynes) *led and clr: hdd 2f out: wknd fnl f* **25/1**	57
50-0	9	2	**Suhayl Star (IRE)**[14] 275 6-9-0 60 RossAtkinson 8 (P Burgoyne) *hld up off the pce in midfield: rdn and effrt over 2f out: hanging and no prog over 1f out: fdd* **13/2**[3]	50
2024	10	¾	**Dickie Le Davoir**[2] 404 6-8-8 57 (v) BillyCray[(3)] 9 (R C Guest) *dwlt: hld up in last pair: no prog 2f out: plugged on* **13/2**[3]	45
30-0	11	2 ½	**One Cool Dream**[35] 21 4-8-8 57 TobyAtkinson[(3)] 2 (P W Hiatt) *dwlt: towards rr: rdn 3f out: sn struggling* **33/1**	39
04-6	12	2 ¼	**Haasem (USA)**[22] 194 7-8-6 57 DannyBrock[(5)] 11 (J R Jenkins) *dwlt: rcvrd into midfield on inner: lost pl over 2f out: btn after* **16/1**	33

1m 24.64s (-0.16) **Going Correction** +0.175s/f (Slow) **12** Ran SP% **115.9**
Speed ratings (Par 101): **107,106,105,105,103 102,101,101,99,98 95,93**
toteswingers: 1&2 £17.70, 1&3 £9.60, 2&3 £25.70 CSF £42.66 CT £266.80 TOTE £5.70: £2.50, £2.90, £3.00; EX 66.80 TRIFECTA Not won..
Owner R J Tufft **Bred** Burton Agnes Stud Co Ltd **Trained** Upper Lambourn, Berks

FOCUS
A modest apprentice handicap run at a good pace. Pretty sound form for the grade.

443 MARRIOTT HOTEL OPENING SPRING 2010 MAIDEN STKS — 7f (P)
2:00 (2:02) (Class 5) 3-Y-0+ **£2,456** (£725; £362) **Stalls** Low

Form				RPR
233-	1		**Ginger Grey (IRE)**[107] 6963 3-8-10 65 DaneO'Neill 5 (D R C Elsworth) *hld up in 5th: pushed along over 2f out: prog over 1f out: styd on to ld last 150yds: in command after* **9/4**[1]	61+
4-	2	¾	**Jodawes (USA)**[37] 7885 3-8-10 0 SteveDrowne 1 (J R Best) *t.k.h early: trckd ldr to wl over 1f out: rdn and effrt to chal 1f out: chsd wnr ins fnl f: a hld* **5/2**[2]	59
000-	3	1	**Trading Nation (USA)**[64] 7627 4-9-13 70 SaleemGolam 6 (P W Hiatt) *s.s: t.k.h early: hld up in 4th: prog towards inner to ld wl over 1f out: edgd rt after: hdd and outpcd last 150yds* **12/1**	61
40-	4	hd	**Lou Bear (IRE)**[37] 7886 3-8-10 0 J-PGuillambert 4 (J Akehurst) *t.k.h early: trckd ldng pair: wdst bnd 2f out and lost pl: rdn and styd on same pce fnl f* **4/1**[3]	55
3646	5	shd	**Tatawor (IRE)**[10] 313 3-8-10 65 (b) StephenCraine 8 (J R Boyle) *hld up in 7th: cl enough over 1f out: looking for room and taken towards outer: rdn and r.o last 100yds: no ch* **13/2**	55
0-6	6	2 ¼	**Yourgolftravel Com**[7] 356 5-9-8 0 TobyAtkinson[(5)] 7 (M Wigham) *plld hrd: hld up in 6th: rdn 2f out: no imp after* **20/1**	54
	7	nse	**Ramble On Love** 3-8-5 0 FrankieMcDonald 3 (P Winkworth) *s.s: rn v green in last: detached 2f out: picked up last 100yds and running on nr fin* **25/1**	44
-664	8	shd	**Maxijack (IRE)**[6] 362 3-8-10 56 ChrisCatlin 2 (G Brown) *led at modest pce: tried to kick on over 2f out: hdd wl over 1f out: sn wknd* **33/1**	49

1m 27.97s (3.17) **Going Correction** +0.175s/f (Slow)
WFA 3 from 4yo+ 17lb **8** Ran SP% **111.9**
Speed ratings (Par 103): **88,87,86,85,85 83,83,82**
toteswingers: 1&2 £2.30, 1&3 £5.20, 2&3 £7.10 CSF £7.64 TOTE £2.70: £1.10, £1.40, £4.00; EX 6.40 Trifecta £31.20 Pool: £449.97 - 10.67 winning units..
Owner T Mohan **Bred** B Kennedy **Trained** Newmarket, Suffolk

FOCUS
An ordinary maiden run at a steady early gallop. The form makes sense amongst the principals but it is doubtful the winner had to improve.
Trading Nation(USA) Official explanation: jockey said gelding hung right
Yourgolftravel Com Official explanation: jockey said gelding ran too free

Ramble On Love Official explanation: jockey said filly ran green

444 CYPRIUM BAR AT MARRIOTT LINGFIELD (S) STKS 1m (P)
2:30 (2:30) (Class 6) 4-Y-0+ £1,774 (£523; £262) Stalls High

Form RPR

345- **1** **Wrighty Almighty (IRE)**[241] 2807 8-8-13 59 JimCrowley 7 66
(P R Chamings) *hld up in last: plenty to do whn effrt on wd outside 2f out: prog over 1f out: r.o u.p fnl f: led post* **8/1**

60- **2** *nse* **Lastkingofscotland (IRE)**[53] 7759 4-8-13 82 (b[1]) PaulDoe 8 66
(Jim Best) *trckd ldr: clr w him over 2f out: rdn to ld over 1f out: hanging and looked awkward: kpt on fnl f: hdd post* **7/2**[2]

4-04 **3** *1* **Ravi River (IRE)**[17] 230 6-9-5 72 (v[1]) J-PGuillambert 2 70
(P D Evans) *racd freely: led: clr w one rival over 2f out: hdd on inner over 1f out: nt qckn fnl f* **3/1**[1]

206- **4** *1 3/4* **Murrin (IRE)**[85] 7362 6-8-13 68 (p) StevieDonohoe 4 59
(R A Mills) *hld up on inner: outpcd fr 3f out: rdn and sme prog over 1f out: nvr rchd ldrs* **4/1**[3]

0-03 **5** *1/2* **Woolston Ferry (IRE)**[12] 289 4-8-13 57 (p) FergusSweeney 3 58
(David Pinder) *chsd ldng pair: rdn and no imp over 2f out: steadily lost pl fnl f* **9/1**

-405 **6** *1/2* **Luisa Tetrazzini (IRE)**[15] 270 4-8-6 53 ow3 MarkCoumbe(5) 5 55
(John A Harris) *rrd bef stalls opened: hld up: prog on outer 3f out to dispute 3rd 2f out: no hdwy over 1f out: fdd* **25/1**

5253 **7** *5* **Lord Deevert**[8] 342 5-8-10 60 (p) WilliamCarson(3) 1 45
(W G M Turner) *hld up in tch: rdn 3f out: sn struggling and bhd* **5/1**

3-64 **8** *7* **Cavalry Guard (USA)**[17] 234 6-8-8 51 (b) AmyBaker(5) 6 28
(T D McCarthy) *chsd ldrs: rdn and struggling 3f out: sn bhd* **16/1**

1m 38.12s (-0.08) **Going Correction** +0.175s/f (Slow) 8 Ran SP% **114.7**
Speed ratings (Par 101): **107,106,105,104,103 103,98,91**
toteswingers: 1&2 £9.50, 1&3 £2.80, 2&3 £3.40 CSF £36.28 TOTE £13.90: £2.90, £1.90, £1.80; EX 31.40 Trifecta £233.40 Pool: £369.07 - 1.17 winning units..There was no bid for the winner. Lastkingofscotland was claimed by J J Best for £6,000.
Owner The Boccy Hall Evans Tyrrell Partnership **Bred** P Heffernan **Trained** Baughurst, Hants
■ Stewards' Enquiry : Mark Coumbe two-day ban: careless riding (Feb 20-21)

FOCUS
The principals started battling up front plenty soon enough here and left themselves vulnerable to a late closer. Pretty muddling form and it is doubtful if the winner had to improve.

445 SIMON MILLER 30TH BIRTHDAY MAIDEN STKS 5f (P)
3:05 (3:05) (Class 5) 3-Y-0 £2,456 (£725; £362) Stalls High

Form RPR

0-43 **1** **Mrs Boss**[15] 257 3-8-12 67 ow3 JamesMillman(3) 3 71
(B R Millman) *best away but sn settled in last: brought wd in st: rdn to ld ent fnl f: sn clr* **5/2**[2]

260- **2** *3 1/4* **Diamond Johnny G (USA)**[212] 3779 3-9-3 83 NeilCallan 4 61
(E J Creighton) *racd three wd: disp ld to over 1f out: nt qckn u.p: plugged on to take 2nd nr fin* **6/5**[1]

50-3 **3** *nk* **Posy Fossil (USA)**[10] 313 3-8-9 62 WilliamCarson(3) 2 55
(S C Williams) *sn disp ld: rdn over 2f out: nt qckn over 1f out: one pce after* **3/1**[3]

60- **4** *hd* **Miss Kitty Grey (IRE)**[184] 4688 3-8-12 0 PatCosgrave 1 55?
(J R Boyle) *sn disp ld on inner: slt advantage over 1f out: hdd ent fnl f: wknd nr fin* **11/1**

60.19 secs (1.39) **Going Correction** +0.175s/f (Slow) 4 Ran SP% **107.4**
Speed ratings (Par 97): **95,89,89,89**
CSF £5.87 TOTE £3.30; EX 6.50.
Owner Mrs L S Millman **Bred** Mrs L S Millman **Trained** Kentisbeare, Devon

FOCUS
No more than a very modest maiden. The favourite was well below form and the race is rated around the winner.

446 MARRIOTT PLAY AND STAY H'CAP 5f (P)
3:35 (3:35) (Class 2) (0-100,98) 4-Y-0+ £10,361 (£3,083; £1,540; £769) Stalls High

Form RPR

-231 **1** **Nickel Silver**[10] 307 5-8-12 92 (v) TomEaves 1 99+
(B Smart) *mde all at gd pce: brought wd in st: hrd pressed ins fnl f: hld on* **6/5**[1]

3023 **2** *nk* **Indian Skipper (IRE)**[6] 365 5-7-13 84 (v[1]) BillyCray(5) 6 90
(R C Guest) *s.i.s: pushed along in 5th early: gng bttr after 2f: rdn and prog over 1f out: wnt 2nd last 100yds: gaining fin* **11/1**

-4 **3** *1/2* **Wotashirtfull (IRE)**[30] 74 5-8-4 84 oh1 (p) NickyMackay 2 88
(J R Boyle) *chsd wnr: rdn and grad clsd fnl f but lost 2nd last 100yds* **7/1**[3]

-305 **4** *2* **Peak District (IRE)**[3] 384 6-8-5 85 (b[1]) ChrisCatlin 4 82
(K A Ryan) *chsd ldng pair: rdn and fnd nil over 1f out: wl btn after* **9/2**[2]

-040 **5** *3/4* **Ebraam (USA)**[7] 358 7-9-4 98 RobertWinston 3 92
(S Curran) *s.s: hld up in last on inner: rdn and no real prog over 1f out* **9/2**[2]

00-0 **6** *1 1/2* **Hoh Hoh Hoh**[20] 212 8-8-12 92 StevieDonohoe 5 81
(R J Price) *s.s: sn chsd ldng trio: rdn to dispute 3rd on inner 2f out: no hdwy fr over 1f out* **14/1**

58.43 secs (-0.37) **Going Correction** +0.175s/f (Slow) 6 Ran SP% **109.3**
Speed ratings (Par 109): **109,108,107,104,103 100**
toteswingers: 1&2 £1.90, 1&3 £2.70, 2&3 £6.90 CSF £14.55 TOTE £1.70: £1.30, £5.00; EX 12.00.
Owner M Barber **Bred** Mrs Sheila White **Trained** Hambleton, N Yorks

FOCUS
This was not a strong race for the grade, but the winner recording a small personal best and the next two were close to their marks.

NOTEBOOK
Nickel Silver, representing a stable in cracking form, broke well and made every yard, bravely holding off strong challengers at the finish. He won off a career-high mark here, but not being taken on for the lead was key, and he won't always find things falling so kindly. He has now won at all four current AW tracks. (op 11-8 tchd 6-4 and 11-10)
Indian Skipper(IRE), wearing a visor for the first time on this drop back to the minimum trip, was better away from the gates but still struggled to go the early pace. He finished well, though, and the experiment could be said to have been a success. (tchd 10-1)
Wotashirtfull(IRE) was 1lb wrong at the weights but he was back at his favourite track and ran right up to his best in defeat. He likes to lead but was denied that role by the winner this time. (op 8-1 tchd 13-2)
Peak District(IRE) was blinkered for the first time in an attempt to get him to rediscover some of his old sparkle, but he was again a little below his best. (op 4-1 tchd 11-2 and 7-2 in places)
Ebraam(USA), who won this race in 2008 and was fifth in it last year, was taken to the inside entering the straight and made no further progress. He needs to drop a few pounds to be of interest. (tchd 4-1 and 5-1)
Hoh Hoh Hoh has now run on the AW four times and has only ever beaten one rival. (op 10-1)

447 GOLF & RACING H'CAP 1m 4f (P)
4:10 (4:10) (Class 2) (0-100,104) 4-Y-0+ £10,361 (£3,083; £1,540; £769) Stalls Low

Form RPR

1 **1** **Buxted (IRE)**[22] 179 4-8-6 88 StevieDonohoe 3 100+
(R A Mills) *trckd ldng pair: wnt 2nd 3f out: shkn up to ld narrowly 1f out: drvn and won gng away at fin* **7/2**[2]

11- **2** *1 1/2* **King's Salute (USA)**[70] 7573 4-8-5 87 JoeFanning 5 96
(M Johnston) *led 1f: trckd ldr: led over 3f out: drvn 2f out: hdd 1f out: styd on wl but wl hld nr fin* **13/8**[1]

4361 **3** *2* **Full Toss**[2] 408 4-8-8 95 6ex AndrewHeffernan(5) 1 101
(P D Evans) *t.k.h early: hld up in 4th: lost pl sltly over 4f out: effrt to chse ldng pair over 2f out: styd on wl u.p but no real imp* **10/1**

3-51 **4** *4 1/2* **Dance The Star (USA)**[16] 252 5-9-0 93 FergusSweeney 2 92
(D M Simcock) *s.s: hld up in last: prog on inner and wl in tch 4f out: wl outpcd fnl 2f* **5/1**[3]

2-21 **5** *6* **Paktolos (FR)**[18] 224 7-8-7 91 (p) MarkCoumbe(5) 7 80
(John A Harris) *hld up in 6th: clsd on wd outside 4f out: drvn over 2f out: wknd wl over 1f out* **16/1**

4-11 **6** *3 1/4* **Mister New York (USA)**[15] 266 5-9-3 96 (b) JimCrowley 4 80
(Noel T Chance) *hld up in 5th: clsd on ldrs 4f out: drvn over 2f out: sn wknd* **7/2**[2]

45-0 **7** *2 1/2* **Valmari (IRE)**[8] 341 7-8-0 86 oh3 (b) CharlotteKerton(7) 6 66
(G Prodromou) *t.k.h: led after 1f to over 3f out: sn dropped out* **80/1**

2m 30.69s (-2.31) **Going Correction** +0.175s/f (Slow)
WFA 4 from 5yo+ 3lb 7 Ran SP% **115.4**
Speed ratings (Par 109): **114,113,111,108,104 102,100**
toteswingers: 1&2 £2.60, 1&3 £5.70, 2&3 £4.20 CSF £9.82 CT £50.08 TOTE £3.90: £2.00, £1.60; EX 9.10 Trifecta £126.10 Pool: £3.70 - 630.93 winning units..
Owner Buxted Partnership **Bred** Ronan Burns **Trained** Headley, Surrey
■ The first winner for Robert Mills, who took over the licence following the recent death of his father Terry.

FOCUS
A good-quality handicap in which all but the rank outsider had won last time out.

NOTEBOOK
Buxted(IRE) sauntered clear of a 65-rated rival (subsequently successful) in winning his maiden on his debut here last time, and despite being given a mark of 88 for his handicap debut he still looked to hold strong claims. He got the better of a progressive sort in King's Salute and looks a smart performer in the making, so it's no great surprise that his connections are thinking about stepping him up to Listed company towards the end of March/beginning of April. (op 3-1 tchd 11-4)
King's Salute(USA), returning from a 70-day break, led them into the straight but couldn't hold off the strong finish of the winner. He bumped into one here, but is fully capable of returning to winning ways against more exposed rivals. (op 5-4 tchd 7-4)
Full Toss came here on the back of a win at Wolverhampton two days earlier, but a 6lb penalty left him vulnerable, especially against a couple of rivals who were relatively unexposed. He ran a solid race in the circumstances. (op 12-1 tchd 8-1)
Dance The Star(USA), 6lb higher than when successful at Wolverhampton last time, stayed on steadily nearest the inside rail, but was another simply unable to land a blow against the first two, who are clearly well ahead of the handicapper. (op 15-2)
Paktolos(FR), raised 7lb for his last-time-out success over almost two furlongs further, didn't have the pace to get involved from the turn in. (op 20-1)
Mister New York(USA), chasing a hat-trick off a career-high mark, was also left flat-footed when the front pair kicked on. (op 11-2)

448 LINGFIELD PARK GOLF CLUB H'CAP 1m (P)
4:45 (4:45) (Class 4) (0-85,78) 3-Y-0 £4,209 (£1,252; £625; £312) Stalls High

Form RPR

5-21 **1** **Monterosso**[14] 274 3-9-7 78 JoeFanning 4 85+
(M Johnston) *trckd ldr: shkn up to ld over 1f out: pushed along and wl in command fnl f* **8/11**[1]

-122 **2** *1 1/2* **Lisahane Bog**[10] 311 3-9-4 75 (v[1]) DaneO'Neill 2 76
(P R Hedger) *hld up bhd ldng pair: rdn over 2f out: styd on to take 2nd ins fnl f: no ch w wnr* **9/2**[3]

14- **3** *3/4* **Tenacestream (CAN)**[38] 7878 3-9-6 77 RobertWinston 6 76
(J R Best) *racd too keenly: led at modest pce: tried to kick on over 2f out: hdd and nt qckn over 1f out: one pce* **3/1**[2]

1 **4** *hd* **Nubar Boy**[17] 236 3-9-5 76 (t) RichardSmith 5 75
(Tom Dascombe) *hld up in last: taken wd and effrt 2f out: nt qckn over 1f out: one pce after* **16/1**

20-1 **5** *3/4* **Kinky Afro (IRE)**[23] 159 3-8-8 70 RossAtkinson(5) 1 67
(J S Moore) *hld up bhd ldng pair: rdn on inner over 2f out: nt qckn over 1f out: no hdwy after* **16/1**

1m 41.42s (3.22) **Going Correction** +0.175s/f (Slow) 5 Ran SP% **112.9**
Speed ratings (Par 99): **90,88,87,87,86**
toteswingers: 1&2 £4.40. CSF £4.67 TOTE £1.60: £1.10, £2.90; EX 4.20 Place 6: £36.95, Place 5: £15.78.
Owner Sheikh Hamdan Bin Mohammed Al Maktoum **Bred** Darley **Trained** Middleham Moor, N Yorks

FOCUS
The top-weight here was rated 7lb below the ceiling for the race, and the early pace was far from frantic, resulting in something of a sprint finish.
Tenacestream(CAN) Official explanation: jockey said colt ran too free
T/Plt: £56.00 to a £1 stake. Pool: £62,253.87. 810.77 winning tickets. T/Qpdt: £21.50 to a £1 stake. Pool: £3,666.84. 125.75 winning tickets. JN

MONT-DE-MARSAN (R-H)
Saturday, February 6

OFFICIAL GOING: Very soft

450a PRIX DE CAMPET (MAIDEN) (C&G) 7f
3:00 (3:00) 3-Y-0 £6,195 (£2,478; £1,858; £1,239; £619)

RPR

1 **Myasun (FR)**[90] 7316 3-9-2 OlivierTrigodet 72
(C Baillet, France)

2 *3* **Katchmore (IRE)**[37] 7885 3-9-2 CharlesNora 65
(Jean-Rene Auvray) *prom: pushed along over 2f out: sn wnt 2nd: styd on: no ch w wnr [no SP]*

3 *3* **Zarly (FR)**[185] 4686 3-9-2 Francois-XavierBertras 57
(F Rohaut, France)

4 *nk* **Takashi (FR)**[213] 3-9-2 56
(J-C Rouget, France)

5 *1* **Proust (FR)** 3-8-12 ... 50
(B De Montzey, France)
6 *½* **Grand Lucius (FR)** 3-8-12 ... 49
(D Guillemin, France)
7 *1½* **Bahatoo** 3-8-12 ... 45
(X Thomas-Demeaulte, France)
8 *8* **Tragagalletas (IRE)** 3-9-2 ...(b) 29
(L A Urbano-Grajales, France)
9 *nk* **Vermentino (FR)**93 7264 3-9-2 ... 28
(M Roussel, France)
10 *shd* **Wolfgang (SPA)**10 3-9-2 ... 28
(M Alonso, Spain)
0 **Skyfly (FR)** 3-8-12 ... —
(T Lemer, France)
0 **Domino Play (FR)** 3-9-2 ... —
(R Avial Lopez, Spain)
0 **Indian Maj (FR)** 3-9-2 ...(b) —
(J Suarez Paniagua, France)
1m 33.98s (93.98) 13 Ran
PARI-MUTUEL (Including 1 Euro stake): WIN 7.50; PL 3.70, 4.00, 2.60;DF 48.30.
Owner Ecurie Jarlan **Bred** Sarl Ecurie Jarlan **Trained** France

398 SOUTHWELL (L-H)
Sunday, February 7

OFFICIAL GOING: Standard
The track favoured front-runners.
Wind: Nil Weather: Misty

451 COME JUMP RACING TOMORROW H'CAP 1m (F)
1:40 (1:41) (Class 5) (0-70,70) 4-Y-O+ **£2,456** (£544; £544) **Stalls** Low

Form RPR
02-3 1 **Trans Sonic**31 75 7-8-8 **60** ... FranciscoDaSilva 5 81
(J Hetherton) *sn led: pushed clr fr over 2f out: styd on wl* **14/1**
325- 2 *8* **Ansells Pride (IRE)**42 7854 7-9-2 **68** ... TomEaves 4 70
(B Smart) *sn pushed along and prom: chsd wnr 3f out: rdn and hung lft over 2f out: styd on same pce* **7/2**1
4413 2 *dht* **General Tufto**3 400 5-8-13 **68** ...(b) KellyHarrison(3) 8 70
(C Smith) *hld up: hdwy u.p over 1f out: nvr nrr* **6/1**
-123 4 *1½* **Miss Bootylishes**3 398 5-8-13 **70** ... AmyBaker(5) 9 69
(A B Haynes) *prom: lost pl over 4f out: hdwy over 1f out: no ex fnl f* **4/1**2
5300 5 *2¾* **Jonnie Skull (IRE)**7 367 4-8-7 **66** ...(vt) LeonnaMayor(7) 7 59
(P S McEntee) *chsd ldrs: shkn up and edgd lft over 2f out: wknd over 1f out* **33/1**
4120 6 *shd* **Carmenero (GER)**6 373 7-8-13 **70** ... BarryMcHugh(5) 10 62
(C R Dore) *hld up: rdn over 3f out: styd on ins fnl f: nrst fin* **16/1**
1-30 7 *1¼* **Convince (USA)**9 348 9-8-7 **59** ...(p) PaulHanagan 6 49
(J L Flint) *stall opened fractionally early: led early: chsd ldrs and sn pushed along: rdn 1/2-way: wknd 3f out* **22/1**
5-21 8 *2¾* **Borasco (USA)**3 398 5-9-4 **70** 6ex ... PhillipMakin 3 53
(T D Barron) *sn pushed along in rr: rdn over 3f out: nvr on terms* **9/2**3
23-0 9 *4½* **Solis**26 144 4-8-8 **60** ... GrahamGibbons 1 33
(J J Quinn) *mid-div: sn pushed along: rdn 1/2-way: wknd over 3f out* **9/2**3
-061 10 *2¾* **Madison Belle**12 297 4-8-11 **63** ... AndrewElliott 2 30
(J R Weymes) *chsd ldr tl rdn 3f out: wknd 2f out* **16/1**
1m 39.17s (-4.53) **Going Correction** -0.35s/f (Stan) 10 Ran SP% **118.6**
Speed ratings (Par 103): **108,100,100,98,95 95,94,91,87,84**PL: Trans Sonic £3.40, Ansells Pride £1.70, General Tufto £1.90 EX: TS&AP £43.00, TS> £82.60 CSF: TS&AP £31.88, TS> £48.64. TC: TS&AP> £168.44, TS>&AP £183.32. toteswingers:TS&AP:£10.00, TS>:£12.00, AP>:£7.00 TOTE £15.40 TRIFECTA Not wo27 Owner.

FOCUS
A modest handicap and few were ever involved. The winner impressed and the time was good for the grade, but the track was favouring pace.

452 BETDAQ ON 0870 178 1221 CLAIMING STKS 1m (F)
2:10 (2:10) (Class 6) 3-Y-O **£1,774** (£523; £262) **Stalls** Low

Form RPR
10-6 1 **Tiger Hawk (USA)**6 372 3-8-3 65 ...(b) AndrewHeffernan(5) 4 69
(P D Evans) *set stdy pce tl qcknd 1/2-way: rdn clr fnl 2f: eased nr fin* **11/4**2
1-21 2 *9* **Inside Track (IRE)**24 168 3-8-10 75 ...(b) TonyCulhane 2 50
(P T Midgley) *chsd wnr: shkn up over 3f out: rdn: hung lft and wknd over 1f out* **4/9**1
0-36 3 *1* **Red Valerian Two (IRE)**12 302 3-8-9 55 ... PaulPickard(5) 1 52
(P T Midgley) *prom: racd keenly: rdn over 3f out: wknd wl over 2f out* **12/1**3
6 4 *2¼* **Maigold Rose**23 189 3-8-4 0 ... DavidProbert 3 37
(J R Weymes) *s.i.s: racd keenly and sn prom: rdn 1/2-way: wknd 3f out* **25/1**
1m 41.85s (-1.85) **Going Correction** -0.35s/f (Stan) 4 Ran SP% **107.5**
Speed ratings (Par 95): **95,86,85,82**
CSF £4.41 TOTE £2.80; EX 6.20.
Owner Freddie Ingram **Bred** Sun Valley Farm **Trained** Pandy, Monmouths

FOCUS
With the track suiting front-runners, Tiger Hawk made all for a wide-margin success. With the favourite below par this took little winning.
Inside Track(IRE) Official explanation: trainer had no explanation for the poor form shown

453 BET PREMIER LEAGUE FOOTBALL-BETDAQ MAIDEN STKS 6f (F)
2:40 (2:41) (Class 5) 3-Y-O **£2,456** (£725; £362) **Stalls** Low

Form RPR
1 **Solstice** 3-8-7 0 ... BarryMcHugh(5) 3 82+
(Julie Camacho) *trckd ldrs: led 2f out: shkn up over 1f out: r.o wl* **9/2**3
2 *1½* **Binthere Dunthat** 3-8-12 0 ... HayleyTurner 7 77+
(M L W Bell) *in tch but pushed along in the early stages: rdn to chse wnr over 1f out: r.o* **5/2**1
3- 3 *4½* **Just Mandy (IRE)**211 3849 3-8-12 0 ... PaulHanagan 5 63
(R A Fahey) *chsd ldr: rdn and ev ch over 2f out: hung lft over 1f out: no ex* **3/1**2
4 *nse* **Fighter Boy (IRE)** 3-9-3 0 ... PhillipMakin 6 68
(T D Barron) *trckd ldrs: racd keenly: hung lft over 1f out: no ex* **3/1**2
0- 5 *17* **Pinewood Polly**85 7396 3-8-7 0 ... TobyAtkinson(5) 4 8
(S A Harris) *s.i.s: sn pushed along in rr: wknd wl over 2f out* **80/1**
4 6 *9* **Fine And Dandie (IRE)**12 301 3-9-3 0 ... AdrianNicholls 2 16
(D Nicholls) *restless in stalls: sn led: rdn and hdd 2f out: sn edgd lft and wknd* **7/1**
1m 14.62s (-1.88) **Going Correction** -0.35s/f (Stan) 6 Ran SP% **110.5**
Speed ratings (Par 97): **98,96,90,89,67 55**
toteswinger:1&2:£2.60, 1&3:£3.00, 2&3:£2.30 CSF £15.61 TOTE £6.20: £2.50, £1.70; EX 9.30.
Owner G B Turnbull Ltd **Bred** The National Stud **Trained** Norton, N Yorks

FOCUS
Not much previous form to go on but this looked a reasonable maiden, and the time was 0.56 seconds quicker than the later 3-y-o seller.
Fine And Dandie(IRE) Official explanation: jockey said gelding had no more to give

454 BET SIX NATIONS RUGBY - BETDAQ (S) STKS 6f (F)
3:10 (3:11) (Class 6) 3-Y-O **£1,774** (£523; £262) **Stalls** Low

Form RPR
0 1 **Moors Gorse**6 372 3-8-9 0 ... GrahamGibbons 5 62
(R Hollinshead) *led: hdd over 4f out: chsd ldr: rdn over 1f out: styd on to ld wl ins fnl f* **10/1**
-323 2 *hd* **Flow Chart (IRE)**6 370 3-9-5 71 ...(b) PhillipMakin 1 71
(T D Barron) *w wnr tl led over 4f out: rdn and edgd rt over 1f out: hdd wl ins fnl f* **6/5**1
2-40 3 *2* **City Gossip (IRE)**27 122 3-8-4 58 ... AshleyMorgan(5) 4 55
(M G Quinlan) *chsd ldrs: rdn over 2f out: styd on same pce fnl f* **14/1**
53-1 4 *hd* **Marjolly (IRE)**27 122 3-9-0 60 ...(p) MatthewDavies(5) 3 64
(George Baker) *s.i.s: in rr: hdwy over 3f out: sn rdn: styd on same pce fnl f* **5/2**2
2334 5 *1¾* **Tamarind Hill (IRE)**3 406 3-9-0 67 ...(b) AndrewMullen 2 53
(A J McCabe) *sn pushed along in rr: sme hdwy u.p over 1f out: no ex fnl f* **9/2**3
1m 15.18s (-1.32) **Going Correction** -0.35s/f (Stan) 5 Ran SP% **108.0**
Speed ratings (Par 95): **94,93,91,90,88**
.There was no bid for the winner. Flow Chart was claimed by Mr P. Grayson for £6,000.\n\x\x
Owner R Hollinshead **Bred** Longdon Stud Ltd **Trained** Upper Longdon, Staffs

FOCUS
Continuing the general theme of the meeting, it proved difficult to make up ground. The time was 0.56 seconds slower than the earlier 3-y-o maiden won by Solstice. Muddling form with the runner-up the best guide.

455 BET NFL SUPERBOWL - BETDAQ H'CAP 7f (F)
3:40 (3:40) (Class 6) (0-60,58) 3-Y-O **£1,774** (£523; £262) **Stalls** Low

Form RPR
-532 1 **Premium Charge**13 288 3-8-13 **53** ... DavidProbert 3 56
(C A Dwyer) *mde virtually all: hrd rdn and jnd over 1f out: styd on gamely: all out* **15/8**1
000- 2 *nse* **Buzz Bird**137 6215 3-8-6 **46** ... FrannyNorton 6 49+
(T D Barron) *hld up: rdn 1/2-way: rdn and hung lft over 1f out: r.o wl towards fin: jst failed* **15/2**
50-0 3 *nk* **Lord's Seat**12 302 3-8-0 **45** ... AndrewHeffernan(5) 1 47
(A Berry) *sn prom: rdn and ev ch fr over 1f out: styd on* **40/1**
0-62 4 *2* **Bertie Buckle (IRE)**10 329 3-8-13 **53** ... HayleyTurner 5 50
(J R Gask) *chsd ldrs: pushed along 1/2-way: chsd wnr over 2f out: rdn and ev ch over 1f out: no ex wl ins fnl f* **4/1**3
46-3 5 *1* **Taper Jean Girl (IRE)**10 329 3-8-11 **51** ... AndrewElliott 2 45
(Mrs R A Carr) *chsd wnr tl rdn over 2f out: styd on same pce fnl f* **11/1**
6-32 6 *1* **D'Urberville**12 302 3-9-4 **58** ... PaulHanagan 4 49
(J R Jenkins) *sn pushed along in rr: rdn over 2f out: no imp* **2/1**2
1m 28.7s (-1.60) **Going Correction** -0.35s/f (Stan) 6 Ran SP% **110.7**
Speed ratings (Par 95): **95,94,94,92,91 90**
toteswinger:1&2:£2.30, 1&3:£7.50, 2&3:£8.40 CSF £15.65 TOTE £2.40: £1.10, £2.50; EX 17.10.
Owner Mrs Shelley Dwyer **Bred** Mrs J A Chapman **Trained** Burrough Green, Cambs
■ Stewards' Enquiry : Andrew Heffernan three-day ban: used whip with excessive frequency (Feb 21-23)
David Probert caution: used whip with excessive frequency.

FOCUS
A very moderate but competitive handicap which was well run. The winner is gradually improving.

456 TRY BETDAQ FOR AN EXCHANGE CLAIMING STKS 1m 6f (F)
4:10 (4:10) (Class 6) 4-Y-O+ **£1,774** (£523; £262) **Stalls** Low

Form RPR
-612 1 **Boundless Prospect (USA)**10 327 11-8-8 68.. AndrewHeffernan(5) 7 64
(P D Evans) *broke wl: stdd and dropped in rr after 1f: rdn over 4f out: hdwy over 3f out: drvn to ld over and edgd lft wl over 1f out: styd on* **13/8**1
-134 2 *2* **Dream In Blue**5 377 5-9-0 67 ...(p) FrederikTylicki 5 62
(J A Glover) *plld hrd: trckd ldr 5f: remained handy: chsd ldr over 4f out: led over 3f out: rdn and hdd wl over 1f out: edgd lft: styd on same pce ins fnl f* **10/3**3
6-33 3 *hd* **Dunaskin (IRE)**10 327 10-8-13 74 ... BarryMcHugh(5) 2 66
(B Ellison) *prom: hmpd over 4f out: shkn up over 3f out: sn rdn: styd on wl towards fin* **9/4**2
3-00 4 *5* **Spiritonthemount (USA)**10 322 5-9-2 47 ...(v1) PhillipMakin 8 57?
(P W Hiatt) *given reminders to ld: rdn and hdd over 3f out: edgd rt and wknd wl over 1f out* **22/1**
0-5 5 *3* **Zaffeu**23 190 9-8-13 57 ... VinceSlattery 6 50
(A G Juckes) *s.i.s: sn prom: chsd ldr 9f out tl rdn over 4f out: wknd wl over 1f out* **7/1**
6 *3* **Ginger's Lad**16 6-8-9 0 ...(t) JamesSullivan(5) 1 47
(M W Easterby) *s.i.s: hld up: rdn and wknd over 3f out* **40/1**
3m 6.57s (-1.73) **Going Correction** -0.35s/f (Stan)
WFA 4 from 5yo+ 5lb 6 Ran SP% **111.2**
Speed ratings (Par 101): **90,88,88,85,84 82**
toteswinger:1&2:£2.10, 1&3:£1.70, 2&3:£2.30 CSF £7.28 TOTE £2.50: £1.80, £2.00; EX 7.50 Trifecta £10.50 Pool: £507.86 - 35.69 winning units..
Owner Diamond Racing Ltd **Bred** Mrs Edgar Scott Jr & Mrs Lawrence Macelree **Trained** Pandy, Monmouths
■ Stewards' Enquiry : Vince Slattery caution: careless riding.

FOCUS
A modest claimer run at a steady pace.

457 BET PREMIER LEAGUE FOOTBALL - BETDAQ H'CAP 1m 3f (F)
4:40 (4:40) (Class 6) (0-60,60) 4-Y-O+ **£1,774** (£523; £262) **Stalls** Low

Form RPR
4-25 1 **All Guns Firing (IRE)**17 246 4-9-4 **60** ... DavidNolan 7 68
(D Carroll) *jst abt mde all: rdn clr over 2f out: edgd rt fnl f: styd on* **7/1**

2016 **2** *1 ¼* **Highland River**[10] 330 4-8-13 **55**........ LeeVickers 3 61
(A Sadik) *chsd ldrs: pushed along 4f out: rdn to chse wnr 2f out: edgd rt fnl f: kpt on* **4/1**[2]

-635 **3** *6* **Mister Frosty (IRE)**[4] 390 4-8-4 **53**........(p) CharlotteKerton(7) 1 49
(G Prodromou) *reminder sn after s: prom: pushed along over 4f out: chsd wnr briefly over 2f out: styd on same pce* **5/1**[3]

060- **4** *¾* **New England**[107] 6998 8-9-2 **56**........ StephenCraine 4 51+
(N J Vaughan) *hld up: hdwy over 3f out: rdn over 1f out: styd on same pce* **9/1**

02-0 **5** *4* **Boy Dancer (IRE)**[13] 290 7-8-6 **46** oh1........(p) PaulHanagan 6 34
(J J Quinn) *prom: lost pl 8f out: hdwy over 4f out: rdn over 3f out: sn outpcd* **9/1**

05-0 **6** *4 ½* **Sudden Impulse**[11] 309 9-9-1 **55**........ TomEaves 2 35
(A D Brown) *hld up: pushed along 1/2-way: rdn over 3f out: nvr on terms* **14/1**

100- **7** *5* **Iceman George**[176] 5035 6-9-1 **60**........(b) TobyAtkinson(5) 10 32
(G C Bravery) *hld up: hdwy 8f out: rdn and wknd over 3f out* **7/1**

3-00 **8** *hd* **Coral Shores**[17] 244 5-9-3 **57**........(v) PhillipMakin 5 28
(P W Hiatt) *chsd ldrs: lost pl over 4f out: wknd over 3f out* **7/2**[1]

00-0 **9** *6* **Lady Longcroft**[27] 131 5-8-13 **53**........ SaleemGolam 9 14
(J Pearce) *chsd ldrs: rdn over 3f out: wknd over 2f out* **17/2**

00-5 **10** *28* **Eyesore**[26] 142 4-8-0 **47** oh1 ow1........ AndrewHeffernan(5) 8 —
(S A Harris) *sn pushed along and a in rr: wknd over 4f out: t.o* **66/1**

2m 25.41s (-2.59) **Going Correction** -0.35s/f (Stan)
WFA 4 from 5yo+ 2lb **10** Ran SP% **122.6**
Speed ratings (Par 101): **95,94,89,89,86 83,79,79,74,54**
toteswinger:1&2:£4.90, 1&3:£4.00, 2&3:£4.90 CSF £37.09 CT £158.29 TOTE £10.30: £2.40, £2.30, £2.20; EX 34.60 Trifecta £74.90 Pool: £550.78 - 5.44 winning units. Place 6: £89.23, Place 5: £36.39.
Owner Miss A Muir **Bred** Jack Ronan And Des Ver Hunt Farm Ltd **Trained** Sledmere, E Yorks

FOCUS
A moderate handicap, and further evidence that front-runners were at an advantage. The race is rated around the runner-up with the winner stepping up on recent form.
All Guns Firing(IRE) Official explanation: trainer said, regarding apparent improvement in form, that the gelding benefited from a more positive ride being allowed to dominate.
T/Plt: £96.10 to a £1 stake. Pool: £57,005.75. 432.71 winning tickets. T/Qpdt: £13.10 to a £1 stake. Pool: £3,758.44. 211.50 winning tickets. CR

332 CAGNES-SUR-MER
Saturday, February 6

OFFICIAL GOING: Heavy

458a PRIX DU CROS DE CAGNES 7f 110y
12:50 (12:55) 4-Y-0+ **£11,062** (£4,425; £3,319; £2,212; £1,106)

RPR
1 **Psy Chic (FR)**[65] 6-8-11 .... DominiqueBoeuf 89
(Robert Collet, France)
2 *1* **Royal Pennekamp (FR)**[119] 7-8-11 .... SebastienMaillot 86
(B Dutruel, France)
3 *2* **Tigron (USA)**[15] 272 9-8-11 ....(b) GaetanMasure 81
(Mme C Barande-Barbe, France)
4 *shd* **All Ways To Rome (FR)**[15] 272 6-9-5 ....(b) 89
(H-A Pantall, France)
5 *5* **Satchmo Bay (FR)**[111] 9-8-11 68
(C Boutin, France)
6 *2* **Royal Power (IRE)**[15] 272 7-8-11 .... IoritzMendizabal 63
(D Nicholls) *cl up early: 5th and pushed along 1/2-way: 7th and one pce st* **11/2**[1]
7 *14* **Heart Attack (FR)**[15] 272 4-8-11 28
(G Martin, Austria)
8 *3* **Botanique (FR)**[137] 4-9-4 28
(M Pimbonnet, France)
9 *4* **Zizany (IRE)**[11] 304 7-8-11 11
(Robert Collet, France)
10 *shd* **Outer Continent (IRE)**[15] 272 5-8-11 ....(b) 11
(X Nakkachdji, France)
11 *dist* **Cafe Mystique (IRE)**[420] 7666 4-8-11 .... —
(P Vovcenko, Germany)

1m 43.71s (103.71) **11** Ran SP% **15.4**
PARI-MUTUEL (Including 1 Euro stake): WIN 3.20 (coupled with Zizany);PL 1.70, 2.50, 3.10; DF 12.90.
Owner Mme Catherine Dubuquoi **Bred** Robert Collet **Trained** Chantilly, France

459a PRIX DE SAINT JEAN (CLAIMER) (WOMEN PROFESSIONALS) 7f 110y
1:50 (1:58) 5-Y-0+ **£6,637** (£2,655; £1,991; £1,327; £664)

RPR
1 **Mikos (FR)**[95] 10-9-5 .... NadegeOuakli 73
(Robert Collet, France)
2 *6* **Daudet (GER)**[15] 273 6-8-11 .... MarieFlahault 50
(H Blume, Germany)
3 *1 ½* **Pauillac (GER)**[136] 9-9-5 ....(b) KarenBeaumard 54
(B Dutruel, France)
4 *2 ½* **Derison (USA)**[11] 303 8-9-4 47
(P Monfort, France)
5 *5* **Wunderkind (GER)**[11] 303 5-9-5 ....(b) 35
(P Chatelain, France)
6 *5* **Val d'Espoir (IRE)**[129] 6-9-4 ....(b) 22
(H-A Pantall, France)
7 *6* **Royal Dignitary (USA)**[15] 273 10-9-1 .... DelphineSantiago 4
(D Nicholls) *led main gp in centre early: in tch in 6th on rail 1/2-way: drvn st: sn btn* **78/10**[1]
8 *4* **Petille (FR)**[145] 5-8-8 .... —
(Robert Collet, France)
9 *8* **Sendish (IRE)**[111] 7-9-1 ....(b) —
(H Billot, France)
10 *6* **Butterfly Flip (FR)**[11] 303 6-8-8 .... —
(J-P Perruchot, France)

1m 45.59s (105.59) **10** Ran SP% **11.4**
PARI-MUTUEL: WIN 3.10 (coupled with Petille); PL 1.60, 2.10, 2.90;DF 10.80.
Owner Mme Christian Wingtans **Bred** Mme Raymonde Wingtans **Trained** Chantilly, France

PAU (R-H)
Sunday, February 7

OFFICIAL GOING: Standard

460a PRIX HOTEL VILLA NAVARRE (LADY AMATEURS) (ALL-WEATHER) 7f 110y
1:50 (1:52) 4-Y-0+ **£6,195** (£2,478; £1,858; £1,239; £619)

RPR
1 **Russian Angel**[51] 7802 6-9-1 .... MlleAnne-SophiePacault 55
(Jean-Rene Auvray) *mde all: rdn 1 1/2f out: hld on wl cl home* **4/1**[1]
2 *snk* **New's Ivoire (FR)**[161] 5-9-7 .... MlleHeleneCorcoral 60
(L A Urbano-Grajales, France)
3 *½* **Proci Road (FR)**[190] 7-9-9 .... MlleStephanieHusser 61
(M Drean, France)
4 *½* **Gran Yago (IRE)**[273] 6-9-7 58
(C Delcher-Sanchez, Spain)
5 *2* **Flying Blue (FR)**[168] 5-9-9 55
(R Martin Sanchez, Spain)
6 *2* **Qui Danse (FR)**[858] 6-9-1 42
(Mlle S Sourd, France)
7 *4* **Desdichas (FR)** 5-9-3 35
(T Mercier, France)
8 *1 ½* **Zariyan (FR)**[50] 7822 7-9-9 38
(Mlle C Nicot, France)
9 *5* **Lonia Blue (FR)**[180] 4-9-3 20
(Mlle C Griolet, France)
10 *2 ½* **Lousard (FR)** 4-9-1 12
(D Barone, France)

1m 33.47s (93.47) **10** Ran SP% **20.0**
PARI-MUTUEL (Including 1 Euro stake): WIN 5.00; PL 2.00, 2.60, 2.80;DF 21.10.
Owner Nigel Kelly And Alison Auvray **Bred** A Harrison **Trained**

ST MORITZ (R-H)
Sunday, February 7

OFFICIAL GOING: Frozen

461a GRAND PRIX GUARDAVAL IMMOBILIEN (SNOW) 1m 1f
1:15 (1:28) 4-Y-0+
£5,029 (£2,515; £1,796; £1,198; £599; £359)

RPR
1 **Winterwind (IRE)**[50] 7821 5-9-4 .... GeorgBocskai 5 —
(Carmen Bocskai, Switzerland)
2 *1 ¼* **Fighting Johan (GER)**[159] 6-9-1 .... DPorcu 1 —
(G Raveneau, Switzerland)
3 *3 ½* **Mannlichen**[65] 7628 4-8-12 .... SteveDrowne 7 —
(M Johnston) **183/10**[1]
4 *1 ¾* **Vlavianus (CZE)**[105] 9-9-4 ....(b) DaneO'Neill 3 —
(M Weiss, Switzerland)
5 *1 ½* **Just That (SLO)** 5-9-0 .... RobertHavlin 11 —
(M Weiss, Switzerland)
6 *1* **Wassiljew (IRE)**[147] 6-9-6 .... VJuracek 8 —
(A Scharer, Germany)
7 *½* **Ziking (FR)**[105] 5-9-6 .... OlivierPlacais 9 —
(A Scharer, Germany)
8 **Atlantic Dancer (GER)**[364] 464 7-8-5 .... ChantalZollet(4) 4 —
(A Schennach, Switzerland)
9 **Buddhist Monk**[135] 6248 5-8-6 .... NoemiHerren(7) 12 —
(Dagmar Geissmann, Switzerland)
10 **Synergistic (IRE)**[860] 5858 5-8-13 .... MKolb 13 —
(A Scharer, Germany)
11 **First Time (GER)**[287] 1555 7-9-0 .... TonyCastanheira 2 —
(Karin Suter, Switzerland)
12 **Song Of Victory (GER)**[217] 6-9-8 .... MiguelLopez 6 —
(M Weiss, Switzerland)
13 **Tellesteem** 5-8-13 ....(b) SNemeth 10 —
(S Szabolcs, Germany)

1m 59.3s (119.30) **13** Ran SP% **5.2**
(Including SFr1 stake): WIN 6.80; PL 2.10, 2.60, 3.40; SF 14.10.
Owner Markus Graff **Bred** Denis & Teresa Bergin **Trained** Switzerland

427 WOLVERHAMPTON (A.W) (L-H)
Monday, February 8

OFFICIAL GOING: Standard
Wind: Moderate against Weather: Cloudy

462 BET MULTIPLES - BETDAQ H'CAP 5f 20y(P)
2:00 (2:00) (Class 6) (0-65,65) 4-Y-0+ **£1,774** (£523; £262) **Stalls** Low

Form RPR
06-5 **1** **Ingleby Star (IRE)**[25] 165 5-9-3 **64**........(p) JimmyQuinn 5 77
(N Wilson) *a.p: swtchd rt wl over 1f out: rdn to ld and edgd lft ins fnl f: r.o* **10/1**

2-44 **2** *1 ½* **Grudge**[10] 349 5-9-4 **65**........(e) FrannyNorton 8 73
(Ollie Pears) *led: rdn and edgd lft 1f out: hdd ins fnl f: nt qckn* **11/4**[1]

4-30 **3** *1 ¼* **Decider (USA)**[12] 306 7-9-1 **62**........(p) JoeFanning 2 66
(R A Harris) *w ldr: ev ch over 1f out: no ex ins fnl f* **8/1**

2-00 **4** *1 ½* **First Order**[16] 275 9-8-10 **62**........(v) AnnStokell(5) 1 60
(Miss A Stokell) *chsd ldrs: n.m.r on ins over 3f out: hung rt over 1f out: rdn and one pce ins fnl f* **20/1**

00-4 **5** *¾* **Bookiesindex Boy**[12] 306 6-9-4 **65**........(b) DaneO'Neill 10 60
(J R Jenkins) *mid-div: hdwy 2f out: bmpd over 1f out: one pce* **10/1**

3-56 **6** *nk* **Tartatartufata**[4] 402 8-8-13 **60**........(v) TomQueally 9 54
(J G Given) *bhd: pushed along 3f out: sme hdwy over 1f out: nvr trbld ldrs* **12/1**

2203 **7** *1* **Kheley (IRE)**[10] 349 4-9-1 **62** LiamJones 7 53
(W M Brisbourne) *mid-div: pushed along over 1f out: no hdwy* **15/2**[3]
105- **8** *½* **Shannon Golden**[67] 7615 4-8-10 **57** LukeMorris 3 46
(S R Bowring) *bhd: rdn over 1f out: n.d* **20/1**
606- **9** *½* **Almaty Express**[51] 7819 8-8-12 **59** (b) ChrisCatlin 4 46+
(J R Weymes) *bmpd s: a in rr* **8/1**
0-40 **10** *nk* **Diddums**[11] 325 4-8-7 **54** DavidProbert 11 40
(P S McEntee) *s.i.s: a in rr* **14/1**
50-3 **11** *4 ½* **Stash**[27] 138 4-9-1 **62** (t) GrahamGibbons 6 32
(R Hollinshead) *prom: pushed along over 2f out: bmpd over 1f out: wknd fnl f* **5/1**[2]

62.04 secs (-0.26) **Going Correction** +0.025s/f (Slow) 11 Ran SP% 119.4
Speed ratings (Par 101): **103,100,98,96,95 94,92,92,91,90 83**
toteswingers: 1&2 £9.30, 1&3 £15.50, 2&3 £6.10 CSF £38.21 CT £239.25 TOTE £14.00: £3.10, £1.70, £2.90; EX 55.50 TRIFECTA Not won..
Owner Renaissance Racing LLC **Bred** Pat Cosgrove **Trained** Sandhutton, N Yorks
■ Stewards' Enquiry : Jimmy Quinn three-day ban: careless riding (Feb 22 to 24)

FOCUS
A moderate sprint handicap in which it proved difficult to make up significant amounts of ground.
Almaty Express Official explanation: jockey said gelding was hampered at start
Stash Official explanation: trainer said gelding finished distressed

463 STAY AT THE WOLVERHAMPTON HOLIDAY INN AWT "HANDS AND HEELS" APPRENTICE SERIES H'CAP 1m 5f 194y(P)
2:30 (2:31) (Class 6) (0-60,56) 4-Y-O+ **£1,774** (£523; £262) **Stalls** Low

Form RPR
-042 **1** **Sir Sandicliffe (IRE)**[4] 409 6-9-3 **51** KierenFox 1 58
(W M Brisbourne) *a.p: pushed along to chse ldr jst over 2f out: led over 1f out: styd on* **7/2**[3]
0-30 **2** *1 ½* **Red Wine**[11] 331 11-8-9 **48** JonathanHinch[(5)] 5 53
(J A Glover) *stdd s: hld up in rr: pushed along and hdwy on outside 2f out: c v wd st: styd on ins fnl f: tk 2nd cl home* **12/1**
00-4 **3** *½* **Desert Hawk**[11] 331 9-8-6 **45** JulieCumine[(5)] 4 49
(P Howling) *racd keenly: prom: lost pl over 3f out: styd on fr over 1f out: tk 3rd last stride* **25/1**
4-62 **4** *nse* **Ardmaddy (IRE)**[12] 309 6-9-4 **55** (b) HarryBentley[(3)] 3 59
(G L Moore) *led 2f: w ldrs: led 3f out: hdd over 1f out: no ex ins fnl f* **5/2**[2]
115- **5** *2 ¼* **Private Equity (IRE)**[57] 7740 4-9-3 **56** RyanClark 7 57
(W Jarvis) *hld up in tch: pushed along wl over 1f out: one pce* **15/8**[1]
-603 **6** *hd* **Free Falling**[6] 376 4-8-8 **47** ow2 (vt) HollyHall 2 48
(A J Lidderdale) *hld up: hdwy over 5f out: led over 4f out to 3f out: lost pl over 2f out: btn whn n.m.r ins fnl f* **20/1**
/46- **7** *1 ¼* **Telling Stories (IRE)**[253] 1441 4-8-10 **49** DavidKenny 8 48
(B D Leavy) *hld up in rr: pushed along and hdwy on ins over 2f out: wknd fnl f* **50/1**
00-0 **8** *2 ½* **April The Second**[18] 244 6-8-11 **45** JohnCavanagh 9 40
(R J Price) *hld up: short-lived effrt over 5f out: bhd fnl 3f* **66/1**
1000 **9** *¾* **Royal Rainbow**[3] 420 6-9-5 **53** MatthewLawson 6 47
(P W Hiatt) *w ldr: led after 2f tl over 4f out: wknd wl over 1f out* **8/1**

3m 9.47s (3.47) **Going Correction** +0.025s/f (Slow)
WFA 4 from 6yo+ 5lb 9 Ran SP% 116.4
Speed ratings (Par 101): **91,90,89,89,88 88,87,86,85**
toteswingers: 1&2 £5.30, 1&3 £9.30, 2&3 £13.20 CSF £41.88 CT £911.10 TOTE £5.30: £1.60, £2.70, £5.80; EX 39.30 Trifecta £300.40 Part won. Pool: £406.06 - 0.10 winning units..
Owner The Blacktoffee Partnership **Bred** James Lombard **Trained** Great Ness, Shropshire

FOCUS
Moderate horses ridden by mainly inexperienced riders, who weren't allowed to use their whips, and they went a muddling pace. This is form to treat with caution.

464 ENJOY THE PARTY PACK GROUP OFFER (S) STKS 7f 32y(P)
3:00 (3:03) (Class 6) 3-Y-O+ **£1,774** (£523; £262) **Stalls** High

Form RPR
-043 **1** **Ravi River (IRE)**[2] 444 6-9-9 72 (v) RichardEvans[(5)] 7 76+
(P D Evans) *hld up in mid-div: nt clr run wl over 1f out: swtchd rt jst over 1f out: r.o ins fnl f: rdn to ld cl home* **9/4**[1]
0300 **2** *½* **Jord (IRE)**[17] 269 6-9-5 59 FrederikTylicki 11 63
(J A Glover) *a.p: rdn wl over 1f out: led wl ins fnl f: hdd cl home* **12/1**
3211 **3** *hd* **Obe Gold**[5] 391 8-10-0 65 J-PGuillambert 2 71
(P Howling) *led early: a.p: pushed along 3f out: rdn to ld jst over 1f out: hdd wl ins fnl f* **10/3**[2]
03-4 **4** *½* **Geezers Colours**[24] 181 5-9-10 65 AndrewElliott 4 66
(J R Weymes) *hld up towards rr: hdwy on ins wl over 1f out: rdn and swtchd rt 1f out: kpt on* **6/1**[3]
0-20 **5** *1 ¼* **Angaric (IRE)**[17] 269 7-9-3 55 AdamCarter[(7)] 3 63
(B Smart) *hld up in mid-div: rdn and hdwy over 1f out: no ex towards fin* **12/1**
6-54 **6** *1 ¼* **Via Mia**[10] 348 4-9-5 63 (p) DaneO'Neill 9 55
(George Baker) *sn chsng ldr: led wl over 1f out: sn hdd: rdn and no ex ins fnl f* **10/1**
0-04 **7** *3* **Tri Chara (IRE)**[24] 195 6-9-10 54 (p) GrahamGibbons 6 53
(R Hollinshead) *hld up in tch: pushed along over 2f out: rdn and wknd ins fnl f* **20/1**
405- **8** *¾* **Where's Killoran**[291] 1476 5-9-5 45 ShaneKelly 8 46
(E J Alston) *sn led: rdn and hdd wl over 1f out: wknd ins fnl f* **100/1**
40-6 **9** *7* **Bentley**[11] 328 6-10-0 57 TomQueally 10 38
(J G Given) *a towards rr* **25/1**
6-10 **10** *16* **Imperial House**[20] 223 4-10-0 67 (b) ChrisCatlin 5 —
(R A Harris) *s.i.s: a in rr* **13/2**

1m 29.75s (0.15) **Going Correction** +0.025s/f (Slow)
WFA 3 from 4yo+ 17lb 10 Ran SP% 115.5
Speed ratings (Par 101): **100,99,99,98,97 95,92,91,83,65**
toteswingers: 1&2 £7.80, 1&3 £3.40, 2&3 £8.80 CSF £30.17 TOTE £3.30: £1.40, £2.60, £1.70; EX 31.40 Trifecta £108.10 Pool: £587.57 - 4.02 winning units..There was no bid for the winner.
Owner J L Guillambert **Bred** Gainsborough Stud Management Ltd **Trained** Pandy, Monmouths

FOCUS
A modest seller and the time was ordinary, being 1.08 seconds slower than the following 61-75 handicap.
Imperial House Official explanation: jockey said colt jumped awkwardly away and never travelled

465 BETDAQ.CO.UK H'CAP 7f 32y(P)
3:30 (3:37) (Class 5) (0-75,74) 4-Y-O+ **£2,456** (£725; £362) **Stalls** High

Form RPR
2-21 **1** **Smalljohn**[7] 373 4-8-12 **68** 6ex (v) TomEaves 3 78
(B Smart) *led over 1f: chsd ldr: led wl over 1f out: drvn out* **15/8**[1]
0-20 **2** *2 ½* **Kensington (IRE)**[7] 373 9-8-13 **69** (p) RobertWinston 7 72
(A J McCabe) *hld up in rr: c wd st: rdn and hdwy over 1f out: r.o to take 2nd wl ins fnl f: nt trble wnr* **14/1**
F2-2 **3** *½* **Seldom (IRE)**[7] 373 4-8-8 **64** JimmyQuinn 1 66
(M Brittain) *s.i.s: sn prom: pushed along over 2f out: hrd rdn jst over 1f out: one pce* **9/4**[2]
6-41 **4** *½* **Kipchak (IRE)**[10] 342 5-8-13 **69** (p) ShaneKelly 5 69
(C R Dore) *chsd ldr: led over 5f out: rdn and hdd wl over 1f out: no ex ins fnl f* **7/1**
030- **5** *3 ½* **Blue Charm**[195] 4400 6-9-2 **72** GregFairley 2 63
(I W McInnes) *s.i.s: sn prom: pushed along over 2f out: wknd wl over 1f out* **40/1**
640- **6** *2 ¼* **Ishiadancer**[52] 7801 5-9-4 **74** PatCosgrave 6 59
(E J Alston) *hld up: pushed along over 1f out: no rspnse* **5/1**[3]
000- **7** *14* **Kingsmaite**[58] 7728 9-8-5 **61** (b) LukeMorris 4 8
(S R Bowring) *hld up in tch: rdn and lost pl over 3f out: no ch fnl 2f* **22/1**

1m 28.67s (-0.93) **Going Correction** +0.025s/f (Slow) 7 Ran SP% 108.2
Speed ratings (Par 103): **106,103,102,102,98 95,79**
toteswingers: 1&2 £5.60, 1&3 £1.30, 2&3 £5.20 CSF £25.29 TOTE £2.40: £1.30, £4.10; EX 26.50.
Owner B Smart **Bred** W H R John And Partners **Trained** Hambleton, N Yorks

FOCUS
The pace was strong and the winning time was 1.08 seconds quicker than the earlier seller won by the 72-rated Ravi River.

466 SPONSOR A RACE BY CALLING 01902 390000 CLAIMING STKS 1m 141y(P)
4:00 (4:04) (Class 6) 4-Y-O+ **£1,774** (£523; £262) **Stalls** Low

Form RPR
15-4 **1** **Plush**[24] 197 7-8-10 81 RossAtkinson[(5)] 4 85
(Tom Dascombe) *stdd s: hld up in rr: pushed along and hdwy on wd outside over 2f out: rdn and hung lft fr 1f out: led ins fnl f: r.o* **5/2**[2]
4-01 **2** *½* **Head First**[14] 295 4-8-6 58 DavidProbert 9 75
(W Jarvis) *hld up towards rr: hdwy over 2f out: rdn over 1f out: carried sltly lft ins fnl f: r.o* **17/2**
0-13 **3** *1 ¾* **Ilie Nastase (FR)**[9] 359 6-9-5 85 NeilCallan 6 84
(D M Simcock) *sn led: rdn wl over 1f out: hdd ins fnl f: no ex* **9/4**[1]
2-23 **4** *½* **New Star (UAE)**[14] 294 6-8-8 73 ShaneKelly 2 72
(W M Brisbourne) *led early: chsd ldr: rdn wl over 1f out: no ex wl ins fnl f* **4/1**[3]
20-4 **5** *6* **Xpres Maite**[32] 71 7-9-2 77 (b) DaneO'Neill 3 66
(S R Bowring) *hld up in mid-div: rdn over 2f out: wknd wl over 1f out* **11/1**
-006 **6** *4 ½* **Hilbre Court (USA)**[18] 245 5-8-13 72 (b) GrahamGibbons 8 53
(B P J Baugh) *prom: rdn 3f out: wknd wl over 1f out* **16/1**
0- **7** *hd* **Sand Tiger (IRE)**[302] 1238 4-9-0 0 LeeTopliss[(7)] 7 60
(R A Fahey) *hld up towards rr: pushed along over 2f out: sn struggling* **14/1**
-624 **8** *10* **Ten Pole Tudor**[13] 298 5-8-11 56 (p) LiamJones 5 27
(R A Harris) *hld up in mid-div: pushed along over 3f out: hung rt bnd over 2f out: sn bhd* **40/1**
060- **9** *4* **Remark (IRE)**[76] 7500 6-8-2 47 (bt[1]) JamesSullivan[(5)] 1 14
(M W Easterby) *hld up in tch: wknd over 2f out* **100/1**
600- **10** *29* **Lastroarofdtiger (USA)**[39] 7891 4-9-1 72 RobertWinston 10 —
(J R Weymes) *hld up in tch: wknd over 2f out* **66/1**

1m 49.97s (-0.53) **Going Correction** +0.025s/f (Slow) 10 Ran SP% 115.7
Speed ratings (Par 101): **103,102,101,100,95 91,91,82,78,52**
toteswingers: 1&2 £4.30, 1&3 £2.40, 2&3 £4.00 CSF £23.90 TOTE £4.10: £1.20, £2.70, £1.10; EX 19.60 Trifecta £55.10 Pool: £481.20 - 6.46 winning units..
Owner John Reed **Bred** Cheveley Park Stud Ltd **Trained** Malpas, Cheshire

FOCUS
A good claimer run at a strong pace, courtesy of Ilie Nastase.
Lastroarofdtiger(USA) Official explanation: jockey said gelding lost its action

467 TRY BETDAQ FOR AN EXCHANGE H'CAP (DIV I) 1m 1f 103y(P)
4:30 (4:36) (Class 6) (0-65,65) 4-Y-O+ **£1,433** (£423; £211) **Stalls** Low

Form RPR
540- **1** **Saviour Sand (IRE)**[276] 1833 6-8-13 **65** (t) KylieManser[(5)] 11 73
(T Keddy) *led after 1f: hrd rdn over 1f out: all out* **40/1**
5-35 **2** *nk* **Spinning Ridge (IRE)**[17] 262 5-9-0 **61** LiamJones 4 68
(R A Harris) *hld up in mid-div: hdwy 2f out: hung lft and rdn over 1f out: r.o ins fnl f* **14/1**
5-36 **3** *shd* **Mutajaaser (USA)**[12] 308 5-9-1 **62** JimmyQuinn 1 69
(K A Morgan) *led 1f: prom: chsd wnr 3f out: sn rdn: r.o ins fnl f* **11/1**
1-40 **4** *1 ¼* **Alf Tupper**[10] 348 7-8-13 **60** RobertWinston 7 64
(Adrian McGuinness, Ire) *hld up towards rr: hdwy wl over 1f out: sn rdn: hung lft ins fnl f: kpt on* **14/1**
3-00 **5** *nk* **Just Timmy Marcus**[7] 373 4-9-3 **64** TonyCulhane 9 68
(B P J Baugh) *hld up towards rr: hdwy over 2f out: rdn jst over 1f out: kpt on towards fin* **8/1**
0430 **6** *1* **Naheell**[12] 309 4-9-1 **62** NeilCallan 2 64
(G Prodromou) *a.p: rdn over 2f out: no ex wl ins fnl f* **10/3**[2]
3-13 **7** *1* **Bestowed**[13] 298 5-8-10 **62** (v) RichardEvans[(5)] 13 62
(P D Evans) *hld up in rr: pushed along over 2f out: rdn wl over 1f out: styd on fnl f: nt rch ldrs* **3/1**[1]
3514 **8** *5* **Bajan Pride**[10] 354 6-8-5 **59** (b[1]) LeeTopliss[(7)] 5 48
(R A Fahey) *hld up towards rr: rdn 3f out: c v wd st: nvr nr ldrs* **10/1**
63-0 **9** *2* **Apotheosis**[9] 361 5-9-2 **63** TomQueally 6 48
(C R Dore) *hld up in mid-div: c wd st: wknd wl over 1f out* **5/1**[3]
500- **10** *3* **Lean Burn (USA)**[94] 7278 4-8-10 **57** (t) FergusSweeney 10 36
(A G Newcombe) *hld up towards rr: rdn over 4f out: struggling fnl 3f* **33/1**
000- **11** *2 ¼* **A Dream Come True**[172] 5195 5-8-13 **65** (v[1]) AndrewHeffernan[(5)] 12 39
(D Burchell) *sn chsng wnr: rdn and lost 2nd over 3f out: wknd over 2f out* **50/1**
-000 **12** *2 ½* **Melt (IRE)**[17] 270 5-8-8 **55** (b) GrahamGibbons 3 24
(M W Easterby) *hld up in tch: wknd wl over 1f out* **33/1**

2m 1.91s (0.21) **Going Correction** +0.025s/f (Slow) 12 Ran SP% 116.9
Speed ratings (Par 101): **100,99,99,98,97 96,96,92,90,87 85,83**
toteswingers: 1&2 £102.70, 1&3 £32.70, 2&3 £18.00 CSF £506.63 CT £6449.44 TOTE £57.40: £14.20, £6.20, £3.50; EX 847.80 TRIFECTA Not won..
Owner A C Maylam **Bred** Michael Munnelly **Trained** Newmarket, Suffolk
■ Stewards' Enquiry : Kylie Manser one-day ban: used whip with excessive frequency (Feb 22)
Liam Jones two-day ban: used whip with excessive frequency (Feb 22-23)

FOCUS
A modest handicap run in a time was 0.38 seconds slower than the second division.
Alf Tupper Official explanation: jockey said gelding hung left in home straight

Bestowed Official explanation: jockey said gelding never travelled

468 HORSERACEBASE.COM HORSE RACING DATABASE SOLUTIONS MAIDEN STKS — 1m 4f 50y(P)
5:00 (5:03) (Class 5) 4-Y-0+ — **£2,456** (£725; £362) Stalls Low

Form — RPR

02-3 **1** **Peace Corps**[14] 291 4-9-3 70........(v) AdamKirby 3 — 76
(J R Fanshawe) *a.p: rdn to ld jst ins fnl f: r.o* — **3/1**[2]

/3-3 **2** *2 ¼* **Hydrant**[10] 352 4-9-3 66........ GregFairley 6 — 73
(P Salmon) *led: rdn and hdd jst ins fnl f: nt qckn* — **7/1**

03-6 **3** *2* **Tropical Blue**[10] 352 4-9-3 72........ JoeFanning 10 — 69
(Jennie Candlish) *t.k.h in tch: wnt 2nd wl over 3f out: ev ch wl over 1f out: sn rdn: one pce* — **9/2**[3]

25-2 **4** *hd* **Capeability (IRE)**[14] 291 4-9-3 70........ ChrisCatlin 1 — 69
(M R Channon) *hld up in mid-div: lost pl on ins over 5f out: sn swtchd rt: hdwy over 3f out: rdn over 1f out: one pce* — **9/4**[1]

0- **5** *4 ½* **Sacco D'Oro**[40] 7882 4-8-12 0........ TomEaves 8 — 57
(M Mullineaux) *hld up in rr: rdn over 2f out: sme prog wl over 1f out: nvr nr ldrs* — **100/1**

63 **6** *nk* **Happy Fleet**[12] 308 7-9-1 0........ DaneO'Neill 5 — 56
(R Curtis) *hld up in rr: rdn over 2f out: sme prog over 1f out: nvr nr ldrs* — **25/1**

7 *3 ¾* **Hunters Belt (IRE)**[344] 6-9-6 0........ AndrewMullen 2 — 55
(N Wilson) *hld up in mid-div: pushed along and hdwy on outside 3f out: rdn and wknd wl over 1f out* — **5/1**

4 **8** *40* **Onegin (SAF)**[12] 308 4-8-9 64........ FergusSweeney 9 — —
(D M Simcock) *hld up towards rr: hdwy 5f out: rdn and wknd 3f out: t.o* — **20/1**

000- **9** *26* **Hilbre Point (USA)**[266] 2126 4-9-3 55........ RobertWinston 7 — —
(N J Vaughan) *sn chsng ldr: lost 2nd and wknd over 3f out: sn eased: t.o* — **40/1**

10 *11* **Raydar**[53] 5-9-6 0........ ShaneKelly 4 — —
(W M Brisbourne) *hld up in tch: pushed along and lost pl over 4f out: sn t.o* — **100/1**

2m 41.15s (0.05) **Going Correction** +0.025s/f (Slow)
WFA 4 from 5yo+ 3lb — 10 Ran SP% **116.1**
Speed ratings (Par 103): **100,98,97,97,94 93,91,64,47,40**
toteswingers: 1&2 £5.30, 1&3 £5.70, 2&3 £4.70 CSF £22.88 TOTE £4.30: £1.80, £1.80, £1.90; EX 25.00 Trifecta £222.00 Pool: £528.07 - 1.76 winning units..
Owner Elite Racing Club **Bred** Cheveley Park Stud Ltd **Trained** Newmarket, Suffolk

FOCUS
A weak maiden and not form to dwell on.
Hilbre Point(USA) Official explanation: jockey said gelding moved poorly throughout

469 TRY BETDAQ FOR AN EXCHANGE H'CAP (DIV II) — 1m 1f 103y(P)
5:30 (5:30) (Class 6) (0-65,65) 4-Y-0+ — **£1,433** (£423; £211) Stalls Low

Form — RPR

1-02 **1** **Make Amends (IRE)**[9] 361 5-9-2 **63**........ GeorgeBaker 4 — 70
(R J Hodges) *hld up in mid-div: hdwy over 2f out: led wl over 1f out: rdn ins fnl f: r.o* — **6/1**[2]

100- **2** *hd* **High Five Society**[143] 6074 6-8-10 **57**........(bt) JimmyQuinn 7 — 64
(S R Bowring) *hld up towards rr: hdwy wl over 1f out: hrd rdn and ev ch wl ins fnl f: r.o* — **66/1**

6-44 **3** *½* **King Of Connacht**[5] 396 7-8-11 **58**........(v) LiamJones 6 — 64
(M Wellings) *hld up towards rr: hdwy 2f out: nt qckn towards fin* — **16/1**

0-26 **4** *3* **Magnitude**[13] 298 5-8-8 **62**........(bt) KierenFox[(7)] 12 — 62
(C C Bealby) *hld up in rr: rdn and hdwy on outside over 2f out: c wd st: one pce fnl f* — **16/1**

041- **5** *¾* **Granny McPhee**[128] 6497 4-8-8 **62**........ NatashaEaton[(7)] 5 — 63+
(A Bailey) *hld up in mid-div: nt clr run on ins over 2f out: plld out ent st: kpt on ins fnl f: nvr trbld ldrs* — **25/1**

61-0 **6** *2 ¾* **Coolnaharan (IRE)**[3] 427 10-8-8 **60**........(p) JamesSullivan[(5)] 13 — 53
(Lee Smyth, Ire) *hld up in rr: swtchd rt to outside ent st: rdn jst over 1f out: n.d* — **33/1**

0-26 **7** *1 ½* **The Graig**[14] 295 6-8-6 **53**........(tp) GregFairley 8 — 43
(J R Holt) *sn w ldr: led over 3f out: rdn and hdd wl over 1f out: wknd ins fnl f* — **25/1**

02-0 **8** *2 ¼* **New World Order (IRE)**[17] 261 6-9-2 **63**........(t) DaneO'Neill 1 — 49
(R Curtis) *led 1f: prom tl wknd 3f out* — **12/1**

-111 **9** *6* **Grey Command (USA)**[3] 427 5-9-1 **62**........ RobertWinston 2 — 37
(M Brittain) *prom: chsd ldr wl over 2f out tl rdn wl over 1f out: sn wknd* — **11/10**[1]

0-34 **10** *½* **Maximus Aurelius (IRE)**[9] 361 5-9-4 **65**........(t) LukeMorris 11 — 39
(J Jay) *prom: rdn 2f out: sn wknd* — **8/1**[3]

350/ **11** *½* **Erdeli (IRE)**[438] 6626 6-9-4 **65**........(t) ChrisCatlin 9 — 38
(P R Webber) *hld up in mid-div: bhd fnl 3f* — **11/1**

000/ **12** *shd* **Petrosian**[60] 6424 6-8-4 **51** oh6........(p) DavidProbert 3 — 24
(D Burchell) *led after 1f tl over 3f out: rdn over 2f out: wknd wl over 1f out* — **40/1**

2m 1.53s (-0.17) **Going Correction** +0.025s/f (Slow) — 12 Ran SP% **115.4**
Speed ratings (Par 101): **101,100,100,97,97 94,93,91,85,85 85,84**
toteswingers: 1&2 £22.20, 1&3 £10.60, 2&3 £38.60 CSF £364.69 CT £5864.66 TOTE £7.80: £2.00, £9.60, £2.90; EX 247.00 TRIFECTA Not won. Place 6: £344.63 Place 5: £156.51.
Owner Miss R Dobson **Bred** Moyglare Stud Farm Ltd **Trained** Charlton Mackrell, Somerset

FOCUS
The winning time was 0.38 seconds quicker than the first division.
Grey Command(USA) Official explanation: jockey said, regarding running, that the horse tired quickly home straight and may have been feeling the effect its previous race; trainer's rep said horse lost its right-fore shoe
T/Plt: £257.70 to a £1 stake. Pool: £62,798.30. 177.86 winning tickets. T/Qpdt: £36.00 to a £1 stake. Pool: £6,157.50. 126.54 winning tickets. KH

451 SOUTHWELL (L-H)
Tuesday, February 9

OFFICIAL GOING: Standard
Wind: Light across Weather: Bright spells and wintry showers

470 ARENA LEISURE PLC AMATEUR RIDERS' H'CAP — 1m 3f (F)
1:50 (1:51) (Class 6) (0-52,52) 4-Y-0+ — **£1,714** (£527; £263) Stalls Low

Form — RPR

32-5 **1** **Jackie Kiely**[28] 139 9-10-10 **51**........(tp) TomDavid[(3)] 2 — 63
(R Brotherton) *hld up in rr: hdwy over 5f out: pushed along and in tch 4f out: effrt to chse ldrs and swtchd lft over 2f out: rdn to ld wl over 1f out: clr ent fnl f* — **11/4**[1]

02-4 **2** *4* **Bright Sparky (GER)**[21] 41 7-10-9 **47**........(vt) MissSBrotherton 11 — 52
(M W Easterby) *hld up towards rr: hdwy over 5f out: effrt 3f out and sn cl up: rdn and ev ch wl over 1f out: drvn and one pce appr last* — **4/1**[2]

6-60 **3** *hd* **Nawamees (IRE)**[4] 426 12-11-0 **52**........(p) MrsEEvans 5 — 57
(P D Evans) *led: rdn along 3f out: jnd over 2f out: drvn and hdd wl over 1f out: kpt on same pce* — **14/1**

0-20 **4** *3* **Cragganmore Creek**[20] 228 7-10-3 **46** oh1........(v) MrBMMorris[(5)] 3 — 46
(D Morris) *trckd ldrs: hdwy 5f out: cl up over 3f out: sn rdn along: drvn 2f out and sn one pce* — **6/1**

/0-5 **5** *2 ¼* **Six Of Clubs**[13] 314 4-10-1 **46** oh1........(b) MrPPrince[(5)] 8 — 42
(W G M Turner) *rapid hdwy on inner to chse ldrs after 2f: rdn along over 3f out: drvn over 2f out and grad wknd* — **14/1**

006- **6** *½* **Bernix**[56] 7761 8-10-1 **46** oh1........(p) MissLWilson[(7)] 4 — 41
(N Tinkler) *chsd ldrs on inner: rdn along over 3f out: plugged on same pce fnl 2f* — **25/1**

00/0 **7** *2* **Bansha (IRE)**[12] 331 4-10-2 **47**........ MrCDavies[(5)] 14 — 39
(A Bailey) *hld up: hdwy on outer to chse ldrs 5f out: rdn along over 3f out: drvn wl over 2f out and sn btn* — **5/1**[3]

00-6 **8** *hd* **Candilejas**[12] 326 4-10-0 **47**........ MissCBoxall[(7)] 12 — 38
(R Curtis) *prom: rdn along 4f out: wknd 3f out* — **22/1**

000/ **9** *8* **Key Partners (IRE)**[596] 3328 9-10-9 **52**........ MrAshleePrice[(5)] 10 — 30
(R Curtis) *stdd s and hld up in rr: hdwy on outer over 5f out: rdn along over 3f out and sn wknd* — **16/1**

6300 **10** *8* **Easy Wonder (GER)**[6] 390 5-10-3 **46** oh1........(v[1]) MrCMartin[(5)] 1 — 10
(I A Wood) *hld up in rr: stdy hdwy 1/2-way: chsd ldrs 4f out: rdn along over 3f out and sn wknd* — **20/1**

06-0 **11** *7* **Flaming Blaze**[5] 407 4-10-1 **48**........(bt[1]) MissCharlotteHolmes[(7)] 13 — —
(P C Haslam) *dwlt and in rr tl rapid hdwy to chse ldrs after 3f: cl up 1/2-way: rdn along over 4f out and sn wknd* — **16/1**

000- **12** *9* **Copper Sovereign**[121] 6703 8-10-3 **46** oh1........ LucyBarry[(5)] 7 — —
(G Brown) *prom: pushed along bef 1/2-way: sn lost pl and bhd fnl 3f* **66/1**

2m 28.04s (0.04) **Going Correction** -0.075s/f (Stan)
WFA 4 from 5yo+ 2lb — 12 Ran SP% **117.2**
Speed ratings (Par 101): **96,93,92,90,89 88,87,87,81,75 70,63**
toteswingers: 1&2 £2.50, 1&3 £5.70, 2&3 £8.40 CSF £12.35 CT £130.66 TOTE £3.30: £1.40, £1.60, £3.30; EX 10.60 Trifecta £17.50 Pool: £365.15 - 15.41 winning units..
Owner Mrs Carol Newman **Bred** Mrs M Chaworth Musters **Trained** Elmley Castle, Worcs

FOCUS
A moderate if competitive amateur riders' handicap containing two of the last three winners of the race. The pace was honest enough. Straightforward form.

471 BET PREMIER LEAGUE FOOTBALL - BETDAQ H'CAP — 5f (F)
2:20 (2:20) (Class 6) (0-65,63) 3-Y-0 — **£1,774** (£523; £262) Stalls High

Form — RPR

5-04 **1** **Sandy Toes**[12] 329 3-8-3 **45**........ AdrianMcCarthy 6 — 48
(J A Glover) *chsd ldrs: hdwy 2f out: rdn wl over 1f out: drvn ent fnl f: kpt on wl to ld nr fin* — **33/1**

3132 **2** *hd* **Turf Time**[6] 387 3-8-11 **53**........ ChrisCatlin 7 — 55
(J A Glover) *in tch towards stands' side: hdwy 2f out and sn rdn: drvn over 1f out: styd on ins fnl f: jst failed* — **4/1**[3]

5226 **3** *shd* **Lady Brickhouse**[6] 387 3-8-6 **48**........ LukeMorris 8 — 50
(M D Squance) *cl up: rdn along 1/2-way: hdd over 1f out: drvn ins fnl f: hdd and no ex towards fin* — **8/1**

5-44 **4** *½* **Pavement Games**[6] 387 3-7-13 **46**........ BillyCray[(5)] 1 — 46
(R C Guest) *sn rdn along and outpcd in rr: hdwy 1/2-way: rdn wl over 1f out and sn ev ch tl drvn and one pce ins fnl f* — **3/1**[2]

00-4 **5** *shd* **Young George**[23] 209 3-8-5 **50**........ KellyHarrison[(3)] 3 — 49
(C W Fairhurst) *chsd ldrs: rdn along 2f out: n.m.r and swtchd rt wl over 1f out: sn drvn and kpt on ins fnl f* — **14/1**

-663 **6** *1 ¼* **Annia Galeria (IRE)**[11] 343 3-8-13 **55**........ DavidProbert 5 — 50
(C A Dwyer) *led: rdn along 1/2-way: drvn and hung lft wl over 1f out: hdd over 1f out: wknd ins fnl f* — **8/1**

01-4 **7** *1 ¾* **Billie Jean**[31] 111 3-9-7 **63**........ MichaelHills 2 — 52
(B W Hills) *cl up on outer: rdn along 2f out: sltly hmpd wl over 1f out and sn btn* — **7/4**[1]

050- **8** *15* **Nidamar**[60] 7707 3-8-3 **45**........(b[1]) JimmyQuinn 4 — —
(Mrs R A Carr) *sn outpcd and bhd fr 1/2-way* — **66/1**

60.64 secs (0.94) **Going Correction** +0.05s/f (Slow) — 8 Ran SP% **114.7**
Speed ratings (Par 95): **94,93,93,92,92 90,87,63**
toteswingers: 1&2 £11.40, 1&3 £14.10, 2&3 £2.90 CSF £160.80 CT £922.01 TOTE £37.20: £4.30, £1.60, £1.80; EX 197.20 Trifecta £218.80 Pool: £390.39 - 1.32 winning units..
Owner Sexy Six Partnership **Bred** Mrs Yvette Dixon **Trained** Babworth, Notts
■ Stewards' Enquiry : Chris Catlin three-day ban: used whip with excessive frequency without giving gelding time to respond (Feb 23-25)

FOCUS
A very modest 3-y-o sprint handicap and a rather messy contest. Six of the eight runners were in a line across the track half a furlong from home and the form looks weak. It resulted in a one-two for Jeremy Glover, but not in the order many would have been expected.
Annia Galeria(IRE) Official explanation: jockey said filly hung left throughout
Billie Jean Official explanation: vet said filly returned lame

472 BETDAQ ON 0870 178 1221 (S) STKS — 5f (F)
2:50 (2:50) (Class 6) 4-Y-0+ — **£1,774** (£523; £262) Stalls High

Form — RPR

00-0 **1** **Spic 'n Span**[4] 431 5-8-12 62........(b) JoeFanning 2 — 69
(R A Harris) *sn led: rdn wl over 1f out: edgd lft ins fnl f: kpt on* — **2/1**[2]

0-21 **2** *½* **Monte Major (IRE)**[26] 165 9-8-5 60........(v) SeanPalmer[(7)] 5 — 67
(D Shaw) *in tch: pushed along 1/2-way: sn rdn and gd hdwy over 1f out: drvn and kpt on ins fnl f* — **15/8**[1]

0-65 **3** *¾* **Guto**[7] 380 7-8-9 67........ KellyHarrison[(3)] 1 — 65
(W J H Ratcliffe) *sn rdn along and outpcd after 1f: hdwy over 2f out: rdn to chse ldng pair over 1f out: drvn and kpt on ins fnl f* — **5/1**[3]

0026 **4** *1 ¾* **Music Box Express**[7] 379 6-8-12 55........(v) TonyCulhane 3 — 58
(George Baker) *cl up: rdn along 2f out: drvn over 1f out: wknd ins fnl f* **6/1**

00-0 **5** *2 ¼* **Fasliyanne (IRE)**[11] 344 4-8-7 55........ AdrianNicholls 4 — 45
(K A Ryan) *chsd ldrs: rdn along over 2f out: drvn wl over 1f out and sn outpcd* — **9/1**

59.78 secs (0.08) **Going Correction** +0.05s/f (Slow) — 5 Ran SP% **109.1**
Speed ratings (Par 101): **101,100,99,96,92**
CSF £6.02 TOTE £2.90: £1.60, £1.50; EX 6.00.There was no bid for the winner.
Owner P Nurcombe **Bred** C A Cyzer **Trained** Earlswood, Monmouths

The Form Book, Raceform Ltd, Compton, RG20 6NL

FOCUS
A moderate seller, but at least three of these usually like to force the pace so a decent gallop was always likely. The winning time was 0.86 seconds faster than the 3-y-o handicap.

473 BACK AND LAY AT BETDAQ MAIDEN STKS 6f (F)
3:20 (3:21) (Class 5) 3-Y-O+ £2,456 (£725; £362) Stalls Low

Form RPR
240- 1 **Loveinthesand (IRE)**153 5763 3-8-12 75 JoeFanning 5 68+
(M Johnston) *prom: hdwy to chal over 2f out and sn led: rdn over 1f out: edgd lft ins fnl f: kpt on towards fin* 4/6[1]
026 2 1 **Ceto**6 392 3-8-7 0 ChrisCatlin 3 60
(P S McEntee) *cl up: rdn to ld briefly 2f out: sn hdd: drvn and ev ch ent fnl f tl no ex last 100yds* 7/1[3]
34-5 3 2 **My Mandy (IRE)**6 392 3-8-7 66 LiamJones 1 54
(R A Harris) *trckd ldrs on inner: hdwy over 2f out: rdn wl over 1f out: drvn and hung lft ent fnl f: sn one pce* 9/2[2]
4-4 4 3/4 **Blades Harmony**19 253 3-8-12 0 GrahamGibbons 6 57+
(E S McMahon) *dwlt: hdwy on outer 1/2-way: chsd ldrs 2f out: sn rdn and one pce ent fnl f* 12/1
50 5 2 1/2 **Blues Forever (IRE)**8 374 3-8-9 0 ow2 RichardEvans(5) 4 51
(P D Evans) *sn rdn along: outpcd and bhd 1/2-way: sme late hdwy* 14/1
0-0 6 3 3/4 **Wings Of Kintyre (IRE)**18 267 6-9-3 0 (p) BillyCray(5) 2 37
(A Berry) *led: rdn along 1/2-way: hdd 2f out: sn drvn and wknd* 50/1

1m 15.61s (-0.89) **Going Correction** -0.075s/f (Stan)
WFA 3 from 6yo 15lb 6 Ran SP% **107.0**
Speed ratings (Par 103): **102,100,98,97,93 88**
toteswingers: 1&2 £2.10, 1&3 £2.00, 2&3 £2.50 CSF £5.19 TOTE £1.50: £1.10, £2.40; EX 5.60.
Owner M Doyle **Bred** M Doyle **Trained** Middleham Moor, N Yorks

FOCUS
A weak and uncompetitive maiden.
Blues Forever(IRE) ◆ Official explanation: jockey said gelding resented kickback

474 PLAY GOLF AT SOUTHWELL GOLF CLUB H'CAP 6f (F)
3:50 (3:50) (Class 3) (0-90,90) 4-Y-O+ £6,799 (£2,023; £1,011; £505) Stalls Low

Form RPR
01-1 1 **Harlech Castle**33 71 5-8-13 85 (b) StephenCraine 6 98
(J R Boyle) *trckd ldr: hdwy over 2f out: rdn to chal over 1f out: led ent fnl f: kpt on* 7/4[1]
2034 2 1 1/4 **Bel Cantor**14 299 7-8-5 80 (p) KellyHarrison(3) 4 89
(W J H Ratcliffe) *led: rdn along 2f out: jnd and drvn over 1f out: hdd ent fnl f: kpt on u.p* 4/1[2]
2154 3 nk **Onceaponatime (IRE)**4 432 5-8-4 76 oh1 LukeMorris 3 84
(M D Squance) *trckd ldrs: hdwy on outer 2f out: rdn over 1f out: drvn and kpt on ins fnl f: nrst fin* 4/1[2]
16-0 4 3 1/4 **Esprit De Midas**16 286 4-9-1 87 (b[1]) NeilCallan 2 85+
(K A Ryan) *trckd ldng pair: effrt over 2f out: sn rdn along: drvn and wknd over 1f out* 4/1[2]
0P0- 5 6 **Dubai Dynamo**120 6732 5-9-4 90 AndrewElliott 5 68
(Mrs R A Carr) *a in rr: rdn along and bhd fr 1/2-way* 22/1
100/ 6 12 **Tawzeea (IRE)**548 4900 5-8-6 78 JoeFanning 1 18
(J D Bethell) *a in rr: outpcd and bhd fnl 2f* 14/1[3]

1m 13.89s (-2.61) **Going Correction** -0.075s/f (Stan) 6 Ran SP% **107.4**
Speed ratings (Par 107): **114,112,111,107,99 83**
toteswingers: 1&2 £1.50, 1&3 £2.20, 2&3 £3.30 CSF £8.09 TOTE £2.30: £1.30, £3.10; EX 6.90.
Owner Elite Racing Club **Bred** Elite Racing Club **Trained** Epsom, Surrey

FOCUS
By far the best race on the card, run at a solid pace.

NOTEBOOK
Harlech Castle, bidding for a C&D hat-trick off a 4lb higher mark, got a nice lead from Bel Cantor in the early stages and although he had to work in order to wrestle the lead from him a furlong out, then strode out well to win with a bit in hand. He relishes these conditions and may not have stopped winning yet. (op 15-8 tchd 13-8 and 2-1 in places)
Bel Cantor was 8lb higher than for his last win but he ran really well from 7lb wrong in a hot C&D handicap last time. Soon in front, he set a decent pace but never gave up and only the in-form favourite was able to get past him. He deserves to get his head back in front. (op 9-2 tchd 7-2)
Onceaponatime(IRE) ◆ had twice been narrowly beaten by Harlech Castle over C&D in recent months, but a subsequent win on Polytrack meant that he was 4lb worse off with him compared to last time. Held up early, he looked a real danger when making an effort coming to the last furlong, but could then make little more impression. He can be given some credit as he was given a patient ride in a race otherwise dominated by prominent racers, but Polytrack may suit him better given that he possesses a decent turn of foot. (op 11-2)
Esprit De Midas, a three-time winner over 7f here around a year ago, was blinkered for the first time. Content to take a lead early, he had every chance until fading inside the last furlong and remains 8lb above his last winning mark, so he may need some more leniency. He was reported to have been struck into. Official explanation: trainer said gelding was struck into (op 9-4)
Dubai Dynamo, who had lost his way completely in his last few starts for Paul Cole, was making a rare appearance over a trip this short on his debut for the yard. He never got into the race, however, and still needs to prove that he retains any of his old ability. (op 16-1)
Tawzeea(IRE), having his first start for the yard and making his sand debut after 19 months off, raced keenly at the back of the field early and was a beaten horse at halfway. He was reported to have hung left. Official explanation: jockey said gelding hung left throughout (op 16-1 tchd 12-1)

475 BOOK YOUR TICKETS ON LINE AT SOUTHWELL-RACECOURSE.CO.UK MAIDEN H'CAP 1m (F)
4:20 (4:21) (Class 6) (0-55,55) 3-Y-O £1,774 (£523; £262) Stalls Low

Form RPR
066- 1 **The Blue Dog (IRE)**52 7816 3-8-9 50 TonyCulhane 1 60+
(George Baker) *trckd ldrs on inner: hdwy 3f out: led 2f out and sn rdn: drvn ent fnl f: kpt on* 2/1[1]
00-0 2 3 **Always Dixie (IRE)**22 216 3-8-13 54 (b[1]) JoeFanning 7 57
(M Johnston) *dwlt: sn trcking ldrs: hdwy over 3f out: rdn to chal 2f out: drvn and ev ch whn edgd lft jst ins fnl f: sn one pce* 6/1
6-30 3 1 **Sternian**11 340 3-8-9 50 LukeMorris 4 51
(M E Rimmer) *hld up in tch: hdwy on inner over 2f out: rdn and ev ch over 1f out: drvn and one pce ins fnl f* 14/1
4540 4 6 **Creevy (IRE)**4 422 3-8-5 46 oh1 (b) DavidProbert 3 34
(S Kirk) *prom: effrt 3f out and sn rdn: drvn 2f out and grad wknd appr fnl f* 7/1
05-4 5 2 1/4 **Little Meadow (IRE)**14 302 3-8-7 53 TobyAtkinson(5) 8 36
(Miss J Feilden) *in rr: hdwy on wd outside 3f out: sn rdn and nvr nr ldrs* 5/1[3]
600- 6 2 1/2 **Alotago (IRE)**123 6639 3-9-0 55 AdrianNicholls 2 32
(D Nicholls) *led: rdn along over 2f out: drvn and hdd wl over 1f out: sn wknd* 20/1
66-5 7 1/2 **Penderyn**14 302 3-8-2 46 oh1 KellyHarrison(3) 6 22
(C Smith) *chsd ldrs: rdn along 1/2-way: sn wknd* 20/1
-356 8 nk **Hathaway (IRE)**15 288 3-8-10 51 ShaneKelly 10 26
(W M Brisbourne) *a towards rr* 4/1[2]
00-5 9 3 **Whip Up (IRE)**13 305 3-8-5 46 oh1 FrankieMcDonald 9 15
(J G Portman) *chsd ldrs on wd outside: rdn along over 3f out and sn wknd* 18/1

1m 43.15s (-0.55) **Going Correction** -0.075s/f (Stan) 9 Ran SP% **118.2**
Speed ratings (Par 95): **99,96,95,89,86 84,83,83,80**
toteswingers: 1&2 £2.10, 1&3 £11.20, 2&3 £7.20 CSF £14.84 CT £129.54 TOTE £2.50: £1.10, £2.40, £3.00; EX 16.60 Trifecta £209.40 Part won. Pool: £283.00 - 0.64 winning units..
Owner Mrs V P Baker & Partners **Bred** Mervyn Stewkesbury **Trained** Moreton Morrell, Warwicks

FOCUS
One gelding up against eight fillies in this dire maiden handicap.

476 MEMBERSHIP AT SOUTHWELL GOLF CLUB MAIDEN H'CAP 1m 3f (F)
4:50 (4:50) (Class 5) (0-75,74) 4-Y-O+ £2,456 (£725) Stalls Low

Form RPR
2 1 **Spruce (USA)**6 396 4-8-6 60 JimmyQuinn 2 72+
(Miss J Feilden) *set stdy pce: qcknd over 3f out: wl clr 2f out: eased ins fnl f: unchal* 2/13[1]
34/5 2 25 **Ivestar (IRE)**12 327 5-8-8 65 (vt[1]) PatrickDonaghy(5) 1 35+
(P C Haslam) *trckd wnr: effrt 4f out: rdn along over 3f out: sn outpcd and wl adrift whn eased over 1f out* 9/2[2]

2m 28.62s (0.62) **Going Correction** -0.075s/f (Stan)
WFA 4 from 5yo 2lb 2 Ran SP% **104.8**
Speed ratings (Par 103): **94,75**
TOTE £1.10 Place 6: £ 21.53 Place 5: £12.21.
Owner Good Company Partnership **Bred** Juddmonte Farms Inc **Trained** Exning, Suffolk

FOCUS
This is as bad as it gets - a 61-75 maiden handicap for 4-y-os and upwards reduced to two runners with the withdrawal of Dr Valentine. Although matches on the AW used to be rare (there were only two in the three years leading up to January) this was the third in a little over three weeks.
T/Plt: £11.30 to a £1 stake. Pool: £60,308.66. 3,871.82 winning tickets. T/Qpdt: £4.00 to a £1 stake. Pool: £3,857.36. 710.82 winning tickets. JR

383 KEMPTON (A.W) (R-H)
Wednesday, February 10

OFFICIAL GOING: Standard
Wind: Moderate, ahead

477 KEMPTON.CO.UK H'CAP 5f (P)
5:10 (5:10) (Class 7) (0-50,50) 4-Y-O+ £1,364 (£403; £201) Stalls High

Form RPR
6-00 1 **Gleaming Spirit (IRE)**19 271 6-8-12 45 (v) AdrianMcCarthy 6 55
(Peter Grayson) *mde all: pushed along over 1f out: kpt on strly: unchal* 20/1
0-00 2 2 1/4 **Taboor (IRE)**19 271 12-8-12 45 SaleemGolam 10 47
(R M H Cowell) *s.i.s towards rr: hdwy 2f out: styd on strly fr over 1f out fin wl to take 2nd last strides but no ch w wnr* 10/1
-446 3 hd **Cocktail Party (IRE)**9 368 4-9-2 49 (v) FergusSweeney 11 50
(J W Unett) *in tch: hdwy on ins to chse wnr over 1f out: no imp on wnr and lost 2nd last strides* 2/1[1]
5-05 4 1 1/2 **Sir Loin**13 319 9-8-7 45 (v) RossAtkinson(5) 3 41
(P Burgoyne) *sn prom: impr to trckd ldrs and edgd rt appr fnl f: rdn ins fnl f and sn hung rt and one pce* 12/1
0-00 5 hd **Romantic Verse**20 249 5-8-9 45 (bt) MichaelStainton(3) 1 40
(R A Harris) *s.i.s towards rr: rdn 1/2-way: styd on strly fnl f: fin wl but nvr a threat* 20/1
50-0 6 hd **Tightrope (IRE)**13 319 4-8-12 45 (b) TomQueally 2 39
(T D McCarthy) *chsd wnr to 1/2-way: sltly outpcd ins fnl 2f: effrt whn hmpd and swtchd lft 1f out: kpt on but nt a threat* 12/1
060 7 1 3/4 **Cheshire Rose**6 402 5-9-0 47 (p) LiamJones 4 35
(A M Hales) *racd on outside: styd on fnl f but nvr gng pce to be competitive* 15/2[2]
50-0 8 shd **Shirley High**20 253 4-8-13 46 PaulDoe 12 39
(P Howling) *chsd ldrs: wnt 2nd 1/2-way tl wl over 1f out: styd in tch tl hmpd and eased wl ins fnl f* 20/1
50-0 9 3/4 **Town House**9 369 8-8-9 45 KellyHarrison(3) 9 30
(B P J Baugh) *t.k.h: chsd ldrs over 3f* 9/1[3]
00-0 10 3/4 **Woodcote (IRE)**21 241 8-8-13 46 (v) AdamKirby 8 28
(Peter Grayson) *slowly away: a in rr* 9/1[3]
000- 11 2 1/2 **Tan Bonita (USA)**63 7689 5-8-12 45 JimCrowley 7 18
(R J Smith) *plld hrd: bhd fr 1/2-way* 12/1
00-0 12 8 **The Magic Of Rio**29 132 4-9-3 50 DaneO'Neill 5 —
(Peter Grayson) *a in rr* 16/1

59.99 secs (-0.51) **Going Correction** -0.05s/f (Stan) 12 Ran SP% **117.4**
Speed ratings (Par 97): **102,98,98,95,95 95,92,92,90,89 85,72**
toteswingers: 1&2 £46.30, 1&3 £8.60, 2&3 £5.90 CSF £200.28 CT £587.28 TOTE £17.30: £7.20, £3.40, £1.30; EX 446.70.
Owner E Grayson & Partner **Bred** Rathasker Stud **Trained** Formby, Lancs

FOCUS
A weak race but the winner made it a good tempo.
Sir Loin Official explanation: jockey said gelding hung badly right
Tightrope(IRE) Official explanation: jockey said gelding suffered interference in runing

478 BOOK NOW FOR RACING POST CHASE DAY H'CAP 5f (P)
5:40 (5:40) (Class 4) (0-85,86) 3-Y-O £4,209 (£1,252; £625; £312) Stalls High

Form RPR
16- 1 **Breathless Kiss (USA)**163 5521 3-8-11 75 JimCrowley 4 81
(K A Ryan) *mde all: drvn along over 1f out: styd on strly fnl f: unchal* 7/2[3]
3-11 2 1 1/4 **Texas Queen**10 363 3-8-12 76 6ex JoeFanning 2 77
(M R Channon) *in tch: racd on outside: rdn and hdwy over 1f out: styd on to take 2nd fnl 75yds but no ch w wnr* 7/2[3]
0-1 3 1 1/4 **Best Trip (IRE)**28 147 3-9-0 78 FrannyNorton 5 75
(R C Guest) *trckd ldrs: wnt 2nd 2f out: no imp on wnr and lost 2nd fnl 75yds* 5/2[1]
540- 4 2 1/2 **Micky's Knock Off (IRE)**67 7636 3-8-3 67 AdrianMcCarthy 3 55
(R C Guest) *towards rr: rdn 1/2-way: mod prog fnl f* 10/1
4-42 5 1 **Italian Tom (IRE)**14 310 3-9-1 79 (p) LukeMorris 1 63
(R A Harris) *chsd wnr 3f: wknd qckly over 1f out* 11/4[2]

59.83 secs (-0.67) **Going Correction** -0.05s/f (Stan) 5 Ran SP% **108.8**
Speed ratings (Par 99): **103,101,99,95,93**
toteswingers: 1&2 £8.90 CSF £15.30 TOTE £4.70: £2.30, £1.10; EX 15.40.
Owner Mrs Angie Bailey **Bred** Don Mattox & Pam Mattox **Trained** Hambleton, N Yorks

FOCUS
For the second race running, the winner made all but the pace was not as strong as the first race and the time was disappointing in comparison considering the better class of this field.
Best Trip(IRE) ◆ Official explanation: jockey said gelding hung right

479 DIGIBET H'CAP 1m 2f (P)
6:10 (6:10) (Class 7) (0-50,50) 4-Y-0+ £1,364 (£403; £201) Stalls High

Form RPR
00-6 1 **Lytham (IRE)**[6] 407 9-9-3 **50** FergusSweeney 10 58
(A W Carroll) *in rr: hdwy over 3f out: str run u.p to ld 1f out: hld on wl* **6/1**[3]
5-34 2 ¾ **Dobravany (IRE)**[12] 353 6-9-2 **49** (p) JimmyQuinn 1 56
(K A Morgan) *in rr: stl plenty to do 2f out: str run appr fnl f: fin wl to take 2nd nr fin: nt rch wnr* **5/1**[1]
4-46 3 hd **Desert Fairy**[12] 354 4-8-6 **47** AlexEdwards(7) 12 54
(J W Unett) *in rr: hdwy on outside fr 2f out: styd on strly fnl f: gng on cl home* **20/1**
-444 4 nk **Inquisitress**[7] 389 6-8-12 **48** MarcHalford(3) 9 54+
(J J Bridger) *in tch: hdwy over 2f out: styd on wl thrght fnl f: gng on cl home* **14/1**
-106 5 nk **Turkish Sultan (IRE)**[12] 347 7-9-2 **49** (b) LukeMorris 4 54
(J M Bradley) *chsd ldrs: drvn to chal fr over 1f out: styd on same pce ins fnl f* **16/1**
0-02 6 ¾ **Midnight Bay**[6] 407 4-9-0 **48** HayleyTurner 7 52
(P D Evans) *chsd ldrs: t.k.h: drvn to take slt advantage appr fnl f: sn hdd: wknd nr fin* **5/1**[1]
00/0 7 ½ **Global Guest**[21] 229 6-8-12 **48** (t) PatrickHills(3) 5 51
(S Curran) *mid-div: hdwy appr fnl f: kpt on ins fnl f but nvr a threat* **16/1**
55-0 8 shd **Corrib (IRE)**[6] 411 7-8-13 **46** DavidProbert 14 49
(B Palling) *chsd ldrs: rdn on ins rail ins fnl 2f: ev ch appr fnl f: wknd fnl 100yds* **12/1**
14-0 9 nk **Jiggalong**[26] 184 4-9-0 **48** PaulDoe 3 50
(Jim Best) *in rr: pushed along 2f out: hdwy appr fnl f: styd on ins fnl f but nvr a threat* **11/2**[2]
-226 10 6 **Crimson Flame (IRE)**[21] 228 7-9-3 **50** TomQueally 13 42
(S Curran) *trckd ldr tl lft in ld after 3f: rdn 2f out: hdd appr fnl f: wknd ins fnl f* **5/1**[1]
040/ 11 1¾ **Shropshirelass**[58] 5020 7-9-0 **47** SamHitchcott 2 36
(Miss Z C Davison) *chsd ldrs 7f* **40/1**
00-0 12 5 **Hatch A Plan (IRE)**[32] 100 9-8-10 **50** RyanClark(7) 6 30
(Mouse Hamilton-Fairley) *v late removing blindfold: wnt lft s and lost 20 l: effrt to latch on to main gp 1/2-way but nt rcvr: dropped away fnl 3f* **16/1**
0-00 R **Gospel Spirit**[14] 308 5-9-3 **50** SimonWhitworth 11 —
(J R Jenkins) *led: t.k.h: rn out after 3f* **80/1**

2m 9.03s (1.03) **Going Correction** -0.05s/f (Stan)
WFA 4 from 5yo+ 1lb 13 Ran SP% **120.1**
Speed ratings (Par 97): **93,92,92,92,91 91,90,90,90,85 84,80,—**
toteswingers: 1&2 £6.10, 1&3 £43.20, 2&3 £26.00 CSF £35.72 CT £575.44 TOTE £8.90: £3.10, £1.10, £7.50; EX 58.20.
Owner Morgan, Clarke & Parris **Bred** Mrs A S O'Brien And Lars Pearson **Trained** Cropthorne, Worcs

FOCUS
Just a medium gallop on the whole, but it was strong enough for the principals to come from off the pace.
Hatch A Plan(IRE) Official explanation: jockey said he had been unable to remove blind on leaving stalls
Gospel Spirit Official explanation: jockey said gelding cocked its jaw turning into back straight

480 DIGIBET.COM H'CAP 1m 2f (P)
6:40 (6:42) (Class 4) (0-85,85) 4-Y-0+ £4,209 (£1,252; £625; £312) Stalls High

Form RPR
502- 1 **King Olav (UAE)**[46] 7233 5-9-5 **85** LukeMorris 2 95
(A W Carroll) *in tch: hdwy 3f out: str run fr over 1f out: styd on strly ins fnl f: led cl home* **3/1**[2]
-512 2 hd **Mister Green (FR)**[12] 341 4-9-3 **84** (b) JoeFanning 10 94
(K McAuliffe) *stdd s: in rr tl hdwy ins fnl 2f: str run fnl f to ld fnl 30yds: hdd cl home* **8/1**
212- 3 ½ **Desert Vision**[45] 7851 6-9-5 **85** (vt) PhillipMakin 9 94
(M W Easterby) *in rr tl hdwy ins fnl 2f: slt ld fnl 100yds: hdd fnl 30yds: hld whn tight for room on line* **6/1**[3]
54-3 4 4½ **Hawaana (IRE)**[7] 394 5-9-0 **80** SteveDrowne 5 81
(Miss Gay Kelleway) *in rr: pushed along 3f out: hdwy over 1f out: r.o fnl f but nvr a threat* **8/1**
44-1 5 nk **Thunderball**[11] 359 4-9-0 **81** ChrisCatlin 3 81
(J A Glover) *led after 2f: rdn over 2f out: hdd & wknd qckly fnl 100yds* **12/1**
1-54 6 1¾ **Free Tussy (ARG)**[12] 341 6-8-12 **78** (bt) PatCosgrave 11 75
(G L Moore) *in tch: hdwy ro chse ldrs ins fnl 3f: rdn and outpcd fnl 2f* **16/1**
60-4 7 ½ **Cry Alot Boy**[21] 231 7-8-10 **76** JimmyQuinn 8 72
(K A Morgan) *slowly away: rdn 2f out and sme late prog* **16/1**
20-0 8 1¾ **Brouhaha**[21] 231 6-9-3 **83** RichardKingscote 6 76
(Tom Dascombe) *disp ld 2f: chsd ldr after tl ins fnl 2f: sn outpcd* **10/1**
131- 9 ½ **Poyle Meg**[63] 7684 4-9-2 **83** (p) JimCrowley 12 75
(R M Beckett) *chsd ldrs 7f* **11/4**[1]
010- 10 7 **Best In Class**[63] 7684 4-8-7 **77** WilliamCarson(3) 7 57
(S C Williams) *slowly away: a in rr* **14/1**
00-0 11 8 **It's Dubai Dolly**[19] 266 4-8-9 **76** WandersonD'Avila 4 41
(A J Lidderdale) *disp ld 2f: chsd ldrs tl wknd over 3f out* **25/1**

2m 4.72s (-3.28) **Going Correction** -0.05s/f (Stan)
WFA 4 from 5yo+ 1lb 11 Ran SP% **127.2**
Speed ratings (Par 105): **111,110,110,106,106 105,104,103,103,97 91**
toteswingers: 1&2 £8.20, 1&3 £5.90, 2&3 £3.40 CSF £30.28 CT £144.94 TOTE £6.50: £2.40, £3.60, £1.80; EX 46.10.
Owner Cover Point Racing **Bred** Darley **Trained** Cropthorne, Worcs

FOCUS
A good gallop eventually brought the hold-up horses into play, but it went to a runner who had been in touch throughout.

481 DIGIBET SPORTS BETTING CLAIMING STKS 7f (P)
7:10 (7:10) (Class 6) 3-Y-0+ £2,047 (£604; £302) Stalls High

Form RPR
-013 1 **Caprio (IRE)**[6] 405 5-9-12 81 NickyMackay 1 82+
(J R Boyle) *mde most: shkn up over 1f out: kpt on ins fnl f under hand riding: readily* **10/11**[1]
-504 2 ½ **Little Pete (IRE)**[16] 292 5-9-10 77 AdamKirby 8 79
(I W McInnes) *chsd ldrs: chsd wnr over 2f out: clsd ins fnl f but a readily hld* **7/4**[2]
14-5 3 5 **Charlie Delta**[20] 251 7-9-7 60 (b) LukeMorris 6 60
(R A Harris) *chsd ldrs: rdn 2f out: wnt 3rd fnl f but wl hld* **14/1**
0-03 4 nk **Gone Hunting**[23] 214 4-9-9 74 (t) SaleemGolam 7 61
(J Pearce) *in tch: hdwy on ins to 2f out: chsd ldrs in 3rd sn after: nvr any ch and outpcd into 3rd fnl f* **9/1**[3]
00- 5 1½ **See Elsie Play**[235] 3161 4-9-8 0 SamHitchcott 5 56?
(Miss Z C Davison) *slowly away: in rr: pushed along over 2f out: green but mod prog over 1f out* **33/1**
00-0 6 8 **Whisky Jack**[9] 373 4-9-11 67 (b) FrannyNorton 2 38
(W R Muir) *chsd wnr tl wknd over 2f out* **25/1**

1m 25.39s (-0.61) **Going Correction** -0.05s/f (Stan) 6 Ran SP% **112.2**
Speed ratings (Par 101): **101,100,94,94,92 83**
toteswingers: 1&2 £1.10, 1&3 £2.50, 2&3 £3.80 CSF £2.69 TOTE £1.90: £1.30, £1.10; EX 3.00.
Owner M Khan X2 **Bred** P Rabbitte **Trained** Epsom, Surrey

FOCUS
After the winner had dictated an unremarkable pace, the top two in the betting dominated this in the last 2f.

482 RAY BUTCHER, YOU'RE MY FAVOURITE H'CAP 1m 4f (P)
7:40 (7:40) (Class 5) (0-75,75) 3-Y-0 £2,590 (£770; £385; £192) Stalls Centre

Form RPR
6-11 1 **Keenes Royale**[20] 254 3-9-2 **70** (t) JimCrowley 3 78+
(R M Beckett) *trckd ldr: t.k.h: shkn up to ld over 2f out: easily* **11/10**[1]
40-3 2 4 **Temple Fair (USA)**[15] 302 3-8-3 **57** GregFairley 5 56
(M Johnston) *led: pushed along 3f out: hdd over 2f out: sn no ch w wnr but hld on for 2nd thrght fnl f* **4/1**[3]
1-12 3 ¾ **Thundering Home**[5] 428 3-9-7 **75** HayleyTurner 4 73
(E A L Dunlop) *towards rr but wl in tch: pushed along and hdwy to trck ldng trio over 2f out: nvr any ch w wnr but styd on to cl on 2nd fnl f* **5/2**[2]
065- 4 10 **Rock Of Eire**[78] 7502 3-8-4 **58** (t) LukeMorris 2 40
(E J Creighton) *in tch: rdn to chse ldrs ins fnl 3f: hung rt and wknd over 2f out* **20/1**
3-31 5 7 **Kathindi (IRE)**[14] 305 3-8-7 **66** RossAtkinson(5) 1 37
(J S Moore) *in tch: rdn to chse ldrs ins fnl 3f: hung lft and wknd wl over 2f out* **15/2**

2m 36.58s (2.08) **Going Correction** -0.05s/f (Stan) 5 Ran SP% **112.7**
Speed ratings (Par 97): **91,88,87,81,76**
CSF £6.13 TOTE £2.20: £1.50, £1.70; EX 8.20.
Owner Mrs R J Jacobs **Bred** Newsells Park Stud Limited **Trained** Whitsbury, Hants

FOCUS
A modest gallop but a progressive winner.
Rock Of Eire Official explanation: vet said gelding lost left-hind shoe

483 DAY TIME, NIGHT TIME, GREAT TIME H'CAP 6f (P)
8:10 (8:13) (Class 5) (0-70,69) 3-Y-0 £2,590 (£770; £385; £192) Stalls High

Form RPR
2612 1 **Freddie's Girl (USA)**[11] 357 3-9-4 **69** AdamKirby 7 77
(Stef Higgins) *mde all: drvn and styd on strly thrght fnl f* **13/8**[1]
300- 2 ¾ **Candyfloss Girl**[109] 7033 3-9-0 **65** DavidProbert 6 71
(H J L Dunlop) *disp 2nd tl chsd wnr over 2f out: rdn and flashed tail fr over 1f out: kpt on fnl f but a hld* **5/1**
433- 3 1½ **Caramelita**[64] 7674 3-9-2 **67** TomQueally 4 68
(J R Jenkins) *disp 2nd tl 2f out: styd on same pce* **4/1**[3]
106- 4 1¼ **Tom Folan**[183] 4868 3-9-3 **68** (p) FrannyNorton 3 66
(H J Collingridge) *s.i.s: sn in tch: drvn and effrt over 2f out: nvr on terms and styd on same pce* **12/1**
05-5 5 2 **Val C**[21] 233 3-8-11 **62** JimmyQuinn 1 54
(M Botti) *in tch: rdn 3f out: wknd 2f out* **7/2**[2]
6465 6 1¼ **Tatawor (IRE)**[4] 443 3-9-0 **65** (b) PatCosgrave 8 53
(J R Boyle) *rdn 3f out: a outpcd* **6/1**

1m 13.86s (0.76) **Going Correction** -0.05s/f (Stan) 6 Ran SP% **119.0**
Speed ratings (Par 97): **92,91,89,87,84 83**
toteswingers: 1&2 £3.70, 1&3 £1.10, 2&3 £2.40 CSF £11.15 CT £28.89 TOTE £2.30: £1.10, £3.00; EX 8.40 Place 6 £58.23, Place 5 £30.27.
Owner Mrs Anne & Fred Cowley **Bred** Respite Farm Inc **Trained** Lambourn, Berks

FOCUS
The tempo was moderate and they quickened considerably in the last 2f after racing in a tight bunch.
T/Plt: £42.10 to a £1 stake. Pool: £75,304.46. 1,303.95 winning tickets. T/Qpdt: £10.50 to a £1 stake. Pool: £7,677.73. 539.50 winning tickets. ST

442 LINGFIELD (L-H)
Wednesday, February 10

OFFICIAL GOING: Standard
Wind: Fresh, against Weather: Snow flurries and bright spells, cold

484 MARRIOTT PLAY & STAY MAIDEN STKS 1m 2f (P)
1:25 (1:26) (Class 5) 3-Y-0 £2,456 (£725; £362) Stalls Low

Form RPR
6- 1 **Bebopalula (IRE)**[110] 6992 3-8-12 0 MichaelHills 9 65+
(B W Hills) *s.i.s: sn rcvrd to chse ldrs on outer: t.k.h: wnt 2nd over 4f out: led wl over 2f out: rdn 2 l clr wl over 1f out: drvn ins fnl f: kpt on and a holding on* **6/4**[1]
02-4 2 ¾ **Christmas Coming**[18] 274 3-9-3 69 DaneO'Neill 2 67
(D R C Elsworth) *t.k.h early: broke wl: stdd into midfield over 8f out: pushed along over 4f out: rdn over 2f out: styd on u.p ins fnl f: wnt 2nd last strides: nt quite pce to rch wnr* **5/1**[3]
3 hd **Atlantic Tiger (IRE)** 3-9-3 0 JoeFanning 5 67+
(M Johnston) *chsd ldr tl led over 8f out: hdd wl over 2f out: rdn and unable qck w wnr wl over 1f out: edgd rt but kpt on again ins fnl f: lost 2nd last strides* **8/1**
4 4 ¾ **Frameit (IRE)**[5] 421 3-9-3 0 LiamKeniry 3 65
(J S Moore) *chsd ldrs: rdn and nt pce of ldng pair ent fnl 2f: styd on steadily u.p ins fnl f: nt quite pce to chal ldrs* **11/1**
04 5 1¼ **Beat Route**[12] 340 3-8-12 0 JemmaMarshall(5) 4 63
(M J Attwater) *t.k.h: led tl over 8f out: hld up wl in tch after: hdwy on inner 2f out: kpt on same pce fnl f* **33/1**
6 ½ **Vulcanite (IRE)** 3-9-3 0 JimCrowley 1 62+
(R M Beckett) *towards rr: pushed along over 4f out: hdwy into midfield over 2f out: rdn and styd on same pce fr over 1f out* **3/1**[2]

00- **7** 2 3/4 **Nurai**[138] 6254 3-8-12 0 TonyCulhane 7 51
(P W D'Arcy) *hld up in last pair: hdwy over 4f out: outpcd and rdn over 2f out: no prog fr wl over 1f out* **66/1**

0-6 **8** 8 **All Right Now**[21] 236 3-8-12 0 LeeNewnes[(5)] 8 40
(S Kirk) *stdd after s: hld up in rr: struggling and rdn wl over 2f out: no ch fnl 2f* **100/1**

006- **9** nk **Lady Hetherington**[83] 7451 3-8-12 60 ChrisCatlin 6 34
(G Brown) *in tch: hdwy to chse ldrs jst over 3f out: wknd u.p ent fnl 2f: wl bhd fnl f* **40/1**

0 **10** 5 **Rosewood Lad**[11] 356 3-9-3 0 LukeMorris 11 29
(J S Moore) *racd in midfield: rdn along over 7f out: lost tch wl over 2f out: wl bhd fnl f* **66/1**

00 **11** 4 1/2 **Big Eric**[25] 206 3-9-3 0 PaulDoe 10 20
(P D Evans) *in tch in midfield: hdwy 5f out: chsd ldrs 3f out: wknd qckly jst over 2f out: wl bhd fnl f* **125/1**

2m 8.13s (1.53) **Going Correction** +0.025s/f (Slow) 11 Ran SP% **111.3**
Speed ratings (Par 97): **94,93,93,92,91 91,89,82,82,78 74**
toteswingers: 1&2 £2.80, 1&3 £4.10, 2&3 £3.60 CSF £8.45 TOTE £2.40: £1.02, £1.70, £3.10; EX 10.00 Trifecta £19.60 Pool: £404.56 - 15.24 winning units..
Owner Phil Cunningham **Bred** William Flynn **Trained** Lambourn, Berks

FOCUS
A fair maiden. The runner-up sets the level.

485 BET ASIAN H'CAPS - BETDAQ HANDICAP 1m 2f (P)
1:55 (1:55) (Class 5) (0-75,75) 4-Y-0+ **£2,456** (£725; £362) **Stalls** Low

Form RPR

64-5 **1** **Officer In Command (USA)**[11] 359 4-9-5 **75** LiamKeniry 1 82
(J S Moore) *led for 1f: chsd clr ldr after: clsd 3f out: ev ch over 1f out: drvn ahd ent fnl f: r.o wl* **7/2**[2]

5-02 **2** 3/4 **Rapid City**[14] 315 7-8-12 **67** PaulDoe 2 73
(P D Evans) *stdd s: t.k.h: hld up in last pair: rdn and hdwy on outer bnd 2f out: chsd ldrs over 1f out: kpt on wl to go 2nd fnl 50yds: unable to rch wnr* **5/1**[3]

30-5 **3** hd **Bid For Glory**[16] 294 6-8-13 **68** (v) JimmyQuinn 6 74
(H J Collingridge) *hld up in midfield: clsd up over 3f out: rdn and effrt over 1f out: styd on ins fnl f: wnt 3rd towards fin: nvr quite pce to chal wnr* **13/2**

12-3 **4** 1/2 **Bolanderi (USA)**[20] 255 5-8-11 **73** AlexEdwards[(7)] 8 78
(Andrew Turnell) *chsd ldng trio: clsd over 3f out: ev ch and rdn jst over 1f out: unable qck ins fnl f: lost 2 pls fnl 50yds* **11/4**[1]

60-0 **5** 3/4 **All About You (IRE)**[16] 294 4-9-1 **71** J-PGuillambert 7 74
(P Howling) *sn pushed up and led after 1f: sn clr: reduced advantage 3f out: hrd pressed wl over 1f out: rdn and hdd ent fnl f: wknd fnl 75yds* **25/1**

516- **6** 1/2 **Black N Brew (USA)**[56] 7777 4-9-3 **73** SteveDrowne 3 75
(J R Best) *stdd after s: hld up in last trio: clsd 3f out: rdn and edging rt over 1f out: nvr gng pce to threaten ldrs* **15/2**

3-33 **7** 1 **Laureldeans Best (IRE)**[13] 330 4-8-4 60 oh1 ChrisCatlin 5 61
(R A Fahey) *chsd clr ldng pair: clsd over 3f out: unable qck u.p jst over 2f out: wknd 1f out* **8/1**

P56- **8** 28 **Trifti**[52] 7823 9-9-2 **71** DaneO'Neill 4 21
(Miss Jo Crowley) *s.i.s: hld up in last pair: clsd on ldrs over 3f out: rdn and no prog ent fnl 2f: eased whn btn fnl f: burst blood vessel* **12/1**

2m 7.07s (0.47) **Going Correction** +0.025s/f (Slow)
WFA 4 from 5yo+ 1lb 8 Ran SP% **113.3**
Speed ratings (Par 103): **99,98,98,97,97 96,96,73**
toteswingers: 1&2 £3.80, 1&3 £6.80, 2&3 £6.10 CSF £20.93 CT £106.88 TOTE £3.50: £1.40, £1.50, £2.30; EX 17.90 Trifecta £85.90 Pool: £328.87 - 2.83 winning units..
Owner N Brunskill & J S Moore **Bred** Blooming Hills Inc **Trained** Upper Lambourn, Berks
■ Stewards' Enquiry : Paul Doe two-day ban: careless riding (Feb 24-25)

FOCUS
A moderate handicap, run at an uneven pace and which resulted in a tight finish.
Trifti Official explanation: vet said gelding had bled

486 TRY BETDAQ FOR AN EXCHANGE H'CAP 7f (P)
2:25 (2:25) (Class 6) (0-65,64) 4-Y-0+ **£1,774** (£523; £262) **Stalls** Low

Form RPR

261- **1** **Copperwood**[73] 7591 5-8-11 **57** DaneO'Neill 8 65
(M Blanshard) *in tch in midfield: rdn and hdwy over 1f out: edgd lft u.p but ev ch ins fnl f: led fnl 75yds: hld on cl home* **10/1**

1-03 **2** nk **Forward Feline (IRE)**[9] 373 4-9-4 **64** DavidProbert 12 71
(B Palling) *in tch in midfield: pushed along 5f out: rdn and effrt wl over 1f out: r.o strly u.p ins fnl f: wnt 2nd last strides: nt quite rch wnr* **12/1**

0-60 **3** nk **Trip Switch**[14] 312 4-8-12 **58** SaleemGolam 4 65
(G Prodromou) *led: pressed and rdn wl over 1f out: kpt on wl: tl hdd fnl 75yds: no ex and lost 2nd nr fin* **25/1**

-253 **4** 1/2 **Bollywood Style**[4] 442 5-8-12 **58** SteveDrowne 9 63
(J R Best) *in tch in midfield on outer: rdn and effrt wl over 1f out: r.o wl fnl 150yds: nt quite rch ldrs* **13/2**[2]

-502 **5** nse **Waterloo Dock**[14] 317 5-8-11 **57** MartinDwyer 6 62
(M Quinn) *chsd ldr: rdn ent fnl 2f: ev ch and drvn wl over 1f out: no ex fnl 75yds* **14/1**

26-5 **6** 1/2 **Teen Ager (FR)**[10] 367 6-9-3 **63** JimmyQuinn 5 67
(P Burgoyne) *hld up wl in tch: effrt to chse ldrs 2f out: rdn and unable qck over 1f out: keeping on same pce and hld whn nt clr run and edging out rt wl ins fnl f* **7/1**[3]

0-11 **7** 1/2 **Stanley Goodspeed**[4] 442 7-8-6 **59** (t) KierenFox[(7)] 14 62+
(J W Hills) *stdd after s: wl bhd in last: hdwy over 2f out: v wd and rdn bnd 2f out: hanging lft over 1f out: styd on fnl f: nvr gng to rch ldrs* **7/4**[1]

-463 **8** nk **Kyle (IRE)**[14] 317 6-9-2 **62** LiamKeniry 2 64
(C R Dore) *hld up in tch in midfield: rdn and effrt wl over 1f out: one pce and no imp fnl f* **12/1**

42/0 **9** shd **Angels Quest**[17] 282 5-8-6 **52** LukeMorris 13 55
(A W Carroll) *sn pushed along in rr: hdwy and swtchd lft over 1f out: drvn and kpt on same pce ins fnl f: n.m.r and eased towards fin* **40/1**

46/5 **10** 2 1/2 **Unlimited**[17] 285 8-9-0 **60** FergusSweeney 3 55
(A W Carroll) *plld hrd: chsd ldrs: drvn and effrt over 1f out: wknd fnl f* **10/1**

0-40 **11** 2 1/4 **Dream Express (IRE)**[29] 135 5-8-11 **57** HayleyTurner 11 47
(P Howling) *stdd s: hld up in last trio: rdn and no prog ent fnl 2f: no ch fnl f* **16/1**

260- **12** 5 **Idle Power (IRE)**[102] 7180 12-9-3 **63** PatCosgrave 10 40
(J R Boyle) *chsd ldrs tl rdn and wknd ent fnl 2f: wl bhd fnl f* **33/1**

0-00 **13** 3/4 **Moral Duty (USA)**[7] 397 5-8-13 **59** TonyCulhane 1 34
(W G M Turner) *s.i.s: a bhd* **66/1**

1m 24.55s (-0.25) **Going Correction** +0.025s/f (Slow) 13 Ran SP% **119.0**
Speed ratings (Par 101): **102,101,101,100,100 100,99,99,99,96 93,87,87**
toteswingers: 1&2 £14.80, 1&3 £37.70, 2&3 £68.60 CSF £120.32 CT £3001.69 TOTE £12.10: £2.90, £4.30, £7.80; EX 175.30 TRIFECTA Not won..
Owner Mrs Rosemary K Wilkerson **Bred** Hertford Offset Press **Trained** Upper Lambourn, Berks
■ Stewards' Enquiry : Dane O'Neill two-day ban: careless riding (Feb 24-25)

FOCUS
A moderate handicap, run at a good pace.
Unlimited Official explanation: jockey said gelding ran too freely

487 MARRIOTT HOTEL OPENING SPRING 2010 H'CAP 1m (P)
2:55 (2:57) (Class 5) (0-75,75) 4-Y-0+ **£2,456** (£725; £362) **Stalls** High

Form RPR

-313 **1** **Aflaam (IRE)**[10] 367 5-8-6 **68** AndrewHeffernan[(5)] 5 77
(R A Harris) *hld up towards rr of main gp: hdwy over 2f out: rdn to chal jst over 1f out: edgd lft u.p but led jst ins fnl f: r.o wl* **12/1**

65-5 **2** 3/4 **Trafalgar Square**[7] 393 8-9-4 **75** GeorgeBaker 4 82
(M J Attwater) *hld up towards rr of main gp: effrt and hanging lft over 1f out: swtchd rt ent fnl f: r.o wl u.p fnl 150yds: wnt 2nd nr fin* **16/1**

-563 **3** nk **I Confess**[7] 393 5-8-4 **68** (v) KevinLundie[(7)] 9 74
(P D Evans) *broke wl: led and grad crossed to inner rail: hdd 7f out: chsd ldr after tl rdn to ld over 1f out: hdd jst ins fnl f: one pce fnl 100yds* **16/1**

1-14 **4** hd **Erinjay (IRE)**[5] 430 4-8-8 **70** TobyAtkinson[(5)] 8 79+
(M Wigham) *rrd s: v.s.a and lost many l: grad clsd and in tch 1/2-way: hdwy on outer bnd 2f out: styd on ins fnl f: nt rch ldrs* **13/8**[1]

35-3 **5** 3/4 **El Libertador (USA)**[14] 315 4-8-11 **68** LiamKeniry 6 72
(E A Wheeler) *hld up towards rr of main gp: hdwy to chse ldrs 2f out: rdn and nt qckn whn n.m.r jst ins fnl f: one pce after* **10/1**

35-0 **6** 3/4 **Bennelong**[21] 231 4-9-4 **75** PaulDoe 3 78
(P D Evans) *chsd ldrs: sltly hmpd over 7f out: rdn and effrt 2f out: n.m.r and swtchd rt jst ins fnl f: one pce after* **9/1**

00-6 **7** shd **Alfresco**[11] 359 6-9-4 **75** (b) SteveDrowne 1 77
(J R Best) *chsd ldng trio: effrt on inner whn n.m.r and swtchd rt 1f out: kpt on u.p fnl 100yds: unable to chal* **12/1**

0315 **8** 2 3/4 **Expensive Problem**[11] 361 7-8-6 **70** KierenFox[(7)] 2 66
(R J Smith) *hld up in rr of main gp: dropped to last and rdn 3f out: n.d fnl 2f* **8/1**[3]

5-1 **9** 1 1/2 **Zerzura**[16] 291 4-8-9 **73** CharlesEddery[(7)] 7 66
(H R A Cecil) *chsd ldr and grad crossed to rail: led after 1f: rdn and hdd over 1f out: wknd fnl f* **9/2**[2]

1m 37.04s (-1.16) **Going Correction** +0.025s/f (Slow) 9 Ran SP% **113.6**
Speed ratings (Par 103): **106,105,104,104,104 103,103,100,98**
toteswingers: 1&2 £24.60, 1&3 £15.60, 2&3 £14.30 CSF £180.90 CT £3052.91 TOTE £14.20: £2.80, £3.30, £4.90; EX 192.20 Trifecta £221.10 Part won. Pool: £298.89 - 0.10 winning units..
Owner The Circle Bloodstock I Limited **Bred** Shadwell Estate Company Limited **Trained** Earlswood, Monmouths
■ Stewards' Enquiry : Andrew Heffernan two-day ban: careless riding (Feb 24-25)

FOCUS
A modest handicap, run at a good pace.
Erinjay(IRE) Official explanation: jockey said gelding had reared and panicked as gates opened
Expensive Problem Official explanation: jockey said gelding ran flat

488 BET PREMIER LEAGUE FOOTBALL - BETDAQ CLAIMING STKS 1m 5f (P)
3:25 (3:27) (Class 6) 4-Y-0+ **£1,774** (£523; £262) **Stalls** Low

Form RPR

0-34 **1** **Doubnov (FR)**[13] 323 7-9-8 72 (p) JoeFanning 2 79
(Ian Williams) *mde all: clr tl jnd over 2f out: rdn along hands and heels and maintained narrow ld fr over 1f out* **13/8**[2]

0-41 **2** nse **Prince Charlemagne (IRE)**[19] 263 7-9-2 71 GeorgeBaker 1 73
(G L Moore) *hld up in 3rd: chsd wnr 3f out: upsides over 2f out: rdn over 1f out: a jst hld fnl f* **1/1**[1]

0-33 **3** 6 **Quince (IRE)**[16] 293 7-9-0 65 (v) SaleemGolam 3 63
(J Pearce) *chsd wnr: rdn over 3f out: sn dropped to last and outpcd by ldng pair* **4/1**[3]

2m 46.67s (0.67) **Going Correction** +0.025s/f (Slow) 3 Ran SP% **108.1**
Speed ratings (Par 101): **98,97,94**
CSF £3.66 TOTE £2.90; EX 3.40.
Owner Dr Marwan Koukash **Bred** Daniel Valley Masson Et Al **Trained** Portway, Worcs

FOCUS
A very tactical affair dominated by the market leaders.

489 GOLF AND RACING H'CAP 6f (P)
3:55 (3:55) (Class 4) (0-85,85) 3-Y-O **£4,209** (£1,252; £625; £312) **Stalls** Low

Form RPR

200- **1** **Raddy 'Ell Pauline (IRE)**[158] 5658 3-9-5 **83** ChrisCatlin 4 88+
(K A Ryan) *t.k.h: mde all: edgd lft jst over 1f out: rdn and styd on wl fnl f* **10/3**[2]

42-2 **2** 1 3/4 **Torres Del Paine**[28] 147 3-8-7 **71** JimmyQuinn 5 71
(J C Fox) *racd in last: rdn 2f out: hdwy 1f out: chsd wnr ins fnl f: no imp fnl 100yds* **12/1**[3]

1- **3** shd **Bowmaker**[106] 7087 3-9-7 **85** JoeFanning 1 88+
(M Johnston) *dwlt: chsd ldng pair: rdn to chse wnr over 1f out: 3/4 l down and trying to chal whn nt clr run and snatched up jst ins fnl f: one pce and unable to rcvr after* **4/9**[1]

60-2 **4** 1 3/4 **Diamond Johnny G (USA)**[4] 445 3-9-5 **83** GeorgeBaker 3 77
(E J Creighton) *t.k.h: chsd wnr tl over 1f out: outpcd fnl f* **14/1**

1m 11.98s (0.08) **Going Correction** +0.025s/f (Slow) 4 Ran SP% **106.7**
Speed ratings (Par 99): **100,97,97,95**
CSF £27.98 TOTE £5.10; EX 17.70.
Owner Mike McGeever & Mrs Theresa Marnane **Bred** Fattoria Di Marcianella Di Razza Del Pian Del Lago **Trained** Hambleton, N Yorks

FOCUS
A dramatic little handicap. The winner and the hampered third ran to the same mark.

490 MARRIOTT PLAY & STAY H'CAP 1m (P)
4:25 (4:25) (Class 5) (0-75,75) 3-Y-O **£2,456** (£725; £362) **Stalls** High

Form RPR

0-15 **1** **Kinky Afro (IRE)**[4] 448 3-8-13 **70** LiamKeniry 5 76+
(J S Moore) *chsd ldrs: rdn and ev ch over 1f out: led 1f out: hld on wl u.p fnl f* **8/1**

15-2 **2** 1/2 **Khanivorous**[10] 366 3-9-4 **75** (p) PatCosgrave 2 80
(J R Boyle) *chsd ldr: rdn to ld over 1f out: hdd 1f out: r.o u.p but a jst hld fnl f* **7/4**[1]

06-1 **3** 2 **Orsett Lad (USA)**[12] 346 3-8-5 **62** DavidProbert 7 63
(J R Best) *stdd after s: hld up in last pair: hdwy on outer jst over 2f out: chsd ldng pair ins fnl f: kpt on* **5/1**[3]

620- **4** 2 1/4 **Fusaichi Flyer (USA)**[44] 7859 3-8-9 **66** SteveDrowne 6 62+
(R Charlton) *stdd after s: hld up in last pair: rdn and effrt ent fnl 2f: swtchd rt over 1f out: styd on ins fnl f: nvr threatened ldrs* **13/2**

53-1 **5** ½ **Pastel Blue (IRE)**[21] 238 3-9-0 71 HayleyTurner 4 66
(M L W Bell) *led: sn clr: rdn ent fnl 2f: hdd over 1f out: wknd fnl f* **5/2**[2]
45-3 **6** 6 **Rathbawn Girl (IRE)**[28] 149 3-8-7 64 JimmyQuinn 1 45
(Miss J Feilden) *t.k.h: chsd ldrs tl rdn and struggling 2f out: wl btn fnl f* **16/1**
060- **7** ½ **Tallawalla (IRE)**[155] 5741 3-8-8 65 ChrisCatlin 3 45
(M R Channon) *in tch in midfield: rdn and struggling over 2f out: no ch fr over 1f out* **14/1**

1m 37.26s (-0.94) **Going Correction** +0.025s/f (Slow) 7 Ran SP% 118.6
Speed ratings (Par 97): **105,104,102,100,99 93,93**
toteswingers: 1&2 £3.90, 1&3 £4.20, 2&3 £3.10 CSF £23.71 TOTE £9.00: £4.70, £1.20; EX 26.40 Place 6 £4,467.85, Place 5 £3,066.11.
Owner Phil Cunningham **Bred** S Couldrige **Trained** Upper Lambourn, Berks

FOCUS
A modest handicap in which the first pair came clear.
T/Plt: £6,505.70 to a £1 stake. Pool: £58,640.49. 6.58 winning tickets. T/Qpdt: £2,139.50 to a £1 stake. Pool: £3,614.10. 1.25 winning tickets. SP

470 SOUTHWELL (L-H)
Wednesday, February 10

OFFICIAL GOING: Standard
An additional meeting consisting of three Flat races and three bumpers, all on the Fibresand.
Wind: Moderate, half against Weather: Very cold, snow showers

491 PLAY GOLF AT SOUTHWELL GOLF CLUB (S) STKS 1m (F)
1:30 (1:30) (Class 6) 4-Y-O+ **£2,047** (£604; £302) **Stalls** Low

Form RPR
-P41 **1** **Castle Myth (USA)**[8] 379 4-8-12 58 (be) BarryMcHugh(5) 5 64+
(B Ellison) *trckd ldr: led 5f out tl 3 f out: styd on fnl f: led nr fin* **11/8**[2]
206 **2** ½ **Mackintosh (IRE)**[5] 427 4-8-6 53 (v) JamesSullivan(5) 1 57
(Patrick Morris) *trckd ldrs: led 3f out: 2 l clr and edgd lft 1f out: hdd nr fin* **7/1**[3]
-226 **3** 2¾ **Special Cuvee**[27] 169 4-8-11 60 (v) GregFairley 3 51
(A B Haynes) *dwlt: trckd ldrs: effrt over 3f out: rdn and hung lft over 2f out: kpt on fnl f* **1/1**[1]
060- **4** 23 **Kneesy Earsy Nosey**[172] 5254 4-8-9 39 ow8 (p) AnnStokell(5) 4 —
(Miss A Stokell) *t.k.h: led: hdd 5f out: sn rdn: lost pl 3f out: sn lft bhd* **40/1**

1m 43.84s (0.14) **Going Correction** 0.0s/f (Stan) 4 Ran SP% 107.0
Speed ratings (Par 101): **99,98,95,72**
CSF £9.80 TOTE £2.70; EX 8.80.There was no bid for the winner.
Owner Locketts Legends **Bred** Mr & Mrs Gerald J Stautberg **Trained** Norton, N Yorks

FOCUS
A poorly contested seller run at a modest pace.

492 SOUTHWELL RACECOURSE FOR CONFERENCES H'CAP 5f (F)
2:05 (2:05) (Class 4) (0-85,84) 4-Y-O+ **£4,209** (£1,252; £625; £312) **Stalls** High

Form RPR
0-05 **1** **Colorus (IRE)**[12] 349 7-8-2 73 (p) PaulPickard(5) 1 81
(W J H Ratcliffe) *mde virtually all: kpt on fnl f: hld on nr fin* **5/1**[3]
1-22 **2** hd **Excellent Show**[20] 250 4-9-2 82 TomEaves 2 89
(B Smart) *w wnr: chal over 2f out: no ex nr fin* **11/10**[1]
-025 **3** ½ **Pawan (IRE)**[12] 350 10-8-9 80 (b) AnnStokell(5) 3 85
(Miss A Stokell) *dwlt: sn drvn along: sn chsng ldrs: outpcd 2f out: kpt on wl ins fnl f* **10/1**
0232 **4** 7 **Indian Skipper (IRE)**[4] 446 5-8-13 84 (v) BillyCray(5) 4 64
(R C Guest) *trckd ldrs stands' side: effrt over 2f out: hung bdly lft and lost pl over 1f out* **2/1**[2]

59.33 secs (-0.37) **Going Correction** +0.075s/f (Slow) 4 Ran SP% 106.7
Speed ratings (Par 105): **105,104,103,92**
CSF £10.86 TOTE £4.70; EX 11.60.
Owner J Sheard & W J S Ratcliffe **Bred** M Ervine **Trained** Newmarket, Suffolk

FOCUS
A small field with only the four runners, but a true run race nonetheless with the front pair batting it out from the start.

493 HOSPITALITY AT SOUTHWELL RACECOURSE H'CAP 1m 4f (F)
2:40 (2:42) (Class 6) (0-60,58) 4-Y-O+ **£2,047** (£604; £302) **Stalls** Low

Form RPR
00/0 **1** **Sarah's Boy**[21] 228 5-8-8 45 GregFairley 2 58+
(D E Pipe) *led: shkn up and qcknd 3f out: rdn clr appr fnl f: unchal* **3/1**[3]
60-6 **2** 6 **Nakoma (IRE)**[26] 198 8-9-2 58 (be[1]) BarryMcHugh(5) 4 61
(B Ellison) *hld up in tch: drvn over 4f out: sn outpcd: kpt on fnl 2f: tk modest 2nd towards fin* **5/2**[2]
2603 **3** 1 **Inside Story (IRE)**[8] 377 8-9-2 53 (b) PJMcDonald 5 55
(C R Dore) *drvn early to sn chse wnr: kpt on same pce fnl 2f* **4/1**
504- **4** 3¼ **Piverina (IRE)**[156] 5732 5-8-8 45 TomEaves 1 42
(Julie Camacho) *trckd ldrs: pushed along 6f out: wknd fnl f* **2/1**[1]
000- **5** 53 **Fan Club**[63] 4034 6-8-3 45 DeanHeslop(5) 6 —
(Mrs R A Carr) *uns rdr and rn loose for abt 7 minutes: covered abt 2 ms bef being ct: hld up in tch: hdwy to chse ldrs over 7f out: wknd 3f out: sn bhd and eased: hopelessly t.o* **50/1**
000- **6** 20 **Tagula Minx (IRE)**[53] 7818 4-8-5 45 AndrewElliott 3 —
(J Pearce) *t.k.h: sn restrained in rr: drvn along 6f out: lost tch over 3f out: sn t.o and eased: eventually completed* **33/1**

2m 40.04s (-0.96) **Going Correction** 0.0s/f (Stan)
WFA 4 from 5yo+ 3lb 6 Ran SP% 111.8
Speed ratings (Par 101): **103,99,98,96,60 47**
toteswingers: 1&2 £4.40, 1&3 £3.70, 2&3 £1.10 CSF £10.83 TOTE £5.00: £2.50, £1.50; EX 14.70.
Owner Ms Sarah Hayes **Bred** J G Davis And Star Pointe Ltd **Trained** Nicholashayne, Devon

FOCUS
A weak 1m 4f handicap run at a modest pace.\n
Sarah's Boy Official explanation: trainer's rep said, regarding apparent improvement in form, having had its first run for a year previously, the gelding had improved and was better suited by the track.

458 CAGNES-SUR-MER
Wednesday, February 10

OFFICIAL GOING: Heavy

494a PRIX WILLIAM ALEXANDRE RUINAT (TURF) 1m 4f 110y
12:50 (12:51) 4-Y-O+ **£11,062** (£4,428; £3,319; £2,212; £1,106)

RPR
1 **La Boum (GER)**[16] 7-8-7 ThomasHuet 87
(Robert Collet, France)
2 4 **Lost Soldier Three (IRE)**[13] 332 9-8-10 (p) IoritzMendizabal 84
(D Nicholls) *disp 2nd on outside tl wnt 2nd 6f out: led narrowly 2f out to 1 1/2f out: outpcd by wnr but kpt on for 2nd* **68/10**[1]
3 5 **Rockawango (FR)**[152] 5851 4-9-2 FranckBlondel 86
(M Pimbonnet, France)
4 3 **Dunaden (FR)**[16] 4-8-9 74
(Y Fouin, France)
5 5 **Rento (FR)**[91] 7-8-10 (p) 63
(W Walton, France)
6 10 **Sight Unseen**[266] 2176 4-8-7 48
(F Vermeulen, France)
7 9 **Marcus (FR)**[477] 5-8-10 33
(F Rohaut, France)

3m 3.10s (183.10)
WFA 4 from 5yo+ 3lb 7 Ran SP% 12.8
PARI-MUTUEL (including 1 Euro stake): WIN 1.80; PL 1.30, 2.60;SF 13.10.
Owner Emmanuel Trussardi **Bred** Gestut Karlshof **Trained** Chantilly, France

477 KEMPTON (A.W) (R-H)
Thursday, February 11

OFFICIAL GOING: Standard
Wind: fresh, behind Weather: dry, cold

495 BET FA CUP - BETDAQ H'CAP 6f (P)
5:00 (5:01) (Class 7) (0-50,50) 4-Y-O+ **£1,364** (£403; £201) **Stalls** High

Form RPR
260- **1** **Boldinor**[136] 6335 7-9-3 50 GeorgeBaker 10 58
(M R Bosley) *chsd ldr tl led over 3f out: rdn wl over 1f out: clr ins fnl f: r.o strly* **12/1**
0-53 **2** 1¼ **Davids Mark**[14] 319 10-9-1 48 (p) SimonWhitworth 1 52
(J R Jenkins) *stdd and dropped in rr after s: in rr: hdwy ent fnl 2f: swtchd lft ent fnl f: r.o wl to go 2nd nr fin: no ch w wnr* **12/1**
0042 **3** nk **Commandingpresence (USA)**[14] 319 4-8-5 45 KierenFox(7) 5 48
(J J Bridger) *in tch: hdwy and rdn to chse ldng pair ent fnl 2f: kpt on same pce fnl f* **7/1**[3]
44-5 **4** nk **Royal Acclamation (IRE)**[20] 264 5-9-1 48 HayleyTurner 12 50
(H J Evans) *hld up towards rr: hdwy towards inner over 2f out: swtchd lft and rdn over 1f out: drvn to chse wnr ins fnl f: no imp and lost 2 pls nr fin* **11/4**[2]
-044 **5** ¾ **Mister Incredible**[7] 403 7-8-7 47 (b) RyanClark(7) 7 47
(J M Bradley) *chsd ldrs: rdn and unable qck ent fnl 2f: kpt on same pce fnl f* **14/1**
-005 **6** 1 **Romantic Verse**[1] 477 5-8-9 45 (vt) MichaelStainton(3) 8 42
(R A Harris) *s.i.s: rdn and effrt on outer ent fnl 2f: styd on u.p fnl f: nvr trbld ldrs* **20/1**
0-42 **7** nk **Jessica Wigmo**[8] 388 7-9-3 50 ShaneKelly 4 46
(A W Carroll) *stdd s: hld up in midfield: swtchd ins and hdwy jst over 2f out: rdn and one pce fr over 1f out* **13/8**[1]
-300 **8** 1 **Sonhador**[6] 423 4-9-3 50 SaleemGolam 11 43
(G Prodromou) *chsd ldrs: chsd wnr over 2f out: rdn wl over 1f out: lost 2nd ins fnl f and wknd fnl 100yds* **12/1**
0-06 **9** 2 **Tightrope (IRE)**[1] 477 4-8-12 45 (b) MartinDwyer 6 38
(T D McCarthy) *led tl over 3f out: wknd over 2f out: wl btn and eased ins fnl f* **16/1**
06-6 **10** ¾ **Desert Dust**[38] 30 7-8-12 45 (b) NickyMackay 9 30
(G C Bravery) *hmpd sn after s: in tch in midfield tl wknd u.p over 1f out* **40/1**
-000 **11** ¾ **Spring Bridge (IRE)**[8] 391 4-8-9 45 (vt[1]) MarcHalford(3) 2 28
(Mrs L C Jewell) *a towards rr: rdn and effrt on outer over 2f out: no prog* **33/1**
000- **12** 3¼ **Winterbourne**[67] 7651 4-8-13 46 JimmyQuinn 3 19
(M Blanshard) *a in rr: wl bhd fnl 2f* **20/1**

1m 12.68s (-0.42) **Going Correction** -0.05s/f (Stan) 12 Ran SP% 127.8
Speed ratings (Par 97): **100,98,97,97,96 95,94,93,90,89 88,84**
toteswinger:1&2:£14.10, 1&3:£15.00, 2&3:£6.50 CSF £151.81 CT £1123.02 TOTE £12.20: £3.60, £6.30, £3.50; EX 131.50.
Owner Ron Collins **Bred** Ron Collins **Trained** Chalfont St Giles, Bucks

FOCUS
This weak sprint handicap was run at a sound pace, but few managed to land a serious blow.
Jessica Wigmo Official explanation: trainer said mare was struck into
Tightrope(IRE) Official explanation: jockey said gelding lost its action and hung left
Spring Bridge(IRE) Official explanation: jockey said gelding hung left on the bend

496 BET SIX NATIONS RUGBY - BETDAQ CLASSIFIED CLAIMING STKS 1m (P)
5:30 (5:30) (Class 6) 4-Y-O+ **£2,047** (£604; £302) **Stalls** High

Form RPR
-024 **1** **Alqaahir (USA)**[11] 367 8-8-7 70 RobertLButler(3) 8 75+
(P Butler) *hld up in tch: smooth hdwy to join ldrs gng wl over 1f out: led ent fnl f: pushed clr: comf* **13/2**[3]
620- **2** 2½ **Having A Ball**[82] 7481 6-8-12 64 DaneO'Neill 12 68
(P D Cundell) *hld up in midfield: rdn and effrt ent fnl 2f: switching rt and hdwy over 1f out: styd on to chse wnr fnl 150yds: no imp after* **8/1**
0/-1 **3** ¾ **Sedgwick**[34] 83 8-8-10 65 StevieDonohoe 1 64
(Ian Williams) *chsd ldrs: shkn up to join ldrs over 2f out: rdn and racd awkwardly over 1f out: plugged on one pce and no ch w wnr fnl f* **5/1**[2]
030- **4** shd **Singleb (IRE)**[211] 3980 6-8-12 67 (p) LukeMorris 11 66
(Miss Gay Kelleway) *sn chsng ldr: led over 2f out: sn rdn: hdd over 1f out: sn outpcd by wnr and lost 2 pls ins fnl f* **20/1**

21-4 **5** 3/4 **Sotik Star (IRE)**20 262 7-8-11 63................................(p) JimmyQuinn 4 63
(K A Morgan) *stdd after s: t.k.h: hld up in last trio: rdn and hdwy on inner over 2f out: chsd ldrs and drvn over 1f out: one pce fnl f* **3/1**1

-060 **6** 3/4 **Resplendent Nova**18 285 8-8-12 64.................................... PaulDoe 7 63
(P Howling) *stdd s: hld up in rr: hdwy over 2f out: kpt on same pce u.p fnl f* **15/2**

4-40 **7** nk **Fine Ruler (IRE)**20 262 6-9-2 57..................................... GeorgeBaker 3 66
(M R Bosley) *racd in midfield on outer: rdn and effrt over 2f out: kpt on same pce and nvr threatened ldrs* **25/1**

60-0 **8** nse **Mountain Pass (USA)**17 289 8-8-2 50 ow1..............(p) FrannyNorton 9 52
(B J Llewellyn) *dwlt: t.k.h: hld up in midfield: shuffled bk towards rr over 2f out: switching rt and hdwy over 1f out: kpt on but nvr trbld ldrs* **50/1**

2254 **9** 2 **Party In The Park**8 397 5-7-11 55............................. NathanAlison(7) 5 49
(J R Boyle) *broke wl: sn stdd to chse ldng pair: rdn and fnd little 2f out: wknd and hung lft ent fnl f* **8/1**

00-6 **10** 3 1/4 **James Pollard (IRE)**17 289 5-7-13 50............. AndrewHeffernan(5) 10 42
(B J Llewellyn) *dwlt: t.k.h: hld up towards rr: n.d* **66/1**

26-6 **11** 1 1/2 **Naxox (FR)**38 32 9-8-4 64...(p) MartinDwyer 13 38
(George Baker) *sn led: clr 5f out: rdn and hdd over 2f out: wknd qckly over 1f out* **33/1**

-123 **12** nk **Shake On It**13 348 6-8-11 65.............................. JamieJones(5) 2 50
(M R Hoad) *stdd and dropped in bhd after s: a bhd* **8/1**

0-35 **13** shd **Apache Moon**16 301 4-8-12 65.................................... J-PGuillambert 6 45
(R Curtis) *t.k.h: hld up in midfield: rdn and lost pl wl over 2f out: wl btn fnl 2f* **25/1**

1m 38.8s (-1.00) **Going Correction** -0.05s/f (Stan) **13** Ran SP% **118.9**
Speed ratings (Par 101): **103,100,99,99,98 98,97,97,95,92 91,90,90**
toteswinger:1&2:£10.90, 1&3:£5.00, 2&3:£8.60 CSF £52.91 TOTE £9.90: £4.10, £4.40, £2.10; EX 51.90.
Owner Mrs E Lucey-Butler **Bred** Shadwell Farm LLC **Trained** East Chiltington, E Sussex
■ Robert Lucey-Butler's first Flat winner as a professional, and first winner since an injury over jumps in the spring.
■ Stewards' Enquiry : Nathan Alison one-day ban: failed to ride to draw (Feb 25)

FOCUS
This open contest was run at a good pace.
Sotik Star(IRE) Official explanation: jockey said gelding was slowly away

497 BET MULTIPLES - BETDAQ CLAIMING STKS 1m 4f (P)
6:00 (6:01) (Class 6) 4-Y-0+ **£2,047** (£604; £302) **Stalls** Centre

Form RPR

4-44 **1** **Hurakan (IRE)**22 239 4-9-0 73..................................(p) J-PGuillambert 3 72+
(P D Evans) *stdd s: hld up in midfield: rdn and hdwy over 2f out: led over 1f out: edgd lft ent fnl f: pushed clr fnl f: eased towards fin* **10/11**1

50-4 **2** 2 1/4 **Farncombe (IRE)**6 429 4-8-0 62......................... AndrewHeffernan(5) 1 57
(R A Harris) *stdd s: hld up in last pair: hdwy to chse ldr and rdn over 2f out: ev ch over 1f out: nt pce of wnr fnl f but kpt on for clr 2nd* **15/2**

00-0 **3** 3 **Cossack Prince**29 148 5-9-6 63......................................(p) IanMongan 8 64
(Mrs L J Mongan) *led: sn clr: reduced advantage 6f out: kicked clr again 4f out: rdn over 2f out: hdd over 1f out: wl btn fnl f* **7/2**2

0-00 **4** 3 **Play Up Pompey**28 160 8-8-6 43.................................... KierenFox(7) 7 52
(J J Bridger) *chsd ldng pair: rdn and unable qck over 2f out: no ch fr over 1f out* **33/1**

00-1 **5** 4 1/2 **Classic Blue (IRE)**34 80 6-8-5 55..........................(vt) SaleemGolam 6 37
(Ian Williams) *chsd ldr tl over 2f out: rdn and btn ent fnl 2f: no ch after* **5/1**3

6 22 **Sazeilla (CZE)**105 5-8-5 45.. LukeMorris 2 —
(J A T De Giles) *a bhd: rdn 8f out: lost tch over 2f out: eased fr over 1f out: t.o* **33/1**

2m 35.31s (0.81) **Going Correction** -0.05s/f (Stan)
WFA 4 from 5yo+ 3lb **6** Ran SP% **108.9**
Speed ratings (Par 101): **95,93,91,89,86 71**
totesinger:1&2:£1.40, 1&3:£1.30, 2&3:£2.30 CSF £7.96 TOTE £2.70: £1.40, £5.50; EX 6.10.
Owner J L Guillambert **Bred** Newberry Stud Company **Trained** Pandy, Monmouths

FOCUS
This was notably weakened by the non-runners.

498 BETDAQ ON 0870 178 1221 H'CAP (DIV I) 7f (P)
6:30 (6:31) (Class 6) (0-58,58) 4-Y-0+ **£1,706** (£503; £252) **Stalls** High

Form RPR

4-46 **1** **Guildenstern (IRE)**22 234 8-9-0 54.............................. JimmyQuinn 7 63
(P Howling) *hld up in tch in midfield: hdwy over 2f out: chsd wnr 1f out: rdn to ld fnl 100yds: r.o wl* **13/2**3

6-05 **2** nk **Sovereignty (JPN)**8 397 8-8-8 53......................... MarkCoumbe(5) 14 61
(D K Ivory) *stdd after s: t.k.h: hld up in rr: stl plenty to do jst over 2f out: gd hdwy on inner over 1f out: pressed wnr fnl 75yds: kpt on* **8/1**

6430 **3** 3/4 **Louisiade (IRE)**20 269 9-8-6 46 oh1......................(p) FrannyNorton 12 52
(R C Guest) *chsd ldrs: rdn to ld over 1f out: hrd drvn and hdd fnl 100yds: one pce after* **16/1**

300- **4** 1/2 **Dancing Welcome**45 7860 4-9-3 57................................(b) LukeMorris 3 62
(J M Bradley) *towards rr: rdn and effrt over 2f out: hdwy u.p ent fnl f: styng on wl towards fin: nt rch ldrs* **14/1**

-050 **5** 3/4 **Whotsit (IRE)**15 318 4-8-9 56................................(b) JohnFahy(7) 2 59
(Miss Amy Weaver) *t.k.h: sn chsng ldr: ev ch and rdn over 2f out: led 2f out: hdd over 1f out: styd on same pce u.p ins fnl f* **16/1**

4-00 **6** nk **Too Grand**20 262 5-8-5 52... KierenFox(7) 10 54
(J J Bridger) *hld up in midfield on inner: swtchd rt off of rail and effrt 2f out: rdn and chsd ldrs 1f out: one pce and no imp after* **25/1**

-640 **7** nk **Cavalry Guard (USA)**5 444 6-8-6 51...................(b) RossAtkinson(5) 9 52
(T D McCarthy) *t.k.h: chsd ldrs: rdn and unable qck jst over 2f out: one pce and hld fnl f* **16/1**

0-60 **8** 3/4 **The Mouse Carroll (IRE)**20 256 6-9-3 57...................... ShaneKelly 5 56
(B R Johnson) *hld up towards rr: bhd a wall of horses and looking for run ent fnl 2f: swtchd rt and hdwy fnl f: n.d* **9/1**

50-3 **9** hd **Silidan**20 269 7-9-0 54...(v1) AdamKirby 4 53
(Miss M E Rowland) *stdd after s: t.k.h: hld up in rr: sme hdwy and rdn ent fnl 2f: nvr threatened ldrs: swtchd lft wl ins fnl f* **9/1**

0-00 **10** hd **One Cool Dream**5 442 4-9-3 57..............................(b1) SaleemGolam 13 55
(P W Hiatt) *in tch in midfield on inner: effrt u.p to chse ldrs over 1f out: btn 1f out* **33/1**

-363 **11** 1 3/4 **Josiah Bartlett (IRE)**8 388 4-8-7 47............................ HayleyTurner 6 40
(Ian Williams) *racd in midfield on outer: rdn and no prog over 2f out: nvr threatened ldrs* **13/2**3

0-13 **12** shd **Musashi (IRE)**22 229 5-9-4 58.......................................(b) IanMongan 1 51
(Mrs L J Mongan) *s.i.s: a towards rr: n.d* **5/1**2

23-0 **13** 1 **Bold Diva**15 312 5-8-7 52...(v) AmyRyan(5) 8 42
(A W Carroll) *t.k.h: chsd ldrs tl wknd u.p ent fnl 2f: n.d fnl f* **10/1**

00/0 **14** 3 **Clearing Sky (IRE)**29 145 9-8-6 46 oh1..................(p) NickyMackay 11 28
(J R Boyle) *led tl rdn and hdd 2f out: wknd over 1f out: eased wl ins fnl f* **66/1**

1m 25.93s (-0.07) **Going Correction** -0.05s/f (Stan) **14** Ran SP% **124.3**
Speed ratings (Par 101): **98,97,96,96,95 95,94,93,93,93 91,91,90,86**
toteswinger:1&2:£10.60, 1&3:£16.00, 2&3:£33.60 CSF £59.00 CT £841.23 TOTE £4.20: £1.20, £4.80, £5.50; EX 40.30.
Owner Brian Johnson **Bred** Peter E Daly **Trained** Newmarket, Suffolk

FOCUS
This low-grade handicap had a wide-open look about it.
Too Grand Official explanation: vet said mare returned lame
Silidan Official explanation: jockey said gelding ran too free

499 BETDAQ ON 0870 178 1221 H'CAP (DIV II) 7f (P)
7:00 (7:03) (Class 6) (0-58,58) 4-Y-0+ **£1,706** (£503; £252) **Stalls** High

Form RPR

041- **1** **Harting Hill**71 7614 5-9-3 57.. GeorgeBaker 9 66+
(M P Tregoning) *trckd ldrs: hdwy to go 2nd over 2f out: led gng wl over 1f out: sn chal and rdn: fnd ex and forged ahd ins fnl f* **15/8**1

0-30 **2** 1/2 **Sendreni (FR)**20 270 6-9-4 58..................................(p) StephenCraine 8 66
(M Wigham) *hld up wl in tch: trckd wnr through 2f out: chal over 1f out: r.o but a jst hld by wnr ins fnl f* **14/1**

/06- **3** 1 1/2 **Eager To Bow (IRE)**220 3672 4-8-12 52................. RichardKingscote 1 56+
(P R Chamings) *hld up towards rr: gd hdwy jst over 2f out: chsd ldng pair ent fnl f: r.o but nvr gng pce to rch ldrs* **28/1**

1-05 **4** 1/2 **Kielty's Folly**17 290 6-8-10 55 ow2.............................. JamieJones(5) 4 59+
(B P J Baugh) *hld up towards rr: swtchd lft and hdwy over 2f out: r.o to press for 3rd ins fnl f: nvr trbld ldng pair* **10/1**

31-0 **5** hd **Signora Frasi (IRE)**20 269 5-8-9 56.......................... DavidKenny(7) 2 58
(A G Newcombe) *s.i.s: bhd: hdwy and edging rt fr over 1f out: pressing for 3rd and r.o fnl f: nvr trbld ldrs* **20/1**

5-16 **6** 2 **Diane's Choice**22 235 7-9-0 54.......................................(b) PaulDoe 10 51
(Miss Gay Kelleway) *stdd s: t.k.h: hld up towards rr: rdn and effrt on outer jst over 2f out: kpt on but nvr gng pce to threaten ldrs* **14/1**

00-0 **7** 1 1/2 **Fortezza**22 242 4-8-12 52... JackMitchell 14 46
(C F Wall) *sn bustled along in midfield: rdn and swtchd lft over 2f out: hdwy u.p 2f out: no prog and btn whn n.m.r 1f out* **6/1**2

00-6 **8** shd **Count Ceprano (IRE)**5 442 6-9-3 57............................... TomQueally 3 50
(C R Dore) *stdd s: hld up towards rr: effrt on inner and rdn ent fnl 2f: nvr trbld ldrs* **6/1**2

02-0 **9** 2 1/4 **King's Sabre**9 378 4-8-13 53....................................(p) FrannyNorton 12 41
(R C Guest) *led at fast gallop: rdn and hdd over 1f out: sn wknd* **13/2**3

406- **10** 1 1/4 **Hilltop Legacy**190 4665 7-7-13 46 oh1........................ DannyBrock(7) 11 31
(J R Jenkins) *dwlt: a towards rr: rdn and no prog over 2f out* **33/1**

0046 **11** 1 3/4 **Grizedale (IRE)**8 388 11-8-1 48 ow1.......................(tp) KierenFox(7) 7 28
(M J Attwater) *t.k.h: chsd ldr tl over 2f out: wknd ent fnl 2f* **20/1**

00-0 **12** 2 3/4 **Affirmatively**10 368 5-8-6 46 oh1..........................(tp) LukeMorris 13 19
(A W Carroll) *in tch: chsd ldrs and rdn 2f out: wknd qckly u.p over 1f out* **50/1**

60/0 **13** 6 **Kims Rose (IRE)**25 211 7-8-1 46 oh1.............(p) AndrewHeffernan(5) 5 4
(J L Flint) *racd keenly: chsd ldrs: wkng whn hmpd over 2f out: wl bhd fnl 2f* **16/1**

1m 25.32s (-0.68) **Going Correction** -0.05s/f (Stan) **13** Ran SP% **122.9**
Speed ratings (Par 101): **101,100,98,98,97 95,93,93,91,89 87,84,77**
toteswinger:1&2:£9.70, 1&3:£30.90, 2&3:£43.00 CSF £30.28 CT £614.24 TOTE £2.70: £1.80, £6.60, £11.70; EX 38.10.
Owner Miss S Sharp **Bred** Stanley J Sharp **Trained** Lambourn, Berks

FOCUS
The second division of the low-grade 7f handicap, run at a fair pace.
King's Sabre Official explanation: jockey said gelding ran too free

500 BET PREMIER LEAGUE FOOTBALL - BETDAQ H'CAP 2m (P)
7:30 (7:31) (Class 4) (0-85,85) 4-Y-0+ **£4,209** (£1,252; £625; £312) **Stalls** High

Form RPR

60-1 **1** **Alsadaa (USA)**22 232 7-9-12 83.. IanMongan 5 91
(Mrs L J Mongan) *mde all: rdn and kicked clr 2f out: fnd ex whn pressed ins fnl f: r.o wl* **6/1**3

-213 **2** 3/4 **Satwa Gold (USA)**8 395 4-8-11 74................................. TomQueally 6 81
(Stef Higgins) *rrd s: stdd and hld up in rr: hdwy jst over 2f out: rdn to chse wnr 1f out: pressed wnr ins fnl f: no ex and hld fnl 50yds* **9/1**

212- **3** 3/4 **Right Stuff (FR)**21 4988 7-10-0 85................................. GeorgeBaker 4 91
(G L Moore) *t.k.h: hld up towards rr: effrt on outer and hung rt over 2f out: kpt edging rt but kpt on to go 3rd ins fnl f: no imp fnl 100yds* **6/1**3

043- **4** 3/4 **Alnwick**104 7151 6-9-6 77.. DaneO'Neill 9 82
(P D Cundell) *chsd wnr: rdn ent fnl 3f: lost 2nd over 1f out: kpt on same pce u.p fnl f* **9/2**2

1-34 **5** hd **Dreamwalk (IRE)**13 352 4-9-1 81..........................(p) AndreaAtzeni(3) 7 86
(R Curtis) *in tch in midfield: effrt and rdn on inner over 2f out: chsd wnr over 1f out tl 1f out: one pce after* **8/1**

124- **6** 1 1/2 **Rose Row**125 6636 6-9-7 78.. HayleyTurner 1 82
(Mrs Mary Hambro) *stdd after s: t.k.h: hld up in rr: effrt and rdn whn hmpd over 2f out: styd on but nvr trbld ldrs* **10/1**

050- **7** 1 1/2 **American Spin**218 3737 6-9-3 74..................................(e) LukeMorris 2 75
(L A Dace) *stdd s: t.k.h: hld up in rr: effrt u.p on inner over 2f out: no real prog and nvr trbld ldrs* **8/1**

4/2- **8** 1 **Bugsy's Boy**80 6622 6-9-0 71.. MartinDwyer 8 72
(George Baker) *chsd ldng trio: rdn 4f out: lost pl and struggling whn hmpd over 2f out: no ch after* **12/1**

140- **9** 2 1/4 **Sweetheart**19 6851 6-9-6 77.. NeilCallan 3 75
(Jamie Poulton) *disp 2nd: rdn over 3f out: lost pl u.p over 2f out: bhd fnl 2f* **7/2**1

3m 26.88s (-3.22) **Going Correction** -0.05s/f (Stan)
WFA 4 from 6yo+ 6lb **9** Ran SP% **118.0**
Speed ratings (Par 105): **106,105,105,104,104 104,103,102,101**
toteswinger:1&2:£3.90, 1&3:£6.80, 2&3:£7.10 CSF £59.86 CT £341.55 TOTE £4.50: £3.00, £3.40, £3.20; EX 24.50.
Owner Mrs P J Sheen **Bred** Shadwell Farm LLC **Trained** Epsom, Surrey

FOCUS
A competitive staying handicap.

501 BETDAQ.CO.UK H'CAP 6f (P)
8:00 (8:01) (Class 5) (0-70,70) 4-Y-0+ **£2,590** (£770; £385; £192) **Stalls** High

Form RPR

5-32 **1** **Secret Witness**7 404 4-9-4 70.......................................(b) LiamJones 6 80
(R A Harris) *jostled leaving stalls: t.k.h: hld up in tch: hdwy to join ldr over 2f out: rdn to ld over 1f out: r.o wl u.p fnl f* **7/2**1

5226 **2** 1 1/4 **Fromsong (IRE)**[15] 306 12-9-1 **67** .... MartinDwyer 3 73
(D K Ivory) *chsd ldr tl led over 2f out: rdn and hdd over 1f out: kpt on same pce fnl f* **9/1**

0-00 **3** 1/2 **The Wee Chief (IRE)**[14] 325 4-8-13 **65** .... RichardKingscote 8 69
(J C Fox) *stdd s: hld up towards rr: nt clr run over 2f out: rdn and hdwy wl over 1f out: chsd ldng pair 1f out: kpt on same pce after* **16/1**

012- **4** nk **Kingsgate Castle**[52] 7834 5-8-10 **62** .... (b) LukeMorris 4 65
(Miss Gay Kelleway) *jostled leaving stalls: towards rr: effrt u.p jst over 2f out: r.o ins fnl f: nt rch ldrs* **7/1**

3-40 **5** 3/4 **Loyal Royal (IRE)**[18] 287 7-8-4 **61** .... (b) AndrewHeffernan(5) 10 62
(J M Bradley) *dwlt: bhd: rdn and effrt on inner 2f out: no imp fnl f* **10/1**

0-42 **6** nk **Peter's Gift (IRE)**[7] 398 4-8-13 **70** .... AmyRyan(5) 7 70
(K A Ryan) *in tch in midfield: n.m.r and lost pl jst over 2f out: kpt on same pce u.p fr over 1f out* **9/2**[2]

6-04 **7** 3/4 **Highland Harvest**[14] 325 6-9-0 **66** .... FrannyNorton 9 63
(Jamie Poulton) *t.k.h: chsd ldrs: rdn and effrt 2f out: wknd jst ins fnl f* **11/2**[3]

4-50 **8** 2 **Resplendent Alpha**[19] 275 6-9-4 **70** .... JimmyQuinn 5 61
(P Howling) *hmpd sn after s: hld up in rr: swtchd lft and rdn over 1f out: nvr trbld ldrs* **13/2**

2-14 **9** 5 **Hollow Jo**[14] 325 10-9-1 **67** .... (v) FergusSweeney 2 42
(J R Jenkins) *mid-div on outer: rdn over 2f out: struggling wl over 1f out: sn btn* **12/1**

000- **10** 2 1/2 **Five Gold Rings (IRE)**[110] 7021 4-8-1 **60** .... KierenFox(7) 1 27
(M G Hazell) *led and sn crossed to rail: rdn and hdd over 2f out: wknd qckly wl over 1f out* **66/1**

1m 12.23s (-0.87) **Going Correction** -0.05s/f (Stan) **10** Ran SP% **115.8**
Speed ratings (Par 103): **103,101,100,100,99 98,97,95,88,85**
toteswinger:1&2:£9.90, 1&3:£28.80, 2&3:£18.30 CSF £35.42 CT £457.35 TOTE £4.20: £1.80, £3.60, £4.00; EX 36.50.
Owner Ridge House Stables Ltd **Bred** Cheveley Park Stud Ltd **Trained** Earlswood, Monmouths

FOCUS
An ordinary sprint handicap.

502 BETDAQ THE BETTING EXCHANGE H'CAP — 6f (P)
8:30 (8:31) (Class 4) (0-80,80) 4-Y-O+ — **£4,209** (£1,252; £625; £312) **Stalls** High

Form — RPR

352- **1** **New Leyf (IRE)**[53] 7828 4-8-11 **73** .... SteveDrowne 3 85+
(J R Gask) *t.k.h: hld up in tch: hdwy to ld ent fnl f: pushed along and in command fnl f: comf* **2/1**[1]

43-4 **2** 1 1/4 **Jake The Snake (IRE)**[18] 286 9-9-2 **78** .... NeilCallan 8 85
(A W Carroll) *wnt lft s: hld up in rr: n.m.r and looking to get out over 2f out: swtchd lft and hdwy jst over 1f out: chsd wnr fnl 50yds: r.o but nvr looked like rching wnr* **7/2**[3]

140- **3** 1 1/4 **Todber**[78] 7518 5-8-7 **69** .... (v) MartinDwyer 5 72
(M P Tregoning) *chsd clr ldr: rdn and clsd over 2f out: ev ch briefly over 1f out: kpt on same pce fnl f* **14/1**

1113 **4** 1 **Divine Force**[6] 432 4-9-1 **77** .... SimonWhitworth 2 77
(M Wigham) *hld up in last pair: rdn and effrt ent fnl 2f: kpt on but nvr gng pce to threaten ldrs* **9/4**[2]

2446 **5** 2 3/4 **Vhujon (IRE)**[18] 286 5-9-4 **80** .... (p) TomQueally 6 71
(P D Evans) *chsd ldng pair: effrt u.p 2f out: wknd ent fnl f* **9/2**

00-0 **6** 1/2 **Bobs Dreamflight**[8] 393 4-8-6 **73** .... MarkCoumbe(5) 1 62
(D K Ivory) *led: sn clr: hdd ent fnl f: sn wknd* **20/1**

1m 12.37s (-0.73) **Going Correction** -0.05s/f (Stan) **6** Ran SP% **115.9**
Speed ratings (Par 105): **102,100,98,97,93 93**
toteswinger:1&2:£2.60, 1&3:£2.80, 2&3:£3.70 CSF £9.88 CT £75.13 TOTE £4.90: £4.20, £4.20; EX 10.80 Place 6: £297.13, Place 5: £73.61.
Owner Horses First Racing Limited **Bred** John Weld **Trained** Sutton Veny, Wilts

FOCUS
A modest handicap, run at a solid pace thanks to the front-running Bobs Dreamflight. Sound form.
T/Plt: £147.50 to a £1 stake. Pool: £83,767.98. 414.33 winning tickets. T/Qpdt: £18.80 to a £1 stake. Pool: £11,352.23. 444.80 winning tickets. SP

491 SOUTHWELL (L-H)
Thursday, February 11

OFFICIAL GOING: Standard to slow
Wind: Moderate across Weather: Bright and dry, but cold

503 BET MULTIPLES - BETDAQ H'CAP — 1m (F)
1:50 (1:56) (Class 6) (0-52,52) 4-Y-O+ — **£1,774** (£523; £262) **Stalls** Low

Form — RPR

000- **1** **Isitcozimcool (IRE)**[236] 3175 5-8-12 **50** .... PatCosgrave 12 58+
(D E Cantillon) *a.p: smooth hdwy 3f out: led 2f out: shkn up: edgd rt over 1f out and sn rdn: drvn ins fnl f: jst hld on* **7/2**[2]

0-3 **2** shd **Granakey (IRE)**[8] 389 7-8-10 **48** ow1 .... StevieDonohoe 4 54
(Ian Williams) *trckd ldrs on inner: hdwy wl over 2f out: rdn to chal over 1f out: drvn ins fnl f and ev ch tl no ex nr fin* **3/1**[1]

0/00 **3** 3/4 **Bansha (IRE)**[2] 470 4-8-4 **47** .... DeclanCannon(5) 14 51
(A Bailey) *pushed along and in tch on outer: hdwy 3f out: rdn over 2f out: drvn to chse ldrs over 1f out: kpt on ins fnl f* **17/2**[3]

040- **4** 1 1/2 **Unconsoled**[65] 7678 4-8-7 **48** .... BarryMcHugh(3) 6 49
(J Hetherton) *hld up towards rr: hdwy and rdn along 3f out: chsd ldrs over 1f out: drvn and ev ch ins fnl f: no ex* **14/1**

6505 **5** 1 **Amber Moon**[13] 347 5-8-6 **49** ow1 .... (b) AnnStokell(5) 8 48
(Miss A Stokell) *in tch: rdn along 3f out: drvn 2f out: kpt on same pce u.p* **20/1**

04-0 **6** nse **Jenny's Pride (IRE)**[41] 7 4-8-10 **48** .... DavidProbert 13 47
(John A Harris) *chsd ldrs on outer: hdwy 3f out: rdn over 2f out: drvn wl over 1f out: one pce appr fnl f* **12/1**

0-64 **7** 1 **Viking Awake (IRE)**[13] 347 4-8-10 **48** .... (t) GrahamGibbons 11 45
(J W Unett) *led: rdn along and hdd 2f out: sn drvn and grad wknd appr last* **9/1**

00-0 **8** 1 1/4 **Doctor Of Music (IRE)**[8] 389 4-8-12 **50** .... (v[1]) TomEaves 5 44
(B Smart) *towards rr tl sme late hdwy* **20/1**

50-5 **9** 2 1/4 **Royal Crest**[40] 21 4-9-0 **52** .... JoeFanning 1 41
(A Crook) *dwlt and towards rr tl sme late hdwy* **12/1**

35-3 **10** 1/2 **Davana**[14] 326 4-8-6 **47** .... (p) KellyHarrison(3) 9 35
(W J H Ratcliffe) *a towards rr* **17/2**[3]

03/5 **11** 3 1/2 **Miss Xu Xia**[16] 297 4-9-0 **52** .... (p) PJMcDonald 10 32
(G R Oldroyd) *trckd ldrs: effrt over 2f out: sn rdn and wknd* **40/1**

103- **12** 6 **Reigning In Rio (IRE)**[62] 1481 4-8-11 **49** .... TonyCulhane 2 16
(P T Midgley) *rdn along 1/2-way: a towards rr* **22/1**

066- **13** 1/2 **Komreyev Star**[56] 7784 8-8-8 **46** oh1 .... ChrisCatlin 3 12
(R E Peacock) *a in rr: bhd fr 1/2-way* **25/1**

000- **14** 18 **Elevate Bobbob**[55] 7796 4-8-3 **46** oh1 .... (v) BillyCray(5) 7 —
(A Berry) *cl up on inner: rdn along over 3f out and sn wknd* **200/1**

1m 45.53s (1.83) **Going Correction** +0.075s/f (Slow) **14** Ran SP% **121.0**
Speed ratings (Par 101): **93,92,92,90,89 89,88,87,85,84 81,75,74,56**
toteswinger:1&2:£3.80, 1&3:£11.20, 2&3:£9.60 CSF £13.12 CT £87.00 TOTE £4.90: £1.80, £1.70, £3.60; EX 13.90 Trifecta £59.80 Pool: £358.82 - 4.44 winning units..
Owner Michael Davies **Bred** D And Mrs D Veitch **Trained** Newmarket, Suffolk

FOCUS
The surface was reckoned to be riding just on the slow side of good but quicker than of late. This was a low-grade 46-52 handicap.
Isitcozimcool(IRE) Official explanation: trainer said, regarding apparent improvement in form, that the gelding had shown a tendency to hang in the past and he also appreciated the step up in trip.
Reigning In Rio(IRE) Official explanation: jockey said filly hung right

504 BET SIX NATIONS RUGBY - BETDAQ H'CAP — 5f (F)
2:20 (2:25) (Class 5) (0-75,70) 4-Y-O+ — **£2,456** (£725; £362) **Stalls** High

Form — RPR

0-15 **1** **Where's Reiley (USA)**[9] 378 4-8-8 **65** .... DeanHeslop(5) 1 74
(T D Barron) *racd wd: pushed along and outpcd after 2f: hdwy 2f out: rdn over 1f out: styd on to ld ins fnl f: kpt on strly* **4/1**[3]

-653 **2** 1 3/4 **Guto**[2] 472 7-8-12 **67** .... KellyHarrison(3) 2 70
(W J H Ratcliffe) *prom: effrt 2f out: rdn to ld briefly over 1f out: drvn and hdd ins fnl f: kpt on same pce* **12/1**

142- **3** 3/4 **First Swallow**[51] 7838 5-8-10 **62** .... (t) FrederikTylicki 5 62
(D H Brown) *led: rdn along 2f out: drvn and hdd over 1f out: kpt on same pce* **6/4**[1]

00-4 **4** 1/2 **Captain Kallis (IRE)**[13] 351 4-8-5 **57** .... DavidProbert 3 55
(D J S Ffrench Davis) *dwlt: sn chsng ldrs: hdwy 2f out and sn rdn: drvn appr fnl f and sn one pce* **7/2**[2]

50-0 **5** 1/2 **La Capriosa**[6] 431 4-9-0 **66** .... RobertWinston 6 62
(J A Glover) *cl up: rdn along 2f out: grad wknd* **11/2**

006- **6** 6 **Miss Thippawan (USA)**[258] 2454 4-7-13 **56** oh11 .... JamesSullivan(5) 4 31
(J Hetherton) *chsd ldrs: rdn along over 2f out: sn drvn and wknd* **66/1**

0-00 **7** 9 **Came Back (IRE)**[9] 380 7-8-13 **70** .... AnnStokell(5) 7 12
(Miss A Stokell) *cl up: rdn along 1/2-way: sn wknd* **40/1**

59.71 secs (0.01) **Going Correction** +0.10s/f (Slow) **7** Ran SP% **109.2**
Speed ratings (Par 103): **103,100,99,98,97 87,73**
toteswinger:1&2:£4.00, 1&3:£1.80, 2&3:£2.80 CSF £44.12 TOTE £4.30: £2.10, £4.30; EX 29.80.
Owner Dovebrace Ltd Air-Conditioning-Projects **Bred** Overbrook Farm **Trained** Maunby, N Yorks

FOCUS
A tight 56-70 sprint handicap.

505 BETDAQEXTRA.COM CLAIMING STKS — 6f (F)
2:50 (2:55) (Class 6) 4-Y-O+ — **£1,774** (£523; £262) **Stalls** Low

Form — RPR

55-2 **1** **Spin Again (IRE)**[9] 379 5-9-5 60 .... AndrewMullen 2 73
(D Nicholls) *cl up: rdn to ld jst over 2f out: sn rdn and edgd lft over 1f out: drvn ins fnl f: kpt on* **7/4**[1]

-545 **2** 2 1/4 **Don Pele (IRE)**[14] 328 8-8-13 58 .... (p) LiamJones 4 60
(R A Harris) *trckd ldrs: hdwy 1/2-way: rdn over 1f out: drvn to chse wnr ent fnl f: no imp* **5/1**[3]

0-33 **3** 1 1/2 **Cornus**[14] 328 8-8-11 59 .... (be) FrederikTylicki 1 54
(J A Glover) *led: rdn along 1/2-way: hdd over 2f out: drvn over 1f out: kpt on same pce* **11/4**[2]

3503 **4** 1 1/4 **Vogarth**[9] 379 6-8-4 57 .... (b) DeclanCannon(5) 5 48
(M C Chapman) *chsd ldng pair: rdn along over 2f out: sn drvn and one pce* **8/1**

1255 **5** 4 **Stonecrabstomorrow (IRE)**[9] 379 7-8-8 70 .... (p) MarkCoumbe(5) 6 40
(John A Harris) *sn rdn along: a in rr* **5/1**[3]

1m 16.89s (0.39) **Going Correction** +0.075s/f (Slow) **5** Ran SP% **107.5**
Speed ratings (Par 101): **100,97,95,93,88**
toteswinger:1&2:£7.60 CSF £10.10 TOTE £2.80: £1.20, £2.40; EX 11.20.Cornus was claimed by A. McCabe for £6,000
Owner Nice To See You Euro-Racing & Partner **Bred** Barry Lyons **Trained** Sessay, N Yorks

FOCUS
A moderate claimer.

506 HOSPITALITY AT SOUTHWELL RACECOURSE H'CAP — 2m (F)
3:20 (3:25) (Class 6) (0-65,71) 4-Y-O+ — **£1,774** (£523; £262) **Stalls** Low

Form — RPR

-55 **1** **Zaffeu**[4] 456 9-9-5 **57** .... (p) VinceSlattery 7 66
(A G Juckes) *hld up: stdy hdwy over 6f out: jnd ldrs 4f out: led 3f out and so0on rdn clr: drvn over 1f out: kpt on gamely u.p ins fnl f: jst hld on* **14/1**

0-51 **2** hd **Victory Quest (IRE)**[7] 401 10-10-5 **71** 6ex .... (v) RobertWinston 8 80
(Mrs S Lamyman) *trckd ldrs: hdwy over 3f out: rdn to chse wnr wl over 1f out: drvn and edgd lft ent fnl f: styd on wl: jst failed* **13/2**[3]

6/06 **3** 1 **Delorain (IRE)**[27] 186 7-8-8 **46** oh1 .... (vt) JerryO'Dwyer 4 54
(W B Stone) *cl up: led after 5f: rdn along over 4f out: hdd 3f out: sn drvn and sltly outpcd: kpt on u.p fnl f* **20/1**

3-22 **4** 3/4 **Spring Breeze**[30] 140 9-8-13 **51** .... (p) GrahamGibbons 9 58
(J J Quinn) *prom: effrt over 3f out: rdn along to chse wnr wl over 2f out: drvn wl over 1f out: kpt on same pce fnl f* **5/4**[1]

0135 **5** 7 **Greenbelt**[7] 401 9-9-3 **55** .... TomEaves 5 53
(G M Moore) *trckd ldrs: effrt over 3f out: rdn along over 2f out: sn drvn and outpcd* **6/1**[2]

500- **6** nk **Davids City (IRE)**[66] 7670 6-8-8 **46** .... FrederikTylicki 6 44
(G A Harker) *hld up in rr: pushed along 5f out: rdn over 3f out: styd on fnl 2f: nrst fin* **13/2**[3]

/320 **7** 27 **Arisea (IRE)**[14] 331 7-8-12 **50** ow2 .... DavidNolan 1 16
(Paul Murphy) *trckd ldrs on inner: rdn along 6f out: wknd over 4f out: sn bhd* **14/1**

00-0 **8** 23 **Trempari**[20] 263 7-8-10 **48** ow2 .... (b) TonyCulhane 3 —
(Mike Murphy) *led 5f: cl up tl rdn along 7f out: sn wknd and bhd* **11/1**

3m 45.04s (-0.46) **Going Correction** +0.075s/f (Slow) **8** Ran SP% **111.8**
Speed ratings (Par 101): **104,103,103,103,99 99,85,74**
totewinger:1&2:£7.20, 1&3:£16.20, 2&3:£9.30 CSF £96.52 CT £1801.55 TOTE £16.10: £2.70, £1.90, £4.90; EX 57.00 Trifecta £308.20 Pool: £720.58 - 1.73 winning units..
Owner Whispering Winds **Bred** Patrick Eddery Ltd **Trained** Abberley, Worcs
■ Stewards' Enquiry : Robert Winston two-day ban: excessive use of whip (Feb 25-26)

FOCUS
A modest 46-71 stayers' handicap and the pace was sound.

507 PLAY GOLF AT SOUTHWELL GOLF CLUB (S) STKS — 7f (F)
3:50 (3:55) (Class 6) 3-Y-O — **£1,774** (£523; £262) **Stalls** Low

Form				RPR
0-61	**1**		**Tiger Hawk (USA)**^{4} [452] 3-9-3 65 ....(b) PatCosgrave 2 (P D Evans) *led: rdn along over 2f out: drvn over 1f out: kpt on wl u.p ins fnl f: jst hld on* **4/5**^{1}	61
6-35	**2**	*nk*	**Taper Jean Girl (IRE)**^{4} [455] 3-8-12 51 .... AndrewElliott 1 (Mrs R A Carr) *trckd ldng pair: hdwy over 2f out: rdn to challoenge over 1f out: drvn ins fnl f and ev ch tl no ex nr fin* **10/1**	55
00-6	**3**	*3 ¼*	**Alotago (IRE)**^{2} [475] 3-8-6 55 .... AndrewMullen 5 (D Nicholls) *cl up: chal wl over 2f out: sn rdn and ev ch tl drvn and one pce appr fnl f* **13/2**^{3}	41
340-	**4**	*15*	**Springwell Giant (IRE)**^{111} [7003] 3-8-6 63 .... DeclanCannon$^{(5)}$ 4 (A J McCabe) *in tch: rdn along 1/2-way: sn outpcd and bhd fnl 2f* **5/2**^{2}	9

1m 31.85s (1.55) **Going Correction** +0.075s/f (Slow) — 4 Ran SP% **106.6**
Speed ratings (Par 95): **94,93,89,72**
CSF £8.45 TOTE £1.50; EX 5.50.The winner was bought in for 4,250gns.

Owner Freddie Ingram **Bred** Sun Valley Farm **Trained** Pandy, Monmouths

FOCUS
A poor and uncompetitive seller.

508 SOUTHWELL RACECOURSE FOR CONFERENCES H'CAP — 7f (F)
4:20 (4:25) (Class 4) (0-80,83) 4-Y-O+ — **£4,209** (£1,252; £625; £312) **Stalls** Low

Form				RPR
030-	**1**		**Tin Cha Woody (USA)**^{59} [7752] 5-8-8 **68** ....(b^{1}) RPCleary 3 (Daniel Mark Loughnane, Ire) *dwlt: pushed along towards rr: hdwy 1/2-way: rdn and qcknd to ld over 2f out: clr over 1f out: styd on strly* **16/1**	81
04-0	**2**	*3 ½*	**Hits Only Jude (IRE)**^{40} [16] 7-9-1 **75** .... DavidNolan 8 (D Carroll) *cl up on outer: effrt and ev ch over 2f out: sn rdn: drvn and edgd lft over 1f out: chsd wnr ins fnl f: sn no imp* **9/2**^{3}	79
4110	**3**	*1 ¾*	**Transmission (IRE)**^{21} [245] 5-9-4 **78** .... TomEaves 2 (B Smart) *trckd ldrs on inner: effrt and ev ch over 2f out: sn rdn: drvn over 1f out and kpt on same pce* **8/1**	78
50-0	**4**	*½*	**Flores Sea (USA)**^{41} [6] 6-8-12 **72** .... PhillipMakin 7 (T D Barron) *towards rr: hdwy on wd outside wl over 2f out: sn rdn: drvn to chse ldrs and edgd lft over 1f out: sn no imp* **11/2**	71
-112	**5**	*4*	**Elusive Warrior (USA)**^{27} [191] 7-8-7 **72** ....(p) DeclanCannon$^{(5)}$ 1 (A J McCabe) *cl up: rdn along 3f out: wknd 2f out* **4/1**^{2}	61
60-1	**6**	*1 ½*	**Gaily Noble (IRE)**^{8} [394] 4-9-4 **83** 6ex .... AmyBaker$^{(5)}$ 4 (A B Haynes) *chsd ldrs: rdn along 1/2-way: drvn over 2f out and sn wknd* **5/1**	68
00-6	**7**	*6*	**Classic Descent**^{13} [350] 5-9-1 **75** .... AndrewElliott 6 (Mrs R A Carr) *s.i.s: a bhd* **33/1**	45
2-05	**8**	*7*	**Apache Ridge (IRE)**^{18} [287] 4-8-8 **68** ....(b^{1}) ChrisCatlin 9 (K A Ryan) *led: rdn along 3f out: drvn and hdd over 2f out and sn wknd* **7/2**^{1}	20

1m 28.65s (-1.65) **Going Correction** +0.075s/f (Slow) — 8 Ran SP% **112.4**
Speed ratings (Par 105): **112,108,106,105,100 99,92,84**
toteswinger:1&2:£14.80, 1&3:£14.70, 2&3:£5.00 CSF £83.30 CT £628.86 TOTE £27.10: £3.40, £1.90, £1.90; EX 138.90 TRIFECTA Not won..

Owner Leo Cox **Bred** D Zuckerman & R Mary Zuckerman As T B E **Trained** Trim, Co Meath

FOCUS
What looked beforehand a competitive 68-83 handicap was turned into a procession by the winner.

Elusive Warrior(USA) Official explanation: jockey said gelding ran flat

509 SOUTHWELL FOR RACING AND GOLF H'CAP — 1m 3f (F)
4:50 (4:55) (Class 5) (0-70,76) 4-Y-O+ — **£2,456** (£725; £362) **Stalls** Low

Form				RPR
-311	**1**		**Charging Indian (IRE)**^{7} [400] 4-9-12 **76** 6ex ....(b) TonyCulhane 7 (P T Midgley) *hld up in tch: hdwy 4f out: chsd ldrs over 2f out: swtchd lft and rdn wl over 1f out: drvn to ld ins fnl f: sn edgd lft: hld on gamely* **9/4**^{2}	83
00-0	**2**	*hd*	**Miss Christophene (IRE)**^{28} [169] 4-9-1 **65** .... AndrewMullen 1 (Mrs S Lamyman) *trckd ldrs on inner: hdwy to ld 3f out: rdn over 2f out: drvn over 1f out: hdd ins fnl f: kpt on wl u.p towards fin* **14/1**	72
40-1	**3**	*1 ½*	**Ask The Oracle**^{28} [166] 4-9-1 **65** .... SteveDrowne 4 (H Morrison) *cl up: led 4f out: rdn along and hdd 3f out: drvn 2f out and ev ch tl one pce ent fnl f* **2/1**^{1}	69
5-11	**4**	*2 ½*	**Slick Mover (IRE)**^{15} [309] 5-9-3 **65** .... DavidProbert 5 (B G Powell) *hld up in rr: hdwy 3f out: rdn along over 2f out: kpt on appr fnl f: n.d* **4/1**^{3}	65
4132	**5**	*¾*	**General Tufto**^{4} [451] 5-9-3 **68** ....(b) KellyHarrison$^{(3)}$ 2 (C Smith) *trckd ldrs: hdwy over 3f out: rdn 2f out and ev ch tl drvn and wknd appr fnl f* **11/1**	67
50-	**6**	*22*	**Drum Major (IRE)**^{174} [5217] 5-9-0 **62** .... AmirQuinn 6 (G L Moore) *chsd ldrs: rdn along over 4f out and sn wknd* **12/1**	26
0-04	**7**	*hd*	**Mullitovermaurice**^{7} [400] 4-8-10 **60** .... RobertWinston 3 (J G Given) *led: rdn along and hdd 4f out: sn wknd* **16/1**	24

2m 28.29s (0.29) **Going Correction** +0.075s/f (Slow)
WFA 4 from 5yo 2lb — 7 Ran SP% **112.7**
Speed ratings (Par 103): **101,100,99,97,97 81,81**
toteswinger:1&2:£7.30, 1&3:£2.20, 2&3:£9.90 CSF £31.29 TOTE £3.30: £1.50, £5.40; EX 27.70 Place 6: £405.07, Place 5: £261.72.

Owner David Mann **Bred** Samac Ltd **Trained** Westow, N Yorks

■ Stewards' Enquiry : Andrew Mullen three-day ban: used whip with excessive frequency without giving filly time to respond (Feb 25-27)

FOCUS
A competitive 60-76 handicap and the pace was sound.

T/Plt: £267.90 to a £1 stake. Pool: £84,643.84. 230.58 winning tickets. T/Qpdt: £32.00 to a £1 stake. Pool: £6,286.76. 145.18 winning tickets. JR

^{434}MEYDAN (L-H)
Thursday, February 11

OFFICIAL GOING: All-weather - standard; turf course - good to firm

510a 4MEN (CONDITIONS RACE) (TAPETA) — 7f
2:30 (2:34) 3-Y-O
£18,518 (£6,172; £3,086; £1,543; £925; £617)

			RPR
1		**Mendip (USA)**^{160} [5637] 3-8-8 90 .... FrankieDettori 3 (Saeed Bin Suroor) *trckd ldrs: rdn to ld 1f out: r.o wl* **11/8**^{1}	90+
2	*½*	**Uncle Tom (BRZ)**^{131} [6505] 4-9-11 96 .... TJPereira 9 (P Bary, France) *in rr of mid-div: r.o wl fnl 1 1/2f: nrst fin* **12/1**	99+
3	*¾*	**Happy Dubai (IRE)**^{34} 3-8-8 85 .... RoystonFfrench 1 (A Al Raihe, UAE) *s.i.s: trckd ldrs: led 2f out: hdd 1f out: kpt on same pce* **33/1**	87
4	*2 ¾*	**Izaaj (USA)**^{34} 3-8-8 85 ....(t) XZiani 11 (M bin Shafya, UAE) *racd in rr: r.o fnl 1 1/2f: n.d* **50/1**	80+
5	*nse*	**Saboteur**^{27} 3-8-8 93 .... JRosales 7 (A bin Huzaim, UAE) *trckd ldrs on outside: ev ch 2f out: led briefly: r.o same pce* **33/1**	79
6	*¼*	**Marine Spirit (GER)**^{4} 3-8-8 87 .... PJSmullen 12 (M bin Shafya, UAE) *nvr bttr than mid-div* **50/1**	79
7	*½*	**Digital (BRZ)**^{194} 4-9-4 101 ....(t) WBlandi 6 (A Cintra Pereira, Brazil) *in rr of mid-div: r.o fnl 1 1/2f: nvr nr to chal* **12/1**	80
8	*1 ½*	**Astonishment (IRE)**^{7} [414] 3-8-8 95 ....(t) KierenFallon 4 (F Nass, Bahrain) *nvr bttr than mid-div* **25/1**	73
9	*½*	**Enak (ARG)**^{264} 4-9-11 110 ....(t) DaraghO'Donohoe 14 (Saeed Bin Suroor) *racd in last: nvr nr to chal* **10/1**^{3}	82
10	*3 ¼*	**Cappiwino (USA)**^{139} 3-8-8 95 ....(bt) MickaelBarzalona 2 (Saeed Bin Suroor) *sn led: rdn and hdd 2f out: wknd* **14/1**	63
11	*4 ¾*	**Timely Jazz (IRE)**^{117} [6849] 3-8-8 101 ....(t) AlanMunro 13 (Niels Petersen, Norway) *nvr nr to chal* **12/1**	50
12	*3 ¾*	**Chaperno (USA)**^{108} [7063] 3-8-8 94 .... AhmedAjtebi 8 (Saeed Bin Suroor) *nvr nr to chal* **14/1**	40
13	*1 ¼*	**Graymalkin (IRE)**^{13} 3-8-8 85 .... WJSupple 5 (M bin Shafya, UAE) *trckd ldrs for 2 1/2f: wknd qckly* **33/1**	37
14	*1 ¼*	**Fareej (USA)**^{120} [6779] 3-8-8 93 .... TedDurcan 10 (Saeed Bin Suroor) *nvr able to chal* **7/2**^{2}	34

1m 24.59s (84.59)
WFA 3 from 4yo 17lb — **14** Ran SP% **126.4**
CFC: £20.17.
Owner Godolphin **Bred** Jayeff B Stables **Trained** Newmarket, Suffolk

FOCUS
The front two look pretty smart, but a few of those close up in behind, namely the likes of Happy Dubai, Izaaj and Marine Spirit, limit the form.

NOTEBOOK
Mendip(USA) looked a decent prospect when defeating a very useful type in a 1m maiden on Polytrack last September, and the choice for Frankie Dettori this time, he was extremely well backed. Like on debut, he required a blanket for stalls entry, but in the race itself he was always handily placed. He seemed to lug left when first coming under pressure in the straight, but was soon balanced and found enough to get on top, before holding off the fast-finishing runner-up. It appears he's far from the finished article, with him having the scope to improve, as well as having some growing up to do mentally.
Uncle Tom(BRZ), a Grade 1 winner over 1m on grass in Brazil last June but off the track since finishing out the back in a Group 2 at Longchamp on Arc weekend, couldn't get as good a position as the winner, being tucked away off the pace towards the inside, and he got going too late. He'll appreciate a return to further, and while it remains to be seen whether next week's Guineas will come too soon, he can be considered for the other two legs of the Triple Crown.
Happy Dubai(IRE), winless in four runs for Bryan Smart last season (including in a visor), has improved this year and built on the promise of his recent Jebel Ali win, gained over 6f on dirt.
Izaaj(USA) couldn't reverse recent form with Happy Dubai but he finished well under a rider with a most unorthodox style.
Saboteur, a maiden winner for Godolphin last year, was produced with every chance and improved on the from he showed on the dirt at Jebel Ali recently.
Enak(ARG), a Grade 1 winner over 1m on turf in Argentina last May, lacked the required pace but made some late headway and will be suited by further.
Fareej(USA) was 2-2 last year, with both wins coming over 1m (the latter on Polytrack), but this drop in trip looked unlikely to suit judged on breeding and, having sweated up beforehand, he ran no sort of race.

511a AQUARIUS (H'CAP) (TAPETA) — 7f
3:05 (3:10) (90-105,105) 3-Y-O+
£40,740 (£13,580; £6,790; £3,395; £2,037; £1,358)

			RPR
1		**Escape Route (USA)**^{46} 6-8-13 98 ....(t) RichardMullen 7 (S Seemar, UAE) *mid-div: smooth prog 2f out: r.o wl: led fnl 110yds* **12/1**	102
2	*1 ¼*	**Swop (IRE)**^{14} [339] 7-9-3 102 .... KierenFallon 8 (L M Cumani) *mid-div: r.o wl fnl 1 1/2f: nrst fin* **13/8**^{1}	103
3	*¼*	**Palazzone (IRE)**^{76} [7566] 4-8-13 98 ....(b) KLatham 3 (G M Lyons, Ire) *trckd ldrs: led and ev ch 1f out: hdd and one pce fnl 110yds* **8/1**	98
4	*½*	**Green Coast (IRE)**^{14} [339] 7-9-2 101 .... TadhgO'Shea 14 (Doug Watson, UAE) *s.i.s: chsd ldrs: n.m.r 1 1/2f out: r.o wl* **13/2**^{2}	100
5	*shd*	**Silverside (USA)**^{123} 4-9-2 101 .... JulienGrosjean 12 (M Delcher-Sanchez, Spain) *in rr of mid-div: gng wl 2 1/2f out: r.o one pce fnl 1 1/2f* **12/1**	100
6	*3*	**Otaared**^{14} [338] 5-9-5 105 ....(t) WilliamBuick 1 (D Selvaratnam, UAE) *mid-div on rail: rdn 2 1/2f out: nvr able to chal* **7/1**^{3}	95
7	*¼*	**Artimino**^{335} 6-8-8 100 .... AntiocoMurgia$^{(7)}$ 2 (I Mohammed, UAE) *nvr bttr than mid-div* **25/1**	90
8	*shd*	**Snow Runner (ARG)**^{14} [339] 7-9-1 100 ....(t) PaulHanagan 13 (Vanja Sandrup, Sweden) *a mid-div* **40/1**	90
9	*1 ¼*	**Greek Renaissance (IRE)**^{39} 7-9-1 100 ....(t) PJSmullen 5 (E Charpy, UAE) *a mid-div* **20/1**	86
10	*¾*	**Halkin (USA)**^{14} [339] 8-9-1 100 .... WayneSmith 9 (F Nass, Bahrain) *sn led: gng wl 2f out: rdn and hdd 1f out: wknd fnl 110yds* **33/1**	84
11	*1 ¾*	**Fateh Field (USA)**^{123} 5-8-13 98 .... JRosales 11 (A bin Huzaim, UAE) *nvr able to chal* **10/1**	78
12	*¼*	**Prince Fasliyev**^{151} 6-9-1 100 .... AlanMunro 6 (Niels Petersen, Norway) *nvr able to chal* **20/1**	79

13 *shd* **Grand Hombre (USA)**[27] 10-9-1 100..................(t) LJurado 10 79
(R Bouresly, Kuwait) *trckd ldng gp tl 2f out: wknd* **40/1**
14 *hd* **Aahaykid (IRE)**[98] 7259 4-9-3 102..................(bt) JimCrowley 4 80
(P D Deegan, Ire) *s.i.s: racd in rr: n.d* **40/1**
1m 24.65s (84.65) **14 Ran SP% 123.1**
CFC: £30.15, TRI: £175.88.
Owner H R H Princess Haya Of Jordan **Bred** Robert N Clay & Serengeti Stable **Trained** United Arab Emirates

FOCUS
This race was full of exposed types and the pace looked modest early on (time slower than earlier 3-y-o conditions race), so not form to dwell on. The form is rated through the third.

NOTEBOOK
Escape Route(USA) won over as far as 1m2f when trained by John Gosden, but his latest win came over 5f on the dirt at Jebel Ali and his speed was an asset in this rather muddling contest. He was reluctant to go into the stalls, and in the race itself he was towards the rear turning into the straight, but he picked up well when getting one clear run on the outside of runners. A rise in the weights might find him out.
Swop(IRE), racing off the same mark as when third to the promising Leahurst (fifth good winner since) over C&D two weeks earlier, could be described as a little unlucky as he never seemed to have that much room in the straight, albeit Fallon never really had to stop riding. Whatever, though, he was under pressure over two furlongs out, and his lack of tactical speed in this steadily run race seemed to be his undoing. He probably won't find a handicap as weak as this one next time, but a return to 1m should help and he did win third-time out (on turf) at last year's carnival.
Palazzone(IRE), 4lb higher than when winning on Polytrack at Dundalk over this trip last October, was always well placed from his inside draw but wasn't quite good enough.
Green Coast(IRE) got going too late and couldn't reverse recent placings with Swop.
Silverside(USA), Spanish trained, had every chance but was swamped by speedier types late on and should be suited by a return to 1m.
Artimino, returning from 335 days off, ran better than his finishing position suggests as, having missed the break, he was denied a clear run in the straight.

512a INSIDEOUT (H'CAP) (TAPETA) 1m 3f
3:45 (3:46) (90-105,104) 3-Y-O+

£40,740 (£13,580; £6,790; £3,395; £2,037; £1,358)

RPR
1 **Highland Glen**[128] 6571 4-8-13 100..................FrankieDettori 11 106+
(Saeed Bin Suroor) *in rr of mid-div: smooth prog 2f out: r.o wl to ld 110yds out* **9/2**[2]
2 *1 3/4* **Monte Alto (IRE)**[6] 436 6-9-1 100..................(t) RichardHills 6 102
(A Al Raihe, UAE) *s.i.s: mid-div on rail: chsd ldrs 2f out: r.o wl: no ch w wnr* **13/2**[3]
3 *hd* **Lion Sands**[14] 335 6-9-1 100..................JRosales 1 102
(A bin Huzaim, UAE) *mid-div: trckd ldr 2f out: led 1 1/2f out: one pce and hdd 110yds out* **33/1**
4 *1 1/4* **Meeriss (IRE)**[13] 5-9-3 102..................WilliamBuick 3 102
(D Selvaratnam, UAE) *trckd ldng duo tl 3f out: sn wknd* **14/1**
5 *4 1/2* **Emerald Wilderness (IRE)**[14] 334 6-9-2 101..................JamieSpencer 7 93
(R M H Cowell) *mid-div: chsd ldrs 1 1/2f out: r.o wl* **11/1**
6 *1 3/4* **Record Breaker (IRE)**[7] 418 6-9-2 101..................(b) KierenFallon 12 90
(M Johnston) *a in mid-div* **14/1**
7 *1 1/4* **Lindner (GER)**[14] 335 5-8-13 98..................AhmedAjtebi 9 85
(Saeed Bin Suroor) *in rr of mid-div: nvr able to chal* **12/1**
8 *3/4* **Bridge Of Gold (USA)**[26] 205 4-9-2 104..................PaulHanagan 4 89
(M A Magnusson) *mid-div: chsd ldrs fnl 1 1/2f* **9/4**[1]
9 *1 3/4* **Colony (IRE)**[14] 335 5-8-7 99..................(b) AntiocoMurgia(7) 2 82
(M Al Subouse, UAE) *sn led: hdd 1 1/2f out: wknd* **50/1**
10 *2 3/4* **Wild Savannah**[326] 8-9-3 102..................(t) PJSmullen 13 80
(E Charpy, UAE) *nvr bttr than mid-div* **33/1**
11 *4 1/2* **Kerashan (IRE)**[11] 8-8-11 97..................(bt) RoystonFfrench 5 66
(A Al Raihe, UAE) *trckd ldr tl 2 1/2f out: wknd* **25/1**
12 *2 1/4* **Lignon's Hero (BRZ)**[193] 5-9-1 100..................(t) WBlandi 14 66
(A Cintra Pereira, Brazil) *nvr bttr than mid-div* **12/1**
13 *23* **Zulu Chief (USA)**[6] 435 5-8-11 97..................KShea 8 23
(M F De Kock, South Africa) *s.i.s: mid-div: rdn 3 1/2f out: sn wknd* **20/1**
14 *dist* **Imvula (AUS)**[14] 334 6-9-0 99..................TedDurcan 10 —
(Saeed Bin Suroor) *settled in last: rdn 4 1/2f out: nvr involved* **10/1**
2m 16.73s (136.73)
WFA 4 from 5yo+ 2lb **14 Ran SP% 124.9**
CFC: £33.29, TRI: £892.27.
Owner Godolphin **Bred** The Queen **Trained** Newmarket, Suffolk

FOCUS
A reasonable handicap, although the favourite ran below expectations. The pace seemed strong.

NOTEBOOK
Highland Glen, who was having his first start since leaving Sir Michael Stoute, has clearly done well since joining these connections. It's true he had won his last two starts, but he was far from convincing on his latest outing, again proving reluctant to go into the stalls (has refused to even enter them in the past) before racing keenly in front. This time, though, it seems he went into the stalls without too much bother, and despite racing enthusiastically, he responded well to hold-up tactics, with the decent gallop obviously helping matters. Taken wide around the final bend to get a clear run, he showed a smart change of pace and ultimately won cosily. He's now 3-3 since being gelded and his new trainer, who described him as being 90% fit, sounded hopeful that he will continue to go the right way. If that's the case, he can yet rate higher.
Monte Alto(IRE) finds winning difficult but he's been in good form at this carnival and his proximity gives the form a solid look.
Lion Sands was given every chance and stepped up massively on his recent outing, but he's another who rarely wins these days.
Meeriss(IRE), fit from racing on the dirt at Jebel Ali, coped with the return to synthetics but was one paced in the straight.
Emerald Wilderness(IRE), who found 1m11/2f an inadequate test around here on his debut for this yard, travelled well for much of the way but found disappointingly little.
Record Breaker(IRE) ran as though in need of further.
Lindner(GER), who was over 7l behind Monte Alto over C&D on his Dubai debut, ran a thoroughly unconvincing race, racing well out the back before plugging on at just the one pace. He looks limited.
Bridge Of Gold(USA) was only 4lb higher than when winning a decent 1m2f handicap on Polytrack at Lingfield last time, a race that's worked out well, but he was disappointing. He was trying his furthest trip to date, but was in trouble as early as leaving the back straight.

513a WHEELS (H'CAP) (TAPETA) 1m 2f
4:20 (4:22) (95-110,108) 3-Y-O+

£44,444 (£14,814; £7,407; £3,703; £2,222; £1,481)

RPR
1 **Lizard's Desire (SAF)**[14] 334 5-9-3 107..................ChristopheSoumillon 9 110+
(M F De Kock, South Africa) *mid-div: smooth prog to trck ldr 2 1/2f out: led 1 1/2f out: comf* **1/1**[1]
2 *2 1/4* **Soy Libriano (ARG)**[7] 415 5-9-1 105..................(t) FrankieDettori 13 103
(Saeed Bin Suroor) *in rr of mid-div: rdn 4f out: r.o wl: no ch w wnr* **8/1**[2]
3 *1/2* **Burdlaz (IRE)**[203] 4256 5-9-2 106..................AhmedAjtebi 7 103
(Saeed Bin Suroor) *settled in rr: r.o wl fnl 2f: nrst fin* **14/1**
4 *1* **Re Barolo (IRE)**[74] 7588 7-9-0 104..................CSandoval 6 99
(A bin Huzaim, UAE) *settled in rr: r.o wl fnl 2f: nrst fin* **8/1**[2]
5 *1 1/4* **We'll Come**[14] 337 6-9-4 108..................JRosales 8 101
(A bin Huzaim, UAE) *in rr of mid-div: r.o wl fnl 1 1/2f: nrst fin* **20/1**
6 *1 3/4* **Antonios (IND)**[109] 5-8-9 99..................SilvestreDeSousa 4 88
(S Shah, India) *trckd ldrs tl wknd 2 1/2f out* **11/1**[3]
7 *1 3/4* **Eddie Jock (IRE)**[14] 337 6-9-1 105..................RichardMullen 5 91
(S Seemar, UAE) *nvr bttr than mid-div* **20/1**
8 *shd* **Celtic Wolf (FR)**[173] 5-9-0 104..................(t) PJSmullen 11 89
(E Charpy, UAE) *a mid-div* **33/1**
9 *6* **Clasp**[14] 334 8-8-5 95..................(vt) TadhgO'Shea 10 68
(Doug Watson, UAE) *trckd ldr: led 3f out tl hdd 1 1/2f out: wknd* **22/1**
10 *1* **Galactic Star**[7] 418 7-9-1 105..................(t) RoystonFfrench 14 76
(A Al Raihe, UAE) *settled in rr: nvr nr to chal* **33/1**
11 *1/4* **Philario (IRE)**[14] 338 5-9-1 105..................JimCrowley 3 76
(P D Deegan, Ire) *nvr bttr than mid-div* **33/1**
12 *13* **Bab Al Salam (USA)**[14] 335 4-8-10 101..................TedDurcan 2 46
(Saeed Bin Suroor) *mid-div on rail tl rdn 2 1/2f out: sn btn* **8/1**[2]
13 *5* **Shopton Lane (USA)**[13] 6-8-5 95..................(t) WJSupple 12 30
(Doug Watson, UAE) *sn led: hdd 3f out: wknd* **50/1**
14 *8 3/4* **Moiqen (IRE)**[220] 3700 5-9-4 108..................RichardHills 1 25
(Doug Watson, UAE) *trckd ldr tl wknd 3f out* **25/1**
2m 3.38s (123.38)
WFA 4 from 5yo+ 1lb **14 Ran SP% 126.8**
CFC: £8.52, TRI: £84.73.
Owner Sheikh Mohammed Bin Khalifa Al Maktoum **Bred** A J Boshoff **Trained** South Africa

FOCUS
A very good handicap. The form is rated around the second and third.

NOTEBOOK
Lizard's Desire(SAF), who had defeated subsequent carnival winner and stablemate King Of Rome over C&D two weeks earlier, showed he remained well handicapped off a 7lb higher mark. He was drawn wider this time, and raced further back as a consequence, but under expert handling he had made good headway to be ideally placed by the top of the straight, before picking up well for a thoroughly convincing victory. It will be interesting to see where he goes next. We know he's also effective on turf at up to 1m4f, so he has plenty of options, but it would be no surprise to see him kept to this surface and distance, seeing as it suits so well, and there's a handicap for horses rated 100 and above on February 25. Should his connections choose to be really ambitious, there is the third round of the Al Maktoum Challenge on March 4 to consider.
Soy Libriano(ARG) ran much better than when looking less than interested over C&D the previous week, and that run clearly brought him on, although he again gave the impression he wasn't fully concentrating. Provided he continues to go the right way, there should be better to come, maybe in headgear.
Burdlaz(IRE), the winner of a weak Listed race in France when last seen 203 days previously, lost some momentum when having to wait for a clear run around the turn into the straight and he should be able to build on this.
Re Barolo(IRE) ◆, having his first start since leaving Marco Botti, was asked to make his move from well off the pace out widest of all around the final bend, and his run unsurprisingly flattened out. He moved like a horse in good form and can do better.
We'll Come ran okay without really improving on his recent fourth, when he was denied a clear run. He's quite a big horse who doesn't seem all that nimble around the bends, and perhaps he'll be worth a try on the turf track.
Antonios(IND) ◆, last year's Indian Derby and St Leger winner, is almost certainly capable of better. Racing over a trip probably shorter than ideal, he went from tracking the leaders down the back straight to just about last of all in a matter of strides before the final bend, having got stuck in behind Moiqen, who was stopping quickly. That cost him his chance, but he did well to recover into sixth and will be of interest off this sort of mark next time, seriously so if stepped up in trip.
Bab Al Salam(USA) again ran disappointingly and is not performing as expected at this carnival.

514a UAE 1000 GUINEAS SPONSORED BY GULF NEWS (FILLIES) (LISTED RACE) (TAPETA) 1m
5:05 (5:06) 3-Y-O

£92,592 (£30,864; £15,432; £7,716; £4,629; £3,086)

RPR
1 **Siyaadah**[131] 6477 3-8-9 83..................AhmedAjtebi 12 103
(Saeed Bin Suroor) *s.i.s: racd in rr: smooth prog out wd over 2f out: r.o to ld cl home* **50/1**
2 *1* **Ayun Tara (FR)**[114] 6929 3-8-9 105..................(p) GregoryBenoist 2 100
(X Nakkachdji, France) *mid-div on rail: chsd ldrs 2f out: r.o wl* **12/1**
3 *1/4* **Berg Bahn (IRE)**[123] 6708 3-8-9 90..................KLatham 7 100
(G M Lyons, Ire) *mid-div: r.o wl fnl 1 1/2f: nt qckn fnl 55yds* **25/1**
4 *3/4* **Raihana (AUS)**[14] 333 4-9-5 107..................ChristopheSoumillon 3 101
(M F De Kock, South Africa) *trckd ldr: led 1f out: r.o: hdd fnl 55yds* **1/1**[1]
5 *3/4* **Bikini Babe (IRE)**[137] 6316 3-8-9 100..................KierenFallon 11 96
(M Johnston) *settled in rr: chsd ldrs 2f out: nt qckn fnl 110yds* **10/1**[3]
6 *2 1/4* **Waasemah (KSA)**[14] 333 3-8-9 99..................TedDurcan 8 91
(B Al Subaie, Saudi Arabia) *chsd ldrs for 4 1/2f: wknd* **14/1**
7 *1/4* **Ishitaki (ARG)**[286] 4-9-5 100..................FrankieDettori 5 94
(Saeed Bin Suroor) *trckd ldrs: rdn 3f out: nt qckn* **4/1**[2]
8 *1/2* **Silver Grey (IRE)**[14] 333 3-8-9 97..................(p) RobertHavlin 6 89
(R Ingram) *nvr bttr than mid-div* **20/1**
9 *1/2* **Talenta (BRZ)**[14] 333 4-9-5 100..................WBlandi 13 91
(A Cintra Pereira, Brazil) *trckd ldrs: ev ch 1f out: nt qckn fnl 110yds* **16/1**
10 *4 1/4* **Muntherah (KSA)**[14] 333 3-8-9 98..................(b) PJSmullen 9 78
(B Al Subaie, Saudi Arabia) *trckd ldr: led briefly 1 1/2f out: one pce fnl f* **33/1**
11 *1/2* **Opera Comica (BRZ)**[131] 6503 4-9-5 101..................(t) TJPereira 1 80
(P Bary, France) *sn led: hdd 2f out: wknd* **20/1**
12 *1* **Mensajera De La Luz (CHI)**[236] 4-9-5 102..................OlivierPeslier 14 78
(J Barton, Saudi Arabia) *in rr of mid-div: nvr able to chal* **10/1**[3]
13 *9* **Absolute Music (USA)**[14] 333 3-8-9 104..................JamieSpencer 4 54
(R M H Cowell) *settled in rr: nvr able to chal* **50/1**
14 *6* **Diamond Laura**[14] 333 3-8-9 83..................TadhgO'Shea 10 41
(Doug Watson, UAE) *nvr able to chal* **100/1**
1m 37.21s (97.21)
WFA 3 from 4yo 19lb **14 Ran SP% 129.6**
CFC: £579.46.
Owner Godolphin **Bred** Lofts Hall Stud **Trained** Newmarket, Suffolk

FOCUS
An eighth winner in ten runnings of the UAE 1,000 Guineas to have been bred in the northern hemisphere, and also a seventh victory in the race for Saeed Bin Suroor. The form of this year's contest needs treating with caution, as the leaders went off too fast, setting this up for those waited with. But even allowing for that, the result would seem to confirm that this year's classic fillies are, in general, an ordinary bunch, although we are still to find out who will turn up for the Oaks.

NOTEBOOK

Siyaadah appeared to have loads to find in this company, having looked no better than useful in three turf runs over 7f last year but, handling the surface well, she clearly benefited considerably from being held up off the overly strong pace. It was clear at the top of the straight she was travelling nicely, and once switched wide into the clear, she picked up, whilst many of those in front of her were beginning to tire. Quite a big filly, she's certainly improved since last year, but she has to be considered flattered the bare result.

Ayun Tara(FR), who was runner-up in Group 3 company over this trip on turf in France last October, ran a big race considering she was never that far away from the strong pace. She had to wait for a run in the straight until about a furlong out, although that may actually have helped her chance.

Berg Bahn(IRE) improved on the form she showed in two runs in Ireland last year, despite getting warm, although she was suited by the way the race unfolded.

Raihana(AUS) paid for racing too close to the strong gallop on this step up in trip, and Mike De Kock is still looking for his first win in this race. Still, the filly managed to confirm form with all of those who re-opposed from last time.

Bikini Babe(IRE) was outpaced for most of the way but stayed on past beaten horses. It remains to be seen what she actually achieved.

Waasemah(KSA), runner-up in the trial, travelled well but didn't find much.

Ishitaki(ARG), who won a couple of Grade 1s in Argentina by an aggregate margin of 14l, had been off since last May, but according to Simon Crisford, first time up was expected to be the time to catch her. After tracking the favourite, she came off the bridle before the straight and didn't pick up.

515a AL SHINDAGHA SPRINT SPONSORED BY XPRESS (GROUP 3) (TAPETA) 6f

5:40 (5:40) 3-Y-O+

£74,074 (£24,691; £12,345; £6,172; £3,703; £2,469)

			RPR
1		**War Artist (AUS)**[60] 7745 7-9-1 115 .... OlivierPeslier 7	119
		(J M P Eustace) *mid-div: trckd ldrs 2 1/2f out: led 2f out: qcknd clr 1 1/2f out: styd on wl* **7/2**[2]	
2	2 ¾	**Gayego (USA)**[96] 7306 5-9-3 115 ....(t) FrankieDettori 2	112
		(Saeed Bin Suroor) *in rr of mid-div: n.m.r over 2f out: r.o wl 1 /1/2f out: kpt on wl* **1/1**[1]	
3	1 ½	**El Cambio (AUS)**[243] 6-8-11 111 ....(b) AhmedAjtebi 3	101
		(Saeed Bin Suroor) *mid-div: r.o wl fnl 2f* **10/1**	
4	¼	**Sir Gerry (USA)**[7] 416 5-8-11 108 .... TedDurcan 4	101
		(J R Best) *in rr of mid-div: r.o wl fnl 2f: nrst fin* **10/1**	
5	1	**Star Crowned (USA)**[6] 437 7-8-11 109 ....(t) LJurado 9	97
		(R Bouresly, Kuwait) *mid-div: chsd ldrs 2 1/2f out: ev ch: one pce fnl f* **16/1**	
6	1 ½	**Instant Recall (IRE)**[6] 434 9-8-11 105 ....(v) WayneSmith 10	93
		(M Al Muhairi, UAE) *trckd ldr: ev ch 2f out: wknd fnl f* **50/1**	
7	hd	**Morgan Drive (IRE)**[102] 7206 5-9-0 107 .... PJSmullen 5	95
		(M Gasparini, Italy) *in rr: nvr gng pce to chal* **16/1**	
8	2 ¼	**Indian Chant (USA)**[579] 7-8-11 101 ....(t) TadhgO'Shea 6	85
		(A Al Raihe, UAE) *mid-div: one pce fnl 1 1/2f* **50/1**	
9	5	**Taqdeyr**[7] 412 5-8-11 98 .... JRosales 11	69
		(A bin Huzaim, UAE) *sn led: hdd 2f out: wknd* **40/1**	
10	¾	**Musaalem (USA)**[14] 336 6-8-11 107 .... RichardHills 12	66
		(Doug Watson, UAE) *s.i.s: mid-div: nvr able to chal* **8/1**[3]	
11	½	**Al Qasi (IRE)**[117] 6848 7-8-11 100 .... RoystonFfrench 1	65
		(A Al Raihe, UAE) *nvr able to chal* **40/1**	
12	5 ½	**Mac Gille Eoin**[7] 416 6-8-11 100 .... JimCrowley 8	47
		(J Gallagher) *nvr bttr than mid-div* **40/1**	

1m 10.74s (70.74) 12 Ran SP% **124.5**

CFC: £7.52.

Owner Rupert Plersch **Bred** S Kirkham **Trained** Newmarket, Suffolk

FOCUS

A decent Group 3 contest run at a strong pace.

NOTEBOOK

War Artist(AUS) ◆ was expected to need this first run since finishing down the field in the Hong Kong Sprint, but he was always travelling really strongly and bounded clear in the straight to record an impressive victory. His trainer had previously considered him to be at his best over a straight 6f, so the Al Quoz Sprint on World Cup night was the main target. That may still be the case, but it would be no surprise if the manner of this success encourages a re-think. The Golden Shaheen, to be run over this C&D on the same day (March 27), offers double the amount of prize money ($2,000,000), and is a Group 1, compared to the turf contest, which is a Group 3.

Gayego(USA) ◆, like the winner, was expected to need this run, his first since finishing fourth in last season's Breeders' Cup Sprint, seeing as he is the "biggest and heaviest horse in the yard" according to Saeed Bin Suroor, and he was conceding weight all round owing to the penalty he picked up for winning a Grade 1 last year (over this trip on synthetics). Held up off the pace, he lacked War Artist's sharpness and could only follow that rival through at a respectful distance.

El Cambio(AUS) ◆, a multiple Group-race winner (although not at the highest level) over 6f-7f in Australia, ran a fine race after 242 days off. He looked a bit unlucky not to finish closer, as he had to wait for a clear run after travelling well, although he was receiving weight from the front pair.

Sir Gerry(USA), whose earlier C&D carnival success came off a mark of 105, ran on from off the strong pace without seriously threatening.

Star Crowned(USA) ran about as well as could have been expected.

Indian Chant(USA) will surely have pleased connections with this comeback from 579 days off.

516a GNADS4U (H'CAP) (TURF) 1m 4f 93y

6:15 (6:15) (100-119,119) 3-Y-O+

£64,814 (£21,604; £10,802; £5,401; £3,240; £2,160)

			RPR
1		**Halicarnassus (IRE)**[14] 337 6-8-11 110 .... AlanMunro 6	111
		(M R Channon) *sn led: rdn over 3f out and kpt on bravely* **9/1**	
2	shd	**Mourilyan (IRE)**[100] 7215 6-9-2 115 ....(t) RyanMoore 7	116
		(H J Brown, South Africa) *s.i.s: settled in rr: prog to chse ldrs 3f out: r.o wl ins fnl f: jst hld* **11/2**[3]	
3	1	**Quijano (GER)**[117] 6873 8-9-6 119 .... AStarke 9	118
		(P Schiergen, Germany) *trckd ldr: ev ch 2 1/2f out: one pce ins fnl f* **8/1**	
4	½	**Claremont (IRE)**[131] 6502 4-8-11 112 .... AhmedAjtebi 3	112
		(Saeed Bin Suroor) *settled in rr: chsd ldrs 2 1/2f out: one pce fnl f* **7/1**	
5	¼	**Once More Dubai (USA)**[99] 7237 5-8-8 107 ....(bt) FrankieDettori 10	105
		(Saeed Bin Suroor) *mid-div: chsd ldrs 3f out: nt qckn fnl f* **5/2**[1]	
6	¼	**Pompeyano (IRE)**[7] 418 5-8-5 104 ....(t) RichardMullen 2	102+
		(S Seemar, UAE) *mid-div: n.m.r after 1f and again 1 1/2f out* **16/1**	
7	shd	**Topclas (FR)**[7] 418 4-8-6 107 .... WJSupple 4	106
		(M bin Shafya, UAE) *nvr bttr than mid-div* **10/1**	
8	1 ¼	**Frozen Fire (GER)**[7] 417 5-9-1 113 ....(t) ChristopheSoumillon 1	110
		(M F De Kock, South Africa) *trckd ldr: ev ch 2 1/2f out: wknd* **9/2**[2]	
9	3	**Illustrious Blue**[110] 7031 7-8-11 110 .... JimCrowley 8	101
		(W J Knight) *s.i.s: settled in rr: nvr able to chal* **16/1**	
10	10	**Mulaqat**[14] 335 7-8-5 102 .... WilliamBuick 5	79
		(D Selvaratnam, UAE) *nvr bttr than mid-div* **33/1**	

2m 44.49s (164.49)

WFA 4 from 5yo+ 3lb 10 Ran SP% **119.5**

CSF: £59.40, TRI: £421.50.

Owner Doric Racing **Bred** Yeomanstown Lodge Stud **Trained** West Ilsley, Berks

FOCUS

A high-class handicap, but form to treat with caution as the winner was allowed his own way in front and set a steady pace.

NOTEBOOK

Halicarnassus(IRE) was allowed his own way in front and set a steady pace. This admirably tough individual showed fine resolution to hang on and claim his second carnival success (won off 108 at Nad Al Sheba last year), but he may struggle to follow up.

Mourilyan(IRE), having his first run since finishing third in last year's Melbourne Cup, had a tongue-tie fitted and ran a terrific race in defeat, in the process displaying an attitude that couldn't be faulted (not always been the case). He was last at the top of the straight, but produced a sustained effort and just failed to get up. Presumably his connections will now choose between the DRC Gold Cup over 2m, a race in which he was runner-up last year, and the Dubai City Of Gold over 1m4f, in which he was second in 2008.

Quijano(GER), who was pulled up in the Canadian International when last seen, raced close up throughout, but even so, the lack of pace in the race didn't suit. He should be capable of better.

Claremont(IRE) ◆, a Group 3 winner over 1m4f in France when with Andre Fabre, but disappointing on his final start for that yard over 1m7f, ran a big race in defeat. He sat last for much of the way, before swinging widest of all into the straight, and having made a big move, his run flattened out late on. There should be improvement forthcoming.

Once More Dubai(USA), a Listed winner over this trip on Polytrack last November, was simply too keen.

Pompeyano(IRE) ◆, unlucky not to go close over 1m6f the previous week, again endured a trouble trip, being badly hampered on the first bend, before being denied a clear run in the straight. He's running out of options at this year's carnival, but could go well at a price if allowed his chance in the DRC Gold Cup on February 25.

Frozen Fire(GER) again offered nothing. He got a bit warm, and was keen, before failing to respond to pressure.

Illustrious Blue was another who didn't settle.

517a GULF NEWS BROADCASTING (H'CAP) (TURF) 1m 1f

6:50 (6:57) (100-119,119) 3-Y-O+

£64,814 (£21,604; £10,802; £5,401; £3,240; £2,160)

			RPR
1		**Pan River (TUR)**[103] 5-8-9 108 .... SelimKaya 4	113+
		(Ayhan Kasar, Turkey) *mid-div: chsd ldrs 2f out: led cl home* **5/1**[3]	
2	1	**Lucky Find (SAF)**[14] 339 7-8-6 105 .... KShea 12	108
		(M F De Kock, South Africa) *mid-div: trckd ldrs 2 1/2f out: led 1 1/2f out: r.o wl: hdd cl homne* **12/1**	
3	1 ½	**Shaweel**[103] 7186 4-9-0 112 .... FrankieDettori 11	113
		(Saeed Bin Suroor) *mid-div: chsd ldrs 2f out: nt qckn cl home* **10/3**[2]	
4	1 ¼	**Spring Of Fame (USA)**[131] 6505 4-8-11 110 .... TedDurcan 7	107
		(Saeed Bin Suroor) *a mid-div* **10/1**	
5	nse	**Al Shemali**[378] 338 6-8-7 106 ....(t) RoystonFfrench 3	103
		(A Al Raihe, UAE) *mid-diviaion on rail: nvr able to chal* **14/1**	
6	2	**Beauchamp Xerxes**[14] 334 4-8-5 100 ....(p) PaulHanagan 10	97
		(G A Butler) *s.i.s: settled in rr: nvr nr to chal* **33/1**	
7	¾	**Autonomy (IND)**[109] 5-8-5 100 ....(bt) WilliamBuick 6	95
		(B Chenoy, India) *trckd ldrs tl 1 1/2f out: one pce fnl f* **11/2**	
8	1 ¾	**McCartney (GER)**[242] 2953 5-8-6 105 ....(t) RichardMullen 1	93
		(S Seemar, UAE) *in rr of mid-div: nvr able to chal* **16/1**	
9	¼	**Alazeyab (USA)**[131] 6480 4-8-5 102 ....(t) TadhgO'Shea 2	91
		(A Al Raihe, UAE) *trckd ldrs to 2f out: wknd* **16/1**	
10	1 ¾	**Rocks Off (ARG)**[6] 441 5-8-5 100 ....(b) DaraghO'Donohoe 9	87
		(M F De Kock, South Africa) *in rr of mid-div: n.d* **33/1**	
11	2 ¾	**Golden Sword**[201] 4298 4-9-6 119 ....(bt) ChristopheSoumillon 5	97
		(M F De Kock, South Africa) *sn led: hdd 2f out: wknd* **5/2**[1]	

1m 51.87s (111.87) 11 Ran SP% **124.8**

Placepot: £254.60. Pool of £14843.90 - 42.55 winning units. Quadpot: £100.70. Pool of £707.70 - 5.20 winning units..

Owner Nevzat Seyok **Bred** N Seyok **Trained** Turkey

FOCUS

The results of the last two races on this international stage paid a noticeable compliment to horse racing in Turkey, highlighting the quality of runners to compete in that country and, more specifically, the worth of one of their most prestigious races, the Bosphorus Cup. The reason being, the one-two in that particular Group 2 contest last year were Halicarnassus, successful in the previous race on this card, and of course Pan River.

NOTEBOOK

Pan River(TUR) showed a good attitude to take this high-class handicap. Returning from over three months off, he was entitled to find this trip a bit sharp, but he stayed on well, having been nicely enough placed in about mid-division for much of the way. There should be more to come, especially when he tackles further, and he might be able to defy a rise.

Lucky Find(SAF), on turf for the first time in over a year, travelled well for a long way and ran on to the line, but the winner was just too good.

Shaweel, trying beyond 1m for the first time, made a satisfactory return. He's been lightly raced since joining this yard, but is entitled to come for the outing and could yet do better.

Spring Of Fame(USA) ran on late from a fair way back. This was an encouraging return from over four months off and he'll be of particular interest next time if switching to the Tapeta, seeing as he's 2-3 on Polytrack (unlucky for the only defeat on that surface).

Al Shemali shaped well after over a year off and is obviously entitled to come on for this.

Beauchamp Xerxes was keen early and only ran on past beaten rivals, although this was a better effort than when he was well held on the Tapeta last time.

Autonomy(IND), a neck too good for Antonios (unlucky sixth off 99 in a 1m2f Tapeta handicap earlier on the card) off level weights in a 1m4f Grade 1 in India last year, couldn't quicken in the straight over a trip short of his optimum.

Golden Sword had a tongue-tie and blinkers fitted on first start for Mike De Kock, but after leading early, he stopped quite quickly in the straight.

[503]SOUTHWELL (L-H)

Friday, February 12

OFFICIAL GOING: Standard

The sixth consecutive day's racing at Southwell.

Wind: Fresh across Weather: Overcast with the odd spot of rain

518 BET SIX NATIONS RUGBY - BETDAQ H'CAP — 1m (F)

1:15 (1:15) (Class 6) (0-60,60) 4-Y-0+ **£1,774** (£523; £262) **Stalls** Low

Form RPR

0-14 **1** **Positivity**[22] 248 4-8-11 **53**....(p) TomEaves 5 60
(B Smart) *a.p: rdn over 2f out: nt clr run and swtchd rt over 1f out: r.o u.p to ld wl ins fnl f* **7/1**

066- **2** *nk* **Tomintoul Star**[173] 5286 4-8-12 **54**.... AndrewElliott 8 60
(Mrs R A Carr) *hld up in tch: hmpd over 3f out: nt clr run over 2f out: r.o wl ins fnl f: jst failed* **12/1**

2263 **3** *½* **Special Cuvee**[2] 491 4-9-4 **60**....(v) PhillipMakin 9 65
(A B Haynes) *hld up: hdwy u.p and hung lft fr over 2f out: led over 1f out: hdd wl ins fnl f* **6/1**

6240 **4** *¾* **Ten Pole Tudor**[4] 466 5-9-0 **56**....(p) LiamJones 10 59
(R A Harris) *prom: rdn over 4f out: ev ch over 1f out: styd on same pce ins fnl f* **17/2**

0-32 **5** *1 ¾* **Granakey (IRE)**[1] 503 7-8-5 **47**.... SaleemGolam 2 46
(Ian Williams) *chsd ldrs: led 3f out: edgd rt 2f out: rdn and hdd over 1f out: no ex ins fnl f* **7/2**[1]

3-30 **6** *1 ¼* **Tobrata**[29] 169 4-9-4 **60**.... RobertWinston 4 57
(M Brittain) *chsd ldrs: rdn over 2f out: no ex fnl f* **5/1**[3]

4-14 **7** *½* **Dontuwishitwereso**[35] 86 4-8-13 **55**....(b) FrannyNorton 6 50
(P W D'Arcy) *s.i.s: sn pushed along in rr: r.o ins fnl f: nvr nrr* **9/2**[2]

020- **8** *3 ¼* **Rub Of The Relic (IRE)**[322] 979 5-8-4 **51**....(v) PaulPickard(5) 3 39
(P T Midgley) *chsd ldr tl led over 3f out: sn rdn and hdd: wknd wl over 1f out* **20/1**

03-0 **9** *3 ¼* **Bob Stock (IRE)**[21] 256 4-9-4 **60**.... TonyCulhane 7 40
(W J Musson) *hld up: a in rr* **11/1**

5034 **10** *16* **Vogarth**[1] 505 6-8-10 **57**....(v) DeclanCannon(5) 1 —
(M C Chapman) *sn pushed along to ld: rdn and hdd over 3f out: sn wknd* **33/1**

1m 43.56s (-0.14) **Going Correction** +0.15s/f (Slow) **10** Ran SP% **118.1**
Speed ratings (Par 101): **106,105,105,104,102 101,100,97,94,78**
toteswingers: 1&2 £19.00, 1&3 £4.30, 2&3 £20.60 CSF £88.57 CT £538.45 TOTE £7.20: £2.20, £5.20, £1.70; EX 106.20 TRIFECTA Not won..
Owner Mrs F Denniff **Bred** Mrs Fiona Denniff **Trained** Hambleton, N Yorks

FOCUS
A poor handicap but competitive enough and there were five in a line across the track inside the final furlong.
Bob Stock(IRE) Official explanation: jockey said gelding never travelled

519 BET FA CUP - BETDAQ H'CAP — 6f (F)

1:45 (1:45) (Class 6) (0-65,71) 3-Y-0 **£1,774** (£523; £262) **Stalls** Low

Form RPR

210- **1** **Eight Hours**[147] 6048 3-9-1 **62**....(b) TonyHamilton 3 68
(R A Fahey) *swvd rt s: chsd ldrs: rdn over 3f out: wnt 2nd over 1f out: led ins fnl f: edgd lft: styd on u.p* **4/1**[3]

2331 **2** *½* **Maoi Chinn Tire (IRE)**[7] 425 3-9-5 **71** 6ex....(p) RossAtkinson(5) 1 76
(J S Moore) *led: edgd rt fr over 2f out: rdn over 1f out: hdd ins fnl f: styd on u.p* **9/4**[1]

104- **3** *4* **Drumpellier (IRE)**[182] 4975 3-8-10 **62**.... PaulPickard(5) 2 55
(P T Midgley) *chsd ldr: ev ch over 2f out: sn rdn: styd on same pce appr fnl f* **15/2**

-041 **4** *shd* **Sandy Toes**[3] 471 3-8-4 **51** 6ex.... AdrianMcCarthy 6 43
(J A Glover) *hmpd s: sn outpcd: styd on ins fnl f: nvr nrr* **3/1**[2]

4-20 **5** *8* **Singingintherain (IRE)**[23] 233 3-9-3 **64**.... JoeFanning 5 32
(R A Mills) *hmpd s: sn pushed along and a in rr* **9/2**

00-0 **6** *13* **Paint By Numbers**[15] 326 3-7-13 **51** oh6.... AndrewHeffernan(5) 4 —
(J A Glover) *s.i.s and hmpd s: outpcd* **28/1**

1m 18.82s (2.32) **Going Correction** +0.15s/f (Slow) **6** Ran SP% **109.2**
Speed ratings (Par 95): **90,89,84,83,73 55**
toteswingers: 1&2 £2.30, 1&3 £3.90, 2&3 £3.10 CSF £12.65 TOTE £5.70: £2.70, £1.20; EX 15.40.
Owner Aidan J Ryan **Bred** Foxlea Farm And Stud **Trained** Musley Bank, N Yorks
■ Stewards' Enquiry : Ross Atkinson three-day ban: used whip with excessive frequency (Feb 26-28)
Adrian McCarthy four-day ban: used whip with excessive frequency (Feb 26-Mar 1)

FOCUS
A rather unsatisfactory contest, decided to some degree at the start where the winner swerved violently away to his right, slamming into Singingintherain, who was almost brought down, and she in turn cannoned into Sandy Toes. Even the other pair had an independent coming together leaving the stalls, so all in all the form has to have a question mark against it.

520 BET IN RUNNING - BETDAQ CLAIMING STKS — 5f (F)

2:20 (2:20) (Class 6) 4-Y-0+ **£1,683** (£501; £250; £125) **Stalls** High

Form RPR

-442 **1** **Grudge**[4] 462 5-8-13 65....(e) FrannyNorton 7 77
(Ollie Pears) *chsd ldrs: led wl over 1f out: sn rdn and hung lft: r.o wl* **11/2**[3]

-121 **2** *2 ¾* **Total Impact**[14] 349 7-9-4 78.... RobertWinston 4 72
(C R Dore) *led 1f: w ldrs: rdn and ev ch over 1f out: nt clr run ins fnl f: styd on same pce* **10/11**[1]

-051 **3** *1 ¾* **Colorus (IRE)**[2] 492 7-8-9 73....(p) PaulPickard(5) 1 62
(W J H Ratcliffe) *chsd ldrs: rdn 1/2-way: ev ch over 1f out: no ex fnl f* **15/8**[2]

-004 **4** *1 ½* **First Order**[4] 462 9-9-0 62....(v) AnnStokell(5) 3 62
(Miss A Stokell) *w ldrs: led over 3f out: rdn and hdd wl over 1f out: wknd fnl f* **40/1**

0-00 **5** *7* **Proud Linus (USA)**[16] 318 5-9-2 55.... DavidNolan 2 33
(D Carroll) *prom and sn pushed along: led 4f out: hdd 3f out: rdn and hung lft 1/2-way: sn wknd* **40/1**

60.83 secs (1.13) **Going Correction** +0.275s/f (Slow) **5** Ran SP% **107.4**
Speed ratings (Par 101): **101,96,93,91,80**
CSF £10.57 TOTE £3.90: £2.00, £1.20; EX 11.50.Grudge was claimed by C. R. Dore for £7000.
Owner K C West **Bred** D H Brailsford **Trained** Norton, N Yorks

FOCUS
A routine Fibresand claimer in which the quintet raced almost in a line until halfway.

521 BOOK YOUR TICKETS ONLINE AT SOUTHWELL-RACECOURSE.CO.UK (S) STKS — 1m 4f (F)

2:55 (2:55) (Class 6) 4-Y-0+ **£1,774** (£523; £262) **Stalls** Low

Form RPR

3-41 **1** **My Mate Mal**[10] 377 6-9-4 63.... BarryMcHugh(3) 3 68
(B Ellison) *mde all: rdn clr over 3f out: styd on u.p* **9/4**[1]

-302 **2** *3* **Jazrawy**[10] 377 8-8-10 51.... DeclanCannon(5) 1 59
(A J McCabe) *chsd wnr over 3f: remained handy tl outpcd over 3f out: rallied to go 2nd again and hung lft over 1f out: styd on: eased whn btn towards fin* **8/1**[2]

60-1 **3** *5* **Friends Hope**[15] 327 9-9-2 67....(b) TonyCulhane 6 51
(R Curtis) *s.i.s: hld up: hdwy 1/2-way: rdn to chse wnr over 2f out tl wknd over 1f out* **9/4**[1]

0-56 **4** *2 ¼* **Anduril**[6] 199 9-9-1 44.... DavidNolan 4 47
(D Carroll) *prom: chsd wnr over 4f out tl rdn and wknd over 2f out* **22/1**[3]

600/ **5** *45* **High Treason (USA)**[854] 6158 8-9-1 77.... PhillipMakin 2 —
(John C McConnell, Ire) *hld up: rdn 1/2-way: wknd over 4f out: eased fnl 3f: t.o* **9/4**[1]

/0-0 **6** *3 ¼* **Itcanbedone Again (IRE)**[14] 353 11-9-1 45.... FergusSweeney 5 —
(J W Unett) *prom: chsd wnr over 8f out tl rdn over 4f out: wknd over 3f out: sn eased: t.o* **100/1**

2m 43.56s (2.56) **Going Correction** +0.15s/f (Slow) **6** Ran SP% **108.8**
Speed ratings (Par 101): **97,95,91,90,60 58**
CSF £20.26 TOTE £3.00: £2.10, £3.90; EX 12.20.There was no bid for the winner.
Owner Koo's Racing Club **Bred** Mrs A M Mallinson **Trained** Norton, N Yorks

FOCUS
A moderate seller, but at least the winner made sure it was run at an honest pace.

522 ARENA LEISURE PLC H'CAP — 1m (F)

3:30 (3:30) (Class 4) (0-85,79) 3-Y-0 **£4,209** (£1,252) **Stalls** Low

Form RPR

1- **1** **Doctor Zhivago**[69] 7638 3-9-6 **79**.... JoeFanning 1 87+
(M Johnston) *mde all: shkn up over 2f out: sn clr: eased towards fin* **2/7**[1]

0-31 **2** *1 ¼* **Purple Gallery (IRE)**[13] 356 3-9-2 **75**....(p) HayleyTurner 2 73
(J S Moore) *chsd wnr: cl enough 3f out: sn rdn: outpcd 2f out: styd on but flattered by proximity to wnr* **11/4**[2]

1m 47.16s (3.46) **Going Correction** +0.15s/f (Slow) **2** Ran SP% **104.4**
Speed ratings (Par 99): **88,86**
TOTE £1.40.
Owner Sheikh Hamdan Bin Mohammed Al Maktoum **Bred** Meon Valley Stud **Trained** Middleham Moor, N Yorks

FOCUS
Yet another AW match, the fourth in four weeks, in which both colts were making their handicap debuts.

523 SOUTHWELL-RACECOURSE.CO.UK MAIDEN STKS — 7f (F)

4:05 (4:05) (Class 5) 3-Y-0+ **£2,456** (£725; £362) **Stalls** Low

Form RPR

1 **Rubi Dia** 3-8-10 0.... JoeFanning 2 66+
(M Johnston) *led at stdy pce tl hdd over 4f out: remained handy: rallied to ld ins fnl f: hung rt: r.o* **7/4**[1]

0-32 **2** *nk* **Turning Circle**[8] 399 4-9-6 0.... JohnCavanagh(7) 3 68
(M Brittain) *trckd ldrs: plld hrd: led over 4f out: rdn over 1f out: hdd ins fnl f: carried rt: r.o* **15/8**[2]

3 *10* **Fillibeg (IRE)** 3-8-4 0 ow2.... BarryMcHugh(3) 4 40+
(R A Fahey) *sn chsng ldrs: rdn and hung rt over 2f out: hung lft and wknd over 1f out* **4/1**[3]

0-02 **4** *6* **Almatlaie (USA)**[22] 249 4-9-8 51.... FergusSweeney 1 20
(J W Unett) *hld up: rdn over 2f out: sn wknd* **8/1**

00- **5** *13* **Sam Jicaro**[194] 4557 3-8-5 0.... RossAtkinson(5) 5 —
(Mrs L Williamson) *s.i.s: hld up: plld hrd: rdn: hung rt and lost tch 1/2-way* **40/1**

1m 30.59s (0.29) **Going Correction** +0.15s/f (Slow)
WFA 3 from 4yo 17lb **5** Ran SP% **104.7**
Speed ratings (Par 103): **104,103,92,85,70**
CSF £4.76 TOTE £2.30: £1.40, £1.40; EX 4.40.
Owner C G Maybury **Bred** Castlemartin Stud And Skymarc Farm **Trained** Middleham Moor, N Yorks

FOCUS
A modest maiden in which the first two pulled a long way clear of the rest.
Rubi Dia ◆ Official explanation: jockey said colt hung right

524 PLAY GOLF BEFORE RACING AT SOUTHWELL H'CAP — 7f (F)

4:40 (4:41) (Class 5) (0-70,70) 3-Y-0 **£2,456** (£725; £362) **Stalls** Low

Form RPR

346- **1** **Demonstrative (USA)**[104] 7168 3-9-4 **70**.... JoeFanning 2 85+
(M Johnston) *dwlt: hdwy over 4f out: chsd ldr 1/2-way: led 2f out: rdn clr fnl f: eased nr fin* **11/4**[1]

5321 **2** *4* **Premium Charge**[5] 455 3-8-1 **60** 6ex ow1.... RyanClark(7) 1 62
(C A Dwyer) *led: rdn and hdd 2f out: edgd lft and styd on same pce fnl f* **7/1**

6-13 **3** *2 ¼* **Novay Essjay (IRE)**[13] 357 3-9-4 **70**.... AndrewMullen 3 66
(D Nicholls) *chsd ldrs: rdn over 2f out: sn outpcd* **11/4**[1]

-264 **4** *4 ½* **Gold Party**[23] 240 3-8-12 **64**....(t) RobertWinston 5 51
(K McAuliffe) *chsd ldrs: pushed along 1/2-way: swtchd lft and shkn up 2f out: nt run on* **5/1**[3]

-430 **5** *nk* **Tealing**[16] 310 3-8-13 **65**.... PhillipMakin 6 49
(R C Guest) *sn outpcd: mod late prog* **6/1**

-321 **6** *3* **Ant Music (IRE)**[8] 399 3-8-11 **68** 6ex....(b) RossAtkinson(5) 4 45
(J S Moore) *chsd ldr tl rdn and hung rt 1/2-way: wknd 2f out* **9/2**[2]

1m 29.61s (-0.69) **Going Correction** +0.15s/f (Slow) **6** Ran SP% **115.0**
Speed ratings (Par 97): **109,104,101,96,96 92**
toteswingers: 1&2 £4.90, 1&3 £3.10, 2&3 £2.70 CSF £22.99 TOTE £4.30: £1.30, £2.80; EX 19.00 Place 6: £30.52 Place 5: £5.18.
Owner Sheikh Hamdan Bin Mohammed Al Maktoum **Bred** Gainsborough Farm Llc **Trained** Middleham Moor, N Yorks

FOCUS
An ordinary handicap, but the winning time was almost a second quicker than the maiden and the winner looks a nice sort.
T/Plt: £14.00 to a £1 stake. Pool: £52,166.33. 2,701.24 winning tickets. T/Qpdt: £3.50 to a £1 stake. Pool: £3,748.16. 774.23 winning tickets. CR

462 WOLVERHAMPTON (A.W) (L-H)

Friday, February 12

OFFICIAL GOING: Standard

Wind: Light against Weather: Fine

525 FREE HORSE RACING TIPS @ BIGTIPS.CO.UK H'CAP 5f 20y(P)

5:15 (5:15) (Class 6) (0-60,60) 4-Y-0+ £2,047 (£453; £453) Stalls Low

Form RPR

-212 1 **Monte Major (IRE)**[3] 472 9-8-11 60 (v) SeanPalmer(7) 5 68
(D Shaw) *towards rr: hdwy wl over 1f out: led wl ins fnl f: r.o* 7/2[1]

-330 2 1 1/4 **Bluebok**[14] 351 9-8-13 55 (bt) LukeMorris 2 59
(J M Bradley) *hld up in tch: rdn jst over 1f out: ev ch wl ins fnl f: nt qckn* 12/1

5-56 2 dht **Monsieur Reynard**[11] 369 5-8-13 55 DavidProbert 4 59
(J M Bradley) *hld up in tch: pushed along wl over 1f out: kpt on towards fin* 4/1[2]

-000 4 3/4 **Triskaidekaphobia**[21] 271 7-8-7 49 (t) PaulFitzsimons 1 50
(Miss J R Tooth) *sn led: rdn over 1f out: hdd wl ins fnl f: no ex* 33/1

26-0 5 3/4 **Metal Guru**[22] 243 6-9-2 58 (p) TomQueally 3 56
(R Hollinshead) *led early: a.p: rdn over 1f out: nt qckn ins fnl f* 10/1

5-10 6 1/2 **Radiator Rooney (IRE)**[14] 351 7-9-4 60 (v) StephenCraine 10 56
(Patrick Morris) *s.i.s: sn swtchd lft: hld up in rr: swtchd lft over 1f out: kpt on ins fnl f: nt rch ldrs* 8/1

4-34 7 3/4 **Best One**[31] 132 6-8-13 55 (b) KevinGhunowa 8 49
(R A Harris) *towards rr: rdn and effrt 1f out: nvr trbld ldrs* 14/1

640- 8 shd **Pinball (IRE)**[53] 7834 4-8-11 53 (v) TomEaves 13 46
(Mrs L Williamson) *s.i.s: rdn fnl f: nvr nrr* 16/1

06-0 9 1 1/4 **Almaty Express**[4] 462 8-9-3 59 (b) GrahamGibbons 6 48
(J R Weymes) *prom: chsd ldr over 3f out tl rdn wl over 1f out: wknd ins fnl firlong* 9/1

-010 10 1 3/4 **Head To Head (IRE)**[14] 344 6-8-11 53 (bt) JimmyQuinn 9 35
(A D Brown) *a towards rr* 16/1

0-03 11 2 **Agnes Love**[23] 242 4-9-0 59 AndreaAtzeni(3) 7 34
(J Akehurst) *hld up in tch: pushed along over 2f out: wknd wl over 1f out* 13/2[3]

62.26 secs (-0.04) **Going Correction** +0.025s/f (Slow) 11 Ran SP% 114.8
Speed ratings (Par 101): **101,99,99,97,96 95,94,94,92,89 86**
PL: Bluebok £3.60, Monsieur Reynard £1.70 EX: Monte Major/Bluebok £20.60, MM/MR £9.80, CSF: MM/B £22.54, MM/MR £8.33 TRI: MM/B/MR £87.17, MM/MR/B £74.54 toteswingers: 1&Bluebok £6.90, 1&Monsieur Reynard £3.30, B&MR £9.20 TOTE £3.70: £1.60.
Owner Derek Shaw **Bred** B Kennedy **Trained** Sproxton, Leics

FOCUS
As if often the case over this C&D, the draw played a big part, with the first five berthed in the lowest five stalls. They went quick enough up front and the winner stepped up marginally on recent form.

526 BET FA CUP - BETDAQ H'CAP 1m 4f 50y(P)

5:45 (5:45) (Class 4) (0-85,82) 4-Y-0+ £4,533 (£1,348; £674; £336) Stalls Low

Form RPR

-332 1 **Kames Park (IRE)**[7] 430 8-8-7 68 oh5 JimmyQuinn 1 76
(R C Guest) *s.i.s: hld up in rr: hdwy 2f out: swtchd lft wl over 1f out: led wl ins fnl f: rdn out* 7/2[3]

10-2 2 nk **Admirable Duque (IRE)**[9] 395 4-8-2 71 (p) BillyCray(5) 2 79
(D J S Ffrench Davis) *hld up: pushed along over 3f out: hdwy over 2f out: rdn to ld ins fnl f: sn hdd: kpt on* 11/4[1]

304- 3 1 1/4 **Aureate**[106] 7137 6-8-13 74 DavidProbert 4 80
(B Forsey) *chsd ldr: led 3f out: rdn over 1f out: hdd ins fnl f: nt qckn* 6/1

0/1- 4 2 1/4 **Transvestite (IRE)**[85] 330 8-8-7 75 KierenFox(7) 6 77
(Miss Tor Sturgis) *hld up: pushed along and sltly outpcd over 2f out: styd on ins fnl f* 15/2

31-0 5 3 1/2 **Rocky's Pride (IRE)**[23] 239 4-8-12 76 NeilCallan 5 73
(A B Haynes) *t.k.h: stdy prog on ins 4f out: rdn over 1f out: wknd fnl f* 13/2

12-3 6 2 1/2 **Profit's Reality (IRE)**[17] 300 8-9-7 82 GeorgeBaker 3 75
(M J Attwater) *led: hdd 3f out: wkng whn hmpd wl over 1f out* 10/3[2]

2m 41.5s (0.40) **Going Correction** +0.025s/f (Slow)
WFA 4 from 6yo+ 3lb 6 Ran SP% 111.4
Speed ratings (Par 105): **99,98,97,96,94 92**
toteswingers: 1&2 £2.40, 1&3 £4.10, 2&3 £3.70 CSF £13.28 TOTE £4.20: £2.70, £1.40; EX 14.90.
Owner Future Racing (Notts) Limited **Bred** Pat Beirne **Trained** Stainforth, S Yorks
■ Stewards' Enquiry : Jimmy Quinn two-day ban: careless riding (Feb 26-27)

FOCUS
There was a fair pace on here.

527 NEW VAUXHALL ASTRA MEDIAN AUCTION MAIDEN STKS 5f 216y(P)

6:15 (6:15) (Class 6) 3-5-Y-O £1,774 (£523; £262) Stalls Low

Form RPR

1 **Slikback Jack (IRE)** 3-8-12 0 FrederikTylicki 10 70+
(J A Glover) *bhd: pushed along 3f out: c wd st: rdn and hdwy over 1f out: sn edgd lft: r.o to ld towards fin* 14/1

364- 2 3/4 **Flaxen Lake**[63] 7708 3-8-12 68 TomQueally 1 68
(R Hollinshead) *led after 1f: rdn and hdd towards fin* 11/8[1]

3 1/2 **Lockantanks** 3-8-12 0 SamHitchcott 2 66
(M R Channon) *a.p: chal over 1f out: sn rdn: nt qckn wl ins fnl f* 13/2[2]

4 2 **Ryan Style (IRE)** 4-9-13 0 TomEaves 4 64
(Mrs L Williamson) *s.i.s: hld up and bhd: hdwy on ins 2f out: rdn and one pce fnl f* 22/1

5 hd **Golden Ratio (IRE)** 3-8-7 0 LukeMorris 9 54+
(J R Gask) *sn outpcd in rr: hdwy wl over 1f out: rdn and edgd lft jst ins fnl f: one pce* 15/2

6 3 1/2 **Starlight Muse (IRE)** 3-8-7 0 GrahamGibbons 7 43
(E S McMahon) *hld up and bhd: pushed along over 2f out: hdwy wl over 1f out: wknd ins fnl f* 8/1

4- 7 1 **Little Weed (IRE)**[104] 7190 3-8-12 0 DavidProbert 6 45
(B Palling) *led 1f: w ldr tl wknd wl over 1f out* 16/1

0- 8 1/2 **French Wind**[56] 7800 3-8-9 0 AndreaAtzeni(3) 8 43
(Pat Eddery) *prom tl rdn and wknd wl over 1f out* 7/1[3]

5 9 6 **Gemma's Delight (IRE)**[18] 288 3-8-7 55 RPCleary 5 19
(Noel Lawlor, Ire) *t.k.h: prom: rdn over 2f out: wknd wl over 1f out* 10/1

1m 15.5s (0.50) **Going Correction** +0.025s/f (Slow)
WFA 3 from 4yo 15lb 9 Ran SP% 116.8
Speed ratings (Par 101): **97,96,95,92,92 87,86,85,77**
toteswingers: 1&2 £8.70, 1&3 £15.90, 2&3 £1.80 CSF £34.13 TOTE £21.30: £4.00, £1.10, £1.90; EX 53.20.
Owner Brian Morton **Bred** Kilfrush Stud **Trained** Babworth, Notts

FOCUS
A modest maiden run at an ordinary early gallop.

528 BET ASIAN H'CAPS - BETDAQ HANDICAP 5f 216y(P)

6:45 (6:45) (Class 2) (0-100,98) 4-Y-£10,723 (£3,209; £1,604; £802; £399) Stalls Low

Form RPR

000- 1 **Flipando (IRE)**[117] 6876 9-8-7 87 GrahamGibbons 2 108+
(T D Barron) *s.i.s: hld up: hdwy on ins over 2f out: led ins fnl f: sn clr: easily* 25/1

20-1 2 5 **Bajan Tryst (USA)**[14] 350 4-8-10 90 NeilCallan 4 96
(K A Ryan) *led: rdn and hdd ins fnl f: sn btn* 5/1[3]

3-30 3 3/4 **Orpsie Boy (IRE)**[19] 286 7-8-8 88 StevieDonohoe 3 92
(N P Littmoden) *bhd: pushed along over 2f out: rdn over 1f out: r.o ins fnl f: tk 3rd towards fin* 9/2[2]

0405 4 1/2 **Ebraam (USA)**[6] 446 7-8-13 98 DeclanCannon(5) 1 100
(S Curran) *a.p: wnt 2nd briefly over 2f out: sn rdn one pce* 12/1

4-11 5 1 1/4 **Tourist**[17] 299 5-8-12 92 JimmyQuinn 6 91
(D Shaw) *s.i.s: sn hld up in mid-div: rdn wl over 1f out: no hdwy* 10/3[1]

406- 6 3/4 **Thebes**[101] 7227 5-8-9 89 GregFairley 5 85
(M Johnston) *chsd ldr tl wl over 1f out: sn rdn and wknd* 9/2[2]

03-5 7 2 3/4 **Shifting Star (IRE)**[29] 177 5-8-12 92 (t) ShaneKelly 8 80
(W R Swinburn) *hld up and bhd: rdn over 2f out: sn struggling* 9/1

-026 8 nk **Flowing Cape (IRE)**[17] 299 5-8-6 91 (tp) PaulPickard(5) 7 78
(R Hollinshead) *sn outpcd* 8/1

-620 9 3 1/2 **Imprimis Tagula (IRE)**[13] 358 6-8-11 98 (v) NatashaEaton(7) 9 75
(A Bailey) *hld up in tch: wknd over 2f out* 16/1

1m 12.91s (-2.09) **Going Correction** +0.025s/f (Slow) 9 Ran SP% 114.6
Speed ratings (Par 109): **114,107,106,105,104 103,99,98,94**
toteswingers: 1&2 £21.30, 1&3 £23.60, 2&3 £4.40 CSF £144.36 CT £679.08 TOTE £29.00: £7.80, £1.60, £2.10; EX 249.80.
Owner Mrs J Hazell **Bred** Denis McDonnell **Trained** Maunby, N Yorks

FOCUS
A good-quality sprint handicap run at a true gallop and won incredibly easily. The winner clocked a time just 0.30sec outside the track record.

NOTEBOOK
Flipando(IRE), who last ran over this trip back in 2004 and for whom this very much looked like a pipe-opener, comes from a stable in good form and had dropped to a good mark. He showed he can be a player in some decent sprints, granted pace, with this win off 87. Well drawn in stall two, the strong gallop allowed him to travel well, and once they turned into the straight he was always going to see the trip out better than anything else. Whether he stays at this distance or reverts to a mile now remains to be seen, but he's clearly more versatile than was once thought. (tchd 28-1)
Bajan Tryst(USA) likes to lead and, in a bid to follow up his recent C&D success, he took them along a real good clip. He set the race up nicely for the winner, but the fact that he held on to second suggests he didn't go much too fast. (op 11-4)
Orpsie Boy(IRE), who could be excused his run at Kempton last time as he was badly hampered, had a good draw but he was being shoved along rounding the turn into the straight. He stayed on well to take third and posted a sound effort, but his losing run now stretches back 25 starts. (op 5-1 tchd 4-1)
Ebraam(USA), already due to be dropped 3lb in the handicap, had the best draw, tracked the leader for much of the way and had no obvious excuse. (op 11-1)
Tourist wasn't up to the task of landing the hat-trick off a 6lb higher mark despite getting the good gallop he needs. (op 9-2)
Thebes won on his reappearance last season, but having shown up prominently to the turn in, he weakened here, and perhaps the outing was needed. (op 6-1 tchd 7-1)
Flowing Cape(IRE) Official explanation: jockey said gelding suffered interference at start

529 NEW VAUXHALL ASTRA H'CAP 1m 5f 194y(P)

7:15 (7:16) (Class 5) (0-70,68) 4-Y-0+ £2,729 (£806; £403) Stalls Low

Form RPR

22-1 1 **Augustus John (IRE)**[18] 293 7-10-0 68 TomEaves 4 76
(R Brotherton) *hld up in mid-div: hrd rdn over 2f out: hdwy over 1f out: styd on u.p to ld nr fin* 5/1[3]

6-45 2 shd **Resplendent Ace (IRE)**[15] 323 6-10-0 68 J-PGuillambert 6 76
(P Howling) *hld up in rr: hdwy wl over 1f out: rdn to ld ins fnl f: hdd nr fin* 16/1

30-4 3 1 3/4 **Weybridge Light**[18] 293 5-9-7 61 FergusSweeney 8 66
(M R Bosley) *hld up in tch: rdn to chse ldr wl over 2f tl wl over 1f out: styd on ins fnl f* 13/2

000- 4 2 1/4 **Motarjm (USA)**[78] 7539 6-9-11 65 (t) SaleemGolam 10 67
(J Pearce) *chsd ldr: led 4f out: rdn over 1f out: hdd ins fnl f: one pce* 8/1

0-55 5 1 **Estate**[18] 293 8-9-8 65 HaddenFrost(3) 1 66
(D E Pipe) *hld up in tch: rdn and wnt 2nd wl over 1f out: wknd ins fnl f* 8/1

3-12 6 shd **Leyte Gulf (USA)**[18] 293 7-9-13 67 DaneO'Neill 9 68
(C C Bealby) *s.i.s: sn hld up in mid-div: rdn and hdwy wl over 1f out: wknd ins fnl f* 7/2[2]

0-50 7 1/2 **Boogie Dancer**[28] 184 6-9-0 54 TomQueally 5 54
(H S Howe) *hld up towards rr: rdn wl over 1f out: sn hung lft: n.d* 40/1

21-3 8 2 **Starburst**[32] 121 5-9-11 65 GeorgeBaker 2 63
(A M Balding) *hld up towards rr: short-lived effrt on ins over 1f out* 9/4[1]

46-0 9 18 **Wabbraan (USA)**[32] 121 5-8-9 54 AmyBaker(5) 7 26
(M Hill) *led: hdd 4f out: wknd over 2f out: eased whn no ch jst over 1f out* 25/1

3m 3.91s (-2.09) **Going Correction** +0.025s/f (Slow) 9 Ran SP% 117.4
Speed ratings (Par 103): **106,105,104,103,103 103,102,101,91**
toteswingers: 1&2 £6.70, 1&3 £6.60, 2&3 £17.20 CSF £81.46 CT £529.15 TOTE £4.70: £1.50, £3.20, £2.30; EX 63.40.
Owner Arthur Clayton **Bred** Rizerie Syndicate **Trained** Elmley Castle, Worcs
■ Stewards' Enquiry : Tom Eaves two-day ban: used whip with excessive frequency (Feb 26 - 27)

FOCUS
A modest staying contest.

530 THE BLACK COUNTRY'S ONLY RACECOURSE H'CAP 7f 32y(P)

7:45 (7:49) (Class 7) (0-50,50) 4-Y-0+ £1,364 (£403; £201) Stalls High

Form RPR

000- 1 **Dhhamaan (IRE)**[60] 7754 5-9-3 50 (b) HayleyTurner 5 57
(Mrs R A Carr) *mde all: hrd rdn fnl f: all out* 14/1

-025 2 hd **Imperial Skylight**[9] 388 4-9-3 50 (v) SamHitchcott 4 56
(M R Channon) *hld up in tch: wnt 2nd 2f out: sn rdn: ev ch wl ins fnl f: r.o* 11/2[3]

0-42 3 hd **Ride A White Swan**[30] 145 5-9-1 48 NeilCallan 10 53
(D Shaw) *s.i.s: hld up in rr: hdwy on ins wl over 1f out: kpt on ins fnl f* 5/1[2]

-003 4 2 3/4 **Mojeerr**[14] 347 4-9-3 50 (v) DavidProbert 11 48
(A J McCabe) *hld up towards rr: rdn over 2f out: styd on ins fnl f: nrst fin* 14/1

3630 **5** *nk* **Josiah Bartlett (IRE)**[1] 498 4-9-0 **47**........................ StevieDonohoe 12 44
(Ian Williams) *hld up in rr: nt clr run briefly wl over 1f out: rdn and r.o ins fnl f: nvr nrr* **8/1**

0-63 **6** *nse* **Berrymead**[21] 264 5-8-10 **48**.. AnnStokell(5) 2 45
(Miss A Stokell) *n.m.r and lost pl sn after s: bhd tl hdwy on ins over 1f out: nvr trbld ldrs* **20/1**

- **7** *1* **Leo's Lucky Angel (IRE)**[497] 6454 5-9-3 **50**...................... ShaneKelly 7 44
(Daniel Mark Loughnane, Ire) *hld up in mid-div: prog on outside 2f out: wknd ins fnl f* **7/2**[1]

/00- **8** *¾* **Blue Cross Boy (USA)**[78] 7543 5-9-2 **49**..........................(b) RPCleary 9 41
(Adrian McGuinness, Ire) *hld up in mid-div: no hdwy fnl 2f* **10/1**

00-0 **9** *2 ¾* **Montmartre (USA)**[9] 388 4-9-3 **50**..........................(b) FergusSweeney 8 35
(David Pinder) *sn chsng ldr: rdn and lost 2nd over 2f out: wknd wl over 1f out* **20/1**

0230 **10** *¾* **All You Need (IRE)**[21] 264 6-8-10 **50**........................(v) DavidKenny(7) 6 33
(R Hollinshead) *prom tl wknd 1f out* **16/1**

56/0 **11** *½* **Mister Beano (IRE)**[17] 296 5-8-12 **50**..............(v) AndrewHeffernan(5) 1 32
(R J Price) *hld up in mid-div: pushed along over 2f out: wknd wl over 1f out* **33/1**

1m 30.11s (0.51) **Going Correction** +0.025s/f (Slow) 11 Ran SP% **106.2**
Speed ratings (Par 97): **98,97,97,94,94 94,92,92,88,88 87**
toteswingers: 1&2 £15.70, 1&3 £10.40, 2&3 £4.40 CSF £70.89 CT £335.96 TOTE £15.90: £3.40, £2.60, £1.70; EX 96.40.
Owner S B Clark **Bred** D Veitch And Musagd Abo Salim **Trained** Huby, N Yorks
■ Neo's Mate was withdrawn with a vet's certificate (15/2, deduct 10p in the £ under R4).

FOCUS
A moderate affair in which the exposed placed horses set a moderate standard.

531 BETDAQ ON 0870 178 1221 H'CAP (DIV I) 5f 216y(P)
8:15 (8:16) (Class 6) (0-60,60) 4-Y-O+ £1,706 (£503; £252) Stalls Low

Form RPR

0-50 **1** **White Shift (IRE)**[16] 312 4-8-11 **60**.................................. KierenFox(7) 5 69
(P Howling) *hld up in mid-div: hdwy 2f out: swtchd lft and rdn to ld wl ins fnl f: r.o* **11/1**

3-40 **2** *1* **Divertimenti (IRE)**[8] 402 6-8-5 **52**....................(b) AndrewHeffernan(5) 3 58
(S R Bowring) *led: edgd rt and rdn over 1f out: hdd wl ins fnl f* **11/1**

1-43 **3** *2 ¼* **Only A Game (IRE)**[14] 351 5-9-1 **57**............................(tp) DaneO'Neill 9 56
(I W McInnes) *hld up in rr: swtchd rt and hdwy over 1f out: rdn and kpt on one pce ins fnl f* **3/1**[2]

650- **4** *¾* **Avoncreek**[142] 6216 6-8-1 **46** oh1................................ KellyHarrison(3) 2 43
(B P J Baugh) *a.p: rdn and ev ch over 1f out: wknd wl ins fnl f* **25/1**

-311 **5** *½* **Albero Di Giuda (IRE)**[11] 369 5-9-0 **59** 6ex............(t) AndreaAtzeni(3) 4 55
(F Sheridan) *t.k.h: hdwy 4f out: rdn and one pce fnl 2f* **2/1**[1]

-603 **6** *3 ½* **Trip Switch**[2] 486 4-8-11 **58**................................. DeclanCannon(5) 8 43
(G Prodromou) *towards rr: rdn over 2f out: c wd st: nvr nr ldrs* **7/1**[3]

40-0 **7** *1 ¾* **Smirfys Systems**[16] 312 11-9-4 **60**............................ StevieDonohoe 7 40
(Mrs D J Sanderson) *prom tl wknd over 1f out* **8/1**

050- **8** *nk* **Myriola**[52] 7839 5-8-4 **46** oh1.. HayleyTurner 1 25
(D Shaw) *hld up in rr: prog on ins over 2f out: wknd over 1f out* **33/1**

5-0 **9** *9* **Acrosstheuniverse (USA)**[41] 14 4-8-12 **54**..................(t) NeilCallan 6 18
(J R Gask) *prom tl rdn and wknd 3f out* **8/1**

000- **10** *4* **Iron Max (IRE)**[62] 7727 4-8-4 **46** oh1.........................(p) DavidProbert 10 —
(Mrs L Williamson) *bhd fnl 3f* **66/1**

1m 15.1s (0.10) **Going Correction** +0.025s/f (Slow) 10 Ran SP% **118.0**
Speed ratings (Par 101): **100,98,95,94,94 89,87,86,74,69**
toteswingers: 1&2 £9.70, 1&3 £6.30, 2&3 £9.80 CSF £124.12 CT £468.42 TOTE £14.10: £3.40, £3.30, £1.20; EX 50.30.
Owner Paul Terry **Bred** Grange Stud **Trained** Newmarket, Suffolk

FOCUS
Moderate handicap run at an ordinary gallop.

532 BETDAQ ON 0870 178 1221 H'CAP (DIV II) 5f 216y(P)
8:45 (8:48) (Class 6) (0-60,60) 4-Y-O+ £1,706 (£503; £252) Stalls Low

Form RPR

00-6 **1** **Doctor Hilary**[14] 351 8-9-2 **58**.......................................(v) RobertHavlin 3 67
(A B Haynes) *a.p: rdn wl over 1f out: led wl ins fnl f: r.o* **7/1**

50-3 **2** *½* **Romantic Queen**[9] 391 4-9-2 **58**................................(t) TonyCulhane 1 65
(George Baker) *s.i.s: pushed along and hdwy over 2f out: led ins fnl f: sn rdn and hdd: kpt on* **7/2**[2]

0-21 **3** *2 ½* **Miss Firefly**[11] 368 5-9-4 **60** 6ex.................................(p) JimmyQuinn 7 60
(R J Hodges) *hld up in mid-div: hdwy on ins wl over 1f out: rdn and one pce ins fnl f* **3/1**[1]

643 **4** *nk* **Muktasb (USA)**[8] 404 9-8-5 **54**...............................(v) SeanPalmer(7) 10 53
(D Shaw) *s.i.s: hdwy over 3f out: rdn 2f out: one pce whn edgd lft ins fnl f* **7/2**[2]

000- **5** *2 ½* **Miacarla**[106] 7136 7-7-13 **46** oh1.................................. DeclanCannon(5) 5 37
(H A McWilliams) *led: rdn over 1f out: hdd & wknd ins fnl f* **50/1**

00-0 **6** *1 ½* **Avonlini**[21] 270 4-8-1 **46** oh1.. KellyHarrison(3) 2 33
(B P J Baugh) *hld up in mid-div: no hdwy fnl 2f* **33/1**

4-53 **7** *½* **Charlie Delta**[2] 481 7-9-4 **60**..(b) LiamJones 4 45
(R A Harris) *prom: pushed along over 2f out: wknd wl over 1f out* **5/1**[3]

000- **8** *1 ¼* **Transcentral**[171] 5326 4-8-4 **46** oh1.................................. DavidProbert 6 27
(T Wall) *s.i.s: rdn over 2f out: a in rr* **33/1**

00-0 **9** *8* **Mandhooma**[41] 8 4-8-12 **54**... LukeMorris 9 11
(P W Hiatt) *prom tl rdn and wknd 2f out* **14/1**

000- **10** *47* **Northern Empire (IRE)**[43] 7890 7-8-11 **53**......................(p) NeilCallan 8 —
(F Jordan) *mid-div: dropped in rr 3f out: sn t.o* **16/1**

1m 15.01s (0.01) **Going Correction** +0.025s/f (Slow) 10 Ran SP% **119.0**
Speed ratings (Par 101): **100,99,96,95,92 90,89,87,77,14**
toteswingers: 1&2 £7.60, 1&3 £7.20, 2&3 £4.10 CSF £32.07 CT £92.66 TOTE £10.10: £2.00, £1.80, £1.40; EX 43.90 Place 6: £93.56 Place 5: £52.41.
Owner double-r-racing.com **Bred** The Lavington Stud **Trained** Limpley Stoke, Bath
■ Stewards' Enquiry : Robert Havlin caution: used whip with excessive frequency

FOCUS
Very marginally the quicker of the two divisions.
T/Plt: £88.90 to a £1 stake. Pool: £89,186.70. 732.05 winning tickets. T/Qpdt: £36.60 to a £1 stake. Pool: £11,213.00. 226.40 winning tickets. KH

[484] LINGFIELD (L-H)
Saturday, February 13

OFFICIAL GOING: Standard
Wind: fresh, against Weather: overcast, cold

533 MARRIOTT PLAY & STAY MAIDEN STKS 1m (P)
1:25 (1:28) (Class 5) 3-Y-O £2,456 (£725; £362) Stalls High

Form RPR

1 **Dream On Buddy (IRE)** 3-8-12 0............................ RobertWinston 12 64+
(B W Hills) *w'like: scope: t.k.h: hld up in tch: hdwy to press ldrs over 2f out: led and rn green over 1f out: kpt on wl fnl f* **7/4**[1]

0-2 **2** *½* **Sunley Spinalonga**[16] 321 3-8-7 0........................... DeclanCannon(5) 6 63+
(D R C Elsworth) *leggy: s.i.s: hld up towards rr: hdwy on outer jst over 2f out: styd on wl u.p fnl f: wnt 2nd fnl 100yds: nvr quite getting to wnr* **9/2**[2]

3 *½* **Lingfield Bound (IRE)** 3-9-3 0.................................... SteveDrowne 10 67
(J R Best) *athletic: lw: hld up in tch on outer: hdwy 3f out: rdn to chse ldrs ent fnl 2f: chsd wnr ins fnl f tl fnl 100yds: kpt on same pce towards fin* **12/1**

0- **4** *¾* **Mejd (IRE)**[120] 6810 3-9-3 0.. ChrisCatlin 8 65
(M R Channon) *t.k.h: hld up towards rr: hdwy ent fnl 2f: chsd ldrs and swtchd lft 1f out: kpt on same pce fnl f* **11/1**

5 *2* **Sheila's Bond** 3-8-12 0... LukeMorris 1 56
(J S Moore) *leggy: s.i.s: sn rcvrd and in tch: rdn and unable qck ent fnl 2f: styd on same pce after* **33/1**

6 *nk* **My Nan Nell (IRE)** 3-8-12 0.. JackMitchell 5 58+
(B J McMath) *leggy: v s.i.s and sn rdn along: in tch in rr after 2f: rdn jst over 2f out: styd on wl fnl f: nvr trbld ldrs* **40/1**

0 **7** *½* **Coxwain (IRE)**[16] 321 3-9-3 0.. JoeFanning 3 59
(M Johnston) *w'like: broke wl: led: rdn and hdd over 1f out: wknd ins fnl f* **9/2**[2]

8 *2 ½* **Broughtons Swinger** 3-8-12 0.................................... TonyCulhane 11 49
(W J Musson) *leggy: in tch in midfield tl dropped in rr over 4f out: kpt on same pce fnl 2f* **33/1**

9 *2 ¼* **Egorr Redfeer** 3-9-3 0.. DaneO'Neill 4 49+
(D R C Elsworth) *lengthy: v.s.a: rn green and detached last tl clsd and in tch over 4f out: kpt on same pce: nvr trbld ldrs* **8/1**[3]

0- **10** *½* **Whitley Bay (USA)**[92] 7376 3-9-0 0.............................. MarcHalford(3) 7 48
(J R Best) *w'like: chsd ldrs tl lost pl u.p over 2f out: n.d fnl 2f* **100/1**

- **11** *5* **Highland Cadett** 3-9-1 0 ow1.................................... JamesMillman(3) 2 38
(B R Millman) *w'like: taken down early: s.i.s: sn in tch in midfield on inner: pushed along 5f out: lost pl over 2f out: wl bhd fnl 2f* **22/1**

0-5 **12** *shd* **Miss Polly Plum**[30] 159 3-8-12 0.................................... JerryO'Dwyer 9 31
(C A Dwyer) *t.k.h: chsd ldr tl ent fnl 2f: sn wknd* **66/1**

1m 40.46s (2.26) **Going Correction** +0.025s/f (Slow) 12 Ran SP% **115.0**
Speed ratings (Par 97): **89,88,88,87,85 84,84,81,79,79 74,74**
toteswingers: 1&2 £1.70, 1&3 £3.90, 2&3 £3.60 CSF £8.35 TOTE £3.10: £1.40, £2.00, £2.20; EX 9.80 Trifecta £28.10 Pool: £271.63 - 7.14 winning units..
Owner J Winston **Bred** Kilcarn Stud **Trained** Lambourn, Berks

FOCUS
An ordinary maiden and the pace was ordinary too, causing a few to pull. There should be winners to come from the race, although the real merit of this race is hard to assess. The winner seems sure to rate higher.
Egorr Redfeer Official explanation: jockey said colt was slowly away

534 LINGFIELD PARK GOLF CLUB (S) STKS 1m (P)
1:55 (1:55) (Class 6) 3-Y-O £1,774 (£523; £262) Stalls High

Form RPR

-133 **1** **Tuscan King**[12] 371 3-9-5 65......................................(b) J-PGuillambert 4 59
(P D Evans) *b: mde all: pushed along and qcknd 2f out: a holding rivals and pushed out fnl f* **4/9**[1]

-400 **2** *1* **Underworld Dandy**[8] 422 3-9-5 54..............................(b) MartinDwyer 6 57
(R T Phillips) *chsd wnr thrght: rdn and sltly outpcd 2f out: styd on same pce u.p after* **7/1**[3]

40-0 **3** *nk* **Better Be Blue (IRE)**[19] 288 3-8-9 52.............................. LukeMorris 5 47+
(A W Carroll) *s.i.s: wl in tch in last: rdn ent fnl 2f: outpcd u.p over 1f out: styd on ins fnl f: wnt 3rd fnl 100yds: nvr gng pce to trble wnr* **12/1**

-265 **4** *1* **Brenda Duke**[12] 372 3-8-9 54..............................(b[1]) FrankieMcDonald 7 44
(J G Portman) *t.k.h: hld up wl in tch: rdn and unable qck 2f out: styd on again ins fnl f* **6/1**[2]

00-5 **5** *½* **Suzybee**[24] 236 3-8-9 42.. AndrewElliott 1 43
(M R Hoad) *in tch: rdn and effrt on inner wl over 1f out: disputing 2nd ent fnl f: no ex and wknd fnl 100yds* **28/1**

1m 41.34s (3.14) **Going Correction** +0.025s/f (Slow) 5 Ran SP% **107.2**
Speed ratings (Par 95): **85,84,83,82,82**
toteswingers: 1&2 £3.90 CSF £3.76 TOTE £1.30: £1.02, £2.90; EX 2.60.There was no bid for the winner.
Owner J L Guillambert **Bred** Horizon Bloodstock Limited **Trained** Pandy, Monmouths
■ Stewards' Enquiry : J-P Guillambert caution: careless riding; one-day ban: failed to ride to draw (Feb 27)

FOCUS
A weak seller, with a winning time 0.88 sec slower than the maiden. The winner did not need to match his recent form and this is a race to be against.

535 MARRIOTT HOTEL OPENING SPRING 2010 H'CAP 6f (P)
2:25 (2:25) (Class 4) (0-85,85) 4-Y-O+ £4,209 (£1,252; £625; £312) Stalls Low

Form RPR

-014 **1** **Billy Red**[15] 345 6-9-3 **84**..(b) FergusSweeney 4 91
(J R Jenkins) *mde all at gd gallop: rdn over 1f out: jst lasted: all out* **9/2**[3]

600- **2** *hd* **Halsion Chancer**[158] 5753 6-8-10 **77**............................ RobertWinston 8 83
(J R Best) *towards rr: rdn over 2f out: hdwy u.p ent fnl f: pressed wnr towards fin: nt quite get up* **12/1**

35-0 **3** *¾* **Methaaly (IRE)**[29] 192 7-8-8 **75**................................(be) GregFairley 1 79
(M Mullineaux) *chsd ldng pair tl wnt 2nd jst over 2f out: drvn and pressed wnr jst over 1f out: kpt on same pce u.p fnl f* **16/1**

40-3 **4** *3* **Incomparable**[15] 345 5-8-13 **80**..............................(p) FrederikTylicki 3 75
(J A Glover) *lw: taken down early: chsd ldng trio: rdn and unable qck over 1f out: wknd ins fnl f* **7/2**[2]

30-1 **5** *½* **Tin Cha Woody (USA)**[2] 508 5-8-7 **74** 6ex.......................(b) RPCleary 7 68
(Daniel Mark Loughnane, Ire) *a struggling to go pce towards rr: rdn over 3f out: no imp fnl 2f* **11/4**[1]

-463 **6** *1 ¾* **Timeteam (IRE)**[10] 384 4-9-0 **81**.................................. RichardHughes 5 69+
(P D Evans) *rel to r: v.s.a: wl bhd: rdn ent fnl 2f: kpt on: nvr any ch* **11/4**[1]

The Form Book, Raceform Ltd, Compton, RG20 6NL

016- 7 *14* **Theatre Street (IRE)**[156] 5805 4-8-10 **77**........................ HayleyTurner 2 23
(S Dow) *chsd wnr tl jst over 2f out: sn wknd: wl bhd and eased ins fnl f* **12/1**

1m 11.17s (-0.73) **Going Correction** +0.025s/f (Slow) **7** Ran SP% **115.0**
Speed ratings (Par 105): **105,104,103,99,99 96,78**
toteswingers: 1&2 £11.60, 1&3 £7.10, 2&3 £10.70 CSF £54.75 CT £790.49 TOTE £6.60: £2.50, £6.20; EX 62.40 Trifecta £160.20 Pool: £331.24 - 1.53 winning units..
Owner Mrs Irene Hampson **Bred** D R Tucker **Trained** Royston, Herts

FOCUS
A competitive sprint handicap on paper but the winner enjoyed the run of the race and the form is limited.
Tin Cha Woody(USA) ◆ Official explanation: trainer said, regarding running, that the gelding was unsuited by the drop in trip and quicker ground.
Timeteam(IRE) Official explanation: jockey said gelding was slowly away

536 LINGFIELD PARK FOURBALL H'CAP 1m 2f (P)
3:00 (3:00) (Class 2) (0-100,97) 4-Y-0+ **£10,361** (£3,083; £1,540; £769) **Stalls** Low

Form RPR
103- **1** **Dalradian (IRE)**[213] 3988 4-8-9 **88**.................................... JimCrowley 2 99+
(W J Knight) *hld up in last trio: stl plenty to do but gng wl jst over 2f out: gd hdwy towards inner over 1f out: rdn to ld wl ins fnl f: r.o wl* **9/1**[3]

2-35 **2** *¾* **Mafeking (UAE)**[14] 360 6-8-8 **86**.................................. AndrewElliott 8 95
(M R Hoad) *lw: hld up in tch in midfield: rdn along over 3f out: hdwy to press ldrs on outer over 2f out: led 1f out: hdd and no ex wl ins fnl f* **16/1**

5122 **3** *1* **Mister Green (FR)**[3] 480 4-8-5 **84**................................(b) LiamJones 3 91+
(K McAuliffe) *t.k.h: hld up towards rr: hdwy over 2f out: jnd ldrs stl on bit ent fnl f: sn rdn: nt pce of ldng pair fnl 100yds* **4/1**[2]

5-61 **4** *½* **Vainglory (USA)**[16] 324 6-8-10 **88**................................. MartinDwyer 7 94
(D M Simcock) *in tch in midfield on inner: effrt u.p over 1f out: ev ch 1f out: kpt on same pce u.p fnl 100yds* **16/1**

00-0 **5** *½* **Raptor (GER)**[14] 360 7-8-12 **90**.................................... RobertWinston 4 95
(M E Rimmer) *hld up towards rr: hdwy on outer over 2f out: rdn wl over 1f out: chsd ldrs ent fnl f: kpt on u.p but nt gng pce to chal ldrs* **50/1**

3613 **6** *nse* **Full Toss**[7] 447 4-9-2 **95**.. RichardHughes 10 100
(P D Evans) *s.i.s: hld up in midfield: effrt on outer bnd 2f out: styd on u.p fnl f: unable to chal* **10/1**

-201 **7** *1 ¼* **Baylini**[14] 360 6-8-12 **90**.. HayleyTurner 5 96+
(Ms J S Doyle) *stdd s: hld up towards rr: effrt whn nt clr run and hmpd over 1f out: kpt on fnl f: nvr able to chal* **10/1**

0-14 **8** *½* **Winter Fever (SAF)**[14] 360 6-8-11 **89**............................ LukeMorris 12 90
(J M P Eustace) *lw: chsd ldrs: rdn to go 2nd over 2f out: stl ev ch 1f out: wknd u.p ins fnl f* **16/1**

3-11 **9** *2* **Thunderstruck**[15] 341 5-8-8 **86**....................................(p) ChrisCatlin 11 83
(J A Glover) *t.k.h: chsd ldr after 1f tl led 5f out: rdn ent fnl 2f: hdd 1f out: sn wknd* **12/1**

2-33 **10** *2 ¾* **Confidentiality (IRE)**[14] 360 6-8-8 **86**......................... SteveDrowne 13 78
(M Wigham) *hld up in tch in midfield on outer: sltly hmpd 3f out: lost pl and towards rr 2f out: rdn over 1f out: no imp fnl f* **20/1**

1 **11** *2 ¼* **Cairnsmore**[17] 308 4-9-3 **96**... JoeFanning 6 83
(M Johnston) *lw: dwlt: t.k.h and sn rcvrd to chse ldrs: rdn and chsd ldr briefly wl over 1f out: wknd qckly ent fnl f* **9/4**[1]

064- **12** *1 ½* **Robby Bobby**[187] 4840 5-8-10 **88**....................................... GregFairley 1 72
(M Johnston) *broke wl and led for 1f: styd handy tl lost pl u.p jst over 2f out: towards rr whn swtchd rt over 1f out: wl btn after* **33/1**

16-6 **13** *5* **Bound By Honour (SAF)**[36] 81 7-9-3 **95**................(b) GeorgeBaker 9 69
(G L Moore) *chsd ldr tl led after 1f: hdd 5f out: chsd ldr over 2f out: sn struggling u.p and wl btn over 1f out* **10/1**

445/ **14** *9* **Donaldson (GER)**[7] 8-9-5 **97**.................................... RichardKingscote 14 53
(Jonjo O'Neill) *stdd s: a in rr: rdn 5f out: sn struggling and lost tch* **50/1**

2m 2.74s (-3.86) **Going Correction** +0.025s/f (Slow)
WFA 4 from 5yo+ 1lb **14** Ran SP% **125.0**
Speed ratings (Par 109): **116,115,114,114,113 113,112,112,110,108 106,105,101,94**
toteswingers: 1&2 £29.90, 1&3 £13.10, 2&3 £15.70 CSF £145.73 CT £678.11 TOTE £12.40: £2.50, £4.80, £2.00; EX 221.70 TRIFECTA Not won..
Owner Canisbay Bloodstock **Bred** Hesmonds Stud Ltd **Trained** Patching, W Sussex
■ Stewards' Enquiry : Liam Jones two-day ban: careless riding (Feb 27-28)

FOCUS
A red-hot handicap, run at a decent pace, in which several of these had met each other recently. There were still plenty in with a chance 1f out and in such a competitive contest the ability to find racing room was crucial. The runner-up is the best guide.

NOTEBOOK
Dalradian(IRE) ◆, whose two previous wins have come over 1m here, was trying this trip for the first time and he won on his seasonal reappearance last year, so the absence since July was unlikely to be a problem. Switched off out the back early, the key to this victory was that he enjoyed a beautiful gap one off the rail turning for home while many of his rivals swung wide, and he made full use of it. The longer distance proved no problem and he should be able to build on this. (op 15-2 tchd 7-1 and 10-1)
Mafeking(UAE), without a win in more than two years despite several near-misses in the meantime, finished behind three of these over C&D last time, though he was beaten less than a length into fifth. Although he was off the bridle half a mile from home, this still looked likely to be his day when he hit the front inside the final furlong, but once again something came from out of the clouds to nail him. He has become very unlucky.
Mister Green(FR), who has been in fine form since stepped up to this trip recently, enjoyed a 2lb pull with Thunderstruck for a neck defeat at Kempton two starts ago and managed to turn that form around at least. He was still on the bridle when brought to challenge 1f out and seemed likely to win, but he just lost out in the run to the line. (op 9-2)
Vainglory(USA), 5lb higher than when scoring over 1m at Kempton last time, had his chance on the inside once into the straight and kept on well, but although he has been placed several times over this trip he has yet to win over it.
Raptor(GER) ◆, without a win since April 2008, was returning from a break when last of ten behind Baylini over C&D last month on his debut for the yard and ran much better here. He was always seeing plenty of daylight on the outside and was forced wide in the home straight, so this was a decent effort under the circumstances.
Full Toss is holding his form extremely well considering his busy schedule, but not for the first time at this track he was forced very wide into the home straight and did well to finish so close. He is now 10lb higher than for his last success in a handicap and this effort is unlikely to result in his mark being dropped much, if at all. (op 14-1 tchd 9-1)
Baylini, racing under her optimum conditions, was put up 1lb for her last-gasp victory over C&D last month. Making her effort from off the pace and still going strongly once in line for home, she went for the same gap as Mister Green, and with the gelding getting there first she got murdered. She would have finished an awful lot closer otherwise. (op 14-1)
Cairnsmore, by far the least exposed in the field, was having his first start in a handicap after slamming the high-class chaser Fix The Rib in a Kempton maiden last month when making his British debut following a lengthy absence. Not best away, he soon pulled himself into a handy position and raced keenly enough but was still among the leaders 1f out before folding completely. Perhaps this competitive contest came soon enough for him, with this being only his fourth start, and he shouldn't be given up on just yet. (tchd 5-2 and 11-4 in places)

537 SUPER 7 CONDITIONS STKS (SUPER 7 QUALIFIER) 7f (P)
3:30 (3:31) (Class 3) 4-Y-0+ **£6,799** (£2,023; £1,011; £505) **Stalls** Low

Form RPR
23-4 **1** **Everymanforhimself (IRE)**[21] 278 6-9-3 92....................(v) NeilCallan 1 101
(K A Ryan) *trckd ldrs on inner: rdn to ld ent fnl f: hrd pressed thrght fnl f: r.o wl* **9/4**[2]

3113 **2** *hd* **Autumn Blades (IRE)**[14] 358 5-9-3 96.......................(p) DavidProbert 3 100
(A Bailey) *lw: dwlt: niggled along early in last: hdwy on outer over 2f out: chal and edgd lft over 1f out: drvn ins fnl f: a jst hld* **13/8**[1]

413/ **3** *1* **Souter's Sister (IRE)**[483] 6818 4-8-12 104.......................... JerryO'Dwyer 2 92
(M Botti) *hld up in last pair: effrt on inner over 1f out: pressed ldrs u.p ins fnl f: one pce fnl 100yds* **3/1**[3]

4363 **4** *1 ¾* **Carcinetto (IRE)**[16] 324 8-9-5 92.................................. RichardHughes 5 95
(P D Evans) *chsd ldr: rdn ent fnl 2f: wknd jst ins fnl f* **9/1**

250- **5** *½* **Beckermet (IRE)**[78] 7558 8-9-3 86... ChrisCatlin 4 91
(R F Fisher) *led: rdn ent fnl 2f: hdd jst over 1f out: wkng whn hmpd and snatched up 1f out* **10/1**

1m 24.02s (-0.78) **Going Correction** +0.025s/f (Slow) **5** Ran SP% **113.0**
Speed ratings (Par 107): **105,104,103,101,101**
CSF £6.54 TOTE £3.20: £1.90, £1.10; EX 7.00.
Owner J Duddy B McDonald & A Heeney **Bred** Denis McDonnell **Trained** Hambleton, N Yorks
■ Stewards' Enquiry : Neil Callan two-day ban: careless riding (Feb 27-28)

FOCUS
A tight little conditions event, run at a fair pace, though the quintet were still tightly packed turning for home, at which point the jockeys all made for the centre of the track. The form makes sense on paper.

NOTEBOOK
Everymanforhimself(IRE), beaten over 3l by Autumn Blades over 1m here last month and 6lb better off, travelled well behind the leaders and, having hit the front over 1f out, proved much more resilient than the runner-up in the battle to the line. This was his first win beyond 6f, which opens up more opportunities. (op 11-4 tchd 3-1)
Autumn Blades(IRE), a four-time winner in handicap company on Polytrack this winter, none of them by more than a neck, was held up early before being set alight around the outside on the home bend. At that stage he looked the most likely winner, but the head went to one side and, although he ran on, at no stage did he look like getting the better of the winner. (op 15-8 tchd 2-1)
Souter's Sister(IRE) ◆, surprise winner of a Group 3 at Newmarket in October 2008 for Richard Hannon, hadn't been seen since later that same month. Best in at the weights and trying this surface for the first time on her debut for her new yard, she had every chance on the inside of the field up the home straight and wasn't beaten until well inside the last furlong. This was an encouraging return. (op 11-4 tchd 2-1 and 10-3 in a place)
Carcinetto(IRE) has been falling just short in this type of event since returned to sand this winter. Again her chance was there, but she had a few pounds to find on these terms and wasn't good enough. (op 8-1 tchd 10-1)
Beckermet(IRE), formerly a Listed-class performer but without a win since September 2007 and worst in at these weights, was allowed an uncontested lead but had run his race when squeezed out between the front pair 1f from home. (op 12-1)

538 LINGFIELDPARK.CO.UK MAIDEN STKS 5f (P)
4:05 (4:05) (Class 5) 3-Y-0+ **£2,456** (£725; £362) **Stalls** Low

Form RPR
/22- **1** **Ajjaadd (USA)**[66] 7686 4-9-13 70...................................... SteveDrowne 5 62
(T E Powell) *lw: t.k.h: chsd ldrs: rdn over 1f out: led and edgd u.p ins fnl f: hrd drvn wl ins fnl f: all out* **4/5**[1]

60-4 **2** *nse* **Miss Kitty Grey (IRE)**[7] 445 3-8-8 59................................. JoeFanning 1 51
(J R Boyle) *chsd ldrs on inner: rdn and ev ch jst over 1f out: kpt on wl u.p wl ins fnl f: jst hld* **15/2**

0-05 **3** *1* **Seek The Cash (USA)**[22] 257 3-8-13 60...................... FrannyNorton 4 52
(M Quinn) *lw: sn led: hrd presed and rdn 2f out: hdd ins fnl f: btn fnl 75yds* **4/1**[2]

004- **4** *hd* **Kalligal**[164] 5566 5-9-8 38.. RobertHavlin 3 53+
(R Ingram) *taken down early: stdd after s: hld up in last pair: swtchd rt and rdn over 1f out: no prog tl r.o strly ins fnl f* **16/1**

44-6 **5** *2* **Starwatch**[24] 233 3-8-10 59... MarcHalford[(3)] 6 44
(J J Bridger) *racd freely: w ldr: rdn ent fnl 2f: wknd jst ins fnl f* **11/2**[3]

-40 **6** *8* **Rightcar Joan (IRE)**[12] 374 3-8-8 0................................. SaleemGolam 2 11
(Peter Grayson) *a in rr: rdn and struggling fr 1/2-way: no ch fnl 2f* **50/1**

0-60 **7** *nk* **Lunaticus**[16] 321 4-9-1 20..(p) KierenFox[(7)] 7 15
(M J Attwater) *t.k.h: chsd ldrs on outer: lost pl on bnd and rdn wl over 1f out: wl btn fnl f* **66/1**

60.00 secs (1.20) **Going Correction** +0.025s/f (Slow)
WFA 3 from 4yo+ 14lb **7** Ran SP% **112.0**
Speed ratings (Par 103): **91,90,89,89,85 73,72**
toteswingers: 1&2 £2.60, 1&3 £1.30, 2&3 £1.90 CSF £7.38 TOTE £1.60: £1.02, £3.70; EX 4.90.
Owner Katy & Lol Pratt **Bred** Darley **Trained** Reigate, Surrey
■ Ted Powell's first winner since 2005.

FOCUS
A very moderate Polytrack maiden run in a poor time, and form to be against.

539 GOLF AND RACING H'CAP 1m 4f (P)
4:40 (4:40) (Class 6) (0-52,51) 4-Y-0+ **£1,774** (£523; £262) **Stalls** Low

Form RPR
4-00 **1** **Jiggalong**[3] 479 4-8-9 **48**.. PaulDoe 5 55
(Jim Best) *hld up in tch in midfield: hdwy to chse ldrs jst over 2f out: chsd ldr over 1f out: flashed tail u.p but rdn to ld ins fnl f: hld on cl home: all out* **5/1**[2]

-004 **2** *hd* **Play Up Pompey**[2] 497 8-8-9 **45**........................... RichardKingscote 14 52
(J J Bridger) *stdd and dropped in bhd after s: stl plenty to do 2f out: gd hdwy over 1f out: drvn to press wnr fnl 50yds: jst hld* **14/1**

053- **3** *1 ½* **Jezza**[66] 7687 4-8-9 **48**.. RichardHughes 13 52
(Karen George) *chsd ldr 10f out tl 9f out: styd chsng ldrs: rdn over 1f out: ev ch u.p 1f out: one pce fnl 150yds* **7/2**[1]

55- **4** *nk* **Crazy Bold (GER)**[164] 4880 7-8-9 **45**.............................. HayleyTurner 3 49
(A W Carroll) *t.k.h: chsd ldr for 2f: styd handy: hdwy to ld ent fnl 2f: rdn over 1f out: hdd ins fnl f: no ex fnl 100yds* **13/2**[3]

00-5 **5** *hd* **Broughtons Point**[8] 420 4-8-6 **45**................................. JamieMackay 2 49
(W J Musson) *in tch in midfield: rdn and effrt over 1f out: chsd ldrs and drvn 1f out: kpt on wl but nvr quite pce to rch ldrs* **12/1**

5-30 **6** ½ **Barbirolli**[27] [210] 8-9-0 **50** .... JerryO'Dwyer 6 53
(W B Stone) *hld up in last trio: hdwy on outer over 2f out: styd on wl ins fnl f: nt rch ldrs* **9/1**

-265 **7** 2¾ **Mid Wicket (USA)**[15] [354] 4-8-12 **51** .... NeilCallan 15 50
(Mouse Hamilton-Fairley) *stdd and dropped in after s: rdn and effrt ent fnl 2fstyd on but nvr gng pce to rch ldrs* **7/1**

500- **8** 2 **Amwell Brave**[47] [6204] 9-8-9 **45** .... RobertWinston 11 41
(J R Jenkins) *dropped in after s: hld up towards rr: rdn and effrt towards inner wl over 1f out: nvr threatened ldrs* **7/1**

56-3 **9** 2¾ **Geoffdaw**[10] [390] 5-8-11 **50** .... RobertLButler(3) 7 42
(Miss Sheena West) *t.k.h: hld up in tch: rdn over 2f out: wknd over 1f out* **9/1**

0/0- **10** 1 **Indian Haze (IRE)**[126] [5873] 4-8-6 **45** ....(p) RPCleary 8 35
(Daniel Mark Loughnane, Ire) *hld up towards rr: rdn 4f out: last and drvn 3f out: n.d after* **33/1**

00-0 **11** 3¾ **Supplementary (IRE)**[30] [160] 8-8-9 **45** .... FergusSweeney 1 30
(M J Coombe) *dwlt: sn rcvrd to ld: hdd ent fnl 2f: wknd qckly over 1f out* **33/1**

000- **12** 6 **Stoic Leader (IRE)**[61] [7754] 10-8-12 **48** .... ChrisCatlin 9 24
(R F Fisher) *t.k.h: pressed ldr 9f out tl over 2f out: sn lost pl: wl bhd fnl f* **16/1**

2m 33.24s (0.24) **Going Correction** +0.025s/f (Slow)
WFA 4 from 5yo+ 3lb 12 Ran SP% **123.3**
Speed ratings (Par 101): **100,99,98,98,98 98,96,95,93,92 90,86**
toteswingers: 1&2 £26.80, 1&3 £5.20, 2&3 £13.20 CSF £76.48 CT £281.02 TOTE £7.80: £2.80, £5.20, £1.70; EX 122.60 TRIFECTA Not won. Place 6: £63.41 Place 5: £46.86 .
Owner M & R Refurbishments Ltd **Bred** Norcroft Park Stud **Trained** Lewes, E Sussex
■ Stewards' Enquiry : Richard Kingscote one-day ban: used whip without giving gelding time to respond (Feb 27)

FOCUS
A competitive handicap, but a poor one, with the joint top-weights rated just 50. Sound, low-grade form.
T/Plt: £82.50 to a £1 stake. Pool: £57,604.27. 509.58 winning tickets. T/Qpdt: £29.80 to a £1 stake. Pool: £3,254.36. 80.76 winning tickets. SP

525 WOLVERHAMPTON (A.W) (L-H)
Saturday, February 13

OFFICIAL GOING: Standard
Wind: Light across Weather: Fine

540 CLEANWASTESOLUTIONS AMATEUR RIDERS' H'CAP (DIV I) 1m 141y(P)
6:20 (6:20) (Class 6) (0-60,60) 4-Y-0+ £1,384 (£425; £212) Stalls Low

Form RPR

44-6 **1** **By Command**[32] [144] 5-10-10 **59** ....(p) MrJoshuaMoore(3) 3 72+
(K A Ryan) *hld up in tch: led on bit over 1f out: sn rdn: drvn out* **9/2[3]**

-054 **2** 1¼ **Kielty's Folly**[2] [499] 6-10-0 **53** .... MissStefaniaGandola(7) 2 60
(B P J Baugh) *hld up in rr: hdwy over 2f out: wnt 2nd jst ins fnl f: pushed along and nt qckn* **4/1[2]**

0-65 **3** 1½ **Cruise Control**[6] [433] 4-10-1 **50** .... MrMPrice(3) 6 53
(R J Price) *hld up in mid-div: pushed along and hdwy over 1f out: rdn and styd on to take 3rd post* **50/1**

-111 **4** nse **Lyrical Intent**[15] [347] 4-10-9 **60** .... MrJPFeatherstone(5) 10 63
(P Howling) *hld up in mid-div: hdwy 3f out: rdn jst over 1f out: kpt on one pce* **9/2[3]**

0-43 **5** 1½ **Royal Society**[15] [354] 4-10-2 **55** .... MissCEReid(7) 9 55
(R A Farrant) *hld up in tch: led jst over 2f out tl over 1f out: no ex ins fnl f* **12/1**

0-21 **6** 1¼ **Barodine**[9] [407] 7-10-4 **55** .... MrPPrince(5) 7 52
(R J Hodges) *hld up in rr: hdwy on outside 2f out: c wd st: rdn wl over 1f out: no further prog* **3/1[1]**

-030 **7** 2 **Foxtrot Bravo (IRE)**[24] [229] 4-9-7 **46** oh1 .... MrTGarner(7) 1 38
(Miss S L Davison) *led early: prom: rdn 2f out: wknd over 1f out* **28/1**

00-3 **8** 8 **Northgate Lodge (USA)**[19] [290] 5-10-0 **46** .... MrSDobson 13 20
(M Brittain) *sn led: rdn and hdd jst over 2f out: wknd over 1f out* **12/1**

00-0 **9** 10 **Machinate (USA)**[15] [347] 8-9-12 **47** .... MrPCollington(3) 4 —
(W M Brisbourne) *hld up in mid-div: pushed along and hdwy 3f out: wknd 2f out* **16/1**

000/ **10** 3¾ **Pont Wood**[11] [11] 6-10-0 **46** oh1 .... MissSBrotherton 5 —
(Mrs N S Evans) *a in rr* **80/1**

660/ **11** 2¼ **Loyal Knight (IRE)**[514] [6036] 5-10-2 **53** .... MissWGibson(5) 12 —
(P T Midgley) *prom tl wknd qckly wl over 2f out* **18/1**

000/ **12** 9 **High Class Problem (IRE)**[465] [7194] 7-9-11 **50** .... MrJPearce(7) 8 —
(D C O'Brien) *a towards rr: t.o fnl 3f* **50/1**

1m 51.7s (1.20) **Going Correction** +0.075s/f (Slow) 12 Ran SP% **116.5**
Speed ratings (Par 101): **97,95,94,94,93 92,90,83,74,70 68,60**
toteswingers: 1&2 £5.50, 1&3 £30.70, 2&3 £27.50 CSF £21.98 CT £793.28 TOTE £6.60: £1.90, £1.70, £4.80; EX 35.90.
Owner Hambleton Racing Ltd XV **Bred** Nawara Stud Co Ltd **Trained** Hambleton, N Yorks

FOCUS
An ordinary handicap and straightforward to rate with the winner back to form and capable of better.
Kielty's Folly Official explanation: vet said gelding returned lame right-fore

541 CE PROPERTY SERVICES GROUP AMATEUR RIDERS' H'CAP (DIV II) 1m 141y(P)
6:50 (6:50) (Class 6) (0-60,59) 4-Y-0+ £1,384 (£425; £212) Stalls Low

Form RPR

6-60 **1** **Flighty Fellow (IRE)**[9] [411] 10-10-3 **53** ....(v) MrJPMcGrath(5) 2 62
(B G Powell) *s.i.s: sn hld up in mid-div: hdwy on ins over 3f out: swtchd rt wl over 2f out: led jst ins fnl f: rdn out* **12/1**

0/03 **2** 1¼ **Wetherby Place (IRE)**[10] [397] 4-10-0 **52** .... MrJMQuinlan(7) 1 58+
(M Wigham) *hld up towards rr: hdwy on ins over 2f out: rdn jst over 1f out: styd on u.p to take 2nd towards fin: nt trble wnr* **5/1[2]**

-432 **3** nk **Alfredtheordinary**[10] [390] 5-10-8 **58** .... MrPPrince(5) 4 63
(M R Channon) *a.p: kpt on ins fnl f* **11/4[1]**

00-2 **4** 2 **Marjury Daw (IRE)**[19] [290] 4-10-11 **56** .... MissSBrotherton 3 57
(J G Given) *led: hdd 6f out: w ldr: led over 3f out: rdn and hdd jst ins fnl f: one pce* **6/1[3]**

06-0 **5** 2¼ **Bobering**[15] [353] 10-9-9 **45** .... MissAWallace(5) 9 41
(B P J Baugh) *hld up in rr: styd on fr over 1f out: nrst fin* **33/1**

565- **6** shd **Persian Tomcat (IRE)**[62] [7737] 4-9-11 **45** ....(v) MrRBirkett(3) 7 40
(Miss J Feilden) *hld up in mid-div: hdwy 3f out: sn rdn: wknd wl over 1f out* **25/1**

5140 **7** shd **Bajan Pride**[5] [467] 6-10-7 **59** ....(v) MissCCundall(7) 8 54
(R A Fahey) *w ldr: led 6f out tl over 3f out: wknd ins fnl f* **8/1**

/00- **8** 1¼ **Coeur Brule (FR)**[19] [5990] 4-9-13 **47** .... MrDavidTurner(3) 10 39
(Miss S L Davison) *hld up in rr: rdn wl over 2f out: nvr nr ldrs* **12/1**

00-4 **9** ½ **Naledi**[19] [295] 6-9-13 **47** ow2 .... MrMPrice(3) 6 38
(R J Price) *a towards rr* **11/1**

5-56 **10** nse **Our Kes (IRE)**[9] [410] 8-10-3 **53** .... MrJBanks(5) 11 44
(P Howling) *a in rr* **8/1**

045- **11** 2½ **Schinken Otto (IRE)**[269] [734] 9-10-2 **50** .... MissRJefferson(3) 5 35
(J M Jefferson) *bhd fnl 3f* **16/1**

056- **12** 17 **Our Fugitive (IRE)**[319] [1055] 8-9-10 **48** .... MrCBevan(7) 12 —
(C Gordon) *t.k.h: prom tl wknd 3f out* **50/1**

1m 51.87s (1.37) **Going Correction** +0.075s/f (Slow) 12 Ran SP% **118.2**
Speed ratings (Par 101): **96,94,94,92,90 90,90,89,89,89 86,71**
toteswingers: 1&2 £12.10, 1&3 £11.50, 2&3 £4.40 CSF £69.79 CT £198.64 TOTE £13.50: £4.20, £2.50, £1.40; EX 101.50.
Owner Mrs J L Le Brocq **Bred** F Hinojosa **Trained** Upper Lambourn, Berks

FOCUS
A weak handicap, confined amateur riders. The form looks fairly sound.
Flighty Fellow(IRE) Official explanation: trainer's rep said, regarding apparent improvement in form, that the gelding appeared to benefit from the shorter distance of 1m 4f.
Marjury Daw(IRE) Official explanation: vet said filly lost a front shoe
Coeur Brule(FR) Official explanation: jockey said gelding was denied a clear run

542 CLEANEVENT (S) STKS 1m 1f 103y(P)
7:20 (7:20) (Class 6) 3-Y-O £1,774 (£523; £262) Stalls Low

Form RPR

4-23 **1** **Vittachi**[23] [254] 3-8-12 52 ....(b) TomQueally 6 57
(J D Bethell) *sn led: rdn and edgd rt ins fnl f: drvn out* **13/8[1]**

4403 **2** 1 **Clayton Flick (IRE)**[12] [372] 3-8-12 57 .... StevieDonohoe 5 55+
(A B Haynes) *hld up in rr: c wd st: hdwy fnl f: tk 2nd nr fin* **6/1[3]**

0- **3** nk **Welcome Bounty**[101] [7243] 3-8-12 0 .... GrahamGibbons 3 54
(R A Farrant) *s.i.s: hld up in mid-div: pushed along and hdwy 2f out: rdn and kpt on ins fnl f* **11/1**

-611 **4** nk **Tiger Hawk (USA)**[2] [507] 3-8-13 62 ....(b) AndrewHeffernan(5) 2 59
(P D Evans) *led early: a.p: pushed along to chse wnr 2f out: rdn over 1f out: nt qckn and lost 2nd wl ins fnl f* **11/4[2]**

000- **5** nk **Whipper's Delight (IRE)**[107] [7130] 3-8-7 55 ....(e[1]) JimmyQuinn 7 48
(D Donovan) *hld up in rr: pushed along 3f out: hdwy on ins wl over 1f out: rdn and kpt on same pce ins fnl f* **12/1**

64 **6** 4 **Maigold Rose**[6] [452] 3-8-7 0 .... LukeMorris 10 39
(J R Weymes) *sn chsng wnr: rdn and lost 2nd 2f out: wknd over 1f out* **50/1**

00-0 **7** nk **Port Hill**[23] [254] 3-8-12 48 .... ShaneKelly 8 44
(W M Brisbourne) *hld up in mid-div: hdwy over 3f out: wknd 2f out* **33/1**

606- **8** 8 **Expensive Legacy**[84] [7474] 3-8-7 49 ....(bt[1]) DavidProbert 4 22
(H J L Dunlop) *bmpd sn after s: hld up towards rr: pushed along over 3f out: rdn and no ch fnl 2f* **8/1**

5560 **9** 2 **Scintillating (IRE)**[12] [372] 3-8-7 42 ....(p) LiamJones 9 18
(R Hollinshead) *prom: wkng whn sltly hmpd over 2f out* **25/1**

2m 3.43s (1.73) **Going Correction** +0.075s/f (Slow) 9 Ran SP% **114.9**
Speed ratings (Par 95): **95,94,93,93,93 89,89,82,80**
toteswingers: 1&2 £2.10, 1&3 £5.00, 2&3 £8.00 CSF £11.67 TOTE £2.70: £1.20, £2.40, £2.90; EX 13.10.The winner was bought in for 4,000gns.
Owner Clarendon Thoroughbred Racing **Bred** London Thoroughbred Services Ltd **Trained** Middleham Moor, N Yorks
■ Stewards' Enquiry : Jimmy Quinn caution: used whip with excessive force.

FOCUS
A routine seller best judged around the first two.
Scintillating(IRE) Official explanation: jockey said filly ran too free early

543 BET FA CUP - BETDAQ H'CAP 1m 141y(P)
7:50 (7:50) (Class 5) (0-75,70) 4-Y-0+ £2,729 (£806; £403) Stalls Low

Form RPR

15-5 **1** **Ella Woodcock (IRE)**[40] [29] 6-9-0 **66** .... ShaneKelly 2 76+
(E J Alston) *a gng wl: led wl ins fnl f: pushed out* **7/1[2]**

2-23 **2** nk **Seldom (IRE)**[5] [465] 4-8-12 **64** .... JimmyQuinn 1 71
(M Brittain) *led: rdn 1f out: hdd wl ins fnl f* **5/2[1]**

5-02 **3** ¾ **Hypnotic Gaze (IRE)**[18] [298] 4-8-9 **68** ....(p) KierenFox(7) 9 74
(J Mackie) *a.p: ev ch over 2f out: rdn wl over 1f out: nt qckn wl ins fnl f* **5/2[1]**

0-30 **4** 2¼ **Sadeek**[10] [383] 6-8-11 **63** .... TomEaves 7 64
(B Smart) *hld up in tch: pushed along over 4f out: rdn wl over 1f out: kpt on same pce ins fnl f* **8/1[3]**

5-00 **5** nk **Fandango Boy**[9] [405] 9-9-3 **69** .... StevieDonohoe 4 69
(Ian Williams) *hld up and bhd: prog on ins wl over 1f out: one pce ins fnl f* **20/1**

00-1 **6** hd **Toolentidhaar (USA)**[20] [284] 6-9-4 **70** .... ChrisCatlin 8 70
(Andrew Turnell) *w ldr: pushed along over 2f out: wknd wl over 1f out* **12/1**

033- **7** nse **Cavendish Road (IRE)**[110] [7065] 4-8-12 **69** .... AndrewHeffernan(5) 6 69
(N J Vaughan) *hld up and bhd: rdn over 2f out: nvr trbld ldrs* **8/1[3]**

000- **8** 3 **Ninth House (USA)**[71] [7633] 8-9-4 **70** ....(t) AndrewElliott 3 64+
(Mrs R A Carr) *s.s: a in rr* **16/1**

00R- **9** 26 **Willie Ever**[332] [868] 6-8-13 **65** .... DavidNolan 5 4
(D G Bridgwater) *dwlt: a bhd: lost tch fnl 2f* **80/1**

1m 50.87s (0.37) **Going Correction** +0.075s/f (Slow) 9 Ran SP% **111.4**
Speed ratings (Par 103): **101,100,100,98,97 97,97,94,71**
toteswingers: 1&2 £2.40, 1&3 £6.20, 2&3 £3.20 CSF £23.58 CT £54.30 TOTE £7.50: £1.90, £1.10, £1.70; EX 24.90.
Owner Derrick Mossop **Bred** Pippa Hackett **Trained** Longton, Lancs

FOCUS
A modest handicap but the winner scored in fair style. The standard looks reliable based around the third and fourth.

544 BETDAQ THE BETTING EXCHANGE FILLIES' H'CAP 7f 32y(P)
8:20 (8:20) (Class 5) (0-75,74) 4-Y-0+ £2,729 (£806; £403) Stalls High

Form RPR

40-6 **1** **Ishiadancer**[5] [465] 5-8-11 **74** .... KierenFox(7) 1 89+
(E J Alston) *mde all: clr wl over 1f out: sn rdn: eased towards fin* **3/1[2]**

6-31 **2** 8 **Fazbee (IRE)**[21] [275] 4-9-1 **71** ....(b) TonyCulhane 4 66
(P W D'Arcy) *hld up: pushed along and hdwy on ins wl over 1f out: sn chsng wnr: no imp* **5/4[1]**

0-65 **3** 2 **Perfect Class**[20] [284] 4-8-13 **69** .... LukeMorris 3 59
(C G Cox) *a.p: chsd wnr over 2f out tl rdn over 1f out: one pce* **11/2**

The Form Book, Raceform Ltd, Compton, RG20 6NL

23-0 **4** 2 1/4 **Mozayada (USA)**[34] 115 6-9-4 **74** RobertWinston 2 58
(M Brittain) *chsd wnr tl rdn over 2f out: wknd wl over 1f out* **14/1**
142- **5** 8 **Montiboli (IRE)**[197] 4496 5-8-9 **70** AmyRyan(5) 5 34
(K A Ryan) *hld up: stdy prog over 5f out: rdn and wknd over 2f out* **5/1**[3]
1m 28.41s (-1.19) **Going Correction** +0.075s/f (Slow) **5** Ran SP% **108.2**
Speed ratings (Par 100): **109,99,97,95,85**
CSF £6.93 TOTE £3.80: £1.80, £1.10; EX 9.40.
Owner Racing Shares Nuppend **Bred** Southern Seafoods **Trained** Longton, Lancs
FOCUS
Little strength in depth here and the winner dictated, allowed a soft time up front. She was impressive all the same and the form could be rated at least 5lb higher.

545 CE RISK, SAFETY & SECURITY MAIDEN FILLIES' STKS 1m 141y(P)
8:50 (8:52) (Class 5) 3-Y-0+ **£2,456** (£725; £362) **Stalls** Low

Form RPR
6 **1** **Myplacelater**[10] 385 3-8-0 0 DeclanCannon(5) 4 81+
(D R C Elsworth) *hld up: hdwy 3f out: led jst over 2f out: rdn over 1f out: drew clr fnl f: r.o wl* **13/2**[3]
230- **2** 8 **Jewelled**[93] 7356 4-9-5 68 KierenFox(7) 9 68
(J W Hills) *led: hdd jst over 2f out: rdn and btn 1f out* **9/4**[2]
0- **3** 1 1/4 **Dane Cottage**[117] 6903 3-8-5 0 LukeMorris 8 60
(Miss Gay Kelleway) *hld up towards rr: pushed along over 3f out: rdn over 2f out: hdwy wl over 1f out: tk 3rd ins fnl f* **33/1**
4 4 **Nadinska** 3-8-5 0 ChrisCatlin 5 54+
(M R Channon) *s.i.s: sn hld up in tch: pushed along over 2f out: rdn and wknd wl over 1f out* **10/11**[1]
0 **5** 11 **Spirited Lady (IRE)**[22] 267 3-8-4 0 ow2 BarryMcHugh(3) 7 30
(R A Fahey) *hdwy over 5f out: rdn and wknd 2f out* **33/1**
00-0 **6** 2 1/4 **Mays Louise**[19] 295 6-9-7 37 JemmaMarshall(5) 2 29
(B P J Baugh) *hld up in rr: rdn over 2f out: sn struggling* **100/1**
0-00 **7** 2 1/4 **Helpmeronda**[15] 354 4-9-12 40 LiamJones 1 24
(W M Brisbourne) *led early: chsd ldr tl rdn and wknd over 2f out* **100/1**
8 9 **Forever Fong** 3-8-5 0 JimmyQuinn 6 —
(J R Weymes) *hdwy over 5f out: n.m.r and wknd over 3f out* **20/1**
-550 **P** **Mrs Slocombe (IRE)**[15] 353 4-9-12 45 (t) DavidProbert 3 —
(Mrs N S Evans) *prom: lost pl over 5f out: p.u lame over 4f out* **28/1**
1m 50.53s (0.03) **Going Correction** +0.075s/f (Slow)
WFA 3 from 4yo+ 21lb **9** Ran SP% **112.6**
Speed ratings (Par 100): **102,94,93,90,80 78,76,68,—**
toteswingers: 1&2 £2.90, 1&3 £9.00, 2&3 £13.40 CSF £19.86 TOTE £7.70: £1.90, £1.10, £7.40; EX 21.00.
Owner D R C Elsworth **Bred** Mrs N A Ward **Trained** Newmarket, Suffolk
FOCUS
A weak maiden overall, but the winner impressed and the form should work out rated through the second.

546 BETDAQ ON 0870 178 1221 H'CAP 1m 4f 50y(P)
9:20 (9:20) (Class 5) (0-75,77) 4-Y-0+ **£2,729** (£806; £403) **Stalls** Low

Form RPR
33/4 **1** **Houston Dynimo (IRE)**[23] 255 5-9-1 **68** TomEaves 5 76
(N G Richards) *stdd s: hld up: pushed along and hdwy on inisde wl over 1f out: sn rdn: r.o to ld post* **15/2**
1-21 **2** shd **Quinsman**[10] 395 4-9-7 **77** LukeMorris 9 85
(J S Moore) *hld up: stdy prog over 5f out: rdn over 1f out: led wl ins fnl f: hdd post* **4/1**[2]
5-23 **3** 1/2 **Benedict Spirit (IRE)**[8] 430 5-9-0 **72** (p) AndrewHeffernan(5) 3 79
(P D Evans) *hld up in tch: wnt 2nd 4f out: led on bit 3f out: rdn over 1f out: sn edgd rt: hdd wl ins fnl f: kpt on* **10/3**[1]
3-36 **4** 3/4 **Vertigo On Course (IRE)**[20] 284 5-8-5 **61** BarryMcHugh(3) 2 67+
(R A Fahey) *hld up in tch: lost pl 4f out: rdn and hdwy 1f out: styng on whn n.m.r towards fin* **6/1**[3]
14-0 **5** 1 **Bramalea**[21] 280 5-8-10 **63** RobertWinston 8 68+
(B W Duke) *hld up: pushed along and hdwy on outside 2f out: c wd st: rdn wl over 1f out: styng on whn nt clr run towards fin* **14/1**
00-0 **6** 1/2 **Whooshka (USA)**[23] 255 4-9-2 **72** JackMitchell 1 76+
(P W Chapple-Hyam) *hld up in tch: n.m.r and bmpd jst over 2f out: rdn wl over 1f out: one pce fnl f* **20/1**
22-0 **7** 10 **Maslak (IRE)**[41] 25 6-9-6 **73** ChrisCatlin 6 62
(P W Hiatt) *chsd ldr: led over 6f out to 3f out: rdn and wknd 1f out* **12/1**
51-2 **8** 2 3/4 **Crazy Chris**[12] 375 5-9-7 **74** DavidProbert 4 59+
(B Palling) *led: hdd over 6f out: n.m.r and bmpd jst over 2f out: wknd wl over 1f out* **10/3**[1]
2m 40.08s (-1.02) **Going Correction** +0.075s/f (Slow)
WFA 4 from 5yo+ 3lb **8** Ran SP% **111.3**
Speed ratings (Par 103): **106,105,105,105,104 104,97,95**
toteswingers: 1&2 £14.50, 1&3 £5.30, 2&3 £2.70 CSF £35.50 CT £115.56 TOTE £8.80: £2.60, £1.70, £1.60; EX 50.10 Place 6: £23.44 Place 5: £6.20.
Owner Norman Ormiston **Bred** Sweetmans Bloodstock **Trained** Greystoke, Cumbria
■ Stewards' Enquiry : Andrew Heffernan caution: careless riding; two-day ban: used whip with excessive frequency (Mar 5, 8)
Jack Mitchell two-day ban: careless riding (Mar 5, 8)
FOCUS
A modest handicap. The winner was thrown in on his old form in Ireland but still some way below that level.
T/Plt: £40.70 to a £1 stake. Pool: £88,015.36. 1,575.62 winning tickets. T/Qpdt: £5.70 to a £1 stake. Pool: £8,236.56. 1,055.29 winning tickets. KH

494 CAGNES-SUR-MER
Saturday, February 13
OFFICIAL GOING: Standard

547a PRIX DES CHEVREFEUILLES (MAIDEN) (C&G) (ALL-WEATHER) 1m 2f (D)
1:20 (1:22) 3-Y-0 **£8,850** (£3,540; £2,655; £1,770; £885)

RPR
1 **Munaawer (USA)**[80] 7529 3-8-13 IoritzMendizabal 76
(J D Bethell) *in tch: 3rd 1/2-way: 4th and pushed along st: 2nd and chalng over 1f out: led jst ins fnl f: styd on wl* **12/1**[1]
2 1 1/2 **Bubble Zack (FR)**[107] 3-9-2 StephanePasquier 76
(D Prod'Homme, France)
3 1 1/2 **Kalidoun (FR)** 3-9-2 GuillaumeMillet 73
(T Larriviere, France)
4 3 **Successful (FR)**[84] 3-8-13 64
(B Goudot, France)
5 1/2 **Da Paolino (FR)** 3-9-2 66
(D Prod'Homme, France)
6 8 **Mundher (IRE)**[16] 3-9-2 50
(J E Hammond, France)
2m 4.37s (124.37) **6** Ran SP% **7.7**
PARI-MUTUEL (Including 1 Euro stake): WIN 13.00; PL 6.50, 3.60;SF 51.20.
Owner Hornblower Racing **Bred** Edward P Evans **Trained** Middleham Moor, N Yorks

548a PRIX DES ANCOLIES (ALL-WEATHER) 1m 2f (D)
1:50 (1:51) 3-Y-0 **£11,947** (£4,779; £3,584; £2,389; £1,195)

RPR
1 **Arlequin**[113] 6993 3-9-1 IoritzMendizabal 67
(J D Bethell) *in tch: 4th 1/2-way: pushed along over 4f out: drvn st: 2nd & chalng over 1f out: rdn to ld 100yds out* **43/10**[1]
2 1/2 **Serva Padrona (IRE)**[28] 3-9-1 DominiqueBoeuf 66
(H-A Pantall, France)
3 3 **Duo Victorieux (FR)** 3-9-4 GuillaumeMillet 63
(T Larriviere, France)
4 hd **Cup Cake (FR)**[92] 3-9-1 (b) 60
(B Dutruel, France)
5 3 **Heart Breaker (FR)**[107] 3-8-10 49
(M Boutin, France)
6 2 **Marina (GER)**[92] 3-9-1 50
(N Bertran De Balanda, France)
2m 6.36s (126.36) **6** Ran SP% **18.9**
PARI-MUTUEL: WIN 5.30; PL 2.30, 1.30; SF 13.70.
Owner Dr Anne J F Gillespie **Bred** Dr A J F Gillespie **Trained** Middleham Moor, N Yorks

549a PRIX DES BOURACHES (ALL-WEATHER) 6f 110y
3:55 (3:58) 4-Y-0+ **£8,850** (£3,540; £2,655; £1,770; £885)

RPR
1 **Cadeau For Maggi**[18] 304 5-9-2 FabriceVeron 82
(H-A Pantall, France)
2 3/4 **Garnica (FR)**[18] 304 7-8-11 (p) IoritzMendizabal 75
(D Nicholls) *in tch: 4th 1/2-way: pushed along over 2f out: 3rd and rdn over 1f out: styd on same pce: wnt 2nd nr fin* **5/1**[1]
3 nk **Heart Attack (FR)**[7] 458 4-8-11 ThierryThulliez 74
(G Martin, Austria)
4 1 1/2 **Kerno (IRE)**[18] 304 6-9-2 (p) 75
(P Monfort, France)
5 snk **Staraco (FR)**[18] 304 6-9-0 72
(Rod Collet, France)
6 nse **Zizany (IRE)**[7] 458 7-8-11 69
(Robert Collet, France)
7 2 1/2 **Smart Diplomacy (USA)**[72] 4-9-4 69
(A De Royer-Dupre, France)
8 5 **Marny (GER)**[18] 304 5-8-10 46
(H Blume, Germany)
1m 16.97s (76.97) **8** Ran SP% **16.7**
PARI-MUTUEL: WIN 3.00; PL 1.40, 1.90, 3.40; DF 8.00.
Owner Michel Perret **Bred** Pontchartrain Stud **Trained** France

495 KEMPTON (A.W) (R-H)
Sunday, February 14
OFFICIAL GOING: Standard
Wind: moderate, against Weather: overcast, cold

550 BET CHAMPIONS LEAGUE FOOTBALL - BETDAQ CLAIMING STKS 6f (P)
2:05 (2:06) (Class 5) 3-Y-0 **£2,590** (£770; £385; £192) **Stalls** High

Form RPR
105- **1** **Little Perisher**[90] 7410 3-9-2 72 TomQueally 6 71
(A P Jarvis) *chsd ldrs: rdn and effrt over 2f out: led over 1f out: clr ins fnl f: kpt on* **5/1**[3]
15-5 **2** 1 **Miss Lesley**[22] 276 3-8-9 70 (b) MartinDwyer 3 61
(D K Ivory) *chsd ldrs: effrt ent fnl 2f: edging rt after but r.o to chse wnr fnl 150yds: kpt on but a hld* **3/1**[2]
6-46 **3** 1 3/4 **Arken Lad**[9] 425 3-8-13 65 (e) JimmyQuinn 4 59
(D Donovan) *racd in midfield: effrt on inner ent fnl 2f: styd on same pce u.p fnl f* **14/1**
-624 **4** 1/2 **Avow (USA)**[16] 343 3-8-8 67 (b) RossAtkinson(5) 5 57
(J S Moore) *wnt lft s: sn led: rdn jst over 2f out: hdd over 1f out: wknd ins fnl f* **5/1**[3]
0-23 **5** 1 1/2 **Coolree Star (IRE)**[18] 310 3-9-7 78 ChrisCatlin 1 61
(J A Glover) *w ldr: rdn jst over 2f out: wknd ent fnl f* **7/4**[1]
6 1/2 **My Meteor** 3-9-4 0 JamesMillman(3) 2 59+
(A G Newcombe) *s.i.s: bhd and rn green early: gd hdwy to chse ldrs but hanging rt wl over 1f out: no prog fnl f* **33/1**
7 6 **Carolina Cherry (IRE)** 3-8-5 0 HayleyTurner 8 24
(Miss Amy Weaver) *sn pushed along and rn green in last pair: rdn and hung lft jst over 2f out: edgd rt ins fnl f: nvr trbld ldrs* **25/1**
4656 **8** 2 1/4 **Tatawor (IRE)**[4] 483 3-8-5 64 (p) JemmaMarshall(5) 7 22
(J R Boyle) *in tch in last trio: rdn jst over 2f out: wknd and lost tch qckly over 1f out* **16/1**
1m 12.98s (-0.12) **Going Correction** -0.025s/f (Stan) **8** Ran SP% **114.0**
Speed ratings (Par 97): **99,97,95,94,92 92,84,81**
toteswinger:1&2:£3.10, 1&3:£8.90, 2&3:£7.20 CSF £20.28 TOTE £6.00: £1.50, £1.10, £4.80; EX 21.90.
Owner A B Parr **Bred** Mrs Ann Jarvis **Trained** Twyford, Bucks
FOCUS
An ordinary claimer, and sound enough form.

551 BET PREMIER LEAGUE FOOTBALL - BETDAQ MEDIAN AUCTION MAIDEN STKS 1m 3f (P)
2:40 (2:40) (Class 6) 3-5-Y-0 **£2,047** (£604; £302) **Stalls** High

Form RPR
1 **Dosti** 3-8-5 0 (p) MartinDwyer 4 66+
(J R Boyle) *chsd ldrs: effrt to ld narrowly 2f out: forged ahd ins fnl f: r.o wl* **9/1**

-3 **2** ½ **Brave Talk**[16] 340 3-8-5 0 DavidProbert 7 66
(S Kirk) *in tch in last trio: swtchd sharply lft jst over 2f out: stl plenty to do over 1f out: str run u.p 1f out: pressed wnr fnl 100yds: r.o but hld towards fin* **9/2**[3]
2223 **3** 1 **The Great Husk (IRE)**[9] 433 3-8-5 64 JimmyQuinn 2 64
(J S Moore) *sn led: rdn and narrowly hdd 2f out: stl ev ch tl no ex fnl 150yds* **5/1**
46-3 **4** shd **Fair Nella**[9] 422 3-8-0 62 FrankieMcDonald 3 59
(J G Portman) *broke wl: t.k.h: stdd to trck ldrs after 1f: effrt on inner over 2f out: ev ch over 1f out: one pce fnl f* **10/3**[2]
24 **5** 1½ **Jan Mayen**[26] 226 4-9-7 0 JoeFanning 1 60+
(M Johnston) *sn chsng ldr: ev ch over 2f out: unable qck u.p and beginning to struggle whn short of room ent fnl f: no prog after* **2/1**[1]
6 7 **Appledore (IRE)** 3-8-5 0 SimonWhitworth 6 52+
(A G Newcombe) *t.k.h: early: hld up in last pair: stl in tch whn hmpd over 2f out: n.d after* **12/1**
5 **7** nk **Kitty Koo (IRE)**[17] 326 3-7-12 0 ow5 MatthewCosham(7) 5 50
(J Jay) *hld up in tch in rr: hdwy on outer 4f out: struggling u.p over 2f out: wl btn fnl 2f* **33/1**

2m 26.37s (4.47) **Going Correction** -0.025s/f (Stan)
WFA 3 from 4yo 23lb **7** Ran SP% **111.9**
Speed ratings (Par 101): **82,81,80,80,79 74,74**
toteswinger:1&2:£8.00, 1&3:£8.80, 2&3:£2.20 CSF £46.57 TOTE £12.40: £6.70, £3.80; EX 51.40.
Owner M Khan X2 **Bred** Berry Racing **Trained** Epsom, Surrey
■ Stewards' Enquiry : David Probert three-day ban: careless riding (Feb 28-Mar 2)

FOCUS
A weakish maiden but interesting enough, with a few that had shown ability up against a couple of interesting newcomers. They went a very steady pace, though, and there were four in a line across the track 2f from home. Solid but limited form.

552 BET IN-RUNNING - BETDAQ H'CAP 7f (P)
3:10 (3:10) (Class 5) (0-75,75) 4-Y-0+ £2,590 (£770; £385; £192) Stalls High

Form RPR
6-12 **1** **Ocean Legend (IRE)**[14] 367 5-9-4 75 NeilCallan 11 84+
(A W Carroll) *trckd ldrs: hdwy to ld 2f out: sn rdn: drvn ent fnl f: r.o wl* **5/2**[1]
02-0 **2** ½ **Monsieur Fillioux (USA)**[20] 292 4-9-3 74 AdamKirby 3 82
(J R Fanshawe) *stdd and dropped in bhd after s: gd hdwy and swtchd ins over 1f out: chsd wnr ins fnl f: r.o but nvr quite getting to wnr* **8/1**
02-4 **3** 1¼ **Another Try (IRE)**[21] 287 5-8-8 65 HayleyTurner 6 70
(A P Jarvis) *t.k.h: hld up in tch towards rr: hdwy jst over 2f out: chsd ldrs and drvn ent fnl f: one pce fnl 150yds* **5/1**[3]
00-2 **4** 2½ **Cut And Thrust (IRE)**[11] 393 4-9-2 73 (p) ChrisCatlin 10 71
(M Wellings) *hld up in midfield: hdwy over 2f out: chsd ldrs and rdn over 1f out: wknd jst ins fnl f* **9/1**
030- **5** 2¼ **Gazboolou**[125] 6725 6-9-3 74 FergusSweeney 13 67
(David Pinder) *chsd ldrs: rdn to ld jst over 2f out: sn hdd: wknd u.p ent fnl f* **16/1**
6-11 **5** dht **Ejeed (USA)**[25] 234 5-8-3 65 ow3 RossAtkinson(5) 8 58
(Miss Z C Davison) *hld up in midfield on outer: reminders 4f out: effrt but hanging rt fnr over 2f out: no imp fr over 1f out* **4/1**[2]
000- **7** 1¾ **Esteem Lord**[235] 3274 4-8-8 65 LiamJones 2 53
(Jamie Poulton) *hld up in last: effrt and swtchd rt wl over 1f out: n.d* **40/1**
01-3 **8** nk **Moojeh (IRE)**[30] 191 4-9-4 75 JerryO'Dwyer 4 65+
(M Botti) *t.k.h: chsd ldrs: rdn and unable qck whn short of room 2f out: n.d after* **7/1**
000- **9** 2 **Auld Arty (FR)**[175] 5283 4-8-13 70 RobertHavlin 12 53
(Miss Jo Crowley) *led tl rdn and hdd jst over 2f out: sn struggling: wl btn fnl f* **20/1**
3005 **10** hd **Jonnie Skull (IRE)**[7] 451 4-8-1 65 (vt) LeonnaMayor(7) 7 47
(P S McEntee) *w ldr tl over 2f out: wknd qckly wl over 1f out: wl bhd fnl f* **33/1**
403- **11** ¾ **Hambledon Hill**[184] 4987 4-8-6 63 JimmyQuinn 9 43
(P Burgoyne) *in tch: effrt and rdn on inner jst over 2f out: wknd jst over 1f out* **20/1**

1m 24.92s (-1.08) **Going Correction** -0.025s/f (Stan) **11** Ran SP% **119.6**
Speed ratings (Par 103): **105,104,103,100,97 97,95,95,92,92 91**
toteswinger:1&2:£7.50, 1&3:£3.40, 2&3:£8.50 CSF £22.57 CT £97.63 TOTE £3.00: £1.10, £4.50, £1.80; EX 29.30.
Owner Ocean Trailers Ltd **Bred** Mark Commins **Trained** Cropthorne, Worcs

FOCUS
A competitive little handicap run at a decent pace thanks to Auld Arty and Jonnie Skull duelling up front, but they may have gone off too quick as they both eventually dropped right out. The form looks solid.
Ejeed(USA) ◆ Official explanation: jockey said gelding hung left and lost a tooth
Esteem Lord Official explanation: jockey said gelding was denied a clear run
Moojeh(IRE) ◆ Official explanation: jockey said filly was denied a clear run

553 BETDAQ.CO.UK LADYBIRD STKS (LISTED RACE) 1m (P)
3:45 (3:45) (Class 1) 4-Y-0+
£22,708 (£8,608; £4,308; £2,148; £1,076; £540) Stalls High

Form RPR
203- **1** **Viva Vettori**[235] 3282 6-9-0 87 DaneO'Neill 11 105
(D R C Elsworth) *hld up wl in tch: swtchd rt and rdn 2f out: rdn to ld ins fnl f: sn clr: eased towards fin* **8/1**
115- **2** 2 **Black Dahlia**[60] 7768 5-8-9 94 FrederikTylicki 12 96
(J A Glover) *hld up in midfield on inner: effrt whn sltly hmpd 2f out: swtchd rt and hdwy over 1f out: r.o wl to chse wnr ins fnl f: kpt on but no threat to wnr* **8/1**
01-2 **3** ½ **Splinter Cell (USA)**[31] 175 4-9-0 94 AndreaAtzeni 4 100
(M Botti) *hld up towards rr: n.m.r and swtchd lft wl over 1f out: rdn and edgd lft over 1f out: r.o wl ins fnl f to go 3rd fnl 50yds: no ch w wnr* **10/1**
113- **4** ½ **Spinning**[56] 7827 7-9-0 95 (b) PhillipMakin 7 98+
(T D Barron) *s.i.s: hld up in rr: stl plenty to do and swtchd ins and qcknd ent fnl 2f: r.o wl to press for placing ins fnl f: no ch w wnr* **9/1**
3634 **5** nk **Carcinetto (IRE)**[1] 537 8-8-9 92 PaulDoe 2 93
(P D Evans) *stdd after s: hld up in last trio: rdn and effrt on outer ent fnl 2f: r.o fnl f: nvr trbld ldrs* **20/1**
636- **6** ¾ **Six Of Hearts**[79] 7565 6-9-0 97 (b) FMBerry 1 96
(Cecil Ross, Ire) *in tch in midfield on outer: hdwy to join ldrs gng wl 2f out: rdn to ld over 1f out: hdd and immediately outpcd by wnr ins fnl f: wknd fnl 100yds* **4/1**[1]
13-1 **7** ¾ **Audemar (IRE)**[25] 231 4-9-0 88 MartinDwyer 6 94
(E F Vaughan) *t.k.h: chsd ldrs: rdn jst over 2f out: struggling over 1f out: wl hld fnl f* **6/1**[2]
05-3 **8** ½ **Plum Pudding (IRE)**[36] 109 7-9-0 102 RichardHughes 5 93
(R Hannon) *chsd ldr tl led over 6f out: rdn wl over 1f out: hdd over 1f out: wknd fnl f* **7/1**
000- **9** ¾ **Yahrab (IRE)**[265] 2327 5-9-0 101 NeilCallan 8 92
(C E Brittain) *t.k.h: chsd ldrs: rdn and unable qck 2f out: wknd jst over 1f out* **13/2**[3]
351- **10** ½ **Victoria Sponge (IRE)**[125] 6731 4-8-9 89 JimCrowley 3 86
(S C Williams) *stdd and dropped in bhd after s: rdn and effrt 2f out: nvr trbld ldrs* **11/1**
146 **11** ¾ **Reve De Nuit (USA)**[23] 266 4-9-0 95 (b[1]) RobertWinston 9 89
(A J McCabe) *t.k.h: hld up in tch: rdn and effrt on outer over 2f out: sltly hmpd and carried lft wl over 1f out: n.d after* **16/1**
16-5 **12** 16 **Alsahil (USA)**[31] 175 4-9-0 85 JoeFanning 10 54
(Micky Hammond) *racd freely: led tl over 1f out: chsd ldr after tl jst after 2f out: sn wknd: wl btn and eased ins fnl f* **33/1**

1m 36.88s (-2.92) **Going Correction** -0.025s/f (Stan) **12** Ran SP% **123.4**
Speed ratings (Par 111): **113,111,110,110,109 108,108,107,106,106 105,89**
toteswinger:1&2:£19.10, 1&3:£25.30, 2&3:£13.40 CSF £73.65 TOTE £9.80: £4.10, £3.10, £4.60; EX 108.70.
Owner Mike Watson **Bred** Stanley Estate And Stud Co **Trained** Newmarket, Suffolk
■ Stewards' Enquiry : Andrea Atzeni two-day ban: careless riding (Feb 28-Mar 1)

FOCUS
A competitive Listed event run at a decent pace and the form looks solid without being a race to go overboard about. A big step up from the winner.

NOTEBOOK
Viva Vettori was racing for the first time since June, but he has a good record fresh and has plenty of winning form around here. A bigger concern was that he had plenty to find on official ratings, but it made no difference and market support beforehand suggested a big run was expected. Having travelled powerfully in midfield, he dived for inside rail after the intersection and produced a telling turn of foot to hit the front and pull well clear. He may be aimed at the Lincoln provided the ground isn't too soft, for which he was given a quote of 20-1 from Hills. (op 12-1)
Black Dahlia, progressive in handicaps prior to a decent effort in a similar race to this over 7f here when last seen in December, finished strongly from the middle of the field, but the winner as already home and hosed. At least this effort shows that she is well up to this level. (tchd 9-1)
Splinter Cell(USA), runner-up in a messy conditions event at Wolverhampton last time, finished strongly from well off the pace but this effort rather confirms the view that he ideally needs further. (op 9-1)
Spinning ◆, a fine third in a hot handicap over course and distance last time when bidding for a hat-trick, lost ground at the start with a slow break and came off the bridle fully 3f from home, but he finished well when switched to the inside rail after the intersection. Next month's Lincoln Trial at Wolverhampton, won by the same owner/trainer's Flipando last year, looks the ideal target for him. (op 13-2)
Carcinetto(IRE), fourth of five in a Lingfield conditions event the previous day, bettered that performance here and made up a lot of late ground, but actually winning races is proving hard for her this winter. (tchd 25-1)
Six Of Hearts, who hadn't been seen since winning a conditions event on the Dundalk Polytrack in November, travelled very well in midfield but also covered plenty of ground by racing wide. He still seemed likely to win when cruising into the lead over a furlong out, but once there his stamina seemed to give out completely. (op 7-1)
Audemar(IRE) didn't seem suited by the switch to positive tactics. (op 9-1)
Plum Pudding(IRE) ran his usual honest race from the front until fading inside the last 2f. He doesn't seem to be at the top of his game at present. (op 6-1 tchd 8-1)
Victoria Sponge(IRE) Official explanation: jockey said filly suffered interference soon after start

554 BETDAQ ON 0870 178 1221 H'CAP 2m (P)
4:20 (4:20) (Class 5) (0-70,66) 4-Y-0+ £2,590 (£770; £385; £192) Stalls High

Form RPR
0-01 **1** **Kristallo (GER)**[17] 322 5-9-6 58 DaneO'Neill 7 65
(P R Webber) *chsd ldrs: rdn to chse ldr 2f out: 2 l down over 1f out: kpt on wl fnl f to ld on post* **7/2**[2]
1/03 **2** nse **Kentmere (IRE)**[17] 322 9-9-11 63 HayleyTurner 6 70
(P R Webber) *led: rdn and kicked 2 l clr wl over 1f out: kpt on wl under hands and heels riding tl worn down fnl 100yds and hdd on post* **12/1**
-202 **3** 1½ **Star Choice**[9] 426 5-9-11 63 RobertHavlin 8 69+
(J Pearce) *hld up in midfield: rdn whn short of room and hmpd jst over 2f out: rallied u.p ent fnl f: r.o wl to snatch 3rd on post* **8/1**
/02- **4** nse **Maraased**[59] 7790 5-9-12 64 IanMongan 3 69
(S Gollings) *hld up in tch: swtchd lft and effrt jst over 2f out: chsd clr ldng pair jst over 1f out: no imp fnl f: lost 3rd on post* **14/1**
0421 **5** 2 **Sir Sandicliffe (IRE)**[6] 463 6-8-8 53 KierenFox(7) 2 56
(W M Brisbourne) *hld up towards rr: rdn ent fnl 3f: no real prog tl styd on u.p fnl f: nvr trbld ldrs* **11/2**[3]
0/6- **6** 1 **Waarid**[18] 300 5-9-10 62 (be) GeorgeBaker 5 64
(G L Moore) *chsd ldr: pushed along 3f out: rdn and nt qckn jst over 2f out: out pce and no threat fr over 1f out* **8/1**
360- **7** nk **Ned Ludd (IRE)**[65] 6692 7-10-0 66 (b[1]) TomQueally 9 67
(J G Portman) *awkward leaving stalls: sn chsng ldrs: rdn and wandered u.p jst over 2f out: no ch w ldrs fr over 1f out* **12/1**
045- **8** 1½ **Go Amwell**[20] 3737 7-9-1 53 (v) LiamJones 4 52
(J R Jenkins) *s.i.s: a towards rr: nvr trbld ldrs* **12/1**
221- **9** 1 **Follow The Dream**[68] 7675 7-9-11 63 RichardHughes 1 62
(Karen George) *stdd and dropped in bhd after s: hld up towards rr: rdn and no real rspnse over 2f out: n.d* **11/4**[1]
-620 **10** ½ **Zuwaar**[9] 426 5-9-5 60 (tp) RobertLButler(3) 10 58
(P Butler) *hld up in rr: effrt towards inner 2f out: nvr trbld ldrs* **20/1**

3m 35.79s (5.69) **Going Correction** -0.025s/f (Stan) **10** Ran SP% **121.0**
Speed ratings (Par 103): **84,83,83,83,82 81,81,80,80,80**
toteswinger:1&2:£9.70, 1&3:£5.40, 2&3:£10.60 CSF £47.12 CT £323.13 TOTE £4.00: £2.10, £4.30, £3.90; EX 51.80.
Owner Iain Russell Watters **Bred** Gestut Hof Ittlingen **Trained** Mollington, Oxon

FOCUS
An ordinary staying handicap, but they went a better early pace than in many staying events around here. It resulted in a 1-2 for trainer Paul Webber and the pair are rated close to their bests.
Follow The Dream Official explanation: jockey said mare was unsuited by the slow pace

555 BET MULTIPLES - BETDAQ H'CAP (DIV I) 6f (P)
4:50 (4:51) (Class 6) (0-65,65) 4-Y-0+ £1,706 (£503; £252) Stalls High

Form RPR
4262 **1** **Sherjawy (IRE)**[16] 344 6-8-6 58 RossAtkinson(5) 4 67
(Miss Z C Davison) *chsd ldrs: grad crossed to rail and led after 1f: rdn wl over 1f out: hrd pressed ins fnl f: hld on gamely* **11/2**[3]
05-6 **2** nk **Love You Louis**[18] 312 4-9-3 64 RichardHughes 9 72
(J R Jenkins) *broke wl: led for 1f: stdd and sltly hmpd over 5f out: chsd ldrs after: effrt to chse wnr jst over 1f out: rdn to chal ins fnl f: no ex and hld fnl 50yds* **10/3**[1]

03-5 **3** ½ **Style Award**[37] 77 5-8-9 **59** KellyHarrison(3) 7 67+
(W J H Ratcliffe) *in tch in midfield: rdn whn short of room and lost pl over 1f out: sn swtchd lft: r.o strly fnl f: nt rch ldng pair* **20/1**
-066 **4** 1 **Titus Gent**[11] 391 5-9-1 **62** LiamJones 11 66+
(R A Harris) *chsd ldrs early: hmpd and lost pl after 1f: towards rr: rdn and stl plenty to do 2f out: gd hdwy ent fnl f: styd on wl but nvr able to chal* **12/1**
-054 **5** ¾ **Sirjosh**[9] 423 4-8-4 **51** oh2 (p) JimmyQuinn 5 52
(D Donovan) *chsd ldr tl 4f out: rdn and unable qck 4f out: one pce u.p fr over 1f out* **20/1**
-400 **6** 1 ¼ **Diddums**[6] 462 4-8-2 **56** ow2 AmyScott(7) 12 54+
(P S McEntee) *stdd s: hld up in rr: looking for run bhd a wall of horses and swtchd ins over 1f out: kpt on fnl f: nvr trbld ldrs* **14/1**
2314 **7** ¾ **Equinity**[11] 391 4-8-8 **55** (t) SaleemGolam 3 50
(J Pearce) *dismntd and led to s: stdd and swtchd sharply rt after s: rdn and effrt 2f out: no imp fnl f* **16/1**
-534 **8** nk **Premier Lad**[31] 170 4-9-4 **65** PhillipMakin 10 59
(T D Barron) *t.k.h: hld up wl in tch: rdn and effrt on inner 2f out: no imp ent fnl f* **4/1**[2]
0-04 **9** ½ **Norse Warrior (USA)**[14] 364 4-9-2 **63** (v) AdamKirby 8 55
(Peter Grayson) *towards rr: reminders 4f out: drvn and no prog over 2f out* **20/1**
-421 **10** nk **Steel City Boy (IRE)**[30] 185 7-8-13 **60** JimCrowley 1 51
(D Shaw) *midfield tl dashed up on outer to press ldr 4f out: rdn ent fnl 2f: wknd u.p ent fnl f* **15/2**
0-56 **11** ¾ **Star Strider**[11] 397 6-8-9 **61** ow2 KylieManser(5) 2 50
(T Keddy) *in tch in midfield on outer: wknd 2f out:* **8/1**
000- **12** 4 **West Leake (IRE)**[212] 4061 4-8-13 **60** TomQueally 6 36
(P Burgoyne) *restless in stalls: in tch tl rdn and wknd qckly ent fnl 2f* **33/1**

1m 12.76s (-0.34) **Going Correction** -0.025s/f (Stan) **12** Ran SP% **118.8**
Speed ratings (Par 101): **101,100,99,98,97 95,94,94,93,93 92,87**
toteswinger:1&2:£5.10, 1&3:£24.70, 2&3:£18.20 CSF £22.76 CT £351.16 TOTE £7.20: £1.80, £2.10, £8.40; EX 30.90.
Owner Charlie's Starrs **Bred** Darley **Trained** Hammerwood, E Sussex
■ Stewards' Enquiry : Ross Atkinson one-day ban: careless riding (Mar 1)

FOCUS
A moderate sprint handicap, but run at a good pace. Limited form.
Style Award ◆ Official explanation: jockey said mare was denied a clear run
Titus Gent Official explanation: jockey said gelding suffered interference soon after start
Equinity Official explanation: jockey said filly suffered interference soon after start
Star Strider Official explanation: jockey said gelding hung badly right

556 BET MULTIPLES - BETDAQ H'CAP (DIV II) 6f (P)
5:20 (5:20) (Class 6) (0-65,65) 4-Y-O+ **£1,706** (£503; £252) **Stalls** High

Form RPR
5452 **1** **Don Pele (IRE)**[3] 505 8-8-11 **58** (b) LiamJones 9 65
(R A Harris) *chsd ldrs: rdn ent fnl 2f: ev ch 1f out: hrd drvn ins fnl f: r.o to ld on post* **5/1**
434 **2** nse **Muktasb (USA)**[2] 532 9-8-0 **54** (v) SeanPalmer(7) 6 61
(D Shaw) *in tch: effrt on inner 2f out: led ent fnl f: edge dlft fnl 100yds: hdd on post* **4/1**[2]
000- **3** 2 ¾ **Sir Geoffrey (IRE)**[124] 6765 4-9-4 **65** FrederikTylicki 10 64
(J A Glover) *led: hrd pressed 2f out: rdn and hdd ent fnl f: wknd fnl 100yds* **10/3**[1]
2030 **4** nk **Kheley (IRE)**[6] 462 4-8-10 **62** DeanHeslop(5) 5 60
(W M Brisbourne) *in tch: rdn and outpcd 2f out: styd on steadily ins fnl f: nvr gng pce to threaten ldrs* **7/1**
0-44 **5** 1 ¼ **Captain Kallis (IRE)**[3] 504 4-8-10 **57** FrankieMcDonald 11 51
(D J S Ffrench Davis) *t.k.h: chsd ldr: ev ch and rdn 2f out: wknd jst ins fnl f* **9/2**[3]
500- **6** ¾ **Shadow Bay (IRE)**[111] 7053 4-8-7 **59** RossAtkinson(5) 2 51
(Miss Z C Davison) *sn outpcd in last: rdn and in tch 3f out: struggling and btn wl over 1f out* **25/1**

1m 12.89s (-0.21) **Going Correction** -0.025s/f (Stan) **6** Ran SP% **94.3**
Speed ratings (Par 101): **100,99,96,95,94 93**
toteswinger:1&2:£3.70, 1&3:£2.70, 2&3:£3.20 CSF £17.24 CT £39.34 TOTE £3.80: £1.60, £1.10; EX 17.10 Place 6 £412.96, Place 5 £185.46.
Owner Robert Bailey **Bred** John J Cosgrave **Trained** Earlswood, Monmouths
■ Valentino Swing was withdrawn after proving unruly at the stalls (9/2, deduct 15p in the £ under R4).

FOCUS
Another moderate sprint handicap and decimated by four non-runners and Valentino Swing being withdrawn at the start. The winning time was 0.13 seconds slower than the first division. Limited form.
Captain Kallis(IRE) Official explanation: jockey said gelding ran too free
T/Plt: £383.10 to a £1 stake. Pool: £73,135.38. 139.35 winning tickets. T/Qpdt: £30.40 to a £1 stake. Pool: £5,651.74. 137.40 winning tickets. SP

557 - 558a (Foreign Racing) - See Raceform Interactive

547 CAGNES-SUR-MER
Sunday, February 14

OFFICIAL GOING: Turf course - heavy; all-weather - standard

559a PRIX DE LA MEDITERRANEE (CLAIMER) (ALL-WEATHER) 1m (F)
2:55 (2:58) 5-Y-O+ **£6,637** (£2,655; £1,991; £1,327; £664)

RPR
1 **Val d'Espoir (IRE)**[8] 459 6-9-3 (b) DominiqueBoeuf 76
(H-A Pantall, France)
2 1 ½ **Alhaprince (IRE)**[658] 6-9-3 IoritzMendizabal 73
(F Seguin, France)
3 2 **Fire Flyer (FR)**[842] 7-9-4 (b) AMuzzi 69
(J C Napoli, France)
4 nse **Crossbill**[157] 7-9-6 71
(Y Fertillet, France)
5 1 ½ **Royal Dignitary (USA)**[8] 459 10-9-3 OfirBenDavid 64
(D Nicholls) *racd in 2nd: rdn st: styd on tl no ex ins fnl f* **9/1**[1]
6 snk **Noblement (GER)**[23] 273 5-9-0 (b) 61
(Mario Hofer, Germany)
7 1 **Lanfranc (FR)**[19] 303 7-9-3 62
(M Gentile, France)
8 2 **Manuelita** 5-9-3 57
(T Larriviere, France)
9 3 **Astrologue**[254] 5-9-0 (p) 47
(K Borgel, France)
10 2 ½ **Isander (USA)**[19] 303 5-9-0 (b) 41
(F Chappet, France)
0 **Wunderkind (GER)**[8] 459 5-9-7 (b) —
(P Chatelain, France)
0 **Butterfly Flip (FR)**[8] 459 6-8-10 (p) —
(J-P Perruchot, France)

1m 35.35s (95.35) **12** Ran SP% **10.0**
PARI-MUTUEL (Including 1 Euro stake): WIN 7.30; PL 2.60, 2.40, 2.10;DF 15.70.
Owner Mme Sibylle Egloff **Bred** Gestut Sohrenhof **Trained** France

560a PRIX D'UFA (H'CAP) (ALL-WEATHER) 6f 110y
3:25 (3:28) 4-Y-O+ **£9,735** (£3,894; £2,920; £1,947; £973)

RPR
1 **Amico Fritz (GER)**[13] 4-8-12 JulienAuge 78
(H-A Pantall, France)
2 nk **Johanan (FR)**[23] 272 4-9-6 StephanePasquier 85
(F-X De Chevigny, France)
3 shd **Allez Bailey (FR)**[67] 7696 4-9-4 CharlesNora 83
(W Walton, France)
4 nk **Desert Ocean (IRE)**[103] 6-9-3 81
(G Collet, France)
5 snk **Loup Normand (FR)**[73] 7-8-5 69
(M Nigge, France)
6 shd **Bonnie Prince Blue**[19] 303 7-8-6 IoritzMendizabal 69
(D Nicholls) *mid-div: 8th and pushed along st: drvn and styd on at one pce fr over 1 1/2f out: nrest at fin* **5/1**[1]
7 ¾ **Maggi Fong**[19] 304 4-8-10 71
(H-A Pantall, France)
8 shd **Agnes Champ (FR)**[97] 4-8-0 (b) 61
(M Boutin, France)
9 nk **Star Val (FR)**[73] 6-8-5 65
(Mme C Barande-Barbe, France)
10 ½ **Pink Candie (FR)**[19] 304 4-9-0 73
(Mlle V Dissaux, France)
0 **Choparlas (FR)**[108] 8-8-6 (b) —
(M Boutin, France)
0 **Bobtail (FR)**[1036] 7-8-12 (p) —
(F Rohaut, France)
0 **Ceodora (GER)**[19] 303 5-8-10 —
(J-P Perruchot, France)
0 **Bacarrita (FR)**[115] 5-8-6 —
(L A Urbano-Grajales, France)
0 **Helipad (FR)**[67] 7696 4-8-5 —
(F-X De Chevigny, France)
0 **Zibeling (IRE)**[42] 28 4-9-1 —
(Robert Collet, France)

1m 17.66s (77.66) **16** Ran SP% **16.7**
PARI-MUTUEL: WIN 15.30; PL 4.90, 4.80, 5.50; DF 97.70.
Owner Alexandre Pereira **Bred** A Pereira **Trained** France

540 WOLVERHAMPTON (A.W) (L-H)
Monday, February 15

OFFICIAL GOING: Standard
Wind: Light behind Weather: Showers

561 BET CHAMPIONS LEAGUE FOOTBALL - BETDAQ H'CAP 5f 20y(P)
2:10 (2:11) (Class 6) (0-52,52) 4-Y-O+ **£1,774** (£523; £262) **Stalls** Low

Form RPR
015- **1** **Straboe (USA)**[56] 7834 4-8-13 **51** SaleemGolam 12 63+
(S C Williams) *hld up in tch: rdn to ld ins fnl f: drvn out* **7/1**[3]
-605 **2** 1 **Maggie Kate**[10] 423 5-8-12 **50** (b) RobertHavlin 6 58
(R Ingram) *hld up in mid-div on ins: hdwy over 1f out: rdn and swtchd rt ins fnl f: fin wl* **12/1**
540- **3** 1 ¼ **Across The Sands**[55] 7838 4-9-0 **52** (b[1]) ChrisCatlin 1 56
(C N Kellett) *led after 1f: rdn and hdd ins fnl f: nt qckn* **9/1**
00-2 **4** hd **The Cuckoo**[11] 402 4-9-0 **52** FrannyNorton 7 55
(M Quinn) *led 1f: w ldr: rdn jst over 1f out: nt qckn wl ins fnl f* **15/2**
3434 **5** 1 ¾ **Truly Divine**[11] 402 5-8-8 **46** oh1 (v) DavidProbert 13 43
(C A Dwyer) *hld up in mid-div: rdn and edgd lft 1f out: kpt on same pce* **14/1**
-003 **6** ½ **Metropolitan Chief**[14] 368 6-8-8 **46** JoeFanning 5 41
(P Burgoyne) *hld up in rr: pushed along and c wd st: hung lft fr over 1f out: nvr trbld ldrs* **9/1**
2/0- **7** ½ **Tune Up The Band**[371] 475 6-9-0 **52** JimmyQuinn 4 46
(R J Hodges) *prom: rdn over 1f out: wknd ins fnl f* **6/1**[2]
3-43 **8** nk **Shakespeare's Son**[10] 423 5-9-0 **52** HayleyTurner 2 47+
(H J Evans) *hld up in rr: nt clr run over 1f out: n.d* **7/2**[1]
6515 **9** nk **Meikle Barfil**[14] 369 8-9-0 **52** (bt) RobertWinston 3 43
(J M Bradley) *hld up in tch: rdn and wknd 1f out* **11/1**
4463 **10** 2 ¾ **Cocktail Party (IRE)**[5] 477 4-8-10 **48** (v) FergusSweeney 8 29
(J W Unett) *t.k.h in rr: pushed along over 1f out: no rspnse* **10/1**
040/ **11** 3 ¼ **Smirfys Gold (IRE)**[504] 6328 6-8-8 **46** oh1 (p) FrederikTylicki 11 16
(Mrs D J Sanderson) *hld up in tch: pushed along and wknd wl over 1f out* **22/1**

61.72 secs (-0.58) **Going Correction** +0.025s/f (Slow) **11** Ran SP% **116.9**
Speed ratings (Par 101): **105,103,101,101,98 97,96,96,95,91 86**
toteswingers: 1&2 £26.20, 1&3 £15.50, 2&3 £30.90 CSF £87.38 CT £778.71 TOTE £10.80: £2.10, £5.60, £2.90; EX 229.30 TRIFECTA Not won..
Owner Brigid & Damian Hennessy-Bourke **Bred** Darley **Trained** Newmarket, Suffolk

FOCUS
A moderate but competitive sprint handicap run at a decent pace. A personal best from the winner, and sound but limited form in behind.
Shakespeare's Son Official explanation: jockey reported gelding missed break and jumped right

562 WOLVERHAMPTON-RACECOURSE.CO.UK (S) STKS 5f 216y(P)
2:40 (2:40) (Class 6) 3-Y-O+ **£1,774** (£523; £262) **Stalls** Low

Form RPR
2-52 **1** **Espy**[12] 391 5-9-8 67 PJMcDonald 2 64
(I W McInnes) *hld up and bhd: hdwy on ins wl over 1f out: led jst ins fnl f: rdn and r.o wl* **3/1**[1]
0-60 **2** 1 ½ **Bentley**[7] 464 6-9-13 57 (v) JimCrowley 6 65
(J G Given) *led: rdn wl over 1f out: hdd jst ins fnl f: nt qckn* **28/1**

35-3 **3** ¾ **Sir Edwin Landseer (USA)**[24] 258 10-9-5 70.(be) MichaelStainton(3) 3 57
(G L Moore) *racd keenly in tch: swtchd lft wl over 1f out: rdn and nt qckn wl ins fnl f* **6/1**[3]

2113 **4** *shd* **Obe Gold**[7] 464 8-9-13 68........ J-PGuillambert 9 65+
(P Howling) *hld up: pushed along 3f out: rdn jst over 1f out: swtchd lft ins fnl f: kpt on: nrst fin* **7/2**[2]

1510 **5** *nk* **Interchoice Star**[17] 351 5-9-13 60........(p) JerryO'Dwyer 5 61
(R Hollinshead) *hld up in tch: rdn wl over 1f out: one pce fnl f* **9/1**

12-0 **6** *nk* **Buy On The Red**[34] 138 9-9-13 67........ AdrianNicholls 7 60
(D Nicholls) *w ldr: rdn and ev ch over 1f out: one pce* **9/1**

3002 **7** *1* **Jord (IRE)**[7] 464 6-9-3 59........ FrederikTylicki 8 47
(J A Glover) *prom: pushed along over 2f out: wknd wl over 1f out* **3/1**[1]

40-6 **8** *2* **Tournedos (IRE)**[17] 349 8-9-8 73........(p) AndrewElliott 1 46
(Mrs R A Carr) *a bhd* **18/1**

1m 15.15s (0.15) **Going Correction** +0.025s/f (Slow)
WFA 3 from 5yo+ 15lb 8 Ran SP% **115.2**
Speed ratings (Par 101): **100,98,97,96,96 96,94,92**
toteswingers: 1&2 £16.50, 1&3 £4.30, 2&3 £14.30 CSF £83.41 TOTE £3.90: £1.40, £4.30, £2.00; EX 75.30 Trifecta £286.80 Part won. Pool: £387.59 - 0.93 winning units..There was no bid for the winner.
Owner Keith Brown Properties (hull) Ltd **Bred** Miss Brooke Sanders **Trained** Catwick, E Yorks

FOCUS
An ordinary seller and they didn't seem to go that quick. The winner was below his best in success.
Obe Gold Official explanation: jockey reported gelding denied a clear run

563 OVER 400 POINTS PROFIT AT BIGTIPS.CO.UK MAIDEN STKS 1m 4f 50y(P)
3:10 (3:10) (Class 5) 4-Y-0+ £2,456 (£725; £362) Stalls Low

Form RPR

4- **1** **Spinning Well (IRE)**[89] 7439 4-8-12 72........(tp) JimCrowley 3 67+
(R M Beckett) *set slow pce: qcknd 2f out: rdn over 1f out: clr ins fnl f: comf* **3/1**[3]

3-63 **2** *6* **Tropical Blue**[7] 468 4-9-3 72........ StephenCraine 5 61
(Jennie Candlish) *hld up: pushed along over 2f out: hdwy on ins wl over 1f out: sn rdn: wnt 2nd 1f out: no ch w wnr* **11/4**[2]

0/6- **3** *1* **Wee Ziggy**[76] 7608 7-9-6 39........ TomEaves 7 59?
(M Mullineaux) *hld up in tch: pushed along 2f out: rdn and btn over 1f out* **80/1**

24-2 **4** *shd* **Monaco Dream (IRE)**[10] 421 4-8-12 72........ JoeFanning 4 54
(W Jarvis) *w wnr: pushed along over 2f out: rdn and btn over 1f out* **5/2**[1]

4/ **5** 1 ¼ **Dawnhill (GER)**[614] 2954 6-9-6 0........ GrahamGibbons 2 57
(J J Quinn) *prom: rdn over 1f out: one pce* **9/2**

/ **6** *5* **Decibel**[641] 6-9-6 0........ FrannyNorton 6 52+
(K A Ryan) *hld up: pushed along and struggling wl over 1f out* **16/1**

00 **7** *5* **Jolly Cooper**[16] 355 7-8-8 0........ BarryAdams(7) 8 36
(Mike Murphy) *hld up: pushed along and bhd fnl 3f* **100/1**

8 *7* **Boa**[7] 5-9-1 0........ HayleyTurner 9 25
(R Hollinshead) *prom tl pushed along and wknd 2f out* **12/1**

2m 42.45s (1.35) **Going Correction** +0.025s/f (Slow)
WFA 4 from 5yo+ 3lb 8 Ran SP% **114.2**
Speed ratings (Par 103): **96,92,91,91,90 87,83,79**
toteswingers: 1&2 £11.90, 2&3 £14.20, 1&3 not won. CSF £11.68 TOTE £4.70: £2.00, £1.50, £6.10; EX 18.80 TRIFECTA Not won..
Owner Ballylinch Stud **Bred** Ballylinch Stud **Trained** Whitsbury, Hants

FOCUS
A really weak maiden run at a steady pace and, with the third-placed finisher rated just 39, this is not form to dwell on. The first two are rated below form.
Boa Official explanation: trainers representative reported mare in season

564 BETDAQ POKER H'CAP 1m 1f 103y(P)
3:40 (3:40) (Class 5) (0-75,70) 3-Y-0 £2,456 (£725; £362) Stalls Low

Form RPR

6-21 **1** *nse* **Bubbly Braveheart (IRE)**[10] 422 3-9-7 70........ RobertWinston 2 70+
(A Bailey) *hld up in 3rd: effrt over 2f out: rdn and carried v wd ent st: rdn over 1f out: r.o ins fnl f: jst failed: fin 2nd, nse: awrdd r* **8/13**[1]

-315 **2** **Kathindi (IRE)**[5] 482 3-8-12 66........ RossAtkinson(5) 3 65
(J S Moore) *led: pushed along whn hung bdly rt and rn v wd ent st: rdn over 1f out: jst hld on: fin first: disq: plcd 2nd* **7/2**[2]

00-2 **3** ¾ **Always De One**[14] 372 3-8-6 55........ JimmyQuinn 1 53+
(Miss J Feilden) *chsd ldr: pushed along and ev ch whn carried v wd and bmpd ent st: rdn over 1f out: kpt on ins fnl f* **5/1**[3]

5-56 **4** *5* **A P Ling**[23] 279 3-8-6 55........ SaleemGolam 4 42
(C N Kellett) *hld up last: missed trble ent st: rdn and effrt over 1f out: wknd ins fnl f* **14/1**

2m 5.14s (3.44) **Going Correction** +0.025s/f (Slow) 4 Ran SP% **107.5**
Speed ratings (Par 97): **84,85,84,79**
CSF £3.01 TOTE £1.50; EX 2.20.
Owner The Champagne Club **Bred** Albert Conneally **Trained** Newmarket, Suffolk
■ Stewards' Enquiry : Robert Winston one-day ban: excessive use of whip (Mar 1)
Ross Atkinson caution: careless riding

FOCUS
This form needs treating with real caution. For a start, they went a muddling gallop, with Kathindi, who had led from the off, slowing the pace down the back straight, and that runner then hung badly right off the bend into the straight, carrying Always De One, who in turn carried Bubbly Braveheart, over to the stands' rail. It was no surprise the latter was awarded the race.

565 BETDAQ.CO.UK APPRENTICE H'CAP 1m 1f 103y(P)
4:10 (4:10) (Class 4) (0-80,80) 4-Y-0+ £4,209 (£1,252; £625; £312) Stalls Low

Form RPR

3151 **1** **Formidable Guest**[14] 375 6-8-11 72........ RyanPowell 10 78
(J Pearce) *hld up and bhd: hdwy over 2f out: rdn to ld and edgd lft ins fnl f: r.o* **9/2**[2]

4-26 **2** ½ **Boo**[25] 255 8-8-6 70........(v) AlexEdwards(3) 6 75
(J W Unett) *a.p: led wl over 1f out: rdn and edgd lft whn hdd ins fnl f: kpt on* **9/1**

145- **3** 1 ½ **Slip**[73] 7628 5-8-7 73........ HarryBentley(5) 5 75
(Tim Vaughan) *hld up in mid-div: hdwy jst over 1f out: kpt on to take 3rd last strides* **5/1**[3]

2-42 **4** *nk* **Ahlawy (IRE)**[10] 429 7-8-9 75........(bt) SeanPalmer(5) 4 76
(F Sheridan) *dwlt: sn hld up in tch: ev ch over 1f out: one pce* **5/1**[3]

/00- **5** 2 ¼ **Holiday Cocktail**[93] 6648 8-8-7 68........ LeeTopliss 9 64
(J J Quinn) *hld up in rr: pushed along and effrt on ins wl over 1f out: wknd ins fnl f* **25/1**

20-0 **6** *shd* **Buddy Holly**[43] 25 5-9-5 80........ RyanClark 7 76
(Pat Eddery) *hld up in mid-div: hdwy over 2f out: c wd st: rdn wl over 1f out: wknd ins fnl f* **8/1**

00-1 **7** 1 ½ **Hannicean**[21] 294 6-8-6 67........ DavidKenny 8 60
(Ian Williams) *s.i.s: hld up and bhd: pushed along over 2f out: rdn and struggling wl over 1f out* **11/4**[1]

662- **8** 1 ¾ **Johnmanderville**[123] 6804 4-8-8 76........ ShirleyTeasdale(7) 2 65
(N Wilson) *led: hdd over 3f out: wknd wl over 1f out* **8/1**

060/ **9** ½ **Harare**[513] 6134 9-8-5 66 oh7........ MatthewLawson 1 54
(R J Price) *w ldr: led over 3f out: rdn over 2f out: hdd wl over 1f out: sn wknd* **28/1**

2m 0.69s (-1.01) **Going Correction** +0.025s/f (Slow) 9 Ran SP% **117.7**
Speed ratings (Par 105): **105,104,103,102,100 100,99,97,97**
toteswingers: 1&2 £8.60, 1&3 £6.30, 2&3 £10.10 CSF £45.35 CT £212.05 TOTE £4.50: £1.70, £3.10, £1.70; EX 38.20 Trifecta £202.90 Part won. Pool: £274.23 - 0.10..
Owner Macniler Racing Partnership **Bred** Kingwood Bloodstock **Trained** Newmarket, Suffolk

FOCUS
A fair apprentice handicap.

566 SPONSOR A RACE BY CALLING 01902 390000 H'CAP 1m 141y(P)
4:40 (4:40) (Class 5) (0-70,67) 3-Y-0 £2,456 (£725; £362) Stalls Low

Form RPR

51-2 **1** **Miami Gator (IRE)**[35] 127 3-8-13 62........ AndrewElliott 4 68
(J R Weymes) *chsd ldr: pushed along over 2f out: led wl over 1f out: sn hdd: r.o u.p to ld last strides* **9/4**[1]

000- **2** *shd* **Pastello**[80] 7551 3-8-7 63........ CharlesEddery(7) 2 69
(R Hannon) *t.k.h in tch: led over 1f out: sn rdn and edgd rt: hdd last strides* **4/1**[3]

1-16 **3** 4 ½ **Wedding Dream**[13] 382 3-9-4 67........ FrannyNorton 3 63
(K A Ryan) *led: pushed along and hdd wl over 1f out: wknd ins fnl f* **6/1**

3345 **4** 3 ¾ **Tamarind Hill (IRE)**[8] 454 3-9-1 64........(b) RobertWinston 1 51
(A J McCabe) *hld up last: pushed along over 2f out: wnt 4th wl over 1f out: no further prog* **11/2**

1-21 **5** *3* **Bookiesindex Girl (IRE)**[18] 329 3-9-2 65........ ShaneKelly 5 45
(J R Jenkins) *t.k.h early: in tch: rdn and wknd 2f out* **5/2**[2]

1m 51.23s (0.73) **Going Correction** +0.025s/f (Slow) 5 Ran SP% **109.0**
Speed ratings (Par 97): **97,96,92,89,86**
CSF £11.13 TOTE £3.50: £1.40, £2.70; EX 10.50.
Owner Mrs Elaine M Burke **Bred** Newlands House Stud **Trained** Middleham Moor, N Yorks

FOCUS
A modest 3-y-o handicap but the form looks fairly sound.

567 BARRIE & JANICE FAULKNER SILVER WEDDING H'CAP (DIV I) 7f 32y(P)
5:10 (5:10) (Class 6) (0-52,56) 4-Y-0+ £1,433 (£423; £211) Stalls High

Form RPR

0-06 **1** **Obe Brave**[31] 193 7-8-9 52........(b) JamesSullivan(5) 1 62
(Lee Smyth, Ire) *led 1f: hld up in tch on ins: swtchd rt jst over 1f out: rdn to ld ins fnl f: drvn out* **7/1**

-423 **2** ¾ **Ride A White Swan**[3] 530 5-8-10 48........ GrahamGibbons 11 56
(D Shaw) *s.s: t.k.h in rr: hdwy wl over 1f out: ev ch ins fnl f: nt qckn* **4/1**[2]

0545 **3** 1 ¾ **Sirjosh**[1] 555 4-8-11 49........(p) JimmyQuinn 12 52
(D Donovan) *hld up: stdy prog over 3f out: c wd st: rdn and one pce ins fnl f* **7/1**

-024 **4** 1 ½ **Almatlaie (USA)**[3] 523 4-8-13 51........ FergusSweeney 4 50
(J W Unett) *hld up in rr: pushed along over 2f out: rdn and hdwy over 1f out: r.o ins fnl f* **12/1**

00-1 **5** ½ **Dhhamaan (IRE)**[3] 530 5-9-4 56 6ex........(b) HayleyTurner 8 54
(Mrs R A Carr) *prom: led over 5f out: rdn jst over 1f out: hdd ins fnl f: no ex* **7/1**

0-00 **6** 1 ½ **Jeannie (IRE)**[26] 242 4-8-1 46 oh1........ RyanClark(7) 3 40
(N P Littmoden) *hld up in tch: lost pl over 3f out: kpt on ins fnl f: n.d* **50/1**

206- **7** *shd* **Herbert Crescent**[60] 7782 5-8-11 52........ BarryMcHugh(3) 10 46
(Ollie Pears) *s.s: hld up in rr: hdwy on outside over 3f out: rdn and edgd lft over 1f out: wknd ins fnl f* **5/1**[3]

0252 **8** 1 ¾ **Imperial Skylight**[3] 530 4-8-12 50........(v) ChrisCatlin 6 39
(M R Channon) *rdn to ld after 1f: sn hdd: prom: rdn over 1f out: wknd fnl f* **3/1**[1]

36-0 **9** *nk* **Stormburst (IRE)**[10] 423 6-8-8 46........ DavidProbert 5 34
(A J Chamberlain) *hld up in tch: rdn over 2f out: wknd wl over 1f out* **33/1**

3-50 **10** 1 ½ **Outer Hebrides**[14] 368 9-8-9 50........(v) KellyHarrison(3) 7 34
(J M Bradley) *hld up in mid-div: hdwy over 4f out: rdn and wkng whn n.m.r over 1f out* **25/1**

00-0 **11** *nk* **Vanatina (IRE)**[18] 320 6-8-9 47........ LiamJones 9 30
(W M Brisbourne) *a bhd* **40/1**

1m 29.54s (-0.06) **Going Correction** +0.025s/f (Slow) 11 Ran SP% **118.0**
Speed ratings (Par 101): **101,100,98,96,95 94,94,92,91,89 89**
toteswingers: 1&2 £10.90, 1&3 £7.90, 2&3 £6.30 CSF £34.29 CT £211.19 TOTE £10.10: £3.40, £2.50, £2.30; EX 40.60 Trifecta £261.30 Part won. Pool: £353.18 - 0.20 winning units..
Owner Mark Devlin **Bred** Helshaw Grange Stud, E Kent & Mrs E Co **Trained** Dungannon, Co Tyrone

FOCUS
A race full of horses who find winning difficult, and the pace was muddling. They looked to go really quick early on, but Hayley Turner aboard Dhhamaan slowed the pace significantly once getting to the front after a couple of furlongs or so. The time was 0.49 seconds slower than the second division.

568 BARRIE & JANICE FAULKNER SILVER WEDDING H'CAP (DIV II) 7f 32y(P)
5:40 (5:40) (Class 6) (0-52,52) 4-Y-0+ £1,433 (£423; £211) Stalls High

Form RPR

6-00 **1** **Pipers Piping (IRE)**[14] 369 4-8-11 52........ MichaelStainton(3) 2 63+
(P Howling) *hld up in tch on ins: rdn to ld jst over 1f out: edgd rt ins fnl f: drvn out* **3/1**[2]

0-54 **2** 3 ¼ **Misterisland (IRE)**[14] 369 5-8-8 46 oh1........ TomEaves 3 49
(M Mullineaux) *s.i.s: hld up in rr: hdwy on ins wl over 1f out: rdn fnl f: kpt on one pce* **9/2**[3]

-625 **3** *nk* **Hard Ball**[20] 296 4-8-13 51........(v) FrannyNorton 5 53
(M Quinn) *hld up in mid-div: hdwy and nt clr run wl over 1f out: sn swtchd rt and rdn: r.o to take 3rd nr fin* **13/2**

0-03 **4** ½ **Megalo Maniac**[34] 142 7-8-8 46........(v) FrederikTylicki 10 47
(R A Fahey) *sn hld up in tch: rdn wl over 1f out: no ex towards fin* **7/1**

500/ **5** *nse* **Motu (IRE)**[420] 7766 9-8-5 48........(v) AndrewHeffernan(5) 9 49
(I W McInnes) *prom: rdn over 2f out: one pce ins fnl f* **22/1**

-402 **6** 1 ¾ **Divertimenti (IRE)**[3] 531 6-8-12 50........(b) JoeFanning 1 47
(S R Bowring) *led: rdn and hdd jst over 1f out: wknd wl ins fnl f* **11/4**[1]

00-2 **7** ½ **Mr Fantozzi (IRE)**[34] 142 5-9-0 52........(bt) JimmyQuinn 11 47
(D Donovan) *sn w ldr: rdn wl over 1f out: sn wknd* **10/1**

00-0 **8** *6* **Sofonisba**[21] 295 4-8-8 49........(p) AndreaAtzeni(3) 6 30
(M Botti) *hld up towards rr: rdn over 3f out: c wd st: struggling wl over 1f out* **20/1**

The Form Book, Raceform Ltd, Compton, RG20 6NL

000 9 2 3/4 **Brazilian Brush (IRE)**[14] 368 5-8-11 **52**.....................(bt) JackDean(3) 7 26
(J M Bradley) *dwlt: a in rr* **25/1**
1m 29.05s (-0.55) **Going Correction** +0.025s/f (Slow) 9 Ran SP% **117.7**
Speed ratings (Par 101): **104,100,99,99,99 97,96,89,86**
toteswingers: 1&2 £6.90, 1&3 £6.10, 2&3 £4.80 CSF £16.82 CT £82.27 TOTE £3.90: £1.80, £1.60, £1.70; EX 18.20 Trifecta £198.00 Pool: £ 535.39 - 2.00 winning units. Place 6: £127.75 Place 5: £35.00 .
Owner C N Wright **Bred** Drumhass Stud **Trained** Newmarket, Suffolk
■ Stewards' Enquiry : Andrew Heffernan referral: used whip with excessive frequency
FOCUS
All the attention was on Pipers Piping. The time was 0.49 seconds quicker than the first division
T/Plt: £182.60 to a £1 stake. Pool: £73,921.33. 295.45 winning tickets. T/Qpdt: £33.50 to a £1 stake. Pool: £5,408.31. 119.30 winning tickets. KH

518 SOUTHWELL (L-H)
Tuesday, February 16

OFFICIAL GOING: Standard
Wind: almost nil Weather: fine and sunny, mild

569 BET CHAMPIONS LEAGUE FOOTBALL - BETDAQ H'CAP 6f (F)
2:00 (2:00) (Class 6) (0-55,55) 4-Y-O+ **£1,774** (£523; £262) **Stalls Low**

Form RPR
03-2 1 **Fuzzy Cat**[21] 296 4-8-9 **55**.. DeanHeslop(5) 4 68
(T D Barron) *dwlt: hdwy on inner over 2f out: led jst ins fnl f: carried hd high and sn hdd: led again nr fin* **15/8**[1]
-531 2 nk **Fulford**[12] 403 5-8-12 **53**.. JimmyQuinn 11 65
(M Brittain) *dwlt and swtchd lft after s: hdwy on ins over 2f out: narrow advantage 100yds out: hdd towards fin* **9/2**[2]
1-32 3 2 1/4 **Angle Of Attack (IRE)**[27] 234 5-9-0 **55**....................(v) RobertWinston 6 60
(A D Brown) *led: pushed 3 l clr over 2f out: hdd jst ins fnl f: no ex* **6/1**[3]
-040 4 2 1/2 **Tri Chara (IRE)**[8] 464 6-8-13 **54**.............................(p) GrahamGibbons 2 51
(R Hollinshead) *in tch: effrt over 2f out: edgd rt over 1f out: kpt on* **14/1**
30-4 5 1/2 **Verinco**[39] 89 4-9-0 **55**..(p) TomEaves 14 50
(B Smart) *chsd ldrs: wnt 2nd 3f out: edgd lft over 1f out: one pce* **10/1**
0-24 6 1 1/4 **Cheery Cat (USA)**[21] 296 6-8-8 **52**........................(p) KellyHarrison(3) 13 43
(J Balding) *chsd ldrs: fdd over 1f out* **12/1**
0003 7 nk **Bertbrand**[12] 403 5-8-7 **48**...(v) SaleemGolam 3 38
(I W McInnes) *chsd ldrs: wknd whn hmpd appr fnl f* **33/1**
0340 8 1 1/2 **Vogarth**[4] 518 6-8-7 **55**..(b) DavidKenny(7) 5 40
(M C Chapman) *in rr: sn drvn along: kpt on fnl 2f: nvr a factor* **40/1**
3-60 9 3/4 **Handsinthemist (IRE)**[12] 402 5-8-6 **47**................. FrankieMcDonald 7 30
(P T Midgley) *in tch: drvn and outpcd over 2f out* **25/1**
-006 10 3/4 **Makshoof (IRE)**[11] 423 6-8-11 **52**..................................(p) NeilCallan 9 33
(I W McInnes) *in tch: effrt over 2f out: fdd over 1f out* **20/1**
50-0 11 2 1/2 **Redwater River**[12] 403 6-8-6 **47**..............................(b) AndrewElliott 8 20
(Mrs R A Carr) *s.i.s: a in rr* **28/1**
440- 12 1/2 **Fashion Icon (USA)**[259] 2581 4-8-12 **53**................. FranciscoDaSilva 12 24
(J Hetherton) *chsd ldrs: wknd 2f out* **20/1**
0-64 13 4 **Great Knight (IRE)**[25] 270 5-8-11 **52**............................ ChrisCatlin 10 10
(John Joseph Hanlon, Ire) *in tch: drvn over 4f out: sn lost pl* **14/1**
1m 14.99s (-1.51) **Going Correction** -0.20s/f (Stan) 13 Ran SP% **119.6**
Speed ratings (Par 101): **102,101,98,95,94 92,92,90,89,88 85,84,79**
toteswingers: 1&2 £3.00, 1&3 £3.10, 2&3 £4.30 CSF £8.42 CT £44.90 TOTE £2.60: £1.20, £2.10, £1.90; EX 11.50 Trifecta £27.60 Pool: £370.79 - 9.92 winning units..
Owner Richard Barnes, Colin Aitken **Bred** Baroness Bloodstock **Trained** Maunby, N Yorks
■ Stewards' Enquiry : Dean Heslop one-day ban: used whip in the incorrect place (Mar 2)
FOCUS
They went a strong pace in this moderate handicap and the first two came from a long way back.

570 BET IN RUNNING - BETDAQ MAIDEN STKS 1m (F)
2:30 (2:30) (Class 5) 3-Y-O+ **£2,456** (£725; £362) **Stalls Low**

Form RPR
5- 1 **Shernando**[132] 6592 3-8-8 0.. JoeFanning 3 84+
(M Johnston) *drvn early to trck ldrs: led over 4f out: shkn up over 2f out: drew rt away: v easily* **4/11**[1]
2 7 **Wrongwayround (IRE)**[76] 4-9-13 0................................ PJMcDonald 5 68
(G A Swinbank) *s.s: hdwy 3f out: wnt 2nd 1f out: no ch w wnr* **10/1**
00- 3 8 **Stratton Banker (IRE)**[162] 5722 3-8-8 0........................ SaleemGolam 1 46
(S C Williams) *hld up in tch: effrt over 2f out: kpt on to take modest 3rd 1f out* **18/1**
55-4 4 2 3/4 **Mydy Easy (USA)**[22] 291 4-9-13 65................................... NeilCallan 4 44
(P T Midgley) *chsd ldrs: sn drvn along: wnt 3rd over 2f out: wknd fnl f* **9/1**[3]
0-5 5 2 1/4 **Shame The Devil (IRE)**[11] 421 5-9-13 0.......................... LeeVickers 8 39
(H J Evans) *trckd ldrs: outpcd over 3f out: wknd 2f out* **33/1**
060 6 1 1/2 **Miereveld**[15] 374 3-8-8 0... StevieDonohoe 6 32
(Sir Mark Prescott) *w ldrs: drvn over 4f out: sn outpcd: lost pl 3f out* **50/1**
7 4 1/2 **Spirit Of Darley (USA)** 3-8-3 0.. ChrisCatlin 7 17
(C E Brittain) *w ldrs: chal 3f out: sn drvn: hung rt and lost pl over 1f out* **11/2**[2]
4-0 8 36 **Owen Jones (USA)**[17] 356 4-9-10 0................................ WilliamCarson(3) 2 —
(P W Hiatt) *led: hdd over 4f out: hung lft and lost pl over 3f out: bhd and eased 2f out: eventually completed: hopelessly t.o* **25/1**
1m 43.13s (-0.57) **Going Correction** -0.20s/f (Stan)
WFA 3 from 4yo+ 19lb 8 Ran SP% **121.8**
Speed ratings (Par 103): **94,87,79,76,74 72,68,6**
toteswingers: 1&2 £3.60, 1&3 £3.70, 2&3 £15.20 CSF £5.95 TOTE £1.40: £1.02, £2.90, £3.70; EX 8.30 Trifecta £79.60 Pool: £690.99 - 6.42 winning units..
Owner The Originals **Bred** Miss K Rausing **Trained** Middleham Moor, N Yorks
FOCUS
A seriously uncompetitive maiden.
Owen Jones(USA) Official explanation: jockey said gelding hung left throughout

571 BETDAQ ON 0870 178 1221 (S) STKS 7f (F)
3:00 (3:00) (Class 6) 4-Y-O+ **£1,774** (£523; £262) **Stalls Low**

Form RPR
0-04 1 **Flores Sea (USA)**[5] 508 6-8-12 72................................... PhillipMakin 7 73+
(T D Barron) *trckd ldr: led 2f out: rdn clr* **11/10**[1]
1134 2 3 3/4 **Obe Gold**[1] 562 8-9-4 68.. J-PGuillambert 9 73
(P Howling) *trckd ldrs on outside: drvn over 3f out: wnt 2nd over 1f out: no imp and eased towards fin* **2/1**[2]
0610 3 8 **Madison Belle**[9] 451 4-8-13 63....................................... PaulHanagan 4 45
(J R Weymes) *led tl 2f out: wknd fnl f* **10/1**
6-10 4 3 3/4 **Zeffirelli**[14] 378 5-9-1 58.. WilliamCarson(3) 5 40
(M Quinn) *sn chsng ldrs: wknd over 1f out* **6/1**[3]
6050 5 4 **Favouring (IRE)**[21] 297 8-8-5 44...................................(b) DavidKenny(7) 6 24
(M C Chapman) *chsd ldrs: hung rt: lost pl 3f out* **100/1**
003- 6 3/4 **Pretty Orchid**[174] 5338 5-8-7 50.............................(p) FrankieMcDonald 8 17
(P T Midgley) *in rr: drvn over 4f out: bhd fnl 3f* **28/1**
0/0- 7 20 **Blushing Dreamer (IRE)**[75] 7615 4-8-0 32...................... RyanClark(7) 3 —
(Miss N A Lloyd-Beavis) *s.i.s: in rr: bhd fnl 3f: t.o: virtually p.u* **150/1**
1m 28.06s (-2.24) **Going Correction** -0.20s/f (Stan) 7 Ran SP% **109.4**
Speed ratings (Par 101): **104,99,90,86,81 80,58**
toteswingers: 1&2 £1.40, 1&3 £2.70, 2&3 £2.10 CSF £3.11 TOTE £1.70: £1.10, £2.90; EX 3.90 Trifecta £7.20 Pool: £731.43 - 74.15 winning units..The winner was bought in for 4,250gns.
Owner T D Barron **Bred** Beckie McLay-Irons **Trained** Maunby, N Yorks
FOCUS
An ordinary seller best rated around the runner-up.
Blushing Dreamer(IRE) Official explanation: jockey said filly lost its action final 1 1/2f.

572 COME JUMPING NEXT TUESDAY H'CAP 1m (F)
3:30 (3:30) (Class 4) (0-85,85) 4-Y-O+ **£4,209** (£1,252; £625; £312) **Stalls Low**

Form RPR
2-31 1 **Trans Sonic**[9] 451 7-7-13 **71** 6ex.............................. JamesSullivan(5) 5 80
(J Hetherton) *sn led: hdd 3f out: led over 1f out: styd on gamely to regain advantage last 100yds* **4/1**[1]
3-04 2 1 1/4 **Mozayada (USA)**[3] 544 6-8-7 **74**................................... FrannyNorton 8 80
(M Brittain) *led early: trckd ldrs: styd on to take narrow advantage jst ins fnl f: sn hdd and no ex* **11/1**
1-14 3 2 3/4 **Ours (IRE)**[12] 408 7-8-13 **85**.................................(p) AndrewHeffernan(5) 6 85
(John A Harris) *dwlt: racd wd in rr: hdwy and hung lft over 2f out: kpt on to take modest 3rd nr fin* **9/2**[2]
0-10 4 1 **Snow Bay**[19] 324 4-9-1 **82**.. GregFairley 9 80
(B Smart) *w ldr: led 3f out: hung lft and hdd over 1f out: wknd towards fin* **4/1**[1]
350- 5 1 **Full Speed (GER)**[66] 6681 5-8-13 **80**............................ RobertWinston 7 76
(G A Swinbank) *chsd ldrs on outside: effrt over 3f out: hung lft one pce fnl 2f* **7/1**
1-50 6 1/2 **Mcconnell (USA)**[27] 231 5-8-11 **81**............................ RobertLButler(3) 1 76
(P Butler) *dwlt: in rr: kpt on fnl 2f: nvr a factor* **12/1**
406- 7 5 **Toby Tyler**[195] 4660 4-8-4 **71**.. JimmyQuinn 3 55
(P T Midgley) *dwlt: sn outpcd and drvn along: sme hdwy 3f out: lost pl and eased over 1f out* **14/1**
-262 8 1 1/4 **Elusive Fame (USA)**[26] 245 4-8-9 **76**..........................(b) JoeFanning 2 57
(M Johnston) *sn chsng ldrs: effrt over 2f out: lost pl over 1f out: eased* **5/1**[3]
1125 9 3/4 **Elusive Warrior (USA)**[5] 508 7-8-5 **72**.....................(p) AndrewMullen 4 51
(A J McCabe) *sn lost nr side cheekpiece: chsd ldrs: drvn over 4f out: wknd over 1f out: eased* **16/1**
1m 41.51s (-2.19) **Going Correction** -0.20s/f (Stan) 9 Ran SP% **115.9**
Speed ratings (Par 105): **102,100,98,97,96 95,90,89,88**
toteswingers: 1&2 £10.60, 1&3 £4.30, 2&3 £8.10 CSF £48.51 CT £206.18 TOTE £4.70: £1.40, £3.30, £2.00; EX 60.30 Trifecta £318.30 Part won. Pool: £430.23 - 0.60 winning units..
Owner Mrs Lynne Lumley **Bred** I A Balding **Trained** Norton, N Yorks
FOCUS
A tight handicap. There was always likely to be a decent tempo and so it proved, but still few got into the race from off the pace. Sound form.

573 BOOK YOUR TICKETS ON LINE AT SOUTHWELL-RACECOURSE.CO.UK H'CAP 7f (F)
4:00 (4:00) (Class 3) (0-95,95) 4-Y-O+ **£6,799** (£2,023; £1,011; £505) **Stalls Low**

Form RPR
0342 1 **Bel Cantor**[7] 474 7-8-1 **81** oh1.................................(p) KellyHarrison(3) 4 88
(W J H Ratcliffe) *mde all: hld on gamely* **11/2**[3]
2-40 2 hd **Seek The Fair Land**[23] 286 4-8-4 **84** ow1............... WilliamCarson(3) 6 91
(J R Boyle) *trckd ldrs on outside: effrt 3f out: hung lft: wnt 2nd 100yds out: jst hld* **15/8**[1]
1543 3 2 **Onceaponatime (IRE)**[7] 474 5-8-4 **81** oh6........................ LukeMorris 1 83
(M D Squance) *trckd ldrs on inner: t.k.h: wnt 2nd over 1f out: one pce ins fnl f* **12/1**
1103 4 2 1/2 **Transmission (IRE)**[5] 508 5-7-13 **81** oh3................ JamesSullivan(5) 5 76
(B Smart) *w wnr: effrt 3f out: sltly hmpd over 1f out: one pce* **7/1**
3-23 5 nse **Nightjar (USA)**[21] 299 5-8-13 **95**................................(b) AmyRyan(5) 3 90
(K A Ryan) *trckd ldrs: effrt 3f out: one pce fnl 2f* **5/2**[2]
22-0 6 6 **Ingleby Arch (USA)**[21] 299 7-9-1 **92**.............................. PhillipMakin 2 72
(T D Barron) *dwlt: sn drvn along in last: reminders over 3f out: c wd over 2f out: sn lost pl and bhd* **7/1**
1m 27.53s (-2.77) **Going Correction** -0.20s/f (Stan) 6 Ran SP% **111.4**
Speed ratings (Par 107): **107,106,104,101,101 94**
toteswingers: 1&2 £3.10, 1&3 £8.40, 2&3 £5.90 CSF £16.05 TOTE £5.90: £2.00, £1.50; EX 20.90.
Owner W J H Ratcliffe **Bred** Henry And Mrs Rosemary Moszkowicz **Trained** Newmarket, Suffolk
FOCUS
A good handicap, but the pace wasn't overly strong.
NOTEBOOK
Bel Cantor was allowed an easy enough lead and was good enough to take advantage. He's equally effective over shorter and should remain competitive. (op 9-2)
Seek The Fair Land, the track record holder over this trip on Kempton's Polytrack, ran up to his best on this first try on Fibresand and was just held, with 1lb overweight clearly not helping. However, it's possible to argue that he might even have won had he not hung left over 1f out, before continuing to be inclined to edge in that direction, and he may yet do better back at Kempton. (op 5-2)
Onceaponatime(IRE) ◆ ran well considering he was 6lb out of the handicap, and is probably best suited by a strongly run 6f on Polytrack. He's one to keep in mind for when he gets his conditions. (tchd 10-1)
Transmission(IRE) was comfortably held and is probably a bit high in the weights now. (op 17-2)
Nightjar(USA) seemed to be intimidated in between rivals turning into the straight and lost his place as a consequence. Prior to that he had been a little keen just off the front-running winner and, all things considered, his apprentice rider would surely have been better off by being more positive. (op 9-4 tchd 11-4)
Ingleby Arch(USA) was simply not in the mood this time. (op 6-1)

574 ARENA LEISURE PLC H'CAP 7f (F)
4:30 (4:30) (Class 6) (0-60,60) 3-Y-O **£1,774** (£523; £262) **Stalls Low**

Form RPR
66-4 1 **Yawary**[18] 346 3-9-4 **60**...(t) NeilCallan 5 80+
(C E Brittain) *w ldrs: led over 4f out: drvn clr 1f out: heavily eased nr fin* **4/1**[3]

00-2 **2** 3 3/4 **Buzz Bird**[9] 455 3-8-4 **46** .... FrannyNorton 1 53
(T D Barron) *dwlt: sn drvn along in rr: hdwy 2f out: kpt on to take 2nd 1f out: no ch w wnr* **2/1**[1]

000- **3** 3 3/4 **Rescent**[60] 7791 3-8-5 **47** .... AndrewElliott 6 44
(Mrs R A Carr) *led tl over 4f out: one pce fnl 2f* **40/1**

35-0 **4** 3/4 **La Toya J (IRE)**[27] 233 3-9-4 **60** .... DaneO'Neill 4 55
(R Curtis) *drvn early to trck ldrs: kpt on to take 2nd over 1f out: sn wknd* **9/4**[2]

0-03 **5** nk **Lord's Seat**[9] 455 3-7-13 **46** oh1 ....(p) AndrewHeffernan(5) 7 40
(A Berry) *chsd ldrs: drvn and stmbld over 4f out: sn outpcd: one pce fnl 2f* **14/1**

205- **6** 6 **Thewinnatakesitall**[61] 7778 3-9-1 **57** .... FrankieMcDonald 2 35
(H J Evans) *t.k.h: trckd ldrs: hung lft and lost pl over 1f out* **16/1**

-534 **7** 1 3/4 **Baby Judge (IRE)**[32] 188 3-8-6 **48** .... ChrisCatlin 8 21
(M C Chapman) *chsd ldrs on outer: rdn and outpcd over 2f out: sn lost pl* **11/1**

-403 **8** 3 1/2 **City Gossip (IRE)**[9] 454 3-8-11 **58** .... JamieJones(5) 3 22
(M G Quinlan) *s.i.s: effrt on outer over 3f out: lost pl over 2f out* **14/1**

1m 28.95s (-1.35) **Going Correction** -0.20s/f (Stan) **8** Ran SP% **114.1**
Speed ratings (Par 95): **99,94,90,89,89 82,80,76**
toteswingers: 1&2 £3.20, 1&3 £17.50, 2&3 £15.90 CSF £12.36 CT £273.17 TOTE £6.10: £1.90, £1.10, £8.30; EX 15.80 Trifecta £221.80 Pool: £512.56 - 1.71 winning units..
Owner Saeed Manana **Bred** Cheveley Park Stud Ltd **Trained** Newmarket, Suffolk

FOCUS
A weak handicap but the winner showed much improved form. The standard is solid but limited in behind.

575 MEMBERSHIP OF SOUTHWELL GOLF CLUB H'CAP — 1m 4f (F)
5:00 (5:00) (Class 6) (0-65,65) 4-Y-O+ — **£1,774** (£523; £262) **Stalls** Low

Form RPR

01-2 **1** **Tyrana (GER)**[35] 139 7-9-3 **58** .... StevieDonohoe 5 69+
(Ian Williams) *trckd ldrs: wnt 2nd 3f out: led and hung lft over 1f out: styd on strly: readily* **9/4**[2]

0/01 **2** 1 3/4 **Sarah's Boy**[6] 493 5-8-10 **51** 6ex .... GregFairley 3 58
(D E Pipe) *led: drvn over 2f out: hung lft and carried hd awkwardly: hdd over 1f out: kpt on same pce* **11/8**[1]

0162 **3** 3 1/4 **Highland River**[9] 457 4-8-12 **56** ow1 .... LeeVickers 1 59
(A Sadik) *chsd ldrs: drvn over 3f out: one pce fnl 2f* **11/1**

125- **4** 1 3/4 **Swords**[73] 7635 8-9-1 **56** .... JoeFanning 4 56
(R E Peacock) *hld up in last: hdwy over 3f out: sn chsng ldrs: one pce fnl 2f* **6/1**[3]

0-12 **5** 1 3/4 **Dan Buoy (FR)**[11] 114 7-8-13 **59** ....(p) RossAtkinson(5) 2 56
(R C Guest) *trckd ldrs: drvn over 7f out: sn lost pl and detached in last: kpt on fnl f* **8/1**

6 12 **Glorybe (GER)**[191] 4-9-7 **65** .... DaneO'Neill 6 44
(C C Bealby) *t.k.h: sn trcking ldrs: lost pl over 2f out: bhd whn eased ins fnl f* **20/1**

2m 38.63s (-2.37) **Going Correction** -0.20s/f (Stan)
WFA 4 from 5yo+ 3lb **6** Ran SP% **111.4**
Speed ratings (Par 101): **99,97,95,94,93 85**
toteswingers: 1&2 £1.10, 1&3 £5.70, 2&3 £4.90 CSF £5.63 TOTE £3.00: £1.90, £1.10; EX 6.00 Place 6: £5.41 Place 5: £4.43.
Owner T Bhoot **Bred** Gestut Brummerhof **Trained** Portway, Worcs

FOCUS
A modest handicap, but fair for the grade with the winner building on his good recent form.
T/Plt: £8.80 to a £1 stake. Pool: £82,078.69. 6,738.24 winning tickets. T/Qpdt: £7.30 to a £1 stake. Pool: £5,534.03. 554.78 winning tickets. WG

550 KEMPTON (A.W) (R-H)
Wednesday, February 17

OFFICIAL GOING: Standard
Wind: Light, across Weather: Fine

576 KEMPTON.CO.UK APPRENTICE H'CAP — 1m 2f (P)
5:10 (5:10) (Class 7) (0-50,54) 4-Y-O+ — **£1,364** (£403; £201) **Stalls** High

Form RPR

0-61 **1** **Lytham (IRE)**[7] 479 9-9-7 **54** 6ex .... AmyBaker 8 62+
(A W Carroll) *t.k.h: hld up in last pair: prog on wd outside fr 3f out: led over 1f out: sn in command: urged along and kpt on* **9/4**[1]

0-00 **2** 1 1/4 **Hatch A Plan (IRE)**[7] 479 9-9-0 **50** .... CharlesEddery(3) 3 56
(Mouse Hamilton-Fairley) *blindfold off in plenty of time and broke on terms: trckd ldng quartet: effrt over 1f out: edgd lft u.p but tk 2nd ins fnl f: no real imp on wnr* **20/1**

1065 **3** 3/4 **Turkish Sultan (IRE)**[7] 479 7-8-10 **48** ....(b) RyanClark(5) 2 53
(J M Bradley) *hld up in last quartet: pushed along 3f out: urged along and prog over 1f out to take 3rd ins fnl f* **11/2**[3]

600- **4** 2 3/4 **Ruwain**[89] 7466 6-8-13 **46** .... AshleyMorgan 6 46
(P J McBride) *mde most: rdn and hdd over 1f out: wknd fnl f* **7/1**

3000 **5** 3/4 **Easy Wonder (GER)**[8] 470 5-8-7 **45** ....(b) MatthewCosham(5) 10 43
(I A Wood) *trckd ldrs: cl enough over 1f out: nt qckn and sn lost pl* **25/1**

0- **6** 1 **Andaman Sunset**[63] 7767 5-9-3 **50** ....(tp) JamieJones 7 47
(J L Spearing) *t.k.h: hld up in last quartet: rdn 3f out: effrt on inner over 1f out: sn no prog* **8/1**

04-4 **7** hd **Sir Haydn**[39] 99 10-8-8 **46** ....(v) DannyBrock(5) 9 42
(J R Jenkins) *w ldr: upsides over 2f out: wknd over 1f out* **15/2**

0-00 **8** 4 1/2 **Clerical (USA)**[14] 397 4-8-11 **48** ....(p) AmyScott(3) 5 36
(R M H Cowell) *trckd ldng pair: lost pl over 2f out: wknd over 1f out* **14/1**

534- **9** 1/2 **Spanish Cross (IRE)**[89] 7466 5-8-10 **48** .... HollyHall(5) 1 35
(G Prodromou) *t.k.h: hld up in last pair: pushed along and no prog over 2f out: sn bhd* **9/2**[2]

2m 7.25s (-0.75) **Going Correction** -0.15s/f (Stan)
WFA 4 from 5yo+ 1lb **9** Ran SP% **115.0**
Speed ratings (Par 97): **97,96,95,93,92 91,91,88,87**
Tote Swingers: 1&2 £17.90, 1&3 £3.60, 2&3 £20.80 CSF £52.17 CT £224.35 TOTE £3.20: £1.70, £10.80, £1.10; EX 41.00.
Owner Morgan, Clarke & Parris **Bred** Mrs A S O'Brien And Lars Pearson **Trained** Cropthorne, Worcs

FOCUS
A weak apprentice handicap. The standard is set around the second and third.

577 BISTRO AT THE PANORAMIC BAR & RESTAURANT H'CAP — 5f (P)
5:40 (5:40) (Class 4) (0-85,81) 3-Y-O — **£4,209** (£1,252; £625; £312) **Stalls** High

Form RPR

-233 **1** **Athwaab**[25] 277 3-8-7 **69** .... WilliamCarson(3) 1 76
(M G Quinlan) *mde all: drvn over 1f out: kpt gng wl and in command fnl f* **10/1**

21-4 **2** 1 3/4 **Lucky Mellor**[25] 277 3-9-7 **80** ....(b) NeilCallan 5 81
(D K Ivory) *hld up bhd ldrs: effrt and cl up on inner over 1f out: sn rdn and nt qckn: no imp on wnr fnl f* **5/2**[2]

16-1 **3** 3/4 **Breathless Kiss (USA)**[7] 478 3-9-3 **81** 6ex ....(b[1]) AmyRyan(5) 3 79+
(K A Ryan) *s.s: keen and sn in tch: prog rnd outside to dispute 2nd 2f out: nt qckn over 1f out: one pce after* **11/4**[3]

-112 **4** 1/2 **Texas Queen**[7] 478 3-8-6 **72** .... CharlesEddery(7) 4 68
(M R Channon) *t.k.h: hld up: dropped to last 1/2-way: nt qckn over 1f out: kpt on last 100yds* **9/4**[1]

-223 **5** 3 1/2 **R Woody**[17] 363 3-9-2 **75** .... SteveDrowne 2 60
(Mrs L C Jewell) *chsd wnr to 2f out: wknd over 1f out* **6/1**

59.79 secs (-0.71) **Going Correction** -0.15s/f (Stan) **5** Ran SP% **109.4**
Speed ratings (Par 99): **99,96,95,94,88**
CSF £34.25 TOTE £12.30: £10.20, £1.10; EX 35.00.
Owner John Hanly **Bred** Shadwell Estate Co Ltd **Trained** Newmarket, Suffolk

FOCUS
The pace was only steady by the usual standards for this distance. It was a fair little race despite the turnout, with the winner recording a personal best.
Breathless Kiss(USA) Official explanation: jockey said filly missed the break

578 DIGIBET.COM H'CAP — 5f (P)
6:10 (6:10) (Class 4) (0-85,85) 4-Y-O+ — **£4,209** (£1,252; £625; £312) **Stalls** High

Form RPR

-366 **1** **Lord Of The Reins (IRE)**[14] 384 6-8-6 **73** .... FrannyNorton 5 82
(J G Given) *hld up in 5th: prog to take 2nd 1f out: shkn up and r.o wl on inner to ld narrowly but decisively last 50yds* **15/2**[3]

-034 **2** hd **Glamorous Spirit (IRE)**[14] 384 4-9-4 **85** .... LiamJones 6 94
(R A Harris) *racd freely: led at str pce: over 2 l clr 1f out: kpt on but hdd last 50yds* **11/4**[2]

01-5 **3** 1 1/4 **Anne Of Kiev (IRE)**[19] 345 5-8-11 **78** ....(t) LukeMorris 4 82
(J R Gask) *s.i.s: hld up last: stl there over 1f out: rdn ent fnl f: wnt 3rd last 100yds and r.o wl: no ch to rch ldng pair* **8/1**

1010 **4** 3 1/2 **Thoughtsofstardom**[14] 384 7-7-11 **71** oh2 .... LeonnaMayor(7) 1 62
(P S McEntee) *t.k.h: chsd ldr: no imp over 1f out: wknd fnl f* **20/1**

5665 **5** 3/4 **Canadian Danehill (IRE)**[12] 432 8-9-0 **81** ....(p) NeilCallan 3 70
(R M H Cowell) *chsd ldng pair to 1/2-way: sn rdn: 3rd again briefly over 1f out: wknd fnl f* **9/1**

1-41 **6** 1/2 **Absa Lutte (IRE)**[14] 384 7-8-11 **78** ....(t) StephenCraine 2 65
(Patrick Morris) *awkward s: rcvrd to chse ldng pair 1/2-way: rdn over 1f out: fdd tamely* **1/1**[1]

58.93 secs (-1.57) **Going Correction** -0.15s/f (Stan) **6** Ran SP% **114.3**
Speed ratings (Par 105): **106,105,103,98,96 96**
Tote Swingers: 1&2 £3.90, 1&3 £4.80, 2&3 £1.10 CSF £29.01 TOTE £11.60: £8.30, £1.70; EX 26.60.
Owner Peter Swann **Bred** C Farrell **Trained** Willoughton, Lincs

FOCUS
A fair sprint handicap run at a good pace. The time was only 0.01 seconds outside the track record, and 0.86 seconds quicker than the earlier 3-y-o handicap for horses rated 66-85. Straightforward form, although the favourite failed to give her running.

579 DIGIBET CLASSIFIED CLAIMING STKS — 7f (P)
6:40 (6:40) (Class 6) 4-Y-O+ — **£2,047** (£604; £302) **Stalls** High

Form RPR

-610 **1** **Lord Fidelio (IRE)**[24] 285 4-9-0 70 .... DavidProbert 6 79+
(A M Balding) *dwlt: settled in 6th: pushed along and prog over 2f out: rdn and clsd qckly to ld over 1f out: sn clr* **3/1**[1]

-120 **2** 4 **Straight Face (IRE)**[16] 373 6-8-10 65 ....(b) J-PGuillambert 4 65
(P D Evans) *chsd ldng pair: pushed along 3f out: kpt on fr over 1f out to take 2nd jst ins fnl f: no ch w wnr* **11/2**

14-0 **3** 1 **Trade Centre**[26] 259 5-9-2 70 ....(b[1]) LiamJones 7 69
(R A Harris) *settled in 5th: rdn 3f out: prog on inner over 1f out: kpt on to take 3rd ins fnl f: n.d* **9/2**[3]

4531 **4** 2 **Dvinsky (USA)**[17] 364 9-9-8 70 ....(b) JimmyQuinn 3 70
(P Howling) *chsd ldr: lost 2nd and rdn over 1f out: no ex ent fnl f: wknd sn after* **4/1**[2]

2144 **5** 4 1/2 **Mocha Java**[19] 342 7-8-3 63 ....(p) AndreaAtzeni(3) 1 42
(Matthew Salaman) *dwlt: hld up in last: pushed along 1/2-way: nvr a factor* **14/1**

0-50 **6** 3/4 **Milne Bay (IRE)**[24] 287 5-8-7 67 ....(t) LauraPike(7) 8 48
(D M Simcock) *led at decent pce: gng easily over 2f out: capitulated and hdd over 1f out: wknd rapidly* **11/2**

1206 **7** 6 **Carmenero (GER)**[10] 451 7-9-4 70 .... RobertWinston 5 47
(C R Dore) *dwlt: chsd ldng trio: rdn 3f out: sn wknd: t.o* **8/1**

1m 24.06s (-1.94) **Going Correction** -0.15s/f (Stan) **7** Ran SP% **111.7**
Speed ratings (Par 101): **105,100,99,97,91 91,84**
Tote Swingers: 1&2 £6.00, 1&3 £3.50, 2&3 £3.10 CSF £18.76 TOTE £5.30: £4.60, £1.20; EX 16.10.Winner was claimed by Mr Ollie Pears for £8,000.
Owner J B Munz **Bred** G S A Bloodstock Ptl Ltd **Trained** Kingsclere, Hants

FOCUS
Only 9lb separated this lot at the weights and this was a fair claimer, with an improved effort from the winner. The pace seemed decent enough.
Carmenero(GER) Official explanation: jockey said gelding hung right; vet said gelding was found to be lame right-hind

580 DIGIBET SPORTS BETTING H'CAP — 7f (P)
7:10 (7:10) (Class 4) (0-85,85) 4-Y-O+ — **£4,209** (£1,252; £625; £312) **Stalls** High

Form RPR

460- **1** **Dingaan (IRE)**[139] 6429 7-9-1 **82** .... DavidProbert 2 89
(A M Balding) *hld up in 7th: rdn and prog on wd outside fr jst over 2f out: styd on to ld narrowly jst ins fnl f: drvn out* **10/1**

0-43 **2** 3/4 **Dinner Date**[37] 123 8-7-13 **73** ow2 .... LauraPike(7) 7 78
(T Keddy) *hld up in 6th: stdy prog over 2f out: pushed along to chal 1f out: r.o but a jst hld by wnr* **20/1**

342- **3** 1/2 **Confuchias (IRE)**[61] 7795 6-9-4 **85** .... LukeMorris 3 89
(J R Gask) *t.k.h: hld up in 5th: rdn over 2f out: clsd grad fr over 1f out: a jst outpcd by ldng pair fnl f* **4/1**[2]

The Form Book, Raceform Ltd, Compton, RG20 6NL

142- **4** 2 **Arachnophobia (IRE)**[109] 7181 4-9-0 **81**...................... RobertWinston 4 80
(Pat Eddery) *chsd ldr: rdn over 2f out: grad clsd u.p and nrly upsides ent fnl f: sn fdd* **7/1[3]**

1-04 **5** ¾ **L'Hirondelle (IRE)**[20] 324 6-9-3 **84**.................................... PaulDoe 5 81
(M J Attwater) *led: urged along over 2f out: hdd & wknd jst ins fnl f* **8/1**

66-5 **6** 24 **Hellbender (IRE)**[23] 292 4-8-9 **76**.......................... RichardKingscote 9 8
(S Kirk) *chsd ldng pair to over 2f out: sn wknd: eased fnl f: t.o* **14/1**

3-10 **7** 24 **Spinning Bailiwick**[12] 432 4-9-1 **82** ow2...................... GeorgeBaker 1 —+
(G L Moore) *hld up in last: bdly hmpd jst over 2f out: virtually p.u after* **14/1**

1-2 **P** **Celtic Sovereign (IRE)**[26] 259 4-8-12 **79**.................... JerryO'Dwyer 6 —
(M G Quinlan) *plld hrd early: hld up bhd ldng pair: clsng whn broke down over 2f out: p.u* **6/4[1]**

1m 24.87s (-1.13) **Going Correction** -0.15s/f (Stan) 8 Ran SP% **110.8**
Speed ratings (Par 105): **100,99,98,96,95 68,40,—**
Tote Swingers: 1&2 £23.60, 1&3 £9.00, 2&3 £12.30 CSF £169.26 CT £901.33 TOTE £13.30: £3.40, £6.60, £1.70; EX 180.10.
Owner Lady C S Cadbury **Bred** Mrs Gill Wilson **Trained** Kingsclere, Hants

FOCUS
A race marred by the horrendous-looking injury Celtic Sovereign suffered just over 2f from the finish. This handicap was obviously not as strong as it might have been and the time was 0.81 secs slower than the earlier claimer won by the 70-rated Lord Fidelio. The form is rated around the principals.
Spinning Bailiwick Official explanation: jockey said filly was badly hampered

581 GOFFS BREEZE UP AT KEMPTON MARCH 12TH H'CAP 6f (P)
7:40 (7:41) (Class 6) (0-55,55) 3-Y-O **£2,047** (£604; £302) **Stalls** High

Form RPR

-023 **1** **Sweet Avon**[19] 346 3-9-0 **53**... ShaneKelly 2 62
(Matthew Salaman) *hld up bhd ldng trio: gng easily over 2f out: prog to ld over 1f out: edgd rt whn pressed fnl f: hld on wl* **7/1**

-432 **2** ¾ **Exceed Power**[26] 265 3-8-10 **52**.................................. AndreaAtzeni(3) 6 59
(D M Simcock) *hld up in 7th and off the pce: clsd over 2f out: rdn to take 2nd jst over 1f out: chal fnl f: kpt on but a hld* **7/2[1]**

660- **3** 3¾ **Roybuoy**[48] 7887 3-9-0 **53**...(b) JimmyQuinn 4 49
(H J L Dunlop) *hld up in 6th: effrt on inner over 2f out: kpt on to take 3rd ins fnl f but ldng pair wl away* **9/1**

-603 **4** 4½ **Dolly Will Do**[14] 387 3-8-4 **46**...................................... KellyHarrison(3) 8 28
(N P Mulholland) *settled in 9th: urged along over 2f out: plugged on to claim remote 4th last stride* **9/1**

400- **5** shd **Back On**[242] 3167 3-8-8 **52**..(v[1]) MarkCoumbe(5) 3 34
(M D Squance) *chsd ldng quartet: drvn and lost pl over 2f out: no ch after: jst lost out in battle for remote 4th* **20/1**

6-60 **6** shd **Princess Shamal**[14] 387 3-8-12 **51**............................. StephenCraine 9 32
(J R Jenkins) *t.k.h: w ldr: led 1/2-way: fnd nil in front and hdd over 1f out: wknd fnl f* **20/1**

004- **7** 2¼ **Old Devil Moon (IRE)**[113] 7089 3-8-13 **52**.................... TomQueally 1 31
(R A Mills) *hld up in last: shkn up over 2f out: keeping on to cl on gp squabbling for remote 4th whn short of room ins fnl f* **9/2[2]**

4-44 **8** ½ **Mind The Monarch**[18] 357 3-8-11 **55**......................... RossAtkinson(5) 7 28
(R A Teal) *pushed along in 8th after 2f and wl off the pce: nvr a factor* **5/1[3]**

00-5 **9** ¾ **Ba Jetstream**[14] 387 3-8-7 **46** oh1.................................(p) JoeFanning 10 17
(F Jordan) *rousted up to ld on inner: hdd and rdn 1/2-way: styd w ldr: upsides over 1f out: wknd rapidly* **16/1**

-624 **10** 5 **Bertie Buckle (IRE)**[10] 455 3-9-0 **53**...........................(b[1]) LukeMorris 5 9
(J R Gask) *plld hrd early bhd ldng pair: wknd rapidly over 2f out* **7/1**

1m 12.74s (-0.36) **Going Correction** -0.15s/f (Stan) 10 Ran SP% **117.5**
Speed ratings (Par 95): **96,95,90,84,83 83,80,80,79,72**
Tote Swingers: 1&2 £3.30, 1&3 £14.00, 2&3 £6.50 CSF £31.98 CT £221.31 TOTE £14.00: £4.20, £1.10, £5.70; EX 26.10.
Owner Brig C K Price **Bred** Brigadier C K Price **Trained** Upper Lambourn, Berks

FOCUS
This lot had run 76 times between them without managing to win and it was obviously a weak race, but the winner's improvement has been taken at face value.
Dolly Will Do Official explanation: jockey said filly suffered interference in running
Old Devil Moon(IRE) Official explanation: jockey said gelding was denied a clear run

582 BOOK NOW FOR RACING POST CHASE DAY H'CAP 1m (P)
8:10 (8:11) (Class 5) (0-70,70) 3-Y-O **£2,590** (£770; £385; £192) **Stalls** High

Form RPR

0-24 **1** **Volatilis (IRE)**[12] 425 3-8-9 **61**.................................... HayleyTurner 3 62
(J W Hills) *mde all: set v stdy pce but nt threatened: rdn and hung lft fr 2f out: drvn and hld on wl fnl f* **7/2[2]**

63-2 **2** nk **Red Yarn**[34] 159 3-9-2 **68** ow1... GeorgeBaker 2 68
(G L Moore) *trckd ldng pair: effrt over 2f out: wnt 2nd over 1f out: tried to chal fnl f but fnd little and easily intimidated: a hld* **5/2[1]**

5-50 **3** ¾ **Layla's Lad (USA)**[28] 233 3-8-8 **60**.............................. JoeFanning 4 59
(D M Simcock) *trckd wnr: effrt over 2f out: hmpd and lost 2nd over 1f out: kpt on one pce after* **13/2**

33-1 **4** nk **Ginger Grey (IRE)**[11] 443 3-9-2 **68**............................. DaneO'Neill 1 66
(D R C Elsworth) *hld up in last pair in slowly run r: urged along fr over 2f out: grad clsd on ldrs but nvr able to throw down meaningful chal* **5/2[1]**

005- **5** 13 **Great Intrigue (IRE)**[139] 6424 3-9-4 **70**........................ TomQueally 5 38
(J S Moore) *hld up in last pair: wknd 2f out: t.o* **4/1[3]**

1m 41.76s (1.96) **Going Correction** -0.15s/f (Stan) 5 Ran SP% **112.7**
Speed ratings (Par 97): **84,83,82,82,69**
CSF £12.89 TOTE £4.80: £2.40, £5.00; EX 11.00 Place 6: £221.33 Place 5: £132.62 .
Owner P Abberley **Bred** G J King **Trained** Upper Lambourn, Berks

FOCUS
Form to treat with caution as the winner was allowed to set a noticeably steady pace (time nearly four seconds slower than standard) in a clear lead, and there was a distinct lack of initiative shown by some of the beaten jockeys. The front three wandered about in the closing stages and came close together, prompting a stewards' inquiry, but it was no real surprise the placings remained unaltered.
Red Yarn Official explanation: jockey said filly hung right
T/Plt: £476.20 to a £1 stake. Pool: £58,068.84. 89.00 winning tickets. T/Qpdt: £65.30 to a £1 stake. Pool: £8,042.41. 91.10 winning tickets. JN

[533]LINGFIELD (L-H)
Wednesday, February 17

OFFICIAL GOING: Standard
Wind: Virtually nil Weather: Sunny

583 MEARNS INTRODUCTION TO RACING MAIDEN STKS 7f (P)
2:00 (2:07) (Class 5) 3-Y-O **£2,456** (£725; £362) **Stalls** Low

Form RPR

0- **1** **Edinburgh Knight (IRE)**[186] 5029 3-9-3 0...................... TonyCulhane 14 80+
(P W D'Arcy) *hld up towards rr: hdwy 3f out: str run appr fnl f: styd on to ld fnl 75yds: pushed out* **11/4[1]**

04- **2** 1¼ **Caracal**[207] 4307 3-9-3 0.. JoeFanning 8 73+
(M Johnston) *led: rdn 2f out: styd on wl fr over 1f out: hdd and outpcd fnl 75yds* **3/1[2]**

4-2 **3** 5 **Jodawes (USA)**[11] 443 3-9-3 0.................................. SteveDrowne 11 60
(J R Best) *chsd ldrs: rdn over 2f out: styd on u.p to take 3rd cl home* **4/1[3]**

44 **4** nk **Merals Choice**[20] 321 3-8-12 0.................................... NickyMackay 3 54
(J R Boyle) *t.k.h: chsd ldrs: rdn 2f out: wl hld 3rd fnl f tl outpcd into 4th cl home* **8/1**

5 ¾ **Heliocentric** 3-9-0 0.. PatrickHills(3) 2 57+
(R Hannon) *in tch: chsd ldrs and rdn ins fnl 3f: styd on same pce insode fnl f* **16/1**

0 **6** hd **Just Say Please**[14] 392 3-8-12 0................................. JimmyQuinn 7 51
(D K Ivory) *chsd ldrs: rdn ins fnl 3f: wknd ins fnl f* **40/1**

7 1¼ **Eywa** 3-8-12 0.. JimCrowley 5 48+
(W Jarvis) *v.s.a and bhd: pushed along over 2f oiut: hdwy on outside over 1f out: styd on wl thrght fnl f: gng on cl home but nvr any threat* **25/1**

000- **8** shd **Securitisation (IRE)**[117] 6991 3-9-3 37.......................... TomQueally 9 53
(B J Curley) *mid-div: pushed along and hung lft ins fnl 3f: pushed along and no ch w ldrs whn edgd lft again fnl f* **50/1**

40-4 **9** nk **Lou Bear (IRE)**[11] 443 3-9-3 64..............................(p) J-PGuillambert 10 52
(J Akehurst) *chsd ldrs: rdn ins fnl 3f: wknd fnl f* **13/2**

10 nk **Single Lady** 3-8-12 0.. LukeMorris 6 46
(J S Moore) *a towards rr* **25/1**

0-0 **11** 1¾ **Bibiana Bay**[37] 128 3-8-12 0.. ShaneKelly 4 41
(B I Case) *rdn 3f out: nvr bttr than mid-div* **200/1**

12 ¾ **Trelicia** 3-8-9 0.. WilliamCarson(3) 13 39
(S C Williams) *sn towards rr: sme prog whn hmpd fnl f* **33/1**

-6 **13** 6 **Madame Bonaparte (IRE)**[32] 206 3-8-12 0.............. JamieMackay 12 23
(P L Gilligan) *t.k.h: sn bhd* **100/1**

1m 26.25s (1.45) **Going Correction** -0.05s/f (Stan) 13 Ran SP% **118.5**
Speed ratings (Par 97): **89,87,81,81,80 80,79,78,78,78 76,75,68**
Tote Swingers: 1&2 £2.70, 1&3 £3.50 2&3 £6.50 CSF £10.39 TOTE £3.80: £1.70, £1.40, £1.70; EX 16.60 Trifecta £17.90 Pool: £393.08 - 16.24 winning units..
Owner Knights Racing **Bred** New England Stud Myriad Norelands **Trained** Newmarket, Suffolk

FOCUS
This looked a fair maiden on paper and the market got it right. The winner is a nice prospect and the form is rated around the third.

584 BET ASIAN H'CAPS - BETDAQ HANDICAP 2m (P)
2:30 (2:34) (Class 6) (0-60,59) 4-Y-O+ **£1,774** (£523; £262) **Stalls** Low

Form RPR

/063 **1** **Delorain (IRE)**[6] 506 7-8-10 **45**.................................(vt) JerryO'Dwyer 14 53
(W B Stone) *mde virtually all: hrd pressed fr 2f out: edgd rt u.p jst ins fnl f: hld on wl* **12/1**

40/2 **2** hd **Poppy Gregg**[12] 420 5-8-6 **46**.......................................(v) AmyBaker(5) 8 54
(Dr J R J Naylor) *in rr tl stdy hdwy 4f out: drvn to chal wl over 1f out: styd on strly ins fnl f but a jst hld by wnr* **14/1**

50 **3** ¾ **Peinture De Guerre (FR)**[14] 390 7-9-3 **52**.................(b) GeorgeBaker 7 59
(G L Moore) *hld up in rr: n.m.r over 5f out: stdy hdwy fr 3f out: drvn to chal over 1f out and edgd lft jst ins fnl f: outpcd fnl 100yds* **33/1**

03/3 **4** 3½ **Hampton Court**[32] 164 5-9-9 **58**..................................... IanMongan 5 61
(J W Mullins) *in tch 1/2-way: rdn and hdwy fr 3f out: styd on fnl 2f but nvr gng pce to rch ldrs* **6/1[2]**

5-03 **5** shd **Colourful Move**[12] 420 5-8-11 **46**..............................(t) RobertHavlin 12 49
(P G Murphy) *chsd ldrs: drvn to chal fr 2f out: upsides and u.p whn hmpd jst ins fnl f: nt rcvr* **13/2[3]**

00-0 **6** 2½ **Bold Adventure**[33] 198 6-9-4 **53**.................................. TonyCulhane 2 53
(W J Musson) *in rr and pushed along over 6f out: rdn and hdwy on outside fr 2f out: kpt on cl home* **6/1[2]**

0- **7** hd **Share Option**[83] 1609 8-9-3 **52**..................................... JimmyQuinn 4 51
(A W Carroll) *mid-div: pushed along and hdwy on ins over 3f out: sn rdn: wknd fnl f* **8/1**

-304 **8** nk **Mymateeric**[15] 376 4-8-8 **49**...................................... SaleemGolam 13 48
(J Pearce) *chsd ldrs: rdn over 3f out: wknd fnl f* **16/1**

9 3¼ **Ajman (IRE)**[131] 6655 5-9-10 **59**................................... StephenCraine 9 54
(Evan Williams) *in rr: hdwy 6f out: pushed along over 2f out: wknd over 1f out* **25/1**

034- **10** 10 **Captain Flack**[171] 5483 4-9-2 **57**................................(b) JimCrowley 3 40
(J A R Toller) *chsd ldrs: rdn fr 6f out: wknd over 2f out* **10/1**

450- **11** 1¼ **The Saucy Snipe**[9] 6446 4-8-9 **50**............................(p) KevinGhunowa 1 32
(D C O'Brien) *rn wout declared tongue tie: a in rr* **40/1**

4-22 **12** 25 **Valkyrie (IRE)**[13] 411 4-8-6 **47**.................................... LukeMorris 11 —
(N P Littmoden) *chsd ldrs 12f* **7/2[1]**

45-3 **13** 3½ **Nyetimber (USA)**[40] 80 4-9-0 **55**................................. ShaneKelly 6 —
(J A Osborne) *rrd stalls and lost 15 l: managed to latch on to main gp 1/2-way: nvr any ch and sn wknd* **20/1**

3m 23.84s (-1.86) **Going Correction** -0.05s/f (Stan)
WFA 4 from 5yo+ 6lb 13 Ran SP% **118.6**
Speed ratings (Par 101): **102,101,101,99,99 98,98,98,96,91 90,78,76**
Tote Swingers: 1&2 £30.50, 1&3 £57.10, 2&3 £38.30 CSF £160.65 CT £5302.67 TOTE £14.60: £4.80, £4.30, £10.10; EX 257.10 TRIFECTA Not won..
Owner Miss Caroline Scott **Bred** Glending Bloodstock **Trained** West Wickham, Cambs

FOCUS
A very ordinary stayers' handicap which has been rated around the winner's recent level.

585 BET WGC MATCH PLAY GOLF - BETDAQ MAIDEN STKS 1m 5f (P)
3:00 (3:02) (Class 5) 4-Y-O+ **£2,456** (£725; £362) **Stalls** Low

Form RPR

6 **1** **Two Oclock John**[21] 316 4-9-3 0.................................. JackMitchell 6 64+
(H J Collingridge) *trckd ldrs: rdn over 2f out: str run fr 1f out: kpt on wl to ld cl home* **7/1[3]**

42-4 **2** ½ **French Hollow**[18] 355 5-9-7 69 .... RobertWinston 5 63
(T J Fitzgerald) *chsd ldrs: rdn to chal fr over 2f out and stl upsides ins fnl f: no ex cl home* **1/1**[1]
3 *nse* **Gordon Road (IRE)**[10] 4-9-3 0 .... JerryO'Dwyer 7 63
(M G Quinlan) *chsd ldrs: rdn to ld appr fnl f: kpt slt ld u.p tl: hdd and no ex cl home* **8/1**
4 ¾ **Uncle Eli (IRE)**[22] 8-9-0 0 .... RichardRowe(7) 8 62
(R Rowe) *towards rr tl stdy ldway ins fnl 2f: styd on wl thrght fnl f: kpt on cl home* **25/1**
5 2½ **Shannon Falls (FR)**[347] 6-9-2 0 .... IanMongan 2 53
(Miss Jo Crowley) *slowly away: bhd tl rpid hdwy to ld 6f out: kpt narrow advantage u.str.p tl hdd appr fnl f: wknd ins fnl f* **66/1**
63-4 **6** ½ **Sure Fire (GER)**[34] 166 5-9-7 63 .... TomQueally 12 62+
(B J Curley) *in rr: pushed along and sme hdwy whn rn wd bnd ins fnl 2f: styd on wl fnl f but nt rch ldrs* **9/2**[2]
406/ **7** 2¾ **Sweet Seville (FR)**[150] 7661 6-9-2 30 .... JimCrowley 3 48
(M D Squance) *slt ld tl hdd 6f out: styd pressing ldrs tl wknd over 1f out* **16/1**
8 ½ **Tanktastic**[62] 8-9-7 0 .... DaneO'Neill 9 53?
(P R Hedger) *chsd ldrs: rdn over 3f out: wknd ins fnl 2f* **16/1**
0 **9** ½ **Hopefull Blue (IRE)**[18] 356 4-8-12 0 .... JimmyQuinn 10 47?
(J W Mullins) *a towards rr* **25/1**
56 **10** 4½ **Randomer**[28] 237 7-9-4 0 ....(p) RobertLButler(3) 4 45?
(P Butler) *chsd ldrs: wknd 3f out* **100/1**
11 33 **Givenn** 6-9-2 0 .... GeorgeBaker 11 —
(Ms J S Doyle) *sn bhd: t.o* **16/1**

2m 51.98s (5.98) **Going Correction** -0.05s/f (Stan)
WFA 4 from 5yo+ 4lb **11** Ran SP% **119.6**
Speed ratings (Par 103): **79,78,78,78,76 76,74,74,74,71 50**
Tote Swingers: 1&2 £3.20, 1&3 £6.80, 2&3 £3.40 CSF £14.29 TOTE £6.30: £2.10, £1.10, £2.00; EX 17.70 Trifecta £270.30 Part won. Pool: £365.32 - 0.44 winning units..
Owner Greenstead Hall Racing Ltd **Bred** Greenstead Hall Racing **Trained** Exning, Suffolk
FOCUS
A poor maiden run at a steady early pace. A race to be negative about.

586 BET CHAMPION LEAGUE FOOTBALL - BETDAQ (S) STKS 1m 2f (P)
3:30 (3:31) (Class 6) 4-6-Y-O **£1,774** (£523; £262) **Stalls** Low

Form RPR
0-53 **1** **Whodunit (UAE)**[14] 396 6-8-10 59 ....(b) WilliamCarson(3) 10 72
(P W Hiatt) *mde all: drvn clr over 2f out: unchal* **6/1**[3]
013- **2** 8 **Fong's Alibi**[132] 5568 4-8-7 73 ....(p) LukeMorris 2 52
(J S Moore) *chsd ldrs: rdn 3f out: styd on u.p to chse wnr ins fnl f but nvr any ch* **7/1**
226- **3** 1 **Hallstatt (IRE)**[169] 4247 4-8-12 80 ....(tp) ShaneKelly 7 55
(Evan Williams) *in tch: hdwy on outside 2f out: styd on to take 3rd ins fnl f but no ch w wnr* **7/2**[2]
-650 **4** ½ **Hold The Bucks (USA)**[12] 426 4-8-7 59 ....(p) RossAtkinson(5) 9 54
(J S Moore) *in tch: rdn and hdwy fr 3f out to chse wnr wl over 1f out but nvr any ch: wknd ins fnl f* **12/1**
31-3 **5** *nk* **Dream Of Fortune (IRE)**[14] 383 6-9-0 73 ....(t) JamieJones(5) 8 59
(M G Quinlan) *slowly away and lost 5 l at s: pushed along over 3f out: sme prog over 1f out and kpt on ins fnl f but nt rcvr* **6/4**[1]
-506 **6** 7 **Meydan Dubai (IRE)**[14] 395 5-8-10 62 ....(v) MarcHalford(3) 1 40
(J R Best) *chsd wnr tl wknd wl over 1f out* **16/1**
-335 **7** 4½ **Big Nige (IRE)**[12] 429 4-8-12 59 .... SaleemGolam 4 32
(J Pearce) *chsd ldrs: rdn over 3f out: wknd ins fnl 2f* **15/2**
8 12 **Slayer**[245] 3936 5-8-13 57 ....(p) VinceSlattery 6 —
(M S Tuck) *rdn 4f out: a in rr* **100/1**
000/ **9** 16 **Savanna's Gold**[486] 6836 6-8-1 0 .... RichardRowe(7) 3 —
(R Rowe) *s.i.s: in rr tl rapid hdwy to chse ldrs 1/2-way: wknd 4f out* **100/1**

2m 4.60s (-2.00) **Going Correction** -0.05s/f (Stan)
WFA 4 from 5yo+ 1lb **9** Ran SP% **116.3**
Speed ratings: **106,99,98,98,98 92,88,79,66**
Tote Swingers: 1&2 £6.30, 1&3 £4.30, 2&3 £3.80 CSF £47.80 TOTE £6.80: £1.70, £1.80, £2.00; EX 55.40 Trifecta £337.30 Part won. Pool: £455.86 winning units..There was no bid for the winner. Dream of Fortune was claimed by Mr P. D. Evans £6,000. Hallstatt was claimed by Mr A. B. Hill £6,000.
Owner Exors of the Late John Hedges **Bred** Darley **Trained** Hook Norton, Oxon
FOCUS
A fair seller. The winner dictated from the front and posted a carrer best, and the form could easily be rated 6lb+ better.

587 MARRIOTT PLAY & STAY H'CAP 1m (P)
4:00 (4:00) (Class 5) (0-70,70) 4-Y-O+ **£2,456** (£725; £362) **Stalls** High

Form RPR
-222 **1** **Charlie Smirke (USA)**[14] 385 4-9-1 67 .... GeorgeBaker 9 79+
(G L Moore) *hld up in tch: stdy hdwy over 1f out: drvn to ld fnl 120yds: kpt on wl* **4/1**[1]
5633 **2** 2¼ **I Confess**[7] 487 5-8-11 68 ....(b) AndrewHeffernan(5) 5 75
(P D Evans) *led tl narrowly hdd 2f out: styd front rn and rallied to chse wnr fnl 75yds but no imp* **5/1**[3]
-032 **3** ½ **Forward Feline (IRE)**[7] 486 4-8-12 64 .... DavidProbert 11 70
(B Palling) *in rr: pushed along 2f out: hdwy fnl f: fin wl but nt rch ldng duo* **7/1**
60-2 **4** *nk* **Lastkingofscotland (IRE)**[11] 444 4-9-0 66 ....(b) PaulDoe 8 71
(Jim Best) *sn drvn to chse ldr: slt ld 2f out: kpt on u.p tl hdd fnl 120yds: wknd fnl 75yds* **4/1**[1]
000- **5** ½ **Efficiency**[80] 7586 4-8-10 62 .... DaneO'Neill 12 66
(M Blanshard) *in rr tl rdn and styd on appr fnl f: fin wl but nvr a threat* **25/1**
06-4 **6** *hd* **Murrin (IRE)**[11] 444 6-9-0 66 ....(p) StevieDonohoe 6 70
(R A Mills) *chsd ldrs: rdn over 2f out: outpcd fnl f* **14/1**
-044 **7** 1 **Grand Honour (IRE)**[16] 373 4-8-10 62 .... JimmyQuinn 7 64
(P Howling) *in rr tl hdwy on ins 2f out: styd on same pce u.p fnl f* **12/1**
600- **8** *hd* **Aviso (GER)**[201] 4502 6-9-4 70 .... TomQueally 2 71
(B J Curley) *hld up in tch: pushed along ins fnl 2f: nvr gng pce to get into contention* **13/2**
5-35 **9** *nk* **El Libertador (USA)**[7] 487 4-9-2 68 .... JimCrowley 4 69
(E A Wheeler) *in rr: rdn over 2f out: nvr gng pce to get into contention* **9/2**[2]
5465 **10** 1¼ **Justcallmehandsome**[13] 405 8-8-12 69 ....(v) BillyCray(5) 1 67
(D J S Ffrench Davis) *chsd ldrs: rdn 3f out: wknd appr fnl f* **50/1**
-044 **11** 1¼ **Durgan**[18] 356 4-8-12 64 .... SteveDrowne 3 59
(Mrs L C Jewell) *chsd ldrs tl wknd 2f out* **25/1**

1m 37.08s (-1.12) **Going Correction** -0.05s/f (Stan) **11** Ran SP% **124.7**
Speed ratings (Par 103): **103,100,100,99,99 99,98,98,97,96 95**
Tote Swingers: 1&2 £5.20, 1&3 £3.80, 2&3 £9.00 CSF £25.25 CT £144.36 TOTE £4.80: £1.60, £2.40, £2.30; EX 25.50 Trifecta £49.10 Pool: £342.51 - 516 winning units..
Owner R E Anderson **Bred** W S Farish & Kilroy Thoroughbred Partnership **Trained** Lower Beeding, W Sussex
FOCUS
A fairly competitive handicap. The winner finally delivered and the form is solid rated around the second and third.

588 LINGFIELDPARK.CO.UK H'CAP 1m 2f (P)
4:30 (4:30) (Class 5) (0-70,74) 4-Y-O+ **£2,456** (£725; £362) **Stalls** Low

Form RPR
61-1 **1** **Franco Is My Name**[24] 282 4-9-5 70 .... DaneO'Neill 13 85+
(P R Hedger) *hld up in rr: swtchd rt and hdwy wl over 1f out: qcknd to ld ins fnl f: readily* **15/8**[1]
41-5 **2** 1¼ **Granny McPhee**[9] 469 4-8-4 62 .... NatashaEaton(7) 5 71
(A Bailey) *in rr tl hdwy 3f out: drvn to take slt ld wl over 1f out: hdd ins fnl f and sn outpcd by wnr but styd on wl for 2nd* **18/1**
0-53 **3** 1¾ **Bid For Glory**[7] 485 6-9-4 68 ....(v) JimmyQuinn 11 74
(H J Collingridge) *in rr tl hdwy on ins over 2f out: drvn to chal wl over 1f out: no ex u.p ins fnl f* **10/1**
-321 **4** 1 **Freedom Fire (IRE)**[21] 316 4-8-12 63 .... PatCosgrave 6 67
(G L Moore) *chsd ldrs tl hmpd and snatched up bnd 2f out: styd on again fr over 1f out but nvr gng pce to get into contention* **7/2**[2]
4-06 **5** 1¾ **Dark Ranger**[18] 361 4-8-5 56 ....(b) LukeMorris 7 57
(T J Pitt) *towards rr: hdwy over 2f out: styng on whn n.m.r and swtchd lft wl over 1f out: kpt on ins fnl f* **12/1**
3131 **6** ½ **Aflaam (IRE)**[7] 487 5-9-5 74 6ex .... AndrewHeffernan(5) 2 74
(R A Harris) *chsd ldrs: rdn over 2f out: no imp: wknd ins fnl f* **4/1**[3]
000- **7** 1 **St Savarin (FR)**[71] 7677 9-8-12 62 .... VinceSlattery 8 60
(M S Tuck) *in rr: rdn along 1/2-way: hdwy on ins 2f out but nvr gng pce to get into contention* **66/1**
005- **8** 1¼ **Diamond Twister (USA)**[84] 7524 4-9-0 65 ....(t) RobertWinston 10 61
(J R Best) *chsd ldrs: drvn along 3f out: wknd over 1f out* **16/1**
0430 **9** ½ **Awatuki (IRE)**[14] 395 7-8-9 59 ....(b) NickyMackay 1 54
(J R Boyle) *chsd ldr 1/2-way: led 4f out: kpt slt ld u.p fr over 2f out: hdd wl over 1f out and wknd qckly* **25/1**
4310 **10** 3½ **Vinces**[18] 361 6-9-2 66 .... HayleyTurner 9 55
(T D McCarthy) *chsd ldrs: rdn over 3f out: wknd 2f out* **10/1**
0/ **11** *nk* **Aah Haa**[851] 6346 5-7-12 55 .... RichardRowe(7) 4 43
(N J Gifford) *t.k.h: slt ld tl narrowly hdd 4f out: styd chalng to 2f out: wknd qckly wl over 1f out* **40/1**

2m 4.65s (-1.95) **Going Correction** -0.05s/f (Stan)
WFA 4 from 5yo+ 1lb **11** Ran SP% **121.8**
Speed ratings (Par 103): **105,104,102,101,100 100,99,98,97,95 94**
Tote Swingers: 1&2 £13.30, 1&3 £5.30, 2&3 £26.50 CSF £42.47 CT £287.84 TOTE £2.90: £1.30, £5.50, £2.90; EX 39.80 TRIFECTA Not won..
Owner P C F Racing Ltd **Bred** J J Whelan **Trained** Dogmersfield, Hampshire
FOCUS
A few of these turned up in good heart and the form looks solid for the grade. The winner looks a bit better than the bare form.

589 GOLF AND RACING AT LINGFIELD PARK H'CAP 1m 2f (P)
5:00 (5:00) (Class 6) (0-65,64) 3-Y-O **£1,774** (£523; £262) **Stalls** Low

Form RPR
000- **1** **Desert Recluse (IRE)**[48] 7885 3-8-2 48 .... AndreaAtzeni(3) 1 52+
(Pat Eddery) *sn led: narrowly hdd 5f out: drvn to take narrow ld again 2f out: edgd rt over 1f out: styd on wl whn strly chal fnl 110yds* **10/3**[3]
000- **2** ¾ **Moonbalej**[119] 6930 3-9-1 58 .... JoeFanning 2 61
(M Johnston) *chsd ldrs: rdn over 2f out: styd on wl to chal fnl 110yds: no ex cl home* **5/2**[1]
-134 **3** 1½ **Glen Lass**[12] 422 3-9-7 64 ....(b) SaleemGolam 4 64
(J Pearce) *in rr but in tch: rdn along 4f out: hdwy over 1f out: styd on ins fnl f but nvr gng pce to rch ldng duo* **6/1**
2-24 **4** *shd* **Captain Cool (IRE)**[33] 183 3-8-8 51 ....(p) DavidProbert 3 51
(R Hannon) *hld up in rr: rdn 3f out: styd on fr 2f out: kpt on ins fnl f: fin wl* **15/2**
2233 **5** 3¼ **The Great Husk (IRE)**[3] 551 3-9-2 64 ....(p) RossAtkinson(5) 6 58
(J S Moore) *disp ld tl led 5f out: rdn 3f out: hdd 2f out: wknd fnl f* **3/1**[2]
06-4 **6** 2½ **Baggsy (IRE)**[32] 206 3-8-9 52 .... AmirQuinn 5 42
(Miss J Feilden) *chsd ldrs: drvn 4f out: wknd 2f out* **4/1**

2m 6.68s (0.08) **Going Correction** -0.05s/f (Stan) **6** Ran SP% **122.7**
Speed ratings (Par 95): **97,96,95,95,92 90**
Tote Swingers: 1&2 £4.00, 1&3 £4.00, 2&3 £4.60 CSF £13.51 TOTE £4.10: £2.30, £2.10; EX 22.00 Place 6: £199.72 Place 5: £161.78 .
Owner Pat Eddery Racing (Storm Bird) **Bred** John Foley & Miss Ann Aungier **Trained** Nether Winchendon, Bucks
FOCUS
A chance could be given to each of the runners. Limited form, with a clear step up from the winner.
T/Plt: £175.30 to a £1 stake. Pool: £64,656.69. 269.19 winning tickets. T/Qpdt: £9.40 to a £1 stake. Pool: £5,685.01. 442.95 winning tickets. ST

576 KEMPTON (A.W) (R-H)
Thursday, February 18
OFFICIAL GOING: Standard
Wind: Virtually nil Weather: Rain

590 TRY BETDAQ FOR AN EXCHANGE APPRENTICE H'CAP 1m 3f (P)
5:30 (5:30) (Class 7) (0-50,60) 4-Y-O+ **£1,364** (£403; £201) **Stalls** High

Form RPR
-611 **1** **Lytham (IRE)**[1] 576 9-9-12 60 12ex .... AmyBaker 9 67
(A W Carroll) *hld up in rr: stdy hdwy on outside fr 3f out to ld appr fnl f: shkn up ins fnl f and kpt on: all out* **3/1**[1]
5-20 **2** *hd* **Turner's Touch**[14] 410 8-8-8 47 ....(be) HarryBentley(5) 1 54
(G L Moore) *s.i.s: bhd tl hdwy on outside fr 3f out: str run to press wnr thrght fnl f: no ex fnl strides* **7/1**
06-4 **3** *shd* **Ocean Of Peace (FR)**[29] 228 7-8-7 46 .... HollyHall(5) 4 53+
(M R Bosley) *in rr gd prog fr 2f out: str run on far side to press ldng duo ins fnl f: no ex last strides* **13/2**
0-43 **4** 3 **Desert Hawk**[10] 463 9-8-4 45 .... JulieCumine(7) 12 47
(P Howling) *mid-div: pushed along and hdwy fr 2f out: styd on fnl f but nt rch ldrs* **15/2**
5-65 **5** *nk* **Noah Jameel**[15] 396 8-8-11 50 .... DavidKenny(5) 10 51
(A G Newcombe) *chsd ldrs: led appr fnl 2f: hdd & wknd ins fnl f* **6/1**[3]
60-0 **6** *nk* **Inn For The Dancer**[29] 228 8-8-9 46 .... CharlesEddery(3) 2 47
(J C Fox) *s.i.s: in rr: hrd drvn and styd on fnl 2f but nvr rchd ldrs* **25/1**

The Form Book, Raceform Ltd, Compton, RG20 6NL

-001 **7** 2 3/4 **Jiggalong**[5] 539 4-9-4 **54** 6ex AndrewHeffernan 13 50
(Jim Best) *chsd ldrs: t.k.h: drvn to chal fnl 2f: wknd ins fnl f* **9/2**[2]

6-05 **8** 1/2 **Bobering**[5] 541 10-8-11 **45** PaulPickard 5 41
(B P J Baugh) *s.i.s: in rr: rdn and sme prog fnl 2f* **25/1**

2260 **9** 2 3/4 **Crimson Flame (IRE)**[8] 479 7-8-12 **49** (b[1]) BillyCray(3) 7 40
(S Curran) *in rr tl hdwy fr 4f out: drvn to chse ldrs over 2f out: wknd over 1f out* **12/1**

40/0 **10** 5 **Shropshirelass**[8] 479 7-8-13 **47** (p) RossAtkinson 11 30
(Miss Z C Davison) *chsd ldrs: rdn 4f out: wknd 3f out* **50/1**

000- **11** 3 1/2 **Mixing**[64] 7766 8-8-10 **47** AmyScott(3) 3 25
(M J Attwater) *chsd ldrs: rdn 3f out: wknd qckly over 1f out* **20/1**

-500 **12** 1 **Sufficient Warning**[18] 367 6-8-11 **45** AshleyMorgan 8 21
(R J Smith) *led tl: tl hdd & wknd appr fnl 2f* **40/1**

2m 24.21s (2.31) **Going Correction** -0.025s/f (Stan)
WFA 4 from 5yo+ 2lb **12** Ran SP% **119.6**
Speed ratings (Par 97): **90,89,89,87,87 87,85,84,82,79 76,75**
toteswingers: 1&2 £6.40, 1&3 £5.50, 2&3 £8.70 CSF £22.91 CT £130.26 TOTE £3.20: £2.00, £1.80, £1.90; EX 35.10.
Owner Morgan, Clarke & Parris **Bred** Mrs A S O'Brien And Lars Pearson **Trained** Cropthorne, Worcs

FOCUS
A low-grade handicap run at a steady pace for the most part, and the fact that the first three were all able to come from well off the pace has much to do with them being relatively well handicapped at this level right now. Solid but very limited form.

591 BET EUROPA LEAGUE - BETDAQ H'CAP 1m (P)
6:00 (6:00) (Class 7) (0-50,56) 4-Y-0+ **£1,364** (£403; £201) **Stalls** High

Form RPR

00-1 **1** **Isitcozimcool (IRE)**[7] 503 5-9-9 **56** 6ex PatCosgrave 13 73+
(D E Cantillon) *trckd ldrs: led gng smoothly wl over 1f out: pushed clr ins fnl f* **10/3**[2]

0-00 **2** 3 1/2 **Mountain Pass (USA)**[7] 496 8-9-3 **50** (p) DavidProbert 8 57
(B J Llewellyn) *s.i.s: in rr tl: hdwy 3f out: rdn and kpt on fr 2f out to chse wnr ins fnl f but nvr any ch* **20/1**

0-05 **3** 1 1/2 **Imperium**[29] 229 9-9-1 **48** (p) DaneO'Neill 3 52
(Jean-Rene Auvray) *in rr: rdn and hdwy over 2f out: styd on u.p fnl f to take wl hld 3rd last stride* **16/1**

0/00 **4** nse **Global Guest**[8] 479 6-8-12 **48** (t) PatrickHills(3) 12 52
(S Curran) *chsd ldrs: rdn over 2f out: nvr on terms w wnr: one pce fr over 1f out: lost wl hld 3rd last stride* **12/1**

-431 **5** 2 3/4 **Hi Spec (IRE)**[15] 389 7-9-3 **50** (p) JimmyQuinn 7 48
(Miss M E Rowland) *t.k.h: chsd ldrs: wnt 2nd over 1f out but nvr any ch w wnr: wknd ins fnl f* **3/1**[1]

0-60 **6** nk **James Pollard (IRE)**[7] 496 5-9-3 **50** LiamKeniry 6 47
(B J Llewellyn) *s.i.s: in rr whn pushed along and prog fr 2f out: nvr rchd ldrs* **40/1**

-026 **7** 1 3/4 **Midnight Bay**[8] 479 4-9-1 **48** HayleyTurner 9 41
(P D Evans) *chsd ldr: led ins fnl 3f: hdd wl over 1f out and sn btn* **7/2**[3]

5350 **8** nk **Reigning Monarch (USA)**[15] 388 7-8-9 **47** RossAtkinson(5) 2 40
(Miss Z C Davison) *in rr: rdn over 2f out: sme prog fnl f* **14/1**

4444 **9** 1/2 **Inquisitress**[8] 479 6-8-12 **48** MarcHalford(3) 4 40
(J J Bridger) *in rr: rdn and sme hdwy 2f out: nvr rchd ldrs: wknd ins fnl f* **10/1**

00-0 **10** 1 3/4 **Rock Art (IRE)**[47] 13 4-9-2 **49** (p) TomQueally 11 37
(Karen George) *led tl hdd ins fnl 3f: wknd appr fnl f* **33/1**

/0-0 **11** 2 **Zazous**[21] 320 9-9-2 **49** SebSanders 5 32
(J J Bridger) *rdn 3f out: nvr nr ldrs* **40/1**

0/0- **12** 3 1/2 **Irish Bay (IRE)**[94] 7411 7-9-3 **50** (t) JerryO'Dwyer 1 26
(Luke Comer, Ire) *chsd ldrs: rdn over 3f out: sn btn* **33/1**

-400 **13** hd **Battimoore (IRE)**[15] 388 4-8-9 **47** (b) AndrewHeffernan(5) 14 22
(I W McInnes) *s.i.s: plld hrd: nvr bttr than mid-div: wknd* **25/1**

1m 39.23s (-0.57) **Going Correction** -0.025s/f (Stan) **13** Ran SP% **119.0**
Speed ratings (Par 97): **101,97,96,95,93 92,91,90,90,88 86,83,82**
toteswingers: 1&2 £19.60, 1&3 £18.40, 2&3 £17.90 CSF £76.45 CT £972.01 TOTE £3.70: £1.10, £4.70, £8.40; EX 76.90.
Owner Michael Davies **Bred** D And Mrs D Veitch **Trained** Newmarket, Suffolk

FOCUS
Another low-grade handicap but one run at a fair pace and producing an impressive winner.
Irish Bay(IRE) Official explanation: jockey said gelding hung right

592 BETDAQ POKER MEDIAN AUCTION MAIDEN STKS 1m (P)
6:30 (6:32) (Class 6) 3-5-Y-0 **£2,047** (£604; £302) **Stalls** High

Form RPR

4 **1** **Peadar Miguel**[35] 161 3-8-8 0 JerryO'Dwyer 9 78+
(M G Quinlan) *trckd ldrs: shkn up and ld appr fnl f: rn green but styd on wl* **7/1**

302- **2** 3/4 **Juicy Pear (IRE)**[99] 7325 3-8-8 78 HayleyTurner 10 76
(M L W Bell) *trckd ldrs: drvn to chse wnr fnl f: kpt on u.p but a hld* **2/1**[1]

3 2 1/4 **Merrqaad** 3-8-8 0 MartinDwyer 4 73+
(M P Tregoning) *chsd ldrs: puhed along 4f out: drvn and styd on to chse ldrs fnl f: kpt on but nvr any threat* **5/2**[2]

6- **4** 2 1/2 **Gra Adhmhar (IRE)**[60] 7825 3-8-8 0 JimmyQuinn 8 69+
(D J Coakley) *t.k.h: chsd ldrs: pushed along and rn green fr 2f out: kpt on wl cl home* **14/1**

0-0 **5** 3 1/2 **Chateau Zara**[29] 238 3-8-3 0 LukeMorris 3 53
(C G Cox) *led tl hdd appr fnl f and sn wknd* **50/1**

6 1 1/2 **Gems** 3-8-3 0 DavidProbert 6 50+
(H J L Dunlop) *s.i.s: in rr and keen early: rdn 3f out: nvr in contention* **8/1**

7 3/4 **Sparkys Gift (IRE)** 3-8-8 0 JackMitchell 2 53+
(P M Phelan) *s.i.s: rdn over 2f out: nvr gng pce to get into contention* **33/1**

8 7 **Manxman (IRE)** 3-8-8 0 JoeFanning 1 38
(M Johnston) *a in rr* **6/1**[3]

0 **9** 3 1/2 **Swindlers Lass (IRE)**[15] 385 3-8-3 0 AdrianMcCarthy 7 25
(Mark Gillard) *chsd ldrs over 5f: nvr gng pce* **100/1**

00- **10** 5 **Public Image**[194] 4786 4-9-8 0 RobertHavlin 5 14
(Jamie Poulton) *s.i.s: a in rr* **40/1**

1m 39.3s (-0.50) **Going Correction** -0.025s/f (Stan)
WFA 3 from 4yo 19lb **10** Ran SP% **114.8**
Speed ratings (Par 101): **101,100,98,95,92 90,89,82,79,74**
toteswingers: 1&2 £1.80, 1&3 £6.50, 2&3 £2.80 CSF £20.79 TOTE £9.60: £2.10, £1.50, £1.70; EX 25.10.
Owner Peter J Moran **Bred** A C M Spalding **Trained** Newmarket, Suffolk
■ Stewards' Enquiry : Luke Morris one-day ban: failed to ride to draw (Mar 4)

FOCUS
Several decent stables represented but with all the newcomers looking in need of the experience to varying degrees, the basic form of this maiden is probably on the weak side and certainly muddling, with a very steady pace complicating matters further.
Gra Adhmhar(IRE) Official explanation: jockey said gelding ran freely early on and ran green
Public Image Official explanation: jockey said gelding hung left

593 BACK OR LAY AT BETDAQ FILLIES' H'CAP 1m (P)
7:00 (7:01) (Class 4) (0-85,80) 4-Y-0+ **£4,209** (£1,252; £625; £312) **Stalls** High

Form RPR

1/1- **1** **Island Sunset (IRE)**[230] 3574 4-9-6 **79** MartinDwyer 4 89
(W R Muir) *trckd ldrs: rdn to dispute ld fr over 1f out and thrght fnl f: asserted last strides* **9/2**[3]

1-30 **2** shd **Moojeh (IRE)**[4] 552 4-9-2 **75** JerryO'Dwyer 3 85
(M Botti) *stdd s: in rr tl hdwy fr 2f out: disp ld over 1f out and thrght fnl f tl no ex last strides* **9/2**[3]

13-5 **3** 2 3/4 **My Best Bet**[36] 150 4-9-7 **80** TomQueally 5 83
(Stef Higgins) *s.i.s: hld up in rr: hdwy and nt clr run over 1f out: swtchd lft styd on fnl f: no imp on ldrs* **4/1**[2]

0/6 **4** nk **Lady Kent (IRE)**[15] 393 4-8-9 **68** JoeFanning 2 71
(J R Boyle) *chsd ldr: led 2f out: hdd over 1f out: wknd ins fnl f* **7/2**[1]

2/1- **5** 3 1/2 **One Slick Chick (IRE)**[369] 556 4-9-7 **80** HayleyTurner 6 75
(M Botti) *in rr: pushed along over 2f out: styd on same pce fnl f* **8/1**

4350 **6** 3/4 **Goodbye Cash (IRE)**[12] 442 6-7-12 **62** AndrewHeffernan(5) 9 55
(P D Evans) *led tl hdd 2f out: sn btn* **10/1**

3-30 **7** 3/4 **Perfect Secret**[21] 321 4-8-2 **61** oh1 DavidProbert 1 52
(A M Balding) *stdd s: pushed along fr 3f out: a outpcd* **7/1**

655- **8** shd **Dubai Gem**[258] 2679 4-8-9 **68** LukeMorris 7 59
(Jamie Poulton) *s.i.s: sn chsng ldrs: wknd 2f out* **16/1**

1m 37.57s (-2.23) **Going Correction** -0.025s/f (Stan) **8** Ran SP% **117.2**
Speed ratings (Par 102): **110,109,107,106,103 102,101,101**
toteswingers: 1&2 £3.30, 1&3 £6.50, 2&3 £9.10 CSF £25.73 CT £88.10 TOTE £3.50: £1.10, £1.70, £1.10; EX 29.40.
Owner Mrs J M Muir **Bred** Rathasker Stud **Trained** Lambourn, Berks

FOCUS
An interesting fillies handicap run at a decent pace and form that looks likely to stand up well with the third on a decent mark and a reliable marker.

594 BET SUPER LEAGUE - BETDAQ CLAIMING STKS 7f (P)
7:30 (7:30) (Class 6) 3-Y-0 **£2,047** (£604; £302) **Stalls** High

Form RPR

05-5 **1** **Craicattack (IRE)**[18] 366 3-8-13 71 (p) LiamKeniry 4 70
(J S Moore) *mde all: qcknd pced fr 2f out: drvn and styd on strly fr ins fnl f* **5/4**[1]

3-14 **2** 3/4 **Marjolly (IRE)**[11] 454 3-8-7 60 (p) MartinDwyer 1 62
(George Baker) *s.i.s: sn chsng wnr: rdn fr 2f out: nvr quite upsides wnr: no imp thrght fnl f* **3/1**[3]

5-45 **3** 1 1/2 **St Ignatius**[17] 370 3-8-2 68 (b) JohnFahy(7) 5 60
(R M Beckett) *t.k.h: trckd ldrs rdn and effrt fr 2f out: nvr rchd wnr and styd on same pce fnl f* **11/4**[2]

5 **4** shd **Zephyron (IRE)**[27] 267 3-8-11 0 JerryO'Dwyer 3 62?
(J R Holt) *in rr: pushed along over 2f out: styd on ins fnl f: kpt on but nvr any threat* **14/1**

00-5 **5** 3 3/4 **Belle Park**[47] 9 3-8-2 55 JimmyQuinn 2 43
(Karen George) *s.i.s: in rr but in tch: rdn 2f out: nvr on terms and wknd over 1f* **12/1**

1m 27.15s (1.15) **Going Correction** -0.025s/f (Stan) **5** Ran SP% **110.5**
Speed ratings (Par 95): **92,91,89,89,85**
CSF £5.32 TOTE £1.60: £1.02, £3.10; EX 5.60.Marjolly was claimed by J. Gallagher for £4,000
Owner W Adams & J S Moore **Bred** A M F Persse **Trained** Upper Lambourn, Berks

FOCUS
A modest claimer won by the horse with the highest official rating who was able to dictate a steady pace.

595 COMMISSION DEALS - BETDAQ H'CAP 6f (P)
8:00 (8:01) (Class 5) (0-75,78) 4-Y-0+ **£2,590** (£770; £385; £192) **Stalls** High

Form RPR

102- **1** **Boho Chic**[121] 6914 4-8-7 **61** ChrisCatlin 8 67
(George Baker) *set mod pce: qcknd pced sharply to asserted over 2f out: drvn and hld on wl fnl f* **11/2**[3]

-321 **2** nk **Secret Witness**[7] 501 4-9-5 **78** 6ex (b) AndrewHeffernan(5) 7 83
(R A Harris) *plld hrd in 2nd off mod pce: rdn whn pce qcknd over 2f out: styd on wl thrght fnl f: clsng on wnr nr fin but a hld* **11/10**[1]

424- **3** 3/4 **Mudhish (IRE)**[150] 6175 5-9-1 **69** (b) SebSanders 5 72
(C E Brittain) *chsd ldrs off mod pce: rdn and one pce whn wnr qcknd over 2f out: styd on thrght fnl f and nvr gng pce cl home to threaten* **3/1**[2]

1-25 **4** 3/4 **Welcome Approach**[14] 404 7-8-9 **63** LukeMorris 4 64+
(J R Weymes) *hld up in rr off mod pce: outpcd whn wnr qcknd over 2f out: styd on u.p fnl f but nvr rchd ldrs* **13/2**

000- **5** 18 **Albaher**[131] 6680 4-8-11 **65** SaleemGolam 6 8
(Peter Grayson) *in rr off mod pce: lost tch whn wnr qcknd over 2f out* **9/1**

1m 13.61s (0.51) **Going Correction** -0.025s/f (Stan) **5** Ran SP% **111.3**
Speed ratings (Par 103): **95,94,93,92,68**
CSF £12.32 TOTE £6.30: £3.60, £1.90; EX 9.30.
Owner P K Gardner **Bred** P K Gardner **Trained** Moreton Morrell, Warwicks

FOCUS
A very different race than the one that looked likely at the overnight stage after the withdrawal of two potential front runners, and that left the way for the only other likely pace setter to steal the race after being allowed to set an unsatisfactorily dawdling gallop.

596 BETDAQ.CO.UK H'CAP 6f (P)
8:30 (8:30) (Class 4) (0-85,82) 3-Y-0 **£4,209** (£1,252; £625; £312) **Stalls** High

Form RPR

30-1 **1** **Ghazwah**[23] 301 3-8-11 **72** MartinDwyer 6 76+
(R A Fahey) *chsd ldrs: drvn and styd on strly ins fnl f to ld fnl 110yds: won gng away* **9/4**[2]

534- **2** 1 1/4 **Kylladdie**[63] 7786 3-8-10 **71** ChrisCatlin 7 69
(S Gollings) *pressed ldr tl led appr fnl 2f: kpt on u.p ins fnl f: hdd and outpcd fnl 110yds* **11/1**

230- **3** 3/4 **Gertmegalush (IRE)**[132] 6643 3-9-7 **82** (b) TomQueally 2 78
(J D Bethell) *in rr: rdn over 2f out: styd on thrght fnl f: gng on cl home* **10/1**

32-3 **4** 1/2 **Barlaman (USA)**[16] 382 3-8-10 **71** (t) NeilCallan 8 65
(C E Brittain) *mde most tl hdd over 2f out: wknd: styd on wl tl wknd fnl 100yds* **7/2**[3]

4-21 **5** *4* **Duellist**[27] 267 3-9-0 **75**........................ JoeFanning 1 57
(M Johnston) *chsd ldrs: rdn over 2f out: btn whn nt clr run over 1f out: sn wknd* **6/4**[1]

1m 12.72s (-0.38) **Going Correction** -0.025s/f (Stan) **5** Ran SP% **110.4**
Speed ratings (Par 99): **101,99,98,97,92**
CSF £23.50 TOTE £3.30: £2.20, £4.00; EX 17.60 Place 6 £29.77, Place 5 £15.67.
Owner Dr Marwan Koukash **Bred** Shadwell Estate Company Limited **Trained** Musley Bank, N Yorks

FOCUS
A fair handicap run at a reasonable tempo, but even though there were only five runners it still produced one hard-luck story with the eventual third unfortunate not to have gone very close. For all that, the second has been in the grip of the assessor, so this probably isn't form to be getting carried away with.
T/Plt: £20.10 to a £1 stake. Pool: £71,320.68. 2,589.71 winning tickets. T/Qpdt: £4.10 to a £1 stake. Pool: £8,149.84. 1,448.88 winning tickets. ST

569 SOUTHWELL (L-H)
Thursday, February 18

OFFICIAL GOING: Standard
Wind: Light, half-against. Weather: Overcast with the odd snow shower

597 BET PREMIER LEAGUE FOOTBALL - BETDAQ H'CAP — 1m (F)
1:50 (1:50) (Class 6) (0-60,60) 3-Y-O — **£1,774** (£523; £262) **Stalls** Low

Form RPR
000- **1** **Step To It (IRE)**[157] 5942 3-8-4 **46** oh1........................ ChrisCatlin 2 51
(K A Ryan) *sn pushed along to chse ldr: rdn over 2f out: led over 1f out: drvn out* **8/1**

000- **2** *3/4* **Magic Millie (IRE)**[155] 5981 3-8-8 **50**........................ FranciscoDaSilva 5 53
(J Hetherton) *chsd ldrs: rdn over 2f out: r.o to go 2nd wl ins fnl f: nt rch wnr* **10/1**

-352 **3** *2 1/2* **Taper Jean Girl (IRE)**[7] 507 3-8-9 **51**........................(p) AndrewElliott 1 49
(Mrs R A Carr) *led: clr 6f out: rdn and hdd over 1f out: no ex ins fnl f* **4/1**[3]

25 **4** *1* **Market Puzzle (IRE)**[17] 371 3-9-4 **60**........................ ShaneKelly 3 55
(W M Brisbourne) *prom: pushed along 1/2-way: rdn over 2f out: styd on same pce appr fnl f* **11/4**[1]

430- **5** *1* **Patachou**[115] 7064 3-8-8 **50**........................ LukeMorris 7 43
(R J Smith) *hld up: rdn over 5f out: styd on u.p fr over 1f out: n.d* **4/1**[3]

50-4 **6** *2 3/4* **Delta Sky (IRE)**[25] 283 3-9-4 **60**........................ HayleyTurner 4 47
(Miss Amy Weaver) *hld up: hdwy over 4f out: outpcd over 3f out: n.d after* **7/2**[2]

1m 44.2s (0.50) **Going Correction** -0.125s/f (Stan) **6** Ran SP% **109.1**
Speed ratings (Par 95): **92,91,88,87,86 84**
toteswingers: 1&2 £6.40, 1&3 £8.30, 2&3 £10.10. CSF £73.09 TOTE £12.70: £3.10, £4.40; EX 100.80.
Owner D W Barker **Bred** P R Bloodstock **Trained** Hambleton, N Yorks

FOCUS
A modest handicap run. The pace was decent but only a few got involved.
Step To It(IRE) Official explanation: trainer said, regarding apparent improvement in form, that the gelding appeared to have matured and strengthened since its previous run in September.

598 BET IN RUNNING - BETDAQ (S) STKS — 1m (F)
2:20 (2:20) (Class 6) 4-Y-O+ — **£1,774** (£523; £262) **Stalls** Low

Form RPR
/-13 **1** **Sedgwick**[7] 496 8-9-3 65........................ StevieDonohoe 2 70
(Ian Williams) *sn led: hdd 7f out: remained w ldr tl led over 3f out: hdd over 2f out: rdn to ld over 1f out: styd on wl* **4/7**[1]

40-4 **2** *6* **Unconsoled**[7] 503 4-8-6 48........................(vt[1]) FranciscoDaSilva 3 46
(J Hetherton) *chsd ldrs: led over 2f out: sn rdn and drifted rt: hung lft and hdd over 1f out: no ex fnl f* **4/1**[2]

4046 **3** *4* **Boss Hog**[16] 377 5-8-11 52........................ PJMcDonald 4 42
(P T Midgley) *chsd ldrs: rdn over 2f out: sn wknd* **4/1**[2]

00/ **4** *36* **Amber May**[73] 980 7-8-6 0........................ GregFairley 6 —
(S G West) *led 7f out: rdn and hdd over 3f out: sn wknd: t.o* **33/1**[3]

1m 42.35s (-1.35) **Going Correction** -0.125s/f (Stan) **4** Ran SP% **106.6**
Speed ratings (Par 101): **101,95,91,55**
CSF £3.08 TOTE £1.80; EX 2.30.There was no bid for the winner
Owner A L R Morton **Bred** G And Mrs Middlebrook **Trained** Portway, Worcs

FOCUS
A seller severely weakened by the withdrawal of 69 and 70-rated pair Heathyards Junior and Miss Bootylishes.

599 BETDAQ.CO.UK MEDIAN AUCTION MAIDEN STKS — 1m 4f (F)
2:55 (2:55) (Class 6) 4-6-Y-O — **£1,774** (£523; £262) **Stalls** Low

Form RPR
003- **1** **Mediterranean Sea (IRE)**[99] 7324 4-8-12 47........................ StephenCraine 5 57
(J R Jenkins) *a.p: chsd ldr over 5f out: led on bit 2f out: sn shkn up: rdn out* **7/2**[3]

-463 **2** *1 3/4* **Desert Fairy**[8] 479 4-8-12 47........................ TomEaves 2 54
(J W Unett) *trckd ldr: racd keenly: led over 6f out: rdn and hdd 2f out: styd on same pce fnl f* **10/3**[2]

-340 **3** *1* **Dovedon Angel**[14] 407 4-8-12 48........................ SteveDrowne 4 53
(Miss Gay Kelleway) *trckd ldrs: plld hrd early: rdn over 3f out: no ex ins fnl f* **3/1**[1]

5-30 **4** *1/2* **Davana**[7] 503 4-8-9 47........................ KellyHarrison(3) 6 52
(W J H Ratcliffe) *hld up: hdwy 5f out: rdn over 3f out: no ex ins fnl f* **8/1**

004- **5** *1/2* **Rock Tech**[64] 7767 5-8-13 46........................ DannyBrock(7) 7 56
(J R Jenkins) *hld up: plld hrd: bhd 7f out: hdwy and hung lft over 1f out: nt rch ldrs* **6/1**

6 *7* **Crazy Gracie (IRE)**[8] 4-8-8 0 ow3........................ AdamBeschizza(7) 3 44
(Miss J Feilden) *set stdy pce: hdd over 6f out: rdn over 4f out: wknd 3f out* **33/1**

5 **7** *12* **Railway Park (IRE)**[12] 166 6-9-6 0........................(v) PJMcDonald 1 28
(J S Wainwright) *s.i.s: hld up: bhd fnl 7f* **15/2**

2m 45.27s (4.27) **Going Correction** -0.125s/f (Stan)
WFA 4 from 5yo+ 3lb **7** Ran SP% **110.4**
Speed ratings: **80,78,78,77,77 72,64**
toteswingers: 1&2 £2.00, 1&3 £2.60, 2&3 £2.10 CSF £14.44 TOTE £4.00: £2.10, £1.90; EX 15.20.
Owner Mrs Wendy Jenkins **Bred** D H W Dobson **Trained** Royston, Herts

FOCUS
A weak maiden. Those who had been assessed were rated only in the 40s. The pace was steady and they were tightly grouped in the early stages.

600 DINE IN THE QUEEN MOTHER RESTAURANT CLAIMING STKS — 1m 4f (F)
3:30 (3:30) (Class 6) 4-Y-O+ — **£1,774** (£523; £262) **Stalls** Low

Form RPR
341 **1** **Doubnov (FR)**[8] 488 7-9-12 72........................ SteveDrowne 6 79
(Ian Williams) *a.p: chsd ldr after 2f: rdn and ev ch fr over 1f out: styd on u.p to ld nr fin* **15/8**[1]

-452 **2** *shd* **Resplendent Ace (IRE)**[6] 529 6-9-6 68........................ J-PGuillambert 5 73
(P Howling) *hld up: hdwy 1/2-way: led wl over 1f out: sn rdn: hdd nr fin* **5/2**[2]

-333 **3** *3 1/2* **Dunaskin (IRE)**[11] 456 10-9-6 74........................(be) TomEaves 3 68
(B Ellison) *led: rdn and hdd wl over 1f out: styd on same pce fnl f* **9/2**[3]

0-13 **4** *23* **Friends Hope**[6] 521 9-8-7 67........................(p) FrankieMcDonald 4 20
(R Curtis) *s.i.s: hld up: rdn 5f out: wknd sn after: t.o* **13/2**

3022 **5** *7* **Jazrawy**[6] 521 8-8-5 55........................(p) DeclanCannon(5) 1 13
(A J McCabe) *chsd ldr 2f: remained handy: rdn over 4f out: sn wknd: t.o* **12/1**

106/ **6** *1* **Corran Ard (IRE)**[502] 5054 9-9-6 0........................ StephenCraine 2 21
(Tim Vaughan) *chsd ldrs: pushed along 7f out: wknd 5f out: t.o* **10/1**

2m 38.75s (-2.25) **Going Correction** -0.125s/f (Stan) **6** Ran SP% **111.7**
Speed ratings (Par 101): **102,101,99,84,79 78**
toteswingers: 1&2 £2.40, 1&3 £1.90, 2&3 £2.60 CSF £6.70 TOTE £3.00: £1.90, £1.30; EX 6.70.
Owner Dr Marwan Koukash **Bred** Daniel Valliery Masson Et Al **Trained** Portway, Worcs

FOCUS
A tight claimer. The first three had BHA ratings between 70 and 74 and pulled miles clear of the rest.

601 MEMBERSHIP AT SOUTHWELL GOLF CLUB H'CAP — 5f (F)
4:05 (4:05) (Class 5) (0-70,71) 4-Y-O+ — **£2,456** (£725; £362) **Stalls** High

Form RPR
-151 **1** **Where's Reiley (USA)**[7] 504 4-9-3 **71** 6ex........................ DeanHeslop(5) 7 79
(T D Barron) *dwlt: sn pushed along in rr: rdn and r.o to ld wl ins fnl f* **9/2**[1]

-426 **2** *nk* **Bo McGinty (IRE)**[13] 431 9-8-11 **60**........................(v) PaulHanagan 1 67
(R A Fahey) *sn pushed along and prom: outpcd 3f out: hdwy u.p over 1f out: r.o* **5/1**[2]

42-3 **3** *3/4* **First Swallow**[7] 504 5-8-13 **62**........................(t) FrederikTylicki 3 66
(D H Brown) *led: hdd over 3f out: led again 2f out: rdn and hdd jst over 1f out: r.o* **6/1**[3]

0-45 **4** *nse* **Bookiesindex Boy**[10] 462 6-9-2 **65**........................(b) StephenCraine 5 69
(J R Jenkins) *hmpd s: hld up: hdwy 1/2-way: led on bit jst over 1f out: shkn up and hdd wl ins fnl f* **16/1**

611- **5** *3/4* **Forever's Girl**[80] 7601 4-9-4 **67**........................ PJMcDonald 6 68
(G R Oldroyd) *s.i.s: hdwy 1/2-way: rdn over 1f out: no ex towards fin* **11/1**

0-05 **6** *1/2* **La Capriosa**[7] 504 4-9-1 **64**........................ ChrisCatlin 9 64
(J A Glover) *chsd ldrs: rdn 1/2-way: styd on* **16/1**

6532 **7** *hd* **Guto**[7] 504 7-8-13 **65**........................ KellyHarrison(3) 4 64
(W J H Ratcliffe) *edgd rt s: sn w ldr: led over 3f out: rdn and hdd 2f out: styd on same pce ins fnl f* **11/1**

3-04 **8** *nk* **Chosen One (IRE)**[16] 378 5-8-11 **60**........................(p) TomEaves 2 58
(B Smart) *chsd ldrs: rdn and ev ch over 1f out: no ex wl ins fnl f* **6/1**[3]

0044 **9** *nk* **First Order**[6] 520 9-8-8 **62**........................(v) AnnStokell(5) 10 59
(Miss A Stokell) *s.i.s: hld up: plld hrd: hdwy u.p over 1f out: nt rch ldrs* **40/1**

0-34 **10** *1* **Figaro Flyer (IRE)**[13] 431 7-9-3 **66**........................ J-PGuillambert 13 59
(P Howling) *hld up: rdn and swtchd lft 1f out: n.d* **11/1**

-115 **11** *shd* **Lujiana**[14] 402 5-8-5 **54**........................ FrannyNorton 8 49
(M Brittain) *chsd ldrs: rdn 1/2-way: nt clr run over 1f out: eased whn btn wl ins fnl f* **10/1**

5-04 **12** *2* **Loose Caboose (IRE)**[38] 125 5-8-6 **60**........................(p) DeclanCannon(5) 12 46
(A J McCabe) *mid-div: rdn 1/2-way: wknd fnl f* **18/1**

06-6 **13** *3 1/4* **Miss Thippawan (USA)**[7] 504 4-8-4 **53** oh8........................ FranciscoDaSilva 11 27
(J Hetherton) *hld up: hdwy 1/2-way: rdn and wknd over 1f out* **125/1**

50-6 **14** *1/2* **Calmdownmate (IRE)**[16] 380 5-9-4 **67**........................ AndrewElliott 14 39
(Mrs R A Carr) *sn outpcd: bhd whn hung lft over 1f out* **25/1**

59.14 secs (-0.56) **Going Correction** -0.025s/f (Stan) **14** Ran SP% **121.6**
Speed ratings (Par 103): **103,102,101,101,100 99,98,98,97,96 96,93,87,87**
toteswingers: 1&2 £6.30, 1&3 £5.90, 2&3 £4.80 CSF £26.23 CT £143.84 TOTE £5.60: £2.40, £2.50, £2.00; EX 33.40 Trifecta £176.30 Part won. Pool: £238.33 - 0.50 winning units..
Owner Dovebrace Ltd Air-Conditioning-Projects **Bred** Overrbrook Farm **Trained** Maunby, N Yorks

FOCUS
A fair handicap run at a frenetic pace. The first five raced up the centre to far side of the track.
Figaro Flyer(IRE) Official explanation: jockey said gelding moved poorly

602 CALL 01636 814481 TO SPONSOR A RACE H'CAP — 7f (F)
4:40 (4:40) (Class 5) (0-70,68) 4-Y-O+ — **£2,456** (£725; £362) **Stalls** Low

Form RPR
-261 **1** **Whatyouwoodwishfor (USA)**[23] 296 4-8-10 **60**........................(b) PaulHanagan 2 69
(R A Fahey) *mde all: clr 3f out: rdn and edgd lft over 1f out: hung rt ins fnl f: styd on* **9/2**[3]

-306 **2** *1 1/2* **Tobrata**[6] 518 4-8-10 **60**........................ FrannyNorton 4 65
(M Brittain) *chsd wnr to 1/2-way: outpcd over 2f out: rallied over 1f out: r.o u.p to go 2nd wl ins fnl f* **7/1**

-202 **3** *nk* **Kensington (IRE)**[10] 465 9-8-13 **68**........................(p) DeclanCannon(5) 6 72
(A J McCabe) *a.p: chsd wnr 1/2-way: rdn over 1f out: styd on: lost 2nd wl ins fnl f* **15/2**

03-3 **4** *nk* **Gentle Guru**[16] 380 6-9-2 **66**........................ SteveDrowne 8 69
(R T Phillips) *sn outpcd: hdwy u.p and edgd lft over 1f out: r.o: nt rch ldrs* **15/2**

62-1 **5** *4* **Young Gladiator (IRE)**[16] 378 5-9-3 **67**........................(b) FrederikTylicki 1 60
(Julie Camacho) *trckd ldrs: racd keenly: rdn 1/2-way: styd on same pce fnl 2f* **7/2**[1]

6-12 **6** *2 1/4* **Charles Parnell (IRE)**[16] 380 7-9-1 **68**........................ MichaelStainton(3) 5 54
(S P Griffiths) *s.i.s: hld up: rdn 1/2-way: n.d* **4/1**[2]

7 *nk* **Way West (IRE)**[99] 7340 4-8-11 **64**........................ PBBeggy(3) 7 50
(Paul W Flynn, Ire) *sn pushed along in rr: rdn over 4f out: wknd over 2f out* **5/1**

300- **8** *4* **Diamond Surprise**[107] 7229 4-9-1 **65**........................ FrankieMcDonald 3 40
(R Curtis) *s.i.s: hld up: rdn and wknd 1/2-way* **28/1**

1m 28.47s (-1.83) **Going Correction** -0.125s/f (Stan) **8** Ran SP% **116.5**
Speed ratings (Par 103): **105,103,102,102,98 95,95,90**
toteswingers: 1&2 £5.50, 1&3 £6.10, 2&3 £12.40 CSF £36.46 CT £234.15 TOTE £5.60: £1.30, £2.30, £1.50; EX 35.10 Trifecta £188.00 Part won. Pool: £254.17 - 0.43 winning units..
Owner Mel Roberts & Ms Nicola Meese 1 **Bred** Manganaro Llc **Trained** Musley Bank, N Yorks

FOCUS
This looked a competitive handicap but the winner ran them into submission and hardly anything got into it from off the pace.

603 ARENA LEISURE PLC APPRENTICE H'CAP — 1m (F)
5:10 (5:10) (Class 6) (0-58,58) 4-Y-0+ — **£1,774** (£523; £262) **Stalls** Low

Form — RPR

600- **1** **Magic Haze**[148] 6217 4-9-0 **55** .... LeeTopliss 4 — 63
(Miss S E Hall) *sn chsng ldr: rdn over 1f out: led ins fnl f: r.o* **10/1**

2062 **2** *1* **Mackintosh (IRE)**[8] 491 4-8-5 **51** .... (v) MatthewCosham(5) 3 — 57
(Patrick Morris) *hld up: hdwy and n.m.r over 4f out: led over 1f out: rdn and hdd ins fnl f: styd on* **7/2**[2]

5055 **3** *hd* **Amber Moon**[7] 503 5-8-7 **48** .... (b) LauraPike 2 — 53
(Miss A Stokell) *led: rdn and hdd over 1f out: styd on* **13/2**

04-0 **4** *shd* **Plenilune (IRE)**[42] 75 5-8-6 **47** .... JohnCavanagh 6 — 52
(M Brittain) *prom: lost pl 5f out: hdwy u.p over 1f out: r.o* **13/2**

3166 **5** *4* **Very Well Red**[18] 367 7-9-3 **58** .... RyanClark 1 — 54
(P W Hiatt) *chsd ldrs: rdn over 3f out: styd on same pce fr over 1f out* **4/1**[3]

00-0 **6** *6* **Dancing Wave**[47] 20 4-8-10 **54** .... AlexEdwards(3) 5 — 37
(M C Chapman) *prom: lost pl 5f out: bhd whn hung rt ent st* **20/1**

23-0 **7** *10* **Holyfield Warrior (IRE)**[27] 256 6-9-3 **58** .... RyanPowell 7 — 19
(R J Smith) *s.i.s: hld up: hdwy over 4f out: rdn and wknd 3f out* **9/4**[1]

1m 42.59s (-1.11) **Going Correction** -0.125s/f (Stan) — **7** Ran **SP% 113.5**
Speed ratings (Par 101): **100,99,98,98,94 88,78**
toteswingers: 1&2 £6.40, 1&3 £9.80, 2&3 £4.30 CSF £44.07 TOTE £14.40: £6.10, £2.20; EX 48.50 Place 6 £350.07, Place 5 £18.70.
Owner Mrs Joan Hodgson **Bred** Miss S E Hall **Trained** Middleham Moor, N Yorks

FOCUS
An ordinary handicap and a race of changing fortunes.
Dancing Wave Official explanation: jockey said filly hung right
Holyfield Warrior(IRE) Official explanation: jockey said gelding ran flat
T/Plt: £1,489.50 to a £1 stake. Pool: £55,501.98. 27.20 winning tickets. T/Qpdt: £21.10 to a £1 stake. Pool: £5,583.37. 195.71 winning tickets. CR

510 MEYDAN (L-H)
Thursday, February 18

OFFICIAL GOING: Standard

604a HAAFHD SPONSORED BY SHADWELL ESTATE (H'CAP) (TAPETA) — 6f
3:05 (3:05) (90-105,105) 3-Y-0+
£40,740 (£13,580; £6,790; £3,395; £2,037; £1,358)

RPR

1 **Frosty Secret (USA)**[13] 434 6-9-2 101 .... KShea 6 — 105
(M F De Kock, South Africa) *trckd ldr: led 2f out: r.o wl: comf* **4/1**[1]

2 *2 ¼* **Lui Rei (ITY)**[116] 4-9-3 102 .... RyanMoore 5 — 99+
(H J Brown, South Africa) *s.i.s: racd in rr: r.o wl fnl 2f: nrest at fin* **15/2**[3]

3 *1* **So Will I**[364] 611 9-9-5 105 .... (t) RichardHills 11 — 98
(Doug Watson, UAE) *racd in mid-div: prog out wd 2 1/2f out: kpt on wl 1 1/2f out: styd on fnl 110yds* **12/1**

4 *shd* **Sol De Angra (BRZ)**[13] 434 5-9-5 105 .... TJPereira 7 — 97
(A Cintra Pereira, Brazil) *trckd ldrs: ev ch 1 1/2f out: nt qckn fnl 110yds* **6/1**[2]

5 *¼* **Calrissian (GER)**[13] 434 6-9-5 105 .... (t) TedDurcan 3 — 96
(Fredrik Reuterskiold, Sweden) *s.i.s: r.o fnl 1 1/2f: nvr able to chal* **25/1**

6 *hd* **Good Control (AUS)**[21] 336 5-9-3 102 .... MNunes 10 — 94
(Pat Lee, Macau) *trckd ldrs on outside: ev ch ent st: one pce* **8/1**

7 *1* **Rileyskeepingfaith**[21] 336 4-9-3 102 .... AlanMunro 9 — 91
(M R Channon) *a in mid-div* **12/1**

8 *½* **Judd Street**[13] 434 8-9-4 104 .... (b) KierenFallon 8 — 90
(Eve Johnson Houghton) *nvr bttr than mid-div* **12/1**

9 *3* **Prohibit**[13] 434 5-9-2 101 .... JamieSpencer 4 — 78
(R M H Cowell) *nvr bttr than mid-div* **6/1**[2]

10 *4 ¼* **Classic Blade (IRE)**[14] 416 4-9-5 105 .... (vt) TadhgO'Shea 2 — 68
(Doug Watson, UAE) *sn led: hdd & wknd 2f out* **20/1**

11 *¾* **Matsunosuke**[13] 434 8-9-5 105 .... PJSmullen 12 — 65
(A B Coogan) *a towards rr: n.d* **14/1**

12 *4 ½* **Prince Tamino**[13] 437 7-9-4 104 .... (t) RoystonFfrench 1 — 50
(A Al Raihe, UAE) *mid-div: chsd ldrs 2f out: wknd 1f out* **8/1**

1m 11.39s (71.39) — **12** Ran **SP% 120.9**
CSF: £34.23, Tricast: £339.50.
Owner Elsadig Elhag **Bred** Carl Bowling **Trained** South Africa

FOCUS
A good sprint handicap. The winner is rated to his mark.

NOTEBOOK
Frosty Secret(USA), who had finished ahead of five of these rivals over C&D on his previous start, took this in straightforward fashion. He was always well placed close to the pace and picked up nicely once getting a clear run in the straight. (op 9-2)
Lui Rei(ITY) ◆ didn't progress after winning the Group 2 Prix Robert Papin as a juvenile, but this was an encouraging Dubai debut. He was left with far too much to do after taking a while to get into his stride and had his chance further compromised when having to wait for a clear run until around a furlong out. But the way he finished suggests he's up to winning a similar race, probably over 7f. (op 8-1)
So Will I kept on steadily from off the pace on his first run for a year.
Sol De Angra(BRZ)'s Grade 1 success in Brazil came over 5f and his stamina seemed to give out in a similar event to this one over C&D on his Dubai debut. It was the same story this time.
Calrissian(GER) had to wait for a run against the inside rail early in the straight, before finishing well.
Good Control(AUS), too keen for his own good when a close fourth over C&D on his Dubai debut, seemed to settle okay this time, but could make no impression. (op 7-1)
Rileyskeepingfaith could have been expected to fare better after his encouraging run over C&D off the back of a long absence, but it would be unfair to judge him too harshly at this stage.
Prohibit was again denied a clear run and, as such, couldn't show his best, but he doesn't appeal as one to keep making excuses for.

605a NAAQOOS SPONSORED BY SHADWELL ESTATE (H'CAP) (TAPETA) — 1m 3f
3:40 (3:40) (90-105,105) 3-Y-0+
£40,740 (£13,580; £6,790; £3,395; £2,037; £1,358)

RPR

1 **Emirates Champion**[13] 436 4-8-9 97 .... (t) FrankieDettori 10 — 103+
(Saeed Bin Suroor) *trckd ldrs: rdn 3f out: led 1 1/2f out: r.o wl* **11/8**[1]

2 *1 ½* **Monte Alto (IRE)**[7] 512 6-9-1 100 .... (t) RichardHills 3 — 104
(A Al Raihe, UAE) *mid-div: chsd ldrs 2f out: kpt on* **13/2**[3]

3 *1 ½* **Captain Webb**[14] 419 5-8-13 98 .... (t) PJSmullen 7 — 99
(E Charpy, UAE) *sn led: qcknd 4f out: hdd 1 1/2f out: kpt on same pce* **33/1**

4 *½* **Titurel (GER)**[14] 418 5-9-5 105 .... KierenFallon 8 — 104
(Manfred Hofer, Germany) *mid-div: r.o wl fnl 2f: n.d* **6/1**[2]

5 *½* **Salute Him (IRE)**[14] 419 7-9-4 104 .... JamieSpencer 12 — 102
(A J Martin, Ire) *s.i.s: in rr of mid-div: kpt on fnl 1 1/2f: nrest at fin* **9/1**

6 *3 ¼* **Mister Fasliyev (IRE)**[13] 441 8-8-9 95 .... (bt) TadhgO'Shea 1 — 88
(E Charpy, UAE) *mid-div on rail: r.o same pce fnl 2f* **20/1**

7 *¼* **Quai D'Orsay**[14] 418 4-8-10 98 .... AhmedAjtebi 6 — 90
(Saeed Bin Suroor) *racd in rr: nvr nr to chal* **20/1**

8 *¼* **Stock Market (USA)**[21] 334 5-8-9 95 .... (t) TedDurcan 13 — 87
(N Al Mandeel, Saudi Arabia) *trckd ldng gp: one pce fnl 2f* **40/1**

9 *shd* **Blaze Of Fire**[6] 4-8-8 96 .... KLatham 4 — 88
(M F De Kock, South Africa) *settled in rr: nvr able to chal* **20/1**

10 *1 ¾* **Hot Six (BRZ)**[14] 419 5-9-5 105 .... TJPereira 14 — 94
(P Bary, France) *mid-div: rn wd 3 1/2f out: sn u.p* **6/1**[2]

11 *1 ¾* **Book Of Music (IRE)**[14] 415 7-8-11 97 .... (t) RyanMoore 2 — 83
(S Seemar, UAE) *nvr bttr than mid-div* **33/1**

12 *nse* **Democrate**[188] 5004 5-8-9 95 .... RichardMullen 11 — 81
(S Seemar, UAE) *nvr bttr than mid-div* **25/1**

13 *nse* **Leitmotiv (IRE)**[39] 7-8-9 95 .... (v) WayneSmith 9 — 81
(M Al Muhairi, UAE) *settled in rr: nvr able to chal* **20/1**

14 *4* **Great Hawk (USA)**[13] 441 7-8-9 95 .... (v) WilliamBuick 5 — 74
(F Nass, Bahrain) *trckd ldr: rdn to chse ldr 3 1/2f out: wknd fnl 2f* **66/1**

2m 19.57s (139.57)
WFA 4 from 5yo+ 2lb — **14** Ran **SP% 126.7**
CSF: £9.29, TRI: £227.29.
Owner Godolphin **Bred** Gainsborough Stud Management Ltd **Trained** Newmarket, Suffolk

FOCUS
The pace was only modest and those who raced handy were at an advantage. The winner was close to his turf best.

NOTEBOOK
Emirates Champion was only 1lb higher than when runner-up to progressive stablemate Anmar (who was the first string) over C&D two weeks previously and, with nothing of that one's calibre in opposition this time, he was able to justify favouritism. He was forced to work plenty hard enough, despite having been beautifully positioned all the way by Dettori, but then again this was only his fifth start. (op 6-4)
Monte Alto(IRE) ran another fine race in defeat and is holding his form really well. He has found only unexposed improvers too good on four carnival starts this year, all over this C&D, including today's winner when third two starts back.
Captain Webb was granted a soft lead and looks flattered.
Titurel(GER) finished a close second (off a 3lb lower mark) over 1m6f on the turf first time up in Dubai, so a steadily run race over 3f shorter was never going to suit and he would surely have benefited from a more positive ride.
Salute Him(IRE) had far too much to do when switching wide at the top of the straight.
Quai D'Orsay, like the fourth-placed finisher, was dropping three furlongs in trip, so he had no chance when just about last turning in, at which point he was denied a clear run.
Blaze Of Fire was another set a lot to do and also didn't get a clear run in the straight.
Hot Six(BRZ) was racing off the same mark as when runner-up to King Of Rome over 1m2f on his Dubai debut, but he suffered a wide trip this time from stall 14 and never featured. (op 11-2)

606a AQLAAM SPONSORED BY SHADWELL ESTATE (H'CAP) (TAPETA) — 6f
4:15 (4:15) (95-110,110) 3-Y-0+
£55,555 (£18,518; £9,259; £4,629; £2,777; £1,851)

RPR

1 **Leahurst (IRE)**[21] 339 4-9-5 109 .... RyanMoore 1 — 117
(J Noseda) *trckd ldrs: gng wl 2 1/2f out: led 1 1/2f out: r.o wl: comf* **4/5**[1]

2 *5 ¾* **Prince Shaun (IRE)**[21] 336 5-8-8 98 .... (t) TadhgO'Shea 9 — 89
(Doug Watson, UAE) *s.i.s: racd in rr: r.o wl fnl 2f: no ch w wnr* **33/1**

3 *¾* **Aranel (IRE)**[21] 339 4-8-10 100 .... JulienGrosjean 6 — 89
(M Delcher-Sanchez, Spain) *mid-div: r.o wl fnl 2f: nrest at fin* **10/1**

4 *1 ¾* **Thor's Echo (USA)**[14] 416 8-8-11 101 .... (bt) RichardMullen 7 — 85
(S Seemar, UAE) *led in centre: hdd and ev ch 1 1/2f out: one pce fnl 110yds* **11/1**

5 *¾* **Star Crowned (USA)**[7] 515 7-9-3 107 .... (t) LJurado 11 — 88
(R Bouresly, Kuwait) *trckd ldrs: one pce fnl 1 1/2f* **16/1**

6 *¼* **Bounty Quest**[20] 8-8-5 95 .... WayneSmith 10 — 76
(Doug Watson, UAE) *trckd ldrs: ev ch 2f out: r.o same pce* **40/1**

7 *¾* **Al Qasi (IRE)**[7] 515 7-8-10 100 .... (t) RoystonFfrench 2 — 78
(A Al Raihe, UAE) *a mid-div* **25/1**

8 *¾* **Capricorn Run (USA)**[14] 413 7-8-10 100 .... (v) PJSmullen 8 — 76
(A J McCabe) *nvr able to chal* **66/1**

9 *3 ¼* **Embalo (BRZ)**[523] 5-8-8 98 .... (t) TedDurcan 5 — 64
(Doug Watson, UAE) *racd in rr: n.d* **20/1**

10 *2 ¾* **Prime Defender**[131] 6661 6-9-2 106 .... RichardHills 4 — 64
(B W Hills) *trckd ldrs: disp ld 4f out tl wknd 2f out* **7/1**[3]

11 *2* **Iguazu Falls (USA)**[14] 416 5-8-5 95 .... (t) WJSupple 12 — 47
(M bin Shafya, UAE) *nvr bttr than mid-div* **40/1**

12 *12* **Aichi (AUS)**[21] 336 5-9-6 110 .... (b) AhmedAjtebi 3 — 26
(Saeed Bin Suroor) *nvr able to chal* **6/1**[2]

1m 10.82s (70.82) — **12** Ran **SP% 123.6**
CSF: £49.36, TRI: £195.02.
Owner Mrs Susan Roy **Bred** D & B Egan **Trained** Newmarket, Suffolk

FOCUS
Mainly exposed sorts for this sprint, with the one exception being Leahurst. He produced another step up but the winning margin was more like 5 lengths.

NOTEBOOK
Leahurst(IRE) ◆ was a hugely impressive winner, extending his unbeaten record on synthetic surfaces to four races. He was a bit keen when successful off a 7lb lower mark on his Dubai debut over 7f, so it was understandable his connections wanted to try him over a sprint trip and it was clear from the off he had sufficient speed. If anything, he was again a bit free, but he got a lovely position from stall one, tracking the leaders, and having briefly looked as though he might struggle for room at the top of the straight, he quickened between rivals to go clear. The one slight concern was the way he edged right under pressure, just as he did last time, but it didn't seem to slow him down. When racing on a track clearly riding slow first time up at the carnival, Leahurst had posted a time that compared very favourably with last week's action, when conditions were noticeably quicker, and while it's true that comparing race times from different meetings is not always a reliable guide, this was clearly another high-class performance on the clock. He was only 0.08 seconds slower than the time War Artist managed in the previous week's Group 3, when carrying 4lb less, and 0.57 seconds quicker than the 101-rated Frosty Secret, carrying 3lb less, managed earlier on this card. There can be no doubt this was the performance of a Group horse and he will presumably be given his chance in the Mahab Al Shimaal over C&D on Super Thursday (March 4), where he could meet the likes of Gayego, and that will tell us whether or not he's Golden Shaheen material. (op 5-6)

Prince Shaun(IRE) finished well out wide for second, but obviously had no chance with the rapidly improving winner. (op 28-1)
Aranel(IRE), over 2l behind Leahurst over 7f last time, met that rival on 7lb better terms but simply couldn't get near him when it mattered.
Thor's Echo(USA), winner of the Breeders' Cup Sprint in 2006, was racing off the same mark as when third over C&D on his return from around 17 months off, and he ran well after disputing the early lead. (op 10-1)
Star Crowned(USA) has nothing in hand off this sort of mark.
Prime Defender ran disappointingly on his return from four months off. (op 13-2)
Aichi(AUS) failed to build on a recent unlucky run.

607a NAYEF SPONSORED BY SHADWELL ESTATE (H'CAP) (TAPETA) 7f

4:55 (4:56) (100-113,113) 3-Y-O+

£64,814 (£21,604; £10,802; £5,401; £3,240; £2,160)

RPR

1 **Sirocco Breeze**[21] 339 5-8-8 104 ... FrankieDettori 10 114+
(Saeed Bin Suroor) *settled in last: smooth prog 2 1/2f out: rdn to ld 1f out: comf* **6/1**[3]

2 2 3/4 **Mutheeb (USA)**[14] 413 5-9-3 112 ... RichardHills 8 114
(M Al Muhairi, UAE) *trckd ldng duo: led 2f out: kpt on wl: no ch w wnr* **10/3**[1]

3 3/4 **Warsaw (IRE)**[14] 413 5-8-5 100 ... (b) DaraghO'Donohoe 12 100
(M F De Kock, South Africa) *mid-div: rdn 2 1/2f out: r.o wl fnl f* **25/1**

4 1/4 **Marching (AUS)**[306] 6-9-0 109 ... AhmedAjtebi 13 108
(Saeed Bin Suroor) *Mid-div: chsd ldrs 3f out: r.o one pce* **12/1**

5 1/4 **Barbecue Eddie (USA)**[13] 438 6-8-5 100 ... (b) WJSupple 2 99+
(Doug Watson, UAE) *rdn to ld: hdd 2f out: n.m.r ins fnl f: nt rcvr* **6/1**[3]

6 shd **Summit Surge (IRE)**[13] 438 6-9-4 113 ... KierenFallon 3 111
(L M Cumani) *a mid-div* **5/1**[2]

7 1/4 **Emmrooz**[260] 2606 5-8-9 105 ... WilliamBuick 9 102
(D Selvaratnam, UAE) *nvr bttr than mid-div* **14/1**

8 1 **Hunting Tower (SAF)**[13] 440 8-9-3 112 ... ChristopheSoumillon 6 107
(M F De Kock, South Africa) *trckd ldrs tl 3f out: one pce fnl 2f* **18/1**

9 1 **Munaddam (USA)**[13] 438 8-9-2 111 ... TadhgO'Shea 1 103
(E Charpy, UAE) *a mid-div* **14/1**

10 nse **Le Drakkar (AUS)**[383] 5-9-1 110 ... CSanchez 5 102
(A bin Huzaim, UAE) *settled in rr: nvr able to chal* **12/1**

11 4 1/4 **Don Renato (CHI)**[55] 7-8-11 107 ... (t) OlivierPeslier 11 87
(J Barton, Saudi Arabia) *nvr nr to chal* **16/1**

12 17 **Atomic Rain (USA)**[200] 4-9-0 109 ... (b) MickaelBarzalona 4 44
(Saeed Bin Suroor) *nvr able to chal* **33/1**

13 11 **Dohasa (IRE)**[64] 7768 5-9-0 109 ... TedDurcan 7 14
(I Mohammed, UAE) *nvr bttr than mid-div* **8/1**

1m 23.95s (83.95) **13 Ran SP% 126.1**
CSF: £27.76, TRI: £491.04.
Owner Godolphin **Bred** Gainsborough Stud Management Ltd **Trained** Newmarket, Suffolk

FOCUS
They went a good pace in this decent handicap. The form is rated through the runner-up and sixth.

NOTEBOOK
Sirocco Breeze ◆, a naturally free-going type who had ruined his chance by pulling too hard when behind the likes of Leahurst and Mutheeb over C&D on his Dubai debut, proved suited by the decent gallop. It was slightly surprising to see the winner kept to 7f, but his connections got it spot on, and so, too, did Frankie Dettori, who managed to get him settled, holding him up in last place early on. The Godolphin first string made good headway around the bend and the result seemed inevitable when he was produced out wide in the straight. This was a smart performance from Sirocco Breeze on only his fifth start and, provided he continues to settle, there should be more to come, maybe over 6f one day.
Mutheeb(USA), who was 8lb higher than when 5l ahead of the potentially smart but unlucky Stoic over C&D last time, produced a noteworthy effort. He was really keen to post, and could probably have settled better in the race itself as well, so he deserves credit for finishing so close to a promising type. (op 7-2)
Warsaw(IRE) stayed at 7f, rather than dropping back to 6f, and he could find only the one pace in the straight.
Marching(AUS), winless since landing a 1m2f Group 2 in Australia in 2007, did well to finish so close as he raced without cover pretty much throughout and was keen early on.
Barbecue Eddie(USA) was allowed a ridiculously easy lead when winning over C&D last time and a repeat performance off a 5lb higher mark always seemed unlikely. He was duly reeled in this time, although the beaten margin was exaggerated when he was squeezed up against the rail by the runner-up around a furlong out. (op 13-2)
Summit Surge(IRE) seems to be a bit high in the weights.
Emmrooz, smart but lightly raced when with Godolphin, was having his first run for 260 days and this trip was surely shorter than ideal. (op 12-1)
Dohasa(IRE) got upset in the stalls and it's easy to excuse his poor run.

608a UAE 2000 GUINEAS SPONSORED BY SHADWELL ESTATE, SAKHEE (GROUP 3) (TAPETA) 1m

5:30 (5:32) 3-Y-O

£92,592 (£30,864; £15,432; £7,716; £4,629; £3,086)

RPR

1 **Musir (AUS)**[14] 414 4-9-5 113 ... ChristopheSoumillon 14 116+
(M F De Kock, South Africa) *mid-div: smooth prog chse ldrs 2 1/2f out: led ins fnl f out: won comf* **1/1**[1]

2 3 1/4 **Frozen Power (IRE)**[14] 414 3-8-9 105 ... AhmedAjtebi 11 106
(Saeed Bin Suroor) *mid-div chsd ldrs 2 1/2f out: ev ch 1 1/2f out: one pce fnl 55yds* **13/2**[2]

3 1 1/4 **Della Barba (CHI)**[236] 4-9-5 99 ... OlivierPeslier 4 105+
(J Barton, Saudi Arabia) *trckd ldrs: n.m.r 2 1/2f out: r.o wl fnl 1 1/2f* **25/1**

4 2 1/4 **Solid Choice (AUS)**[14] 414 4-9-5 102 ... KShea 13 100
(M F De Kock, South Africa) *mid-div: trckd ldrs 2f out: r.o wl fnl 1 1/2f* **12/1**

5 1/2 **Jardim (BRZ)**[14] 414 4-9-5 102 ... RichardMullen 10 99
(A Cintra Pereira, Brazil) *mid-div: r.o wl fnl 2f: nrst fin* **33/1**

6 hd **Oroveso (BRZ)**[14] 414 4-9-5 102 ... TJPereira 1 98
(P Bary, France) *a mid-div* **16/1**

7 1/4 **Maroon Machine (IRE)**[99] 7346 3-8-9 100 ... KierenFallon 5 96
(E J O'Neill, France) *nvr bttr than mid-div* **16/1**

8 1 1/4 **Storm Chispazo (ARG)**[96] 4-9-5 104 ... RyanMoore 8 95
(H J Brown, South Africa) *trckd ldrs: led briefly 4f out: one pce fnl f* **12/1**

9 2 1/2 **Rock Jock (IRE)**[14] 414 3-8-9 99 ... PJSmullen 12 87
(A Manuel, UAE) *racd in rr: r.o fnl 2f: nvr nr to chal* **66/1**

10 2 1/4 **Quartier Latin (ARG)**[124] 4-9-5 104 ... RichardHills 3 84
(Doug Watson, UAE) *trckd ldrs: t.k.h: ev ch whn n.m.r 2 1/2f out: wknd fnl 1 1/2f* **10/1**[3]

11 shd **Dubai Miracle (USA)**[145] 6268 3-8-9 99 ... WilliamBuick 2 82
(D M Simcock) *nvr bttr than mid-div* **25/1**

12 1/4 **Real Secret (BRZ)**[164] 4-9-5 104 ... WBlandi 6 83
(A Cintra Pereira, Brazil) *settled in last: nvr nr to chal* **12/1**

13 4 1/4 **Olympic Danz (BRZ)**[14] 414 4-9-5 98 ... MNunes 9 73
(A Cintra Pereira, Brazil) *trckd ldrs tl 2 1/2f out: sn btn* **50/1**

14 4 3/4 **El Amarillista (ARG)**[14] 414 4-9-5 102 ... (t) WJSupple 7 62
(J Barton, Saudi Arabia) *sn led: hdd 2 1/2f out: wknd* **40/1**

1m 37.46s (97.46)
WFA 3 from 4yo 19lb **14 Ran SP% 123.8**
CSF: £7.03.
Owner Sheikh Mohammed Bin Khalifa Al Maktoum **Bred** Sh Mohd Bin Khalifa Al Maktoum **Trained** South Africa

FOCUS
The tenth running of this Classic. Horses bred in the southern hemisphere seemed to be at an advantage according to the trends, having landed five of the previous renewals from just 30 representatives, including three of the last four, whereas the northern hemisphere's four winners came from a total of 73 runners. The second and third are rated to their best.

NOTEBOOK
Musir(AUS) became the fifth trial winner in the last six years to follow up in the main event. He had defied a penalty when just too good for Frozen Power over 7f two weeks earlier and showed himself in a different league to his rivals, in the process providing Mike De Kock with a fourth win in the race. A wide draw probably wasn't ideal, but he travelled well in about mid-division and it was noticeable that he was still going best early in the straight. Once asked to stretch, he found plenty and was an impressive winner. Presumably the middle leg of the UAE Triple Crown will be on Musir's agenda now - on this evidence the extra 300m should just about be within his grasp - and, while the competition may get a little tougher in that contest, and/or in the Derby on World Cup night, it will clearly take a pretty good one to beat him. (op 10-11)
Frozen Power(IRE) was 7lb worse off with the winner this time and never looked like reversing form. This was a decent effort in defeat, but Godolphin has a few better three-year-olds than him in their stable. (op 7-1)
Della Barba(CHI), Grade 1 placed in Chile, travelled nicely for much of the way, but he lost his place turning in and that cost him his chance. Still, he finished well when in the clear and should be suited by the extra 300m in the next two legs of the Triple Crown. (op 20-1)
Solid Choice(AUS), fourth in the trial, ran well this time considering he was stuck wide throughout from stall 13.
Jardim(BRZ), sixth in the trial, finished well without threatening.
Oroveso(BRZ), third in the trial, didn't seem to have much room towards the inside in the second half of the contest, but he didn't look unlucky. (op 14-1)
Maroon Machine(IRE), who didn't run badly in the Dewhurst on his penultimate start considering the trip was too short, also seemed to find this distance inadequate, finishing well but much too late.
Storm Chispazo(ARG), last seen winning the Argentine Derby over an extended 1m4f in November, was given a handy ride but still got outpaced in the straight.

609a AL MAKTOUM CHALLENGE R2 SPONSORED BY SHADWELL ESTATE (GROUP 3) (TAPETA) 1m 1f 110y

6:05 (6:06) 3-Y-O+

£74,074 (£24,691; £12,345; £6,172; £3,703; £2,469)

RPR

1 **Allybar (IRE)**[13] 435 4-9-4 112 ... AhmedAjtebi 3 117
(Saeed Bin Suroor) *s.i.s: settled in rr: smooth prog 2 1/2f out: led ins fnl f: r.o wl* **10/1**

2 1/2 **Crowded House**[14] 417 4-9-4 118 ... JamieSpencer 10 116+
(B J Meehan) *settled in rr: trckd wnr 2f out: r.o wl ins fnl f: nrst fin* **15/8**[1]

3 3 1/4 **Calvados Blues (FR)**[146] 6327 4-9-4 110 ... TedDurcan 6 109
(Saeed Bin Suroor) *mid-div: r.o wl fnl 2f: nrst fin* **14/1**

4 3/4 **Mr Brock (SAF)**[14] 415 7-9-4 112 ... KShea 12 107
(M F De Kock, South Africa) *in rr of mid-div: smooth prog to ld 2f out: r.o same pce* **10/1**

5 1/4 **Snaafy (USA)**[13] 440 6-9-4 119 ... (v) RichardHills 11 106
(M Al Muhairi, UAE) *mid-div: ev ch bhd ldrs 1 1/2f out: wknd fnl 110yds* **11/4**[2]

6 8 **Jalil (USA)**[350] 771 6-9-4 106 ... (t) FrankieDettori 8 89
(Saeed Bin Suroor) *a mid-div* **10/1**

7 1/4 **Perfect Stride**[148] 6202 5-9-4 112 ... RyanMoore 4 89
(Sir Michael Stoute) *mid-div: n.m.r 2 1/2f out: r.o same pce* **9/1**[3]

8 1/4 **Jet Express (SAF)**[20] 8-9-4 107 ... RoystonFfrench 5 88
(A Al Raihe, UAE) *trckd ldrs tl 2 1/2f out: wknd* **33/1**

9 10 **Storm Sir (USA)**[21] 5-9-4 95 ... OlivierPeslier 7 67
(B Al Abed, Bahrain) *trckd ldr tl 3f out: wknd* **66/1**

10 7 1/4 **Bon Grain (FR)**[79] 5-9-4 108 ... WJSupple 2 52
(M bin Shafya, UAE) *sn led: hdd 2 1/2f out: wknd fnl 2f* **25/1**

11 1 3/4 **Poet**[13] 440 5-9-4 116 ... PJSmullen 9 48
(E Charpy, UAE) *nvr bttr than mid-div* **16/1**

12 1/2 **Mr. Crazy Boy (ARG)**[14] 414 4-8-10 98 ... (b) ChristopheSoumillon 1 40
(M F De Kock, South Africa) *mid-div on rail: n.m.r 2 1/2f out: nt rcvr* **22/1**

1m 57.05s (117.05) **12 Ran SP% 123.9**
CSF: £29.46.
Owner Godolphin **Bred** Wertheimer Et Frere **Trained** Newmarket, Suffolk

FOCUS
This went to subsequent World Cup winner Moon Ballad in 2003, but it's hard to know exactly what to make of this year's race. The pace seemed strong, and those held up dominated, but even so, several runners were short of room when the field bunched up at the top of the straight.

NOTEBOOK
Allybar(IRE) hammered Presvis in a three-runner handicap off a mark of 108 over 1m2f around here on his debut for Godolphin, but that was muddling form. It was hard to know what to expect this time, but he proved himself to be very smart with a hard-fought success, certainly improving on the solid but unspectacular form he showed when trained in France. He was well ridden, being held up well off the decent pace, before swinging wide into the straight to ensure a clear run, and that meant he got first run on the slightly unlucky runner-up. It's clear plenty went his way and, while he's certainly progressing, he'll probably come up short next time, presumably in either the third round of this series, or the World Cup.
Crowded House looked worth a shot in a race like this to test his World Cup credentials after running well on his return from an absence over an inadequate (and slowly run) 1m1f on turf last time, and the surface promised to suit seeing as he won his maiden on Polytrack. He sat last early after taking a while to get into his stride, but that wasn't a concern considering the pace was strong. More of a problem was that he had nowhere to go when looking to make a move early in the straight, and he was forced to switch markedly right, only getting in the clear around a furlong out and very much allowing the winner first run. He finished well, suggesting he might have won with an uninterrupted trip, although he didn't help himself by hanging left. His form is currently well short of World Cup standard, but he can be expected to come on again for this, especially over a little further, and he's certainly worth his place in the third round of this series on Super Thursday. That will tell us more. (op 9-4)
Calvados Blues(FR), a dual Group 3 winner when trained in France, got a better run into the straight than some of these but was no match for the front two. This was a good effort after 146 days off.
Mr Brock(SAF), a clear-cut winner over 1m2f off a mark of106 on his return to Dubai, looks the best guide to the form. He swung wide into the straight and had his chance. (op 8-1)

Snaafy(USA), a winner on turf over 1m off a mark of 116 on his reappearance, was trying synthetics for the first time and was unproven over a trip this far. He didn't have a great deal of room in the closing stages, but wasn't unlucky and these conditions basically failed to bring out the best in him. (op 5-2)
Jalil(USA), lightly raced and disappointing since winning round three of this challenge in 2008, offered some encouragement. He lost his place and any chance, when short of room turning into the straight, but kept on steadily once in the open.
Perfect Stride, winner of the Wolferton Handicap off a mark of 108 at Royal Ascot last year, was probably held when a bit short of room in the straight. (op 17-2)
Storm Sir(USA) had no room against the inside rail when trying to stay on in the straight and is better than he showed.

610a MUHTATHIR SPONSORED BY SHADWELL ESTATE (H'CAP) (TAPETA) 1m

6:40 (6:47) (90-105,105) 3-Y-0+

£40,740 (£13,580; £6,790; £3,395; £2,037; £1,358)

RPR

1 **Calming Influence (IRE)**[13] [440] 5-9-4 105 AhmedAjtebi 14 117+
(Saeed Bin Suroor) *in rr of mid-div: rdn to chse ldrs 3f out: led 1f out: r.o wl: comf* **9/1**[3]
2 6 1/4 **Beauchamp Viceroy**[13] [441] 6-9-3 104 (p) RyanMoore 10 102
(G A Butler) *mid-div: r.o wl fnl 2f* **16/1**
3 nse **Balcarce Nov (ARG)**[14] [412] 5-9-2 102 JamieSpencer 11 101
(T P Tate) *settled in rr: r.o wl fnl 2f* **6/1**[2]
4 1 **Aspectus (IRE)**[14] [415] 7-9-4 105 KierenFallon 7 101
(J A Osborne) *mid-div: rdn 2 1/2f out: one pce fnl 1 1/2f* **10/1**
5 1 1/4 **Blues Ballad**[20] 6-9-0 100 (t) RichardMullen 5 94
(S Seemar, UAE) *slowly away: mid-div on rail: r.o wl fnl 1 1/2f* **10/1**
6 1/4 **Derbaas (USA)**[13] [438] 4-9-2 102 RichardHills 1 95
(A Al Raihe, UAE) *a mid-div* **20/1**
7 1/2 **Yasoodd**[13] [440] 7-9-1 101 (e) WilliamBuick 8 93
(D Selvaratnam, UAE) *wl away: a mid-div* **4/1**[1]
8 1/2 **Philario (IRE)**[7] [513] 5-8-13 102 MartinLane(3) 12 93
(P D Deegan, Ire) *nvr bttr than mid-div* **50/1**
9 6 3/4 **Codigo De Honor (ARG)**[55] 6-9-2 102 PJSmullen 9 77
(B Al Subaie, Saudi Arabia) *sn led: hdd 2 1/2f out: wknd* **20/1**
10 3 3/4 **Echoes Rock (GER)**[13] [440] 7-9-4 105 (t) WJSupple 3 71
(Doug Watson, UAE) *trckd ldr tl 2 1/2f out: wknd* **20/1**
11 2 **Alazeyab (USA)**[7] [517] 4-9-2 102 (t) TadhgO'Shea 2 64
(A Al Raihe, UAE) *nvr bttr than mid-div* **33/1**
12 3 3/4 **Perfectly (ARG)**[34] 5-9-3 104 (t) OlivierPeslier 6 56
(J Barton, Saudi Arabia) *nvr able to chal* **16/1**
13 3/4 **Aahaykid (IRE)**[7] [511] 4-9-2 102 KLatham 4 54
(P D Deegan, Ire) *nvr able to chal* **12/1**

1m 37.1s (97.10) **13** Ran SP% **101.1**
CSF: £75.05, TRI: £368.87.
Owner Godolphin **Bred** Mrs Helen Lyons **Trained** Newmarket, Suffolk

FOCUS
This race was delayed by around seven or eight minutes when Sovereign Remedy got loose. That one's withdrawal weakened what was already an ordinary looking handicap by carnival standards. The pace seemed honest enough.

NOTEBOOK
Calming Influence(IRE) improved significantly on the form he showed when fourth off this mark on the turf on his return from around a year off. That recent outing obviously brought him on significantly and he clearly also relished this first try over a synthetic course, as he absolutely bolted up. He's due a hefty weights rise, and things will be tougher when he's faced with less exposed rivals, but he is clearly an improved performer.
Beauchamp Viceroy, with cheekpieces on in place of blinkers, appreciated the drop in trip and ran well.
Balcarce Nov(ARG) looked to be set too much to do over C&D last time and it is the same story, if not even more pronounced, on this occasion. He wouldn't have troubled the winner whatever the case, though.
Aspectus(IRE) was produced with every chance and improved on the form he showed first time up in Dubai.
Blues Ballad didn't help himself with a slow start and this was a respectable effort in the circumstances. (op 9-1)
Derbaas(USA) was short of room late on and could have finished a little closer.
Yasoodd could not confirm recent turf placings with today's winner and remains hard to win with.

[583]LINGFIELD (L-H)
Friday, February 19

OFFICIAL GOING: Standard
Wind: Fresh, across towards stands Weather: Fine

611 LINGFIELDPARK.CO.UK APPRENTICE (S) STKS 1m 4f (P)

12:55 (12:55) (Class 6) 4-Y-0+ **£1,774** (£523; £262) **Stalls** Low

Form RPR

-264 1 **Magnitude**[11] [469] 5-9-5 62 (bt) WilliamCarson 6 64
(C C Bealby) *trckd ldr to 1/2-way: 2nd again 4f out: led over 3f out: over 3 l clr and wl in command over 2f out: drvn out fnl f* **7/4**[1]
-410 2 4 **Playful Asset (IRE)**[21] [354] 4-8-9 53 JulieCumine(7) 1 58
(P Howling) *hld up in last: prog fr 3f out but wnr already clr: pushed into 2nd over 1f out: no imp* **13/2**[3]
2-F6 3 1/2 **Seaquel**[19] [190] 4-8-8 47 AshleyHamblett(3) 7 52
(A B Haynes) *led at mod pce: hdd over 3f out: no ch w wnr over 2f out: lost 2nd over 1f out: kpt on* **16/1**
03-0 4 4 1/2 **Bertie Smalls**[16] [396] 4-8-13 50 (b) AshleyMorgan(3) 4 51
(M H Tompkins) *trckd ldrs: effrt 3f out but sn outpcd: n.d fnl 2f* **16/1**
06-6 5 2 **Kings Topic (USA)**[16] [390] 10-9-2 59 (p) AmyBaker(3) 3 48
(A B Haynes) *in tch: rdn over 4f out: wknd 3f out: sn bhd* **7/1**
0-42 6 4 1/2 **Farncombe (IRE)**[8] [497] 4-8-13 62 RossAtkinson(3) 5 41
(R A Harris) *plld hrd: cl up: wnt 2nd 1/2-way to 4f out: wknd over 2f out* **5/2**[2]
/00- 7 8 **Highland Homestead**[100] [7328] 5-9-2 55 JamieJones(3) 2 29
(M R Hoad) *in tch: rdn 5f out: wknd over 3f out: sn wl bhd* **10/1**

2m 34.35s (1.35) **Going Correction** +0.05s/f (Slow)
WFA 4 from 5yo+ 3lb **7** Ran SP% **111.6**
Speed ratings (Par 101): **97,94,94,91,89 86,81**
toteswingers: 1&2 £2.00, 1&3 £9.20, 2&3 £19.30 CSF £13.03 TOTE £2.20: £1.10, £3.10; EX 14.30.The winner was sold to R Harris for 5,600gns
Owner Chris Hamilton **Bred** Cheveley Park Stud Ltd **Trained** Barrowby, Lincs

FOCUS
Not form to dwell on for too long.

612 BREATHE SPA AT MARRIOTT LINGFIELD H'CAP 1m 5f (P)

1:25 (1:26) (Class 6) (0-65,63) 4-Y-0+ **£1,774** (£523; £262) **Stalls** Low

Form RPR

605- 1 **Hucking Hero (IRE)**[17] [7515] 5-9-2 57 PatCosgrave 1 63
(Tim Vaughan) *trckd ldr 2f: lost pl sltly 3f out: rdn whn pce lifted over 2f out: wnt 2nd over 1f out: hrd drvn and styd on to ld last strides* **7/2**[1]
2U1- 2 shd **Carlton Scroop (FR)**[275] [871] 7-9-5 63 (b) AndreaAtzeni(3) 5 69
(J Jay) *t.k.h: pressed ldr after 3f: rdn to ld over 2f out: kpt on u.p: hdd last strides* **5/1**[3]
/52- 3 3/4 **Alternative Choice (USA)**[326] [1036] 4-9-1 60 J-PGuillambert 7 65
(N P Littmoden) *hld up in last pair: effrt on inner 2f out: styd on fnl f: nvr quite able to chal* **7/1**
50- 4 1 **Sotelo**[132] [6668] 8-9-8 63 IanMongan 4 67
(S Gollings) *hld up in last pair: reminder 2f out: nt clr run over 1f out and swtchd rt: reminders and r.o ins fnl f: nvr rchd ldrs* **16/1**
0-55 5 2 **Choral Festival**[23] [309] 4-9-0 62 MarcHalford(3) 2 63
(J J Bridger) *mde most at modest pce: drvn and hdd over 2f out: wknd over 1f out* **6/1**
46/5 6 22 **Nelson Vettori**[23] [316] 6-8-12 53 SteveDrowne 6 37
(C E Longsdon) *hld up in tch: effrt 3f out: wknd rapidly and virtually p.u over 1f out* **4/1**[2]
4-16 P **Fantasy Ride**[14] [420] 8-8-12 53 SaleemGolam 3 —
(J Pearce) *t.k.h: cl up tl broke down bdly over 2f out and p.u* **5/1**[3]

2m 47.36s (1.36) **Going Correction** +0.05s/f (Slow)
WFA 4 from 5yo+ 4lb **7** Ran SP% **108.2**
Speed ratings (Par 101): **97,96,96,95,94 81,—**
toteswingers: 1&2 £3.40, 1&3 £6.80, 2&3 £3.30 CSF £18.73 TOTE £3.30: £1.10, £3.10; EX 11.10.
Owner M Khan X2 **Bred** Mrs A Hughes **Trained** Aberthin, Vale of Glamorgan

FOCUS
A modest handicap.
Nelson Vettori Official explanation: jockey said gelding lost its action

613 BETDAQ POKER (S) STKS 7f (P)

1:55 (1:55) (Class 6) 3-Y-0+ **£1,774** (£523; £262) **Stalls** Low

Form RPR

0431 1 **Ravi River (IRE)**[11] [464] 6-10-0 70 (v) J-PGuillambert 5 74
(P D Evans) *restrained into last after s but trckd ldng pair after 2f: rdn 2f out: wnt 2nd jst over 1f out: hrd drvn and styd on to ld last 75yds* **11/8**[1]
5025 2 1 1/4 **Waterloo Dock**[9] [486] 5-9-8 57 SebSanders 8 64
(M Quinn) *led 1f: pressed ldr: led over 3f out: drvn over 1f out: hdd and outpcd last 75yds* **4/1**[3]
1P0- 3 1 1/2 **Lindoro**[76] [7645] 5-9-9 85 JamieJones(5) 7 66
(M G Quinlan) *trckd ldng pair: cl enough 2f out: rdn and nt qckn over 1f out: one pce after* **9/4**[2]
0-60 4 hd **Count Ceprano (IRE)**[8] [499] 6-9-3 55 DeclanCannon(5) 3 60+
(C R Dore) *hld up in last pair: effrt over 2f out: rdn and kpt on fnl f: nrly snatched 3rd* **16/1**
5066 5 6 **Meydan Dubai (IRE)**[2] [586] 5-9-8 62 (v) SteveDrowne 1 45
(J R Best) *led after 1f to over 3f out: wknd rapidly over 1f out* **10/1**
040- 6 1 3/4 **Ishibee (IRE)**[107] [7239] 6-9-0 46 (p) MarcHalford(3) 4 35
(J J Bridger) *hld up in last pair: shkn 3f out: no prog and btn over 1f out* **66/1**

1m 25.63s (0.83) **Going Correction** +0.05s/f (Slow) **6** Ran SP% **109.3**
Speed ratings (Par 101): **97,95,93,93,86 84**
CSF £6.87 TOTE £2.20: £1.20, £2.20; EX 5.70 Trifecta £9.60 Pool: £414.67 - 31.81 winning units.There was no bid for the winner. Lindoro was claimed by Peter Moran for £6,000
Owner J L Guillambert **Bred** Gainsborough Stud Management Ltd **Trained** Pandy, Monmouths

FOCUS
Selling grade stuff and the form horse going into the contest, Ravi River, proved too strong and was able to follow up his recent Wolverhampton win.

614 TRY BETDAQ FOR AN EXCHANGE H'CAP (DIV I) 7f (P)

2:25 (2:26) (Class 6) (0-60,60) 4-Y-0+ **£1,433** (£423; £211) **Stalls** Low

Form RPR

2534 1 **Bollywood Style**[9] [486] 5-9-2 58 SteveDrowne 4 66
(J R Best) *trckd ldrs: effrt over 2f out: drvn on outer over 1f out: r.o to ld jst ins fnl f: kpt on wl* **7/2**[1]
00-4 2 1/2 **Dancing Welcome**[8] [498] 4-8-12 57 (b) JackDean(3) 12 64
(J M Bradley) *wl in rr: rdn 3f out: stl in last quartet over 1f out: r.o fnl f: fin wl to take 2nd last strides* **13/2**[3]
00-0 3 nk **Our Day Will Come**[16] [397] 4-8-8 55 DeclanCannon(5) 3 61
(B Palling) *wl plcd bhd ldrs: effrt in cl 5th 2f out: nt qckn over 1f out: chsd wnr last 100yds: a hld: lost 2nd fnl strides* **16/1**
-600 4 shd **Dynamo Dave (USA)**[23] [318] 5-7-12 47 (b) RyanPowell(7) 9 53
(M D I Usher) *towards rr: pushed along over 2f out: effrt on outer over 1f out: r.o ins fnl f: nrst fin* **20/1**
0-00 5 3/4 **Suhayl Star (IRE)**[13] [442] 6-9-2 58 AdamKirby 11 62
(P Burgoyne) *t.k.h: trckd ldng pair: wnt 2nd over 2f out: rdn to ld jst over 1f out: hdd jst ins fnl f: no ex and lost pls nr fin* **15/2**
6400 6 3 1/4 **Cavalry Guard (USA)**[8] [498] 6-8-4 51 (b) AmyBaker(5) 1 46
(T D McCarthy) *hld up in last pair: bmpd along over 2f out: kpt on one pce fr over 1f out* **20/1**
0-21 7 hd **Copper King**[16] [388] 6-8-10 52 LiamKeniry 2 46
(Miss Tor Sturgis) *hld up in midfield: effrt on inner over 2f out: one pce and no imp over 1f out* **7/2**[1]
00-0 8 nk **Winterbourne**[8] [495] 4-8-4 46 (b[1]) AdrianMcCarthy 6 40
(M Blanshard) *plld hrd: trckd ldr to over 2f out: wknd fnl f* **33/1**
-530 9 1 **Charlie Delta**[7] [532] 7-8-11 60 (b) JakePayne(7) 10 51
(R A Harris) *racd freely: led at str pce: hdd jst over 1f out: wknd rapidly* **20/1**
3100 10 nk **Elusive Ronnie (IRE)**[22] [325] 4-9-3 59 (b) JoeFanning 7 49
(R A Teal) *hld up in last pair: pushed along on inner 2f out: modest late prog: nvr nr ldrs* **11/1**
450 11 1 3/4 **Oceans Edge**[22] [321] 4-9-4 60 PatCosgrave 8 45
(J R Boyle) *fractious preliminaries: slowest away and reminder sn after s: racd wd thrght in midfield: no prog over 2f out: struggling after* **5/1**[2]
00-0 12 3/4 **Transcentral**[7] [532] 4-8-3 48 oh1 ow2 MarcHalford(3) 5 31
(T Wall) *nvr bttr than midfield: no prog over 2f out: sn lost pl* **66/1**

1m 24.96s (0.16) **Going Correction** +0.05s/f (Slow) **12** Ran SP% **119.1**
Speed ratings (Par 101): **101,100,100,99,99 95,95,94,93,93 91,90**
toteswingers: 1&2 £3.10, 1&3 £12.80, 2&3 £30.80 CSF £24.54 CT £330.89 TOTE £4.00: £1.40, £2.40, £6.00; EX 20.20 Trifecta £164.70 Part won. Pool: £222.65 - 0.50 winning units..

Owner Miss Sara Furnival **Bred** Baroness Bloodstock & Redmyre Bloodstock **Trained** Hucking, Kent
■ Stewards' Enquiry : Jake Payne one-day ban: failed to ride to draw (Mar 5)

FOCUS
A strong pace to this low-grade handicap and the finish was dominated by horses who were held up.

615 TRY BETDAQ FOR AN EXCHANGE H'CAP (DIV II) 7f (P)
3:00 (3:00) (Class 6) (0-60,60) 4-Y-0+ **£1,433** (£423; £211) **Stalls** Low

Form RPR
-001 **1** **Pipers Piping (IRE)**[4] 568 4-8-13 **58** 6ex.............. MichaelStainton(3) 4 67
(P Howling) *trckd ldrs: squeezed through to go 2nd wl over 1f out: drvn ahd 1f out: sn jnd: battled on wl* **6/4**[1]

3-24 **2** *shd* **Towy Boy (IRE)**[18] 368 5-8-10 **52**......................(b) NeilCallan 5 61
(I A Wood) *t.k.h: hld up bhd ldrs: cruising 2f out: pushed up to join wnr ent fnl f: fnd nil and wouldn't overtake* **11/2**[2]

0-01 **3** *nk* **Top Flight Splash**[29] 249 4-8-9 **51**......................(v) StevieDonohoe 6 59
(P D Evans) *led at decent pce: drvn 2f out: hdd 1f out: battled on wl but jst hld* **16/1**

/050 **4** *3 ½* **Contented (IRE)**[22] 319 8-7-11 **46**......................(tp) RyanPowell(7) 3 45
(Mrs L C Jewell) *hld up in midfield on inner: prog fr 2f out: cl up on inner jst over 1f out: sn rdn and nt qckn* **40/1**

-350 **5** *nk* **Bold Rose**[16] 397 4-8-8 **55**......................(p) LeeNewnes(5) 1 54
(M D I Usher) *dwlt: hld up in rr on inner: gng strly over 2f out: effrt over 1f out but one pce after* **33/1**

0423 **6** *1* **Commandingpresence (USA)**[8] 495 4-8-3 **48** oh1 ow2 MarcHalford(3) 10 44
(J J Bridger) *mounted on crse: dwlt: hld up in last quartet: rdn over 2f out: kpt on fr over 1f out: no ch* **20/1**

/023 **7** *¾* **Castleburg**[23] 318 4-9-4 **60**...................... FergusSweeney 8 54
(G L Moore) *hld up in midfield: nt qckn 2f out: no prog fr over 1f out* **12/1**

40-0 **8** *½* **Ever Cheerful**[13] 442 9-9-3 **59**......................(p) SebSanders 7 52
(A B Haynes) *chsd ldr to wl over 1f out: wknd* **6/1**[3]

-052 **9** *¾* **Sovereignty (JPN)**[8] 498 8-8-10 **52**...................... MartinDwyer 9 46+
(D K Ivory) *taken down early: hld up in last quartet: shkn up wl over 2f out: no prog over 1f out: trapped bhd rivals nr fin* **15/2**

6-00 **10** *shd* **Stormburst (IRE)**[4] 567 6-8-4 **46**......................(p) AdrianMcCarthy 12 37
(A J Chamberlain) *chsd ldng pair to 2f out: wknd* **50/1**

05-5 **11** *1* **Amber Sunset**[23] 312 4-9-1 **60**...................... AndreaAtzeni(3) 11 48
(J Jay) *hld up in midfield and racd on wd outside: lost grnd whn v wd bnd 2f out: wknd* **12/1**

0-66 **12** *1* **Yourgolftravel Com**[13] 443 5-9-1 **57**......................(t) StephenCraine 2 43
(M Wigham) *awkward to post: dwlt: hld up in wl in rr: last over 2f out: cajoled along and hd high: no prog* **25/1**

1m 23.53s (-1.27) **Going Correction** +0.05s/f (Slow) **12** Ran SP% **118.7**
Speed ratings (Par 101): **109,108,108,104,104 103,102,101,100,100 99,98**
toteswingers: 1&2 £3.80, 1&3 £7.30, 2&3 £18.00 CSF £8.80 CT £97.61 TOTE £2.50: £1.20, £2.00, £4.60; EX 12.30 Trifecta £273.70 Pool: £421.67 - 1.14 winning units.
Owner C N Wright **Bred** Drumhass Stud **Trained** Newmarket, Suffolk
■ Stewards' Enquiry : Michael Stainton one-day ban: failed to ride to draw (Mar 5)

FOCUS
Not as much depth as the first division and, unlike that race, this was dominated by horses that raced close to the speed.

616 MARRIOTT PLAY & STAY H'CAP 6f (P)
3:35 (3:36) (Class 4) (0-80,75) 4-Y-0+ **£4,209** (£1,252; £625; £312) **Stalls** Low

Form RPR
0-60 **1** **Vintage (IRE)**[26] 286 6-9-2 **73**...................... IanMongan 2 81
(J Akehurst) *trckd ldng pair: effrt and hanging over 1f out: drvn to chal fnl f: led post* **9/4**[1]

-222 **2** *shd* **Handsome Cross (IRE)**[14] 431 9-8-10 **67**......................(v) StevieDonohoe 3 74
(W J Musson) *hld up in last pair: effrt over 1f out: brought w wl-timed chal fnl f between rivals: led last 50yds: hdd post* **15/2**

520- **3** *¾* **Whiskey Junction**[132] 6666 6-9-4 **75**...................... SebSanders 4 80
(M Quinn) *trckd ldr: led 2f out: hrd rdn and hdd last 50yds: no ex* **10/3**[2]

2262 **4** *nk* **Fromsong (IRE)**[8] 501 12-8-10 **67**...................... MartinDwyer 1 71
(D K Ivory) *taken down early: trckd ldng pair: effrt on inner over 1f out: tried to chal fnl f: nt qckn last 100yds* **5/1**[3]

-424 **5** *nk* **Rondeau (GR)**[16] 393 5-9-2 **73**...................... LiamKeniry 6 76
(P R Chamings) *hld up in last pair: nt gng that wl most of way: effrt on outer over 1f out: styd on fnl f: nrst fin* **10/3**[2]

0104 **6** *7* **Thoughtsofstardom**[2] 578 7-8-12 **69**...................... JoeFanning 5 50
(P S McEntee) *led at str pce: hdd 2f out: wknd rapidly* **16/1**

1m 11.11s (-0.79) **Going Correction** +0.05s/f (Slow) **6** Ran SP% **111.2**
Speed ratings (Par 105): **107,106,105,105,105 95**
toteswingers: 1&2 £3.80, 1&3 £2.20, 2&3 £4.70 CSF £19.03 TOTE £3.60: £2.10, £2.10; EX 21.50.
Owner Taylor And Sheldon Partners **Bred** Mountarmstrong Stud **Trained** Epsom, Surrey

FOCUS
A strong pace thanks to Thoughtsofstardom who blitzed from the gates and that helped a few of these to settle.

617 MARRIOTT HOTEL OPENING SPRING 2010 H'CAP 1m (P)
4:10 (4:10) (Class 4) (0-85,82) 3-Y-0 **£4,209** (£1,252; £625; £312) **Stalls** High

Form RPR
05-1 **1** **Ginger Jack**[16] 385 3-9-2 **77**...................... JoeFanning 2 88+
(M Johnston) *mde all: dictated mod pce: wound it up fr over 2f out: stretched clr fnl f* **7/4**[1]

0-11 **2** *2 ¾* **Marosh (FR)**[25] 288 3-8-11 **72**...................... J-PGuillambert 3 75+
(R M H Cowell) *plld hrd: hld up: n.m.r and dropped to last 1/2-way: effrt 2f out: nt clr run briefly 1f out: wnt 2nd last 100yds: no ch w wnr* **15/2**

6-11 **3** *nk* **Ostentation**[17] 382 3-9-0 **75**...................... LiamKeniry 4 76
(R A Teal) *hld up in tch: effrt 2f out: drvn to chse wnr over 1f out: no imp: lost 2nd last 100yds: kpt on* **6/1**

5-22 **4** *nk* **Khanivorous**[9] 490 3-9-3 **78**......................(p) PatCosgrave 5 79
(J R Boyle) *hld up in last: effrt on outer 2f out: rdn and styd on same pce fr over 1f out* **3/1**[2]

5534 **5** *2* **Transfixed (IRE)**[14] 424 3-9-2 **77**...................... StevieDonohoe 1 73
(P D Evans) *t.k.h: trckd wnr over 2f: styd cl up: shkn up to press for 2nd over 1f out: fdd fnl f* **25/1**

032- **6** *1 ¾* **Muwalla**[151] 6173 3-9-7 **82**...................... NeilCallan 6 74
(C E Brittain) *plld hrd: trckd wnr over 5f out to over 1f out: wknd* **9/2**[3]

1m 37.94s (-0.26) **Going Correction** +0.05s/f (Slow) **6** Ran SP% **109.4**
Speed ratings (Par 99): **103,100,99,99,97 95**
toteswingers: 1&2 £3.00, 1&3 £2.90, 2&3 £5.00 CSF £14.56 TOTE £3.10: £1.50, £3.30; EX 16.30.
Owner Sheikh Hamdan Bin Mohammed Al Maktoum **Bred** Darley **Trained** Middleham Moor, N Yorks

FOCUS
A muddling race in which the early pace was a dawdle.
Marosh(FR) Official explanation: jockey said colt ran too free
Muwalla Official explanation: jockey said colt hung left

618 BET SUPER LEAGUE - BETDAQ MEDIAN AUCTION MAIDEN STKS 1m 2f (P)
4:45 (4:45) (Class 5) 3-Y-0 **£2,456** (£725; £362) **Stalls** Low

Form RPR
1 **Tajaarub** 3-9-3 0...................... MichaelHills 1 80+
(B W Hills) *trckd ldng pair: shkn up 2f out: wnt 2nd over 1f out: r.o to ld last 100yds: won gng away* **5/1**[3]

3 **2** *1 ¼* **Atlantic Tiger (IRE)**[9] 484 3-9-3 0...................... JoeFanning 4 79
(M Johnston) *led: awkward bnd after 1f: jnd and kicked on over 2f out: hdd and nt qckn last 100yds* **4/6**[1]

0 **3** *3 ¼* **Corres (IRE)**[16] 385 3-9-3 0...................... LiamKeniry 5 73+
(D R C Elsworth) *hld up last: wnt 4th 3f out but sn outpcd and pushed along: styd on fnl f* **15/8**[2]

544- **4** *3* **Larkrise Star**[219] 3979 3-8-13 68 ow1...................... AdamKirby 6 61
(D K Ivory) *trckd ldr: rdn to chal and upsides over 2f out: wknd rapidly over 1f out* **14/1**

5 *5* **Mister Pleau (USA)** 3-9-0 0...................... MarcHalford(3) 3 55
(J R Best) *hld up in 4th: nudged by rival over 4f out: wknd wl over 2f out* **25/1**

2m 7.21s (0.61) **Going Correction** +0.05s/f (Slow) **5** Ran SP% **122.0**
Speed ratings (Par 97): **99,98,95,93,89**
toteswingers: 1&2 £3.00, 1&3 £2.90, 2&3 £5.00 CSF £9.99 TOTE £5.90: £2.90, £1.10; EX 11.40 Place 6 £26.12, Place 5 £14.73.
Owner Hamdan Al Maktoum **Bred** Minster Stud **Trained** Lambourn, Berks

FOCUS
The writing looked on the wall again as Joe Fanning was allowed to dictate at steady fractions on short priced favourite Atlantic Tiger, but he has bumped into a decent newcomer.
T/Plt: £18.30 to a £1 stake. Pool: £52,771.99. 2,098.24 winning tickets. T/Qpdt: £6.70 to a £1 stake. Pool: £4,882.83. 535.88 winning tickets. JN

561 WOLVERHAMPTON (A.W) (L-H)
Friday, February 19

OFFICIAL GOING: Standard
Wind: Nil Weather: Fine

619 ENJOY THE PARTY PACK GROUP OFFER H'CAP 5f 20y(P)
5:15 (5:15) (Class 6) (0-60,55) 3-Y-0 **£1,774** (£523; £262) **Stalls** Low

Form RPR
4322 **1** **Exceed Power**[2] 581 3-9-1 **52**...................... HayleyTurner 6 60
(D M Simcock) *hld up in rr: hdwy on outside jst over 1f out: sn rdn: led wl ins fnl f: r.o* **2/1**[1]

460- **2** *1* **Dower Glen**[156] 5976 3-9-4 **55**...................... AndrewMullen 2 59
(N Wilson) *chsd ldr: chal 2f out: rdn to ld 1f out: hdd wl ins fnl f* **16/1**

0-51 **3** *1 ½* **Duke Of Rainford**[28] 265 3-9-3 **54**...................... TonyCulhane 3 53
(M Herrington) *hld up: hdwy on ins over 2f out: rdn and nt qckn ins fnl f* **9/4**[2]

2263 **4** *½* **Lady Brickhouse**[10] 471 3-8-11 **48**...................... LukeMorris 7 45
(M D Squance) *hld up and bhd: pushed along and hdwy on ins wl over 1f out: sn rdn: nt qckn ins fnl f* **8/1**

0-45 **5** *½* **Young George**[10] 471 3-8-13 **50**...................... PJMcDonald 4 45
(C W Fairhurst) *hld up: hdwy over 1f out: sn rdn: one pce ins fnl f* **11/1**

1322 **6** *¾* **Turf Time**[10] 471 3-9-4 **55**...................... ChrisCatlin 5 48
(J A Glover) *prom tl pushed along and wknd wl over 1f out* **4/1**[3]

6636 **7** *4 ½* **Annia Galeria (IRE)**[10] 471 3-9-4 **55**......................(p) DavidProbert 1 32
(C A Dwyer) *led: rdn wl over 1f out: hdd 1f out: wknd ins fnl f* **14/1**

62.87 secs (0.57) **Going Correction** +0.10s/f (Slow) **7** Ran SP% **116.1**
Speed ratings (Par 95): **99,97,95,94,93 92,85**
toteswingers: 1&2 £11.70, 1&3 £1.70, 2&3 £27.70 CSF £34.84 TOTE £2.70: £1.90, £4.50; EX 43.40.
Owner Dr Ali Ridha **Bred** Rabbah Bloodstock Limited **Trained** Newmarket, Suffolk
■ Stewards' Enquiry : Andrew Mullen two day ban: used whip with excessive frequency (Mar 5, 6)

FOCUS
Two and a half inches of overnight snowfall meant the meeting had to survive two morning inspections. A moderate handicap but, although the gallop was sound, the winning time was over two and a half seconds slower than the Racing Post standard. The winner came down the centre in the straight. The form is rated around the first two.

620 BET MULTIPLES - BETDAQ H'CAP 1m 5f 194y(P)
5:45 (5:45) (Class 3) (0-95,90) 4-Y-0 **£6,938** (£2,076; £1,038; £519; £258) **Stalls** Low

Form RPR
0-22 **1** **Admirable Duque (IRE)**[7] 526 4-8-3 **75**...................... BillyCray(5) 4 83
(D J S Ffrench Davis) *t.k.h in tch: rdn to ld jst over 1f out: styd on wl* **10/1**

3321 **2** *4 ½* **Kames Park (IRE)**[7] 526 8-8-9 **70** 6ex...................... JimmyQuinn 1 73
(R C Guest) *stdd s: hld up in rr: hdwy wl over 1f out: rdn and chsd wnr jst ins fnl f: no imp* **6/1**

00/6 **3** *1* **Palomar (USA)**[2] 239 8-9-2 **78**...................... TomQueally 5 79
(N G Richards) *hld up and bhd: hdwy to chse ldr over 8f out: chal over 2f out: rdn over 1f out: one pce fnl f* **5/2**[2]

-215 **4** *1 ½* **Paktolos (FR)**[13] 447 7-9-9 **90**......................(p) MarkCoumbe(5) 2 89
(John A Harris) *hld up in tch: rdn wl over 1f out: one pce fnl f* **5/1**[3]

26-2 **5** *11* **Coeur De Lionne (IRE)**[29] 252 6-9-9 **85**...................... HayleyTurner 6 70
(E A L Dunlop) *set slow pce: qcknd over 7f out: rdn jst over 2f out: hdd jst over 1f out: wknd fnl f* **15/8**[1]

002/ **6** *6* **Southern Regent (IND)**[475] 5892 9-8-11 **80**...................... IanBrennan(7) 3 55
(J J Quinn) *t.k.h: prom: lost pl 8f out: pushed along over 3f out: sn struggling* **14/1**

3m 8.81s (2.81) **Going Correction** +0.10s/f (Slow)
WFA 4 from 6yo+ 5lb **6** Ran SP% **110.1**
Speed ratings (Par 107): **95,92,91,91,84 81**
toteswingers: 1&2 £3.60, 2&3 £2.60 CSF £63.04 TOTE £12.20: £3.30, £2.30; EX 33.40.
Owner Brian W Taylor **Bred** Airlie Stud And R N Clay **Trained** Lambourn, Berks
■ Stewards' Enquiry : Mark Coumbe four-day ban: used whip with excessive frequency (Mar 5, 8)

FOCUS
Exposed sorts in a useful handicap but a very slow pace means this isn't reliable form. The winner came down the centre in the straight.

The Form Book, Raceform Ltd, Compton, RG20 6NL

NOTEBOOK

Admirable Duque(IRE) travelled strongly without his usual cheekpieces and showed much the best turn of foot in a slowly run race to win with plenty in hand. However this doesn't look form to take at face value and his short-term future will depend on how the handicapper views this contest. (op 9-1 tchd 12-1)

Kames Park(IRE), who will be 1lb higher in future, failed to settle in this very messy race and is almost certainly a bit better than he was able to show. A decent gallop around middle distances suits him well and he's worth another chance when it looks as though there will be some pace on. (op 5-1)

Palomar(USA) is better known as a capable performer over jumps and was third in a hurdle at Musselburgh two days earlier but, although he had the run of the race to a greater degree than a few of these, had his limitations exposed in a slowly run race. He'll be seen to better effect granted a stiffer test of stamina but he has little margin for error from this mark. (op 11-4 tchd 3-1)

Paktolos(FR), a course-and-distance winner in January, was another that would have preferred a greater test of stamina, but he is likely to remain vulnerable to the more progressive or the better handicapped sorts from his current mark of 90. (op 4-1)

Coeur De Lionne(IRE), a well-backed favourite, was the disappointment of the race and dropped out very tamely when pressure was applied in a race that he had been allowed to control. He tends to run the odd poor race and is not one to be taking too short a price about. (op 9-4)

Southern Regent(IND), a winning hurdler, was soundly beaten on this first run since late 2008 on this first start for his new stable and he'll have to show a fair bit more before he is a solid betting proposition. (op 20-1 tchd 25-1)

621 WOLVERHAMPTON HOSPITALITY - A PLEASURE H'CAP 1m 5f 194y(P)

6:15 (6:17) (Class 6) (0-60,58) 4-Y-0+ **£2,047** (£604; £302) **Stalls** Low

Form RPR

04-6 **1** **Paint The Town Red**[25] 293 5-9-7 **56** JackMitchell 2 63
(H J Collingridge) *hld up in rr: smooth prog on outside over 2f out: led wl over 1f out: drvn out* **10/1**

46-4 **2** 1 ½ **Lisbon Lion (IRE)**[15] 411 5-9-4 **53** FrederikTylicki 9 58
(James Moffatt) *hld up in mid-div: pushed along and hdwy wl over 1f out: rdn and chsd wnr fnl f: nt qckn* **8/1**[3]

3-12 **3** nk **Fine Tolerance**[30] 228 4-9-3 **57** DavidProbert 3 61
(Miss S L Davison) *s.s: hld up in rr: pushed along over 2f out: rdn and hdwy jst over 1f out: styd on ins fnl f* **10/1**

4-33 **4** nk **They All Laughed**[15] 411 7-9-4 **53** (p) PJMcDonald 4 57
(Mrs Marjorie Fife) *hld up towards rr: pushed along 3f out: c v wd st: rdn wl over 1f out: styd on wl towards fin: nvr nrr* **5/1**[2]

463- **5** hd **Smarties Party**[70] 7557 7-9-9 **58** TomEaves 6 62
(C W Thornton) *sn hld up in mid-div: lost pl over 3f out: rdn and hdwy jst over 1f out: rdn and styd on ins fnl f* **25/1**

636- **6** 2 **Dantari (IRE)**[118] 4168 5-9-9 **58** ShaneKelly 7 59
(Evan Williams) *hld up in mid-div: pushed along 3f out: rdn 2f out: hdwy jst over 1f out: one pce ins fnl f* **8/1**[3]

0000 **7** ½ **Royal Rainbow**[11] 463 6-9-2 **51** ChrisCatlin 12 51
(P W Hiatt) *prom: rdn over 1f out: wknd ins fnl f* **33/1**

25-4 **8** nk **Swords**[3] 575 8-9-2 **56** AndrewHeffernan(5) 11 56
(R E Peacock) *hld up in rr: stdy hdwy on outside over 5f out: led jst over 2f out: sn rdn: hdd wl over 1f out: wknd ins fnl f* **12/1**

-436 **9** hd **Supernoverre (IRE)**[23] 309 4-9-1 **55** JimmyQuinn 1 59+
(P Howling) *hld up in tch on ins: pushed along and lost pl 3f out: nt clr run over 2f out: hdwy on ins over 1f out: sn rdn: wknd wl ins fnl f* **4/1**[1]

5-51 **10** 2 ¼ **Dazzling Begum**[15] 411 5-9-3 **52** RobertHavlin 13 48
(J Pearce) *hld up in mid-div: hdwy 3f out: pushed along and wknd jst over 1f out* **12/1**

/2-1 **11** 1 ¾ **Shandelight (IRE)**[15] 410 6-9-5 **57** BarryMcHugh(3) 10 51
(Julie Camacho) *hld up in tch: pushed along over 2f out: wknd wl over 1f out* **8/1**[3]

0-05 **12** 8 **Treeko (IRE)**[15] 409 5-8-12 **50** (b[1]) RussKennemore(3) 5 33
(P A Kirby) *led early: chsd ldr tl over 3f out: wknd over 2f out* **33/1**

20-1 **13** ¾ **Mekong Miss**[33] 210 4-8-11 **58** MatthewCosham(7) 8 40
(J Jay) *sn led: hdd jst over 2f out: wknd wl over 1f out* **16/1**

3m 7.15s (1.15) **Going Correction** +0.10s/f (Slow)
WFA 4 from 5yo+ 5lb **13** Ran SP% **119.2**
Speed ratings (Par 101): **100,99,98,98,98 97,97,97,96,95 94,90,89**
toteswingers: 1&2 £20.10, 1&3 £15.90, 2&3 £12.70 CSF £85.97 CT £826.38 TOTE £10.30: £3.20, £3.10, £2.70; EX 113.20.
Owner Miss C Fordham **Bred** Snailwell Stud Co Ltd **Trained** Exning, Suffolk

FOCUS

A moderate handicap but, although the gallop was an ordinary one to the home straight, those held up came to the fore late on. The winner came down the centre in the straight.

Smarties Party Official explanation: vet said mare lost a near-fore shoe

Swords Official explanation: jockey said gelding had been hanging right

Supernoverre(IRE) Official explanation: jcokey said gelding had been denied a clear run on the final bend

Treeko(IRE) Official explanation: jockey said gelding had been hanging left in the straight

Mekong Miss Official explanation: jockey said filly had been hanging right throughout

622 WOLVERHAMPTON HOLIDAY INN H'CAP 1m 4f 50y(P)

6:45 (6:45) (Class 7) (0-50,50) 4-Y-0+ **£1,364** (£403; £201) **Stalls** Low

Form RPR

600- **1** **Gamesters Lady**[88] 4861 7-9-0 **47** (b) PaulDoe 1 61+
(Jim Best) *led early: chsd clr ldr: led over 4f out: clr over 3f out: rdn over 1f out: unchal* **5/1**[3]

-302 **2** 5 **Red Wine**[11] 463 11-9-1 **48** FrederikTylicki 3 55
(J A Glover) *stdd s: hld up in rr: pushed along and hdwy on outside over 2f out: wnt 2nd ins fnl f: no ch w wnr* **7/2**[1]

52/5 **3** ½ **Trysting Grove (IRE)**[15] 410 9-9-3 **50** PaulFitzsimons 6 56
(E G Bevan) *s.i.s: hld up in rr: hdwy to chse wnr over 2f out: rdn wl over 1f out: no ex and lost 2nd ins fnl f* **10/1**

0-43 **4** 4 ½ **John Potts**[15] 410 5-8-13 **46** TonyCulhane 2 45
(B P J Baugh) *hld up: pushed along and hdwy over 2f out: wknd ins fnl f* **7/1**

0-60 **5** 2 ¾ **Bubses Boy**[15] 411 4-8-11 **47** HayleyTurner 9 42
(P Howling) *hld up in rr: pushed along 4f out: styd on fr wl over 1f out: nvr nr ldrs* **10/1**

04-4 **6** 7 **Piverina (IRE)**[9] 493 5-8-12 **45** TomEaves 11 29
(Julie Camacho) *hld up towards rr: sme prog over 5f out: pushed along over 5f out: wknd wl over 1f out* **8/1**

-342 **7** 6 **Dobravany (IRE)**[9] 479 6-9-2 **49** (p) JimmyQuinn 5 24
(K A Morgan) *hld up: sme prog over 3f out: wknd over 2f out* **4/1**[2]

510- **8** 11 **Suitably Accoutred (IRE)**[231] 3561 4-9-0 **50** TomQueally 7 9
(Mrs A Duffield) *chsd ldrs: pushed along and wnt 2nd briefly over 2f out: wknd wl over 1f out* **14/1**

500/ **9** 10 **Border Fox**[13] 3755 7-9-3 **50** (b[1]) GregFairley 10 —
(P Salmon) *t.k.h: sn led and clr: hdd over 4f out: wknd wl over 2f out* **33/1**

200- **10** 26 **Roisin's Prince (IRE)**[82] 3617 8-9-0 **50** (tp) BarryMcHugh(3) 4 —
(M Sheppard) *chsd ldrs tl wknd over 5f out: t.o* **16/1**

2m 40.83s (-0.27) **Going Correction** +0.10s/f (Slow)
WFA 4 from 5yo+ 3lb **10** Ran SP% **116.2**
Speed ratings (Par 97): **104,100,100,97,95 90,86,79,72,55**
toteswingers: 1&2 £5.80, 1&3 £21.20, 2&3 £10.30 CSF £22.76 CT £169.14 TOTE £6.90: £2.30, £1.40, £3.40; EX 25.30.
Owner M & R Refurbishments Ltd **Bred** D Timmis **Trained** Lewes, E Sussex

FOCUS

A very moderate handicap in which the pace was sound. The winner continued the trend of coming down the centre in the straight.

Piverina(IRE) Official explanation: jockey said mare had run flat

623 BET WGC GOLF - BETDAQ CLAIMING STKS 1m 1f 103y(P)

7:15 (7:15) (Class 5) 4-Y-0+ **£2,729** (£806; £403) **Stalls** Low

Form RPR

-133 **1** **Ilie Nastase (FR)**[11] 466 6-9-2 85 PaulHanagan 3 84
(D M Simcock) *hld up: wnt 2nd over 3f out: rdn 2f out: r.o to ld last stride* **7/4**[2]

5-41 **2** shd **Plush**[11] 466 7-8-11 81 RossAtkinson(5) 2 84
(Tom Dascombe) *stdd s: t.k.h in rr: hdwy to ld over 4f out: hdd wl over 1f out: sn rdn: led wl ins fnl f: hdd last stride* **10/11**[1]

-544 **3** ¾ **Atacama Sunrise**[28] 261 4-8-5 65 SaleemGolam 1 71
(J Pearce) *chsd ldr: led wl over 1f out: rdn and hdd wl ins fnl f* **6/1**[3]

626- **4** 6 **United Nations**[69] 7723 9-8-7 71 AndrewMullen 5 62
(N Wilson) *led: hdd over 4f out: nt clr run on ins over 3f out: wknd 2f out* **25/1**

2m 15.33s (13.63) **Going Correction** +0.10s/f (Slow) **4** Ran SP% **106.9**
Speed ratings (Par 103): **43,42,42,36**
CSF £3.65 TOTE £2.80; EX 3.40.Ilie Nastase was claimed by C. R. Dore for £14,000
Owner Dr Marwan Koukash **Bred** Deln Limited **Trained** Newmarket, Suffolk
■ Stewards' Enquiry : Ross Atkinson two-day ban: used whip with excessive frequency (Mar 5 & 8)
Paul Hanagan two-day ban: used whip with excessive frequency (Mar 5 & 8)

FOCUS

A race lacking in depth and a farcically slow early pace means this is another result to treat with caution. The first three raced centre to far side in the closing stages.

624 JOHN NORMAN "SINGING PLUMBER" MAIDEN FILLIES' STKS 7f 32y(P)

7:45 (7:46) (Class 5) 3-Y-0+ **£2,456** (£725; £362) **Stalls** High

Form RPR

56- **1** **Areeda (IRE)**[224] 3820 3-8-7 0 ChrisCatlin 9 77+
(C E Brittain) *chsd ldr: led over 2f out: rdn over 1f out: drvn out* **7/2**[2]

2 **2** hd **Binthere Dunthat**[12] 453 3-8-7 0 HayleyTurner 3 76+
(M L W Bell) *a.p: wnt 2nd wl over 1f out: rdn and sustained chal fnl f: kpt on* **10/11**[1]

3-3 **3** 7 **Just Mandy (IRE)**[12] 453 3-8-7 0 PaulHanagan 11 57
(R A Fahey) *a.p: rdn over 1f out: wknd ins fnl f* **9/1**

0- **4** 5 **Glan Y Mor (IRE)**[169] 5605 3-8-7 0 LukeMorris 7 44
(F J Brennan) *t.k.h in mid-div: rdn wl over 1f out: sn btn* **40/1**

5 1 ½ **Swift Steel** 3-8-7 0 JackMitchell 10 40
(Mrs A Duffield) *s.i.s: pushed along over 3f out: a bhd* **50/1**

-263 **6** ¾ **Fine Silk (USA)**[16] 392 4-9-5 67 JamieJones(5) 5 44
(M G Quinlan) *led: hdd over 2f out: wknd wl over 1f out* **15/2**

64- **7** 4 ½ **Revoltinthedesert**[212] 4194 3-8-4 0 AndreaAtzeni(3) 4 25
(M Botti) *hld up in mid-div: effrt over 2f out: wknd wl over 1f out* **7/1**[3]

0- **8** 8 **Sparkle Park**[50] 7886 3-8-7 0 MartinDwyer 8 4
(B J Meehan) *a in rr: pushed along over 3f out: sn struggling* **50/1**

60- **9** 4 **Cheshire Lady (IRE)**[230] 3633 3-8-9 0 ow2 ShaneKelly 6 —
(W M Brisbourne) *dwlt: t.k.h: sn mid-div: wknd 2f out* **100/1**

1m 29.93s (0.33) **Going Correction** +0.10s/f (Slow)
WFA 3 from 4yo 17lb **9** Ran SP% **116.2**
Speed ratings (Par 100): **102,101,93,88,86 85,80,71,66**
toteswingers: 1&2 £2.60, 1&3 £1.60, 2&3 £3.30 CSF £7.04 TOTE £4.80: £1.70, £1.10, £2.40; EX 8.80.
Owner Saeed Manana **Bred** Knockainey Stud **Trained** Newmarket, Suffolk
■ Stewards' Enquiry : Hayley Turner one-day ban: used whip with excessive frequency (Mar 5)

FOCUS

A race lacking anything in the way of strength in depth. The gallop was an ordinary one and the first two pulled clear in the straight. The winner came down the centre.

Revoltinthedesert Official explanation: jockey said filly had moved poorly in the straight

625 BET PREMIER LEAGUE FOOTBALL - BETDAQ H'CAP 7f 32y(P)

8:15 (8:16) (Class 5) (0-75,76) 3-Y-O **£2,914** (£867; £433; £216) **Stalls** High

Form RPR

225- **1** **Rjeef (IRE)**[171] 5542 3-9-4 **74** SebSanders 1 88
(C E Brittain) *mde all: pushed clr wl over 1f out: drvn out* **9/2**[3]

46-1 **2** ¾ **Demonstrative (USA)**[7] 524 3-9-6 **76** 6ex GregFairley 4 88
(M Johnston) *s.i.s: bhd: sn pushed along: hdwy on ins 2f out: rdn and wnt 2nd wl over 1f out: r.o towards fin: nt rch wnr* **1/1**[1]

2-06 **3** 9 **Itsthursdayalready**[19] 366 3-9-0 **70** TomQueally 7 58
(J G Given) *hld up and bhd: pushed along and hdwy 1f out: rdn and r.o to take 3rd towards fin: no ch w ldng pair* **20/1**

524- **4** ½ **Libertino (IRE)**[93] 7430 3-8-11 **67** MartinDwyer 2 53
(B J Meehan) *prom: chsd wnr over 2f out tl rdn wl over 1f out: sn wknd* **12/1**

14 **5** 1 **The Glamour Cat (IRE)**[23] 311 3-8-13 **72** AndreaAtzeni(3) 3 56
(M Botti) *hld up in tch: rdn wl over 1f out: sn wknd* **7/2**[2]

02-1 **6** 3 ¼ **Reallymissgreeley (USA)**[32] 219 3-9-3 **73** (b) StephenCraine 6 48
(K A Ryan) *chsd wnr tl pushed along over 2f out: rdn and wknd wl over 1f out* **33/1**

342- **7** 2 ½ **Count Bertoni (IRE)**[108] 7218 3-9-0 **70** (p) IanMongan 8 38
(S Gollings) *prom tl rdn and wknd wl over 1f out* **16/1**

024- **8** dist **Going French (IRE)**[76] 7637 3-9-1 **71** (b[1]) TonyCulhane 5 —
(R Curtis) *s.v.s: a wl in rr: t.o fnl 3f* **33/1**

1m 29.27s (-0.33) **Going Correction** +0.10s/f (Slow) **8** Ran SP% **114.6**
Speed ratings (Par 97): **105,104,93,93,92 88,85,—**
toteswingers: 1&2 £3.00, 1&3 £4.10, 2&3 £5.60 CSF £9.24 CT £76.64 TOTE £6.90: £1.40, £1.30, £3.80; EX 12.30 Place 6 £514.71, Place 5 £215.45.
Owner Saeed Manana **Bred** K Lee **Trained** Newmarket, Suffolk

FOCUS

A couple of previous winners in a fair handicap. The gallop was a reasonable one and the first two pulled a long way clear. The winner ended up against the inside rail late on.

T/Plt: £309.80 to a £1 stake. Pool: £79,864.73. 188.14 winning tickets. T/Qpdt: £31.30 to a £1 stake. Pool: £12,327.22. 291.34 winning tickets. KH

[604] MEYDAN (L-H)

Friday, February 19

OFFICIAL GOING: All-weather - standard; turf course - good to firm

626a AL DANA SPONSORED BY COMMERCIAL BANK OF DUBAI (H'CAP) (TAPETA) 7f

2:55 (2:55) (95-110,110) 3-Y-O+

£44,444 (£14,814; £7,407; £3,703; £2,222; £1,481)

RPR

1 **Green Coast (IRE)**[8] 511 7-8-11 101 .... TadhgO'Shea 9 108
(Doug Watson, UAE) *settled in rr: smooth prog 2 1/2f out: led 1 1/2f out: r.o wl* **6/1**[2]

2 3/4 **Silverside (USA)**[8] 511 4-8-11 101 .... JulienGrosjean 8 106+
(M Delcher-Sanchez, Spain) *trckd ldrs: n.m.r 2f out: r.o wl once clr: nrst fin* **15/2**[3]

3 1 1/2 **Al Khaleej (IRE)**[15] 413 6-8-10 100 .... TedDurcan 4 101
(E A L Dunlop) *mid-div: r.o wl fnl 1 1/2f* **12/1**

4 shd **Kalahari Gold (IRE)**[15] 417 5-9-3 107 .... RichardHills 1 108
(Doug Watson, UAE) *trckd ldrs: ev ch 1 1/2f out: nt qckn fnl 110yds* **9/2**[1]

5 1/4 **Lovelace**[15] 413 6-9-3 107 .... RoystonFfrench 3 107
(M Johnston) *mid-div on rail: nvr able to chal* **12/1**

6 1 1/4 **Gallagher**[15] 413 4-9-3 107 .... JamieSpencer 14 104
(B J Meehan) *trckd ldrs tl fnl f: wknd* **8/1**

7 1/2 **Across The Rhine (USA)**[15] 413 4-8-9 99 .... PJSmullen 13 94
(A Manuel, UAE) *mid-div: n.m.r 1 1/2f out: nt rcvr* **33/1**

8 1/2 **Desuetude (AUS)**[14] 437 5-9-2 106 .... AhmedAjtebi 5 100
(Saeed Bin Suroor) *sn led: hdd 2f out: wknd* **14/1**

9 1/4 **Ocean's Minstrel**[15] 412 4-8-10 100 .... AlanMunro 12 93
(J Ryan) *trckd ldr tl 2 1/2f out: wknd* **50/1**

10 1 1/4 **Awinnersgame (IRE)**[15] 416 4-8-13 102 .... RyanMoore 7 93
(J Noseda) *in rr of mid-div: nvr able to chal* **8/1**

11 4 **Artimino**[8] 511 6-8-4 100 ....(b) AntiocoMurgia(7) 2 79
(I Mohammed, UAE) *slowly away: nvr able to chal* **33/1**

12 1/2 **Ceremonial Jade (UAE)**[15] 412 7-9-1 105..(p) ChristopheSoumillon 10 83
(M Botti) *nvr able to chal* **14/1**

13 3/4 **Axiom**[22] 336 6-9-1 105 .... KierenFallon 11 81
(L M Cumani) *nvr bttr than mid-div* **9/2**[1]

14 2 1/4 **McCartney (GER)**[8] 517 5-8-13 102 ....(t) RichardMullen 6 73
(S Seemar, UAE) *in rr of mid-div: nvr nr to chal* **25/1**

1m 24.23s (84.23) **14 Ran SP% 125.0**
CSF: £51.12, TRI: £541.06.
Owner Mohsin Al Tajir **Bred** Hadi Al Tajir **Trained** United Arab Emirates

FOCUS
A case could be made for quite a few of these and this was a competitive handicap.

NOTEBOOK
Green Coast(IRE) got going too late when unsuited by a steady pace last time, but he had previously finished a good fourth in a decent handicap containing the likes of subsequent winners Mutheeb, Leahurst and Sirocco Breeze, and was a worthy winner. It's true some of those in behind didn't get the best of runs, but things didn't exactly go the winner's way either, as he was forced to swing much wider than ideal around the turn into the straight when making his move from the rear.
Silverside(USA), one place behind today's winner last time, ran a fine race considering he was denied a clear run until around a furlong out, which point he finished well but just too late.
Al Khaleej(IRE) didn't always have that much room towards the inside when staying on from off the pace, but he was still able to produce a decent finishing effort and wasn't unlucky.
Kalahari Gold(IRE), fifth in a 1m1f Group 3 on the turf last time, when the ground was possibly a bit too quick, promised to be suited by the drop in trip and switch to Tapeta, but he was slightly disappointing. It's possible he over raced a little bit early on when tracking the leaders, but even so, his finishing effort was tame.
Lovelace was blocked in his run against the inside rail early in the straight, but he could only find the one pace once in the clear and wasn't unlucky.
Gallagher had today's fourth and fifth-placed finishers behind him when a promising third in a good race over C&D on his Dubai debut, but he failed to build on that and was disappointing. Having been well placed, he didn't pick up and gave the impression he may want dropping back to 6f. (op 8-1tchd 9-1)
Axiom, a bit unlucky over 6f on his Dubai debut, proved disappointing on this step up in trip. (op 11-2 tchd 5-1)

627a CBD FINANCIAL SERVICES SPONSORED BY COMMERCIAL BANK OF DUBAI (H'CAP) (TAPETA) 1m 3f

3:30 (3:30) (95-110,107) 3-Y-O+

£44,444 (£14,814; £7,407; £3,703; £2,222; £1,481)

RPR

1 **Drunken Sailor (IRE)**[22] 335 5-9-1 104 ....(b) KierenFallon 8 104
(L M Cumani) *mid-div: rdn to ld fnl f: r.o wl: jst hld on* **5/2**[1]

2 1/2 **King Of Rome (IRE)**[15] 419 5-9-4 107 .... KShea 11 106
(M F De Kock, South Africa) *mid-div: chsd ldrs 2f out: r.o wl: jst failed* **3/1**[2]

3 1/2 **Northern Glory**[14] 436 7-9-4 107 .... KKerekes 7 105
(W Figge, Germany) *Mid-div: chsd ldrs and ev ch 2f out: one pce fnl 110yds* **25/1**

4 1/2 **Hello Morning (FR)**[14] 441 5-8-6 95 .... TadhgO'Shea 4 92
(E Charpy, UAE) *trckd ldrs: led 2f out: r.o wl: hdd fnl 55yds* **16/1**

5 1 1/2 **Espiritu (FR)**[14] 441 4-8-13 104 ....(p) FrankieDettori 5 99
(Saeed Bin Suroor) *s.i.s: settled in rr: rdn 3 1/2f out: nt qckn* **11/2**[3]

6 1 3/4 **Dr Faustus (IRE)**[15] 419 5-8-7 96 ow1 ....(t) PatDobbs 9 87
(Doug Watson, UAE) *settled in rr: gng wl 2 1/2f out: n.m.r 2f out: nt rcvr* **10/1**

7 3/4 **Mashaahed**[14] 436 7-9-3 106 ....(t) RichardHills 1 97
(E Charpy, UAE) *in rr of mid-div: rdn 3 1/2f out: one pce* **10/1**

8 11 **Detonator (IRE)**[40] 5-9-1 104 .... WayneSmith 2 76
(M Al Muhairi, UAE) *sn led: t.k.h: hdd 2f out: wknd* **6/1**

9 4 3/4 **Distinctive Image (USA)**[22] 335 5-8-6 95 ....(p) TedDurcan 6 59
(G A Butler) *trckd ldr tl 2 1/2f out: wknd* **25/1**

10 16 **Stubbs Art (IRE)**[14] 438 5-8-10 99 ow1 .... ChristopheSoumillon 10 35
(M F De Kock, South Africa) *broke awkwardly: t.k.h in rr: mid-div 7f out: wknd fnl 3 1/2f* **20/1**

2m 18.48s (138.48)
WFA 4 from 5yo+ 2lb **10 Ran SP% 119.8**
CSF: £10.02, TRI: £147.45.
Owner Samanda Racing **Bred** Cyril Kiernan **Trained** Newmarket, Suffolk

FOCUS
A decent handicap containing a couple of runners who were already carnival winners this year, and that pair finished first and second. The pace seemed just ordinary.

NOTEBOOK
Drunken Sailor(IRE), raised 7lb for an impressive win over C&D on his debut in Dubai, was forced to work harder this time, although it's possible he's the type who keeps a little bit back for himself. He travelled with his usual enthusiasm in about mid-division, and once Fallon found a gap early in the straight, he picked up sufficiently, despite again edging out to his right. It seems unlikely the winner will go up more than 6lb, so an identical race to this one on March 5 could be a suitable target. (op 3-1 tchd 11/4)
King Of Rome(IRE) was just held off a mark 5lb higher than when winning over 1m2f on his previous start. He was forced to swing wide into the straight, which didn't help his cause, and he just took too long to pick up.
Northern Glory was just held when intimidated by the winner, and more specifically, the winning rider's whip.
Hello Morning(FR) was always well placed and had his chance. (op 14-1)
Espiritu(FR), 2lb higher than when runner-up over 1m2f on his Dubai debut, was trying his furthest trip to date and could make no impression. He's one to avoid.
Stubbs Art(IRE) refused to settle on this step up in trip, looking a thoroughly awkward ride.

628a ATTIJARI AL ISLAMI SPONSORED BY COMMERCIAL BANK OF DUBAI (H'CAP) (TAPETA) 6f

4:05 (4:05) (95-110,108) 3-Y-O+

£44,444 (£14,814; £7,407; £3,703; £2,222; £1,481)

RPR

1 **Global City (IRE)**[15] 416 4-8-11 101 ....(t) FrankieDettori 10 107+
(Saeed Bin Suroor) *trckd ldrs: rdn to ld 110yds out: r.o wl* **3/1**[2]

2 1 1/4 **Montpellier (IRE)**[15] 416 7-9-3 107 ....(t) RoystonFfrench 12 109
(A Al Raihe, UAE) *trckd ldrs: led 2f out: r.o wl: hdd 110yds out* **7/1**[3]

3 1 **Jaasoos (IRE)**[22] 339 6-8-13 102 .... WilliamBuick 8 102
(D Selvaratnam, UAE) *mid-div: rdn to chse ldrs 2 1/2f out: r.o wl: nrst fin* **25/1**

4 1 1/4 **Oasis Star (IND)**[14] 434 6-9-3 107 .... YSrinath 4 102
(C Katrak, India) *trckd ldr: nt qckn 2f out: r.o same pce* **2/1**[1]

5 shd **Sir Gerry (USA)**[8] 515 5-9-4 108 .... TedDurcan 11 102
(J R Best) *settled in rr: r.o wl fnl 2f: nrst fin* **9/1**

6 shd **Five Star Junior (USA)**[14] 434 4-8-8 98 .... KierenFallon 6 92
(Mrs L Stubbs) *a mid-div* **16/1**

7 hd **Mrs Boss (BRZ)**[328] 4-8-13 106 ....(t) WBlandi 1 97
(A Cintra Pereira, Brazil) *sn led: v keen: hdd 2f out: wknd* **15/2**

8 1 1/4 **Tawaassol (USA)**[12] 7-8-6 96 ....(bt) TadhgO'Shea 7 86
(E Charpy, UAE) *nvr bttr than mid-div* **25/1**

9 3/4 **Alsadeek (IRE)**[15] 416 5-8-7 97 .... PatDobbs 2 84
(Doug Watson, UAE) *nvr bttr than mid-div* **20/1**

10 3/4 **League Champion (USA)**[14] 437 7-8-7 97 .... DaraghO'Donohoe 5 82
(R Bouresly, Kuwait) *trckd ldrs: led briefly 2 1/2f out: sn hdd & wknd* **22/1**

11 3 1/2 **Almajd (IRE)**[358] 696 5-8-10 100 .... RichardHills 3 74
(M Al Muhairi, UAE) *s.i.s: nvr able to chal* **20/1**

12 4 3/4 **Shallal**[126] 6815 5-8-6 96 .... WJSupple 9 54
(Doug Watson, UAE) *nvr bttr than mid-div* **25/1**

1m 11.34s (71.34) **12 Ran SP% 123.9**
CSF: £22.50, TRI: £441.53.
Owner Godolphin **Bred** Mrs Monica Hackett **Trained** Newmarket, Suffolk

FOCUS
This is not strong form, with Global City and Montpellier, 4lb and 3lb higher respectably than when separated by only a nose over C&D two weeks earlier, the one-two again. The pace wasn't overly quick and it proved hard to make up ground.

NOTEBOOK
Global City(IRE), 4lb higher than his C/D win, benefited from being ridden closer to the pace this time and won with more authority on his previous start. A higher mark in better company will probably find him out.
Montpellier(IRE), a pound better off with Global City than when beaten a nose by him last time, did well to finish so close considering he was very free early on.
Jaasoos(IRE) found this easier than the hot 7f handicap he contested in January and ran well.
Oasis Star(IND) was disappointing off a mark 2lb higher than when runner-up over C&D on her debut in Dubai. She handled the bend better this time, but failed to pick up.
Sir Gerry(USA), 3lb higher than when winning over C&D in January, was stuck wide for a lot of the way from his double-figure stall.
Five Star Junior(USA) would have wanted a quicker pace to chase.
Mrs Boss(BRZ) was unbeaten in three runs on dirt in Brazil, including a couple of Grade 2s, but she had been off since March 2009, and was very keen on this return. All things considered, this was a respectable performance. (op 15-2)

629a CBD VISA INFINITE CARD SPONSORED BY COMMERCIAL BANK OF DUBAI (H'CAP) (TAPETA) 1m 2f

4:50 (4:50) (95-110,109) 3-Y-O+

£44,444 (£14,814; £7,407; £3,703; £2,222; £1,481)

RPR

1 **Al Shemali**[8] 517 6-9-2 105 ....(t) RoystonFfrench 4 106
(A Al Raihe, UAE) *mid-div: smooth prog 2f out: r.o wl: led 110yds out* **20/1**

2 1/4 **Firebet (IRE)**[172] 5508 4-9-4 108 .... FrankieDettori 9 109
(Saeed Bin Suroor) *in rr of mid-div: chsd ldrs 2f out: r.o fnl f* **11/10**[1]

3 shd **Naval Officer (USA)**[15] 417 4-9-4 108 ....(tp) OlivierPeslier 1 108
(J Barton, Saudi Arabia) *trckd ldng duo: ev ch 2 1/2f out: nt qckn fnl 55yds* **16/1**

4 3/4 **Clasp**[8] 513 8-8-7 96 ow1 ....(vt) PatDobbs 7 94
(Doug Watson, UAE) *mid-div: chsd ldrs 2 1/2f out: n.m.r 1 1/2f out: r.o wl* **25/1**

5 1 3/4 **Wonder Lawn (SAF)**[14] 438 7-8-8 97 .... KShea 12 92
(M F De Kock, South Africa) *in rr of mid-div: chsd runner-up 2f out: one pce fnl f* **16/1**

6 1 3/4 **Jaroslaw (SAF)**[22] 334 7-8-11 100 .... WilliamBuick 6 92
(D M Simcock) *trckd ldng duo: ev ch 1 1/2f out: one pce* **11/2**[3]

7 1/4 **Walzertraum (USA)**[15] 415 5-9-4 107 ....(p) ChristopheSoumillon 3 98
(Manfred Hofer, Germany) *nvr bttr than mid-div* **14/1**

8 5 1/2 **Royal Prince**[15] 415 9-8-6 95 .... TadhgO'Shea 8 75
(Doug Watson, UAE) *nvr bttr than mid-div* **25/1**

9 hd **Falcativ**[61] 7827 5-8-6 95 .... TedDurcan 11 75
(I Mohammed, UAE) *s.i.s: nvr able to chal* **5/1**[2]

10 3/4 **Master Of Arts (USA)**[14] 440 5-8-11 100 .... KierenFallon 13 78
(M Johnston) *mid-div: n.d* **20/1**

11 1 1/4 **Trois Rois (FR)**[147] 6327 5-9-6 109 .... AhmedAjtebi 10 85
(Saeed Bin Suroor) *s.i.s: settled rr: nvr able to chal* **14/1**

The Form Book, Raceform Ltd, Compton, RG20 6NL

12 2 1/4 **Beauchamp Xerxes**[8] 517 4-8-10 100............................(p) PJSmullen 2 71
(G A Butler) *trckd ldrs: led 2 1/2f out: hdd 2f out* **33/1**

13 30 **Lucky Ray (ARG)**[15] 415 7-8-6 95......................(vt) DaraghO'Donohoe 5 6
(Doug Watson, UAE) *sn led: rdn 3f out: trckd 2 1/2f out: wknd* **28/1**

2m 3.94s (123.94)
WFA 4 from 5yo+ 1lb **13** Ran SP% **128.4**
CSF: £42.38, TRI: £426.70.

Owner Sheikh Hamdan Bin Mohammed Al Maktoum **Bred** Minster Stud **Trained** UAE

FOCUS
A good handicap run at a decent pace.

NOTEBOOK
Al Shemali improved significantly on the form he showed when returning from around a year off on the turf a week earlier, adding to his carnival success from 2008. Plenty went his way, though, and a rise might find him out. (op 18-1)

Firebet(IRE), a tough and most progressive sort at up to 1m4f on turf for Richard Fahey last year, was just held on his first run for Godolphin. He looked the winner when produced wide with his challenge from off the pace in the straight, but he had been forced to cover a lot of ground and couldn't find extra. He's entitled to improve from this. (op 11-8 tchd 6-5)

Naval Officer(USA) didn't run much of a race in Group 3 company on turf when returning from an absence two weeks earlier, but the ground might well have been too quick for him then, and he may also have needed the run. Whatever the case, he handled this surface well and was just held, with the cheekpieces appearing to help.

Clasp didn't have that much room in the straight, but he wasn't unlucky. This was an improvement on his recent efforts.

Wonder Lawn(SAF), back up in trip, got going too late after being blocked in his run at the top of the straight. (op 14-1)

Jaroslaw(SAF), who got going too late when third to Lizard's Desire and King Of Rome (both winners since) over 1m1 1/2f around here on his Dubai debut, was given a more positive ride on this slight step up in trip, but he failed to see his race out, having looked the winner at the top of the straight. It was hard to tell whether he simply didn't go through with his effort, or got tired after chasing a strong pace. (op 5-1)

Falcativ had won both his starts for Marco Botti after being bought out of Luca Cumani's yard, the latest coming off a mark of 91, but he was back up in trip on his debut for another new yard and offered little. (op 9/2)

630a CBD WORLDMASTER CARD SPONSORED BY COMMERCIAL BANK OF DUBAI (CONDITIONS RACE) (TAPETA) 1m
5:25 (5:25) 3-Y-O+

£40,740 (£13,580; £6,790; £3,395; £2,037; £1,358)

RPR

1 **Skysurfers**[124] 6880 4-9-3 95.. FrankieDettori 13 116+
(Saeed Bin Suroor) *disp: kicked clr 2f out: r.o wl comf* **9/1**

2 3 1/4 **Eagle Mountain**[68] 7747 6-8-11 120.. KShea 11 101+
(M F De Kock, South Africa) *in rr of mid-div: smooth prog 3f out: r.o fnl 1 1/2f: no ch w wnr* **1/1**[1]

3 1 1/4 **Consul General**[22] 338 6-9-3 110.................................... KierenFallon 7 104
(N Al Mandeel, Saudi Arabia) *trckd ldr: nt qckn 1 1/2f out: r.o same pce* **7/1**[2]

4 1/2 **Stoic (IRE)**[15] 413 4-9-3 98.. RyanMoore 12 103
(J Noseda) *mid-div: chsd ldrs 2 1/2f out: r.o wl* **8/1**

5 1 3/4 **Cat Junior (USA)**[14] 440 5-8-11 113..........................(t) JamieSpencer 2 93
(B J Meehan) *in rr of mid-div: r.o fnl 2f: n.d* **7/1**[2]

6 1 3/4 **Fourpenny Lane**[14] 439 5-8-13 102.................................. PJSmullen 14 91
(Ms Joanna Morgan, Ire) *s.i.s: nvr able to chal: r.o fnl 1 1/2f* **20/1**

7 1 1/2 **King Jock (USA)**[15] 412 9-8-11 97................................ TadhgO'Shea 1 85
(A Manuel, UAE) *s.i.s: racd in rr: n.d* **66/1**

8 shd **Hattan (IRE)**[334] 8-8-11 111.. WayneSmith 9 85
(M Al Muhairi, UAE) *disp in centre: hdd 3f out: one pce fnl 2f* **14/1**

9 3/4 **Without A Prayer (IRE)**[22] 338 5-9-3 112....................... JimCrowley 8 90
(R M Beckett) *trckd ldrs: one pce fnl 2f* **15/2**[3]

10 1/4 **Lelah Dorak (KSA)**[56] 4-9-3 100.................................. TedDurcan 3 89
(B Al Shaibani, Saudi Arabia) *a mid-div* **33/1**

11 2 1/2 **Bab Al Bahrain (USA)**[10] 6-9-3 97...(t) LJurado 4 83
(R Bouresly, Kuwait) *disp on rail: tl 4f out: sn rdn and btn* **66/1**

12 2 1/4 **Fervent Prince**[47] 5-8-11 95.. CSanchez 10 72
(A bin Huzaim, UAE) *nvr bttr than mid-div* **66/1**

13 3/4 **Foolin Myself**[126] 6815 5-9-3 97....................................... WilliamBuick 5 76
(D Selvaratnam, UAE) *in rr of mid-div: nvr nr to chal* **66/1**

1m 36.97s (96.97) **13** Ran SP% **128.2**
CSF: £42.38.

Owner Godolphin **Bred** Darley **Trained** Newmarket, Suffolk

FOCUS
A fascinating conditions contest in which the once-raced Skysurfers produced a high-class performance.

NOTEBOOK
Skysurfers ◆ produced a high-class performance. It's true the runner-up was below his very best, but this is still really solid form, with the 110-rated third looking a good guide following a decent run over C&D last time, and while some might argue the fourth horse, rated only 98, limits the level, that one has looked a smart type in the making for a while now. The winner was taking a marked step up in class, having won his maiden on Fibresand at Southwell, albeit he absolutely hacked up, but he was always going well on the pace, racing enthusiastically. Once asked to stretch in the straight, he quickened impressively, before being eased off the final few yards. This was quite an achievement from Skysurfers considering his profile, and it will be a surprise if he isn't up to winning Group races. With his stable having no stand-out World Cup contender, they may want to test this one's credentials in the third round of the Al Maktoum Challenge. However, he's clearly a horse with plenty of speed, and would be no sure thing to get 1m2f on breeding, so the Burj Nahaar, over this C&D on the same day (March 4), may be the best option, ahead of a possible tilt at the Godolphin Mile.

Eagle Mountain was off the turf for the first time and racing over a trip short of optimum after 68 days off, although he was getting weight from some of these, including the winner. He was understandably below form, but still didn't run badly behind the promising winner and much better can be expected in the third round of the Al Maktoum Challenge on Super Thursday.

Consul General, third in the first round of the Al Maktoum Challenge over C&D last time, ran his race but simply found a couple too good.

Stoic(IRE) had loads to find with some of these at the weights, but he had looked much better than the bare form when running on well from an unpromising position over an inadequate 7f first time up in Dubai and duly proved himself better than his current mark, although he didn't help himself by appearing to hang left. He presumably ran here because he couldn't make the cut for a suitable handicap, however, and with his rating now set to go up, he might not be that easy to place.

Fourpenny Lane was not up to this class.

631a AL FAHIDI FORT SPONSORED BY COMMERCIAL BANK OF DUBAI (GROUP 2) (TURF) 1m
6:00 (6:00) 3-Y-O+

£92,592 (£30,864; £15,432; £7,716; £4,629; £3,086)

RPR

1 **Bankable (IRE)**[156] 5995 6-8-11 115.................................(t) RyanMoore 3 114
(H J Brown, South Africa) *settled in rr: chsd ldrs 2f out: r.o wl: led last 55yds* **7/2**[2]

2 shd **Imbongi (SAF)**[14] 438 6-9-0 115....................... ChristopheSoumillon 11 117
(M F De Kock, South Africa) *in rr of mid-div: smooth prog 2f out: r.o wl* **7/2**[2]

3 hd **Ibn Battuta (USA)**[21] 5-8-11 105...................................... WayneSmith 5 114
(M Al Muhairi, UAE) *mid-div: n.m.r 2 1/2f out: r.o wl once clr: jst failed* **20/1**

4 3 **Tam Lin**[15] 417 7-8-11 110...(t) WJSupple 10 107
(M bin Shafya, UAE) *led main gp: rdn 3f out: r.o same pce* **14/1**

5 nse **Fravashi (AUS)**[307] 5-9-0 112...(p) TedDurcan 8 110
(Saeed Bin Suroor) *nvr bttr than mid-div* **14/1**

6 1 **Justenuffhumor (USA)**[104] 7308 5-9-1 120.................. FrankieDettori 1 108
(Saeed Bin Suroor) *in rr of mid-div: nvr able to chal* **5/2**[1]

7 1 3/4 **Premio Loco (USA)**[22] 338 6-9-1 116............................ GeorgeBaker 7 104
(C F Wall) *a mid-div* **8/1**[3]

8 1/4 **Ibn Khaldun (USA)**[657] 1808 5-8-11 113......................... AhmedAjtebi 4 100
(Saeed Bin Suroor) *s.i.s: a in rr* **16/1**

9 3 **Debussy (IRE)**[187] 5084 4-9-1 113................................... WilliamBuick 6 97
(J H M Gosden) *sn led: hdd 2 1/2f out: wknd* **16/1**

10 1 1/2 **Dunelight (IRE)**[14] 440 7-8-11 109...............................(v) KierenFallon 9 89
(C G Cox) *trckd ldrs: rdn 2 1/2f out: one pce fnl 1 1/2f* **22/1**

1m 38.5s (98.50) **10** Ran SP% **118.3**
CSF: £16.49.

Owner Ramzan Kadyrov **Bred** Barronstown Stud & Cobra **Trained** South Africa

FOCUS
This has been a good trial for the Duty Free in recent years, with Gladiatorus taking both races last season, 2008 winner Archipenko going on to finish third, and Linngari, successful in 2007, subsequently second in that aforementioned Group 1 contest. However, this year's race looks short of that level - the winner was a well-beaten fifth in the Duty Free last year and the third was rated just 105 - and it will be a surprise if one of these wins on World Cup night. The pace was strong, with Debussy, a Group 2 winner over 1m2f in France last year, kept honest up front by Dunelight.

NOTEBOOK
Bankable(IRE), last seen winning a 1m Listed race at Sandown for Gary Moore in September, was getting weight from a few of his main rivals. He picked up well from a fair way, having had the race run to suit, but idled once in a share of the lead and nearly missed out. He's entitled to come on for this, and the Group 2 Zabeel Mile on March 5 could be a suitable target.

Imbongi(SAF) had been in good form at some of the other tracks in the UAE lately, but he looked to have loads to find at this level. However, he ran a terrific race and could even be considered slightly unlucky as he was denied a clear run when first looking to make his move early in the straight.

Ibn Battuta(USA) had been in good form at some of the other tracks in the UAE lately, but he looked to have loads to find at this level. However, he ran a terrific race and could even be considered slightly unlucky as he was denied a clear run when first looking to make his move early in the straight.

Tam Lin wasn't good enough.

Fravashi(AUS), a multiple Group-race winner in Australia, including a 7f Group 3 on easy ground when last seen in April 2009, shaped nicely on his debut for Saeed Bin Suroor and is open to improvement.

Justenuffhumor(USA), a dual Grade 2 winner in the US who was last seen finishing third behind Goldikova in the Breeders' Cup Mile, could make no impression under his penalty.

Premio Loco(USA), not at his best on the Tapeta in the first round of the Al Maktoum challenge, was disappointing on this return to turf. (op 9-1)

Ibn Khaldun(USA), the 2007 Racing Post Trophy winner, well beaten in the following year's Newmarket 2,000 Guineas on his only start since then, didn't pick up for pressure and offered little. However, he's obviously entitled to come on a good deal for this.

632a COMMERCIAL BANK OF DUBAI (H'CAP) (TAPETA) 1m 1f 110y
6:35 (6:39) (90-105,105) 3-Y-O+

£40,740 (£13,580; £6,790; £3,395; £2,037; £1,358)

RPR

1 **Roman's Run (USA)**[63] 6-8-13 98...............................(t) TadhgO'Shea 12 100
(Doug Watson, UAE) *mid-div: smooth prog 2 1/2f out: led fnl 55yds* **28/1**

2 1/2 **Don Velez (ARG)**[42] 5-9-3 102....................................(t) OlivierPeslier 10 103
(J Barton, Saudi Arabia) *mid-div: chsd ldrs 2 1/2f out: led 1 1/2f out: hdd cl home* **12/1**

3 1/2 **Roman Republic (FR)**[204] 4455 4-8-13 99..................... FrankieDettori 6 99
(Saeed Bin Suroor) *mid-div: chsd ldrs 1 1/2f out: one pce fnl 110yds* **5/4**[1]

4 1 1/4 **Kal Barg**[14] 441 5-9-2 101.. WilliamBuick 9 98
(D Selvaratnam, UAE) *in rr of mid-div: r.o wl fnl 1 1/2f: nrst fin* **6/1**[2]

5 1 1/2 **Red Rock Canyon (IRE)**[15] 418 6-9-1 100...........................(t) KShea 3 94
(M F De Kock, South Africa) *settled last: nvr able to chal* **20/1**

6 1/2 **Art Of War (SAF)**[14] 441 6-9-2 101...................... ChristopheSoumillon 2 94
(M F De Kock, South Africa) *sn led: hdd 4f out: ev ch 1 1/2f out: wknd* **11/1**

7 1/4 **Proponent (IRE)**[22] 334 6-8-13 98..................................(t) KierenFallon 1 91
(R Charlton) *trckd ldrs on rail: nt qckn fnl 2f* **10/1**[3]

8 3/4 **Thaky (KSA)**[98] 6-9-3 102.. JamieSpencer 8 93
(B Al Shaibani, Saudi Arabia) *broke awkwardly: settled rr: r.o wl fnl 1 1/2f: nvr able to chal* **20/1**

9 3 1/4 **Golden Arrow (IRE)**[21] 7-9-5 105....................................(bt) PJSmullen 5 88
(E Charpy, UAE) *in rr of mid-div: nvr able to chal* **14/1**

10 1 3/4 **Atila Sher Danon (GER)**[14] 441 4-8-11 98........................ ADeVries 7 78
(W Hickst, Germany) *trckd ldrs: led 3 1/2 out: rdn and grad wknd* **40/1**

11 nse **Indiana Gal (IRE)**[14] 439 5-9-0 99...................................(p) TedDurcan 14 79
(Patrick Martin, Ire) *in rr of mid-div: nvr able to chal* **12/1**

12 nse **Alcomo (BRZ)**[22] 335 7-9-3 102..(t) WBlandi 4 82
(A Cintra Pereira, Brazil) *mid-div: n.d* **33/1**

13 3/4 **Black Eagle (IRE)**[15] 417 4-9-3 104.................................. JRosales 11 82
(A bin Huzaim, UAE) *nvr able to chal* **10/1**[3]

14 4 **Tasteyville (USA)**[22] 334 7-9-0 99................................ RichardHills 13 69
(E Charpy, UAE) *trckd ldrs: wd: wknd 2f out* **33/1**

1m 58.36s (118.36) **14** Ran SP% **128.6**
CSF: £331.34, TRI: £774.92.

Owner Elsadig Elhag **Bred** WinStar Farm LLC **Trained** United Arab Emirates

FOCUS
Mainly exposed runners and this was one of the weaker handicaps run at this year's carnival.

NOTEBOOK

Roman's Run(USA) is a bleeder, so credit to connections for getting him spot on for this assignment after a two-month break. He proved suited by the trip, the furthest he has tried to date, and also acted well on the synthetic surface at the first attempt. It would be no surprise if he gets a bit of confidence from this.

Don Velez(ARG), a winner in Argentina, and more recent Saudi Arabia, was just denied on his Dubai debut.

Roman Republic(FR) had been off the track since winning a 1m2f handicap for Mark Johnston at Glorious Goodwood last July. He travelled strongly for a long way, but didn't have that much room early in the straight and failed to pick up sufficiently when in the clear. There should be plenty of improvement to come. (op 11-8)

Kal Barg, 5lb higher than when winning over C&D on his previous start, was another who didn't get much of a run in the straight and he's capable of a bit better. (op 13-2)

Red Rock Canyon(IRE) seemed to have less room than any of these when trying to stay on towards the inside in the straight and was unlucky not to finish a good deal closer. Whilst he's not one to make excuses for, this was not the first time at this carnival that he's hinted he might be able to win a similar race this. (op 18-1)

Proponent(IRE) was a bit short of room towards the inside at the top of the straight, but he didn't look unlucky.

611 LINGFIELD (L-H)

Saturday, February 20

OFFICIAL GOING: Standard

Wind: Fairly modest, behind Weather: Bright, partly cloudy, chilly

633 LINGFIELDPARK.CO.UK CLAIMING STKS — 1m (P)

1:45 (1:45) (Class 6) 3-Y-O — **£1,774** (£523; £262) **Stalls** High

Form — RPR

2-51 **1** **Kirsty's Boy (IRE)**[15] [424] 3-8-10 75 .... LiamKeniry 2 — 68+
(J S Moore) *mde all: rdn and qcknd wl over 1f out: in command fnl f: r.o wl* **5/4**[1]

1331 **2** *1 ¼* **Tuscan King**[7] [534] 3-8-6 65 .... (b) AndrewHeffernan(5) 1 — 66
(P D Evans) *trckd ldng pair: rdn and effrt wl over 1f out: kpt on u.p to chse wnr ins fnl f: nvr gng pce to chal* **5/2**[2]

6-40 **3** *nk* **Sunrise Lyric (IRE)**[24] [313] 3-8-7 68 .... (p) JoeFanning 5 — 61
(P F I Cole) *hld up wl in tch in last pair: effrt and wd bnd 2f out: kpt on ins fnl f: no threat to wnr* **4/1**[3]

3216 **4** *nse* **Ant Music (IRE)**[8] [524] 3-8-10 65 .... (b) RichardHughes 3 — 64
(J S Moore) *t.k.h: trckd wnr: rdn and nt pce of wnr wl over 1f out: styd on same pce fnl f* **7/1**

0 **5** *1* **Broughtons Swinger**[7] [533] 3-8-6 0 .... JamieMackay 4 — 58
(W J Musson) *hld up wl in tch in last pair: rdn ent fnl 2f: one pce and no prog after* **28/1**

1m 41.4s (3.20) **Going Correction** +0.125s/f (Slow) — 5 Ran SP% **109.0**

Speed ratings (Par 95): **89,87,87,87,86**

CSF £4.50 TOTE £2.20: £1.60, £1.10; EX 3.80.

Owner F J Stephens **Bred** Edmond Kent **Trained** Upper Lambourn, Berks

FOCUS

Just a run-of-the-mill claimer, but the small field looked quite closely matched.

634 PATRICIA HUSH 50TH BIRTHDAY MAIDEN STKS — 1m (P)

2:20 (2:20) (Class 5) 3-Y-O — **£2,456** (£725; £362) **Stalls** High

Form — RPR

1 **Rebel Soldier (IRE)** 3-9-3 0 .... GeorgeBaker 4 — 87+
(J Noseda) *hld up in tch in midfield: hdwy to trck ldng pair jst over 2f out: shkn up to ld over 1f out: readily c clr fnl f: easily* **5/4**[1]

06- **2** *3 ½* **Gumnd (IRE)**[241] [3270] 3-9-3 0 .... SebSanders 5 — 77
(C E Brittain) *chsd ldr: rdn ent fnl 2f: led over 1f out: hdd ent fnl f: no ch w wnr but kpt on for clr 2nd* **8/1**

4 **3** *2* **Blues Music (IRE)**[19] [374] 3-9-3 0 .... MichaelHills 1 — 72+
(B W Hills) *s.i.s: sn chsng ldrs: rdn ent fnl 2f: outpcd and swtchd rt over 1f out: styd on ins fnl f: no threat to ldng pair* **11/4**[2]

3 **4** *hd* **Understory (USA)**[35] [201] 3-9-3 0 .... JoeFanning 2 — 72
(M Johnston) *chsd ldrs: rdn and unable qck jst over 2f out: one pce and wl hld fnl f* **14/1**

40-2 **5** *¾* **Banks And Braes**[42] [106] 3-9-3 73 .... RichardHughes 3 — 70
(R Hannon) *led: rdn ent fnl 2f: hdd over 1f out: wknd fnl f* **7/2**[3]

0 **6** *½* **Mack's Sister**[17] [385] 3-8-12 0 .... JimmyQuinn 6 — 64
(D K Ivory) *t.k.h: hld up in tch towards rr: rdn and outpcd jst over 2f out: n.d after: kpt on ins fnl f* **66/1**

0-0 **7** *11* **Whitley Bay (USA)**[7] [533] 3-9-0 0 .... MarcHalford(3) 7 — 44
(J R Best) *a bhd and sn rdn along: lost tch over 2f out* **100/1**

1m 37.09s (-1.11) **Going Correction** +0.125s/f (Slow) — 7 Ran SP% **113.6**

Speed ratings (Par 97): **110,106,104,104,103 103,92**

Tote Swingers: 1&2 £14.70, 1&3 £18.20, 2&3 £13.70 CSF £12.45 TOTE £2.30: £1.60, £4.10; EX 17.40.

Owner The Honorable Earle I Mack **Bred** En Garde Syndicate **Trained** Newmarket, Suffolk

FOCUS

An interesting maiden for the time of year, and the winner looks to have a bright future.

635 GOLF AND RACING H'CAP — 1m (P)

2:50 (2:50) (Class 2) (0-100,100) 4-Y-O+ **£10,361** (£3,083; £1,540; £769) **Stalls** High

Form — RPR

000- **1** **Mahadee (IRE)**[161] [5863] 5-9-4 100 .... (b) NeilCallan 3 — 109
(C E Brittain) *in tch in midfield: hdwy to chse ldrs over 2f out: wnt 2nd jst over 1f out: rdn to ld ins fnl f: kpt on u.p* **12/1**

4-02 **2** *½* **Benandonner (USA)**[28] [278] 7-8-5 90 .... BarryMcHugh(3) 2 — 98
(Mike Murphy) *led: rdn ent fnl 2f: drvn jst over 1f out: hdd and kpt on same pce ins fnl f* **8/1**

3-10 **3** *1* **Audemar (IRE)**[6] [553] 4-8-3 88 .... MartinLane(3) 4 — 94
(E F Vaughan) *t.k.h: chsd ldrs: rdn to chse ldr 2f out tl jst over 1f out: styd on same pce u.p fnl f* **11/2**[3]

6345 **4** *1* **Carcinetto (IRE)**[6] [553] 8-8-10 92 .... PaulDoe 10 — 96
(P D Evans) *stdd after s: hld up towards rr: gd hdwy towards inner wl over 1f out: chsd ldrs and drvn ent fnl f: no imp ins fnl f* **20/1**

006- **5** *½* **Orchard Supreme**[78] [7626] 7-8-5 87 .... FrankieMcDonald 8 — 90
(R Hannon) *towards rr: rdn and gd hdwy over 2f out: styd on same pce ins fnl f* **33/1**

12-5 **6** *shd* **Mr Willis**[21] [358] 4-8-9 91 .... SteveDrowne 6 — 93
(J R Best) *hld up in tch: effrt and swtchd rt bnd 2f out: styd on u.p but nvr gng pce to threaten ldrs* **9/2**[2]

1132 **7** *1 ¼* **Autumn Blades (IRE)**[7] [537] 5-9-0 96 .... FrannyNorton 9 — 100+
(A Bailey) *towards rr: effrt on outer whn hmpd and pushed v wd bnd 2f out: n.d after: r.o ins fnl f* **11/2**[3]

-614 **8** *shd* **Vainglory (USA)**[7] [536] 6-8-6 88 .... MartinDwyer 11 — 90+
(D M Simcock) *hld up in tch in midfield: rdn whn hmpd and pushed rt bnd 2f out: n.d after: r.o ins fnl f* **7/2**[1]

-303 **9** *nk* **Orpsie Boy (IRE)**[8] [528] 7-8-5 87 .... HayleyTurner 12 — 86
(N P Littmoden) *stdd and dropped in bhd after s: rdn and hdwy over 1f out: swtchd lft jst ins fnl f: kpt on but rtrbld ldrs* **16/1**

/50- **10** *3 ¾* **Cry Of Freedom (USA)**[311] [1291] 4-8-5 87 .... JoeFanning 5 — 78
(M Johnston) *chsd ldr tl 2f out: wknd u.p over 1f out: eased whn no ch wl ins fnl f* **16/1**

2324 **11** *1 ¼* **Indian Skipper (IRE)**[10] [492] 5-8-4 86 oh1 .... (p) JimmyQuinn 1 — 75
(R C Guest) *t.k.h: hld up towards inner: gd hdwy on inner 2f out: wknd ent fnl f* **33/1**

015- **12** *1 ½* **The Kyllachy Kid**[85] [7558] 4-8-5 87 .... ChrisCatlin 7 — 71
(S Gollings) *chsd ldrs: rdn whn rdn and hung rt bnd 2f out: no ch after* **16/1**

1m 36.24s (-1.96) **Going Correction** +0.125s/f (Slow) course record **12** Ran SP% **118.3**

Speed ratings (Par 109): **114,113,112,111,111 110,109,109,109,105 104,102**

Tote Swingers: 1&2 £14.70, 1&3 £18.20, 2&3 £13.70 CSF £102.30 CT £448.83 TOTE £16.50: £4.50, £2.60, £2.20; EX 135.80 Trifecta £274.60 Part won. Pool: £371.18 - 0.10 winning units..

Owner Saeed Manana **Bred** Darley **Trained** Newmarket, Suffolk

FOCUS

A decent prize and much the largest turnout on the card. On paper, it looked a very competitive handicap.

NOTEBOOK

Mahadee(IRE) failed to show much on turf last season, but had previously proved useful on this surface and returned to form with a game effort. Never far off the pace, he came with a determined run in the home straight and was driven out to lead in the closing stages. Whether he will be able to overcome a rise in the ratings remains to be seen, though, as his winning mark here of 100 represents a career-high. (tchd 14-1)

Benandonner(USA), beaten just a short head by Autumn Blades here in January and markedly better off at the weights, seemed to have a leading chance and is probably the soundest guide to the form. He led or disputed the lead from the outset and fought on bravely after being headed by the winner.

Audemar(IRE) ◆, three times a winner at Kempton, was taking a drop in grade after contesting at Listed event on his latest outing. He was another who was in the front rank throughout and this game display suggests he can collect again in the not-too-distant future. (op 7-1)

Carcinetto(IRE) is not particularly well handicapped, but she usually gives a decent account of herself, despite not having won for a while. (op 16-1)

Orchard Supreme has not been very consistent lately, but the peaks of his form gave him a solid chance and this was among his better efforts, as he made ground in the home straight and was not beaten far. (op 40-1)

Mr Willis, four times successful in 2009, was having his second run after a midwinter break. He had been below par on his comeback, but perhaps needed that race, as this was reasonably encouraging. He might well notch another victory soon. (op 4-1)

Autumn Blades(IRE) has been in good form this winter but his chance here was compromised when he was carried very wide by The Kyllachy Kid on the home turn. (tchd 5-1)

Vainglory(USA) travelled strongly but was hampered at a crucial stage of the race. Official explanation: jockey said horse suffered interference in running (op 4-1 tchd 10-3)

636 BREATHE SPA AT MARRIOTT LINGFIELD H'CAP — 1m 4f (P)

3:20 (3:20) (Class 4) (0-85,81) 4-Y-O+ — **£4,209** (£1,252; £625; £312) **Stalls** Low

Form — RPR

21 **1** **Spruce (USA)**[11] [476] 4-8-4 67 oh1 .... JimmyQuinn 6 — 77+
(Miss J Feilden) *chsd ldr tl 7f out: rdn to chse ldr again and swtchd rt wl over 1f out: drvn ins fnl f: led fnl 75yds: r.o wl* **2/1**[1]

/116 **2** *¾* **Gargano (IRE)**[16] [400] 5-8-9 69 .... JoeFanning 2 — 78
(M Johnston) *led: rdn ent fnl 2f: clr w wnr ins fnl f: hdd and no ex fnl 75yds* **6/1**[3]

-233 **3** *4* **Benedict Spirit (IRE)**[7] [546] 5-8-8 73 .... AndrewHeffernan(5) 3 — 76
(P D Evans) *t.k.h early: chsd ldrs: effrt u.p to press ldrs over 2f out: outpcd by ldng pair 1f out* **6/1**[3]

050- **4** *1* **Encircled**[131] [6724] 6-9-7 81 .... RichardHughes 7 — 82
(J R Jenkins) *stdd and dropped in bhd after s: effrt and clsd ent fnl 2f: sn no prog and no ch w ldrs fr over 1f out* **11/1**

0-00 **5** *hd* **War Of The Roses (IRE)**[22] [341] 7-9-4 78 .... TomEaves 4 — 79
(R Brotherton) *stdd s: t.k.h: hld up in last pair: clsd and in tch 3f out: wknd u.p wl over 1f out* **15/2**

-212 **6** *3 ¾* **Quinsman**[7] [546] 4-9-2 79 .... LiamKeniry 5 — 74
(J S Moore) *t.k.h: chsd ldrs tl wnt 2nd 7f out tl wl over 1f out: sn wknd* **5/2**[2]

2m 33.17s (0.17) **Going Correction** +0.125s/f (Slow)

WFA 4 from 5yo+ 3lb — 6 Ran SP% **110.6**

Speed ratings (Par 105): **104,103,100,100,100 97**

Tote Swingers: 1&2 £1.40, 1&3 £3.20, 2&3 £4.40 CSF £13.85 TOTE £2.90: £1.70, £2.90; EX 11.10.

Owner Good Company Partnership **Bred** Juddmonte Farms Inc **Trained** Exning, Suffolk

FOCUS

An ordinary handicap, with the top weight rated 81, but none could be completely dismissed.

637 MARRIOTT HOTEL OPENING SPRING 2010 H'CAP — 1m 2f (P)

3:55 (3:55) (Class 4) (0-85,85) 4-Y-O+ — **£4,209** (£1,252; £625; £312) **Stalls** Low

Form — RPR

06-2 **1** **December Draw (IRE)**[31] [239] 4-9-1 82 .... ShaneKelly 1 — 90+
(W J Knight) *chsd ldr: rdn and edging lft over 1f out: rdn to ld ins fnl f: r.o wl* **2/1**[1]

4-51 **2** *¾* **Officer In Command (USA)**[10] [485] 4-8-11 78 .... (p) LiamKeniry 2 — 85
(J S Moore) *led at stdy gallop: rdn and qcknd wl over 1f out: hdd and no ex ins fnl f* **4/1**[3]

62-0 **3** *3 ¾* **Basra (IRE)**[31] [239] 7-8-13 79 .... IanMongan 5 — 79
(Miss Jo Crowley) *stdd and stmbld s: t.k.h: hld up in last pair: rdn and swtchd rt over 1f out: kpt on to chse ldng pair ins fnl f: no threat to ldng pair* **11/1**

0-21 **4** *1 ¾* **Cupid's Glory**[17] [383] 8-8-10 76 .... RichardHughes 3 — 73
(G L Moore) *t.k.h: chsd ldng pair tl 6f out: rdn and nt pce of ldrs wl over 1f out: no ch w ldrs fnl f* **6/1**

030- **5** *2* **Ramona Chase**[124] [5915] 5-9-1 81 .... (t) AdamKirby 6 — 74
(M J Attwater) *stdd s: t.k.h: hld up in last pair: short-lived effrt and clsd 2f out: sn no prog and wl btn fnl f* **16/1**

3/60 **6** *nk* **Hazzard County (USA)**[21] [360] 6-9-2 85 .... MartinLane(3) 4 — 78
(D M Simcock) *t.k.h: chsd ldrs: rdn and edgd lft wl over 1f out: sn wknd* **5/2**[2]

2m 8.07s (1.47) **Going Correction** +0.125s/f (Slow)

WFA 4 from 5yo+ 1lb — 6 Ran SP% **110.4**

Speed ratings (Par 105): **99,98,95,94,92 92**

Tote Swingers: 1&2 £1.90, 1&3 £3.40, 2&3 £6.40 CSF £9.96 TOTE £3.00: £1.80, £1.70; EX 10.40.

Owner Brook House **Bred** Wardstown Stud Ltd **Trained** Patching, W Sussex

The Form Book, Raceform Ltd, Compton, RG20 6NL

FOCUS
Some solid handicappers lined up, even if one or two had a bit to prove, and the result was predictable enough.

638 MARRIOTT PLAY AND STAY MAIDEN STKS 6f (P)
4:30 (4:30) (Class 5) 3-Y-O+ £2,456 (£725; £362) Stalls Low

Form RPR
6-44 1 **Mint Whip (IRE)**24 310 3-8-6 62 FrannyNorton 6 59
(R Hannon) *hld up in tch: effrt and edging lft over 1f out: r.o u.p to ld fnl 100yds: jst hld on* 9/1
2 2 *nse* **Pippbrook Ministar**17 392 3-8-6 0 HayleyTurner 7 59
(J R Boyle) *bhd: niggled along over 4f out: plld out over 1f out: str run u.p fnl f: ev ch fnl 75yds: jst failed* 7/4[1]
556- 3 1 ½ **England (IRE)**238 3403 3-8-11 63 NeilCallan 2 59
(N P Littmoden) *t.k.h: chsd ldrs: rdn wl over 1f out: led jst ins fnl f: hdd and nt pce of ldng pair fnl 100yds* 7/1
0-3 4 *nk* **Penrod Ballantyne (IRE)**19 374 3-8-11 0 MartinDwyer 8 58
(B J Meehan) *hld up in tch: effrt towards inner over 1f out: drvn to press ldr ins fnl f: nt pce of ldng pair fnl 100yds* 10/3[3]
00-3 5 ¾ **Trading Nation (USA)**14 443 4-9-12 65 SaleemGolam 4 60
(P W Hiatt) *taken down early: short of room sn after s: in tch: edging out rt over 1f out: styd on same pce fnl f* 16/1
-060 6 2 **Tightrope (IRE)**9 495 4-9-7 44 (b) AmyBaker(5) 1 54?
(T D McCarthy) *led: rdn wl over 1f out: hdd jst ins fnl f: wknd fnl 150yds* 66/1
0-60 7 2 **Divine White**23 319 7-9-7 42 (p) AdamKirby 3 43
(G P Enright) *sn pushed up to chse ldr: wknd u.p jst over 1f out* 66/1
225 8 2 **Takajan (IRE)**17 385 3-8-11 73 RichardHughes 5 44+
(S Kirk) *t.k.h: chsd ldrs: rdn and unable qck whn short of room and squeezed out over 1f out: no ch after* 5/2[2]

1m 12.08s (0.18) **Going Correction** +0.125s/f (Slow)
WFA 3 from 4yo+ 15lb 8 Ran SP% **119.4**
Speed ratings (Par 103): **103,102,100,100,99 96,94,91**
Tote Swingers: 1&2 £5.10, 1&3 £6.40, 2&3 £4.10 CSF £26.41 TOTE £11.80: £3.10, £1.02, £2.50; EX 31.40 Trifecta £231.10 Pool: £696.51 - 2.23 winning units..
Owner Ballylinch Stud **Bred** Ballylinch Stud **Trained** East Everleigh, Wilts
■ Stewards' Enquiry : Saleem Golam one-day ban: careless riding (Mar 8)

FOCUS
An ordinary sprint maiden, seemingly lacking strength in depth, and a few were hard to fancy.

639 VIEW OUR 2010 FIXTURES AT LINGFIELDPARK.CO.UK H'CAP 5f (P)
5:05 (5:05) (Class 2) (0-100,91) 4-Y-O+ £10,361 (£3,083; £1,540; £769) Stalls Low

Form RPR
100- 1 **Le Toreador**126 6843 5-9-4 **91** (tp) NeilCallan 3 101
(K A Ryan) *mde all: jnd 3f out: rdn wl over 1f out: forged ahd ent fnl f: r.o wl* 11/8[1]
26-2 2 1 ¾ **Ivory Silk**34 212 5-9-0 **87** (b) LukeMorris 2 91
(J R Gask) *chsd ldng pair: rdn and effrt 2f out: chsd wnr ins fnl f: no imp after* 7/4[2]
0-06 3 2 **Hoh Hoh Hoh**14 446 8-9-1 **88** RichardHughes 4 85
(R J Price) *chsd wnr: jnd wnr 3f out: rdn wl over 2f out: struggling ent fnl f: btn and lost 2nd ins fnl f* 4/1[3]
0253 4 1 ¾ **Pawan (IRE)**10 492 10-8-7 **85** ow5 (b) AnnStokell(5) 1 75
(Miss A Stokell) *s.i.s: a last and sn bustled along: rdn over 2f out: nvr gng pce to trble ldrs* 8/1

58.25 secs (-0.55) **Going Correction** +0.125s/f (Slow) 4 Ran SP% **109.6**
Speed ratings (Par 109): **109,106,103,100**
CSF £4.15 TOTE £2.50; EX 4.30 Place 6 £30.36, Place 5 £25.28.
Owner Guy Reed **Bred** G Reed **Trained** Hambleton, N Yorks

FOCUS
Just four runners, and not strong for a Class 2 event, but the winner scored decisively.

NOTEBOOK
Le Toreador, seven times a winner and proven on this surface, was just 1lb higher than for his latest success at Wolverhampton in October, so his chance was obvious. He made virtually all the running, being headed briefly going into the home turn, and, after quickening into the straight, he never looked likely to be caught. He will go up the ratings for this victory, but may overcome a small rise. (op 11-10 tchd 6-4)
Ivory Silk had been raised 1lb for finishing second at Wolverhampton on her most recent outing, making her 7lb higher than for her latest victory, and she was unable to make the required leap. She battled on bravely close home, though, and is at the top of her game. (op 5-2)
Hoh Hoh Hoh was better off at the weights after finishing behind Ivory Silk in January, but his record on all-weather tracks does not make pretty reading and he seemed up against it in his bid to reverse the form. So it proved and he may have to wait for the turf season to regain the winning thread. (op 9-2 tchd 7-2)
Pawan(IRE) is consistent on Southwell's Fibresand surface, but his Polytrack record is less convincing and he carried 5lb overweight. Given those circumstances, he was not disgraced, even though he was always last. (tchd 7-1 and 9-1)
T/Plt: £74.10 to a £1 stake. Pool: £67,578.02. 665.20 winning tickets. T/Qpdt: £31.00 to a £1 stake. Pool: £4,403.54. 104.96 winning tickets. SP

557 CAGNES-SUR-MER
Saturday, February 20

OFFICIAL GOING: Standard

640a PRIX DES REMPARTS (ALL-WEATHER) 7f 110y
1:35 (1:34) 4-Y-O+ £11,062 (£4,425; £3,319; £2,212; £1,106)

RPR
1 **Source Bleue (FR)**482 4-8-8 TonyPiccone 3 85
(J C Napoli, France)
2 ¾ **Crindegun (FR)**163 4-8-7 JulienMarquestau(8) 1 91
(P Khozian, France)
3 1 **Garnica (FR)**7 549 7-8-11 (p) Francois-XavierBertras 6 84
(D Nicholls) *racd in 4th on outside: rdn and ev ch 1 1/2f out: one pce fnl f* 14/5[1]
4 *nse* **Tigron (USA)**14 458 9-8-11 (b) GaetanMasure 5 84
(Mme C Barande-Barbe, France)
5 *nk* **Royal Pennekamp (FR)**14 458 7-8-11 SebastienMaillot 4 83
(B Dutruel, France)
6 ¾ **Psy Chic (FR)**14 458 6-9-3 DominiqueBoeuf 2 87
(Robert Collet, France)
7 1 **Satchmo Bay (FR)**14 458 9-8-11 AlexisBadel 7 79
(C Boutin, France)

1m 36.23s (96.23) 7 Ran SP% **26.3**
PARI-MUTUEL (including 1 Euro stake): WIN 19.10; PL 3.10, 1.50, 1.60; SF 29.50.
Owner Georges Hermans **Bred** P Jeanneret **Trained** France

597 SOUTHWELL (L-H)
Sunday, February 21

645 Meeting Abandoned - Snow

651 - 654a (Foreign Racing) - See Raceform Interactive

633 LINGFIELD (L-H)
Monday, February 22

OFFICIAL GOING: Standard
Wind: fresh, against Weather: dull, but dry now

655 LINGFIELDPARK.CO.UK MAIDEN STKS 1m (P)
2:25 (2:26) (Class 5) 3-Y-O+ £2,590 (£770; £385; £192) Stalls High

Form RPR
232- 1 **Call To Arms (IRE)**160 5958 3-8-9 78 AdrianNicholls 8 82+
(M Johnston) *t.k.h: mde all: set stdy gallop tl pushed clr wl over 1f out: wl clr fnl f: v easily* 5/6[1]
3 2 4 ½ **Lingfield Bound (IRE)**9 533 3-8-6 0 MarcHalford(3) 7 68
(J R Best) *sn chsng wnr: rdn and nt pce of wnr wl over 1f out: wl hld after but kpt on for clr 2nd* 7/4[2]
5 3 4 **Sheila's Bond**9 533 3-8-4 0 LukeMorris 6 53
(J S Moore) *chsd ldrs: rdn to chse ldng pair over 2f out: wl outpcd by ldrs 2f out: n.d after* 7/1[3]
6- 4 3 ¾ **Court Drinking (USA)**81 7618 3-8-10 0 ow1 TonyCulhane 3 50
(J R Best) *dwlt: sn chsng ldrs: rdn and struggling over 2f out: no ch fnl 2f* 14/1
00- 5 3 ¼ **Eclipsed (USA)**133 6737 3-8-4 0 RossAtkinson(5) 1 41
(J R Best) *t.k.h: hld up wl in tch in midfield: rdn and struggling over 2f out: wl hld fnl 2f* 25/1
0P- 6 1 ¼ **Roar Talent (USA)**125 6913 3-8-9 0 JackMitchell 5 38
(J R Best) *chsd ldrs: rdn and struggling over 3f out: wl bhd fnl 2f* 33/1
00-5 7 ½ **Back On**5 581 3-8-11 52 ow2 TomEaves 4 39
(M D Squance) *hld up in tch in rr: rdn and struggling 3f out: sn wl bhd* 25/1
0 8 ¾ **Givenn**5 585 6-9-9 0 GeorgeBaker 2 30
(Ms J S Doyle) *hld up in tch in last trio: swtchd off rail and rdn over 2f out: sn wl btn* 66/1

1m 38.59s (0.39) **Going Correction** +0.225s/f (Slow)
WFA 3 from 6yo 19lb 8 Ran SP% **122.2**
Speed ratings (Par 103): **107,102,98,94,91 90,89,89**
toteswingers: 1&2 £1.10, 1&3 £3.20, 2&3 £1.50 CSF £2.65 TOTE £1.70: £1.02, £1.10, £1.90; EX 2.40.
Owner Sheikh Hamdan Bin Mohammed Al Maktoum **Bred** Darley **Trained** Middleham Moor, N Yorks

FOCUS
There was not much strength in depth in this maiden but the favourite did the job in good style and his main rival finished a long way clear of the third, so the form looks solid enough. The winner can rate a good deal higher and the next two ran similarly to when making their debuts in the same race.

656 GOLF AND RACING H'CAP 1m (P)
2:55 (2:55) (Class 6) (0-60,60) 4-Y-O+ £2,047 (£604; £302) Stalls High

Form RPR
0500 1 **Binnion Bay (IRE)**31 261 9-8-9 51 (b) RichardKingscote 4 58
(J J Bridger) *s.i.s: hld up in tch in rr: rdn and effrt over 1f out: swtchd lft and hdwy ent fnl f: r.o wl to ld towards fin* 9/1
-032 2 *hd* **Wavertree Warrior (IRE)**17 427 8-9-4 60 (b) LukeMorris 6 67
(N P Littmoden) *chsd ldrs: rdn and effrt whn n.m.r and jostled wl over 1f out: chal ent fnl f: led wl ins fnl f: sn hdd and no ex towards fin* 11/4[1]
00-0 3 *nk* **Sapphire Prince (USA)**50 23 4-9-3 59 GeorgeBaker 2 65
(J R Best) *led after 1f and set stdy gallop: rdn ent fnl 2f: kpt on wl tl hdd and no ex wl ins fnl f* 4/1[2]
0-10 4 1 ¼ **Prince Valentine**19 389 9-8-7 49 (p) AmirQuinn 9 52
(G L Moore) *chsd ldr over 6f out: jnd ldr 3f out: rdn wl over 1f out: one pce ins fnl f* 16/1
034- 5 ½ **Ermine Grey**135 6668 9-8-10 57 AmyBaker(5) 5 59+
(A W Carroll) *s.i.s: in tch towards rr: rdn and effrt v wd bnd 2f out: edgd lft and no imp over 1f out: swtchd rt jst ins fnl f: r.o but nvr able to chal* 15/2[3]
-130 6 *nk* **Musashi (IRE)**11 498 5-9-2 58 (b) IanMongan 7 61
(Mrs L J Mongan) *v.s.a: bhd: hdwy on outer over 2f out: rdn and no imp fr over 1f out* 11/4[1]
3500 7 1 ½ **Reigning Monarch (USA)**4 591 7-8-3 50 ow3 (p) RossAtkinson(5) 3 48
(Miss Z C Davison) *t.k.h: hld up wl in tch: swtchd to outer and rdn over 2f out: no prog and btn over 1f out* 16/1
3-40 8 2 **Batchworth Blaise**22 367 7-8-4 53 RichardRowe(7) 8 47
(E A Wheeler) *stdd s: t.k.h: hld up towards rr: hdwy to join ldrs 3f out: rdn and edgd lft wl over 1f out: wknd ent fnl f* 12/1
300- 9 3 ½ **Amwell House**348 802 5-8-4 46 oh1 AdrianMcCarthy 1 31
(J R Jenkins) *broke wl: led for 1f: stdd and in midfield over 4f out: lost pl and rdn over 2f out: wl bhd fnl f* 50/1

1m 40.05s (1.85) **Going Correction** +0.225s/f (Slow) 9 Ran SP% **116.5**
Speed ratings (Par 101): **99,98,98,97,96 96,94,92,89**
toteswingers: 1&2 £7.30, 1&3 £8.30, 2&3 £3.90 CSF £34.34 CT £118.25 TOTE £12.80: £2.60, £1.10, £2.10; EX 32.30.
Owner J J Bridger **Bred** Fieldspring Ltd **Trained** Liphook, Hants

FOCUS
An ordinary handicap. The pace was very steady and there was a tight finish. The form looks weak but is straightforward enough.

657 MARRIOTT HOTEL OPENING SPRING 2010 H'CAP 7f (P)
3:30 (3:30) (Class 4) (0-85,80) 4-Y-O+ £4,533 (£1,348; £674; £336) Stalls Low

Form RPR
2156 1 **Prince Of Thebes (IRE)**19 394 9-8-12 74 LukeMorris 1 81
(M J Attwater) *sn led and set stdy gallop: rdn and qcknd over 2f out: hrd drvn and hdd fnl 100yds: rallied to ld again on post* 9/2[3]
3-42 2 *nse* **Jake The Snake (IRE)**11 502 9-8-11 78 AmyBaker(5) 2 85
(A W Carroll) *stdd s: t.k.h: hld up in last: rdn whn pce qcknd over 2f out: swtchd lft and gd hdwy over 1f out: led narrowly fnl 100yds: hdd on post* 9/4[1]

5-41 3 nk **Billberry**[26] 317 5-8-7 69 (t) JackMitchell 4 75
(S C Williams) *t.k.h: hld up in 3rd: rdn over 2f out: drvn to press ldrs ins fnl f: kpt on wl* 11/4[2]
00-2 4 1 **Halsion Chancer**[9] 535 6-9-0 79 MarcHalford(3) 3 82
(J R Best) *chsd ldr: rdn over 2f out: lost 2nd ent fnl f and one pce after* 11/4[2]
-100 5 1 1/4 **Spinning Bailiwick**[5] 580 4-9-4 80 GeorgeBaker 5 80
(G L Moore) *t.k.h: hld up in tch: rdn over 2f out: one pce and no imp fr over 1f out* 8/1

1m 27.49s (2.69) **Going Correction** +0.225s/f (Slow) 5 Ran SP% **113.4**
Speed ratings (Par 105): **93,92,92,91,90**
CSF £15.43 TOTE £6.60: £3.10, £1.20; EX 18.40.
Owner Canisbay Bloodstock **Bred** Mrs A Rothschild & London Thoroughbred Services L **Trained** Epsom, Surrey

FOCUS
A fair handicap and an interesting tactical affair. The time was over four seconds above standard and the form is limited.

658 MARRIOTT PLAY AND STAY H'CAP 6f (P)
4:05 (4:05) (Class 5) (0-70,67) 4-Y-O+ **£2,590** (£770; £385; £192) **Stalls** Low

Form RPR
-140 1 **Hollow Jo**[11] 501 10-9-2 65 (v) StephenCraine 4 72
(J R Jenkins) *hld up in tch in rr: hdwy on outer 2f out: rdn and r.o wl fnl f to ld last stride* 4/1[3]
2621 2 shd **Sherjawy (IRE)**[8] 555 6-8-10 64 6ex RossAtkinson(5) 2 71
(Miss Z C Davison) *led: rdn wl over 1f out: battled on wl tl hdd last stride* 5/2[2]
445- 3 1 1/2 **Bold Ring**[115] 7158 4-8-4 60 JohnFahy(7) 5 62
(E J Creighton) *hld up in tch: rdn and effrt over 1f out: chsd ldr ins fnl f tl fnl 100yds: no ex* 14/1
12-4 4 1 1/2 **Kingsgate Castle**[11] 501 5-8-13 62 (b) LukeMorris 3 61
(Miss Gay Kelleway) *chsd ldrs: rdn to chse ldr over 1f out: sn hung lft u.p: wknd ins fnl f* 7/4[1]
600- 5 1/2 **Millfields Dreams**[186] 5182 11-9-4 67 (p) TomEaves 6 63
(M D Squance) *chsd ldr tl wl over 1f out: sn unable qck u.p: one pce and btn fnl f* 16/1
0-06 6 1 **Bobs Dreamflight**[11] 502 4-8-13 67 MarkCoumbe(5) 1 60
(D K Ivory) *broke wl: sn stdd and hld up in tch in rr: rdn and effrt wl over 1f out: no prog* 6/1

1m 12.68s (0.78) **Going Correction** +0.225s/f (Slow) 6 Ran SP% **111.8**
Speed ratings (Par 103): **103,102,100,98,98 96**
toteswingers: 1&2 £2.00, 1&3 £5.80, 2&3 £3.80 CSF £14.27 TOTE £4.30: £2.90, £1.90; EX 14.70.
Owner Mrs Wendy Jenkins **Bred** K J Reddington **Trained** Royston, Herts

FOCUS
They went a fair pace for this sprint handicap and there was a very tight finish. Sound but limited form.

659 LINGFIELD PARK FOURBALL (S) STKS 5f (P)
4:40 (4:40) (Class 6) 4-Y-O+ **£2,047** (£604; £302) **Stalls** High

Form RPR
1000 1 **Elusive Ronnie (IRE)**[3] 614 4-9-5 59 (b) JackMitchell 6 65
(R A Teal) *dwlt: sn outpcd and rdn along in rr: drvn and stl plenty to do over 1f out: str run ins fnl f to ld nr fin* 7/2[2]
5-33 2 hd **Sir Edwin Landseer (USA)**[7] 562 10-9-1 70 ow1 (be) GeorgeBaker 3 60
(G L Moore) *chsd ldrs: rdn to chal over 1f out: led and hung lft ins fnl f: clr fnl 100yds: hdd nr fin* 4/5[1]
-450 3 1 3/4 **Nawaaff**[17] 423 5-9-0 47 SebSanders 7 53
(M Quinn) *hld up in tch towards rr: rdn and hdwy towards inner wl over 1f out: chsd ldrs and drvn over 1f out: kpt on one pce ins fnl f* 14/1
4-06 4 1 1/4 **Sweet Applause (IRE)**[24] 344 4-8-10 58 ow1 (p) TonyCulhane 2 46
(G Prodromou) *chsd ldr tl wl over 1f out: keeping on same pce and btn whn sltly hmpd ins fnl f* 9/2[3]
0-50 5 3/4 **Magic Glade**[31] 271 11-9-0 43 (b) AdrianMcCarthy 4 46
(Peter Grayson) *taken down early: dwlt: sn rcvrd to chse ldrs: rdn to ld on inner wl over 1f out: drvn and hdd ins fnl f: wknd fnl 100yds* 66/1
-001 6 3 1/4 **Gleaming Spirit (IRE)**[12] 477 6-9-5 52 (v) TomEaves 1 39
(Peter Grayson) *led: rdn and hdd wl over 1f out: wknd qckly over 1f out* 8/1
00-0 7 9 **Tan Bonita (USA)**[12] 477 5-8-9 42 LukeMorris 5 —
(R J Smith) *in tch in midfield: rdn and struggling over 2f out: wl btn over 1f out: eased wl ins fnl f* 50/1

59.40 secs (0.60) **Going Correction** +0.225s/f (Slow) 7 Ran SP% **117.2**
Speed ratings (Par 101): **104,103,100,98,97 92,78**
toteswingers: 1&2 £1.80, 1&3 £7.40, 2&3 £3.80 CSF £6.95 TOTE £4.90: £2.30, £1.10; EX 7.50.There was no bid for the winner.
Owner R J Ryan **Bred** The Ginger Group **Trained** Ashtead, Surrey

FOCUS
An ordinary seller run at a decent pace. It was a race of wildly changing fortunes and in-running drama. The winner, third and fifth set the level.

660 LINGFIELD PARK GOLF CLUB H'CAP 1m 4f (P)
5:10 (5:10) (Class 5) (0-75,63) 4-Y-O+ **£2,590** (£770; £385; £192) **Stalls** Low

Form RPR
60- 1 **Bariolo (FR)**[357] 734 6-9-7 63 GeorgeBaker 6 74
(Noel T Chance) *stdd s: hld up in last pair: smooth hdwy to chse ldng pair over 2f out: rdn to ld 1f out: styd on wl to forge ahd ins fnl f* 11/4[2]
2023 2 1 3/4 **Star Choice**[8] 554 5-9-7 63 SebSanders 1 71
(J Pearce) *dwlt: sn pushed up to chse ldr: led 10f out: hrd pressed and rdn wl over 2f out: drvn and hdd over 1f out: one pce ins fnl f* 1/1[1]
46-0 3 hd **Venir Rouge**[45] 83 6-9-1 60 RobertLButler(3) 4 68
(Matthew Salaman) *chsd ldrs: rdn wl over 1f out: outpcd over 1f out: styd on to go 3rd ins fnl f: pressing for 2nd nr fin: no threat to wnr* 8/1
-555 4 3 1/4 **Choral Festival**[7] 612 4-9-3 62 RichardKingscote 3 65
(J J Bridger) *led for 2f: chsd ldr after: jnd ldr and rdn wl over 2f out: wknd u.p ent fnl f* 7/2[3]
00-0 5 2 **Amwell Brave**[9] 539 9-8-7 49 oh4 AdrianMcCarthy 2 49
(J R Jenkins) *hld up wl in tch: rdn and effrt ent fnl 2f: one pce and btn over 1f out* 16/1
50/- 6 42 **Just Beware**[10] 3437 8-8-3 50 oh4 ow1 (p) RossAtkinson(5) 5 —
(Miss Z C Davison) *dwlt: a last: rdn and no rspnse 5f out: t.o and eased fnl 2f* 25/1

2m 35.93s (2.93) **Going Correction** +0.225s/f (Slow)
WFA 4 from 5yo+ 3lb 6 Ran SP% **119.7**
Speed ratings (Par 103): **99,97,97,95,94 66**
toteswingers: 1&2 £1.80, 1&3 £4.40, 2&3 £3.10 CSF £6.43 TOTE £4.30: £2.40, £1.10; EX 8.00
Place 6 £7.55, Place 5 £7.18.
Owner Neil Campbell & Noel Chance Racing Club **Bred** Mrs Elisabeth Gane **Trained** Upper Lambourn, Berks

FOCUS
The leaders attacked from some way out in this fair handicap and it was probably an advantage to race just off the pace. The winner is rated back to his French form with the third to his recent best.
T/Plt: £15.30 to a £1 stake. Pool: £81,806.32. 3,903.15 winning tickets. T/Qpdt: £8.40 to a £1 stake. Pool: £5,592.43. 492.35 winning tickets. SP

619 WOLVERHAMPTON (A.W) (L-H)
Monday, February 22

OFFICIAL GOING: Standard
Wind: Moderate against Weather: Cloudy

661 SPONSOR A RACE AT WOLVERHAMPTON AMATEUR RIDERS' H'CAP 1m 4f 50y(P)
2:10 (2:10) (Class 6) (0-52,52) 4-Y-O+ **£1,714** (£527; £263) **Stalls** Low

Form RPR
2-42 1 **Bright Sparky (GER)**[13] 470 7-10-8 46 (vt) MissSBrotherton 11 58+
(M W Easterby) *hld up in tch: led wl over 2f out: rdn wl over 1f out: drvn out* 9/4[1]
403- 2 3/4 **Amical Risks (FR)**[118] 7085 6-10-11 49 MrSWalker 6 60+
(Joss Saville) *hld up in mid-div: rdn and hdwy over 3f out: chsd wnr 2f out: rdn over 1f out: styd on ins fnl f* 9/1
66-0 3 6 **Stravita**[38] 199 6-10-4 47 (p) MissRKneller(5) 9 49
(R Hollinshead) *hld up in mid-div: hdwy 2f out: rdn over 1f out: one pce* 12/1
-560 4 1/2 **Our Kes (IRE)**[9] 541 8-10-13 51 MrJoshuaMoore 12 52
(P Howling) *stdd s: sn swtchd lft: hld up in rr: pushed along and hdwy on outside over 2f out: rdn wl over 1f out: one pce* 9/1
30/5 5 3/4 **Go On Ahead (IRE)**[33] 228 10-10-10 48 MrsMRoberts 8 49
(M J Coombe) *t.k.h: chsd ldr to 7f out: wknd over 2f out* 14/1
0-06 6 1/2 **Inn For The Dancer**[4] 590 8-10-3 46 MrsSarah-JaneFox(5) 4 45
(J C Fox) *hld up in rr: pushed along over 2f out: rdn wl over 1f out: nvr nr ldrs* 33/1
-434 7 shd **Desert Hawk**[4] 590 9-10-3 46 oh1 MrJPFeatherstone(5) 5 48+
(P Howling) *ducked and rdr slow to remove blindfold: s.s: hld up in rr: pushed along over 3f out: rdn wl over 1f out: n.d* 5/1[2]
0-05 8 hd **Solo Choice**[18] 411 4-10-6 47 MrSDobson 1 46
(I W McInnes) *hld up in mid-div: lost pl over 4f out: bhd fnl 3f* 16/1
02-0 9 2 1/2 **Under Fire (IRE)**[26] 309 7-10-9 52 MrMWall(5) 10 47
(A W Carroll) *led: hdd over 4f out: rdn 2f out: wknd ins fnl f* 22/1
-306 10 1/2 **Barbirolli**[9] 539 8-10-4 49 MissCScott(7) 2 43
(W B Stone) *prom: wnt 2nd 7f out: led over 4f out tl wl over 2f out: wknd wl over 1f out* 10/1
/003 11 3/4 **Bansha (IRE)**[11] 503 4-10-1 47 MrCDavies(5) 7 40
(A Bailey) *hld up in tch: wknd over 3f out* 8/1[3]

2m 48.71s (7.61) **Going Correction** +0.175s/f (Slow)
WFA 4 from 6yo+ 3lb 11 Ran SP% **115.2**
Speed ratings (Par 101): **81,80,76,76,75 75,75,75,73,73 72**
toteswingers: 1&2 £4.80, 1&3 £12.80, 2&3 £15.80 CSF £22.41 CT £199.88 TOTE £3.10: £1.30, £3.00, £3.70; EX 21.30 Trifecta £154.30 Part won. Pool: £208.58 - 0.54 winning units..
Owner Rupert Armitage & Graham Sparkes **Bred** Graf Und Grafin Von Stauffenberg **Trained** Sheriff Hutton, N Yorks

FOCUS
A moderate amateur riders' handicap run at a steady pace. The first two finished clear and this is strong form for the grade which could be rated up to 5lb higher.

662 BET CHAMPIONS LEAGUE FOOTBALL - BETDAQ H'CAP 5f 20y(P)
2:40 (2:40) (Class 5) (0-75,72) 3-Y-O **£2,456** (£725; £362) **Stalls** Low

Form RPR
00-1 1 **Lewyn**[34] 222 3-9-4 72 FergusSweeney 6 85+
(K A Ryan) *chsd ldr: rdn to ld 1f out: r.o wl* 9/4[1]
-513 2 3 1/2 **Duke Of Rainford**[3] 619 3-8-4 58 oh3 (p) PaulHanagan 7 58
(M Herrington) *hld up in rr: hdwy whn swtchd rt 1f out: rdn and wnt 2nd wl ins fnl f: nt trble wnr* 7/1
40-4 3 3/4 **Micky's Knock Off (IRE)**[12] 478 3-8-10 64 FrannyNorton 3 61
(R C Guest) *chsd ldrs: pushed along over 3f out: rdn jst over 1f out: kpt on one pce ins fnl f* 7/2[2]
-431 4 1/2 **Mrs Boss**[16] 445 3-9-1 72 JamesMillman(3) 5 68
(B R Millman) *hld up: c wd st: rdn over 1f out: kpt on towards fin: tk 4th post* 13/2
64-2 5 shd **Flaxen Lake**[10] 527 3-9-2 70 GrahamGibbons 2 65
(R Hollinshead) *prom: rdn jst over 1f out: one pce* 9/2[3]
5-4 6 shd **Your Gifted (IRE)**[18] 399 3-8-1 60 JamesSullivan(5) 1 55
(Patrick Morris) *hld up: hdwy on ins wl over 1f out: rdn and one pce fnl f* 8/1
-032 7 4 **Blue Neptune**[24] 343 3-9-0 68 MartinDwyer 4 48
(W R Muir) *led: rdn and hdd 1f out: wknd ins fnl f* 16/1

62.60 secs (0.30) **Going Correction** +0.175s/f (Slow) 7 Ran SP% **114.0**
Speed ratings (Par 97): **104,98,97,96,96 96,89**
toteswingers: 1&2 £3.40, 1&3 £3.20, 2&3 £6.70 CSF £18.48 TOTE £3.40: £1.60, £3.90; EX 17.60.
Owner N Cable & M Smith **Bred** Mrs S J Walker **Trained** Hambleton, N Yorks

FOCUS
A modest handicap anmd limited but solid form behind the progressive winner, who is better than this grade.

663 HOTEL & CONFERENCING AT WOLVERHAMPTON (S) STKS 1m 141y(P)
3:10 (3:10) (Class 6) 4-Y-O+ **£1,774** (£523; £262) **Stalls** Low

Form RPR
-260 1 **Well Of Echoes**[38] 193 4-8-4 47 (tp) DeclanCannon(5) 10 66
(A J McCabe) *hld up and bhd: hdwy over 3f out: led over 2f out: rdn over 1f out: rdn out* 18/1
3-44 2 3/4 **Geezers Colours**[14] 464 5-9-0 65 AndrewElliott 6 69
(J R Weymes) *a.p: rdn and kpt on to take 2nd wl ins fnl f* 7/2[2]
1202 3 1/2 **Straight Face (IRE)**[5] 579 6-9-6 65 (b) HayleyTurner 8 74
(P D Evans) *chsd ldr: ev ch over 2f out: rdn over 1f out: nt qckn ins fnl f* 5/1
1230 4 1 3/4 **Shake On It**[11] 496 6-9-1 65 JamieJones(5) 5 70
(M R Hoad) *hld up in mid-div: smooth prog 2f out: hung lft over 1f out: one pce ins fnl f* 4/1[3]
1-45 5 nk **Sotik Star (IRE)**[11] 496 7-9-0 62 (p) PatCosgrave 7 64
(K A Morgan) *s.i.s: hld up and bhd: rdn and hdwy 1f out: kpt on towards fin* 5/2[1]

60-0 **6** 5 **Remark (IRE)**14 466 6-8-9 45 (t) JamesSullivan(5) 3 52
(M W Easterby) *hld up and bhd: rdn over 2f out: nvr nr ldrs* **40/1**

0/20 **7** ¾ **Kathleen Kennet**19 389 10-8-9 48 LiamKeniry 4 45
(M R Bosley) *led: hdd over 2f out: rdn and wknd over 1f out* **16/1**

-400 **8** 1 ¼ **Fine Ruler (IRE)**11 496 6-9-6 59 VinceSlattery 1 53
(M R Bosley) *hld up in mid-div: pushed along over 3f out: bhd fnl 2f* **16/1**

00-0 **9** ¾ **La Diosa (IRE)**28 289 4-8-9 48 ChrisCatlin 9 41
(Mrs S Lamyman) *hld up: sn in tch: pushed along and wknd 3f out* **40/1**

0R-0 **10** 92 **Willie Ever**9 543 6-9-0 61 DavidNolan 2 —
(D G Bridgwater) *v rel to r: a wl t.o* **66/1**

1m 52.7s (2.20) **Going Correction** +0.175s/f (Slow) 10 Ran SP% **110.9**
Speed ratings (Par 101): **97,96,95,94,94 89,88,87,87,5**
toteswingers: 1&2 £7.30, 1&3 £8.30, 2&3 £3.90 CSF £75.77 TOTE £16.60: £3.30, £1.70, £1.30; EX 64.20 Trifecta £293.30 Part won. Pool: £396.40 - 0.50 winning units..There was no bid for the winner.
Owner M Shirley **Bred** Plantation Stud **Trained** Averham Park, Notts

FOCUS
A moderate seller. The winner bounced back to her best.

664 DINE IN THE HORIZONS RESTAURANT MAIDEN STKS 1m 1f 103y(P)
3:45 (3:46) (Class 5) 3-Y-O+ £2,456 (£725; £362) Stalls Low

Form RPR

45- **1** **Mercoliano**100 7400 3-8-2 0 AndreaAtzeni(3) 9 76+
(M Botti) *mde all: pushed clr wl over 1f out: sn edgd lft: eased towards fin* **6/1[3]**

505 **2** 9 **Blues Forever (IRE)**13 473 3-8-6 63 ow1 PaulDoe 4 60+
(P D Evans) *hld up: pushed along over 3f out: rdn and hdwy over 1f out: edgd lft and wnt 2nd ins fnl f: no ch w wnr* **14/1**

44 **3** 2 ¾ **Frameit (IRE)**12 484 3-8-5 0 MartinDwyer 7 53
(J S Moore) *sn chsng wnr: lost 2nd 4f out: rdn over 2f out: sn btn* **12/1**

40- **4** nk **Heading To First**229 3750 3-8-5 0 ChrisCatlin 1 52
(C E Brittain) *prom: rdn and btn over 2f out* **1/1[1]**

3 **5** 1 ¼ **Ancient Times (USA)**20 381 3-8-5 0 JoeFanning 8 50
(M Johnston) *hld up in tch: wnt 2nd 4f out: pushed along and ev ch over 2f out: btn wl over 1f out* **3/1[2]**

- **6** 25 **Sir Mark (IRE)**87 6-9-12 0 (t) RobertHavlin 2 7
(M A Peill) *hld up: pushed along over 3f out: sn struggling* **100/1**

0-0 **7** 20 **Minimusic**21 374 3-8-0 0 DavidProbert 5 —
(B Palling) *bhd fnl 4f: t.o* **100/1**

2m 2.20s (0.50) **Going Correction** +0.175s/f (Slow)
WFA 3 from 4yo+ 21lb 7 Ran SP% **105.6**
Speed ratings (Par 103): **104,96,93,93,92 69,52**
toteswingers: 1&2 £7.20, 1&3 £4.60, 2&3 £7.30 CSF £65.61 TOTE £5.20: £2.10, £4.00; EX 47.80 Trifecta £327.30 Part won. Pool: £442.36 - 0.30 winning units..
Owner Giuliano Manfredini **Bred** Mystic Meg Limited **Trained** Newmarket, Suffolk
■ Danderek was withdrawn after his stall was damaged (8/1, deduct 10p in the £ under R4).

FOCUS
With the front two in the betting running below expectations, this was an ordinary maiden, but still, there was a potentially very useful winner. The runner-up produced a personal best too.

665 BETDAQ THE BETTING EXCHANGE H'CAP (DIV I) 1m 1f 103y(P)
4:20 (4:20) (Class 6) (0-65,65) 4-Y-O+ £1,433 (£423; £211) Stalls Low

Form RPR

6/2- **1** **Matjar (IRE)**66 7798 7-9-0 61 LiamKeniry 7 72+
(Joseph Quinn, Ire) *hld up in mid-div: hdwy wl over 1f out: led ins fnl f: r.o* **9/4[1]**

2-04 **2** ½ **King's Icon (IRE)**17 427 5-8-11 58 (p) NickyMackay 4 68
(M Wigham) *hld up in tch: rdn to chal ins fnl f: nt qckn* **5/1[2]**

-363 **3** 1 ¼ **Mutajaaser (USA)**14 467 5-9-1 62 (p) PatCosgrave 3 69
(K A Morgan) *chsd ldr: led 2f out: rdn over 1f out: hdd ins fnl f: no ex* **11/2[3]**

-216 **4** 1 **Barodine**9 540 7-8-7 54 JoeFanning 5 59
(R J Hodges) *hld up towards rr: hdwy whn swtchd rt 1f out: kpt on ins fnl f* **7/1**

6305 **5** nse **Josiah Bartlett (IRE)**10 530 4-8-1 51 oh5 AndreaAtzeni(3) 9 56
(Ian Williams) *hld up towards rr: c wd st: rdn and hdwy over 1f out: one pce ins fnl f* **25/1**

000- **6** nk **Singbella**253 2947 4-9-4 65 AdamKirby 10 69
(C G Cox) *hld up in mid-div: hdwy over 2f out: rdn and edgd lft 1f out: one pce ins fnl f* **8/1**

-601 **7** 1 **Flighty Fellow (IRE)**9 541 10-8-9 56 (v) HayleyTurner 8 58
(B G Powell) *stdd s: hld up in rr: rdn wl over 1f out: styng on whn nt clr run wl ins fnl f* **12/1**

60-0 **8** 1 ½ **Mighty Mover (IRE)**49 34 8-8-5 52 DavidProbert 6 51
(B Palling) *prom: ev ch over 2f out: rdn wl over 1f out: nt qckn whn carried lft ins fnl f* **14/1**

4-16 **9** ¾ **King's Jester (IRE)**24 353 8-8-2 54 (b) JamesSullivan(5) 1 51
(Lee Smyth, Ire) *hld up in mid-div: pushed along over 2f out: rdn and wkng whn sltly hmpd ins fnl f* **25/1**

3353 **10** 12 **Join Up**24 353 4-8-6 53 MartinDwyer 2 25
(W M Brisbourne) *led: hdd 2f out: wknd over 1f out: eased ins fnl f* **10/1**

2m 3.07s (1.37) **Going Correction** +0.175s/f (Slow) 10 Ran SP% **117.6**
Speed ratings (Par 101): **100,99,98,97,97 97,96,95,94,83**
toteswingers: 1&2 £4.80, 1&3 £3.80, 2&3 £9.20 CSF £13.23 CT £53.89 TOTE £3.30: £1.20, £1.50, £2.40; EX 26.00 Trifecta £88.00 Pool: £695.03 - 5.84 winning units..
Owner Ms Aine Brodbin **Bred** Shadwell Estate Ltd **Trained** Sixmilebridge, Co. Clare

FOCUS
A moderate handicap run in a time almost identical to the second division. The winner can rate higher.
Singbella Official explanation: jockey said filly hung left closing stages
Join Up Official explanation: jockey said gelding ran too free

666 BETDAQ THE BETTING EXCHANGE H'CAP (DIV II) 1m 1f 103y(P)
4:55 (4:55) (Class 6) (0-65,64) 4-Y-O+ £1,433 (£317; £317) Stalls Low

Form RPR

1-52 **1** **Granny McPhee**5 588 4-9-2 62 RobertWinston 6 72+
(A Bailey) *hld up towards rr: stdy prog over 5f out: led wl over 1f out: pushed out* **1/1[1]**

66-1 **2** 1 ¼ **The City Kid (IRE)**28 290 7-8-8 54 SaleemGolam 2 58
(G D Blake) *hld up in mid-div: hdwy over 2f out: chsd wnr over 1f out: rdn and kpt on same pce ins fnl f* **7/1[2]**

5-00 **2** dht **Corrib (IRE)**12 479 7-8-4 50 oh5 (p) DavidProbert 10 54
(B Palling) *hld up in mid-div: c wd st: rdn and hdwy wl over 1f out: kpt on ins fnl f* **25/1**

1-06 **4** 1 ¾ **Coolnaharan (IRE)**14 469 10-8-6 57 (p) JamesSullivan(5) 9 57
(Lee Smyth, Ire) *hld up in rr: c wd st: rdn over 1f out: styd on ins fnl f: nvr nrr* **16/1**

2-40 **5** ¾ **Blackstone Vegas**18 409 4-8-4 53 (v[1]) MartinLane(3) 4 52
(D Shaw) *prom: rdn and squeezed through over 2f out: one pce whn edgd lft ins fnl f* **16/1**

2213 **6** 1 ¾ **Kirstys Lad**18 407 8-8-5 51 GregFairley 5 47
(M Mullineaux) *led: hdd 7f out: w ldr: led jst over 3f out: rdn and hdd wl over 1f out: wknd ins fnl f* **7/1[2]**

00- **7** shd **Forced Opinion (USA)**122 6998 5-8-3 52 AndreaAtzeni(3) 8 47
(K A Morgan) *s.i.s: hld up in rr: pushed along over 2f out: short-lived effrt wl over 1f out* **40/1**

20-0 **8** 1 ¾ **New Beginning (IRE)**28 294 6-9-4 64 AndrewMullen 7 58
(Mrs S Lamyman) *prom: rdn whn hmpd and lost pl over 2f out* **15/2[3]**

2/0- **9** 2 **The Last Bottle (IRE)**79 7648 5-8-2 55 SeanPalmer(7) 1 43
(W M Brisbourne) *w ldr: led 7f out tl jst over 3f out: rdn and wknd over 1f out* **22/1**

-546 **10** 4 **Via Mia**14 464 4-9-0 60 (p) ChrisCatlin 3 41
(George Baker) *hld up in rr: pushed along over 3f out: sn struggling* **12/1**

2m 3.11s (1.41) **Going Correction** +0.175s/f (Slow) 10 Ran SP% **116.9**
TOTE £2.00: £1.10 TRIFECTA DHT: 2-6-10 £29.30 Pool: £496.5427 Owner.
■ Stewards' Enquiry : Martin Lane three-day ban: careless riding (Mar 8-10)

FOCUS
The time was virtually identical to the first division. This was a pretty weak handicap but the form is sound enough.

667 FREE HORSE RACING TIPS @ BIGTIPS.CO.UK MAIDEN STKS 7f 32y(P)
5:25 (5:26) (Class 5) 3-Y-O+ £2,456 (£725; £362) Stalls High

Form RPR

0- **1** **Midfielder (USA)**131 6772 3-8-9 0 RobertHavlin 6 75+
(J H M Gosden) *hld up in mid-div: smooth prog wl over 1f out: rdn to ld ins fnl f: r.o wl* **2/1[1]**

2 1 ¾ **West Emirates (USA)** 4-9-12 0 AdamKirby 4 74+
(C G Cox) *led: rdn over 1f out: hdd ins fnl f: nt qckn* **3/1[3]**

3 ¾ **Jawal** 3-8-9 0 ChrisCatlin 3 66+
(C E Brittain) *s.i.s: hld up in rr: pushed along and hdwy 2f out: c wd st: rdn and no ex ins fnl f* **5/2[2]**

450- **4** 3 ½ **Hill Of Miller (IRE)**54 7871 3-8-9 70 (t) MartinDwyer 7 57
(Rae Guest) *hld up and bhd: hdwy wl over 1f out: rdn and wknd ins fnl f* **4/1**

000/ **5** 5 **A Nod And A Wink (IRE)**881 5708 6-9-7 43 LiamKeniry 8 44
(S Lycett) *hld up in tch: jnd ldr 5f out: ev ch 2f out: sn rdn: wknd over 1f out* **33/1**

6 **6** 4 **Boxer Shorts**49 31 4-9-12 0 GregFairley 5 38
(M Mullineaux) *chsd ldr 2f: prom tl rdn and wknd wl over 1f out* **80/1**

00- **7** 3 **Billy Simmonds**158 6022 5-9-5 0 AdamBeschizza(7) 1 30
(Miss J Feilden) *prom: rdn wl over 1f out: wknd fnl f* **100/1**

0- **8** 12 **Dunfishin (IRE)**56 7859 3-8-9 0 VinceSlattery 9 —
(M S Tuck) *s.i.s: a bhd: lost tch fnl 2f* **100/1**

1m 30.65s (1.05) **Going Correction** +0.175s/f (Slow)
WFA 3 from 4yo+ 17lb 8 Ran SP% **113.1**
Speed ratings (Par 103): **101,99,98,94,88 83,80,66**
toteswingers: 1&2 £3.20, 1&3 £2.40, 2&3 £2.70 CSF £8.15 TOTE £3.10: £1.10, £1.30, £1.30; EX 9.20 Trifecta £12.20 Pool: £716.12 - 43.38 winning units..
Owner H R H Princess Haya Of Jordan **Bred** Rock River Enterprises Limited **Trained** Newmarket, Suffolk

FOCUS
Not much strength in depth, and the time was 1.21 seconds slower than the following Class 5 handicap, but the front three looked quite promising. The fifth limits the form.

668 BET IN RUNNING - BETDAQ H'CAP 7f 32y(P)
5:55 (5:55) (Class 5) (0-70,70) 4-Y-O+ £2,456 (£725; £362) Stalls High

Form RPR

153- **1** **Global Village (IRE)**197 4824 5-8-13 65 SaleemGolam 11 75
(G C Bravery) *hld up towards rr: hdwy over 3f out: rdn to ld wl ins fnl f: jst hld on* **9/1**

60/0 **2** hd **Harare**7 565 9-8-4 59 (v) AndreaAtzeni(3) 8 68
(R J Price) *s.i.s: hld up in rr: c v wd st: hdwy fnl f: rdn and r.o towards fin: jst failed* **25/1**

114 **3** 1 ¼ **Headache**16 442 5-9-0 66 (bt) RobertWinston 10 72
(B W Duke) *sn chsng ldr: led 2f out: rdn over 1f out: hdd wl ins fnl f: no ex* **9/2[2]**

3-40 **4** 2 **Kersivay**21 373 4-9-3 69 PaulDoe 1 69
(P D Evans) *hld up in tch on ins: pushed along over 2f out: rdn over 1f out: one pce ins fnl f* **6/1[3]**

505- **5** 2 **Border Owl (IRE)**73 7711 5-8-9 61 GregFairley 7 56
(P Salmon) *sn led: hdd 2f out: rdn over 1f out: wknd wl ins fnl f* **9/1**

054- **6** ¾ **Hyde Lea Flyer**77 7672 5-8-13 65 GrahamGibbons 4 58
(E S McMahon) *t.k.h: prom: rdn wl over 1f out: wknd ins fnl f* **8/1**

663 **7** 2 ½ **Gracie's Gift (IRE)**31 270 8-8-5 57 FrannyNorton 3 45
(R C Guest) *hld up in mid-div: lost pl 5f out: rdn and sme hdwy over 1f out: eased whn btn towards fin* **20/1**

131- **8** 1 ¾ **Orangeleg**54 7877 4-8-5 60 WilliamCarson(3) 5 41
(S C Williams) *hld up towards rr: hdwy over 3f out: rdn over 2f out: wknd wl over 1f out* **7/4[1]**

0-06 **9** 3 ¾ **El Potro**31 264 8-8-4 56 oh11 NickyMackay 6 27
(J R Holt) *hld up in mid-div: pushed along over 3f out: bhd fnl 2f* **100/1**

30-5 **10** 4 **Blue Charm**14 465 6-9-4 70 StevieDonohoe 9 30
(I W McInnes) *dwlt: a in rr* **25/1**

05-0 **11** 3 **Shannon Golden**14 462 4-8-4 56 oh1 PaulHanagan 2 8
(S R Bowring) *led early: prom: pushed along and wknd 2f out* **40/1**

1m 29.44s (-0.16) **Going Correction** +0.175s/f (Slow) 11 Ran SP% **115.8**
Speed ratings (Par 103): **107,106,105,103,100 99,97,95,90,86 82**
toteswingers: 1&2 £28.40, 1&3 £6.50, 2&3 £15.20 CSF £213.36 CT £850.22 TOTE £15.60: £3.40, £6.30, £1.90; EX 273.00 TRIFECTA Part won. Pool: £832.21 - 0.10 winning units. Place 6 £194.00, Place 5 £93.77..
Owner Mrs Janice Jones **Bred** Kilfrush Stud **Trained** Cowlinge, Suffolk

FOCUS
A modest but competitive handicap. The form is rated around the second to fourth.
Shannon Golden Official explanation: jockey said gelding lost its action behind
T/Jkpt: £7,100.00 to a £1 stake. Pool: £10,000.00. 1.00 winning ticket. T/Plt: £121.70 to a £1 stake. Pool: £104,075.94. 624.26 winning tickets. T/Qpdt: £34.20 to a £1 stake. Pool: £8,065.89. 174.50 winning tickets. KH

655 LINGFIELD (L-H)

Tuesday, February 23

OFFICIAL GOING: Standard

Wind: fresh, across Weather: dull, light rain

669 BET IN RUNNING - BETDAQ MAIDEN STKS — 1m 4f (P)

2:10 (2:11) (Class 5) 4-Y-O+ £2,456 (£725; £362) Stalls Low

Form RPR

2 **1** **Cashpoint**[24] 355 5-9-6 0 LiamKeniry 5 69+
(A Middleton) *t.k.h early: chsd ldr for 1f: in tch in midfield: hdwy to chse ldr over 2f out: drvn to ld ent fnl f: forged ahd fnl 150yds* 2/1[1]

/0-3 **2** 1 1/2 **Sinchiroka (FR)**[18] 421 4-9-3 70 GeorgeBaker 2 65
(R J Smith) *led at stdy gallop: rdn and qcknd ent fnl 2f: hdd ent fnl f: one pce fnl 150yds* 12/1

3 **3** 1 1/4 **Gordon Road (IRE)**[6] 585 4-9-3 0 JerryO'Dwyer 4 63
(M G Quinlan) *hld up in tch in last trio: shkn up over 2f out: hdwy on inner to chse ldng pair wl over 1f out: one pce and no imp fnl f* 5/1[3]

4 4 **Yemeni Princess (IRE)**[15] 4-8-12 0 StevieDonohoe 1 52
(B G Powell) *trckd ldrs: rdn and unable qck over 2f out: outpcd by ldng trio over 1f out and wl btn after* 5/1[3]

5 1/2 **National Theatre (USA)** 4-8-12 0 KylieManser(5) 8 56?
(T Keddy) *stdd s: hld up in tch in last: effrt and hdwy on inner 2f out: no imp fr over 1f out* 20/1

6 5 **Tehente Son**[11] 5-9-6 0 JoeFanning 3 48?
(Andrew Turnell) *v.s.a and bustled along early: in tch in last trio: rdn and effrt ent fnl 2f: sn outpcd and wl btn over 1f out* 50/1

0/ **7** 12 **Lyster (IRE)**[515] 4821 11-9-6 0 PaulDoe 7 29?
(P D Evans) *chsd ldng pair: rdn and struggling 3f out: wl bhd fnl 2f: eased ins fnl f* 33/1

0- **8** 1 **Prince Pippin (IRE)**[17] 5987 4-9-3 0 (t) JimCrowley 6 27?
(S Curran) *chsd ldr after 1f tl over 2f out: sn rdn and lost pl: wl bhd over 1f out: eased ins fnl f* 11/4[2]

030 **R** **Always The Sun**[19] 410 4-8-5 46 RyanPowell(7) 10 —
(P Leech) *ref to r* 25/1

2m 37.2s (4.20) **Going Correction** +0.15s/f (Slow)
WFA 4 from 5yo+ 3lb 9 Ran SP% 114.5
Speed ratings (Par 103): **92,91,90,87,87 83,75,75,—**
toteswingers: 1&2 £7.50, 1&3 £2.80, 2&3 £4.40 CSF £25.65 TOTE £2.90: £1.10, £2.30, £1.80; EX 19.60 Trifecta £22.50 Pool: £477.09 - 15.67 winning units..
Owner Macable Partnership **Bred** Stowell Park Stud **Trained** Granborough, Bucks

FOCUS
There was plenty of jumps form on offer in this Flat maiden, which was probably a fair race of its type for the time of year. They went a very steady pace and the time was over seven seconds above standard.

670 BREATHE SPA AT MARRIOTT LINGFIELD CLAIMING STKS — 1m 2f (P)

2:40 (2:40) (Class 6) 3-Y-O £1,774 (£523; £262) Stalls Low

Form RPR

4-50 **1** **Yorksters Prince (IRE)**[18] 422 3-8-9 56 DavidProbert 3 62
(M G Quinlan) *in tch in midfield: rdn to chse ldr 2f out: hung lft wl over 1f out: drvn to ld ins fnl f: hdd fnl 50yds: r.o to ld again last strides* 10/1

3312 **2** hd **Tuscan King**[3] 633 3-8-10 65 (b) HayleyTurner 1 63
(P D Evans) *trckd ldrs: rdn and effrt over 1f out: drvn and ev ch ins fnl f: led narrowly fnl 50yds: hdd last strides* 4/6[1]

6226 **3** 1 1/4 **Magic Spirit**[18] 422 3-8-2 57 (b[1]) LukeMorris 5 53
(J S Moore) *dwlt: sn rcvrd to chse ldr: led over 2f out: rdn and hung lft over 1f out: hdd ins fnl f: wknd towards fin* 7/1[2]

4032 **4** 3 3/4 **Clayton Flick (IRE)**[10] 542 3-8-8 56 ow1 StevieDonohoe 2 51
(A B Haynes) *v.s.a: hld up in rr: sme hdwy and nudged along wl over 1f out: no ch w ldrs fnl f* 11/1

-0 **5** hd **Highland Cadett**[10] 533 3-8-13 0 JamesMillman(3) 4 59
(B R Millman) *t.k.h early: hld up in tch: effrt and rdn ent fnl 2f: outpcd over 1f out: wl hld fnl f* 33/1

4002 **6** 8 **Underworld Dandy**[10] 534 3-8-4 60 ow1 (b) WilliamCarson(3) 6 34
(R T Phillips) *led: rdn and hdd over 2f out: wknd qckly over 1f out: wl btn fnl f* 12/1

0 **7** 1 1/4 **Egorr Redfeer**[10] 533 3-8-6 0 DeclanCannon(5) 7 39+
(D R C Elsworth) *s.i.s: in tch in last pair: rdn 3f out: sn struggling: wl bhd fr over 1f out* 8/1[3]

2m 9.18s (2.58) **Going Correction** +0.15s/f (Slow) 7 Ran SP% 111.7
Speed ratings (Par 95): **95,94,93,90,90 84,83**
toteswingers: 1&2 £2.90, 1&3 £5.20, 2&3 £1.70 CSF £16.43 TOTE £11.70: £4.20, £1.10; EX 24.00.Yorksters Prince was claimed by G. Prodromou for £8000.
Owner Wexford Racing **Bred** Lady Legard & Sir Tatton Sykes **Trained** Newmarket, Suffolk
■ Stewards' Enquiry : Hayley Turner caution: used whip with excessive frequency

FOCUS
A moderate claimer run at an ordinary pace. Weak form, rated around the winner and third.
Clayton Flick(IRE) Official explanation: jockey said colt was slowly away

671 BET MULTIPLES - BETDAQ MEDIAN AUCTION MAIDEN STKS — 1m (P)

3:10 (3:13) (Class 5) 3-4-Y-O £2,456 (£725; £362) Stalls High

Form RPR

3- **1** **Pentominium**[146] 6382 3-8-8 0 JoeFanning 3 72+
(M Johnston) *led: jnd over 2f out: rdn and hdd narrowly wl over 1f out: led again ins fnl f: rdn out* 2/9[1]

0-22 **2** nk **Sunley Spinalonga**[10] 533 3-7-12 60 DeclanCannon(5) 2 65
(D R C Elsworth) *chsd wnr: jnd ldr over 2f out: rdn ent fnl 2f: led narrowly wl over 1f out: hdd ins fnl f: kpt on but hld towards fin* 4/1[2]

3 9 **In A Fortnight** 3-8-8 0 JackMitchell 1 49
(H J Collingridge) *dwlt: in tch in last: rdn 3f out: sn struggling: wl btn wl over 1f out* 25/1[3]

1m 40.9s (2.70) **Going Correction** +0.15s/f (Slow) 3 Ran SP% 105.7
Speed ratings (Par 103): **92,91,82**
CSF £1.38 TOTE £1.30; EX 1.20.
Owner Sheikh Hamdan Bin Mohammed Al Maktoum **Bred** J G And Mrs Davis **Trained** Middleham Moor, N Yorks
■ Ramble On Love (33/1) was withdrawn (ref to ent stalls).

FOCUS
Just the three runners, but they went an honest-enough pace. The form has been rated through the runner-up but is not easy to pin down.

672 BET ASIAN H'CAPS - BETDAQ HANDICAP — 1m (P)

3:40 (3:41) (Class 4) (0-85,85) 4-Y-O+ £4,209 (£1,252; £625; £312) Stalls High

Form RPR

0-60 **1** **Alfresco**[13] 487 6-8-6 73 (b) LukeMorris 3 83
(J R Best) *broke wl to chse ldrs early: stdd and grad dropped towards rr: gd hdwy towards inner to chal on bit 1f out: rdn to ld ins fnl f: rdn out* 7/1

021- **2** 1/2 **Pegasus Again (USA)**[55] 7883 5-9-4 85 JoeFanning 9 94
(R A Mills) *led and grad crossed to rail: hrd pressed and rdn wl over 1f out: kpt on wl tl hdd and no ex fnl 100yds* 9/4[1]

2-26 **3** 1 1/4 **Den's Gift (IRE)**[26] 324 6-9-3 84 (b) AdamKirby 4 90
(C G Cox) *chsd ldr for 2f: styd chsng ldrs: rdn and ev ch 2f out tl one pce ins fnl f* 13/2

-344 **4** 1/2 **Gallantry**[20] 394 8-8-9 76 PaulDoe 1 81
(P Howling) *hld up in last pair: rdn and hdwy on inner to chse ldrs over 1f out: no ex u.p fnl 150yds* 14/1

0541 **5** 1/2 **Red Somerset (USA)**[19] 405 7-9-2 83 (b) GeorgeBaker 6 87
(R J Hodges) *t.k.h: hld up in tch in midfield: rdn and effrt bnd 2f out: kpt on fnl f but nvr gng pce to trble ldrs* 11/2[3]

4-15 **6** hd **Thunderball**[13] 480 4-9-0 81 FrederikTylicki 7 84
(J A Glover) *chsd ldrs: rdn and ev ch 2f out: outpcd over 1f out: one pce and btn fnl f* 3/1[2]

5-52 **7** 1 1/4 **Trafalgar Square**[13] 487 8-8-9 76 DavidProbert 8 76
(M J Attwater) *hld up in last trio: rdn and effrt ent fnl 2f: kpt on but nvr trbld ldrs* 12/1

4465 **8** 9 **Vhujon (IRE)**[12] 502 5-8-5 79 KevinLundie(7) 5 59+
(P D Evans) *s.i.s: t.k.h: hld up towards rr: hdwy on outer 3f out: v wd and lost pl bnd 2f out: wl btn after* 25/1

3/P- **9** 11 **Fifty Cents**[417] 17 6-9-1 82 SteveDrowne 2 36
(M F Harris) *t.k.h: hdwy to chse ldr after tl wknd qckly ent fnl 2f: wl bhd and eased ins fnl f* 66/1

1m 36.88s (-1.32) **Going Correction** +0.15s/f (Slow) 9 Ran SP% 116.7
Speed ratings (Par 105): **112,111,110,109,109 109,107,98,87**
toteswingers: 1&2 £6.60, 1&3 £10.00, 2&3 £3.60 CSF £23.39 CT £110.09 TOTE £8.50: £2.40, £1.40, £1.90; EX 36.70 Trifecta £158.20 Pool: £615.88 - 2.88 winning units..
Owner Mrs A M Riney **Bred** Usk Valley Stud **Trained** Hucking, Kent

FOCUS
A fair handicap run at a reasonable pace. The second, third and fourth help set the level.

673 MARRIOTT HOTEL OPENING SPRING 2010 FILLIES' H'CAP — 7f (P)

4:10 (4:10) (Class 5) (0-70,68) 4-Y-O+ £2,456 (£725; £362) Stalls Low

Form RPR

0/64 **1** **Lady Kent (IRE)**[5] 593 4-9-4 68 PatCosgrave 8 75
(J R Boyle) *chsd ldr: rdn to ld narrowly over 1f out: drvn ent fnl f: hdd briefly ins fnl f: sn led again and outbattled runner-up* 11/8[1]

0230 **2** hd **Castleburg**[4] 615 4-8-10 60 (be[1]) FergusSweeney 5 67
(G L Moore) *t.k.h: hld up in tch towards rr: hdwy wl over 1f out: shkn up to chal and racd awkardly 1f out: rdn to ld briefly ins fnl f: sn hdd: edgd lft and nt qckn nr fin* 16/1

0/3 **3** nk **Roshina (IRE)**[20] 385 4-9-1 65 IanMongan 1 71
(Miss Jo Crowley) *dwlt: sn rcvrd to chse ldrs: ev ch u.p over 1f out: unable qck towards fin* 3/1[2]

3505 **4** 1 3/4 **Bold Rose**[4] 615 4-8-5 55 (p) LukeMorris 4 56
(M D I Usher) *s.i.s: bhd and sn pushed along: clsd on inner ent fnl 2f: drvn to chse ldrs over 1f out: no imp fnl 150yds* 20/1

3506 **5** nk **Goodbye Cash (IRE)**[5] 593 6-8-12 62 PaulDoe 2 63
(P D Evans) *led: hrd pressed and rdn 2f out: hdd over 1f out: no ex fnl 150yds* 6/1[3]

244- **6** 2 **Monashee Rock (IRE)**[74] 7716 5-9-0 64 LiamKeniry 3 60
(Matthew Salaman) *in tch in last pair: pushed along over 4f out: in tch but bhd a wall of horses over 1f out: no imp fnl f* 11/1

40-6 **7** 1 1/4 **Ivory Lace**[52] 11 9-8-13 66 WilliamCarson(3) 6 59
(S Woodman) *in tch in midfield on outer: rdn and lost pl whn wd bnd 2f out: n.d after: styd on ins fnl f* 16/1

30-2 **8** nse **Jewelled**[10] 545 4-8-13 68 KierenFox(5) 7 60
(J W Hills) *t.k.h: hld up wl in tch: trckd ldrs over 2f out: rdn and unable qck wl over 1f out: wknd fnl f* 8/1

1m 24.31s (-0.49) **Going Correction** +0.15s/f (Slow) 8 Ran SP% 117.4
Speed ratings (Par 100): **108,107,107,105,105 102,101,101**
toteswingers: 1&2 £6.50, 1&3 £2.20, 2&3 £4.60 CSF £27.54 CT £61.38 TOTE £2.20: £1.10, £3.10, £1.80; EX 32.10 Trifecta £219.60 Pool: £451.24 - 1.52 winning units..
Owner J-P Lim & Allen B Pope **Bred** Tally-Ho Stud **Trained** Epsom, Surrey

FOCUS
A modest fillies' handicap run at a strong pace. The winner was close to her Irish best but the form is limited with the field compressed.

674 LINGFIELDPARK.CO.UK H'CAP — 6f (P)

4:40 (4:42) (Class 6) (0-55,58) 4-Y-O+ £1,774 (£523; £262) Stalls Low

Form RPR

-166 **1** **Diane's Choice**[12] 499 7-8-13 53 (b) DavidProbert 1 62
(Miss Gay Kelleway) *chsd ldrs: clsd over 2f out: drvn to ld ins fnl f: styd on wl* 7/1

1002 **2** 1 **Tamino (IRE)**[22] 368 7-9-1 55 ShaneKelly 2 61
(P Howling) *chsd ldng pair: clsd over 2f out: drvn to press ldrs over 1f out: kpt on to go 2nd nr fin* 10/3[1]

500- **3** nk **Cardinal**[102] 7370 5-8-12 52 JackMitchell 8 57
(N P Moore) *off pce in midfield: hdwy towards inner 2f out: chsd ldrs and drvn ent fnl f: kpt on same pce fnl 100yds* 16/1

6-00 **4** shd **Hatman Jack (IRE)**[25] 344 4-8-10 53 RussKennemore(3) 3 58
(B G Powell) *chsd ldr: clsd over 2f out: drvn to ld over 1f out: hdd and one pce ins fnl f* 10/1

030- **5** nk **Sign Of The Cross**[111] 7239 6-9-0 54 EddieAhern 10 58
(C R Dore) *off the pce in midfield: hdwy jst over 2f out: swtchd lft jst over 1f out: drvn and styd on same pce fnl f* 10/1

260 **6** 1/2 **Spoof Master (IRE)**[33] 251 6-9-1 55 (t) LiamKeniry 11 57
(C R Dore) *led at fast gallop: rdn and hdd over 1f out: no ex and btn jst ins fnl f* 14/1

4342 **7** nk **Muktasb (USA)**[9] 556 9-8-13 53 ow1 (v) AdamKirby 12 60+
(D Shaw) *rrd at s: sn swtchd lft: wl bhd: clsd on inner jst over 2f out: nt clr run fr over 1f out: travelling strly fnl f but nvr any room: nvr able to chal* 7/2[2]

-445 **8** ½ **Captain Kallis (IRE)**[9] 556 4-9-1 **55**........ HayleyTurner 9 61+
(D J S Ffrench Davis) *chsd ldrs: clsd over 2f out: rdn and chsng ldrs whn short of room and eased ins fnl f: unable to chal* **11/2**[3]

4006 **9** *nk* **Diddums**[9] 555 4-8-5 **52**........ AmyScott(7) 5 54
(P S McEntee) *wl off the pce towards rr: hdwy wl over 1f out: styng on whn nt clr run jst ins fnl f: swtchd rt ins fnl f: nvr able to chal* **9/1**

04-4 **10** *6* **Kalligal**[10] 538 5-8-12 **52**........ RobertHavlin 7 33
(R Ingram) *a in rr: rdn and effrt over 2f out: nvr trbld ldrs* **25/1**

00-0 **11** *44* **Crystal B Good (USA)**[52] 8 4-9-0 **54**........ RobertWinston 6 —
(J R Best) *bhd: lost tch 1/2-way: virtually p.u fnl 2f: t.o* **40/1**

1m 11.84s (-0.06) **Going Correction** +0.15s/f (Slow) 11 Ran SP% **120.2**
Speed ratings (Par 101): **106,104,104,104,103 103,102,102,101,93 34**
toteswingers: 1&2 £8.10, 1&3 £40.00, 2&3 £26.50 CSF £31.26 CT £375.69 TOTE £10.60: £2.50, £1.30, £6.20; EX 36.40 TRIFECTA Not won..
Owner The Dark Side, Gay Kelleway **Bred** Green Pastures Farm **Trained** Exning, Suffolk

FOCUS
They went a noticeably strong pace, yet there was only around 3l covering the first nine at the finish, and three of these still found significant trouble in running. As such, the bare result needs treating with caution.
Muktasb(USA) Official explanation: jockey said gelding was denied a clear run
Captain Kallis(IRE) Official explanation: jockey said gelding was denied a clear run
Crystal B Good(USA) Official explanation: jockey said filly had a breathing problem

675 CYPRIUM BAR AT MARRIOTT LINGFIELD FILLIES' H'CAP — 1m 2f (P)
5:10 (5:10) (Class 5) (0-70,68) 4-Y-O+ — **£2,456** (£725; £362) **Stalls** Low

Form RPR

-021 **1** **Make Amends (IRE)**[15] 469 5-9-5 **67**........ GeorgeBaker 3 75
(R J Hodges) *chsd ldrs: rdn over 1f out: led 1f out: styd on wl u.p fnl f* **6/1**[3]

-012 **2** *nk* **Head First**[15] 466 4-9-5 **68**........ DavidProbert 8 76
(W Jarvis) *hld up in tch in last trio: hdwy and nt clr run jst over 2f out tl swtchd rt over 1f out: r.o wl fnl f: wnt 2nd towards fin* **7/1**

5443 **3** ¾ **Atacama Sunrise**[4] 623 4-9-2 **65**........ SaleemGolam 1 71
(J Pearce) *in tch in midfield: hdwy on inner wl over 1f out: ev ch and drvn 1f out: no ex fnl 100yds* **5/1**[2]

36-5 **4** 1 ½ **Where's Susie**[16] 263 5-8-10 **58**........ RobertHavlin 7 61
(M Madgwick) *chsd ldr tl unable qck u.p over 1f out: styd on same pce fnl f* **10/1**

-521 **5** 1 ½ **Granny McPhee**[1] 666 4-9-5 **68** 6ex........ RobertWinston 9 68
(A Bailey) *hld up in tch in last trio: hdwy 4f out: chsd ldrs and wd u.p bnd 2f out: no imp after* **11/10**[1]

2134 **6** *shd* **Look Officer (USA)**[22] 375 4-9-5 **68**........ TravisBlock 4 68
(Miss M E Rowland) *led: rdn over 1f out: hdd 1f out: wknd qckly ins fnl f* **33/1**

003- **7** 1 ¼ **My Sweet Georgia (IRE)**[67] 7797 4-9-2 **65**........ AdamKirby 5 62
(Stef Higgins) *in tch in midfield: effrt and rdn jst over 2f out: no prog u.p ent fnl f* **15/2**

634- **8** 1 ¼ **Foreign Investment (IRE)**[214] 4266 4-9-3 **66**........ PaulDoe 10 61
(P D Evans) *stdd s: hld up in rr: rdn and effrt on outer bnd 2f out: no prog* **25/1**

2m 7.43s (0.83) **Going Correction** +0.15s/f (Slow)
WFA 4 from 5yo+ 1lb 8 Ran SP% **118.7**
Speed ratings (Par 100): **102,101,101,99,98 98,97,96**
toteswingers: 1&2 £2.80, 1&3 £2.30, 2&3 £4.40 CSF £48.98 CT £228.68 TOTE £4.10: £2.10, £1.90, £2.00; EX 28.30 Trifecta £134.80 Pool: £559.24 - 3.07 winning units. Place 6: £8.93 Place 5: £5.03.
Owner Miss R Dobson **Bred** Moyglare Stud Farm Ltd **Trained** Charlton Mackrell, Somerset

FOCUS
An ordinary fillies' handicap run at a modest pace. The consistent second and third set the level.
My Sweet Georgia(IRE) Official explanation: jockey said filly hung right
T/Plt: £11.70 to a £1 stake. Pool: £62,397.45. 3,884.17 winning tickets. T/Qpdt: £6.20 to a £1 stake. Pool: £4,060.39. 479.31 winning tickets. SP

590 KEMPTON (A.W) (R-H)
Wednesday, February 24

OFFICIAL GOING: Standard
Wind: Virtualy nil Weather: Rain

676 GOFFS BREEZE UP AT KEMPTON MARCH 12TH H'CAP — 1m 2f (P)
5:30 (5:33) (Class 5) (0-75,76) 4-Y-O+ — **£2,590** (£770; £385; £192) **Stalls** High

Form RPR

1-11 **1** **Franco Is My Name**[7] 588 4-9-6 **76** 6ex........ FergusSweeney 9 88+
(P R Hedger) *hld up in mid-div: hdwy on outside over 1f out: str run to ld fnl 120yds: comf* **5/4**[1]

-531 **2** 1 ¾ **Whodunit (UAE)**[7] 586 6-8-7 **65** 6ex........(b) WilliamCarson(3) 6 72
(P W Hiatt) *led: rdn 3 l clr over 2f out: one pce whn hdd ins fnl 120yds* **10/1**

-022 **3** *1* **Rapid City**[14] 485 7-8-13 **68**........ RobertWinston 8 73
(P D Evans) *in tch: rapid hdwy 3f out to chse ldrs 2f out: disp 2nd over 1f out: styd on same pce ins fnl f* **16/1**

6-21 **4** *1* **Zero Cool (USA)**[21] 396 6-8-8 **63**........(p) LiamKeniry 4 66
(G L Moore) *chsd ldrs: disp 2nd u.p over 1f out: styd on same pce ins fnl f* **5/1**[2]

0-40 **5** 1 ¾ **Cry Alot Boy**[14] 480 7-9-5 **74**........ PatCosgrave 1 74+
(K A Morgan) *stdd s: in rr tl hdwy on outside fr 2f out: str run fnl f but nt rch ldrs* **16/1**

50-6 **6** *1* **Drum Major (IRE)**[13] 509 5-7-12 **60**........ HarryBentley(7) 11 58
(G L Moore) *in rr tl hdwy 2f out: styd on fnl f but nt rch ldrs* **50/1**

010- **7** ¾ **Mr Hichens**[79] 7664 5-8-13 **68**........(p) SteveDrowne 13 65
(Karen George) *chsd ldrs: t.k.h: rdn over 2f out: wknd wl over 1f out* **33/1**

1-12 **8** ½ **Chalice Welcome**[37] 220 7-9-5 **74**........ HayleyTurner 5 70
(N B King) *in rr: pushed along over 2f out: sme prog fr over 1f out: nvr a threat* **8/1**[3]

20-2 **9** *1* **Having A Ball**[13] 496 6-8-10 **65**........ MartinDwyer 10 59
(P D Cundell) *chsd ldrs: rdn 3f out: wknd wl over 1f out* **25/1**

/0-0 **10** ½ **Outofoil (IRE)**[35] 239 4-9-4 **74**........(b[1]) JimCrowley 3 67
(R M Beckett) *chsd ldr: rdn 3f out: wknd wl over 1f out* **16/1**

0-05 **11** ¾ **All About You (IRE)**[14] 485 4-8-11 **70**........ MichaelStainton(3) 14 68+
(P Howling) *hld up in rr: stdy hdwy on ins fr 2f out: nvr in contention and eased ins fnl f* **40/1**

603- **12** 3 ½ **Cold Turkey**[309] 1435 10-8-13 **68**........ AmirQuinn 12 54
(G L Moore) *towards rr most of way* **40/1**

10-0 **13** *5* **Best In Class**[14] 480 4-9-5 **75**........ JoeFanning 2 54
(S C Williams) *chsd ldrs tl wknd fr 3f out* **20/1**

560- **14** *dist* **Murhee (USA)**[193] 5035 4-8-9 **65** oh1........ EddieAhern 7 —
(Mrs A M Thorpe) *a towards rr* **33/1**

2m 6.02s (-1.98) **Going Correction** 0.0s/f (Stan)
WFA 4 from 5yo+ 1lb 14 Ran SP% **120.3**
Speed ratings (Par 103): **107,105,104,104,102 101,101,100,100,99 99,96,92,—**
toteswingers: 1&2 £2.00, 1&3 £8.30, 2&3 £26.80 CSF £13.17 CT £147.16 TOTE £1.70: £1.10, £4.00, £5.60; EX 15.20.
Owner P C F Racing Ltd **Bred** J J Whelan **Trained** Dogmersfield, Hampshire
■ Stewards' Enquiry : Michael Stainton ten-day ban: failed to take all reasonable and permissible measures (Mar 10-13, 16-20, 22)

FOCUS
This looked to be a competitive handicap for the class but few got into it from off the pace. The winner can rate higher and the third and fourth set the level.
Mr Hichens Official explanation: jockey said gelding ran free
All About You(IRE) Official explanation: jockey said, regarding running and riding, that his orders were to drop the gelding in and give it every chance, it failed to get a clear run early in the straight, and when a gap appeared on the rails he was concerned that the horse in front may roll back on him; trainer said, gelding finished distressed on its previous run.

677 KEMPTON.CO.UK MEDIAN AUCTION MAIDEN STKS — 1m 3f (P)
6:00 (6:05) (Class 6) 3-5-Y-O — **£2,047** (£604; £302) **Stalls** High

Form RPR

0- **1** **Chink Of Light**[112] 7244 3-8-5 0........ DavidProbert 8 68+
(A M Balding) *trckd ldrs in 3rd: shkn up over 2f out: drvn and qcknd over 1f out to ld ins fnl f: c clr fnl 100yds: comf* **11/10**[1]

300/ **2** 2 ½ **Byblos**[22] 4985 5-10-0 69........(v[1]) JimCrowley 7 68
(W J Greatrex) *trckd ldr: chal fr 3f out tl led wl over 1f out: hdd ins fnl f and sn no ch w wnr but kpt on wl for 2nd* **12/1**

-244 **3** 2 ¾ **Captain Cool (IRE)**[7] 589 3-8-5 51........(p) FrannyNorton 3 60
(R Hannon) *led tl hdd wl over 1f out: wknd ins fnl f* **11/1**

-32 **4** *nk* **Brave Talk**[10] 551 3-8-5 0........ MartinDwyer 2 59+
(S Kirk) *in rr: shake up and styd on wl fr over 1f out: gng on clsng stages* **2/1**[2]

6-34 **5** 3 ½ **Fair Nella**[10] 551 3-8-1 62 ow1........ FrankieMcDonald 4 50
(J G Portman) *mid-div: rdn and effrt over 2f out: nvr any threat: wknd ins fnl f* **10/1**[3]

0 **6** 1 ¾ **Zafeen's Pearl**[21] 385 3-8-0 0........ AdrianMcCarthy 5 46
(D K Ivory) *mid-div and rdn 3f out: nvr any threat and sn btn* **33/1**

7 4 ½ **Prickles**[248] 5-9-9 0........ SteveDrowne 10 43
(Karen George) *in rr: rdn and sme prog on ins fr 3f out: nvr anywhere nr ldrs and wknd 2f out* **33/1**

8 2 ¼ **Coombeshead Lass** 3-8-0 0........ LukeMorris 9 35
(J Gallagher) *rdn and green early: a bhd* **33/1**

5-0 **9** *19* **Kingston Folly**[40] 189 3-8-5 0........ KevinGhunowa 1 10
(A B Haynes) *t.k.h: chsd ldrs on outside: rdn 4f out: wknd 3f out* **66/1**

2m 23.43s (1.53) **Going Correction** 0.0s/f (Stan)
WFA 3 from 4yo 23lb 4 from 5yo 2lb 9 Ran SP% **116.4**
Speed ratings (Par 101): **94,92,90,89,87 86,82,81,67**
toteswingers: 1&2 £5.60, 1&3 £3.00, 2&3 £8.60 CSF £15.98 TOTE £2.20: £1.10, £3.30, £2.60; EX 16.80.
Owner David Brownlow **Bred** Floors Farming And Christopher J Heath **Trained** Kingsclere, Hants

FOCUS
This poor maiden was run at an uneven pace and being held up was a disadvantage.

678 DIGIBET CLAIMING STKS — 6f (P)
6:30 (6:32) (Class 6) 3-Y-O+ — **£2,047** (£604; £302) **Stalls** High

Form RPR

20 **1** **Valentino Swing (IRE)**[31] 287 7-9-8 63........ AdamKirby 6 69
(Miss T Spearing) *in rr: hdwy and nt clr run ins fnl 2f: sn swtchd rt and qcknd to take slt ld 1f out: drvn out* **9/1**

314 **2** ¾ **Dvinsky (USA)**[7] 579 9-9-10 70........(b) RobertWinston 5 69
(P Howling) *chsd ldrs: rdn and hung lft ins fnl 2f: drvn to take slt ld wl over 1f out: sn hdd: hung rt and one pce cl home* **9/4**[1]

0304 **3** 1 ¾ **Kheley (IRE)**[10] 556 4-8-11 61........ KierenFox(5) 9 55
(W M Brisbourne) *in tch: rdn and hdwy to chal over 1f out: styd on same pce ins fnl f* **14/1**

-642 **4** 1 ¼ **Misaro (GER)**[24] 364 9-9-8 69........(b) LiamJones 2 57
(R A Harris) *sn chsng ldr: rdn and hung lft over 1f out: wknd ins fnl f* **5/1**

-300 **5** *shd* **The Tatling (IRE)**[21] 384 13-9-5 78........ JackDean(3) 4 57
(J M Bradley) *wnt lft s: sn in tch: rdn and effrt over 1f out: nvr rchd ldrs and styd on same pce ins fnl f* **4/1**[2]

06-4 **6** *nse* **Tom Folan**[14] 483 3-8-2 65........(p) LukeMorris 3 48
(Andrew Reid) *hmpd s and bhd: hdwy fr 2f out: styd on fnl f but nvr gng pce to rch ldrs* **10/1**

-521 **7** 2 ¾ **Espy**[9] 562 5-9-6 67........ PJMcDonald 7 46
(I W McInnes) *outpcd most of way* **9/2**[3]

005- **8** *nk* **Ballyvonane (USA)**[91] 7514 3-8-5 48........(b) FrannyNorton 1 41
(L A Dace) *sn led: rdn and hung bdly rt fr 2f out: hdd wl over 1f out and sn wknd* **66/1**

1m 11.91s (-1.19) **Going Correction** 0.0s/f (Stan)
WFA 3 from 4yo+ 15lb 8 Ran SP% **112.9**
Speed ratings (Par 101): **107,106,103,102,101 101,98,97**
toteswingers: 1&2 £5.50, 1&3 £13.80, 2&3 £4.10 CSF £28.87 TOTE £10.30: £2.90, £1.30, £3.10; EX 36.70.
Owner D J Oseman **Bred** Sean P Bourke **Trained** Alcester, Warwicks

FOCUS
There was a solid early pace in this moderate claimer.

679 DIGIBET.COM H'CAP — 6f (P)
7:00 (7:00) (Class 4) (0-85,81) 4-Y-O+ — **£4,209** (£1,252; £625; £312) **Stalls** High

Form RPR

01-1 **1** **Sutton Veny (IRE)**[31] 287 4-8-13 **76**........ AdamKirby 1 88+
(J R Gask) *led: stdd pce over 3f out: qcknd again over 2f out: drvn clr over 1f out: eased nr fin* **1/1**[1]

01-6 **2** 1 ¾ **Lujeanie**[46] 102 4-9-4 **81**........(p) JimCrowley 5 88
(D K Ivory) *plld hrd in rr: hdwy on outside as pce qcknd over 2f out: styd on to chse wnr over 1f out but nvr any ch* **10/3**[2]

5-03 **3** 1 ½ **Methaaly (IRE)**[11] 535 7-8-12 **75**........(be) JoeFanning 2 78
(M Mullineaux) *awkward s: sn chsng ldrs: upsides as pce stdd 3f out: rdn and chsd wnr 2f out: wknd into 3rd over 1f out* **8/1**

4636 **4** 2 ½ **Timeteam (IRE)**[11] 535 4-9-4 **81**........ IanMongan 3 76
(P D Evans) *slowly away and rel to r early: impr to press ldrs whn pce stdd 3f out: wknd wl over 1f out* **9/2**[3]

326- 5 8 **Tous Les Deux**[315] 1283 7-9-3 **80**........ GeorgeBaker 4 51
(G L Moore) *t.k.h: hdwy on ins over 2f out and racd alone: wknd u.p wl over 1f out* **11/2**

1m 12.37s (-0.73) **Going Correction** 0.0s/f (Stan) 5 Ran SP% **117.8**
Speed ratings (Par 105): **104,101,99,96,85**
CSF £5.16 TOTE £2.20: £1.30, £2.20; EX 5.60.

Owner The Sutton Veny Syndicate **Bred** Rathbarry Stud **Trained** Sutton Veny, Wilts

FOCUS
A tight little handicap, run at an uneven pace.

680 DIGIBET SPORTS BETTING H'CAP 1m 4f (P)
7:30 (7:30) (Class 4) (0-85,80) 3-Y-O **£4,209** (£1,252; £625) **Stalls** Centre

Form RPR

21 1 **Into Wain (USA)**[19] 433 3-8-10 **69**........ MartinDwyer 4 78+
(D M Simcock) *trckd ldr: pushed along over 2f out: drvn and styd on fnl f to ld fnl 120yds: sn in command: comf* **5/4**[2]

431- 2 ¾ **Exemplary**[149] 6331 3-9-7 **80**........ JoeFanning 2 86+
(M Johnston) *led: pushed along over 2f out: rdn fnl f: hdd and no ex fnl 120yds* **1/1**[1]

045 3 2 ¼ **Beat Route**[14] 484 3-8-2 **66**........ JemmaMarshall(5) 1 68
(M J Attwater) *racd in 3rd tl rdn and hdwy 2f out to dispute cl 2nd wl over 1f out: wknd ins fnl f* **8/1**[3]

2m 42.74s (8.24) **Going Correction** 0.0s/f (Stan) 3 Ran SP% **105.6**
Speed ratings (Par 99): **72,71,70**
CSF £2.81 TOTE £1.90; EX 2.50.

Owner Ahmad Al Shaikh **Bred** Don M Robinson **Trained** Newmarket, Suffolk

FOCUS
With Danger Mulally a non-runner this was always going to be a tactical affair. The top weight was rated 5lb lower than the race's ceiling, so it didn't appear a strong race for the grade. However, each of the three runners were open to improvement.

681 BISTRO IN THE PANORAMIC H'CAP 7f (P)
8:00 (8:00) (Class 4) (0-85,81) 3-Y-O **£4,209** (£1,252; £625; £312) **Stalls** High

Form RPR

110- 1 **Niran (IRE)**[230] 3779 3-9-8 **80**........ SebSanders 5 85+
(C E Brittain) *trckd ldrs: rdn and styd on to ld jst ins fnl f: kpt on strly* **2/1**[1]

0-13 2 nk **Tiradito (USA)**[33] 268 3-9-3 **75**........(p) MartinDwyer 2 79
(M Botti) *in rr: rdn and hdwy fr 2f out: str run fnl f to chse wnr nr fin but a hld* **5/1**[3]

5345 3 2 **Transfixed (IRE)**[5] 617 3-9-5 **77**........ IanMongan 1 76
(P D Evans) *led: rdn and kpt slt ld whn strly chal fr over 2f out: hdd jst ins fnl f: wknd cl home* **20/1**

21-2 4 ¾ **Robust Wish (USA)**[20] 406 3-9-9 **81**........(b) EddieAhern 4 78
(B J Meehan) *hld up in rr: rdn and hdwy on ins fr 2f out: nvr quite on terms w ldrs and styd on same pce ins fnl f* **10/3**[2]

02-1 5 hd **Seamster**[34] 247 3-8-13 **71**........ JoeFanning 3 67
(M Johnston) *chsd ldr: chal fr over 2f out tl over 1f out: wknd ins fnl f* **2/1**[1]

1m 25.71s (-0.29) **Going Correction** 0.0s/f (Stan) 5 Ran SP% **111.2**
Speed ratings (Par 99): **101,100,98,97,97**
CSF £12.40 TOTE £2.00: £1.10, £5.20; EX 9.40.

Owner Saeed Manana **Bred** Miss Audrey F Thompson **Trained** Newmarket, Suffolk

FOCUS
An interesting three-year-old handicap, run at an average pace.

682 ALL-WEATHER "HANDS AND HEELS" APPRENTICE H'CAP 1m (P)
8:30 (8:30) (Class 7) (0-50,50) 4-Y-O+ **£1,364** (£403; £201) **Stalls** High

Form RPR

0-00 1 **Machinate (USA)**[11] 540 8-8-12 **45**........ KierenFox 11 54
(W M Brisbourne) *stdd towards rr: hdwy over 2f out: drvn to ld 1f out: pushed clr* **8/1**

00-0 2 3 ½ **Red Current**[38] 211 6-8-10 **46**........ JakePayne(3) 1 46
(R A Harris) *trckd ldrs: led over 2f out: rdn and hdd 1f out: styd on same pce ins fnl f* **14/1**

00/5 3 1 **Motu (IRE)**[9] 568 9-9-1 **48**........(v) LeeTopliss 4 46
(I W McInnes) *disp ld tl slt advantage 3f out: hdd over 2f out: styd on one pce fr over 1f out* **11/2**[2]

0-00 4 1 **Montmartre (USA)**[12] 530 4-9-0 **47**........ DavidKenny 9 43
(David Pinder) *broke wl: stdd towards rr: hdwy over 2f out: styd on fr over 1f out but nvr any threat* **10/1**

50/6 5 2 ¼ **Edin Burgher (FR)**[34] 248 9-8-7 **45**........(v) JessicaSteven(5) 10 36
(T T Clement) *disp ld tl 3f out: styd pressing ldr tl ins fnl 2f: wknd fnl f* **33/1**

-000 6 nse **Stark Contrast (USA)**[26] 347 6-8-12 **45**........ HollyHall 8 36+
(M D I Usher) *awkwards stalls and slowly away: hung rt 3f out: sme prog fr over 1f our: nvr any threat* **6/1**[3]

050- 7 nk **My Jeanie (IRE)**[79] 7660 6-8-13 **46**........ RichardRowe 6 36
(J C Fox) *chsd ldrs: hmpd on ins over 2f out: wknd over 1f out* **6/1**[3]

60-4 8 2 ½ **My Mirasol**[20] 407 6-9-1 **48**........(p) MatthewLawson 3 33+
(D E Cantillon) *slowly away: in rr tl rapid hdwy on outside to chse ldrs over 4f out: wknd 2f out* **2/1**[1]

0005 9 3 ¾ **Easy Wonder (GER)**[7] 576 5-8-9 **45**........(b) MatthewCosham(3) 12 21
(I A Wood) *in tch whn hmpd on ins wl over 4f out: sme prog on ins fr 3f out: nvr on terms and wknd 2f out* **8/1**

000/ 10 13 **Definite Honey**[513] 6333 4-8-12 **45**........(p) RyanClark 7 —
(J M Bradley) *a in rr* **16/1**

1m 40.55s (0.75) **Going Correction** 0.0s/f (Stan) 10 Ran SP% **124.1**
Speed ratings (Par 97): **96,92,91,90,88 88,87,85,81,68**
toteswingers: 1&2 £22.00, 1&3 £8.00, 2&3 £26.50 CSF £120.59 CT £695.49 TOTE £9.30: £2.90, £3.20, £2.10; EX 81.00 Place 6 £24.87, Place 5 £15.74.

Owner Mark Brisbourne **Bred** Gaines-Gentry Thoroughbreds & William Condren **Trained** Great Ness, Shropshire

■ Stewards' Enquiry : Richard Rowe two-day ban: careless riding (Mar 10-11)

FOCUS
A dire "hands and heels" handicap for apprentice riders.

Easy Wonder(GER) Official explanation: jockey said mare suffered interference in running

T/Plt: £41.50 to a £1 stake. Pool: £79,644.73. 1,397.86 winning tickets. T/Qpdt: £17.40 to a £1 stake. Pool: £5,457.30. 232.00 winning tickets. ST

669 LINGFIELD (L-H)
Wednesday, February 24

OFFICIAL GOING: Standard
Wind: fresh, behind Weather: mainly cloudy

683 BET IN RUNNING - BETDAQ MEDIAN AUCTION MAIDEN STKS 6f (P)
1:40 (1:40) (Class 5) 3-5-Y-O **£2,456** (£725; £362) **Stalls** Low

Form RPR

023- 1 **Noble Greek (USA)**[145] 6443 3-8-9 82........ RobertWinston 4 70
(J R Best) *led early: sn stdd and hld up in tch: pressed ldr over 2f out: rdn and unable qck over 1f out: styd on u.p ins fnl f to ld nr fin* **1/4**[1]

33-3 2 nk **Caramelita**[14] 483 3-8-4 66........ NickyMackay 1 64
(J R Jenkins) *sn led: rdn wl over 1f out: looked wnr ins fnl f tl worn down nr fin* **4/1**[2]

3 2 ¾ **Force To Spend** 3-8-4 0........ LukeMorris 3 56+
(N P Littmoden) *chsd ldrs: rdn and chsd ldng pair jst over 2f out: outpcd jst ins fnl f: kpt on* **25/1**[3]

0-0 4 2 ¼ **French Wind**[12] 527 3-8-9 0........ DavidProbert 2 54+
(Pat Eddery) *wl in tch: rdn and outpcd in last over 2f out: one pce and no imp after* **33/1**

1m 12.77s (0.87) **Going Correction** +0.275s/f (Slow) 4 Ran SP% **106.8**
Speed ratings (Par 103): **105,104,100,97**
CSF £1.50 TOTE £1.10; EX 1.10.

Owner Hucking Horses **Bred** Helen Barbazon & Joseph Barbazon **Trained** Hucking, Kent

FOCUS
A modest maiden run at a steady early pace. The wind was behind them in the home straight. The winner was below par and the form is best viewed through the second and fourth.

684 BREATHE SPA AT MARRIOTT LINGFIELD H'CAP 6f (P)
2:10 (2:10) (Class 6) (0-65,65) 4-Y-O+ **£1,774** (£523; £262) **Stalls** Low

Form RPR

-064 1 **Sweet Applause (IRE)**[2] 659 4-8-4 **58**........ CharlotteKerton(7) 4 65
(G Prodromou) *t.k.h: hld up wl in tch: hdwy to chse ldr and edgd rt over 1f out: rdn to ld 1f out: r.o wl* **25/1**

0-32 2 nk **Romantic Queen**[12] 532 4-8-13 **60**........(t) TonyCulhane 5 66
(George Baker) *stdd s: t.k.h: hld up in tch in rr: gd hdwy ent fnl f: ev ch fnl 100yds: r.o but a jst hld* **9/1**

6-10 3 1 ¼ **Raimond Ridge (IRE)**[20] 404 4-8-11 **65**........ MatthewCosham(7) 8 67+
(J Jay) *stdd s and sn swtchd lft: t.k.h: hld up in tch in rr: hdwy on outer over 1f out: r.o strly fnl f: wnt 3rd fnl 75yds: nt rch ldng pair* **12/1**

3153 4 1 **The Geester**[28] 312 6-8-13 **60**........ AdamKirby 1 59
(Stef Higgins) *led at stdy gallop: rdn and qcknd ent fnl 2f: hdd 1f out: outpcd fnl 150yds* **11/4**[1]

6-56 5 nk **Teen Ager (FR)**[14] 486 6-9-1 **62**........ LiamKeniry 6 60
(P Burgoyne) *t.k.h: hld up wl in tch: effrt to press ldrs ent fnl f: sn rdn and fnd little: one pce fnl 150yds* **7/2**[2]

-405 6 ½ **Loyal Royal (IRE)**[13] 501 7-8-10 **60**........(b) JackDean(3) 7 57
(J M Bradley) *stdd s: t.k.h: hld up in tch in rr: rdn and unable qck 2f out: styng on but stl plenty to do whn nt clr run and swtchd lft jst ins fnl f: nvr trbld ldrs* **9/1**

5341 7 ¾ **Bollywood Style**[5] 614 5-9-3 **64** 6ex........ SteveDrowne 3 58
(J R Best) *chsd ldrs: wnt 2nd 4f out: rdn ent fnl 2f: wkng whn short of room and sltly hmpd over 1f out: n.d after* **7/2**[2]

0-11 8 ½ **Bishopbriggs (USA)**[26] 351 5-9-2 **63**........ TravisBlock 2 56
(M G Quinlan) *chsd ldr tl 4f out: chsd ldrs after tl wknd u.p ent fnl f* **6/1**[3]

1m 13.16s (1.26) **Going Correction** +0.275s/f (Slow) 8 Ran SP% **116.9**
Speed ratings (Par 101): **102,101,99,98,98 97,96,95**
toteswingers: 1&2 £31.40, 1&3 £40.90, 2&3 £13.20 CSF £232.93 CT £2854.97 TOTE £26.20: £6.70, £1.70, £4.20; EX 172.40 TRIFECTA Not won..

Owner Matt Bartram **Bred** Castlemartin Stud And Skymarc Farm **Trained** East Harling, Norfolk

■ Stewards' Enquiry : Charlotte Kerton one-day ban: careless riding (Mar 10)

FOCUS
They didn't go much of a pace and there were a few racing keenly early. Pretty limited form.

Teen Ager(FR) Official explanation: vet said gelding bled from the nose

685 LINGFIELDPARK.CO.UK (S) STKS 1m 2f (P)
2:45 (2:47) (Class 6) 4-Y-O+ **£1,774** (£523; £262) **Stalls** Low

Form RPR

6504 1 **Hold The Bucks (USA)**[7] 586 4-9-0 59........(p) LukeMorris 10 63
(J S Moore) *mde all: rdn and wnt 2 l clr over 1f out: styd on wl fnl f* **7/1**

13-2 2 1 ¼ **Fong's Alibi**[7] 586 4-8-9 73........(p) LiamKeniry 8 58+
(J S Moore) *chsd wnr tl over 8f out: rdn to chse wnr again over 1f out: kpt on but no real imp fnl f* **15/8**[1]

4026 3 shd **Hip Hip Hooray**[21] 383 4-8-9 62........ FrannyNorton 3 58+
(L A Dace) *hld up in tch: rdn and hdwy to chse ldng pair over 1f out: kpt on to press for 2nd ins fnl f: nvr gng pce to rch wnr* **4/1**[2]

6-65 4 3 ¼ **Kings Topic (USA)**[5] 611 10-9-1 59........(p) StevieDonohoe 5 55
(A B Haynes) *dwlt: sn bustled along and chsng ldrs: rdn and unable qck jst over 2f out: no ch w wnr over 1f out: styd on again ins fnl f* **15/2**

000- 5 1 ¼ **Artreju (GER)**[79] 7668 7-8-12 45........ RobertLButler(3) 6 52
(P Butler) *awkward leaving stalls: t.k.h: hld up in rr: hdwy on outer over 2f out: rdn and no prog over 1f out: plugged on ins fnl f: nvr threatened wnr* **100/1**

0-00 6 hd **Lady Longcroft**[17] 457 5-8-10 50........ SaleemGolam 2 47
(J Pearce) *t.k.h: in tch whn nt clr run on bnd over 2f out: rdn and no imp ins fnl f* **25/1**

6010 7 nse **Flighty Fellow (IRE)**[2] 665 10-9-1 56........(v) RossAtkinson(5) 1 57
(B G Powell) *hld up in rr: hmpd bnd 9f out: rdn and effrt wl over 1f out: sn edging rt and no prog: plugged on ins fnl f: nvr trbld ldrs* **11/2**[3]

0042 8 ½ **Play Up Pompey**[11] 539 8-9-1 47........ RichardKingscote 7 51
(J J Bridger) *hld up in tch in midfield: rdn and unable to over 2f out: no prog u.p fnl 2f* **14/1**

9 nse **Flight Wise**[116] 6-8-12 0........ RussKennemore(3) 9 51
(N R Mitchell) *dwlt: sn rcvrd and chsd wnr over 8f out: rdn jst over 2f out: btn over 1f out: wknd fnl f* **250/1**

0/ 10 1 ¼ **Narcisco (GER)**[295] 5-9-1 85........(t) SteveDrowne 4 51
(N J Hawke) *hld up towards rr: rdn and no prog ent fnl 2f: no ch whn n.m.r and eased wl ins fnl f* **12/1**

2m 10.0s (3.40) **Going Correction** +0.275s/f (Slow)
WFA 4 from 5yo+ 1lb 10 Ran SP% **114.0**
Speed ratings (Par 101): **97,96,95,93,92 92,92,91,91,90**
toteswingers: 1&2 £5.40, 1&3 £10.40, 2&3 £2.20 CSF £19.94 TOTE £9.00: £2.90, £1.20, £1.80; EX 23.50 Trifecta £138.40 Pool: £652.85 - 3.49 winning units..The winner was bought in for 4,000gns

The Form Book, Raceform Ltd, Compton, RG20 6NL

Owner E Moore & J S Moore **Bred** David E Hager II **Trained** Upper Lambourn, Berks
FOCUS
Once again the early gallop was far from frantic, and the place to be was on the front end. Hold The Bucks made all under a good ride but the fifth holds down the form.
Narcisco(GER) Official explanation: trainer said gelding bled from the nose

686 MARRIOTT HOTEL OPENING SPRING 2010 H'CAP 1m 2f (P)
3:20 (3:20) (Class 4) (0-85,83) 3-Y-O **£4,209** (£1,252; £625; £312) **Stalls** Low

Form RPR
-211 **1** **Rock A Doodle Doo (IRE)**[32] 279 3-8-12 **74**.................. JimCrowley 1 80+
(W Jarvis) *trckd ldrs: rdn to chal wl over 1f out: led jst ins fnl f: edgd lft u.p last 100yds: r.o wl* **4/5**[1]

4121 **2** *nk* **Exceedthewildman**[21] 386 3-9-0 **81**..............................(p) KierenFox(5) 4 84
(J S Moore) *hld up in rr: trckd ldrs at 1/2-way: ev ch 2f out: sltly bmpd ins fnl f r.o wl last 110yds but a hld by wnr* **7/1**[3]

40-1 **3** *2* **Whippers Love (IRE)**[19] 428 3-9-7 **83**............................. JoeFanning 3 85+
(M Johnston) *chsd ldr tl rdn to ld 2f out: hdd jst ins fnl f: stl ev ch but keeping on one pce whn squeezed out and hmpd fnl 100yds: eased after* **15/8**[2]

24-1 **4** *5* **Ana Moutabahi**[31] 283 3-8-9 **71**................................. StevieDonohoe 2 61
(P D Evans) *led: rdn over 2f out: hdd 2f out: wknd over 1f out* **16/1**

2m 10.41s (3.81) **Going Correction** +0.275s/f (Slow) 4 Ran SP% **108.7**
Speed ratings (Par 99): **95,94,93,89**
CSF £6.71 TOTE £1.50; EX 5.20.
Owner The Doodle Doo Partnership **Bred** Mrs A S O'Brien And Lars Pearson **Trained** Newmarket, Suffolk
■ Stewards' Enquiry : Jim Crowley four-day ban: careless riding (Mar 10-13)
FOCUS
A decent little handicap featuring four last-time-out winners, but once again the early pace was steady and it turned into a bit of a tactical affair. The winner is progressive.

687 GOLF AND RACING AT LINGFIELD PARK CLAIMING STKS 5f (P)
3:55 (3:55) (Class 6) 4-Y-0+ **£1,774** (£523; £262) **Stalls** High

Form RPR
2222 **1** **Handsome Cross (IRE)**[5] 616 9-8-13 67...............(v) StevieDonohoe 1 72+
(W J Musson) *stdd s: hld up in last: hdwy to chse ldng pair 1/2-way: led on bit ent fnl f: pushed clr fnl 150yds: easily* **2/5**[1]

2005 **2** *1 ½* **Ten Down**[26] 344 5-8-10 54.. MartinDwyer 4 60
(M Quinn) *led tl 3f out: styd pressing ldr: rdn over 2f out: ev ch 1f out: easily brushed aside by wnr fnl 150yds* **11/4**[2]

4345 **3** *2 ¾* **Truly Divine**[9] 561 5-8-1 45...(v) RyanClark(7) 3 48
(C A Dwyer) *w ldr tl led 3f out: rdn and hung lft over 1f out: hdd ent fnl f: sn fdd* **14/1**[3]

0000 **4** *3* **Spring Bridge (IRE)**[13] 495 4-8-9 43.........................(vt) SteveDrowne 5 38
(Mrs L C Jewell) *chsd clr ldng pair: rdn and no prog 1/2-way: nvr trbld ldrs* **33/1**

0-00 **5** *10* **Tan Bonita (USA)**[2] 659 5-8-4 42..................................... LukeMorris 2 —
(R J Smith) *chsd clr ldng pair: rdn and dropped to last 1/2-way: lost tch 2f out: eased fnl f* **50/1**

58.79 secs (-0.01) **Going Correction** +0.275s/f (Slow) 5 Ran SP% **109.7**
Speed ratings (Par 101): **111,108,104,99,83**
CSF £1.74 TOTE £1.40: £1.10, £1.30; EX 1.90.
Owner McHugh & Partners II **Bred** Keith Wills **Trained** Newmarket, Suffolk
FOCUS
A claimer that couldn't have been set up any better for the winner, who was much too good for some modest opponents. Solid but limited form.

688 BET MULTIPLES - BETDAQ H'CAP 2m (P)
4:25 (4:25) (Class 4) (0-85,81) 4-Y-0+ **£4,209** (£1,252; £625; £312) **Stalls** Low

Form RPR
32-1 **1** **Sinbad The Sailor**[20] 409 5-9-1 **68**..............................(v) TonyCulhane 8 76+
(George Baker) *led tl 10f out: chsd ldr after: ev ch and drvn over 1f out: led ins fnl f: styd on wl* **7/4**[1]

24-6 **2** *½* **Rose Row**[13] 500 6-9-11 **78**...................................... RichardKingscote 7 85
(Mrs Mary Hambro) *stdd s: hld up in last pair: clsd 5f out: rdn and hdwy over 1f out: drvn and ev ch ins fnl f: unable qck towards fin* **11/2**

50-0 **3** *hd* **American Spin**[13] 500 6-9-5 **72**...................................(e) RobertHavlin 2 79
(L A Dace) *t.k.h: chsd ldrs tl hdwy to ld 10f out: rdn over 2f out: drvn and hrd pressed over 1f out: hdd ins fnl f: kpt on same pce fnl 100yds* **12/1**

2132 **4** *1 ½* **Satwa Gold (USA)**[13] 500 4-9-3 **76**................................. AdamKirby 4 81
(Stef Higgins) *t.k.h: in tch: rdn and effrt on inner 2f out: ev ch and hrd drvn ent fnl f: no ex fnl 150yds* **7/2**[2]

01-6 **5** *nk* **Dani's Girl (IRE)**[35] 232 7-9-8 **80**................................. KierenFox(5) 3 85
(P M Phelan) *stdd s: t.k.h: hld up in last trio: clsd 5f out: rdn and chsd ldrs 2f out: styd on same pce fr over 1f out* **16/1**

412 **6** *2 ½* **Prince Charlemagne (IRE)**[14] 488 7-9-3 **70**................ GeorgeBaker 1 73
(G L Moore) *chsd wnr tl 10f out: chsd ldrs after: rdn ent fnl 2f: wknd u.p over 1f out* **9/2**[3]

7 *1 ¾* **Morar**[106] 4-9-8 **81**.. IanMongan 5 81
(Mrs L J Mongan) *hld up in midfield: rdn and effrt on outer bnd 2f out: wknd over 1f out: n.d fnl f* **10/1**

5-00 **8** *6* **Valmari (IRE)**[18] 447 7-9-6 **80**.............................. CharlotteKerton(7) 6 73
(G Prodromou) *stdd s: t.k.h: hld up in last trio: hdwy on outer 5f out: dropped to last over 2f out and sn btn: hung lft bnd jst over 2f out* **40/1**

3m 39.11s (13.41) **Going Correction** +0.275s/f (Slow)
WFA 4 from 5yo+ 6lb 8 Ran SP% **117.3**
Speed ratings (Par 105): **77,76,76,75,75 74,73,70**
toteswingers: 1&2 £2.60, 1&3 £5.40, 2&3 £7.30 CSF £12.29 CT £89.54 TOTE £2.30: £1.30, £1.80, £4.30; EX 13.10 Trifecta £371.90 Pool: £598.10 - 1.19 winning units..
Owner Sir Alex Ferguson **Bred** Sir Eric Parker **Trained** Moreton Morrell, Warwicks
FOCUS
The top-weight in this handicap was rated 5lb below the ceiling for the race. They ambled round before sprinting from the run down the hill second time around, and it proved a big advantage to be handy. Straightforward form, rated around the second and third.

689 BET ASIAN H'CAPS - BETDAQ HANDICAP 6f (P)
4:55 (4:55) (Class 5) (0-70,70) 3-Y-O **£2,456** (£725; £362) **Stalls** Low

Form RPR
00-2 **1** **Candyfloss Girl**[14] 483 3-9-2 **68**....................................... SebSanders 3 74
(H J L Dunlop) *chsd ldr: rdn and upsides ldr 2f out: led over 1f out: flashed tail u.p but r.o wl fnl f* **4/1**[3]

241- **2** *1 ¾* **Kummel Excess (IRE)**[72] 7748 3-8-9 **66**................. MatthewDavies(5) 7 67
(George Baker) *chsd ldrs: rdn and effrt ent fnl 2f: drvn to chse wnr jst ins fnl f: no imp after* **10/3**[1]

5-52 **3** *1 ½* **Miss Lesley**[10] 550 3-8-13 **70**..................................(b) MarkCoumbe(5) 1 66
(D K Ivory) *awkward leaving stalls' and s.i.s: sn rcvrd to chse ldrs: rdn ent fnl 2f: drvn and one pce fnl f* **5/1**

-622 **4** *½* **May Chorus (IRE)**[19] 425 3-8-7 **59**................................. NickyMackay 2 53+
(J R Boyle) *led: rdn ent fnl 2f: hdd over 1f out: outpcd fnl f* **7/2**[2]

400- **5** *nse* **Yeah**[139] 6610 3-7-13 **56** oh3...................................(b[1]) JamesSullivan(5) 6 50+
(Patrick Morris) *stdd s and wnt lft s: t.k.h: hld up in last pair: rdn and effrt wl over 1f out: stl plenty to do whn nt clr run ins fnl f: sn swtchd rt: styd on: nvr trbld ldrs* **7/1**

-053 **6** *¾* **Seek The Cash (USA)**[11] 538 3-8-11 **63**.......................... ShaneKelly 4 55
(M Quinn) *t.k.h: hld up wl in tch: rdn and unable qck over 1f out: one pce and wl hld fnl f* **13/2**

55-5 **7** *1* **Future Regime (IRE)**[47] 85 3-8-0 **57** oh2 ow1............. KierenFox(5) 5 46
(Patrick Morris) *s.i.s: in tch in rr: rdn over 2f out: no prog fnl 2f* **14/1**

1m 13.78s (1.88) **Going Correction** +0.275s/f (Slow) 7 Ran SP% **114.5**
Speed ratings (Par 97): **98,95,93,93,92 91,90**
toteswingers:1&2:£2.70, 2&3:£4.10, 1&3:£2.50 CSF £17.76 CT £66.90 TOTE £5.10: £3.20, £2.10; EX 22.70 Trifecta £51.70 Pool: £410.73 - 5.87 winning units. Place 6 £42.65, Place 5 £32.86..
Owner Stephen J Buckmaster **Bred** Baroness Bloodstock **Trained** Lambourn, Berks
FOCUS
A modest sprint handicap and the slowest of the three races run over the C&D on the card. Pretty weak form but a personal best from the decisive winner.
Seek The Cash(USA) Official explanation: trainer said colt choked
Future Regime(IRE) Official explanation: jockey said filly was slowly away
T/Plt: £49.50 to a £1 stake. Pool: £45,981.59. 677.16 winning tickets. T/Qpdt: £5.00 to a £1 stake. Pool: £3,781.91. 552.88 winning tickets. SP

640 CAGNES-SUR-MER
Wednesday, February 24
OFFICIAL GOING: Standard

690a PRIX DE SAINT-RAPHAEL (H'CAP) (ALL-WEATHER) 1m (F)
4:10 (4:17) 4-Y-0+ **£10,177** (£4,071; £3,053; £2,035; £1,018)

RPR
1 **Vestris (IRE)**[33] 273 5-9-1 .... MathiasSautjeau —
(Y Fertillet, France)

2 *1* **Chicaya (FR)**[476] 6-9-2 .... ThomasMessina —
(F Vermeulen, France)

3 *snk* **Evergrey (FR)**[153] 5-9-0 .... MickaelForest —
(C Boutin, France)

4 *1* **Bella Nueva (FR)** 4-8-10 .... —
(F Rohaut, France)

5 *hd* **Cuando Cuanto (FR)**[668] 6-9-3 .... —
(B Goudot, France)

6 *1* **Loup Normand (FR)**[10] 560 7-9-0 .... —
(M Nigge, France)

7 *1 ½* **Lasse (GER)**[67] 7821 7-8-13 .... —
(P Vovcenko, Germany)

8 *½* **Royal Dignitary (USA)**[10] 559 10-8-13 .... IoritzMendizabal —
(D Nicholls) *prom: 3rd 1/2-way: rdn over 2f out: styd on tl no ex ins fnl f* **31/1**[1]

9 *1* **Torronto (FR)**[33] 273 7-8-11 ....(p) —
(P Monfort, France)

10 *½* **Bacarrita (FR)**[10] 560 5-9-0 .... —
(L A Urbano-Grajales, France)

0 **Cape Velvet (IRE)**[83] 6-9-0 .... —
(Mme J Bidgood, Spain)

0 **Kiss Senora (FR)**[317] 6-9-2 .... —
(A Bonin, France)

0 **Rock And Chop (FR)**[129] 5-9-0 ....(b) —
(C Boutin, France)

0 **Wait And See (FR)**[132] 5-9-1 .... —
(Robert Collet, France)

0 **Star Val (FR)**[10] 560 6-9-0 .... —
(Mme C Barande-Barbe, France)

0 **Chico Del Sol (FR)**[83] 5-9-6 ....(p) —
(J Rossi, France)

0 **American Mail (FR)**[225] 4-8-10 ....(b) —
(T Doumen, France)

0 **Family Story (FR)**[129] 5-8-12 .... —
(J-J Napoli, France)

1m 34.59s (94.59) 18 Ran SP% **3.1**
PARI-MUTUEL (Including 1 Euro stake): WIN 14.90; PL 5.40, 3.60, 5.50;DF 60.20.
Owner Mme France Fertillet **Bred** Ecurie Skymarc Farm **Trained** France

676 KEMPTON (A.W) (R-H)
Thursday, February 25
OFFICIAL GOING: Standard
Wind: Brisk behind Weather: Rain

691 BET EUROPA LEAGUE - BETDAQ H'CAP 7f (P)
5:40 (5:40) (Class 7) (0-50,50) 4-Y-0+ **£1,364** (£403; £201) **Stalls** High

Form RPR
20/2 **1** **King Canute (IRE)**[22] 389 6-9-3 **50**................................... JoeFanning 5 59+
(D Morris) *mde virtually all: drvn along over 2f out: styd on strly fnl f* **9/4**[1]

2/00 **2** *1* **Angels Quest**[15] 486 5-9-3 **50**... LukeMorris 11 56
(A W Carroll) *pushed along in mid-div over 3f out and one pce 2f out: styd on u.p and hung rt over 1f out: r.o ins fnl f to take 2nd cl home but no imp on wnr* **3/1**[2]

-314 **3** *1 ¼* **Clever Omneya (USA)**[22] 388 4-9-3 **50**................. RichardHughes 10 52
(J R Jenkins) *chsd ldrs: rdn over 2f out: styd on to chse wnr ins fnl f but no imp: lost 2nd cl home* **9/2**[3]

50-0 **4** *hd* **Yakama (IRE)**[45] 124 5-9-3 **50**...(b) AdamKirby 4 52
(Mrs C A Dunnett) *chsd ldrs: rdn and c to r alone on stands' side fr 2f out: kpt on fnl f but nvr any ch w wnr* **25/1**

4232 **5** *hd* **Ride A White Swan**[10] 567 5-9-0 **50**.......................... MartinLane(3) 3 51
(D Shaw) *in rr: pushed along and hung rt fr over 2f out but stl styd thrght fnl f: nt rch wnr* **6/1**

0504 **6** 2 **Contented (IRE)**[6] 615 8-8-10 **46**........................(tp) RobertLButler(3) 14 42
(Mrs L C Jewell) *in rr: hdwy on ins fr 3f out to chse ldrs 2f out: one pce fnl f* **20/1**

0/53 **7** *nk* **Motu (IRE)**[1] 682 9-9-1 **48**........................(v) DanielTudhope 12 44
(I W McInnes) *chsd wnr: rdn over 2f out: wknd ins fnl f* **11/1**

00-0 **8** 1/2 **Flamestone**[43] 145 6-9-0 **47**........................ StevieDonohoe 8 41
(A E Price) *s.i.s: bhd: drvn and styd on fnl f: nvr rchd ldrs* **33/1**

-053 **9** 3/4 **Imperium**[7] 591 9-9-1 **48**........................(p) ShaneKelly 9 41
(Jean-Rene Auvray) *in rr: rdn and hdwy over 2f out: pushed rt appr fnl f: kpt on ins fnl f but nvr a threat* **14/1**

0460 **10** 1 1/4 **Grizedale (IRE)**[14] 499 11-8-8 **46**........................(tp) KierenFox(5) 2 35
(M J Attwater) *sn chsng ldrs: rdn over 2f out: wknd whn pushed rt over 1f out* **40/1**

0056 **11** 1 3/4 **Romantic Verse**[14] 495 5-8-9 **45**........................(bt) MichaelStainton(3) 7 32
(R A Harris) *plld hrd: chsd ldrs: rdn over 2f out: btn whn hmpd over 1f out* **25/1**

/00- **12** 2 1/2 **Devon Diva**[127] 6934 4-8-9 **47**........................ MarkCoumbe(5) 13 26
(J F Panvert) *bhd most of way* **40/1**

0-00 **13** *nk* **Zazous**[7] 591 9-9-2 **49**........................ RichardKingscote 6 27
(J J Bridger) *a towards rr* **50/1**

1m 26.35s (0.35) **Going Correction** 0.0s/f (Stan) **13** Ran SP% **125.5**
Speed ratings (Par 97): **98,96,95,95,94 92,92,91,90,89 87,84,84**
toteswingers: 1&2 £3.50, 1&3 £5.80, 2&3 £6.30 CSF £8.63 CT £30.75 TOTE £2.40: £1.10, £3.10, £2.20; EX 15.00.
Owner R Nunn **Bred** Tower Bloodstock **Trained** Baxter's Green, Suffolk
■ Stewards' Enquiry : Martin Lane one-day ban: careless riding (Mar 11)

FOCUS
An ordinary handicap run at a decent pace. The market leaders filled the first three positions and the form could work out.
Grizedale(IRE) Official explanation: jockey said gelding ran too free

692 BET SIX NATIONS RUGBY - BETDAQ MEDIAN AUCTION MAIDEN STKS 7f (P)
6:10 (6:12) (Class 6) 3-5-Y-0 **£2,047** (£604; £302) **Stalls** High

Form RPR

066- **1** **Durham Town (IRE)**[197] 4915 3-8-11 62........................ MartinDwyer 3 68
(D K Ivory) *s.i.s: in rr but in tch: pushed along 2f out: no imp on ldrs appr fnl f tl qckng ins fnl f: fin strly to ld fnl 50yds: won gng away* **33/1**

2 1/2 **Bohemian Melody** 3-8-11 0........................ JerryO'Dwyer 5 67+
(M Botti) *dwlt: sn trcking ldrs: pushed along: green and hung lft wnt over 1f out: qckng fnl f to ld fnl 120yds: hdd and no ex fnl 50yds* **8/11**[1]

230- **3** 1 **Swift Return**[121] 7096 3-8-11 76........................ AdamKirby 2 64
(S C Williams) *sn led: jnd 3f out: rdn over 2f out and sn asserted: hdd and outpcd fnl 120yds* **3/1**[2]

00- **4** *nk* **Fancy Star**[208] 4524 3-8-11 0........................ MichaelHills 1 63+
(B W Hills) *wnt lft s: sn chsng ldr: upsides over 3f out tl rdn over 2f out: hung bdly lft over 1f out but stl in contention ins fnl f: no ex cl home* **4/1**[3]

0 **5** 10 **Sparkys Gift (IRE)**[7] 592 3-8-11 0........................ IanMongan 6 36
(P M Phelan) *outpcd* **25/1**

1m 26.71s (0.71) **Going Correction** 0.0s/f (Stan)
WFA 3 from 4yo 17lb **5** Ran SP% **109.7**
Speed ratings (Par 101): **95,94,93,92,81**
CSF £59.09 TOTE £29.00: £14.40, £1.10; EX 43.10.
Owner K T Ivory **Bred** Shane O'Dwyer **Trained** Radlett, Herts

FOCUS
A modest maiden. It produced a tight finish and was a race of wildly changing fortunes. It is very hard to know what to make of the form.

693 BETDAQ THE BETTING EXCHANGE H'CAP (DIV I) 6f (P)
6:40 (6:40) (Class 6) (0-55,64) 4-Y-0+ **£1,706** (£503; £252) **Stalls** High

Form RPR

05F- **1** **Replicator**[265] 2686 5-8-13 **55**........................(e[1]) AshleyHamblett(5) 4 71+
(P L Gilligan) *sn led: pushed along and styd on to go clr 2f out: hung lft ins fnl f* **25/1**

06-3 **2** 3 1/2 **Eager To Bow (IRE)**[14] 499 4-9-1 **52**........................ RichardKingscote 5 56
(P R Chamings) *in rr: pushed along and hdwy fr over 2f out: styd on to go 2nd fnl 120yds but no ch w wnr* **5/2**[1]

30-5 **3** 1 1/2 **Sign Of The Cross**[2] 674 6-9-3 **54**........................ LiamKeniry 9 53
(C R Dore) *t.k.h: chsd ldrs: wnt 2nd over 2f out but nvr any ch w wnr: outpcd into 3rd fnl 120yds* **9/2**[3]

1661 **4** 1/2 **Diane's Choice**[2] 674 7-9-8 **59** 6ex........................(b) DavidProbert 10 57
(Miss Gay Kelleway) *t.k.h: stdd in rr: hdwy on ins over 2f out: chsd ldrs and rdn over 1f out and styd alone far side: wknd ins fnl f* **3/1**[2]

0036 **5** 1 1/2 **Metropolitan Chief**[10] 561 6-8-9 **46**........................ SteveDrowne 8 41
(P Burgoyne) *t.k.h: chsd ldrs tl n.m.r and lost position bnd 3f out: styd on again fnl f but nvr a threat* **9/1**

0060 **6** 1/2 **Diddums**[2] 674 4-8-8 **52**........................ AmyScott(7) 12 44
(P S McEntee) *in rr: hdwy towards far side over 2f out: styd on same pce fr over 1f out* **6/1**

40-6 **7** 1 **Dualagi**[30] 296 6-9-3 **54**........................ GeorgeBaker 2 43
(M R Bosley) *t.k.h: chsd ldrs: rdn 3f out: wknd qckly 2f out* **7/1**

3-00 **8** 1/2 **Bold Diva**[14] 498 5-8-13 **50**........................(v) LukeMorris 6 37
(A W Carroll) *in rr: hdwy to cl on ldrs over 2f out: nvr on terms: sn rdn: wknd appr fnl f* **7/1**

0-06 **9** 3 3/4 **Avonlini**[13] 532 4-8-4 **46** oh1........................ JemmaMarshall(5) 7 22
(B P J Baugh) *t.k.h: chsd ldrs tl rn wd bnd 3f out: wknd over 2f out* **66/1**

1m 11.98s (-1.12) **Going Correction** 0.0s/f (Stan) **9** Ran SP% **126.4**
Speed ratings (Par 101): **107,102,100,99,97 97,95,95,90**
toteswingers: 1&2 £10.70, 1&3 £19.10, 2&3 £4.20 CSF £95.42 CT £361.16 TOTE £39.60: £10.00, £1.10, £1.10; EX 155.70.
Owner Linton Doolan **Bred** R And Mrs Heathcote **Trained** Newmarket, Suffolk

FOCUS
A low-grade sprint handicap run at very steady pace and not many got into it.

694 BETDAQ THE BETTING EXCHANGE H'CAP (DIV II) 6f (P)
7:10 (7:11) (Class 6) (0-55,55) 4-Y-0+ **£1,706** (£503; £252) **Stalls** High

Form RPR

434- **1** **Short Cut**[70] 7787 4-8-13 **50**........................(t) StevieDonohoe 7 58
(Ian Williams) *chsd ldrs: hrd drvn over 1f out: str run ins fnl f to ld last strides* **7/1**

606 **2** *nk* **Spoof Master (IRE)**[2] 674 6-9-4 **55**........................(t) LiamKeniry 8 62
(C R Dore) *led tl hdd over 4f out: styd pressing ldr tl led again ins fnl 2f: styd on ins fnl f: ct last strides* **14/1**

0022 **3** 1 1/4 **Tamino (IRE)**[2] 674 7-9-4 **55**........................ ShaneKelly 5 58
(P Howling) *led over 4f out: rdn and hdd ins fnl 2f: styd cl 2nd ins fnl f: lost 2nd and outpcd fnl 50yds* **4/1**[2]

3420 **4** 1/2 **Muktasb (USA)**[2] 674 9-8-8 **52**........................(v) SeanPalmer(7) 2 54+
(D Shaw) *s.i.s: in rr: pushed along over 2f out: styd on fnl f: gng on cl home but nvr a threat* **7/2**[1]

-420 **5** 4 **Jessica Wigmo**[14] 495 7-8-13 **50**........................ LukeMorris 6 40
(A W Carroll) *s.i.s: in rr: drvn along over 2f out: styd on u.p fnl f but nvr in contention* **11/2**[3]

60-1 **6** 3/4 **Boldinor**[14] 495 7-9-3 **54**........................ GeorgeBaker 11 42
(M R Bosley) *chsd ldrs: rdn over 2f out: nvr on terms and wknd fnl f* **4/1**[2]

4652 **7** *nk* **Hart Of Gold**[20] 423 6-9-3 **54**........................(b) LiamJones 10 41
(R A Harris) *s.i.s: t.k.h early: rdn over 2f out: a outpcd* **9/1**

50-4 **8** 4 **Avoncreek**[13] 531 6-8-4 **46** oh1........................ JemmaMarshall(5) 3 21
(B P J Baugh) *rn wd bnd 3f out: a bhd* **33/1**

2-50 **9** 3 1/4 **Grand Palace (IRE)**[29] 312 7-9-3 **54**........................(v) AdamKirby 9 19
(H J Evans) *in tch: rdn wl over 2f out: sn btn: b.b.v* **9/1**

0/00 **10** 1 **Clearing Sky (IRE)**[14] 498 9-8-9 **46** oh1........................(p) SaleemGolam 12 8
(J R Boyle) *plld hrd and bmpd rail sn after s: chsd ldrs tl wknd wl over 2f out* **40/1**

1m 12.22s (-0.88) **Going Correction** 0.0s/f (Stan) **10** Ran SP% **122.2**
Speed ratings (Par 101): **105,104,102,102,96 95,95,90,85,84**
toteswingers: 1&2 £16.80, 1&3 £8.30, 2&3 £16.30 CSF £104.59 CT £453.24 TOTE £6.70: £1.70, £6.30, £1.10; EX 103.30.
Owner Philip Holden **Bred** David Brown & G B Turnbull Ltd **Trained** Portway, Worcs
■ Stewards' Enquiry : Liam Keniry two-day ban: careless riding (Mar 11-12)

FOCUS
A modest handicap run at a decent pace, but the hold-up performers struggled to get involved. The first four pulled clear of the rest.
Boldinor Official explanation: trainer said gelding had been struck into behind
Grand Palace(IRE) Official explanation: jockey said gelding hung left-handed from 3f out; trainer said gelding bled from the nose

695 BETDAQ.CO.UK CLAIMING STKS 7f (P)
7:40 (7:40) (Class 6) 3-Y-0+ **£2,047** (£604; £302) **Stalls** High

Form RPR

5042 **1** **Little Pete (IRE)**[15] 481 5-9-12 77........................ AdamKirby 7 83
(I W McInnes) *led 2f: styd trcking ldr tl led again wl over 2f out: rdn and wandered u.p ins fnl f: styd on strly* **7/2**[3]

6101 **2** 1 3/4 **Lord Fidelio (IRE)**[8] 579 4-9-12 70........................ SebSanders 1 78
(Ollie Pears) *in rr: shkn up 2f out: drvn and str run appr fnl f: styd on to take 2nd cl home but no ch w wnr* **15/8**[1]

0-30 **3** *hd* **Seasider**[26] 358 5-9-11 83........................ MartinLane(3) 2 79
(D M Simcock) *s.i.s: in rr tl: stdy hdwy fr 2f out: drvn to chse wnr appr fnl f: no imp ins fnl f and lost 2nd cl home* **5/1**

0241 **4** 2 3/4 **Alqaahir (USA)**[14] 496 8-9-8 70........................ RobertLButler(3) 3 69
(P Butler) *chsd ldrs: rdn 2f out: wknd ins fnl f* **11/1**

00-6 **5** *shd* **Shadow Bay (IRE)**[11] 556 4-9-2 59........................ RossAtkinson(5) 9 65?
(Miss Z C Davison) *chsd ldrs: wnt 2nd 2f out but no imp on wnr: outpcd appr fnl f: wknd ins fnl f* **50/1**

-100 **6** 1 **Imperial House**[17] 464 4-9-7 67........................(b) LiamJones 5 62
(R A Harris) *in rr: pushed along over 2f out: nvr gng pce to get into contention* **20/1**

456- **7** 7 **Esteem Machine (USA)**[86] 7603 6-9-10 75........................(v) RichardHughes 6 46
(P D Evans) *plld hrd: led after 2f: hdd over 2f out and sn btn* **3/1**[2]

1m 26.05s (0.05) **Going Correction** 0.0s/f (Stan) **7** Ran SP% **113.7**
Speed ratings (Par 101): **99,97,96,93,93 92,84**
toteswingers: 1&2 £1.60, 1&3 £3.30, 2&3 £3.10 CSF £10.38 TOTE £2.60: £1.10, £2.40; EX 11.40.Little Pete was claimed by C Bjorling for £10,000.
Owner Keith Brown Properties (hull) Ltd **Bred** Larry Ryan **Trained** Catwick, E Yorks
■ Stewards' Enquiry : Adam Kirby two-day ban: used whip in incorrect place (Mar 11-12)

FOCUS
A competitive claimer. Five of the runners held BHA ratings between 70 and 83.
Esteem Machine(USA) Official explanation: jockey said gelding ran too free

696 BET CHELTENHAM FESTIVAL - BETDAQ H'CAP 7f (P)
8:10 (8:10) (Class 5) (0-75,81) 4-Y-0+ **£2,590** (£770; £385; £192) **Stalls** High

Form RPR

-121 **1** **Ocean Legend (IRE)**[11] 552 5-9-10 **81** 6ex........................ AdamKirby 4 91
(A W Carroll) *chsd ldrs: led over 1f out: drvn and styd on strly thrght fnl f* **3/1**[1]

-432 **2** 1 1/4 **Dinner Date**[8] 580 8-8-7 **71**........................ LauraPike(7) 5 78
(T Keddy) *in tch: hdwy over 2f out: drvn and styd on to chse wnr ins fnl f: no imp but hld on wl to hold 2nd* **13/2**[3]

215- **3** *hd* **Berbice (IRE)**[122] 7054 5-9-4 **75**........................(e[1]) RichardHughes 8 81
(S Donohoe, Ire) *hld up towards rr: stdy hdwy over 2f out: drvn to dispute 2nd fnl f but no imp on wnr: dropped to 3rd last strides* **4/1**[2]

53-1 **4** 1 3/4 **Art Market (CAN)**[44] 135 7-8-11 **68** ow1........................(p) IanMongan 3 69
(Miss Jo Crowley) *trckd ldr: led over 2f out: rdn and hdd over 1f out: wknd fnl 120yds* **14/1**

544- **5** 1 3/4 **Chief Exec**[69] 7801 8-8-12 **74**........................(b) KierenFox(5) 9 71
(J R Gask) *in rr: stl last ins fnl 3f: gd prog on ins to chse ldrs ins fnl 2f to chse ldrs 1f out: no imp and sn wknd* **9/1**

41-1 **6** 3/4 **Harting Hill**[14] 499 5-8-5 **62**........................ HayleyTurner 7 57
(M P Tregoning) *stdd s: in rr: rdn over 2f out: nvr gng pce to get into contention* **3/1**[1]

60-0 **7** 1 3/4 **Idle Power (IRE)**[15] 486 12-8-5 **62** ow1........................ MartinDwyer 1 52
(J R Boyle) *chsd ldrs tl wknd qckly over 2f out* **25/1**

0440 **8** 2 1/2 **Grand Honour (IRE)**[8] 587 4-8-5 **62**........................ SaleemGolam 10 45
(P Howling) *led tl hdd over 2f out: sn btn* **20/1**

24-3 **9** 2 1/4 **Mudhish (IRE)**[7] 595 5-8-12 **69**........................(b) SebSanders 2 46
(C E Brittain) *s.i.s: in rr: rdn and effrt on outside 3f out: nvr rchd ldrs and sn wknd* **10/1**

1m 24.73s (-1.27) **Going Correction** 0.0s/f (Stan) **9** Ran SP% **117.7**
Speed ratings (Par 103): **107,105,105,103,101 100,98,95,93**
toteswingers: 1&2 £6.30, 1&3 £4.30, 2&3 £7.30 CSF £23.59 CT £79.64 TOTE £4.60: £1.80, £1.70, £2.10; EX 27.40.
Owner Ocean Trailers Ltd **Bred** Mark Commins **Trained** Cropthorne, Worcs

FOCUS
A fair handicap, involving three last-time-out winners. It again seemed an advantage to raise near the pace and the hold-up runners had trouble getting into it.

Dinner Date Official explanation: trainer said gelding lost both front shoes

697 BET MULTIPLES - BETDAQ H'CAP 1m 4f (P)
8:40 (8:41) (Class 3) (0-95,93) 4-Y-0+

£6,542 (£1,959; £979; £490; £244; £122) **Stalls** Centre

Form RPR

02-1 **1** **King Olav (UAE)**[15] 480 5-9-3 **91** LukeMorris 3 98
(A W Carroll) *trckd ldrs in 3rd tl chsd ldr ins fnl 3f: drvn to ld wl over 1f out: drvn out* **3/1**[2]

-514 **2** *1* **Dance The Star (USA)**[19] 447 5-9-4 **92** EddieAhern 6 97
(D M Simcock) *hld up in rr: gd hdwy 2f out: str run to chse wnr ins fnl f: no imp and jst hld on for 2nd* **7/1**[3]

-546 **3** *nse* **Free Tussy (ARG)**[15] 480 6-8-5 **79** oh2 (bt) DavidProbert 1 84
(G L Moore) *in rr: hdwy fr 2f out: str run fr over 1f out: fin wl to press for 2nd cl home but no imp on wnr* **20/1**

2010 **4** *½* **Baylini**[12] 536 6-9-2 **90** HayleyTurner 5 94
(Ms J S Doyle) *t.k.h in rr: hdwy fr 2f out: styd on u.p to cl on ldrs nr fin but no ch w wnr* **14/1**

0-40 **5** *hd* **Samarinda (USA)**[26] 360 7-9-0 **88** JerryO'Dwyer 2 92
(Mrs P Sly) *in rr tl: rdn and styd on fr 2f out: kpt on wl cl home but no imp on wnr* **33/1**

45/0 **6** *3 ¾* **Donaldson (GER)**[12] 536 8-9-5 **93** GeorgeBaker 7 91
(Jonjo O'Neill) *led: rdn and qcknd 3f out: hdd over 1f out and sn wknd* **40/1**

11-2 **7** *90* **King's Salute (USA)**[19] 447 4-8-13 **90** JoeFanning 8 —
(M Johnston) *trckd ldr: rdn 3f out and wknd qckly: t.o dismntd* **4/6**[1]

2m 35.19s (0.69) **Going Correction** 0.0s/f (Stan)
WFA 4 from 5yo+ 3lb **7** Ran SP% **114.3**
Speed ratings (Par 107): **97,96,96,95,95 93,—**
toteswingers: 1&2 £2.60, 1&3 £8.40, 2&3 £10.70 CSF £23.20 CT £352.34 TOTE £3.20: £1.20, £3.50; EX 23.50.
Owner Cover Point Racing **Bred** Darley **Trained** Cropthorne, Worcs

FOCUS
A decent handicap. The pace was sedate and the hot favourite was very disappointing.

NOTEBOOK
King Olav(UAE) landed a gamble over 1m2f here last time after a brief spell hurdling. He had a 6lb higher mark to deal with in a tougher race over a longer trip but moved well for a long way and displayed a determined attitude to fight off a queue of challengers after hitting the front approaching the furlong marker. He will rise to another career-high mark but is probably not fully exposed yet and has an excellent record of 1120211 on Polytrack.The Rosebery Handicap here could be his next target. (op 4-1)
Dance The Star(USA) took his form to a new high when storming clear after getting first run in a Wolverhampton handicap two runs back. Things did not go to plan last time but he bounced back with a decent effort in a race that did not set up for his hold-up style. The relatively lightly raced five-year-old has a steadily progressive profile on Polytrack, and may be able to elevate his form another notch to justify a mark in the low-90s. (op 15-2 tchd 8-1)
Free Tussy(ARG) took a keen grip in the early stages but did well to snatch third from out of the weights.
Baylini was free early on but stuck to the task on the step back up to 1m4f. She has a modest conversion rate but all of her four wins have been at Lingfield and she should be suited by the return to a strongly run 1m2f handicap at that track. (op 12-1)
Samarinda(USA) ran respectably on his belated first try at 1m4f but didn't conclusively prove his stamina in a slowly run race.
King's Salute(USA) suffered his first defeat since arriving from France when finding an unbeaten and potentially smart colt too strong at this trip at Lingfield last time. The odds-on favourite didn't have to worry about any handicap blots in this race but he stopped alarmingly quickly and finished very distressed. Official explanation: vet said colt returned distressed (op 4-7)

698 BETDAQ.CO.UK H'CAP 1m (P)
9:10 (9:10) (Class 5) (0-70,68) 3-Y-O **£2,590** (£770; £385; £192) **Stalls** High

Form RPR

00-2 **1** **Pastello**[10] 566 3-8-13 **63** RichardHughes 10 69+
(R Hannon) *t.k.h: hld up in rr: stdy hdwy fr 2f out: drvn and qcknd to ld ins fnl f: styd on strly* **4/1**[2]

066- **2** *¾* **Azlak (USA)**[166] 5864 3-8-9 **59** MartinDwyer 3 62
(C E Brittain) *led: drvn and qcknd ins fnl 3f: hdd ins fnl f: nt gng pce of wnr but styd on wl for 2nd* **3/1**[1]

066- **3** *1 ¼* **Tamtara**[134] 6781 3-9-2 **66** EddieAhern 6 66
(Mrs A J Perrett) *in tch: hdwy whn nt clr run over 1f out: drven and qcknd to chse ldrs ins fnl f: tk 3rd nr fin but no ch w ldng duo* **14/1**

02-2 **4** *½* **Katchmore (IRE)**[19] 450 3-9-2 **66** ShaneKelly 12 65+
(Jean-Rene Auvray) *in rr: hdwy on outside over 1f put: styd on wl fnl f: gng on cl home* **9/1**

3-22 **5** *nk* **Red Yarn**[8] 582 3-9-3 **67** (p) GeorgeBaker 7 65
(G L Moore) *chsd ldrs: wnt 2nd u.p over 1f out: edgd lft and wknd ins fnl f* **7/1**

100- **6** *1 ¼* **Dr Mathias**[125] 7003 3-9-4 **68** DavidProbert 9 63
(P D Evans) *in tch: hdwy to chse ldrs over 2f out: sn rdn: wknd ins fnl f* **20/1**

03-1 **7** *2* **Highland Bridge**[28] 321 3-9-3 **67** LiamKeniry 4 57
(D R C Elsworth) *chsd ldr: rdn over 2f out: wknd appr fnl f* **5/1**[3]

221- **8** *½* **Chocolate Cookie (IRE)**[99] 7435 3-9-4 **68** AdamKirby 13 58
(Miss M E Rowland) *in rr tl stdy hdwy fr 3f out: styng on whn hmpd over 1f out: sn drvn but nvr a danger after* **8/1**

9 *3 ¾* **The Bay Bandit**[110] 7298 3-8-4 **54** oh1 FrankieMcDonald 11 36+
(S Donohoe, Ire) *t.k.h in rr: sme hdwy whn nt clr run over 2f out: nvr a factor after* **50/1**

6-13 **10** *2* **Orsett Lad (USA)**[15] 490 3-8-12 **62** SteveDrowne 8 37
(J R Best) *chsd ldrs: wnt 2nd and rdn over 2f out: wknd qckly over 1f out* **12/1**

05-0 **11** *2* **Barastar**[20] 422 3-8-12 **62** PatCosgrave 5 32
(J R Boyle) *chsd ldrs: rdn 3f out: wknd over 2f out* **33/1**

005- **12** *11* **Drubinca**[149] 6364 3-8-7 **57** SaleemGolam 2 1
(S C Williams) *hmpd s: a in rr* **33/1**

65-0 **13** *6* **Egyptology (IRE)**[25] 366 3-9-0 **64** (b¹) JoeFanning 1 —
(M Johnston) *t.k.h: chsd ldrs tl wknd qckly wl over 2f out: dropping away whn bdly hmpd sn after* **12/1**

1m 40.55s (0.75) **Going Correction** 0.0s/f (Stan) **13** Ran SP% **129.9**
Speed ratings (Par 97): **96,95,94,93,93 91,89,89,85,83 81,70,64**
toteswingers: 1&2 £6.10, 1&3 £15.00, 2&3 £16.60 CSF £17.44 CT £170.53 TOTE £7.00: £2.30, £2.20, £6.50; EX 24.60 Place 6: £20.96 Place 5: £17.07.
Owner Longview Stud & Bloodstock Ltd **Bred** Wyck Hall Stud Ltd **Trained** East Everleigh, Wilts

FOCUS
They went a steady pace for this handicap for 3-y-os. The winner was fairly impressive and could be one to follow.
Red Yarn Official explanation: jockey said filly hung right-handed
Drubinca Official explanation: jockey said gelding hung right-handed

T/Plt: £52.40 to a £1 stake. Pool: £81,370.24. 1,132.11 winning tickets. T/Qpdt: £23.30 to a £1 stake. Pool: £7,848.55. 248.90 winning tickets. ST

597 SOUTHWELL (L-H)
Thursday, February 25

OFFICIAL GOING: Standard
Wind: Light against Weather: Overcast

699 BET EUROPA LEAGUE - BETDAQ MEDIAN AUCTION MAIDEN STKS 5f (F)
2:10 (2:15) (Class 6) 3-5-Y-O **£1,774** (£523; £262) **Stalls** High

Form RPR

63- **1** **Fair Passion**[115] 7213 3-8-8 0 JimmyQuinn 2 59+
(D Shaw) *trckd ldrs: plld hrd: led over 3f out: hdd 1/2-way: rdn to ld 1f out: edgd lft: r.o* **11/8**[1]

0-45 **2** *½* **Verinco**[9] 569 4-9-13 55 (v¹) TomEaves 9 67
(B Smart) *chsd ldrs: led 1/2-way: rdn and hdd 1f out: r.o* **12/1**

20-3 **3** *2 ½* **Irish Music (IRE)**[25] 364 5-9-13 59 DarrylHolland 6 58
(A P Jarvis) *led: hdd over 3f out: rdn over 1f out: styd on same pce* **5/1**[2]

004- **4** *shd* **Rain On The Wind (IRE)**[155] 6207 3-8-10 70 WilliamCarson(3) 10 56+
(S C Williams) *prom: outpcd 1/2-way: rallied and edgd lft over 1f out: r.o* **5/1**[2]

5 *3* **Bird Call (IRE)** 3-8-3 0 DeanHeslop(5) 1 37
(T D Barron) *swvd lft s: sn pushed along in rr: r.o ins fnl f: nt trble ldrs* **13/2**[3]

6 *nk* **Carrie's Magic** 3-8-8 0 FrannyNorton 5 36
(T D Barron) *mid-div: edgd rt and outpcd over 3f out: r.o ins fnl f: b.b.v* **14/1**

/0-0 **7** *1 ½* **Steel Mask (IRE)**[21] 403 5-9-6 45 JohnCavanagh(7) 8 40+
(M Brittain) *s.i.s: outpcd: styd on ins fnl f* **66/1**

0- **8** *1 ¾* **Bahamian Bolt**[110] 7289 3-8-8 0 LeeNewnes(5) 3 30
(R Bastiman) *chsd ldrs: rdn 1/2-way: sn wknd* **33/1**

050- **9** *2 ¾* **Sally's Swansong**[216] 4281 4-9-3 39 GaryBartley(5) 7 19
(E J Alston) *mid-div: nt clr run and lost pl wl over 3f out: sn hung lft: n.d after* **50/1**

2634 **10** *¾* **Lady Brickhouse**[6] 619 3-8-3 49 PaulPickard(5) 11 12
(M D Squance) *prom: rdn over 3f out: wknd 1/2-way* **22/1**

11 *2 ¼* **Ignore** 3-8-13 0 AndrewElliott 4 9
(Mrs R A Carr) *dwlt: outpcd* **50/1**

60.45 secs (0.75) **Going Correction** +0.175s/f (Slow)
WFA 3 from 4yo+ 14lb **11** Ran SP% **115.8**
Speed ratings (Par 101): **101,100,96,96,91 90,88,85,81,79 76**
toteswingers: 1&2 £5.60, 1&3 £2.30, 2&3 £5.30 CSF £18.86 TOTE £2.40: £1.10, £2.90, £1.60; EX 17.40 Trifecta £56.10 Pool: £496.97 - 6.55 winning units..
Owner Angie Conway / Whiteman Partnership **Bred** D R Tucker **Trained** Sproxton, Leics

FOCUS
A moderate maiden and, as is usually the case over this straight 5f, all the action took place down the centre of the track.
Carrie's Magic Official explanation: jockey said filly bled from the nose
Ignore Official explanation: jockey said gelding hung left throughout

700 TRY BETDAQ FOR AN EXCHANGE (S) STKS 1m 4f (F)
2:40 (2:45) (Class 6) 4-Y-O+ **£1,774** (£523; £262) **Stalls** Low

Form RPR

3333 **1** **Dunaskin (IRE)**[7] 600 10-8-11 72 BarryMcHugh(3) 6 66
(B Ellison) *mde all: rdn over 2f out: styd on u.p* **8/15**[1]

1342 **2** *2 ¾* **Dream In Blue**[18] 456 5-9-5 65 (p) FrederikTylicki 1 67
(J A Glover) *a.p: chsd wnr over 4f out: rdn over 3f out: no ex wl ins fnl f* **2/1**[2]

-304 **3** *11* **Davana**[7] 599 4-8-1 47 PaulPickard(5) 7 40
(W J H Ratcliffe) *chsd ldrs: wknd over 4f out: wnt mod 3rd over 3f out* **16/1**[3]

00-5 **4** *53* **Fan Club**[15] 493 6-8-9 35 DeanHeslop(5) 5 —
(Mrs R A Carr) *hld up: effrt over 4f out: sn wknd: t.o* **100/1**

0-06 **5** *41* **Rony Dony (IRE)**[27] 342 6-9-0 42 (bt) NickyMackay 4 —
(M E Rimmer) *chsd wnr tl rdn over 4f out: sn wknd: t.o* **66/1**

000/ **6** *92* **James Junior**[526] 6008 4-8-11 0 TomEaves 3 —
(P D Niven) *hld up: bhd fnl 8f: sn t.o* **28/1**

2m 39.91s (-1.09) **Going Correction** -0.05s/f (Stan)
WFA 4 from 5yo+ 3lb **6** Ran SP% **110.4**
Speed ratings (Par 101): **101,99,91,56,29 —**
toteswingers: 1&2 £1.10, 1&3 £1.90, 2&3 £1.30 CSF £1.72 TOTE £1.60: £1.10, £1.30; EX 1.90.There was no bid for the winner.
Owner Koo's Racing Club **Bred** J P And Miss M Mangan **Trained** Norton, N Yorks
■ Stewards' Enquiry : Barry McHugh caution: used whip with excessive frequency.

FOCUS
As weak and uncompetitive a seller as it's possible to get.

701 BET SIX NATIONS RUGBY - BETDAQ H'CAP 2m (F)
3:15 (3:15) (Class 5) (0-75,72) 4-Y-O+ **£2,456** (£725; £362) **Stalls** Low

Form RPR

-512 **1** **Victory Quest (IRE)**[14] 506 10-9-13 **72** (v) DarrylHolland 4 82+
(Mrs S Lamyman) *mde all: rdn over 4f out: hung rt fnl 2f: clr over 1f out: stvd on u.p: eased towards fin* **6/5**[1]

0-62 **2** *8* **Nakoma (IRE)**[15] 493 8-8-9 **57** BarryMcHugh(3) 3 55
(B Ellison) *prom: chsd wnr 1/2-way: rdn over 4f out: wknd over 1f out* **6/4**[2]

-125 **3** *4* **Dan Buoy (FR)**[9] 575 7-8-9 **59** (p) RossAtkinson(5) 5 53
(R C Guest) *trckd ldrs: reminders over 9f out: lost pl and reluctant over 7f out: sn t.o: r.o ins fnl f* **9/2**[3]

4 *36* **Super Ross (IRE)**[14] 2019 7-8-8 **53** oh8 (b) FrankieMcDonald 1 3
(C R Dore) *chsd ldrs tl wknd 1/2-way: sn t.o* **25/1**

3m 44.81s (-0.69) **Going Correction** -0.05s/f (Stan) **4** Ran SP% **107.5**
Speed ratings (Par 103): **99,95,93,75**
CSF £3.27 TOTE £1.80; EX 3.30.
Owner Mrs S Lamyman **Bred** Miss Veronica Henley **Trained** Ruckland, Lincs

FOCUS
An ordinary staying handicap.

702 COME JUMPING AT SOUTHWELL IN MARCH CLASSIFIED CLAIMING STKS 6f (F)
3:45 (3:45) (Class 6) 3-Y-O £1,774 (£523; £262) Stalls Low

Form RPR
400- 1 Set Back[110] 7289 3-8-8 58 AdrianNicholls 4 71
(D Nicholls) chsd ldr: pushed along 1/2-way: rdn to ld over 1f out: r.o 7/1
020- 2 3/4 Thaliwarru[140] 6609 3-8-2 60 JimmyQuinn 5 63
(J R Gask) hld up: racd keenly: hdwy over 2f out: rdn to chse wnr fnl f: r.o 5/1[3]
1213 3 3 Anjomarba (IRE)[20] 424 3-8-5 68 (p) WilliamCarson(3) 1 61
(W G M Turner) led: rdn and hdd over 1f out: styd on same pce fnl f: eased whn btn nr fin 2/1[1]
2-31 4 3 Il Forno[29] 313 3-8-9 70 JohnFahy(7) 3 59
(D Nicholls) plld hrd and prom: rdn over 2f out: edgd rt over 1f out: wknd ins fnl f 3/1[2]
3454 5 3/4 Tamarind Hill (IRE)[10] 566 3-7-11 62 (b) DeclanCannon(5) 6 43
(A J McCabe) prom: rdn over 2f out: wknd fnl f 5/1[3]
00-4 6 12 Alphacino[35] 247 3-8-2 59 (p) FrannyNorton 2 7
(B M R Haslam) chsd ldrs tl rdn and wknd over 2f out 14/1
1m 16.84s (0.34) Going Correction -0.05s/f (Stan) 6 Ran SP% 110.8
Speed ratings (Par 95): 95,94,90,86,85 69
toteswingers: 1&2 £5.90, 1&3 £3.40, 2&3 £3.80 CSF £39.50 TOTE £7.40: £2.50, £1.90; EX 52.10.
Owner D W Barker Bred Mrs S E Barclay Trained Sessay, N Yorks

FOCUS
A moderate claimer.
Alphacino Official explanation: jockey said gelding resented kickback

703 PLAY GOLF AT SOUTHWELL GOLF CLUB H'CAP 6f (F)
4:20 (4:20) (Class 5) (0-75,75) 4-Y-O+ £2,456 (£725; £362) Stalls Low

Form RPR
4-02 1 Hits Only Jude (IRE)[14] 508 7-9-4 75 DavidNolan 3 85
(D Carroll) prom and sn pushed along: rdn 1/2-way: swtchd lft over 1f out: r.o to ld wl ins fnl f 7/2[2]
1212 2 1 Total Impact[13] 520 7-9-1 75 BarryMcHugh(3) 2 82
(C R Dore) trckd ldrs: rdn to ld over 1f out: edgd lft and hdd wl ins fnl f 9/2[3]
013- 3 2 Punching[96] 7483 6-9-1 72 FrankieMcDonald 1 73
(C R Dore) trckd ldrs: racd keenly: led over 4f out: rdn and hdd over 1f out: no ex ins fnl f 14/1
-426 4 nk Peter's Gift (IRE)[14] 501 4-8-13 70 (p) DarryllHolland 6 70
(K A Ryan) sn outpcd: r.o ins fnl f: nvr nrr 9/2[3]
65-1 5 1/2 Wyatt Earp (IRE)[21] 404 9-9-2 73 (p) GregFairley 4 71
(P Salmon) sn pushed along to ld: hdd over 4f out: chsd ldr: rdn over 2f out: styd on same pce appr fnl f 3/1[1]
-002 6 8 Westwood[23] 378 5-8-6 63 NickyMackay 5 35
(D Haydn Jones) chsd ldrs: rdn over 2f out: wknd over 1f out: b.b.v 7/2[2]
1m 15.63s (-0.87) Going Correction -0.05s/f (Stan) 6 Ran SP% 112.5
Speed ratings (Par 103): 103,101,99,98,97 87
toteswingers: 1&2 £3.30, 2&3 £3.80, 1&3 not won. CSF £19.35 TOTE £4.80: £2.70, £1.70; EX 20.40.
Owner Yummy Mummy's Racing Club Bred Swordlestown Stud Trained Sledmere, E Yorks
■ Stewards' Enquiry : David Nolan one-day ban: used whip with excessive frequency (Mar 11)

FOCUS
A fair little sprint handicap in which the leaders may have gone off too quick and set it up for the closers. The form looks straightforward and pretty solid.
Westwood Official explanation: trainer said gelding bled from the nose

704 CALL 01636 814481 TO SPONSOR A RACE H'CAP 7f (F)
4:50 (4:51) (Class 6) (0-65,65) 4-Y-O+ £1,774 (£523; £262) Stalls Low

Form RPR
0606 1 Resplendent Nova[14] 496 8-9-1 62 DarryllHolland 8 71
(P Howling) prom: pushed along 1/2-way: rdn over 2f out: styd on u.p to ld post 3/1[2]
5312 2 shd Fulford[9] 569 5-8-6 53 FrannyNorton 6 62
(M Brittain) hld up: hdwy over 2f out: rdn to ld ins fnl f: hdd post 5/2[1]
1445 3 1 3/4 Mocha Java[8] 579 7-8-11 63 (p) DeclanCannon(5) 9 67
(Matthew Salaman) led: hdd over 4f out: led again 1/2-way: rdn over 1f out: hdd and unable qck ins fnl f 11/1
60-4 4 5 Kladester (USA)[34] 269 4-8-13 60 TonyCulhane 7 51
(M Herrington) prom: rdn 1/2-way: hung lft over 1f out: wknd fnl f 9/1
56-2 5 3 War And Peace (IRE)[19] 442 6-8-11 65 (e) LewisWalsh(7) 10 47
(Jane Chapple-Hyam) hld up: pushed along over 2f out: nvr trbld ldrs 10/3[3]
040- 6 3 3/4 Island Chief[122] 7057 4-8-11 63 (p) AmyRyan(5) 4 35
(K A Ryan) chsd ldrs: rdn over 2f out: wknd over 1f out 10/1
-461 7 3 1/4 Guildenstern (IRE)[14] 498 8-8-10 57 JimmyQuinn 5 21
(P Howling) hld up: rdn 1/2-way: a in rr 10/1
00/0 8 1 1/2 African Blues[24] 369 7-7-13 51 oh6 (t) BillyCray(5) 2 10
(D J S Ffrench Davis) chsd ldr tl led over 4f out: rdn and hdd 1/2-way: wknd wl over 1f out 100/1
-000 9 13 Moral Duty (USA)[15] 486 5-8-4 54 ow2 WilliamCarson(3) 1 —
(W G M Turner) sn pushed along and prom: lost pl over 4f out: bhd fnl 3f: t.o 50/1
1m 29.23s (-1.07) Going Correction -0.05s/f (Stan) 9 Ran SP% 116.1
Speed ratings (Par 101): 104,103,101,96,92 88,84,83,68
toteswingers: 1&2 £7.30, 2&3 £8.80, 1&3 not won. CSF £11.01 CT £70.99 TOTE £5.20: £1.70, £1.60, £2.30; EX 14.30 Trifecta £67.00 Pool: £741.35 - 8.18 winning units..
Owner The Oh So Sharp Racing Partnership Bred A Turner Trained Newmarket, Suffolk
■ Stewards' Enquiry : Darryll Holland two-day ban: used whip with excessive frequency down shoulder and in the forehand (Mar 11-12)
Franny Norton four-day ban: used whip with excessive frequency without giving gelding time to respond (Mar 11, 13 -16)

FOCUS
A modest handicap, but they went a decent early pace and the field finished well spread out.

705 SOUTHWELL RACECOURSE FOR CONFERENCES H'CAP 1m (F)
5:20 (5:21) (Class 6) (0-55,60) 4-Y-O+ £1,774 (£523; £262) Stalls Low

Form RPR
3/3- 1 Pendragon (USA)[16] 7855 7-9-0 55 BarryMcHugh(3) 9 66
(B Ellison) hld up: hdwy 1/2-way: led 2f out: sn rdn: hung lft fnl f: styd on 11/1[3]
26-3 2 1 Fitzolini[31] 290 4-9-2 54 (p) JimmyQuinn 13 63
(A D Brown) chsd ldrs tl led over 2f out: sn rdn and hdd: styd on 12/1
00-1 3 1 3/4 Magic Haze[7] 603 4-8-10 55 LeeTopliss(7) 4 61
(Miss S E Hall) chsd ldrs: rdn over 2f out: swtchd rt over 1f out: styd on 7/1[2]
4-04 4 1 3/4 Plenilune (IRE)[7] 603 5-8-9 47 FrannyNorton 8 48
(M Brittain) broke wl: lost pl after 1f: hdwy u.p over 1f out: no imp ins fnl f 16/1
00-0 5 5 Captain Imperial (IRE)[20] 426 4-8-12 55 LeeNewnes(5) 2 46+
(R Bastiman) chsd ldr tl led 1/2-way: rdn and hdd over 2f out: wknd over 1f out 7/1[2]
0-40 6 1 1/2 Naledi[12] 541 6-8-3 46 oh1 DeclanCannon(5) 3 33
(R J Price) s.i.s: hdwy 5f out: rdn and lost pl over 3f out: n.d after 66/1
40-5 7 1 Meml[37] 227 4-8-8 46 TomEaves 5 31
(J D Bethell) sn pushed along to ld: hdd 1/2-way: rdn and wknd over 1f out 25/1
20-0 8 1 1/4 Rub Of The Relic (IRE)[13] 518 5-8-7 50 (v) PaulPickard(5) 7 32
(P T Midgley) sn outpcd and bhd: nvr nrr 33/1
0-50 9 3 1/4 Royal Crest[14] 503 4-8-12 50 GregFairley 12 25
(A Crook) plld hrd and prom: rdn over 3f out: wknd over 2f out 33/1
001- 10 1 Hint Of Honey[60] 7855 4-8-8 53 DavidKenny(7) 1 26
(A G Newcombe) hld up: rdn over 3f out: sn wknd 14/1
0-00 11 3/4 Redwater River[9] 569 6-8-4 47 (b) DeanHeslop(5) 6 18
(Mrs R A Carr) hld up: a in rr: bhd fnl 3f 100/1
05-0 12 6 Where's Killoran[17] 464 5-8-1 46 oh1 LewisWalsh(7) 10 —
(E J Alston) mid-div: wknd 1/2-way: bhd fnl 3f 50/1
0-11 13 1 1/2 Isitcozimcool (IRE)[7] 591 5-9-8 60 6ex PatCosgrave 11 14
(D E Cantillon) sn prom: rdn over 3f out: hung rt and wknd over 2f out: eased ins fnl f 8/11[1]
1m 43.4s (-0.30) Going Correction -0.05s/f (Stan) 13 Ran SP% 125.7
Speed ratings (Par 101): 99,98,96,94,89 88,87,85,82,81 80,74,73
toteswingers: 1&2 £10.00, 1&3 £10.10, 2&3 £17.00 CSF £135.54 CT £1039.11 TOTE £12.80: £3.20, £3.10, £2.80; EX 134.20 TRIFECTA Not won. Place 6: £66.40 Place 5: 45.63.
Owner Mrs Claire Ellison Bred Flaxman Holdings Ltd Trained Norton, N Yorks

FOCUS
A poor contest to end the card, though a couple of these looked well handicapped beforehand. The early pace was decent, though, with three vying for the advantage until well past halfway.
Isitcozimcool(IRE) Official explanation: jockey said gelding never travelled
T/Plt: £173.30 to a £1 stake. Pool: £68,145.15. 286.99 winning tickets. T/Qpdt: £144.70 to a £1 stake. Pool: £4,262.87. 21.80 winning tickets. CR

626 MEYDAN (L-H)
Thursday, February 25

OFFICIAL GOING: All-weather - standard; turf course - good to firm

706a MEYDAN HOTEL (H'CAP) (TAPETA) 1m 3f
2:35 (2:35) (90-105,104) 3-Y-O+
£40,740 (£13,580; £6,790; £3,395; £2,037; £1,358)

RPR
1 Antinori (IRE)[21] 419 4-8-8 96 (v) AhmedAjtebi 2 104+
(Saeed Bin Suroor) settled in last: smooth prog 3f out: r.o wl to ld 55yds out 3/1[1]
2 1 1/2 Marinous (FR)[110] 7302 4-8-13 100 (t) WayneSmith 3 104
(M Al Muhairi, UAE) mid-div on rail: trckd ldr 3f out: led 1 1/2f out: hdd fnl 55yds 12/1
3 1/2 Kal Barg[6] 632 5-9-1 100 WilliamBuick 1 103
(D Selvaratnam, UAE) settled in rr: rdn 3f out: r.o wl: nrst fin 9/1
4 1 1/4 Captain Webb[7] 605 5-8-13 98 (t) PJSmullen 5 99
(E Charpy, UAE) sn led: hdd 1 1/2f out: r.o gamely 8/1
5 2 1/4 Wonder Lawn (SAF)[6] 629 7-8-11 97 ChristopheSoumillon 8 93
(M F De Kock, South Africa) bmpd s: nvr bttr than mid-div: one pce fnl 1 1/2f 7/1
6 3/4 Record Breaker (IRE)[14] 512 6-9-1 100 (b) KierenFallon 6 96
(M Johnston) a mid-div 12/1
7 1 1/4 Alcomo (BRZ)[6] 632 7-9-1 100 (t) WBlandi 4 94
(A Cintra Pereira, Brazil) in rr of mid-div: r.o fnl 1 1/2f: n.d 33/1
8 6 1/4 Red Rock Canyon (IRE)[6] 632 6-9-0 99 (t) KShea 12 83+
(M F De Kock, South Africa) settled in rr: one pce fnl 1 1/2f: n.d 9/2[2]
9 2 1/4 Bridge Of Gold (USA)[14] 512 4-9-2 104 (b) PaulHanagan 10 84+
(M A Magnusson) bmpd at s: nvr bttr than mid-div 11/2[3]
10 1/4 Galactic Star[14] 513 7-9-3 102 (t) RoystonFfrench 14 82+
(A Al Raihe, UAE) mid-div: rn wd: nvr able to chal 33/1
11 4 1/4 Wild Savannah[14] 512 8-9-1 100 (t) TadhgO'Shea 13 73+
(E Charpy, UAE) nvr bttr than mid-div 33/1
12 3 1/4 Blaze Of Fire[7] 605 4-8-8 96 KLatham 11 63+
(M F De Kock, South Africa) trckd ldr: rdn 4 1/2f out: sn wknd 25/1
13 3 3/4 Hopes And Fears (IRE)[530] 5927 5-8-10 96 TedDurcan 9 57
(M Al Muhairi, UAE) broke awkwardly: nvr bttr than mid-div 20/1
14 3 3/4 Big Bound (USA)[153] 6327 4-9-1 102 RichardMullen 7 58
(B Al Subaie, Saudi Arabia) trckd ldrs: t.k.h: rdn 4f out: sn btn 20/1
2m 16.35s (136.35)
WFA 4 from 5yo+ 2lb 14 Ran SP% 129.8
CSF: £40.89, Tricast: £305.14..
Owner Godolphin Bred Peter Harris Trained Newmarket, Suffolk

FOCUS
An ordinary handicap for the level. The pace increased early in the back straight.

NOTEBOOK
Antinori(IRE) built on the form he showed when third over 1m2f on his debut for this yard. He was set a lot to do under a confident ride, sitting last early and still having seven-plus lengths to make up 2f out, and he was kept towards the inside for an ambitious run. However, he got the gaps when needed and picked up really well to ultimately win cosily. He could run out of options at this year's carnival, unless he goes again next week, but whatever, he's clearly smart. (op 3-1 tchd 10-3)
Marinous(FR), last seen winning a 1m3f Listed race on heavy ground in France in November, fared best of those to race close to the pace and emerges with plenty of credit. He travelled strongly for a long way, only to be picked off late on, and this was a smart performance.
Kal Barg, 4lb higher than when winning over 1m2f on his penultimate outing and trying his furthest trip to date, ran on from a long way back out wide without being able to match the winner's speed.
Captain Webb, who enjoyed the run of the race in front when third over C&D the previous week, was unable to dominate this time but still ran well.
Wonder Lawn(SAF) plugged on without threatening.
Record Breaker(IRE) continues below his best.
Red Rock Canyon(IRE) found himself last of all with less than 2f to go after having to switch extremely wide for a clear run and couldn't get involved.

Bridge Of Gold(USA), tried in blinkers for the first time, was squeezed out at the start, before racing keenly when wide with no cover, so he had excuses, but he basically looks to have gone the wrong way since winning at Lingfield last month.

707a MEYDAN MUSEUM (H'CAP) (TAPETA) 6f

3:10 (3:11) (95-110,107) 3-Y-O+

£44,444 (£14,814; £7,407; £3,703; £1,851; £1,851)

RPR

1 — **Star Crowned (USA)**[7] 606 7-9-2 106....................(t) RoystonFfrench 7 111
(R Bouresly, Kuwait) *mid-div: r.o wl fnl 2f: led 110yds out: hld on bravely* **14/1**

2 hd **Good Control (AUS)**[7] 604 5-8-11 101................................ MNunes 5 105
(Pat Lee, Macau) *mid-div: trckd ldrs 2f out: r.o wl fnl f* **10/1**

3 ¾ **Alo Pura**[21] 416 6-8-10 100..(e) WilliamBuick 2 102
(D Selvaratnam, UAE) *racd in rr: r.o wl fnl 1 1/2f: nrst fin* **10/1**

4 shd **Rileyskeepingfaith**[7] 604 4-8-10 100.............................(v) AlanMunro 9 102
(M R Channon) *mid-div: r.o wl fnl 1 1/2f: nrst fin* **16/1**

5 ½ **Escape Route (USA)**[14] 511 6-8-13 102..................(t) RichardMullen 8 103
(S Seemar, UAE) *mid-div: chsd ldrs and ev ch 1 1/2f out: nt qckn* **4/1**[1]

5 dht **Morgan Drive (IRE)**[14] 515 5-9-3 107........................... MircoDemuro 1 108+
(M Gasparini, Italy) *settled in rr: r.o wl fnl 1 1/2f: nrst fin* **12/1**

7 1 **So Shiny (ARG)**[20] 434 5-9-1 105...............................(t) OlivierPeslier 11 102
(J Barton, Saudi Arabia) *sn led: hdd 1 1/2f out: wknd* **4/1**[1]

8 1 **Prime Defender**[7] 606 6-9-2 106....................................... RichardHills 4 100
(B W Hills) *in rr of mid-div: nvr able to chal* **14/1**

9 ½ **Aichi (AUS)**[7] 606 5-9-3 107... AhmedAjtebi 3 100
(Saeed Bin Suroor) *settled in rr: nvr nr to chal* **8/1**[3]

10 5½ **Barney McGrew (IRE)**[159] 6091 7-9-3 107........................ PhillipMakin 6 83
(M Dods) *nvr able to chal* **13/2**[2]

11 ¼ **Instant Recall (IRE)**[14] 515 9-8-13 102...................(v) FrankieDettori 12 79
(M Al Muhairi, UAE) *trckd ldrs: wknd 1 1/2f out* **14/1**

12 8 **Conquest (IRE)**[385] 418 6-9-1 105.................................. WayneSmith 10 57
(M Al Muhairi, UAE) *bmpd s: in rr of mid-div: chsd ldrs 2 1/2f out: one pce fnl 1 1/2f out* **25/1**

1m 11.98s (71.98) **12** Ran SP% **120.0**
CSF: £148.84, Tricast: £1500.82.
Owner Bouresly Racing Syndicate **Bred** Carl Rosen Associates **Trained** Kuwait

FOCUS
Most of these looked poorly handicapped and this wasn't a strong race. The pace was decent early on.

NOTEBOOK
Star Crowned(USA) was one of those who didn't seem to have much at all in hand off his current sort of mark, but he was a game winner on his fifth carnival start this year.
Good Control(AUS) raced with his usual enthusiasm, before staying on towards the inside to have every chance.
Alo Pura, set too much to do over C&D last time, again finished well under strong pressure but was never quite getting there.
Rileyskeepingfaith looked the winner when bursting through between rivals inside the final furlong, but he didn't go through with his effort. He seemed intimidated by his rivals, not least the winner, with that one's jockey's whip possibly hitting him in the face late on, although he was held at that point.
Escape Route(USA), 4lb higher than when winning over a steadily run 7f on this track last time, sweated up beforehand and got fractious in the stalls. He then never travelled in the race itself, so this wasn't a bad effort in the circumstances.
Morgan Drive(IRE), well held at Group 3 level behind War Artist over C&D on his Dubai debut, made his move wider than ideal.
So Shiny(ARG), 5lb higher than when winning over C&D on her return to Dubai, was hassled up front and seemed to get lit up, racing keenly into the straight.
Prime Defender ran a little better than he did the previous week and would have been slightly closer with a better trip.
Barney McGrew(IRE), 4lb higher than when runner-up in the Ayr Gold Cup, gave trouble at the stalls, by no means for the first time. In the race, he probably lost his chance when hampered around the final bend. (op- 6-1 tchd 13-2)

708a MEYDAN HORIZONS (H'CAP) (TAPETA) 1m 2f

3:50 (3:50) (100-111,111) 3-Y-O+

£64,814 (£21,604; £10,802; £5,401; £3,240; £2,160)

RPR

1 — **Mr Brock (SAF)**[7] 609 7-9-1 110.. KShea 4 115+
(M F De Kock, South Africa) *trckd ldr: rdn to ld 1 1/2f out: comf* **10/11**[1]

2 1¾ **Meeriss (IRE)**[14] 512 5-8-6 101.................................(t) WilliamBuick 6 103
(D Selvaratnam, UAE) *trckd ldng pair: ev ch 2 1/2f out: one pce fnl f* **7/1**[3]

3 2¼ **Hattan (IRE)**[6] 630 8-9-2 111...(t) WayneSmith 5 108
(M Al Muhairi, UAE) *broke awkwardly: in rr of mid-div: r.o fnl 1 1/2f: n.d* **14/1**

4 shd **Emerald Wilderness (IRE)**[14] 512 6-8-5 100........... RoystonFfrench 1 97
(R M H Cowell) *mid-div on rail: r.o wl fnl 2f: nrst fin* **16/1**

5 ½ **Eddie Jock (IRE)**[14] 513 6-8-8 104...........................(b) RichardMullen 3 99
(S Seemar, UAE) *in rr of mid-div: one pce fnl 1 1/2f* **25/1**

6 1¼ **Hunting Tower (SAF)**[7] 607 8-9-1 110............. ChristopheSoumillon 7 103
(M F De Kock, South Africa) *settled in rr: nvr able to chal* **17/2**

7 6¼ **Trois Rois (FR)**[6] 629 5-9-0 109.................................... AhmedAjtebi 2 90
(Saeed Bin Suroor) *sn led: t.k.h: kicked clr 4f out: hdd 1 1/2f out: wknd* **11/1**

8 ¼ **Re Barolo (IRE)**[14] 513 7-8-8 104................................... CSanchez 9 83
(A bin Huzaim, UAE) *mid-div: nvr able to chal* **11/2**[2]

9 2¼ **We'll Come**[14] 513 6-8-11 107... JRosales 8 82
(A bin Huzaim, UAE) *settled in rr: rdn 3f out: n.d* **14/1**

2m 5.06s (125.06) **9** Ran SP% **122.2**
CSF: £8.64, Tricast: £61.37.
Owner Mme Serge Seenyen **Bred** Mrs B D Oppenheimer **Trained** South Africa

FOCUS
An ordinary handicap, and a steady pace meant those held up were disadvantaged.

NOTEBOOK
Mr Brock(SAF), fourth behind the likes of Allybar and Crowded House in the second round of the Al Maktoum Challenge the previous week, gave that form a boost. He found this all rather straightforward, racing just off the leader before running on best in the straight. (op 6-4 tchd 10-11)
Meeriss(IRE), 1lb lower than when fourth over 1m3f on his previous start, was tried in a tongue-tie this time but he never seriously threatened the winner.
Hattan(IRE) raced out the back after starting slowly and, although nipping through towards the inside rail in the straight, he was never dangerous. (op 12-1 tchd 14-1)
Emerald Wilderness(IRE) probably would have preferred a stronger-run race, but he's not one to make too many excuses for. (op 12-1 tchd 16-1)
Eddie Jock(IRE) couldn't get involved from off the pace. (op 20-1 tchd 25-1)
Trois Rois(FR) looked a horrible ride, hanging around the bends and racing keenly in front. (op 10-1 tchd 11-1)
Re Barolo(IRE) had shaped well on his Dubai debut but this was a poor effort. (op 6-1 tchd 11-2)

709a UAE OAKS SPONSORED BY MEYDAN (FILLIES) (LISTED RACE) (TAPETA) 1m 1f 110y

4:25 (4:26) 3-Y-O

£92,592 (£30,864; £15,432; £7,716; £4,629; £3,086)

RPR

1 — **Raihana (AUS)**[14] 514 4-9-5 107......................... ChristopheSoumillon 3 111+
(M F De Kock, South Africa) *broke awkwardly: settled in rr: smooth prog to trck runner-up 1/2f out: led last 55yds* **11/4**[2]

2 1¼ **Bikini Babe (IRE)**[14] 514 3-8-9 102................................. KierenFallon 1 106
(M Johnston) *trckd ldr: led 2f out: hdd 55yds out* **5/1**[3]

3 4½ **Siyaadah**[14] 514 3-8-9 108... AhmedAjtebi 8 100+
(Saeed Bin Suroor) *settled in rr: trckd wnr 4f out: nt qckn fnl 1 1/2f* **11/8**[1]

4 1¾ **Berg Bahn (IRE)**[14] 514 3-8-9 105.. KLatham 2 94
(G M Lyons, Ire) *mid-div on rail: r.o one pce fnl 1 1/2f* **6/1**

5 ½ **Jodi (ARG)**[13] 4-9-5 85.. KShea 7 96
(M F De Kock, South Africa) *sn led: t.k.h: hdd 2f out: wknd* **40/1**

6 15 **Talenta (BRZ)**[14] 514 4-9-5 98..................................... FrankieDettori 5 68
(A Cintra Pereira, Brazil) *in rr of mid-div: nvr able to chal* **16/1**

7 2¾ **Mensajera De La Luz (CHI)**[14] 514 4-9-5 102..........(v) OlivierPeslier 6 62
(J Barton, Saudi Arabia) *trckd ldr tl 3f out: wknd* **16/1**

8 20 **Flowers In Spring (FR)**[18] 3-8-9 88............................. WilliamBuick 4 21
(D Selvaratnam, UAE) *t.k.h: plld way to dispute ld after 2f: dropped to rr 5f out* **80/1**

1m 58.71s (118.71)
WFA 3 from 4yo 21lb **8** Ran SP% **115.2**
CSF: £17.14.
Owner Sheikh Mohammed Bin Khalifa Al Maktoum **Bred** Sheikh Mohammed Bin Khalifa Al Maktoum **Trained** South Africa

FOCUS
Of the eight who lined up, six had contested the Guineas a couple of weeks earlier, and considering that didn't look a great race at the time, it's difficult to be overly enthusiastic about this contest. The pace was honest enough.

NOTEBOOK
Raihana(AUS) had been on edge in the paddock but she settled well under a hold-up ride. Her chance was compromised by racing close to an overly strong pace when fourth in the Guineas, so the switch to more patient tactics suited, and she had no problem with this longer trip, getting on top gradually. In doing so, she became only the third filly bred in the southern hemisphere to win this from ten runnings. She'll now be aimed at the UAE Derby, a race her trainer had mentioned as a likely target pre-carnival, but it will be a surprise if she's good enough to follow up. (op 10-3 tch 11-4)
Bikini Babe(IRE), a staying-on fifth in the Guineas, proved suited by this step up to her furthest trip to date. She was given every chance under a good ride, but the winner was simply the better filly.
Siyaadah looked flattered by the bare result of her Guineas win, when she benefited from being held up well off the pace, and this effort would seem to confirm that view. It's true she covered more ground than the front two when going wide into the straight this time, but she wasn't going well enough to follow that pair through and only ran on past beaten rivals. She looked a doubtful stayer on breeding and it's hard to know for sure whether she truly got the trip, but whatever, she is likely to continue to find things tough from now on.
Berg Bahn(IRE) was not sure to stay and she was below the form she showed when third in Guineas. (op 11-2 tchd 6-1)
Jodi(ARG), officially rated 85, limits the form.
Talenta(BRZ) has gone backwards since shaping well in the Guineas trial. (op 14-1 tchd 16-1)
Mensajera De La Luz(CHI) won a Grade 1 in Chile last year but she has so far shown little in Dubai.

710a MEYDAN METROPOLIS (CONDITIONS RACE) (TAPETA) 7f

5:00 (5:01) 3-Y-O+

£40,740 (£13,580; £6,790; £3,395; £2,037; £1,358)

RPR

1 — **Midshipman (USA)**[28] 338 4-9-5 113.......................(vt) FrankieDettori 6 118+
(Saeed Bin Suroor) *mid-div: smooth prog to ld 1 1/2f out: r.o wl* **4/5**[1]

2 3¼ **Asset (IRE)**[20] 437 7-9-2 110..(b) TedDurcan 11 107
(Saeed Bin Suroor) *in rr of mid-div: r.o wl fnl 1 1/2f: nrst fin* **7/1**[3]

3 1¼ **Alazeyab (USA)**[7] 610 4-9-2 100..................................(t) TadhgO'Shea 2 104
(A Al Raihe, UAE) *trckd ldr: ev ch 2f out: kpt on one pce fnl 1 1/2f* **33/1**

4 ¾ **Laa Rayb (USA)**[162] 5995 6-9-5 110................................(e) WilliamBuick 1 105
(D Selvaratnam, UAE) *in rr of mid-div: r.o wl fnl 2f: nrst fin* **8/1**

5 ¼ **Codigo De Honor (ARG)**[7] 610 6-9-5 100................. RichardMullen 5 104
(B Al Subaie, Saudi Arabia) *trckd ldr: nt qckn fnl 2f* **66/1**

6 1 **Commander Cave (USA)**[21] 412 5-9-0 98.................(t) PJSmullen 14 97
(E Charpy, UAE) *settled in rr: r.o wl fnl 1 1/2f: nvr able to chal* **33/1**

7 1¼ **Opera Comica (BRZ)**[14] 514 4-9-0 101............................ TJPereira 13 94
(P Bary, France) *sn led: hdd 2 1/2f out: wknd* **33/1**

8 1¼ **Across The Rhine (USA)**[6] 626 4-9-5 99...................... TomQueally 4 96
(A Manuel, UAE) *trckd ldr tl 2 1/2f out: wknd* **40/1**

9 4¾ **Lovelace**[6] 626 6-9-0 107... KierenFallon 3 79
(M Johnston) *trckd ldrs: one pce fnl 2 1/2f* **6/1**[2]

10 3 **Swift Gift**[21] 412 5-9-5 98... JamieSpencer 8 76
(B J Meehan) *nvr nr to chal* **8/1**

11 1 **Digital (BRZ)**[14] 510 4-8-11 101...(t) WBlandi 9 66
(A Cintra Pereira, Brazil) *settled in rr: n.d* **33/1**

12 shd **Olympic Election (BRZ)**[20] 440 5-9-11 101.... ChristopheSoumillon 12 79
(R Solanes, Brazil) *settled in rr: n.d* **33/1**

13 ¼ **Bab Al Bahrain (USA)**[6] 630 6-9-5 97...............................(t) LJurado 10 73
(R Bouresly, Kuwait) *nvr nr to chal* **66/1**

14 7½ **Almajd (IRE)**[6] 628 5-9-0 100..................................(v) RichardHills 7 49
(M Al Muhairi, UAE) *in rr of mid-div: n.d* **33/1**

1m 23.39s (83.39) **14** Ran SP% **127.6**
CSF: £6.80.
Owner Godolphin **Bred** Stonerside Stable **Trained** Newmarket, Suffolk

FOCUS
This was a decent conditions contest and they went a strong pace.

NOTEBOOK
Midshipman(USA) was too fresh when racing freely over 1m in the first round of the Al Maktoum Challenge on his return from a short break, but he proved a different proposition on this drop in both distance and grade. His supporters were entitled to be concerned when he was forced to swing very wide around the turn into the straight, when still at least 3l off the lead, but the good gallop up front was in his favour and he produced an impressive finishing effort to reel in inferior rivals. Considering the ground he covered, this was no mean feat. The 2008 Breeders' Cup Juvenile winner is a class act when in this sort of form and he'll now be aimed at the Godolphin Mile on World Cup night. He will surely go there with a live chance, although he will need to relax to give himself a chance of seeing his race out. (op 10-11 tchd 8-11 and 4-5)

Asset(IRE) ran his usual sort of race, travelling well a fair way off the pace but not finding enough to win. In fairness, though, his successful stablemate is quite simply a superior horse.
Alazeyab(USA) surprised in finishing so close considering he raced up with the strong pace early on and was under pressure around the turn into the straight to hold his position. This was an improvement on his two previous carnival efforts.
Laa Rayb(USA) tried eye-shields for the first time instead of the blinkers he had on when last seen for Mark Johnston. He had a toughish task with the front two at the weights and could only find the one pace after briefly being denied a clear run around 300m out. (op 15-2 tchd 8-1)
Codigo De Honor(ARG), a Grade 1 winner in South America, was always prominent and improved on the form he showed first time up at the carnival.
Lovelace was disappointing.
Swift Gift had a bit too much to find.

711a BALANCHINE SPONSORED BY MEYDAN (FILLIES (GROUP 3) (TURF) 1m 1f

5:45 (5:45) 3-Y-0+

£74,074 (£24,691; £12,345; £6,172; £3,703; £2,469)

			RPR
1		**Deem (IRE)**[48] 5-8-13 112 ow2 .... OlivierPeslier 4	112
		(J Barton, Saudi Arabia) *settled in rr: r.o wl fnl 2f: led cl home* 6/1[3]	
2	shd	**Aspectoflove (IRE)**[20] 439 4-8-11 105 .... FrankieDettori 1	110
		(Saeed Bin Suroor) *in rr of mid-div: chsd ldrs 2 1/2f out: led over 1f out: hdd cl home* 5/4[1]	
3	1 ½	**Zirconeum (SAF)**[20] 439 5-9-3 107 .... KShea 5	113
		(M F De Kock, South Africa) *mid-div: trckd ldr 3 1/2f out: led 2f out: hdd over 1f out: r.o wl* 6/4[2]	
4	4 ½	**Purple Sage (IRE)**[20] 439 4-8-11 102 .... KierenFallon 6	97
		(F Nass, Bahrain) *set stdy pce: qcknd 5f out: hdd 2f out: one pce after* 16/1	
5	½	**Rockette (FR)**[20] 441 5-8-11 95 .... PJSmullen 3	96
		(E J O'Neill, France) *mid-div on rail: nvr able to chal* 50/1	
6	¾	**Ahla Wasahl**[20] 439 4-8-11 104 .... AhmedAjtebi 2	94
		(D M Simcock) *settled in rr: nvr nr to chal* 16/1	
7	¼	**Vattene (IRE)**[20] 439 5-8-11 100 .... MircoDemuro 8	94
		(M Gasparini, Italy) *s.i.s: chsd ldrs for 7 1/2f: wknd* 40/1	
8	1 ½	**Estrela Anki (BRZ)**[21] 418 5-9-3 99 .... TJPereira 7	96
		(P Bary, France) *trckd ldr tl 3 1/2f out: sn wknd* 66/1	

1m 53.93s (113.93) **8** Ran SP% **116.4**
CSF: 14.21.
Owner Prince Sultan Mohammed Saud Al Kabeer **Bred** Prince Sultan Al Kabeer **Trained** Saudi Arabia

FOCUS
Not a bad Group 3, but the race lacked strength in depth and they went a steady pace. Six of the eight runners had contested the Cape Verdi earlier in the carnival.

NOTEBOOK
Deem(IRE) landed the Cape Verdi on her Dubai debut last year (before running fifth in this race), and she repeated the trick of going in first time up at the carnival. She has won on the dirt in Saudi Arabia, where her trainer is usually based, but it's no surprise the grass suits so well considering her turf pedigree. This was a noteworthy performance considering she was held up in a slowly-run race and it would be no surprise were to she improve on last year's seventh placing in the Sheema Classic. (op 5-1 tchd 6-1)
Aspectoflove(IRE)'s jockey gave the impression he felt he had the race in safe keeping late on, once his filly had readily mastered Zirconeum, taking two looks over his left shoulder at that rival near the line, and putting his whip down after the first glance. However, the winner was looming on the other side, and it appeared that Dettori only noticed that rival's threat when looking over to the right just strides from the post, at which point he became slightly more vigorous, but was still caught. At no point did Dettori stop riding, and it's debatable whether his filly would have won under further pressure from the whip, but it obviously didn't look good and supporters of the favourite will understandably be less than pleased. Whatever the case, Aspectoflove, who ran second in the Cape Verdi, had been given a good ride until that point, looking the winner when taking over halfway up the straight, and this was another smart performance in defeat.
Zirconeum(SAF) had excuses when failing to justify her lofty reputation in the Cape Verdi (trip was short of her optimum, received a bump in the straight and was short of peak fitness), but while it's true not everything went her way this time either, this was slightly disappointing. She was conceding 6lb to all bar one of her rivals, and there is no doubt she needs more of a stamina test, but the first two went past her pretty easily and it remains to be seen whether she's quite as good as some people thought. (op 13-8 tchd 6-4)
Purple Sage(IRE), a staying on fifth in the Cape Verdi, raced a little keenly under restraint in front, setting a modest pace, and she was outclassed when the going got serious. (op 14-1 tchd 16-1)
Rockette(FR) failed to prove herself up to this level. (op 50-1 tchd 40-1)
Ahla Wasahl could make no impression after being held up and swinging wide into the straight.

712a DRC GOLD CUP SPONSORED BY MEYDAN (CONDITIONS RACE) (TURF) 2m

6:20 (6:20) 3-Y-0+

£64,814 (£21,604; £10,802; £5,401; £3,240; £2,160)

			RPR
1		**Sabotage (UAE)**[21] 418 4-8-8 100 .... MickaelBarzalona 4	111
		(Saeed Bin Suroor) *trckd ldng duo: rdn 3f out: r.o wl to ld fnl 110yds* 20/1	
2	¼	**Age Of Reason (UAE)**[21] 418 5-9-0 110 .... FrankieDettori 3	111
		(Saeed Bin Suroor) *trckd ldr: led 2 1/2f out: r.o wl: hdd fnl 100yds* 11/4[2]	
3	1 ¾	**Pompeyano (IRE)**[14] 516 5-9-0 104 .... (t) RichardMullen 12	109
		(S Seemar, UAE) *mid-div: n.m.r 2 1/2f out: r.o wl fnl 1 1/2f: nrst fin* 12/1	
4	¼	**Whispering Gallery**[28] 337 4-8-8 115 .... TedDurcan 7	109
		(Saeed Bin Suroor) *sn led: sst stdy pce: qcknd 5f out: hdd 2 1/2f out: r.o same pce* 6/4[1]	
5	1 ¾	**Topclas (FR)**[14] 516 4-8-8 107 .... WJSupple 11	107
		(M bin Shafya, UAE) *mid-div: trckd ldr 7f out: chal 2f out: no ex* 20/1	
6	½	**Titurel (GER)**[7] 605 5-9-0 105 .... OlivierPeslier 9	106
		(Manfred Hofer, Germany) *in rr of mid-div: n.m.r 2 1/2f out: r.o same pce* 9/1[3]	
7	shd	**Frozen Fire (GER)**[14] 516 5-9-0 111 .... (t) ChristopheSoumillon 2	106
		(M F De Kock, South Africa) *s.i.s: settled in rr: rdn 4f out: nvr nr to chal* 14/1	
8	shd	**Montaff**[21] 418 4-8-8 102 .... AlanMunro 5	106
		(M R Channon) *mid-div on rail: one pce fnl 2f* 20/1	
9	1 ¾	**Mojave Moon**[21] 418 4-8-8 108 .... (v) AhmedAjtebi 8	104
		(Saeed Bin Suroor) *s.i.s: settled in rr: nvr nr to chal* 9/1[3]	
10	¼	**Princess Taylor**[28] 335 6-8-9 98 .... (t) PJSmullen 1	98
		(D K Weld, Ire) *nvr bttr than mid-div* 25/1	
11	8 ½	**Lion Sands**[14] 512 6-9-0 100 .... JRosales 10	93
		(A bin Huzaim, UAE) *nvr bttr than mid-div* 33/1	
12	6 ½	**Lignon's Hero (BRZ)**[14] 512 5-9-0 100 .... (t) KierenFallon 6	85
		(A Cintra Pereira, Brazil) *mid-div: t.k.h: n.d* 33/1	

3m 29.42s (209.42)
WFA 4 from 5yo+ 6lb **12** Ran SP% **125.0**
CSF: 73.12.
Owner Sheikh Hamdan Bin Mohammed Al Maktoum **Bred** Darley **Trained** Newmarket, Suffolk

FOCUS
The second running of this staying contest and it was a competitive race, but somewhat predictably, the pace was modest. As a result, it paid to race handy.

NOTEBOOK
Sabotage(UAE) improved significantly on the form he showed when fourth in the 1m6f trial on his first start for this yard. He was worse off at the weights this time, but was always well placed and stayed on best after being switched early in the straight under a stylish ride. While his stamina was not properly tested, he looked strong at the line.
Age Of Reason(UAE) won the 1m6f handicap trial for this off 106 and had a decent chance at these weights. He got a good lead off Whispering Gallery, but simply couldn't resist the winner's challenge. His stamina for this trip, the furthest he had tried to date, was not severely tested. (op 5-2 tchd 11-4)
Pompeyano(IRE) seemed again to be left with too much to do after being held up, but it's possible his effort was beginning to flatten out at the line. He would have preferred a stronger pace.
Whispering Gallery, an impressive winner over 1m2f on the Tapeta off a mark of 107 on his Dubai debut, was trying this trip for the first time, but he's bred to stay. He was allowed a soft lead for much of the way, but Topclas pressured him down the back straight and he couldn't offer much when it mattered. (op 15-8 tchd 6-4)
Titurel(GER) ◆ is considerably better than he showed. The steady pace was no use to him, as he was keen early and left with a lot to do, but he was just beginning to pick up when denied a clear run towards the inside rail late on. He would probably have been in the first three with a better trip, and may even have won had the race been run to suit. (op 8-1 tchd 9-1)
Frozen Fire(GER) plugged on without ever looking that keen to get involved. (op 12-1 tchd 14-1)
Montaff went for the same gap as Titurel and was himself short of room.

713a IMAX CUP (H'CAP) (TAPETA) 1m

6:55 (6:56) (95-110,110) 3-Y-0+

£44,444 (£14,814; £7,407; £3,703; £2,222; £1,481)

			RPR
1		**Lucky Find (SAF)**[14] 517 7-9-1 105 .... KShea 1	108
		(M F De Kock, South Africa) *in rr of mid-div: smooth prog 2f out: led 1 1/2f out: r.o wl* 8/1	
2	¼	**Vesuve (IRE)**[159] 6132 4-9-4 108 .... WayneSmith 8	110
		(M Al Muhairi, UAE) *trckd ldrs: ev ch 1 1/2f out: nt qckn fnl f* 28/1	
3	2 ¼	**Le Drakkar (AUS)**[7] 607 5-9-6 110 .... CSanchez 14	108
		(A bin Huzaim, UAE) *sn led: hdd 1 1/2f out: r.o same pce* 40/1	
4	¾	**Jet Express (SAF)**[7] 609 8-9-3 107 .... RoystonFfrench 10	103
		(A Al Raihe, UAE) *trckd ldrs: r.o same pce fnl 1 1/2f* 20/1	
5	¼	**Swop (IRE)**[14] 511 7-8-13 102 .... KierenFallon 13	100+
		(L M Cumani) *in rr of mid-div: r.o fnl 2f: nrst fin* 10/3[2]	
6	¼	**Derbaas (USA)**[7] 610 4-8-13 102 .... RichardHills 2	98+
		(A Al Raihe, UAE) *nvr able to chal* 20/1	
7	½	**Fourpenny Lane**[6] 630 5-8-13 102 .... PJSmullen 11	97
		(Ms Joanna Morgan, Ire) *nvr able to chal* 16/1	
8	1 ¼	**Khor Dubai (IRE)**[21] 413 4-8-13 102 .... JRosales 5	94
		(A bin Huzaim, UAE) *nvr bttr than mid-div* 25/1	
9	nse	**Stoic (IRE)**[6] 630 4-9-1 105 .... RyanMoore 12	96
		(J Noseda) *nvr bttr than mid-div* 9/4[1]	
10	¼	**Raise Your Heart (IRE)**[20] 436 7-9-3 107 .... (e) KLatham 3	97
		(Ms Joanna Morgan, Ire) *racd in rr: nvr nr to chal* 25/1	
11	1	**Sovereign Remedy (USA)**[21] 412 4-8-13 102 .... FrankieDettori 6	91
		(Saeed Bin Suroor) *mid-div on rail: ev ch 1 1/2f out: nt qckn* 4/1[3]	
12	1 ½	**Liberation (IRE)**[21] 412 4-8-10 100 .... AhmedAjtebi 9	85
		(Saeed Bin Suroor) *trckd ldr: hrd rdn 3 1/2f out: wknd* 25/1	
13	1	**Emmrooz**[7] 607 5-9-1 105 .... WilliamBuick 7	88
		(D Selvaratnam, UAE) *mid-div: n.m.r 2f out: nt rcvr* 16/1	
14	11	**Masaalek**[21] 412 5-8-9 99 .... (v) TadhgO'Shea 4	57
		(Doug Watson, UAE) *s.i.s: n.d* 40/1	

1m 36.7s (96.70) **14** Ran SP% **126.1**
CSF: 222.37 Tricast: 8216.04.Placepot: £48.20 to a £1 stake. Pool: £12,149.45. 183.65 winning tickets. Quadpot: £2.00 to a £1 stake. Pool: £687.20. 252.60 winning tickets..
Owner Sh Ahmed bin Mohd bin Khalifa Al Maktoum **Bred** Oldlands Stud **Trained** South Africa

FOCUS
A good, competitive handicap.

NOTEBOOK
Lucky Find(SAF), off the same mark as when runner-up over 1m1f on turf last time, didn't mind the return to synthetics and gained his third carnival success, adding to his two Nad Al Sheba victories from 2008. Incidentally, he was the fifth winner to come out of the 7f handicap won by Leahurst here on January 28, but there probably isn't much more for him in Dubai this year considering he's no longer Group class.
Vesuve(IRE), last year's French Derby seventh, joined these connections for 150,000 euros in October. He was always well positioned and this was an encouraging first start for his new trainer, especially as he ought to benefit from a step back up in trip.
Le Drakkar(AUS) didn't shape too badly on his return from a long absence and first start since joining these connections over 7f the previous week and he stepped up on that effort, despite racing a bit freely in front. He was pretty decent when trained in South Africa, winning their Guineas and placing in the Derby, and there could yet be more to come. (op 33-1 tchd 40-1)
Jet Express(SAF) appreciated the drop in trip and ran well.
Swop(IRE) shaped as though a return to this trip would suit, and had won third time up at the carnival last year, but he had no chance after enduring a wide trip throughout from stall 13.
Stoic(IRE), 8lb higher than when an unlucky second over 7f on his Dubai debut, had no hope after being pitched wide the whole way around from a double-figure stall.
Sovereign Remedy(USA), who had burst through the stalls and covered about a lap of the track loose ahead of his intended start in a similar race the previous week, was nicely positioned for most of the way, tucked way towards the inside in about mid-division, but he found nothing for pressure. He returned having bled from both nostrils. (op 9-2 tchd 4-1)
Emmrooz didn't have much room in the straight and is better than he showed.

699 SOUTHWELL (L-H)

Friday, February 26

OFFICIAL GOING: Standard

Wind: Fresh behind Weather: Raining

714 BET PREMIER LEAGUE FOOTBALL - BETDAQ CLAIMING STKS 1m 6f (F)

2:00 (2:00) (Class 6) 4-Y-O+ **£1,774** (£523) **Stalls** Low

Form RPR

4522 1 **Resplendent Ace (IRE)**[8] [600] 6-9-2 70 MichaelStainton(3) 3 77
(P Howling) *trckd ldr: pushed along 3f out: effrt and cl up 2f out: rdn and styd best to ld ins fnl f* **9/4**[2]

411 2 ¾ **Doubnov (FR)**[8] [600] 7-9-6 75 SteveDrowne 1 77
(Ian Williams) *set stdy pce: qcknd 3f out: pushed along and jnd wl over 1f out: sn rdn: drvn: edgd lft and hdd ins fnl f: no ex* **4/11**[1]

3m 5.15s (-3.15) **Going Correction** -0.225s/f (Stan) **2** Ran SP% **104.1**

Speed ratings (Par 101): **100,99**

Tote Swingers: 1&2 £4.20, 1&3 £11.60, 2&3 £4.90 TOTE £2.50.

Owner Paul Howling **Bred** Newlands House Stud **Trained** Newmarket, Suffolk

FOCUS

The time was surprisingly quick for a match race, being just over two seconds above standard.

715 BET SIX NATIONS RUGBY - BETDAQ H'CAP 1m (F)

2:30 (2:31) (Class 5) (0-70,70) 4-Y-O+ **£2,456** (£725; £362) **Stalls** Low

Form RPR

1325 1 **General Tufto**[15] [509] 5-8-13 68 (b) MartinLane(3) 8 81
(C Smith) *hld up: smooth hdwy 3f out: swtchd lft over 2f out and sn cl up: led over 1f: sn rdn clr and styd on strly* **9/1**

P411 2 4½ **Castle Myth (USA)**[16] [491] 4-8-5 60 (be) BarryMcHugh(3) 4 63
(B Ellison) *hld up in tch: hdwy 3f out: chsd ldrs 2f out: rdn and ev ch over 1f out: drvn and one pce ent fnl f* **13/2**[3]

66-2 3 1½ **Tomintoul Star**[14] [518] 4-8-4 56 (p) AndrewElliott 11 56
(Mrs R A Carr) *chsd ldrs: hdwy on wd outside to ld over 3f out: rdn along over 2f out: drvn and hdd over 1f out: kpt on same pce* **7/1**

1-10 4 1¼ **Heathyards Junior**[36] [255] 4-9-3 69 ShaneKelly 6 66
(A J McCabe) *trckd ldrs: hdwy on outer 1/2-way: rdn to chse ldrs over 2f out and ch tl drvn and wknd over 1f out* **14/1**

-005 5 3 **Fandango Boy**[13] [543] 9-9-3 69 StevieDonohoe 9 59
(Ian Williams) *hld up: hdwy over 2f out: rdn and kpt on appr fnl f: nvr nr ldrs* **25/1**

-023 6 4 **Hypnotic Gaze (IRE)**[13] [543] 4-8-11 68 (p) KierenFox(5) 5 50
(J Mackie) *t.k.h: cl up: rdn along wl over 2f out and grad wknd* **3/1**[1]

05-0 7 1¼ **Provost**[31] [298] 6-8-1 58 (b[1]) JamesSullivan(5) 10 37
(M W Easterby) *dwlt: a in rr* **6/1**[2]

-304 8 2 **Sadeek**[13] [543] 6-8-10 62 GregFairley 7 36
(B Smart) *slt ld: rdn along and hdd over 3f out: drvn over 2f out and sn wknd* **7/1**

101- 9 4½ **Cheers For Thea (IRE)**[151] [6349] 5-9-4 70 (bt) DavidNolan 1 35
(T D Easterby) *trckd ldrs on inner: hdwy and cl up 1/2-way: rdn along over 2f out and sn wknd* **22/1**

0066 10 4 **Hilbre Court (USA)**[18] [466] 5-9-3 69 (p) GrahamGibbons 3 25
(B P J Baugh) *prom: rdn along over 3f out and sn wknd* **9/1**

00-6 11 2¼ **Bookiebasher Babe (IRE)**[22] [398] 5-9-1 67 FrannyNorton 2 18
(M Quinn) *midfield: rdn along to join ldrs after 1f: rdn along 1/2-way and sn wknd* **33/1**

1m 41.47s (-2.23) **Going Correction** -0.225s/f (Stan) **11** Ran SP% **115.4**

Speed ratings (Par 103): **102,97,96,94,91 87,86,84,80,76 73**

Tote Swingers: 1&2 £1.80, 1&3 £2.80, 2&3 £5.10 CSF £63.62 CT £445.45 TOTE £12.90: £2.20, £1.70, £2.40; EX 58.50 Trifecta £294.80 Part won. Pool: £398.48 - 0.84 winning units..

Owner Phil Martin & Trev Sleath **Bred** Hascombe And Valiant Studs **Trained** Temple Bruer, Lincs

FOCUS

A modest handicap run at a decent pace.

716 BET SUPER LEAGUE - BETDAQ (S) STKS 6f (F)

3:05 (3:05) (Class 6) 3-Y-O+ **£1,774** (£523; £262) **Stalls** Low

Form RPR

-423 1 **Not My Choice (IRE)**[24] [378] 5-9-8 62 (t) AdamKirby 5 68
(J Balding) *rdn along in early stages and a cl up: effrt to ld over 2f out: rdn wl over 1f out: drvn and edgd lft ins fnl f: kpt on* **1/1**[1]

4262 2 1¼ **Bo McGinty (IRE)**[8] [601] 9-9-8 60 (v) FrederikTylicki 3 65
(R A Fahey) *trckd ldrs: hdwy over 2f out: rdn to chse wnr over 1f out: drvn and n.m.r on inner ins fnl f: sn one pce* **9/4**[2]

200- 3 6 **Sea Land (FR)**[132] [6861] 6-9-5 60 (be[1]) BarryMcHugh(3) 4 45
(B Ellison) *in tch: hdwy over 2f out and sn rdn: drvn over 1f out: kpt on same pce* **13/2**[3]

6-60 4 shd **Miss Thippawan (USA)**[8] [601] 4-8-12 39 JamesSullivan(5) 8 39
(J Hetherton) *hld up towards rr: hdwy wl over 2f out: swtchd rt to wd outside wl over 1f out and sn rdn: drvn and kpt on ins fnl f: nrst fin* **66/1**

-600 5 6 **Handsinthemist (IRE)**[10] [569] 5-8-12 47 PaulPickard(5) 12 20
(P T Midgley) *a in rr* **33/1**

-006 6 2¾ **Owed**[22] [403] 8-9-1 42 (tp) MatthewLawson(7) 11 16
(R Bastiman) *chsd ldrs: rdn along 1/2-way: sn wknd* **50/1**

212/ 7 hd **Dendor**[571] [4683] 6-9-8 52 (p) DanielTudhope 1 16
(A Dickman) *cl up on inner: led after 1f: rdn along and hdd over 2f out: sn edgd lft and wknd* **9/1**

0-60 8 2½ **Tournedos (IRE)**[11] [562] 8-9-8 73 (p) AndrewElliott 10 8
(Mrs R A Carr) *led 1f: cl up tl rdn along over 3f out and sn wknd* **20/1**

1m 15.0s (-1.50) **Going Correction** -0.225s/f (Stan) **8** Ran SP% **115.3**

Speed ratings (Par 101): **101,99,91,91,83 79,79,75**

Tote Swingers: 1&2 £1.80, 1&3 £2.80, 2&3 £5.10 CSF £3.30 TOTE £2.10: £1.10, £1.10, £2.10; EX 4.00 Trifecta £18.20 Pool: £669.38 - 27.11 winning units..No bid for the winner.

Owner D Kilpatrick W McKay **Bred** Alan Dargan **Trained** Scrooby, Notts

FOCUS

This seller was weakened by five non-runners and it was a moderate contest.

Tournedos(IRE) Official explanation: trainer said gelding had a breathing problem

717 GOLF AND RACING AT SOUTHWELL H'CAP 1m (F)

3:40 (3:42) (Class 6) (0-60,59) 3-Y-O **£1,774** (£523; £262) **Stalls** Low

Form RPR

005- 1 **Dazakhee**[107] [7335] 3-8-13 54 TonyCulhane 10 62+
(P T Midgley) *hld up in rr: hdwy 3f out: chsd ldrs 2f out: rdn to ld and edgd lft appr fnl f: drvn out* **16/1**

00-2 2 2¼ **Moonbalej**[9] [589] 3-9-3 58 AdrianNicholls 8 61
(M Johnston) *trckd ldrs: hdwy 3f out: effrt 2f out and sn cl: rdn to ld 1 1/2f out: sn put hd in air and hung bdly lft: hdd appr fnl f and one pce* **7/4**[1]

463- 3 2 **Princess Mandy (IRE)**[90] [7584] 3-8-13 54 DarryllHolland 1 53+
(K A Ryan) *prom: rdn along: n.m.r and outpcd wl over 2f out: rallied u.p appr fnl f: sn drvn and kpt on towards fin* **3/1**[2]

00-2 4 ½ **Magic Millie (IRE)**[8] [597] 3-8-4 50 JamesSullivan(5) 9 48
(J Hetherton) *in tch hdwy on outer over 2f out: sn rdn and kpt on same pce appr fnl f* **7/1**

00-3 5 nk **Rescent**[10] [574] 3-8-1 47 PaulPickard(5) 5 44
(Mrs R A Carr) *led: rdn along 3f out: hdd 2f out and sn drvn: grad wknd* **16/1**

436- 6 nse **As Brave As You (IRE)**[88] [7597] 3-8-7 51 BarryMcHugh(3) 6 48
(B Ellison) *in tch: hdwy over 3f out: rdn along over 2f out: kpt on same pce* **4/1**[3]

005- 7 1½ **Bitter Honey**[77] [7713] 3-8-13 59 KierenFox(5) 2 52
(E J Alston) *cl up: rdn to ld briefly 2f out: sn drvn: hdd 1 1/2f out: n.m.r and wknd appr fnl f* **12/1**

500- 8 11 **Moonlight Blaze**[130] [6901] 3-9-2 57 PJMcDonald 7 26
(C W Fairhurst) *cl up: rdn along 3f out and sn wknd* **33/1**

1m 43.22s (-0.48) **Going Correction** -0.225s/f (Stan) **8** Ran SP% **116.3**

Speed ratings (Par 95): **93,90,88,88,87 87,86,75**

Tote Swingers: 1&2 £6.50, 1&3 £8.60, 2&3 £2.30 CSF £45.33 CT £113.64 TOTE £17.90: £3.90, £1.10, £1.70; EX 58.90 Trifecta £307.80 Pool: £736.39 - 1.77 winning units..

Owner Darren & Annaley Yates **Bred** M Kerr-Dineen **Trained** Westow, N Yorks

FOCUS

A moderate 3-y-o handicap run in a time 1.75 seconds slower than the earlier Class 5 handicap for older horses.

718 SOUTHWELL-RACECOURSE.CO.UK MAIDEN STKS 1m 3f (F)

4:15 (4:16) (Class 5) 3-Y-O+ **£2,456** (£725; £362) **Stalls** Low

Form RPR

3-32 1 **Hydrant**[18] [468] 4-9-7 70 BillyCray(5) 8 70+
(P Salmon) *t.k.h: chsd ldr: pushed along and sltly outpcd 2f out: swtchd rt and rdn over 1f out: drvn ins fnl f and styd on wl to ld nr line* **11/4**[2]

0 2 shd **Hunters Belt (IRE)**[18] [468] 6-10-0 0 DanielTudhope 2 70
(N Wilson) *hld up in tch: hdwy over 3f out: rdn to ld over 1f out: drvn and hdd nr fin* **8/1**

2 3 1 **Wrongwayround (IRE)**[10] [570] 4-9-12 0 PJMcDonald 6 68
(G A Swinbank) *trckd ldrs: hdwy to chse ldr over 4f out: rdn to ld 2f out: drvn and hdd over 1f out: kpt on u.p ins fnl f* **7/4**[1]

0-5 4 6 **Sacco D'Oro**[18] [468] 4-9-2 0 DeanHeslop(5) 3 54+
(M Mullineaux) *in tch on inner: rdn along over 3f out: plugged on same pce u.p fnl 2f* **33/1**

/6 5 3 **Decibel**[11] [563] 6-10-0 0 FrannyNorton 7 53
(K A Ryan) *t.k.h: led: rdn along over 3f out: hdd and drvn 2f out: grad wknd* **16/1**

6 1¼ **Major Pop (USA)** 3-8-4 0 ow2 BarryMcHugh(3) 4 49
(R A Fahey) *dwlt: hdwy to chse ldng pair after 3f: rdn along 4f out: wknd wl over 2f out* **3/1**[3]

6- 7 6 **Light The City (IRE)**[162] [6033] 3-8-0 0 DeclanCannon(5) 5 37
(Mrs R A Carr) *in tch: rdn along over 3f out: sn wknd* **40/1**

0-00 8 20 **Doctor Of Music (IRE)**[15] [503] 4-9-5 47 (v) AdamCarter(7) 1 7
(B Smart) *sn rdn along: a in rr: bhd fnl 4f* **80/1**

2m 26.59s (-1.41) **Going Correction** -0.225s/f (Stan)

WFA 3 from 4yo 23lb 4 from 6yo 2lb **8** Ran SP% **111.6**

Speed ratings (Par 103): **96,95,95,90,88 87,83,68**

Tote Swingers: 1&2 £3.90, 1&3 £2.00, 2&3 £4.10 CSF £23.25 TOTE £3.10: £1.10, £2.90, £1.30; EX 20.10 Trifecta £56.90 Pool: £978.05 - 12.70 winning units..

Owner The Waterboys **Bred** Lord Halifax **Trained** Kirk Deighton, West Yorks

■ Stewards' Enquiry : Billy Cray three-day ban: careless riding (Mar 12-13,16)

Adam Carter one-day ban: used whip when out of contention (Mar 12)

FOCUS

An ordinary maiden run at a modest pace. The time was 1.76 seconds slower than the following handicap won by the rated 70-rated Bosamcliff.

719 PLAY GOLF AT SOUTHWELL GOLF CLUB H'CAP 1m 3f (F)

4:45 (4:45) (Class 5) (0-70,70) 4-Y-O+ **£2,456** (£725; £362) **Stalls** Low

Form RPR

3022 1 **Bosamcliff (IRE)**[12] [400] 5-9-1 70 AndrewHeffernan(5) 3 79
(P D Evans) *hld up in rr: stdy hdwy 5f out: chsd ldr 4f out: rdn 2f out: sn chal and drvn to ld ent fnl f: kpt on* **7/4**[1]

-411 2 1½ **My Mate Mal**[14] [521] 6-9-0 67 BarryMcHugh(3) 6 74
(B Ellison) *led and sn clr: pushed along 3f out: rdn 2f out: drvn and hdd ent fnl f: kpt on same pce* **7/2**[3]

-364 3 3 **Vertigo On Course (IRE)**[13] [546] 5-8-11 61 TonyHamilton 4 63
(R A Fahey) *t.k.h: chsd ldng pair: rdn along and outpcd 4f out: drvn and kpt on fnl 2f* **5/2**[2]

21-4 4 8 **Lava Steps (USA)**[50] [76] 4-9-2 68 TonyCulhane 1 57
(P T Midgley) *trckd ldrs: rdn along and outpcd 5f out: hdwy u.p 3f out: sn drvn and btn* **9/2**

605- 5 39 **Mister Fizzbomb (IRE)**[86] [6236] 7-9-0 64 (v) GrahamGibbons 2 —
(J S Wainwright) *chsd ldr: rdn along over 4f out: drvn and wknd over 3f out* **25/1**

2m 24.83s (-3.17) **Going Correction** -0.225s/f (Stan)

WFA 4 from 5yo+ 2lb **5** Ran SP% **109.2**

Speed ratings (Par 103): **102,100,98,92,—**

CSF £8.03 TOTE £2.50: £1.30, £2.90; EX 7.40.

Owner W Clifford **Bred** London Thoroughbred Services Ltd **Trained** Pandy, Monmouths

FOCUS

A modest handicap run in a time 1.76 seconds quicker than the earlier maiden won by the 70-rated Hydrant.

720 SOUTHWELL RACECOURSE FOR CONFERENCES H'CAP 1m 4f (F)

5:15 (5:15) (Class 6) (0-60,60) 4-Y-O+ **£1,774** (£523; £262) **Stalls** Low

Form RPR

600- 1 **Bivouac (UAE)**[86] [5953] 6-9-0 53 DarryllHolland 1 64
(G A Swinbank) *trckd ldrs gng wl: smooth hdwy 3f out: led 2f out: rdn over 1f out: styd on wl* **8/1**[3]

2-51 2 4½ **Jackie Kiely**[17] [470] 9-9-3 56 (tp) JackMitchell 7 60
(R Brotherton) *hld up in rr: stdy hdwy 5f out: rdn to chse wnr wl over 1f out: sn drvn and no imp fnl f* **7/2**[2]

6353 3 3¾ **Mister Frosty (IRE)**[19] [457] 4-8-2 51 (p) CharlotteKerton(7) 12 50
(G Prodromou) *chsd ldrs: hdwy to ld after 4f: rdn along over 3f out: drvn 2f out: kpt on same pce u.p* **10/1**

12-2 **4** hd **Merrion Tiger (IRE)**[24] 376 5-9-0 **60**.......... IanBrennan(7) 10 59+
(A G Foster) *in rr and sn rdn along: hdwy over 3f out: drvn 2f out: kpt on appr fnl f: nrst fin* **13/8**[1]

303- **5** 2 1/4 **Golden Future**[28] 6845 7-8-11 **50**.......... (t) TonyHamilton 13 45
(P D Niven) *prom: chsd ldr 1/2-way: rdn along 3f out: drvn 2f out and sn one pce* **12/1**

00-0 **6** 7 **Lean Burn (USA)**[18] 467 4-8-12 **54**.......... (t) TravisBlock 9 38
(A G Newcombe) *towards rr: hdwy 4f out: rdn 3f out: drvn 2f out and sn no imp* **40/1**

1623 **7** 1/2 **Highland River**[10] 575 4-9-3 **59**.......... LeeVickers 2 43
(A Sadik) *trckd ldrs on inner: rdn along and outpcd 4f out: no ch after* **12/1**

6/00 **8** 3 3/4 **Mandalay Prince**[22] 410 6-8-11 **50**.......... TonyCulhane 11 28
(W J Musson) *towards rr: stdy hdwy on outer 1/2-way: in tch 4f out: rdn along over 3f out and sn outpcd* **28/1**

03-0 **9** 1 3/4 **Reigning In Rio (IRE)**[15] 503 4-8-1 **48**.......... PaulPickard(5) 14 23
(P T Midgley) *hld up: a towards rr* **33/1**

0-42 **10** shd **Unconsoled**[8] 598 4-8-0 **47**.......... (v) JamesSullivan(5) 3 22
(J Hetherton) *hld up: hdwy and in tch 4f out: rdn along 3f out and sn btn* **20/1**

/53- **11** 8 **Royal Max (IRE)**[104] 3511 4-8-3 **50**.......... DeclanCannon(5) 6 13
(M C Chapman) *chsd ldrs: rdn along over 5f out and sn wknd* **16/1**

000/ **12** 3 1/4 **Surdoue**[517] 3131 10-8-7 **46** oh1.......... FrannyNorton 8 —
(M J Scudamore) *led 4f: cl up tl rdn along over 3f out and wknd wl over 2f out* **50/1**

00-0 **13** 24 **Iceman George**[19] 457 6-9-4 **57**.......... PatCosgrave 4 —
(G C Bravery) *chsd ldrs: rdn along 1/2-way: sn wknd* **25/1**

2m 36.83s (-4.17) **Going Correction** -0.225s/f (Stan)
WFA 4 from 5yo+ 3lb **13** Ran SP% **121.2**
Speed ratings (Par 101): **104,101,98,98,96 92,91,89,88,88 82,80,64**
Tote Swingers: 1&2 £6.10, 1&3 £8.10, 2&3 £6.70 CSF £34.05 CT £293.01 TOTE £8.90: £3.20, £2.10, £1.90; EX 40.10 Trifecta £208.60 Part won. Pool: £282.02 - 0.66 winning units. Place 6: £38.14 Place 5: £7.55.
Owner Mrs J M Penney **Bred** Darley **Trained** Melsonby, N Yorks

FOCUS
A moderate handicap run at a decent pace.
T/Plt: £13.60 to a £1 stake. Pool: £75,431.11. 4,020.31 winning tickets. T/Qpdt: £1.80 to a £1 stake. Pool: £7,380.94. 2,894.12 winning tickets. JR

661 WOLVERHAMPTON (A.W) (L-H)
Friday, February 26

OFFICIAL GOING: Standard
Wind: Moderate behind Weather: Fine

721 SPONSOR A RACE BY CALLING 01902 390000 APPRENTICE H'CAP 5f 216y(P)
5:10 (5:11) (Class 7) (0-50,54) 4-Y-O+ **£1,706** (£503; £252) **Stalls** Low

Form RPR

1 **Saddlers Bend (IRE)**[221] 4160 4-8-7 **45**.......... NathanAlison(3) 8 65+
(George Baker) *hld up and bhd: hdwy on ins over 2f out: plld out ent st: led ins fnl f: eased cl home* **9/2**[2]

4-54 **2** 2 3/4 **Royal Acclamation (IRE)**[15] 495 5-8-13 **48**.......... (p) DavidKenny 4 57
(H J Evans) *s.i.s: sn mid-div: hdwy over 2f out: ev ch ins fnl f: rdn and nt qckn* **13/2**[3]

-222 **3** 3 1/2 **Tag Team (IRE)**[22] 403 9-8-10 **50**.......... (p) MatthewCosham(5) 2 48
(John A Harris) *led: hdd over 3f out: led over 2f out: rdn wl over 1f out: hdd ins fnl f: one pce* **85/40**[1]

636 **4** nk **Berrymead**[14] 530 5-8-13 **48**.......... LauraPike 1 45
(Miss A Stokell) *hld up in tch on ins: ev ch 1f out: rdn and one pce* **8/1**

-500 **5** 4 **Outer Hebrides**[11] 567 9-9-5 **54** ow4.......... (v) ShaneRyan 6 39
(J M Bradley) *hld up in mid-div: pushed along wl over 1f out: no hdwy* **16/1**

-532 **6** 3/4 **Davids Mark**[15] 495 10-8-9 **49**.......... (p) DannyBrock(5) 11 32
(J R Jenkins) *s.i.s: outpcd: hdwy on ins wl over 1f out: rdn and no further prog fnl f* **8/1**

00-0 **7** nk **Latin Connection (IRE)**[28] 349 4-8-10 **45**.......... (p) SoniaEaton 9 27
(Lee Smyth, Ire) *outpcd: pushed along over 2f out: nvr nr ldrs* **40/1**

030- **8** 1 1/4 **Red Dagger (IRE)**[163] 5998 4-8-12 **47**.......... RichardRowe 5 25
(R J Price) *hld up and bhd: rdn wl over 1f out: nvr nr ldrs* **10/1**

0445 **9** 3/4 **Mister Incredible**[15] 495 7-8-11 **46**.......... (b) RyanClark 12 22
(J M Bradley) *chsd ldr: led over 3f out tl over 2f out: sn rdn: wknd jst over 1f out* **16/1**

4000 **10** 3 **Battimoore (IRE)**[8] 591 4-8-12 **47**.......... (p) LeeTopliss 13 14
(I W McInnes) *s.i.s: outpcd* **18/1**

0560 **11** 1/2 **Romantic Verse**[1] 691 5-8-3 **45**.......... (t[1]) LeonnaMayor(7) 10 10
(R A Harris) *prom tl wknd over 2f out* **22/1**

000- **12** 3 3/4 **Wavertree Princess (IRE)**[114] 7241 5-8-7 **49**.......... JulieCumine(7) 3 3
(A J Lidderdale) *prom tl wknd over 2f out* **25/1**

1m 14.19s (-0.81) **Going Correction** -0.075s/f (Stan) **12** Ran SP% **122.5**
Speed ratings (Par 97): **102,98,93,93,87 86,86,84,83,79 79,74**
Tote Swingers: 1&2 £8.40, 1&3 £4.90, 2&3 £4.20 CSF £34.46 CT £82.51 TOTE £5.80: £1.90, £1.90, £1.30; EX 63.70.
Owner Mrs Christine Cone **Bred** J F Tuthill **Trained** Moreton Morrell, Warwicks
■ Stewards' Enquiry : Leonna Mayor one-day ban: did not keep straight from stalls (Mar 12)

FOCUS
There was 5mm of overnight rain and the track was worked up to a depth of 4 inches prior to being reinstated. A very moderate handicap featuring a host of infrequent winners and inconsistent sorts. The gallop was sound throughout (time just over a second outside Racing Post standard) and the winner raced in the centre in the straight. This was a surprisingly strong race for the grade and the winner was value for extra.
Saddlers Bend(IRE) ◆ Official explanation: trainer's representative said, regarding the running and riding, that it was the filly's first appearence from Mr Baker's yard, and appeared to have been well suited by the polytrack and running over a reduced distance of 6f.

722 BETDAQ THE BETTING EXCHANGE H'CAP 5f 216y(P)
5:40 (5:40) (Class 3) (0-95,90) 4-Y-O+ **£6,938** (£2,076; £1,038; £519; £258) **Stalls** Low

Form RPR

06-6 **1** **Thebes**[14] 528 5-9-2 **88**.......... GregFairley 9 99
(M Johnston) *chsd ldr: led 2f out: rdn over 1f out: r.o* **11/2**[3]

5433 **2** nk **Onceaponatime (IRE)**[10] 573 5-8-4 **76** oh1.......... LukeMorris 5 86
(M D Squance) *hld up in tch: rdn over 1f out: chal ins fnl f: kpt on* **6/1**

P0-5 **3** 1/2 **Dubai Dynamo**[17] 474 5-9-2 **88**.......... AndrewElliott 1 96
(Mrs R A Carr) *s.i.s: hld up towards rr: hdwy on ins wl over 1f out: kpt on ins fnl f* **40/1**

52-1 **4** nk **New Leyf (IRE)**[15] 502 4-8-5 **77**.......... HayleyTurner 7 84
(J R Gask) *hld up towards rr: rdn over 1f out: hdwy fnl f: kpt on* **11/4**[2]

0-12 **5** 1 1/4 **Rocket Rob (IRE)**[30] 307 4-8-13 **85**.......... SebSanders 2 88
(M Botti) *a.p: rdn over 1f out: no ex wl ins fnl f* **9/4**[1]

0260 **6** 1/2 **Flowing Cape (IRE)**[14] 528 5-9-4 **90**.......... (tp) AdamKirby 3 92
(R Hollinshead) *hld up in mid-div: rdn and hdwy over 1f out: fdd ins fnl f* **8/1**

-033 **7** 1 **Methaaly (IRE)**[2] 679 7-7-12 **77** oh1 ow1.......... (be) MatthewLawson(7) 4 76
(M Mullineaux) *s.i.s: hld up in rr: c wd st: rdn wl over 1f out: n.d* **16/1**

0141 **8** 6 **Billy Red**[13] 535 6-9-1 **87**.......... (b) FergusSweeney 8 66
(J R Jenkins) *led: hdd 2f out: rdn over 1f out: wknd fnl f* **14/1**

1m 13.68s (-1.32) **Going Correction** -0.075s/f (Stan) **8** Ran SP% **113.2**
Speed ratings (Par 107): **105,104,103,103,101 101,99,91**
Tote Swingers: 1&2 £6.80, 1&3 £13.20, 2&3 £20.00 CSF £37.39 CT £1190.64 TOTE £5.10: £1.80, £1.30, £8.60; EX 37.10.
Owner Sheikh Hamdan Bin Mohammed Al Maktoum **Bred** Whitsbury Manor Stud And Mrs M E Slade **Trained** Middleham Moor, N Yorks

FOCUS
A useful handicap and a decent gallop returned a time half a second quicker than the opening handicap. The winner raced in the centre in the straight and is rated back to his best form here.

NOTEBOOK
Thebes has a patchy record since his last win but he returned to something like his best and, although edging both ways under pressure, stuck on in tenacious fashion to notch his second win over course and distance. He seems to like it here but will find life tougher after reassessment, especially against the more progressive types. (op 7-1 tchd 5-1)
Onceaponatime(IRE) is a reliable yardstick who got a good tow into the race and ran right up to his best. He is equally effective on Fibresand and should continue to go well either over this trip or over 7f. (op 13-2 tchd 11-2)
Dubai Dynamo ◆, who won four times from 6f to 1m for Paul Cole, fared much better than on his first run for Ruth Carr returned to Polytrack. He has little margin for error from this mark but should be suited by the return to 7f and appeals as the type to win a race for his current yard.
New Leyf(IRE) may not be entirely straightforward as he tends to race with the choke out and carry his head high but he's a fair sprinter who ran creditably in a race where the leaders weren't stopping in the straight. There are definitely more races to be won with him. (tchd 5-2 and 3-1)
Rocket Rob(IRE) had the run of the race but failed to reproduce his last two efforts returned to this longer trip and the slight interference he suffered late on made no difference to the result. Although he has won over this trip all his best form is over the minimum trip. (tchd 5-2)
Flowing Cape(IRE), again sporting the cheekpieces, bettered the form of his two previous starts but was again below the level he showed over course and distance in mid-January. He will have to show a bit more before he is a solid betting proposition. (op 12-1 tchd 7-1)

723 BET IN RUNNING - BETDAQ H'CAP (DIV I) 5f 20y(P)
6:10 (6:11) (Class 6) (0-65,65) 4-Y-O+ **£1,433** (£423; £211) **Stalls** Low

Form RPR

4210 **1** **Steel City Boy (IRE)**[12] 555 7-8-10 **60**.......... MartinLane(3) 4 72
(D Shaw) *s.i.s: hld up in rr: hdwy on ins wl over 1f out: edgd rt and led wl ins fnl f: r.o* **8/1**

00-3 **2** 1 3/4 **Sir Geoffrey (IRE)**[12] 556 4-9-4 **65**.......... FrederikTylicki 1 71
(J A Glover) *led early: a.p: rdn wl over 1f out: ev ch wl ins fnl f: nt qckn* **5/1**[2]

06-0 **3** 1/2 **Wreningham**[45] 137 5-8-5 **55**.......... WilliamCarson(3) 9 59
(S C Williams) *sn led: rdn over 1f out: hdd wl ins fnl f: no ex* **13/2**[3]

0440 **4** 1/2 **First Order**[8] 601 9-8-8 **60**.......... (v) AnnStokell(5) 3 62
(Miss A Stokell) *hld up towards rr: hdwy wl over 1f out: sn rdn: kpt on one pce ins fnl f* **12/1**

00-0 **5** 1 1/4 **Lucky Art (USA)**[21] 431 4-9-1 **62**.......... AndrewElliott 5 60
(Mrs R A Carr) *hld up in mid-div: hdwy over 2f out: rdn and one pce fnl f* **16/1**

0-01 **6** 1 1/2 **Spic 'n Span**[17] 472 5-9-3 **64**.......... (b) LiamJones 2 56
(R A Harris) *hld up in tch: pushed along and wnt 2nd over 2f out: wknd wl ins fnl f* **9/2**[1]

003- **7** 1 1/2 **Leftontheshelf (IRE)**[120] 7136 4-9-4 **65**.......... AdamKirby 7 52
(Miss T Spearing) *hld up towards rr: pushed along over 2f out: rdn over 1f out: nvr trbld ldrs* **13/2**[3]

4026 **8** shd **Divertimenti (IRE)**[11] 568 6-8-7 **54**.......... (b) LukeMorris 8 41
(S R Bowring) *hld up towards rr: rdn over 2f out: n.d* **14/1**

-454 **9** 2 1/2 **Bookiesindex Boy**[8] 601 6-9-3 **64**.......... (b) StephenCraine 6 42
(J R Jenkins) *hld up in mid-div: wknd 2f out* **5/1**[2]

300- **10** 3/4 **Dodaa (USA)**[66] 7839 7-8-5 **52**.......... SaleemGolam 10 27
(N Wilson) *prom tl wknd wl over 1f out* **22/1**

00-5 **11** 11 **Miacarla**[14] 532 7-8-4 **51** oh6.......... FrankieMcDonald 11 —
(H A McWilliams) *hld up in mid-div: pushed along over 2f out: sn bhd* **80/1**

61.57 secs (-0.73) **Going Correction** -0.075s/f (Stan) **11** Ran SP% **115.1**
Speed ratings (Par 101): **102,99,98,97,95 93,90,90,86,85 67**
Tote Swingers: 1&2 £8.30, 1&3 £9.70, 2&3 £8.00 CSF £46.70 CT £282.52 TOTE £8.80: £3.00, £1.80, £2.30; EX 23.20.
Owner J Medley **Bred** Mrs A B McDonnell **Trained** Sproxton, Leics

FOCUS
Division one of a modest handicap and one run at a good gallop throughout. The whole field swung wide into the straight, enabling the winner (who edged into the centre late on) to make ground on the inside of the bunch. The form is rated around the second to fourth.

724 BET MULTIPLES - BETDAQ CLASSIFIED CLAIMING STKS 1m 4f 50y(P)
6:40 (6:41) (Class 5) 4-Y-O+ **£2,456** (£725; £362) **Stalls** Low

Form RPR

-131 **1** **Sedgwick**[8] 598 8-8-12 65.......... StevieDonohoe 2 70+
(Ian Williams) *hld up towards rr: stdy hdwy over 3f out: led over 1f out: sn rdn: r.o* **6/4**[1]

2/0- **2** 1/2 **Drizzi (IRE)**[66] 7842 9-8-12 57.......... SaleemGolam 4 69+
(J Pearce) *hld up: hdwy on ins wl over 1f out: rdn and kpt on ins fnl f* **12/1**

2641 **3** 4 1/2 **Magnitude**[7] 611 5-8-11 60.......... (t) LiamJones 8 60
(R A Harris) *chsd ldr: pushed along over 2f out: ev ch over 1f out: wknd ins fnl f* **15/8**[2]

60-4 **4** 4 **New England**[19] 457 8-8-11 54.......... LukeMorris 1 54
(N J Vaughan) *prom tl rdn and wknd over 1f out* **6/1**[3]

-404 **5** 1 **Alf Tupper**[18] 467 7-8-3 60.......... LeeTopliss(7) 6 51
(Lee Smyth, Ire) *hld up in tch: wknd over 2f out* **16/1**

/000 **6** hd **Solarias Quest**[30] 309 8-8-9 59.......... ShaneKelly 5 50
(W M Brisbourne) *led: rdn and hdd over 1f out: wknd fnl f* **33/1**

00/0 **7** 10 **Key Partners (IRE)**[17] 470 9-8-8 50.......... KevinGhunowa 3 34
(R Curtis) *hld up in rr: rdn and struggling over 2f out* **66/1**

2m 43.03s (1.93) **Going Correction** -0.075s/f (Stan) **7** Ran SP% **107.1**
Speed ratings (Par 103): **90,89,86,84,83 83,76**
CSF £17.67 TOTE £2.40: £1.90, £4.40; EX 18.40.
Owner A L R Morton **Bred** G And Mrs Middlebrook **Trained** Portway, Worcs

FOCUS
A modest claimer in which a steady gallop to the home straight means this bare form is not entirely reliable, although it does appear to make sense. The winner was another to race in the centre and the first two pulled clear.
Alf Tupper Official explanation: jockey said gelding hung left and stopped very quickly

725 BET SIX NATIONS RUGBY - BETDAQ H'CAP — 1m 1f 103y(P)
7:10 (7:10) (Class 4) (0-85,85) 4-Y-0+ — **£4,533** (£1,348; £674; £336) **Stalls** Low

Form — RPR
-600 **1** **Stand Guard**[29] 324 6-8-12 **84** ..... AndrewHeffernan(5) 5 — 93
(P Howling) *mde all: hrd rdn over 1f out: drvn out* **5/1**[3]
1511 **2** ½ **Formidable Guest**[11] 565 6-8-5 **72** ..... SaleemGolam 3 — 80+
(J Pearce) *hld up: pushed along and hdwy over 1f out: chsd wnr ins fnl f: rdn and kpt on* **6/4**[1]
5-51 **3** 2½ **Ella Woodcock (IRE)**[13] 543 6-7-13 **71** oh1 ..... KierenFox(5) 2 — 74
(E J Alston) *a.p: chsd wnr over 1f out tl ins fnl f: one pce* **7/2**[2]
1356 **4** *shd* **Follow The Flag (IRE)**[22] 405 6-8-12 **79** ..... (p) FrederikTylicki 6 — 82
(A J McCabe) *hld up last: pushed along over 2f out: rdn wl over 1f out: styd on wl towards fin: nvr nrr* **12/1**
0-0 **5** 1½ **Sand Tiger (IRE)**[18] 466 4-8-6 **80** ..... LeeTopliss(7) 1 — 80
(R A Fahey) *hld up: pushed along over 2f out: n.d* **20/1**
0-34 **6** ½ **Just Bond (IRE)**[22] 405 8-9-3 **84** ..... PJMcDonald 4 — 83
(G R Oldroyd) *t.k.h: prom: rdn and wknd ins fnl f* **9/1**
1-65 **7** 6 **Scamperdale**[22] 408 8-9-4 **85** ..... GrahamGibbons 8 — 73
(B P J Baugh) *prom: chsd wnr over 6f out: rdn over 2f out: lost 2nd wl over 1f out: sn wknd* **8/1**

1m 59.9s (-1.80) **Going Correction** -0.075s/f (Stan) — 7 Ran SP% **112.5**
Speed ratings (Par 105): **105,104,102,102,100 100,95**
Tote Swingers: 1&2 £2.60, 1&3 £5.10, 2&3 £1.60 CSF £12.51 CT £28.52 TOTE £7.20: £2.40, £1.30; EX 13.40.
Owner The Circle Bloodstock I Limited **Bred** Juddmonte Farms Ltd **Trained** Newmarket, Suffolk

FOCUS
Mainly exposed performers in a fair handicap. The gallop was a steady one though and the way things unfolded suited the winner more than the runner-up. Both came down the centre in the straight. The winner was back to something like his best and the second remains in good form.

726 BETDAQ ON 0870 178 1221 H'CAP — 5f 20y(P)
7:40 (7:41) (Class 7) (0-50,49) 4-Y-0+ — **£1,364** (£403; £201) **Stalls** Low

Form — RPR
1-00 **1** **Mr Funshine**[36] 243 5-9-0 **49** ..... MartinLane(3) 3 — 56+
(D Shaw) *hld up in mid-div: hdwy on ins over 2f out: led jst ins fnl f: pushed out* **12/1**
3000 **2** 1¼ **Sonhador**[15] 495 4-9-2 **48** ..... SaleemGolam 4 — 51
(G Prodromou) *hld up and bhd: hdwy on ins wl over 1f out: rdn and kpt on ins fnl f* **8/1**
0030 **3** *shd* **Bertbrand**[10] 569 5-9-2 **48** ..... (v) LiamKeniry 1 — 50
(I W McInnes) *led: hdd over 2f out: led wl over 1f out: rdn and hdd jst ins fnl f: kpt on* **5/1**[2]
002 **4** 1¼ **Taboor (IRE)**[16] 477 12-8-13 **45** ..... GrahamGibbons 6 — 43
(R M H Cowell) *hld up in tch: pushed along over 2f out: rdn over 1f out: one pce ins fnl f* **9/1**
05- **5** 1 **Grand Minstrel (IRE)**[198] 4894 6-8-6 **45** ..... MatthewLawson(7) 9 — 39
(P J Lally, Ire) *s.i.s: sn prom: led over 2f out: rdn and hdd wl over 2f out: one pce ins fnl f* **12/1**
054 **6** *hd* **Sir Loin**[16] 477 9-8-8 **45** ..... (v) KierenFox(5) 13 — 38
(P Burgoyne) *racd keenly: a.p: rdn and one pce ins fnl f* **22/1**
4630 **7** *hd* **Cocktail Party (IRE)**[11] 561 4-9-2 **48** ..... (v) ShaneKelly 11 — 41
(J W Unett) *hld up in tch: rdn and one pce ins fnl f* **12/1**
56-0 **8** 2¼ **Our Fugitive (IRE)**[13] 541 8-9-1 **47** ..... (p) HayleyTurner 8 — 32
(C Gordon) *chsd ldr 2f: wknd wl over 1f out* **16/1**
6-22 **9** ½ **Admiral Bond (IRE)**[35] 271 5-9-3 **49** ..... (p) PJMcDonald 12 — 32
(G R Oldroyd) *bhd fnl 2f* **6/1**[3]
000- **10** *hd* **Walragnek**[184] 5345 6-9-3 **49** ..... (b) LukeMorris 5 — 31
(J G M O'Shea) *s.i.s: a in rr* **22/1**
3453 **11** *nse* **Truly Divine**[2] 687 5-8-13 **45** ..... (b[1]) DavidProbert 7 — 27
(C A Dwyer) *s.i.s: a bhd* **3/1**[1]

62.38 secs (0.08) **Going Correction** -0.075s/f (Stan) — 11 Ran SP% **114.7**
Speed ratings (Par 97): **96,94,93,91,90 89,89,86,85,84 84**
Tote Swingers: 1&2 £22.80, 1&3 £15.60, 2&3 £4.60 CSF £102.05 CT £420.38 TOTE £16.80: £2.90, £3.00, £2.00; EX 90.40.
Owner Unity Farm Holiday Centre Ltd **Bred** Unity Farm Holiday Centre Ltd **Trained** Sproxton, Leics

FOCUS
A very moderate handicap run at a decent gallop, in which the two of the market leaders disappointed. The pace was sound and the winner raced centre to far side in the straight. Low draws dominated.

727 BET IN RUNNING - BETDAQ H'CAP (DIV II) — 5f 20y(P)
8:10 (8:10) (Class 6) (0-65,65) 4-Y-0+ — **£1,433** (£423; £211) **Stalls** Low

Form — RPR
206- **1** **Ridley Didley (IRE)**[252] 3111 5-8-3 **55** ..... PaulPickard(5) 2 — 65
(N Wilson) *led after 1f: rdn fnl f: r.o* **15/2**
5105 **2** 1¼ **Interchoice Star**[11] 562 5-8-13 **60** ..... (p) JerryO'Dwyer 11 — 66+
(R Hollinshead) *hld up in rr: hdwy jst over 1f out: r.o wl ins fnl f: nt rch wnr* **12/1**
2121 **3** ½ **Monte Major (IRE)**[14] 525 9-8-10 **64** ..... (v) SeanPalmer(7) 9 — 68
(D Shaw) *hld up towards rr: hdwy 2f out: sn rdn: kpt on ins fnl f* **9/2**[2]
5-62 **4** 1¼ **Love You Louis**[12] 555 4-9-3 **64** ..... StephenCraine 3 — 64
(J R Jenkins) *a.p: pushed along and chsd wnr over 2f out: rdn over 1f out: no imp: lost 2nd and no ex towards fin* **5/2**[1]
-303 **5** 1¼ **Decider (USA)**[18] 462 7-9-1 **62** ..... (p) LiamJones 7 — 57
(R A Harris) *hld up in mid-div: hdwy over 2f out: rdn and no imp fnl f* **13/2**
005- **6** *nse* **Rabbit Fighter (IRE)**[133] 6825 6-8-9 **59** ..... MartinLane(3) 5 — 54+
(D Shaw) *s.i.s: hld up in rr: hdwy on ins over 2f out: no further prog fnl f* **16/1**
40-3 **7** 2 **Across The Sands**[11] 561 4-8-5 **52** ..... (b) FrankieMcDonald 6 — 40
(C N Kellett) *prom: rdn over 1f out: wknd ins fnl f* **10/1**
-562 **8** ½ **Monsieur Reynard**[14] 525 5-8-8 **55** ..... DavidProbert 10 — 41
(J M Bradley) *bhd fnl 2f* **5/1**[3]
0-00 **9** 10 **Town House**[16] 477 8-7-11 **51** oh6 ..... DannyBrock(7) 8 — 1
(B P J Baugh) *led 1f: wknd over 2f out* **66/1**

61.85 secs (-0.45) **Going Correction** -0.075s/f (Stan) — 9 Ran SP% **112.7**
Speed ratings (Par 101): **100,98,97,95,93 93,89,89,73**
Tote Swingers: 1&2 £12.10, 1&3 £9.20, 2&3 £7.10 CSF £89.89 CT £451.45 TOTE £10.00: £2.90, £2.70, £1.40; EX 100.40.
Owner Feenan & Tobin **Bred** Peter Molony **Trained** Sandhutton, N Yorks

FOCUS
A modest handicap run at a decent gallop throughout. the winner raced close to the inside rail all the way round.
Across The Sands Official explanation: jockey said gelding hung left

728 BET PREMIER LEAGUE FOOTBALL - BETDAQ MAIDEN STKS — 1m 141y(P)
8:40 (8:41) (Class 5) 3-Y-O — **£2,456** (£725; £362) **Stalls** Low

Form — RPR
32-6 **1** **Muwalla**[7] 617 3-9-3 82 ..... (t) SebSanders 1 — 82+
(C E Brittain) *mde all: rdn clr wl over 1f out: eased cl home* **5/6**[1]
0-3 **2** 7 **Dane Cottage**[13] 545 3-8-12 0 ..... LukeMorris 4 — 61
(Miss Gay Kelleway) *hld up in tch: rdn to chse wnr 2f out: no imp* **12/1**
3 8 **Dubai Moonlight** 3-8-12 0 ..... ShaneKelly 5 — 45
(Jane Chapple-Hyam) *chsd wnr tl rdn 2f out: wknd over 1f out* **11/4**[2]
000- **4** *hd* **Sweet Mirasol (IRE)**[130] 6901 3-8-12 48 ..... AdamKirby 3 — 44
(Miss M E Rowland) *hld up in tch: rdn and wknd over 2f out* **80/1**
5 52 **Musical Mark** 3-9-3 0 ..... JerryO'Dwyer 2 — —
(M Botti) *s.s: sn pushed along in rr: eased whn no ch over 2f out* **9/2**[3]

1m 50.0s (-0.50) **Going Correction** -0.075s/f (Stan) — 5 Ran SP% **108.3**
Speed ratings (Par 97): **99,92,85,85,39**
CSF £11.38 TOTE £1.70: £1.10, £2.90; EX 7.50 Place 6: £118.07 Place 5: £81.33 .
Owner Saeed Manana **Bred** S P Burke **Trained** Newmarket, Suffolk

FOCUS
An uncompetitive maiden and one weakened further with the newcomers (both single-figure odds) both disappointing. The pace was only fair and the winner came down the centre in the straight. The form makes sense.
Musical Mark Official explanation: jockey said gelding ran green and hung left
T/Plt: £305.20 to a £1 stake. Pool: £82,263.10. 196.75 winning tickets. T/Qpdt: £60.90 to a £1 stake. Pool: £11,110.64. 134.82 winning tickets. KH

729 - 733a (Foreign Racing) - See Raceform Interactive

683 LINGFIELD (L-H)
Saturday, February 27

OFFICIAL GOING: Standard
Wind: Moderate across Weather: Overcast

734 BET IN RUNNING - BETDAQ MAIDEN STKS — 1m 4f (P)
2:10 (2:15) (Class 5) 3-Y-O — **£2,456** (£725; £362) **Stalls** Low

Form — RPR
32 **1** **Atlantic Tiger (IRE)**[8] 618 3-9-3 0 ..... JoeFanning 2 — 69+
(M Johnston) *mde all: set mod pce tl jnd and qcknd over 4f out: pushed along 2f out: rdn clr appr fnl f: comf* **4/6**[1]
2-42 **2** 3½ **Christmas Coming**[17] 484 3-9-3 70 ..... KierenFallon 3 — 63+
(D R C Elsworth) *t.k.h early off mod pce: drvn and styd on to chse wnr wl over 1f out: sn no ch and one pce ins fnl f* **13/8**[2]
53 **3** 2 **Pascalina**[28] 356 3-8-12 0 ..... ChrisCatlin 1 — 54
(J Akehurst) *in rr but in tch: pushed along and one pce over 2f out: styd on fr over 1f out to take 3rd wl ins fnl f but nvr a threat to ldng duo* **25/1**[3]
5 **4** ½ **Mister Pleau (USA)**[8] 618 3-9-3 0 ..... RobertWinston 4 — 58?
(J R Best) *chsd ldr off mod pce: chal whn pce qcknd over 4f out and stl upsides whn rdn over 2f out: lost 2nd wl over 1f out and styd on same pce ins fnl f* **40/1**
0- **5** *shd* **Tallulah Mai**[85] 7622 3-8-12 0 ..... SaleemGolam 5 — 53
(Matthew Salaman) *in rr but in tch: pushed along over 2f out: kpt on fr over 1f out but nvr a threat* **50/1**

2m 35.39s (2.39) **Going Correction** 0.0s/f (Stan) — 5 Ran SP% **106.3**
Speed ratings (Par 97): **92,89,88,88,87**
CSF £1.77 TOTE £1.50: £1.10, £1.10; EX 1.90.
Owner Atlantic Racing Limited **Bred** Darley **Trained** Middleham Moor, N Yorks

FOCUS
A modest maiden and a two-horse race according to the market. The early pace was steady and it didn't pick up until around 4f from home.

735 TONY "KAZY" ED ORCHARD H'CAP — 1m 5f (P)
2:40 (2:45) (Class 5) (0-70,73) 4-Y-0+ — **£2,456** (£725; £362) **Stalls** Low

Form — RPR
211 **1** **Spruce (USA)**[7] 636 4-9-7 **73** ..... JimCrowley 1 — 85+
(Miss J Feilden) *racd in 2nd tl drvn to ld over 2f out: pushed clr over 1f out: easily* **4/9**[1]
4-50 **2** 2½ **Mustajed**[22] 426 9-9-2 **67** ..... (b) JamesMillman(3) 2 — 74
(B R Millman) *disp 3rd fr 1/2-way: pushed along and outpcd 3f out: styd on fr over 1f out: edgd rt and chsd wnr ins fnl f but nvr gng pce of wnr* **16/1**
-333 **3** *nk* **Quince (IRE)**[17] 488 7-9-2 **64** ..... (v) SaleemGolam 6 — 70
(J Pearce) *stdd s and hld up in rr: pushed along and checked bnd into st styd on up centre crse to take 3rd fnl f: clsng on 2nd nr fin but no ch w wnr* **16/1**
235- **4** 7 **Sir Liam (USA)**[25] 871 6-8-8 **56** ..... JoeFanning 4 — 52
(Tim Vaughan) *led tl hdd over 2f out: sn no ch w wnr: wknd fnl f* **11/2**[2]
651- **5** ¾ **Sitwell**[18] 6758 4-8-11 **63** ..... (b[1]) HayleyTurner 5 — 58
(A King) *disp 3rd 1/2-way and disp 2nd over 3f out tl over 2f out: sn no ch w wnr and wknd appr fnl f* **13/2**[3]

2m 46.97s (0.97) **Going Correction** 0.0s/f (Stan)
WFA 4 from 6yo+ 4lb — 5 Ran SP% **109.7**
Speed ratings (Par 103): **97,95,95,90,90**
CSF £8.89 TOTE £1.50: £1.10, £4.40; EX 7.40.
Owner Good Company Partnership **Bred** Juddmonte Farms Inc **Trained** Exning, Suffolk

FOCUS
A moderate staying handicap in which the punters only wanted to know one horse. The early pace was better than many long-distance races around here, though it did slow at around halfway.

736 BET SIX NATIONS RUGBY - BETDAQ H'CAP — 5f (P)
3:15 (3:20) (Class 4) (0-85,85) 4-Y-0+ — **£4,209** (£1,252; £625; £312) **Stalls** High

Form — RPR
0342 **1** **Glamorous Spirit (IRE)**[10] 578 4-9-4 **85** ..... ChrisCatlin 7 — 95
(R A Harris) *mde all: rdn whn chal appr fnl f: sn asserted and styd on strly ins fnl f* **4/1**[2]
3054 **2** 1¾ **Peak District (IRE)**[21] 446 6-9-2 **83** ..... (t) KierenFallon 4 — 87
(K A Ryan) *chsd ldrs: sltly hmpd over 3f out: rdn 2f out: styd on fnl f to take 2nd nr fin but no imp on wnr* **15/8**[1]
04-0 **3** *nk* **Stolt (IRE)**[44] 172 6-8-11 **78** ..... DarryllHolland 2 — 81
(N Wilson) *sn chsng wnr: edgd rt over 3f out: rdn to chal appr fnl f: sn outpcd ins fnl f and lost 2nd nr fin* **15/2**

13-0 **4** *1* **Step It Up (IRE)**[31] 307 6-8-9 **76**.................................. StephenCraine 8 75
(J R Boyle) *in rr: pushed along and styd on fr over 1f out: kpt on cl home but nvr gng pce to get into contention* **11/2**[3]

1046 **5** *¾* **Thoughtsofstardom**[8] 616 7-7-11 **71** oh3................ LeonnaMayor(7) 5 67
(P S McEntee) *in rr but in tch: shkn up and hdwy appr fnl f: kpt on ins fnl f but nvr gng pce to get into contention* **33/1**

0513 **6** *1* **Colorus (IRE)**[15] 520 7-8-2 **74**...................................(p) PaulPickard(5) 6 67
(W J H Ratcliffe) *chsd ldrs: rdn over 2f out: wknd over 1f out* **16/1**

-410 **7** *2¾* **Even Bolder**[22] 431 7-8-4 **76**... KierenFox(5) 3 59
(E A Wheeler) *in rr: sme prog on ins wl over 1f out: nvr on terms and wknd ins fnl f: bled* **4/1**[2]

57.74 secs (-1.06) **Going Correction** 0.0s/f (Stan) **7** Ran SP% **110.8**
Speed ratings (Par 105): **108,105,104,103,101 100,95**
toteswingers: 1&2 £1.80, 1&3 £6.00, 2&3 £3.70 CSF £11.15 CT £48.93 TOTE £4.60: £1.80, £1.70; EX 8.20 Trifecta £24.90 Pool: £749.02 - 22.23 winning units..
Owner Robert Bailey **Bred** Carlo Soria **Trained** Earlswood, Monmouths
■ Stewards' Enquiry : Leonna Mayor £290 fine: used mobile phone outside of designated area
Darryll Holland one-day ban: careless riding (Mar 13)

FOCUS
A decent sprint handicap and with several trailblazers in opposition a strong pace was a near certainty. As it turned out this race was dominated by those that raced handily and nothing else got into it.
Stolt(IRE) Official explanation: jockey said gelding was slowly away
Even Bolder Official explanation: trainer said gelding bled from the nose

737 BETDAQ.CO.UK CLEVES STKS (LISTED RACE) 6f (P)
3:50 (3:55) (Class 1) 4-Y-0+
£22,708 (£8,608; £4,308; £2,148; £1,076; £540) **Stalls** Low

Form RPR
001- **1** **Jaconet (USA)**[98] 7488 5-8-12 102...................................(b) PhillipMakin 7 111+
(T D Barron) *sn led: rdn and styd on strly over 1f out: c readily clr ins fnl f* **11/10**[1]

140- **2** *3½* **Green Manalishi**[98] 7488 9-9-0 104.................................. KierenFallon 6 102
(K A Ryan) *chsd ldrs: rdn over 2f out: styd on u.p to chse wnr ins fnl f but nvr any ch: hld on wl for 2nd cl home* **8/1**

13/ **3** *nk* **Mullionmileanhour (IRE)**[620] 3105 4-9-0 0................... SteveDrowne 4 101+
(J R Best) *hmpd sn after s: in rr: pushed along 2f out: plenty to whn mde hdwy wl over 1f out: swtchd lft and qcknd ins fnl f: fin wl to press for 2nd cl home but nvr any ch w wnr* **6/1**[3]

15-1 **4** *nk* **Arganil (USA)**[44] 163 5-9-3 108..................................... DarryllHolland 2 103
(K A Ryan) *sn chsng wnr: rdn over 2f out: no ch w wnr wl over 1f out: one pce and lost 2nd ins fnl f* **3/1**[2]

5/6- **5** *2¼* **Smarten Die (IRE)**[34] 7-9-0 0... StefanieHofer 3 93
(Frau E Mader, Germany) *wnt rt sn after s and plld hrd: towards rr: pushed along over 2f out: sme hdwy appr fnl f: nvr on terms and one pce* **20/1**

3421 **6** *2¼* **Bel Cantor**[11] 573 7-9-0 80..(p) HayleyTurner 1 86
(W J H Ratcliffe) *chsd ldrs: rdn 3f out: wknd appr fnl f* **25/1**

4054 **7** *½* **Ebraam (USA)**[15] 528 7-9-0 95..................................... RobertWinston 5 84
(S Curran) *hmpd sn after s and in rr: rdn ins fnl 3f: effrt fr 2f out: nvr gng pce to get into contention* **10/1**

000- **8** *10* **Brunelleschi**[119] 7189 7-9-0 75.......................................(b) PaulHanagan 8 52
(P L Gilligan) *broke wl: rdn and in rr fr 1/2-way* **80/1**

1m 10.12s (-1.78) **Going Correction** 0.0s/f (Stan) course record **8** Ran SP% **116.9**
Speed ratings (Par 111): **111,106,105,105,102 99,98,85**
CSF £11.19 TOTE £2.30: £1.10, £2.20, £2.40; EX 11.20 Trifecta £53.10 Pool: £1055.01 - 14.70 winning units..
Owner R G Toes **Bred** Team Block **Trained** Maunby, N Yorks

FOCUS
Probably not the strongest Listed race ever run here, but a keen betting heat with a couple well supported against the favourite. The pace was very strong, however.

NOTEBOOK
Jaconet(USA) had been successful in her last two starts over C&D, including when having three of today's rivals behind her in a similar contest in November, and has won after a layoff before so the three-month absence since then should not have been a problem. Just as when winning those two races here, she set a furious pace and, having been brought wide into the straight, had established a significant advantage on reaching the furlong pole. She seems to be getting better and better. (op 10-11 tchd 6-4 and 13-8 in a place)
Green Manalishi, not seen since running very disappointingly behind Jaconet here in November, is much better than that and proved it with a much better performance here. He could never get anywhere near the mare, but battled on gamely to snatch second. (op 15-2 tchd 7-1)
Mullionmileanhour(IRE) ◆ hadn't been seen since finishing third behind his stable-companion Flashmans Papers in the 2008 Windsor Castle. He had shown when winning impressively on his Kempton debut that he handled Polytrack, but his trainer had warned beforehand that he could have done with another couple of weeks with him. Having been held up well off the pace early, he was only given one crack with the whip but finished in great style to grab third and this was surely a precursor to better things to come. (op 10-1)
Arganil(USA), fifth behind Jaconet and Ebraam here in November, attracted market support and was always handy, but he could never get to the winner and does look best over 5f. (op 4-1 tchd 11-4)
Smarten Die(IRE), unplaced in two previous attempts at this level in this country, both over course and distance, travelled well but could not pick up and wasn't good enough.
Bel Cantor has been in decent form in handicap company on sand this winter, but he had a mountain to climb on these terms and was firmly put in his place. (op 22-1)
Ebraam(USA) had a bit to find with a few of these at the weights, but he is capable of running well at this level as he showed when chasing Jaconet home here in November. He did get messed about after a furlong and was knocked back to the rear of the field, but how much that affected his performance is hard to say. (op 11-1 tchd 9-1)

738 BETDAQ THE BETTING EXCHANGE WINTER DERBY TRIAL STKS (LISTED RACE) 1m 2f (P)
4:20 (4:28) (Class 1) 4-Y-0+
£22,708 (£8,608; £4,308; £2,148; £1,076; £540) **Stalls** Low

Form RPR
211- **1** **Gitano Hernando**[140] 6687 4-9-6 120.............................. KierenFallon 6 115+
(M Botti) *stdd towards rr: pushed along and hdwy ins fnl 3f: str run to ld over 1f out: c clr ins fnl f: in n.d whn pricked ears and idled fnl 55yds* **1/2**[1]

32-2 **2** *4½* **Suits Me**[28] 360 7-9-0 106... DarryllHolland 7 95+
(T P Tate) *led: jnd fr over 5f out: pushed along over 2f out: hdd over 1f out whn reminder and flashed tail: sn no ch w wnr but hld on for 2nd cl home* **3/1**[2]

1223 **3** *½* **Mister Green (FR)**[14] 536 4-8-13 89..............................(b) EddieAhern 4 95
(K McAuliffe) *hld up towards rr: hdwy over 1f out: styd on ins fnl f to cl on 2nd nr fin but nvr any ch w wnr* **20/1**

00-0 **4** *¾* **Yahrab (IRE)**[13] 553 5-9-0 100... SebSanders 8 93
(C E Brittain) *chsd ldr: chalng 5f out: rdn along over 2f out: styd on same pce ins fnl f* **13/2**[3]

-330 **5** *2¾* **Confidentiality (IRE)**[14] 536 6-8-9 85.......................... NickyMackay 3 83
(M Wigham) *in tch: rdn and styd on over 2f out: nvr gng pce to rch ldrs and wknd appr fnl f* **50/1**

51-0 **6** *2¼* **Victoria Sponge (IRE)**[13] 553 4-8-8 89........................... ChrisCatlin 1 79
(S C Williams) *s.i.s: rdn over 3f out: a in rr* **40/1**

/5 **7** *47* **Mesa Marauder**[30] 324 6-9-0 89...................................(p) JerryO'Dwyer 5 —
(M Botti) *chsd ldrs: rdn over 3f out: sn wknd: eased whn no ch ins fnl 2f* **66/1**

2m 1.97s (-4.63) **Going Correction** 0.0s/f (Stan) course record
WFA 4 from 5yo+ 1lb **7** Ran SP% **115.7**
Speed ratings (Par 111): **118,114,114,113,111 109,—**
toteswingers: 1&2 £1.60, 1&3 £2.30, 2&3 £2.10 CSF £2.28 TOTE £1.50: £1.30, £1.40; EX 3.00 Trifecta £8.80 Pool: £1485.30 - 123.73 winning units..
Owner Team Valor International & Gary Barber **Bred** Newsells Park Stud Ltd **Trained** Newmarket, Suffolk

FOCUS
Zanay (2000), Adiemus (2002), Parasol (2003) and Eccentric (2005) won this before going on to take the Winter Derby itself, whilst Scintillo finished third in this race before winning the big prize last year. The pace was very decent thanks to established front-runner Suits Me and the winning time was only 0.34 seconds outside the course record.

NOTEBOOK
Gitano Hernando ◆, racing for the first time since winning the Grade 1 Goodwood Stakes at Santa Anita in October, was unbeaten in two previous domestic AW outings, winning both very impressively, and he had apparently been working well on Polytrack at home. Switched off early, he had to be nudged along to take closer order approaching the home bend, but then produced a devastating turn of foot to lead a furlong out and was soon clear. He did half-hesitate well inside the last furlong and pricked his ears, but it made no difference to his superiority. This outing was in order to put him right for a tilt at the Dubai World Cup next month, as his trainer only considered him 80 per cent to 90 per cent fit for this, and it certainly served its purpose. (op 8-13 tchd 4-6)
Suits Me, placed in six of his eight starts over course and distance and narrowly beaten in this race last year, established his usual front-running role and set a decent pace, but the winner cut him down to size a furlong from home. He was clear second best in at the weights, so he has run his race. (op 10-3 tchd 4-1)
Mister Green(FR) ◆, running consistently well in handicaps on sand this winter, had plenty to find on these terms but he stayed on well over the last couple of furlongs to take third place. Hopefully he hasn't ruined his handicap mark with this effort, as there are more races to be won with him around here otherwise. (op 16-1)
Yahrab(IRE), successful at a similar level over C&D on his last visit here in November 2008, was entitled to need his recent return from nine months off. Never far away, he had every chance a furlong out but like the others was swept aside by the favourite. (op 8-1)
Confidentiality(IRE) is very effective around here in handicap company, but she had a lot to find on these terms and could never make her presence felt in this company. (op 40-1)
Victoria Sponge(IRE), well beaten when stepped up to this level on her debut for the yard at Kempton earlier this month, was trying beyond 1m for the first time but was beaten fully 3f from home. (op 33-1)

739 TRY BETDAQ FOR AN EXCHANGE H'CAP (SUPER 7 QUALIFIER) 7f (P)
4:55 (4:55) (Class 2) (0-100,104) 4-Y-0+ **£6,722** (£6,722; £1,540; £769) **Stalls** Low

Form RPR
00-1 **1** **Mahadee (IRE)**[7] 635 5-9-8 **104**....................................(b) SebSanders 5 111
(C E Brittain) *in rr but in tch: rdn ins fnl 2f: plenty to do whn u.p and hung lft over 1f out: plld rt to outside 1f out and str run ins fnl f to force dead heat* **3/1**[2]

-402 **1** *dht* **Seek The Fair Land**[11] 573 4-8-4 **86** oh2...................(p) NickyMackay 6 93
(J R Boyle) *trckd ldrs: chal fr over 3f out tl rdn to take slt ld appr fnl 2f: hld on wl u.p ins fnl f tl ct for dead heat* **4/1**[3]

0-11 **3** *nk* **Elna Bright**[27] 365 5-8-12 **94**.. LiamKeniry 2 100
(B R Johnson) *in tch: hdwy fr 2f out: rdn and str run ins fnl f to go 2nd nr fin: outpcd into 3rd by dead heater fnl strides* **7/4**[1]

-115 **4** *1½* **Tourist**[15] 528 5-8-9 **91**.. RobertWinston 1 94
(D Shaw) *chsd ldrs: rdn 2f out: outpcd over 1f out: styd on again ins fnl f but nt rch ldng trio* **12/1**

0-61 **5** *nk* **Ishiadancer**[14] 544 5-7-13 **86**... KierenFox(5) 3 88
(E J Alston) *sn led: jnd fr 3f out: rdn over 2f out: hdd appr fnl f: wknd wl ins fnl f* **15/2**

510- **6** *5* **Kyllachy Star**[112] 7294 4-8-10 **92**..................................... PaulHanagan 4 81
(R A Fahey) *in tch: chsd ldrs 1/2-way: wknd wl over 1f out* **7/1**

1m 24.4s (-0.40) **Going Correction** 0.0s/f (Stan) **6** Ran SP% **113.3**
Speed ratings (Par 109): **102,102,101,99,99 93**
TOTE WIN: Mahadee £1.90 Seek the Fair Land £10.30 PL: M £2.20, SFL £2.00 EX: M/SFL £10.30 SFL/M £8.90 CSF: M/SFL £7.77 SFL/M £8.31. toteswingers: Mahadee&3 £1.10, Mahadee & Seek the Fair Land £2.80 Seek the Fair Land&3 £2.60.
Owner Chris Watkins And David N Reynolds **Bred** Raimon Bloodstock **Trained** Epsom, Surrey
Owner Saeed Manana **Bred** Darley **Trained** Newmarket, Suffolk

FOCUS
A decent handicap, but the early pace wasn't that strong and it developed into a bit of a sprint.

NOTEBOOK
Mahadee(IRE), put up 4lb for his success in a hot handicap here seven days earlier when returning from a break, was given a patient ride and took time to gather stride when switched to the wide outside after turning in, but he produced a smart turn of foot to force a dead heat. All seven of his previous career successes were over at least 1m, so this was a good effort over an inadequate trip in a race not really run to suit. (tchd 7-2)
Seek The Fair Land hasn't enjoyed the best of luck since winning twice on Polytrack in December and being 2lb wrong here meant he was still 11lb higher than for his last success. He could probably have done with a stronger pace here too, but he was always in a good position. Having taken time to get the better of the leader Ishiadancer, he looked likely to win outright inside the last furlong, but was joined on the line and had to be content with a share of the spoils. (tchd 7-2)
Elna Bright, successful in his last two outings over course and distance and bidding for a hat-trick, finished well from off the pace and wasn't beaten far by the front pair, but he is now 4lb higher than for his last win in a handicap. (tchd 13-8 and 15-8 in places)
Tourist has gained his last three wins over 6f, though he has won over this trip. He didn't help himself by taking a grip early and although he stayed on, it was never going to be enough. The handicapper may have his measure now. (op 10-1)
Ishiadancer is most effective when allowed an uncontested lead and was able to enjoy that luxury again here. She battled back very gamely when joined by Seek The Fair Land 2f out, but eventually had to admit defeat. She was put up 12lb for her Wolverhampton demolition a fortnight earlier and that may well have anchored her. (op 7-1 tchd 13-2 and 8-1)

Kyllachy Star, successful off 4lb lower over course and distance in his only previous try here back in October, hadn't been seen since disappointing on turf the following month. He dropped right out here, but was entitled to need it. (tchd 6-1)

740 BET CARLING CUP FINAL - BETDAQ CONDITIONS STKS 1m (P)

5:25 (5:27) (Class 3) 4-Y-0+ **£6,799** (£2,023; £1,011; £505) **Stalls** High

Form				RPR
03-1	1		**Dalradian (IRE)**[14] 536 4-9-3 94 ... JimCrowley 7 (W J Knight) *hld up in rr tl rapid hdwy on rails wl over 1f out to ld ins fnl f: drvn out* **11/10**[1]	97+
5415	2	½	**Red Somerset (USA)**[4] 672 7-9-1 84 ow1 ... GeorgeBaker 6 (R J Hodges) *chsd ldrs: chal ins fnl 2f: rdn over 1f out and one pce: styd on again to chse wnr ins fnl f and kpt on but a hld* **8/1**	94
3454	3	¾	**Carcinetto (IRE)**[7] 635 8-8-11 92 ... AndrewHeffernan(5) 3 (P D Evans) *in rr but in tch: rdn along fr 2f out: styd on fnl f and gng on cl home but a hld by ldng duo* **18/1**	93+
440-	4	nk	**Advanced**[116] 7232 7-9-0 105 ... KierenFallon 1 (K A Ryan) *chsd ldrs: rdn whn n.m.r and checked jst ins fnl f: kpt on again cl home* **6/1**[3]	92+
600-	5	nk	**Abbondanza (IRE)**[147] 6487 7-9-0 108 ...(p) DarryllHolland 2 (N Wilson) *led: rdn whn jnd fr 2f out: kpt slt advantage u.p tl hdd ins fnl f: wknd fnl 50yds* **7/2**[2]	90
3-53	6	½	**My Best Bet**[9] 593 4-8-9 80 ... ChrisCatlin 8 (Stef Higgins) *in rr: rdn over 2f out: styd on u.p fr over 1f out but nvr any threat* **25/1**	84
0-05	7	nk	**Raptor (GER)**[14] 536 7-9-0 89 ... RobertWinston 5 (M E Rimmer) *trckd ldr: chal over 2f out: btn whn n.m.r wl over 1f out* **11/1**	88

1m 37.88s (-0.32) **Going Correction** 0.0s/f (Stan) 7 Ran SP% **112.7**
Speed ratings (Par 107): **101,100,99,99,99 98,98**
toteswingers: 1&2 £3.00, 1&3 £6.00, 2&3 £7.10 CSF £10.54 TOTE £2.10: £1.20, £3.30; EX 7.30 Trifecta £91.40 Pool: £838.89 - 6.79 winning units. Place 6 £4.43, Place 5 £4.41.
Owner Canisbay Bloodstock **Bred** Hesmonds Stud Ltd **Trained** Patching, W Sussex

FOCUS

An interesting conditions event, but another race in which they didn't appear to go a great pace early.

NOTEBOOK

Dalradian(IRE) ◆ seemed to face a stiff task in conceding weight to some higher-rated rivals, but at least he came into this at the top of his game. Held up early, as was the case when he scored over 2f further here a fortnight earlier he was presented with a gap on the inside turning in as the leaders ran wide, and he made full use of it. He continues to go from strength to strength and may reappear at Wolverhampton on Thursday, whilst he might yet also take his chance in the Winter Derby. (op 6-5 tchd Evens and 5-4 in places)

Red Somerset(USA) was worst in at the weights, but having been handy from the off, he put in a strong challenge once into the straight and was just outbattled. Much will depend on what the handicapper makes of this performance. (op 10-1 tchd 14-1)

Carcinetto(IRE), not for the first time, finished strongly if far too late. She tries her hardest despite her very busy schedule, but continues on her lengthy losing run. (op 16-1)

Advanced, having only his fourth try on sand and returning from almost four months off, had a decent chance at the weights but he was trying 1m for the first time in his 43rd start. He was still in with some sort of chance when getting short of room inside the last furlong, but he can't be described as unlucky. (op 9-2)

Abbondanza(IRE), making his debut for the yard after nearly five months off, was successful in his last three visits to this track last spring, making just about all each time. Best in at the weights, he was able to enjoy an uncontested lead once again here and tried to quicken from the front approaching the home turn, but he was collared passing the furlong pole and had no more to offer. (op 9-2)

My Best Bet is effective under these conditions, but she had a lot to find at the weights and could never offer a threat from off the pace. (op 16-1)

Raptor(GER), on a lengthy losing run, ran better when fifth behind Dalradian here last time, but he seemed to have run his race when getting hampered over a furlong from home. (op 12-1)

T/Plt: £8.20 to a £1 stake. Pool: £77,820.26. 6,922.51 winning tickets. T/Qpdt: £5.80 to a £1 stake. Pool: £4,982.42. 629.33 winning tickets. ST

690 CAGNES-SUR-MER

Saturday, February 27

OFFICIAL GOING: Turf course - heavy; all-weather - standard

741a PRIX POLICEMAN (LISTED RACE) (ALL-WEATHER) 1m 2f (D)

1:05 (1:07) 3-Y-0 **£24,336** (£9,735; £7,301; £4,867; £2,434)

			RPR
1		**Paris Vegas (USA)**[30] 3-8-11 ... ThierryThulliez 7 (F Chappet, France)	94
2	1 ½	**Querry Boy (FR)**[17] 3-8-11 ... FabriceVeron 6 (H-A Pantall, France)	91
3	1 ½	**Ucandri (IRE)**[17] 3-8-11 ... JulienAuge 1 (C Ferland, France)	88
4	1 ½	**Bahamian Box**[105] 7407 3-8-11 ...(b) FranckBlondel 4 (T Larriviere, France)	85
5	1 ½	**Tagar Bere (FR)**[13] 557 3-8-11 ... DominiqueBoeuf 5 (M Pimbonnet, France)	82
6	1 ½	**Arlequin**[14] 548 3-8-11 ... IoritzMendizabal 3 (J D Bethell) *racd in 4th bhd slow pce: rdn over 3f out: btn 2f out* **9/2**[1]	79
7	snk	**Munaawer (USA)**[14] 547 3-8-11 ... StephanePasquier 2 (J D Bethell) *racd in 6th bhd slow pce: rdn 3f out: unable qck fr 2f out* **11/1**[2]	79

2m 2.76s (122.76) 7 Ran SP% **26.5**
PARI-MUTUEL (including 1 Euro stake): WIN 3.20; PL 2.00, 2.80;SF 17.90.
Owner Aleksandar Pavlovic **Bred** Ocala Horses Llc **Trained** France

742a GRAND PRIX DU CONSEIL GENERAL DES ALPES MARITIMES (LISTED RACE) (TURF) 1m 4f 110y

2:45 (2:47) 4-Y-0+ **£33,186** (£13,274; £9,956; £6,637; £3,319)

			RPR
1		**Tangaspeed (FR)**[13] 558 5-8-9 ... DavyBonilla 4 (R Laplanche, France)	85
2	1	**Rento (FR)**[17] 494 7-8-13 ...(p) Francois-XavierBertras 2 (W Walton, France)	88
3	1 ½	**Poincon De France (IRE)**[118] 6-8-13 ... FranckBlondel 5 (P Monfort, France)	85
4	¾	**Lost Soldier Three (IRE)**[17] 494 9-8-13 ...(p) IoritzMendizabal 3 (D Nicholls) *led to 1 1/2f out: one pce* **17/2**[1]	84
5	shd	**Wysiwyg Lucky (FR)**[33] 7-8-9 ... StephanePasquier 11 (J-L Gay, France)	80
6	nk	**Griraz (FR)** 5-8-13 ... PhilippeSogorb 7 (J-L Dubord, France)	84
7	2 ½	**Cape Martin (IRE)**[41] 8-8-13 ... GBietolini 6 (Gianluca Bietolini, Italy)	80
8	7	**Dunaden (FR)**[17] 494 4-8-9 ... ThierryThulliez 12 (Y Fouin, France)	70
9	hd	**Andrei Roublev (USA)**[109] 9-8-13 ...(p) SebastienMaillot 1 (D Windrif, France)	70
10	dist	**Golden Clou (FR)**[13] 558 4-8-6 ...(p) GregoryBenoist 8 (P Demercastel, France)	—
11		**Black Crystal (USA)**[302] 1657 4-8-6 ... DominiqueBoeuf 10 (Robert Collet, France)	—

2m 58.8s (178.80)
WFA 4 from 5yo+ 3lb 11 Ran SP% **10.5**
PARI-MUTUEL: WIN 7.30; PL 2.50, 3.00, 4.60; DF 47.60.
Owner R Pires & Mme L Gagneux **Bred** Mme Laurence Gagneux **Trained** France

743a PRIX SKY LAWYER (ALL-WEATHER) 6f 110y

4:20 (4:21) 4-Y-0+ **£13,274** (£5,310; £3,982; £2,655; £1,327)

			RPR
1		**Livandar (FR)**[57] 4-8-9 ... FranckBlondel 13 (C Theodorakis, Greece) **227/10**[2]	96
2	3	**Parfum Des Dieux**[32] 304 5-8-13 ... IoritzMendizabal 7 (J-C Rouget, France)	92
3	nse	**Cadeau For Maggi**[14] 549 5-8-11 ... FabriceVeron 11 (H-A Pantall, France)	90
4	shd	**Magic Box (ITY)**[189] 7-8-9 ... DavyBonilla 2 (F & S Brogi, Italy)	88
5	snk	**Psy Chic (FR)**[7] 640 6-8-13 ... DominiqueBoeuf 12 (Robert Collet, France)	91
6	1	**Kerno (IRE)**[14] 549 6-8-9 ...(p) StephanePasquier 5 (P Monfort, France)	84
7	nk	**Garnica (FR)**[7] 640 7-8-9 ...(p) Francois-XavierBertras 6 (D Nicholls) *midfield: disputing 6th st: disputing 3rd whn rdn over 1f out: sn btn* **6/1**[1]	84
8	snk	**Film Set (USA)**[32] 304 4-8-9 ... Jean-BernardEyquem 4 (F Vermeulen, France)	83
9	½	**Zibeling (IRE)**[13] 560 4-8-6 ... SebastienMaillot 8 (Robert Collet, France)	79
10	½	**Secret Affair**[140] 8-8-9 ...(p) FabienLefebvre 10 (Mme C Vergne & D Sicaud, France)	80
0		**Royal Power (IRE)**[21] 458 7-8-9 ... GaetanMasure 3 (D Nicholls) *towards rr: rdn 2f out: nvr a factor* **51/1**[3]	—
0		**Black Out (GER)**[167] 5-8-11 ... KKerekes 9 (W Figge, Germany)	—
0		**Allez Bailey (FR)**[13] 560 4-8-9 ... CharlesNora 1 (W Walton, France)	—

1m 16.12s (76.12) 13 Ran SP% **20.4**
PARI-MUTUEL: WIN 23.70; PL 4.60, 1.40, 1.40; DF 49.10.
Owner Christos Theodorakis **Bred** Haras De S A Aga Khan Scea **Trained** Greece

691 KEMPTON (A.W) (R-H)

Sunday, February 28

OFFICIAL GOING: Standard

Wind: fresh, across Weather: overcast, dry after heavy rain this morning

744 BET CARLING CUP FINAL - BETDAQ MAIDEN STKS 6f (P)

2:20 (2:21) (Class 5) 3-Y-O **£2,590** (£770; £385; £192) **Stalls** High

Form				RPR
5-	1		**Progress (IRE)**[135] 6809 3-8-12 0 ... ShaneKelly 2 (J Noseda) *s.i.s: in tch in midfield: edgd rt and hmpd wl over 3f out: rdn along 3f out: rdn to chse ldrs and plenty to do 2f out: kpt wanting to edge rt but r.o wl to ld towards fin* **5/6**[1]	71+
2-22	2	½	**Torres Del Paine**[18] 489 3-9-3 71 ... JimmyQuinn 4 (J C Fox) *chsd ldr: pushed along to chal 2f out: rdn to ld over 1f out: kpt on u.p tl hdd and no ex towards fin* **15/2**	74
3-32	3	2	**Caramelita**[4] 683 3-8-12 66 ... JimCrowley 1 (J R Jenkins) *led at set gd gallop: rdn and hdd over 1f out: wknd fnl 100yds* **13/2**[3]	63
	4	5	**Rock With You** 3-8-12 0 ... LukeMorris 6 (J R Gask) *in tch in midfield tl dropped to last trio and outpcd over 3f out: no threat to ldrs after: swtchd lft over 2f out: kpt on fnl f* **20/1**	47
	5	1 ½	**Madlool (IRE)** 3-9-3 0 ... JoeFanning 3 (W J Haggas) *chsd ldrs: rdn and unable qck over 2f out: sn struggling: wl btn over 1f out* **7/2**[2]	47
	6	3 ½	**Piccolo Blue** 3-8-12 0 ... AdamKirby 5 (C G Cox) *sn outpcd and rdn along in last pair: lost tch over 2f out* **16/1**	31
	7	3 ¼	**Higenius** 3-9-3 0 ... VinceSlattery 7 (D Burchell) *s.i.s: sn rdn along and struggling in last pair: lost tch wl over 2f out* **66/1**	26
00-6	8	1 ¾	**Cockney Colonel (USA)**[23] 424 3-9-1 0 ow1 ...(t) AlanCreighton(3) 8 (E J Creighton) *chsd ldng pair: rdn 3f out: wknd over 2f out: wl bhd fnl f* **66/1**	21

1m 13.04s (-0.06) **Going Correction** +0.025s/f (Slow) 8 Ran SP% **115.5**
Speed ratings (Par 97): **101,100,97,91,89 84,80,77**
toteswingers: 1&2 £2.40, 1&3 £2.60, 2&3 £2.10 CSF £8.06 TOTE £1.80: £1.10, £1.70, £1.20; EX 7.00.
Owner The Honorable Earle I Mack **Bred** Darley **Trained** Newmarket, Suffolk

FOCUS

A fair 3-y-o maiden featuring a few that had already shown ability up against a couple of interesting newcomers. The third sets the level.

745 BET IN RUNNING - BETDAQ H'CAP 6f (P)

2:50 (2:50) (Class 6) (0-60,60) 3-Y-O **£2,047** (£604; £302) **Stalls** High

Form				RPR
0-33	1		**Posy Fossil (USA)**[22] 445 3-9-1 60 ...(t) WilliamCarson(3) 7 (S C Williams) *handy in main gp: rdn and swtchd lft over 1f out: styd on wl u.p to ld fnl 100yds: sn clr: eased nr fin* **11/1**	66

3226 **2** 1 ½ **Turf Time**[9] [619] 3-8-12 **54**........ ChrisCatlin 10 55
(J A Glover) *racd wl off the pce in midfield: rdn and hdwy ent fnl 2f: r.o wl fnl f: wnt 2nd fnl 75yds: no imp on wnr after* **9/2**[1]

60-3 **3** hd **Roybuoy**[11] [581] 3-8-9 **51**........(b) JimmyQuinn 11 52
(H J L Dunlop) *hmpd sn after s and sn bhd: rdn and swtchd ins and hdwy ent fnl 2f: r.o wl to press for 2nd fnl 50yds: nt rch wnr* **5/1**[2]

5-55 **4** nk **Val C**[18] [483] 3-9-4 **60**........(b[1]) SebSanders 12 60
(M Botti) *led: wnt clr 4f out: wl clr 1/2-way: rdn wl 1f out: tired and hdd fnl 100yds: lost 2 pls fnl 75yds* **11/2**[3]

05-0 **5** ½ **Ballyvonane (USA)**[4] [678] 3-8-6 **48**........(b) LukeMorris 1 46
(L A Dace) *chsd ldr: rdn over 2f out: clsd u.p over 1f out: kpt on same pce ins fnl f* **6/1**

-441 **6** ½ **Rightcar**[25] [387] 3-9-2 **58**........ RobertWinston 8 54
(Peter Grayson) *awkward leaving stalls and s.i.s: hld up in rr: hdwy towards inner over 2f out: chsd ldrs jst ins fnl f: no ex fnl 100yds* **11/2**[3]

060- **7** ½ **Pursuit Of Gold**[95] [7513] 3-8-13 **55**........ SteveDrowne 4 50
(J R Best) *racd wl off the pce in midfield: rdn and no prog over 2f out: styd on ins fnl f: nvr gng pce to rch ldrs* **16/1**

0-55 **8** 2 ¼ **Belle Park**[10] [594] 3-8-13 **55**........ JamieMackay 5 43
(Karen George) *s.i.s: a wl off the pce in rr: rdn over 2f out: no prog and nvr trbld ldrs* **33/1**

0- **9** 1 ¼ **Mac Tiernan (IRE)**[95] [7529] 3-8-5 **50**........ KellyHarrison(3) 6 34
(P J Lally, Ire) *racd keenly: chsd ldrs: rdn over 2f out: wknd wl over 1f out* **8/1**

04-0 **10** 8 **Old Devil Moon (IRE)**[11] [581] 3-8-10 **52**........ StevieDonohoe 2 13
(R A Mills) *sn rdn along in midfield: lost pl u.p 3f out: wl bhd and eased ins fnl f* **10/1**

50-0 **11** 1 ¼ **Joan's Legacy**[25] [387] 3-8-8 **50**........ RichardSmith 9 7
(J C Fox) *chsd ldr tl wknd u.p ent fnl 2f: wl bhd and eased ins fnl f* **20/1**

1m 13.65s (0.55) **Going Correction** +0.025s/f (Slow) **11** Ran SP% **122.0**
Speed ratings (Par 95): **97,95,94,94,93 93,92,89,87,77 75**
toteswingers: 1&2 £9.90, 1&3 £9.20, 2&3 £3.90 CSF £62.30 CT £288.46 TOTE £13.00: £5.40, £1.70, £1.10; EX 51.90.
Owner J W Parry **Bred** London Thoroughbred Services Ltd **Trained** Newmarket, Suffolk

FOCUS
A very moderate sprint handicap and only two of these had won. They went a furious early pace, but it collapsed and the winning time was 0.61 seconds slower than the maiden. The runner-up is the best guide to the level.
Roybuoy Official explanation: jockey said gelding suffered interference at start
Rightcar Official explanation: jockey said colt jumped awkwardly on leaving stalls

746 BETDAQ THE BETTING EXCHANGE CLAIMING STKS 1m 3f (P)
3:20 (3:21) (Class 6) 4-Y-O+ **£2,047** (£604; £302) **Stalls** High

Form RPR
-441 **1** **Hurakan (IRE)**[17] [497] 4-9-3 73........(p) J-PGuillambert 8 72+
(P D Evans) *trckd ldrs: effrt between horses to chal over 1f out: led jst ins fnl f: a doing enough after: pushed out* **5/4**[2]

0006 **2** 1 **Solarias Quest**[2] [724] 8-8-11 59........ ShaneKelly 1 62
(W M Brisbourne) *stdd s: hld up in tch in last pair: effrt ent fnl 2f: swtchd rt jst over 1f out: kpt on to snatch 2nd on post: nt pce to chal wnr* **20/1**

550- **3** nse **Sahrati**[62] [5170] 6-9-3 75........ EddieAhern 2 68
(A King) *trckd ldr: rdn to ld 2f out: hdd jst ins fnl f: kpt on same pce after: lost 2nd on post* **1/1**[1]

4 4 **Escardo (GER)**[119] 7-9-7 67........ DavidNolan 5 66
(D G Bridgwater) *wl in tch in midfield: rdn and effrt to press ldrs over 2f out: wknd jst ins fnl f* **20/1**

-002 **5** nse **Hatch A Plan (IRE)**[11] [576] 9-8-3 52........ CharlesEddery(7) 6 55
(Mouse Hamilton-Fairley) *hld up wl in tch in last pair: rdn and effrt towards inner wl over 1f out: outpcd over 1f out and no ch w ldrs fnl f* **16/1**

00P- **6** 10 **State General (IRE)**[19] [6680] 4-8-13 77........ JimCrowley 7 44
(Miss J Feilden) *led tl rdn and hdd 2f out: wknd qckly over 1f out: eased whn no ch ins fnl f* **10/1**[3]

/0-0 **7** 7 **Macademy Royal (USA)**[39] [235] 7-8-7 35........(t) LindseyWhite(7) 4 32
(Miss N A Lloyd-Beavis) *chsd ldrs: rdn over 2f out: struggling whn rdr dropped whip 2f out: sn wl bhd: eased ins fnl f* **80/1**

2m 25.2s (3.30) **Going Correction** +0.025s/f (Slow)
WFA 4 from 6yo+ 2lb **7** Ran SP% **120.2**
Speed ratings (Par 101): **89,88,88,85,85 78,72**
toteswingers:1&2:£5.30, 1&3:£1.10, 2&3:£6.60 CSF £28.82 TOTE £2.70: £1.30, £9.70; EX 41.30.Sahrati was claimed by A. B. Haynes for £12,000
Owner J L Guillambert **Bred** Newberry Stud Company **Trained** Pandy, Monmouths
■ Stewards' Enquiry : David Nolan caution: used whip down shoulder in the forehand.

FOCUS
A moderate claimer, with question marks against many of these, and a two-horse race according to the market. They went a very steady early pace and the race developed into a sprint. The second, fifth and seventh govern the level of the form.
Escardo(GER) Official explanation: jockey said gelding hung right

747 BETDAQ ON 0870 178 1221 H'CAP 7f (P)
3:55 (3:55) (Class 4) (0-80,79) 4-Y-O+ **£4,209** (£1,252; £625; £312) **Stalls** High

Form RPR
-414 **1** **Kipchak (IRE)**[20] [465] 5-8-8 **69**........(p) LiamKeniry 4 79
(C R Dore) *taken down early: mde all: clr 4f out: rdn ent fnl 2f: styd on wl fnl f: unchal* **5/1**

404- **2** 3 ¼ **Last Sovereign**[145] [6564] 6-9-3 **78**........ ShaneKelly 8 80
(Jane Chapple-Hyam) *chsd wnr: swtchd lft and rdn wl over 1f out: no imp fnl f* **4/1**[3]

00-5 **3** nk **Millfields Dreams**[6] [658] 11-8-6 **67**........ LukeMorris 3 68
(M D Squance) *hld up towards rr: rdn and hdwy over 2f out: chsd ldng pair over 1f out: kpt on to press for 2nd fnl 100yds: nvr trbld wnr* **25/1**

066- **4** 1 ¾ **Priti Fabulous (IRE)**[60] [7872] 5-8-6 **72**........(p) DeclanCannon(5) 1 69
(A J McCabe) *s.i.s: hld up in rr: swtchd lft and effrt over 2f out: kpt on to go 4th jst ins fnl f: nvr trbld ldrs* **2/1**[1]

2060 **5** 3 ¼ **Carmenero (GER)**[11] [579] 7-8-8 **69**........ EddieAhern 7 58
(C R Dore) *chsd ldrs: wknd u.p wl over 1f out: wl btn fnl f* **25/1**

0-34 **6** nk **Ray Of Joy**[30] [350] 4-9-2 **77**........ StephenCraine 6 65
(J R Jenkins) *chsd ldrs: effrt and rdn to dispute 2nd over 2f out: wknd u.p over 1f out* **8/1**

4-20 **7** 1 ½ **Sunshine Always (IRE)**[25] [394] 4-9-4 **79**........ JimCrowley 5 63
(T D McCarthy) *racd in midfield: drvn and effrt on inner over 2f out: sn no imp and wl btn fnl f* **11/4**[2]

0-24 **8** 24 **Cut And Thrust (IRE)**[14] [552] 4-8-12 **73**........(p) ChrisCatlin 2 —
(M Wellings) *sn bhd: lost tch qckly and t.o 1/2-way* **8/1**

1m 25.51s (-0.49) **Going Correction** +0.025s/f (Slow) **8** Ran SP% **126.6**
Speed ratings (Par 105): **103,99,98,96,93 92,91,63**
toteswingers:1&2:£5.30, 1&3:£18.10, 2&3:£14.10 CSF £28.31 CT £475.51 TOTE £6.80: £1.80, £1.70, £5.40; EX 30.90.
Owner Liam Breslin **Bred** Miss Mary Davidson & Mrs Steffi Von Schilcher **Trained** Cowbit, Lincs
■ Stewards' Enquiry : Shane Kelly one-day ban: careless riding (Mar 16)

FOCUS
A fair handicap on paper, but many of these have found winning difficult recently. The pace was a fair one, but the race was dominated by those that raced prominently and nothing got into it from off the pace. The winner has been rated back to his better form.

748 BET CHELTENHAM FESTIVAL - BETDAQ H'CAP 2m (P)
4:25 (4:25) (Class 6) (0-65,65) 4-Y-O+ **£2,047** (£604; £302) **Stalls** High

Form RPR
00-4 **1** **Coda Agency**[20] [263] 7-9-9 **63**........ JimCrowley 7 70
(D W P Arbuthnot) *hld up in tch in midfield: hdwy 4f out: rdn to ld 2f out: styd on gamely u.p fnl f* **4/1**[1]

636 **2** ½ **Happy Fleet**[20] [468] 7-9-4 **58**........ FergusSweeney 10 64
(R Curtis) *in tch in midfield: hdwy on inner 3f out: swtchd lft over 2f out: chal 2f out: ev ch u.p after: unable qck fnl f* **11/1**

0/22 **3** hd **Poppy Gregg**[11] [584] 5-8-3 **48**........(v) AmyBaker(5) 11 54+
(Dr J R J Naylor) *stdd s: hld up in rr: swtchd to outer 5f out: rdn and v wd bnd 3f out: stl 10th and plenty to do 2f out: r.o strly after and wnt 3rd last strides: nt quite rch ldrs* **15/2**[3]

2-01 **4** hd **Isle De Maurice**[17] [420] 8-9-8 **62**........(b) GeorgeBaker 2 68
(G L Moore) *dwlt: sn bustled up to r in midfield: rdn and effrt over 2f out: chsd ldng pair jst over 1f out: kpt on but nvr quite pce to chal ldrs: lost 3rd last strides* **7/1**[2]

566/ **5** 2 ½ **Golden Alchemist**[99] [3347] 7-8-6 **46** oh1........ LukeMorris 3 49
(M D I Usher) *towards rr: pushed along bnd over 8f out: rdn and hdwy into midfield 4f out: plugged on steadily u.p fnl 2f: nvr able to rch ldrs* **14/1**

3/6- **6** 1 ¼ **Watch Out**[20] [7154] 6-8-3 **46** oh1........(tp) KellyHarrison(3) 8 47
(D Burchell) *hld up towards rr: sltly hmpd over 5f out: hdwy towards inner over 2f out: chsd ldrs and drvn over 1f out: no prog fnl f* **20/1**

0-16 **7** 3 ½ **Purely By Chance**[37] [263] 5-9-0 **54**........(b) SaleemGolam 13 51
(J Pearce) *chsd ldrs: lost pl and dropped towards rr 4f out: rdn over 3f out: styd on same pce fr over 2f out* **8/1**

4215 **8** 2 ½ **Sir Sandicliffe (IRE)**[14] [554] 6-8-9 **54**........ KierenFox(5) 6 48
(W M Brisbourne) *hld up towards rr: rdn and no real prog 3f out: plugged on one pce after: nvr trbld ldrs* **10/1**

0-03 **9** 4 **Cossack Prince**[17] [497] 5-9-9 **63**........ IanMongan 1 52
(Mrs L J Mongan) *racd wd: chsd ldrs: wnt 2nd over 5f out tl over 2f out: wknd qckly u.p 2f out* **16/1**

600- **10** hd **Royal Premier (IRE)**[74] [7767] 7-8-7 **47**........(v) PaulDoe 4 36
(H J Collingridge) *chsd ldr tl led over 7f out: rdn and hdd 2f out: wknd qckly over 1f out* **33/1**

21-0 **11** 3 ¼ **Follow The Dream**[14] [554] 7-9-9 **63**........ ChrisCatlin 5 48
(Karen George) *hld up in rr: hdwy into midfield 4f out: rdn and struggling 3f out: wl btn fnl 2f* **10/1**

125/ **12** 6 **Quarrymount**[41] [6335] 9-9-11 **65**........ LiamKeniry 12 43
(C Gordon) *chsd ldrs tl wknd qckly u.p over 2f out: wl bhd fnl f* **16/1**

-060 **13** 40 **Try Cat**[32] [316] 4-8-0 **46** oh1........(b[1]) JimmyQuinn 9 —
(Sir Mark Prescott) *in tch in midfield: rdn and lost pl qckly over 3f out: t.o and eased fnl f* **7/1**[2]

06/0 **14** 69 **Sweet Seville (FR)**[11] [585] 6-8-7 **47**........ JoeFanning 14 —
(M D Squance) *led tl over 7f out: dropped out rapidly over 5f out: t.o and virtually p.u fnl 3f* **25/1**

3m 29.55s (-0.55) **Going Correction** +0.025s/f (Slow)
WFA 4 from 5yo+ 6lb **14** Ran SP% **124.4**
Speed ratings (Par 101): **102,101,101,101,100 99,97,96,94,94 92,89,69,35**
toteswingers: 1&2 £15.20, 1&3 £14.10, 2&3 £39.70 CSF £49.28 CT £330.03 TOTE £4.20: £1.90, £4.90, £2.20; EX 74.30.
Owner Banfield, Thompson **Bred** Baydon House Stud **Trained** Compton, Berks

FOCUS
A moderate staying handicap, but quite a competitive race. However, they didn't go a great gallop early, so this wasn't the test of stamina it might have been. The form looks solid but limited.
Try Cat Official explanation: jockey said filly stopped quickly
Sweet Seville(FR) Official explanation: jockey said mare hung left

749 BET MULTIPLES - BETDAQ H'CAP 1m (P)
4:55 (4:55) (Class 4) (0-85,85) 4-Y-O+ **£4,209** (£1,252; £625; £312) **Stalls** High

Form RPR
3444 **1** **Gallantry**[5] [672] 8-8-6 **76**........ MichaelStainton(3) 7 84+
(P Howling) *hld up in last trio: effrt on outer 2f out: edgd rt but str run u.p to ld ins fnl f: r.o wl* **9/2**[2]

21-2 **2** 1 **Pegasus Again (USA)**[5] [672] 5-9-4 **85**........ JoeFanning 5 91
(R A Mills) *led: rdn jst over 2f out: hdd fnl f: battled on gamely but a hld by wnr after* **13/8**[1]

1331 **3** ¾ **Ilie Nastase (FR)**[9] [623] 6-9-4 **85**........ LiamKeniry 4 89
(C R Dore) *stdd s: hld up in last pair: rdn and hdwy over 1f out: wnt between horses to chse ldng pair ins fnl f: kpt on but nt rch ldrs* **10/1**

-300 **4** ½ **Istiqdaam**[25] [394] 5-8-2 **74**........(b) JamesSullivan(5) 2 77
(M W Easterby) *t.k.h: disp 2nd pl: rdn ent fnl 2f: keeping on same pce and btn whn n.m.r towards fin* **10/1**

5-06 **5** 2 **Bennelong**[18] [487] 4-8-7 **74**........(v[1]) PaulDoe 6 72
(P D Evans) *t.k.h: dispted 2nd pl: rdn and hanging rt over 1f out: wknd jst ins fnl f* **6/1**

-520 **6** ½ **Trafalgar Square**[5] [672] 8-8-9 **76**........ LukeMorris 3 73
(M J Attwater) *stdd s: hld up in last pair: effrt on inner jst over 2f out: no imp ins fnl f* **12/1**

-506 **7** ½ **Mcconnell (USA)**[12] [572] 5-8-9 **79**........ RobertLButler(3) 1 75
(P Butler) *chsd ldng trio: rdn and unable qck 2f out: one pce and hld whn n.m.r ins fnl f* **25/1**

-112 **8** 13 **Hereford Boy**[25] [394] 6-8-13 **80**........(p) RobertHavlin 8 45
(D K Ivory) *hld up in tch in midfield: rdn and no rspnse jst over 2f out: wl btn over 1f out* **5/1**[3]

1m 39.03s (-0.77) **Going Correction** +0.025s/f (Slow) **8** Ran SP% **116.9**
Speed ratings (Par 105): **104,103,102,101,99 99,98,85**
toteswingers: 1&2 £2.90, 1&3 £3.90, 2&3 £2.40 CSF £12.55 CT £69.57 TOTE £5.10: £1.30, £1.20, £2.30; EX 11.70 Place 6 £72.12, Place 5 £53.37.
Owner The Circle Bloodstock I Limited **Bred** Cheveley Park Stud Ltd **Trained** Newmarket, Suffolk

FOCUS
A fair little handicap, but the early pace looked modest, which caused a couple to pull. The runner-up has been rated close to his recent good run, and the third to his recent best.

Bennelong Official explanation: jockey said gelding hung right
T/Jkpt: Not won. T/Plt: £48.00 to a £1 stake. Pool: £71,995.17. 1,093.29 winning tickets. T/Qpdt: £20.40 to a £1 stake. Pool: £5,192.96. 187.54 winning tickets. SP

721 WOLVERHAMPTON (A.W) (L-H)

Monday, March 1

OFFICIAL GOING: Standard changing to standard to fast after race 1 (2.10)
Wind: Light across Weather: Fine and sunny

750 WOLVERHAMPTON-RACECOURSE.CO.UK H'CAP 5f 20y(P)
2:10 (2:10) (Class 5) (0-75,75) 4-Y-0+ £2,456 (£725; £362) Stalls Low

Form RPR
42-2 **1** **Desperate Dan**[31] 349 9-8-13 **70**....(v) NeilCallan 6 79
(A B Haynes) *a.p: pushed along early: shkn up over 1f out: edgd lft and r.o to ld nr fin* **8/1**
6-51 **2** ½ **Ingleby Star (IRE)**[21] 462 5-8-13 **70**....(p) JimmyQuinn 4 77
(N Wilson) *led: rdn over 1f out: hdd nr fin* **3/1**[2]
0-03 **3** ¾ **Brierty (IRE)**[24] 431 4-9-3 **74**.... DavidNolan 1 78
(D Carroll) *prom: rdn 1/2-way: r.o* **2/1**[1]
2122 **4** hd **Total Impact**[4] 703 7-9-4 **75**.... LiamKeniry 9 78
(C R Dore) *hld up: hdwy over 1f out: sn rdn: r.o* **7/2**[3]
13-3 **5** nk **Punching**[4] 703 6-8-10 **72**.... DeclanCannon(5) 8 74
(C R Dore) *trckd ldr: rdn and hung lft over 1f out: styd on* **11/1**
2-45 **6** 3 **Lithaam (IRE)**[33] 306 6-8-12 **69**....(p) LukeMorris 5 60
(J M Bradley) *hld up: rdn 1/2-way: nvr trbld ldrs* **14/1**
2-24 **7** 2 **Bahamian Kid**[24] 431 5-9-1 **72**....(v) JerryO'Dwyer 7 56
(R Hollinshead) *chsd ldrs: rdn 1/2-way: wknd over 1f out* **12/1**

61.34 secs (-0.96) **Going Correction** 0.0s/f (Stan) **7** Ran SP% **114.4**
Speed ratings (Par 103): **107,106,105,104,104 99,96**
toteswingers: 1&2 £4.00, 1&3 £4.30, 2&3 £2.70 CSF £32.19 CT £66.71 TOTE £7.00: £3.30, £2.20; EX 27.50 Trifecta £202.90 Pool: £548.59 - 2.00 winning units..
Owner Joe McCarthy **Bred** Sheikh Amin Dahlawi **Trained** Limpley Stoke, Bath

FOCUS
The official going description was changed to standard to fast following this race, but the times throughout the card don't support that decision. Ordinary handicap form, with the winner back towards his best.

751 GREAT OFFERS AT WOLVERHAMPTON-RACECOURSE.CO.UK MAIDEN STKS 5f 216y(P)
2:40 (2:40) (Class 5) 3-Y-0+ £2,456 (£725; £362) Stalls Low

Form RPR
1 **Shearman (IRE)** 3-8-12 0.... GrahamGibbons 2 86+
(E S McMahon) *trckd ldrs: plld hrd: led on bit over 1f out: r.o wl* **3/1**[3]
62- **2** 3 **Hot Spark**[149] 6493 3-8-12 0.... NeilCallan 6 71
(K A Ryan) *led: racd keenly: rdn and hdd over 1f out: styd on same pce ins fnl f* **13/8**[1]
4 **3** ¾ **Fighter Boy (IRE)**[22] 453 3-8-7 0.... DeanHeslop(5) 3 69
(T D Barron) *trckd ldr: plld hrd: rdn and hung lft over 1f out: styd on same pce* **12/1**
2-2 **4** hd **Bandstand**[34] 301 4-9-12 0.... TomEaves 5 68
(B Smart) *chsd ldrs: outpcd 2f out: styd on ins fnl f* **7/4**[2]
5 3¾ **Lucas Pitt** 3-8-12 0.... StephenCraine 1 56
(M J Scudamore) *s.s: hdwy over 3f out: sn rdn: outpcd fnl 2f* **40/1**
6 30 **Shawkantango** 3-8-5 0.... SeanPalmer(7) 7 —
(D Shaw) *s.s: outpcd* **100/1**

1m 14.26s (-0.74) **Going Correction** 0.0s/f (Stan)
WFA 3 from 4yo 14lb **6** Ran SP% **110.6**
Speed ratings (Par 103): **104,100,99,98,93 53**
toteswingers: 1&2 £1.80, 1&3 £2.80, 2&3 £2.40 CSF £8.04 TOTE £4.20: £2.30, £1.50; EX 11.20.
Owner J C Fretwell **Bred** Thomas Cahalan & Sophie Hayley **Trained** Lichfield, Staffs

FOCUS
Just an ordinary maiden. Tricky form to pin down, with the second granted a soft lead but still beaten easily.

752 ENJOY THE PARTY PACK GROUP OFFER APPRENTICE H'CAP 1m 1f 103y(P)
3:10 (3:11) (Class 5) (0-75,74) 4-Y-0+ £2,456 (£725; £362) Stalls Low

Form RPR
636- **1** **Satwa Moon (USA)**[179] 5614 4-9-3 **72**.... AshleyHamblett 11 85+
(E A L Dunlop) *chsd ldrs: chalng whn hmpd over 1f out: led ins fnl f: rdn and r.o* **7/2**[2]
4-61 **2** 2½ **By Command**[16] 540 5-8-10 **65**....(p) AmyRyan 3 73
(K A Ryan) *a.p: chsd ldr over 3f out: hmpd over 1f out: led briefly ins fnl f: styd on same pce* **5/2**[1]
1110 **3** 1¼ **Grey Command (USA)**[21] 469 5-8-6 **66**.... JohnCavanagh(5) 1 72
(M Brittain) *led: clr over 6f out: rdn: hung lft and hmpd rivals over 1f out: hdd and no ex ins fnl f* **7/1**
-041 **4** 1¼ **Bavarica**[24] 426 8-8-11 **73**.... AdamBeschizza(7) 9 77
(Miss J Feilden) *hld up: hdwy u.p over 1f out: styd on: nt rch ldrs* **20/1**
025- **5** 1 **Nisaal (IRE)**[143] 6640 5-8-10 **68**....(p) IanBrennan(3) 7 70
(J J Quinn) *hld up in tch: stdd and lost pl over 7f out: plenty to do 2f out: r.o ins fnl f: nt trble ldrs* **7/1**
-262 **6** 1 **Boo**[14] 565 8-8-12 **72**....(v) DavidKenny(5) 4 73+
(J W Unett) *rrd s: bhd: last and rdn turning for home: nt clr run wl over 1f out: r.o ins fnl f: nrst fin* **15/2**
26-4 **7** 2½ **United Nations**[10] 623 9-8-8 **70**.... ShirleyTeasdale(7) 10 65
(N Wilson) *s.s: hld up: hdwy over 5f out: rdn over 2f out: wknd over 1f out* **66/1**
0-16 **8** 1¾ **Toolentidhaar (USA)**[16] 543 6-8-10 **70**.... AlexEdwards(5) 6 62
(Andrew Turnell) *chsd ldr tl rdn over 3f out: wknd over 1f out* **20/1**
1316 **9** 1½ **Aflaam (IRE)**[12] 588 5-9-2 **71**.... DeclanCannon 2 60
(R A Harris) *hld up: rdn over 3f out: wknd over 2f out* **5/1**[3]

2m 1.36s (-0.34) **Going Correction** 0.0s/f (Stan) **9** Ran SP% **115.2**
Speed ratings (Par 103): **101,98,97,96,95 94,92,91,89**
toteswingers: 1&2 £4.10, 1&3 £7.00, 2&3 £3.90 CSF £12.35 CT £56.87 TOTE £5.40: £2.00, £1.10, £2.60; EX 23.20 Trifecta £76.20 Pool:£288.48 - 2.80 winning units..
Owner The Lamprell Partnership **Bred** Charles H Deters **Trained** Newmarket, Suffolk
■ Stewards' Enquiry : John Cavanagh two-day ban: careless riding (Mar 16-17)

FOCUS
They were soon strung out in this modest apprentice handicap and those who got behind had no chance. Solid form which should work out, with a decent effort from the winner.

753 SPONSOR A RACE BY CALLING 01902 390000 H'CAP (DIV I) 1m 141y(P)
3:40 (3:40) (Class 6) (0-60,60) 4-Y-0+ £1,433 (£423; £211) Stalls Low

Form RPR
2601 **1** **Well Of Echoes**[7] 663 4-8-6 **53** 6ex....(tp) DeclanCannon(5) 5 67+
(A J McCabe) *dwlt: hld up: hdwy over 2f out: rdn and hung lft fr over 1f out: led ins fnl f: r.o* **12/1**
4323 **2** 1½ **Alfredtheordinary**[16] 541 5-8-11 **58**.... AndrewHeffernan(5) 7 67
(M R Channon) *mid-div: hmpd 7f out: hdwy sn after: rdn and ev ch ins fnl f: styd on same pce* **13/2**[2]
0-15 **3** 2¾ **Dhhamaan (IRE)**[14] 567 5-8-11 **53**....(b) HayleyTurner 13 56
(Mrs R A Carr) *led: rdn and hdd ins fnl f: no ex* **22/1**
2136 **4** 1¼ **Kirstys Lad**[7] 666 8-8-6 **51**.... KellyHarrison(3) 1 51
(M Mullineaux) *prom: rdn over 2f out: styd on same pce fnl f* **11/1**[3]
000- **5** shd **Never Sold Out (IRE)**[122] 5211 5-8-6 **48**.... LukeMorris 11 48
(J G M O'Shea) *hld up: rdn over 2f out: r.o ins fnl f: nvr nrr* **100/1**
-160 **6** nse **King's Jester (IRE)**[7] 665 8-8-9 **54**....(bt) BarryMcHugh(3) 9 54
(Lee Smyth, Ire) *hld up: hdwy over 2f out: rdn and hung lft over 1f out: styd on same pce fnl f* **16/1**
0/02 **7** ½ **Harare**[7] 668 9-8-13 **58**....(v) WilliamCarson(3) 8 59+
(R J Price) *trckd ldrs: hmpd and lost pl 7f out: rdn over 2f out: styd on ins fnl f* **11/4**[1]
0542 **8** nse **Kielty's Folly**[16] 540 6-8-13 **55**.... TonyCulhane 2 56
(B P J Baugh) *hld up: hdwy over 1f out: nt clr run and swtchd rt ins fnl f: nvr trbld ldrs* **11/4**[1]
/44- **9** ½ **Feeling (IRE)**[80] 7719 6-8-0 **47** oh1 ow1.... KierenFox(5) 3 44
(D Burchell) *prom: chsd ldr 6f out: rdn over 2f out: hung lft and wknd fnl f* **25/1**
-006 **10** ¾ **Jeannie (IRE)**[14] 567 4-8-4 **46** oh1.... FrannyNorton 4 42
(N P Littmoden) *chsd ldr over 2f: remained handy tl rdn over 2f out: wknd over 1f out* **50/1**
30-0 **11** 7 **Stateside (CAN)**[29] 367 5-9-4 **60**.... PaulHanagan 6 40
(R A Fahey) *prom: edgd lft 7f out: rdn over 3f out: wknd over 1f out* **14/1**
0-30 **12** 3½ **Northgate Lodge (USA)**[16] 540 5-8-4 **46** oh1.... JimmyQuinn 10 17
(M Brittain) *hld up: hdwy u.p over 2f out: sn wknd* **20/1**
-141 **13** 2½ **Positivity**[17] 518 4-9-0 **56**....(p) TomEaves 12 22
(B Smart) *hld up: rdn and wknd over 2f out* **11/1**[3]

1m 49.73s (-0.77) **Going Correction** 0.0s/f (Stan) **13** Ran SP% **119.5**
Speed ratings (Par 101): **103,101,99,98,98 97,97,97,97,96 90,87,84**
toteswingers: 1&2 £17.40, 1&3 £50.90, 2&3 £26.70 CSF £83.41 CT £1779.06 TOTE £16.30: £4.20, £2.40, £7.50; EX 101.50 Trifecta £105.60 Pool: £285.45 - 2.00 winning units..
Owner M Shirley **Bred** Plantation Stud **Trained** Averham Park, Notts

FOCUS
A moderate handicap run in a time 0.25 seconds faster than the second division. The winner is in the form of his life and could build from here.

754 STAY AT THE WOLVERHAMPTON HOLIDAY INN MEDIAN AUCTION MAIDEN STKS 1m 141y(P)
4:10 (4:12) (Class 5) 3-4-Y-0 £2,456 (£725; £362) Stalls Low

Form RPR
00- **1** **Power Series (USA)**[199] 5000 3-8-8 0.... RobertHavlin 5 75+
(J H M Gosden) *hld up: hdwy over 1f out r.o to ld post: value for much more than the winning margin* **9/4**[2]
4 **2** nse **Nadinska**[16] 545 3-8-3 0.... LukeMorris 2 69+
(M R Channon) *chsd ldrs: led over 1f out: hdd ins fnl f: r.o u.p* **9/2**[3]
02-2 **3** nse **Juicy Pear (IRE)**[11] 592 3-8-8 78.... HayleyTurner 4 74
(M L W Bell) *trckd ldr: led over 3f out: rdn and hdd over 1f out: rallied to ld ins fnl f: hdd post* **4/6**[1]
0 **4** 1 **Manxman (IRE)**[11] 592 3-8-8 0.... JoeFanning 1 72
(M Johnston) *led: rdn and hdd over 3f out: outpcd 2f out: rallied fnl f: r.o* **20/1**
0/3- **5** 8 **Dr Valentine (FR)**[83] 2293 4-10-0 74.... SebSanders 3 54
(Mrs A Duffield) *s.s: hdwy over 4f out: rdn and ev ch over 2f out: wknd over 1f out* **25/1**

1m 52.54s (2.04) **Going Correction** 0.0s/f (Stan)
WFA 3 from 4yo 20lb **5** Ran SP% **117.5**
Speed ratings (Par 103): **90,89,89,89,81**
CSF £13.37 TOTE £4.20: £1.70, £2.60; EX 16.90.
Owner K Abdulla **Bred** Juddmonte Farms Inc **Trained** Newmarket, Suffolk
■ Stewards' Enquiry : Hayley Turner two-day ban: used whip with excessive frequency (Mar 16-17)

FOCUS
This looked an interesting maiden, but a steady pace resulted in a slow time. There was controversy over the winning jockey's ride and it is hard to pin down the level of the form.

755 DINE IN THE HORIZONS RESTAURANT MAIDEN STKS 1m 1f 103y(P)
4:40 (4:42) (Class 5) 3-Y-0 £2,456 (£725; £362) Stalls Low

Form RPR
06-2 **1** **Gumnd (IRE)**[9] 634 3-9-3 73.... SebSanders 4 82
(C E Brittain) *mde all: pushed clr over 2f out: rdn and edgd lft fnl f: all out* **4/9**[1]
2 hd **Beneath** 3-9-3 0.... TomQueally 6 81+
(Pat Eddery) *a.p: rdn to chse wnr over 2f out: r.o wl towards fin: jst failed* **12/1**
3 7 **Beggar's Opera (IRE)** 3-9-3 0....(t) RobertHavlin 5 70+
(J H M Gosden) *rn green in rr: drvn along over 4f out: outpcd 3f out: hung lft and styd on to go 3rd ins fnl f: n.d* **6/1**[3]
- **4** 2¾ **Omaruru (IRE)** 3-9-3 0.... JoeFanning 1 61
(M Johnston) *chsd wnr tl rdn over 2f out: hung lft and wknd sn after* **5/1**[2]
6 **5** 3¾ **Gems**[11] 592 3-8-12 0.... JimmyQuinn 3 48
(H J L Dunlop) *chsd ldrs tl rdn and wknd over 2f out* **25/1**
6 13 **Roxy Spirit (IRE)** 3-8-12 0.... TomEaves 2 21
(M Mullineaux) *hld up: rdn over 5f out: wknd over 3f out* **100/1**

2m 2.89s (1.19) **Going Correction** 0.0s/f (Stan) **6** Ran SP% **112.7**
Speed ratings (Par 98): **94,93,87,85,81 70**
toteswingers: 1&2 £2.20, 1&3 £2.00, 2&3 £2.90 CSF £7.44 TOTE £1.50: £1.10, £2.90; EX 7.50.
Owner Saeed Manana **Bred** Tullamaine Castle Stud **Trained** Newmarket, Suffolk

FOCUS
An interesting maiden than should produce some winners. The winner is rated to his recent Lingfield form. The pace was just ordinary and the time was 1.53 seconds slower than the earlier Class 5 handicap for older horses.

756 THE BLACK COUNTRY'S ONLY RACECOURSE H'CAP 1m 4f 50y(P)
5:10 (5:10) (Class 5) (0-75,75) 4-Y-0+ £2,456 (£725; £362) Stalls Low

Form RPR
2333 1 **Benedict Spirit (IRE)**[9] 636 5-8-10 72............(v[1]) AndrewHeffernan(5) 3 84
(P D Evans) *trckd ldrs: racd keenly: wnt 2nd over 2f out: led wl over 1f out: edgd rt: rdn out* 10/3[1]
-632 2 3 **Tropical Blue**[14] 563 4-8-9 68.............................. StephenCraine 2 75
(Jennie Candlish) *hld up in tch: chsd wnr wl over 1f out: sn rdn and hung lft: nt run on* 15/2
10-4 3 nk **Ahmedy (IRE)**[42] 220 7-8-9 73.............................. IanBrennan(7) 6 80
(J J Quinn) *hmpd sn after s: hld up: plld hrd: hdwy over 2f out: sn rdn: styd on same pce fnl f* 7/1
6/2- 4 2 ½ **Gremlin**[252] 3223 6-8-5 67.............................. KierenFox(5) 5 70
(D Burchell) *hmpd sn after s: hld up: rdn and hung lft over 1f out: nt trble ldrs* 12/1
212 5 1 ½ **Kames Park (IRE)**[10] 620 8-8-10 72.............................. BillyCray(5) 9 73+
(R C Guest) *s.s: hld up: r.o ins fnl f: nvr nrr* 5/1[3]
1-05 6 1 **Rocky's Pride (IRE)**[17] 526 4-9-1 74.............................. NeilCallan 1 73
(A B Haynes) *hld up: hdwy over 1f out: sn rdn: wknd ins fnl f* 12/1
04-3 7 8 **Aureate**[17] 526 6-8-13 75.............................. DeclanCannon(5) 7 61
(B Forsey) *wnt lft s: chsd ldr tl led over 5f out: hdd over 3f out: rdn and wknd over 2f out* 7/1
36-0 8 ½ **Street Devil (USA)**[40] 231 5-9-2 73.............................. TonyCulhane 8 58
(R Curtis) *led: hdd over 5f out: led again over 3f out: rdn and hdd wl over 1f out: wknd fnl f* 33/1
123- 9 28 **Safebreaker**[133] 6900 5-8-8 70..............................(p) AmyRyan(5) 4 11
(K A Ryan) *chsd ldrs tl rdn and wknd wl over 3f out: t.o* 9/2[2]

2m 40.32s (-0.78) **Going Correction** 0.0s/f (Stan)
WFA 4 from 5yo+ 2lb 9 Ran SP% **113.0**
Speed ratings (Par 103): **102,100,99,98,97 96,91,90,72**
toteswingers: 1&2 £3.60, 1&3 £7.10, 2&3 £12.20 CSF £28.02 CT £162.12 TOTE £4.90: £1.80, £2.10, £2.70; EX 35.10 Trifecta £218.80 Part won. Pool: £295.80 - 0.20 winning units..
Owner Jason Tucker **Bred** Allevamento Pian Di Neve Srl **Trained** Pandy, Monmouths

FOCUS
A modest handicap run an ordinary pace. The form makes plenty of sense.
Kames Park(IRE) Official explanation: jockey said gelding was denied a clear run
Safebreaker Official explanation: jockey said gelding hung right-handed throughout

757 SPONSOR A RACE BY CALLING 01902 390000 H'CAP (DIV II) 1m 141y(P)
5:40 (5:40) (Class 6) (0-60,60) 4-Y-0+ £1,433 (£423; £211) Stalls Low

Form RPR
1 1 **Saddlers Bend (IRE)**[3] 721 4-8-4 46 oh1.............................. JimmyQuinn 2 55+
(George Baker) *hld up in tch: led over 1f out: sn rdn: all out* 11/10[1]
-042 2 shd **King's Icon (IRE)**[7] 665 5-9-2 58..............................(b) NickyMackay 9 67
(M Wigham) *hld up in tch: lost pl over 3f out: hdwy 2f out: r.o wl ins fnl f* 11/2[3]
3530 3 2 **Join Up**[7] 665 4-8-6 53.............................. KierenFox(5) 11 58
(W M Brisbourne) *led: rdn and hdd over 1f out: styd on same pce fnl f* 22/1
0322 4 2 ½ **Wavertree Warrior (IRE)**[7] 656 8-9-4 60..............................(b) NeilCallan 4 60
(N P Littmoden) *chsd ldrs: rdn over 2f out: styd on same pce appr fnl f* 11/2[3]
0-24 5 nk **Marjury Daw (IRE)**[16] 541 4-8-13 55.............................. TomQueally 3 54+
(J G Given) *dwlt: hld up: rdn over 3f out: last and plenty to do turning for home: hung lft and r.o wl ins fnl f: nvr nrr* 14/1
-064 6 ¾ **Coolnaharan (IRE)**[7] 666 10-8-10 57..............................(p) JamesSullivan(5) 5 55+
(Lee Smyth, Ire) *hld up: last but one and plenty to do turning for home: hung lft and r.o ins fnl f: n.d* 22/1
00-0 7 hd **Desert Mile (IRE)**[58] 21 7-8-13 55.............................. PJMcDonald 12 52
(Ollie Pears) *hld up in tch: rdn over 2f out: no imp fnl f* 9/2[2]
-000 8 1 ½ **King Of Rhythm (IRE)**[31] 354 7-8-4 53.............................. NeilFarley(7) 13 47
(D Carroll) *prom: racd keenly: chsd ldr over 5f out: rdn and ev ch over 2f out: wknd fnl f* 33/1
0034 9 ½ **Mojeerr**[17] 530 4-8-3 50..............................(b[1]) DeclanCannon(5) 10 43
(A J McCabe) *hld up: hdwy over 3f out: rdn over 2f out: hung lft and wknd over 1f out* 25/1
-640 10 2 ½ **Viking Awake (IRE)**[18] 503 4-8-7 49 ow1..............................(t) GrahamGibbons 7 37+
(J W Unett) *hld up: rdn and nt clr run wl over 1f out: n.d* 40/1
-050 11 1 ¼ **Bobering**[11] 590 10-8-2 47 oh1 ow1.............................. KellyHarrison(3) 1 32
(B P J Baugh) *hld up: effrt over 2f out: n.d* 66/1
-000 12 2 ¼ **One Cool Dream**[18] 498 4-8-8 53..............................(b) WilliamCarson(3) 8 33
(P W Hiatt) *led: hdd over 7f out: chsd ldrs: rdn and wkng whn hung lft over 1f out:* 40/1

1m 50.02s (-0.48) **Going Correction** 0.0s/f (Stan) 12 Ran SP% **125.1**
Speed ratings (Par 101): **102,101,100,97,97 96,96,95,95,92 91,89**
toteswingers: 1&2 £3.40, 1&3 £12.30, 2&3 £13.80 CSF £7.35 CT £97.52 TOTE £2.50: £1.10, £2.00, £4.80; EX 11.20 Trifecta £91.20 Pool: £537.74 - 4.36 winning units. Place 6: £95.19 Place 5: £37.65 .
Owner Mrs Christine Cone **Bred** J F Tuthill **Trained** Moreton Morrell, Warwicks

FOCUS
The time was 0.25 seconds slower than the first division. Solid form which should work out.
Wavertree Warrior(IRE) Official explanation: jockey said gelding hung right
T/Plt: £126.10 to a £1 stake. Pool: £67,645.18. 391.56 winning tickets. T/Qpdt: £22.30 to a £1 stake. Pool: £5,463.89. 181.06 winning tickets. CR

734 LINGFIELD (L-H)
Tuesday, March 2

OFFICIAL GOING: Standard
Wind: Almost nil Weather: Fine, pleasant

758 MARRIOTT HOTEL OPENING SPRING 2010 MAIDEN STKS 7f (P)
2:10 (2:10) (Class 5) 3-Y-0+ £2,456 (£725; £362) Stalls Low

Form RPR
333- 1 **Mawaddah (IRE)**[111] 7326 3-8-10 76.............................. FrankieMcDonald 8 80+
(R Hannon) *prom: led over 4f out: 2 l clr over 2f out: pushed along and styd on wl fr over 1f out* 5/4[1]
2 2 ¼ **Magic Omen (USA)** 3-8-10 0.............................. JoeFanning 4 74+
(M Johnston) *wl in tch: chsd wnr wl over 2f out: sn shkn up: styd on wl but no imp fnl f* 9/2[2]
5 3 4 ½ **Army Of Stars (IRE)**[40] 253 4-9-12 0.............................. ShaneKelly 2 65
(J A Osborne) *dwlt: hld up in tch in rr: plenty to do whn effrt on outer 2f out: styd on to take modest 3rd ent fnl f: no ch ldng pair* 50/1
6-4 4 1 ¾ **Court Drinking (USA)**[8] 655 3-8-10 0.............................. SteveDrowne 3 54
(J R Best) *dwlt: hld up in tch: sltly awkward but prog over 2f out: chsd clr ldng pair over 1f out tl ent fnl f: one pce* 22/1
0- 5 3 ½ **Asterrlini (IRE)**[165] 6066 3-8-5 0.............................. HayleyTurner 6 40
(C E Brittain) *prom: rdn and lost pl sn after 1/2-way: struggling 2f out: modest late prog* 10/1
6 shd **Southern Cape (IRE)** 3-8-10 0.............................. JimmyQuinn 9 45
(D J Coakley) *s.s: detached in last and pushed along: no prog tl kpt on fnl f* 6/1[3]
50- 7 2 ¼ **Tislimeen**[129] 7033 3-8-5 0.............................. ChrisCatlin 5 34
(M R Channon) *led to over 4f out: lost pl over 2f out: wknd over 1f out* 9/2[2]
00/0 8 1 **Savanna's Gold**[13] 586 6-9-0 34.............................. RichardRowe(7) 7 37
(R Rowe) *racd wd: wl in tch: rdn to chse ldng pair over 2f out to over 1f out: wknd rapidly* 250/1
00 9 6 **Givenn**[8] 655 6-9-7 0.............................. GeorgeBaker 1 21
(Ms J S Doyle) *hld up in tch on inner: effrt over 2f out: wknd rapidly over 1f out* 100/1

1m 25.73s (0.93) **Going Correction** +0.05s/f (Slow)
WFA 3 from 4yo+ 16lb 9 Ran SP% **111.9**
Speed ratings (Par 103): **96,93,88,86,82 82,79,78,71**
toteswingers: 1&2 £2.50, 1&3 £7.70, 2&3 £10.20 CSF £6.64 TOTE £2.10: £1.30, £1.50, £6.90; EX 9.20 Trifecta £85.50 Pool:£487.72 - 4.22 winning units..
Owner Malih L Al Basti **Bred** J Beckett **Trained** East Everleigh, Wilts

FOCUS
A modest maiden run at a steady pace. The first two did well to pull clear.

759 LINGFIELDPARK.CO.UK MAIDEN STKS 6f (P)
2:40 (2:40) (Class 5) 3-Y-O £2,456 (£725; £362) Stalls Low

Form RPR
1 **Srda (USA)** 3-8-12 0.............................. SebSanders 4 68+
(C E Brittain) *hld up in last pair: prog on inner 2f out: drvn and styd on fnl f to ld last 100yds* 2/1[1]
22 2 ½ **Pippbrook Ministar**[10] 638 3-8-12 0.............................. HayleyTurner 1 67
(J R Boyle) *t.k.h early: trckd ldng pair: shkn up over 2f out: effrt and drvn to chal 1f out: upsides but nt qckn w wnr last 100yds* 2/1[1]
5-26 3 ½ **Neduardo**[33] 321 3-9-3 69.............................. RobertHavlin 3 70
(P W Chapple-Hyam) *led: 2 l clr 2f out: drvn and pressed 1f out: hdd and one pce last 100yds* 5/1[2]
3 4 1 ¾ **Lockantanks**[18] 527 3-9-3 0.............................. ChrisCatlin 2 64
(M R Channon) *chsd ldr to wl over 1f out: nt qckn after* 12/1
4-53 5 hd **My Mandy (IRE)**[21] 473 3-8-12 64.............................. LiamJones 5 59
(R A Harris) *cl up: pushed along 1/2-way: wl in tch over 1f out: rdn and nt qckn* 20/1
0- 6 10 **Bob Goes Electric (IRE)**[304] 1669 3-9-3 0.............................. RobertWinston 6 32
(J R Best) *t.k.h: racd wd: chsd ldrs tl wknd 2f out* 8/1[3]
03- 7 5 **Marius Maximus (IRE)**[158] 6246 3-9-3 0.............................. JoeFanning 7 16
(M Johnston) *s.i.s: t.k.h early and hld up in last: wknd rapidly 2f out* 12/1

1m 11.95s (0.05) **Going Correction** +0.05s/f (Slow) 7 Ran SP% **114.6**
Speed ratings (Par 98): **101,100,99,97,97 83,77**
toteswingers:1&2:£2.00, 1&3:£3.90, 2&3:£2.90 CSF £5.86 TOTE £4.30: £3.20, £1.10; EX 8.20.
Owner Saeed Manana **Bred** Brushwood Stable **Trained** Newmarket, Suffolk

FOCUS
A modest maiden, run at a fair pace.
Bob Goes Electric(IRE) Official explanation: jockey said colt ran free to post

760 CYPRIUM BAR AT MARRIOTT LINGFIELD (S) STKS 1m 2f (P)
3:10 (3:10) (Class 6) 3-Y-O £1,774 (£523; £262) Stalls Low

Form RPR
400- 1 **Nom De La Rosa (IRE)**[156] 6305 3-8-7 66.............................. FergusSweeney 5 57
(G L Moore) *in tch: chsd ldng pair 3f out: sn rdn: styd on fr over 1f out to ld last 150yds* 5/2[2]
2263 2 1 ¼ **Magic Spirit**[7] 670 3-8-7 57..............................(b) LukeMorris 4 55
(J S Moore) *s.i.s: led after 1f tl after 2f: led again over 4f out: hrd rdn on inner over 1f out: hdd and no ex last 150yds* 13/2
2164 3 1 **Ant Music (IRE)**[10] 633 3-9-4 65.............................. LiamKeniry 1 64
(J S Moore) *in tch: dropped to last and struggling over 3f out: plugged on again fr over 1f out* 10/3[3]
06-0 4 1 **Expensive Legacy**[17] 542 3-8-7 49.............................. JimmyQuinn 3 51
(H J L Dunlop) *led after 2f to over 4f out: pushed along and struggling over 3f out: plugged on fnl f* 25/1
-345 5 ½ **Fair Nella**[6] 677 3-8-7 62.............................. JoeFanning 6 50
(J G Portman) *led 1f: styd cl up: trckd ldr 4f out: looked dangerous over 1f out: effrt petered out ent fnl f* 2/1[1]
30-5 6 6 **Patachou**[12] 597 3-8-2 48..............................(v[1]) KierenFox(5) 7 39
(R J Smith) *racd wd: hld up in last pair: effrt over 3f out: wknd 2f out* 14/1

2m 9.44s (2.84) **Going Correction** +0.05s/f (Slow) 6 Ran SP% **108.8**
Speed ratings (Par 96): **90,89,88,87,87 82**
.The winner was bought in for 3,200gns. Magic Spirit was claimed by F. W. K. Griffin for £6,000
Owner Tony Bloom **Bred** Maddenstown Equine Enterprise Ltd **Trained** Lower Beeding, W Sussex
■ Stewards' Enquiry : Fergus Sweeney caution: careless riding

FOCUS
A weak seller and the winner did not need to match her 2yo peak.

761 SHOVELSTRODE H'CAP 6f (P)
3:40 (3:40) (Class 4) (0-85,85) 4-Y-0+ £4,209 (£1,252; £625; £312) Stalls Low

Form RPR
00/- 1 **Lucky Redback (IRE)**[493] 6979 4-9-1 82.............................. JimmyFortune 4 91
(R Hannon) *detached in last and pushed along early: stl last and hanging rt over 1f out: picked up wl fnl f on wd outside: r.o to ld last strides* 5/2[1]
3212 2 ½ **Secret Witness**[12] 595 4-8-11 78..............................(b) LiamJones 2 85
(R A Harris) *trckd ldng pair: effrt 2f out: rdn to ld ins fnl f: styd on: hdd last strides* 5/2[1]
660- 3 ½ **Beat The Bell**[90] 7613 5-9-1 82.............................. ShaneKelly 5 88
(J A Osborne) *trckd ldng pair: effrt 2f out: rdn to ld 1f out: hdd and outpcd ins fnl f* 15/2
0542 4 4 **Peak District (IRE)**[3] 736 6-9-2 83..............................(t) StephenCraine 6 76
(K A Ryan) *trckd ldr: led wl over 1f out: hdd & wknd rapidly 1f out* 7/2[2]

0-24 **5** 1 1/2 **Halsion Chancer**[8] 657 6-8-12 **79** .... RobertWinston 3 67
(J R Best) *led: drvn and hdd wl over 1f out: sn wknd* **9/2**[3]
1m 10.79s (-1.11) **Going Correction** +0.05s/f (Slow) 5 Ran SP% **109.3**
Speed ratings (Par 105): **109,108,107,102,100**
CSF £8.81 TOTE £3.20: £1.90, £1.50; EX 8.70.
Owner Amblestock Partnership **Bred** M J Wiley **Trained** East Everleigh, Wilts

FOCUS
A fair little handicap, run at a sound pace.

762 MARRIOTT HOTEL COMING SOON H'CAP 1m 2f (P)
4:10 (4:10) (Class 6) (0-65,65) 3-Y-O £1,774 (£523; £262) Stalls Low

Form RPR
300- **1** **Usquaebach**[131] 6970 3-8-11 **55** .... FergusSweeney 13 61+
(P M Phelan) *hld up and sn last: gd prog on wd outside fr 3f out: clsd on ldrs over 1f out: kpt on fnl f to ld last strides* **100/1**
2443 **2** *nk* **Captain Cool (IRE)**[6] 677 3-8-0 **51** ....(p) CharlesEddery(7) 1 56
(R Hannon) *hld up in midfield: prog on inner 3f out: nowhere to go briefly over 2f out: rdn and styd on to ld narrowly ins fnl f: hdd last strides* **9/2**[3]
000- **3** *nk* **Mnarani (IRE)**[91] 7604 3-9-7 **65** .... LiamKeniry 3 69
(J S Moore) *prom: led gng strly over 2f out: drvn over 1f out: hdd ins fnl f: nt qckn nr fin* **14/1**
0-23 **4** 3 1/2 **Always De One**[15] 564 3-8-11 **55** .... JimmyQuinn 6 53
(Miss J Feilden) *settled midfield: rdn 3f out: prog 2f out: clsd on ldrs over 1f out: nt qckn and btn fnl f* **4/1**[2]
-302 **5** 3/4 **New Den**[25] 422 3-9-5 **63** ....(v) NickyMackay 5 59
(J R Boyle) *disp 2nd pl: drvn 5f out: railled over 3f out: upsides over 2f out: wknd over 1f out: fin lame* **15/2**
0-05 **6** *shd* **Chateau Zara**[12] 592 3-8-12 **56** .... AdamKirby 11 52
(C G Cox) *hld up wl in rr: stdy prog on inner over 2f out: rdn and nt qckn over 1f out: one pce after* **16/1**
60-0 **7** *hd* **Tallawalla (IRE)**[20] 490 3-9-2 **60** .... ChrisCatlin 10 55
(M R Channon) *drvn fr wd draw early but sn hld up in rr: gng easily 3f out bhd rivals: rdn and fnd nil 2f out: plodded on* **12/1**
600- **8** 1 1/2 **Dinkie Short**[146] 6586 3-8-11 **55** ....(p) HayleyTurner 12 47
(B De Haan) *dwlt: mostly in last pair: rdn 3f out: modest late prog* **18/1**
20-4 **9** 3 3/4 **Fusaichi Flyer (USA)**[20] 490 3-9-4 **62** .... SteveDrowne 9 47
(R Charlton) *hld up wl in tch: cl up on outer 3f out: wknd tamely 2f out* **9/4**[1]
-625 **10** 2 3/4 **Royal Torbo (ISR)**[28] 381 3-8-11 **60** .... MatthewDavies(5) 8 39
(George Baker) *nvr bttr than midfield: struggling on outer 3f out: sn btn* **33/1**
65-4 **11** 1/2 **Rock Of Eire**[20] 482 3-8-11 **55** ....(t) EddieCreighton 4 33
(E J Creighton) *led: drvn and hdd over 2f out: wknd rapidly over 1f out* **40/1**
26-4 **12** 7 **Spice Fair**[25] 433 3-9-2 **65** .... LeeNewnes(5) 7 29
(M D I Usher) *disp 2nd pl to 3f out: sn wknd* **12/1**
2m 5.95s (-0.65) **Going Correction** +0.05s/f (Slow) 12 Ran SP% **120.3**
Speed ratings (Par 96): **104,103,103,100,100 100,99,98,95,93 93,87**
toteswingers:1&2:£56.50, 1&3:£196.50, 2&3:£15.70 CSF £520.00 CT £6726.08 TOTE £99.40: £14.80, £1.90, £4.40; EX 464.70 TRIFECTA Not won..
Owner KFM Partnership **Bred** R P Williams **Trained** Epsom, Surrey
■ Stewards' Enquiry : Jimmy Quinn one-day ban: careless riding (Mar 16)

FOCUS
A moderate handicap and a real shock but there was no fluke about it. The second and fourth set a modest but solid level.
New Den Official explanation: vet said colt finished lame right fore
Rock Of Eire Official explanation: jockey said gelding hung right in straight

763 BREATHE SPA AT MARRIOTT LINGFIELD H'CAP 7f (P)
4:40 (4:40) (Class 6) (0-55,55) 4-Y-O+ £1,774 (£523; £262) Stalls Low

Form RPR
0-53 **1** **Sign Of The Cross**[5] 693 6-9-2 **54** .... RobertWinston 2 62
(C R Dore) *hld up in midfield: gng strly 2f out: asked for effrt and sed hanging w hd to one side over 1f out: cajoled along and styd on fnl f: led last strides* **9/1**
-013 **2** *hd* **Top Flight Splash**[11] 615 4-8-9 **52** ....(v) AndrewHeffernan(5) 11 59
(P D Evans) *prom: chsd ldr 4f out: rdn to ld narrowly over 1f out: kpt on fnl f: hdd last strides* **4/1**[2]
0223 **3** 1 3/4 **Tamino (IRE)**[5] 694 7-9-3 **55** .... JimmyQuinn 9 58
(P Howling) *led: drvn and narowly hdd over 1f out: one pce ins fnl f* **3/1**[1]
0/0 **4** 1 **Aah Haa**[13] 588 5-9-0 **52** .... J-PGuillambert 7 53
(N J Gifford) *chsd ldrs: pushed along fr 1/2-way: effrt 2f out: nt qckn over 1f out: kpt on* **20/1**
5000 **5** *nk* **Reigning Monarch (USA)**[8] 656 7-8-3 **46** ....(p) RossAtkinson(5) 12 46
(Miss Z C Davison) *dropped in fr wd draw: hld up towards rr: rdn in 7th 2f out: nt qckn over 1f out: kpt on fnl f* **16/1**
000- **6** 1/2 **Takitwo**[141] 6719 7-9-0 **52** ....(v) SimonWhitworth 4 51
(P D Cundell) *hld up in rr: stl there 2f out: reminders and sme prog over 1f out: rdn and kpt on one pce fnl f: nvr rchd ldrs* **33/1**
4450 **7** *hd* **Captain Kallis (IRE)**[7] 674 4-9-2 **54** .... HayleyTurner 6 52
(D J S Ffrench Davis) *chsd ldr 3f: styd cl up: effrt on inner over 1f out: wknd fnl f* **9/1**
2520 **8** 1 3/4 **Imperial Skylight**[15] 567 4-9-0 **52** ....(v) ChrisCatlin 8 46
(M R Channon) *trckd ldrs: gng easily over 2f out: rdn and fnd nil wl over 1f out: btn after* **16/1**
-600 **9** *nk* **The Mouse Carroll (IRE)**[19] 498 6-9-3 **55** .... FrankieMcDonald 3 48
(B R Johnson) *a in rr: rdn on inner over 2f out: no real prog* **13/2**[3]
4600 **10** *nk* **Grizedale (IRE)**[5] 691 11-8-3 **46** ....(tp) KierenFox(5) 5 38
(M J Attwater) *hld up in last: no prog 2f out: btn after* **50/1**
2325 **11** *hd* **Ride A White Swan**[5] 691 5-8-12 **50** .... KevinGhunowa 14 42
(D Shaw) *dropped in fr wd draw: hld up: effrt on outer 2f out: fnd nil* **7/1**
0-03 **12** 11 **Our Day Will Come**[11] 614 4-8-12 **55** .... DeclanCannon(5) 13 19
(B Palling) *nvr bttr than midfield: rdn on outer 3f out: wknd: t.o* **12/1**
1m 24.48s (-0.32) **Going Correction** +0.05s/f (Slow) 12 Ran SP% **120.0**
Speed ratings (Par 101): **103,102,100,99,99 98,98,96,96,95 95,83**
toteswingers:1&2:£8.30, 1&3:£7.10, 2&3:£2.80 CSF £44.65 CT £139.39 TOTE £13.60: £3.20, £2.90, £1.10; EX 57.90 Trifecta £171.20 Pool:£289.31 - 1.25 winning units..
Owner Mrs Louise Marsh **Bred** T R G Vestey **Trained** Cowbit, Lincs

FOCUS
A weak handicap where the first two pulled clear. Limited form, pitched around the principals.

764 LINGFIELDPARK.CO.UK APPRENTICE H'CAP 2m (P)
5:10 (5:11) (Class 5) (0-75,70) 4-Y-O+ £2,456 (£725; £362) Stalls Low

Form RPR
0232 **1** **Star Choice**[8] 660 5-9-7 **63** ....(b[1]) AshleyMorgan 2 71
(J Pearce) *trckd ldng pair: chal on inner to ld over 2f out: rdn and wl in command fnl f* **9/4**[1]
000/ **2** 3 **Himba**[58] 4576 7-8-6 **51** oh2 .... RichardRowe(3) 6 54
(N J Gifford) *trckd ldr: chal on outer over 2f out: chsd wnr after: kpt on but no imp* **66/1**
510- **3** 3 3/4 **Gandalf**[145] 6622 8-9-11 **70** .... JohnFahy(3) 3 69
(Miss Amy Weaver) *s.s: hld up in rr: wl in tch 3f out: nudged along as ldng pair wnt clr 2f out: rdn and one pce ins fnl f: no ch w front pair* **7/2**[3]
12-0 **4** 3 1/2 **Strikemaster (IRE)**[13] 330 4-8-13 **60** .... AndrewHeffernan 5 55
(B Ellison) *hld up in rr: pushed along 3f out: sn outpcd: rdn to take 4th ins fnl f* **3/1**[2]
10-0 **5** *nk* **K'Gari (USA)**[13] 15 4-8-4 **51** oh3 ....(be) DeclanCannon 4 45
(B Ellison) *led: rdn and hdd over 2f out: wknd over 1f out* **16/1**
3m 30.87s (5.17) **Going Correction** +0.05s/f (Slow)
WFA 4 from 5yo+ 5lb 5 Ran SP% **85.4**
Speed ratings (Par 103): **89,87,85,83,83**
CSF £44.65 TOTE £2.50: £1.60, £8.60; EX 29.50 Place 6 £39.66, Place 5 £25.79.
Owner Macniler Racing Partnership **Bred** B J Warren **Trained** Newmarket, Suffolk
■ Prince Charlemagne was withdrawn after breaking out of the stalls (5/2, deduct 25p in the 3 under R4).

FOCUS
This was weakened by the late withdrawal and due to the moderate pace the form is suspect. The winner and fourth set the level.
T/Plt: £73.00 to a £1 stake. Pool: £73,929.20. 739.26 winning tickets. T/Qpdt: £52.30 to a £1 stake. Pool: £5,054.52. 71.40 winning tickets. JN

744 KEMPTON (A.W) (R-H)
Wednesday, March 3

OFFICIAL GOING: Standard
Wind: Fresh, across (towards stands) Weather: Cloudy

765 KEMPTON.CO.UK H'CAP 1m 2f (P)
5:45 (5:45) (Class 4) (0-80,79) 4-Y-O+ £4,209 (£1,252; £625; £312) Stalls High

Form RPR
0-54 **1** **Taaresh (IRE)**[28] 383 5-8-6 **67** .... JoeFanning 8 75
(K A Morgan) *trckd ldrs: wnt 2nd 3f out: effrt to ld over 1f out: sn 2 l clr: readily* **7/1**
0-06 **2** 1 1/4 **Buddy Holly**[16] 565 5-9-3 **78** .... AdamKirby 2 85
(Pat Eddery) *led at stdy pce for over 3f: trckd ldng pair 2f out: trapped bhd wkng rival over 1f out and n.m.r sn after: got through to take 2nd last 100yds: wnr already home* **11/4**[1]
-214 **3** 3/4 **Cupid's Glory**[11] 637 8-8-13 **74** .... LiamKeniry 7 79
(G L Moore) *hld up in last trio: prog over 2f out: rdn to chse wnr jst over 1f out: no imp: lost 2nd last 100yds* **12/1**
5112 **4** 2 1/2 **Formidable Guest**[5] 725 6-9-1 **76** .... RobertHavlin 3 76
(J Pearce) *hld up in last trio: pushed along over 2f out: plugged on u.p to take 4th ins fnl f: no ch* **9/2**[3]
30-5 **5** 1 1/2 **Ramona Chase**[11] 637 5-9-4 **79** ....(t) MartinDwyer 4 76
(M J Attwater) *dwlt: t.k.h and prog to ld after 4f: hdd & wknd rapidly over 1f out* **20/1**
0223 **6** 1 1/4 **Rapid City**[7] 676 7-8-7 **68** .... PaulDoe 9 69
(P D Evans) *hld up in last trio: sme prog on inner 2f out: keeping on but only ch of pl whn no room against rail fnl f* **13/2**
4-34 **7** 1 1/4 **Hawaana (IRE)**[21] 480 5-9-3 **78** .... SteveDrowne 6 71
(Miss Gay Kelleway) *trckd ldrs: rdn and wknd 2f out* **3/1**[2]
40-3 **8** 17 **Watchmaker**[26] 429 7-8-6 **67** .... ChrisCatlin 1 29
(Miss Tor Sturgis) *prom: led briefly over 6f out: wknd rapidly wl over 2f out: t.o* **14/1**
2m 7.92s (-0.08) **Going Correction** -0.05s/f (Stan) 8 Ran SP% **114.8**
Speed ratings (Par 105): **98,97,96,94,93 92,91,77**
toteswingers: 1&2 10.90, 1&3 £5.70, 2&3 £12.10 CSF £26.74 CT £228.79 TOTE £8.20: £2.90, £2.10, £4.60; EX 34.50.
Owner P Doughty **Bred** Shadwell Estate Company Limited **Trained** Newmarket, Suffolk

FOCUS
A modest and open-looking handicap. It was run at a steady pace until two went on going out onto the back straight and the overall form is worth treating with a degree of caution, although the winner did it quite well.

766 BOOK KEMPTON TICKETS ON 0844 579 3008 CLAIMING STKS 6f (P)
6:15 (6:17) (Class 6) 3-Y-O £2,047 (£604; £302) Stalls High

Form RPR
3312 **1** **Maoi Chinn Tire (IRE)**[19] 519 3-8-12 74 ....(p) LiamKeniry 3 75
(J S Moore) *mde virtually all: def advantage over 2f out: strly drvn to maintain advantage fr over 1f out* **5/2**[2]
-235 **2** 2 1/2 **Coolree Star (IRE)**[17] 550 3-9-3 78 .... JimCrowley 4 72
(J A Glover) *w wnr to 1/2-way: sn rdn: 2 l down by 2f out and no imp after* **9/4**[1]
604- **3** 2 3/4 **Reach For The Sky (IRE)**[135] 6906 3-8-0 65 .... CharlotteKerton(7) 5 54
(G Prodromou) *chsd ldng pair: outpcd over 2f out: bmpd along furiously and no imp after* **20/1**
0-34 **4** 3/4 **Penrod Ballantyne (IRE)**[11] 638 3-9-3 63 .... MartinDwyer 6 62+
(B J Meehan) *stdd s: hld up last: t.k.h for 1f but sn pushed along: sme prog fnl 2f: nvr a threat* **9/2**[3]
410- **5** *nk* **Chandrayaan**[146] 6609 3-8-12 67 ....(v) SamHitchcott 2 56
(J E Long) *towards rr: drvn over 2f out: limited prog wl over 1f out and nt look v willing* **20/1**
530- **6** 4 **Petrocelli**[205] 4858 3-8-11 72 .... ShaneKelly 7 43
(A J McCabe) *settled in rr: rdn and no prog over 2f out: wknd fnl f* **7/1**
0 **7** 7 **Carolina Cherry (IRE)**[17] 550 3-8-1 0 .... FrankieMcDonald 8 12
(Miss Amy Weaver) *chsd ldrs: wknd rapidly fnl 2f* **50/1**
-425 **8** 1 **Italian Tom (IRE)**[21] 478 3-9-3 79 .... ChrisCatlin 1 25
(R A Harris) *chsd ldrs: wknd rapidly over 2f out* **7/1**
1m 11.86s (-1.24) **Going Correction** -0.05s/f (Stan) 8 Ran SP% **114.0**
Speed ratings (Par 96): **106,102,99,98,97 92,82,81**
toteswingers: 1&2 £1.60, 1&3 £13.70, 2&3 £20.80 CSF £8.30 TOTE £2.00: £1.02, £2.00, £8.00; EX 9.20.
Owner W Adams & J S Moore **Bred** Mrs E Thompson **Trained** Upper Lambourn, Berks

FOCUS
An ordinary claimer and limited form, based around the second and fourth.
Petrocelli Official explanation: jockey said gelding hung left

767 DIGIBET H'CAP 6f (P)
6:45 (6:50) (Class 5) (0-75,75) 4-Y-O+ £2,590 (£770; £385; £192) Stalls High

Form RPR
-404 **1** **Kersivay**[9] 668 4-8-7 **69**..........(v[1]) AndrewHeffernan(5) 11 76
(P D Evans) *rrd bef stalls opened: mde virtually all: gng strly 2f out: hrd rdn whn chal jst over 1f out: hld on* **4/1**[1]

-254 **2** *nk* **Welcome Approach**[13] 595 7-8-5 **62**.......... LukeMorris 10 68
(J R Weymes) *prom: wnt 2nd 2f out: rdn to chal over 1f out: nt qckn and a jst hld fnl f* **12/1**

-034 **3** *hd* **Gone Hunting**[21] 481 4-8-13 **70**..........(t) DaneO'Neill 12 75
(J Pearce) *s.i.s: sn chsd ldrs on inner: effrt 2f out: drvn to go 3rd over 1f out: styd on fnl f: a jst hld* **12/1**

4245 **4** *1* **Rondeau (GR)**[12] 616 5-9-1 **72**.......... JimCrowley 8 74
(P R Chamings) *hld up in 8th: prog jst over 2f out: wnt 4th jst over 1f out: kpt on same pce* **13/2**

2-43 **5** *nk* **Another Try (IRE)**[17] 552 5-8-4 **66** ow1.......... MatthewDavies(5) 1 67+
(A P Jarvis) *dropped in fr wd draw: hld up: last 2f out: taken to wd outside and gd prog over 1f out: kpt on fnl f: no ch to throw down a chal* **6/1**[3]

40-3 **6** *1 3/4* **Todber**[20] 502 5-8-11 **68**..........(v) MartinDwyer 4 63
(M P Tregoning) *pressed wnr: veered lft after 1f: lost 2nd 2f out: grad fdd* **10/1**

01 **7** *1* **Valentino Swing (IRE)**[7] 678 7-9-0 **71** 6ex ow2.......... AdamKirby 5 63+
(Miss T Spearing) *settled in 9th: pushed along over 2f out: rn into trble briefly over 1f out: nt persevered w whn little ch fnl f* **10/1**

30-5 **8** *3/4* **Gazboolou**[17] 552 6-9-1 **72**.......... FergusSweeney 7 62
(David Pinder) *trckd ldrs: wl plcd over 2f out: rdn and no rspnse wl over 1f out: sn btn* **16/1**

66-4 **9** *3/4* **Priti Fabulous (IRE)**[3] 747 5-9-1 **72**.......... ShaneKelly 2 59
(A J McCabe) *dropped in fr wd draw and hld up in last trio: shkn up and no real prog over 2f out* **9/1**

20-3 **10** *1/2* **Whiskey Junction**[12] 616 6-9-4 **75**.......... SebSanders 3 61
(M Quinn) *chsd ldng pair: rdn wl over 2f out: sn lost pl and btn* **9/2**[2]

-056 **11** *3/4* **La Capriosa**[13] 601 4-8-5 **62**.......... ChrisCatlin 6 45
(J A Glover) *trckd ldrs on outer: rdn over 2f out: sn lost pl and btn* **25/1**

6-00 **12** *hd* **Princess Valerina**[26] 432 6-9-1 **72**.......... FrankieMcDonald 9 55
(D Haydn Jones) *fractious on to crse and led to post: s.s: a in last trio: rdn and no prog 2f out* **20/1**

1m 12.31s (-0.79) **Going Correction** -0.05s/f (Stan) 12 Ran SP% **123.9**
Speed ratings (Par 103): **103,102,102,101,100 98,96,95,94,94 93,93**
toteswingers: 1&2 £12.70, 1&3 £21.30, 2&3 £31.30 CSF £55.48 CT £421.81 TOTE £7.20: £2.50, £3.90, £4.80; EX 64.40.
Owner Mrs I M Folkes **Bred** Brook Stud Bloodstock Ltd **Trained** Pandy, Monmouths

FOCUS
Things do not come much more open than this moderate sprint handicap. There was an average pace on and it was another race where it paid to race handily. High draws dominated and the form is solid but limited.

768 DIGIBET.COM MAIDEN FILLIES' STKS 1m (P)
7:15 (7:18) (Class 5) 3-Y-O+ £2,590 (£770; £385; £192) Stalls High

Form RPR
0- **1** **Tafawut**[187] 5398 3-8-9 0.......... LukeMorris 8 73+
(C G Cox) *s.i.s: sn in midfield: smooth prog fr 3f out: shkn up to cl and ld jst over 1f out: edgd lft but readily drew clr* **11/4**[2]

44-4 **2** *3 1/2* **Larkrise Star**[12] 618 3-8-9 66.......... ChrisCatlin 3 62
(D K Ivory) *chsd ldr: effrt to ld 2f out: hdd and edgd lft jst over 1f out: outpcd after* **9/1**

3 *1* **Jumeirah Palm (USA)** 3-8-9 0.......... HayleyTurner 13 62+
(D M Simcock) *s.i.s: towards rr on inner: sltly checked 3f out and sn rousted along: signs of greenness but styd on fr 2f out: wnt 3rd ins fnl f: nrst fin* **6/1**[3]

06- **4** *3* **Lady Willa (IRE)**[163] 6163 3-8-9 0.......... MichaelHills 1 52+
(B W Hills) *racd wd: cl up: chsd ldng pair 1/2-way to over 2f out: rn green and outpcd: kpt on again ins fnl f* **15/8**[1]

5 *nk* **Engaging**[210] 4-9-13 0.......... SebSanders 9 58
(P D Cundell) *led to 2f out: steadily fdd* **20/1**

5-04 **6** *1/2* **La Toya J (IRE)**[15] 574 3-8-9 58.......... FergusSweeney 7 50
(R Curtis) *prom: chsd ldng pair briefly over 2f out and cl enough: wknd over 1f out* **14/1**

7 *nk* **Rock D'Argent (IRE)** 3-8-9 0.......... TravisBlock 10 50+
(H Morrison) *s.s: wl in rr: sme prog on inner over 2f out: shkn up over 1f out: n.d but kpt on* **11/1**

00-5 **8** *2* **See Elsie Play**[21] 481 4-9-6 60.......... GemmaGracey-Davison(7) 5 51
(Miss Z C Davison) *racd wd in midfield: u.p 3f out: steadily outpcd after* **33/1**

4-40 **9** *2* **Kalligal**[8] 674 5-9-13 52.......... RobertHavlin 6 46
(R Ingram) *wl in rr: pushed along and sme prog fr over 2f out: no ch w ldrs: wknd fnl f* **80/1**

50 **10** *1* **Kitty Koo (IRE)**[17] 551 3-8-2 0.......... MatthewCosham(7) 12 38
(J Jay) *a in rr: struggling over 2f out* **100/1**

0- **11** *3 1/2* **Annacaboe (IRE)**[203] 4906 3-8-9 0.......... AdrianMcCarthy 11 29
(D K Ivory) *chsd ldng pair to 1/2-way: lost pl u.p after* **100/1**

12 *hd* **Adoyen Spice** 3-8-9 0.......... MartinDwyer 4 29
(Mike Murphy) *v s.i.s: rn green in last: nvr a factor* **20/1**

0-0 **13** *2 1/4* **Melting Bob (USA)**[37] 291 4-9-13 0.......... ShaneKelly 2 23
(Dr J D Scargill) *a towards rr: wknd over 2f out* **33/1**

1m 40.85s (1.05) **Going Correction** -0.05s/f (Stan)
WFA 3 from 4yo+ 18lb 13 Ran SP% **119.4**
Speed ratings (Par 100): **92,88,87,84,84 83,83,81,79,78 74,74,72**
toteswingers:1&2 £3.30, 1&3 £6.20, 2&3 £4.10 CSF £26.01 TOTE £4.70: £2.00, £2.40, £2.20; EX 36.30.
Owner Barry Taylor **Bred** Barry Taylor **Trained** Lambourn, Berks

FOCUS
A moderate fillies' maiden, run at an ordinary pace. The winner impressed but the bare form is limited by the likes of the sixth and ninth.

769 DIGIBET CASINO H'CAP 1m (P)
7:45 (7:47) (Class 3) (0-95,92) 4-Y-O+
£6,542 (£1,959; £979; £490; £244; £122) Stalls High

Form RPR
1 **Starluck (IRE)**[67] 4357 5-9-4 **92**.......... LiamKeniry 7 103+
(A Fleming) *hld up in 6th: stdy prog over 2f out: couple of sharp reminders over 1f out: wnt 2nd ent fnl f: clsd to ld last 75yds: pushed out* **7/2**[1]

0-16 **2** *1/2* **Gaily Noble (IRE)**[20] 508 4-8-8 **82**.......... FergusSweeney 3 91
(A B Haynes) *trckd ldng pair: effrt to ld wl over 1f out: styd on wl but hdd and outpcd last 75yds* **20/1**

000- **3** *1 1/4* **Wise Dennis**[136] 6876 8-8-8 **82**.......... ShaneKelly 9 88+
(A P Jarvis) *stdd s but sn pushed along to stay in tch in rr: drvn and prog on inner over 2f out: styd on to take 3rd ins fnl f: nrst fin* **12/1**

6140 **4** *2* **Vainglory (USA)**[11] 635 6-9-0 **88**.......... MartinDwyer 5 90
(D M Simcock) *chsd ldng trio: shkn up over 2f out: drvn and one pce fr over 1f out: losing grnd nr fin* **7/2**[1]

214- **5** *2 1/4* **Jesse James (IRE)**[171] 5914 4-8-13 **87**.......... SteveDrowne 8 84
(J R Gask) *chsd ldr to jst over 2f out: steadily wknd* **7/1**[3]

-156 **6** *nk* **Thunderball**[8] 672 4-8-7 **81**..........(p) ChrisCatlin 6 77
(J A Glover) *led to wl over 1f out: wknd rapidly fnl f* **15/2**

0-52 **7** *5* **Councellor (FR)**[34] 324 8-9-2 **90**..........(t) MickyFenton 1 75
(Stef Higgins) *a in last trio: pushed along on outer 1/2-way: struggling u.p over 2f out* **10/1**

/606 **8** *1/2* **Hazzard County (USA)**[11] 637 6-8-9 **83**.......... HayleyTurner 2 67
(D M Simcock) *stdd s: hld up in detached last: effrt over 2f out: sn no prog and btn* **13/2**[2]

50-0 **9** *3 1/4* **Cry Of Freedom (USA)**[11] 635 4-8-9 **83**.......... JoeFanning 4 60
(M Johnston) *chsd ldng quartet: u.p over 3f out: sn dropped to rr and btn* **7/1**[3]

1m 37.17s (-2.63) **Going Correction** -0.05s/f (Stan) 9 Ran SP% **116.1**
Speed ratings (Par 107): **111,110,109,107,105 104,99,99,95**
toteswingers: 1&2 £14.70, 1&3 £11.90, 2&3 £14.90 CSF £79.63 CT £765.26 TOTE £3.90: £1.60, £7.20, £6.00; EX 70.50.
Owner A T A Wates **Bred** Castlemartin Stud And Skymarc Farm **Trained** Beare Green, Surrey

FOCUS
This looked a pretty tight handicap featuring some useful performers. Starluck can do considerably better if taking the Flat seriously, and the runner-up is the key to this form.

NOTEBOOK
Starluck(IRE) was having his prep for the Festival and did the business in ready fashion. Unraced as a juvenile, he had experience of Polytrack when trained in Ireland but had yet to run over a trip this short. The fair early pace helped his cause, though, and he travelled sweetly as he always does over hurdles. He hit a brief flat spot when asked for his effort, but picked up strongly to get on top and had something in hand at the finish. The abandonment of Wincanton's Kingwell Hurdle last month now looks a blessing in disguise as this should put him spot on for the Champion Hurdle, for which he can be backed at 16-1. He proved himself on that stiff track in October and his trainer reckons he is much stronger this year, but that was against weak opposition and it will be surprising if he sees it out best of all later this month. (op 3-1 tchd 4-1)
Gaily Noble(IRE) was never far away and made a bold bid, but the winner was always going to reel in him. This effort confirms he is best kept to Polytrack and it was probably a career-best effort in defeat. (op 25-1)
Wise Dennis stayed on with purpose from a fair way back. He is very likely going to come on a deal for the run and is now very well handicapped on his previous best efforts, so can be placed to resume winning ways before that long. (op 16-1)
Vainglory(USA) lacked the pace to make a significant impact, but still ran close to his previous level and helps to set the standard. (tchd 3-1)
Jesse James(IRE) should be all the better for this debut for his new connections and is one to keep an eye on. (op 6-1)

770 SPONSOR AT KEMPTON H'CAP (DIV I) 1m 4f (P)
8:15 (8:18) (Class 6) (0-65,65) 4-Y-O+ £1,706 (£503; £252) Stalls Centre

Form RPR
355- **1** **Turjuman (USA)**[151] 6473 5-9-6 **65**.......... StevieDonohoe 10 76+
(W J Musson) *stdd s: hld up in last trio: effrt and gd run through fr wl over 1f out: r.o wl to ld last 100yds* **6/1**[3]

/0-2 **2** *1/2* **Drizzi (IRE)**[5] 724 9-8-12 **57**.......... SaleemGolam 2 65
(J Pearce) *hld up in last trio: prog on inner over 2f out: sustained effrt to ld briefly ins fnl f: r.o but jst outpcd by wnr* **5/1**[2]

5554 **3** *1 1/2* **Choral Festival**[9] 660 4-8-13 **60**..........(p) RichardKingscote 4 66
(J J Bridger) *hld up in midfield: prog over 2f out to go 2nd over 1f out and looked threatening: sn rdn and nt qckn: kpt on* **12/1**

2-00 **4** *nk* **New World Order (IRE)**[23] 469 6-9-1 **60**..........(t) DaneO'Neill 3 65
(R Curtis) *led: fought on quite wl fr 2f out: hdd and outpcd ins fnl f* **20/1**

4306 **5** *1/2* **Naheell**[23] 467 4-8-13 **60**..........(p) AmirQuinn 9 64
(G Prodromou) *stdd s: hld up in last trio: trbld passage fr 2f out to jst over 1f out: prog after but no ch to catch ldrs* **10/1**

4-22 **6** *2 1/4* **On Terms (USA)**[35] 316 4-8-8 **55**.......... HayleyTurner 1 56
(S Dow) *trckd ldrs on outer: rdn over 3f out: stl chsng over 1f out: fdd* **7/1**

3214 **7** *hd* **Freedom Fire (IRE)**[14] 588 4-9-2 **63**.......... GeorgeBaker 11 63
(G L Moore) *trckd ldng pair: wnt 2nd 2f out to over 1f out: nt qckn and wknd fnl f* **7/2**[1]

-500 **8** *nk* **Boogie Dancer**[19] 529 6-8-6 **51** oh1.......... JoeFanning 7 51
(H S Howe) *trckd ldrs: cl up towards inner 2f out: nt pce to hold pl over 1f out and hmpd sn after: no ch fnl f* **20/1**

-114 **9** *2 3/4* **Slick Mover (IRE)**[20] 509 5-9-5 **64**.......... SteveDrowne 5 60
(B G Powell) *sn trckd ldr: pushed along 3f out: lost 2nd 2f out and gng worse than most: sn wknd* **7/2**[1]

00-0 **10** *1/2* **Mixing**[13] 590 8-8-1 **51** oh6..........(p) JemmaMarshall(5) 8 46
(M J Attwater) *trckd ldrs tl wknd over 1f out* **100/1**

2m 33.14s (-1.36) **Going Correction** -0.05s/f (Stan)
WFA 4 from 5yo+ 2lb 10 Ran SP% **115.2**
Speed ratings (Par 101): **102,101,100,100,100 98,98,98,96,96**
toteswingers: 1&2 £5.20, 1&3 £18.30, 2&3 £22.70 CSF £34.82 CT £349.31 TOTE £9.00: £3.00, £2.30, £4.40; EX 38.00.
Owner I Johnson & John D Jacques **Bred** Shadwell Farm LLC **Trained** Newmarket, Suffolk

FOCUS
A good handicap for the class which was dominated by horses coming from off the pace. Solid form.
New World Order(IRE) Official explanation: jockey said gelding hung right

Slick Mover(IRE) Official explanation: jockey said mare had no more to give

771 SPONSOR AT KEMPTON H'CAP (DIV II) 1m 4f (P)
8:45 (8:47) (Class 6) (0-65,64) 4-Y-0+ £1,706 (£503; £252) Stalls High

Form RPR
U1-2 **1** **Carlton Scroop (FR)**[12] 612 7-9-3 **64**.....................(b) AndreaAtzeni(3) 5 72
(J Jay) *hld up in last pair: gd prog on inner fr over 2f out: pushed into ld over 1f out: wl in command after: readily* **9/4**[1]
20-0 **2** *1 ¼* **Little Sark (IRE)**[51] 121 5-8-7 **56**......................... AndrewHeffernan(5) 2 62
(P D Evans) *hld up in 7th: effrt over 2f out: sn rdn and nt qckn: styd on u.p over 1f out: tk 2nd last stride* **16/1**
060- **3** *nse* **Blue Tango (IRE)**[31] 6910 4-9-3 **63**...............................(b) JimmyQuinn 7 69
(Mrs A J Perrett) *hld up in 6th: effrt over 2f out towards inner: chal over 1f out: chsd wnr after: readily hld fnl f: lost 2nd last stride* **16/1**
01-0 **4** *1 ½* **Champagne Fizz (IRE)**[38] 282 4-8-9 **55**.................. FergusSweeney 6 59
(Miss Jo Crowley) *stdd s: hld up in last trio: cruising bhd ldng gp over 2f out: pushed along and no rspnse wl over 1f out: rdn and styd on fnl f: nvr gng to threaten* **14/1**
6-54 **5** *nk* **Where's Susie**[8] 675 5-9-0 **58**............................... RobertHavlin 3 61
(M Madgwick) *trckd ldng quartet: effrt on outer to ld 2f out: hdd over 1f out: fdd fnl f* **7/1**
3533 **6** *5* **Mister Frosty (IRE)**[5] 720 4-7-12 **51**..................(p) CharlotteKerton(7) 8 47
(G Prodromou) *t.k.h early: trckd ldr: led over 3f out to 2f out: bmpd along and wknd fnl f* **14/1**
00-0 **7** *5* **Lough Beg (IRE)**[27] 411 7-8-7 **51**.................................(t) ChrisCatlin 10 39
(Miss Tor Sturgis) *trckd ldng pair: cl enough to chal over 2f out: wknd rapidly over 1f out* **13/2**[3]
52-3 **8** *4 ½* **Alternative Choice (USA)**[12] 612 4-9-0 **60**............... J-PGuillambert 4 41
(N P Littmoden) *trckd ldng trio: wknd over 2f out* **9/1**
9 *¾* **Helium (FR)**[108] 5-9-3 **61**... JimCrowley 9 41
(N J Gifford) *led to over 3f out: rdn and lost pl over 2f out: wknd rapidly over 1f out* **5/1**[2]
265- **10** *nk* **Broughtons Paradis (IRE)**[72] 7831 4-8-13 **59**........... StevieDonohoe 1 39
(W J Musson) *s.i.s: hld up in last trio: shuffled along on outer over 2f out: wknd wl over 1f out* **11/1**

2m 34.32s (-0.18) **Going Correction** -0.05s/f (Stan)
WFA 4 from 5yo+ 2lb 10 Ran SP% 116.7
Speed ratings (Par 101): **98,97,97,96,95 92,89,86,85,85**
toteswingers: 1&2 £8.70, 1&3 £20.90, 2&3 £45.30 CSF £42.53 CT £473.56 TOTE £3.00: £1.80, £2.80, £7.40; EX 42.10.
Owner Joe Singh **Bred** Jonathan Jay **Trained**

FOCUS
Like the first division of the 1m4f handicap this was run to suit the closers, despite the early pace not appearing to be strong. The form is rated around the second to fourth, with a personal best from the winner.

772 KEMPTON FOR OUTDOOR EVENTS H'CAP 7f (P)
9:15 (9:16) (Class 4) (0-85,91) 3-Y-O £4,209 (£1,252; £625; £312) Stalls High

Form RPR
206- **1** **Amary (IRE)**[152] 6447 3-9-7 **85**... SebSanders 4 87+
(C E Brittain) *hld up in last pair: prog on outer 2f out: drvn to ld jst ins fnl f: styd on wl* **9/4**[2]
100- **2** *nk* **Green Earth (IRE)**[132] 6963 3-8-9 **73**.............................. JimmyQuinn 2 75
(Mrs A J Perrett) *trckd ldng trio: effrt 2f out: drvn to ld briefly 1f out: pressed wnr after: a jst hld* **10/1**
3453 **3** *hd* **Transfixed (IRE)**[7] 681 3-8-6 **75**......................... AndrewHeffernan(5) 5 76
(P D Evans) *trckd ldng pair: rdn to chal fr 2f out: stl pressing u.p fnl f: a jst hld* **16/1**
041- **4** *1 ¼* **Yer Woman (IRE)**[97] 7536 3-9-13 **91**............................ JimmyFortune 6 90
(R Hannon) *dwlt: hld up in last pair: effrt over 2f out: pressed ldrs jst over 1f out: nt qckn and looked hld whn nowhere to go ins fnl f: kpt on* **5/1**[3]
3-11 **5** *shd* **Admiral Cochrane (IRE)**[49] 149 3-9-7 **85**...................... JoeFanning 7 87+
(W Jarvis) *hld up in 5th: gng easily whn nt clr run 2f out to 1f out: styd on at jst the same pce whn in the clr fnl f* **15/8**[1]
05-1 **6** *½* **Little Perisher**[17] 550 3-8-11 **75**.. DaneO'Neill 1 71
(A P Jarvis) *trckd ldr: rdn to take narrow advantage 2f out to 1f out: fdd* **16/1**
5-51 **7** *5* **Craicattack (IRE)**[13] 594 3-8-9 **73**...................................(p) LiamKeniry 3 57
(J S Moore) *led to 2f out: wknd rapidly over 1f out* **7/1**

1m 25.48s (-0.52) **Going Correction** -0.05s/f (Stan) 7 Ran SP% 115.6
Speed ratings (Par 100): **100,99,99,98,97 97,91**
toteswingers: 1&2 £6.30, 1&3 £56.70, 2&3 £20.20 CSF £25.11 TOTE £5.10: £3.30, £3.90; EX 31.90 Place 6 £190.18, Place 5 £77.56.
Owner Saeed Manana **Bred** Marie & Mossy Fahy **Trained** Newmarket, Suffolk
■ Stewards' Enquiry : Andrew Heffernan three-day ban: one for careless riding (Mar 17) and two for excessive use of the whip (Mar 18-19)

FOCUS
An interesting little 3yo handicap featuring four last-time-out winners. There were some hard-luck stories in the race and the third is the best guide to the form.
Admiral Cochrane(IRE) Official explanation: jockey said colt colt was denied a run
T/Plt: £292.60 to a £1 stake. Pool: £85,920.83. 214.30 winning tickets. T/Qpdt: £130.50 to a £1 stake. Pool: £8,433.97. 47.80 winning tickets. JN

750 WOLVERHAMPTON (A.W) (L-H)
Wednesday, March 3

OFFICIAL GOING: Standard
Wind: Moderate half against Weather: Fine

773 GREAT OFFERS AT WOLVERHAMPTON-RACECOURSE.CO.UK H'CAP 5f 216y(P)
2:30 (2:31) (Class 6) (0-55,55) 4-Y-0+ £1,774 (£523; £262) Stalls Low

Form RPR
-246 **1** **Cheery Cat (USA)**[15] 569 6-8-11 **52**...........................(p) LukeMorris 11 58
(J Balding) *led early: chsd ldrs: pushed along over 3f out: rdn wl over 1f out: led jst ins fnl f: drvn out* **12/1**
-400 **2** *½* **Dream Express (IRE)**[21] 486 5-8-11 **55**............ MichaelStainton(3) 10 60
(P Howling) *half-rrd s: hld up and bhd: c wd st: rdn and hdwy 1f out: r.o ins fnl f: tk 2nd last stride* **16/1**
00-1 **3** *shd* **Cwmni**[26] 423 4-8-13 **54**.. DavidProbert 13 58
(B Palling) *mid-div: pushed along over 2f out: rdn and hdwy over 1f out: r.o ins fnl f* **10/1**
6520 **4** *1* **Hart Of Gold**[6] 694 6-8-13 **54**...................................(b) LiamJones 12 55
(R A Harris) *sn led: rdn over 1f out: hdd jst ins fnl f: no ex towards fin* **20/1**
062 **5** *½* **Spoof Master (IRE)**[6] 694 6-9-0 **55**.................................(t) LiamKeniry 8 55
(C R Dore) *sn w ldr: rdn over 1f out: one pce fnl f* **8/1**
-660 **6** *nk* **Yourgolftravel Com**[12] 615 5-9-0 **55**........................... StephenCraine 9 54
(M Wigham) *s.i.s: towards rr: hung lft and hdwy over 1f out: kpt on ins fnl f* **33/1**
7 *½* **Withnail (IRE)**[98] 7525 6-9-0 **55**... AdamKirby 3 52
(Stef Higgins) *in rr: pushed along over 1f out: rdn fnl f: nvr trbld ldrs* **3/1**[1]
-323 **8** *1 ½* **Angle Of Attack (IRE)**[15] 569 5-9-0 **55**.................(v) GrahamGibbons 7 49
(A D Brown) *prom tl rdn and wknd wl ins fnl f* **6/1**[3]
-205 **9** *shd* **Angaric (IRE)**[23] 464 7-8-7 **55**...................................... AdamCarter(7) 6 48
(B Smart) *chsd ldrs: rdn wl over 1f out: wknd ins fnl f* **10/1**
4204 **10** *3 ½* **Muktasb (USA)**[6] 694 9-8-11 **55**..................................(v) MartinLane(3) 5 37+
(D Shaw) *s.s: a in rr* **4/1**[2]
00-3 **11** *nk* **Cardinal**[8] 674 5-8-11 **52**... JackMitchell 1 33+
(N P Moore) *bhd fnl 3f: sddle slipped* **8/1**

1m 15.81s (0.81) **Going Correction** +0.20s/f (Slow) 11 Ran SP% 121.0
Speed ratings (Par 101): **102,101,101,99,99 98,98,96,96,91 90**
toteswingers: 1&2 £50.80, 1&3 £27.90, 2&3 £52.50 CSF £193.63 CT £1313.76 TOTE £15.60: £3.80, £8.40, £3.90; EX 213.60 Trifecta £224.60 Part won. Pool: £303.59 - 0.10 winning units..
Owner The Cataractonium Racing Syndicate **Bred** K L Ramsay & Sarah K Ramsay **Trained** Scrooby, Notts

FOCUS
The leaders went off too quick in this handicap and the principals came from off the pace. Limited but solid form.
Muktasb(USA) Official explanation: jockey said gelding was slow out of the stalls
Cardinal Official explanation: jockey said saddle slipped

774 HOTEL & CONFERENCING AT WOLVERHAMPTON (S) STKS 5f 20y(P)
3:00 (3:01) (Class 6) 4-Y-0+ £1,774 (£523; £262) Stalls Low

Form RPR
1213 **1** **Monte Major (IRE)**[5] 727 9-8-12 64..........................(v) SeanPalmer(7) 4 66
(D Shaw) *chsd ldrs: rdn to ld wl ins fnl f: r.o* **9/4**[2]
2622 **2** *hd* **Bo McGinty (IRE)**[5] 716 9-9-0 62..........................(v) FrederikTylicki 6 60
(R A Fahey) *chsd ldrs: led over 1f out: rdn and hdd wl ins fnl f: r.o* **10/11**[1]
3302 **3** *2* **Bluebok**[19] 525 9-9-0 55...(bt) LukeMorris 5 53
(J M Bradley) *bhd: rdn and hdwy over 1f out: kpt on to take 3rd last strides* **12/1**
-040 **4** *hd* **Ronnie Howe**[27] 402 6-8-7 43....................................(bt) LeeTopliss(7) 7 52
(S R Bowring) *bhd: hdwy and nt clr run on ins over 2f out: n.m.r briefly wl over 1f out: ev ch ins fnl f: rdn and nt qckn* **50/1**
50-0 **5** *1 ¾* **Sally's Swansong**[6] 699 4-8-9 39.................................(b[1]) FrannyNorton 1 41
(E J Alston) *w ldrs: rdn and wknd ins fnl f* **66/1**
-600 **6** *½* **Tournedos (IRE)**[5] 716 8-9-0 67..............................(b[1]) AndrewElliott 10 44
(Mrs R A Carr) *s.i.s: in rr: nt clr run on ins and swtchd rt over 1f out: nvr trbld ldrs* **14/1**
5150 **7** *4 ½* **Meikle Barfil**[16] 561 8-8-12 51......................................(bt) RyanClark(7) 2 33
(J M Bradley) *w ldr: led over 3f out: rdn and hdd over 1f out: wknd ins fnl f* **33/1**
50-0 **8** *nk* **Myriola**[19] 531 5-8-6 40.. MartinLane(3) 3 22
(D Shaw) *led over 1f: rdn and wkng whn n.m.r over 1f out* **50/1**
0-30 **9** *8* **Stash**[23] 462 4-9-0 60...(p) GrahamGibbons 9 —
(R Hollinshead) *chsd ldrs: c wd st: wknd over 1f out* **10/1**[3]

63.29 secs (0.99) **Going Correction** +0.20s/f (Slow) 9 Ran SP% 115.0
Speed ratings (Par 101): **100,99,96,96,93 92,85,84,72**
toteswingers: 1&2 £1.50, 1&3 £4.30, 2&3 £3.30 CSF £4.50 TOTE £3.00: £1.10, £1.10, £2.90; EX 5.10 Trifecta £21.10 Pool: £550.57 - 19.23 winning units..There was no bid for the winner.
Owner Derek Shaw **Bred** B Kennedy **Trained** Sproxton, Leics
■ Stewards' Enquiry : Sean Palmer one-day ban: careless riding (Mar 17)

FOCUS
The betting suggested this seller was a two-horse race, and the market was proved correct. Weak form, with the winner basically to form.
Tournedos(IRE) ◆ Official explanation: jockey said gelding was denied a clear run
Stash Official explanation: vet said gelding bled from nose

775 SPONSOR A RACE BY CALLING 01902 390000 H'CAP 1m 4f 50y(P)
3:30 (3:30) (Class 6) (0-65,64) 3-Y-O £1,774 (£523; £262) Stalls Low

Form RPR
00-1 **1** **Desert Recluse (IRE)**[14] 589 3-8-6 **52**...................... AndreaAtzeni(3) 9 67+
(Pat Eddery) *chsd ldr: led 3f out: rdn over 1f out: clr fnl f: easily* **13/8**[1]
4-66 **2** *6* **Second Brook (IRE)**[41] 254 3-8-12 **55**........................ RobertWinston 6 56
(R Hollinshead) *hld up in tch: chsd wnr 2f out: sn rdn: no imp* **28/1**
00-0 **3** *¾* **The Mighty Mod (USA)**[26] 422 3-8-8 **51**......................... GregFairley 4 51
(M Johnston) *hld up in mid-div: pushed along over 3f out: hdwy over 1f out: styd on to take 3rd wl ins fnl f* **25/1**
00-0 **4** *½* **Nurai**[21] 484 3-8-13 **56**.. TonyCulhane 10 55
(P W D'Arcy) *hld up towards rr: pushed along and hdwy over 2f out: sn rdn: one pce* **13/2**[3]
5052 **5** *3 ½* **Blues Forever (IRE)**[9] 664 3-9-5 **62**............................. PaulHanagan 3 56
(P D Evans) *prom: rdn over 2f out: wknd over 1f out* **3/1**[2]
0-00 **6** *1* **Port Hill**[18] 542 3-8-0 **48**.. KierenFox(5) 8 40
(W M Brisbourne) *t.k.h in mid-div: rdn and c wd st: nvr nr ldrs* **50/1**
1343 **7** *¾* **Glen Lass**[14] 589 3-9-7 **64**..(b) SaleemGolam 2 55
(J Pearce) *bmpd s: hld up in mid-div: bhd fnl 3f* **8/1**
00-5 **8** *7* **Cordiality**[51] 118 3-9-0 **57**.. GrahamGibbons 11 38
(P G Murphy) *prom: rdn over 2f out: wknd wl over 1f out* **33/1**
00-5 **9** *4* **Sam Jicaro**[19] 523 3-8-0 **48**...................................... JamesSullivan(5) 12 23
(Mrs L Williamson) *wnt rt s: a in rr* **80/1**
2335 **10** *7* **The Great Husk (IRE)**[14] 589 3-9-2 **64**...................... RossAtkinson(5) 7 28
(J S Moore) *led: hdd 3f out: rdn and wknd 2f out* **10/1**
00-5 **11** *1 ¾* **Whipper's Delight (IRE)**[18] 542 3-8-9 **52**..................(e) JimmyQuinn 1 14
(D Donovan) *hld up in mid-div: pushed along over 3f out: sn bhd* **28/1**
646 **12** *½* **Maigold Rose**[18] 542 3-8-2 **45**... LukeMorris 5 6
(J R Weymes) *prom: pushed along over 3f out: sn wknd* **100/1**

2m 43.78s (2.68) **Going Correction** +0.20s/f (Slow) 12 Ran SP% 114.5
Speed ratings (Par 96): **99,95,94,94,91 91,90,86,83,78 77,77**
toteswingers: 1&2 £13.00, 1&3 £7.90, 2&3 £31.10 CSF £58.46 CT £839.10 TOTE £2.40: £1.40, £4.70, £4.70; EX 64.50 TRIFECTA Not won..
Owner Pat Eddery Racing (Storm Bird) **Bred** John Foley & Miss Ann Aungier **Trained** Nether Winchendon, Bucks

FOCUS
Some unexposed performers in this 3-y-o handicap, including the winner who scored with a lot in hand. The form is rated around the next three home.

Port Hill Official explanation: jockey said gelding hung right

776 ENJOY THE PARTY PACK GROUP OFFER MDN FILLIES' STKS 1m 1f 103y(P)
4:00 (4:01) (Class 5) 3-Y-O+ **£2,456** (£725; £362) **Stalls** Low

Form RPR

53 **1** **Sheila's Bond**[9] 655 3-8-5 0 LukeMorris 9 56+
(J S Moore) *w ldr: led wl over 1f out: drvn out* **25/1**

6-23 **2** *nk* **Tomintoul Star**[5] 715 4-9-11 56 AndrewElliott 7 61
(Mrs R A Carr) *hld up in rr: swtchd rt and gd hdwy on outside to ld over 2f out: hdd wl over 1f out: rdn and kpt on ins fnl f* **8/1**[3]

0 **3** *1 1/2* **Single Lady**[14] 583 3-8-5 0 FrannyNorton 2 52+
(J S Moore) *a.p: rdn over 1f out: kpt on same pce* **40/1**

-303 **4** *1 1/4* **Sternian**[22] 475 3-8-5 50 NickyMackay 8 49
(M E Rimmer) *hld up in tch: rdn and one pce ins fnl f* **33/1**

562- **5** *6* **Angelena Ballerina (IRE)**[137] 6858 3-8-5 65 (p) JimmyQuinn 4 37
(Karen George) *hld up towards rr: sme prog over 2f out: swtchd lft wl over 1f out: wknd ins fnl f* **4/1**[2]

-000 **6** *3/4* **Helpmeronda**[18] 545 4-9-11 37 (t) GeorgeBaker 3 41
(W M Brisbourne) *hld up and bhd: c wd st: no imp whn edgd lft 1f out* **200/1**

7 *1 1/4* **One Cool Pussy (IRE)** 4-9-11 0 RPCleary 6 38
(Daniel Mark Loughnane, Ire) *s.s: hld up: rdn and struggling over 1f out* **33/1**

8 *1 3/4* **Floridita (USA)** 3-8-5 0 GregFairley 1 29
(M Johnston) *rn green: led: pushed along and hdd over 2f out: sn wknd* **4/7**[1]

/- **9** *2 1/2* **Smackeroo (USA)** 4-9-4 0 IanBrennan(7) 5 30
(J J Quinn) *s.i.s: sn hld up in tch: rdn and wknd over 2f out* **16/1**

2m 8.98s (7.28) **Going Correction** +0.20s/f (Slow)
WFA 3 from 4yo 20lb **9** Ran SP% **113.3**
Speed ratings (Par 100): **75,74,73,72,66 66,65,63,61**
toteswingers: 1&2 £5.50, 1&3 £33.70, 2&3 £27.10 CSF £196.71 TOTE £15.20: £3.40, £2.10, £6.20; EX 65.70 Trifecta £452.90 Part won. Pool: £612.16 - 0.45 winning units..
Owner Ray Styles **Bred** Mrs Anita R Dodd **Trained** Upper Lambourn, Berks

FOCUS
A moderate and uncompetitive fillies' maiden but some interest regarding the debutantes, and one of them was sent off at odds on. The second and fourth are the best guides.

777 THE HORIZONS RESTAURANT, THE PLACE TO DINE H'CAP 1m 5f 194y(P)
4:30 (4:31) (Class 6) (0-65,65) 4-Y-O+ **£1,774** (£523; £262) **Stalls** Low

Form RPR

0-55 **1** **Broughtons Point**[18] 539 4-8-2 46 oh1 JamieMackay 6 59+
(W J Musson) *hld up in mid-div: hdwy to ld over 1f out: reminder and edgd lft whn wnt clr ins fnl f: easily* **14/1**

63-5 **2** *3 1/2* **Smarties Party**[12] 621 7-9-4 58 PJMcDonald 3 63
(C W Thornton) *hld up in rr: smooth prog 3f out: swtchd rt ent st: rdn and chsd wnr ins fnl f: no imp* **7/1**

60-6 **3** *nk* **Lastroseofsummer (IRE)**[26] 421 4-9-0 58 DavidProbert 9 63+
(Rae Guest) *towards rr: pushed along briefly 7f out: rdn and hdwy over 1f out: styd on wl ins fnl f* **33/1**

500- **4** *2 1/4* **Rare Coincidence**[16] 7751 9-8-10 50 (p) PaulHanagan 4 52
(R F Fisher) *sn led: rdn 2f out: hdd over 1f out: wknd ins fnl f* **25/1**

5-40 **5** *1 3/4* **Swords**[12] 621 8-8-11 54 MartinLane(3) 7 53
(R E Peacock) *hld up in rr: hdwy wl over 1f out: sn rdn: no imp fnl f* **12/1**

0-43 **6** *7* **Weybridge Light**[19] 529 5-9-7 61 GeorgeBaker 13 51
(M R Bosley) *led early: hld up in tch: rdn and wnt 2nd over 3f out: wknd over 1f out* **9/2**[2]

15-5 **7** *2 3/4* **Private Equity (IRE)**[23] 463 4-8-12 56 J-PGuillambert 5 42
(W Jarvis) *prom: rdn over 1f out: eased whn btn ins fnl f* **11/2**[3]

/6-3 **8** *7* **Wee Ziggy**[16] 563 7-9-6 60 TomEaves 12 36
(M Mullineaux) *hld up in mid-div: pushed along over 3f out: rdn and wknd 2f out* **40/1**

00-4 **9** *4 1/2* **Motarjm (USA)**[19] 529 6-9-10 64 (t) SaleemGolam 11 34
(J Pearce) *hld up in tch: pushed along over 3f out: wknd wl over 1f out* **3/1**[1]

35/4 **10** *3/4* **Hope Road**[26] 186 6-9-11 65 RichardKingscote 2 34
(A B Haynes) *hld up in rr: pushed along over 3f out: eased whn btn over 1f out* **16/1**

4-05 **11** *19* **Bramalea**[18] 546 5-9-9 63 RobertWinston 1 5
(B W Duke) *hld up in tch: rdn and wknd over 3f out: eased whn no ch over 1f out* **8/1**

00-0 **12** *2 1/2* **Hilbre Point (USA)**[23] 468 4-8-8 52 (v1) JimmyQuinn 8 —
(N J Vaughan) *sn chsng ldr: wknd over 3f out: eased whn no ch wl over 1f out* **100/1**

50-4 **13** *36* **Sotelo**[12] 612 8-9-9 63 PatCosgrave 10 —
(S Gollings) *hld up in tch: rdn and wknd wl over 1f out: eased over 2f out* **12/1**

3m 5.46s (-0.54) **Going Correction** +0.20s/f (Slow)
WFA 4 from 5yo+ 4lb **13** Ran SP% **120.3**
Speed ratings (Par 101): **109,107,106,105,104 100,98,94,92,91 81,79,59**
toteswingers: 1&2 £28.20, 1&3 £28.20, 2&3 £43.80 CSF £107.16 CT £3189.32 TOTE £16.00: £5.40, £3.20, £2.30; EX 175.30 TRIFECTA Not won..
Owner Broughton Thermal Insulation **Bred** Broughton Bloodstock **Trained** Newmarket, Suffolk

FOCUS
The leaders went a decent gallop and the principals came from behind.
Broughtons Point Official explanation: trainer's rep said, regarding the apparent improvement in form shown, filly was better suited by the step up in trip to a mile and six furlongs and that she has improved throughout the season
Sotelo Official explanation: vet said horse bled from nose

778 STAY AT THE WOLVERHAMPTON HOLIDAY INN H'CAP 5f 20y(P)
5:00 (5:02) (Class 6) (0-60,66) 4-Y-O+ **£1,774** (£523; £262) **Stalls** Low

Form RPR

15-1 **1** **Straboe (USA)**[16] 561 4-8-12 57 (v1) WilliamCarson(3) 1 69+
(S C Williams) *hld up towards rr: hdwy on outside over 2f out: c wd st: rdn over 1f out: sn hung lft: led ins fnl f: r.o* **11/8**[1]

50-0 **2** *2 1/2* **Trick Or Two**[33] 351 4-9-1 57 AndrewElliott 11 60
(Mrs R A Carr) *sn chsng ldr: hung lft over 3f out: ev ch ins fnl f: nt qckn* **50/1**

00-0 **3** *hd* **Riflessione**[29] 378 4-9-4 60 (b) LiamJones 8 62
(R A Harris) *hld up in mid-div: hdwy 3f out: rdn over 1f out: hmpd briefly ins fnl f: r.o* **22/1**

2101 **4** *3/4* **Steel City Boy (IRE)**[5] 723 7-9-7 66 6ex MartinLane(3) 4 65
(D Shaw) *s.i.s: hld up in rr: rdn over 1f out: r.o ins fnl f: nrst fin* **6/1**[3]

3043 **5** *shd* **Kheley (IRE)**[7] 678 4-8-13 60 KierenFox(5) 7 60
(W M Brisbourne) *hld up in rr: rdn and hdwy over 1f out: nt clr run briefly ins fnl f: kpt on* **12/1**

4404 **6** *1 3/4* **First Order**[5] 723 9-8-13 60 (v) AnnStokell(5) 13 53
(Miss A Stokell) *in rr: rdn over 1f out: late prog: nrst fin* **33/1**

06-1 **7** *1* **Ridley Didley (IRE)**[5] 727 5-9-0 61 6ex PaulPickard(5) 3 50
(N Wilson) *led: rdn jst over 1f out: hdd ins fnl f: wknd* **4/1**[2]

6-05 **8** *1 1/4* **Metal Guru**[19] 525 6-8-12 57 (p) RussKennemore(3) 10 44
(R Hollinshead) *prom tl rdn and wknd over 1f out* **25/1**

6-00 **9** *nk* **Almaty Express**[19] 525 8-8-13 55 JimmyQuinn 5 38
(J R Weymes) *prom: n.m.r on ins over 3f out: wknd over 2f out* **25/1**

-040 **10** *1 1/2* **Chosen One (IRE)**[13] 601 5-9-2 58 (p) TomEaves 2 36
(B Smart) *bhd fnl 2f* **8/1**

5620 **P** **Monsieur Reynard**[5] 727 5-8-13 55 DavidProbert 6 —
(J M Bradley) *hld up in mid-div: lost pl 2f out: p.u lame wl over 1f out* **12/1**

62.87 secs (0.57) **Going Correction** +0.20s/f (Slow) **11** Ran SP% **119.8**
Speed ratings (Par 101): **103,99,98,97,97 94,92,90,90,88** —
toteswingers: 1&2 £29.50, 1&3 £13.00, 2&3 £55.10 CSF £112.03 CT £1156.77 TOTE £2.50: £1.20, £10.70, £2.40; EX 116.10 TRIFECTA Not won..
Owner Brigid & Damian Hennessy-Bourke **Bred** Darley **Trained** Newmarket, Suffolk
■ Stewards' Enquiry : William Carson three-day ban: careless riding (Mar 17-19)

FOCUS
An ordinary sprint handicap. The winner is in top form and the form looks sound enough.
Kheley(IRE) Official explanation: jockey said filly was denied a clear run
First Order Official explanation: jockey said gelding hung right on bend
Metal Guru Official explanation: jockey said mare was struck into

779 WOLVERHAMPTON-RACECOURSE.CO.UK H'CAP 7f 32y(P)
5:30 (5:30) (Class 4) (0-85,85) 4-Y-O+ **£4,209** (£1,252; £625; £312) **Stalls** High

Form RPR

42-4 **1** **Arachnophobia (IRE)**[14] 580 4-9-0 81 RobertWinston 3 88
(Pat Eddery) *chsd ldr over 5f out: led over 2f out: rdn over 1f out: jst hld on* **2/1**[1]

62-0 **2** *nse* **Johnmanderville**[16] 565 4-8-5 75 MartinLane(3) 8 82
(N Wilson) *hld up in tch: rdn over 2f out: r.o ins fnl f: jst failed* **20/1**

1134 **3** *3 1/2* **Divine Force**[20] 502 4-8-11 78 SimonWhitworth 6 76
(M Wigham) *s.i.s: hld up: hdwy 2f out: sn rdn: one pce ins fnl f* **2/1**[1]

-211 **4** *1* **Smalljohn**[23] 465 4-8-7 74 (v) TomEaves 7 70
(B Smart) *led: pushed along and hdd over 2f out: rdn wl over 1f out: wknd ins fnl f* **4/1**[2]

5-36 **5** *1 1/2* **Carnivore**[37] 292 8-8-6 78 DeanHeslop(5) 9 70
(T D Barron) *s.i.s: hld up: effrt 2f out: c wd st: rdn over 1f out: no imp* **14/1**[3]

2023 **6** *1* **Kensington (IRE)**[13] 602 9-7-13 71 oh1 (p) DeclanCannon(5) 2 61
(A J McCabe) *chsd ldr over 1f: prom tl rdn and wknd over 1f out* **14/1**[3]

0-15 **7** *28* **Tin Cha Woody (USA)**[18] 535 5-8-9 76 (b) RPCleary 4 —
(Daniel Mark Loughnane, Ire) *a in rr: pushed along over 4f out: sn lost tch* **14/1**[3]

1m 29.45s (-0.15) **Going Correction** +0.20s/f (Slow) **7** Ran SP% **111.4**
Speed ratings (Par 105): **108,107,103,102,101 99,67**
toteswingers: 1&2 £5.40, 1&3 £1.60, 2&3 £6.90 CSF £42.18 CT £85.83 TOTE £3.40: £1.60, £6.50; EX 36.00 Trifecta £302.90 Part won. Pool: £409.35 - 0.45 winning units..
Owner Pat Eddery Racing (Sharpo) **Bred** Michael Staunton **Trained** Nether Winchendon, Bucks

FOCUS
There was a solid gallop to this handicap, which featured a number of horses more or less in the grip of the handicapper. Limited but sound form.
Tin Cha Woody(USA) Official explanation: jockey said gelding was reluctant to race

780 ALL WEATHER "HANDS AND HEELS" APPRENTICE SERIES H'CAP 1m 141y(P)
6:00 (6:00) (Class 6) (0-58,63) 4-Y-O+ **£1,774** (£523; £262) **Stalls** Low

Form RPR

6011 **1** **Well Of Echoes**[2] 753 4-9-4 59 12ex (tp) JohnFahy 2 68
(A J McCabe) *hld up in rr: hdwy wl over 1f out: led wl ins fnl f: r.o* **7/4**[1]

-330 **2** *3/4* **Laureldeans Best (IRE)**[21] 485 4-9-3 58 LeeTopliss 11 65
(R A Fahey) *hld up towards rr: pushed along over 2f out: hdwy wl over 1f out: led 1f out: hdd wl ins fnl f* **3/1**[2]

0553 **3** *1* **Amber Moon**[13] 603 5-8-7 48 (b) LauraPike 4 53
(Miss A Stokell) *t.k.h: led early: a.p: ev ch 1f out: nt qckn wl ins fnl f* **10/1**

-001 **4** *1 1/4* **Machinate (USA)**[7] 682 8-8-10 51 6ex KierenFox 6 54
(W M Brisbourne) *hld up in mid-div: lost pl over 4f out: pushed along over 2f out: swtchd rt over 1f out: styd on fnl f: nt rch ldrs* **12/1**

00-0 **5** *nk* **Stoic Leader (IRE)**[18] 539 10-8-2 46 NoelGarbutt(3) 1 48
(R F Fisher) *a prominent: pushed along over 2f out: one pce fnl f* **14/1**

1-05 **6** *3/4* **Signora Frasi (IRE)**[20] 499 5-9-1 56 DavidKenny 12 56
(A G Newcombe) *hld up towards rr: stdy prog on ins 3f out: pushed along and ev ch 1f out: fdd towards fin* **15/2**[3]

00-5 **7** *1* **Saving Grace**[26] 427 4-8-7 48 RyanClark 5 46
(E J Alston) *sn led: hdd over 6f out: led over 2f out: hdd 1f out: wknd wl ins fnl f* **20/1**

50-0 **8** *3 1/4* **My Jeanie (IRE)**[7] 682 6-8-5 46 RichardRowe 8 38
(J C Fox) *sn chsng ldr: led over 6f out tl over 2f out: wknd over 1f out* **33/1**

500- **9** *2 3/4* **Portrush Storm**[203] 4887 5-8-9 50 JohnCavanagh 13 36
(R E Peacock) *hld up in rr: stdy hdwy on outside over 3f out: c wd st: wknd wl over 1f out* **50/1**

5041 **10** *3/4* **Hold The Bucks (USA)**[7] 685 4-9-5 63 6ex (p) GillianDawson(3) 3 47
(J S Moore) *hld up in tch: wknd over 3f out* **10/1**

050- **11** *14* **Protiva**[139] 5063 4-8-11 57 (p) AdamBeschizza(5) 10 12
(Karen George) *a in rr: pushed along 4f out: sn lost tch* **66/1**

1m 53.87s (3.37) **Going Correction** +0.20s/f (Slow) **11** Ran SP% **116.8**
Speed ratings (Par 101): **93,92,91,90,90 89,88,85,83,82 70**
toteswingers: 1&2 £3.20, 1&3 £6.80, 2&3 £4.80 CSF £6.42 CT £40.10 TOTE £2.70: £1.20, £1.70, £4.00; EX 11.20 Trifecta £92.20 Pool: £314.01 - 2.52 winning units. Place 6: £3,651.55, Place 5: £267.22..
Owner M Shirley **Bred** Plantation Stud **Trained** Averham Park, Notts

FOCUS
A very moderate race but the winner is in great form.
Machinate(USA) Official explanation: jockey said gelding suffered interference in running
T/Plt: £1,419.10 to a £1 stake. Pool: £73,428.43. 37.77 winning tickets. T/Qpdt: £186.10 to a £1 stake. Pool: £6,790.90. 27.00 winning tickets. KH

[714]SOUTHWELL (L-H)

Thursday, March 4

OFFICIAL GOING: Standard

Wind: Light, across. Weather: Fine and dry

781 CALL 01636 814481 TO SPONSOR A RACE H'CAP — 1m (F)

2:10 (2:11) (Class 5) (0-75,74) 3-Y-O — **£2,331** (£693; £346; £173) **Stalls** Low

Form — RPR

13-2 **1** **Sweet Child O'Mine**[62] 4 3-9-2 **72** ... FrannyNorton 5 — 79
(R C Guest) *dwlt: sn pushed along to chse ldrs: hdwy on inner 3f out: rdn to chal whn hmpd over 1f out: sn led and edgd rt ins fnl f: drvn out* **13/8**[1]

00-1 **2** *1 1/4* **First Post (IRE)**[30] 381 3-9-1 **71** ... DaneO'Neill 6 — 75
(D Haydn Jones) *hld up: hdwy on outer 3f out: rdn to chse ldrs over 1f out: styd on to chse wnr ins fnl f: no imp towards fin* **9/2**[3]

6114 **3** *1/2* **Tiger Hawk (USA)**[19] 542 3-8-4 **65** ...(b) AndrewHeffernan(5) 3 — 68
(P D Evans) *cl up: led over 3f out: rdn over 2f out: drvn and edgd lft over 1f out: kpt on same pce u.p ins fnl f* **10/1**

-314 **4** *3 1/4* **Paintball (IRE)**[30] 382 3-9-0 **73** ... AndreaAtzeni(3) 1 — 69
(W R Muir) *in tch: pushed along over 3f out: sn rdn and kpt on same pce fnl 2f* **13/2**

643- **5** *1 1/4* **Cloudy City (USA)**[187] 5428 3-9-4 **74** ... JoeFanning 4 — 67
(M Johnston) *trckd ldng pair: hdwy to chse ldr 3f out: rdn over 2f out and sn btn* **5/2**[2]

-163 **6** *14* **Wedding Dream**[17] 566 3-8-10 **66** ...(p) TomEaves 2 — 28
(K A Ryan) *led: rdn along and hdd over 3f out: sn wknd* **22/1**

1m 41.41s (-2.29) **Going Correction** -0.10s/f (Stan) — **6** Ran SP% **111.6**

Speed ratings (Par 98): **107,105,105,102,100 86**

Tote Swingers: 1&2 £2.00, 1&3 £3.10, 2&3 £6.10 CSF £9.24 TOTE £2.40: £1.40, £2.40; EX 10.00.

Owner EERC **Bred** A Reid **Trained** Stainforth, S Yorks

■ Stewards' Enquiry : Andrew Heffernan one-day ban: careless riding (Apr 6)

FOCUS

A fair handicap run at just an ordinary pace. The first two looked well weighted and the third looked the best guide to the form.

782 DINE IN THE QUEEN MOTHER RESTAURANT CLAIMING STKS — 7f (F)

2:40 (2:41) (Class 6) 3-Y-O — **£1,774** (£523; £262) **Stalls** Low

Form — RPR

00-1 **1** **Set Back**[7] 702 3-8-12 58 ... AdrianNicholls 10 — 69
(D Nicholls) *prom on outer: hdwy 1/2-way: led over 2f out: rdn wl over 1f out: drvn ins fnl f and kpt on strly* **5/2**[2]

4305 **2** *1 3/4* **Tealing**[20] 524 3-8-10 64 ...(e1) FrannyNorton 6 — 63
(R C Guest) *in tch: hdwy 3f out: rdn wl over 1f out: chsd wnr ent fnl f: sn drvn and no imp* **12/1**

2-3 **3** *1 3/4* **Golden Tiger**[28] 399 3-9-5 0 ... MickyFenton 4 — 67
(T P Tate) *sn pushed along towards rr: rdn along: lost pl and bhd 1/2-way: rn wd st and hdwy 2f out: kpt on wl u.p appr fnl f: tk 3rd on line* **12/1**

4 *shd* **Cardiff Boy (USA)** 3-9-8 0 ... EddieAhern 1 — 70
(B J Meehan) *towards rr: hdwy on inner wl over 2f out: rdn to chse ldng pair over 1f out: one pce ins fnl f: lost 3rd on line* **14/1**

-212 **5** *4* **Inside Track (IRE)**[25] 452 3-8-10 75 ...(v1) TonyCulhane 3 — 48
(P T Midgley) *led: rdn along and hdd over 2f out: drvn wl over 1f out and grad wknd* **5/1**[3]

10-1 **6** *nk* **Eight Hours**[20] 519 3-9-0 67 ...(b) PaulHanagan 5 — 51
(R A Fahey) *trckd ldrs: cl up 1/2-way: rdn to chal 3f out: drvn over 2f out and sn wknd* **9/4**[1]

5340 **7** *1 1/2* **Baby Judge (IRE)**[16] 574 3-8-5 46 ... AndrewHeffernan(5) 8 — 44
(M C Chapman) *cl up: rdn along over 3f out and sn wknd* **50/1**

4-46 **8** *shd* **Captain Bluebird (IRE)**[31] 371 3-8-10 62 ...(v1) JimmyQuinn 9 — 43
(D Donovan) *hld up in tch: effrt over 2f out: sn rdn: edgd lft and wknd* **8/1**

00-0 **9** *1/2* **Isle Of Ellis (IRE)**[37] 301 3-8-7 40 ... ChrisCatlin 2 — 39
(J A Glover) *chsd ldrs on inner: rdn along 3f out: sn wknd* **100/1**

10 *1* **Account Closed** 3-8-2 0 ... JamesSullivan(5) 7 — 37
(C A Mulhall) *a in rr* **66/1**

1m 29.66s (-0.64) **Going Correction** -0.10s/f (Stan) — **10** Ran SP% **113.6**

Speed ratings (Par 96): **99,97,95,94,90 89,88,88,87,86**

Tote Swingers: 1&2 £9.60, 1&3 £5.60, 2&3 £10.20 CSF £31.52 TOTE £3.50: £1.10, £3.10, £2.30; EX 35.30 Trifecta £340.80 Part won. Pool £460.63 - 0.20 winning units..

Owner D W Barker **Bred** Mrs S E Barclay **Trained** Sessay, N Yorks

FOCUS

Typical claiming form, with a couple of these open to further improvement. The winner is rated to the level of his recent course win.

783 JEFF ORANGE BIRTHDAY H'CAP — 5f (F)

3:10 (3:10) (Class 4) (0-85,85) 3-Y-O — **£4,100** (£1,227; £613; £306; £152) **Stalls** High

Form — RPR

-111 **1** **Love Delta (USA)**[36] 310 3-9-7 **85** ... JoeFanning 2 — 97+
(M Johnston) *cl up gng wl: led 2f out: rdn and qcknd clr over 1f out: comf* **5/2**[2]

-112 **2** *3* **Boogie Waltzer**[32] 363 3-7-11 **66** oh1 ... AmyBaker(5) 5 — 67
(S C Williams) *cl up: led briefly 1/2-way: rdn and hdd 2f out: drvn over 1f out and kpt on same pce* **12/1**

6-13 **3** *1/2* **Breathless Kiss (USA)**[15] 577 3-8-10 **79** ...(b) AmyRyan(5) 7 — 78
(K A Ryan) *s.i.s: sn chsng ldrs: edgd rt to stands' rail wl over 1f out: sn drvn kpt on same pce* **9/1**

1-42 **4** *1 3/4* **Lucky Mellor**[15] 577 3-9-2 **80** ...(b) AdamKirby 3 — 73
(D K Ivory) *trckd ldrs: pushed along and sltly outpcd 1/2-way: rdn and hdwy 2f out: drvn wl over 1f out and sn no imp* **2/1**[1]

2-34 **5** *1 1/2* **Barlaman (USA)**[14] 596 3-8-5 **69** ...(t) ChrisCatlin 4 — 57
(C E Brittain) *prom: rdn along over 2f out and sn wknd* **9/1**

0-25 **6** *1 1/2* **Ramamara (IRE)**[52] 122 3-8-4 **73** ... AndrewHeffernan(5) 6 — 55
(P D Evans) *led: rdn along and hdd 1/2-way: sn wknd* **20/1**

0-13 **7** *2 1/2* **Best Trip (IRE)**[22] 478 3-9-0 **78** ... FrannyNorton 9 — 51
(R C Guest) *in tch: rdn along and bhd fr 1/2-way* **8/1**[3]

524- **8** *nk* **Dazeen**[188] 5392 3-8-10 **74** ... TonyCulhane 1 — 46
(P T Midgley) *wnt lft s: a towards rr* **16/1**

58.77 secs (-0.93) **Going Correction** -0.10s/f (Stan) — **8** Ran SP% **111.4**

Speed ratings (Par 100): **103,98,97,94,92 89,85,85**

Tote Swingers: 1&2 £3.70, 1&3 £5.00, 2&3 £9.00 CSF £30.31 CT £225.64 TOTE £3.20: £1.30, £2.60, £3.60; EX 25.10 Trifecta £42.10 Pool £424.18 - 7.45 winning units..

Owner Crone Stud Farms Ltd **Bred** Palides Investments N V Inc & Hair 'Em Corporation **Trained** Middleham Moor, N Yorks

FOCUS

A decent sprint handicap and there were five in a line across the track at halfway. As usual the main action took place down the centre. Solid enough foem which could be rated up to 5lb higher.

Lucky Mellor Official explanation: jockey said colt moved poorly

784 HOSPITALITY AT SOUTHWELL RACECOURSE MAIDEN STKS — 5f (F)

3:40 (3:40) (Class 5) 3-Y-O — **£2,331** (£693; £346; £173) **Stalls** High

Form — RPR

-453 **1** **St Ignatius**[14] 594 3-9-3 66 ...(b) RichardKingscote 3 — 72+
(R M Beckett) *trckd ldng pair: hdwy 2f out: rdn to ld 1 1/2f out: clr ent fnl f and kpt on wl* **7/2**[2]

3-33 **2** *4 1/2* **Just Mandy (IRE)**[13] 624 3-8-12 62 ... PaulHanagan 2 — 53+
(R A Fahey) *in tch: sn rdn along and outpcd 1/2-way: hdwy wl over 1f out: drvn and kpt on ent fnl f: nt trble wnr* **7/4**[1]

46 **3** *1 3/4* **Fine And Dandie (IRE)**[25] 453 3-9-3 0 ... AdrianNicholls 6 — 50
(D Nicholls) *cl up: rdn along 2f out and ev ch tl drvn and outpcd appr fnl f* **12/1**

00- **4** *2 1/4* **Bombay Mist**[113] 7331 3-8-12 0 ... FrannyNorton 9 — 37
(R C Guest) *led: rdn along 2f out: hdd and drvn 1 1/2f out: grad wknd* **80/1**

5 *1/2* **Coal Miner (IRE)** 3-9-3 0 ... AndrewElliott 1 — 40
(Mrs R A Carr) *s.i.s: hdwy on outer to chse ldrs after 1f: rdn along 2f out: sn drvn and btn over 1f out* **20/1**

4-44 **6** *1* **Blades Harmony**[23] 473 3-9-3 64 ... GrahamGibbons 7 — 36
(E S McMahon) *s.i.s: hdwy and in tch 1/2-way: sn rdn and n.d* **11/2**[3]

0 **7** *7* **Killing Moon (USA)**[29] 385 3-9-3 0 ... ChrisCatlin 4 — 11
(K A Ryan) *s.i.s: a in rr* **11/2**[3]

0-42 **8** *2 1/4* **Miss Kitty Grey (IRE)**[19] 538 3-8-12 61 ... PatCosgrave 5 — —
(J R Boyle) *s.i.s: a in rr* **6/1**

59.77 secs (0.07) **Going Correction** -0.10s/f (Stan) — **8** Ran SP% **117.3**

Speed ratings (Par 98): **95,87,85,81,80 79,67,64**

Tote Swingers: 1&2 £3.00, 1&3 £8.50, 2&3 £6.00 CSF £10.35 TOTE £4.60: £1.70, £1.50, £2.70; EX 13.30 Trifecta £54.10 Pool £217.26 - 2.97 winning units..

Owner A W A Partnership **Bred** Simon And Helen Plumbly **Trained** Whitsbury, Hants

FOCUS

A modest maiden and again the centre of the track was the place to be. The winning time was exactly a second slower than the preceding handicap. The winner scored with something to spare.

Miss Kitty Grey(IRE) Official explanation: trainer's rep said filly struck into herself

785 SOUTHWELL-RACECOURSE.CO.UK H'CAP — 1m 4f (F)

4:10 (4:10) (Class 4) (0-85,79) 4-Y-O+ **£4,100** (£1,227; £613; £306; £152) **Stalls** Low

Form — RPR

2111 **1** **Spruce (USA)**[5] 735 4-9-6 **79** 6ex ... JimmyQuinn 6 — 92+
(Miss J Feilden) *set stdy pce: qcknd 3f out: rdn clr wl over 1f out: easily* **8/11**[1]

60-1 **2** *4 1/2* **Bariolo (FR)**[10] 660 6-8-12 **69** 6ex ... HayleyTurner 5 — 74
(Noel T Chance) *hld up in rr: hdwy on outer after 4f: trckd wnr 1/2-way: chal 3f out: rdr over 2f out drvn and one pce appr fnl f* **13/2**[3]

1 **3** *1 3/4* **Reverend Green (IRE)**[35] 326 4-9-0 **78** ... AmyRyan(5) 3 — 80
(K A Ryan) *hld up in tch: hdwy over 3f out: rdn along over 2f out: drvn over 1f out and kpt on same pce* **3/1**[2]

000- **4** *1 3/4* **Hollow Green (IRE)**[117] 7291 4-9-4 **77** ... PaulHanagan 4 — 77
(P D Evans) *chsd wnr: rdn along over 3f out: drvn over 2f out and sn wknd* **16/1**

300- **5** *1 3/4* **Moheebb (IRE)**[168] 6013 6-9-3 **77** ...(b) BarryMcHugh(3) 7 — 74
(Mrs R A Carr) *trckd ldng pair: pushed along over 3f out: rdn over 2f out and sn one pce* **14/1**

2m 40.51s (-0.49) **Going Correction** -0.10s/f (Stan)

WFA 4 from 5yo+ 2lb — **5** Ran SP% **108.8**

Speed ratings (Par 105): **97,94,92,91,90**

CSF £5.86 TOTE £1.80: £1.10, £2.00; EX 3.80.

Owner Good Company Partnership **Bred** Juddmonte Farms Inc **Trained** Exning, Suffolk

FOCUS

A fair little handicap run at an ordinary early pace, but it was turned into a one-horse race by Spruce, who took another step up. Sound form.

786 MEMBERSHIP OF SOUTHWELL GOLF CLUB FILLIES' H'CAP — 1m 3f (F)

4:40 (4:40) (Class 5) (0-75,71) 4-Y-O+ — **£2,331** (£693; £346; £173) **Stalls** Low

Form — RPR

0-06 **1** **Whooshka (USA)**[19] 546 4-9-6 **71** ... ChrisCatlin 4 — 79
(P W Chapple-Hyam) *trckd ldrs: hdwy over 3f out: rdn to ld 2f out: drvn and hdd over 1f out: edgd lft ins fnl f: rallied u.p to ld last 75yds* **7/2**[3]

0-02 **2** *1 1/2* **Miss Christophene (IRE)**[21] 509 4-9-2 **67** ... AndrewMullen 3 — 73
(Mrs S Lamyman) *hld up in tch: hdwy over 4f out: pushed along to chse ldng pair 3f out: rdn to chal 2f out: drvn to ld over 1f out: hdd and no ex last 75yds* **2/1**[2]

1346 **3** *12* **Look Officer (USA)**[9] 675 4-9-3 **68** ... AdamKirby 5 — 61+
(Miss M E Rowland) *hld up in rr: rapid hdwy to ld 7f out: rdn along 3f out: hdd and drvn 2f out: sn outpcd* **7/1**

5533 **4** *4* **Amber Moon**[1] 780 5-7-13 **56** oh8 ...(b) LauraPike(7) 1 — 36
(Miss A Stokell) *led 4f: chsd ldr: rdn along over 3f out and sn wknd* **18/1**

5-53 **5** *3 1/4* **Bushy Dell (IRE)**[31] 375 5-8-8 **63** ... AmyBaker(5) 2 — 38
(Miss J Feilden) *hld up towards rr: pushed along over 5f out: rdn over 4f out: sn outpcd and bhd* **15/8**[1]

2m 25.67s (-2.33) **Going Correction** -0.10s/f (Stan)

WFA 4 from 5yo 1lb — **5** Ran SP% **108.1**

Speed ratings (Par 100): **104,102,94,91,88**

CSF £10.49 TOTE £4.90: £1.70, £1.10; EX 8.90.

Owner C G P Wyatt **Bred** Northwest Farms Llc **Trained** Newmarket, Suffolk

FOCUS

A modest fillies' handicap and a rather muddling race with Look Officer injecting a sudden change of pace before halfway which changed the whole complexion of the contest. The first two came well clear and produced sound form.

Look Officer(USA) Official explanation: jcokey said filly had no more to give

Bushy Dell(IRE) Official explanation: jockey said mare was never travelling

787 PLAY GOLF BEFORE RACING AT SOUTHWELL APPRENTICE H'CAP — 1m (F)

5:10 (5:10) (Class 5) (0-75,74) 4-Y-O+ — **£2,331** (£693; £346; £173) **Stalls** Low

Form — RPR

05-5 **1** **Border Owl (IRE)**[10] 668 5-8-6 **61** ... BillyCray 4 — 69
(P Salmon) *set stdy pce: qcknd 3f out: rdn 2f out: drvn and edgd lft ins fnl f: kpt on* **9/1**

234 **2** *1/2* **Miss Bootylishes**[25] 451 5-9-0 **69** ... JohnFahy 8 — 76
(A B Haynes) *trckd ldng pair: hdwy to chse wnr over 2f out: rdn wl over 1f out: drvn and kpt on ins fnl f* **11/4**[2]

-041 **3** 1 ¾ **Flores Sea (USA)**[16] 571 6-9-1 **70**....................(p) KierenFox 6 73
(Mrs R A Carr) *trckd wnr: effrt 3f out: rdn 2f out: drvn and one pce appr fnl f* **5/1**[3]

3251 **4** 1 **General Tufto**[6] 715 5-9-2 **74** 6ex....................(b) RichardRowe(3) 2 75
(C Smith) *stdd s: hld up and bhd: hdwy wl over 2f out and sn rdn: styd on to chse ldrs over 1f out: drvn and no imp ins fnl f* **6/4**[1]

200- **5** ¾ **Horsley Warrior**[248] 3466 4-8-10 **68**.................... DavidKenny(3) 7 67
(E S McMahon) *chsd ldrs: rdn along over 2f out: sn drvn and kpt on same pce* **10/1**

42-5 **6** 9 **Montiboli (IRE)**[19] 544 5-8-6 **68**....................(p) MarkPower(7) 3 48
(K A Ryan) *t.k.h: trckd ldrs: pushed along 3f out: sn rdn and wknd over 2f out* **28/1**

155- **7** nk **Heroes**[17] 4434 6-9-2 **74**.................... NathanAlison(3) 5 53
(J R Boyle) *dwlt: hld up in tch: effrt 3f out: sn rdn and nvr a factor* **12/1**

1m 43.65s (-0.05) **Going Correction** -0.10s/f (Stan) **7** Ran SP% **113.6**
Speed ratings (Par 103): **96,95,93,92,92 83,82**
Tote Swingers: 1&2 £3.60, 1&3 £5.60, 2&3 £2.60 CSF £33.50 CT £138.88 TOTE £8.80: £3.00, £1.80; EX 51.20 Trifecta £235.10 Pool £463.95 - 1.46 winning units. Place 6 £44.59, Place 5 £25.63..
Owner Viscount Environmental **Bred** Gainsborough Stud Management Ltd **Trained** Kirk Deighton, West Yorks

FOCUS
A modest apprentice handicap, dominated by those that raced handily, and the first three held those positions throughout. Sound form.
T/Plt: £40.60 to a £1 stake. Pool: £63,283.83. 1,137.06 winning tickets. T/Qpdt: £6.80 to a £1 stake. Pool: £4,346.60. 467.35 winning tickets. JR

773 WOLVERHAMPTON (A.W) (L-H)
Thursday, March 4

OFFICIAL GOING: Standard
Wind: Almost nil Weather: Fine

788 ADELE MULLEN STILL PUNTING AT 87 H'CAP — 5f 216y(P)
5:20 (5:21) (Class 6) (0-65,64) 3-Y-O **£2,047** (£604; £302) **Stalls** Low

Form RPR

403- **1** **Cookie Galore**[134] 6938 3-8-9 **52**.................... FrederikTylicki 6 58
(J A Glover) *s.i.s: hld up in rr: hdwy on ins wl over 1f out: sn rdn: led ins fnl f: edgd rt and bmpd: r.o* **5/1**[3]

0-43 **2** 1 ¾ **Micky's Knock Off (IRE)**[10] 662 3-9-0 **64**..........(e[1]) CharlesEddery(7) 4 64
(R C Guest) *t.k.h: w ldr after 1f: led 3f out: rdn over 1f out: hdd and edgd rt ins fnl f: sn bmpd: nt qckn* **4/1**[2]

0-50 **3** 1 **Miss Polly Plum**[19] 533 3-8-2 **45**.................... NickyMackay 2 42
(C A Dwyer) *hld up: hdwy on ins 2f out: rdn jst over 1f out: kpt on same pce* **20/1**

06-0 **4** 1 ½ **Lady Hetherington**[22] 484 3-8-11 **57**.................... RobertLButler(3) 3 49+
(G Brown) *hld up in tch: pushed along over 2f out: outpcd wl over 1f out: sn swtchd rt: kpt on towards fin* **20/1**

06-5 **5** ½ **True Red (IRE)**[46] 208 3-8-7 **50**....................(p) DavidProbert 8 41
(Mrs N S Evans) *broke wl: led: hdd 3f out: rdn jst over 2f out: wknd ins fnl f* **16/1**

0231 **6** hd **Sweet Avon**[15] 581 3-9-3 **60**.................... ShaneKelly 1 50
(Matthew Salaman) *chsd ldr 1f: prom: pushed along over 2f out: rdn and wknd over 1f out* **7/4**[1]

56-3 **7** ½ **England (IRE)**[12] 638 3-9-6 **63**.................... J-PGuillambert 7 51
(N P Littmoden) *hld up: sme prog over 3f out: sn rdn: wknd over 2f out* **4/1**[2]

6034 **8** 2 ¼ **Dolly Will Do**[15] 581 3-8-0 **46**.................... KellyHarrison(3) 5 27
(N P Mulholland) *bhd fnl 3f* **14/1**

1m 15.95s (0.95) **Going Correction** +0.125s/f (Slow) **8** Ran SP% **115.1**
Speed ratings (Par 96): **98,95,94,92,91 91,90,87**
Tote Swingers: 1&2 £4.10, 1&3 £15.40, 2&3 £23.10 CSF £25.49 CT £362.68 TOTE £5.10: £1.90, £2.10, £5.80; EX 34.80.
Owner Dixon, Denniff, Youdan **Bred** Mrs Fiona Denniff **Trained** Babworth, Notts

FOCUS
A weak handicap run at a fast pace, and a step forward from the winner.

789 STAY AT THE WOLVERHAMPTON HOLIDAY INN (S) STKS — 5f 216y(P)
5:50 (5:50) (Class 6) 4-Y-O+ **£1,774** (£523; £262) **Stalls** Low

Form RPR

0664 **1** **Titus Gent**[18] 555 5-9-6 62.................... DavidProbert 2 67
(R A Harris) *hld up in tch: rdn wl over 1f out: r.o to ld last strides* **6/1**

4231 **2** nk **Not My Choice (IRE)**[6] 716 5-9-0 62....................(t) PaulDoe 6 60
(J Balding) *led: clr over 1f out: rdn ins fnl f: hdd last strides* **11/4**[1]

-602 **3** nk **Bentley**[17] 562 6-9-6 57....................(v) GeorgeBaker 7 65
(J G Given) *chsd ldr: rdn over 1f out: kpt on ins fnl f* **16/1**

342 **4** 2 ¾ **Obe Gold**[16] 571 8-9-6 68.................... J-PGuillambert 8 56
(P Howling) *hld up and bhd: pushed along over 3f out: rdn and kpt on fnl f: nvr trbld ldrs* **3/1**[2]

0-61 **5** 1 ¼ **Doctor Hilary**[20] 532 8-9-0 62....................(v) RobertHavlin 11 46
(A B Haynes) *hld up in tch: pushed along over 2f out: btn over 1f out* **15/2**

00-0 **6** ¾ **Monsieur Harvey**[41] 264 4-9-0 43.................... TomEaves 3 44
(B Smart) *hld up in mid-div: rdn and hdwy on ins wl over 1f out: wknd ins fnl f* **33/1**

2-00 **7** 1 **King's Sabre**[21] 499 4-8-7 52....................(e[1]) CharlesEddery(7) 10 41
(R C Guest) *rrd and s.s: hld up in rr: c wd st: n.d* **28/1**

00-5 **8** nk **Albaher**[14] 595 4-9-0 60....................(b[1]) SaleemGolam 1 40
(Peter Grayson) *prom tl rdn and wknd 1f out* **33/1**

5210 **9** 17 **Espy**[8] 678 5-9-0 67....................(p) PJMcDonald 9 —
(I W McInnes) *a bhd: eased whn no ch ins fnl f* **7/2**[3]

1m 15.28s (0.28) **Going Correction** +0.125s/f (Slow) **9** Ran SP% **115.2**
Speed ratings (Par 101): **103,102,102,98,96 95,94,94,71**
Tote Swingers: 1&2 £6.50, 1&3 £12.40, 2&3 £7.50 CSF £22.44 TOTE £6.30: £1.40, £1.40, £3.60; EX 30.10.There was no bid for the winner.
Owner Alan & Adam Darlow, A Darlow Productions **Bred** Heather Raw **Trained** Earlswood, Monmouths
■ Stewards' Enquiry : Paul Doe three-day ban: used whip with excessive frequency and without giving mount time to respond (Mar 18-20)

FOCUS
A fairly competitive seller, five of the runners had BHA ratings between 62 and 73. The first three were always prominent and the hold-up runners struggled to get involved. Typical form for the grade.

790 WEATHERBYS PRINTING H'CAP — 1m 1f 103y(P)
6:20 (6:20) (Class 3) (0-95,92) 4-Y-O **£6,938** (£2,076; £1,038; £519; £258) **Stalls** Low

Form RPR

-352 **1** **Mafeking (UAE)**[19] 536 6-9-1 **89**.................... AndrewElliott 10 99
(M R Hoad) *sn w ldr: led 6f out: rdn and edgd rt ins fnl f: r.o* **11/1**

6-21 **2** nk **December Draw (IRE)**[12] 637 4-8-13 **87**.................... ShaneKelly 6 96+
(W J Knight) *hld up in mid-div: stdy hdwy over 3f out: rdn: wnt 2nd and hung lft wl ins fnl f: r.o* **14/1**

1/1- **3** 2 ½ **Perpetually (IRE)**[322] 1303 4-9-3 **91**.................... JoeFanning 1 95
(M Johnston) *led: hdd 6f out: pushed along over 2f out: rdn wl over 1f out: one pce ins fnl f* **8/11**[1]

3305 **4** ½ **Confidentiality (IRE)**[5] 738 6-8-11 **85**.................... NickyMackay 3 88
(M Wigham) *prom: lost pl sltly over 3f out: sn pushed along: rallied wl over 1f out: sn rdn: one pce ins fnl f* **10/1**[3]

4543 **5** ½ **Carcinetto (IRE)**[5] 740 8-8-13 **92**.................... AndrewHeffernan(5) 2 94
(P D Evans) *hld up in mid-div: lost pl on ins over 5f out: pushed along over 2f out: rdn and styd on fnl f* **25/1**

4152 **6** 1 ½ **Red Somerset (USA)**[5] 740 7-8-9 **83**.................... RichardKingscote 4 83
(R J Hodges) *t.k.h early in tch: lost pl on ins 5f out: rdn and hdwy wl over 1f out: eased whn btn towards fin* **14/1**

243- **7** ½ **Rainbow Mirage (IRE)**[189] 5375 6-9-0 **88**.................... GrahamGibbons 7 87
(E S McMahon) *hld up towards rr: n.d* **16/1**

6-42 **8** ¾ **Snow Dancer (IRE)**[28] 408 6-8-3 **82**.................... JamesSullivan(5) 9 79
(H A McWilliams) *hld up in rr: rdn over 2f out: no rspnse* **28/1**

-121 **9** ½ **Chosen Forever**[27] 430 5-8-10 **84**.................... JimmyQuinn 8 80
(G R Oldroyd) *prom tl rdn and wknd over 1f out* **5/1**[2]

4650 **10** 5 **Justcallmehandsome**[15] 587 8-7-11 **78** oh11..........(v) NoelGarbutt(7) 5 65
(D J S Ffrench Davis) *s.i.s: t.k.h towards rr: prog on outside over 4f out: wknd over 2f out* **100/1**

2m 1.88s (0.18) **Going Correction** +0.125s/f (Slow) **10** Ran SP% **119.5**
Speed ratings (Par 107): **104,103,101,101,100 99,98,98,97,93**
Tote Swingers: 1&2 £10.30, 1&3 £3.50, 2&3 £4.10 CSF £153.42 CT £252.77 TOTE £10.90: £2.00, £3.30, £1.10; EX 75.60.
Owner Mrs J E Taylor **Bred** Darley **Trained** Lewes, E Sussex

FOCUS
A hot handicap involving three last-time-out winners and five others who were placed on their latest run. The pace was steady and the first two pulled clear of the rest. Sound form.

NOTEBOOK
Mafeking(UAE) arrived here after five consecutive near-misses in 1m2f Polytrack handicaps. He had a career-high mark to deal with and was keen up with the pace from his wide draw but he kept battling away, despite shifting to the right, and just had enough to fend off a fast finisher. This first win since January 2008 should boost his morale but he was allowed to dictate in a steadily run race and will take another move up the weights after this success. (op 15-2)
December Draw(IRE) finished well from just off the pace but could not quite get there in his attempt to defy a 5lb rise for his win in a 1m2f Lingfield handicap last time. He is a steadily progressive and tactically versatile type who should be able to win more races. (op 12-1)
Perpetually(IRE) went in at 9-1 in a Yarmouth maiden on his debut in 2008 and shrugged off a 12-month absence when swooping late in a 1m2f Newmarket handicap last April. He had another layoff and an 8lb higher mark to overcome on his AW debut, was in trouble soon after forfeiting the lead to the eventual winner at the halfway stage and could only plug on after that. This was still a decent enough effort in race where things did not really go to plan and he should be sharper next time. (op 5-4)
Confidentiality(IRE), out of her depth behind Gitano Hernando in a Listed race last week, bounced back with a fair effort but her current mark is probably near the ceiling of her ability. (op 8-1)
Carcinetto(IRE) deserves some credit for doing best of the hold-up horses. The consistent 8-y-o posted a number of good efforts during the winter and is 3lb lower than when winning at Chester last August, but his losing run has now stretched to 20. (op 20-1)
Red Somerset(USA) had every chance against the far rail but could not sustain his effort. (op 10-1)
Chosen Forever has proved a revelation since switched to this track but he was too keen up with the pace this time and faded in a bid to make it five wins in the last six. (op 11-2 tchd 6-1)

791 ENJOY THE LINCOLN TRIAL - 13TH MARCH H'CAP (DIV I) — 1m 1f 103y(P)
6:50 (6:51) (Class 6) (0-55,55) 4-Y-O+ **£1,706** (£503; £252) **Stalls** Low

Form RPR

-406 **1** **Naledi**[7] 705 6-8-1 **47** oh1 ow1.................... AndrewHeffernan(5) 4 55
(R J Price) *t.k.h early in mid-div: pushed along over 2f out: brought wd st: rdn and hdwy over 1f out: r.o u.p to ld cl home* **12/1**

/032 **2** ¾ **Wetherby Place (IRE)**[19] 541 4-8-7 **53**.................... TobyAtkinson(5) 2 59
(M Wigham) *a.p: rdn wl over 1f out: ev ch wl ins fnl f: kpt on* **7/4**[1]

-654 **3** nk **Kings Topic (USA)**[8] 685 10-9-0 **55**....................(p) RobertHavlin 9 60
(A B Haynes) *sn prom: rdn 2f out: ev ch wl ins fnl f: kpt on* **10/1**

0025 **4** ¾ **Hatch A Plan (IRE)**[4] 746 9-8-4 **52**.................... CharlesEddery(7) 8 56
(Mouse Hamilton-Fairley) *hld up in mid-div: hdwy on ins to ld over 1f out: sn rdn: hdd and no ex cl home* **16/1**

6-12 **5** ¾ **The City Kid (IRE)**[10] 666 7-8-13 **54**.................... SaleemGolam 10 56
(G D Blake) *hld up and bhd: pushed along and hdwy 2f out: one pce ins fnl f* **4/1**[2]

-606 **6** 1 ¼ **James Pollard (IRE)**[14] 591 5-8-7 **48**.................... DavidProbert 6 48
(B J Llewellyn) *t.k.h early: hld up and bhd: rdn wl over 1f out: styd on ins fnl f: nt rch ldrs* **15/2**

006/ **7** 3 ½ **Noble Edge**[26] 4559 7-8-0 **46** oh1....................(t) PaulPickard(5) 5 38
(L R James) *prom tl wknd 3f out* **66/1**

55-3 **8** 1 **Roundthetwist (IRE)**[44] 227 5-8-5 **46**....................(v) AndrewElliott 1 36
(J R Weymes) *led: hdd over 4f out: rdn over 1f out: wknd ins fnl f* **5/1**[3]

6006 **9** 6 **Djalalabad (FR)**[29] 389 6-8-5 **46** oh1....................(tp) AdrianMcCarthy 11 24
(Mrs C A Dunnett) *hld up: hdwy over 6f out: led over 4f out: hdd over 1f out: sn rdn: wknd fnl f* **22/1**

00-0 **10** 8 **Chicamia**[41] 270 6-8-5 **46** oh1.................... NickyMackay 3 7
(M Mullineaux) *bhd fnl 3f* **50/1**

2m 3.47s (1.77) **Going Correction** +0.125s/f (Slow) **10** Ran SP% **115.3**
Speed ratings (Par 101): **97,96,96,95,94 93,90,89,84,77**
Tote Swingers: 1&2 £14.00, 1&3 £15.60, 2&3 £5.80 CSF £32.65 CT £226.57 TOTE £15.20: £2.80, £1.40, £2.70; EX 71.20.
Owner Mrs Janice Thompson **Bred** Genesis Green Stud Ltd **Trained** Ullingswick, H'fords

FOCUS
A poor handicap, involving a number of longstanding maidens. They finished in a bit of a bunch but the second and third set a solid enough level.

The Form Book, Raceform Ltd, Compton, RG20 6NL

Djalalabad(FR) Official explanation: jockey said mare hung right

792 WOLVERHAMPTON-RACECOURSE.CO.UK H'CAP 1m 141y(P)

7:20 (7:20) (Class 4) (0-85,81) 3-Y-O £4,533 (£1,348; £674; £336) Stalls Low

Form RPR

-151 **1** **Kinky Afro (IRE)**[22] 490 3-9-0 **74**........ LiamKeniry 2 83
(J S Moore) *mde all: pushed along and qcknd clr wl over 1f out: sn rdn: r.o wl* **5/1**[2]

6-12 **2** *5* **Demonstrative (USA)**[13] 625 3-9-6 **80**........ JoeFanning 1 78
(M Johnston) *s.i.s: sn hld up in tch: rdn and sltly outpcd over 2f out: styd on to take 2nd towards fin: no ch w wnr* **4/11**[1]

1-21 **3** *½* **Miami Gator (IRE)**[17] 566 3-8-6 **66**........ AndrewElliott 3 63
(J R Weymes) *chsd wnr: ev ch over 2f out: outpcd and lost 2nd wl over 1f out: kpt on one pce fnl f* **12/1**

1-24 **4** *½* **Robust Wish (USA)**[8] 681 3-9-7 **81**........(b) EddieAhern 4 77
(B J Meehan) *a.p: rdn over 2f out: chsd wnr wl over 1f out: no imp* **10/1**[3]

1m 51.21s (0.71) **Going Correction** +0.125s/f (Slow) **4** Ran SP% **106.8**
Speed ratings (Par 100): **101,96,96,95**
CSF £7.40 TOTE £4.40; EX 11.60.
Owner Phil Cunningham **Bred** S Couldrige **Trained** Upper Lambourn, Berks

FOCUS
A decent but very tactical handicap, and it is probably bedst to treat the form with caution.

793 ENJOY THE PARTY PACK GROUP OFFER MAIDEN FILLIES' STKS 7f 32y(P)

7:50 (7:51) (Class 5) 3-Y-O+ £2,456 (£725; £362) Stalls High

Form RPR

22 **1** **Binthere Dunthat**[13] 624 3-8-8 0........ HayleyTurner 2 71+
(M L W Bell) *a.p: shkn up to ld 1f out: r.o* **2/9**[1]

6 **2** *1* **Starlight Muse (IRE)**[20] 527 3-8-8 0........ GrahamGibbons 7 68+
(E S McMahon) *chsd ldr after 1f: led 2f out: rdn and hdd 1f out: nt qckn* **25/1**

4056 **3** *6* **Luisa Tetrazzini (IRE)**[26] 444 4-9-5 53........(b[1]) MarkCoumbe(5) 3 58
(John A Harris) *hld up and bhd: stdy prog over 2f out: swtchd rt ent st: rdn and tk 3rd ins fnl f: no ch w ldng pair* **20/1**

3 **4** *¾* **Fillibeg (IRE)**[20] 523 3-8-8 0........ PaulHanagan 6 50
(R A Fahey) *hld up in tch: pushed along over 2f out: rdn and wknd over 1f out* **7/1**[2]

00- **5** *3 ¾* **Alhena (IRE)**[159] 6284 3-8-8 0........ FergusSweeney 5 40+
(K A Ryan) *bhd: rdn and effrt 3f out: c wd st: wknd wl over 1f out* **12/1**[3]

0-05 **6** *¾* **Izzi Mill (USA)**[28] 398 4-9-10 63........ ShaneKelly 4 44
(A J McCabe) *led: hdd 2f out: rdn and wknd over 1f out* **12/1**[3]

5 **7** *¾* **Swift Steel**[13] 624 3-8-8 0........ JackMitchell 8 36
(Mrs A Duffield) *a in rr* **33/1**

0-4 **8** *3 ½* **Glan Y Mor (IRE)**[13] 624 3-8-8 0........ LiamKeniry 9 26
(F J Brennan) *t.k.h in mid-div: hdwy over 3f out: wknd wl over 1f out* **22/1**

000/ **9** *7* **Park Run**[18] 5653 5-9-10 44........ AdamKirby 1 13
(J L Spearing) *chsd ldrs: pushed along over 3f out: wknd wl over 2f out* **50/1**

1m 30.4s (0.80) **Going Correction** +0.125s/f (Slow)
WFA 3 from 4yo+ 16lb **9** Ran SP% **127.6**
Speed ratings (Par 100): **100,98,92,91,86 86,85,81,73**
Tote Swingers: 1&2 £2.80, 1&3 £4.20, 2&3 £40.00 CSF £17.58 TOTE £1.30: £1.02, £3.20, £5.90; EX 6.00.
Owner R L W Frisby **Bred** Palm Tree Thoroughbreds **Trained** Newmarket, Suffolk

FOCUS
A fillies' maiden that lacked strength in depth. The first two pulled a long way clear of the rest and the hot favourite was value for a bit more than the winning margin. The form looks to make sense.
Alhena(IRE) Official explanation: jockey said filly suffered interference in running

794 WOLVERHAMPTON HOSPITALITY - A PLEASURE H'CAP 7f 32y(P)

8:20 (8:21) (Class 7) (0-50,51) 4-Y-O+ £1,364 (£403; £201) Stalls High

Form RPR

-002 **1** **Mountain Pass (USA)**[14] 591 8-9-3 **50**........(p) DavidProbert 5 57
(B J Llewellyn) *hld up in tch: led wl over 1f out: sn rdn: drvn and hld on wl ins fnl f* **12/1**

-000 **2** *hd* **Bold Diva**[7] 693 5-9-3 **50**........(v) JimmyQuinn 4 58
(A W Carroll) *hld up in mid-div: nt clr run on ins wl over 1f out: sn swtchd rt and hdwy: rdn and ev ch ins fnl f: r.o* **25/1**

11 **3** *nse* **Saddlers Bend (IRE)**[3] 757 4-8-13 **51** 6ex........ MatthewDavies(5) 8 57
(George Baker) *a.p: c wd st: ev ch fr over 1f out: rdn and r.o ins fnl f* **4/6**[1]

0-04 **4** *hd* **Yakama (IRE)**[7] 691 5-9-3 **50**........ AdamKirby 1 56
(Mrs C A Dunnett) *a.p: rdn over 1f out: ev ch ins fnl f: kpt on* **18/1**

660- **5** *¾* **Imperial Djay (IRE)**[181] 5633 5-9-0 **47**........ JoeFanning 10 51
(Mrs R A Carr) *hld up in rr: hdwy wl over 1f out: rdn and r.o ins fnl f* **20/1**

/530 **6** *½* **Motu (IRE)**[7] 691 9-8-10 **48**........(v) AndrewHeffernan(5) 6 51
(I W McInnes) *t.k.h: chsd ldr: led jst over 2f out tl wl over 1f out: sn rdn: no ex ins fnl f* **20/1**

0244 **7** *6* **Almatlaie (USA)**[17] 567 4-9-3 **50**........ FergusSweeney 7 38
(J W Unett) *hld up in mid-div: rdn over 1f out: no hdwy* **10/1**[3]

-0 **8** *¾* **Leo's Lucky Angel (IRE)**[20] 530 5-9-0 **50**........ GFCarroll(3) 12 36
(Daniel Mark Loughnane, Ire) *a towards rr* **10/1**[3]

20-1 **9** *1 ¾* **Russian Angel**[25] 460 6-9-1 **48**........ LiamKeniry 2 30
(Jean-Rene Auvray) *led: hdd jst over 2f out: wknd wl over 1f out* **11/2**[2]

4-54 **10** *1* **Montego Breeze**[35] 326 4-9-1 **48**........ MickyFenton 11 28
(John A Harris) *a in rr* **40/1**

6/00 **11** *¾* **Mister Beano (IRE)**[20] 530 5-9-0 **47**........(v) SaleemGolam 9 25
(R J Price) *a towards rr* **50/1**

1m 31.49s (1.89) **Going Correction** +0.125s/f (Slow) **11** Ran SP% **124.3**
Speed ratings (Par 97): **94,93,93,93,92 92,85,84,82,81 80**
Tote Swingers: 1&2 £9.60, 1&3 £4.90, 2&3 £14.60 CSF £285.36 CT £478.80 TOTE £17.40: £3.30, £4.40, £1.10; EX 229.70.
Owner B J Llewellyn **Bred** Marablue Farm **Trained** Fochriw, Caerphilly
■ Stewards' Enquiry : G F Carroll one-day ban: careless riding (Mar 18)

FOCUS
A low-grade handicap. The pace was steady and there was a very tight finish but the first six did pull a long way clear of the rest.

795 ENJOY THE LINCOLN TRIAL - 13TH MARCH H'CAP (DIV II) 1m 1f 103y(P)

8:50 (8:50) (Class 6) (0-55,55) 4-Y-O+ £1,706 (£503; £252) Stalls Low

Form RPR

1 **Sworn Tigress (GER)**[131] 5-8-6 **46**........ JimmyQuinn 6 65+
(George Baker) *prom: chsd ldr over 6f out: led 3f out: clr wl over 1f out: rdn out* **6/4**[1]

5303 **2** *6* **Join Up**[3] 757 4-8-8 **53**........ RossAtkinson(5) 2 58
(W M Brisbourne) *hld up in tch: chsd wnr over 2f out: rdn wl over 1f out: no imp* **4/1**[3]

2164 **3** *2 ¼* **Barodine**[10] 665 7-9-1 **55** ow1........ GeorgeBaker 8 56
(R J Hodges) *hld up: prog whn n.m.r over 2f out: rdn over 1f out: one pce* **5/2**[2]

0-30 **4** *1 ¾* **Silidan**[21] 498 7-9-0 **54**........ AdamKirby 4 51
(Miss M E Rowland) *chsd ldrs tl over 6f out: prom: rdn 2f out: sn wknd* **16/1**

5-53 **5** *3* **Fitzwarren**[38] 295 9-8-5 **45**........(tp) DavidProbert 3 37
(A D Brown) *hld up: pushed along and prog on ins over 2f out: rdn and btn over 1f out* **12/1**

-000 **6** *6* **Redwater River**[7] 705 6-8-5 **45**........(b) AndrewElliott 5 25
(Mrs R A Carr) *led: hdd 3f out: rdn over 2f out: wknd wl over 1f out* **50/1**

-653 **7** *5* **Cruise Control**[19] 540 4-8-4 **49**........ AndrewHeffernan(5) 9 20
(R J Price) *hld up: pushed along and short-lived effrt on outside whn bmpd over 2f out* **8/1**

0050 **8** *29* **Easy Wonder (GER)**[8] 682 5-8-5 **45**........(b) JoeFanning 1 —
(I A Wood) *hld up in tch: wknd over 3f out: lost action and eased wl over 1f out* **40/1**

0-20 **9** *4* **Space Pirate**[13] 354 5-8-6 **46**........(b) SaleemGolam 7 —
(J Pearce) *dwlt: a in rr: rdn and t.o fnl 4f* **33/1**

2m 1.02s (-0.68) **Going Correction** +0.125s/f (Slow) **9** Ran SP% **120.6**
Speed ratings (Par 101): **108,102,100,99,96 91,86,60,57**
Tote Swingers: 1&2 £4.20, 1&3 £2.20, 2&3 £4.30 CSF £8.27 CT £14.69 TOTE £2.20: £1.20, £1.90, £1.50; EX 11.80 Place 6 £144.47, Place 5 £36.09..
Owner Sir Alex Ferguson **Bred** Gestut Wittekindshof **Trained** Moreton Morrell, Warwicks

FOCUS
A massive gamble was landed in emphatic style in this modest handicap.
Easy Wonder(GER) Official explanation: jockey said mare lost its action
T/Plt: £181.10 to a £1 stake. Pool: £75,679.75. 304.94 winning tickets. T/Qpdt: £26.00 to a £1 stake. Pool: £10,035.20. 285.55 winning tickets. KH

[706]MEYDAN (L-H)

Thursday, March 4

OFFICIAL GOING: All-weather - standard; turf course - good to firm

796a AL BASTAKIYA SPONSORED BY DERRINSTOWN STUD , BAHRI (LISTED RACE) (TAPETA) 1m 1f 110y

3:35 (3:36) 3-Y-O

£92,592 (£30,864; £15,432; £7,716; £4,629; £3,086)

RPR

1 **Mendip (USA)**[21] 510 3-8-7 100........ FrankieDettori 14 110+
(Saeed Bin Suroor) *trckd ldr: led gng wl 2f out: r.o wl: easily* **11/4**[2]

2 *6 ¼* **Della Barba (CHI)**[14] 608 4-9-4 106........ OlivierPeslier 4 100
(J Barton, Saudi Arabia) *led and set stdy gallop: rdn and hdd 2f out: r.o gamely: no ch w wnr* **11/2**[3]

3 *¼* **Enak (ARG)**[21] 510 4-9-11 108........(t) TedDurcan 2 106
(Saeed Bin Suroor) *trckd ldr: ev ch 2 1/2f out: r.o same pce* **20/1**

4 *¼* **Izaaj (USA)**[21] 510 3-8-7 90........(t) WJSupple 7 95
(M bin Shafya, UAE) *mid-div: r.o wl fnl 1 1/2f: nrest at fin* **66/1**

5 *½* **Vale Of York (IRE)**[117] 7307 3-9-0 118........ AhmedAjtebi 8 101
(Saeed Bin Suroor) *mid-div: t.k.h: chsd wnr 3f out: one pce fnl 1 1/2f* **5/2**[1]

6 *½* **Solid Choice (AUS)**[14] 608 4-9-4 102........ KShea 6 97
(M F De Kock, South Africa) *mid-div: n.d* **6/1**

7 *¼* **Uncle Tom (BRZ)**[21] 510 4-9-11 104........ TJPereira 13 104
(P Bary, France) *in rr of mid-div: r.o one pce fnl 2f* **12/1**

8 *shd* **Maroon Machine (IRE)**[14] 608 3-8-7 100........ KierenFallon 5 92
(E J O'Neill, France) *mid-div: n.d: r.o fnl 2f* **33/1**

9 *1 ¾* **Saboteur**[21] 510 3-8-7 90........ JRosales 3 89
(A bin Huzaim, UAE) *a mid-div* **66/1**

10 *½* **Landowner**[18] 3-8-7 90........ CSanchez 1 88
(A bin Huzaim, UAE) *nvr bttr than mid-div* **20/1**

11 *¼* **Kona Coast**[152] 6478 3-8-7 93........ WilliamBuick 10 88
(J H M Gosden) *in rr of mid-div: n.d* **16/1**

12 *hd* **Storm Chispazo (ARG)**[14] 608 4-9-11 104........ RyanMoore 12 98
(H J Brown, South Africa) *settled in rr: nvr able to chal* **16/1**

13 *1 ¼* **Jardim (BRZ)**[14] 608 4-9-6 102........ RichardMullen 11 91
(A Cintra Pereira, Brazil) *s.i.s: n.d* **20/1**

14 *7 ½* **Moran Gra (USA)**[18] 3-8-7 95........(e) TadhgO'Shea 9 71
(D Selvaratnam, UAE) *in rr of mid-div: n.d* **66/1**

1m 59.42s (119.42)
WFA 3 from 4yo 20lb **14** Ran SP% **126.1**
CSF: £17.99..
Owner Godolphin **Bred** Jayeff B Stables **Trained** Newmarket, Suffolk

FOCUS
The middle leg of the colts' Triple Crown was weakened by the withdrawal of UAE 2,000 Guineas winner Musir, and a steady pace meant those held up were at a disadvantage, with the first three racing in the front three throughout. The lack of a true gallop tempers enthusiasm for the form, but Mendip was very impressive.

NOTEBOOK
Mendip(USA) ◆ extended his unbeaten record to three races in impressive style. Just as on his two previous outings, he required a blanket for stalls entry, but he did everything asked of him and already looks to have matured mentally since winning a 7f conditions contest on his Dubai debut three weeks earlier. He had lugged left when first coming under pressure last time, but he looked a thoroughly uncomplicated ride on this occasion, gradually getting across into a handy position from his unfavourable stall, before readily drawing clear when asked for an effort. It is true he was well placed considering how the race unfolded, but he does not look flattered, and he is now a leading contender for the UAE Derby, which will be run over this C&D on World Cup night. He will probably clash with Mendip in that contest, but the Godolphin horse's proven stamina could give him the edge. (op 10-3)
Della Barba(CHI) seemed to find 1m too short when third in the Guineas, but there were no excuses this time. He was allowed a soft lead but basically proved no match at all for the winner, and time may show he faced a near impossible task with that rival.
Enak(ARG), a Grade 1 winner in Argentina last year, had found 7f an inadequate test when well behind Mendip on his debut in Dubai and this was a little better. (op 16-1)
Izaaj(USA) was the subject of a positive jockey change and ran well considering he came a little wide into the straight, yet was still able to fare best of those who raced off the pace.
Vale Of York(IRE) was a major disappointment on his first start since landing last year's Breeders' Cup Juvenile, although the signs were ominous beforehand. He was keen on the way to the post, even appearing to fly-leap at one stage, and he refused to settle early on in the race itself. He was beaten before the straight and his connections will be hoping this run takes the freshness out of him, as well as brings him on fitness-wise. (op 9-4)
Solid Choice(AUS) seemed unsuited by either the step up in trip of the lack of pace in the race. (op 11-2)

Uncle Tom(BRZ), a 1/2l second to Mendip over 7f last time, got going too late and never threatened.
Maroon Machine(IRE) was keen early and didn't pick up.

797a MAHAB AL SHIMAAL SPONSORED BY DERRINSTOWN STUD, ELNADIM (GROUP 3) (TAPETA) 6f

4:15 (4:15) 3-Y-O+

£74,074 (£24,691; £12,345; £6,172; £3,703; £2,469)

RPR

1 **Desert Party (USA)**[306] [1688] 4-9-5 113........................(t) FrankieDettori 2 118
(Saeed Bin Suroor) *mid-div: smooth prog to ld 2f out: r.o wl* **9/2**[2]

2 1 1/4 **Mutheeb (USA)**[14] [607] 5-9-5 112.................................. RichardHills 12 114+
(M Al Muhairi, UAE) *in rr of mid-div: smooth prog 2f out: r.o wl: no ch w wnr* **7/1**[3]

3 2 **Sir Gerry (USA)**[13] [628] 5-9-5 107.. TedDurcan 9 108
(J R Best) *settled in rr: r.o wl fnl 2f: nrest at fin* **16/1**

4 1/4 **Prince Shaun (IRE)**[14] [606] 5-9-5 98..............................(t) RyanMoore 4 107
(Doug Watson, UAE) *nvr nr to chal: r.o wl fnl 1 1/2f* **66/1**

5 shd **War Artist (AUS)**[21] [515] 7-9-8 116.............................. OlivierPeslier 7 109
(J M P Eustace) *mid-div: rdn 2 1/2f out: r.o one pce* **10/11**[1]

6 2 **Palazzone (IRE)**[21] [511] 4-9-5 98.......................................(b) KLatham 1 100
(G M Lyons, Ire) *hld up: r.o fnl 1 1/2f: nvr able to chal* **33/1**

7 3/4 **Barbecue Eddie (USA)**[14] [607] 6-9-5 99....................(b) TadhgO'Shea 3 100
(Doug Watson, UAE) *s.i.s: settled in rr: nvr able to chal* **33/1**

8 3/4 **Force Freeze (USA)**[27] [437] 5-9-5 112...........................(t) PatDobbs 10 95
(Doug Watson, UAE) *a mid-div* **15/2**

9 1 1/4 **Snow Runner (ARG)**[21] [511] 7-9-5 97..........................(t) PJSmullen 11 91
(Vanja Sandrup, Sweden) *sn rdn in rr: nvr involved* **100/1**

10 3/4 **Montpellier (IRE)**[13] [628] 7-9-5 108.........................(t) RoystonFfrench 8 89
(A Al Raihe, UAE) *trckd ldr tl 2 1/2f out: one pce fnl 1 1/2f* **12/1**

11 1 1/4 **Mrs Boss (BRZ)**[13] [628] 4-8-13 106......................................(t) WBlandi 5 79
(A Cintra Pereira, Brazil) *sn led: hdd 2f out: wknd fnl f* **33/1**

12 3/4 **El Amarillista (ARG)**[14] [608] 4-9-3 100...............................(t) WRamos 6 80
(J Barton, Saudi Arabia) *trckd ldr tl 3f out: wknd fnl 1 1/2f* **50/1**

1m 10.82s (70.82)
WFA 3 from 4yo+ 14lb **12** Ran SP% **121.7**
CSF: £35.46..
Owner Godolphin **Bred** David Smith & Steven Sinatra **Trained** Newmarket, Suffolk

FOCUS
This Golden Shaheen trial was not a strong race for the grade, with the proximity of, among others, the 98-rated Prince Shaun limiting the form. That said, connections of Leahurst, who trounced that runner 53/4l when conceding 11lb over C&D last time, will obviously be encouraged ahead of World Cup night. The form is sound enough.

NOTEBOOK
Desert Party(USA) produced a fine performance on his first start since picking up an injury in last season's Kentucky Derby. He apparently returned from his run at Churchill Downs with filling and soreness in his left-front ankle and a displaced chip that was to require surgery. However, dropped back in trip and returned to synthetics (won his maiden on Polytrack over 41/2f), he justified good market support on his return to action. He showed sufficient speed to track the leaders towards the inside and stayed on well after saving ground into the straight. He is clearly a versatile horse and it remains to be seen where he goes next. The Golden Shaheen, back over C&D on March 27, is probably the most obvious target, provided that does not come too soon. He will almost certainly need to improve a good deal on this performance, but that is not out of the question. (op 5-1)
Mutheeb(USA), too buzzed up over 7f here last time, proved suited by this drop in trip, as his breeding (by Danzig, out of a winning sprinter) suggested. His effort is all the more creditable considering he had to come wide into the straight. (op 6-1)
Sir Gerry(USA) raced off the pace and never looked like winning at any stage, but he kept on to take the separate race for third.
Prince Shaun(IRE) ran well but his proximity does little for the form.
War Artist(AUS) had looked good when winning the Group 3 Al Shindagha Sprint (Sir Gerry fourth) over C&D on his first start in Dubai, but he was a major disappointment this time. A penalty for that win meant he was conceding between 3lb and 15lb, but that is no excuse; he basically failed to pick up, despite having again tanked along through the early stages. His connections were sure that he was going to have come on for his reappearance fitness-wise, but it seems that last performance left its mark. (op Evs)
Palazzone(IRE) is another who does little for the form.
Barbecue Eddie(USA), who could not dominate on this drop in trip, is a little better than he showed considering he was denied a clear run in the straight.
Force Freeze(USA) failed to progress from a decent win first time up at the carnival. (op 6-1)

798a BURJ NAHAAR SPONSORED BY DERRINSTOWN STUD, ALHAARTH (GROUP 3) (TAPETA) 1m

4:50 (4:52) 3-Y-O+

£74,074 (£24,691; £12,345; £6,172; £3,703; £2,469)

RPR

1 **Cat Junior (USA)**[13] [630] 5-9-0 113...........................(bt) RichardHills 11 117
(B J Meehan) *sn led: rdn 2f out: r.o strly: hld on wl* **25/1**

2 1 1/4 **Green Coast (IRE)**[13] [626] 7-9-0 105.............................. TadhgO'Shea 9 114
(Doug Watson, UAE) *mid-div: r.o wl fnl 2f: nrest at fin* **25/1**

3 1/2 **Calming Influence (IRE)**[14] [610] 5-9-0 113................... AhmedAjtebi 7 113
(Saeed Bin Suroor) *mid-div: ev ch bhd wnr 1 1/2f out: wknd fnl 110yds* **7/1**[3]

4 1 1/4 **Jet Express (SAF)**[7] [713] 8-9-0 107........................... RoystonFfrench 1 110
(A Al Raihe, UAE) *trckd ldr: kpt on same pce fnl 1 1/2f* **40/1**

5 1 1/4 **Skysurfers**[13] [630] 4-9-0 116..................................... FrankieDettori 6 107
(Saeed Bin Suroor) *mid-div: rdn 3f out: r.o at one pce fnl f* **8/11**[1]

6 3/4 **Vesuve (IRE)**[7] [713] 4-9-0 112... WayneSmith 13 105
(M Al Muhairi, UAE) *trckd ldr: ev ch 2f out: one pce fnl f* **25/1**

7 1/4 **Forgotten Voice (IRE)**[35] [338] 5-9-0 115........................ RyanMoore 5 105
(J Noseda) *mid-div: rdn 3f out: r.o same pce fnl 1 1/2f* **9/2**[2]

8 nse **Fravashi (AUS)**[13] [631] 5-9-2 112.................................(p) TedDurcan 14 107
(Saeed Bin Suroor) *settled in rr: chsd ldrs 3f out: nt qckn fnl 1 1/2f* **25/1**

9 1/4 **Biarritz (SAF)**[364] [774] 7-9-0 108...(b) KShea 2 104
(M F De Kock, South Africa) *settled in rr: nvr able to chal: r.o fnl 1 1/2f* **25/1**

10 1 1/4 **Al Arab (BRZ)**[28] [412] 5-9-0 109.. WBlandi 4 101
(A Cintra Pereira, Brazil) *a mid-div* **14/1**

11 2 **Laa Rayb (USA)**[7] [710] 6-9-0 108.................................(e) WilliamBuick 3 97
(D Selvaratnam, UAE) *nvr bttr than mid-div* **20/1**

12 1 **Don Renato (CHI)**[14] [607] 7-9-0 107..................................(bt) WRamos 10 94
(J Barton, Saudi Arabia) *in rr of mid-div: nvr able to chal* **40/1**

13 3/4 **Soneva (USA)**[27] [439] 4-8-11 111...................... ChristopheSoumillon 12 90
(M Botti) *broke awkwardly: settled in rr: nvr able to chal* **11/1**

14 5 1/2 **We'll Come**[7] [708] 6-9-0 104.. JRosales 8 80
(A bin Huzaim, UAE) *mid-div: rn wd: n.d* **66/1**

1m 35.95s (95.95) **14** Ran SP% **133.9**
CSF: £545.18..
Owner Roldvale Ltd & Gold Property Investments **Bred** March Thoroughbreds **Trained** Manton, Wilts

FOCUS
With the front two in the betting, Skysurfers and Forgotten Voice, both disappointing, this is ordinary form for the grade, although the time was quick.

NOTEBOOK
Cat Junior(USA) had appeared to be set too much to do by Jamie Spencer on his two previous starts in Dubai this year, albeit he was hampered in the early stages on the first occasion and the switch to front-running tactics, as well as the fitting of blinkers for the first time, clearly suited. He was allowed a relatively soft lead and took full advantage, staying on well to end a losing run stretching back to his debut maiden success in 2007. Although he had not won for a long time, he had shown plenty of smart form in defeat, recording a three-figure RPR on eight different occasions, and this performance proved he is capable when things go his way. The Godolphin Mile is likely to be a tougher test, though.
Green Coast(IRE), the winner of a 7f handicap off a mark of 101 on his previous start, ran a fine race on this step up in grade, improving on his third placing in this last year. His effort is all the more creditable considering a stronger pace would probably have suited better.
Calming Influence(IRE), a wide-margin winner off a mark of 105 over C&D last time, raced handily throughout, although he was caught a bit wide. (op 15-2)
Jet Express(SAF) kept on towards the inside without ever really threatening.
Skysurfers looked a near-certain future Group-race winner when landing a conditions contest over C&D on only his second start, but he ran below expectations on this rise in class, basically appearing a bit flat, and this probably came too soon. (op Evs)
Forgotten Voice(IRE) was expected to have come on for his fast-finishing second in the first round of the Al Maktoum Challenge over this C&D, but he found little for pressure.
Fravashi(AUS) was dropped in from his wide draw and would have preferred a stronger pace. (op 22-1)
Biarritz(SAF) made some late headway out extremely wide and offered some encouragement on his first start for a year. (op 20-1)
Al Arab(BRZ) was much too keen.
Soneva(USA), who had a penalty to carry for her success in the Group 3 Cape Verdi on the turf, gave trouble at the stalls, unshipping her jockey before going forward, and then losing ground when starting awkwardly.

799a DUBAI CITY OF GOLD SPONSORED BY DERRINSTOWN STUD, MARJU (GROUP 2) (TURF) 1m 4f 93y

5:35 (5:36) 3-Y-O+

£92,592 (£30,864; £15,432; £7,716; £4,629; £3,086)

RPR

1 **Campanologist (USA)**[138] [6850] 5-9-0 115..................... FrankieDettori 2 116+
(Saeed Bin Suroor) *mid-div on rail: smooth prog 3f out: rdn 2f out: led nr fin* **6/1**[3]

2 1/4 **Pan River (TUR)**[21] [517] 5-9-0 110....................................... SelimKaya 9 116
(Ayhan Kasar, Turkey) *mid-div: rdn 2f out: r.o wl: nrest at fin* **8/1**

3 1/2 **Golden Sword**[21] [517] 4-8-11 119..................... ChristopheSoumillon 10 114
(M F De Kock, South Africa) *sn led: trckd ldr after 1 1/2f: smooth prog to ld again 1 1/2f out: hdd and lost 2nd nr fin* **11/2**[2]

4 1 1/4 **Pompeyano (IRE)**[7] [712] 5-9-0 108............................(t) RichardMullen 3 113
(S Seemar, UAE) *mid-div: r.o wl fnl 2f: nvr able to chal* **50/1**

5 1/4 **Anmar (USA)**[27] [436] 4-8-11 113...................................... AhmedAjtebi 4 112
(Saeed Bin Suroor) *settled in rr: n.m.r 2 1/2f out: r.o fnl 1 1/2f: nrest at fin* **11/4**[1]

6 shd **Claremont (IRE)**[21] [516] 4-8-11 112.................................... TedDurcan 7 111
(Saeed Bin Suroor) *in rr of mid-div: r.o fnl 1 1/2f: n.d* **10/1**

7 6 1/4 **Quijano (GER)**[21] [516] 8-9-5 119.. AStarke 12 108
(P Schiergen, Germany) *in rr of mid-div: r.o same pce fnl 2f* **7/1**

8 2 **Frozen Fire (GER)**[7] [712] 5-9-0 110..(t) KLatham 11 100
(M F De Kock, South Africa) *led after 1 1/2f: rdn 4f out: hdd 1 1/2f out: wknd* **20/1**

9 1/2 **Titurel (GER)**[7] [712] 5-9-0 107... OlivierPeslier 13 99
(Manfred Hofer, Germany) *trckd ldrs tl 2f out: wknd* **20/1**

10 9 1/2 **Perfect Stride**[14] [609] 5-9-0 112.. RyanMoore 1 85
(Sir Michael Stoute) *mid-div on rail: nvr able to chal* **12/1**

11 1/2 **Topclas (FR)**[7] [712] 4-8-11 107... WJSupple 8 83
(M bin Shafya, UAE) *settled in rr: nvr able to chal* **50/1**

12 23 **King Of Rome (IRE)**[13] [627] 5-9-0 109....................................... KShea 14 50
(M F De Kock, South Africa) *nvr bttr than mid-div* **14/1**

P **Halicarnassus (IRE)**[21] [516] 6-9-3 112.................................... AlanMunro 5 —
(M R Channon) *nvr bttr than mid-div: p.u* **14/1**

2m 37.36s (157.36)
WFA 4 from 5yo+ 2lb **13** Ran SP% **123.5**
CSF: £53.24..
Owner Godolphin **Bred** Darley **Trained** Newmarket, Suffolk

FOCUS
A competitive trial for the Sheema Classic, but using the likes of the 110-rated runner-up, and the fourth, who had an official mark of 108, as a guide, the form is short of Group 1 standard. The winner is rated close to his best. As is usually the case on the Meydan turf track, the pace seemed just ordinary.

NOTEBOOK
Campanologist(USA) has now won first time out in three of the four years he has been racing, although that's not to say he won't progress. This was a game performance on his first start since finishing down the field in the Champion Stakes and he is certainly worth his place in the Sheema Classic. Being a quite a big, strong horse, who is entitled to be getting better, it would not be a surprise to see him pick up an ordinary Group 1 at some stage this year, although it remains to be seen whether that will be on World Cup night. (op 13-2)
Pan River(TUR), a winner off 108 over a trip shorter than ideal (1m1f) on his Dubai debut, ran a fine race, just being held after staying on well from the rear. Like the winner, he is worth his place in the Sheema Classic, although he will probably find at least a couple too good.
Golden Sword stopped quickly when last behind Pan River on his debut for this yard, but he went without the tongue-tie and blinkers this time and fared better back over a more suitable trip. Having got a good lead off stablemate Frozen Fire, he travelled well for a long way, before being run out of it in the straight, and it wouldn't be a surprise to see him do better again next time, which will presumably be World Cup night. (op 5-1)
Pompeyano(IRE) was ridden a bit more handily than is often the case and responded with what was surely a career best.
Anmar(USA), who impressed when defeating a subsequent winner on the Tapeta over 1m3f off a mark of 106 on his Dubai debut, was set too much to do on this return to turf and only got going when the race was as good as over after meeting trouble at the top of the straight. It would be no surprise to see him fare better if he makes the cut for the Sheema Classic. (op 3-1)
Claremont(IRE) was blocked in his run early in the straight, and being just a one-paced galloper, he could not recover. He could yet do better, particularly off a stronger pace.

Quijano(GER), appearing in this race for the fourth time (won in 2007, fifth 08 and second 09), had it all to do conceding weight all round and could make no impression out wide. (op 13-2 tchd 6-1)
Frozen Fire(GER) ran a bit better than of late after being allowed a soft lead.

800a AL MAKTOUM CHALLENGE R3 SPONSORED BY DERRINSTOWN STUD, INTIKHAB (GROUP 2) (TAPETA) — 1m 2f

6:10 (6:11) 3-Y-O+

£111,111 (£37,037; £18,518; £9,259; £5,555; £3,703)

RPR

1 — **Red Desire (JPN)**[95] 7593 4-8-10 116 ow1 .... OlivierPeslier 13 — 118+
(Mikio Matsunaga, Japan) *settled in rr: stl in rr 2 1/2f out: r.o wl: led nr line* — **8/1**

2 — ¼ — **Gloria De Campeao (BRZ)**[35] 338 7-9-0 120 .... TJPereira 5 — 120
(P Bary, France) *sn led: rdn 2 1/2f out: r.o wl: hdd on line* — **6/1**[3]

3 — ¾ — **Mr Brock (SAF)**[7] 708 7-9-0 115 .... KShea 3 — 119
(M F De Kock, South Africa) *trckd ldrs: ev ch 1 1/2f out: nt qckn fnl 110yds* — **10/1**

4 — shd — **Allybar (IRE)**[14] 609 4-9-0 117 .... AhmedAjtebi 2 — 118+
(Saeed Bin Suroor) *s.i.s: in rr of mid-div: r.o fnl 2f: nrest at fin* — **13/2**

5 — ¼ — **Lizard's Desire (SAF)**[21] 513 5-9-0 115 .... ChristopheSoumillon 1 — 118
(M F De Kock, South Africa) *mid-div on rail: nvr able to chal* — **7/1**

6 — 1½ — **Al Shemali**[13] 629 6-9-0 108 .... (t) RoystonFfrench 4 — 115
(A Al Raihe, UAE) *mid-div: r.o wl fnl 2f: nvr able to chal* — **33/1**

7 — ¼ — **Cavalryman**[151] 6526 4-9-0 125 .... FrankieDettori 11 — 114
(Saeed Bin Suroor) *mid-div: chsd ldrs 2 1/2f out: one pce fnl 1 1/2f* — **5/2**[1]

8 — 1¼ — **Vodka (JPN)**[95] 7593 6-8-9 120 .... Christophe-PatriceLemaire 8 — 107
(Katsuhiko Sumii, Japan) *mid-div: chsd ldrs 2 1/2f out: one pce fnl f* — **4/1**[2]

9 — ½ — **Joe Louis (ARG)**[20] 7-9-0 109 .... (t) WRamos 14 — 111
(J Barton, Saudi Arabia) *settled in last: a in rr* — **50/1**

10 — ½ — **Debussy (IRE)**[13] 631 4-9-0 113 .... WilliamBuick 10 — 110
(J H M Gosden) *in rr of mid-div: n.d* — **25/1**

11 — 3½ — **Le Drakkar (AUS)**[7] 713 5-9-0 110 .... CSanchez 9 — 103
(A bin Huzaim, UAE) *in rr of mid-div: n.d* — **50/1**

12 — 6 — **Raise Your Heart (IRE)**[7] 713 7-9-0 105 .... (e) PJSmullen 6 — 91
(Ms Joanna Morgan, Ire) *settled in rr: n.d* — **66/1**

13 — 8 — **Re Barolo (IRE)**[7] 708 7-9-0 102 .... JRosales 12 — 75
(A bin Huzaim, UAE) *mid-div: t.k.h: nvr involved* — **66/1**

14 — 4¼ — **Bon Grain (FR)**[14] 609 5-9-0 108 .... WJSupple 7 — 66
(M bin Shafya, UAE) *trckd ldrs tl 3f out: sn btn* — **100/1**

2m 2.62s (122.62) — **14** Ran SP% **123.6**
CSF: £55.24..
Owner Tokyo Horse Racing **Bred** Shadai Farm **Trained** Japan

FOCUS
An inconclusive World Cup trial, and the big race remains wide open. Three of the last ten winners of this - Dubai Millennium, Street Cry and Electrocutionist - followed up in the main event, and this year's race looked strong, with six Grade/Group 1 winners joined by some promising, in-form contenders. However, the pace was only modest, resulting in a bunch finish, and the bare form is short of what will surely be required come March 27.

NOTEBOOK
Red Desire(JPN), who was last seen finishing third behind Vodka in the Japan Cup last November, carried 1lb overweight and overcame being held up in a slowly run race, showing a tremendous turn of foot when switched wide at the top of the straight to get up in the final strides. While it is hard to know exactly what to make of this form, Red Desire, if taking her chance in the big one, will surely go there with as good a chance as any, as there should be improvement to come, and she is likely to be even better suited by a stronger pace. Interestingly, her jockey Olivier Peslier is the regular rider these days of Vision D'Etat, who is joint-favourite in some lists for the World Cup. When asked which race this filly should go for next, Peslier said the Sheema Classic, but that is no surprise considering he obviously wouldn't want to give up the ride on either runner.
Gloria De Campeao(BRZ), the winner of the first round of this series, was allowed a soft enough lead and had every chance, but he was just caught. This performance would seem to suggest he will come up short in the World Cup.
Mr Brock(SAF), fourth behind Allybar in the second round but subsequently a winner off a mark of 110, was always nicely positioned and can have no excuse whatsoever.
Allybar(IRE), who had defeated Presvis in a muddling three-runner race on his debut for this yard before winning the second leg of this series, gave the impression he is slightly better than he showed as he never had much room when trying to stay on from off the pace against the inside rail in the straight. Although not as classy as some, he'll be worth his place in the World Cup and could run well at a price if things go his way.
Lizard's Desire(SAF), a dual handicap winner off marks of 100 and 107 on this surface earlier in the carnival, is better than he showed as he was continually blocked in his run in the straight. It is guesswork to know where he would have finished with a clear run, but he would not have been that far away.
Al Shemali found this tougher than the C&D handicap he won last time but ran about as well as could have been expected.
Cavalryman, last seen running third in the Arc when with Andre Fabre, seemed to find this too much of a test of speed. He should do better back on turf. According to Simon Crisford, the Sheema Classic is now the aim. (op 11-4)
Vodka(JPN), who bled from the nose after winning the Japan Cup when last seen, could not confirm form with Red Desire and was found to have bled from the nose again. She has been retired to stud in Ireland and will be covered by Sea The Stars.

801a JEBEL HATTA SPONSORED BY DERRINSTOWN STUD, HAATEL (GROUP 2) (TURF) — 1m 1f

6:45 (6:47) 3-Y-O+

£92,592 (£30,864; £15,432; £7,716; £4,629; £3,086)

RPR

1 — **Presvis**[27] 435 6-9-5 120 .... RyanMoore 1 — 122+
(L M Cumani) *s.i.s: settled in last: smooth prog 2f out: led cl home* — **4/1**[2]

2 — 1½ — **Alexandros**[28] 417 5-9-0 115 .... FrankieDettori 3 — 114
(Saeed Bin Suroor) *mid-div: smooth prog to ld 1 1/2f out: hdd cl home* — **5/6**[1]

3 — 1 — **Tam Lin**[13] 631 7-9-0 110 .... (t) WJSupple 4 — 112
(M bin Shafya, UAE) *sn led: hdd & wknd 2f out* — **25/1**

4 — ¼ — **Ibn Battuta (USA)**[13] 631 5-9-0 113 .... WayneSmith 6 — 112
(M Al Muhairi, UAE) *trckd ldrs: led 2f out: hdd 1 1/2f out: r.o same pce* — **10/1**

5 — 1½ — **Justenuffhumor (USA)**[13] 631 5-9-3 120 .... TedDurcan 8 — 112
(Saeed Bin Suroor) *mid-div: chsd ldrs 2 1/2f out: nt qckn fnl 1 1/2f* — **9/1**[3]

6 — shd — **Lahaleeb (IRE)**[138] 6872 4-9-1 116 .... JohnEgan 5 — 109
(F Nass, Bahrain) *a mid-div: nvr involved* — **16/1**

7 — 2¼ — **Black Eagle (IRE)**[13] 632 4-9-0 104 .... JRosales 2 — 104
(A bin Huzaim, UAE) *s.i.s: nvr involved* — **50/1**

8 — 2¾ — **Ibn Khaldun (USA)**[13] 631 5-9-0 113 .... AhmedAjtebi 10 — 98
(Saeed Bin Suroor) *nvr bttr than mid-div* — **18/1**

9 — hd — **Naval Officer (USA)**[13] 629 4-9-0 110 .... (tp) OlivierPeslier 12 — 98
(J Barton, Saudi Arabia) *settled in rr: rdn 4f out: n.d* — **25/1**

10 — ½ — **War Monger (USA)**[28] 415 6-9-0 108 .... RichardHills 9 — 97
(Doug Watson, UAE) *in rr of mid-div: n.d* — **66/1**

11 — 1¼ — **Zirconeum (SAF)**[7] 711 5-9-1 107 .... KShea 7 — 95
(M F De Kock, South Africa) *mid-div: trckd ldrs 2 1/2f out: sn wknd* — **12/1**

12 — 3¼ — **With Interest**[35] 337 7-9-0 105 .... (t) RoystonFfrench 11 — 88
(A Al Raihe, UAE) *n.d* — **66/1**

1m 52.93s (112.93) — **12** Ran SP% **125.1**
CSF: 7.83. Placepot: £452.20 to a £1 stake. Pool: £14,310.50. 23.10 winning tickets. Quadpot: £194.70 to a £1 stake. Pool: £842.00. 3.20 winning tickets..
Owner Leonidas Marinopoulos **Bred** Mrs M Campbell-Andenaes **Trained** Newmarket, Suffolk

FOCUS
They went a steady pace in this Dubai Duty Free prep, and that can't have been ideal for Presvis, so it's to his credit he was able to win. He is rated right back to his best.

NOTEBOOK
Presvis had underperformed in three runs since returning from a summer break, but he looks back to something like his best judged on this performance, particularly as he was conceding weight all round. There are plenty of theories as to why he has not been at his best lately, including that he might not be suited to synthetics (two of his last three defeats came away from the grass), and that Kieren Fallon (by that rider's own admission) simply doesn't get on with him. Whatever the case, though, he dispelled the view that he's lost his pace. Returned to turf with Ryan Moore back aboard, in truth he looked to have been set plenty to do after starting slowly, particularly considering the modest gallop. However, he enjoyed a good run against the inside rail early in the straight, displaying the sort of speed that had seen him progress so well around this time last year, without having to be really asked, before bursting through when getting a gap to ultimately win cosily. He will surely stick to the turf now and try and better last season's second placing in the Duty Free (back over this C&D), but frustratingly for his connections, he probably won't have the assistance of Ryan Moore, who is presumably going to be claimed by Sir Michael Stoute for Confront in the same race. Perhaps that will tempt Luca Cumani to switch this gelding back to the Tapeta for the World Cup, and he was trimmed by some firms to a best price of 12/1 for that contest, but it is still hard to see.
Alexandros escaped a penalty for his win in the Group 3 Al Rashidiya, but he proved slightly disappointing. Much like last time, he was well placed in a steadily run race, and travelled strongly, but on this occasion he didn't lengthen when coming under pressure. Being a horse who probably doesn't want the ground too quick, and who is maybe stretched by 1m1f (even though he won over the distance last time), perhaps his connections will consider the Godolphin Mile, as Tapeta should suit.
Tam Lin was allowed the run of the race in front and finished much closer to Alexandros than he had managed two starts back.
Ibn Battuta(USA) ruined his chance by sweating up and racing keenly early on. He is a talented individual, but he seemingly needs to learn to relax.
Justenuffhumor(USA) looked to be hanging right in the straight and did not let himself down under pressure. (op 8-1)
Lahaleeb(IRE), sold out of Mick Channon's yard for 1,000,000gns after winning the Grade 1 E P Taylor Stakes at Woodbine last October, did not have that much room in the straight and is a little better than she showed.
Ibn Khaldun(USA), eighth in the Al Fahidi Fort on his first run for nearly two years, was another who was short of room in the straight. (op 16-1)
Zirconeum(SAF) ran poorly and has failed to live up to expectations.

[758]LINGFIELD (L-H)

Friday, March 5

OFFICIAL GOING: Standard
Wind: medium, half against Weather: bright, chilly breeze

802 MARRIOTT HOTEL OPENING SOON H'CAP (DIV I) — 7f (P)

1:20 (1:20) (Class 5) (0-70,75) 4-Y-O+ — **£2,115** (£624; £312) **Stalls** Low

Form — RPR

0252 — 1 — **Waterloo Dock**[14] 613 5-8-6 **57** .... (v[1]) FrannyNorton 3 — 64
(M Quinn) *racd keenly: led for 1f: pressed ldr tl led again 3f out: clr over 1f out: 3 l clr ins fnl f: tiring fnl 100yds: jst lasted: all out* — **8/1**

-413 — 2 — hd — **Billberry**[11] 657 5-9-4 **69** .... (t) AdamKirby 10 — 75
(S C Williams) *stdd s: bhd: stiil plenty do and rdn on inner over 1f out: hdwy to chse clr wnr ins fnl f: r.o wl: nt quite get up* — **7/2**[3]

000- — 3 — ½ — **Pha Mai Blue**[65] 7876 5-8-9 **60** .... NickyMackay 8 — 65
(J R Boyle) *hld up in last trio: effrt on outer bnd 2f out: edgd lft but kpt on wl u.p fnl f: nt quite rch wnr* — **11/4**[2]

03-0 — 4 — 3¾ — **Hambledon Hill**[19] 552 4-8-9 **60** .... SteveDrowne 1 — 55
(P Burgoyne) *s.i.s: hld up in last trio: rdn and effrt wl over 1f out: plugged on fnl f: nvr trbld ldrs: fin 5th: plcd 4th* — **20/1**

4141 — 5 — 1 — **Kipchak (IRE)**[5] 747 5-9-10 **75** 6ex .... (p) LiamKeniry 2 — 68
(C R Dore) *taken down early: dwlt: sn pushed up to ld after 1f: hdd and rdn 3f out: drvn and btn wl over 1f out: fdd fnl f: fin 6th: plcd 5th* — **13/8**[1]

000- — 6 — 1¼ — **Hazytoo**[91] 7627 6-9-4 **69** .... FergusSweeney 6 — 59
(P J Makin) *chsd ldrs: rdn to chse ldng pair jst over 2f out: wknd u.p over 1f out: wl btn fnl f: fin 7th: plcd 6th* — **16/1**

00-0 — 7 — 27 — **Auld Arty (FR)**[19] 552 4-9-3 **68** .... RobertHavlin 7 — —
(Miss Jo Crowley) *chsd ldrs: pushed along over 4f out: dropped to last over 2f out: sn lost tch: virtually p.u fr wl over 1f out: t.o: fin 8th: plcd 7th* — **20/1**

0050 — D — nk — **Jonnie Skull (IRE)**[19] 552 4-8-4 **62** .... (vt) LeonnaMayor[(7)] 4 — 67
(P S McEntee) *in tch in midfield: pushed along ent fnl 2f: chsd clr wnr over 1f out tl ins fnl f: kpt on but nvr quite getting to wnr: fin 4th: disqualified - jockey failed to weigh-in* — **33/1**

1m 23.57s (-1.23) **Going Correction** -0.075s/f (Stan) — **8** Ran SP% **116.4**
Speed ratings (Par 103): **104,103,103,98,97 96,65,102**
Tote Swingers: 1&2 £2.10, 1&3 £4.20, 2&3 £3.10 CSF £35.83 CT £98.29 TOTE £6.90: £1.60, £1.20, £1.50; EX 15.50 Trifecta £65.70 Pool: £346.67 - 3.90 winning units..
Owner M J Quinn **Bred** Norman Court Stud **Trained** Newmarket, Suffolk
■ Stewards' Enquiry : Adam Kirby one-day ban: used whip without giving mount time to respond (Mar 19)
Leonna Mayor three-day ban: in breach of rule (B)67.9 (Mar 19, 20, 22)

FOCUS
An interesting little handicap.
Kipchak(IRE) Official explanation: vet said gelding lost a shoe
Auld Arty(FR) Official explanation: jockey said gelding banged his head on the stalls

803 LINGFIELDPARK.CO.UK MAIDEN STKS — 1m 4f (P)

1:50 (1:51) (Class 5) 3-Y-O+ — **£2,456** (£725; £362) **Stalls** Low

Form — RPR

6 — 1 — **Vulcanite (IRE)**[23] 484 3-8-5 0 .... RichardKingscote 10 — 74+
(R M Beckett) *mde all: clr 2f out: rdn and edgd lft over 1f out: styd on wl fnl f* — **1/1**[1]

4 **2** *2 1/4* **Yemeni Princess (IRE)**[10] 669 4-9-7 0 .... StevieDonohoe 7 69
(B G Powell) *in tch: rdn and hdwy to chse ldng pair wl over 2f out chsd clr wnr wl over 1f out: kpt on but nvr gng pce to chal wnr* **25/1**

3 *5* **Barrel Of Fun (IRE)**[134] 6604 4-9-12 77 .... PaulDoe 6 66
(Jim Best) *chsd wnr: rdn and unable qck over 2f out: 3rd and wl btn fr over 1f out* **6/1**[3]

343- **4** *2 1/4* **Bussell Along (IRE)**[227] 4177 4-9-7 51 .... AdamKirby 2 58
(Stef Higgins) *in tch in midfield: rdn outpcd 3f out: wnt modest 4th over 2f out: kpt on same pce fnl 2f* **50/1**

5 *1 1/4* **Parhelion** 3-8-5 0 .... JoeFanning 8 58+
(M Johnston) *s.i.s: sn pushed along and rn green in rr: rdn and struggling 4f out: sme hdwy over 2f out: kpt on fnl f: n.d* **13/2**

4 **6** *1/2* **Uncle Eli (IRE)**[16] 585 8-9-7 0 .... RichardRowe(7) 4 61
(R Rowe) *hld up towards rr: sme hdwy into midfield 3f out: swtchd wd over 2f out: hmpd and swtchd wdr bnd 2f out: kpt on fnl f: n.d* **33/1**

7 *14* **Badster (IRE)**[319] 5-10-0 0 .... J-PGuillambert 12 40
(N J Gifford) *s.i.s: t.k.h early: hld up towards rr: hdwy into midfield and rdn over 4f out: sn outpcd and wl btn whn hmpd bnd 2f out* **100/1**

00 **8** *3/4* **Hopefull Blue (IRE)**[16] 585 4-9-7 0 .... LiamKeniry 9 33
(J W Mullins) *stdd s: hld up in rr: rdn and struggling over 4f out: sn lost tch* **150/1**

0 **9** *2 3/4* **Flight Wise**[9] 685 6-9-11 0 .... RussKennemore(3) 1 34
(N R Mitchell) *wnt rt s: chsd ldrs: rdn and wknd over 3f out: wl bhd fnl 2f* **250/1**

0- **10** *2 1/2* **Bristol Delauriere (FR)**[162] 6225 6-9-7 0 .... LindseyWhite(7) 3 30
(Miss N A Lloyd-Beavis) *t.k.h: hld up in rr: rdn and lost tch over 3f out* **250/1**

11 *7* **Swiss Guard**[144] 6750 4-9-12 78 .... SebSanders 11 20
(Tim Vaughan) *chsd ldrs: rdn over 3f out: wknd qckly and wd bnd 2f out: virtually p.u fnl f* **11/4**[2]

P **Ba Bonanza** 3-8-5 0 .... ChrisCatlin 5 —
(M R Channon) *s.i.s: rn green and sn pushed along in last tl lost action and p.u qckly 5f out* **50/1**

2m 32.99s (-0.01) **Going Correction** -0.075s/f (Stan) 12 Ran SP% **117.4**
WFA 3 from 4yo 23lb 4 from 5yo+ 2lb
Speed ratings (Par 103): **97,95,92,90,89 89,80,79,77,76 71,—**
Tote Swingers: 1&2 £8.10, 1&3 £3.30, 2&3 £10.60 CSF £35.52 TOTE £2.20: £1.50, £3.40, £2.00; EX 33.10 Trifecta £231.40 Part won. Pool: £312.82 - 0.75 winning units..
Owner Mrs Barbara Facchino **Bred** Barouche Stud Ireland Ltd **Trained** Whitsbury, Hants
■ Stewards' Enquiry : Lindsey White two-day ban: used whip when out of contention (Mar 19-20)
Russ Kennemore caution: used whip when out of contention

FOCUS
A fair maiden won very nicely by the well-supported favourite.
Flight Wise Official explanation: jockey said gelding ducked right at the start
Swiss Guard Official explanation: jockey said colt lost its action

804 CYPRIUM BAR AT MARRIOTT LINGFIELD (S) STKS 1m (P)
2:25 (2:25) (Class 6) 4-Y-0+ **£1,774** (£523; £262) **Stalls** High

Form RPR

0-24 **1** **Lastkingofscotland (IRE)**[16] 587 4-8-12 66 ....(b) PaulDoe 4 75
(Jim Best) *racd keenly: led after 1f: mde rest: pushed clr ent fnl 2f: wl clr and in n.d after* **11/10**[1]

0263 **2** *4* **Hip Hip Hooray**[9] 685 4-8-8 62 ow1 .... RobertHavlin 3 63+
(L A Dace) *chsd ldrs: rdn to chse clr wnr 2f out: no imp after* **15/2**

45-1 **3** *6* **Wrighty Almighty (IRE)**[27] 444 8-9-4 66 .... GeorgeBaker 7 59
(P R Chamings) *taken down early: stdd s: hld up in rr: rdn and effrt whn carried v wd bnd 2f out: no ch after: wnt poor 3rd over 1f out* **11/2**[3]

2F/- **4** *5* **Kaballero (GER)**[583] 4529 9-8-12 63 .... PatCosgrave 8 42
(S Gollings) *chsd ldrs: wnt 2nd over 3f out tl 2f out: sn hung bdly rt and rn wd bnd wl over 1f out: wl btn after* **11/1**

4311 **5** *1/2* **Ravi River (IRE)**[14] 613 6-9-4 70 ....(v) J-PGuillambert 1 47+
(P D Evans) *stdd s: hld up in last pair: outpcd over 2f out: no ch fr wl over 1f out: b.b.v* **10/3**[2]

0-06 **6** *10* **Whisky Jack**[23] 481 4-8-12 63 ....(b) FrannyNorton 9 19
(W R Muir) *t.k.h: in tch on outer: rdn and btn over 2f out: wl bhd and eased ins fnl f* **25/1**

000- **7** *nk* **Spin Sister**[141] 6788 4-8-7 40 ....(t) ChrisCatlin 2 13
(J Gallagher) *led for 1f: chsd wnr after tl over 3f out: sn struggling: wl btn fnl 2f* **100/1**

1m 36.83s (-1.37) **Going Correction** -0.075s/f (Stan) 7 Ran SP% **111.0**
Speed ratings (Par 101): **103,99,93,88,87 77,77**
Tote Swingers: 1&2 £2.80, 1&3 £2.30, 2&3 £3.30 CSF £9.64 TOTE £2.10: £1.40, £2.50; EX 10.10 Trifecta £41.70 Pool: £606.32 - 10.74 winning units..There was no bid for the winner.
Owner M & R Refurbishments Ltd **Bred** Baronrath Stud **Trained** Lewes, E Sussex

FOCUS
A modest handicap and limited form.
Wrighty Almighty(IRE) Official explanation: jockey said gelding was carried wide on the final bend
Ravi River(IRE) Official explanation: trainer said gelding bled from the nose

805 LINGFIELDPARK.CO.UK H'CAP 1m (P)
3:00 (3:00) (Class 6) (0-60,62) 3-Y-O **£1,774** (£523; £262) **Stalls** High

Form RPR

66-2 **1** **Azlak (USA)**[8] 698 3-9-3 59 .... NeilCallan 10 76+
(C E Brittain) *trckd ldr tl over 6f out: styd handy: swtchd rt and hdwy between horses jst over 2f out: led wl over 1f out: clr 1f out: r.o wl: easily* **10/11**[1]

050- **2** *6* **Not In The Clock (USA)**[64] 7886 3-9-3 59 .... RobertWinston 1 62+
(J R Best) *hld up in tch towards rr: rdn and effrt to go modest 3rd over 1f out: r.o up fnl f to go 2nd towards fin: no ch w wnr* **20/1**

-501 **3** *1/2* **Yorksters Prince (IRE)**[10] 670 3-9-1 62 6ex .... KierenFox(5) 7 62
(G Prodromou) *in tch: swtchd rt and hdwy over 2f out: led ent fnl 2f: hdd wl over 1f out: no ch w wnr 1f out: lost 2nd towards fin* **14/1**

145- **4** *8* **Sultan's Choice**[184] 5573 3-9-3 59 .... PaulDoe 3 40
(P D Evans) *hld up in last trio: rdn and effrt jst over 2f out: sn wl outpcd by ldrs: wnt poor 4th jst ins fnl f: n.d* **16/1**

444 **5** *1/2* **Merals Choice**[16] 583 3-9-2 58 .... PatCosgrave 2 38
(J R Boyle) *awkward leaving stalls and stdd s: hld up in rr: rdn and effrt 2f out: sn wl outpcd by ldrs: n.d* **16/1**

61-5 **6** *3/4* **Whipperway (IRE)**[28] 422 3-8-10 55 .... RobertLButler(3) 9 33
(Miss Sheena West) *in tch in midfield on outer: sn niggled along: struggling u.p over 2f out: no ch fr wl over 1f out* **16/1**

-503 **7** *nk* **Layla's Lad (USA)**[16] 582 3-9-4 60 .... EddieAhern 4 37
(D M Simcock) *hld up in last trio: effrt whn nt clr run ent fnl 2f: n.d* **9/1**[3]

3212 **8** *3/4* **Premium Charge**[21] 524 3-9-1 60 .... AndreaAtzeni(3) 6 35
(C A Dwyer) *broke wl: racd freely: led tl jst over 2f out: sn hung rt and wknd* **7/2**[2]

6640 **9** *1* **Maxijack (IRE)**[27] 443 3-9-0 56 .... AdamKirby 5 29
(G Brown) *in tch in midfield on inner: reminders over 4f out: struggling jst over 2f out: wl btn fr wl over 1f out* **25/1**

0-55 **10** *19* **Suzybee**[20] 534 3-8-4 46 .... ChrisCatlin 8 —
(M R Hoad) *awkward leaving stalls and dwlt: sn rcvrd and pressed ldr over 6f out tl over 2f out: sn dropped out: t.o fnl f* **66/1**

1m 36.71s (-1.49) **Going Correction** -0.075s/f (Stan) 10 Ran SP% **119.0**
Speed ratings (Par 96): **104,98,97,89,89 88,87,87,86,67**
Tote Swingers: 1&2 £7.10, 1&3 £4.90, 2&3 £23.60 CSF £26.95 CT £179.02 TOTE £1.80: £1.20, £3.80, £2.70; EX 25.50 Trifecta £195.40 Pool: £623.30 - 2.36 winning units..
Owner Saeed Manana **Bred** Rabbah Bloodstock Llc **Trained** Newmarket, Suffolk
■ Stewards' Enquiry : Robert Winston one-day ban: careless riding (Mar 19)

FOCUS
A pretty weak handicap for 3yos, but the first pair came clear and produced solid form. Much improved form from the winner.
Premium Charge Official explanation: jockey said gelding lost its action on the final bend

806 JOAN GRAINGER LIFETIME IN RACING H'CAP 5f (P)
3:35 (3:35) (Class 5) (0-70,70) 4-Y-0+ **£2,456** (£725; £362) **Stalls** High

Form RPR

-103 **1** **Raimond Ridge (IRE)**[9] 684 4-8-10 65 .... AndreaAtzeni(3) 2 74
(J Jay) *v.s.a: bhd: rdn and hdwy on outer over 1f out: str run fnl f to ld nr fin* **7/1**[2]

51-1 **2** *1/2* **Brynfa Boy**[44] 241 4-9-4 70 .... TonyCulhane 8 77
(P W D'Arcy) *taken down early: t.k.h: hld up off pce towards rr: pushed along and hdwy wl over 1f out: led fnl 100yds: edgd lft u.p and hdd nr fin* **6/5**[1]

2624 **3** *3/4* **Fromsong (IRE)**[14] 616 12-9-1 67 ....(p) EddieAhern 3 71
(D K Ivory) *taken down early: towards rr: swtchd ins and effrt over 1f out: drvn to chse ldrs ins fnl f: one pce fnl 75yds* **11/1**

5-65 **4** *1/2* **Chjimes (IRE)**[41] 275 6-9-4 70 .... LiamKeniry 9 73
(C R Dore) *t.k.h: hld up in tch: rdn and effrt 2f out: hung lft 1f out: kpt on u.p fnl f* **12/1**

-340 **5** *1 1/4* **Figaro Flyer (IRE)**[15] 601 7-8-13 65 .... ShaneKelly 1 63
(P Howling) *racd in midfield: effrt but n.m.r over 1f out: nt clr run jst ins fnl f tl hmpd and snatched up fnl 150yds: sn swtchd rt: r.o towards fin: unable to rcvr* **11/1**

4-10 **6** *1* **Silver Prelude**[44] 241 9-9-2 68 ....(t) AdamKirby 4 62
(S C Williams) *led at fast gallop: rdn ent 2f out: clr over 1f out: hdd fnl 100yds: sn wknd* **10/1**[3]

22-1 **7** *1 3/4* **Ajjaadd (USA)**[20] 538 4-9-4 70 .... SteveDrowne 10 58
(T E Powell) *sn chsng ldng pair: rdn to chse ldr over 1f out tl ins fnl f: sn wknd* **12/1**

0-00 **8** *1/2* **Simple Rhythm**[35] 345 4-9-4 70 .... JerryO'Dwyer 7 56
(J Ryan) *wl bhd in last pair: styd on ins fnl f: nvr trbld ldrs* **66/1**

0465 **9** *shd* **Thoughtsofstardom**[6] 736 7-9-2 68 .... ChrisCatlin 6 54
(P S McEntee) *chsd ldrs tl wknd u.p ent fnl f* **20/1**

10-6 **10** *4* **Edith's Boy (IRE)**[44] 241 4-9-2 68 .... NeilCallan 5 40
(S Dow) *dwlt: sn pushed up to chse ldr: rdn ent fnl 2f: lost 2nd over 1f out: fdd fnl f* **11/1**

58.30 secs (-0.50) **Going Correction** -0.075s/f (Stan) 10 Ran SP% **113.7**
Speed ratings (Par 103): **101,100,99,98,96 94,91,91,90,84**
Tote Swingers: 1&2 £7.40, 1&3 £5.10, 2&3 £3.30 CSF £15.28 CT £93.99 TOTE £7.40: £1.90, £1.30, £2.70; EX 18.80 Trifecta £143.20 Pool: £667.92 - 3.45 winning units..
Owner David Fremel **Bred** Myles And Mrs Joan Doyle **Trained**
■ Stewards' Enquiry : Liam Keniry one-day ban: careless riding (Mar 19)

FOCUS
A tight sprint handicap with only 5lb covering the ten runners, but they bet 7-1 bar one. Fast and furious stuff thanks to habitual trailblazer Silver Prelude, but it played into the hands of the hold-up horses with the first three all coming from well off the pace. Straightforward form.
Chjimes(IRE) Official explanation: jockey said gelding hung left
Figaro Flyer(IRE) Official explanation: jockey said gelding suffered interference in the straight

807 LINGFIELD PARK SPORTING MEMBERSHIP H'CAP 6f (P)
4:10 (4:10) (Class 4) (0-85,79) 3-Y-O **£4,209** (£1,252; £625; £312) **Stalls** Low

Form RPR

-013 **1** **Private Olley**[28] 425 3-8-6 64 .... JoeFanning 5 70
(J Akehurst) *chsd ldr: rdn to chal jst over 1f out: r.o wl to ld wl ins fnl f* **6/1**

6121 **2** *3/4* **Freddie's Girl (USA)**[23] 483 3-9-2 74 .... AdamKirby 6 77
(Stef Higgins) *led: rdn and c centre st: hrd pressed and drvn jst over 1f out: hdd and no ex wl ins fnl f* **4/1**[3]

56-1 **3** *3/4* **Areeda (IRE)**[14] 624 3-9-3 75 .... NeilCallan 4 76
(C E Brittain) *chsd ldrs: rdn to chse ldng pair 2f out: drvn ent fnl f: one pce fnl 150yds* **9/4**[1]

34-2 **4** *1 3/4* **Kylladdie**[15] 596 3-8-13 71 .... ChrisCatlin 3 67
(S Gollings) *hld up in last pair: rdn and effrt over 1f out: kpt on same pce u.p ins fnl f* **7/2**[2]

131- **5** *1 1/2* **Vito Volterra (IRE)**[88] 7661 3-8-12 70 .... TonyCulhane 2 61
(A B Haynes) *chsd ldrs: rdn and unable qck wl over 1f out: wknd jst ins fnl f* **7/2**[2]

0-24 **6** *3 1/2* **Diamond Johnny G (USA)**[23] 489 3-9-7 79 ....(t) EddieCreighton 1 60
(E J Creighton) *taken down early: blind removed late and v.s.a: sn nudged along to rcvr: in tch and plld hrd after 1f: swtchd to outer and pushed along over: no prog and hung lft 1f out* **20/1**

1m 11.25s (-0.65) **Going Correction** -0.075s/f (Stan) 6 Ran SP% **114.3**
Speed ratings (Par 100): **101,100,99,96,94 90**
Tote Swingers: 1&2 £2.60, 1&3 £3.10, 2&3 £2.10 CSF £30.40 TOTE £9.00: £3.50, £1.80; EX 31.70.
Owner David S M Caplin **Bred** Bearstone Stud **Trained** Epsom, Surrey

FOCUS
A fair handicap, although the top-weight was rated 6lb below the ceiling for the race. A personal best from the winner. It paid to race handily.
Diamond Johnny G(USA) Official explanation: jockey said he was slow to pull the blind off the colt

808 MARRIOTT HOTEL OPENING SOON H'CAP (DIV II) 7f (P)
4:45 (4:45) (Class 5) (0-70,75) 4-Y-0+ **£2,115** (£624; £312) **Stalls** Low

Form RPR

0-03 **1** **Sapphire Prince (USA)**[11] 656 4-8-4 59 .... AndreaAtzeni(3) 2 67
(J R Best) *dwlt: sn bustled up to chse ldrs: rdn ent fnl 2f: drvn ent fnl f: chsd ldr ins fnl f: styd on wl to ld last strides* **4/1**[2]

44-0 **2** *hd* **Hypnotist (UAE)**[30] 393 4-9-1 67 ....(b[1]) NeilCallan 4 74
(C E Brittain) *led: rdn ent fnl 2f: hung lft u.p 1f out: clr ins fnl f: hrd drvn and hdd last strides* **4/1**[2]

2302 **3** *1/2* **Castleburg**[10] 673 4-8-6 58 ....(be) SamHitchcott 9 64
(G L Moore) *hld up in last trio: hdwy on outer bnd 2f out: chsd ldrs 1f out: drvn and edging lft ins fnl f: kpt on towards fin* **7/1**

The Form Book, Raceform Ltd, Compton, RG20 6NL

-110 **4** ½ **Stanley Goodspeed**[23] 486 7-8-11 **68**.........................(t) KierenFox(5) 8 73
(J W Hills) *chsd ldrs on outer: rdn and unable qck 2f out: rallied 1f out: kpt on u.p ins fnl f* **5/1**[3]

4056 **5** 1 ¾ **Loyal Royal (IRE)**[9] 684 7-8-8 **60**.........................(b) JoeFanning 3 60
(J M Bradley) *stdd s: hld up in rr: effrt on outer 2f out: n.m.r jst over 1f out: styd on same pce ins fnl f* **14/1**

3-00 **6** 2 ¾ **Apotheosis**[25] 467 5-8-8 **60**......................... LiamKeniry 1 53
(C R Dore) *hld up in rr: rdn and no prog jst over 2f out: nvr gng pce to threaten ldrs* **14/1**

4041 **7** nk **Kersivay**[2] 767 4-9-9 **75** 6ex.........................(v) PaulDoe 6 68
(P D Evans) *t.k.h: chsd ldr: rdn ent fnl 2f: carried rt sn bnd sn after: hrd drvn and btn ent fnl f: lost 2nd and wknd qckly ins fnl f* **9/4**[1]

0-35 **8** 1 ¼ **Trading Nation (USA)**[13] 638 4-8-11 **63**......................... ChrisCatlin 5 52
(P W Hiatt) *t.k.h: hld up in tch: lost pl and pushed along ent fnl 2f: wl btn 1f out* **16/1**

1m 24.08s (-0.72) **Going Correction** -0.075s/f (Stan) 8 Ran SP% **119.2**
Speed ratings (Par 103): **101,100,100,99,97 94,94,92**
Tote Swingers: 1&2 £6.30, 1&3 £3.20, 2&3 £3.30 CSF £21.39 CT £111.15 TOTE £5.90: £2.00, £1.70, £1.90; EX 28.50 Trifecta £99.60 Pool: £269.28 - 2 winning units..
Owner Ian Beach & John Fletcher **Bred** Bruce Moriarty & Jill Moriarty **Trained** Hucking, Kent
■ Nacho Libre was withdrawn (4/1, arrived at s with incorrect headgear). Deduct 20p in the £ under R4. New market formed.

FOCUS
The slower of the two divisions by 0.51sec. Sound but limited form.
Kersivay Official explanation: jockey said gelding ran too free

809 MARRIOTT HOTEL PLAY AND STAY H'CAP 7f (P)
5:15 (5:17) (Class 5) (0-70,74) 3-Y-O **£2,456** (£725; £362) **Stalls** Low

Form RPR

43-4 **1** **Honest Broker (IRE)**[57] 73 3-8-11 **62**......................... JoeFanning 5 65
(M Johnston) *in tch in midfield: rdn and effrt ent fnl 2f: styd on u.p to chal ins fnl f: styd on wl to ld towards fin* **12/1**

-241 **2** hd **Volatilis (IRE)**[16] 582 3-8-7 **63**......................... KierenFox(5) 12 65
(J W Hills) *dropped in towards rr after s: effrt on outer bnd wl over 1f out: str run ins fnl f: pressed wnr towards fin: nt quite rch wnr* **8/1**

040- **3** nk **Slasi**[149] 6590 3-8-8 **59**......................... ChrisCatlin 14 60
(C E Brittain) *chsd ldrs: rdn and ev ch over 1f out: drvn to ld ins fnl f: hdd and no ex towards fin* **25/1**

6224 **4** ½ **May Chorus (IRE)**[9] 689 3-8-8 **59**......................... FergusSweeney 13 59
(J R Boyle) *stdd and dropped in bhd after s: stl last over 1f out: hdwy whn n.m.r and swtchd rt jst ins fnl f: r.o wl fnl 150yds: nt rch ldrs* **16/1**

24-4 **5** ½ **Libertino (IRE)**[14] 625 3-9-2 **67**......................... EddieAhern 8 65
(B J Meehan) *towards rr: rdn over 2f out: hdwy over 1f out: chsd ldrs and rdn ins fnl f: keeping on same pce and hld whn n.m.r towards fin* **4/1**[1]

2-22 **6** hd **Knightfire (IRE)**[43] 247 3-8-10 **61**......................... ShaneKelly 2 59
(W R Swinburn) *chsd ldrs: rdn and effrt towards inner over 1f out: drvn and ev ch 1f out: one pce fnl 150yds* **11/2**[2]

3-15 **7** nse **Pastel Blue (IRE)**[23] 490 3-9-4 **69**......................... PatCosgrave 4 67
(M L W Bell) *led: rdn ent fnl 2f: hrd pressed and drvn ent fnl f: hdd ins fnl f: no ex fnl 150yds* **9/1**

0-21 **8** ½ **Candyfloss Girl**[9] 689 3-9-9 **74** 6ex......................... SebSanders 10 70
(H J L Dunlop) *in tch in midfield on outer: effrt to chse ldrs ent fnl 2f: flashed tail u.p fr over 1f out: one pce and hld whn n.m.r and eased: towards fin* **15/2**[3]

5-36 **9** 1 **Rathbawn Girl (IRE)**[23] 490 3-8-6 **64**......................... AdamBeschizza(7) 9 58
(Miss J Feilden) *t.k.h: hld up towards rr: n.m.r 5f out: rdn and effrt over 1f out: kpt on fnl f: nevr trbld ldrs* **40/1**

344- **10** 1 **Slip Sliding Away (IRE)**[69] 7846 3-8-11 **62**......................... RobertWinston 6 53
(J R Best) *chsd ldr tl over 1f out: wknd u.p ins fnl f* **11/2**[2]

00-5 **11** 3 **Bell's Ocean (USA)**[34] 357 3-8-12 **63**......................... MichaelHills 1 46
(J Ryan) *chsd ldrs: rdn and unable qck 2f out: wknd fnl f* **20/1**

21-0 **12** ¾ **Chocolate Cookie (IRE)**[8] 698 3-9-3 **68**......................... AdamKirby 7 49
(Miss M E Rowland) *stdd s: hld up in tch in midfield: rdn and no prog over 1f out: wl hld fnl f* **15/2**[3]

-142 **13** nk **Marjolly (IRE)**[15] 594 3-9-0 **65**.........................(p) NeilCallan 11 45
(J Gallagher) *stdd s: hld up towards rr: rdn and effrt wl over 1f out: no prog* **16/1**

04-3 **14** 1 **Reach For The Sky (IRE)**[2] 766 3-8-7 **65**........(v[1]) CharlotteKerton(7) 3 42
(G Prodromou) *in tch in midfield: nudged along and lost pl 2f out: bhd fnl f* **20/1**

1m 24.56s (-0.24) **Going Correction** -0.075s/f (Stan) 14 Ran SP% **130.7**
Speed ratings (Par 98): **98,97,97,96,96 96,96,95,94,93 89,88,88,87**
Tote Swingers: 1&2 £35.10, 1&3 £62.30, 2&3 £79.80 CSF £108.98 CT £2483.02 TOTE £11.40: £3.10, £3.20, £6.10; EX 148.20 TRIFECTA Not won. Place 6: £60.63 Place 5: £22.27 .
Owner F Towey **Bred** Frank Towey **Trained** Middleham Moor, N Yorks

FOCUS
A competitive heat run at a good pace, and a tight finish. They finished in a heap and the form is limited.
Slip Sliding Away(IRE) Official explanation: jockey said colt hung left
T/Plt: £24.80 to a £1 stake. Pool: £58,317.47. 1,714.35 winning tickets. T/Qpdt: £10.50 to a £1 stake. Pool: £5,163.38. 363.03 winning tickets. SP

788 WOLVERHAMPTON (A.W) (L-H)
Friday, March 5

OFFICIAL GOING: Standard changing to standard to fast after race 1 (5.35)
Wind: Moderate across Weather: Fine

810 PARADE RESTAURANT CLASSIFIED CLAIMING STKS 5f 20y(P)
5:35 (5:35) (Class 5) 4-Y-O+ **£2,456** (£725; £362) **Stalls** Low

Form RPR

2131 **1** **Monte Major (IRE)**[2] 774 9-8-2 64.........................(v) JimmyQuinn 4 68
(D Shaw) *hld up in tch: rdn to ld ins fnl f: r.o* **9/4**[2]

6424 **2** shd **Misaro (GER)**[9] 678 9-8-6 69.........................(b) DavidProbert 3 72
(R A Harris) *chsd ldr: rdn over 1f out: led briefly ins fnl f: r.o* **15/8**[1]

-633 **3** 2 ¼ **Cape Royal**[29] 402 10-8-6 58.........................(bt) KevinGhunowa 2 64
(J M Bradley) *led: rdn and hdd ins fnl f: sn n.m.r: no ex* **20/1**

2-44 **4** ¾ **Kingsgate Castle**[11] 658 5-8-2 62.........................(b) LukeMorris 6 57
(Miss Gay Kelleway) *bhd: rdn over 2f out: hdwy over 1f out: one pce ins fnl f* **10/1**

2-21 **5** ½ **Desperate Dan**[4] 750 9-8-3 70.........................(v) AmyBaker(5) 8 61
(A B Haynes) *hld up and bhd: sme hdwy wl over 1f out: kpt on one pce ins fnl f* **5/2**[3]

040 **6** 7 **Norse Warrior (USA)**[19] 555 4-8-8 60.........................(v) AdrianMcCarthy 5 36
(Peter Grayson) *chsd ldrs tl rdn and wknd over 2f out* **33/1**

00-0 **7** hd **Wavertree Princess (IRE)**[7] 721 5-8-7 49......... WandersonD'Avila 1 34
(A J Lidderdale) *prom tl rdn and wknd over 1f out* **100/1**

61.31 secs (-0.99) **Going Correction** +0.025s/f (Slow) 7 Ran SP% **111.9**
Speed ratings (Par 103): **108,107,104,103,102 91,90**
Tote Swingers: 1&2 £1.50, 1&3 £7.80, 2&3 £5.70 CSF £6.53 TOTE £3.10: £1.10, £2.10; EX 8.50.
Owner Derek Shaw **Bred** B Kennedy **Trained** Sproxton, Leics

FOCUS
A tight sprint run at decent pace with the older horses dominating proceedings. Straightforward form.

811 WOLVERHAMPTON-RACECOURSE.CO.UK H'CAP 2m 119y(P)
6:05 (6:05) (Class 3) (0-95,82) 4-Y-O+ **£6,938** (£2,076; £1,038; £519; £258) **Stalls** Low

Form RPR

3331 **1** **Benedict Spirit (IRE)**[4] 756 5-9-5 **78** 6ex.........................(v) MartinLane(3) 8 87
(P D Evans) *hld up: hdwy over 3f out: n.m.r and squeezed through over 2f out: rdn to ld wl over 1f out: styd on* **9/2**[2]

2222 **2** 1 ½ **Calculating (IRE)**[29] 401 6-8-10 **71** ow1......................... LeeNewnes(5) 6 78
(M D I Usher) *sn chsng ldr: led 3f out: rdn and hdd wl over 1f out: nt qckn ins fnl f* **6/1**[3]

26-3 **3** 1 ¾ **Silk Hall (UAE)**[43] 252 5-9-12 **82**......................... JimmyFortune 3 87
(A King) *a.p: ev ch wl over 1f out: sn rdn and hung rt: one pce ins fnl f* **9/2**[2]

4-62 **4** ¾ **Rose Row**[9] 688 6-9-8 **78**......................... LukeMorris 5 82
(Mrs Mary Hambro) *hld up in tch: rdn 3f out: one pce fnl 2f* **3/1**[1]

14-0 **5** 2 **Stagecoach Emerald**[59] 41 8-8-4 **65** oh15 ow2..(b) TobyAtkinson(5) 7 67
(T T Clement) *in rr: rdn over 3f out: nvr trbld ldrs* **50/1**

43-4 **6** 1 ¾ **Alnwick**[22] 500 6-9-7 **77**......................... DaneO'Neill 4 77
(P D Cundell) *led: hdd 3f out: sn rdn and edgd rt and bmpd: wknd wl over 1f out* **6/1**[3]

-221 **7** 7 **Admirable Duque (IRE)**[14] 620 4-9-0 **80**......................... BillyCray(5) 2 71
(D J S Ffrench Davis) *hld up towards rr: pushed along over 3f out: hung rt bnd over 2f out: wknd wl over 1f out* **13/2**

/1-4 **8** 22 **Transvestite (IRE)**[21] 526 8-9-4 **74**......................... DavidProbert 1 39
(Miss Tor Sturgis) *hld up: rdn and struggling over 3f out* **20/1**

3m 38.8s (-3.00) **Going Correction** +0.025s/f (Slow)
WFA 4 from 5yo+ 5lb 8 Ran SP% **110.0**
Speed ratings (Par 107): **108,107,106,106,105 104,101,90**
Tote Swingers: 1&2 £3.60, 1&3 £4.90, 2&3 £4.80 CSF £28.97 CT £117.95 TOTE £4.20: £1.60, £2.40, £1.60; EX 23.40.
Owner Jason Tucker **Bred** Allevamento Pian Di Neve Srl **Trained** Pandy, Monmouths
■ Stewards' Enquiry : Martin Lane two-day ban: careless riding (Mar 19-20)

FOCUS
A competitive staying handicap run at a steady pace with no guaranteed pacemaker in the field. Sound enough form.

NOTEBOOK
Benedict Spirit(IRE) had done all his winning on the Fibresand before winning over 1m4f here on Monday in a first-time visor and stayed on powerfully over this longer trip to collect again. Sitting behind the leaders, he moved through for his effort only to meet with interference from the fading Alnwick but soon hit the front and drew clear. On a career high with his 6lb penalty but this looked a comfortable success and the application of the headgear appears to be doing the trick. (op 11-2)
Calculating(IRE) tracked the leader before taking the lead momentarily entering the straight but could only stay on at the same pace. He is paying for his consistency after being runner-up the last four times and keeps creeping up the weights. This was a solid effort in a better grade and staying is his forte but, unfortunately, he will yet again suffer for this effort. (op 8-1)
Silk Hall(UAE) travelled sweetly behind the front pair before laying down his effort when coming wide entering the straight. He stayed on at the same pace with the only slight concern being that he hung to his right. This was being used as a prep run before the festival, where he is being aimed at the Coral Cup, and it was a satisfactory performance which he should benefit from, although he did look well in the preliminaries. (op 11-4)
Rose Row was ridden a bit closer to the pace than she has been in the past, but when asked to make her effort could only muster the same pace and was well held before hanging left inside the distance. (tchd 11-4)
Stagecoach Emerald was a long way out of the handicap and was in trouble a fair way out but he did stay on well inside the final furlong without ever threatening to get to the leaders.
Alnwick tried to cut out much of the running but was fading when losing out in a barging match entering the straight. (tchd 13-2)

812 DINE IN THE HORIZONS RESTAURANT CLAIMING STKS 1m 141y(P)
6:35 (6:36) (Class 5) 3-Y-O **£3,070** (£906; £453) **Stalls** Low

Form RPR

3122 **1** **Tuscan King**[10] 670 3-8-13 67.........................(b) JimmyFortune 3 68
(P D Evans) *hld up: hdwy over 1f out: rdn to ld wl ins fnl f: r.o* **3/1**[2]

-403 **2** ½ **Sunrise Lyric (IRE)**[13] 633 3-8-6 64......................... GregFairley 2 60
(P F I Cole) *hld up: hdwy on ins to ld wl over 1f out: sn rdn and edgd rt: hdd wl ins fnl f* **5/2**[1]

-213 **3** 2 **Miami Gator (IRE)**[1] 792 3-9-2 66......................... AndrewElliott 1 65
(J R Weymes) *led: a.p: rdn and nt qckn whn n.m.r wl ins fnl f* **5/2**[1]

-231 **4** 5 **Vittachi**[20] 542 3-8-8 58.........................(b) JimmyQuinn 4 46
(J D Bethell) *sn led: hdd wl over 1f out: rdn and wknd ins fnl f* **4/1**[3]

05 **5** 9 **Broughtons Swinger**[13] 633 3-8-8 0......................... JamieMackay 5 25
(W J Musson) *hld up last: pushed along wl over 1f out: sn struggling* **14/1**

000- **6** 6 **Kings Aphrodite**[288] 2187 3-8-11 54......................... LukeMorris 6 14
(Miss Gay Kelleway) *prom: chsd ldr over 5f out: rdn over 2f out: wknd wl over 1f out* **25/1**

1m 50.95s (0.45) **Going Correction** +0.025s/f (Slow) 6 Ran SP% **112.7**
Speed ratings (Par 98): **99,98,96,92,84 79**
Tote Swingers: 1&2 £2.60, 1&3 £2.30, 2&3 £2.70 CSF £11.02 TOTE £3.50: £2.00, £2.40; EX 8.80.
Owner J L Guillambert **Bred** Horizon Bloodstock Limited **Trained** Pandy, Monmouths

FOCUS
A small field for this competitive claimer run at a fair pace with the front three pulling clear. Sound but limited form.

813 SPONSOR A RACE BY CALLING 01902 390000 APPRENTICE H'CAP 1m 4f 50y(P)
7:05 (7:06) (Class 6) (0-55,56) 4-Y-O+ **£1,774** (£523; £262) **Stalls** Low

Form RPR

03-2 **1** **Amical Risks (FR)**[11] 661 6-8-7 **49**......................... DavidKenny(3) 9 55
(Joss Saville) *stdd s: hld up in rr: stdy hdwy on outside over 4f out: rdn over 2f out: led ins fnl f: all out* **4/1**[2]

-405 **2** shd **Blackstone Vegas**[11] 666 4-8-7 **53**.........................(v) SeanPalmer(5) 7 59
(D Shaw) *led: rdn and edgd lft jst over 1f out: hdd ins fnl f: r.o* **13/2**

0-44 **3** 1 ¼ **New England**[7] 724 8-8-8 **54**......................... JulieCumine(7) 10 58
(N J Vaughan) *s.s: plld hrd: sn in tch: wnt 2nd over 5f out: chal over 2f out: sn rdn: no ex towards fin* **20/1**

000- **4** ½ **Tar (IRE)**23 7499 6-8-4 **46**.............................. NathanAllison(3) 6 49
(Tim Vaughan) *chsd ldr tl over 5f out: pushed along and ev ch whn hmpd jst over 1f out: kpt on towards fin* **20/1**

-510 **5** ½ **Dazzling Begum**14 621 5-8-9 **51**.............................. RyanClark(3) 4 53
(J Pearce) *hld up: pushed along and hdwy over 2f out: rdn fnl f: styd on towards fin* **6/1**3

0-60 **6** nk **Jordan's Light (USA)**9 309 7-8-5 **51**.............................. KevinLundie(7) 12 52
(P D Evans) *hld up towards rr: rdn over 2f out: styd on ins fnl f: nvr nrr* **12/1**

06-0 **7** nk **Hammer**19 121 5-8-9 **55**..............................(tp) FrancisHayes(7) 2 56
(Mrs A M Thorpe) *hld up in rr: styd on ins fnl f: nrst fin* **8/1**

-334 **8** 2½ **They All Laughed**14 621 7-8-6 **52**..............................(p) LewisWalsh(7) 8 49
(Mrs Marjorie Fife) *hld up in tch: nt clr run briefly over 3f out: rdn and lost pl over 2f out* **3/1**1

/0-0 **9** ½ **The Last Bottle (IRE)**11 666 5-9-0 **56** ow1.............................. ShaneRyan(3) 3 52
(W M Brisbourne) *hld up in mid-div: prog over 4f out: rdn and wknd over 2f out* **7/1**

2m 44.32s (3.22) **Going Correction** +0.025s/f (Slow)
WFA 4 from 5yo+ 2lb **9 Ran SP% 113.4**
Speed ratings (Par 101): **90,89,89,88,88 88,88,86,86**
Tote Swingers: 1&2 £3.60, 1&3 £14.90, 2&3 £29.90 CSF £29.58 CT £453.59 TOTE £4.40: £1.30, £1.70, £5.80; EX 30.70.
Owner Ownaracehorse.co.uk (Lowbeck) **Bred** Francois A Petit , J & Mme I Andre **Trained** Middleham, N Yorks
■ Stewards' Enquiry : Sean Palmer four-day ban: careless riding (Mar 19-20, 22, 24)

FOCUS
A low-grade apprentice handicap run at a pedestrian early pace with the tempo only steadily increasing down the back straight. The winner did not quite reproduce his recent level.

814 GREAT OFFERS AT WOLVERHAMPTON-RACECOURSE.CO.UK H'CAP — 1m 1f 103y(P)
7:35 (7:36) (Class 5) (0-70,70) 4-Y-0+ — £2,729 (£806; £403) Stalls Low

Form RPR

0422 **1** **King's Icon (IRE)**4 757 5-8-6 **58**..............................(b) NickyMackay 1 69
(M Wigham) *hld up in tch: led over 1f out: rdn and edgd rt ins fnl f: drvn out* **13/8**1

4433 **2** 2½ **Atacama Sunrise**10 675 4-9-0 **66**.............................. DaneO'Neill 10 72
(J Pearce) *hld up in tch: rdn and chsd wnr fnl f: nt qckn* **7/1**

40-1 **3** ½ **Saviour Sand (IRE)**25 467 6-8-11 **68** ow2..............................(t) KylieManser(5) 5 73
(T Keddy) *s.i.s: hld up in rr: swtchd lft and hdwy over 1f out: rdn and kpt on ins fnl f* **10/1**

-040 **4** 3¾ **Mullitovermaurice**22 509 4-8-4 **56**.............................. FrannyNorton 4 54
(J G Given) *a.p: pushed along over 2f out: n.m.r wl over 1f out: rdn and one pce fnl f* **14/1**

25-2 **5** 2¾ **Eastern Gift**42 256 5-9-1 **67**.............................. LukeMorris 8 60
(Miss Gay Kelleway) *hld up in rr: pushed along over 2f out: rdn whn swtchd rt ins fnl f: nvr nr ldrs* **13/2**3

000- **6** 1¾ **Nesno (USA)**94 6862 7-8-7 **59**.............................. GrahamGibbons 2 50
(J D Bethell) *prom: rdn and wkng whn n.m.r wl over 1f out* **50/1**

154- **7** ½ **Business Class (BRZ)**108 7423 5-8-10 **62**.............................. PJMcDonald 6 51
(Mrs Marjorie Fife) *led: hdd over 2f out: sn rdn: wknd over 1f out* **12/1**

-352 **8** ½ **Spinning Ridge (IRE)**25 467 5-8-9 **61**..............................(b1) LiamJones 9 49
(R A Harris) *plld hrd: prom: wnt 2nd over 5f out: led over 2f out: rdn and hdd over 1f out: wknd ins fnl f* **12/1**

-533 **9** 5 **Bid For Glory**16 588 6-9-3 **69**..............................(v) JimmyQuinn 7 49
(H J Collingridge) *hld up towards rr: pushed along over 2f out: no imp whn hmpd over 1f out* **11/2**2

000- **10** 4½ **Tenjack King**27 7867 5-9-4 **70**..............................(t) MickyFenton 3 40
(Joss Saville) *hld up towards rr: pushed along over 2f out: rdn and struggling whn hmpd on ins over 1f out* **50/1**

2m 0.48s (-1.22) **Going Correction** +0.025s/f (Slow) **10 Ran SP% 114.4**
Speed ratings (Par 103): **106,103,103,100,97 96,95,95,90,86**
Tote Swingers: 1&2 £2.40, 1&3 £6.80, 2&3 £8.40 CSF £12.92 CT £83.97 TOTE £2.60: £1.10, £2.30, £3.50; EX 13.50.
Owner A Dunmore, John Williams **Bred** C J Foy **Trained** Newmarket, Suffolk

FOCUS
Plenty returning to form in this ordinary handicap run at a fair pace. Straightforward form.

815 HOTEL AND CONFERENCING AT WOLVERHAMPTON MAIDEN STKS — 1m 141y(P)
8:05 (8:06) (Class 5) 3-Y-0+ — £2,456 (£725; £362) Stalls Low

Form RPR

34 **1** **Understory (USA)**13 634 3-8-7 0.............................. GregFairley 2 68
(M Johnston) *led 1f: a.p: rdn to ld over 1f out: edgd rt ins fnl f: r.o wl* **2/1**2

2 **2** 2 **West Emirates (USA)**11 667 4-9-13 0.............................. SteveDrowne 6 69
(C G Cox) *led after 1f: rdn and hdd over 1f out: nt qckn ins fnl f* **11/8**1

0-32 **3** 1 **Adam De Beaulieu (USA)**32 374 3-8-7 69..............................(t) TomEaves 5 61
(B M R Haslam) *hld up in tch: chal over 2f out: rdn over 1f out: one pce ins fnl f* **7/1**3

04-0 **4** 2¼ **Pachakutek (USA)**56 83 4-9-13 60..............................(p) WandersonD'Avila 10 62
(A J Lidderdale) *prom: chsd ldr over 6f out: ev ch over 2f out: sn rdn: wknd wl over 1f out* **20/1**

5 hd **Forsyth** 3-8-7 0.............................. PJMcDonald 4 58+
(G A Swinbank) *s.i.s: in rr: pushed along and styd on fr over 1f out: nrst fin* **25/1**

40- **6** ½ **Al Dafa (USA)**171 5966 3-8-0 0.............................. IanBurns(7) 9 54
(M L W Bell) *hld up: stdy hdwy over 5f out: pushed along over 2f out: wknd wl over 1f out* **9/1**

7 2¼ **Ferney Boy** 4-9-13 0.............................. JimmyQuinn 11 55
(G A Swinbank) *s.s: a in rr* **33/1**

0 **8** 1 **Maree Prince (IRE)**54 113 9-9-6 0.............................. LeeTopliss(7) 1 53
(Ferdy Murphy) *s.i.s: pushed along over 2f out: c wd st: a towards rr* **100/1**

9 3¾ **Idol Deputy (FR)**21 4-9-8 0.............................. LeeNewnes(5) 8 44
(M D I Usher) *s.s: hld up towards rr: pushed along over 2f out: sn struggling* **100/1**

60- **10** 1¼ **Agricultural**37 4014 4-9-10 0.............................. BarryMcHugh(3) 3 41
(Mrs L B Normile) *hld up in mid-div: pushed along over 3f out: rdn and bhd fnl 2f* **100/1**

6 **11** ½ **Appledore (IRE)**19 551 3-8-7 0.............................. SimonWhitworth 7 34
(A G Newcombe) *hld up in mid-div: short-lived effrt over 2f out* **25/1**

1m 51.37s (0.87) **Going Correction** +0.025s/f (Slow)
WFA 3 from 4yo+ 20lb **11 Ran SP% 116.3**
Speed ratings (Par 103): **97,95,94,92,92 91,89,88,85,84 83**
Tote Swingers: 1&2 £1.80, 1&3 £3.00, 2&3 £2.30 CSF £4.68 TOTE £3.50: £1.30, £1.10, £1.70; EX 7.00.
Owner Sheikh Hamdan Bin Mohammed Al Maktoum **Bred** Darley **Trained** Middleham Moor, N Yorks

FOCUS
A maiden lacking any real strength in depth which was run at a decent pace with little coming from off the pace. The form is limited.

816 BE MERRY IN THE HORIZONS RESTAURANT H'CAP — 1m 1f 103y(P)
8:35 (8:35) (Class 7) (0-50,59) 4-Y-0+ — £1,364 (£403; £201) Stalls Low

Form RPR

00-5 **1** **Querido (GER)**29 407 6-8-11 **49**..............................(p) TobyAtkinson(5) 12 58+
(M Wigham) *hld up towards rr: hdwy over 2f out: nt clr run: swtchd lft and squeezed through jst ins fnl f: sn rdn to ld: r.o* **13/2**3

54-0 **2** ½ **Duneen Dream (USA)**47 210 5-8-12 **45**.............................. DavidProbert 1 52
(Mrs N S Evans) *led early: chsd ldr tl over 3f out: rdn 2f out: bmpd and carried lft ins fnl f: sn rdn and ev ch: nt qckn cl home* **12/1**

0653 **3** nk **Turkish Sultan (IRE)**16 576 7-8-9 **49**..............................(b) RyanClark(7) 10 55
(J M Bradley) *a.p: wnt 2nd over 3f out: led jst over 2f out: sn rdn: hdd ins fnl f: kpt on* **18/1**

0111 **4** 1 **Well Of Echoes**2 780 4-9-7 **59** 12ex..............................(tp) DeclanCannon(5) 11 63
(A J McCabe) *stdd s: hld up in rr: stdy hdwy on outside over 3f out: rdn and hung lft over 1f out: sn bmpd: nt qckn ins fnl f* **2/1**1

0-40 **5** ¾ **My Mirasol**9 682 6-9-1 **48**..............................(p) DaneO'Neill 4 50
(D E Cantillon) *sn led: hdd jst over 2f out: rdn wl over 1f out: ev ch whn carried lft ins fnl f: fdd towards fin* **13/2**3

55-4 **6** 1¾ **Crazy Bold (GER)**20 539 7-8-12 **45**.............................. LukeMorris 7 48+
(A W Carroll) *hld up in mid-div: hdwy over 3f out: rdn over 2f out: bdly hmpd over 1f out: nt rcvr* **3/1**2

4632 **7** 4 **Desert Fairy**15 599 4-9-1 **48**.............................. TomEaves 6 38
(J W Unett) *hld up in mid-div: lost pl 4f out: bhd fnl 3f* **8/1**

404/ **8** 4 **Janet's Delight**359 5575 5-9-0 **50**.............................. PatrickHills(3) 8 32
(S Curran) *a in rr* **16/1**

5-30 **9** 2¼ **Roundthetwist (IRE)**1 791 5-8-13 **46**..............................(v) AndrewElliott 3 23
(J R Weymes) *hld up in tch: pushed along 3f out: wkng whn n.m.r on ins briefly jst over 2f out* **33/1**

2m 2.41s (0.71) **Going Correction** +0.025s/f (Slow) **9 Ran SP% 117.9**
Speed ratings (Par 97): **97,96,96,95,94 93,89,86,84**
CSF £82.28 CT £1341.66 TOTE £7.30: £2.20, £4.10, £4.30; EX 122.90 Place 6: £20.61 Place 5: £16.09.
Owner Inglethorpe **Bred** Gestut Brummerhof **Trained** Newmarket, Suffolk
■ Stewards' Enquiry : Toby Atkinson one-day ban: careless riding (Mar 19)
Declan Cannon two-day ban: careless riding (Mar 19-20)

FOCUS
A modest heat run at a good pace. Weak form with the winner back to his best.
T/Plt: £20.90 to a £1 stake. Pool: £91,966.68. 3,208.72 winning tickets. T/Qpdt: £4.60 to a £1 stake. Pool: £10,567.13. 1,666.21 winning tickets. KH

796 MEYDAN (L-H)
Friday, March 5

OFFICIAL GOING: All-weather - standard; turf course - good to firm

817a MEYDAN MASTERS LEG 1 THE MEYDAN HOTEL (H'CAP) (TAPETA) — 6f
3:05 (3:06) (95-110,106) 4-Y-0+
£44,444 (£14,814; £7,407; £3,703; £2,222; £1,481)

RPR

1 **Alazeyab (USA)**8 710 4-9-3 102..............................(t) AGryder 3 107
(A Al Raihe, UAE) *sn led: hdd after 1 1/2f out: r.o wl fnl f: led cl home* **20/1**

2 ¾ **Warsaw (IRE)**15 607 5-9-0 99..............................(b) OlivierPeslier 7 102
(M F De Kock, South Africa) *mid-div: r.o wl fnl 2f: nrst fin* **10/1**

3 shd **Rileyskeepingfaith**8 707 4-9-1 100......(v) Christophe-PatriceLemaire 4 102
(M R Channon) *trckd ldr: r.o wl fnl f: nrst fin* **10/1**

4 ¾ **So Will I**15 604 9-9-5 105..............................(t) KDesormeaux 9 104
(Doug Watson, UAE) *trckd ldr: ev ch 1f out: one pce fnl f* **12/1**

5 hd **Gallagher**14 626 4-9-5 105.............................. AhmedAjtebi 6 104
(B J Meehan) *led after 1 1/2f: clr 3f out: hdd 50yds out: wknd* **14/1**

6 ½ **Global City (IRE)**14 628 4-9-6 106..............................(t) TedDurcan 10 103
(Saeed Bin Suroor) *a mid-div* **9/4**1

7 ½ **Lui Rei (ITY)**15 604 4-9-3 102.............................. RichardHills 5 99
(H J Brown, South Africa) *settled in rr: r.o fnl f: nvr able to chal* **5/1**2

8 1¾ **Good Control (AUS)**8 707 5-9-3 102.............................. NorihiroYokoyama 8 93
(Pat Lee, Macau) *a mid-div* **9/1**

9 1 **Prime Defender**8 707 6-9-4 104.............................. RyanMoore 1 91
(B W Hills) *mid-div: nvr able to chal* **14/1**

10 1¼ **Thor's Echo (USA)**15 606 8-9-2 101..............................(t) FrankieDettori 11 86
(S Seemar, UAE) *in rr: n.d* **8/1**3

11 ½ **Morgan Drive (IRE)**8 707 5-9-6 106.............................. CoreyBrown 12 88
(M Gasparini, Italy) *in rr: nvr able to chal* **14/1**

12 ¼ **Ceremonial Jade (UAE)**14 626 7-9-3 102..............................(t) JamieSpencer 2 84
(M Botti) *in rr: nvr involved* **25/1**

1m 11.05s (71.05) **12 Ran SP% 123.0**
CSF: £214.71 Tricast: £2,144.35.
Owner Hamdan Al Maktoum **Bred** Shadwell Farm LLC **Trained** UAE

FOCUS
A good, competitive handicap. None of the runners appeared that keen to lead through the first furlong, but Gallagher soon pulled his way to the front and set a good pace. The winner is rated to his mark.

NOTEBOOK
Alazeyab(USA) had never previously raced over shorter than 7f and this trip seemed unlikely to suit judged on his breeding, but he displayed sufficient speed to build on his third behind Midshipman from the previous week. Well drawn, he was never too far away and ran on strongly for pressure in the straight. (op 16-1)
Warsaw(IRE) had been shaping as though in need of a drop back to this trip recently and he duly ran well, keeping on nicely from off the pace.
Rileyskeepingfaith never had that much room in the straight, and only really got a clear shot around a furlong out, but he still stepped up on his recent C&D effort.
So Will I ran well to be third over C&D on his return from a year off last time and he confirmed that promise with another solid effort, although he clearly has little in hand off his current sort of mark. (op 10-1 tchd 11-1)
Gallagher appeared suited by the drop back in trip, looking the winner for much of the straight, but he had been keen in front early on and those exertions told near the finish.
Global City(IRE) had won both his previous starts over C&D, but he was found out by a further 5lb rise.

Lui Rei(ITY) was off the same mark as when a staying-on second (in front of the likes of Rileyskeepingfaith and So Will I) over C&D two weeks earlier, but he had shaped then as though in need of another furlong and he was never going the pace this time after missing the break.
Good Control(AUS) was weak on Betfair and ran nowhere near the form he showed when runner-up in a similar event on his previous start. (op 8-1)
Thor's Echo(USA) ran no sort of race without his usual blinkers and the decision to remove the headgear seems strange.

818a MEYDAN MASTERS LEG 2 MEYDAN MUSEUM (H'CAP) (TAPETA) 7f

3:40 (3:43) (95-110,110) 4-Y-0+

£44,444 (£14,814; £7,407; £3,703; £2,222; £1,481)

RPR

1 **Sirocco Breeze**[15] 607 5-9-11 110 .... RichardHills 11 117+
(Saeed Bin Suroor) *settled in rr: smooth prog 2 1/2f out: led 1f out: easily* **2/1**[1]

2 *2 1/2* **Swop (IRE)**[8] 713 7-9-3 102 .... CoreyBrown 7 102
(L M Cumani) *settled in rr: r.o wl fnl 1 1/2f: nrst fin* **15/2**

3 *1 3/4* **Consul General**[14] 630 6-9-11 110 ....(t) AGryder 5 105
(N Al Mandeel, Saudi Arabia) *mid-div: chsd ldrs 2 1/2f out: led 1 1/2f out: hdd 1f out: kpt on same pce* **10/1**

4 *shd* **Silverside (USA)**[14] 626 4-9-4 104 .... FrankieDettori 9 98
(M Delcher-Sanchez, Spain) *mid-div: chsd ldrs 2f out: r.o wl nrst fin* **7/2**[2]

5 *hd* **Beauchamp Viceroy**[15] 610 6-9-4 104 ....(p) KDesormeaux 10 97
(G A Butler) *trckd ldr tl 3f out: wknd* **14/1**

6 *1/4* **Balcarce Nov (ARG)**[15] 610 5-9-3 102 .... TedDurcan 6 96
(T P Tate) *s.i.s: mid-div: r.o fnl 1 1/2f: nrst fin* **12/1**

7 *1 1/4* **Munaddam (USA)**[15] 607 8-9-10 109 .... NorihiroYokoyama 4 101+
(E Charpy, UAE) *mid-div* **25/1**

8 *nse* **Marching (AUS)**[15] 607 6-9-8 108 .... Christophe-PatriceLemaire 1 99+
(Saeed Bin Suroor) *mid-div* **7/1**[3]

9 *1* **Abbashiva (GER)**[29] 412 5-9-4 104 ....(t) AhmedAjtebi 3 91
(T Mundry, Germany) *sn led: kicked clr 3 1/2f out: hdd 1 1/2f out: wknd* **16/1**

10 *3 1/2* **Desuetude (AUS)**[14] 626 5-9-4 104 .... RyanMoore 12 81
(Saeed Bin Suroor) *mid-div: nvr able to chal* **25/1**

11 *2 1/4* **Al Muheer (IRE)**[160] 6270 5-9-5 105 .... JamieSpencer 2 76
(M Al Subouse, UAE) *nvr bttr than mid-div* **16/1**

1m 22.95s (82.95) **12 Ran SP% 122.7**
CSF: £18.59 Tricast: £127.16.
Owner Godolphin **Bred** Gainsborough Stud Management Ltd **Trained** Newmarket, Suffolk

FOCUS
A decent handicap run at a strong pace, with Abbashiva racing freely in a clear lead. The winner has the scope to do better.

NOTEBOOK
Sirocco Breeze had the race run to suit and impressed off a 6lb higher mark than when winning over C&D (race working out well) on his previous start. The key to this horse is getting him settled, and he responded well to a confident hold-up ride once dropped in from stall 11. He was forced to switch off the rail and go wide at the top of the straight, at which point he only had one rival behind him, but he produced a really smart change of pace, a move that was all the more taking considering he required mainly only hand riding. He's clearly Group class, although it remains to be seen whether there is a suitable race for him on World Cup night. The Godolphin Mile is an option, but he may not be fully effective over that trip, and his stable already has a few possibles for the race. Perhaps he'll drop back to 6f, for he certainly seems to have sufficient speed, and while the Golden Shaheen might be asking a bit much of him, he would be interesting if turning up in the Al Quoz Sprint on the turf. The only slight question mark there would be his ability to handle really quick ground seeing as he has had problems with his hoofs in the past. Whatever the case, Richard Hills thinks he'll be up to winning decent races back in Europe.
Swop(IRE) ran an honest race in defeat but simply lacked the winner's speed. (op 8-1)
Consul General probably just paid for chasing the strong pace but still ran well, posting his third smart effort of the carnival.
Silverside(USA) finished a good second to Green Coast (runner-up in the Group 3 Burj Nahaar next time) on his previous start, but he never looked like defying a 3lb higher mark. (op 4-1)
Beauchamp Viceroy was always handy and proved vulnerable to the closers.
Balcarce Nov(ARG) compromised his chance with a slow start and doesn't seem to be fully applying himself in his race, suggesting headgear might be needed.
Marching(AUS) probably would have been a length or two closer with a clear run in the straight.

819a MEYDAN CLASSIC (CONDITIONS RACE) (TURF) 1m

4:15 (4:15) 3-Y-0

£55,555 (£18,518; £9,259; £4,629; £2,777; £1,851)

RPR

1 **Frozen Power (IRE)**[15] 608 3-8-7 108 .... AhmedAjtebi 10 104+
(Saeed Bin Suroor) *mid-div: smooth prog 2f out: led 1f out: easily* **13/8**[1]

2 *1 1/4* **Timely Jazz (IRE)**[22] 510 3-8-7 101 ....(vt) Per-AndersGraberg 7 99
(Niels Petersen, Norway) *sn led: rdn clr 2 1/2f out: hdd 1f out: r.o wl: no ch w wnr* **25/1**

3 *2 3/4* **Oroveso (BRZ)**[15] 608 4-9-4 102 .... TJPereira 12 98
(P Bary, France) *trckd ldr: ev ch 2f out: one pce fnl f* **13/2**[3]

4 *2 1/4* **Black Snowflake (USA)**[29] 414 3-8-7 97 .... RoystonFfrench 2 88
(Saeed Bin Suroor) *mid-div on rail: r.o fnl 2f: n.d* **12/1**

5 *nse* **Mr. Crazy Boy (ARG)**[15] 609 4-9-8 98 ....(b) ChristopheSoumillon 8 97
(M F De Kock, South Africa) *mid-div: rdn 3f out: r.o wl fnl f: nrst fin* **12/1**

6 *1 3/4* **Astonishment (IRE)**[22] 510 3-8-7 95 ....(t) WayneSmith 9 84
(F Nass, Bahrain) *trckd ldr: ev ch 2f out: wknd fnl 50yds* **20/1**

7 *1/2* **Anzas (IRE)**[112] 7384 3-8-7 97 ....(b) RichardMullen 3 83
(S Seemar, UAE) *mid-div* **14/1**

8 *shd* **Dubai Miracle (USA)**[15] 608 3-8-7 99 .... WilliamBuick 6 83
(D M Simcock) *mid-div* **16/1**

9 *5* **Olympic Danz (BRZ)**[15] 608 4-9-4 98 .... KierenFallon 5 77
(A Cintra Pereira, Brazil) *nvr able to chal* **25/1**

10 *1/2* **Tahitian Warrior (USA)**[61] 3-8-7 100 .... FrankieDettori 4 71
(Saeed Bin Suroor) *nvr able to chal* **3/1**[2]

11 *2 1/4* **Real Secret (BRZ)**[15] 608 4-9-11 104 .... WBlandi 1 78
(A Cintra Pereira, Brazil) *mid-div: n.d* **20/1**

12 *7* **Coeur Loyal (CHI)**[29] 414 4-9-6 95 ....(b) TedDurcan 11 57
(Saeed Bin Suroor) *nvr nr to chal* **20/1**

1m 38.22s (98.22)
WFA 3 from 4yo 18lb **12 Ran SP% 126.3**
CSF: £205.06 Tricast: £566.68.
Owner Godolphin **Bred** Rathbarry Stud **Trained** Newmarket, Suffolk

FOCUS
The form of this conditions event looks pretty useful (time 0.42 seconds quicker than the 6-y-o Imbongi recorded in later Group 2), although Timely Jazz was allowed a soft enough lead and had his rivals on the stretch when sent clear rounding the turn into the straight. The winner was value for extra.

NOTEBOOK
Frozen Power(IRE) had around 5l on the 101-rated runner-up at the top of the straight and did well to win this. He has the option of switching back to Tapeta for UAE Derby, but he would be no sure thing to stay the 1m1 1/2f trip, and his earlier carnival efforts behind Musir suggest he would come up short in any case. Plus, this was his third tough race of the year. Whatever, though, he looks set to make a solid Group 3 type of horse back in Europe.
Timely Jazz(IRE) was a talented juvenile for Brian Meehan last year, and with a first-time visor helping him focus, he took a fair bit of pegging back.
Oroveso(BRZ) was held by Frozen Power on their two previous meeting this year, but he still ran respectably. (op 6-1)
Black Snowflake(USA) seems short of this level.
Mr. Crazy Boy(ARG) didn't help himself with a slow start but still ran better than of late, proving suited by the return to turf.
Tahitian Warrior(USA), acquired by these connections after winning a 6f maiden on the dirt on debut in the US in early January, was well backed but he never featured. Simon Crisford had warned punters beforehand that he didn't fancy him, reasoning that the gelding was running in this race because he was not fit enough to contest the previous day's Al Bastakiya. (op 10-3)

820a MEYDAN MASTERS LEG 3 MEYDAN CITY CORPORATION (H'CAP) (TAPETA) 1m 3f

4:50 (4:50) (95-110,110) 4-Y-0+

£44,444 (£14,814; £7,407; £3,703; £2,222; £1,481)

RPR

1 **Once More Dubai (USA)**[22] 516 5-9-6 107 ....(bt) KDesormeaux 9 112
(Saeed Bin Suroor) *settled in rr: rdn 2 1/2f out: r.o wl fnl f: led fnl 50yds* **14/1**

2 *1 1/4* **Salute Him (IRE)**[15] 605 7-9-3 104 .... RichardHills 11 107
(A J Martin, Ire) *mid-div: trckd ldr 2f out: led 1f out: hdd cl home* **14/1**

3 *1/2* **Firebet (IRE)**[14] 629 4-9-8 110 .... OlivierPeslier 10 112
(Saeed Bin Suroor) *trckd ldr: led m out: rdn 2f out: hdd 1f out: kpt on* **2/1**[1]

4 *1/4* **Marinous (FR)**[8] 706 4-9-0 101 ....(bt) FrankieDettori 5 104
(M Al Muhairi, UAE) *mid-div: r.o fnl 1 1/2f: nrst fin* **7/1**[3]

5 *3/4* **Drunken Sailor (IRE)**[14] 627 5-9-7 108 ....(b) TedDurcan 6 109
(L M Cumani) *mid-div: r.o fnl 1 1/2f: nrst fin* **5/1**[2]

6 *3/4* **Northern Glory**[14] 627 7-9-7 108 .... CoreyBrown 4 107
(W Figge, Germany) *a mid-div* **16/1**

7 *1/2* **Meeriss (IRE)**[8] 708 5-9-1 101 ....(t) AhmedAjtebi 1 101
(D Selvaratnam, UAE) *mid-div: n.d: r.o fnl 2f* **16/1**

8 *1 1/4* **Burdlaz (IRE)**[22] 513 5-9-5 106 .... NorihiroYokoyama 2 103
(Saeed Bin Suroor) *settled in rr: nvr able to chal* **7/1**[3]

9 *1/4* **Illustrious Blue**[22] 516 7-9-10 110 .... Christophe-PatriceLemaire 8 107
(W J Knight) *s.i.s: settled in rr: r.o fnl 2f: nrst fin* **33/1**

10 *1 1/2* **Mashaahed**[14] 627 7-9-3 104 ....(t) JamieSpencer 12 98
(E Charpy, UAE) *sn led: hdd m out: u.p fnl 2f* **33/1**

11 *5* **Autonomy (IND)**[22] 517 5-9-0 100 .... AGryder 3 87
(B Chenoy, India) *nvr bttr than mid-div* **16/1**

12 *11* **Soy Libriano (ARG)**[22] 513 5-9-5 106 ....(t) RyanMoore 7 74
(Saeed Bin Suroor) *trckd ldr: hrd rdn 4f out: wknd* **7/1**[3]

2m 15.78s (135.78)
WFA 4 from 5yo+ 1lb **12 Ran SP% 124.4**
CSF: £205.06 Tricast: £566.68.
Owner Godolphin **Bred** Cashel Stud Inc **Trained** Newmarket, Suffolk

FOCUS
A good handicap run at a decent enough pace. Straightforward form.

NOTEBOOK
Once More Dubai(USA) was too keen when a beaten favourite over 1m4f on turf last time, but he settled better on this occasion and picked up really well late on, having had only two rivals behind him at the top of the straight. Although he's not always been the most likable type, he has produced smart winning performances on three of his last four starts. (op 12-1)
Salute Him(IRE) was ridden much closer to the pace than on his two previous starts this year and he responded with an improved display.
Firebet(IRE), 2lb higher than when runner-up over 1m2f on his debut for this yard, looked to run too freely early on, tanking his way into the lead after a couple of furlongs or so. He settled okay once in front and by no means ran badly, but his early exertions still told late on. (op 9-4)
Marinous(FR) didn't help himself by racing keenly.
Drunken Sailor(IRE), a dual C&D winner, was up a further 4lb on his hat-trick bid and found only the one pace after travelling well.
Northern Glory was 3lb better off with Drunken Sailor than when 1l behind that rival last time but he couldn't reverse form.
Burdlaz(IRE) didn't build on the form he showed when third to Lizard's Desire over slightly shorter on his Dubai debut, but he still reversed form with the disappointing Soy Libriano.

821a MEYDAN MASTERS LEG 4 IMAX (H'CAP) (TAPETA) 1m 2f

5:30 (5:29) (95-112,112) 4-Y-0+

£55,555 (£18,518; £9,259; £4,629; £2,777; £1,851)

RPR

1 **Kal Barg**[8] 706 5-8-12 100 .... Christophe-PatriceLemaire 1 104
(D Selvaratnam, UAE) *mid-div: smooth prog on rail 2f out: r.o to ld fnl 50yds* **10/1**

2 *1 1/4* **Emerald Wilderness (IRE)**[8] 708 6-8-11 99 ....(p) RyanMoore 10 101
(R M H Cowell) *trckd ldr: led 2f out: rdn 2f out: hdd 1f out: r.o gamely* **14/1**

3 *shd* **Monte Alto (IRE)**[15] 605 6-8-13 100 ....(t) RichardHills 4 104
(A Al Raihe, UAE) *mid-div: trckd ldrs 2 1/2f out: n.m.r 2f out: r.o wl fnl f* **7/1**[2]

4 *1 1/4* **Walzertraum (USA)**[14] 629 5-9-4 106 ....(p) OlivierPeslier 7 105
(Manfred Hofer, Germany) *mid-div: r.o fnl f: nrst fin* **25/1**

5 *1/4* **Calvados Blues (FR)**[15] 609 4-9-8 110 .... NorihiroYokoyama 2 109
(Saeed Bin Suroor) *settled in rr: r.o fnl 2f: nrst fin* **8/1**[3]

6 *2 1/2* **Roman's Run (USA)**[14] 632 6-9-1 102 ....(t) AhmedAjtebi 11 97
(Doug Watson, UAE) *broke awkwardly: mid-div: nvr able to chal* **8/1**[3]

7 *hd* **Fiery Lad (IRE)**[28] 436 5-9-7 109 .... FrankieDettori 8 103
(L M Cumani) *trckd ldr: ev ch 3f out: one pce fnl f* **11/1**

8 *2 1/4* **Jaroslaw (SAF)**[14] 629 7-8-11 99 .... CoreyBrown 3 89
(D M Simcock) *settled in rr: nvr nr to chal* **20/1**

9 *nse* **Roman Republic (FR)**[14] 632 4-8-13 100 .... KDesormeaux 9 91
(Saeed Bin Suroor) *mid-div: nvr nr to chal* **6/4**[1]

10 *hd* **Front House (IRE)**[29] 417 5-9-11 112 .... TedDurcan 5 103
(M F De Kock, South Africa) *trckd ldr: ev ch 2f out: wknd fnl f* **14/1**

11 *2* **Celtic Wolf (FR)**[22] 513 5-9-2 104 ....(t) JamieSpencer 6 90
(E Charpy, UAE) *settled in rr: no room 2 1/2f out: n.d* **33/1**

12 *1/4* **Hattan (IRE)**[8] 708 8-9-8 110 .... AGryder 12 95
(M Al Muhairi, UAE) *wl away: sn led: t.k.h: hdd 7f out: wknd fnl 2f* **14/1**

2m 3.81s (123.81) **12 Ran SP% 123.7**
CSF: £144.34 Tricast: £1061.78.
Owner Sheikh Ahmed Al Maktoum **Bred** Mrs C G Gardiner **Trained** United Arab Emirates

FOCUS
An ordinary carnival handicap run at a decent pace. Pretty straightforward form.
NOTEBOOK
Kal Barg, just as when winning over slightly shorter around here three starts back, was suited a strong gallop and he picked up well after enjoying a ground-saving trip against the inside rail.
Emerald Wilderness(IRE) doesn't always find that much for pressure, but the return to front tactics suited surprisingly well. The fitting of cheekpieces also helped, and this was a decent effort in defeat, especially considering he had to work to get to the lead.
Monte Alto(IRE) made it five places from five carnival starts this year. The way he has held his form is a credit to his connections, but he is hard to win with and failed to convince that he wanted to get to the front once in the clear around a furlong out.
Walzertraum(USA) got going too late to threaten.
Calvados Blues(FR), third in the second round of the Al Maktoum Challenge on his first run since joining these connections from France, is better than he showed. His rider opted to switch him extremely wide at the top of the straight, rather than stick to the inside rail and follow the winner through. (op 7-1)
Roman's Run(USA), 4lb higher than when winning over slightly shorter on his previous start, suffered a wide trip and unsurprisingly failed to feature.
Roman Republic(FR) was disappointing off a mark 1lb higher than when third behind Roman's Run (Kal Barg fourth) over slightly shorter last time, and this second run back after a lengthy absence seemingly came too soon. (op 13-8)

822a THE MEYDAN RACECOURSE (CONDITIONS RACE) (TURF) 6f
6:10 (6:10) 3-Y-O+

£64,814 (£21,604; £10,802; £5,401; £3,240; £2,160)

RPR
1 **Judd Street**[15] 604 8-9-2 102 (v) KierenFallon 1 110
(Eve Johnson Houghton) *trckd ldrs: r.o wl fnl 2f: led line* **28/1**
2 *nse* **Star Crowned (USA)**[8] 707 7-9-2 109 (t) RoystonFfrench 7 110
(R Bouresly, Kuwait) *s.i.s: prom in centre: led 1 1/f out: hdd line* **11/1**
3 *3 1/4* **Dohasa (IRE)**[15] 607 5-9-2 109 PJSmullen 8 100
(I Mohammed, UAE) *mid-div: r.o wl fnl 2f* **16/1**
4 *1/4* **Calrissian (GER)**[15] 604 6-9-2 104 (t) TedDurcan 6 99
(Fredrik Reuterskiold, Sweden) *settled in rr: swtchd far side 3f out: r.o same pce* **25/1**
5 *2 3/4* **Frosty Secret (USA)**[15] 604 6-9-2 108 KShea 12 91
(M F De Kock, South Africa) *trckd ldr tl 2 1/2f out: wknd* **5/1**[3]
6 *1/4* **Musaalem (USA)**[22] 515 6-9-2 107 RichardHills 4 90
(Doug Watson, UAE) *settled in rr: t.k.h: r.o one pce fnl f* **14/1**
7 *shd* **Barney McGrew (IRE)**[8] 707 7-9-2 107 PhillipMakin 2 90
(M Dods) *slowly away: n.d* **12/1**
8 *shd* **Classic Blade (IRE)**[15] 604 4-9-2 105 TadhgO'Shea 10 90
(Doug Watson, UAE) *nvr nr to chal* **33/1**
9 *3 1/4* **Sol De Angra (BRZ)**[15] 604 5-9-7 105 TJPereira 11 85
(A Cintra Pereira, Brazil) *led nr side: hdd 2f out: wknd* **33/1**
10 *4 1/2* **Aichi (AUS)**[8] 707 5-9-2 107 AhmedAjtebi 3 67
(Saeed Bin Suroor) *mid-div: nvr able to chal* **12/1**
11 *1/2* **El Cambio (AUS)**[22] 515 6-9-2 111 (b) FrankieDettori 5 65
(Saeed Bin Suroor) *nvr bttr than mid-div* **11/4**[2]
12 *15* **Oasis Star (IND)**[14] 628 6-8-11 106 RyanMoore 9 15
(C Katrak, India) *settled in rr: n.d* **5/2**[1]
1m 11.46s (71.46) 12 Ran SP% **121.3**
CSF: £306.36.
Owner R F Johnson Houghton **Bred** R F Johnson Houghton **Trained** Blewbury, Oxon
■ The first race to be run over the straight 6f on the Meydan turf.
FOCUS
They all raced up the middle of the track early on, but the front two ended up towards the stands' side rail. Mainly exposed runners for this conditions contest, and several of the main contenders underperformed, leaving this form looking short of what will be required in the Al Quoz Sprint back over C&D on World Cup night. The pace seemed just steady for the distance through the first half furlong or so.
NOTEBOOK
Judd Street seemed to run slightly above his official mark of 102. Kieren Fallon said the plan had been to try and get some cover, but the gelding showed good speed from the off and, despite being inclined to edge right, produced a game effort under a strong ride. This was a second carnival success for Judd Street following a win at Nad Al Sheba last year. (op 25-1)
Star Crowned(USA), a handicap winner off 106 on the Tapeta the previous week, ran a game race in defeat on what was his sixth carnival start of the year. (op 10-1)
Dohasa(IRE) ran no sort of race after getting upset in the stalls on his debut for this yard but this was better.
Calrissian(GER) kept on from off the pace after being switched but never seriously threatened.
Frosty Secret(USA), a winner on the Tapeta off 101 on his previous start, was trying turf for the first time and wasn't at his best. (op 11-2)
Musaalem(USA) was too keen.
Barney McGrew(IRE) was below the pick of his British form.
El Cambio(AUS) weakened quite quickly and failed to confirm the promise he showed in a Group 3 on the Tapeta on his first run since leaving Australia. (op 9-4, tchd 5-2)
Oasis Star(IND) promised to be suited by the switch to turf, as well as the straight track, but she was simply never going. Sadly, she collapsed and died after the race.

823a ZABEEL MILE SPONSORED BY MEYDAN (GROUP 2) (TURF) 1m
6:45 (6:47) 3-Y-O+

£92,592 (£30,864; £15,432; £7,716; £4,629; £3,086)

RPR
1 **Imbongi (SAF)**[14] 631 6-9-2 115 ChristopheSoumillon 10 113+
(M F De Kock, South Africa) *mid-div: rdn to chse ldrs 2 1/2f out: r.o to ld fnl 50yds* **9/4**[2]
2 *1/4* **Kalahari Gold (IRE)**[14] 626 5-9-0 107 TadhgO'Shea 8 110
(Doug Watson, UAE) *mid-div: smooth prog 2f out: led briefly 1 1/2f out: r.o wl: hdd cl home* **14/1**
3 *1/2* **Summit Surge (IRE)**[15] 607 6-9-2 112 (t) KierenFallon 9 111
(L M Cumani) *mid-div: r.o wl fnl 2f: nrst fin* **8/1**
4 *1/2* **Purple Sage (IRE)**[8] 711 4-8-9 102 OlivierPeslier 12 103
(F Nass, Bahrain) *in rr: n.d* **33/1**
5 *3/4* **Hunting Tower (SAF)**[8] 708 8-9-0 108 (t) KShea 6 107
(M F De Kock, South Africa) *trckd ldrs: ev ch 2f out: nt qckn fnl f* **20/1**
6 *3/4* **Dunelight (IRE)**[14] 631 7-9-0 109 (v) RyanMoore 3 105
(C G Cox) *trckd ldr tl 3f out: ev ch fnl f: wknd* **28/1**
7 *3/4* **Snaafy (USA)**[15] 609 6-9-0 119 (v) RichardHills 4 107
(M Al Muhairi, UAE) *mid-div: chsd ldrs and ev ch 2f out: n.m.r 1/2f out and 1f out: nt rcvr* **2/1**[1]
8 *hd* **Yasoodd**[15] 610 7-9-0 101 (e) WilliamBuick 7 103
(D Selvaratnam, UAE) *sn led: hdd 1 1/2f out: wknd* **33/1**
9 *1 1/2* **Ocean's Minstrel**[14] 626 4-9-0 100 AlanMunro 5 100
(J Ryan) *nvr bttr than mid-div* **66/1**
10 *2* **Echoes Rock (GER)**[15] 610 7-9-0 105 (t) PatDobbs 2 95
(Doug Watson, UAE) *v s.i.s: n.d* **50/1**
11 *3 1/4* **Without A Prayer (IRE)**[14] 630 5-9-0 110 JimCrowley 11 88
(R M Beckett) *nvr bttr than mid-div* **16/1**
12 *28* **Rio De La Plata (USA)**[140] 6812 5-9-0 113 FrankieDettori 1 26
(Saeed Bin Suroor) *s.i.s: in rr of mid-div: sn u.p* **5/1**[3]
1m 38.64s (98.64) 12 Ran SP% **122.0**
CSF: £32.01.
Owner Sh Mohd Khalifa Al Maktoum & B Clements **Bred** Summerhill Stud Ltd **Trained** South Africa
FOCUS
A weak, uncompetitive Group 2 (the runner-up was rated 107 and the fourth 102) and poor race planning was surely to blame. This year's contest was run a week later than had been the case at the last two carnivals, resulting in something of a clash with the Jebel Hatta, a race of the same class over 1m1f on turf the previous day, and to a lesser extent the Burj Nahaar, a 1m Tapeta Group 3 that was also run 24 hours earlier. They seemed to go a decent enough pace, but the final time was a disappointing 0.42 seconds slower than the 3-y-o Frozen Power, carrying 8st7lb, recorded in the earlier conditions event. Limited form.
NOTEBOOK
Imbongi(SAF), beaten a short-head by Bankable in the Al Fahidi Fort over C&D on his previous start, found this slightly easier. He showed a good attitude when getting a run against the inside rail in the straight and will be worth his place in the Duty Free, but it will be a surprise if he's good enough to win that race.
Kalahari Gold(IRE) stayed on well out wide but was just held. This was a fine effort in defeat, but it's worth remembering this was a soft race for the level. (op 12-1)
Summit Surge(IRE), with a tongue-tie re-fitted, simply took too long to get going. He shapes as though worth another try at around 1m2f (was a 3-y-o only previous time he attempted that distance), and there is stamina in his pedigree considering one of his half-brothers won over 2m, as well as over hurdles. Either that or he needs headgear to sharpen him up. (op 7-1)
Purple Sage(IRE) hadn't run badly in the Cape Verdi and the Balanchine against her own sex, but her form did not suggest she was up to this level and her proximity seems to confirm this wasn't a strong race. She was again seen flashing her tail at one point, but it didn't seem to halt her momentum and she may even have been slightly closer with a clearer run. (op 40-1)
Hunting Tower(SAF) ran respectably with a tongue-tie fitted.
Dunelight(IRE) didn't run badly considering he was taken on up front by Yasoodd. (op 25-1)
Snaafy(USA) was blocked in his run when trying to pick up around a furlong out and would have been quite a bit closer with a clear run, but that said, he basically didn't seem to be going well enough to take the gap before it closed, so he couldn't be called an unlucky loser. (tchd 9-4)
Rio De La Plata(USA) was heavily eased and something was presumably amiss.

AQUEDUCT (L-H)
Saturday, March 6

OFFICIAL GOING: Fast

824a GOTHAM STKS (GRADE 3) (DIRT) 1m 110y
10:12 (12:00) 3-Y-O

£92,593 (£30,864; £15,432; £7,716; £4,630; £617)

RPR
1 **Awesome Act (USA)**[119] 7304 3-8-4 JRLeparoux 4 106
(J Noseda) *held up in mid-division, headway 3f out, switched outside & close 4th 2f out, led 1f out, ran on well* **57/20**[1]
2 *1 1/4* **Yawanna Twist (USA)**[27] 3-8-6 EPrado 2 106
(Richard Dutrow Jr, U.S.A) **77/20**[2]
3 *1 3/4* **Nacho Friend (USA)**[219] 3-8-4 JBravo 3 100
(Kelly Breen, U.S.A) **41/5**
4 *1 1/4* **Turf Melody (USA)**[42] 3-8-8 RADominguez 8 102
(H Graham Motion, U.S.A) **112/10**
5 *1/2* **Shrimp Dancer (USA)**[132] 3-8-4 (b) GSaez 7 97
(David Donk, U.S.A) **24/1**
6 *hd* **Peppi Knows (USA)**[28] 3-8-8 RMigliore 6 100
(Timothy Kreiser, U.S.A) **73/10**
7 *11* **I've Got The Fever (USA)** 3-8-4 (b) CHill 5 74
(John Terranova II, U.S.A) **156/10**
8 *hd* **Wow Wow Wow (USA)**[47] 3-8-4 (b) CNakatani 10 74
(D Wayne Lukas, U.S.A) **9/2**[3]
9 *2* **Three Day Rush (USA)**[28] 3-8-4 FJara 1 70
(Todd Pletcher, U.S.A) **89/10**
10 *6* **Afleet Again (USA)**[28] 3-8-4 (b) KCarmouche 9 58
(Robert E Reid Jr, U.S.A) **25/1**
1m 43.85s (103.85) 10 Ran SP% **119.9**
PARI-MUTUEL (including $2 stakes): WIN 7.70; PL (1-2) 5.10, 5.90;SHOW (1-2-3) 3.80, 4.70, 6.80; SF 39.60.
Owner Mrs Susan Roy and Vinery Stables **Bred** Flaxman Holdings Ltd **Trained** Newmarket, Suffolk

NOTEBOOK
Awesome Act(USA), running on dirt for the first time, travelled well and won comfortably. He will remain in America, still in the care of Noseda, and is likely to run in the Wood Memorial at Aqueduct before a planned crack at the Kentucky Derby.

802 LINGFIELD (L-H)
Monday, March 8

OFFICIAL GOING: Standard
Wind: Fresh, half against Weather: Fine, chilly

825 LINGFIELDPARK.CO.UK MAIDEN STKS 1m (P)
2:10 (2:10) (Class 5) 3-Y-O **£2,456** (£725; £362) **Stalls** High

Form RPR
3 1 **Merrqaad**[18] 592 3-9-3 0 WilliamBuick 8 79+
(M P Tregoning) *led 1f: trckd ldng pair: plld out and rdn over 1f out: flashed tail but r.o last 150yds to ld fnl strides* **5/2**[2]
2 *nk* **Al Farahidi (USA)** 3-9-3 0 JoeFanning 6 78+
(M Johnston) *t.k.h: led briefly after 1f: trckd ldr: rdn to ld over 1f out: styd on fnl f: hdd last strides* **10/1**
0-4 3 *hd* **Mejd (IRE)**[23] 533 3-9-3 0 ChrisCatlin 4 78+
(M R Channon) *cl up bhd ldrs: shkn up and effrt 2f out: urged along and styd on fnl f: nrly snatched 2nd* **16/1**
4 *1 3/4* **Danehill Sunset (IRE)** 3-9-3 0 MichaelHills 5 74+
(B W Hills) *s.s: plld hrd and led over 5f out: hdd over 1f out: kpt on tl wknd last 50yds* **9/1**
-05 5 *10* **Highland Cadett**[13] 670 3-9-0 0 JamesMillman(3) 3 51
(B R Millman) *hld up in last pair: nudged along over 2f out: sn lft bhd by ldrs* **100/1**

4- **6** 2 ½ **Head Hunted**[124] 7243 3-9-3 0 .... TomQueally 1 45
(E A L Dunlop) *dwlt: a in last pair: pushed along 4f out: lft bhd fr over 2f out* **13/2**[3]

3 **7** 2 ½ **Jawal**[14] 667 3-9-3 0 .... SebSanders 2 39
(C E Brittain) *trckd ldrs on outer: rdn and no rspnse over 2f out: hanging and wknd rapidly over 1f out* **11/8**[1]

1m 37.97s (-0.23) **Going Correction** +0.10s/f (Slow) **7** Ran SP% **110.0**
Speed ratings (Par 98): **105,104,104,102,92 90,87**
toteswingers: 1&2 £4.40, 1&3 £7.50, 2&3 £9.50 CSF £24.79 TOTE £2.90: £1.90, £3.70; EX 29.10 Trifecta £137.90 Pool: 727.12 - 3.90 winning units..
Owner Hamdan Al Maktoum **Bred** Cheveley Park Stud Ltd **Trained** Lambourn, Berks

FOCUS
An interesting maiden, but they went a modest pace. There is improvement to come from the principals.
Al Farahidi(USA) Official explanation: jockey said colt hung left
Danehill Sunset(IRE) Official explanation: jockey said colt hung left

826 MARRIOTT HOTEL OPENING SPRING 2010 (S) STKS 6f (P)
2:40 (2:40) (Class 6) 3-Y-O **£1,774** (£523; £262) **Stalls** Low

Form RPR
6244 **1** **Avow (USA)**[22] 550 3-8-13 66 .... (b) LiamKeniry 5 68
(J S Moore) *mde all: drvn 2 l clr 2f out: kpt on u.p fnl f: unchal* **11/2**

-523 **2** 2 ¼ **Miss Lesley**[12] 689 3-9-0 68 .... (b) NeilCallan 2 61
(D K Ivory) *chsd wnr: rdn and no imp 2f out: wl hld whn wandered rt and lft ins fnl f* **3/1**[3]

460- **3** *shd* **Kenswick**[119] 7317 3-8-5 55 .... AndreaAtzeni(3) 1 55
(Pat Eddery) *hld up in 4th: rdn and nt qckn 2f out: plugged on fnl f and nrly snatched 2nd* **15/8**[1]

3232 **4** *nk* **Flow Chart (IRE)**[29] 454 3-9-5 71 .... (b) AdamKirby 4 65
(Peter Grayson) *reminders in last over 4f out: in tch: rdn and nt qckn 2f out: kpt on last 150yds to cl on wilting rivals* **11/1**

2133 **5** ¾ **Anjomarba (IRE)**[11] 702 3-8-11 67 .... (p) JackDean(3) 6 58
(W G M Turner) *disp 2nd pl to over 1f out: folded u.p* **11/4**[2]

1m 12.86s (0.96) **Going Correction** +0.10s/f (Slow) **5** Ran SP% **110.2**
Speed ratings (Par 96): **97,94,93,93,92**
CSF £21.84 TOTE £7.10: £3.00, £1.90; EX 25.30.There was no bid for the winner
Owner Two Bucks Stable **Bred** J D Squires **Trained** Upper Lambourn, Berks

FOCUS
No more than a fair seller and the time was unsurprisingly the slowest of the three races run over this trip. The winner looks the best guide.

827 LINGFIELD PARK FOURBALL CLAIMING STKS 1m 2f (P)
3:15 (3:15) (Class 6) 4-Y-O+ **£1,774** (£523; £262) **Stalls** Low

Form RPR
4411 **1** **Hurakan (IRE)**[8] 746 4-9-3 73 .... (p) J-PGuillambert 9 69+
(P D Evans) *stdd s: hld up last: looking for room over 1f out: prog ent fnl f: urged along w no recrse of whip to ld last 100yds: a fending off rival* **15/8**[2]

3313 **2** *nk* **Ilie Nastase (FR)**[8] 749 6-9-7 85 .... LiamKeniry 6 73+
(C R Dore) *hld up in 7th: effrt on outer over 1f out: drvn to chal and upsides ins fnl f: nt qckn u.p nr fin* **5/4**[1]

4-32 **3** 2 ¼ **Dichoh**[38] 342 7-9-2 75 .... (v) GeorgeBaker 5 64+
(M Madgwick) *hld up in 6th: prog on outer 2f out: drvn to ld 1f out: hdd and outpcd last 100yds* **11/2**[3]

-426 **4** *nk* **Farncombe (IRE)**[17] 611 4-8-3 58 .... DavidProbert 1 50
(R A Harris) *t.k.h: hld up in tch: trckd ldrs 2f out: rdn to chal over 1f out: nt qckn and sn btn* **14/1**

002- **5** 1 **Felicia**[91] 7660 5-8-5 48 ow1 .... SamHitchcott 2 51
(J E Long) *trckd ldrs: cl enough 2f out: squeezed out over 1f out: n.d after* **50/1**

06/6 **6** *nk* **Corran Ard (IRE)**[18] 600 9-8-11 74 .... FergusSweeney 3 56
(Tim Vaughan) *t.k.h: prom: wnt 2nd 6f out: drvn to chal over 1f out: fnd nil and sn btn* **33/1**

0410 **7** ½ **Hold The Bucks (USA)**[5] 780 4-8-11 60 .... (p) LukeMorris 8 55
(J S Moore) *led over 2f: rdn over 4f out: sn lost pl on inner: tried to rally over 1f out and cl enough: sn outpcd* **20/1**

200- **8** *hd* **Shared Moment (IRE)**[159] 6394 4-8-9 59 .... (p) ChrisCatlin 4 52
(J Gallagher) *t.k.h early: led over 7f out to 1f out: sn btn* **33/1**

2m 7.23s (0.63) **Going Correction** +0.10s/f (Slow) **8** Ran SP% **113.9**
Speed ratings (Par 101): **101,100,98,98,97 97,97,97**
toteswingers:1&2:£1.60, 1&3:£2.90, 2&3:£2.40 CSF £4.35 TOTE £2.80: £1.10, £1.10, £2.00; EX 6.10 Trifecta £15.80 Pool: 447.86 - 20.91 winning units..
Owner J L Guillambert **Bred** Newberry Stud Company **Trained** Pandy, Monmouths
■ Stewards' Enquiry : J-P Guillambert one day ban: careless riding

FOCUS
A fair claimer, but they went a muddling pace. The first three are capable of better than the bare form.

828 AT THE RACES FILLIES' H'CAP 6f (P)
3:50 (3:50) (Class 5) (0-75,73) 4-Y-O+ **£2,456** (£725; £362) **Stalls** Low

Form RPR
500- **1** **Orange Pip**[182] 5719 5-9-4 73 .... SebSanders 7 86+
(P J Makin) *mde all: hanging rt much of way: edgd rt fr over 1f out but styd on strly: in n.d fnl f* **7/2**[2]

-322 **2** 3 ¼ **Romantic Queen**[12] 684 4-8-7 62 .... (t) ChrisCatlin 4 65
(George Baker) *hld up in last: prog on wd outside over 1f out: wnt 2nd ins fnl f: no imp on wnr* **5/1**[3]

-501 **3** ¾ **White Shift (IRE)**[24] 531 4-8-5 65 .... KierenFox(5) 1 66
(P Howling) *hld up in tch: lost pl and pushed along over 2f out: effrt over 1f out: kpt on to take 3rd ins fnl f* **8/1**

03-0 **4** 1 **Leftontheshelf (IRE)**[10] 723 4-8-7 62 .... (p) LiamJones 5 60
(Miss T Spearing) *hld up in tch: effrt on outer over 2f out: one pce and no prog over 1f out* **8/1**

2636 **5** ½ **Fine Silk (USA)**[17] 624 4-8-12 67 .... JerryO'Dwyer 2 63
(M G Quinlan) *chsd wnr: rdn and no imp over 1f out: wknd ins fnl f* **10/1**

45-3 **6** 1 ¼ **Bold Ring**[14] 658 4-8-4 59 .... HayleyTurner 3 52
(E J Creighton) *hld up in 6th: gng wl 2f out: effrt on inner over 1f out: sn rdn and nt qckn: wknd last 150yds* **5/1**[3]

-312 **7** 1 ¾ **Fazbee (IRE)**[23] 544 4-9-2 71 .... (b) TonyCulhane 6 58
(P W D'Arcy) *chsd ldng pair to jst over 1f out: wknd* **11/4**[1]

1m 11.84s (-0.06) **Going Correction** +0.10s/f (Slow) **7** Ran SP% **113.5**
Speed ratings (Par 100): **104,99,98,97,96 95,92**
toteswingers:1&2:£5.40, 1&3:£5.70, 2&3:£5.10 CSF £20.88 TOTE £3.40: £2.30, £2.70; EX 21.70.
Owner Lady Whent **Bred** Raffin Bloodstock **Trained** Ogbourne Maisey, Wilts

FOCUS
An uncompetitive fillies' handicap in which few were ever involved. The time was the quickest of three 6f races on the card, although the other two contests over the trip were a seller and a claimer. The winner is rated back to form.

829 LINGFIELDPARK.CO.UK CLAIMING STKS 6f (P)
4:25 (4:26) (Class 6) 4-Y-O+ **£1,774** (£523; £262) **Stalls** Low

Form RPR
000- **1** **Prince Namid**[131] 7119 8-8-5 69 .... LukeMorris 6 66+
(J A T De Giles) *hld up in last trio: prog on wd outside over 1f out: hung lft but r.o to ld ins fnl f: in command after* **10/1**

1224 **2** 1 **Total Impact**[7] 750 7-9-3 76 .... RobertWinston 3 75+
(C R Dore) *mostly pressed ldr: cruising 2f out: led over 1f out: rdn and limited rspnse ent fnl f: sn hdd and outpcd* **5/6**[1]

0-03 **3** *nk* **Riflessione**[5] 778 4-8-9 60 .... (b) LiamJones 1 66
(R A Harris) *chsd ldrs: effrt on outer over 2f out: rdn over 1f out: keeping on whn checked ins fnl f: styd on to press for 2nd nr fin* **9/2**[2]

26-5 **4** 1 ¼ **Tous Les Deux**[12] 679 7-9-3 78 .... GeorgeBaker 2 70
(G L Moore) *stdd s: hld up in last trio: prog on inner over 2f out cl up over 1f out: reminder and nt qckn* **7/1**[3]

4236 **5** 1 ¼ **Commandingpresence (USA)**[17] 615 4-8-0 45 ow2
FrankieMcDonald 8 49
(J J Bridger) *gave trble to s and ent stalls: dwlt: hld up in last trio: effrt and in tch over 1f out: fdd ins fnl f* **33/1**

000- **6** *shd* **Briannsta (IRE)**[82] 7774 8-8-5 50 .... SamHitchcott 5 54
(J E Long) *chsd ldrs on outer: rdn over 2f out: nt qckn over 1f out: no imp after* **25/1**

620- **7** 2 ½ **Come On Buckers (IRE)**[125] 7224 4-8-4 58 ow1 .... (v) HayleyTurner 7 45
(E J Creighton) *mde most to over 1f out: wknd fnl f* **15/2**

-006 **8** 2 ¼ **Place The Duchess**[39] 319 4-8-2 45 ow2 .... (bt) WandersonD'Avila 4 35
(A J Lidderdale) *t.k.h: w ldrs: lost pl 2f out: sn btn* **50/1**

1m 12.27s (0.37) **Going Correction** +0.10s/f (Slow) **8** Ran SP% **114.8**
Speed ratings (Par 101): **101,99,99,97,95 95,92,89**
toteswingers:1&2:£4.70, 1&3:£8.10, 2&3:£2.00 CSF £18.80 TOTE £17.70: £3.90, £1.10, £1.20; EX 43.80 Trifecta £152.70 Pool: 577.98 - 2.80 winning units..
Owner T Gould **Bred** Mrs R D Peacock **Trained** Stanton Fitzwarren, Wilts
■ Stewards' Enquiry : Luke Morris two-day ban: careless riding (22, 24)

FOCUS
A modest claimer run in a time 0.43 seconds slower than the earlier handicap won by the 73-rated Orange Pip. The winner is better than the bare form.

830 AT THE RACES H'CAP 1m 4f (P)
5:00 (5:00) (Class 5) (0-75,73) 3-Y-O **£2,456** (£725; £362) **Stalls** Low

Form RPR
31 **1** **Beyond (IRE)**[38] 340 3-9-2 71 .... GeorgeBaker 1 81+
(J Noseda) *cl up: led on inner over 1f out: pushed clr: smoothly* **8/11**[1]

40-4 **2** 2 ½ **Heading To First**[14] 664 3-9-1 70 .... SebSanders 5 70
(C E Brittain) *led: jinked bnd over 9f out: tried to kick on over 2f out: hdd over 1f out: easily outpcd* **8/1**

0-22 **3** *hd* **Moonbalej**[10] 717 3-8-5 60 .... (b[1]) JoeFanning 4 60
(M Johnston) *t.k.h early: sn trckd ldr: asked to chal wl over 1f out: hd high and wouldn't overtake* **4/1**[2]

0-40 **4** 3 ¼ **Fusaichi Flyer (USA)**[6] 762 3-8-7 62 .... ChrisCatlin 3 57
(R Charlton) *stdd s: hld up last: outpcd over 2f out: shkn up and no imp over 1f out* **20/1**

-212 **5** *hd* **Bubbly Braveheart (IRE)**[21] 564 3-9-4 73 .... RobertWinston 2 68
(A Bailey) *plld hrd: hld up in 4th: rdn over 2f out: sn outpcd and btn* **11/2**[3]

2m 35.34s (2.34) **Going Correction** +0.10s/f (Slow) **5** Ran SP% **109.2**
Speed ratings (Par 98): **96,94,94,92,91**
CSF £7.07 TOTE £1.60: £1.10, £3.30; EX 5.90.
Owner The Honorable Earle I Mack **Bred** Pat Fullam **Trained** Newmarket, Suffolk

FOCUS
An interesting 3-y-o handicap, although the pace was predictably steady. The well treated winner won easily.
Bubbly Braveheart(IRE) Official explanation: jockey said gelding ran too free

831 FURLONGS & FAIRWAYS H'CAP 5f (P)
5:30 (5:30) (Class 6) (0-60,58) 3-Y-O **£1,774** (£523; £262) **Stalls** High

Form RPR
5-05 **1** **Ballyvonane (USA)**[8] 745 3-8-8 48 .... (b) LukeMorris 7 52
(L A Dace) *s.i.s: rcvrd to take 2nd over 3f out: brought wd in st: rdn to ld jst ins fnl f: drvn out* **7/1**

030- **2** ¾ **Tulip Explosion**[180] 5776 3-8-8 48 .... JimmyQuinn 1 50
(D Shaw) *t.k.h early: chsd ldr to over 3f out: shkn up over 1f out: styd on to take 2nd again last 100yds: a hld* **5/1**

5132 **3** ¾ **Duke Of Rainford**[14] 662 3-9-3 57 .... (p) TonyCulhane 4 56
(M Herrington) *hld up in 6th: effrt over 1f out: urged along and prog to take 3rd wl ins fnl f: kpt on same pce after* **4/1**[2]

6360 **4** 1 **Annia Galeria (IRE)**[17] 619 3-8-13 53 .... DavidProbert 6 48
(C A Dwyer) *led: rdn over 1f out: hdd and fdd jst ins fnl f* **20/1**

05-6 **5** *shd* **Thewinnatakesitall**[20] 574 3-9-1 55 .... (p) FrankieMcDonald 5 50
(H J Evans) *t.k.h: hld up in tch: rdn and nt qckn over 1f out: kpt on nr fin* **33/1**

3221 **6** *shd* **Exceed Power**[17] 619 3-9-4 58 .... HayleyTurner 2 57+
(D M Simcock) *s.s: hld up in last pair: pushed along on inner over 1f out: no ch whn nt clr run ins fnl f: swtchd rt and styd on* **15/8**[1]

-444 **7** 1 ½ **Pavement Games**[27] 471 3-8-6 46 .... (p) FrannyNorton 8 35
(R C Guest) *racd awkwardly: in tch: hanging and nt qckn over 1f out: no ch ins fnl f* **9/2**[3]

60.15 secs (1.35) **Going Correction** +0.10s/f (Slow) **7** Ran SP% **109.8**
Speed ratings (Par 96): **93,91,90,89,88 88,86**
toteswingers:1&2:£6.50, 1&3:£2.70, 2&3:£5.20 CSF £38.05 CT £147.25 TOTE £5.20: £2.80, £3.80; EX 39.60 TRIFECTA Not won. Place 6 £40.15, Place 5 £13.52.
Owner M C S D Racing Partnership **Bred** Tenlane Farm & Trackside Farm **Trained** Five Oaks, W Sussex

FOCUS
A moderate 3-y-o sprint handicap and weak form.
T/Plt: £39.90 to a £1 stake. Pool: £64,659.80. 1,182.26 winning tickets. T/Qpdt: £4.90 to a £1 stake. Pool: £5,484.70. 816.95 winning tickets. JN

[781]SOUTHWELL (L-H)

Tuesday, March 9

OFFICIAL GOING: Standard

Wind: Light half-behind Weather: Overcast

832 BEST EQUESTRIAN SHOPPING AT RIDEAWAY.CO.UK H'CAP 5f (F)

2:10 (2:11) (Class 5) (0-75,74) 4-Y-0+ **£2,456** (£725; £362) **Stalls** High

Form RPR

1511 **1** **Where's Reiley (USA)**[19] 601 4-9-4 **74**.................... GrahamGibbons 3 88+
(T D Barron) *s.i.s: hdwy over 3f out: led over 1f out: shkn up and r.o wl* **7/4**[1]

-016 **2** *3* **Spic 'n Span**[11] 723 5-8-8 **64**..(b) JoeFanning 1 67
(R A Harris) *awkward leaving stalls: led 4f out: rdn and hdd over 1f out: styd on same pce ins fnl f* **7/2**[2]

5136 **3** *3 1/2* **Colorus (IRE)**[10] 736 7-9-1 **74**..................................(p) KellyHarrison(3) 4 65
(W J H Ratcliffe) *chsd ldrs: rdn 1/2-way: styd on same pce appr fnl f* **11/2**[3]

610- **4** *1 1/2* **Spirit Of Coniston**[115] 7398 7-8-9 **65**.............................. TonyCulhane 7 50
(P T Midgley) *in tch and sn drvn along: hmpd 1/2-way: sn outpcd: rdn and hung lft over 1f out: n.d after* **22/1**

2-33 **5** *1 1/2* **First Swallow**[19] 601 5-8-6 **62**....................................(t) AndrewMullen 6 42
(D H Brown) *led 1f: chsd ldrs: rdn whn hmpd and lost pl 1/2-way: hung lft over 1f out: n.d after* **6/1**

0-60 **6** *nse* **Calmdownmate (IRE)**[19] 601 5-8-8 **64**........................... LukeMorris 8 44
(Mrs R A Carr) *s.i.s: sn drvn along in rr: hmpd 2f out: n.d* **20/1**

40-1 **7** *1/2* **Sir Nod**[32] 432 8-9-3 **73**.. PaulHanagan 5 51
(Julie Camacho) *s.i.s: sn chsng ldrs: rdn and hung rt 1/2-way: hung lft over 1f out: sn wknd* **7/2**[2]

60.22 secs (0.52) **Going Correction** +0.20s/f (Slow) 7 Ran SP% **119.6**
Speed ratings (Par 103): **103,98,92,90,87 87,86**
toteswingers:1&2:£2.50, 1&3:£3.20, 2&3:£4.70 CSF £8.75 CT £28.55 TOTE £2.80: £1.50, £2.20; EX 10.70 Trifecta £50.50 Pool: 835.40 - 12.23 winning units..
Owner Dovebrace Ltd Air-Conditioning-Projects **Bred** Overrbook Farm **Trained** Maunby, N Yorks

FOCUS
A modest handicap run at a sound pace. The winner is going from strength to strength.
Spirit Of Coniston Official explanation: jockey said that gelding hung left throughout.
Sir Nod Official explanation: jockey said gelding hung right throughout.

833 DIAMOND RACING'S BOUNDLESS PROSPECT HAPPY RETIREMENT CLAIMING STKS 1m 6f (F)

2:40 (2:40) (Class 6) 4-Y-0+ **£1,774** (£523; £262) **Stalls** Low

Form RPR

206- **1** **Three Boars**[84] 7760 8-8-13 57.................................(b) DavidProbert 4 62
(S Gollings) *chsd ldr tl led over 2f out: rdn over 1f out: styd on wl* **17/2**[3]

3422 **2** *4 1/2* **Dream In Blue**[12] 700 5-8-13 67..................................(p) FrederikTylicki 1 56
(J A Glover) *led at stdy pce: rdn and hdd over 2f out: no ex fnl f* **15/8**[2]

0-06 **3** *4 1/2* **Lean Burn (USA)**[11] 720 4-8-7 51..................................(t) FergusSweeney 5 47
(A G Newcombe) *trckd ldrs: racd keenly: rdn and hung lft over 2f out: wknd over 1f out* **20/1**

5221 **4** *7* **Resplendent Ace (IRE)**[11] 714 6-9-6 73............... MichaelStainton(3) 3 50
(P Howling) *hld up in tch: racd keenly: rdn over 3f out: wknd over 2f out* **8/11**[1]

4 **5** *42* **Super Ross (IRE)**[12] 701 7-9-9 40..(b) LiamKeniry 2 —
(C R Dore) *s.i.s: hld up in tch: rdn over 6f out: wknd over 5f out: t.o* **50/1**

3m 12.48s (4.18) **Going Correction** +0.15s/f (Slow)
WFA 4 from 5yo+ 4lb 5 Ran SP% **109.9**
Speed ratings (Par 101): **94,91,88,84,60**
CSF £24.76 TOTE £8.40: £1.90, £1.10; EX 20.80.
Owner P Whinham **Bred** J M Greetham **Trained** Scamblesby, Lincs
■ Boundless Prospect was injured and had to miss what was to have been his swansong.
■ Stewards' Enquiry : Liam Keniry caution; used whip when out of contention

FOCUS
A weak claimer run at a steady pace. The winner is rated to his best form of recent years.
Resplendent Ace(IRE) Official explanation: trainer was unable to offer any explanation into poor running

834 PLAY GOLF BEFORE RACING AT SOUTHWELL (S) STKS 1m 3f (F)

3:10 (3:10) (Class 6) 4-Y-0+ **£1,774** (£523; £262) **Stalls** Low

Form RPR

3331 **1** **Dunaskin (IRE)**[12] 700 10-8-12 69.......................... BarryMcHugh(3) 4 68
(B Ellison) *chsd ldr over 9f out: led over 4f out: hrd rdn fr over 2f out: styd on: eased last strides* **4/11**[1]

6413 **2** *3/4* **Magnitude**[11] 724 5-8-11 60..(t) LiamJones 6 63
(R A Harris) *chsd ldrs and sn pushed along: wnt 2nd over 4f out: hrd rdn and ev ch fr over 2f out: unable qck towards fin* **11/2**[2]

/3-5 **3** *11* **Dr Valentine (FR)**[8] 754 4-8-10 74.................................... JackMitchell 3 45
(Mrs A Duffield) *s.i.s: racd keenly and sn trcking ldrs: rdn over 3f out: edgd rt and wknd fr over 2f out* **8/1**[3]

255- **4** *24* **Desert Destiny**[246] 3679 10-8-11 62............................ TonyHamilton 1 7
(C Grant) *hld up: rdn and wknd over 4f out: t.o* **16/1**

00/0 **5** *23* **Surdoue**[11] 720 10-8-11 42... MickyFenton 5 —
(M J Scudamore) *led: hdd over 4f out: sn rdn: wknd over 3f out: t.o* **50/1**

2m 28.86s (0.86) **Going Correction** +0.15s/f (Slow)
WFA 4 from 5yo+ 1lb 5 Ran SP% **107.7**
Speed ratings (Par 101): **102,101,93,76,59**
CSF £2.59 TOTE £1.50: £1.40, £1.60; EX 2.70.There was no bid for the winner.
Owner Koo's Racing Club **Bred** J P And Miss M Mangan **Trained** Norton, N Yorks
■ Stewards' Enquiry : Barry McHugh one-day ban; used whip with excessive frequency (24th Mar)

FOCUS
They went a good pace, but this is not form to dwell on.

835 SOUTHWELL-RACECOURSE.CO.UK H'CAP 1m 4f (F)

3:40 (3:40) (Class 6) (0-65,65) 4-Y-0+ **£1,774** (£523; £262) **Stalls** Low

Form RPR

212/ **1** **Veloso (FR)**[482] 7280 8-9-6 **65**.................................... FrederikTylicki 2 79+
(J A Glover) *led early: trckd ldr tl led over 4f out: rdn clr fnl 2f* **4/1**[2]

060- **2** *8* **Orkney (IRE)**[116] 4737 5-9-5 **64**.. TomEaves 5 66
(Julie Camacho) *hld up: reminders over 6f out: hrd drvn over 4f out: outpcd 3f out: styd on u.p to go 2nd ins fnl f: nvr any ch w wnr* **15/2**[3]

6-21 **3** *nk* **Cozy Tiger (USA)**[47] 246 5-9-6 **65**............................ TonyCulhane 3 67
(W J Musson) *hld up in tch: rdn to chse wnr over 2f out: styd on same pce: lost 2nd ins fnl f* **6/4**[1]

1-12 **4** *5* **Dart**[63] 41 6-9-6 **65**.. RobertWinston 1 59+
(Mrs S Lamyman) *hld up: detached 7f out: rdn over 4f out: n.d* **4/1**[2]

-251 **5** *2 3/4* **All Guns Firing (IRE)**[30] 457 4-9-4 **65**.......................... DavidNolan 6 55
(D Carroll) *sn drvn along to ld: rdn and hdd over 4f out: wknd 2f out* **4/1**[2]

2m 43.28s (2.28) **Going Correction** +0.15s/f (Slow)
WFA 4 from 5yo+ 2lb 5 Ran SP% **111.8**
Speed ratings (Par 101): **98,92,92,89,87**
CSF £30.68 TOTE £5.40: £2.40, £3.30; EX 42.30.
Owner Brian Morton **Bred** Jean Louis Pariente **Trained** Babworth, Notts

FOCUS
None of the five runners could be safely ruled out beforehand and this was a reasonable race for the grade. They went a good pace. The winner won easily and the level in behind could be 3lb out either way.

836 SOUTHWELL RACECOURSE FOR CONFERENCES H'CAP (DIV I) 6f (F)

4:10 (4:10) (Class 6) (0-60,60) 4-Y-0+ **£1,433** (£423; £211) **Stalls** Low

Form RPR

6103 **1** **Madison Belle**[21] 571 4-9-1 **57**...................................... PaulHanagan 3 64
(J R Weymes) *led: hdd over 4f out: led again over 2f out: sn rdn: styd on gamely* **7/1**[3]

4303 **2** *nk* **Louisiade (IRE)**[26] 498 9-8-4 **46**..................................(p) FrannyNorton 4 52
(R C Guest) *s.i.s: sn pushed along in rr: hdwy over 4f out: rdn over 2f out: r.o* **4/1**[1]

0066 **3** *nk* **Owed**[11] 716 8-7-12 **47** oh1 ow1............................(tp) MatthewLawson(7) 5 52
(R Bastiman) *chsd ldrs: rdn and ev ch fr over 2f out: styd on* **66/1**

0-30 **4** *1/2* **Cardinal**[6] 773 5-8-10 **52**.. JackMitchell 9 56
(N P Moore) *prom: lost pl 5f out: hdwy over 2f out: sn rdn: n.m.r ins fnl f: r.o* **7/1**[3]

005- **5** *3* **Exceedingly Good (IRE)**[191] 5468 4-9-2 **58**..........(t) FergusSweeney 10 52
(S R Bowring) *sn prom: rdn: hung lft and swished tail over 1f out: styd on same pce* **22/1**

3115 **6** *1/2* **Albero Di Giuda (IRE)**[25] 531 5-8-13 **58**...............(t) AndreaAtzeni(3) 11 50
(F Sheridan) *s.i.s: hld up: hdwy over 2f out: rdn and hung lft over 1f out: nt trble ldrs* **4/1**[1]

320 **7** *2 1/2* **Kings Ace (IRE)**[40] 328 4-8-13 **55**................................ AdrianNicholls 6 39
(A Berry) *prom: lost pl over 3f out: styd on ins fnl f* **8/1**

0-10 **8** *2* **Jul's Lad (IRE)**[39] 351 4-9-0 **56**.......................................(b) DavidNolan 1 34
(D Carroll) *s.i.s: sn pushed along: a in rr* **9/2**[2]

350- **9** *9* **Lake Chini (IRE)**[142] 6877 8-8-13 **55**.........................(b) GrahamGibbons 8 4
(M W Easterby) *sn drvn along in rr: bhd fr 1/2-way* **12/1**

-350 **10** *9* **Apache Moon**[26] 496 4-9-4 **60**..(b[1]) KevinGhunowa 2 —
(R Curtis) *s.i.s: hdwy to ld over 4f out: rdn and hdd over 2f out: sn wknd* **12/1**

1m 17.53s (1.03) **Going Correction** +0.15s/f (Slow) 10 Ran SP% **115.5**
Speed ratings (Par 101): **99,98,98,97,93 92,89,86,74,62**
toteswingers:1&2:£6.10, 1&3:£17.60, 2&3:£13.60 CSF £34.80 CT £1705.65 TOTE £8.60: £2.50, £2.60, £9.20; EX 29.50 TRIFECTA Not won..
Owner Mrs Elaine M Burke **Bred** Paul Sweeting **Trained** Middleham Moor, N Yorks
■ Stewards' Enquiry : Jack Mitchell two-day ban; used whip with excessive frequency. (24-25 Mar)
David NolanD three-day ban; weighed in two pounds over. (24-27 Mar)

FOCUS
A bvery moderate but competitive sprint handicap run at a strong pace. The second and third limit the form.

837 BOOK TICKETS ON LINE AT SOUTHWELL-RACECOURSE.CO.UK H'CAP 1m (F)

4:40 (4:41) (Class 4) (0-85,82) 4-Y-0+ **£4,209** (£1,252; £625; £312) **Stalls** Low

Form RPR

-311 **1** **Trans Sonic**[21] 572 7-8-3 **74**..................................... LeeTopliss(7) 10 91
(J Hetherton) *led over 6f out: rdn clr fr over 2f out: styd on wl* **7/2**[1]

0-45 **2** *2 3/4* **Xpres Maite**[29] 466 7-8-11 **75**.................................(b) FergusSweeney 6 86
(S R Bowring) *prom: hrd rdn over 3f out: sn outpcd: rallied to chse wnr over 1f out: r.o* **10/1**

533- **3** *4 1/2* **Daaweitza**[87] 7724 7-8-7 **71**..(be) TomEaves 8 72+
(B Ellison) *mid-div: reminders and lost pl 5f out: bhd and plenty to do over 3f out: swtchd rt over 2f out: hdwy u.p over 1f out: nt rch ldrs* **9/1**

060- **4** *1* **Kidlat**[138] 6973 5-8-8 **72**.. JoeFanning 4 71
(A Bailey) *in rr and pushed along: hdwy u.p fnl 2f: n.d* **14/1**

000- **5** *2 1/4* **Mangham (IRE)**[169] 6168 5-9-2 **80**............................. FrederikTylicki 5 74
(D H Brown) *prom: pushed along 1/2-way: rdn to chse wnr briefly over 1f out: wknd fnl f* **10/1**

2514 **6** *2 1/4* **General Tufto**[5] 787 5-8-9 **76**...................................(b) AndreaAtzeni(3) 1 65
(C Smith) *sn outpcd: rdn over 2f out: nvr nrr* **5/1**[2]

554- **7** *3/4* **Exit Smiling**[173] 6014 8-9-0 **78**....................................... TonyCulhane 7 68
(P T Midgley) *prom: chsd wnr over 3f out: sn rdn: wknd over 1f out* **8/1**

40-2 **8** *6* **Bolodenka (IRE)**[53] 196 8-8-13 **77**............................... PaulHanagan 9 51
(R A Fahey) *hld up: sme hdwy u.p over 1f out: sn wknd* **25/1**

-042 **9** *2* **Mozayada (USA)**[21] 572 6-8-10 **74**............................. FrannyNorton 2 44
(M Brittain) *mid-div: rdn 1/2-way: wknd 2f out* **17/2**

430- **10** *3 1/2* **Smarty Socks (IRE)**[194] 5375 6-9-4 **82**........................ PJMcDonald 11 44
(P T Midgley) *s.s: a bhd* **25/1**

-065 **11** *1 1/2* **Bennelong**[9] 749 4-8-10 **74**..(p) PaulDoe 12 33
(P D Evans) *prom: chsd wnr over 4f out tl rdn over 3f out: wknd 2f out* **11/2**[3]

010- **12** *3/4* **Avertis**[72] 7854 5-8-12 **76**..(t) MickyFenton 3 33
(Stef Higgins) *led: hdd over 6f out: rdn over 3f out: wknd 2f out* **22/1**

1m 42.53s (-1.17) **Going Correction** +0.15s/f (Slow) 12 Ran SP% **122.8**
Speed ratings (Par 105): **111,108,103,102,100 98,97,91,89,86 84,83**
toteswingers:1&2:£13.20, 1&3:£10.60, 2&3:£28.90 CSF £40.00 CT £296.23 TOTE £4.70: £1.80, £4.30, £2.60; EX 61.10 TRIFECTA Not won..
Owner Mrs Lynne Lumley **Bred** I A Balding **Trained** Norton, N Yorks

FOCUS
A fair, competitive handicap. The winner impressed again with the runner-up helping set the level.
Exit Smiling Official explanation: jockey said that the gelding had no more to give.

838 HOSPITALITY AT SOUTHWELL RACECOURSE H'CAP 7f (F)

5:10 (5:10) (Class 6) (0-52,52) 4-Y-0+ **£1,774** (£523; £262) **Stalls** Low

Form RPR

0002 **1** **Bold Diva**[5] 794 5-8-10 **48**...(v) LukeMorris 2 66
(A W Carroll) *hld up: hdwy over 2f out: rdn to ld and edgd lft ins fnl f: r.o* **11/2**[2]

000- **2** *3/4* **Scruffy Skip (IRE)**[140] 6926 5-8-9 **47**.........................(p) JerryO'Dwyer 14 63
(Mrs C A Dunnett) *led 6f out: rdn over 1f out: edgd lft and hdd ins fnl f: unable qck towards fin* **66/1**

0404 **3** 4 ½ **Tri Chara (IRE)**21 569 6-9-0 52 (p) GrahamGibbons 5 56
(R Hollinshead) *prom: rdn 1/2-way: styd on same pce appr fnl f* 6/1³

-442 **4** hd **Nabeeda**36 369 5-9-0 52 RobertWinston 7 55
(M Brittain) *chsd ldrs: rdn 1/2-way: styd on same pce fr over 1f out* 6/1³

00/0 **5** nk **Border Fox**18 622 7-8-9 47 (t) GregFairley 8 50
(P Salmon) *mid-div: rdn over 4f out: r.o ins fnl f: nvr nrr* 25/1

0-05 **6** 1 ¼ **Captain Imperial (IRE)**12 705 4-9-0 52 DanielTudhope 1 51
(R Bastiman) *hld up: pushed along over 2f out: hdwy and hung lft over 1f out: nt trble ldrs* 6/1³

5453 **7** ½ **Sirjosh**22 567 4-8-5 48 DeanHeslop(5) 9 46
(D Donovan) *s.i.s: hdwy u.p over 1f out: n.d* 13/2

03-6 **8** 2 ¾ **Pretty Orchid**21 571 5-8-12 50 (p) PJMcDonald 12 40
(P T Midgley) *mid-div: hdwy over 4f out: rdn over 2f out: sn wknd* 50/1

065- **9** 1 ¼ **Danish Art (IRE)**174 5982 5-8-10 51 BarryMcHugh(3) 13 38
(M W Easterby) *s.i.s: hld up: rdn over 2f out: a in rr* 14/1

3400 **10** 2 ½ **Vogarth**21 569 6-8-7 52 (b) DavidKenny(7) 4 32
(M C Chapman) *led: hdd 6f out: remained handy: rdn 1/2-way: wknd 2f out* 33/1

6253 **11** 1 ¾ **Hard Ball**22 568 4-8-13 51 (v) FrannyNorton 11 27
(M Quinn) *sn prom: rdn 1/2-way: wknd 2f out: eased fnl f* 10/3¹

-500 **12** 6 **Royal Crest**12 705 4-8-3 48 ow1 LeeTopliss(7) 10 7
(A Crook) *chsd ldrs: lost pl 5f out: sn bhd* 16/1

100- **13** 9 **Union Jack Jackson (IRE)**150 6674 8-8-6 47 (b) KellyHarrison(3) 3 —
(John A Harris) *mid-div: hdwy 1/2-way: hung lft and wknd over 2f out* 25/1

1m 30.83s (0.53) **Going Correction** +0.15s/f (Slow) 13 Ran SP% **121.3**
Speed ratings (Par 101): **102,101,96,95,95 94,93,90,88,86 84,77,66**
toteswingers:1&2:£51.70, 1&3:£6.50, 2&3:£56.10 CSF £351.24 CT £2341.44 TOTE £7.30: £2.70, £15.80, £3.10; EX 200.90 TRIFECTA Not won..
Owner Mrs P Izamis **Bred** Peter Balding **Trained** Cropthorne, Worcs

FOCUS
A weak handicap run at a decent pace. Sound enough form with the first pair clear.

839 SOUTHWELL RACECOURSE FOR CONFERENCES H'CAP (DIV II) 6f (F)
5:40 (5:40) (Class 6) (0-60,60) 4-Y-O+ £1,433 (£423; £211) Stalls Low

Form RPR

630 **1** **Gracie's Gift (IRE)**15 668 8-9-0 56 GrahamGibbons 5 66
(R C Guest) *led 1f: chsd ldrs: led again wl over 1f out: drvn out* 22/1

3122 **2** ½ **Fulford**12 704 5-9-1 57 FrannyNorton 6 65
(M Brittain) *mid-div: hdwy over 2f out: rdn to chse wnr ins fnl f: r.o* 15/8¹

4500 **3** 2 ¼ **Captain Kallis (IRE)**7 763 4-8-12 54 (be¹) FrederikTylicki 10 55
(D J S Ffrench Davis) *trckd ldrs: led 2f out: sn rdn and hdd: styd on same pce ins fnl f* 5/1²

521 **4** nk **Don Pele (IRE)**23 556 8-9-4 60 (b) LiamJones 8 60
(R A Harris) *chsd ldrs: led over 2f out: sn rdn and hdd: styd on same pce ins fnl f* 8/1

-030 **5** 1 ½ **Cape Of Storms**33 402 7-9-3 59 (b) TomEaves 3 54
(R Brotherton) *trckd ldrs: rdn over 2f out: styd on same pce appr fnl f* 17/2

/50- **6** shd **Reprieved**348 972 5-8-4 46 oh1 ChrisCatlin 9 44+
(J J Quinn) *dwlt: racd in last pl: stl there 2f out: r.o ins fnl f: nrst fin* 22/1

-104 **7** 4 ½ **Zeffirelli**21 571 5-9-2 58 (v¹) SebSanders 1 38
(M Quinn) *drvn along to ld 5f out: hdd over 2f out: wknd over 1f out* 10/1

-433 **8** nk **Only A Game (IRE)**25 531 5-9-1 57 (tp) AdamKirby 2 36
(I W McInnes) *prom: rdn over 2f out: wknd over 1f out* 6/1³

-000 **9** 3 ½ **Conjecture**32 423 8-7-12 47 MatthewLawson(7) 4 15
(R Bastiman) *sn pushed along: a in rr* 40/1

-604 **10** 2 ¼ **Miss Thippawan (USA)**11 716 4-8-4 46 oh1 FranciscoDaSilva 7 7
(J Hetherton) *sn outpcd* 28/1

0-40 **11** 5 **Royal Envoy (IRE)**39 351 7-8-13 55 JimmyQuinn 11 —
(P Howling) *sn pushed along in rr: bhd fr 1/2-way* 18/1

1m 16.98s (0.48) **Going Correction** +0.15s/f (Slow) 11 Ran SP% **116.3**
Speed ratings (Par 101): **102,101,98,97,95 95,89,89,84,81 75**
toteswingers:1&2:£9.50, 1&3:£17.20, 2&3:£4.70 CSF £60.73 CT £258.30 TOTE £20.40: £4.80, £1.40, £2.00; EX 76.90 Trifecta £281.80 Place 6 £123.13, Place 5 £77.04. Pool: 571.39 - 1.50 winning units..
Owner S Hussey **Bred** Richard O'Hara **Trained** Stainforth, S Yorks

FOCUS
The time was 0.55 seconds quicker than the first division. Straightforward form.
Royal Envoy(IRE) Official explanation: jockey said that the gelding did not face the kick-back.
T/Plt: £367.90 to a £1 stake. Pool: £64,848.11. 128.65 winning tickets. T/Qpdt: £46.90 to a £1 stake. Pool: £4,667.25. 73.50 winning tickets. CR

825 LINGFIELD (L-H)
Wednesday, March 10

OFFICIAL GOING: Standard
Wind: Strong, against Weather: Fine

840 ASHFORD ENVIRONMENTAL H'CAP 1m 2f (P)
2:00 (2:00) (Class 4) (0-85,89) 3-Y-O £4,209 (£1,252; £625; £312) Stalls Low

Form RPR

1212 **1** **Exceedthewildman**14 686 3-9-0 83 (p) KierenFox(5) 4 84
(J S Moore) *stdd s: hld up in last pair: effrt 2f out: cajoled along to cl on ldrs 1f out: led last 100yds: full value for winning margin* 4/1²

10- **2** ½ **Bint Doyen**144 6852 3-9-2 80 NeilCallan 5 80
(C E Brittain) *hld up in 4th: effrt to join ldng pair over 2f out: drvn into narrow ld 1f out: hdd and one pce last 100yds* 5/1

03-3 **3** ½ **Epic (IRE)**53 203 3-8-8 72 GregFairley 2 72
(M Johnston) *trckd ldng pair to over 3f out: cl enough on inner but nt qckn wl over 1f out: plld out and styd on wl to take 3rd and gaining nr fin* 9/2³

110- **4** 1 ½ **Stags Leap (IRE)**151 6664 3-9-11 89 RichardHughes 1 85
(R Hannon) *led at mod pce: jnd 3f out: hdd and one pce u.p 1f out* 7/4¹

00-3 **5** nse **Mnarani (IRE)**8 762 3-8-2 66 oh1 LukeMorris 3 62
(J S Moore) *trckd ldr: upsides fr 3f out: drvn and nt overtake fr 2f out: stl upsides 1f out: outpcd fnl f* 9/2³

5013 **6** hd **Yorksters Prince (IRE)**5 805 3-8-2 66 oh1 KirstyMilczarek 6 62
(G Prodromou) *t.k.h: hld up in last pair: nt qckn on outer 2f out and lost grnd: styd on ins fnl f* 16/1

2m 9.13s (2.53) **Going Correction** +0.20s/f (Slow) 6 Ran SP% **115.3**
Speed ratings (Par 100): **97,96,96,95,94 94**
toteswingers: 1&2 £3.80, 1&3 £2.70, 2&3 £6.30 CSF £24.54 TOTE £4.90: £2.30, £2.90; EX 31.20.
Owner E Moore & J S Moore **Bred** Horizon Bloodstock Limited **Trained** Upper Lambourn, Berks

FOCUS
A headwind was blowing into the runners' faces in the home straight and the time for the opener was over five seconds outside the standard. This was a decent handicap, but it was a steadily run affair which turned into a sprint in the straight, and the form looks a little suspect. The winner did it well though and the runner-up built on her good debut last year.
Epic(IRE) Official explanation: jockey said that the gelding was denied a clear run

841 TAGWORLDWIDE.COM CLAIMING STKS 1m 4f (P)
2:30 (2:30) (Class 6) 4-Y-O+ £1,774 (£523; £262) Stalls Low

Form RPR

-005 **1** **War Of The Roses (IRE)**18 636 7-9-5 76 TomEaves 3 76+
(R Brotherton) *stdd s: hld up in 4th: moved up 3f out to chse ldr over 2f out: led over 1f out: wl in command fnl f* 7/2²

4111 **2** 1 **Hurakan (IRE)**2 827 4-9-1 73 (p) J-PGuillambert 2 73+
(P D Evans) *stdd s: hld up in 3rd: trapped by wnr coming up on outer whn pce lifted wl over 2f out: styd on fnl 2f to take 2nd last 75yds: a too much to do* 2/5¹

6111 **3** 1 **Lytham (IRE)**20 590 9-8-8 63 AmyBaker(5) 5 67+
(A W Carroll) *stdd s: hld up last: lft wl bhd whn r began in earnest 3f out: urged along and styd on fr over 1f out: tk 3rd nr fin: too much to do* 15/2³

10-0 **4** hd **Strong Storm (USA)**33 426 4-8-11 61 ow1 (p) DaneO'Neill 4 60
(Andrew Reid) *stdd s but sn trckd ldr: led wl over 2f out: hdd and nt qckn over 1f out: lost 2 pls last 75yds* 16/1

0/0 **5** 22 **Turnham Green**12 326 4-8-6 0 (b¹) KirstyMilczarek 1 22
(S Curran) *led at mod pce to wl over 2f out: immediately btn* 100/1

2m 37.36s (4.36) **Going Correction** +0.20s/f (Slow)
WFA 4 from 7yo+ 2lb 5 Ran SP% **112.3**
Speed ratings (Par 101): **93,92,91,91,76**
CSF £5.47 TOTE £4.10: £1.30, £1.10; EX 7.00.Hurakan was claimed by G. Baker for £14,000.
Owner P S J Croft **Bred** Mrs Jane Bailey **Trained** Elmley Castle, Worcs
■ Stewards' Enquiry : J-P Guillambert one-day ban: used whip with excessive frequency

FOCUS
No more than a fair claimer. The pace was pretty steady and the race only developed off the home turn, but they finished in the order they should have done according to BHA ratings. Not form to take too seriously.

842 OYSTER PARTNERSHIP H'CAP 1m 5f (P)
3:00 (3:00) (Class 5) (0-70,69) 4-Y-O+ £2,456 (£725; £362) Stalls Low

Form RPR

2321 **1** **Star Choice**8 764 5-8-12 63 (b) SimonPearce(5) 9 73+
(J Pearce) *hld up in midfield: prog 4f out: led over 2f out: cruising and wl in command over 1f out: v readily* 3/1²

-502 **2** 2 ½ **Mustajed**11 735 9-9-4 67 (b) JamesMillman(3) 4 74
(B R Millman) *dwlt: hld up in last pair: prog fr 4f out: chsng ldrs whn nt clr run and snatched up over 2f out: effrt again over 1f out: r.o to take 2nd nr fin* 9/1

26 **3** 1 ¼ **Prince Charlemagne (IRE)**14 688 7-9-9 69 GeorgeBaker 1 74
(G L Moore) *hld up in last: sltly hmpd 4f out: smooth prog on outer over 2f out: wnt 2nd over 1f out: sn rdn and no imp on wnr: lost 2nd nr fin* 2/1¹

03-0 **4** 6 **Cold Turkey**14 676 10-9-6 66 AmirQuinn 10 62
(G L Moore) *prog to ld after 2f: hdd 7f out: led again 3f out to over 2f out: easily outpcd after* 14/1

15-6 **5** hd **Sagunt (GER)**33 426 7-9-8 68 JimmyFortune 3 64
(S Curran) *trckd ldrs: effrt to go 3rd over 2f out: rdn and hanging over 1f out: wknd* 7/2³

00-0 **6** ¾ **Royal Premier (IRE)**10 748 7-8-9 55 oh8 (v) JerryO'Dwyer 2 50
(H J Collingridge) *reminder sn after s: in tch: rdn over 3f out: sn wl outpcd: plugged on fnl f* 50/1

34-0 **7** ½ **Captain Flack**21 584 4-8-6 55 (b) KirstyMilczarek 8 49
(J A R Toller) *towards rr: rdn on outer over 3f out: sn outpcd: plugged on fnl f* 16/1

00/2 **8** 1 **Byblos**14 677 5-9-9 69 (v) RichardHughes 5 62
(W J Greatrex) *led 2f: styd prom: hrd rdn over 3f out: wknd 2f out* 8/1

000- **9** 21 **Man Of Gwent (UAE)**242 3847 6-9-6 66 J-PGuillambert 7 30
(P D Evans) *in tch: dropped to last 4f out: sn u.p and wknd: t.o* 28/1

004- **10** 1 ½ **Granski (IRE)**104 7546 4-8-6 55 oh5 (p) SamHitchcott 6 16
(D M Fogarty, Ire) *led 7f out and injected pce: hdd & wknd rapidly 3f out: t.o* 40/1

2m 46.51s (0.51) **Going Correction** +0.20s/f (Slow)
WFA 4 from 5yo+ 3lb 10 Ran SP% **122.1**
Speed ratings (Par 103): **106,104,103,100,99 99,99,98,85,84**
toteswingers: 1&2 £4.40, 1&3 £2.80, 2&3 £3.50 CSF £31.51 CT £68.05 TOTE £3.60: £1.60, £2.00, £1.30; EX 32.40 Trifecta £70.20 Pool: £247.90 - 2.61 winning units..
Owner Macniler Racing Partnership **Bred** B J Warren **Trained** Newmarket, Suffolk

FOCUS
A modest handicap run at a fair pace. The first three home filled the last three positions with a circuit still to cover and the form has a sound look to it, rated through the third. The easy winner was possibly value for extra.
Granski(IRE) Official explanation: jockey said that the gelding ran too freely

843 NICHOLAS HALL MAIDEN STKS 7f (P)
3:30 (3:30) (Class 5) 3-Y-O £2,456 (£725; £362) Stalls Low

Form RPR

223- **1** **Shamir**116 7388 3-9-3 79 FergusSweeney 4 80
(Miss Jo Crowley) *n.m.r briefly over 5f out: trckd ldng pair: wnt 2nd 2f out gng wl: rdn to ld jst ins fnl f: styd on wl* 4/1³

2 **2** ¾ **Magic Omen (USA)**8 758 3-9-3 0 GregFairley 8 78
(M Johnston) *led 2f: chsd ldr to 2f out: styd on again over 1f out to take 2nd ins fnl f: a hld* 5/2²

4- **3** 1 **Aetos**225 4410 3-9-3 0 MartinDwyer 6 75
(M P Tregoning) *t.k.h and allowed to ld after 2f: shkn up and hanging over 1f out: hdd and nt qckn jst ins fnl f* 11/10¹

30- **4** 3 ¾ **Thereafter (USA)**170 6164 3-8-12 0 SteveDrowne 2 60
(R Charlton) *hld up in 5th: effrt to chse ldng trio 2f out: sn pushed along and outpcd* 16/1

5 1 ¾ **Sayyedati Storm (USA)** 3-8-12 0 MichaelHills 1 55+
(B W Hills) *dwlt: mostly in 6th: outpcd wl over 2f out: pushed along and no real prog after* 9/1

6 ¾ **Amends (USA)** 3-9-0 0 MarcHalford(3) 7 58+
(J R Best) *s.i.s: t.k.h and hld up in last pair: outpcd fr 3f out: rn green 2f out: pushed along and kpt on* 66/1

7 nk **Green Secret** 3-8-12 0 FrederikTylicki 3 52
(A J McCabe) *hld up in last pair: outpcd wl over 2f out: shkn up and no prog* 25/1

06 **8** ½ **Just Say Please**[21] 583 3-8-12 0 JimmyQuinn 5 51
(D K Ivory) *t.k.h: chsd ldng trio to 2f out: steadily wknd* **66/1**

1m 26.45s (1.65) **Going Correction** +0.20s/f (Slow) 8 Ran SP% **118.9**
Speed ratings (Par 98): **98,97,96,91,89 88,88,87**
toteswingers: 1&2 £1.80, 1&3 £2.70, 2&3 £2.20 CSF £15.01 TOTE £4.50: £1.30, £1.10, £1.20; EX 19.50 Trifecta £29.30 Pool: £585081.00 -14.78 winning units..
Owner Kilstone Limited **Bred** Plantation Stud **Trained** Whitcombe, Dorset

FOCUS
A good maiden for the time of yerar in which the first three, who finished clear, look pretty useful. Shamir is rated to last year's mark and winners should come out of the race.

844 ARROWS REMOVAL OF LONDON H'CAP (DIV I) 7f (P)
4:00 (4:03) (Class 6) (0-60,61) 4-Y-0+ £1,433 (£423; £211) Stalls Low

Form RPR

61-1 **1** **Copperwood**[28] 486 5-9-3 **59** DaneO'Neill 2 66
(M Blanshard) *t.k.h: hld up bhd ldrs: drvn over 1f out: styd on wl fnl f to ld post* **9/2**[2]

6036 **2** *shd* **Trip Switch**[26] 531 4-8-11 **58** KierenFox(5) 11 65
(G Prodromou) *hld up wl in rr: stl there jst over 1f out: rapid prog past packed field fnl f: tk 2nd post: jst failed* **16/1**

3032 **3** *nse* **Louisiade (IRE)**[1] 836 9-8-4 **46** (p) FrannyNorton 1 53
(R C Guest) *trckd ldrs on inner: shkn up 2f out: clsd 1f out: poked hd in front wl ins fnl f: hdd post* **16/1**

0132 **4** ½ **Top Flight Splash**[8] 763 4-8-10 **52** (v) GregFairley 8 58
(P D Evans) *led 2f: trckd ldr: effrt to ld again narrowly wl over 1f out: hdd wl ins fnl f: no ex last strides* **6/1**[3]

00-3 **5** ½ **Pha Mai Blue**[5] 802 5-9-4 **60** PatCosgrave 10 64
(J R Boyle) *rdn to go prom early: effrt on outer to press ldrs 2f out: cl enough ent fnl f: nt qckn* **5/2**[1]

-333 **6** ½ **Cornus**[27] 505 8-9-1 **57** (be) JamesDoyle 7 60
(A J McCabe) *settled midfield: effrt 2f out: drvn and kpt on fr over 1f out: nt pce to chal* **20/1**

-242 **7** 1 **Towy Boy (IRE)**[19] 615 5-8-12 **54** (b) RichardHughes 5 59+
(I A Wood) *hld up in last pair: gng strly 2f out: looking for room fr over 1f out but nowhere to go: no ch* **6/1**[3]

113 **8** *shd* **Saddlers Bend (IRE)**[6] 794 4-9-5 **61** 6ex TonyCulhane 3 62
(George Baker) *s.i.s: settled towards rr: rdn 3f out: effrt u.p into midfield 1f out: no ex* **15/2**

3410 **9** *hd* **Bollywood Style**[14] 684 5-9-4 **60** SteveDrowne 12 59
(J R Best) *hld up in last pair: u.p and struggling over 2f out: one pce and no imp after* **20/1**

2233 **10** 1¼ **Tamino (IRE)**[8] 763 7-8-13 **55** JimmyQuinn 4 51
(P Howling) *led after 2f: narrowly hdd wl over 1f out: stl cl enough on inner ent fnl f: wknd rapidly* **14/1**

005 **11** ½ **Suhayl Star (IRE)**[19] 614 6-8-12 **57** WilliamCarson(3) 6 52
(P Burgoyne) *t.k.h: trckd ldng pair: chal and upsides 2f out: wknd rapidly 1f out* **14/1**

1m 25.35s (0.55) **Going Correction** +0.20s/f (Slow) 11 Ran SP% **121.7**
Speed ratings (Par 101): **104,103,103,103,102 102,100,100,100,99 98**
toteswingers: 1&2 £33.30, 1&3 £12.40, 2&3 £37.10 CSF £77.05 CT £1077.00 TOTE £5.60: £2.10, £6.50, £3.40; EX 109.00 TRIFECTA Not won..
Owner Mrs Rosemary K Wilkerson **Bred** Hertford Offset Press **Trained** Upper Lambourn, Berks

FOCUS
The first division of this low-grade handicap had an open look to it beforehand and that was how it turned out, with the entire field covered by less than five lengths at the finish. As such the form may not prove entirely reliable. The winner was rated to form in completing the hat-trick, with the next three helping set the level.
Cornus Official explanation: jockey said the gelding was denied a clear run
Towy Boy(IRE) Official explanation: jockey said that the gelding ran too freely and was denied a clear run

845 ARROWS REMOVAL OF LONDON H'CAP (DIV II) 7f (P)
4:30 (4:31) (Class 6) (0-60,60) 4-Y-0+ £1,433 (£423; £211) Stalls Low

Form RPR

-035 **1** **Woolston Ferry (IRE)**[32] 444 4-9-1 **57** (p) FergusSweeney 8 67
(David Pinder) *trckd ldrs: cl up 2f out: rdn to ld over 1f out on outer: styd on effectively enough* **13/2**

-342 **2** 1¾ **Lopinot (IRE)**[35] 397 7-9-4 **60** (v) GeorgeBaker 9 65
(M R Bosley) *stdd s: hld up in last prog gng wl 2f out: swtchd to inner to chal jst over 1f out: nt pce of wnr* **4/1**[3]

4400 **3** *hd* **Grand Honour (IRE)**[13] 696 4-9-4 **60** JimmyQuinn 11 65
(P Howling) *hld up in rr: sme prog on outer 2f out: shkn up as ldrs wnt for home over 1f out: r.o fnl f and nrly snatched 2nd* **7/2**[2]

0/21 **4** 1¾ **King Canute (IRE)**[13] 691 6-8-13 **55** MickyFenton 10 55
(D Morris) *pressed ldr: rdn to chal 2f out: stl in contention over 1f out: outpcd* **2/1**[1]

0020 **5** 1½ **Jord (IRE)**[23] 562 6-9-3 **59** FrederikTylicki 4 55
(J A Glover) *mde most: drvn 2f out: hdd over 1f out: fdd ins fnl f* **15/2**

00-0 **6** *nse* **West Leake (IRE)**[24] 555 4-9-1 **57** DaneO'Neill 3 53
(P Burgoyne) *trckd ldrs: cl up and gng wl enough 2f out: effrt on inner over 1f out: sn wknd* **25/1**

0004 **7** ½ **Spring Bridge (IRE)**[14] 687 4-8-4 **49** oh1 ow3 (vt) MarcHalford(3) 7 43
(Mrs L C Jewell) *hld up wl in rr: effrt on wd outside 2f out: sn lft bhd by ldrs: plugged on* **66/1**

-000 **8** ¾ **King's Sabre**[6] 789 4-8-10 **52** (e) FrannyNorton 5 44
(R C Guest) *plld hrd: hld up in midfield: lost pl 2f out: nudged along and n.d after* **20/1**

0-00 **9** 1½ **Ever Cheerful**[19] 615 9-9-1 **57** (p) SteveDrowne 6 45
(A B Haynes) *sn chsd ldng pair: rdn over 2f out: lost pl and btn over 1f out* **12/1**

000- **10** 8 **Kings On The Roof**[217] 4648 4-8-5 **47** AdrianMcCarthy 1 14
(M D Squance) *hld up on inner: rdn 3f out: no real prog: wknd rapidly over 1f out* **40/1**

1m 24.97s (0.17) **Going Correction** +0.20s/f (Slow) 10 Ran SP% **120.9**
Speed ratings (Par 101): **107,105,104,102,101 101,100,99,97,88**
totewingers: 1&2 £4.30, 1&3 £7.80, 2&3 £4.20 CSF £32.86 CT £104.35 TOTE £6.80: £1.80, £1.40, £2.50; EX 36.80 Trifecta £167.50 Part won. Pool: £226.43 - 0.10 winning units..
Owner Ms L Burns **Bred** Tim Taylor **Trained** Kingston Lisle, Oxon

FOCUS
This looked the weaker of the two divisions but it was run in a slightly quicker time and the form may stand up better. The winner will look well treated on his oldf form even after reassessment.
King's Sabre Official explanation: jockey said the gelding ran too freely

846 PREMIER SHOWFREIGHT H'CAP 5f (P)
5:00 (5:00) (Class 4) (0-85,83) 4-Y-0+ £4,209 (£1,252; £625; £312) Stalls High

Form RPR

6212 **1** **Sherjawy (IRE)**[16] 658 6-8-5 **70** oh4 ow1 SamHitchcott 3 76
(Miss Z C Davison) *w ldr: rdn 2f out: persistent chal fnl f: led post* **10/1**

43 **2** *nse* **Wotashirtfull (IRE)**[32] 446 5-9-4 **83** (p) PatCosgrave 4 89
(J R Boyle) *mde most: drvn and v narrow advantage fnl f: hdd post* **10/11**[1]

4650 **3** *nk* **Vhujon (IRE)**[15] 672 5-8-12 **77** RichardHughes 2 82
(P D Evans) *hld up bhd ldng pair: pushed along fr 1/2-way: tried to chal u.p fnl f: kpt on but a hld* **10/3**[3]

3-04 **4** 1¼ **Step It Up (IRE)**[11] 736 6-8-10 **75** StephenCraine 1 75
(J R Boyle) *hld up bhd ldng pair: effrt over 1f out: sn rdn and nt qckn: wl hld fnl f* **3/1**[2]

59.72 secs (0.92) **Going Correction** +0.20s/f (Slow) 4 Ran SP% **109.6**
Speed ratings (Par 105): **100,99,99,97**
CSF £20.25 TOTE £6.60; EX 13.40.
Owner Charlie's Starrs **Bred** Darley **Trained** Hammerwood, E Sussex

FOCUS
There was no depth to this small-field sprint and this is form to forget. Sherjawy produced another career-best on the face of things.

847 MARRIOTT HOTEL LINGFIELD OPENING SOON APPRENTICE H'CAP 1m (P)
5:35 (5:35) (Class 6) (0-55,55) 4-Y-0+ £1,774 (£523; £262) Stalls High

Form RPR

040- **1** **Athboy Auction**[101] 7591 5-8-1 **46** NatashaEaton(5) 12 54+
(H J Collingridge) *dropped in fr wd draw: hld up in rr: gd prog over 1f out: pushed into ld last 100yds: r.o wl* **33/1**

3032 **2** 1 **Join Up**[6] 795 4-8-12 **52** DeanHeslop 10 57
(W M Brisbourne) *racd wd in midfield: hanging and lost grnd over 1f out: rdn and r.o fnl f: tk 2nd last strides* **7/4**[1]

6533 **3** *hd* **Turkish Sultan (IRE)**[5] 816 7-8-4 **49** (b) RyanClark(5) 3 54
(J M Bradley) *pressed ldr: led 2f out: hrd pressed 1f out: hdd and no ex last 100yds* **4/1**[2]

540- **4** *hd* **Gold Rock (FR)**[345] 1042 5-8-8 **55** GeorgeDowning(7) 9 60
(A W Carroll) *t.k.h: cl up: wnt 3rd 2f out gng wl: urged along 1f out: nt qckn* **10/1**

5001 **5** ¾ **Binnion Bay (IRE)**[16] 656 9-9-0 **54** (b) AshleyMorgan 5 57
(J J Bridger) *hld up in midfield: rdn over 1f out: styd on same pce after: nvr able to chal* **9/1**[3]

-104 **6** 1 **Prince Valentine**[16] 656 9-8-4 **49** (p) HarryBentley(5) 4 50
(G L Moore) *hld up in midfield on inner: clsd on ldrs 2f out: ch ent fnl f: fdd and lost pls nr fin* **12/1**

300- **7** *nk* **Baba Ghanoush**[94] 7652 8-8-3 **46** oh1 (v) KierenFox(3) 7 46
(M J Attwater) *chsd ldrs: pushed along fr 1/2-way: effrt to go 3rd briefly over 2f out: lost pl over 1f out: keeping on whn no room and snatched up last 75yds* **20/1**

0014 **8** ¾ **Machinate (USA)**[7] 780 8-8-9 **52** JohnFahy(3) 11 50
(W M Brisbourne) *settled towards rr: effrt 2f out: rdn and one pce fr over 1f out: n.d* **12/1**

035- **9** ½ **Ardent Prince**[70] 7877 7-8-6 **46** AmyBaker 1 43
(A B Haynes) *s.s: mostly in last pair: urged along on inner over 1f out: one pce* **10/1**

004 **10** *nk* **Dynamo Dave (USA)**[19] 614 5-8-4 **47** (b) AmyScott(3) 8 44
(M D I Usher) *hld up in last pair: rdn bhd 2f out and stl last: no prog* **10/1**

000- **11** 1 **Iron Man Of Mersey (FR)**[161] 6399 4-8-6 **46** oh1 SophieDoyle 2 40
(A W Carroll) *t.k.h: led to 2f out: wknd fnl f* **11/1**

0500 **12** 3 **Easy Wonder (GER)**[6] 795 5-8-1 **46** oh1 (b) MatthewCosham(5) 6 34
(I A Wood) *t.k.h: pressed ldng pair to over 2f out: sn pushed along: wknd rapidly over 1f out* **50/1**

1m 39.33s (1.13) **Going Correction** +0.20s/f (Slow) 12 Ran SP% **127.0**
Speed ratings (Par 101): **102,101,100,100,99 98,98,97,97,97 96,93**
toteswingers: 1&2 £22.20, 1&3 £42.00, 2&3 £3.80 CSF £95.92 CT £318.13 TOTE £55.90: £10.90, £1.50, £1.80; EX 327.60 Trifecta £123.70 Pool: £302.59- 1.81 winning units. Place 6: £50.92 Place 5: £13.05.
Owner John Dover **Bred** Llety Stud **Trained** Exning, Suffolk

FOCUS
A very moderate apprentice handicap. The pace was just fair and they finished in something of a heap. The winner found form from somewhere and did it really well.
T/Plt: £30.20 to a £1 stake. Pool: £54,507.05. 1,313.56 winning tickets. T/Qpdt: £17.00 to a £1 stake. Pool: £4,920.28. 213.05 winning tickets. JN

810 WOLVERHAMPTON (A.W) (L-H)
Wednesday, March 10

OFFICIAL GOING: Standard
Wind: Almost nil Weather: Fine

848 WOLVERHAMPTON HOSPITALITY - A PLEASURE CLAIMING STKS 5f 20y(P)
5:30 (5:30) (Class 6) 4-Y-0+ £1,774 (£523; £262) Stalls Low

Form RPR

4242 **1** **Misaro (GER)**[5] 810 9-8-7 65 (b) DavidProbert 5 74
(R A Harris) *chsd ldr: led wl over 1f out: rdn out* **5/4**[1]

1311 **2** 1¾ **Monte Major (IRE)**[5] 810 9-7-12 64 (v) SeanPalmer(7) 4 66
(D Shaw) *a.p: chsd wnr fnl f: rdn and kpt on same pce* **5/2**[2]

00-6 **3** 3¾ **Klynch**[33] 432 4-8-9 77 (b) AndrewElliott 2 57
(Mrs R A Carr) *bhd: kpt on to take 3rd ins fnl f: no ch w ldng pair* **7/1**

016/ **4** 1 **Pennyspider (IRE)**[543] 5902 5-8-5 62 LukeMorris 7 49
(M S Saunders) *bhd: rdn and hdwy over 1f out: one pce fnl f* **33/1**

-654 **5** 2¼ **Chjimes (IRE)**[5] 806 6-8-12 70 LiamKeniry 3 48
(C R Dore) *prom tl rdn and wknd fnl f* **4/1**[3]

0-00 **6** ¾ **Wavertree Princess (IRE)**[5] 810 5-7-12 45 JulieCumine(7) 6 33
(A J Lidderdale) *hld up in tch: wknd 2f out* **100/1**

0-50 **7** 5 **Miacarla**[12] 723 7-8-5 40 (b[1]) ChrisCatlin 1 20
(H A McWilliams) *led: hdd wl over 1f out: wknd fnl f* **150/1**

62.08 secs (-0.22) **Going Correction** +0.125s/f (Slow) 7 Ran SP% **110.1**
Speed ratings (Par 101): **106,103,97,95,92 90,82**
toteswingers: 1&2 £1.10, 1&3 £1.90, 2&3 £2.80 CSF £4.19 TOTE £2.40: £2.00, £1.70; EX 4.60.
Owner Messrs Criddle Davies Dawson & Villa **Bred** Wilhelm Fasching **Trained** Earlswood, Monmouths

FOCUS
This looked another match between Misaro and Monte Major, the pair having fought out the finish of a similar race over C&D just five days earlier. Straightforward form.

849 BEST ODDS GUARANTEED AT LADBROKES.COM MAIDEN STKS 5f 216y(P)
6:00 (6:02) (Class 5) 3-Y-O+ **£2,456** (£725; £362) **Stalls** Low

Form				RPR
45-	**1**		**Sir Frank Wappat**[161] 6386 3-8-9 0 .... JoeFanning 12 (M Johnston) *a.p: wnt 2nd 3f out: rdn to ld jst over 1f out: sn edgd lft: rdn out* **5/2**[1]	68+
5	**2**	1 1/2	**Golden Ratio (IRE)**[26] 527 3-8-4 0 .... LukeMorris 10 (J R Gask) *chsd ldrs: pushed along over 3f out: rdn wl over 1f out: kpt on to take 2nd last strides: nt trble wnr* **9/2**	58
0-05	**3**	*hd*	**Sally's Swansong**[7] 774 4-8-13 39 ....(b) GaryBartley(5) 7 (E J Alston) *led: hdd jst over 1f out: swtchd rt jst ins fnl f: rdn and no ex: lost 2nd last strides* **33/1**	61
454-	**4**	3 1/4	**Zinjbar (USA)**[173] 6063 3-8-4 68 .... ChrisCatlin 5 (C E Brittain) *chsd ldrs: pushed along over 3f out: outpcd over 2f out: kpt on ins fnl f* **3/1**[2]	47
5	**5**	1/2	**Lucas Pitt**[9] 751 3-8-9 0 .... JamieMackay 11 (M J Scudamore) *bhd: c wd st: kpt on fr over 1f out: n.d* **12/1**	51
60-0	**6**	1 3/4	**Cheshire Lady (IRE)**[19] 624 3-8-4 0 .... LiamJones 8 (W M Brisbourne) *bhd: pushed along over 3f out: sme prog wl over 1f out: nvr nr ldrs* **50/1**	41
66	**7**	3/4	**Boxer Shorts**[16] 667 4-9-9 0 .... TomEaves 4 (M Mullineaux) *mid-div: pushed along over 2f out: no hdwy* **50/1**	47+
00-	**8**	1 3/4	**Born A Dancer (IRE)**[166] 6241 3-8-4 0 .... HayleyTurner 1 (J W Hills) *sn hld up in mid-div: pushed along wl over 1f out: no rspnse* **7/2**[3]	33
	9	2 1/2	**Aim'Ees Star** 3-8-4 0 .... DavidProbert 2 (John A Harris) *s.i.s: a in rr* **20/1**	26
00-	**10**	3	**Greenore Gordon**[230] 4219 3-8-9 0 .... VinceSlattery 3 (M S Saunders) *a bhd* **33/1**	22
600/	**11**	11	**Marron Flore**[1133] 321 7-9-4 35 ....(tp) WandersonD'Avila 6 (A J Lidderdale) *chsd ldr to 3f out: rdn over 2f out: sn wknd* **66/1**	—

1m 16.06s (1.06) **Going Correction** +0.125s/f (Slow)
WFA 3 from 4yo+ 14lb 11 Ran SP% **117.7**
Speed ratings (Par 103): **97,95,94,90,89 87,86,84,80,76 62**
CSF £13.28 TOTE £3.90: £1.90, £2.00, £8.10; EX 16.60.
Owner Paul Dean **Bred** Itchen Valley Stud **Trained** Middleham Moor, N Yorks

FOCUS
Rather a weak maiden, the form being held down by the third. The winner was well on top and the form is rated around the second, sixth and seventh.

850 LADBROKESPOKER.COM H'CAP 7f 32y(P)
6:30 (6:31) (Class 3) (0-95,91) 4-Y-O+ **£6,938** (£2,076; £1,038; £519; £258) **Stalls** High

Form				RPR
0-53	**1**		**Dubai Dynamo**[12] 722 5-9-2 **89** .... AndrewElliott 6 (Mrs R A Carr) *a.p: rdn to ld jst over 1f out: r.o wl* **18/1**	100
-615	**2**	3 1/4	**Ishiadancer**[11] 739 5-8-13 **86** .... EddieAhern 5 (E J Alston) *sn chsng ldr: led 3f out: rdn and hdd jst over 1f out: one pce* **13/2**[2]	88
104-	**3**	1 3/4	**Shaws Diamond (USA)**[208] 5005 4-8-5 **78** .... DavidProbert 3 (D Shaw) *hld up and bhd: pushed along over 2f out: rdn wl over 1f out: kpt on to take 3rd wl ins fnl f* **16/1**	75
15-0	**4**	*nk*	**The Kyllachy Kid**[18] 635 4-8-13 **86** ....(p) ChrisCatlin 4 (S Gollings) *sn led: hdd 3f out: wknd 2f out* **7/1**[3]	82
100-	**5**	1 1/2	**Rulesn'regulations**[127] 7227 4-9-4 **91** .... LiamKeniry 1 (Matthew Salaman) *hld up and bhd: pushed along over 2f out: rdn over 1f out: no rspnse* **7/1**[3]	83
232-	**6**	3 3/4	**Cheviot (USA)**[256] 3375 4-9-1 **88** .... NeilCallan 2 (M A Jarvis) *prom: hung lft and rdn over 1f out: eased whn btn wl ins fnl f* **8/11**[1]	70

1m 28.96s (-0.64) **Going Correction** +0.125s/f (Slow) 6 Ran SP% **107.4**
Speed ratings (Par 107): **108,104,102,101,100 95**
toteswingers: 1&2 £4.60, 1&3 £5.80, 2&3 £9.40 CSF £112.90 TOTE £12.40: £3.40, £2.50; EX 18.30.
Owner The Bottom Liners **Bred** T K & Mrs P A Knox **Trained** Huby, N Yorks

FOCUS
This looked a decent handicap and it was run at a true pace. The standard is sensible with the winner back to his very best form.

NOTEBOOK
Dubai Dynamo had shaped pleasingly over 6f at the course latest, and was expected to be suited by the return to 7f, which made his major market drift rather puzzling. Always going strongly, he went on over 1f out and won with plenty in hand. He is in again here on Saturday, this time over 6f, and may take some stopping under a penalty in this form. (op 9-1)
Ishiadancer, a C&D winner off 12lb lower two starts back, did not run too badly at Lingfield last time and she appreciated the return to this track, getting the outright lead past halfway and keeping on as best she could once headed. (op 11-2)
Shaws Diamond(USA) ran well in a few good handicaps last turf season, but she has plenty of placed form at this course and it was no surprise to see her run well, keeping on late having been outpaced. Her best efforts have come when ridden more positively and she looks capable of winning off this mark. (op 25-1)
The Kyllachy Kid, sporting first-time cheekpieces for his in-form yard, was just 1lb higher than when winning here in November, but he was quickly brushed aside and it emerged he had lost a shoe. As a result he deserves another chance. Official explanation: vet said gelding lost its right fore shoe (op 11-1)
Rulesn'regulations, a lightly raced sort who won his maiden here (5f), had never gone this far before, but he was beaten well before stamina became an issue. (op 15-2 tchd 8-1)
Cheviot(USA), who was very strong at the head of the market, ran a dire race. A winner on his only previous AW start at Kempton, he was going without the cheekpieces he wore on his last two starts and looked an awkward ride in the straight, finding little for pressure and being eased. This was clearly not his form and his rider reported he hung badly left in the straight. Official explanation: jockey said, regarding the running and riding, that the gelding was hanging badly left handed in the final two furlongs (op 4-6)

851 ENJOY THE PARTY PACK GROUP OFFER CLAIMING STKS 7f 32y(P)
7:00 (7:02) (Class 6) 3-Y-O+ **£1,774** (£523; £262) **Stalls** High

Form				RPR
0-03	**1**		**Cobo Bay**[34] 408 5-10-0 85 ....(b) NeilCallan 2 (K A Ryan) *sn led: pushed along wl over 1f out: rdn ins fnl f: r.o* **11/10**[1]	88
-303	**2**	*nk*	**Seasider**[13] 695 5-9-10 80 .... WilliamBuick 5 (D M Simcock) *s.i.s: sn hld up in mid-div: rdn over 2f out: c wd st: hdwy over 1f out: wnt 2nd and edgd lft wl ins fnl f: r.o* **6/1**[2]	84
-216	**3**	1 3/4	**Bonnie Prince Blue**[24] 560 7-9-10 75 .... AdrianNicholls 6 (D Nicholls) *sn prom: chsd wnr over 5f out: rdn wl over 1f out: no imp: lost 2nd wl ins fnl f* **7/1**[3]	79
3115	**4**	*nk*	**Ravi River (IRE)**[5] 804 6-9-6 70 ....(v) J-PGuillambert 7 (P D Evans) *hld up in rr: pushed along over 3f out: kpt on u.p to take 4th wl ins fnl f* **10/1**	74
-463	**5**	2 1/4	**Arken Lad**[24] 550 3-8-3 65 ....(e) PaulHanagan 3 (D Donovan) *led early: prom: rdn wl over 1f out: wknd wl ins fnl f* **20/1**	61
1012	**6**	1/2	**Lord Fidelio (IRE)**[13] 695 4-9-10 75 .... SebSanders 9 (Ollie Pears) *hld up in rr: hdwy on ins wl over 1f out: sn rdn: wknd wl ins fnl f* **6/1**[2]	71
6641	**7**	1/2	**Titus Gent**[6] 789 5-9-6 62 .... DavidProbert 1 (R A Harris) *hld up in tch: pushed along over 2f out: rdn over 1f out: wknd ins fnl f* **12/1**	65
510-	**8**	1 1/2	**Athaakeel (IRE)**[119] 7330 4-9-0 64 .... LiamJones 8 (R A Harris) *dwlt: sn swtchd lft: sn hld up in tch: ev ch over 2f out: wknd fnl f* **50/1**	55

1m 29.78s (0.18) **Going Correction** +0.125s/f (Slow)
WFA 3 from 4yo+ 16lb 8 Ran SP% **112.2**
Speed ratings (Par 101): **103,102,100,100,97 97,96,94**
toteswingers: 1&2 £2.00, 1&3 £2.20, 2&3 £14.60 CSF £7.67 TOTE £1.80: £1.10, £1.90, £2.00; EX 7.00.
Owner The C H F Partnership **Bred** The C H F Partnership **Trained** Hambleton, N Yorks

FOCUS
A fair claimer that should produce winners. The winner was best in and the fifth governs the form.

852 WATCH LIVE SPORT AT LADBROKES.COM H'CAP 1m 4f 50y(P)
7:30 (7:30) (Class 5) (0-75,72) 4-Y-O+ **£3,070** (£906; £453) **Stalls** Low

Form				RPR
3-15	**1**		**Jeer (IRE)**[40] 352 6-9-6 **72** ....(b) GrahamGibbons 6 (M W Easterby) *mde all: hrd rdn over 1f out: hld on wl ins fnl f* **11/2**[3]	81
0-10	**2**	*nk*	**Hannicean**[23] 565 6-9-1 **67** .... StevieDonohoe 2 (Ian Williams) *t.k.h: hdwy to chse wnr 8f out: rdn over 1f out: chal ins fnl f: kpt on* **16/1**	76
36-1	**3**	6	**Satwa Moon (USA)**[9] 752 4-9-4 **72** .... PaulHanagan 4 (E A L Dunlop) *hld up: hdwy on ins over 3f out: rdn 2f out: wknd ins fnl f* **4/5**[1]	72+
3/41	**4**	3/4	**Houston Dynimo (IRE)**[25] 546 5-9-4 **70** .... TomEaves 5 (N G Richards) *hld up in rr: rdn wl over 1f out: tk 4th jst ins fnl f: n.d* **3/1**[2]	68+
3333	**5**	1/2	**Quince (IRE)**[11] 735 7-8-7 **64** ....(b[1]) SimonPearce(5) 1 (J Pearce) *chsd wnr 4f: hld up: hdwy over 3f out: wknd wl over 1f out* **12/1**	62+
4	**6**	16	**Escardo (GER)**[10] 746 7-9-1 **67** .... DavidNolan 3 (D G Bridgwater) *hld up: pushed along over 2f out: sn struggling* **33/1**	41+

2m 45.28s (4.18) **Going Correction** +0.125s/f (Slow)
WFA 4 from 5yo+ 2lb 6 Ran SP% **112.5**
Speed ratings (Par 103): **91,90,86,86,85 75**
toteswingers: 1&2 £10.50, 1&3 £4.30, 2&3 £2.30 CSF £76.33 TOTE £7.10: £2.60, £5.60; EX 77.60.
Owner Mrs Jean Turpin **Bred** Floors Farming And Side Hill Stud **Trained** Sheriff Hutton, N Yorks

FOCUS
Just a modest handicap, in which the early gallop was a sedate one, and the front two held their positions throughout. The runner-up is the key to the form, which is very suspect.
Satwa Moon(USA) Official explanation: jockey said colt hung left throughout

853 LADBROKESCASINO.COM H'CAP (DIV I) 1m 141y(P)
8:00 (8:01) (Class 5) (0-70,70) 4-Y-O+ **£2,729** (£806; £403) **Stalls** Low

Form				RPR
4-26	**1**		**Dajen**[45] 285 4-8-9 **61** .... WilliamBuick 5 (D M Simcock) *hld up in mid-div: rdn and hdwy on outside 1f out: r.o wl to ld wl ins fnl f* **4/1**[2]	69
4221	**2**	1	**King's Icon (IRE)**[5] 814 5-9-0 **66** 6ex ....(b) NickyMackay 10 (M Wigham) *hld up towards rr: hdwy wl over 1f out: rdn and r.o ins fnl f* **9/4**[1]	72
0-44	**3**	1 1/4	**Kladester (USA)**[13] 704 4-8-6 **58** .... PaulHanagan 8 (M Herrington) *sn chsng ldr: ev ch 2f out: rdn over 1f out: nt qckn wl ins fnl f* **40/1**	61
4-03	**4**	*nse*	**Trade Centre**[21] 579 5-9-2 **68** ....(p) LiamJones 3 (R A Harris) *led: rdn and hdd wl ins fnl f: no ex* **10/1**	71
2414	**5**	1 3/4	**Alqaahir (USA)**[13] 695 8-9-0 **69** .... RobertLButler(3) 7 (P Butler) *hld up in tch: pushed along and one pce ins fnl f* **12/1**	69
02-0	**6**	1 1/2	**Dr Wintringham (IRE)**[67] 11 4-8-9 **61** .... ChrisCatlin 9 (Karen George) *hld up in rr: rdn and kpt on fnl f: n.d* **25/1**	57
34-5	**7**	1/2	**Ermine Grey**[16] 656 9-8-5 **57** .... LukeMorris 6 (A W Carroll) *hld up in mid-div: rdn jst over 2f out: no hdwy* **7/1**	52
0323	**8**	1 1/4	**Forward Feline (IRE)**[21] 587 4-8-13 **65** .... DavidProbert 2 (B Palling) *prom: rdn wl over 1f out: wknd ins fnl f* **13/2**[3]	58
-050	**9**	2 3/4	**All About You (IRE)**[14] 676 4-9-4 **70** .... J-PGuillambert 11 (P Howling) *a in rr* **16/1**	57
540-	**10**	1/2	**Minturno (USA)**[169] 6178 4-9-1 **67** .... SilvestreDeSousa 1 (Mrs A Duffield) *hld up in tch: pushed along over 2f out: wknd wl over 1f out* **10/1**	53
4-04	**11**	3/4	**Pachakutek (USA)**[5] 815 4-8-8 **60** ....(p) WandersonD'Avila 4 (A J Lidderdale) *bhd fnl 2f* **20/1**	44

1m 52.63s (2.13) **Going Correction** +0.125s/f (Slow) 11 Ran SP% **119.4**
Speed ratings (Par 103): **95,94,93,92,91 90,89,88,86,85 84**
toteswingers: 1&2 £3.80, 1&3 £54.00, 2&3 £10.70 CSF £13.29 CT £324.46 TOTE £6.90: £1.60, £1.30, £5.90; EX 18.20.
Owner Tick Tock Partnership **Bred** Miss D Fleming **Trained** Newmarket, Suffolk

FOCUS
Another race in which the early pace was just a steady one. The winner is less exposed than most of these and should have more to offer.
Forward Feline(IRE) Official explanation: jockey said the filly hung right

854 GREAT OFFERS AT WOLVERHAMPTON-RACECOURSE.CO.UK H'CAP 1m 141y(P)
8:30 (8:30) (Class 7) (0-50,52) 4-Y-O+ **£1,364** (£403; £201) **Stalls** Low

Form				RPR
1	**1**		**Sworn Tigress (GER)**[6] 795 5-9-5 **52** 6ex .... TonyCulhane 12 (George Baker) *hld up in mid-div: hdwy on outside 3f out: pushed along over 1f out: led ins fnl f: rdn and r.o wl* **1/2**[1]	72+
0-50	**2**	4	**Saving Grace**[7] 780 4-9-1 **48** .... GrahamGibbons 3 (E J Alston) *led: pushed along and hdd wl over 1f out: rdn and ev ch jst ins fnl f: one pce* **25/1**	58

-044 **3** 2 ¾ **Yakama (IRE)**[6] 794 5-9-3 **50**......(b) AdamKirby 1 54
(Mrs C A Dunnett) *chsd ldr tl over 6f out: prom: led wl over 1f out: sn rdn: hdd ins fnl f: wknd* **11/1**[3]

1364 **4** 1 ¼ **Kirstys Lad**[9] 753 8-9-0 **50**...... KellyHarrison(3) 10 51
(M Mullineaux) *prom: chsd ldr over 6f out to 2f out: wknd over 1f out* **16/1**

6-25 **5** 1 ¼ **Stanley Rigby**[35] 389 4-9-2 **49**...... JackMitchell 5 48
(C F Wall) *hld up in tch: rdn over 2f out: sn wknd* **13/2**[2]

-002 **6** nse **Corrib (IRE)**[16] 666 7-9-3 **50**......(p) DavidProbert 6 48
(B Palling) *prom tl rdn and wknd wl over 1f out* **14/1**

-542 **7** 1 ¼ **Misterisland (IRE)**[23] 568 5-8-13 **46**...... TomEaves 13 42
(M Mullineaux) *hld up in rr: pushed along and sme hdwy wl over 1f out: sn rdn: no further prog* **16/1**

30-0 **8** ¾ **Red Dagger (IRE)**[12] 721 4-8-13 **46**...... LiamJones 11 40
(R J Price) *a in rr* **50/1**

4315 **9** 1 ½ **Hi Spec (IRE)**[20] 591 7-9-3 **50**......(p) NeilCallan 9 41
(Miss M E Rowland) *hld up towards rr: short-lived effrt over 2f out* **20/1**

00/5 **10** ½ **A Nod And A Wink (IRE)**[16] 667 6-9-1 **48**...... LiamKeniry 7 38
(S Lycett) *hld up towards rr: rdn over 2f out: sn struggling* **40/1**

2440 **11** hd **Almatlaie (USA)**[6] 794 4-9-3 **50**...... StevieDonohoe 2 40
(J W Unett) *a towards rr* **50/1**

00-5 **12** shd **Artreju (GER)**[14] 685 7-8-12 **48**...... RobertLButler(3) 4 37
(P Butler) *hld up towards rr: short-lived effrt on ins over 2f out* **100/1**

1m 51.09s (0.59) **Going Correction** +0.125s/f (Slow) 12 Ran SP% **122.7**
Speed ratings (Par 97): **102,98,96,94,93 93,92,91,90,90 90,89**
toteswingers: 1&2 £14.20, 1&3 £4.40, 2&3 £36.10 CSF £26.32 CT £92.15 TOTE £1.60: £1.10, £8.50, £2.40; EX 18.30.
Owner Sir Alex Ferguson **Bred** Gestut Wittekindshof **Trained** Moreton Morrell, Warwicks

FOCUS
A low-grade handicap. Sworn Tigress is better than this grade and can win again.

855 LADBROKESCASINO.COM H'CAP (DIV II) 1m 141y(P)
9:00 (9:00) (Class 5) (0-70,70) 4-Y-0+ **£2,729** (£806; £403) **Stalls** Low

Form RPR

10-0 **1** **Mr Hichens**[14] 676 5-9-1 **67**...... ChrisCatlin 2 79
(Karen George) *chsd ldr: led over 1f out: rdn and edgd lft jst ins fnl f: r.o* **12/1**

3520 **2** nk **Spinning Ridge (IRE)**[5] 814 5-8-9 **61**...... LiamJones 5 73
(R A Harris) *a.p: chsd wnr fnl f: kpt on* **7/1**[3]

036- **3** 2 ½ **Tevez**[197] 5329 5-8-7 **59**...... LukeMorris 4 65
(D Donovan) *awkward leaving stalls: hld up in mid-div: hdwy on ins over 2f out: rdn and one pce fnl f* **16/1**

-513 **4** 2 ½ **Ella Woodcock (IRE)**[12] 725 6-9-4 **70**...... EddieAhern 9 70
(E J Alston) *hld up towards rr: styd on ins fnl f: tk 4th nr fin* **4/1**[2]

00-0 **5** 1 **Ninth House (USA)**[25] 543 8-9-2 **68**......(t) SilvestreDeSousa 8 66
(Mrs R A Carr) *hld up and bhd: rdn and hdwy over 1f out: swtchd lft jst ins fnl f: nvr trbld ldrs* **8/1**

-612 **6** ¾ **By Command**[9] 752 5-8-13 **65**......(p) NeilCallan 10 61
(K A Ryan) *hld up in mid-div: stdy hdwy over 3f out: rdn over 1f out: wknd ins fnl f* **5/2**[1]

3-00 **7** 1 ¾ **Bob Stock (IRE)**[26] 518 4-8-8 **60**...... TonyCulhane 3 52
(W J Musson) *hld up and bhd: stdy prog on outside over 3f out: c wd st: rdn and wknd over 1f out* **10/1**

00-0 **8** nse **Prince Rossi (IRE)**[38] 367 6-8-6 **58**......(v) PaulHanagan 1 50
(A E Price) *led: rdn and hdd over 1f out: wknd ins fnl f* **22/1**

00-5 **9** ¾ **Efficiency**[21] 587 4-8-10 **62**...... LiamKeniry 6 52
(M Blanshard) *hld up in tch: wknd wl over 1f out* **7/1**[3]

0-50 **10** 1 ¾ **Blue Charm**[16] 668 6-9-2 **68**...... StevieDonohoe 7 54
(I W McInnes) *a in rr* **40/1**

1m 50.44s (-0.06) **Going Correction** +0.125s/f (Slow) 10 Ran SP% **114.1**
Speed ratings (Par 103): **105,104,102,100,99 98,97,97,96,94**
toteswingers: 1&2 £24.30, 1&3 £28.10, 2&3 £7.70 CSF £91.39 CT £1349.07 TOTE £15.90: £3.30, £3.10, £4.10; EX 130.60 Place 6: £295.39 Place 5: £228.63 .
Owner Eastington Racing Club **Bred** C A Green **Trained** Higher Eastington, Devon

FOCUS
The pace was more generous than it had been in the first division. Routine and solid form, rated through the runner-up.
T/Plt: £276.90 to a £1 stake. Pool: £74,914.36. 197.47 winning tickets. T/Qpdt: £77.40 to a £1 stake. Pool: £8,291.32. 79.20 winning tickets. KH

832 SOUTHWELL (L-H)
Thursday, March 11

OFFICIAL GOING: Standard
Wind: Light behind Weather: Overcast

856 PLAY GOLF AT SOUTHWELL GOLF CLUB H'CAP 6f (F)
2:20 (2:21) (Class 5) (0-70,69) 3-Y-0 **£2,456** (£725; £362) **Stalls** Low

Form RPR

41-2 **1** **Kummel Excess (IRE)**[15] 689 3-8-12 **68**...... MatthewDavies(5) 3 75+
(George Baker) *mde virtually all: shkn up over 1f out: r.o wl* **9/2**[3]

4545 **2** 2 ¼ **Tamarind Hill (IRE)**[14] 702 3-8-8 **59**......(b) GrahamGibbons 5 60
(A J McCabe) *hmpd s: sn chsng wnr: rdn over 1f out: styd on same pce* **14/1**

04-4 **3** ½ **Rain On The Wind (IRE)**[14] 699 3-8-13 **67**...... WilliamCarson(3) 7 66
(S C Williams) *edgd lft s: racd keenly and sn trcking ldrs: rdn and edgd lft over 1f out: r.o* **9/4**[1]

3052 **4** 3 **Tealing**[7] 782 3-8-13 **64**......(e) JimmyQuinn 8 54
(R C Guest) *hld up: shkn up over 1f out: nvr nr to chal* **15/2**

325- **5** 3 ¾ **Babylonian**[244] 3820 3-9-4 **69**...... JoeFanning 2 48
(M Johnston) *trckd ldrs: rdn over 2f out: edgd lft and wknd over 1f out* **5/2**[2]

030- **6** 5 **Bandear (IRE)**[161] 6418 3-8-12 **63**...... SebSanders 6 27
(C E Brittain) *hmpd s: sn drvn along in rr: wknd over 2f out* **8/1**

50-4 **7** 3 ½ **Hill Of Miller (IRE)**[17] 667 3-9-3 **68**......(t) MartinDwyer 1 21
(Rae Guest) *prom: rdn over 2f out: sn wknd* **14/1**

1m 17.26s (0.76) **Going Correction** +0.10s/f (Slow) 7 Ran SP% **113.7**
Speed ratings (Par 98): **98,95,94,90,85 78,74**
toteswingers:1&2:£10.50, 1&3:£2.80, 2&3:£8.80 CSF £60.51 CT £175.96 TOTE £6.20: £3.00, £5.10; EX 48.60 Trifecta £302.20 Part won. Pool: £408.44 - 0.91 winning units..
Owner Mrs V P Baker & Partners **Bred** John Donegan **Trained** Moreton Morrell, Warwicks

FOCUS
A modest 3-y-o sprint handicap and few got involved. The runner-up limits the form.

857 PLAY GOLF BEFORE RACING AT SOUTHWELL H'CAP 1m 3f (F)
2:50 (2:50) (Class 5) (0-75,77) 4-Y-0+ **£2,331** (£693; £346; £173) **Stalls** Low

Form RPR

4-23 **1** **Eseej (USA)**[42] 323 5-8-11 **70**...... WilliamCarson(3) 5 79
(P W Hiatt) *mde all: hung rt fr 1/2-way: rdn over 2f out: styd on* **11/4**[1]

-061 **2** 1 **Whooshka (USA)**[7] 786 4-9-6 **77** 6ex...... ChrisCatlin 2 84
(P W Chapple-Hyam) *a.p: rdn to chse wnr over 3f out: styd on u.p* **6/1**

042- **3** 1 ¾ **Almahaza (IRE)**[84] 7784 6-8-5 **61**...... DavidProbert 6 69+
(A J Chamberlain) *stdd s: hld up: hdwy and nt clr run over 3f out: sn rdn: no ex towards fin* **5/1**[3]

-104 **4** 3 **Heathyards Junior**[13] 715 4-8-10 **67**...... GrahamGibbons 4 67
(A J McCabe) *hld up: rdn over 4f out: sn outpcd: styd on wl u.p to go 4th nr fin* **9/2**[2]

134- **5** nk **Veiled Applause**[118] 7014 7-8-12 **75**...... IanBrennan(7) 7 74
(J J Quinn) *pushed along in rr: hdwy over 4f out: sn rdn: hung lft 2f out: styd on same pce fnl f* **8/1**

6-32 **6** 1 ¼ **Fitzolini**[14] 705 4-8-4 **61** oh5......(p) JimmyQuinn 1 58
(A D Brown) *chsd ldrs: rdn over 4f out: styd on same pce u.p appr fnl f* **10/1**

06-0 **7** 1 **Toby Tyler**[23] 572 4-8-12 **69**...... PJMcDonald 3 65
(P T Midgley) *s.i.s: hld up: bhd 1/2-way: rdn and hung lft fnl 2f: n.d* **12/1**

131- **8** 22 **Amazing Blue Sky**[217] 4715 4-9-4 **75**...... AndrewMullen 8 36
(Mrs R A Carr) *chsd wnr tl rdn and wknd over 3f out: t.o* **10/1**

2m 28.72s (0.72) **Going Correction** +0.10s/f (Slow)
WFA 4 from 5yo+ 1lb 8 Ran SP% **112.8**
Speed ratings (Par 103): **101,100,99,96,96 95,94,78**
toteswingers:1&2:£3.30, 1&3:£3.40, 2&3:£4.10 CSF £18.87 CT £76.58 TOTE £4.00: £1.30, £2.20, £2.20; EX 17.70 Trifecta £71.70 Pool: £362.74 - 3.74 winning units..
Owner P W Hiatt **Bred** Shadwell Farm LLC **Trained** Hook Norton, Oxon

FOCUS
A few of these had their stamina to prove, but not Eseej, who set a good pace and still had enough to hold on.

858 MEMBERSHIP OF SOUTHWELL GOLF CLUB MEDIAN AUCTION MAIDEN STKS 1m (F)
3:25 (3:25) (Class 6) 3-5-Y-0 **£1,683** (£501; £250; £125) **Stalls** Low

Form RPR

2-23 **1** **Juicy Pear (IRE)**[10] 754 3-8-8 78...... HayleyTurner 7 74
(M L W Bell) *trckd ldrs: plld hrd: stdd and dropped in rr after 1f: hdwy 3f out: rdn to ld ins fnl f: hung lft: r.o* **5/6**[1]

3- **2** 1 ¼ **Privy Speech (IRE)**[83] 7792 3-8-3 0...... DavidProbert 3 64
(Rae Guest) *hld up in tch: led 2f out: sn rdn: hdd 1f out: styd on same pce* **11/4**[2]

0-32 **3** nse **Dane Cottage**[13] 728 3-8-3 65...... LukeMorris 8 64
(Miss Gay Kelleway) *chsd ldrs: pushed along 3f out: rdn to ld 1f out: sn edgd lft and hdd: no ex towards fin* **15/2**

345- **4** 13 **Oskari**[198] 5329 5-9-7 63...... PaulPickard(5) 2 41
(P T Midgley) *led: rdn and hdd 2f out: sn wknd* **4/1**[3]

000/ **5** 5 **Without Equal**[579] 4873 4-9-7 25...... DanielTudhope 5 25
(A Dickman) *hld up: a in rr: rdn over 3f out: sn wknd* **100/1**

0 **6** 1 ½ **Ignore**[14] 699 3-8-8 0...... AndrewElliott 6 26
(Mrs R A Carr) *chsd ldr tl rdn over 2f out: sn hung lft and wknd* **100/1**

50 **7** 10 **Swift Steel**[7] 793 3-8-3 0...... JimmyQuinn 1 —
(Mrs A Duffield) *s.i.s: sn prom: rdn over 4f out: wknd 3f out* **40/1**

1m 44.51s (0.81) **Going Correction** +0.10s/f (Slow)
WFA 3 from 4yo+ 18lb 7 Ran SP% **117.4**
Speed ratings (Par 101): **99,97,97,84,79 78,68**
toteswingers:1&2:£1.60, 1&3:£2.30, 2&3:£1.90 CSF £3.62 TOTE £2.20: £1.50, £1.50; EX 4.50 Trifecta £4.70 Pool: £620.64 - 96.65 winning units..
Owner Billy Maguire **Bred** Ballyhane Stud **Trained** Newmarket, Suffolk

FOCUS
A modest maiden with the winner setting a fair standard and the runner-up progressing from debut.
Swift Steel Official explanation: trainer said filly scoped dirty after the race

859 SOUTHWELL RACECOURSE FOR CONFERENCES H'CAP 6f (F)
3:55 (3:55) (Class 4) (0-85,85) 4-Y-0+
£4,050 (£1,212; £606; £303; £151; £76) **Stalls** Low

Form RPR

4332 **1** **Onceaponatime (IRE)**[13] 722 5-8-8 **78**...... WilliamCarson(3) 6 87
(M D Squance) *hld up: swtchd rt and hdwy over 1f out: sn rdn: r.o to ld nr fin* **11/4**[1]

3-35 **2** hd **Punching**[10] 750 6-8-4 **71** oh1...... HayleyTurner 5 79
(C R Dore) *hld up in tch: plld hrd: rdn to ld over 1f out: edgd rt u.p ins fnl f: hdd nr fin* **3/1**[2]

-021 **3** 1 ¼ **Hits Only Jude (IRE)**[14] 703 7-8-5 **79**...... NeilFarley(7) 1 83
(D Carroll) *pushed along to ld 5f out: rdn: edgd rt and hdd over 1f out: styd on same pce* **5/1**[3]

4216 **4** 1 ¾ **Bel Cantor**[12] 737 7-9-1 **85**......(p) KellyHarrison(3) 3 83
(W J H Ratcliffe) *disp ld tl 1f: chsd ldrs: rdn over 2f out: styd on same pce fnl f* **3/1**[2]

03-1 **5** ¾ **Jack Rackham**[42] 325 6-8-5 **72**......(v) PaulHanagan 2 68
(B Smart) *disp ld tl 1f: chsd ldr: rdn over 2f out: no ex fnl f* **7/1**

433- **6** 16 **Frognal (IRE)**[146] 6815 4-9-4 **85**...... AndrewElliott 4 30
(Mrs R A Carr) *sn pushed along in rr: rdn and wknd over 2f out* **12/1**

1m 15.83s (-0.67) **Going Correction** +0.10s/f (Slow) 6 Ran SP% **113.5**
Speed ratings (Par 105): **108,107,106,103,102 81**
toteswingers:1&2:£2.60, 1&3:£3.00, 2&3:£4.40 CSF £11.54 TOTE £3.60: £1.90, £2.20; EX 12.20.
Owner M D Squance **Bred** Dermot O'Rourke **Trained** Newmarket, Suffolk

FOCUS
A fair sprint handicap run at a decent pace and the form is sound but limited.

860 QUEEN MOTHER RESTAURANT H'CAP 5f (F)
4:30 (4:30) (Class 6) (0-55,56) 4-Y-0+ **£1,774** (£523; £262) **Stalls** High

Form RPR

-001 **1** **Mr Funshine**[13] 726 5-8-11 **56** ow2...... GaryBartley(5) 1 63
(D Shaw) *chsd ldrs: rdn to ld ins fnl f: r.o* **9/4**[1]

3230 **2** nk **Angle Of Attack (IRE)**[8] 773 5-9-1 **55**......(v) DanielTudhope 3 61
(A D Brown) *edgd rt s: led: hdd 1/2-way: led again 2f out: rdn and hdd ins fnl f: r.o* **11/4**[2]

The Form Book, Raceform Ltd, Compton, RG20 6NL

-430 **3** *2* **Shakespeare's Son**[24] 561 5-8-12 **52**................. FrankieMcDonald 10 51
(H J Evans) *s.i.s: hld up: hdwy over 1f out: rdn and hung lft ins fnl f: styd on same pce* **8/1**

5-00 **4** *3 1/4* **Shannon Golden**[17] 668 4-8-12 **52**........................(bt[1]) KevinGhunowa 8 39
(S R Bowring) *chsd ldrs: rdn 1/2-way: wknd fnl f* **11/1**

5204 **5** *1* **Hart Of Gold**[8] 773 6-9-0 **54**..(b) StephenCraine 5 37
(R A Harris) *s.i.s and hmpd s: in rr: shkn up over 1f out: nvr nrr* **7/2**[3]

40-0 **6** *1 1/4* **Fashion Icon (USA)**[23] 569 4-8-10 **50**......................... AndrewMullen 9 29
(J Hetherton) *chsd ldrs: rdn 1/2-way: wknd fnl f* **20/1**

263- **7** *1/2* **You'relikemefrank**[169] 6206 4-8-10 **50**..........................(p) DuranFentiman 4 27
(J Balding) *hmpd s: sn chsng ldrs: led 1/2-way: rdn and hdd 2f out: hmpd over 1f out: wknd ins fnl f* **20/1**

040/ **8** *7* **Retaliate**[158] 4514 6-8-3 **46** oh1....................................... KellyHarrison(3) 6 —
(M D Squance) *hmpd s: outpcd* **66/1**

000- **9** *3/4* **Red Cell (IRE)**[156] 6553 4-8-7 **50**...............................(b) BarryMcHugh(3) 7 —
(I W McInnes) *hung lft leaving stalls: sn outpcd: hung rt 1/2-way* **20/1**

60.29 secs (0.59) **Going Correction** +0.15s/f (Slow) **9** Ran SP% **114.9**

Speed ratings (Par 101): **101,100,97,92,90 88,87,76,75**

toteswingers:1&2:£2.20, 1&3:£5.80, 2&3:£5.50 CSF £8.02 CT £40.35 TOTE £3.10: £1.30, £1.20, £2.40; EX 9.90 Trifecta £43.70 Pool: £402.80 - 6.81 winning units..

Owner Unity Farm Holiday Centre Ltd **Bred** Unity Farm Holiday Centre Ltd **Trained** Sproxton, Leics

■ Stewards' Enquiry : Daniel Tudhope caution: used whip down shoulder in the forehand position

FOCUS

A moderate sprint handicap but the in-form winner sets the level.

Red Cell(IRE) Official explanation: trainer said gelding didn't handle the kick back

861 SOUTHWELL-RACECOURSE.CO.UK APPRENTICE H'CAP 7f (F)

5:00 (5:01) (Class 6) (0-60,60) 3-Y-O **£1,774** (£523; £262) **Stalls** Low

Form RPR

2120 **1** **Premium Charge**[6] 805 3-9-0 **60**.................................... RyanClark(5) 8 72+
(C A Dwyer) *broke wl and mde all: rdn clr fnl f: comf* **3/1**[2]

0414 **2** *5* **Sandy Toes**[27] 519 3-8-5 **46**.. SimonPearce 2 44
(J A Glover) *hld up: hdwy over 1f out: sn rdn: edgd lft and styd on same pce fnl f* **8/1**

20-2 **3** *1 1/2* **Thaliwarru**[14] 702 3-9-2 **60**... JohnFahy(3) 5 54
(J R Gask) *pushed along in rr early: hdwy 3f out: rdn and hung lft fr over 1f out: nt run on: wnt 3rd nr fin* **85/40**[1]

00-1 **4** *hd* **Step To It (IRE)**[21] 597 3-8-10 **51**.. AmyRyan 1 45+
(K A Ryan) *sn pushed along in mid-div: hdwy u.p over 2f out: wnt 2nd over 1f out: wknd ins fnl f* **7/2**[3]

3523 **5** *4* **Taper Jean Girl (IRE)**[21] 597 3-9-0 **55**.......................(p) DeanHeslop 3 39
(Mrs R A Carr) *chsd wnr tl rdn over 2f out: wknd fnl f* **10/1**

00-6 **6** *1 3/4* **Kings Aphrodite**[6] 812 3-8-13 **54**................................... AshleyMorgan 7 33
(Miss Gay Kelleway) *prom: chsd wnr over 2f out: sn rdn: wknd fnl f* **20/1**

0-35 **7** *6* **Rescent**[13] 717 3-8-5 **46** oh1.. PaulPickard 4 10
(Mrs R A Carr) *chsd ldrs: rdn 1/2-way: wknd over 2f out* **12/1**

0-60 **8** *4* **Luminosa**[47] 274 3-8-5 **46** oh1.. DeclanCannon 6 —
(D Donovan) *prom: rdn 1/2-way: wknd over 2f out* **20/1**

1m 31.2s (0.90) **Going Correction** +0.10s/f (Slow) **8** Ran SP% **116.6**

Speed ratings (Par 96): **98,92,90,90,85 83,76,72**

toteswingers:1&2:£5.10, 1&3:£3.10, 2&3:£3.30 CSF £27.75 CT £59.75 TOTE £4.30: £1.40, £2.30, £1.40; EX 27.60 Trifecta £328.80 Part won. Pool: £444.39 - 0.91 winning units. Place 6 £24.61, Place 5 £3.35.

Owner Mrs Shelley Dwyer **Bred** Mrs J A Chapman **Trained** Burrough Green, Cambs

FOCUS

A moderate handicap and the winner was the third on the day to make all. The form is rated negatively around the placed horses.

T/Plt: £29.70 to a £1 stake. Pool: £68,439.23. 1,679.01 winning tickets T/Qpdt: £4.50 to a £1 stake. Pool: £4,687.00. 769.83 winning tickets CR

848 WOLVERHAMPTON (A.W) (L-H)

Thursday, March 11

OFFICIAL GOING: Standard

Wind: Almost nil Weather: Fine

862 GREAT OFFERS AT WOLVERHAMPTON-RACECOURSE.CO.UK CLAIMING STKS 1m 141y(P)

5:30 (5:30) (Class 6) 4-Y-O+ **£2,047** (£604; £302) **Stalls** Low

Form RPR

113- **1** **Fremen (USA)**[178] 5944 10-8-11 82.................................. AdrianNicholls 6 75+
(D Nicholls) *s.i.s: sn rcvrd: led over 6f out: rdn and edgd lft over 1f out: r.o wl* **5/2**[2]

2023 **2** *1 1/4* **Straight Face (IRE)**[17] 663 6-8-11 65 ow2..............(b) J-PGuillambert 4 72
(P D Evans) *hld up in tch: rdn over 1f out: r.o to take 2nd wl ins fnl f: nt trble wnr* **7/1**

351/ **3** *2 1/4* **Bazroy (IRE)**[459] 7594 6-8-8 88.............................(v) AndrewHeffernan(5) 1 69+
(P D Evans) *hld up: rdn and hdwy over 1f out: styd on to take 3rd towards fin* **3/1**[3]

130- **4** *1 3/4* **Appalachian Trail (IRE)**[79] 7837 9-9-1 92.......................(b) TomEaves 3 67+
(N Wilson) *led early: chsd wnr over 5f out: rdn over 1f out: lost 2nd and wknd towards fin* **2/1**[1]

2304 **5** *1* **Shake On It**[17] 663 6-8-9 64... ChrisCatlin 2 59
(M R Hoad) *a bhd* **12/1**

0-00 **6** *2* **Flamestone**[14] 691 6-8-8 45.. GrahamGibbons 7 53
(A E Price) *sn led: hdd over 6f out: rdn and wknd wl over 1f out* **66/1**

1m 51.12s (0.62) **Going Correction** +0.05s/f (Slow) **6** Ran SP% **108.6**

Speed ratings (Par 101): **99,97,95,94,93 91**

toteswingers:1&2:£2.70, 1&3:£2.20, 2&3:£4.40 CSF £18.30 TOTE £3.70: £2.20, £4.30; EX 17.50.

Owner Middleham Park Racing XXXV C King A Seed **Bred** Flaxman Holdings Ltd **Trained** Sessay, N Yorks

FOCUS

A fair claimer in which three horses - the winner, third and fourth - dominated at the weights. The winning jockey slowed the pace after 2f and controlled the race from then on. The form is limited by the runner-up and sixth.

863 WOLVERHAMPTON-RACECOURSE.CO.UK H'CAP 1m 1f 103y(P)

6:00 (6:00) (Class 2) (0-100,91) 4-Y-O+

£10,592 (£3,172; £1,586; £793; £396; £198) **Stalls** Low

Form RPR

06-5 **1** **Orchard Supreme**[19] 635 7-8-13 **86**.............................. MartinDwyer 2 93
(R Hannon) *hld up and bhd: hdwy on ins wl over 1f out: rdn to ld wl ins fnl f: r.o* **5/2**[1]

-110 **2** *hd* **Thunderstruck**[26] 536 5-8-13 **86**....................................(p) ChrisCatlin 9 92
(J A Glover) *led after 1f: rdn wl over 1f out: hdd wl ins fnl f: r.o* **13/2**

-140 **3** *hd* **Winter Fever (SAF)**[26] 536 6-9-1 **88**................................ LukeMorris 3 94
(J M P Eustace) *a.p: rdn jst over 2f out: ev ch ins fnl f: kpt on* **4/1**[2]

0104 **4** *1 1/4* **Baylini**[14] 697 6-9-2 **89**.. JamesDoyle 1 92
(Ms J S Doyle) *hld up in mid-div: pushed along wl over 1f out: rdn and kpt on ins fnl f* **7/1**

3054 **5** *1* **Confidentiality (IRE)**[7] 790 6-8-12 **85**.......................... NickyMackay 8 86
(M Wigham) *hld up in rr: rdn over 1f out: swtchd rt ins fnl f: r.o: nvr nrr* **15/2**

154- **6** *shd* **Tartan Gunna**[152] 6665 4-9-4 **91**.. JoeFanning 4 92
(M Johnston) *hld up in mid-div: hdwy over 2f out: rdn over 1f out: one pce* **6/1**[3]

-346 **7** *1 3/4* **Just Bond (IRE)**[13] 725 8-8-9 **83** oh1............................ PJMcDonald 7 79
(G R Oldroyd) *hld up and bhd: c wd st: n.d* **22/1**

6001 **8** *nk* **Stand Guard**[13] 725 6-8-10 **88**............................ AndrewHeffernan(5) 5 84
(P Howling) *led 1f: chsd ldr tl rdn wl over 1f out: wknd wl ins fnl f* **9/1**

400- **9** *14* **Wigwam Willie (IRE)**[173] 6094 8-9-2 **89**..........................(tp) NeilCallan 6 53
(K A Ryan) *hld up in tch: wknd wl over 1f out* **25/1**

2m 0.56s (-1.14) **Going Correction** +0.05s/f (Slow) **9** Ran SP% **118.6**

Speed ratings (Par 109): **107,106,106,105,104 104,103,102,90**

toteswingers:1&2:£6.30, 1&3:£5.10, 2&3:£3.40 CSF £19.87 CT £64.44 TOTE £3.70: £2.00, £2.20, £1.70; EX 29.80.

Owner Brian C Oakley **Bred** Mrs M H Goodrich **Trained** East Everleigh, Wilts

FOCUS

A good turnout for a valuable prize. The pace was a routine one, with the runner-up quickening it on the run to the straight. The form is reasonable although limited for the grade.

NOTEBOOK

Orchard Supreme has an excellent record at Wolverhampton, this last-gasp win giving him two seconds and three wins at the track. Though not at his best for over a year, he has been slipping in the weights as a result and Dwyer's run up the rail was timed to perfection. (op 10-3 tchd 7-2)

Thunderstruck is on a stiff mark at present, but he has been in cracking form in recent months and continues to improve. Bouncing back from a below-par effort last time, when he pulled too hard under restraint, and returning to the front-running tactics which suit him ideally, he only went under late on. (op 15-2 tchd 8-1)

Winter Fever(SAF) continues to look useful and this sort of mark should not be beyond him in the coming months. (op 5-1)

Baylini ran much better than on her only previous visit to Wolverhampton, when the 1m4f trip stretched her stamina. Her favourite track is Lingfield but connections admit that there are not enough races there for her. (op 15-2 tchd 8-1)

Confidentiality(IRE) is battling the handicapper at present, but she was doing some good late work as befits a mare who has been running with credit at the full 1m2f. (op 13-2)

Tartan Gunna had been off the track since October but gave notice that he is one to consider for the turf season after a pretty good time of it in decent company last year. (op 9-2)

Just Bond(IRE), a regular round here these days, has not been quite at his best of late and this was a tough race in which to attempt a form revival. (op 20-1)

Stand Guard found this to be a better-class race than when making all last time. (tchd 10-1)

864 PARADE RESTAURANT MEDIAN AUCTION MAIDEN STKS 1m 1f 103y(P)

6:30 (6:31) (Class 5) 3-Y-O **£2,729** (£806; £403) **Stalls** Low

Form RPR

6 **1** **My Nan Nell (IRE)**[26] 533 3-8-12 0.................................. JackMitchell 5 72+
(T Keddy) *hld up and bhd: hdwy jst over 1f out: led wl ins fnl f: r.o wl* **9/1**

6-4 **2** *2 1/4* **Gra Adhmhar (IRE)**[21] 592 3-9-3 0................................... EddieAhern 4 72+
(D J Coakley) *hld up in mid-div: smooth hdwy 2f out: led jst over 1f out: edgd rt ins fnl f: sn hdd: nt qckn* **9/2**[3]

04 **3** *1/2* **Manxman (IRE)**[10] 754 3-9-3 0... JoeFanning 7 71
(M Johnston) *chsd ldr after 1f tl wl over 1f out: one pce ins fnl f* **4/1**[2]

243- **4** *1* **Dr Finley (IRE)**[147] 6786 3-9-3 74................................ HayleyTurner 6 69
(M L W Bell) *hld up in tch: awkward hd carriage 2f out: one pce fnl f* **15/8**[1]

000- **5** *1 3/4* **Stadium Of Light (IRE)**[140] 6965 3-9-3 44.......................(t) TravisBlock 1 65
(H Morrison) *a.p: rdn and ev ch over 1f out: wknd wl ins fnl f* **25/1**

0-5 **6** *1 1/4* **Asterrlini (IRE)**[9] 758 3-8-12 0...................................... SebSanders 2 60+
(C E Brittain) *led: rdn and hdd jst over 1f out: hmpd ins fnl f: sn wknd* **12/1**

00 **7** *3 3/4* **Swindlers Lass (IRE)**[21] 592 3-8-12 0........................... DavidProbert 8 50
(Mark Gillard) *hld up in mid-div: pushed along over 3f out: c wd st: rdn and wknd wl over 1f out* **150/1**

8 *6* **Rannoch Moor** 3-9-3 0.. MartinDwyer 3 42
(M P Tregoning) *rn green in rr: no ch fnl 3f* **5/1**

2m 4.49s (2.79) **Going Correction** +0.05s/f (Slow) **8** Ran SP% **111.8**

Speed ratings (Par 98): **89,87,86,85,84 83,79,74**

toteswingers:1&2:£9.80, 1&3:£6.50, 2&3:£2.70 CSF £46.90 TOTE £11.50: £2.20, £1.80, £1.30; EX 52.70.

Owner A C Maylam **Bred** Hong Kong Breeders Club **Trained** Newmarket, Suffolk

FOCUS

The first three were unexposed and set the standard, but the fourth had solid maiden form on turf.

865 NAME A RACE TO ENHANCE YOUR BRAND H'CAP 1m 4f 50y(P)

7:00 (7:02) (Class 7) (0-50,52) 4-Y-O+ **£1,364** (£403; £201) **Stalls** Low

Form RPR

11 **1** **Sworn Tigress (GER)**[1] 854 5-9-2 **52** 12ex........... MatthewDavies(5) 2 81+
(George Baker) *a gng wl: led wl over 1f out: pushed clr fnl f: easily* **1/2**[1]

4052 **2** *9* **Blackstone Vegas**[6] 813 4-8-11 **50**................................(v) NeilCallan 9 59
(D Shaw) *led 1f: chsd ldr: led wl over 2f out: rdn and hdd wl over 1f out: one pce* **9/1**[3]

-551 **3** *1 1/2* **Broughtons Point**[8] 777 4-8-12 **51** 6ex........................ JamieMackay 1 58
(W J Musson) *hld up in tch: lost pl 7f out: hdwy over 2f out: rdn wl over 1f out: edgd lft ent fnl f: one pce* **9/2**[2]

2/53 **4** *nk* **Trysting Grove (IRE)**[20] 622 9-8-13 **50**.................... PaulFitzsimons 12 56
(E G Bevan) *s.s: hld up and bhd: sme prog over 2f out: c wd st: rdn jst over 1f out: one pce* **16/1**

3055 **5** *hd* **Josiah Bartlett (IRE)**[17] 665 4-8-3 **49**......................... AlexEdwards(7) 8 55
(Ian Williams) *hld up in rr: sme prog wl over 1f out: swtchd rt 1f out: one pce* **22/1**

340 **6** *1* **Mojeerr**[10] 757 4-8-11 **50**.. GrahamGibbons 10 54
(A J McCabe) *hld up towards rr: hdwy on ins wl over 1f out: sn rdn: no further prog* **25/1**

5336 **7** *5* **Mister Frosty (IRE)**[8] 771 4-8-3 **49**........................ CharlotteKerton(7) 11 45
(G Prodromou) *led after 1f: hdd wl over 2f out: wknd wl over 1f out* **25/1**

5604 **8** *2* **Our Kes (IRE)**[17] 661 8-8-13 **50**.. JimmyQuinn 5 43
(P Howling) *hld up in tch: rdn and wknd wl over 1f out* **14/1**

/66- 9 34 **Shouldntbethere (IRE)**[391] 528 6-8-10 **47**.................... JackMitchell 3 —
(Mrs P N Dutfield) *s.i.s: plld hrd: hdwy 8f out: wknd qckly wl over 2f out: t.o* **50/1**

2m 40.24s (-0.86) **Going Correction** +0.05s/f (Slow)
WFA 4 from 5yo+ 2lb **9** Ran SP% **121.4**
Speed ratings (Par 97): **104,98,97,96,96 96,92,91,68**
toteswingers:1&2:£2.30, 1&3:£1.30, 2&3:£2.70 CSF £6.23 CT £13.70 TOTE £1.50: £1.10, £1.90, £1.30; EX 6.50.
Owner Sir Alex Ferguson **Bred** Gestut Wittekindshof **Trained** Moreton Morrell, Warwicks

FOCUS
A useful recruit to all-weather racing annihilated her rivals for the third time in a week and the form looks reasonable.

866 THE HORIZONS RESTAURANT, THE PLACE TO DINE H'CAP 5f 216y(P)
7:30 (7:32) (Class 7) (0-50,50) 4-Y-0+ **£883** (£883; £201) **Stalls** Low

Form RPR

0365 **1** **Metropolitan Chief**[14] 693 6-8-12 **45**.................... RobertHavlin 5 57
(P Burgoyne) *hld up in mid-div: hdwy on ins wl over 1f out: rdn to ld ins fnl f: edgd rt towards fin: jnd post* **11/1**

3250 **1** *dht* **Ride A White Swan**[9] 763 5-9-3 **50**....................(p) NeilCallan 12 62
(D Shaw) *hld up in rr: hdwy wl over 1f out: r.o to force dead heat post* **13/2**

-542 **3** *1 ½* **Royal Acclamation (IRE)**[13] 721 5-8-9 **49**.............(p) DavidKenny(7) 6 56
(H J Evans) *a.p: wnt 2nd 2f out: rdn and kpt on same pce fnl f* **4/1**[1]

60-5 **4** *½* **Imperial Djay (IRE)**[7] 794 5-9-0 **47**.................... JoeFanning 10 53
(Mrs R A Carr) *hld up in mid-div: hdwy 2f out: rdn and nt qckn ins fnl f* **11/2**[3]

/0-0 **5** *1 ¾* **Tune Up The Band**[24] 561 6-9-3 **50**.................... GeorgeBaker 8 50
(R J Hodges) *led: rdn over 1f out: hdd ins fnl f: fdd* **8/1**

0303 **6** *½* **Bertbrand**[13] 726 5-9-2 **49**....................(v) DaneO'Neill 9 47
(I W McInnes) *a.p: rdn and no imp fnl f* **12/1**

0002 **7** *1* **Sonhador**[13] 726 4-9-2 **49**.................... TonyCulhane 2 44
(G Prodromou) *hld up in mid-div: rdn wl over 1f out: no hdwy* **12/1**

60-0 **8** *½* **Commander Wish**[38] 368 7-8-11 **47**....................(p) RussKennemore(3) 3 41
(Lucinda Featherstone) *stmbld sn after s: towards rr whn pushed along over 3f out: c wd st: rdn wl over 1f out: no imp whn hung lft ins fnl f* **16/1**

-034 **9** *1 ¼* **Megalo Maniac**[24] 568 7-8-12 **45**....................(v) PaulHanagan 7 35
(R A Fahey) *s.i.s: rdn wl over 1f out: a bhd* **8/1**

5-00 **10** *6* **Acrosstheuniverse (USA)**[27] 531 4-9-3 **50**...........(b[1]) SteveDrowne 11 20
(J R Gask) *chsd ldr to 2f out: sn wknd* **20/1**

4205 **11** *4* **Jessica Wigmo**[14] 694 7-9-2 **49**.................... LukeMorris 13 7
(A W Carroll) *rdn wl over 1f out: a in rr* **5/1**[2]

/000 **12** *6* **Mister Beano (IRE)**[7] 794 5-8-11 **47**....................(v) JackDean(3) 1 —
(R J Price) *chsd ldrs tl rdn and wknd over 2f out* **66/1**

1m 14.98s (-0.02) **Going Correction** +0.05s/f (Slow) **12** Ran SP% **123.5**
Speed ratings (Par 97): **102,102,100,99,97 96,95,94,92,84 79,71**WIN: Ride A White Swan, £3.20 Metroplitan Chief £6.70 PL: RWS £2.10, MC £3.70, RA £1.70 EX: RWS/MC £51.20, MC/RWS £40.60 CSF: RWS/MC £39.74 MC/RWS £42.13. T/C: RWS/MC/RA £167.65, MC/RWS/RA £175.25. toteswinger: RWS/RA £4.90, RWS/MC £16.90, RA/MC £13.70 TOTE £27: £Owner, £L Tomlin, £Bred, £J A Prescott And C M OakshottTrained Shepton Montague, Somerset.
Owner N Morgan **Bred** Michael John Williamson **Trained** Sproxton, Leics

FOCUS
A dead-heat between a 28-race maiden and a runner who had not won for three years suggests this was not a classic. Metropolitan Chief is rated to his recent best.

867 STAY AT THE WOLVERHAMPTON HOLIDAY INN H'CAP 7f 32y(P)
8:00 (8:00) (Class 5) (0-75,81) 4-Y-0+ **£2,914** (£867; £433; £216) **Stalls** High

Form RPR

053- **1** **Fol Liam**[187] 5676 4-8-2 **64**....................(p) DeclanCannon(5) 3 71
(A J McCabe) *hld up in tch: led 2f out: rdn over 1f out: r.o* **14/1**

/020 **2** *½* **Harare**[10] 753 9-8-1 **63** ow1....................(v) AndrewHeffernan(5) 1 69
(R J Price) *hld up in rr: pushed along over 2f out: c wd st: rdn and r.o wl ins fnl f: nt rch wnr* **11/2**

44-5 **3** *½* **Chief Exec**[14] 696 8-8-11 **73**....................(b) KierenFox(5) 8 78
(J R Gask) *bmpd s: hld up in rr: pushed along over 2f out: c v wd st: hdwy over 1f out: sn hung lft: kpt on ins fnl f* **7/2**[3]

2114 **4** *2 ¼* **Smalljohn**[8] 779 4-9-3 **74**....................(v) TomEaves 5 73
(B Smart) *led: hdd 2f out: rdn over 1f out: one pce* **11/4**[2]

4264 **5** *½* **Peter's Gift (IRE)**[14] 703 4-8-11 **68**.................... NeilCallan 10 66
(K A Ryan) *a.p: rdn wl over 1f out: one pce* **9/1**

4441 **6** *1* **Gallantry**[11] 749 8-9-10 **81** 6ex.................... GeorgeBaker 7 77
(P Howling) *bmpd s: hld up towards rr: hdwy over 2f out: rdn over 1f out: no imp fnl f* **2/1**[1]

030- **7** *3 ½* **Avontuur (FR)**[139] 6984 8-8-6 **68**....................(b) DeanHeslop(5) 6 55
(Mrs R A Carr) *hld up in mid-div: pushed along over 2f out: wknd over 1f out* **22/1**

606- **8** *1 ¼* **Seneschal**[190] 5566 9-8-11 **73**.................... AmyBaker(5) 2 57
(A B Haynes) *chsd ldrs: pushed along over 2f out: rdn and wknd over 1f out* **50/1**

/P-0 **9** *3 ½* **Fifty Cents**[16] 672 6-9-4 **75**.................... SteveDrowne 9 50
(M F Harris) *sn chsng ldr: ev ch over 2f out: wknd wl over 1f out* **22/1**

1m 29.2s (-0.40) **Going Correction** +0.05s/f (Slow) **9** Ran SP% **124.9**
Speed ratings (Par 103): **104,103,102,100,99 98,94,93,89**
toteswingers:1&2:£9.60, 1&3:£9.80, 2&3:£6.00 CSF £93.95 CT £344.30 TOTE £19.00: £3.50, £2.40, £1.70; EX 104.40.
Owner A C Timms **Bred** Adrian Smith **Trained** Averham Park, Notts

FOCUS
A good gallop made this a fair test, but by the time the hold-up horses began to run on it was just too late to catch the winner. The form is ordinary.

868 ENJOY THE PARTY PACK GROUP OFFER H'CAP 1m 1f 103y(P)
8:30 (8:33) (Class 6) (0-65,65) 4-Y-0+ **£2,047** (£604; £302) **Stalls** Low

Form RPR

253/ **1** **Scary Movie (IRE)**[559] 5477 5-9-1 **62**.................... EddieAhern 1 74+
(D J Coakley) *led 1f: a.p: rdn to ld wl over 1f out: r.o* **6/1**[3]

-220 **2** *1 ¼* **Alfie Tupper (IRE)**[54] 202 7-9-2 **63**.................... PatCosgrave 3 70
(J R Boyle) *a.p: chsd wnr fnl f: kpt on* **4/1**[1]

41/ **3** *2 ½* **Blue Eyed Eloise**[705] 1210 8-9-1 **62**.................... JackMitchell 6 64
(B J McMath) *hld up in mid-div: hdwy on ins over 1f out: sn rdn: one pce ins fnl f* **8/1**

00-6 **4** *¾* **Singbella**[17] 665 4-9-2 **63**.................... LukeMorris 4 63
(C G Cox) *a.p: rdn wl over 1f out: one pce* **9/1**

3065 **5** *¾* **Naheell**[8] 770 4-8-13 **60**....................(p) TonyCulhane 7 60
(G Prodromou) *hld up towards rr: hdwy over 1f out: nvr trbld ldrs* **7/1**

024- **6** *nk* **Seventh Hill**[106] 7524 5-8-13 **60**.................... NeilCallan 11 58
(M Blanshard) *hld up in mid-div: pushed along 2f out: rdn over 1f out: no real prog* **10/1**

-340 **7** *nk* **Maximus Aurelius (IRE)**[31] 469 5-9-2 **63**....................(t) ChrisCatlin 12 61
(J Jay) *led after 1f: hdd wl over 1f out: wknd ins fnl f* **10/1**

2-66 **8** *3 ½* **Hector Spectre (IRE)**[56] 162 4-9-2 **63**....................(p) DavidProbert 9 53
(Mrs N S Evans) *hld up in mid-div: pushed along over 2f out: rdn and btn jst over 1f out* **25/1**

34-0 **9** *hd* **Foreign Investment (IRE)**[16] 675 4-8-13 **65**.... AndrewHeffernan(5) 10 55
(P D Evans) *hld up towards rr: stdy prog 6f out: rdn and wknd fnl f* **11/1**

245 **10** *2 ½* **Jan Mayen**[25] 551 4-8-11 **58**.................... JoeFanning 8 43
(M Johnston) *s.i.s: sn hld up in tch: wknd wl over 1f out* **5/1**[2]

4045 **11** *2 ½* **Alf Tupper**[13] 724 7-8-4 **58**.................... LeeTopliss(7) 5 37
(Lee Smyth, Ire) *dwlt: a in rr* **20/1**

300- **12** *¾* **Khun John (IRE)**[117] 6640 7-9-2 **63**.................... StevieDonohoe 13 41
(W J Musson) *a towards rr: pushed along and no ch fnl 3f* **16/1**

2m 2.27s (0.57) **Going Correction** +0.05s/f (Slow) **12** Ran SP% **125.6**
Speed ratings (Par 101): **99,97,95,95,94 94,93,90,90,88 86,85**
toteswingers:1&2:£5.80, 1&3:£9.30, 2&3:£4.40 CSF £32.13 CT £202.77 TOTE £8.10: £2.10, £2.30, £3.00; EX 52.70.
Owner J G Mountford **Bred** Mrs T Brudenell **Trained** West Ilsley, Berks

FOCUS
A run-of-the-mill gallop made it hard to come from behind but the form looks solid enough for the level. The race was notable for the appearances of the similarly-named Alfie Tupper and Alf Tupper, but they finished at opposite ends of the field.
T/Plt: £119.10 to a £1 stake. Pool: £81,822.31. 501.10 winning tickets. T/Qpdt: £23.90 to a £1 stake. Pool: £8,972.87. 277.20 winning tickets. KH

862 WOLVERHAMPTON (A.W) (L-H)
Friday, March 12

OFFICIAL GOING: Standard
Wind: Almost nil Weather: Fine

869 SPONSOR A RACE BY CALLING 01902 390000 H'CAP 5f 20y(P)
5:50 (5:50) (Class 5) (0-70,70) 4-Y-0+ **£2,914** (£867; £433; £216) **Stalls** Low

Form RPR

0-32 **1** **Sir Geoffrey (IRE)**[14] 723 4-8-13 **65**....................(p) FrederikTylicki 6 74
(J A Glover) *mde all: rdn over 1f out: edgd rt ins fnl f: drvn out* **4/1**[1]

1014 **2** *nk* **Steel City Boy (IRE)**[9] 778 7-8-11 **66**.................... MartinLane(3) 3 74
(D Shaw) *bmpd s: hld up in rr: hdwy wl over 1f out: sn rdn: wnt 2nd towards fin: nt rch wnr* **4/1**[1]

11-5 **3** *1 ¼* **Forever's Girl**[22] 601 4-9-1 **67**.................... PJMcDonald 5 70
(G R Oldroyd) *hld up in mid-div: hdwy over 1f out: sn rdn: kpt on ins fnl f* **6/1**[2]

6222 **4** *nk* **Bo McGinty (IRE)**[9] 774 9-8-10 **62**....................(v) PaulHanagan 10 64
(R A Fahey) *a.p: rdn whn carried sltly rt over 1f out: kpt on same pce ins fnl f* **7/1**

0-02 **5** *½* **Trick Or Two**[9] 778 4-8-5 **57**.................... AndrewElliott 4 58
(Mrs R A Carr) *chsd ldrs: rdn over 1f out: swtchd lft ins fnl f: one pce* **6/1**[2]

1052 **6** *hd* **Interchoice Star**[14] 727 5-8-10 **62**....................(p) JerryO'Dwyer 2 62
(R Hollinshead) *bmpd s: hld up in rr: prog on ins over 1f out: rdn and one pce fnl f* **13/2**[3]

-066 **7** *1 ¼* **Bobs Dreamflight**[18] 658 4-8-7 **64** ow1................(b[1]) MarkCoumbe(5) 7 59
(D K Ivory) *chsd ldrs: pushed along over 2f out: c wd st: no hdwy fnl f* **16/1**

0546 **8** *3 ¾* **Sir Loin**[14] 726 9-8-4 **56** oh11....................(v) LukeMorris 8 38
(P Burgoyne) *s.i.s: t.k.h: sn rcvrd: jnd wnr over 3f out: edgd rt over 1f out: wknd ins fnl f* **66/1**

-110 **9** *nk* **Bishopbriggs (USA)**[16] 684 5-8-11 **63**.................... MickyFenton 1 44
(M G Quinlan) *wnt rt s: a in rr* **10/1**

62.18 secs (-0.12) **Going Correction** +0.125s/f (Slow) **9** Ran SP% **110.9**
Speed ratings (Par 103): **105,104,102,102,101 100,98,92,92**
Tote Swingers: 1&2 £15.50, 1&3 £16.10, 2&3 £23.50 CSF £18.21 CT £88.92 TOTE £3.60: £1.70, £1.10, £2.90; EX 24.60.
Owner Dixon, Howlett & The Chrystal Maze Ptn **Bred** P Rabbitte **Trained** Babworth, Notts

FOCUS
The track had been power-harrowed and rolled back, but the going was still officially standard. A modest sprint. The first two were closely matched on previous C/D form.

870 GREAT OFFERS AT WOLVERHAMPTON-RACECOURSE.CO.UK H'CAP 5f 216y(P)
6:20 (6:21) (Class 6) (0-55,55) 3-Y-0 **£2,047** (£604; £302) **Stalls** Low

Form RPR

00-4 **1** **Sweet Mirasol (IRE)**[14] 728 3-8-8 **48**....................(t) JimmyQuinn 4 54
(Miss M E Rowland) *hld up in tch: wnt 2nd 2f out: led jst over 1f out: drvn out* **20/1**

64-0 **2** *1 ½* **Nabrina (IRE)**[60] 127 3-8-4 **51** ow1.................... JohnCavanagh(7) 9 52
(M Brittain) *led: rdn and hdd jst over 1f out: kpt on same pce* **10/1**

2262 **3** *nk* **Turf Time**[12] 745 3-9-0 **54**.................... ChrisCatlin 10 54
(J A Glover) *a.p: rdn over 1f out: kpt on one pce fnl f* **5/2**[2]

05-0 **4** *nk* **Drubinca**[15] 698 3-8-10 **53**....................(v[1]) WilliamCarson(3) 5 52
(S C Williams) *hld up and bhd: rdn over 2f out: c wd st: hung rt to stands' rail fr wl over 1f out: r.o ins fnl f: nrst fin* **2/1**[1]

3-06 **5** *2 ¼* **Moonlight Serenade**[42] 346 3-8-11 **54**....................(p) JackDean(3) 6 46
(W G M Turner) *hld up in tch: pushed along 3f out: rdn over 1f out: one pce* **12/1**

0-50 **6** *3* **Ba Jetstream**[23] 581 3-8-6 **46** oh1.................... JoeFanning 2 28
(F Jordan) *bhd: pushed along whn sltly hmpd jst over 2f out: rdn jst over 1f out: n.d* **20/1**

00-5 **7** *shd* **Yeah**[16] 689 3-8-13 **53**.................... StephenCraine 1 35
(Patrick Morris) *hld up in tch on ins: nt clr run jst over 2f out tl wl over 1f out: btn whn rdn jst over 1f out* **6/1**[3]

5600 **8** *4 ½* **Scintillating (IRE)**[27] 542 3-8-6 **46** oh1....................(v[1]) DuranFentiman 7 14
(R Hollinshead) *s.i.s: outpcd* **33/1**

-503 **9** *4* **Miss Polly Plum**[8] 788 3-8-3 **46** oh1.................... KellyHarrison(3) 3 1
(C A Dwyer) *w ldr tl pushed along over 2f out: wknd wl over 1f out* **8/1**

1m 15.96s (0.96) **Going Correction** +0.125s/f (Slow) **9** Ran SP% **116.5**
Speed ratings (Par 96): **98,96,95,95,92 88,88,82,76**
Tote Swingers: 1&2 £32.90, 1&3 £10.60, 2&3 £6.00 CSF £200.96 CT £686.11 TOTE £23.20: £4.00, £3.10, £1.20; EX 325.00.
Owner Miss M E Rowland **Bred** Paul Kavanagh **Trained** Lower Blidworth, Notts

FOCUS
A poor handicap, only livened by a big gamble on Drubinca. It was well run but this is not form to be too positive about.

The Form Book, Raceform Ltd, Compton, RG20 6NL

Drubinca Official explanation: jockey said gelding hung right

871 HOTEL & CONFERENCING AT WOLVERHAMPTON H'CAP 1m 4f 50y(P)
6:50 (6:50) (Class 4) (0-85,82) 4-Y-0+ **£4,533** (£1,348; £674; £336) **Stalls** Low

Form				RPR
0414	1		**Bavarica**[11] 752 8-8-4 73 AdamBeschizza(7) 5 (Miss J Feilden) *hld up in tch: rdn wl over 1f out: r.o u.p to ld post* **20/1**	78
2111	2	nse	**Clear Sailing**[44] 314 7-9-2 78 StevieDonohoe 6 (P Leech) *a.p: led wl over 1f out: rdn fnl f: hdd post* **9/1**	83
124-	3	nk	**Demolition**[154] 6644 6-9-6 82 PaulHanagan 1 (R A Fahey) *led: rdn and hdd wl over 1f out: ev ch fnl f: r.o* **5/2**[2]	86
26-3	4	1 1/4	**Hallstatt (IRE)**[23] 586 4-8-9 73 GrahamGibbons 2 (J Mackie) *hld up: rdn and hdwy on ins over 2f out: kpt on same pce fnl f* **14/1**	75
/2-4	5	shd	**Gremlin**[11] 756 6-8-6 68 oh1 DavidProbert 3 (D Burchell) *hld up: pushed along over 2f out: rdn over 1f out: styd on towards fin* **6/1**[3]	70
125	6	5	**Kames Park (IRE)**[11] 756 8-8-10 72 JimmyQuinn 4 (R C Guest) *dwlt: hld up in rr: nt clr run on ins wl over 3f out: short-lived effrt on ins wl over 1f out* **8/1**	66
1162	7	10	**Gargano (IRE)**[20] 636 5-8-12 74 JoeFanning 7 (M Johnston) *chsd ldr tl pushed along over 2f out: sn wknd* **7/4**[1]	52

2m 40.94s (-0.16) **Going Correction** +0.125s/f (Slow)
WFA 4 from 5yo+ 2lb 7 Ran SP% **111.8**
Speed ratings (Par 105): **105,104,104,103,103 100,93**
Tote Swingers: 1&2 £9.60, 1&3 £14.10, 2&3 £3.90 CSF £172.03 TOTE £23.80: £7.20, £2.00; EX 163.80.
Owner Miss J Feilden **Bred** Juddmonte Farms **Trained** Exning, Suffolk
■ Adam Beschizza's first winner.

FOCUS
A fairly competitive little handicap, and it was won by the rank outsider. The pace was steady and they finished in something of a bunch, so it's hard to view the form positively.
Gargano(IRE) Official explanation: jockey said, regarding running, that the gelding found nothing in home straight

872 THE BLACK COUNTRY'S ONLY RACECOURSE MEDIAN AUCTION MAIDEN STKS 1m 4f 50y(P)
7:20 (7:21) (Class 6) 3-5-Y-O **£1,774** (£523; £262) **Stalls** Low

Form				RPR
5	1		**Parhelion**[7] 803 3-8-5 0 JoeFanning 11 (M Johnston) *a.p: led over 2f out: rdn wl over 1f out: edgd rt ins fnl f: r.o* **2/1**[2]	67+
-006	2	1 1/4	**Port Hill**[9] 775 3-8-5 48 LukeMorris 10 (W M Brisbourne) *hld up in rr: rdn over 2f out: c wd st: hdwy over 1f out: r.o to take 2nd wl ins fnl f: nt trble wnr* **50/1**	65
0	3	2	**Boa**[25] 563 5-9-9 0 GrahamGibbons 4 (R Hollinshead) *hld up in tch: chsd wnr 2f out: rdn over 1f out: no ex and lost 2nd wl ins fnl f* **16/1**	60
0-54	4	3 1/2	**Sacco D'Oro**[14] 718 4-9-7 56 TomEaves 9 (M Mullineaux) *s.i.s: hld up and bhd: nt clr run over 2f out: hdwy wl over 1f out: sn rdn: wknd ins fnl f* **16/1**	54
06	5	3 3/4	**Zafeen's Pearl**[16] 677 3-8-0 0 AdrianMcCarthy 5 (D K Ivory) *hung rt: racd wd: hld up in mid-div: rdn and hdwy over 3f out: ev ch over 2f out: wknd over 1f out* **33/1**	45
65	6	3 1/4	**Gems**[11] 755 3-8-0 0 JimmyQuinn 7 (H J L Dunlop) *hld up towards rr: pushed along and hdwy over 3f out: rdn over 2f out: wknd over 1f out* **9/1**[3]	40
	7	9	**Demo Jo** 4-9-7 0 StephenCraine 8 (M Wigham) *led: hdd over 2f out: wknd qckly wl over 1f out* **28/1**	28
000-	8	25	**The Coach**[105] 7557 4-9-5 42 JoshWall(7) 1 (T Wall) *a in rr: t.o fnl 2f* **125/1**	—
3034	9	3 1/2	**Sternian**[9] 776 3-8-0 50 NickyMackay 2 (M E Rimmer) *hld up in tch on ins: wknd over 3f out: t.o* **14/1**	—
-324	10	7	**Brave Talk**[16] 677 3-8-5 0 DavidProbert 6 (S Kirk) *w ldr tl pushed along over 3f out: rdn and wknd qckly wl over 2f out: t.o* **11/10**[1]	—

2m 42.83s (1.73) **Going Correction** +0.125s/f (Slow)
WFA 3 from 4yo 23lb 4 from 5yo 2lb 10 Ran SP% **118.5**
Speed ratings (Par 101): **99,98,96,94,92 89,83,67,64,60**
Tote Swingers: 1&2 £11.80, 1&3 £6.30, 2&3 £14.10 CSF £109.71 TOTE £3.40: £1.40, £6.70, £3.80; EX 159.10.
Owner Sheikh Hamdan Bin Mohammed Al Maktoum **Bred** Sheikh Abdulla Bin Isa Al-Khalifa **Trained** Middleham Moor, N Yorks

FOCUS
A modest maiden run in a time 1.89sec slower than the preceding handicap. The form is hard to pin down and does not look too solid.
Zafeen's Pearl Official explanation: jockey said filly hung right
Brave Talk Official explanation: jockey said gelding failed to travel from halfway

873 WOLVERHAMPTON-RACECOURSE.CO.UK H'CAP 1m 141y(P)
7:50 (7:51) (Class 4) (0-80,80) 4-Y-0+ **£4,533** (£1,348; £674; £336) **Stalls** Low

Form				RPR
01-0	1		**Cheers For Thea (IRE)**[14] 715 5-8-7 69 (bt) DuranFentiman 9 (T D Easterby) *hld up in mid-div: c wd st: hdwy over 1f out: sn rdn: r.o to ld nr fin* **16/1**	79
201-	2	1/2	**Mosqueras Romance**[240] 3981 4-9-1 80 AndreaAtzeni(3) 4 (M Botti) *led: hdd 6f out: chsd ldr: led over 1f out: rdn wl ins fnl f: hdd nr fin* **10/3**[1]	88
60-4	3	shd	**Kidlat**[3] 837 5-8-10 72 JoeFanning 1 (A Bailey) *a.p: pushed along over 2f out: rdn and r.o ins fnl f* **7/2**[2]	80
6500	4	1/2	**Justcallmehandsome**[8] 790 8-8-2 67 (v) KellyHarrison(3) 10 (D J S Ffrench Davis) *prom: led 6f out tl over 1f out: sn rdn: kpt on same pce* **14/1**	74
16/	5	2 1/4	**Coral Creek (IRE)**[119] 7380 6-8-9 78 JohnFahy(7) 6 (M J Grassick, Ire) *hld up towards rr: hdwy over 1f out: rdn and one pce fnl f* **33/1**	80
-232	6	1/2	**Seldom (IRE)**[27] 543 4-8-4 66 JimmyQuinn 11 (M Brittain) *hld up in mid-div: hdwy 2f out: rdn over 1f out: one pce* **9/1**[3]	67
0-55	7	1	**Ramona Chase**[9] 765 5-9-3 79 (t) GeorgeBaker 7 (M J Attwater) *stdd s: hld up in rr: sme late prog ins fnl f: n.d* **18/1**	77
1114	8	1/2	**Well Of Echoes**[7] 816 4-7-13 63 6ex (tp) DeclanCannon(5) 3 (A J McCabe) *hld up in rr: pushed along 3f out: nvr nr ldrs* **11/1**	63
-536	9	1 1/4	**My Best Bet**[13] 740 4-9-4 80 MickyFenton 5 (Stef Higgins) *hld up in mid-div: pushed along over 3f out: rdn and wknd ins fnl f* **11/1**	74
2-02	10	4 1/2	**Johnmanderville**[9] 779 4-8-10 75 MartinLane(3) 8 (N Wilson) *prom: rdn wl over 1f out: eased whn btn jst ins fnl f* **10/3**[1]	65

1m 50.39s (-0.11) **Going Correction** +0.125s/f (Slow) 10 Ran SP% **115.8**
Speed ratings (Par 105): **105,104,104,104,102 101,100,100,99,95**
Tote Swingers: 1&2 £14.40, 1&3 £22.50, 2&3 £6.80 CSF £68.47 CT £239.96 TOTE £18.40: £5.40, £2.00, £1.10; EX 88.10.
Owner Ron George **Bred** Crone Stud Farms Ltd **Trained** Great Habton, N Yorks

FOCUS
A fairly competitive handicap, and another steadily run race with a bunch finish. A personal best from the winner with the next four close to their marks.
Justcallmehandsome Official explanation: jockey said gelding faded rapidly in the final furlong
Ramona Chase Official explanation: jockey said gelding was denied a clear run

874 NAME A RACE TO ENHANCE YOUR BRAND H'CAP 2m 119y(P)
8:20 (8:22) (Class 5) (0-70,70) 4-Y-0+ **£2,914** (£867; £433; £216) **Stalls** Low

Form				RPR
0-06	1		**Bold Adventure**[23] 584 6-8-9 51 oh1 TonyCulhane 6 (W J Musson) *hld up in mid-div: smooth prog 3f out: led 1f out: edgd rt: pushed out* **2/1**[1]	62+
3-52	2	2 1/4	**Smarties Party**[9] 777 7-9-2 58 PJMcDonald 11 (C W Thornton) *hld up towards rr: smooth hdwy over 2f out: rdn and chsd wnr ins fnl f: no imp* **7/1**[3]	66
-555	3	1 3/4	**Estate**[28] 529 8-9-7 63 JamesDoyle 7 (D E Pipe) *hld up in mid-div: hdwy over 4f out: led wl over 2f out: rdn whn edgd rt and hdd 1f out: no ex* **16/1**	69
/2-0	4	5	**Bugsy's Boy**[17] 500 6-9-9 70 (p) MatthewDavies(5) 8 (George Baker) *sn led: hdd after 2f: chsd ldr: ev ch 3f out: rdn over 1f out: wknd fnl f* **7/2**[2]	70
3-	5	2	**Torina (IRE)**[90] 7732 5-9-1 57 EddieAhern 4 (M J Grassick, Ire) *led early: prom: rdn jst over 3f out: wknd wl over 1f out* **7/2**[2]	55
/223	6	3/4	**Poppy Gregg**[12] 748 5-8-2 51 oh3 (v) MatthewCosham(7) 2 (Dr J R J Naylor) *hld up towards rr: rdn 3f out: nvr nr ldrs* **10/1**	48
500-	7	6	**Tabaran (FR)**[16] 2429 7-8-12 54 (tp) ChrisCatlin 3 (Mrs A M Thorpe) *hld up in tch: wknd wl over 2f out* **18/1**	44
41-4	8	7	**M'Lady Rousseur (IRE)**[43] 322 4-8-12 59 DaneO'Neill 10 (C C Bealby) *led after 2f tl wl over 2f out: sn wknd* **9/1**	40
600-	9	5	**Transfered (IRE)**[105] 7557 4-8-4 51 oh5 (p) AndrewElliott 5 (Lucinda Featherstone) *unruly and tried to unseat rdr sn after s: a in rr* **50/1**	26

3m 43.18s (1.38) **Going Correction** +0.125s/f (Slow)
WFA 4 from 5yo+ 5lb 9 Ran SP% **122.5**
Speed ratings (Par 103): **101,99,99,96,95 95,92,89,87**
Tote Swingers: 1&2 £6.10, 1&3 £10.40, 2&3 £6.50 CSF £18.30 CT £185.71 TOTE £3.80: £1.70, £2.20, £3.90; EX 26.50.
Owner W J Musson **Bred** Bricklow Ltd **Trained** Newmarket, Suffolk

FOCUS
With no obvious front-runner, there was a danger this would be a tactical affair but M'lady Rousseur was sent to the front for a change and set a sound gallop. The winner had slipped to a good mark.
Torina(IRE) Official explanation: jockey said mare hung left

875 STAY AT THE WOLVERHAMPTON HOLIDAY INN H'CAP 1m 4f 50y(P)
8:50 (8:50) (Class 6) (0-65,70) 4-Y-0+ **£2,047** (£604; £302) **Stalls** Low

Form				RPR
0-	1		**Lady Mickataine (USA)**[91] 7719 4-8-9 55 EddieAhern 6 (M J Grassick, Ire) *chsd ldr tl over 5f out: led jst over 2f out tl wl over 1f out: sn rdn: led ins fnl f: r.o* **11/2**	62
3-21	2	1	**Amical Risks (FR)**[7] 813 6-8-9 53 GregFairley 7 (Joss Saville) *s.i.s: hld up and bhd: hdwy 6f out: led wl over 1f out: sn rdn: hdd ins fnl f: nt qckn* **6/4**[1]	58
0404	3	1 1/2	**Mullitovermaurice**[7] 814 4-8-10 56 (p) PaulHanagan 8 (J G Given) *hld up in tch: lost pl 7f out: hdwy over 2f out: rdn wl over 1f out: one pce ins fnl f* **9/2**[3]	59
6-30	4	2 1/4	**Wee Ziggy**[9] 777 7-9-2 60 TomEaves 9 (M Mullineaux) *hld up: hdwy 7f out: led over 4f out: hdd jst over 2f out: rdn over 1f out: wknd ins fnl f* **25/1**	59
6-00	5	hd	**Hammer**[7] 813 5-8-11 55 (tp) ChrisCatlin 4 (Mrs A M Thorpe) *hld up in tch: pushed along over 2f out: rdn and one pce fnl f* **10/3**[2]	54
620-	6	3 3/4	**Sparkaway**[130] 7214 4-8-10 56 StevieDonohoe 5 (W J Musson) *hld up and bhd: rdn over 2f out: no rspnse* **10/1**	49
600-	7	2	**Sweet Request**[38] 3798 6-7-13 50 oh4 (v[1]) MatthewCosham(7) 1 (Dr J R J Naylor) *led: hdd over 4f out: rdn and wknd 2f out* **33/1**	40

2m 46.37s (5.27) **Going Correction** +0.125s/f (Slow)
WFA 4 from 5yo+ 2lb 7 Ran SP% **112.5**
Speed ratings (Par 101): **87,86,85,83,83 81,79**
Tote Swingers: 1&2 £3.20, 1&3 £5.30, 2&3 £2.80 CSF £13.74 CT £39.18 TOTE £6.70: £2.50, £1.50; EX 19.60 Place 6: £1294.67 Place 5: £823.56.
Owner Michael O'Flynn **Bred** Robert J Sullivan Et Al **Trained** Pollardstown, Co Kildare

FOCUS
A moderate affair run in a poor time. The top two in the weights (9-8 and 9-6) were non-runners. Muddling form.
T/Plt: £198.50 to a £1 stake. Pool: £101,508.57. 373.17 winning tickets. T/Qpdt: £81.00 to a £1 stake. Pool: £8,952.46. 81.70 winning tickets. KH

876 - 882a (Foreign Racing) - See Raceform Interactive

869 WOLVERHAMPTON (A.W) (L-H)
Saturday, March 13

OFFICIAL GOING: Standard
Wind: Fresh across Weather: Overcast

883 WILLIAMHILL.COM LADY WULFRUNA STKS (LISTED RACE) 7f 32y(P)
2:15 (2:17) (Class 1) 4-Y-0+
£22,708 (£8,608; £4,308; £2,148; £1,076; £540) **Stalls** High

Form				RPR
-006	1		**Dunelight (IRE)**[8] 823 7-9-3 105 (v) RyanMoore 7 (C G Cox) *chsd ldr tl led over 1f out: sn rdn: r.o* **5/1**	110
212-	2	nk	**Mia's Boy**[126] 7294 6-9-3 106 EddieAhern 1 (C A Dwyer) *hld up in tch: ev ch ent fnl f: sn rdn: r.o* **11/4**[1]	109
0550	3	3/4	**Lovelace**[16] 710 6-9-3 0 JoeFanning 10 (M Johnston) *chsd ldrs: rdn and ev ch fr over 1f out: r.o* **10/1**	107

300- **4** ½ **Redford (IRE)**[168] 6270 5-9-3 101 .... JamieSpencer 2 106+
(K A Ryan) *hld up: hmpd bnd 6f out: disputing last and plenty to do over 2f out: hdwy over 1f out: rdn and r.o: nt rch ldrs* **7/2**[2]

5435 **5** 9 **Carcinetto (IRE)**[9] 790 8-8-12 90 .... PatCosgrave 4 77
(P D Evans) *hld up: hmpd bnd 6f out: styd on ins fnl f: nvr nrr* **33/1**

30-4 **6** hd **Appalachian Trail (IRE)**[2] 862 9-9-3 92 ....(b) TomEaves 9 81
(N Wilson) *hld up: last 3f out: rdn over 1f out: n.d* **50/1**

0000 **7** ¾ **Ocean's Minstrel**[8] 823 4-9-6 0 .... JerryO'Dwyer 3 82
(J Ryan) *chsd ldrs: rdn over 3f out: wknd over 1f out* **20/1**

13/3 **8** 2 **Souter's Sister (IRE)**[28] 537 4-8-12 104 .... JimmyFortune 11 69
(M Botti) *mid-div: rdn over 2f out: sn wknd* **12/1**

0-11 **9** hd **Mahadee (IRE)**[14] 739 5-9-3 106 ....(b) NeilCallan 8 73
(C E Brittain) *mid-div: hdwy 1/2-way: rdn over 2f out: wknd wl over 1f out* **9/2**[3]

00-5 **10** 1½ **Abbondanza (IRE)**[14] 740 7-9-3 108 ....(p) PaulMulrennan 6 69
(N Wilson) *led: clr over 5f out: rdn over 2f out: hdd & wknd over 1f out* **18/1**

0-00 **11** 12 **Capricorn Run (USA)**[23] 606 7-9-3 98 ....(v) SebSanders 5 37
(A J McCabe) *sn drvn along in rr: wknd over 2f out* **50/1**

1m 27.8s (-1.80) **Going Correction** +0.05s/f (Slow) 11 Ran SP% **117.4**
Speed ratings (Par 111): **112,111,110,110,99 99,98,96,96,94 80**
toteswingers: 1&2 £2.70, 1&3 £9.60, 2&3 £11.00 CSF £18.49 TOTE £6.10: £1.80, £1.80, £3.20; EX 22.00 Trifecta £226.40 Pool: £443.65 - 1.45 winning units..
Owner Mr And Mrs P Hargreaves **Bred** D And B Egan **Trained** Lambourn, Berks

FOCUS
A decent Listed race run at a strong pace, with Appalachian Trail going off much too fast. Interestingly, two of the first three finishers had recently returned from Dubai. Ordinary form for the grade.

NOTEBOOK
Dunelight(IRE) had been comfortably held in good company at Meydan recently, including eight days ago, but he's clearly well forward following his spell in the sun and benefited from the drop in grade. He was sensibly ridden, being restrained in second early on rather take on the leader, and he stayed on well in the straight to record his first victory over this distance. He's not in the Lincoln. (tchd 11-2)
Mia's Boy ◆, returning from more than four months off, ran a fine Lincoln trial, splitting a couple of race-fit rivals who were fresh from Dubai. It will be a big ask to defy a mark of 106 at Doncaster but he was a close second in a big-field handicap off just a 1lb lower rating when last seen in 2009 and won't be top weight if Expresso Star lines up (which is said to be the plan). He was trimmed by most firms, but 16-1 is still available. (op 3-1)
Lovelace was disappointing in Dubai but this was better. He had every chance but was just held. (op 17-2)
Redford(IRE), bought out of Michael Bell's yard for 130,000gns since he was last seen, apparently worked well at Southwell five days earler although, according to Jamie Spencer, he has always been a good worker. Returning from 168 days off, he was left with too much to do after starting slowly and then soon being squeezed for room, allowing the front three to get a start on him. He did pick up well to finish clear of the remainder, and this was a promising start for his new connections but, considering his overall profile, it might be unwise to get carried away. (op 5-1)
Carcinetto(IRE) had plenty to find and was well held after meeting a bit of trouble early on. (tchd 40-1)
Appalachian Trail(IRE) ran better than when beaten in a claimer two days earlier but still made no impression.
Mahadee(IRE) got up on the line to dead-heat over this trip last time, but he's better suited by further and weakened after getting outpaced around the turn into the straight. (op 5-1)

884 WILLIAMHILL.COM - POKER H'CAP 7f 32y(P)
2:50 (2:51) (Class 4) (0-85,84) 3-Y-O **£4,209** (£1,252; £625; £312) **Stalls High**

Form RPR

0-1 **1** **Edinburgh Knight (IRE)**[24] 583 3-9-0 77 .... TonyCulhane 5 93+
(P W D'Arcy) *hld up: smooth hdwy on outer over 2f out: led over 1f out: shkn up and r.o wl* **8/13**[1]

-132 **2** 2¾ **Tiradito (USA)**[17] 681 3-9-1 78 ....(p) MartinDwyer 1 82
(M Botti) *chsd ldrs: led briefly wl over 1f out: outpcd ins fnl f* **20/1**

1 **3** 1¼ **Slikback Jack (IRE)**[29] 527 3-8-9 72 .... FrederikTylicki 6 73+
(J A Glover) *fly-leapt and nrly uns rdr s: hld up: plld hrd: hdwy over 1f out: r.o* **22/1**

531- **4** 2¼ **Kumbeshwar**[130] 7218 3-9-5 82 .... RyanMoore 10 77
(P D Evans) *chsd ldrs: outpcd over 2f out: rallied fnl f: r.o* **33/1**

1 **5** ½ **Solstice**[34] 453 3-8-12 78 .... BarryMcHugh(3) 7 71
(Julie Camacho) *s.i.s: hdwy 6f out: rdn and ev ch over 1f out: no ex ins fnl f* **16/1**

001- **6** nk **Amenable (IRE)**[165] 6356 3-9-0 77 .... AndrewMullen 9 69
(D Nicholls) *sn led: hdd over 4f out: led again wl over 1f out: sn hdd: no ex fnl f* **40/1**

1 **7** 1 **Burghley**[61] 128 3-9-6 83 .... HayleyTurner 2 73
(M L W Bell) *hld up: hdwy over 2f out: shkn up and swtchd rt over 1f out: swtchd lft ins fnl f: nt trble ldrs* **4/1**[2]

533 **8** 1 **Transfixed (IRE)**[10] 772 3-8-13 76 .... JimmyFortune 4 63
(P D Evans) *chsd ldr tl led over 4f out: rdn and hdd wl over 1f out: wknd and eased fnl f* **33/1**

10-1 **9** shd **Niran (IRE)**[17] 681 3-9-7 84 .... SebSanders 3 71
(C E Brittain) *mid-div: rdn over 2f out: wknd over 1f out* **9/1**[3]

30-3 **10** 1½ **Gertmegalush (IRE)**[23] 596 3-9-5 82 ....(b) TomQueally 11 65
(J D Bethell) *s.i.s: hld up: rdn 1/2-way: a in rr* **33/1**

346- **11** 13 **Electric City (IRE)**[183] 5841 3-8-9 72 ow2 .... JerryO'Dwyer 8 20
(M G Quinlan) *rdn over 3f out: a in rr: bhd fnl 3f* **100/1**

1m 29.19s (-0.41) **Going Correction** +0.05s/f (Slow) 11 Ran SP% **119.2**
Speed ratings (Par 100): **104,100,99,96,96 95,94,93,93,91 76**
CSF £20.82 CT £169.38 TOTE £1.50: £1.10, £4.60, £3.80; EX 17.80 Trifecta £228.90 Pool: £417.74 - 1.35 winning units..
Owner Knights Racing **Bred** New England Stud Myriad Norelands **Trained** Newmarket, Suffolk

FOCUS
This looked a good, competitive three-year-old handicap beforehand but the winner was a class apart and looked a fair bit better than the bare form. The pace was strong, with Amenable and Transfixed taking each other on, and those two had little hope of seeing the race out.

885 WILLIAMHILL.COM LINCOLN TRIAL H'CAP 1m 141y(P)
3:25 (3:26) (Class 2) (0-105,100) 4-Y-O+
£31,155 (£9,330; £4,665; £2,335; £1,165; £585) **Stalls Low**

Form RPR

405- **1** **Vitznau (IRE)**[152] 6732 6-9-2 93 .... RichardHughes 9 104
(R Hannon) *hld up: hdwy over 2f out: rdn to ld wl ins fnl f: readily* **9/1**

203- **2** ¾ **Fanunalter**[120] 7375 4-9-3 94 .... RyanMoore 3 103
(M Botti) *hld up: hdwy to ld 1f out: sn rdn and hung rt: hdd wl ins fnl f* **5/2**[1]

423- **3** nk **Albaqaa**[245] 3873 5-9-4 95 .... PaulHanagan 7 103
(R A Fahey) *a.p: racd keenly: rdn over 2f out: r.o* **12/1**

001- **4** 1¼ **Extraterrestrial**[175] 6094 6-9-2 100 .... LeeTopliss(7) 13 105
(R A Fahey) *hld up: hdwy over 1f out: swtchd lft ins fnl f: r.o* **33/1**

66 **5** nk **Noble Citizen (USA)**[36] 438 5-9-3 94 ....(be) HayleyTurner 10 99
(D M Simcock) *led at stdy pce: qcknd over 2f out: rdn: drifted rt and hdd 1f out: styd on* **33/1**

1320 **6** ¾ **Autumn Blades (IRE)**[21] 635 5-9-5 96 .... DavidProbert 12 99
(A Bailey) *hld up: hdwy over 2f out: rdn over 1f out: nt clr run and rdr dropped reins ins fnl f: kpt on* **18/1**

2-52 **7** 1½ **Tartan Gigha (IRE)**[37] 415 5-9-6 97 .... JoeFanning 6 97
(M Johnston) *sn trcking ldr: racd keenly: rdn over 2f out: edgd rt and no ex ins fnl f* **13/2**[3]

13-4 **8** 1 **Spinning**[27] 553 7-9-4 95 ....(b) JimmyFortune 11 92
(T D Barron) *dwlt: hld up: rdn over 1f out: styd on ins fnl f: nvr nrr* **10/1**

6136 **9** shd **Full Toss**[28] 536 4-9-0 94 .... MartinLane(3) 5 91
(P D Evans) *chsd ldrs: rdn over 2f out: wknd ins fnl f* **20/1**

00-1 **10** shd **Flipando (IRE)**[29] 528 9-9-6 97 .... JamieSpencer 2 94
(T D Barron) *trckd ldrs: rdn over 2f out: wknd over 1f out* **11/4**[2]

15-2 **11** ¾ **Black Dahlia**[27] 553 5-9-3 94 .... FrederikTylicki 8 89
(J A Glover) *prom: rdn over 2f out: wknd fnl f* **10/1**

1m 50.07s (-0.43) **Going Correction** +0.05s/f (Slow) 11 Ran SP% **120.4**
Speed ratings (Par 109): **103,102,102,100,100 100,98,97,97,97 96**
toteswingers: 1&2 £8.30, 1&3 £14.60, 2&3 £6.10 CSF £31.89 CT £283.71 TOTE £12.70: £3.00, £1.40, £3.80; EX 49.50 Trifecta £578.20 Part won. Pool: £781.40 - 0.20 winning units..
Owner Louis Stalder **Bred** John McLoughlin **Trained** East Everleigh, Wilts

FOCUS
Last season Flipando became the first winner of this race in seven years to contest the Lincoln, finishing third, although Very Wise was pulled up in the 2007 running before taking the main event. Looking further back, 2001 Lincoln winner Nimello had landed the consolation trial, while the 2000 victor John Ferneley was third in this contest. This year's race looked really competitive and the form is likely to be well represented at Doncaster later this month despite the modest pace. The form is taken at face value.

NOTEBOOK
Vitznau(IRE) hadn't won since April 2008, but he was clearly well handicapped considering he was runner-up in the 7f Listed race on this card last year, and he returned to form after five months off. This was his first success over a trip this far and he looked to have something to spare near the line although it's possible the runner-up was idling. The plan now is to aim him at the Lincoln and he will still look reasonably treated on his best form under a 5lb penalty seeing he was once rated 104. While this win may boost his confidence and the likely strong pace as well as the big field should suit, it's worth noting his top six RPRs prior to this success were gained around a bend, and he is yet to win on a straight course. Plus, he was only tenth in the race in 2008 off a mark of 97. (op 12-1)
Fanunalter, gelded since his last run, was well ridden in defeat, saving ground towards the inside turning into the straight, and he looked the winner when taking over around a furlong out but his finishing effort was disappointing. That may sound harsh considering this was such a competitive handicap, and it may well be that he simply got tired on this first run for four months, but the suspicion is he did not help his rider once in front - his ears were pricked and he seemed to idle. He's obviously entitled to come on for this and he has the potential to be pretty good (contested last year's Italian Derby), but it's possible he is a difficult ride who needs to be saved as late as possible. He is not in the Lincoln. (op 7-2)
Albaqaa, returning from eight months off, was well placed considering the way the race unfolded, although he raced a bit keenly, and duly posted a decent effort. He's entitled to come on for this and should go well in the Lincoln. (op 10-1 tchd 9-1)
Extraterrestrial, seventh in this last year off a mark of 92, had to run off 100 this time after being raised 5lb for winning at Ayr last September, although he had a decent claimer taking weight off. This was a pleasing return considering he was left with a lot to do after being dropped in from the widest stall, and had to wait for a run around the turn into the straight. Like his stable companion in third he should run a good race in the Lincoln, with this outing likely to put him spot on.
Noble Citizen(USA), back from a brief spell in Dubai, was yet to win over a trip this far and didn't see the race out after racing keenly in the lead.
Autumn Blades(IRE) plugged on, despite his rider briefly dropping his reins late on, but was never dangerous. (tchd 16-1 and 20-1)
Tartan Gigha(IRE), who was off the same mark as when runner-up to improving subsequent winner Mr Brock in Dubai at the beginning of February, was a shade disappointing. (op 6-1 tchd 7-1)
Spinning was beaten a long way out but kept on near the finish. (tchd 11-1)
Flipando(IRE)'s success in this last year came off a mark of 93, but he was off 97 this time following a 10lb rise for an impressive reappearance win over 6f. The lack of pace did not help and he failed to pick up after taking a grip. Perhaps he's worth another try over a sprint trip. (op 9-2 tchd 5-1 in places)

886 WILLIAMHILL.COM - CASINO CLAIMING STKS 5f 20y(P)
4:00 (4:00) (Class 5) 3-Y-O **£2,590** (£770; £385; £192) **Stalls Low**

Form RPR

0320 **1** **Blue Neptune**[19] 662 3-8-7 64 .... MartinDwyer 5 64
(W R Muir) *mde all: hrd rdn ins fnl f: all out* **8/1**

-314 **2** nk **Il Forno**[16] 702 3-8-12 69 .... JamieSpencer 4 68
(D Nicholls) *sn chsng wnr: rdn 2f out: r.o* **2/1**[1]

1-16 **3** hd **Magenta Strait**[40] 370 3-8-4 62 .... DavidProbert 7 59+
(R Hollinshead) *hld up: hdwy over 1f out: r.o ins fnl f: edgd lft nr fin* **6/1**

10-3 **4** hd **Clear Ice (IRE)**[70] 17 3-8-8 72 ....(b¹) AndrewMullen 2 62
(D Nicholls) *chsd ldrs: rdn 1/2-way: r.o* **9/2**[3]

-432 **5** 1¼ **Micky's Knock Off (IRE)**[9] 788 3-8-10 66 ....(e) JimmyQuinn 3 60
(R C Guest) *prom: rdn 1/2-way: styng on same pce whn n.m.r towards fin* **3/1**[2]

006- **6** 6 **Crystal Glass**[116] 7420 3-8-9 33 .... BarryMcHugh(3) 8 40
(T D Easterby) *sn outpcd: nvr nrr* **33/1**

5 **7** ½ **Bird Call (IRE)**[16] 699 3-8-7 0 .... GrahamGibbons 6 34
(T D Barron) *chsd ldrs: rdn and hung rt 1/2-way: sn wknd* **16/1**

6 **8** 11 **Shawkantango**[12] 751 3-8-11 0 .... MartinLane(3) 1 1
(D Shaw) *s.s: outpcd* **100/1**

62.73 secs (0.43) **Going Correction** +0.05s/f (Slow) 8 Ran SP% **111.7**
Speed ratings (Par 98): **98,97,97,96,94 85,84,66**
toteswingers: 1&2 £3.40, 1&3 £4.80, 2&3 £3.20 CSF £23.29 TOTE £9.70: £2.30, £1.30, £2.10; EX 36.10 Trifecta £106.00 Pool: £613.09 - 4.28 winning units..Blue Neptune was claimed by A. Bailey for £5000.
Owner Martin P Graham **Bred** T E Pocock And C M Oakshott **Trained** Lambourn, Berks

FOCUS
A modest three-year-old claimer and there was not much between the front five at the weights. The form is rated around the principals.

887 WILLIAMHILL.COM - BINGO H'CAP 5f 216y(P)
4:35 (4:35) (Class 2) (0-100,97) 4-Y-0+
£9,969 (£2,985; £1,492; £747; £372; £187) **Stalls** Low

Form				RPR
-114	**1**		**Tiddliwinks**[42] 358 4-9-3 **96** .... JamieSpencer 12 (K A Ryan) *hld up: hdwy u.p over 1f out: hung lft ins fnl f: r.o to ld last strides* **3/1**[1]	107+
6-61	**2**	*nk*	**Thebes**[15] 722 5-8-12 **91** .... GregFairley 6 (M Johnston) *led early: chsd ldr tl led again over 3f out: rdn over 1f out: edgd rt and hdd last strides* **9/2**[2]	101
0540	**3**	*2 ½*	**Ebraam (USA)**[14] 737 7-9-0 **93** .... JimmyFortune 2 (S Curran) *hld up in tch: racd keenly: rdn over 1f out: styd on* **14/1**	95
0-66	**4**	*hd*	**Five Star Junior (USA)**[22] 628 4-9-4 **97** .... TomEaves 9 (Mrs L Stubbs) *chsd ldrs: rdn over 1f out: styd on* **25/1**	98
-531	**5**	*nse*	**Dubai Dynamo**[3] 850 5-9-2 **95** 6ex .... AndrewElliott 1 (Mrs R A Carr) *sn chsng ldrs: rdn over 1f out: styd on* **9/1**	96
132-	**6**	*½*	**Prime Exhibit**[152] 6732 5-8-12 **91** .... PaulHanagan 10 (R A Fahey) *hld up: hdwy and nt clr run over 1f out: running on whn n.m.r ins fnl f: nvr able to chal* **6/1**[3]	94+
4-02	**7**	*nk*	**Orpenindeed (IRE)**[41] 365 7-8-9 **88** ....(p) JerryO'Dwyer 8 (M Botti) *hld up in tch: rdn over 2f out: styd on same pce fnl f* **16/1**	87
42-3	**8**	*nk*	**Confuchias (IRE)**[24] 580 6-8-6 **85** ....(b[1]) LukeMorris 13 (J R Gask) *hld up: rdn over 2f out: r.o ins fnl f: nvr trbld ldrs* **18/1**	83
0-12	**9**	*nk*	**Bajan Tryst (USA)**[29] 528 4-8-11 **90** .... NeilCallan 4 (K A Ryan) *sn led: hdd over 3f out: rdn and ev ch over 1f out: no ex fnl f* **8/1**	87
000-	**10**	*1 ½*	**Northern Dare (IRE)**[140] 7015 6-8-8 **87** .... EddieAhern 7 (D Nicholls) *chsd ldrs: rdn over 2f out: wknd fnl f* **11/1**	79
1154	**11**	*2 ¼*	**Tourist**[14] 739 5-8-12 **91** .... JimmyQuinn 5 (D Shaw) *s.s: hld up: a in rr* **10/1**	76
2-06	**12**	*¾*	**Ingleby Arch (USA)**[25] 573 7-8-11 **90** .... GrahamGibbons 11 (T D Barron) *sn drvn along in rr: wknd over 2f out* **50/1**	72
-504	**13**	*2*	**Fathsta (IRE)**[41] 365 5-8-5 **87** .... MartinLane(3) 3 (D M Simcock) *s.s: a in rr* **10/1**	63

1m 13.62s (-1.38) **Going Correction** +0.05s/f (Slow) **13** Ran SP% **128.7**
Speed ratings (Par 109): **111,110,107,107,106 106,105,105,105,103 100,99,96**
toteswingers: 1&2 £5.00, 1&3 £12.10, 2&3 £23.80 CSF £17.02 CT £181.95 TOTE £4.40: £1.70, £1.90, £4.10; EX 15.70 Trifecta £281.20 Pool: £399.10 - 1.05 winning units..
Owner Guy Reed **Bred** Guy Reed **Trained** Hambleton, N Yorks

FOCUS
A decent sprint handicap but despite the pace appearing quite strong few got involved. The runner-up is probably the best guide to the form.

NOTEBOOK
Tiddliwinks produced a smart performance to overcome his wide draw, picking up well out wide from a long way back to reel in the positively ridden runner-up, with a gap back to the remainder. He still had around two or three lengths to make up on Thebes a furlong out and, just like last time, wanted to hang left but still managed to get there. He's now three from three over 6f and there could be more to come, although he still has to prove himself on turf. The plan now is to aim him at a Listed race, and connections think he'll have the speed for 5f (there's a 5f Listed race at Lingfield on Winter Derby day), although he is unlikely to appreciate soft ground on turf. (op 9-2)
Thebes, winner of this race last year off 88, was off 91 this time after being raised 3lb for another success over this C&D recently. Given his usual positive ride, he joined the early leader at about halfway and looked to have done plenty of running but he stuck on really well, ultimately finding only one too strong. This was a game effort in defeat. (op 13-2)
Ebraam(USA) had every chance towards the inside and kept on despite carrying his head a little high. (tchd 16-1)
Five Star Junior(USA), well held in a couple of runs in Dubai recently, travelled well but found only the one pace and is held off his current sort of mark. (op 28-1 tchd 22-1)
Dubai Dynamo, carrying a penalty for his recent 7f course win, had the pace to sit handy but could make no impression in the straight. (op 7-1)
Prime Exhibit ◆, sold out of Roger Charlton's yard for 28,000gns last October, was trying 6f for the first time after five months off and took a while to find his stride. He ended up racing enthusiastically off the pace but was blocked in his run when staying on around a furlong out before finishing well once in the clear. This was a pleasing start for his new connections and not a bad Lincoln trial. He should make the cut at Doncaster and could go well if the ground is not too quick. (op 10-1)
Bajan Tryst(USA) was taken on up front by the runner-up at about halfway and soon faded. Official explanation: jockey said gelding had no more to give (op 13-2)

888 WILLIAMHILL.COM - VEGAS H'CAP 1m 5f 194y(P)
5:10 (5:10) (Class 4) (0-85,88) 4-Y-0+ **£4,209** (£1,252; £625; £312) **Stalls** Low

Form				RPR
256	**1**		**Kames Park (IRE)**[1] 871 8-8-11 **71** .... JimmyQuinn 2 (R C Guest) *hld up: hdwy on bit over 2f out: led ins fnl f: r.o wl* **15/2**	79
50-1	**2**	*2 ¼*	**William's Way**[70] 15 8-8-12 **72** .... NeilCallan 4 (I A Wood) *hld up: hdwy over 2f out: rdn and hung rt ins fnl f: styd on to go 2nd nr fin* **9/1**	76
2-11	**3**	*1*	**Augustus John (IRE)**[29] 529 7-8-11 **71** .... TomEaves 3 (R Brotherton) *hld up: rdn over 2f out: styd on to go 3rd post: nvr nrr* **3/1**[2]	74
50-4	**4**	*shd*	**Encircled**[21] 636 6-9-5 **79** .... RichardHughes 7 (J R Jenkins) *chsd ldrs: led over 1f out: sn rdn: hdd and no ex ins fnl f: lost 2 pls cl home* **4/1**[3]	82
3311	**5**	*½*	**Benedict Spirit (IRE)**[8] 811 5-9-6 **83** ....(v) MartinLane(3) 8 (P D Evans) *chsd ldrs: rdn over 2f out: styd on same pce fr over 1f out* **11/4**[1]	85
4112	**6**	*3 ¾*	**Doubnov (FR)**[15] 714 7-9-2 **76** ....(p) JamieSpencer 1 (Ian Williams) *trckd ldr: racd keenly: led over 2f out: rdn: drifted rt and hdd over 1f out: wknd ins fnl f* **7/1**	73
-000	**7**	*2 ¾*	**Valmari (IRE)**[17] 688 7-8-9 **76** .... RichardOld(7) 6 (G Prodromou) *stdd s: hld up: racd in last pl tl passed one rival ins fnl f: nvr on terms* **50/1**	69
5/06	**8**	*6*	**Donaldson (GER)**[16] 697 8-10-0 **88** .... GeorgeBaker 5 (Jonjo O'Neill) *set stdy pce tl rdn and hdd over 2f out: wknd over 1f out* **20/1**	73

3m 4.58s (-1.42) **Going Correction** +0.05s/f (Slow) **8** Ran SP% **112.7**
Speed ratings (Par 105): **106,104,104,104,103 101,100,96**
toteswingers: 1&2 £6.00, 1&3 £5.30, 2&3 £3.20 CSF £69.56 CT £245.47 TOTE £8.20: £2.40, £2.60, £1.40; EX 37.70 Trifecta £330.00 Pool: £472.75 - 1.06 winning units..
Owner Future Racing (Notts) Limited **Bred** Pat Beirne **Trained** Stainforth, S Yorks

FOCUS
A fair staying handicap. The form is ordinary but sound enough.

889 WILLIAMHILL.COM - BETTING MAIDEN STKS 1m 141y(P)
5:40 (5:41) (Class 5) 3-Y-0+ **£2,729** (£806; £403) **Stalls** Low

Form				RPR
43	**1**		**Fighter Boy (IRE)**[12] 751 3-8-9 0 ow1 .... JamieSpencer 10 (T D Barron) *stdd s: hld up: smooth hdwy over 1f out: led on bit ins fnl f: comf* **4/1**[2]	76+
324-	**2**	*1 ½*	**Amtaar**[172] 6181 3-8-3 66 .... ChrisCatlin 7 (C E Brittain) *w ldr tl led 7f out: rdn over 1f out: hung lft and hdd ins fnl f: one pce* **11/2**[3]	61
04-	**3**	*½*	**Rainbow Six**[112] 7491 3-8-8 0 .... JerryO'Dwyer 4 (M Botti) *hld up: hdwy over 1f out: edgd lft and r.o ins fnl f* **22/1**	65
-4	**4**	*hd*	**Omaruru (IRE)**[12] 755 3-8-8 0 .... JoeFanning 9 (M Johnston) *chsd ldrs: shkn up over 2f out: edgd lft ins fnl f: r.o* **14/1**	64+
5	**5**	*hd*	**Heliocentric**[24] 583 3-8-8 0 .... RichardHughes 8 (R Hannon) *chsd ldr 7f out: rdn and ev ch over 1f out: edgd lft and no ex ins fnl f* **10/11**[1]	64
4/5	**6**	*¾*	**Dawnhill (GER)**[26] 563 6-10-0 0 .... GrahamGibbons 3 (J J Quinn) *hld up: racd keenly: hdwy over 1f out: nt clr run ins fnl f: styd on same pce* **25/1**	68?
443-	**7**	*¾*	**Layla's Boy**[152] 6727 3-8-8 74 .... PaulHanagan 1 (R A Fahey) *led: hdd 7f out: chsd ldrs: rdn over 1f out: styd on same pce* **15/2**	60
00-	**8**	*¾*	**Denton Ryal**[144] 6920 3-8-3 0 .... NickyMackay 2 (M E Rimmer) *prom: racd keenly: rdn and n.m.r over 1f out: no ex fnl f* **50/1**	54
0	**9**	*½*	**Rock D'Argent (IRE)**[10] 768 3-8-3 0 .... JimmyQuinn 6 (H Morrison) *hld up: hdwy 5f out: rdn over 1f out: hung lft and wknd ins fnl f* **18/1**	53
0	**10**	*8*	**Idol Deputy (FR)**[8] 815 4-9-9 0 .... LeeNewnes(5) 5 (M D I Usher) *hld up: a in rr: wknd over 2f out* **100/1**	45

1m 53.29s (2.79) **Going Correction** +0.05s/f (Slow)
WFA 3 from 4yo+ 20lb **10** Ran SP% **122.6**
Speed ratings (Par 103): **89,87,87,87,86 86,85,84,84,77**
toteswingers: 1&2 £5.80, 1&3 £12.10, 2&3 £12.20 CSF £27.01 TOTE £7.20: £1.90, £1.80, £4.00; EX 29.90 Trifecta £293.70 Pool: £718.47 - 1.81 winning units. Place 6: £39.43, Place 5: £19.29..
Owner A G Greenwood **Bred** Rockhart Trading Ltd **Trained** Maunby, N Yorks

FOCUS
An interesting maiden but they went a steady pace and, using the 66-rated runner-up as a guide, the bare form is modest. Fighter Boy impressed though and is rated a 4l winner.
T/Plt: £64.20 to a £1 stake. Pool: £92,605.78. 1,052.87 winning tickets. T/Qpdt: £24.40 to a £1 stake. Pool: £5,213.17. 157.55 winning tickets. CR

856 SOUTHWELL (L-H)
Tuesday, March 16

OFFICIAL GOING: Standard
Wind: Light across Weather: Cloudy with sunny spells

892 32REDBET.COM H'CAP 6f (F)
1:20 (1:20) (Class 5) (0-70,70) 4-Y-0+ **£2,331** (£693; £346; £173) **Stalls** Low

Form				RPR
-352	**1**		**Punching**[5] 859 6-9-4 **70** .... LiamKeniry 4 (C R Dore) *trckd ldrs: rdn to ld ins fnl f: styd on u.p* **15/8**[1]	78
5-21	**2**	*¾*	**Spin Again (IRE)**[33] 505 5-9-2 **68** .... AdrianNicholls 5 (D Nicholls) *led: rdn over 2f out: hdd ins fnl f: styd on* **5/1**[3]	74
1222	**3**	*½*	**Fulford**[7] 839 5-8-5 **57** ....(v) JoeFanning 8 (M Brittain) *trckd ldrs: racd keenly: rdn and ev ch over 1f out: styd on same pce ins fnl f* **9/4**[2]	61
140-	**4**	*7*	**Efisio Princess**[93] 7738 7-8-12 **67** .... NataliaGemelova(3) 2 (J E Long) *plld hrd and sn prom: rdn over 2f out: hung rt and wknd over 1f out* **20/1**	49
0504	**5**	*hd*	**Jonnie Skull (IRE)**[11] 802 4-8-10 **62** ....(vt) ChrisCatlin 6 (P S McEntee) *chsd ldr tl rdn over 2f out: wknd over 1f out* **14/1**	43
-606	**6**	*1*	**Calmdownmate (IRE)**[7] 832 5-8-12 **64** .... SilvestreDeSousa 1 (Mrs R A Carr) *s.i.s: sme hdwy 2f out: sn swtchd rt and wknd* **16/1**	42
0011	**7**	*1 ¾*	**Pipers Piping (IRE)**[25] 615 4-8-2 **61** .... JulieCumine(7) 7 (P Howling) *s.i.s: hld up: hdwy over 2f out: wkng whn hmpd over 1f out* **9/1**	34
-000	**8**	*22*	**Came Back (IRE)**[33] 504 7-8-9 **66** ow1 .... AnnStokell(5) 3 (Miss A Stokell) *s.i.s: hld up: racd keenly: rdn and wknd 2f out* **50/1**	—

1m 16.5s **Going Correction** +0.075s/f (Slow) **8** Ran SP% **111.5**
Speed ratings (Par 103): **103,102,101,92,91 90,88,58**
toteswingers:1&2:£2.80, 1&3:£1.60, 2&3:£2.70 CSF £11.09 CT £20.75 TOTE £2.00: £1.10, £2.20, £1.20; EX 8.30 Trifecta £27.60 Pool: £396.60 - 10.64 winning units..
Owner Liam Breslin **Bred** Cheveley Park Stud Ltd **Trained** Cowbit, Lincs
■ Stewards' Enquiry : Natalia Gemelova two-day ban: careless riding (Mar 31-Apr 1)
Adrian Nicholls two-day ban: careless riding (Mar 31-Apr 1)

FOCUS
A modest sprint handicap dominated by those who raced handily. Straightforward form with the winner rated pretty much to his best.

893 £320 FREE AT 32RED.COM CLASSIFIED CLAIMING STKS 1m (F)
1:55 (1:55) (Class 6) 4-Y-0+ **£1,774** (£523; £262) **Stalls** Low

Form				RPR
0-00	**1**		**Rub Of The Relic (IRE)**[19] 705 5-7-13 48 ....(be) PaulPickard(5) 3 (P T Midgley) *chsd ldr 7f out: rdn fr over 3f out: led 2f out: hdd ins fnl f: rallied to ld towards fin* **50/1**	62'
-312	**2**	*hd*	**Sir George (IRE)**[46] 348 5-8-6 65 .... PaulHanagan 9 (Ollie Pears) *hld up in tch: jnd ldrs 2f out: rdn to ld ins fnl f: sn edgd lft: hdd towards fin* **7/2**[2]	64
4132	**3**	*2 ½*	**Magnitude**[7] 834 5-8-6 60 ....(vt[1]) LiamJones 7 (R A Harris) *sn pushed along and prom: drvn 1/2-way: outpcd 3f out: hdwy u.p and hung lft fr over 1f out: styd on* **7/2**[2]	58
4453	**4**	*3*	**Mocha Java**[19] 704 7-7-13 63 ....(p) DeclanCannon(5) 2 (Matthew Salaman) *led 7f out: rdn and hdd 2f out: no ex fnl f* **7/1**[3]	49
2633	**5**	*1 ½*	**Special Cuvee**[32] 518 4-8-7 60 ow3 ....(v) RobertHavlin 1 (A B Haynes) *s.i.s: hdwy over 6f out: rdn over 2f out: styd on same pce appr fnl f* **12/1**	48
03-0	**6**	*1 ¼*	**My Sweet Georgia (IRE)**[21] 675 4-8-12 64 ow1 ....(b) AdamKirby 4 (Stef Higgins) *led 1f: chsd ldrs: rdn over 2f out: sn outpcd* **9/1**	51

4112 **7** 1 1/4 **Castle Myth (USA)**[18] 715 4-8-5 60 ow2..............(be) BarryMcHugh(3) 8 44
(B Ellison) *sn pushed along in rr: rdn 1/2-way: nvr on terms* **9/4**[1]

0-60 **8** 14 **Bookiebasher Babe (IRE)**[18] 715 5-8-12 64.................. GregFairley 5 15
(M Quinn) *mid-div: sn drvn along: wknd over 3f out* **28/1**

6/ **9** 11 **King Zeal (IRE)**[876] 6387 6-8-4 58..................... JoeFanning 10 —
(B D Leavy) *hld up in tch: pushed along 1/2-way: wknd over 3f out* **20/1**

2-56 **10** 3 1/2 **Montiboli (IRE)**[12] 787 5-8-5 65..........................(p) AmyRyan(5) 6 —
(K A Ryan) *s.i.s: sn pushed along in rr: lost tch over 3f out* **25/1**

1m 43.39s (-0.31) **Going Correction** +0.075s/f (Slow) **10** Ran SP% **119.4**
Speed ratings (Par 101): **104,103,101,98,96 95,94,80,69,65**
toteswingers:1&2:£25.60, 1&3:£32.00, 2&3:£4.50 CSF £217.62 TOTE £80.30: £12.80, £1.70, £1.60; EX 215.50 TRIFECTA Not won..Magnitude was claimed by B Baugh for £6,000.
Owner O R Dukes **Bred** M J Wiley **Trained** Westow, N Yorks

FOCUS
A modest claimer and a real shocker for punters. The form is rated around the runner-up.
Rub Of The Relic(IRE) Official explanation: trainer said, regarding apparent improvement in form, that the gelding tends to be unpredictable and has benefited from the change of headgear, first time eye shield and blinkers.
Castle Myth(USA) Official explanation: jockey said gelding lost its action shortly after start

894 32RED.COM MAIDEN STKS 6f (F)
2:30 (2:31) (Class 5) 3-Y-O **£2,729** (£806; £403) **Stalls** Low

Form RPR

-263 **1** **Neduardo**[14] 759 3-9-3 73..................................... RobertHavlin 5 79
(P W Chapple-Hyam) *mde all: pushed clr fnl 2f: eased towards fin* **5/1**[3]

30- **2** 7 **Layla's Lexi**[181] 5977 3-8-12 0... PaulHanagan 8 52
(D Nicholls) *chsd ldrs: rdn over 2f out: sn outpcd: hung lft and wnt 2nd ins fnl f: no ch w wnr* **10/1**

3 hd **Blue Moon** 3-8-12 0.. SilvestreDeSousa 4 51+
(K A Ryan) *s.i.s: hld up: hdwy over 1f out: nrst fin* **18/1**

06- **4** 3 1/2 **Tell Halaf**[129] 7288 3-9-3 0.. JamieSpencer 1 45
(M L W Bell) *trckd ldrs: shkn up over 2f out: edgd lft and wknd over 1f out* **10/3**[2]

5 **5** 1 1/2 **Coal Miner (IRE)**[12] 784 3-9-3 0.................................. AndrewElliott 7 40
(Mrs R A Carr) *chsd wnr: rdn over 2f out: wknd over 1f out* **40/1**

0- **6** 1 1/4 **I'Lldoit**[216] 4888 3-9-3 0.. FrankieMcDonald 3 36
(H J Evans) *sn outpcd* **100/1**

43- **7** 3/4 **Excellent Vision**[158] 6646 3-9-3 0...................................... TomEaves 2 34
(B Smart) *s.i.s: hdwy over 3f out: rdn: hung lft and wknd 2f out* **8/11**[1]

0 **8** 2 1/2 **Account Closed**[12] 782 3-8-7 0................................ JamesSullivan(5) 6 21
(C A Mulhall) *sn outpcd: bhd fr 1/2-way* **80/1**

1m 17.13s (0.63) **Going Correction** +0.075s/f (Slow) **8** Ran SP% **116.7**
Speed ratings (Par 98): **98,88,88,83,81 80,79,75**
toteswingers:1&2:£4.20, 1&3:£4.70, 2&3:£6.70 CSF £52.83 TOTE £6.20: £1.40, £1.90, £3.10; EX 41.10 Trifecta £118.20 Pool: £488.91 - 3.06 winning units..
Owner G Roeder & D Baldwin **Bred** Bond Thoroughbred Corporation **Trained** Newmarket, Suffolk

FOCUS
An uncompetitive maiden in which only half the field counted as far as the market was concerned. With the favourite running poorly the winner had little to beat, although he is rated as improving by 8lb. The winning time was 0.63 seconds slower than the opening handicap.
Excellent Vision Official explanation: jockey said colt never travelled

895 BET AT 32RED.COM (S) STKS 7f (F)
3:05 (3:05) (Class 6) 3-Y-O+ **£1,774** (£523; £262) **Stalls** Low

Form RPR

5050 **1** **Royal Dignitary (USA)**[20] 690 10-9-8 0...................... AdrianNicholls 4 73
(D Nicholls) *led: hdd over 4f out: led again over 2f out: sn rdn: clr over 1f out: all out* **15/8**[1]

40-6 **2** 1 **Island Chief**[19] 704 4-9-8 60.......................................(p) TonyHamilton 8 70
(K A Ryan) *s.i.s: sn chsng ldrs: rdn over 3f out: outpcd and hung lft fr over 2f out: rallied to chse wnr over 1f out: styd on* **10/1**

0413 **3** 1 **Flores Sea (USA)**[12] 787 6-10-0 69....................(p) SilvestreDeSousa 3 73
(Mrs R A Carr) *sn outpcd: hdwy u.p over 1f out: nt rch ldrs* **11/4**[2]

200 **4** 3 1/2 **Kings Ace (IRE)**[7] 836 4-9-1 55............................ CharlotteKerton(7) 2 58
(A Berry) *prom: racd keenly: rdn over 2f out: styd on* **33/1**

600- **5** 2 1/2 **Haroldini (IRE)**[246] 3929 8-9-8 52...................................(p) ChrisCatlin 5 51
(J Balding) *hld up: rdn over 3f out: sme hdwy over 1f out: wknd fnl f* **20/1**

00-3 **6** 1 3/4 **Sea Land (FR)**[18] 716 6-9-5 59.........................(be) BarryMcHugh(3) 6 46
(B Ellison) *prom: rdn 1/2-way: wknd over 2f out* **7/1**

-150 **7** 1 **Tin Cha Woody (USA)**[13] 779 5-10-0 76......................(b) LiamJones 1 50
(R A Harris) *s.i.s: sn chsng ldrs: led over 4f out: rdn and hdd over 2f out: wknd over 1f out* **4/1**[3]

1m 30.95s (0.65) **Going Correction** +0.075s/f (Slow) **7** Ran SP% **110.7**
Speed ratings (Par 101): **99,97,96,92,89 87,86**
toteswingers:1&2:£4.30, 1&3:£2.10, 2&3:£4.60 CSF £20.16 TOTE £2.70: £1.50, £2.90; EX 13.00 Trifecta £33.30 Pool: £427.67 - 9.49 winning units..There was no bid for the winner
Owner Middleham Park Racing XXXVI **Bred** Bentley Smith, J Michael O'Farrell Jr , Joan Thor **Trained** Sessay, N Yorks
■ Stewards' Enquiry : Charlotte Kerton two-day ban: used whip with excessive frequency without giving gelding time to respond (Mar 31-Apr 1)

FOCUS
A routine Fibresand seller in which few got involved. The form looks sound for the grade judged around the runner-up and the fourth.

896 32RED CASINO OF THE DECADE H'CAP 5f (F)
3:45 (3:45) (Class 6) (0-60,60) 4-Y-O+ **£1,774** (£523; £262) **Stalls** High

Form RPR

1150 **1** **Lujiana**[26] 601 5-8-11 53.. JoeFanning 4 61
(M Brittain) *prom: pushed along 1/2-way: rdn to ld 1f out: jst hld on* **4/1**[1]

4046 **2** nk **First Order**[13] 778 9-8-11 58.......................................(v) AnnStokell(5) 1 65
(Miss A Stokell) *rdr lost iron leaving stalls: in rr: hdwy 1/2-way: rdn over 1f out: r.o* **14/1**

-452 **3** 1 1/4 **Verinco**[19] 699 4-9-4 60...(v) TomEaves 9 62
(B Smart) *a.p: led and edgd lft 2f out: sn rdn: hdd 1f out: styd on same pce* **7/1**[3]

260- **4** nse **Cavitie**[153] 6777 4-8-8 53 ow1................................. RussKennemore(3) 14 55+
(Andrew Reid) *prom: outpcd 3f out: rallied and hung lft over 1f out: r.o* **25/1**

0435 **5** 1 **Kheley (IRE)**[13] 778 4-8-12 59....................................... KierenFox(5) 5 58
(W M Brisbourne) *mid-div: sn pushed along: hdwy over 1f out: bmpd sn after: styd on* **10/1**

04-1 **6** 2 **After The Show**[46] 344 9-9-4 60.................................. MartinDwyer 2 51
(Rae Guest) *s.i.s: outpcd: rdn 1/2-way: nvr nrr* **11/2**[2]

0560 **7** 1 1/4 **La Capriosa**[13] 767 4-9-4 60.............................(p) FrederikTylicki 12 47
(J A Glover) *chsd ldrs: rdn 2f out: wknd fnl f* **8/1**

060- **8** 1/2 **Sills Vincero**[325] 1529 4-9-0 56....................................... PaulHanagan 3 41
(Miss M E Rowland) *prom: lost pl over 3f out: n.d after* **40/1**

00-0 **9** 1 **Dodaa (USA)**[18] 723 7-8-4 49.............................(v[1]) AshleyHamblett(3) 7 31
(N Wilson) *led: rdn and hdd 2f out: wknd fnl f* **10/1**

214 **10** 1/2 **Don Pele (IRE)**[7] 839 8-9-4 60..................................(v[1]) LiamJones 10 40
(R A Harris) *hung lft s: outpcd* **9/1**

-025 **11** 1 1/4 **Trick Or Two**[4] 869 4-9-1 57.................................(b) AndrewElliott 13 32
(Mrs R A Carr) *s.i.s: hdwy over 3f out: wknd fnl f* **12/1**

4303 **12** hd **Shakespeare's Son**[5] 860 5-8-10 52...................... FrankieMcDonald 8 27
(H J Evans) *s.i.s: outpcd* **12/1**

-040 **13** 6 **Loose Caboose (IRE)**[26] 601 5-8-8 57....................(b) ConorQuish(7) 6 10
(A J McCabe) *s.s: hdwy into mid-div over 3f out: wknd 1/2-way* **16/1**

60.20 secs (0.50) **Going Correction** +0.125s/f (Slow) **13** Ran SP% **121.4**
Speed ratings (Par 101): **101,100,98,98,96 93,91,90,89,88 86,86,76**
toteswingers:1&2:£14.70, 1&3:£5.70, 2&3:£25.70 CSF £63.18 CT £402.06 TOTE £4.30: £1.40, £4.20, £2.90; EX 72.90 Trifecta £113.90 Pool: £280.24 - 1.82 winning units..
Owner Mel Brittain **Bred** Bearstone Stud **Trained** Warthill, N Yorks
■ Stewards' Enquiry : Russ Kennemore two-day ban: careless riding (Mar 31-Apr 1)

FOCUS
A competitive if modest sprint handicap and the action ultimately unfolded towards the far side of the track. The first two are rated in line with their winter form.
Trick Or Two Official explanation: jockey said gelding hung both ways
Loose Caboose(IRE) Official explanation: trainer said mare bled from the nose

897 32REDPOKER.COM H'CAP 1m 4f (F)
4:25 (4:25) (Class 5) (0-75,76) 4-Y-O+ **£3,412** (£1,007; £504) **Stalls** Low

Form RPR

33-3 **1** **Daaweitza**[7] 837 7-9-2 71...(be) TomEaves 7 78
(B Ellison) *a.p: led 2f out: sn rdn: styd on* **85/40**[1]

02/6 **2** 2 3/4 **Southern Regent (IND)**[25] 620 9-8-13 75.................. IanBrennan(7) 8 78
(J J Quinn) *hld up in tch: rdn over 3f out: chsd wnr over 1f out: styd on same pce ins fnl f* **20/1**

-231 **3** 1 1/2 **Eseej (USA)**[5] 857 5-9-4 76 6ex............................... WilliamCarson(3) 5 76
(P W Hiatt) *led: hung rt fr over 5f out: rdn and hdd 2f out: no ex fnl f* **9/4**[2]

055- **4** 1/2 **Bandanaman (IRE)**[111] 2662 4-8-8 65............................ PJMcDonald 2 64
(G A Swinbank) *hld up: hdwy over 1f out: nt rch ldrs* **20/1**

06-0 **5** 1 **La Columbina**[36] 174 5-8-7 62................................ FrankieMcDonald 4 60
(H J Evans) *hld up: rdn over 3f out: styd on ins fnl f: nrst fin* **66/1**

320- **6** 2 3/4 **Tilos Gem (IRE)**[123] 7373 4-9-4 75.................................. JoeFanning 3 68
(M Johnston) *sn chsng ldr: rdn over 2f out: wknd fnl f* **3/1**[3]

235- **7** 12 **Dispol Diva**[228] 4506 4-8-4 61...(v) ChrisCatlin 6 35
(P T Midgley) *chsd ldrs: rdn over 4f out: wknd 3f out* **12/1**

-056 **8** 22 **Rocky's Pride (IRE)**[15] 756 4-9-1 72........................... RobertHavlin 1 11
(A B Haynes) *stdd s: hld up: bhd fnl 7f: t.o* **16/1**

2m 41.72s (0.72) **Going Correction** +0.075s/f (Slow)
WFA 4 from 5yo+ 2lb **8** Ran SP% **112.4**
Speed ratings (Par 103): **100,98,97,96,96 94,86,71**
toteswingers:1&2:£9.60, 1&3:£2.00, 2&3:£10.60 CSF £44.89 CT £102.61 TOTE £3.00: £1.10, £3.50, £1.70; EX 45.40 Trifecta £246.20 Pool: £449.25 - 1.35 winning units..
Owner Mrs Andrea M Mallinson **Bred** C Mallinson **Trained** Norton, N Yorks

FOCUS
An ordinary middle-distance handicap, run at an even pace. The winner is rated in line with his best winter efforts but this form may be unreliable.

898 £10 FREE BINGO AT 32RED APPRENTICE H'CAP 1m 4f (F)
5:05 (5:05) (Class 6) (0-55,54) 4-Y-O+ **£1,774** (£523; £262) **Stalls** Low

Form RPR

656- **1** **Dulce Domum**[239] 4142 4-8-6 45...................................... DeclanCannon 9 57
(A B Haynes) *drvn along early to chse ldrs: led 3f out: sn rdn clr: styd on wl* **33/1**

3340 **2** 5 **They All Laughed**[11] 813 7-9-0 51..............................(p) DeanHeslop 13 55+
(Mrs Marjorie Fife) *hld up: hdwy over 5f out: rdn over 2f out: hung lft and styd on same pce* **9/4**[1]

0-55 **3** 2 1/4 **Six Of Clubs**[35] 470 4-8-6 45...................................(b) MatthewDavies 2 45
(W G M Turner) *prom: rdn and hung lft over 1f out: styd on same pce* **25/1**

4-46 **4** 6 **Piverina (IRE)**[25] 622 5-8-8 45................................(p) JamesSullivan 10 36
(Julie Camacho) *hld up: hdwy over 5f out: rdn over 2f out: sn wknd* **14/1**

565- **5** 1 **Ba Dreamflight**[32] 5873 5-8-8 45.. SimonPearce 6 34
(H Morrison) *hld up: drvn along 1/2-way: nvr nrr* **13/2**

4340 **6** 3/4 **Desert Hawk**[22] 661 9-8-1 45.................................... JulieCumine(7) 5 33
(P Howling) *mid-div: hdwy to chse ldr over 6f out: led over 4f out: hdd 3f out: wknd 2f out* **20/1**

6036 **7** 1 3/4 **Free Falling**[36] 463 4-8-1 45...............................(vt) NathanAlison(5) 4 30
(A J Lidderdale) *s.s: nvr nrr* **20/1**

0-51 **8** 4 1/2 **Querido (GER)**[11] 816 6-8-13 53..............................(p) TobyAtkinson(3) 1 31
(M Wigham) *hld up: pushed along over 4f out: n.d* **5/2**[2]

-063 **9** nk **Lean Burn (USA)**[7] 833 4-8-7 51................................(t) DavidKenny(5) 8 29
(A G Newcombe) *prom: rdn over 3f out: wknd over 2f out* **6/1**[3]

5-30 **10** 6 **Nyetimber (USA)**[27] 584 4-9-1 54...................................... SophieDoyle 11 22
(J A Osborne) *chsd ldr tl led over 8f out: hdd over 4f out: rdn and wknd over 2f out* **14/1**

3-00 **11** 30 **Reigning In Rio (IRE)**[18] 720 4-8-6 45.............................. PaulPickard 7 —
(P T Midgley) *led: hdd over 8f out: rdn and wknd over 3f out* **40/1**

2m 41.32s (0.32) **Going Correction** +0.075s/f (Slow)
WFA 4 from 5yo+ 2lb **11** Ran SP% **119.0**
Speed ratings (Par 101): **101,97,96,92,91 91,89,86,86,82 62**
toteswingers:1&2:£10.70, 1&3:£2.30, 2&3:£1.30 CSF £103.09 CT £1992.24 TOTE £46.70: £5.70, £2.20, £6.80; EX 370.60 TRIFECTA Not won. Place 6 £62.70, Place 5 £54.32.
Owner The Villains **Bred** Coln Valley Stud **Trained** Limpley Stoke, Bath

FOCUS
A weak apprentice handicap with over half the field wrong at the weights. It was run at a fair pace and they finished very well spread out. The winning time was 0.4 seconds faster than the preceding contest. An improved effort from the winner with the second close to recent form.
Desert Hawk Official explanation: trainer said gelding finished distressed
Querido(GER) Official explanation: trainer said gelding resented the kickback
Reigning In Rio(IRE) Official explanation: jockey said filly hung right throughout
T/Plt: £98.70 to a £1 stake. Pool: £50,593.38. 373.83 winning tickets. T/Qpdt: £38.80 to a £1 stake. Pool: £3,908.55. 74.40 winning tickets. CR

765 KEMPTON (A.W) (R-H)

Wednesday, March 17

OFFICIAL GOING: Standard

Wind: virtually nil Weather: dry, overcast

899 KEMPTON.CO.UK CLASSIFIED CLAIMING STKS 5f (P)

5:50 (5:50) (Class 6) 3-Y-O+ £2,047 (£604; £302) Stalls High

Form				RPR
6243	1		**Fromsong (IRE)**[12] 806 12-9-8 67 (p) MartinDwyer 1 *(D K Ivory) taken down early: chsd ldng pair: chsd ldr wl over 1f out: rdn to ld ins fnl f: kpt on and a holding on* 7/2[2]	76
2421	2	nk	**Misaro (GER)**[7] 848 9-9-5 65 (b) DavidProbert 5 *(R A Harris) mid-div: pushed along 1/2-way: hdwy over 1f out: rdn and r.o ins fnl f: clsng on wnr towards fin but nvr threatening* 6/5[1]	72
216-	3	3/4	**Lethal**[94] 7738 7-9-1 65 RussKennemore(3) 2 *(Andrew Reid) led: sn hdd: chsd ldr tl led again 2f out: rdn over 1f out: hdd ins fnl f: kpt on same pce* 6/1[3]	68
2224	4	2 1/2	**Bo McGinty (IRE)**[5] 869 9-9-4 60 (b) TonyHamilton 7 *(R A Fahey) taken down early: awkward leaving stalls and s.i.s: towards rr: swtchd lft and effrt over 1f out: kpt on but nvr gng pce to rch ldrs* 7/2[2]	59
4530	5	6	**Truly Divine**[10] 726 5-9-1 44 CathyGannon 6 *(C A Dwyer) restless in stalls: awkward leaving stalls and s.i.s: a in rr: rdn and no rspnse 2f out: wl btn fnl f* 50/1	35
0016	6	7	**Gleaming Spirit (IRE)**[23] 659 6-9-1 50 (v) AdrianMcCarthy 4 *(Peter Grayson) sn led: rdn and hdd 2f out: wknd over 1f out: wl btn fnl f* 33/1	9
0-50	7	3 1/2	**Albaher**[13] 789 4-9-3 54 DaneO'Neill 3 *(Peter Grayson) sn outpcd in rr: n.d* 25/1	—

60.26 secs (-0.24) **Going Correction** +0.05s/f (Slow) 7 Ran SP% **112.9**

Speed ratings (Par 101): **103,102,101,97,87 76,70**

Tote Swingers: 1&2 £1.30, 1&3 £2.40, 2&3 £2.30 CSF £7.90 TOTE £4.60: £3.60, £2.90; EX 8.50.

Owner Dean Ivory **Bred** Mrs Teresa Bergin **Trained** Radlett, Herts

FOCUS

Competitive, despite the small field.

Albaher Official explanation: jockey said colt moved poorly

900 MIX BUSINESS WITH PLEASURE MEDIAN AUCTION MAIDEN STKS 6f (P)

6:20 (6:21) (Class 5) 3-5-Y-O £2,590 (£770; £385; £192) Stalls High

Form				RPR
2	1		**Dominium (USA)**[45] 362 3-9-1 0 LukeMorris 8 *(J R Gask) hld in last pair: swtchd lft and effrt wl over 1f out: str run fnl f to ld towards fin* 3/1[3]	76
33-	2	1/2	**Lago Indiano (IRE)**[133] 7234 3-9-1 0 NeilCallan 5 *(Mrs A J Perrett) sn bustled up to ld: rdn and hdd over 2f out: drvn and ev ch over 1f out: led again fnl 100yds: hdd and no ex towards fin* 9/4[2]	74
-323	3	3/4	**Caramelita**[17] 744 3-8-10 66 RichardHughes 2 *(J R Jenkins) t.k.h early: hld up wl in tch: swtchd lft and effrt 2f out: drvn 1f out: kpt on same pce after* 9/2	67
	4	3/4	**Arctic Lynx (IRE)** 3-9-1 0 SteveDrowne 3 *(J R Best) chsd ldr after 1f: led over 2f out: rdn wl over 1f out: hdd fnl 100yds: wknd towards fin* 16/1	69
004-	5	3/4	**Master Mylo (IRE)**[149] 6903 3-9-1 67 JimCrowley 7 *(D K Ivory) hld up in tch: pushed along and effrt ent fnl 2f: kpt on same pce fnl f* 11/1	67
0-6	6	4	**Bob Goes Electric (IRE)**[15] 759 3-8-12 0 MarcHalford(3) 6 *(J R Best) t.k.h: hld up in tch: rdn and rn green over 2f out: wl hld fnl f* 33/1	54
020-	7	4 1/2	**Quaestor (IRE)**[179] 6104 3-9-1 79 RichardKingscote 1 *(Tom Dascombe) led tl over 2f out: wknd qckly u.p over 1f out: wl btn fnl f* 7/4[1]	40
	8	15	**Titch (IRE)** 4-9-9 0 AdrianMcCarthy 4 *(Peter Grayson) a in rr: lost tch over 2f out: tailing off whn rn green over 1f out* 50/1	—

1m 12.92s (-0.18) **Going Correction** +0.05s/f (Slow)

WFA 3 from 4yo 13lb 8 Ran SP% **129.4**

Speed ratings (Par 103): **103,102,101,100,99 94,88,68**

Tote Swingers: 1&2 £2.00, 1&3 £3.20, 2&3 £2.60 CSF £11.86 TOTE £5.50: £1.20, £1.10, £1.10; EX 10.10.

Owner Richard L Page **Bred** Corbett Farm **Trained** Sutton Veny, Wilts

FOCUS

An ordinary maiden, run at a strong pace.

901 DIGIBET.COM H'CAP 6f (P)

6:50 (6:51) (Class 4) (0-85,90) 3-Y-O £4,209 (£1,252; £625; £312) Stalls High

Form				RPR
213-	1		**Jarrow (IRE)**[110] 7552 3-9-5 83 JoeFanning 7 *(M Johnston) dwlt and bustled along leaving stalls: bhd: swtchd lft and effrt over 2f out: str run to ld ent fnl f: clr fnl 100yds: comf* 5/4[1]	96+
410-	2	2	**Dusty Spirit**[130] 7290 3-8-7 74 (t) JackDean(3) 5 *(W G M Turner) chsd ldrs for 1f: midfield after: rdn and effrt on inner jst over 2f out: drvn and chsd ldrs over 1f out: chsd clr wnr ins fnl f: no imp* 25/1	77
41-4	3	hd	**Yer Woman (IRE)**[14] 772 3-9-9 90 PatrickHills(3) 8 *(R Hannon) hld up in last pair: swtchd lft and gd hdwy ent fnl f: r.o to press for 2nd nr fin: no ch w wnr* 9/2[2]	93
5-16	4	1 1/2	**Little Perisher**[14] 772 3-8-11 75 TomQueally 6 *(A P Jarvis) towards rr: rdn over 2f out: styd on u.p fnl f: nvr gng pce to threaten ldrs* 14/1	73
4-24	5	1 1/4	**Kylladdie**[12] 807 3-8-7 71 oh1 DavidProbert 1 *(S Gollings) sn bustled along to press ldr: led 4f out: drvn and hdd ent fnl f: wknd fnl 150yds* 8/1	65
5330	6	3/4	**Transfixed (IRE)**[4] 884 3-8-12 76 CathyGannon 9 *(P D Evans) t.k.h: hld up in tch in midfield: rdn and effrt to chse ldrs over 1f out: wknd fnl f* 16/1	68
1212	7	3 1/2	**Freddie's Girl (USA)**[12] 807 3-8-12 76 AdamKirby 2 *(Stef Higgins) led tl 4f out: styd prom tl wknd u.p wl over 1f out* 9/1	56
0131	8	3 3/4	**Private Olley**[12] 807 3-8-7 71 oh3 ChrisCatlin 4 *(J Akehurst) wnt lft s: bhd tl gd hdwy on outer to chse ldrs over 3f out: wknd u.p over 2f out* 15/2[3]	39
2331	9	nk	**Athwaab**[28] 577 3-8-5 74 TobyAtkinson(5) 3 *(M G Quinlan) t.k.h: chsd ldrs: w ldr over 3f out tl wknd qckly wl over 1f out* 10/1	41

1m 12.51s (-0.59) **Going Correction** +0.05s/f (Slow) 9 Ran SP% **121.0**

Speed ratings (Par 100): **105,102,102,100,98 97,92,87,87**

Tote Swingers: 1&2 £25.40, 1&3 £5.60, 2&3 £2.70 CSF £42.26 CT £122.27 TOTE £3.00: £1.40, £8.80, £1.90; EX 48.30.

Owner Sheikh Hamdan Bin Mohammed Al Maktoum **Bred** Derek Veitch **Trained** Middleham Moor, N Yorks

FOCUS

This was an interesting 3-y-o handicap. The leaders went off plenty fast enough and set things up for the closers.

902 DIGIBET CASINO H'CAP 7f (P)

7:20 (7:21) (Class 4) (0-85,85) 4-Y-O+ £4,209 (£1,252; £625; £312) Stalls High

Form				RPR
04-2	1		**Last Sovereign**[17] 747 6-8-11 78 ShaneKelly 5 *(Jane Chapple-Hyam) mde all: rdn and qcknd over 2f out: kpt on wl and a holding rival fnl f* 4/1[2]	86
0131	2	1/2	**Caprio (IRE)**[35] 481 5-9-1 82 NickyMackay 7 *(J R Boyle) chsd ldrs: rdn and pressed wnr 2f out: r.o wl but a hld fnl f* 7/1[3]	89
0/-1	3	1 1/2	**Lucky Redback (IRE)**[15] 761 4-9-4 85 RichardHughes 4 *(R Hannon) t.k.h: chsd wnr tl rdn and sltly outpcd over 2f out: rallied to chse ldng pair 1f out: kpt on same pce after* 13/8[1]	88
000-	4	1/2	**Ra Junior (USA)**[153] 6795 4-9-4 85 AndrewMullen 1 *(D Nicholls) hld up in tch in rr: rdn and effrt wl over 2f out: hdwy to chse ldrs over 1f out: no imp fnl f* 12/1	86
-422	5	1 1/4	**Jake The Snake (IRE)**[23] 657 9-8-7 79 AmyBaker(5) 2 *(A W Carroll) stdd and v.s.a: t.k.h and in tch in last after 2f: c v wd bnd wl over 2f out: sn rdn: styd on ins fnl f: no ch* 7/1[3]	77
5/10	6	1	**Noble Jack (IRE)**[46] 359 4-8-8 75 LiamKeniry 9 *(G L Moore) chsd wnr tl 2f out: wknd u.p ent fnl f* 16/1	70
6364	7	1/2	**Timeteam (IRE)**[21] 679 4-8-13 80 JimmyFortune 6 *(P D Evans) t.k.h: hld up in tch towards rr: rdn and effrt ent fnl 2f: unable qck and no prog after* 20/1	74
1343	8	3 1/2	**Divine Force**[14] 779 4-8-6 78 TobyAtkinson(5) 8 *(M Wigham) t.k.h: stdd after s and hld up in tch in midfield: swtchd ins short-lived effrt u.p ent 2f out: wknd over 1f out* 17/2	62
3240	9	7	**Indian Skipper (IRE)**[25] 635 5-9-4 85 (v) FrannyNorton 3 *(R C Guest) in tch in midfield on outer: rdn and nt qckn ent fnl 2f: sn btn and wl bhd fnl f* 11/1	50

1m 26.33s (0.33) **Going Correction** +0.05s/f (Slow) 9 Ran SP% **120.3**

Speed ratings (Par 105): **100,99,97,97,95 94,94,90,82**

Tote Swingers: 1&2 £5.60, 1&3 £3.00, 2&3 £2.30 CSF £33.64 CT £63.88 TOTE £3.50: £1.10, £2.90, £1.90; EX 35.70.

Owner Howard Spooner **Bred** Gestut Hof Ittlingen & Cheveley Park Stud Ltd **Trained** Dalham, Suffolk

FOCUS

Another fair handicap, this time for older horses. There was no real pace on early, though, which caught the out the majority of runners and the overall form is a little suspect.

Divine Force Official explanation: jockey said gelding ran too freely

903 DIGIBET DRAGONFLY STKS (LISTED RACE) 1m 4f (P)

7:50 (7:50) (Class 1) 4-Y-O+

£22,708 (£8,608; £4,308; £2,148; £1,076; £540) Stalls Centre

Form				RPR
11	1		**Buxted (IRE)**[39] 447 4-9-0 96 StevieDonohoe 3 *(R A Mills) hld up in last trio: rdn along over 2f out: 4th and stl plenty to do jst over 1f out: r.o strly ins fnl f to ld towards fin: won gng away* 5/2[1]	108+
-066	2	1	**Record Breaker (IRE)**[20] 706 6-9-2 98 (b) JoeFanning 2 *(M Johnston) chsd ldrs: rdn to ld over 1f out: clr ins fnl f: r.o wl tl mown by wnr towards fin* 5/1[3]	103
614-	3	2 1/4	**Heliodor (USA)**[144] 7031 4-9-0 107 RichardHughes 7 *(R Hannon) led tl narrowly hdd 3f out: rdn and stl ev ch wl over 1f out: outpcd by ldr 1f out: lost 2nd ins fnl f* 3/1[2]	99
0-00	4	1 1/2	**Illustrious Blue**[12] 820 7-9-7 108 JimCrowley 6 *(W J Knight) t.k.h early: hld up in last pair: rdn and effrt ent fnl f: racd awkwardly u.p over 1f out: kpt on but nvr gng pce to threaten ldrs* 5/2[1]	102
1111	5	nse	**Spruce (USA)**[13] 785 4-9-0 90 JimmyQuinn 1 *(Miss J Feilden) stdd and dropped in after s: hdwy to chse ldr 10f out: led narrowly 3f out: rdn over 2f out: hdd over 1f out: wknd ent fnl f* 8/1	97
0-	6	1	**Porgy**[159] 6658 5-9-2 96 TonyHamilton 4 *(R A Fahey) stdd s: hld up in last pair: rdn and racd awkwardly ent fnl 2f: nt qckn and plugged on same pce* 33/1	95
0-50	7	1/2	**Kaolak (USA)**[40] 441 4-9-0 93 ChrisCatlin 9 *(J Ryan) t.k.h: chsd ldr tl 10f out: chsd ldrs after tl wknd u.p over 1f out* 33/1	95
4141	8	3 3/4	**Bavarica**[5] 871 8-8-11 72 Louis-PhilippeBeuzelin 5 *(Miss J Feilden) hld up in midfield: rdn and wknd 2f out* 33/1	84?

2m 33.09s (-1.41) **Going Correction** +0.05s/f (Slow)

WFA 4 from 5yo+ 2lb 8 Ran SP% **118.7**

Speed ratings (Par 111): **106,105,103,102,102 102,101,99**

Tote Swingers: 1&2 £5.40, 1&3 £2.80, 2&3 £4.80 CSF £16.04 TOTE £4.10: £1.10, £2.10, £1.90; EX 14.40.

Owner Buxted Partnership **Bred** Ronan Burns **Trained** Headley, Surrey

FOCUS

A good contest.

NOTEBOOK

Buxted(IRE) made it three wins from as many outings despite finding little go his way through the race. Making his debut in Listed company and having his first run away from Lingfield, he was held up off just an average pace early on. He got caught a little flat-footed when the race got serious two furlongs out, but found a fine turn of foot down the centre of the track and was always going to get up. This lightly raced four-year-old certainly looks a Group performer in the making. (op 9-4 tchd 2-1 and 3-1 in a place)

Record Breaker(IRE) was well placed when the tempo began to quicken up and shot the front in the home straight. He gave his all, but was a sitting duck for the classy winner. (op 6-1)

Heliodor(USA) had to be of interest and he held a solid chance on official figures. Returning from a 144-day break, he was able to dictate from an early stage but lacked the required turn of foot when asked to quicken and still has to prove he stays this far. (op 5-2)

Illustrious Blue, returning from Dubai, was backed despite being saddled with a 7lb penalty. He wasn't at all suited by being held up off the ordinary pace and was staying on too late in the home straight. (op 7-2 tchd 4-1)

904 BOOK KEMPTON TICKETS ON 0844 579 3008 H'CAP 1m 4f (P)

8:20 (8:20) (Class 5) (0-75,75) 3-Y-O £2,590 (£770; £385; £192) Stalls Centre

Form RPR

0-11 **1** **Desert Recluse (IRE)**[14] 775 3-8-5 **66** LeeTopliss(7) 5 76
(Pat Eddery) *chsd ldr tl led 4f out: mde rest: rdn clr wl over 1f out: styd on wl* **5/2**[2]

0-1 **2** 1 ¼ **Chink Of Light**[21] 677 3-9-7 **75** JimmyFortune 1 83
(A M Balding) *s.i.s: racd in midfield: rdn over 3f out: no real hdwy tl drvn to chse clr wnr jst over 1f out: kpt edging rt u.p: styd on but nvr gng pce to threaten wnr* **6/4**[1]

0-32 **3** 6 **Temple Fair (USA)**[35] 482 3-8-4 **58** JoeFanning 4 56
(M Johnston) *led tl 4f out: chsd wnr tl unable qck u.p 2f out: wknd over 1f out: wl btn fnl f* **6/1**[3]

-234 **4** ½ **Always De One**[15] 762 3-8-2 **56** oh1 JimmyQuinn 6 53
(Miss J Feilden) *hld up in last pair: pushed and hdwy over 4f out: drvn and unable qck jst over 2f out: wknd over 1f out: wl btn fnl f* **10/1**

0136 **5** nk **Yorksters Prince (IRE)**[7] 840 3-8-4 **65** CharlotteKerton(7) 7 62
(G Prodromou) *chsd ldrs: rdn and unable qck over 2f out: hung lft and wl hld fr over 1f out* **16/1**

5030 **6** 21 **Layla's Lad (USA)**[12] 805 3-8-6 **60** MartinDwyer 3 23
(D M Simcock) *stdd s: hld up in last pair: rdn and lost tch over 2f out: t.o fr over 1f out* **15/2**

2m 34.47s (-0.03) **Going Correction** +0.05s/f (Slow) **6** Ran SP% **109.6**
Speed ratings (Par 98): **102,101,97,96,96 82**
Tote Swingers: 1&2 £1.10, 1&3 £1.10, 2&3 £3.80 CSF £6.30 TOTE £2.10: £1.30, £1.10; EX 6.40.
Owner Pat Eddery Racing (Storm Bird) **Bred** John Foley & Miss Ann Aungier **Trained** Nether Winchendon, Bucks

FOCUS
This modest three-year-old handicap was run at a fair early pace which saw them strung out on the back straight, before things slowed right up nearing the home turn.

905 LEVY BOARD H'CAP 6f (P)

8:50 (8:51) (Class 4) (0-85,85) 4-Y-O+ £4,209 (£1,252; £625; £312) Stalls High

Form RPR

2-14 **1** **New Leyf (IRE)**[19] 722 4-8-10 **77** SteveDrowne 5 88
(J R Gask) *t.k.h: hld up in tch: plld out and effrt wl over 1f out: rdn and edgd rt but r.o wl to ld fnl 100yds: sn in command* **11/4**[1]

-346 **2** 1 ¼ **Ray Of Joy**[17] 747 4-8-8 **75** NickyMackay 6 82
(J R Jenkins) *t.k.h: trckd ldrs: hdwy to ld and rdn wl over 1f out: hdd and nt pce of wnr fnl 100yds* **10/1**

030 **3** nk **Orpsie Boy (IRE)**[25] 635 7-9-4 **85** NeilCallan 8 91
(N P Littmoden) *t.k.h: hld up wl in tch on inner: rdn and effrt 2f out: kpt on wl u.p fnl f* **9/2**[2]

2163 **4** nk **Bonnie Prince Blue**[7] 851 7-8-8 **75** (b) AndrewMullen 7 80
(D Nicholls) *dwlt and hmpd s: t.k.h: hld up wl in tch in midfield: rdn and effrt wl over 1f out: kpt on wl u.p fnl f* **14/1**

324- **5** nk **Bahamian Lad**[77] 7875 5-9-1 **82** JerryO'Dwyer 9 86
(R Hollinshead) *wnt bdly lft s: sn led and set stdy gallop: qcknd over 2f out: rdn and hdd wl over 1f out: kpt on one pce fnl f* **17/2**

2122 **6** nse **Secret Witness**[15] 761 4-8-12 **79** LiamJones 4 83
(R A Harris) *chsd ldrs: rdn and unable qck 2f out: styng on same pce and hld whn n.m.r ins fnl f* **6/1**[3]

1-62 **7** 1 **Lujeanie**[21] 679 4-9-0 **81** JimCrowley 2 82
(D K Ivory) *stdd and dropped in bhd after s: t.k.h: hld up in rr: rdn and gd hdwy on inner to chse ldrs over 1f out: wknd fnl f* **8/1**

6503 **8** 1 ¼ **Vhujon (IRE)**[7] 846 5-8-10 **77** RichardHughes 1 74
(P D Evans) *stdd and dropped in s: t.k.h: hld up in tch in last trio: rdn ent fnl 2f: styd on same pce after* **10/1**

600/ **9** 4 ½ **Financial Times (USA)**[669] 2188 8-9-1 **82** (t) TomQueally 11 64
(Stef Higgins) *restless in stalls: t.k.h: chsd ldr tl rdn and wknd over 1f out: bhd fnl f* **20/1**

543- **10** ¾ **Bertoliver**[77] 7872 6-8-12 **79** DaneO'Neill 10 59
(S C Williams) *t.k.h: hld up in tch in rr: rdn and no hdwy ent fnl 2f: wl btn fnl f* **7/1**

1m 13.11s (0.01) **Going Correction** +0.05s/f (Slow) **10** Ran SP% **122.9**
Speed ratings (Par 105): **101,99,98,98,98 98,96,95,89,88**
Tote Swingers: 1&2 £13.20, 1&3 £6.40, 2&3 £18.20 CSF £33.73 CT £125.89 TOTE £2.60: £1.10, £4.00, £2.00; EX 53.20 Place 6: £5.26 Place 5: £3.71 .
Owner Horses First Racing Limited **Bred** John Weld **Trained** Sutton Veny, Wilts

FOCUS
A competitive sprint handicap for the class. It was yet another race on the night run at a messy early pace, however, and there were plenty of chances as a result.
T/Plt: £8.50 to a £1 stake. Pool: £58,294.02. 4,973.67 winning tickets. T/Qpdt: £3.60 to a £1 stake. Pool: £5,979.88. 1,216.22 winning tickets. SP

892 SOUTHWELL (L-H)

Wednesday, March 17

OFFICIAL GOING: Standard
Wind: Light across Weather: Cloudy and dry

906 32REDBET.COM H'CAP 5f (F)

1:55 (1:56) (Class 6) (0-65,64) 3-Y-O £1,774 (£523; £262) Stalls High

Form RPR

226- **1** **Liberty Lady (IRE)**[94] 7736 3-9-6 **63** DavidProbert 12 69
(D Donovan) *wnt lft s: sn chsng ldrs: hdwy 2f out: rdn over 1f out: styd on to ld jst ins fnl f: edgd rt and kpt on* **10/1**

0-04 **2** ¾ **Lets Move It**[62] 167 3-8-2 **45** (v) LukeMorris 2 48
(D Shaw) *in tch: rdn along 2f out: drvn to chse ldrs over 1f out: kpt on wl u.p ins fnl f* **16/1**

-065 **3** ½ **Silver Linnet (IRE)**[40] 425 3-8-10 **56** (b) AndreaAtzeni(3) 5 57+
(M G Quinlan) *led: rdn clr wl over 1f out: drvn and hdd jst ins fnl f: one pce* **7/1**

5-65 **4** 3 ¼ **Thewinnatakesitall**[9] 831 3-8-12 **55** (b[1]) FrankieMcDonald 9 44
(H J Evans) *sltly hmpd s: in tch and rdn along 1/2-way: styng on whn edgd lft and bmpd over 1f out: kpt on same pce* **40/1**

5452 **5** nk **Tamarind Hill (IRE)**[6] 856 3-9-2 **59** (b) SebSanders 3 47
(A J McCabe) *dwlt and sn rdn along towards rr: hdwy 2f out: drvn over 1f out: kpt on same pce* **5/1**[3]

34-5 **6** ½ **Caol Ila (IRE)**[62] 167 3-8-11 **54** PaulMulrennan 8 40
(J G Given) *chsd ldrs: rdn along over 2f out: drvn and edgd rt over 1f out: kpt on same pce* **33/1**

-455 **7** ¾ **Young George**[26] 619 3-8-3 **49** KellyHarrison(3) 6 33
(C W Fairhurst) *midfield: effrt and sme hdwy 1/2-way: swtchd lft and rdn 2f out: swtchd rt over 1f out: kpt on u.p ins fnl f: nvr nr ldrs* **16/1**

0-4 **8** 1 **Bombay Mist**[13] 784 3-8-2 **45** FrannyNorton 4 25
(R C Guest) *prom: rdn along over 2f out: grad wknd* **25/1**

-535 **9** 3 ½ **My Mandy (IRE)**[15] 759 3-9-7 **64** LiamJones 7 32
(R A Harris) *dwlt: sn rdn along and a towards rr* **10/1**

003- **10** 1 ¼ **Vanilla Loan (IRE)**[147] 6947 3-9-3 **60** JerryO'Dwyer 10 23
(M Botti) *dwlt sltly and hmpd s: rdn along 1/2-way: a bhd* **9/2**[2]

04-3 **11** ½ **Drumpellier (IRE)**[33] 519 3-8-12 **60** PaulPickard(5) 13 21
(P T Midgley) *chsd ldrs on outer: rdn along 2f out: sn wknd* **14/1**

03-0 **12** ¾ **Marius Maximus (IRE)**[15] 759 3-8-6 **49** GregFairley 1 8
(M Johnston) *in tch on wd outside: hdwy to chse ldrs 1/2-way: rdn 2f out: drvn over 1 1/2f out and wknd qckly* **10/3**[1]

463 **13** 33 **Fine And Dandie (IRE)**[13] 784 3-8-9 **52** AdrianNicholls 11 —
(D Nicholls) *hmpd s: in rr whn hung bdly lft 1/2-way: bhd and eased wl over 1f out* **12/1**

60.01 secs (0.31) **Going Correction** -0.025s/f (Stan) **13** Ran SP% **124.0**
Speed ratings (Par 96): **96,94,94,88,88 87,86,84,79,77 76,75,22**
Tote Swingers: 1&2 £25.20, 1&3 £18.20, 2&3 £38.50 CSF £162.96 CT £1245.16 TOTE £16.00: £3.60, £4.50, £1.90; EX 237.00 TRIFECTA Not won..
Owner Mark Jones **Bred** Chris Giblett **Trained** Newmarket, Suffolk

FOCUS
A moderate 3-y-o sprint handicap in which few got involved. Probably not form to rate too positively.
Thewinnatakesitall Official explanation: jockey said filly hung badly left under pressure
Fine And Dandie(IRE) Official explanation: jockey said gelding hung left throughout

907 32RED CASINO OF DECADE H'CAP 7f (F)

2:30 (2:30) (Class 5) (0-75,72) 4-Y-O+ £2,456 (£725; £362) Stalls Low

Form RPR

5045 **1** **Jonnie Skull (IRE)**[1] 892 4-8-8 **62** (vt) ChrisCatlin 1 69
(P S McEntee) *trckd ldrs on inner: pushed along and outpcd after 3f: rdn and bhd 3f out: rdn and hdwy 2f out: swtchd rt and drvn over 1f out: styd on strly to ld fnl 75yds* **14/1**

2-15 **2** 1 ¾ **Young Gladiator (IRE)**[27] 602 5-8-12 **66** (b) FrederikTylicki 4 69
(Julie Camacho) *chsd ldrs: hdwy 3f out: rdn to chse ldng pair 2f out: drvn over 1f out: styd on to chal ins fnl f: kpt on same pce* **7/2**[2]

3 hd **Academy Blues (USA)**[250] 3831 5-9-0 **68** AdrianNicholls 2 70
(D Nicholls) *trckd ldrs: hdwy 3f out: chsd ldr over 2f out: rdn to ld over 1f out: sn drvn: hdd and no ex last 75yds* **9/2**

2611 **4** 3 ¼ **Whatyouwoodwishfor (USA)**[27] 602 4-8-11 **65** (b) PaulHanagan 3 58
(R A Fahey) *set str pce: rdn along on inner 2f out: drvn and hdd wl over 1f out: wknd ent fnl f* **5/2**[1]

1250 **5** 7 **Elusive Warrior (USA)**[29] 572 7-8-11 **70** (p) DeclanCannon(5) 5 44
(A J McCabe) *chsd ldrs on outer: rdn along 3f out: wknd over 2f out* **13/2**

0-60 **6** 4 ½ **Classic Descent**[34] 508 5-9-4 **72** AndrewElliott 6 34
(Mrs R A Carr) *s.i.s: a bhd* **22/1**

4-02 **7** 6 **Hypnotist (UAE)**[12] 808 4-9-1 **69** (b) SebSanders 7 15
(C E Brittain) *chsd ldrs on outer: rdn along bef 1/2-way and sn wknd* **4/1**[3]

1m 31.19s (0.89) **Going Correction** +0.15s/f (Slow) **7** Ran SP% **113.3**
Speed ratings (Par 103): **100,98,97,94,86 80,74**
Tote Swingers: 1&2 £6.20, 1&3 £6.10, 2&3 £3.70 CSF £61.10 TOTE £11.60: £4.90, £3.00; EX 82.50.
Owner Mrs Rebecca McEntee **Bred** Canice Farrell Jnr **Trained** Newmarket, Suffolk

FOCUS
They went a really strong pace in this modest handicap and they all finished tired. The winner is rated back to his best.
Jonnie Skull(IRE) Official explanation: trainer said, regarding apparent improvement in form, that the gelding benefited from the fast-run pace.

908 32RED.COM H'CAP 1m (F)

3:05 (3:06) (Class 5) (0-75,75) 4-Y-O+ £2,729 (£806; £403) Stalls Low

Form RPR

/3-1 **1** **Pendragon (USA)**[20] 705 7-8-4 **61** oh2 PaulHanagan 5 76+
(B Ellison) *trckd ldrs: pushed along briefly 3f out: hdwy on bit 2f out and sn cl up: led 1f out: sn rdn and edgd lft ins fnl f: rdn out* **5/2**[1]

2620 **2** 2 **Elusive Fame (USA)**[29] 572 4-9-4 **75** (b) GregFairley 8 85
(M Johnston) *led: hdd over 3f out: led again over 2f out: rdn wl over 1f out: drvn and hdd 1f out: kpt on same pce ins fnl f* **7/2**[2]

110- **3** 1 ¼ **Just Five (IRE)**[139] 7141 4-9-4 **75** PhillipMakin 2 82
(M Dods) *a.p: effrt 2f out and sn cl up: rdn and ev ch over 1f out: drvn and one pce ins fnl f* **8/1**

6-00 **4** ½ **Street Devil (USA)**[16] 756 5-8-13 **70** TonyCulhane 9 76
(R Curtis) *hld up: swtchd ins and hdwy wl over 2f out: sn rdn and styd on appr fnl f: nrst fin* **11/1**

1034 **5** 3 ½ **Transmission (IRE)**[29] 573 5-9-4 **75** TomEaves 6 73
(B Smart) *prom on outer: rdn along wl over 2f out: grad wknd* **11/2**[3]

5060 **6** 4 **Mcconnell (USA)**[17] 749 5-9-1 **75** RobertLButler(3) 4 64
(P Butler) *a towards rr* **7/1**

5-51 **7** 6 **Border Owl (IRE)**[13] 787 5-8-2 **64** BillyCray(5) 3 39
(P Salmon) *sn chsng ldr on inner: hdwy to ld over 3f out: rdn and hdd over 2f out: sn drvn and wknd* **10/1**

0-55 **8** 2 ¼ **Shame The Devil (IRE)**[29] 570 5-8-6 **63** FrankieMcDonald 10 33
(H J Evans) *s.i.s: a bhd* **66/1**

500- **9** nk **Bahiano (IRE)**[299] 2243 9-8-10 **67** (p) SebSanders 7 36
(C E Brittain) *a towards rr* **11/1**

4-55 **10** ¾ **West End Lad**[50] 298 7-8-3 **63** (b) MartinLane(3) 1 30
(S R Bowring) *towards rr: rdn along 1/2-way and sn bhd* **16/1**

1m 42.77s (-0.93) **Going Correction** +0.15s/f (Slow) **10** Ran SP% **122.9**
Speed ratings (Par 103): **110,108,106,106,102 98,92,90,90,89**
Tote Swingers: 1&2 £2.70, 1&3 £5.20, 2&3 £9.30 CSF £11.83 CT £65.58 TOTE £3.30: £1.80, £1.90, £2.60; EX 15.00 Trifecta £146.00 Pool: £374.95 - 1.90 winning units..
Owner Mrs Claire Ellison **Bred** Flaxman Holdings Ltd **Trained** Norton, N Yorks

FOCUS
A fair handicap in which it paid to race prominently. The unexposed winner was 2lb wrong under his penalty and is likely to do better again. The runner-up is a pretty solid guide.

The Form Book, Raceform Ltd, Compton, RG20 6NL

Shame The Devil(IRE) Official explanation: jockey said gelding missed the break

909 BET AT 32RED.COM (S) STKS 1m (F)
3:45 (3:45) (Class 6) 3-Y-O £1,774 (£523; £262) Stalls Low

Form RPR
-332 1 **Just Mandy (IRE)**13 784 3-8-7 62 PaulHanagan 7 60
(R A Fahey) *trckd ldrs: hdwy 3f out: rdn to chse ldr wl over 1f out: drvn ent fnl f: styd on to ld fnl 100yds* 15/8²
2125 2 1 ¼ **Inside Track (IRE)**13 782 3-8-13 74 PaulPickard(5) 5 68
(P T Midgley) *trckd ldr: hdwy over 3f out: led over 2f out: rdn clr wl over 1f out: drvn and edgd lft ent fnl f: hdd and no ex last 100yds* 11/2³
1143 3 3 ¼ **Tiger Hawk (USA)**13 781 3-8-13 65 (b) RichardEvans(5) 1 61
(P D Evans) *led: rdn along 3f out: hdd and drvn over 2f out: kpt on same pce* 7/4¹
0-14 4 1 ¼ **Step To It (IRE)**6 861 3-9-4 51 (p) ChrisCatlin 4 58
(K A Ryan) *in tch on outer: rdn along and outpcd over 3f out: drvn and kpt on fnl 2f: n.d* 9/1
36-6 5 2 **As Brave As You (IRE)**19 717 3-8-9 50 BarryMcHugh(3) 3 47
(B Ellison) *dwlt: a towards rr* 8/1
6-0 6 4 **Light The City (IRE)**19 718 3-8-12 0 AndrewElliott 6 38
(Mrs R A Carr) *dwlt: hdwy to chse ldrs 1/2-way: rdn along over 3f out and sn wknd* 50/1
000- 7 5 **Micky's Bird**96 7706 3-8-7 42 PaulEddery 2 21
(R C Guest) *chsd ldrs on inner: rdn along 1/2-way: sn wknd* 100/1
1m 46.04s (2.34) **Going Correction** +0.15s/f (Slow) 7 Ran SP% 110.6
Speed ratings (Par 96): **94,92,89,88,86 82,77**
Tote Swingers: 1&2 £2.70, 1&3 £1.40, 2&3 £2.10 CSF £11.76 TOTE £3.10: £1.60, £2.20; EX 13.90.Winner bought in for 8,500gns.
Owner Dr Marwan Koukash **Bred** Mick McGinn **Trained** Musley Bank, N Yorks

FOCUS
Sound form, with the first three not bad for the grade. It is doubtful he had to improve much on recent efforts.

910 £320 FREE AT 32RED.COM H'CAP 1m 6f (F)
4:25 (4:25) (Class 5) (0-75,73) 4-Y-O+ £3,412 (£1,007; £504) Stalls Low

Form RPR
12/1 1 **Veloso (FR)**8 835 8-9-9 71 6ex FrederikTylicki 2 77
(J A Glover) *mde most: rdn along over 2f out and sn jnd: drvn and hdd 1f out: rallied u.p to ld nr fin* 5/4¹
1044 2 shd **Heathyards Junior**6 857 4-8-10 67 DeclanCannon(5) 7 73
(A J McCabe) *hld up: hdwy 4f out: chal 2f out: rdn to ld 1f out: drvn ins fnl f: hdd and no ex nr fin* 8/1
40-2 3 1 ¼ **Chocolate Caramel (USA)**61 190 8-9-11 73 PaulHanagan 5 77
(R A Fahey) *trckd ldrs: cl up 4f out: rdn 2f out: sltly outpcd over 1f out: drvn and rallied ins fnl f: no ex towards fin* 4/1²
0-26 4 16 **My Friend Fritz**50 300 10-9-4 66 PhillipMakin 6 48
(P W Hiatt) *chsd ldrs: rdn along 4f out: drvn 3f out and sn outpcd* 9/1
1-44 5 1 ½ **Lava Steps (USA)**19 719 4-9-1 67 TonyCulhane 3 47
(P T Midgley) *chsd ldrs: rdn along 4f out: drvn 3f out and sn outpcd* 16/1
015- 6 12 **Hi Dancer**8 3450 7-9-0 67 PatrickDonaghy(5) 1 30
(B M R Haslam) *cl up on inner: rdn along 5f out: wknd 4f out and sn bhd* 11/2³
-535 7 28 **Bushy Dell (IRE)**13 786 5-8-7 62 AdamBeschizza(7) 4 —
(Miss J Feilden) *a in rr: outpcd and bhd fnl 5f* 25/1
3m 9.59s (1.29) **Going Correction** +0.15s/f (Slow)
WFA 4 from 5yo+ 4lb 7 Ran SP% 110.7
Speed ratings (Par 103): **102,101,101,92,91 84,68**
Tote Swingers: 1&2 £3.80, 1&3 £2.20, 2&3 £6.60 CSF £11.25 TOTE £2.40: £2.00, £3.50; EX 16.40.
Owner Brian Morton **Bred** Jean Louis Pariente **Trained** Babworth, Notts
■ Stewards' Enquiry : Frederik Tylicki two-day ban: used whip with excessive frequency (Mar 31-Apr 1)

FOCUS
A fair staying handicap. The winner is rated to a similar level to his recent course win and the second ran his best race yet.
Hi Dancer Official explanation: jockey said gelding ran flat

911 32REDPOKER.COM MAIDEN STKS 6f (F)
5:05 (5:05) (Class 5) 3-Y-O+ £2,456 (£725; £362) Stalls Low

Form RPR
2- 1 **Xilerator (IRE)**137 7167 3-8-13 0 AdrianNicholls 3 72
(D Nicholls) *led: jnd 2f out and sn rdn along: hdd 1f out: sn drvn and edgd lft ins fnl f: rallied wl to ld fnl 75yds* 1/2¹
2 1 **Philosophers Stone (FR)** 3-8-13 0 PhillipMakin 6 69
(T D Barron) *cl up: effrt 2f out: rdn to ld 1f out: drvn: hdd and no ex fnl 75yds* 10/1
3062 3 2 ¼ **Tobrata**27 602 4-9-12 62 AlanMunro 2 66
(M Brittain) *trckd ldrs on inner: effrt over 2f out: sn rdn and kpt on same pce* 7/1²
4 ¾ **Mirza** 3-8-13 0 SebSanders 7 59
(Rae Guest) *cl up on outer: rdn along over 2f out: kpt on same pce* 16/1
5 3 ¼ **Special Quality (USA)** 3-8-13 0 TomEaves 4 49
(R M H Cowell) *in tch: rdn along 1/2-way: n.d* 8/1³
/-0 6 1 ¾ **Smackeroo (USA)**14 776 4-9-0 0 IanBrennan(7) 1 42
(J J Quinn) *s.i.s: a in rr* 50/1
1m 16.77s (0.27) **Going Correction** +0.15s/f (Slow)
WFA 3 from 4yo 13lb 6 Ran SP% 107.2
Speed ratings (Par 103): **104,102,99,98,94 92**
Tote Swingers: 1&2 £1.50, 1&3 £1.10, 2&3 £5.90 CSF £5.58 TOTE £1.50: £1.50, £2.50; EX 5.50.
Owner Ian Hewitson **Bred** Denis And Mrs Teresa Bergin **Trained** Sessay, N Yorks

FOCUS
The bare form is no better than fair, but this was still a relatively interesting maiden. The form is rated around the exposed third but could be underrated.

912 CASINO AT 32RED.COM H'CAP 6f (F)
5:40 (5:40) (Class 6) (0-60,60) 4-Y-O+ £1,774 (£523; £262) Stalls Low

Form RPR
5003 1 **Captain Kallis (IRE)**8 839 4-8-10 52 (be) FrederikTylicki 10 63
(D J S Ffrench Davis) *trckd ldrs: hdwy on outer 1/2-way: rdn to ld wl over 1f out: drvn ins fnl f: jst hld on* 4/1¹
00-2 2 shd **Scruffy Skip (IRE)**8 838 5-8-5 47 (p) AndrewElliott 6 58
(Mrs C A Dunnett) *led over 2f: cl up tl led again over 2f out: sn rdn and hdd wl over 1f out: drvn and rallied wl ins fnl f: jst failed* 4/1¹
0340 3 shd **Megalo Maniac**6 866 7-8-4 46 oh1 (v) PaulHanagan 2 56
(R A Fahey) *towards rr: pushed along and hdwy 2f out: rdn over 1f out: styd on strly ins fnl f* 5/1²
2050 4 2 ¾ **Angaric (IRE)**14 773 7-8-5 54 (p) AdamCarter(7) 9 56
(B Smart) *trckd ldrs: effrt towards outer over 2f out: sn rdn and one pce fr over 1f out* 12/1
4424 5 nk **Nabeeda**8 838 5-8-10 52 AlanMunro 4 53
(M Brittain) *trckd ldrs on inner: hdwy over 2f out: rdn to chse ldng pair over 1f out: sn drvn and kpt on same pce* 5/1²
0000 6 1 ½ **King's Sabre**7 845 4-8-10 52 (e) PaulEddery 5 48
(R C Guest) *in tch: rdn along and sltly outpcd over 2f out: kpt on u.p appr fnl f: n.d* 20/1
3-60 7 1 ¾ **Pretty Orchid**8 838 5-8-3 50 (p) PaulPickard(5) 7 40
(P T Midgley) *chsd ldrs: rdn along wl over 2f out: sn drvn and wknd* 22/1
0663 8 1 **Owed**8 836 8-7-11 46 oh1 (tp) MatthewLawson(7) 1 33
(R Bastiman) *cl up on inner: led over 3f out: rdn along and hdd over 2f out: sn wknd* 12/1
05-5 9 1 ½ **Exceedingly Good (IRE)**8 836 4-9-2 58 (t) FergusSweeney 8 40
(S R Bowring) *a towards rr* 16/1
-444 10 1 ¾ **Kingsgate Castle**12 810 5-9-4 60 (b) TomEaves 11 37
(Miss Gay Kelleway) *dwlt: racd wd: a in rr* 7/1³
00-0 11 16 **Billy Simmonds**23 667 5-8-1 50 oh1 ow4 AdamBeschizza(7) 3 —
(Miss J Feilden) *reminders after s: a in rr: bhd fr 1/2-way* 33/1
1m 16.95s (0.45) **Going Correction** +0.15s/f (Slow) 11 Ran SP% 119.2
Speed ratings (Par 101): **103,102,102,99,98 96,94,93,91,88 67**
Tote Swingers: 1&2 £4.00, 1&3 £5.70, 2&3 £6.30 CSF £19.27 CT £84.24 TOTE £5.60: £2.20, £1.50, £2.00; EX 18.80 Trifecta £40.70 Pool: £212.22 - 3.85 winning units. Place 6: £93.93 Place 5: £18.46 .
Owner Hargood Limited **Bred** Pipe View Stud **Trained** Lambourn, Berks
■ Stewards' Enquiry : Andrew Elliott one-day ban: used whip with excessive frequency (Mar 31)

FOCUS
A moderate but competitive handicap.
T/Plt: £512.70 to a £1 stake. Pool: £41,262.51. 58.75 winning tickets. T/Qpdt: £7.20 to a £1 stake. Pool: £3,962.34. 407.19 winning tickets. JR

906 SOUTHWELL (L-H)
Thursday, March 18

OFFICIAL GOING: Standard
Wind: Light across Weather: Overcast

913 BET AT 32RED.COM H'CAP 5f (F)
2:30 (2:30) (Class 5) (0-70,68) 4-Y-O+ £2,934 (£866; £433) Stalls High

Form RPR
4540 1 **Bookiesindex Boy**20 723 6-9-0 64 (b) StephenCraine 8 74+
(J R Jenkins) *hld up: smooth hdwy over 1f out: led on bit wl ins fnl f: easily* 14/1
0162 2 1 ½ **Spic 'n Span**9 832 5-9-0 64 (b) ChrisCatlin 2 69
(R A Harris) *led: rdn over 1f out: hdd and unable qck wl ins fnl f* 11/2³
1501 3 nse **Lujiana**2 896 5-8-9 59 6ex JoeFanning 1 63
(M Brittain) *chsd ldrs: rdn over 1f out: styd on* 4/1²
4421 4 nk **Grudge**34 520 5-9-4 68 (e) SebSanders 3 71
(C R Dore) *s.i.s: rcvrd to chse ldr over 3f out: rdn over 1f out: styd on* 9/4¹
3-53 5 2 ½ **Style Award**32 555 5-8-6 59 KellyHarrison(3) 4 53
(W J H Ratcliffe) *prom: rdn and hung lft over 1f out: styd on same pce* 9/1
4650 6 3 ½ **Thoughtsofstardom**13 806 7-8-10 67 (be) LeonnaMayor(7) 5 49
(P S McEntee) *prom: rdn over 1f out: sn wknd* 28/1
000- 7 ¾ **Guest Connections**166 6489 7-8-12 62 AndrewMullen 7 41
(D Nicholls) *s.s: outpcd: t.o 1/2-way: r.o ins fnl f* 25/1
3405 8 1 **Figaro Flyer (IRE)**13 806 7-9-1 65 ShaneKelly 10 40
(P Howling) *s.i.s: outpcd* 13/2
6006 9 1 **Tournedos (IRE)**15 774 8-9-1 65 (b) AndrewElliott 6 37
(Mrs R A Carr) *sn outpcd* 40/1
16/4 10 4 ½ **Pennyspider (IRE)**8 848 5-8-12 62 LukeMorris 11 18
(M S Saunders) *prom: rdn 1/2-way: wknd wl over 1f out* 25/1
410- 11 8 **Hitches Dubai (BRZ)**222 4772 5-9-1 65 AdrianNicholls 9 —
(D Nicholls) *dwlt: outpcd* 10/1
59.35 secs (-0.35) **Going Correction** 0.0s/f (Stan) 11 Ran SP% 118.8
Speed ratings (Par 103): **102,99,99,99,95 89,88,86,85,77 65**
toteswingers:1&2:£16.60, 1&3:£11.10, 2&3:£4.40 CSF £86.71 CT £378.84 TOTE £26.00: £4.40, £1.70, £1.90; EX 86.50 TRIFECTA Not won..
Owner Robin Stevens **Bred** D R Tucker **Trained** Royston, Herts

FOCUS
An ordinary sprint handicap and, as usual, the action all took place centre-to-far side.

914 CASINO AT 32RED.COM CLASSIFIED CLAIMING STKS 6f (F)
3:05 (3:05) (Class 6) 3-Y-O+ £1,942 (£578; £288; £144) Stalls Low

Form RPR
-133 1 **Novay Essjay (IRE)**34 524 3-8-5 70 AdrianNicholls 2 71
(D Nicholls) *mde all: rdn over 2f out: styd on gamely* 11/4²
3521 2 shd **Punching**2 892 6-9-7 70 LiamKeniry 5 78
(C R Dore) *trckd ldrs: hmpd sn after s: rdn and ev ch fr over 1f out: kpt on* 5/4¹
2312 3 2 ¾ **Not My Choice (IRE)**14 789 5-9-4 62 (t) AdamKirby 3 66
(J Balding) *sn rdn to chse wnr: ev ch fr over 2f out tl no ex wl ins fnl f* 5/1³
3224 4 4 ½ **Whitbarrow (IRE)**44 379 11-9-2 69 (b) JamesMillman(3) 4 52
(B R Millman) *trckd ldrs: rdn over 1f out: wknd fnl f* 9/1
4330 5 2 ¼ **Only A Game (IRE)**9 839 5-8-9 57 (tp) LeeTopliss(7) 7 42
(I W McInnes) *sn pushed along in rr: rdn and hung lft over 1f out: n.d* 33/1
0-33 6 4 **Irish Music (IRE)**21 699 5-9-4 57 ShaneKelly 6 31
(A P Jarvis) *chsd ldrs: rdn over 2f out: wknd over 1f out* 16/1
2555 7 2 ¾ **Stonecrabstomorrow (IRE)**35 505 7-8-13 63 (p) MarkCoumbe(5) 1 23
(John A Harris) *sn outpcd* 28/1
1m 15.34s (-1.16) **Going Correction** -0.175s/f (Stan)
WFA 3 from 5yo+ 13lb 7 Ran SP% 110.0
Speed ratings (Par 101): **100,99,96,90,87 81,78**
toteswingers:1&2:£1.90, 1&3:£1.70, 2&3:£2.20 CSF £6.02 TOTE £2.90: £2.10, £1.30; EX 6.60.Novay Essjay was claimed by C. R. Dore for £8,000
Owner Middleham Park Racing XXXI **Bred** Camogue Stud Ltd **Trained** Sessay, N Yorks
■ Stewards' Enquiry : Adrian Nicholls caution: used whip down shoulder in the forehand

FOCUS
A modest claimer.

915 POKER AT 32RED.COM MEDIAN AUCTION MAIDEN STKS 7f (F)
3:45 (3:47) (Class 5) 3-5-Y-O **£2,934** (£866; £433) Stalls Low

Form RPR
1 **Don't Call Me (IRE)** 3-8-11 0......(t) TomEaves 9 70+
(B Smart) *s.i.s: hdwy over 5f out: rdn over 2f out: hung lft over 1f out: led and rn green ins fnl f: rdn and r.o wl towards fin* **7/1**
53 2 2 1/4 **Army Of Stars (IRE)**[16] 758 4-9-12 0...... ShaneKelly 10 69
(J A Osborne) *chsd ldrs: rdn and ev ch fr over 1f out: styd on same pce wl ins fnl f* **9/2**[2]
-322 3 3/4 **Turning Circle**[34] 523 4-9-5 62...... JohnCavanagh(7) 4 67
(M Brittain) *hld up in tch: racd keenly: led 2f out: rdn over 1f out: hdd and no ex ins fnl f* **5/2**[1]
54 4 4 **Zephyron (IRE)**[28] 594 3-8-11 0...... NickyMackay 13 51
(J R Holt) *chsd ldrs: rdn 1/2-way: wknd over 1f out* **11/1**
5 3/4 **Mark To Market (IRE)** 3-8-6 0...... SophieDoyle(5) 5 49
(J A Osborne) *mid-div: hdwy 1/2-way: rdn and wknd over 1f out* **16/1**
00- 6 3 1/4 **Zambuka (FR)**[313] 1866 3-8-6 0...... KevinGhunowa 8 35
(R Curtis) *stdd s: hld up: plld hrd: nvr nrr* **20/1**
00 7 2 1/4 **Coxwain (IRE)**[33] 533 3-8-11 0...... GregFairley 3 34
(M Johnston) *pushed along early then rn keen tl rdn over 4f out: sn outpcd* **13/2**[3]
06 8 1 1/4 **Ignore**[7] 858 3-8-11 0...... AndrewElliott 7 31
(Mrs R A Carr) *led: rdn hung lft and hdd 2f out: sn wknd* **125/1**
9 1/2 **Collect Art (IRE)** 3-8-11 0...... HayleyTurner 1 30
(M L W Bell) *prom: rdn 1/2-way: wknd 2f out* **9/2**[2]
10 17 **Presidium Galaxy** 3-8-6 0...... ChrisCatlin 11 —
(G M Moore) *s.s: outpcd* **20/1**
11 nk **Some Yarn (IRE)** 3-8-8 0...... RobertLButler(3) 2 —
(Mrs L C Jewell) *s.s: outpcd* **50/1**

1m 29.37s (-0.93) **Going Correction** -0.175s/f (Stan)
WFA 3 from 4yo 15lb 11 Ran SP% **117.3**
Speed ratings (Par 103): **98,95,94,90,89 85,82,81,80,61 61**
toteswingers:1&2:£5.70, 1&3:£4.30, 2&3:£1.90 CSF £37.11 TOTE £11.30: £3.40, £1.80, £1.20; EX 44.00 Trifecta £117.30 Pool: £396.36 - 2.50 winning units..
Owner H E Sheikh Rashid Bin Mohammed **Bred** Darley **Trained** Hambleton, N Yorks

FOCUS
An ordinary-looking maiden with the third horse rated 62 and they finished well spread out.

916 RUMMY AT 32RED.COM H'CAP 5f (F)
4:25 (4:25) (Class 3) (0-95,95) 4-Y-0+ **£7,771** (£2,312; £1,155; £577) Stalls Low

Form RPR
112- 1 **Arthur's Edge**[131] 7292 6-9-2 93...... DavidProbert 4 105
(B Palling) *chsd ldrs: rdn to ld over 1f out: r.o wl* **9/1**
3321 2 1 3/4 **Onceaponatime (IRE)**[7] 859 5-8-7 84 6ex...... LukeMorris 5 90
(M D Squance) *sn pushed along in rr: gd hdwy u.p fr over 1f out: fin wl: wnt 2nd nr fin* **6/1**[3]
00-5 3 nse **Luscivious**[51] 299 6-8-10 87......(b) FrederikTylicki 14 93
(J A Glover) *chsd ldrs: rdn 1/2-way: styd on* **33/1**
515- 4 hd **Captain Carey**[208] 5245 4-8-4 81...... LiamJones 7 86
(M S Saunders) *chsd ldrs: rdn and ev ch over 1f out: styd on same pce ins fnl f* **33/1**
5111 5 1 **Where's Reiley (USA)**[9] 832 4-8-4 80 6ex...... ChrisCatlin 6 82
(T D Barron) *s.i.s: outpcd: swtchd lft over 3f out: rdn 1/2-way: r.o fr over 1f out: nvr nrr* **13/2**
52-1 6 1 **Rebel Duke (IRE)**[76] 2 6-9-0 94...... BarryMcHugh(3) 1 92
(Ollie Pears) *prom: rdn over 1f out: styd on same pce fnl f* **3/1**[1]
304- 7 hd **Fol Hollow (IRE)**[173] 6283 5-8-11 88...... AdrianNicholls 10 85
(D Nicholls) *led: rdn and hdd over 1f out: no ex* **7/1**
356- 8 1 1/4 **Something (IRE)**[159] 6675 8-9-2 93...... PaulQuinn 3 85
(D Nicholls) *s.s: hdwy over 3f out: wknd fnl f* **16/1**
-063 9 1/2 **Hoh Hoh Hoh**[26] 639 8-8-5 85...... MartinLane(3) 2 76
(R J Price) *chsd ldrs: rdn 1/2-way: wknd over 1f out* **16/1**
-612 10 3 **Thebes**[5] 887 5-9-0 91...... GregFairley 12 71
(M Johnston) *mid-div: drvn along 3f out: sn wknd* **4/1**[2]
505- 11 1 **Saucy Brown (IRE)**[215] 5025 4-9-1 92...... AndrewMullen 9 68
(D Nicholls) *dwlt: outpcd* **28/1**
2534 12 nk **Pawan (IRE)**[26] 639 10-8-7 89 oh1 ow8......(b) AnnStokell(5) 8 64
(Miss A Stokell) *chsd ldrs: rdn and lost pl over 3f out: sn bhd* **50/1**
060- 13 3 1/2 **Rievaulx World**[231] 4456 4-9-4 95...... NeilCallan 11 58
(K A Ryan) *chsd ldrs: rdn 1/2-way: wknd over 1f out* **25/1**

58.81 secs (-0.89) **Going Correction** 0.0s/f (Stan) 13 Ran SP% **122.0**
Speed ratings (Par 107): **107,104,104,103,102 100,100,98,97,92 91,90,85**
toteswingers:1&2:£7.40, 1&3:£32.30, 2&3:£53.80 CSF £60.53 CT £1784.76 TOTE £12.80: £3.40, £2.00, £7.00; EX 66.50 Trifecta £272.20 Part won. Pool: £367.97 - 0.50 winning units..
Owner Christopher & Annabelle Mason **Bred** Christopher J Mason **Trained** Tredodridge, Vale Of Glamorgan

FOCUS
A decent and competitive sprint handicap. The pace was strong and the winning time was 0.54 seconds faster than the opener.

NOTEBOOK
Arthur's Edge, who attracted market support here despite returning from four months off, was making his Fibresand debut and trying the minimum trip for the first time in his 23rd start. Now 13lb higher for his last success, he was handy from the off but was needing to be ridden along to hold his position at halfway. However, he forged his way to the front over a furlong from home and fairly bounded clear. He will now be aimed at the Cammidge Trophy at Doncaster on the opening day of the turf season. (op 14-1)
Onceaponatime(IRE), carrying a 6lb penalty for his success over a subsequent winner here seven days earlier (officially raised 2lb for that effort), was having only his third try over the minimum trip and seemed to find this C&D an inadequate test when third here in November. Well backed, he hit a flat spot at halfway before finishing strongly to grab second late on and will appreciate a return to 6f. (op 10-1)
Luscivious ◆ had the worst of the draw, but ran a blinder against the stands' rail and was always there or thereabouts. He handles these conditions and there should be another day.
Captain Carey, absent since August, did well to show to the fore for as long as he did and this was a decent effort off a 16lb higher mark than when successful on his last sand outing over C&D almost a year ago. (op 25-1)
Where's Reiley(USA), successful in all four starts over C&D this year, had to carry a 6lb penalty for his success here nine days earlier but was still 3lb well in compared to his new mark. However, he faced an impossible task when dropping to last at halfway and, although he stayed on once switched to the far rail, he had too much ground to make up. (tchd 6-1)
Rebel Duke(IRE), a four-time winner over C&D, was 8lb higher than when successful here on New Year's Day, but although he tried to put in an effort towards the far side over a furlong from home, it came to little. (op 4-1 tchd 9-2)
Fol Hollow(IRE) ◆ has a decent record first time out so the absence since September shouldn't have been a problem, but he had run moderately in two previous tries here so was off a 7lb lower mark than on turf. He showed decent speed for a long way this time, however, and may be one to look out for in the early weeks of the turf season. (op 5-1)
Something(IRE) ◆ also has a fine record fresh, but he was making his Fibresand debut and having only his third try over the minimum trip. He didn't run at all badly, though, and is another to watch out for back over further. (tchd 14-1 and 20-1)
Thebes Official explanation: trainer said, regarding running, that he was unable to explain the poor form but was of the opinion that this could be the gelding's form.
Rievaulx World Official explanation: jockey said gelding had no more to give

917 BINGO AT 32RED.COM H'CAP 1m 3f (F)
5:05 (5:05) (Class 4) (0-85,80) 4-Y-0+ **£5,459** (£1,612; £806) Stalls Low

Form RPR
50-5 1 **Full Speed (GER)**[30] 572 5-9-6 80...... PJMcDonald 5 95
(G A Swinbank) *a.p: led over 1f out: rdn clr* **11/2**[3]
43-2 2 5 **Kingsdale Orion (IRE)**[30] 300 6-9-1 75...... TomEaves 2 82
(B Ellison) *pushed along to ld: after 1f: rdn and hdd over 1f out: edgd rt and styd on same pce* **9/4**[1]
0612 3 2 **Whooshka (USA)**[7] 857 4-9-1 76...... AlanMunro 4 79
(P W Chapple-Hyam) *led 1f: chsd ldr: rdn over 3f out: ev ch over 2f out: no ex fr over 1f out* **9/4**[1]
365- 4 1 1/2 **Country Road (IRE)**[147] 6974 4-8-10 71...... PaulMulrennan 1 72
(M W Easterby) *hld up: hdwy over 3f out: rdn over 2f out: styd on same pce* **12/1**
13 5 18 **Reverend Green (IRE)**[14] 785 4-9-2 77...... NeilCallan 3 47
(K A Ryan) *chsd ldrs: rdn over 3f out: wknd over 2f out: eased over 1f out* **10/3**[2]

2m 25.01s (-2.99) **Going Correction** -0.175s/f (Stan)
WFA 4 from 5yo+ 1lb 5 Ran SP% **107.7**
Speed ratings (Par 105): **103,99,97,96,83**
CSF £7.34 TOTE £6.50: £2.60, £1.60; EX 21.50.
Owner The County Set Three **Bred** Dr K Schulte **Trained** Melsonby, N Yorks

FOCUS
A fair little middle-distance handicap on paper, but a very impressive winner.
Reverend Green(IRE) Official explanation: trainer had no explanation for the poor form shown

918 SPREADBET AT 32RED.COM H'CAP 1m (F)
5:35 (5:35) (Class 6) (0-60,65) 4-Y-0+ **£2,047** (£604; £302) Stalls Low

Form RPR
3-11 1 **Pendragon (USA)**[1] 908 7-9-6 65 6ex...... BarryMcHugh(3) 9 78
(B Ellison) *chsd ldrs: led over 1f out: edgd lft and rdn clr ins fnl f* **1/1**[1]
0021 2 3 1/2 **Bold Diva**[9] 838 5-9-0 56 6ex......(v) LukeMorris 12 61
(A W Carroll) *a.p: chsd wnr over 1f out: sn rdn: no ex ins fnl f* **14/1**
1410 3 4 **Positivity**[17] 753 4-9-0 56......(p) TomEaves 10 51
(B Smart) *mid-div: rdn 1/2-way: hdwy u.p over 1f out: edgd lft fnl f: nt trble ldrs* **16/1**
-001 4 1 **Rub Of The Relic (IRE)**[2] 893 5-8-12 54 6ex......(v) FrankieMcDonald 7 47
(P T Midgley) *prom: nt clr run over 3f out: sn outpcd: styd on fnl f* **8/1**[3]
62-4 5 nk **Lilly Grove**[42] 398 5-9-1 57...... PJMcDonald 13 49
(G A Swinbank) *hld up: rdn over 2f out: hdwy over 1f out: nvr nrr* **9/1**
0/05 6 hd **Border Fox**[9] 838 7-8-5 47......(t) GregFairley 8 39
(P Salmon) *plld hrd: led 7f out: rdn over 2f out: hdd & wknd over 1f out* **14/1**
5334 7 1/2 **Amber Moon**[14] 786 5-8-7 54 ow6......(b) AnnStokell(5) 14 45
(Miss A Stokell) *prom: chsd ldr over 4f out to over 3f out: wknd over 1f out* **33/1**
F/-4 8 1 **Kaballero (GER)**[13] 804 9-9-4 60...... IanMongan 4 48
(S Gollings) *prom: rdn and wknd over 2f out* **33/1**
1400 9 2 **Bajan Pride**[33] 541 6-8-8 57......(v) MarzenaJeziorek(7) 1 41
(R A Fahey) *s.s: hdwy 6f out: wknd over 1f out* **25/1**
6335 10 5 **Special Cuvee**[2] 893 4-9-4 60......(v) SebSanders 11 32
(A B Haynes) *s.s: rdn over 2f out: a in rr* **13/2**[2]
1665 11 3 1/4 **Very Well Red**[28] 603 7-9-0 56...... SilvestreDeSousa 5 21
(P W Hiatt) *led 1f: chsd ldrs: rdn over 3f out: wknd over 2f out* **16/1**
0-00 12 1 1/2 **Son Of Monsieur**[42] 410 4-8-4 46 oh1...... DuranFentiman 6 7
(G R Oldroyd) *sn outpcd* **50/1**
0-00 13 1 1/2 **Red Dagger (IRE)**[8] 854 4-8-4 46...... HayleyTurner 3 4
(R J Price) *hld up: rdn over 3f out: sn lost tch* **40/1**

1m 41.49s (-2.21) **Going Correction** -0.175s/f (Stan) 13 Ran SP% **123.7**
Speed ratings (Par 101): **104,100,96,95,95 95,94,93,91,86 83,81,80**
toteswingers:1&2:£5.80, 1&3:£3.50, 2&3:£16.90 CSF £17.18 CT £164.52 TOTE £2.00: £1.30, £3.30, £4.40; EX 15.20 Trifecta £64.80 Pool: £157.65 - 1.80 winning units. Place 6 £57.86, Place 5 £19.12.
Owner Mrs Claire Ellison **Bred** Flaxman Holdings Ltd **Trained** Norton, N Yorks

FOCUS
A moderate handicap, but three of these were carrying penalties for recent course victories.
Rub Of The Relic(IRE) Official explanation: jockey said gelding was denied a clear run
Red Dagger(IRE) Official explanation: trainer said gelding scoped badly after race
T/Plt: £125.30 to a £1 stake. Pool: £48,101.41. 280.23 winning tickets. T/Qpdt: £49.10 to a £1 stake. Pool: £3,868.74. 58.20 winning tickets. CR

883 WOLVERHAMPTON (A.W) (L-H)
Thursday, March 18

OFFICIAL GOING: Standard
Wind: Moderate half behind Weather: Fine

919 32REDBET.COM H'CAP 5f 20y(P)
5:45 (5:45) (Class 4) (0-85,81) 3-Y-0 **£4,209** (£1,252; £625; £312) Stalls Low

Form RPR
63-1 1 **Fair Passion**[21] 699 3-8-7 67...... JimmyQuinn 2 77
(D Shaw) *mde all: drvn out ins fnl f* **85/40**[2]
0-11 2 1 1/4 **Lewyn**[24] 662 3-9-7 81...... FergusSweeney 5 87
(K A Ryan) *a chsng wnr: rdn and nt qckn ins fnl f* **2/1**[1]
21-3 3 3 1/2 **Maldon Prom (IRE)**[67] 117 3-9-0 74...... JerryO'Dwyer 1 67
(C A Dwyer) *chsd ldrs: hrd rdn over 1f out: one pce* **7/2**[3]
1323 4 3 1/4 **Duke Of Rainford**[10] 831 3-7-11 62 oh5......(p) PaulPickard(5) 4 43
(M Herrington) *hld up: sme prog on ins over 2f out: wknd ins fnl f* **5/1**
24-0 5 11 **Dazeen**[14] 783 3-8-12 72...... TonyCulhane 6 14
(P T Midgley) *hld up: pushed along and outpcd 3f out* **16/1**

62.05 secs (-0.25) **Going Correction** +0.125s/f (Slow) 5 Ran SP% **110.1**
Speed ratings (Par 100): **107,105,99,94,76**
CSF £6.79 TOTE £2.90: £3.60, £1.10; EX 5.70.
Owner Angie Conway / Whiteman Partnership **Bred** D R Tucker **Trained** Sproxton, Leics

FOCUS
Just the five runners, but the front two are fair types.

920 32RED.COM (S) STKS — 1m 141y(P)
6:15 (6:15) (Class 6) 4-Y-O+ £1,774 (£523; £262) Stalls Low

Form RPR
11-6 **1** **What's Up Doc (IRE)**[75] 19 9-8-12 70 DaneO'Neill 4 69
(Mrs Lawney Hill) *mde all: rdn clr over 1f out: r.o* **4/1**[3]
0232 **2** *nk* **Straight Face (IRE)**[7] 862 6-9-4 65 (b) J-PGuillambert 7 74
(P D Evans) *hld up in tch: pushed along over 2f out: c wd st: rdn over 1f out: wnt 2nd and edgd lft wl ins fnl f: r.o* **13/2**
0-46 **3** *3 ½* **Appalachian Trail (IRE)**[5] 883 9-9-4 92 (b) JimmyQuinn 3 66
(N Wilson) *s.i.s: sn hld up in mid-div: hdwy over 2f out: rdn whn swtchd lft 1f out: one pce* **2/1**[1]
-234 **4** *1 ½* **New Star (UAE)**[38] 466 6-8-12 72 ShaneKelly 5 57
(W M Brisbourne) *chsd wnr: rdn over 1f out: one pce fnl f* **5/2**[2]
0100 **5** *1 ½* **Flighty Fellow (IRE)**[22] 685 10-8-13 56 KylieManser(5) 8 59
(T Keddy) *hld up and bhd: hdwy on ins over 1f out: no imp fnl f* **40/1**
6 *nk* **Seriy Tzarina**[149] 4-8-7 0 FergusSweeney 6 47
(A G Newcombe) *hld up and bhd: rdn over 2f out: sn struggling* **66/1**
12-6 **7** *nk* **Desert Bump**[58] 225 4-8-4 70 AndreaAtzeni(3) 1 47
(E F Vaughan) *prom: rdn wl over 1f out: wknd ins fnl f* **8/1**
0-06 **8** *11* **Remark (IRE)**[24] 663 6-8-7 46 (t) JamesSullivan(5) 2 26
(M W Easterby) *a in rr: no ch fnl 4f* **66/1**

1m 51.25s (0.75) **Going Correction** +0.125s/f (Slow) **8** Ran SP% **111.8**
Speed ratings (Par 101): **101,100,97,96,94 94,94,84**
toteswingers:1&2:£5.70, 1&3:£2.70, 2&3:£3.00 CSF £28.20 TOTE £4.90: £1.50, £1.30, £1.10; EX 19.20.There was no bid for the winner
Owner M B Clarke **Bred** James J Monaghan **Trained** Aston Rowant, Oxon

FOCUS
A modest seller

921 32RED CASINO OF DECADE H'CAP — 1m 1f 103y(P)
6:45 (6:45) (Class 3) (0-95,95) 4-Y-O+ £6,623 (£1,982; £991; £495; £246) Stalls Low

Form RPR
212 **1** **December Draw (IRE)**[14] 790 4-8-13 **90** ShaneKelly 6 102
(W J Knight) *a.p: edgd lft and led 1f out: r.o wl* **11/4**[2]
1102 **2** *2* **Thunderstruck**[7] 863 5-8-9 **86** (p) ChrisCatlin 1 94
(J A Glover) *led: rdn and hdd 1f out: nt qckn wl ins fnl f* **7/2**[3]
0545 **3** *¾* **Confidentiality (IRE)**[7] 863 6-8-7 **84** NickyMackay 5 90
(M Wigham) *a.p: rdn and ev ch over 1f out: nt qckn fnl f* **8/1**
-050 **4** *1 ¾* **Raptor (GER)**[19] 740 7-8-10 **87** MickyFenton 7 90+
(M E Rimmer) *s.i.s: hld up in rr: rdn and r.o fnl f: nvr trbld ldrs* **14/1**
/1-3 **5** *nk* **Perpetually (IRE)**[14] 790 4-9-0 **91** JoeFanning 8 93
(M Johnston) *sn chsng ldr: ev ch over 2f out: btn whn n.m.r briefly over 1f out* **7/4**[1]
4355 **6** *¾* **Carcinetto (IRE)**[5] 883 8-8-12 **89** PatCosgrave 2 89
(P D Evans) *hld up: rdn over 2f out: no hdwy* **16/1**
1526 **7** *3 ½* **Red Somerset (USA)**[14] 790 7-8-11 **88** JimmyQuinn 4 81
(R J Hodges) *hld up: pushed along over 2f out: bhd whn rdn wl over 1f out* **20/1**

2m 0.13s (-1.57) **Going Correction** +0.125s/f (Slow) **7** Ran SP% **113.7**
Speed ratings (Par 107): **111,109,108,107,106 106,102**
toteswingers:1&2:£1.70, 1&3:£4.80, 2&3:£5.40 CSF £12.67 CT £66.24 TOTE £3.40: £1.80, £2.10; EX 14.10.
Owner Brook House **Bred** Wardstown Stud Ltd **Trained** Patching, W Sussex

FOCUS
An ordinary handicap for the class. The pace seemed no more than fair.

NOTEBOOK
December Draw(IRE) had four of these rivals behind him when runner-up in a similar race over course and distance on his previous start and he confirmed form quite readily, despite edging left under pressure in the straight. This was only his 11th start and he's improving. (tchd 3-1)
Thunderstruck, who was 2lb well in, was allowed to dominate and ran to form in defeat. (op 4-1)
Confidentiality(IRE) travelled well into the straight but found only the one pace and couldn't reverse recent form with Thunderstruck. (op 9-1)
Raptor(GER) raced out the back after starting slowly and, although making some progress in the straight, he never looked like winning.
Perpetually(IRE) ran below the form he showed when 21/2l behind today's winner over course and distance on his return from the best part of a year off the track and seemingly found this coming too soon. (op 6-4)

922 BET AT 32RED.COM MAIDEN STKS — 1m 1f 103y(P)
7:15 (7:15) (Class 5) 3-Y-O+ £2,456 (£725; £362) Stalls Low

Form RPR
2 **1** **Beneath**[17] 755 3-8-4 0 MartinLane(3) 4 78+
(Pat Eddery) *chsd ldr: led wl over 1f out: sn pushed along: readily* **4/9**[1]
400- **2** *1 ¼* **Iptkaar (USA)**[166] 6477 3-8-3 75 ow1 (b[1]) ChrisCatlin 10 69
(C E Brittain) *led: pushed along and hdd wl over 1f out: rdn and nt qckn fnl f* **7/1**[2]
5 **3** *2 ½* **Musical Mark**[20] 728 3-8-4 0 (b[1]) AndreaAtzeni(3) 9 68
(M Botti) *hld up in mid-div: hdwy over 2f out: rdn over 1f out: one pce* **20/1**
4 *1 ½* **Lady Eclair (IRE)** 4-9-7 0 JoeFanning 2 65
(M Johnston) *a.p: pushed along over 3f out: rdn over 2f out: one pce* **8/1**[3]
05 **5** *1 ¾* **Spirited Lady (IRE)**[33] 545 3-8-2 0 JimmyQuinn 3 56
(R A Fahey) *hld up in mid-div: pushed along and wknd wl over 1f out* **50/1**
4-6 **6** *2 ¼* **Head Hunted**[10] 825 3-8-9 0 ow2 TomQueally 1 58
(E A L Dunlop) *hld up in rr: rdn and btn wl over 1f out* **10/1**
03 **7** *nk* **Single Lady**[15] 776 3-8-2 0 FrannyNorton 5 51
(J S Moore) *s.i.s: a in rr* **16/1**
8 *11* **Suli Blew** 4-9-7 0 GeorgeBaker 7 32
(T Keddy) *s.i.s: hld up in mid-div: bhd fnl 2f* **33/1**
9 *17* **Ellie's Prince**[43] 7-9-12 0 TravisBlock 8 —
(S C Burrough) *dwlt: hld up in rr: pushed along 3f out: sn lost tch: t.o* **100/1**

2m 4.50s (2.80) **Going Correction** +0.125s/f (Slow)
WFA 3 from 4yo+ 19lb **9** Ran SP% **118.5**
Speed ratings (Par 103): **92,90,88,87,85 83,83,73,58**
toteswingers:1&2:£2.00, 1&3:£7.40, 2&3:£19.80 CSF £4.19 TOTE £1.30: £1.02, £1.90, £4.80; EX 5.10.
Owner K Abdulla **Bred** Millsec Limited **Trained** Nether Winchendon, Bucks

FOCUS
An uneventful maiden, with the pace modest (time over six seconds above standard) and few getting involved, but the form looks fair.

923 £320 FREE AT 32RED.COM CLASSIFIED CLAIMING STKS — 1m 4f 50y(P)
7:45 (7:45) (Class 6) 4-Y-O+ £1,774 (£523; £262) Stalls Low

Form RPR
1311 **1** **Sedgwick**[20] 724 8-8-6 67 JoeFanning 3 70
(Ian Williams) *chsd ldr tl over 5f out: wnt 2nd again wl over 1f out: led ent fnl f: easily* **11/10**[1]
3335 **2** *3 ½* **Quince (IRE)**[8] 852 7-8-0 64 (v) SimonPearce(5) 5 63
(J Pearce) *hld up in tch: chsd ldr over 5f out tl wl over 1f out: sn rdn and sltly outpcd: kpt on to take 2nd post* **4/1**[3]
4112 **3** *nse* **My Mate Mal**[20] 719 6-8-2 70 JamesSullivan(5) 4 65
(B Ellison) *led: rdn wl over 1f out: hdd ent fnl f: no ex and lost 2nd post* **7/4**[2]
6-40 **4** *7* **United Nations**[17] 752 9-8-4 67 (p) JimmyQuinn 7 51
(N Wilson) *s.s whn rdr slow to remove blindfold: hld up and bhd: rdn and short-lived effrt wl over 1f out* **10/1**
600/ **5** *1 ½* **Vintage Quest**[450] 7776 8-8-4 40 (b) DavidProbert 6 49?
(D Burchell) *hld up in tch: rdn and wknd wl over 1f out* **40/1**
600/ **6** *3* **I Feel Fine**[547] 6015 7-8-1 42 PaulPickard(5) 8 46?
(A Kirtley) *stdd s: hld up in rr: pushed along over 2f out: sn struggling* **66/1**

2m 46.77s (5.67) **Going Correction** +0.125s/f (Slow) **6** Ran SP% **117.0**
Speed ratings (Par 101): **86,83,83,78,77 75**
toteswingers:1&2:£1.60, 1&3:£1.10, 2&3:£1.60 CSF £6.54 TOTE £2.30: £1.20, £1.90; EX 4.10.
Owner A L R Morton **Bred** G And Mrs Middlebrook **Trained** Portway, Worcs

FOCUS
A modest claimer run at a steady pace and the final time was over ten seconds above standard.

924 32REDPOKER.COM H'CAP — 5f 216y(P)
8:15 (8:17) (Class 5) (0-75,74) 4-Y-O+ £2,456 (£725; £362) Stalls Low

Form RPR
5F-1 **1** **Replicator**[21] 693 5-8-3 **62** (e) AshleyHamblett(3) 2 71
(P L Gilligan) *led: rdn and hdd 1f out: led nr fin* **5/1**[2]
-033 **2** *hd* **Brierty (IRE)**[17] 750 4-9-4 **74** DavidNolan 3 82
(D Carroll) *hld up in tch: led 1f out: rdn and edgd rt ins fnl f: hdd nr fin* **6/1**[3]
2542 **3** *1 ¼* **Welcome Approach**[15] 767 7-8-7 **63** LukeMorris 5 67
(J R Weymes) *hld up in tch: rdn and edgd rt 1f out: kpt on* **4/1**[1]
142 **4** *1 ½* **Dvinsky (USA)**[22] 678 9-8-13 **69** (b) JimmyQuinn 1 69
(P Howling) *chsd wnr tl wl over 1f out: rdn and one pce fnl f* **4/1**[1]
356- **5** *1 ¼* **Fault**[120] 7432 4-8-13 **69** (t) MickyFenton 6 65
(Stef Higgins) *s.i.s: hld up: no hdwy fnl 2f* **5/1**[2]
0330 **6** *1* **Methaaly (IRE)**[20] 722 7-9-4 **74** GeorgeBaker 4 66
(M Mullineaux) *s.s: hld up in rr: pushed along over 1f out: nvr nr ldrs* **13/2**
-240 **7** *¾* **Bahamian Kid**[17] 750 5-9-0 **70** (v) AdamKirby 7 60
(R Hollinshead) *t.k.h towards rr: no imp whn rdn ins fnl f* **14/1**
-506 **8** *shd* **Milne Bay (IRE)**[29] 579 5-8-5 **64** (t) MartinLane(3) 8 54
(D M Simcock) *hld up towards rr: rdn and edgd lft jst over 1f out: n.d after* **14/1**

1m 14.64s (-0.36) **Going Correction** +0.125s/f (Slow) **8** Ran SP% **114.3**
Speed ratings (Par 103): **107,106,105,103,101 100,99,98**
toteswingers:1&2:£9.00, 1&3:£5.30, 2&3:£5.70 CSF £34.78 CT £130.74 TOTE £7.30: £1.70, £2.70, £1.40; EX 45.90.
Owner Linton Doolan **Bred** R And Mrs Heathcote **Trained** Newmarket, Suffolk
■ Stewards' Enquiry : Ashley Hamblett three-day ban: used whip with excessive frequency down shoulder in the forehand (Apr 1, 3-4)

FOCUS
The pace seemed just ordinary and those held up couldn't get involved.

925 £10 FREE BINGO AT 32RED H'CAP — 1m 141y(P)
8:45 (8:46) (Class 5) (0-70,67) 4-Y-O+ £2,456 (£725; £362) Stalls Low

Form RPR
-261 **1** **Dajen**[8] 853 4-8-11 **67** 6ex LauraPike(7) 4 79+
(D M Simcock) *hld up in rr: hdwy 3f out: sn pushed along: rdn over 1f out: led jst ins fnl f: r.o* **9/4**[1]
5004 **2** *1 ¼* **Justcallmehandsome**[6] 873 8-9-1 **67** (v) KellyHarrison(3) 3 76
(D J S Ffrench Davis) *led: rdn and edgd rt over 1f out: hdd jst ins fnl f: kpt on same pce* **7/2**[3]
-455 **3** *1 ¾* **Sotik Star (IRE)**[24] 663 7-8-12 **61** (p) JimmyQuinn 1 66+
(K A Morgan) *prom: lost pl over 4f out: rdn and kpt on fr over 1f out: tk 3rd wl ins fnl f* **11/2**
-443 **4** *1 ½* **Kladester (USA)**[8] 853 4-8-9 **58** TonyCulhane 5 60
(M Herrington) *sn chsng ldr: ev ch over 2f out: rdn and lost 2nd wl over 1f out: hld whn sn sltly hmpd* **9/1**
0/0- **5** *¾* **Kilkenny Bay**[306] 2082 4-8-8 **57** JoeFanning 8 57
(W Jarvis) *hld up in rr: pushed along and struggling over 2f out: sme late prog* **20/1**
5215 **6** *shd* **Granny McPhee**[23] 675 4-8-11 **67** NatashaEaton(7) 2 67
(A Bailey) *prom tl wknd 2f out* **7/1**
0055 **7** *3* **Fandango Boy**[20] 715 9-9-4 **67** StevieDonohoe 7 68+
(Ian Williams) *hld up: hdwy over 6f out: pushed along over 2f out: rdn over 1f out: eased whn btn ins fnl f* **11/4**[2]

1m 50.52s (0.02) **Going Correction** +0.125s/f (Slow) **7** Ran SP% **122.3**
Speed ratings (Par 103): **104,102,101,100,99 99,96**
toteswingers:1&2:£2.40, 1&3:£2.90, 2&3:£4.30 CSF £11.58 CT £40.32 TOTE £3.10: £2.10, £2.40; EX 12.20 Place 6 £10.26, Place 5 £8.07.
Owner Tick Tock Partnership **Bred** Miss D Fleming **Trained** Newmarket, Suffolk
■ Stewards' Enquiry : Tony Culhane two-day ban: careless riding (Apr 1,3)
Laura Pike one-day ban: careless riding (Apr 1)

FOCUS
A modest handicap run at a decent enough gallop.
T/Plt: £11.20 to a £1 stake. Pool: £67,718.21. 4,383.52 winning tickets. T/Qpdt: £4.10 to a £1 stake. Pool: £7,567.94. 1,358.60 winning tickets. KH

28 DEAUVILLE (R-H)
Thursday, March 18

OFFICIAL GOING: Standard

926a PRIX RONDE DE NUIT (LISTED RACE) (FILLIES) (ALL-WEATHER) 6f 110y
2:15 (2:18) 3-Y-O £24,336 (£9,735; £7,301; £4,912; £2,434)

RPR
1 **Evading Tempete**[24] 3-8-12 ....(p) Jean-BernardEyquem 3 95
(F Rohaut, France) 6/1[1]
2 2 ½ **Calina Salsa (FR)**[105] 3-8-12 .... DominiqueBoeuf 8 87
(Y Barberot, France)
3 1 **Okapina (FR)**[99] 3-8-12 .... MaximeGuyon 1 84
(Mlle S-V Tarrou, France)
4 ½ **Coreliev (IRE)**[32] 557 3-8-12 .... FranckBlondel 5 83
(F Rossi, France)
5 hd **Red Love (USA)**[40] 3-8-12 .... ChristopheSoumillon 7 82
(J-C Rouget, France)
6 nse **Kelty In Love (FR)**[122] 7441 3-9-2 .... Christophe-PatriceLemaire 6 86
(T Larriviere, France)
7 snk **Ascot Glory (IRE)**[135] 7231 3-8-12 .... RaphaelMarchelli 9 82
(S Wattel, France)
8 1 ½ **Ghazwah**[28] 596 3-8-12 .... EddieAhern 2 77
(R A Fahey) *prom on ins early: 5th 1/2-way: pushed along st: nvr able to chal* 9/1[2]
9 ½ **Elisheba (FR)**[135] 7230 3-8-12 .... ThierryThulliez 4 76
(F Doumen, France)

1m 21.0s (81.00) 9 Ran SP% 24.3
PARI-MUTUEL (including 1 Euro stake): WIN 7.00; PL 2.30, 2.90, 4.50;DF 28.70.
Owner A Mouknass & A Forde **Bred** Wentworth Racing (pty) Ltd **Trained** Sauvagnon, France

927a PRIX MONTENICA (LISTED RACE) (C&G) (ALL-WEATHER) 6f 110y
2:50 (2:53) 3-Y-O £24,336 (£9,735; £7,301; £4,912; £2,434)

RPR
1 **Too Nice Name (FR)**[99] 3-8-12 .... OlivierPeslier 1 98
(Robert Collet, France)
2 snk **Thyan (FR)**[26] 3-8-12 .... GaetanMasure 4 98
(Mlle M Henry, France)
3 nk **Army Scout (USA)**[24] 3-8-12 .... ChristopheSoumillon 3 97
(J-C Rouget, France)
4 2 ½ **Layla's Hero (IRE)**[145] 7016 3-9-2 .... EddieAhern 5 93
(D Nicholls) *in tch: cl 3rd 1/2-way: rdn early st: unable qck* 43/10[1]
5 snk **Tall Chief (IRE)**[6] 3-8-12 .... StephanePasquier 2 89
(Mlle V Dissaux, France)
6 10 **Stormy Montlioux (FR)** 3-8-12 ....(b) Jean-BernardEyquem 6 60
(Y Durepaire, Spain)

1m 19.7s (79.70) 6 Ran SP% 18.9
PARI-MUTUEL: WIN 17.90; PL 8.20, 8.80; SF 197.20.
Owner Mlle Micheline Vidal **Bred** Remi Boucret **Trained** Chantilly, France

840 LINGFIELD (L-H)
Friday, March 19

OFFICIAL GOING: Standard
Wind: medium, half behind Weather: dull, light rain

928 BREATHE SPA AT MARRIOTT LINGFIELD MAIDEN STKS 1m 4f (P)
1:55 (1:56) (Class 5) 3-Y-O £2,456 (£725; £362) Stalls Low

Form RPR
3 1 **Beggar's Opera (IRE)**[18] 755 3-9-3 0.........................(t) RobertHavlin 3 82+
(J H M Gosden) *chsd ldrs: wnt 2nd over 9f out: pushed into ld ent fnl 2f: rdn clr over 1f out: comf* 10/11[1]
4-33 2 2 ¾ **Septemberintherain**[58] 240 3-9-3 72.....................(v[1]) StevieDonohoe 4 75
(R A Mills) *dwlt: pushed up to ld after 1f: rdn and hdd ent fnl 2f: btn over 1f out: plugged on same pce* 9/4[2]
443 3 10 **Frameit (IRE)**[25] 664 3-9-3 68...(p) LukeMorris 5 59
(J S Moore) *t.k.h: hld up in tch: rdn and wl outpcd by ldng pair over 3f out: no ch fr wl over 2f out: plugged on* 5/1[3]
0- 4 nk **Sweet Caroline (IRE)**[125] 7396 3-8-12 0......................... MichaelHills 2 54
(B W Hills) *led for 1f: chsd ldng pair fr over 9f out: drvn and wl outpcd by ldng pair over 3f out: no ch fr over 2f out: plugged on* 12/1
00 5 1 ½ **Rosewood Lad**[37] 484 3-9-3 0................................... FergusSweeney 6 56
(J S Moore) *in tch in rr of main gp: rdn and struggling 4f out: no ch fnl 2f* 66/1
6 dist **Blues Buddy** 3-8-12 0.. ChrisCatlin 1 —
(M A Allen) *v.s.a: sn detached in last: t.o fnl 6f: virtually p.u fnl 3f* 50/1

2m 31.65s (-1.35) **Going Correction** -0.025s/f (Stan) 6 Ran SP% 111.0
Speed ratings (Par 98): **103,101,94,94,93** —
toteswingers: 1&2 £1.10, 1&3 £1.50, 2&3 £1.20 CSF £3.07 TOTE £1.80: £1.40, £1.30; EX 3.40.
Owner H R H Princess Haya Of Jordan **Bred** T R G Vestey **Trained** Newmarket, Suffolk

FOCUS
Only three with any worthwhile form in this maiden.
Rosewood Lad Official explanation: jockey said gelding hung left in straight

929 MARRIOTT HOTEL LINGFIELD CLASSIFIED CLAIMING STKS 1m 2f (P)
2:30 (2:32) (Class 6) 4-Y-O+ £1,774 (£523; £262) Stalls Low

Form RPR
2202 1 **Alfie Tupper (IRE)**[8] 868 7-8-3 63................................ NickyMackay 5 67
(J R Boyle) *hld up in tch in last trio: hdwy jst over 2f out: rdn to chal over 1f out: led narrowly ins fnl f: hld hd high but a holding rival after* 3/1[2]
51-5 2 shd **Pyrus Time (IRE)**[6] 162 4-8-10 67....................................... LukeMorris 2 74
(J S Moore) *chsd ldrs: rdn to ld over 1f out: narrowly hdd jst ins fnl f: nt qckn u.p and a jst hld after* 11/1
4332 3 1 ¾ **Atacama Sunrise**[14] 814 4-8-1 66........................... SimonPearce(5) 3 69+
(J Pearce) *chsd ldrs: nt clr run and shuffled bk jst over 2f out: swtchd rigth and clr run 1f out: r.o wl to go 3rd nr fin: nvr able to chal* 9/2[3]
2143 4 hd **Cupid's Glory**[16] 765 8-8-10 74.. RyanMoore 4 70
(G L Moore) *hld up in tch in last trio: effrt on inner wl over 1f out: chsd ldrs jst ins fnl f: wknd fnl 100yds* 13/8[1]
0-04 5 3 ½ **Strong Storm (USA)**[9] 841 4-7-13 61......................(p) AndreaAtzeni(3) 6 55
(Andrew Reid) *chsd ldr tl over 1f out: wknd u.p fnl f* 12/1
4100 6 1 **Hold The Bucks (USA)**[11] 827 4-8-4 60 ow2........(b[1]) AdrianNicholls 1 55
(J S Moore) *led: c off rail and rdn over 2f out: hdd over 1f out: wkng whn nt clr run and swtchd lft jst ins fnl f: n.d after* 40/1
-323 7 1 ½ **Dichoh**[11] 827 7-9-2 75..(v) GeorgeBaker 8 64
(M Madgwick) *stdd s: hld up in last: rdn and effrt on outer wl over 1f out: no prog and nvr trbld ldrs* 9/1
4264 8 4 **Farncombe (IRE)**[11] 827 4-8-2 57.................................. DavidProbert 7 42
(R A Harris) *in tch: rdn and unable qck over 2f out: bhd fr over 1f out* 33/1

2m 7.13s (0.53) **Going Correction** -0.025s/f (Stan) 8 Ran SP% 112.7
Speed ratings (Par 101): **96,95,94,94,91 90,89,86**
toteswingers: 1&2 £5.00, 1&3 £2.50, 2&3 £5.50 CSF £34.29 TOTE £4.60: £1.50, £2.20, £1.40; EX 33.00 Trifecta £260.50 Pool: £507.11 - 1.44 winning units..Pyrus Time was claimed by R. A. Harris for £10,000.
Owner Epsom Equine Spa Partnership **Bred** Stone Ridge Farm **Trained** Epsom, Surrey

FOCUS
Just an ordinary claimer and the gallop wasn't overly strong, but two pulled clear in the final furlong.
Atacama Sunrise Official explanation: jockey said filly was denied a clear run

930 MARRIOTT HOTEL OPENING SPRING 2010 MAIDEN STKS 1m (P)
3:05 (3:06) (Class 5) 3-Y-O £2,456 (£725; £362) Stalls High

Form RPR
1 **Capponi (IRE)** 3-9-3 0.. JoeFanning 4 83+
(M Johnston) *chsd ldrs: pressed ldr and clr ent fnl 2f: led 1f out: styd on strly to go clr fnl f: easily* 9/2[3]
43 2 3 ¾ **Blues Music (IRE)**[27] 634 3-9-3 0.................................... MichaelHills 3 74
(B W Hills) *s.i.s: sn pushed up to chse ldr: led over 3f out: clr w wnr ent fnl 2f: rdn and hdd 1f out: nt pce of wnr fnl f* 7/4[1]
32 3 2 ¼ **Lingfield Bound (IRE)**[25] 655 3-9-3 0............................ SteveDrowne 9 69
(J R Best) *hld up in tch in midfield: rdn and effrt jst over 2f out: disp modest 3rd fr wl over 1f out: kpt on same pce* 6/1
6- 4 ½ **Streets Of War (USA)**[146] 7034 3-9-3 0........................ RobertHavlin 2 67
(P W Chapple-Hyam) *in tch on inner: rdn to chse clr ldng pair jst over 2f out: no prog and no threat to ldng pair fr wl over 1f out* 10/1
0 5 4 ½ **Trelicia**[30] 583 3-8-12 0... JimCrowley 7 52
(S C Williams) *hld up in last trio: rdn and sme hdwy jst over 2f out: sn wl outpcd and n.d after: plugged on* 80/1
06 6 ½ **Mack's Sister**[27] 634 3-8-12 0.. HayleyTurner 10 50
(D K Ivory) *stdd and dropped in bhd after s: struggling u.p wl over 2f out: nvr trbld ldrs* 25/1
7 1 ¼ **The Wonga Coup (IRE)** 3-9-3 0.. IanMongan 5 52
(P M Phelan) *s.i.s: a bhd: struggling and rdn over 2f out: n.d* 20/1
5- 8 ½ **Sheila Toss (IRE)**[179] 6164 3-8-12 0......................... FrankieMcDonald 6 46
(R Hannon) *awkward leaving satlls: in tch: rdn and lost pl jst over 3f out: wl btn fnl 2f* 9/4[2]
060- 9 13 **Gazamali (IRE)**[153] 6842 3-9-3 44.................................. FergusSweeney 1 20
(H J Evans) *sn led: hdd over 3f out: wknd u.p over 2f out: wl bhd fnl f* 100/1
00- 10 80 **Sirri**[197] 5605 3-8-12 0.. SebSanders 8 —
(C E Brittain) *in tch on outer: rdn over 4f out: lost pl and virtually p.u fr over 2f out* 33/1

1m 37.9s (-0.30) **Going Correction** -0.025s/f (Stan) 10 Ran SP% 122.5
Speed ratings (Par 98): **100,96,94,93,89 88,87,86,73,—**
toteswingers: 1&2 £2.10, 1&3 £4.10, 2&3 £2.40 CSF £13.06 TOTE £5.60: £1.40, £1.20, £2.20; EX 16.20 Trifecta £51.30 Pool: £476.18 - 6.86 winning units..
Owner Sheikh Hamdan Bin Mohammed Al Maktoum **Bred** Darley **Trained** Middleham Moor, N Yorks

FOCUS
Not much depth to this maiden in terms of what those with experience had achieved, but the first two came clear to mark themselves down as decent, especially the winner who was making his racecourse debut.
Sirri Official explanation: jockey said filly lost its action

931 LINGFIELD PARK FOURBALL FILLIES' H'CAP 1m (P)
3:45 (3:45) (Class 5) (0-70,70) 4-Y-O+ £1,591 (£1,591; £181; £181) Stalls High

Form RPR
0/33 1 **Roshina (IRE)**[24] 673 4-8-13 **65**.. IanMongan 4 73
(Miss Jo Crowley) *in tch: n.m.r bnd ent fnl 2f: rdn to chal over 1f out: led jst ins fnl f: kpt on u.p jnd nr post* 4/1[2]
3023 1 dht **Castleburg**[14] 808 4-8-8 **60**.....................................(be) FergusSweeney 7 68
(G L Moore) *stdd after s: hld up in tch: hdwy 2f out: rdn to chal and edging lft ins fnl f: jnd wnr nr fin* 11/2[3]
0-60 3 1 ¼ **Ivory Lace**[24] 673 9-8-13 **65**... JimCrowley 10 71+
(S Woodman) *hld up towards rr: rdn over 2f out: hdwy and swtchd rt 1f out: running on and clsng on ldrs whn nt clr run ins fnl f: unable to rcvr* 20/1
2632 3 dht **Hip Hip Hooray**[14] 804 4-8-8 **60** ow1.............................. RobertHavlin 5 65
(L A Dace) *chsd ldr: rdn to ld over 1f out: hdd jst ins fnl f: kpt on same pce fnl 100yds* 8/1
-160 5 3 ¼ **Toolentidhaar (USA)**[18] 752 6-9-3 **69**............................ HayleyTurner 6 66
(Andrew Turnell) *chsd ldr tl rdn to ld over 2f out: hdd over 1f out: wknd fnl f* 14/1
145- 6 ½ **Aphrodisia**[258] 3627 6-9-3 **69**.. StevieDonohoe 9 65+
(Ian Williams) *v.s.a: detached in last and sn pushed along: rdn and no hdwy over 2f out: styd on fnl f: nvr trbld ldrs* 3/1[1]
/641 7 hd **Lady Kent (IRE)**[24] 673 4-9-4 **70**..................................... PatCosgrave 3 66
(J R Boyle) *dwlt: sn in tch: rdn and effrt 2f out: wknd u.p jst ins fnl f* 3/1[1]
2365 8 1 **Commandingpresence (USA)**[11] 829 4-8-4 **56** oh11
FrankieMcDonald 8 49
(J J Bridger) *s.i.s: hld up in rr: effrt on inner over 1f out: kpt on but nvr gng pce to threaten ldrs* 50/1
0-50 9 hd **Efficiency**[9] 855 4-8-12 **64** ow2...(p) NeilCallan 2 57
(M Blanshard) *in tch in midfield: rdn and unable qck jst over 2f out: no threat to ldrs after* 20/1
5 10 16 **Engaging**[16] 768 4-8-7 **59**.. MartinDwyer 1 13
(P D Cundell) *led tl hdd over 2f out: wknd qckly u.p wl over 1f out: wl btn and eased ins fnl f* 16/1

1m 37.9s (-0.30) **Going Correction** -0.025s/f (Stan) 10 Ran SP% 120.5
27 Trifecta £Owner D J Deer Bred.
Owner Kilstone Limited **Bred** D H W Dobson **Trained** Whitcombe, Dorset
■ A rare instance of dead-heats for both first and third place.

The Form Book, Raceform Ltd, Compton, RG20 6NL

FOCUS
A very ordinary handicap. The dead-heaters for first had lost a combined total of 30 races prior to this.
Ivory Lace ◆ Official explanation: jockey said mare was denied a clear run
Aphrodisia ◆ Official explanation: jockey said mare was keen to post

932 LINGFIELD PARK SPORTING MEMBERSHIP CLAIMING STKS 7f (P)
4:25 (4:26) (Class 6) 3-Y-O £1,774 (£523; £262) Stalls Low

Form RPR
34 **1** **Lockantanks**[17] 759 3-8-11 0 ChrisCatlin 5 73
(M R Channon) *chsd ldr tl led 3f out: rdn wl over 1f out: clr ent fnl f: r.o wl: comf* **6/1**[3]
145- **2** 3 ¾ **Giulietta Da Vinci**[94] 7756 3-8-1 64 KellyHarrison(3) 6 56
(S C Williams) *hld up in tch in last trio: hdwy on outer over 2f out: rdn wl over 1f out: chsd clr wnr ins fnl f: no imp* **13/2**
-510 **3** 1 ½ **Craicattack (IRE)**[16] 772 3-9-3 73 (p) RyanMoore 4 65
(J S Moore) *led tl 3f out: drvn ent fnl 2f: nt pce of wnr ent fnl f: lost 2nd ins fnl f* **2/1**[1]
2324 **4** 1 ½ **Flow Chart (IRE)**[11] 826 3-8-9 71 (b) AdrianMcCarthy 8 53
(Peter Grayson) *hld up in rr: hdwy and rdn over 2f out: drvn to chse ldrs over 1f out: no prog and wl hld fnl f* **8/1**
4-45 **5** ½ **Libertino (IRE)**[14] 809 3-9-1 67 MartinDwyer 1 58
(B J Meehan) *in tch in midfield on inner: rdn and unable qck ent fnl 2f: n.d and one pce after* **7/2**[2]
-344 **6** 2 **Penrod Ballantyne (IRE)**[16] 766 3-8-13 65 EddieAhern 2 50
(B J Meehan) *hld up in tch towards rr: rdn and no hdwy 2f out: n.d* **15/2**
2441 **7** 2 ¼ **Avow (USA)**[11] 826 3-8-2 66 (b) GillianDawson(7) 3 40
(J S Moore) *t.k.h: chsd ldrs: rdn and struggling over 2f out: wl btn fr wl over 1f out* **10/1**
6400 **8** 11 **Maxijack (IRE)**[14] 805 3-8-7 53 (v1) SamHitchcott 7 8
(G Brown) *in tch in midfield on outer: rdn whn short of room and hmpd bnd jst over 2f out: wl btn after* **66/1**

1m 24.56s (-0.24) **Going Correction** -0.025s/f (Stan) **8 Ran SP% 116.6**
Speed ratings (Par 96): **100,95,94,92,91 89,86,74**
toteswingers: 1&2 £3.30, 1&3 £3.70, 2&3 £6.60 CSF £45.27 TOTE £9.00: £2.60, £1.80, £1.10; EX 43.80 Trifecta £186.80 Pool: £363.58 - 1.44 winning units..Giulietta da Vinci was claimed by S. Woodman for £6000. Lockantanks was claimed by A. B. Haynes for £7000.
Owner M Channon **Bred** Jeremy Green And Sons **Trained** West Ilsley, Berks
FOCUS
A modest but open claimer in which several had a chance at the weights.
Avow(USA) Official explanation: jockey said gelding hung left

933 MARRIOTT PLAY & STAY H'CAP 7f (P)
5:05 (5:05) (Class 5) (0-70,70) 3-Y-O £2,456 (£725; £362) Stalls Low

Form RPR
002- **1** **Mount Juliet (IRE)**[172] 6347 3-9-0 66 MartinDwyer 1 68
(M Botti) *in tch in midfield: hdwy to trck ldrs and nt clr run bnd 2f out: rdn to ld jst over 1f out: drvn fnl 100yds: hld on* **5/1**[3]
063- **2** hd **Welsh Artist**[113] 7538 3-9-2 68 NeilCallan 4 69+
(Mrs A J Perrett) *chsd ldrs: rdn over 2f out: n.m.r and barging match w rivals wl over 1f out: chsd wnr fnl 100yds: styd on wl and clsng on wnr fin* **8/1**
-441 **3** nk **Mint Whip (IRE)**[27] 638 3-8-12 64 RyanMoore 7 64
(R Hannon) *in tch in midfield: rdn and effrt 2f out: drvn and chsd ldrs ent fnl f: kpt on wl fnl 100yds* **7/2**[1]
-345 **4** 2 ½ **Barlaman (USA)**[15] 783 3-9-2 68 (bt1) SebSanders 2 61
(C E Brittain) *w ldr tl led over 2f out: edgd rt and rdn wl over 1f out: hdd jst over 1f out: wknd ins fnl f* **10/1**
-130 **5** nk **Orsett Lad (USA)**[22] 698 3-8-7 62 MarcHalford(3) 14 55+
(J R Best) *stdd s: hld up in rr: rdn and effrt on outer bnd 2f out: styd on u.p ins fnl f: nvr able to chal* **20/1**
10-5 **6** ¾ **Chandrayaan**[16] 766 3-8-13 65 (v) SamHitchcott 3 56
(J E Long) *stdd s: hld up towards rr: stdy hdwy 3f out: chsd ldrs over 1f out: drvn and wknd jst ins fnl f* **25/1**
1201 **7** 2 ¾ **Premium Charge**[8] 861 3-8-1 60 RyanClark(7) 5 43
(C A Dwyer) *w ldrs: ev ch and rdn 2f out: struggling whn bmpd over 1f out: sn wknd* **9/2**[2]
06-2 **8** ½ **Abhar (USA)**[76] 9 3-9-1 67 SteveDrowne 12 49
(J R Best) *in tch in midfield on outer: rdn along over 4f out: no prog over 2f out: no ch fnl 2f* **10/1**
-323 **9** 1 ¾ **Adam De Beaulieu (USA)**[14] 815 3-9-3 69 (t) TomEaves 10 46
(B M R Haslam) *a towards rr: bhd and rdn over 2f out: n.d* **16/1**
31-5 **10** 8 **Vito Volterra (IRE)**[14] 807 3-9-4 70 TonyCulhane 11 26
(A B Haynes) *led on outer: hdd and rdn over 2f out: wknd qckly 2f out* **16/1**
660- **11** 14 **Bathwick Xaara**[156] 6775 3-8-10 62 HayleyTurner 8 —
(J G Portman) *in tch in midfield tl rdn and btn jst over 2f out: wl bhd and eased ins fnl f* **33/1**
2244 **12** 1 ¼ **May Chorus (IRE)**[14] 809 3-8-7 59 JoeFanning 9 —
(J R Boyle) *a in rr: rdn and no rspnse over 2f out: wl bhd and eased ins fnl f* **17/2**

1m 24.96s (0.16) **Going Correction** -0.025s/f (Stan) **12 Ran SP% 120.2**
Speed ratings (Par 98): **98,97,97,94,94 93,90,89,87,78 62,61**
toteswingers: 1&2 £5.50, 1&3 £3.40, 2&3 £4.10 CSF £44.37 CT £163.38 TOTE £4.60: £2.50, £2.80, £1.80; EX 43.10 Trifecta £122.10 Pool: £435.73 - 2.64 winning units..
Owner J Barton & C Pizarro **Bred** Forenaghts Stud **Trained** Newmarket, Suffolk
FOCUS
A modest handicap.
May Chorus(IRE) Official explanation: trainer said filly made a noise

934 LINGFIELDPARK.CO.UK H'CAP 1m (P)
5:40 (5:40) (Class 5) (0-75,75) 3-Y-O £2,456 (£725; £362) Stalls High

Form RPR
1 **1** **Dream On Buddy (IRE)**[34] 533 3-8-6 63 MartinDwyer 8 75+
(B W Hills) *stdd s: hld up in last trio: hdwy on inner over 2f out: chal over 1f out: edgd rt but rdn to ld ins fnl f: r.o wl* **11/8**[1]
-215 **2** ½ **Duellist**[29] 596 3-9-3 74 JoeFanning 10 85+
(M Johnston) *t.k.h: pressed ldr tl rdn to ld over 1f out: clr w wnr 1f out: hdd and no ex ins fnl f* **10/1**
00-2 **3** 2 ¾ **Green Earth (IRE)**[16] 772 3-9-3 74 JimCrowley 3 78
(Mrs A J Perrett) *sn chsng ldrs: rdn and nt pce of ldng pair over 1f out: kpt on u.p fnl f* **8/1**[3]
0-21 **4** ¾ **Pastello**[22] 698 3-8-12 69 RyanMoore 2 72
(R Hannon) *t.k.h: hld up in tch in midfield: rdn and effrt ent fnl 2f: nt clr run and swtchd lft jst over 1f out: styd on same pce fnl f* **3/1**[2]
40-3 **5** 2 **Slasi**[14] 809 3-8-4 61 oh1 ChrisCatlin 6 59
(C E Brittain) *t.k.h: led at stdy gallop: rdn ent fnl 2f: hdd over 1f out: wknd fnl f* **14/1**
141- **6** ½ **Al Khimiya (IRE)**[89] 7824 3-9-3 74 HayleyTurner 5 71
(S Woodman) *t.k.h: hld up in tch in midfield: rdn and no hdwy jst over 2f out: kpt on u.p fnl f: nvr gng pce to trble ldrs* **12/1**
4-23 **7** 1 ¾ **Jodawes (USA)**[30] 583 3-8-8 65 SteveDrowne 4 57
(J R Best) *in tch: rdn and unable qck ent fnl 2f: wl btn fr over 1f out* **16/1**
216- **8** shd **Dance For Julie (IRE)**[180] 6134 3-9-3 74 TomEaves 7 66
(B M R Haslam) *stdd s: plld hrd: hld up in rr: n.d* **33/1**
14 **9** 2 **Nubar Boy**[41] 448 3-9-4 75 (t) RichardKingscote 9 62
(Tom Dascombe) *stdd s: t.k.h: chsd ldrs on outer: rdn 2f out: wknd u.p ent fnl f* **10/1**
44-0 **10** shd **Slip Sliding Away (IRE)**[14] 809 3-8-4 61 oh1 AdrianNicholls 1 48
(J R Best) *stdd s: plld hrd and hld up in last: n.d* **33/1**

1m 39.2s (1.00) **Going Correction** -0.025s/f (Stan) **10 Ran SP% 122.5**
Speed ratings (Par 98): **94,93,90,90,88 87,85,85,83,83**
toteswingers: 1&2 £4.70, 1&3 £4.10, 2&3 £10.10 CSF £18.10 CT £88.62 TOTE £2.20: £1.20, £2.90, £1.60; EX 23.30 Trifecta £150.00 Pool: £421.73 - 2.08 winning units. Place 6: £23.52 Place 5: £19.94.
Owner J Winston **Bred** Kilcarn Stud **Trained** Lambourn, Berks
FOCUS
A decent gallop to this handicap and once again the winner got a dream run up the inside.
Dance For Julie(IRE) Official explanation: jockey said filly ran too free
T/Plt: £24.40 to a £1 stake. Pool: £47,059.52. 1,404.39 winning tickets. T/Qpdt: £7.80 to a £1 stake. Pool: £3,854.33. 361.56 winning tickets. SP

919 WOLVERHAMPTON (A.W) (L-H)
Friday, March 19

OFFICIAL GOING: Standard
Wind: Fresh against changing to light behind for the final 3 races Weather: Raining

935 32REDBET.COM H'CAP 5f 20y(P)
5:50 (5:52) (Class 4) (0-80,78) 4-Y-O+ £4,533 (£1,348; £674; £336) Stalls Low

Form RPR
0-32 **1** **Master Lightfoot**[49] 345 4-9-1 75 ShaneKelly 5 84
(W R Swinburn) *a.p: chsd ldr over 3f out: rdn over 1f out: r.o to ld wl ins fnl f* **9/2**[3]
2221 **2** shd **Handsome Cross (IRE)**[23] 687 9-8-8 68 (v) JamieMackay 1 77+
(W J Musson) *hld up: hdwy and swtchd rt over 1f out: r.o* **9/2**[3]
4-03 **3** ¾ **Stolt (IRE)**[20] 736 6-9-3 77 DarryllHolland 4 83
(N Wilson) *led: rdn and hdd wl ins fnl f: styd on same pce* **5/2**[1]
1-53 **4** 1 ¼ **Anne Of Kiev (IRE)**[30] 578 5-9-4 78 (t) JerryO'Dwyer 6 79
(J R Gask) *s.i.s: hld up: hdwy 1/2-way: rdn over 1f out: hung lft ins fnl f: styd on same pce* **11/2**
0142 **5** nk **Steel City Boy (IRE)**[7] 869 7-8-6 66 PaulHanagan 3 66
(D Shaw) *chsd ldrs: rdn 1/2-way: sn outpcd: styd on ins fnl f* **4/1**[2]
520- **6** shd **Caranbola**[179] 6159 4-8-5 65 JimmyQuinn 2 65
(M Brittain) *chsd ldr to over 3f out: remained handy: rdn over 1f out: styd on same pce* **11/2**

61.90 secs (-0.40) **Going Correction** 0.0s/f (Stan) **6 Ran SP% 115.7**
Speed ratings (Par 105): **103,102,101,99,99 99**
toteswingers: 1&2 £5.30, 1&3 £2.80, 2&3 £5.00 CSF £25.48 TOTE £8.00: £2.30, £2.00; EX 22.60.
Owner P W Harris & Miss V Palmer **Bred** Bottisham Heath Stud **Trained** Aldbury, Herts
FOCUS
A fair handicap run but one run at just an ordinary gallop. Winner and second came down the centre in the straight.

936 32RED CASINO OF THE DECADE MAIDEN STKS 5f 20y(P)
6:20 (6:22) (Class 5) 3-Y-O+ £2,456 (£725; £362) Stalls Low

Form RPR
0- **1** **Addictive Dream (IRE)**[191] 5778 3-8-12 0 ShaneKelly 4 74+
(W R Swinburn) *hld up: hdwy over 1f out: swtchd lft sn after: r.o to ld wl ins fnl f: comf* **15/2**
-554 **2** 2 **Val C**[19] 745 3-8-7 61 (b) NickyMackay 2 62
(M Botti) *led: clr 1/2-way: rdn and hdd wl ins fnl f* **9/4**[1]
0-05 **3** 3 ¼ **Tune Up The Band**[8] 866 6-9-10 50 GeorgeBaker 8 60
(R J Hodges) *chsd ldrs: hung lft 1/2-way: sn rdn: styd on same pce fr over 1f out* **9/1**
4 nk **Sulis Minerva (IRE)** 3-8-7 0 LukeMorris 1 49+
(J R Gask) *hld up: hdwy: hmpd and swtchd rt jst over 2f out: sn rdn styd on: nt trble ldrs* **33/1**
-053 **5** ¾ **Sally's Swansong**[9] 849 4-9-2 40 (b) GaryBartley(3) 7 51
(E J Alston) *chsd ldrs: hmpd jst over 2f out: sn rdn: styd on same pce* **16/1**
60-2 **6** nk **Dower Glen**[28] 619 3-8-7 58 JimmyQuinn 9 45
(N Wilson) *prom: rdn 1/2-way: no imp fnl 2f* **6/1**[3]
60 **7** nse **Shawkantango**[6] 886 3-8-12 0 DaneO'Neill 5 50
(D Shaw) *dwlt: outpcd: r.o ins fnl f: nvr nrr* **100/1**
55 **8** ½ **Lucas Pitt**[9] 849 3-8-12 0 StephenCraine 10 48+
(M J Scudamore) *sn outpcd: r.o ins fnl f: nrst fin* **20/1**
5-23 **9** 1 **Blue Zephyr**[47] 362 3-8-12 67 DarryllHolland 3 45
(W R Muir) *chsd ldrs: pushed along and swtchd rt 3f out: hmpd and lost pl jst over 2f out: n.d after* **3/1**[2]
10 nse **Murura (IRE)** 3-8-12 0 PaulMulrennan 11 44+
(J G Given) *sn outpcd: nt clr run over 1f out: n.d* **10/1**
0-00 **11** 10 **Shirley High**[37] 477 4-8-12 44 JohnFahy(7) 13 8
(P Howling) *prom: hmpd jst over 2f out: sn wknd* **66/1**
50- **12** 6 **Princess Lexi (IRE)**[164] 6556 3-8-7 0 SilvestreDeSousa 12 —
(K A Ryan) *sn outpcd* **20/1**

61.71 secs (-0.59) **Going Correction** 0.0s/f (Stan)
WFA 3 from 4yo+ 12lb **12 Ran SP% 121.7**
Speed ratings (Par 103): **104,100,95,95,93 93,93,92,90,90 74,65**
toteswingers: 1&2 £7.20, 1&3 £25.10, 2&3 £5.90 CSF £24.27 TOTE £9.90: £2.30, £1.60, £2.30; EX 33.70.
Owner Caveat Emptor Partnership **Bred** Eugene Matthews **Trained** Aldbury, Herts

FOCUS
A modest maiden in which a couple of the market leaders disappointed and a race that is unlikely to be throwing up many winners. The pace was sound and the winner ended up just off the inside rail.

937 32RED.COM H'CAP 7f 32y(P)
6:50 (6:50) (Class 6) (0-60,60) 4-Y-0+ £1,774 (£523; £262) Stalls High

Form RPR

50 **1** **Unlimited**[37] 486 8-9-3 **59** ... LukeMorris 5 70
(A W Carroll) *hld up: hdwy u.p over 1f out: hung lft ins fnl f: r.o to ld post* **7/1**

5202 **2** nse **Spinning Ridge (IRE)**[9] 855 5-9-4 **60** ... (v[1]) LiamJones 9 71
(R A Harris) *led: clr over 2f out: rdn over 1f out: hdd post* **11/2**[3]

36-3 **3** 1 1/4 **Tevez**[9] 855 5-8-10 **59** ... MJMurphy(7) 12 67
(D Donovan) *dwlt: hld up: hdwy over 1f out: r.o* **12/1**

5-46 **4** 1 1/4 **Quiet Mountain (IRE)**[45] 378 5-8-11 **56** ... BarryMcHugh(3) 2 60
(Ollie Pears) *hld up: hdwy over 1f out: sn rdn: styng on same pce whn n.m.r wl ins fnl f* **6/1**

50-0 **5** 1 **Lake Chini (IRE)**[10] 836 8-8-8 **55** ... (b) JamesSullivan(5) 3 57
(M W Easterby) *s.i.s: hld up: r.o ins fnl f: nrst fin* **50/1**

0-42 **6** 2 1/4 **Dancing Welcome**[28] 614 4-9-2 **58** ... (b) NickyMackay 1 53
(J M Bradley) *chsd ldrs: rdn over 2f out: styd on same pce appr fnl f* **5/1**[2]

0362 **7** 1/2 **Trip Switch**[9] 844 4-8-9 **58** ... CharlotteKerton(7) 7 52
(G Prodromou) *s.i.s: pushed along thrght in rr tl r.o ins fnl f: nvr nrr* **12/1**

-531 **8** 1 1/2 **Sign Of The Cross**[17] 763 6-9-2 **58** ... PhillipMakin 6 48
(C R Dore) *prom: racd keenly: chsd clr ldr over 2f out: sn rdn: wknd fnl f* **15/2**

4003 **9** 4 **Grand Honour (IRE)**[9] 845 4-9-4 **60** ... JimmyQuinn 8 39
(P Howling) *hld up: hdwy over 2f out: sn rdn: wknd over 1f out* **7/2**[1]

-030 **10** 4 **Our Day Will Come**[17] 763 4-8-13 **55** ... DavidProbert 11 23
(B Palling) *prom: rdn over 3f out: wknd over 2f out* **22/1**

-056 **11** 2 **Izzi Mill (USA)**[15] 793 4-8-9 **58** ... (p) JohnFahy(7) 10 21
(A J McCabe) *chsd ldr tl rdn over 2f out: wknd over 1f out* **22/1**

1m 28.74s (-0.86) **Going Correction** 0.0s/f (Stan) 11 Ran SP% **118.9**
Speed ratings (Par 101): **104,103,102,101,99 97,96,95,90,85 83**
toteswingers: 1&2 £13.80, 1&3 £21.90, 2&3 £8.60 CSF £44.86 CT £470.99 TOTE £6.90: £2.80, £2.60, £5.10; EX 51.30.
Owner M B Clarke **Bred** J Wise **Trained** Cropthorne, Worcs
■ Stewards' Enquiry : Luke Morris one-day ban: careless riding (Apr 3)

FOCUS
A moderate handicap in which a reasonable gallop increased leaving the back straight. The winner came down the centre in the straight.
Dancing Welcome Official explanation: jockey said filly was denied a clear run
Trip Switch Official explanation: jockey said gelding was denied a clear run
Our Day Will Come Official explanation: jockey said filly hung right

938 BET AT 32RED.COM H'CAP 2m 119y(P)
7:20 (7:20) (Class 4) (0-85,78) 4-Y-0+ £4,533 (£1,348; £674; £336) Stalls Low

Form RPR

2-45 **1** **Gremlin**[7] 871 6-8-12 **67** ... KierenFox(5) 3 73
(D Burchell) *hld up in tch: led wl over 1f out: sn rdn: hung lft ins fnl f: all out* **6/1**

2-11 **2** hd **Sinbad The Sailor**[23] 688 5-9-4 **73** ... (v) MatthewDavies(5) 1 79
(George Baker) *set stdy pce tl hdd over 9f out: led again 5f out: rdn and hdd wl over 1f out: styd on* **7/4**[1]

300/ **3** 1/2 **Dancing Sword**[49] 7009 5-8-10 **60** ... DavidProbert 6 65
(D Burchell) *hld up: hdwy over 3f out: rdn over 1f out: styd on* **40/1**

2222 **4** 1 1/4 **Calculating (IRE)**[14] 811 6-9-4 **73** ... LeeNewnes(5) 2 77
(M D I Usher) *chsd ldr over 6f: remained handy: outpcd over 5f out: rallied over 1f out: r.o* **4/1**[3]

3211 **5** 15 **Star Choice**[9] 842 5-9-3 **72** 6ex ... (b) SimonPearce(5) 4 58
(J Pearce) *chsd ldrs: rdn over 3f out: wknd over 2f out* **11/4**[2]

1112 **6** 50 **Clear Sailing**[7] 871 7-10-0 **78** ... ShaneKelly 5 65
(P Leech) *stdd s: racd keenly and sn trcking ldrs: led over 9f out: hdd 5f out: rdn and wknd over 2f out: eased fnl f: t.o* **10/1**

3m 43.22s (1.42) **Going Correction** 0.0s/f (Stan) 6 Ran SP% **108.8**
Speed ratings (Par 105): **96,95,95,95,88 64**
toteswingers: 1&2 £3.20, 1&3 £7.50, 2&3 £24.30 CSF £15.95 TOTE £6.80: £2.70, £1.10; EX 26.00.
Owner Jason Tucker **Bred** Catridge Farm Stud Ltd **Trained** Briery Hill, Blaenau Gwent

FOCUS
A fair handicap but a steady pace means this bare form may not be entirely reliable. The winner raced centre to far side in the straight.
Star Choice Official explanation: trainer said gelding finished distresed
Clear Sailing Official explanation: jockey said gelding tired from 2f out

939 £320 FREE AT 32RED.COM H'CAP (DIV I) 1m 141y(P)
7:50 (7:50) (Class 6) (0-55,55) 4-Y-0+ £1,433 (£423; £211) Stalls Low

Form RPR

-245 **1** **Marjury Daw (IRE)**[18] 757 4-9-0 **54** ... PaulMulrennan 4 64
(J G Given) *broke wl: stdd and lost pl after 1f: hdwy over 3f out: led ins fnl f: rdn out* **5/1**[3]

-535 **2** 2 **Fitzwarren**[15] 795 9-8-6 **46** oh1 ... (tp) SilvestreDeSousa 6 51
(A D Brown) *sn led: rdn over 1f out: hdd and unable qck ins fnl f* **16/1**

-260 **3** 1 1/4 **The Graig**[39] 469 6-8-10 **50** ... (t) JerryO'Dwyer 5 52
(J R Holt) *prom: pushed along 3f out: hrd rdn fr over 1f out: no ex ins fnl f* **13/2**

1606 **4** hd **King's Jester (IRE)**[18] 753 8-8-8 **53** ... (b) JamesSullivan(5) 7 55
(Lee Smyth, Ire) *prom: racd keenly: rdn over 1f out: styd on same pce* **12/1**

-004 **5** 2 1/4 **Montmartre (USA)**[23] 682 4-8-1 **46** oh1 ... SimonPearce(5) 12 43
(David Pinder) *chsd ldr: rdn and ev ch wl over 1f out: wknd ins fnl f* **28/1**

225- **6** 3/4 **Mr Chocolate Drop (IRE)**[357] 979 6-9-1 **55** ... (b) JimmyQuinn 9 52
(Miss M E Rowland) *s.i.s: hld up: hmpd over 1f out: r.o ins fnl f: nvr rchd ldrs* **10/1**

6066 **7** hd **James Pollard (IRE)**[15] 791 5-8-6 **46** ... DavidProbert 3 41
(B J Llewellyn) *s.s: sn pushed along in rr: styd on ins fnl f: nvr nrr* **18/1**

40-4 **8** nk **Gold Rock (FR)**[9] 847 5-9-1 **55** ... LukeMorris 2 49
(A W Carroll) *trckd ldrs: nt clr run jst over 2f out: sn rdn: wknd fnl f* **5/2**[1]

100- **9** 1 1/2 **Molly The Witch (IRE)**[159] 6705 4-9-1 **55** ... JamieMackay 1 46
(W J Musson) *hld up: effrt whn hmpd ins fnl f: n.d* **10/1**

0322 **10** 1 1/2 **Join Up**[9] 847 4-8-7 **52** ... RossAtkinson(5) 8 39
(W M Brisbourne) *hld up: hdwy 1/2-way: rdn over 2f out: wknd over 1f out* **7/2**[2]

1m 50.54s (0.04) **Going Correction** 0.0s/f (Stan) 10 Ran SP% **121.3**
Speed ratings (Par 101): **99,97,96,95,93 93,93,92,91,90**
toteswingers: 1&2 £18.00, 1&3 £6.50, 2&3 £19.00 CSF £84.73 CT £535.92 TOTE £6.20: £1.80, £4.20, £2.30; EX 138.70.
Owner Danethorpe Racing Partnership **Bred** Mulhime Ltd Marston Stud & D Bonnycastle **Trained** Willoughton, Lincs

FOCUS
A moderate handicap run at an ordinary gallop. The winner raced towards the centre in the straight.
Mr Chocolate Drop(IRE) Official explanation: jockey said gelding was denied a clear run

940 £320 FREE AT 32RED.COM H'CAP (DIV II) 1m 141y(P)
8:20 (8:20) (Class 6) (0-55,55) 4-Y-0+ £1,433 (£423; £211) Stalls Low

Form RPR

5-00 **1** **Provost**[21] 715 6-9-1 **55** ... (b) GrahamGibbons 1 65
(M W Easterby) *s.i.s: hld up: hdwy over 1f out: rdn to ld wl ins fnl f* **14/1**

1643 **2** 1/2 **Barodine**[15] 795 7-9-1 **55** ow2 ... GeorgeBaker 12 64
(R J Hodges) *sn led: rdn over 1f out: hdd wl ins fnl f* **4/1**[1]

40-1 **3** 1 3/4 **Athboy Auction**[9] 847 5-7-13 **46** ... NatashaEaton(7) 11 51
(H J Collingridge) *s.i.s: hld up: disputing last turning for home and plenty to do: hdwy on ins over 1f out: r.o* **12/1**

0-05 **4** hd **Stoic Leader (IRE)**[16] 780 10-8-6 **46** oh1 ... FrannyNorton 4 51
(R F Fisher) *chsd ldrs: rdn over 2f out: styd on* **20/1**

-006 **5** 1/2 **Flamestone**[8] 862 6-8-6 **46** oh1 ... JimmyQuinn 3 49
(A E Price) *chsd ldr 5f: rdn to go 2nd again 2f out: no ex fnl f* **20/1**

0021 **6** 1/2 **Mountain Pass (USA)**[15] 794 8-8-11 **51** ... (p) DavidProbert 9 53
(B J Llewellyn) *s.i.s: hld up: hdwy over 2f out: rdn over 1f out: styd on* **7/1**[3]

5333 **7** nse **Turkish Sultan (IRE)**[9] 847 7-8-10 **50** ... (b) NickyMackay 2 52
(J M Bradley) *prom: rdn over 2f out: edgd rt fr over 1f out: one pce fnl f* **10/1**

3644 **8** 1 **Kirstys Lad**[9] 854 8-8-7 **50** ... KellyHarrison(3) 10 50
(M Mullineaux) *chsd ldrs: wnt 2nd over 3f out: tl rdn 2f out: no ex fnl f* **10/1**

0140 **9** shd **Machinate (USA)**[9] 847 8-8-7 **52** ... KierenFox(5) 6 52
(W M Brisbourne) *hld up: rdn over 1f out: nvr trbld ldrs* **18/1**

0322 **10** nk **Wetherby Place (IRE)**[15] 791 4-9-0 **54** ... StephenCraine 8 57+
(M Wigham) *hld up: effrt and nt clr run twice ins fnl f: nvr nr to chal* **15/2**

0-00 **11** 9 **My Jeanie (IRE)**[16] 780 6-8-6 **46** oh1 ... LiamJones 7 24
(J C Fox) *hld up: drvn along over 3f out: a in rr* **33/1**

-435 **12** 6 **Royal Society**[11] 540 4-9-1 **55** ... DaneO'Neill 13 19
(R A Farrant) *hld up in tch: rdn over 2f out: sn wknd* **12/1**

/002 **P** **Angels Quest**[22] 691 5-8-13 **53** ... LukeMorris 5 —
(A W Carroll) *in rr and pushed along 7f out: p.u 5f out* **9/2**[2]

1m 51.22s (0.72) **Going Correction** 0.0s/f (Stan) 13 Ran SP% **120.4**
Speed ratings (Par 101): **96,95,94,93,93 92,92,92,91,91 83,78,—**
toteswingers: 1&2 £67.00, 1&3 £107.20, 2&3 £14.70 CSF £68.05 CT £735.75 TOTE £15.10: £6.30, £1.90, £4.20; EX 80.20.
Owner A G Black **Bred** Charlie Wyatt **Trained** Sheriff Hutton, N Yorks

FOCUS
The second division of this moderate handicap. The gallop was an ordinary one and the winner raced centre to far side in the straight.
Provost Official explanation: trainer's rep had no explanation for the apparen t improvement in form

941 32REDPOKER.COM H'CAP 1m 1f 103y(P)
8:50 (8:51) (Class 5) (0-70,72) 4-Y-0+ £2,729 (£806; £403) Stalls Low

Form RPR

4-62 **1** **Danderek**[42] 433 4-9-2 **66** ... PaulHanagan 7 77+
(R A Fahey) *mde all: rdn clr over 2f out: styd on wl* **14/1**[3]

111 **2** 2 1/2 **Sworn Tigress (GER)**[8] 865 5-9-3 **72** 12ex ... MatthewDavies(5) 11 78+
(George Baker) *hld up: hdwy over 2f out: sn rdn: wnt 2nd ins fnl f: nt rch wnr* **8/13**[1]

036- **3** 1 3/4 **Waahej**[95] 7752 4-9-0 **64** ... LukeMorris 8 66
(P W Hiatt) *hld up in tch: rdn over 3f out: styd on u.p: nt trble ldrs* **25/1**

-214 **4** hd **Zero Cool (USA)**[23] 676 6-9-1 **65** ... (p) GeorgeBaker 12 67
(G L Moore) *prom: chsd wnr over 2f out: sn rdn: hung lft and no ex fnl f* **10/1**[2]

014- **5** nk **King's Masque**[148] 6968 4-9-4 **68** ... DavidProbert 3 69
(B J Llewellyn) *chsd ldrs: rdn over 2f out: styd on same pce fnl f* **22/1**

4-24 **6** 1 1/2 **Monaco Dream (IRE)**[32] 563 4-9-4 **68** ... (p) AlanMunro 2 66
(W Jarvis) *hld up: rdn over 2f out: styd on fr over 1f out: n.d* **22/1**

2156 **7** 3/4 **Granny McPhee**[1] 925 4-8-10 **67** ... NatashaEaton(7) 4 63+
(A Bailey) *hld up: hmpd over 7f out: r.o ins fnl f: nvr nrr* **20/1**

1103 **8** 1 **Grey Command (USA)**[18] 752 5-8-8 **65** ... JohnCavanagh(7) 9 59
(M Brittain) *prom: lost pl over 6f out: rdn over 2f out: n.d after* **20/1**

36- **9** 1/2 **Enlist**[349] 1133 6-9-1 **65** ... FergusSweeney 10 58
(B G Powell) *chsd wnr tl rdn over 2f out: wknd fnl f* **16/1**

00-0 **10** 1 1/4 **Aviso (GER)**[30] 587 6-9-3 **67** ... TomQueally 5 58
(B J Curley) *s.i.s: hld up: nvr on terms* **14/1**[3]

-133 **11** 1/2 **Moscow Oznick**[55] 280 5-8-10 **67** ... (p) MJMurphy(7) 6 56
(D Donovan) *mid-div: hmpd and dropped in rr over 7f out: n.d* **25/1**

4-55 **12** 3 1/2 **Supercast (IRE)**[42] 430 7-8-13 **68** ... (t) SimonPearce(5) 13 50
(N J Vaughan) *mid-div: hdwy over 5f out: rdn and wknd over 2f out* **14/1**[3]

2m 0.75s (-0.95) **Going Correction** 0.0s/f (Stan) 12 Ran SP% **122.8**
Speed ratings (Par 103): **104,101,100,100,99 98,97,96,96,95 94,91**
toteswingers: 1&2 £2.80, 1&3 £35.10, 2&3 £11.60 CSF £21.58 CT £251.70 TOTE £14.70: £3.10, £1.10, £6.80; EX 38.30.
Owner Derek Rowlands & Daniel Keenan **Bred** Mrs Maureen Buckley **Trained** Musley Bank, N Yorks

FOCUS
A one-sided event judging by the market but an improved effort in a run-of-the-mill handicap from the winner, who dictated an ordinary gallop and raced centre to far side in the straight.
Aviso(GER) Official explanation: jockey said gelding hung left

942 £10 FREE BINGO AT 32RED H'CAP 1m 4f 50y(P)
9:20 (9:20) (Class 7) (0-50,50) 4-Y-0+ £1,364 (£403; £201) Stalls Low

Form RPR

000/ **1** **Me Fein**[447] 7787 6-9-1 **50** ... TomQueally 10 67+
(B J Curley) *hld up: nt clr run over 3f out: hdwy over 2f out: rdn over 1f out: r.o to ld post* **5/6**[1]

53-3 **2** shd **Jezza**[34] 539 4-8-11 **48** ... DarryllHolland 8 59
(Karen George) *led: pushed clr over 2f out: rdn over 1f out: edgd rt ins fnl f: hdd post* **9/2**[2]

/534 **3** *2¼* **Trysting Grove (IRE)**[8] 865 9-8-10 **50**.......................... KierenFox(5) 11 57
(E G Bevan) *s.i.s: hld up: hdwy over 3f out: rdn to chse ldr over 2f out: styd on same pce ins fnl f* **14/1**

6-43 **4** *8* **Ocean Of Peace (FR)**[29] 590 7-8-13 **48**.................. FergusSweeney 12 43
(M R Bosley) *hld up: hdwy over 1f out: nt rch ldrs* **10/1**[3]

00-4 **5** *3* **Tar (IRE)**[14] 813 6-8-11 **46**.. PaulHanagan 6 36
(Tim Vaughan) *chsd ldr 4f: remained handy: rdn over 2f out: wknd over 1f out* **14/1**

406 **6** *2* **Mojeerr**[8] 865 4-8-5 **49**...(p) NoraLooby(7) 4 36
(A J McCabe) *plld hrd and prom: trckd ldr 8f out tl rdn over 2f out: wknd over 1f out* **50/1**

5105 **7** *hd* **Dazzling Begum**[14] 813 5-8-10 **50**............................. SimonPearce(5) 9 36
(J Pearce) *hld up: rdn over 2f out: nvr on terms* **12/1**

/06- **8** *2¼* **Marieschi (USA)**[332] 1442 6-8-11 **46**............................ FrannyNorton 5 29
(R F Fisher) *trckd ldrs: racd keenly: rdn over 3f out: wknd over 2f out* **33/1**

6-03 **9** *¾* **Stravita**[25] 661 6-8-10 **45**...(p) DaneO'Neill 3 26
(R Hollinshead) *hld up: rdn over 2f out: a in rr* **11/1**

256- **10** *3* **King's Fable (USA)**[176] 6226 7-9-1 **50**.........................(p) JerryO'Dwyer 2 27
(Karen George) *hld up: a in rr* **28/1**

/000 **11** *1¾* **Mandalay Prince**[12] 720 6-8-11 **46**............................. StevieDonohoe 7 20
(W J Musson) *s.i.s: hld up: pushed along 5f out: wknd 3f out* **33/1**

00-0 **12** *32* **Forced Opinion (USA)**[25] 666 5-9-1 **50**......................... JimmyQuinn 1 —
(K A Morgan) *prom: rdn over 3f out: sn wknd: t.o* **16/1**

2m 40.91s (-0.19) **Going Correction** 0.0s/f (Stan)
WFA 4 from 5yo+ 2lb **12** Ran SP% **128.4**
Speed ratings (Par 97): **100,99,98,93,91 89,89,88,87,85 84,63**
toteswingers: 1&2 £2.90, 1&3 £8.50, 2&3 £14.20 CSF £4.97 CT £37.69 TOTE £1.90: £1.10, £2.60, £2.80; EX 5.90 Place 6: £326.50 Place 5: £106.64.
Owner Curley Leisure **Bred** Irish National Stud **Trained** Newmarket, Suffolk

FOCUS
A very moderate handicap and one run at an ordinary gallop till the pace lifted passing the 3f pole. The winner raced centre to far side in the straight.
Tar(IRE) Official explanation: jockey said gelding hung left throughout
Forced Opinion(USA) Official explanation: jockey said horse stopped quickly
T/Plt: £1,146.90 to a £1 stake. Pool: £82,253.06. 52.35 winning tickets. T/Qpdt: £80.50 to a £1 stake. Pool: £9,395.83. 86.30 winning tickets. CR

928 LINGFIELD (L-H)
Saturday, March 20

OFFICIAL GOING: Standard
Wind: strong behind

943 SPORTINGBET SUPPORTS HEROS ALL WEATHER "HANDS AND HEELS" APPRENTICE SERIES FINAL H'CAP 1m (P)
1:55 (1:56) (Class 4) (0-85,85) 4-Y-O+ **£5,180** (£1,541; £770; £384) **Stalls** High

Form RPR

-162 **1** **Gaily Noble (IRE)**[17] 769 4-9-4 **85**.................................... ShaneRyan 8 95
(A B Haynes) *in tch: pushed along and wd bnd 2f out: chsd ldr 1f out: led fnl 100yds: r.o wl* **6/1**[3]

1561 **2** *nk* **Prince Of Thebes (IRE)**[26] 657 9-8-9 **76**........................... KierenFox 1 85
(M J Attwater) *chsd ldrs: rdn to ld jst over 2f out: hdd whn unable qck fnl 100yds* **11/1**

3564 **3** *3* **Follow The Flag (IRE)**[22] 725 6-8-6 **78**...................(p) ConorQuish(5) 3 80
(A J McCabe) *in tch: effrt in barging match over 1f out: styd on same pce fnl f* **25/1**

2221 **4** *hd* **Charlie Smirke (USA)**[31] 587 4-8-4 **74**.................. HarryBentley(3) 9 76
(G L Moore) *hld up in tch of midfield: hdwy 2f out: kpt on fnl f: nt pce to rch ldrs* **5/1**[1]

-263 **5** *1½* **Den's Gift (IRE)**[25] 672 6-8-12 **84**..........................(b) ThomasDyer(5) 12 82
(C G Cox) *chsd ldr: ev ch over 2f out: wknd ent fnl f* **5/1**[1]

0-43 **6** *½* **Kidlat**[8] 873 5-8-3 **73**... NatashaEaton(3) 6 70
(A Bailey) *led tl jst over 2f out: wknd ent fnl f* **11/2**[2]

1104 **7** *¾* **Stanley Goodspeed**[15] 808 7-8-4 **71** oh3..................(t) NathanAlison 2 66
(J W Hills) *in tch in midfield: effrt on inner wl over 1f out: no further prog fnl f* **22/1**

0650 **8** *4½* **Bennelong**[11] 837 4-8-0 **72**... KevinLundie(5) 10 57
(P D Evans) *s.i.s: sn pushed along: a in rr: lost tch 2f out* **14/1**

6-54 **9** *2¼* **Tous Les Deux**[12] 829 7-8-8 **75**....................................... LeeTopliss 11 55
(G L Moore) *stdd s: t.k.h: hld up in rr: rdn and no prog fnl 2f* **12/1**

10/- **10** *8* **Longoria (IRE)**[673] 2149 5-8-10 **77**..................................... DavidKenny 7 38
(Lucinda Featherstone) *a towards rr: rdn over 3f out: no ch fnl 2f* **40/1**

60-1 **11** *2½* **Dingaan (IRE)**[31] 580 7-8-13 **85**.................................. FrancisHayes(5) 4 41
(A M Balding) *awkward leaving stalls and v.s.a: racd wd: a in rr* **8/1**

1m 36.89s (-1.31) **Going Correction** +0.025s/f (Slow) **11** Ran SP% **107.4**
Speed ratings (Par 105): **107,106,103,103,102 101,100,96,94,86 83**
toteswingers: 1&2 £10.90, 1&3 £26.00, 2&3 £27.50 CSF £56.38 CT £1136.89 TOTE £6.50: £1.90, £2.60, £6.30; EX 52.20 Trifecta £161.80 Part won. Pool: £218.69 - 0.45 winning units..
Owner Athos Racing **Bred** Garry Chong **Trained** Limpley Stoke, Bath
■ Alfresco was withdrawn (unruly in stalls, 8/1). Deduct 10p in the £ under R4.

FOCUS
The final of this 'hands and heels' apprentices' handicap series was an open betting race and fell to one of those backed late.
Dingaan(IRE) Official explanation: jockey said gelding was slowly away

944 SPORTINGBET SUPPORTS HEROS "SUPER 7" H'CAP FINAL 7f (P)
2:25 (2:27) (Class 2) 4-Y-O+
£31,155 (£9,330; £4,665; £2,335; £1,165; £585) **Stalls** Low

Form RPR

5-22 **1** **Bravo Echo**[49] 358 4-9-2 **89**.. LukeMorris 8 98
(M J Attwater) *chsd ldr: rdn ent fnl 2f: led ins fnl f: r.o strly* **4/1**[2]

3206 **2** *1¼* **Autumn Blades (IRE)**[7] 885 5-9-8 **95**........................(v) DavidProbert 9 101
(A Bailey) *hld up in tch in midfield: effrt whn rdn over 1f out: pressed wnr ins fnl f: nt qckn and btn fnl 100yds* **8/1**

4021 **3** *½* **Seek The Fair Land**[21] 739 4-9-1 **88**........................(p) PatCosgrave 1 92
(J R Boyle) *chsd ldrs: rdn and unable qck 2f out: kpt on again fnl f: nt quite able to reel in ldng pair* **8/1**

1540 **4** *¾* **Tourist**[7] 887 5-9-3 **90**.. JimmyQuinn 2 92
(D Shaw) *led: rdn and fnd ex over 1f out: hdd ins fnl f: one pce after* **25/1**

3556 **5** *1* **Carcinetto (IRE)**[2] 921 8-9-2 **89**................................. RichardHughes 5 89
(P D Evans) *in tch in midfield: rdn and unable qck 2f out: rallied u.p fnl f: styd on towards fin* **16/1**

0-02 **6** *1½* **Wigram's Turn (USA)**[55] 286 5-9-3 **90**...................(v) JimmyFortune 6 86
(A M Balding) *stdd s: hld up in last trio: hmpd and lost tch over 4f out: n.d after* **12/1**

10-6 **7** *¾* **Kyllachy Star**[21] 739 4-9-3 **90**..(p) PaulHanagan 7 83
(R A Fahey) *s.i.s: towards rr: hmpd and lost tch over 4f out: nvr bk on terms* **20/1**

3-41 **8** *4½* **Everymanforhimself (IRE)**[35] 537 6-9-10 **97**..............(v) NeilCallan 10 78
(K A Ryan) *chsd ldrs: rdn and nt qckn 2f out: wl btn over 1f out* **9/1**

0-31 **9** *2* **The Scorching Wind (IRE)**[49] 358 4-9-6 **93**................(t) RyanMoore 4 69+
(S C Williams) *hld up in rr: hmpd and lost tch over 4f out: nvr bk on terms* **3/1**[1]

-113 **10** *dist* **Elna Bright**[21] 739 5-9-8 **95**.. KierenFallon 3 —
(B R Johnson) *hld up in midfield whn hmpd and lost action 5f out: sn eased: virtually p.u fnl 3f* **5/1**[3]

1m 23.91s (-0.89) **Going Correction** +0.025s/f (Slow) **10** Ran SP% **116.1**
Speed ratings (Par 109): **106,104,104,103,102 100,99,94,92,—**
toteswingers: 1&2 £7.10, 1&3 £6.80, 2&3 £14.20 CSF £35.92 CT £249.90 TOTE £4.90: £2.00, £2.60, £2.20; EX 41.90 Trifecta £178.20 Pool: £949.16 - 3.94 winning units..
Owner Canisbay Bloodstock **Bred** Juddmonte Farms Ltd **Trained** Epsom, Surrey

FOCUS
A very competitive final of this series and a number of these have clashed several times over the winter.

NOTEBOOK
Bravo Echo, narrowly beaten by today's favourite last time, deserved this success and confirmed previous form from that race with the runner-up on worse terms. He looks progressive and the sort to run well in some big handicaps on turf this spring and summer, with the Victoria Cup appealing as a possible race for him. (tchd 7-2 and 9-2)
Autumn Blades(IRE) was 4lb better off with today's winner for a two-length beating over course and distance at the end of January and looked the likely winner when cruising onto the heels of the leaders going into the home turn. However, he could not find as much as the winner in the closing stages. (op 10-1)
Seek The Fair Land chased the leaders throughout and ran on all the way to the line without being able to narrow the gap on the first two. He maintains his form well, but is now 15lb higher than when gaining the first of his three wins this winter in December. (op 10-1 tchd 12-1)
Tourist is another who has climbed the handicap this winter, being 20lb higher than when scoring in October. He made a brave effort from the front and tried to steal it off the bend, but he had nothing more to give inside the last furlong. (tchd 28-1)
Carcinetto(IRE), having her 23rd race since last winning back in August, keeps running well in defeat and was one of several staying on well when the race was over. (op 18-1)
Wigram's Turn(USA) was out the back for much of the way, but hit top gear in the straight and ran on past beaten horses. (op 11-1)
Kyllachy Star was another to run on from the back when the race was over. (op 12-1)
Everymanforhimself(IRE) faded disappointingly having been up with the leaders early. (op 11-1)
The Scorching Wind(IRE) was carried back through the field after being hampered by the lame Elna Bright and lost all chance. (op 11-4 tchd 7-2)
Elna Bright appeared to go lame and hampered the favourite as his rider attempted to pull up.
Official explanation: vet said gelding was struck into right-hind

945 SPORTINGBET SUPPORTS HEROS SPRING CUP (LISTED RACE) 7f (P)
3:00 (3:00) (Class 1) 3-Y-O
£34,062 (£12,912; £6,462; £3,222; £1,614; £810) **Stalls** Low

Form RPR

10- **1** **Classic Colori (IRE)**[147] 7030 3-9-1 95.................... RichardKingscote 8 101
(Tom Dascombe) *taken down early: stdd s and sn swtchd lft: midfield: effrt over 1f out: wnt between horses and r.o strly ins fnl f: led post* **7/1**[3]

2111 **2** *nse* **Greyfriarschorista**[44] 406 3-9-1 96.................................. JoeFanning 6 101
(M Johnston) *chsd ldr: rdn to ld over 1f out: battled on wl: ct post* **15/8**[1]

352- **3** *nse* **Stargaze (IRE)**[91] 7806 3-9-1 103.................................... DavidProbert 7 101
(A Bailey) *in tch: rdn and hdwy over 1f out: r.o strly ins fnl f: nt quite get up* **10/1**

435- **4** *1½* **Jira**[168] 6477 3-8-12 98.. SebSanders 1 94
(C E Brittain) *s.i.s: sn rcvrd to chse ldrs: ev ch u.p 1f out: no ex fnl 100yds* **12/1**

240- **5** *nse* **Fratellino**[161] 6660 3-9-1 95.. RobertWinston 3 97
(A J McCabe) *led: rdn ent fnl 2f: hdd over 1f out: kpt on wl tl no ex fnl 100yds* **50/1**

410- **6** *2¾* **Hanson'D (IRE)**[147] 7017 3-9-1 100....................................... NeilCallan 12 89
(K A Ryan) *awkward s: s.i.s: hld up in last pair: rdn and prog 2f out: kpt on u.p fnl f: nt rch ldrs* **13/2**[2]

222- **7** *½* **Ongoodform (IRE)**[135] 7251 3-9-1 89................................ TonyCulhane 2 88
(P W D'Arcy) *t.k.h: chsd ldrs: effrt u.p wl over 1f out: wknd fnl f* **25/1**

126- **8** *2½* **Haadeeth**[141] 7150 3-9-1 90... MartinDwyer 13 81+
(M P Tregoning) *stdd s: hld up in last pair: sme prog on inner over 1f out: nvr trbld ldrs* **14/1**

-256 **9** *3¾* **Ramamara (IRE)**[16] 783 3-8-10 71................................... CathyGannon 10 66
(P D Evans) *towards rr: rdn 4f out: sme prog over 2f out: wknd over 1f out* **100/1**

215- **10** *1¾* **Duplicity**[159] 6752 3-9-3 100.. RichardHughes 4 73
(R Hannon) *t.k.h: hld up in midfield: struggling 2f out: eased whn wl btn ins fnl f* **11/1**

06-1 **11** *½* **Amary (IRE)**[17] 772 3-8-10 87.. ChrisCatlin 9 60
(C E Brittain) *rdn 3f out: a towards rr* **18/1**

0-00 **12** *nk* **Dubai Miracle (USA)**[15] 819 3-9-1 0.............................(b[1]) JimCrowley 5 64
(D M Simcock) *t.k.h: hld up towards rr: rdn and effrt 2f out: sn no further prog: wl btn fnl f* **25/1**

02-0 **13** *¾* **Kona Coast**[16] 796 3-9-1 0..(p) WilliamBuick 11 62
(J H M Gosden) *a towards rr: struggling bdly 3f out* **11/1**

1m 23.54s (-1.26) **Going Correction** +0.025s/f (Slow) **13** Ran SP% **116.6**
Speed ratings (Par 106): **108,107,107,106,106 102,102,99,95,93 92,92,91**
toteswingers: 1&2 £4.30, 1&3 £20.50, 2&3 £5.80 CSF £19.29 TOTE £9.90: £2.80, £1.20, £3.60; EX 32.40 Trifecta £429.10 Part won. Pool: £579.99 - 0.20 winning units..
Owner The Classic Strollers Partnership **Bred** Frank Dunne **Trained** Malpas, Cheshire

FOCUS
The last three winners had all been making their seasonal debuts and that trend continued. They appeared to go a good pace from the start, being fractionally slower than the preceding handicap, and it produced a desperate finish.

NOTEBOOK
Classic Colori(IRE) had beaten nine subsequent winners when scoring on his debut at Windsor last July. In his only subsequent race three and a half months later, he appeared not handle soft ground in a Group 3 at Newbury. He handled this ground well though and, after tracking the pace from the start, ran on really well under pressure to get up close home. He is apparently quirky but can improve again back on turf and still has an entry in the French Guineas. (tchd 15-2)
Greyfriarschorista has been impressive in lesser company when making the running but was unable to get to the front early. He did lead eventually but after sticking on well for pressure was caught near the line. He looks progressive still but the handicapper will not be giving him much rope after this. (op 9-4 tchd 7-4 and 5-2 in a place)

Stargaze(IRE), third in the Richmond Stakes last season for Andrew Balding, had been beaten at odds-on when making his debut for his current yard before Christmas. He came to have every chance inside the final furlong but went down narrowly, and should be up to scoring at this level before long. (op 12-1)
Jira, a Listed winner last season, represented a trainer with a good record in this race. She was never far away but could not match the colts in the last furlong and has yet to conclusively prove that this trip suits her as well as 6f. (op 9-1)
Fratellino was trying this trip for the first time, having looked best at 5f as a juvenile. He made the running at a good pace and did well to keep going once headed, so might be worth another go at this distance.
Hanson'D(IRE) was settled in the rear from his high draw before running on late. He looks likely to appreciate further in time. (op 8-1)
Ongoodform(IRE) chased the leaders from the start before fading in the straight. He had a stiff task at the weights so this was a creditable effort. (tchd 28-1)
Haadeeth was drawn widest of all and was held up before his rider switched to the inside in the straight. He could make no impression though and is likely to do better in handicaps. (op 16-1)
Duplicity was far too keen early on, and stopped quickly, according to his rider. Official explanation: jockey said colt stopped quickly (op 13-2)

946 SPORTINGBET SUPPORTS HEROS WINTER DERBY (GROUP 3) 1m 2f (P)
3:35 (3:38) (Class 1) 4-Y-O+

£56,770 (£21,520; £10,770; £5,370; £2,690; £1,350) **Stalls** Low

Form RPR
311- **1** **Tranquil Tiger**[91] 7809 6-9-0 112........(b) TomQueally 7 113+
(H R A Cecil) *broke wl: led tl over 8f out: trckd ldr: pushed ahd over 1f out: idled and drifted rt ins fnl 100yds: a doing enough* **11/8**[1]
2-22 **2** ¾ **Suits Me**[21] 738 7-9-0 106........ DarryllHolland 12 111
(T P Tate) *chsd ldr: led over 8f out: pushed along 3f out: hdd whn outpcd by wnr over 1f out: rallied as wnr idled ins fnl f but a being hld* **9/1**
000- **3** nk **Pallodio (IRE)**[34] 558 5-9-0 105........ YannLerner 10 110
(J E Hammond, France) *hld up in tch: outpcd 2f out: rallied to go 3rd ins fnl f: styng on wl at fin* **20/1**
246- **4** hd **Stotsfold**[155] 6812 7-9-3 116........ AdamKirby 9 113+
(W R Swinburn) *hld up off pce towards rr: effrt ent fnl 2f: stl plenty to do whn drvn over 1f out: running on wl whn sltly hmpd nr fin but nvr gng to rch ldrs* **9/2**[2]
0-04 **5** 2 **Yahrab (IRE)**[21] 738 5-9-0 100........(b[1]) NeilCallan 2 106
(C E Brittain) *t.k.h: hld up in midfield: drvn and effrt wl over 1f out: one pce fnl f* **20/1**
2233 **6** 1 ¾ **Mister Green (FR)**[21] 738 4-9-0 89........(b) EddieAhern 1 103
(K McAuliffe) *chsd ldrs: sltly hmpd 8f out: rdn to chse ldng pair 2f out: wknd fnl f* **25/1**
1025 **7** hd **Beauchamp Viceroy**[15] 818 6-9-0 103........(p) RyanMoore 4 102
(G A Butler) *in tch in midfield: rdn whn unable qck and wd bnd 2f out: styd on same pce* **20/1**
3-11 **8** 1 **Dalradian (IRE)**[21] 740 4-9-0 96........ JimCrowley 5 100
(W J Knight) *hld up wl off pce towards rr: hdwy whn nt clr run briefly wl over 1f out: swtchd rt ent fnl f: nvr able to chal* **8/1**[3]
/30- **9** nse **Soul City (IRE)**[277] 2992 4-9-0 113........ RichardHughes 6 100
(R Hannon) *chsd ldrs: rdn 4f out: sn wknd* **8/1**[3]
1360 **10** 1 ¾ **Full Toss**[7] 885 4-9-0 94........ JimmyFortune 14 97
(P D Evans) *stdd s: hld up wl off pce in last trio: lost tch 2f out* **50/1**
0000 **11** ½ **Ocean's Minstrel**[7] 883 4-9-0 101........ AlanMunro 11 96
(J Ryan) *hld up wl off pce towards rr: nvr a factor* **50/1**
2-00 **12** 8 **Fiery Lad (IRE)**[15] 821 5-9-0 108........ KierenFallon 13 80
(L M Cumani) *hld up wl off pce in last trio: lost tch 2f out* **14/1**
050- **13** 1 **Bon Spiel**[12] 6795 6-9-0 100........ ChrisCatlin 8 78
(C Gordon) *stdd s: hld up wl bhd in last trio: lost tch 2f out* **100/1**

2m 3.27s (-3.33) **Going Correction** +0.025s/f (Slow) **13** Ran SP% **122.2**
Speed ratings (Par 113): **114,113,113,113,111 110,109,109,109,107 107,100,100**
toteswingers: 1&2 £4.00, 1&3 £6.90, 2&3 £17.10 CSF £13.69 TOTE £2.20: £1.10, £2.80, £4.80; EX 13.20 Trifecta £118.50 Pool: £1,690.15 - 10.55 winning units..
Owner K Abdulla **Bred** Juddmonte Farms Ltd **Trained** Newmarket, Suffolk

FOCUS
The biggest race of the all-weather season and another competitive-looking contest. Generally winners have come into this having already scored in the current season, and only two fitted that category this time, but they could not uphold the statistic.

NOTEBOOK
Tranquil Tiger ◆ has taken really well to Polytrack and maintained his unbeaten sequence, having won twice at Listed level before Christmas. Heavily backed beforehand, his rider had him in the right place in a contest not run at that strong a gallop, and kicked on early in the straight. He began to pay for his exertions, having been keen early inside the last furlong, and those in the frame were closing fast near the finish, but too late. He should remain a force in similar company on this surface. (op 2-1 tchd 9-4 in places)
Suits Me had been touched off by today's winner over course and distance before Christmas and ran close to that form on 2lb worse terms. His rider settled the pace once in front and, although he could not initially respond when the winner committed rallied well and was closing again near the line. He has now been runner-up in his last four starts in the top all-weather company and really deserves to win again. (op 11-1)
Pallodio(IRE), the French challenger, and a dual winner at Cagnes-Sur-Mer this year, was a market drifter. He chased the leading group from the start but did not pick up straight away once in line for home, then stayed on well inside the last furlong to finish just a lengths behind the winner. (op 12-1)
Stotsfold ◆ was settled off the pace in a race run at not that strong a gallop, and his rider was still sitting motionless some way off the pace on the run down towards the straight. He still had five lengths to find on the winner approaching the final furlong but picked up really well, was beaten barely a length and was in front half a dozen strides after the line. It is difficult to avoid the impression that he was given too much to do. (op 6-1)
Yahrab(IRE) chased the leaders from the start and kept going at the one speed in the straight. Along with the first two he helps set the level of the form. (tchd 18-1)
Mister Green(FR) had a fair bit to do judged on official ratings and never got involved, despite appearing to run his race. (op 33-1)
Beauchamp Viceroy has been running creditably at Meydan and stayed on well enough, but is arguably best given a more positive ride back at a mile.
Dalradian(IRE) was another held up and failed to get into contention. (op 17-2 tchd 10-1)
Soul City(IRE) ◆ did not fare too badly on his first start since Royal Ascot last year. He showed up early but gradually faded in the closing stages and his rider held him together and let him come home in his own time once beaten. Formerly a useful juvenile, the kindness could pay dividends in the future. (op 13-2 tchd 9-1)

947 SPORTINGBET.COM SUPPORTS HEROS H'CAP 1m 4f (P)
4:10 (4:10) (Class 3) (0-95,92) 4-Y-O+ **£6,799** (£2,023; £1,011; £505) **Stalls** Low

Form RPR
21 **1** **Cashpoint**[25] 669 5-8-6 78 oh3........ ChrisCatlin 6 89
(A Middleton) *t.k.h: trckd ldng pair: wnt upsides 3f out: hrd drvn over 1f out: tk narrow advantage ins fnl f: hld on gamely: all out* **14/1**
421- **2** nse **Becausewecan (USA)**[155] 6816 4-9-2 **90**........ JoeFanning 4 101
(M Johnston) *led: jnd over 2f out: sn rdn: narrowly hdd ins fnl f: kpt on gamely: jst hld* **6/4**[1]
5142 **3** 6 **Dance The Star (USA)**[23] 697 5-9-6 **92**........ JamieSpencer 3 93
(D M Simcock) *stdd s: hld up last: effrt to press ldrs on outer over 2f out: drvn and wknd ent fnl f* **7/4**[2]
-405 **4** ½ **Samarinda (USA)**[23] 697 7-9-1 **87**........ MickyFenton 1 88
(Mrs P Sly) *broke wl: sn stdd in 4th: effrt over 2f out: rdn and wknd ent fnl f* **8/1**
5 4 ½ **Cluain Alainn (IRE)**[162] 6654 4-8-11 **85**........ StevieDonohoe 5 78
(Ian Williams) *chsd ldr: pushed along over 8f out: rdn and dropped to last over 2f out: bhd fnl f* **6/1**[3]

2m 31.54s (-1.46) **Going Correction** +0.025s/f (Slow)
WFA 4 from 5yo+ 2lb **5** Ran SP% **108.4**
Speed ratings (Par 107): **105,104,100,100,97**
CSF £34.68 TOTE £8.70: £2.30, £2.00; EX 16.10.
Owner Macable Partnership **Bred** Stowell Park Stud **Trained** Granborough, Bucks

FOCUS
Following two withdrawals this handicap was contested by just five but still did not appear that easy to solve and produced a very close finish.

NOTEBOOK
Cashpoint was the outsider of the quintet but had won his maiden over course and distance and a bumper for Henrietta Knight over 2m here in November, after which he was sold for just £6,000. Despite being 3lb out of the handicap, he was always travelling well and threw down his challenge to the favourite in the straight. He had to work really hard as his rival fought back and in the end only won on the nod. Whatever he does in the future, he already looks a bargain. (op 10-1)
Becausewecan(USA) had not been out of the first two in three previous starts on Polytrack and Fibresand and made the running. Like many of his stable companions he found plenty when challenged and was unlucky to go down by the minimum margin. He will be of interest on soft ground once the turf season starts. (op 13-8)
Dance The Star(USA) has had a pretty good winter and, after being held up, made ground to be close enough on the run to the straight. However, he was under pressure soon after and could not go with the principals, although winning the battle for third. (tchd 13-8)
Samarinda(USA) is not quite as good as he once was, but had his chance on the home turn. He faded once in line for home and it looks as if he does not stay this far in a truly-run race. (tchd 15-2)
Cluain Alainn(IRE) was making his debut for the yard, having been with John Oxx last season. He showed up early, but was under pressure on the run down to the straight and was the first beaten. (op 13-2 tchd 7-1)

948 SPORTINGBET SUPPORTS HEROS HEVER SPRINT STKS (LISTED RACE) 5f (P)
4:45 (4:46) (Class 1) 4-Y-O+

£22,708 (£8,608; £4,308; £2,148; £1,076; £540) **Stalls** High

Form RPR
5-14 **1** **Arganil (USA)**[21] 737 5-9-3 105........(b[1]) NeilCallan 1 113
(K A Ryan) *chsd ldrs: rdn 2f out: wnt 2nd 1f out: r.o wl u.str.p to ld post* **4/1**[2]
3421 **2** shd **Glamorous Spirit (IRE)**[21] 736 4-8-9 90........ ChrisCatlin 2 105
(R A Harris) *led at fast gallop: hrd drvn fnl f: kpt on: ct post* **16/1**
01-1 **3** 1 **Jaconet (USA)**[21] 737 5-8-12 106........(b) PhillipMakin 3 104
(T D Barron) *chsd ldr for 2f: c wd and outpcd on bnd wl over 1f out: rallied fnl f: kpt on towards fin* **11/8**[1]
355- **4** hd **Inxile (IRE)**[170] 6427 5-9-3 105........ AdrianNicholls 5 108
(D Nicholls) *t.k.h: hld up in midfield early: hdwy on outer to chse ldr 3f out tl 1f out: kpt on u.p* **7/1**[3]
010- **5** 2 ¼ **Rowe Park**[119] 7488 7-9-0 104........ RyanMoore 4 97
(Mrs L C Jewell) *off the pce in midfield: drvn and effrt on inner over 1f out: kpt on but nt pce to rch ldrs* **15/2**
-100 **6** 1 **Matsunosuke**[30] 604 8-9-0 105........ TonyCulhane 6 94
(A B Coogan) *hld up towards rr: rdn and effrt over 1f out: kpt on but nt pce to rch ldrs: b.b.v* **15/2**
000- **7** nk **Moorhouse Lad**[192] 5765 7-9-0 103........ TomEaves 7 93
(B Smart) *chsd ldrs: rdn and unable qck wl over 1f out: kpt on same pce* **25/1**
6-22 **8** 1 **Ivory Silk**[28] 639 5-8-9 87........(b) LukeMorris 9 84
(J R Gask) *a in last trio* **28/1**
0-00 **9** 3 ½ **Mac Gille Eoin**[37] 515 6-9-0 97........ JimCrowley 10 76
(J Gallagher) *a outpcd towards rr* **25/1**
26P- **10** hd **Crimson Fern (IRE)**[287] 2704 6-8-9 93........ RichardHughes 8 71
(M S Saunders) *hld up towards rr: hdwy on inner into midfield 2f out: sn rdn: wknd fnl f* **50/1**

57.49 secs (-1.31) **Going Correction** +0.025s/f (Slow) **10** Ran SP% **117.1**
Speed ratings (Par 111): **111,110,109,108,105 103,103,101,96,95**
toteswingers: 1&2 £8.50, 1&3 £2.70, 2&3 £3.70 CSF £61.43 TOTE £4.30: £2.10, £3.20, £1.10; EX 63.30 Trifecta £59.80 Pool: £ 898.17 - 11.10 winning units..
Owner The Big Moment **Bred** The Big Moment **Trained** Hambleton, N Yorks
■ Stewards' Enquiry : Neil Callan two-day ban: used whip with excessive frequency without giving gelding time to respond (Apr 3-4)
Chris Catlin two-day ban: used whip with excessive frequency without giving filly time to respond (Apr 3-4)

FOCUS
A competitive Listed sprint.

NOTEBOOK
Arganil(USA) ◆ was bidding to repeat last year's success. He had been beaten twice by the favourite around here this winter, but both of those races were over 6f, and he's arguably best over the minimum trip. Fitted with blinkers for the first time, he had the inside stall and got a good tow into the race, then found just enough under pressure to deny the long-time leader. He is smart on this surface and might be able to find another race on turf given cut in the ground this spring. (op 6-1)
Glamorous Spirit(IRE) ◆ is a real speedball and, in a race with plenty of pacey performers, flew out of the stalls and attempted to make all. She refused to give in when the winner drew alongside and deserves plenty of credit for this effort. A sharp track suits her ideally, and she now has two wins and two seconds from four starts here. The black type she earned will also increase her stud value, and she will be of interest if aimed at races around Chester this season, as she has won there before. (tchd 14-1)
Jaconet(USA) came into this having won all five starts at 6f on Polytrack (including being 3-3 here), although she had won at 5f on fast ground. She jumped well enough but was unable to go with the runner-up and it was not until the final furlong that she began to make an impression. She looks more than capable of winning at this level on turf, and there are a number of fillies-only sprints that might suit her. (op 5-4 tchd 6-4)
Inxile(IRE) was having his first try on Polytrack and ran pretty well on his first outing since October. He was kicking out in the stalls beforehand and did not jump as well as the principals. However, he made good ground to challenge on the home turn and was only seen off entering the last furlong. He looks set for another good season, and perhaps can win at Group level, having lost a Group 3 in the stewards' room last season. (op 8-1)

Rowe Park is another who had a fair bit to find with the favourite, but performed with credit on his first run since November. This should put his straight for a turf campaign, when 5f and fast ground will be his optimum conditions. (op 10-1)
Matsunosuke, who has been running in Dubai, had the race run to suit but could make little impression in the straight. He is not quite as good on turf as Polytrack, but is suited by a stiff 5f and Listed races at Sandown could offer him the best opportunities. Official explanation: vet said gelding had bled from the nose (op 6-1)
Moorhouse Lad showed good pace on this seasonal debut to show the ability remains, but is more effective on Fibresand or a fast 5f on turf. (op 33-1)
Crimson Fern(IRE), having her first run since breaking a blood-vessel last summer, showed some pace before blowing up.

949 SPORTINGBET SUPPORTS HEROS MAIDEN STKS — 1m 2f (P)
5:20 (5:21) (Class 4) 3-Y-O — £4,209 (£1,252; £625; £312) Stalls Low

Form — RPR
0- **1** **Gomrath (IRE)**[231] 4524 3-9-3 0 ... KierenFallon 5 78+
(M R Channon) *t.k.h: trckd ldr: upsides over 2f out: led over 1f out: rdn ins fnl f: forged clr fnl 100yds* **7/4**[2]
423- **2** *1 1/4* **Deauville Post (FR)**[204] 5399 3-9-3 82 ... RichardHughes 2 76
(R Hannon) *led at stdy gallop: jnd over 2f out: drvn whn hdd over 1f out: no ex fnl 100yds* **8/11**[1]
35 **3** *nk* **Ancient Times (USA)**[26] 664 3-9-3 0 ... JoeFanning 4 75
(M Johnston) *chsd ldng pair: rdn ent fnl f: one pce fnl 100yds* **10/1**[3]
0453 **4** *5* **Beat Route**[24] 680 3-8-12 65 ... JemmaMarshall(5) 1 65
(M J Attwater) *dwlt: hld up in last pair in tch: rdn ent fnl 2f: sn outpcd by ldrs: edgd rt over 1f out* **16/1**
5 *24* **Mujdy (IRE)** 3-9-3 0 ... JackMitchell 3 17
(D C O'Brien) *a in last pair: rn green and pushed along early: rdn wl over 2f out: wl bhd fr over 1f out* **66/1**

2m 8.06s (1.46) **Going Correction** +0.025s/f (Slow) **5 Ran SP% 110.7**
Speed ratings (Par 100): **95,94,93,89,70**
CSF £3.38 TOTE £2.60: £1.30, £1.10; EX 3.30.
Owner Jon and Julia Aisbitt **Bred** Kilfrush Stud **Trained** West Ilsley, Berks
FOCUS
A small-field maiden and a steady early pace but a good finish.

950 SPORTINGBET.COM SUPPORTS HEROS MAIDEN STKS — 1m (P)
5:50 (5:52) (Class 4) 3-Y-O+ — £4,209 (£1,252; £625; £312) Stalls High

Form — RPR
2 **1** **Al Farahidi (USA)**[12] 825 3-8-10 0 ... JoeFanning 10 85+
(M Johnston) *mde all: rdn and fnd ex whn jnd chal over 1f out: clr ins fnl f: eased towards fin* **10/3**[2]
0-43 **2** *3* **Mejd (IRE)**[12] 825 3-8-10 74 ... KierenFallon 6 78
(M R Channon) *in tch: pressed ldng pair whn drvn 2f out: outpcd over 1f out: styd on again to go 2nd nr the fin* **11/2**
2- **3** *hd* **Balducci**[94] 7764 3-8-10 0 ... DavidProbert 9 77
(A M Balding) *chsd ldng pair: wnt 2nd 3f out chal over 1f out: sn rdn: fnd little: lost 2nd towards fin* **6/5**[1]
0- **4** *1 1/2* **Bin Shamardal (IRE)**[231] 4524 3-8-10 0 ... MichaelHills 5 74
(B W Hills) *in tch: rdn to chse ldng trio ent fnl 2f: one pce fr over 1f out* **5/1**[3]
5 *4 1/2* **Yashrid (USA)** 3-8-10 0 ... NeilCallan 3 63+
(M A Jarvis) *dwlt: sn pushed along: hdwy into midfield 5f out: rdn and unable qck 2f out: hld after* **14/1**
46 **6** *2 3/4* **Uncle Eli (IRE)**[5] 803 8-9-6 0 ... RichardRowe(7) 8 61
(R Rowe) *s.i.s: bhd: hdwy on outer into midfield over 2f out: wknd wl over 1f out* **66/1**
0 **7** *1 1/4* **Eywa**[31] 583 3-8-5 0 ... HayleyTurner 7 48
(W Jarvis) *hld up towards rr: sme modest hdwy over 2f out: sn rdn: wl hld fr over 1f out* **25/1**
8 *1/2* **Hatta Stream (IRE)**[14] 4-9-8 0 ... SimonPearce(5) 2 57
(J Pearce) *chsd wnr tl 3f out: sn wknd* **66/1**
0 **9** *4 1/2* **Adoyen Spice**[17] 768 3-8-5 0 ... CathyGannon 4 36
(Mike Murphy) *rdn and no rspnse fr 4f out: a towards rr* **100/1**
00- **10** *3 1/4* **Katie The Hatter (IRE)**[90] 7826 4-9-8 0 ... JimCrowley 11 34
(Mike Murphy) *a bhd: lost tch over 2f out* **50/1**
11 *14* **Liberty Point (IRE)** 4-9-13 0 ... SebSanders 1 —
(I A Wood) *a towards rr: rdn 4f out: t.o* **66/1**

1m 37.92s (-0.28) **Going Correction** +0.025s/f (Slow)
WFA 3 from 4yo+ 17lb **11 Ran SP% 118.5**
Speed ratings (Par 105): **102,99,98,97,92 90,88,88,83,80 66**
toteswingers: 1&2 £2.90, 1&3 £4.20, 2&3 £1.70 CSF £21.52 TOTE £5.20: £1.30, £2.20, £1.40; EX 15.30 Trifecta £25.60 Pool £433.25 - 12.51 winning units. Place 6 £100.35, Place 5 £13.75..
Owner Sheikh Hamdan Bin Mohammed Al Maktoum **Bred** Gainsborough Farm Llc **Trained** Middleham Moor, N Yorks
FOCUS
Quite an interesting maiden with several big yards represented. Four dominated the betting market and they filled the first four places.
T/Plt: £97.50 to a £1 stake. Pool: £104,120.68. 779.36 winning tickets. T/Qpdt: £3.50 to a £1 stake. Pool: £6,587.18. 1,380.85 winning tickets. SP

890 SAINT-CLOUD (L-H)
Saturday, March 20

OFFICIAL GOING: Very soft

952a PRIX ROSE DE MAI (LISTED RACE) (FILLIES) — 1m 2f 110y
1:35 (1:37) 3-Y-O — £24,336 (£9,735; £7,301; £4,912; £2,434)

RPR
1 **Sandbar**[12] 3-8-11 ... Francois-XavierBertras 6 96
(F Rohaut, France)
2 *shd* **Sound Of Summer (USA)**[23] 3-8-11 ... ChristopheSoumillon 1 96
(J-C Rouget, France)
3 *2 1/2* **Scandola (USA)**[116] 3-8-11 ... OlivierPeslier 4 91
(S Wattel, France)
4 *1/2* **Marie De Medici (USA)**[140] 7187 3-8-11 ... GregFairley 3 90
(M Johnston) *prom on outside: 3rd st: rdn 2 1/2f out: outpcd over 2f out: rallied to regain 3rd briefly ins fnl f: one pce* **8/1**[1]
5 *1/2* **Plume Rose**[127] 3-8-11 ... Christophe-PatriceLemaire 9 89
(Y De Nicolay, France)
6 *3/4* **Terra Nova (FR)**[12] 3-8-11 ... AnthonyCrastus 5 88
(Robert Collet, France)
7 *1/2* **Balerina (FR)**[38] 3-8-11 ... TonyPiccone 8 87
(K Borgel, France)
8 *4* **Foundation Filly**[119] 3-8-11 ... ThierryThulliez 7 79
(F Doumen, France)
9 *nk* **Ruler Of My Heart (IRE)**[34] 557 3-8-11 ... FranckBlondel 2 78
(F Rossi, France)

2m 22.7s (3.10) **Going Correction** +0.40s/f (Good) **9 Ran SP% 11.1**
Speed ratings: **104,103,102,101,101 100,100,97,97**
PARI-MUTUEL: WIN 3.70; PL 1.40, 1.40, 2.20; DF 4.60.
Owner Lady O'Reilly **Bred** Petra Bloodstock Agency **Trained** Sauvagnon, France

953a PRIX EXBURY (GROUP 3) — 1m 2f
2:40 (2:39) 4-Y-O+ — £35,398 (£14,159; £10,619; £7,080; £3,540)

RPR
1 **Chinchon (IRE)**[176] 6327 5-9-0 ... (p) ChristopheSoumillon 9 112
(C Laffon-Parias, France) *a cl up: 3rd st: led 1 1/2f out: eased cl home* **41/10**[2]
2 *2* **Starlish (IRE)**[97] 7747 5-9-0 ... AnthonyCrastus 3 108
(E Lellouche, France) *racd in 4th on ins: n.m.r and squeezed through narrow gap 1 1/2f out: wnt 2nd ins fnl f: jst hld on for 2nd* **11/1**
3 *nse* **La Boum (GER)**[38] 494 7-8-8 ... ThomasHuet 7 102
(Robert Collet, France) *hld up: 7th st: styd on fr over 1f out: jst missed 2nd* **47/10**[3]
4 *3/4* **Eire**[34] 558 6-8-6 ... LaurentHuart 2 98
(M Nigge, France) *in rr: 8th st: styd on steadily down outside fnl 2f* **97/10**
5 *3/4* **Court Canibal**[126] 7406 5-9-0 ... OlivierPeslier 1 105
(M Delzangles, France) *led to 1 1/2f out: one pce* **63/10**
6 *nk* **Capitaine Courage (IRE)**[126] 7408 5-8-12 ... ThierryThulliez 5 102
(F Doumen, France) *pressed ldr in 2nd: one pce form over 1 1/2f out* **10/1**
7 *nk* **Ashalanda (FR)**[97] 7747 4-8-13 ... Christophe-PatriceLemaire 6 103
(A De Royer-Dupre, France) *in rr: last st: stl last appr fnl f: sme late hdwy* **5/2**[1]
8 *1/2* **Terre Du Vent (FR)**[15] 4-8-8 ... StephanePasquier 4 97
(Y De Nicolay, France) *midfield: 5th st: rdn and one pce under 2f out* **16/1**
9 *1 1/2* **Tangaspeed (FR)**[21] 742 5-8-6 ... DavyBonilla 8 92
(R Laplanche, France) *hld up: 6th st: btn over 1f out* **11/1**

2m 16.6s (0.60) **Going Correction** +0.40s/f (Good) **9 Ran SP% 120.4**
Speed ratings: **113,111,111,110,110 109,109,109,108**
PARI-MUTUEL: WIN 5.10; PL 1.80, 2.50, 1.90; DF 23.60.
Owner Sarl Darpat France **Bred** Zubieta Limited **Trained** Chantilly, France

CURRAGH (R-H)
Sunday, March 21

OFFICIAL GOING: Soft

954a TALLY HO STUD EUROPEAN BREEDERS FUND MAIDEN — 5f
2:15 (2:17) 2-Y-O — £11,907 (£2,761; £1,207; £690)

RPR
1 **High Award (IRE)** 2-9-3 ... WMLordan 12 84+
(T Stack, Ire) *trckd ldrs on outer: 4th 1/2-way: impr to chal under 1 1/2f out: led ins fnl f: r.o wl* **9/2**[2]
2 *3/4* **Suntan (IRE)** 2-9-3 ... KJManning 3 81
(J S Bolger, Ire) *cl up on stands' rail: 2nd 1/2-way: disp ld fr under 2f out: hdd ins fnl f: kpt on* **10/1**
3 *nk* **Clondinnery (IRE)** 2-9-3 ... KLatham 8 80
(G M Lyons, Ire) *sn led: rdn and jnd under 2f out: hdd ins fnl f: kpt on same pce* **12/1**
4 *1* **Flic Flac (IRE)** 2-8-12 ... PJSmullen 5 72+
(D K Weld, Ire) *hld up: 7th 1/2-way: 6th 1f out: kpt on* **10/1**
5 *1/2* **Madeira Man (IRE)** 2-9-3 ... DPMcDonogh 10 75
(Kevin Prendergast, Ire) *cl up in 3rd: chal 1 1/2f out: no ex ins fnl f* **6/1**[3]
6 *1/2* **Future Impact (IRE)** 2-9-3 ... FMBerry 4 73+
(P D Deegan, Ire) *chsd ldrs in 5th: effrt 1 1/2f out: no imp ins fnl f* **6/1**[3]
7 *3* **Emperor Hadrian (IRE)** 2-9-3 ... JMurtagh 2 62+
(A P O'Brien, Ire) *hld up in tch: 6th 1/2-way: rdn and no imp fr 1 1/2f out* **4/1**[1]
8 *1/2* **Stoichkhov (IRE)** 2-9-3 ... WJLee 7 60
(K J Condon, Ire) *chsd ldrs in 6th: no imp fr 1 1/2f out* **33/1**
9 *6* **Wrekin Rock (IRE)** 2-9-3 ... CDHayes 6 39
(J T Gorman, Ire) *s.i.s and reminders: a towards rr:* **33/1**
10 *3/4* **Julius Geezer (IRE)** 2-9-3 ... RichardKingscote 9 36+
(Tom Dascombe) *upset in stalls: dwlt sltly: a towards rr: eased fnl f* **4/1**[1]
11 *1* **Pirateer (IRE)** 2-8-10 ... JPO'Brien(7) 1 33
(A P O'Brien, Ire) *chsd ldrs on stands' rail: sn rdn: bhd fr 2f out* **8/1**

66.71 secs (4.21) **Going Correction** +0.60s/f (Yiel) **11 Ran SP% 129.6**
Speed ratings: **84,82,82,80,79 79,74,73,63,62 61**
CSF £54.74 TOTE £5.90: £2.40, £2.70, £3.30; DF 135.10.
Owner Mrs John Magnier **Bred** Mrs T Stack And Mrs Jane Rowli **Trained** Golden, Co Tipperary
FOCUS
An interesting 2-y-o maiden to kick off the season and it would be a surprise if it didn't prove to be an informative race.
NOTEBOOK
High Award(IRE) got well worked up beforehand, was reluctant to load and sweated freely, but it didn't affect him in the race. Handy towards the outside off a good pace, he picked up well when asked a furlong out and forged his way to the front late on to win with a bit of authority. He wants at least another furlong and already looks a stakes horse as he overcame a bit of adversity to land this. (op 5/1 tchd 11/2)
Suntan(IRE) certainly knew his job at the first time of asking, jumping out in front and quickly grabbing the inside rail. While he wasn't able to get away he did keep on well all the way to the line, although how much improvement there is to come would be debatable. He certainly is good enough to win a maiden though.
Clondinnery(IRE) is likely to be heading towards Dundalk sooner or later but like the runner-up he was professional and knew his job. An extra furlong might be interesting as well. He jumped out smartly and was more or less upsides the winner most of the way until he was run out of it inside the last. (op 14/1)
Flic Flac(IRE) will also appreciate an extra furlong and should improve a good bit for this experience. She was tucked away behind the leaders and while she couldn't quicken over a furlong out she did keep on nicely under hands and heels inside the last and will progress.
Madeira Man(IRE) ran well but was just unable to sustain his effort inside the last furlong. He should improve. (op 6/1 tchd 7/1)
Emperor Hadrian(IRE) ◆ was slightly outpaced, ran green, and while never able to make an impression he did run on inside the last and one would imagine he'll improve significantly. (op 5/2)

Julius Geezer(IRE) probably left his race at the start as he got very upset in the stalls, had to be taken out and reloaded and was never a factor in the race having been slightly slowly into his stride. Official explanation: jockey said colt became upset in the stalls and did not act on today's ground (op 7/2)
Pirateer(IRE) Official explanation: jockey said colt became unbalanced and ran green

957a LODGE PARK STUD EUROPEAN BREEDERS FUND PARK EXPRESS STKS (GROUP 3) (FILLIES) 1m

3:55 (4:00) 3-Y-0+ **£48,318** (£14,123; £6,690; £2,230)

RPR

1 **Pollen (IRE)**[136] 7259 5-9-10 98 .... WJLee 4 105
(T Stack, Ire) *hld up in tch: 6th after 1/2-way: 4th travelling wl under 3f out: led over 1 1/2f out: sn rdn and strly pressed: kpt on wl u.p: all out* **6/1**[3]

2 *hd* **Devoted To You (IRE)**[227] 4726 3-8-11 104 ow2 .... JMurtagh 5 104
(A P O'Brien, Ire) *trckd ldrs: 5th 3f out: sn drvn along: impr into 2nd and chal 1 1/2f out: kpt on wl u.p ins fnl f: jst failed* **2/1**[1]

3 *3* **Latin Love (IRE)**[154] 6884 4-9-10 102 .... WMLordan 3 99
(David Wachman, Ire) *rrd up leaving stalls and s.i.s: hld up in tch: prog into 4th under 1 1/2f out: kpt on same pce fnl f* **10/1**

4 *1* **Akdarena**[161] 6708 3-8-9 94 ....(b[1]) KJManning 2 93
(J S Bolger, Ire) *prom: 3rd 1/2-way: 2nd 3f out: sn rdn: 4th and no ex fnl f* **9/2**[2]

5 *4* **Danehill's Pearl (IRE)**[239] 4334 4-9-10 .... RichardKingscote 6 87
(Tom Dascombe) *trckd ldrs in 5th: hdwy on outer 1/2-way: rdn to ld 3f out: hdd over 1 1/2f out: 5th and no ex fnl f* **6/1**[3]

6 *1* **Indiana Gal (IRE)**[30] 632 5-9-10 97 ....(p) DPMcDonogh 9 84
(Patrick Martin, Ire) *hld up towards rr: no imp fr 2f out: kpt on same pce* **25/1**

7 *2 1/2* **Fourpenny Lane**[24] 713 5-9-10 100 ....(p) FMBerry 8 79
(Ms Joanna Morgan, Ire) *a towards rr: no ex fr under 2f out* **14/1**

8 *3* **Lady Lupus (IRE)**[161] 6708 3-8-9 99 .... JPO'Brien 7 69
(A P O'Brien, Ire) *led and disp: hdd 3f out: sn wknd* **7/1**

9 *20* **Rare Ransom**[176] 6298 4-9-10 96 ....(b[1]) PJSmullen 1 26
(D K Weld, Ire) *disp ld: rdn and hdd appr 1/2-way: sn wknd: eased fr 1 1/2f out: t.o* **14/1**

1m 49.69s (3.69) **Going Correction** +0.60s/f (Yiel)
WFA 3 from 4yo+ 17lb 9 Ran SP% **118.9**
Speed ratings: **105,104,101,100,96 95,93,90,70**
CSF £18.98 TOTE £6.80: £1.80, £1.30, £3.10; DF 20.00.
Owner Gerard O'Brien **Bred** Jerry O'Brien **Trained** Golden, Co Tipperary

FOCUS
The fourth is the best guide to the form.

NOTEBOOK
Pollen(IRE), who landed the Irish Lincoln on this day last year, kept on for a game success here to round off an incredible day for the stable. Covered up behind the early lead off an even gallop, she travelled up towards the outside to throw down her challenge a furlong out and in the end the bigger and stronger mare just got the better of her 3-y-o counterpart inside the last 50 yards. This race was described as her Derby by winning connections - it probably wouldn't be a huge surprise if she was retired to the paddocks fairly soon - and her value as a broodmare is assured after this tough display. (op 7/1)
Devoted To You(IRE) ◆ was the best of the Classic generation in this field. Coming from these quarters one would expect her to show plenty of improvement for this initial outing. Never far from the pace, she improved over a furlong out and travelled well between horses to produce her effort a furlong down. In fairness to her she battled well as the first two drew clear but the winner just had fractionally too many guns for her. It was a very good performance by a 3-y-o against an older filly this early in the season and it does augur well for the coming weeks and months. (op 6/4)
Latin Love(IRE) missed the break slightly before getting back into contention before halfway, and although she was never able to get into a challenging position she did run on well enough inside the last over a trip probably fractionally short of her best.
Akdarena had a little bit to find on official ratings but she ran well although probably paid the price for racing a fraction too keen early on. She had her head in front or close to it from the outset and had every chance when bagging the stands' rail over a furlong out before weakening up the hill. (op 4/1)
Danehill's Pearl(IRE) ◆ hadn't run since last July and ran as though she needed it. Racing just off the pace, she was ridden through to challenge and led over a furlong out but emptied quite quickly under pressure inside the last. (op 6/1 tchd 13/2)
Indiana Gal(IRE) kept on again inside the last having been the first filly under pressure just after halfway.
Rare Ransom ran as if something was quite amiss, dropping right away once headed over 3f out and finishing tailed off. (op 12/1)

958 - 960a (Foreign Racing) - See Raceform Interactive

[935]WOLVERHAMPTON (A.W) (L-H)

Monday, March 22

OFFICIAL GOING: Standard
Wind: Moderate half behind Weather: Light rain until after 3.20

961 SPONSOR A RACE BY CALLING 01902 390000 H'CAP (DIV I) 5f 216y(P)

2:20 (2:21) (Class 6) (0-60,60) 4-Y-0+ **£1,433** (£423; £211) **Stalls** Low

Form RPR

2040 1 **Muktasb (USA)**[19] 773 9-8-12 54 ....(v) GrahamGibbons 9 64
(D Shaw) *s.i.s: sn hld up in tch: pushed along wl over 1f out: led ent fnl f: sn rdn: edgd rt towards fin: r.o* **8/1**[3]

150- 2 *1/2* **Charles Darwin (IRE)**[131] 7330 7-9-4 60 .... FrannyNorton 8 68
(M Blanshard) *hld up in tch: led jst over 1f out: sn hdd: kpt on* **16/1**

4002 3 *1 1/2* **Dream Express (IRE)**[19] 773 5-9-0 56 .... RobertWinston 4 59
(P Howling) *s.i.s: hld up in rr: hdwy whn nt clr run over 1f out: sn swtchd rt: rdn and kpt on ins fnl f* **11/2**[2]

6614 4 *3/4* **Diane's Choice**[25] 693 7-9-0 56 ....(b) DavidProbert 3 57
(Miss Gay Kelleway) *s.i.s: hld up in mid-div: hdwy whn nt clr run briefly wl over 1f out: rdn and kpt on one pce fnl f* **8/1**[3]

223- 5 *3/4* **Who's Winning (IRE)**[166] 6587 9-8-10 55 ....(t) RussKennemore[(3)] 5 53
(B G Powell) *hld up in mid-div: hdwy on ins wl over 1f out: one pce ins fnl f* **14/1**

3336 6 *nk* **Cornus**[12] 844 8-9-0 56 ....(be) JamesDoyle 2 58+
(A J McCabe) *s.i.s: hld up in rr: hdwy on ins whn nt clr run jst over 1f out: plld out ins fnl f: nt rch ldrs* **11/2**[2]

0565 7 *hd* **Loyal Royal (IRE)**[17] 808 7-8-13 58 ....(bt) JackDean[(3)] 11 55
(J M Bradley) *hld up and bhd: c wd st: rdn and kpt on ins fnl f: n.d* **11/1**

0-06 8 *1 1/4* **West Leake (IRE)**[12] 845 4-8-13 55 .... DaneO'Neill 1 48
(P Burgoyne) *sn led: rdn and hdd wl over 1f out: wknd ins fnl f* **18/1**

1324 9 *3/4* **Top Flight Splash**[12] 844 4-8-6 55 ....(v) MatthewCosham[(7)] 6 45
(P D Evans) *led early: w ldr: led wl over 1f out: sn rdn and hdd: wknd ins fnl f* **7/2**[1]

5-36 10 *2 3/4* **Bold Ring**[14] 828 4-9-1 57 .... EddieCreighton 10 39
(E J Creighton) *hld up in mid-div: pushed along over 2f out: rdn and wknd wl over 1f out* **20/1**

2140 11 *2 1/4* **Don Pele (IRE)**[6] 896 8-9-4 60 ....(p) LiamJones 7 34
(R A Harris) *w ldrs: wkng whn n.m.r over 1f out* **9/1**

0305 12 *nk* **Cape Of Storms**[13] 839 7-9-2 58 ....(b) TomEaves 12 31
(R Brotherton) *w ldrs on outside: wknd 2f out* **22/1**

1m 15.7s (0.70) **Going Correction** +0.05s/f (Slow) 12 Ran SP% **120.5**
Speed ratings (Par 101): **97,96,94,93,92 91,91,90,89,85 82,81**
toteswingers: 1&2 £31.90, 1&3 £9.20, 2&3 £17.90 CSF £131.06 CT £783.72 TOTE £10.80: £3.10, £5.70, £1.80; EX 157.10 Trifecta £156.20 Part won. Pool: £211.21 - 0.30 winning units..
Owner Miss Claire Comery **Bred** Shadwell Farm LLC **Trained** Sproxton, Leics

FOCUS
A competitive sprint run in a time 0.44 seconds slower than the second division. The form looks straightforward, rated around the first two,
Cornus Official explanation: jockey said gelding was denied a clear run

962 NAME A RACE TO ENHANCE YOUR BRAND (S) STKS 5f 20y(P)

2:50 (2:51) (Class 6) 3-Y-O **£1,774** (£523; £262) **Stalls** Low

Form RPR

4-25 1 **Flaxen Lake**[28] 662 3-8-12 68 ....(p) GrahamGibbons 5 68
(R Hollinshead) *chsd ldr: rdn over 1f out: led ins fnl f: drvn out* **11/4**[2]

3201 2 *2 1/2* **Blue Neptune**[9] 886 3-9-1 65 .... KellyHarrison[(3)] 6 65
(P D Evans) *led: rdn and hdd ins fnl f: no ex* **9/2**[3]

0-34 3 *nk* **Clear Ice (IRE)**[9] 886 3-9-4 70 ....(b) AdrianNicholls 2 64
(D Nicholls) *hld up and bhd: hdwy on ins wl over 1f out: sn rdn: kpt on same pce ins fnl f* **5/2**[1]

5350 4 *1 1/2* **My Mandy (IRE)**[5] 906 3-8-7 64 .... LiamJones 8 48
(R A Harris) *hld up and bhd: hdwy on outside 2f out: c wd st: rdn and no imp fnl f* **11/2**

034- 5 *1/2* **Madam Isshe**[196] 5714 3-8-7 60 .... FergusSweeney 1 46
(M S Saunders) *prom tl rdn and wknd wl over 1f out* **15/2**

4-30 6 *1/2* **Reach For The Sky (IRE)**[17] 809 3-8-6 61 .... CharlotteKerton[(7)] 3 50
(G Prodromou) *hld up in tch: wknd wl over 1f out* **9/1**

00 7 *6* **Carolina Cherry (IRE)**[19] 766 3-8-7 0 .... HayleyTurner 7 22
(Miss Amy Weaver) *a in rr* **80/1**

05 8 *nk* **Captain Tony (IRE)**[50] 362 3-8-12 0 ....(b[1]) LiamKeniry 4 26
(Matthew Salaman) *hld up in mid-div: pushed along over 2f out: wknd wl over 1f out* **40/1**

63.05 secs (0.75) **Going Correction** +0.05s/f (Slow) 8 Ran SP% **114.2**
Speed ratings (Par 96): **96,92,91,89,88 87,77,77**
toteswingers: 1&2 £2.70, 1&3 £2.60, 2&3 £2.80 CSF £15.58 TOTE £3.30: £1.30, £1.30, £1.60; EX 15.90 Trifecta £23.70 Pool: £689.73 - 21.52 winning units..The winner was bought by C. Hunt for 6,000 guineas.
Owner M Johnson **Bred** R Hollinshead And M Johnson **Trained** Upper Longdon, Staffs

FOCUS
A modest seller rated around the first and second.

963 GREAT OFFERS AT WOLVERHAMPTON-RACECOURSE.CO.UK MAIDEN STKS 1m 4f 50y(P)

3:20 (3:23) (Class 5) 3-Y-O+ **£2,456** (£725; £362) **Stalls** Low

Form RPR

1 **Shut The Bar**[110] 5-9-8 0 .... MatthewDavies[(5)] 4 73
(George Baker) *hld up in mid-div: hdwy on ins over 7f out: led wl over 1f out: sn rdn: drvn out* **10/1**

2 *nk* **Mongoose Alert (IRE)**[117] 8-9-13 0 .... AdamKirby 8 72
(Stef Higgins) *hld up towards rr: smooth prog over 2f out: chsd wnr over 1f out: rdn ins fnl f: kpt on* **15/2**

33 3 *6* **Gordon Road (IRE)**[27] 669 4-9-11 0 .... JerryO'Dwyer 2 62
(M G Quinlan) *a.p: led over 7f out: hrd rdn over 2f out: hdd wl over 1f out: wknd ins fnl f* **7/2**[2]

4 *nk* **Dancing Dude (IRE)** 3-8-5 0 .... JoeFanning 6 60+
(M Johnston) *led over 3f: prom: pushed along over 3f out: wkng whn rdn and jinked rt 1f out* **5/2**[1]

0 5 *3 3/4* **Ferney Boy**[17] 815 4-9-11 0 .... RobertWinston 12 56
(G A Swinbank) *hld up in mid-div: pushed along over 2f out: rdn and btn wl over 1f out* **22/1**

23 6 *shd* **Wrongwayround (IRE)**[24] 718 4-9-11 0 .... PJMcDonald 9 56
(G A Swinbank) *chsd ldr: led over 8f out tl over 7f out: ev ch over 2f out: wknd over 1f out* **5/1**[3]

03 7 *1/2* **Boa**[10] 872 5-9-8 0 .... GrahamGibbons 10 50
(R Hollinshead) *prom: ev ch over 2f out: wknd over 1f out* **12/1**

5 8 *5* **National Theatre (USA)**[27] 669 4-9-6 0 .... KylieManser[(5)] 5 47
(T Keddy) *a in rr* **20/1**

6 9 *hd* **Major Pop (USA)**[24] 718 3-8-5 0 .... PaulHanagan 11 45
(R A Fahey) *hld up in mid-div: rdn 4f out: wknd wl over 2f out* **14/1**

10 *3 1/4* **Street Runner**[238] 4-9-11 0 .... ChrisCatlin 1 42
(R Hollinshead) *bhd fnl 4f* **16/1**

11 *6* **El Passos (IRE)**[35] 6-9-13 0 .... DaneO'Neill 7 42
(R Curtis) *s.s: a in rr* **66/1**

12 *32* **Titanic Mill** 3-8-0 0 .... JamesSullivan[(5)] 3 —
(Mrs L Williamson) *a towards rr: rdn over 4f out: sn t.o* **100/1**

2m 42.56s (1.46) **Going Correction** +0.05s/f (Slow)
WFA 3 from 4yo 22lb 4 from 5yo+ 2lb 12 Ran SP% **120.1**
Speed ratings (Par 103): **97,96,92,92,90 90,89,86,86,84 80,58**
toteswingers: 1&2 £14.50, 1&3 £7.10, 2&3 £7.80 CSF £81.58 TOTE £11.80: £3.80, £3.10, £1.50; EX 125.00 Trifecta £295.70 Part won. Pool: £399.61 - 0.75 winning units..
Owner Mrs D Mitchell **Bred** Mrs D L Mitchell **Trained** Moreton Morrell, Warwicks

FOCUS
A modest maiden run at an ordinary gallop. The third and fifth offer the best guides in race with little solid to go on.
Dancing Dude(IRE) Official explanation: jockey said colt ran green

964 RINGSIDE CONFERENCE SUITE, 700 THEATRE STYLE H'CAP 1m 1f 103y(P)

3:50 (3:50) (Class 5) (0-75,74) 3-Y-O **£2,456** (£725; £362) **Stalls** Low

Form RPR

1 1 **Srda (USA)**[20] 759 3-9-1 71 .... SebSanders 5 89+
(C E Brittain) *hld up: hdwy to ld wl over 1f out: rdn and edgd rt ent fnl f: sn clr: readily* **1/1**[1]

1221 2 *7* **Tuscan King**[17] 812 3-8-12 68 ....(b) JamieSpencer 3 68
(P D Evans) *hld up: rdn over 2f out: hdwy over 1f out: wnt 2nd ins fnl f: no ch w wnr* **15/2**[3]

431- 3 *nk* **Crunched**[142] 7193 3-9-2 72 .... HayleyTurner 2 71
(M L W Bell) *led early: hld up in tch: ev ch wl over 1f out: sn rdn: one pce* **4/1**[2]

043 **4** 1 **Manxman (IRE)**[11] 864 3-9-4 **74**.......... JoeFanning 7 71
(M Johnston) *hld up in rr: pushed along over 2f out: hdwy over 1f out: no further prog fnl f* **11/1**

6250 **5** ¾ **Royal Torbo (ISR)**[20] 762 3-8-4 **60** oh2.......... ChrisCatlin 1 56
(George Baker) *prom: pushed along over 2f out: wknd wl over 1f out* **50/1**

2125 **6** 5 **Bubbly Braveheart (IRE)**[14] 830 3-9-1 **71**.......... RobertWinston 8 56
(A Bailey) *sn w ldr: led over 2f out tl wl over 1f out: sn wknd* **15/2**[3]

050- **7** 4½ **Kingsdine (IRE)**[203] 5499 3-7-13 **60** oh3.......... SimonPearce(5) 6 36
(M S Saunders) *sn led: hdd over 2f out: wknd wl over 1f out* **40/1**

3151 **8** 10 **Kathindi (IRE)**[35] 564 3-8-11 **67**.......... LiamKeniry 4 22
(J S Moore) *hld up and bhd: pushed along over 3f out: no ch fnl 2f* **20/1**

2m 1.22s (-0.48) **Going Correction** +0.05s/f (Slow) **8** Ran SP% **111.0**
Speed ratings (Par 98): **104,97,97,96,95 91,87,78**
toteswingers: 1&2 £3.00, 1&3 £2.50, 2&3 £2.90 CSF £8.47 CT £20.19 TOTE £2.30: £1.10, £1.80, £1.70; EX 8.90 Trifecta £18.20 Pool: £512.22 - 20.78 winning units..
Owner Saeed Manana **Bred** Brushwood Stable **Trained** Newmarket, Suffolk

FOCUS
A fair 3-y-o handicap won in impression fashion by Oaks entrant Srda. The form looks pretty sound rated around the placed horses.

965 WOLVERHAMPTON HOSPITALITY - A PLEASURE H'CAP 7f 32y(P)
4:20 (4:20) (Class 6) (0-65,65) 4-Y-0+ £1,774 (£523; £262) Stalls High

Form RPR

1040 **1** **Zeffirelli**[13] 839 5-8-10 **57**.......... MartinDwyer 4 65
(M Quinn) *led: hdd 3f out: rdn 2f out: rallied u.p to ld cl home* **50/1**

2022 **2** hd **Spinning Ridge (IRE)**[3] 937 5-9-4 **65**.......... (b) LiamJones 11 72
(R A Harris) *t.k.h: sn prom: wnt 2nd over 5f out: led 3f out: sn pushed along: rdn and edgd rt jst over 1f out: hdd cl home* **5/1**[2]

6126 **3** ½ **By Command**[12] 855 5-9-3 **64**.......... (tp) JamieSpencer 8 70+
(K A Ryan) *s.i.s: sn swtchd lft: hld up in rr: rdn over 2f out: hdwy over 1f out: r.o ins fnl f: nrst fin* **13/2**[3]

6-25 **4** shd **War And Peace (IRE)**[25] 704 6-8-11 **65**.......... (e) LewisWalsh(7) 2 71
(Jane Chapple-Hyam) *hld up in tch: wnt 2nd over 1f out: ev ch ins fnl f: nt qckn towards fin* **10/1**

1-16 **5** ½ **Harting Hill**[25] 696 5-9-1 **62**.......... GeorgeBaker 1 66
(M P Tregoning) *prom tl rdn and wknd over 1f out* **3/1**[1]

1140 **6** 1¼ **Well Of Echoes**[10] 873 4-8-11 **63**.......... (tp) DeclanCannon(5) 7 64
(A J McCabe) *dwlt: hld up in rr: pushed along over 2f out: rdn and sme prog on ins wl over 1f out: nvr trbld ldrs* **16/1**

44-6 **7** 1 **Monashee Rock (IRE)**[27] 673 5-9-1 **62**.......... LiamKeniry 12 60
(Matthew Salaman) *in rr: rdn over 1f out: n.d* **12/1**

660- **8** 1 **Fiefdom (IRE)**[113] 7587 8-9-0 **61**.......... DanielTudhope 3 57
(I W McInnes) *hld up in mid-div: no hdwy fnl 2f* **40/1**

04-1 **9** 1¼ **Munich (IRE)**[61] 235 6-9-2 **63**.......... (p) DaneO'Neill 5 55
(R Curtis) *a bhd* **3/1**[1]

3230 **10** 5 **Forward Feline (IRE)**[12] 853 4-9-4 **65**.......... DavidProbert 6 44
(B Palling) *prom: rdn over 2f out: wknd wl over 1f out* **17/2**

040- **11** 24 **Polar Annie**[203] 5502 5-9-3 **64**.......... FergusSweeney 9 —
(M S Saunders) *prom tl hung rt and lost pl 3f out: sn eased* **40/1**

1m 30.23s (0.63) **Going Correction** +0.05s/f (Slow) **11** Ran SP% **120.0**
Speed ratings (Par 101): **98,97,97,97,96 95,93,92,91,85 58**
toteswingers: 1&2 £21.70, 1&3 £27.20, 2&3 £8.30 CSF £290.50 CT £1926.98 TOTE £50.60: £8.30, £1.90, £2.80; EX 217.20 TRIFECTA Not won..
Owner A G MacLennan **Bred** J Spearing And Kate Ive **Trained** Newmarket, Suffolk

FOCUS
A moderate handicap in which it paid to race prominently. The winner is rated back to his best with the fourth and fifth to recent marks.
Zeffirelli Official explanation: trainer said, regarding apparent improvement in form, that the gelding may have benefited from the removal of the headgear which it wore previously.
Munich(IRE) Official explanation: trainer said, regarding running, that the gelding was unsuited by the track
Polar Annie Official explanation: jockey said mare was unsteerable around final bend

966 STAY AT THE WOLVERHAMPTON HOLIDAY INN H'CAP 1m 141y(P)
4:50 (4:50) (Class 5) (0-75,74) 4-Y-0+ £2,456 (£725; £362) Stalls Low

Form RPR

0-01 **1** **Mr Hichens**[12] 855 5-9-2 **72**.......... JamieSpencer 4 83+
(Karen George) *sn led: swvd rt and hdd wl over 1f out: hrd rdn and rallied to ld cl home* **3/1**[2]

6322 **2** ¾ **Tropical Blue**[21] 756 4-9-0 **70** ow1.......... (p) StephenCraine 5 77
(Jennie Candlish) *t.k.h in tch: wnt 2nd 5f out: rdn whn lft in ld wl over 1f out: hdd cl home* **9/2**[3]

3045 **3** 4 **Shake On It**[11] 862 6-8-7 **63**.......... ChrisCatlin 6 61
(M R Hoad) *s.i.s: hld up in rr: hdwy 1f out: rdn and kpt on to take 3rd towards fin* **20/1**

0211 **4** nk **Make Amends (IRE)**[27] 675 5-9-1 **71**.......... GeorgeBaker 3 68
(R J Hodges) *a.p: pushed along over 2f out: rdn over 1f out: one pce* **11/4**[1]

0-35 **5** 3¼ **Pha Mai Blue**[12] 844 5-8-4 **60**.......... NickyMackay 8 50
(J R Boyle) *hld up: pushed along and effrt over 2f out: rdn over 1f out: wknd ins fnl f* **6/1**

55-0 **6** 1½ **Heroes**[18] 787 6-9-0 **70**.......... (v) PatCosgrave 2 56
(J R Boyle) *hld up: rdn over 2f out: hdwy wl over 1f out: wknd ins fnl f* **11/1**

0-05 **7** 2¼ **Ninth House (USA)**[12] 855 8-8-10 **66**.......... (t) PJMcDonald 7 47
(Mrs R A Carr) *hld up in rr: pushed along over 3f out: no rspnse* **15/2**

310- **8** 6 **Mr Udagawa**[154] 6907 4-9-4 **74**.......... DavidProbert 1 41
(B J Llewellyn) *led early: prom: rdn over 2f out: wknd over 1f out* **14/1**

1m 49.94s (-0.56) **Going Correction** +0.05s/f (Slow) **8** Ran SP% **115.7**
Speed ratings (Par 103): **104,103,99,99,96 95,93,87**
toteswingers: 1&2 £4.60, 1&3 £6.50, 2&3 £14.10 CSF £17.21 CT £226.76 TOTE £5.20: £1.40, £1.60, £3.00; EX 25.70 Trifecta £216.30 Pool: £526.23 - 1.80 winning units..
Owner Eastington Racing Club **Bred** C A Green **Trained** Higher Eastington, Devon

FOCUS
A modest handicap in which those who raced handy seemed to be at an advantage. The form is rated around the first two but looks modest.

967 WOLVERHAMPTON-RACECOURSE.CO.UK H'CAP 5f 20y(P)
5:20 (5:20) (Class 6) (0-65,62) 4-Y-0+ £1,774 (£523; £262) Stalls Low

Form RPR

-033 **1** **Riflessione**[14] 829 4-9-4 **62**.......... (b) LiamJones 1 75
(R A Harris) *hld up in tch on ins: swtchd rt over 2f out: c wd st: rdn to ld towards fin* **7/2**[1]

02-1 **2** 2¼ **Boho Chic**[32] 595 4-8-13 **62**.......... (p) MatthewDavies(5) 9 67
(George Baker) *stdd s: sn swtchd lft: hld up in rr: hdwy on ins over 2f out: rdn to ld jst ins fnl f: hdd towards fin* **13/2**[3]

-000 **3** shd **Almaty Express**[19] 778 8-8-5 **52**.......... (b) AshleyHamblett(3) 2 57
(J R Weymes) *led: rdn wl over 1f out: hdd jst ins fnl f: nt qckn* **8/1**

5600 **4** 2¼ **La Capriosa**[6] 896 4-9-2 **60**.......... RobertWinston 3 57
(J A Glover) *w ldr: rdn over 1f out: one pce* **15/2**

0641 **5** 3¼ **Sweet Applause (IRE)**[26] 684 4-8-10 **61**.......... CharlotteKerton(7) 10 46
(G Prodromou) *hld up: rdn over 1f out: nvr trbld ldrs* **11/1**

3023 **6** nk **Bluebok**[19] 774 9-8-8 **55**.......... (bt) JackDean(3) 5 39+
(J M Bradley) *prom: bdly hmpd and lost pl over 3f out: pushed along over 2f out: n.d after* **14/1**

6333 **7** 1¼ **Cape Royal**[17] 810 10-9-0 **58**.......... (bt) KevinGhunowa 8 37
(J M Bradley) *w ldrs tl wknd wl over 1f out* **12/1**

0011 **8** 1¾ **Mr Funshine**[11] 860 5-8-13 **60**.......... MartinLane(3) 6 33+
(D Shaw) *hld up: nt clr run over 3f out: sn bhd* **4/1**[2]

0052 **9** 4½ **Ten Down**[26] 687 5-8-10 **54**.......... MartinDwyer 7 11+
(M Quinn) *prom: bdly hmpd and lost pl over 3f out: bhd fnl 2f* **9/1**

-004 **10** 6 **Hatman Jack (IRE)**[27] 674 4-8-8 **55** ow2.......... (p) RussKennemore(3) 11 —
(B G Powell) *prom tl pushed along and wknd over 2f out* **14/1**

61.87 secs (-0.43) **Going Correction** +0.05s/f (Slow) **10** Ran SP% **117.8**
Speed ratings (Par 101): **105,101,101,97,92 91,89,87,79,70**
toteswingers: 1&2 £4.20, 1&3 £4.40, 2&3 £11.30 CSF £26.71 CT £176.14 TOTE £4.40: £1.60, £2.00, £3.00; EX 34.50 Trifecta £118.60 Pool: £248.46 - 1.55 winning units..
Owner Paul Moulton **Bred** Tom & Evelyn Yates **Trained** Earlswood, Monmouths
■ Stewards' Enquiry : Kevin Ghunowa five-day ban: careless riding (Apr 5-9)

FOCUS
Moderate form and quite a rough race. Despite that the form looks sound amongst the principals.
Mr Funshine Official explanation: jockey said gelding suffered interference in running
Hatman Jack(IRE) Official explanation: jockey said gelding hung badly right-handed throughout

968 SPONSOR A RACE BY CALLING 01902 390000 H'CAP (DIV II) 5f 216y(P)
5:50 (5:51) (Class 6) (0-60,60) 4-Y-0+ £1,433 (£423; £211) Stalls Low

Form RPR

3140 **1** **Equinity**[36] 555 4-8-8 **55**.......... (t) SimonPearce(5) 7 63
(J Pearce) *hld up: hdwy over 1f out: led jst ins fnl f: rdn out* **12/1**

4610 **2** hd **Guildenstern (IRE)**[25] 704 8-9-1 **57**.......... RobertWinston 3 64
(P Howling) *hmpd sn after s: hld up and bhd: hdwy on ins wl over 1f out: sn rdn: ev ch ins fnl f: r.o* **14/1**

6023 **3** 1 **Bentley**[18] 789 6-9-4 **60**.......... (v) PaulMulrennan 4 64
(J G Given) *a.p: rdn whn carried rt jst over 1f out: kpt on ins fnl f* **6/1**

4355 **4** 1¼ **Kheley (IRE)**[6] 896 4-8-12 **59**.......... KierenFox(5) 1 59
(W M Brisbourne) *a.p: swtchd rt jst over 1f out: rdn and nt qckn ins fnl f* **13/2**

0-00 **5** nk **Smirfys Systems**[38] 531 11-9-2 **58**.......... (p) JoeFanning 13 57
(Mrs D J Sanderson) *sn led: edgd rt jst over 1f out: rdn and hdd jst ins fnl f: no ex* **16/1**

0 **6** 1¼ **Withnail (IRE)**[19] 773 6-8-13 **55**.......... (t) AdamKirby 10 50
(Stef Higgins) *hld up in rr: pushed along over 2f out: rdn and kpt on fnl f: nvr trbld ldrs* **9/2**[3]

2461 **7** ¾ **Cheery Cat (USA)**[19] 773 6-8-6 **55**.......... (p) DavidKenny(7) 2 48
(J Balding) *hld up in tch: rdn over 2f out: btn over 1f out* **4/1**[2]

05-6 **8** ½ **Rabbit Fighter (IRE)**[24] 727 6-8-13 **58**.......... (v) MartinLane(3) 9 49
(D Shaw) *dwlt: rdn over 1f out: nvr nr ldrs* **7/2**[1]

60-0 **9** 3¾ **Sills Vincero**[6] 896 4-9-0 **56**.......... PaulHanagan 11 35
(Miss M E Rowland) *led early: hld up in tch: wknd wl over 2f out* **25/1**

10-0 **10** ¾ **Athaakeel (IRE)**[12] 851 4-9-4 **60**.......... LiamJones 12 37
(R A Harris) *prom: ev ch over 2f out: sn pushed along: btn whn bmpd jst over 1f out: eased wl ins fnl f* **10/1**

1m 15.26s (0.26) **Going Correction** +0.05s/f (Slow) **10** Ran SP% **121.2**
Speed ratings (Par 101): **100,99,98,96,96 94,93,93,88,87**
toteswingers: 1&2 £29.60, 1&3 £8.00, 2&3 £13.10 CSF £173.14 CT £1121.07 TOTE £17.20: £3.40, £3.40, £2.20; EX 143.70 Trifecta £277.10 Part won. Pool: £374.49 - 0.20 winning units. Place 6: £83.05 Place 5: £27.12.
Owner M B Clarke **Bred** Whitwell Bloodstock **Trained** Newmarket, Suffolk

FOCUS
The time was 0.44 seconds quicker than the first division. The form looks straightforward rated around the placed horses.
T/Plt: £92.40 to a £1 stake. Pool: £69,378.00. 547.69 winning tickets. T/Qpdt: £21.10 to a £1 stake. Pool: £5,798.58. 203.11 winning tickets. KH

899 KEMPTON (A.W) (R-H)
Wednesday, March 24

OFFICIAL GOING: Standard
Wind: Light, across Weather: Fine, mild

969 KEMPTON.CO.UK H'CAP (DIV I) 1m 2f (P)
5:50 (5:50) (Class 6) (0-60,60) 4-Y-0+ £1,706 (£503; £252) Stalls High

Form RPR

45-2 **1** **Carr Hall (IRE)**[69] 162 7-8-13 **55**.......... NeilCallan 3 62
(A W Carroll) *trckd ldrs in abt 6th: prog 2f out: drvn to ld jst over 1f out: jst hld on* **9/2**[3]

3232 **2** hd **Alfredtheordinary**[23] 753 5-9-4 **60**.......... SamHitchcott 12 67
(M R Channon) *hld up towards rr on inner: sltly checked 2f out: prog against rail over 1f out: wnt 2nd last 100yds: clsd on wnr: jst failed* **8/1**

600- **3** 1½ **Rosy Dawn**[139] 7250 5-8-4 **46** oh1.......... HayleyTurner 5 50
(J J Bridger) *trckd ldrs: effrt 2f out: disp 2nd over 1f out: one pce after* **40/1**

-045 **4** nk **Strong Storm (USA)**[5] 929 4-9-1 **60**.......... (v) RussKennemore(3) 1 63
(Andrew Reid) *hld up in last pair fr wdst draw: pushed along 3f out: effrt on wd outside 2f out: prog 1f out: no ex last 100yds: no ch* **12/1**

600- **5** ½ **Dawson Creek (IRE)**[105] 7693 6-8-11 **53**.......... ChrisCatlin 9 55
(B Gubby) *led 1f: pressed ldr: led over 2f out: drvn and hdd jst over 1f out: fdd* **20/1**

3-05 **6** nk **Hambleden Hill**[19] 802 4-9-1 **57**.......... SteveDrowne 7 58+
(P Burgoyne) *stdd s: hld up wl in rr: taken wdst of all 2f out: gd prog fnl f: no ch to rch ldrs* **16/1**

0-10 **7** ½ **Gheed (IRE)**[56] 309 5-9-2 **58**.......... (t) JimmyQuinn 6 58
(K A Morgan) *hld up towards rr: effrt on outer over 2f out: rdn and nt qckn over 1f out: one pce after* **22/1**

6/04 **8** ½ **Catholic Hill (USA)**[49] 390 5-8-12 **54**.......... (b) EddieAhern 8 53+
(C J Mann) *stdd s: hld up in midfield: brief effrt over 1f out: no ch whn n.m.r ins fnl f: eased* **9/1**

66-0 **9** ½ **Shouldntbethere (IRE)**[13] 865 6-7-13 **46** oh1.......... AmyBaker(5) 11 44
(Mrs P N Dutfield) *s.s: hld up in last pair: effrt over 2f out: n.m.r between rivals wl over 1f out: one pce fnl f* **33/1**

-004 **10** ½ **New World Order (IRE)**[21] 770 6-9-4 **60**..................(tp) DaneO'Neill 10 57
(R Curtis) *trckd ldrs on inner: trapped bhd wkng rival over 2f out and lost pl: renewed effrt and cl up over 1f out: fdd ins fnl f* **11/4**[1]
502- **11** 17 **Major Promise**[102] 7733 5-8-13 **55**.................................. ShaneKelly 2 18
(Jane Chapple-Hyam) *s.s: pushed up to press ldng pair after 3f: racd awkwardly whn asked for effrt over 2f out: wknd rapidly over 1f out: t.o* **7/2**[2]
0-00 **12** 26 **Chicamia**[20] 791 6-8-4 **46** oh1.. NickyMackay 4 —
(M Mullineaux) *led after 1f to over 2f out: wknd v rapidly: t.o* **66/1**
2m 8.64s (0.64) **Going Correction** +0.125s/f (Slow) **12** Ran SP% **117.7**
Speed ratings (Par 101): **102,101,100,100,100 99,99,98,98,98 84,63**
toteswingers: 1&2 £4.60, 1&3 £41.40, 2&3 £28.00 CSF £37.55 CT £1282.03 TOTE £6.90: £3.30, £2.70, £7.00; EX 22.20.
Owner A W Carroll **Bred** R Cody **Trained** Cropthorne, Worcs
■ Stewards' Enquiry : Hayley Turner one-day ban: careless riding (7 Apr)
FOCUS
A moderate contest as the first ten finished in a bit of a heap but the form looks straightforward. The time was 2.33 seconds quicker than the second division, but that was slowly run.
Catholic Hill(USA) Official explanation: jockey said gelding had been denied a clear run
Chicamia Official explanation: jockey said mare stopped quickly

970 KEMPTON.CO.UK H'CAP (DIV II) 1m 2f (P)
6:20 (6:20) (Class 6) (0-60,60) 4-Y-O+ **£1,706** (£503; £252) **Stalls** High

Form RPR
1306 **1** **Musashi (IRE)**[30] 656 5-9-1 **57**.......................................(b) IanMongan 2 66
(Mrs L J Mongan) *plld hrd early: trckd ldr after 2f: led over 2f out and sn drew more than 2 l clr: unchal after* **5/1**[2]
2451 **2** 2 **Marjury Daw (IRE)**[5] 939 4-9-4 **60** 6ex........................ PaulMulrennan 1 65+
(J G Given) *trckd ldr 2f: mostly 3rd after: rdn to go 2nd jst over 1f out: styd on but wnr already clr* **6/1**[3]
3220 **3** 2¾ **Wetherby Place (IRE)**[5] 940 4-8-12 **54**...................... StephenCraine 5 54
(M Wigham) *trckd ldrs: wnt 3rd over 2f out but already outpcd by wnr: hanging and lost pl over 1f out: kpt on to snatch 3rd again post* **5/1**[2]
2640 **4** hd **Farncombe (IRE)**[5] 929 4-8-13 **55**..............................(p) DavidProbert 6 54
(R A Harris) *led and allowed to set mod pce: tried to kick on 3f out: hdd over 2f out: lost 2nd jst over 1f out: fdd* **9/1**
4-40 **5** nse **Sir Haydn**[35] 576 10-7-11 **46** oh1...............................(v) DannyBrock[(7)] 7 45
(J R Jenkins) *t.k.h: hld up bhd ldrs: pushed along 3f out: effrt on inner over 1f out: plugged on* **20/1**
0062 **6** 1 **Solarias Quest**[24] 746 8-9-3 **59**... ShaneKelly 8 56
(W M Brisbourne) *hld up towards rr: no ch after pce lifted over 2f out and lft w plenty to do: no real prog: kpt on fnl f* **12/1**
011- **7** 1¾ **Lunar Limelight**[100] 7754 5-9-4 **60**.................................... SebSanders 9 54+
(P J Makin) *hld up in last trio: last and wl off the pce over 2f out: no ch after: plugged on* **11/4**[1]
0254 **8** 1¾ **Hatch A Plan (IRE)**[20] 791 9-8-3 **52**...................... CharlesEddery[(7)] 11 42+
(Mouse Hamilton-Fairley) *hld up in last: taken wd over 2f out: nvr any ch of making prog* **14/1**
000- **9** 1 **Warrior Nation (FR)**[102] 7732 4-9-0 **56**......................... NeilChalmers 3 44
(A J Chamberlain) *stdd s: t.k.h: hld up in rr: brief effrt over 2f out: sn no ch* **50/1**
0015 **10** 3¾ **Binnion Bay (IRE)**[14] 847 9-8-12 **54**...................(b) RichardKingscote 4 35
(J J Bridger) *dwlt: t.k.h: wl in tch after 4f: wd and rdn 3f out: sn wknd* **10/1**
2m 10.97s (2.97) **Going Correction** +0.125s/f (Slow) **10** Ran SP% **114.5**
Speed ratings (Par 101): **93,91,89,89,89 88,86,85,84,81**
toteswingers: 1&2 £7.60, 1&3 £6.20, 2&3 £6.30 CSF £34.40 CT £157.00 TOTE £6.40: £2.30, £1.60, £1.80; EX 52.30.
Owner Mrs P J Sheen **Bred** Corduff Stud & J Corcorcan **Trained** Epsom, Surrey
FOCUS
They went a steady gallop - the time was 2.33 seconds slower than the first division - and it paid to race handily. Not form to be too positive about.

971 MIX BUSINESS WITH PLEASURE AT KEMPTON MAIDEN STKS 1m 2f (P)
6:50 (6:51) (Class 5) 3-Y-O+ **£2,590** (£770; £385; £192) **Stalls** High

Form RPR
344- **1** **Ebiayn (FR)**[26] 6475 4-10-0 75... JamieSpencer 6 77
(A King) *trckd ldrs: quick move to ld over 4f out and grabbed inner: rdn and drew away fr over 1f out* **12/1**[3]
0/5- **2** 3½ **Celtic Commitment**[427] 231 4-10-0 64............................ SebSanders 5 70
(S Dow) *led after 2f: narrowly hdd over 4f out: pressed wnr tl readily outpcd over 1f out* **33/1**
3 **3** 1¼ **Jumeirah Palm (USA)**[21] 768 3-8-3 0........................... HayleyTurner 3 59
(D M Simcock) *awkward s: keen early: trckd ldrs on outer: pushed along 4f out: effrt and hanging sltly 2f out: one pce after* **4/1**[2]
20- **4** 2½ **Texan Star (IRE)**[235] 4524 3-8-8 0.................................... RobertHavlin 2 59
(J H M Gosden) *led 2f: trckd ldr tl dropped to 3rd over 4f out: rdn and nt qckn over 1f out: fdd* **2/5**[1]
5 nk **Bethlehem (IRE)** 3-8-8 0... TravisBlock 7 58
(H Morrison) *in tch: pushed along and outpcd over 3f out: kpt on fnl f* **20/1**
3 **6** 7 **In A Fortnight**[29] 671 3-8-8 0.. JimmyQuinn 4 44
(H J Collingridge) *hld up last: wl outpcd fr over 3f out: toiling after* **33/1**
7 33 **True Union (USA)** 4-10-0 0... AlanMunro 8 —
(A P Jarvis) *puilled hrd early: hld up in tch: wknd 4f out: wl t.o* **33/1**
2m 9.16s (1.16) **Going Correction** +0.125s/f (Slow)
WFA 3 from 4yo 20lb **7** Ran SP% **112.7**
Speed ratings (Par 103): **100,97,96,94,93 88,61**
toteswingers: 1&2 £9.20, 1&3 £2.80, 2&3 £11.70 CSF £271.17 TOTE £12.60: £4.80, £6.50; EX 136.00.
Owner Winter Madness **Bred** Team Valor And Gary Barber **Trained** Barbury Castle, Wilts
FOCUS
A weak maiden best rated through the runner-up.

972 DIGIBET.COM H'CAP 5f (P)
7:20 (7:21) (Class 4) (0-85,83) 4-Y-O+ **£4,209** (£1,252; £625; £312) **Stalls** High

Form RPR
3661 **1** **Lord Of The Reins (IRE)**[35] 578 6-8-10 **75**............... PaulMulrennan 2 85
(J G Given) *settled off the pce in 4th: clsd over 1f out: eased out and decisive effrt to ld last 150yds: r.o* **7/2**[2]
2121 **2** 1 **Sherjawy (IRE)**[14] 846 6-8-6 **71**...................................... SamHitchcott 1 77
(Miss Z C Davison) *drvn in last trio bef 1/2-way: fnlly clsd over 1f out: wnt 2nd last 100yds: no imp on wnr nr fin* **15/2**
32 **3** nk **Wotashirtfull (IRE)**[14] 846 5-9-4 **83**............................(p) PatCosgrave 6 88
(J R Boyle) *disp ld at str pce and clr of rest: sitting duck whn pack clsd over 1f out: hdd and outpcd last 150yds* **2/1**[1]
500- **4** 1¼ **The Jobber (IRE)**[153] 6972 9-8-12 **77**.................................. DaneO'Neill 5 77
(M Blanshard) *rdn in last trio bef 1/2-way: tried to cl over 1f out: kpt on one pce* **7/1**
6506 **5** ¾ **Thoughtsofstardom**[6] 913 7-7-11 **69** oh2................ LeonnaMayor[(7)] 4 67
(P S McEntee) *disp ld at str pce to 1f out: fdd* **25/1**
662- **6** ½ **Ocean Blaze**[153] 6972 6-9-0 **79**... ChrisCatlin 3 75
(B R Millman) *stdd s: hld up in last and wl off the pce: pushed along on inner over 1f out: kpt on but nvr nr ldrs: rdr nvr used whip* **11/2**[3]
1425 **7** ¾ **Steel City Boy (IRE)**[5] 935 7-8-1 **69**........................... MartinLane[(3)] 7 69+
(D Shaw) *trckd clr ldng pair: clsd over 1f out but then trapped bhd them: nowhere to go and lost pl fnl f* **6/1**
59.66 secs (-0.84) **Going Correction** +0.125s/f (Slow) **7** Ran SP% **113.3**
Speed ratings (Par 105): **105,103,102,100,99 98,97**
toteswingers: 1&2 £4.60, 1&3 £2.10, 2&3 £2.40 CSF £28.72 TOTE £6.30: £4.50, £5.80; EX 22.20.
Owner Danethorpe Racing Partnership **Bred** C Farrell **Trained** Willoughton, Lincs
FOCUS
A tight sprint, run at a decent pace with the placed horses setting the standard.
Steel City Boy(IRE) Official explanation: jockey said gelding had been denied a clear

973 DIGIBET CHALLENGE STKS (CONDITIONS RACE) 1m 1f 110y(P)
7:50 (7:50) (Class 2) 3-Y-O
£9,969 (£2,985; £1,492; £747; £372; £187) **Stalls** High

Form RPR
121- **1** **Middle Club**[188] 6045 3-8-12 108.................................. RichardHughes 3 88+
(R Hannon) *trckd ldng trio: prog to go 2nd over 1f out: clsd to ld ins fnl f: hrd rdn and jst hld on* **10/11**[1]
61 **2** shd **Myplacelater**[39] 545 3-8-12 82..................................... DaneO'Neill 6 88+
(D R C Elsworth) *hld up in 5th: ct out whn pce lifted over 2f out: gd prog jst over 1f out: clsd on wnr last 100yds: pipped on the nod* **9/1**
51- **3** ½ **Rumool**[294] 2599 3-9-3 89... NeilCallan 2 92
(C E Brittain) *led at mod pce: kicked on over 2f out: hdd and nt qckn ins fnl f* **6/1**[2]
1511 **4** 1¼ **Kinky Afro (IRE)**[20] 792 3-8-12 83...................................... LiamKeniry 7 84
(J S Moore) *trckd ldng pair: rdn and nt qckn over 1f out: one pce after* **8/1**[3]
5 1 **Velikiy Zevs (USA)**[164] 3-9-3 0.. JoeFanning 4 87
(M Johnston) *hld up in 6th: outpcd and wd 2f out: kpt on fnl f: n.d* **14/1**
2121 **6** 1¼ **Exceedthewildman**[14] 840 3-9-3 86.............................(p) GeorgeBaker 5 84
(J S Moore) *s.s and lft abt 4 l: hld up last: effrt and tried to cl on ldrs over 1f out: wknd fnl f* **17/2**
7 3¼ **Hemera (USA)**[164] 3-8-12 0.. GregFairley 1 72
(M Johnston) *pressed ldr tl wknd 2f out* **16/1**
2m 3.29s (123.29) **7** Ran SP% **110.9**
toteswingers: 1&2 £4.30, 1&3 £2.30, 2&3 £6.50 CSF £9.24 TOTE £1.80: £1.40, £5.10; EX 7.70.
Owner R J McCreery **Bred** Stowell Hill Ltd **Trained** East Everleigh, Wilts
FOCUS
This conditions event was steadily run and the 108-rated winner ran well below her mark. The races is probably best rated around the fourth and sixth.
NOTEBOOK
Middle Club, a Group 3 winner in France on her final juvenile outing, clearly ran some way below her official mark of 108. She picked up quite readily after coming three wide into the straight to have every chance a furlong out, but Hughes initially seemed reluctant to give her a hard time and she didn't clear away as one might have expected, ultimately requiring pressure form the whip to just hold on. Her connections felt she needed the run and she certainly gave the impression she'll come on a fair bit for this. The plan now is apparently a Group 3 at Saint-Cloud in April, in which she will avoid a penalty. (op 5-6)
Myplacelater didn't beat much when winning her maiden by 8l at Wolverhampton last time, but she proved herself to be pretty useful with a decent performance in defeat. The winner got first run, but this filly still had her chance and only just missed out. (op 10-1 tchd 11-1)
Rumool looked a handful when winning his maiden over 6f around here last June, bolting before the start and then veering badly left under pressure in the straight. Up in trip for his return, he was allowed to dominate and proved more straightforward this time, although he did carry his head high once again. He doesn't appeal as one for maximum confidence, but clearly possesses plenty of ability and is entitled to improve again. (op 5-1)
Kinky Afro(IRE), a progressive handicapper whose latest win came by 5l off a mark of 74, found this company a bit hot but still ran well.
Velikiy Zevs(USA), previously trained in Russia, is a brother to Shamardal and offered some encouragement after 164 days off. He lacked the pace of some of these both at the start and in the latter stages, but kept on for pressure out wide in the straight and shaped as though he might get further. (op 16-1)
Exceedthewildman, a handicap winner of 83 last time, lost around 3l at the start, but the steadying of the pace at halfway helped him. He basically just didn't seem quite good enough. Official explanation: jockey said colt missed the berak (op 10-1)
Hemera(USA), like Velikiy Zevs, was having her first start since coming over from Russia, but she dropped out tamely in the straight. (op 20-1)

974 DIGIBET SPORTS BETTING H'CAP 1m 4f (P)
8:20 (8:20) (Class 4) (0-85,83) 4-Y-O+ **£4,209** (£1,252; £625; £312) **Stalls** Centre

Form RPR
55-1 **1** **Turjuman (USA)**[21] 770 5-8-11 **72**............................... StevieDonohoe 9 81+
(W J Musson) *hld up in 5th decisive move on inner to ld 2f out: sn at least 2 l clr: reduced advantage ins fnl f but a holding on* **9/2**[2]
0-14 **2** ¾ **Oxford City (IRE)**[7] 426 6-8-9 **70**................................(t) LiamKeniry 7 75
(P M Phelan) *trckd ldng trio: nt qckn and outpcd 2f out: kpt on fr over 1f out to take 2nd ins fnl f: clsng at fin* **7/1**
-345 **3** nk **Dreamwalk (IRE)**[41] 500 4-9-4 **81**................................(v) JimCrowley 3 86
(R Curtis) *trckd ldr after 3f tl jst over 2f out: sn rdn and nt qckn: kpt on to take 2nd again briefly ins fnl f: nvr able to chal* **5/2**[1]
113- **4** ½ **Akbabend**[149] 7066 4-9-6 **83**... JoeFanning 1 87
(M Johnston) *led after 1f and set modest pce: hdd and nt qckn 2f out: kpt on same pce after* **11/2**[3]
006- **5** 1¼ **Valdan (IRE)**[158] 6855 6-8-11 **72**..................................(t) SteveDrowne 8 74
(M A Barnes) *hld up in 6th: outpcd and nudged along 2f out: shkn up over 1f out: kpt on: no ch* **25/1**
0051 **6** nk **War Of The Roses (IRE)**[14] 841 7-9-1 **76**........................ TomEaves 5 78
(R Brotherton) *hld up in 7th: effrt 2f out but sn outpcd: one pce fnl f* **10/1**
-550 **7** nk **Ramona Chase**[12] 873 5-9-2 **77**................................(t) GeorgeBaker 2 78+
(M J Attwater) *s.s: t.k.h: hld up last: lft trailing once pce lifted over 2f out: taken to wd outside and styd on fnl f: no ch* **14/1**
4-30 **8** 3¼ **Aureate**[23] 756 6-8-12 **73**... NeilChalmers 4 69
(B Forsey) *led 1f: 3rd after 3f tl wknd 2f out* **16/1**
2m 39.4s (4.90) **Going Correction** +0.125s/f (Slow)
WFA 4 from 5yo+ 2lb **8** Ran SP% **100.1**
Speed ratings (Par 105): **88,87,87,86,86 85,85,83**
toteswingers: 1&2 £2.80, 1&3 £2.30, 2&3 £3.00 CSF £26.79 CT £62.97 TOTE £2.80: £1.02, £3.40, £2.20; EX 24.10.

Owner I Johnson & John D Jacques **Bred** Shadwell Farm LLC **Trained** Newmarket, Suffolk

FOCUS

A fair handicap but muddling form despite the winning being rated back to his best.

975 BOOK NOW FOR THIS SATURDAY H'CAP 1m (P)

8:50 (8:52) (Class 5) (0-75,74) 4-Y-O+ £2,590 (£770; £385; £192) Stalls High

Form RPR

264- **1** **Striding Edge (IRE)**[172] 6496 4-9-4 **74** MartinDwyer 2 83
(W R Muir) *hld up wl in rr in strly run r: prog over 2f out: chal over 1f out: gained upper hand ins fnl f: styd on wl* **6/1**[2]

0-20 **2** ½ **Having A Ball**[28] 676 6-8-9 **65** ChrisCatlin 13 73
(P D Cundell) *hld up in rr in strly run r: prog over 2f out: drvn to ld jst over 1f out: styd on but hdd and hld ins fnl f* **16/1**

000- **3** 2¼ **Jazacosta (USA)**[161] 6784 4-8-7 **63** ow1 FergusSweeney 12 66+
(Miss Jo Crowley) *hld up in 5th: edgd towards nr side in st: clsd and narrow ld briefly over 1f out: one pce fnl f* **9/1**

6061 **4** nk **Resplendent Nova**[27] 704 8-8-11 **67** DarryllHolland 6 69
(P Howling) *hld up in last trio: prog on inner 2f out: drvn to cl on ldrs 1f out: edgd lft and one pce after* **12/1**

0-00 **5** 1½ **Outofoil (IRE)**[28] 676 4-9-0 **70** (b) JimCrowley 11 69
(R M Beckett) *hld up in 6th: prog on inner over 2f out: upsides over 1f out: fdd fnl f* **15/2**[3]

/23- **6** nse **Cross The Line (IRE)**[357] 1067 8-9-1 **71** RichardHughes 9 69
(A P Jarvis) *hld up off the pce in midfield: nt asked for effrt tl over 1f out: shkn up and one pce* **6/1**[2]

3160 **7** ½ **Aflaam (IRE)**[23] 752 5-8-12 **71** MichaelStainton(3) 10 68
(R A Harris) *rousted along early to rch abt 9th after 2f: effrt u.p 2f out: kpt on but nvr gng pce to threaten* **12/1**

0500 **8** 3¾ **All About You (IRE)**[14] 853 4-8-12 **68** SteveDrowne 3 57
(P Howling) *hld up in last pair: shkn up and modest prog 2f out: nvr on terms* **25/1**

-031 **9** 1¾ **Sapphire Prince (USA)**[19] 808 4-8-3 **62** AndreaAtzeni(3) 8 47
(J R Best) *chsd clr ldng pair: hung lft over 2f out: wknd over 1f out* **12/1**

000- **10** 3¾ **Pedasus (USA)**[223] 4930 4-8-9 **65** LiamKeniry 5 41
(T Keddy) *racd wd in midfield: hanging after 2f: no real prog 2f out: sn wknd* **10/1**

00-0 **11** 2½ **Esteem Lord**[38] 552 4-8-6 **62** LiamJones 14 32
(Jamie Poulton) *chsd ldng trio: rdn fr 1/2-way: wknd rapidly 2f out* **16/1**

0-00 **12** 6 **Best In Class**[28] 676 4-9-3 **73** (v¹) NeilCallan 7 29
(S C Williams) *chsd clr ldr and wl ahd of rest: upsides wl over 1f out: hung lft and wknd rapidly* **10/1**

5312 **13** 2½ **Whodunit (UAE)**[28] 676 6-8-9 **68** (b) WilliamCarson(3) 4 19
(P W Hiatt) *led at str pce and sn clr: hung lft over 2f out: hdd & wknd rapidly over 1f out* **5/1**[1]

1m 39.15s (-0.65) **Going Correction** +0.125s/f (Slow) **13** Ran SP% **123.9**

Speed ratings (Par 103): **108,107,105,104,103 103,102,99,97,93 91,85,82**

toteswingers: 1&2 £23.00, 1&3 £18.00, 2&3 £34.70 CSF £102.23 CT £905.38 TOTE £5.00: £1.20, £3.50, £3.80; EX 122.20.

Owner Linkslade Racing **Bred** G Prendergast **Trained** Lambourn, Berks

FOCUS

A modest handicap but run at a good gallop and the fourth sets the level of the form.

976 LEVY BOARD H'CAP 7f (P)

9:20 (9:21) (Class 7) (0-50,50) 4-Y-O+ £1,364 (£403; £201) Stalls High

Form RPR

5423 **1** **Royal Acclamation (IRE)**[13] 866 5-8-9 **49** (p) DavidKenny(7) 11 58
(H J Evans) *trckd ldrs: gng easily over 2f out: produced to ld over 1f out: idled and sn pressed: fnd jst enough ins fnl f to hold on* **9/1**

0443 **2** shd **Yakama (IRE)**[14] 854 5-9-3 **50** (b) AdamKirby 7 59
(Mrs C A Dunnett) *hld up in rr: stdy prog on inner fr over 2f out: chal over 1f out: w wnr fnl f: jst hld last strides* **7/1**[2]

4-43 **3** 1½ **Black Draft**[70] 146 8-8-8 **46** SophieDoyle(5) 6 51
(B Forsey) *hld up wl in rr: rdn and prog fr over 2f out: styd on wl fnl f to take 3rd nr fin* **25/1**

06-0 **4** ½ **Herbert Crescent**[37] 567 5-9-3 **50** (b) PaulMulrennan 14 54
(Ollie Pears) *rrd s: hld up towards rr: prog on inner over 2f out: tried to chal over 1f out: fdd ins fnl f* **7/1**[2]

3143 **5** nk **Clever Omneya (USA)**[27] 691 4-9-3 **50** RichardHughes 5 53
(J R Jenkins) *hld up bhd ldrs: shkn up 2f out: clsd grad 1f out: jst pushed out last 100yds whn no ch of winning* **11/2**[1]

0323 **6** ¾ **Louisiade (IRE)**[14] 844 9-9-1 **48** (p) FrannyNorton 8 49
(R C Guest) *t.k.h: disp ld to over 1f out: grad fdd* **15/2**[3]

3651 **7** ½ **Metropolitan Chief**[13] 866 6-9-2 **49** RobertHavlin 12 48
(P Burgoyne) *s.i.s: sn trckd ldrs: cl up 2f out: rdn and nt qckn: one pce after* **14/1**

5200 **8** 2 **Imperial Skylight**[22] 763 4-9-3 **50** (v) ChrisCatlin 10 44
(M R Channon) *disp ld to over 1f out: losing pl whn n.m.r ent fnl f* **9/1**

060- **9** 1¾ **Flute Magic**[172] 6497 4-9-0 **50** JamesMillman(3) 2 39
(B R Millman) *pressed ldng pair but racd on outer fr wd draw: rdn over 2f out: steadily wknd over 1f out* **9/1**

5420 **10** ½ **Misterisland (IRE)**[14] 854 5-8-13 **46** NickyMackay 4 34
(M Mullineaux) *chsd ldrs: u.p over 2f out: steadily wknd* **20/1**

4006 **11** ½ **Cavalry Guard (USA)**[33] 614 6-8-11 **49** (b) AmyBaker(5) 13 36
(T D McCarthy) *rrd s: a in rr: pushed along and struggling over 2f out* **12/1**

35-0 **12** 11 **Ardent Prince**[14] 847 7-8-13 **46** FergusSweeney 9 3
(A B Haynes) *s.i.s: a in rr: t.o* **9/1**

2050 **13** 1¾ **Jessica Wigmo**[13] 866 7-8-9 **47** (t) MarkCoumbe(5) 3 —
(A W Carroll) *reluctant to go to post: rel to r: a bhd: t.o* **12/1**

1m 26.52s (0.52) **Going Correction** +0.125s/f (Slow) **13** Ran SP% **122.8**

Speed ratings (Par 97): **102,101,100,99,99 98,97,95,93,92 92,79,77**

toteswingers: 1&2 £21.40, 1&3 £45.10, 2&3 £15.80 CSF £72.78 CT £1548.92 TOTE £13.40: £3.70, £3.00, £11.50; EX 90.40 Place 6 £832.93, Place 5 £252.55.

Owner Mrs J Evans **Bred** The Susie Syndicate **Trained** Broadwas, Worcs

FOCUS

A poor handicap but the time was reasonable for the grade. The form looks straightforward and reliable at a low level.

Metropolitan Chief Official explanation: jockey said gelding bumped its head on leaving stalls

Flute Magic Official explanation: jockey said gelding hung left

Jessica Wigmo Official explanation: jockey said mare had resented the tongue strap

T/Plt: £115.40 to a £1 stake. Pool: £73,223.50. 463.01 winning tickets. T/Qpdt: £26.50 to a £1 stake. Pool: £7,197.60. 200.90 winning tickets. JN

[969]KEMPTON (A.W) (R-H)

Thursday, March 25

OFFICIAL GOING: Standard

Wind: MODERATE BEHIND Weather: OVERCAST/RAIN

977 ESSEX RACING CLUB WESTWOOD WANDERERS CC CLAIMING STKS 1m (P)

5:50 (5:51) (Class 6) 3-Y-O £2,047 (£604; £302) Stalls High

Form RPR

2212 **1** **Tuscan King**[3] 964 3-9-0 68 (b) J-PGuillambert 3 69
(P D Evans) *hld up in rr: stdy hdwy ins fnl 3f to ld ins fnl 2f: carried hd to one side and hdd over 1f out: rallied strly u.p ins fnl f to ld fnl 75yds: hld on all out* **7/4**[1]

1643 **2** shd **Ant Music (IRE)**[23] 760 3-8-11 65 (b) LiamKeniry 5 66
(J S Moore) *towards rr tl gd hdwy over 2f out to ld over 1f out: sn rdn: hdd fnl 75yds: kpt on wl: jst failed* **8/1**

00 **3** 4½ **Rock D'Argent (IRE)**[12] 889 3-8-5 0 JimmyQuinn 2 49
(H Morrison) *slowly away: hld up in rr tl stdy hdwy over 2f out: sn chsng ldrs: outpcd by ldng duo fnl f* **10/1**

00-6 **4** 6 **Dr Mathias**[28] 698 3-8-13 65 DavidProbert 6 44
(P D Evans) *chsd ldrs: rdn over 2f out: wknd appr fnl f* **7/2**[2]

3321 **5** ½ **Just Mandy (IRE)**[8] 909 3-8-7 62 PaulHanagan 8 36
(R A Fahey) *led hdd ins fnl 2f: wknd over 1f out* **4/1**[3]

000- **6** 2¾ **Flotate (USA)**[199] 5722 3-8-9 55 RobertHavlin 7 32
(Jane Chapple-Hyam) *chsd ldrs tl wknd qckly wl over 1f out* **20/1**

-046 **7** 1¼ **La Toya J (IRE)**[22] 768 3-8-7 58 FergusSweeney 1 27
(R Curtis) *chsd ldrs tl rn wd bnd 3f out: n.d after* **14/1**

000- **8** 2½ **Rivitivo**[246] 4188 3-8-2 42 LukeMorris 9 17
(W M Brisbourne) *a in rr* **100/1**

0-46 **9** 13 **Delta Sky (IRE)**[35] 597 3-8-5 60 (b¹) ChrisCatlin 4 —
(Miss Amy Weaver) *s.i.s: sn rcvrd to chse ldrs: wknd qckly 3f out* **14/1**

1m 40.82s (1.02) **Going Correction** +0.10s/f (Slow) **9** Ran SP% **117.9**

Speed ratings (Par 96): **98,97,93,87,86 84,82,80,67**

toteswingers: 1&2 £14.30, 1&3 £3.50, 2&3 £6.40 CSF £17.44 TOTE £2.00: £1.10, £2.00, £4.20; EX 12.60.Rock D'argent was claimed by Andrew Haynes for £6,000.

Owner J L Guillambert **Bred** Horizon Bloodstock Limited **Trained** Pandy, Monmouths

FOCUS

A tight claimer with not much between the principals at these weights. The pace did not appear to be strong, but the front-runners fared badly and the hold-up horses quickly came into play in the home straight. The first two are rated to near their best.

Rock D'Argent(IRE) Official explanation: jockey said filly reared as gates opened

978 ESSEX RACING CLUB JEFFREY GREEN RUSSELL MAIDEN FILLIES' STKS (DIV I) 1m (P)

6:20 (6:20) (Class 5) 3-Y-O+ £2,266 (£674; £337; £168) Stalls High

Form RPR

46- **1** **Carioca (IRE)**[229] 4792 3-8-7 0 AndreaAtzeni(3) 1 78+
(M Botti) *led after 1f: pushed clr fr 2f out: v easily* **11/4**[2]

45- **2** 6 **Miss Miracle**[188] 6062 3-8-10 0 LukeMorris 5 63
(C G Cox) *chsd wnr after 2f: rdn and effrt wl over 2f out: nvr on terms and sn lft bhd by wnr but styd on for clr 2nd* **13/8**[1]

060- **3** 2½ **Bideeya (USA)**[168] 6609 3-8-10 65 (p) NeilCallan 4 57
(C E Brittain) *chsd ldrs: t.k.h: rdn over 2f out: nvr any ch w wnr and wknd ins fnl f* **14/1**

0-50 **4** 1 **See Elsie Play**[22] 768 4-9-13 57 SamHitchcott 8 60
(Miss Z C Davison) *in tch: rdn over 2f out: kpt on fr over 1f out but nvr any threat* **66/1**

00- **5** nk **Tammela**[168] 6607 3-8-10 0 AlanMunro 10 54+
(A P Jarvis) *broke wl: stdd in rr: pushed along 3f out: styd on fr over 1f out but nvr any threat* **33/1**

6 1¾ **Oh Two** 3-8-7 0 WilliamCarson(3) 9 50+
(S C Williams) *s.i.s: in rr: green whn pushed along 2f out: sme hdwy fr over 1f out* **66/1**

3 **7** 1 **Dubai Moonlight**[27] 728 3-8-3 0 LewisWalsh(7) 2 48
(Jane Chapple-Hyam) *towards rr: hdwy on outside bnd 3f out: nvr in contention: wknd and hung lft over 1f out* **25/1**

2- **8** ½ **Jounce (USA)**[131] 7396 3-8-10 0 RobertHavlin 11 46
(J H M Gosden) *broke wl: outpcd over 4f out: pushed along and sme hdwy 3f out: nvr in contention and wknd ins fnl 2f* **3/1**[3]

62-5 **9** nk **Angelena Ballerina (IRE)**[22] 776 3-8-10 62 ChrisCatlin 7 46
(Karen George) *led 1f: rdn and hung rt on rails ins fnl 3f: wknd over 2f out* **10/1**

10 ¾ **Gifted Lady (IRE)** 3-8-3 0 RichardRowe(7) 6 44
(P M Phelan) *s.i.s: wnt wd bnd 3f out: a towards rr* **66/1**

0- **11** 5 **Swain's Quest (USA)**[96] 7816 3-8-3 0 AmyScott(7) 12 32
(Eve Johnson Houghton) *t.k.h: in tch: sme hdwy 3f out: sn wknd* **80/1**

1m 41.24s (1.44) **Going Correction** +0.10s/f (Slow)

WFA 3 from 4yo 17lb **11** Ran SP% **118.0**

Speed ratings (Par 100): **96,90,87,86,86 84,83,82,82,81 76**

toteswingers: 1&2 £2.40, 1&3 £9.90, 2&3 £8.50 CSF £7.39 TOTE £3.70: £1.20, £1.60, £3.90; EX 9.50.

Owner The Great Partnership **Bred** John Doyle **Trained** Newmarket, Suffolk

FOCUS

They went no pace and it proved impossible to come from behind, with the field finishing well stretched out and the first three having been prominent throughout. An impressive winner but the form is limited by the proximity of the fourth.

979 ESSEX RACING CLUB JEFFREY GREEN RUSSELL MAIDEN FILLIES' STKS (DIV II) 1m (P)

6:50 (6:51) (Class 5) 3-Y-O+ £2,266 (£674; £337; £168) Stalls High

Form RPR

2- **1** **Clairvoyance (IRE)**[126] 7450 3-8-10 0 NickyMackay 10 81+
(J H M Gosden) *t.k.h: trckd ldr tl led over 5f out: pushed clr wl over 2f out: easily* **9/4**[2]

4- **2** 6 **Goolagong (IRE)**[216] 5220 3-8-10 0 JimCrowley 11 67
(R M Beckett) *led tl hdd over 5f out: styd chsng wnr: rdn ins fnl 3f: no imp and readily outpcd fnl 2f* **8/11**[1]

0- **3** ½ **Double Fortune**[99] 7764 3-8-10 0 LiamJones 3 66
(Jamie Poulton) *chsd ldrs: rdn 3f out: styd on fr over 1f out to cl on 2nd nr fin but nvr any ch w wnr* **33/1**

4 1½ **White Finch (USA)** 3-8-10 0 DavidProbert 2 62+
(A M Balding) *s.i.s: in rr: stl plenty to do ins fnl 3f and sn hung rt: hdwy and green ins fnl 2f: kpt on fnl f* **14/1**

00- **5** 1/2 **Babycakes (IRE)**[131] 7388 3-8-10 0 HayleyTurner 1 61+
(M L W Bell) *in rr: hdwy over 2f out: nvr anywhere nr wnr and styd on same pce fr wl over 1f out* **33/1**

6 6 **Shades Of Grey** 3-8-10 0 LukeMorris 6 46
(C G Cox) *s.i.s: in rr: green and pushed along over 2f out: nvr gng pce to get into contention* **25/1**

0006 **7** 2 1/4 **Helpmeronda**[22] 776 4-9-13 39 (t) GeorgeBaker 9 46
(W M Brisbourne) *s.i.s: sn prom: wknd over 2f out* **66/1**

8 4 1/2 **Seminova** 3-8-10 0 JoeFanning 5 30
(M Johnston) *chsd ldrs tl wknd over 3f out* **12/1**[3]

0- **9** 14 **Isabel's Pet**[129] 7411 4-9-13 0 ChrisCatlin 7 —
(Karen George) *bhd fr 1/2-way* **66/1**

1m 40.49s (0.69) **Going Correction** +0.10s/f (Slow)
WFA 3 from 4yo+ 17lb **9** Ran SP% **115.7**
Speed ratings (Par 100): **100,94,93,92,91 85,83,78,64**
toteswingers: 1&2 £1.10, 1&3 £19.70, 2&3 £9.30 CSF £4.05 TOTE £3.00: £1.10, £1.10, £7.10; EX 4.00.
Owner H R H Princess Haya Of Jordan **Bred** Old Carhue Stud **Trained** Newmarket, Suffolk

FOCUS
The shape of the race was remarkably similar to the earlier division, with the prominent runners dominating and the winner taking control early in the straight following an almost indentically modest tempo. However, the time was 0.75 second faster, and it was the quickest of the three 1m contests run to this point.

980 STUARTWILLIAMSRACING.CO.UK MAIDEN STKS 7f (P)
7:20 (7:22) (Class 5) 3-Y-O **£2,590** (£770; £385; £192) **Stalls** High

Form RPR

2 **1** **Bohemian Melody**[28] 692 3-9-3 0 JerryO'Dwyer 8 83+
(M Botti) *trckd ldrs: drvn to ld over 1f out: pushed clr ins fnl f: comf* **11/4**[2]

2- **2** 2 **Point Out (USA)**[152] 7024 3-9-3 0 RobertHavlin 2 76
(J H M Gosden) *trckd ldrs: pushed along 2f out: styd on wl to chse wnr thrght fnl f and kpt on wl but a readily hld* **15/8**[1]

4 **3** 1 **Rock With You**[25] 744 3-8-12 0 LukeMorris 12 68
(J R Gask) *chsd ldrs: rdn 3f out: drvn and ev ch 1f out: one pce ins fnl f* **12/1**

4 1 **Island Rhapsody** 3-8-12 0 DavidProbert 11 66
(A M Balding) *wnt lft s: chsd ldrs: rdn over 2f out: styd on same pce fnl f* **12/1**

5- **5** 2 **Aqua Vitae (IRE)**[196] 5800 3-8-12 0 JoeFanning 13 60
(M Johnston) *led rdn over 2f out: hdd over 1f out: wknd ins fnl f* **11/2**[3]

6 2 **Jo Boy** 3-9-3 0 MartinDwyer 10 60+
(D M Simcock) *bmpd s and s.i.s: in rr: pushed along over 2f out: styd on fnl f but nvr a threat* **20/1**

5 **7** 3 1/2 **Madlool (IRE)**[25] 744 3-9-3 0 LiamJones 3 50+
(W J Haggas) *wnt rt: s.i.s: plld hrd in rr: pushed along over 2f out: sme prog fnl f* **10/1**

04- **8** 1 **Arnie Guru**[199] 5722 3-8-12 0 KierenFox(5) 1 48
(M J Attwater) *unruly in stalls: sn chsng ldrs: rdn over 3f out: styd in tch tl wknd over 1f out* **40/1**

9 1/2 **Michael's Nook** 3-9-3 0 FergusSweeney 14 46+
(W S Kittow) *v.s.a: wl bhd: pushed along 3f out: styd on fr 2f out: gng on cl home but nvr a threat* **50/1**

6 **10** shd **Southern Cape (IRE)**[23] 758 3-9-3 0 RobertWinston 4 46+
(D J Coakley) *bmpd s: a towards rr* **33/1**

0- **11** 1 **Spirit Of Normandy**[127] 7430 3-8-12 0 SteveDrowne 7 38
(R Ingram) *in tch: rdn 3f out: wknd ins fnl 2f* **100/1**

12 3/4 **Rubbinghouse Com** 3-9-3 0 IanMongan 5 41
(P M Phelan) *towards rr most of way* **66/1**

0-0 **13** 17 **Dunfishin (IRE)**[31] 667 3-9-3 0 NeilChalmers 6 —
(M S Tuck) *a in rr* **100/1**

1m 26.92s (0.92) **Going Correction** +0.10s/f (Slow) **13** Ran SP% **116.9**
Speed ratings (Par 98): **98,95,94,93,91 88,84,83,83,83 81,81,61**
toteswingers: 1&2 £1.10, 1&3 £8.00, 2&3 £9.40 CSF £7.67 TOTE £2.70: £1.10, £1.30, £3.50; EX 7.40.
Owner Mrs L Botti **Bred** Ivan W Allan **Trained** Newmarket, Suffolk

FOCUS
Little experience on show, but these late developers should win a few races between them. This looks a fair race with the runner-up the best guide.
Michael's Nook Official explanation: jockey said gelding had been very slowly away

981 ESSEXRACINGCLUB.CO.UK H'CAP 7f (P)
7:50 (7:51) (Class 4) (0-85,85) 4-Y-O+ **£4,209** (£1,252; £625; £312) **Stalls** High

Form RPR

4225 **1** **Jake The Snake (IRE)**[8] 902 9-8-12 79 NeilCallan 2 87
(A W Carroll) *s.i.s: in rr: hdwy and nt clr run 2f out: drvn and str run ins fnl f: hmpd fnl 50yds: led nr fin* **7/1**

4322 **2** nk **Dinner Date**[28] 696 8-8-7 74 LiamKeniry 8 81
(T Keddy) *hld up towards rr: hdwy over 2f out: slt ld appr fnl f: hung lft u.p fnl 75yds: hdd nr fin* **11/2**[3]

1312 **3** 1/2 **Caprio (IRE)**[8] 902 5-9-1 82 NickyMackay 7 88
(J R Boyle) *trckd ldrs: slt ld ins fnl 2f: narrowly hdd appr fnl f: stl ev ch thrght fnl f: no ex nr fin* **11/4**[1]

/-13 **4** 1 1/4 **Lucky Redback (IRE)**[8] 902 4-9-4 85 (b[1]) RichardHughes 1 87
(R Hannon) *in rr: pushed along on outside over 2f out: hdwy over 1f out: styng on whn hung bdly rt u.p fnl 50yds and stmbld: nt rcvr* **7/2**[2]

4416 **5** 1 1/2 **Gallantry**[14] 867 8-8-10 80 MichaelStainton(3) 4 80+
(P Howling) *in rr: hdwy and nt clr run ins fnl 3f: hdwy fr 2f out: styng on to press ldrs whn bdly hmpd and stmbld fnl 50yds: nt rcvr* **11/1**

4132 **6** hd **Billberry**[20] 802 5-8-1 71 oh1 (t) AndreaAtzeni(3) 6 69
(S C Williams) *led tl hdd ins fnl 2f: styd pressing ldrs tl fading whn bdly hmpd and stmbld fnl 50yds* **15/2**

0-00 **7** 13 **Cry Of Freedom (USA)**[22] 769 4-8-11 78 (b) JoeFanning 5 41
(M Johnston) *chsd ldrs: rdn over 2f out: sn wknd* **9/1**

000- **8** 14 **Aroundthebay**[147] 7132 4-9-4 85 SebSanders 3 10
(H J L Dunlop) *chsd ldr: chal 4f out tl 3f out: wknd over 2f out* **11/1**

1m 26.19s (0.19) **Going Correction** +0.10s/f (Slow) **8** Ran SP% **115.2**
Speed ratings (Par 105): **102,101,101,99,97 97,82,66**
toteswingers: 1&2 £5.80, 1&3 £9.20, 2&3 £4.60 CSF £45.35 CT £132.37 TOTE £10.00: £2.80, £2.70, £1.10; EX 48.90.
Owner D Morgan & M B Clarke **Bred** J F Tuthill **Trained** Cropthorne, Worcs
■ Stewards' Enquiry : Michael Stainton two-day ban: caresless riding (Apr 8-9)
Richard Hughes three-day ban: careless riding (Apr 19-21)

FOCUS
The pace could have been better but the two pacemakers were well beaten and the winner needs a good gallop, so the race panned out as if it had been stronger. The form is a bit muddling and most of these are exposed.
Gallantry Official explanation: jockey said gelding suffered interference in running

982 ESSEX RACING CLUB BAILEYS HORSE FEEDS H'CAP 2m (P)
8:20 (8:22) (Class 6) (0-65,63) 4-Y-O+ **£2,047** (£604; £302) **Stalls** High

Form RPR

3-04 **1** **Cold Turkey**[15] 842 10-9-11 62 GeorgeBaker 5 74+
(G L Moore) *hld up in rr: stdy hdwy over 3f out: str run to ld appr fnl f: sn in command: comf* **2/1**[1]

-226 **2** 1 **On Terms (USA)**[22] 770 4-8-11 53 HayleyTurner 3 64
(S Dow) *chsd ldr after 4f: led over 3f out: sn rdn: hdd over 1f out: styd on but a readily hld by wnr* **12/1**

-035 **3** 3 **Colourful Move**[36] 584 5-8-9 46 (t) FergusSweeney 9 53
(P G Murphy) *in tch: chsd ldrs 1/2-way: rdn 3f out: kpt on fnl 2f but nvr gng pce of ldng duo* **6/1**[2]

-160 **4** 4 1/2 **Purely By Chance**[25] 748 5-8-11 53 (b) SimonPearce(5) 14 55
(J Pearce) *chsd ldrs: chal over 3f out tl 2f out: wknd over 1f out* **14/1**

2236 **5** 3 3/4 **Poppy Gregg**[13] 874 5-8-5 47 (v) AmyBaker(5) 4 44
(Dr J R J Naylor) *s.i.s: in rr: styd on fnl 2f but nvr a threat* **7/1**[3]

-220 **6** 2 1/4 **Valkyrie (IRE)**[36] 584 4-8-5 47 LukeMorris 1 41
(N P Littmoden) *in rr: pushed along 5f out: styd on fnl 2f but nvr any threat* **14/1**

513- **7** 2 **Sunny Spells**[86] 7867 5-9-9 63 WilliamCarson(3) 10 55
(S C Williams) *in rr: rdn over 4f out: sme prog fnl 3f* **6/1**[2]

-004 **8** 4 **Spiritonthemount (USA)**[46] 456 5-8-13 50 (b) ChrisCatlin 12 37
(P W Hiatt) *chsd ldrs: rdn 6f out: wknd fr 3f out* **28/1**

236- **9** 6 **Whitcombe Spirit**[25] 6692 5-9-4 55 RobertHavlin 13 35
(Jamie Poulton) *in tch: rdn over 4f out: wknd 3f out* **14/1**

640- **10** 1/2 **La Polka**[208] 5430 4-9-6 62 SteveDrowne 11 41
(H Morrison) *chsd ldrs tl wknd over 4f out* **12/1**

6200 **11** 18 **Zuwaar**[39] 554 5-9-3 57 (tp) RobertLButler(3) 7 15
(P Butler) *a towards rr* **33/1**

4-00 **12** 2 1/4 **Captain Flack**[15] 842 4-8-10 52 (b) LiamKeniry 6 7
(J A R Toller) *t.k.h in rr: nvr bttr than mid-div* **33/1**

00/2 **13** 25 **Himba**[15] 764 7-9-1 52 RichardHughes 8 —
(N J Gifford) *led: rdn over 4f out: hdd over 3f out: sn wknd: eased fnl f* **20/1**

1253 **14** 10 **Dan Buoy (FR)**[19] 701 7-9-0 56 (p) RossAtkinson(5) 2 —
(R C Guest) *chsd ldrs to 1/2-way: eased fnl 3f* **25/1**

3m 28.79s (-1.31) **Going Correction** +0.10s/f (Slow)
WFA 4 from 5yo+ 5lb **14** Ran SP% **127.7**
Speed ratings (Par 101): **107,106,105,102,100 99,98,96,93,93 84,83,70,65**
toteswingers: 1&2 £9.20, 1&3 £4.10, 2&3 £12.00 CSF £28.25 CT £134.24 TOTE £3.20: £1.70, £2.40, £2.90; EX 42.40.
Owner A Grinter **Bred** Worksop Manor Stud **Trained** Lower Beeding, W Sussex

FOCUS
A decent pace for 2m set the race up perfectly for the winner. The form looks sound.
Himba Official explanation: jockey said gelding stopped quickly
Dan Buoy(FR) Official explanation: jockey said gelding stopped quickly

983 ESSEX RACING CLUB BLUE TIGER MARKETING H'CAP 1m 4f (P)
8:50 (8:52) (Class 6) (0-60,60) 4-Y-O+ **£2,047** (£604; £302) **Stalls** Centre

Form RPR

0-22 **1** **Drizzi (IRE)**[22] 770 9-9-0 59 SimonPearce(5) 9 68+
(J Pearce) *in rr tl hdwy fr 5f out: str run fr over 2f out: sn chsd wnr over 1f out: led fnl 120yds: styd on strly* **4/1**[2]

-545 **2** 1 1/2 **Where's Susie**[22] 771 5-9-2 56 RobertHavlin 10 63
(M Madgwick) *towards mid-div: hdwy over 2f out: styd on wl fnl f to take 2nd cl home but no ch w wnr* **15/2**

0040 **3** nk **New World Order (IRE)**[1] 969 6-9-6 60 (tp) DaneO'Neill 3 66
(R Curtis) *sn led: rdn over 2f out: hdd and outpcd fnl 120yds: lost 2nd cl home* **13/2**[3]

0655 **4** 2 **Naheell**[14] 868 4-9-3 59 (p) TonyCulhane 12 62+
(G Prodromou) *in rr: pushed along over 3f out: styd on fr over 1f out: kpt on cl home but nvr a danger* **13/2**[3]

003- **5** 2 1/2 **Super Fourteen**[19] 6370 4-9-2 58 NeilCallan 1 57
(R H York) *chsd ldrs: rdn 3f out: styd on same pce fnl 2f* **16/1**

0-66 **6** nk **Drum Major (IRE)**[29] 676 5-9-4 58 GeorgeBaker 2 56
(G L Moore) *t.k.h: hld up in tch: pushed along and hd to one side over 2f out: sn btn* **7/2**[1]

356- **7** 3/4 **December**[94] 7831 4-9-4 60 RobertWinston 11 57
(Mrs C A Dunnett) *sn chsng ldr: rdn over 2f out: wknd appr fnl f* **20/1**

4-40 **8** hd **Dovedon Earl**[57] 316 4-9-0 56 LiamKeniry 8 53
(T Keddy) *in rr tl styd on fnl 2f: nvr a threat* **25/1**

0-00 **9** 1 1/2 **Stateside (CAN)**[24] 753 5-9-2 56 PaulHanagan 13 51
(R A Fahey) *chsd ldrs: rdn fr 3f out: wknd qckly appr fnl f* **25/1**

514- **10** nk **Largem**[174] 6446 4-9-1 57 RichardHughes 7 51
(J R Jenkins) *bhd most of way* **4/1**[2]

11 3/4 **Tifoso (FR)**[18] 5-9-1 55 (e[1]) PaulEddery 4 48
(R C Guest) *in rr: hdwy 4f out: in tch and rdn over 2f out: sn wknd* **66/1**

4-06 **12** 1 3/4 **Academy Gigsnreels (USA)**[48] 429 5-8-10 57 CPHoban(7) 5 47
(Seamus Fahey, Ire) *nvr bttr than mid-div* **33/1**

/56- **13** 3 1/4 **Minder**[256] 2320 4-9-4 60 PatCosgrave 6 45
(J G Portman) *in rr: effrt over 3f out: sn wknd* **20/1**

000/ **14** nk **What's For Tea**[346] 7506 5-8-11 54 (p) RobertLButler(3) 14 38
(P Butler) *chsd ldrs: rdn over 3f out: wknd qckly over 2f out* **100/1**

2m 34.77s (0.27) **Going Correction** +0.10s/f (Slow)
WFA 4 from 5yo+ 2lb **14** Ran SP% **129.2**
Speed ratings (Par 101): **103,102,101,100,98 98,98,97,96,96 96,95,92,92**
toteswingers: 1&2 £7.80, 1&3 £7.20, 2&3 £10.30 CSF £34.30 CT £202.98 TOTE £4.90: £2.50, £4.30, £1.10; EX 36.70.
Owner Eagle Bloodstock & Racing **Bred** Azienda Agricola La Vigna **Trained** Newmarket, Suffolk

FOCUS
They were soon stetched out, but it looked an ordinary gallop for the trip. Despite that the form looks sound rated around the winner and third.

984 ESSEXRACINGCLUB.CO.UK ACTION FOR FAMILY CARERS H'CAP 1m (P)
9:20 (9:20) (Class 7) (0-50,50) 4-Y-O+ **£1,364** (£403; £201) **Stalls** High

Form RPR

050- **1** **Lady Lam**[245] 4246 4-9-2 49 DavidProbert 2 59
(S Kirk) *chsd ldrs: hdwy on outside over 2f out: str run fnl f to ld fnl 120yds: drvn out* **14/1**

0065 **2** 1 1/4 **Flamestone**[6] 940 6-9-1 48 StevieDonohoe 6 55
(A E Price) *in tch: hdwy on ins to ld ins fnl 2f: styd on u.p tl hdd and outpcd fnl 120yds* **12/1**

4432 **3** ½ **Yakama (IRE)**[1] 976 5-9-3 **50**......(b) AdamKirby 14 56
(Mrs C A Dunnett) *in rr tl hdwy over 2f out: styd on to press ldrs ins fnl f: no ex fnl 120yds* **11/4**[1]

6-04 **4** 1 ¾ **Herbert Crescent**[1] 976 5-9-3 **50**......(b) PaulMulrennan 1 52+
(Ollie Pears) *plunged s and v.s.a: stdy hdwy over 2f out: kpt on fnl f but nvr quite gng pce to rch ldrs* **5/1**[2]

00-6 **5** ¾ **Takitwo**[23] 763 7-9-3 **50**......(v) SimonWhitworth 8 50
(P D Cundell) *mid-div: pushed along over 2f out: kpt on ins fnl f but nvr rchd ldrs* **5/1**[2]

02 **6** ½ **Red Current**[29] 682 6-8-6 **46**......(p) JakePayne(7) 13 45
(R A Harris) *chsd ldrs: n.m.r: swtchd lft and lost position over 2f out: styd on again fnl f but nvr a threat* **8/1**[3]

306 **7** hd **Motu (IRE)**[21] 794 9-9-0 **47**......(b) DanielTudhope 10 45
(I W McInnes) *chsd ldr: led briefly 2f out: sn hdd: wknd ins fnl f* **12/1**

0045 **8** 2 ¼ **Montmartre (USA)**[6] 939 4-8-7 **45**...... SimonPearce(5) 3 38
(David Pinder) *in tch: hdwy towards outside 3f out: rdn and wknd 2f out* **16/1**

3150 **9** nse **Hi Spec (IRE)**[15] 854 7-9-3 **50**......(p) JimmyQuinn 5 43
(Miss M E Rowland) *in rr: sme prog fnl 2f* **8/1**[3]

0-50 **10** 1 ¾ **Artreju (GER)**[15] 854 7-8-6 **46** ow1......(p) KaseyLoftus(7) 4 35
(P Butler) *a towards rr* **40/1**

0000 **11** ½ **One Cool Dream**[24] 757 4-9-3 **50**...... ChrisCatlin 7 38
(P W Hiatt) *led tl hdd & wknd 2f out* **16/1**

-400 **12** 3 ¾ **Kalligal**[22] 768 5-9-3 **50**...... RobertHavlin 11 29
(R Ingram) *bhd most of way* **25/1**

1m 41.1s (1.30) **Going Correction** +0.10s/f (Slow) **12** Ran SP% **122.3**
Speed ratings (Par 97): **97,95,95,93,92 92,92,89,89,88 87,83**
toteswingers: 1&2 £32.60, 1&3 £12.40, 2&3 £8.30 CSF £177.03 CT £616.80 TOTE £26.20: £8.50, £5.60, £1.10; EX 147.80 Place 6: £5.85, Place 5: £3.13..
Owner J B J Richards **Bred** J B J Richards **Trained** Upper Lambourn, Berks

FOCUS
A routine gallop, but some of these modest sorts probably couldn't have gone any faster anyway. The form looks straightforward overall.
Lady Lam Official explanation: trainer said, regarding apparent improvement in form, that this was the filly's first run for the yard.
Herbert Crescent Official explanation: jockey said gelding had reared and was slowly away
Montmartre(USA) Official explanation: jockey said gelding hung right
T/Jkpt: £2,727.60 to a £1 stake. Pool: £13,446.27. 3.50 winning tickets. T/Plt: £8.80 to a £1 stake. Pool: £88,113.34. 7,291.19 winning tickets. T/Qpdt: £4.00 to a £1 stake. Pool: £8,394.40. 1,549.60 winning tickets. ST

943 LINGFIELD (L-H)
Friday, March 26

OFFICIAL GOING: Standard
All four races at up to 7f were won by horses ridden from the front, with a strong wind behind the runners in the straight no doubt playing its part.
Wind: strong, behind Weather: overcast, breezy

985 MARRIOTT HOTEL OPENING SPRING 2010 MAIDEN FILLIES' STKS 7f (P)
2:05 (2:07) (Class 5) 3-Y-O+ **£2,729** (£806; £403) **Stalls** Low

Form RPR

00- **1** **Faited To Pretend (IRE)**[135] 7326 3-8-9 0...... MartinDwyer 7 70
(M Botti) *t.k.h: chsd ldr tl led over 5f out: mde rest: pushed clr jst over 1f out: rdn fnl f: a gng to hold on* **10/1**

62- **2** ½ **Picnic Party**[128] 7436 3-8-9 0...... DaneO'Neill 14 69
(D R C Elsworth) *t.k.h: chsd ldrs: wnt 2nd 5f out: rdn and nt pce of wnr wl over 1f out: styd on u.p fnl 100yds: nt quite gng to rch wnr* **9/4**[1]

3 nk **Spicewood (USA)** 3-8-9 0...... RobertHavlin 4 68+
(J H M Gosden) *dwlt: sn in tch in midfield: rdn to chse ldrs ent fnl 2f: outpcd over 1f out: rallied ins fnl f: r.o strly to go 3rd nr fin* **10/3**[2]

62 **4** 1 **Starlight Muse (IRE)**[22] 793 3-8-9 0...... GrahamGibbons 10 65
(E S McMahon) *chsd ldrs: wnt 3rd and rdn jst over 2f out: rdn and hung lft over 1f out: styd on same pce after* **7/2**[3]

0- **5** 3 **Weeping Willow (IRE)**[235] 4603 3-8-9 0...... NickyMackay 5 57+
(J H M Gosden) *hld up in tch towards rr: outpcd 2f out: styd on steadily fnl f: nvr trbld ldrs* **15/2**

0- **6** 3 ½ **Auburn Place**[149] 7106 3-8-9 0...... LiamKeniry 3 47
(E F Vaughan) *led tl over 5f out: chsd ldrs after: rdn and unable qck over 2f out: wknd qckly wl over 1f out* **100/1**

7 1 **Najam** 3-8-9 0...... ChrisCatlin 13 45
(C E Brittain) *sn niggled along towards rr: rdn and outpcd over 2f out: plugged on ins fnl f: nvr gng pce to trble ldrs* **9/1**

8 nk **Hope She Does (USA)** 3-8-6 0...... MarcHalford(3) 9 44
(Mrs L C Jewell) *s.i.s: hld up in tch in rr: pushed along over 2f out: rdn and hdwy over 1f out: nvr gng pce to threaten ldrs* **150/1**

9 nk **Polynesian Queen (IRE)** 3-8-9 0...... JerryO'Dwyer 12 43
(M G Quinlan) *stdd and dropped in s: t.k.h: hld up towards rr: swtchd wd 3f out: rdn and no prog 2f out* **66/1**

10 1 ¾ **Faraday's Fancy (IRE)** 4-9-10 0...... TravisBlock 6 38
(Miss A M Newton-Smith) *s.i.s: hld up in tch towards rr: rdn and unable qck over 2f out: no ch fnl 2f* **100/1**

11 ¾ **Yehonala (USA)** 3-8-9 0...... RobertWinston 1 36
(J R Best) *in tch in midfield: pushed along 4f out: rdn and struggling wl over 2f out: bhd fr wl over 1f out* **25/1**

1m 25.97s (1.17) **Going Correction** 0.0s/f (Stan)
WFA 3 from 4yo 15lb **11** Ran SP% **114.9**
Speed ratings (Par 100): **93,92,92,90,87 83,82,82,81,79 78**
toteswingers:1&2:£6.00, 1&3:£7.90, 2&3:£2.80 CSF £31.90 TOTE £13.50: £2.70, £1.20, £1.80; EX 49.40 TRIFECTA Not won..
Owner Frontier Racing Group **Bred** Rozelle Bloodstock **Trained** Newmarket, Suffolk

FOCUS
The pace was modest early and there was a strong wind behind the runners in the straight, meaning those who raced prominently were at an advantage (the first four races were won by front runners). Still, this looked an interesting fillies' maiden that should produce some winners. The form is rated around the fourth.

986 MARRIOTT PLAY & STAY CLAIMING STKS 6f (P)
2:40 (2:40) (Class 6) 4-Y-O+ **£2,047** (£604; £302) **Stalls** Low

Form RPR

4212 **1** **Misaro (GER)**[9] 899 9-8-10 69......(b) DavidProbert 1 68
(R A Harris) *mde all: hrd pressed and rdn 2f out: hung lft u.p 1f out: forged ahd ins fnl f: kpt on wl* **9/4**[2]

323 **2** 1 ¾ **Wotashirtfull (IRE)**[2] 972 5-9-9 83......(p) PatCosgrave 3 76
(J R Boyle) *chsd ldrs: rdn 2f out: swtchd ins and effrt over 1f out: kpt on same pce u.p fnl f: wnt 2nd fnl 50yds* **11/10**[1]

000- **3** nk **Mutamared (USA)**[110] 7656 10-8-9 70......(t) RussKennemore(3) 10 64
(Andrew Reid) *chsd wnr: ev ch and rdn wl over 1f out: no ex and btn fnl 100yds: lost 2nd fnl 50yds* **10/1**

23-5 **4** ½ **Who's Winning (IRE)**[4] 961 9-8-9 55......(t) HayleyTurner 5 59
(B G Powell) *chsd ldrs: rdn and outpcd wl over 2f out: rallied ins fnl f: gng on fin: nvr to rch wnr* **14/1**

424 **5** 1 ¼ **Dvinsky (USA)**[8] 924 9-8-13 69......(b) DarryllHolland 7 59
(P Howling) *dwlt: sn bustled up to chse ldrs: rdn and unable qck jst over 2f out: edgd lft u.p over 1f out: wknd ins fnl f* **11/2**[3]

00-0 **6** 1 ¾ **Public Image**[36] 592 4-8-6 41...... LiamJones 6 46
(Jamie Poulton) *s.i.s: wl outpcd in last trio: pushed along over 1f out: kpt on steadily ins fnl f: nvr trbld ldrs* **40/1**

000- **7** 4 **Coeur Courageux (FR)**[347] 1258 8-8-13 54...... MickyFenton 4 41
(W De Best-Turner) *s.i.s: a bhd: nvr on terms* **66/1**

0/00 **8** 5 **Savanna's Gold**[24] 758 6-7-10 34...... RichardRowe(7) 9 15
(R Rowe) *s.i.s: a wl bhd* **100/1**

1m 11.61s (-0.29) **Going Correction** 0.0s/f (Stan) **8** Ran SP% **114.5**
Speed ratings (Par 101): **101,98,98,97,95 93,88,81**
toteswingers:1&2:£1.40, 1&3:£5.30, 2&3:£4.00 CSF £5.06 TOTE £3.60: £1.10, £1.20, £2.60; EX 5.90 Trifecta £52.10 Pool: £629.21 - 8.92 winning units..
Owner Messrs Criddle Davies Dawson & Villa **Bred** Wilhelm Fasching **Trained** Earlswood, Monmouths

FOCUS
Once again the wind was strong behind the runners in the straight. The 55-rated Who's Winning and the 41-rated Public Image limit the form. So does the final time which was 1.51 seconds second slower than the following handicap won by the 82-rated Beat The Bell.
Dvinsky(USA) Official explanation: jockey said gelding missed the break
Public Image Official explanation: jockey said filly hung left
Coeur Courageux(FR) Official explanation: jockey said gelding missed the break and hung left down the hill
Savanna's Gold Official explanation: jockey said mare missed the break

987 LINGFIELD PARK OWNERS CLUB H'CAP 6f (P)
3:15 (3:16) (Class 4) (0-85,85) 4-Y-O+ **£4,209** (£1,252; £625; £312) **Stalls** Low

Form RPR

60-3 **1** **Beat The Bell**[24] 761 5-9-1 **82**...... GeorgeBaker 8 93
(J A Osborne) *sn led and clr: rdn jst over 1f out: kpt on wl* **4/1**[2]

-245 **2** 1 **Halsion Chancer**[24] 761 6-8-11 **78**...... RobertWinston 3 86
(J R Best) *prom in chsng gp: rdn to go 3rd ent fnl 2f: kpt on wl u.p fnl f: wnt 2nd fnl 50yds: nvr gng to rch wnr* **14/1**

460- **3** ½ **Viking Spirit**[143] 7227 8-9-4 **85**...... AdamKirby 4 91
(W R Swinburn) *led: sn hdd: chsd clr wnr after: rdn and no imp 2f out: styd on ins fnl f but nvr gng to rch wnr: lost 2nd fnl 50yds* **4/1**[2]

1226 **4** 2 ¾ **Secret Witness**[9] 905 4-8-12 **79**......(b) LiamJones 5 77
(R A Harris) *hld up off the pce in midfield: rdn and effrt wl over 1f out: kpt on but nvr gng pce to rch ldrs* **7/2**[1]

-044 **5** 3 **Step It Up (IRE)**[16] 846 6-8-6 **73**...... NickyMackay 2 61
(J R Boyle) *stdd s: hld up wl bhd in last pair: rdn and sme hdwy over 1f out: no imp fnl f* **14/1**

00/0 **6** 1 **Financial Times (USA)**[9] 905 8-9-1 **82**......(t) MickyFenton 1 67
(Stef Higgins) *hld up wl off the pce towards rr: hdwy on inner ent fnl 2f: no prog over 1f out: wl btn fnl f* **33/1**

500- **7** 2 ¼ **Archie Rice (USA)**[166] 6702 4-8-13 **80**...... LiamKeniry 7 58
(T Keddy) *prom in main gp: rdn wl over 2f out: no prog and wknd 2f out: wl btn fnl f* **10/1**[3]

303 **8** 1 ¾ **Orpsie Boy (IRE)**[9] 905 7-9-4 **85**...... J-PGuillambert 9 57
(N P Littmoden) *racd wl off the pce towards rr: rdn and no rspnse 4f out: nvr on terms* **4/1**[2]

650- **9** 3 **Phantom Whisper**[153] 7026 7-8-8 **75**...... AlanMunro 6 37
(B R Millman) *hld up in last pair: struggling in last and rdn 3f out: wl bhd fnl 2f* **14/1**

1m 10.1s (-1.80) **Going Correction** 0.0s/f (Stan) course record **9** Ran SP% **114.3**
Speed ratings (Par 105): **112,110,110,106,102 101,98,95,91**
toteswingers:1&2:£5.60, 1&3:£5.30, 2&3:£9.40 CSF £57.22 CT £238.72 TOTE £6.60: £1.80, £2.80, £1.50; EX 39.80 Trifecta £258.00 Part won. Pool: £348.73 - 0.65 winning units..
Owner D J P Turner **Bred** D J P Turner **Trained** Upper Lambourn, Berks

FOCUS
Form to treat with caution as there was again a strong wind behind the runners in the straight and Beat The Bell benefited from a shrewd ride from George Baker, becoming the third straight winner on the card to go from the front. The form has been rated at face value.

988 BIG GERRY HEGARTY MEMORIAL H'CAP 5f (P)
3:50 (3:50) (Class 6) (0-65,63) 3-Y-O **£2,047** (£604; £302) **Stalls** High

Form RPR

0653 **1** **Silver Linnet (IRE)**[9] 906 3-8-11 **56**......(b) JerryO'Dwyer 3 67+
(M G Quinlan) *mde all: clr fr over 2f out: rdn and kpt on wl over 1f out: eased towards fin* **10/3**[2]

0-44 **2** 2 ¼ **Papageno**[54] 363 3-9-4 **63**...... JimCrowley 6 64
(J R Jenkins) *chsd ldng pair: rdn to chse clr wnr over 2f out: hrd drvn and kpt on same pce fr over 1f out* **15/2**

160- **3** 1 ¾ **Pherousa**[176] 6418 3-9-3 **62**...... DaneO'Neill 1 60+
(M Blanshard) *in tch towards rr: swtchd rt and effrt 2f out: chsd ldng pair and drvn 1f out: kpt on same pce after* **8/1**

-051 **4** 2 **Ballyvonane (USA)**[18] 831 3-8-7 **52**......(b) LiamKeniry 9 40
(L A Dace) *in tch in midfield: rdn and effrt ent fnl 2f: hrd drvn and no prog over 1f out: wl hld fnl f* **15/8**[1]

3604 **5** 3 **Annia Galeria (IRE)**[18] 831 3-8-7 **52**...... CathyGannon 8 29
(C A Dwyer) *racd in last pair: rdn and struggling 3f out: nvr on terms* **20/1**

5030 **6** ½ **Miss Polly Plum**[14] 870 3-8-1 **49** oh4...... AndreaAtzeni(3) 7 24
(C A Dwyer) *dwlt: a in rr: n.d* **22/1**

0536 **7** 4 **Seek The Cash (USA)**[30] 689 3-9-3 **62**...... FrannyNorton 4 23
(M Quinn) *in tch in midfield: rdn and unable qck over 2f out: bhd wl over 1f out* **10/1**

30-2 **8** 8 **Tulip Explosion**[18] 831 3-8-1 **49**...... MartinLane(3) 5 —
(D Shaw) *chsd wnr tl over 2f out: sn wknd: wl bhd and eased ins fnl f* **5/1**[3]

58.62 secs (-0.18) **Going Correction** 0.0s/f (Stan) **8** Ran SP% **115.6**
Speed ratings (Par 96): **101,97,94,91,86 85,79,66**
toteswingers:1&2:£4.40, 1&3:£5.90, 2&3:£6.50 CSF £28.75 CT £186.55 TOTE £3.90: £1.70, £1.80, £2.50; EX 21.10 Trifecta £174.20 Pool: £456.73 - 1.94 winning units..
Owner Donal Flynn **Bred** L Mulryan **Trained** Newmarket, Suffolk
■ Stewards' Enquiry : Andrea Atzeni caution: used whip without giving filly sufficient time to respond.

FOCUS
Modest form and this was all rather straightforward for Silver Linnet, who became the fourth straight winner on the card to be ridden from the front, no doubt benefiting from, among other things, the wind being behind her in the straight. The runner-up looks the best guide to the form.

989 LINGFIELDPARK.CO.UK H'CAP — 1m 5f (P)
4:25 (4:25) (Class 5) (0-75,70) 4-Y-O+ £2,729 (£806; £403) Stalls Low

Form RPR
410- **1** **Mr Plod**[100] 7767 5-8-7 56 ... MartinDwyer 6 63+
(Andrew Reid) *hld up in midfield: rdn and hdwy over 2f out: chsd ldng pair ent fnl f: r.o wl to ld fnl 50yds* 9/2[2]

024- **2** ½ **Sumani (FR)**[177] 6376 4-9-1 67 ... HayleyTurner 8 73
(S Dow) *led tl 10f out: led again wl over 3f out: rdn ent fnl 2f: kpt on wl u.p tl hdd and no ex fnl 50yds* 6/1[3]

642- **3** nse **Soundbyte**[143] 7222 5-9-1 64 ... FergusSweeney 1 70
(J Gallagher) *chsd ldrs: wnt 2nd and rdn wl over 2f out: unable qck and drvn over 1f out: styd on wl ins fnl f* 9/2[2]

2214 **4** 6 **Resplendent Ace (IRE)**[17] 833 6-9-7 70 ... RobertWinston 7 67
(P Howling) *dropped in bhd after s: hld up in rr: rdn and no real prog 3f out: sme modest hdwy on outer fnl f: nvr trbld ldrs* 10/1

63 **5** 2½ **Prince Charlemagne (IRE)**[16] 842 7-9-6 69 ... GeorgeBaker 2 62
(G L Moore) *hld up in last trio: hdwy over 3f out: chsd ldrs and rdn ent fnl 2f: btn over 1f out: eased whn no ch wl ins fnl f* 2/1[1]

123- **6** 1¾ **Extremely So**[115] 7608 4-8-6 58 ... ChrisCatlin 4 49
(P J McBride) *t.k.h: chsd ldrs tl rdn over 2f out: wknd wl over 1f out: wl btn fnl f* 13/2

032/ **7** 18 **Sensible**[463] 7713 5-8-13 62 ... DarryllHolland 5 26
(H J Collingridge) *chsd ldr tl led 10f out: hdd wl over 3f out: sn struggling: wl bhd fnl 2f: eased ins fnl f* 16/1

2-30 **8** 8 **Alternative Choice (USA)**[23] 771 4-8-4 59 ... AndreaAtzeni(3) 3 11
(N P Littmoden) *dropped in bhd after s: a bhd: lost tch 3f out: eased fr wl over 1f out* 11/1

2m 46.21s (0.21) **Going Correction** 0.0s/f (Stan)
WFA 4 from 5yo+ 3lb 8 Ran SP% **120.6**
Speed ratings (Par 103): **99,98,98,94,93 92,81,76**
toteswingers:1&2:£5.80, 1&3:£5.00, 2&3:£5.10 CSF £33.41 CT £131.37 TOTE £6.70: £1.80, £1.80, £1.90; EX 31.30 Trifecta £201.70 Part won. Pool: £272.65 - 0.20 winning units..
Owner A S Reid **Bred** A S Reid **Trained** Mill Hill, London NW7

FOCUS
A modest handicap run at a muddling sort of gallop. The bias towards front runners noted in the four earlier races at up to 7f was non-existent over this much longer trip. The form has a sound look to it.

990 LINGFIELD PARK SPORTING MEMBERSHIP H'CAP — 1m 2f (P)
5:00 (5:00) (Class 4) (0-85,85) 4-Y-O+ £4,533 (£1,348; £674; £336) Stalls Low

Form RPR
/1-1 **1** **Island Sunset (IRE)**[36] 593 4-9-4 85 ... MartinDwyer 3 92
(W R Muir) *hld up in tch: hdwy to ld wl over 1f out: sn hrd pressed and rdn: kpt on gamely u.p fnl f* 1/1[1]

04-0 **2** nk **Herschel (IRE)**[51] 394 4-8-2 72 ... Louis-PhilippeBeuzelin(3) 1 78
(G L Moore) *trckd ldrs: effrt to chal wl over 1f out: drvn and edgd rt fnl f: nt qckn and a jst hld* 8/1

5453 **3** nk **Confidentiality (IRE)**[8] 921 6-9-3 84 ... (p) NickyMackay 6 89
(M Wigham) *hld up in tch: nt clr run 2f out: sn swtchd rt and rdn: pressed ldrs and drvn ins fnl f: keeping on whn hit on nose by rivals whip fnl 50yds: no imp after* 11/4[2]

5206 **4** 2 **Trafalgar Square**[26] 749 8-8-7 74 ... AlanMunro 5 75
(M J Attwater) *stdd s: hld up in tch in last: rdn and effrt on outer 2f out: kpt on same pce ins fnl f* 25/1

-512 **5** 7 **Officer In Command (USA)**[34] 637 4-9-1 82 ... (p) LiamKeniry 4 69
(J S Moore) *sn chsng ldr: rdn and lost pl jst over 2f out: wknd over 1f out* 4/1[3]

210- **6** 1 **Negotiation (IRE)**[208] 5475 4-9-4 85 ... FrannyNorton 2 70
(M Quinn) *led tl rdn and hdd wl over 1f out: wknd jst over 1f out* 14/1

2m 5.83s (-0.77) **Going Correction** 0.0s/f (Stan) 6 Ran SP% **118.3**
Speed ratings (Par 105): **103,102,102,100,95 94**
toteswingers:1&2:£3.50, 1&3:£2.60, 2&3:£2.50 CSF £11.08 TOTE £2.30: £1.30, £3.10; EX 16.00 Place 6 £35.96, Place 5 £21.99.
Owner Mrs J M Muir **Bred** Rathasker Stud **Trained** Lambourn, Berks

FOCUS
There was a bunch finish and the form is muddling and probably ordinary for the grade. The form is rated through the winner.
T/Plt: £40.90 to a £1 stake. Pool: £64,830.18. 1,154.33 winning tickets. T/Qpdt: £16.30 to a £1 stake. Pool: £4,196.84. 189.76 winning tickets. SP

961 WOLVERHAMPTON (A.W) (L-H)
Friday, March 26

OFFICIAL GOING: Standard
Wind: Almost nil Weather: Fine

991 CE PROPERTY SERVICES GROUP H'CAP — 5f 216y(P)
5:40 (5:40) (Class 6) (0-65,62) 3-Y-O £1,774 (£523; £262) Stalls Low

Form RPR
-226 **1** **Knightfire (IRE)**[21] 809 3-9-3 61 ... (t) ShaneKelly 3 74
(W R Swinburn) *hld up in tch: pushed along to ld 1f out: drew clr ins fnl f: easily* 13/8[1]

-360 **2** 4 **Rathbawn Girl (IRE)**[21] 809 3-8-11 62 ... AdamBeschizza(7) 2 62
(Miss J Feilden) *s.i.s: hld up in rr: hdwy wl over 1f out: sn rdn: r.o u.p to take 2nd wl ins fnl f: no ch w wnr* 9/1

5-46 **3** 4½ **Your Gifted (IRE)**[32] 662 3-9-0 58 ... StephenCraine 4 44
(Patrick Morris) *t.k.h: sn led: hdd 1f out: rdn and wknd ins fnl f* 18/1

05-0 **4** 1 **Bitter Honey**[28] 717 3-8-13 57 ... EddieAhern 1 39
(E J Alston) *prom: rdn and chsd wnr 2f out tl over 1f out: wknd ins fnl f* 13/2[2]

-446 **5** ½ **Blades Harmony**[22] 784 3-9-4 62 ... GrahamGibbons 7 43
(E S McMahon) *prom: rdn over 2f out: wknd over 1f out* 8/1[3]

0-41 **6** shd **Sweet Mirasol (IRE)**[14] 870 3-8-10 54 ... (t) JimmyQuinn 9 34
(Miss M E Rowland) *broke wl: sn stdd: hdwy on outside 3f out: c wd st: wknd over 1f out* 13/2[2]

4440 **7** 1½ **Pavement Games**[18] 831 3-8-4 48 oh3 ... (p) PaulEddery 5 24
(R C Guest) *led early: prom: rdn and wkng whn edgd rt over 1f out* 20/1

000- **8** nk **Silver In The Sand**[184] 6215 3-8-11 55 ... PaulHanagan 6 30
(J D Bethell) *a bhd* 12/1

4416 **9** 1¼ **Rightcar**[26] 745 3-9-0 58 ... NeilCallan 8 29
(Peter Grayson) *hld up in tch: nt clr run fr wl over 1f out tl ins fnl f: n.d after* 10/1

1m 15.07s (0.07) **Going Correction** +0.025s/f (Slow) 9 Ran SP% **112.7**
Speed ratings (Par 96): **100,94,88,87,86 86,84,84,82**
toteswingers:1&2:£4.80, 1&3:£9.10, 2&3:£17.50 CSF £16.45 CT £189.12 TOTE £2.50: £1.20, £3.10, £4.90; EX 19.90.
Owner The Castle Guards **Bred** J Owens **Trained** Aldbury, Herts

FOCUS
A moderate 3-y-o handicap. There was a sound pace on and the form looks straightforward, with improvement from the winner.
Rightcar Official explanation: jockey said colt hung right-handed throughout

992 BETFAIR ALL WEATHER FORUM COMPETITION H'CAP — 5f 20y(P)
6:10 (6:10) (Class 3) (0-95,95) 4-Y-O+ £6,938 (£2,076; £1,038; £519; £258) Stalls Low

Form RPR
414- **1** **Medicean Man**[168] 6645 4-8-6 83 ... JimmyQuinn 4 95+
(J R Gask) *s.i.s: c wd st: str run ins fnl f: hrd rdn and edgd lft towards fin: led last strides* 10/1

531- **2** shd **Gilt Edge Girl**[130] 7414 4-8-13 90 ... LukeMorris 1 102
(C G Cox) *a.p: rdn to ld ins fnl f: hdd last strides* 11/4[1]

00-1 **3** 2¼ **Le Toreador**[34] 639 5-9-4 95 ... (tp) NeilCallan 7 99
(K A Ryan) *wnt lft s: led: rdn and hdd ins fnl f: no ex* 10/3[3]

100- **4** hd **Noverre To Go (IRE)**[182] 6240 4-9-2 93 ... (t) RichardKingscote 5 96+
(Tom Dascombe) *s.i.s: hld up in rr: hdwy on ins over 1f out: one pce ins fnl f* 15/2

460- **5** 1 **Cerito**[121] 7511 4-8-5 82 ... GregFairley 3 82
(J R Boyle) *hld up in tch: pushed along wl over 1f out: rdn and no hdwy fnl f* 22/1

311- **6** ½ **Royal Intruder**[155] 6972 5-8-11 88 ... RichardHughes 2 86
(S Donohoe, Ire) *t.k.h: hdwy over 1f out: wknd wl ins fnl f* 3/1[2]

0-53 **7** nse **Luscivious**[8] 916 6-8-10 87 ... (b) FrederikTylicki 6 85
(J A Glover) *carried sltly lft s: chsd ldr tl wl over 1f out: rdn and wknd ins fnl f* 8/1

61.15 secs (-1.15) **Going Correction** +0.025s/f (Slow) 7 Ran SP% **111.1**
Speed ratings (Par 107): **110,109,106,105,104 103,103**
toteswingers:1&2:£7.20, 1&3:£8.20, 2&3:£2.60 CSF £35.51 TOTE £13.20: £4.50, £2.00; EX 47.60.
Owner Stuart Dobb & Miss Kate Dobb **Bred** Barry Taylor **Trained** Sutton Veny, Wilts

FOCUS
A decent little sprint handicap. It was run at just an average pace and interestingly the majority of runners headed for the centre of the home straight. The first three are generally progressive and this is form to view positively.

NOTEBOOK
Medicean Man was making his AW debut and had yet to run over the minimum trip. Held up early on, he was pulled widest of all off the home bend and began to motor passing the furlong pole. Despite showing a slightly awkward head carriage, he got up for a last-gasp success and has obviously wintered well. Considering he came from behind off an average pace this was a taking success and, a horse with few miles on the clock for his age, he is entitled to improve a deal for the run. (op 8-1)
Gilt Edge Girl was 5lb higher than when winning over C&D on her previous outing 130 days earlier. She made a slightly awkward start, but was soon racing in the box seat and looked all over the winner once sent to the front. She was mugged late on, but it should rate a career-best in defeat and there will be other days for this likeable filly. (op 4-1)
Le Toreador came into this 4lb higher than when scoring at Lingfield last month and had won on his last run over C&D. He had the run of things out in front and gave his all, but the handicapper just looks to have his measure now. (op 3-1 tchd 7-2)
Noverre To Go(IRE), returning from a six-month absence, made a sluggish start and got a very patient ride. He was the only one that kept to the far side in the home straight and shaped as though he would come on plenty for the run. Returning to 6f should also only see him get closer again. (op 17-2 tchd 7-1)
Cerito travelled well and was only found out by his lack of a recent run from the furlong marker. He ought to prove sharper next time and can find less competitive assignments. (tchd 20-1 and 25-1)
Royal Intruder found little once asked for his effort and probably needed the run (op 11-4)
Luscivious dropped out after proving too free for his own good. (tchd 7-1)

993 CLEANEVENT H'CAP (DIV I) — 7f 32y(P)
6:40 (6:40) (Class 6) (0-55,55) 3-Y-O £1,433 (£423; £211) Stalls High

Form RPR
-550 **1** **Belle Park**[26] 745 3-8-4 52 ... AdamBeschizza(7) 7 55
(Karen George) *hld up towards rr: rdn and hdwy over 1f out: r.o to ld cl home* 33/1

-065 **2** ¾ **Moonlight Serenade**[14] 870 3-8-9 53 ... (b[1]) JackDean(3) 9 54
(W G M Turner) *hld up and bhd: c wd st: rdn and hdwy over 1f out: r.o under stands' rail ins fnl f: tk 2nd last strides* 14/1

-525 **3** hd **Novillero**[56] 346 3-8-6 47 ... LukeMorris 10 48
(J C Fox) *hld up in mid-div: hdwy wl over 1f out: sn rdn: kpt on ins fnl f* 7/2[2]

040- **4** shd **Charmaxjoanne**[113] 7616 3-8-2 46 oh1 ... (v[1]) KellyHarrison(3) 5 46
(B M R Haslam) *led early: a.p: rdn to ld jst over 1f out: hdd cl home* 66/1

-350 **5** ½ **Rescent**[15] 861 3-8-5 46 oh1 ... AndrewElliott 6 45
(Mrs R A Carr) *led after 1f: sn hdd: w ldr: ev ch wl over 1f out: rdn and kpt on same pce fnl f* 25/1

000- **6** ½ **Motty's Gift**[121] 7513 3-8-11 52 ... (v[1]) ShaneKelly 3 50
(W R Swinburn) *hld up in mid-div: pushed along 3f out: rdn and hdwy on ins over 1f out: ev ch ins fnl f: no ex towards fin* 6/1

60-0 **7** 1¾ **Pursuit Of Gold**[26] 745 3-8-13 54 ... SteveDrowne 1 47
(J R Best) *prom: stdd and lost pl on ins after 1f: pushed along 3f out: rdn and hdwy jst over 1f out: one pce ins fnl f* 12/1

000- **8** shd **Catawollow**[111] 7638 3-8-5 46 oh1 ... PaulEddery 8 39
(R C Guest) *hld up in tch: rdn and wknd 1f out* 33/1

4142 **9** 1½ **Sandy Toes**[15] 861 3-8-0 46 ... SimonPearce(5) 4 35
(J A Glover) *s.i.s: a in rr* 4/1[3]

00-0 **10** 2½ **Born A Dancer (IRE)**[16] 849 3-9-0 55 ... EddieAhern 2 37
(J W Hills) *prom: led over 5f out: rdn and hdd jst over 1f out: wknd ins fnl f* 8/1

63-3 **11** 7 **Princess Mandy (IRE)**[28] 717 3-8-13 54 ... (p) NeilCallan 11 17
(K A Ryan) *s.i.s: hdwy on outside over 5f out: rdn over 2f out: wknd wl over 1f out: fin lame* 3/1[1]

1m 31.19s (1.59) **Going Correction** +0.025s/f (Slow) 11 Ran SP% **118.2**
Speed ratings (Par 96): **91,90,89,89,89 88,86,86,84,81 73**
toteswingers:1&2:£45.80, 1&3:£29.90, 2&3:£6.90 CSF £426.02 CT £2037.89 TOTE £47.40: £9.70, £4.20, £1.70; EX 164.10.
Owner Eastington Racing Club **Bred** C A Green **Trained** Higher Eastington, Devon

FOCUS
This was a very weak 3-y-o handicap and there were a host of chances inside the final furlong, resulting in a bunch finish. Not a race to view positively.

Princess Mandy(IRE) Official explanation: vet said filly finished lame

994 MIKE SMITH MAGNUS SUPPLIES CLAIMING STKS — 1m 1f 103y(P)

7:10 (7:10) (Class 5) 4-Y-0+ — **£2,729** (£806; £403) **Stalls** Low

Form — RPR

14-5 **1** **King's Masque**[7] [941] 4-8-13 68 .... DavidProbert 1 — 75
(B J Llewellyn) *hld up: squeezed through and hdwy wl over 1f out: rdn ins fnl f: led cl home* **9/2**[3]

0236 **2** ½ **Hypnotic Gaze (IRE)**[28] [715] 4-8-11 67 ....(p) GrahamGibbons 2 — 72
(J Mackie) *chsd ldr: shkn up to ld 1f out: rdn and hdd cl home* **5/2**[2]

P-00 **3** 2½ **Fifty Cents**[15] [867] 6-8-9 70 ....[1] SteveDrowne 5 — 65
(M F Harris) *led: rdn and hdd 1f out: no ex ins fnl f* **25/1**

1126 **4** 6 **Doubnov (FR)**[13] [888] 7-8-11 73 .... EddieAhern 6 — 54
(Ian Williams) *prom: rdn whn bmpd wl over 1f out: sn wknd* **10/11**[1]

6/66 **5** ¾ **Corran Ard (IRE)**[18] [827] 9-8-10 69 .... StevieDonohoe 3 — 52
(Tim Vaughan) *hld up: pushed along 3f out: rdn whn swtchd lft and hdwy over 1f out: wknd fnl f* **20/1**

00-0 **6** 54 **Man Of Gwent (UAE)**[16] [842] 6-8-8 62 ....(p) PaulHanagan 4 — —
(P D Evans) *prom tl wknd over 3f out: sn lost tch: t.o* **28/1**

2m 0.10s (-1.60) **Going Correction** +0.025s/f (Slow) — **6** Ran SP% **111.2**

Speed ratings (Par 103): **108,107,105,100,99 51**

toteswingers:1&2:£1.10, 1&3:£6.90, 2&3:£5.10 CSF £15.55 TOTE £6.90: £2.30, £1.20; EX 19.40.

Owner B J Llewellyn **Bred** Deerfield Farm **Trained** Fochriw, Caerphilly

FOCUS

This poor claimer was run at a fair gallop and the first pair fought it out soon after the furlong marker. The form is best viewed around them.

Fifty Cents Official explanation: jockey said gelding hung right throughout

995 GREAT OFFERS ONLINE AT WOLVERHAMPTON-RACECOURSE.CO.UK H'CAP — 1m 1f 103y(P)

7:40 (7:40) (Class 7) (0-50,50) 4-Y-0+ — **£1,364** (£403; £201) **Stalls** Low

Form — RPR

4-02 **1** **Duneen Dream (USA)**[21] [816] 5-8-11 **46** .... DavidProbert 2 — 54
(Mrs N S Evans) *led early: chsd ldr: rdn wl over 1f out: r.o to ld last stride* **7/2**[1]

003- **2** *nse* **Home**[102] [7751] 5-9-1 **50** ....(vt) AdamKirby 7 — 58
(C Gordon) *sn led: rdn wl over 1f out: hdd last stride* **7/2**[1]

6-50 **3** ¾ **Time To Play**[16] [198] 5-9-1 **50** .... SamHitchcott 6 — 56+
(G Brown) *hld up in mid-div: hdwy on ins wl over 1f out: sn rdn: kpt on ins fnl f* **28/1**

-655 **4** 1 **Noah Jameel**[36] [590] 8-8-13 **48** .... SteveDrowne 1 — 52
(A G Newcombe) *a.p: rdn wl over 1f out: kpt on one pce ins fnl f* **5/1**[2]

-255 **5** *nk* **Stanley Rigby**[16] [854] 4-8-13 **48** .... JackMitchell 11 — 52+
(C F Wall) *hld up in rr: pushed along over 3f out: c wd st: hdwy over 1f out: sn rdn: r.o ins fnl f: nt rch ldrs* **9/1**

4061 **6** 1½ **Naledi**[22] [791] 6-9-1 **50** .... ShaneKelly 12 — 50
(R J Price) *hld up towards rr: kpt on fnl f: n.d* **11/1**

65-0 **7** *shd* **Danish Art (IRE)**[17] [838] 5-8-10 **50** ....(b[1]) JamesSullivan[(5)] 3 — 50
(M W Easterby) *hld up towards rr: hdwy on ins wl over 1f out: no further prog fnl f* **16/1**

0660 **8** 1¾ **James Pollard (IRE)**[7] [939] 5-8-11 **46** ....(t) LukeMorris 10 — 43
(B J Llewellyn) *hld up towards rr: nt clr run wl over 1f out: nvr nr ldrs* **20/1**

6440 **9** 1½ **Kirstys Lad**[7] [940] 8-8-11 **49** .... KellyHarrison[(3)] 4 — 42
(M Mullineaux) *broke wl: racd keenly in tch: rdn over 2f out: wknd over 1f out* **6/1**[3]

4-06 **10** 1 **Jenny's Pride (IRE)**[43] [503] 4-8-12 **47** .... SebSanders 9 — 38
(John A Harris) *hld up in mid-div: hung lft and wknd over 1f out* **12/1**

000- **11** 1¾ **Calypso Girl (IRE)**[200] [5716] 4-8-11 **46** .... StevieDonohoe 13 — 34
(P Leech) *t.k.h in mid-div: wknd 2f out* **33/1**

-060 **12** 8 **Remark (IRE)**[8] [920] 6-8-11 **46** ....(t) GrahamGibbons 8 — 17
(M W Easterby) *prom tl wknd wl over 1f out* **22/1**

2m 2.47s (0.77) **Going Correction** +0.025s/f (Slow) — **12** Ran SP% **122.8**

Speed ratings (Par 97): **97,96,96,95,95 93,93,92,90,89 88,81**

toteswingers:1&2:£3.80, 1&3:£30.80, 2&3:£32.90 CSF £14.81 CT £306.56 TOTE £4.40: £1.70, £2.20, £6.60; EX 23.00.

Owner John Berry (Gwent) **Bred** Wayne G Lyster III Et Al **Trained** Pandy, Monmouths

FOCUS

A bottom-drawer handicap and unsurprisingly wide open. It was a race in which it paid to race handy and being held up was a definite disadvantage. The first two are the best guide to the form.

Jenny's Pride(IRE) Official explanation: jockey said filly hung left in home straight

Remark(IRE) Official explanation: jockey said gelding had a breathing problem

996 CE RISK, SAFETY & SECURITY H'CAP — 1m 5f 194y(P)

8:10 (8:10) (Class 5) (0-75,71) 4-Y-0+ — **£2,729** (£806; £403) **Stalls** Low

Form — RPR

6-04 **1** **Prince Picasso**[51] [395] 7-9-8 **68** ....(b[1]) PaulHanagan 6 — 79
(R A Fahey) *mde virtually all: rdn 2f out: clr 1f out: styd on wl* **8/1**

/414 **2** 5 **Houston Dynimo (IRE)**[16] [852] 5-9-9 **69** .... PhillipMakin 1 — 73+
(N G Richards) *hld up: pushed along over 2f out: hdwy 1f out: styd on to take 2nd wl ins fnl f: no ch w wnr* **9/2**

-113 **3** *nk* **Augustus John (IRE)**[13] [888] 7-9-11 **71** .... TomEaves 5 — 75
(R Brotherton) *hld up in tch: rdn and sltly outpcd 2f out: styd on ins fnl f* **3/1**[2]

004- **4** ½ **First To Call**[106] [7701] 6-9-8 **68** .... SebSanders 4 — 71
(P J Makin) *chsd wnr: chal over 2f out: rdn wl over 1f out: sn btn* **9/4**[1]

602/ **5** 1¾ **Simone Martini (IRE)**[287] [2901] 5-8-10 **56** ....(t) SteveDrowne 3 — 59
(M F Harris) *hld up in tch: rdn and sltly outpcd over 2f out: eased whn btn towards fin* **33/1**

4-61 **6** 1¼ **Paint The Town Red**[35] [621] 5-8-13 **59** .... JackMitchell 2 — 58
(H J Collingridge) *hld up and bhd: short lived effrt over 2f out* **7/2**[3]

3463 **7** 8 **Look Officer (USA)**[22] [786] 4-9-1 **65** .... AdamKirby 7 — 53
(Miss M E Rowland) *a in rr* **18/1**

3m 9.14s (3.14) **Going Correction** +0.025s/f (Slow)

WFA 4 from 5yo+ 4lb — **7** Ran SP% **115.5**

Speed ratings (Par 103): **92,89,88,88,87 86,82**

toteswingers:1&2:£6.20, 1&3:£3.30, 2&3:£2.20 CSF £44.26 TOTE £9.00: £4.70, £2.90; EX 48.30.

Owner Aidan J Ryan **Bred** Cheveley Park Stud Ltd **Trained** Musley Bank, N Yorks

FOCUS

This was an open little staying handicap. The uneven pace dictated it was another race where it was a disadvantage being held up, though. The winner may not have had to improve on his winter form to score.

997 CLEANWASTESOLUTIONS MAIDEN STKS — 5f 216y(P)

8:40 (8:41) (Class 5) 3-Y-0+ — **£2,456** (£725; £362) **Stalls** Low

Form — RPR

0 **1** **Murura (IRE)**[7] [936] 3-9-0 0 .... PaulMulrennan 7 — 77+
(J G Given) *hld up in tch: rdn to ld wl ins fnl f: r.o* **11/2**[2]

4 **2** 1½ **Ryan Style (IRE)**[42] [527] 4-9-13 0 .... TomEaves 9 — 76
(Mrs L Williamson) *led over 2f: led 2f out: rdn jst over 1f out: hdd wl ins fnl f: nt qckn* **13/2**[3]

5 **3** 2½ **Special Quality (USA)**[9] [911] 3-9-0 0 .... GrahamGibbons 3 — 64
(R M H Cowell) *w ldrs: rdn and ev ch over 1f out: no ex ins fnl f* **13/2**[3]

3 **4** ½ **Blue Moon**[10] [894] 3-8-9 0 .... NeilCallan 8 — 57+
(K A Ryan) *s.i.s: hld up and bhd: hdwy over 2f out: rdn over 1f out: one pce* **9/2**[1]

6 **5** 1 **My Meteor**[40] [550] 3-8-11 0 .... JamesMillman[(3)] 5 — 59+
(A G Newcombe) *a.p: nt clr run briefly wl over 1f out: sn btn* **13/2**[3]

6 4½ **True Pleasure (IRE)** 3-8-9 0 .... JimmyQuinn 11 — 40+
(J D Bethell) *s.i.s: outpcd in rr: swtchd lft jst ins fnl f: nrst fin* **25/1**

7 2 **Khateer** 3-9-0 0 .... SebSanders 4 — 38
(E F Vaughan) *w ldr: led over 3f out to 2f out: wknd over 1f out* **9/2**[1]

60- **8** 1 **Otterton**[238] [4503] 3-8-9 0 .... PaulEddery 1 — 30
(R Hollinshead) *mid-div: pushed along over 3f out: wknd over 1f out* **66/1**

0- **9** *nk* **Miracle Wish (IRE)**[300] [2494] 3-8-9 0 .... JimCrowley 13 — 29
(R M Beckett) *hld up in tch: wknd 2f out* **8/1**

55 **10** 2 **Coal Miner (IRE)**[10] [894] 3-9-0 0 .... AndrewElliott 12 — 28
(Mrs R A Carr) *hld up and bhd: short-lived effrt on outside 3f out* **20/1**

0 **11** 3¾ **Higenius**[26] [744] 3-9-0 0 .... VinceSlattery 10 — 16
(D Burchell) *a bhd* **100/1**

12 5 **Haf (IRE)** 3-8-9 0 .... SaleemGolam 2 — —
(Peter Grayson) *s.i.s: a bhd* **80/1**

0 **13** 2½ **Titch (IRE)**[9] [900] 4-9-8 0 .... AdrianMcCarthy 6 — —
(Peter Grayson) *mid-div: pushed along over 3f out: wknd wl over 2f out* **100/1**

1m 15.14s (0.14) **Going Correction** +0.025s/f (Slow)

WFA 3 from 4yo 13lb — **13** Ran SP% **116.2**

Speed ratings (Par 103): **100,98,94,94,92 86,84,82,82,79 74,67,64**

toteswingers:1&2:£8.20, 1&3:£9.00, 2&3:£11.80 CSF £38.17 TOTE £7.90: £2.30, £2.90, £2.10; EX 54.20.

Owner The Living Legend Racing Partnership **Bred** Corrin Stud **Trained** Willoughton, Lincs

FOCUS

A modest maiden, but it was well run. The winner showed big improvement and the second stepped up too.

True Pleasure(IRE) Official explanation: jockey said filly missed the break and ran green

Coal Miner(IRE) Official explanation: jockey said gelding hung both ways

998 CLEANEVENT H'CAP (DIV II) — 7f 32y(P)

9:10 (9:10) (Class 6) (0-55,55) 3-Y-0 — **£1,433** (£423; £211) **Stalls** High

Form — RPR

565- **1** **Destiny's Dancer**[216] [5253] 3-8-1 **47** .... PatrickDonaghy[(5)] 1 — 53+
(B M R Haslam) *prom: nt clr run on ins and lost pl sn after s: hld up towards rr: hdwy wl over 1f out: swtchd rt ent fnl f: rdn to ld last stride* **7/2**[3]

0 **2** *shd* **The Bay Bandit**[29] [698] 3-8-12 **53** .... RichardHughes 9 — 59
(S Donohoe, Ire) *hld up in tch: hrd rdn to ld jst over 1f out: hdd last stride* **9/4**[1]

0-33 **3** 1 **Roybuoy**[26] [745] 3-8-11 **52** ....(b) JimmyQuinn 8 — 55
(H J L Dunlop) *hld up in tch: ev ch jst over 1f out: rdn and nt qckn ins fnl f* **6/1**

000- **4** *hd* **Jigajig**[171] [6555] 3-8-5 **46** oh1 .... PaulHanagan 11 — 48
(K A Ryan) *sn chsng ldr: lost 2nd wl over 1f out: sn rdn and hung lft: hung lft again wl ins fnl f: nt qckn* **20/1**

2623 **5** 1 **Turf Time**[14] [870] 3-9-0 **55** .... FrederikTylicki 5 — 55
(J A Glover) *led: rdn and hdd over 1f out: one pce* **3/1**[2]

6-04 **6** ½ **Lady Hetherington**[22] [788] 3-8-13 **54** .... SamHitchcott 3 — 52
(G Brown) *led early: prom: rdn to ld over 1f out: sn hdd: fdd wl ins fnl f* **11/1**

6340 **7** ½ **Lady Brickhouse**[29] [699] 3-8-5 **49** ow1 .... WilliamCarson[(3)] 6 — 46
(M D Squance) *hld up towards rr: pushed along over 2f out: rdn and effrt over 1f out: nvr trbld ldrs* **25/1**

000- **8** 1¼ **Gulf Punch**[178] [6367] 3-8-5 **46** oh1 .... FrannyNorton 10 — 40
(M F Harris) *hld up in mid-div: pushed along and no hdwy fnl 2f* **16/1**

5-50 **9** 1¼ **Future Regime (IRE)**[30] [689] 3-8-12 **53** .... StephenCraine 2 — 43
(Patrick Morris) *a bhd* **16/1**

00-0 **10** 3½ **Micky's Bird**[9] [909] 3-8-5 **46** oh1 .... PaulEddery 7 — 27
(R C Guest) *a bhd* **100/1**

006- **11** 1½ **Redoubtable Grace**[108] [7674] 3-8-5 **46** oh1 .... AndrewElliott 4 — 23
(Mrs R A Carr) *hmpd sn after s: a in rr* **100/1**

1m 31.03s (1.43) **Going Correction** +0.025s/f (Slow) — **11** Ran SP% **123.0**

Speed ratings (Par 96): **92,91,90,90,89 88,88,86,85,81 79**

toteswingers:1&2:£5.40, 1&3:£4.80, 2&3:£4.30 CSF £12.10 CT £48.08 TOTE £2.50: £1.02, £2.00, £3.70; EX 17.70 Place 6 £503.92, Place 5 £268.56.

Owner Mark James **Bred** Plantation Stud **Trained** Middleham Moor, N Yorks

FOCUS

This second division of the 7f handicap was the stronger of the two. There was a solid pace on and the form should work out, with the fifth setting a pretty sound level.

T/Plt: £506.10 to a £1 stake. Pool: £81,967.73. 118.21 winning tickets. T/Qpdt: £38.30 to a £1 stake. Pool: £10,355.75. 199.60 winning tickets. KH

999 - 1005a (Foreign Racing) - See Raceform Interactive

DONCASTER (L-H)

Saturday, March 27

OFFICIAL GOING: Soft (good to soft in places; 5.4)

Wind: moderate 1/2 against Weather: fine but chilly

1006 WILLIAM HILL SPRING MILE (H'CAP) 1m (S)

2:00 (2:02) (Class 2) 4-Y-0+

£31,155 (£9,330; £4,665; £2,335; £1,165; £585) **Stalls** High

Form RPR

340- **1** **Irish Heartbeat (IRE)**[168] 6678 5-9-8 **89** .... PaulHanagan 19 101+
(R A Fahey) *hld up stands' side: smooth hdwy 1/2-way: trckd ldrs on bit over 2f out: effrt to ld over 1f out: shkn up and hung rt ins fnl f: sn drvn and edgd lft: kpt on towards fin* **4/1**[1]

005- **2** *hd* **Sohcahtoa (IRE)**[101] 7226 4-9-2 **83** .... NeilCallan 10 92
(R Hannon) *in tch stands' side: hdwy 2f out: rdn to chse ldrs over 1f out: swtchd rt and drvn ins fnl f: kpt on wl: 2nd of 13 in gp* **16/1**

404- **3** *¾* **Lucky Dance (BRZ)**[98] 7810 8-9-5 **86** .... RobertHavlin 12 93
(A G Foster) *a.p stands' side: effrt to ld over 2f out: sn rdn and hdd over 1f out: drvn and kpt on ins fnl f: 3rd of 13 in gp* **25/1**

/50- **4** *1* **Ben Chorley**[259] 3873 6-9-7 **88** .... CathyGannon 18 93
(P D Evans) *in tch stands' side: gd hdwy to chse ldrs over 2f out: rdn and ev ch over 1f out: drvn ent fnl f and kpt on same pce: 4th of 13 in gp* **9/1**[3]

322- **5** *¾* **Kiwi Bay**[140] 7287 5-9-6 **87** .... TomEaves 7 90+
(M Dods) *hld up in rr far side: hdwy over 3f out: rdn to ld that gp 2f out: drvn over 1f out: kpt on ins fnl f: 1st of 6 in gp* **10/1**

54-6 **6** *1 ¼* **Tartan Gunna**[16] 863 4-9-10 **91** .... JoeFanning 22 91
(M Johnston) *dwlt and in rr: hdwy wl over 2f out: sn rdn and hung lft over 1f out: kpt on ins fnl f: 5th of 13 in gp* **20/1**

426- **7** *2 ¼* **Laudatory**[173] 6535 4-9-2 **83** .... AdamKirby 13 78
(W R Swinburn) *dwlt and towards rr stands' side: hdwy 1/2-way: swtchd lft and rdn to chse ldrs 2f out: sn drvn and no imp appr fnl f: 6th of 13 in gp* **11/1**

-103 **8** *4 ½* **Audemar (IRE)**[35] 635 4-9-7 **88** .... MartinDwyer 11 73
(E F Vaughan) *in tch stands' side: effrt over 3f out: rdn to chse ldrs over 2f out: sn drvn and kpt on same pce: 7th of 13 in gp* **10/1**

220- **9** *1* **Billy Dane (IRE)**[168] 6675 6-9-8 **89** ....(p) JMurtagh 14 71
(F P Murtagh) *overall ldr stands' side: rdn along over 3f out: hdd over 2f out and grad wknd: 8th of 13 in gp* **18/1**

100- **10** *½* **Marajaa (IRE)**[175] 6480 8-9-8 **89** .... TonyCulhane 21 70
(W J Musson) *nvr bttr than midfield stands' side: 9th of 13 in gp* **40/1**

000- **11** *2 ¼* **Joseph Henry**[168] 6675 8-9-8 **89** .... FrannyNorton 15 65
(D Nicholls) *chsd ldrs stands' side: rdn along wl over 2f out: sn wknd: 10th of 13 in gp* **33/1**

130- **12** *hd* **Mountain Cat (IRE)**[175] 6485 6-9-3 **84** .... RobertWinston 17 59
(G A Swinbank) *chsd ldrs stands' side: rdn along over 3f out: grad wknd: 11th of 13 in gp* **20/1**

000- **13** *1 ¾* **The Osteopath (IRE)**[140] 7294 7-9-9 **90** .... PhillipMakin 3 61
(M Dods) *trckd ldr far side: hdwy 3f out: rdn to ld briefly over 2f out: sn hdd & wknd: 2nd of 6 in gp* **14/1**

101- **14** *9* **Captain Macarry (IRE)**[157] 6944 5-9-8 **89** ....(v) GrahamGibbons 20 40
(J J Quinn) *chsd ldrs stands' side to 1/2-way: sn wknd and bhd fnl 2f: 12th of 13 in gp* **16/1**

040- **15** *3 ¼* **Dhaular Dhar (IRE)**[105] 7294 8-9-9 **90** .... DanielTudhope 2 33
(J S Goldie) *trckd ldrs far side: hdwy 1/2-way: rdn wl over 2f out and sn wknd: 3rd of 6 in gp* **20/1**

050- **16** *2 ¼* **Moynahan (USA)**[134] 7375 5-9-8 **89** .... AlanMunro 6 27
(P F I Cole) *chsd ldng pair far side: rdn along over 3f out: sn wknd and bhd: 4th of 6 in gp* **8/1**[2]

-022 **17** *7* **Benandonner (USA)**[35] 635 7-9-6 **90** .... AndreaAtzeni(3) 1 12
(Mike Murphy) *led far side gp: rdn along over 3f out: hdd over 2f out and sn wknd: 5th of 6 in gp* **12/1**

6-50 **18** *3 ¾* **Alsahil (USA)**[41] 553 4-9-4 **85** .... FrederikTylicki 16 —
(Micky Hammond) *cl up stands' side: rdn along 1/2-way: sn wknd: last of 13 in gp* **50/1**

012- **19** *½* **Conry (IRE)**[144] 7220 4-9-4 **85** .... StephenCraine 4 —
(Patrick Morris) *in tch far side: rdn along over 3f out: sn wknd and bhd: last of 6 in gp* **16/1**

1m 45.43s (6.13) **Going Correction** +0.75s/f (Yiel) **19** Ran SP% **130.4**

Speed ratings (Par 109): **99,98,98,97,96 95,92,88,87,86 84,84,82,73,70 68,61,57,56**

toteswingers:1&2:£22.80, 1&3:£46.60, 2&3:£111.90 CSF £67.49 CT £1519.03 TOTE £5.40: £1.80, £4.90, £4.80, £2.30; EX 204.60 TRIFECTA Not won..

Owner M A Leatham & G H Leatham **Bred** P D Savill **Trained** Musley Bank, N Yorks

■ Stewards' Enquiry : Robert Havlin two-day ban: used whip with excessive frequency (Apr 10,12)

Neil Callan four-day ban: used whip with excessive frequency (Apr 10,12-14)

Adam Kirby one-day ban: careless riding (Apr 14)

FOCUS

After a week of mixed weather the going was described as 'tacky, holding ground'. Another competitive edition of the Spring Mile, and a tight-knit field separated by only 8lb on BHA ratings. It was not quite as classy as the 2009 race, with the top-weight running off 91 compared with 94 a year ago. The field quickly split into two groups, with 13 of them in the main bunch racing centre-to-stands' side, although keeping away from the rail, and the other half dozen isolated up the far side. The larger group held the call, with only fifth-placed Kiwi Bay of the far-side six finishing in the first 12. It appeared to be a case of the near-side group being where the pace was rather than any draw bias.

NOTEBOOK

Irish Heartbeat(IRE), formerly trained in Ireland by David Myerscough, who has handed in his licence, won his maiden over a mile at three but has done most of his racing since as a sprinter and won a valuable handicap over 5f at the Curragh last September. Well supported, he travelled up very strongly in the larger bunch but, after striking the front, did not win as easily as he had promised, instead pricking his ears and idling before rather scrambling home. Value for a greater margin of victory, he saw out the trip well in the ground but obviously has plenty of speed and will not mind dropping back in distance if need be. Newbury's Spring Cup, over this trip, could be next for him. (op 11-2 tchd 6-1 in a place)

Sohcahtoa(IRE) failed to go on after finishing third in the Kentucky Derby Challenge at Kempton a year ago, and even had a run over hurdles in December, but is down to his last winning mark now. He was taken to race with the larger group rather than go with the six on his immediate left down the far side, and that proved the correct decision. Under pressure on the far flank of his group with around 3f to run, he responded and was closing down the winner at the line.

Lucky Dance(BRZ) struck the front over 2f out and kept on well, but had no chance with the winner and was caught for second late on. Fifth in this race a year ago when 6lb higher, he failed to get his head in front in 11 subsequent starts but this was a pleasing effort.

Ben Chorley had not been seen since finishing last in the John Smith's Cup at York last July when trained by David Lanigan. Still with his former owners, he had underfoot conditions to suit and ran well from his high draw, just failing to quicken up inside the last. He has a good record fresh and it remains to be seen if he can build on this. (op 10-1)

Kiwi Bay ◆ had no chance as it turned out from his low draw, but finished a mile clear of the other five who raced down the far side despite having nothing to race with in the last furlong and a half. He progressed last term and has reportedly strengthened up during the winter, and there could be a nice handicap to be won with him this year. (tchd 9-1)

Tartan Gunna was sharper for his recent return on the sand and ran respectably from the highest draw. Ideally he needs slightly further and better ground.

Laudatory ran a fair race on the outside of the main group on this seasonal return and first try on soft. (op 16-1)

Audemar(IRE), having only his third run on turf, was another encountering soft ground for the first time. (op 16-1)

Billy Dane(IRE)'s wins have all come on a quick surface and he faded after showing prominently on this first start since the autumn. (op 16-1)

The Osteopath(IRE) had ground conditions to suit but has never won off a mark this high and could only finish a remote second in the far-side sextet. (op 12-1)

Moynahan(USA) is down to a career-low mark but remains disappointing despite the excuse of a low draw. (op 12-1)

1007 WILLIAMHILL.COM - LIVE CASINO CAMMIDGE TROPHY (LISTED RACE) 6f

2:35 (2:35) (Class 1) 3-Y-0+

£22,708 (£8,608; £4,308; £2,148; £1,076; £540) **Stalls** High

Form RPR

55-4 **1** **Inxile (IRE)**[7] 948 5-9-5 105 .... PaulHanagan 14 111
(D Nicholls) *led after 1f: kpt on wl ins fnl f: gamely* **17/2**

-000 **2** *½* **Prime Defender**[22] 817 6-9-2 105 .... RobertWinston 10 106
(B W Hills) *in rr: hdwy over 2f out: chal 1f out: no ex wl ins fnl f* **12/1**

/1-3 **3** *1* **Fitz Flyer (IRE)**[85] 2 4-9-2 98 .... JMurtagh 13 103
(D H Brown) *in rr: hdwy over 2f out: styd on fnl f* **16/1**

630- **4** *1 ½* **Damien (IRE)**[262] 3747 4-9-2 99 .... MichaelHills 8 98
(B W Hills) *hld up towards rr: hdwy over 2f out: chsng ldrs appr fnl f: kpt on same pce* **5/1**[2]

2-00 **5** *1 ½* **Barney McGrew (IRE)**[22] 822 7-9-2 106 .... PhillipMakin 9 96+
(M Dods) *hld up towards rr: effrt and nt clr run 2f out: styd on fnl f* **16/1**

12-1 **6** *½* **Arthur's Edge**[9] 916 6-9-2 100 .... DavidProbert 4 92
(B Palling) *mid-div: effrt over 2f out: nvr trbld ldrs* **7/1**[3]

024- **7** *½* **Evens And Odds (IRE)**[189] 6091 6-9-2 102 .... WilliamCarson 3 90+
(D Nicholls) *trckd ldrs: effrt over 2f out: kpt on one pce* **11/1**

110- **8** *1 ¾* **Fullandby (IRE)**[126] 7488 8-9-5 99 .... AlanMunro 15 87
(T J Etherington) *s.i.s: sn bhd: kpt on fnl 2f: nvr nr ldrs* **16/1**

00-4 **9** *4 ½* **Redford (IRE)**[14] 883 5-9-2 103 .... NeilCallan 11 70
(K A Ryan) *hld up in rr: hdwy over 2f out: wknd fnl f* **9/2**[1]

/24- **10** *nse* **Swiss Franc**[399] 633 5-9-2 98 .... DaneO'Neill 12 70
(D R C Elsworth) *chsd ldrs: effrt over 2f out: wknd appr fnl f* **25/1**

000- **11** *nk* **Star Rover (IRE)**[168] 6660 3-8-6 102 .... CathyGannon 6 72
(P D Evans) *chsd ldrs: lost pl over 1f out* **66/1**

500- **12** *11* **Pusey Street Lady**[162] 6814 6-8-11 90 .... JoeFanning 1 29
(J Gallagher) *racd wd: led 1f: chsd ldrs: lost pl over 1f out: bhd and eased ins fnl f* **9/1**

040- **13** *1 ½* **Tax Free (IRE)**[174] 6522 8-9-2 112 .... FrannyNorton 5 29
(D Nicholls) *chsd ldrs: lost pl over 1f out: bhd and eased ins fnl f* **7/1**[3]

1m 16.31s (2.71) **Going Correction** +0.75s/f (Yiel)

WFA 3 from 4yo+ 13lb **13** Ran SP% **119.4**

Speed ratings (Par 111): **111,110,109,107,105 104,103,101,95,95 94,80,78**

toteswingers:1&2:£20.50, 1&3:£24.40, 2&3:£40.40 CSF £106.47 TOTE £12.60: £3.80, £4.80, £2.70; EX 131.60 Trifecta £1051.90 Part won. Pool: £1421.49 - 0.45 winning units..

Owner Ian Hewitson **Bred** Denis & Mrs Teresa Bergin **Trained** Sessay, N Yorks

FOCUS

A well-established Listed sprint featuring mostly battle-hardened sprinters. Barry Hills, who had won two of the previous five runnings, was doubly represented and both ran with credit.

NOTEBOOK

Inxile(IRE) handles soft ground but all his wins had been at 5f. He had run well on his return in a similar race over 5f on Polytrack the previous weekend, and showed the benefit with a game all-the way success, despite connections feeling another run might be needed. He looked sure to be beaten when the runner-up ranged alongside but refused to give way. He took a while to pull up, looks one to keep on-side in the short term, and could head for a race at Fontainebleau next week. (op 16-1)

Prime Defender, last year's winner, had not scored since but came here fit from running in Dubai. He travelled well and looked sure to repeat last year's success entering the last furlong but the winner proved far more resolute. He is clearly in good heart and should continue to run his race at a similar level, although his strike-rate is not that good. (op 14-1)

Fitz Flyer(IRE), a lightly raced 4-y-o, was back from a break and ran pretty well. However, his effort flattened out in the final furlong and the impression is that the minimum trip suits ideally. (op 14-1)

Damien(IRE), the stable companion of the runner-up, was a decent juvenile but struggled in a light campaign last season. He was the subject of a gamble on this first start since July, and came to have his chance but had nothing in reserve in the closing stages. (op 11-2 tchd 9-2 and 6-1 in a place)

Barney McGrew(IRE) ◆, who caught an infection in Dubai, had shown his best form on fast ground and sand but stays further than this. He was noted doing his best work late and will be interesting back in handicaps on a sound surface. (op 12-1)

Arthur's Edge improved considerably last autumn and showed he has retained his form by winning a 5f handicap at Southwell off 93 earlier in the month. He chased the leaders throughout and stuck to his task, but could make little impression. (op 17-2 tchd 13-2)

Evens And Odds(IRE), a stablemate of the winner, was runner-up in the Stewards' Cup and fourth in the Ayr Gold Cup last season. He goes well fresh and came to challenge over 1f out before tiring in the closing stages. He should be better for the outing. (op 10-1)

Fullandby(IRE) beat Arthur's Edge a head in a similar race here at the end of last season but was 3lb worse off. He usually goes well first time out but was taken off his feet early before running on past beaten horses. (op 14-1)

Redford(IRE) has gained his wins over 7f and 1m, but was not beaten far in the Ayr Gold Cup last season. However, he was another who was unable to go the early pace and never figured. (op 4-1 tchd 5-1)

Star Rover(IRE) showed early pace before fading.

Tax Free(IRE) was allowed to come home in his own time and should be better for the outing. He is likely to go for the Palace House Stakes, which he won in 2007. (op 13-2 tchd 11-2)

1008 WILLIAM HILL LINCOLN (HERITAGE H'CAP) 1m (S)

3:10 (3:15) (Class 2) 4-Y-O+

£77,887 (£23,325; £11,662; £5,837; £2,912; £1,462) Stalls High

Form	Pos	Dist	Horse	Jockey	RPR
212-	1		**Penitent**[160] 6876 4-9-2 **98** (W J Haggas) *trckd ldrs: smooth hdwy over 2f out and sn cl up: effrt to ld ent fnl f: sn rdn and kpt on strly* **3/1**[1]	JMurtagh 1	115
32-6	2	2 ½	**Prime Exhibit**[14] 887 5-8-6 **91** (R A Fahey) *a.p: hdwy to ld over 2f out: rdn over 1f out: drvn and hdd ent fnl f: kpt on same pce* **12/1**	WilliamCarson(3) 5	102
301-	3	3 ¾	**Mull Of Killough (IRE)**[183] 6249 4-9-0 **96** (J L Spearing) *hld up towards rr: hdwy whn n.m.r and swtchd lft over 2f out: rdn wl over 1f out: styd on strly ins fnl f: tk 3rd nr fin* **11/1**	AdamKirby 10	98
005-	4	nk	**Smokey Oakey (IRE)**[143] 7245 6-9-1 **97** (M H Tompkins) *hld up towards rr: gd hdwy over 3f out: chsd ldrs over 2f out: rdn wl over 1f out: kpt on same pce ent fnl f* **20/1**	JimmyQuinn 14	99
01-4	5	½	**Extraterrestrial**[14] 885 6-8-11 **100** (R A Fahey) *in tch: stdy hdwy 3f out: chsd ldng pair wl over 1f out: rdn and ch appr fnl f: sn drvn and wknd* **18/1**	LeeTopliss(7) 3	101
12-2	6	1	**Mia's Boy**[14] 883 6-9-10 **106** (C A Dwyer) *in tch: hdwy to chse ldng trio 2f out: sn rdn and no imp* **11/1**	EddieAhern 6	104
23-3	7	6	**Albaqaa**[14] 885 5-8-13 **95** (R A Fahey) *dwlt and in rr: hdwy 3f out: rdn along 2f out: kpt on appr fnl f: nvr nr ldrs* **6/1**[2]	PaulHanagan 19	79
03-1	8	½	**Viva Vettori**[41] 553 6-8-10 **92** 5ex (D R C Elsworth) *towards rr: hdwy over 2f out and sn rdn: kpt on appr fnl f: nvr nr ldrs* **16/1**	DaneO'Neill 8	75
615-	9	2	**Harrison George (IRE)**[168] 6675 5-8-10 **95** (R A Fahey) *in tch: rdn along wl over 2f out: sn no hdwy* **16/1**	BarryMcHugh(3) 17	74
530-	10	1 ½	**Ishetoo**[161] 6843 6-8-11 **93** (Ollie Pears) *t.k.h: hld up in rr: hdwy wl over 2f out: shkn up fnl 2f: nvr nr ldrs* **100/1**	FrannyNorton 11	68
000-	11	3 ¼	**Huzzah (IRE)**[166] 6732 5-8-11 **93** (B W Hills) *dwlt: a towards rr* **10/1**[3]	MichaelHills 20	61
05-1	12	nse	**Vitznau (IRE)**[14] 885 6-9-2 **98** 5ex (R Hannon) *a in rr* **25/1**	SteveDrowne 15	66
1460	13	nse	**Reve De Nuit (USA)**[41] 553 4-8-8 **95** (A J McCabe) *in rr and rdn along 1/2-way: nvr a factor* **66/1**	DeclanCannon(5) 12	63
114-	14	½	**Tiger Reigns**[189] 6094 4-8-11 **93** (M Dods) *a towards rr* **12/1**	PhillipMakin 13	59
3600	15	shd	**Full Toss**[7] 946 4-8-12 **94** (P D Evans) *in tch: rdn along 1/2-way: sn wknd* **100/1**	CathyGannon 4	60
311-	16	1	**Collateral Damage (IRE)**[140] 7294 7-9-0 **96** (T D Easterby) *chsd ldrs: rdn along over 3f out: sn wknd* **14/1**	(t) DavidAllan 16	60
40-4	17	19	**Advanced**[28] 740 7-9-4 **105** (K A Ryan) *cl up: rdn along 3f out: sn wknd* **50/1**	AmyRyan(5) 18	25
-500	18	7	**Kaolak (USA)**[10] 903 4-8-11 **93** (J Ryan) *led: rdn along over 3f out: hdd & wknd over 2f out* **50/1**	(v) RobertWinston 2	—
100-	19	2	**Dubai's Touch**[231] 4768 6-9-2 **98** (M Johnston) *swtchd lft at s and sn in tch: rdn along over 3f out and sn wknd* **66/1**	(b) JoeFanning 9	—
600-	20	5	**Lang Shining (IRE)**[189] 6094 6-8-13 **95** (J A Osborne) *in tch: rdn along 1/2-way: sn wknd* **18/1**	MartinDwyer 7	—
640-	21	2	**Mister Hardy**[140] 7294 5-8-10 **92** (R A Fahey) *a in rr: bhd fr 1/2-way* **28/1**	FrederikTylicki 21	—

1m 43.31s (4.01) **Going Correction** +0.75s/f (Yiel) **21** Ran SP% **130.3**

Speed ratings (Par 109): **109,106,102,102,101 100,94,94,92,90 87,87,87,87,87 86,67,60,58,53 51**

toteswingers:1&2:£18.90, 1&3:£11.40, 2&3:£103.00 CSF £37.93 CT £381.01 TOTE £4.50: £1.90, £3.60, £3.00, £4.70; EX 58.60 Trifecta £748.90 Pool: £15,637.37 - 15.45 winning units..

Owner Cheveley Park Stud **Bred** Cheveley Park Stud Ltd **Trained** Newmarket, Suffolk

■ Stewards' Enquiry : Paul Hanagan two-day ban: careless riding (Apr 10,12)

FOCUS

A typically competitive renewal of this traditional turf season opening feature on paper, although the pace did not appear that strong early. However, the time was 2.12secs faster than the consolation race that opened the card, and only three had a chance of winning in the last quarter-mile. The earlier Spring Mile was dominated by horses drawn in double figures that came centre to stands' side, but the first two here were drawn one and five and finished up nearer the far rail.

NOTEBOOK

Penitent ◆, lightly raced and unexposed but 12lb higher than for his latest success, was the subject of a major gamble and duly obliged. Never far away, he tracked the runner-up 2f out before going on entering the last furlong and won with the minimum of fuss. He will go up a fair amount but is clearly up to winning at Listed level at least if going on from this. (op 4-1)

Prime Exhibit, another who is lightly raced, was 9lb above his last winning mark but looked unlucky in running on his return in a 6f Polytrack handicap. He did by far the best of the Fahey quintet and was the only one to give the winner a race in the last 2f. He looks capable of winning a decent handicap on slightly better ground.

Mull Of Killough(IRE), yet another who had been lightly raced, acts well on fast ground and had never tackled soft. On his first run since September, he was held up before running on late and could prove a standard bearer for his yard this year. (op 10-1 tchd 12-1)

Smokey Oakey(IRE), winner of this race in 2008 and a Group 3 winner after, had struggled since as a result of which he had dropped back to just 2lb above his winning mark of two years ago. Well suited by soft ground, he ran on from off the pace, making up two places inside the last furlong to reach the frame. He might be able to win again off this sort of mark, given a soft surface. (op 18-1 tchd 16-1)

Extraterrestrial, a stable companion of the runner-up racing over his optimum trip, having been runner-up in the Spring Mile in 2009, had run well in the Lincoln Trial at Wolverhampton and the ground was no problem. He came to have every chance 2f out but then shifted left and tired in the closing stages, being run out of the places near the finish. (op 20-1)

Mia's Boy, fourth last year on fast going, had finished runner-up in a Listed race on his recent return. He had a good course record here - two wins and not out of the first five in three other starts - but was racing off his highest-ever mark. He tracked the pace throughout but was another who was treading water from well over 1f out. (op 14-1)

Albaqaa, a close third in the Lincoln trial, did not help his chance by dwelling in the stalls and did well to run on and reach his final position. He can be given another chance. (op 10-1)

Viva Vettori, a three-time winner on Polytrack, including a Listed race last time, had been placed on his only run on soft. He never got competitive despite running on and the impression is that he is a more effective tool on synthetics.

Harrison George(IRE), a course winner who had been successful at 6f and 7f but who was trying this trip for the first time, was 5lb above his last winning mark. He ran his race on his first start since October without convincing that he lasted the longer distance. (op 14-1)

Ishetoo, a useful sprinter who had looked best at 5f on fast ground, was another stepping up to this trip on his first run for Ollie Pears. He was never in contention but had more behind than in front of him.

Huzzah(IRE), a big-handicap regular and fifth in this in 2009, goes well fresh, having won on his seasonal debut in 2008, and had dropped back to his last winning mark. However, he spoilt his chance by rearing in the stalls and missing the break. Official explanation: jockey said gelding missed the break (tchd 11-1)

Vitznau(IRE), who won Wolverhampton's Lincoln trial in cosy fashion with Albaqaa and Extraterrestrial behind, was 5lb worse off with that pair but never reached a challenging position, having been held up at the back. He has still to convince he stays this far in a truly-run race on turf. (op 20-1)

Reve De Nuit(USA), ex-French and a winner over 1m on his British debut on Fibresand, had the blinkers he wore last time left off. He was being ridden along before halfway and lost his place, so he was last of all 3f out before staying on again. Headgear is likely to be back on next time and a step up in trip might be worth trying. (op 80-1)

Tiger Reigns, progressive last year when he won five times and his rating rose from 68 to 93, scored first time out in 2009 but this time around failed to pick up under pressure.

Collateral Damage(IRE) had won six of his last seven starts and beat Mia's Boy over 7f here in November. However, he made little impression on this first outing since. (tchd 12-1 and 16-1)

Mister Hardy, a 6f and 7f winner who acts on soft ground, was back to his last winning mark but trying a new trip on his first run since November. However, he was under pressure a long way out, before the longer distance became an issue. (tchd 33-1)

1009 WILLIAMHILL.COM - PLAY POKER BROCKLESBY CONDITIONS STKS 5f

3:40 (3:48) (Class 4) 2-Y-O

£12,952 (£3,854; £1,926; £962) Stalls High

Form	Pos	Dist	Horse	Jockey	RPR
	1		**Chiswick Bey (IRE)** 2-8-11 0 (R A Fahey) *chsd ldrs: edgd lft and led over 1f out: edgd rt ins fnl f: hld on towards fin* **6/1**[2]	PaulHanagan 10	84+
	2	hd	**Lady Brookie** 2-8-3 0 (W G M Turner) *led: hdd over 1f out: rallied ins fnl f: no ex nr fin* **16/1**	JackDean(3) 2	78
	3	3 ¼	**Squires Gate (IRE)** 2-8-11 0 (B W Hills) *racd stands' side: trckd ldrs: edgd lft 2f out: chal 1f out: one pce whn hmpd ins fnl f* **11/2**[1]	MichaelHills 16	72+
	4	nk	**Diamond Geezah (IRE)** 2-8-11 0 (B W Hills) *in rr: hdwy 2f out: kpt on wl fnl f: will improve* **11/2**[1]	RobertWinston 9	71+
	5	3 ½	**Little Libretto (IRE)** 2-8-6 0 (P D Evans) *chsd ldrs: wknd 1f out* **66/1**	CathyGannon 1	53
	6	nse	**Saucy Buck (IRE)** 2-8-11 0 (M R Channon) *s.i.s: hdwy over 2f out: kpt on fnl f* **18/1**	TonyCulhane 8	58
	7	nse	**Mayhab** 2-8-11 0 (C E Brittain) *chsd ldrs stands' side: kpt on same pce over 1f out* **6/1**[2]	NeilCallan 15	58+
	8	1 ¾	**Sky Diamond (IRE)** 2-8-11 0 (J G Given) *uns rdr and rn loose in paddock: prom: swtchd lft after 1f: wknd over 1f out* **25/1**	PaulMulrennan 7	51
	9	hd	**Sir Lunchalott** 2-8-11 0 (J S Moore) *in rr: sme hdwy over 1f out: nvr nr ldrs* **40/1**	StevieDonohoe 4	51
	10	1 ¾	**Mirror Lad** 2-8-11 0 (Tom Dascombe) *led stands' side: wknd over 1f out* **11/2**[1]	RichardKingscote 13	44
	11	nk	**The Best Mode (IRE)** 2-8-11 0 (P D Evans) *sn chsng ldrs: wknd over 1f out* **16/1**	EddieAhern 3	43
	12	1	**Majestic Style (IRE)** 2-8-6 0 (A P Jarvis) *chsd ldrs: lost pl over 1f out* **33/1**	AlanMunro 6	35
	13	1	**Las Verglas Star (IRE)** 2-8-4 0 (R A Fahey) *s.i.s: hdwy stands' side to chse ldrs over 2f out: edgd lft and lost pl over 1f out* **25/1**	LeeTopliss(7) 11	36
	14	2 ½	**Diplomasi** 2-8-11 0 (C E Brittain) *in rr and sn drvn along* **11/1**[3]	SebSanders 5	27

64.35 secs (3.85) **Going Correction** +0.75s/f (Yiel) **14** Ran SP% **114.7**

Speed ratings (Par 94): **99,98,93,93,87 87,87,84,84,81 80,79,77,73**

toteswingers:1&2:£13.40, 1&3:£2.90, 2&3:£10.80 CSF £87.86 TOTE £6.50: £2.50, £3.60, £2.10; EX 82.40 Trifecta £252.50 Part won. Pool: £341.25 - 0.90 winning units..

Owner Mrs H Steel **Bred** Mrs Kay Egan **Trained** Musley Bank, N Yorks

FOCUS

An open Brocklesby, but the field was reduced by two after a couple became upset in the stalls. Last year's race was won by subsequent Group 1 winner Hearts Of Fire from the useful pair Archers Road and Swilly Ferry, and although this edition may not turn out to be as classy there should still be plenty of winners coming out of it in the next few weeks. A group of four raced down the stands' side initially with the remainder down the centre, but the two groups converged not much after halfway.

NOTEBOOK

Chiswick Bey(IRE)'s trainer won this three years ago with Mister Hardy. Out of a an unraced half-sister to last year's Group 2-placed French juvenile Ascot Glory, he was much the most expensive of these sold at public auction, costing £90,000 as a yearling (the second time he went through the ring). He came with a steady run to lead, appearing to be hanging left at the same time, then edged right under pressure before his rider pulled his stick through and he held off the runner-up. He looks a decent juvenile, but it remains to be seen how much improvement there is to come from him. (op 11-2)

Lady Brookie's trainer Bill Turner often targets this race and has won it four times all told. The filly broke well and tacked over from her low draw to race prominently. She could not hold off the winner, but ran all the way to the line to go down fighting and looks certain to go one better in the near future. (op 20-1)

Squires Gate(IRE), from the stable of the aforementioned Swilly Ferry, did best of the quartet to race up the rail. He travelled up smoothly but could not put his head in front and was just held when he was squeezed out entering the final furlong. His stamina failed him ultimately in this tacky ground, but he looks another who will have no problem winning. (op 7-2 tchd 6-1)

Diamond Geezah(IRE) ◆ had to be switched before running on very nicely under hands and heels. He looks sure to win a race or two and another furlong will not be a problem. (op 15-2)

Little Libretto(IRE), the longer priced of the David Evans pair, showed plenty of pace before fading in the final furlong. (op 80-1)

Saucy Buck(IRE), sold for £24,000 as a yearling, was slowly away but kept on as he got the hang of things. (op 20-1 tchd 16-1)

Mayhab is bred for speed, being a half-brother to useful sprinter Dazed And Amazed out of a sister to high-class sprinter Bishops Court. He made late progress near the stands' rail and should improve for the run. (op 7-1 tchd 15-2)

Sky Diamond(IRE), a 20,000 euro yearling, got loose in the paddock. He showed a bit of pace but may need more time. (op 33-1)

Sir Lunchalott was a cheap buy, but he came home quite well after looking green through the early parts. (op 100-1)

Mirror Lad, whose trainer had a 2-y-o runner at the Curragh last weekend, is a half-brother to winners at 1m to 1m4f. He showed pace against the stands' rail before fading. The runners either side of him in the stalls were withdrawn after playing up, which might have affected him. (op 7-1 tchd 5-1)

Las Verglas Star(IRE), a stablemate of the winner, did not get home after chasing the pace. (op 20-1 tchd 18-1)

1010 BOB BEEVERS MEMORIAL MAIDEN STKS 1m 2f 60y
4:15 (4:18) (Class 5) 3-Y-O £4,533 (£1,348; £674; £336) Stalls Low

Form RPR

0- 1 **Senate**[126] 7491 3-9-3 0 RobertHavlin 12 86+
(J H M Gosden) *hld up in tch: hdwy 1/2-way: swtchd rt and effrt to chse ldrs 3f out: rdn to ld 1 1/2f out: sn clr: eased towards fin* 5/1[3]

2 2 ½ **Goodlukin Lucy** 3-8-9 0 MartinLane(3) 5 73+
(Pat Eddery) *hld up towards rr: hdwy over 4f out: rdn to chse ldrs 2f out: kpt on u.p ins fnl f* 40/1

03 3 4 **Corres (IRE)**[36] 618 3-9-3 0 EddieAhern 3 70+
(D R C Elsworth) *trckd ldrs: hdwy 4f out: rdn to chse ldng pair over 2f out: drvn over 1f out and sn no imp* 7/2[2]

30- 4 2 ¼ **Chain Of Events**[198] 5793 3-9-3 0 MichaelHills 2 66
(B W Hills) *trckd ldrs: hdwy 4f out: led over 2f out: rdn and hdd 1 1/2f out: sn drvn: edgd rt and wknd ins fnl f* 11/8[1]

6-50 5 3 **Penderyn**[46] 475 3-8-7 40 PaulPickard(5) 11 55?
(C Smith) *led and sn clr: rdn along over 3f out: hdd over 2f out and grad wknd* 100/1

6 2 ¾ **Thingathong (FR)** 3-8-12 0 RichardKingscote 7 50
(Tom Dascombe) *s.i.s and in rr: hdwy over 3f out: sn rdn: nvr rchd ldrs* 13/2

7 6 **Rumballina** 3-8-12 0 JerryO'Dwyer 6 38
(Miss Amy Weaver) *midfield: rdn along 4f out: sn btn* 20/1

8 1 ¼ **Enchanting Smile (FR)** 3-8-12 0 ShaneKelly 9 36
(A J McCabe) *a in rr* 50/1

0- 9 3 **Sharakti (IRE)**[189] 6125 3-8-12 0 DeclanCannon(5) 8 35
(A J McCabe) *a towards rr* 100/1

10 ¾ **Three White Socks (IRE)** 3-9-3 0 TomEaves 10 34
(B Ellison) *a in rr* 18/1

2- 11 15 **Inlovingmemory (IRE)**[299] 2541 3-8-12 0 ow5 RichardEvans(5) 1 —
(M A Barnes) *chsd clr ldr: rdn along over 4f out: sn wknd and bhd fnl 2f* 33/1

4- 12 24 **Golden Gates (IRE)**[173] 6533 3-9-3 0 TonyCulhane 4 —
(Mrs A Duffield) *chsd ldrs: rdn along 1/2-way: sn wknd and bhd fnl 3f* 14/1

2m 18.04s (8.64) **Going Correction** +0.625s/f (Yiel) 12 Ran SP% 120.3
Speed ratings (Par 98): **97,95,91,90,87 85,80,79,77,76 64,45**
toteswingers:1&2:£36.00, 1&3:£5.40, 2&3:£29.10 CSF £200.37 TOTE £6.30: £2.20, £7.00, £1.70; EX 258.80 TRIFECTA Not won..
Owner H R H Princess Haya Of Jordan **Bred** Watership Down Stud **Trained** Newmarket, Suffolk
■ Stewards' Enquiry : Eddie Ahern one-day ban: careless riding (Apr 10)

FOCUS
Little strength in depth to this maiden. The fifth home set a fair pace and was soon clear but was largely ignored by the remainder.
Penderyn Official explanation: jockey said filly was unsuited by the soft (good to soft places) ground
Golden Gates(IRE) Official explanation: jockey said gelding had a breathing problem

1011 WILLIAMHILL.COM - PLAY BINGO H'CAP (DIV I) 1m 2f 60y
4:50 (4:50) (Class 4) (0-85,85) 4-Y-O+ £6,152 (£1,830; £914; £456) Stalls Low

Form RPR

363- 1 **Red Jade**[169] 6648 5-9-0 81 PaulHanagan 3 95
(R A Fahey) *trckd ldr: shkn up to ld over 1f out: styd on strly: readily* 7/2[1]

00-4 2 1 ¾ **Hollow Green (IRE)**[23] 785 4-8-8 75 CathyGannon 2 85
(P D Evans) *s.i.s: hdwy over 2f out: wnt 2nd 1f out: kpt on wl: no imp* 9/1

026- 3 1 ¼ **Aspro Mavro (IRE)**[140] 7287 4-8-11 78 RobertHavlin 1 86
(J H M Gosden) *led: hdd over 1f out: kpt on same pce* 7/2[1]

006- 4 7 **Charlie Cool**[119] 7583 7-8-13 80 (b) RobertWinston 7 74
(Mrs R A Carr) *hld up in rr: hdwy to chse ldrs 3f out: wknd fnl f* 16/1

-062 5 6 **Buddy Holly**[24] 765 5-8-5 75 MartinLane(3) 9 57
(Pat Eddery) *prom: effrt and swtchd rt over 3f out: one pce* 6/1[2]

-436 6 2 ½ **Kidlat**[7] 943 5-8-6 73 JoeFanning 5 50
(A Bailey) *sn chsng ldrs: hung lft over 2f out: wknd over 1f out* 12/1

025- 7 9 **Best Prospect (IRE)**[213] 5334 8-8-12 79 (t) PhillipMakin 6 38
(M Dods) *hld up towards rr: nt clr run over 3f out: lost pl 2f out* 14/1

/32- 8 7 **Spirit Of A Nation (IRE)**[191] 6014 5-9-4 85 FrederikTylicki 11 30
(D H Brown) *in rr: sme hdwy whn hmpd over 2f out: lost pl over 1f out* 13/2[3]

9 6 **Spahi (FR)**[94] 4-8-1 73 JamesSullivan(5) 4 6
(J Hetherton) *sn chsng ldrs: lost pl over 2f out* 80/1

06- 10 2 ½ **Opera Prince**[159] 6907 5-8-10 77 SebSanders 10 5
(Lady Herries) *in rr: hdwy into midfield 7f out: wknd and eased wl over 1f out* 15/2

646- 11 2 ¼ **Red Kestrel (USA)**[182] 6281 5-8-13 80 NeilCallan 8 3
(K A Ryan) *swtchd lft after s: in rr: hdwy into midfield 9f out: chsng ldrs and effrt over 2f out: sn wknd and eased* 16/1

2m 14.78s (5.38) **Going Correction** +0.625s/f (Yiel) 11 Ran SP% 121.2
Speed ratings (Par 105): **110,108,107,102,97 95,88,82,77,75 73**
toteswingers:1&2:£8.50, 1&3:£5.70, 2&3:£12.80 CSF £37.53 CT £121.35 TOTE £3.60: £1.90, £3.50, £1.50; EX 47.50 Trifecta £194.20 Pool: £315.00 - 1.20 winning units..
Owner Keep Racing **Bred** Darley **Trained** Musley Bank, N Yorks
■ Stewards' Enquiry : Martin Lane one-day ban: careless riding (Apr 10)

FOCUS
Formerly a race for 3-y-os, this handicap was first run as a contest for older horses in 2007. The division of the race meant that the field was smaller than had previously been the case but the time was 3.24secs faster than the preceding maiden.
Opera Prince Official explanation: jockey said gelding had no more to give

1012 UNIVERSALRECYCLINGCOMPANY.CO.UK APPRENTICE H'CAP 1m 4f
5:20 (5:20) (Class 5) (0-70,70) 4-Y-O+ £3,412 (£1,007; £504) Stalls Low

Form RPR

544- 1 **Leslingtaylor (IRE)**[105] 5698 8-9-4 70 IanBrennan(3) 10 80
(J J Quinn) *trckd ldrs: effrt over 2f out: rdn to chal over 1f out: drvn and styd on to ld ins fnl f: edge lft and kpt on* 15/2[3]

460- 2 1 ¼ **Royal Straight**[409] 500 5-8-3 57 ow1 LeeTopliss(5) 2 65+
(R A Fahey) *hld up: hdwy 4f out: trckd ldrs 3f out: chal over 2f out: rdn to ld wl over 1f out: drvn and edgd rt ent fnl f: sn hdd and kpt on same pce* 6/1[2]

002- 3 ¾ **Agglestone Rock**[136] 7084 5-9-3 66 DeanHeslop 12 73
(P A Kirby) *chsd ldr: hdwy to ld over 3f out: rdn wl over 2f out: hdd wl over 1f out: kpt on u.p ins fnl f* 12/1

-212 4 1 ½ **Amical Risks (FR)**[15] 875 6-8-7 56 oh3 PatrickDonaghy 14 61
(Joss Saville) *hld up in rr: stdy hdwy over 3f out: rdn along 2f out: styd on appr fnl f: nrst fin* 18/1

112- 5 ¾ **Ghufa (IRE)**[86] 7888 6-8-1 57 SophieSilvester(7) 3 61
(J Pearce) *bmpd s and in rr tl gd hdwy on inner over 4f out: chsd ldrs over 2f out: kpt on same pce* 14/1

00-5 6 6 **Holiday Cocktail**[40] 565 8-8-9 65 ShaneBKelly(7) 1 60
(J J Quinn) *hld up in midfield: hdwy 4f out: rdn along 3f out: no imp fnl 2f* 28/1

3022 7 1 ½ **Red Wine**[36] 622 11-8-3 59 JonathanHinch(7) 18 51
(J A Glover) *rrd s and towards rr: wd st: hdwy 4f out: rdn along 3f out: plugged on same pce fnl 2f* 9/2[1]

654- 8 shd **Astrolibra**[106] 7712 6-8-8 57 AshleyMorgan 7 49
(M H Tompkins) *in tch: hdwy 4f out: rdn along 3f out and sn btn* 20/1

35-0 9 2 ½ **Dispol Diva**[11] 897 4-8-7 58 (v) PaulPickard 8 46
(P T Midgley) *chsd ldrs: rdn along over 3f out and sn wknd* 25/1

1140 10 1 **Slick Mover (IRE)**[24] 770 5-9-0 63 RossAtkinson 6 50
(B G Powell) *trckd ldrs: hdwy to chse ldng pair 1/2-way: rdn along over 3f out: hung rt and wknd over 2f out* 25/1

060- 11 2 ¼ **Polish Power (GER)**[175] 6498 10-9-1 64 SimonPearce 16 47
(P G Murphy) *a towards rr* 16/1

051- 12 2 ¼ **Oddsmaker (IRE)**[126] 7118 9-9-6 69 (t) RichardEvans 15 49
(M A Barnes) *led and sn clr: rdn along 4f out: hdd over 3f out and grad wknd* 25/1

0/1- 13 4 ½ **Warne's Way (IRE)**[15] 7036 7-9-5 68 MatthewDavies 4 41
(B G Powell) *a in rr* 8/1

1-30 14 1 ¼ **Starburst**[43] 529 5-8-8 64 HobieGill(7) 13 35
(A M Balding) *towards rr: hdwy on wd outside 5f out: rdn along over 3f out and sn wknd* 16/1

00- 15 ½ **Comrade Cotton**[290] 2824 6-8-6 58 RosieJessop(3) 9 29
(J Ryan) *a towards rr* 20/1

20-6 16 1 **Sparkaway**[15] 875 4-8-4 58 TobyAtkinson(3) 17 27
(W J Musson) *s.i.s: a bhd* 17/2

0442 17 28 **Heathyards Junior**[10] 910 4-9-5 70 DeclanCannon 5 —
(A J McCabe) *in tch: rdn along over 4f out and sn wknd* 11/1

2m 43.21s (8.31) **Going Correction** +0.625s/f (Yiel)
WFA 4 from 5yo+ 2lb 17 Ran SP% 130.1
Speed ratings (Par 103): **97,96,95,94,94 90,89,89,87,86 85,83,80,79,79 78,60**
toteswingers:1&2:£15.00, 1&3:£24.90, 2&3:£28.20 CSF £49.73 CT £561.16 TOTE £10.50: £2.70, £1.90, £3.20, £4.80; EX 81.30 Trifecta £203.20 Part won. Pool: £274.69 - 0.10 winning units..
Owner Mrs Marie Taylor **Bred** Mrs Peggy Kelly **Trained** Settrington, N Yorks

FOCUS
A moderate apprentice handicap which was not run at a particularly strong pace.
Red Wine Official explanation: trainer's rep had no explanation for the poor form shown
Sparkaway Official explanation: jockey said gelding was slow away
Heathyards Junior Official explanation: jockey said gelding was unsuited by the soft (good to soft places) ground

1013 WILLIAMHILL.COM - PLAY BINGO H'CAP (DIV II) 1m 2f 60y
5:55 (5:56) (Class 4) (0-85,82) 4-Y-O+ £6,152 (£1,830; £914; £456) Stalls Low

Form RPR

004- 1 **Rosbay (IRE)**[67] 6648 6-8-10 74 DuranFentiman 5 82
(T D Easterby) *s.i.s: hdwy on ins over 2f out: led jst ins fnl f: styd on* 9/1

430- 2 1 ¼ **Embsay Crag**[155] 6996 4-9-2 80 (p) PaulMulrennan 6 86
(Mrs K Walton) *hld up towards rr: swtchd rt over 3f out: styd on fnl 2f: tk 2nd nr fin* 12/1

34-5 3 ¾ **Veiled Applause**[16] 857 7-8-7 78 IanBrennan(7) 8 83
(J J Quinn) *hld up in rr: hdwy 7f out: swtchd lft over 3f out: led over 2f out: hdd jst ins fnl f: no ex* 6/1[3]

1- 4 1 ¼ **Abayaan**[100] 7780 4-9-2 80 ShaneKelly 2 82
(Jane Chapple-Hyam) *mid-div: dropped in rr after 3f: hdwy on ins to chse ldrs whn hmpd over 3f out: styd on same pce appr fnl f* 7/2[2]

333- 5 2 ½ **Andhaar**[114] 7620 4-8-13 77 DavidProbert 3 74
(S Gollings) *trckd ldrs: chal over 2f out: one pce appr fnl f* 10/1

412- 6 3 ¼ **Starla Dancer (GER)**[154] 7014 4-9-1 79 PaulHanagan 4 70+
(R A Fahey) *in tch: effrt over 3f out: fdd appr fnl f* 3/1[1]

6-34 7 ¾ **Hallstatt (IRE)**[15] 871 4-8-9 73 GrahamGibbons 11 63
(J Mackie) *sn chsng ldrs: wknd over 1f out* 12/1

3111 8 ¾ **Trans Sonic**[18] 837 7-8-13 82 JamesSullivan(5) 9 70
(J Hetherton) *led 1f: chsd ldr: led over 3f out: hdd over 1f out: sn wknd* 8/1

200- 9 21 **Wind Shuffle (GER)**[37] 4102 7-8-13 77 DanielTudhope 7 26
(J S Goldie) *in rr: hdwy and prom 4f out: wknd 2f out: eased whn bhd ins fnl f* 18/1

31-0 10 3 ½ **Amazing Blue Sky**[16] 857 4-8-11 75 AndrewMullen 10 17
(Mrs R A Carr) *drvn to chse ldr: led after 1f: hdd over 3f out: wknd over 2f out: eased whn bhd ins fnl f* 20/1

2m 15.96s (6.56) **Going Correction** +0.625s/f (Yiel) 10 Ran SP% 117.1
Speed ratings (Par 105): **105,104,103,102,100 97,97,96,79,77**
toteswingers:1&2:£20.10, 1&3:£12.60, 2&3:£10.70 CSF £111.73 CT £704.45 TOTE £12.20: £2.80, £3.40, £2.40; EX 138.80 Trifecta £137.80 Part won. Pool: £186.32 - 0.10 winning units.
Place 6 £493.08, Place 5 £152.48.
Owner Croft, Taylor & Hebdon Partnership **Bred** Alan Dargan **Trained** Great Habton, N Yorks
■ Stewards' Enquiry : Ian Brennan one-day ban: careless riding (tbn)

FOCUS
The second division of this handicap was run 1.18secs slower than the first leg. They might have gone too fast early as they seemed to go a good gallop from the off, and the first four were the last four turning into the straight.
T/Jkpt: Not won. T/Plt: £2,177.00 to a £1 stake. Pool: £165,009.16. 55.33 winning tickets.
T/Qpdt: £24.20 to a £1 stake. Pool: £10,735.13. 326.95 winning tickets. JR

977 KEMPTON (A.W) (R-H)
Saturday, March 27

OFFICIAL GOING: Standard
Wind: virtually nil Weather: overcast with showers

1014 WILLIAMHILL.COM - POKER CONDITIONS STKS 6f (P)
2:20 (2:20) (Class 3) 3-Y-O+ £6,542 (£1,959; £979; £490; £244) Stalls High

Form RPR

640 1 **Prohibit**[37] 604 5-9-4 99 PatCosgrave 5 107
(R M H Cowell) *trckd ldrs: swtchd rt at cutaway over jst 2f out: shkn up to ld over 1f out: r.o wl* 6/1[3]

255- **2** ½ **Elnawin**[316] 2035 4-9-4 105 RichardHughes 2 106
(R Hannon) *racd keenly: led: rdn and hdd over 1f out: kpt on ins fnl f* **9/4**[2]

1141 **3** 4 **Tiddliwinks**[14] 887 4-9-4 103 JimmyFortune 3 93
(K A Ryan) *racd in cl 4th: rdn whn sltly outpcd over 2f out: sn hung lft: r.o ins fnl f but nvr a threat to ldng pair* **11/10**[1]

224- **4** 1¼ **Son Of The Cat (USA)**[126] 7488 4-9-4 93 (t) JimCrowley 4 89
(B Gubby) *trckd ldrs: effrt over 2f out: kpt on same pce* **6/1**[3]

-006 **5** 19 **Wavertree Princess (IRE)**[17] 848 5-8-13 45 HayleyTurner 1 23
(A J Lidderdale) *racd in cl 5th tl outpcd over 2f out* **125/1**

1m 11.57s (-1.53) **Going Correction** -0.075s/f (Stan) **5** Ran SP% **107.8**
Speed ratings (Par 107): **107,106,101,99,74**
CSF £18.90 TOTE £9.00: £2.80, £1.60; EX 27.70.
Owner Dasmal,Rix,Barr,Morley,Penney **Bred** Juddmonte Farms Ltd **Trained** Six Mile Bottom, Cambs

FOCUS
An interesting little conditions sprint and basically a four-horse race. The form is rated around the winner and the second to last year's form.

NOTEBOOK
Prohibit had been winless since scoring at Great Leighs in October 2008 when with John Gosden and didn't enjoy much luck in three outings at Meydan this year for his current yard. However, he attracted market support on this return to these shores and the betting was proved right. He threatened to pull too hard early, but then settled when getting a lead from the runner-up and travelled much better thereafter. Produced on the inside after the intersection, he found plenty under pressure and this was a good effort as he had a bit to find with a couple of these at the weights. (op 8-1 tchd 11-2)
Elnawin, best in at the weights and winner of the Group 3 Sirenia Stakes over C&D as a 2-y-o, hadn't been seen since last May. Soon in front, he took quite a grip and though he battled back gamely after the winner headed him a furlong out, his earlier exertions can't have helped. This should have taken the freshness out of him and the outing can only bring him on. Official explanation: jockey said colt hung left throughout (op 2-1 tchd 15-8)
Tiddliwinks, winner of three of his last four starts, came into this 3-3 over this distance including two wins over C&D, but having been held up he didn't find as much as had looked likely under pressure and appeared to hang. He was 2-2 at this venue coming into this, so the track shouldn't have been a problem and there must have been another reason for this tame effort. (op Evens tchd 6-5 and 5-4 in a place)
Son Of The Cat(USA), absent since November, came into this 0-9 on sand but he has run some creditable races on the surface. Another to attract market support, he raced in a good position on the shoulder of the leader for much of the way but was finding it all too much from over a furlong out. To be fair to him, he had plenty to find with his three main rivals at the weights. (op 8-1 tchd 11-2)
Wavertree Princess(IRE), officially rated 45, cantered around in her own time to pick up a bit of prizemoney. (op 100-1)

1015 WILLIAMHILL.COM ROSEBERY H'CAP 1m 3f (P)
2:50 (2:50) (Class 2) (0-105,99) 4-Y-0+
£21,808 (£6,531; £3,265; £1,634; £815; £409) **Stalls** High

Form RPR

004- **1** **Dansili Dancer**[181] 6302 8-9-3 **99** JohnFahy(7) 9 112
(C G Cox) *mid-div: smooth hdwy fr 3f out: qcknd up wl to ld over 1f out: sn clr: pushed out* **8/1**[3]

2-11 **2** 6 **King Olav (UAE)**[30] 697 5-9-5 **94** LukeMorris 8 97
(A W Carroll) *trckd ldrs: rdn over 3f out: led briefly 2f out: kpt on but nt pce of wnr sn after* **7/2**[1]

3521 **3** ¾ **Mafeking (UAE)**[23] 790 6-9-4 **93** AndrewElliott 14 95
(M R Hoad) *trckd ldrs: rdn and ev ch 2f out: kpt on but nt pce of wnr sn after* **8/1**[3]

1044 **4** ½ **Baylini**[16] 863 6-9-0 **89** JamesDoyle 5 90
(Ms J S Doyle) *mid-div: hdwy over 2f out: sn rdn to chse ldrs: kpt on fnl f* **12/1**

21-2 **5** 1 **Becausewecan (USA)**[7] 947 4-9-5 **95** DarryllHolland 11 94
(M Johnston) *led: rdn and hdd 2f out: no ex fnl f* **8/1**[3]

330- **6** nse **Martyr**[260] 3826 5-9-0 **89** RichardHughes 6 88
(R Hannon) *mid-div: outpcd over 2f out: styd on fnl f: nrst fin* **8/1**[3]

215- **7** nse **Red Cadeaux**[203] 5660 4-9-0 **90** JimCrowley 4 89+
(E A L Dunlop) *hld up towards rr: rdn wl over 2f out: styd on fnl f: nvr nrr* **11/1**

0-6 **8** shd **Porgy**[10] 903 5-9-6 **95** PJMcDonald 10 94
(R A Fahey) *s.i.s: towards rr: pushed along and stdy prog fr 2f out: sltly hmpd sn after: styd on ins fnl f* **25/1**

1124 **9** 5 **Formidable Guest**[24] 765 6-8-0 **75** FrankieMcDonald 12 65
(J Pearce) *mid-div: hdwy whn nt clr run and snatched up over 1f out: no further imp* **33/1**

10 **10** 1¼ **Cairnsmore**[42] 536 4-9-5 **95** GregFairley 7 83
(M Johnston) *prom: rdn and ev ch 2f out: sn wknd* **15/2**[2]

140- **11** 6 **Pevensey (IRE)**[140] 7293 8-9-4 **93** (p) GeorgeBaker 1 71
(J J Quinn) *s.i.s: a towards rr* **33/1**

24-3 **12** 2½ **Demolition**[15] 871 6-8-9 **84** TonyHamilton 13 58
(R A Fahey) *mid-div: rdn over 3f out: wknd wl over 1f out* **8/1**[3]

0010 **13** ¾ **Stand Guard**[16] 863 6-8-9 **87** MichaelStainton(3) 2 59
(P Howling) *trckd ldrs: rdn over 3f out: wknd over 2f out* **33/1**

06- **14** 24 **Liszt (IRE)**[220] 5178 4-9-9 **99** PatCosgrave 3 30
(Ian Williams) *a towards rr: eased fr 2f out* **16/1**

2m 17.2s (-4.70) **Going Correction** -0.075s/f (Stan)
WFA 4 from 5yo+ 1lb **14** Ran SP% **124.1**
Speed ratings (Par 109): **114,109,109,108,108 107,107,107,104,103 98,97,96,79**
toteswingers:1&2:£22.10, 1&3:£21.20, 2&3:£4.30 CSF £35.94 CT £236.94 TOTE £12.40: £3.20, £2.00, £3.10; EX 53.00 Trifecta £211.60 Pool: £300.37 - 1.05 winning units..
Owner The Loyal Troupers **Bred** The Magic Slipper Partnership **Trained** Lambourn, Berks
■ Stewards' Enquiry : James Doyle two-day ban: careless riding (Apr 10,12)

FOCUS
This was run at a decent pace thanks to Becausewecan and they took over half a second off the course record, but what had looked a competitive event on paper was turned into a rout. The form is rated around the sdolid placed horses.

NOTEBOOK
Dansili Dancer ◆ hadn't been seen since September, but was back down to his last winning mark. Having only his fourth try on sand, for a horse who stays further than this the strong pace was ideal and he travelled beautifully just behind the leaders before moving closer off the final bend. Switched out wide passing the intersection, he quickened up very smartly and had no problem in pulling right away from a decent field. This was an impressive performance under top weight, but he may be forced back into Listed company once he is reassessed. (op 10-1)
King Olav(UAE), bidding for a course hat-trick off a 3lb higher mark, was always handy but he was needing to be shoved along to hold his place before the end of the back straight. To his credit, he stayed in the thick of the action until the winner was unleashed over a furlong out and all he could do from then on was battle on to win the separate race for second. (op 9-2)
Mafeking(UAE) perhaps doesn't win the number of races his talent suggests he should, but he got it right at Wolverhampton last time. Off a 4lb higher mark here, he was always close up and had every chance towards the inside after the intersection but, like all the others, he was blown away by the winner. This was yet another solid effort from him. (op 9-1)
Baylini, 1lb lower than when a close fourth in this race last year, travelled well off the pace and looked a possible threat when diving to the inside after the intersection, but she could never land a telling blow. Despite this solid effort, she does look better at Lingfield. (op 14-1 tchd 11-1)
Becausewecan(USA), 5lb higher than when narrowly denied at Lingfield seven days earlier when returning from five months off, may have done too much too soon and had little left once headed well over a furlong out. (op 6-1)
Martyr, having his first outing since July, made some late progress and is entitled to have benefited from the run. (op 10-1)
Red Cadeaux ◆, having his first start since September, raced near the back of the field early and came off the bridle before the home straight, but he eventually responded to pressure and finished strongly. He needs a stiffer test than this now and is one to watch for back over a more suitable trip. (op 12-1)
Porgy, sixth of eight in a 1m4f Listed contest here on his debut for the yard ten days earlier, didn't look straightforward that day and though he stayed on well over the last 2f here, his high head-carriage again left something to be desired. (op 20-1)
Formidable Guest, already successful three times this year, would have been a bit closer had she not been squeezed out between Baylini and the weakening Demolition passing the 2f pole. (op 28-1)

1016 WILLIAMHILL.COM MAGNOLIA STKS (LISTED RACE) 1m 2f (P)
3:25 (3:26) (Class 1) 4-Y-0+
£22,708 (£8,608; £4,308; £2,148; £1,076; £540) **Stalls** High

Form RPR

216- **1** **South Easter (IRE)**[281] 3087 4-8-13 105 (t) LiamJones 6 107+
(W J Haggas) *trckd ldrs: kpt in on bnd by runner up turning for home: sn rdn: r.o to ld fnl 100yds: rdn out* **13/8**[1]

230- **2** ½ **Safari Sunup (IRE)**[140] 7293 5-8-13 97 JimCrowley 2 106
(P Winkworth) *hld up last of 6 but cl up: tk clsr order 3f out: rdn 2f out: kpt on w wnr fr over 1f out: a being jst hld: wnt 2nd nr fin* **20/1**

121 **3** ½ **December Draw (IRE)**[9] 921 4-8-13 90 HayleyTurner 1 105
(W J Knight) *trckd ldrs: rdn into narrow ld wl over 1f out: hdd fnl 100yds: edgd lft nr fin: kpt on* **9/1**

210- **4** ½ **Honimiere (IRE)**[162] 6813 4-8-8 94 PJMcDonald 3 99
(G A Swinbank) *hld up in cl 5th: tk clsr order over 2f out: sn rdn: nvr quite able to chal: styd on* **20/1**

-222 **5** 1½ **Suits Me**[7] 946 7-8-13 106 DarryllHolland 5 101
(T P Tate) *trckd ldr: led after 3f: rdn and hdd wl over 1f out: kpt pressing ldr tl no ex fnl 100yds* **7/4**[2]

14-3 **6** 1¾ **Heliodor (USA)**[10] 903 4-8-13 107 RichardHughes 4 98
(R Hannon) *led: hdd whn squeezed up on rails after 3f: trckd ldr: rdn 2f out: no ex ins fnl f* **11/2**[3]

2m 5.90s (-2.10) **Going Correction** -0.075s/f (Stan) **6** Ran SP% **109.4**
Speed ratings (Par 111): **105,104,104,103,102 101**
toteswingers:1&2:£14.50, 1&3:£2.40, 2&3:£26.60 CSF £29.54 TOTE £2.70: £2.00, £1.60; EX 33.50.
Owner Markus Jooste & Bernard Kantor **Bred** Tarworth Bloodstock Investments Ltd **Trained** Newmarket, Suffolk
■ Stewards' Enquiry : Darryll Holland one-day ban: careless riding (Apr 10)
Hayley Turner caution: careless riding

FOCUS
An interesting Listed event and the pace looked decent with a couple of confirmed front-runners in opposition, but with the highest-rated pair filling the last two places, it's hard to get a handle on the value of the form. The form is muddling with the winner rated to last year's Dee Stakes form but likely to do better.

NOTEBOOK
South Easter(IRE) was the only one of the sextet with any real pretensions to being better than this level. Not seen since posting a tame effort in the King Edward VII Stakes at Royal Ascot last June, he had narrowly got the better of a rather unlucky Gitano Hernando in the Dee Stakes at Chester prior to that and the market suggested he was thought ready for this return to action. Having travelled well in the middle of the field, there was a moment turning for home when it looked like he might get short of room, but the gap appeared in time and he quickened up well to forge ahead well inside the last furlong. He is still totally unexposed and it will be fascinating to see how he progresses. The Huxley Stakes back at Chester is a possible target. (op 2-1 tchd 6-4)
Safari Sunup(IRE), without a win since October 2008 and returning from four months off, made his move around the outside of the field on the home bend and stayed on all the way to the line. This was an encouraging return and he deserves to get his head back in front. (op 16-1 tchd 25-1)
December Draw(IRE) came into this in fine form on Polytrack, but this was a different proposition as he would have been upwards of 7lb better off with his five rivals in a handicap. He looked the likely winner when sent to the front over a furlong from home, but couldn't quite see it out. This was a decent effort on these terms and he remains at the top of his game. (op 10-1)
Honimiere(IRE), not seen since finishing well beaten on his first try in Listed company at Newmarket in October, was making his sand debut. Held up out the back, he stayed on up the home straight to finish on the heels of the principals and is entitled to come on for it. (op 16-1)
Suits Me, runner-up in his last four outings including in the Winter Derby seven days earlier, was successful in his only previous try over this C&D. Admittedly, he had to work in order to get to the front after 2f, but it was still disappointing the way he capitulated over a furlong from home. Perhaps this came too soon after his big effort at Lingfield. (op 6-4 tchd 15-8 and 2-1 in a place)
Heliodor(USA), marginally best in at the weights and back down to a more suitable trip after his encouraging return to action in a similar contest over 2f further here ten days earlier, was even more disappointing. Admittedly he didn't have a great deal of room to play with against the inside rail in the home straight, but it wasn't enough to explain this modest effort. (op 5-1 tchd 9-2)

1017 WILLIAMHILL.COM - BINGO EBF MAIDEN STKS 5f (P)
4:00 (4:00) (Class 4) 2-Y-0 **£4,533** (£1,348; £674; £336) **Stalls** High

Form RPR

1 **Takeaway** 2-9-3 0 RichardHughes 3 75+
(R Hannon) *travelled wl trcking ldrs: led over 1f out: r.o wl: readily* **7/2**[1]

2 1½ **Beach Patrol (IRE)** 2-9-3 0 EddieCreighton 5 66
(M R Channon) *led: rdn and hdd over 1f out: kpt on but nt pce of wnr* **14/1**

3 ¾ **Iztaccihuatl** 2-8-12 0 PatCosgrave 4 58+
(M J Scudamore) *s.i.s: sn in tch: rdn over 2f out: r.o ent fnl f: wnt 3rd nring fin* **22/1**

4 nk **Master Macho (IRE)** 2-9-3 0 ChrisCatlin 7 62
(M R Channon) *sn pushed along in tch: rdn to chse ldrs ent st: kpt on but nt pce to mount chal* **5/1**[2]

5 1¼ **Pick A Little** 2-9-3 0 KevinGhunowa 6 57
(B W Duke) *s.i.s: towards rr: rdn over 2f out: styd on fr over 1f out: nt rch ldrs* **16/1**

6 ¾ **Johnny Hancocks (IRE)** 2-9-3 0 JimmyFortune 2 54
(P D Evans) *prom: rdn over 2f out: fdd ent fnl f* **15/2**

7 1 1/4 **Ivan's A Star (IRE)** 2-9-3 0 .... LiamKeniry 1 49
(J S Moore) *s.i.s: rn wd on bnd over 2f out: nvr bttr than mid-div* **20/1**

8 nk **Jibouti (IRE)** 2-9-3 0 .... DarryllHolland 10 48
(C E Brittain) *s.i.s: a towards rr* **7/2**^{1}

9 1 1/2 **Bold Deceiver** 2-8-5 0 .... LeonnaMayor(7) 8 37
(P S McEntee) *chsd ldrs: rdn over 2f out: wknd over 1f out* **33/1**

10 10 **Unknown Rebel (IRE)** 2-9-3 0 .... JimCrowley 9 2
(K A Ryan) *a towards rr* **6/1**^{3}

11 nk **Huckle Duckle (IRE)** 2-8-12 0 .... (b1) TomMcLaughlin 12 —
(P S McEntee) *a towards rr* **25/1**

62.59 secs (2.09) **Going Correction** -0.075s/f (Stan) **11** Ran SP% **115.6**
Speed ratings (Par 94): **80,77,76,75,73 72,70,70,67,51 51**
toteswingers:1&2:£6.30, 1&3:£32.60, 2&3:£32.60 CSF £50.99 TOTE £3.80: £1.90, £3.50, £6.70; EX 44.00.
Owner S Mahal, R Morecombe & D Anderson **Bred** Redhill Bloodstock Limited **Trained** East Everleigh, Wilts

FOCUS
No previous form to go on, but a familiar result with the prize going to a yard with a rich tradition with its juveniles. Not many ever got into this.

NOTEBOOK
Takeaway, a 20,000euros foal but only a £5,000 yearling, is out of a winning sprinter on dirt. He certainly knew his job as he travelled smoothly close to the pace and his rider even had the luxury of taking a pull on him after turning in. Once unleashed, he found plenty and this April foal is likely to be kept on the go in the early weeks of the turf season. (op 4-1 tchd 3-1)
Beach Patrol(IRE), a £26,000 half-brother to three winners at up to 1m, showed good speed out in front and though he had no answer to the winner, he kept on going to hold on to second. A May foal, he is entitled to progress with racing.
Iztaccihuatl, a half-sister to the 1m2f winner Addwaitya, was being niggled along in the middle of the field from some way out, but she finished in good style and her breeding suggests she will appreciate further in due course. (op 20-1)
Master Macho(IRE), a £5,000 half-brother to two winners at up to 1m6f, was never far away and had every chance. He too is likely to get further in time. (op 6-1)
Pick A Little, a £6,000 colt out of a winner over 1m in the US, showed ability and was staying on at the line. There should be a small race in him. (op 20-1)
Johnny Hancocks(IRE), a 7,000euros half-brother to three winners at up to 1m including Waterline Twenty who won twice at this track for the same stable, had to do plenty of early running from his low draw to take a handy position and that eventually told. This May foal is probably capable of better. (op 6-1)
Jibouti(IRE), out of a half-sister to the high-class Lover's Knot, is a January foal and was therefore the oldest in the field, but after having missed the break he looked absolutely clueless and is surely better than this. (tchd 4-1)

1018 WILLIAMHILL.COM - CASINO H'CAP (LONDON MILE QUALIFIER) 1m (P)
4:35 (4:35) (Class 3) (0-95,88) 3-Y-O

£6,542 (£1,959; £979; £490; £244; £122) **Stalls** High

Form RPR

513- **1** **Huygens**^{108} [7685] 3-9-3 **84** .... DarryllHolland 2 98+
(D J Coakley) *hld up bhd: stl last whn gd hdwy at cutaway over 2f out: str run ins fnl f: led fnl 75yds: won gng away* **7/1**

30- **2** 1 3/4 **Navajo Chief**^{154} [7030] 3-9-7 **88** .... JimCrowley 5 95
(A P Jarvis) *trckd ldrs: rdn over 2f out: kpt on ins fnl f: wnt 2nd fnl strides* **20/1**

2152 **3** hd **Duellist**^{8} [934] 3-8-12 **79** .... GregFairley 6 86
(M Johnston) *prom: rdn to ld wl over 1f out: hdd fnl 75yds: no ex whn lost 2nd fnl strides* **5/1**^{3}

0-1 **4** 3 **Midfielder (USA)**^{33} [667] 3-8-11 **78** .... JimmyFortune 3 78
(J H M Gosden) *mid-div: rdn over 2f out: little imp tl styd on fnl f* **11/4**^{1}

6-13 **5** 3/4 **Areeda (IRE)**^{22} [807] 3-8-8 **75** .... ChrisCatlin 10 73
(C E Brittain) *led: rdn and hdd wl over 1f out: no ex ins fnl f* **13/2**

-112 **6** nk **Marosh (FR)**^{36} [617] 3-8-7 **74** .... SaleemGolam 8 72
(R M H Cowell) *hld up towards rr: rdn over 2f out: sme late prog: nvr a danger* **10/1**

46-1 **7** nk **Highland Quaich**^{55} [366] 3-9-0 **81** .... LiamKeniry 4 78
(D R C Elsworth) *hld up towards rr: sme late prog u.p: nvr trbld ldrs* **4/1**^{2}

300- **8** 3/4 **Avon River**^{200} [5742] 3-8-13 **80** .... RichardHughes 9 75
(R Hannon) *stdd s: in rr: sme hdwy 2f out: sn rdn: no further imp: fdd ins fnl f* **14/1**

-231 **9** 2 1/4 **Juicy Pear (IRE)**^{16} [858] 3-8-10 **77** .... HayleyTurner 7 67
(M L W Bell) *trckd ldrs: rdn over 2f out: wknd over 1f out* **16/1**

1m 39.05s (-0.75) **Going Correction** -0.075s/f (Stan) **9** Ran SP% **115.6**
Speed ratings (Par 102): **100,98,98,95,94 94,93,92,90**
toteswingers:1&2:£39.30, 1&3:£7.60, 2&3:£30.80 CSF £132.71 CT £765.59 TOTE £8.90: £2.40, £3.30, £2.20; EX 98.90.
Owner Chris Van Hoorn **Bred** R F And Mrs Knipe **Trained** West Ilsley, Berks

FOCUS
Some progressive 3-y-os took part in this decent handicap, but it was run at a rather muddling early pace. The third sets the level and the form makes sense overall.

NOTEBOOK
Huygens ◆ was last seen finishing third in a nursery over C&D in December and three of his six rivals that day went on to win their next starts. He put up a remarkable effort here for, having been held up out the back early, he made for the inside rail after the intersection and then had to weave his way through his rivals to get a run, but he still managed to produce a devastating turn of foot to hit the front half a furlong from home. He is one to follow and could make up into a very nice type. (op 13-2 tchd 8-1)
Navajo Chief, tried in Pattern company in his last couple of starts at two, was making his sand and handicap debuts after five months off, but he did attract support at long odds. Never far away, he kept staying on and responded to pressure to snatch second place on the line. He looks capable of winning off this sort of mark. (op 33-1)
Duellist, 5lb higher than when narrowly beaten over this trip at Lingfield eight days earlier, was always on the shoulder of the leader before being sent for home passing the 2f pole, but he could do nothing to repel the winner's dazzling turn of foot and lost second on the line. The handicapper may have him now, but he is yet to race on turf so it would be interesting to see how he copes with that. (op 6-1)
Midfielder(USA), making his handicap debut after winning a Wolverhampton maiden on his second start last month which hasn't really worked out, offered a brief threat when produced down the outside in the home straight but his effort didn't really amount to much. This performance would suggest that he was allocated a stiff-enough opening handicap mark. (op 5-2 tchd 2-1 and 3-1 in a place)
Areeda(IRE), trying this trip for the first time, was allowed to dictate at her own pace but folded rather tamely once headed 2f from home. It looked as though she didn't stay. (op 7-1 tchd 15-2 and 8-1 in a place)
Marosh(FR), thwarted in his hat-trick bid off 2lb lower at Lingfield last month, never landed a blow and he looks to be in the handicapper's grip now. Official explanation: jockey said gelding was awkward around the bend and hung under pressure (tchd 11-1)
Highland Quaich, a dual winner over 7f at this track, was 8lb higher than when overcoming trouble in running to score here last time out. Having taken a grip at the rear of the field early, his response when asked to get closer was very limited and he wouldn't have won at any trip. (op 9-2 tchd 6-1)

1019 WILLIAMHILL.COM - VEGAS H'CAP 6f (P)
5:10 (5:10) (Class 2) (0-105,98) 3-Y-O

£9,969 (£2,985; £1,492; £747; £372; £187) **Stalls** High

Form RPR

1-43 **1** **Yer Woman (IRE)**^{10} [901] 3-8-10 **90** .... PatrickHills(3) 2 95
(R Hannon) *patiently rdn in last pair: shkn up over 1f out: r.o strly: led fnl 60yds: all out* **9/2**^{3}

141- **2** hd **Edgewater (IRE)**^{87} [7878] 3-8-7 **84** .... ChrisCatlin 4 88
(J Akehurst) *hld up: swtchd rt and hdwy over 2f out: rdn to ld ent fnl f: hdd fnl 60yds: kpt on wl* **9/1**

15-0 **3** 2 1/4 **Duplicity**^{7} [945] 3-9-7 **98** .... RichardHughes 7 95
(R Hannon) *trckd ldrs: rdn 2f out: ev ch ent fnl f: kpt on same pce* **10/3**^{2}

000- **4** 1/2 **Ghostwing**^{168} [6677] 3-9-0 **91** .... HayleyTurner 1 87
(J Gallagher) *trckd ldr: rdn and ev ch ent fnl f: kpt on same pce* **25/1**

1111 **5** 3/4 **Love Delta (USA)**^{23} [783] 3-9-4 **95** .... GregFairley 5 88
(M Johnston) *chsd ldrs: rdn over 2f out: nt pce to mount chal* **15/8**^{1}

00-1 **6** 2 3/4 **Raddy 'Ell Pauline (IRE)**^{45} [489] 3-8-10 **87** .... JimmyFortune 6 71
(K A Ryan) *led: rdn and hdd ent fnl f: wknd* **6/1**

45- **7** 12 **Kingdom Of Munster (IRE)**^{217} [5275] 3-9-4 **95** .... PatCosgrave 3 41
(Ian Williams) *s.i.s: a in rr* **11/1**

1m 11.95s (-1.15) **Going Correction** -0.075s/f (Stan) **7** Ran SP% **112.5**
Speed ratings (Par 104): **104,103,100,100,99 95,79**
toteswingers:1&2:£5.60, 1&3:£3.60, 2&3:£4.00 CSF £41.58 TOTE £4.10: £2.70, £5.00; EX 33.80.
Owner Jim McArdle **Bred** Mrs Clodagh McStay **Trained** East Everleigh, Wilts
■ Stewards' Enquiry : Chris Catlin one-day ban: careless riding (Apr 10)

FOCUS
A decent little sprint handicap run at a true pace. The first two are generally progressive and the third is rated to his juvenile form.

NOTEBOOK
Yer Woman(IRE) ◆ hadn't enjoyed the rub of the green in either start since winning off 8lb lower over C&D in November, but she got it right this time. Given a patient ride, she travelled well before being brought with her effort widest of all and battled on gamely to just get the better of the persistent runner-up. She can't be put up much for this and is capable of winning again on this surface when the cards fall her way. (op 10-3)
Edgewater(IRE) ◆, 3lb higher than when winning a four-runner event at Lingfield when last seen in December, was taking on better company here. He looked the likely winner when produced to hit the front against the inside rail entering the last furlong and battled back very gamely after the filly had headed him. He should be sharper next time. (op 17-2 tchd 8-1)
Duplicity, who pulled too hard on his return to action in the Spring Cup at Lingfield seven days earlier, travelled well behind the leaders and had every chance a furlong out, but could then find no extra. He still looks to be paying for his success in a soft-ground Listed event at Newbury last summer and needs to drop a few pounds more. (op 7-1 tchd 8-1)
Ghostwing was extremely highly tried after winning an Ayr maiden for Richard Fahey last June. Making his sand and handicap debuts for his new yard after five months off, he was sent to the front coming to the last furlong but didn't last there long and was run out of it. This was still a fair effort and he should come on for it. (tchd 20-1)
Love Delta(USA), winner of all four starts so far this year including one over C&D, had every chance passing the intersection but was already making hard work of it by that stage and the 10lb higher mark proved beyond him. (op 2-1 tchd 7-4)
Raddy 'Ell Pauline(IRE), a C&D winner at two, was possibly fortunate to win a four-runner event off 4lb lower at Lingfield last month. After making the early running, she was comfortably picked off approaching the last furlong. (op 5-1 tchd 4-1)

1020 WILLIAMHILL.COM QUEEN'S PRIZE (H'CAP) 2m (P)
5:40 (5:41) (Class 2) (0-105,95) 4-Y-O+

£9,969 (£2,985; £1,492; £747; £372; £187) **Stalls** High

Form RPR

204- **1** **Gala Evening**^{284} [2994] 8-9-7 **90** .... RichardHughes 4 101+
(J A B Old) *trckd ldrs: jnd ldr travelling wl ent fnl f: nudged ahd: comf* **5/2**^{1}

12-3 **2** 1 1/4 **Right Stuff (FR)**^{44} [500] 7-9-3 **86** .... GeorgeBaker 7 94
(G L Moore) *led: sn 5 l clr: rdn 2f out: jnd ent fnl f: sn hdd: no ch w wnr* **3/1**^{2}

-624 **3** 2 3/4 **Rose Row**^{22} [811] 6-8-10 **79** .... HayleyTurner 2 83
(Mrs Mary Hambro) *stdd s: in rr: smooth hdwy to trck ldr 3f out: sn rdn: styd on same pce* **12/1**

1423 **4** 1 **Dance The Star (USA)**^{7} [947] 5-9-8 **91** .... DarryllHolland 8 94
(D M Simcock) *hld up: c wd ent st 3f out: sn rdn: styd on same pce: nvr threatened* **15/2**

402- **5** 3/4 **Yellowstone (IRE)**^{154} [7038] 6-9-7 **90** .... JimCrowley 3 92
(P F I Cole) *in tch: rdn over 2f out: styd on same pce: nvr threatened* **15/2**

1-65 **6** 15 **Dani's Girl (IRE)**^{14} [688] 7-8-6 **80** .... KierenFox(5) 1 64
(P M Phelan) *racd keenly: in tch tl hung lft and wknd over 2f out* **12/1**

231/ **7** 24 **Silver Suitor (IRE)**^{686} [1984] 6-9-12 **95** .... JimmyFortune 5 50
(D R C Elsworth) *trckd ldr tl 3f out: sn wknd: eased fnl 2f* **4/1**^{3}

3m 30.66s (0.56) **Going Correction** -0.075s/f (Stan) **7** Ran SP% **112.5**
Speed ratings (Par 109): **95,94,93,92,92 84,72**
toteswingers:1&2:£2.10, 1&3:£5.90, 2&3:£7.20 CSF £9.83 CT £71.10 TOTE £2.80: £1.40, £1.90; EX 11.10 Place 6 £512.22, Place 5 £190.56.
Owner W E Sturt **Bred** Juddmonte Farms **Trained** Barbury Castle, Wilts

FOCUS
A fair staying handicap, though weakened by the withdrawal of the forecast favourite Alsadaa which left the race without a confirmed front-runner. Moderate form for the grade but the winner has an excellent course record.

NOTEBOOK
Gala Evening loomed large entering the final furlong with his rider sitting motionless and when the button was pressed, the response was instant. Runner-up off 2lb lower in this race last year, he had been successful in all three outings over this C&D before that, but each of those wins came off the back of a recent outing and he was returning from nine months off here. It made no difference to him, however, and this was a decent effort after such a long absence. (op 7-2)
Right Stuff(FR) was allowed the luxury of a very soft lead and it looked as though he would take some catching passing the 3f pole, as he still held a significant advantage. However, a look in the mirrors over a furlong out would have seen the winner looming large and there was nothing he could do about it. He did his best, but it probably wasn't ideal that he was forced to do his own donkeywork. (op 10-3 tchd 7-2)
Rose Row, whose last success came over C&D off 13lb lower in September, had plenty to find with Right Stuff on their meeting here last month. She was keen enough early and though she was within striking distance coming to the last 2f, she couldn't then find a change of gear. (op 8-1)
Dance The Star(USA), consistent on Polytrack but trying 2f further than he had ever attempted before, was switched off out the back early. Although he stayed on over the last couple of furlongs, he was never doing enough. The jury is still out over his stamina for the trip. (op 7-1 tchd 8-1)

Yellowstone(IRE), without a win since July 2008 and making his sand debut on his 26th start after five months off, is now 27lb lower than in his prime but he never made much impression from mid-division. (op 7-1 tchd 8-1)
Dani's Girl(IRE), still 5lb higher than when winning over C&D in December, was back on the Flat after finishing well beaten in the Imperial Cup, but she was too keen on the outside of the field and dropped right out. (op 11-1 tchd 9-1)
Silver Suitor(IRE), making his sand debut after an absence of nearly two years, raced in second until appearing to blow up passing the 3f pole. Official explanation: jockey said gelding had no more to give (op 7-2 tchd 9-2)
T/Plt: £842.90 to a £1 stake. Pool: £64,816.07. 56.13 winning tickets. T/Qpdt: £65.60 to a £1 stake. Pool: £3,186.80. 35.90 winning tickets. TM

817 MEYDAN (L-H)

Saturday, March 27

OFFICIAL GOING: Turf course - good to firm; all-weather - standard

1021a AL QUOZ SPRINT SPONSORED BY EMIRATES NBD (GROUP 3) (TURF) 6f

1:20 (1:20) 3-Y-0+

£370,370 (£123,456; £61,728; £30,864; £18,518; £12,345)

RPR

1 **Joy And Fun (NZ)**[34] 652 7-9-0 117 (p) BrettDoyle 6 120
(D Cruz, Hong Kong) *trckd ldr: rdn to ld fnl 55yds: r.o wl* **12/1**

2 3/4 **Fravashi (AUS)**[23] 798 5-9-0 110 (b) AhmedAjtebi 7 118
(Saeed Bin Suroor) *mid-div: chsd ldrs 2 1/2f out: r.o wl ins fnl f* **33/1**

3 1/4 **California Flag (USA)**[104] 7745 6-9-0 118 (bt) JTalamo 8 117
(Brian Koriner, U.S.A) *sn led: hdd 55yds out: r.o same pce* **4/1**[1]

4 1 1/2 **War Artist (AUS)**[23] 797 7-9-0 116 OlivierPeslier 9 112
(J M P Eustace) *mid-div: rdn 3f out: r.o one pce* **9/1**

5 1/4 **All Silent (AUS)**[21] 7-9-0 119 (bt) CoreyBrown 4 111
(Grahame Begg, Australia) *mid-div: r.o fnl 2f: n.d* **6/1**[3]

6 1 3/4 **Judd Street**[22] 822 8-9-0 110 (v) KierenFallon 16 106+
(Eve Johnson Houghton) *nvr bttr than mid-div* **33/1**

7 1/4 **Sirocco Breeze**[22] 818 5-9-0 116 FrankieDettori 3 105
(Saeed Bin Suroor) *a in mid-div* **9/2**[2]

8 1/4 **Finjaan**[203] 5657 4-9-0 117 RichardHills 11 104
(M P Tregoning) *nvr bttr than mid-div* **10/1**

9 2 **Mariol (FR)**[175] 6503 7-9-0 113 Christophe-PatriceLemaire 1 98
(Robert Collet, France) *nvr able to chal* **25/1**

10 3/4 **Asset (IRE)**[30] 710 7-9-0 108 (b) TedDurcan 2 95
(Saeed Bin Suroor) *nvr bttr than mid-div* **28/1**

11 1/2 **Terrific Challenge (USA)**[15] 8-9-0 106 (vt) RichardMullen 15 94
(S Seemar, UAE) *nvr able to chal* **33/1**

12 1/4 **Sir Gerry (USA)**[23] 797 5-9-0 107 RyanMoore 12 93
(J R Best) *nvr able to chal* **25/1**

13 1/4 **Our Giant (AUS)**[251] 7-9-0 115 (b) KShea 5 92
(M F De Kock, South Africa) *a in rr* **6/1**[3]

14 3/4 **Star Crowned (USA)**[22] 822 7-9-0 109 (t) RoystonFfrench 14 90
(R Bouresly, Kuwait) *led: nr side gp: rdn 3f out: one pce fnl 1 1/2f* **33/1**

15 6 1/4 **Prince Shaun (IRE)**[23] 797 5-9-0 106 (t) TadhgO'Shea 10 70
(Doug Watson, UAE) *rrd as stalls opened: racd in rr: n.d* **40/1**

16 3/4 **Dohasa (IRE)**[15] 5-9-0 105 PJSmullen 13 67
(I Mohammed, UAE) **33/1**

69.80 secs (69.80) **16** Ran SP% **121.8**
CSF: £368.37.
Owner Mr & Mrs Johnny Wong Chun Nam **Bred** L Williams **Trained** Hong Kong

FOCUS
It was questionable whether this race would be worthy of its place on the World Cup card (for the first time) seeing as the meeting already stages a Group 1 sprint now run on a surface not too dissimilar to turf. However, it proved to be a popular alternative to its more prestigious relative, with greatly increased prize money (although still only half the value of the Golden Shaheen) rewarded with a big field. The quantity was certainly matched with quality, too. On the downside, though, it could be argued that the Golden Shaheen suffered slightly in terms of strength in depth as a consequence. This was only the second race to be run over the straight 6f at Meydan and a middle draw proved advantageous. They split into two groups early, with five horses racing towards the stands' side, but all the pace was with the main bunch up the centre of the track. The time 1.66 seconds quicker than Judd Street recorded in the only previous race run over the track and trip.

NOTEBOOK
Joy And Fun(NZ) often gets behind in his races, but he applied himself well through the early stages this time and that enabled him to make the most of his good draw by keeping tabs on early leader California Flag. He went off quickly to do so, but being a winner at up to 1m, his stamina was assured, and he duly kept on really strongly. His running-on third behind Sacred Kingdom in last December's Hong Kong Sprint represented top form and he was able to build on that to pick up this decent prize.
Fravashi(AUS) didn't run much of a race from the widest draw over 1m on Tapeta last time, but he had previously shaped well on his Dubai debut when fifth in a Group 2 on turf. A triple Group-race winner (although not at the highest level) over 7f in Australia, he had the blinkers back on (in place of cheekpieces) for this switch to sprinting and ran a fine race in defeat. It's true that, like the winner, he was well drawn, but this is rock-solid form and he could have a good season if coming to Europe.
California Flag(USA), last year's Breeders' Cup Turf Sprint winner, had run a blinder in the Hong Sprint when last seen (hassled up front but still managed fifth) and ran another big race in defeat. His undoing was simply not having a bend to race around, which would have allowed him to get in a crucial breather. He showed his customary early speed, but Joe Talamo said he struggled to get the gelding to change his legs (this would have come naturally with a bend to race around), and that when he did manage it, the horse switched them straight back again. Unsurprisingly, this 6-y-o simply ran out of energy in the last half-furlong. There are more big races to be won with him when he gets his conditions.
War Artist(AUS) looked really good when winning a 6f Group 3 on the Tapeta first time up in Dubai, but having subsequently disappointed in a similar race, he was aimed at this contest, rather than the Golden Shaheen. Drawn favourably, he was never too far away, but although keeping on, he failed to pick up as well as one might have hoped and couldn't reverse Hong Kong Sprint form with today's winner and third. This performance was short of his best form and he has not gone on as expected from that impressive success in February.
All Silent(AUS), poorly drawn when behind today's winner and third in the Hong Kong Sprint, warmed up for this with a satisfactory effort in the Newmarket Handicap in his native Australia. However, he was again not helped by his stall position, as he ended up out wide of the main group up the centre and could make no real impression.
Judd Street, the only previous winner over this straight track, ran a huge ran in defeat. He raced well away from the main action in the group of five towards the near side through the opening stages and comfortably beat the others who were in that bunch.
Sirocco Breeze, the winner of a couple of 7f handicaps on Tapeta at the carnival, was up in class and faced with quite different conditions, and he simply lacked the necessary pace from halfway. He kept on, though, and may yet prove himself up to this level. (op: 4/1)
Finjaan, off the track since presumably being unsuited by soft ground in the Haydock Sprint Cup, had little chance after racing in the stands'-side bunch early on and this is easily excused.
Asset(IRE) was never going the pace.
Sir Gerry(USA) could make no impression.
Our Giant(AUS), who had been off since winning a Grade 1 in South Africa last July, and who missed the Mahab Al Shimaal after apparently getting cast in box, was never going.
Prince Shaun(IRE) lost his race when rearing badly coming out of the stalls.

1022a GODOLPHIN MILE SPONSORED BY ETISALAT (GROUP 2) (TAPETA) 1m

1:55 (1:58) 3-Y-0+

£370,370 (£123,456; £61,728; £30,864; £18,518; £12,345)

RPR

1 **Calming Influence (IRE)**[23] 798 5-9-0 110 AhmedAjtebi 4 118
(Mahmood Al Zarooni) *trckd ldr: led 1/2f out: r.o wl: hld on gamely* **14/1**

2 1 **Green Coast (IRE)**[23] 798 7-9-0 111 TadhgO'Shea 14 115
(Doug Watson, UAE) *settled in rr: rdn 2 1/2f out: r.o wl fnl f: nrst fin* **20/1**

3 1 **Skysurfers**[23] 798 4-9-0 116 TedDurcan 12 113
(Saeed Bin Suroor) *mid-div: r.o wl fnl f: nrst fin* **11/2**[2]

4 1 1/2 **Glorious Noah (JPN)**[34] 654 4-9-0 110 ShinichiroKobayashi 5 110
(Yoshito Yahagi, Japan) *mid-div: rdn 3f out: r.o wl fnl f* **25/1**

5 3/4 **Forgotten Voice (IRE)**[23] 798 5-9-0 115 RyanMoore 10 108
(J Noseda) *sn rdn in rr: r.o fnl 2f: nrst fin* **10/1**

6 3/4 **Kalahari Gold (IRE)**[22] 823 5-9-0 112 RichardHills 1 106
(Doug Watson, UAE) *mid-div: smooth prog 3f out: ev ch 1 1/2f out: nt qckn* **16/1**

7 3/4 **Lucky Find (SAF)**[30] 713 7-9-0 110 KShea 6 104
(M F De Kock, South Africa) *nvr bttr than mid-div* **14/1**

8 1/4 **Vesuve (IRE)**[23] 798 4-9-0 112 WayneSmith 8 104
(M Al Muhairi, UAE) *racd in rr: nvr able to chal* **25/1**

9 shd **Cat Junior (USA)**[23] 798 5-9-0 115 (bt) JamieSpencer 2 104
(B J Meehan) *s.i.s: trckd ldng duo tl 2 1/2f out: sn btn* **7/1**[3]

10 2 1/4 **Le Drakkar (AUS)**[23] 800 5-9-0 110 CSanchez 3 98
(A bin Huzaim, UAE) *sn led: hdd & wknd 2 1/2f out* **40/1**

11 1 3/4 **Desert Party (USA)**[23] 797 4-9-0 116 (t) FrankieDettori 11 94
(Saeed Bin Suroor) *in rr of mid-div: rdn 2 1/2f out: n.d* **13/8**[1]

12 1 1/4 **Summit Surge (IRE)**[22] 823 6-9-0 113 (t) KierenFallon 13 91
(L M Cumani) *nvr bttr than mid-div* **12/1**

13 hd **Consul General**[22] 818 6-9-0 110 AGryder 7 91
(N Al Mandeel, Saudi Arabia) *nvr able to chal* **33/1**

14 3 **Jet Express (SAF)**[23] 798 8-9-0 108 RoystonFfrench 9 84
(A Al Raihe, UAE) *nvr bttr than mid-div* **33/1**

1m 36.57s (96.57) **14** Ran SP% **122.8**
CSF: £276.86.
Owner Godolphin **Bred** Mrs Helen Lyons **Trained** Newmarket, Suffolk
■ A first winner from his first runner for Godolphin's new trainer, Mahmood Al Zarooni.

FOCUS
Not a strong Group 2 on paper, as apart from rank outsider Le Drakkar, who won at Grade 1 level as a 3-y-o, and Desert Party, who could boast Grade 2 winning form, the field consisted of only four other horses successful at Group/Graded level, and all at a notch below this class.

NOTEBOOK
Calming Influence(IRE) won his first race above Listed class and showed improved form on his previous best, which included a third place in the Burj Nahaar last time out. Prominent from the outset, he sat behind the leader before kicking for home on the turn into the straight, and that move proved decisive as the closers just couldn't make up the lost ground. He hasn't run in Europe since the end of his 3-y-o season but looks a solid enough performer, and very adaptable, having won when held up, when racing near the pace, on soft and firm ground, and of course on this artificial surface, too. (op 12-1)
Green Coast(IRE) finished one place and half a length in front of the winner when they met in the Burj Nahaar, but having been held up at the back of the field and seen the winner get first run on them all, his strong finishing effort came just too late this time. He has proved himself very effective on this surface this season. (op 16-1)
Skysurfers, who may have bounced when a beaten favourite in the Burj Nahaar, didn't run badly from his wide draw. He enjoyed a trouble-free run through the pack up the straight and, as a colt having just his fourth career start, should still be capable of better still in future. (op 6-1)
Glorious Noah(JPN), a Grade 3 winner on dirt in Japan, got a bit outpaced before running on again at the finish. He was fourth in the Grade 1 Japan Dirt Derby over 1m2f last year and perhaps he'll appreciate returning to that sort of distance.
Forgotten Voice(IRE) had shaped well over this C&D in the first round of the Al Maktoum challenge, but disappointed in the Burj Naahar. Dropped in from his wide draw, he saved some ground on the inside before finishing his race out wider, but by the time he got going the race was all but over. (op 9-1)
Kalahari Gold(IRE), switching back to the Tapeta, enjoyed a nice trip on the inside but didn't see his race out as well as might have been expected. His good run over a mile last time came in a steadily run affair and it's likely his best trip is 7f. (op 14-1)
Lucky Find(SAF) confirmed recent C&D form with Vesuve and Le Drakkar, but that handicap form proved below the standard required in this contest.
Cat Junior(USA) beat the first two here when successful in the Burj Nahaar but he was slowly away this time, denied the lead and raced keenly in behind the pace. As a result of the way the race unfolded he wasn't seen at his best.
Desert Party(USA) made a successful return to action over 6f here earlier this month, but he was drawn wide this time and raced keenly as Dettori tried to get some cover. This was clearly not his true form. (op 2-1)
Summit Surge(IRE), another poorly drawn, was asked to make an early move around the outside to get a prominent pitch. He soon paid for that effort. (op 11-1)

1023a UAE DERBY SPONSORED BY THE SAEED & MOHAMMED AL NABOODAH GROUP (GROUP 2) (TAPETA) 1m 1f 110y

2:35 (2:35) 3-Y-0

£740,740 (£246,913; £123,456; £61,728; £37,037; £24,691)

RPR

1 **Musir (AUS)**[37] 608 4-9-5 117 ChristopheSoumillon 9 122+
(M F De Kock, South Africa) *settled in rr: smooth prog 3f out: swtchd to rail 1 1/2f out: rdn to ld 110yds out* **11/8**[1]

2 1 3/4 **Raihana (AUS)**[30] 709 4-9-1 110 KShea 3 113
(M F De Kock, South Africa) *mid-div rdn to chse ldrs 3f out: led ins fnl f whn hdd 110yds out: r.o wl* **12/1**[3]

3 1 1/4 **Mendip (USA)**[23] 796 3-8-8 115 FrankieDettori 5 111
(Saeed Bin Suroor) *s.i.s: mid-div: smooth prog to ld 2f out: hdd ins fnl f: kpt on* **9/4**[2]

4 2 1/4 **Enak (ARG)**[23] 796 4-9-5 108 (t) TedDurcan 2 110
(Saeed Bin Suroor) *mid-div: r.o wl: fnl 2f* **20/1**

5 1/4 **Frozen Power (IRE)**[22] 819 3-8-8 110 AhmedAjtebi 7 106
(Mahmood Al Zarooni) *in rr of mid-div: r.o one pce fnl 1 1/2f* **14/1**

6 1/4 **Siyaadah**[30] 709 3-8-4 108 .... AGryder 6 102
(Mahmood Al Zarooni) *nvr able to chal* **25/1**

7 1 1/4 **Oroveso (BRZ)**[22] 819 4-9-5 102 .... TJPereira 1 106
(P Bary, France) *nvr able to chal* **33/1**

8 4 1/2 **Della Barba (CHI)**[23] 796 4-9-5 106 .... OlivierPeslier 4 97
(J Barton, Saudi Arabia) *trckd ldr: hmpd 4f out: n.m.r 2 1/2f out: r.o one pce* **20/1**

9 3 1/2 **Izaaj (USA)**[23] 796 3-8-8 100 .... (t) WJSupple 11 87
(M bin Shafya, UAE) *mid-div: trckd ldrs: n.m.r 1 1/2f out: nt rcvr* **50/1**

10 11 **Makaanah (KSA)**[29] 3-8-4 98 .... JBarria 10 61
(J Barton, Saudi Arabia) *n.d* **50/1**

11 3 1/4 **Uncle Tom (BRZ)**[23] 796 4-9-5 104 .... KierenFallon 8 62
(P Bary, France) *racd in rr: nvr able to chal* **20/1**

12 6 3/4 **Mr. Crazy Boy (ARG)**[22] 819 4-9-5 102 .... (b) CoreyBrown 14 48
(M F De Kock, South Africa) *in rr of mid-div: nvr able to chal* **40/1**

13 13 **Solid Choice (AUS)**[23] 796 4-9-5 102 .... (bt) KLatham 12 22
(M F De Kock, South Africa) *sn led: keen: hdd & wknd 3f out* **50/1**

P **Timely Jazz (IRE)**[22] 819 3-8-8 107 .... (vt) Per-AndersGraberg 13 —
(Niels Petersen, Norway) *trckd ldrs tl p.u 4f out* **25/1**

1m 57.44s (117.44)
WFA 3 from 4yo 19lb **14** Ran SP% **120.5**
CSF: £16.84.

Owner Sheikh Mohammed Bin Khalifa Al Maktoum **Bred** Sh Mohd Bin Khalifa Al Maktoum **Trained** South Africa

FOCUS

The ten previous runnings of this classic had been completely and utterly dominated by Godolphin (six wins) and Mike De Kock (four wins) and it would have been a major shock had that trend not continued. That stat considered, it was hardly surprising to note that six of the previous winners were bred in the northern hemisphere, although they were gained from a total of 80 representatives, compared to four southern hemisphere victories from only 47 runners. This year's Derby, the first to be run on a synthetic surface, looked a good race, and although it was a bit rough, not helped by Timely Jazz unfortunately going wrong inside the final half-mile, the form should prove solid. The pace was really strong, thanks to a stablemate of the winner, Solid Choice, who recovered from a slow start to lead after going wide around the first bend.

NOTEBOOK

Musir(AUS), held up last of all off the quick gallop for much of the way, stuck towards the inside, meaning he missed the trouble when Timely Jazz dropped away. Having made good headway around the final bend, he had little room in which to make his move at the top of the straight, but Soumillon went for a gap between the inside rail and Mendip, and his mount was good enough to take it, although the weakening Izaaj was badly hampered as a result. Once in the clear, Musir dispelled any stamina doubts with a strong staying effort, readily seeing off Godolphin's main hope, and always doing enough to keep his own trainer's filly, Raihana, at bay. The winner, now 3-3 in Dubai following victories in the Guineas trial and the Guineas itself (Frozen Power second both times), is considered by Mike De Kock to be the "classiest" of his four previous Derby winners. The plan now is apparently for him to continue his career in Australia, where he was bred, with David Payne, and the Cox Plate is his main aim.

Raihana(AUS), the UAE Oaks winner, ran a tremendous race in defeat. Another to benefit from the strong pace, she came through to have every chance but simply found one too good. Like Musir, she is expected to go to Australia in due course.

Mendip(USA) was visually impressive when winning the Al Bastakiya over C&D last time, but he got the run of the race that day and the final time was slow (1.98 seconds slower than this race). Faced with tougher company and a quite obviously stronger gallop, he came up short, but he still emerges with a deal of credit considering he raced slightly closer to the pace than the front two, and was checked in his run when just getting going. He gives the impression he still has some maturing to do and he looks a fine long-term prospect. (op:5/2)

Enak(ARG) finished closer to Mendip than he had in the Al Bastakiya, benefiting from the stronger pace this time. He came under pressure quite early, and then didn't have much room around the bend into the straight, but he basically wasn't quite good enough.

Frozen Power(IRE), twice second to Musir on this surface prior to winning a decent conditions race over 1m on the turf, came wide into the straight from well off the pace and didn't see his race out. His stamina was far from guaranteed and he looked a non-stayer, although he has had quite a few hard races now.

Siyaadah, who looked flattered to win the UAE 1000 Guineas, seemed to run to the same sort of level as when third to Raihana in the Oaks.

Oroveso(BRZ) didn't have a great deal of room around the bend into the straight, after which he was one-paced.

Della Barba(CHI) probably did too much too soon in chasing the strong pace, but that said, he basically doesn't look good enough for this sort of level.

Makaanah(KSA), a Group 1 winner in Saudi Arabia last time, is probably better than she showed seeing as she was hampered leaving the back straight.

1024a DUBAI GOLDEN SHAHEEN SPONSORED BY GULF NEWS (GROUP 1) (TAPETA) 6f

3:15 (3:15) 3-Y-0+

£740,740 (£246,913; £123,456; £61,728; £37,037; £24,691)

RPR

1 **Kinsale King (USA)**[63] 5-9-0 113 .... (bt) GKGomez 7 124
(Carl O'Callaghan, U.S.A) *trckd ldr: led 2f out: r.o wl: comf* **7/1**[3]

2 1/2 **Rocket Man (AUS)**[48] 5-9-0 121 .... RFradd 6 122+
(Patrick Shaw, Singapore) *trckd ldr: ev ch whn n.m.r 2 1/2f out: r.o wl fnl 2f* **7/4**[1]

3 2 **One World (AUS)**[34] 652 6-9-0 118 .... (t) DarrenBeadman 1 116
(J Moore, Hong Kong) *mid-div: rdn 3f out: r.o fnl f* **11/1**

4 1 1/2 **Laurel Guerreiro (JPN)**[34] 654 6-9-0 115 .... (b) ShinjiFujita 4 111
(Mitsugu Kon, Japan) *rdn to ld: hdd 2 1/2f out: wknd fnl f* **33/1**

5 1/4 **Eagle Falls (AUS)**[21] 5-9-0 115 .... (tp) CoreyBrown 2 110
(David Hayes, Australia) *racd in rr: n.d* **11/1**

6 hd **Benbaun (IRE)**[174] 6522 9-9-0 115 .... (v) PJSmullen 3 110
(K A Ryan) *in rr: nvr nr to chal* **16/1**

7 1/2 **Mutheeb (USA)**[23] 797 5-9-0 112 .... RichardHills 10 108
(M Al Muhairi, UAE) *mid-div: rdn to chse ldrs 2f out: nt qckn fnl f* **12/1**

8 1 1/4 **Gayego (USA)**[44] 515 5-9-0 115 .... (t) FrankieDettori 8 104
(Saeed Bin Suroor) *in rr: nvr able to chal* **3/1**[2]

9 1/2 **Force Freeze (USA)**[23] 797 5-9-0 112 .... (t) TadhgO'Shea 5 103
(Doug Watson, UAE) *trckd ldrs: rdn 3f out: wknd fnl f* **25/1**

10 1 1/2 **Regal Parade**[203] 5657 6-9-0 118 .... AdrianNicholls 9 98
(D Nicholls) *nvr able to chal* **12/1**

1m 10.89s (70.89) **10** Ran SP% **118.6**
CSF: £19.95.

Owner Sheehy LLC **Bred** Marvin Little Jr **Trained** North America

FOCUS

While the Al Quoz Sprint proved a success, its new place on the World Cup card has surely had a slightly negative impact on the Golden Shaheen, with most horses equally effective on turf and Tapeta. It's true there were some top-notch sprinters in this line up, but the race lacked depth and there were a number of runners in the earlier sprint who would by no means have been out of place in this field. Certainly something is not quite right when a $2,000,000 Group 1 cannot attract a maximum field of 12. The American dominance (six-time winners since the race attained Group 1 status in 2002) was expected to be under serious threat now that the event is staged on a synthetic surface, rather than dirt. However, the sole challenger from US proved good enough, thanks in no small part to a fine ride from the excellent Garrett Gomez, who was at his absolute best, whilst the runner-up's jockey was not.

NOTEBOOK

Kinsale King(USA), a dual Graded winner (but not at the highest level) on synthetics, most recently at Santa Anita in January, proved himself in Group 1 company with a game performance. Having shown good speed pretty much from the off, he was caught three-wide early on, but his chance was helped when Rocket Man was restrained just in behind the pace. As a consequence, he got first run on that rival and responded well to strong pressure to hold on. Regardless of the runner-up's somewhat troubled trip, this was a high-class performance from the winner, who is apparently going to be aimed at the Golden Jubilee at Royal Ascot.

Rocket Man(AUS) ◆, extremely well backed, might have won under a more positive ride, although that said, it's entirely possible Kinsale King would have pulled out more if joined. The main issue was Robbie Fradd's decision to give up his position between pacesetter Laurel Guerreiro and the winner after a couple of furlongs or so. That resulted in the 5-y-o being short of room at the top of the straight and he had to wait until about 300m out to get a clear run, by which time the winner had gone. It's to the horse's credit that he was able to recover his momentum and stay on for second. Rocket Man had to be operated for a condylar fracture of the off-side cannon bone last year, but it's clear he retains all of his ability. Trained in Singapore, his only previous defeat came when failing by just a neck to the great Sacred Kingdom in the International Sprint at Kranji last May, and he must have a huge chance of going one place better in that race this time around, especially with his old rival not sure to line up. (op 2-1)

One World(AUS), who had finished behind Sacred Kingdom on his last three starts, with the pick of those efforts probably coming when second in the Hong Kong Sprint, ran another honourable race in defeat. Having raced off the pace towards the inside from stall one, he was only in the clear 250m out, although the runner-up had to wait a similar length of time for his run.

Laurel Guerreiro(JPN), dual Grade 1 winner in Japan, didn't go off quite as fast as some might have expected and he stuck on reasonably well for fourth.

Eagle Falls(AUS) ◆, a Group 2 winner in Australia last year who was second in the prestigious Group 1 Newmarket Handicap last time, is better than he showed. Set a lot to do, he had nowhere to go at the top of the straight and faced an impossible task by the time he was in the clear, finishing well but much too late.

Benbaun(IRE) has a good record when fresh but he hasn't won over 6f since 2007 and he was simply too keen.

Mutheeb(USA) had a bit to find in this company and a wide trip from stall ten didn't help matters.

Gayego(USA) seemed badly in need of the run when second to War Artist over C&D in February (first outing since close fourth in the Breeders' Cup Sprint), and was expected to have come on a good deal. However, he was never travelling and failed to make any impression. This was disappointing. (op 11-4)

Regal Parade, who finished last season with victory in the Group 1 Haydock Sprint Cup, was stuck out widest and never threatened to get competitive.

1025a DUBAI DUTY FREE SPONSORED BY DUBAI DUTY FREE (GROUP 1) (TURF) 1m 1f

3:55 (3:58) 3-Y-0+

£1,851,851 (£617,283; £308,641; £154,320; £92,592; £61,728)

RPR

1 **Al Shemali**[23] 800 6-9-0 113 .... (t) RoystonFfrench 7 121
(A Al Raihe, UAE) *mid-div: rdn 3 1/2f out: chsd ldrs 2 1/2f out: led 1 1/2f out: r.o wl* **40/1**

2 1 1/2 **Bankable (IRE)**[36] 631 6-9-0 115 .... (t) KShea 8 118
(H J Brown, South Africa) *in rr of mid-div: rdn 2 1/2f out: r.o wl fnl 2f: nrst fin* **12/1**

3 3 1/4 **Imbongi (SAF)**[22] 823 6-9-0 115 .... ChristopheSoumillon 1 111
(M F De Kock, South Africa) *in rr of mid-div: r.o wl fnl 1 1/2f* **12/1**

4 1/4 **The Usual Q. T. (USA)**[56] 4-9-0 116 .... VEspinoza 9 110
(James Cassidy, U.S.A) *trckd ldng duo: ev ch 1 1/2f out: nt qckn* **20/1**

5 1/4 **Take The Points (USA)**[49] 4-9-0 117 .... (b) EPrado 10 110
(Todd Pletcher, U.S.A) *trckd ldr: led 3 1/2f out: hdd 1 1/2f out: r.o same pce* **14/1**

6 shd **Lahaleeb (IRE)**[23] 801 4-8-9 116 .... JohnEgan 13 105
(F Nass, Bahrain) *in rr of mid-div: r.o wl fnl 1 1/2f* **40/1**

7 3/4 **Ibn Battuta (USA)**[23] 801 5-9-0 113 .... WayneSmith 4 108
(M Al Muhairi, UAE) *nvr able to chal* **33/1**

8 1/4 **Good Ba Ba (USA)**[27] 8-9-0 122 .... (t) WCMarwing 2 107
(D Cruz, Hong Kong) *nvr bttr than mid-div* **7/1**[2]

9 1/2 **Courageous Cat (USA)**[35] 4-9-0 122 .... (t) GKGomez 5 106
(William Mott, U.S.A) *trckd ldng duo: ev ch 3f out: wknd fnl f* **8/1**[3]

10 1/4 **Calvados Blues (FR)**[22] 821 4-9-0 110 .... AhmedAjtebi 16 106
(Mahmood Al Zarooni) *settled in rr: nvr nr to chal* **50/1**

11 1/2 **Presvis**[23] 801 6-9-0 120 .... Christophe-PatriceLemaire 15 105
(L M Cumani) *in rr of mid-div: nvr able to chal* **15/8**[1]

12 3/4 **Snaafy (USA)**[22] 823 6-9-0 119 .... (v) RichardHills 14 103
(M Al Muhairi, UAE) *a mid-div: n.m.r 1 1/2f out* **33/1**

13 1/2 **Confront**[104] 7746 5-9-0 115 .... RyanMoore 12 102
(Sir Michael Stoute) *trckd ldrs: n.m.r 2f out: nt rcvr* **10/1**

14 1 1/2 **Alexandros**[23] 801 5-9-0 115 .... FrankieDettori 11 99
(Saeed Bin Suroor) *nvr bttr than mid-div* **7/1**[2]

15 2 1/4 **Justenuffhumor (USA)**[23] 801 5-9-0 116 .... TedDurcan 3 94
(Saeed Bin Suroor) *nvr able to chal* **25/1**

16 41 **Tam Lin**[23] 801 7-9-0 110 .... (t) WJSupple 6 3
(M bin Shafya, UAE) *sn led: hdd & wknd 3 1/2f out* **50/1**

1m 50.84s (110.84) **16** Ran SP% **125.3**
CSF: £452.62.

Owner Sheikh Hamdan Bin Mohammed Al Maktoum **Bred** Minster Stud **Trained** UAE

FOCUS

This race looked pretty much up to standard on paper, with the second, third, fifth and sixth from last year re-opposing, and taken on by some interesting newcomers to racing in Dubai, in the shape of Breeders' Cup Mile runner-up Courageous Cat, multiple Group/Grade 1 winners Good Ba Ba and Take The Points, and Confront, a progressive gelding representing Sir Michael Stoute. However, there looked to be a lack of pace in the race, and sure enough it turned into something of a tactical affair, with a result to delight the layers.

NOTEBOOK

Al Shemali, who was hovering around the 200 to 250 mark on Betfair prior to the race, had no chance on paper, having been well held in each of his previous five starts in Group company. His sixth when running on late off a steady pace in the third round of the Al Maktoum Challenge last time out wasn't a bad effort, but it would have taken a leap of faith to imagine he'd be able to beat a number of genuine Group 1 performers here. Having tracked the pace in around fifth place, he quickened up really well in the straight to go clear, and was always holding the late challenge of Bankable, but all in all this is probably one of those results that should be filed under 'wacky'.

Bankable(IRE) won the Al Fahidi Fort on his debut for his current connections and improved on his fifth in this race last year when trained by Mike de Kock with a strong-finishing second place. A better all-round gallop would undoubtedly have suited him, but it was a good effort from this very consistent 6-y-o.

Imbongi(SAF), beaten narrowly by Bankable in the Al Fahidi Fort and a winner of the Zabeel Mile since, has four wins to his name in Group 2 company but has been beaten on each of his five starts at Group 1 level. He tracked the winner through for much of the race but couldn't match his turn of foot from a furlong out.

The Usual Q. T.(USA) didn't take to the Pro-Ride when well beaten at Santa Anita last time but he'd previously looked progressive on turf and appreciated the return to this surface. Despite racing keenly off the ordinary early gallop, he was well placed just behind the leaders to make a dash for home once they swung into the straight.

Take The Points(USA), first past the post but later disqualified in a Grade 1 at Gulfstream last month, disputed the lead from an early stage and was another who benefited from the lack of pace in the race. He had every chance.

Lahaleeb(IRE) didn't run badly behind Presvis in the Jebel Hatta on her debut for new connections, but this looked more competitive. She had plenty to do turning into the straight and hung in on Alexandros a furlong out, but once straightened up she kept on well. Easier ground suits her ideally.

Ibn Battuta(USA), who looked to have a bit to find at this level, was in last place turning in but was brought with his challenge widest of all, thereby avoiding most of the trouble on his inner.

Good Ba Ba(USA) is a top-class performer at Sha Tin in Hong Kong, but that's a right-handed track, and he'd run below his best on his previous two starts outside that country, when sent to Japan, so the question was whether he would be as effective here as he is at home. It may be that he doesn't travel well, but not too much should be read into this performance as he's a classic hold-up performer, best off a decent gallop, and he simply didn't have the race run to suit. (op:7/1 tchd:13/2)

Courageous Cat(USA)'s second in the Breeders' Cup Mile was a big step up on anything he'd done before, but he won a Grade 3 race on his reappearance and came here with a progressive profile. Well placed tracking the leader on the rail, it's difficult to make too many excuses for him given the way the race unfolded. (op:10/1)

Calvados Blues(FR), back on turf and drawn widest of all, got chopped for room as Ibn Battuta hung into him a furlong out. He would have finished a little closer with a clear run.

Presvis, runner-up to all-the-way-winner Gladiatorus in this race last year, arrived here on the back of an impressive success over the C&D in the Jebel Hatta, where he gave 5lb and a beating to Alexandros. He wasn't done many favours by the draw, but as a hold-up performer that need not have been a huge concern. The prospect of a steady early pace was, though, as he needs luck when trying to find a way through and it helps if his rivals up front are weakening. Trying to make up ground from behind in the straight, he ran into a wall of horses and crossed the line having not been asked a serious question. He is very talented but needs the breaks, and is certainly vulnerable when there is no pace up front. It's also worth noting that Ryan Moore gets on particularly well with him, winning five times from seven starts, while other riders are now 1-10 on him. Apparently the plan is to return to Hong Kong next month to try and win the QEII Cup again. (op:9/4)

Snaafy(USA), who was drawn and raced wide, didn't get home. He's more effective at distances up to a mile.

Confront had the look of a typical improving older horse from the Stoute stable. A winner in Listed and Group 3 company before being beaten less than two lengths by Good Ba Ba in the Hong Kong Mile on his final start last season, he's bred to improve with age. He was just keeping on one-paced when hampered inside the final furlong and wasn't knocked about afterwards, and a more galloping track will suit him in future.

Alexandros is quite a keen-going sort and, although he was squeezed up inside the last, he didn't seem to be going anywhere fast at the time. He's probably at his best bossing lesser rivals in lower grade. (op:13/2)

1026a DUBAI SHEEMA CLASSIC SPONSORED BY GUANGSHA GROUP (GROUP 1) (TURF) 1m 4f 11y

4:35 (5:08) 3-Y-O+

£1,851,851 (£617,283; £308,641; £154,320; £92,592; £61,728)

Pos	Dist	Horse / Trainer / Comment	Jockey	SP	RPR
1		**Dar Re Mi**^{140} [7310] 5-8-9 120 (J H M Gosden) *mid-div: smooth prog 2 1/2f out: rdn to ld 1f out: r.o wl*	WilliamBuick 14	**9/1**^{3}	120
2	3/4	**Buena Vista (JPN)**^{35} 4-8-9 118 ow1 (Hiroyoshi Matsuda, Japan) *in rr: r.o wl fnl 2f: nrst fin*	OlivierPeslier 10	**6/1**^{1}	120
3	hd	**Spanish Moon (USA)**^{104} [7744] 6-9-0 120 (Sir Michael Stoute) *in rr: chsd ldrs 2f out: nt qckn fnl 50yds*	RyanMoore 13	**6/1**^{1}	123
4	3/4	**Deem (IRE)**^{30} [711] 5-8-9 110 (J Barton, Saudi Arabia) *mid-div: chsd ldrs 2 1/2f out: nt qckn fnl 100yds*	JRLeparoux 11	**50/1**	117
5	1 3/4	**Cavalryman**^{23} [800] 4-8-13 125 (Saeed Bin Suroor) *a mid-div*	FrankieDettori 16	**6/1**^{1}	120
6	1/2	**Eastern Anthem (IRE)**^{181} [6324] 6-9-0 117 (Mahmood Al Zarooni) *settled in rr: nvr nr to chal: r.o fnl 2f*	(t) AhmedAjtebi 2	**12/1**	118
7	3/4	**Pan River (TUR)**^{23} [799] 5-9-0 115 (Ayhan Kasar, Turkey) *settled in rr: nvr able to chal: r.o fnl 1 1/2f*	SelimKaya 4	**16/1**	117
8	1/4	**Youmzain (IRE)**^{104} [7744] 7-9-0 125 (M R Channon) *in rr: nvr able to chal*	KierenFallon 7	**7/1**^{2}	117
9	1 1/4	**Campanologist (USA)**^{23} [799] 5-9-0 116 (Saeed Bin Suroor) *in rr: nvr able to chal*	TedDurcan 15	**14/1**	115
10	2 3/4	**Pompeyano (IRE)**^{23} [799] 5-9-0 113 (S Seemar, UAE) *mid-div: chsd ldrs 3f out: sn btn*	(vt) RichardMullen 6	**66/1**	110
11	3/4	**Anmar (USA)**^{23} [799] 4-8-13 113 (Mahmood Al Zarooni) *nvr bttr than mid-div*	RichardHills 3	**25/1**	110
12	4 1/4	**Quijano (GER)**^{23} [799] 8-9-0 118 (P Schiergen, Germany) *nvr bttr than mid-div*	AStarke 5	**40/1**	102
13	8	**Mourilyan (IRE)**^{44} [516] 6-9-0 116 (H J Brown, South Africa) *s.i.s: in rr: n.d*	(t) KShea 12	**20/1**	89
14	13	**Golden Sword**^{23} [799] 4-8-13 117 (M F De Kock, South Africa) *trckd ldr: led 3f out: hdd 2f out: wknd*	ChristopheSoumillon 8	**20/1**	70
15	2 1/4	**Jukebox Jury (IRE)**^{161} [6873] 4-8-13 118 (M Johnston) *led main gp: chsd ldrs 3f out: sn rdn and btn*	RoystonFfrench 1	**12/1**	66
16	1/2	**Presious Passion (USA)**^{27} 7-9-0 123 (Mary Hartmann, U.S.A) *sn led: hdd & wknd 3f out*	(b) ElvisTrujillo 9	**12/1**	64

2m 31.84s (151.84)
WFA 4 from 5yo+ 2lb **16** Ran SP% **120.2**
CSF: £56.58.
Owner Lord Lloyd-Webber **Bred** Watership Down Stud **Trained** Newmarket, Suffolk

FOCUS

A competitive field featuring nine individual Group/Grade 1 winners. With the trail-blazing Presious Passion in the line-up, there was never any doubt that the race would be run at a strong gallop, and the form looks very solid for the grade.

NOTEBOOK

Dar Re Mi developed into a high-class performer last season, the best of her sex in Europe, and this was yet another career-high, as she reversed Arc form with Youmzain and Cavalryman, while also confirming Breeders' Cup Turf form with Spanish Moon. Given a fine ride by William Buick, who could not have kicked off his first season as stable jockey to John Gosden any better, the mare enjoyed a trouble-free run, swept five wide off the final bend and kept on strongly to edge ahead around half a furlong out. She's clearly now a very valuable broodmare prospect but she continues in training this season, with the Breeders' Cup again the long-term target, although the Filly & Mare Turf rather than the Turf is favoured by her trainer this time. On this showing, though, she's well up to taking on the boys in races like the Coronation Cup and King George, and she's likely to be given entries for both.

Buena Vista(JPN), winner of the Japanese Guineas and Oaks last year and successful in her prep race five weeks earlier, made it a one-two for the girls. Given a patient ride, she was denied some racing room by Deem around a furlong out but saw her race out well inside the last half furlong and looks to have run right up to her best.

Spanish Moon(USA), denied by the narrowest of margins in this race last year, had been off the track since December, but he goes well fresh. He picked up well alongside the winner once the gap came for him a furlong and a half out, but couldn't quite see her off. He's become a consistent performer at the top level.

Deem(IRE) was only seventh in this race last year but looks to have improved since. Quite versatile regarding distance, she won the Balanchine over 1m1f on her reappearance, but recorded a career-best on this return to 1m4f.

Cavalryman, the Arc third, ran acceptably on his debut for Godolphin in the third round of the Al Maktoum Challenge, and the return to turf coupled with a step up to 1m4f promised to suit him. He hit the front inside the final 2f, but edged left and weakened inside the last. It was a fair effort but he'll need to step up if he's to compete for the top middle-distance prizes in Europe this summer.

Eastern Anthem(IRE), last year's winner, had the benefit of coming into the race on the back of a successful carnival last season. This time he was asked to win it first time up, and although the tongue tie, missing for his last three starts, was back on, he wasn't quite up to repeating. He did finish well down the outside, though. (op 14-1)

Pan River(TUR), who ran Campanologist to a neck in a Group 2 here last time, managed to reverse that form despite being slightly hampered at one stage early in the straight.

Youmzain(IRE), three times an Arc runner-up, had run with credit in this race the previous three years, but had never had a strong gallop to run off before. With Presious Passion taking them along at a really good pace, he looked to have the race set up for his trademark late finish, but for some reason he failed to deliver, despite being brought to have his chance down the outside in the straight.

Campanologist(USA) is not quite up to Group 1 standard, but he will no doubt pay his way at a slightly lower level again this season. He cannot have the ground too fast.

Quijano(GER), who has 14 wins to his name, has never won on ground quicker than good. These conditions were probably on the fast side for him.

Mourilyan(IRE) is another not quite up to this level, at least over this distance. He stays 2m well and just found things happening too quickly in this high-class race.

Golden Sword paid for chasing the strong gallop set by Breeders' Cup Turf runner-up Presious Passion.

Jukebox Jury(IRE), who likes to be up there, led the chasing pack behind the front two, but was another beaten on the turn in. This ground might have been quick enough for him, and he's entitled to come on for this first run since October.

Presious Passion(USA) only knows one way to race and soon built up his customary early advantage, but try as he might to get a breather into him, his rider was unable to conserve enough of the gelding's energy, and he was headed and beaten before the turn in.

1027a DUBAI WORLD CUP SPONSORED BY EMIRATES AIRLINE (GROUP 1) (TAPETA) 1m 2f

5:45 (5:53) 3-Y-O+

£3,703,703 (£1,234,567; £617,283; £308,641; £185,185; £123,456)

Pos	Dist	Horse / Trainer / Comment	Jockey	SP	RPR
1		**Gloria De Campeao (BRZ)**^{23} [800] 7-9-0 120 (P Bary, France) *sn led: rdn clr 2 1/2f out: r.o wl: jst hld on*	TJPereira 5	**16/1**	122
2	nse	**Lizard's Desire (SAF)**^{23} [800] 5-9-0 116 (M F De Kock, South Africa) *in rr of mid-div: smooth prog 3 1/2f out: r.o wl: jst failed*	KShea 7	**33/1**	122
3	shd	**Allybar (IRE)**^{23} [800] 4-9-0 117 (Mahmood Al Zarooni) *trckd ldrs: ev ch 1 1/2f out: nt qckn fnl 110yds*	AhmedAjtebi 1	**16/1**	121
4	1 1/4	**Gio Ponti (USA)**^{35} [651] 5-9-0 125 (Christophe Clement, U.S.A) *in rr of mid-div: r.o fnl 1 1/2f: nrst fin*	RADominguez 4	**5/1**^{2}	119+
5	shd	**Mastery**^{141} [7281] 4-9-0 117 (Saeed Bin Suroor) *trckd ldrs: nt qckn fnl 2f*	FrankieDettori 12	**16/1**	119
6	3/4	**Gitano Hernando**^{28} [738] 4-9-0 120 (M Botti) *a in mid-div*	KierenFallon 2	**10/3**^{1}	120+
7	1/4	**Richard's Kid (USA)**^{48} 5-9-0 119 (Bob Baffert, U.S.A) *settled in rr: nvr nr to chal*	(bt) GKGomez 10	**16/1**	117+
8	1/4	**Mr Brock (SAF)**^{23} [800] 7-9-0 117 (M F De Kock, South Africa) *trckd ldrs: ev ch 1 1/2f out: wknd fnl 110yds*	RyanMoore 13	**40/1**	117
9	1/4	**Crowded House**^{37} [609] 4-9-0 118 (B J Meehan) *settled in rr: nvr nr to chal*	JRVelazquez 9	**11/1**	116
10	hd	**Twice Over**^{140} [7311] 5-9-0 123 (H R A Cecil) *a in mid-div*	TomQueally 11	**11/2**^{3}	116
11	2 3/4	**Red Desire (JPN)**^{23} [800] 4-8-9 116 (Mikio Matsunaga, Japan) *nvr bttr than mid-div*	ChristopheSoumillon 3	**6/1**	105
12	1 1/4	**Vision D'Etat (FR)**^{104} [7747] 5-9-0 123 (E Libaud, France) *a mid-div*	OlivierPeslier 6	**13/2**	108
13	1/2	**Amor De Pobre (CHI)**^{43} 5-9-0 113 (J Barton, Saudi Arabia) *trckd ldr: rdn 3f out: sn btn*	AGryder 14	**66/1**	107
14	4 1/2	**Furthest Land (USA)**^{48} 5-9-0 115 (Michael J Maker, U.S.A) *in rr of mid-div: nvr able to chal*	(b) JRLeparoux 8	**40/1**	98

2m 3.83s (123.83) **14** Ran SP% **123.9**
CSF: £480.71. Placepot: £5,286.10 to a £1 stake. Pool: £9413.75. 1.30 winning tickets. Quadpot: £305.60 to a £1 stake. Pool: £413.00. 0.10 winning tickets..

Owner Estrela Energia Stables **Bred** Haras Santarem **Trained** Chantilly, France

■ This was the first year that the World Cup was staged at Meydan on a synthetic surface.

FOCUS

While the race can obviously no longer expect to attract the top American dirt performers (there had been eight previous US-trained winners, including true greats like Cigar and Curlin), it was a shame Zenyatta, so brilliant on similar synthetic surfaces, didn't represent the States. In that one's absence, the pre-race impression was that there was no genuinely top-class runner on show, with the highest official mark on offer being 125, and the top RPR being 127 (both Gio Ponti). Therefore a far more open race than has often been the case was expected, and that is exactly how it turned out. From a form perspective it was a highly unsatisfactory contest, with the winner allowed to set a modest pace (time only the fourth quickest of nine thoroughbred races to be run over the trip so far at Meydan), resulting in a bunch finish and many of the leading contenders being inconvenienced. However, while far from being an ideal punting medium, this was certainly not a race to be completely negative about - it provided a thrilling international spectacle for the neutral. Between them the 14 runners were trained in seven different countries and had amassed a total of 17 victories around the world at the highest level. And with there being so little between them on form, combined with the lack of pace, there was a tremendous finish, with any number of these in with a chance at the top of the straight, before three of them crossed the line almost as one in a bid to capture to richest prize in horse racing. It was the domestic form that proved the key, and more specifically, the main C&D trial, the third round of the Al Maktoum Challenge. Indeed, the first three finishers had all contested that prep race. Gloria Di Campeao is the lowest rated winner in the race's history on RPRs.

NOTEBOOK

Gloria De Campeao(BRZ) was only just caught by Red Desire last time, and with the Japanese filly below form, confirming placings with the three runners who were behind him that day proved good enough. He was beaten 14l into second in this race 12 months ago, having managed only eighth the season before that, but he proved himself a better horse away from the dirt when winning a Singapore Group 1 on turf last May and has really taken to the Tapeta since returning to Dubai this year. However, while this was a magnificent achievement for all concerned, from a form perspective this 7-y-o must be considered flattered by the bare result. He's tough and honest, but by no means top class and will probably struggle to ever repeat such a performance. Incidentally, Gloria De Campeao became the first winner of this race not trained in either America or by Godolphin since Singspiel in 1997.

Lizard's Desire(SAF) has made tremendous progress in Dubai this year, winning a couple of handicaps before a slightly unlucky fifth (might have been second at least) in the third round of the Al Maktoum Challenge, and this was his best performance so far. He lost out literally on the nod and emerges with a deal of credit considering he came from a fair way back, although he did enjoy a clearer trip than some.

Allybar(IRE) progressed extremely well on this surface at the carnival, winning twice before a close fourth in the trial, and he showed himself to still be very much on the way up. He didn't get in the clear until about 200m out, and although perhaps slightly unlucky not to beat the winner, the runner-up finished that bit stronger than him.

Gio Ponti(USA) couldn't match the form he showed when second to Zenyatta in the Breeders' Cup Classic, but the way the race unfolded didn't allow him to. The steady pace wasn't much use to him and he simply couldn't quicken sufficiently once taken to the outside in the straight, although he still finished well. (op: 6/1)

Mastery, last year's St Leger winner, had gained experience of a synthetic surface when third in the Breeders' Cup Marathon and ran a fine race over a trip surely short of his optimum. He managed to get a handy position from a wide draw, but the lack of pace in the race certainly didn't help his chance and, although having to be switched around 200m out, he simply lacked the speed of those who finished ahead of him.

Gitano Hernando ◆, the winner of his four previous starts on synthetics, came into this off the same sort of preparation as he had prior to his win in the Grade 1 Goodwood at Santa Anita last year, and he was extremely well backed in the UK. However, nothing went his way and it's to his credit he was able to finish so close. For starters, the steady pace was never going to suit such a big, powerful galloper, and while he did well to still be in with some sort of a shout early in the straight, he was continually blocked in his run. His momentum was completely halted just over 200m out, and the manner in which he picked afterwards once finally in the open suggests he was a bit unlucky. There should be another decent prize in this colt. (op:7/2)

Richard's Kid(USA) was just about last when swinging widest of all at the top of the straight but finished strongly. He has shown high-class form on synthetics in the US and this was a noteworthy performance. (op:14/1)

Mr Brock(SAF) had little to find with the front three, but he suffered a wide trip in trying to get a handy position form stall 13.

Crowded House should have been thereabouts judged on carnival form, but he ran a lacklustre race, again taking an age to get into his stride, before failing to make much progress for pressure, even allowing for the lack of pace in the race.

Twice Over, reappearing after his hard race behind Gio Ponti in the Breeders' Cup Classic, wasn't helped by his draw and raced too freely out wide down the back straight. (op:5/1)

Red Desire(JPN) had picked up well off a similarly modest tempo when defeating today's front three over C&D on her Dubai debut, but she was unable to produce the same kind of finishing kick this time.

Vision D'Etat(FR) had to be examined by the Vet on the morning of the race prior to be allowed to take his chance, with there reportedly being a concern about slight stiffness in the horse. There was, though, a similar scare prior to his Hong Kong Cup victory. After racing keenly off the pace, the response was limited when he came under pressure. (op:6/1)

Furthest Land(USA) has struggled since winning last year's Breeders' Cup Dirt Mile and was too keen this time.

1006 DONCASTER (L-H)

Sunday, March 28

OFFICIAL GOING: Good to soft (soft in places; 6.3)

Wind: Fresh 1/2 against Weather: Fine, breezy and cold

1028 AJA GENTLEMAN AMATEUR RIDERS' H'CAP — 1m 2f 60y

2:00 (2:00) (Class 5) (0-70,70) 4-Y-0+ — **£2,498** (£774; £387; £193) **Stalls** Low

Form — RPR

600- **1** — **Blue Spinnaker (IRE)**[160] [6900] 11-10-2 **58** .... MrOGreenall 4 — 72
(M W Easterby) *hld up in rr: smooth hdwy on inner over 3f out: led 2f out: rdn clr appr fnl f: styd on wl* **10/3**[1]

25-5 **2** *3 ¼* **Nisaal (IRE)**[27] [752] 5-10-10 **66** .... (p) MrSWalker 1 — 74
(J J Quinn) *trckd ldrs on inner: swtchd rt and hdwy over 2f out: rdn over 1f out: chsd wnr ins fnl f: no impm* **11/2**[2]

0-36 **3** *1 ¼* **Sea Land (FR)**[12] [895] 6-9-7 **56** oh9 .... MrJohnWilley(7) 10 — 61+
(B Ellison) *hld up towards rr: hdwy over 2f out: sn rdn and styd on strly ent fnl f: nrst fin* **50/1**

0-13 **4** *1* **Magic Haze**[31] [705] 4-10-2 **58** .... MrHarryChalloner 5 — 62
(Miss S E Hall) *trckd ldrs: swtchd ins and rdn over 2f out: kpt on ins fnl f: nrst fin* **12/1**

613- **5** *1 ¾* **Crystal Feather**[209] [5524] 4-10-1 **62** .... MrJPFeatherstone(5) 7 — 62
(E F Vaughan) *t.k.h: a.p: effrt 3f out: rdn to ld briefly over 2f out: hdd and drvn 2f out: grad wknd* **16/1**

560- **6** *1* **Wovoka (IRE)**[159] [6924] 7-11-0 **70** .... MrAJBerry 6 — 68
(K A Ryan) *hld up in rr: stdy hdwy 4f out: chsd ldrs 2f out: sn rdn and kpt on same pce* **14/1**

4-50 **7** *1 ¾* **Ermine Grey**[18] [853] 9-9-11 **56** oh1 .... MrRJKirk(3) 13 — 51
(A W Carroll) *t.k.h: midfield: hdwy and in tch whn edgd rt over 4f out: rdn to chse ldrs over 2f out: sn drvn and btn* **16/1**

23-3 **8** *¾* **Onemoreandstay**[11] [76] 5-10-4 **67** .... MrJMQuinlan(7) 14 — 61
(H J Collingridge) *chsd ldrs: pushed along 4f out: rdn wl over 2f out and sn no imp* **14/1**

46-0 **9** *nk* **Nayessence**[82] [42] 4-9-7 **56** oh6 .... (t) LukeStrong(7) 8 — 49
(M W Easterby) *prom: led after 2f: rdn along 3f out: hdd over 2f out: grad wknd* **100/1**

5134 **10** *2 ¼* **Ella Woodcock (IRE)**[18] [855] 6-10-13 **69** .... MrSDobson 3 — 58
(E J Alston) *hld up towards rr: hdwy over 4f out: rdn along over 3f out and n.d* **11/1**

000- **11** *½* **Monfils Monfils (USA)**[91] [7851] 8-9-13 **60** .... AdamWedge(5) 12 — 48
(R E Barr) *midfield: hdwy on outer whn bmpd over 4f out: rdn over 3f out and sn wknd* **20/1**

36-3 **12** *2 ½* **Waahej**[9] [941] 4-10-5 **64** .... MrPCollington(3) 16 — 47
(P W Hiatt) *in tch: hdwy to chse ldrs 1/2-way: rdn along 3f out: sn drvn and wknd* **14/1**

5022 **13** *1 ¼* **Mustajed**[18] [842] 9-10-2 **63** .... (b) MrPMillman(5) 15 — 44
(B R Millman) *hld up towards rr: gd hdwy 1/2-way: effrt towards to chse ldrs over 3f out: sn rdn and btn over 2f out* **8/1**[3]

4222 **14** *2 ½* **Dream In Blue**[19] [833] 5-9-7 **56** oh11 .... (p) MrATBrook(7) 9 — 32
(J A Glover) *hld up in rr: sme hdwy on wd outside over 4f out: sn rdn and nvr a factor* **16/1**

425- **15** *3 ¾* **Everaard (USA)**[47] [6975] 4-10-5 **68** .... HenryBrooke(7) 11 — 37
(Mrs K Walton) *a towards rr* **50/1**

066 **16** *9* **Mojeerr**[9] [942] 4-9-9 **56** oh10 .... (p) MrBMMorris(5) 18 — 8
(A J McCabe) *chsd ldrs: rdn along 5f out: sn wknd* **40/1**

0P-6 **17** *nk* **State General (IRE)**[28] [746] 4-10-3 **62** .... (b1) MrRBirkett(3) 2 — 13
(Miss J Feilden) *led 2f: prom tl rdn along 4f out and sn wknd* **25/1**

2m 19.05s (9.65) **Going Correction** +0.475s/f (Yiel) — **17** Ran SP% **119.2**

Speed ratings (Par 103): **87,84,83,82,81 80,79,78,78,76 75,73,72,70,67 60,60**

toteswingers: 1&2 £6.20, 1&3 £46.30, 2&3 £79.50 CSF £17.75 CT £782.22 TOTE £3.90: £1.70, £1.60, £8.30, £3.00; EX 26.20 TRIFECTA Not won..

Owner T C Dewhirst **Bred** M3 Elevage And Haras D'Etreham **Trained** Sheriff Hutton, N Yorks

FOCUS

Following a dry night the ground had dried out slightly and was officially described as good to soft, soft in places. An ordinary amateur riders' handicap and they didn't appear to go that quick.

1029 CROWNHOTEL-BAWTRY.COM MAIDEN STKS — 7f

2:30 (2:34) (Class 4) 3-Y-O — **£4,533** (£1,348; £674; £336) **Stalls** High

Form — RPR

1 — **Bullwhip (IRE)** 3-9-3 0 .... RobertHavlin 14 — 93+
(J H M Gosden) *w'like: cmpt: lw: swvd rt s: sn trcking ldrs: smooth hdwy to ld 2f out: sn wnt rt away: eased fnl 50yds* **7/1**[3]

2 *7* **African Wave (USA)** 3-9-3 0 .... WilliamBuick 6 — 74
(J H M Gosden) *w'like: cmpt: mid-div: hdwy to chse wnr over 1f out: kpt on same pce* **3/1**[2]

0- **3** *½* **Fifty Moore**[288] [2936] 3-9-3 0 .... AndrewElliott 16 — 73
(Jedd O'Keeffe) *chsd ldrs: wnt 3rd 1f out: styd on same pce* **66/1**

36- **4** *1 ¾* **Cultivar**[208] [5542] 3-9-3 0 .... MichaelHills 8 — 68
(B W Hills) *lw: trckd ldrs: effrt 2f out: kpt on same pce* **2/1**[1]

0- **5** *4 ½* **Brananx (USA)**[156] [6990] 3-9-3 0 .... JamieSpencer 11 — 56+
(K A Ryan) *swvd rt s: hld up in rr: nt clr run over 3f out: kpt on steadily fnl 2f* **10/1**

36- **6** *1 ¾* **Monkton Vale (IRE)**[156] [6982] 3-9-3 0 .... PaulHanagan 4 — 51
(R A Fahey) *in rr-div: styd on fnl 2f: nvr nr ldrs* **9/1**

26- **7** *shd* **Battle Study (IRE)**[135] [7376] 3-8-12 68 .... DeclanCannon(5) 13 — 51
(A J McCabe) *dwlt: sn chsng ldrs: outpcd fnl 2f* **50/1**

P00- **8** *6* **Dovedon Diva**[141] [7288] 3-8-12 0 .... SaleemGolam 10 — 30
(T Keddy) *t.k.h in rr: sme hdwy 2f out: nvr on terms* **150/1**

250- **9** *½* **Tislaam (IRE)**[192] [6009] 3-9-3 79 .... PaulMulrennan 17 — 33
(J S Wainwright) *dwlt: hld up in rr: kpt on fnl 2f: nvr a factor* **33/1**

04- **10** *¾* **Yes Chef**[156] [6990] 3-9-3 0 .... FergusSweeney 7 — 31
(J Gallagher) *led: hdd 2f out: sn wknd* **20/1**

11 *½* **Marteau** 3-9-3 0 .... NeilCallan 9 — 30
(K A Ryan) *rangy unf: scope: hld up in rr: sme hdwy over 2f out: nvr on terms* **25/1**

0- **12** *½* **Russian Brigadier**[156] [6990] 3-9-3 0 .... AlanMunro 2 — 29
(M Brittain) *uns rdr and rn loose to s: trckd ldrs: t.k.h: lost pl 2f out* **100/1**

0 **13** *3 ¼* **Collect Art (IRE)**[10] [915] 3-8-10 0 .... IanBurns(7) 5 — 20
(M L W Bell) *rrd s: sn chsng ldrs: rdr dropped reign over 2f out: wknd over 1f out* **50/1**

14 *1* **Raktiman (IRE)** 3-9-3 0 .... RichardKingscote 3 — 17
(Tom Dascombe) *rangy: unf: mid-div: rdn and lost pl over 2f out* **16/1**

15 *14* **Eviction (IRE)** 3-9-3 0 .... GrahamGibbons 1 — —
(E S McMahon) *leggy: unf: scope: unruly s: s.s: sn chsng ldrs: wknd 2f out: bhd and eased ins fnl f* **16/1**

00- **16** *17* **Media Jury**[170] [6646] 3-9-3 0 .... DavidNolan 12 — —
(J S Wainwright) *swvd rt s: rr-div: drvn over 2f out: bhd and eased ins fnl f* **200/1**

1m 32.15s (5.85) **Going Correction** +0.575s/f (Yiel) — **16** Ran SP% **120.8**

Speed ratings (Par 100): **89,81,80,78,73 71,71,64,63,62 62,61,58,56,40 21**

toteswingers: 1&2 £5.60, 1&3 £53.30, 2&3 £34.70 CSF £26.42 TOTE £8.10: £3.10, £1.90, £12.60; EX 19.10 TRIFECTA Not won..

Owner H R H Princess Haya Of Jordan **Bred** John O'Connor **Trained** Newmarket, Suffolk

FOCUS

Quite an interesting maiden, even though the betting suggested it wasn't that competitive. They raced as a group down the centre of the track and eventually finished spread out all over Town Moor. It resulted in a one-two for trainer John Gosden.

1030 WILLIAMHILL.COM - PLAY BLACKJACK H'CAP — 7f

3:00 (3:03) (Class 4) (0-85,85) 4-Y-O+ — **£4,533** (£1,348; £674; £336) **Stalls** High

Form — RPR

644- **1** — **Deadly Encounter (IRE)**[241] [4459] 4-8-12 **79** .... PaulHanagan 7 — 91
(R A Fahey) *trckd ldrs: hdwy over 2f out: rdn and hung rt over 1f out: drvn ins fnl f and styd on to ld nr line* **5/1**[3]

000- **2** *hd* **Internationaldebut (IRE)**[168] [6702] 5-9-4 **85** .... TonyCulhane 17 — 96+
(P T Midgley) *hld up towards rr: gd hdwy 1/2-way: effrt and pushed wd over 2f out: qcknd to ld wl over 1f out: drvn and edgd rt ins fnl f: hdd nr line* **25/1**

5315 **3** *1* **Dubai Dynamo**[15] [887] 5-9-3 **84** .... AndrewElliott 15 — 93
(Mrs R A Carr) *hld up in rr: swtchd rt and gd hdwy 2f out: rdn over 1f out and ev ch tl drvn and nt qckn ins fnl f* **12/1**

The Form Book, Raceform Ltd, Compton, RG20 6NL

405- **4** *2* **Toto Skyllachy**[115] 7617 5-8-10 **77** .... KierenFallon 14 80
(J O'Reilly) *midfield: pushed along 1/2-way: swtchd lft and rdn over 2f out: styd on appr fnl f: nrst fin* **4/1**[2]

240- **5** *3* **Legal Legacy**[170] 6645 4-8-12 **79** .... PhillipMakin 13 74
(M Dods) *in tch: hdwy over 2f out: effrt and ev ch wl over 1f out: sn rdn: edgd lft and wknd ent fnl f* **12/1**

160- **6** *1* **Regeneration (IRE)**[148] 7189 4-8-9 **76** .... JamieSpencer 19 69
(M L W Bell) *hld up towards rr: hdwy over 2f out: rdn over 1f out: kpt on ins fnl f: nvr nr ldrs* **3/1**[1]

0-00 **7** *1* **Carlitos Spirit (IRE)**[63] 285 6-8-9 **76** .... TomEaves 11 66
(I W McInnes) *wnt rt s and towards rr: hdwy over 2f out: sn rdn and kpt on appr fnl f: nvr nr ldrs* **100/1**

056- **8** *nk* **Captain Dancer (IRE)**[156] 6997 4-8-6 **73** .... RobertWinston 1 62
(B W Hills) *prom: effrt over 2f out: sn rdn and ev ch tl edgd lft and wknd over 1f out* **13/2**

600- **9** *hd* **Zomerlust**[153] 7060 8-9-4 **85** .... GrahamGibbons 16 74
(J J Quinn) *in tch: pushed along 1/2-way: kpt on same pce fnl 2f* **20/1**

000- **10** *2 1/2* **Game Lad**[180] 6361 8-8-5 **72** ....(t) DuranFentiman 9 54+
(T D Easterby) *midfield: effrt and n.m.r over 2f out: sn rdn and no hdwy* **20/1**

200- **11** *1/2* **Violent Velocity (IRE)**[145] 7220 7-8-2 **76** .... IanBrennan(7) 5 56
(J J Quinn) *chsd ldrs: rdn along over 2f out and grad wknd* **33/1**

10-1 **12** *1/2* **Steel Stockholder**[62] 292 4-8-4 **71** oh1 .... JimmyQuinn 12 50
(M Brittain) *in tch: effrt to chse ldrs wl over 2f out: sn rdn and wknd wl over 1f out* **12/1**

6152 **13** *3/4* **Ishiadancer**[18] 850 5-9-4 **85** .... EddieAhern 6 62
(E J Alston) *led: rdn along over 2f out: hdd & wknd wl over 1f out* **20/1**

400- **14** *1 1/4* **Bid For Gold**[141] 7287 6-7-12 **72** .... EleanorMcGowan(7) 10 46
(Jedd O'Keeffe) *prom: rdn along wl over 2f out and sn wknd* **100/1**

000- **15** *hd* **Knavesmire (IRE)**[170] 6645 4-8-10 **77** .... AlanMunro 2 50
(M Brittain) *a in rr* **40/1**

-014 **16** *2* **Ponting (IRE)**[54] 380 4-8-3 **75** .... PaulPickard(5) 8 43
(P T Midgley) *cl up: rdn along over 2f out: wknd whn hmpd wl over 1f out* **33/1**

30-0 **17** *2* **Smarty Socks (IRE)**[19] 837 6-9-1 **82** .... PJMcDonald 4 44
(P T Midgley) *v.s.a and a bhd* **40/1**

1120 **18** *hd* **Hereford Boy**[28] 749 6-8-13 **80** ....(p) RobertHavlin 18 42
(D K Ivory) *a in rr* **33/1**

33-6 **19** *13* **Frognal (IRE)**[17] 859 4-9-4 **85** .... PaulMulrennan 3 12
(Mrs R A Carr) *chsd ldrs: rdn along over 2f out: sn wknd* **40/1**

1m 30.75s (4.45) **Going Correction** +0.575s/f (Yiel) **19** Ran SP% **134.3**
Speed ratings (Par 105): **97,96,95,93,89 88,87,87,87,84 83,83,82,80,80 78,75,75,60**
toteswingers: 1&2 £37.70, 1&3 £14.80, 2&3 £62.70 CSF £137.64 CT £1520.63 TOTE £5.80: £2.00, £4.40, £3.60, £1.60; EX 149.80 Trifecta £167.40 Part won. Pool: £226.29 - 0.50 winning units..
Owner Mrs M W Kenyon & S Bradley **Bred** R A Fahey **Trained** Musley Bank, N Yorks

FOCUS
A competitive handicap and again the field raced as one group down the centre. There were several still in with a chance coming to the last furlong and the winning time was 1.4 seconds faster than the maiden.
Game Lad Official explanation: jockey said gelding was denied a clear run
Smarty Socks(IRE) Official explanation: jockey said gelding was slowly away

1031 WILLIAMHILL.COM - PLAY ROULETTE DONCASTER SHIELD (CONDITIONS STKS) 1m 4f
3:35 (3:35) (Class 2) 4-Y-O+ **£12,952** (£3,854; £1,926; £962) **Stalls** Low

Form RPR
061- **1** **Merchant Of Dubai**[128] 7465 5-9-0 99 .... RobertWinston 7 107
(G A Swinbank) *led 2f: led 8f out: chal over 1f out: hld on gamely* **9/2**

1115 **2** *nk* **Spruce (USA)**[11] 903 4-8-12 95 .... JimmyQuinn 6 106
(Miss J Feilden) *trckd ldrs: wnt 2nd over 2f out: hung lft and chal appr fnl f: no ex nr fin* **16/1**

164- **3** *12* **Hidden Brief**[109] 7697 4-8-8 94 ow1 .... NeilCallan 2 83
(M A Jarvis) *w ldr: t.k.h: led after 2f: hdd 8f out: drvn 3f out: wandered and wknd over 1f out* **7/2**[2]

0662 **4** *6* **Record Breaker (IRE)**[11] 903 6-9-0 100 ....(b) RichardHills 4 77
(M Johnston) *lw: in tch: pushed along over 5f out: sn chsng ldrs: wknd appr fnl f* **4/1**[3]

110- **5** *12* **Furmigadelagiusta**[260] 3874 6-9-6 108 .... PaulHanagan 8 64
(R A Fahey) *sn chsng ldrs: effrt over 3f out: wknd over 2f out: eased ins fnl f* **15/8**[1]

3-31 **6** *12* **Daaweitza**[12] 897 7-9-0 84 .... TomEaves 1 39
(B Ellison) *chsd ldrs: drvn along 6f out: lost pl 3f out* **50/1**

7 *73* **Prince Apollo**[208] 5-9-4 95 .... JamieSpencer 5 —
(Ian Williams) *lw: stdd s: t.k.h detached in last: drvn 6f out: lost pl over 3f out: sn bhd and eased: wl t.o* **14/1**

2m 36.51s (1.61) **Going Correction** +0.475s/f (Yiel)
WFA 4 from 5yo+ 2lb **7** Ran SP% **109.7**
Speed ratings (Par 109): **114,113,105,101,93 85,37**
toteswingers: 1&2 £6.00, 1&3 £3.70, 2&3 £5.20 CSF £62.57 TOTE £5.30: £2.20, £4.20; EX 58.80 Trifecta £322.20 Part won. Pool: £435.47 - 0.10 winning units..
Owner Highland Racing 2 **Bred** A Smith **Trained** Melsonby, N Yorks

FOCUS
This race had only been won once by a four-year-old in the last eight runnings at Doncaster and that trend continued, if only just. The runners came up the centre of the track after turning in, but despite the early pace only looking steady it developed into a thrilling match over the last couple of furlongs.

NOTEBOOK
Merchant Of Dubai hadn't been seen since winning a decent handicap at Wolverhampton in November, but he has shown that he can go well fresh. Having grabbed the race by the scruff of the neck half a mile from home, he faced a stern challenge from the runner-up throughout the last couple of furlongs but his stamina came into play and he just managed to hold on to win with nothing to spare. He may go for a Group 3 at Cologne next. (op 10-3)
Spruce(USA) has been a revelation on sand this winter, but he was around four lengths behind Record Breaker at Kempton earlier this month and showed little in three outings on turf in France. However, he travelled very well behind the leaders and tried his hardest to get to the winner but, despite giving it his all, he came up against a very determined rival. This proved once and for all that he can handle grass which opens up all sorts of options for him, though his handicap mark may suffer as a result of this.
Hidden Brief was returning from three months off. She set the early pace, but she was struggling as soon as the winner went for home half a mile out and could merely plug on for third from that point. She had questions to answer over this longer trip in the ground and this didn't really answer them. (op 9-2 tchd 5-1 in places)
Record Breaker(IRE), fit from a spell at Meydan when chasing home a progressive sort in a Listed contest at Kempton earlier this month, was still travelling well passing the 3f pole but found nothing like as much off the bridle as had seemed likely. He probably needs better ground. (op 5-1 tchd 7-2)
Furmigadelagiusta, second and third in the last two runnings of this and best in at the weights, was making his debut for the yard on this first start since July, but he was having to be niggled along soon after turning for home and found nothing. Official explanation: trainer's rep had no explanation for the poor form shown (op 7-4 tchd 2-1)
Daaweitza came into this off the back of a win in a modest Southwell handicap, but he was worst in at the weights and was finding this too tough from some way out. (op 40-1)

1032 WILLIAMHILL.COM - IN PLAY H'CAP 6f
4:10 (4:11) (Class 2) (0-100,100) 4-Y-O+ **£10,361** (£3,083; £1,540; £769) **Stalls** High

Form RPR
211- **1** **Kaldoun Kingdom (IRE)**[169] 6678 5-9-3 **99** .... PaulHanagan 2 107
(R A Fahey) *in tch: hdwy on wd outside wl over 1f out: rdn to ld ins fnl f: sn drvn and kpt on wl towards fin* **6/1**[2]

05-0 **2** *1/2* **Saucy Brown (IRE)**[10] 916 4-8-8 **90** .... FrannyNorton 16 96
(D Nicholls) *trckd ldrs: hdwy 2f out and sn cl up: rdn and ev ch ent fnl f: sn drvn and kpt on* **33/1**

204- **3** *hd* **One Way Or Another (AUS)**[121] 7560 7-8-1 **90** .... JohnFahy(7) 8 98+
(J R Gask) *hld up towards rr: gd hdwy over 2f out: chsd ldrs over 1f out: rdn and ev ch ent fnl f whn hmpd and hit twice in face by opponents whip: kpt on wl towards fin* **20/1**

000- **4** *shd* **Baldemar**[156] 6994 5-8-8 **90** .... TonyHamilton 13 95
(R A Fahey) *hld up in rr: swtchd rt and hdwy 2f out: chsd ldrs ent fnl f: kpt on towards fin* **16/1**

214- **5** *1/2* **Hotham**[156] 6994 7-8-4 **89** .... BarryMcHugh(3) 12 93
(N Wilson) *trckd ldrs: hdwy and cl up over 2f out: rdn to ld over 1f out: drvn and hdd appr fnl f: hmpd and no ex last 100yds* **28/1**

412- **6** *1/2* **Jonny Mudball**[127] 7486 4-8-8 **90** .... RichardKingscote 4 92
(Tom Dascombe) *hld up in tch: gd hdwy 2f out: rdn to ld briefly appr fnl f: sn hung rt and hdd: drvn and wknd towards fin* **5/2**[1]

000- **7** *hd* **Zidane**[141] 7294 8-9-0 **96** .... EddieAhern 17 98
(J R Fanshawe) *hld up in rr: hdwy 2f out: rdn to chse ldrs over 1f out: kpt on ins fnl f: nrst fin* **12/1**

050- **8** *1 1/2* **Sonny Red (IRE)**[183] 6270 6-8-13 **100** .... MichaelO'Connell(5) 5 97
(D Nicholls) *trckd ldrs: hdwy 2f out and sn ev ch: rdn and hld whn n.m.r ent fnl f* **12/1**

100- **9** *2 1/2* **Haajes**[168] 6694 6-7-13 **86** oh1 ....(t) PaulPickard(5) 7 75
(P T Midgley) *in rr: hdwy towards outer 2f out: rdn and kpt on appr fnl f: nvr nr ldrs* **22/1**

000- **10** *1* **Protector (SAF)**[141] 7292 9-8-4 **86** oh1 ....(t) AndrewMullen 18 72
(A G Foster) *nvr bttr than midfield* **25/1**

000- **11** *3/4* **Courageous (IRE)**[155] 7019 4-8-13 **95** .... TomEaves 3 78
(B Smart) *chsd ldrs: hdwy to ld wl over 2f out: rdn and hung rt wl over 1f out: sn hdd & wknd* **16/1**

060- **12** *1* **Coleorton Choice**[145] 7227 4-8-5 **87** .... DavidProbert 1 67
(R Hollinshead) *chsd ldrs: rdn along 1/2-way: sn wknd* **50/1**

232- **13** *3 3/4* **Fantasy Explorer**[129] 7454 7-8-7 **89** ow1 .... JamieSpencer 6 57
(J J Quinn) *nvr bttr than midfield* **16/1**

5404 **14** *hd* **Tourist**[8] 944 5-8-4 **86** oh2 .... JimmyQuinn 9 53
(D Shaw) *awkward s: a towards rr* **16/1**

000- **15** *2* **Jobe (USA)**[225] 5032 4-8-7 **89** .... JoeFanning 10 50
(K A Ryan) *disp ld tl led 1/2-way: sn rdn and hdd wl over 2f out: wknd* **22/1**

100- **16** *nk* **Aldermoor (USA)**[141] 7294 4-8-5 **87** .... SaleemGolam 15 47
(S C Williams) *in tch to 1/2-way: sn wknd* **50/1**

2-30 **17** *8* **Confuchias (IRE)**[15] 887 6-8-6 **88** ....(b) LukeMorris 19 22
(J R Gask) *bhd fr 1/2-way* **8/1**[3]

100- **18** *16* **Pavershooz**[162] 6843 5-8-10 **92** .... DuranFentiman 11 —
(N Wilson) *plld hrd: disp ld to 1/2-way: sn rdn and wknd qckly: bhd fr wl over 1f out: b.b.v* **20/1**

1m 15.7s (2.10) **Going Correction** +0.575s/f (Yiel) **18** Ran SP% **125.3**
Speed ratings (Par 109): **109,108,108,107,107 106,106,104,101,99 98,97,92,92,89 89,78,57**
toteswingers: 1&2 £25.90, 1&3 £29.70, 2&3 £43.30 CSF £203.44 CT £3821.02 TOTE £8.70: £2.00, £4.90, £4.50, £4.20; EX 233.70 TRIFECTA Not won..
Owner P D Smith Holdings Ltd **Bred** Gainsborough Stud Management Ltd **Trained** Musley Bank, N Yorks

FOCUS
A very competitive sprint handicap in which several still held a chance a furlong from home.

NOTEBOOK
Kaldoun Kingdom(IRE), gelded since winning his last two starts of last season, was 6lb higher on this return from five months off but he was representing a stable that can do no wrong at this meeting. He was always travelling powerfully behind the leaders on the far side of the field and found plenty when asked to hit the front inside the last furlong. The operation obviously hasn't done him any harm and he may be capable of further improvement. (op 5-1 tchd 13-2)
Saucy Brown(IRE) found the minimum trip totally inadequate on his debut for the yard following an absence at Southwell ten days earlier, but ran much better over this more suitable distance. He did especially well to keep on for second as he was always close to the pace and probably prefers a sounder surface.
One Way Or Another(AUS) ◆, returning from four months off, did win over this trip in Australia in 2007 but he has been running over further in recent seasons. Nonetheless he was possibly unlucky not to go very close here as he travelled well off the pace but never saw much daylight, and when he did eventually find a gap to go through he took an almighty crack across the nose from a rival's whip which not surprisingly caused him to hesitate. He deserves compensation. (op 33-1)
Baldemar, a stablemate of the winner and returning from five months off, can go well fresh but he was given plenty to do here and, although he finished well when switched stands' side, he had too much ground to make up. (op 20-1)
Hotham, another returning from five months off and still 5lb above his last winning mark, gave himself every chance and this was an encouraging return to action.
Jonny Mudball ◆, returning from four months off, was by far the least exposed in the field having only made his racecourse debut in October, but was nonetheless sent off a warm favourite. He came through to just about force his head in front a furlong out, but couldn't stamp his authority on the contest and was run out of it. This was a stiff test at this stage of his career and he remains open to improvement. (op 3-1tchd 7-2 in places)
Zidane ◆, whose success in a C&D conditions event in similar ground last August was by far his best effort of the season, was another returning from four months off but he ran on well from the rear of the field and has become well handicapped now. (op 11-1)
Sonny Red(IRE), not seen since September, likes to get his toe in and he does stay this trip even though all four career wins have come over the minimum. Backed earlier in the day, he briefly hit the front over a furlong out but had already been overhauled when hampered inside the last. (op 11-1 tchd 14-1)
Confuchias(IRE) Official explanation: jockey said horse lost its actiion

Pavershooz Official explanation: jockey said gelding bled from the nose

1033 ROBINHOODAIRPORT.COM H'CAP — 1m 2f 60y

4:45 (4:45) (Class 3) (0-90,83) 3-Y-O — £6,799 (£2,023; £1,011; £505) — Stalls Low

Form — RPR

3144 **1** — **Paintball (IRE)**[24] 781 3-8-6 71 .... MartinDwyer 4 — 83
(W R Muir) *lw: hld up in last: effrt 3f out: chal 1f out: styd on to ld post* — **12/1**

10-3 **2** shd **Miss Starlight**[51] 428 3-8-13 78 .... EddieCreighton 3 — 90
(P J McBride) *chsd ldrs: led over 2f out: edgd rt over 1f out: hdd post* — **33/1**

2111 **3** 4 ½ **Rock A Doodle Doo (IRE)**[32] 686 3-8-12 77 .... J-PGuillambert 1 — 80
(W Jarvis) *in tch: hdwy to chse ldrs 6f out: effrt over 3f out: one pce fnl 2f* — **4/1[3]**

661- **4** 2 ¼ **Green Lightning (IRE)**[144] 7244 3-9-3 82 .... JoeFanning 2 — 81
(M Johnston) *lw: dwlt: sn led: hdd after 2f: chal over 3f out: wknd fnl f* — **7/4[1]**

510- **5** 1 **Sharaayeen**[156] 6993 3-9-0 79 .... RichardHills 5 — 76
(B W Hills) *trckd ldrs: led 4f out: hdd over 2f out: hung lft and wknd over 1f out* — **2/1[2]**

31-4 **6** 14 **Kumbeshwar**[15] 884 3-8-12 82 .... RichardEvans(5) 6 — 52
(P D Evans) *led early: t.k.h: led after 2f: hdd 4f out: lost pl over 2f out: sn bhd* — **12/1**

2m 15.28s (5.88) **Going Correction** +0.475s/f (Yiel) — **6** Ran SP% **108.0**
Speed ratings (Par 102): **102,101,98,96,95 84**
toteswingers: 1&2 £7.90, 1&3 £2.50, 2&3 £6.40 CSF £231.16 TOTE £11.20: £3.50, £4.80; EX 68.40.
Owner Mrs J M Muir **Bred** James Waldron **Trained** Lambourn, Berks

FOCUS
A race won last year by Gitano Hernando off a mark of 84, but it seems highly unlikely that any of these will reach his level. The early pace was modest, but even so the finish was dominated by two horses that were held up out the back early.

NOTEBOOK
Paintball(IRE), twice disappointing since winning a Southwell maiden in January, was making his turf debut and trying beyond 1m for the first time, but he proved to be much improved by the different surface. Held up out the back early, he produced a telling turn of foot down the outside to snatch the race from the filly on the line and it already seems likely that he will achieve much more on grass than he has on sand. (op 10-1 tchd 9-1)
Miss Starlight ◆, a well-beaten third of four on her return to action at Wolverhampton last month, was unproven in these conditions but she ran her socks off and looked likely to win when taking over in front towards the inside of the track 2f from home, but the winner just wore her down. She shouldn't take long in going one better. (op 25-1)
Rock A Doodle Doo(IRE), unplaced in three turf maidens at two, was bidding for a four-timer off a 3lb higher mark after winning three Polytrack handicaps earlier this year. He made his effort entering the last 2f and tried his best, but could do nothing to stop the front pair from scampering clear of him. The handicapper may have him now. (op 9-2)
Green Lightning(IRE), making his handicap debut having ended last season with victory in a soft-ground Nottingham maiden, is bred to relish this longer trip. Having always been close up, he had every chance up the home straight but was inclined to hold his head rather high and was made to look one-paced late on. It may be a case of him still being green and he is worth another chance. (op 6-4)
Sharaayeen, not seen since enduring a troubled passage in a 1m nursery here in October, was sent for home passing the 4f pole but faded very tamely once headed entering the last quarter-mile. Official explanation: jockey said colt hung left (op 11-4)
Kumbeshwar, proven in soft ground, was trying beyond 7f for the first time but he did far too much in front early and had shot his bolt half a mile from home. Official explanation: jockey said gelding ran too free early (op 10-1)

1034 SOCIETY LIFESTYLE & LEISURE MAGAZINE FILLIES' H'CAP — 1m (S)

5:15 (5:15) (Class 4) (0-85,85) 4-Y-O+ — £4,533 (£1,348; £674; £336) — Stalls High

Form — RPR

002- **1** — **Paquerettza (FR)**[169] 6680 4-9-0 81 .... FrederikTylicki 6 — 88
(D H Brown) *trckd ldrs: led over 1f out: edgd lft ins fnl f: hld on towards fin* — **15/8[1]**

0122 **2** ½ **Head First**[33] 675 4-8-4 71 .... DavidProbert 5 — 77
(W Jarvis) *hld up in rr: effrt 3f out: edgd rt jst ins fnl f: styd on wl: fin strly* — **12/1**

100- **3** hd **Saturn Girl (IRE)**[188] 6174 4-8-7 74 ow1 .... JamieSpencer 2 — 79
(M L W Bell) *chsd ldrs: effrt over 3f out: chal 2f out: edgd rt 1f out: no ex last 75yds* — **15/2**

100- **4** 3 **Faldal**[257] 3968 4-9-4 85 .... FrankieDettori 4 — 84
(Miss Gay Kelleway) *trckd ldrs: effrt over 2f out: one pce whn eased towards fin* — **11/4[2]**

342 **5** 5 **Miss Bootylishes**[24] 787 5-8-4 71 oh1 .... JoeFanning 1 — 58
(A B Haynes) *led: qcknd over 3f out: hdd over 1f out: sn wknd* — **9/2[3]**

140- **6** 3 **Chadwell Spring (IRE)**[176] 6474 4-8-4 71 oh1 .... JimmyQuinn 8 — 51
(Miss J Feilden) *hld up effrt over 2f out: wknd over 1f out* — **25/1**

101- **7** 2 ¼ **Wiseman's Diamond (USA)**[192] 6023 5-7-13 71 oh1.. PaulPickard(5) 7 — 46
(P T Midgley) *chsd ldrs: pushed along over 3f out: lost pl 2f out* — **10/1**

1m 45.23s (5.93) **Going Correction** +0.575s/f (Yiel) — **7** Ran SP% **112.0**
Speed ratings (Par 102): **93,92,92,89,84 81,79**
toteswingers: 1&2 £3.90, 1&3 £4.30, 2&3 £6.50 CSF £24.31 CT £135.94 TOTE £2.80: £1.40, £3.40; EX 19.00 Trifecta £156.80 Pool: £654.78 - 3.09 winning units. Place 6: £10,662.71, Place 5: £4,531.24..
Owner J B Smith & J M Smith **Bred** Newsells Park Stud **Trained** Maltby, S Yorks

FOCUS
An ordinary fillies' handicap. The field threatened to split into two early, but the two groups had merged after a furlong and they came down the centre. The pace looked modest.
T/Jkpt: Not won. T/Plt: £15,352.70 to a £1 stake. Pool: £118,825.87. 5.65 winning tickets. T/Qpdt: £948.10 to a £1 stake. Pool: £7,559.54. 5.90 winning tickets. JR

1035 - (Foreign Racing) - See Raceform Interactive

LEOPARDSTOWN (L-H)

Sunday, March 28

OFFICIAL GOING: Soft

1036a LEOPARDSTOWN 1,000 GUINEAS TRIAL STKS (GROUP 3) (FILLIES) — 7f

2:55 (2:59) 3-Y-O — £28,761 (£8,407; £3,982; £1,327)

RPR

1 — **Lady Springbank (IRE)**[182] 6316 3-9-0 101 .... JimCrowley 11 — 102+
(P D Deegan, Ire) *chsd ldrs: 4th 1/2-way: impr to ld over 1 1/2f out: rdn clr over 1f out: kpt on strly: comf* — **8/1**

2 1 ½ **Duchess Of Foxland (IRE)**[7] 959 3-9-0 88 .... EJMcNamara 8 — 97
(Mark L Fagan, Ire) *mid-div: 9th 1/2-way: rdn in 8th 2f out: styd on in 5th 1 1/2f out: 2nd 1f out: no ch w wnr: kpt on same pce* — **10/1**

3 1 ¾ **Crystal Gal (IRE)**[168] 6708 3-9-0 91 .... DPMcDonogh 6 — 92
(Kevin Prendergast, Ire) *chsd ldrs: 5th 1/2-way: rdn in 4th 2f out: 3rd 1f out: kpt on same pce fnl f* — **10/1**

4 3 ½ **Karasiyra (IRE)**[143] 7256 3-9-0 .... FMBerry 12 — 83
(John M Oxx, Ire) *chsd ldrs: 6th 1/2-way: rdn and lost pl ent st: 10th 2f out: 9th 1f out: kpt on fnl f* — **7/2[2]**

5 1 **Miss Laa Di Da**[227] 4959 3-9-0 87 .... PJSmullen 10 — 80
(Noel Meade, Ire) *hld up towards rr: rdn in 10th over 1f out: kpt on fnl f* — **20/1**

6 nk **Pluirin (USA)**[16] 877 3-9-0 .... KJManning 2 — 79?
(J S Bolger, Ire) *chsd ldrs: 3rd 1/2-way: rdn in 5th 2f out: no ex over 1f out* — **12/1**

7 1 ¾ **Queen Of Troy (IRE)**[170] 6651 3-9-0 94 .... SMLevey 7 — 74
(A P O'Brien, Ire) *led: rdn and chal 2 1/2f out: hdd over 1 1/2f out: no ex in 4th 1f out: kpt on one pce* — **25/1**

8 1 **Ice Empress (IRE)**[143] 7256 3-9-0 .... CO'Donoghue 4 — 72
(A P O'Brien, Ire) *mid-div: 8th 1/2-way: rdn in 7th 2f out: no ex 1 1/2f out: kpt on same pce* — **10/1**

9 ½ **You'll Be Mine (USA)**[183] 6269 3-9-0 105 .... JAHeffernan 1 — 70
(A P O'Brien, Ire) *mid-div: 7th 1/2-way: rdn in 6th 2f out: no imp over 1f out: wknd fnl f* — **6/1[3]**

10 3 **Famous (IRE)**[182] 6319 3-9-0 105 .... JMurtagh 9 — 62
(A P O'Brien, Ire) *chsd ldrs: 2nd 1/2-way: rdn to chal 2 1/2f out: no ex over 1f out: wknd* — **2/1[1]**

11 13 **Wrong Answer**[153] 7072 3-9-0 101 .... CDHayes 5 — 27
(Kevin Prendergast, Ire) *dwlt: a towards rr* — **8/1**

1m 33.91s (5.21) **Going Correction** +0.80s/f (Soft) — **11** Ran SP% **135.6**
Speed ratings: **102,100,98,94,93 92,90,89,89,85 70**
CSF £98.83 TOTE £9.30: £2.40, £3.70, £3.40; DF 88.90.
Owner Mark Gittins **Bred** Mrs M P V Gittins **Trained** The Curragh, Co Kildare

FOCUS
Lady Springbank continued a flying start to the season for trainer Paul Deegan with a fine performance on her first encounter with soft ground. The winning time was slower than the following C&D handicap and the race, dominated by reasonably unexposed types, has been rated around the fifth to her maiden win.

NOTEBOOK
Lady Springbank(IRE) left little doubt that she is a genuine Pattern-class filly with this display. Though it took her a while to work her way into a challenging position from her wide draw, she was travelling best by the 2f pole and was in control from over a furlong out. She will have no trouble staying another furlong, and having won on good to firm ground there will be no shortage of options for her. (op 7/1)
Duchess Of Foxland(IRE) was well supported and made sustained headway through the last quarter-mile, vindicating her trainer's decision to take this big step up in class after her win in the Madrid Handicap at the Curragh a week earlier. A 20-1 maiden winner at Naas on her fourth and final start last season, she seems to be improving in leaps and bounds.
Crystal Gal(IRE) ran a solid race to confirm last season's initial promise, when she beat Free Judgement first time out in a maiden. A Galileo filly out of an unraced half-sister to Derby runner-up Walk In The Park, she should be able to build on this and can prosper over further in due course. (op 14/1)
Karasiyra(IRE) should also do better when she tackles 1m plus. (op 4/1)
Miss Laa Di Da emerged with some credit.
You'll Be Mine(USA), whose big drift in the market signalled she was not expected to be at home on the ground, never looked like making a serious impact. (op 9/2)
Famous(IRE) folded tamely after running up with the pace supplied by her stablemate. (op 11/4)
Wrong Answer Official explanation: jocket said filly became upset in the stalls and did not act on today's ground

1038a LEOPARDSTOWN 2,000 GUINEAS TRIAL STKS (GROUP 3) (C&G) — 1m

4:05 (4:06) 3-Y-O — £28,761 (£8,407; £3,982; £1,327)

RPR

1 — **Noll Wallop (IRE)**[168] 6712 3-9-0 .... WMLordan 4 — 111
(T Stack, Ire) *settled bhd ldrs: 5th 1/2-way: hdwy in 4th 2f out: impr to ld 1 1/2f out: sn rdn clr: kpt on strly fnl f: comf* — **7/2[2]**

2 3 ½ **Viscount Nelson (USA)**[141] 7304 3-9-0 110 .... CO'Donoghue 1 — 103+
(A P O'Brien, Ire) *disp early: sn chsd ldrs: 3rd 1/2-way: rdn in 5th 2f out: kpt on in 3rd 1f out: styd on to 2nd ins fnl f: no ch w wnr* — **7/1**

3 1 **Famous Warrior (IRE)**[170] 6651 3-9-0 105 .... DPMcDonogh 5 — 101
(Kevin Prendergast, Ire) *hld up towards rr: rdn in 7th 2f out: styd on in 4th 1f out: kpt on same pce fnl f* — **12/1**

4 hd **Fighting Brave (USA)**[170] 6651 3-9-0 .... JAHeffernan 2 — 102+
(A P O'Brien, Ire) *mid-div: 6th 1/2-way: rdn 2f out: 5th 1f out: kpt on same pce fnl f* — **14/1**

5 shd **Black Quartz (FR)**[239] 4553 3-9-0 103 .... JMurtagh 7 — 100
(A P O'Brien, Ire) *sn led: chal 3f out: rdn and hdd 1 1/2f out: no ex in 2nd 1f out: kpt on one pce fnl f* — **7/2[2]**

6 4 **Free Judgement (USA)**[153] 7072 3-9-0 110 .... KJManning 3 — 91
(J S Bolger, Ire) *chsd ldrs: 4th 1/2-way: rdn in 3rd 2f out: no ex in 4th 1 1/2f out: wknd over 1f out* — **2/1[1]**

7 hd **Sebastian Flyte**[178] 6426 3-9-0 107 .... WJSupple 8 — 90
(Francis Ennis, Ire) *chsd ldr: chal 3f out: rdn in 3rd and no ex 1 1/2f out: 5th 1f out: kpt on one pce* — **13/2[3]**

8 shd **Purple Land (USA)**[329] 1711 3-9-0 .... DJMoran 6 — 90?
(J S Bolger, Ire) *a towards rr* — **33/1**

1m 47.15s (5.95) **Going Correction** +0.80s/f (Soft) — **8** Ran SP% **120.9**
Speed ratings: **102,98,97,97,97 93,93,92**
CSF £29.95 TOTE £4.80: £1.80, £2.90, £3.20; DF 34.90.
Owner Roger O'Byrne **Bred** Eugenia Farms **Trained** Golden, Co Tipperary

FOCUS
Having taken the Curragh by storm a week earlier, Tommy Stack continued his magnificent start to the season thanks to a convincing display by the gambled-on Noll Wallop. The race has been rated around the third and fifth, with the winner rated to a big personal best.

NOTEBOOK
Noll Wallop(IRE) was a narrow winner of a maiden at the Curragh last October on the second of two starts at two, but he showed no sign of being inconvenienced here, proving considerably superior to his rivals. Clearly the stable's general wellbeing is an important factor at the moment, but this was an encouraging reintroduction by a colt who will appreciate better ground. Bought for just €22,000 as a yearling, he looks a bargain. (op 5/1)
Viscount Nelson(USA), who ended last season with an outing in the Breeders' Cup Juvenile Turf, confirmed a fair standard of ability by taking second.
Famous Warrior(IRE) upheld form with a couple of those who had finished behind him when he was second in a Listed race at Dundalk last October. (op 9/1)
Free Judgement(USA) was prominent to under 2f out before dropping out of contention, with the going possibly the main factor in his eclipse. (op 11/8)

1039 - 1041a (Foreign Racing) - See Raceform Interactive

985 **LINGFIELD** (L-H)

Monday, March 29

OFFICIAL GOING: Standard

Wind: Light, behind Weather: Overcast with occasional showers

1042 PICK A WINNER WITH BLUE SQUARE ICARD (S) STKS 1m (P)
2:10 (2:10) (Class 6) 3-Y-O+ **£2,047** (£604; £302) **Stalls High**

Form				RPR
546-	1		**The Mumbo**[130] 7456 4-9-3 59 (b) AlanMunro 6 *(W Jarvis) cl up: chsd ldr 3f out: drvn 2f out: styd on fnl f to ld last strides* **14/1**	66
0-50	2	hd	**Abbondanza (IRE)**[16] 883 7-9-8 106 (p) FrankieDettori 3 *(N Wilson) led 2f: trckd ldr: led again over 3f out: tried to draw away 2f out: drvn fnl f: hdd last strides* **1/4**[1]	71
1154	3	1	**Ravi River (IRE)**[19] 851 6-10-0 70 (v) J-PGuillambert 4 *(P D Evans) hld up: trckd ldrs 2f out: rdn and swtchd rt over 1f out: drvn and kpt on fnl f: nt rch ldng pair* **10/1**[3]	74
-540	4	hd	**Tous Les Deux**[9] 943 7-9-8 70 RyanMoore 8 *(G L Moore) hld up: gng strly bhd ldrs over 2f out: rdn and edgd rt fr over 1f out: styd on* **7/1**[2]	68
/200	5	3 ¼	**Kathleen Kennet**[35] 663 10-8-12 46 SimonPearce(5) 7 *(M R Bosley) racd wd: in tch: lost grnd whn wd bnd 2f out: nt on terms after* **50/1**	55
00	6	15	**Flight Wise**[24] 803 6-9-5 0 RussKennemore(3) 1 *(N R Mitchell) dwlt: chsd ldr 2f: rdn and wknd over 3f out: t.o* **50/1**	24
-066	7	22	**Whisky Jack**[24] 804 4-9-8 60 (b) MartinDwyer 2 *(W R Muir) t.k.h: hld up tl allowed to ld after 2f: hdd over 3f out: wknd rapidly 2f out: t.o* **33/1**	—

1m 38.27s (0.07) **Going Correction** +0.05s/f (Slow) **7 Ran SP% 115.1**
Speed ratings (Par 101): **101,100,99,99,96 81,59**
toteswingers: 1&2 £2.80, 1&3 £5.50, 2&3 £2.00 CSF £18.68 TOTE £20.60: £6.10, £1.10; EX 34.90 Trifecta £227.30 Pool: £629.73 - 2.05 winning units..There was no bid for the winner. Abbondanza was claimed by D. Nicholls £6000.
Owner Willie W Robertson **Bred** Mount Coote Partnership **Trained** Newmarket, Suffolk
■ Stewards' Enquiry : Alan Munro two-day ban: careless riding (Apr 12-13); caution: used whip without giving filly time to respond.

FOCUS
They didn't go much of a pace in this seller, although it was still the quickest of the three C&D times. The winner and fifth are more likely guides to the form than the second, third and fourth, all of whom have doubts over their current form.
Flight Wise Official explanation: jockey said gelding hung right early stages

1043 BLUESQUARE.COM MAIDEN AUCTION FILLIES' STKS 5f (P)
2:40 (2:41) (Class 6) 2-Y-O **£2,047** (£604; £302) **Stalls High**

Form				RPR
	1		**Primo Lady** 2-8-2 0 (v1) LukeMorris 8 *(Miss Gay Kelleway) nt that wl away but sn wl in tch: trckd ldng pair 2f out: green sn after but shkn up to ld 1f out: scooted clr* **12/1**	76+
	2	3 ½	**Scarlet Rocks (IRE)** 2-8-6 0 RobertWinston 9 *(P D Evans) pressed ldr after 1f: narrow ld over 1f out: hdd and easily outpcd 1f out: kpt on* **12/1**	67
	3	½	**Bajan Bullet** 2-8-4 0 CathyGannon 4 *(P D Evans) sn in rr: wd bnd 2f out and plenty to do after: r.o wl fnl f: nrly snatched 2nd* **15/2**	64+
	4	nk	**Wotsthehurry** 2-8-2 0 FrannyNorton 6 *(M R Channon) led after 1f to over 1f out: sn outpcd* **7/2**[2]	61
	5	¾	**Mandy's Princess (IRE)** 2-8-3 0 PaulHanagan 7 *(R A Fahey) chsd ldrs: effrt to dispute 3rd over 2f out: no imp over 1f out: fdd* **11/4**[1]	59
	6	1 ½	**Crazy In Love** 2-8-2 0 KirstyMilczarek 1 *(W G M Turner) led 1f: lost pl by 1/2-way: rdn and no prog 2f out* **14/1**	52
	7	nk	**Sheila's Star (IRE)** 2-8-7 0 LiamKeniry 10 *(J S Moore) dwlt: outpcd and sn detached in last: styd on fr over 1f out: nrst fin* **11/2**[3]	56+
	8	1	**Tupelo (IRE)** 2-7-12 0 AndreaAtzeni(3) 2 *(P W D'Arcy) in rr whn hmpd on inner over 3f out: nvr on terms w ldrs* **8/1**	47
	9	1 ¾	**Indian Dip** 2-8-2 0 ow1 KevinGhunowa 5 *(R Curtis) t.k.h in midfield: snatched up over 3f out and dropped to rr: struggling fnl 2f* **16/1**	41
	10	3 ½	**Tessa (IRE)** 2-8-2 0 AdrianMcCarthy 3 *(Peter Grayson) dwlt: in tch to 1/2-way: wknd 2f out* **80/1**	29

60.32 secs (1.52) **Going Correction** +0.05s/f (Slow) **10 Ran SP% 116.3**
Speed ratings (Par 87): **89,83,82,82,80 78,78,76,73,68**
toteswingers: 1&2 £12.40, 1&3 £39.80, 2&3 £18.00 CSF £146.25 TOTE £11.60: £3.10, £9.20, £4.60; EX 105.60 TRIFECTA Not won..
Owner K Jarvis, G Hodson, P Moule **Bred** Mr And Mrs L Baker **Trained** Exning, Suffolk
■ Primo Lady is the first winner of a £10,000 Racing Post Yearling Bonus.

FOCUS
No form to go on. This was probably just an ordinary fillies' maiden, but the race ought to produce some winners.

NOTEBOOK
Primo Lady cost £5,000 and is bred to be precocious, being a sister to dual 5f winning juvenile Lucky Mellor, out of a 6f 2-y-o winner. This was a nice performance on debut, although she had apparently already been to Lingfield for a racecourse gallop, and she had a visor on, so she knew her job better than most. Although perhaps not open to a great deal of improvement, she obviously has a fair amount of ability. (op 14-1 tchd 10-1)
Scarlet Rocks(IRE), a 15,000euros purchase out of a winning juvenile, raced prominently throughout and, although no match for the winner, she kept on reasonably well. (op 8-1)
Bajan Bullet ◆, a 9,000gns half-sister to, among others, 1m winner Khalafa, was outpaced for much of the way and swung extremely wide into the straight, but she finished well. She's open to a deal of improvement. (op 10-1)
Wotsthehurry, £5,500 first foal of a 1m2f winner, showed loads of speed but lost her chance when running quite green around the bend into the straight. (op 4-1 tchd 9-2)
Mandy's Princess(IRE), a 8,500gns half-sister to Potaro, a 7f Group 3 winner at two, found only the one pace in the straight and looks limited. (op 15-8)
Crazy In Love could make no impression. (tchd 10-1)
Sheila's Star(IRE) ◆ was a major eyecatcher. This 20,000euros half-sister to dual 7f winner Magic Mornings raced in a detached last for most of the way after starting slowest of all, but she really got going in the straight. She's in need of a stiffer test of stamina, but whatever, she is open to a significant amount of improvement. (op 9-1)
Tupelo(IRE) was hampered after a furlong or so when the keen-running Indian Dip was squeezed for room. (op 10-1)

1044 BLUE SQUARE EXCLUSIVE LIVE SHOW PRICES H'CAP 6f (P)
3:10 (3:10) (Class 5) (0-75,75) 4-Y-O+ **£2,729** (£806; £403) **Stalls Low**

Form				RPR
056-	1		**Quasi Congaree (GER)**[144] 7254 4-8-8 65 (t) PaulHanagan 7 *(I A Wood) trckd ldrs and racd on inner: effrt to go 2nd over 1f out: styd on to ld ins fnl f* **20/1**	76
600-	2	¾	**For Life (IRE)**[113] 7656 8-8-10 70 NataliaGemelova(3) 1 *(J E Long) led after 100yds: urged along over 1f out: hdd ins fnl f: kpt on* **33/1**	79
2454	3	1 ½	**Rondeau (GR)**[26] 767 5-9-1 72 JimCrowley 3 *(P R Chamings) settled in midfield: effrt over 2f out: prog on inner over 1f out to chse ldng pair fnl f: no imp* **6/1**[3]	76
00-1	4	1	**Prince Namid**[21] 829 8-8-12 69 LukeMorris 12 *(J A T De Giles) blindfold off sltly late and dwlt: towards rr on outer: effrt 2f out: hanging over 1f out: styd on ins fnl f* **15/2**	70+
535-	5	hd	**Poppanan (USA)**[88] 7891 4-8-12 69 TonyCulhane 2 *(S Dow) stdd s: hld up in last pair: shuffled along 2f out: sme prog on inner 1f out: shkn up and kpt on* **13/2**	69
2431	6	1	**Fromsong (IRE)**[12] 899 12-8-10 67 MartinDwyer 4 *(D K Ivory) taken down early: hld up: gng strly over 2f out: shkn up and no rspnse over 1f out* **11/2**[2]	64
1416	7	¾	**Kipchak (IRE)**[24] 802 5-9-4 75 (p) LiamKeniry 8 *(C R Dore) taken down early: v fast away but led for only 100yds: chsd ldr to over 1f out: wknd* **13/2**	69
606-	8	½	**Comadoir (IRE)**[113] 7656 4-9-4 75 FergusSweeney 10 *(Miss Jo Crowley) chsd ldng pair on outer: rdn over 2f out: wknd over 1f out* **14/1**	68
-601	9	hd	**Vintage (IRE)**[38] 616 6-9-4 75 IanMongan 9 *(J Akehurst) chsd ldrs: rdn over 2f out: hanging and wknd over 1f out* **11/4**[1]	67
00-0	10	3 ½	**Brunelleschi**[30] 737 7-9-4 75 (b) KirstyMilczarek 6 *(P L Gilligan) hld up: a last: pushed along and no prog 2f out* **16/1**	56

1m 12.04s (0.14) **Going Correction** +0.05s/f (Slow) **10 Ran SP% 115.0**
Speed ratings (Par 103): **101,100,98,96,96 95,94,93,93,88**
toteswingers: 1&2 £47.70, 1&3 £23.50, 2&3 £29.00 CSF £523.62 CT £4461.36 TOTE £22.00: £5.50, £8.30, £2.00; EX 746.90 TRIFECTA Not won..
Owner M Forbes & C R Lamborne **Bred** Graf And Grafin Von Stauffenberg **Trained** Upper Lambourn, Berks

FOCUS
A modest sprint handicap which was not strong run. The runner-up looks the best guide to the form.
Brunelleschi Official explanation: jockey said gelding never travelled

1045 BLUE SQUARE'S NEW IPHONE APP H'CAP 7f (P)
3:40 (3:40) (Class 4) (0-85,81) 3-Y-O **£4,533** (£1,348; £674; £336) **Stalls Low**

Form				RPR
25-1	1		**Rjeef (IRE)**[38] 625 3-9-4 81 SebSanders 6 *(C E Brittain) pressed ldrs: shkn up on outer 2f out: led jst over 1f out: powered away fnl f* **5/2**[2]	93+
14-3	2	4 ½	**Tenacestream (CAN)**[51] 448 3-8-13 76 RobertWinston 4 *(J R Best) mostly pressed ldr: rdn to ld briefly over 1f out: kpt on but no match for wnr* **12/1**	75
5-1	3	½	**Progress (IRE)**[29] 744 3-8-8 71 WilliamBuick 7 *(J Noseda) hld up in 6th: effrt on outer 2f out: drvn and hanging over 1f out: kpt on fnl f to take 3rd post* **11/4**[3]	69+
1-	4	shd	**Thrust Control (IRE)**[175] 6544 3-9-3 80 SamHitchcott 2 *(M R Channon) hld up in 5th: rdn to trck ldrs 2f out: cl enough over 1f out: sn outpcd* **14/1**	78
341	5	1	**Lockantanks**[10] 932 3-9-1 78 RyanMoore 5 *(A B Haynes) t.k.h early: hld up last: stl last and outpcd 2f out: kpt on fnl f* **11/1**	73
3306	6	½	**Transfixed (IRE)**[12] 901 3-8-11 74 CathyGannon 3 *(P D Evans) led to over 1f out: wknd fnl f* **33/1**	68
1-	7	5	**Secretive**[97] 7836 3-9-0 77 FrankieDettori 1 *(M Johnston) prom: pushed along 1/2-way and sn lost pl: no prog 2f out: wknd and eased* **9/4**[1]	57

1m 24.62s (-0.18) **Going Correction** +0.05s/f (Slow) **7 Ran SP% 111.6**
Speed ratings (Par 100): **103,97,97,97,96 95,89**
toteswingers: 1&2 £5.70, 1&3 £2.60, 2&3 £4.00 CSF £29.76 TOTE £2.90: £1.10, £5.10; EX 33.60.
Owner Saeed Manana **Bred** K Lee **Trained** Newmarket, Suffolk

FOCUS
A fair 3-y-o handicap. The winner stepped up on his good Wolverhampton win and the form could be rated a length higher.

1046 BET NOW AT BLUESQUARE.COM MAIDEN STKS 1m 2f (P)
4:10 (4:10) (Class 5) 3-Y-O **£2,729** (£806; £403) **Stalls Low**

Form				RPR
024-	1		**Street Entertainer (IRE)**[124] 7522 3-9-3 79 JimCrowley 1 *(Mrs A J Perrett) pressed ldr: led 3f out: rdn clr over 1f out: in n.d after* **5/4**[1]	83
	2	3 ¼	**Zuider Zee (GER)** 3-9-3 0 WilliamBuick 5 *(J H M Gosden) s.i.s: hld up last: prog into 3rd over 2f out but ldng pair away: styd on to take 2nd ins fnl f: no imp on wnr* **15/8**[2]	77+
353	3	4 ½	**Ancient Times (USA)**[9] 949 3-9-3 74 FrankieDettori 4 *(M Johnston) trckd ldng pair: chal on outer 3f out: rdn and nt qckn 2f out: wknd and lost 2nd ins fnl f* **7/2**[3]	68
54	4	10	**Mister Pleau (USA)**[30] 734 3-9-3 0 RobertWinston 3 *(J R Best) stdd s: hld up in 4th: pushed along over 3f out: sn struggling: t.o* **20/1**	48
0	5	½	**The Wonga Coup (IRE)**[10] 930 3-9-3 0 IanMongan 2 *(P M Phelan) led: sn stdd pce: rdn and hdd 3f out: wknd: t.o* **33/1**	47

2m 7.77s (1.17) **Going Correction** +0.05s/f (Slow) **5 Ran SP% 109.2**
Speed ratings (Par 98): **97,94,90,82,82**
CSF £3.79 TOTE £2.60: £1.20, £1.10; EX 4.00.
Owner George Materna **Bred** Marston Stud And Fleming Thoroughbreds **Trained** Pulborough, W Sussex

FOCUS
An uncompetitive maiden run at a modest gallop. The winner was the clear form pick and might not have had to improve, but has been rated a small personal best.

1047 BET ON YOUR IPHONE WITH BLUE SQUARE H'CAP — 1m (P)
4:40 (4:41) (Class 5) (0-75,74) 4-Y-0+ £2,729 (£806; £403) Stalls High

Form — RPR

2214 **1** **Charlie Smirke (USA)**[9] 943 4-9-4 **74** ... RyanMoore 3 — 83+
(G L Moore) *settled in rr: last 1/2-way: pushed along and prog fr 2f out: wl-timed run fnl f to ld last 75yds: won gng away* — **2/1**[1]

-241 **2** 1 **Lastkingofscotland (IRE)**[24] 804 4-8-13 **69** ...(b) JimmyFortune 4 — 76
(Jim Best) *led at stdy pce to 1/2-way: led again wl over 2f out: kicked over a l clr over 1f out: hdd and outpcd last 75yds* — **9/4**[2]

510- **3** shd **Markhesa**[150] 7149 4-8-4 **60** ... NickyMackay 5 — 68+
(J R Boyle) *trckd ldrs: looking for clr run fr wl over 1f out: swtchd to inner and effrt fnl f: styd on but nt pce of wnr* — **18/1**

3422 **4** 1 **Lopinot (IRE)**[19] 845 7-7-13 **60** ...(v) SimonPearce(5) 6 — 64
(M R Bosley) *trckd ldrs: rdn to chse ldr over 1f out to ins fnl f: one pce* — **5/1**[3]

-565 **5** 2 1/4 **Teen Ager (FR)**[33] 684 6-8-5 **61** ... LukeMorris 2 — 60+
(P Burgoyne) *rrd s: t.k.h: hld up in last trio: no room on inner 2f out: swtchd rt fnl f: styd on but no ch* — **10/1**

-350 **6** 1 1/4 **El Libertador (USA)**[40] 587 4-8-10 **66** ... SteveCarson 7 — 64+
(E A Wheeler) *trckd ldr to 1/2-way: wnt 2nd again over 2f out to over 1f out: wkng whn short of room ins fnl f* — **9/1**

2322 **7** 1 1/2 **Straight Face (IRE)**[11] 920 6-8-12 **68** ...(b) J-PGuillambert 1 — 65+
(P D Evans) *restless stalls: trckd ldrs: rdn and nt qckn over 1f out: wkng whn short of room ins fnl f* — **14/1**

5-13 **8** 2 1/2 **Wrighty Almighty (IRE)**[24] 804 8-8-10 **66** ... JimCrowley 9 — 52
(P R Chamings) *dropped in fr wd draw: hld up in last trio and t.k.h: rdn over 2f out: no prog and btn after* — **18/1**

-000 **9** nk **Simple Rhythm**[24] 806 4-8-4 **67** ... StephanieThewlis(7) 8 — 53
(J Ryan) *racd v wd: plld hrd: prog to ld 1/2-way to wl over 2f out: sn btn* — **100/1**

1m 39.13s (0.93) **Going Correction** +0.05s/f (Slow) 9 Ran SP% **118.0**
Speed ratings (Par 103): **97,96,95,94,92 91,89,87,87**
toteswingers: 1&2 £2.00, 1&3 £10.70, 2&3 £15.00 CSF £6.86 CT £60.74 TOTE £2.50: £1.20, £1.10, £7.80; EX 7.30 Trifecta £72.60 Pool: £427.13 - 4.35 winning units..

Owner R E Anderson **Bred** W S Farish & Kilroy Thoroughbred Partnership **Trained** Lower Beeding, W Sussex

■ Stewards' Enquiry : Nicky Mackay three-day ban: careless riding (Apr 12-14)

FOCUS
A modest handicap run at a steady pace. The time was 0.86 seconds slower than the 59-rated The Mumbo recorded in the earlier seller. The form is rated around the runner-up.

1048 BLUE SQUARE SUPPORTING MARIE CURIE CANCER CARE H'CAP — 1m (P)
5:10 (5:11) (Class 6) (0-60,60) 3-Y-0 £2,047 (£604; £302) Stalls High

Form — RPR

00-1 **1** **Usquaebach**[27] 762 3-9-3 **59** ... IanMongan 6 — 62+
(P M Phelan) *mde most: wd bnd 2f out: narrowly hdd fnl f: styd on wl to ld again post* — **8/1**

000 **2** shd **Coxwain (IRE)**[11] 915 3-9-2 **58** ... FrankieDettori 2 — 61
(M Johnston) *pressed ldr: lft upsides bnd 2f out: narrow ld on inner fnl f: hdd post* — **11/2**[3]

4032 **3** nk **Sunrise Lyric (IRE)**[24] 812 3-9-4 **60** ... RyanMoore 1 — 62
(P F I Cole) *hld up early: stdy prog on inner to trck ldrs 1/2-way: cl up 2f out: rdn to chal fnl f and upsides: nt qckn nr fin* — **5/1**[2]

4 nk **Buona Sarah (IRE)**[136] 7378 3-9-4 **60** ... PatCosgrave 12 — 62+
(J R Boyle) *settled midfield: eased out and effrt over 1f out: rdn and r.o fnl f: unable to rch ldrs* — **10/1**

000- **5** 1 **Tregony Bridge**[149] 7177 3-8-8 **50** ... FergusSweeney 10 — 49
(M Blanshard) *hld up wl in rr: effrt 2f out: cajoled along w hd high and hanging: styd on but nvr chal* — **40/1**

60-3 **6** 3/4 **Kenswick**[21] 826 3-8-10 **59** ... LeeTopliss(7) 3 — 57
(Pat Eddery) *towards rr: drvn and dropped to last pair 5f out: sed gng bttr 3f out: prog on inner over 1f out: drvn again and one pce* — **14/1**

30-6 **7** 1/2 **Bandear (IRE)**[18] 856 3-9-4 **60** ... SebSanders 4 — 56+
(C E Brittain) *w ldrs: carried wd bnd 2f out: shkn up and nt qckn over 1f out: pushed along and one pce fnl f* — **20/1**

531 **8** shd **Sheila's Bond**[26] 776 3-9-0 **56** ... LukeMorris 9 — 52
(J S Moore) *towards rr on outer: u.p fr 3f out and struggling: kpt on fnl f: no ch* — **4/1**[1]

540- **9** hd **Baileys Vision**[153] 7079 3-9-4 **60** ... JimmyFortune 8 — 56
(C A Dwyer) *settled in last trio: effrt on inner 2f out: hrd rdn over 1f out: no hdwy fnl f* — **25/1**

036- **10** 5 1/2 **Take My Hand**[173] 6590 3-9-0 **56** ... AlanMunro 11 — 39
(M R Channon) *racd wd thrght: hld up in last trio: nudged along 2f out: nvr remotely involved: eased fnl f* — **6/1**

000- **11** 3/4 **Liebelei (USA)**[159] 6931 3-8-8 **50** ...(b[1]) MartinDwyer 7 — 31
(H J L Dunlop) *mostly in midfield: rdn over 2f out: wknd over 1f out* — **20/1**

45-4 **12** shd **Sultan's Choice**[24] 805 3-9-1 **57** ...(p) CathyGannon 5 — 38
(P D Evans) *chsd ldrs: rdn over 2f out: wknd over 1f out* — **14/1**

1m 39.37s (1.17) **Going Correction** +0.05s/f (Slow) 12 Ran SP% **115.7**
Speed ratings (Par 96): **96,95,95,95,94 93,93,92,92,92 91,91**
toteswingers: 1&2 £9.30, 1&3 £7.00, 2&3 £4.40 CSF £47.66 CT £247.30 TOTE £9.70: £2.90, £1.60, £2.60; EX 53.20 Trifecta £102.40 Pool: £360.02 - 2.60 winning units. Place 6: £156.20 Place 5: £129.38 .

Owner KFM Partnership **Bred** R P Williams **Trained** Epsom, Surrey

FOCUS
A moderate handicap run at a steady pace and the time was the slowest of three races over 1m on the card. Limited but sound form.

Liebelei(USA) Official explanation: jockey said filly jumped right

T/Plt: £266.20 to a £1 stake. Pool: £60,948.40. 167.10 winning tickets. T/Qpdt: £28.40 to a £1 stake. Pool: £4,912.23. 127.70 winning tickets. JN

991 WOLVERHAMPTON (A.W) (L-H)
Monday, March 29

OFFICIAL GOING: Standard
Wind: Variable Weather: Light rain for 2.50 and 3.20

1049 WOLVERHAMPTON HOSPITALITY - A PLEASURE CLAIMING STKS — 7f 32y(P)
2:20 (2:21) (Class 6) 4-Y-0+ £1,774 (£523; £262) Stalls High

Form — RPR

-031 **1** **Cobo Bay**[19] 851 5-9-6 85 ...(b) NeilCallan 2 — 91
(K A Ryan) *sn led: clr over 1f out: rdn ins fnl f: r.o* — **15/8**[1]

5-04 **2** 1/2 **The Kyllachy Kid**[19] 850 4-9-6 85 ...(p) DavidProbert 3 — 90
(S Gollings) *led early: chsd wnr: rdn wl over 1f out: kpt on towards fin* — **9/4**[2]

3032 **3** 1 1/4 **Seasider**[19] 851 5-8-12 79 ... MartinLane(3) 7 — 82
(D M Simcock) *s.i.s: sn hld up in tch: rdn wl over 1f out: kpt on one pce ins fnl f* — **6/1**[3]

-254 **4** 1 3/4 **War And Peace (IRE)**[7] 965 6-8-2 65 ...(p) LewisWalsh(7) 6 — 71
(Jane Chapple-Hyam) *hld up and bhd: prog on outside 2f out: c wd st: edgd lft ins fnl f: no imp* — **25/1**

51/3 **5** 4 **Bazroy (IRE)**[18] 862 6-8-13 85 ...(b) TomQueally 1 — 64
(P D Evans) *hld up and bhd: rdn wl over 1f out: no rspnse* — **13/2**

000- **6** 6 **Silver Wind**[157] 6994 5-9-3 83 ...(v) JamieSpencer 4 — 52
(P D Evans) *prom tl pushed along and wknd wl over 1f out* — **15/2**

-040 **7** 7 **Pachakutek (USA)**[19] 853 4-8-12 59 ...(p) KierenFallon 5 — 28
(A J Lidderdale) *s.i.s: hld up: hdwy over 3f out: wknd over 2f out* — **40/1**

1m 30.24s (0.64) **Going Correction** +0.175s/f (Slow) 7 Ran SP% **111.2**
Speed ratings (Par 101): **103,102,101,99,94 87,79**
toteswingers: 1&2 £2.10, 1&3 £2.80, 2&3 £3.90 CSF £5.92 TOTE £2.40: £1.20, £1.90; EX 7.40.War And Peace was claimed by J. Babb for £4000.
Owner The C H F Partnership **Bred** The C H F Partnership **Trained** Hambleton, N Yorks

FOCUS
A decent little claimer. The fourth limits the form and the winner probably didn't need to improve much on his recent efforts.

1050 DINE IN THE HORIZONS RESTAURANT MAIDEN STKS — 7f 32y(P)
2:50 (2:51) (Class 5) 3-Y-0+ £2,331 (£693; £346; £173) Stalls High

Form — RPR

3- **1** **Red Gulch**[123] 7537 3-8-12 0 ... KierenFallon 8 — 75+
(E A L Dunlop) *t.k.h: a.p: wnt 2nd over 5f out: led 2f out: edgd lft jst over 1f out: sn clr: readily* — **6/4**[1]

22 **2** 2 1/4 **West Emirates (USA)**[24] 815 4-9-13 0 ... AdamKirby 5 — 68
(C G Cox) *w ldr: led after 1f to 2f out: kpt on same pce* — **9/2**[3]

0-54 **3** 1 1/4 **Imperial Djay (IRE)**[18] 866 5-9-13 47 ... JimmyQuinn 6 — 65
(Mrs R A Carr) *hld up and bhd: pushed along and hdwy over 1f out: kpt on to take 3rd wl ins fnl f* — **50/1**

060- **4** nk **Catbells (IRE)**[177] 6481 3-8-7 72 ... DavidProbert 2 — 54
(A Bailey) *a.p: rdn over 2f out: one pce* — **3/1**[2]

06- **5** 2 3/4 **Gojeri (IRE)**[150] 7145 3-8-12 0 ... NeilCallan 1 — 52
(M A Jarvis) *hld up: no hdwy fnl 2f* — **8/1**

0- **6** 3 1/2 **Stay On Track (IRE)**[294] 2771 3-8-12 0 ... JamieSpencer 7 — 42
(E F Vaughan) *s.i.s: c wd st: a in rr* — **16/1**

7 nk **Skyfire** 3-8-12 0 ... JoeFanning 4 — 42
(M Johnston) *led 1f: prom: pushed along over 2f out: wknd over 1f out* — **10/1**

1m 30.99s (1.39) **Going Correction** +0.175s/f (Slow)
WFA 3 from 4yo+ 15lb 7 Ran SP% **111.2**
Speed ratings (Par 103): **99,96,95,94,91 87,87**
toteswingers: 1&2 £2.20, 1&3 £6.40, 2&3 £6.80 CSF £8.08 TOTE £2.60: £1.80, £1.90; EX 4.80.
Owner R J Arculli **Bred** Cheveley Park Stud Ltd **Trained** Newmarket, Suffolk

FOCUS
A weakish maiden with the third holding down the form. The winner was left with little to beat but did it nicely.

1051 WOLVERHAMPTON-RACECOURSE.CO.UK H'CAP — 1m 141y(P)
3:20 (3:20) (Class 4) (0-80,78) 4-Y-0+ £4,209 (£1,252; £625; £312) Stalls Low

Form — RPR

4366 **1** **Kidlat**[2] 1011 5-9-0 **73** ... AdamKirby 9 — 82
(A Bailey) *sn prom: led 7f out: rdn 2f out: drvn out* — **4/1**[3]

650- **2** 1 1/4 **Sarwin (USA)**[161] 6900 7-8-6 **65** ... JimmyQuinn 6 — 71+
(G A Swinbank) *hld up: hdwy on ins wl over 1f out: hrd rdn and wnt 2nd ins fnl f: no ex cl home* — **18/1**

-011 **3** 3/4 **Mr Hichens**[7] 966 5-9-5 **78** 6ex ... DarryllHolland 3 — 83
(Karen George) *a.p: ev ch over 2f out: rdn over 1f out: nt qckn* — **3/1**[2]

0042 **4** nk **Justcallmehandsome**[11] 925 8-8-6 **68** ...(v) KellyHarrison(3) 2 — 72
(D J S Ffrench Davis) *led over 1f: prom: rdn wl over 1f out: kpt on one pce* — **9/1**

-340 **5** 1/2 **Hawaana (IRE)**[26] 765 5-9-3 **76** ... SteveDrowne 8 — 79+
(Miss Gay Kelleway) *hld up: rdn over 2f out: kpt on ins fnl f: nt rch ldrs* — **11/1**

160- **6** 1 1/2 **Standpoint**[268] 3643 4-9-4 **77** ... GrahamGibbons 4 — 76
(R Hollinshead) *hld up in tch: rdn wl over 1f out: fdd ins fnl f* — **16/1**

534- **7** 2 1/4 **Una Pelota (IRE)**[311] 2229 4-9-4 **77** ... RichardKingscote 7 — 71
(Tom Dascombe) *hld up: hdwy over 3f out: wknd wl over 1f out* — **5/2**[1]

4133 **8** 1/2 **Flores Sea (USA)**[13] 895 6-8-10 **69** ...(b) SilvestreDeSousa 5 — 62
(Mrs R A Carr) *hld up in tch: rdn and wknd 2f out* — **16/1**

0202 **9** hd **Harare**[18] 867 9-8-2 **64** ...(v) MartinLane(3) 1 — 57
(R J Price) *a in rr* — **16/1**

1m 50.77s (0.27) **Going Correction** +0.175s/f (Slow) 9 Ran SP% **114.8**
Speed ratings (Par 105): **105,103,103,102,102 101,99,98,98**
toteswingers: 1&2 £15.80, 1&3 £4.20, 2&3 £12.90 CSF £71.32 CT £245.30 TOTE £6.90: £2.80, £6.20, £1.80; EX 68.90.
Owner John Stocker **Bred** Darley **Trained** Newmarket, Suffolk

FOCUS
Few got into this muddling handicap, another race on the card to go to a prominent runner. The fourth looks a fair guide to the form.

1052 STAY AT THE WOLVERHAMPTON HOLIDAY INN H'CAP — 5f 216y(P)
3:50 (3:50) (Class 4) (0-85,84) 3-Y-0 £4,209 (£1,252; £625; £312) Stalls Low

Form — RPR

0-10 **1** **Niran (IRE)**[16] 884 3-9-4 **84** ... NeilCallan 6 — 89
(C E Brittain) *a.p: rdn to ld wl ins fnl f: edgd lft: r.o* — **3/1**[1]

The Form Book, Raceform Ltd, Compton, RG20 6NL

10-2 **2** *nk* **Dusty Spirit**[12] 901 3-8-5 **74** JackDean(3) 2 78
(W G M Turner) *a.p: led over 1f out: rdn and edgd rt ins fnl f: sn hdd: r.o* **3/1**[1]

-133 **3** *nk* **Breathless Kiss (USA)**[25] 783 3-8-13 **79** JamieSpencer 4 82+
(K A Ryan) *s.i.s: hld up and bhd: c wd st: hdwy over 1f out: rdn and nt qckn towards fin* **3/1**[1]

1331 **4** *3 1/4* **Novay Essjay (IRE)**[11] 914 3-8-5 **71** JimmyQuinn 1 64
(C R Dore) *led: hdd over 1f out: sn rdn: wknd ins fnl f* **9/2**[2]

106- **5** *4 1/2* **Iron Velvet (USA)**[191] 6099 3-8-9 **75** JoeFanning 5 53
(M Johnston) *w ldr tl rdn over 1f out: wknd fnl f* **8/1**[3]

20-0 **6** *1* **Quaestor (IRE)**[12] 900 3-8-10 **76** RichardKingscote 3 51
(Tom Dascombe) *hld up and bhd: short-lived effrt on ins over 1f out* **8/1**[3]

1m 15.65s (0.65) **Going Correction** +0.175s/f (Slow) **6** Ran SP% **115.4**
Speed ratings (Par 100): **102,101,101,96,90 89**
toteswingers: 1&2 £2.20, 1&3 £2.70, 2&3 £2.30 CSF £12.64 TOTE £5.40: £4.00, £2.00; EX 14.60.
Owner Saeed Manana **Bred** Miss Audrey F Thompson **Trained** Newmarket, Suffolk
■ Stewards' Enquiry : Neil Callan caution: used whip without giving colt sufficient time to respond

FOCUS
A decent little sprint handicap and probably reasonable form for the grade. The winner built on his penultimate Kempton win.
Niran(IRE) Official explanation: trainers rep had no explanation regarding the apparent improvement in form

1053 COMBINE BUSINESS WITH PLEASURE H'CAP 2m 119y(P)
4:20 (4:20) (Class 5) (0-75,73) 4-Y-O+ **£2,456** (£725; £362) Stalls Low

Form RPR
-451 **1** **Gremlin**[10] 938 6-9-3 **69** KierenFox(5) 2 78
(D Burchell) *chsd ldr: led over 2f out: rdn ins fnl f: styd on wl* **5/2**[1]

2115 **2** *2 1/2* **Star Choice**[10] 938 5-9-9 **70** (b) RobertHavlin 4 76
(J Pearce) *hld up: stdy prog over 3f out: chsd wnr 2f out: rdn over 1f out: no imp* **7/2**[3]

5513 **3** *4* **Broughtons Point**[18] 865 4-8-2 **54** oh1 JamieMackay 3 55
(W J Musson) *hld up in tch: rdn and edgd lft 1f out: one pce* **11/4**[2]

6230 **4** *4 1/2* **Highland River**[10] 720 4-8-2 **54** JimmyQuinn 1 50
(A Sadik) *led: rdn and hdd over 2f out: wknd wl over 1f out* **20/1**

0-12 **5** *3 1/2* **William's Way**[16] 888 8-9-12 **73** NeilCallan 5 65
(I A Wood) *hld up in rr: pushed along and short-lived effrt on ins wl over 1f out* **11/4**[2]

3m 51.35s (9.55) **Going Correction** +0.175s/f (Slow)
WFA 4 from 5yo+ 5lb **5** Ran SP% **108.9**
Speed ratings (Par 103): **84,82,80,78,77**
CSF £11.17 TOTE £2.60: £1.10, £3.70; EX 9.10.
Owner Jason Tucker **Bred** Catridge Farm Stud Ltd **Trained** Briery Hill, Blaenau Gwent

FOCUS
A low-grade and slowly run handicap. It has been rated around the runner-up.

1054 SPONSOR A RACE BY CALLING 01902 390000 H'CAP 1m 4f 50y(P)
4:50 (4:50) (Class 6) (0-60,60) 3-Y-O **£1,774** (£523; £262) Stalls Low

Form RPR
060- **1** **Il Portico**[197] 5907 3-8-11 **53** KierenFallon 4 61
(M R Channon) *a.p: wnt 2nd over 6f out: led over 3f out: rdn over 1f out: r.o* **4/1**[3]

0062 **2** *hd* **Port Hill**[17] 872 3-9-2 **58** ShaneKelly 1 65
(W M Brisbourne) *hld up in tch: chal over 2f out: rdn and nt qckn ins fnl f* **8/1**

2505 **3** *7* **Royal Torbo (ISR)**[7] 964 3-8-11 **58** MatthewDavies(5) 8 54
(George Baker) *hld up towards rr: pushed along and hdwy over 2f out: rdn over 1f out: wknd ins fnl f* **9/1**

2314 **4** *3* **Vittachi**[24] 812 3-9-2 **58** (b) TomQueally 5 49
(J D Bethell) *hld up in rr: hdwy on outside 3f out: rdn and wknd over 1f out* **9/1**

-662 **5** *1 1/2* **Second Brook (IRE)**[26] 775 3-9-1 **57** AdamKirby 6 46
(R Hollinshead) *hld up in rr: hrd rdn and short-lived effrt over 2f out* **10/3**[1]

-323 **6** *10* **Temple Fair (USA)**[12] 904 3-9-1 **57** JoeFanning 2 30
(M Johnston) *chsd ldr tl over 6f out: wknd over 2f out* **7/2**[2]

-223 **7** *6* **Moonbalej**[21] 830 3-9-4 **60** (b) GregFairley 9 23
(M Johnston) *led: hdd over 3f out: sn wknd* **11/2**

6-06 **8** *2 1/2* **Light The City (IRE)**[12] 909 3-8-5 **47** AndrewElliott 3 6
(Mrs R A Carr) *hld up: pushed along over 3f out: sn bhd* **40/1**

2m 42.74s (1.64) **Going Correction** +0.175s/f (Slow) **8** Ran SP% **114.2**
Speed ratings (Par 96): **101,100,96,94,93 86,82,80**
toteswingers: 1&2 £7.50, 1&3 £7.50, 2&3 £10.80 CSF £35.52 CT £269.85 TOTE £4.70: £2.20, £3.20, £4.30; EX 50.50 Place 6: £44.27 Place 5: £33.67 .
Owner Derek And Jean Clee **Bred** D D And Mrs Jean P Clee **Trained** West Ilsley, Berks

FOCUS
This was a weakish handicap with several below par. It has been rated around the third with the first pair showing improvement.
Il Portico Official explanation: trainer's rep said, regarding apparent improvement in form, that the gelding was a backward two-year-old which had benefited from the step up in trip.
Second Brook(IRE) Official explanation: jockey said gelding hung left from 3f out
T/Plt: £129.60 to a £1 stake. Pool: £60,604.13. 341.28 winning tickets. T/Qpdt: £50.90 to a £1 stake. Pool: £4,031.54. 58.60 winning tickets. KH

951 SAINT-CLOUD (L-H)
Monday, March 29

OFFICIAL GOING: Heavy

1055a PRIX DE NANTES (CLAIMER) 1m
2:40 (2:41) 4-Y-O **£7,965** (£3,186; £2,389; £1,593; £796)

RPR
1 **Accord Secret (FR)**[135] 4-9-4 ChristopheSoumillon 82
(J-C Rouget, France)

2 *1 1/2* **Lady Aline**[164] 4-8-7 (b) FlavienPrat(5) 73
(T Clout, France)

3 *2* **Vitassana (IRE)**[191] 4-8-8 Christophe-PatriceLemaire 64
(J-P Gallorini, France)

4 *1 1/2* **Lady's Art (FR)**[166] 6771 4-8-12 (b) 65
(S Wattel, France)

5 *1 1/2* **Grand Palais (IRE)**[293] 4-8-8 58
(C Lerner, France)

6 *1 1/2* **Aden Gulf (IRE)**[211] 4-9-1 61
(P Schiergen, Germany)

7 *1/2* **Marechale (FR)**[136] 7385 4-8-8 53
(Mme C Head-Maarek, France)

8 *shd* **Palea (GER)**[62] 303 4-8-9 54
(S Jesus, France)

9 *hd* **Stay Cool (FR)**[136] 7386 4-8-13 (b) 57
(D Smaga, France)

10 *1/2* **Lisselan Hurricane (USA)**[160] 4-8-11 54
(Mme J Bidgood, Spain)

0 **Sunniva Duke (IRE)**[180] 4-9-1 —
(D Prod'Homme, France)

0 **Marangu (IRE)**[151] 4-9-0 —
(W Hickst, Germany)

0 **Good Star (FR)**[110] 7696 4-8-8 —
(B Dutruel, France)

0 **Big Brown Tsar (FR)**[145] 4-8-11 —
(M Delzangles, France)

0 **Grand Nordique (USA)**[116] 4-8-4 —
(N Clement, France)

1m 47.5s **15** Ran
PARI-MUTUEL: WIN 1.60; PL 1.20, 2.60, 3.30; DF 9.40.
Owner Frank A McNulty **Bred** Haras D'Etreham **Trained** Pau, France

COMPIEGNE (L-H)
Tuesday, March 30

OFFICIAL GOING: Heavy

1056a PRIX DE COURTIEUX (CLAIMER) 1m 4f
3:40 (3:46) 5-Y-O+ **£7,522** (£3,009; £2,257; £1,504; £752)

RPR
1 **Sybelio (FR)**[17] 6-9-5 ChristopheSoumillon 86
(J Rossi, France)

2 *3* **Sunrise Spirit (FR)**[17] 9-8-13 AnthonyCaramanolis(5) 80
(F Doumen, France)

3 *1* **Group Captain**[126] 8-9-4 OlivierPeslier 79
(Alex Fracas, France)

4 *1 1/2* **Lost Soldier Three (IRE)**[31] 742 9-9-1 (p) 73
(Mme J Bidgood, Spain)

5 *2 1/2* **Lady Di (GER)**[14] 6-8-12 66
(J De Roualle, France)

6 *10* **Beaubahhare (FR)**[126] 5-9-1 (b) 53
(J-P Delaporte, France)

7 *5* **Figo (GER)**[257] 10-9-2 46
(P Lefevre, France)

8 *1/2* **Cuban (FR)**[151] 7-9-3 (b) 46
(J-P Delaporte, France)

9 *2* **Godfreyson (IRE)**[102] 5-9-10 50
(A Trybuhl, Germany)

10 *1/2* **Beau Marchand (FR)**[194] 6-9-4 43
(Mlle Y Vollmer, France)

0 **Pocketwood**[398] 6983 8-9-4 GaetanMasure —
(Jean-Rene Auvray) *cl up tl lost pl bef 1/2-way: kpt to ins in st but sn wl btn* **33/1**[1]

0 **Carlix (FR)**[169] 8-8-11 —
(J-L Gay, France)

0 **Saalewuste (GER)**[17] 5-8-12 (p) —
(J-P Gallorini, France)

2m 59.56s (179.56) **13** Ran SP% **2.9**
PARI-MUTUEL (including 1 Euro stake): WIN 3.80; PL 1.70, 7.30, 3.20;DF 72.20.
Owner Charley Rossi **Bred** Gestut Eulenberger Hof **Trained** France

1014 KEMPTON (A.W) (R-H)
Wednesday, March 31

OFFICIAL GOING: Standard
Wind: Brisk, half against Weather: Changeable, rain Race 1; cold

1057 KEMPTON.CO.UK CLAIMING STKS 6f (P)
5:30 (5:31) (Class 6) 3-Y-O **£2,047** (£604; £302) Stalls High

Form RPR
3310 **1** **Athwaab**[14] 901 3-8-9 74 RyanMoore 2 69
(M G Quinlan) *fast away fr wd draw: t.k.h: mde all and sn crossed to rail: shkn up 2f out: kpt on wl enough fnl f* **4/5**[1]

4325 **2** *1 1/4* **Micky's Knock Off (IRE)**[18] 886 3-8-10 65 (e) KierenFallon 3 66
(R C Guest) *chsd ldng trio: effrt on outer over 2f out: hung rt and wnt 2nd over 1f out: stl hanging and ref to throw down a proper chal* **11/2**[2]

4410 **3** *1 1/2* **Avow (USA)**[12] 932 3-8-8 70 (b) LiamKeniry 4 58
(J S Moore) *trckd wnr: nt qckn and hld whn hmpd over 1f out: plugged on ins fnl f* **8/1**

-306 **4** *1/2* **Reach For The Sky (IRE)**[9] 962 3-7-13 61 KierenFox(5) 5 52
(G Prodromou) *chsd ldng trio on inner: shkn up to dispute 2nd 2f out: nt qckn over 1f out: one pce* **8/1**

0514 **5** *1/2* **Ballyvonane (USA)**[5] 988 3-8-8 52 (b) LukeMorris 6 55
(L A Dace) *chsd ldrs in 6th: rdn over 2f out: kpt on fr over 1f out: n.d* **12/1**

2012 **6** *3* **Blue Neptune**[9] 962 3-8-5 65 AndreaAtzeni(3) 9 44
(P D Evans) *trckd ldng pair: disp 2nd 2f out: short of room sn after: wknd fnl f* **6/1**[3]

7 *1/2* **Avonside (IRE)** 3-9-8 0 DaneO'Neill 1 56
(Pat Eddery) *s.s: a in 7th: nvr on terms w ldrs: pushed along 2f out: keeping on nr fin* **25/1**

400- **8** *8* **Impressioniste (IRE)**[162] 6927 3-9-4 0 StevieDonohoe 7 23
(Luke Comer, Ire) *a in last pair and sn bhd: t.o* **28/1**

00 **9** *2* **Account Closed**[15] 894 3-8-12 0 PaulMulrennan 8 10
(C A Mulhall) *fractious bef ent stalls: dwlt: mostly in last and a bhd: t.o* **100/1**

1m 13.83s (0.73) **Going Correction** +0.05s/f (Slow) **9** Ran SP% **123.4**
Speed ratings (Par 96): **97,95,93,92,92 88,87,76,74**
toteswingers: 1&2 £3.20, 1&3 £2.80, 2&3 £6.00 CSF £6.22 TOTE £2.10: £1.20, £1.50, £2.10; EX 8.30.
Owner John Hanly **Bred** Shadwell Estate Co Ltd **Trained** Newmarket, Suffolk

FOCUS
A modest claimer and the winner performed below her mark. The runner-up is rated to her winter best.
Ballyvonane(USA) Official explanation: jockey said gelding suffered interference in the early stages

1058 PANORAMIC BAR & RESTAURANT H'CAP — 6f (P)
6:00 (6:01) (Class 5) (0-70,69) 3-Y-O — **£2,590** (£770; £385; £192) **Stalls** High

Form — RPR
45-1 **1** **Sir Frank Wappat**[21] 849 3-9-0 **65** FrankieDettori 7 75
(M Johnston) *trckd ldng pair: clsd to ld jst over 1f out: shkn up and sn in command: r.o wl* **3/1**[1]
04-5 **2** 1 ¼ **Master Mylo (IRE)**[14] 900 3-9-2 **67** JimCrowley 3 73
(D K Ivory) *nt that wl away: hld up in last trio: gd prog fr 2f out: wnt 2nd ins fnl f: r.o but unable to chal* **12/1**
-230 **3** 2 ½ **Blue Zephyr**[12] 936 3-8-13 **64** MartinDwyer 12 62
(W R Muir) *chsd ldrs in 6th on inner: pushed along bef 1/2-way: tried to cl over 1f out: styd on to take 3rd last 100yds* **14/1**
4413 **4** ¾ **Mint Whip (IRE)**[12] 933 3-9-2 **67** RichardHughes 10 63
(R Hannon) *trckd ldrs: gng easily 2f out: no rspnse whn asked for effrt wl over 1f out: plugged on* **6/1**[3]
560- **5** ½ **Mellifera**[132] 7453 3-9-4 **69** AdamKirby 6 63
(W R Swinburn) *hld up in abt 7th: shuffled along 2f out: only 8th ins fnl f: r.o last 100yds: fin wl* **16/1**
-063 **6** shd **Itsthursdayalready**[40] 625 3-9-3 **68** PaulMulrennan 8 62
(J G Given) *hld up in 9th: stdy prog on inner fr over 2f out: clsd on ldrs over 1f out: no ex fnl f* **15/2**
3142 **7** ½ **Il Forno**[18] 886 3-9-4 **69** EddieAhern 5 61
(Ian Williams) *led to jst over 1f out: wknd rapidly ins fnl f* **8/1**
546- **8** 1 **Do More Business (IRE)**[197] 5967 3-8-4 **62** RichardRowe(7) 11 51
(P M Phelan) *hld up in last trio: nudged along on inner fr 2f out: kpt on steadily: nvr nr ldrs* **16/1**
100- **9** shd **Royal Blade (IRE)**[208] 5650 3-9-3 **68** AlanMunro 4 57
(A P Jarvis) *chsd ldr to over 1f out: wknd rapidly ins fnl f* **12/1**
4-43 **10** ¾ **Rain On The Wind (IRE)**[20] 856 3-8-12 **66**(t) WilliamCarson(3) 9 52
(S C Williams) *v awkward s: hld up in last: taken to wd outside in st: hanging and one reminder 2f out: kpt on but nvr on terms* **7/2**[2]
0-40 **11** nk **Lou Bear (IRE)**[42] 583 3-8-12 **63** J-PGuillambert 1 48
(J Akehurst) *wnt lft s: racd wd in abt 8th: rdn over 2f out: no prog after* **20/1**
0-56 **12** nk **Chandrayaan**[12] 933 3-8-12 **63**(v) RichardThomas 2 47
(J E Long) *restless in stalls: chsd ldng quartet: hanging and fnd nil whn rdn over 2f out: wknd fnl f* **25/1**

1m 13.27s (0.17) **Going Correction** +0.05s/f (Slow) **12** Ran SP% **126.8**
Speed ratings (Par 98): **100,98,95,94,93 93,92,91,91,90 89,89**
toteswingers: 1&2 £11.40, 1&3 £12.70, 2&3 £19.80 CSF £43.81 CT £470.60 TOTE £4.00: £2.10, £6.30, £6.10; EX 60.90.
Owner Paul Dean **Bred** Itchen Valley Stud **Trained** Middleham Moor, N Yorks
FOCUS
Probably a fair race for the grade and the form has been rated on the positive side, through the fourth.
Rain On The Wind(IRE) Official explanation: jockey said gelding hung right

1059 DIGIBET MEDIAN AUCTION MAIDEN STKS — 1m 3f (P)
6:30 (6:30) (Class 6) 3-Y-O — **£2,047** (£604; £302) **Stalls** High

Form — RPR
0434 **1** **Manxman (IRE)**[9] 964 3-9-3 74 (b[1]) FrankieDettori 6 74
(M Johnston) *mde all: rdn 2f out: looked ungainly but kpt on wl to assert fnl f* **9/4**[2]
034- **2** ¾ **High On A Hill (IRE)**[145] 7267 3-9-3 70 LiamKeniry 5 72
(S Kirk) *chsd ldng trio for 4f: rdn in 5th over 3f out: looked to be struggling after tl styd on wl u.p fr over 1f out: tk 2nd nr fin and clsd on wnr* **16/1**
43-0 **3** ¾ **Layla's Boy**[18] 889 3-9-3 72 EddieAhern 1 71
(Ian Williams) *trckd wnr: rdn to chal 2f out: drvn upsides 1f out: btn off last 100yds: lost 2nd nr fin* **15/2**
0-42 **4** 1 ¼ **Heading To First**[23] 830 3-9-3 70 SebSanders 7 69
(C E Brittain) *trckd ldng pair: cl enough 2f out whn sharp reminder and nt qckn: kpt on same pce after* **10/3**[3]
5 2 ¼ **Zigato** 3-9-3 0 WilliamBuick 9 65+
(J H M Gosden) *s.i.s: rn green in last: pushed along and no prog over 2f out on outer: fnlly picked up fnl f: bttr for experience* **13/8**[1]
6 ¾ **Miss Formidable (IRE)** 3-8-9 0 AndreaAtzeni(3) 10 58
(Luke Comer, Ire) *in tch in midfield: effrt on inner over 2f out: no prog over 1f out: fdd* **66/1**
0-5 **7** ¾ **Tallulah Mai**[32] 734 3-8-12 0 SaleemGolam 4 57
(Matthew Salaman) *dwlt: hld up in last pair: sme prog over 2f out: shkn up and no hdwy over 1f out* **33/1**
000- **8** 5 **Aintgottaname**[117] 7624 3-8-12 40 ShaneKelly 2 48?
(M J McGrath) *chsd ldng trio after 4f: rdn and wknd 2f out* **66/1**
00- **9** 7 **Lady Christie**[162] 6912 3-8-12 0 DaneO'Neill 3 35
(M Blanshard) *in tch in midfield tl wknd over 2f out* **33/1**

2m 22.32s (0.42) **Going Correction** +0.05s/f (Slow) **9** Ran SP% **118.5**
Speed ratings (Par 96): **100,99,98,98,96 95,95,91,86**
toteswingers: 1&2 £7.40, 1&3 £2.70, 2&3 £7.70 CSF £36.49 TOTE £3.30: £1.20, £2.90, £2.30; EX 42.00.
Owner Sh Hamdan Bin Mohammed Al Makt **Bred** Glending Bloodstock **Trained** Middleham Moor, N Yorks
■ Stewards' Enquiry : Eddie Ahern two-day ban: used whip in an incorrect place (Apr 14-15)
FOCUS
A moderate maiden where the winner dictated and posted a small personal best, with the next three close to their marks.
Zigato Official explanation: jockey said colt ran green

1060 DIGIBET.COM H'CAP — 1m 3f (P)
7:00 (7:00) (Class 4) (0-80,76) 3-Y-O — **£4,209** (£1,252; £625; £312) **Stalls** High

Form — RPR
4534 **1** **Beat Route**[11] 949 3-8-5 **65** JemmaMarshall(5) 7 68
(M J Attwater) *trckd ldng pair: shkn up to chse ldr over 2f out to over 1f out: wnt 2nd again sn after: styd on wl to ld nr fin* **16/1**
-123 **2** nk **Thundering Home**[49] 482 3-9-7 **76** RyanMoore 5 78
(E A L Dunlop) *hld up in 5th: prog over 2f out to ld over 1f out: drvn fnl f: worn down nr fin* **7/4**[1]
51 **3** ½ **Parhelion**[19] 872 3-9-1 **70** FrankieDettori 3 72
(M Johnston) *trckd ldng trio: rdn 3f out: tried to cl over 1f out: styd on but nvr quite able to chal* **15/8**[2]
00-5 **4** 1 ½ **Stadium Of Light (IRE)**[20] 864 3-8-10 **65**(t) TravisBlock 6 64
(H Morrison) *hld up in last: detached and rdn 3f out: no prog tl picked up wl fnl f: nrst fin* **20/1**
4432 **5** 1 ½ **Captain Cool (IRE)**[29] 762 3-8-2 **57** oh2(b[1]) FrankieMcDonald 2 53
(R Hannon) *t.k.h early: hld up in 6th: rdn over 2f out: nt qckn and no real imp* **10/1**
00-2 **6** 1 ¾ **Iptkaar (USA)**[13] 922 3-9-3 **72**(b) ChrisCatlin 1 65
(C E Brittain) *nt that wl away but sn pressed ldr: rdn 3f out: lost pl over 2f out: sn btn* **11/2**[3]
1 **7** 1 ½ **Dosti**[45] 551 3-9-0 **69**(p) PatCosgrave 4 60
(J R Boyle) *led: edgd lft over 2f out: hdd & wknd over 1f out* **15/2**

2m 24.3s (2.40) **Going Correction** +0.05s/f (Slow) **7** Ran SP% **118.0**
Speed ratings (Par 100): **93,92,92,91,90 88,87**
toteswingers: 1&2 £8.70, 1&3 £9.10, 2&3 £1.90 CSF £46.63 TOTE £29.90: £9.80, £2.00; EX 79.00.
Owner Canisbay Bloodstock **Bred** Canisbay Bloodstock Ltd **Trained** Epsom, Surrey
FOCUS
A fairly tight handicap, run at an uneven pace. The form looks pretty weak.

1061 DIGIBET CASINO H'CAP (LONDON MILE QUALIFIER) — 1m (P)
7:30 (7:33) (Class 5) (0-75,75) 3-Y-O — **£2,590** (£770; £385; £192) **Stalls** High

Form — RPR
022- **1** **Calypso Star (IRE)**[140] 7335 3-8-11 **68** RichardHughes 5 77+
(R Hannon) *hld up in 6th off str pce: clsd on ldrs over 2f out: effrt on inner over 1f out: shkn up to ld ins fnl f: readily* **11/4**[2]
1-24 **2** ¾ **Capricornus (USA)**[68] 268 3-9-3 **74** FrankieDettori 4 80
(M Johnston) *hld up in 4th off str pce: clsng whn sltly checked 3f out: prog to ld over 1f out: hdd ins fnl f: r.o but hld after* **13/2**
433- **3** 2 ¾ **Sheer Force (IRE)**[173] 6627 3-9-4 **75** ShaneKelly 1 75+
(W J Knight) *hld up in last pair: pushed along and prog 2f out: shkn up and styd on to take 3rd ins fnl f: no ch w ldng pair* **9/2**[3]
4-42 **4** 1 ½ **Larkrise Star**[28] 768 3-8-7 **69** ow1 MarkCoumbe(5) 8 66
(D K Ivory) *chsd clr ldng pair: clsd to ld over 2f out to over 1f out: fdd fnl f* **33/1**
41-6 **5** nk **Al Khimiya (IRE)**[12] 934 3-9-2 **73** JimCrowley 3 68
(S Woodman) *hld up in last pair off str pce: rdn and effrt on outer over 2f out: nt qckn over 1f out: fdd ins fnl f: fin 6th, plcd 5th* **7/1**
425- **6** 1 ¼ **Joe Packet**[193] 6104 3-9-3 **74** TomQueally 9 66
(J G Portman) *hld up in 5th off str pce: clsd and wl in tch over 2f out: lost pl sn after: fdd fnl f: fin 7th, plcd 6th* **9/1**
04-3 **7** 3 ¾ **Rainbow Six**[18] 889 3-8-10 **70** AndreaAtzeni(3) 7 53
(M Botti) *chsd clr ldr's str pce: hung lft briefly bnd 3f out: upsides over 2f out: wknd rapidly over 1f out: fin 8th, plcd 7th* **16/1**
46-0 **8** 20 **Electric City (IRE)**[18] 884 3-8-11 **68** AdamKirby 10 5
(M G Quinlan) *sn pushed up to ld and set str pce: hdd & wknd rapidly over 2f out: t.o: fin 9th, plcd 8th* **66/1**
13 **D** ½ **Slikback Jack (IRE)**[18] 884 3-9-3 **74** ChrisCatlin 6 74+
(J A Glover) *hld up in 7th off str pce: effrt and nowhere to go on inner over 2f out: prog and nt clr run over 1f out: styd on; fin 5th disq* **7/4**[1]

1m 39.82s (0.02) **Going Correction** +0.05s/f (Slow) **9** Ran SP% **127.4**
Speed ratings (Par 98): **101,100,97,96,95 93,90,70,95**
toteswingers: 1&2 £4.90, 1&3 £3.10, 2&3 £6.20 CSF £23.83 CT £83.86 TOTE £4.10: £1.80, £3.10, £2.10; EX 25.20.
Owner A C Pickford & N A Woodcock **Bred** Lisieux Stud **Trained** East Everleigh, Wilts
FOCUS
A modest handicap, run at a frantic pace. An interesting race for the grade with the winner picking up on his progressive 2yo form.
Slikback Jack(IRE) Official explanation: jockey said gelding was denied a clear run

1062 FAMILY FUN DAY EASTER SATURDAY H'CAP — 1m 4f (P)
8:00 (8:00) (Class 4) (0-85,85) 4-Y-O+ — **£4,209** (£1,252; £625; £312) **Stalls** Centre

Form — RPR
-151 **1** **Jeer (IRE)**[21] 852 6-8-11 **76**(b) GrahamGibbons 8 84
(M W Easterby) *mde all: set mod pce but sn wl clr w one rival: rdn 2f out: edgd lft u.p: hld on* **2/1**[2]
01-5 **2** ½ **Trachonitis (IRE)**[64] 300 6-8-11 **76** FrankieDettori 9 83+
(J R Jenkins) *hld up in last pair and wl off the pce: prog to 3rd over 1f out: rdn and clsd on ldng pair: tk 2nd post: too much to do* **9/2**[3]
/060 **3** shd **Donaldson (GER)**[18] 888 8-9-6 **85** GeorgeBaker 7 92
(Jonjo O'Neill) *pressed wnr and sn wl clr of rest: pushed along wl over 2f out: rdr waved whip a lot but only one reminder ins fnl f: nt qckn and lost 2nd post* **12/1**
5463 **4** 5 **Free Tussy (ARG)**[34] 697 6-9-0 **79**(bt) RyanMoore 4 78
(G L Moore) *hld up in 4th and wl off the pce: chsd ldng pair over 2f out: no imp: lost 3rd over 1f out* **11/8**[1]
0000 **5** 1 ¼ **Valmari (IRE)**[18] 888 7-8-4 **76** ow3 RichardOld(7) 5 73
(G Prodromou) *plld hrd: hld up: brief effrt over 2f out: sn no prog* **33/1**
000- **6** 19 **Court Wing (IRE)**[314] 2192 4-8-3 **75** oh26 ow4 MatthewDavies(5) 2 41
(George Baker) *w ldng pair 1f: sn restrained: rdn 3f out: wknd over 2f out: t.o* **40/1**

2m 36.05s (1.55) **Going Correction** +0.05s/f (Slow)
WFA 4 from 6yo+ 2lb **6** Ran SP% **108.5**
Speed ratings (Par 105): **96,95,95,92,91 78**
toteswingers: 1&2 £2.10, 1&3 £5.30, 2&3 £7.20 CSF £10.52 CT £70.98 TOTE £3.60: £1.90, £1.80; EX 9.50.
Owner Mrs Jean Turpin **Bred** Floors Farming And Side Hill Stud **Trained** Sheriff Hutton, N Yorks
FOCUS
A funny race in that despite the pace not being strong two broke clear and only the runner-up made any significant inroads on the pair. Suspect form which shouldn't be taken at face value.
Trachonitis(IRE) Official explanation: jockey said, regarding running and riding, his instructions were to drop in the rear as the gelding is known to pull hard in its races. He added that throughout the race he was conscious of the need to keep the gelding settled. He decided to track the favourite Free Tussy, but when he realized that that horse was beaten he then launched his effort.

1063 BOOK KEMPTON TICKETS ON 0844 579 3008 H'CAP (DIV I) — 7f (P)
8:30 (8:30) (Class 5) (0-75,75) 4-Y-O+ — **£2,266** (£674; £337; £168) **Stalls** High

Form — RPR
6323 **1** **Hip Hip Hooray**[12] 931 4-8-4 **61** oh1 ChrisCatlin 11 70
(L A Dace) *hld up in abt 7th: prog over 2f out and sn trckd ldrs: effrt to ld 1f out: styd on wl* **14/1**
01 **2** 2 **Unlimited**[12] 937 8-8-6 **63** LukeMorris 10 67
(A W Carroll) *s.i.s and squeezed out s: hld up in last trio: rdn and prog fr 2f out: styd on fnl f to take 2nd last strides* **11/2**[3]
4245 **3** nk **Dvinsky (USA)**[5] 986 9-8-12 **69**(b) KierenFallon 4 72
(P Howling) *w ldr: rdn to ld over 2f out: hdd 1f out: kpt on u.p* **7/1**

115 **4** ½ **Ejeed (USA)**[45] 552 5-8-5 **62**......(p) SamHitchcott 5 63
(Miss Z C Davison) *t.k.h: hld up bhd ldng trio: effrt to go 2nd over 1f out and sn upsides: fnd nil then folded tamely last 100yds* **13/2**

1143 **5** 1¼ **Headache**[37] 668 5-8-9 **66**......(bt) DaneO'Neill 2 64
(B W Duke) *racd on outer: trckd ldng trio: effrt and cl up over 2f out: nt qckn over 1f out* **7/2**[1]

4-53 **6** ¾ **Chief Exec**[20] 867 8-9-2 **73**......(b) AdamKirby 1 69
(J R Gask) *s.i.s and dropped in fr wd draw: hld up in last but sn detached and pushed along: styd on fr over 2f out: no ch to rch ldrs* **7/1**

56-5 **7** nk **Fault**[13] 924 4-8-11 **68**......(t) MickyFenton 7 63
(Stef Higgins) *hld up in last trio: effrt on wd outside over 2f out: sme prog over 1f out: one pce after* **6/1**

/00- **8** 5 **Mister Ross**[314] 2188 5-9-4 **75**...... PatCosgrave 9 57
(J R Boyle) *wnt rt s: hld up in rr: u.p gng nowhere over 2f out: btn after* **12/1**

06-0 **9** 1¾ **Seneschal**[20] 867 9-8-8 **70**...... AmyBaker(5) 3 47
(A B Haynes) *racd wdst of ldng trio: wknd over 2f out* **40/1**

1100 **10** nk **Bishopbriggs (USA)**[19] 869 5-8-5 **62**...... JamieMackay 8 38
(M G Quinlan) *trckd ldng trio: cl up 2f out: sn rdn and wknd rapidly* **33/1**

-100 **11** 15 **Nacho Libre**[56] 393 5-8-13 **70**......(b) GrahamGibbons 6 6
(M W Easterby) *racd freely: mde most to over 2f out: wknd rapidly and eased: t.o* **4/1**[2]

1m 25.75s (-0.25) **Going Correction** +0.05s/f (Slow) **11 Ran SP% 130.0**
Speed ratings (Par 103): **103,100,100,99,98 97,97,91,89,89 71**
toteswingers: 1&2 £18.90, 1&3 £13.30, 2&3 £9.50 CSF £98.61 CT £623.67 TOTE £14.70: £3.30, £2.60, £2.40; EX 88.20.
Owner M C S D Racing Partnership **Bred** Mrs R S Evans **Trained** Five Oaks, W Sussex
■ Stewards' Enquiry : Chris Catlin one-day ban: careless riding (Apr 14)

FOCUS
A wide-open handicap and a clear-cut winner. It was the quicker of the two divisions but the form looks pretty ordinary.
Nacho Libre Official explanation: jockey said gelding finished distressed

1064 BOOK KEMPTON TICKETS ON 0844 579 3008 H'CAP (DIV II) 7f (P)
9:00 (9:00) (Class 5) (0-75,73) 4-Y-O+ **£2,266** (£674; £337; £168) **Stalls** High

Form RPR

/00- **1** **Print (IRE)**[316] 2160 4-8-13 **68**...... AlanMunro 9 75
(M R Channon) *plld hrd: hld up bhd ldng pair: effrt to ld over 1f out: swished tail and looked vulnerable ent fnl f: kpt on wl* **6/1**[3]

0-50 **2** 1 **Gazboolou**[28] 767 6-8-8 **70**...... DavidKenny(7) 8 75
(David Pinder) *hld up bhd ldrs: effrt over 2f out: chsd wnr over 1f out: looked dangerous ent fnl f: fnd nil and hld after* **10/1**

645- **3** 1 **Steel Free (IRE)**[159] 6997 4-9-3 **72**...... RobertHavlin 5 74
(M Madgwick) *hld up in last trio: effrt on outer over 2f out: rdn and kpt on fr over 1f out to take 3rd nr fin* **16/1**

1-11 **4** ½ **Copperwood**[21] 844 5-8-8 **63** ow1...... DaneO'Neill 6 64
(M Blanshard) *stdd s: hld up in last trio: prog over 2f out: disp 2nd over 1f out and jinked briefly: nt qckn after* **6/4**[1]

021- **5** 2¼ **Ede's Dot Com (IRE)**[154] 7105 6-8-2 **62**...... KierenFox(5) 7 57
(P M Phelan) *stdd s: hld up in last: pushed along 3f out: sme prog into midfield over 1f out: fdd ins fnl f* **9/4**[2]

06-0 **6** 3¼ **Musical Script (USA)**[82] 78 7-8-8 **63**......(b) ChrisCatlin 4 49
(Mouse Hamilton-Fairley) *t.k.h on outer and sn trckd ldr: rdn to ld over 2f out to over 1f out: wknd rapidly* **14/1**

005- **7** 5 **Perfect Friend**[174] 6621 4-9-4 **73**...... EddieAhern 10 45
(S Kirk) *cl up on inner: effrt over 2f out: wknd rapidly over 1f out* **8/1**

0000 **8** 13 **Simple Rhythm**[2] 1047 4-8-12 **67**...... KierenFallon 2 4
(J Ryan) *led to over 2f out: wknd: eased: t.o* **20/1**

1m 26.25s (0.25) **Going Correction** +0.05s/f (Slow) **8 Ran SP% 122.6**
Speed ratings (Par 103): **100,98,97,97,94 90,85,70**
toteswingers: 1&2 £6.90, 2&3 £21.60, 1&3 £12.40 CSF £67.76 CT £945.47 TOTE £9.40: £2.10, £3.10, £4.10; EX 56.20 Place 6: £77.35 Place 5: £58.78 .
Owner Highclere Thoroughbred Racing (Ormonde) **Bred** Victor Stud Bloodstock Ltd **Trained** West Ilsley, Berks

FOCUS
The second division of the 7f handicap and it was run at a fair pace. It was slower than the first division but the form looks stronger.
Simple Rhythm Official explanation: jockey said filly stopped quickly
T/Jkpt: Not won. T/Plt: £209.40 to a £1 stake. Pool: £92,442.99. 322.15 winning tickets. T/Qpdt: £36.30 to a £1 stake. Pool: £8,885.03. 180.70 winning tickets. JN

913 SOUTHWELL (L-H)
Wednesday, March 31

OFFICIAL GOING: Standard
The was a tailwind in the straight.
Wind: Light behind Weather: Overcast and cold

1065 SOUTHWELL-RACECOURSE.CO.UK MAIDEN STKS (DIV I) 5f (F)
2:00 (2:00) (Class 5) 2-Y-O **£2,456** (£725; £362) **Stalls** High

Form RPR

1 **Jamesway (IRE)** 2-9-3 0...... PaulHanagan 5 85+
(R A Fahey) *mde all: clr wl over 1f out: comf* **9/4**[1]

2 1½ **Mappin Time (IRE)** 2-9-3 0...... DavidAllan 2 78+
(T D Easterby) *midfield: swtchd lft and hdwy 2f out: rdn to chse wnr over 1f out: kpt on ins fnl f* **12/1**

3 7 **Callipygos** 2-8-5 0...... LeonnaMayor(7) 3 43
(P S McEntee) *a.p: chsd wnr after 2f: rdn along 2f out: kpt on same pce* **100/1**

4 1½ **Trading** 2-9-3 0...... DuranFentiman 8 42
(T D Easterby) *prom: chsd wnr 2f out: sn rdn and one pce* **33/1**

5 ½ **Merjaan** 2-9-3 0...... NeilCallan 4 40
(C E Brittain) *midfield: effrt 1/2-way: rdn along and edgd rt wl over 1f out: sn no imp* **5/2**[2]

6 nk **Be A Good Lady** 2-8-7 0...... PaulPickard(5) 10 34+
(P T Midgley) *s.i.s: wl bhd: gd hdwy over 1f out: kpt on ins fnl f: nvr rch ldrs* **25/1**

7 3¼ **Bobby Smith (IRE)** 2-9-3 0...... AdamKirby 6 26
(M G Quinlan) *dwlt and towards rr: hdwy and in tch 1/2-way: sn rdn and wknd wl over 1f out* **8/1**[3]

0 **8** ½ **Huckle Duckle (IRE)**[4] 1017 2-8-12 0......(b) TomMcLaughlin 11 19
(P S McEntee) *chsd ldrs: rdn along 2f out: grad wknd* **20/1**

9 ¾ **Roodee Queen** 2-8-12 0...... StephenCraine 9 16
(Patrick Morris) *dwlt and in rr: hdwy nr stands' rails after 2f and sn chsng ldrs: rdn along 2f out and sn wknd* **10/1**

10 2 **Moving Picture** 2-9-3 0...... PhillipMakin 7 13
(B M R Haslam) *a towards rr* **16/1**

11 7 **Wotitis** 2-9-0 0...... JackDean(3) 1 —
(W G M Turner) *sn outpcd and bhd fr 1/2-way* **12/1**

58.54 secs (-1.16) **Going Correction** -0.375s/f (Stan) **11 Ran SP% 113.3**
Speed ratings (Par 92): **94,91,80,78,77 76,71,70,69,66 55**
toteswingers: 1&2 £6.70, 1&3 £28.90, 2&3 £42.70 CSF £27.68 TOTE £2.90: £1.20, £3.40, £13.30; EX 27.40 Trifecta £161.50 Part won. Pool: £218.32 - 0.45 winning units..
Owner Middleham Park Racing Xix **Bred** Yeomanstown Stud **Trained** Musley Bank, N Yorks

FOCUS
Probably a modest maiden, but the front two finished clear. The time was 0.69 seconds slower than the second division, which was won by Richard Fahey's Arctic Feeling.

NOTEBOOK
Jamesway(IRE) is bred to be a fast 2-y-o considering he's a brother to the smart Star Rover, who won five juvenile races over this trip last year, out of a Brocklesby winner, and he didn't disappoint. He went sharply right on leaving the stalls, and was inclined to go in that direction pretty much throughout, but the rail, although not always the place to be over this C&D, was a help, and he showed good speed. Ultimately a comfortable winner, there was plenty to like about this performance, not least that he took an age to pull up after the line. He was, though, still proving head-strong when being cantered back and is evidently an out-and-out speedster, so it's hoped he goes the right way. (op 11-4)
Mappin Time(IRE), a £16,000 purchase, got behind early after struggling to go the pace, but he picked up well in the latter stages and was the only one to give the winner some sort of a race. (op 9-1)
Callipygos, a sister to dual 1m2f-1m5f winner La Gessa, and Marvin Gardens, a 6f winner, out of a dual 6f-1m2f scorer, showed early speed up the centre of the track but was left behind by the front two. (tchd 80-1)
Trading, a £2,500 first foal of a dual winner over 1m-1m1f, showed a bit of early speed but was beaten just after halfway.
Merjaan, a 70,000gns purchase, who is closely related to 1m-1m1f winner Ensnare, was pushed along pretty much throughout and lacked the required speed and know how. (op 11-4)
Be A Good Lady ◆ made little appeal on breeding, but this was an eyecatching debut. Having started slowly, she was soon detached in last place and being pushed along, looking set to finish well beaten, but she got the idea in the closing stages and finished reasonably well.

1066 SOUTHWELL-RACECOURSE.CO.UK MAIDEN STKS (DIV II) 5f (F)
2:30 (2:31) (Class 5) 2-Y-O **£2,456** (£725; £362) **Stalls** High

Form RPR

1 **Arctic Feeling (IRE)** 2-9-3 0...... PaulHanagan 11 85+
(R A Fahey) *mde all: rdn and edgd lft over 1f out: kpt on wl fnl f:* **6/5**[1]

2 1½ **Style And Panache (IRE)** 2-8-12 0...... CathyGannon 6 74+
(P D Evans) *cl up: rdn along 2f out: drvn and ev ch over 1f out: kpt on same pce ins fnl f* **10/1**

3 5 **Daas Rite (IRE)** 2-9-3 0...... NeilCallan 4 59
(K A Ryan) *in tch: hdwy over 2f out: swtchd lft and rdn to chse ldng pair over 1f out: hung rt and kpt on same pce ent fnl f* **11/1**

4 2¼ **Peppercorn Rent (IRE)** 2-8-12 0...... DavidAllan 1 45
(T D Easterby) *chsd ldng pair: rdn along over 2f out: edgd rt over 1f out: sn one pce* **16/1**

5 nk **Mishtaag** 2-9-3 0...... ChrisCatlin 3 49
(C E Brittain) *chsd ldng pair: rdn along over 2f out: sn wknd* **5/1**[2]

6 2¼ **Barista (IRE)** 2-8-12 0...... DeclanCannon(5) 9 40
(A J McCabe) *chsd ldrs: rdn along 2f out and sn no hdwy* **7/1**[3]

0 **7** 4½ **Bold Deceiver**[4] 1017 2-8-12 0...... TomMcLaughlin 5 17
(P S McEntee) *in tch: rdn along 1/2-way: sn outpcd* **8/1**

8 1½ **Cruise Tothelimit (IRE)** 2-9-3 0...... StephenCraine 8 16
(Patrick Morris) *s.i.s: a in rr* **33/1**

9 1½ **Soviet Bolt (IRE)** 2-9-3 0...... PJMcDonald 10 10+
(P T Midgley) *s.i.s: a in rr* **25/1**

10 nk **Sailor Boy (IRE)** 2-8-10 0...... MJMurphy(7) 7 9
(D Donovan) *s.i.s: a in rr* **25/1**

57.85 secs (-1.85) **Going Correction** -0.375s/f (Stan) 2y crse rec **10 Ran SP% 119.7**
Speed ratings (Par 92): **99,96,88,85,84 80,73,71,68,68**
toteswingers: 1&2 £5.10, 1&3 £4.20, 2&3 £13.10 CSF £14.73 TOTE £2.30: £1.50, £2.70, £2.10; EX 17.50 Trifecta £199.60 Pool: £388.60 - 1.44 winning units..
Owner Percy/Green Racing 2 **Bred** John McEnery **Trained** Musley Bank, N Yorks

FOCUS
The time, which was a 0.69 seconds than Richard Fahey's Jamesway recorded in the first division, was a new juvenile course record, although there was a tailwind.

NOTEBOOK
Arctic Feeling(IRE), a 17,000euros purchase, is a half-brother to Ponting, a triple 6f winner on Fibresand, and his dam was a dual 7f-1m winner on Fibresand, so it was no surprise he handled this surface well. Extremely well backed, he certainly knew his job, showing plenty of speed from the off, and he needed only one flick with the whip to keep the runner-up at bay. He looks useful, but will have to prove himself on turf. (op 5-4 tchd 6-4 and 11-8 in places)
Style And Panache(IRE), a 60,000euros half-brother to 7f juvenile winner Putra Laju, showed good early pace and, although coming under pressure by about halfway, she kept on reasonably well. Clear of the remainder, she should find a similar race. (op 12-1)
Daas Rite(IRE), a £5,000 half-brother to dual middle-distance winner Shanghai Star, out of a dual 1m1f scorer, simply lacked the speed of the front two. (op 10-1)
Peppercorn Rent(IRE), a half-sister to a 7f juvenile winner, out of a dam who also won over 7f at two, could not make much impression in the face of kickback in the last couple of furlongs, ending up stands' side from stall one after being switched, but she showed ability.
Mishtaag, a 26,000gns purchase, out of a 1m2f winner, was under pressure and struggling by halfway. (op 11-2)

1067 ENJOY THE LUCKY 7 GROUP OFFER MEDIAN AUCTION MAIDEN STKS 1m 4f (F)
3:00 (3:01) (Class 5) 3-5-Y-O **£2,729** (£806; £403) **Stalls** Low

Form RPR

50- **1** **Sir Pitt**[158] 7029 3-8-5 0...... NickyMackay 2 75+
(J H M Gosden) *trckd ldng pair on inner: hdwy over 3f out and sn pushed along: effrt to chal 2f out: sn rdn and kpt on to ld 1 1/2f out: sn hung bdly rt: clr ins fnl f* **8/13**[1]

000- **2** 3 **Ibn Hiyyan (USA)**[168] 6772 3-8-5 **60**...... JoeFanning 7 70
(M Johnston) *t.k.h: cl up: led over 3f out: rdn along 2f out: drvn and hdd over 1f out: sn swtchd lft and kpt on same pce* **5/2**[2]

040- **3** 12 **Deportista**[102] 7818 4-8-13 **48**...... DavidKenny(7) 6 48
(J A Pickering) *trckd ldng pair: effrt over 3f out: rdn along wl over 2f out: sn drvn and plugged on same pce* **66/1**

60-0 **4** 14 **Flute Magic**[7] 976 4-9-8 **50**...... JamesMillman(3) 4 31
(B R Millman) *led: rdn along and hdd over 3f out: sn wknd* **28/1**

5 1½ **Rosie Raymond**[24] 5-9-5 0...... MartinLane(3) 3 23
(C Smith) *in tch: rdn along 5f out: sn wknd* **66/1**

6 23 **Pennfield Pirate** 3-8-5 0 .... JimmyQuinn 1 —
(H Morrison) *s.i.s: green and reminders sn after s: in rr tl swtchd wd and hdwy to chse ldrs over 6f out: rdn along over 4f out and wknd qckly* **15/2**[3]

0- 7 6 **Mik**[276] [3425] 4-9-11 0 .... FergusSweeney 5 —
(Dr J R J Naylor) *in tch: rdn along 5f out: sn wknd and bhd* **100/1**

2m 37.85s (-3.15) **Going Correction** -0.10s/f (Stan)
WFA 3 from 4yo 22lb 4 from 5yo 2lb 7 Ran SP% **109.7**
Speed ratings (Par 103): **106,104,96,86,85 70,66**
toteswingers: 1&2 £1.50, 1&3 £4.80, 2&3 £7.60 CSF £2.08 TOTE £1.40: £1.10, £1.60; EX 2.80.
Owner A E Oppenheimer **Bred** Hascombe And Valiant Studs **Trained** Newmarket, Suffolk

FOCUS
A weak maiden, but it was well run and the form has been rated on the positive side.

1068 DINE IN THE QUEEN MOTHER RESTAURANT H'CAP (DIV I) 5f (F)
3:30 (3:30) (Class 6) (0-60,60) 4-Y-0+ **£1,706** (£503; £252) **Stalls** High

Form RPR

6004 1 **La Capriosa**[9] [967] 4-9-2 **58** .... RobertWinston 4 71
(J A Glover) *chsd clr ldr: rdn along 2f out: styd on to ld jst ins fnl f: sn drvn and kpt on* **5/1**[3]

0-06 2 2 1/4 **Fashion Icon (USA)**[20] [860] 4-8-0 **47** .... JamesSullivan(5) 7 52
(J Hetherton) *in tch: pushed along and sltly outpcd 1/2-way: rdn and hdwy 2f out: styd on wl u.p ent fnl f: tk 2nd nr line* **33/1**

0250 3 nk **Trick Or Two**[15] [896] 4-9-0 **56** ....(b) SilvestreDeSousa 5 60
(Mrs R A Carr) *led and sn clr: rdn along wl over 1f out: hdd jst ins fnl f: sn drvn and kpt on same pce: lost 2nd nr line* **10/1**

0110 4 1 1/2 **Mr Funshine**[9] [967] 5-9-1 **60** .... GaryBartley(3) 8 59
(D Shaw) *dwlt and towards rr: hdwy 1/2-way: rdn to chse ldrs wl over 1f out: sn drvn and no imp ins fnl f* **8/1**

340 5 1/2 **Best One**[47] [525] 6-8-12 **54** ....(b) ChrisCatlin 3 51
(R A Harris) *dwlt: sn in tch: swtchd lft and hdwy 1/2-way: rdn to chse ldrs wl over 1f out: sn drvn and one pce* **13/2**

2302 6 hd **Angle Of Attack (IRE)**[20] [860] 5-9-2 **58** ....(v) GrahamGibbons 6 54
(A D Brown) *chsd ldrs and sn pushed along: rdn over 2f out: sn drvn and grad wknd* **4/1**[1]

2244 7 nk **Bo McGinty (IRE)**[14] [899] 9-9-4 **60** ....(v) PaulHanagan 11 55
(R A Fahey) *racd on stands' rails: rdn along and bhd 1/2-way: edgd lft and hdwy over 1f out: kpt on ins fnl f: nt rch ldrs* **9/2**[2]

505 8 3 3/4 **Magic Glade**[37] [659] 11-8-4 **46** oh1 ....(b) AdrianMcCarthy 9 28
(Peter Grayson) *rdn along 1/2-way and a towards rr* **40/1**

0-24 9 4 **The Cuckoo**[44] [561] 4-8-10 **52** .... FrannyNorton 1 19
(M Quinn) *chsd ldng pair: rdn along 1/2-way: sn wknd* **4/1**[1]

000 10 1 1/2 **Givenn**[29] [758] 6-8-4 **46** oh1 ....(bt[1]) DavidProbert 2 8
(Ms J S Doyle) *a outpcd and bhd* **50/1**

-500 11 2 3/4 **Miacarla**[21] [848] 7-7-13 **46** oh1 .... DeclanCannon(5) 10 —
(H A McWilliams) *a outpcd and bhd* **100/1**

57.69 secs (-2.01) **Going Correction** -0.375s/f (Stan) 11 Ran SP% **116.7**
Speed ratings (Par 101): **101,97,96,94,93 93,92,86,80,78 73**
toteswingers: 1&2 £38.80, 1&3 £11.00, 2&3 £31.70 CSF £160.06 CT £1589.21 TOTE £6.30: £2.00, £8.80, £4.50; EX 158.70 TRIFECTA Not won..
Owner Paul J Dixon **Bred** Slatch Farm Stud **Trained** Babworth, Notts

FOCUS
A typically competitive 5f handicap for the course. The time was under standard and 0.39 seconds quicker than the second division, although there was a tailwind. The first two showed their best form for some time, with the third the best guide.
Bo McGinty(IRE) Official explanation: jockey said gelding never travelled

1069 MEMBERSHIP OF SOUTHWELL GOLF CLUB H'CAP 1m 6f (F)
4:00 (4:00) (Class 3) (0-90,90) 4-Y-0+ **£7,123** (£2,119; £1,059; £529) **Stalls** Low

Form RPR

116- 1 **Stanstill (IRE)**[193] [6095] 4-9-9 **89** .... RobertWinston 4 101+
(G A Swinbank) *tk gd hold on heels of ldrs: hdwy 3f out: chal 2f out: rdn to ld 1 1/2f out: kpt on wl u.p ins fnl f* **9/2**[3]

211- 2 1 3/4 **Lucky Punt**[116] [7640] 4-9-10 **90** .... FergusSweeney 5 96
(B G Powell) *trckd ldng pair: hdwy to ld 6f out: rdn along 3f out: drvn and hdd 1 1/2f out: kpt on same pce u.p ins fnl f* **11/4**[1]

2224 3 shd **Calculating (IRE)**[12] [938] 6-8-10 **72** .... DavidProbert 2 78
(M D I Usher) *led: hdd 6f out: rdn along on inner and cl up 3f out: drvn wl over 1f out: kpt on* **10/1**

166- 4 5 **Swiss Act**[339] [1555] 6-9-13 **89** .... JoeFanning 8 88
(M Johnston) *trckd ldrs: effrt over 3f out: sn rdn and one pce fnl 2f* **11/1**

142- 5 1/2 **Bin End**[314] [2189] 4-9-5 **85** .... JamieSpencer 7 83
(M L W Bell) *heavily restrained s and dropped out in rr: hdwy on outer over 3f out: rdn to chse ldrs 2f out: sn hrd drvn and no imp* **3/1**[2]

3115 6 2 1/2 **Benedict Spirit (IRE)**[12] [888] 5-9-3 **82** ....(v) MartinLane(3) 6 77
(P D Evans) *hld up in tch on inner: hdwy 4f out: rdn along over 3f out: sn wknd* **17/2**

/22- 7 22 **Heathyards Pride**[426] [330] 10-9-7 **83** .... GrahamGibbons 1 47
(R Hollinshead) *hld up in tch: effrt 4f out: rdn along and wknd over 3f out* **50/1**

0-23 8 7 **Chocolate Caramel (USA)**[14] [910] 8-8-12 **74** .... PaulHanagan 3 28
(R A Fahey) *cl up: rdn along over 3f out: sn wknd and bhd* **9/1**

3m 4.42s (-3.88) **Going Correction** -0.10s/f (Stan)
WFA 4 from 5yo+ 4lb 8 Ran SP% **109.8**
Speed ratings (Par 107): **107,106,105,103,102 101,88,84**
toteswingers: 1&2 £4.10, 1&3 £9.40, 2&3 £6.90 CSF £15.84 CT £105.33 TOTE £6.40: £2.20, £1.60, £1.30; EX 20.40 Trifecta £327.70 Part won. Pool: £442.85 - 0.85 winning units..
Owner The Twopin Partnership **Bred** E J Daly **Trained** Melsonby, N Yorks

FOCUS
A decent staying handicap in which it paid to race handily. The winner was value for double the margin and the third looks the best guide.

NOTEBOOK
Stanstill(IRE), trying Fibresand for the first time on his return from 193 days off, won tidily, despite racing keenly down the back straight. He progressed well last year and is clearly still improving. Now very useful, he should have a good season back on turf. (op 7-1)
Lucky Punt came into this 5-6 on Fibresand and this was a fine effort in defeat off a 6lb higher mark than for his latest success. He had been off for 116 days and is entitled to be sharper next time. (op 9-4)
Calculating(IRE) ran to form but simply struggled against a couple of more progressive types. (op 17-2)
Swiss Act, returning from 339 days off, came off the bridle around the bend into the straight, lacking the sharpness of the front three, and simply got going too late. He should come a good deal for this. (op 14-1)
Bin End, gelded since he was last seen in May of last year, was set a lot to do on his return to action and could make no impression in the straight. He had looked quite a promising type and it's too early to give up on him seeing as he may have simply failed to act on Fibresand. (op 5-2)
Benedict Spirit(IRE), runner-up over hurdles latest, was 3-8 on this surface, but he proved disappointing. (op 12-1 tchd 8-1)

1070 CONFERENCING AT SOUTHWELL RACECOURSE H'CAP 7f (F)
4:30 (4:32) (Class 5) (0-75,75) 3-Y-0 **£2,590** (£770; £385; £192) **Stalls** Low

Form RPR

6-41 1 **Yawary**[43] [574] 3-9-3 **74** ....(t) NeilCallan 5 87
(C E Brittain) *trckd ldrs: pushed along 3f out: hdwy to chal 2f out: rdn to ld 1 1/2f out: drvn clr ent fnl f: styd on wl* **2/1**[1]

3230 2 5 **Adam De Beaulieu (USA)**[12] [933] 3-8-11 **68** ....(t) PhillipMakin 8 67
(B M R Haslam) *trckd ldrs: hdwy on outer 3f out: rdn to chse wnr over 1f out: sn drvn and edgd lft ent fnl f: sn one pce* **14/1**

2-15 3 3/4 **Seamster**[35] [681] 3-9-0 **71** .... JoeFanning 1 68
(M Johnston) *mde most on inner: rdn along and jnd 2f out: drvn and hdd 1 1/2f out: kpt on same pce* **6/1**[3]

0-11 4 1 1/4 **Set Back**[27] [782] 3-8-11 **68** .... AndrewMullen 2 62
(D Nicholls) *cl up: rdn along over 2f out: drvn wl over 1f out and sn one pce* **11/4**[2]

454- 5 nse **Deely Plaza**[163] [6895] 3-8-11 **68** .... RobertWinston 3 61
(J A Glover) *chsd ldrs on inner: rdn along 3f out: drvn over 2f out and sn one pce* **11/1**

03-5 6 20 **Tukitinyasok (IRE)**[55] [406] 3-9-4 **75** .... PaulHanagan 4 14
(R F Fisher) *s.i.s: a bhd* **14/1**

1252 7 4 **Inside Track (IRE)**[14] [909] 3-8-10 **72** .... PaulPickard(5) 6 —
(P T Midgley) *cl up: rdn along 1/2-way: wknd over 2f out: sn bhd and eased* **16/1**

1m 29.0s (-1.30) **Going Correction** -0.10s/f (Stan) 7 Ran SP% **101.8**
Speed ratings (Par 98): **103,97,96,95,94 72,67**
toteswingers: 1&2 £7.40, 1&3 £2.30, 2&3 £10.00 CSF £23.52 CT £96.61 TOTE £1.90: £1.10, £6.40; EX 31.30 Trifecta £148.50 Pool: £301.70 - 1.50 winning units..
Owner Saeed Manana **Bred** Cheveley Park Stud Ltd **Trained** Newmarket, Suffolk
■ Premium Charge was withdrawn after proving unruly in the stalls. R4 applies, deduct 10p in the £.

FOCUS
A modest handicap but pretty solid form at face value, with a biggish step up from the winner.
Tukitinyasok(IRE) Official explanation: jockey said gelding missed the break

1071 GREAT OFFERS AT SOUTHWELL-RACECOURSE.CO.UK H'CAP 2m (F)
5:00 (5:01) (Class 6) (0-65,65) 4-Y-0+ **£2,047** (£604; £302) **Stalls** Low

Form RPR

3-05 1 **Mountain Forest (GER)**[57] [376] 4-8-2 **45** .... JimmyQuinn 2 60+
(H Morrison) *a.p: smooth hdwy over 3f out: led on bit wl over 2f out: sn clr: easily* **13/2**[2]

3043 2 6 **Davana**[34] [700] 4-8-0 **46** .... KellyHarrison(3) 5 51
(W J H Ratcliffe) *a.p: rdn along and sltly outpcd over 3f out: drvn and rallied over 2f out: kpt on ins fnl f: no ch w wnr* **33/1**

00-4 3 1 1/4 **Rare Coincidence**[20] [777] 9-8-11 **49** ....(p) PaulHanagan 9 53
(R F Fisher) *led: rdn along 4f out: hdd wl over 2f out: drvn fr wl over 1f out and kpt on same pce* **5/1**[1]

551 4 4 1/2 **Zaffeu**[48] [506] 9-9-8 **60** ....(p) VinceSlattery 12 58
(A G Juckes) *in tch: hdwy to chse ldrs over 6f out: rdn along over 3f out: drvn over 2f out and plugged on same pce* **7/1**[3]

46-0 5 nk **Telling Stories (IRE)**[35] [463] 4-8-4 **47** ....(t) SilvestreDeSousa 4 45
(B D Leavy) *hld up: hdwy 6f out: rdn along over 3f out: plugged on fnl 2f: n.d* **16/1**

55-4 6 5 **Bandanaman (IRE)**[15] [897] 4-9-8 **65** .... PJMcDonald 1 57
(G A Swinbank) *trckd ldrs: effrt 4f out: rdn along over 3f out and sn wknd* **13/2**[2]

-204 7 25 **Cragganmore Creek**[50] [470] 7-8-7 **45** .... JoeFanning 3 7
(D Morris) *trckd ldrs: rdn along over 6f out: sn wknd* **14/1**

56-1 8 3 1/2 **Dulce Domum**[15] [898] 4-8-5 **53** .... DeclanCannon(5) 6 11
(A B Haynes) *rrd and awkward s: in rr tl hdwy to trck ldrs after 4f: rdn along 7f out: lost pl over 5f out and sn bhd* **5/1**[1]

60-2 9 6 **Orkney (IRE)**[22] [835] 5-9-12 **64** .... TomEaves 11 14
(Julie Camacho) *a in rr: rdn along 1/2-way and sn bhd* **13/2**[2]

000- 10 1 1/4 **Just Dan**[193] [6098] 4-8-4 **47** ow2 .... KevinGhunowa 10 —
(D W Thompson) *a in rr: bhd fnl 4f* **66/1**

4-05 11 9 **Stagecoach Emerald**[26] [811] 8-8-12 **55** ....(b) TobyAtkinson(5) 8 —
(T T Clement) *a in rr: wl bhd fnl 5f* **7/1**[3]

3m 41.97s (-3.53) **Going Correction** -0.10s/f (Stan)
WFA 4 from 5yo+ 5lb 11 Ran SP% **115.3**
Speed ratings (Par 101): **104,101,100,98,97 95,82,81,78,77 73**
toteswingers: 1&2 £19.10, 1&3 £7.40, 2&3 £30.80 CSF £192.17 CT £1156.60 TOTE £7.20: £2.40, £7.30, £1.20; EX 164.80 TRIFECTA Not won..
Owner H Morrison **Bred** Gestut Isarland **Trained** East Ilsley, Berks

FOCUS
A weak staying handicap run in a slow time. Big improvement from the winner, but the form makes sense around the placed horses.
Dulce Domum Official explanation: trainer had no explanation for the poor form shown

1072 DINE IN THE QUEEN MOTHER RESTAURANT H'CAP (DIV II) 5f (F)
5:35 (5:35) (Class 6) (0-60,60) 4-Y-0+ **£1,706** (£503; £252) **Stalls** High

Form RPR

60-4 1 **Cavitie**[15] [896] 4-8-11 **53** .... DarryllHolland 9 61+
(Andrew Reid) *in tch: rdn along 2f out: swtchd rt and drvn over 1f out: styd on strly ins fnl f to ld on line* **11/4**[1]

6066 2 shd **Calmdownmate (IRE)**[15] [892] 5-9-3 **59** .... PJMcDonald 3 67
(Mrs R A Carr) *racd wd: chsd ldrs: hdwy 2f out: rdn over 1f out: ev ch ent fnl f: drvn to ld last 40yds: hdd on line* **11/2**[3]

0031 3 hd **Captain Kallis (IRE)**[14] [912] 4-9-0 **56** ....(be) JamieSpencer 7 63
(D J S Ffrench Davis) *led 1f: cl up tl led again 2f out and sn rdn: drvn ins fnl f: hdd and no ex last 40yds* **3/1**[2]

4503 4 1 1/2 **Nawaaff**[37] [659] 5-8-5 **47** .... FrannyNorton 2 49
(M Quinn) *cl up: effrt 2f out and ev ch tl rdn and one pce ent fnl f* **17/2**

-004 5 2 1/4 **Shannon Golden**[20] [860] 4-8-3 **50** ....(t) SimonPearce(5) 1 44
(S R Bowring) *chsd ldrs: rdn along 2f out: drvn over 1f out and grad wknd* **9/1**

0400 6 nk **Chosen One (IRE)**[28] [778] 5-9-0 **56** ....(v[1]) TomEaves 10 48
(B Smart) *cl up towards stands' rail: led after 1f: rdn along and hdd 2f out: sn drvn and grad wknd* **8/1**

0-00 7 3 3/4 **Athaakeel (IRE)**[9] [968] 4-9-4 **60** .... LiamJones 5 39
(R A Harris) *cl up: rdn along 2f out: drvn and wknd over 1f out* **20/1**

00-0 8 5 **Iron Max (IRE)**[47] [531] 4-8-4 **46** oh1 .... PaulHanagan 6 7
(Mrs L Williamson) *a in rr* **100/1**

000- 9 11 **Mr Rooney (IRE)**[148] [7219] 7-8-0 **47** oh1 ow1 .... BillyCray(5) 4 —
(A Berry) *a in rr: bhd fr 1/2-way* **28/1**

The Form Book, Raceform Ltd, Compton, RG20 6NL

5-60 F **Rabbit Fighter (IRE)**[9] 968 6-8-13 58........................(v) MartinLane(3) 8 —
(D Shaw) *dwlt and in rr: rdn along 1/2-way: bhd whn swvd bdly lft ins fnl f and crashed through rails: fell* **20/1**

58.08 secs (-1.62) **Going Correction** -0.375s/f (Stan) **10** Ran SP% **112.7**
Speed ratings (Par 101): **97,96,96,94,90 90,84,76,58,—**
toteswingers: 1&2 £5.60, 2&3 £3.50, 1&3 not won. CSF £16.57 CT £47.49 TOTE £3.50: £2.00, £1.60, £1.70; EX 17.40 Trifecta £46.30 Pool: £275.39 - 4.40 winning units. Place 6: £55.93 Place 5: £25.63 .
Owner A S Reid **Bred** A S Reid **Trained** Mill Hill, London NW7

FOCUS
The time was 0.39 seconds slower than the first division. An improvement from the winner, with the race best rated around the third.
T/Plt: £57.00 to a £1 stake. Pool: £70,951.20. 908.10 winning tickets. T/Qpdt: £16.10 to a £1 stake. Pool: £6,325.08. 289.62 winning tickets. JR

FOLKESTONE (R-H)
Thursday, April 1

OFFICIAL GOING: Heavy (4.1)
Wind: Fresh, half-behind Weather: overcast, chilly

1073 LADBROKES.COM EUROPEAN BREEDERS' FUND MAIDEN STKS 5f
2:10 (2:16) (Class 5) 2-Y-O **£3,497** (£1,040; £520; £259) **Stalls** Low

Form RPR
1 **Novabridge** 2-9-3 0.. JamieSpencer 3 71+
(A B Haynes) *mde all: sn crossed to r on stands' rail: rdn and edgd rt fr over 1f out: styd on wl to go clr ent fnl f: eased towards fin* **6/1**

2 *3 1/4* **Calormen** 2-9-3 0.. KierenFallon 4 59
(M R Channon) *chsd ldrs: rdn and unable qck wl over 1f out: no ch w wnr fnl f: kpt on to go 2nd nr fin* **11/2**[3]

3 *nk* **Molly Mylenis** 2-8-12 0.. CathyGannon 2 53+
(P D Evans) *v.s.a: bhd and sn rdn along: hdwy into midfield and reminders 1/2-way: sn outpcd by ldrs: styd on fnl f: wnt 3rd nr fin* **10/3**[2]

4 *nk* **Shafgaan** 2-9-3 0.. NeilCallan 1 57
(C E Brittain) *chsd wnr: chal 2f out: sn rdn and nt qckn w wnr: edgd rt and wl hld fnl f: lost 2 pls nr fin* **3/1**[1]

5 *5* **Helen Of Toy** 2-8-12 0.. FergusSweeney 10 34
(B G Powell) *in tch tl shkn up and unable qck ent fnl 2f: wl btn fr wl over 1f out* **14/1**

6 *2 1/2* **Imperial Waltzer** 2-9-3 0... AlanMunro 8 30
(M R Channon) *s.i.s: sn bustled along in rr: nvr trbld ldrs* **10/1**

7 *2* **Danehill Deb** 2-8-12 0... PatDobbs 6 18
(B De Haan) *broke wl: chsd ldrs and flashing tail: rdn and wknd ent fnl 2f: wl btn fnl f* **14/1**

8 *13* **Terrys Flutter** 2-8-12 0.. J-PGuillambert 5 —
(M A Allen) *v.s.a: rn green and a detached in last: t.o fr 1/2-way* **50/1**

64.89 secs (4.89) **Going Correction** +0.725s/f (Yiel) **8** Ran SP% **102.1**
Speed ratings (Par 92): **89,83,83,82,74 70,67,46**
toteswingers: 1&2 £3.20, 1&3 £4.10, 2&3 £3.00 CSF £30.41 TOTE £6.70: £2.30, £1.10, £1.70; EX 22.70 Trifecta £75.10 Pool: £407.49 - 4.01 winning units..
Owner Dajam Ltd **Bred** Bishopswood Bloodstock & Trickledown Stud **Trained** Limpley Stoke, Bath
■ Tigelise was withdrawn (13/2, unruly in stalls). Deduct 10p in the £ under R4.

FOCUS
There was no overnight rain, but the ground remained heavy for Folkestone's first Flat meeting of the year. In fact, clerk of the course Andy Waitt said the GoingStick average of 4.1 was about as bad as you would want it. He also felt the best ground was close to the stands' rail and the evidence of this opener supported that view. No form to go on but this was probably a modest maiden. The time was 5.59 seconds outside standard, confirming conditions were testing.

NOTEBOOK
Novabridge failed to attract a bid as a yearling but had cost 8,000gns as a foal. A half-brother to, among others, multiple sprint winner Brunelleschi, out of a 5f juvenile winner, he looked well educated, breaking sharply to lead against the possibly favoured nearside rail, and he found plenty for a few smacks with the whip, ultimately being eased down when drifting towards the centre of the track in the final strides. He evidently has a fair amount of ability, but this is not form to get carried away with. (op 7-1)
Calormen ◆, the first foal of a 5f juvenile selling winner, needed this experience. He ran on well without being given anything like a hard time and should improve. (op 4-1)
Molly Mylenis, a £6,500 first foal of a multiple 5f-7f winner, lost about 3l at the start and soon received a reminder. She gradually got the idea, responding to pressure to claim third, although she did race towards the likely favoured near rail. (op 4-1)
Shafgaan, a 17,000gns half-brother to, among others, smart triple 7f-1m2f winner Rosa Grace, out of a successful sprinter, seemed to know his job early on, showing speed, but he faded in the closing stages. It might be that he failed to handle the ground, but his trainer is yet to have a 2-y-o placed from six runners and it seems his youngsters are needing a run. (tchd 4-1)
Helen Of Toy, drawn in stall ten, was caught wide and never featured. (tchd 16-1)
Imperial Waltzer was not best away and could make no impression. (op 8-1)

1074 LADBROKESBINGO.COM H'CAP 5f
2:40 (2:45) (Class 5) (0-75,74) 4-Y-O+ **£3,070** (£906; £453) **Stalls** Low

Form RPR
-624 1 **Love You Louis**[34] 727 4-8-9 65.................................. RichardHughes 4 80
(J R Jenkins) *mde all and sn crossed to stands' rail: rdn clr jst over 1f out: in command ins fnl f: eased towards fin* **5/2**[1]

100- 2 *3* **Ginobili (IRE)**[159] 7028 4-8-12 68.................................. SebSanders 1 69
(Andrew Reid) *taken down early: t.k.h: trckd ldng pair: rdn and unable qck wl over 1f out: plugged on u.p ins fnl f to go 2nd nr fin: no ch w wnr* **6/1**

410- 3 *nk* **Pocket's Pick (IRE)**[91] 7890 4-8-9 65............................... RyanMoore 6 65
(G L Moore) *chsd wnr: rdn and unable qck wl over 1f out: btn jst ins fnl f: wknd fnl 100yds and lost 2nd nr fin* **10/1**

060- 4 *5* **Kyllachy Storm**[163] 6915 6-9-0 70................................ DarryllHolland 7 52
(R J Hodges) *hld up in tch: swtchd rt off of rail and effrt jst over 2f out: sn wl outpcd and no ch after* **9/2**[3]

065- 5 *2* **Lucky Leigh**[118] 7634 4-9-4 74...................................... KierenFallon 9 49
(M R Channon) *chsd ldrs: rdn over 2f out: wknd u.p 2f out: wl btn over 1f out* **12/1**

405- 6 *4* **Rocker**[161] 6964 6-9-4 74.. GeorgeBaker 8 34
(G L Moore) *racd in last pair: rdn and no rspnse 2f out: sn wl bhd* **5/1**

5-11 7 *6* **Straboe (USA)**[29] 778 4-8-5 64.............................. WilliamCarson(3) 5 3
(S C Williams) *stdd s: hld up in rr: lost tch over 2f out* **4/1**[2]

63.13 secs (3.13) **Going Correction** +0.725s/f (Yiel) **7** Ran SP% **114.5**
Speed ratings (Par 103): **103,98,97,89,86 80,70**
toteswingers: 1&2 £3.30, 1&3 £5.40, 2&3 £14.50 CSF £17.98 CT £126.49 TOTE £3.10: £1.90, £3.70; EX 18.90 Trifecta £134.10 Pool: £351.76 - 1.94 winning units..
Owner J Pepper **Bred** Mrs Wendy Jenkins **Trained** Royston, Herts
■ Desperate Dan (12/1) was withdrawn after refusing to leave the paddock. Deduct 5p in the £ under R4. New market formed.

FOCUS
Just like in the opener, the winner made all against the stands'-side rail and those who raced elsewhere had little hope. This is modest form.
Straboe(USA) Official explanation: trainer had no explanation for the poor form shown

1075 LADBROKES.COM MAIDEN FILLIES' STKS 6f
3:10 (3:15) (Class 5) 3-Y-O **£2,729** (£806; £403) **Stalls** Low

Form RPR
3233 1 **Caramelita**[15] 900 3-9-0 66... RyanMoore 7 68
(J R Jenkins) *trckd ldrs: effrt to ld 2f out: rdn clr over 1f out: eased towards fin: easily* **1/1**[1]

60- 2 *6* **Rio Mist**[281] 3271 3-9-0 0.. RichardHughes 6 49
(R Hannon) *in tch: chsd clr wnr over 1f out: no imp after: eased towards fin* **11/4**[2]

0 3 *1 3/4* **Dreamacha**[64] 313 3-8-11 0.................................... WilliamCarson(3) 8 43
(S C Williams) *in tch in last trio: rdn ent fnl 2f: wnt modest 3rd over 1f out: kpt on same pce fnl f* **9/1**

005- 4 *8* **Silvee**[198] 5967 3-9-0 42.. NeilChalmers 2 18
(J J Bridger) *led tl rdn and hdd 2f out: wknd qckly over 1f out: wl btn fnl f* **50/1**

5 *7* **Masteeat (USA)** 3-9-0 0.. SteveDrowne 1 —
(J R Best) *s.i.s: a towards rr: rdn and lost tch over 2f out* **11/2**[3]

440- 6 *6* **Aldorable**[169] 6775 3-9-0 59.. JackMitchell 5 —
(R A Teal) *taken down early: s.i.s: a bhd: racd awkwadly and lost tch over 2f out: t.o* **14/1**

0- 7 *11* **Lucky Flyer**[301] 2636 3-9-0 0... JamesDoyle 3 —
(S Kirk) *chsd ldr tl jst over 2f out: sn wknd and wl bhd: t.o* **25/1**

1m 16.72s (4.02) **Going Correction** +0.725s/f (Yiel) **7** Ran SP% **114.5**
Speed ratings (Par 95): **102,94,91,81,71 63,49**
toteswingers: 1&2 £1.60, 1&3 £2.80, 2&3 £3.50 CSF £3.91 TOTE £2.00: £1.10, £1.70; EX 5.10 Trifecta £21.80 Pool: £ 589.45 - 19.98 winning units..
Owner La Senoritas **Bred** R B Hill **Trained** Royston, Herts

FOCUS
A really weak maiden and they finished strung out.

1076 LADBROKESPOKER.COM H'CAP 6f
3:40 (4:06) (Class 4) (0-85,84) 4-Y-O+ **£4,857** (£1,445; £722; £360)

Form RPR
440- 1 **Spitfire**[118] 7626 5-9-4 84... KierenFallon 7 92
(J R Jenkins) *sn trckd ldrs on rail fr flag s: despite supposed to be drawn wd: swtchd rt off of rail 2f out: rdn to ld ent fnl f: clr ins fnl f: r.o wl* **4/1**[2]

620- 2 *2 1/4* **Kerrys Requiem (IRE)**[172] 6694 4-9-4 84.......................... ChrisCatlin 1 85
(M R Channon) *in tch in midfield: swtchd rt and effrt wl over 1f out: kpt on u.p to chse wnr fnl 100yds: no imp after* **20/1**

031- 3 *1 1/4* **Daddy's Gift (IRE)**[120] 7613 4-8-12 78........................ RichardHughes 5 75
(R Hannon) *led: pressed over 2f out: rdn wl over 1f out: hdd ent fnl f: sn outpcd by wnr: lost 2nd fnl 100yds* **9/2**[3]

3640 4 *1/2* **Timeteam (IRE)**[15] 902 4-8-9 75...................................... CathyGannon 6 70
(P D Evans) *taken down early: t.k.h: chsd ldr: ev ch over 2f out: rdn 2f out: outpcd by wnr ent fnl f: plugged on same pce after* **16/1**

130- 5 *2 1/4* **Kingswinford (IRE)**[145] 7287 4-8-4 77...................... MatthewCosham(7) 8 65
(P D Evans) *hld up in tch towards rr: rdn and effrt ent fnl 2f: wknd and edgd lft jst over 1f out* **6/1**

0-00 6 *2 1/2* **Idle Power (IRE)**[35] 696 12-8-1 72.............................. KierenFox(5) 3 52
(J R Boyle) *chsd ldrs: lost pl and pushed along 1/2-way: no prog wl over 1f out* **10/1**

7 *3* **Signore Momento (IRE)**[214] 5489 4-8-11 77.................. HayleyTurner 2 48
(Miss Amy Weaver) *a bhd: rdn along 1/2-way: wl btn fnl 2f* **3/1**[1]

1m 15.0s (2.30) **7** Ran SP% **97.2**
CSF £51.21 CT £194.53 TOTE £4.20: £2.00, £6.10; EX 41.70 Trifecta £217.60 Pool: £391.22 - 1.33 winning units..
Owner The Spitfire Partnership **Bred** R B Hill **Trained** Royston, Herts
■ Harlech Castle was withdrawn (7/2, unruly and injured in stalls). Deduct 20p in the £ under R4. Race hand timed.

FOCUS
There was a delay of over 25 minutes (albeit the race had already been put back five minutes) after Harlech Castle, who was subsequently withdrawn, seemed to get stuck in his stall, having been quite fractious. As a consequence of that incident, there was eventually a flag start, but it was a bit of a shambles. After walking around to the front of the stalls, the runners were allowed to set off almost immediately with no apparent attempt to line them up, let alone get them into the correct order. All things considered, this is form to treat with real caution. With this race being run short of the advertised distance, no speed figures have been allocated.

1077 LADBROKESCASINO.COM H'CAP 1m 4f
4:10 (4:45) (Class 5) (0-75,74) 4-Y-O+ **£3,070** (£906; £453)

Form RPR
/40- 1 **Hawridge Star (IRE)**[160] 6995 8-8-10 64............................ AlanMunro 4 74
(W S Kittow) *hld up in rr: pushed along over 3f out: stl plenty to do 2f out: hdwy and swtchd lft over 1f out: chal jst ins fnl f: led fnl 75yds: r.o wl* **9/4**[2]

640- 2 *3/4* **Goodwood Starlight (IRE)**[162] 6936 5-9-3 74............... RobertLButler(3) 5 83
(Miss Sheena West) *t.k.h: hld up in last pair: swtchd to outer and hdwy ent jst over 2f out: rdn to ld over 1f out: hdd and no ex fnl 75yds* **12/1**

1-54 3 *8* **I'm In The Pink (FR)**[28] 300 6-9-6 74............................ JamieSpencer 7 71
(P D Evans) *hld up in main gp: clsd on ldr over 3f out: rdn and effrt on inner 2f out: ev ch over 1f out: sn hung lft: wknd fnl f* **13/8**[1]

2313 4 *1 1/4* **Eseej (USA)**[16] 897 5-9-6 74.. ChrisCatlin 1 69
(P W Hiatt) *racd keenly: led and sn wl clr: reduced advantage over 3f out: rdn ent fnl 2f: hdd and sltly hmpd over 1f out: sn wknd* **15/2**

5543 5 *6* **Choral Festival**[29] 770 4-8-7 62...................................... HayleyTurner 6 48
(J J Bridger) *chsd clr ldr: clsd over 3f out: rdn ent fnl 2f: sn lost pl and wknd qckly* **8/1**

2114 6 *24* **Make Amends (IRE)**[10] 966 5-9-3 71................................ GeorgeBaker 2 21
(R J Hodges) *t.k.h: hld up in last trio: hdwy on outer over 3f out: chsd ldrs and rdn over 2f out: wknd qckly over 1f out: eased ins fnl f* **7/1**[3]

36-0 7 *18* **Enlist**[13] 941 6-8-9 63.. FergusSweeney 3 —
(B G Powell) *prom in main gp tl wknd qckly u.p 3f out: t.o and eased fr over 1f out* **25/1**

2m 58.8s (17.90) **Going Correction** +1.575s/f (Heav)
WFA 4 from 5yo+ 1lb **7** Ran SP% **115.8**
Speed ratings (Par 103): **103,102,97,96,92 76,64**
toteswingers: 1&2 £6.00, 1&3 £2.60, 2&3 £6.70 CSF £29.28 CT £54.37 TOTE £3.00: £2.00, £4.50; EX 28.80 Trifecta £125.40 Pool: £564.65 - 3.33 winning units..
Owner Eric Gadsden **Bred** Seamus Murphy **Trained** Blackborough, Devon

FOCUS
The stalls were out of action following an incident in an earlier race and a flag start was needed, although it didn't matter too much over this distance. The race was hand timed. They went a strong pace in this modest handicap and it proved to be a real test in the conditions.

1078 LADBROKES.COM H'CAP — 1m 1f 149y
4:40 (5:17) (Class 6) (0-60,58) 4-Y-0+ — **£2,047** (£604; £302)

Form — RPR

-306 **1** **Golden Prospect**[69] [270] 6-9-3 **57**............................ PaulFitzsimons 14 — 66
(Miss J R Tooth) *t.k.h: hld up in tch in rr: stl plenty to do but travelling strly over 2f out: swtchd to outer and rdn over 1f out: chal and edgd lft 1f out: led fnl 75yds: edgd rt u.p towards fin* **33/1**

2322 **2** ½ **Alfredtheordinary**[8] [969] 5-9-1 **55**.............................. ChrisCatlin 1 — 63
(M R Channon) *chsd ldrs: wnt 2nd wl over 2f out: led 2f out: sn rdn: edgd lft u.p ent fnl f: hdd fnl 75yds: one pce and carried rt towards fin* **4/1**[2]

02-5 **3** 4½ **Felicia**[24] [827] 5-8-10 **50**.. SamHitchcott 8 — 49
(J E Long) *wl in tch in midfield: effrt 3f out: rdn to chse ldrs jst over 2f out: wnt 2nd over 1f out tl ent fnl f: one pce after* **14/1**

000- **4** ¾ **Mick Is Back**[155] [7127] 6-9-1 **55**...................................(p) TomQueally 13 — 52
(G G Margarson) *chsd ldrs: rdn over 2f out: drvn and one pce fr over 1f out* **13/2**[3]

00-0 **5** 7 **Amwell House**[38] [656] 5-8-5 **45**.............................. AdrianMcCarthy 10 — 27
(J R Jenkins) *t.k.h: hld up wl in tch towards rr: hdwy to chse ldrs over 2f out: no prog u.p wl over 1f out: wl hld fnl f* **25/1**

000- **6** 10 **Steady Gaze**[364] [1081] 5-8-2 **45**...................... Louis-PhilippeBeuzelin(3) 5 — 6
(G L Moore) *in tch in midfield: lost pl but stl in tch towards rr 1/2-way: rdn and no rspnse wl over 2f out* **7/2**[1]

00-3 **7** 1¾ **Rosy Dawn**[8] [969] 5-8-8 **48**.. HayleyTurner 2 — 17
(J J Bridger) *sn chsng ldr tl led over 3f out: rdn and hdd 2f out: wknd qckly: wl btn and eased ins fnl f* **11/1**

000- **8** 5 **Illicit**[127] [7512] 5-9-4 **58**...(t) SteveDrowne 3 — 5
(J R Holt) *hld up in tch in rr: rdn and no rspnse 3f out: sn wl bhd: eased ins fnl f* **14/1**

000/ **9** 1¾ **Mamichor**[590] [5166] 7-8-0 **45**.. KierenFox(5) 12 — —
(Mrs L J Mongan) *led tl over 3f out: wknd qckly u.p over 2f out: eased ins fnl f* **18/1**

00/0 **10** ½ **High Class Problem (IRE)**[47] [540] 7-8-5 **50**.........(p) SimonPearce(5) 6 — —
(D C O'Brien) *t.k.h: hld up in midfield on outer: rdn 4f out: wknd qckly 3f out: eased fnl f* **66/1**

3-00 **11** 3¾ **Holyfield Warrior (IRE)**[42] [603] 6-9-3 **57**.................. RichardHughes 4 — —
(R J Smith) *hld up in tch in rr: rdn and no prog wl over 2f out: t.o and eased fnl f* **12/1**

6432 **12** 9 **Barodine**[13] [940] 7-9-3 **57**.. GeorgeBaker 9 — —
(R J Hodges) *chsd ldrs tl rdn and btn over 2f out: virtually p.u fr over 1f out: t.o* **4/1**[2]

2m 22.4s (17.50) **Going Correction** +1.575s/f (Heav) — **12** Ran SP% **118.5**
Speed ratings (Par 101): **93,92,89,88,82 74,73,69,68,67 64,57**
toteswingers: 1&2 £14.90, 1&3 £33.40, 2&3 £10.10 CSF £159.67 CT £1987.40 TOTE £37.20: £7.20, £2.00, £3.40; EX 163.80 TRIFECTA Not won. Place 6: £140.65 Place 5: £80.22.
Owner Miss J R Tooth **Bred** D E And Mrs J Cash **Trained** Upper Lambourn, Berks

FOCUS
The stalls remained out of action, so another flag start was needed. The race was hand timed. This was just a moderate handicap, but they went a reasonable pace.
Illicit Official explanation: jockey said gelding lost its action
Mamichor Official explanation: jockey said gelding hung left
Holyfield Warrior(IRE) Official explanation: jockey said gelding lost its action
Barodine Official explanation: jockey said gelding was unsuited by the heavy ground
T/Jkpt: Not won. T/Plt: £460.70 to a £1 stake. Pool: £118,339.10. 187.51 winning tickets. T/Qpdt: £58.20 to a £1 stake. Pool: £9,473.20. 120.30 winning tickets. SP

FONTAINEBLEAU
Friday, April 2

OFFICIAL GOING: Very soft

1081a PRIX COR DE CHASSE (LISTED RACE) (3YO+) (TURF) — 5f 110y
1:35 (12:00) 3-Y-0+ — **£23,008** (£9,203; £6,902; £4,601; £2,300)

RPR

1 **Amico Fritz (GER)**[10] 4-9-7 0.. MaximeGuyon 7 — 101
(H-A Pantall, France) **51/10**[3]

2 nk **Bluster (FR)**[134] [7458] 4-9-11 0.............................. ChristopheSoumillon 6 — 104
(Robert Collet, France) **15/1**

3 1½ **Tiza (SAF)**[134] [7458] 8-10-0 0.....................................(p) DominiqueBoeuf 5 — 102
(A De Royer-Dupre, France) **6/1**

4 snk **Manzila (FR)**[123] 7-9-4 0...(b) RonanThomas 3 — 92
(Mme C Barande-Barbe, France) **44/1**

5 hd **Best Joking (GER)**[123] 5-9-7 0.. JohanVictoire 4 — 94
(W Hefter, Germany) **14/1**

6 1½ **Salut L'Africain (FR)**[120] [7621] 5-9-11 0...........................(p) ThomasHuet 10 — 93
(Robert Collet, France) **7/2**[1]

7 2 **Planet Five (USA)**[178] [6579] 4-9-7 0.......... Christophe-PatriceLemaire 11 — 82
(P Bary, France) **44/5**

8 ½ **Blue Cayenne (FR)**[134] [7458] 5-9-7 0.............................. RaphaelMarchelli 9 — 81
(Mlle S-V Tarrou, France) **9/2**[2]

9 4 **Contest (IRE)**[178] [6579] 6-9-11 0.......................................(b) GregoryBenoist 8 — 71
(C Theodorakis, Greece) **25/1**

10 1½ **Livandar (FR)**[34] [743] 4-9-7 0.. DavyBonilla 2 — 63
(C Theodorakis, Greece) **11/1**

11 **Isabella Grey**[301] [2673] 4-9-4 0.............................. StephanePasquier 1 — 60
(K A Ryan) *showed early spd: forced to r wdst of all as field swtchd to stands' rail: grad fdd: wl btn* **20/1**

66.60 secs (66.60) — **11** Ran SP% **113.4**
WIN (incl. 1 euro stake): 6.10. PLACES: 2.40, 4.70, 2.50. DF: 41.20. SF: 68.40.
Owner Alexandre Pereira **Bred** A Pereira **Trained** France

[1057] KEMPTON (A.W) (R-H)
Saturday, April 3

OFFICIAL GOING: Standard
Wind: Moderate behind Weather: Overcast

1082 32RED.COM FILLIES' CONDITIONS STKS — 1m (P)
2:05 (2:06) (Class 2) 3-Y-O
£12,462 (£3,732; £1,866; £934; £466; £234) **Stalls** High

Form — RPR

13- **1** **Pipette**[161] [7033] 3-8-12 96.. JimmyFortune 2 — 100+
(A M Balding) *in tch: pushed along and qcknd over 2f out to ld appr fnl f: pushed along ins fnl f: readily* **13/8**[1]

154- **2** 1¼ **Bella Swan**[183] [6447] 3-8-12 90.. AdamKirby 3 — 97
(W R Swinburn) *in rr but in tch: swtchd lft over 2f out: styd on wl appr fnl f and fin wl to take 2nd last strides but nvr no imp on wnr* **8/1**

153- **3** hd **Clarietta**[154] [7187] 3-8-12 95.. RyanMoore 4 — 97
(J L Dunlop) *trckd ldr: pushed along over 2f out: rdn over 1f out: styd on again to chse wnr ins fnl f but no imp: lost 2nd last strides* **7/2**[2]

2-1 **4** 1¾ **Clairvoyance (IRE)**[9] [979] 3-8-12 85.............................. WilliamBuick 6 — 93
(J H M Gosden) *sn led: pushed along over 2f out: hdd appr fnl f: wknd fnl 120yds* **7/2**[2]

612 **5** hd **Myplacelater**[10] [973] 3-8-12 82.. DaneO'Neill 5 — 92
(D R C Elsworth) *chsd ldrs: rdn along wl over 2f out: styd on same pce* **7/1**[3]

10-2 **6** 4½ **Bint Doyen**[24] [840] 3-8-12 82.. SebSanders 1 — 82
(C E Brittain) *chsd ldrs: rdn 3f out: wknd over 2f out* **22/1**

1m 38.62s (-1.18) **Going Correction** +0.05s/f (Slow) — **6** Ran SP% **110.5**
Speed ratings (Par 101): **107,105,105,103,103 99**
toteswingers:1&2:£2.40, 1&3:£1.90, 2&3:£4.50 CSF £14.83 TOTE £2.30: £1.20, £3.60; EX 15.90.
Owner George Strawbridge **Bred** George Strawbridge **Trained** Kingsclere, Hants

FOCUS
Something of a replacement for the Masaka Stakes, which held Listed status, and a decent little conditions contest, not far off Listed-class form. The winner is rated to her Radley Stakes third.

NOTEBOOK
Pipette was the only Guineas entry in the line-up. She showed plenty of ability in two starts last year but was always going to be more of a three-year-old and, having been nudged along rounding the turn into the straight, really found her stride inside the final furlong and a half to eventually win cosily. A daughter of Pivotal out of a Sadler's Wells mare, the winner is not going to want quick ground on turf, but if getting some cut she could yet turn up for the Guineas, for which she was trimmed to 33-1. She's sure to stay further than 1m in time, though, and it's not out of the question that she'll get the Oaks trip, so one of the recognised trials is an alternative target for her. She's now a best price 50-1 for Epsom. (tchd 15-8)
Bella Swan, who wasn't disgraced in Group 3 company on her final two starts last year, was a bit keen early held up off the pace, and had to wait for a gap to challenge in the straight, but she finished well once in the clear. She certainly looks capable of picking up some black type somewhere. (op 9-1)
Clarietta, fifth in the May Hill and third to Oaks favourite Timepiece in a Listed race at Newmarket in her last starts at two, hardly boosted the form of those two races, but she's entitled to come on for the outing. (tchd 10-3)
Clairvoyance(IRE), who had race-fitness on her side having taken a maiden here in style nine days earlier, enjoyed the run of the race in front and briefly looked to have stolen a march when quickening early in the straight. It wasn't a bad effort on this step up in class. (op 10-3 tchd 3-1)
Myplacelater lacked the pace to get involved and will appreciate a return to further. (op 12-1)
Bint Doyen, another dropping back in distance, was on her toes beforehand. She raced widest of all and flashed her tail under pressure. (op 20-1)

1083 BET AT 32RED.COM CONDITIONS STKS — 1m (P)
2:40 (2:40) (Class 2) 3-Y-O
£12,462 (£3,732; £1,866; £934; £466; £234) **Stalls** High

Form — RPR

1 **Aldovrandi (IRE)**[147] 3-8-12 0.. RyanMoore 5 — 102+
(M Botti) *t.k.h: in tch: pushed along over 2f out: drvn: swtchd rt and qcknd appr fnl f to ld ins fnl f: drvn out* **8/1**[3]

214- **2** 1 **Azizi**[175] [6664] 3-8-12 98...(b[1]) RichardHills 6 — 100
(W J Haggas) *trckd ldrs: wnt 2nd 3f out: drvn to ld ins fnl 2f: edgd lft appr fnl f and hdd ins fnl f: kpt on but a hld* **11/10**[1]

30-2 **3** 2¼ **Navajo Chief**[7] [1018] 3-8-12 88.. JimCrowley 4 — 95
(A P Jarvis) *led tl hdd ins fnl 2f: outpcd by ldng duo fnl f* **8/1**[3]

10-1 **4** 4½ **Classic Colori (IRE)**[14] [945] 3-9-6 100.................. RichardKingscote 2 — 92
(Tom Dascombe) *t.k.h: stdd in rr: pushed along 3f out and no imp on ldrs 2f out: sme prog fnl f but nvr any threat* **9/2**[2]

210- **5** 1 **Planet Red (IRE)**[228] [5133] 3-8-12 86.............................. RichardHughes 3 — 82
(R Hannon) *chsd ldr 5f: styd wl there tl wknd appr fnl f* **9/2**[2]

6-21 **6** 4½ **Gumnd (IRE)**[33] [755] 3-8-12 77.. SebSanders 1 — 72
(C E Brittain) *s.i.s: t.k.h and sn trcking ldrs on outside: pushed along over 2f out: wknd over 1f out* **18/1**

1m 39.62s (-0.18) **Going Correction** +0.05s/f (Slow) — **6** Ran SP% **111.5**
Speed ratings (Par 104): **102,101,98,94,93 88**
toteswingers:1&2:£2.80, 1&3:£6.70, 2&3:£2.70 CSF £17.19 TOTE £9.30: £3.50, £1.40; EX 19.70.
Owner Tenuta Dorna Di Montaltuzzo SRL **Bred** A Panetta **Trained** Newmarket, Suffolk

FOCUS
This race used to carry Listed status when run as the Easter Stakes, and was regarded as a Classic trial, but none of these six runners held a Guineas entry. The early pace wasn't great and the winning time a second slower than the earlier race for fillies. The form is decent if a bit muddling, with the second and third the best guides.

NOTEBOOK
Aldovrandi(IRE) made a really good impression and the Italian 2,000 Guineas might now be on the agenda for him. He came into the race a maiden, having finished second on his debut last year at San Siro, but market support suggested he was expected to cope with this step up in class. A half-brother to multiple sprint winner Rasaman out of a half-sister to Rakti, the winner pulled hard to the first turn and in the circumstances did well to quicken up in the straight and deny the favourite. There's more to come from him in a stronger-run race and he should be suited by quick ground on turf. (op 12-1)
Azizi, officially best in at the weights, boasts a very attractive pedigree and was a well-backed favourite. He hung left on more than one occasion last term, though, and the application of blinkers was clearly an attempt to put that right. Having been sent on approaching the final furlong and given every chance, though, he again edged left under pressure and gave best. (op 5-4)
Navajo Chief, who had the benefit of a run a week earlier, was slightly edgy in the prelims, but he settled well in front in the race itself and enjoyed the run of things. He had no excuses the way the race worked out and was simply outclassed. (op 9-1 tchd 10-1)

The Form Book, Raceform Ltd, Compton, RG20 6NL

Classic Colori(IRE), on his toes beforehand, like the winner didn't settle through the early stages. He could have done with a stronger pace but still faced a stiff task under his 8lb penalty for winning a Listed race last time out. (op 3-1 tchd 5-1)
Planet Red(IRE) settled in a prominent position and was well placed considering the way the race worked out, but he didn't get home, and it has to be likely that he'll prove to be at his best this year over shorter. His pedigree certainly supports that view. (op 6-1)
Gumnd(IRE), on the other hand, was dropping back in distance after winning his maiden at Wolverhampton over 1m1½f. A stronger gallop over a longer trip is going to suit him. (op 12-1 tchd 20-1)

1084 32RED CASINO SNOWDROP FILLIES' STKS (LISTED RACE) 1m (P)
3:15 (3:16) (Class 1) 4-Y-0+
£22,708 (£8,608; £4,308; £2,148; £1,076; £540) **Stalls** High

Form RPR
250- **1** **Shamwari Lodge (IRE)**[182] 6505 4-8-12 **105** .... RichardHughes 5 107
(R Hannon) *trckd ldrs: wnt 2nd 3f out: shkn up and qcknd appr fnl f led and wnt rt fnl 150yds: styd on strly* **13/8**[1]
01-2 **2** 1 ¼ **Mosqueras Romance**[22] 873 4-8-12 **82**............. RyanMoore 2 104
(M Botti) *led after 1f: drvn and qcknd 2f out: hdd and outpcd fnl 120yds* **17/2**
346- **3** 4 ½ **Chantilly Tiffany**[160] 7044 6-8-12 **100**............................ WilliamBuick 12 94
(J H M Gosden) *hld up towards rr: rdn and hdwy on ins over 2f out: styd on u.p to take 3rd 1f out but run flattened out and no further prog* **5/2**[2]
1-11 **4** ¾ **Island Sunset (IRE)**[8] 990 4-8-12 **85**.............................. MartinDwyer 1 92
(W R Muir) *chsd ldrs: drvn along fr 3f out and one pce 2f out: styd on again u.p fnl f* **9/1**
000- **5** 1 **Please Sing**[189] 6272 4-8-12 **97**.. KierenFallon 3 90
(M R Channon) *mid-div: pushed along ins fnl 3f: styd on fr over 1f out but nvr any threat* **8/1**[3]
5565 **6** ¾ **Carcinetto (IRE)**[14] 944 8-8-12 **88**.............................. CathyGannon 10 88
(P D Evans) *in rr: rdn along over 2f out: styd on fnl f but nvr gng pce to get into contention* **40/1**
000- **7** 1 ¼ **Charlotte Point (USA)**[166] 6907 4-8-12 **80**........................ EddieAhern 6 85
(P F I Cole) *sn chsng ldrs: rdn over 2f out: wknd appr fnl f* **66/1**
1-06 **8** 1 ¼ **Victoria Sponge (IRE)**[35] 738 4-8-12 **86**....................... DaneO'Neill 11 82
(S C Williams) *s.i.s in rr: pushed along and sme prog over 2f out: nvr any threat* **40/1**
464- **9** hd **Seradim**[227] 5175 4-8-12 **92**..(p) JimmyFortune 4 82
(P F I Cole) *led 1f: styd trcking ldrs tl wknd over 1f out* **18/1**
5-20 **10** 1 ¼ **Black Dahlia**[21] 885 5-8-12 **92**..................................... FrederikTylicki 7 79
(J A Glover) *a towards rr* **14/1**
4533 **11** 7 **Confidentiality (IRE)**[8] 990 6-8-12 **84**.....................(b[1]) NickyMackay 8 63
(M Wigham) *chsd ldrs until wknd qckly over 2f out* **40/1**
1m 38.07s (-1.73) **Going Correction** +0.05s/f (Slow) **11** Ran SP% **119.0**
Speed ratings (Par 108): **110,108,104,103,102 101,100,99,99,97 90**
toteswingers:1&2:£6.40, 1&3:£2.50, 2&3:£6.60 CSF £16.61 TOTE £2.70: £1.40, £2.40, £1.40; EX 19.80 Trifecta £46.20 Pool: £1,396.18 - 22.36 winning units..
Owner Andrew Russell **Bred** Pier House Stud **Trained** East Everleigh, Wilts

FOCUS
This Listed race, run at a modest early gallop, didn't look as competitive as the numbers suggested, with the market judging two horses to be some way clear of the rest. They finished first and third. The form is rated around the winner and fourth.

NOTEBOOK
Shamwari Lodge(IRE) looked fit beforehand and won first time out for the second season in succession. Best in at the weights, she has met trouble in running in the past when trying to make up ground from off the pace, but on this occasion she was ridden far more prominently, tracking the leader for much of the race before quickening up nicely inside the last to win cosily. Clearly just as effective on Polytrack as she is on turf, the bare form is nothing outstanding, but the winner looks to have resumed as good as ever and her connections will no doubt be hopeful she can progress to Group company at some point this term. (tchd 6-4 and 7-4)
Mosqueras Romance, second off 80 in a handicap at Wolverhampton on her reappearance, puts the form in context. A progressive filly on Polytrack, she enjoyed the run of things out in front, being allowed to set an ordinary gallop, and in the circumstances second place was as good as she could hope for. (op 8-1 tchd 10-1)
Chantilly Tiffany, second in this race last year, has switched stables. Although second-best in at the weights, the race wasn't really run to suit her as she was held up off the modest gallop and the first two got first run on her. (op 11-4 tchd 3-1)
Island Sunset(IRE), for whom the drop back from 1m2f wasn't ideal, had the worst of the draw, too, on this step up in class. Forced quite wide, she was readily outpaced when the sprint for home began. (op 8-1 tchd 10-1 in places)
Please Sing, who was placed at Group 3 level last season, could be given a chance at the weights, but she was another inconvenienced by the way the race was run. (op 12-1)
Carcinetto(IRE) is a confirmed hold-up performer and needs the leaders to go off quick and come back to her to be seen at her best. (op 33-1)
Seradim Official explanation: jockey said filly ran too free
Confidentiality(IRE) was on her toes in the paddock. (op 33-1)

1085 32RED.COM H'CAP 7f (P)
3:50 (3:56) (Class 2) (0-105,102) 4-Y-0+
£31,155 (£9,330; £4,665; £2,335; £1,165; £585) **Stalls** High

Form RPR
0250 **1** **Beauchamp Viceroy**[14] 946 6-9-10 **102**.......................(b) RyanMoore 8 110
(G A Butler) *broke wl and edgd rt after 1f: trckd ldrs and wnt 2nd over 2f out: led appr fnl f: drvn out* **20/1**
030- **2** ½ **Dunn'o (IRE)**[190] 6249 5-8-8 **93**.. JohnFahy(7) 3 100
(C G Cox) *broke wl: sn ld: rdn 2f out: hdd appr fnl f: kpt on ins fnl f but nt pce of wnr: jst hld on for 2nd cl home* **12/1**
060- **3** hd **Kay Gee Be (IRE)**[182] 6480 6-8-12 **90**............................ KierenFallon 16 96+
(W Jarvis) *bmpd after 1f: chsd ldrs: rdn and one pce 2f out: styd on wl thrght fnl f and rallying to press for 2nd last strides: nt rch wnr* **6/1**[1]
-221 **4** nk **Bravo Echo**[14] 944 4-9-2 **94**... JimCrowley 10 100
(M J Attwater) *prom: chsd ldr over 4f out: rdn 2f out: kpt on wl thrght fnl f but nvr gng pce to chal* **6/1**[1]
216- **5** shd **Light From Mars**[161] 7019 5-9-5 **100**.......................... JamesMillman(3) 5 105+
(B R Millman) *slowly away and lost 4 l s: stl plenty to do over 2f out: hdwy appr fnl f: rapid hdwy ins fnl f: fin wl but nt rch wnr* **15/2**[2]
5-10 **6** 1 **Vitznau (IRE)**[7] 1008 6-9-5 **97**....................................... RichardHughes 15 100+
(R Hannon) *hmpd after 1f: in rr: hdwy and nt clr run 2f out: gd hdwy 1f out: fin wl: gng on cl home* **15/2**[2]
0000 **7** ¾ **Ceremonial Jade (UAE)**[29] 817 7-9-5 **100**..........(t) AndreaAtzeni(3) 14 101
(M Botti) *chsng ldrs whn hmpd after 1f and sn mid-div: gd hdwy over 2f out to chse ldrs over 1f out: no ex ins fnl f* **14/1**
0043 **8** ¾ **Rileyskeepingfaith**[29] 817 4-9-9 **101**............................ AlanMunro 12 100+
(M R Channon) *hmpd after 1f and in rr: hdwy on outside and hanging lft fr 2f out: styd on ins fnl f but nvr a threat* **14/1**
2062 **9** ½ **Autumn Blades (IRE)**[14] 944 5-9-5 **97**........................(v) DavidProbert 1 94
(A Bailey) *hmpd after 1f: hdwy 3f out: hung rt over 2f: styd on same pce fnl f* **20/1**
-310 **10** ½ **The Scorching Wind (IRE)**[14] 944 4-8-12 **93**......(t) WilliamCarson(3) 6 89
(S C Williams) *wnt lft s and s.i.s: t.k.h in mid-div: hdwy on ins 2f out: chsd ldrs over 1f out: wknd ins fnl f* **8/1**[3]
0-60 **11** 1 ½ **Kyllachy Star**[14] 944 4-8-12 **90**...................................(b[1]) PaulHanagan 9 82
(R A Fahey) *hmpd after 1f: chsd ldrs: rdn over 2f out: wknd fnl f* **12/1**
0220 **12** nk **Benandonner (USA)**[7] 1006 7-8-11 **92**.................... BarryMcHugh(3) 11 83
(Mike Murphy) *hmpd after 1f: in tch: rdn over 2f out: wknd over 1f out* **20/1**
212- **13** 1 ¼ **Servoca (CAN)**[151] 7227 4-9-1 **93**.................................... MartinDwyer 2 81
(Mike Murphy) *rdn along 3f out: nvr bttr than mid-div* **14/1**
00-0 **14** 4 ½ **Dubai's Touch**[7] 1008 6-9-4 **96**...................................(v[1]) JoeFanning 7 72
(M Johnston) *chsd ldrs: rdn 3f out: wknd ins fnl 2f* **20/1**
1m 25.07s (-0.93) **Going Correction** +0.05s/f (Slow) **14** Ran SP% **117.6**
Speed ratings (Par 109): **107,106,106,105,105 104,103,102,102,101 100,99,98,93**
toteswingers:1&2:£54.80, 1&3:£36.70, 2&3:£26.50 CSF £214.32 CT £1428.13 TOTE £24.50: £6.10, £4.90, £2.60; EX 355.30 Trifecta £2764.50 Pool: £26,674.02 - 7.14 winning units..
Owner Erik Penser **Bred** E Penser **Trained** Newmarket, Suffolk
■ Thebes (10/1, broke out of stalls, deduct 5p in the £ under R4) and Capricorn Run (66/1, inj in stalls) were withdrawn.

FOCUS
A decent, competitive handicap, run for massively increased prize-money compared with the previous year, as a result of the BHA's attempt to improve the quality of racing over the Easter weekend. The race was delayed after two horses' stalls burst open early. The first four were always prominent and the winner posted a clear personal best, with the form rated around the next three.

NOTEBOOK
Beauchamp Viceroy, who faced some stiff tasks in Dubai and in a Group 3 at Lingfield last time out, found this more his cup of tea, and enjoyed a great trip, tracking the leader on the rail having broken well from his middle draw. All seven of his wins have come on Polytrack and there's little sign to date that he's anywhere near as good on turf, so opportunities might be limited in the near future. (op 16-1)
Dunn'o(IRE) was left with a tactical advantage when both Thebes and Capricorn Run burst the stalls and were withdrawn. The defection of the former left him as the likely front-runner in the race and, despite having a difficult draw to overcome, he did so and got to the front without too much bother by the time they reached the first turn. Able to set no more than a fair gallop, ensuring that not much got into it from behind, he was ideally placed to quicken in the straight, but he was just unable to keep the winner at bay. (op 14-1)
Kay Gee Be(IRE), who has a history of going well fresh, had a good draw and Fallon in the saddle. Tucked in on the rail behind the eventual winner, he took a while to pick up and was a bit short of room inside the last, but ran a solid race. (op 15-2)
Bravo Echo had race-fitness on his side and, having held a prominent pitch just behind the leader throughout, had no excuse. This was a good effort off a career-high mark, though, and he remains progressive. (op 7-1)
Light From Mars ◆, dropped in on the rail from his low draw, was given plenty to do in a race where the leaders didn't come back. He finished better than anything, though, and remains capable of winning a nice pot back on turf when getting a stronger pace to run at. The Victoria Cup might fit the bill, although he ran poorly on his only previous visit to Ascot. Official explanation: jockey said gelding missed the break (op 14-1)
Vitznau(IRE), not at home in the soft ground at Doncaster last week, promised to be suited by the return to Polytrack, but the lack of pace was against him and he didn't enjoy the clearest of runs as he tried to make up ground in the straight.
Ceremonial Jade(UAE), who didn't shine in Dubai, had a good draw but didn't make best use of it. (tchd 12-1)
Rileyskeepingfaith, on his toes beforehand, struggled to get competitive from off the pace but should not be too harshly judged given the way the race was run.
Servoca(CAN) was on his toes in the paddock.

1086 32REDPOKER.COM H'CAP 7f (P)
4:20 (4:22) (Class 4) (0-85,85) 3-Y-O **£4,209** (£1,252; £625; £312) **Stalls** High

Form RPR
1523 **1** **Duellist**[7] 1018 3-9-0 **81**.. FrankieDettori 6 91
(M Johnston) *mid-div: hdwy whn n.m.r and swtchd lft ins fnl 2f: str run fnl f to ld fnl 120yds: comf* **11/4**[1]
431- **2** 1 ¾ **Gallant Eagle (IRE)**[197] 6071 3-8-12 **79**.......................... RyanMoore 11 84
(S Kirk) *in rr: hdwy on outside and hrd rdn fr 2f out: stl hanging and styd on strly fnl f to take 2nd cl home but no ch w wnr* **9/2**[2]
23-1 **3** ½ **Shamir**[24] 843 3-8-12 **79**.. FergusSweeney 12 82
(Miss Jo Crowley) *in rr tl hdwy over 2f out: styd on to press ldrs ins fnl f: one pce cl home* **13/2**[3]
034- **4** nse **Jack My Boy (IRE)**[147] 7290 3-8-11 **78**......................... RobertWinston 3 81
(P D Evans) *chsd ldrs: chal 2f out: slt ld appr fnl f: hdd and outpcd fnl 120yds* **16/1**
160- **5** shd **Tewin Wood**[118] 7654 3-8-6 **73**... DavidProbert 9 76
(A Bailey) *disp ld early: slt advantage fr 4f out: hrd drvn whn chal fr 2f out: hdd appr fnl f: wknd fnl 120yds* **25/1**
21 **6** 1 ½ **Dominium (USA)**[17] 900 3-8-10 **77**................................ SteveDrowne 14 76
(J R Gask) *in rr: hdwy: over 1f out: styd on wl fnl f but nt rch ldrs* **9/1**
140 **7** nk **Nubar Boy**[15] 934 3-8-7 **74**...................................(t) RichardKingscote 2 72
(Tom Dascombe) *stdd s in rr: nt clr run over 2f out: rdn and hdwy over 1f out and sn chsng ldrs: nvr quite upsides and wknd fnl 120yds* **33/1**
41 **8** 1 ¼ **Peadar Miguel**[44] 592 3-8-12 **79**................................... JerryO'Dwyer 13 74
(M G Quinlan) *chsd ldrs: rdn over 2f out: wknd fnl f* **12/1**
-164 **9** 1 ¼ **Little Perisher**[17] 901 3-8-7 **74**.. WilliamBuick 7 65
(A P Jarvis) *chsd ldrs: rdn 2f out: wknd over 1f out* **33/1**
3066 **10** 1 ¾ **Transfixed (IRE)**[5] 1045 3-8-7 **74**................................ CathyGannon 10 61
(P D Evans) *chsd ldrs: wknd over 1f out* **33/1**
012- **11** 1 ¾ **Pullyourfingerout (IRE)**[170] 6793 3-8-6 **73**.................. HayleyTurner 5 55
(B G Powell) *chsd ldrs: rdn 3f out: wknd 2f out* **16/1**
064- **12** 2 ¼ **Magnus Thrax (USA)**[159] 7063 3-8-12 **79**..................... RichardHughes 4 55
(R Hannon) *stdd s: nvr bttr than mid-div* **15/2**
-115 **13** hd **Admiral Cochrane (IRE)**[31] 772 3-9-4 **85**....................... JoeFanning 1 60
(W Jarvis) *mid-div: rdn and effrt on outside 3f out: nvr rchd ldrs and sn wknd* **12/1**
2352 **14** 2 ¾ **Coolree Star (IRE)**[31] 766 3-8-10 **77**................................ JimCrowley 8 45
(J A Glover) *disp ld 3f: styd chsng ldrs tl wknd wl over 2f out* **16/1**
1m 24.87s (-1.13) **Going Correction** +0.05s/f (Slow) **14** Ran SP% **125.6**
Speed ratings (Par 100): **108,106,105,105,105 103,103,101,100,98 96,93,93,90**
toteswingers:1&2:£4.10, 1&3:£4.70, 2&3:£8.30 CSF £14.27 CT £77.10 TOTE £3.80: £1.60, £1.60, £2.60; EX 17.50.
Owner Sh Hamdan Bin Mohammed Al Makt **Bred** Darley **Trained** Middleham Moor, N Yorks

FOCUS
It was impossible to rule many of these out and it looked a fairly decent contest. The winning time was 0.20sec quicker than the preceding all-aged handicap over the same distance and this is form to view fairly positively.

1087 32RED ONLINE CASINO H'CAP 2m (P)
4:55 (4:55) (Class 4) (0-85,78) 4-Y-0+ £4,209 (£1,252; £625; £312) Stalls High

Form RPR
42-3 1 **Soundbyte**[8] 989 5-9-0 67 FergusSweeney 7 77
(J Gallagher) *trckd ldrs: drvn and hdwy ins fnl 3f: styd on to ld wl over 1f out: c clr ins fnl f: readily* 9/4[2]
-142 2 5 **Oxford City (IRE)**[10] 974 6-9-3 70 (t) IanMongan 2 74
(P M Phelan) *in tch: hdwy to cl on ldrs 1/2-way: chal 4f out tl slt ld ins fnl 3f: sn rdn: hdd wl over 1f out and sn no ch w wnr but kpt on for clr 2nd* 5/2[3]
130- 3 3 1/4 **Epsom Salts**[182] 6473 5-9-4 78 RichardRowe(7) 6 78
(P M Phelan) *in rr but in tch: pushed along 3f out: hdwy 2f out and styd on to take 3rd fnl f but nvr any ch* 12/1
-011 4 2 1/2 **Kristallo (GER)**[48] 554 5-8-8 61 ow1 DaneO'Neill 4 58
(P R Webber) *trckd ldr: slt ld 4f out: narrowly hdd ins fnl 3f: styd rt there tl wknd over 2f out* 15/8[1]
0/20 5 29 **Byblos**[24] 842 5-9-0 67 (v) JimCrowley 3 29
(W J Greatrex) *led tl narrowly hdd 4f out: styd upsides tl wknd qckly over 2f out: eased whn no ch* 11/1
3m 33.19s (3.09) **Going Correction** +0.05s/f (Slow) 5 Ran SP% **110.1**
Speed ratings (Par 105): **94,91,89,88,74**
CSF £8.26 TOTE £3.20: £1.60, £1.90; EX 8.60.
Owner Oliver Parsons **Bred** Mrs R J Gallagher **Trained** Chastleton, Oxon
FOCUS
Just a fair staying handicap, with the top-weight coming in rated 7lb below the ceiling for the race.

1088 32RED.COM CASINO H'CAP (LONDON MILE QUALIFIER) 1m (P)
5:25 (5:26) (Class 4) (0-85,85) 4-Y-0+ £4,209 (£1,252; £625; £312) Stalls High

Form RPR
550- 1 **Highly Regal (IRE)**[129] 7523 5-9-0 81 (b) RyanMoore 13 91
(R A Teal) *mid-div: rdn 2f out: str run fnl f: led cl home* 8/1
322- 2 1/2 **Chapter And Verse (IRE)**[127] 7560 4-9-1 85 AndreaAtzeni(3) 10 94
(Mike Murphy) *in tch: rdn: styd on and edgd lft over 1f out: r.o u.p to take a slt ld fnl 50yds: hdd cl home* 16/1
241- 3 1/2 **Desert Kiss**[204] 5833 5-9-3 84 AdamKirby 3 92+
(W R Swinburn) *mid-div: rdn and gd hdwy fr 2f out: qcknd to ld ins fnl f: hdd and one pce fnl 50yds* 10/1
5612 4 1 1/2 **Prince Of Thebes (IRE)**[14] 943 9-8-8 80 KierenFox(5) 4 85
(M J Attwater) *chsd ldrs: rdn and pushed lft 1f out: wknd fnl 100yds* 16/1
4-21 5 3/4 **Last Sovereign**[17] 902 6-9-0 81 FrankieDettori 1 84
(Jane Chapple-Hyam) *led and racd wd 3f: rdn 2f out: hdd ins fnl f: wknd fnl 100yds* 13/2[2]
0-15 6 1/2 **Totally Focussed (IRE)**[59] 394 5-8-13 80 HayleyTurner 14 84+
(S Dow) *stdd s: towards rr: hmpd 5f out: styng on whn hmpd 1f out: wnt rt: r.o again cl home* 10/1
2635 7 nse **Den's Gift (IRE)**[14] 943 6-8-10 84 (b) JohnFahy(7) 8 86
(C G Cox) *chsd ldrs: rdn 2f out: wknd fnl 120yds* 10/1
310- 8 hd **Getcarter**[142] 7356 4-8-13 80 RichardHughes 6 81+
(R Hannon) *in rr: hdwy fr 2f out: swtchd rt and bmpd ins fnl f: fin wl* 16/1
020- 9 hd **Block Party**[171] 6773 4-8-13 80 WilliamBuick 12 81
(D M Simcock) *in tch whn hmpd 5f out: sn in tch: rdn over 2f out: styd on same pce* 14/1
00-3 10 hd **Wise Dennis**[31] 769 8-9-1 82 ShaneKelly 11 82
(A P Jarvis) *s.i.s: hmpd in rr 5f out: hdwy fr 2f out but nvr nr ldrs* 9/2[1]
3132 11 3/4 **Ilie Nastase (FR)**[26] 827 6-9-4 85 LiamKeniry 16 83
(C R Dore) *chsd ldrs: rdn 2f out: wkng whn bmpd ins fnl f* 25/1
340- 12 3/4 **Sonning Gate**[315] 2273 4-9-4 85 DaneO'Neill 9 82
(D R C Elsworth) *a towards rr* 16/1
60- 13 shd **Elliptical (USA)**[170] 6795 4-9-4 85 EddieAhern 15 88+
(G A Butler) *chsd ldrs rdn 2f out: fading whn hmpd 1f out: eased* 7/1[3]
1200 14 1 1/4 **Hereford Boy**[6] 1030 6-8-13 80 (p) RobertHavlin 7 74
(D K Ivory) *a towards rr* 40/1
4165 15 3/4 **Gallantry**[9] 981 8-8-9 79 MichaelStainton(3) 2 71
(P Howling) *a towards rr* 33/1
306- 16 21 **Calypso Bay (IRE)**[308] 2488 4-9-4 85 GeorgeBaker 5 29
(Jonjo O'Neill) *chsd ldrs tl wknd ins fnl 3f: eased whn btn* 33/1
1m 39.05s (-0.75) **Going Correction** +0.05s/f (Slow) 16 Ran SP% **124.8**
Speed ratings (Par 105): **105,104,104,102,101 101,101,101,100,100 99,99,99,97,97 76**
toteswingers:1&2:£33.80, 1&3:£16.40, 2&3:£22.60 CSF £128.46 CT £1363.37 TOTE £11.20: £3.20, £3.50, £2.80, £3.30; EX 191.20 Place 6 £30.83, Place 5 £14.33.
Owner J Morton **Bred** Mervyn Stewkesbury **Trained** Ashtead, Surrey
■ Stewards' Enquiry : Andrea Atzeni two-day ban: careless riding (Apr 17,19)
FOCUS
A competitive handicap run at a really good pace, and it was set up for those coming from behind.
Getcarter Official explanation: jockey said colt was denied a clear run
T/Jkpt: Not won. T/Plt: £77.80 to a £1 stake. Pool: £136,614.19. 1,281.01 winning tickets. T/Qpdt: £30.60 to a £1 stake. Pool: £7,339.15. 177.20 winning tickets. ST

1089 - 1090a (Foreign Racing) - See Raceform Interactive

999 DUNDALK (A.W) (L-H)
Saturday, April 3

OFFICIAL GOING: Standard

1091a CROWNE PLAZA LEADING JOCKEY & TRAINER CHAMPIONSHIP RACE 5f (P)
3:35 (3:36) 3-Y-0+ £10,075 (£2,336; £1,022; £584)

RPR
1 **Sole Power**[136] 7446 3-8-12 97 PJSmullen 3 101
(Edward Lynam, Ire) *chsd ldrs: 3rd 1/2-way: rdn to ld over 1f out: kpt on wl fnl f* 11/2[3]
2 1 1/4 **Luisant**[149] 7259 7-9-9 108 FMBerry 4 101+
(J A Nash, Ire) *mid-div: 7th 1/2-way: rdn 1 1/2f out: kpt on wl fnl f to 2nd on line* 6/1
3 shd **Six Of Hearts**[13] 956 6-9-4 98 (b) MHarley(5) 8 101+
(Cecil Ross, Ire) *chsd ldrs: 5th 1/2-way: rdn in 6th 2f out: 5th 1f out: kpt on fnl f to 2nd: lost 2nd on line* 10/1
4 1 3/4 **Santo Padre (IRE)**[162] 7007 6-9-9 102 CO'Donoghue 7 94
(David Marnane, Ire) *chsd ldrs: 4th 1/2-way: cl 3rd 2f out: rdn in 4th 1 1/2f out: kpt on same pce* 9/2[2]
5 nk **Calm Bay (IRE)**[155] 7161 4-9-2 90 (t) DCByrne(7) 10 93
(H Rogers, Ire) *chsd ldrs: 3rd 1/2-way: chal 2f out: rdn in 3rd 1f out: no ex fnl f* 33/1
6 1/2 **Invincible Ash (IRE)**[141] 7380 5-8-11 95 (p) JulieBurke(7) 2 86
(M Halford, Ire) *towards rr: sme late hdwy fnl f: n.d* 14/1
7 hd **Atlantic Cycle (IRE)**[282] 3323 3-8-2 BACurtis(5) 9 81
(K J Condon, Ire) *nvr a factor* 14/1
8 hd **Green Manalishi**[35] 737 9-9-9 (p) JMurtagh 1 90
(K A Ryan) *mid-div: 6th 1/2-way: rdn over 1f out: no imp fnl f* 11/8[1]
9 1 1/2 **An Tadh (IRE)**[36] 733 7-9-9 95 KLatham 5 85
(G M Lyons, Ire) *led: rdn and hdd over 1f out: no ex ins fnl f* 8/1
10 4 1/2 **Just For Mary**[203] 5889 6-9-9 86 RPCleary 6 68
(Daniel Mark Loughnane, Ire) *s.i.s: a towards rr* 25/1
57.46 secs (57.46)
WFA 3 from 4yo+ 11lb 10 Ran SP% **130.3**
CSF £43.46 TOTE £8.50: £1.80, £2.10, £3.00; DF 69.60.
Owner Mrs S Power **Bred** G Russell **Trained** Dunshaughlin, Co Meath

NOTEBOOK
Sole Power, one of only two 3-y-os in the line-up, was a maiden winner over the C&D late last season before being beaten at odds-on over 6f here on his final juvenile start. He tracked the leaders and availed of a gap between horses to come through and lead over 1f out. He ran on well and has the makings of a useful sprinter. (op 5/1)
Luisant, a five-time winner whose three victories last season included two over 6f at this track, was always going to find this trip on the sharp side on his first start of the year. Ridden along and slightly outpaced in sixth place before the straight, he began to warm to his task entering the final furlong and finished well to snatch second on the line. A useful sort, he will appreciate going back up in distance.
Six Of Hearts, having his fourth run of the year, had won over 7f here in February before finishing fifth over 6f on soft ground in a handicap on the Curragh. He chased the leaders and, after coming under pressure in fourth over 1f out, ran on to go second well inside the final furlong. (op 8/1)
Santo Padre(IRE), a four-time winner and successful in the Portland Handicap in September before ending his campaign by running fourth in a Listed race over this C&D, was making his reappearance. He raced prominently but, after coming under pressure in second almost 2f out, could raise no extra from over 1f out, although he did keep on in the closing stages. (op 4/1)
Calm Bay(IRE), whose two wins were achieved over this C&D, performed creditably considering he had plenty on at the weights. Soon close up on the outside, he was second before the straight and, after dropping to third 2f out, could raise no extra from over 1f out.
Green Manalishi, all but two of whose 14 wins have been over this trip, has two victories on the Lingfield AW to his credit. Runner-up in a 6f Listed event at Lingfield on his reappearance, he had cheekpieces back on here and, after breaking reasonably well from his inside draw, soon found himself in behind horses. While that situation continued he was never going well enough to make any impression on the leaders. (op 6/4)

1092 - 1096a (Foreign Racing) - See Raceform Interactive

824 AQUEDUCT (L-H)
Saturday, April 3

OFFICIAL GOING: Dirt: fast

1097a WOOD MEMORIAL STKS (GRADE 1) (3YO) (DIRT) 1m 1f (D)
10:12 (10:15) 3-Y-0
£277,777 (£92,592; £46,296; £23,148; £13,888; £9,259)

RPR
1 **Eskendereya (USA)**[42] 3-8-11 0 JRVelazquez 3 119+
(Todd Pletcher, U.S.A) 1/2[1]
2 9 3/4 **Jackson Bend (USA)**[42] 3-8-11 0 CHBorel 5 100
(Nicholas Zito, U.S.A) 77/10[3]
3 hd **Awesome Act (USA)**[28] 824 3-8-11 0 JRLeparoux 2 100
(J Noseda) 27/10[2]
4 1 1/2 **Schoolyard Dreams (USA)**[21] 3-8-11 0 (b) RADominguez 4 97
(Derek S Ryan, U.S.A) 87/10
5 2 1/2 **Carnivore (USA)** 3-8-11 0 (b) JustinShepherd 6 92
(Joseph W Delozier III, U.S.A) 33/1
6 nk **Most Happy Fella (USA)** 3-8-11 0 (b) AnnaNapravnik 1 92
(William Badgett Jr, U.S.A) 69/1
1m 49.97s (0.27) 6 Ran SP% **119.9**
PARI-MUTUEL (all including $2 stake): WIN 3.00; PLACE (1-2) 2.30, 3.90; SHOW (1-2-3) 2.10, 2.60, 2.20; SF 11.60.
Owner Zayat Stables LLC **Bred** Sanford R Robertson **Trained** USA
FOCUS
A slowly run race.
NOTEBOOK
Eskendereya(USA) won in fine style and is now a short-priced favourite for the Kentucky Derby, but it may be unwise to get carried for the time being seeing as this is muddling form.
Awesome Act(USA) didn't build on his Gotham Stakes win, but he can be excused. Not only did he lose a shoe coming out of the stalls, but the steady pace was no use to him and he pulled much too hard. He should have much better in the Kentucky Derby, where the likely strong gallop will suit.

MUSSELBURGH (R-H)
Sunday, April 4

OFFICIAL GOING: Good to soft (soft in places; 5.4)
Wind: Virtually nil Weather: Bright & dry

1098 TOTEPLACEPOT (S) STKS 1m 1f
2:20 (2:22) (Class 6) 3-Y-0+ £2,590 (£770; £385; £192) Stalls High

Form RPR
13-1 1 **Fremen (USA)**[24] 862 10-10-0 82 AdrianNicholls 9 85
(D Nicholls) *trckd ldr: cl up 4f out: led 3f out: rdn over 1f out and kpt on wl* 2/1[2]
164- 2 1 3/4 **Wind Star**[281] 3374 7-9-10 88 RobertWinston 7 78
(G A Swinbank) *in tch hdwy to trck ldrs 1/2-way: effrt to chse wnr 2f out: sn rdn: drvn and edgd rt ins fnl f: no imp towards fin* 5/4[1]
0-62 3 3 **Island Chief**[19] 895 4-9-10 69 (p) JamieSpencer 10 71
(K A Ryan) *t.k.h: trckd ldrs on inner: swtchd lft and hdwy over 2f out: sn rdn and chsd ldng pair over 1f out: drvn: edgd righr and no imp ent fnl f* 5/1[3]
356- 4 6 **Birkside**[158] 7118 7-9-10 62 PhillipMakin 6 58
(Miss L A Perratt) *dwlt and in rr: hdwy and pushed along over 2f out: sn rdn and kpt on ins fnl f: nvr nr ldrs* 16/1
001- 5 1 1/2 **Intersky Charm (USA)**[10] 6640 6-10-0 69 (v) PaulMulrennan 3 59
(Mrs S C Bradburne) *led: rdn along and hdd over 3f out: grad wknd* 33/1

The Form Book, Raceform Ltd, Compton, RG20 6NL

100- **6** 2 1/2 **Middlemarch (IRE)**[22] 7014 10-9-7 69........................(v) GaryBartley(3) 4 49
(J S Goldie) *chsd ldng pair: rdn along 3f out: drvn and wknd fnl 2f* **14/1**

000- **7** 3 3/4 **Primo Way**[195] 6157 9-9-10 53........................ DuranFentiman 8 41
(D A Nolan) *a towards rr* **100/1**

5-44 **8** 5 **Mydy Easy (USA)**[47] 570 4-9-5 64........................ PaulPickard(5) 2 30
(P T Midgley) *t.k.h: chsd ldrs on outer: rdn along 3f out and sn wknd* **33/1**

400- **9** 15 **Jim Martin**[155] 7173 5-9-5 55........................ JamesSullivan(5) 1 —
(D A Nolan) *a in rr: bhd fr over 2f out* **80/1**

2m 0.10s (6.20) **Going Correction** +0.55s/f (Yiel) **9** Ran SP% **115.1**
Speed ratings (Par 101): **98,96,93,88,87 84,81,77,63**
Tote Swingers: 1&2 £1.70, 1&3 £3.30, 2&3 £3.20 CSF £4.74 TOTE £2.90: £1.10, £1.10, £3.00; EX 5.40.There was no bid for the winner.
Owner Middleham Park Racing XXXV C King A Seed **Bred** Flaxman Holdings Ltd **Trained** Sessay, N Yorks

FOCUS
A fair seller, but the pace was just modest and it paid to race handy.

1099 TOTESWINGER H'CAP 5f
2:50 (2:50) (Class 4) (0-85,85) 4-Y-O+
£6,231 (£1,866; £933; £467; £233; £117) **Stalls** Low

Form RPR

-530 **1** **Luscivious**[9] 992 6-8-9 73........................(b) FrederikTylicki 5 89
(J A Glover) *mde virtually all: rdn and qcknd clr ent fnl f: kpt on wl* **5/1**[2]

050- **2** 2 3/4 **Highland Warrior**[159] 7081 11-7-11 66 oh3........................ PaulPickard(5) 2 72
(P T Midgley) *s.i.s and bhd: gd hdwy on inner over 1f out: rdn and styd on strly ins fnl f: tk 2nd nr line* **50/1**

010- **3** shd **Rasaman (IRE)**[177] 6647 6-9-1 82........................ GaryBartley(3) 3 88+
(J S Goldie) *towards rr: pushed along and hdwy wl over 1f out: rdn and styd on ins fnl f* **14/1**

220- **4** 1 1/4 **Sirenuse (IRE)**[191] 6253 4-9-2 80........................ TomEaves 6 81
(B Smart) *cl up: rdn and ev ch wl over 1f out: drvn appr fnl f and grad wknd* **10/1**

000- **5** 1/2 **River Falcon**[162] 7015 10-9-7 85........................ DanielTudhope 1 84
(J S Goldie) *towards rr: pushed along 1/2-way: hdwy 2f out: swtchd rt and rdn ent fnl f: kpt on towards fin* **10/1**

635- **6** 1 **Lucky Numbers (IRE)**[201] 5959 4-9-7 85........................ SilvestreDeSousa 4 81
(Paul Green) *chsd ldrs: rdn 2f out: grad wknd* **12/1**

-512 **7** 1/2 **Ingleby Star (IRE)**[34] 750 5-8-7 71........................(p) JimmyQuinn 9 65
(N Wilson) *t.k.h: chsd ldrs: rdn along 2f out: sn drvn and grad wknd* **14/1**

15/- **8** 1 3/4 **Haigh Hall**[676] 2497 4-9-2 80........................ PaulHanagan 7 68
(R A Fahey) *trckd ldng pair: effrt 2f out: sn rdn and ch tl drvn and wknd appr fnl f* **4/1**[1]

065- **9** 1 1/4 **Solar Spirit (IRE)**[172] 6776 5-8-10 79........................ IanBrennan(5) 12 62+
(J J Quinn) *chsd ldrs: rdn along 2f out: sn wknd* **5/1**[2]

1115 **10** 2 3/4 **Where's Reiley (USA)**[17] 916 4-8-12 76........................ GrahamGibbons 10 49
(T D Barron) *sn rdn along and outpcd: a towards rr* **15/2**[3]

050- **11** 7 **Rothesay Dancer**[167] 6902 7-8-12 79........................ KellyHarrison(3) 8 27
(J S Goldie) *dwlt: a in rr* **20/1**

316- **12** 2 1/2 **Euston Square**[165] 6944 4-9-6 84........................ AdrianNicholls 11 23
(D Nicholls) *sn rdn along in rr: outpcd and bhd fnl 2f* **12/1**

62.50 secs (2.10) **Going Correction** +0.55s/f (Yiel) **12** Ran SP% **118.7**
Speed ratings (Par 105): **105,100,100,98,97 96,95,92,90,86 74,70**
Tote Swingers: 1&2 £55.80, 1&3 £32.40, 2&3 £51.50 CSF £222.25 CT £3275.65 TOTE £6.80: £2.20, £13.50, £9.90; EX 340.10.
Owner Paul J Dixon & Brian Morton **Bred** R J Turner **Trained** Babworth, Notts

FOCUS
A fair sprint handicap, although Luscivious may have been at an advantage in being given a forward ride, tight against the near-side rail on this rain-softened ground. As such, a few of the beaten runners ought to be capable of better in due course, and it's probably worth noting that this race produced loads of winners last year.

1100 TOTEQUADPOT MAIDEN STKS 7f 30y
3:20 (3:20) (Class 5) 3-Y-O+ **£2,590** (£770; £385; £192) **Stalls** High

Form RPR

0 **1** **Skyfire**[6] 1050 3-8-13 0........................ JoeFanning 6 76
(M Johnston) *led 1f: trckd ldr tl hdwy to chal and carried bdly lft 2f out: rdn to ld 1 1/2f out: edgd rt ins fnl f: drvn and hld on wl towards fin* **11/1**[3]

44- **2** nk **Chushka**[202] 5949 3-8-8 0........................ TomEaves 9 70
(B Smart) *t.k.h: trckd ldrs on inner: hdwy over 2f out: rdn to chal ent fnl f and ev ch tl drvn and no ex towards fin* **3/1**[2]

3 5 **Bajan Flash** 3-8-13 0........................ GregFairley 8 62
(B Smart) *hld up in rr: hdwy 3f out: rdn to chse ldrs 2f out: kpt on ins fnl f: tk 3rd nr line* **12/1**

3- **4** hd **Jack O'Lantern**[163] 6991 3-8-13 0........................ PaulHanagan 4 61
(R A Fahey) *cl up: led after 1f pushed along and jnd over 2f out: sn rdn and hung lft: drvn and hdd 1 1/2f out: sn btn* **8/13**[1]

000- **5** 10 **Dubara Reef (IRE)**[135] 7463 3-8-13 0........................ SilvestreDeSousa 1 34
(Paul Green) *chsd ldng pair: rdn along 3f out: drvn and wknd fnl 2f* **50/1**

6 1/2 **I'm Frank**[22] 4-9-13 0........................ PJMcDonald 2 38
(G A Swinbank) *a towards rr* **12/1**

7 3 **Hong Kong Island (IRE)** 3-8-13 0........................ PaulMulrennan 5 25
(J Barclay) *a in rr* **50/1**

0- **8** 2 1/4 **One Cat Diesel (IRE)**[163] 6982 3-8-13 0........................ DuranFentiman 7 19
(N Wilson) *in tch: hdwy to chse ldrs over 3f out: sn rdn and wknd* **80/1**

1m 34.0s (5.00) **Going Correction** +0.55s/f (Yiel)
WFA 3 from 4yo 14lb **8** Ran SP% **115.8**
Speed ratings (Par 103): **100,99,93,93,82 81,78,75**
Tote Swingers: 1&2 £4.00, 1&3 £6.20, 2&3 £4.80 CSF £44.56 TOTE £10.80: £2.70, £1.20, £3.10; EX 50.70.
Owner Sheikh Hamdan Bin Mohammed Al Maktoum **Bred** Darley **Trained** Middleham Moor, N Yorks

FOCUS
Probably an ordinary maiden. The time was 0.97 seconds quicker than She's In The Money, an 80-rated 4-y-o, recorded in a later handicap, although the ground will have been more cut up by that stage.

1101 TOTESUPER7 MUSSELBURGH GOLD CUP (HANDICAP STKS) 1m 6f
3:50 (3:50) (Class 4) (0-85,85) 4-Y-O+
£12,462 (£3,732; £1,866; £934; £466; £234) **Stalls** High

Form RPR

0/0- **1** **My Arch**[133] 6681 8-8-13 77........................ BarryMcHugh(3) 8 86
(Ollie Pears) *hld up in rr: hdwy 4f out: rdn to chse ldrs over 1f out: swtchd lft and drvn ent fnl f: styd on wl to ld nr line* **11/1**

2/11 **2** shd **Veloso (FR)**[18] 910 8-9-0 75........................ FrederikTylicki 14 84
(J A Glover) *a.p: effrt to chal over 2f out: rdn to ld 1 1/2f out: drvn ins fnl f: hdd and no ex nr line* **16/1**

004- **3** nk **Bogside Theatre (IRE)**[25] 7091 6-9-0 75........................ PJMcDonald 4 84
(G M Moore) *cl up: effrt over 4f out: led 3f out: rdn over 2f out: drvn and hdd 1 1/2f out: rallied u.p ins fnl f and ev ch tl no ex nr fin* **4/1**[1]

000- **4** 3 1/4 **Highland Legacy**[148] 7293 6-9-8 83........................(v) JamieSpencer 10 87
(M L W Bell) *hld up in midfield: hdwy 5f out: effrt 3f out: sn rdn and chsd ldrs over 1f out: drvn and one pce ins fnl f* **4/1**[1]

245- **5** 3 1/4 **Dazzling Light (UAE)**[158] 7117 5-8-12 76........................ GaryBartley(3) 1 75+
(J S Goldie) *hld up in rr: swtchd wd and hdwy over 2f out: rdn to chse ldrs over 1f out and ch tl drvn and wknd ins fnl f* **22/1**

363- **6** 5 **Puy D'Arnac (FR)**[155] 7170 7-8-12 73........................ RobertWinston 9 65
(G A Swinbank) *hld up in midfield: gd hdwy over 5f out: chsd ldrs 3f out: rdn and ch 2f out: sn drvn and wknd appr fnl f* **7/1**[3]

001- **7** 3/4 **Sphinx (FR)**[8] 7170 12-8-13 74........................(b) PaulMulrennan 5 65
(E W Tuer) *hld up in midfield: effrt 3f out: rdn along over 2f out and sn no imp* **18/1**

461- **8** nk **Gordonsville**[67] 7117 7-9-10 85........................ DanielTudhope 7 76
(J S Goldie) *midfield: hdwy over 4f out: in tch 3f out and sn rdn: drvn over 1f out and no imp* **15/2**

3-11 **9** 1 1/2 **Wicked Daze (IRE)**[74] 237 7-9-5 80........................ PhillipMakin 13 69
(Miss L A Perratt) *led: rdn along over 4f out: hdd 3f out: drvn and wknd over 2f out* **28/1**

-041 **10** 8 **Prince Picasso**[9] 996 7-9-0 75........................(b) PaulHanagan 3 53
(R A Fahey) *trckd ldrs: pushed along 6f out: rdn along 3f out: drvn and wknd over 2f out* **12/1**

230/ **11** 5 **Planetarium**[56] 3719 5-9-0 75........................ TonyHamilton 11 46
(P Monteith) *a in rr: bhd fnl 3f* **100/1**

222- **12** 3 1/2 **Outrageous Request**[96] 7867 4-8-7 78........................(p) LeeTopliss(7) 12 44
(Pat Eddery) *in tch: hdwy 4f out: rdn along 3f out: wknd over 2f out* **13/2**[2]

1620 **13** 3 1/2 **Gargano (IRE)**[23] 871 5-8-13 74........................ JoeFanning 6 35
(M Johnston) *chsd ldrs: rdn along over 5f out: wknd over 3f out* **25/1**

3-22 **14** 2 1/2 **Kingsdale Orion (IRE)**[17] 917 6-9-0 75........................ TomEaves 2 32
(B Ellison) *a bhd* **22/1**

3m 11.1s (5.80) **Going Correction** +0.55s/f (Yiel)
WFA 4 from 5yo+ 3lb **14** Ran SP% **121.7**
Speed ratings (Par 105): **105,104,104,102,101 98,97,97,96,92 89,87,85,83**
Tote Swingers: 1&2 £17.80, 1&3 £11.70, 2&3 £17.20 CSF £166.07 CT £836.17 TOTE £12.30: £2.50, £5.00, £2.30; EX 273.40 Trifecta £340.50 Part won. Pool: £460.20 - 0.10 winning units..
Owner J D Spensley & Mrs M A Spensley **Bred** J And A Spensley **Trained** Norton, N Yorks
■ Stewards' Enquiry : Barry McHugh five-day ban: used whip with excessive frequency (Apr 19-23)
P J McDonald caution: used whip with excessive frequency.

FOCUS
A fair, competitive staying handicap run at a good pace in the conditions.
Sphinx(FR) Official explanation: jockey said gelding was denied a clear run

1102 BET TOTEPOOL AT TOTESPORT.COM EASTER H'CAP 7f 30y
4:20 (4:20) (Class 4) (0-85,85) 4-Y-O+
£6,231 (£1,866; £933; £467; £233; £117) **Stalls** High

Form RPR

512- **1** **She's In The Money**[189] 6311 4-8-13 80........................ PaulHanagan 6 87
(R A Fahey) *in tch: hdwy to chse ldrs over 2f out: rdn to ld whn hung bdly lft to stands rail 1 1/2f out: drvn and styd on strly fnl f* **7/4**[1]

000- **2** 2 1/4 **Toledo Gold (IRE)**[48] 6485 4-8-8 75........................ DavidAllan 1 76
(E J Alston) *trckd ldrs: hdwy over 2f out: rdn: n.m.r and swtchd lft 1 1/2f out: kpt on u.p ins fnl f: tk 2nd nr line* **33/1**

30-0 **3** nk **Mountain Cat (IRE)**[8] 1006 6-9-3 84........................ RobertWinston 8 84
(G A Swinbank) *cl up: led 2 1/2f out: rdn and hdd whn hmpd 1 1/2f out: swtchd rt and drvn whn edgd rt ins fnl f: one pce lost 2nd nr line* **4/1**[3]

00-4 **4** 1 **Ra Junior (USA)**[18] 902 4-9-4 85........................ AdrianNicholls 5 82
(D Nicholls) *in tch: hdwy over 2f out: rdn to chse ldrs over 1f out: swtchd lft ent fnl f and kpt on same pce* **3/1**[2]

200- **5** 2 3/4 **Floor Show**[253] 4326 4-9-1 82........................ DanielTudhope 3 72
(N Wilson) *t.k.h: set str pce: rdn along and hdd 2 1/2f out: grad wknd* **9/1**

423- **6** 4 1/2 **Stellite**[155] 7171 10-8-1 71 oh1........................ KellyHarrison(3) 4 49
(J S Goldie) *hld up: a towards rr* **15/2**

-302 **7** 4 1/2 **Sendreni (FR)**[52] 499 6-8-6 73........................(p) AndrewMullen 2 39
(Mrs J C McGregor) *dwlt: a in rr* **40/1**

300- **8** 8 **Summer Dancer (IRE)**[190] 6278 6-9-1 82........................ PhillipMakin 7 26
(P T Midgley) *dwlt and towards rr: effrt and sme hdwy over 3f out: sn rdn and wknd* **12/1**

1m 34.97s (5.97) **Going Correction** +0.55s/f (Yiel) **8** Ran SP% **116.2**
Speed ratings (Par 105): **95,92,92,90,87 82,77,68**
Tote Swingers: 1&2 £9.70, 1&3 £3.50, 2&3 £15.30 CSF £64.75 CT £214.46 TOTE £2.80: £1.10, £9.80, £1.10; EX 50.30.
Owner Cavan Pickering & Stewart Whitehead **Bred** Hermes Services Ltd **Trained** Musley Bank, N Yorks

FOCUS
A fair handicap run at a strong pace in the conditions, and the runners ended up middle to stands' side in the straight. The time was 0.97 seconds slower than the three-year-old Skyfire recorded in an earlier maiden, although the ground will have been more chewed up by this stage.

1103 BET TOTEPOOL 0800 221 221 MAIDEN STKS 1m 4f 100y
4:50 (4:50) (Class 5) 3-Y-O+ **£2,590** (£770; £385; £192) **Stalls** High

Form RPR

2 **1** **Goodlukin Lucy**[8] 1010 3-8-0 0 ow1........................ MartinLane(3) 1 71+
(Pat Eddery) *trckd ldrs on outer: hdwy on outside over 2f out: rdn to ld over 1f out: kpt on ins fnl f* **1/1**[1]

4 **2** 1 3/4 **Dancing Dude (IRE)**[13] 963 3-8-7 0........................ JoeFanning 2 72+
(M Johnston) *chsd ldr: cl up 4f out: led over 2f out: rdn and hung bdly lft over 1f out and sn hdd: drvn: edgd rt and kpt on same pce ins fnl f* **7/2**[3]

02 **3** 7 **Hunters Belt (IRE)**[37] 718 6-10-0 0........................ DanielTudhope 6 64+
(N Wilson) *hld up in rr: smooth hdwy 3f out: n.m.r 2f out: rdn to chse ldrs over 1f out: swtchd rt ent fnl f and kpt on same pce* **3/1**[2]

60 **4** 1 1/2 **Major Pop (USA)**[13] 963 3-8-7 0........................ PaulHanagan 3 60
(R A Fahey) *led: rdn along over 4f out: hdd over 2f out: sn drvn and wknd over 1f out* **22/1**

6/ **5** 7 **Tuxsumdoin**[458] 1 6-9-9 0........................ PaulMulrennan 8 46?
(J R Weymes) *hdwy 3f out: rdn and in tch 2f out: sn wknd* **80/1**

60-0 **6** 3/4 **Agricultural**[30] 815 4-9-10 52........................ BarryMcHugh(3) 5 50?
(Mrs L B Normile) *a in rr* **66/1**

543- **7** 13 **Dean Iarracht (IRE)**[121] 7632 4-9-10 56........................ KellyHarrison(3) 7 31
(Miss Tracy Waggott) *a towards rr: rdn along and outpcd over 2f out* **20/1**

0-3 **8** *26* **Welcome Bounty**[50] [542] 3-8-7 0................................ GrahamGibbons 4 —
(Miss L A Perratt) *chsd ldrs: rdn along 3f out: sn wknd* **20/1**

2m 56.63s (14.63) **Going Correction** +0.55s/f (Yiel)
WFA 3 from 4yo 21lb 4 from 6yo 1lb **8** Ran SP% **113.8**
Speed ratings (Par 103): **73,71,67,66,61 61,52,35**
Tote Swingers: 1&2 £2.00, 1&3 £2.00, 2&3 £2.10 CSF £4.38 TOTE £1.90: £1.20, £1.10, £1.50; EX 5.10.
Owner Evergreen Racing **Bred** Moretail Ventures **Trained** Nether Winchendon, Bucks

FOCUS
No more than a fair maiden, with little strength in depth, but it should produce the odd winner.
Welcome Bounty Official explanation: trainer said colt had a breathing problem

1104 BET TOTEPOOL ON ALL UK RACING H'CAP 5f
5:20 (5:20) (Class 5) (0-75,73) 3-Y-O **£3,238** (£963; £481; £240) **Stalls** Low

Form RPR
321- **1** **Esuvia (IRE)**[114] [7708] 3-9-4 **70**................................ TomEaves 4 87
(B Smart) *mde most: rdn clr appr fnl f: styd on strly* **9/4**[2]
406- **2** *2 1/2* **Diman Waters (IRE)**[151] [7242] 3-9-0 **66**................................ DavidAllan 3 74
(E J Alston) *trckd ldrs: hdwy 2f out: sn rdn: chsd wnr ins fnl f: no imp* **2/1**[1]
4-05 **3** *2 1/4* **Dazeen**[17] [919] 3-8-10 **67**................................ PaulPickard(5) 2 67
(P T Midgley) *hld up in rr: hdwy 2f out: swtchd rt and rdn over 1f out: styd on ins fnl f: nrst fin* **16/1**
0-26 **4** *2 1/2* **Dower Glen**[16] [936] 3-8-6 **58**................................ JimmyQuinn 6 49
(N Wilson) *prom: rdn along 2f out and ch tl drvn and wknd ent fnl f* **12/1**
156- **5** *7* **Hold On Tiger (IRE)**[169] [6841] 3-9-7 **73**................................ PaulMulrennan 1 39
(J Barclay) *cl up: rdn along 2f out: wknd over 1f out* **16/1**
010- **6** *1* **Royal Holiday (IRE)**[170] [6829] 3-9-7 **73**................................ PJMcDonald 10 35
(B Ellison) *a towards rr* **28/1**
020- **7** *3* **Blue Avon**[202] [5938] 3-8-4 **56**................................ PaulHanagan 9 7
(R A Fahey) *a towards rr* **8/1**[3]
436- **8** *6* **Bronze Beau**[153] [7213] 3-9-6 **72**................................ TonyHamilton 8 —
(Mrs L Stubbs) *prom: rdn along over 2f out: sn wknd* **8/1**[3]
000- **U** **Koo And The Gang (IRE)**[156] [7156] 3-8-12 **67**........... BarryMcHugh(3) 5 —
(B Ellison) *stmbld s and uns rdr w blind stl in pl* **9/1**

62.00 secs (1.60) **Going Correction** +0.55s/f (Yiel) **9** Ran SP% **119.2**
Speed ratings (Par 98): **109,105,101,97,86 84,79,70,—**
Tote Swingers: 1&2 £1.80, 1&3 £8.30, 2&3 £9.80 CSF £7.46 CT £56.85 TOTE £3.40: £1.60, £1.40, £5.30; EX 8.90 Place 6: £60.64 Place 5: £56.13.
Owner Ceffyl Racing **Bred** Round Hill Stud **Trained** Hambleton, N Yorks

FOCUS
A fair three-year-old sprint handicap and Esuvia had her rivals well strung out, winning in a manner that suggests she's better than this grade. The time - 0.50 seconds quicker than 73-rated six-year-old Luscivious managed earlier on the card - supports that view, for although the ground may have dried out a bit, it was surely also pretty chewed up by this point.
T/Jkpt: Part won. £41,219.60 to a £1 stake. Pool: £58,055.87. 0.50 winning tickets. T/Plt: £403.80 to a £1 stake. Pool: £77,953.49. 140.90 winning tickets. T/Qpdt: £43.90 to a £1 stake. Pool: £4,471.86. 75.33 winning tickets. JR

1105 - 1110a (Foreign Racing) - See Raceform Interactive

[1079]SAINT-CLOUD (L-H)
Sunday, April 4

OFFICIAL GOING: Turf:very heavy

1111a PRIX EDMOND BLANC (GROUP 3) (4YO+) (TURF) 1m
2:40 (12:00) 4-Y-0+ **£35,398** (£14,159; £10,619; £7,079; £3,539)

RPR
1 **Gris De Gris (IRE)**[22] [890] 6-9-0 0................ Christophe-PatriceLemaire 115
(A De Royer-Dupre, France) *led fr s: qcknd wl in st (field switching to stands' rail): styd on wl: comf* **10/11**[1]
2 *2* **Skins Game**[22] [890] 4-8-11 0................................ ChristopheSoumillon 107
(J-C Rouget, France) *racd in midfield: qcknd to chse ldr in st: styd on wl to hold 2nd* **11/4**[2]
3 *1/2* **Liang Kay (GER)**[141] [7406] 5-9-0 0................................ MaximeGuyon 109
(Uwe Ostmann, Germany) *in rr fr s: proged in st: styd on to chal for 2nd: no ex ins fnl 110yds* **10/1**[3]
4 *6* **Cheyrac (FR)**[58] [439] 4-8-8 0................................ GregoryBenoist 89
(X Nakkachdji, France) *racd in 2nd fr s: rdn early in st: dropped bk to 4th: no ex* **12/1**
5 *2 1/2* **Vertigineux (FR)**[338] [1658] 6-9-2 0................................ PhilippeSogorb 92
(Mme C Dufreche, France) *racd bhd ldrs fr s: failed to qckn in st: fdd* **10/1**[3]
6 *nk* **Diableside (FR)**[13] 4-8-11 0................................ OlivierPeslier 86
(Y Durepaire, Spain) *a in rr: rdn early in st: no ex* **14/1**
7 *5* **Konig Bernard (FR)**[148] [7302] 4-8-11 0................................ DominiqueBoeuf 75
(W Baltromei, Germany) *prom tl st: rdn: no ex: fdd* **12/1**

1m 50.3s (2.80) **Going Correction** +0.675s/f (Yiel) **7** Ran SP% **119.3**
Speed ratings: **113,111,110,104,102 101,96**
WIN (incl. 1 euro stake): 2.00; PLACES: 1.10, 1.10, 1.50; DF: 2.30; SF 3.00.
Owner Jean-Claude Seroul **Bred** Jean-Claude Seroul **Trained** Chantilly, France

REDCAR (L-H)
Monday, April 5

OFFICIAL GOING: Soft (good to soft in places; 5.8)

1112 MARKET CROSS JEWELLERS FILLIES' H'CAP 5f
2:00 (2:00) (Class 5) (0-70,66) 4-Y-0+ **£2,396** (£712; £267; £267) **Stalls** Centre

Form RPR
0041 **1** **La Capriosa**[5] [1068] 4-9-5 **64** 6ex................................ RobertWinston 5 73
(J A Glover) *cl up: led after 2f: rdn clr ent fnl f: kpt on* **9/4**[1]
535- **2** *1 1/4* **Dispol Kylie (IRE)**[213] [5626] 4-9-6 **65**................................ PhillipMakin 6 70
(P T Midgley) *hld up: hdwy 2f out: sn rdn: styd on ins fnl f: nrst fin* **10/1**
0535 **3** *1* **Sally's Swansong**[17] [936] 4-8-5 **50**................................(b) DuranFentiman 4 51
(E J Alston) *dwlt and towards rr: swtchd lft and hdwy 2f out: sn rdn: kpt on ins fnl f: nrst fin* **8/1**
524- **3** *dht* **Comptonspirit**[187] [6379] 6-9-1 **60**................................ J-PGuillambert 7 61
(B P J Baugh) *chsd ldrs: hdwy 2f out: sn rdn and styd on ins fnl f* **15/2**[3]
6364 **5** *1* **Berrymead**[38] [721] 5-8-6 **56** ow1................................ AnnStokell(5) 10 53
(Miss A Stokell) *wnt rt s: towards rr: pushed along 2f out: rdn over 1f out: kpt on ins fnl f: nrst fin* **40/1**

1-53 **6** *shd* **Forever's Girl**[24] [869] 4-8-10 **55**................................ PJMcDonald 2 52
(G R Oldroyd) *cl up: effrt and ev ch 2f out: sn rdn and wknd ent fnl f* **11/2**[2]
5013 **7** *shd* **Lujiana**[18] [913] 5-9-0 **59**................................ DavidAllan 3 56
(M Brittain) *prom: rdn along 2f out: sn drvn and wknd over 1f out* **11/2**[2]
3554 **8** *shd* **Kheley (IRE)**[14] [968] 4-9-1 **65**................................ DeanHeslop(5) 8 61
(W M Brisbourne) *cl up on outer: rdn along over 2f out: sn drvn and grad wknd* **12/1**
600- **8** *dht* **City For Conquest (IRE)**[256] [4225] 7-8-2 **47** oh2.........(b) AndrewElliott 9 43
(John A Harris) *sn outpcd and pushed along in rr: swtchd rt 1/2-way: rdn wl over 1f out: kpt on ins fnl f: nrst fin* **40/1**
030- **10** *3 1/2* **Darcy's Pride (IRE)**[150] [7280] 6-8-11 **56**................................(t) TonyHamilton 1 40
(P T Midgley) *led 2f: cl up tl rdn along and wknd 2f out* **14/1**

61.10 secs (2.50) **Going Correction** +0.60s/f (Yiel) **10** Ran SP% **112.7**
Speed ratings (Par 100): **104,102,100,100,98 98,98,98,98,92**PL: Comptonspirit £1.20, Sally's Swansong £1.30 TC: La Capriosa, Dispol Kylie, Comptonspirit £70.95: La Capriosa, Dispol Kylie, Sally's Swansong £75.12. toteswingers:LC&DK:£4.20, DK&CS:£6.60, LC&SS:£2.60, DK&SS:£5.70, LC&CS:£2.80 CSF £25.13 TOTE £2.90: £1.30, £3.2027, £Owner, £Paul J DixonBred Slatch Farm Stud Trifecta £Trained Babworth, Notts.

FOCUS
There was 2mm of rain overnight and the going remained soft, good to soft in places. Robert Winston, who won the first race, reported it as being tacky, puddingy ground. A modest fillies' handicap but straightforward form with the winner rated to last year's best, backed up by the second.

1113 WIN A VIP DAY OUT @ REDCARRACING.CO.UK H'CAP 2m 4y
2:35 (2:35) (Class 6) (0-65,63) 4-Y-0+ **£1,748** (£520; £260; £129) **Stalls** Low

Form RPR
5/1- **1** **Sendali (FR)**[23] [5734] 6-8-12 50................................ PaulHanagan 14 59
(J D Bethell) *hld up towards rr: stdy hdwy over 4f out: trckd ldrs 3f out: swtchd rt and effrt 2f out: rdn to ld 1f out: drvn ins fnl f and hld on wl* **7/1**[3]
550- **2** *hd* **Born To Perform**[225] [5289] 5-9-5 57................................ RobertWinston 12 66+
(G A Swinbank) *hld up in tch: smooth hdwy over 5f out: trckd ldrs on bit over 3f out: led 2f out: rdn and hdd 1f out: drvn and edgd lft: rallied and ev ch ins fnl f: no ex nr fin* **11/2**[2]
0631 **3** *3* **Delorain (IRE)**[47] [584] 7-8-10 48................................(vt) JerryO'Dwyer 7 53
(W B Stone) *trcks ldng pair: hdwy 4f out: rdn along over 2f out: drvn and ch over 1f out: sn one pce* **14/1**
640/ **4** *6* **Graysland**[279] [6330] 4-7-12 45................................(p) PaulPickard(5) 10 43
(P A Kirby) *hld up and bhd: hdwy 5f out: rdn along 3f out: drvn over 2f out: kpt on to take 4th ins fnl f: fin lame* **20/1**
33-0 **5** *1 1/4* **Front Rank (IRE)**[8] [376] 10-8-12 50................................ FrederikTylicki 15 46
(Mrs Dianne Sayer) *chsd ldr: hdwy to ld 4f out: rdn 3f out: drvn and hdd 2f out: grad wknd* **40/1**
011- **6** *8* **Unawatuna**[174] [6767] 5-9-4 59................................ KellyHarrison(3) 4 46
(Mrs K Walton) *trckd ldrs: pushed along 5f out: effrt and rdn 3f out: grad wknd fnl 2f* **4/1**[1]
350- **7** *3/4* **Mister Pete (IRE)**[16] [3068] 7-8-13 56................................(p) AmyRyan(5) 13 42
(C Grant) *chsd ldrs: rdn along over 3f out: drvn over 2f out and sn wknd* **15/2**
432- **8** *5* **Flora's Pride**[26] [7085] 6-9-3 55................................ TonyCulhane 8 35
(K G Reveley) *hld up in rr: sme hdwy over 3f out: sn rdn and nvr nr ldrs* **17/2**
00-0 **9** *15* **Waterloo Corner**[20] [331] 8-8-12 50................................ DavidAllan 2 12
(R Craggs) *towards rr: rdn along over 7f out: sme hdwy on wd outside 3f out: nvr a factor* **20/1**
360- **10** *1* **Master Nimbus**[214] [5600] 10-9-11 63................................ GrahamGibbons 6 24
(J J Quinn) *trckd ldrs: effrt 4f out: rdn along over 3f out: wknd over 2f out* **16/1**
-050 **11** *25* **Solo Choice**[10] [661] 4-8-4 46................................ RoystonFfrench 11 —
(I W McInnes) *hld up towards rr: hdwy into midfield 1/2-way: rdn along over 3f out and nvr a factor* **33/1**
5-14 **12** *5* **Mehendi (IRE)**[60] [401] 4-9-3 59................................ TomEaves 16 —
(B Ellison) *stdd s and hld up: a bhd* **9/1**
2/0- **13** *4* **Mt Desert**[26] [7505] 8-9-6 58................................ PaulMulrennan 9 —
(E W Tuer) *led: rdn along over 4f out: sn hdd & wknd* **33/1**
000- **14** *13* **Drop The Hammer**[171] [6822] 4-8-10 52................................ SilvestreDeSousa 5 —
(J Hetherton) *chsd ldrs on inner: rdn along over 4f out and sn wknd* **16/1**
2-24 **15** *22* **Merrion Tiger (IRE)**[38] [720] 5-9-7 59................................(p) AndrewMullen 3 —
(A G Foster) *a towards rr: bhd fnl 3f* **20/1**
400- **16** *19* **Bogula (IRE)**[174] [6766] 4-8-8 50................................ FrannyNorton 1 —
(Mrs A Duffield) *in tch: pushed along and lost pl 1/2-way: bhd fnl 4f* **50/1**

3m 47.13s (15.73) **Going Correction** +1.025s/f (Soft)
WFA 4 from 5yo+ 4lb **16** Ran SP% **123.2**
Speed ratings (Par 101): **101,100,99,96,95 91,91,88,81,80 68,65,63,57,46 36**
toteswingers:1&2:£10.20, 1&3:£10.50, 2&3:£21.70 CSF £41.75 CT £540.89 TOTE £7.50: £2.40, £2.00, £3.10, £4.20; EX 62.80.
Owner Elliott Brothers And Peacock **Bred** Sarl Haras Du Taillis Et Al **Trained** Middleham Moor, N Yorks
■ Stewards' Enquiry : Robert Winston one-day ban: used whip with excessive frequency (Apr 19)
Paul Pickard Vet said filly returned lame

FOCUS
An ordinary staying handicap in which the third looks the best guide to the form.
Solo Choice Official explanation: jockey said gelding had no more to give
Mt Desert Official explanation: jockey said gelding had no more to give
Drop The Hammer Official explanation: jockey said filly had no more to give
Merrion Tiger(IRE) Official explanation: jockey said gelding hung right throughout

1114 RACING UK ON SKY 432 (S) STKS 7f
3:10 (3:10) (Class 6) 3-Y-0+ **£1,748** (£520; £260; £129) **Stalls** Centre

Form RPR
-600 **1** **Pretty Orchid**[19] [912] 5-8-9 50................................(p) PaulPickard(5) 9 56
(P T Midgley) *hld up: stdy hdwy 1/2-way: effrt over 2f out: rdn to ld 1 1/2f out: hung bdly lft 1f out: wandered ins fnl f: kpt on towards fin* **16/1**
1120 **2** *1 3/4* **Castle Myth (USA)**[20] [893] 4-9-6 53................................ IanBrennan(5) 7 62
(B Ellison) *trckd ldrs: pushed along and outpcd wl over 2f out: sn rdn and hdwy over 1f out: keeping on whn n.m.r and swtchd rt ins fnl f: sn drvn and styd on same pce* **5/1**[3]
-060 **3** *1/2* **Jenny's Pride (IRE)**[10] [995] 4-8-9 46................................ MarkCoumbe(5) 4 50
(John A Harris) *trckd ldrs: hdwy 3f out: rdn wl over 1f out and ev ch tl drvn and one pce ent fnl f* **13/2**
-560 **4** *2 1/4* **Montiboli (IRE)**[20] [893] 5-8-9 68................................(p) AmyRyan(5) 1 44
(K A Ryan) *dwlt: sn chsng ldrs: hdwy to ld 3f out: rdn and hdd 1 1/2f out: sn drvn and wknd* **9/2**[2]
003/ **5** *3 1/2* **Frank Crow**[49] [3214] 7-9-5 59................................ SilvestreDeSousa 8 39
(N Tinkler) *in rr and sn pushed along: hdwy wl over 1f out: kpt on ins fnl f: nvr a factor* **7/2**[1]

60-4 **6** *6* **Kneesy Earsy Nosey**[54] [491] 4-8-9 35 (p) AnnStokell(5) 5 18
(Miss A Stokell) *chsd ldrs: rdn along 3f out: sn wknd* **40/1**

2000 **7** *8* **Imperial Skylight**[12] [976] 4-9-5 43 SamHitchcott 3 —
(M R Channon) *chsd ldrs: rdn along 3f out: sn wknd* **6/1**

0- **8** *1 1/2* **Fleetwoodsands (IRE)**[284] [3292] 3-8-5 0 RoystonFfrench 10 —
(Miss Tracy Waggott) *cl up: rdn along 1/2-way: sn wknd* **28/1**

022- **9** *14* **Musigny (USA)**[167] [6924] 4-9-5 59 PaulHanagan 6 —
(Miss S E Hall) *led: rdn along and hdd 3f out: wknd qckly* **9/2**[2]

1m 29.73s (5.23) **Going Correction** +0.60s/f (Yiel)
WFA 3 from 4yo+ 14lb **9** Ran SP% **114.6**
Speed ratings (Par 101): **94,92,91,88,84 78,68,67,51**
toteswingers:1&2:£11.10, 1&3:£11.40, 2&3:£9.80 CSF £93.27 TOTE £17.70: £4.90, £1.10, £2.50; EX 98.50.There was no bid for the winner
Owner K L Man **Bred** Southill Stud **Trained** Westow, N Yorks

FOCUS
The betting rightly suggested this was a competitive affair. The winner is rated back to her best.

1115 BUY YOUR TICKETS ON-LINE @ REDCARRACING.CO.UK H'CAP 7f
3:45 (3:46) (Class 5) (0-70,68) 4-Y-O+ **£2,396** (£712; £356; £177) **Stalls** Centre

Form RPR

3 **1** **Academy Blues (USA)**[19] [907] 5-9-4 68 AdrianNicholls 9 81+
(D Nicholls) *prom: led over 2f out: drvn out fnl f* **15/2**[3]

6-00 **2** *1 1/4* **Toby Tyler**[25] [857] 4-8-12 62 TonyCulhane 14 72
(P T Midgley) *hld up: hdwy and hung lft over 2f out: chsd wnr 1f out: kpt on* **16/1**

1330 **3** *1* **Flores Sea (USA)**[7] [1051] 6-9-0 64 (b) SilvestreDeSousa 3 71
(Mrs R A Carr) *prom: drvn and outpcd over 2f out: rallied over 1f out: kpt on fnl f* **9/1**

-152 **4** *nk* **Young Gladiator (IRE)**[19] [907] 5-9-2 66 (b) FrederikTylicki 7 72
(Julie Camacho) *led to over 2f out: sn rdn: kpt on same pce ins fnl f* **5/1**[1]

022- **5** *7* **Many Welcomes**[167] [6925] 5-8-2 57 JemmaMarshall(5) 1 45
(B P J Baugh) *hld up: hdwy 3f out: shkn up and no imp fr 2f out* **20/1**

50-2 **6** *nse* **Sarwin (USA)**[7] [1051] 7-9-1 65 RobertWinston 8 52
(G A Swinbank) *cl up: led briefly over 2f out: rdn and wknd appr fnl f* **11/2**[2]

300- **7** *shd* **Silly Gilly (IRE)**[132] [7500] 6-8-6 56 PaulHanagan 4 43
(R E Barr) *cl up tl rdn and wknd fr over 2f out* **14/1**

330- **8** *3/4* **Coole Dodger (IRE)**[188] [6358] 5-8-4 54 RoystonFfrench 11 39
(B Ellison) *t.k.h: hld up: outpcd over 2f out: sme late hdwy: nvr on terms* **20/1**

050- **9** *2* **Dabbers Ridge (IRE)**[115] [7719] 8-8-13 66 GaryBartley(3) 6 46
(I W McInnes) *in tch: drvn and outpcd over 2f out: n.d after* **20/1**

050- **10** *3/4* **Film Festival (USA)**[310] [2505] 7-9-1 68 BarryMcHugh(3) 15 46
(B Ellison) *hld up: rdn over 2f out: sn btn* **16/1**

245- **11** *nk* **Northern Flyer (GER)**[195] [6182] 4-9-1 65 GrahamGibbons 12 42
(J J Quinn) *in tch: rdn and outpcd over 2f out: sn n.d* **11/1**

0345 **12** *9* **Transmission (IRE)**[19] [908] 5-9-2 66 TomEaves 13 19
(B Smart) *sn towards rr and outpcd: no ch fr 1/2-way* **5/1**[1]

025- **13** *3* **Star Addition**[164] [6988] 4-8-5 55 DuranFentiman 5 —
(E J Alston) *hld up: rdn along 1/2-way: btn fnl 2f* **12/1**

0420 **14** *9* **Mozayada (USA)**[27] [837] 6-9-1 65 DavidAllan 2 —
(M Brittain) *chsd ldrs: rdn along 1/2-way: sn lost pl* **25/1**

000- **15** *6* **Barataria**[164] [6987] 8-8-11 68 MatthewLawson(7) 10 —
(R Bastiman) *s.s: a bhd* **66/1**

1m 28.37s (3.87) **Going Correction** +0.60s/f (Yiel) **15** Ran SP% **124.6**
Speed ratings (Par 103): **101,99,98,98,90 90,89,89,86,85 85,75,71,61,54**
toteswingers:1&2:£27.40, 1&3:£17.20, 2&3:£36.40 CSF £115.89 CT £1141.45 TOTE £10.50: £2.70, £7.00, £4.60; EX 136.70.
Owner Bulldog Racing **Bred** Kinghaven Farms Ltd **Trained** Sessay, N Yorks

FOCUS
A modest handicap run at a decent pace, and the first four finished clear, suggesting this is sound form for the grade.
Barataria Official explanation: jockey said gelding missed the break due to difficulty in removing blindfold

1116 REDCAR RACECOURSE CONFERENCE & EVENTS VENUE MAIDEN STKS (DIV I) 1m 1f
4:20 (4:21) (Class 5) 3-Y-O+ **£2,072** (£616; £308; £153) **Stalls** Low

Form RPR

02- **1** **Dandino**[159] [7121] 3-8-11 0 PaulMulrennan 8 69+
(J G Given) *prom: swtchd ins and hdwy 3f out: led 2f out and sn rdn: drvn ins fnl f: kpt on wl towards fin* **2/1**[2]

055- **2** *1 3/4* **Brockfield**[243] [4660] 4-9-7 58 JohnCavanagh(7) 1 69
(M Brittain) *prom: hdwy to ld 3f out: rdn and hdd 2f out: ev ch tl drvn and no ex fnl 100yds* **33/1**

-6 **3** *1 3/4* **Sir Mark (IRE)**[42] [664] 6-10-0 0 DanielTudhope 9 65
(M A Peill) *trckd ldrs: hdwy to chse ldr 1/2-way: rdn along and sltly outpcd 3f out: kpt on u.p fnl 2f* **66/1**

4 *1 3/4* **Kataragama**[353] 4-9-6 0 KellyHarrison(3) 2 56+
(Mrs K Walton) *in tch: effrt over 3f out and sn rdn along: kpt on u.p fnl 2f: tk 4th nr line* **25/1**

33- **5** *nse* **Palawi (IRE)**[159] [7116] 3-8-11 0 GrahamGibbons 4 57
(J J Quinn) *led: rdn along 4f out: hdd 3f out and sn drvn: wknd fnl 2f: sltly eased nr fin* **11/8**[1]

6 *9* **Robbie Burnett** 3-8-11 0 RobertWinston 10 37
(G A Swinbank) *dwlt: hdwy and in tch 1/2-way: rdn along wl over 3f out and sn outpcd* **12/1**

7 *4* **Offspring** 3-8-6 0 DuranFentiman 3 24
(T D Easterby) *in tch: effrt to chse ldrs 4f out: rdn along over 3f out and sn wknd* **20/1**

8 *4 1/2* **I Got Music** 3-8-6 0 AndrewElliott 5 14
(K G Reveley) *dwlt: a in rr* **40/1**

9 *6* **Fantastic Favour** 3-8-6 0 PatrickDonaghy(5) 6 —
(Jedd O'Keeffe) *a towards rr: rdn along and outpcd fnl 3f* **25/1**

- **10** *53* **Fluster (USA)** 4-9-9 0 RoystonFfrench 7 —
(M Johnston) *chsd ldrs: rdn along after 3f: drvn and lost pl over 4f out: sn bhd and virtually p.u 2f out* **13/2**[3]

2m 2.73s (9.73) **Going Correction** +1.025s/f (Soft)
WFA 3 from 4yo+ 17lb **10** Ran SP% **115.8**
Speed ratings (Par 103): **97,95,93,92,92 84,80,76,71,—**
toteswingers:1&2:£11.20, 1&3:£26.70, 2&3:£29.40 CSF £74.02 TOTE £2.40: £1.10, £8.20, £12.60; EX 64.20.
Owner Elite Racing Club **Bred** Elite Racing Club **Trained** Willoughton, Lincs
■ Stewards' Enquiry : Graham Gibbons ten-day ban: (2nd offence) failed to ride out for 4th (Apr 19-28)

FOCUS
Modest maiden form and hard to be positive about it with doubts over those in the frame behind the winner.

1117 JOHN SMITH'S REDCAR STRAIGHT-MILE CHAMPIONSHIP H'CAP (QUALIFIER) 1m
4:55 (4:55) (Class 4) (0-85,84) 4-Y-O+ **£4,209** (£1,252; £625; £312) **Stalls** Centre

Form RPR

54-0 **1** **Exit Smiling**[27] [837] 8-9-1 81 TonyCulhane 3 91
(P T Midgley) *cl up: led over 2f out: edgd rt and drvn out fnl f* **12/1**

505- **2** *3/4* **Happy Anniversary (IRE)**[149] [7287] 4-8-13 79 SilvestreDeSousa 7 87
(Mrs D J Sanderson) *chsd ldrs: wnt 2nd and effrt over 2f out: kpt on ins fnl f* **14/1**

60-6 **3** *1 1/2* **Wovoka (IRE)**[8] [1028] 7-8-4 70 PaulHanagan 1 75
(K A Ryan) *hld up: hdwy u.p over 2f out: r.o ins fnl f* **13/2**[3]

-111 **4** *hd* **Pendragon (USA)**[18] [918] 7-8-3 72 BarryMcHugh(3) 11 76
(B Ellison) *hld up: rdn 3f out: hdwy to chse ldrs 2f out: sn edgd lft: one pce fnl f* **15/2**

5 *1* **Alakhan (IRE)**[171] [6834] 4-9-0 80 StevieDonohoe 9 82
(Ian Williams) *dwlt: hld up: rdn 3f out: plenty to do and hdwy appr fnl f: kpt on: nrst fin* **18/1**

3153 **6** *1 3/4* **Dubai Dynamo**[8] [1030] 5-9-4 84 AndrewElliott 5 82
(Mrs R A Carr) *dwlt: hld up: hdwy and in tch over 2f out: outpcd appr fnl f* **5/1**[2]

0/4- **7** *1/2* **Glenmuir (IRE)**[214] [5598] 7-8-1 72 IanBrennan(5) 10 69
(J J Quinn) *t.k.h in midfield: lost pl 3f out: shkn up: carried hd high and rallied 2f out: no imp fnl f: nvr nr ldrs* **33/1**

035- **8** *4 1/2* **Charlie Tipple**[58] [7060] 6-9-2 82 (p) PaulMulrennan 12 69
(T D Easterby) *prom: drvn 1/2-way: wknd over 2f out* **12/1**

12- **9** *nk* **Mr Rainbow**[175] [6731] 4-9-4 84 RobertWinston 8 70
(G A Swinbank) *t.k.h: prom: effrt and ev ch briefly over 2f out: wknd over 1f out* **7/4**[1]

220- **10** *1 1/2* **Sir Royal (USA)**[285] [3265] 5-8-8 74 PJMcDonald 2 56
(G A Swinbank) *led to over 2f out: sn rdn and wknd* **16/1**

4/56 **11** *18* **Dawnhill (GER)**[23] [889] 6-8-4 70 RoystonFfrench 4 11
(J J Quinn) *prom: drvn 3f out: sn lost pl: t.o* **66/1**

510- **12** *1* **Lakeman (IRE)**[132] [5598] 4-8-9 75 TomEaves 6 14
(B Ellison) *hld up in midfield: outpcd 1/2-way: wknd over 2f out: t.o* **40/1**

1m 41.8s (3.80) **Going Correction** +0.60s/f (Yiel) **12** Ran SP% **118.2**
Speed ratings (Par 105): **105,104,102,102,101 99,99,94,94,93 75,74**
toteswingers:1&2:£26.40, 1&3:£15.80, 2&3:£16.40 CSF £166.38 CT £1215.56 TOTE £16.10: £4.70, £4.10, £2.70; EX 173.60.
Owner Peter Mee **Bred** Mrs D O Joly **Trained** Westow, N Yorks

FOCUS
A fair, reasonably competitive handicap. The first two raced prominently throughout but the form looks straightforward with the winner and fourth setting the level.
Charlie Tipple Official explanation: jockey said gelding never travelled
Mr Rainbow Official explanation: jockey said gelding pulled right-handed from halfway

1118 18 GREAT DAYS RACING AHEAD H'CAP 5f
5:30 (5:30) (Class 6) (0-60,60) 3-Y-O **£1,748** (£520; £260; £129) **Stalls** Centre

Form RPR

500- **1** **Sir Louis**[178] [6646] 3-8-13 55 PaulHanagan 1 66
(R A Fahey) *cl up: led after 2f: rdn clr appr last: kpt on strly* **3/1**[1]

4-30 **2** *3* **Drumpellier (IRE)**[19] [906] 3-8-10 57 PaulPickard(5) 6 57
(P T Midgley) *dwlt: sn swtchd lft to outer: hdwy 1/2-way: swtchd rt and rdn wl over 1f out: styd on to chse wnr ins fnl f: sn no imp* **10/1**

04-0 **3** *3/4* **Gower Sophia**[81] [167] 3-8-12 54 (v) DavidAllan 3 51
(M Brittain) *a.p: rdn along 2f out: drvn over 1f out: kpt on same pce* **10/1**

000- **4** *1* **Whispered Times (USA)**[139] [7419] 3-9-4 60 RobertWinston 11 54
(Miss Tracy Waggott) *wnt rt s: towards rr and pushed along after 1f: hdwy 1/2-way: rdn to chse ldrs over 1f out: edgd rt and one pce ins fnl f* **16/1**

000- **5** *hd* **Eeny Mac (IRE)**[236] [4888] 3-8-6 48 FrannyNorton 4 41
(N Bycroft) *chsd ldrs: sn pushed along: outpcd and in rr after 1 1/2f: rdn 2f out: styd on appr last: nrst fin* **20/1**

0-34 **6** *3* **Vilnius**[78] [213] 3-9-0 56 SamHitchcott 9 38
(M R Channon) *chsd ldrs: rdn along 2f out: grad wknd* **7/1**[2]

355- **7** *1 1/2* **Luv U Noo**[160] [7089] 3-9-2 58 TomEaves 5 35
(B Ellison) *prom: rdn along 1/2-way: sn wknd* **22/1**

0-50 **8** *1* **Yeah**[24] [870] 3-8-10 52 (b) JerryO'Dwyer 7 25
(Patrick Morris) *chsd ldrs: rdn along 1/2-way: sn wknd* **14/1**

030- **9** *nk* **Hot Rod Mamma (IRE)**[145] [7331] 3-8-12 54 FrederikTylicki 8 26
(Mrs Dianne Sayer) *in tch: rdn along over 2f out: sn wknd* **14/1**

4-56 **10** *shd* **Caol Ila (IRE)**[19] [906] 3-8-10 52 PaulMulrennan 13 24
(J G Given) *a towards rr* **14/1**

060 **11** *1/2* **Ignore**[18] [915] 3-8-4 46 oh1 AndrewElliott 2 16
(Mrs R A Carr) *led 2f: cl up and rdn along 1/2-way: sn wknd* **50/1**

3234 **12** *1/2* **Duke Of Rainford**[18] [919] 3-9-1 57 TonyCulhane 10 25
(M Herrington) *chsd ldrs: rdn along over 2f out and sn wknd* **11/1**

-463 **13** *1 1/4* **Your Gifted (IRE)**[10] [991] 3-8-10 55 BarryMcHugh(3) 12 19
(Patrick Morris) *in tch on wd outside: effrt to chse ldrs 2f out: sn rdn and wknd qckly over 1f out* **15/2**[3]

4630 **14** *29* **Fine And Dandie (IRE)**[19] [906] 3-8-10 52 (b1) AdrianNicholls 15 —
(D Nicholls) *cl up: reminders after 1f: rdn along 1/2-way: sn hung lft and wknd: bhd and eased appr last* **11/1**

61.34 secs (2.74) **Going Correction** +0.60s/f (Yiel) **14** Ran SP% **121.1**
Speed ratings (Par 96): **102,97,96,94,94 89,86,85,84,84 83,83,81,34**
toteswingers:1&2:£9.20, 1&3:£17.10, 2&3:£17.50 CSF £32.18 CT £275.61 TOTE £4.50: £2.30, £3.50, £3.80; EX 32.80.
Owner P Ashton **Bred** Brigadier C K Price **Trained** Musley Bank, N Yorks

FOCUS
One or two unexposed horses in this line-up and it was one of them who came out on top. The form looks sound but limited, rated around the placed horses.
Sir Louis ◆ Official explanation: trainer's rep said, regarding apparent improvement in form, that the gelding was very immature last year and thrived through the winter.
Fine And Dandie(IRE) Official explanation: jockey said gelding hung left throughout

1119 REDCAR RACECOURSE CONFERENCE & EVENTS VENUE MAIDEN STKS (DIV II) 1m 1f
6:00 (6:00) (Class 5) 3-Y-O+ **£2,072** (£616; £308; £153) **Stalls** Low

Form RPR

0- **1** **Bear Tobouggie**[149] [7288] 3-8-6 0 PJMcDonald 1 73
(G A Swinbank) *hld up in tch: drvn and outpcd over 3f out: rallied 2f out: drvn to ld wl ins fnl f: styd on wl* **14/1**

0- **2** *nk* **Warling (IRE)**[156] 7183 3-8-6 0 ...... RoystonFfrench 8 72
(J Noseda) *s.i.s: sn hld up in tch: drvn and green over 4f out: no imp tl gd hdwy to ld over 1f out: hrd rdn and hdd wl ins fnl f: r.o* **11/4**[2]

240- **3** *4* **Gritstone**[184] 6478 3-8-11 72 ...... PaulHanagan 5 69+
(R A Fahey) *broke wl and early ldr: chsd ldr: led briefly wl over 1f out: one pce u.p fnl f* **15/8**[1]

642- **4** *8* **Danceintothelight**[164] 6982 3-8-11 72 ...... PhillipMakin 6 51
(K A Ryan) *racd keenly: sn led and set decent gallop: hdd wl over 1f out: sn wknd* **10/3**[3]

5 *shd* **Hail Tiberius** 3-8-11 0 ...... GrahamGibbons 9 51
(T D Walford) *t.k.h: trckd ldrs: effrt and rdn over 2f out: wknd over 1f out* **20/1**

6 *1 1/4* **Trojan Gift (USA)** 3-8-11 0 ...... TomEaves 2 48+
(Julie Camacho) *hld up: outpcd 1/2-way: shkn up and styd on steadily fnl 2f: nvr nr ldrs* **16/1**

7 *31* **Benamy Boy** 4-10-0 0 ...... FrannyNorton 4 —
(N Bycroft) *bhd: struggling 1/2-way: nvr on terms: eased whn no ch fnl 2f* **40/1**

03- **8** *3/4* **Prime Circle**[276] 3590 4-9-9 0 ...... DeanHeslop(5) 7 —
(A D Brown) *s.i.s: bhd: struggling fr 1/2-way: eased whn no ch last 2f* **20/1**

0- **9** *1 1/4* **Broctune Papa Gio**[171] 6821 3-8-11 0 ...... TonyCulhane 3 —
(K G Reveley) *hld up towards rr: rn green and outpcd 1/2-way: no ch after: eased last 2f* **66/1**

10 *6* **Fantastic Times** 4-9-7 0 ......(v[1]) JohnCavanagh(7) 10 —
(M Brittain) *trckd ldrs: rdn over 4f out: wknd over 3f out: eased whn no ch* **40/1**

2m 2.93s (9.93) **Going Correction** +1.025s/f (Soft)
WFA 3 from 4yo 17lb **10** Ran SP% **113.0**
Speed ratings (Par 103): **96,95,92,85,84 83,56,55,54,49**
toteswingers:1&2:£6.10, 1&3:£10.70, 2&3:£9.40 CSF £48.45 TOTE £17.40: £3.60, £1.80, £1.30; EX 58.00 Place 6 £1,112.10, Place 5 £650.34.
Owner The Three Bears **Bred** F K M Ent, W R N & R Wilne **Trained** Melsonby, N Yorks

FOCUS
The leaders went too quick in the conditions and the winning time was 0.20sec slower than the first division. The level is a bit fluid but the first two are unexposed.
T/Jkpt: Not won. T/Plt: £768.60 to a £1 stake. Pool: £70,551.07. 67.00 winning tickets. T/Qpdt: £108.10 to a £1 stake. Pool: £3,376.47. 23.10 winning tickets. JR

WARWICK (L-H)
Monday, April 5
1120 Meeting Abandoned - Waterlogged

YARMOUTH (L-H)
Monday, April 5

OFFICIAL GOING: Soft
Wind: Fresh across Weather: Overcast

1127 BEST ODDS GUARANTEED @TOTESPORT.COM MAIDEN STKS — 1m 3y
1:45 (1:47) (Class 5) 3-Y-O+ **£3,154** (£944; £472; £236; £117) **Stalls** High

Form RPR

1 **Admission** 3-8-12 0 ...... HayleyTurner 3 83+
(M L W Bell) *s.i.s: hdwy 1/2-way: chsd ldr over 1f out: shkn up to ld ins fnl f: r.o* **10/1**[3]

2- **2** *2 1/4* **Clockmaker (IRE)**[352] 1355 4-9-13 0 ...... WilliamBuick 9 82
(J H M Gosden) *sn led: rdn and hdd ins fnl f: styd on same pce* **4/5**[1]

- **3** *2 1/4* **Heaven Forbid** 3-8-7 0 ...... LiamKeniry 1 68+
(J R Fanshawe) *s.i.s: hld up: swtchd rt over 2f out: hdwy over 1f out: hung lft and r.o ins fnl f: nt trble ldrs* **33/1**

0- **4** *3/4* **Desert Liaison**[240] 4797 3-8-7 0 ...... ShaneKelly 11 66+
(J Noseda) *hld up in tch: rdn over 1f out: styd on same pce ins fnl f* **10/1**[3]

5- **5** *1 1/2* **Khajaaly (IRE)**[179] 6607 3-8-12 0 ...... RichardHills 12 68
(E A L Dunlop) *s.i.s: racd keenly and hdwy over 5f out: rdn over 1f out: nt clr run: edgd lft and wknd ins fnl f* **12/1**

50- **6** *1 3/4* **Silent Majority (IRE)**[143] 7376 3-8-12 0 ...... KierenFallon 8 64+
(E A L Dunlop) *hld up: pushed along over 3f out: nvr trbld ldrs* **25/1**

00 **7** *1/2* **Eywa**[16] 950 3-8-7 0 ...... EddieAhern 2 57+
(W Jarvis) *mid-div: rdn over 1f out: wknd fnl f* **80/1**

0- **8** *1 3/4* **Fasette**[303] 2699 3-8-7 0 ...... JimmyQuinn 15 53
(M H Tompkins) *s.i.s: hld up: rdn over 2f out: n.d* **100/1**

5 **9** *1/2* **Yashrid (USA)**[16] 950 3-8-12 0 ...... NeilCallan 13 59+
(M A Jarvis) *chsd ldr over 3f: remained handy: wnt 2nd again over 2f out: rdn and edgd lft over 1f out: wkng whn hmpd ins fnl f* **12/1**

00- **10** *4 1/2* **Tumbled Again**[155] 7199 3-8-12 0 ...... JamieMackay 6 47
(M E Rimmer) *prom: rdn 1/2-way: wknd over 2f out* **200/1**

00-0 **11** *1 1/2* **Denton Ryal**[23] 889 3-8-7 60 ...... NickyMackay 7 39
(M E Rimmer) *prom: chsd ldr over 4f out tl rdn over 2f out: wknd wl over 1f out* **150/1**

12 *15* **Silver Astralis** 3-8-7 0 ...... SaleemGolam 4 4
(Mrs C A Dunnett) *s.s: outpcd* **200/1**

13 *1* **Ancient Greece** 3-8-12 0 ...... FrankieDettori 14 7
(M Johnston) *chsd ldrs: rdn over 3f out: wknd over 2f out: eased fnl f* **11/2**[2]

14 *1 1/2* **Chez Vrony** 4-9-13 0 ...... JackMitchell 10 7
(D Morris) *s.i.s: a in rr: lost tch over 2f out* **200/1**

1m 45.18s (4.58) **Going Correction** +0.60s/f (Yiel)
WFA 3 from 4yo 15lb **14** Ran SP% **115.7**
Speed ratings (Par 103): **101,98,96,95,94 92,92,90,89,85 83,68,67,66**
toteswingers:1&2:£4.40, 1&3:£33.90, 2&3:£10.80 CSF £17.51 TOTE £12.70: £3.30, £1.10, £6.80; EX 29.50 Trifecta £149.30 Part won. Pool: £201.76 - 0.50 winning units..
Owner Highclere Thoroughbred Racing (Eve) **Bred** Highclere Stud **Trained** Newmarket, Suffolk

FOCUS
The ground was officially described as soft and there was a fairly stiff cross-wind, so a test of stamina ensued, especially for these inexperienced types. The form looks sound and pretty decent, with the runner-up the best guide.

1128 FREE RACING POST FORM @TOTESPORT.COM H'CAP — 1m 3y
2:15 (2:16) (Class 5) (0-75,73) 4-Y-O+ **£2,719** (£809; £404; £202) **Stalls** High

Form RPR

2611 **1** **Dajen**[18] 925 4-8-10 72 ...... LauraPike(7) 6 85+
(D M Simcock) *hld up in tch: led over 1f out: shkn up and styd on wl* **13/2**

/16- **2** *1 1/2* **Brushing**[200] 6015 4-8-10 70 ...... AshleyMorgan(5) 11 80+
(M H Tompkins) *hld up: hdwy over 2f out: rdn over 1f out: edgd lft: r.o* **10/1**

000- **3** *3* **Mishrif (USA)**[164] 6996 4-9-3 72 ......(v) KierenFallon 10 75
(J R Jenkins) *prom: hung lft and led over 2f out: rdn and hdd over 1f out: no ex fnl f* **9/2**[2]

00-3 **4** *5* **Saturn Girl (IRE)**[8] 1034 4-9-4 73 ...... JamieSpencer 5 64
(M L W Bell) *s.i.s: sn pushed along in rr: hdwy u.p 2f out: sn hung lft: wknd ins fnl f* **3/1**[1]

533- **5** *1 1/4* **Land Hawk (IRE)**[188] 6365 4-8-6 66 ...... SimonPearce(5) 1 54
(J Pearce) *dwlt: hdwy over 5f out: led 3f out: hdd over 2f out: rdn and wknd over 1f out* **17/2**

065- **6** *4 1/2* **Green Agenda**[160] 7101 4-9-1 70 ...... FrankieDettori 7 48
(M Johnston) *hld up: rdn over 3f out: wknd over 1f out* **6/1**[3]

5000 **7** *17* **All About You (IRE)**[12] 975 4-8-11 66 ...... SaleemGolam 9 5
(P Howling) *prom: rdn over 3f out: wknd over 2f out: t.o* **33/1**

200- **8** *2* **King Columbo (IRE)**[156] 7189 5-8-9 71 ...... AdamBeschizza(7) 3 5
(Miss J Feilden) *chsd ldrs: rdn over 2f out: sn wknd: t.o* **9/1**

000- **9** *2 3/4* **Cordell (IRE)**[167] 6924 5-8-12 67 ...... EddieAhern 8 —
(P D Evans) *led 5f: wknd over 2f out: t.o* **16/1**

5-10 **10** *2 3/4* **Zerzura**[54] 487 4-9-4 73 ...... TomQueally 12 —
(H R A Cecil) *plld hrd: trckd ldrs: rdn over 2f out: sn wknd: t.o* **11/1**

1m 44.65s (4.05) **Going Correction** +0.60s/f (Yiel) **10** Ran SP% **117.6**
Speed ratings (Par 103): **103,101,98,93,92 87,70,68,66,63**
toteswingers:1&2:£5.30, 1&3:£4.40, 2&3:£6.10 CSF £70.24 CT £332.03 TOTE £8.80: £3.10, £2.80, £2.40; EX 129.60 TRIFECTA Not won..
Owner Tick Tock Partnership **Bred** Miss D Fleming **Trained** Newmarket, Suffolk

FOCUS
A few of these are open to improvement this term but they couldn't live with the winner. The form looks fair for the grade with the first two on the up.
Saturn Girl(IRE) Official explanation: jockey said filly never travelled
All About You(IRE) Official explanation: trainer said gelding was unsuited by the soft ground

1129 TOTESPORT 0800 221 221 H'CAP (DIV I) — 7f 3y
2:50 (2:50) (Class 6) (0-65,65) 4-Y-O+ **£1,748** (£520; £260; £129) **Stalls** High

Form RPR

1263 **1** **By Command**[14] 965 5-9-3 **64** ......(tp) JamieSpencer 2 74
(K A Ryan) *mid-div: sn pushed along: hdwy over 2f out: rdn over 1f out: styd on u.p to ld wl ins fnl f* **15/8**[1]

1-0 **2** *1/2* **Woolfall Sovereign (IRE)**[93] 12 4-9-4 **65** ...... SebSanders 1 74
(G G Margarson) *a.p: rdn to ld 1f out: hdd wl ins fnl f* **9/1**

6-33 **3** *2 1/4* **Tevez**[17] 937 5-8-8 **62** ...... MJMurphy(7) 5 65
(D Donovan) *mid-div: hdwy 1/2-way: rdn over 1f out: styd on same pce ins fnl f* **7/1**[3]

060- **4** *2 1/2* **Moon Lightning (IRE)**[152] 7246 4-9-0 **61** ...... JimmyQuinn 9 57
(M H Tompkins) *hld up: rdn over 2f out: styd on ins fnl f: nvr nrr* **9/1**

5 **5** *1/2* **Sir Mozart (IRE)**[80] 194 7-8-13 **60** ...... TomQueally 6 55
(B J Curley) *stdd s: hld up: hdwy 2f out: no imp fnl f* **10/1**

-504 **6** *2* **See Elsie Play**[11] 978 4-8-6 **58** ...... RossAtkinson(5) 11 48
(Miss Z C Davison) *s.s: sn pushed along in rr: rdn 1/2-way: n.d* **20/1**

2530 **7** *nk* **Hard Ball**[27] 838 4-8-1 **51** ......(v) Louis-PhilippeBeuzelin(3) 4 40
(M Quinn) *led 1f: chsd ldr tl rdn over 2f out: wknd fnl f* **7/1**[3]

0505 **8** *nk* **Whotsit (IRE)**[53] 498 4-8-1 **55** ......(b) LauraPike(7) 3 43
(Miss Amy Weaver) *plld hrd: led 6f out: rdn and hdd 1f out: wknd ins fnl f* **5/1**[2]

000- **9** *1 1/2* **Bahama Baileys**[160] 7094 5-8-4 **51** oh6 ...... HayleyTurner 8 35
(C A Dwyer) *chsd ldrs: rdn over 2f out: wknd over 1f out* **33/1**

1435 **10** *26* **Clever Omneya (USA)**[12] 976 4-8-4 **51** oh1 ...... NickyMackay 10 —
(J R Jenkins) *s.i.s: rdn 1/2-way: wknd over 2f out: t.o* **10/1**

0-00 **11** *15* **Billy Simmonds**[19] 912 5-8-1 **55** oh6 ow4 ...... AdamBeschizza(7) 7 —
(Miss J Feilden) *mid-div: rdn 4f out: sn lost pl: t.o* **66/1**

1m 31.55s (4.95) **Going Correction** +0.60s/f (Yiel) **11** Ran SP% **123.8**
Speed ratings (Par 101): **95,94,91,89,88 86,85,85,83,54 36**
toteswingers:1&2:£5.30, 1&3:£4.40, 2&3:£6.10 CSF £20.96 CT £105.54 TOTE £2.30: £1.10, £3.80, £3.60; EX 19.70 Trifecta £70.80 Pool: £135.95 - 1.42 winning units..
Owner Hambleton Racing Ltd XV **Bred** Nawara Stud Co Ltd **Trained** Hambleton, N Yorks

FOCUS
The feature of this particularly modest 7f handicap was the frantic pace and that helped to set things up for the hold-up horses. The form looks pretty solid.

1130 TOTESPORT 0800 221 221 H'CAP (DIV II) — 7f 3y
3:25 (3:25) (Class 6) (0-65,65) 4-Y-O+ **£1,748** (£520; £260; £129) **Stalls** High

Form RPR

0-00 **1** **Aviso (GER)**[17] 941 6-9-4 **65** ...... TomQueally 7 73
(B J Curley) *s.s: hld up: hdwy 2f out: rdn and hung rt fr over 1f out: styd on to ld wl ins fnl f* **6/1**[3]

030- **2** *1 1/4* **Eye For The Girls**[172] 6787 4-8-7 **54** ...... KierenFallon 1 59
(M R Channon) *chsd ldrs: rdn to ld and hung rt fr over 2f out: hdd wl ins fnl f* **3/1**[2]

0-65 **3** *2 1/4* **Shadow Bay (IRE)**[39] 695 4-8-3 **55** ...... RossAtkinson(5) 10 54
(Miss Z C Davison) *hld up: rdn 1/2-way: hdwy u.p over 1f out: nt rch ldrs* **12/1**

14- **4** *1/2* **Big Boom**[243] 4668 5-9-1 **62** ...... PatCosgrave 6 59
(M Quinn) *chsd ldrs: rdn over 2f out: sn outpcd: styd on fnl f* **3/1**[2]

0060 **5** *2* **Djalalabad (FR)**[32] 791 6-8-5 **52** oh6 ow1 ...... SaleemGolam 9 44
(J Pearce) *hld up in tch: plld hrd: rdn over 1f out: wknd ins fnl f* **28/1**

0110 **6** *3* **Pipers Piping (IRE)**[20] 892 4-8-11 **61** ...... MichaelStainton(3) 5 45
(P Howling) *led: rdn and hdd over 2f out: hmpd over 1f out: sn wknd* **11/1**

0451 **7** *3 1/4* **Jonnie Skull (IRE)**[19] 907 4-8-10 **57** ......(vt) FrankieDettori 11 32
(P S McEntee) *prom: rdn 1/2-way: wknd 2f out* **11/4**[1]

06-0 **8** *11* **Hilltop Legacy**[53] 499 7-8-4 **51** oh1 ...... NickyMackay 2 —
(J R Jenkins) *prom: rdn and hung lft 4f out: wknd 3f out: eased fnl f* **16/1**

1m 32.4s (5.80) **Going Correction** +0.60s/f (Yiel) **8** Ran SP% **116.3**
Speed ratings (Par 101): **90,88,86,85,83 79,76,63**
toteswingers:1&2:£6.20, 1&3:£13.80, 2&3:£14.60 CSF £24.83 CT £213.24 TOTE £9.70: £3.40, £2.40, £4.90; EX 37.70 TRIFECTA Not won..
Owner Curley Leisure **Bred** Gestut Schlenderhan **Trained** Newmarket, Suffolk

FOCUS
Just as uncompetitive as the first division, but another close finish in which the front pair finished nicely clear. this looks the weaker of the two divisions with the winner rated to last year's form.

Jonnie Skull(IRE) Official explanation: trainer said gelding was unsuited by the soft ground

1131 MORE LIVE FOOTBALL BETTING @TOTESPORT.COM H'CAP 5f 43y
4:00 (4:00) (Class 6) (0-60,60) 4-Y-O+ £2,072 (£616; £308; £153) Stalls High

Form RPR

6-03 **1** **Wreningham**[38] 723 5-8-7 52 WilliamCarson(3) 5 64
(S C Williams) *led centre gp: racd keenly: overall ldr 1/2-way: edgd rt ins fnl f: rdn out* 5/1[3]

1104 **2** ½ **Mr Funshine**[5] 1068 5-8-10 52 NeilCallan 3 62
(D Shaw) *racd centre: prom: racd keenly: swtchd rt wl over 1f out: chsd wnr fnl f: r.o* 9/1

0606 **3** 3¾ **Diddums**[39] 693 4-9-4 60 (b) KierenFallon 4 57
(P S McEntee) *racd centre: hld up: pushed along 1/2-way: hdwy u.p over 1f out: styd on same pce fnl f* 10/1

6144 **4** 1 **Diane's Choice**[14] 961 7-9-0 56 (b) FrankieDettori 9 49+
(Miss Gay Kelleway) *s.i.s: racd stands' side: hld up: jnd centre gp 1/2-way: hdwy sn after: rdn over 1f out: edgd rt: styd on same pce* 4/1[2]

442- **5** ¾ **Rough Rock (IRE)**[160] 7100 5-8-6 53 TobyAtkinson(5) 8 43+
(C A Dwyer) *overall ldr stands' side tl jnd centre gp 1/2-way: sn rdn: no ex fnl f* 8/1

5401 **6** ½ **Bookiesindex Boy**[18] 913 6-9-2 58 (b) StephenCraine 2 46
(J R Jenkins) *racd centre: trckd ldrs: racd keenly: shkn up fnl f: fnd nil* 3/1[1]

003- **7** 2 **Russian Rocket (IRE)**[160] 7100 8-9-4 60 TomMcLaughlin 1 41
(Mrs C A Dunnett) *racd centre: s.i.s: hdwy 1/2-way: rdn over 1f out: wknd ins fnl f* 17/2

0024 **8** shd **Taboor (IRE)**[38] 726 12-8-4 46 oh1 HayleyTurner 6 27
(R M H Cowell) *trckd ldrs in centre: rdn whn hmpd wl over 1f out: sn wknd* 25/1

0625 **9** 7 **Spoof Master (IRE)**[33] 773 6-9-1 57 (t) LiamKeniry 7 13
(C R Dore) *racd stands' side: prom: jnd centre 1/2-way: sn rdn and wknd* 9/1

000- **10** 7 **Mugeba**[160] 7100 9-8-4 46 oh1 NickyMackay 11 —
(C A Dwyer) *racd stands' side: chsd ldrs tl rdn and wknd 2f out* 50/1

0065 **11** nk **Wavertree Princess (IRE)**[9] 1014 5-7-11 46 oh1 (p) RosieJessop(7) 10 —
(A J Lidderdale) *racd stands' side: prom to 1/2-way* 14/1

66.70 secs (4.00) **Going Correction** +0.60s/f (Yiel) 11 Ran SP% 124.9
Speed ratings (Par 101): **88,87,81,79,78 77,74,74,63,51 51**
toteswingers:1&2:£9.30, 1&3:£9.40, 2&3:£11.80 CSF £52.98 CT £448.87 TOTE £6.20: £1.80, £3.90, £3.40; EX 54.10 Trifecta £164.40 Part won. Pool: £222.29 - 0.20 winning units..
Owner Mervyn Ayers **Bred** Executive Bloodlines Ltd **Trained** Newmarket, Suffolk

FOCUS
A modest sprint handicap and pretty straightforward form with the first two close to their all-weather marks.

1132 TOTESPORTGAMES.COM MEDIAN AUCTION MAIDEN STKS 1m 2f 21y
4:35 (4:37) (Class 6) 3-5-Y-O £2,331 (£693; £346; £173) Stalls Low

Form RPR

26-3 **1** **Aspro Mavro (IRE)**[9] 1011 4-9-11 78 WilliamBuick 2 72
(J H M Gosden) *chsd ldrs: rdn to ld over 1f out: hdd 1f out: rallied to ld ins fnl f: edgd rt: r.o* 6/5[1]

44- **2** 1½ **Zenarinda**[160] 7099 3-8-1 0 JimmyQuinn 8 60
(M H Tompkins) *prom: rdn to ld 1f out: hdd and unable qck ins fnl f* 8/1

033 **3** ½ **Corres (IRE)**[9] 1010 3-8-6 72 EddieAhern 1 64+
(D R C Elsworth) *led: hdd wl over 3f out: hmpd and outpcd sn after: rallied over 1f out: styd on* 5/1[3]

4 shd **Marrimeclaire (IRE)** 3-8-1 0 JamieMackay 5 59+
(B J McMath) *s.i.s: hld up: shkn up and hung rt over 2f out: swtchd lft and r.o ins fnl f: nrst fin* 150/1

6- **5** nk **Widezain (IRE)**[199] 6066 3-8-6 0 KierenFallon 7 63
(M R Channon) *chsd ldr: chal 4f out: sn rdn: hmpd over 2f out: sn outpcd: rallied fnl f* 3/1[2]

0340 **6** ½ **Sternian**[24] 872 3-8-1 48 NickyMackay 6 57
(M E Rimmer) *chsd ldrs: led wl over 3f out: rdn and hdd over 1f out: no ex ins fnl f* 100/1

35- **7** 1 **Inpursuitoffreedom**[170] 6858 3-8-1 0 PaulQuinn 3 55
(P J McBride) *hld up in tch: plld hrd: rdn over 1f out: no ex ins fnl f* 14/1

8 12 **Two Certainties** 3-8-6 0 SaleemGolam 4 36
(S C Williams) *unruly in stalls: hld up: rdn over 3f out: stmbld and wknd over 2f out* 66/1

9 12 **Zakeeta (IRE)** 3-7-12 0 Louis-PhilippeBeuzelin(3) 9 7
(J Noseda) *s.s: a in rr: lost tch fnl 4f* 14/1

2m 17.4s (6.90) **Going Correction** +0.60s/f (Yiel)
WFA 3 from 4yo 19lb 9 Ran SP% 114.7
Speed ratings (Par 101): **96,94,94,94,94 93,92,83,73**
toteswingers:1&2:£2.60, 1&3:£2.20, 2&3:£5.20 CSF £12.07 TOTE £2.00: £1.10, £2.80, £1.40; EX 9.80 Trifecta £27.70 Pool: £335.55 - 8.94 winning units..
Owner M Kerr-Dineen,Mrs C Waters & Ptnrs **Bred** T Kimura **Trained** Newmarket, Suffolk

FOCUS
A low-grade maiden in which only around two lengths separated six horses behind the winner, and it might be unwise to get too carried away with this form, with the pace muddling.

1133 TOTESPORTCASINO.COM H'CAP 1m 2f 21y
5:10 (5:10) (Class 5) (0-75,75) 4-Y-O+ £2,719 (£809; £404; £202) Stalls Low

Form RPR

0504 **1** **Raptor (GER)**[18] 921 7-9-4 75 NickyMackay 2 86
(M E Rimmer) *chsd ldrs: led 3f out: rdn over 1f out: styd on* 9/4[1]

303- **2** ¾ **Daredevil Dan**[172] 6789 4-8-3 65 AshleyMorgan(5) 6 74
(M H Tompkins) *hld up: hdwy to chse wnr over 2f out: rdn over 1f out: edgd lft: styd on* 8/1

0-00 **3** 6 **It's Dubai Dolly**[54] 480 4-9-4 75 TomQueally 1 72
(A J Lidderdale) *hld up: hdwy 7f out: rdn over 2f out: wknd fnl f* 10/1

06-0 **4** 4 **Opera Prince**[9] 1011 5-9-4 75 SebSanders 5 64
(Lady Herries) *hld up: hdwy over 3f out: sn rdn: wknd over 1f out* 4/1[3]

56-0 **5** 10 **December**[11] 983 4-8-1 61 oh4 Louis-PhilippeBeuzelin(3) 3 30
(Mrs C A Dunnett) *led: rdn and hdd 3f out: sn wknd* 14/1

5-24 **6** 2 **Capeability (IRE)**[56] 468 4-8-12 69 KierenFallon 4 34
(M R Channon) *prom: lost pl over 5f out: rdn over 3f out: sn wknd* 5/2[2]

3633 **7** 33 **Mutajaaser (USA)**[42] 665 5-8-5 62 (p) JimmyQuinn 7 —
(K A Morgan) *chsd ldr after 1f tl rdn over 3f out: sn wknd: eased fnl 2f: t.o* 15/2

2m 14.87s (4.37) **Going Correction** +0.60s/f (Yiel) 7 Ran SP% 118.0
Speed ratings (Par 103): **106,105,100,97,89 87,57**
toteswingers:1&2:£4.80, 1&3:£7.00, 2&3:£9.80 CSF £21.85 TOTE £2.60: £1.10, £7.10; EX 21.30.
Owner Winning Circle Partnership **Bred** Gestut Rheinberg Ag **Trained** Newmarket, Suffolk
■ Stewards' Enquiry : Ashley Morgan caution: used whip with excessive frequency.

FOCUS
This concerned only the front pair from 2f out. The winner has raced off higher marks on the all-weather and could defy a penalty.
Capeability(IRE) Official explanation: jockey said gelding lost its action

1134 TOTESPORTBINGO.COM H'CAP 1m 3f 101y
5:45 (5:46) (Class 6) (0-65,63) 4-Y-O+ £2,072 (£616; £308; £153) Stalls Low

Form RPR

00-0 **1** **Khun John (IRE)**[25] 868 7-9-1 60 WilliamBuick 2 68
(W J Musson) *a.p: led 2f out: sn rdn: styd on wl* 4/1[1]

000- **2** 1¼ **Group Leader (IRE)**[19] 7246 4-9-4 63 FrankieDettori 3 69
(J R Jenkins) *prom: lost pl over 4f out: rallied over 2f out: sn ev ch: unable qck towards fin* 4/1[1]

5-50 **3** nk **Private Equity (IRE)**[33] 777 4-8-8 53 HayleyTurner 7 59
(W Jarvis) *hld up: hdwy over 3f out: nt clr run over 2f out: r.o* 7/1

0-40 **4** ½ **Motarjm (USA)**[17] 777 6-9-3 62 (t) SaleemGolam 12 67
(J Pearce) *hld up: hdwy over 2f out: rdn over 1f out: r.o* 16/1

005- **5** 3 **Sanctum**[239] 4828 4-8-7 55 Louis-PhilippeBeuzelin(3) 1 55
(Dr J D Scargill) *led: hdd 10f out: chsd ldrs: rdn over 1f out: no ex* 16/1

3-46 **6** 10 **Sure Fire (GER)**[47] 585 5-9-1 60 TomQueally 8 43
(B J Curley) *hld up: rdn 1/2-way: n.d* 11/2[2]

32/0 **7** shd **Sensible**[10] 989 5-8-12 57 JackMitchell 11 40
(H J Collingridge) *hld up: hdwy over 4f out: wknd over 2f out* 20/1

0454 **8** 1¼ **Strong Storm (USA)**[12] 969 4-8-11 59 (p) RussKennemore(3) 9 40
(Andrew Reid) *prom: led 3f out: hdd 2f out: sn wknd* 9/1

2144 **9** 2 **Resplendent Ace (IRE)**[10] 989 6-9-0 59 KierenFallon 10 36
(P Howling) *hdwy to ld 10f out: rdn and hdd 3f out: wknd over 1f out* 10/1

0-46 **10** 1¾ **Bromhead (USA)**[17] 314 4-8-5 50 JimmyQuinn 4 24
(K A Morgan) *prom: rdn over 2f out: sn wknd* 6/1[3]

0-60 **11** 1 **Sparkaway**[9] 1012 4-8-11 56 JamieMackay 6 29
(W J Musson) *s.s: hld up: a in rr: eased over 1f out: stirrup leather broke* 12/1

2m 38.35s (9.65) **Going Correction** +0.60s/f (Yiel) 11 Ran SP% 125.5
Speed ratings (Par 101): **88,87,86,86,84 77,76,76,74,73 72**
toteswingers:1&2:£6.10, 1&3:£10.70, 2&3:£9.40 CSF £20.69 CT £114.48 TOTE £5.30: £1.90, £2.20, £3.20; EX 32.50 TRIFECTA Not won. Place 6 £86.85, Place 5 £57.88..
Owner The Strawberries To A Donkey Partnership **Bred** Sti Engineering Srl **Trained** Newmarket, Suffolk

FOCUS
A weak handicap best rated around the first two.
Strong Storm(USA) Official explanation: jockey said gelding hung badly right
Sparkaway Official explanation: jockey said leather broke
T/Plt: £122.90 to a £1 stake. Pool: £59,692.50. 354.56 winning tickets. T/Qpdt: £30.60 to a £1 stake. Pool: £3,293.34. 79.60 winning tickets. CR

FFOS LAS (L-H)
Tuesday, April 6

OFFICIAL GOING: Good to soft (7.5) changing to good to soft (soft in places) after race 5 (4:35)
Wind: strong across Weather: overcast with light showers, persistent rain from the 3rd race

1136 TRUSTMARK DESIGN AND PRINT MAIDEN STKS 5f
2:20 (2:22) (Class 5) 2-Y-O £2,729 (£806; £403) Stalls High

Form RPR

1 **Bathwick Bear (IRE)** 2-9-3 0 JimmyFortune 7 82
(P D Evans) *sn chsng ldrs: rdn to ld over 2f out: r.o wl fnl f: rdn out* 9/1[3]

2 **2** 1 **Scarlet Rocks (IRE)**[8] 1043 2-8-12 0 DavidProbert 6 73
(P D Evans) *prom: rdn and ev ch fr over 2f out: kpt on but no ex ins fnl f* 14/1

0 **3** 4 **Ivan's A Star (IRE)**[10] 1017 2-9-3 0 LukeMorris 8 64
(J S Moore) *s.i.s: towards rr: hdwy wl over 2f out: edgd lft u.p fr over 1f out: r.o towards fin* 22/1

4 nk **Dingle View (IRE)** 2-8-12 0 CathyGannon 1 58+
(P D Evans) *mid-div: rdn and no imp 3f out: r.o fnl f* 33/1

2 **5** 1¼ **Lady Brookie**[10] 1009 2-8-9 0 JackDean(3) 3 53
(W G M Turner) *chsd ldrs: rdn wl over 2f out: one pce after: lost 2 pls ins fnl f* 4/5[1]

6 1¼ **Babich Bay (IRE)** 2-9-3 0 GrahamGibbons 2 54
(R Curtis) *chsd ldrs: rdn wl over 2f out: wknd over 1f out* 14/1

7 nk **Rosina Grey** 2-8-10 0 ow1 JamesMillman(3) 4 49
(B R Millman) *mid-div tl squeezed out 3f out: nvr bk on terms* 33/1

8 4½ **Belle Bayardo (IRE)** 2-9-3 0 LiamJones 10 37
(R A Harris) *s.i.s: a towards rr* 40/1

2 **9** 1 **Beach Patrol (IRE)**[10] 1017 2-9-3 0 KierenFallon 9 33
(M R Channon) *led tl over 2f out: sn wknd* 3/1[2]

10 9 **Snapshott (IRE)** 2-9-3 0 JoeFanning 5 —
(R A Harris) *mid-div: effrt 3f out: wknd 2f out* 100/1

59.22 secs (1.82) **Going Correction** +0.275s/f (Good) 10 Ran SP% 117.5
Speed ratings (Par 92): **96,94,88,87,85 83,83,75,74,59**
toteswingers:1&2:£7.30, 1&3:£16.30, 2&3:£12.20 CSF £115.19 TOTE £13.70: £2.70, £2.80, £4.90; EX 60.90 TRIFECTA Not won..
Owner W Clifford **Bred** D Veitch & R O'Callaghan **Trained** Pandy, Monmouths
■ Stewards' Enquiry : Graham Gibbons three-day ban: careless riding (Apr 23-25)

FOCUS
Three of the four with previous experience had finished runner-up on their debuts, so this looked a fair maiden for the time of year. It was a relatively uncompetitive betting heat, although two newcomers were quite well supported. The placed horses are rated as improvers and this could be a fair contest.

NOTEBOOK
Bathwick Bear(IRE) ◆ is a 21,000euros half-brother to a couple of juvenile winners out of a 5f 2-y-o winner. He clearly knew his job first time and, after switching to the rail early on, he came through to lead 2f out and stuck on resolutely to hold off his more experienced stable companion. He should improve for the run and could well follow up under a penalty, but will be aimed at the Lily Agnes Stakes at Chester in May. (op 7-1)
Scarlet Rocks(IRE) had made a promising debut on Polytrack and ran another solid race, only losing out to her stable companion who came up the rail, but drawing clear of the rest. She should be able to win a race before long. (op 16-1)
Ivan's A Star(IRE) built on his debut despite again missing the break and should be capable of better if getting away on terms. (op 28-1)
Dingle View(IRE), a 20,000euros sister to the useful Vhujon, was unfancied in the betting but ran on late from the rear despite being hampered and only narrowly failed to complete a clean sweep for her stable. She will know a lot more next time.

Lady Brookie finished a head second in the Brocklesby on her debut and was sent off at odds-on to go one better. She broke well and had every chance towards the centre of the track, but weakened over a furlong out. This was disappointing and casts doubt over the quality of the Doncaster race. (op Evens)
Babich Bay(IRE) is bred to be more effective over further in time but showed ability despite displaying signs of inexperience. He could be the sort to make his mark in nurseries over further later in the season. His rider picked up a three-day ban for careless riding. Official explanation: jockey said colt hung right (op 9-1)
Beach Patrol(IRE), runner-up on his debut on Polytrack when making the pace, he tried to do the same again on this switch to turf but was in trouble before being headed at around the 2f pole. (op 7-2 tchd 11-4)

1137 RWYTH CABS MAIDEN STKS 6f
2:55 (2:56) (Class 5) 3-Y-0+ **£2,590** (£770; £385; £192) **Stalls** High

Form RPR
0- **1** **Fayre Bella**[157] [7182] 3-8-8 0 TadhgO'Shea 7 71
(J Gallagher) *slowly away: towards rr: hdwy whn nt clr run 3f out: stdy prog fr over 2f out: r.o wl fnl f: led fnl 50yds: rdn out* **100/1**
05- **2** *nk* **Superior Edge**[221] [5380] 3-8-8 0 DavidProbert 4 70
(B Palling) *prom: persistent chal u.p fr 2f out: led fnl 100yds: no ex whn hdd fnl 50yds* **14/1**
252- **3** *1¼* **Bonheurs Art (IRE)**[169] [6905] 3-8-9 72 ow1 MichaelHills 6 67
(B W Hills) *led: rdn and hrd pressed fr over 2f out: no ex whn hdd fnl 100yds* **4/9**[1]
0- **4** *1¾* **Easy Terms**[321] [2175] 3-8-5 0 AndreaAtzeni(3) 8 60
(B R Millman) *trckd ldrs: rdn over 2f out: kpt on same pce* **16/1**
4 **5** *3* **Mirza**[20] [911] 3-8-13 0 MartinDwyer 5 59+
(Rae Guest) *trckd ldrs: struggling to hold pl whn squeezed out over 2f out: nvr bk on terms* **6/1**[3]
6 *5* **British Sea Power (IRE)** 3-8-6 0 JohnFahy(7) 1 40
(J R Gask) *mid-div tl outpcd after 2f* **33/1**
7 *12* **Hedonist (IRE)** 3-8-13 0 LukeMorris 2 1
(J R Gask) *t.k.h early in mid-div: outpcd after 2f: hung lft: sn bhd* **33/1**
8 *6* **Music Festival (USA)** 3-8-13 0 FrankieDettori 3 —
(M Johnston) *trckd ldrs: rdn 3f out: wknd 2f out* **5/1**[2]

1m 10.93s (1.23) **Going Correction** +0.275s/f (Good) 8 Ran SP% **119.6**
Speed ratings (Par 103): **102,101,99,97,93 86,70,62**
toteswingers:1&2:£32.20, 1&3:£12.30, 2&3:£3.30 CSF £1128.61 TOTE £118.20: £15.80, £3.60, £1.10; EX 864.70 TRIFECTA Not won..
Owner R Biggs **Bred** Mrs R J Gallagher **Trained** Chastleton, Oxon
■ Stewards' Enquiry : Tadhg O'Shea one-day ban: careless riding (Apr 20)

FOCUS
Very limited experience amongst the runners in this 3-y-o sprint maiden and they went 14-1 bar three. The winner is rated close to his juvenile form.

1138 WEATHERBYS BANK H'CAP 1m 4f (R)
3:30 (3:30) (Class 4) (0-85,81) 3-Y-0 **£4,533** (£1,348; £674; £336) **Stalls** High

Form RPR
211 **1** **Into Wain (USA)**[41] [680] 3-8-13 73 MartinDwyer 4 91+
(D M Simcock) *hld up bhd ldng trio: trckd ldr 3f out: pushed into ld over 1f out: drifted rt: rdn and styd on wl* **7/1**[3]
0-12 **2** *1* **Chink Of Light**[20] [904] 3-9-6 80 JimmyFortune 5 96
(A M Balding) *trckd ldr tl dropped to 4th over 5f out: rdn and stdy prog fr 3f out: chsd wnr ent fnl f: hld fnl 75yds* **11/4**[2]
31-2 **3** *3½* **Exemplary**[41] [680] 3-9-6 80 FrankieDettori 6 90
(M Johnston) *led: qcknd pce 4f out: rdn and hdd over 1f out: sn veered rt: no ex* **11/4**[2]
145- **4** *15* **Leitzu (IRE)**[188] [6391] 3-8-9 69 AlanMunro 1 55
(M R Channon) *hld up in last pair: effrt over 3f out: wnt 4th but no ch w ldin g trio over 2f out: sn wknd* **7/1**[3]
200- **5** *5* **The Starboard Bow**[173] [6805] 3-9-7 81 DavidProbert 2 59
(S Kirk) *hld up in last pair: effrt over 3f out: wknd over 2f out* **20/1**
-111 **6** *19* **Keenes Royale**[55] [482] 3-9-5 79 JimCrowley 3 27
(R M Beckett) *trckd ldr: rdn over 3f out: wknd 2f out: eased* **5/2**[1]

2m 39.65s (2.85) **Going Correction** +0.275s/f (Good) 6 Ran SP% **111.7**
Speed ratings (Par 100): **101,100,98,88,84 72**
toteswingers:1&2:£2.80, 1&3:£2.80, 2&3:£2.90 CSF £26.16 TOTE £6.50: £3.80, £2.50; EX 22.50.
Owner Ahmad Al Shaikh **Bred** Don M Robinson **Trained** Newmarket, Suffolk

FOCUS
A small field but an interesting handicap with a number having shown form on the all-weather already. That quartet dominated the betting market. The third sets the level.

1139 WEATHERBYS BETTRENDS.CO.UK H'CAP 2m (R)
4:05 (4:05) (Class 2) (0-105,100) 4-Y-0+ **£10,092** (£3,020; £1,510; £755; £376) **Stalls** Low

Form RPR
310- **1** **Yes Mr President (IRE)**[171] [6851] 5-9-11 100 JoeFanning 5 108+
(M Johnston) *disp tl clr ldr after 2f tl over 8f out: regained ld 2f out: forged clr fnl f: easily* **3/1**[3]
04-1 **2** *5* **Gala Evening**[10] [1020] 8-9-7 96 RichardHughes 4 96
(J A B Old) *hld up bhd ldrs: wnt 4th 4f out: sn rdn: styd on: wnt 2nd ent fnl f: no ch w easy wnr* **9/4**[2]
006- **3** *1* **Hindu Kush (IRE)**[170] [6875] 5-8-3 81 oh3 AndreaAtzeni(3) 6 80
(Ian Williams) *plld hrd: hld up: plld way through to join ldr 6f out: led over 4f out: rdn and hdd 2f out: styd on same pce* **11/8**[1]
4 *2½* **Manjam (IRE)**[60] 6-8-1 81 oh4 (t) SimonPearce(5) 1 77
(A P Boxhall) *disp ld for 2f: trckd ldrs: outpcd 5f out: styd on fr over 2f out but nt a threat to ldrs* **33/1**
1-1 **5** *13* **Sheshali (IRE)**[51] [352] 6-8-13 88 JimmyFortune 2 68
(Evan Williams) *disp ld for 2f: trckd wnr: led over 8f out tl over 4f out: sn rdn: fdd fr 2f out* **7/1**

3m 40.54s (10.54) **Going Correction** +0.275s/f (Good) 5 Ran SP% **113.3**
Speed ratings (Par 109): **84,81,81,79,73**
CSF £10.48 TOTE £4.90: £3.20, £1.10; EX 8.20.
Owner T J Monaghan **Bred** T J Monaghan **Trained** Middleham Moor, N Yorks

FOCUS
A decent handicap although not that competitive an event for the prizemoney. The form is muddling but the winner looks progressive.

NOTEBOOK
Yes Mr President(IRE) ◆ was the second market drifter to oblige in successive races. He made the early running, but Fanning was content to settle him in when he was taken on for the lead before halfway. He cruised up to challenge in the straight and, when asked, put distance between himself and the rest with minimal effort. Already rated 100, he will go up again for this and Listed races probably beckon now. However, he will still be of interest if taking his chance in the big staying handicaps later in the year, such as the Ebor. (op 15-8)
Gala Evening returned to form when scoring on Polytrack last time on his first start since June. He chased the winner home without threatening and looks much more effective around Kempton. (op 11-4)
Hindu Kush(IRE), making his debut for the yard and having been gelded since his last start, was a well-backed favourite. However, he spoilt his chance by being far too keen, eventually pulling his way up to join the leader leaving the back straight. It was no surprise that he failed to last home, and it is to be hoped the run will take the freshness out of him. Official explanation: jockey said gelding ran too freely (op 9-4)
Manjam(IRE) won twice on soft ground over hurdles in the autumn, but had not run on the Flat since leaving France. He was the complete outsider and looked beaten turning in before staying on quite well in the last 2f. Official explanation: jockey said gelding lost its action on top bend
Sheshali(IRE) stays well over hurdles and had won his last two on the Flat including on Polytrack. He was ridden positively, but was in trouble early in the straight. His best form has been on a sound surface and this softer ground clearly did not suit. (op 15-2 tchd 13-2)

1140 BURNS PET NUTRITION H'CAP 5f
4:35 (4:36) (Class 4) (0-80,80) 3-Y-0 **£4,533** (£1,348; £674; £336) **Stalls** High

Form RPR
6531 **1** **Silver Linnet (IRE)**[11] [988] 3-8-9 68 (b) AlanMunro 7 72
(M G Quinlan) *broke wl: mde all: r.o wl whn pressed ent fnl f: rdn out* **5/2**[1]
046- **2** *1½* **Leleyf (IRE)**[172] [6827] 3-9-1 74 KierenFallon 1 73
(M R Channon) *chsd wnr: rdn and ev ch ent fnl f: no ex fnl 100yds* **5/1**[2]
2216 **3** *½* **Exceed Power**[29] [831] 3-7-13 61 oh3 AndreaAtzeni(3) 3 58
(D M Simcock) *towards rr: swtchd out for effrt 2f out: r.o fnl f: nt quite rch ldng pair* **15/2**
4314 **4** *2* **Mrs Boss**[43] [662] 3-8-10 72 JamesMillman(3) 5 62
(B R Millman) *chsd ldrs: rdn 3f out: kpt on same pce fnl 2f* **11/2**[3]
304- **5** *¾* **Avonvalley**[227] [5241] 3-9-3 76 FergusSweeney 4 63
(M S Saunders) *s.i.s: towards rr: sme late prog: nvr a factor* **20/1**
4250 **6** *1¾* **Italian Tom (IRE)**[34] [766] 3-9-5 78 LukeMorris 6 59
(R A Harris) *chsd ldrs: rdn 3f out: fdd jst over 1f out* **16/1**
100- **7** *11* **Avongate**[160] [7108] 3-9-0 73 LiamJones 8 14
(R A Harris) *sn struggling in rr* **14/1**
200- **8** *2¾* **The Hermitage (IRE)**[185] [6486] 3-9-7 80 FrankieDettori 2 12
(M Johnston) *chsd ldrs: rdn 3f out: wknd over 1f out* **5/2**[1]

58.54 secs (1.14) **Going Correction** +0.275s/f (Good) 8 Ran SP% **118.3**
Speed ratings (Par 100): **101,98,97,94,93 90,73,68**
toteswingers:1&2:£3.80, 1&3:£3.40, 2&3:£4.80 CSF £16.05 CT £83.97 TOTE £2.60: £1.10, £1.70, £3.20; EX 21.70 Trifecta £57.50 Pool: £297.74 - 3.83 winning units..
Owner Donal Flynn **Bred** L Mulryan **Trained** Newmarket, Suffolk

FOCUS
A fair sprint handicap in which three-quarters of the field were fillies and they filled the first five places. The third sets the level, despite racing from out of the weights.
Avonvalley Official explanation: jockey said filly was slowly away

1141 KEVIN THOMAS PHARMACY FILLIES' H'CAP 1m (R)
5:05 (5:05) (Class 5) (0-70,70) 4-Y-0+ **£2,914** (£867; £433; £216) **Stalls** Low

Form RPR
3425 **1** **Miss Bootylishes**[9] [1034] 5-8-13 70 AmyBaker(5) 2 78
(A B Haynes) *cl up: rdn to ld over 2f out: hld on gamely towards fin: drvn out* **6/1**[3]
10-3 **2** *hd* **Markhesa**[8] [1047] 4-8-8 60 NickyMackay 4 68
(J R Boyle) *trckd ldrs: rdn to chse wnr ent fnl f: kpt on: clsng at fin* **11/4**[1]
544- **3** *4* **Light Dubai (IRE)**[259] [4166] 4-9-0 66 TonyCulhane 1 64
(M R Channon) *hld up: hdwy to chse ldrs and effrt 2f out: kpt on same pce fnl f* **13/2**
2-06 **4** *½* **Dr Wintringham (IRE)**[27] [853] 4-8-8 60 RichardHughes 6 57+
(Karen George) *hld up: hdwy over 3f out to chse ldrs: rdn 2f out: styd on same pce* **7/2**[2]
050- **5** *¾* **Second To Nun (IRE)**[128] [7587] 4-8-4 56 oh5 DavidProbert 9 51
(Jean-Rene Auvray) *trckd ldr: rdn and ev ch fr 2f out tl ent fnl f: kpt on same pce* **11/1**
0-20 **6** *3¼* **Jewelled**[42] [673] 4-8-13 70 KierenFox(5) 7 58
(J W Hills) *led: rdn and hdd over 2f out: wknd ent fnl f* **12/1**
00-0 **7** *nk* **Shared Moment (IRE)**[29] [827] 4-8-6 58 (p) TadhgO'Shea 5 45
(J Gallagher) *hld up: rdn over 2f out: unable to get on terms* **9/1**
041- **8** *½* **Aine's Delight (IRE)**[169] [6910] 4-8-6 63 SimonPearce(5) 3 49
(Andrew Turnell) *t.k.h early: cl up: rdn 3f out: wknd over 1f out* **13/2**
2/0- **9** *32* **Navene (IRE)**[322] [2166] 6-8-13 65 (t) FergusSweeney 8 —
(M R Bosley) *t.k.h: hld up last: wknd 2f out* **25/1**

1m 45.08s (4.58) **Going Correction** +0.575s/f (Yiel) 9 Ran SP% **119.7**
Speed ratings (Par 100): **100,99,95,95,94 91,91,90,58**
toteswingers:1&2:£4.90, 1&3:£7.30, 2&3:£3.80 CSF £23.79 CT £114.03 TOTE £3.10: £1.10, £2.90, £3.20; EX 21.60 Trifecta £171.80 Pool: £241.58 - 1.04 winning units. Place 6 £142.94, Place 5 £22.97.
Owner Mrs H Adams & Miss C Berry **Bred** T P Young And D Hanson **Trained** Limpley Stoke, Bath

FOCUS
Rain which started before the previous race eased the ground and it was changed to Good to Soft, Soft in places. A modest fillies' handicap with question marks over several and the form is best rated through the runner-up to her latest Lingfield form.
T/Plt: £177.80 to a £1 stake. Pool: £60,368.86. 247.74 winning tickets. T/Qpdt: £8.80 to a £1 stake. Pool: £5,774.45. 483.58 winning tickets. TM

1065 SOUTHWELL (L-H)
Tuesday, April 6

OFFICIAL GOING: Standard
Wind: fresh across Weather: Cloudy but dry

1142 PLAY POKER AT LADBROKES.COM H'CAP (DIV I) 7f (F)
2:10 (2:10) (Class 6) (0-55,55) 4-Y-0+ **£1,706** (£503; £252) **Stalls** Low

Form RPR
4043 **1** **Tri Chara (IRE)**[28] [838] 6-8-10 53 ow2 (p) RussKennemore(3) 10 64
(R Hollinshead) *sn led: rdn along 2f out: hdd over 1f out: drvn and rallied ins fnl f to ld last 50yds* **9/1**
3403 **2** *1* **Megalo Maniac**[20] [912] 7-8-8 48 (v) PaulHanagan 11 56
(R A Fahey) *in tch: gd hdwy 2f out: rdn to ld over 1f out: drvn ins fnl f: hdd and no ex last 50yds* **6/1**[3]
3236 **3** *2* **Louisiade (IRE)**[13] [976] 9-8-8 48 (p) FrannyNorton 6 51
(R C Guest) *hld up: hdwy 2f out: rdn to chse ldrs over 1f out: kpt on ins fnl f: nrst fin* **8/1**
4000 **4** *1* **Vogarth**[28] [838] 6-8-4 51 ow1 DavidKenny(7) 9 51
(M C Chapman) *prom: effrt over 2f out: rdn wl over 1f out: kpt on same pce appr fnl f* **50/1**

The Form Book, Raceform Ltd, Compton, RG20 6NL

0563 **5** *nk* **Luisa Tetrazzini (IRE)**[33] 793 4-8-10 **55**..............(b) MarkCoumbe(5) 12 54
(John A Harris) *prom: rdn along wl over 1f out: drvn and wknd appr fnl f* **20/1**

4103 **6** *1 1/2* **Positivity**[19] 918 4-9-1 **55**..............(p) TomEaves 7 50
(B Smart) *s.i.s and bhd: pushed along 1/2-way: rdn and hdwy 2f out: kpt on u.p ins fnl f: nt rch ldrs* **10/1**

50-6 **7** *hd* **Reprieved**[28] 839 5-8-1 **46** oh1.............. IanBrennan(5) 4 41
(J J Quinn) *s.i.s and bhd tl sme late hdwy* **4/1**[2]

3340 **8** *3/4* **Amber Moon**[19] 918 5-8-5 **50** ow3..............(b) AnnStokell(5) 8 43
(Miss A Stokell) *nvr bttr than midfield* **20/1**

622 **9** *7* **Mackintosh (IRE)**[47] 603 4-8-12 **52**..............(b) JamieSpencer 5 26
(Patrick Morris) *trckd ldrs: effrt over 2f out: sn rdn and btn* **5/2**[1]

25-6 **10** *4* **Mr Chocolate Drop (IRE)**[18] 939 6-9-0 **54**..............(b) AdamKirby 3 17
(Miss M E Rowland) *a in rr* **10/1**

0006 **11** *2 1/2* **Redwater River**[33] 795 6-8-6 **46** oh1..............(b) AndrewElliott 1 2
(Mrs R A Carr) *a in rr* **40/1**

1m 29.66s (-0.64) **Going Correction** -0.075s/f (Stan) 11 Ran SP% **116.1**
Speed ratings (Par 101): **100,98,96,95,95 93,93,92,84,79 76**
toteswingers:1&2:£6.70, 1&3:£12.60, 2&3:£9.90 CSF £58.67 CT £461.69 TOTE £10.50: £2.90, £1.70, £2.70; EX 51.10.
Owner The Tri Chara Partnership **Bred** High Bramley Grange Stud **Trained** Upper Longdon, Staffs

FOCUS
A moderate handicap run in a time 0.17 seconds quicker than the second division and sound form for the grade, rated around the placed horses.
Mackintosh(IRE) Official explanation: jockey said gelding hung left throughout
Mr Chocolate Drop(IRE) Official explanation: jockey said gelding never travelled

1143 BEST ODDS GUARANTEED AT LADBROKES.COM MAIDEN STKS 1m (F)
2:40 (2:40) (Class 5) 3-Y-O £2,729 (£806; £403) **Stalls** Low

Form RPR

0- **1** **Staff Sergeant**[139] 7429 3-9-3 0.............. RoystonFfrench 5 76+
(M Johnston) *led after 1f: pushed along and hdd 3f out: sn rdn and rallied to ld 1 1/2f out: clr ent fnl f and styd on strly* **7/1**[3]

2 *3* **Widow Bird (IRE)** 3-8-12 0.............. SteveDrowne 6 64+
(H Morrison) *s.i.s and in rr: hdwy 1/2-way: wd st and sn chsng ldrs: rdn along wl over 1f out: kpt on wl ent fnl f: nt rch wnr* **16/1**

5 **3** *3* **Mark To Market (IRE)**[19] 915 3-8-12 0.............. SophieDoyle(5) 7 62
(J A Osborne) *prom: wd st: rdn 2f out: drvn over 1f out: kpt on same pce* **20/1**

63-2 **4** *shd* **Welsh Artist**[18] 933 3-9-3 72.............. NeilCallan 2 62
(Mrs A J Perrett) *led 1f: cl up on inner tl led again 3f out: rdn over 2f out: hdd 1 1/2f out: sn drvn and wknd* **15/8**[2]

05- **5** *8* **Halyard (IRE)**[203] 5966 3-9-3 0.............. AdamKirby 1 44
(W R Swinburn) *trckd ldrs: hdwy 3f out: rdn wl over 2f out and sn btn* **11/10**[1]

0- **6** *3* **Countrycraft**[276] 3606 3-9-3 0.............. TonyHamilton 9 37
(Miss S E Hall) *towards rr: sme hdwy 3f out: rdn and edgd rt wl over 1f out: nvr nr ldrs* **80/1**

7 *6* **Gyrate** 3-9-3 0.............. FrederikTylicki 3 23
(J A Glover) *s.i.s: a bhd* **25/1**

060- **8** *1* **Bravo Blue (IRE)**[165] 6991 3-8-12 25.............. ChrisCatlin 8 16
(T H Caldwell) *cl up: rdn along over 3f out and sn wknd* **150/1**

0 **9** *3 1/4* **Three White Socks (IRE)**[10] 1010 3-9-3 0.............. TomEaves 4 13
(B Ellison) *sn rdn along in rr: bhd fr 1/2-way* **66/1**

1m 42.57s (-1.13) **Going Correction** -0.075s/f (Stan) 9 Ran SP% **112.8**
Speed ratings (Par 98): **102,99,96,95,87 84,78,77,74**
toteswingers:1&2:£4.20, 1&3:£7.50, 2&3:£8.30 CSF £91.66 TOTE £5.80: £1.70, £2.20, £3.20; EX 38.30.
Owner Sheikh Hamdan Bin Mohammed Al Maktoum **Bred** Darley **Trained** Middleham Moor, N Yorks

FOCUS
An ordinary maiden but about average for the grade and thefirst two can do better.
Halyard(IRE) Official explanation: trainer's rep said, regarding running, that the colt failed to act on the Fibresand surface.

1144 SOUTHWELL-RACECOURSE.CO.UK (S) STKS 1m (F)
3:10 (3:11) (Class 6) 3-Y-O £1,774 (£523; £262) **Stalls** Low

Form RPR

1433 **1** **Tiger Hawk (USA)**[20] 909 3-9-2 65..............(b) JamieSpencer 1 67+
(P D Evans) *mde all: jnd 2f out and sn rdn: drvn over 1f out: kpt on u.p ins fnl f* **1/4**[1]

-035 **2** *4 1/2* **Lord's Seat**[49] 574 3-8-12 49 ow1.............. DanielTudhope 5 50
(A Berry) *trckd wnr to 1/2-way: effrt 3f out: rdn to chal 2f out and ev ch tl drvn: edgd lft and wknd ent fnl f* **9/1**[3]

60-0 **3** *4* **Otterton**[11] 997 3-8-6 47.............. ChrisCatlin 3 34
(R Hollinshead) *trckd ldng pair: hdwy to chse wnr 1/2-way: rdn along 3f out and sn one pce* **16/1**

0-50 **4** *7* **Whipper's Delight (IRE)**[34] 775 3-8-1 49.............. IanBrennan(5) 4 18
(D Donovan) *sn pushed along in rr: rdn over 3f out and sn outpcd* **7/1**[2]

1m 43.64s (-0.06) **Going Correction** -0.075s/f (Stan) 4 Ran SP% **108.4**
Speed ratings (Par 96): **97,92,88,81**
CSF £3.18 TOTE £1.40; EX 2.20.The winner was bought in for 4,000gns.
Owner Freddie Ingram **Bred** Sun Valley Farm **Trained** Pandy, Monmouths

FOCUS
A poor 3-y-o seller with the winner having to work hard to beat inferior rivals.

1145 PLAY ROULETTE AT LADBROKES.COM H'CAP 1m 4f (F)
3:45 (3:46) (Class 6) (0-60,60) 3-Y-O £2,047 (£604; £302) **Stalls** Low

Form RPR

00-2 **1** **Ibn Hiyyan (USA)**[6] 1067 3-9-4 **60**.............. RoystonFfrench 1 73+
(M Johnston) *mde all: rdn clr 2f out: kpt on wl* **5/6**[1]

005 **2** *4 1/2* **Rosewood Lad**[18] 928 3-8-8 **50**.............. LiamKeniry 3 53
(J S Moore) *hld up in rr: stdy hdwy 4f out: rdn to chse ldrs 3f out: kpt on u.p to take 2nd ins fnl f: no ch w wnr* **16/1**

005- **3** *3 1/4* **Blinka Me**[136] 7474 3-9-1 **57**..............(b) JimmyQuinn 7 54
(M H Tompkins) *trckd ldrs: hdwy 4f out: chsd wnr 3f out: rdn over 2f out: drvn wl over 1f out and kpt on same pce* **8/1**[3]

-363 **4** *13* **Red Valerian Two (IRE)**[58] 452 3-8-11 **53**.............. MickyFenton 2 30
(P T Midgley) *bhd: sme hdwy over 4f out: rdn along 3f out: plugged on fnl 2f: nvr a factor* **20/1**

000- **5** *1 1/2* **Bollin Andrew**[204] 5951 3-8-8 **50**.............. DavidAllan 6 24
(T D Easterby) *chsd ldrs: rdn along after 4f: drvn and outpcd over 4f out: wd st and n.d* **3/1**[2]

0-00 **6** *2 3/4* **Micky's Bird**[11] 998 3-8-4 **46** oh1.............. FrannyNorton 5 16
(R C Guest) *sn pushed along in rr: bhd fr 1/2-way* **100/1**

000 **7** *8* **Swindlers Lass (IRE)**[26] 864 3-8-10 **52**.............. NeilChalmers 8 9
(Mark Gillard) *prom: rdn along 5f out: sn wknd and bhd fnl 3f* **100/1**

6625 **8** *14* **Second Brook (IRE)**[8] 1054 3-9-1 **57**..............(v[1]) RobertWinston 9 —
(R Hollinshead) *chsd ldrs and rn wd bnd after 2f: sn cl up: rdn along over 3f out and sn wknd* **9/1**

600- **9** *10* **Hotgrove Boy**[175] 6763 3-8-10 **52**.............. AndrewMullen 4 —
(A G Foster) *a in rr: bhd fnl 4f* **20/1**

2m 41.37s (0.37) **Going Correction** -0.075s/f (Stan) 9 Ran SP% **118.1**
Speed ratings (Par 96): **95,92,89,81,80 78,73,63,57**
toteswingers:1&2:£5.70, 1&3:£3.90, 2&3:£9.20 CSF £17.31 CT £72.45 TOTE £2.00: £1.10, £4.00, £1.90; EX 18.90.
Owner Sheikh Hamdan Bin Mohammed Al Maktoum **Bred** Two Sisters' Farm Inc **Trained** Middleham Moor, N Yorks

FOCUS
An uncompetitive 3-y-o handicap and they were soon strung out, with a few of these looking extremely limited. The runner-up is rated close to his maiden form.
Second Brook(IRE) Official explanation: trainer said gelding had a breathing problem

1146 MEMBERSHIP OF SOUTHWELL GOLF CLUB (S) STKS 5f (F)
4:20 (4:20) (Class 6) 3-Y-O+ £2,047 (£604; £302) **Stalls** High

Form RPR

1363 **1** **Colorus (IRE)**[28] 832 7-9-5 73..............(p) PaulPickard(5) 1 64
(W J H Ratcliffe) *cl up: led 2f out: rdn ent fnl f and kpt on wl* **8/13**[1]

405 **2** *2* **Best One**[6] 1068 6-9-10 54..............(b) ChrisCatlin 4 57
(R A Harris) *led: rdn along and hdd 2f out: drvn ent fnl f and kpt on same pce* **13/2**[3]

4525 **3** *nk* **Tamarind Hill (IRE)**[20] 906 3-8-3 59..............(b) DeclanCannon(5) 6 46
(A J McCabe) *chsd ldrs: rdn 2f out: drvn and edgd lft ent fnl f: kpt on towards fin* **10/3**[2]

0-06 **4** *1/2* **Monsieur Harvey**[33] 789 4-9-5 43.............. TomEaves 3 49
(B Smart) *chsd ldng pair: rdn along wl over 1f out: sn drvn and one pce* **18/1**

0600 **5** *3 3/4* **Remark (IRE)**[11] 995 6-9-0 42..............(t) JamesSullivan(5) 5 36
(M W Easterby) *cl up: rdn along after 1 1/2f: drvn and wkng whn hung rt 2f out* **33/1**

00-0 **6** *1 3/4* **Mr Rooney (IRE)**[6] 1072 7-9-0 39..............(b[1]) MarkCoumbe(5) 2 29
(A Berry) *a in rr* **50/1**

60.51 secs (0.81) **Going Correction** +0.075s/f (Slow)
WFA 3 from 4yo+ 11lb 6 Ran SP% **108.5**
Speed ratings (Par 101): **98,94,94,93,87 84**
toteswingers:1&2:£1.90, 1&3:£1.60, 2&3:£1.50 CSF £4.82 TOTE £1.80: £1.50, £1.10; EX 3.70.The winner was bought in for 5,500gns.
Owner J Sheard & W J S Ratcliffe **Bred** M Ervine **Trained** Newmarket, Suffolk

FOCUS
An ordinary seller run in a time 1.10 seconds slower than the 68-rated Grudge recorded in the following handicap. The winner wwas below his best and the runner-up sets the level.

1147 BET IN PLAY AT LADBROKES.COM H'CAP 5f (F)
4:50 (4:50) (Class 5) (0-75,74) 3-Y-O+ £2,590 (£770; £385; £192) **Stalls** High

Form RPR

4214 **1** **Grudge**[19] 913 5-9-8 **68**..............(be[1]) RobertWinston 10 78
(C R Dore) *cl up: led 1/2-way: rdn over 1f out: drvn ins fnl f: jst hld on* **9/1**

111- **2** *nse* **Diamond Blade**[119] 7681 4-9-3 **63**..............(p) DuranFentiman 7 73+
(T D Easterby) *dwlt: sn chsng ldrs: swtchd lft and effrt wl over 1f out: rdn to chal ent fnl f: sn drvn and ev ch: jst hld* **8/1**

5212 **3** *2 1/4* **Punching**[19] 914 6-10-0 **74**.............. LiamKeniry 6 76
(C R Dore) *chsd ldrs: rdn and sltly outpcd wl over 1f out: styd on ins fnl f* **7/2**[2]

16-3 **4** *1/2* **Lethal**[20] 899 7-9-0 **63**.............. RussKennemore(3) 9 63
(Andrew Reid) *led to 1/2-way: cl up tl rdn wl over 1f out and grad wknd appr fnl f* **6/1**

0662 **5** *nk* **Calmdownmate (IRE)**[6] 1072 5-9-0 **60** oh1.............. PJMcDonald 5 59
(Mrs R A Carr) *prom: rdn 2f out and ev ch tl drvn and wknd ent fnl f* **10/3**[1]

4630 **6** *2 3/4* **Kyle (IRE)**[55] 486 6-8-11 **62**.............. DeclanCannon(5) 2 51
(C R Dore) *towards rr: hdwy wl over 1f out: sn rdn and nvr nr ldrs* **18/1**

0605 **7** *1 1/4* **Carmenero (GER)**[37] 747 7-9-7 **67**.............. FrankieMcDonald 1 51
(C R Dore) *a towards rr* **40/1**

0462 **8** *2 3/4* **First Order**[21] 896 9-8-11 **62**..............(v) AnnStokell(5) 11 37
(Miss A Stokell) *chsd ldrs: rdn along over 2f out: sn wknd* **25/1**

5320 **9** *1/2* **Guto**[47] 601 7-9-2 **65**.............. KellyHarrison(3) 8 38
(W J H Ratcliffe) *chsd ldrs: rdn along 1/2-way: drvn and wknd wl over 1f out* **12/1**

1-21 **10** *4 1/2* **Kummel Excess (IRE)**[26] 856 3-8-12 **74**.............. MatthewDavies(5) 4 26
(George Baker) *s.i.s: a bhd* **11/2**[3]

59.21 secs (-0.49) **Going Correction** +0.075s/f (Slow)
WFA 3 from 4yo+ 11lb 10 Ran SP% **115.3**
Speed ratings (Par 103): **106,105,102,101,101 96,94,90,89,82**
toteswingers:1&2:£6.70, 1&3:£4.60, 2&3:£5.50 CSF £78.02 CT £301.84 TOTE £13.10: £3.70, £3.20, £1.10; EX 50.90.
Owner Mrs Jennifer Marsh **Bred** D H Brailsford **Trained** Cowbit, Lincs

FOCUS
A modest but competitive handicap. The time was 1.10 seconds quicker than the 73-rated Colorus recorded in the earlier seller and the form is ordinary with the third to his best 5f form.
Lethal Official explanation: trainer said gelding was struck into
Kummel Excess(IRE) Official explanation: jockey said filly missed the break and never travelled

1148 PLAY POKER AT LADBROKES.COM H'CAP (DIV II) 7f (F)
5:20 (5:20) (Class 6) (0-55,55) 4-Y-O+ £1,706 (£503; £252) **Stalls** Low

Form RPR

0-22 **1** **Scruffy Skip (IRE)**[20] 912 5-8-11 **51**..............(p) TomMcLaughlin 10 64
(Mrs C A Dunnett) *chsd clr ldr: hdwy over 2f out: rdn to ld wl over 1f out: clr ent fnl f and r.o* **7/2**[2]

4000 **2** *4* **Bajan Pride**[19] 918 6-9-1 **55**.............. PaulHanagan 7 57
(R A Fahey) *chsd ldng pair: rdn over 2f out: drvn to chse wnr appr fnl f: no imp* **4/1**[3]

030- **3** *shd* **Kingaroo (IRE)**[160] 7127 4-8-10 **50**.............. RobertWinston 1 52
(G Woodward) *chsd ldrs: hdwy 2f out: sn rdn and kpt on ins fnl f* **20/1**

6630 **4** *1/2* **Owed**[20] 912 8-8-1 **48**..............(tp) MatthewLawson(7) 8 49
(R Bastiman) *t.k.h: hld up: hdwy over 2f out: sn rdn and kpt on appr fnl f: nrst fin* **40/1**

040- **5** *1/2* **Crocodile Bay (IRE)**[237] 4887 7-9-1 **55**..............(b) FrannyNorton 11 54
(R C Guest) *led and sn clr: rdn over 2f out: drvn and hdd over 1f out: wknd ins fnl f* **7/1**

325 **6** *1 1/2* **Granakey (IRE)**[53] 518 7-8-10 **50**.............. StevieDonohoe 3 45
(Ian Williams) *towards rr: hdwy 2f out: sn rdn and n.d* **11/4**[1]

00-5 **7** *hd* **Haroldini (IRE)**[21] 895 8-8-12 **52**................................(p) ChrisCatlin 5 47
(J Balding) *a towards rr* **14/1**
4200 **8** *8* **Misterisland (IRE)**[13] 976 5-8-8 **47** ow2............................ TomEaves 6 21
(M Mullineaux) *dwlt: a in rr* **22/1**
/214 **9** *hd* **King Canute (IRE)**[27] 845 6-9-1 **55**............................ MickyFenton 9 28
(N P Mulholland) *chsd ldrs: rdn along wl over 2f out: sn wknd* **13/2**
00-0 **10** *4* **Michael Collins (IRE)**[94] 19 4-8-8 **48**.................. FrankieMcDonald 4 10
(G J Smith) *chsd ldrs: rdn along wl over 2f out and sn wknd* **100/1**
3060 **11** *8* **Motu (IRE)**[12] 984 9-8-6 **46**......................................(v) RoystonFfrench 2 —
(I W McInnes) *sn rdn along: a bhd* **33/1**

1m 29.83s (-0.47) **Going Correction** -0.075s/f (Stan) **11** Ran SP% **116.9**
Speed ratings (Par 101): **99,94,94,93,93 91,91,82,81,77 68**
toteswingers:1&2:£4.90, 1&3:£7.30, 2&3:£3.80 CSF £16.76 CT £248.40 TOTE £5.00: £2.00, £2.60, £6.00; EX 21.40 Place 6 £93.84, Place 5 £31.24.
Owner C Dunnett, D Cooper, R Clarke & J Power **Bred** Darley **Trained** Hingham, Norfolk

FOCUS
They went a very strong pace, but few got involved and the time was 0.17 seconds slower than the first division. The winner could rate higher but there are doubts over some of the others.
Granakey(IRE) Official explanation: jockey said mare never travelled
T/Plt: £46.70 to a £1 stake. Pool: £54,196.16. 846.33 winning tickets. T/Qpdt: £3.70 to a £1 stake. Pool: £4,900.13. 970.37 winning tickets. JR

CATTERICK (L-H)

Wednesday, April 7

OFFICIAL GOING: Good to soft (soft in places; 6.4)
Wind: almost nil Weather: fine and very mild

1149 YORKSHIRE4X4.COM ADVENTURE ACTIVITIES CLAIMING STKS 7f

2:10 (2:10) (Class 6) 3-Y-O+ **£1,774** (£523; £262) **Stalls** Low

Form RPR
3122 **1** **Sir George (IRE)**[22] 893 5-9-5 65.............................. BarryMcHugh(3) 1 79
(Ollie Pears) *sn trcking ldrs: smooth hdwy over 2f out: led jst ins fnl f: pushed out* **9/2**[2]
30-5 **2** *1* **Kingswinford (IRE)**[6] 1076 4-9-12 77.......................... RobertWinston 8 80
(P D Evans) *mid-div: effrt over 2f out: swtchd rt over 1f out: styd on same pce ins fnl f* **7/4**[1]
0501 **3** *1* **Royal Dignitary (USA)**[22] 895 10-9-10 71................. AdrianNicholls 5 75
(D Nicholls) *sn chsng ldrs: kpt on same pce fnl f* **9/1**
600- **4** *4* **Nuit Sombre (IRE)**[114] 7754 10-9-9 62.................... SilvestreDeSousa 9 64
(G A Harker) *led tl hdd & wknd jst ins fnl f* **20/1**
-623 **5** *1 ½* **Island Chief**[3] 1098 4-9-10 69..(p) TonyHamilton 2 60+
(K A Ryan) *s.i.s and sn hmpd: in rr and pushed along: styd on fnl 2f: could nt rch ldrs* **5/1**[3]
4160 **6** *½* **Kipchak (IRE)**[9] 1044 5-9-12 75................................(p) PJMcDonald 10 61
(C R Dore) *charged gate and stall opened fractionally early: w ldrs: hung lft and wknd fnl f* **11/1**
001- **7** *4 ½* **Whispering Spirit (IRE)**[215] 5621 4-9-3 59..................(p) MickyFenton 6 40
(Mrs A Duffield) *chsd ldrs: hung rt and wknd over 1f out* **9/1**
0- **8** *2 ¼* **Its Beyond Me**[28] 2527 6-9-0 0................................ PatrickDonaghy(5) 4 36
(F P Murtagh) *sn outpcd and in rr: sme hdwy 2f out: nvr a factor* **200/1**
65-0 **9** *2* **Pacific Bay (IRE)**[36] 36 4-8-9 57................................ IanBrennan(5) 11 25
(D McCain Jnr) *mid-div: lost pl over 2f out* **40/1**
034- **10** *2* **Highly Acclaimed**[224] 5336 4-8-9 49.............................. AmyRyan(5) 3 20
(Mrs A Duffield) *mid-div: drvn over 2f out: sn lost pl* **80/1**
100- **11** *2 ¼* **Lytton**[200] 6103 5-9-6 60..(v) DavidAllan 7 20
(R Ford) *hood removed v late and s.s: sme hdwy on outer over 2f out: sn wknd* **28/1**
420- **12** *4 ½* **Soto**[172] 6847 7-9-10 59.. LeeVickers 12 12
(M W Easterby) *w ldrs: lost pl over 2f out* **40/1**

1m 30.72s (3.72) **Going Correction** +0.675s/f (Yiel) **12** Ran SP% **114.4**
Speed ratings (Par 101): **105,103,102,98,96 95,90,88,85,83 81,75**
toteswingers: 1&2 £3.30, 1&3 £7.60, 2&3 £5.90 CSF £11.61 TOTE £6.10: £1.60, £1.20, £3.00; EX 16.50.Sir George was subject to a friendly claim.
Owner Ian Bishop **Bred** Bernard Colclough **Trained** Norton, N Yorks

FOCUS
A reasonable claimer run at a good pace, and the time was 0.32 seconds quicker than the later handicap won by the 74-rated Academy Blues. They raced middle to far side in the straight. The form is rated around the placed horses.

1150 CATTERICKBRIDGE.CO.UK H'CAP 1m 5f 175y

2:40 (2:40) (Class 5) (0-75,73) 4-Y-O+ **£2,331** (£693; £346; £173) **Stalls** Low

Form RPR
0220 **1** **Red Wine**[11] 1012 11-8-10 **57**.. DavidAllan 11 66
(J A Glover) *hld up in rr: hdwy over 5f out: smooth hdwy to ld last 100yds: pushed out* **5/1**[1]
432- **2** *1 ¾* **Patavium (IRE)**[32] 6769 7-8-11 **58**............................ TonyHamilton 9 65
(E W Tuer) *trckd ldrs: drvn and hung rt over 4f out: slt ld jst ins fnl f: sn hdd and no ex* **9/1**
300- **3** *½* **Amir Pasha (UAE)**[24] 3617 5-8-4 **54** oh2.................(p) KellyHarrison(3) 3 61+
(Micky Hammond) *trckd ldrs: effrt over 2f out: nt clr run over 1f out: swtchd rt ins fnl f: kpt on wl* **12/1**
451- **4** *1 ¾* **Royal Trooper (IRE)**[155] 7222 4-9-7 **71**........................... LeeVickers 4 75
(J G Given) *led: hdd jst ins fnl f: no ex* **5/1**[1]
145- **5** *3 ¼* **Miss Keck**[215] 5625 6-9-6 **67**.. PJMcDonald 8 66
(G A Swinbank) *w ldr: upsides over 1f out: sn wknd* **7/1**[2]
344- **6** *½* **Classic Contours (USA)**[175] 5952 4-9-2 **71**.................. IanBrennan(5) 2 70
(J J Quinn) *trckd ldrs: t.k.h: fdd fnl f* **15/2**[3]
515- **7** *shd* **Bijou Dan**[148] 3728 9-9-2 **68**................................ PatrickDonaghy(5) 6 66
(G M Moore) *mid-div: kpt on one pce fnl 2f: nvr nr to chal* **14/1**
042- **8** *13* **Saloon (USA)**[120] 7675 6-9-5 **73**..............................(p) LewisWalsh(7) 10 53
(Jane Chapple-Hyam) *hld up in rr: bhd fnl 3f* **12/1**
5-46 **9** *½* **Bandanaman (IRE)**[7] 1071 4-9-1 **65**............................ RobertWinston 7 45
(G A Swinbank) *sn in rr: drvn 7f out: hung bdly lft and bit slipped rt through mouth: eased and lost pl 4f out* **5/1**[1]
400- **10** *10* **Call Of Duty (IRE)**[197] 6184 5-8-9 **56**...................... DuranFentiman 1 22
(Mrs Dianne Sayer) *mid-div: lost pl over 3f out: sn bhd* **20/1**
1330 **11** *29* **Moscow Oznick**[19] 941 5-9-6 **67**..............................(p) MickyFenton 5 —
(D Donovan) *sn trcking ldrs: lost pl 3f out: sn bhd and eased: t.o* **20/1**

3m 13.7s (10.10) **Going Correction** +0.675s/f (Yiel)
WFA 4 from 5yo+ 3lb **11** Ran SP% **115.8**
Speed ratings (Par 103): **98,97,96,95,93 93,93,86,85,80 63**
toteswingers: 1&2 £10.10, 1&3 £8.60, 2&3 £24.40 CSF £49.30 CT £504.86 TOTE £4.40: £2.20, £2.80, £3.60; EX 44.00.
Owner Paul J Dixon **Bred** Genesis Green Stud Ltd **Trained** Babworth, Notts
■ Stewards' Enquiry : Lewis Walsh one-day ban: used whip when out of contention (Apr 21)

FOCUS
A modest handicap run at a reasonable pace. They stayed towards the far side in the straight and the placed horses offer the best guide to the form.
Bandanaman(IRE) Official explanation: jockey said gelding hung badly left and the bit slipped through its mouth

1151 TED THOMPSON 81ST BIRTHDAY H'CAP 1m 3f 214y

3:10 (3:10) (Class 3) (0-95,95) 4-Y-O+ **£6,799** (£2,023; £1,011; £505) **Stalls** Low

Form RPR
124- **1** **Trip The Light**[138] 7465 5-8-10 **87**........................(v) MarzenaJeziorek(7) 3 94
(R A Fahey) *trckd ldrs: effrt on ins over 2f out: led jst ins fnl f: styd on* **12/1**
433- **2** *1 ½* **Ella**[151] 7293 6-9-6 **90**.. RobertWinston 6 95
(G A Swinbank) *trckd ldrs: chal over 5f out: drvn over 3f out: led over 2f out: edgd lft and hdd jst ins fnl f: no ex* **11/8**[1]
1-25 **3** *½* **Becausewecan (USA)**[11] 1015 4-9-10 **95**........................ GregFairley 4 99
(M Johnston) *w ldr: led after 3f: hdd over 2f out: rallied ins fnl f: styd on towards fin* **7/2**[2]
100- **4** *½* **Rangefinder**[151] 7293 6-9-4 **88**.................................. TonyHamilton 9 91+
(Jane Chapple-Hyam) *hld up in rr: hdwy over 4f out: kpt on fnl 2f: nvr really threatened* **11/1**
/60- **5** *2 ¼* **Folk Tune (IRE)**[32] 6095 7-8-5 **80**.............................. IanBrennan(5) 8 80
(J J Quinn) *hld up in rr: hdwy over 4f out: one pce fnl 2f* **33/1**
524- **6** *4 ½* **Bollin Felix**[299] 2895 6-9-3 **87**..(p) DavidAllan 5 80
(T D Easterby) *dwlt: in rr: drvn along 7f out: sme hdwy over 2f out: wknd over 1f out* **8/1**[3]
202- **7** *6* **Crackentorp**[184] 6546 5-9-9 **93**.............................. DuranFentiman 7 76
(T D Easterby) *dwlt: in rr: pushed along 6f out: sme hdwy on outside over 2f out: wknd over 1f out* **17/2**
043- **8** *10* **Just Lille (IRE)**[184] 6536 7-9-3 **90**.......................... BarryMcHugh(3) 2 57
(Mrs A Duffield) *led 3f: w ldr: lost pl over 5f out: bhd fnl 3f* **22/1**
010- **9** *10* **Kimberley Downs (USA)**[177] 6734 4-8-12 **86**.............. GaryBartley(3) 1 37
(N Wilson) *trckd ldrs: lost pl 3f out: sn bhd* **22/1**

2m 46.4s (7.50) **Going Correction** +0.675s/f (Yiel)
WFA 4 from 5yo+ 1lb **9** Ran SP% **113.6**
Speed ratings (Par 107): **102,101,100,100,98 95,91,85,78**
toteswingers: 1&2 £6.00, 1&3 £7.20, 2&3 £2.50 CSF £27.92 CT £72.75 TOTE £12.60: £3.80, £1.10, £1.20; EX 39.10.
Owner The Matthewman One Partnership **Bred** Darley **Trained** Musley Bank, N Yorks
■ Stewards' Enquiry : Marzena Jeziorek three-day ban: used whip with excessive frequency in incorrect position (Apr 21-23)

FOCUS
A good handicap, although the first three were always prominent. The main action took place far side in the straight and again the placed horses set the level.

NOTEBOOK
Trip The Light defied an absence of 138 days to win decisively for his in-form yard, proving himself on easy ground in the process. His first success came off a mark of just 46, but he continues to improve and looks set for another good year. (op 17-2)
Ella, off the track since finishing third in the November Handicap, looked straight enough for her return, and she travelled well on the speed for much of the way, but she simply found one too good. She looks capable of making further progress this year. (op 15-8 tchd 2-1 in a place)
Becausewecan(USA) had a race-fitness edge over the first two, but he had to work in order to be able to dominate. He kept on well when headed, though, and this was a decent effort in defeat off top weight. (op 4-1 tchd 9-2)
Rangefinder, down the field in the November Handicap on his debut for this yard, made a creditable reappearance, faring best of those waited with, and he's entitled to improve for the run. (op 14-1)
Folk Tune(IRE), a winner over fences last October, was well held on this rare Flat outing and he probably wants better ground, as well as possibly a stiffer test. (op 25-1)
Bollin Felix, back after 299 days off, ran as though he'll do better back over further with the benefit of this outing. (op 15-2)

1152 GODS SOLUTION H'CAP 7f

3:40 (3:41) (Class 5) (0-75,74) 4-Y-O+ **£2,590** (£770; £385; £192) **Stalls** Low

Form RPR
31 **1** **Academy Blues (USA)**[2] 1115 5-9-4 **74** 6ex................ AdrianNicholls 4 88
(D Nicholls) *trckd ldrs: effrt over 2f out: led 1f out: drvn out* **5/2**[1]
0213 **2** *2* **Hits Only Jude (IRE)**[27] 859 7-7-13 **62**......................... NeilFarley(7) 9 71+
(D Carroll) *racd wd: lost pl over 4f out: hdwy over 2f out: styd on to take 2nd last 50yds* **13/2**
3004 **3** *2 ¼* **Istiqdaam**[38] 749 5-9-4 **74**..(b) RobertWinston 10 77
(M W Easterby) *chsd ldrs: led over 2f out: hdd 1f out: kpt on same pce* **6/1**[3]
051- **4** *5* **Gap Princess (IRE)**[121] 7673 6-9-3 **73**.................... SilvestreDeSousa 7 63
(G A Harker) *trckd ldrs: effrt over 2f out: wknd over 1f out* **22/1**
-606 **5** *1 ¾* **Classic Descent**[21] 907 5-8-12 **68**..............................(t) AndrewElliott 3 53
(Mrs R A Carr) *s.s: detached in last: styd on fnl 2f: nvr nr ldrs* **40/1**
6114 **6** *4* **Whatyouwoodwishfor (USA)**[21] 907 4-8-9 **65**.......(b) TonyHamilton 2 39
(R A Fahey) *w ldr: led over 3f out: hdd over 2f out: wknd over 1f out* **10/1**
350- **7** *¾* **Chief Red Cloud (USA)**[188] 6437 4-8-5 **64**.............. BarryMcHugh(3) 8 36
(J R Weymes) *hld up in rr: drvn over 2f out: nvr a factor* **22/1**
122- **8** *3 ½* **Nufoudh (IRE)**[200] 6103 6-8-1 **60** oh2........................ KellyHarrison(3) 1 23
(Miss Tracy Waggott) *gave problems in stalls: led tl over 3f out: lost pl over 1f out* **10/1**
2645 **9** *2* **Peter's Gift (IRE)**[27] 867 4-8-2 **63**.................................. AmyRyan(5) 5 20
(K A Ryan) *chsd ldrs: outpcd over 3f out: sme hdwy 2f out: sn wknd* **8/1**
3- **10** *12* **Spavento (IRE)**[191] 6351 4-8-12 **68**.................................. DavidAllan 6 —
(E J Alston) *s.i.s: in rr: bhd whn eased ins fnl f* **9/2**[2]

1m 31.04s (4.04) **Going Correction** +0.675s/f (Yiel) **10** Ran SP% **114.8**
Speed ratings (Par 103): **103,100,98,92,90 85,85,81,78,65**
toteswingers: 1&2 £5.40, 1&3 £4.30, 2&3 £7.10 CSF £18.07 CT £89.82 TOTE £2.80: £1.10, £2.10, £2.50; EX 23.60.
Owner Bulldog Racing **Bred** Kinghaven Farms Ltd **Trained** Sessay, N Yorks

FOCUS
A modest handicap in which they went a strong pace, although the time was 0.32 seconds slower than the earlier claimer won by 65-rated Sir George. They raced towards the far side in the straight. The winner is one of the few solid performers in the race.

1153 TOYTOP MAIDEN STKS 5f 212y

4:10 (4:10) (Class 5) 3-Y-O+ **£2,331** (£693; £346; £173) **Stalls** Low

Form RPR
2- **1** **Johannesgray (IRE)**[200] 6096 3-8-13 0......................... AdrianNicholls 1 70+
(D Nicholls) *trckd ldrs: t.k.h: effrt over 2f out: narrow ld over 1f out: hld on towards fin* **5/4**[1]
60- **2** *nk* **Transmit (IRE)**[222] 5408 3-8-13 0.. DavidAllan 5 69
(T D Easterby) *t.k.h: w ldrs: upsides over 1f out: kpt on wl towards fin* **16/1**

3/0- **3** *nk* **Grand Stitch (USA)**[320] 2250 4-9-11 70 .... DanielTudhope 4 71
(D Carroll) *led tl over 3f out: upsides 1f out: no ex wl ins fnl f* **20/1**

225- **4** *½* **Ventura Cove (IRE)**[319] 2260 3-8-13 78 .... TonyHamilton 3 66
(R A Fahey) *w ldr: led over 3f out tl over 1f out: kpt on same pce fnl 150yds* **9/4**[2]

5 *2* **Barnstorm** 3-8-13 0 .... GregFairley 6 60+
(M Johnston) *dwlt: sn chsng ldrs: upsides over 1f out: fdd last 150yds* **7/2**[3]

6 **6** *15* **Plum Mac**[69] 327 6-9-6 0 .... PaulQuinn 2 10
(N Bycroft) *s.i.s: lost pl over 3f out: sn wl bhd* **100/1**

03- **7** *3* **Falcon's Tribute (IRE)**[189] 6390 8-9-1 0 .... TobyAtkinson(5) 7 —
(P Salmon) *chsd ldrs on outside: drvn over 3f out: lost pl over 2f out: sn bhd and eased ins fnl f* **33/1**

1m 19.25s (5.65) **Going Correction** +0.675s/f (Yiel)
WFA 3 from 4yo+ 12lb 7 Ran SP% **112.0**
Speed ratings (Par 103): **89,88,88,87,84 64,60**
toteswingers: 1&2 £4.10, 1&3 £4.20, 2&3 £8.20 CSF £21.50 TOTE £1.40: £1.02, £10.30; EX 25.90.
Owner Brian Morton **Bred** Trish Olsen **Trained** Sessay, N Yorks

FOCUS
A more interesting maiden that might appear the case at first glance, and the race ought to produce the odd nice winner. The main action took place up the centre of the track in the straight. The proximity of the placed horses rather limits the form.

1154 GORACING.CO.UK H'CAP 5f
4:40 (4:40) (Class 6) (0-65,65) 4-Y-0+ **£2,047** (£604; £302) **Stalls** Low

Form RPR

400- **1** **Dispol Grand (IRE)**[219] 5517 4-9-2 63 .... RobertWinston 2 74
(P T Midgley) *swvd rt s: chsd ldrs: styd on to ld 100yds out* **14/1**

0-05 **2** *1 ¼* **Fasliyanne (IRE)**[57] 472 4-8-5 52 .... (b) AndrewMullen 1 59
(K A Ryan) *chsd clr ldr: hrd rdn and kpt on to chal ins fnl f: no ex* **11/1**

-062 **3** *2* **Fashion Icon (USA)**[7] 1068 4-8-1 53 oh4 ow2 .... IanBrennan(5) 11 52
(J Hetherton) *mid-div: hdwy over 1f out: styd on to take 3rd last 50yds* **12/1**

2503 **4** *1 ¼* **Trick Or Two**[7] 1068 4-8-9 56 .... (b) SilvestreDeSousa 7 51
(Mrs R A Carr) *led and sn clr: wknd and hdd 100yds out* **5/1**[2]

3036 **5** *½* **Bertbrand**[27] 866 5-8-4 51 oh2 .... (v) AndrewElliott 9 44
(I W McInnes) *mid-div: hdwy 2f out: kpt on fnl f* **20/1**

10-4 **6** *1 ¾* **Spirit Of Coniston**[29] 832 7-8-11 63 .... PaulPickard(5) 4 50
(P T Midgley) *chsd ldrs: kpt on same pce fnl 2f* **9/4**[1]

610- **7** *¾* **Mayoman (IRE)**[160] 7138 5-8-7 61 .... NeilFarley(7) 14 45+
(D Carroll) *hmpd s: racd wd: styd on fnl 2f: nvr nr ldrs* **17/2**

00-0 **8** *3 ¼* **Red Cell (IRE)**[27] 860 4-8-1 51 oh1 .... (b) KellyHarrison(3) 3 23
(I W McInnes) *hmpd s: in rr: kpt on fnl 2f: nvr on terms* **33/1**

000- **9** *nk* **Officer Mor (USA)**[162] 7082 4-8-5 52 .... DuranFentiman 6 23
(Mrs Dianne Sayer) *dwlt: sn mid-div: nvr a factor* **17/2**

0130 **10** *3 ½* **Lujiana**[2] 1112 5-8-5 59 .... JohnCavanagh(7) 12 18
(M Brittain) *swvd rt s: r wd: nvr on terms* **8/1**[3]

4250 **11** *3* **Steel City Boy (IRE)**[14] 972 7-9-4 65 .... PJMcDonald 10 13
(D Shaw) *a towards rr* **14/1**

060- **12** *2 ½* **Rightcar Dominic**[99] 7869 5-8-5 52 oh6 ow1 .... GregFairley 8 —
(Peter Grayson) *s.s: a in rr* **100/1**

0020 **13** *nk* **Sonhador**[27] 866 4-8-4 51 oh2 .... PaulQuinn 5 —
(A Berry) *a in rr* **20/1**

0-00 **14** *6* **Iron Max (IRE)**[7] 1072 4-7-11 51 oh6 .... MatthewLawson(7) 13 —
(Mrs L Williamson) *hmpd s: r wd: a bhd* **100/1**

63.20 secs (3.40) **Going Correction** +0.725s/f (Yiel) 14 Ran SP% **123.4**
Speed ratings (Par 101): **101,99,95,93,93 90,89,83,83,77 72,68,68,58**
toteswingers: 1&2 £13.60, 1&3 £13.70, 2&3 £8.30 CSF £156.42 CT £1969.74 TOTE £18.30: £5.40, £3.90, £4.20; EX 86.40.
Owner W B Imison **Bred** Martyn J McEnery **Trained** Westow, N Yorks

■ Stewards' Enquiry : Andrew Mullen five-day ban: used whip with excessive frequency (Apr 21-25)

FOCUS
A moderate sprint handicap run at a very fast pace. The form is best rated around the winner and third.
Sonhador Official explanation: jockey said gelding lost its action

1155 RACINGUK.COM H'CAP 5f
5:10 (5:10) (Class 6) (0-60,60) 3-Y-O **£2,047** (£604; £302) **Stalls** Low

Form RPR

4630 **1** **Your Gifted (IRE)**[2] 1118 3-8-13 55 .... DanielTudhope 2 56
(Patrick Morris) *swvd rt s: w ldrs: led over 3f out: edgd rt fnl f: jst lasted* **4/1**[2]

-460 **2** *nse* **Captain Bluebird (IRE)**[34] 782 3-9-4 60 .... MickyFenton 1 61
(D Donovan) *rrd s and sn given reminders: jnd wnr over 3f out: styd on ins fnl f: jst failed* **11/2**

523- **3** *½* **Sharp Shoes**[184] 6542 3-8-11 56 .... BarryMcHugh(3) 3 55
(Mrs A Duffield) *chsd ldrs: effrt 2f out: styd on wl ins fnl f* **4/1**[2]

4-02 **4** *3 ½* **Nabrina (IRE)**[26] 870 3-8-3 52 .... JohnCavanagh(7) 7 39
(M Brittain) *chsd ldrs: rdn over 2f out: fdd fnl f* **5/2**[1]

0-20 **5** *2 ½* **Tulip Explosion**[12] 988 3-8-6 48 .... SilvestreDeSousa 9 26
(D Shaw) *swvd rt s: sn chsng ldrs: outpcd over 2f out: edgd lft and lost pl over 1f out* **5/1**[3]

300- **6** *6* **Kirkby's Gem**[183] 6555 3-8-7 49 .... PJMcDonald 5 5
(A Berry) *led over 1f: lost pl over 2f out: sn bhd* **8/1**

64.43 secs (4.63) **Going Correction** +0.725s/f (Yiel) 6 Ran SP% **111.7**
Speed ratings (Par 96): **91,90,90,84,80 70**
toteswingers: 1&2 £3.10, 1&3 £2.80, 2&3 £3.30 CSF £25.19 CT £90.49 TOTE £6.40: £5.10, £4.90; EX 23.80 Place 6: £87.69 Place 5: £60.92 .
Owner Morris, Walsh & D&D Coatings Ltd **Bred** Rathasker Stud **Trained** Tarporley, Cheshire

■ Stewards' Enquiry : Barry McHugh caution: used whip with excessive frequency.

FOCUS
Moderate form and not a race to treat positively.
T/Jkpt: £136,781.00 to a £1 stake. Pool: £192,649.34. 1.00 winning ticket. T/Plt: £93.60 to a £1 stake. Pool: £65,750.10. 512.33 winning tickets. T/Qpdt: £16.20 to a £1 stake. Pool: £3,910.80. 177.60 winning tickets. WG

1082 KEMPTON (A.W) (R-H)
Wednesday, April 7

OFFICIAL GOING: Standard
Wind: Brisk, against Weather: Overcast

1156 BOOK KEMPTON TICKETS ON 0844 579 3008 H'CAP 1m 2f (P)
5:30 (5:30) (Class 4) (0-85,83) 4-Y-0+ **£4,209** (£1,252; £625; £312) **Stalls** High

Form RPR

3661 **1** **Kidlat**[9] 1051 5-8-13 78 6ex .... PatCosgrave 8 85
(A Bailey) *mde all and set sensible pce: urged along to up the tempo over 2f out: drvn over 1f out: kpt on gamely* **6/1**[3]

132- **2** *¾* **Plymouth Rock (IRE)**[196] 6203 4-9-4 83 .... RyanMoore 6 89
(J Noseda) *a 2nd: rdn to chal over 1f out: nrly upsides ent fnl f: nvr finding enough to go past* **2/1**[1]

322- **3** *nk* **Absinthe (IRE)**[203] 5997 4-9-0 79 .... AdamKirby 1 84
(W R Swinburn) *trckd ldng trio: rdn over 1f out: styd on fnl f but nvr able to throw down decisive chal* **11/4**[2]

45-6 **4** *hd* **Aphrodisia**[19] 931 6-8-4 69 .... TadhgO'Shea 3 74+
(Ian Williams) *t.k.h early: led 1f: looking for room and swtchd lft then rt over 1f out: styd on fnl f: a jst too much to do* **16/1**

-541 **5** *½* **Taaresh (IRE)**[35] 765 5-8-4 72 .... AndreaAtzeni(3) 2 76
(K A Morgan) *hld up in midfield: taken wd and prog over 3f out: disp 3rd over 1f out: hd to one side and nt qckn: kpt on* **8/1**

2064 **6** *nk* **Trafalgar Square**[12] 990 8-8-2 72 .... JemmaMarshall(5) 7 75
(M J Attwater) *t.k.h: hld up in 7th: effrt on wd outside 2f out: styd on fr over 1f out: nvr posed a real threat* **25/1**

504- **7** *3 ¼* **Mount Hadley (USA)**[152] 7271 6-9-4 83 .... NickyMackay 9 79
(G A Butler) *trckd ldng pair: drvn on inner over 1f out: lost pl ent fnl f: wknd rapidly last 100yds* **10/1**

5 **8** *1 ¼* **Cluain Alainn (IRE)**[18] 947 4-9-3 82 .... StevieDonohoe 5 76
(Ian Williams) *hld up in last: rdn and detached fr over 2f out: no ch after* **25/1**

1434 **9** *shd* **Cupid's Glory**[19] 929 8-8-4 72 .... Louis-PhilippeBeuzelin(3) 4 66
(G L Moore) *mostly in 5th on inner: rdn over 1f out: sn wknd* **20/1**

2m 7.37s (-0.63) **Going Correction** +0.025s/f (Slow) 9 Ran SP% **112.8**
Speed ratings (Par 105): **103,102,102,102,101 101,98,97,97**
toteswingers: 1&2 £3.60, 1&3 £4.20, 2&3 £1.50 CSF £17.46 CT £39.49 TOTE £5.50: £2.00, £1.10, £1.60; EX 23.40.
Owner John Stocker **Bred** Darley **Trained** Newmarket, Suffolk

FOCUS
A couple of unexposed sorts in a fair handicap. The gallop was a modest one and those held up were at a disadvantage. The winner raced against the inside rail throughout but the form is muddling, with the fourth the best guide.
Aphrodisia Official explanation: jockey said mare was denied a clear run

1157 PANORAMIC BAR & RESTAURANT MAIDEN STKS 1m 3f (P)
6:00 (6:00) (Class 5) 3-4-Y-O **£2,590** (£770; £385; £192) **Stalls** High

Form RPR

2/0- **1** **Swindler (IRE)**[253] 4405 4-9-13 0 .... JimmyFortune 6 76
(A M Balding) *t.k.h 1f: restrained bhd ldrs: wnt 2nd 3f out: sltly outpcd 2f out: shkn up to cl over 1f out: two sharp reminders and led last 75yds* **4/9**[1]

53 **2** *½* **Musical Mark**[20] 922 3-8-4 0 .... (b) AndreaAtzeni(3) 2 72
(M Botti) *t.k.h: led after 3f: shkn up and fnd ex 2f out: hrd rdn and edgd lft over 1f out: hdd last 75yds* **10/3**[2]

00- **3** *6* **Lauberhorn**[209] 5787 3-8-7 0 .... EddieAhern 8 62
(Eve Johnson Houghton) *hld up in 6th: prog towards inner 3f out: edgd lft but wnt 3rd 2f out: shkn up and lft bhd by ldng pair: kpt on* **9/1**[3]

006- **4** *9* **Suhailah**[129] 7590 4-9-3 40 .... JemmaMarshall(5) 1 45
(M J Attwater) *hld up in tch: prog on outer to dispute 2nd 3f out: wknd over 2f out* **66/1**

0- **5** *13* **Platinum Bounty**[313] 2433 4-9-8 0 .... JerryO'Dwyer 4 23
(N P Mulholland) *in tch tl wknd rapidly over 2f out: t.o* **66/1**

6 *12* **Tooprague**[72] 4-9-8 0 .... DaneO'Neill 3 —
(P R Hedger) *s.v.s: hld up in last: wknd wl over 2f out: t.o* **33/1**

0 **7** *12* **Juniper Prince**[67] 355 4-9-13 0 .... VinceSlattery 5 —
(G P Enright) *led after 1f tl after 3f: pushed along over 4f out: wknd rapidly 3f out: wl t.o* **66/1**

2m 21.29s (-0.61) **Going Correction** +0.025s/f (Slow)
WFA 3 from 4yo 20lb 7 Ran SP% **109.7**
Speed ratings (Par 103): **103,102,98,91,82 73,64**
toteswingers: 1&2 £1.10, 1&3 £1.60, 2&3 £1.90 CSF £1.90 TOTE £1.50: £1.10, £1.50; EX 2.00.
Owner Mr & Mrs P McMahon & Mr & Mrs R Gorell **Bred** G Callanan **Trained** Kingsclere, Hants

FOCUS
A most uncompetitive maiden in which the gallop was steady until 2f out and the bare form, rated through the runner-up, does not look reliable. The first two came down the centre in the straight.

1158 DIGIBET.COM H'CAP 1m 3f (P)
6:30 (6:30) (Class 6) (0-60,60) 3-Y-O **£2,047** (£604; £302) **Stalls** High

Form RPR

045- **1** **Shelfah (IRE)**[174] 6792 3-9-2 58 .... FrankieDettori 5 68+
(M A Jarvis) *trckd ldng pair: wnt 2nd over 2f out: pushed into ld wl over 1f out: pressed ent fnl f: rdn and styd on wl* **3/1**[1]

640- **2** *¾* **Big Wave Bay (IRE)**[201] 6046 3-9-4 60 .... KierenFallon 11 69+
(A P Jarvis) *hld up in 5th on inner: effrt over 2f out: shkn up to chse wnr 1f out: styd on but no imp last 100yds* **5/1**[3]

055- **3** *3* **Red Amy**[230] 5192 3-9-1 57 .... RyanMoore 6 61+
(M L W Bell) *hld up in midfield: prog fr 3f out: rdn and styd on to take 3rd jst ins fnl f: no imp on ldng pair* **4/1**[2]

0622 **4** *1 ¾* **Port Hill**[9] 1054 3-9-2 58 .... ShaneKelly 2 59
(W M Brisbourne) *chsd ldng trio: effrt on outer 3f out: rdn and nt qckn 2f out: grad fdd* **5/1**[3]

000- **5** *1 ¼* **Oak Leaves**[165] 7029 3-9-1 57 .... PatCosgrave 9 56
(J G Portman) *chsd clr ldr to over 2f out: nt qckn u.p: fdd over 1f out* **40/1**

5310 **6** *1* **Sheila's Bond**[9] 1048 3-9-0 56 .... LukeMorris 3 53
(J S Moore) *a in midfield: rdn over 2f out: one pce and no real prog* **12/1**

504- **7** *1 ¼* **Mini Max**[163] 7056 3-9-3 59 .... DaneO'Neill 8 54
(B W Duke) *settled in 9th: effrt over 2f out: hanging and limited repsonse whn rdn: n.d over 1f out* **25/1**

413- **8** *¾* **Miss Whippy**[195] 6232 3-9-0 56 .... JimmyQuinn 4 50
(P Howling) *s.i.s: hld up in rr: plenty of tail swishing and no prog over 2f out: modest late hdwy* **9/1**

0-00 **9** *nk* **Tallawalla (IRE)**[36] 762 3-9-0 **56** .... SamHitchcott 7 49
(M R Channon) *led and sn clr: 8 l ahd 4f out: c bk over 2f out: hdd wl over 1f out: wknd rapidly fnl f* **14/1**

1-56 **10** *½* **Whipperway (IRE)**[33] 805 3-8-10 **55** .... RobertLButler(3) 12 47
(Miss Sheena West) *hld up in last trio: shkn up and no prog over 2f out: no real prog after* **20/1**

5-45 **11** *1 ¼* **Little Meadow (IRE)**[57] 475 3-8-1 **50** .... AdamBeschizza(7) 1 40
(Miss J Feilden) *racd wd in midfield: lost grnd and in last trio by 3f out: no ch after* **40/1**

0-60 **12** *2* **All Right Now**[56] 484 3-8-6 **48** .... DavidProbert 10 35
(S Kirk) *dwlt: racd v awkwardly in last most of the r: nvr a factor* **33/1**

0-03 **13** *5* **Better Be Blue (IRE)**[53] 534 3-8-7 **49** .... KirstyMilczarek 13 27
(A W Carroll) *trckd ldrs on inner: no prog over 2f out: wknd rapidly over 1f out* **16/1**

2m 22.5s (0.60) **Going Correction** +0.025s/f (Slow) **13 Ran SP% 125.0**
Speed ratings (Par 96): **98,97,95,94,93 92,91,90,90,90 89,87,84**
toteswingers: 1&2 £6.30, 2&3 £6.40, 1&3 £4.50 CSF £17.66 CT £63.04 TOTE £3.10: £1.10, £3.80, £2.90; EX 17.70.
Owner Sheikh Ahmed Al Maktoum **Bred** Darley **Trained** Newmarket, Suffolk

FOCUS
A moderate handicap run at no more than a reasonable gallop and one in which four of the five places were filled by horses making their handicap debuts. The winner and runner-up finished clear and raced centre to far side in the straight and the form appears sound enough.

1159 DIGIBET FILLIES' H'CAP 1m (P)
7:00 (7:01) (Class 4) (0-85,78) 3-Y-O **£4,209** (£1,252; £625; £312) **Stalls** High

Form RPR

01- **1** **Totally Ours**[158] 7177 3-9-5 **76** .... MartinDwyer 4 85
(W R Muir) *trckd ldr: shkn up whn sltly outpcd 2f out: clsd fnl f: styd on wl to ld nr fin* **12/1**

1- **2** *nk* **Gracious Melange**[112] 7763 3-9-5 **76** .... KierenFallon 7 84
(M Botti) *plld hrd early: led at modest pce: bttr tempo fr 1/2-way: stretched 2 l clr 2f out: rdn fnl f: worn down nr fin* **11/10**[1]

1- **3** *1* **Dubai Bounty**[102] 7844 3-8-12 **69** .... NickyMackay 2 75+
(G A Butler) *hld up in 7th: outpcd and shkn up on outer 2f out: prog over 1f out: styd on to take 3rd last strides* **10/1**

11 **4** *hd* **Dream On Buddy (IRE)**[19] 934 3-9-1 **72** .... MichaelHills 8 77+
(B W Hills) *quite keen early: hld up in 5th: effrt on inner over 2f out: chsd ldng pair fnl f: kpt on but lost 3rd last strides* **9/2**[2]

-222 **5** *1* **Sunley Spinalonga**[43] 671 3-8-0 **62** .... DeclanCannon(5) 10 65
(D R C Elsworth) *s.i.s: quite keen and sn trckd ldng pair: nt qckn 2f out: one pce after* **16/1**

052- **6** *½* **Ice Diva**[152] 7277 3-8-12 **69** .... TonyCulhane 6 71+
(P W D'Arcy) *hld up in 8th: gng strly 3f out: outpcd 2f out: shkn up and kpt on steadily fr over 1f out: could improve* **7/1**[3]

0-1 **7** *2 ¼* **Tafawut**[35] 768 3-9-7 **78** .... LukeMorris 9 74
(C G Cox) *t.k.h in 5th: stmbld and wnt lft over 5f out: wknd 2f out* **12/1**

530- **8** *5* **Lenkiewicz**[177] 6727 3-9-2 **76** .... JamesMillman(3) 5 60
(B R Millman) *hld up in last: outpcd fr 1/2-way: pushed along and rchd 8th 2f out: no prog over 1f out: wknd* **25/1**

036- **9** *½* **Gobama**[149] 7320 3-9-1 **72** .... SebSanders 3 55
(J W Hills) *plld hrd: sn hld up in 9th: rdn and no prog over 2f out* **28/1**

01- **10** *6* **Ravens Rose**[187] 6441 3-8-8 **65** .... SaleemGolam 1 34
(J G Portman) *plld hrd: sn trckd ldng trio on outer: bmpd over 5f out: wknd rapidly over 2f out: t.o* **50/1**

1m 40.99s (1.19) **Going Correction** +0.025s/f (Slow) **10 Ran SP% 117.9**
Speed ratings (Par 97): **95,94,93,93,92 92,89,84,84,78**
toteswingers: 1&2 £3.30, 1&3 £21.50, 2&3 £3.40 CSF £25.57 CT £152.35 TOTE £23.20: £11.50, £3.50, £10.40; EX 33.00.
Owner Foursome Thoroughbreds **Bred** W Muir And Foursome Thoroughbreds **Trained** Lambourn, Berks

FOCUS
A host of previous winners in a useful fillies' handicap. A steady gallop only picked up around the 2f pole and the winner and second ended up just off the inside rail in the closing stages. Not totally reliable form but worth treating positively.

1160 DIGIBET CASINO H'CAP 2m (P)
7:30 (7:30) (Class 5) (0-70,68) 4-Y-0+ **£2,590** (£770; £385; £192) **Stalls** High

Form RPR

-051 **1** **Mountain Forest (GER)**[7] 1071 4-8-5 **51** 6ex .... JimmyQuinn 5 61
(H Morrison) *trckd ldrs: smooth effrt to ld 2f out and sn kicked at least 2 l clr: drvn and styd on wl fnl f* **10/3**[2]

041 **2** *¾* **Cold Turkey**[13] 982 10-9-12 **68** .... RyanMoore 8 77+
(G L Moore) *hld up in 8th: prog over 2f out: chsd clr wnr over 1f out: styd on wl and grad clsd but nvr gng to get there: lame* **11/8**[1]

15-4 **3** *5* **Calzaghe (IRE)**[37] 182 6-9-8 **67** .... RobertLButler(3) 12 70+
(Jim Best) *hld up in last trio: dropped to last 4f out: gng wl enough but stl in rr as r unfolded 2f out: rdn and prog after: styd on to snatch modest 3rd on post* **12/1**

13-0 **4** *shd* **Sunny Spells**[13] 982 5-8-13 **62** .... RyanClark(7) 10 65
(S C Williams) *cl up on inner: outpcd fr 2f out: kpt on to chse ldng pair 1f out: no imp: lost 3rd on post* **16/1**

466 **5** *2 ½* **Uncle Eli (IRE)**[18] 950 8-9-0 **63** .... RichardRowe(7) 9 63
(R Rowe) *hld up last: taken to outer 7f out and racd keenly: rapid prog rnd field to ld 3f out: hdd and fdd 2f out* **33/1**

-60 **6** *3 ½* **Pocket Too**[12] 322 7-9-11 **67** ....(p) KirstyMilczarek 2 63
(Matthew Salaman) *cl up: wnt 2nd 5f out: led briefly over 3f out: wl outpcd fr 2f out* **14/1**

0-40 **7** *3* **Set Em Up Mo**[70] 316 4-7-12 **49** oh4 ....(p) KierenFox(5) 7 41
(M J Attwater) *t.k.h: hld up in midfield: wl outpcd fr 2f out* **50/1**

0-41 **8** *3 ½* **Coda Agency**[12] 748 7-9-8 **64** .... FrankieDettori 6 52
(D W P Arbuthnot) *trckd ldrs: easily outpcd fr over 2f out: fdd* **13/2**[3]

03-5 **9** *¾* **Super Fourteen**[13] 983 4-8-7 **56** .... MartinLane(3) 1 43
(R H York) *trckd ldr to 5f out: wknd fr 3f out* **40/1**

/36- **10** *nse* **Attainable**[167] 6975 4-9-6 **66** .... SebSanders 4 53
(J A B Old) *hld up in last pair: wd bnd 3f out and outpcd: n.d after* **14/1**

0403 **11** *2 ½* **New World Order (IRE)**[13] 983 6-9-4 **60** ....(t) KierenFallon 3 44
(R Curtis) *led at mostly mod pce and racd keenly: hdd over 3f out: grad fdd and eased* **14/1**

3m 31.79s (1.69) **Going Correction** +0.025s/f (Slow)
WFA 4 from 5yo+ 4lb **11 Ran SP% 119.4**
Speed ratings (Par 103): **96,95,93,93,91 90,88,86,86,86 85**
toteswingers: 1&2 £2.20, 1&3 £9.70, 2&3 £9.30 CSF £8.29 CT £49.02 TOTE £4.40: £1.30, £1.10, £5.80; EX 7.40.
Owner H Morrison **Bred** Gestut Isarland **Trained** East Ilsley, Berks

FOCUS
A modest handicap and another race on the card to be run at a steady gallop (nearly 8 seconds above Racing Post Standard) to the intersection. The first two, who finished clear, raced centre to far side in the closing stages. The form looks pretty sound rated around the fourth and fifth.
Cold Turkey Official explanation: vet said gelding returned lame

1161 KEMPTON FOR OUTDOOR EVENTS H'CAP 1m 4f (P)
8:00 (8:01) (Class 4) (0-85,85) 4-Y-0+ **£4,209** (£1,252; £625; £312) **Stalls** Centre

Form RPR

434- **1** **Sherman McCoy**[189] 6388 4-8-9 **79** .... JamesMillman(3) 6 86
(B R Millman) *led after 1f and set mod gallop: shkn up over 2f out: jnd on all sides over 1f out: gained upper hand ins fnl f: hld on wl* **25/1**

0-44 **2** *hd* **Encircled**[25] 888 6-8-13 **79** .... EddieAhern 3 86+
(J R Jenkins) *hld up in last trio: effrt on wd outside over 2f out: r.o over 1f out: wnt 2nd last 100yds: jst hld* **14/1**

343- **3** *½* **Curacao**[189] 6388 4-8-9 **76** .... JimCrowley 1 82
(Mrs A J Perrett) *pressed wnr after 1f: rdn and upsides over 1f out: n.m.r ent fnl f: kpt on but a jst lacking ex* **12/1**

111- **4** *¾* **Rowan Tiger**[180] 6634 4-8-7 **74** .... NickyMackay 4 79
(J R Boyle) *t.k.h: trckd ldrs: effrt to chal and upsides over 1f out: nt qckn fnl f* **8/1**[3]

-111 **5** *nk* **Franco Is My Name**[42] 676 4-9-4 **85** .... DaneO'Neill 10 89+
(P R Hedger) *hld up and sn last: prog on inner over 2f out: rdn to chal and upsides over 1f out tl ins fnl f: fdd* **9/4**[2]

1410 **6** *nk* **Bavarica**[21] 903 8-8-3 **76** .... AdamBeschizza(7) 7 80
(Miss J Feilden) *t.k.h: hld up in tch: chsd ldrs and cl up over 1f out: kpt on but nvr able to chal* **25/1**

610- **7** *1 ¾* **It's A Date**[125] 4988 5-8-13 **79** .... JimmyFortune 8 80
(A King) *led 1f: trckd ldng pair after: cl up and rdn 2f out: hld 1f out: fdd* **25/1**

614- **8** *nk* **King's Song (IRE)**[201] 6059 4-8-8 **75** ow2 .... RyanMoore 9 79+
(Sir Michael Stoute) *hld up in rr: prog over 2f out: rdn to chal and upsides over 1f out: lost pl and fdd fnl f* **13/8**[1]

3453 **9** *39* **Dreamwalk (IRE)**[14] 974 4-9-0 **81** ....(v) KierenFallon 2 19
(R Curtis) *trckd ldrs on outer: wnt wd fr 4f out: dropped out qckly 3f out: eased: t.o* **14/1**

2m 32.97s (-1.53) **Going Correction** +0.025s/f (Slow)
WFA 4 from 5yo+ 1lb **9 Ran SP% 112.5**
Speed ratings (Par 105): **106,105,105,105,104 104,103,103,77**
toteswingers:1&2 £23.10, 2&3 £14.10, 1&3 £26.10 CSF £315.77 CT £4345.92 TOTE £37.40: £6.00, £5.60, £4.60; EX 416.90.
Owner Mustajed Partnership **Bred** Horizon Bloodstock Limited **Trained** Kentisbeare, Devon
■ Stewards' Enquiry : Eddie Ahern two-day ban: used whip with excessive frequency without giving mare time to respond (Apr 21-22)
Nicky Mackay two-day ban: careless riding (Apr 21-22)

FOCUS
A useful handicap on paper but another race that turned into a two furlong sprint and the bare form is dubious and hard to rate positively. The winner raced towards the centre in the straight.

1162 JUMP RACING HERE ON FRIDAY H'CAP (DIV I) 7f (P)
8:30 (8:31) (Class 6) (0-60,60) 3-Y-O **£1,706** (£503; £252) **Stalls** High

Form RPR

00-6 **1** **Motty's Gift**[12] 993 3-8-9 **51** ....(v) ShaneKelly 10 57
(W R Swinburn) *chsd ldr: rdn over 2f out: lost pl sltly over 1f out: rallied fnl f: led nr fin* **11/1**

36-0 **2** *½* **Take My Hand**[9] 1048 3-9-0 **56** .... KierenFallon 8 61
(M R Channon) *trckd ldrs: effrt to go 2nd over 1f out: hrd rdn and sustained chal after: led last 75yds: sn hdd and no ex* **7/2**[1]

055- **3** *hd* **Show Willing (IRE)**[158] 7177 3-8-11 **58** .... MatthewDavies(5) 11 62
(A P Jarvis) *led at decent pce and racd freely: rdn over 1f out: kpt on but hdd last 75yds* **16/1**

00-5 **4** *¾* **Tregony Bridge**[9] 1048 3-8-8 **50** .... FergusSweeney 3 52+
(M Blanshard) *hld up last: stdy prog over 2f out: urged along and wnt 4th fnl f: rdn and nt qckn after* **10/1**

4400 **5** *2 ½* **Pavement Games**[12] 991 3-8-4 **46** oh1 .... DavidProbert 12 41
(R C Guest) *chsd ldrs: rdn 2f out: disp 4th and nt qckn over 1f out: one pce after* **10/1**

045- **6** *hd* **Chinese Democracy (USA)**[168] 6938 3-8-13 **55** .... FrankieDettori 1 50
(P F I Cole) *hld up in last pair: shkn up and sme prog over 2f out: one pce and nvr bttr than midfield after* **7/1**

003 **7** *1 ½* **Rock D'Argent (IRE)**[13] 977 3-9-3 **59** .... RyanMoore 2 50
(A B Haynes) *hld up in rr: swtchd towards inner and effrt over 2f out: no imp on ldrs over 1f out* **5/1**[2]

000- **8** *1* **Seeking Stardom**[201] 6054 3-9-4 **60** .... IanMongan 6 48
(P M Phelan) *towards rr: pushed along firmly fr 3f out: limited prog 2f out: no hdwy over 1f out* **11/1**

0652 **9** *shd* **Moonlight Serenade**[12] 993 3-8-8 **53** ....(b) JackDean(3) 9 41
(W G M Turner) *awkward s: hld up towards rr: prog on inner over 2f out: chsd ldrs over 1f out: racd awkwardly and wknd tamely* **12/1**

1420 **10** *nk* **Sandy Toes**[12] 993 3-7-13 **46** oh1 .... SimonPearce(5) 5 33
(J A Glover) *a in rr: rdn on outer and no prog over 2f out* **20/1**

060 **11** *2 ¼* **Just Say Please**[28] 843 3-9-0 **56** .... JimmyQuinn 4 37
(D K Ivory) *chsd ldng pair to 3f out: edgd lft and wknd over 2f out* **20/1**

5145 **12** *¾* **Ballyvonane (USA)**[7] 1057 3-8-9 **51** ....(b) LukeMorris 7 30
(L A Dace) *chsd ldrs: u.p and losing pl over 2f out: sn in rr* **11/2**[3]

1m 26.11s (0.11) **Going Correction** +0.025s/f (Slow) **12 Ran SP% 124.7**
Speed ratings (Par 96): **100,99,99,98,95 95,93,92,92,91 89,88**
toteswingers:1&2 £11.60, 2&3 £24.90, 1&3 £56.00 CSF £51.94 CT £634.95 TOTE £15.40: £5.40, £1.10, £9.90; EX 94.00.
Owner Mrs A Motson **Bred** Grasshopper 2000 Ltd **Trained** Aldbury, Herts

FOCUS
Division one of a moderate handicap and, although a reasonable gallop this time, those held up were at a disadvantage. The principals raced towards the centre in the straight and the third is the best guide to the level.
Motty's Gift Official explanation: trainer said, regarding apparent improvement in form, that it had been gelded and was its second run in visor.

1163 JUMP RACING HERE ON FRIDAY H'CAP (DIV II) 7f (P)
9:00 (9:00) (Class 6) (0-60,60) 3-Y-O **£1,706** (£503; £252) **Stalls** High

Form RPR

000- **1** **Decency (IRE)**[149] 7317 3-8-13 **55** .... KierenFallon 11 59+
(E A L Dunlop) *stmbld s: hld up in tch: prog on inner 2f out: rdn to ld 1f out: drvn out to hold on* **7/2**[2]

5253 **2** *hd* **Novillero**[12] 993 3-8-5 **47** .... LukeMorris 8 50+
(J C Fox) *hld up towards rr: lost pl 2f out: nt clr run and swtchd lft over 1f out: gd prog after: wnt 2nd ins fnl f and clsd on wnr fin* **8/1**

0306 **3** 1/2 **Miss Polly Plum**[12] 988 3-8-1 **46** oh1 .... KellyHarrison(3) 2 48
(C A Dwyer) *plld hrd: hld up in last pair: prog on outer over 1f out: styd on to dispute 2nd ins fnl f: nt qckn after* **40/1**

6235 **4** 1 1/4 **Turf Time**[12] 998 3-8-12 **54** .... DaneO'Neill 3 53
(J A Glover) *racd freely: led: rdn and hdd 1f out: fdd and lost 2 pls last 100yds* **15/2**[3]

4160 **5** 1 1/4 **Rightcar**[12] 991 3-9-1 **57** .... AdamKirby 7 52
(Peter Grayson) *rrd s and reminder sn after: in last pair tl effrt on inner 2f out: hrd rdn over 1f out: one pce* **20/1**

03-1 **6** nk **Cookie Galore**[34] 788 3-9-3 **59** .... FrederikTylicki 9 53
(J A Glover) *dwlt: sn trckd ldng pair: rdn and fnd nil 2f out: one pce after* **3/1**[1]

0323 **7** 3/4 **Sunrise Lyric (IRE)**[9] 1048 3-9-4 **60** .... RyanMoore 6 52
(P F I Cole) *hld up in midfield: effrt on outer over 2f out: nt qckn over 1f out: n.d after* **3/1**[1]

603- **8** 4 **Goodison Goal (IRE)**[97] 7884 3-8-9 **51** .... StephenCraine 10 33
(Patrick Morris) *trckd ldrs: gng easily over 2f out: cl up over 1f out: sn rdn and wknd rapidly* **16/1**

5-04 **9** 1 3/4 **Drubinca**[26] 870 3-8-11 **53** ....(v) SaleemGolam 5 30
(S C Williams) *chsd ldr: rdn and reluctant over 2f out: sn lost pl* **10/1**

1m 26.8s (0.80) **Going Correction** +0.025s/f (Slow) **9** Ran SP% **117.3**
Speed ratings (Par 96): **96,95,95,93,92 92,91,86,84**
toteswingers:1&2 £6.80, 2&3 £21.00, 1&3 £42.60 CSF £32.20 CT £965.20 TOTE £7.50: £3.80, £4.10, £16.90; EX 29.50 Place 6: £25.33 Place 5: £21.12.
Owner Highclere Thoroughbred Racing-St SimonII **Bred** Mohammed Al Sulaim **Trained** Newmarket, Suffolk

FOCUS
Another moderate handicap and one run at just an ordinary gallop. The winner edged just off the inside rail late on and is up a stone on her maiden form, although the level looks fluid.
Decency(IRE) Official explanation: trainer's rep said, regarding apparent improvement in form, that the filly had matured well over the winter and had been impressive in its work.
T/Plt: £49.50 to a £1 stake. Pool: £70,444.48. 1,038.70 winning tickets. T/Qpdt: £47.90 to a £1 stake. Pool: £6,013.70. 92.90 winning tickets. JN

1042 LINGFIELD (L-H)
Wednesday, April 7

OFFICIAL GOING: Standard
Wind: fairly modest, half against Weather: overcast

1164 BLUE SQUARE INTERNATIONAL TRIAL HERE ON SATURDAY MAIDEN STKS (DIV I) 7f (P)
2:00 (2:02) (Class 5) 3-Y-O **£2,388** (£705; £352) **Stalls** Low

Form RPR

52- **1** **Illustrious Prince (IRE)**[159] 7145 3-9-3 0 .... WilliamBuick 5 66+
(J Noseda) *chsd ldng pair: rdn and swtchd ins wl over 1f out: qcknd to chal 1f out: sn led: r.o wl* **11/10**[1]

2- **2** 3/4 **Cabal**[145] 7376 3-8-12 0 .... RyanMoore 10 59
(Sir Michael Stoute) *chsd ldr: rdn to chal ent fnl 2f: led ent fnl f: sn hdd: edgd lft and no ex ins fnl f* **13/8**[2]

6- **3** nk **Dizziness (USA)**[285] 3356 3-8-12 0 .... SteveDrowne 8 58+
(R Charlton) *bmpd s: t.k.h: hld up in tch in midfield: effrt wl over 1f out: swtchd rt over 1f out: kpt on wl ins fnl f* **14/1**

0- **4** 2 3/4 **Compton Park**[132] 7538 3-9-3 0 .... ShaneKelly 9 56+
(W J Knight) *stdd and hmpd s: t.k.h: hld up in last pair: rdn over 1f out: kpt on wl ins fnl f: nvr trbld ldrs* **33/1**

50 **5** nk **Madlool (IRE)**[13] 980 3-9-3 0 .... TadhgO'Shea 2 55
(W J Haggas) *racd keenly: sn led: rdn and pressed 2f out: hdd ent fnl f: wknd fnl 100yds* **20/1**

6 nk **Majestatic** 3-9-3 0 .... LukeMorris 1 54
(S W James) *t.k.h: hld up in tch towards rr: rdn wl over 1f out: kpt on ins fnl f: nt pce to rch ldrs* **100/1**

00- **7** nse **Mount Athos (IRE)**[165] 7029 3-9-3 0 .... MichaelHills 4 54
(J W Hills) *in tch in midfield: rdn and styd on same pce fnl 2f* **33/1**

8 1 **Concurrence (USA)** 3-9-3 0 .... RoystonFfrench 6 51
(M Johnston) *chsd ldrs: pushed along wl over 2f out: rdn and lost pl bnd 2f out: n.d after* **9/1**[3]

00- **9** shd **Vert Chapeau**[177] 6722 3-8-12 0 .... LiamKeniry 7 46+
(E F Vaughan) *stdd and wnt rt s: t.k.h: hld up towards rr: styd on same pce fnl 2f* **50/1**

60-0 **10** 1 **Gazamali (IRE)**[19] 930 3-9-3 44 .... FrankieMcDonald 11 48?
(H J Evans) *s.i.s: a in last pair: rdn and no prog fr wl over 1f out* **100/1**

1m 27.49s (2.69) **Going Correction** +0.075s/f (Slow) **10** Ran SP% **117.0**
Speed ratings (Par 98): **87,86,85,82,82 81,81,80,80,79**
toteswingers: 1&2 £1.10, 1&3 £3.20, 2&3 £4.80 CSF £2.87 TOTE £2.20: £1.20, £1.10, £2.80; EX 3.00 Trifecta £20.10 Pool: £455.94 - 16.40 winning units..
Owner Saeed Suhail **Bred** Rathbarry Stud **Trained** Newmarket, Suffolk

FOCUS
A decent maiden. It was run at a solid pace and the two clear market leaders filled the first two positions. The time was the slowest of those run over the trip on the day and the form looks weak.

1165 BLUE SQUARE INTERNATIONAL TRIAL HERE ON SATURDAY MAIDEN STKS (DIV II) 7f (P)
2:30 (2:31) (Class 5) 3-Y-O **£2,388** (£705; £352) **Stalls** Low

Form RPR

0- **1** **Falakee**[166] 6990 3-9-3 0 .... RyanMoore 7 74
(P W Chapple-Hyam) *led: rdn and narrowly hdd 2f out: kpt on gamely to ld again ins fnl f: kpt on wl* **9/1**[3]

530- **2** 1/2 **Soho Theatre**[162] 7095 3-9-3 74 ....(p) DaneO'Neill 5 73+
(D R C Elsworth) *chsd ldrs: rdn and effrt on inner jst over 1f out: nt clr run and swtchd rt ins fnl f: r.o wl towards fin* **10/1**

02- **3** hd **Frequency**[169] 6913 3-9-3 0 .... KierenFallon 2 72
(E A L Dunlop) *w ldr: led narrowly 2f out: rdn over 1f out: hdd and edgd lft u.p ins fnl f: one pce fnl 100yds* **1/2**[1]

60 **4** 2 3/4 **Southern Cape (IRE)**[13] 980 3-9-3 0 .... JimmyQuinn 8 65
(D J Coakley) *chsd ldrs: pushed along and outpcd by ldng trio wl over 1f out: kpt on again ins fnl f: nt pce to rch ldrs* **33/1**

5 4 **Mush Mir (IRE)** 3-9-3 0 .... PatCosgrave 6 54+
(J R Boyle) *rn green in last trio: rdn along over 4f out: kpt on ins fnl f: nvr trbld ldrs* **33/1**

0-0 **6** shd **Annacaboe (IRE)**[35] 768 3-8-12 0 .... AdrianMcCarthy 9 49
(D K Ivory) *racd in midfield: rdn along and outpcd by ldrs over 2f out: n.d after* **100/1**

0-6 **7** 1 3/4 **Stay On Track (IRE)**[9] 1050 3-9-3 0 .... LiamKeniry 10 49+
(E F Vaughan) *t.k.h: hld up towards rr: rdn and outpcd whn carried rt bnd 2f out: no ch w ldrs after* **25/1**

8 1 **Togoaviking** 3-9-3 0 .... LiamJones 1 47
(W J Haggas) *s.i.s: sn in midfield: rdn and outpcd whn edgd rt bnd 2f out: wl hld after* **8/1**[2]

000- **9** 1/2 **No Complaining (IRE)**[162] 7096 3-8-12 40 .... JerryO'Dwyer 11 40
(B J Curley) *in tch on outer: pushed along and carried rt bnd 2f out: wl btn after* **50/1**

10 6 **Sula Two** 3-8-12 0 .... SteveDrowne 4 24
(R J Hodges) *a in rr: rdn and struggling over 2f out: sn wl bhd* **66/1**

11 5 **Captain John Nixon** 3-9-3 0 .... DarryllHolland 3 15
(Pat Eddery) *s.i.s: rn green and sn rdn along in rr: nvr on terms: lost tch and wd bnd 2f out* **12/1**

1m 26.3s (1.50) **Going Correction** +0.075s/f (Slow) **11** Ran SP% **118.7**
Speed ratings (Par 98): **94,93,93,90,85 85,83,82,81,74 69**
toteswingers:1&2 £7.00, 2&3 £2.70, 1&3 £2.00 CSF £88.75 TOTE £7.90: £3.00, £2.60, £1.02; EX 108.60 Trifecta £297.90 Part won. Pool: £402.57 - 0.20 winning units..
Owner Ziad A Galadari **Bred** Galadari Sons Stud Company Limited **Trained** Newmarket, Suffolk

FOCUS
This looked quite a bit weaker than the first division. The hot favourite was turned over but the first three were clear of the fourth who was a long way ahead of the rest, and the form could work out. The form looks more reliable than the first division.

1166 £66 OF FREE BETS AT BLUESQUARE.COM H'CAP 6f (P)
3:00 (3:00) (Class 6) (0-60,60) 4-Y-O+ **£2,047** (£604; £302) **Stalls** Low

Form RPR

2521 **1** **Waterloo Dock**[33] 802 5-9-3 **59** ....(v) MartinDwyer 6 68
(M Quinn) *chsd ldrs: wnt 2nd 1/2-way: led wl over 1f out: sn rdn: kpt on wl u.p ins fnl f* **9/2**[2]

0660 **2** 1/2 **Bobs Dreamflight**[26] 869 4-8-13 **60** ....(b) MarkCoumbe(5) 4 67
(D K Ivory) *chsd ldr tl 1/2-way: shuffled bk and lost pl ent fnl 2f: swtchd rt and hdwy u.p ent fnl f: r.o wl to go 2nd towards fin* **20/1**

252- **3** 1/2 **Green Velvet**[127] 7602 5-9-4 **60** .... TravisBlock 8 66
(P J Makin) *chsd ldrs: rdn ent fnl 2f: drvn over 1f out: chsd wnr fnl 100yds: kpt on same pce and lost 2nd towards fin* **3/1**[1]

106 **4** 1 **Radiator Rooney (IRE)**[54] 525 7-9-3 **59** ....(v) StephenCraine 3 62
(Patrick Morris) *stdd s: hld up in midfield: hdwy on bit on inner to chse wnr over 1f out: rdn ent fnl f: fnd little and btn fnl 100yds* **20/1**

0401 **5** nse **Muktasb (USA)**[16] 961 9-9-2 **58** ....(v) JimmyQuinn 1 60
(D Shaw) *s.i.s: bhd: hdwy on inner wl over 1f out: chsd ldrs 1f out: kpt on same pce u.p ins fnl f* **12/1**

155- **6** 1 **Ask Jenny (IRE)**[109] 7815 8-9-4 **60** .... RyanMoore 11 59+
(Patrick Morris) *stdd s: hld up in last trio: hdwy and n.m.r over 1f out: hdwy between horses 1f out: no imp fnl 100yds* **15/2**

3-04 **7** nk **Leftontheshelf (IRE)**[30] 828 4-9-1 **60** ....(b[1]) JackDean(3) 7 58
(Miss T Spearing) *in tch in midfield: rdn and effrt 2f out: kpt on same pce u.p fnl f* **7/1**

1400 **8** nk **Don Pele (IRE)**[16] 961 8-9-3 **59** ....(b) LiamJones 10 56+
(R A Harris) *stdd s: hld up in last trio: hdwy wl over 1f out: n.m.r ins fnl f: styd on fnl 100yds: nvr trbld ldrs* **20/1**

0001 **9** 1 1/4 **Elusive Ronnie (IRE)**[44] 659 4-9-3 **59** ....(b) JackMitchell 2 52
(R A Teal) *sn in last and rdn along: c wd st: sme late hdwy but nvr on terms* **9/1**

1401 **10** shd **Equinity**[16] 968 4-8-11 **58** ....(t) SimonPearce(5) 9 51
(J Pearce) *taken down early: hld up towards rr: rdn and wd bnd 2f out: no prog after* **12/1**

1534 **11** nk **The Geester**[42] 684 6-9-4 **60** .... AdamKirby 5 52
(Stef Higgins) *chsd ldrs tl lost pl jst over 2f out: no ch w ldrs fr over 1f out* **11/2**[3]

130- **12** 1 3/4 **Blessed Place**[238] 4907 10-9-1 **57** .... FergusSweeney 12 43
(D J S Ffrench Davis) *sn led and crossed to rail: hdd 2f out: wknd qckly over 1f out* **33/1**

1m 11.84s (-0.06) **Going Correction** +0.075s/f (Slow) **12** Ran SP% **125.4**
Speed ratings (Par 101): **103,102,101,100,100 98,98,98,96,96 95,93**
toteswingers: 1&2 £29.60, 1&3 £4.70, 2&3 £7.20 CSF £99.94 CT £322.38 TOTE £6.00: £1.80, £8.40, £2.00; EX 153.80 TRIFECTA Not won..
Owner M J Quinn **Bred** Norman Court Stud **Trained** Newmarket, Suffolk
■ Stewards' Enquiry : Jack Mitchell one-day ban: used whip with excessive frequency (Apr 21)

FOCUS
A low-grade handicap but there were four last-time-out winners in the line-up. The pace was decent and the form is straightforward and could prove reliable.
Don Pele(IRE) Official explanation: jockey said gelding suffered interference on leaving stalls
Blessed Place Official explanation: jockey said gelding lost its action inside final furlong

1167 BLUE SQUARE'S NEW IPHONE APP (S) STKS 6f (P)
3:30 (3:30) (Class 6) 3-Y-O+ **£2,047** (£604; £302) **Stalls** Low

Form RPR

6545 **1** **Chjimes (IRE)**[28] 848 6-9-8 68 .... LiamKeniry 4 71
(C R Dore) *chsd ldrs: effrt on inner to ld wl over 1f out: edgd rt u.p and hdd ins fnl f: rallied fnl 50yds to ld again nr fin* **9/2**[3]

00-3 **2** hd **Mutamared (USA)**[12] 986 10-9-5 67 ....(t) RussKennemore(3) 9 70
(Andrew Reid) *chsd ldrs on outer: hdwy to press ldrs 2f out: ev ch over 1f out: edgd lft u.p and led ins fnl f: hdd and no ex nr fin* **9/2**[3]

3-54 **3** 2 1/4 **Who's Winning (IRE)**[12] 986 9-9-8 55 ....(t) KirstyMilczarek 5 63
(B G Powell) *in tch in midfield: rdn and effrt ent fnl 2f: chsd ldng pair ins fnl f: no imp fnl 100yds* **11/1**

P0-3 **4** 2 **Lindoro**[47] 613 5-9-13 80 ....(bt) JerryO'Dwyer 8 62
(T T Clement) *in tch in midfield on outer: rdn and effrt wl over 1f out: hrd drvn and nt qckn ent fnl f: no ch w ldng pair ins fnl f* **2/1**[1]

0-0 **5** 3/4 **Soul Murmur (IRE)**[64] 377 5-9-5 59 ....(bt) AndreaAtzeni(3) 1 54
(F Sheridan) *awkward leaving stalls and dwlt: racd freely: hdwy to ld after 1f: hdd and rdn wl over 1f out: wknd ins fnl f* **33/1**

00-0 **6** nk **Coeur Courageux (FR)**[12] 986 8-9-5 52 .... PatrickHills(3) 11 53
(W De Best-Turner) *stdd s: hld up towards rr: hdwy towards inner over 1f out: no imp u.p ins fnl f* **66/1**

-332 **7** 2 **Sir Edwin Landseer (USA)**[44] 659 10-9-8 63 ....(be) RyanMoore 10 47
(G L Moore) *hld up towards rr: hdwy ent fnl 2f: swtchd lft and rdn over 1f out: no prog and nvr trbld ldrs* **3/1**[2]

00-6 **8** 3 1/4 **Briannsta (IRE)**[30] 829 8-9-13 49 .... RichardThomas 2 41
(J E Long) *in tch in midfield: rdn and struggling over 2f out: wknd wl over 1f out* **33/1**

245- **9** 4 **Unbelievable Jeff**[199] 6140 4-9-3 48 .... RossAtkinson(5) 6 24
(J S Moore) *midfield tl lost pl and rdn over 2f out: no ch after* **14/1**

1500 **10** 2 **Tin Cha Woody (USA)**[22] 895 5-9-13 74 ....(p) LiamJones 12 22
(R A Harris) *a bhd: lost tch 1/2-way* **16/1**

000- **11** ½ **Hayley's Girl**[119] 7689 4-8-12 40..............(b) AmyBaker(5) 3 11
(S W James) *led for 1f: chsd ldr after tl over 2f out: wknd qckly wl over 1f out* **100/1**

0000 **12** 2 ¼ **Givenn**[7] 1068 6-9-3 37..............(bt) JamesDoyle 7 3
(Ms J S Doyle) *s.i.s: a bhd: lost tch over 2f out: eased whn wl btn ins fnl f* **100/1**

1m 11.72s (-0.18) **Going Correction** +0.075s/f (Slow) **12** Ran SP% **124.9**
Speed ratings (Par 101): **104,103,100,98,97 96,94,89,84,81 81,78**
toteswingers: 1&2 £6.40, 1&3 £7.70, 2&3 £8.10 CSF £26.20 TOTE £4.30: £1.10, £2.10, £2.80; EX 22.60 Trifecta £142.10 Pool: £334.13 - 1.74 winning units..There was no bid for the winner.

Owner Sean J Murphy **Bred** Morgan O'Flaherty **Trained** Cowbit, Lincs

FOCUS
A fair seller run at a reasonable pace. The first two held BHA ratings of 68 and 67, so the form looks solid enough, with the third the best guide.

Unbelievable Jeff Official explanation: jockey said gelding hung left

1168 PICK A WINNER WITH ICARD H'CAP 7f (P)
4:00 (4:01) (Class 5) (0-70,70) 3-Y-O **£3,070** (£906; £453) **Stalls** Low

Form RPR

605- **1** **Sonny G (IRE)**[97] 7884 3-8-1 56 oh3.............. AndreaAtzeni(3) 8 63
(J R Best) *mde all: rdn and clr over 1f out: tiring fnl 100yds: jst lasted: all out* **33/1**

323 **2** *hd* **Lingfield Bound (IRE)**[19] 930 3-8-13 68.............. MarcHalford(3) 2 74
(J R Best) *chsd ldrs: rdn to chse ldng pair wl over 1f out: chsd wnr ins fnl f: r.o wl u.str.p fnl 100yds: nt quite rch wnr* **13/2**

550- **3** 1 ¾ **Kajima**[159] 7146 3-9-3 69.............. RyanMoore 6 71+
(R Hannon) *stdd s: hld up in rr: stl plenty to do wl over 1f out: gd hdwy ent fnl f: r.o but nvr gng to rch ldng pair* **5/2**[1]

3-41 **4** *nk* **Honest Broker (IRE)**[33] 809 3-8-13 65.............. RoystonFfrench 7 66
(M Johnston) *in tch in midfield: rdn over 2f out: unable qck and no prog 2f out: kpt on wl ins fnl f: nt pce to rch ldrs* **8/1**

3-14 **5** 1 ½ **Ginger Grey (IRE)**[49] 582 3-9-1 67..............(p) DaneO'Neill 12 64+
(D R C Elsworth) *hld up towards rr on outer: hdwy 2f out: drvn jst over 1f out: kpt on but nvr able to rch ldrs* **8/1**

3064 **6** 1 **Reach For The Sky (IRE)**[7] 1057 3-8-1 58.............. KierenFox(5) 10 52+
(G Prodromou) *hld up in rr: hdwy over 1f out: r.o ins fnl f: nvr trbld ldrs* **33/1**

510- **7** ½ **Dream Number (IRE)**[149] 7320 3-9-4 70.............. MartinDwyer 9 63
(W R Muir) *in tch tl rdn and unable qck ent fnl 2f: no ch w ldrs fr over 1f out* **14/1**

500- **8** ¾ **Boga (IRE)**[226] 5310 3-8-4 56 oh1.............. JimmyQuinn 1 47
(R J Hodges) *t.k.h: chsd wnr: rdn and unable qck over 1f out: lost 2nd ins fnl f: wknd qckly after* **66/1**

213- **9** *shd* **Newbury Street**[166] 6983 3-9-3 69.............. FrederikTylicki 5 59
(R A Fahey) *in tch in midfield: rdn and effrt on inner wl over 1f out: no prog and wl hld after* **7/2**[2]

510- **10** 2 **Pintura**[178] 6693 3-9-3 69.............. WilliamBuick 3 54
(D M Simcock) *a in rr: nvr trbld ldrs* **11/2**[3]

6-44 **11** 2 ½ **Court Drinking (USA)**[36] 758 3-8-5 57.............. LukeMorris 4 35
(J R Best) *chsd ldrs tl wknd u.p wl over 1f out: wl btn fnl f* **25/1**

-230 **12** 1 ¼ **Jodawes (USA)**[19] 934 3-8-11 63.............. SteveDrowne 11 38
(J R Best) *a towards rr: rdn and no rspnse ent fnl 2f: wl bhd fr over 1f out* **20/1**

1m 24.85s (0.05) **Going Correction** +0.075s/f (Slow) **12** Ran SP% **124.4**
Speed ratings (Par 98): **102,101,99,99,97 96,96,95,95,92 89,88**
toteswingers: 1&2 £51.30, 1&3 £34.80, 2&3 £6.60 CSF £236.68 CT £767.84 TOTE £54.10: £12.10, £1.20, £1.10; EX 276.60 Trifecta £249.20 Part won. Pool: £336.89 - 0.10 winning units..

Owner Martin Long **Bred** G G Racing **Trained** Hucking, Kent

■ Stewards' Enquiry : Kieren Fox two-day ban: careless riding (Apr 21-22)

Andrea Atzeni one-day ban: failed to ride to draw (Apr 21)

FOCUS
A fair handicap for 3-y-os but hardly anything got into it from behind and there was a surprise winner. The time was the best of the race run over the trip and the third and fourth set the level.

Sonny G(IRE) Official explanation: trainer said, regarding apparent improvement in form, that the colt is maturing and strengthening and expected it to run better on its previous run.

1169 BET NOW AT BLUESQUARE.COM H'CAP 1m 4f (P)
4:30 (4:30) (Class 5) (0-75,75) 4-Y-O+ **£3,070** (£906; £453) **Stalls** Low

Form RPR

-120 **1** **Chalice Welcome**[19] 676 7-9-3 73.............. EddieAhern 9 84
(N B King) *hld up in tch in midfield: rdn and effrt jst over 2f out: led over 1f out: clr ins fnl f: rdn out* **12/1**

60-2 **2** 1 **Red Hot Desert**[74] 280 4-8-13 70.............. ShaneKelly 3 79+
(W R Swinburn) *hld up in rr: rdn and stl plenty to do over 1f out: hdwy 1f out: chsd wnr ins fnl f: kpt on and edgd lft towards fin* **5/2**[1]

140- **3** 1 ½ **Bell Island**[119] 7695 6-8-11 67..............(v) SebSanders 2 74
(Lady Herries) *led: rdn 4f out: jnd 3f out: forged ahd again ent fnl 2f: hdd over 1f out: styd on same pce fnl f* **4/1**[3]

0516 **4** 1 ¾ **War Of The Roses (IRE)**[14] 974 7-9-5 75.............. WilliamBuick 1 79
(R Brotherton) *chsd ldng pair: effrt and rdn to press ldrs over 1f out: unable qck ent fnl f: one pce after* **13/2**

10-1 **5** ¾ **Mr Plod**[12] 989 5-8-5 61 oh1.............. MartinDwyer 7 64
(Andrew Reid) *hld up in last pair: clsd over 2f out: rdn to chse ldrs on inner over 1f out: btn 1f out: wknd ins fnl f* **11/4**[2]

40-0 **6** 6 **Bomber Brown (IRE)**[55] 174 4-9-1 72.............. JackMitchell 8 65
(P W Chapple-Hyam) *chsd ldr: jnd ldr 3f out: rdn and unable qck over 2f out: wknd qckly over 1f out: wl bhd fnl f* **12/1**

06-5 **7** 3 ¼ **Valdan (IRE)**[14] 974 6-8-10 71..............(t) AndrewHeffernan(5) 6 59
(M A Barnes) *racd in midfield: pushed along over 3f out: rdn and dropped to rr over 2f out: wl bhd fnl 2f* **16/1**

2m 32.24s (-0.76) **Going Correction** +0.075s/f (Slow)
WFA 4 from 5yo+ 1lb **7** Ran SP% **109.8**
Speed ratings (Par 103): **105,104,103,102,101 97,95**
toteswingers: 1&2 £6.50, 1&3 £7.70, 2&3 £3.20 CSF £38.92 CT £133.62 TOTE £11.20: £5.30, £3.10; EX 39.10 Trifecta £206.50 Pool: £346.14 - 1.24 winning units..

Owner The Dyball Partnership **Bred** The Dyball Partnership **Trained** Newmarket, Suffolk

FOCUS
This was weakened by three withdrawals but it still looked fairly competitive. The form is not that strong though, with the fourth the best guide.

1170 TONIGHT'S CHAMPIONS LEAGUE BETTING AT BLUESQUARE.COM H'CAP (DIV I) 7f (P)
5:00 (5:01) (Class 6) (0-60,60) 4-Y-O+ **£1,706** (£503; £252) **Stalls** Low

Form RPR

4224 **1** **Lopinot (IRE)**[9] 1047 7-9-4 60..............(v) GeorgeBaker 8 68
(M R Bosley) *stdd s: hld up in tch towards rr: swtchd rt and gd hdwy: hung lft fr over 1f out: led ins fnl f: kpt hanging lft but r.o* **11/2**[2]

-400 **2** ½ **Royal Envoy (IRE)**[29] 839 7-8-8 53.............. MichaelStainton(3) 1 60
(P Howling) *hld up in tch in midfield: hdwy on inner jst over 1f out: ev ch ins fnl f: unable qck fnl 75yds* **33/1**

0212 **3** 1 **Bold Diva**[20] 918 5-9-0 56..............(v) LukeMorris 5 60+
(A W Carroll) *hld up in tch: nt clr run jst over 1f out tl swtchd rt jst ins fnl f: r.o but unable to rch ldng pair* **5/1**[1]

-000 **4** 1 **Bob Stock (IRE)**[28] 855 4-9-2 58.............. JamieMackay 10 60+
(W J Musson) *stdd s: hld up in last trio: hdwy jst over 1f out: nt clr run ins fnl f: swtchd rt and r.o wl fnl 75yds: nt rch ldrs* **16/1**

3620 **5** ½ **Trip Switch**[19] 937 4-8-13 60.............. KierenFox(5) 12 60
(G Prodromou) *stdd and dropped in bhd after s: hdwy on inner jst over 1f out: kpt on ins fnl f: nvr rchd ldrs* **11/2**[2]

0006 **6** *nk* **King's Sabre**[21] 912 4-8-7 49..............(e) PaulEddery 2 48
(R C Guest) *taken down early: t.k.h: sn led: rdn over 1f out: hrd drvn and hdd ins fnl f: wknd towards fin* **50/1**

2501 **7** *shd* **Ride A White Swan**[27] 866 5-8-9 54..............(p) MartinLane(3) 9 53+
(D Shaw) *taken down early: stdd s: hld up in tch in rr: effrt and nt clr run 1f out tl wl ins fnl f: r.o towards fin: nvr able to chal* **14/1**

6606 **8** *nk* **Yourgolftravel Com**[35] 773 5-8-12 54.............. StephenCraine 11 52
(M Wigham) *hld up in tch: rdn and hld hd awkwardly over 1f out: nt qckn and one pce fnl f* **20/1**

222- **9** *nse* **Sermons Mount (USA)**[163] 7052 4-9-3 59.............. WilliamBuick 14 57
(Mouse Hamilton-Fairley) *t.k.h: chsd ldrs: rdn wl over 1f out: styd on one pce u.p fnl f* **5/1**[1]

000- **10** 1 **Purus (IRE)**[129] 7586 8-9-4 60.............. LiamKeniry 7 56
(R A Teal) *t.k.h: hld up in tch in midfield on outer: lost pl and rdn along jst over 2f out: kpt on again ins fnl f: nvr trbld ldrs* **10/1**

46-0 **11** *shd* **Ymir**[95] 11 4-8-13 55.............. LiamJones 4 54+
(M J Attwater) *chsd ldrs: rdn wl over 1f out: keeping on same pce whn nt clr run and hmpd ins fnl f: no ch after* **14/1**

4231 **12** ½ **Royal Acclamation (IRE)**[14] 976 5-8-4 51..............(p) SimonPearce(5) 3 49+
(H J Evans) *hld up in tch towards rr: hdwy to chse ldrs ent fnl f: nt clr run ins fnl f and nvr able to chal* **8/1**[3]

040- **13** ¾ **Polemica (IRE)**[251] 4452 4-9-3 59.............. JamesDoyle 13 51
(F Sheridan) *t.k.h: chsd ldr after 1f: drvn wl over 1f out: wknd jst ins fnl f: wl btn whn nt clr run and eased towards fin* **22/1**

0-13 **14** 1 **Athboy Auction**[19] 940 5-8-0 49.............. NatashaEaton(7) 6 38
(H J Collingridge) *chsd ldrs: rdn and unable qck over 1f out: wknd ins fnl f* **20/1**

1m 25.6s (0.80) **Going Correction** +0.075s/f (Slow) **14** Ran SP% **122.3**
Speed ratings (Par 101): **98,97,96,95,94 94,94,93,92 92,91,91,89**
toteswingers: 1&2 £46.80, 1&3 £4.00, 2&3 £42.50 CSF £189.13 CT £1006.09 TOTE £5.90: £1.40, £12.20, £2.30; EX 206.30 TRIFECTA Not won..

Owner Mrs Jean M O'Connor **Bred** G And Mrs Middlebrook **Trained** Chalfont St Giles, Bucks

■ Stewards' Enquiry : William Buick one-day ban: failed to ride to draw (Apr 21)

FOCUS
A modest handicap. It got a bit messy in the straight and there were a few hard luck stories, so the form may not prove that reliable.

Trip Switch Official explanation: vet said gelding returned lame right-fore
Ride A White Swan Official explanation: jockey said gelding was denied a clear run
Ymir Official explanation: jockey said gelding was denied a clear run closing stages
Athboy Auction Official explanation: trainer said mare swallowed its tongue

1171 TONIGHT'S CHAMPIONS LEAGUE BETTING AT BLUESQUARE.COM H'CAP (DIV II) 7f (P)
5:35 (5:35) (Class 6) (0-60,60) 4-Y-O+ **£1,706** (£503; £252) **Stalls** Low

Form RPR

-400 **1** **Batchworth Blaise**[44] 656 7-8-3 50.............. KierenFox(5) 5 58
(E A Wheeler) *stdd s: hld up in rr: effrt on outer bnd 2f out: str run fnl f to ld fnl 75yds: r.o wl* **33/1**

-604 **2** *nk* **Count Ceprano (IRE)**[47] 613 6-8-7 54.............. SimonPearce(5) 12 61
(J Pearce) *hld up in last pair: hdwy and rdn on outer bnd 2f out: ev ch fnl 100yds: kpt on wl* **8/1**

6-32 **3** ¾ **Eager To Bow (IRE)**[41] 693 4-8-10 52.............. RichardKingscote 6 57+
(P R Chamings) *wl in tch in midfield: rdn to chal over 1f out: hrd drvn to ld fnl 100yds: sn hdd and one pce after* **7/2**[1]

540- **4** 1 **West Kirk**[110] 7803 4-9-4 60.............. J-PGuillambert 14 62
(W Jarvis) *sn led and crossed to rail: rdn wl over 1f: hrd drvn ent fnl f: hdd fnl 100yds: no ex* **20/1**

4100 **5** *shd* **Bollywood Style**[28] 844 5-9-3 59.............. SteveDrowne 8 61
(J R Best) *in tch: rdn and effrt over 1f out: drvn and ev ch ins fnl f: one pce fnl 100yds* **9/1**

1130 **6** ½ **Saddlers Bend (IRE)**[28] 844 4-8-11 58.............. MatthewDavies(5) 1 59
(George Baker) *trckd ldrs on inner: rdn to chal over 1f out: hrd drvn and styd on same pce fnl f* **5/1**[2]

650- **7** ¾ **Desert Pride**[154] 7241 5-8-12 54.............. IanMongan 10 53
(W S Kittow) *chsd ldrs: rdn wl over 1f out: hrd drvn ent fnl f: wknd fnl 150yds* **8/1**

60-0 **8** *shd* **Fiefdom (IRE)**[16] 965 8-9-2 58.............. DarryllHolland 11 57
(I W McInnes) *stdd s: hld up in rr: hdwy and n.m.r over 1f out: swtchd lft ent fnl f: r.o but nvr able to rch ldrs* **16/1**

4-60 **9** ½ **Monashee Rock (IRE)**[16] 965 5-9-4 60..............(p) LiamKeniry 3 57
(Matthew Salaman) *hld up in tch in midfield: rdn and effrt on inner wl over 1f out: kpt on same pce ins fnl f* **12/1**

0-65 **10** ¾ **Takitwo**[13] 984 7-8-7 49..............(v) LiamJones 7 44
(P D Cundell) *hld up towards rr: rdn and hdwy over 1f out: nvr much room fnl f: nvr trbld ldrs* **16/1**

2363 **11** *nk* **Louisiade (IRE)**[1] 1142 9-8-6 48..............(p) PaulEddery 4 42
(R C Guest) *w ldr: rdn 2f out: wknd u.p ins fnl f* **13/2**[3]

0-40 **12** 4 **Gold Rock (FR)**[19] 939 5-8-6 55.............. GeorgeDowning(7) 9 39
(A W Carroll) *wl in tch in midfield: rdn 2f out: wknd over 1f out* **12/1**

1m 25.56s (0.76) **Going Correction** +0.075s/f (Slow) **12** Ran SP% **119.3**
Speed ratings (Par 101): **98,97,96,95,95 94,94,94,93,92 92,87**
toteswingers: 1&2 £36.10, 1&3 £32.10, 2&3 £8.60 CSF £280.59 CT £1196.17 TOTE £34.90: £9.20, £4.10, £1.10; EX 190.40 TRIFECTA Not won. Place 6: £25.07 Place 5: £21.25 .

Owner Astrod TA Austin Stroud & Co **Bred** Mrs D Price **Trained** Whitchurch-on-Thames, Oxon

FOCUS
An ordinary handicap. They finished in a bunch and the form looks a bit suspect, with the second rated to his selling-race form.
T/Plt: £40.90 to a £1 stake. Pool: £60,720.42. 1,083.09 winning tickets. T/Qpdt: £47.40 to a £1 stake. Pool: £3,676.74. 57.40 winning tickets. SP

NOTTINGHAM (L-H)
Wednesday, April 7

OFFICIAL GOING: Soft (5.2)
All races run on inner course.
Wind: Virtually nil Weather: Overcast and light showers

1172 BET TOTEPOOL ON 0800 221 221 H'CAP (DIV I) 1m 75y
1:50 (1:51) (Class 6) (0-65,65) 4-Y-O+ £1,619 (£481; £240; £120) Stalls Low

Form RPR
6650 1 **Very Well Red**[20] 918 7-9-0 64 WilliamCarson(3) 14 78
(P W Hiatt) *led 2f: cl up tl led again wl over 2f out: rdn clr appr fnl f: kpt on strly* **12/1**
13-5 2 3 ½ **Crystal Feather**[10] 1028 4-9-1 62 TomQueally 13 67
(E F Vaughan) *t.k.h: in tch: hdwy over 3f out: rdn to chse ldng pair over 2f out: kpt on u.p ins fnl f: nt rch wnr* **9/2**[2]
00-5 3 2 **Horsley Warrior**[34] 787 4-8-11 65 (b[1]) DavidKenny(7) 10 66
(E S McMahon) *dwlt and in rr: stdy hdwy 1/2-way: chsd ldrs wl over 2f out: rdn wl over 1f out: kpt on ins fnl f: nrst fin* **12/1**
4512 4 1 **Marjury Daw (IRE)**[14] 970 4-8-13 60 PaulMulrennan 6 59
(J G Given) *chsd ldng pair: hdwy to chal over 3f out: rdn along 2f out: and ev ch tl drvn and wknd over 1f out* **11/1**
/-40 5 3 **Kaballero (GER)**[20] 918 9-8-10 57 FrankieDettori 9 49
(S Gollings) *chsd ldrs: rdn over 2f out: sn drvn and no imp* **8/1**[3]
530- 6 2 ¼ **Mohawk Ridge**[172] 6860 4-9-4 65 PhillipMakin 3 52
(M Dods) *dwlt and in rr: hdwy 3f out: shkn up over 2f out: kpt on: nt rch ldrs* **8/1**[3]
566- 7 5 **Tanforan**[196] 6217 8-9-4 65 RichardHughes 12 40
(B P J Baugh) *t.k.h: hld up towards rr: hdwy over 3f out and sn pushed along: rdn 2f out and sn no imp* **9/1**
-502 8 ¾ **Saving Grace**[28] 854 4-8-4 51 oh3 FrannyNorton 7 24
(E J Alston) *chsd wnr: led after 2f: rdn along and hdd 3f out: drvn over 2f out and sn wknd* **14/1**
00-0 9 1 **Iron Man Of Mersey (FR)**[28] 847 4-8-1 53 oh6 ow2 SophieDoyle(5) 2 24
(A W Carroll) *in tch: rdn along over 3f out and sn no hdwy* **33/1**
/05- 10 7 **Starlight Gazer**[116] 7728 7-9-2 63 PatDobbs 1 18
(J C Fox) *chsd ldr: led after 2f: rdn along over 3f out: hdd wl over 2f out and sn wknd* **20/1**
-202 11 3 ¼ **Having A Ball**[14] 975 6-8-8 55 ChrisCatlin 5 —
(P D Cundell) *a in rr* **4/1**[1]
0-00 12 31 **Esteem Lord**[14] 975 4-8-12 59 NeilCallan 8 —
(Jamie Poulton) *t.k.h in rr: pushed along and sme hdwy over 3f out: sn rdn and wknd* **20/1**
0000 13 nse **Admirals Way**[63] 388 5-8-0 52 BillyCray(5) 4 —
(C N Kellett) *chsd ldrs: rdn along 1/2-way: sn wknd: bhd and eased over 1f out* **50/1**
060- 14 64 **Catchmeifyoucan (FR)**[23] 6910 4-9-0 61 PaulHanagan 11 —
(Andrew Turnell) *in tch on wd outside: rdn along 1/2-way: sn wknd and bhd fnl 2f* **50/1**

1m 52.12s (2.52) **Going Correction** +0.35s/f (Good) 14 Ran SP% **117.2**
Speed ratings (Par 101): **101,97,95,94,91 89,84,83,82,75 72,41,41,—**
toteswingers: 1&2 £17.30, 1&3 £30.90, 2&3 £10.40 CSF £59.92 CT £497.03 TOTE £13.80: £4.40, £2.10, £3.30; EX 76.30.
Owner Phil Kelly **Bred** Butts Enterprises Limited **Trained** Hook Norton, Oxon

FOCUS
Following a dry night, the going was officially described as Soft all round. This was a very moderate handicap with few ever getting into it and the winning time was over ten seconds above standard. The winner is probably the best guide to the form.
Very Well Red Official explanation: trainer's rep said, regarding apparent improvement in form, that he could not explain the poor run last time.
Having A Ball Official explanation: jockey said gelding was unsuited by the soft ground
Esteem Lord Official explanation: jockey said gelding was unsuited by the soft ground
Admirals Way Official explanation: jockey said gelding ran too free
Catchmeifyoucan(FR) Official explanation: jockey said gelding had a breathing problem

1173 EUROPEAN BREEDERS' FUND TOTEPLACEPOT NOVICE STKS 5f 13y
2:20 (2:20) (Class 4) 2-Y-O £4,630 (£1,377; £688; £343) Stalls Centre

Form RPR
5 1 **Little Libretto (IRE)**[11] 1009 2-8-9 0 PaulHanagan 5 72
(P D Evans) *mde all: rdn over 1f out: drvn ins fnl f: kpt on wl towards fin* **25/1**
3 2 ½ **Bajan Bullet**[9] 1043 2-8-9 0 CathyGannon 7 70
(P D Evans) *cl up: effrt over 1f out: sn rdn and ev ch tl drvn: edgd rt and no ex last 50yds* **15/2**[3]
2 3 ½ **Style And Panache (IRE)**[7] 1066 2-8-9 0 JamieSpencer 3 68
(P D Evans) *trckd ldng pair: hdwy and cl up 2f out: rdn over 1f out: ev ch and drvn ins fnl f: no ex last 100yds* **8/11**[1]
1 4 2 **Takeaway**[11] 1017 2-9-5 0 RichardHughes 1 71
(R Hannon) *trckd ldrs: effrt over 1f out: rdn and n.m.r ent ins fnl f: sn one pce* **3/1**[2]
4 5 22 **Wotsthehurry**[9] 1043 2-8-9 0 AlanMunro 6 —
(M R Channon) *rrd s: in tch: rdn along 2f out: sn outpcd and eased* **12/1**

65.06 secs (4.06) **Going Correction** +0.70s/f (Yiel) 5 Ran SP% **106.2**
Speed ratings (Par 94): **95,94,93,90,55**
CSF £162.54 TOTE £25.80: £7.20, £2.20; EX 44.00.
Owner Mrs I M Folkes **Bred** Agricola Dell 'Olmo Srl **Trained** Pandy, Monmouths

FOCUS
An interesting little novice event in which David Evans was responsible for three of the five remaining runners and they finished 1-2-3, though not in the order most would have expected. The field raced down the centre of the track and the order barely changed throughout the contest. The form does not appear that strong.

NOTEBOOK
Little Libretto(IRE) had finished fifth in the Brocklesby on debut and the second from that race hadn't done much for the form at Ffos Las the previous day, but she showed good early speed at Doncaster and did the same here, dominating from the off and showing real guts to hold off her two stable companions. (op 16-1)
Bajan Bullet, a promising third on her Lingfield Polytrack debut despite not appearing to handle the track, was always handy and stuck to her task after coming off the bridle inside the last 2f, but she could never quite get the better of her stablemate. She already looks as though she could do with an extra furlong. (op 13-2 tchd 10-1)
Style And Panache(IRE), clear of the third when runner-up to a nice prospect on her Southwell debut, looked the stable's number one according to the market but she was keen enough early and, despite plenty of assistance from the saddle, she was never quite doing enough. She may not have liked this ground. Official explanation: jockey said filly was unsuited by the soft ground (op 11-10)
Takeaway, the only colt in the field and easy winner of a Kempton Polytrack maiden on debut, travelled well enough after missing the break but didn't pick up when asked. He faced a stiff task under his penalty, but may prefer a sounder surface. (op 15-8 tchd 13-8)
Wotsthehurry, just behind Bajan Bullet when fourth on her Lingfield debut and 2lb worse off, was the first beaten. Official explanation: jockey said filly was unsuited by the soft ground (op 14-1)

1174 TOTESWINGER CONDITIONS STKS 5f 13y
2:50 (2:50) (Class 3) 3-Y-O+ £6,799 (£2,023; £1,011; £505) Stalls Centre

Form RPR
050- 1 **Wi Dud**[165] 7015 6-9-1 97 JamieSpencer 3 109
(K A Ryan) *hld up: hdwy 1/2-way: swtchd lft and effrt over 1f out: rdn and qcknd to ld ins fnl f: kpt on strly* **9/2**[3]
00-0 2 2 ¼ **Moorhouse Lad**[18] 948 7-9-1 100 TomEaves 1 101
(B Smart) *a.p: hdwy 2f out: rdn to ld over 1f out: drvn and hdd ins fnl f: kpt on same pce* **8/1**
2-16 3 1 **Rebel Duke (IRE)**[20] 916 6-8-8 94 LeeTopliss(7) 8 97
(Ollie Pears) *prom: hdwy and cl up 2f out: rdn and ev ch over 1f out: edgd lft and one pce ins fnl f* **10/1**
560- 4 2 ¾ **Angus Newz**[172] 6843 7-8-10 82 FrannyNorton 7 82
(M Quinn) *prom: pushed along 2f out: sn rdn and kpt on same pce appr fnl f* **25/1**
641- 5 1 **Quest For Success (IRE)**[165] 7015 5-9-1 99 PaulHanagan 2 84
(R A Fahey) *trckd ldrs: effrt 2f out: sn rdn and wknd ent fnl f* **15/8**[1]
142- 6 nk **Noble Storm (USA)**[188] 6427 4-9-10 105 GrahamGibbons 5 92
(E S McMahon) *t.k.h: chsd ldrs tl led after 1f: rdn along 2f out: hdd over 1f out: wknd ins fnl f* **3/1**[2]
5340 7 ½ **Pawan (IRE)**[20] 916 10-8-10 80 (p) AnnStokell(5) 4 81
(Miss A Stokell) *dwlt: a in rr* **66/1**
240- 8 1 ¾ **Mattamia (IRE)**[214] 5654 4-8-12 93 JamesMillman(3) 6 75
(B R Millman) *led 1f: prom and rdn along 1/2-way: sn wknd* **9/1**

63.31 secs (2.31) **Going Correction** +0.70s/f (Yiel) 8 Ran SP% **113.5**
Speed ratings (Par 107): **109,105,103,99,97 97,96,93**
toteswingers: 1&2 £5.10, 1&3 £13.30, 2&3 £10.20 CSF £39.21 TOTE £7.70: £2.70, £2.20, £2.40; EX 40.20.
Owner J Duddy,L Duddy,P McBride,Mrs J Ryan **Bred** D R Botterill **Trained** Hambleton, N Yorks

FOCUS
An interesting conditions sprint in which the favourite had won five of the last seven runnings. The runner-up is rated to last year's best.

NOTEBOOK
Wi Dud had every chance at the weights, but he was behind Quest For Success when last seen in October and was without a win since the 2006 Flying Childers. However, he was always cruising behind the leaders under Spencer here and found plenty when switched wide to hit the front inside the last furlong. His rider reported that he won despite not liking the ground and he is now likely to head for the Temple Stakes. (tchd 4-1)
Moorhouse Lad, marginally best in at the weights but disappointing since finishing runner-up in the 2008 Prix de l'Abbaye, ran much better here and had every chance before the winner pounced. He can win races if stepping forward from this. (op 10-1 tchd 7-1)
Rebel Duke(IRE), better known as a Fibresand sprinter, was always up there and had every chance until well inside the last furlong. He wasn't disgraced in his one start on turf last year and has winning form on soft ground, so this decent effort wasn't a surprise. (op 9-1 tchd 12-1)
Angus Newz, off since October and without a win since September 2008, has plenty of winning form on this sort of ground but she faced a stiff task at these weights. She will probably be better off back in races confined to her own sex. (op 22-1)
Quest For Success(IRE), not seen since winning an ultra-competitive Doncaster handicap in October, was proven on a testing surface and had every chance on these terms, but he failed to pick up for pressure and was a bit disappointing. (op 7-4 tchd 2-1)
Noble Storm(USA), a most progressive sprinter last season and twice successful on soft ground as a juvenile, ran fast until over a furlong out and may have just needed it. (op 4-1)
Pawan(IRE), badly in at the weights just as he was when narrowly beaten in this race last year, was taken off his feet throughout. (op 80-1)
Mattamia(IRE), who won the following handicap on his reappearance at this meeting last year, showed up for a while but his trainer had warned that the soft ground was against him so this effort is easily forgiven. (tchd 8-1 and 10-1)

1175 TOTEEXACTA H'CAP 5f 13y
3:20 (3:21) (Class 5) (0-70,70) 3-Y-O £2,590 (£770; £385; £192) Stalls Centre

Form RPR
-245 1 **Kylladdie**[21] 901 3-9-4 70 FrankieDettori 3 80
(S Gollings) *cl up: slt ld 1/2-way: rdn and hung rt over 1f out: drvn clr ins fnl f* **13/8**[1]
1122 2 3 ¼ **Boogie Waltzer**[34] 783 3-8-12 67 WilliamCarson(3) 2 65
(S C Williams) *wnt lft s: racd wd: chsd ldrs: hdwy 2f out: ev ch and rdn over 1f out: drvn: edgd lft and one pce ins fnl f* **9/4**[2]
210- 3 1 ½ **Tell Me A Story**[166] 6983 3-9-3 69 AlanMunro 5 62
(M Brittain) *prom: effrt 2f out: sn rdn and ev ch tl wknd appr fnl f* **15/2**
1-40 4 2 ½ **Billie Jean**[57] 471 3-8-11 63 RichardHills 7 47
(B W Hills) *chsd ldrs: rdn over 2f out: sn one pce* **6/1**[3]
1- 5 2 ¾ **Midget**[301] 2800 3-8-11 63 DavidNolan 6 37
(D Carroll) *led to 1/2-way: sn rdn along: wknd wl over 1f out* **11/1**
U60- 6 3 ½ **Proper Littlemadam**[177] 6721 3-8-11 63 TomQueally 4 24
(C N Kellett) *a in rr: outpcd fr 1/2-way* **40/1**

65.26 secs (4.26) **Going Correction** +0.825s/f (Soft) 6 Ran SP% **105.7**
Speed ratings (Par 98): **98,92,90,86,82 76**
toteswingers: 1&2 £1.20, 1&3 £3.10, 2&3 £2.90 CSF £4.73 CT £13.58 TOTE £1.90: £2.60, £1.10; EX 4.70.
Owner P S Walter **Bred** Horizon Bloodstock Limited **Trained** Scamblesby, Lincs

FOCUS
An ordinary 3-y-o sprint handicap with one gelding against five fillies and the runners used the full width of the track. The winner is rated to his early juvenile form.

1176 TOTEPOOL "FURTHER FLIGHT" STKS (LISTED RACE) 1m 6f 15y
3:50 (3:50) (Class 1) 4-Y-O+
£22,708 (£8,608; £4,308; £2,148; £1,076; £540) Stalls Low

Form RPR
101- 1 **Opinion Poll (IRE)**[179] 6662 4-8-11 104 FrankieDettori 2 116+
(M A Jarvis) *trckd ldrs: smooth hdwy over 4f out: led on bit 2f out: sn wl clr: heavily eased ins fnl f* **11/8**[1]
4-00 2 4 **Montaff**[41] 712 4-8-11 0 AlanMunro 6 100
(M R Channon) *midfield: hdwy on outer 4f out: rdn to chse ldrs over 2f out: drvn to chse wnr and hung lft over 1f out: sn no imp* **12/1**

330- **3** 1 1/4 **Halla San**[46] 3143 8-9-0 97 .... PaulHanagan 7 98
(R A Fahey) *towards rr: pushed along over 6f out: hdwy over 3f out: sn rdn: kpt on appr fnl f: n.d* **33/1**

521- **4** 3 1/2 **Deportment**[162] 7101 4-8-6 82 .... WilliamCarson 11 88
(S C Williams) *led: rdn 4f out: drvn 3f out: hdd 2f out and grad wknd* **25/1**

550/ **5** shd **Raincoat**[30] 4508 6-9-0 95 .... TedDurcan 10 93
(F J Brennan) *hld up and bhd: hdwy on outer over 3f out: sn rdn: nvr rchd ldrs* **125/1**

21P/ **6** 8 **Shipmaster**[700] 1916 7-9-0 0 .... JamieSpencer 1 82
(A King) *cl up: rdn along 4f out: drvn over 3f out and grad wknd* **11/1**

025- **7** 3/4 **Drill Sergeant**[165] 7031 5-9-0 106 .... JoeFanning 5 81
(M Johnston) *trckd ldrs: effrt 4f out: rdn along 3f out: drvn over 2f out and sn btn* **15/2**[3]

130- **8** 18 **Swingkeel (IRE)**[172] 6851 5-9-0 96 .... JimmyFortune 9 55
(J L Dunlop) *hld up towards rr: hdwy over 4f out: rdn to chse ldrs 3f out: sn drvn and wknd* **11/1**

9 nk **Carnac (IRE)**[176] 4-8-11 81 .... PaulMulrennan 4 55
(J S Wainwright) *midfield: effrt 4f out: sn rdn and wknd* **100/1**

320- **10** 32 **Tastahil (IRE)**[151] 7293 6-9-0 109 .... RichardHills 8 10
(B W Hills) *trckd ldrs: hdwy and cl up 1/2-way: rdn over 4f out: wknd qckly: bhd and eased fnl 3f* **5/2**[2]

3m 16.97s (9.67) **Going Correction** +0.475s/f (Yiel)
WFA 4 from 5yo+ 3lb **10** Ran SP% **115.4**
Speed ratings (Par 111): **91,88,88,86,85 81,80,70,70,52**
toteswingers: 1&2 £5.40, 1&3 £8.40, 2&3 £20.00 CSF £19.40 TOTE £2.40: £1.30, £2.50, £5.00; EX 19.50.
Owner Sheikh Ahmed Al Maktoum **Bred** Darley **Trained** Newmarket, Suffolk

FOCUS
This race had been won by a 4-y-o four times in the past five years, but although that age-group made up only 40% of this field they once again provided the first two home. The pace seemed generous enough in the conditions and it all proved too much for a few, with the runners finishing very well spread out. The winner is progressive although there is some doubt about what he has beaten.

NOTEBOOK
Opinion Poll(IRE) ◆, who was a progressive handicapper last year, handles this ground and was stepping up 2f in trip for this return to action. He had reportedly done plenty of work, however, and he looked the winner from a long way out as his rider was sitting motionless whilst his rivals were hard at it. Once the button was pressed 2f from home he was soon away and clear and, though the form could be viewed as dubious with his main market rival running a shocker, the margin of victory gives no indication as to his superiority. He now looks ready for something even better, and a step up to 2m for the Sagaro Stakes may be an option. (tchd 6-4)
Montaff, proven in testing ground and not disgraced in two starts at Meydan in February, stayed on from the middle of the field over the last 4f to finish a clear second best, but was never in the same parish as the winner. He may not be the easiest to place this season. (op 14-1 tchd 11-1)
Halla San, having his first outing on the Flat since last June but very disappointing in two starts over hurdles since then, was given plenty to do and though he stayed on all the way up the home straight, he never had a hope of getting there. He needs an even greater test of stamina than this. (tchd 28-1)
Deportment, last seen winning a Yarmouth handicap for James Fanshawe in October, was trying further than 1m2f for the first time on this reappearance. Keen enough in front, she nonetheless did very well to hang in there until the winner swooped past on her inside passing the 2f pole. Lack of peak fitness rather than lack of stamina may have been the issue and she faced a stiff task at the weights in any case, so much will depend on how the Handicapper interprets this.
Raincoat, a shadow of the horse that won the 2007 Blue Riband Trial Stakes, was having his first start on the Flat since July 2008 and hasn't looked a natural in five tries over hurdles in the meantime. He stayed on down the outside over the last 3f and wasn't disgraced, but this looked a case of him running on past beaten rivals and he will need to back this up before he becomes a betting proposition. (op 200-1)
Shipmaster, winner of the 2008 Group 3 Sagaro Stakes but not seen since pulling up in the Chester Cup the following month, loves these conditions and was only beaten a whisker in this race two years ago. Having attracted some market support, he showed up prominently until understandably blowing up over 2f from home, and this should have done him the world of good. (op 16-1)
Drill Sergeant, well in at the weights, has won first time out in the past and goes in the ground so the way he faded after coming off the bridle on the home turn was disappointing. (op 9-1 tchd 7-1)
Swingkeel(IRE), not seen since beaten a very long way in the Cesarewitch, made a short-lived effort coming to the last 2f and ideally needs further than this. Official explanation: jockey said gelding was unsuited by the soft ground (op 12-1 tchd 10-1)
Tastahil(IRE), last seen finishing in mid-division on the November Handicap, won first time out last year, likes these conditions, and was best in at the weights so he had plenty going for him, but he came under pressure starting the turn for home and gradually dropped right out. His rider reported that he had lost his action. Official explanation: jockey said gelding lost its action (tchd 9-4 and 11-4)

1177 TOTESUPER7 H'CAP 1m 2f 50y
4:20 (4:20) (Class 5) (0-70,68) 4-Y-0+ **£2,590** (£770; £385; £192) **Stalls** Low

Form RPR

55-2 **1** **Brockfield**[2] 1116 4-8-8 58 .... AlanMunro 9 72
(M Brittain) *chsd ldng pair: hdwy 3f out: rdn to chal 2f out: drvn to ld appr fnl f: r.o wl* **9/1**[3]

00-1 **2** 1 1/4 **Blue Spinnaker (IRE)**[10] 1028 11-8-9 64 6ex .... JamesSullivan(5) 13 76+
(M W Easterby) *hld up in rr: hdwy on outer 3f out: rdn 2f out: styd on ins fnl f: nt rch wnr* **7/2**[2]

60-2 **3** 2 3/4 **Royal Straight**[11] 1012 5-8-8 58 .... PaulHanagan 10 64
(R A Fahey) *trckd ldrs: effrt over 2f out: rdn wl over 1f out and sn one pce* **7/4**[1]

3120 **4** 4 1/2 **Whodunit (UAE)**[14] 975 6-9-1 68 .... (b) WilliamCarson(3) 4 66
(P W Hiatt) *led: rdn along 3f out: drvn 2f out: hdd over 1f out: grad wknd* **33/1**

403- **5** 3/4 **Highkingofireland**[154] 7247 4-8-11 61 .... TomQueally 7 57
(J R Weymes) *hld up towards rr: gd hdwy on inner 4f out: chsd ldrs 3f out: rdn 2f out: kpt on same pce* **16/1**

442- **6** 1 3/4 **Inspirina (IRE)**[165] 7020 6-9-3 67 .... RichardHughes 14 60
(R Ford) *t.k.h in tch: hdwy 3f out: sn rdn: nvr nr ldrs* **9/1**[3]

025- **7** 3/4 **Croeso Cusan**[154] 7248 5-8-2 57 .... SophieDoyle(5) 1 49
(J L Spearing) *chsd ldr: rdn over 3f out: drvn over 2f out: sn wknd* **25/1**

65-0 **8** 2 1/2 **Broughtons Paradis (IRE)**[35] 771 4-8-10 60 .... ChrisCatlin 15 47
(W J Musson) *nvr bttr than mid-div* **22/1**

55-0 **9** shd **Dubai Gem**[48] 593 4-9-0 64 .... NeilCallan 12 51
(Jamie Poulton) *in tch: effrt on outer over 3f out: sn rdn and n.d* **25/1**

-452 **10** 14 **Xpres Maite**[29] 837 7-9-1 65 .... (p) PhillipMakin 6 25
(S R Bowring) *chsd ldrs: rdn along over 3f out: sn wknd* **16/1**

51-5 **11** 14 **Sitwell**[39] 735 4-8-12 62 .... (v) JamieSpencer 5 —
(A King) *hld up towards rr: effrt 4f out: sn rdn and nvr a factor* **25/1**

155- **12** nk **Kyle Of Bute**[161] 7127 4-8-12 62 .... TedDurcan 11 —
(B P J Baugh) *a in rr* **33/1**

55-5 **13** 12 **Silken Sands (IRE)**[93] 31 4-8-0 57 ow2 .... JohnFahy(7) 2 —
(C G Cox) *a towards rr* **16/1**

600- **14** 2 1/4 **Pitbull**[176] 6761 7-7-13 54 .... (p) BillyCray(5) 3 —
(A Berry) *a in rr: bhd fr 1/2-way* **66/1**

2m 21.61s (7.31) **Going Correction** +0.475s/f (Yiel) **14** Ran SP% **119.5**
Speed ratings (Par 103): **89,88,85,82,81 80,79,77,77,66 55,54,45,43**
toteswingers: 1&2 £9.60, 1&3 £8.90, 2&3 £2.90 CSF £37.09 CT £82.80 TOTE £10.00: £2.50, £2.10, £1.30; EX 73.80.
Owner Mel Brittain **Bred** Cheveley Park Stud Ltd **Trained** Warthill, N Yorks

FOCUS
An ordinary handicap dominated by those at the head of the market. The runner-up is rated in line with last season's best efforts.
Croeso Cusan Official explanation: jockey said mare ran too free
Broughtons Paradis(IRE) Official explanation: jockey said filly never travelled
Pitbull Official explanation: jockey said gelding was unsuited by the soft ground

1178 BET TOTEPOOL AT TOTESPORT.COM H'CAP 1m 75y
4:50 (4:51) (Class 5) (0-70,70) 3-Y-O **£2,590** (£770; £385; £192) **Stalls** Low

Form RPR

300- **1** **Lord Raglan (IRE)**[156] 7210 3-8-10 62 .... TomQueally 6 67
(J R Weymes) *midfield: gd hdwy on inner over 3f out: chal 2f out: rdn to ld ins fnl f: sn drvn and kpt on wl* **40/1**

-056 **2** 3/4 **Chateau Zara**[36] 762 3-8-0 59 ow3 .... JohnFahy(7) 11 62
(C G Cox) *cl up: led 3f out: rdn over 1f out: drvn and hdd ins fnl f: one pce* **16/1**

05-3 **3** 2 1/2 **Tilsworth Glenboy**[81] 206 3-8-13 65 .... RichardHughes 3 69+
(J R Jenkins) *hld up in rr: gd hdwy on inner over 3f out: trckd ldrs over 2f out: swtchd rt and rdn to chal whn hung bdly lft and then rt ins fnl f: one pce after* **11/1**

000- **4** 5 **Choc'A'Moca (IRE)**[162] 7079 3-8-4 56 oh11 .... CathyGannon 7 42
(D Carroll) *led: rdn and hdd 3f out: drvn 2f out and grad wknd* **66/1**

06-4 **5** 7 **Tell Halaf**[22] 894 3-8-13 65 .... JamieSpencer 12 35
(M L W Bell) *plld hrd: in tch: rdn 3f out: swtchd lft over 2f out: plugged on same pce* **5/2**[1]

435- **6** 4 1/2 **Interakt**[204] 5970 3-9-3 69 .... AlanMunro 2 29
(M R Channon) *hld up in rr: hdwy 4f out: rdn to chse ldrs over 2f out: sn drvn and no imp* **8/1**

066- **7** 3 1/2 **All Moving Parts (USA)**[169] 6923 3-9-4 70 .... PaulMulrennan 5 22
(J S Wainwright) *in rr: sme hdwy on inner over 3f out: sn rdn and nvr a factor* **66/1**

500- **8** 2 3/4 **High Holborn (IRE)**[211] 5742 3-9-1 67 .... (b[1]) PaulFitzsimons 13 12
(Miss J R Tooth) *t.k.h: chsd ldrs on outside: rdn over 3f out: sn wknd* **18/1**

6-04 **9** 1/2 **Sixties Rock**[72] 288 3-8-5 57 .... ChrisCatlin 1 —
(J A Glover) *t.k.h: chsd ldrs: rdn 3f out: sn wknd* **22/1**

1 **10** 6 **Rubi Dia**[54] 523 3-8-13 65 .... JoeFanning 8 —
(M Johnston) *chsd ldrs: rdn over 3f out: drvn and wknd wl over 2f out* **3/1**[2]

00-3 **11** 9 **Stratton Banker (IRE)**[50] 570 3-8-13 65 .... (t) TedDurcan 4 —
(S C Williams) *hld up: a towards rr* **20/1**

500- **12** 1 1/4 **On The Cusp (IRE)**[166] 6990 3-9-4 70 .... NeilCallan 10 —
(M A Jarvis) *chsd ldrs: rdn over 3f out: sn wknd* **11/1**

032- **13** 4 1/2 **Primo De Vida (IRE)**[171] 6874 3-9-2 68 .... JimCrowley 9 —
(R M Beckett) *chsd ldrs: rdn 1/2-way: sn wknd* **7/1**[3]

1m 55.78s (6.18) **Going Correction** +0.475s/f (Yiel) **13** Ran SP% **119.5**
Speed ratings (Par 98): **88,87,84,79,72 68,64,62,61,55 46,45,40**
toteswingers: 1&2 £70.70, 1&3 £18.40, 2&3 £27.80 CSF £561.76 CT £7566.47 TOTE £48.60: £12.40, £6.30, £4.90; EX 681.00.
Owner John A Duffy **Bred** Skymarc Farm **Trained** Middleham Moor, N Yorks
■ Stewards' Enquiry : John Fahy one-day ban: used whip with excessive frequency (Apr 21)

FOCUS
A modest event in which only one of the 13 runners had won a race before, but several of these were unknown quantities and/or making their handicap debuts. Again it was an advantage to be handy, even though the winner came from off the pace. Not a race to be positive about.
Tell Halaf Official explanation: jockey said colt hung left-handed throughout

1179 BET TOTEPOOL ON 0800 221 221 H'CAP (DIV II) 1m 75y
5:20 (5:20) (Class 6) (0-65,65) 4-Y-O+ **£1,619** (£481; £240; £120) **Stalls** Low

Form RPR

-550 **1** **West End Lad**[21] 908 7-8-10 60 .... (b) AshleyHamblett(3) 5 72
(S R Bowring) *chsd ldr: led 3f out: rdn clr 2f out: hld on wl towards fin* **9/2**[2]

-500 **2** hd **Ermine Grey**[10] 1028 9-8-9 56 ow1 .... JamieSpencer 3 68
(A W Carroll) *trckd ldrs: swtchd rt 3f out: rdn to chse wnr and edgd lft 2f out: sn drvn and styd on u.p ins fnl f: jst failed* **3/1**[1]

036- **3** 8 **Full Victory (IRE)**[168] 6937 8-9-4 65 .... GrahamGibbons 2 59
(R A Farrant) *hld up in rr: gd hdwy on inner 4f out: chsd ldrs over 2f out: sn rdn and no imp* **9/1**

-600 **4** 4 **Bookiebasher Babe (IRE)**[22] 893 5-8-6 53 .... FrannyNorton 4 37
(M Quinn) *led: rdn along and hdd 3f out: grad wknd* **22/1**

0-53 **5** 14 **Millfields Dreams**[38] 747 11-9-4 65 .... (p) TomMcLaughlin 12 17
(P Leech) *midfield: effrt 4f out: rdn along 3f out: nvr nr ldrs* **20/1**

450- **6** 3 1/4 **Lilly Royal (IRE)**[154] 7246 4-9-2 63 .... RichardHughes 7 8
(B Palling) *towards rr: sme hdwy over 3f out: nvr a factor* **15/2**

0400 **7** 1 3/4 **Pachakutek (USA)**[9] 1049 4-8-12 59 .... (v[1]) AlanMunro 8 —
(A J Lidderdale) *chsd ldrs: rdn along 4f out: sn wknd* **40/1**

0-00 **8** 1 1/4 **Affirmatively**[55] 499 5-8-0 54 oh6 ow3 .... (bt) JohnFahy(7) 9 —
(A W Carroll) *a bhd* **40/1**

3061 **9** 2 1/4 **Golden Prospect**[6] 1078 6-9-2 63 6ex .... PaulFitzsimons 10 —
(Miss J R Tooth) *s.i.s: a bhd* **7/1**

505- **10** 13 **Big Whitfield**[161] 7126 4-9-1 62 .... PhillipMakin 13 —
(M Dods) *a in rr: bhd fr 1/2-way* **5/1**[3]

540- **11** 14 **Eyes Like A Hawk (IRE)**[209] 5806 4-8-11 58 .... PaulHanagan 1 —
(Jedd O'Keeffe) *chsd ldrs: rdn along over 4f out: sn wknd* **14/1**

1m 53.06s (3.46) **Going Correction** +0.475s/f (Yiel) **11** Ran SP% **114.8**
Speed ratings (Par 101): **101,100,92,88,74 71,69,68,66,53 39**
toteswingers: 1&2 £5.00, 1&3 £11.20, 2&3 £9.00 CSF £17.06 CT £113.47 TOTE £4.60: £1.40, £1.30, £1.60; EX 17.80 Place 6: £402.66 Place 5: £123.82.
Owner K Nicholls **Bred** Keith Nicholls **Trained** Edwinstowe, Notts

FOCUS
A moderate handicap and another race in which it paid to be up there from the start. Again very few ever got into it and the winning time was just under a second slower than the first division. The runner-up looks the best guide to the level.
Golden Prospect Official explanation: jockey said gelding ran flat
T/Plt: £420.60 to a £1 stake. Pool: £57,289.10. 99.42 winning tickets. T/Qpdt: £16.20 to a £1 stake. Pool: £4,300.46. 196.10 winning tickets. JR

LEICESTER (R-H)

Thursday, April 8

OFFICIAL GOING: Soft (heavy in places; 5.4)

Wind: virtually nil Weather: bright and sunny

1180 LADBROKES.COM KNIGHTON MEDIAN AUCTION MAIDEN STKS 5f 2y

2:15 (2:15) (Class 5) 2-Y-O **£2,590** (£770; £385; £192) **Stalls** Low

Form RPR

1 **Mayfair Princess** 2-8-12 0 ChrisCatlin 2 65
(P S McEntee) *chsd ldrs: led after 1f: mde rest: shkn up and hung rt fr over 1f out: rdn and hung rt across crse ins fnl f: hld on* **40/1**

3 2 ½ **Molly Mylenis**[7] 1073 2-8-12 0 CathyGannon 9 65+
(P D Evans) *disp ld for 1f: chsd ldng pair after: rdn over 2f out: chsd wnr over 1f out: trying to chal whn carried rt fnl 150yds: hmpd fnl 75yds: kpt on* **10/3**[2]

3 2 ½ **Mollyow (IRE)** 2-8-12 0 DavidProbert 3 54
(B Palling) *dwlt: bhd: rdn over 3f out: styd on steadily fnl f to go 3rd nr fin: nvr trbld ldrs* **9/1**

0 4 nk **Unknown Rebel (IRE)**[12] 1017 2-9-3 0 NeilCallan 4 58
(K A Ryan) *chsd ldrs: rdn over 3f out: kpt on same pce u.p fr over 1f out: nvr gng pce to threaten ldrs* **20/1**

0 5 nse **Sky Diamond (IRE)**[12] 1009 2-9-3 0 PaulMulrennan 8 58
(J G Given) *sn rdn along in midfield: hdwy u.p ent fnl f: wnt 3rd fnl 100yds: no imp and lost 2 pls nr fin* **7/2**[3]

6 ½ **Zarazar** 2-8-12 0 AndrewHeffernan[(5)] 1 56
(P D Evans) *s.i.s: sn bhd and rn green: styd on wl fnl f: nvr trbld ldrs* **28/1**

0 7 ½ **The Best Mode (IRE)**[12] 1009 2-9-3 0 JamieSpencer 7 54
(P D Evans) *disp ld for 1f: chsd wnr after tl over 1f out: wknd fnl f* **8/1**

2 8 1 **Calormen**[7] 1073 2-9-3 0 KierenFallon 6 51
(M R Channon) *dwlt: sn pushed along in midfield: rdn and no prog wl over 1f out: no ch w ldrs fnl f* **2/1**[1]

0 9 24 **Sailor Boy (IRE)**[8] 1066 2-9-0 0 AndreaAtzeni[(3)] 5 —
(D Donovan) *a towards rr: rdn and struggling 3f out: t.o fnl f* **66/1**

66.32 secs (6.32) **Going Correction** +0.825s/f (Soft) 9 Ran SP% **111.9**
Speed ratings (Par 92): **82,81,77,76,76 75,75,73,35**
toteswingers: 1&2 £21.90, 1&3 £21.80, 2&3 £6.00 CSF £161.02 TOTE £35.40: £5.30, £1.40, £2.40; EX 132.00 TRIFECTA Not won..
Owner Mrs Rebecca McEntee **Bred** P Balding **Trained** Newmarket, Suffolk

FOCUS
Difficult to gauge, but this was probably just an ordinary event of its type and those with form did not seem to set an especially high standard.

NOTEBOOK
Mayfair Princess, a daughter of speedy stallion Superior Premium out of mare who won several times from 5-9f, was quickly out of the gates and made all. She started to drift right shortly after the furlong pole and, despite her rider using his whip in the correct hand, eventually veered right across the track, taking the second with her. The stewards considered her antics did not affect the placings and let the result stand, but backers of the runner-up may well feel aggrieved. (tchd 50-1)
Molly Mylenis, only a neck behind Calormen when both had made their debut seven days earlier, renewed rivalry on the same terms and comfortably reversed those placings. Never far off the pace, she made her challenge on the far side of Mayfair Princess and was pushed across the course for the last half-furlong. Her rider had to snatch up close home and she can be considered an unlucky loser. (op 7-2 tchd 5-2)
Mollyow(IRE), an inexpensively-purchased half-sister to 5f juvenile winner, lost ground at the start. She gradually clawed back the deficit however, and was staying on at the finish. She should improve for this experience. (op 14-1)
Unknown Rebel(IRE) had beaten only one home on his Kempton debut, but showed a good deal more switched to turf. His form here is probably not good enough to indicate he will take a maiden in the near future, but he clearly has some ability. (op 14-1)
Sky Diamond(IRE), a nine-length eighth in the Brocklesby at Doncaster after getting loose in the paddock, did not do a great deal for that Town Moor form. (op 9-2 tchd 5-1)
Zarazar has a pedigree suggesting longer trips will ultimately suit and, given his breeding, he did not fare too badly. (op 22-1)
Calormen, a staying-on second in this sort of ground at Folkestone a week previously, seemed likely to be suited by the stiffer course here, but appeared not to progress from that first outing. (op 13-8)

1181 LADBROKES.COM (S) STKS 5f 218y

2:50 (2:51) (Class 6) 3-Y-O **£1,942** (£578; £288; £144) **Stalls** Low

Form RPR

0-23 1 **Thaliwarru**[28] 861 3-9-0 60 SteveDrowne 9 65
(J R Gask) *hld up in tch: hdwy 1/2-way: rdn to chal wl over 1f out: led jst over 1f out: edged lft u.p fnl f: kpt on wl* **9/2**[2]

4635 2 1 **Arken Lad**[29] 851 3-9-2 64 (p) AndreaAtzeni[(3)] 6 67
(D Donovan) *led: rdn and racd awkwardly 2f out: hdd jst over 1f out: kpt on same pce u.p ins fnl f: edgd rt nr fin* **7/1**

0-40 3 4 **Hill Of Miller (IRE)**[28] 856 3-9-0 65 (t) MartinDwyer 3 49
(Rae Guest) *s.i.s: bhd: hdwy and swtchd lft over 2f out: kpt plugging on to 3rd ins fnl f: nvr gng pce to threaten ldrs* **8/1**

600- 4 2 ½ **Monte Mayor One**[160] 7156 3-9-0 57 DaneO'Neill 8 41
(D Haydn Jones) *in tch: chsd ldr jst over 2f out tl wl over 1f out: wknd u.p over 1f out* **11/1**

6-46 5 6 **Tom Folan**[43] 678 3-9-0 68 (p) RobertWinston 4 22
(Andrew Reid) *s.i.s: sn in mdifield: rdn and no prog ent fnl 2f: wl btn over 1f out* **15/8**[1]

400- 6 5 **Special Betty**[99] 7871 3-8-9 48 (v[1]) FrankieMcDonald 2 —
(D Haydn Jones) *chsd ldrs: rdn wl over 2f out: sn struggling: wl bhd fr wl over 1f out* **50/1**

4550 7 nk **Young George**[22] 906 3-8-11 47 KellyHarrison[(3)] 5 —
(C W Fairhurst) *t.k.h: hld up in last trio: rdn and btn wl over 2f out* **33/1**

-343 8 4 **Clear Ice (IRE)**[17] 962 3-9-5 63 AdrianNicholls 7 —
(D Nicholls) *chsd ldr tl jst over 2f out: sn rdn and wknd: wl bhd and eased ins fnl f* **11/2**[3]

0-66 9 7 **Kings Aphrodite**[28] 861 3-9-0 50 LukeMorris 1 —
(Miss Gay Kelleway) *a towards rr: rdn and btn wl over 2f out: wl bhd and eased ins fnl f* **20/1**

1m 17.73s (4.73) **Going Correction** +0.825s/f (Soft) 9 Ran SP% **110.0**
Speed ratings (Par 96): **101,99,94,91,83 76,75,70,61**
toteswingers: 1&2 £5.00, 1&3 £6.20, 2&3 £6.70 CSF £32.69 TOTE £5.80: £2.00, £1.70, £2.20; EX 31.80 Trifecta £261.80 Pool: £367.95- 1.04 winning units..There was no bid for the winner.
Owner Tony Bloom **Bred** Mr & Mrs Kevan Watts **Trained** Sutton Veny, Wilts

FOCUS
A run-of-the-mill seller, with the top-rated runner on a BHA mark of 68. The front pair are the most likely guide to the form.

Tom Folan Official explanation: jockey said filly lost right front shoe

1182 LADBROKES.COM KIBWORTH H'CAP 1m 1f 218y

3:25 (3:27) (Class 3) (0-95,90) 3-Y-O **£6,799** (£2,023; £1,011; £505) **Stalls** High

Form RPR

0-32 1 **Miss Starlight**[11] 1033 3-8-9 78 EddieCreighton 4 89
(P J McBride) *sn niggled along in last pair: hdwy over 3f out: rdn to press ldng pair over 1f out: led ins fnl f: kpt on wl u.p* **9/2**[2]

002- 2 nk **Alrasm (IRE)**[167] 6993 3-9-7 90 RichardHills 3 100+
(M A Jarvis) *t.k.h: chsd ldr tl led over 8f out: settled in front and set stdy gallop: jnd over 2f out: rdn jst over 1f out: hdd ins fnl f: kpt on but a hld by wnr* **2/1**[1]

1441 3 2 ½ **Paintball (IRE)**[11] 1033 3-8-8 77 6ex MartinDwyer 1 82
(W R Muir) *chsd ldr: jnd ldr over 2f out: rdn wl over 1f out: hrd drvn and unable qck ent fnl f: kpt on same pce after* **6/1**[3]

43-4 4 2 ¼ **Dr Finley (IRE)**[28] 864 3-8-4 73 HayleyTurner 5 74
(M L W Bell) *broke wl: led tl over 8f out: t.k.h and trckd ldng pair after: rdn 2f out: wknd u.p over 1f out* **11/1**

310- 5 13 **Tut (IRE)**[201] 6088 3-8-8 77 AndrewElliott 8 52
(J R Weymes) *t.k.h: chsd ldrs early: sn stdd and racd in last pair: reminder 4f out: rdn and btn 3f out: wl bhd and eased fnl f* **33/1**

235- 6 hd **King's Parade**[180] 6672 3-8-1 73 Louis-PhilippeBeuzelin[(3)] 7 48
(Sir Michael Stoute) *in tch: rdn and effrt over 2f out: wknd ent fnl 2f: wl bhd fnl f* **9/2**[2]

51- 7 20 **Jibrrya**[223] 5407 3-9-0 83 AlanMunro 2 18
(M R Channon) *t.k.h: hld up wl in tch: shkn up and hung rt over 2f out: sn wl btn: eased fr over 1f out: t.o* **6/1**[3]

2m 15.56s (7.66) **Going Correction** +0.825s/f (Soft) 7 Ran SP% **109.5**
Speed ratings (Par 102): **102,101,99,97,87 87,71**
toteswingers: 1&2 £3.50, 1&3 £2.60, 2&3 £4.00 CSF £12.72 CT £47.74 TOTE £5.20: £2.50, £1.30; EX 15.60 Trifecta £48.50 Pool: £423.26 - 6.45 winning units..
Owner Maelor Racing **Bred** T J Cooper **Trained** Newmarket, Suffolk

FOCUS
Some of the shine was taken off this when Dante Stakes entry Rigidity was withdrawn in the morning, but it was competitive and the form looks sound. It has been rated around the winner and third who reproduced their Doncaster form at the revised weights.

NOTEBOOK
Miss Starlight was 6lb better off with the penalised Paintball following her short-head defeat by that rival over this distance at Doncaster 11 days earlier and she made that weight turnaround tell with a game victory. Held up in the early stages, she made progress approaching 2f out and quickened up nicely to overhaul the pace-setting runner-up. A rise in the ratings will make it tougher for her - and she is due to go up 5lb immediately after this - but she has an admirable attitude and, according to her jockey, may stay a little farther. (op 4-1 tchd 5-1)
Alrasm(IRE), raised 3lb after his length second over 1m at Doncaster on the last of his two-year-old outings, was not, on breeding at least, an obvious candidate for a step up to this trip. He had stayed on well that day, though, and his rider did not seem to have any doubts about his stamina, as he set out to make all the running. He saw out the trip, even trying to fight back in the closing stages, but he was not quite good enough on these terms. (op 7-4 tchd 9-4)
Paintball(IRE), an all-weather maiden winner in January, had shown improved form when switched to turf and upped in trip at Doncaster last time out. He was carrying a 6lb penalty for that victory, however, and it proved too much. As he appears more or less to have reproduced his Town Moor form here, he will probably find it hard to win again his current mark. (tchd 7-1)
Dr Finley(IRE) is still a maiden and, although in a prominent position early on here, he was unable to hold his place in the home straight. His overall record does not indicate he is progressing with racing and, that being the case, he may need some help from the handicapper. (op 16-1)
Tut(IRE), the outsider of the line-up, made a little late progress after being held up in the early stages, but he was never really in contention. (tchd 40-1)
King's Parade had been beaten just a neck on his debut over 7f at this venue last term and, though his two subsequent efforts were slightly disappointing, he seemed to have scope for improvement stepped up to this distance. He ran moderately, though, never figuring in a seriously challenging position and fading away tamely in the final furlong. (op 5-1 tchd 7-2)

1183 LADBROKES.COM GRANBY MAIDEN STKS 1m 3f 183y

4:00 (4:00) (Class 5) 3-Y-O+ **£2,914** (£867; £433; £216) **Stalls** High

Form RPR

1 **Oscar Close (IRE)**[103] 5-9-9 0 MatthewDavies[(5)] 2 68+
(George Baker) *mde all: rdn wl over 1f out: edgd rt and styd on wl ins fnl f* **2/5**[1]

606- 2 2 **Mohanad (IRE)**[160] 3575 4-9-10 62 RobertLButler[(3)] 4 65
(Miss Sheena West) *trckd wnr: rdn 2f out: edgd lft u.p over 1f out: kpt on same pce ins fnl f* **5/2**[2]

5- 3 16 **Frankie Falco**[117] 7725 4-9-8 0 SimonPearce[(5)] 1 39
(G Fierro) *trckd ldrs: effrt to press ldrs 3f out: hung rt u.p and btn wl over 1f out* **33/1**[3]

0-0 4 10 **Bristol Delauriere (FR)**[34] 803 6-9-7 0 LindsayWhite[(7)] 3 23
(Miss N A Lloyd-Beavis) *dwlt: sn t.k.h and cl up: rdn and edgd rt over 3f out: sn struggling: wl bhd fnl 2f* **80/1**

2m 50.22s (16.32) **Going Correction** +0.825s/f (Soft)
WFA 4 from 5yo+ 1lb 4 Ran SP% **104.2**
Speed ratings (Par 103): **78,76,66,59**
CSF £1.45 TOTE £1.40; EX 1.30.
Owner Wayne Hennessey **Bred** Mrs E Moore **Trained** Moreton Morrell, Warwicks

FOCUS
A very disappointing turn-out, with no 3yos, for a contest that sometimes features a smart performer. The winner is entitled to do better on his jumps form.

1184 LADBROKES.COM CONDITIONS STKS 5f 218y

4:35 (4:36) (Class 3) 3-Y-O **£6,623** (£1,982; £991) **Stalls** Low

Form RPR

541- 1 **Falasteen (IRE)**[194] 6275 3-9-0 93 TonyHamilton 4 93
(R A Fahey) *led: clr 4f out: pressed and rdn over 1f out: narrowly hdd 1f out: kpt on gamely fnl f to ld again on post* **15/8**[2]

042- 2 shd **Singeur (IRE)**[166] 7016 3-9-2 100 DanielTudhope 3 95
(R Bastiman) *t.k.h: hld up in last: clsd and trckd wnr wl over 1f out: pushed along to ld narrowly 1f out: rdn ins fnl f: kpt on but hdd on post* **8/13**[1]

010- 3 6 **Ginger Ted (IRE)**[215] 5658 3-8-7 77 KellyHarrison[(3)] 2 70
(R C Guest) *chsd wnr: shkn up and wanting to hang over 2f out: lost 2nd wl over 1f out: hung rt and btn over 1f out* **10/1**[3]

1m 17.1s (4.10) **Going Correction** +0.825s/f (Soft) 3 Ran SP% **105.8**
Speed ratings (Par 102): **105,104,96**
CSF £3.44 TOTE £2.50; EX 3.20.
Owner Dr Marwan Koukash **Bred** Mrs Anne Marie Burns **Trained** Musley Bank, N Yorks

FOCUS
Another disappointing turn-out, at least numerically, but each of the contestants had solid form. The winner produced a personal best but this form is hardly convincing.

NOTEBOOK

Falasteen(IRE), who made all before holding on gamely to land a Chester nursery from a mark of 86 last September, again showed great tenacity on this first start for the yard. Setting the pace for more than half a mile, he fought back bravely when challenged and overtaken approaching the furlong pole. He had been raised 7lb since that Roodee victory and probably ran to something like his official assessment in winning this, despite not appearing entirely happy on the ground. He may well get another hike in the ratings now, which will not make life easy for him, but courage is in his favour. (tchd 2-1)

Singeur(IRE), successful four times as a two-year-old and beaten just a head at Listed level on his final outing of 2009, set a decent standard. He had to give weight to both his rivals, but his official rating of 100 suggested that should not be beyond him. On the face of it, then, this defeat was disappointing, but, in mitigation, it can be argued that he disliked the ground and did not quite get home. A furlong out he looked like collecting, but he was worried out of first prize close home and will surely be better off on a quicker surface. A drop to 5f is likely to help, too. (op 4-7 tchd 1-2)

Ginger Ted(IRE), winner of two nurseries over this distance in 2009, was already proven in testing conditions. He looked up against it in this event, though, even in receipt of weight from the opposition, and his finishing position was entirely predictable. (op 16-1)

1185 LADBROKES.COM H'CAP — 7f 9y

5:10 (5:12) (Class 4) (0-85,85) 4-Y-O+ **£4,209** (£1,252; £625; £312) **Stalls** Low

Form				RPR
000-	1		**Guilded Warrior**[164] 7060 7-9-3 **84** ... FergusSweeney 1	93
			(W S Kittow) *racd stands' side: mde all: rdn ent fnl 2f: kpt on wl u.p fnl f* **7/1**	
223-	2	3/4	**Lochan Mor**[160] 7155 4-8-12 **79** ... JamieSpencer 2	86
			(M L W Bell) *racd stands' side: trckd ldrs: rdn and effrt 2f out: rdn to chal wl over 1f out: no ex u.p fnl 75yds: 2nd of 4 in gp* **7/2**[3]	
000-	3	2 1/2	**Slugger O'Toole**[152] 7287 5-8-5 **75** ... WilliamCarson(3) 4	75
			(S C Williams) *racd stands' side: hld up in tch: rdn and effrt ent fnl 2f: drvn and styd on same pce fr over 1f out: wnt 3rd ins fnl f: 3rd of 4 in gp* **10/3**[2]	
560-	4	2 3/4	**Dancing Maite**[126] 7617 5-8-5 **75** ... AshleyHamblett(3) 5	68
			(S R Bowring) *racd stands' side: chsd wnr: rdn over 2f out: lost 2nd wl over 1f out: edgd rt and btn 1f out: 4th of 4 in gp* **20/1**	
421-	5	3/4	**Jordaura**[152] 7287 4-9-0 **81** ... JerryO'Dwyer 10	72+
			(J R Holt) *racd far side: t.k.h: hld up wl in tch: hdwy over 2f out: rdn and chsng overall ldrs 2f out: rdr dropped whip over 1f out: wknd fnl f: 1st of 5 in gp* **14/1**	
-042	6	3 1/2	**The Kyllachy Kid**[10] 1049 4-9-4 **85** ... (p) DarryllHolland 7	70+
			(S Gollings) *rring in stalls: racd far side: led that gp: rdn wl over 2f out: wknd u.p over 1f out: 2nd of 5 in gp* **14/1**	
05-4	7	16	**Toto Skyllachy**[11] 1030 5-8-10 **77** ... KierenFallon 9	15
			(J O'Reilly) *racd far side: in tch: shkn up and hung lft into centre of crse ent fnl 2f: wl btn and eased ent fnl f: 3rd of 5 in gp* **5/2**[1]	
2-02	8	1/2	**Monsieur Fillioux (USA)**[53] 552 4-8-10 **77** ... EddieAhern 6	14
			(J R Fanshawe) *racd far side: chsd ldr of that gp: rdn and btn over 2f out: eased fr over 1f out: 4th of 5 in gp* **14/1**	
033-	9	1 3/4	**Emeebee**[147] 7356 4-8-9 **76** ... StevieDonohoe 8	8
			(W J Musson) *racd far side: awkward leaving stalls and slowly away: a in rr: lost tch over 2f out: eased fr over 1f out: 5th of 5 in gp* **20/1**	

1m 30.95s (4.75) **Going Correction** +0.825s/f (Soft) 9 Ran SP% **115.9**

Speed ratings (Par 105): **105,104,101,98,97 93,75,74,72**

toteswingers: 1&2 £5.60, 1&3 £9.40, 2&3 £6.50 CSF £31.86 CT £93.75 TOTE £9.50: £2.60, £1.60, £2.20; EX 37.40 Trifecta £233.90 Pool of £347.69 - 1.10 winning units..

Owner The Racing Guild **Bred** Manor Farm Packers Ltd **Trained** Blackborough, Devon

FOCUS

A competitive handicap, with the top-weight rated 85, and the field split into two groups. The stands' side contingent were well on top at the finish. The winner looks the best guide to the form.

Toto Skyllachy Official explanation: trainer had no explanation for the poor form shown

1186 LADBROKES.COM BARKBY MAIDEN STKS — 1m 1f 218y

5:40 (5:40) (Class 5) 3-Y-O+ **£2,914** (£867; £433; £216) **Stalls** High

Form				RPR
	1		**Maxim Gorky (IRE)** 3-8-8 0 ... RyanMoore 1	84+
			(Sir Michael Stoute) *t.k.h early: trckd ldr: pushed along to go upsides over 2f out: rdn to ld over 1f out: pushed clr under hands and heels 1f out: comf* **5/4**[1]	
3222	2	2 3/4	**Tropical Blue**[17] 966 4-9-13 72 ... (p) JoeFanning 5	77
			(Jennie Candlish) *led: jnd over 2f out: sn rdn: hdd over 1f out: plugged on same pce and no ch w wnr fnl f* **11/4**[2]	
	3	27	**Setter's Princess**[25] 4-9-8 0 ... GeorgeBaker 3	30
			(R J Hodges) *wl in tch in last: stmbld over 4f out: rdn and lost tch w ldng pair over 2f out: eased wl ins fnl f* **8/1**[3]	
	4	40	**Tower** 3-8-8 0 ... (b[1]) RobertHavlin 2	—
			(J H M Gosden) *dwlt: sn handy: pushed along over 3f out: rdn and lost tch qckly wl over 2f out: wl t.o and eased ins fnl f* **11/4**[2]	

2m 15.92s (8.02) **Going Correction** +0.825s/f (Soft)

WFA 3 from 4yo 19lb 4 Ran SP% **108.9**

Speed ratings (Par 103): **100,97,76,44**

CSF £4.96 TOTE £2.50; EX 4.80 Place 6: £90.21 Place 5: £31.97.

Owner Mrs John Magnier, M Tabor & D Smith **Bred** Ecurie De Meautray, Skymarc Farm & Castl **Trained** Newmarket, Suffolk

FOCUS

Just one runner with previous form - and that no better than fair - but two of the newcomers looked potentially interesting.

T/Plt: £148.20 to a £1 stake. Pool: £40,218.80. 198.08 winning tickets. T/Qpdt: £28.20 to a £1 stake. Pool: £3,162.43. 82.92 winning tickets. SP

1049 WOLVERHAMPTON (A.W) (L-H)

Thursday, April 8

OFFICIAL GOING: Standard

Wind: Moderate, behind Weather: Bright and sunny

1187 DINE IN THE HORIZONS RESTAURANT CLAIMING STKS — 5f 20y(P)

5:50 (5:50) (Class 6) 3-Y-O **£2,047** (£604; £302) **Stalls** Low

Form				RPR
3101	1		**Athwaab**[8] 1057 3-8-11 74 ... NeilCallan 7	73
			(M G Quinlan) *t.k.h early: pressed ldr: led 2f out: pushed clr fnl f* **1/1**[1]	
6-55	2	5	**True Red (IRE)**[35] 788 3-8-5 48 ... (b[1]) DavidProbert 3	49
			(Mrs N S Evans) *led to 2f out: sn drvn: kpt on same pce fnl f* **14/1**	
-163	3	nk	**Magenta Strait**[26] 886 3-8-6 61 ... ChrisCatlin 8	49
			(R Hollinshead) *s.i.s: last but in tch: effrt over 1f out: swtchd rt ins fnl f: no imp* **9/2**[3]	
6045	4	hd	**Annia Galeria (IRE)**[13] 988 3-8-2 48 ... FrannyNorton 1	44
			(C A Dwyer) *trckd ldrs: effrt 2f out: kpt on same pce fnl f* **20/1**	
450-	5	2 1/2	**Ishipink**[223] 5380 3-8-7 0 ... JimmyQuinn 2	40
			(R J Hodges) *t.k.h: hld up in tch: rdn wl over 1f out: edgd lft and sn no imp* **25/1**	
-321	6	1/2	**Wanchai Whisper**[69] 343 3-9-0 68 ... DaneO'Neill 6	45
			(P R Hedger) *dwlt: sn in tch: effrt 2f out: wknd ins fnl f* **3/1**[2]	
0	7	23	**Haf (IRE)**[13] 997 3-8-5 0 ... AdrianMcCarthy 4	—
			(Peter Grayson) *in tch: drvn and outpcd after 2f: sn struggling: t.o* **66/1**	

62.62 secs (0.32) **Going Correction** +0.10s/f (Slow) 7 Ran SP% **109.9**

Speed ratings (Par 96): **101,93,92,92,88 87,50**

toteswingers: 1&2 £3.50, 1&3 £1.90, 2&3 £3.90 CSF £15.31 TOTE £2.00: £1.50, £4.00; EX 8.40.

Owner John Hanly **Bred** Shadwell Estate Co Ltd **Trained** Newmarket, Suffolk

FOCUS

There was not much strength in depth in this claimer. The favourite ran out an emphatic winner but the 48-rated second holds the form down.

1188 BUSCADOR H'CAP (DIV I) — 1m 4f 50y(P)

6:20 (6:20) (Class 6) (0-60,60) 4-Y-O+ **£1,433** (£423; £211) **Stalls** Low

Form				RPR
6-00	1		**Nayessence**[11] 1028 4-8-9 **50** ... (t) GrahamGibbons 2	63
			(M W Easterby) *mde all: drew clr w runner-up fr 4f out: drvn and kpt on gamely fnl f* **20/1**	
0-62	2	2 1/4	**Colonel Sherman (USA)**[63] 410 5-9-3 **57** ... FrankieDettori 9	66
			(P A Kirby) *t.k.h: chsd wnr thrght: clr of remainder fr 4f out: effrt over 2f out: one pce fnl f: eased whn hld towards fin* **5/4**[1]	
000-	3	3 1/4	**Fulfilment (IRE)**[180] 6673 4-8-13 **54** ... TonyCulhane 8	58
			(W J Musson) *hld up in midfield: drvn and outpcd over 3f out: rallied 2f out: chsd ldrs ins fnl f: kpt on: no imp* **7/2**[2]	
5343	4	nk	**Trysting Grove (IRE)**[20] 942 9-8-4 **49** ... KierenFox(5) 1	52+
			(E G Bevan) *dwlt: hld up: effrt whn nt clr run over 3f out: rdn and styd on fnl 2f: nrst fin* **7/1**[3]	
40-3	5	3	**Deportista**[8] 1067 4-8-7 **48** ... JimmyQuinn 7	47
			(J A Pickering) *prom: effrt over 3f out: outpcd and lost 3rd ins fnl f* **25/1**	
04-5	6	4 1/2	**Rock Tech**[49] 599 5-8-3 **50** ... DannyBrock(7) 5	41
			(J R Jenkins) *t.k.h early: hld up: rdn over 3f out: nvr able to chal* **33/1**	
006-	7	1 3/4	**Zalkani (IRE)**[170] 6918 10-8-7 **52** ... (v[1]) SimonPearce(5) 4	41
			(J Pearce) *hld up: effrt whn nt clr run over 3f out: nvr on terms* **25/1**	
0-64	8	3	**Singbella**[28] 868 4-8-12 **60** ... JohnFahy(7) 10	44
			(C G Cox) *chsd ldng pair: rdn over 3f out: wknd fnl 2f* **9/1**	
660-	9	6	**Turbo Shandy**[25] 7495 7-8-11 **51** ... DavidProbert 11	25
			(D Burchell) *dwlt: t.k.h in rr: struggling over 3f out: sn btn* **18/1**	
2140	10	11	**Sunset Boulevard (IRE)**[62] 426 7-9-5 **59** ... ChrisCatlin 6	16
			(Miss Tor Sturgis) *prom: rdn over 4f out: wknd over 3f out* **22/1**	
-056	11	21	**Hambledon Hill**[15] 969 4-9-2 **57** ... LiamKeniry 3	—
			(P Burgoyne) *hld up: struggling 4f out: sn btn: t.o* **16/1**	
-304	12	1 3/4	**Wee Ziggy**[27] 875 7-9-1 **55** ... AlanMunro 12	—
			(M Mullineaux) *midfield on outside: struggling 4f out: sn wknd: t.o* **33/1**	

2m 40.26s (-0.84) **Going Correction** +0.10s/f (Slow)

WFA 4 from 5yo+ 1lb 12 Ran SP% **123.0**

Speed ratings (Par 101): **106,104,102,102,100 97,95,93,89,82 68,67**

toteswingers: 1&2 £12.50, 1&3 £23.60, 2&3 £2.80 CSF £44.14 CT £120.47 TOTE £39.00: £6.80, £1.10, £1.90; EX 132.50.

Owner Steve Hull **Bred** Gainsborough Stud Management Ltd **Trained** Sheriff Hutton, N Yorks

FOCUS

A modest handicap run at a steady pace. The first two were in those positions all the way round and nothing got into it from behind.

1189 STAY AT THE WOLVERHAMPTON HOLIDAY INN H'CAP — 1m 1f 103y(P)

6:50 (6:50) (Class 4) (0-80,80) 3-Y-O **£4,209** (£1,252; £625; £312) **Stalls** Low

Form				RPR
6-21	1		**Azlak (USA)**[34] 805 3-9-1 **74** ... NeilCallan 1	80
			(C E Brittain) *trckd ldrs gng wl: hdwy to ld appr fnl f: edgd rt: drvn out ins fnl f* **9/2**[2]	
0-23	2	nk	**Green Earth (IRE)**[20] 934 3-9-1 **74** ... JimCrowley 7	79+
			(Mrs A J Perrett) *hld up in tch: effrt wl over 1f out: kpt on u.p fnl f: wnt 2nd towards fin but a hld* **12/1**	
306-	3	1/2	**Argaum (IRE)**[157] 7209 3-8-13 **72** ... AdamKirby 2	76
			(W R Swinburn) *dictated ordinary gallop: rdn and hdd appr fnl f: kpt on: lost 2nd towards fin* **7/2**[1]	
221-	4	1	**White Dart**[190] 6373 3-9-3 **76** ... AlanMunro 9	78+
			(M R Channon) *t.k.h: hld up: hdwy over 1f out: kpt on fnl f: nrst fin* **7/2**[1]	
122-	5	nse	**Nave (USA)**[120] 7685 3-8-13 **72** ... FrankieDettori 6	74
			(M Johnston) *cl up: chal 1/2-way: rdn over 2f out: nt qckn fnl f* **5/1**[3]	
31-3	6	2 3/4	**Crunched**[17] 964 3-8-13 **72** ... HayleyTurner 4	68
			(M L W Bell) *t.k.h: in tch: effrt 2f out: no imp fnl f* **6/1**	
1222	7	shd	**Lisahane Bog**[61] 448 3-9-3 **76** ... DaneO'Neill 5	72
			(P R Hedger) *dwlt: hld up: drvn over 3f out: effrt ent st: nvr able to chal* **14/1**	
041-	8	1 1/2	**Sounds Of Thunder**[129] 7597 3-8-12 **71** ... DavidProbert 3	64
			(H J L Dunlop) *prom: drvn over 2f out: sn outpcd: n.d after* **22/1**	
10	9	nk	**Munaawer (USA)**[40] 741 3-9-7 **80** ... (b[1]) PaulHanagan 8	72
			(J D Bethell) *t.k.h: cl up: rdn over 2f out: hung* **20/1**	

2m 3.90s (2.20) **Going Correction** +0.10s/f (Slow) 9 Ran SP% **117.0**

Speed ratings (Par 100): **94,93,93,92,92 89,89,88,88**

toteswingers: 1&2 £9.40, 1&3 £5.20, 2&3 £12.60 CSF £57.57 CT £211.54 TOTE £5.20: £1.40, £3.60, £2.00; EX 46.20.

Owner Saeed Manana **Bred** Rabbah Bloodstock Llc **Trained** Newmarket, Suffolk

■ Stewards' Enquiry : Neil Callan caution: careless riding

FOCUS

A decent handicap for 3yos. The market leaders were all involved in the finish and the form could be worth following.

White Dart Official explanation: jockey said gelding was denied a clear run

1190 ENJOY THE PARTY PACK GROUP OFFER MAIDEN STKS — 5f 20y(P)

7:20 (7:20) (Class 5) 3-Y-O+ **£2,456** (£725; £362) **Stalls** Low

Form				RPR
42	1		**Ryan Style (IRE)**[13] 997 4-9-11 0 ... TomEaves 6	82
			(Mrs L Williamson) *chsd ldrs: led 2f out: drvn and styd on strly fnl f* **7/2**[3]	
22-	2	2 1/2	**South African (USA)**[208] 5882 4-9-6 0 ... PaulHanagan 4	68
			(M A Magnusson) *dwlt: sn in tch: effrt and edgd lft over 1f out: kpt on fnl f: wnt 2nd cl home: no ch w wnr* **3/1**[2]	
62-2	3	hd	**Hot Spark**[38] 751 3-9-0 79 ... NeilCallan 3	67
			(K A Ryan) *chsd ldr: chal briefly 2f out: one pce fnl f: lost 2nd cl home* **6/5**[1]	

4 *8* **Prince Of Nama (IRE)** 3-8-11 0 AshleyHamblett(3) 1 38+
(P L Gilligan) *s.i.s: outpcd: shortlived effrt 2f out: edgd lft and sn btn* **15/2**
00 5 *12* **Titch (IRE)**[13] 997 4-9-6 0 AdrianMcCarthy 7 —
(Peter Grayson) *sn outpcd and drvn along: no ch fr 1/2-way: t.o* **200/1**
660/ 6 *14* **Lunar Lass**[883] 6722 5-9-6 41 (b[1]) GrahamGibbons 5 —
(D C Griffiths) *t.k.h: set str pce to 2f out: wknd qckly: t.o* **66/1**
62.55 secs (0.25) **Going Correction** +0.10s/f (Slow)
WFA 3 from 4yo+ 11lb **6 Ran SP% 106.4**
Speed ratings (Par 103): **102,98,97,84,65 43**
toteswingers: 1&2 £2.20, 1&3 £1.20, 2&3 £1.10 CSF £12.79 TOTE £6.30: £3.80, £3.60; EX 13.10.
Owner The Castle Bend Syndicate **Bred** Johnny Kent **Trained** Saighton, Cheshire
FOCUS
They went a decent pace in this maiden and the three market leaders pulled a long way clear of the rest.
Prince Of Nama(IRE) Official explanation: jockey said colt was slowly away
Lunar Lass Official explanation: jockey said mare ran too freely

1191 SPONSOR A RACE BY CALLING 01902 390000 H'CAP 5f 216y(P)
7:50 (7:53) (Class 4) (0-85,83) 3-Y-O **£4,209** (£1,252; £625; £312) **Stalls** Low

Form RPR
-112 1 **Lewyn**[21] 919 3-9-4 **83** FergusSweeney 1 87
(K A Ryan) *s.i.s: hld up: hdwy on outside 2f out: led ins fnl f: kpt on wl* **9/1**
-210 2 *nk* **Candyfloss Girl**[34] 809 3-8-10 **75** DavidProbert 6 78
(H J L Dunlop) *hld up in tch: effrt 2f out: pressed wnr and flashed tail ins fnl f: r.o* **10/1**
651- 3 *3/4* **Tres Amigos**[172] 6874 3-8-11 **76** AdrianNicholls 3 77
(D Nicholls) *led tl rdn and hdd ins fnl f: kpt on same pce towards fin* **6/1[3]**
001- 4 *shd* **Little Garcon (USA)**[167] 7001 3-9-1 **83** AndreaAtzeni(3) 2 83
(M Botti) *t.k.h: cl up: chal over 1f out to ent fnl f: kpt on same pce last 100yds* **5/2[2]**
2631 5 *3* **Neduardo**[23] 894 3-9-0 **79** RobertHavlin 8 70
(P W Chapple-Hyam) *cl up: outpcd and edgd lft wl over 1f out: no imp fnl f* **9/1**
5-11 6 *3/4* **Sir Frank Wappat**[8] 1058 3-8-6 **71** 6ex JoeFanning 4 59
(M Johnston) *t.k.h early: trckd ldrs: effrt ent st: wknd ent fnl f* **5/4[1]**
0-30 7 *1/2* **Gertmegalush (IRE)**[26] 884 3-9-1 **80** (v[1]) TomQueally 5 67
(J D Bethell) *prom: drvn and outpcd 1/2-way: no imp fnl 2f* **16/1**
1m 14.96s (-0.04) **Going Correction** +0.10s/f (Slow) **7 Ran SP% 122.3**
Speed ratings (Par 100): **104,103,102,102,98 97,96**
toteswingers: 1&2 £9.90, 1&3 £7.80, 2&3 £10.60 CSF £97.66 CT £595.06 TOTE £11.10: £4.80, £5.70; EX 82.90.
Owner N Cable & M Smith **Bred** Mrs S J Walker **Trained** Hambleton, N Yorks
FOCUS
A hot-looking handicap involving four last-time-out winners. The leaders went hard up front and set it up for the finishers.
Sir Frank Wappat Official explanation: trainer had no explanation for the poor form shown

1192 WOLVERHAMPTON-RACECOURSE.CO.UK H'CAP 5f 216y(P)
8:20 (8:21) (Class 4) (0-85,85) 4-Y-O+ **£4,209** (£1,252; £625; £312) **Stalls** Low

Form RPR
200- 1 **Mo Mhuirnin (IRE)**[217] 5607 4-9-2 **83** PaulHanagan 3 93
(R A Fahey) *dwlt: midfield on outside: effrt ent st: edgd lft and led wl ins fnl f: kpt on wl* **10/1**
-534 2 *1/2* **Anne Of Kiev (IRE)**[20] 935 5-8-10 **77** (t) LukeMorris 9 85
(J R Gask) *hld up: hdwy and swtchd lft ent fnl f: pressed wnr wl ins fnl f: r.o* **11/2[2]**
0332 3 *3/4* **Brierty (IRE)**[21] 924 4-8-10 **77** DavidNolan 5 83
(D Carroll) *cl up: rdn and led briefly ins fnl f: kpt on: hld nr fin* **7/1**
60-3 4 *1 1/4* **Viking Spirit**[13] 987 8-9-4 **85** AdamKirby 6 87
(W R Swinburn) *sn led: edgd rt and hdd ins fnl f: kpt on same pce* **7/2[1]**
5040 5 *nk* **Fathsta (IRE)**[26] 887 5-9-4 **85** EddieAhern 8 87
(D M Simcock) *t.k.h: prom on outside: effrt over 1f out: keeping on whn nt clr run ins fnl f: no imp* **15/2**
-222 6 *1/2* **Weet A Surprise**[62] 432 5-8-11 **78** (v) GrahamGibbons 4 77
(J W Unett) *midfield: drvn over 2f out: kpt on u.p fnl f: no imp* **7/1**
3306 7 *1* **Methaaly (IRE)**[21] 924 7-8-6 **73** (be) AlanMunro 2 69
(M Mullineaux) *plld hrd in midfield: rdn over 2f out: no imp over 1f out* **14/1**
0/06 8 *hd* **Financial Times (USA)**[13] 987 8-8-11 **78** (t) TomQueally 10 74
(Stef Higgins) *hld up: effrt ent st: nvr able to chal* **25/1**
24-5 9 *hd* **Bahamian Lad**[22] 905 5-9-0 **81** JerryO'Dwyer 1 76
(R Hollinshead) *broke wl and early ldr: cl up tl rdn and no ex over 1f out* **13/2[3]**
3430 10 *1* **Divine Force**[22] 902 4-8-10 **77** (b[1]) SimonWhitworth 11 69
(M Wigham) *s.s: bhd: rdn 2f out: nvr rchd ldrs* **14/1**
0-63 11 *1/2* **Klynch**[29] 848 4-8-8 **75** (b) AndrewElliott 7 65
(Mrs R A Carr) *sn w ldr: rdn and wknd appr fnl f* **33/1**
1m 15.19s (0.19) **Going Correction** +0.10s/f (Slow) **11 Ran SP% 116.9**
Speed ratings (Par 105): **102,101,100,98,98 97,96,96,95,94 93**
toteswingers: 1&2 £11.40, 1&3 £17.00, 2&3 £4.20 CSF £63.80 CT £424.19 TOTE £10.70: £4.90, £2.30, £2.90; EX 87.40.
Owner Shevlin-Whelan Syndicate **Bred** John McEnery **Trained** Musley Bank, N Yorks
■ Stewards' Enquiry : Paul Hanagan two-day ban: careless riding (Apr 22-23)
FOCUS
A competitive sprint handicap. The pace was fairly sedate early on.

1193 THE BLACK COUNTRY'S ONLY RACETRACK H'CAP 1m 141y(P)
8:50 (8:51) (Class 6) (0-55,55) 4-Y-O+ **£1,683** (£501; £250; £125) **Stalls** Low

Form RPR
-464 1 **Quiet Mountain (IRE)**[20] 937 5-8-12 **55** BarryMcHugh(3) 7 65
(Ollie Pears) *prom chsng gp: smooth hdwy to ld appr 2f out: rdn out fnl f* **7/1**
5002 2 *3/4* **Ermine Grey**[1] 1179 9-9-1 **55** LukeMorris 13 63
(A W Carroll) *midfield chsng gp: effrt over 2f out: styd on to chse wnr towards fin* **6/1[3]**
5-60 3 *1* **Mr Chocolate Drop (IRE)**[2] 1142 6-9-0 **54** (b) JimmyQuinn 6 60
(Miss M E Rowland) *t.k.h: in tch chsng gp: hdwy to chse wnr wl over 1f out: one pce and lost 2nd towards fin* **16/1**
5420 4 *1 3/4* **Kielty's Folly**[38] 753 6-9-1 **55** TonyCulhane 11 57
(B P J Baugh) *hld up: effrt on outside ent st: hung lft and one pce fnl f* **12/1**
0216 5 *nse* **Mountain Pass (USA)**[20] 940 8-8-11 **51** (tp) LiamKeniry 9 53
(B J Llewellyn) *hld up: hdwy over 2f out: kpt on u.p fnl f* **14/1**
046- 6 *2* **Al Rayanah**[160] 7152 7-8-7 **52** (p) KierenFox(5) 1 49
(G Prodromou) *hld up: effrt and hdwy 2f out: no imp fnl f* **20/1**
/0 7 *2 1/2* **King Zeal (IRE)**[23] 893 6-9-1 **55** HayleyTurner 12 46
(B D Leavy) *dwlt: bhd: rdn over 3f out: styd on fr 2f out: nvr rchd ldrs* **33/1**
300- 8 *1 1/4* **Aggbag**[195] 6256 6-8-9 **52** AndreaAtzeni(3) 5 40
(J Jay) *prom chsng gp: outpcd over 2f out: n.d after* **12/1**
50-1 9 *1* **Lady Lam**[14] 984 4-9-0 **54** DavidProbert 3 40
(S Kirk) *prom chsng gp: rdn over 2f out: wknd over 1f out* **7/2[1]**
0-0 10 *1* **Comrade Cotton**[12] 1012 6-8-12 **55** (v) MarcHalford(3) 4 39
(J Ryan) *hld up: drvn along over 2f out: nvr on terms* **28/1**
03-2 11 *2* **Home**[13] 995 5-8-12 **52** (vt) AdamKirby 10 31
(C Gordon) *chsd clr ldr to ent st: sn wknd* **5/1[2]**
1400 12 *1 3/4* **Machinate (USA)**[20] 940 8-8-10 **50** LiamJones 2 25
(W M Brisbourne) *midfield: struggling over 2f out: sn btn* **33/1**
/040 13 *13* **Catholic Hill (USA)**[15] 969 5-9-0 **54** (b) EddieAhern 8 —
(C J Mann) *t.k.h: led: clr after 2f to over 2f out: sn hdd: qckly lost pl: eased whn no ch* **13/2**
1m 51.1s (0.60) **Going Correction** +0.10s/f (Slow) **13 Ran SP% 121.0**
Speed ratings (Par 101): **101,100,99,97,97 96,93,92,91,90 89,87,76**
toteswingers: 1&2 £20.00, 1&3 £75.90, 2&3 £38.30 CSF £47.28 CT £677.66 TOTE £8.00: £2.40, £1.60, £4.40; EX 61.30.
Owner O'Brien, Moll, Spencer, Vaux, Davies **Bred** Mrs P Grubb **Trained** Norton, N Yorks
FOCUS
A low-grade handicap run at a solid pace.
Kielty's Folly Official explanation: jockey said gelding hung left in straight

1194 BUSCADOR H'CAP (DIV II) 1m 4f 50y(P)
9:20 (9:20) (Class 6) (0-60,60) 4-Y-O+ **£1,433** (£423; £211) **Stalls** Low

Form RPR
005- 1 **Peintre D'Argent (IRE)**[120] 7688 4-8-7 **48** WilliamBuick 6 55
(W J Knight) *cl up: led over 2f out: drvn out fnl f* **3/1[1]**
14-0 2 *3/4* **Largem**[14] 983 4-9-0 **55** SimonWhitworth 5 61+
(J R Jenkins) *hld up: hdwy on outside over 2f out: edgd lft and chsd wnr ins fnl f: r.o* **10/1**
6554 3 *1 1/4* **Naheell**[14] 983 4-8-12 **58** (p) KierenFox(5) 1 62+
(G Prodromou) *hld up: hdwy ent st: styd on fnl f to take 3rd cl home* **7/2[2]**
4043 4 *shd* **Mullitovermaurice**[27] 875 4-8-13 **54** (p) PaulMulrennan 12 58
(J G Given) *prom: effrt over 2f out: kpt on same pce fnl f* **12/1**
0626 5 *shd* **Solarias Quest**[15] 970 8-9-4 **58** ShaneKelly 11 61
(W M Brisbourne) *hld up: hdwy and prom after 5f: effrt and chsd wnr 2f out to ins fnl f: edgd lft and one pce* **20/1**
-443 6 *hd* **New England**[34] 813 8-8-13 **53** LukeMorris 9 58+
(N J Vaughan) *t.k.h: hld up: nt clr run ent st: swtchd rt and styd on fnl f: nrst fin* **9/1**
003- 7 *3/4* **Ready To Crown (USA)**[15] 5015 6-8-4 **49** (p) DeclanCannon(5) 7 51
(J Mackie) *midfield: dropped in rr 1/2-way: rallied against ins rail over 1f out: no imp fnl f* **7/1**
1050 8 *1/2* **Dazzling Begum**[20] 942 5-8-8 **48** RobertHavlin 2 49
(J Pearce) *in tch: rdn ent st: one pce fnl f* **10/1**
-300 9 *2 3/4* **Nyetimber (USA)**[23] 898 4-8-4 **50** SophieDoyle(5) 4 47
(J A Osborne) *set stdy pce 3f: chsd ldrs tl wknd over 1f out* **25/1**
-660 10 *3/4* **Hector Spectre (IRE)**[28] 868 4-9-5 **60** (p) DavidProbert 8 56
(Mrs N S Evans) *t.k.h: midfield: rdn over 2f out: wknd over 1f out* **14/1**
23-6 11 *1* **Extremely So**[13] 989 4-9-1 **56** ChrisCatlin 10 50
(P J McBride) *bhd: hdwy to ld and maintained stdy gallop after 3f: hdd over 2f out: sn wknd* **13/2[3]**
2m 45.35s (4.25) **Going Correction** +0.10s/f (Slow)
WFA 4 from 5yo+ 1lb **11 Ran SP% 124.2**
Speed ratings (Par 101): **90,89,88,88,88 88,87,87,85,85 84**
toteswingers:1&2 £25.80, 2&3 £9.70, 1&3 £4.50 CSF £36.26 CT £114.69 TOTE £5.20: £2.50, £1.80, £2.30; EX 59.10 Place 6: £452.18 Place 5: £272.10.
Owner The Pro-Claimers **Bred** D Couper Snr **Trained** Patching, W Sussex
■ Stewards' Enquiry : Declan Cannon two-day ban: careless riding (Apr 22-23)
FOCUS
An ordinary handicap . It was run at a modest pace and became tactical.
T/Plt: £568.90 to a £1 stake. Pool: £61,418.76. 78.80 winning tickets. T/Qpdt: £79.40 to a £1 stake. Pool: £7,146.50. 66.60 winning tickets. RY

MAISONS-LAFFITTE (R-H)
Thursday, April 8
OFFICIAL GOING: Turf: very soft

1195a PRIX DJEBEL (GROUP 3) (C&G) (TURF) 7f (S)
1:35 (12:00) 3-Y-O **£35,398** (£14,159; £10,619; £7,079; £3,539)

RPR
1 **Makfi**[132] 3-9-2 0 Christophe-PatriceLemaire 3 110
(M Delzangles, France) *w.w in rr: smooth prog at 1/2-way: qcknd wl to ld 2f out: sn drew clr 1f out: easily* **63/10[3]**
2 *3* **Too Nice Name (FR)**[7] 1079 3-9-2 0 OlivierPeslier 2 102
(Robert Collet, France) *t.k.h early: sn swtchd to outer: qcknd wl ins fnl f to take 2nd cl home* **12/1**
3 *3/4* **Silver Black (USA)**[28] 3-9-2 0 IoritzMendizabal 7 100
(J-C Rouget, France) *led fr s: swtchd to stands' rail: hdd 2f out: r.o wl: lost 2nd cl home* **15/1**
4 *1* **Boltcity (FR)**[27] 3-9-2 0 ChristopheSoumillon 1 97
(J-C Rouget, France) *w.w: proged to cl on ldrs at 1/2-way: rdn 2f out: no ex* **9/10[1]**
5 *2* **Bling (FR)**[13] 3-9-2 0 ThomasHuet 4 92
(C Ferland, France) *chsd ldr after 2f: failed to qckn ins fnl 2f: styd on* **23/1**
6 *3* **Ricci (FR)**[17] 3-9-2 0 StephanePasquier 5 84
(R Gibson, France) *prom on outer fr s: rdn 3f out to join ldrs: no ex* **3/1[2]**
7 *hd* **Thyan (FR)**[21] 927 3-9-2 0 GaetanMasure 8 83
(Mlle M Henry, France) *qckly away on outer: swtchd to stands' rail to chse ldrs: failed to qckn: fdd* **29/1**
8 *2* **Billy Boy Blue (IRE)**[45] 3-9-2 0 GeraldMosse 6 78
(J E Hammond, France) *cl up fr s: rdn at 1/2-way: no ex: fdd* **17/1**
1m 29.0s (0.70) **8 Ran SP% 118.3**
WIN (incl. 1 euro stake): 7.30. PLACES: 2.60, 3.30, 4.20. DF: 25.50. SF: 71.90.
Owner Mathieu Offenstadt **Bred** Shadwell Estate Company Limited **Trained** France

NOTEBOOK

Makfi, whose only previous run resulted in success in similarly testing conditions at Fontainebleau last autumn, stepped up in class on his reappearance and put up a taking display. Out of a half-sister to champion 2yo Alhaarth, he will be considered for both the Poule d'Essai des Poulains and 2000 Guineas, and the bookmakers rate him a 66-1 chance for the latter.

1196a PRIX IMPRUDENCE (GROUP 3) (FILLIES) (TURF) — 7f (S)

2:10 (12:00) 3-Y-O £35,398 (£14,159; £10,619; £7,079; £3,539)

RPR

1 **Joanna (IRE)**[186] 6523 3-9-0 0 .... ChristopheSoumillon 5 111
(J-C Rouget, France) *pursued ldr on outer fr s: mde her move to chal 2 1/2f out: qcknd to ld 1f out: r.o wl* 13/5[2]

2 ½ **Evading Tempete**[21] 926 3-9-0 0 ....(p) Jean-BernardEyquem 2 110
(F Rohaut, France) *cl up on rail fr s: qcknd wl 2 1/2f out: r.o wl ins fnl f: clsng on ldr ins fnl 55yds* 10/1

3 ½ **Special Duty**[188] 6449 3-9-0 0 .... StephanePasquier 7 108
(Mme C Head-Maarek, France) *led fr s on outside: stl in front 1 1/2f out: qckly hdd 1f out: no ex* 9/10[1]

4 6 **Wonderfilly (FR)**[156] 7230 3-9-0 0 .... FlavienPrat 4 92
(P Demercastel, France) *racd bhd ldrs early on: outpcd at 1/2-way: styd on for 4th* 37/1

5 1 **Ascot Glory (IRE)**[21] 926 3-9-0 0 .... RaphaelMarchelli 6 89
(S Wattel, France) *cl up: failed to qckn at 1/2-way: lost 4th in clsng stages* 26/1

6 2 **Lixirova (FR)**[156] 7230 3-9-0 0 .... GregoryBenoist 3 84
(D Smaga, France) *qckly away on stands' rails: racing freely: no ex ins fnl 1 1/2f: fdd* 68/10[3]

7 3 **Saying (USA)**[172] 6888 3-9-0 0 ....(b[1]) OlivierPeslier 1 76
(F Head, France) *cl up: failed to qckn at 1/2-way: fdd* 10/1

1m 28.6s (0.30) 7 Ran SP% 117.7
WIN (incl. 1 euro stake): 3.60. PLACES: 2.30, 4.00. SF: 28.00.
Owner Hamdan Al Maktoum **Bred** Giovanni Faldutto **Trained** Pau, France

NOTEBOOK

Joanna(IRE), third in the Marcel Boussac on her last start at two, coped well with the testing conditions and quickened up well past the favourite a furlong out. The Poule d'Essai des Pouliches is firmly on the agenda for her, where the return to a mile should be very much in her favour.

Evading Tempete ran on late up the rail to take second. She had the benefit of race-fitness over the winner and third, having been on the go on the AW since February and successful in a Listed race at Deauville last time out.

Special Duty, trying a trip beyond 6f for the first time and running on the softest ground she had ever encountered, made most of the running but the first two saw the trip out better. Her trainer had warned that she would need her reappearance and the ground was almost certainly softer than she would care for, but on the back of this defeat she has drifted out to 4-1 for the 1000 Guineas. The Newmarket Classic remains the aim, however, and while her trainer expects her to be much better for the run, those who decide to take her on can point to question marks over whether she's trained on and whether she has the requisite stamina for a mile.

[1098] MUSSELBURGH (R-H)

Friday, April 9

OFFICIAL GOING: Good to soft (good in places; 6.4)

Weather: Overcast

1198 EUROPEAN BREEDERS' FUND MAIDEN STKS — 5f

2:15 (2:16) (Class 5) 2-Y-O £3,885 (£1,156; £577) Stalls Low

Form RPR

0 1 **Las Verglas Star (IRE)**[13] 1009 2-9-3 0 .... PaulHanagan 1 68+
(R A Fahey) *mde all: shkn up and edgd rt over 1f out: drew clr ins fnl f: eased towards fin* 8/11[1]

2 2 **Mica Mika (IRE)** 2-9-3 0 .... TonyHamilton 2 58
(R A Fahey) *dwlt and wnt rt s: chsd ldrs: effrt 1/2-way: styd on to chse wnr wl ins fnl f: no imp* 7/2[3]

3 1½ **Gartsherrie** 2-8-12 0 .... TonyCulhane 3 47+
(P T Midgley) *pressed wnr: effrt over 1f out: rn green: outpcd ins fnl f: lost 2nd wl ins fnl f* 5/2[2]

65.00 secs (4.60) **Going Correction** +0.175s/f (Good) 3 Ran SP% 108.7
Speed ratings (Par 92): **70,66,64**
CSF £3.48 TOTE £1.40; EX 3.10.
Owner CBWS Partnership **Bred** Brendan Holland And P Connell **Trained** Musley Bank, N Yorks

FOCUS

A poor turnout for this juvenile contest and it went the way of the only runner with previous experience but the time was slow, even for an early season juvenile race and probably a weak race.

NOTEBOOK

Las Verglas Star(IRE), whose half-brother Inventor was third in the Grade 2 at Aintree a few minutes earlier, had finished out the back in the Brocklesby but that experience gave him an advantage here, and he made all to score easing down. (op Evens)

Mica Mika(IRE), the winner's stable companion, was slowly into stride and green during the race, but was getting the hang of things near the finish. (op 11-4 tchd 4-1)

Gartsherrie, a cheaply bought filly, showed pace on the outside of the winner before fading under pressure. She can do better against her own sex with this behind her. (tchd 9-4 and 11-4)

1199 TURFTV (S) STKS — 1m 4f 100y

2:50 (2:50) (Class 6) 4-Y-O+ £1,942 (£578; £288; £144) Stalls High

Form RPR

5-06 1 **Sudden Impulse**[61] 457 9-8-8 53 .... SilvestreDeSousa 3 66
(A D Brown) *hld up in tch: hdwy to chse ldr over 2f out: led 1f out: edgd rt: drvn out* 16/1

51-0 2 ½ **Oddsmaker (IRE)**[13] 1012 9-8-8 67 ....(t) AndrewHeffernan[(5)] 4 70
(M A Barnes) *t.k.h: w ldr: led 1/2-way: clr over 3f out: hdd 1f out: rallied: hld towards fin* 5/4[1]

56-4 3 8 **Birkside**[5] 1098 7-8-13 62 .... PhillipMakin 5 57
(Miss L A Perratt) *hld up: hdwy over 2f out: rdn and sn no imp* 10/3[3]

000- 4 1¼ **Along The Nile**[17] 7248 8-8-13 60 ....(b) TonyCulhane 1 55
(K G Reveley) *dwlt: bhd and sn niggled along: effrt on outer over 2f out: edgd rt and sn no imp* 3/1[2]

01-5 5 19 **Intersky Charm (USA)**[5] 1098 6-8-13 69 .... TomEaves 6 25
(Mrs S C Bradburne) *chsd ldrs: wnt 2nd over 3f out to over 2f out: sn wknd: t.o* 12/1

10-0 6 12 **Suitably Accoutred (IRE)**[49] 622 4-8-7 48 .... PaulMulrennan 2 —
(Mrs A Duffield) *hld up in tch: effrt over 5f out: wknd fnl 3f: t.o* 25/1

000- 7 2¾ **Strevelyn**[177] 3711 4-8-12 39 .... TonyHamilton 7 —
(Mrs A Duffield) *t.k.h: led to 1/2-way: wknd over 3f out: t.o* 66/1

2m 47.05s (5.05) **Going Correction** +0.375s/f (Good)
WFA 4 from 6yo+ 1lb 7 Ran SP% 111.4
Speed ratings (Par 101): **98,97,92,91,78 70,69**
toteswingers:1&2:£4.20, 1&3:£3.60, 2&3:£1.90 CSF £34.90 TOTE £11.70: £3.80, £1.90; EX 30.90.There was no bid for the winner.
Owner A D Brown **Bred** Sagittarius Bloodstock Associates Ltd **Trained** Yedingham, N Yorks

FOCUS

A modest seller but reasonably competitive judged on official ratings. However, there was surprise result.

1200 TURFTV BETTING SHOP SERVICE H'CAP — 5f

3:25 (3:26) (Class 4) (0-80,79) 4-Y-O+ £5,180 (£1,541; £770; £384) Stalls Low

Form RPR

50-2 1 **Highland Warrior**[5] 1099 11-8-2 63 .... PaulPickard[(5)] 5 78
(P T Midgley) *dwlt: bhd: gd hdwy to ld ent fnl f: sn clr* 7/2[2]

5120 2 5 **Ingleby Star (IRE)**[5] 1099 5-8-12 71 ....(p) MartinLane[(3)] 4 68
(N Wilson) *w ldrs: led briefly appr fnl f: kpt on ins fnl f: no ch w wnr* 6/1[3]

020- 3 ½ **Mandarin Spirit (IRE)**[118] 7735 10-8-12 68 ....(b) TonyHamilton 2 63
(Miss L A Perratt) *midfield: effrt over 1f out: kpt on fnl f: no imp* 16/1

224- 4 ¾ **Grissom (IRE)**[157] 7220 4-9-9 79 .... JoeFanning 7 72+
(A Berry) *prom on outside: rdn over 2f out: one pce fr over 1f out* 6/1[3]

400- 5 shd **The Bear**[160] 7171 7-8-2 63 .... AndrewHeffernan[(5)] 8 55+
(Miss L A Perratt) *led tl edgd rt and hdd appr fnl f: sn one pce* 25/1

-321 6 ¾ **Sir Geoffrey (IRE)**[28] 869 4-8-12 68 ....(p) FrederikTylicki 1 57
(J A Glover) *chsd ldrs: drvn 1/2-way: one pce over 1f out* 10/3[1]

501- 7 ¾ **Northern Bolt**[157] 7219 5-9-5 75 .... PJMcDonald 11 62
(I W McInnes) *dwlt: bhd and pushed along: styd on ins fnl f: nvr rchd ldrs* 12/1

030- 8 1¼ **Musical Bridge**[148] 7355 4-8-10 66 .... TomEaves 12 48
(Mrs L Williamson) *in tch: drvn 1/2-way: no ex over 1f out* 12/1

0-05 9 1¼ **Lucky Art (USA)**[42] 723 4-9-0 70 .... SilvestreDeSousa 6 48
(Mrs R A Carr) *w ldrs tl wknd over 1f out* 8/1

002- 10 1 **Hosanna**[190] 6410 4-8-4 60 oh13 .... PaulHanagan 3 34
(J Barclay) *hld up in tch: drvn 1/2-way: wknd over 1f out* 50/1

103- 11 1¼ **Distant Sun (USA)**[163] 7119 6-9-0 70 .... PhillipMakin 10 40
(Miss L A Perratt) *bhd and sn outpcd: no ch fr 1/2-way* 22/1

60.59 secs (0.19) **Going Correction** +0.175s/f (Good) 11 Ran SP% 116.4
Speed ratings (Par 105): **105,97,96,95,94 93,92,90,88,86 84**
toteswingers:1&2:£6.70, 1&3:£18.00, 2&3:£19.70 CSF £24.07 CT £297.05 TOTE £4.00: £1.90, £2.10, £4.30; EX 29.40.
Owner R Wardlaw **Bred** Rowcliffe Stud **Trained** Westow, N Yorks
■ Stewards' Enquiry : Andrew Heffernan caution: careless riding

FOCUS

A fair sprint featuring a number of seasonal debutants against others fit from the AW or a recent turf outing.

1201 EDINBURGH EVENING NEWS H'CAP — 7f 30y

4:00 (4:03) (Class 5) (0-70,69) 3-Y-O £3,238 (£963; £481; £240) Stalls High

Form RPR

026- 1 **Orpen Arms (IRE)**[165] 7055 3-8-10 58 .... PaulHanagan 9 64
(R A Fahey) *mde all: rdn 2f out: edgd lft and styd on wl fnl f* 9/4[1]

606- 2 1½ **Coolella (IRE)**[202] 6125 3-8-3 54 .... MartinLane[(3)] 10 56
(J R Weymes) *trckd ldrs: edgd lft and chsd wnr over 1f out: kpt on ins fnl f* 12/1

555- 3 1¾ **So Bazaar (IRE)**[202] 6096 3-9-0 62 .... PJMcDonald 4 59
(G A Swinbank) *hld up in tch: effrt over 2f out: edgd rt appr fnl f: one pce ins fnl f* 10/3[2]

630- 4 1¼ **Frontline Boy (IRE)**[186] 6534 3-9-7 69 .... AndrewElliott 11 63
(J R Weymes) *hld up: hdwy on ins over 2f out: effrt and edgd rt over 1f out: kpt on same pce fnl f* 17/2

020- 5 ½ **Ochilview Warrior (IRE)**[160] 7168 3-8-6 54 .... SilvestreDeSousa 6 46
(R Bastiman) *t.k.h: w wnr: rdn over 2f out: lost 2nd and no ex over 1f out* 8/1

00-5 6 8 **Alhena (IRE)**[36] 793 3-8-7 55 .... TomEaves 7 26
(K A Ryan) *trckd ldrs: rdn over 2f out: wknd wl over 1f out* 6/1[3]

000- 7 26 **Sydney Bridge**[168] 6983 3-8-9 57 .... PaulMulrennan 3 —
(J Barclay) *prom: drvn 3f out: wknd 2f out* 12/1

400- 8 1¾ **Kristen Jane (USA)**[168] 6983 3-8-2 50 oh2 .... DuranFentiman 5 —
(Miss L A Perratt) *hld up in tch: drvn over 3f out: wknd over 2f out* 20/1

1m 32.94s (3.94) **Going Correction** +0.375s/f (Good) 8 Ran SP% 109.9
Speed ratings (Par 98): **99,97,95,93,93 84,54,52**
toteswingers:1&2:£7.20, 1&3:£2.50, 2&3:£8.30 CSF £27.93 CT £81.61 TOTE £3.20: £2.10, £5.30, £1.02; EX 25.00.
Owner Derwent Arms Racing Club Malton **Bred** Mrs Teresa Bergin **Trained** Musley Bank, N Yorks

FOCUS

A modest handicap.

1202 SCOTTISH RACING H'CAP — 1m

4:35 (4:35) (Class 4) (0-85,85) 4-Y-O+ £5,180 (£1,541; £770; £384) Stalls High

Form RPR

522- 1 **Goliaths Boy (IRE)**[179] 6733 4-9-1 82 .... PaulHanagan 5 93
(R A Fahey) *t.k.h early: trckd ldrs: rdn over 2f out: led over 1f out: hld on gamely fnl f* 5/2[1]

00-2 2 1 **Internationaldebut (IRE)**[12] 1030 5-9-4 85 .... TonyCulhane 6 94
(P T Midgley) *t.k.h: hld up: smooth hdwy to trck wnr appr fnl f: sn rdn: kpt on fnl f but a hld* 5/2[1]

25-2 3 6 **Ansells Pride (IRE)**[61] 451 7-8-4 71 oh1 .... GregFairley 8 66
(B Smart) *led tl rdn and hdd over 1f out: sn outpcd by first two* 9/2[2]

1566 4 ¾ **Thunderball**[37] 769 4-8-13 80 .... FrederikTylicki 2 73
(J A Glover) *hld up in tch: drvn along 3f out: edgd rt and no imp fnl 2f* 8/1[3]

-020 5 3¾ **Johnmanderville**[28] 873 4-8-10 80 ....(t) MartinLane[(3)] 4 65
(N Wilson) *prom: drvn over 2f out: edgd rt and wknd over 1f out* 12/1

306- 6 1½ **Silver Rime (FR)**[160] 7169 5-8-12 79 .... PhillipMakin 7 60
(Miss L A Perratt) *hld up in tch: effrt on ins over 2f out: wknd over 1f out* 17/2

00-0 7 2¼ **Wind Shuffle (GER)**[13] 1013 7-8-8 75 .... JoeFanning 1 51
(J S Goldie) *pressed ldr tl rdn and wknd fr 2f out* 16/1

1m 43.08s (1.88) **Going Correction** +0.375s/f (Good) 7 Ran SP% 110.5
Speed ratings (Par 105): **105,104,98,97,93 92,89**
toteswingers:1&2:£1.60, 1&3:£2.50, 2&3:£2.90 CSF £7.99 CT £23.20 TOTE £2.90: £2.30, £1.10; EX 7.00.
Owner Dr Marwan Koukash **Bred** Mrs O M E McKeever **Trained** Musley Bank, N Yorks

FOCUS
A fair handicap.

1203 TURFTV SHOWING BEST RACECOURSES MAIDEN STKS 1m 1f
5:10 (5:10) (Class 5) 3-Y-O+ £2,590 (£770; £385; £192) Stalls High

Form RPR
324- **1** **High Office**[311] 2571 4-10-0 75 PaulHanagan 2 77
(R A Fahey) *mde all: hrd pressed and drvn fr 2f out: kpt on gamely ins fnl f* **4/5**[1]

5-52 **2** 1 ¼ **Nisaal (IRE)**[12] 1028 5-9-9 66 (p) IanBrennan(5) 1 74
(J J Quinn) *t.k.h early: pressed wnr: effrt and ev ch fr over 1f out: kpt on fnl f: hld towards fin* **5/2**[2]

05 **3** 8 **Ferney Boy**[18] 963 4-10-0 0 PJMcDonald 3 56
(G A Swinbank) *prom: effrt over 2f out: edgd rt and outpcd by first two fr over 1f out* **14/1**[3]

2-0 **4** 6 **Inlovingmemory (IRE)**[13] 1010 3-8-1 0 AndrewHeffernan(5) 6 38
(M A Barnes) *t.k.h: trckd ldrs tl rdn and wknd fr 2f out* **20/1**

4- **5** 3 ¼ **Brootommitty (IRE)**[226] 5330 3-8-3 0 MartinLane(3) 5 31
(N Wilson) *dwlt: plld hrd: last but in tch: struggling over 2f out: sn btn* **16/1**

6 1 ½ **Orpenia (IRE)** 4-9-9 0 FrederikTylicki 7 28
(Miss L A Perratt) *t.k.h: hld up in tch: rdn over 2f out: sn btn* **14/1**[3]

1m 58.69s (4.79) **Going Correction** +0.375s/f (Good)
WFA 3 from 4yo+ 17lb 6 Ran SP% **108.1**
Speed ratings (Par 103): **97,95,88,83,80 79**
toteswingers:1&2:£1.20, 1&3:£3.00, 2&3:£1.90 CSF £2.64 TOTE £1.40: £1.10, £1.80; EX 2.40.
Owner R A Fahey **Bred** Genesis Green Stud Ltd **Trained** Musley Bank, N Yorks

FOCUS
Mark Johnston newcomer Bay Willow was withdrawn, which took away much of the interest in this maiden.

1204 TURFTV APPRENTICE H'CAP 1m
5:40 (5:41) (Class 6) (0-60,60) 4-Y-O+ £2,590 (£770; £385; £192) Stalls High

Form RPR
221- **1** **Zaplamation (IRE)**[175] 6817 5-9-4 60 IanBrennan(3) 7 71
(J J Quinn) *hld up: hdwy on outside over 2f out: led over 1f out: drifted rt: kpt on wl* **5/2**[1]

3302 **2** 2 ¼ **Laureldeans Best (IRE)**[37] 780 4-9-2 60 LeeTopliss(5) 5 66
(R A Fahey) *hld up in tch: hdwy over 2f out: chsd wnr 1f out: kpt on: no imp* **7/2**[2]

000- **3** 1 ¾ **Cigalas**[200] 6157 5-9-6 59 PatrickDonaghy 6 61
(Mrs J C McGregor) *t.k.h: hld up: hdwy on ins over 2f out: kpt on fnl f: no imp* **20/1**

404- **4** nk **Red Skipper (IRE)**[160] 7174 5-8-9 55 ShirleyTeasdale(7) 4 56
(N Wilson) *led: c wd st: rdn and hdd over 1f out: kpt on same pce* **10/1**

-056 **5** ½ **Captain Imperial (IRE)**[31] 838 4-8-6 50 (t) MatthewLawson(5) 8 50
(R Bastiman) *t.k.h: trckd ldr: effrt over 2f out: ev ch over 1f out: one pce fnl f* **11/1**

-001 **6** ¾ **Provost**[21] 940 6-9-6 59 (b) JamesSullivan 3 57
(M W Easterby) *hld up: pushed along over 2f out: kpt on fnl f: nvr able to chal* **9/1**[3]

-363 **7** ¾ **Sea Land (FR)**[12] 1028 6-8-8 47 AmyRyan 9 44
(B Ellison) *trckd ldrs: effrt and ev ch over 1f out: no ex fnl f* **5/2**[1]

60/0 **8** 11 **Loyal Knight (IRE)**[55] 540 5-8-11 50 (t) PaulPickard 1 21
(P T Midgley) *plld hrd: in tch on outside: effrt over 3f out: wknd over 2f out* **18/1**

660- **9** 13 **Cold Quest (USA)**[168] 6984 6-9-7 60 MichaelO'Connell 2 —
(Miss L A Perratt) *prom: rdn 3f out: wknd 2f out* **33/1**

1m 44.88s (3.68) **Going Correction** +0.375s/f (Good) 9 Ran SP% **119.8**
Speed ratings (Par 101): **96,93,92,91,91 90,89,78,65**
toteswingers:1&2:£3.40, 1&3:£13.70, 2&3:£13.20 CSF £11.86 CT £144.96 TOTE £2.30: £1.30, £1.10, £7.40; EX 14.50 Place 6 £9.84, Place 5 £5.60.
Owner Andrew Turton & David Barker **Bred** Mesnil Investments Ltd And Deerpark Stud **Trained** Settrington, N Yorks

FOCUS
A moderate apprentices' handicap but competitive nonetheless and a number were in with a chance 2f out.
T/Plt: £13.30 to a £1 stake. Pool: £33,993.19. 1,862.77 winning tickets. T/Qpdt: £4.10 to a £1 stake. Pool: £3,326.52. 598.62 winning tickets. RY

1187 WOLVERHAMPTON (A.W) (L-H)
Friday, April 9

OFFICIAL GOING: Standard
Wind: virtually nil Weather: dry

1205 BEST ODDS AT LADBROKES.COM H'CAP 5f 216y(P)
6:15 (6:16) (Class 6) (0-60,60) 3-Y-O £1,774 (£523; £262) Stalls Low

Form RPR
-505 **1** **Mary's Pet**[71] 321 3-9-2 58 SebSanders 2 65+
(J Akehurst) *mde all: rdn and wnt clr 2f out: edgd rt over 1f out: kpt on wl* **11/4**[1]

0-06 **2** 1 ½ **Cheshire Lady (IRE)**[30] 849 3-8-3 50 DeclanCannon(5) 7 52
(W M Brisbourne) *in tch: hdwy to chse ldng pair ent fnl 2f: nt pce of wnr 2f out: kpt on to chse wnr ins fnl f: nvr gng pce to rch wnr* **33/1**

3400 **3** ¾ **Lady Brickhouse**[14] 998 3-8-4 46 LukeMorris 4 46
(M D Squance) *in tch in midfield: rdn to chse clr ldr wl over 1f out: hrd drvn and no imp ent fnl f: lost 2nd ins fnl f* **16/1**

432- **4** hd **Dimaire**[116] 7748 3-9-2 58 DaneO'Neill 3 57
(D Haydn Jones) *hld up wl in tch: rdn and nt qckn 2f out: edging lft fr over 1f out: kpt on fnl 100yds* **11/2**[3]

0-60 **5** nk **Bandear (IRE)**[11] 1048 3-9-4 60 NeilCallan 5 58+
(C E Brittain) *s.i.s: sn rdn along and outpcd in rr: drvn over 3f out: hdwy into midfield over 2f out: kpt on fnl f but nvr gng pce to rch ldrs* **6/1**

-420 **6** 2 ¼ **Miss Kitty Grey (IRE)**[36] 784 3-9-4 60 PatCosgrave 8 51
(J R Boyle) *in tch in midfield: rdn and effrt ent 2f out: one pce and wl hld after* **25/1**

600 **7** 1 **Shawkantango**[21] 936 3-8-8 50 JimCrowley 10 38+
(D Shaw) *s.i.s: sn wl outpcd in last: sme hdwy fnl f: nvr on terms* **4/1**[2]

50 **8** ½ **Gemma's Delight (IRE)**[56] 527 3-8-10 52 GrahamGibbons 6 38
(J W Unett) *sn chsng wnr tl wl over 1f out: sn wknd u.p* **18/1**

-333 **9** 3 ½ **Roybuoy**[14] 998 3-8-10 52 (b) SteveDrowne 9 27
(H J L Dunlop) *in tch on outer: rdn and nt qckn 2f out: no ch fnl f* **8/1**

0-00 **10** 14 **Born A Dancer (IRE)**[14] 993 3-8-10 52 MichaelHills 1 —
(J W Hills) *s.i.s: a in rr: lost tch 2f out: t.o fnl f* **12/1**

1m 15.88s (0.88) **Going Correction** +0.075s/f (Slow) 10 Ran SP% **113.1**
Speed ratings (Par 96): **97,95,94,93,93 90,89,88,83,65**
toteswingers:1&2:£12.70, 1&3:£11.70, 2&3:£36.50 CSF £96.72 CT £1244.15 TOTE £4.80: £3.20, £12.50, £10.30; EX 61.40.
Owner Mrs I Marshall **Bred** Green Pastures Farm **Trained** Epsom, Surrey

FOCUS
A low-grade handicap in which only two of the runners had been placed last time out. With no obvious front runner, the early pace was muddling and it turned into something of a dash from the home turn.
Mary's Pet Official explanation: trainer's rep said, regarding apparent improvement in form, that the filly had benefited from a drop in class and a more positive ride.

1206 PLAY POKER AT LADBROKES.COM H'CAP 5f 216y(P)
6:45 (6:47) (Class 2) (0-100,100) 4-Y-O+
£10,592 (£3,172; £1,586; £793; £396; £198) Stalls Low

Form RPR
20/- **1** **Secret Asset (IRE)**[538] 6810 5-8-1 90 [1] LewisWalsh(7) 11 101
(Jane Chapple-Hyam) *t.k.h: chsd ldrs on outer: hdwy to join ldr 4f out: rdn 2f out: led ins fnl f: r.o: rdr stood up in irons and eased nr fin* **33/1**

0-10 **2** nk **Flipando (IRE)**[27] 885 9-8-13 95 GrahamGibbons 8 105+
(T D Barron) *stdd s: in tch in rr: hdwy and rdn jst over 1f out: r.o strly to press wnr nr fin: nt quite rch wnr* **13/2**[3]

04-0 **3** 1 **Fol Hollow (IRE)**[22] 916 5-8-4 86 AdrianNicholls 3 93
(D Nicholls) *led: jnd 4f out: rdn ent 2f out: hdd ins fnl f: btn fnl 50yds* **7/1**

0002 **4** ¾ **Prime Defender**[13] 1007 6-9-4 100 MichaelHills 5 104
(B W Hills) *in tch in midfield: rdn and outpcd wl over 1f out: rallied u.p fnl f: styd on* **9/2**[2]

00-4 **5** nk **Baldemar**[12] 1032 5-8-5 90 BarryMcHugh(3) 6 93+
(R A Fahey) *in tch: n.m.r and shuffled bk wl over 1f out: swtchd rt ent fnl f: r.o fnl 100yds: nvr able to chal* **4/1**[1]

0-31 **6** nk **Beat The Bell**[14] 987 5-8-5 87 WilliamBuick 1 90
(J A Osborne) *trckd ldrs on inner: rdn and effrt over 1f out: unable qck u.p 1f out: wknd towards fin* **10/1**

0000 **7** ½ **Ceremonial Jade (UAE)**[6] 1085 7-9-4 100 (t) SebSanders 7 101+
(M Botti) *in tch in rr: swtchd rt and rdn wl over 1f out: kpt on fnl f: nvr trbld ldrs* **10/1**

-664 **8** ¾ **Five Star Junior (USA)**[27] 887 4-9-0 96 KierenFallon 4 95
(Mrs L Stubbs) *hld up in tch in rr: rdn wl over 1f out: n.m.r jst over 1f out tl ins fnl f: kpt on: nvr trbld ldrs* **12/1**

32-0 **9** 1 ¾ **Fantasy Explorer**[12] 1032 7-8-9 91 ow1 DarryllHolland 12 84
(J J Quinn) *t.k.h: chsd ldrs: rdn and unable qck wl over 1f out: wknd ent fnl f* **14/1**

24-0 **10** 1 ¾ **Swiss Franc**[13] 1007 5-9-1 97 JimmyFortune 10 84
(D R C Elsworth) *t.k.h: chsd ldr for 2f: styd handy tl rdn and wknd over 1f out* **12/1**

6200 **11** ½ **Imprimis Tagula (IRE)**[56] 528 6-8-8 97 (v) NatashaEaton(7) 2 83
(A Bailey) *dwlt: sn in tch in midfield: rdn and no hdwy 2f out: n.d fnl f* **40/1**

5403 **12** 1 **Ebraam (USA)**[27] 887 7-8-6 93 DeclanCannon(5) 9 76
(S Curran) *in tch in midfield on outer: pushed along 4f out: rdn and nt qckn 2f out: no ch w ldrs after* **18/1**

6P-0 **13** 11 **Crimson Fern (IRE)**[20] 948 6-8-8 90 FergusSweeney 13 37
(M S Saunders) *hld up in tch in rr on outer: rdn 2f out: sn btn and eased fnl f* **40/1**

1m 13.67s (-1.33) **Going Correction** +0.075s/f (Slow) 13 Ran SP% **117.3**
Speed ratings (Par 109): **111,110,109,108,107 107,106,105,103,101 100,99,84**
toteswingers:1&2:£56.00, 1&3:£23.60, 2&3:£13.10 CSF £230.30 CT £1756.03 TOTE £44.80: £8.70, £3.70, £1.30; EX 212.30.
Owner Simon Pierpoint & Paul Salisbury **Bred** Mrs C Hartery **Trained** Dalham, Suffolk
■ Lewis Walsh's first winner.
■ Stewards' Enquiry : Darryll Holland two-day ban: careless riding (Apr 23-24); one-day ban: failed to ride to draw (Apr 25)

FOCUS
A cracking handicap on paper but something of an unsatisfactory affair all the same in that it was run at a steady gallop and the advantage was very much with those that raced close to the pace.

NOTEBOOK
Secret Asset(IRE) ran out something of a shock winner on his first run since autumn 2008, giving his rider his first winner, and though he was favoured by being ridden prominently in a race most weren't, he still deserves credit considering how hardly pulled early on. Previously raced only at 5f, this win opens up more options for him but it might not be form to take at face value.
Flipando(IRE) ◆ deserves plenty of credit considering he was held up in a race not run at a strong enough gallop to bring his stamina into play, closing fast at the finish but just finding the line coming too soon. For all he goes well here, there won't be much for him from now on and he might be interesting given his new-found versatility if given a stiff 6f on turf. (op 6-1)
Fol Hollow(IRE) had every chance adopting his normal positive tactics but might just be better these days at the minimum trip. This run seems to confirm he's not quite as good on AW as turf, but is certainly better on the surface than Fibresand. (op 10-1)
Prime Defender had won his only previous start here but seemed to find the emphasis on speed this time too much and never really threatened. His last run suggests he is as good as ever, but he has a modest strike rate for one of his ability. (op 4-1)
Baldemar ◆ was unable to repeat his good Doncaster effort, but almost certainly found this an insufficient test, only getting going late, and given the form of his stable is sure to remain of interest giving given a more appropriate test back on turf. (op 5-1 tchd 7-2)
Beat The Bell ran well considering he was up in the weights as well as grade after his all-the-way Lingfield win, but was another favoured by holding a prominent position throughout. (tchd 12-1)
Ceremonial Jade(UAE) was inconvenienced by the steady gallop and never promised to get competitive from off the pace. (tchd 11-1)
Five Star Junior(USA) was another who didn't have the race run to suit. (op 10-1 tchd 14-1)
Fantasy Explorer might have been expected to have done better considering he was well placed turning in and it looks as though he still hasn't come to himself yet.

1207 ENJOY THE PARTY PACK GROUP OFFER H'CAP 1m 5f 194y(P)
7:15 (7:18) (Class 6) (0-65,62) 4-Y-O+ £1,774 (£523; £262) Stalls Low

Form RPR
6-03 **1** **Venir Rouge**[46] 660 6-9-11 61 WilliamBuick 4 70+
(Matthew Salaman) *hld up wl bhd in last trio: swtchd rt and effrt over 3f out: 7th and stl plenty to do wl over 1f out: str run fnl f to ld nr fin: won gng away* **15/2**[3]

-001 **2** ½ **Nayessence**[1] 1188 4-9-3 56 6ex (t) GrahamGibbons 7 64
(M W Easterby) *led tl 8f out: chsd ldr after: wnt clr w ldr 4f out: led wl over 2f out and sn rdn clr: drvn over 1f out: kpt on whn pressed ins fnl f: hdd and no ex nr fin* **9/2**[2]

10-F **3** 3/4 **Altos Reales**[79] 228 6-8-13 **49** PatCosgrave 13 56
(M J Scudamore) *dwlt: sn hld up in midfield: rdn and outpcd by ldng pair 4f out: wnt 3rd over 2f out: pressed ldr ins fnl f: nt qckn and no imp fnl 75yds* **20/1**

2/0- **4** 1 1/4 **Jubilant Note (IRE)**[242] 2351 8-9-12 **62** (v) DJCondon 1 68
(Gordon Elliott, Ire) *hld up bhd in last trio: rdn and outpcd by ldrs 4f out: hdwy to chse ldrs and racd awkwardly 1f out: edgd lft and plugged on fnl f: nvr able to rch ldrs* **3/1**[1]

3-32 **5** 2 **Jezza**[21] 942 4-8-11 **50** DarryllHolland 10 53
(Karen George) *racd keenly: chsd ldr after 1f: led 8f out: drew clr w wnr 4f out: rdn and hdd wl over 2f out: flashed tail u.p and lost 2nd ins fnl f: wknd fnl 100yds* **3/1**[1]

4630 **6** 4 **Look Officer (USA)**[14] 996 4-9-2 **62** LeonnaMayor(7) 2 59
(Miss M E Rowland) *hld up in midfield: rdn and outpcd by ldrs 4f out: hdwy and chsd ldrs over 1f out: one pce and no imp fnl f* **40/1**

242- **7** 3 1/4 **Kings Maiden (IRE)**[266] 4068 7-9-12 **62** RoystonFfrench 11 55
(James Moffatt) *hld up bhd in last trio: outpcd and rdn 4f out: nvr trbld ldrs* **9/1**

02/5 **8** 6 **Simone Martini (IRE)**[14] 996 5-9-5 **55** (t) SteveDrowne 12 39
(M F Harris) *in tch: rdn and outpcd by ldng pair 4f out: wl bhd fnl 2f* **16/1**

-544 **9** 10 **Sacco D'Oro**[28] 872 4-9-2 **55** AlanMunro 8 25
(M Mullineaux) *chsd ldrs: rdn and outpcd by ldng pair 4f out: wl bhd fnl 2f: eased fnl f: t.o* **25/1**

443- **10** 5 **Party Palace**[267] 3997 6-9-2 **52** CathyGannon 9 15
(H S Howe) *chsd ldr for 1f: chsd ldrs after tl rdn and wknd 4f out: t.o fnl 2f* **20/1**

450/ **11** 7 **Summerofsixtynine**[736] 1165 7-9-0 **50** LukeMorris 5 3
(J G M O'Shea) *stdd s: hld up wl in rr: rdn and lost tch 4f out: t.o fnl 2f* **33/1**

12 45 **Sharift (IRE)**[149] 7340 4-8-11 **50** NeilCallan 6 —
(David William O'Connor, Ire) *hld up in tch in midfield: rdn and btn 4f out: t.o 2f out: eased fnl f* **25/1**

3m 5.45s (-0.55) **Going Correction** +0.075s/f (Slow) 12 Ran SP% **118.4**
WFA 4 from 5yo+ 3lb
Speed ratings (Par 101): **104,103,103,102,101 99,97,93,88,85 81,55**
toteswingers:1&2:£8.60, 1&3:£41.30, 2&3:£17.40 CSF £37.22 CT £658.80 TOTE £9.50: £3.30, £2.30, £8.40; EX 48.20.
Owner A Byrne & Partners **Bred** Marshalla Salaman **Trained** Upper Lambourn, Berks

FOCUS
A modest handicap and one run at no more than a fair pace for a long way. The right horses were thereabouts at the finish and the form seems likely to stand up.
Simone Martini(IRE) Official explanation: jockey said gelding hung left

1208 HOTEL & CONFERENCING AT WOLVERHAMPTON CLAIMING STKS 1m 1f 103y(P)
7:45 (7:46) (Class 6) 4-Y-0+ £1,774 (£523; £262) Stalls Low

Form RPR

-412 **1** **Plush**[49] 623 7-8-12 **81** RossAtkinson(5) 1 88
(Tom Dascombe) *stdd s: hld up in last: hdwy on outer over 3f out: chal over 1f out: rdn to ld ins fnl f: kpt on* **3/1**[2]

6000 **2** hd **Full Toss**[13] 1008 4-8-12 **93** RichardEvans(5) 7 87
(P D Evans) *chsd ldrs tl wnt 2nd 4f out: rdn to ld wl over 1f out: sn jnd: hdd ins fnl f: kpt on u.p but a jst hld* **5/6**[1]

3323 **3** 3 **Atacama Sunrise**[21] 929 4-8-1 **67** SimonPearce(5) 2 70
(J Pearce) *hld up in last trio: hdwy 3f out: rdn over 1f out: chsd ldng pair jst ins fnl f: no prog and wl hld fnl 150yds* **7/1**[3]

-003 **4** 3 3/4 **Fifty Cents**[14] 994 6-8-9 **65** SteveDrowne 8 65
(M F Harris) *racd keenly: led after 1f: hdd and rdn wl over 1f out: wknd over 1f out* **20/1**

65-4 **5** 2 3/4 **Country Road (IRE)**[22] 917 4-9-4 **70** GrahamGibbons 4 68
(M W Easterby) *led for 1f: chsd ldr tl 7f out: rdn and lost pl 4f out: no ch fnl 3f* **14/1**

223- **6** nk **Bold Indian (IRE)**[118] 6488 6-8-5 **56** BarryMcHugh(3) 5 58
(M E Sowersby) *t.k.h: hld up in last trio: hdwy to chse ldrs 3f out: wknd u.p over 1f out* **33/1**

00-5 **7** 2 **Never Sold Out (IRE)**[39] 753 5-8-7 **47** LukeMorris 3 53?
(J G M O'Shea) *chsd ldr 7f out tl 4f out: wknd qckly wl over 1f out* **66/1**

2m 1.81s (0.11) **Going Correction** +0.075s/f (Slow) 7 Ran SP% **107.9**
Speed ratings (Par 101): **102,101,99,95,93 93,91**
.Full Toss was claimed by J. S. Goldie for £14,000\n\x\x
Owner John Reed **Bred** Cheveley Park Stud Ltd **Trained** Malpas, Cheshire
■ Stewards' Enquiry : Richard Evans two-day ban: used whip down shoulder in the forehand (Apr 23-24)

FOCUS
An uncompetitive claimer dominated by the two market leaders, much as ratings suggested it would be. The pace wasn't strong and the field was still well bunched 3f out.
Fifty Cents Official explanation: jockey said gelding hung right-handed

1209 WATCH LIVE FOOTBALL AT LADBROKES.COM H'CAP 1m 141y(P)
8:15 (8:15) (Class 6) (0-60,60) 3-Y-0 £1,774 (£523; £262) Stalls Low

Form RPR

4 **1** **Buona Sarah (IRE)**[11] 1048 3-9-4 **60** PatCosgrave 8 67+
(J R Boyle) *t.k.h: chsd ldr after 1f: rdn to ld 2f out: kpt on wl u.p fnl f* **2/1**[1]

000- **2** 1/2 **Celtic Ransom**[165] 7050 3-9-2 **58** MichaelHills 5 64+
(J W Hills) *t.k.h early: hld up in tch: rdn to chse wnr ent fnl f: hrd drvn and pressed wnr ins fnl f: kpt on but a hld* **2/1**[1]

50-0 **3** 2 1/2 **Kingsdine (IRE)**[18] 964 3-9-0 **56** FergusSweeney 3 56
(M S Saunders) *t.k.h: led briefly: sn hld up wl in tch: effrt and n.m.r briefly over 1f out: chsd ldng pair and drvn jst ins fnl f: no imp after* **8/1**[3]

00-6 **4** 2 1/2 **Flotate (USA)**[15] 977 3-8-10 **52** (p) RobertHavlin 1 46
(Jane Chapple-Hyam) *hld up in tch: rdn and outpcd 2f out: plugged on same pce fnl f* **14/1**

00-0 **5** 2 **Gulf Punch**[14] 998 3-8-4 **46** oh1 FrannyNorton 7 36
(M F Harris) *sn led: rdn and hdd 2f out: lost 2nd ent fnl f: sn wknd* **16/1**

235- **6** 3/4 **Firetrap**[225] 5358 3-9-3 **59** SebSanders 6 47
(Mrs A Duffield) *hld up in last: rdn and short-lived effrt over 1f out: no ch fnl f* **9/2**[2]

00-0 **7** 4 **Rivitivo**[15] 977 3-8-4 **46** oh1 LiamJones 4 25
(W M Brisbourne) *stdd and hmpd sn after s: rdn and no prog over 3f out: wl bhd fnl 2f* **40/1**

1m 54.13s (3.63) **Going Correction** +0.075s/f (Slow) 7 Ran SP% **110.9**
Speed ratings (Par 96): **86,85,83,81,79 78,75**
toteswingers:1&2:£1.10, 1&3:£3.70, 2&3:£4.50 CSF £5.49 CT £21.98 TOTE £4.10: £3.80, £3.40; EX 6.90.
Owner Mrs Pippa Boyle **Bred** Peter J Doyle Bloodstock Ltd **Trained** Epsom, Surrey

FOCUS
A weak handicap run at no more than a fair pace, but the first two have something to recommend them at a modest level.

1210 PLAY BINGO AT LADBROKES.COM H'CAP 1m 141y(P)
8:45 (8:45) (Class 4) (0-85,85) 3-Y-0 £4,209 (£1,252; £625; £312) Stalls Low

Form RPR

322- **1** **Fonterutoli (IRE)**[286] 3376 3-8-1 **71** AndreaAtzeni(3) 3 77+
(M Botti) *chsd ldrs: rdn over 2f out: edgd lft u.p but chal ent fnl f: led ins fnl f: r.o wl u.p* **15/8**[1]

00-1 **2** shd **Power Series (USA)**[39] 754 3-9-4 **85** WilliamBuick 2 91
(J H M Gosden) *t.k.h: sn w ldr on inner: led wl over 1f out: sn rdn: hdd ins fnl f: r.o u.p but a jst hld* **5/2**[2]

3-21 **3** 1 **Sweet Child O'Mine**[36] 781 3-8-10 **77** FrannyNorton 1 80
(R C Guest) *mounted on crse: t.k.h: hld up wl in tch: rdn and effrt on inner over 1f out: no ex fnl 100yds* **9/2**

100- **4** 5 **Damietta (USA)**[211] 5797 3-8-10 **77** FrankieDettori 4 72
(M Johnston) *sn led: hdd and rdn wl over 1f out: btn and eased ins fnl f* **3/1**[3]

1m 51.11s (0.61) **Going Correction** +0.075s/f (Slow) 4 Ran SP% **106.5**
Speed ratings (Par 100): **100,99,99,94**
CSF £6.56 TOTE £5.80; EX 5.50.
Owner Scuderia Rencati Srl **Bred** Massimo Parri **Trained** Newmarket, Suffolk

FOCUS
Just the four runners but an interesting handicap and it produced an exciting finish after something of a stop-start pace put the emphasis on finishing speed.

1211 STAY AT THE WOLVERHAMPTON HOLIDAY INN MEDIAN AUCTION MAIDEN STKS 7f 32y(P)
9:15 (9:17) (Class 6) 3-4-Y-0 £1,774 (£523; £262) Stalls High

Form RPR

3- **1** **Prince Of Vasa (IRE)**[227] 5325 3-8-13 **0** FrankieDettori 3 77+
(M Johnston) *mde all: rdn and drew clr w rival over 1f out: kpt on wl fnl f* **11/10**[1]

33-2 **2** nk **Lago Indiano (IRE)**[23] 900 3-8-13 **76** JimCrowley 5 74
(Mrs A J Perrett) *chsd wnr: rdn and clr of field over 1f out: kpt on steadily u.p ins fnl f: nvr quite getting to wnr* **2/1**[2]

52 **3** 4 1/2 **Golden Ratio (IRE)**[30] 849 3-8-8 **0** LukeMorris 4 57
(J R Gask) *chsd ldng pair: rdn wl over 2f out: outpcd and wl btn over 1f out: no ch w ldng pair fnl f* **15/2**[3]

0- **4** hd **Mahlak (IRE)**[224] 5397 3-8-8 **0** ChrisCatlin 7 56+
(C E Brittain) *in tch in midfield: pushed along and struggling over 3f out: rdn and dropped to rr 3f out: no ch fnl 2f: plugged on fnl f* **10/1**

5 3 **Crinan Classic** 3-8-6 **0** JohnFahy(7) 2 53+
(C G Cox) *dwlt: hld up in rr: racd awkwardly bnd over 3f out: bhd and pushed along over 1f out: rdn and kpt on same pce fnl f* **20/1**

6 1/2 **Wadi Wanderer (IRE)** 3-8-13 **0** LiamKeniry 1 52
(E F Vaughan) *dwlt: hld up in last trio: rdn and wl outpcd by ldrs 2f out: one pce and wl btn after* **40/1**

7 2 1/4 **Baxter (IRE)** 3-8-13 **0** MichaelHills 6 46
(J W Hills) *stdd s: hld up in last trio: hdwy to chse ldrs and rdn ent fnl 2f: sn outpcd and btn: wknd fnl f* **20/1**

1m 30.65s (1.05) **Going Correction** +0.075s/f (Slow) 7 Ran SP% **113.8**
Speed ratings (Par 101): **97,96,91,91,87 87,84**
toteswingers:1&2:£1.30, 1&3:£4.00, 2&3:£2.00 CSF £3.37 TOTE £3.20: £3.60, £1.10; EX 4.20 Place 6 £101.65, Place 5 £38.74.
Owner Sheikh Hamdan Bin Mohammed Al Maktoum **Bred** E O'Gorman **Trained** Middleham Moor, N Yorks

FOCUS
Probably no better than fair form in this maiden, though the winner will rate higher in time and a couple in behind ran better than their finishing positions suggest. The pace was a decent one before the eventual winner, out in front at the time, was given a breather.
T/Plt: £460.20 to a £1 stake. Pool: £72,535.57. 115.06 winning tickets. T/Qpdt: £28.40 to a £1 stake. Pool: £7,429.71. 193.34 winning tickets. SP

1212 - 1218a (Foreign Racing) - See Raceform Interactive

1164 LINGFIELD (L-H)
Saturday, April 10

OFFICIAL GOING: Standard
Wind: fairly modest, across Weather: bright

1219 BLUE SQUARE PAY 5 IN THE NATIONAL H'CAP 7f (P)
2:10 (2:14) (Class 3) (0-90,89) 4-Y-0+ £7,771 (£2,312; £1,155; £577) Stalls Low

Form RPR

624- **1** **Spirit Of Sharjah (IRE)**[163] 7133 5-9-4 **89** MichaelHills 8 99
(Miss J Feilden) *hld up towards rr: rdn and hdwy over 1f out: str run to ld wl ins fnl f* **14/1**

000- **2** 3/4 **Crown Choice**[161] 7185 5-9-4 **89** JimmyFortune 2 97
(W R Swinburn) *trckd ldrs: rdn to chal and edgd rt over 1f out: led ins fnl f: hdd and no ex wl ins fnl f* **4/1**[1]

0213 **3** 1 **Seek The Fair Land**[21] 944 4-9-4 **89** (p) PatCosgrave 1 94
(J R Boyle) *chsd ldr: rdn and pressed ldr over 1f out: hrd drvn and edgd lft ins fnl f: one pce fnl 100yds* **7/1**

00-5 **4** hd **Rulesn'regulations**[31] 850 4-9-4 **89** TomQueally 4 94
(Matthew Salaman) *in tch in midfield: nt clr run 2f out: rdn and hdwy on inner over 1f out: chsd ldrs 1f out: kpt on same pce u.p fnl 100yds* **22/1**

1320 **5** 1/2 **Ilie Nastase (FR)**[7] 1088 6-8-12 **83** LiamKeniry 11 86
(C R Dore) *dwlt: dropped in bhd after s: hld up in last pair: rdn and hdwy on inner over 1f out: kpt on fnl f: nt rch ldrs* **28/1**

300- **6** 3/4 **Celtic Sultan (IRE)**[154] 7294 6-9-3 **88** MickyFenton 9 89
(T P Tate) *led and grad crossed to rail: rdn and hrd pressed over 1f out: hdd ins fnl f: keeping on same pce and btn whn short of room wl ins fnl f* **16/1**

5260 **7** 1 **Red Somerset (USA)**[23] 921 7-9-1 **86** GeorgeBaker 10 85
(R J Hodges) *s.i.s: dropped in bhd after s: nt clr run over 1f out: r.o ins fnl f: nvr trbld ldrs* **25/1**

220- **8** nk **Satwa Laird**[181] 6702 4-9-2 **87** KierenFallon 3 85
(E A L Dunlop) *in tch: rdn ent fnl 2f: drvn and unable qck over 1f out: one pce fnl f* **13/2**[3]

1211 **9** 1 **Ocean Legend (IRE)**[44] 696 5-9-1 **86** FrankieDettori 7 81
(A W Carroll) *in tch in midfield: rdn and unable qck ent fnl 2f: no prog u.p fr over 1f out* **9/2**[2]

435- **10** 1/2 **Masai Moon**[171] 6949 6-8-13 **87** JamesMillman(3) 5 81
(B R Millman) *a in rr: last and rdn over 2f out: effrt on inner over 1f out: n.d* **8/1**

1-22 **11** 1/2 **Pegasus Again (USA)**41 749 5-8-10 **88** .... JohnFahy(7) 12 80
(R A Mills) *in tch: rdn jst over 2f out: drvn and btn over 1f out* **9/1**

50-5 **12** 7 **Beckermet (IRE)**56 537 8-9-1 **86** .... SteveDrowne 6 60
(R F Fisher) *prom tl wknd qckly wl over 1f out: wl btn fnl f* **20/1**

2-41 **13** 1 1/2 **Arachnophobia (IRE)**38 779 4-9-2 **87** .... RobertWinston 13 57
(Pat Eddery) *in tch in midfield on outer: wd and struggling bnd 2f out: wl btn fnl f* **10/1**

1m 23.74s (-1.06) **Going Correction** +0.05s/f (Slow) **13** Ran SP% **123.2**
Speed ratings (Par 107): **108,107,106,105,105 104,103,102,101,101 100,92,90**
Tote Swingers: 1&2 £20.70, 1&3 £14.30, 2&3 £21.10 CSF £68.07 CT £457.71 TOTE £14.80: £3.40, £2.10, £2.10; EX 112.90 TRIFECTA Not won..
Owner A Dee **Bred** Mrs Kathleen Reynolds **Trained** Exning, Suffolk
■ Stewards' Enquiry : Jimmy Fortune one-day ban: careless riding (Apr 24)

FOCUS
A decent and competitive handicap, run at a solid pace.

NOTEBOOK
Spirit Of Sharjah(IRE), not seen since a couple of decent efforts over C&D last October, was always travelling well in the middle of the field. Brought with his effort on the outside turning for home, he produced a strong challenge to hit the front inside the last furlong. He remains unexposed on sand and may step up into Listed company next. (op 12-1 tchd 16-1)
Crown Choice ◆, a dual winner over this trip at Kempton a year ago, ended last season on a low note but he was well backed for this return. He was always going well in a good position and briefly hit the front a furlong out, but didn't stay there for long once the winner arrived. He should go one better soon. (op 13-2)
Seek The Fair Land has been in good form at this trip on Polytrack of late and ran his race. He had every chance and stayed on but he continues to creep up the weights which won't make things any easier. (op 13-2 tchd 11-2 and 15-2)
Rulesn'regulations, disappointing after a successful belated return to action at Ascot in September, had still to prove his stamina for this trip but he was putting in some good late work and this was a step back in the right direction. (op 20-1)
Ilie Nastase(FR), who has gained his two victories this winter in small-field claimers, was given plenty to do but he finished strongly along the inside rail so is by no means a lost cause off this mark. (op 25-1)
Celtic Sultan(IRE), making his sand debut on his 35th start and returning from five months off, set a decent pace until swamped a furlong from home. He may be worth a try at another AW track suited more to front-runners.
Red Somerset(USA) ◆ is well handicapped on his very best form, but is still 9lb higher than when last successful. However, he can be considered unfortunate not to have finished closer here as he was hampered when trying to launch an effort turning for home and when he did get through it was far too late. (op 33-1)
Ocean Legend(IRE) was up another 5lb having won three of his past four starts, but he was being ridden along fully 3f from home and perhaps Kempton suits him better. (op 4-1 tchd 5-1)
Arachnophobia(IRE), raised 6lb after scraping home by a nose over this trip at Wolverhampton last month, was disappointing but he was always seeing too much daylight from the outside stall. (op 9-1 tchd 11-1)

1220 FAIR AND SQUARE AT BLUESQUARE.COM H'CAP 1m 4f (P)
2:45 (2:47) (Class 2) (0-105,103) 4-Y-0+ **£10,361** (£3,083; £1,540; £769) **Stalls** Low

Form RPR

15-0 **1** **Red Cadeaux**14 1015 4-8-10 **90** .... KierenFallon 3 101+
(E A L Dunlop) *hld up in tch in midfield: swtchd rt off of inner and hdwy over 2f out: rdn to chse ldr over 1f out: drvn to ld ins fnl f: r.o wl* **7/1**2

132- **2** nk **Tinaar (USA)**166 7066 4-8-8 **88** .... RyanMoore 7 99
(G A Butler) *chsd ldrs: rdn to ld 2f out: drvn over 1f out: hdd ins fnl f: kpt on u.p* **15/8**1

-004 **3** 2 1/4 **Illustrious Blue**24 903 7-9-3 **103** .... JohnFahy(7) 12 110
(W J Knight) *stdd and dropped in bhd after s: gd hdwy on outer to chse ldrs 3f out: rdn to chse ldng pair ent fnl f: no imp after* **9/1**3

530- **4** 1 3/4 **Jedi**252 4520 4-8-1 **84** oh1 .... Louis-PhilippeBeuzelin(3) 2 92+
(Sir Michael Stoute) *in tch in midfield: nt clr run over 2f out tl 2f out: rdn over 1f out: kpt on same pce fnl f* **14/1**

6624 **5** 1/2 **Record Breaker (IRE)**13 1031 6-9-7 **100** ....(b) JoeFanning 11 104
(M Johnston) *towards rr: rdn and effrt ent fnl 2f: styd on u.p fnl f: nvr trbld ldrs* **14/1**

500- **6** 1/2 **Topolski (IRE)**234 5170 4-8-7 **87** .... DavidProbert 5 90+
(A M Balding) *hld up in tch in midfield: rdn over 2f out: sltly hmpd bnd jst over 2f out: drvn and kpt on fnl f: nvr able to chal* **20/1**

100- **7** 3 **Press The Button (GER)**28 6106 7-9-1 **94** .... StephenCraine 6 92
(J R Boyle) *w ldr tl led over 2f out: hdd 2f out: wknd u.p over 1f out* **20/1**

0444 **8** nk **Baylini**14 1015 6-8-9 **88** .... HayleyTurner 4 86
(Ms J S Doyle) *stdd s: hld up in rr: nvr trbld ldrs* **20/1**

-112 **9** 3 1/2 **King Olav (UAE)**14 1015 5-9-1 **94** .... LukeMorris 9 86
(A W Carroll) *chsd ldrs: rdn 3f out: wknd u.p over 1f out: wl btn fnl f* **7/1**2

5213 **10** 3 1/4 **Mafeking (UAE)**14 1015 6-9-0 **93** .... AndrewElliott 1 80
(M R Hoad) *led tl hdd over 2f out: wknd qckly 2f out* **16/1**

211 **11** 1/2 **Cashpoint**21 947 5-8-2 **84** .... AndreaAtzeni(3) 13 70
(A Middleton) *in tch in midfield: rdn and struggling whn wd bnd 2f out: wl btn over 1f out* **7/1**2

030- **12** 25 **Unleashed (IRE)**182 6662 5-9-5 **98** .... TedDurcan 10 44
(C J Mann) *a in rr: rdn and lost tch over 3f out: t.o and eased fnl 2f* **20/1**

2m 28.89s (-4.11) **Going Correction** +0.05s/f (Slow) course record
WFA 4 from 5yo+ 1lb **12** Ran SP% **120.5**
Speed ratings (Par 109): **115,114,113,112,111 111,109,109,106,104 104,87**
Tote Swingers: 1&2 £4.90, 1&3 £17.50, 2&3 £9.00 CSF £19.45 CT £118.03 TOTE £9.50: £3.70, £1.10, £3.70; EX 25.10 Trifecta £104.50 Pool: £480.35 - 3.40 winning units..
Owner R J Arculli **Bred** Foursome Thoroughbreds **Trained** Newmarket, Suffolk

FOCUS
A hot handicap with four of these having contested the Rosebery a fortnight earlier. The pace was decent with Press The Button and Mafeking disputing the advantage for much of the way. The front pair pulled nicely clear of the rest.

NOTEBOOK
Red Cadeaux ◆, who was an eyecatcher when a staying-on seventh on his return to action in the Rosebery, appreciated the extra furlong and reversed the form with the trio that finished ahead of him at Kempton. He travelled strongly throughout and, having moved into a challenging position on the home bend, hit the front over a furlong out. He may have got there too soon as he was inclined to idle and hung over to the inside rail, but he kept on finding under pressure. He may come on again from this. (tchd 8-1)
Tinaar(USA) ◆, an unexposed and progressive handicapper on turf and Polytrack in the second half of last year, was returning from six months off but she was backed off the boards. She held a good position throughout until poking her head in front passing the 2f pole, but the winner collared her on his inside a furlong later. To her credit, she battled back gamely and her winning turn is merely delayed. (op 7-2)
Illustrious Blue, 0-10 on the AW coming into this, didn't do a lot right as he pulled hard early and, after making a rapid move into contention around the wide outside running to the home turn, was noticeably hanging rounding the bend. He still kept going to finish a clear third, however, so emerges with credit and will always remain of interest back at his beloved Goodwood. (tchd 8-1 and 10-1)
Jedi ◆, making his sand debut after an eight-month absence and gelded since last seen, can be rated a bit better than his final position as he was short of room against the inside rail rounding the home bend before running on again. (op 11-1)
Record Breaker(IRE), having only his fourth try on sand and still 4lb above his last winning mark, didn't get going until it was far too late. (op 10-1)
Topolski(IRE) ◆, making his debut for the yard and on sand on this first outing in eight months, was disappointing on his last two starts for Mark Johnston but he was by no means disgraced here and is entitled to come on for it. (op 16-1)
Press The Button(GER), back on the Flat after being well beaten on his return to action in last month's Imperial Cup, is fully effective under these conditions and helped force the pace until headed passing the 2f pole, but he still lasted longer than fellow pace-setter Mafeking.
Baylini reportedly lost a shoe. Official explanation: trainer said mare lost a shoe (op 16-1)
King Olav(UAE), winner of his only previous outing here, was in a handy position when coming off the bridle half a mile from home, but he hung in there until finding it all too much from over a furlong out. Despite his course victory, he may prefer the right-handed track at Kempton. Official explanation: jockey said gelding had no more to give (op 13-2 tchd 6-1)

1221 BLUE SQUARE INTERNATIONAL TRIAL STKS (LISTED RACE) 1m (P)
3:15 (3:15) (Class 1) 3-Y-0 **£22,708** (£8,608; £4,308; £2,148; £1,076) **Stalls** High

Form RPR

615- **1** **Lord Zenith**274 3817 3-9-0 **96** .... JimmyFortune 1 100
(A M Balding) *stdd s: t.k.h: hld up wl in tch: rdn and effrt on inner over 1f out: r.o wl to ld fnl 75yds: hung rt towards fin* **5/2**3

41- **2** 1/2 **Zaahy (USA)**220 5580 3-9-0 **92** .... TomQueally 3 99
(P W Chapple-Hyam) *dwlt: hld up wl in tch: rdn to press ldrs on outer ent fnl f: kpt on wl fnl 100yds* **7/1**

011- **3** 1/2 **Carnaby Street (IRE)**168 7030 3-9-0 **105** .... RyanMoore 4 98
(R Hannon) *led: sn hdd but styd w ldr: rdn and hanging lft into ldr fr wl over 1f out: no ex and btn wl ins fnl f* **9/4**2

210- **4** 1 1/4 **Musaafer (IRE)**168 7017 3-9-0 **98** .... RichardHills 2 98+
(M A Jarvis) *sn led and set stdy gallop: rdn wl over 1f out: kpt on tl hdd fnl 75yds: styng on same pce whn short of room and hmpd wl ins fnl f: eased after* **6/4**1

266- **5** 18 **Florio Vincitore (IRE)**204 6063 3-9-0 **82** .... EddieCreighton 5 51
(E J Creighton) *t.k.h: chsd ldrs on outer: rdn and struggling over 2f out: lost tch 2f out* **66/1**

1m 38.43s (0.23) **Going Correction** +0.05s/f (Slow) **5** Ran SP% **113.3**
Speed ratings (Par 106): **100,99,99,97,79**
CSF £19.30 TOTE £3.40: £1.70, £3.00; EX 20.30.
Owner Mrs M E Wates **Bred** Langton Stud And G E M Wates **Trained** Kingsclere, Hants
■ Stewards' Enquiry : Jimmy Fortune four-day ban: careless riding (Apr 25-28)

FOCUS
The joint smallest field for the race since its inception in 2002 and all five participants lacked a recent run. The pace disputed by Carnaby Street and Musaafer was modest and this developed into a sprint, so it remains to be seen how strong the form is.

NOTEBOOK
Lord Zenith, not seen since finishing unplaced in a Newmarket Group 2 last July, travelled particularly well behind the leaders and when asked to go through the gap on the inside entering the final furlong, he quickened smartly. He did hang markedly away to his right under pressure close home, but was the best horse on merit. Described as still green and raw by his trainer, he should have learned from this and, provided the ground is fast, he may take his chance in the Guineas. (op 3-1tchd 10-3 in places)
Zaahy(USA) ◆, the least exposed in the field and last seen beating a subsequent winner in a 7f novice event here last September, had an uninterrupted run around the outside and finished well to press the winner close to home. He can still improve further. (op 4-1)
Carnaby Street(IRE), winner of the Horris Hill on his final start at two and with upwards of 7lb in hand of his rivals on official ratings, helped set the steady pace but seemed to get slightly outpaced when the tempo quickened on the home turn. He kept staying on despite hanging, but was beaten when intimidated by the winner near the line. Official explanation: jockey said colt hung left (op 10-3 tchd 4-1 in a place)
Musaafer(IRE), last seen finishing ninth of the 11 runners in the Racing Post Trophy after pulling hard, was the other to dispute the pace and held a slight advantage passing the 2f pole. However, he couldn't get clear, was swamped inside the last furlong, and was already beaten when the winner ran across him in the last few yards. He probably needs a stiffer test or a stronger gallop. (op 13-8 tchd 7-4 and 15-8 in a place)
Florio Vincitore(IRE) is effective on this surface, but had a mountain to climb at this level and only lasted as long as he did due to the steady tempo, though he reportedly finished lame. Official explanation: trainer said gelding finished lame (op 50-1)

1222 0-0 SEMI FINAL CASH BACK AT BLUESQUARE.COM MAIDEN STKS 6f (P)
3:50 (3:53) (Class 5) 3-Y-0 **£2,729** (£806; £403) **Stalls** Low

Form RPR

4-3 **1** **Aetos**31 843 3-9-3 0 .... PatDobbs 8 92
(M P Tregoning) *wnt lft s: mde all: rdn clr over 1f out: r.o strly: easily* **7/2**3

302- **2** 5 **Dherghaam (IRE)**172 6922 3-9-3 77 .... RichardHills 9 76
(E A L Dunlop) *chsd ldrs: wnt 2nd over 4f out: rdn and fnd little wl over 1f out: no ch w wnr fnl f* **6/4**1

20- **3** 2 1/2 **Katy's Secret**113 7799 3-8-5 0 .... Mary-AnnParkin(7) 4 63+
(W Jarvis) *hld up in tch on outer: pushed along and outpcd by ldng pair ent fnl 2f: styd on steadily fnl f: no ch w ldng pair* **20/1**

4 2 **Sennockian Storm (USA)** 3-8-12 0 .... JoeFanning 5 57+
(M Johnston) *chsd wnr tl over 4f out: rdn and nt pce of ldng pair ent fnl 2f: no ch w ldng pair fr over 1f out* **2/1**2

60- **5** 1/2 **Winifred Jo**180 6722 3-8-12 0 .... LukeMorris 10 55
(J R Gask) *chsd ldrs: rdn and unable qck 2f out: no ch w ldrs fr over 1f out* **50/1**

6 1/2 **Crazy Parachute** 3-9-3 0 .... GeorgeBaker 6 64+
(G L Moore) *rrd leaving stalls and s.i.s: hld up in rr: hdwy whn nt clr run jst over 1f out tl ins fnl f: n.d* **16/1**

- **7** 1/2 **Thalia Grace** 3-8-12 0 .... AlanMunro 7 52
(L Montague Hall) *pushed lft s: chsd ldrs: rdn and outpcd jst over 2f out: no ch fr over 1f out* **50/1**

0-6 **8** nk **I'Lldoit**25 894 3-9-3 0 .... FrankieMcDonald 1 56
(H J Evans) *sn wl outpcd and rdn along: modest hdwy fnl f: n.d* **66/1**

9 3/4 **Bianco Boy (USA)** 3-9-0 0 .... MarcHalford(3) 3 58+
(J R Best) *sn outpcd in rr of main gp: rdn over 2f out: hdwy on inner whn nt clr run over 1f out tl ins fnl f: n.d* **28/1**

10 18 **Bravo Tango** 3-9-3 0 .... JimCrowley 2 —
(D W P Arbuthnot) *sn wl outpcd in last: t.o after 2f* **33/1**

1m 12.57s (0.67) **Going Correction** +0.05s/f (Slow) **10** Ran SP% **118.0**
Speed ratings (Par 98): **97,90,87,84,83 83,82,81,80,56**
Tote Swingers: 1&2 £2.00, 1&3 £5.70, 2&3 £7.40 CSF £8.81 TOTE £4.10: £1.20, £1.10, £4.30; EX 9.80.
Owner Sir Alex Ferguson & Sotirios Hassiakos **Bred** Paramount Bloodstock **Trained** Lambourn, Berks

FOCUS
An uncompetitive maiden and few ever got into it.
Winifred Jo Official explanation: jockey said filly hung left
Crazy Parachute ◆ Official explanation: jockey said gelding was denied a clear run

1223 BLUE SQUARE'S NEW IPHONE APP MAIDEN AUCTION STKS 5f (P)
4:35 (4:42) (Class 6) 2-Y-O **£2,047** (£604; £302) **Stalls** High

Form				RPR
	1		**Shewalksinbeauty (IRE)** 2-8-7 0 ow1 .... RyanMoore 1 (R Hannon) *s.i.s: in tch: rdn ent fnl 2f: swtchd rt ins fnl f: r.o wl fnl 100yds to ld nr fin* **6/4**[1]	69+
0	2	½	**Sir Lunchalott**[14] 1009 2-8-9 0 .... LiamKeniry 2 (J S Moore) *chsd ldrs: rdn and ev ch fr over 1f out: kpt on one pce fnl 100yds* **13/8**[2]	66
	3	nse	**Stunning In Purple (IRE)** 2-7-13 0 .... AmyBaker(5) 5 (A B Haynes) *led: rdn over 1f out: hdd towards fin* **7/1**[3]	61
	4	3	**Mini Bon Bon** 2-8-4 0 .... JamieMackay 8 (A Bailey) *chsd ldrs: rdn wl over 1f out: wknd ins fnl f* **10/1**	50
0	5	5	**Tessa (IRE)**[12] 1043 2-8-4 0 .... LukeMorris 9 (Peter Grayson) *in tch: rdn wl over 1f out: wknd ent fnl f: eased towards fin* **66/1**	32
6	6	9	**Crazy In Love**[12] 1043 2-8-4 0 .... KirstyMilczarek 7 (W G M Turner) *sn wl outpcd in last* **10/1**	—

61.42 secs (2.62) **Going Correction** +0.05s/f (Slow) 6 Ran SP% **110.3**
Speed ratings (Par 90): **81,80,80,75,67 52**
Tote Swingers: 1&2 £1.20, 1&3 £2.50, 2&3 £2.80 CSF £4.05 TOTE £2.40: £1.30, £1.50; EX 4.30.
Owner Mrs J Wood **Bred** John And Mrs Susan Flavin **Trained** East Everleigh, Wilts

FOCUS
A modest maiden auction weakened further when two of the intended runners, Fit for Purpose and Hannah Cann, got loose in the paddock and had to be withdrawn, while Stacey was also taken out after kicking open the back gate of her stall. No R4 deductions. The winner is probably capable of better.

NOTEBOOK
Shewalksinbeauty(IRE), carrying 1lb overweight, completely missed the break though, to be fair, she was in the stalls a long time due to the shenanigans of some of her rivals, and a victory seemed unlikely. However, she picked up well once in line for home and produced a smart turn of foot to hit the front close to the line. An £8,000 half-sister to five winners from 7f to 1m6f, including the smart stayer First Ballot, she should have little difficulty getting a bit further. (tchd 11-8 and 13-8 and 7-4 in a place)
Sir Lunchalott, who shaped with some promise though only ninth in the Brocklesby, raced keenly enough up with the pace and took a narrow lead passing the 2f pole, but he couldn't put the race to bed and had no answer to the winner's late burst. He already looks in need of a stiffer test. (op 15-8 tchd 6-4)
Stunning In Purple(IRE), a 2,800euros half-sister to eight winners, including the smart Thanksgiving, pinged the gates and to her credit rallied gamely when challenged rounding the turn for home. There should be a small race in her. (op 8-1 tchd 13-2)
Mini Bon Bon, a half-sister to two winners, including the useful Eastern Gift, proved awkward to load but she showed up for a long way and the outing should have done her some good. (op 14-1)
Tessa(IRE) ended up well beaten though she was in the stalls for longer than any of her rivals.
Crazy In Love was reportedly never travelling. Official explanation: jockey said filly never travelled (op 12-1 tchd 14-1)

1224 US MASTERS IN-RUNNING AT BLUESQUARE COM H'CAP 7f (P)
5:10 (5:10) (Class 5) (0-70,70) 4-Y-O+ **£3,070** (£906; £453) **Stalls** Low

Form				RPR
-114	1		**Copperwood**[10] 1064 5-8-10 **62** .... TomQueally 5 (M Blanshard) *hld up in midfield: effrt and swtchd rt over 1f out: sn rdn to chse ldng pair: r.o u.p to ld wl ins fnl f* **10/1**	73
2544	2	1	**War And Peace (IRE)**[12] 1049 6-8-8 **65** .... AndrewHeffernan(5) 2 (P D Evans) *chsd ldrs: wnt 2nd over 2f out: drvn to ld ins fnl f: hdd and no ex wl ins fnl f* **6/1**[3]	73
1326	3	nk	**Billberry**[16] 981 5-9-4 **70** .... (t) RyanMoore 9 (S C Williams) *hld up towards rr: gd hdwy on inner jst over 1f out: rdn to press ldrs ins fnl f: no ex fnl 50yds* **9/4**[1]	77
6-50	4	1 ¼	**Fault**[10] 1063 4-9-0 **66** .... (t) MickyFenton 7 (Stef Higgins) *in tch in midfield: rdn and unable qck over 1f out: styd on u.p fnl 100yds* **16/1**	70
2412	5	nk	**Lastkingofscotland (IRE)**[12] 1047 4-9-3 **69** .... (b) JoeFanning 4 (Jim Best) *led: rdn over 1f out: drvn and hdd ins fnl f: wknd fnl 75yds* **7/2**[2]	72
60-5	6	3 ½	**Learo Dochais (USA)**[91] 110 4-9-0 **66** .... WilliamBuick 10 (M A Jarvis) *hld up in lastr trio: rdn and effrt over 1f out: nvr gng pce to rch ldrs* **12/1**	60
12	7	hd	**Unlimited**[10] 1063 8-8-11 **63** .... LukeMorris 6 (A W Carroll) *in tch: rdn and nt qckn over 1f out: wl btn fnl f* **11/1**	56
060-	8	nk	**My Learned Friend (IRE)**[189] 6476 6-8-10 **69** .... ThomasBrown(7) 3 (A M Balding) *chsd ldr tl over 2f out: wknd ent fnl f* **25/1**	61
1005	9	1 ¼	**Bollywood Style**[3] 1171 5-8-7 **59** .... SteveDrowne 11 (J R Best) *t.k.h: hld up in last rio: rdn and effrt on outer over 1f out: no prog* **16/1**	48
3-14	10	5	**Art Market (CAN)**[44] 696 7-9-1 **67** .... (p) IanMongan 8 (Miss Jo Crowley) *chsd ldrs tl wknd 2f out: wl btn and eased ins fnl f* **7/1**	42
-603	11	3 ¼	**Ivory Lace**[22] 931 9-9-0 **66** .... JimCrowley 1 (S Woodman) *hld up in midfield: hmpd and lost pl over 4f out: bhd after: lost tch 2f out: eased ins fnl f* **14/1**	33

1m 24.5s (-0.30) **Going Correction** +0.05s/f (Slow) 11 Ran SP% **127.2**
Speed ratings (Par 103): **103,101,101,100,99 95,95,95,93,88 84**
Tote Swingers: 1&2 £15.30, 1&3 £6.30, 2&3 £5.10 CSF £74.69 CT £191.98 TOTE £12.80: £2.90, £2.60, £1.30; EX 138.40.
Owner Mrs Rosemary K Wilkerson **Bred** Hertford Offset Press **Trained** Upper Lambourn, Berks

FOCUS
An ordinary handicap run at just a fair pace, and the winning time was 0.76 seconds slower than the earlier handicap over the same trip.

1225 BET NOW AT BLUESQUARE.COM H'CAP (DIV I) 1m 2f (P)
5:45 (5:45) (Class 6) (0-65,65) 4-Y-O+ **£1,706** (£503; £252) **Stalls** Low

Form				RPR
325-	1		**Beaubrav**[189] 5286 4-9-2 **63** .... (t) LiamKeniry 10 (M Madgwick) *hld up towards rr: stdy hdwy fr 4f out: chsd ldrs and rdn 2f out: chal ins fnl f: led fnl 100yds: r.o wl* **12/1**	73
05-0	2	1 ¾	**Diamond Twister (USA)**[52] 588 4-9-2 **63** .... (t) RobertWinston 7 (J R Best) *in tch: rdn to chse ldrs 2f out: hrd drvn to ld 1f out: hdd fnl 100yds: nt pce of wnr after: kpt on* **14/1**	70
3061	3	2	**Musashi (IRE)**[17] 970 5-9-1 **62** .... (b) IanMongan 3 (Mrs L J Mongan) *stdd s: hld up in last trio: hdwy 3f out: n.m.r over 1f out: swtchd rt jst ins fnl f: r.o wl to snatch 3rd on line* **15/2**	65
3222	4	nse	**Alfredtheordinary**[9] 1078 5-8-10 **62** .... AndrewHeffernan(5) 8 (M R Channon) *hld up in midfield: hdwy over 2f out: drvn to chse ldrs ent fnl f: one pce fnl 150yds* **7/2**[2]	64
150-	5	nk	**Goose Green (IRE)**[149] 4300 6-9-1 **62** .... GeorgeBaker 14 (R J Hodges) *hld up in rr: gd hdwy on inner over 1f out: chsd ldrs and drvn ent fnl f: one pce last 150yds* **16/1**	64+
6-00	6	nk	**Siena Star (IRE)**[66] 390 12-8-10 **57** .... MickyFenton 13 (Stef Higgins) *hld up in rr: hdwy on outer over 1f out: rdn ent fnl f: kpt on but nvr gng pce to threaten ldrs* **20/1**	58
4-10	7	½	**Litenup (IRE)**[85] 184 4-8-8 **55** .... (t) WandersonD'Avila 5 (A J Lidderdale) *led and set gd gallop: pressed and rdn 2f out: hrd drvn and hdd 1f out: sn wknd* **40/1**	55
5-21	8	1 ¼	**Carr Hall (IRE)**[17] 969 7-8-11 **58** ow1 .... StephenCraine 11 (A W Carroll) *hld up in last trio: hdwy into midfield over 1f out: no prog fr over 1f out* **5/1**[3]	56
245-	9	2 ½	**The Grey One (IRE)**[111] 7823 7-9-4 **65** .... (p) LukeMorris 12 (J M Bradley) *chsd ldrs: wnt 2nd over 3f out: chal ent fnl 2f: rdn and hld hd high wl over 1f out: wknd qckly over 1f out* **16/1**	58
-000	10	28	**Holyfield Warrior (IRE)**[9] 1078 6-8-9 **56** .... HayleyTurner 6 (R J Smith) *chsd ldrs: rdn and wknd over 2f out: eased fr over 1f out: t.o* **25/1**	—
0400	11	2 ¼	**Catholic Hill (USA)**[2] 1193 5-8-7 **54** .... (b) SteveDrowne 4 (C J Mann) *t.k.h: chsd ldr tl over 3f out: wkng and towards rr whn sltly hmpd bnd jst over 2f out: wl bhd and eased fr over 1f out* **16/1**	—
11-0	12	3 ¾	**Lunar Limelight**[17] 970 5-8-12 **59** .... SebSanders 1 (P J Makin) *hld up in midfield: pushed along over 2f out: nt clr run and shuffled bk to rr bnd jst over 2f out: no ch after: eased fr over 1f out: t.o* **11/4**[1]	—+
-500	13	14	**Efficiency**[22] 931 4-8-13 **60** .... TedDurcan 2 (M Blanshard) *in tch in midfield: pushed along 8f out: rdn and dropped to rr over 3f out: t.o and eased fnl 2f* **25/1**	—

2m 5.69s (-0.91) **Going Correction** +0.05s/f (Slow) 13 Ran SP% **124.2**
Speed ratings (Par 101): **105,103,102,101,101 101,101,100,98,75 73,70,59**
Tote Swingers: 1&2 £26.80, 1&3 £17.50, 2&3 £17.00 CSF £167.88 CT £1365.91 TOTE £16.00: £3.60, £4.20, £4.30; EX 198.30.
Owner The B B Partnership **Bred** Star Pointe Ltd,Brosnan And Williamson **Trained** Denmead, Hants

FOCUS
A very moderate handicap, but at least this was run at a strong pace.
Lunar Limelight Official explanation: jockey said gelding had no more to give

1226 BET NOW AT BLUESQUARE.COM H'CAP (DIV II) 1m 2f (P)
6:15 (6:17) (Class 6) (0-65,63) 4-Y-O+ **£1,706** (£503; £252) **Stalls** Low

Form				RPR
60-3	1		**Blue Tango (IRE)**[38] 771 4-9-4 **63** .... (b) JimCrowley 3 (Mrs A J Perrett) *mde virtually all: rdn clr wl over 1f out: in command fnl f: rdn out* **9/2**[2]	73
00-0	2	1 ¾	**Pedasus (USA)**[17] 975 4-9-3 **62** .... (b[1]) LiamKeniry 13 (T Keddy) *in tch in midfield: rdn and effrt 2f out: racd awkwardly but kpt on to chse wnr ins fnl f: styd on* **12/1**	69+
500-	3	2 ¾	**Filun**[18] 6226 5-8-6 **56** .... (t) AndrewHeffernan(5) 5 (A Middleton) *chsd ldrs: rdn and unable qck wl over 1f out: hld hd high u.p: no ch w wnr fnl f but plugged on to go 3rd last strides* **14/1**	57
604/	4	hd	**Laconicos (IRE)**[159] 5838 8-8-12 **57** .... (t) JerryO'Dwyer 12 (W B Stone) *chsd ldrs: hdwy to join ldrs 7f out: rdn over 2f out: lost pl bnd 2f out: styd on again u.p fnl 150yds* **16/1**	58
100	5	nk	**Gheed (IRE)**[17] 969 5-8-6 **58** .... (t) RyanClark(7) 9 (K A Morgan) *chsd wnr: rdn and nt gng pce of wnr wl over 1f out: lost 2nd ins fnl f* **16/1**	58
1113	6	hd	**Lytham (IRE)**[31] 841 9-8-13 **63** .... AmyBaker(5) 7 (A W Carroll) *t.k.h: hld up in last trio: pushed along and effrt on inner over 1f out: kpt on but nvr any ch of getting to ldrs* **13/2**	63+
000-	7	1 ½	**Pab Special (IRE)**[304] 2807 7-9-4 **63** .... LukeMorris 1 (B R Johnson) *t.k.h: trckd ldrs: rdn and nt qckn wl over 1f out: no ch w wnr fnl f* **20/1**	60
6543	8	½	**Kings Topic (USA)**[37] 791 10-8-11 **56** .... (p) StevieDonohoe 4 (A B Haynes) *in tch in midfield: lost pl 4f out: rdn wl over 1f out: swtchd ins 1f out: nvr trbld ldrs* **12/1**	52
60-0	9	shd	**Polish Power (GER)**[14] 1012 10-9-2 **61** .... SteveDrowne 6 (P G Murphy) *dwlt: in tch in rr: rdn over 1f out: kpt on fnl f but nvr gng pce to threaten ldrs* **5/1**[3]	56
-550	10	1 ¼	**Shame The Devil (IRE)**[24] 908 5-9-1 **60** .... FrankieMcDonald 11 (H J Evans) *hld up in tch: losing pl whn racd awkwardly bnd 2f out: no ch after* **16/1**	53
6-00	11	1	**Enlist**[9] 1077 6-9-1 **60** .... (t) RobertWinston 8 (B G Powell) *hld up in last pair: rdn and effrt on outer jst over 2f out: no prog: wl btn fnl f* **14/1**	51
400-	12	1 ½	**Rehabilitation**[159] 7212 5-9-3 **62** .... (p) TedDurcan 14 (W R Swinburn) *in tch in midfield: rdn and struggling wl over 2f out: bhd fr wl over 1f out* **11/4**[1]	50

2m 7.52s (0.92) **Going Correction** +0.05s/f (Slow) 12 Ran SP% **126.0**
Speed ratings (Par 101): **98,96,94,94,94 93,92,92,92,91 90,89**
Tote Swingers: 1&2 £15.20, 1&3 £30.90, 2&3 £54.10 CSF £61.84 CT £726.74 TOTE £4.00: £1.20, £6.40, £7.70; EX 86.30 Place 6: £30.31 Place 5: £11.52.
Owner The Green Dot Partnership **Bred** Paul Ennis **Trained** Pulborough, W Sussex

FOCUS
Unlike the first division, this was run at a very steady pace and those that raced handily were at a major advantage. The winning time was 1.83 seconds slower.
Polish Power(GER) Official explanation: jockey said horse missed the break
T/Plt: £52.60 to a £1 stake. Pool: £66,421.85. 920.47 winning tickets. T/Qpdt: £14.00 to a £1 stake. Pool: £3,569.41. 188.33 winning tickets. SP

NEWCASTLE (L-H)
Saturday, April 10
1227 Meeting Abandoned - Waterlogged

1205 WOLVERHAMPTON (A.W) (L-H)

Saturday, April 10

OFFICIAL GOING: Standard

Wind: Almost nil Weather: Overcast, warm

1234 FREEBETS.CO.UK GRAND NATIONAL FREE BETS H'CAP 5f 20y(P)

5:30 (5:31) (Class 6) (0-60,60) 4-Y-0+ **£1,774** (£523; £262) **Stalls** Low

Form RPR

0-30 **1** **Across The Sands**43 727 4-8-10 **52**.................(bt) GrahamGibbons 10 60
(C N Kellett) *in tch: effrt and edgd lft over 1f out: led last 100yds: kpt on wl: collapsed after line: dead* **12/1**

2440 **2** *nk* **Bo McGinty (IRE)**10 1068 9-9-4 **60**..........................(v) FrederikTylicki 11 67
(R A Fahey) *hld up: hdwy on outside over 1f out: edgd lft u.p and kpt on wl fnl f: jst hld* **10/3**1

5034 **3** ½ **Trick Or Two**3 1154 4-9-0 **56**................................. SilvestreDeSousa 13 61
(Mrs R A Carr) *pressed ldrs: drvn and led 1f out: edgd lft: hdd last 100yds: no ex cl home* **4/1**2

5540 **4** 1¼ **Kheley (IRE)**5 1112 4-8-10 **57**.. KierenFox(5) 9 58
(W M Brisbourne) *in tch: effrt 2f out: kpt on same pce towards fin* **9/2**3

0003 **5** *nk* **Almaty Express**19 967 8-8-11 **53**.................................(b) TomEaves 4 52+
(J R Weymes) *bhd and outpcd: gd hdwy over 1f out: n.m.r and swtchd rt ins fnl f: kpt on: nrst fin* **4/1**2

1500 **6** 1 **Meikle Barfil**38 774 8-8-8 **50**.....................................(bt) NickyMackay 7 46
(J M Bradley) *blkd s: towards rr: stdy hdwy 1/2-way: effrt over 1f out: no imp* **40/1**

63-0 **7** 1½ **You'relikemefrank**30 860 4-8-6 **48**...............................(p) LiamJones 1 38
(J Balding) *unruly bef s: mde most at str pce to 1f out: sn no ex* **20/1**

6/40 **8** ¾ **Pennyspider (IRE)**23 913 5-9-2 **58**........................ TomMcLaughlin 12 46
(M S Saunders) *trckd ldrs: effrt and rdn 2f out: wknd fnl f* **33/1**

600- **9** ¾ **Blushing Maid**193 6362 4-8-12 **54** ow1............................ DaneO'Neill 6 39
(H S Howe) *blkd s: bhd: hdwy 1/2-way: hung rt and no ex over 1f out* **33/1**

004 **10** *nk* **Triskaidekaphobia**57 525 7-8-6 **48**..........................(t) PaulFitzsimons 8 32
(Miss J R Tooth) *midfield: outpcd over 2f out: sn btn* **18/1**

60-0 **11** 1½ **Rightcar Dominic**3 1154 5-8-5 **47** oh1 ow1.................. SaleemGolam 3 26
(Peter Grayson) *bhd and sn struggling: sme late hdwy: nvr on terms* **100/1**

020- **12** 1½ **Wibbadune (IRE)**242 4886 6-9-2 **58**................................ JimmyQuinn 5 31
(Miss M E Rowland) *bhd and sn outpcd: nvr on terms* **20/1**

060- **13** 1½ **Double Carpet (IRE)**261 4225 7-9-2 **58**..................... FergusSweeney 2 26
(G Woodward) *disp ld tl wknd appr fnl f* **20/1**

62.53 secs (0.23) **Going Correction** +0.075s/f (Slow) **13** Ran SP% **117.8**
Speed ratings (Par 101): **101,100,99,97,97 95,93,92,90,90 87,85,83**
Tote Swingers: 1&2 £8.50, 2&3 £5.30 CSF £47.24 CT £177.16 TOTE £20.40: £5.20, £1.20, £2.80; EX 80.70.
Owner G C Chipman **Bred** Juddmonte Farms Ltd **Trained** Appleby Magna, Derbys

FOCUS
A modest handicap but one predictably run at a strong pace with several front runners in opposition.
Bo McGinty(IRE) Official explanation: vet said gelding bled from the nose

1235 FREEBETS.CO.UK GRAND NATIONAL BEST FREE BETS H'CAP (DIV I) 5f 216y(P)

6:00 (6:05) (Class 6) (0-55,57) 4-Y-0+ **£1,433** (£423; £211) **Stalls** Low

Form RPR

5010 **1** **Ride A White Swan**3 1170 5-8-10 **54**........................(p) GaryBartley(3) 9 68
(D Shaw) *stdd s: hld up: smooth hdwy over 1f out: led ins fnl f: kpt on strly* **9/2**2

350- **2** 2 **Namu**171 6933 7-8-11 **55**... JackDean(3) 11 62
(Miss T Spearing) *bhd: rdn over 2f out: hdwy on outside over 1f out: chsd wnr ins fnl f: r.o* **16/1**

0431 **3** ½ **Tri Chara (IRE)**4 1142 6-8-13 **57** 6ex..................(p) RussKennemore(3) 3 63
(R Hollinshead) *hld up: hdwy over 1f out: kpt on ins fnl f: nrst fin* **11/4**1

2045 **4** ½ **Hart Of Gold**30 860 6-8-11 **52**...(b) LiamJones 6 56
(R A Harris) *t.k.h: led tl edgd lft and hdd ins fnl f: no ex* **7/1**3

-300 **5** ¾ **Carnival Dream**65 404 5-8-11 **52**............................ PatrickMathers 12 54
(H A McWilliams) *midfield: effrt over 2f out: kpt on same pce fnl f* **66/1**

0045 **6** 1½ **Shannon Golden**10 1072 4-8-4 **48**.......................(t) AshleyHamblett(3) 1 45
(S R Bowring) *chsd ldrs: effrt over 2f out: kpt on same pce fnl f* **12/1**

-433 **7** 1½ **Black Draft**17 976 8-8-0 **46**....................................... SophieDoyle(5) 7 38
(B Forsey) *prom: rdn over 2f out: outpcd fnl f* **12/1**

0365 **8** *nse* **Bertbrand**3 1154 5-8-8 **49**...(v) AndrewElliott 10 41
(I W McInnes) *in tch: rdn ent st: no imp fnl f* **20/1**

-000 **9** 1 **Affirmatively**3 1179 5-8-5 **46** oh1...............................(bt) FrannyNorton 4 35
(A W Carroll) *bhd: rdn over 2f out: nvr able to chal* **33/1**

450- **10** 1¼ **Roodee King**166 7052 4-8-6 **47**.................................... SaleemGolam 8 32
(Patrick Morris) *midfield: effrt on ins 2f out: sn no imp* **40/1**

000- **11** 2½ **Fortina's Boy (USA)**140 7484 4-9-0 **55**.......................... ShaneKelly 13 32
(W R Swinburn) *prom tl rdn and wknd over 1f out* **7/1**3

0-00 **12** ¾ **Sills Vincero**19 968 4-8-11 **52**..................................(b1) JimmyQuinn 2 26
(Miss M E Rowland) *chsd ldr tl rdn and wknd over 1f out* **33/1**

1m 15.09s (0.09) **Going Correction** +0.075s/f (Slow) **12** Ran SP% **105.7**
Speed ratings (Par 101): **102,99,98,98,97 95,93,92,91,89 86,85**
CSF £54.78 CT £175.48 TOTE £4.00: £1.50, £10.10, £1.10; EX 75.60.Boldinor was withdrawn. Price at time of withdrawal 9/1. Rule 4 applies to all bets. Deduction - 10p in the pound.
Owner N Morgan **Bred** Michael John Williamson **Trained** Sproxton, Leics
■ Stewards' Enquiry : Liam Jones two-day ban: careless riding (Apr 24-25)

FOCUS
A low level handicap, but one that was run at a good pace with no obvious hard luck stories. Horses held up dominated the finish but two of them were the market leaders and no one group seemed favoured over the rest.

1236 FREEBETS.CO.UK GRAND NATIONAL BEST FREE BETS H'CAP (DIV II) 5f 216y(P)

6:30 (6:31) (Class 6) (0-55,55) 4-Y-0+ **£1,433** (£423; £211) **Stalls** Low

Form RPR

-543 **1** **Imperial Djay (IRE)**12 1050 5-9-0 **55**............................... JimmyQuinn 4 66
(Mrs R A Carr) *dwlt hld up: hdwy on ins ent st: rdn to ld ins fnl f: kpt on wl* **10/3**1

6510 **2** 1½ **Metropolitan Chief**17 976 6-8-10 **51** ow2.............. TomMcLaughlin 5 57
(P Burgoyne) *midfield: effrt and hung lft over 1f out: ev ch ins fnl f: kpt on: nt pce of wnr* **10/1**

0-60 **3** 1¼ **Dualagi**44 693 6-8-11 **52**.. FergusSweeney 1 54
(M R Bosley) *midfield: effrt whn nt clr run 1f out: styd on wl to take 3rd cl home: nt rch first two* **16/1**

0260 **4** *hd* **Divertimenti (IRE)**43 723 6-8-8 **52**......................(b) AshleyHamblett(3) 6 53
(S R Bowring) *t.k.h early: trckd ldrs: effrt over 2f out: led briefly ins fnl f: one pce* **7/1**

4610 **5** ½ **Cheery Cat (USA)**19 968 6-9-0 **55**..............................(p) KierenFallon 9 55
(J Balding) *trckd ldrs: effrt and edgd rt ent st: edgd lft and rallied appr fnl f: one pce ins fnl f* **13/2**3

2330 **6** ½ **Tamino (IRE)**31 844 7-8-13 **54**.................................... J-PGuillambert 2 52
(P Howling) *bhd tl gd hdwy fnl f: nrst fin* **9/1**

- **7** 1¼ **Moonlight Ridge (IRE)**20 955 5-8-7 **48**..................... FrannyNorton 11 42
(Miss Julie Weston, Ire) *pressed ldr: rdn over 2f out: rallied: wknd ins fnl f* **9/2**2

3305 **8** *nk* **Only A Game (IRE)**23 914 5-9-0 **55**......................(tp) FrederikTylicki 8 48
(I W McInnes) *midfield: drvn and outpcd over 2f out: rallied ins fnl f: nvr rchd ldrs* **15/2**

000 **9** ½ **Brazilian Brush (IRE)**54 568 5-8-9 **50**...................(bt) DavidProbert 10 42
(J M Bradley) *led to ins fnl f: sn wknd* **20/1**

-000 **10** 1 **Red Dagger (IRE)**23 918 4-8-2 **46** oh1.................(p) AndreaAtzeni(3) 13 34
(R J Price) *prom: rdn over 2f out: wknd wl over 1f out* **28/1**

0-00 **11** 2¾ **Transcentral**50 614 4-8-5 **46** oh1................................(b1) LiamJones 7 26
(T Wall) *bhd on outside: drvn over 2f out: nvr on terms* **66/1**

0-05 **12** ¾ **Lake Chini (IRE)**22 937 8-8-12 **53**..........................(b) PaulMulrennan 12 30
(M W Easterby) *sn bhd: rdn 1/2-way: nvr on terms* **12/1**

1m 15.25s (0.25) **Going Correction** +0.075s/f (Slow) **12** Ran SP% **121.2**
Speed ratings (Par 101): **101,99,97,97,96 95,94,93,93,91 88,87**
Tote Swingers: 1&2 £19.40, 1&3 £2.40, 2&3 £12.70 CSF £37.90 CT £381.77 TOTE £4.20: £1.70, £4.70, £8.40; EX 40.10.
Owner Hollinbridge Partnership **Bred** D Veitch And Musagd Abo Salim **Trained** Huby, N Yorks

FOCUS
Another low-grade handicap that saw some bunching in the straight but the placed horses arguably finished in the correct order. The early pace wasn't as strong as the first division, and the final time was nearly 0.3 secs slower.
Tamino(IRE) Official explanation: jockey said gelding was unsuited by being unable to make the running

1237 FREEBETS.CO.UK GRAND NATIONAL BETTING OFFERS CLAIMING STKS 5f 216y(P)

7:00 (7:00) (Class 5) 3-Y-0 **£2,729** (£806; £403) **Stalls** Low

Form RPR

4103 **1** **Avow (USA)**10 1057 3-8-8 68..(b) KierenFallon 5 67
(J S Moore) *chsd ldng pair: hrd rdn over 2f out: styd on to ld ins fnl f* **3/1**2

3430 **2** ½ **Clear Ice (IRE)**2 1181 3-8-5 68... BillyCray(5) 4 67
(D Nicholls) *slt ld tl ins fnl f: kpt on* **9/2**3

01 **3** 1¾ **Moors Gorse**62 454 3-8-7 62.................................... GrahamGibbons 7 59
(R Hollinshead) *in tch in 4th: rdn 3f out: kpt on to take 3rd ins fnl f* **5/2**1

504 **4** 3¼ **My Mandy (IRE)**19 962 3-8-5 60.. LiamJones 1 46
(R A Harris) *pressed ldr on rail tl no ex over 1f out* **16/1**

30-6 **5** 1¼ **Petrocelli**38 766 3-8-5 67...(p) JohnFahy(7) 6 49
(A J McCabe) *sn outpcd in 5th: no imp fnl 2f* **11/1**

64-0 **6** 1½ **Revoltinthedesert**50 624 3-8-8 0........................... AndreaAtzeni(3) 3 44
(M Botti) *s.i.s: a outpcd in 6th* **15/2**

3244 **7** 26 **Flow Chart (IRE)**22 932 3-8-12 69..........................(b) SaleemGolam 2 —
(Peter Grayson) *rrlng in stalls bef s: s.i.s: a last and outpcd: no ch fnl 2f* **15/2**

1m 15.71s (0.71) **Going Correction** +0.075s/f (Slow) **7** Ran SP% **109.5**
Speed ratings (Par 98): **98,97,95,90,89 87,52**
Tote Swingers: 1&2 £3.00, 1&3 £1.40, 2&3 £4.60 CSF £15.33 TOTE £4.40: £2.60, £1.10; EX 12.90.
Owner Two Bucks Stable **Bred** J D Squires **Trained** Upper Lambourn, Berks

FOCUS
A modest claimer. The pace was a true one and the form should hold up.
Flow Chart(IRE) Official explanation: jockey said gelding hung right throughout

1238 FREEBETS.CO.UK GRAND NATIONAL BETTING TIPS H'CAP 7f 32y(P)

7:30 (7:33) (Class 5) (0-75,73) 4-Y-0+ **£2,456** (£725; £362) **Stalls** High

Form RPR

0424 **1** **Justcallmehandsome**12 1051 8-8-8 **68**.......................(v) BillyCray(5) 11 77
(D J S Ffrench Davis) *wd: hdwy 5f out: led over 3f out: rdn clr over 1f out: hld on wl fnl f* **12/1**

53-1 **2** ¾ **Fol Liam**30 867 4-8-12 **67**.......................................(p) JamieSpencer 6 74+
(A J McCabe) *mid-div: hdwy and wd into st: r.o to take 2nd ins fnl f: clsd on wnr: a hld* **5/2**1

-240 **3** 2½ **Cut And Thrust (IRE)**41 747 4-8-11 **71**...................... KierenFox(5) 10 71
(M Wellings) *mde most tl over 3f out: one pce fnl f* **25/1**

-502 **4** ½ **Gazboolou**10 1064 6-9-2 **71**.. FergusSweeney 4 70
(David Pinder) *chsd ldrs: rdn over 2f out: kpt on same pce* **7/1**

2020 **5** ½ **Harare**12 1051 9-8-6 **64**.......................................(v) AndreaAtzeni(3) 7 62+
(R J Price) *dwlt: bhd: wd st: drvn along and styd on fnl 2f: nvr nrr* **11/1**

-034 **6** *nse* **Trade Centre**31 853 5-8-13 **68**...................................(p) LiamJones 3 65
(R A Harris) *plld hrd: prom tl no ex over 1f out* **11/2**3

0000 **7** ½ **All About You (IRE)**5 1128 4-8-11 **66**......................... SaleemGolam 2 62
(P Howling) *chsd ldrs: n.m.r after 1f: lost pl 4f out: n.d after* **33/1**

-536 **8** *hd* **Chief Exec**10 1063 8-8-10 **72**...(b) JohnFahy(7) 9 68
(J R Gask) *s.s: bhd: pushed along on ins rail and styd on appr fnl f: n.d* **8/1**

111- **9** 2 **Topcroft**114 7784 4-8-10 **72**..(v) LeeTopliss(7) 1 62
(D Shaw) *reluctant to load: dwlt: hdwy to join ldr after 1f: wknd over 2f out* **9/2**2

1/0- **10** 4 **Ajara (IRE)**442 276 4-9-2 **71**...................................... RichardKingscote 5 50
(Tom Dascombe) *t.k.h in midfield: outpcd 3f out: sn struggling* **16/1**

1m 30.03s (0.43) **Going Correction** +0.075s/f (Slow) **10** Ran SP% **114.4**
Speed ratings (Par 103): **100,99,96,95,95 95,94,94,92,87**
Tote Swingers: 1&2 £19.50, 1&3 £13.00, 2&3 £26.00 CSF £41.38 CT £751.72 TOTE £18.70: £5.50, £1.10, £12.00; EX 56.10.
Owner Mrs J E Taylor **Bred** Mrs J E Taylor **Trained** Lambourn, Berks
■ Stewards' Enquiry : Lee Topliss caution: careless riding.

FOCUS
A competitive handicap, but one that ended up being run at a steady pace and against those held up and the form promises to be muddling.

1239 FREEBETS.CO.UK GRAND NATIONAL FREE BETTING (S) STKS 1m 141y(P)
8:00 (8:00) (Class 6) 4-Y-0+ £1,774 (£523; £262) Stalls Low

Form RPR

06-6 **1** **Bernix**[60] 470 8-8-12 43..........(p) KierenFallon 2 66
(N Tinkler) *chsd ldrs: hrd rdn and edgd lft over 1f out: drvn to ld fnl 75yds* **16/1**

1-61 **2** 3/4 **What's Up Doc (IRE)**[23] 920 9-9-4 70..........DaneO'Neill 3 70
(Mrs Lawney Hill) *sn led: rdn over 2f out: hdd fnl 75yds: kpt on* **11/4**[1]

4553 **3** 1/2 **Sotik Star (IRE)**[23] 925 7-8-12 60..........(p) JimmyQuinn 7 66+
(K A Morgan) *hld up towards rr: hdwy on rail 2f out: cl 3rd whn nt clr run and swtchd rt ins fnl f: r.o* **6/1**[2]

-000 **4** 3 **Athaakeel (IRE)**[10] 1072 4-8-7 57..........LiamJones 11 51
(R A Harris) *stdd s: held up towards rr: gd hdwy and wd st: no ex over 1f out* **33/1**

055- **5** 1/2 **Swiss Art (IRE)**[103] 7858 4-8-12 67..........GrahamGibbons 12 55
(R Hollinshead) *in tch: rdn and outpcd 3f out: swtchd wd in st: styng on at fin* **16/1**

3220 **6** 2 1/2 **Straight Face (IRE)**[12] 1047 6-9-4 68..........(b) J-PGuillambert 6 55
(P D Evans) *broke wl: prom tl wknd 2f out* **10/1**[3]

1406 **7** 3 **Well Of Echoes**[19] 965 4-8-8 62..........(tp) DeclanCannon(5) 9 43
(A J McCabe) *s.s: bhd: rdn over 3f out: modest late hdwy* **10/1**[3]

4000 **8** 1/2 **Pachakutek (USA)**[3] 1179 4-8-7 57..........(p) JemmaMarshall(5) 10 41
(A J Lidderdale) *chsd ldrs: wnt 2nd 4f out: wknd 2f out* **40/1**

00-0 **9** 2 1/2 **Kingsmaite**[61] 465 9-8-9 59..........(b) AshleyHamblett(3) 1 35
(S R Bowring) *sn towards rr: struggling fnl 3f* **16/1**

6600 **10** nk **James Pollard (IRE)**[15] 995 5-8-12 45..........(t) DavidProbert 8 35
(B J Llewellyn) *in tch tl wknd 3f out* **16/1**

1m 50.49s (-0.01) **Going Correction** +0.075s/f (Slow) **10** Ran SP% **88.0**
Speed ratings (Par 101): **103,102,101,99,98 96,93,93,91,90**
Tote Swingers: 1&2 £14.80, 1&3 £13.20, 2&3 £3.10 CSF £33.72 TOTE £14.50: £2.80, £1.10, £1.30; EX 64.70.No bid for the winner.
Owner Danum Racing **Bred** M Lagardere **Trained** Langton, N Yorks

FOCUS
A modest seller weakened further by the late withdrawal at the start of the highest rated horse Bazroy. The pace was a modest one, leading to a surprise result, and it looks unreliable form.
Well Of Echoes Official explanation: jockey said filly was slowly away and never travelled

1240 FREEBETS.CO.UK GRAND NATIONAL BETTING MEDIAN AUCTION MAIDEN STKS 1m 141y(P)
8:30 (8:31) (Class 5) 3-Y-0 £2,456 (£725; £362) Stalls Low

Form RPR

432- **1** **Serafina's Flight**[183] 6638 3-8-12 71..........MartinDwyer 4 74
(W R Muir) *flashed tail thrght: hld up in 3rd: effrt 2f out: r.o to ld ins fnl f: edgd lft: styd on* **5/1**[3]

-432 **2** 2 **Mejd (IRE)**[21] 950 3-9-3 76..........KierenFallon 1 74
(M R Channon) *trckd ldr: disp ld 5f out: rdn over 2f out: edgd lft over 1f out: hdd and one pce ins fnl f* **2/1**[2]

43- **3** 1/2 **High Importance (USA)**[170] 6962 3-9-3 0..........ShaneKelly 3 73
(J Noseda) *led: jnd 5f out: rdn over 2f out: n.m.r on rail 1f out: hdd and no ex ins fnl f* **5/6**[1]

00 **4** 66 **Haf (IRE)**[2] 1187 3-8-12 0..........SaleemGolam 2 —
(Peter Grayson) *stdd s: a last: outpcd and no ch fnl 4f* **66/1**

1m 52.11s (1.61) **Going Correction** +0.075s/f (Slow) **4** Ran SP% **106.0**
Speed ratings (Par 98): **95,93,92,34**
CSF £14.50 TOTE £3.10; EX 6.70.
Owner M J Caddy **Bred** Horizon Bloodstock Limited **Trained** Lambourn, Berks

FOCUS
A fair maiden that turned into something of a cat and mouse affair with the emphasis on the day being more on finishing speed than stamina.

1241 FREEBETS.CO.UK GRAND NATIONAL BEST ODDS H'CAP 1m 1f 103y(P)
9:00 (9:01) (Class 5) (0-75,73) 4-Y-0+ £2,456 (£725; £362) Stalls Low

Form RPR

-621 **1** **Danderek**[22] 941 4-9-4 73..........FrederikTylicki 4 86+
(R A Fahey) *mde all: qcknd 4f out: hld on wl whn pressed by runner-up fnl f* **7/4**[1]

4-51 **2** nk **King's Masque**[15] 994 4-8-13 68..........DavidProbert 7 80+
(B J Llewellyn) *in tch disputing 5th: effrt over 2f out: r.o to press wnr fnl f: jst hld nr fin* **5/1**[3]

2-20 **3** 3 1/2 **Fujin Dancer (FR)**[86] 174 5-8-10 65..........JamieSpencer 9 70
(K A Ryan) *mid-div: wd and effrt in centre st: styd on fnl f* **15/2**

244- **4** shd **Oriental Cavalier**[105] 7847 4-9-3 72..........(p) GrahamGibbons 2 76
(R Hollinshead) *chsd ldrs: rdn 4f out: no ex fnl f* **10/1**

2212 **5** 1 3/4 **King's Icon (IRE)**[31] 853 5-9-0 69..........(b) NickyMackay 8 70
(M Wigham) *towards rr: rdn and styd on fnl 3f: nt rch ldrs* **9/2**[2]

240- **6** 2 **Lunar River (FR)**[147] 7399 7-8-12 67..........(t) FergusSweeney 11 64
(David Pinder) *hld up in rr: rdn and styd on appr fnl f: nvr nrr* **33/1**

0-30 **7** 1/2 **Watchmaker**[38] 765 7-8-11 66 ow1..........DaneO'Neill 3 62
(Miss Tor Sturgis) *t.k.h: prom tl wknd over 1f out* **33/1**

0453 **8** 3/4 **Shake On It**[19] 966 6-8-6 61..........AndrewElliott 10 55
(M R Hoad) *stdd s: t.k.h in rr: mod effrt over 1f out: n.d* **16/1**

46 **9** 10 **Escardo (GER)**[31] 852 7-8-1 63..........JamesRogers(7) 5 36
(D G Bridgwater) *a towards rr: struggling fnl 3f* **50/1**

454- **10** 4 1/2 **Bere Davis (FR)**[16] 6987 5-8-13 68..........KierenFallon 6 31
(M A Barnes) *chsd wnr: rdn 4f out: sn wknd* **14/1**

0/-0 **11** 4 **Longoria (IRE)**[21] 943 5-8-11 73..........DavidKenny(7) 1 28
(Lucinda Featherstone) *in tch disputing 5th: wknd over 3f out: sn bhd* **33/1**

2m 0.90s (-0.80) **Going Correction** +0.075s/f (Slow) **11** Ran SP% **115.4**
Speed ratings (Par 103): **106,105,102,102,100 99,98,98,89,85 81**
CSF £9.65 CT £51.91 TOTE £2.00: £1.10, £1.40, £2.60; EX 12.20 Place 6: £48.62 Place 5: £27.55 .
Owner Derek Rowlands & Daniel Keenan **Bred** Mrs Maureen Buckley **Trained** Musley Bank, N Yorks

FOCUS
An ordinary handicap in which the unexposed winner was able to dictate just a fair pace.
Bere Davis(FR) Official explanation: jockey said gelding hung badly left
T/Plt: £43.70 to a £1 stake. Pool: £51,163.14. 854.12 winning tickets. T/Qpdt: £14.00 to a £1 stake. Pool: £6,366.51. 335.20 winning tickets. RY

OAKLAWN PARK (L-H)
Saturday, April 10

OFFICIAL GOING: Dirt: fast

1242a APPLE BLOSSOM INVITATIONAL H'CAP (GRADE 1) (4YO+ FILLIES & MARES) (DIRT) 1m 1f
12:25 (12:33) 4-Y-0+ £185,185 (£61,728; £30,864; £15,432; £9,259)

RPR

1 **Zenyatta (USA)**[28] 6-8-11 0..........MESmith 4 123+
(John Shirreffs, U.S.A) *last: hdwy on wd outside 3f out: led and wnt clr 2f out: easily* **1/20**[1]

2 4 1/4 **Taptam (USA)**[35] 5-8-5 0..........MCBerry 2 104
(W Bret Calhoun, U.S.A) *pressed ldr: led briefly appr 2f out: no ch w wnr* **35/1**

3 1 1/2 **Be Fair (USA)**[154] 4-8-8 0..........CHBorel 1 104
(D Wayne Lukas, U.S.A) *led tl hdd appr 2f out: kpt on one pce* **15/1**[2]

4 1/2 **Just Jenda (USA)**[35] 4-8-8 0..........TJThompson 5 103
(Cindy Jones, U.S.A) *settled in 4th: short-lived effrt 2f out: sn one pce* **189/10**[3]

5 2 1/4 **War Echo (USA)**[35] 4-8-8 0..........SXBridgmohan 3 99
(Steven Asmussen, U.S.A) *chsd ldrs tl rdn and fdd ins fnl 2f* **198/10**

1m 50.71s (110.71) **5** Ran SP% **114.1**
PARI-MUTUEL (all including $2 stake): WIN 2.10; PLACE (1-2) 2.10, 6.40; SF 18.00.
Owner Mr & Mrs Jerome S Moss **Bred** Maverick Production Limited **Trained** USA

NOTEBOOK
Zenyatta(USA), back on the dirt, totally outclassed some vastly inferior rivals to land her second Apple Blossom and in the process equal the 16-conseuctive win streak of Cigar and Citation.

1243 - 1245a (Foreign Racing) - See Raceform Interactive

954 CURRAGH (R-H)
Sunday, April 11

OFFICIAL GOING: Round course - soft to heavy; straight course - heavy

1246a WWW.THETOTE.COM GLADNESS STKS (GROUP 3) 7f
3:45 (3:45) 4-Y-0+ £34,513 (£10,088; £4,778; £1,592)

RPR

1 **Kargali (IRE)**[21] 958 5-9-0 107..........(t) JMurtagh 7 105
(Luke Comer, Ire) *sn racd in 5th: clsr in 3rd 2f out: rdn to chal in 2nd 1 1/2f out: jst led and kpt on wl ins fnl f* **10/1**

2 3/4 **Rayeni (IRE)**[157] 7259 4-9-0 112..........FMBerry 6 103
(John M Oxx, Ire) *prom: t.k.h early: led u.p 1 1/2f out: sn strly pressed: sltly hmpd ins fnl f: kpt on wout matching wnr* **6/4**[1]

3 1/2 **Croisultan (IRE)**[196] 6320 4-9-0 101..........CO'Donoghue 5 102
(Liam McAteer, Ire) *sn in rr: rdn into mod 4th 1 1/2f out: 3rd and kpt on wout rching 1st 2 ins fnl f* **25/1**

4 3 **Jumbajukiba**[117] 6867 7-9-0 109..........(b) WJSupple 2 94
(Mrs John Harrington, Ire) *sn led: strly pressed 2f out: sn hdd: dropped to 3rd 1 1/2f out: no ex fnl f* **7/1**

5 1 **The Tooth Fairy (IRE)**[21] 956 4-9-0 92..........GFCarroll 4 91
(Michael Mulvany, Ire) *towards rr: no imp u.p and kpt on same pce fr 1 1/2f out* **20/1**

6 7 **Libano (IRE)**[157] 7259 4-9-3 113..........PJSmullen 3 75
(D K Weld, Ire) *cl up: lost pl and no imp u.p fr 2f out: eased ins fnl f* **9/4**[2]

7 11 **Vocalised (USA)**[210] 5921 4-9-3 110..........(t) KJManning 1 45
(J S Bolger, Ire) *chsd ldrs: 4th over 3f out: no ex u.p fr under 2f out: eased fnl f* **6/1**[3]

1m 33.03s (2.23) **Going Correction** +0.65s/f (Yiel) **7** Ran SP% **115.3**
Speed ratings: **113,112,111,108,107 99,86**
CSF £25.99 TOTE £9.80: £3.50, £1.80; DF 37.00.
Owner Mrs Margaret Comer **Bred** H H The Aga Khan's Studs Sc **Trained** Dunboyne, Co Meath

FOCUS
A reason for the winner's improved form compared with his Dundalk run was sought by the stewards and the explanation, that the tongue-tie being applied over the bit after becoming dislodged on the way to the start and might have affected his running, was accepted. The fifth has been rated to his best and the third to a small personal best.

NOTEBOOK
Kargali(IRE), a three-time winner for John Oxx and bought by his present connections for 51,000euros at Goffs in November, left a moderate effort at Dundalk last month behind him to land this Group 3 event on ground similar to what he had won on in the past. Held up, he began his effort 2f out and went to the front inside the final furlong, keeping on despite edging left under pressure. Official explanation: trainer's rep said, regarding the apparent improvement in form, that horse on its previous run had the tongue strap applied over the bit after it had become dislodged on the way to the start and reapplied at the start.
Rayeni(IRE), runner-up in last year's Irish 2,000 Guineas and whose three wins were all achieved on soft ground, led and raced keenly early on. Always in the front rank, he was back in front 1 1/2f out and, although slightly hampered after being headed inside the final furlong, was well held by the winner. Had he settled better there might have been a different result. (op 6/4 tchd 7/4)
Croisultan(IRE), whose winning form is over 5f and 6f, had made little impact on his previous attempts over this trip and had plenty on at the weights He handles this type of ground and, after being held up at the back, began to close 2f out and kept on quite well.
Jumbajukiba, an eight-time winner who goes on most types of ground but is most effective on testing, was, as usual, soon in front and led until 1 1/2f out, from where he could raise no extra.
Libano(IRE), another with smart form on testing ground, tracked the leaders but was done with almost 2f out and was eased when beaten. (op 2/1)
Vocalised(USA), who won the Loughbrown Stakes on this card, the Greenham Stakes and the Tetrarch Stakes, all over this trip and on ground ranging from yielding to heavy early last season, was never a threat and was eased when all hope had gone. (op 4/1)

1247a NEW TOTE SPORTS LOUNGE ALLEGED STKS (LISTED RACE) 1m 2f
4:15 (4:16) 4-Y-0+ £24,446 (£7,146; £3,384; £1,128)

RPR

1 **She's Our Mark**[21] 958 6-9-3 106..........DMGrant 9 105
(Patrick J Flynn, Ire) *sn towards rr: prog u.p fr 2f out: 4th 1f out: styd on wl fnl f to ld cl home* **12/1**[3]

2 1 **Popmurphy**[276] 3778 4-9-1 95..........(b[1]) JimCrowley 7 101
(P D Deegan, Ire) *sn disp ld: led fr 3f out: rdn clr over 1f out: kpt on wl: ct cl home* **12/1**[3]

3 2 **Fame And Glory**[176] 6850 4-9-8 128 JMurtagh 10 105+
(A P O'Brien, Ire) *sn mid-div: prog to trck ldrs and pushed along fr 2f out: chsd ldr over 1f out: clsd and kpt on same pce ins fnl f* **2/5**[1]
4 1 **Dixie Music (IRE)**[336] 1908 4-9-1 100 JAHeffernan 2 95
(A P O'Brien, Ire) *chsd ldrs: 4th 2f out: kpt on same pce u.p fr over 1f out* **12/1**[3]
5 nk **Precious Gem (IRE)**[175] 4-8-12 92 PJSmullen 6 91
(D K Weld, Ire) *sn mid-div: rdn into 5th 1f out: sn no imp and kpt on same pce* **20/1**
6 2 **Raise Your Heart (IRE)**[26] 800 7-9-4 106 RPCleary 1 93
(Ms Joanna Morgan, Ire) *trckd ldrs: rdn in 4th fr 3f out: kpt on same pce fr under 2f out* **20/1**
7 shd **Big Robert**[21] 958 6-9-1 93 (p) KTO'Neill 5 90
(P D Deegan, Ire) *towards rr: last appr st: rdn to chse ldrs 2f out: sn no imp and kpt on same pce* **16/1**
8 4 1/2 **Baron De'L (IRE)**[35] 5894 7-9-4 98 (b) FMBerry 8 84
(Edward P Harty, Ire) *sn disp ld: rdn and hdd fr 3f out: no imp fr 2f out* **20/1**
9 3/4 **Gan Amhras (IRE)**[196] 6320 4-9-1 117 KJManning 3 80
(J S Bolger, Ire) *prom: chal 2f out: wknd fr over 1f out* **6/1**[2]
10 2 **Estephe (IRE)**[16] 1004 4-8-12 86 WMLordan 4 73
(T Stack, Ire) *towards rr: 8th appr st: no ex u.p fr 2f out* **20/1**

2m 23.04s (10.44) **Going Correction** +1.10s/f (Soft) **10** Ran SP% **133.7**
Speed ratings: **111,110,108,107,107 105,105,102,101,100**
CSF £154.14 TOTE £12.60: £2.70, £4.30, £1.10; DF 474.30.
Owner B & M Syndicate **Bred** M Barrett And Redmyre Bloodstock **Trained** Carrick-On-Suir, Co Waterford

FOCUS
The theory that this race was between two horses was blown completely out of the water. The runner-up and fifth have been rated as running small personal bests, with the winner close to her mark.

NOTEBOOK
She's Our Mark came with quite a sustained run to challenge inside the last, and without the rider really having to pick up the stick she won going away. It was a good performance, but one imagines that she won't be running in many more handicaps after this. (op 10/1)
Popmurphy was in first-time blinkers, which appeared to bring about improvement. Taking over the lead early, he had enough in reserve to kick on over 2f out and kept going until the winner overhauled him close home. This will be a hard enough one for the handicapper to evaluate but he's likely to get a stiffer penalty than the winner.
Fame And Glory ran a couple of stones below his best. He had a reasonable position in the race but didn't pick up when he was asked to and once Murtagh knew he wasn't going to win he wasn't at all hard on him. He obviously needed the run badly and judgement must be reserved on him until he's seen out again. (op 1/2)
Dixie Music(IRE) was running for the first time since his maiden win last May and ran very well. He was always just chasing the pace and, while he never looked likely to win, he stuck to his task well. (op 10/1)
Precious Gem(IRE) ran similarly well without threatening, keeping on at the same pace inside the final quarter mile having tracked the pace most of the way. (op 16/1)
Gan Amhras(IRE) tracked the pace and appeared to travel well to the 2f pole but once asked for his effort he found nil and dropped right away. He is a shadow of the horse he was when finishing third in the Stan James 2,000 Guineas last year. (op 5/1)

1248 - 1249a (Foreign Racing) - See Raceform Interactive

DUSSELDORF (R-H)
Sunday, April 11

OFFICIAL GOING: Turf: soft

1250a HENKEL-STUTENPREIS LISTENRENNEN (LISTED RACE) (FILLIES) 1m
3:45 (12:00) Class F 3-Y-O **£10,619** (£3,893; £2,123; £1,061)

RPR
1 **Ronja (USA)** 3-9-1 0 ASchikora 4 101
(W Hickst, Germany) **58/10**
2 shd **Kinky Afro (IRE)**[18] 973 3-8-11 0 LiamKeniry 10 97
(J S Moore) *broke wl: racd in 5th: swtchd to outer in st: rdn and r.o wl to join ldrs 1 1/2f out: chal ldr strly ins fnl f: jst failed* **184/10**
3 1/2 **Reine Heureuse (GER)**[161] 3-9-1 0 PJWerning 5 100
(Uwe Ostmann, Germany) **118/10**
4 1 3/4 **Prakasa (FR)**[168] 7045 3-9-1 0 APietsch 3 96
(W Hickst, Germany) **26/5**[3]
5 3/4 **Devilish Lips (GER)**[196] 3-9-3 0 (b) THellier 12 96
(Andreas Lowe, Germany) **8/1**
6 1 1/2 **Artica (GER)**[168] 7045 3-9-1 0 AndreBest 7 91
(T Mundry, Germany) **248/10**
7 1 1/2 **Anking (GER)**[14] 3-9-1 0 HenkGrewe 9 87
(S Smrczek, Germany) **143/10**
8 1 3/4 **Nianga (GER)**[168] 7045 3-9-1 0 AStarke 6 83
(P Schiergen, Germany) **19/10**[1]
9 1/2 **Top Act (FR)**[168] 7045 3-9-1 0 AGoritz 8 82
(P Schiergen, Germany) **143/10**
10 1 1/2 **Alyshakeys (DEN)** 3-9-3 0 WilliamBuick 2 81
(Wido Neuroth, Norway) **43/10**[2]
11 2 **Genovesa (GER)** 3-9-1 0 SHellyn 1 74
(C Von Der Recke, Germany) **132/10**

1m 41.79s (0.63) **11** Ran SP% **132.3**
WIN (incl. 10 euro stake): 68. PLACES: 24, 42, 36. DF: 2,076. SF: 21,589..
Owner Stall Domstadt **Bred** Lochlow Farm **Trained** Germany

FRANKFURT (L-H)
Sunday, April 11

OFFICIAL GOING: Turf: soft

1251a FRANKFURTER MEILE - FRUHJAHRSPREIS DER STADT FRANKFURT (GROUP 3) (TURF) 1m
4:05 (12:00) 4-Y-O+ **£28,318** (£8,849; £4,424; £2,654)

RPR
1 **Enzio (GER)**[19] 4-8-11 0 DominiqueBoeuf 10 103
(N Milliere, France) *racd in midfield: hdwy 2 1/2f out: qcknd wl: ct ldrs ins fnl 110yds: comf* **69/10**[3]
2 3/4 **Sehrezad (IRE)**[154] 7312 5-9-2 0 JiriPalik 2 107
(Andreas Lowe, Germany) *broke wl: racd in 3rd: hmpd on turn into st: rcvrd wl: hit front ins fnl f: hdd 110yds out: hld on wl for 2nd* **43/10**[2]
3 nk **Beltanus (GER)**[152] 6-8-11 0 JanPalik 4 101
(T Potters, Germany) *prom thrght: stmbld ent st: rcvrd: ev ch fnl 110yds: r.o wl clsng stages* **57/1**
4 3 **Golden Tirol (GER)**[168] 4-9-0 0 LASorrentino 7 97
(T Kluczynski, Poland) *racd in midfield: gd prog early in st: failed to qckn clsng stages* **26/1**
5 nk **Abbashiva (GER)**[37] 818 5-8-11 0 EFrank 14 93
(T Mundry, Germany) *racd in midfield: no prog in st* **164/10**
6 1 **Querari (GER)**[203] 6152 4-9-2 0 EPedroza 5 96
(A Wohler, Germany) *broke wl and racd in 5th: qcknd in st: no ex fnl f* **11/5**[1]
7 1/2 **King Of Sydney (USA)**[161] 7208 4-9-4 0 StefanieHofer 15 97
(Mario Hofer, Germany) *slowly away: racd in rr: sme prog in st: no ex fnl f* **132/10**
8 nk **Sanjii Danon (GER)**[164] 4-9-0 0 JBojko 13 92
(W Hickst, Germany) *racd in midfield: threatened briefly in st: fdd* **107/10**
9 nk **Atlantic Sport (USA)**[288] 3388 5-8-11 0 FilipMinarik 8 89
(P Schiergen, Germany) *racd freely early on: making prog whn hmpd on fnl turn: one pce in st* **232/10**
10 hd **Handsome Hawk (IRE)**[198] 4-9-0 0 Jan-ErikNeuroth 3 91
(Wido Neuroth, Norway) *racd in midfield: moved to 3rd bef st: fdd* **246/10**
11 dist **Konig Concorde (GER)**[196] 6323 5-9-0 0.. LennartHammer-Hansen 16 —
(C Sprengel, Germany) *in rr: rdn bef st: no imp* **122/10**
12 3/4 **Usbeke (GER)**[161] 7208 4-9-0 0 HanaMouchova 12 —
(J-P Carvalho, Germany) *racd in midfield: failed to qckn in st: fdd* **28/1**
13 nk **Torres (GER)**[182] 6713 4-8-11 0 VSchulepov 11 —
(Frau E Mader, Germany) *racd in midfield: failed to qckn: fdd* **40/1**
14 nk **Smooth Operator (GER)**[168] 7044 4-9-2 0 AHelfenbein 6 —
(Mario Hofer, Germany) *nvr a factor* **91/10**
15 5 **Mharadono (GER)**[252] 4582 7-8-11 0 WPanov 9 —
(P Hirschberger, Germany) *led fr s: hdd early in st: fdd bdly* **68/1**
16 3/4 **Schutzenjunker (GER)**[161] 7208 5-9-2 0 DPorcu 1 —
(Uwe Ostmann, Germany) *broke wl: pursued ldr: faltered at 1/2-way: fdd* **10/1**

1m 36.52s (96.52) **16** Ran SP% **131.5**
WIN (incl. 10 euro stake): 79. PLACES: 25, 25, 139. DF: 505. SF: 28,716..
Owner Comte Reginald Von Norman **Bred** Manfred Jurgensmeyer Et Al **Trained** France

SAN SIRO (R-H)
Sunday, April 11

OFFICIAL GOING: Good

1252a PREMIO SEREGNO (LISTED RACE) (FILLIES) 1m
4:25 (4:25) Class F 3-Y-O **£24,778** (£10,902; £5,946; £2,973)

RPR
1 **Carioca (IRE)**[17] 978 3-8-11 MircoDemuro 7 103
(M Botti) *slowly into stride, soon with leaders, led after 2f, quickened halfway and ridden clear, eased final 100yds* **6/5**[1]
2 3 **Cronsa (GER)**[154] 3-9-2 UmbertoRispoli 4 101+
(S Botti, Italy) **27/4**
3 1 1/2 **Lovisa Beat**[7] 3-8-11 DVargiu 2 93
(B Grizzetti, Italy) **23/10**[2]
4 nk **Paloma Varga (IRE)**[154] 3-9-2 MEsposito 3 97
(G Miliani, Italy) **9/2**[3]
5 4 1/2 **Fairy Oasis** 3-8-11 SUrru 5 82
(B Grizzetti, Italy) **23/10**[2]
6 1 1/4 **Biancarosa (IRE)**[154] 3-9-2 FBossa 8 84
(B Grizzetti, Italy) **46/1**
7 snk **Snake River (IRE)**[190] 3-8-11 LManiezzi 1 79
(M Weiss, Switzerland) **147/10**
8 8 **Zauberin (IRE)** 3-8-11 FabioBranca 6 60
(J-P Carvalho, Germany) **6/1**

1m 38.8s (-3.30) **8** Ran SP% **159.9**
WIN 2.18; PL 1.24, 1.64, 1.31; DF 9.61.
Owner The Great Partnership **Bred** John Doyle **Trained** Newmarket, Suffolk

1253 - (Foreign Racing) - See Raceform Interactive

1135 LONGCHAMP (R-H)
Sunday, April 11

OFFICIAL GOING: Turf: soft

1254a PRIX NOAILLES (GROUP 2) (3YO COLTS & FILLIES) (TURF) 1m 2f 110y
2:40 (12:00) 3-Y-O **£65,575** (£25,309; £12,079; £8,053; £4,026)

RPR
1 **Planteur (IRE)**[199] 3-9-2 0 AnthonyCrastus 2 113
(E Lellouche, France) *2nd fr s: cruised to the front early in st: qcknd wl 2f out: wnt clr: comf* **7/4**[1]
2 1 1/2 **Rewilding**[153] 3-9-2 0 MaximeGuyon 9 110+
(A Fabre, France) *racd in 6th to st: chsd ldr: mde grnd wout threatening wnr* **4/1**[3]
3 5 **Ivory Land (FR)**[22] 951 3-9-2 0 GeraldMosse 4 101
(A De Royer-Dupre, France) *in rr tl st: swtchd to outer: r.o wl: n.d to first two* **14/1**
4 3/4 **Dara Tango (FR)**[29] 3-9-2 0 ThierryJarnet 5 100
(Mlle S-V Tarrou, France) *racd in 4th: chsd ldrs in st: wnt 3rd: no ex in clsng stages: lost 3rd cl home* **20/1**
5 1 1/2 **Tenacious Spring (FR)**[34] 3-9-2 0 IoritzMendizabal 6 97
(T Lemer, France) *led fr s: stl in front ent st: rdn and sn hdd: fnd no ex: fdd* **13/2**
6 2 **Laristan (FR)**[24] 3-9-2 0 Christophe-PatriceLemaire 10 93
(J-C Rouget, France) *in rr fr s: mde move on outside early in st: no ex fnl f* **7/2**[2]
7 3/4 **Casa Battlo (FR)**[22] 951 3-9-2 0 OlivierPeslier 3 91
(Robert Collet, France) *racd in 5th fr s: no ex in st: fdd* **20/1**
8 3/4 **Meer Royal (FR)**[10] 1079 3-9-2 0 (b[1]) StephanePasquier 8 90
(P Demercastel, France) *in rr fr s: rdn early in st: failed to qckn: fdd* **20/1**

9 *15* **Paris Vegas (USA)**[43] 741 3-9-2 0 ThierryThulliez 7 62
(F Chappet, France) *towards rr fr s: fnd nthing in st: fdd* **8/1**
10 *6* **Nova Med (IRE)**[13] 3-9-2 0 ChristopheSoumillon 1 50
(Y Durepaire, Spain) *racd in 3rd fr s: dropped away early in st* **16/1**
2m 12.04s (1.84) **Going Correction** +0.375s/f (Good) **10** Ran SP% **129.9**
Speed ratings: **108,106,103,102,101 100,99,99,88,83**
WIN (incl. 1 euro stake): 2.70. PLACES: 1.50, 1.90, 3.00. DF: 6.10. SF: 7.70. CSF: £9.82.
Owner Ecurie Wildenstein **Bred** Dayton Investments Ltd **Trained** Lamorlaye, France

NOTEBOOK
Planteur(IRE) tracked the leader for much of the way and found a nice turn of foot to go clear in the straight. He looks a high-class prospect and the Prix du Jockey Club is the main aim, with an outing in the Prix Hocquart, back here in May, likely beforehand. (tchd 9-4)
Rewilding, who is a half-brother to nine winners, six of them smart at least, including leading middle-distance filly Dar Re Mi and high-class middle-distance performers Darazari and Diaghilev, was held up further back in the pack than Planteur. He quickened up well to go in pursuit of the winner and, while he couldn't bridge the gap, he put distance into the rest of the field, and there's the promise of better to come when he steps up to 1m4f. (tchd 9-2)

1255a PRIX D'HARCOURT (GROUP 2) (4YO+) (TURF) 1m 2f
3:10 (12:00) 4-Y-O+ **£65,575** (£25,309; £12,079; £8,053; £4,026)

RPR
1 **Cutlass Bay (UAE)**[334] 1979 4-9-1 0 MaximeGuyon 5 117
(A Fabre, France) *racd in 6th fr s: mde gd prog early in st: qcknd into ld 1 1/2f out: wnt clr: jst hld on in clsng stages* **5/4**[1]
2 *nk* **Court Canibal**[22] 953 5-8-11 0 OlivierPeslier 7 112
(M Delzangles, France) *in rr early: hmpd early in st whn making move: swtchd to outer: fin strly: jst failed* **12/1**
3 *3/4* **Celimene (IRE)**[165] 7128 4-8-8 0 ChristopheSoumillon 4 108
(C Lerner, France) *towards rr fr s: rdn early in st: r.o wl to claim 3rd cl home* **5/1**[2]
4 *3/4* **On Est Bien (IRE)**[364] 1239 4-8-11 0 JohanVictoire 3 109
(E Lellouche, France) *racd in midfield along rail fr s: rdn early in st: styd on wl* **7/1**[3]
5 *nk* **La Boum (GER)**[22] 953 7-8-8 0 ThierryJarnet 1 105
(Robert Collet, France) *racd bhd ldrs along rail fr s: rdn 2f out: r.o wl: no ex ins fnl 55yds* **10/1**
6 *1 1/2* **Starlish (IRE)**[22] 953 5-8-11 0 AnthonyCrastus 2 105
(E Lellouche, France) *led fr s and stl in front early in st: rdn: hdd and no ex fnl 1 1/2f* **5/1**[2]
7 *5* **The Bogberry (USA)**[175] 6890 5-8-11 0 StephanePasquier 6 95
(A Savujev, Czech Republic) *racd cl to ldrs fr s: rdn early in st: failed to qckn: fdd* **14/1**
8 *3/4* **Validor (FR)**[148] 7408 4-8-11 0 (b) Christophe-PatriceLemaire 8 94
(H-A Pantall, France) *racd cl to ldr fr s: rdn early in st: grad fdd* **20/1**
2m 3.86s (-0.14) **Going Correction** +0.375s/f (Good) **8** Ran SP% **118.5**
Speed ratings: **115,114,114,113,113 112,108,107**
WIN (incl. 1 euro stake): 2.20. PLACES: 1.30, 2.20, 1.70. DF: 18.20. SF: 17.90. CSF: £19.36..
Owner Godolphin SNC **Bred** Darley **Trained** Chantilly, France

NOTEBOOK
Cutlass Bay(UAE), running for the first time since taking the Prix Greffulhe last May, showed he retains plenty of ability by quickening up well to score. They were closing him down at the finish but it was his burst of acceleration that won the day, and this son of Halling will likely bid to retain his unbeaten record in the Prix Ganay on May 2. One would have to think that the Arc, for which he's 25-1 with Hills, will be the long-term target.

1073 FOLKESTONE (R-H)
Monday, April 12
OFFICIAL GOING: Good to soft (good in places; 6.5)
Wind: fresh, half-against Weather: bright and breezy

1256 DIGIBET.COM MEDIAN AUCTION MAIDEN STKS 5f
2:00 (2:02) (Class 6) 2-Y-O **£2,729** (£806; £403) **Stalls** Low

Form RPR
1 **Cape To Rio (IRE)** 2-9-3 0 DaneO'Neill 6 91+
(R Hannon) *chsd ldng trio: hdwy to ld wl over 1f out: rdn clr jst over 1f out: eased wl ins fnl f: v easily* **8/1**[3]
2 *3 3/4* **Cocohatchee** 2-9-3 0 IanMongan 1 74
(P M Phelan) *dwlt: sn rcvrd to chse ldrs: rdn 2f 1/2-way: ev ch 2f out: nt pce of wnr jst over 1f out: wl btn after but kpt on for clr 2nd* **10/1**
6 3 *5* **Saucy Buck (IRE)**[16] 1009 2-9-3 0 SamHitchcott 3 56
(M R Channon) *chsd ldr tl 1/2-way: sn rdn: ev ch 2f out: sn outpcd by ldng pair: wl btn fnl f* **10/11**[1]
32 4 *2 3/4* **Bajan Bullet**[5] 1173 2-8-7 0 AndrewHeffernan(5) 2 41
(P D Evans) *led: rdn and edgd rt 2f out: sn hdd & wknd qckly* **3/1**[2]
5 *hd* **Lady Excellentia (IRE)** 2-8-12 0 SebSanders 4 40+
(A B Haynes) *s.i.s: racd wl off the pce in midfield: nvr on terms w ldrs* **20/1**
6 *6* **Enrichment** 2-8-12 0 JimmyQuinn 9 19
(H J L Dunlop) *s.i.s: a wl off the pce towards rr* **33/1**
7 *3 3/4* **Bishops Moon** 2-8-12 0 JerryO'Dwyer 8 5
(M G Quinlan) *v.s.a: a wl bhd* **20/1**
8 *12* **Night Witch (IRE)** 2-8-12 0 EddieCreighton 5 —
(E J Creighton) *v.s.a: sn wl bhd: t.o after 2f* **50/1**
9 *3 1/4* **Major Return (IRE)** 2-9-3 0 RobertWinston 7 —
(A J McCabe) *broke wl: chsd ldrs for 1f: sn lost pl: bhd 1/2-way: eased fr wl over 1f out: t.o* **33/1**
61.75 secs (1.75) **Going Correction** +0.35s/f (Good) **9** Ran SP% **115.0**
Speed ratings (Par 90): **100,94,86,81,81 71,65,46,41**
Tote Swingers: 1&2 £7.00, 1&3 £2.80, 2&3 £3.50 CSF £73.26 TOTE £7.20: £2.00, £3.50, £1.10; EX 81.00.
Owner Kennet Valley Thoroughbreds I **Bred** Paul Hensey **Trained** East Everleigh, Wilts
FOCUS
There were seven newcomers among the field of nine, but the two with previous experience finished well beaten in third and fourth, and the winner looked useful. This was probably a better than average race for the track.
NOTEBOOK
Cape To Rio(IRE), a £26,000 half-brother to a 6f winner, looked a relaxed sort in the paddock but he moved well to post and knew his job. Trainer Richard Hannon won this race last year with the high-class Monsieur Chevalier and this likeable newcomer looks capable of winning in higher grade. (op 7-1 tchd 9-1)
Cocohatchee, "ready to run", according to trainer Pat Phelan, had the benefit of the rail but still did well to chase home the winner with the third some way behind. His dam won twice over 5f as a 2yo and on this showing he could pick up a similar event. (op 17-2 tchd 8-1 and 11-1)
Saucy Buck(IRE) again showed some promise, as he had done in the Brocklesby, but he failed to justify the market support and was only a modest third. However, he did enough to suggest he can hold his own in similar early-season events, and a step up to 6f should not be a problem when the time comes. (op 6-5 tchd 11-8 and 6-4 in places)
Bajan Bullet had two previous races to her name but was unable to cash in on that edge in experience. She has plenty of early speed, but her breeding suggests that she will be more effective with a greater test of stamina as the season progresses. Official explanation: jockey said filly hung right (op 10-3 tchd 7-2 and 11-4 in places)
Lady Excellentia(IRE), an £11,000 half-sister to an Italian sprint winner, missed the break and never became competitive, though it was clear from some way out that she would be best of the rest. She needs more time.
Enrichment, who is not very big, is by the the speedy Iffraaj but she appears to need more time and at least 6f. (op 20-1)
Major Return(IRE) Official explanation: jockey said colt ran green and was hanging

1257 BRIAN BARNES 65TH BIRTHDAY CELEBRATION MEDIAN AUCTION MAIDEN STKS 6f
2:30 (2:31) (Class 6) 3-Y-O **£2,729** (£806; £403) **Stalls** Low

Form RPR
63- 1 **Free For All (IRE)**[186] 6616 3-9-3 0 StephenCraine 1 79
(S Kirk) *chsd ldr tl led wl over 1f out: sn rdn and hrd pressed: forged ahd ins fnl f: styd on wl fnl 100yds* **5/2**[2]
4 2 *1 3/4* **Sulis Minerva (IRE)**[24] 936 3-8-12 0 (t) LukeMorris 7 68
(J R Gask) *dwlt: sn chsng ldrs: rdn to chal and edgd lft wl over 1f out: ev ch tl no ex and btn fnl 100yds* **11/1**
3 *2 1/4* **Flighty Frances (IRE)** 3-8-12 0 DaneO'Neill 9 61+
(D R C Elsworth) *v.s.a: sn rdn along and wl in rr: hdwy over 1f out: modest 6th ent fnl f: styd on wl to go 3rd nr fin* **16/1**
520- 4 *hd* **Marafong**[236] 5166 3-8-10 79 AdamBeschizza(7) 5 65
(Miss J Feilden) *in tch in midfield tl outpcd and pushed along over 3f out: wl btn 2f out: kpt on ins fnl f* **8/1**[3]
322- 5 *1 1/4* **Flouncing (IRE)**[163] 7177 3-8-12 78 LiamJones 6 56
(W J Haggas) *t.k.h: led and sn crossed towards rail: rdn and hdd wl over 1f out: 3rd and wl btn 1f out: lost 2 pls wl ins fnl f* **6/5**[1]
05-4 6 *2* **Silvee**[11] 1075 3-8-12 42 HayleyTurner 8 50?
(J J Bridger) *chsd ldrs: struggling wl over 2f out: no ch w ldrs fnl 2f* **66/1**
05 7 *2* **Trelicia**[24] 930 3-8-9 0 WilliamCarson(3) 3 44
(S C Williams) *stdd s: a bhd* **25/1**
00- 8 *1 1/2* **Torran Sound**[135] 7571 3-9-3 0 MickyFenton 4 44
(J M P Eustace) *s.i.s: sn rdn along in rr: nvr on terms* **66/1**
6 9 *5* **Piccolo Blue**[43] 744 3-8-12 0 SteveDrowne 2 23
(C G Cox) *a towards rr: wl bhd fnl 2f* **14/1**
1m 14.99s (2.29) **Going Correction** +0.35s/f (Good) **9** Ran SP% **112.9**
Speed ratings (Par 96): **98,95,92,92,90 88,85,83,76**
Tote Swingers: 1&2 £4.50, 1&3 £8.80, 2&3 £18.60 CSF £28.72 TOTE £3.00: £1.30, £3.60, £6.40; EX 40.10.
Owner J C Smith **Bred** Miss A R Byrne **Trained** Upper Lambourn, Berks
FOCUS
The field was soon stretched out, and the third caught the eye in coming from a long way back. Weakish form with the favourite disappointing, rated around the winner with the sixth limiting the form to an extent.

1258 ASHFORD DESIGNER OUTLET LADIES DAY 7TH JUNE H'CAP 6f
3:00 (3:02) (Class 5) (0-75,72) 4-Y-O+ **£3,070** (£906; £453) **Stalls** Low

Form RPR
000- 1 **King's Caprice**[304] 2883 9-9-1 **69** RichardThomas 3 78
(J C Fox) *hld up in tch: effrt over 1f out: rdn to chse ldr ent fnl f: hld hd awkwardly but kpt on to ld fnl 50yds* **20/1**
0026 2 *1/2* **Westwood**[46] 703 5-8-13 **67** DaneO'Neill 4 74
(D Haydn Jones) *led: rdn wl over 1f out: kpt on wl tl hdd and no ex fnl 50yds* **8/1**
210- 3 *3/4* **Simla Sunset (IRE)**[112] 7830 4-9-2 **70** (t) LukeMorris 14 75+
(J R Gask) *hld up towards rr: hdwy on outer wl over 1f out: rdn over 1f out: chsd ldng pair ins fnl f: edgd lft and no imp fnl 75yds* **16/1**
2452 4 *shd* **Halsion Chancer**[17] 987 6-9-4 **72** RobertWinston 10 77
(J R Best) *stdd s and swtchd lft to r towards stands' rail: bhd: rdn and hdwy wl over 1f out: swtchd lft ent fnl f: r.o wl to chse ldrs ins fnl f: nt clr run towards fin* **8/1**
-110 5 *2 3/4* **Straboe (USA)**[11] 1074 4-8-7 **64** (v) WilliamCarson(3) 6 60
(S C Williams) *chsd ldr after 1f: rdn over 1f out: lost 2nd ent fnl f: wknd fnl f* **20/1**
0445 6 *hd* **Step It Up (IRE)**[17] 987 6-9-0 **68** StephenCraine 12 63+
(J R Boyle) *stdd and swtchd lft to r towards stands' rail: hld up towards rr: swtchd out rt looking for run 2f out: rdn to chse ldrs ent fnl f: wknd fnl 100yds* **14/1**
-615 7 *3/4* **Doctor Hilary**[39] 789 8-8-8 **62** (bt) ChrisCatlin 7 55
(M R Hoad) *in tch in midfield: rdn and unable qck 2f out: plugged on same pce fnl f* **20/1**
000- 8 *2 1/2* **Rio Royale (IRE)**[152] 7329 4-8-11 **65** EddieCreighton 13 50
(Mrs A J Perrett) *in tch in midfield: rdn and effrt 2f out: no prog and btn ent fnl f* **20/1**
3-34 9 *nse* **Gentle Guru**[53] 602 6-8-12 **66** SteveDrowne 11 51
(R T Phillips) *dismntd and led to s: stdd s: hld up in rr: rdn over 1f out: nvr on terms* **10/1**
425- 10 *3 1/2* **Space Station**[103] 7876 4-9-2 **70** HayleyTurner 9 43
(S Dow) *in tch on outer: rdn wl over 1f out: wknd over 1f out* **11/2**[2]
060- 11 *8* **Ken's Girl**[182] 6739 6-8-12 **66** MickyFenton 8 14
(W S Kittow) *chsd ldr for 1f: chsd ldrs tl rdn and btn ent fnl 2f: wl btn and eased ins fnl f* **13/2**[3]
56-1 12 *6* **Quasi Congaree (GER)**[14] 1044 4-9-2 **70** (t) SebSanders 1 —
(I A Wood) *chsd ldrs on stands' rail: rdn 2f out: sn btn: eased ins fnl f* **10/3**[1]
000- 13 *4* **Miss Hollybell**[138] 7518 4-9-2 **70** TedDurcan 5 —
(J Gallagher) *nvr gng wl: a in rr: wl bhd fnl 2f: eased ins fnl f* **18/1**
1m 14.29s (1.59) **Going Correction** +0.35s/f (Good) **13** Ran SP% **120.0**
Speed ratings (Par 103): **103,102,101,101,97 97,96,92,92,88 77,69,64**
Tote Swingers: 1&2 £38.20, 1&3 £62.40, 2&3 £20.20 CSF £164.40 CT £2696.35 TOTE £46.50: £11.10, £3.70, £6.60; EX 181.20.
Owner Exors of the Late Miss B Swire **Bred** Miss B Swire **Trained** Collingbourne Ducis, Wilts
FOCUS
They raced as one group in the stands' side half of the course, and a good sprint gallop soon had them strung out. The winner had slipped to a career-low mark and the second ran his best races this time last year.

Quasi Congaree(GER) Official explanation: trainer had no explanation for the poor form shown

1259 ASHFORD DESIGNER OUTLET OPEN TILL 8PM WEEKNIGHTS (S) STKS 7f (S)

3:30 (3:30) (Class 6) 3-Y-O **£2,047** (£604; £302) **Stalls** Low

Form RPR

6- **1** **Catherines Call (IRE)**[220] 5638 3-8-4 0 AndreaAtzeni[(3)] 6 60+
(D Donovan) *hld up in tch in last trio: shkn up and hdwy ent fnl 2f: jnd ldrs gng much the best over 1f out: nudged ahd fnl 50yds: cleverly* **17/2**

0 **2** *nk* **Avonside (IRE)**[12] 1057 3-8-12 0 DaneO'Neill 7 61
(Pat Eddery) *chsd ldrs: rdn to ld over 1f out: drvn ins fnl f: hdd fnl 50yds* **3/1**[2]

-403 **3** *½* **Hill Of Miller (IRE)**[4] 1181 3-8-12 65 (t) ChrisCatlin 2 60
(Rae Guest) *stdd s: t.k.h: hld up in tch in rr: hdwy 3f out: rdn to chse ldng trio jst over 1f out: no imp tl kpt on fnl 75yds* **4/1**[3]

1-50 **4** *nk* **Vito Volterra (IRE)**[24] 933 3-9-3 68 SebSanders 5 64
(A B Haynes) *chsd ldr tl led over 3f out: rdn and hdd over 1f out: kpt on one pce fnl f* **6/4**[1]

4331 **5** *12* **Tiger Hawk (USA)**[6] 1144 3-8-12 65 (b) AndrewHeffernan[(5)] 4 31
(P D Evans) *bustled along early: chsd ldr over 3f out: rdn and wknd qckly 2f out* **8/1**

0-60 **6** *25* **Cockney Colonel (USA)**[43] 744 3-8-12 40 (t) EddieCreighton 1 —
(E J Creighton) *taken down early: racd freely: led tl over 3f out: sn dropped out: t.o fr wl over 1f out* **66/1**

-506 **7** *3* **Ba Jetstream**[31] 870 3-8-12 42 JimmyQuinn 3 —
(F Jordan) *in tch: rdn and struggling over 3f out: lost tch oover 2f out: t.o* **40/1**

1m 29.91s (2.61) **Going Correction** +0.35s/f (Good) 7 Ran SP% **110.6**
Speed ratings (Par 96): **99,98,98,97,84 55,52**
Tote Swingers: 1&2 £4.20, 1&3 £4.80, 2&3 £3.10 CSF £31.88 TOTE £14.30: £6.20, £1.90; EX 34.10.The winner was bought in for £5,200. Vito Volterra bought by Mrs Sandra Smith for £6,000.
Owner Philip Mclaughlin **Bred** K Maginn **Trained** Newmarket, Suffolk

FOCUS
Nothing much on paper, but the first two were unexposed and the winner came home in style. Not easy form to assess but the third and fourth were probably below par. The winner was value for a bit further.

1260 JOHN ELLIOTT MAIDEN STKS 7f (S)

4:00 (4:02) (Class 5) 3-Y-O+ **£2,729** (£806; £403) **Stalls** Low

Form RPR

232- **1** **Whirly Dancer**[177] 6844 3-8-7 72 JimmyQuinn 2 86
(H R A Cecil) *trckd ldrs: clr in ldng trio fr 1/2-way: swtchd rt ent fnl 2f: pushed into ld wl over 1f out: clr fr over 1f out: pushed out* **3/1**[2]

023- **2** *5* **Spa's Dancer (IRE)**[173] 6931 3-8-12 84 RichardHills 12 77
(J W Hills) *chsd ldr tl led over 2f out: hdd and rdn wl over 1f out: hld hd awkwardly u.p and btn over 1f out* **2/1**[1]

0 **3** *5* **Edition**[68] 392 3-8-12 0 SteveDrowne 14 64
(J R Gask) *swtchd lft and dropped in after s: towards rr: hdwy into midfield 4f out: wnt modest 3rd 1f out: nvr trbld ldrs* **66/1**

0 **4** *4* **Hatta Stream (IRE)**[23] 950 4-9-12 0 DaneO'Neill 10 57+
(J Pearce) *wl off the pce towards rr: lost tch 1/2-way: hdwy ent fnl 2f: nt clr run and hmpd ins fnl f: wnt modest 4th fnl 100yds: n.d* **66/1**

322- **5** *1 ¾* **Mountrath**[182] 6735 3-8-12 77 SebSanders 1 48
(B R Johnson) *led tl rdn and hdd over 2f out: 3rd and wl btn over 1f out: lost 2 pls fnl f* **8/1**

00- **6** *3 ¾* **Scarcity (IRE)**[182] 6729 3-8-9 0 ow2 TomMcLaughlin 8 35
(E A L Dunlop) *in tch: outpcd by ldng trio and pushed along 1/2-way: n.d after* **40/1**

00- **7** *shd* **Consider Yourself (USA)**[206] 6062 3-8-7 0 HayleyTurner 11 33
(M L W Bell) *stdd and dropped in bhd after s: wl bhd: lost tch 1/2-way: modest late hdwy: nvr on terms* **16/1**

60- **8** *shd* **Specialising**[173] 6930 3-8-7 0 EddieCreighton 5 32
(M R Channon) *chsd ldrs tl rdn and outpcd 1/2-way: no ch fnl 2f* **33/1**

25- **9** *nse* **Aquarius Star (IRE)**[246] 4817 3-8-8 0 ow1 RobertWinston 7 33
(Pat Eddery) *bhd: pushed along and racd awkwardly 4f out: sn lost tch: modest late hdwy: nvr on terms* **8/1**

0 **10** *7* **Michael's Nook**[18] 980 3-8-12 0 ChrisCatlin 4 18
(W S Kittow) *s.i.s: a bhd: lost tch 4f out:* **50/1**

0 **11** *7* **Faraday's Fancy (IRE)**[17] 985 4-9-7 0 FrankieMcDonald 6 —
(Miss A M Newton-Smith) *chsd ldrs tl 4f out: sn wl outpcd: wl bhd fnl 2f* **200/1**

032- **12** *¾* **Old Money**[188] 6561 3-8-7 78 TedDurcan 13 —
(H J L Dunlop) *chsd ldrs tl over 4f out: sn struggling and dropped out: wl btn and eased fr over 1f out* **5/1**[3]

- **13** *3 ¼* **Bowsers Brave (USA)** 4-9-5 0 KatiaScallan[(7)] 3 —
(M P Tregoning) *s.i.s: a wl bhd: t.o fnl 3f* **16/1**

0- **14** *½* **Star Of Soho (IRE)**[163] 7182 3-8-7 0 SamHitchcott 9 —
(E J Creighton) *s.i.s: racd off the pce in midfield: rdn and toiling 4f out: t.o fnl 2f* **100/1**

1m 28.1s (0.80) **Going Correction** +0.35s/f (Good)
WFA 3 from 4yo 14lb 14 Ran SP% **120.8**
Speed ratings (Par 103): **109,103,97,93,91 86,86,86,86,78 70,69,65,65**
Tote Swingers: 1&2 £2.70, 1&3 £22.50, 2&3 £30.70 CSF £9.20 TOTE £3.40: £1.10, £2.20, £11.50; EX 12.00.
Owner Woodcote Stud Ltd **Bred** Woodcote Stud Ltd **Trained** Newmarket, Suffolk

FOCUS
They went a decent pace, with the runners soon strung out, but the first two were always prominent and those who tried to come from behind made no impression. Another personal best from the clear-cut winner.
Aquarius Star(IRE) Official explanation: jockey said filly was outpaced and unbalanced first 4f
Michael's Nook Official explanation: jockey said gelding ran green
Old Money Official explanation: jockey said filly stopped quickly

1261 STERLINGSERVICE.CO.UK CHAUFFEUR H'CAP 1m 1f 149y

4:30 (4:31) (Class 5) (0-70,70) 3-Y-O **£3,070** (£906; £453) **Stalls** Centre

Form RPR

004- **1** **On Khee**[152] 7325 3-8-10 62 SteveDrowne 8 66+
(H Morrison) *t.k.h: hld up in tch: chsd ldr over 2f out: rdn to ld over 1f out: r.o wl fnl f* **5/2**[1]

406- **2** *2* **One Cool Poppy (IRE)**[177] 6858 3-8-4 56 oh3 LukeMorris 9 54
(H J L Dunlop) *in tch in midfield: rdn 5f out: drvn and bmpd 2f out: kpt on u.p fnl f to go 2nd towards fin: no threat to wnr* **16/1**

1256 **3** *nk* **Bubbly Braveheart (IRE)**[21] 964 3-9-4 70 RobertWinston 10 67
(A Bailey) *t.k.h: led for 1f: stdd and hld up in tch after: rdn and swtchd lft 2f out: chsd wnr jst over 1f out: no imp: lost 2nd towards fin* **8/1**

020- **4** *1 ¼* **Rose Alba (IRE)**[206] 6067 3-8-13 65 TedDurcan 6 60+
(J L Dunlop) *t.k.h: chsd ldr tl led after 1f: hdd over 7f out: chsd ldrs after: rdn and nt clr run 2f out: swtchd lft and drvn over 1f out: kpt on same pce fnl f* **9/2**[2]

533 **5** *½* **Pascalina**[44] 734 3-8-8 60 J-PGuillambert 1 54+
(J Akehurst) *v.s.a: hld up in last trio: hdwy 3f out: pushed along and chsng ldrs over 1f out: kpt on same pce fnl f: swtchd lft towards fin* **20/1**

065- **6** *shd* **Varachi**[172] 6962 3-9-0 66 TomMcLaughlin 11 60+
(E A L Dunlop) *bustled along leaving stalls: in tch: hmpd after 1f hld up in tch towards rr after: hdwy to chse ldrs over 2f out: kpt on same pce u.p fnl f* **7/1**[3]

00-6 **7** *9* **Zambuka (FR)**[25] 915 3-8-4 56 oh4 HayleyTurner 4 30
(R Curtis) *chsd ldrs tl led over 7f out: rdn and hdd wl over 1f out: wknd qckly ent fnl f* **14/1**

1305 **8** *6* **Orsett Lad (USA)**[24] 933 3-8-10 62 JimmyQuinn 3 24
(J R Best) *hld up in rr: rdn and struggling over 2f out: sn wl bhd eased ins fnl f* **16/1**

006- **9** *3 ¾* **Atakora (IRE)**[193] 6416 3-8-8 60 EddieCreighton 2 14
(Mrs A J Perrett) *t.k.h: hdwy to chse ldr over 6f out tl over 2f out: wkng whn bmpd 2f out: wl btn and eased ins fnl f* **7/1**[3]

3-10 **10** *1 ¼* **Highland Bridge**[46] 698 3-9-1 67 DaneO'Neill 7 18
(D R C Elsworth) *in tch: rdn and effrt 3f out: wkng and btn whn hmpd 2f out: bhd and eased ins fnl f* **14/1**

6-20 **11** *¾* **Abhar (USA)**[24] 933 3-9-0 66 SebSanders 5 16
(J R Best) *a in rr: struggling 3f out: wl bhd fnl 2f: eased ins fnl f* **14/1**

2m 10.37s (5.47) **Going Correction** +0.50s/f (Yiel) 11 Ran SP% **119.4**
Speed ratings (Par 98): **98,96,96,95,94 94,87,82,79,78 78**
Tote Swingers: 1&2 £14.70, 1&3 £6.90, 2&3 £17.90 CSF £47.40 CT £289.49 TOTE £3.40: £1.10, £6.20, £1.80; EX 58.30.

Owner Rory Sweet **Bred** Miss B Swire **Trained** East Ilsley, Berks

■ Stewards' Enquiry : Robert Winston two-day ban: careless riding (Apr 26-27)

FOCUS
A good gallop set things up nicely for the winner, who was keen early on and might have burnt herself out if they had gone more slowly. Modest form rated around the third, with the winner up 6lb.

Pascalina Official explanation: jockey said filly was denied a clear run

Atakora(IRE) Official explanation: jockey said filly hung badly left

1262 BOB CHAMPION 60:60 CHALLENGE 20TH APRIL H'CAP 1m 4f

5:00 (5:01) (Class 6) (0-60,60) 4-Y-O+ **£2,047** (£604; £302) **Stalls** Low

Form RPR

03-0 **1** **Karky Schultz (GER)**[23] 121 5-9-6 59 LeeTopliss 2 67+
(J M P Eustace) *stdd and dropped in bhd after s: t.k.h: hld up towards rr: hdwy over 3f out: rdn to chal over 1f out: led 1f out: kpt on wl* **10/3**[1]

360- **2** *½* **Act Three**[187] 6584 6-9-2 55 (t) RichardRowe 1 62
(Mouse Hamilton-Fairley) *stdd and dropped in bhd after s: hld up towards rr: rn wd bnd over 8f out: hdwy 5f out: ev ch and rdn over 1f out: no ex wl ins fnl f* **14/1**

3060 **3** *nk* **Barbirolli**[49] 661 8-8-7 46 LauraPike 13 52
(W B Stone) *t.k.h: in tch in midfield: lost pl and dropped to rr over 4f out: switching to outer over 3f out: effrt and n.m.r wl over 1f out: rdn ent fnl f: r.o wl: nt rch ldrs* **8/1**[3]

000- **4** *1 ½* **Uncle Keef (IRE)**[172] 6974 4-9-1 60 KatiaScallan[(5)] 9 64+
(M P Tregoning) *chsd ldrs: grad lost pl fr 7f out: bhd 3f out: hdwy towards inner over 1f out: edging rt to pass wkng rival ins fnl f: r.o: nt rch ldrs* **11/2**[2]

-00 **5** *½* **Comrade Cotton**[4] 1193 6-8-9 55 StevenPearce[(7)] 5 58
(J Ryan) *hld up in rr and racd wd: hdwy 3f out: nudged along and edgd rt over 1f out: no prog tl styd on ins fnl f: nvr rchd ldrs* **33/1**

-553 **6** *nk* **Six Of Clubs**[27] 898 4-8-2 45 (b) JakePayne[(3)] 8 48
(W G M Turner) *t.k.h: chsd ldrs: wnt 2nd over 3f out: ev ch ent fnl 2f: rdn and fnd nil over 1f out: wknd ins fnl f* **20/1**

010 **7** *1* **Jiggalong**[53] 590 4-8-6 51 MatthewCosham[(5)] 6 52
(Jim Best) *t.k.h: in tch: hdwy to ld over 7f out: hrd pressed and rdn ent fnl 2f: hdd 1f out: wknd ins fnl f* **14/1**

12-5 **8** *½* **Ghufa (IRE)**[16] 1012 6-8-11 57 SophieSilvester[(7)] 3 60+
(J Pearce) *hld up in rr: detached last over 3f out: hdwy on inner over 1f out: chsng ldrs and styng on whn nt clr run and snatched up fnl 100yds: nvr able to chal* **10/3**[1]

2-40 **9** *nk* **Achromatic**[91] 131 4-8-8 53 AdamBeschizza[(5)] 10 53
(W R Swinburn) *t.k.h: chsd ldrs: rdn wl over 1f out: wknd ent fnl f* **12/1**

404- **10** *¾* **Good Buy Dubai (USA)**[174] 6918 4-8-7 54 KaseyLoftus[(7)] 11 53
(C Gordon) *in tch in midfield: pushed along and unable qck over 2f out: nt clr run 2f out: no prog after* **11/1**

00-6 **11** *2* **Steady Gaze**[11] 1078 5-8-1 45 HarryBentley[(5)] 12 40
(G L Moore) *led tl over 7f out: chsd ldr after tl over 3f out: wknd jst over 2f out* **14/1**

0-10 **12** *½* **Mekong Miss**[52] 621 4-8-12 57 NoelGarbutt[(5)] 7 52
(J Jay) *stdd s: t.k.h: hld up towards rr: hdwy 7f out: chsd ldrs over 4f out: wknd 2f out* **16/1**

2m 50.91s (10.01) **Going Correction** +0.50s/f (Yiel)
WFA 4 from 5yo+ 1lb 12 Ran SP% **122.3**
Speed ratings (Par 101): **86,85,85,84,84 83,83,82,82,82 80,80**
Tote Swingers: 1&2 £10.80, 1&3 £10.00, 2&3 £40.90 CSF £55.77 CT £358.60 TOTE £4.00: £2.30, £6.50, £3.20; EX 78.10 Place 6: £261.59 Place 5: £183.88.

Owner Harold Nass **Bred** B Fassbender **Trained** Newmarket, Suffolk

■ Stewards' Enquiry : Katia Scallan two-day ban: careless riding (Apr 26-27)

FOCUS
A fair gallop gave all the runners a chance, with the hold-up performers getting into it around the home turn.

T/Plt: £542.80 to a £1 stake. Pool: £52,823.66. 71.04 winning tickets. T/Qpdt: £123.30 to a £1 stake. Pool: £4,574.08. 27.45 winning tickets. SP

WINDSOR (R-H)

Monday, April 12

OFFICIAL GOING: Good (good to firm in places; 9.0)

Straight at full width and top bend dolled out 2yds from innermost line adding 7yds to races of a mile and over.

Wind: Brisk, against Weather: Fine but cloudy

1263 EUROPEAN BREEDERS' FUND MAIDEN STKS — 5f 10y

2:20 (2:22) (Class 5) 2-Y-O — £3,480 (£1,027; £514) Stalls High

Form — RPR

1 **Zebedee** 2-9-3 0 .... RichardHughes 15 — 84+
(R Hannon) *trckd ldng pair: wnt 2nd 1/2-way: cruised up to ldr over 1f out: pushed into ld ins fnl f: fnd enough* **4/6**[1]

22 2 ½ **Scarlet Rocks (IRE)**[6] 1136 2-8-12 0 .... JamieSpencer 3 — 73
(P D Evans) *gd spd to ld fr wd draw and crossed to nr side rail: hdd ins fnl f: styd on but readily hld* **7/2**[2]

3 1¼ **Littleportnbrandy (IRE)** 2-8-5 0 .... KevinLundie(7) 8 — 68+
(P D Evans) *chsd ldrs and sn wl clr of main pack: rn green but wnt 3rd over 1f out: styd on steadily* **40/1**

4 5 **Straight Line (IRE)** 2-9-3 0 .... RichardKingscote 2 — 53+
(A P Jarvis) *s.i.s: rcvrd to chse ldng quintet but nowhere nr them: kpt on fnl f* **25/1**

5 3¾ **Decimate** 2-9-0 0 .... RussKennemore(3) 4 — 38
(Andrew Reid) *chsd ldng trio: rn green 1/2-way: no imp over 1f out: wknd fnl f* **40/1**

6 3 **Russian Ice** 2-8-7 0 .... MarkCoumbe(5) 6 — 21
(D K Ivory) *dwlt and rrd after s: wl bhd and outpcd: styd on fr over 1f out* **66/1**

7 1¼ **Ad Vitam (IRE)** 2-9-3 0 .... LiamKeniry 5 — 21
(S Kirk) *dwlt: rn green in last trio and sn wl bhd: styd on ins fnl f: nrst fin* **80/1**

8 hd **Valency (IRE)** 2-9-3 0 .... TravisBlock 13 — 20
(A G Newcombe) *s.s: wl bhd in rr gp: sme late prog* **100/1**

9 ½ **Maxiyow (IRE)** 2-8-12 0 .... DavidProbert 12 — 13
(B Palling) *dwlt: rn green and wl bhd: modest late prog* **33/1**

10 ½ **No Peace (IRE)** 2-8-12 0 .... TomQueally 9 — 11
(G G Margarson) *sn wl off the pce despite being in abt 7th: no prog 1/2-way* **66/1**

11 nk **Triple Agent (IRE)** 2-9-3 0 ....(v[1]) PatCosgrave 14 — 15
(A Bailey) *gd spd to chse ldr to 1/2-way: wknd rapidly over 1f out* **14/1**[3]

12 nse **Galtymore Lad** 2-9-3 0 .... TonyCulhane 1 — 15
(M R Channon) *restless in stalls: sn wl bhd in last trio: nvr a factor: kpt on fnl f* **25/1**

13 ½ **Joyously** 2-8-12 0 .... CathyGannon 11 — 8
(P D Evans) *dwlt: rn green and a wl bhd* **50/1**

14 5 **Silly Billy (IRE)** 2-9-3 0 .... EddieAhern 7 — —
(S Kirk) *sn outpcd: rn green whn pushed along 1/2-way: wknd over 1f out* **25/1**

15 3¼ **Regal Bullet (IRE)** 2-9-3 0 .... AdrianMcCarthy 10 — —
(D K Ivory) *dwlt: rn green and a wl bhd: sadlle slipped* **40/1**

62.27 secs (1.97) **Going Correction** +0.225s/f (Good) — **15** Ran SP% **117.8**

Speed ratings (Par 92): **93,92,90,82,76 71,69,69,68,67 67,66,66,58,52**

Tote Swingers: 1&2 £1.50, 1&3 £17.10, 2&3 £23.10 CSF £2.23 TOTE £1.70: £1.20, £1.10, £9.20; EX 4.00 Trifecta £59.60 Pool: £289.24 - 3.59 winning units..

Owner Mrs J Wood **Bred** Hascombe & Valiant Studs **Trained** East Everleigh, Wilts

FOCUS

No strength in depth here and the front three finished clear. The winner looked a decent recruit and the second has been afforded minor improvement from her debut.

NOTEBOOK

Zebedee, a 70,000gns purchase out a smart 1m2f winner, had apparently worked with Takeaway before that one won on debut at Kempton. Extremely well backed, he showed good speed to track Scarlet Rocks and was still cruising when ranging upsides that rival a furlong out. Once asked, he didn't find quite as much as he had looked likely, but still did enough to win cosily and is probably better than the bare form. A horse with size, he should improve and connections will now look for a conditions race. (op 8-11 tchd 4-5 in places and 10-11 in places)

Scarlet Rocks(IRE), runner-up on her first two starts, again had to settle for second but she did nothing wrong. She put her experience to good use, showing loads of natural speed to get across from her low draw, but she was simply beaten by a better rival. A modest race should come her way. (op 3-1 tchd 11-4)

Littleportnbrandy(IRE) ◆, a 13,000euros half-sister to a triple 6f-1m winner in Italy, and 1m winner Ailsa Craig, showed some speed to chase the pace and kept on gradually under her inexperienced rider. With improvement to come, she should soon be winning. (tchd 50-1)

Straight Line(IRE), a 2,700gns purchase as a foal, who was due to be partnered by Kieren Fallon, kept on from about mid-division without being given too hard a time and should be better for the experience. (op 20-1)

Decimate ◆, an already gelded brother to the stable's modest 5f Fibresand winner Cavitie, was green early, needing a slap down his left shoulder not long after leaving the stalls to prevent him from wandering, but he showed speed and has ability.

Regal Bullet(IRE) Official explanation: jockey said saddle slipped

1264 TRAINERMAGAZINE.COM CLAIMING STKS — 1m 2f 7y

2:50 (2:50) (Class 5) 3-Y-O — £2,456 (£725; £362) Stalls Low

Form — RPR

3430 1 **Glen Lass**[40] 775 3-8-2 61 ....(b) SimonPearce(5) 1 — 55
(J Pearce) *hld up in last: stdy prog on outer fr 4f out: wnt 2nd over 2f out: shkn up to ld over 1f out: cajoled along and styd on* **7/2**[2]

4325 2 ¾ **Captain Cool (IRE)**[12] 1060 3-9-5 55 ....(b) RichardHughes 6 — 66
(R Hannon) *hld up in rr: gng easily over 3f out: prog to chse ldrs 2f out: drvn and kpt on to take 2nd fnl f: no imp on wnr* **3/1**[1]

1510 3 1 **Kathindi (IRE)**[21] 964 3-8-12 66 ....(b[1]) LiamKeniry 4 — 57
(J S Moore) *led: edgd lft u.p 2f out: hdd and nt qckn over 1f out: kpt on* **6/1**

044- 4 2¼ **Sassanian (IRE)**[121] 7731 3-8-12 57 ....[1] ShaneKelly 10 — 52
(Jane Chapple-Hyam) *trckd ldr for 3f: racd in 3rd after: losing pl whn squeezed out 2f out: swtchd wd and kpt on* **9/2**[3]

0-05 5 2¼ **Gulf Punch**[3] 1209 3-8-1 40 .... Louis-PhilippeBeuzelin(3) 9 — 40
(M F Harris) *chsd ldrs: pushed along over 3f out: no imp 2f out: fdd* **18/1**

046- 6 1¼ **Spirit Land (IRE)**[142] 7482 3-8-7 52 .... AshleyMorgan(5) 3 — 45
(M H Tompkins) *sn chsd ldrs: cl enough 3f out: rdn over 2f out: grad fdd* **16/1**

0-50 7 8 **Cordiality**[40] 775 3-9-0 55 .... FergusSweeney 8 — 31
(P G Murphy) *hld up: struggling in last pair over 3f out: no prog 2f out: wknd* **22/1**

0026 8 6 **Underworld Dandy**[48] 670 3-8-9 60 ....(b) MartinDwyer 5 — 14
(R T Phillips) *chsd ldr after 3f: rn wd bnd sn after: wknd rapidly over 2f out* **16/1**

003- 9 5 **Cuts Both Ways (USA)**[168] 7056 3-9-2 52 ....(p) RyanMoore 7 — 11
(P F I Cole) *hld up: struggling in last pair over 3f out: sn bhd: t.o* **11/2**

2m 8.51s (-0.19) **Going Correction** -0.025s/f (Good) — **9** Ran SP% **116.5**

Speed ratings (Par 98): **99,98,97,95,94 93,86,81,77**

Tote Swingers: 1&2 £2.20, 1&3 £4.50, 2&3 £5.90 CSF £14.59 TOTE £3.90: £1.10, £2.20, £1.30; EX 14.40 TRIFECTA Pool: £219.12 - 2.61 winning units..Glen Lass was claimed by Mr J. E. Snowden for £8,000.

Owner Ian Bishop **Bred** Limestone And Tara Studs **Trained** Newmarket, Suffolk

FOCUS

A weak claimer. The form is rated around the front three, with apparent improvement from the runner-up.

1265 AW CREATIVE H'CAP — 1m 67y

3:20 (3:21) (Class 4) (0-85,83) 4-Y-O+ — £4,857 (£1,445; £722; £360) Stalls High

Form — RPR

063- 1 **Tudor Key (IRE)**[191] 6474 4-9-3 82 .... RyanMoore 1 — 89
(Mrs A J Perrett) *mde most: drvn 2f out: narrowly hdd jst over 1f out: edgd lft but styd on to ld wl ins fnl f* **9/2**[1]

220- 2 nk **Hail Promenader (IRE)**[185] 6645 4-9-4 83 .... MichaelHills 4 — 89
(B W Hills) *trckd ldng trio: clsd 3f out: shkn up to ld narrowly jst over 1f out: kpt on but hdd wl ins fnl f* **8/1**[3]

0113 3 nk **Mr Hichens**[14] 1051 5-8-13 78 .... DarryllHolland 13 — 84+
(Karen George) *trckd ldrs in 5th: cl enough and looking for room 2f out: swtchd ins over 1f out: hung lft but styd on fnl f* **8/1**[3]

006- 4 1¼ **Edgeworth (IRE)**[163] 7189 4-8-11 76 .... KierenFallon 2 — 79
(B G Powell) *taken down early: hld up in 6th: clsd on ldrs over 2f out: sn shkn up: kpt on fr over 1f out but nvr gng pce to chal* **12/1**

64-1 5 ½ **Striding Edge (IRE)**[19] 975 4-9-0 79 .... MartinDwyer 9 — 81+
(W R Muir) *hld up in 8th: lost pl and rdn 3f out: in last pair 2f out: styd on fr over 1f out: gaining at fin* **11/2**[2]

006- 6 nk **Ellemujie**[172] 6973 5-9-3 82 .... PatCosgrave 11 — 83
(D K Ivory) *hld up in 9th: sme prog over 2f out to midfield over 1f out: rdn and kpt on fnl f: nrst fin* **10/1**

640- 7 nk **Smart Endeavour (USA)**[249] 4715 4-9-1 80 .... ShaneKelly 12 — 80
(W R Swinburn) *trckd ldng pair: cl enough fr 3f out: nt qckn 2f out: fdd ins fnl f* **17/2**

106 8 3½ **Noble Jack (IRE)**[26] 902 4-9-1 80 .... LiamKeniry 8 — 72
(G L Moore) *s.s: hld up in last trio: stl there 2f out: shkn up and sme modest late prog* **28/1**

314- 9 ½ **Cheam Forever (USA)**[189] 6545 4-8-12 77 .... RichardKingscote 10 — 68
(R Charlton) *hld up in 10th: effrt on outer 3f out: no prog wl over 1f out: fdd* **11/1**

235- 10 hd **Rock Anthem (IRE)**[160] 7229 6-8-7 79 ow3 .... BarryAdams(7) 5 — 70
(Mike Murphy) *hld up in last trio: effrt on wd outside 3f out: no prog 2f out: wknd* **33/1**

6-51 11 2 **Orchard Supreme**[32] 863 7-8-13 78 .... RichardHughes 3 — 64
(R Hannon) *hld up in last trio: shkn up 3f out: no real prog* **8/1**[3]

00-0 12 ¾ **Charlotte Point (USA)**[9] 1084 4-9-1 80 .... EddieAhern 14 — 64
(P F I Cole) *hld up in midfield: nt qckn whn shkn up 2f out: fdd over 1f out* **14/1**

041- 13 1¾ **Calahonda**[230] 5329 4-8-11 76 .... TonyCulhane 6 — 56
(P W D'Arcy) *w ldr to 2f out: wknd u.p* **18/1**

1m 43.33s (-1.37) **Going Correction** -0.025s/f (Good) — **13** Ran SP% **120.9**

Speed ratings (Par 105): **105,104,104,103,102 102,102,98,98,97 95,95,93**

Tote Swingers: 1&2 £8.60, 1&3 £9.60, 2&3 £16.60 CSF £40.40 CT £295.11 TOTE £4.00: £1.30, £3.80, £3.70; EX 48.50 TRIFECTA Not won..

Owner Coombelands Racing Syndicate **Bred** Gainsborough Stud Management Ltd **Trained** Pulborough, W Sussex

■ Stewards' Enquiry : Michael Hills one-day ban: used whip with excessive frequency (Apr 26)

FOCUS

A fair handicap in which it paid to race prominently. The form makes sense around the first four.

1266 JOIN ROYAL WINDSOR RACING CLUB H'CAP (DIV I) — 5f 10y

3:50 (3:51) (Class 4) (0-80,80) 4-Y-O+ — £4,209 (£1,252; £625; £312) Stalls High

Form — RPR

500- 1 **Efistorm**[198] 6279 9-9-2 78 .... LiamKeniry 9 — 87
(C R Dore) *trckd ldrs: effrt 2f out: rdn to ld narrowly fnl f: styd on wl* **12/1**

05-6 2 ½ **Rocker**[11] 1074 6-8-11 73 .... RyanMoore 10 — 80
(G L Moore) *led 1f: styd cl up: drvn against rail to ld over 1f out: hdd and hld fnl f* **8/1**

260- 3 ½ **Make My Dream**[120] 7739 7-8-9 71 .... TadhgO'Shea 1 — 76
(J Gallagher) *pressed ldr after 1f: chal towards centre 2f out: styd on u.p: a jst hld* **11/1**

1-12 4 1½ **Brynfa Boy**[38] 806 4-8-10 72 .... TonyCulhane 4 — 72
(P W D'Arcy) *hld up in last quartet: taken towards outer 1/2-way: urged along and styd on same pce over 1f out* **6/1**[3]

00-4 5 ½ **The Jobber (IRE)**[19] 972 9-9-1 77 .... TomQueally 11 — 75
(M Blanshard) *hld up in last quartet: effrt 2f out: swtchd lft ins fnl f and rdn: kpt on: nvr nr to chal* **16/1**

-220 6 nk **Ivory Silk**[23] 948 5-8-5 74 ....(b) JohnFahy(7) 3 — 71
(J R Gask) *hld up in last quartet: taken to wd outside 1/2-way: no imp on ldrs over 1f out* **7/2**[2]

203- 7 2¼ **Green Lagonda (AUS)**[179] 6791 8-8-7 69 .... CathyGannon 8 — 58
(P D Evans) *hld up in last quartet: effrt 2f out: no hdwy fr jst over 1f out* **25/1**

3212 8 1½ **Onceaponatime (IRE)**[25] 916 5-8-13 75 .... JamieSpencer 5 — 59
(M D Squance) *hld up bhd ldrs: nt clr run towards outer 2f out and lost grnd: nvr on terms after* **9/4**[1]

540- 9 hd **Supermassive Muse (IRE)**[192] 6459 5-8-8 70 ....(p) GrahamGibbons 7 — 53
(E S McMahon) *racd keenly: led after 1f to over 1f out: wknd* **10/1**

-620 10 2½ **Lujeanie**[26] 905 4-9-4 80 .... JimCrowley 2 — 54
(D K Ivory) *pressed ldrs tl wknd 2f out* **12/1**

60.79 secs (0.49) **Going Correction** +0.225s/f (Good) — **10** Ran SP% **120.9**

Speed ratings (Par 105): **105,104,103,101,100 99,96,93,93,89**

Tote Swingers: 1&2 £14.30, 1&3 £15.00, 2&3 £10.80 CSF £108.15 CT £1133.93 TOTE £16.80: £3.70, £2.80, £2.80; EX 89.30 Trifecta £301.70 Part won. Pool: £407.89 - 0.44 winning units..

Owner Sean J Murphy **Bred** E Duggan And D Churchman **Trained** Cowbit, Lincs

FOCUS
A competitive sprint, and sound form amongst the principals.

1267 JOIN ROYAL WINDSOR RACING CLUB H'CAP (DIV II) 5f 10y
4:20 (4:21) (Class 4) (0-80,80) 4-Y-O+ **£4,209** (£1,252; £625; £312) **Stalls** High

Form RPR
-321 **1** **Master Lightfoot**[24] 935 4-8-10 **72** .... ShaneKelly 6 82
(W R Swinburn) *cl up: effrt to ld over 1f out: drvn out* **9/2**[2]
00-2 **2** ¾ **Ginobili (IRE)**[11] 1074 4-8-6 **68** .... MartinDwyer 8 75
(Andrew Reid) *taken down early: trckd ldrs: effrt 2f out: chsd wnr fnl f: rdn and nt qckn last 150yds* **7/1**
6241 **3** ¾ **Love You Louis**[11] 1074 4-8-13 **75** .... RichardHughes 9 80
(J R Jenkins) *trckd ldng quartet: effrt over 1f out: wnt 3rd ins fnl f and tried to cl: nt qckn* **13/2**
313- **4** ¾ **Magical Speedfit (IRE)**[166] 7123 5-8-9 **71** .... RyanMoore 11 73+
(G G Margarson) *hld up in rr and off the pce: effrt over 1f out: styd on fnl f: nvr able to chal* **4/1**[1]
6404 **5** 1 ¼ **Timeteam (IRE)**[11] 1076 4-8-11 **73** .... CathyGannon 10 70
(P D Evans) *taken down early: s.s and rousted along early: wl in rr: drvn and kpt on fr over 1f out: n.d* **13/2**
210- **6** ½ **Taurus Twins**[149] 7395 4-9-0 **76** .... (b) JimCrowley 5 72
(R J Price) *taken down early: led to over 1f out: wknd* **5/1**[3]
000- **7** 4 ½ **Memphis Man**[167] 7083 7-8-3 **72** .... KevinLundie(7) 7 51
(P D Evans) *taken down early: s.s and rousted along early: outpcd in last: taken v wd 1/2-way: passed two rival fnl f* **16/1**
430- **8** 1 ¼ **Sharpened Edge**[184] 6666 4-9-2 **78** .... DavidProbert 3 67
(B Palling) *pressed ldr: wandered u.p fr 1/2-way: wknd over 1f out: eased fnl f* **7/1**
000- **9** nk **Zowington**[163] 7189 8-9-4 **80** .... (v) SaleemGolam 1 54
(S C Williams) *blindfold removed by stalls' handler: s.s: a struggling in rr* **20/1**

60.68 secs (0.38) **Going Correction** +0.225s/f (Good) 9 Ran SP% **117.2**
Speed ratings (Par 105): **105,103,102,101,99 98,91,89,88**
Tote Swingers: 1&2 £7.30, 1&3 £4.20, 2&3 £9.10 CSF £36.53 CT £205.62 TOTE £4.60: £1.60, £2.20, £1.90; EX 46.50 Trifecta £58.80 Pool: £275.79 - 3.47 winning units..
Owner P W Harris & Miss V Palmer **Bred** Bottisham Heath Stud **Trained** Aldbury, Herts

FOCUS
Another competitive sprint, run in a quicker time than the first division. Straightforward, sound form.

1268 ATTHERACES.COM MAIDEN STKS 1m 2f 7y
4:50 (4:55) (Class 5) 3-Y-O **£2,729** (£806; £403) **Stalls** Low

Form RPR
1 **Heddwyn (IRE)** 3-9-3 0 .... MartinDwyer 7 79+
(M P Tregoning) *hld up in midfield: clsd on ldrs on inner over 2f out: looking for room tl swtchd lft 1f out: shkn up and r.o to ld fnl strides* **50/1**
02- **2** hd **Protaras (USA)**[181] 6759 3-9-3 0 .... TomQueally 4 79
(H R A Cecil) *trckd ldrs: rdn to chal 2f out: led ins fnl f: hdd last strides* **5/2**[2]
0- **3** ¾ **Alfonso The Wise (IRE)**[186] 6620 3-9-3 0 .... ShaneKelly 12 78
(J Noseda) *trckd ldrs: pushed along 4f out: effrt 2f out: styd on fr over 1f out: jst outpcd* **18/1**
3- **4** nse **Kronful**[226] 5417 3-8-12 0 .... FrankieDettori 13 72
(M A Jarvis) *mde most: hrd pressed fr over 2f out: hdd and no ex ins fnl f* **7/1**[3]
6- **5** 1 **Dynamic Drive (IRE)**[180] 6772 3-9-3 0 .... JimmyFortune 3 75
(W R Swinburn) *sn hld up towards rr: prog on wd outside fr over 2f out: kpt on same pce fr over 1f out* **50/1**
04- **6** hd **Bombadero (IRE)**[170] 7034 3-9-3 0 .... EddieAhern 5 75
(J L Dunlop) *hld up in midfield: prog on outer over 4f out: pressed ldrs 3f out: nt qckn over 1f out: kpt on* **20/1**
5- **7** nk **Regal Park (IRE)**[186] 6617 3-9-3 0 .... GeorgeBaker 10 74+
(J Noseda) *hld up towards rr: effrt against rail fr 3f out: looking for room over 2f out: no real run tl styd on fnl f: nrst fin* **9/1**
52- **8** nk **Plato (JPN)**[184] 6672 3-9-3 0 .... IanMongan 9 74
(H R A Cecil) *chsd ldrs: pushed along over 3f out: cl enough fr 2f out tl fdd fnl f* **16/1**
9 ½ **Sunny Game** 3-9-3 0 .... PatCosgrave 8 73
(M L W Bell) *s.s: hld up wl in rr: pushed along fr 3f out: kpt on steadily wout threatening: nrst fin* **100/1**
4- **10** nk **Nibani (IRE)**[178] 6810 3-9-3 0 .... RyanMoore 1 72
(Sir Michael Stoute) *w ldr: rdn over 2f out: nt qckn over 1f out: fdd and eased ins fnl f* **6/5**[1]
05 **11** 5 **The Wonga Coup (IRE)**[14] 1046 3-8-12 0 .... KierenFox(5) 14 62?
(P M Phelan) *stdd s: hld up in last pair: sme prog over 2f out and swtchd to outer: shuffled along and on heels of ldng gp over 1f out: fdd* **200/1**
5 **12** 4 ½ **Bethlehem (IRE)**[19] 971 3-9-3 0 .... TravisBlock 11 53
(H Morrison) *a wl in rr: struggling over 3f out: sn bhd* **100/1**
13 19 **Playground** 3-9-3 0 .... JamieSpencer 2 15
(M L W Bell) *fractious preliminaries: hld up in last pair: lft bhd fr 4f out: t.o* **33/1**
60 **14** 4 **Appledore (IRE)**[38] 815 3-9-3 0 .... FergusSweeney 6 7
(A G Newcombe) *a in rr: wknd over 3f out: t.o* **100/1**

2m 8.14s (-0.56) **Going Correction** -0.025s/f (Good) 14 Ran SP% **122.8**
Speed ratings (Par 98): **101,100,100,100,99 99,99,98,98,98 94,90,75,72**
Tote Swingers: 1&2 £39.50, 1&3 £82.60, 2&3 £10.80 CSF £175.14 TOTE £52.90: £14.00, £1.70, £5.30; EX 461.70 TRIFECTA Not won..
Owner J A Tabet **Bred** Austin Lyons **Trained** Lambourn, Berks

FOCUS
This looked a fascinating maiden, but the pace was steady, resulting in a bunch finish, and the bare form needs treating with some caution. Several of the principals are likely to rate higher but the form is limited by the likes of the eleventh.

1269 DOMINO'S PIZZA CLASSIFIED STKS 6f
5:20 (5:22) (Class 5) 3-Y-O **£2,729** (£806; £403) **Stalls** High

Form RPR
41- **1** **Key Light (IRE)**[134] 7585 3-9-0 73 .... KierenFallon 2 75
(J W Hills) *hld up towards rr: prog on outer over 2f out: rdn to chal over 1f out: narrow ld ins fnl f: drvn out* **7/1**
624 **2** hd **Starlight Muse (IRE)**[17] 985 3-9-0 68 .... GrahamGibbons 3 74
(E S McMahon) *trckd ldrs: rdn to ld narrowly over 1f out: kpt on wl but hdd and jst hld ins fnl f* **16/1**
410- **3** nk **Ferris Wheel (IRE)**[206] 6055 3-9-0 75 .... RyanMoore 1 73
(P F I Cole) *sn last: taken to outer and hanging lft fr over 2f out: drvn and styd on wl fnl f: nrst fin* **6/1**[3]
636- **4** ½ **Kerchak (USA)**[178] 6809 3-9-0 75 .... JimCrowley 7 72
(W Jarvis) *dwlt: mostly in last pair: stdy prog fr 2f out: clsd on ldrs fnl f: shuffled along and nvr chal* **15/2**
21- **5** nk **Basle**[163] 7190 3-9-0 73 .... FrankieDettori 5 71
(Miss Gay Kelleway) *hld up in midfield: prog over 2f out: rdn to chal over 1f out and upsides: nt qckn ent fnl f: pushed along and fdd* **11/4**[1]
032- **6** 1 **Olney Lass**[156] 7289 3-8-9 71 .... PaulPickard(5) 9 68
(W J H Ratcliffe) *hld up in midfield on inner: swtchd arnd most of field fr 2f out: styd on fnl f: nvr able to rch ldrs* **10/1**
163- **7** 3 ¼ **Katehari (IRE)**[193] 6418 3-9-0 75 .... JimmyFortune 8 57
(A M Balding) *pressed ldr: led 1/2-way: hdd & wknd over 1f out* **3/1**[2]
044- **8** ¾ **Kings 'n Dreams**[137] 7537 3-9-0 72 .... PatCosgrave 4 55+
(D K Ivory) *hld up: nt clr run on inner over 2f out: stl litte room over 1f out: sn eased* **28/1**
056- **9** ½ **Strike Shot**[235] 5194 3-9-0 72 .... MartinDwyer 6 53
(W R Muir) *prom tl wknd 2f out* **20/1**
0-06 **10** 6 **Quaestor (IRE)**[14] 1052 3-9-0 74 .... RichardKingscote 10 34
(Tom Dascombe) *led to 1/2-way: sn wknd* **20/1**

1m 14.38s (1.38) **Going Correction** +0.225s/f (Good) **10** Ran SP% **118.2**
Speed ratings (Par 98): **99,98,98,97,97 95,91,90,89,81**
Tote Swingers: 1&2 £15.20, 1&3 £6.90, 2&3 £17.00 CSF £108.79 TOTE £9.30: £3.40, £5.40, £1.70; EX 114.70 Trifecta £671.20 Pool: £997.74 - 1.10 winning units. Place 6: £201.98 Place 5: £166.12..
Owner Mrs P De W Johnson **Bred** Castlemartin Stud And Skymarc Farm **Trained** Upper Lambourn, Berks

FOCUS
A competitive contest with just 7lb separating them on official figures and only 4lb on pre-race RPRs bar the runner-up. The form seems sound enough.
Kings 'n Dreams Official explanation: jockey said gelding was denied a clear run.
T/Jkpt: Not won. T/Plt: £498.00 to a £1 stake. Pool: £67,856.65. 99.46 winning tickets. T/Qpdt: £198.40 to a £1 stake. Pool: £4,318.51. 16.10 winning tickets. JN

PONTEFRACT (L-H)
Tuesday, April 13

OFFICIAL GOING: Good (good to soft in places for races over further than 1 1/2 miles; 7.0)
Wind: light half behind Weather: Cloudy and cool

1270 ANNUAL BADGE HOLDERS H'CAP (DIV I) 6f
2:20 (2:21) (Class 5) (0-70,70) 4-Y-O+ **£2,590** (£770; £385; £96; £96) **Stalls** Low

Form RPR
330- **1** **Tangerine Trees**[140] 7506 5-9-3 **69** .... TomEaves 10 79
(B Smart) *chsd ldrs: hdwy over 2f out: rdn to ld 1f out: drvn ins fnl f: kpt on wl towards fin* **13/2**[3]
600- **2** hd **Sea Crest**[172] 6988 4-8-4 **56** oh1 .... FrannyNorton 2 65
(M Brittain) *chsd ldrs: hdwy over 2f out: rdn to chal over 1f out and ev ch tl drvn ins fnl f and no ex towards fin* **40/1**
2132 **3** 3 ¼ **Hits Only Jude (IRE)**[6] 1152 7-8-3 **62** .... NeilFarley(7) 1 61+
(D Carroll) *in tch on inner: hdwy over 2f out: rdn to chse ldrs over 1f out: drvn and kpt on ins fnl f* **7/2**[1]
00-0 **4** 4 **Guest Connections**[26] 913 7-8-8 **60** .... (v) AdrianNicholls 5 46
(D Nicholls) *midfield: hdwy 1/2-way: rdn to chse ldrs over 1f out: drvn ins fnl f and kpt on same pce* **13/2**[3]
00-6 **4** dht **He's A Humbug (IRE)**[89] 171 6-8-13 **65** .... JamieSpencer 13 51
(J O'Reilly) *towards rr: hdwy over 2f out: sn rdn: styd on wl fnl f: nrst fin* **20/1**
6050 **6** ½ **Carmenero (GER)**[7] 1147 7-9-1 **67** .... LiamKeniry 7 52
(C R Dore) *towards rr: hdwy on wd outside 2f out: sn rdn and kpt on ins fnl f: nrst fin* **22/1**
3026 **7** 1 ¼ **Angle Of Attack (IRE)**[13] 1068 5-8-4 **56** .... (v) GrahamGibbons 12 37
(A D Brown) *led: rdn along over 2f out: drvn over 1f out: sn hdd & wknd* **14/1**
8 4 ½ **Running Flame (IRE)**[522] 7237 4-8-10 **69** ow1 .... ConorQuish(7) 4 35
(A J McCabe) *hld up in rr: sme hdwy on inner 2f out: n.d* **40/1**
000- **9** nse **Mey Blossom**[164] 7191 5-8-7 **59** .... PaulQuinn 9 25
(R M Whitaker) *chsd ldrs: rdn and hdwy 2f out: drvn and wknd appr fnl f* **11/1**
0140 **10** 1 **Ponting (IRE)**[16] 1030 4-8-13 **70** .... PaulPickard(5) 3 33
(P T Midgley) *dwlt: a in rr* **8/1**
240- **11** ¾ **Ask Dan (IRE)**[172] 6985 4-8-4 **56** oh1 .... (p) PaulHanagan 11 16
(M Dods) *cl up: rdn along 1/2-way: sn wknd* **11/1**
0240 **12** shd **Dickie Le Davoir**[66] 442 6-8-11 **68** .... (p) BillyCray(5) 8 28
(R C Guest) *s.i.s: a bhd* **20/1**
000- **13** 42 **Alpha Tauri (USA)**[248] 4786 4-9-0 **69** .... (t) AndreaAtzeni(3) 6 —
(F Sheridan) *prom: rdn along 1/2-way: sn wknd and bhd* **11/2**[2]

1m 18.04s (1.14) **Going Correction** +0.10s/f (Good) 13 Ran SP% **117.5**
Speed ratings (Par 103): **96,95,91,86,86 85,83,77,77,76 75,75,35**
toteswingers:1&2:£44.80, 1&3:£5.50, 2&3:£19.40 CSF £254.11 CT £1084.41 TOTE £8.60: £2.40, £9.90, £1.50; EX 257.20.
Owner Tangerine Trees Partnership **Bred** Mrs B A Matthews **Trained** Hambleton, N Yorks

FOCUS
After 10 days without rain, the ground had dried out and was largely described as 'lovely ground if a bit dead'. A competitive 56-70 sprint handicap run half a second slower than division II. Pretty straightforward form, rated around the winner.
Carmenero(GER) Official explanation: jockey said gelding was denied a clear run
Alpha Tauri(USA) Official explanation: jockey said gelding ran too free

1271 HIGH-RISE MEDIAN AUCTION MAIDEN STKS 1m 2f 6y
2:50 (2:52) (Class 4) 3-Y-O **£4,533** (£1,348; £674; £336) **Stalls** Low

Form RPR
2 **1** **Zuider Zee (GER)**[15] 1046 3-9-3 0 .... RobertHavlin 3 68+
(J H M Gosden) *trckd ldrs: hdwy on outer over 2f out: rdn over 1f out: drvn and styd on wl fnl f to ld nr line* **2/1**[2]
5 **2** shd **Forsyth**[39] 815 3-9-3 0 .... PJMcDonald 10 68
(G A Swinbank) *led: rdn along over 2f out: edgd rt ent fnl f: sn drvn: hdd on line* **14/1**
5- **3** nk **Moose Moran (USA)**[186] 6629 3-9-3 0 .... TomQueally 4 67+
(H R A Cecil) *trckd ldrs on inner: hdwy 2f out: effrt and n.m.r over 1f out: rdn and kpt on ins fnl f* **1/1**[1]
0-0 **4** 1 ¾ **Sharakti (IRE)**[17] 1010 3-8-12 0 .... DeclanCannon(5) 7 64?
(A J McCabe) *trckd ldrs: hdwy 1/2-way: chsd ldr over 3f out: rdn to chal over 2f out: drvn appr fnl f and grad wknd* **100/1**
6- **5** 13 **Gay Mirage (GER)**[160] 7243 3-8-12 0 .... MichaelHills 1 33
(M A Jarvis) *in tch: pushed along 4f out: rdn over 3f out and n.d* **9/2**[3]

6 9 **On The Right Path** 3-9-3 0 .... DanielTudhope 5 20
(Paul Murphy) *stdd s: hld up: a in rr* **40/1**

0 7 2 ½ **I Got Music**[8] 1116 3-8-12 0 .... AndrewElliott 2 10
(K G Reveley) *a in rr* **100/1**

0-0 8 21 **Broctune Papa Gio**[8] 1119 3-9-0 0 .... GaryBartley(3) 6 —
(K G Reveley) *dwlt: sn chsng ldrs: hdwy and cl up 1/2-way: rdn along over 3f out and sn wknd* **100/1**

2m 18.02s (4.32) **Going Correction** +0.10s/f (Good) **8** Ran SP% **113.6**
Speed ratings (Par 100): **86,85,85,84,73 66,64,47**
toteswingers:1&2:£3.30, 1&3:£1.50, 2&3:£3.90 CSF £27.19 TOTE £3.10: £1.10, £3.30, £1.10; EX 20.80.
Owner H R H Princess Haya Of Jordan **Bred** Graf U Grafin V Stauffenberg **Trained** Newmarket, Suffolk

FOCUS
An ordinary maiden lacking any strength in depth and the pace was very steady until the final half-mile. Probably not form to be too positive about.

1272 DALBY STAND H'CAP 1m 4y
3:20 (3:20) (Class 3) (0-95,95) 4-Y-0+
£6,854 (£2,052; £1,026; £513; £256; £128) **Stalls** Low

Form RPR

15-0 1 **Harrison George (IRE)**[17] 1008 5-9-4 **95** .... PaulHanagan 3 111
(R A Fahey) *trckd ldrs: hdwy over 2f out: led 1 1/2f out and sn rdn clr: edgd lft ins fnl f: kpt on strly* **11/2**[2]

050- 2 7 **Marvo**[164] 7185 6-8-5 **82** .... SaleemGolam 8 82
(M H Tompkins) *hld up in rr: hdwy over 2f out: swtchd rt and rdn over 1f out: styd on ins fnl f: no ch w wnr* **16/1**

4-66 3 ½ **Tartan Gunna**[17] 1006 4-8-13 **90** .... JoeFanning 15 89+
(M Johnston) *s.i.s and hld up in rr: swtchd rt and hdwy 2f out: rdn over 1f out: styd on ins fnl f* **15/2**[3]

22-5 4 nk **Kiwi Bay**[17] 1006 5-8-10 **87** .... PhillipMakin 13 85+
(M Dods) *hld up in rr: hdwy over 2f out: sn swtchd wd and rdn to chse ldrs over 1f out: kpt on ins fnl f* **3/1**[1]

14-5 5 ½ **Jesse James (IRE)**[41] 769 4-8-9 **86** .... SteveDrowne 7 83
(J R Gask) *trckd ldrs on inner: hdwy over 2f out: rdn and ev ch 1 1/2f out: sn drvn and one pce ins fnl f* **8/1**

230- 6 hd **Persian Peril**[151] 7375 6-8-6 **83** .... PJMcDonald 6 79
(G A Swinbank) *midfield: hdwy 3f out: rdn along over 2f out: drvn and kpt on same pce appr fnl f* **20/1**

43-0 7 ¾ **Rainbow Mirage (IRE)**[40] 790 6-8-9 **86** .... GrahamGibbons 12 81
(E S McMahon) *hld up and bhd: hdwy over 1f out: kpt on ins fnl f: nvr nr ldrs* **14/1**

100- 8 ¾ **Medici Pearl**[185] 6675 6-8-11 **88** .... DavidAllan 9 81
(T D Easterby) *hld up in rr: hdwy 2f out: swtchd ins ent fnl f and kpt on: nvr nr ldrs* **25/1**

105- 9 1 ¼ **Handsome Falcon**[164] 7194 6-8-4 **84** ow3 .... BarryMcHugh(3) 11 74
(R A Fahey) *trckd ldrs: hdwy over 2f out: rdn wl over 1f out: drvn and wknd appr fnl f* **16/1**

613- 10 shd **Fastnet Storm (IRE)**[164] 7185 4-9-0 **91** .... MickyFenton 5 81
(T P Tate) *led: rdn along over 2f out: hdd 1 1/2f out and sn wknd* **8/1**

-316 11 ¾ **Daaweitza**[16] 1031 7-8-5 **82** ....(b) RoystonFfrench 10 70
(B Ellison) *chsd ldrs on outer: rdn along 2f out: edgd lft and n.m.r over 1f out: sn wknd* **33/1**

635- 12 1 ¾ **Ezdeyaad (USA)**[186] 6645 6-8-4 **81** oh1 .... AndrewElliott 14 65
(G A Swinbank) *sn cl up: rdn along 3f out and sn wknd* **20/1**

00-0 13 7 **Wigwam Willie (IRE)**[33] 863 8-8-10 **87** ....(tp) PaulMulrennan 2 55
(K A Ryan) *chsd ldrs: rdn along over 2f out and sn wknd* **66/1**

00-5 14 2 ½ **Moheebb (IRE)**[40] 785 6-8-13 **90** ....(b) SilvestreDeSousa 1 52
(Mrs R A Carr) *chsd ldrs on inner: rdn along over 3f out: wknd over 2f out* **25/1**

-360 15 9 **Royal Power (IRE)**[45] 743 7-8-5 **82** ow1 .... AdrianNicholls 4 24
(D Nicholls) *t.k.h: chsd ldrs: pushed along bef 1/2-way and sn btn* **12/1**

1m 44.51s (-1.39) **Going Correction** +0.10s/f (Good) **15** Ran SP% **122.1**
Speed ratings (Par 107): **110,103,102,102,101 101,100,100,98,98 97,96,89,86,77**
toteswingers:1&2:£23.10, 1&3:£8.50, 2&3:£40.80 CSF £82.33 CT £688.48 TOTE £6.20: £2.50, £6.40, £3.10; EX 97.70.
Owner P D Smith Holdings Ltd **Bred** R P Ryan **Trained** Musley Bank, N Yorks

FOCUS
A highly competitive 81-95 handicap run at a strong pace, but in the end a one-horse race. Harrision George's performance was bordering on listed class. The form is rated around the second and third.

NOTEBOOK
Harrison George(IRE), whose first handicap success at three came from a mark of just 79, defied 95 on just his second try over a mile. He burst to the front and went right away for a most impressive success. He looks likely to take a double-digit rise, so Listed races or the top handicaps like the Royal Hunt Cup beckon, with a trip to York next month also likely. Official explanation: trainer said regarding horses improvement gelding was suited by a better pace and saw to much daylight at Doncaster. (op 8-1)
Marvo progressed nicely at five, winning three times, the latest at Hamilton in August from a mark of 76. Resuming from a mark of 82, he made his effort on the outer turning in and stayed on in pleasing fashion to take second spot. He is best with give underfoot. (op 18-1 tchd 20-1)
Tartan Gunna, who fluffed his lines at the start, was another to come wide in the home straight. He was putting in some solid work at the line and a bit further suits him better. (op 8-1 tchd 17-2)
Kiwi Bay, fifth when poorly drawn in the Spring Mile, came from a long way back on the wide outside. He is 9lb higher than his last success at four, but will surely add to his record this time. (op 7-2 tchd 4-1 in a place)
Jesse James(IRE), who came in for plenty of support in the morning, was hard at work going into the final turn and never really threatened. (tchd 9-1)
Persian Peril made a satisfactory return and is better over further. (tchd 18-1)
Rainbow Mirage(IRE), who had just three outings last year, showed that he retains much of his ability. (tchd 18-1 in a place)
Medici Pearl, just 1lb higher than her last winning mark, made an encouraging return.
Fastnet Storm(IRE), a winner three times last year, took them along but seemed to blow up just inside the last. A natural front-runner, he is better suited by a mile and a quarter. (op 9-1)

1273 JAMAICAN FLIGHT H'CAP 2m 1f 216y
3:50 (3:50) (Class 5) (0-75,75) 4-Y-0+ **£3,238** (£963; £481; £240) **Stalls** Low

Form RPR

2530 1 **Dan Buoy (FR)**[19] 982 7-8-3 **57** ....(b) BillyCray(5) 3 67
(R C Guest) *mde all: sn clr: rdn along 3f out: drvn ins fnl f: hld on gamely towards fin* **20/1**[3]

-061 2 ½ **Bold Adventure**[32] 874 6-8-7 **56** .... TonyCulhane 7 65
(W J Musson) *hld up towards rr: hdwy 3f out: str run to chse wnr wl over 1f out and sn rdn: drvn ent fnl f: grad clsd on wnr tl no imp towards fin* **2/1**[1]

660- 3 18 **Luna Landing**[55] 5252 7-9-3 **66** ....(b[1]) PaulHanagan 2 56
(Jedd O'Keeffe) *chsd wnr effrt and clsd up 4f out: rdn wl over 2f out: drvn wl over 1f out and sn wknd* **7/1**[2]

-112 4 15 **Sinbad The Sailor**[25] 938 5-9-12 **75** ....(v) TedDurcan 6 48
(George Baker) *hld up in tch: effrt and sme hdwy 4f out: rdn along 3f out and n.d* **2/1**[1]

-522 5 2 **Smarties Party**[32] 874 7-8-11 **60** .... PJMcDonald 4 31
(C W Thornton) *chsd ldng pair but 20 l adrift: hdwy over 4f out: rdn 3f out: sn drvn and btn* **7/1**[2]

45-0 6 70 **Go Amwell**[58] 554 7-8-7 **56** oh4 .... LiamJones 5 —
(J R Jenkins) *hld up: effrt and sme hdwy 5f out: rdn along over 3f out: sn wknd and t.o fnl 2f* **7/1**[2]

00/6 7 29 **I Feel Fine**[26] 923 7-8-2 **56** oh11 .... PaulPickard(5) 1 —
(A Kirtley) *dwlt: a bhd: t.o fnl 2f* **100/1**

4m 3.97s (7.77) **Going Correction** +0.10s/f (Good) **7** Ran SP% **109.9**
Speed ratings (Par 103): **103,102,94,88,87 73,61**
toteswingers:1&2:£8.10, 1&3:£8.80, 2&3:£3.50 CSF £55.82 TOTE £20.90: £8.00, £1.20; EX 80.40.
Owner Bamboozelem **Bred** London Thoroughbred Services **Trained** Stainforth, S Yorks

FOCUS
The opening heat in the annual and popular Pontefract Stayers' Championship. A 56-75 handicap run at a furious pace thanks to Dan Buoy, who just hung on. The form is rated around the runner-up.
Sinbad The Sailor Official explanation: jockey said gelding was unsuited by good/soft ground

1274 PADDOCK PACKAGE H'CAP 1m 2f 6y
4:20 (4:22) (Class 2) (0-105,103) 4-Y-0+
£10,592 (£3,172; £1,586; £793; £396; £198) **Stalls** Low

Form RPR

3-30 1 **Albaqaa**[17] 1008 5-8-13 **95** .... PaulHanagan 6 104
(R A Fahey) *dwlt and towards rr: hdwy 1/2-way: rdn to chse ldrs over 2f out: drvn over 1f out: styd on to ld ins fnl f: kpt on gamely* **9/4**[1]

011- 2 ¾ **Distant Memories (IRE)**[169] 7077 4-9-7 **103** .... JamieSpencer 10 110
(T P Tate) *trckd ldrs: hdwy over 2f out: rdn to chal wl over 1f out: sn led: drvn and hdd ins fnl f: kpt on* **8/1**

1-13 3 ½ **Shadows Lengthen**[68] 401 4-8-5 **92** ....(b) JamesSullivan(5) 4 98
(M W Easterby) *led: pushed along 3f out: rdn 2f out: drvn and hdd over 1f out: ev ch tl no ex wl ins fnl f* **25/1**

640- 4 ½ **Classic Vintage (USA)**[185] 6662 4-9-0 **96** .... JimCrowley 5 101+
(Mrs A J Perrett) *trckd ldrs on inner: pushed along and sltly outpcd 3f out: swtchd rt and hdwy 2f out: n.m.r and swtchd lft ent fnl f: sn drvn and kpt on* **13/2**[2]

0/0- 5 1 ¾ **Sirgarfieldsobers (IRE)**[193] 6468 4-8-6 **88** .... RoystonFfrench 3 90
(B S Rothwell) *towards rr: hdwy 3f out: rdn along over 2f out: kpt on ins fnl f: nrst fin* **14/1**

-520 6 1 **Tartan Gigha (IRE)**[31] 885 5-9-0 **96** .... JoeFanning 2 96
(M Johnston) *prom on inner: effrt over 2f out and sn rdn: drvn: edgd rt and bmpd ent fnl f: sn one pce* **14/1**

230- 7 1 ½ **Mystery Star (IRE)**[185] 6662 5-9-2 **98** .... TedDurcan 16 95
(M H Tompkins) *hld up in rr: stdy hdwy over 2f out: rdn along wl over 1f out: kpt on ins fnl f: nrst fin* **28/1**

00-0 8 2 ¾ **Unbreak My Heart (IRE)**[56] 278 5-8-4 **89** ow1 .... BarryMcHugh(3) 11 80
(R A Fahey) *in tch: hdwy on outer 3f out: wd st and sn rdn: drvn and wknd appr fnl f* **25/1**

64-3 9 nk **Hidden Brief**[16] 1031 4-8-10 **92** .... MichaelHills 9 84
(M A Jarvis) *prom: effrt to chal over 3f out: rdn along over 2f out: drvn wl over 1f out and sn wknd* **9/1**

4600 10 shd **Reve De Nuit (USA)**[17] 1008 4-8-8 **90** ....(p) JamesDoyle 12 80
(A J McCabe) *towards rr: effrt and sme hdwy on outer over 3f out: rdn and wknd over 2f out* **22/1**

2/4- 11 7 **Ouster (GER)**[356] 1459 4-8-9 **91** ....(t) DaneO'Neill 8 67
(D R C Elsworth) *trckd ldrs: effrt over 2f out: sn rdn and wknd wl over 1f out* **15/2**[3]

014- 12 1 ¼ **Mull Of Dubai**[255] 4517 7-8-12 **94** .... AdrianNicholls 13 68
(D Nicholls) *stdd and swtchd lft s: hld up: a in rr* **28/1**

440- 13 ½ **Camps Bay (USA)**[171] 7018 6-8-6 **88** .... PaulQuinn 1 61
(D Nicholls) *dwlt: a in rr* **20/1**

0-51 14 1 **Full Speed (GER)**[26] 917 5-8-6 **88** .... PJMcDonald 15 59
(G A Swinbank) *midfield: effrt over 3f out: sn rdn along and n.d* **20/1**

0/ 15 21 **Track Record**[53] 5-8-12 **94** .... RichardKingscote 7 23
(Jonjo O'Neill) *midfield: hdwy and in tch 3f out: rdn along over 2f out and sn wknd* **40/1**

000/ 16 4 ½ **Solent (IRE)**[60] 5494 8-8-6 **88** .... GrahamGibbons 14 8
(J J Quinn) *a towards rr: bhd and eased fnl 2f* **50/1**

2m 13.22s (-0.48) **Going Correction** +0.10s/f (Good) **16** Ran SP% **123.2**
Speed ratings (Par 109): **105,104,104,103,102 101,100,98,97,97 92,91,90,89,73 69**
toteswingers:1&2:£6.70, 1&3:£13.30, 2&3:£14.40 CSF £16.63 CT £375.99 TOTE £3.30: £1.70, £1.60, £4.80, £2.10; EX 21.10.
Owner Mrs Josephine Tattersall **Bred** C Eddington And Partners **Trained** Musley Bank, N Yorks

FOCUS
A highly competitive 88-103 handicap run at a strong pace. Pretty solid form with personal bests from the first two.

NOTEBOOK
Albaqaa, who had a setback and couldn't reappear after his third in the John Smith's Cup at York in July, sat down in the stalls when only seventh in the Lincoln. Settled towards the rear, he made his effort on the outer once in line for home and really knuckled down to do just enough and give Richard Fahey his fourth winner in this event in the last six years. Better than ever, he should continue to give a good account of himself with a race at York's May meeting next on the agenda. (op 5-2)
Distant Memories(IRE) reappeared off 13lb higher than his last handicap success after finishing runner-up in a Listed race at Leopardstown on his final start at three. As usual he went down fighting and, an admirable type, he looks sure to go close again next time. (tchd 9-1)
Shadows Lengthen, who ran up a six-timer on the AW, returned to turf on a 40lb higher mark. He made a valiant attempt to make every yard and is a credit to his stable. (tchd 22-1)
Classic Vintage(USA), 6lb higher than winning over 1m4f at Goodwood in July, finished with quite a flourish and is worth noting when stepped back up in trip. (op 17-2 tchd 9-1)
Sirgarfieldsobers(IRE), a brother to Authorized, was his trainer's first runner since his return to Malton after a couple of years working at Ballydoyle. Blanketed for stalls entry, he stayed on late and there is no doubt the potential is there. (op 9-1)
Tartan Gigha(IRE), pipped in the Cambridgeshire from a 6lb lower mark, was back on turf. A slight drop in trip will play more to his strengths but the Handicapper looks to have his measure at present. (tchd 12-1)

Unbreak My Heart(IRE) lost his way after taking this from a 1lb higher mark a year ago. This was a slightly more encouraging effort. (op 28-1)

1275 PONTEFRACT-RACES.CO.UK MAIDEN FILLIES' STKS 6f
4:50 (4:51) (Class 5) 3-Y-O £2,914 (£867; £433; £216) Stalls Low

Form RPR
5- **1** **Maid In Heaven (IRE)**[153] 7326 3-9-0 0 ShaneKelly 8 78+
(W R Swinburn) *in tch on outer: hdwy over 2f out: rdn along over 1f out: n.m.r and swtchd rt ins fnl f: drvn and styd on wl to ld nr line* **4/1**[2]
2 *hd* **Fairy Shoes** 3-9-0 0 PaulHanagan 9 77
(R A Fahey) *chsd ldrs: rdn along wl over 1f out: styd on to ld ins fnl f: sn drvn: hdd and no ex nr line* **6/1**[3]
6 **3** *1 1/4* **Carrie's Magic**[47] 699 3-9-0 0 PhillipMakin 3 73
(T D Barron) *towards rr: hdwy over 2f out: rdn to chse ldrs over 1f out: kpt on wl u.p ins fnl f* **25/1**
4- **4** *hd* **Song Of Parkes**[164] 7167 3-9-0 0 DavidAllan 6 72
(E J Alston) *prom: effrt 2f out: rdn to ld over 1f out and rn green: hung lft and hdd ins fnl f: kpt on same pce* **40/1**
62-2 **5** *4* **Picnic Party**[18] 985 3-9-0 71 DaneO'Neill 1 60
(D R C Elsworth) *mde most on inner: rdn along 2f out: drvn and hdd over 1f out: grad wknd* **9/4**[1]
60-4 **6** *3* **Catbells (IRE)**[15] 1050 3-9-0 68 TomQueally 4 50
(A Bailey) *chsd ldrs on inner: rdn along over 2f out: sn wknd* **7/1**
260- **7** *2 1/2* **A Pocketful Of Rye (IRE)**[172] 7003 3-9-0 68 AdrianNicholls 11 42
(D Nicholls) *cl up on outer: rdn along 3f out: wd st and sn wknd* **9/1**
5-5 **8** *8* **Aqua Vitae (IRE)**[19] 980 3-9-0 0 JoeFanning 10 16
(M Johnston) *cl up: rdn along over 2f out: drvn wl over 1f out and sn wknd* **8/1**
0 **9** *2 1/2* **Green Secret**[34] 843 3-9-0 0 JamesDoyle 2 8
(A J McCabe) *chsd ldrs: pushed along 1/2-way: rdn over 2f out and sn wknd* **28/1**
P **Ming Meng (IRE)** 3-9-0 0 MickyFenton 7 —
(M L W Bell) *s.i.s and bhd whn lost action and p.u after 1f* **16/1**

1m 18.89s (1.99) **Going Correction** +0.10s/f (Good) 10 Ran SP% 114.3
Speed ratings (Par 95): **90,89,88,87,82 78,75,64,61,—**
toteswingers:1&2:£6.90, 1&3:£26.20, 2&3:£54.50 CSF £27.05 TOTE £5.00: £1.60, £2.90, £9.60; EX 36.40.
Owner Delightful Dozen **Bred** Mrs C Hartery **Trained** Aldbury, Herts

FOCUS
Probably just an ordinary maiden fillies' race with little to choose between the first four at the line, but some likely big improvers particularly the first two.
Green Secret Official explanation: jockey said filly had breathing problem
Ming Meng(IRE) Official explanation: jockey said filly was pulled up after losing its action

1276 ANNUAL BADGE HOLDERS H'CAP (DIV II) 6f
5:20 (5:20) (Class 5) (0-70,70) 4-Y-0+ £2,590 (£770; £385; £192) Stalls Low

Form RPR
3366 **1** **Cornus**[22] 961 8-7-13 56 (be) DeclanCannon(5) 3 71
(A J McCabe) *dwlt and in rr: hdwy into midfield 1/2-way: rdn wl over 1f out: str run ent fnl f: styd on wl to ld last 75yds* **6/1**[2]
030- **2** *1 3/4* **Mr Wolf**[178] 6847 9-8-10 67 IanBrennan(5) 13 76
(J J Quinn) *led: rdn clr wl over 1f out: drvn ins fnl f: hdd and no ex last 75yds* **11/1**
2400 **3** *3 1/2* **Bahamian Kid**[26] 924 5-9-3 69 (v) TomQueally 11 67
(R Hollinshead) *trckd ldrs: smooth hdwy over 2f out: rdn wl over 1f out: kpt on same pce ins fnl f* **20/1**
21- **4** *3/4* **Watch Amigo (IRE)**[122] 7730 4-9-3 69 ShaneKelly 9 65+
(W R Swinburn) *towards rr: hdwy on wd outside 1/2-way: rdn 2f out: kpt on ins fnl f: nrst fin* **4/1**[1]
2123 **5** *3/4* **Punching**[7] 1147 6-8-10 62 LiamKeniry 7 55
(C R Dore) *trckd ldrs: smooth hdwy 2f out: rdn wl over 1f out: drvn and wknd ent fnl f* **4/1**[1]
2453 **6** *3/4* **Dvinsky (USA)**[13] 1063 9-8-9 64 (b) MichaelStainton(3) 10 55
(P Howling) *prom: rdn to chse ldr 1/2-way: drvn along and edgd rt over 1f out: sn wknd* **8/1**[3]
00-0 **7** *2 3/4* **Bid For Gold**[16] 1030 6-8-11 70 LanaChambers(7) 6 52
(Jedd O'Keeffe) *hld up: effrt and hdwy on inner whn n.m.r wl over 1f out: kpt on same pce after* **20/1**
2223 **8** *2 3/4* **Fulford**[28] 892 5-8-7 59 (v) FrannyNorton 4 32
(M Brittain) *dwlt: a in rr* **10/1**
/50- **9** *6* **Cherri Fosfate**[301] 2998 6-9-2 68 DavidNolan 2 22
(D Carroll) *a in rr* **33/1**
414- **10** *nk* **The History Man (IRE)**[168] 7086 7-8-6 58 (p) LiamJones 8 11
(B D Leavy) *hld up: a in rr* **11/1**
220- **11** *2 1/4* **Future Gem**[179] 6824 4-9-0 66 DanielTudhope 5 12
(A Dickman) *prom on inner: rdn along 1/2-way: sn wknd* **16/1**
25-0 **12** *5* **Star Addition**[8] 1115 4-8-4 56 oh1 (b[1]) DuranFentiman 12 —
(E J Alston) *prom: rdn along wl over 2f out: sn wknd* **12/1**

1m 17.52s (0.62) **Going Correction** +0.10s/f (Good) 12 Ran SP% 117.2
Speed ratings (Par 103): **99,96,92,91,90 89,85,81,73,73 70,63**
toteswingers:1&2:£14.60, 1&3:£15.80, 2&3:£26.10 CSF £67.51 CT £1263.04 TOTE £5.60: £2.30, £4.00, £6.70; EX 74.40.
Owner Triple A Partnership **Bred** G Russell **Trained** Averham Park, Notts

FOCUS
A modest 56-70 sprint handicap run quicker than the first division. The first two have both slipped to good marks.

1277 RACING NEXT MONDAY APPRENTICE H'CAP 1m 4f 8y
5:50 (5:51) (Class 5) (0-75,73) 4-Y-0+ £2,590 (£770; £385; £192) Stalls Low

Form RPR
/50- **1** **Woody Waller**[142] 6053 5-9-1 70 LeeTopliss(3) 6 80
(J Howard Johnson) *hld up towards rr: stdy hdwy 3f out: chsd ldrs 2f out: rdn and styd on on inner to ld nr fin* **8/1**
550- **2** *1* **King Fingal (IRE)**[185] 6681 5-9-7 73 DuilioDaSilva 8 81
(J J Quinn) *hld up in tch: hdwy on outer 3f out: rdn to chal wl over 1f out and ev ch drvn and one pce ins fnl f* **4/1**[1]
020- **3** *5* **Maybe I Wont**[225] 5532 5-8-10 62 DavidKenny 7 62
(Lucinda Featherstone) *hld up in tch: hdwy 3f out: rdn to chse ldrs 2f out: ev ch over 1f out: kpt on same pce ins fnl f* **16/1**
3134 **4** *3/4* **Eseej (USA)**[12] 1077 5-9-4 73 JohnCavanagh(3) 5 72
(P W Hiatt) *led and sn clr: rdn along over 2f out: hdd wl over 1f out: sn hung rt and kpt on same pce* **7/1**[3]
20-6 **5** *2 1/4* **Tilos Gem (IRE)**[28] 897 4-9-5 72 JohnFahy 3 68
(M Johnston) *chsd clr ldr: hdwy 3f out: rdn to ld wl over 1f out: drvn and hdd ent fnl f: sn wknd* **9/2**[2]
15/- **6** *3/4* **Night Cruise (IRE)**[1109] 844 7-9-2 73 AlexEdwards(5) 4 67
(Ian Williams) *t.k.h: prom: chsd clr ldr 5f out: rdn along over 2f out: sn wknd* **4/1**[1]
-140 **7** *1 1/4* **Mehendi (IRE)**[8] 1113 4-8-3 59 (b) MatthewLawson(3) 1 51
(B Ellison) *towards rr: rdn along 3f out: sn outpcd* **14/1**
050- **8** *7* **Sgt Schultz (IRE)**[123] 7720 7-9-6 72 RyanClark 2 53
(J S Moore) *hld up in tch: hdwy 3f out: rdn along 2f out: wknd qckly 1 1/2f out: fin lame* **9/2**[2]

2m 42.26s (1.46) **Going Correction** +0.10s/f (Good)
WFA 4 from 5yo+ 1lb 8 Ran SP% 112.5
Speed ratings (Par 103): **99,98,95,94,93 92,91,87**
toteswingers:1&2:£4.90, 1&3:£14.90, 2&3:£9.90 CSF £38.66 CT £497.90 TOTE £10.60: £3.20, £1.40, £5.40; EX 50.40 Place 6 £79.80, Place 5 £37.23.
Owner W M G Black & Mrs S Johnson **Bred** P M Hicks **Trained** Billy Row, Co Durham

FOCUS
A modest 59-73 apprentice handicap and the leader seemed to go off very strong. The winner is rated in line with the best view of his old form.
Mehendi(IRE) Official explanation: jockey said gelding hung left
Sgt Schultz(IRE) Official explanation: jockey said gelding finished lame
T/Plt: £174.30 to a £1 stake. Pool: £69,313.24. 290.23 winning tickets. T/Qpdt: £75.20 to a £1 stake. Pool: £3,386.50. 33.30 winning tickets. JR

1127 YARMOUTH (L-H)
Tuesday, April 13

OFFICIAL GOING: Good (7.4)
Wind: fresh, behind Weather: bright and breezy

1278 MATTHEW CLARK MEDIAN AUCTION MAIDEN FILLIES' STKS 1m 3y
2:30 (2:31) (Class 5) 3-5-Y-O £3,497 (£1,040; £520; £259) Stalls High

Form RPR
1 **I'm A Dreamer (IRE)** 3-8-12 0 PatCosgrave 14 74+
(D M Simcock) *s.i.s: hld up towards rr: hdwy into midfield 1/2-way: rdn and wanting to hang lft over 1f out: swtchd rt ins fnl f: r.o strly fnl 100yds to ld last stride* **14/1**
0- **2** *shd* **Towbaat**[175] 6920 3-8-12 0 FrankieDettori 2 74
(M A Jarvis) *in tch: rdn to chse ldrs wl over 1f out: drvn and r.o fnl f to ld fnl 50yds: hdd last stride* **9/2**[1]
3 *3/4* **Law Of The Range** 3-8-12 0 KirstyMilczarek 10 72
(M Botti) *hld up in tch: rdn and effrt wl over 1f out: r.o fnl f: sltly hmpd fnl 75yds: kpt on wl towards fin* **22/1**
64- **4** *1* **Athenian Garden (USA)**[173] 6965 3-8-12 0 EddieAhern 9 70+
(H R A Cecil) *hld up in tch midfield: hdwy over 3f out: led 2f out: sn rdn: kpt on tl hdd fnl 50yds: fdd towards fin* **9/2**[1]
36- **5** *3/4* **Granite Girl**[175] 6920 3-8-12 0 EddieCreighton 13 68
(P J McBride) *hld up towards rr on stands' side of field: hdwy but hanging lft fr over 2f out: chsd ldrs on far side of field and rdn ins fnl f: kpt on: nt rch ldrs* **11/1**
42 **6** *3/4* **Nadinska**[43] 754 3-8-12 0 KierenFallon 4 67
(M R Channon) *chsd ldrs: pressed ldr and rdn wl over 1f out: ev ch after tl wknd fnl 75yds* **10/1**
55- **7** *4* **Alsufooh (USA)**[164] 7167 3-8-12 0 RichardHills 5 57
(M Johnston) *led tl 2f out: sn rdn: wknd ent fnl f* **16/1**
02- **8** *nk* **Bonnie Brae**[173] 6962 3-8-12 0 ChrisCatlin 8 57
(G G Margarson) *chsd ldrs: rdn and unable qck 2f out: wknd ent fnl f* **10/1**
4- **9** *3/4* **Top Tigress**[158] 7276 3-8-12 0 RyanMoore 11 55
(Sir Michael Stoute) *in tch in midfield: pushed along over 3f out: struggling over 2f out: no threat to ldrs after* **13/2**[2]
0-5 **10** *shd* **Weeping Willow (IRE)**[18] 985 3-8-12 0 WilliamBuick 12 55
(J H M Gosden) *in tch in midfield: lost pl and rdn 3f out: hung lft and btn over 2f out* **15/2**[3]
0- **11** *nk* **Blue Again**[138] 7537 3-8-12 0 SebSanders 16 54
(W R Swinburn) *stdd s: hld up towards rr: hdwy into midfield 1/2-way: rdn to chse ldrs ent fnl 2f: wknd qckly over 1f out* **33/1**
0-0 **12** *1* **Fasette**[8] 1127 3-8-12 0 JimmyQuinn 6 52
(M H Tompkins) *chsd ldrs tl 1/2-way: sn lost pl: no ch fnl 2f* **22/1**
0-6 **13** *nk* **Auburn Place**[18] 985 3-8-12 0 HayleyTurner 3 51
(E F Vaughan) *in tch in midfield: rdn over 2f out: wkng whn stmbld 2f out: no ch after* **50/1**
14 *3/4* **Asterales** 3-8-12 0 StevieDonohoe 7 49
(W J Musson) *s.i.s: a bhd* **100/1**
0 **15** *15* **Yehonala (USA)**[18] 985 3-8-12 0 RobertWinston 15 15
(J R Best) *t.k.h: in tch: rdn and wknd qckly 3f out: wl bhd fnl f* **100/1**
16 *2* **Red Smokey (IRE)** 3-8-7 0 AshleyMorgan(5) 1 10
(M H Tompkins) *in tch in midfield tl 1/2-way: sn bhd* **66/1**

1m 37.91s (-2.69) **Going Correction** -0.50s/f (Hard) 16 Ran SP% 117.6
Speed ratings (Par 100): **93,92,92,91,90 89,85,85,84,84 84,83,82,82,67 65**
toteswingers:1&2:£26.20, 1&3:£90.40, 2&3:£34.40 CSF £69.82 TOTE £23.50: £6.40, £1.40, £10.10; EX 175.10 TRIFECTA Not won..
Owner Tick Tock Partnership **Bred** Sean Murphy **Trained** Newmarket, Suffolk

FOCUS
An ordinary fillies' maiden, though it will no doubt produce winners, particularly in handicaps.

1279 LINDLEY CATERING - OFFICIAL RACECOURSE CATERERS H'CAP 7f 3y
3:00 (3:01) (Class 4) (0-85,85) 3-Y-O £4,533 (£1,348; £674; £336) Stalls High

Form RPR
221- **1** **Horseradish**[180] 6796 3-8-9 76 HayleyTurner 2 90
(M L W Bell) *chsd ldrs: wnt 2nd and rdn over 1f out: drvn to ld ins fnl f: r.o wl* **6/1**[3]
21- **2** *nk* **Rule Of Nature**[175] 6922 3-8-8 75 RyanMoore 7 88
(Sir Michael Stoute) *led: rdn wl over 1f out: hdd ins fnl f: kpt on but a jst hld after* **5/2**[2]
510- **3** *2* **Subtefuge**[171] 7013 3-8-3 77 CharlesEddery(7) 8 85
(H R A Cecil) *in tch in midfield: effrt 3f out: rdn to chse ldr 2f out tl over 1f out: styd pressing ldng pair tl no ex fnl 100yds* **10/1**
1126 **4** *3 1/2* **Marosh (FR)**[17] 1018 3-8-7 74 EddieAhern 12 72
(R M H Cowell) *hld up in tch in rr: hdwy 2f out: hanging bdly lft after: wnt modest 4th ins fnl f: nvr gng pce to threaten ldrs* **28/1**
612- **5** *3 1/4* **Fly Silca Fly (IRE)**[235] 5208 3-9-2 83 KierenFallon 3 73
(M R Channon) *chsd ldrs: rdn ent fnl 2f: drvn and btn over 1f out: no ch fnl f* **20/1**
60-5 **6** *2 1/2* **Tewin Wood**[10] 1086 3-7-13 73 NatashaEaton(7) 6 56
(A Bailey) *chsd ldr tl 2f out: wknd u.p over 1f out: no ch w ldrs fnl f* **20/1**

310- **7** ½ **Excellent Guest**[238] 5136 3-8-13 **80** .... SebSanders 10 61
(G G Margarson) *hld up in tch in rr: hdwy 1/2-way: in tch and rdn 2f out: sn outpcd and wl btn over 1f out* **16/1**

4-32 **8** ¾ **Tenacestream (CAN)**[15] 1045 3-8-9 **76** .... RobertWinston 11 55
(J R Best) *in tch in midfield: rdn over 3f out: wl btn whn carried lft and sltly hmpd over 1f out* **12/1**

310- **9** 2¼ **Abriachan**[219] 5692 3-8-11 **78** .... JerryO'Dwyer 9 51
(M G Quinlan) *hld up in tch towards rr: rdn and no hdwy over 2f out: wl btn fnl 2f* **40/1**

113- **10** ½ **Imjin River (IRE)**[138] 7536 3-8-5 **77** .... AshleyMorgan(5) 4 49
(M H Tompkins) *hld up in tch in rr: rdn and effrt over 2f out: sn struggling: n.d fnl 2f* **28/1**

21 **11** 3 **Al Farahidi (USA)**[24] 950 3-9-4 **85** .... FrankieDettori 1 49
(M Johnston) *dwlt: in tch in midfield: rdn and btn over 2f out: eased fnl f* **9/4**[1]

20-4 **12** 14 **Texan Star (IRE)**[20] 971 3-8-13 **80** .... WilliamBuick 5 6
(J H M Gosden) *in tch in midfield: rdn and losing pl 4f out: wl bhd and eased fr over 1f out: t.o* **20/1**

1m 23.04s (-3.56) **Going Correction** -0.50s/f (Hard) **12** Ran SP% **119.9**
Speed ratings (Par 100): **100,99,97,93,89 86,86,85,82,82 78,62**
toteswingers:1&2:£4.40, 1&3:£11.40, 2&3:£9.90 CSF £19.46 CT £154.70 TOTE £5.50: £1.40, £2.10, £3.20; EX 30.90 Trifecta £201.00 Part won. Pool: £271.69 - 0.64 winning units..
Owner Mrs G Rowland-Clark **Bred** Mrs F A Veasey **Trained** Newmarket, Suffolk

FOCUS
No more than a fair 3-y-o handicap.
Marosh(FR) Official explanation: jockey said gelding hung left
Tenacestream(CAN) Official explanation: trainer said colt was unsuited by the good ground
Al Farahidi(USA) Official explanation: jockey said colt lost its action
Texan Star(IRE) Official explanation: jockey said colt lost its action

1280 MATTHEW CLARKE H'CAP 6f 3y
3:30 (3:30) (Class 5) (0-70,70) 3-Y-O **£3,238** (£963; £481; £240) **Stalls** High

Form RPR

03-0 **1** **Vanilla Loan (IRE)**[27] 906 3-8-8 **60** .... WilliamBuick 1 73+
(M Botti) *dwlt: travelled strly and sn trcking ldrs: chal 2f out: rdn to ld over 1f out: r.o strly to draw wl clr fnl 150yds* **5/1**[3]

050- **2** 4½ **Danzoe (IRE)**[184] 6693 3-9-2 **68** .... TomMcLaughlin 9 67
(Mrs C A Dunnett) *in tch: rdn and effrt over 2f out: led wl over 1f out: sn hdd and hung lft: no ch w wnr ins fnl f* **20/1**

00-1 **3** hd **Sir Louis**[8] 1118 3-8-9 **61** 6ex .... TonyHamilton 6 59
(R A Fahey) *led: rdn and hdd wl over 1f out: stl disputing 2nd but outpcd by wnr whn bmpd over 1f out: styd on same pce after* **15/8**[1]

205- **4** 2¾ **Young Simon**[160] 7234 3-9-0 **66** .... SebSanders 3 56
(G G Margarson) *w ldr: rdn ent fnl 2f: struggling whn bmpd over 1f out: wl hld fnl f* **16/1**

2261 **5** 2¾ **Knightfire (IRE)**[18] 991 3-9-4 **70** ....(t) RyanMoore 5 51
(W R Swinburn) *in tch towards rr: rdn and unable qck over 3f out: outpcd over 2f out: no threat to ldrs after: plugged on fnl f* **3/1**[2]

120- **6** 2¾ **Stef And Stelio**[155] 7320 3-9-0 **66** ....(b) FrankieDettori 2 38
(G A Butler) *chsd ldrs: rdn and wl outpcd 2f out: no ch fnl f* **13/2**

000- **7** 2½ **Ellen Vannin (IRE)**[176] 6905 3-8-6 **58** .... HayleyTurner 7 22
(Eve Johnson Houghton) *in tch in rr: rdn ent fnl 2f: sn btn* **20/1**

050- **8** nk **Singin' The Blues**[157] 7288 3-8-13 **65** .... LukeMorris 4 28
(J M P Eustace) *in tch towards rr: rdn and lost tch over 2f out* **20/1**

6000 **9** 4 **Shawkantango**[4] 1205 3-8-4 **56** oh6 .... JimmyQuinn 8 6
(D Shaw) *dwlt: in tch in rr: reminder over 2f out: sn toiling and wl btn fnl 2f* **33/1**

1m 11.39s (-3.01) **Going Correction** -0.50s/f (Hard) **9** Ran SP% **112.9**
Speed ratings (Par 98): **100,94,93,90,86 82,79,79,73**
toteswingers:1&2:£14.00, 1&3:£4.60, 2&3:£9.60 CSF £98.01 CT £252.41 TOTE £6.60: £2.30, £4.90, £1.80; EX 71.90 Trifecta £319.40 Part won. Pool: £431.66 - 0.10 winning units..
Owner Noel O'Callaghan **Bred** Mountarmstrong Stud **Trained** Newmarket, Suffolk

FOCUS
A moderate 3-y-o sprint handicap.

1281 LINDLEY CATERING H'CAP 5f 43y
4:00 (4:01) (Class 3) (0-90,88) 3-Y-O
£7,851 (£2,351; £1,175; £588; £293; £147) **Stalls** High

Form RPR

150- **1** **Monsieur Joe (IRE)**[185] 6660 3-9-7 **88** .... RyanMoore 1 92
(W R Swinburn) *dwlt: pushed along early: in tch in last trio: rdn over 2f out: chsd ldrs and drvn 1f out: str run fnl 100yds to ld on post* **3/1**[1]

1-33 **2** nse **Maldon Prom (IRE)**[26] 919 3-8-6 **73** ....(v) EddieAhern 4 76
(C A Dwyer) *chsd ldrs: rdn and hld hd high wl over 1f out: ev ch 1f out: led ins fnl f: hdd on post* **7/1**

120- **3** 1½ **Yurituni**[185] 6660 3-9-3 **84** .... FrankieDettori 8 82
(Eve Johnson Houghton) *in tch: rdn and effrt wl over 1f out: chsd ldrs 1f out: keeping on but hld whn nt clr run nr fin* **6/1**

46-2 **4** hd **Leleyf (IRE)**[7] 1140 3-8-7 **74** .... KierenFallon 3 71
(M R Channon) *led: edgd rt ent fnl 2f: rdn wl over 1f out: hdd ins fnl f: wknd towards fin* **5/1**

34-4 **5** ½ **Jack My Boy (IRE)**[10] 1086 3-8-6 **78** .... AndrewHeffernan(5) 5 73+
(P D Evans) *chsd ldr tl over 1f out: unable qck and n.m.r ent fnl f: one pce after* **9/2**[3]

5311 **6** 5 **Silver Linnet (IRE)**[7] 1140 3-8-7 **74** 6ex ....(b) WilliamBuick 7 51
(M G Quinlan) *chsd ldrs: rdn and unable qck 2f out: wknd u.p over 1f out* **8/1**

3-11 **7** 2¼ **Fair Passion**[26] 919 3-8-6 **73** .... JimmyQuinn 9 42
(D Shaw) *restless in stalls: a bhd: hung lft and wl btn over 1f out* **4/1**[2]

53-1 **8** 1¾ **The Strig**[72] 362 3-8-9 **79** .... WilliamCarson(3) 6 42
(S C Williams) *stdd s: hld up in last: shkn up 2f out: no rspnse and sn wl btn* **16/1**

60.96 secs (-1.74) **Going Correction** -0.50s/f (Hard) **8** Ran SP% **115.9**
Speed ratings (Par 102): **89,88,86,86,85 77,73,71**
toteswingers:1&2:£11.80, 1&3:£4.60, 2&3:£12.50 CSF £64.35 CT £344.38 TOTE £4.00: £1.40, £5.30, £3.20; EX 54.90 TRIFECTA Not won..
Owner Mrs Helen Checkley **Bred** Nicola And Eleanor Kent **Trained** Aldbury, Herts

FOCUS
A decent little sprint.

NOTEBOOK
Monsieur Joe(IRE) just got up in time. A progressive juvenile who finished in mid-division in the Cornwallis on his final outing, he needed to have improved to win off a mark of 88 (10lb above his last winning mark), and he clearly has. He will presumably take his chance in a good handicap now, possibly at Newmarket's Guineas meeting, and he is expected to improve for 6f. (op 5-1)
Maldon Prom(IRE), in fair form on the AW and receiving 15lb from the winner, had the visor back on but carried his head a bit high in the finish, and would have won if he had given his rider more assistance. He can continue to pay his way. (op 16-1)
Yurituni, twice a winner at two (11lb higher than the last one here) and behind the winner in the Cornwallis, was a bit short of room close home, but it didn't affect her finishing position. This was a decent effort. (op 8-1)
Leleyf(IRE), runner-up to Silver Linnet at Ffos Las on her reappearance, looked to be going well when brought to the stands' rail, but could find no extra late on. (op 6-1 tchd 9-2)
Jack My Boy(IRE) was not helped by the drop in trip. (tchd 4-1)
Silver Linnet(IRE), chasing the hat-trick, couldn't lead and she failed to reproduce her best form. (op 13-2)
Fair Passion, making her turf debut, failed to live up to expectations with the latter stopping quickly and hanging. (tchd 7-2)

1282 LINDLEYCATERING.CO.UK H'CAP 1m 2f 21y
4:30 (4:30) (Class 3) (0-90,90) 4-Y-O+
£8,723 (£2,612; £1,306; £653; £326; £163) **Stalls** Low

Form RPR

400- **1** **Bugaku**[185] 6681 5-8-8 **80** .... RyanMoore 5 87
(Sir Michael Stoute) *chsd ldr tl 4f out: rdn to press ldr wl over 1f out: led over 1f out: kpt on wl* **10/3**[1]

510/ **2** ¾ **Managua**[641] 3920 4-8-8 **80** .... KierenFallon 1 86
(M R Channon) *t.k.h: chsd ldrs: wnt 2nd 4f out: led gng wl jst over 2f out: rdn wl over 1f out: hdd over 1f out: kpt on but a hld ins fnl f* **10/1**

163- **3** ½ **Alcalde**[171] 7018 4-9-3 **89** .... FrankieDettori 2 94
(M Johnston) *led at stdy gallop: qckn pce 4f out: rdn and hdd jst over 2f out: edgd rt and kpt on same pce fnl f* **7/2**[2]

0-42 **4** ½ **Hollow Green (IRE)**[17] 1011 4-8-0 **77** .... AndrewHeffernan(5) 9 81
(P D Evans) *stdd s: hld up in tch: effrt u.p on inner 3f out: kpt on one pce fnl f* **6/1**

5041 **5** 1 **Raptor (GER)**[8] 1133 7-8-9 **81** 6ex .... JamieMackay 6 83
(M E Rimmer) *hld up in tch in last trio: rdn and effrt 2f out: no real imp and keeping on same pce whn swtchd rt ins fnl f* **5/1**[3]

222- **6** nk **Omokoroa (IRE)**[183] 6734 4-8-9 **81** .... JimmyQuinn 3 82
(M H Tompkins) *t.k.h: hld up in tch: shkn up and outpcd 2f out: kpt on ins fnl f: nvr gng pce to threaten ldrs* **7/1**

00-0 **7** 1½ **Lang Shining (IRE)**[17] 1008 6-9-4 **90** .... EddieAhern 4 88
(J A Osborne) *stdd s: hld up in tch in last: shkn up and effrt 2f out: rdn ent fnl f: no imp and hld whn hmpd ins fnl f* **11/1**

402- **8** 11 **Manshoor (IRE)**[291] 3361 5-8-5 **77** .... WilliamBuick 8 53
(Mrs L Wadham) *t.k.h: chsd ldrs: rdn over 2f out: drvn and btn over 1f out: eased ins fnl f* **11/1**

2m 10.4s (-0.10) **Going Correction** +0.10s/f (Good) **8** Ran SP% **114.5**
Speed ratings (Par 107): **104,103,103,102,101 101,100,91**
toteswingers:1&2:£12.10, 1&3:£4.60, 2&3:£4.90 CSF £36.63 CT £123.11 TOTE £4.50: £1.90, £3.30, £1.70; EX 89.50 Trifecta £138.20 Part won. Pool: £186.78 - 0.44 winning units..
Owner Mrs Denis Haynes **Bred** Wretham Stud **Trained** Newmarket, Suffolk

FOCUS
A competitive handicap.

NOTEBOOK
Bugaku, lightly raced for a horse of his age, looked of interest having come down 5lb in the weights from last year, with improvement anticipated this year. He took a while to get going, but always looked the winner having gone on over 1f out and may well have more to offer as he goes back up in trip. (op 4-1)
Managua hadn't been seen since beating only one home in a Group 2 at Newmarket as a juvenile. He travelled strongly on this step up in trip, but Fallon seemed keen not to give him a hard time and accepted the situation once the pair were headed. He should improve considerably for this and will be of obvious interest next time. (op 18-1 tchd 20-1)
Alcalde boxed on best he could having been headed, but shall remain vulnerable off this mark unless improving. (op 3-1)
Hollow Green(IRE), a good second at Doncaster, ran well considering softer ground is ideal. (op 9-2)
Raptor(GER), penalised for his recent C&D success, stilled looked well treated on old form but didn't prove as effective on this quicker ground. He would appreciated a stronger gallop. (op 13-2 tchd 7-1)
Omokoroa(IRE) lacked the pace to get involved and is another who wouldn't have been suited by the early lack of pace. (op 11-1)
Lang Shining(IRE) travelled well in behind runners, but found little once asked for his effort. (op 9-1 tchd 17-2)

1283 M R KING H'CAP 2m
5:00 (5:00) (Class 5) (0-70,67) 4-Y-O+ **£3,238** (£963; £481; £240) **Stalls** High

Form RPR

5133 **1** **Broughtons Point**[15] 1053 4-8-5 **51** .... JamieMackay 1 63+
(W J Musson) *stdd s: hld up in last: hdwy 3f out: swtchd rt wl over 1f out: led gng wl over 1f out: pushed clr ins fnl f: comf* **12/1**

530- **2** 1½ **Any Given Moment (IRE)**[209] 5990 4-8-6 **52** .... WilliamBuick 10 58+
(D M Simcock) *sn chsng ldr tl led 4f out: rdn and hdd over 2f out: outpcd by ldng pair ent fnl f: kpt on again fnl 100yds to go 2nd again nr fin* **10/3**[1]

1604 **3** nk **Purely By Chance**[19] 982 5-8-5 **52** ....(b) SimonPearce(5) 2 58
(J Pearce) *hld up towards rr: hdwy 1/2-way: chsd ldrs 6f out: wnt 2nd 4f out: rdn to ld over 2f out tl over 1f out: one pce and btn fnl f: lost 2nd nr fin* **10/1**

056- **4** 3 **Astroleo**[153] 7336 4-8-2 **48** oh2 .... JimmyQuinn 7 50
(M H Tompkins) *in tch in midfield: pushed and hdwy to chse ldrs 4f out: rdn ent fnl 2f: styd on one pce after* **8/1**

5-43 **5** 5 **Calzaghe (IRE)**[6] 1160 6-9-11 **67** .... RyanMoore 9 63
(Jim Best) *hld up in last trio: rdn and no prog 3f out: kpt on ins fnl f: nvr trbld ldrs* **7/2**[2]

-400 **6** 2 **Dovedon Earl**[19] 983 4-8-7 **53** .... ChrisCatlin 5 47
(T Keddy) *hld up towards rr: gd hdwy to chse ldrs 4f out: rdn over 2f out: wknd u.p over 1f out* **22/1**

3-04 **7** 2½ **Sunny Spells**[6] 1160 5-9-3 **62** .... WilliamCarson(3) 6 53
(S C Williams) *chsd ldrs: rdn and struggling 3f out: wl btn fnl 2f* **6/1**[3]

6313 **8** ½ **Delorain (IRE)**[8] 1113 7-7-7 **49** ow1 ....(vt) JerryO'Dwyer 4 39
(W B Stone) *in tch in midfield: lost pl and bhd whn nt clr run on inner ent fnl 3f: no ch after* **13/2**

0-06 **9** 1¾ **Royal Premier (IRE)**[34] 842 7-8-6 **48** oh3 ....(v) CathyGannon 11 36
(H J Collingridge) *chsd ldrs: rdn and unable qck 3f out: wknd over 2f out: wl btn fnl f* **25/1**

0432 **10** 14 **Davana**[13] 1071 4-7-13 **48** .... KellyHarrison(3) 3 19
(W J H Ratcliffe) *hld up in last trio: rdn and lost tch over 2f out: eased ins fnl f* **20/1**

040- **11** 10 **Present**[147] 7124 6-8-3 **48** oh3 .... Louis-PhilippeBeuzelin(3) 8 7
(Mrs C A Dunnett) *led tl 4f out: sn struggling and lost pl u.p: t.o and eased ins fnl f* **50/1**

060- **12** *44* **Siena**[397] 813 5-8-6 48 oh3 .... LukeMorris 12 —
(Mrs C A Dunnett) *in tch tl rdn and wknd qckly over 3f out: wl t.o fnl 2f*
66/1

3m 33.95s (-0.65) **Going Correction** +0.10s/f (Good)
WFA 4 from 5yo+ 4lb **12** Ran SP% **117.2**
Speed ratings (Par 103): **105,104,104,102,100 99,97,97,96,89 84,62**
toteswingers:1&2:£11.20, 1&3:£27.40, 2&3:£8.70 CSF £48.55 CT £426.32 TOTE £9.80: £4.00, £2.60, £4.10; EX 52.30 TRIFECTA Not won. Place 6 £75.34, Place 5 £22.76.
Owner Broughton Thermal Insulation **Bred** Broughton Bloodstock **Trained** Newmarket, Suffolk

FOCUS
A moderate staying handicap.
T/Jkpt: Not won. T/Plt: £207.70 to a £1 stake. Pool: £76,919.55. 270.27 winning tickets. T/Qpdt: £20.10 to a £1 stake. Pool: £5,738.70. 210.38 winning tickets. SP

BEVERLEY (R-H)
Wednesday, April 14

OFFICIAL GOING: Good (7.7)
Wind: Fresh, across Weather: Overcast and cold

1292 RACING UK ON SKY 432 MAIDEN AUCTION STKS (DIV I) 5f
1:30 (1:34) (Class 5) 2-Y-O **£2,590** (£770; £385; £192) **Stalls** High

Form RPR

2 **1** **Mappin Time (IRE)**[14] 1065 2-9-2 0 .... DavidAllan 2 72
(T D Easterby) *cl up: effrt 2f out: rdn to ld 1 1/2f out: drvn ins fnl f: hld on gamely* **7/4**[1]

2 *shd* **Lovat Lane** 2-8-4 0 .... SilvestreDeSousa 7 60
(Eve Johnson Houghton) *sn chsng ldrs: effrt and n.m.r whn swtchd lft 2f out: sn rdn and chal over 1f out: drvn and ev ch ins fnl f: no ex nr line* **14/1**

3 *3/4* **Saltergate** 2-8-9 0 .... AndrewElliott 6 62+
(N Tinkler) *dwlt and towards rr: rdn along 1/2-way: hdwy on outer wl over 1f out: styd on strly ins fnl f: nrst fin* **33/1**

4 *1* **Glenns Princess** 2-8-4 0 .... PaulHanagan 10 53
(R A Fahey) *cl up on inner: rdn along and sltly outpcd 1/2-way: kpt on u.p appr fnl f* **4/1**[3]

3 **5** *1* **Daas Rite (IRE)**[14] 1066 2-8-9 0 .... PaulMulrennan 5 56
(K A Ryan) *chsd ldrs: hdwy whn n.m.r 2f out: sn rdn and hung rt over 1f out: kpt on same pce* **11/4**[2]

6 *5* **Dubai Celebration** 2-8-11 0 .... PatrickDonaghy(5) 1 44
(Jedd O'Keeffe) *cl up on outer: effrt to chal over 2f out: sn rdn and ev ch tl hung lft and wknd over 1f out* **7/1**

7 *1 3/4* **Chester Deelyte (IRE)** 2-8-5 0 ow1 .... RoystonFfrench 9 26
(Mrs L Williamson) *sn led: pushed along and edgd rt 2f out: sn rdn and hdd 1 1/2f out: wknd ent fnl f* **20/1**

8 *2 1/2* **Phair Winter** 2-8-4 0 .... GrahamGibbons 3 16+
(A D Brown) *s.i.s: a bhd* **33/1**

64.94 secs (1.44) **Going Correction** -0.15s/f (Firm) **8** Ran SP% **112.8**
Speed ratings (Par 92): **82,81,80,79,77 69,66,62**
toteswingers: 1&2 £7.60, 1&3 £12.00, 2&3 £38.80 CSF £26.73 TOTE £1.90: £1.02, £4.10, £10.30; EX 29.00.
Owner P Baillie **Bred** J Jamgotchian **Trained** Great Habton, N Yorks
■ Stewards' Enquiry : Silvestre De Sousa two-day ban: careless riding (Apr 28-29)

NOTEBOOK
Mappin Time(IRE), a son of 2002 Breeders' Cup Sprint winner Orientate, put his previous experience to good use to get off the mark at the second time of asking. Nicely clear of the rest when runner-up at Southwell on his debut, he built on that, clinging on at the finish from a strong challenge from Lovat Lane. Apparently a lazy type, there might be a bit more to come. (op 9-4)
Lovat Lane was weak in the betting beforehand, but is a half-sister to Judd Street and shaped with a deal of promise on her debut. She didn't enjoy the clearest of runs, showed signs of greenness, and shouldn't be long in going one better. (op 9-1)
Saltergate, an already gelded half-brother to four winners, was clueless through the first half of the race, but saw his race out really well once the penny dropped. He should come on quite a bit for this experience. (tchd 40-1)
Glenns Princess, a cheap purchase bred to be a sprinter, was representing a stable in form but wasn't up to the task on her debut. She'll need to improve for this run to get off the mark. (op 11-4)
Daas Rite(IRE), who didn't run badly on his Fibresand debut, struggled a little with the early pace and a longer trip is likely to suit him in time. (op 7-2 tchd 4-1)
Dubai Celebration had the worst of the draw but was prominent towards the outer from the start and ran a bit better than his finishing position suggests. (op 15-2 tchd 6-1)

1293 WELCOME BACK TO BEVERLEY (S) STKS 1m 100y
2:00 (2:00) (Class 5) 3-Y-O+ **£2,590** (£770; £385; £192) **Stalls** High

Form RPR

50-0 **1** **Dabbers Ridge (IRE)**[9] 1115 8-9-10 66 .... GaryBartley(3) 3 73
(I W McInnes) *switcehd rt s and hld up in rr: hdwy on wd outside 2f out: rdn over 1f out: styd on strly ins fnl f to ld nr fin* **25/1**

0-36 **2** *hd* **Kenswick**[16] 1048 3-8-1 58 .... (b[1]) FrannyNorton 11 58
(Pat Eddery) *hld up: hdwy over 3f out: effrt and edgd lft 2f out: rdn over 1f out: styd on to ld ins fnl f: sn drvn: hdd and no ex nr fin* **14/1**

5013 **3** *2 1/2* **Royal Dignitary (USA)**[7] 1149 10-9-13 71 .... AdrianNicholls 4 67
(D Nicholls) *led: rdn along 2f out: drvn ent fnl f: sn hdd and kpt on same pce* **7/2**[1]

000- **4** *1/2* **Rowan Lodge (IRE)**[121] 7755 8-9-13 60 .... (b) PJMcDonald 13 66
(Ollie Pears) *hld up in midfield: smooth hdwy and in tch over 2f out: effrt and carried sltly lft wl over 1f out: sn rdn: swtchd rt and styd on ins fnl f: nrst fin* **4/1**[2]

103- **5** *1 1/2* **Whipma Whopma Gate (IRE)**[173] 6999 5-9-1 55 .... (b) NeilFarley(7) 8 57
(D Carroll) *cl up: rdn along over 2f out and ev ch tl drvn and wknd appr fnl f* **12/1**

1202 **6** *1 1/4* **Castle Myth (USA)**[9] 1114 4-9-6 53 .... DaleSwift(7) 9 59
(B Ellison) *chsd ldrs: rdn along over 2f out: wknd wl over 1f out* **20/1**

6235 **7** *2 1/4* **Island Chief**[7] 1149 4-9-8 69 .... (p) AmyRyan(5) 1 54
(K A Ryan) *midfield on outer: pushed along and sltly outpcd over 3f out: rdn 2f out and nvr rchd ldrs* **12/1**

-440 **8** *nk* **Mydy Easy (USA)**[10] 1098 4-9-7 64 .... TonyCulhane 6 47
(P T Midgley) *hld up: hdwy and in tch 3f out: sn rdn and btn* **40/1**

2603 **9** *4 1/2* **The Graig**[26] 939 6-9-13 49 .... (bt) GrahamGibbons 5 43
(J R Holt) *chsd ldrs: rdn along wl over 2f out: sn wknd* **33/1**

40-4 **10** *1/2* **West Kirk**[7] 1171 4-9-7 71 .... J-PGuillambert 10 41
(W Jarvis) *trckd ldrs on inner: rdn along over 2f out and sn wknd* **5/1**[3]

0014 **11** *1/2* **Rub Of The Relic (IRE)**[27] 918 5-9-8 58 .... (v) PaulPickard(5) 12 41
(P T Midgley) *a towards rr* **10/1**

400- **12** *2 3/4* **Lady Florence**[9] 7840 5-9-8 60 .... RoystonFfrench 14 29
(A B Coogan) *dwlt: a in rr* **14/1**

-405 **13** *28* **Kaballero (GER)**[7] 1172 9-9-7 57 .... PaulHanagan 7 —
(S Gollings) *prom: rdn along 3f out: wknd over 2f out* **20/1**

1m 46.3s (-1.30) **Going Correction** -0.15s/f (Firm)
WFA 3 from 4yo+ 15lb **13** Ran SP% **115.4**
Speed ratings (Par 103): **100,99,97,96,95 94,91,91,87,86 86,83,55**
toteswingers: 1&2 £78.30, 1&3 £22.90, 2&3 £20.90 CSF £311.63 TOTE £35.10: £7.30, £3.40, £1.90; EX 317.60.There was no bid for the winner.
Owner G Parkinson **Bred** Franco Castelfranci **Trained** Catwick, E Yorks

FOCUS
An ordinary seller in which the early pace proved sufficiently strong for the winner to come from last to score. The form is rated around the fourth and fifth.
West Kirk Official explanation: jockey said gelding had no more to give
Rub Of The Relic(IRE) Official explanation: jockey said gelding suffered interference at start
Lady Florence Official explanation: jockey said mare never travelled
Kaballero(GER) Official explanation: trainer's rep said gelding finished distressed

1294 RACING UK ON SKY 432 MAIDEN AUCTION STKS (DIV II) 5f
2:35 (2:39) (Class 5) 2-Y-O **£2,590** (£770; £385; £192) **Stalls** High

Form RPR

1 **Above The Stars** 2-8-8 0 .... PaulHanagan 4 79+
(R A Fahey) *cl up: led over 1f out: rdn and edgd lft ins fnl f: kpt on wl* **3/1**[1]

2 *1/2* **Whisper Louise (IRE)** 2-8-6 0 .... SilvestreDeSousa 8 75+
(Mrs P Sly) *in rr: swtchd outside 1/2-way: hdwy wl over 1f out: sn rdn and styd on to chal ins fnl f: no ex last 50yds* **13/2**[3]

4 **3** *2* **Master Macho (IRE)**[18] 1017 2-8-9 0 .... SamHitchcott 7 71
(M R Channon) *led: rdn along 2f out: drvn and hdd over 1f out: kpt on same pce ins fnl f* **3/1**[1]

0 **4** *6* **Roodee Queen**[14] 1065 2-8-3 0 .... BarryMcHugh(3) 6 46
(Patrick Morris) *in tch: hdwy to chse ldrs 2f out: rdn over 1f out and sn no imp* **18/1**

5 *1/2* **Minch Man** 2-8-9 0 .... AndrewElliott 3 48+
(J R Weymes) *in tch: rdn along and outpcd 1/2-way: swtchd rt wl over 1f out: kpt on u.p ins fnl f* **16/1**

6 *3/4* **Surely This Time (IRE)** 2-8-13 0 .... RichardMullen 10 49+
(K A Ryan) *trckd ldrs: effrt on inner and n.m.r 2f out: sn rdn and one pce* **11/2**[2]

4 **7** *2 1/4* **Mini Bon Bon**[4] 1223 2-8-4 0 .... JamieMackay 1 32
(A Bailey) *t.k.h: cl up: rdn along 2f out: sn wknd* **9/1**

8 *3 1/4* **Anddante (IRE)** 2-9-2 0 .... DavidAllan 9 32
(T D Easterby) *trckd ldrs: rdn 2f out: wknd over 1f out* **12/1**

9 *7* **Dispol Snapper (IRE)** 2-8-11 0 .... TonyCulhane 2 —
(P T Midgley) *a towards rr* **18/1**

10 *1 1/2* **Reel Amber** 2-8-4 0 .... DuranFentiman 5 —
(T D Easterby) *a towards rr* **33/1**

63.75 secs (0.25) **Going Correction** -0.15s/f (Firm) **10** Ran SP% **115.8**
Speed ratings (Par 92): **92,91,88,78,77 76,72,67,56,54**
toteswingers: 1&2 £7.20, 1&3 £3.10, 2&3 £4.20 CSF £22.60 TOTE £3.50: £1.70, £2.80, £1.10; EX 16.60.
Owner Miss K R Harrison **Bred** Manor Farm Stud (rutland) **Trained** Musley Bank, N Yorks

FOCUS
The quicker of the two divisions by 1.19sec.

NOTEBOOK
Above The Stars, representing a stable that can do little wrong at present, is on the small side but has a real sprinting pedigree and knew her job first time up. Travelling strongly and away from the seemingly unfavoured far rail 2f out, she picked up well once her rider went for the whip, and looked very professional. She could be the type to stick with in the early stage of the season. (op 5-2 tchd 9-4)
Whisper Louise(IRE), a half-sister to Patagarrau, a ten-time winner in Italy, and Bankrobber, a 6f winner at two, was green through the early part of the race but, once switched widest of all 2f out, really found her stride and pushed the winner fairly close. She'll have learnt a lot from this. (op 10-1 tchd 11-1 in a place)
Master Macho(IRE), who had the benefit of previous experience, showed up well throughout, although racing nearer the far-side rail than the first two was perhaps not ideal. (op 5-2 tchd 10-3)
Roodee Queen, a half-sister to three-time sprint winner Riflessione, clearly needed her debut and shaped better this time. (op 16-1)
Minch Man was green but showed some ability. (op 22-1)
Surely This Time(IRE), who is out of a mare who won over 1m5f at three, should appreciate another furlong in due course. (op 8-1)

1295 SPRING INTO RACING AT BEVERLEY H'CAP 5f
3:10 (3:11) (Class 3) (0-95,95) 4-Y-O+ **£7,641** (£2,273; £1,136; £567) **Stalls** High

Form RPR

136- **1** **Lenny Bee**[200] 6283 4-8-8 85 .... FrederikTylicki 17 98
(D H Brown) *trckd ldr: led appr fnl f: r.o strly: readily* **4/1**[2]

000- **2** *1 1/2* **Tajneed (IRE)**[200] 6282 7-8-6 88 .... BillyCray(5) 12 96
(D Nicholls) *trckd ldrs: styd on to take 2nd last 75yds: no imp* **14/1**

000- **3** *1 1/2* **Hamish McGonagall**[172] 7015 5-9-1 92 .... DavidAllan 5 94+
(T D Easterby) *swvd lft s: hdwy over 2f out: kpt on ins fnl f* **20/1**

4-03 **4** *1 1/2* **Fol Hollow (IRE)**[5] 1206 5-9-4 95 .... AdrianNicholls 13 92
(D Nicholls) *led: hdd appr fnl f: fdd ins fnl f* **7/2**[1]

004- **5** *shd* **Indian Trail**[226] 5507 10-8-9 86 .... PaulQuinn 14 83
(D Nicholls) *stdd s: mid-div: hdwy over 1f out: keeping on at fin* **25/1**

005- **6** *1 1/4* **Parisian Pyramid (IRE)**[172] 7015 4-8-12 89 .... PaulMulrennan 7 81+
(K A Ryan) *mid-div: stdy hdwy over 1f out: r.o* **28/1**

/03- **7** *nse* **Master Rooney (IRE)**[177] 6897 4-8-11 88 .... RichardMullen 8 80+
(B Smart) *chsd ldrs: effrt and outpcd on outer 2f out: edgd rt and styd on ins fnl f* **14/1**

14-1 **8** *hd* **Medicean Man**[19] 992 4-8-12 89 .... JimmyQuinn 11 80
(J R Gask) *s.i.s: sn drvn into mid-div: swtchd lft over 2f out: n.m.r and edgd rt over 1f out: nvr trbld ldrs* **9/2**[3]

6611 **9** *1 1/2* **Lord Of The Reins (IRE)**[21] 972 6-8-4 81 oh1 .... PaulHanagan 4 67
(J G Given) *hmpd s: swtchd rt after s: in rr: kpt on fnl 2f: nvr nr ldrs* **25/1**

003- **10** *hd* **Abraham Lincoln (IRE)**[286] 3524 6-9-1 92 .... LiamJones 10 77
(R A Harris) *chsd ldrs: wknd appr fnl f* **33/1**

660- **11** *2* **Oldjoesaid**[200] 6283 6-8-13 95 .... AmyRyan(5) 3 73
(K A Ryan) *hmpd s: swtchd rt after s: in rr: sme hdwy over 1f out: nvr a factor* **20/1**

410- **12** *1/2* **The Nifty Fox**[172] 7015 6-8-12 89 .... DuranFentiman 9 65
(T D Easterby) *in tch: drvn over 2f out: wknd over 1f out* **66/1**

23-4 **13** *hd* **Equuleus Pictor**[103] 2 6-8-5 85 .... JackDean(3) 1 60
(J L Spearing) *sn chsng ldrs on outside: wknd over 1f out* **50/1**

30-0 **14** *shd* **Ishetoo**[18] 1008 6-9-1 92 .... FrannyNorton 16 67
(Ollie Pears) *mid-div: wknd over 1f out* **7/1**

026- **15** *1* **Excusez Moi (USA)**[158] [7294] 8-9-2 **93**.................(p) SilvestreDeSousa 6 64
(Mrs R A Carr) *in rr: nvr on terms* **20/1**

1006 **16** *4 ½* **Matsunosuke**[25] [948] 8-9-4 **95**....................................... TonyCulhane 15 50
(A B Coogan) *mid-div: wkng whn hmpd on ins over 1f out: bhd whn eased towards fin* **20/1**

61.72 secs (-1.78) **Going Correction** -0.15s/f (Firm) **16** Ran SP% **122.8**
Speed ratings (Par 107): **108,105,103,100,100 98,98,98,95,95 92,91,91,89 82**
toteswingers: 1&2 £10.00, 1&3 £67.00, 2&3 £85.80 CSF £50.18 CT £1066.76 TOTE £4.80: £1.10, £3.80, £4.20, £1.60; EX 87.80.

Owner Ron Hull **Bred** Whitsbury Manor Stud & Pigeon House Stud **Trained** Maltby, S Yorks

FOCUS
A competitive-looking handicap and the form should work out.

NOTEBOOK
Lenny Bee, who was well backed beforehand, was drawn highest of all and prominent from the start towards the leader's outside. Going better than anything approaching the final furlong, he picked up well for pressure. He looks to have improved from three to four and clearly this ground, which was a little on the dead side, caused him no problems. (tchd 9-2)
Tajneed(IRE) was not the stable's first string judged by jockey bookings but he shaped well on his reappearance and is on a competitive mark considering his last win came in the Great St Wilfrid off 92. (op 18-1 tchd 20-1)
Hamish McGonagall, who went without a win last year but dropped 8lb in the handicap as a result, didn't have a great draw but kept on well to take third and will have to be of interest for something similar in the coming weeks. (op 22-1)
Fol Hollow(IRE), who won this race last year off an 1lb lower mark, just held on to fourth place after making the running next to the far rail. (op 10-3)
Indian Trail didn't run badly considering he needs the ground quicker than this to be seen at his best. (op 28-1)
Parisian Pyramid(IRE), who was kept in check by the handicapper last year, is now with a new stable. He wasn't knocked about while staying on for sixth, and any drop in the weights will no doubt be welcomed by connections. Official explanation: jockey said, regarding running and riding, that his orders were to drop the gelding in from a poor draw and do the best he could, adding that it was always outpaced off a strong pace and ran on through beaten horses and thinks it could be suited by a longer trip. (op 33-1)
Master Rooney(IRE) settled better than he has in the past and didn't run badly from a modest draw. He remains open to further improvement. (op 12-1)
Medicean Man, successful over this trip at Wolverhampton on his reappearance, was disappointing on this return to turf. He missed the break again and was always playing catch-up. (op 5-1)

1296 RAPID LAD STKS (H'CAP) — 1m 1f 207y
3:45 (3:47) (Class 5) (0-70,70) 4-Y-O+ **£2,590** (£770; £385; £192) **Stalls** High

Form RPR

21-1 **1** **Zaplamation (IRE)**[5] [1204] 5-8-3 **60**................................ IanBrennan(5) 3 75+
(J J Quinn) *hld up in midfield: smooth hdwy 3f out: bmpd 2f out: sn swtchd lft and effrt over 1f out: rdn ent fnl f: styd on wl to ld last 100yds* **3/1**[1]

0-12 **2** *½* **Blue Spinnaker (IRE)**[7] [1177] 11-8-13 **65**.................. PaulMulrennan 15 76
(M W Easterby) *hld up towards rr: hdwy 1/2-way: effrt on outer and hung rt 2f out: sn rdn and edgd rt over 1f out: chal ins fnl f and ev ch tl no ex towards fin* **10/3**[2]

5-21 **3** *1 ½* **Brockfield**[7] [1177] 4-8-12 **64** 6ex... DavidAllan 5 72
(M Brittain) *trckd ldrs: hdwy 3f out: rdn over 1f out: led ent fnl f: sn hdd and kpt on same pce* **11/2**[3]

30-0 **4** *3* **Coole Dodger (IRE)**[9] [1115] 5-8-4 **56** oh2.................... PaulHanagan 12 58
(B Ellison) *in rr: hdwy wl over 2f out: rdn over 1f out: styd on appr fnl f: nrst fin* **11/1**

606- **5** *2 ¾* **King's Counsel (IRE)**[21] [6342] 4-7-13 **56** oh3.......(v) JamesSullivan(5) 10 53
(J Hetherton) *led: rdn 2f out: drvn over 1f out: hdd ent fnl f and wknd* **12/1**

030 **6** *nk* **Boa**[23] [963] 5-8-1 **58**.. PaulPickard(5) 4 54
(R Hollinshead) *trckd ldrs: hdwy on outer 3f out: rdn wl over 1f out: drvn and wknd ent fnl f* **20/1**

500/ **7** *2* **Gulf Coast**[497] [6551] 5-8-7 **59**...................................... GrahamGibbons 13 51
(T D Walford) *towards rr on inner: hdwy over 2f out: rdn along wl over 1f out: no imp* **14/1**

530- **8** *nk* **Active Asset (IRE)**[109] [7847] 8-8-5 **57**...........................(p) PJMcDonald 2 48
(J A Glover) *trckd ldrs: hdwy 3f out: rdn along 2f out and sn btn* **16/1**

5352 **9** *5* **Fitzwarren**[26] [939] 9-8-4 **56** oh10..........................(tp) SilvestreDeSousa 6 37
(A D Brown) *hmpd and squeezed out s: towards rr: gd hdwy on outer 3f out: rdn over 2f out and sn wknd* **50/1**

010- **10** *16* **Toujours Souriante**[77] [4988] 4-9-4 **70**.......................... AndrewMullen 7 19
(Miss Tracy Waggott) *hmpd s: a towards rr* **50/1**

05-5 **11** *4 ½* **Mister Fizzbomb (IRE)**[8] [719] 7-8-9 **61**.................(v) FrederikTylicki 14 —
(J S Wainwright) *a in rr* **9/1**

/01- **12** *8* **Bollin Freddie**[308] [2803] 6-8-4 **56**................................... DuranFentiman 9 —
(A J Lockwood) *chsd ldr: rdn along 3f out: drvn over 2f out and sn wknd* **20/1**

2515 **13** *14* **All Guns Firing (IRE)**[36] [835] 4-8-11 **63**.......................... DavidNolan 1 —
(D Carroll) *chsd ldrs: rdn along 3f out: wknd over 2f out* **28/1**

360- **14** *½* **Green Passion (USA)**[193] [6490] 4-9-1 **67**.................. RoystonFfrench 11 —
(M Johnston) *prom: rdn along 3f out: wknd over 2f out* **18/1**

2m 4.99s (-2.01) **Going Correction** -0.15s/f (Firm) **14** Ran SP% **124.2**
Speed ratings (Par 103): **102,101,100,98,95 95,93,93,89,76 73,66,55,55**
toteswingers: 1&2 £3.70, 1&3 £4.80, 2&3 £5.70 CSF £12.34 CT £54.36 TOTE £3.60: £1.90, £1.90, £2.60; EX 11.10.

Owner Andrew Turton & David Barker **Bred** Mesnil Investments Ltd And Deerpark Stud **Trained** Settrington, N Yorks

■ Stewards' Enquiry : David Nolan two-day ban: used whip continually slapping down shoulder when out of contention (Apr 28-29)

FOCUS
They went a decent gallop in what was a modest handicap. The form looks solid rated around the placed horses.

Coole Dodger(IRE) Official explanation: jockey said gelding hung right-handed

1297 RACING UK H'CAP — 1m 1f 207y
4:20 (4:20) (Class 4) (0-80,80) 3-Y-O **£4,727** (£1,406; £702; £351) **Stalls** High

Form RPR

503- **1** **Music Of The Moor (IRE)**[162] [7218] 3-8-8 **70**.................. MickyFenton 1 76
(T P Tate) *hld up in rr: hdwy on outer 2f out: rdn over 1f out: styd on ins fnl f to ld towards fin* **8/1**[3]

025- **2** *nk* **I'm Super Too (IRE)**[210] [5981] 3-8-6 **68**........................... PJMcDonald 6 73
(G A Swinbank) *hld up in rr: hdwy over 2f out: rdn over 1f out: led ins fnl f: sn drvn: hdd and no ex nr fin* **9/1**

14- **3** *2 ½* **Layla's Dancer**[173] [6993] 3-9-2 **78**................................... PaulHanagan 2 78
(R A Fahey) *led: pushed clr over 2f out: sn rdn: drvn and hdd ins fnl f: one pce* **4/5**[1]

-122 **4** *½* **Demonstrative (USA)**[41] [792] 3-9-4 **80**...................... RoystonFfrench 4 79
(M Johnston) *trckd ldrs: effrt 3f out: rdn along 2f out: sn one pce* **7/2**[2]

301- **5** *1* **Tamanaco (IRE)**[271] [4067] 3-9-3 **79**............................ GrahamGibbons 3 76
(T D Walford) *chsd ldr: rdn along wl over 2f out: drvn over 1f out and grad wknd* **14/1**

210- **6** *17* **Saxby (IRE)**[190] [6557] 3-8-8 **70**................................. SilvestreDeSousa 5 33
(G A Harker) *t.k.h: chsd ldng pair: rdn along over 2f out and sn wknd* **20/1**

2m 6.91s (-0.09) **Going Correction** -0.15s/f (Firm) **6** Ran SP% **110.3**
Speed ratings (Par 100): **94,93,91,91,90 76**
toteswingers: 1&2 £3.60, 1&3 £1.60, 2&3 £1.80 CSF £69.05 TOTE £10.00: £3.50, £2.40; EX 49.70.

Owner The Ivy Syndicate **Bred** Snig Elevage **Trained** Tadcaster, N Yorks

FOCUS
They went a fair pace and the first two came from the back of the field. The winner is rated to his early juvenile form.

Saxby(IRE) Official explanation: jockey said gelding ran too free

1298 WHISTLEJACKETS CAFE STKS (H'CAP) — 7f 100y
4:55 (4:56) (Class 5) (0-70,70) 3-Y-O **£2,590** (£770; £385; £192) **Stalls** High

Form RPR

660- **1** **Tribal Myth (IRE)**[223] [5595] 3-8-5 **57**........................ SilvestreDeSousa 6 65
(K A Ryan) *prom: lft in ld after 1f: rdn along 2f out: drvn ent fnl f and kpt on gamely* **7/1**[3]

640- **2** *1 ¾* **Fibs And Flannel**[235] [5256] 3-8-12 **64**........................ DuranFentiman 13 68+
(T D Easterby) *in rr: hdwy over 2f out: swtchd rt wl over 1f out: swtchd lft and rdn over 1f out: styd on ins fnl f: nrst fin* **18/1**

05-1 **3** *shd* **Dazakhee**[47] [717] 3-8-9 **61**... TonyCulhane 5 65
(P T Midgley) *hld up in tch: hdwy over 2f out: rdn to chse wnr over 1f out: drvn ins fnl f and kpt on same pce* **12/1**

00-5 **4** *2 ¾* **Eeny Mac (IRE)**[9] [1118] 3-8-4 **56** oh8.............................. FrannyNorton 11 53
(N Bycroft) *wnt lft s: prom: sn chsng wnr: rdn along 2f out: drvn over 1f out: kpt on same pce* **12/1**

0-24 **5** *nk* **Magic Millie (IRE)**[47] [717] 3-7-13 **56** oh4............... JamesSullivan(5) 14 52+
(J Hetherton) *midfield: effrt whn nt clr run on inner 2f out: sn lost pl and bhd whn swtchd wd over 1f out: rdn and styd on strly ins fnl f: nrst fin* **14/1**

-040 **6** *2* **Sixties Rock**[7] [1178] 3-8-5 **57**.. PJMcDonald 9 48
(J A Glover) *hmpd s and bhd: hdwy on outer 2f out: rdn over 1f out: kpt on ins fnl f: nt rch ;ldrs* **9/1**

04- **7** *1* **Refuse To Wait (IRE)**[225] [5550] 3-8-13 **65**.......................... DavidAllan 8 54
(T D Easterby) *hld up in rr: hdwy over 2f out: sn rdn and n.d* **13/2**[2]

441- **8** *3 ½* **Hoof It**[252] [4652] 3-9-2 **68**.. PaulMulrennan 4 48
(M W Easterby) *t.k.h: prom: rdn along over 2f out and sn wknd* **3/1**[1]

0-02 **9** *3* **Always Dixie (IRE)**[64] [475] 3-8-4 **56**.......................(b) RoystonFfrench 3 28
(M Johnston) *chsd ldrs: rdn along wl over 2f out: sn wknd* **11/1**

040- **10** *¾* **Classical Piece (USA)**[158] [7289] 3-9-1 **70**.............. BarryMcHugh(3) 10 41
(Mrs D J Sanderson) *trckd ldrs on inner: rdn over 2f out and grad wknd* **14/1**

300- **11** *6* **Scarboro Warning (IRE)**[166] [7146] 3-9-2 **68**........... GrahamGibbons 12 24
(J O'Reilly) *t.k.h: chsd ldrs: hmpd after 1f: rdn along 3f out: sn wknd* **12/1**

-114 **F** **Set Back**[14] [1070] 3-9-2 **68**.. AdrianNicholls 7 —
(D Nicholls) *qckly away and led tl struck into fr bhd and fell after 1f: dead* **8/1**

1m 33.41s (-0.39) **Going Correction** -0.15s/f (Firm) **12** Ran SP% **122.0**
Speed ratings (Par 98): **96,94,93,90,90 88,86,82,79,78 71,—**
toteswingers: 1&2 £38.90, 1&3 £22.50, 2&3 £27.10 CSF £129.60 CT £1524.13 TOTE £11.10: £3.20, £7.80, £3.60; EX 225.10.

Owner Mr & Mrs K Hughes and Dr J Gozzard **Bred** Norelands Stallions **Trained** Hambleton, N Yorks

FOCUS
An ordinary handicap, whose result was affected by an early incident when Scarboro Warning clipped the heels of leader Set Back, causing the latter to fall. The pair hampered a number of rivals, causing many of them to be pushed out wide and to lose ground. The form is messy and the fourth and fifth were close enough from out of the handicap.

Tribal Myth(IRE) Official explanation: trainer said, regarding apparent improvement in form, that the gelding was a weak 2yo and had matured and strengthened over the inter.

Hoof It Official explanation: jockey said gelding ran too free

1299 RACING HERE AGAIN NEXT THURSDAY H'CAP — 1m 4f 16y
5:30 (5:30) (Class 5) (0-75,75) 3-Y-O **£2,590** (£770; £385; £192) **Stalls** High

Form RPR

551- **1** **Corsica (IRE)**[173] [6982] 3-9-3 **74**................................... RoystonFfrench 1 88
(M Johnston) *led 2f: cl up tl led again 3f out: rdn and edgd lft wl over 1f out: drvn ins fnl f: kpt on gamely towards fin* **7/2**[2]

561- **2** *½* **Beat The Rush**[177] [6901] 3-8-11 **71**............................. BarryMcHugh(3) 4 84
(Julie Camacho) *trckd ldrs: hdwy over 2f out: n.m.r and swtchd rt wl over 1f out: rdn to chal ent fnl f and ev ch tl drvn and no ex towards fin* **7/2**[2]

-111 **3** *2 ½* **Desert Recluse (IRE)**[28] [904] 3-8-11 **75**...................... LeeTopliss(7) 3 84
(Pat Eddery) *hld up in rr: hdwy on outer over 2f out: rdn and ch over 1f out: sn edgd rt and one pce ent fnl f* **6/1**

406- **4** *hd* **Domination**[159] [7266] 3-8-8 **65**.. TravisBlock 2 74
(H Morrison) *trckd ldng pair: hdwy 3f out: rdn and ev ch 2f out: drvn and one pce fr over 1f out* **9/2**[3]

50-1 **5** *23* **Sir Pitt**[14] [1067] 3-8-13 **70**.. PaulHanagan 5 42
(J H M Gosden) *cl up: led after 2f: rdn along and hdd 3f out: wknd over 2f out* **15/8**[1]

2m 38.03s (-1.77) **Going Correction** -0.15s/f (Firm) **5** Ran SP% **111.7**
Speed ratings (Par 98): **103,102,101,100,85**
CSF £15.95 TOTE £4.00: £1.10, £3.60; EX 20.00 Place 6 £153.14, Place 5 £63.41.

Owner Sheikh Hamdan Bin Mohammed Al Maktoum **Bred** Epona Bloodstock Ltd And P A Byrne **Trained** Middleham Moor, N Yorks

FOCUS
An interesting little handicap. The first three are all slight improvers.

Sir Pitt Official explanation: trainer had no explanation for the poor form shown

T/Plt: £213.80 to a £1 stake. Pool: £53,025.96. 181.00 winning tickets. T/Qpdt: £16.60 to a £1 stake. Pool: £4,298.02. 190.60 winning tickets. JR

[1156]KEMPTON (A.W) (R-H)

Wednesday, April 14

OFFICIAL GOING: Standard

Wind: Moderate, half against Weather: Fine

1300 KEMPTON.CO.UK H'CAP 6f (P)

5:35 (5:35) (Class 6) (0-65,64) 4-Y-0+ £2,047 (£604; £302) Stalls High

Form RPR

60-4 **1** **Kyllachy Storm**[13] 1074 6-9-3 **63**.................... GeorgeBaker 11 71
(R J Hodges) *mde all: drvn 2 l clr ent fnl f: kpt on* **12/1**

6-06 **2** *1* **Musical Script (USA)**[14] 1064 7-9-0 **60**....................(b) LiamKeniry 4 65
(Mouse Hamilton-Fairley) *hld up in midfield: prog over 2f out: rdn to go 2nd over 1f out: styd on: a hld* **8/1**

6602 **3** *1* **Bobs Dreamflight**[7] 1166 4-8-9 **60**....................(b) MarkCoumbe[(5)] 8 62
(D K Ivory) *settled bhd ldrs: prog over 2f out: wnt 3rd 1f out: kpt on: nt pce to chal* **7/1[3]**

3-21 **4** *1 ¼* **Fuzzy Cat**[57] 569 4-8-9 **60**.................... DeanHeslop[(5)] 7 58
(T D Barron) *trckd ldng pair: fnd nil whn asked for effrt over 2f out: lost pl: kpt on again fnl f* **5/2[1]**

2-12 **5** *¾* **Boho Chic**[23] 967 4-8-12 **63**.................... MatthewDavies[(5)] 9 59
(George Baker) *chsd wnr: edgd lft and nt qckn wl over 1f out: fdd sn after* **6/1[2]**

6410 **6** *nk* **Titus Gent**[35] 851 5-9-2 **62**.................... DavidProbert 6 57+
(R A Harris) *blindfold off as stalls opened and dwlt: settled in 9th: rdn 2f out: styd on: nvr nrr* **10/1**

5060 **7** *1 ½* **Milne Bay (IRE)**[27] 924 5-8-9 **62**....................(t) LauraPike[(7)] 1 52
(D M Simcock) *racd wd: sn pressed ldrs: nt qckn 2f out: wknd jst over 1f out* **16/1**

50-2 **8** *1 ¼* **Charles Darwin (IRE)**[23] 961 7-9-2 **62**.................... FergusSweeney 12 48
(M Blanshard) *trckd ldrs on inner: shkn up 2f out: wknd over 1f o ut* **10/1**

5013 **9** *1 ½* **White Shift (IRE)**[37] 828 4-8-11 **64**.................... JohnFahy[(7)] 5 45
(P Howling) *hld up and sn in last trio: shkn up over 2f out: no real prog* **14/1**

1000 **10** *¾* **Bishopbriggs (USA)**[14] 1063 5-9-1 **61**.................... JerryO'Dwyer 10 40
(M G Quinlan) *stdd s: hld up in last: pushed along over 2f out: nvr involved* **20/1**

0010 **11** *½* **Elusive Ronnie (IRE)**[7] 1166 4-8-13 **59**....................(b) SebSanders 2 36
(R A Teal) *racd wd: a in last trio: nvr gng wl: struggling u.p 1/2-way* **16/1**

5340 **12** *shd* **The Geester**[7] 1166 6-9-0 **60**....................(v[1]) StephenCraine 3 37
(Stef Higgins) *t.k.h: hld up bhd ldrs: wknd over 2f out* **12/1**

1m 12.24s (-0.86) **Going Correction** -0.05s/f (Stan) 12 Ran SP% **123.2**
Speed ratings (Par 101): **103,101,100,98,97 97,95,93,91,90 89,89**
toteswingers: 1&2 £23.20, 1&3 £20.90, 2&3 £12.90 CSF £108.92 CT £752.77 TOTE £15.70: £4.80, £2.40, £1.80; EX 58.70.
Owner Mrs Angela Hart **Bred** Sir Eric Parker **Trained** Charlton Mackrell, Somerset

FOCUS
A moderate handicap.

1301 PANORAMIC BAR & RESTAURANT CLAIMING STKS 1m (P)

6:05 (6:05) (Class 6) 4-Y-0+ £2,047 (£604; £302) Stalls High

Form RPR

2600 **1** **Red Somerset (USA)**[4] 1219 7-9-3 86.................... GeorgeBaker 5 81
(R J Hodges) *s.i.s: sn trckd ldrs in 5th: clsd smoothly to ld wl over 1f out: sn clr: comf* **5/4[1]**

3230 **2** *3 ¾* **Dichoh**[26] 929 7-9-3 73....................(v) LiamKeniry 7 72
(M Madgwick) *t.k.h: hld up and sn 6th: prog 2f out: rdn to take 2nd ins fnl f: no ch w wnr* **10/1**

0323 **3** *¾* **Seasider**[16] 1049 5-8-12 78.................... MartinLane[(3)] 8 68
(D M Simcock) *s.s: hld up in last trio: taken to outer and effrt over 2f out: hanging but prog over 1f out: one pce ins fnl f* **2/1[2]**

00- **4** *½* **Douchkette (FR)**[53] 4057 4-8-5 0.................... LukeMorris 9 57
(John Berry) *dwlt: hld up and sn last: rdn over 2f out: sme prog over 1f out: keeping on whn sltly checked ins fnl f* **50/1**

2206 **5** *½* **Straight Face (IRE)**[4] 1239 6-8-4 68....................(b) MatthewCosham[(7)] 4 61
(P D Evans) *trckd ldng trio: rdn over 2f out: wnt 3rd over 1f out: fdd fnl f* **16/1**

0605 **6** *2 ¼* **Djalalabad (FR)**[9] 1130 6-8-5 44.................... SaleemGolam 3 50
(J Pearce) *t.k.h: trckd ldr after 2f: led over 2f out to wl over 1f out: wknd fnl f* **40/1**

1/35 **7** *1 ¼* **Bazroy (IRE)**[16] 1049 6-8-6 80....................(v) AndrewHeffernan[(5)] 2 53
(P D Evans) *t.k.h: restrained into last trio after s: effrt over 2f out: fnd nil and no prog over 1f out* **15/2[3]**

00-5 **8** *3* **Dawson Creek (IRE)**[21] 969 6-8-11 53.................... SebSanders 6 46
(B Gubby) *led to over 2f out: wknd* **22/1**

/00- **9** *11* **Ledgerwood**[296] 3215 5-8-10 40....................(p) NeilChalmers 10 18
(A J Chamberlain) *chsd ldr 2f: wknd over 2f out: t.o* **125/1**

1m 39.05s (-0.75) **Going Correction** -0.05s/f (Stan) 9 Ran SP% **114.1**
Speed ratings (Par 101): **101,97,96,96,95 93,92,89,78**
toteswingers: 1&2 £4.00, 1&3 £1.80, 2&3 £4.10 CSF £14.58 TOTE £2.80: £1.20, £1.10, £2.30; EX 14.10.The winner was claimed by Mr M. Murphy £12,000.
Owner R J Hodges **Bred** Haras D'Etreham **Trained** Charlton Mackrell, Somerset

FOCUS
An uncompetitive claimer.

1302 DIGIBET.COM MEDIAN AUCTION MAIDEN STKS 1m 4f (P)

6:35 (6:36) (Class 6) 3-5-Y-0 £2,047 (£604; £302) Stalls Centre

Form RPR

433- **1** **Ipswich Lad**[126] 7683 3-8-7 74....................(v) DavidProbert 5 78
(A M Balding) *led over 10f out to over 8f out: trckd ldr: led over 5f out: drew clr 4f out: tired but in n.d fr over 1f out* **5/1[2]**

423- **2** *3 ½* **Ebony Boom (IRE)**[164] 7199 3-8-7 76.................... JimmyQuinn 14 72
(H R A Cecil) *trckd ldrs: rdn to go 3rd over 3f out: chsd clr wnr wl over 1f out: kpt on but only modest inroads* **6/4[1]**

3 *4* **Sophies Trophy (IRE)**[24] 5-10-0 0.................... IanMongan 6 68+
(P M Phelan) *trckd ldrs: rdn in 4th over 3f out but outpcd: kpt on same pce fr 2f out to take 3rd nr fin* **6/1[3]**

4 **4** *½* **Marrimeclaire (IRE)**[9] 1132 3-7-11 0.................... AmyBaker[(5)] 3 60
(B J McMath) *hld up in rr: prog to go 5th over 3f out but outpcd: bmpd along and kpt on fnl 2f: chal fr 3rd nr fin* **14/1**

/5-2 **5** *¾* **Celtic Commitment**[21] 971 4-9-13 67.................... SebSanders 10 66
(S Dow) *led over 1f: trckd ldrs after: rdn to go 2nd over 4f out: no imp on wnr over 2f out: fdd over 1f out* **15/2**

6 *7* **Drummers Drumming (USA)** 4-9-13 0.................... ShaneKelly 8 54
(J A Osborne) *s.s: sn midfield: wnt 6th over 3f out but wl outpcd: no hdwy after* **40/1**

346- **7** *1 ½* **Milnagavie**[188] 6607 3-8-2 72.................... FrankieMcDonald 11 45
(R Hannon) *nvr beyond midfield: rdn 1/2-way: poor 9th 3f out: plugged on* **7/1**

8 *3 ¾* **Indian Ghyll (IRE)**[39] 4-9-13 0.................... LiamKeniry 13 46
(R A Teal) *s.s: a wl in rr: no ch fnl 3f: plugged on* **40/1**

6 **9** *14* **Miss Formidable (IRE)**[14] 1059 3-7-13 0.................... AndreaAtzeni[(3)] 7 17
(Luke Comer, Ire) *prom: outpcd in 7th over 3f out: wknd: t.o* **25/1**

0 **10** *9* **Prickles**[49] 677 5-9-9 0.................... DarryllHolland 2 4
(Karen George) *a wl in rr: no ch fr 4f out: t.o* **66/1**

00- **11** *4* **Houda (IRE)**[243] 4980 3-8-2 0.................... LukeMorris 1 —
(J G Portman) *nvr beyond midfield: wknd 4f out: t.o* **50/1**

0 **12** *11* **Demo Jo**[33] 872 4-9-8 0.................... StephenCraine 4 —
(M Wigham) *prog fr midfield to ld over 8f out: hdd over 5f out: wknd 4f out: t.o* **100/1**

13 *3 ¼* **Grey Gauntlet** 3-8-7 0.................... RichardThomas 9 —
(R Ingram) *s.s: a wl in rr: t.o* **100/1**

6 **14** *4 ½* **Tooprague**[7] 1157 4-9-8 0.................... FergusSweeney 12 —
(P R Hedger) *dwlt: a towards rr: wknd over 4f out: t.o* **100/1**

2m 32.17s (-2.33) **Going Correction** -0.05s/f (Stan)
WFA 3 from 4yo 21lb 4 from 5yo 1lb 14 Ran SP% **117.0**
Speed ratings (Par 101): **105,102,100,99,99 94,93,91,81,75 73,65,63,60**
toteswingers: 1&2 £2.70, 1&3 £9.40, 2&3 £4.80 CSF £12.00 TOTE £6.90: £1.90, £1.70, £1.10; EX 14.20.
Owner Marcus Evans **Bred** Darley **Trained** Kingsclere, Hants
■ Stewards' Enquiry : David Probert caution: careless riding

FOCUS
Ordinary maiden form.
Sophies Trophy(IRE) Official explanation: jockey said gelding was hampered after 2f

1303 DIGIBET CASINO H'CAP 1m 4f (P)

7:05 (7:08) (Class 5) (0-70,70) 4-Y-0+ £2,590 (£770; £385; £192) Stalls Centre

Form RPR

-622 **1** **Colonel Sherman (USA)**[6] 1188 5-8-2 **57**.......... AndrewHeffernan[(5)] 12 66
(P A Kirby) *racd freely: mde all and allowed easy ld: kicked on over 2f out: jnd over 1f out: kpt on wl* **3/1[1]**

0-22 **2** *1* **Red Hot Desert**[7] 1169 4-9-5 **70**.................... ShaneKelly 9 77
(W R Swinburn) *a 2nd: urged along to cl on wnr fr 2f out: upsides jst over 1f out: fnd nil and easily btn off* **5/1**

-221 **3** *½* **Drizzi (IRE)**[20] 983 9-8-8 **63**.................... SimonPearce[(5)] 10 70
(J Pearce) *hld up in midfield: gng easily in 6th 3f out: outpcd sn after: shkn up to cl on ldng pair 1f out: nvr fnd enough* **4/1[2]**

-21 **4** *½* **Carlton Scroop (FR)**[42] 771 7-9-0 **67**....................(b) AndreaAtzeni[(3)] 6 73
(J Jay) *awkward s: hld up in 9th: prog fr 3f out: rdn to take 3rd over 1f out: nt qckn after* **9/2[3]**

4665 **5** *½* **Uncle Eli (IRE)**[7] 1160 8-8-6 **63**.................... RichardRowe[(7)] 4 68?
(R Rowe) *trckd ldng trio: wnt 3rd 1/2-way to over 1f out: one pce after* **22/1**

130- **6** *¾* **Squad**[125] 7699 4-9-4 **69**.................... HayleyTurner 7 73+
(S Dow) *stdd s: hld up in last: pushed along and prog over 2f out: kpt gng but no hope of rching ldrs* **16/1**

00/3 **7** *shd* **Dancing Sword**[26] 938 5-8-11 **61**.................... DavidProbert 8 65
(D Burchell) *dwlt: plld hrd early: hld up in last trio: rdn over 3f out: kpt on but n.d* **12/1**

0220 **8** *¾* **Mustajed**[17] 1028 9-9-1 **68**....................(b) JamesMillman[(3)] 1 70
(B R Millman) *hld up: prog to go 5th 1/2-way: shkn up 3f out: sn lost pl: plugged on after* **10/1**

1440 **9** *4 ½* **Resplendent Ace (IRE)**[9] 1134 6-9-2 **69**.............. MichaelStainton[(3)] 5 64
(P Howling) *t.k.h: hld up in 7th: brought wd bnd 3f out: sn wknd* **14/1**

00-0 **10** *22* **Devon Diva**[48] 691 4-8-1 **59** oh10 ow4.............. AdamBeschizza[(7)] 11 19
(J F Panvert) *chsd ldng pair to 1/2-way: rdn and wknd over 4f out: t.o* **150/1**

2m 34.1s (-0.40) **Going Correction** -0.05s/f (Stan)
WFA 4 from 5yo+ 1lb 10 Ran SP% **114.2**
Speed ratings (Par 103): **99,98,98,97,97 96,96,96,93,78**
toteswingers: 1&2 £3.00, 1&3 £4.60, 2&3 £6.10 CSF £17.57 CT £59.52 TOTE £4.70: £2.50, £2.90, £1.10; EX 18.70.
Owner K Sivills, Preesall Garage & The Dublins **Bred** Fred M Allor **Trained** Castleton, N Yorks
■ Stewards' Enquiry : Andrew Heffernan two-day ban: careless riding (Apr 28-29)

FOCUS
A moderate handicap and another race where it paid to race handy.

1304 DIGIBET H'CAP (DIV I) 7f (P)

7:35 (7:37) (Class 6) (0-65,65) 4-Y-0+ £1,706 (£503; £252) Stalls High

Form RPR

532 **1** **Army Of Stars (IRE)**[27] 915 4-9-4 **65**....................(p) ShaneKelly 1 75
(J A Osborne) *wl away fr lowest draw: pressed ldr: effrt to ld jst over 2f out: rdn clr fnl f* **14/1**

-153 **2** *1 ¾* **Dhhamaan (IRE)**[44] 753 5-8-5 **52**....................(b) HayleyTurner 13 57
(Mrs R A Carr) *t.k.h: led at mod pce: hdd jst over 2f out: pressed wnr tl no ex ins fnl f* **12/1**

-165 **3** *shd* **Harting Hill**[23] 965 5-9-0 **61**.................... GeorgeBaker 10 68+
(M P Tregoning) *hld up disputing 6th: trbld passage fr 4f out and lost pl: 10th 2f out: effrt over 1f out: styd on wl and nrly snatched 2nd* **13/2[2]**

154 **4** *nk* **Ejeed (USA)**[14] 1063 5-9-0 **61**....................(p) SamHitchcott 11 65
(Miss Z C Davison) *t.k.h: trckd ldng pair: nt qckn 2f out: kpt on one pce after* **8/1[3]**

2123 **5** *nk* **Bold Diva**[7] 1170 5-8-9 **56**....................(v) LukeMorris 4 59
(A W Carroll) *dropped in fr wd draw and hld up wl in rr: prog on inner over 2f out: clsd on ldrs over 1f out: one pce fnl f* **11/2[1]**

215- **6** *½* **Cadeaux Fax**[177] 6909 5-9-0 **64**.................... JamesMillman[(3)] 3 66
(B R Millman) *t.k.h: hld up disputing 6th: prog to dispute 3rd 2f out: pushed along and nt qckn over 1f out* **8/1[3]**

-000 **7** *1 ¼* **Esteem Lord**[7] 1172 4-8-9 **59**....................(b[1]) MartinLane[(3)] 7 57
(Jamie Poulton) *hld up in last: taken to outer over 2f out and urged along: styd on fnl f: nrst fin* **50/1**

0030 **8** *nk* **Grand Honour (IRE)**[26] 937 4-8-13 **60**.................... JimmyQuinn 5 58
(P Howling) *dropped in fr wd draw and hld up in rr: prog on inner over 2f out: clsd on ldrs over 1f out: wknd ins fnl f* **16/1**

00-3 **9** *¾* **Jazacosta (USA)**[21] 975 4-9-1 **62**.................... IanMongan 8 58
(Miss Jo Crowley) *hld up in 9th: wd bnd 3f out: in tch and rdn 2f out: nt qckn and no prog* **8/1[3]**

2420 **10** 1 1/4 **Towy Boy (IRE)**^{35} 844 5-8-7 **54**....................(t) LiamKeniry 6 46
(I A Wood) *hld up in rr: pushed along and limited prog fr 2f out: fdd fnl f*
10/1

-543 **11** 3/4 **Who's Winning (IRE)**^{7} 1167 9-8-8 **55**....................(t) KirstyMilczarek 12 45
(B G Powell) *t.k.h: cl up: nt qckn 2f out: losing pl whn sltly checked over 1f out*
12/1

3231 **12** 3 1/4 **Hip Hip Hooray**^{14} 1063 4-9-4 **65**.................... KierenFallon 2 46
(L A Dace) *hld up in rr: c v wd bnd 3f out: no prog and sn btn* **11/2**^{1}

0000 **13** 1 **One Cool Dream**^{20} 984 4-8-5 **52** oh3 ow1.................... SaleemGolam 9 31
(P W Hiatt) *trckd ldng quartet on outer: wknd 2f out* **40/1**

1m 25.56s (-0.44) **Going Correction** -0.05s/f (Stan) **13** Ran SP% **118.9**
Speed ratings (Par 101): **100,98,97,97,97 96,95,94,94,92 91,88,86**
toteswingers: 1&2 £36.80, 1&3 £16.50, 2&3 £16.00 CSF £171.32 CT £1243.67 TOTE £22.30: £9.50, £6.60, £1.20; EX 112.60.
Owner J A Osborne **Bred** D Johnson **Trained** Upper Lambourn, Berks
■ Stewards' Enquiry : Sam Hitchcott two-day ban: careless riding (Apr 28-29)
Shane Kelly caution: careless riding.

FOCUS
A weak handicap where it was hard to get involved from out the back.
Harting Hill Official explanation: jockey said gelding was denied a clear run
Cadeaux Fax Official explanation: jockey said gelding hung left in home straight
Who's Winning(IRE) Official explanation: jockey said gelding suffered interference in running

1305 DIGIBET H'CAP (DIV II) 7f (P)

8:05 (8:06) (Class 6) (0-65,65) 4-Y-O+ **£1,706** (£503; £252) **Stalls** High

Form RPR

5655 **1** **Teen Ager (FR)**^{16} 1047 6-8-13 **60**.................... TomMcLaughlin 7 66
(P Burgoyne) *t.k.h: trckd ldr: led over 2f out: kicked 2 l clr 1f out: pushed out to hold on* **6/1**^{3}

21-5 **2** nk **Ede's Dot Com (IRE)**^{14} 1064 6-8-9 **61**.................... KierenFox$^{(5)}$ 1 66+
(P M Phelan) *hld up in 9th: prog fr 2f out: rdn and styd on wl fnl f to take 2nd nr fin* **7/1**

6-05 **3** nk **December**^{9} 1133 4-8-10 **57**....................(vt^{1}) SebSanders 4 61
(Mrs C A Dunnett) *sn trckd ldng pair: rdn to chse wnr wl over 1f out: clsd grad fnl f: lost 2nd nr fin* **10/1**

6530 **4** 1/2 **Cruise Control**^{41} 795 4-7-13 **51** oh3.................... AndrewHeffernan$^{(5)}$ 9 54
(R J Price) *t.k.h: trckd ldrs on outer: nt qckn 2f out: kpt on same pce after* **16/1**

-500 **5** 1/2 **Blue Charm**^{35} 855 6-9-4 **65**.................... DarryllHolland 5 67+
(I W McInnes) *hld up in last pair: stl there 2f out: jst pushed along after but styd on steadily: nrst fin* **25/1**

6102 **6** 1 **Guildenstern (IRE)**^{23} 968 8-8-12 **59**.................... JimmyQuinn 14 58+
(P Howling) *t.k.h: hld up in midfield: stuck bhd rivals fr 2f out: swtchd to inner fnl f: no ch* **5/1**^{2}

0231 **7** shd **Castleburg**^{26} 931 4-9-2 **63**....................(be) GeorgeBaker 12 62
(G L Moore) *t.k.h: hld up bhd ldrs: effrt 2f out: rdn and nt qckn over 1f out: one pce after* **7/2**^{1}

-653 **8** nk **Shadow Bay (IRE)**^{9} 1130 4-8-8 **55**.................... SamHitchcott 10 53
(Miss Z C Davison) *t.k.h: cl up on inner: drvn to dispute 3rd over 1f out: nt qckn: fdd last 100yds* **10/1**

2140 **9** 6 **King Canute (IRE)**^{8} 1148 6-8-8 **55**.................... KierenFallon 8 37
(N P Mulholland) *led to over 2f out: wknd over 1f out: eased* **6/1**^{3}

00-0 **10** 1 1/2 **Warrior Nation (FR)**^{21} 970 4-8-6 **53**.................... NeilChalmers 3 31
(A J Chamberlain) *s.s: a in last trio: wknd 2f out* **66/1**

0652 **11** 3/4 **Flamestone**^{20} 984 6-8-4 **51** oh1.................... DavidProbert 6 27
(A E Price) *t.k.h: trckd ldrs: lost pl after 2f: struggling in rr 3f out* **12/1**

1m 26.13s (0.13) **Going Correction** -0.05s/f (Stan) **11** Ran SP% **117.1**
Speed ratings (Par 101): **97,96,96,95,95 94,93,93,86,85 84**
toteswingers: 1&2 £9.40, 1&3 £14.80, 2&3 £9.80 CSF £47.46 CT £424.01 TOTE £8.80: £2.70, £2.00, £5.00; EX 46.70.
Owner L Tomlin **Bred** Haras De Beauvoir **Trained** Shepton Montague, Somerset
■ Stewards' Enquiry : Neil Chalmers one-day ban: used whip when out of contention (Apr 28)

FOCUS
The second division of the poor 7f handicap and once more it was an advantage to be handy.
Blue Charm Official explanation: jockey said gelding was denied a clear run
Guildenstern(IRE) Official explanation: jockey said gelding was denied a clear run

1306 KEMPTON FOR OUTDOOR EVENTS H'CAP 7f (P)

8:35 (8:35) (Class 4) (0-85,85) 4-Y-O+ **£4,209** (£1,252; £625; £312) **Stalls** High

Form RPR

2251 **1** **Jake The Snake (IRE)**^{20} 981 9-9-1 **82**.................... SebSanders 7 89+
(A W Carroll) *sn hld up in midfield: plenty to do over 1f out: str run fnl f to ld post* **15/2**^{3}

01- **2** hd **Brother Cha (IRE)**^{237} 5181 4-8-12 **79**.................... KierenFallon 1 85+
(L M Cumani) *plld hrd early: led after 1f: rdn over 1f out: looked in command fnl f: collared post* **7/4**^{1}

0-10 **3** 1/2 **Dingaan (IRE)**^{25} 943 7-9-4 **85**.................... DavidProbert 3 90
(A M Balding) *t.k.h: trckd ldrs: rdn over 2f out: kpt on fr over 1f out wout qckning: nrst fin* **16/1**

-365 **4** 1 **Carnivore**^{42} 779 8-8-5 **77**.................... DeanHeslop$^{(5)}$ 4 79
(T D Barron) *awkward s: chsd ldr over 4f out: rdn and kpt on same pce fr over 1f out: lost 2 pls ins fnl f* **20/1**

014- **5** 1 3/4 **Hurricane Spirit (IRE)**^{187} 6633 6-9-3 **84**.................... SteveDrowne 5 82
(J R Best) *hld up in midfield: shkn up over 2f out: wnt 5th fnl f: no imp on ldrs* **10/1**

1650 **6** 1 1/4 **Gallantry**^{11} 1088 8-8-8 **78**.................... MichaelStainton$^{(3)}$ 10 72
(P Howling) *hld up in rr on inner: shkn up 2f out: no real prog* **25/1**

6202 **7** nse **Elusive Fame (USA)**^{28} 908 4-8-9 **76**....................(b) FrankieDettori 9 70
(M Johnston) *s.s: hld up in last pair: pushed along 2f out: nt clr run and swtchd ins fnl f: nvr a real factor* **8/1**

6124 **8** 1/2 **Prince Of Thebes (IRE)**^{11} 1088 9-8-13 **80**.................... LukeMorris 8 73
(M J Attwater) *towards rr: u.p wl over 2f out: no prog* **11/1**

20-0 **9** 3/4 **Block Party**^{11} 1088 4-8-11 **78**....................(p) JamieSpencer 2 69
(D M Simcock) *led 1f: chsd ldr to over 4f out: wknd wl over 1f out* **9/2**^{2}

00-0 **10** 1 1/4 **Archie Rice (USA)**^{19} 987 4-8-10 **77**.................... LiamKeniry 6 64
(T Keddy) *a in last pair: shkn up and no prog 2f out* **25/1**

1m 25.23s (-0.77) **Going Correction** -0.05s/f (Stan) **10** Ran SP% **113.2**
Speed ratings (Par 105): **102,101,101,100,98 96,96,96,95,93**
toteswingers: 1&2 £3.20, 1&3 £6.40, 2&3 £6.50 CSF £19.78 CT £206.79 TOTE £10.20: £2.90, £1.90, £6.00; EX 27.10.
Owner D Morgan & M B Clarke **Bred** J F Tuthill **Trained** Cropthorne, Worcs

FOCUS
A fair handicap.
Elusive Fame(USA) Official explanation: jockey said gelding reared leaving stalls
Block Party Official explanation: jockey said gelding was struck into 2f out

1307 BISTRO FROM £37 IN THE PANORAMIC H'CAP (LONDON MILE QUALIFIER) 1m (P)

9:05 (9:06) (Class 4) (0-80,80) 3-Y-O **£4,209** (£1,252; £625; £312) **Stalls** High

Form RPR

002- **1** **Gold Rules**^{235} 5253 3-9-2 **78**.................... KierenFallon 3 87+
(L M Cumani) *hld up: prog over 2f out: darted to inner and led over 1f out: sn rdn clr: in n.d fnl f* **5/2**^{2}

2220 **2** 2 **Lisahane Bog**^{6} 1189 3-9-0 **76**....................(v) DaneO'Neill 8 80
(P R Hedger) *dwlt and rousted along early in last: prog on outer over 2f out: styd on wl to take 2nd last 100yds: no ch w wnr* **9/1**

411- **3** 1 1/4 **Soul Heaven**^{277} 3842 3-8-13 **75**.................... JamieSpencer 7 76
(M L W Bell) *hld up in rr: prog 2f out: chsd wnr over 1f out: no imp: lost 2nd last 100yds* **9/4**^{1}

342- **4** 1/2 **White Devil**^{216} 5801 3-9-3 **79**.................... LiamKeniry 4 79
(A M Balding) *led briefly after 1f: trckd ldr: led wl over 2f out to over 1f out: outpcd fnl f* **9/1**

33-3 **5** 2 **Sheer Force (IRE)**^{14} 1061 3-8-13 **75**.................... ShaneKelly 6 70
(W J Knight) *led 1f: restrained bhd ldrs: cruised up 2f out: sn shkn up and fnd nil: wknd tamely fnl f* **5/1**^{3}

1-4 **6** 7 **Thrust Control (IRE)**^{16} 1045 3-9-4 **80**.................... AlanMunro 5 59
(M R Channon) *taken down early: trckd ldrs: cl enough on outer 2f out: sn wknd rapidly* **10/1**

0 **7** 14 **Hemera (USA)**^{21} 973 3-9-4 **80**.................... FrankieDettori 2 27
(M Johnston) *a in rr: struggling 3f out: t.o* **12/1**

4-14 **8** 2 **Ana Moutabahi**^{49} 686 3-8-4 **71**....................(v^{1}) AndrewHeffernan$^{(5)}$ 1 13
(P D Evans) *racd v wd early: rushed up to ld wl over 6f out: hdd & wknd rapidly wl over 2f out: t.o* **20/1**

1m 37.93s (-1.87) **Going Correction** -0.05s/f (Stan) **8** Ran SP% **117.6**
Speed ratings (Par 100): **107,105,103,103,101 94,80,78**
toteswingers: 1&2:£7.20, 1&3:£2.10, 2&3:£5.10 CSF £26.09 CT £58.11 TOTE £4.20: £2.40, £4.40, £1.40; EX 18.40 Place 6 £101.35, Place 5 £27.51.
Owner Leonidas Marinopoulos **Bred** Langham Hall Stud **Trained** Newmarket, Suffolk

FOCUS
A tight-looking 3-y-o handicap. It was run at a decent pace and therefore the closers were able to get seriously involved, so the form should work out.
T/Plt: £220.40 to a £1 stake. Pool: £64,832.24. 214.65 winning tickets. T/Qpdt: £41.90 to a £1 stake. Pool: £8,833.84. 155.68 winning tickets. JN

NEWMARKET (Rowley Mile) (R-H)

Wednesday, April 14

OFFICIAL GOING: Good (good to firm in places; 8.3)
Far side track used.
Wind: Fresh, across Weather: Cloudy with sunny spells

1308 ALEX SCOTT MAIDEN STKS (C&G) 7f

1:50 (1:52) (Class 4) 3-Y-O **£5,180** (£1,541; £770; £384) **Stalls** High

Form RPR

2-3 **1** **Balducci**^{25} 950 3-9-0 0.................... WilliamBuick 11 82
(A M Balding) *mde all: set stdy pce tl qcknd over 1f out: rdn and hung lft ins fnl f: r.o* **8/1**

4- **2** 1/2 **Harvest Dancer (IRE)**^{243} 4986 3-9-0 0.................... MartinDwyer 7 81+
(B J Meehan) *s.i.s: sn hld up in tch: rdn over 1f out: r.o* **2/1**^{1}

502- **3** 1 **Count Of Anjou (USA)**^{139} 7537 3-9-0 76.................... RichardHughes 10 78
(R Hannon) *trckd ldrs: shkn up over 2f out: r.o* **14/1**

00- **4** 1/2 **State Gathering**^{166} 7145 3-9-0 0.................... DaneO'Neill 8 77
(H Candy) *prom: racd keenly: rdn over 1f out: r.o* **50/1**

5 nk **Timeless Stride (IRE)** 3-9-0 0.................... RyanMoore 5 76
(Sir Michael Stoute) *sn chsng wnr: rdn and ev ch fr over 1f out tl no ex wl ins fnl f* **12/1**

32- **6** 1/2 **Esaar (USA)**^{194} 6451 3-9-0 0.................... RichardHills 2 75
(B W Hills) *trckd ldrs: racd keenly: rdn over 1f out: styd on same pce* **9/4**^{2}

7 1 1/2 **Excellent Aim** 3-9-0 0.................... ShaneKelly 9 71+
(Jane Chapple-Hyam) *s.i.s: hld up: rdn over 2f out: nvr trbld ldrs* **20/1**

8 nk **Safwaan** 3-9-0 0.................... TadhgO'Shea 3 70+
(W J Haggas) *s.s: hld up: nvr trbld ldrs* **11/2**^{3}

1m 27.51s (2.11) **Going Correction** +0.275s/f (Good) **8** Ran SP% **111.7**
Speed ratings (Par 100): **98,97,96,95,95 94,93,92**
toteswingers: 1&2 £3.70, 1&3 £6.50, 2&3 £5.40 CSF £23.27 TOTE £8.80: £2.30, £1.10, £3.30; EX 27.50.
Owner McMahon/Gorell/Pausewang/Russell **Bred** G Russell **Trained** Kingsclere, Hants

FOCUS
The ground, which had been watered, was described as good, good to firm in places, with a GoingStick reading of 8.3. A decent maiden which should supply a few winners; six of the the first seven home last year ran again and all of them won. The pace was fairly steady though, so the form is a bit muddling and best rated around the winner and third.

1309 SALINITY CONDITIONS STKS 5f

2:25 (2:25) (Class 3) 2-Y-O **£7,771** (£2,312; £1,155; £577) **Stalls** High

Form RPR

1 **Retainer (IRE)** 2-8-10 0 ow1.................... RichardHughes 6 95+
(R Hannon) *w ldr and a gng wl: led over 1f out: shkn up and qcknd clr ins fnl f: impressive* **6/5**^{1}

2 4 1/2 **Sikeeb (IRE)** 2-8-9 0.................... SebSanders 5 79
(C E Brittain) *chsd ldrs: rdn over 1f out: styd on same pce: wnt 2nd ins fnl f* **7/1**

3 1 3/4 **Ocean Bay** 2-8-9 0.................... JerryO'Dwyer 4 73+
(J Ryan) *s.s: in rr: shkn up over 1f out: r.o to go 3rd nr fin: nvr nrr* **14/1**

0 **4** 1/2 **Julius Geezer (IRE)**^{24} 954 2-8-12 0.................... RichardKingscote 1 74
(Tom Dascombe) *wnt rt s: led: rdn and hdd over 1f out: no ex ins fnl f* **9/2**^{2}

5 1/2 **Bilko Pak (IRE)** 2-8-9 0.................... RyanMoore 3 69
(R Hannon) *chsd ldrs: rdn over 1f out: styd on same pce* **6/1**^{3}

6 8 **Early Applause** 2-8-9 0.................... MichaelHills 2 40
(B W Hills) *s.s: sn pushed along in rr: lost tch 1/2-way* **7/1**

60.88 secs (1.78) **Going Correction** +0.275s/f (Good) **6** Ran SP% **109.6**
Speed ratings (Par 96): **96,88,86,85,84 71**
toteswingers: 1&2 £2.90, 1&3 £5.10, 2&3 £4.70 CSF £9.61 TOTE £1.90: £1.60, £3.00; EX 8.50.
Owner B Bull **Bred** Des Vere Hunt & Jack Ronan Farming Co **Trained** East Everleigh, Wilts

The Form Book, Raceform Ltd, Compton, RG20 6NL

FOCUS
Some smart types have taken this in recent years, with the last five subsequently successful at Listed level or above, including Royal Ascot winners Gilded and Art Connoisseur. Just like in the opener, the winner raced against the far rail, and so too did the runner-up. The third also raced against the fence for some of the way.

NOTEBOOK
Retainer(IRE) ◆ was probably on the best ground against the rail, but he was still impressive and looks potentially smart. A £26,000 half-brother to three winning sprinters, out of a fast, useful juvenile in France, he looked well educated, breaking sharply, and he showed loads of natural speed, racing freely on the pace. He was still keen inside the final 2f, but he lengthened in good style when coming under just hand pressure to quickly draw clear and provide his trainer with a fifth win in this race in the last seven years. He looks all over a Norfolk type, but Richard Hannon said he would like to see him settle better and may give him a month or two off to grow up. (op 11-10 tchd 5-4)
Sikeeb(IRE), a 66,000gns half-brother to 7f juvenile winner Gypsy Queen, was green in the paddock but shaped nicely, becoming the first of seven juvenile runners from this yard in 2010 to finish in the places. He should find easier opportunities. (op 8-1)
Ocean Bay ◆ ran an eyecatching race on debut. Described by his trainer beforehand as "a bit of a handful", he was noisy in the paddock, started slowly and ran green out the back for much of the way, but he finished in taking fashion between runners, without being hit with the whip, to get up for third. Out of a smart multiple 5f-1m1f winner, he's open to a deal of improvement and could turn out to be quite useful for a yard that did well with their juveniles last year. (op 16-1)
Julius Geezer(IRE) was sent off joint-favourite for his debut at the Curragh in March, but he got upset in the stalls that day, having to be taken out and reloaded, and failed to run much of a race. The only one with previous experience this time, he performed better, but he still didn't convince with his attitude, racing freely and, on occasions, carrying his head lower than ideal. He's obviously well regarded and has ability, but for now at least he doesn't appeal as one to follow. (op 11-2 tchd 6-1 in places)
Bilko Pak(IRE), a 25,000euros purchase, wasn't given a hard time and is open to improvement. (op 5-1)
Early Applause, a 50,000gns first foal of a dual 1m2f winner, showed little. (tchd 15-2)

1310 £250000 TATTERSALLS TIMEFORM 3-Y-O TROPHY 1m 2f
3:00 (3:00) (Class 2) 3-Y-O

£135,425 (£55,400; £24,650; £12,300; £6,150; £2,450) **Stalls** High

Form				RPR
10-	**1**		**Coordinated Cut (IRE)**[172] 7017 3-9-3 95 .... JamieSpencer 12 (M L W Bell) *swtchd to r centre sn after s: hld up in tch: jnd far side gp 6f out: led 3f out: rdn and hdd whn hmpd over 1f out: rallied to ld post* **9/1**	107+
113-	**2**	*hd*	**Ameer (IRE)**[187] 6656 3-9-3 100 .... FrankieDettori 1 (Saeed Bin Suroor) *hld up in centre gp: jnd far side 6f out: hdwy over 2f out: led and hung rt over 1f out: sn rdn: hdd post* **7/1**	106+
216-	**3**	*6*	**Hot Prospect**[177] 6898 3-9-3 92 .... KierenFallon 8 (M A Jarvis) *racd centre: hld up in tch: plld hrd: jnd far side 6f out: rdn over 2f out: styd on* **8/1**	92
140-	**4**	*1 ¼*	**High Twelve (IRE)**[179] 6849 3-9-3 105 .... WilliamBuick 7 (J H M Gosden) *racd centre: chsd ldrs: jnd far side 6f out: rdn over 1f out: no ex fnl f* **9/2**[2]	90
150-	**5**	*½*	**Cracking Lass (IRE)**[193] 6477 3-8-12 81 .... MartinDwyer 5 (R A Fahey) *racd centre: hld up: jnd far side gp 6f out: rdn over 2f out: r.o ins fnl f: nvr nrr* **50/1**	84+
35-4	**6**	*1*	**Jira**[25] 945 3-8-12 96 .... SebSanders 4 (C E Brittain) *racd centre: hld up: jnd far side 6f out: hdwy over 2f out: sn rdn: wknd ins fnl f* **16/1**	82
25-	**7**	*hd*	**Mark Twain (IRE)**[160] 7258 3-9-3 86 .... PJSmullen 6 (D M Simcock) *racd centre: hld up: jnd far side 6f out: rdn over 2f out: r.o ins fnl f: nrst fin* **100/1**	86
011-	**8**	*nk*	**Karaka Jack**[175] 6948 3-9-3 90 .... GregFairley 2 (M Johnston) *racd centre: prom: jnd far side gp 6f out: rdn over 2f out: wknd fnl f* **28/1**	86
010-	**9**	*¾*	**Sunarise (IRE)**[165] 7187 3-8-12 80 .... RichardHughes 11 (R Hannon) *hld up: racd far side: nt clr run over 2f out: swtchd lft over 1f out: nvr trbld ldrs* **50/1**	79
32-	**10**	*nk*	**Longliner**[169] 7095 3-9-3 0 .... RyanMoore 15 (Sir Michael Stoute) *racd far side: chsd ldrs: rdn over 2f out: sn outpcd: n.m.r 1f out: styd on* **10/3**[1]	83
4-	**11**	*¾*	**Don Carlos (GER)**[151] 7404 3-9-3 105 .... JMurtagh 13 (A P O'Brien, Ire) *overall ldr far side tl rdn and hdd 3f out: wknd fnl f* **6/1**[3]	82
1-	**12**	*shd*	**Next Move (IRE)**[154] 7326 3-9-3 0 .... TedDurcan 14 (Saeed Bin Suroor) *racd far side: dwlt: hld up: hdwy over 3f out: rdn over 2f out: wknd over 1f out* **16/1**	82
1-1	**13**	*¾*	**Doctor Zhivago**[61] 522 3-9-3 88 .... JoeFanning 16 (M Johnston) *racd far side: chsd ldr to 1/2-way: sn rdn: wkng whn n.m.r 2f out* **16/1**	80
506-	**14**	*1 ¾*	**Ice Viking (IRE)**[181] 6793 3-9-3 65 .... TomQueally 10 (J G Given) *racd centre: hld up: jnd far side gp 6f out: effrt over 3f out: wknd over 2f out* **100/1**	77?
30-4	**15**	*2 ¾*	**Chain Of Events**[18] 1010 3-9-3 72 .... MichaelHills 3 (B W Hills) *racd centre: dwlt: hld up: jnd far side gp 6f out: rdn and hung rt fr over 2f out: sn wknd* **66/1**	71
2-00	**16**	*1 ¼*	**Kona Coast**[25] 945 3-9-3 92 .... (p) RobertHavlin 9 (J H M Gosden) *racd centre: led that gp tl jnd far side 6f out: rdn over 2f out: sn wknd* **33/1**	69

2m 6.81s (1.01) **Going Correction** +0.275s/f (Good) **16 Ran SP% 120.6**
Speed ratings (Par 104): **106,105,101,100,99 98,98,98,97,97 97,96,96,94,92 91**
toteswingers: 1&2 £7.00, 1&3 £17.70, 2&3 £11.30 CSF £67.86 TOTE £11.20: £3.80, £1.60, £3.30; EX 90.50.
Owner Lawrie Inman **Bred** Hascombe And Valiant Studs **Trained** Newmarket, Suffolk

FOCUS
A valuable sales event even with the prize money reduction since the inaugural running last year. It produced a good field and the first two, who finished six lengths clear, are a couple of smart colts and both are rated a bit better than the bare form, which is sound overall. Five of the runners raced in a bunch near the far rail with the others down the centre, before the groups merged after half a mile.

NOTEBOOK
Coordinated Cut(IRE) ◆, formerly trained by Peter Chapple-Hyam, was promoted to Derby favouritism after his successful debut at the St Leger meeting, but his reputation was dented when he beat only one home in the Racing Post Trophy back at Doncaster. Always prominent and travelling well on this reappearance, he struck the front with three to run but was quickly tackled and headed by the runner-up, who tightened him up against the rail causing Spencer to stop riding for a couple of strides. He was left with two lengths to make up entering the final furlong, but produced a strong run to salvage things on the line. Available at around 16/1 for the Derby, we will know more after he has run in a trial, with the Dante at York the preferred option. He is a bright prospect and he should certainly get 1m4f. (op 10-1)
Ameer(IRE) lost his unbeaten record in a Saint-Cloud Group 3 on his final start at two. Ridden differently and held up on the outside of the pack, he quickened very smartly to lead but hung across to the rail as he did so, hampering Coordinated Cut. He looked to be in command, but the winner came back at him to snatch the race on the post. Another who is in the Dante and the Derby, he can make his mark in better company than this although he is evidently not straightforward. Official explanation: jockey said colt hung right (op 6-1 tchd 15-2)
Hot Prospect boiled over at Pontefract on his final run last year but behaved better in the preliminaries this time, although he still took a keen hold. He ran a thoroughly respectable race in third, if having no chance with the first pair, and looks worth stepping up to 1m4f.
High Twelve(IRE), who was joint top-rated on official figures, was taken early to post, as he had been in the Dewhurst on his last start at two. He was never far from the pace, but was unable to go with the front two in the final furlong and a half. (op 4-1)
Cracking Lass(IRE) ◆ ran on really well from the back to grab fifth, staying this longer trip surprisingly well. Connections will no doubt be keen to secure some black type for her.
Jira had the benefit of a recent run and performed respectably without entirely convincing she stayed this far. A mile would be no problem.
Mark Twain(IRE), who has been gelded since last season and was running in Britain for the first time, made late progress without ever threatening the principals.
Karaka Jack, who was put up a stone for winning a Southwell nursery on his final start at two, did the better of the Johnston pair without ever looking like winning. (op 25-1)
Longliner held Dante and Irish Derby entries but was somewhat disappointing and has now been a beaten favourite on all three of his starts. (op 4-1 tchd 3-1, 9-2 and 5-1 in places)
Don Carlos(GER), Aidan O'Brien's first runner of the year in Britain, was the other joint top-rated on BHB figures. He made the running alongside the rail before fading. (op 7-1)

1311 BLUESQUARE.COM EUROPEAN FREE H'CAP (LISTED RACE) 7f
3:35 (3:35) (Class 1) 3-Y-O

£22,708 (£8,608; £4,308; £2,148; £1,076; £540) **Stalls** High

Form				RPR
103-	**1**		**Red Jazz (USA)**[279] 3779 3-9-6 **107** .... MichaelHills 3 (B W Hills) *mde all: rdn over 1f out: edgd lft ins fnl f: styd on gamely* **11/2**	114
112-	**2**	*¾*	**Quadrille**[186] 6663 3-9-1 **102** .... RichardHughes 4 (R Hannon) *chsd wnr: rdn over 1f out: r.o* **10/3**[1]	107+
233-	**3**	*2 ½*	**Mata Keranjang (USA)**[185] 6716 3-9-5 **106** .... JamieSpencer 7 (P F I Cole) *chsd ldrs: rdn over 1f out: styd on to go 3rd nr fin* **7/1**	104+
143-	**4**	*hd*	**Audacity Of Hope**[172] 7030 3-9-3 **104** .... (t) KierenFallon 2 (P J McBride) *chsd ldrs: rdn over 1f out: no ex ins fnl f* **7/2**[2]	102
041-	**5**	*5*	**Fremont (IRE)**[196] 6397 3-8-13 **100** .... RyanMoore 5 (R Hannon) *dwlt: hld up: rdn over 2f out: wknd over 1f out* **4/1**[3]	84
634-	**6**	*shd*	**Iver Bridge Lad**[172] 7030 3-9-7 **108** .... AlanMunro 6 (J Ryan) *hld up: racd keenly: rdn over 2f out: wknd fnl f* **16/1**	92
10-6	**7**	*5*	**Hanson'D (IRE)**[25] 945 3-8-13 **100** .... PJSmullen 1 (K A Ryan) *s.i.s: racd keenly and sn trcking ldrs: rdn over 2f out: wknd over 1f out* **17/2**	70

1m 26.55s (1.15) **Going Correction** +0.275s/f (Good) **7 Ran SP% 109.6**
Speed ratings (Par 106): **104,103,100,100,94 94,88**
toteswingers: 1&2 £3.70, 1&3 £4.80, 2&3 £5.70 CSF £22.05 TOTE £6.90: £3.50, £2.40; EX 15.90.
Owner R J Arculli **Bred** William F Murphy & Annabel Murphy **Trained** Lambourn, Berks

FOCUS
A race that has had little bearing on the Newmarket 2000 Guineas in recent years, but Irish Guineas winner Indian Haven took this in 2003, while the last two runnings have gone to subsequent Group-race victors Stimulation (Challenge Stakes) and Ouqba (Jersey Stakes). The bare form of this year's race doesn't look anything special, with the pace just modest (time 1.12 seconds slower than Nell Gwyn) and the winner making all, tight against the favoured far rail for much of the way, and some of these might not be easy to place in the short term. The form has not been rated too positively.

NOTEBOOK
Red Jazz(USA), who had been off the track since finishing third in the July Stakes after apparently coughing, as well as having what Barry Hills described as "niggly problems", obviously had plenty in his favour on his return, being allowed a soft time up front on the best part of the track, and he found enough for pressure to take advantage, despite edging left late on. Entries in both the Duke of York and the Guineas suggests his connections are unsure what his optimum trip will be, and this performance hardly helped to clarify matters. He is said to be unlikely to go for the Guineas, with the Hills team thinking he may be more of a Jersey type. (op 5-1 tchd 9-2)
Quadrille, the winner of his first two starts before finishing second in a conditions contest over this trip at Ascot last October, made a pleasing return. Like the winner, he raced near the rail for much of the way and kept on well when switched into clear. This Guineas entrant should stay further. (tchd 3-1 and 7-2)
Mata Keranjang(USA) is still a maiden, but he has yet to race at a lower level than Listed company and posted several fine efforts in defeat last year. He never looked like winning on this return to action, but kept on all the way to the line and gave the impression he'll be better for the outing. He's a smart type, but may benefit from dropping in grade to gain a confidence-boosting success. (op 8-1 tchd 9-1)
Audacity Of Hope, a tough and progressive juvenile last year who was last seen finishing third in the Horris Hill, seemed to be well enough placed but he didn't pick up as well as one might have and was not given a hard time. (op 9-2)
Fremont(IRE), returning from 196 days off, was left with too much to do in this steadily run race after missing the break.
Iver Bridge Lad, fourth in the Horris Hill on his first try at this trip when last seen in October, was conceding weight all round and never got involved after racing keenly. (op 12-1)
Hanson'D(IRE), who was thought good enough to contest the Racing Post Trophy last season (seventh, beaten 10l), ran poorly. (op 8-1 tchd 15-2)

1312 LESLIE HARRISON MEMORIAL NELL GWYN STKS (GROUP 3) (FILLIES) 7f
4:10 (4:11) (Class 1) 3-Y-O

£36,900 (£13,988; £7,000; £3,490; £1,748; £877) **Stalls** High

Form				RPR
101-	**1**		**Music Show (IRE)**[179] 6852 3-9-1 110 .... KierenFallon 11 (M R Channon) *hld up: swtchd lft and hdwy over 2f out: led over 1f out: edgd rt: drvn out* **6/1**[2]	113+
125-	**2**	*½*	**Blue Maiden**[194] 6447 3-8-12 102 .... RichardHughes 8 (P J McBride) *chsd ldrs: nt clr run: lost pl and stone last over 2f out: hdwy over 1f out: rdn and r.o wl* **12/1**	109+
1-	**3**	*2 ½*	**Principal Role (USA)**[176] 6921 3-8-12 82 .... TomQueally 4 (H R A Cecil) *hld up: hdwy over 2f out: rdn over 1f out: styd on same pce fnl f* **13/2**[3]	102
3-	**4**	*1 ¼*	**Safina**[165] 7183 3-8-12 0 .... RyanMoore 2 (Sir Michael Stoute) *hld up: hdwy and swtchd lft over 2f out: nt clr run and swtchd rt over 1f out: r.o: nt rch ldrs* **8/1**	99+
121-	**5**	*nk*	**Hafawa (IRE)**[183] 6756 3-8-12 90 .... RichardHills 3 (M Johnston) *hld up: hdwy 1/2-way: jnd ldrs: over 2f out: rdn and ev ch over 1f out: no ex fnl f* **9/1**	98

110- **6** *nk* **Distinctive**[179] 6852 3-8-12 102 .... TomEaves 10 97
(B Smart) *hld up: hdwy over 2f out: rdn and n.m.r over 1f out: swtchd lft fnl f: styd on u.p* **16/1**

210- **7** *3 1/4* **Jacqueline Quest (IRE)**[172] 7033 3-8-12 97 .... IanMongan 5 88
(H R A Cecil) *chsd ldr tl led 1/2-way: rdn and hdd over 1f out: wknd ins fnl f* **14/1**

522- **8** *3* **Atasari (IRE)**[179] 6852 3-8-12 109 .... KJManning 6 80
(J S Bolger, Ire) *prom: rdn and hung rt over 1f out: wknd and eased fnl f* **7/2**[1]

215- **9** *4* **Dyna Waltz**[200] 6269 3-8-12 103 .... WilliamBuick 7 69
(J H M Gosden) *chsd ldrs: rdn over 2f out: sn wknd* **10/1**

131- **10** *1 1/4* **Queen's Grace**[166] 7147 3-8-12 100 .... SteveDrowne 1 66
(H Morrison) *hld up: hdwy 1/2-way: rdn over 1f out: wknd fnl f* **9/1**

11 **11** *10* **Srda (USA)**[23] 964 3-8-12 86 .... AhmedAjtebi 9 39
(C E Brittain) *led: edgd rt fr over 4f out: hdd 1/2-way: wknd wl over 2f out* **14/1**

1m 25.43s (0.03) **Going Correction** +0.275s/f (Good) **11** Ran SP% **117.0**
Speed ratings (Par 105): **110,109,106,105,104 104,100,97,92,91 79**
toteswingers: 1&2 £13.40, 1&3 £7.40, 2&3 £19.90 CSF £75.40 TOTE £5.70: £2.00, £4.50, £2.60; EX 84.80.
Owner Jaber Abdullah **Bred** Darley **Trained** West Ilsley, Berks

FOCUS
An open and up-to-scratch renewal of the Nell Gwyn, one of the principal trials for the 1000 Guineas, although Speciosa in 2006 is the only filly in the last 24 years to win both races. It was something of a messy affair and the first two did well to finish clear of the rest after having to come from the rear. They are both rated better than the bare form.

NOTEBOOK
Music Show(IRE) ◆ was penalised 3lb for last autumn's Rockfel Stakes win here and produced a very useful performance to successfully give the weight away. Drawn on the rail, she raced behind the leaders for a time, but had to be pulled out to get a run and found herself at the back of the field. Producing a strong run down the outside to lead, her advantage was being reduced by the runner-up as she got a bit tired, but she always looked in command. Now a winner of four of her five starts, she is sure to come on a good deal for the outing and is well worth her place in the Guineas field, particularly with doubts over ante-post favourite Special Duty following her defeat at Maisons-Laffitte. (op 5-1 tchd 7-1)
Blue Maiden lost her pitch after encountering an interrupted passage and dropped to the rear before bursting through and closing down the winner, who also came from the back. There is improvement to come from her over 1m on easier ground, and connections favour a tilt at the Irish 1000 Guineas. (op 20-1)
Principal Role(USA) created a good impression when winning a Yarmouth maiden on her only start at two and she confirmed herself a useful filly, keeping on well for third. A return to 1m will see her in an even better light, but she does look to have her quirks. (op 11-2)
Safina ◆, whose dam Russian Rhythm won the Guineas seven years ago, was the only maiden in the field. She stayed on steadily once in the clear and should improve considerably for this experience. (op 15-2 tchd 9-1)
Hafawa(IRE) has her share of temperament but she is a useful filly too. She duelled for the lead with the eventual seventh before fading inside the last. (op 10-1 tchd 17-2)
Distinctive had Music Show behind when landing Ayr's Firth Of Clyde Stakes last September, but was favoured by the draw that day and could not confirm the form in the Rockfel. She ran respectably on this seasonal return and seemed to get the trip, but she may not prove easy to place this year.
Jacqueline Quest(IRE), her yard's second string, got to the front at halfway but was soon tackled for the lead, and had no answers once headed. (op 18-1 tchd 20-1)
Atasari(IRE), runner-up to Music Show in the Rockfel in the autumn, was 3lb better off for a neck and was sent off favourite, but after chasing the pace she came under pressure with 3f to run and weakened steadily. She has plenty to prove now. (op 5-1)
Dyna Waltz, whose dam won this race in 1999, was one of the first beaten and will be suited by returning to 1m. (op 11-1)
Queen's Grace, who is only small, did all her racing at two over 6f and did not appear to get home. (tchd 10-1)
Srda(USA), a dual Polytrack winner taking a steep rise in grade on this turf debut, made the early running before dropping right away in the final quarter mile. (op 12-1)

1313 BLUE SQUARE FEILDEN STKS (LISTED RACE) 1m 1f
4:45 (4:46) (Class 1) 3-Y-O

£22,708 (£8,608; £4,308; £2,148; £1,076; £540) **Stalls** High

Form RPR

1- **1** **Rumoush (USA)**[151] 7388 3-8-8 0 .... RichardHills 3 106+
(M P Tregoning) *dwlt: hld up: hdwy over 2f out: led over 1f out: edgd rt: r.o* **7/2**[2]

431 **2** *2 1/2* **Fighter Boy (IRE)**[32] 889 3-8-13 83 .... JamieSpencer 9 106
(T D Barron) *stdd s: hld up and bhd: hdwy 2f out: rdn and hung rt over 1f out: styd on to go 2nd post: no ch w wnr* **40/1**

24-4 **3** *hd* **Marie De Medici (USA)**[25] 952 3-8-8 104 .... FrankieDettori 4 100
(M Johnston) *led to 1/2-way: led again over 2f out: rdn and edgd rt: hdd over 1f out: styd on same pce ins fnl f* **8/1**[3]

211- **4** *1 1/2* **Timepiece**[165] 7187 3-8-11 99 .... TomQueally 2 103+
(H R A Cecil) *hld up in tch: effrt and n.m.r 2f out: edgd rt fr over 1f out: styng on same pce whn nt clr run wl ins fnl f* **2/1**[1]

321- **5** *5* **Mufarrh (IRE)**[183] 6754 3-8-13 92 .... TadhgO'Shea 8 91
(J L Dunlop) *plld hrd and prom: led over 3f out: hdd over 2f out: wknd fnl f* **12/1**

15- **6** *6* **Prizefighting (USA)**[164] 7207 3-8-13 106 .... WilliamBuick 5 78
(J H M Gosden) *prom: rdn over 3f out: wknd over 2f out* **7/2**[2]

541- **7** *8* **Gallic Star (IRE)**[177] 6898 3-8-11 98 .... KierenFallon 1 58
(M R Channon) *chsd ldrs: rdn over 3f out: wknd 2f out* **16/1**

5-54 **8** *1* **Black Snowflake (USA)**[40] 819 3-8-13 97 ....(v[1]) AhmedAjtebi 6 58
(Mahmood Al Zarooni) *s.i.s: hld up: hdwy to ld over 4f out: hdd over 3f out: sn rdn: wknd wl over 1f out* **16/1**

10-4 **9** *19* **Stags Leap (IRE)**[35] 840 3-8-13 89 .... RichardHughes 7 16
(R Hannon) *chsd ldrs tl rdn and wknd over 3f out* **33/1**

1m 51.98s (0.28) **Going Correction** +0.275s/f (Good) **9** Ran SP% **113.7**
Speed ratings (Par 106): **109,106,106,105,100 95,88,87,70**
toteswingers: 1&2 £14.80, 1&3 £7.50, 2&3 £10.30 CSF £121.00 TOTE £4.90: £2.00, £5.90, £1.30; EX 140.70.
Owner Hamdan Al Maktoum **Bred** Shadwell Farm LLC **Trained** Lambourn, Berks

FOCUS
In recent years both Rebel Rebel and Olympian Odyssey were beaten in this race ahead of placing in the 2000 Guineas, while Bollin Eric was third in the 2002 running before landing that year's St Leger. This year's race looked fascinating beforehand, and plenty of intrigue remained after the event. The true worth of the form is difficult to get a handle on, but for now it may be worth assuming Fighter Boy is better than his official mark 83, and instead use Marie De Medici as the benchmark. The first two finishers came from well back, but the third was always prominent and it seems they simply went a good, even gallop. The impressive Rumoush looks well up to a better grade.

NOTEBOOK
Rumoush(USA) ◆, who created a good impression when winning a 1m Polytrack maiden on debut (runner-up, third and seventh successful since), is a half-sister to Ghanaati and Mawatheeq, and she showed herself to be pretty smart in her own right. Held up out the back after taking time to get into her stride, she produced a sustained effort from over 3f out and ultimately only needed to be hit with the whip when inside the final furlong. Considering her inexperience, and that Marcus Tregoning has been quoted as saying she is "already as tall as her close relative Nayef", there is every reason to believe she can progress into a high-class filly. The question now is whether she goes for an Oaks trial, or drops back in trip for the Guineas. There is stamina in her pedigree (sister won over 1m4f), but there's also plenty of speed and she certainly looks a filly with pace. All things considered (not least her ability to act on this track), she deserves to take her chance in the 1000 Guineas, but makes less appeal as an Oaks filly at this stage. (op 4-1 tchd 9-2)
Fighter Boy(IRE) didn't have to come off the bridle when winning his maiden at Wolverhampton last time and it had to be significant that such a good trainer of handicappers opted to go for a Listed race, rather than try to exploit an official mark of 83. Another to start slowly, he was being niggled along out the back over 4f out, but he gradually responded and stayed on well when coming under more serious pressure inside the final 2f. He looks sure to be suited by even further and appeals as the type to go alright in a Derby trial at around 1m4f - maybe the Chester Vase or the Lingfield Derby Trial - if given the chance.
Marie De Medici(USA), fourth in a 1m21/2f Listed race on testing ground on her reappearance, ran well considering she raced more prominently than the front pair. This is her sort of level. (op 9-1 tchd 10-1)
Timepiece ◆ ran in this to establish whether she has the speed for the Guineas, but it's clear she almost certainly doesn't and this was actually a perfectly respectable Oaks trial. She had every chance over 2f out, but simply lacked the speed of Rumoush and was soon hemmed in when that rival swept by, ultimately being short of room and eased inside the final furlong. Although by no means an unlucky loser, she probably would have stayed on into second with one clear run and shaped as though there will be more to come when she steps up in trip. She should go well in a traditional Oaks trial next time and remains of interest for Epsom. (op 6-4)
Mufarrh(IRE), 4l too good for the potentially decent Official Style over 7f at Leicester on his final juvenile start, was too keen and failed to see his race out. (op 14-1 tchd 10-1)
Prizefighting(USA) really impressed when winning a Polytrack maiden on debut last year, but it seemed a strange decision to run him on testing ground in a French Group 1 just a week later, for all that he didn't perform badly. This was a disappointing return to the track. (op 4-1 tchd 9-2 in places)
Black Snowflake(USA) was the first runner in Britain for Godolphin's new second trainer. (op 20-1)

1314 BLUESQUARE.COM I-CARD MAIDEN STKS 1m 2f
5:20 (5:22) (Class 4) 3-Y-O **£5,180** (£1,541; £770; £384) **Stalls** High

Form RPR

1 **Desert Myth (USA)** 3-9-3 0 .... RyanMoore 5 95+
(Sir Michael Stoute) *hld up: hdwy over 2f out: shkn up to ld ins fnl f: r.o* **6/1**[3]

23-2 **2** *1 1/4* **Deauville Post (FR)**[25] 949 3-9-3 82 .... RichardHughes 9 89
(R Hannon) *chsd clr ldr tl led over 2f out: rdn over 1f out: hdd and unable qck ins fnl f* **5/1**[2]

0- **3** *shd* **Awsaal**[166] 7146 3-9-3 0 .... TadhgO'Shea 6 89
(J L Dunlop) *s.s: sn prom: ev ch fr over 2f out: rdn over 1f out: styd on same pce wl ins fnl f* **14/1**

30- **4** *6* **Theology**[180] 6810 3-9-3 0 .... FrankieDettori 4 77+
(J Noseda) *hld up: hdwy and hmpd over 2f out: rdn over 1f out: wknd ins fnl f* **15/2**

5 *3/4* **Usailaan** 3-9-3 0 .... RichardHills 3 75+
(M P Tregoning) *hld up: rdn over 3f out: nvr on terms* **10/1**

6 *6* **Sarbaaz (IRE)** 3-9-3 0 .... JackMitchell 1 63+
(M A Jarvis) *s.i.s: hld up: rdn over 4f out: nvr on terms* **25/1**

0- **7** *2 1/2* **Out Of Eden**[172] 7034 3-9-3 0 .... TomQueally 7 58
(H R A Cecil) *prom: rdn whn hmpd over 2f out: wknd over 1f out* **14/1**

34- **8** *hd* **Lunar Victory (USA)**[188] 6620 3-9-3 0 .... WilliamBuick 10 58
(J H M Gosden) *prom: rdn over 2f out: edgd rt: wknd over 1f out* **11/8**[1]

0- **9** *2 1/2* **Kathleen Frances**[169] 7099 3-8-7 0 .... AshleyMorgan(5) 2 48
(M H Tompkins) *hld up: rdn over 4f out: wknd over 3f out* **100/1**

53- **10** *35* **Cape D'Or (IRE)**[291] 3376 3-9-3 0 .... JohnEgan 8 —
(J L Hassett, Ire) *led and sn clr: wknd and hdd over 2f out: eased: t.o* **25/1**

2m 6.56s (0.76) **Going Correction** +0.275s/f (Good) **10** Ran SP% **115.9**
Speed ratings (Par 100): **107,106,105,101,100 95,93,93,91,63**
toteswingers: 1&2 £5.50, 1&3 £15.80, 2&3 £13.20 CSF £35.28 TOTE £6.30: £1.50, £1.20, £5.30; EX 36.80.
Owner Saeed Suhail **Bred** Edward P Evans **Trained** Newmarket, Suffolk

FOCUS
An interesting maiden in which the first three came clear. Cape D'Or went off far too quickly, with the rest letting him do his own thing. The runner-up is probably the best guide and the winner is a smart prospect.

1315 BET@BLUESQUARE.COM H'CAP 6f
5:55 (5:55) (Class 2) (0-100,100) 3-Y-O **£11,656** (£3,468; £1,733; £865) **Stalls** High

Form RPR

215- **1** **Mister Hughie (IRE)**[193] 6486 3-9-4 95 .... AlanMunro 5 102
(M R Channon) *racd stands' side: hld up: hdwy over 1f out: r.o to ld nr fin* **25/1**

100- **2** *nk* **Pastoral Player**[166] 7150 3-9-1 92 .... SteveDrowne 11 98+
(H Morrison) *racd far side: hld up: hdwy over 1f out: led overall ins fnl f: hdd nr fin: 1st of 14 in gp* **7/1**[2]

310- **3** *shd* **Sunraider (IRE)**[216] 5795 3-8-9 86 .... RobertWinston 1 91
(B W Hills) *racd stands' side: chsd ldr: led that bunch over 1f out: hdd towards fin: 2nd of 5 in gp* **16/1**

213- **4** *3/4* **Racy**[170] 7063 3-8-9 86 .... RyanMoore 3 89
(Sir Michael Stoute) *racd stands' side: chsd ldrs: rdn and ev ch that gp over 1f out: styd on: 3rd of 5 in gp* **13/2**[1]

100- **5** *nk* **Swilly Ferry (USA)**[186] 6677 3-9-4 95 .... MichaelHills 19 97+
(B W Hills) *racd far side: hld up: hdwy and nt clr run over 1f out: hmpd ins fnl f: r.o: nvr able to chal: 2nd of 14 in gp* **14/1**

40-5 **6** *nk* **Fratellino**[25] 945 3-9-5 96 .... JamesDoyle 16 97
(A J McCabe) *overall ldr far side: rdn over 1f out: hdd ins fnl f: styd on: 3rd of 14 in gp* **16/1**

41-2 **7** *nse* **Edgewater (IRE)**[18] 1019 3-8-10 87 .... DaneO'Neill 7 88
(J Akehurst) *racd far side: hld up: rdn over 2f out: r.o ins fnl f: nrst fin: 4th of 14 in gp* **16/1**

1115 **8** *1/2* **Love Delta (USA)**[18] 1019 3-9-4 95 .... JoeFanning 2 94
(M Johnston) *racd stands' side: chsd ldrs: rdn over 1f out: styd on: 4th of 5 in gp* **25/1**

51-1 **9** *nk* **Clifton Bridge**[81] 277 3-8-4 81 .... RichardKingscote 20 79
(R M Beckett) *racd far side: chsd ldrs: rdn and ev ch over 1f out: hung rt and no ex ins fnl f: 5th of 14 in gp* **16/1**

313- **10** *shd* **Folly Bridge**[196] 6397 3-8-1 **81** .... Louis-PhilippeBeuzelin(3) 18 79
(R Charlton) *racd far side: chsd ldrs: rdn over 2f out: no ex ins fnl f: 6th of 14 in gp* **10/1**

162- **11** *nk* **Kaptain Kirkup (IRE)**[193] 6486 3-9-4 **95** .... TomEaves 17 92+
(M Dods) *s.i.s: racd far side: hld up: hdwy and nt clr run over 1f out: nvr trbld ldrs: 7th of 14 in gp* **14/1**

5-03 **12** *3/4* **Duplicity**[18] 1019 3-9-9 **100** .... RichardHughes 10 95
(R Hannon) *racd far side: chsd ldr: rdn and ev ch over 1f out: no ex ins fnl f: 8th of 14 in gp* **20/1**

316- **13** *3/4* **Swiss Cross**[172] 7013 3-8-4 **81** .... MartinDwyer 9 73
(G A Butler) *racd far side: hld up in tch: plld hrd: rdn over 1f out: no ex ins fnl f: 9th of 14 in gp* **8/1**[3]

00-4 **14** *hd* **Ghostwing**[18] 1019 3-8-13 **90** .... TadhgO'Shea 6 82
(J Gallagher) *led stands' side over 4f: no ex: last of 5 in gp* **25/1**

365- **15** *1/2* **Colonel Mak**[172] 7016 3-9-1 **92** .... PhillipMakin 14 89+
(T D Barron) *racd far side: mid-div: rdn over 1f out: no ex fnl f: 10th of 14 in gp* **16/1**

22-0 **16** *1/2* **Ongoodform (IRE)**[25] 945 3-8-12 **89** .... WilliamBuick 12 77
(P W D'Arcy) *racd far side: hld up in tch: rdn over 1f out: no ex fnl f: 11th of 14 in gp* **12/1**

101- **17** *4* **Comedy Hall (USA)**[191] 6541 3-9-1 **92** .... FrankieDettori 15 74
(M Johnston) *chsd ldrs: rdn over 1f out: wknd and eased ins fnl f: 12th of 14 in gp* **9/1**

1150 **18** *3* **Admiral Cochrane (IRE)**[11] 1086 3-8-7 **84** .... RobertHavlin 8 50
(W Jarvis) *racd far side: hld up in tch: rdn over 2f out: wknd over 1f out: 13th of 14 in gp* **50/1**

45-0 **19** *8* **Kingdom Of Munster (IRE)**[18] 1019 3-9-3 **94** .... TomQueally 13 34
(Ian Williams) *racd far side: bhd fr 1/2-way: last of 14 in gp* **80/1**

1m 13.14s (0.94) **Going Correction** +0.275s/f (Good) 19 Ran SP% **126.0**
Speed ratings (Par 104): **104,103,103,102,102 101,101,100,100,100 100,99,98,97,97 96,91,87,76**
toteswingers: 1&2 £44.00, 1&3 £41.40, 2&3 £24.70 CSF £184.16 CT £3003.48 TOTE £29.40: £6.60, £2.70, £5.10, £2.30; EX 330.10 Place 6 £234.50, Place 5 £118.22.
Owner Liam Mulryan **Bred** Mcmac Syndicate **Trained** West Ilsley, Berks

FOCUS
A very competitive 3-y-o sprint handicap. Three of the first four raced in the bunch of five towards the stands' side, but there wasn't much between the two groups.

NOTEBOOK
Mister Hughie(IRE) gained his first success in selling company, but he progressed well to take nurseries off 70 and 79 respectively and he showed he's still improving with a very useful performance after 193 days off. He'll be rated around 100 once reassessed and his connections may look for a Listed race. (op 33-1)
Pastoral Player didn't go on as expected after winning on debut last year, not helped by having a problem with the stalls (refused to enter them ahead of the Redcar Two-Year-Old Trophy) and being a keen type. Gelded since his last run, he was free for a couple of furlongs on the way to the start, but still managed to post a very useful effort, faring best of those in the larger far-side group. His trainer, who won this with Sakhee's Secret in 2007, thinks a bit of him, and he's evidently decent, but it remains to be seen which way he will go. (op 11-2)
Sunraider(IRE) ◆, dropped in trip on his return from 216 days off, showed good speed, tight against the stands' rail, and had every chance. This was only his fourth start and he's open to improvement. (op 20-1)
Racy ◆ ran a pleasing race after 170 days off, showing enough to suggest he can improve past his current mark of 86. (op 6-1)
Swilly Ferry(USA) ◆, reappearing after around six months off, looked an unlucky loser as he was travelling well against the far rail but had nowhere to go for most of the closing stages, only getting in the clear around half a furlong out. Official explanation: jockey said colt was denied a clear run (op 16-1)
Fratellino ran well for a long way under a positive ride on the far side of the track, although unlike the five who finished ahead of him, he had the benefit of a recent outing. Official explanation: jockey said colt lost a shoe
Kaptain Kirkup(IRE) didn't get the best of runs and might be better than he showed.
Duplicity Official explanation: jockey said colt raced too keen
Swiss Cross was too keen.
T/Plt: £186.70 to a £1 stake. Pool: £82,215.18. 321.30 winning tickets. T/Qpdt: £51.80 to a £1 stake. Pool: £5,590.72. 79.74 winning tickets. CR

1300 KEMPTON (A.W) (R-H)
Thursday, April 15

OFFICIAL GOING: Standard
Wind: Brisk, against Weather: Fine

1316 FAMILY FUN DAY MAY 3RD H'CAP — 5f (P)
5:40 (5:40) (Class 6) (0-65,70) 3-Y-O — **£2,047** (£604; £302) **Stalls** High

Form RPR

46-0 **1** **Do More Business (IRE)**[15] 1058 3-9-0 **60** .... JackMitchell 6 64
(P M Phelan) *tended to hang lft: cl up on inner: rdn over 1f out: swtchd lft ent fnl f and sn chsd ldr: r.o to ld last 50yds* **9/4**[1]

-442 **2** *3/4* **Papageno**[20] 988 3-9-3 **63** .... ShaneKelly 4 65
(J R Jenkins) *led: rdn over a l clr 1f out: hdd and fdd last 50yds* **3/1**[2]

3602 **3** *1/2* **Rathbawn Girl (IRE)**[20] 991 3-8-8 **61** .... AdamBeschizza(7) 2 61
(Miss J Feilden) *dwlt: sn in tch and racd wd: effrt over 1f out: kpt on same pce to take 3rd ins fnl f* **7/1**

-205 **4** *hd* **Tulip Explosion**[8] 1155 3-8-4 **50** oh2 .... JimmyQuinn 5 49
(D Shaw) *hld up in last pair: brought wd bnd 2f out: shkn up and prog to dispute 3rd ins fnl f: kpt on same pce* **20/1**

60-3 **5** *1/2* **Pherousa**[20] 988 3-9-2 **62** .... DaneO'Neill 3 59
(M Blanshard) *cl up: chsd ldr wl over 1f out: no imp: wknd ins fnl f* **8/1**

0-66 **6** *1 1/2* **Bob Goes Electric (IRE)**[29] 900 3-8-11 **57** .... SteveDrowne 7 49
(J R Best) *t.k.h: hld up in last pair: shkn up over 1f out: no prog* **4/1**[3]

-042 **7** *1 1/2* **Lets Move It**[29] 906 3-8-4 **50** oh3 ....(v) LukeMorris 1 36
(D Shaw) *dwlt: hanging lft but chsd ldr to wl over 1f out: wknd* **12/1**

61.40 secs (0.90) **Going Correction** 0.0s/f (Stan) 7 Ran SP% **111.8**
Speed ratings (Par 96): **92,90,90,89,88 86,84**
toteswingers: 1&2 £3.50, 1&3 £5.70, 2&3 £3.20 CSF £8.71 CT £37.62 TOTE £5.70: £4.30, £1.10; EX 12.00.
Owner Timesquare Ltd **Bred** Hardys Of Kilkeel Ltd **Trained** Epsom, Surrey

FOCUS
A modest handicap that lost much of its interest with the late defection of likely market leader Silver Linnet. The gallop was just an ordinary one and the winner edged off the inside rail in the closing stages. The first two set the level.

Tulip Explosion Official explanation: jockey said filly ran too freely

1317 BISTRO IN THE PANORAMIC RESTAURANT CLASSIFIED STKS — 1m 2f (P)
6:10 (6:10) (Class 5) 3-Y-O — **£2,590** (£770; £385; £192) **Stalls** High

Form RPR

100- **1** **Dromore (IRE)**[174] 6993 3-9-0 75 .... DavidProbert 5 81
(A M Balding) *t.k.h early: trckd ldr after 4f: chal 2f out: hung fire over 1f out: urged ahd last 150yds: hld on* **9/2**[3]

22-1 **2** *nk* **Calypso Star (IRE)**[15] 1061 3-9-0 75 .... PatDobbs 6 80
(R Hannon) *led 1f: dropped to 3rd after 4f: pushed along 3f out and sn outpcd by ldng pair: no imp tl styd on wl fnl f to take 2nd and cl on wnr fin* **15/8**[1]

-232 **3** *1 1/2* **Green Earth (IRE)**[7] 1189 3-9-0 74 .... JimmyQuinn 4 77
(Mrs A J Perrett) *led after 1f: pressed 2f out: kpt on u.p tl hdd and no ex last 150yds* **7/2**[2]

301- **4** *2 1/2* **Gifted Apakay (USA)**[132] 7624 3-9-0 75 .... SteveDrowne 3 72
(E A L Dunlop) *hld up in 4th: appeared gng wl enough over 2f out: shkn up and nt qckn over 1f out* **8/1**

351- **5** *2* **Maristar (USA)**[176] 6947 3-9-0 75 .... NickyMackay 1 68
(G A Butler) *hld up in last: shkn up and no rspnse 2f out: n.d after* **7/2**[2]

2m 8.15s (0.15) **Going Correction** 0.0s/f (Stan) 5 Ran SP% **108.5**
Speed ratings (Par 98): **99,98,97,95,93**
CSF £12.97 TOTE £14.10: £6.00, £1.10; EX 14.10.
Owner I G Burbidge **Bred** Mount Eaton Stud **Trained** Kingsclere, Hants

FOCUS
A tightly knit classified event on paper but a modest gallop only picked up turning for home. The winner raced just off the inside rail in the straight and rates an improver with the third and fourth the best guides.

1318 DIGIBET.COM CLAIMING STKS — 1m 2f (P)
6:40 (6:40) (Class 6) 4-Y-O+ — **£2,047** (£604; £302) **Stalls** High

Form RPR

3111 **1** **Sedgwick**[28] 923 8-8-13 71 .... StevieDonohoe 4 68
(Ian Williams) *trckd ldr: pushed along over 2f out: effrt to ld wl over 1f out and sn clr: pushed out and in n.d fnl f* **5/2**[2]

60-4 **2** *1 1/2* **Cactus King**[97] 80 7-8-4 62 .... KierenFox(5) 2 61
(P M Phelan) *stdd s: t.k.h: hld up last: gd prog fr 2f out to take 2nd last 150yds: styd on but wnr already home* **12/1**

4340 **3** *1 3/4* **Cupid's Glory**[8] 1156 8-8-13 72 .... PatDobbs 11 61
(G L Moore) *hld up in abt 5th: effrt over 2f out and sn 4th: rdn and kpt on same pce to dispute 2nd briefly ins fnl f* **3/1**[3]

-246 **4** *1 1/4* **Monaco Dream (IRE)**[27] 941 4-8-9 65 ....(p) AlanMunro 3 55
(W Jarvis) *led and allowed unchal ld: hdd wl over 1f out: sn btn* **13/2**

3233 **5** *3/4* **Atacama Sunrise**[6] 1208 4-8-6 67 .... SimonPearce(5) 6 55
(J Pearce) *t.k.h: racd wd: trckd ldrs: wnt 3rd over 2f out: nt qckn over 1f out: fdd* **9/4**[1]

2540 **6** *1/2* **Hatch A Plan (IRE)**[22] 970 9-8-12 50 .... DaneO'Neill 10 55
(Mouse Hamilton-Fairley) *hld up in last trio: gng wl enough over 2f out: shkn up and no prog over 1f out* **40/1**

4102 **7** *3* **Playful Asset (IRE)**[55] 611 4-8-8 53 .... KirstyMilczarek 5 45
(P Howling) *hld up in last trio: shuffled along fr 2f out: nvr a factor* **16/1**

0420 **8** *1 3/4* **Play Up Pompey**[50] 685 8-8-12 47 .... JerryO'Dwyer 9 46
(J J Bridger) *trckd ldrs: drvn over 2f out: sn lost pl and btn* **40/1**

-000 **9** *24* **Wicklewood**[76] 353 4-8-11 44 ....(v) TomMcLaughlin 1 —
(Mrs C A Dunnett) *disp 2nd pl tl wknd rapidly 3f out: t.o* **100/1**

2m 7.04s (-0.96) **Going Correction** 0.0s/f (Stan) 9 Ran SP% **117.1**
Speed ratings (Par 101): **103,101,100,99,98 98,96,94,75**
toteswingers: 1&2 £8.60, 1&3 £3.30, 2&3 £5.70 CSF £32.50 TOTE £2.30: £1.02, £6.90, £2.30; EX 32.10.
Owner A L R Morton **Bred** G And Mrs Middlebrook **Trained** Portway, Worcs

FOCUS
A couple of fair sorts in just an ordinary claimer. The gallop was a moderate one and the winner ended up close to the inside rail in the closing stages. The winner is the most reliable guide.

1319 DIGIBET MAIDEN AUCTION STKS — 5f (P)
7:10 (7:10) (Class 5) 2-Y-O — **£2,590** (£770; £385; £192) **Stalls** High

Form RPR

5 **1** **Pick A Little**[19] 1017 2-8-11 0 .... DaneO'Neill 7 68
(B W Duke) *mde virtually all: gained def advantage over 1f out: styd on* **4/1**[2]

03 **2** *1/2* **Ivan's A Star (IRE)**[9] 1136 2-8-9 0 .... LiamKeniry 6 64
(J S Moore) *trckd ldng pair: wnt 2nd over 1f out on inner: n.m.r sn after: swtchd lft and styd on last 100yds* **5/2**[1]

0 **3** *1/2* **Belle Bayardo (IRE)**[9] 1136 2-8-9 0 .... LiamJones 8 62+
(R A Harris) *dwlt: bdly outpcd and virtually t.o after 2f: picked up fnl f: flashed past 4 rivals last 75yds* **16/1**

0 **4** *1* **Mirror Lad**[19] 1009 2-8-11 0 .... RichardKingscote 5 61
(Tom Dascombe) *disp ld w wnr to 1/2-way: hrd rdn and nt qckn wl over 1f out: readily hld after* **5/2**[1]

0 **5** *1/2* **Bobby Smith (IRE)**[15] 1065 2-8-11 0 .... JerryO'Dwyer 2 59
(M G Quinlan) *chsd ldng pair to 2f out: nt qckn u.p over 1f out: plugged on* **12/1**

6 *nse* **Ruby Alexander (IRE)** 2-8-7 0 ow1 .... JackMitchell 1 55
(R M Beckett) *settled in rr but in tch: shkn up and no real prog over 1f out: plugged on* **5/1**[3]

7 *1/2* **Lady On Top (IRE)** 2-8-1 0 .... AmyBaker(5) 4 52
(Mrs P N Dutfield) *in tch in rr: bmpd along and no imp over 1f out: plugged on* **14/1**

61.65 secs (1.15) **Going Correction** 0.0s/f (Stan) 7 Ran SP% **114.1**
Speed ratings (Par 92): **90,89,88,86,86 85,85**
toteswingers: 1&2 £2.60, 1&3 £4.50, 2&3 £13.70 CSF £14.37 TOTE £7.40: £6.00, £1.10; EX 15.80.
Owner K B Hodges **Bred** D R Tucker **Trained** Lambourn, Berks

FOCUS
A maiden with little strength in depth. The gallop was reasonable and the winner raced just off the inside rail in the straight.

NOTEBOOK
Pick A Little's debut run has taken a few knocks form-wise but he bettered that effort and showed a good attitude in the closing stages. This was not a strong maiden and he had the rub of things but there's no reason why he shouldn't be able to go on a little from this. (op 9-2)
Ivan's A Star(IRE), the most experienced of these, jumped off much better this time and ran up to his best, despite edging away from the inside rail late on. He's vulnerable to an improver in this type of event but may be able to pick up a small race in due course. (tchd 11-4)
Belle Bayardo(IRE) ◆, whose chance was again compromised with a slow start, made up a considerable amount of ground down the centre in the closing stages to finish on the heels of the first two. He'll stay 6f and can win a similar event, especially when jumping off on terms.

Mirror Lad, the subject of support in the day, again showed speed and fared better on this surface than he had in soft ground in the Brocklesby. He'll have to up his game again if he's to win in this grade, though. (op 11-4)

Bobby Smith(IRE) bettered his Fibresand debut form but is likely to remain vulnerable in this type of event. (op 16-1)

Ruby Alexander(IRE), who is related to a couple of juvenile winners, was not disgraced on this racecourse debut and is entitled to improve for the experience. (op 9-2 tchd 4-1)

1320 DIGIBET CASINO H'CAP 5f (P)

7:40 (7:40) (Class 5) (0-75,74) 4-Y-0+ **£2,590** (£770; £385; £192) **Stalls** High

Form RPR

2121 **1** **Misaro (GER)**[20] [986] 9-8-13 **69**..........(b) DavidProbert 3 79
(R A Harris) *pressed ldr: clr of rest over 1f out: rdn to ld jst ins fnl f: sn drew clr* **5/2**[1]

4016 **2** *2 1/4* **Bookiesindex Boy**[10] [1131] 6-9-1 **71**..........(b) StephenCraine 5 73
(J R Jenkins) *racd freely: led: hld together over 1f out: hdd and nudged along jst ins fnl f: no rspnse* **13/2**

4316 **3** *1 3/4* **Fromsong (IRE)**[17] [1044] 12-8-7 **68** ow1..........(p) MarkCoumbe(5) 6 64
(D K Ivory) *chsd ldng pair: pushed along over 1f out and sn outpcd: jst hld on for 3rd* **3/1**[3]

/0-0 **4** *hd* **Bosun Breese**[90] [192] 5-8-13 **74**.......... DeanHeslop(5) 4 69
(T D Barron) *dwlt: off the pce in 5th: rdn over 1f out: kpt on same pce: nvr threatened* **11/4**[2]

1106 **5** *nk* **Pipers Piping (IRE)**[10] [1130] 4-7-12 **61**.......... JulieCumine(7) 1 55+
(P Howling) *dwlt: dropped in fr wd draw and sn wl bhd: c wd bnd 2f out: styd on wl fnl f: nrly snatched 3rd* **16/1**

2500 **6** *3/4* **Steel City Boy (IRE)**[8] [1154] 7-8-12 **68**.......... DaneO'Neill 2 59
(D Shaw) *chsd ldng pair: rdn and nt qckn over 1f out: lost pl fnl f* **10/1**

60.40 secs (-0.10) **Going Correction** 0.0s/f (Stan) 6 Ran SP% **108.5**
Speed ratings (Par 103): **100,96,93,93,92 91**
toteswingers: 1&2 £3.40, 1&3 £1.80, 2&3 £5.10 CSF £17.44 TOTE £2.70: £1.10, £5.80; EX 20.60.
Owner Messrs Criddle Davies Dawson & Villa **Bred** Wilhelm Fasching **Trained** Earlswood, Monmouths

FOCUS
A fair handicap and one run and an ordinary gallop saw those right up with the pace hold an edge. The winner came down the centre in the straight and the form is rated at face value ostensibly through the runner-up.
Pipers Piping(IRE) ◆ Official explanation: jockey said gelding lost an off-fore shoe

1321 TAG RUGBY DEVELOPMENT TRUST H'CAP 6f (P)

8:10 (8:11) (Class 4) (0-80,80) 4-Y-0+ **£4,209** (£1,252; £625; £312) **Stalls** High

Form RPR

030- **1** **Peter Island (FR)**[175] [6964] 7-8-8 **70**..........(v) ChrisCatlin 4 78
(J Gallagher) *mde all and set blistering pce: clr and rdn 2f out: tired fnl f: hld on* **7/1**

054- **2** *3/4* **Thunderous Mood (USA)**[134] [7613] 4-9-2 **78**.......... DaneO'Neill 6 84
(P F I Cole) *chsd ldrs in 6th and off the pce: effrt 2f out: styd on fr over 1f out to take 2nd nr fin* **7/2**[1]

0-30 **3** *nk* **Whiskey Junction**[43] [767] 6-8-13 **75**.......... SebSanders 9 80
(M Quinn) *chsd wnr: drvn over 2f out: clsd grad fr over 1f out: lost 2nd nr fin* **13/2**

2264 **4** *nk* **Secret Witness**[20] [987] 4-9-2 **78**..........(b) LiamJones 3 82
(R A Harris) *dwlt: sn pushed up to dispute 2nd: drvn over 2f out: grad clsd on wnr but no ex fnl f* **13/2**

3462 **5** *nk* **Ray Of Joy**[29] [905] 4-9-0 **76**.......... NickyMackay 2 79
(J R Jenkins) *chsd ldng trio: swtchd off rail 2f out: drvn and clsd grad: nvr able to chal* **8/1**

6200 **6** *1/2* **Lujeanie**[3] [1266] 4-9-4 **80**.......... JimCrowley 8 81+
(D K Ivory) *stdd s and sn wl bhd in last pair: styd on fr over 1f out on inner: rdn fnl f: nrst fin* **5/1**[3]

/060 **7** *1 1/2* **Financial Times (USA)**[7] [1192] 8-9-2 **78**..........(t) PatCosgrave 7 74
(Stef Higgins) *chsd ldng quartet: n.m.r and lost pl 2f out: no prog over 1f out and btn after* **18/1**

1212 **8** *1/2* **Sherjawy (IRE)**[22] [972] 6-8-10 **72**.......... SamHitchcott 5 67
(Miss Z C Davison) *dwlt: rdn in 7th and off the pce: kpt on u.p fr over 1f out: nvr a factor* **4/1**[2]

-500 **9** *7* **Resplendent Alpha**[63] [501] 6-8-6 **68**.......... JimmyQuinn 10 40
(P Howling) *outpcd and wl bhd in last: styd there* **16/1**

1m 12.08s (-1.02) **Going Correction** 0.0s/f (Stan) 9 Ran SP% **120.3**
Speed ratings (Par 105): **106,105,104,104,103 103,101,100,91**
toteswingers: 1&2 £8.00, 1&3 £20.40, 2&3 £6.90 CSF £33.17 CT £173.11 TOTE £7.90: £2.00, £3.60, £1.70; EX 43.80.
Owner C R Marks (banbury) **Bred** Earl Elevage De La Source **Trained** Chastleton, Oxon
■ Stewards' Enquiry : Nicky Mackay two-day ban: careless riding (Apr 29-30)

FOCUS
A fair handicap and one run at a decent gallop throughout and the third looks the best guide to the form. The winner raced centre to far side in the straight.
Sherjawy(IRE) Official explanation: jockey said gelding was slowly away

1322 PRE BOOK THE BISTRO MENU H'CAP (DIV I) 1m (P)

8:40 (8:40) (Class 5) (0-70,70) 4-Y-0+ **£2,266** (£674; £337; £168) **Stalls** High

Form RPR

4145 **1** **Alqaahir (USA)**[36] [853] 8-8-9 **68**.......... KaseyLoftus(7) 8 76
(P Butler) *trckd ldng pair: wnt 2nd over 3f out and led over 2f out: nudged along and styd on steadily* **14/1**

5404 **2** *1 3/4* **Tous Les Deux**[17] [1042] 7-9-1 **67**.......... GeorgeBaker 10 71
(G L Moore) *stdd s: t.k.h: hld up in 5th: prog to chse wnr 2f out: kpt on but no real imp fr over 1f out* **2/1**[1]

-504 **3** *3/4* **Fault**[5] [1224] 4-9-0 **66**..........(t) PatCosgrave 4 68
(Stef Higgins) *hld up in 6th: prog 2f out to take 3rd over 1f out: kpt on same pce after* **6/1**

011- **4** *1* **Final Drive (IRE)**[162] [7239] 4-9-0 **66**.......... EddieCreighton 5 66+
(E J Creighton) *t.k.h: hld up in last trio: prog on inner over 2f out: rchd 4th over 1f out: no imp after* **15/2**

5046 **5** *3/4* **See Elsie Play**[10] [1129] 4-8-7 **59** ow1.......... SamHitchcott 2 57
(Miss Z C Davison) *t.k.h: hld up last: rdn and prog over 2f out: wnt 5th over 1f out: one pce after* **25/1**

502- **6** *7* **Beauchamp Wizard**[195] [6454] 5-9-4 **70**.......... DaneO'Neill 1 52
(G A Butler) *t.k.h: hld up in last trio: shkn up and lft bhd fr 2f out* **4/1**[2]

0310 **7** *nse* **Sapphire Prince (USA)**[22] [975] 4-8-10 **62**.......... SteveDrowne 6 44
(J R Best) *trckd ldng trio: shkn up and lost pl over 2f out: sn no ch* **12/1**

/0-0 **8** *1/2* **Navene (IRE)**[9] [1141] 6-8-13 **65**.......... FergusSweeney 9 46
(M R Bosley) *led to over 2f out: sn wknd* **33/1**

000- **9** *5* **Northern Spy (USA)**[129] [7662] 6-8-11 **70**.......... NathanAlison(7) 7 39
(S Dow) *chsd ldr to over 3f out: wknd rapidly* **11/2**[3]

1m 39.57s (-0.23) **Going Correction** 0.0s/f (Stan) 9 Ran SP% **115.9**
Speed ratings (Par 103): **101,99,98,97,96 89,89,89,84**
toteswingers: 1&2 £7.80, 1&3 £8.60, 2&3 £3.20 CSF £42.53 CT £195.34 TOTE £13.00: £4.70, £2.10, £1.10; EX 54.00.
Owner M D Loftus **Bred** Shadwell Farm LLC **Trained** East Chiltington, E Sussex

FOCUS
A modest handicap in which the early gallop was on the modest side and this was another race on the card to favour those up with the pace, so the form is muddling. The winner came down the centre in the straight.

1323 PRE BOOK THE BISTRO MENU H'CAP (DIV II) 1m (P)

9:10 (9:10) (Class 5) (0-70,70) 4-Y-0+ **£2,266** (£674; £337; £168) **Stalls** High

Form RPR

-535 **1** **Millfields Dreams**[8] [1179] 11-8-8 **65**..........(p) MarkCoumbe(5) 1 74
(P Leech) *dwlt: t.k.h: hld up in last pair: gd prog on inner over 2f out: clsd over 1f out: styd on wl to ld ins fnl f* **33/1**

33-5 **2** *1 3/4* **Land Hawk (IRE)**[10] [1128] 4-8-9 **66**.......... SimonPearce(5) 10 71
(J Pearce) *t.k.h: hld up bhd ldrs: prog over 2f out: led over 1f out: hdd and one pce ins fnl f* **9/4**[2]

2020 **3** *1* **Having A Ball**[8] [1172] 6-9-2 **68**.......... ChrisCatlin 6 71
(P D Cundell) *mostly in 8th: rdn and struggling wl over 2f out: prog on outer again over 1f out: carried lft but styd on wl to take 3rd nr fin* **10/1**

446- **4** *1* **Altimatum (USA)**[129] [7671] 4-8-11 **63**..........(t) AlanMunro 2 64
(P F I Cole) *towards rr: pushed along fr 1/2-way: outpcd and struggling bdly over 2f out: styd on strly again fnl f* **20/1**

3150 **5** *nk* **Expensive Problem**[64] [487] 7-9-3 **69**.......... GeorgeBaker 9 69
(R J Smith) *s.s: hld up in last pair: stdy prog fr 3f out: rdn to cl fr 2f out: disp 3rd ins fnl f: one pce* **20/1**

5-25 **6** *shd* **Eastern Gift**[41] [814] 5-9-1 **67**..........(b[1]) LukeMorris 4 67
(Miss Gay Kelleway) *hld up bhd ldrs: smooth prog over 2f out: shkn up and hung bdly lft fnl f: fnd nil* **12/1**

1435 **7** *1 1/4* **Headache**[15] [1063] 5-9-0 **66**..........(bt) DaneO'Neill 3 63
(B W Duke) *led: kicked 2l clr over 2f out: hdd & wknd over 1f out* **7/1**[3]

1600 **8** *1/2* **Aflaam (IRE)**[22] [975] 5-9-1 **70**.......... MichaelStainton(3) 5 66
(R A Harris) *chsd ldr after 2f: hrd rdn over 2f out: lost 2nd sn after: wknd jst over 1f out* **16/1**

450- **9** *3* **Burnbrake**[162] [7236] 5-8-6 **58**..........(v) DavidProbert 7 47
(L Montague Hall) *chsd ldrs: rdn over 2f out: wknd wl over 1f out* **16/1**

0-32 **10** *3* **Markhesa**[9] [1141] 4-8-8 **60**.......... NickyMackay 8 42
(J R Boyle) *chsd ldr 2f: styd prom: rdn and effrt over 2f out: wknd over 1f out: eased* **2/1**[1]

1m 38.51s (-1.29) **Going Correction** 0.0s/f (Stan) 10 Ran SP% **117.6**
Speed ratings (Par 103): **106,104,103,102,101 101,100,100,97,94**
toteswingers:1&2:£42.10, 2&3:£7.40, 1&3:£30.70 CSF £105.66 CT £860.87 TOTE £51.60: £23.90, £1.10, £6.10; EX 267.00 Place 6: £32.94 Place 5: £22.40.
Owner L Audus **Bred** T G Price **Trained** Exning, Suffolk

FOCUS
Division two of a modest handicap. The gallop was a reasonable one and the winner edged off the inside rail in the closing stages. Despite a surprise result, the form looks fair enough with the third and fourth the best guides.
Eastern Gift Official explanation: jockey said gelding hung left
Markhesa Official explanation: jockey said filly had no more to give
T/Plt: £74.50 to a £1 stake. Pool: £69,240.26. 677.62 winning tickets. T/Qpdt: £23.50 to a £1 stake. Pool: £7,505.88. 235.90 winning tickets. JN

1308
NEWMARKET (Rowley Mile) (R-H)
Thursday, April 15

OFFICIAL GOING: Good to firm (8.7)
Far side track used.
Wind: Fresh across Weather: Hazy sunshine

1324 EUROPEAN BREEDERS FUND MAIDEN FILLIES' STKS 5f

1:50 (1:51) (Class 4) 2-Y-0 **£5,180** (£1,541; £770; £384) **Stalls** Low

Form RPR

1 **Penny's Pearl (IRE)** 2-9-0 0.......... RichardHughes 11 83+
(R Hannon) *str: lw: chsd ldrs: led 1/2-way: hung lft over 1f out: rdn out* **4/1**[2]

2 *1 3/4* **Yarooh (USA)** 2-9-0 0.......... ChrisCatlin 9 77
(C E Brittain) *w'like: chsd ldrs: led over 3f out: hdd 1/2-way: rdn over 1f out: styd on* **9/1**[3]

3 *1/2* **Golden Shine** 2-9-0 0.......... KierenFallon 3 75+
(M R Channon) *str: hld up in tch: racd keenly: swtchd rt over 1f out: n.m.r ins fnl f: r.o* **9/4**[1]

4 *hd* **Emma's Gift (IRE)** 2-9-0 0.......... JimmyQuinn 8 74
(Miss J Feilden) *str: s.i.s: sn chsng ldrs: rdn over 1f out: edgd lft: r.o* **11/1**

5 *1* **Phoebs** 2-9-0 0.......... StevieDonohoe 7 71
(R A Mills) *str: prom: rdn over 1f out: styd on same pce ins fnl f* **16/1**

6 *3/4* **Mother Jones** 2-9-0 0.......... FrederikTylicki 6 68
(D H Brown) *leggy: prom: rdn over 1f out: no ex ins fnl f* **12/1**

7 *1 1/2* **Lady Morganna (IRE)** 2-9-0 0.......... LukeMorris 13 62
(Miss Gay Kelleway) *str: s.i.s: hdwy 1/2-way: rdn over 1f out: wknd fnl f* **16/1**

8 *3/4* **On Wings Of Love (IRE)** 2-9-0 0.......... DavidProbert 2 66+
(A Bailey) *neat: bit bkwd: s.s: hld up: hdwy 1/2-way: effrt whn hmpd ins fnl f: nt rcvr* **14/1**

5 **9** *9* **Helen Of Toy**[14] [1073] 2-9-0 0.......... FergusSweeney 12 27
(B G Powell) *w'like: led: hdd over 3f out: rdn and wknd over 1f out* **14/1**

3 **10** *3* **Callipygos**[15] [1065] 2-8-7 0.......... LeonnaMayor(7) 1 17
(P S McEntee) *w'like: hld up: hung rt and wknd 1/2-way* **33/1**

00 **11** *3/4* **Bold Deceiver**[15] [1066] 2-9-0 0.......... NeilCallan 4 14
(P S McEntee) *neat: prom to 1/2-way* **66/1**

00 **12** *14* **Huckle Duckle (IRE)**[15] [1065] 2-9-0 0.......... TomMcLaughlin 10 —
(P S McEntee) *leggy: s.s: rn green and outpcd* **250/1**

60.75 secs (1.65) **Going Correction** +0.075s/f (Good) 12 Ran SP% **106.7**
Speed ratings (Par 91): **89,86,85,85,83 82,79,78,64,59 58,35**
toteswingers: 1&2 £4.40, 1&3 £1.40, 2&3 £4.60 CSF £32.19 TOTE £3.30: £1.80, £2.60, £1.10; EX 33.40.
Owner Malcolm Brown & Mrs Penny Brown **Bred** Liam O'Neill **Trained** East Everleigh, Wilts

FOCUS
Often a hot race, with recent winners including Wunders Dream (subsequently landed Molecomb and Flying Childers), Flashy Wings (Queen Mary and Lowther), and Silk Blossom (Lowther), while Habaayib was third last year before taking the Albany.

NOTEBOOK

Penny's Pearl(IRE) ◆, a £30,000 breeze-up purchase, half-sister to 1m2f winner Breathing Fire (later very useful hurdler), out of a 5f juvenile winner who was successful at up to 2m, was yet another well-educated Hannon 2-y-o, his sixth such winner of the season. After showing good speed up the middle of the track, she gradually edged left under pressure, ending up with the rail to help inside the final furlong, and stayed on well to record a convincing success. For all that she knew her job, Richard Hannon revealed afterwards that he's only had her for about a month, so there should be plenty of improvement forthcoming, and she looks above average. She has the potential to be Royal Ascot class and a step up in grade awaits. (tchd 9-2)

Yarooh(USA), a $100,000 first foal of a winner in the US, showed plenty of pace and, after gradually getting across towards the stands' side from her high draw, she had the rail to run against over 2f out, but the winner was too good. She should have no trouble finding a similar race before going up in grade. (op 11-1)

Golden Shine ◆, a half-sister to smart sprinter Falcon Hill, and Raine's Cross, a very useful juvenile last year over 5f-1m, shaped nicely on debut. She didn't help her rider by racing enthusiastically in behind the leaders towards the near rail, and then lost her place when not having much room around 2f out. Only in the clear around 1f out, she had too much ground to make up on the winner, but she kept on well without being given a hard time (only hit once with the whip) and gave the impression there will be plenty of improvement to come. Her trainer won this in 2005 with Flashy Wings and this one could be quite useful in time. (tchd 5-2)

Emma's Gift(IRE) ◆ has apparently been working with older horses, being Julia Feilden's only 2-y-o in full work at the moment. An 11,000gns half-sister to a few winners, including The Scorching Wind, who is very useful at around 7f, notably on Polytrack, she recovered from a slow start to travel quite nicely, close to the pace towards the middle of the track, before running green under pressure. There should be a fair amount of improvement to come. (op 12-1)

Phoebs ◆ is bred to be really quick, being either a sister or half-sister to a number of multiple sprint winners, and out of a fast type who won plenty of races. Her trainer's late father did particularly well with some of this one's family, not least the sire and dam, and she showed enough to suggest she'll make quite a nice type. She displayed good speed, but lacked the knowhow of some of these under pressure.

Mother Jones ◆, a £10,000 half-sister to the speedy Fast Freddie, out of a triple sprint juvenile winner, looks pretty fast herself. She showed loads of natural pace and if anything was a bit keen early on. There are races to be won with her over this trip. (tchd 10-1)

Lady Morganna(IRE), a £5,000 purchase, was described as "a bit quirky" by her trainer. Not helped by the widest stall, she ran green throughout and can improve.

On Wings Of Love(IRE), an 8,500euros half-sister to a number of winners, mainly over middle-distances, lost a few lengths with a slow start but she was keeping on gradually when hampered and then clipping heels inside the final furlong. (op 16-1 tchd 12-1)

1325 NGK SPARK PLUGS COACHMAKERS WOOD DITTON STKS 1m

2:25 (2:25) (Class 4) 3-Y-O £6,476 (£1,927; £963; £481) Stalls Low

Form	Pos	Dist	Horse	RPR
	1		**Diescentric (USA)** 3-9-3 0 TomQueally 6 — (H R A Cecil) *str: lengthy: lw: w ldr tl led over 2f out: rdn out* 4/1[1]	84
	2	1 ½	**Soviet Secret** 3-9-3 0 KierenFallon 3 — (P J McBride) *led over 5f: rdn over 1f out: styd on* 13/2[3]	81
	3	2	**Squall** 3-9-3 0 FrankieDettori 10 — (J Noseda) *cmpt: chsd ldrs: rdn over 1f out: styd on same pce fnl f* 9/2[2]	76
	4	3 ½	**Seyaaq (USA)** 3-9-3 0 RichardHills 2 — (B W Hills) *lengthy: bit bkwd: s.i.s: sn prom: rdn over 1f out: styd on same pce* 9/2[2]	68+
	5	1	**Chiefdom Prince (IRE)** 3-9-3 0 RyanMoore 5 — (Sir Michael Stoute) *tall: unf: lw: prom: rdn over 2f out: wknd fnl f* 4/1[1]	66
	6	3	**New Code** 3-9-3 0 MartinDwyer 7 — (W R Muir) *tall: lengthy: hld up in tch: rdn over 2f out: wknd over 1f out* 20/1	59
	7	¾	**Glacial** 3-9-3 0 SebSanders 9 — (E F Vaughan) *athletic: lengthy: prom: rdn over 2f out: sn hung lft: and eased* 16/1	60
	8	2 ½	**Best Of Broadway (IRE)** 3-9-3 0 TedDurcan 8 — (D R Lanigan) *cmpt: bit bkwd: s.s: hld up: rdn over 3f out: a in rr* 14/1	51
	9	2 ¾	**Resolute Road** 3-9-3 0 MichaelHills 4 — (B W Hills) *w'like: leggy: b.hind: s.i.s: hld up: racd keenly: rdn and wknd over 2f out* 12/1	45

1m 39.67s (1.07) **Going Correction** +0.075s/f (Good) **9 Ran SP% 114.7**

Speed ratings (Par 100): **97,95,93,90,89 86,85,82,80**

toteswingers: 1&2 £6.80, 1&3 £3.40, 2&3 £8.40 CSF £29.98 TOTE £4.10: £1.30, £2.60, £1.90; EX 37.80.

Owner Axom (XVIII) **Bred** Morgan's Ford Farm **Trained** Newmarket, Suffolk

FOCUS

Always an informative maiden, the Wood Ditton can often throw up a decent prospect, and it's interesting to note that seven of the previous 11 winners this century (two divisions in 2008) went on to be officially rated in three figures later in their careers. However, the betting was quite open, suggesting no stars in the line-up, and a fairly steady early gallop, resulting in nothing getting into the race from off the pace, casts doubt on the merit of the form. This is probably an up to scratch renewal.

Glacial Official explanation: jockey said gelding hung badly left

1326 CONNAUGHT ACCESS FLOORING ABERNANT STKS (LISTED RACE) 6f

3:00 (3:00) (Class 1) 3-Y-0+ £22,708 (£8,608; £4,308; £2,148; £1,076; £540) Stalls Low

Form	Pos	Dist	Horse	RPR
050-	1		**Equiano (FR)**[193] [6522] 5-9-5 106 MichaelHills 2 — (B W Hills) *lw: sn led: hung rt fr over 1f out: sn rdn: jst hld on* 11/4[1]	114
13/3	2	shd	**Mullionmileanhour (IRE)**[47] [737] 4-9-5 99 SteveDrowne 6 — (J R Best) *lw: a.p: pushed along 1/2-way: rdn to chse wnr fnl f: lost out on the nod* 5/1[3]	114
310-	3	2	**Doncaster Rover (USA)**[242] [5079] 4-9-5 104 FrederikTylicki 3 — (D H Brown) *lw: chsd ldrs: pushed along and lost pl over 4f out: rallied and edgd rt over 1f out: r.o* 7/2[2]	107
24-0	4	¾	**Evens And Odds (IRE)**[19] [1007] 6-9-5 102 AdrianNicholls 8 — (D Nicholls) *chsd ldrs: rdn over 1f out: styd on same pce ins fnl f* 5/1[3]	105
-005	5	1 ¼	**Barney McGrew (IRE)**[19] [1007] 7-9-5 105 PhillipMakin 1 — (M Dods) *s.i.s: sn chsng ldrs: rdn over 1f out: styd on same pce* 12/1	101
310-	6	shd	**Golden Stream (IRE)**[187] [6661] 4-9-4 103 RyanMoore 4 — (Sir Michael Stoute) *swtg: chsd wnr: rdn over 2f out: no ex fnl f* 8/1	100
255-	7	½	**Able Master (IRE)**[159] [7292] 4-9-5 105 TomQueally 7 — (J R Gask) *lw: hld up: hdwy over 2f out: outpcd over 1f out: styd on ins fnl f* 8/1	99
40/0	8	25	**Retaliate**[35] [860] 6-9-0 45 SaleemGolam 5 — (P Leech) *dwlt: racd in last pl: lost tch fr over 3f out* 200/1	14

1m 11.07s (-1.13) **Going Correction** +0.075s/f (Good) **8 Ran SP% 112.6**

Speed ratings (Par 111): **110,109,107,106,104 104,103,70**

toteswingers: 1&2 £2.90, 1&3 £2.90, 2&3 £3.60 CSF £16.27 TOTE £3.60: £1.70, £1.80, £1.70; EX 17.80.

Owner J Acheson **Bred** Ecurie Skymarc Farm **Trained** Lambourn, Berks

FOCUS

A disappointing turnout numerically with eight runners representing the smallest field since Arakan defeated seven rivals in 2004. The form is pretty straightforward for the grade.

NOTEBOOK

Equiano(FR) struggled (unplaced in eight consecutive Group races) after finishing second in last year's race, but the return to this grade saw him gain a narrow success after 193 days off. Allowed to dominate against the stands' rail, he almost ruined his chance by edging all the way across to the middle of the track under pressure, but he got the verdict on the nod. Considering his record last year, it would be easy enough to assume that he'll struggle again from now on. However, he was a high-class type when he won the King's Stand back in 2008 and it was fascinating to hear Michael Hills say afterwards that the colt has had a wind operation since last season, resulting in him apparently being a much happier horse. The jockey also felt a return to 5f will help, reasoning that he felt like a faster horse than last year, and that was certainly the visual impression. The Palace House Stakes back here over the minimum trip on Guineas day is an option, but according to Barry Hills there is a race at Chantilly that the owner may be keen to go for. Whatever the case, a return to Royal Ascot for another crack at the King's Stand is the main aim. (op 10-3 tchd 5-2 and 7-2 in places)

Mullionmileanhour(IRE), who was having his first run since finishing third in the 2008 Windsor Castle when filling the same position in a Polytrack Listed race in February, ran another fine race in defeat, showing he has gone the right way. He was outpaced and under pressure by halfway, but stayed on gradually up the centre of the track, ultimately only just failing. He gave the impression he'll be sharper again next time and is now likely to aimed at the Duke of York Stakes, before a tilt at the Golden Jubilee. (op 4-1 tchd 11-2 and 6-1 in a place)

Doncaster Rover(USA), who impressed when winning a Chester Listed race on his penultimate start last year, shaped nicely on his return from 242 days off. He was outpaced for much of the way, very much giving the impression this was needed both fitness-wise and mentally. (op 4-1)

Evens And Odds(IRE), seventh in the Cammidge Trophy on his reappearance, was a bit free on the pace and could make little impression when under pressure. (tchd 11-2 in a place)

Barney McGrew(IRE) was too keen and this small field didn't play to his strengths. (op 9-1 tchd 14-1 in places)

Golden Stream(IRE), despite being a sister to Oaks runner-up Flight Of Fancy, was a dual 7f Listed winner last year (4lb penalty this time as a result), and she showed early speed on this drop in trip after 187 days off, but her head was a bit high under pressure. She's not an easy filly to work out. (tchd 9-1)

Able Master(IRE), making his debut for the yard, was stuck out wider than ideal for some of the way and lacked the sharpness of some of these after 159 days off. (op 10-1)

1327 RACING POST BREEZEUPBONUS.COM CRAVEN STKS (GROUP 3) (C&G) 1m

3:35 (3:37) (Class 1) 3-Y-O £36,900 (£13,988; £7,000; £3,490; £1,748; £877) Stalls Low

Form	Pos	Dist	Horse	RPR
112-	1		**Elusive Pimpernel (USA)**[173] [7017] 3-8-12 115 RyanMoore 6 — (J L Dunlop) *h.d.w: lw: trckd ldrs: outpcd briefly 3f out: led over 1f out: rdn and r.o wl* 10/11[1]	116+
214-	2	4	**Dancing David (IRE)**[173] [7017] 3-8-12 110 MartinDwyer 9 — (B J Meehan) *chsd ldrs: led over 2f out: rdn and hdd over 1f out: styd on same pce fnl f* 6/1[2]	106
315-	3	1	**Critical Moment (USA)**[173] [7030] 3-8-12 100 MichaelHills 8 — (B W Hills) *lw: racd wd tl passed 1/2-way: w ldr: rdn and ev ch 2f out: sn edgd lft: styd on same pce fnl f* 12/1	104
360-	4	nk	**Dubawi Phantom**[173] [7030] 3-8-12 100 AhmedAjtebi 1 — (D M Simcock) *swtg: chsd ldrs: nt clr run and lost pl over 2f out: rallied fnl f: r.o* 25/1	103
215-	5	3 ¼	**Morana (IRE)**[173] [7017] 3-8-12 107 AlanMunro 2 — (P W Chapple-Hyam) *led: qcknd 3f out: hdd over 2f out: wknd over 1f out* 10/1[3]	96
431-	6	hd	**Lucky General (IRE)**[200] [6317] 3-8-12 112 RichardHughes 4 — (R Hannon) *prom: rdn over 3f out: wknd over 1f out* 14/1	95
31-	7	5	**Mont Agel**[192] [6548] 3-8-12 93 JamieSpencer 3 — (M L W Bell) *bit bkwd: unruly prior to the s: s.s: hld up: hdwy on outer over 2f out: rdn: hung lft and wknd over 1f out* 14/1	84
210-	8	¾	**Markazzi**[194] [6478] 3-8-12 92 RichardHills 5 — (Sir Michael Stoute) *lw: hld up: rdn over 2f out: wknd wl over 1f out* 11/1	82
0-11	9	13	**Edinburgh Knight (IRE)**[33] [884] 3-8-12 90 TonyCulhane 7 — (P W D'Arcy) *rangy: lw: hld up: racd keenly: hdwy 1/2-way: rdn and hung rt over 2f out: sn wknd and eased* 12/1	52

1m 37.16s (-1.44) **Going Correction** +0.075s/f (Good) **9 Ran SP% 116.7**

Speed ratings (Par 108): **110,106,105,104,101 101,96,95,82**

toteswingers: 1&2 £2.10, 1&3 £4.50, 2&3 £8.50 CSF £6.69 TOTE £1.60: £1.10, £2.30, £3.90; EX 4.80.

Owner Windflower Overseas Holdings Inc **Bred** Windflower Overseas Holdings Inc **Trained** Arundel, W Sussex

FOCUS

Each of these runners holds an entry in the 2,000 Guineas but, apart from the winner, who was rated a 16-1 shot for the first Classic coming into the race, the rest were considered rags, quoted at no shorter than 40-1 by the bookmakers beforehand. The favourite had to put up a big performance to prove himself a true Guineas contender, and he did just that. The early pace was decent, resulting in a fast time, 2.51secs quicker than the Wood Ditton, and the form looks solid, with the Racing Post Trophy being given a nice boost in the process.

NOTEBOOK

Elusive Pimpernel(USA) ◆ set the standard on his 2-y-o form, which included a second-place finish in the Racing Post Trophy behind impressive winner St Nicholas Abbey, but the ground was softer than ideal and he was done for toe that day in a race not run at a strong early gallop. The way this race was run suited him much better and despite momentarily being niggled along around 3f out, he soon responded to pressure and was disputing the lead a furlong later. His stamina then kicked in and he powered away for an impressive success, being kept up to his work all the way to the line. He always looked the type to improve physically from two to three and one couldn't have asked for more from his reappearance, so it was no surprise to see the bookmakers slash his price for the Guineas to 6-1. If one was looking for negatives, though, it could be pointed out that he had quite a hard race here in a truly run contest, there's only 16 days to the Guineas, and he didn't beat Dancing David much further than in the Racing Post Trophy. Being out of a mare who stayed 1m6f it would be a surprise if he didn't get further than a mile in time, although his trainer doesn't see him as a Derby horse at all. (op 11-10 tchd 6-5 and 5-4 in places)

Dancing David(IRE) ◆, fourth and just under three lengths behind Elusive Pimpernel in the Racing Post Trophy on his final start last season, did well to cross over from his wide draw and race one off the rail. The winner was much too strong for him but he kept on well to take second, has clearly trained on from two to three and will surely be placed to win in Group company. A step up to 1m2f looks likely and the French Derby will apparently be considered. (op 13-2 tchd 11-2)

Critical Moment(USA), an unlucky-in-running fifth in the Horris Hill on his final start at two when the soft ground wouldn't have been ideal, had conditions more to his liking here. Quickly away from his wide draw, he soon took up a prominent position and helped set a decent gallop away from the rail. He eventually tacked over to race with the rest and kept on well to hold on to third. There should be better to come from him and a Derby trial at Chester is now the plan. (op 16-1 tchd 25-1 in a place)

Dubawi Phantom looked to improve for the fitting of blinkers (missing here) when third in the Solario Stakes, but was well held in similar company afterwards, albeit on softer ground. A return to a quicker surface clearly helped him, but the fact that his trainer had stated that he was pretty fit for this suggests there might not be a great deal of improvement to come, and he could prove difficult to place. (tchd 33-1 in a place)

Morana(IRE), who won the Autumn Stakes before finishing fifth in the Racing Post Trophy, was quite a keen-going sort last term. Allowed to stride on from his low draw, he set a good gallop and, while he didn't have the pace to live with the winner when he quickened away, he kept on and is very likely to come on quite a bit for the outing, just as his trainer had predicted. A longer trip should suit him on pedigree. (op 12-1 tchd 14-1 in places)

Lucky General(IRE), winner of the Goffs Million Sprint last term, had his stamina to prove over this trip, having gone 3-4 over 6f but 0-4 over 7f last term. The way he ran suggests he'll be happier back over shorter. (tchd 16-1 in a place)

Mont Agel, who proved troublesome before the start and was slowly away, showed ability but this company proved too hot for him. He'll appreciate dropping down in grade. (op 11-1 tchd 10-1)

Markazzi looked a smart prospect when winning at Leicester on his second start and, although on the face of it he was disappointing when finishing in midfield in the Tattersalls Timeform Million, he was drawn on the wrong side that day and was lame behind and in front afterwards. Weak in the betting here, he might well have needed the run, but there's a fair amount of speed in his pedigree and perhaps he'll eventually prove more effective over shorter. (op 9-1 tchd 12-1)

Edinburgh Knight(IRE) was restricted to just the one start at two due to a stress fracture in his hip, but made very good impression in winning twice on the Polytrack this spring. Taking a step up in distance and a giant leap in class, he didn't settle through the early stages of the race despite a decent gallop, and burnt himself out. His trainer suggested that the colt would now drop back to sprinting, and he could yet find further improvement in that sphere. (op 8-1 tchd 14-1)

1328 WEATHERBYS BLOODSTOCK RACECARD EARL OF SEFTON STKS (GROUP 3) 1m 1f

4:10 (4:10) (Class 1) 4-Y-O+

£36,900 (£13,988; £7,000; £3,490; £1,748; £877) **Stalls** Low

Form RPR

150- **1** **Sri Putra**[158] 7313 4-8-12 110 NeilCallan 7 115
(M A Jarvis) *racd centre: lft chsng ldr over 7f out: led overall over 2f out: edgd lft and hdd over 1f out: rallied to ld wl ins fnl f* **11/2**

11-1 **2** *1* **Tranquil Tiger**[26] 946 6-9-1 112 (b) TomQueally 8 116
(H R A Cecil) *lw: racd centre tl swtchd to stands' side over 7f out: sn chsng ldr of that gp: overall ldr over 1f out: sn rdn: edgd rt and hdd wl ins fnl f* **3/1**[1]

463- **3** *1 1/4* **Palavicini (USA)**[181] 6812 4-8-12 112 JimmyFortune 6 111
(J L Dunlop) *lw: racd centre tl swtchd to ld stands' side gp over 7f out: rdn and hung rt fr over 1f out: sn hdd: eased whn unsteerable towards fin* **7/2**[2]

501- **4** *2 3/4* **Steele Tango (USA)**[181] 6812 5-9-1 113 LiamKeniry 3 108
(R A Teal) *racd stands' side: chsd ldrs: rdn over 2f out: outpcd over 1f out: styd on ins fnl f* **6/1**

224- **5** *6* **Pachattack (USA)**[137] 7589 4-8-9 101 RichardHughes 4 89
(G A Butler) *racd stands' side: hld up: rdn over 2f out: wknd over 1f out* **33/1**

/23- **6** *1/2* **Sans Frontieres (IRE)**[336] 2014 4-8-12 112 FrankieDettori 1 91
(J Noseda) *racd stands' side: hld up: effrt over 3f out: wknd over 1f out* **6/1**

233- **7** *1* **Kingdom Of Fife**[200] 6303 5-8-12 112 (v) RyanMoore 2 89
(Sir Michael Stoute) *racd stands' side: led that gp tl over 7f out: chsd ldrs: rdn over 3f out: wknd over 1f out* **9/2**[3]

-045 **8** *11* **Yahrab (IRE)**[26] 946 5-8-12 100 (b) SebSanders 5 66
(C E Brittain) *racd centre: overall ldr tl over 2f out: sn wknd* **25/1**

1m 49.33s (-2.37) **Going Correction** +0.075s/f (Good) **8** Ran SP% **116.1**
Speed ratings (Par 113): **113,112,111,108,103 102,101,92**
toteswingers: 1&2 £5.60, 1&3 £6.10, 2&3 £4.40 CSF £22.78 TOTE £6.80: £2.30, £2.10, £1.50; EX 29.20.

Owner H R H Sultan Ahmad Shah **Bred** Glebe Stud And Partners **Trained** Newmarket, Suffolk

FOCUS

This is usually a hot contest for the grade, indeed the race has produced a subsequent Group 1 winner (2005 Valixir 3rd, 06 Notnowcato 1st, 07 Manduro 1st, and 09 Twice Over 3rd) in four of the last five years. It was something of a muddling contest this time, however, with the field splitting into two groups early on. Initially the split was even, but Tranquil Tiger and Palavicini switched to join those stands' side after a furlong or so, leaving only Sri Putra and Yahrab up the middle. The runner-up and third then went right under pressure, meaning the main action took place centre-field after all. Despite all of that, the pace seemed decent enough. The form is a bit messy but the third is rated to last year's course form.

NOTEBOOK

Sri Putra ◆ produced a likeable performance after 158 days off and looks set for a good year. Having travelled strongly, he was only able to get a lead from Yahrab until just inside the final 3f, and he had to do a lot of work on his own until joined a furlong out. At that point he seemed to be ever so slightly headed by Tranquil Tiger, but he proved more resolute than Henry Cecil's runner and knuckled down really well to ultimately win nicely. A Group 2 winner in France last year (for which he escaped a penalty), he has done well from three to four, looking a really powerful type now, and he's fully expected to go on from this, not least considering there should be more to come when he steps back up in trip. Michael Jarvis is unsure where he'll send him next time, but will apparently be tempted by Singapore (presumably the International Cup in May) if he gets an invitation. (op 6-1 tchd 7-1)

Tranquil Tiger enjoyed a fine winter on the Lingfield Polytrack, landing two Listed races, as well as the Group 3 Winter Derby (picked up 3lb penalty), and this was another smart effort on the figures. However, he's a quirky sort who, not for the first time, didn't convince with his attitude. Although last off the bridle, one suspects Tom Queally was forced to go for go for his mount sooner than he wanted, with Palavicini carrying him right, and after finding enough to at least get upsides the winner, this 6-y-o was worried out of it. (op 11-4 tchd 7-2 in a place and 10-3 in places)

Palavicini(USA), a half-brother to the Craven winner Elusive Pimpernel, escaped a penalty for last year's Group 3 success, had conditions to suit, and eventually managed to dominate against the stands' rail, but he ruined his chance by hanging badly right under pressure. He was so wayward that Jimmy Fortune eventually had to ease him off when held late on. Official explanation: jockey said colt hung right (op 9-2 tchd 5-1)

Steele Tango(USA), runner-up in this last year, was penalised for his success in the Group 3 Darley Stakes over C&D when last seen in October and never threatened on his return to action. (op 13-2 tchd 5-1)

Pachattack(USA) had something to find with most of these but didn't run badly on her reappearance. (tched 40-1 in a place)

Sans Frontieres(IRE), who was runner-up in last year's Craven but had been off since finishing third in the Dante, ran as though badly in need of the run and also gave the impression this was an inadequate test of stamina. He probably needs 1m4f and can be given another chance. Incidentally, he went without the sheepskin noseband he had fitted when last seen.

Kingdom Of Fife, who progressed from handicap company to place in a couple of Group 3s last year, had the visor re-fitted for his return, but he showed little. He will surely do better, probably back over further. (tchd 5-1 in a place)

1329 ROSSDALES MAIDEN FILLIES' STKS 7f

4:45 (4:46) (Class 4) 3-Y-O **£5,180** (£1,541; £770; £384) **Stalls** Low

Form RPR

6- **1** **Eldalil**[223] 5639 3-9-0 0 RichardHills 8 86+
(Sir Michael Stoute) *lw: chsd ldrs: led over 1f out: edgd lft: pushed out and a doing enough* **9/4**[1]

0- **2** *nk* **Dance East**[234] 5317 3-9-0 0 RyanMoore 4 82
(J Noseda) *w'like: scope: tall: chsd ldrs: rdn over 1f out: r.o* **16/1**

200- **3** *3/4* **Nimue (USA)**[190] 6582 3-9-0 78 JamieSpencer 11 80
(P F I Cole) *lw: s.s: hld up: nt clr run over 2f out: hdwy over 1f out: rdn and r.o* **10/1**

220- **4** *1 3/4* **Faithful One (IRE)**[173] 7033 3-9-0 83 TedDurcan 9 75
(D R Lanigan) *a.p: rdn and ev ch over 1f out: no ex wl ins fnl f* **10/3**[2]

04- **5** *1 3/4* **Dubai Media (CAN)**[168] 7135 3-9-0 0 MartinDwyer 1 71+
(D M Simcock) *hld up: hdwy over 2f out: hmpd over 1f out: n.m.r ins fnl f: r.o* **10/1**

3 **6** *1 1/2* **Spicewood (USA)**[20] 985 3-9-0 0 WilliamBuick 10 67
(J H M Gosden) *athletic: leggy: lw: s.s: hdwy 1/2-way: rdn over 2f out: styd on same pce fr over 1f out* **9/2**[3]

0- **7** *1/2* **That's My Style**[174] 6992 3-9-0 0 RobertHavlin 5 65+
(J H M Gosden) *lengthy: tall: bit bkwd: s.s: hld up: hdwy over 2f out: n.m.r and lost pl sn after: r.o ins fnl f* **22/1**

00- **8** *shd* **Jemimaville (IRE)**[166] 7183 3-9-0 0 TravisBlock 12 65?
(G C Bravery) *hld up in tch: rdn over 2f out: no ex fnl f* **150/1**

6- **9** *1 1/4* **Fetching**[155] 7325 3-9-0 0 MichaelHills 3 62
(B W Hills) *b.hind: led: rdn and hdd over 1f out: sn hung lft: wknd ins fnl f* **10/1**

54- **10** *5* **First Term**[234] 5318 3-9-0 0 RichardHughes 2 59
(R Hannon) *chsd ldr tl rdn over 2f out: hung rt and hmpd over 1f out and hmpd ins fnl f: eased* **22/1**

30 **11** *3 3/4* **Dubai Moonlight**[21] 978 3-8-7 0 LewisWalsh(7) 6 38
(Jane Chapple-Hyam) *unf: bit bkwd: hld up: bhd fr 1/2-way* **100/1**

12 *1/2* **Dolphin's Dream** 3-9-0 0 KierenFallon 7 37
(B J Meehan) *str: bit bkwd: s.s: hdwy 1/2-way: rdn and wknd 2f out* **25/1**

1m 26.28s (0.88) **Going Correction** +0.075s/f (Good) **12** Ran SP% **119.4**
Speed ratings (Par 97): **97,96,95,93,91 90,89,89,87,82 77,77**
toteswingers: 1&2 £8.10, 1&3 £6.10, 2&3 £20.60 CSF £39.97 TOTE £3.10: £1.50, £4.50, £3.30; EX 42.80.

Owner Hamdan Al Maktoum **Bred** Genesis Green Stud Ltd **Trained** Newmarket, Suffolk

■ Stewards' Enquiry : Martin Dwyer two-day ban: careless riding (Apr 29-30)

FOCUS

An interesting fillies' maiden in which the 78-rated third and 83-rated fourth help give the form a solid look. The third is rated to her debut form backed up by the fourth and sixth.

First Term Official explanation: jockey said filly hung right

1330 BOOK FOR THE IRISH CLASSICS AT CURRAGH.IE H'CAP 1m 2f

5:20 (5:20) (Class 3) (0-95,88) 3-Y-O **£9,066** (£2,697; £1,348; £673) **Stalls** Low

Form RPR

015- **1** **Wigmore Hall (IRE)**[187] 6663 3-9-4 **88** JamieSpencer 2 106+
(M L W Bell) *lw: hld up: hdwy over 2f out: led on bit over 1f out: canter* **10/1**

315- **2** *1 3/4* **Right Step**[210] 6011 3-8-13 **83** TomQueally 8 93
(A P Jarvis) *lw: hld up: hdwy over 2f out: rdn over 1f out: styd on same pce ins fnl f* **25/1**

21- **3** *1* **Tamaathul**[174] 6990 3-9-3 **87** RichardHills 1 95
(B W Hills) *lw: hld up: hdwy 2f out: rdn and ev ch over 1f out: no ex ins fnl f* **3/1**[1]

141- **4** *1 1/4* **Contract Caterer (IRE)**[219] 5742 3-9-1 **85** FrankieDettori 4 90+
(Pat Eddery) *lw: trckd ldrs: racd keenly: rdn over 2f out: styd on* **10/1**

032- **5** *1* **Official Style**[184] 6754 3-8-11 **81** RyanMoore 9 84
(Sir Michael Stoute) *lw: trckd ldrs: racd keenly: led over 2f out: rdn and hdd over 1f out: no ex fnl f* **7/2**[2]

0-16 **6** *3/4* **Arlequin**[47] 741 3-8-11 **81** DarryllHolland 6 83
(J D Bethell) *hld up in tch: rdn and ev ch over 2f out: hung lft over 1f out: styd on same pce* **40/1**

211- **7** *2 1/2* **Spanish Duke (IRE)**[182] 6805 3-8-13 **83** JimmyFortune 3 80
(J L Dunlop) *plld hrd and prom: rdn and edgd lft over 1f out: wknd fnl f* **12/1**

031- **8** *4* **First In The Queue (IRE)**[160] 7277 3-8-9 **78** ow1 RichardHughes 12 68
(S Kirk) *hld up: hdwy 4f out: wknd over 2f out* **40/1**

61 **9** *nse* **Vulcanite (IRE)**[41] 803 3-8-8 **78** JimCrowley 5 66
(R M Beckett) *lw: s.i.s: plld hrd: hdwy over 7f out: rdn over 2f out: sn wknd* **10/1**

2-61 **10** *4* **Muwalla**[48] 728 3-8-12 **82** (t) NeilCallan 7 62
(C E Brittain) *s.i.s: sn led: rdn and hdd over 2f out: wknd over 1f out* **28/1**

121- **11** *6* **Diam Queen (GER)**[148] 7434 3-9-3 **87** KierenFallon 13 55
(L M Cumani) *hood removed late: s.s: pushed along over 4f out: hdwy over 3f out: wknd 2f out* **9/2**[3]

0-13 **12** *7* **Whippers Love (IRE)**[50] 686 3-8-13 **83** JoeFanning 11 37
(M Johnston) *chsd ldr: rdn and wknd over 2f out* **20/1**

2m 5.30s (-0.50) **Going Correction** +0.075s/f (Good) **12** Ran SP% **117.3**
Speed ratings (Par 102): **105,103,102,101,101 100,98,95,95,91 87,81**
toteswingers: 1&2 £30.30, 1&3 £7.00, 2&3 £19.90 CSF £240.60 CT £931.46 TOTE £10.60: £2.60, £7.20, £2.00; EX 186.50 Place 6: £8.40 Place 5: £6.27.

Owner M B Hawtin **Bred** K And Mrs Cullen **Trained** Newmarket, Suffolk

FOCUS

Five of the last eight winners of this handicap for 3-y-os have gone on to score at Pattern level and, despite the top-weight being rated 7lb below the ceiling, on paper this looked as strong a renewal as ever, with three Group race entrants among the line-up. It looks sure to throw up several winners. The early pace wasn't overly strong but the form is rated positively and looks fairly sound.

NOTEBOOK

Wigmore Hall(IRE) looked good winning his maiden over a mile here last September, and had an excuse (lost two shoes) when last of five on his final start. Gelded in the off-season, he travelled strongly at the back of the field before edging to the outer and shadowing Official Style. Cruising to the front approaching the final furlong, he quickened up for minimal pressure and came home without being extended. He looked every inch a Pattern-class performer in the making here, although even a stiff rise in the weights will leave him interesting for another handicap, with a race such as the London Gold Cup at Newbury on Lockinge day looking a suitable target. (op 7-1)

Right Step ◆, below his best when racing keenly on easy ground on his final start at two, appreciated the return to a quicker surface and settled better. He ran right to the line, appreciating the step up in trip, and looks fully capable of winning something similar. (op 40-1)

Tamaathul ◆, who holds Guineas, Dante and Derby entries, had good maiden form at two, finishing runner-up to Dancing David on his debut and making every yard when dropped back to 7f second time out. That shorter trip wouldn't have suited him as he's very much a middle-distance horse on breeding, and this test was expected to be right up his street. Keen enough early on, he picked up really well from 2f out along the stands' rail, while his main rivals raced wider out, and finished to good effect. Softer ground should suit him, he ought to get another 2f in time, and he looks sure to win races. (tchd 11-4 and 10-3 in a place)
Contract Caterer(IRE), winner of a Goodwood nursery on his final start at two, was keeping on really well at the finish and appreciated this greater test of stamina. A stronger all-round gallop would undoubtedly have suited him better. (op 14-1 tchd 16-1 in a place)
Official Style ◆ was well fancied, especially as he'd been apparently galloping with the previous day's maiden winner Desert Myth. He did his chances no good by failing to settle early on, though, and it's to his credit that he was still on the premises at the finish. He can certainly win off his current mark in a race run at a stronger gallop. (op 10-3 tchd 4-1)
Arlequin, a winner over this trip on the AW at Cagnes-Sur-Mer in February, was another who was a little keen early on and shaped encouragingly enough. (op 66-1)
Spanish Duke(IRE) has plenty of stamina in his pedigree and will arguably be suited by further than this in time. This race wasn't run to suit him and he's another who can do better off an end-to-end gallop. (op 14-1 tchd 16-1 in a place)
First In The Queue(IRE) showed improvement for a switch to Polytrack last autumn, but couldn't build on that here, back on turf. (tchd 50-1 in a place)
Vulcanite(IRE), an all-the-way winner of a 1m4f Lingfield maiden last month, had more on his plate in this company and, given the way the race was run and the fact that there's lots of stamina on the dam's side of his pedigree, it's easy to see why he got outpaced in the latter stages. (tchd 8-1 and 12-1 in a place)
Muwalla Official explanation: jockey said colt pulled too hard
Diam Queen(GER), who holds an Oaks entry, was well backed beforehand but proved disappointing, failing to settle early on. She's yet another who can show this form to be all wrong in a stronger-run race. (op 11-2)
T/Plt: £15.20 to a £1 stake. Pool: £80,692.56. 3,871.03 winning tickets. T/Qpdt: £6.40 to a £1 stake. Pool: £5,267.95. 601.01 winning tickets. CR

RIPON (R-H)
Thursday, April 15

OFFICIAL GOING: Good (7.8)
Rail on bottom bend into home straight moved out 6 metres.
Wind: moderate 1/2 against Weather: overcast, breezy and very chilly

1331 E B F EAT SLEEP & DRINK AT NAGS HEAD PICKHILL MAIDEN STKS 5f
2:00 (2:01) (Class 5) 2-Y-O **£3,561** (£1,059; £529; £264) **Stalls** Low

Form	Pos	Dist	Horse / comment	RPR
	1		**Cocktail Charlie** 2-9-3 0 .... DavidAllan 6 (T D Easterby) *trckd ldrs: swtchd outside over 2f out: led over 1f out: edgd lft: styd on strly* **10/3**[1]	73+
	2	1 1/2	**Meandmyshadow** 2-8-12 0 .... GrahamGibbons 8 (A D Brown) *chsd ldrs: kpt on to take 2nd last 75yds* **25/1**	63
	3	3/4	**Bachelor Knight (IRE)** 2-9-3 0 .... PaulHanagan 2 (R A Fahey) *w ldrs: led over 2f out: hdd appr fnl f: kpt on same pce* **4/1**[2]	65
	4	2	**Just For Leo (IRE)** 2-8-12 0 .... AndrewHeffernan(5) 11 (P D Evans) *swvd rt s: t.k.h: w ldrs: led after 1f: hdd over 2f out: fdd ins fnl f* **11/2**[3]	58+
	5	3/4	**Blind Stag (IRE)** 2-9-3 0 .... PaulMulrennan 9 (P T Midgley) *hdwy 3f out: sn chsng ldrs: edgd lft and outpcd* **7/1**	55
	6	hd	**Dreamweaving (IRE)** 2-8-12 0 .... SilvestreDeSousa 4 (N Tinkler) *dwlt: mid-div: effrt over 2f out: n.m.r over 1f out: styd on ins fnl f* **14/1**	49+
	7	1 3/4	**Losing Draw (IRE)** 2-8-7 0 .... PaulPickard(5) 5 (P T Midgley) *t.k.h in rr: hdwy and n.m.r over 1f out: nvr nr ldrs* **20/1**	43
	8	hd	**Hoppy's Flyer (FR)** 2-8-12 0 .... RichardSmith 10 (Tom Dascombe) *hmpd s: mid-div: hdwy on outside over 2f out: wknd over 1f out* **12/1**	42+
	9	6	**Kheya (IRE)** 2-8-12 0 .... PJMcDonald 3 (G M Moore) *led 1f: w ldrs: wknd over 1f out* **13/2**	21
	10	17	**Love Club** 2-9-3 0 .... J-PGuillambert 7 (B P J Baugh) *in rr: bhd fnl 2f* **20/1**	—
	11	6	**Cono (IRE)** 2-9-3 0 .... RoystonFfrench 1 (Miss Tracy Waggott) *s.s: sn wl bhd* **25/1**	—

62.61 secs (1.91) **Going Correction** +0.175s/f (Good) **11** Ran SP% **115.9**
Speed ratings (Par 92): **91,88,87,84,83 82,79,79,69,42 33**
toteswingers: 1&2 £22.50, 1&3 £2.90, 2&3 £18.00 CSF £94.29 TOTE £3.70: £1.10, £7.60, £1.80; EX 107.80 Trifecta £225.10 Part won. Pool: £304.24 - 0.44 winning units..
Owner Habton Farms **Bred** Habton Farms **Trained** Great Habton, N Yorks

FOCUS
Another success for Tim Easterby in this ordinary maiden.

NOTEBOOK
Cocktail Charlie was certainly nothing special on breeding, but made favourite none the less, it was clear from 2f out that he was going best and, having gone on and edged across to the stands' rail, he just had to be ridden out hands and heels to score. He is clearly a useful prospect, and will presumably go for a conditions race next. (op 11-4 tchd 7-2)
Meandmyshadow, who is very much bred to be suited by 1m plus, had to be niggled to hold her position in behind the leaders, but she did stay on well from over 1f out. This was a very pleasing start from a filly who will relish an extra furlong, and looks a winner in waiting. (tchd 22-1)
Bachelor Knight(IRE) ◆, whose yard has made a tremendous start to the season, including with their juveniles, was soon on the pace, but he tended to hang and looked a little green. He should learn from it and can win something similar. (op 7-2)
Just For Leo(IRE), from a yard that has made a bright start with its juveniles, went right out of the gate, but knew his job and was soon showing in front from his wide draw. He was quickly brushed aside by the winner, though, and just missed out on the places. (op 6-1 tchd 13-2)
Blind Stag(IRE), a half-brother to several winners, was backed beforehand and showed enough to suggest he will be winning, with this experience now behind him. (op 18-1)

1332 COPT HEWICK H'CAP 6f
2:35 (2:41) (Class 4) (0-85,85) 4-Y-O+ **£4,209** (£1,252; £625; £312) **Stalls** Low

Form	Pos	Dist	Horse / comment	RPR
000-	1		**Bond City (IRE)**[170] 7083 8-8-13 **80** .... PJMcDonald 13 (G R Oldroyd) *racd far side: trckd ldr: led jst ins fnl f: hld on wl towards fin: 1st of 6 that gp* **50/1**	90
6-04	2	1/2	**Esprit De Midas**[65] 474 4-9-4 **85** .... TonyHamilton 11 (K A Ryan) *racd far side: trckd ldrs: styd on to take 2nd ins fnl f: no ex towards fin: 2nd of 6 that gp* **20/1**	93
2164	3	2 1/2	**Bel Cantor**[35] 859 7-9-0 **84** .... (p) KellyHarrison(3) 15 (W J H Ratcliffe) *led 5 others far side: hdd jst ins fnl f: no ex: 3rd of 6 that gp* **10/1**	84
500-	4	2 1/2	**Favourite Girl (IRE)**[170] 7083 4-8-12 **79** .... DavidAllan 12 (T D Easterby) *racd far side: chsd ldrs: one pce appr fnl f: 4th of 6 that gp* **8/1**[3]	71
-060	5	2 1/4	**Ingleby Arch (USA)**[33] 887 7-8-5 **72** .... GrahamGibbons 14 (T D Barron) *racd far side: chsd ldrs: sn drvn along: one pce fnl 2f: 5th of 6 that gp* **16/1**	57
110-	6	1 1/2	**Turnkey**[209] 6050 8-8-8 **80** .... MichaelO'Connell(5) 1 (D Nicholls) *racd stands' side: in tch swtchd rt 2f out: r.o to ld that side jst ins fnl f: 1st of 10 that gp* **14/1**	60
000-	7	3/4	**Pearly Wey**[126] 7702 7-8-13 **80** .... DanielTudhope 3 (I W McInnes) *racd stands' side: in rr: effrt and nt clr run over 2f out: styd on to take 2nd that side ins fnl f: 2nd of 10 that gp* **25/1**	58+
00-0	8	2 1/4	**Haajes**[18] 1032 6-9-3 **84** .... (t) MickyFenton 8 (P T Midgley) *racd stands' side: in rr: kpt on fnl 2f: nvr a threat: 3rd of 10 that gp* **9/1**	54+
450-	8	dht	**Mrs Penny (AUS)**[108] 7862 6-9-2 **83** .... PaulHanagan 7 (J R Gask) *racd stands' side: sn in rr: styd on wl ins fnl f: 3rd of 10 that gp* **11/1**	53
3-60	10	3/4	**Frognal (IRE)**[18] 1030 4-9-2 **83** .... PaulMulrennan 16 (Mrs R A Carr) *off fore shoe removed at s: racd far side: chsd ldrs: lost pl over 1f out: last of 6 that gp* **33/1**	51
504-	11	1/2	**Mandurah (IRE)**[178] 6902 6-9-1 **82** .... J-PGuillambert 5 (B P J Baugh) *led 9 others stands' side: hdd that side jst ins fnl f: wknd: eased nr fin: 5th of 10 that gp* **33/1**	48
40-5	12	3/4	**Legal Legacy**[18] 1030 4-8-12 **79** .... TomEaves 9 (M Dods) *dwlt: racd stands' side: sn chsng ldrs: wknd appr fnl f: 6th of 10 that gp* **7/1**[1]	43
000-	13	nk	**Maze (IRE)**[181] 6830 5-8-10 **77** .... AndrewMullen 2 (D Nicholls) *racd stands' side: trckd ldrs: wknd over 1f out: 7th of 10 that gp* **7/1**[1]	40
0	14	1/2	**Signore Momento (IRE)**[14] 1076 4-8-10 **77** .... HayleyTurner 10 (Miss Amy Weaver) *racd stands' side: mid-disvsion: drvn over 2f out: sn outpcd: 8th of 10 that gp* **12/1**	38
000-	15	4	**Van Bossed (CAN)**[221] 5697 5-8-10 **77** .... FrannyNorton 6 (D Nicholls) *racd stands' side: chsd ldrs: effrt over 2f out: lost pl over 1f out: 9th of 10 that gp* **10/1**	35+
-655	16	21	**Earlsmedic**[78] 307 5-8-12 **82** .... (e) WilliamCarson(3) 4 (S C Williams) *dwlt: in rr stands' side: hung rt and lost pl over 2f out: sn wl bhd: last of 10 that gp* **15/2**[2]	—

1m 13.47s (0.47) **Going Correction** +0.175s/f (Good) **16** Ran SP% **121.1**
Speed ratings (Par 105): **103,102,99,95,92 90,89,86,86,85 85,84,83,82,77 49**
toteswingers: 1&2 £89.40, 1&3 £93.40, 2&3 £32.40 CSF £817.18 CT £5685.43 TOTE £88.70: £10.90, £5.10, £3.30, £2.60; EX 2019.40 TRIFECTA Not won..
Owner R C Bond **Bred** David Ryan **Trained** Brawby, N Yorks

FOCUS
A competitive sprint. The fair side dominated and the third is the best guide to the form.
Mandurah(IRE) Official explanation: jockey said gelding had no more to give

1333 RIPON SILVER BOWL CONDITIONS STKS 1m 1f 170y
3:10 (3:11) (Class 3) 4-Y-O+ **£6,567** (£1,983; £1,004; £514; £269) **Stalls** High

Form	Pos	Dist	Horse / comment	RPR
045-	1		**Kings Gambit (SAF)**[188] 6644 6-9-0 110 .... MickyFenton 1 (T P Tate) *w ldr: led over 3f out: styd on wl fnl f* **2/1**[2]	111
010-	2	1 1/2	**Almiqdaad**[194] 6480 4-9-0 99 .... TadhgO'Shea 5 (M A Jarvis) *hld up: effrt over 4f out: chal over 3f out: almost upsides and rdn over 1f out: kpt on same pce* **11/8**[1]	108
420-	3	4 1/2	**Serva Jugum (USA)**[205] 6198 4-9-0 111 .... TomEaves 3 (P F I Cole) *hld up: hdwy to trck ldrs 4f out: effrt over 2f out: wknd over 1f out* **6/1**[3]	98
4-01	4	8	**Exit Smiling**[10] 1117 8-8-9 81 .... PaulPickard(5) 2 (P T Midgley) *t.k.h: set stdy pce: qcknd over 5f out: hdd over 3f out: wknd 2f out* **10/1**	82
130-	5	1 1/4	**Bencoolen (IRE)**[194] 6480 5-8-9 93 .... MichaelO'Connell(5) 6 (D Nicholls) *rrd s: sn w ldrs: lost pl 3f out* **12/1**	79
	U		**Bagutta Sun**[578] 4-8-9 0 .... RichardSmith 4 (Tom Dascombe) *fly j. s leaving stalls and uns rdr* **20/1**	—

2m 4.62s (-0.78) **Going Correction** +0.175s/f (Good) **6** Ran SP% **111.3**
Speed ratings (Par 107): **110,108,105,98,97** —
toteswingers: 1&2 £1.50, 1&3 £1.60, 2&3 £2.10 CSF £5.02 TOTE £3.50: £2.60, £1.10; EX 5.30.
Owner Mrs Fitri Hay **Bred** Danika Stud **Trained** Tadcaster, N Yorks

FOCUS
A messy race, with a steady early pace on. The winner did it cosily, however. The third is rated in line with his British form with the third stepping up on last year.

NOTEBOOK
Kings Gambit(SAF) received a fine ride from Fenton to score. Sent on with 3f to run, he was always pulling out more and actually won with a bit to spare, Fenton not getting having to get too serious with him. He isn't the easiest to place, however, and similar races to this are likely to continue to provide him with his best chance of winning. (op 7-2)
Almiqdaad, who finished 11th when joint-favourite for last season's Cambridgeshire, was made favourite despite having a bit to find on official figures, and he came to have every chance, but was always being held. This was a pleasing enough first run back, and he should improve (op 11-10)
Serva Jugum(USA), sporting the winning owner's first colours, had finished ahead of Kings Gambit towards the end of last term, and he travelled strongly on this seasonal return, but didn't find as much as expected and ended up well held. (op 9-2 tchd 13-2)
Exit Smiling stood little chance with a rating of just 81, and he was quickly left trailing. (tchd 17-2 and 12-1)
Bencoolen(IRE) pulled hard and didn't offer much. (tchd 10-1)

1334 RIPON "COCK O' THE NORTH" H'CAP 1m
3:45 (3:46) (Class 3) (0-95,95) 3-Y-O
£7,477 (£2,239; £1,119; £560; £279; £140) **Stalls** High

Form	Pos	Dist	Horse / comment	RPR
-211	1		**Monterosso**[68] 448 3-8-9 **83** .... RoystonFfrench 7 (M Johnston) *sn drvn along: ungainly: hmpd and lost pl bnd over 5f out: reminders 4f out: hdwy and n.m.r over 1f out: burst through to ld last 50yds* **11/2**[2]	89+
601-	2	nk	**Eleanora Duse (IRE)**[147] 7451 3-8-1 **78** .... Louis-PhilippeBeuzelin(3) 2 (Sir Michael Stoute) *hld up: effrt on outer over 3f out: styd on to chal wl ins fnl f: no ex* **11/2**[2]	83+
561-	3	1 1/2	**Jupiter Fidius**[169] 7116 3-7-13 **76** oh1 .... KellyHarrison(3) 1 (Mrs K Walton) *w ldr: led over 3f out: hdd fnl 50yds: no ex* **16/1**	78
110-	4	nk	**William Morgan (IRE)**[217] 5795 3-8-4 **78** .... PaulHanagan 8 (R A Fahey) *t.k.h: led: hdd over 3f out: kpt on wl ins fnl f* **10/3**[1]	79
331-	5	1/2	**Antoniola (IRE)**[174] 6993 3-8-7 **81** .... DavidAllan 3 (T D Easterby) *trckd ldrs: effrt over 2f out: hung lft and sn chsng ldr: styd on same pce fnl f* **10/3**[1]	81

1-46 **6** *2* **Kumbeshwar**[18] 1033 3-8-2 **81** .... AndrewHeffernan(5) 6 76
(P D Evans) *t.k.h: trckd ldrs: one pce fnl 2f* **14/1**

511- **7** *3 1/4* **New Christmas (USA)**[118] 7804 3-8-6 **80** .... TadhgO'Shea 9 68
(B J Meehan) *mid-div: drvn to chse ldrs over 3f out: outpcd over 2f out: wknd ins fnl f* **17/2**

153- **8** *8* **Syrian**[210] 6011 3-9-7 **95** .... HayleyTurner 4 65
(M L W Bell) *dwlt: tk fierce hold in rr: rdn 3f out: no rspnse and sn bhd* **8/1**[3]

160- **9** *2 3/4* **Celestial Tryst**[186] 6693 3-8-4 **78** .... PJMcDonald 5 41
(G M Moore) *in rr: bhd fnl 3f* **33/1**

1m 42.62s (1.22) **Going Correction** +0.175s/f (Good) **9** Ran SP% **114.1**
Speed ratings (Par 102): **100,99,98,97,97 95,92,84,81**
toteswingers: 1&2 £7.40, 1&3 £12.10, 2&3 £16.70 CSF £35.28 CT £454.57 TOTE £4.40: £1.40, £3.10, £4.80; EX 30.90 Trifecta £288.30 Part won. Pool: £389.64 - 0.44 winning units..
Owner Sheikh Hamdan Bin Mohammed Al Maktoum **Bred** Darley **Trained** Middleham Moor, N Yorks

FOCUS
This is usually a decent 3-y-o handicap, and the race should once again work out and is rated positively.

NOTEBOOK
Monterosso ◆ completed a hat-trick on this turf debut, despite having far from a trouble-free trip. The 5lb rise he incurred for winning over this distance at Lingfield looked fair, but he found himself a bit behind, having been hampered, and was under pressure turning in. However, despite being denied a clear run when trying to close, the horse produced a strong burst inside the final furlong, and actually got there in plenty of time. He can be rated value for further than the winning margin, and looks a horse to keep on-side. (op 4-1)
Eleanora Duse(IRE) ◆, winner of a 1m maiden at Kempton on her final outing at two, looked on a very fair mark for this handicap debut, so it was surprising not to see much confidence behind her in the betting. She ran a race full of promise, though, keeping on in the manner of a horse likely to be suited by further, and she is another to keep on-side. (op 5-1 tchd 13-2)
Jupiter Fidius, another to have won on his final start at two, was always well placed and briefly looked the winner, having kicked for home, but he was chased down by two classier types late on. This was a good return from 1lb 'wrong'. (op 25-1)
William Morgan(IRE), twice a winner at two, needed to have improved from two to three, and he was a little keen on this first try at 1m, but saw it out well enough to suggest he could win something similar off this sort of mark. (op 4-1 tchd 3-1)
Antoniola(IRE), 5lb higher than when winning on his handicap debut at Doncaster last backend, travelled well enough, but couldn't quicken and would probably have benefited from a stronger gallop. Official explanation: jockey said gelding hung left in straight (op 7-2)
Syrian Official explanation: jockey said gelding run too freely

1335 SKELTON MAIDEN STKS (DIV I) 1m
4:20 (4:27) (Class 5) 3-Y-O £2,266 (£674; £337; £168) Stalls High

Form RPR

26- **1** **Much Acclaimed (IRE)**[174] 6991 3-9-3 0 .... MickyFenton 2 85
(T P Tate) *swtchd rt after s: drvn to ld: edgd lft 1f out: styd on strly* **15/2**

022- **2** *5* **Finest Reserve (IRE)**[203] 6235 3-9-3 76 .... PaulHanagan 9 73
(M R Channon) *chsd ldrs: chal 2f out: styng on same pce whn swtchd rt ins fnl f* **5/1**[3]

6- **3** *3* **Florentine Ruler (USA)**[169] 7121 3-9-3 0 .... IanMongan 11 66+
(H R A Cecil) *s.s: hdwy 4f out: swtchd lft over 1f out: styd on wl* **5/2**[2]

4 *1 1/4* **Elle Est** 3-8-12 0 .... DavidAllan 6 58
(E J Alston) *mid-div: rn wd bnd 6f out: hdwy over 3f out: sn chsng ldrs: edgd rt and clr 3rd over 1f out: wknd ins fnl f* **40/1**

0-5 **5** *4* **Brananx (USA)**[18] 1029 3-9-3 0 .... PaulMulrennan 8 54
(K A Ryan) *trckd wnr: wknd over 1f out* **25/1**

6 *2 1/2* **Smarty Sam (USA)** 3-9-3 0 .... PJMcDonald 13 54+
(G A Swinbank) *chsd ldrs: sltly hmpd 2f out: sn wknd over 1f out* **20/1**

7 *4 1/2* **Princess Of Troy (IRE)** 3-8-7 0 .... AndrewHeffernan(5) 10 33
(P D Evans) *chsd ldrs: wknd over 1f out* **20/1**

8 *3* **Forks** 3-9-3 0 .... TomEaves 4 31
(B Smart) *s.s: hdwy into mid-div 6f out: drvn 4f out: wknd over 2f out* **40/1**

55- **9** *3 1/2* **Cosmic Orbit**[264] 4308 3-9-3 0 .... FrankieMcDonald 5 23
(R Curtis) *hmpd s: bhd and drvn 3f out* **100/1**

53- **10** *7* **Ultravox (USA)**[246] 4908 3-9-3 0 .... TadhgO'Shea 12 7
(B J Meehan) *in rr: drvn 4f out: hung rt: nvr on terms* **9/4**[1]

00- **11** *10* **Star Cruiser (USA)**[260] 4430 3-9-3 0 .... DuranFentiman 3 —
(T D Easterby) *in tch: drvn 4f out: sn lost pl and bhd* **100/1**

12 *4* **Central Bank (IRE)** 3-9-3 0 .... RoystonFfrench 7 —
(M Johnston) *s.i.s: sn drvn along and bhd: t.o 4f out* **12/1**

1m 42.73s (1.33) **Going Correction** +0.175s/f (Good) **12** Ran SP% **115.7**
Speed ratings (Par 98): **100,95,92,90,86 84,79,76,73,66 56,52**
toteswingers: 1&2 £5.20, 1&3 £4.40, 2&3 £3.50 CSF £40.79 TOTE £8.00: £1.80, £1.20, £1.50; EX 49.00 Trifecta £166.00 Pool: £323.08 - 1.44 winning units..
Owner T P Tate **Bred** Glending Bloodstock **Trained** Tadcaster, N Yorks

FOCUS
A fair maiden The form is rated through the runner-up with the third to his debut mark.
Florentine Ruler(USA) ◆ Official explanation: jockey said colt missed the break
Elle Est Official explanation: jockey said filly hung right final 2f
Cosmic Orbit Official explanation: jockey said gelding missed the break
Ultravox(USA) Official explanation: jockey said colt never travelled
Central Bank(IRE) Official explanation: jockey said gelding ran green throughout

1336 SKELTON MAIDEN STKS (DIV II) 1m
4:55 (5:03) (Class 5) 3-Y-O £2,266 (£674; £337; £168) Stalls High

Form RPR

0- **1** **Celendine**[206] 6154 3-8-12 0 .... PJMcDonald 7 80
(G A Swinbank) *prom: smooth hdwy over 3f out: led over 1f out: styd on strly* **10/1**

4- **2** *4 1/2* **Strong Vigilance (IRE)**[174] 6991 3-9-3 0 .... HayleyTurner 2 75
(M L W Bell) *s.i.s: hdwy over 3f out: styd on to take 2nd ins fnl f: no imp* **11/8**[1]

3 *1* **Laverre (IRE)** 3-8-12 0 .... DavidAllan 12 68+
(T D Easterby) *s.i.s: stdy hdwy over 3f out: styd on fnl 2f: tk 3rd nr fin* **12/1**

4 *hd* **Ezra Church (IRE)** 3-9-3 0 .... GrahamGibbons 13 72
(T D Barron) *prom: effrt over 3f out: kpt on same pce fnl 2f* **8/1**

00 **5** *5* **Killing Moon (USA)**[42] 784 3-9-3 0 .... SilvestreDeSousa 3 61
(K A Ryan) *t.k.h: w ldr: led over 4f out: hdd over 1f out: hung rt and wknd ins fnl f* **28/1**

0- **6** *3/4* **Myraid**[181] 6821 3-9-3 0 .... PaulMulrennan 5 59+
(Ollie Pears) *stdd s: racd in last: hdwy over 2f out: nvr a factor* **50/1**

7 *1/2* **Frontline Phantom (IRE)** 3-9-3 0 .... AndrewElliott 6 58
(J R Weymes) *in tch: lost pl over 5f out: sme hdwy over 3f out: nvr a factor* **40/1**

0-0 **8** *9* **Russian Brigadier**[18] 1029 3-9-3 0 .... FrannyNorton 1 37
(M Brittain) *in rr: t.k.h: bhd fnl 2f* **40/1**

9 *4 1/2* **Khandaq (USA)** 3-9-3 0 .... TadhgO'Shea 11 27
(M Johnston) *unruly gave seriuous problems and delayed s: led: hdd over 4f out: lost pl 2f out: eased whn bhd* **7/2**[2]

10 *1* **Director General (USA)** 3-9-3 0 .... TomEaves 9 25
(Julie Camacho) *mid-div: effrt over 3f out: hung lft: wknd over 2f out* **15/2**[3]

11 *1/2* **Marsh's Gift** 3-9-0 0 .... BarryMcHugh(3) 4 23
(R E Barr) *reluctant to load: s.s: in rr: sme hdwy 3f out: sn wknd* **50/1**

00- **12** *25* **Reel Love**[290] 3468 3-9-3 0 .... J-PGuillambert 8 —
(J R Holt) *chsd ldrs: lost pl over 2f out: bhd whn eased over 1 1/2f out: t.o* **100/1**

0-5 **13** *39* **Pinewood Polly**[67] 453 3-8-12 0 .... RoystonFfrench 10 —
(S A Harris) *t.k.h: trckd ldrs: lost pl over 3f out: bhd and virtually p.u 2f out: hopelessly t.o* **100/1**

1m 42.82s (1.42) **Going Correction** +0.175s/f (Good) **13** Ran SP% **118.2**
Speed ratings (Par 98): **99,94,93,93,88 87,87,78,73,72 72,47,8**
toteswingers: 1&2 £4.30, 1&3 £18.70, 2&3 £7.60 CSF £23.22 TOTE £14.60: £3.50, £1.60, £4.90; EX 34.70 Trifecta £193.30 Part won. Pool: £261.35 -0.10 winning units..
Owner R H Hall **Bred** Miss K Rausing **Trained** Melsonby, N Yorks

FOCUS
The second division of the 1m maiden and not many got into it. The form is best rated through the winner.
Killing Moon(USA) Official explanation: jockey said gelding hung right
Khandaq(USA) Official explanation: jockey said colt had no more to give
Director General(USA) Official explanation: jockey said gelding had been unsuited by the track
Reel Love Official explanation: jockey said colt had no more to give
Pinewood Polly Official explanation: jockey said filly had failed to handle undulations

1337 SHARROW APPRENTICE H'CAP 5f
5:25 (5:30) (Class 5) (0-70,71) 4-Y-O+ £2,590 (£770; £385; £192) Stalls Low

Form RPR

4523 **1** **Verinco**[30] 896 4-8-4 60 .... (v) AdamCarter(8) 3 68
(B Smart) *racd stands' side: w ldrs: led that side 1f out: edgd rt: led overall last 75yds: 1st of 5 that gp* **13/2**

405- **2** *1 1/4* **Kyzer Chief**[194] 6489 5-8-10 61 .... LeeTopliss(3) 1 65
(R E Barr) *uns rdr and rn loose gng to s: led stands' side gp: hdd that side 1f out: edgd rt: kpt on: 2nd of 5 that gp* **6/1**

00-2 **3** *hd* **Sea Crest**[2] 1270 4-8-4 58 oh1 ow2 .... JohnCavanagh(6) 6 61
(M Brittain) *racd far side: chsd ldr: led that gp 75yds out: no ex: 1st of 5 that gp* **4/1**[3]

0343 **4** *2 1/4* **Trick Or Two**[5] 1234 4-8-8 56 .... (b) RyanClark 9 51
(Mrs R A Carr) *swtchd lft s: led 4 others far side: 3 l clr that gp over 1f out: hdd overall and wknd wl ins fnl f: 2nd of 5 that gp* **11/4**[1]

0411 **5** *2* **La Capriosa**[10] 1112 4-9-9 71 6ex .... IanBrennan 8 58
(J A Glover) *racd far side: chsd ldr: wknd over 1f out: 3rd of 5 that gp* **7/2**[2]

3200 **6** *nk* **Guto**[9] 1147 7-9-8 70 .... DavidKenny 10 56
(W J H Ratcliffe) *racd far side: sn outpcd in rr: hdwy 2f out: nvr a threat: 4th of 5 that gp* **16/1**

260- **7** *3 1/4* **King Of Swords (IRE)**[178] 6897 6-9-3 70 .... (p) NoraLooby(5) 2 45
(N Tinkler) *racd stands' side: w ldrs: wknd over 1f out: 3rd of 5 that gp* **14/1**

260- **8** *3* **Maison Dieu**[181] 6825 7-8-7 60 .... NeilFarley(5) 7 24
(A Berry) *racd far side: sn outpcd and in rr: last of 5 that gp* **33/1**

100- **9** *4 1/2* **Caledonia Princess**[132] 7634 4-9-4 66 .... (b) JohnFahy 4 14
(R Curtis) *s.i.s: racd stands' side: sn chsng ldrs: lost pl 2f out: 4th of 5 that gp* **14/1**

0-06 **10** *17* **Wings Of Kintyre (IRE)**[65] 473 6-8-5 56 oh6 ..(b[1]) MatthewLawson(3) 5 —
(A Berry) *racd stands' side: in rr: lost pl over 2f out: sn wl bhd: last of 5 that gp* **66/1**

61.14 secs (0.44) **Going Correction** +0.175s/f (Good) **10** Ran SP% **120.2**
Speed ratings (Par 103): **103,101,100,97,93 93,88,83,76,49**
toteswingers: 1&2 £6.50, 1&3 £4.70, 2&3 £6.10 CSF £46.76 CT £183.33 TOTE £8.20: £2.40, £2.40, £1.10; EX 90.70 Trifecta £120.90 Part won. Pool: £163.39 - 0.60 winning units. Place 6: £71.22 Place 5: £42.70.
Owner B Smart **Bred** Mrs M Gutkin **Trained** Hambleton, N Yorks
■ Stewards' Enquiry : Ryan Clark one-day ban: failed to ride to draw (Apr 29)

FOCUS
A moderate sprint and this time the place to be was on the stands' side. The winner is rated in line with last year's best.
T/Plt: £50.00 to a £1 stake. Pool: £55,409.43. 808.39 winning tickets. T/Qpdt: £8.40 to a £1 stake. Pool: £4,240.65. 369.74 winning tickets. WG

1338 - 1344a (Foreign Racing) - See Raceform Interactive

1316 KEMPTON (A.W) (R-H)
Friday, April 16

OFFICIAL GOING: Standard
Wind: fresh, across Weather: bright and breezy

1345 BETDAQ ON 0870 178 1221 MEDIAN AUCTION MAIDEN STKS 5f (P)
6:25 (6:25) (Class 5) 3-5-Y-O £2,590 (£770; £385; £192) Stalls High

Form RPR

0-0 **1** **Lucky Flyer**[15] 1075 3-8-9 0 .... LiamKeniry 3 68
(S Kirk) *mde all: rn wd bnd over 3f out: rdn clr over 1f out: styd on wl and in n.d fnl f* **16/1**[3]

-246 **2** *1 3/4* **Diamond Johnny G (USA)**[42] 807 3-9-0 78 .... (t) EddieCreighton 5 67
(E J Creighton) *dwlt: sn bustled along and in tch in midfield: rdn 3f out: outpcd by wnr over 1f out: wnt 2nd 1f out: kpt on but nvr threatened wnr* **11/8**[2]

203- **3** *3 3/4* **Lexi's Layla (IRE)**[176] 6971 3-8-9 68 .... JamieSpencer 2 49
(D M Simcock) *sn chsng wnr: carried wd bnd over 3f out: rdn and hanging rt over 1f out: sn outpcd by wnr: lost 2nd 1f out: wl btn fnl f* **1/1**[1]

F60/ **4** *6* **Emma's Secrets**[920] 6093 5-9-2 0 .... MartinLane(3) 4 27
(D Shaw) *sn bustled along in midfield: rdn and struggling ent fnl 2f: wl btn over 1f out* **20/1**

60/6 **5** *4* **Lunar Lass**[8] 1190 5-9-0 41 .... AndrewHeffernan(5) 6 13
(D C Griffiths) *plld hrd: chsd ldrs: flashed tail u.p and wknd wl over 1f out: wl btn fnl f* **33/1**

-600 **6** *6* **Lunaticus**[62] 538 4-9-0 29 .... (p) JemmaMarshall(5) 1 —
(M J Attwater) *a in last pair: rdn 3f out: sn struggling and wl bhd fnl 2f* **50/1**

60.56 secs (0.06) **Going Correction** -0.075s/f (Stan)
WFA 3 from 4yo+ 10lb **6** Ran SP% **107.7**
Speed ratings (Par 103): **96,93,87,77,71 61**
toteswingers:1&2:£2.40, 1&3:£2.10, 2&3:£1.10 CSF £35.85 TOTE £10.80: £2.40, £1.60; EX 62.50.
Owner Gracelands Stud Partnership **Bred** R V Young **Trained** Upper Lambourn, Berks

FOCUS
This looked a two-horse race on paper but there was a surprise result. It has been rated on the negative side with doubts about how much ability the runner-up retains.

1346 BETDAQ.CO.UK H'CAP 1m 2f (P)
7:00 (7:00) (Class 5) (0-75,73) 4-Y-O+ **£2,590** (£770; £385; £192) **Stalls** High

Form RPR

504- **1** **Penchesco (IRE)**[81] 6594 5-9-0 **69** .... JimCrowley 10 79
(Mrs A J Perrett) *chsd ldrs: rdn and effrt 2f out: chal over 1f out: led ins fnl f: forged ahd fnl 75yds* **9/1**

222 **2** *1 1/4* **West Emirates (USA)**[18] 1050 4-9-2 **71** .... AdamKirby 14 79
(C G Cox) *chsd ldng pair: swtchd lft off of rail 2f out: rdn and ev ch over 1f out: led 1f out: hdd ins fnl f: no ex and btn fnl 75yds* **7/1**[3]

2-01 **3** *nk* **Resentful Angel**[76] 361 5-8-12 **72** .... TobyAtkinson(5) 2 79+
(Pat Eddery) *hld up towards rr: rdn and hdwy on outer over 3f out: chsd ldrs over 1f out: kpt on wl to go 3rd wl ins fnl f: nt rch ldng pair* **15/2**

0560 **4** *1 1/4* **Rocky's Pride (IRE)**[31] 897 4-8-13 **68** ....(p) NeilCallan 5 73
(A B Haynes) *in tch in midfield: rdn and effrt on inner 2f out: ev ch jst over 1f out: wknd ins fnl f* **20/1**

4-02 **5** *hd* **Herschel (IRE)**[21] 990 4-9-4 **73** .... GeorgeBaker 9 77
(G L Moore) *chsd ldr: rdn to ld wl over 1f out: hdd 1f out: edgd lft and wknd ins fnl f* **5/2**[1]

166- **6** *3 1/2* **Love In The Park**[213] 5964 5-8-12 **67** .... JackMitchell 4 65+
(R Brotherton) *hld up in rr: rdn and hdwy 3f out: hung rt over 1f out: kpt on: nvr trbld ldrs* **14/1**

1240 **7** *1 1/2* **Formidable Guest**[20] 1015 6-9-4 **73** .... RobertHavlin 8 68
(J Pearce) *bustled along early: sn in tch in midfield: rdn over 2f out: wknd u.p over 1f out* **13/2**[2]

00-0 **8** *2* **Mister Ross**[16] 1063 5-9-2 **71** .... PatCosgrave 13 62
(J R Boyle) *hld up in midfield: rdn and unable qck over 2f out: no ch w ldrs fr over 1f out* **20/1**

0646 **9** *4* **Trafalgar Square**[9] 1156 8-8-12 **72** .... JemmaMarshall(5) 3 55
(M J Attwater) *s.i.s: bhd: hdwy on outer into midfield 1/2-way: rdn and btn over 2f out* **22/1**

0005 **10** *1 1/2* **Valmari (IRE)**[16] 1062 7-8-10 **72** .... CharlotteKerton(7) 7 53
(G Prodromou) *stdd s: bhd: reminder after 1f: t.k.h after and hld up in rr: lost tch over 2f out: nvr on terms* **33/1**

000- **11** *1 1/2* **Baycat (IRE)**[326] 2329 4-9-3 **72** .... TomQueally 1 50
(J G Portman) *in tch in midfield: rdn and struggling 3f out: wl btn fnl 2f* **33/1**

1204 **12** *3/4* **Whodunit (UAE)**[9] 1177 6-8-10 **68** ....(b) WilliamCarson(3) 6 44
(P W Hiatt) *racd keenly: led tl wl over 1f out: sn wknd: wl btn and eased ins fnl f* **8/1**

0606 **13** *3 3/4* **Mcconnell (USA)**[30] 908 5-9-0 **72** ....(p) RobertLButler(3) 12 41
(P Butler) *in tch in midfield: rdn and lost pl qckly over 2f out: wl bhd fnl f* **14/1**

2m 5.77s (-2.23) **Going Correction** -0.075s/f (Stan) **13** Ran SP% **120.4**
Speed ratings (Par 103): **105,104,103,102,102 99,98,97,93,92 91,90,87**
toteswingers:1&2:£10.20, 1&3:£9.90, 2&3:£4.50 CSF £65.92 CT £501.84 TOTE £12.80: £4.50, £2.20, £1.30; EX 53.30.
Owner Mrs Karen Hancock **Bred** Patrick J Dempsey **Trained** Pulborough, W Sussex
■ Stewards' Enquiry : Charlotte Kerton forty-two day ban; In breach of Rule (B) 59.2 (May 10-Jun 20)

FOCUS
They went a solid gallop but it proved hard to come from too far back in the short home straight. The form looks sound enough, with the fourth rated to his recent best for his current yard.
Valmari(IRE) Official explanation: The Disciplinary Panel of the BHA enquired into the running and riding of Valmari who finished unplaced. The jockey said her orders were to drop the mare out, get it to settle as it had been keen previously, then make a move coming into the straight, but it missed the kick and then ran in snatches and had not faced the kickback, she thought that it needed further but not on the all-weather. Having heard their evidence and viewed the video recordings of the race, they found the jockey in breach of Rule (B)59.2 and the trainer in breach of Rule (C)45.4. They suspended Kerton 42 days: May 10th to June 20th. They fined Mr Prodromu £7,5000 and suspended the gelding from running in any race for 40 days from Wednesday, 5th May to Sunday, 13th June

1347 BETDAQ THE BETTING EXCHANGE CLASSIFIED STKS 6f (P)
7:30 (7:31) (Class 5) 3-Y-O **£2,590** (£770; £385; £192) **Stalls** High

Form RPR

01 **1** **Murura (IRE)**[21] 997 3-9-0 67 .... PaulMulrennan 1 70+
(J G Given) *wnt lft s: bhd: stl last over 2f out: rdn and hdwy wl over 1f out: swtchd rt and rdn to go between horses: led ins fnl f: rdn out hands and heels and r.o wl fnl 100yds* **4/1**[2]

020- **2** *1/2* **Kilmanseck**[191] 6590 3-9-0 70 .... NeilCallan 4 68
(Eve Johnson Houghton) *stdd s: in tch: hdwy to chse ldrs 3f out: drvn and ev ch over 1f out: unable qck fnl 100yds* **33/1**

215- **3** *hd* **Kilt Rock (IRE)**[182] 6829 3-9-0 70 .... TomQueally 8 67
(R A Mills) *t.k.h: sn chsng ldrs: rdn and nt qckn wl over 1f out: hdwy u.p to chse ldrs ins fnl f: kpt on* **3/1**[1]

1420 **4** *3/4* **Marjolly (IRE)**[42] 809 3-9-0 65 ....(p) TadhgO'Shea 3 65
(J Gallagher) *t.k.h: hld up towards rr: hdwy on inner over 2f out: rdn to chal over 1f out: led 1f out: hdd ins fnl f: btn fnl 100yds* **25/1**

4-52 **5** *1 1/4* **Master Mylo (IRE)**[16] 1058 3-9-0 70 .... JimCrowley 6 61
(D K Ivory) *in tch in midfield: effrt u.p ent fnl 2f: no prog tl kpt on u.p fnl 150yds: nt pce to rch ldrs* **4/1**[2]

024- **6** *1/2* **Love Match**[184] 6775 3-8-7 66 .... JohnFahy(7) 5 59
(R Charlton) *hld up in last trio: rdn and no prog jst over 2f out: kpt on ins fnl f: nvr gng pce to rch ldrs* **12/1**

033- **7** *nse* **Autocracy**[183] 6802 3-9-0 68 .... LiamJones 7 59
(W J Haggas) *t.k.h: sn chsng ldrs: rdn and unable qck jst over 2f out: one pce fr over 1f out* **9/2**[3]

6352 **8** *shd* **Arken Lad**[8] 1181 3-8-8 64 ow1 ....(v[1]) MJMurphy(7) 9 60
(D Donovan) *racd keenly: chsd ldr tl led after 1f: rdn and hdd 2f out: plugging on same pce and hld whn n.m.r and edgd lft ins fnl f* **16/1**

2316 **9** *1/2* **Sweet Avon**[43] 788 3-9-0 60 .... ShaneKelly 10 57
(Matthew Salaman) *t.k.h: led for 1f: chsd ldr after tl led again 2f out: sn rdn: hdd 1f out: wknd fnl f* **20/1**

2331 **10** *11* **Caramelita**[15] 1075 3-9-0 68 .... FrankieDettori 2 22
(J R Jenkins) *wnt lft s: in tch in midfield on outer: rdn and lost pl over 2f out: btn over 1f out: eased ins fnl f* **7/1**

1m 12.74s (-0.36) **Going Correction** -0.075s/f (Stan) **10** Ran SP% **120.8**
Speed ratings (Par 98): **99,98,98,97,95 94,94,94,93,79**
toteswingers:1&2:£41.80, 1&3:£5.00, 2&3:£36.10 CSF £135.45 TOTE £6.00: £2.50, £17.50, £1.20; EX 76.20.
Owner J G Given **Bred** Corrin Stud **Trained** Willoughton, Lincs

FOCUS
The pace was nothing special for a 6f sprint, so the winner did well to get up from the rear. The form looks slightly muddling but has been taken at face value for now, rated around the third.

1348 BET MULTIPLES - BETDAQ H'CAP 1m 4f (P)
8:00 (8:00) (Class 4) (0-85,85) 4-Y-O+ **£4,209** (£1,252; £625; £312) **Stalls** Centre

Form RPR

1201 **1** **Chalice Welcome**[9] 1169 7-8-13 **79** 6ex .... JackMitchell 5 88+
(N B King) *hld up towards rr: effrt and swtchd rt looking for run over 1f out: str run on inner fnl f to ld nr fin* **12/1**

-650 **2** *nk* **Scamperdale**[49] 725 8-8-12 **83** .... KierenFox(5) 9 90
(B P J Baugh) *chsd ldng pair: rdn and qcknd to ld over 1f out: clr 1f out: drvn ins fnl f: hdd and rdr dropped reins nr fin* **20/1**

521- **3** *3/4* **Incendo**[190] 6613 4-8-11 **78** ....(t) HayleyTurner 7 84+
(J R Fanshawe) *t.k.h: hld up towards rr: rdn and effrt 2f out: sn swtchd lft: kpt on to chse ldrs and drvn ins fnl f: no imp fnl 50yds* **10/3**[2]

0100 **4** *1 1/4* **Stand Guard**[20] 1015 6-9-0 **85** .... AndrewHeffernan(5) 6 89
(P Howling) *t.k.h: rdn and unsble to qckn ent fnl 2f: kpt on same pce u.p fnl f* **20/1**

2561 **5** *3/4* **Kames Park (IRE)**[34] 888 8-8-10 **76** .... JamieSpencer 1 79
(R C Guest) *stdd and dropped in after s: hld up in rr: swtchd rt and gd hdwy on inner 2f out: no imp ins fnl f* **8/1**

635- **6** *1/2* **Relative Strength (IRE)**[202] 6273 5-8-6 **72** ....(v) LiamKeniry 10 74
(A M Balding) *led: rdn ent fnl 2f: hdd and nt pce of ldr over 1f out: one pce and btn fnl f* **5/2**[1]

4634 **7** *nk* **Free Tussy (ARG)**[16] 1062 6-8-12 **78** ....(bt) FergusSweeney 8 79
(G L Moore) *hld up in midfield: rdn and effrt 2f out: edgd lft u.p and no prog 1f out* **14/1**

102 **8** *1 3/4* **Hannicean**[37] 852 6-8-5 **71** .... ChrisCatlin 3 70
(Ian Williams) *v slow away: t.k.h: hld up in last trio: rdn and one pce fnl 2f* **11/1**

250- **9** *1/2* **Phoenix Flight (IRE)**[20] 7151 5-9-0 **80** .... SebSanders 4 78
(H J Evans) *t.k.h: rdn and hung rt over 2f out: wknd ent fnl 2f* **10/1**

1-52 **10** *4* **Trachonitis (IRE)**[16] 1062 6-8-12 **78** .... FrankieDettori 2 69
(J R Jenkins) *stdd s: hld up in rr: effrt on outer 3f out: btn ent fnl 2f* **6/1**[3]

2m 37.66s (3.16) **Going Correction** -0.075s/f (Stan)
WFA 4 from 5yo+ 1lb **10** Ran SP% **118.4**
Speed ratings (Par 105): **86,85,85,84,83 83,83,82,81,79**
toteswingers:1&2:£22.50, 1&3:£8.70, 2&3:£12.60 CSF £227.71 CT £978.22 TOTE £7.90: £1.80, £7.30, £2.00; EX 136.40.
Owner The Dyball Partnership **Bred** The Dyball Partnership **Trained** Newmarket, Suffolk

FOCUS
They were soon strung out, but the tempo was moderate until lifting around the bend, theoretically making it hard to make ground from the rear. The form looks muddling but has been rated around the runner-up for the time being.

1349 BET MANCHESTER DERBY - BETDAQ H'CAP 6f (P)
8:30 (8:30) (Class 3) (0-95,95) 4-Y-O+
£6,542 (£1,959; £979; £490; £244; £122) **Stalls** High

Form RPR

120- **1** **Street Power (USA)**[140] 7558 5-8-11 **88** .... SteveDrowne 9 96
(J R Gask) *in tch in midfield: swtchd lft and hdwy ent fnl f: r.o wl to ld towards fin* **11/4**[1]

102- **2** *nk* **We Have A Dream**[175] 6994 5-8-9 **86** .... MartinDwyer 2 93
(W R Muir) *led: hrd pressed and rdn 2f out: kpt on gamely tl hdd and no ex towards fin* **7/1**[3]

-020 **3** *nk* **Orpenindeed (IRE)**[34] 887 7-8-10 **87** .... SebSanders 7 93
(M Botti) *chsd ldrs: rdn and ev ch wl over 1f out: kpt on u.p fnl f* **15/2**

0405 **4** *shd* **Fathsta (IRE)**[8] 1192 5-8-8 **85** .... TomQueally 8 92+
(D M Simcock) *t.k.h: hld up in tch towards rr: hdwy and nt clr run over 1f out tl ins fnl f: r.o towards fin: nvr able to chal* **8/1**

00-0 **5** *nse* **Pusey Street Lady**[20] 1007 6-8-12 **89** .... ChrisCatlin 5 95
(J Gallagher) *chsd ldr: rdn and ev ch wl over 1f out: kpt on same pce u.p ins fnl f* **16/1**

/06- **6** *1 1/4* **Captain Ramius (IRE)**[328] 2278 4-9-4 **95** .... JamieSpencer 4 97
(K A Ryan) *chsd ldrs: rdn and effrt 2f out: drvn and unable qck ent fnl f: hld after* **3/1**[2]

030- **7** *2* **Baby Strange**[177] 6944 6-8-3 **83** .... MartinLane(3) 6 78
(D Shaw) *stdd s: hld up in rr: hdwy on inner 2f out: no prog ent fnl f* **14/1**

065- **8** *1/2* **Macdillon**[166] 7202 4-8-10 **87** .... FergusSweeney 1 81
(W S Kittow) *wnt bdly lft s: in tch in midfield on outer: rdn and unable qck over 2f out: no threat to ldrs after* **12/1**

214- **9** *3/4* **Avertor**[294] 3362 4-8-6 **83** .... HayleyTurner 3 74
(R Charlton) *stdd s: t.k.h: hld up in last pair: rdn over 2f out: no prog* **14/1**

1m 11.48s (-1.62) **Going Correction** -0.075s/f (Stan) **9** Ran SP% **114.0**
Speed ratings (Par 107): **107,106,106,106,106 104,101,101,100**
toteswingers:1&2:£5.30, 1&3:£5.60, 2&3:£9.40 CSF £22.11 CT £128.89 TOTE £3.40: £1.10, £1.20, £3.10; EX 23.50.
Owner Horses First Racing Limited **Bred** John Hawkins **Trained** Sutton Veny, Wilts

FOCUS
A fair gallop gave everyone a chance and produced a tight finish to this decent-quality sprint. It has been rated around the runner-up and third.

NOTEBOOK
Street Power(USA) was disappointing when last seen in November, but generally he is a reliable sort and this suggests he is in for another good season. Looking ready to run in the paddock, he showed he can handle this higher mark and he appeals as one who will improve a bit more. (tchd 3-1)

We Have A Dream had an excellent 2009 and that means he starts this season on a challenging official rating. However, he seems to be thriving and this should have set him up for a successful campaign. (tchd 13-2)

Orpenindeed(IRE) has not been beaten far in recent races and again ran well. He may yet defy this mark one day. (op 10-1)

Fathsta(IRE) had to wait for a gap but flew home when it opened. He wins rarely these days but is attractively weighted and cannot be ruled out on Polytrack or turf. Official explanation: jockey said gelding was denied a clear run (tchd 9-1)

Pusey Street Lady took on some decent company last year but she has slipped in the weights after failing to win for two years. Mounted on the course and headstrong to post, she put in a good effort which suggests she is worth trying again on Polytrack despite having been campaigned only rarely on it in the past.

Captain Ramius(IRE), on his toes in the paddock, put in a good first run for nearly a year but looked particularly effective over 7f last season. (tchd 10-3)

1350 BET SCOTTISH NATIONAL - BETDAQ H'CAP — 7f (P)

9:00 (9:00) (Class 5) (0-70,71) 4-Y-O+ — **£2,590** (£770; £385; £192) **Stalls** High

Form — RPR

53-1 **1** **Global Village (IRE)**[53] 668 5-9-0 **69**....................... WilliamCarson(3) 9 — 82+
(G C Bravery) *mde all: set stdy gallop: rdn and qcknd 2f out: r.o strly fnl f: comf* **6/4**[1]

-333 **2** 2 ¾ **Tevez**[11] 1129 5-8-4 **59**....................... MartinLane(3) 3 — 65
(D Donovan) *stdd and dropped in after s: hld up in tch: gd hdwy on inner 2f out: chsd wnr and drvn jst over 1f out: no imp* **9/2**[2]

500- **3** ¾ **Russian Rave**[187] 6699 4-9-1 **67**....................... TomQueally 10 — 71
(J G Portman) *plld hrd: chsd ldrs: rdn and nt pce of wnr wl over 1f out: kpt on same pce fnl f* **13/2**

10 **4** 2 **Valentino Swing (IRE)**[44] 767 7-8-13 **68**....................... JackDean(3) 6 — 67
(Miss T Spearing) *t.k.h: hld up in last trio: rdn and effrt 2f out: swtchd rt over 1f out: no imp fnl f* **17/2**

6415 **5** nk **Sweet Applause (IRE)**[25] 967 4-8-2 **61**....................... CharlotteKerton(7) 8 — 59
(G Prodromou) *plld hrd: chsd ldr tl over 1f out: rdn and wknd ent fnl f* **18/1**

05-0 **6** 1 ½ **Perfect Friend**[16] 1064 4-8-13 **70**....................... LeeNewnes(5) 2 — 64
(S Kirk) *wnt lft s: t.k.h: hld up in tch towards rr: rdn and no prog 2f out* **12/1**

410- **7** 1 ¼ **Annes Rocket (IRE)**[172] 7051 5-8-8 **60**....................... LiamKeniry 7 — 50
(J C Fox) *plld hrd: stdd after s: hld up in last pair: rdn and no prog ent fnl 2f* **12/1**

0614 **8** ¾ **Resplendent Nova**[23] 975 8-9-1 **67**....................... DarryllHolland 1 — 55
(P Howling) *in tch: rdn and unable qck over 2f out: wl btn fnl f* **6/1**[3]

1m 27.42s (1.42) **Going Correction** -0.075s/f (Stan) — **8** Ran SP% **117.0**
Speed ratings (Par 103): **88,84,84,81,81 79,78,77**
toteswingers:1&2:£1.60, 1&3:£4.10, 2&3:£6.20 CSF £8.56 CT £34.26 TOTE £2.40: £1.10, £1.10, £3.30; EX 10.40 Place 6 £104.36, Place 5 £44.23.
Owner Mrs Janice Jones **Bred** Kilfrush Stud **Trained** Cowlinge, Suffolk

FOCUS
The early pace was feeble, with the entire field pulling hard, and the front-running winner was in the right place to strike. The winner continues to impress but some aspects of the form may prove to be unreliable. It has been rated around the runner-up.
Annes Rocket(IRE) Official explanation: jockey said horse ran too free
T/Plt: £80.10 to a £1 stake. Pool: £56,174.25. 511.35 winning tickets. T/Qpdt: £10.30 to a £1 stake. Pool: £6,133.01. 440.50 winning tickets. SP

NEWBURY (L-H)

Friday, April 16

OFFICIAL GOING: Good (good to soft in places on round course; 7.5)
Rails set out wide increasing distance on round course by 30 metres.
Wind: Brisk behind Weather: Overcast

1351 ERIK PENSER BANK E B F MAIDEN STKS — 5f 34y

1:35 (1:38) (Class 4) 2-Y-O — **£5,180** (£1,541; £770; £384) **Stalls** High

Form — RPR

1 **Klammer** 2-9-3 0....................... ShaneKelly 5 — 86+
(Jane Chapple-Hyam) *wnt rt s: sn in tch: hdwy over 1f out str run fnl f to ld last strides* **9/2**[2]

2 hd **Royal Exchange** 2-9-3 0....................... RichardHughes 3 — 85+
(R Hannon) *sn w ldr: led over 1f out: edgd lft ins fnl f: kpt on: hdd last strides* **9/4**[1]

4 **3** 2 ½ **Shafgaan**[15] 1073 2-9-3 0....................... NeilCallan 7 — 77+
(C E Brittain) *hmpd s: sn rcvrd to press ldrs and slt ld on rails 2f out: hdd over 1f out: outpcd ins fnl f* **9/2**[2]

4 1 ½ **Memen (IRE)** 2-9-3 0....................... JamieSpencer 4 — 69
(P F I Cole) *sn slt ld: hdd 2f out: styd chalng tl wknd ins fnl f* **20/1**

5 4 **Red Marling (IRE)** 2-9-3 0....................... MichaelHills 9 — 56+
(B W Hills) *wnt lft s: sn in tch: pushed along 2f out: hung lft 2f out and wknd over 1f out* **9/1**[3]

6 6 **Rojo Boy** 2-9-3 0....................... DavidProbert 1 — 29
(A M Balding) *s.i.s and wnt lft s: sn in tch: rdn 2f out: sn btn* **12/1**

7 1 ¾ **Prophet In A Dream** 2-9-3 0....................... KierenFallon 6 — 22
(M R Channon) *wnt rt s: sn rcvrd to chse ldrs: wknd 2f out* **10/1**

8 2 ½ **Honourable Knight (IRE)** 2-9-3 0....................... MartinDwyer 8 — 19+
(M D I Usher) *bdly hmpd s: sn wl bhd and outpcd* **50/1**

61.96 secs (0.56) **Going Correction** -0.075s/f (Good) — **8** Ran SP% **100.6**
Speed ratings (Par 94): **92,91,87,85,78 69,66,62**
toteswingers:1&2:£2.70, 1&3:£3.20, 2&3:£2.60 CSF £11.60 TOTE £5.40: £1.30, £1.50, £1.50; EX 14.80.
Owner Yan Wah Wu **Bred** Ermyn Lodge Stud Limited **Trained** Dalham, Suffolk

FOCUS
This maiden lost some of its interest when Foghorn Leghorn, due to represent the same trainer and owner combination who took this with Winker Watson in 2007, was withdrawn after getting upset in the stalls. The race should still produce winners, though.

NOTEBOOK
Klammer ◆, a 16,000gns purchase, is bred to stay on the dam's side of his pedigree, being a half-sister to dual 1m6f winner Adage, out of a 1m4f winner, but he's clearly inherited plenty of speed from his sire. He has apparently been working with older horses, as his trainer has only a limited number of 2-y-os, and he was well backed. Although going right on leaving the stalls, and coming under pressure by halfway, he overcame his greenness to get on top in the final strides, having been switched towards the centre of the track over 1f out. He can do even better with the benefit of this experience, as well as when upped in trip in time and, all things considered, he's potentially very useful. Jane Chapple-Hyam wants to aim him at the Coventry. (op 7-1 tchd 8-1 in places)
Royal Exchange, a brother to Royal Box, who didn't progress after winning a maiden for this stable on his second start last year, out of a multiple 1m-1m1f winner, was solid in the market and a good run was clearly expected, with the owner in attendance. He showed good speed, but was stuck towards the outer of those on the pace, which might not have been ideal, and was picked off late on. Open to improvement, he should win before long. (op 15-8 tchd 5-2)
Shafgaan, who showed speed on heavy ground first time up before fading into fourth, was carried right on leaving the stalls, but he soon recovered and was never too far away from the near rail. He again showed good pace but simply found a couple too strong and needs his sights lowered. (op 5-1)
Memen(IRE), a 65,000gns half-brother to, among others, one-time smart sprinter Night Prospector, out of a 7f winner, was green in the paddock but showed speed in the race itself, before fading. (op 25-1)
Red Marling(IRE), a 100,000euros half-brother to, among others, 6f Listed winner Mugharreb, out of Marling, champion filly as a 2-y-o and 3-y-o, was slightly hampered when not that quick out of the stalls, and he was basically never going the required pace. (op 8-1)
Rojo Boy, a 20,000gns purchase, ran green throughout. (op 14-1)
Honourable Knight(IRE) was never competitive after starting slowly and soon being slightly hampered, but his trainer was quoted beforehand as saying he expects him "to come on considerably for the run and be difficult to beat next time."

1352 DUBAI DUTY FREE FULL OF SURPRISES H'CAP — 7f (S)

2:10 (2:10) (Class 3) (0-95,93) 3-Y-O
£7,477 (£2,239; £1,119; £560; £279; £140) **Stalls** High

Form — RPR

01- **1** **Meezaan (IRE)**[184] 6781 3-8-12 **87**....................... RichardHills 4 — 103+
(J H M Gosden) *racd towards centre crse: trckd ldrs: led ins fnl 2f: pushed clr ins fnl f: comf* **5/1**[2]

3-1 **2** 2 ½ **High Constable**[102] 31 3-8-12 **87**....................... SteveDrowne 12 — 96
(R Charlton) *t.k.h: in tch: hdwy 2f out: drvn to chse wnr jst fnl f: kpt on but no imp* **5/1**[2]

451- **3** 1 ¼ **Gramercy (IRE)**[158] 7317 3-8-10 **85**....................... JamieSpencer 2 — 91
(M L W Bell) *racd in centre: in tch: hdwy 2f out: styd on to take 3rd ins fnl f but no imp on ldng duo* **9/1**[3]

5-11 **4** ½ **Rjeef (IRE)**[18] 1045 3-9-1 **90**....................... NeilCallan 3 — 94
(C E Brittain) *racd centre crse: trckd ldr: slt ld appr fnl 2f: hdd sn after: outpcd ins fnl f* **14/1**

021- **5** hd **Oasis Dancer**[195] 6478 3-9-4 **93**....................... JimCrowley 7 — 97
(R M Beckett) *chsd ldrs: rdn over 2f out: one pce fnl f* **11/1**

1-3 **6** 2 ½ **Bowmaker**[65] 489 3-8-13 **88**....................... FrankieDettori 1 — 85
(M Johnston) *slt ld in centre crse tl narrowly hdd over 2f out: wknd fnl f* **14/1**

1 **7** 1 **Rebel Soldier (IRE)**[55] 634 3-8-13 **88**....................... JimmyFortune 8 — 82
(J Noseda) *in rr: rdn along 1/2-way and little rspnse: sme prog fr over 1f out* **3/1**[1]

01- **8** 2 **Mr Irons (USA)**[195] 6484 3-8-7 **81** ow1....................... RyanMoore 9 — 71
(Sir Michael Stoute) *in rr: pushed along 3f out: styd on fnl f but nvr any threat* **10/1**

130- **9** nse **Be Invincible (IRE)**[174] 7013 3-8-5 **80**....................... TadhgO'Shea 11 — 69
(B W Hills) *chsd ldrs 5f* **20/1**

510- **10** nk **Russian Rock (IRE)**[304] 2995 3-8-11 **86**....................... SebSanders 14 — 74
(R A Teal) *towards rr most of way* **66/1**

31-2 **11** 1 ¼ **Gallant Eagle (IRE)**[13] 1086 3-8-6 **81**....................... DavidProbert 13 — 66
(S Kirk) *chsd ldrs over 4f* **14/1**

140- **12** 2 ½ **Wisecraic**[209] 6105 3-8-11 **86**....................... RichardKingscote 5 — 64
(Tom Dascombe) *s.i.s: sn rcvrd: swtchd lft and wknd ins fnl 2f* **28/1**

10-5 **13** ½ **Planet Red (IRE)**[13] 1083 3-8-11 **86**....................... RichardHughes 6 — 62
(R Hannon) *bhd fr 1/2-way* **12/1**

1m 23.82s (-1.88) **Going Correction** -0.075s/f (Good) — **13** Ran SP% **123.2**
Speed ratings (Par 102): **107,104,102,102,101 99,97,95,95,95 93,90,90**
toteswingers:1&2:£5.20, 1&3:£8.80, 2&3:£12.70 CSF £30.67 CT £234.68 TOTE £5.70: £2.40, £1.90, £4.20; EX 35.00.
Owner Hamdan Al Maktoum **Bred** Epona Bloodstock Ltd **Trained** Newmarket, Suffolk

FOCUS
The last three runnings of this handicap have produced a host of nice winners, indeed the subsequent Britannia victor was among the beaten runners in both 2008 and 09. This season's race, in which they went a good pace, looked a really strong contest and this is potentially red-hot form. The main action took place up the middle of the track. It has been rated positively around the fourth to the best view of his previous Lingfield win.

NOTEBOOK
Meezaan(IRE) ◆, on the wrong side of the track when well behind Oasis Dancer in a Newmarket sales race on debut, before landing a Polytrack maiden (runner-up, fifth and ninth subsequently successful), impressed on his return. An entry in the 2000 Guineas gave a good indication to the regard in which he is held, and he won this in the manner of a colt who will be better than a handicapper before long. According to Richard Hills, he'll now be trained for the Jersey Stakes. (op 9-2)
High Constable ◆ was beaten at odds of 1-2 over this trip at Wolverhampton on debut, but he justified odds-on favouritism over 1m1/2f at the same track next time and that form is working out really well, with the runner-up and third having subsequently landed five races between them. This half-brother to Group 1 winner Right Approach, returning from 102 days off, was a bit keen early on, but he settled soon enough and ran well behind the potentially smart winner. He shaped as though he'll be suited by a return to further and is himself a smart type in the making. (op 7-1)
Gramercy(IRE) ◆, a non-runner at Newmarket earlier in the week (good, good to firm considered unsuitable), had been off since landing a 6f Polytrack maiden in November (second, third, fourth, sixth and eighth-placed finishers have won since). Set a bit to do, he was outpaced when coming under pressure over 2f out and took a while to close, ultimately plugging on into third without threatening the front two. He shaped as though he won't mind a more forward ride and is a very useful prospect. Official explanation: vet said colt lost a right-fore shoe
Rjeef(IRE) had been raised 9lb for his latest convincing win on Polytrack and time is likely to show he faced a very stiff task conceding weight to the front three. He travelled well on the pace for a long way and looks a horse with more to offer.
Oasis Dancer, who was on the best part of the track when winning a valuable sales race at Newmarket last October, ran well for a long way under top weight on his reappearance, but ultimately shaped as though this first run in 195 days was needed. (op 10-1)
Bowmaker, a winner first time up over 6f on Fibresand last October, before enduring a troubled trip when beaten at 4-9 over the same distance on Polytrack in February, was in trouble over 2f out. He did plug to finish a respectable sixth, though, and might do better over further. (tchd 16-1)
Rebel Soldier(IRE) won impressively over a 1m on Polytrack (runner-up and fourth have won since) first time up, but he was one of the first beaten this time, making only limited progress after coming under pressure as early as halfway. Official explanation: jockey said colt never travelled (op 7-2)
Mr Irons(USA), last seen winning a maiden at Redcar (third and fifth both successful since) in October, lacked the required speed and might need further. (op 11-1)

1353 DUBAI DUTY FREE DOUBLE MILLIONAIRE H'CAP — 5f 34y

2:40 (2:40) (Class 2) (0-110,109) 4-Y-O+
£12,462 (£3,732; £1,866; £934; £350; £350) **Stalls** High

Form — RPR

100- **1** **Blue Jack**[209] 6091 5-8-6 **97**....................... RichardKingscote 8 — 112
(Tom Dascombe) *s.i.s: hld up towards rr: stdy hdwy over 1f out: qcknd to ld jst ins fnl f: pushed out* **10/1**

55-2 **2** 2 ½ **Elnawin**[20] 1014 4-8-13 **104**....................... RichardHughes 9 — 110
(R Hannon) *trckd ldrs: shkn up over 1f out: drvn and styd on fnl f to take 2nd nr fin but no ch w wnr* **7/2**[1]

200- **3** nk **Judge 'n Jury**[174] 7015 6-8-8 **99**.......................(t) LiamJones 3 — 104
(R A Harris) *pressed ldr tl slt advantage appr fnl 2f: rdn sn after: hdd jst ins fnl f: sn outpcd by wnr: lost 2nd nr fin* **14/1**

10-5 **4** 1 ½ **Rowe Park**[27] 948 7-8-12 **103**....................... RyanMoore 4 — 103
(Mrs L C Jewell) *s.i.s: bhd: pushed along 2f out: rdn and qcknd fnl f: fin wl but nvr a threat* **9/1**

200- **5** *hd* **Sohraab**[194] 6522 6-8-7 **98** .... TravisBlock 10 97
(H Morrison) *stdd s: in tch: styd on fr over 1f out but nvr gng pce to get into contention* **5/1**[3]

5/0- **5** *dht* **Desert Phantom (USA)**[160] 7292 4-8-4 **95** .... MartinDwyer 2 94
(D M Simcock) *chsd ldrs: pushed along 2f out: wknd ins fnl f* **25/1**

120- **7** *3 1/2* **Cheveton**[174] 7015 6-8-6 **97** .... RobertWinston 6 83
(R J Price) *chsd ldrs: rdn over 2f out: wknd wl over 1f out* **10/1**

120- **8** *1/2* **Tamagin (USA)**[188] 6661 7-9-4 **109** .... StevieDonohoe 1 93
(J Pearce) *chsd ldrs over 3f* **12/1**

032- **9** *4* **Jargelle (IRE)**[228] 5507 4-8-8 **98** ow1 .... JamieSpencer 7 69
(K A Ryan) *slt advantage tl hdd appr fnl 2f: wknd appr fnl f* **8/1**

10-0 **10** *7* **Fullandby (IRE)**[20] 1007 8-8-8 **98** ow1 .... KierenFallon 5 44
(T J Etherington) *slowly away: nvr travelling and sn wl bhd* **4/1**[2]

59.80 secs (-1.60) **Going Correction** -0.075s/f (Good) **10** Ran SP% **116.4**
Speed ratings (Par 109): **109,105,104,102,101 101,96,95,89,77**
toteswingers:1&2:£8.40, 1&3:£31.50, 2&3:£13.50 CSF £44.92 CT £511.62 TOTE £11.10: £3.60, £1.10, £3.90; EX 51.70 Trifecta £282.60 Part won. Pool: £381.90 - 0.10 winning units..
Owner A Black & M Owen **Bred** Miss S N Ralphs **Trained** Malpas, Cheshire

FOCUS
A high-quality handicap - virtually Listed class - that has produced a number of smart performers in recent seasons, the best of whom was subsequent champion sprinter Kyllachy. Once again it looked a decent contest and produced an impressive winner. He has been rated as running a clear personal best, with the runner-up back to his 2-y-o form and the third close to last year's best.

NOTEBOOK
Blue Jack ◆ recorded a time under standard. A progressive type last season for William Muir, when he went up 21lb in the handicap, the blinkers he wore during that period were left off this time but it made no difference. He missed the break slightly but his rider was in no hurry and, when asked for his effort, he made up his ground quickly, looking to have the race in safe keeping soon after getting to the front. On this evidence he is Group class but he is likely to go to Chester next. (op 16-1)
Elnawin was keen on his return to action over 6f on Polytrack, so this drop to 5f in a race with guaranteed pace looked sure to suit. He travelled well on the heels of the leaders but, despite winning the race for second, had no answer to the winner's change of gear. He can win races at this trip. (op 9-2)
Judge 'n Jury is a very capable performer at this trip but likes to lead and got in a three-way duel. He came out best of that trio and should win his share of good races this year, especially when allowed to dominate. (op 12-1)
Rowe Park came into this with a run under his belt but could not go the early pace. He stayed on well in the closing stages and should find another winning opportunity before long.
Desert Phantom(USA), making his handicap debut, ran well on what was just his second start since finishing down the field at Longchamp in October 2008. He showed plenty of pace on the outside of his field and should be all the better for the outing. (tchd 28-1)
Sohraab, second in this race last year off a 3lb lower mark, was dropping in grade and appeared to get a good lead in the early stages, but failed to produce his usual finishing kick. The race he won last year at Chester could be on the agenda next, although he might have to take on the winner again. (tchd 28-1)
Fullandby(IRE) was disappointing. He had finished third in this for the last two years but missed the break and was taken off his feet in the early stages, so much so that by halfway he was completely detached. Soft ground and an extra furlong is more in his favour these days. (op 9-2 tchd 5-1 in places)

1354 DUBAI DUTY FREE GOLF WORLD CUP CONDITIONS STKS 1m 2f 6y
3:15 (3:16) (Class 3) 3-Y-O
£7,477 (£2,239; £1,119; £560; £279; £140) **Stalls** Centre

Form RPR

6125 **1** **Myplacelater**[13] 1082 3-8-3 88 .... DeclanCannon(5) 1 103
(D R C Elsworth) *plld hrd: hmpd after 1f: stdd in rr 6f out: shkn up 4f out: str run on outside fr wl over 1f out: styd on to ld fnl 20yds: won gng away* **16/1**

1- **2** *1/2* **Bullet Train**[171] 7099 3-8-13 0 .... TomQueally 5 107
(H R A Cecil) *t.k.h towards rr: stdy hdwy fr 4f out: pushed along over 2f out: rdn and styd on to ld fnl 120yds: hdd and outpcd fnl 20yds* **3/1**[2]

1 **3** *1 3/4* **Admission**[11] 1127 3-8-13 0 .... HayleyTurner 6 103
(M L W Bell) *wnt lft after 1f: chsd ldrs: pushed along and one pce over 2f out: styd in tch: kpt on wl fnl f to take 3rd nr fin but no imp on ldng duo* **7/2**[3]

51- **4** *shd* **Rasmy**[177] 6930 3-8-13 87 .... RichardHills 9 103
(M P Tregoning) *sn trcking ldr: upsides fr 4f out until drvn to ld ins fnl 2f: kpt on fnl f tl hdd fnl 120yds: wknd into 4th cl home* **9/4**[1]

016- **5** *1 1/2* **Gardening Leave**[153] 7404 3-8-13 97 .... JimmyFortune 8 100
(A M Balding) *sn led: jnd fr 4f out: rdn 3f out: narrowly hdd ins fnl 2f: wknd ins fnl f* **6/1**

204- **6** *2* **Private Story (USA)**[167] 7184 3-8-13 92 .... RichardHughes 4 96
(R Hannon) *hld up towards rr: pushed along over 2f out: nvr gng pce to get into contention* **11/1**

51- **7** *nk* **Tipperary Boutique (IRE)**[167] 7167 3-8-8 80 .... MichaelHills 2 90?
(B W Hills) *s.i.s: plld hrd and hmpd after 1f: hld up in rr: shkn up and sme hdwy 2f out: nvr gng pce to get into contention* **16/1**

0-23 **8** *4* **Navajo Chief**[13] 1083 3-8-13 93 .... JimCrowley 7 87
(A P Jarvis) *plld hrd: chsd ldrs over 7f* **22/1**

2m 9.85s (1.05) **Going Correction** +0.05s/f (Good) **8** Ran SP% **116.7**
Speed ratings (Par 102): **97,96,95,95,93 92,92,88**
toteswingers:1&2:£9.60, 1&3:£11.80, 2&3:£4.20 CSF £65.17 TOTE £25.10: £4.10, £1.30, £2.10; EX 101.60.
Owner A J Thompson **Bred** Mrs N A Ward **Trained** Newmarket, Suffolk

FOCUS
This conditions race has been contested by some smart types in years gone by, namely the likes of High Heeled (1st 2009), Father Time (3rd 09), Palavicini (4th 09), Patkai (3rd 08), Light Shift (1st 07), The Geezer (1st 05), and Let The Lion Roar (1st 04). The pace seemed just moderate and the time was 6.85 seconds outside standard, but it was still over two seconds faster than both divisions of the later fillies' maidens (won by Pink Symphony and Gertrude Bell). The form looks decent enough.

NOTEBOOK
Myplacelater was unsuited by the drop back to 1m at Kempton last time, but even so, this victory still paid a nice compliment to 1000 Guineas-bound Pipette. Making her turf debut, and back over a more suitable distance, she was keen early on when tucked away towards the inside, but she picked up really well after being switched out around a furlong from the finish. Her connections are entitled to look for some black type races now.
Bullet Train ◆, winner of a 1m maiden at Yarmouth on his only previous start last October, was representing a trainer who has run some smart types in this over the years, and he looked set to win when mastering Rasmy, but he was then himself picked off in the final strides. He had raced wide without cover for a lot of the way, which wasn't ideal, and can do a lot better. Entries in the Dante and Derby confirm the regard in which he is held. (op 11-4 tchd 5-2)
Admission ◆, who impressed when winning first time out over 1m on soft ground at Yarmouth, travelled powerfully but simply lacked the speed of some of these in a steadily run race on quicker going than he encountered on debut. He kept on reasonably well, however, suggesting as though he can do better when there is more emphasis on stamina, be it a stronger-run race, easier ground, or more distance. He certainly has the physical scope to go on improving. (tchd 10-3)
Rasmy ◆, a Guineas and Derby entrant who had been off the track since landing a 1m maiden at Bath by 5l last October, looked the winner when travelling well for much of the straight, but he didn't find as much as had seemed likely, with his stride noticeably shortening inside the final furlong. Perhaps he'll appreciate a return to shorter, but the way he moved for a lot of the contest still suggests he has the ability to do better. (op 3-1)
Gardening Leave, well beaten in a French Group 1 over this trip on testing ground when last seen in November, could have been expected to fare better considering he was allowed a soft time up front. (op 7-1)
Tipperary Boutique(IRE) pulled too hard.

1355 BRIDGET MAIDEN FILLIES' STKS 7f (S)
3:50 (3:55) (Class 4) 3-Y-O
£5,180 (£1,541; £770; £384) **Stalls** High

Form RPR

1 **Funky Lady (USA)** 3-9-0 0 .... RichardHughes 12 81+
(R Hannon) *trckd ldrs: rdn over 1f out: str run fnl f to ld fnl 75yds: comf* **7/4**[1]

2 *1* **Qudwah (IRE)** 3-9-0 0 .... RichardHills 9 78
(M A Jarvis) *sn led: rdn and qcknd over 1f out: hdd and outpcd fnl 75yds* **10/1**

3 *1 3/4* **Titivation** 3-9-0 0 .... JamieSpencer 7 75+
(M L W Bell) *pressed ldr over 2f: styd in cl 2nd: rdn and edgd lft 1f out: styd on same pce ins fnl f: no ch w ldng duo whn sltly hmpd nr fin* **13/2**[3]

4 *2* **Belgique (IRE)** 3-9-0 0 .... RyanMoore 3 68+
(R Hannon) *towards rr: hdwy: hung lft and green 2f out: kpt on fnl f but no ch w ldrs* **20/1**

5 *3 3/4* **Sonnellino** 3-9-0 0 .... WilliamBuick 4 58+
(J H M Gosden) *s.i.s: green and pushed along in rr: hdwy over 1f out: styd on ins fnl f: gng on cl home* **10/1**

6 *shd* **Sooraah** 3-9-0 0 .... MichaelHills 16 58
(W J Haggas) *chsd ldrs: rdn over 2f out: wknd fnl f* **18/1**

7 *nk* **Fashion Flow** 3-9-0 0 .... TomQueally 10 57
(H R A Cecil) *chsd ldrs: hung lft: green and lost position over 2f out: kpt on again ins fnl f* **9/2**[2]

8 *1 3/4* **Saigon Kitty (IRE)** 3-9-0 0 .... RobertWinston 2 52
(J R Best) *chsd ldrs: rdn: green and hung bdly lft over 2f out: sn btn* **66/1**

9 *1/2* **Balatoma (IRE)** 3-9-0 0 .... PatDobbs 8 51
(M P Tregoning) *s.i.s: sn chsng ldrs: outpcd 1/2-way: n.d after* **16/1**

10 *3 1/2* **Ayam Zainah** 3-9-0 0 .... ChrisCatlin 5 41
(M R Channon) *sn chsng ldrs: rdn over 2f out: sn btn* **16/1**

11 *3/4* **Nahab** 3-9-0 0 .... TedDurcan 14 39
(D R Lanigan) *s.i.s: a towards rr* **33/1**

12 *1* **Alnaseem (USA)** 3-9-0 0 .... TadhgO'Shea 1 37
(J L Dunlop) *s.i.s: in rr: sme hdwy 1/2-way: rn green: hung lft and wknd over 2f out* **28/1**

13 *1 1/2* **Floating Angel (USA)** 3-9-0 0 .... SteveDrowne 13 33
(J R Best) *a towards rr* **50/1**

14 *1 1/2* **Western Eyes (IRE)** 3-9-0 0 .... MartinDwyer 11 29
(B J Meehan) *a towards rr* **28/1**

1m 25.77s (0.07) **Going Correction** -0.075s/f (Good) **14** Ran SP% **121.1**
Speed ratings (Par 97): **96,94,92,90,86 86,85,83,83,79 78,77,75,73**
toteswingers:1&2:£6.70, 1&3:£20.80, 2&3:£34.30 CSF £18.88 TOTE £2.60: £1.40, £3.20, £1.90; EX 24.80.
Owner Patrick J Fahey **Bred** Haras D'Etreham And Vision Bloodstock **Trained** East Everleigh, Wilts

FOCUS
In recent seasons this fillies' maiden has gone to subsequent Group-race winners Promising Lead, Silver Touch and Illustrious Miss, but the quality can vary, with the average winner given an RPR of 83. It paid to race prominently in this year's contest.

1356 ROBERT SANGSTER MEMORIAL MAIDEN FILLIES' STKS (DIV I) 1m 2f 6y
4:25 (4:26) (Class 4) 3-Y-O
£4,857 (£1,445; £722; £360) **Stalls** Centre

Form RPR

524- **1** **Pink Symphony**[195] 6477 3-9-0 87 .... JamieSpencer 8 84+
(P F I Cole) *sn trcking ldr: led ins fnl 3f: drvn clr and hung sharply lft to rail 2f out: continue to hang but a in command and drvn out* **5/2**[1]

5- **2** *2* **Mujdeya**[178] 6921 3-9-0 0 .... RichardHills 12 80+
(J H M Gosden) *in rr tl hdwy on outside 3f out: shkn up and hung bdly lft 2f out: continued to hang bdly but r.o to chse wnr fnl f but a wl hld* **7/2**[2]

00- **3** *3 1/2* **Swish Dish (CAN)**[167] 7183 3-9-0 0 .... RichardHughes 9 73
(R Hannon) *chsd ldrs: drvn to dispute 2nd fr over 1f out but no ch w wnr: wknd into 3rd ins fnl f* **33/1**

4 *hd* **Bakongo (IRE)** 3-9-0 0 .... HayleyTurner 4 73+
(M L W Bell) *s.i.s: in rr: pushed along and hdwy on outside fr 2f out: styd on wl thrght fnl f but nvr a threat* **20/1**

5 *3/4* **Blast Furnace (IRE)** 3-9-0 0 .... JimmyFortune 10 71
(P W Chapple-Hyam) *sn led: hdd ins fnl 3f: styd disputing wl hld 2nd tl wknd ins fnl f* **13/2**[3]

4- **6** *1* **Mausin (IRE)**[198] 6389 3-9-0 0 .... TravisBlock 3 69
(H Morrison) *chsd ldrs: rdn over 2f out: wknd wl over 1f out* **33/1**

0- **7** *1 1/4* **Saggiatore**[210] 6062 3-9-0 0 .... RyanMoore 1 67
(E A L Dunlop) *sn in tch: chsd ldrs fr 3f out: sn rdn and no imp: wknd 2f out* **11/1**

8 *3* **Tymora (USA)** 3-9-0 0 .... TomQueally 7 61
(H R A Cecil) *t.k.h: wl in tch tl pushed along 3f out: wknd 2f out* **7/1**

0- **9** *2 1/4* **High Ransom**[174] 7034 3-9-0 0 .... (p) NeilCallan 5 56
(M A Jarvis) *t.k.h: sme prog in bhd ldrs 3f out: sn drvn: wknd appr fnl 2f* **7/1**

10 *4 1/2* **Gakalina (IRE)** 3-9-0 0 .... DarryllHolland 2 47
(J Noseda) *s.i.s: towards rr most of way* **16/1**

11 *4* **Five Bells (IRE)** 3-9-0 0 .... ChrisCatlin 6 39
(M R Channon) *s.i.s: a in rr* **40/1**

2m 12.09s (3.29) **Going Correction** +0.05s/f (Good) **11** Ran SP% **116.4**
Speed ratings (Par 97): **88,86,83,83,82 82,81,78,76,73 70**
toteswingers:1&2:£2.20, 1&3:£15.20, 2&3:£22.00 CSF £10.35 TOTE £3.00: £1.10, £2.00, £8.30; EX 8.30.
Owner Mrs Fitri Hay **Bred** Ronchalon Racing Uk Ltd **Trained** Whatcombe, Oxon

FOCUS
Some high-class fillies' have won a division of this maiden in recent years, namely Clowance in 2008, Folk Opera 2007, Eswarah 2005 and Islington 2002. They went steady and the time was 0.18 seconds slower than the second division, won by Gertrude Bell, and 2.24 seconds slower than Myplacelater managed in the earlier conditions race. It has been rated around the front pair for now, but the third, sixth and seventh showed big improvement on their 2-y-o form and there's a chance one or two may be flattered by the bare result.

1357 BATHWICK TYRES H'CAP 2m
4:55 (4:55) (Class 4) (0-85,80) 4-Y-O+ £4,533 (£1,348; £674; £336) Stalls High

Form				RPR
1324	1		**Satwa Gold (USA)**[51] 688 4-9-5 76 TomQueally 7 (Stef Higgins) *hld up in rr: hdwy on bit fr 3f out: drvn to ld jst ins fnl 2f: drvn out ins fnl f* **25/1**	87
200-	2	1 1/4	**Devil To Pay**[44] 6995 4-9-3 74 RichardHughes 5 (A King) *hld up in tch: hdwy on bit to trck ldrs fr 3f out: drvn to chal 2f out: styd on u.p but nt pce of wnr thrght fnl f* **13/2**[2]	84
06-3	3	4 1/2	**Hindu Kush (IRE)**[10] 1139 5-9-11 78 JamieSpencer 10 (Ian Williams) *stdd s and hld up in rr: hdwy on outside over 3f out: rdn to chse ldrs whn hung lft fr 2f out: nt keen: btn fnl f* **2/1**[1]	82
40-0	4	2 1/4	**Sweetheart**[64] 500 6-9-8 75 NeilCallan 6 (Jamie Poulton) *chsd ldrs: drvn along 6f out: led 3f out: kpt on u.p tl hdd jst ins fnl 2f: wknd over 1f out* **17/2**[3]	76
2-42	5	2	**French Hollow**[58] 585 5-9-0 67 JimmyFortune 13 (T J Fitzgerald) *in rr: hdwy over 3f out: sn rdn to chse ldrs but nvr quite on terms: wknd wl over 1f out* **16/1**	66
60-0	6	3 3/4	**Ned Ludd (IRE)**[42] 554 7-8-11 64 JimCrowley 9 (J G Portman) *in tch: rdn and effrt on outside 3f out: nvr on terms and no ch fnl 2f* **14/1**	59
2-31	7	1 3/4	**Soundbyte**[13] 1087 5-9-5 72 FergusSweeney 2 (J Gallagher) *chsd ldrs: rdn over 3f out: wknd over 2f out* **9/1**	64
1264	8	4 1/2	**Doubnov (FR)**[21] 994 7-9-4 71 (p) WilliamBuick 8 (Ian Williams) *led tl hdd 3f out: sn btn* **22/1**	58
4511	9	9	**Gremlin**[18] 1053 6-9-1 73 KierenFox(5) 12 (D Burchell) *chsd ldrs: rdn over 3f out: wknd qckly over 2f out* **12/1**	49
-300	10	nk	**Aureate**[23] 974 6-8-7 65 SophieDoyle(5) 1 (B Forsey) *bhd most of way* **33/1**	41
315-	11	6	**Sally Forth**[198] 6388 4-9-9 80 SteveDrowne 4 (R Charlton) *chsd ldrs tl wknd qckly over 3f out* **10/1**	49
226-	12	38	**Duke Of Burgundy (FR)**[69] 6595 7-9-5 72 RyanMoore 3 (Jennie Candlish) *bhd: mod prog into mid-div 4f out: sn rdn and wknd: eased whn no ch: t.o* **9/1**	—

3m 30.68s (-1.32) **Going Correction** +0.05s/f (Good)
WFA 4 from 5yo+ 4lb 12 Ran SP% **117.7**
Speed ratings (Par 105): **105,104,102,101,100 98,97,95,90,90 87,—**
toteswingers:1&2:£23.50, 1&3:£12.20, 2&3:£4.10 CSF £175.82 CT £482.47 TOTE £30.50: £5.00, £2.00, £1.10; EX 244.20.

Owner Mrs Anne & Fred Cowley **Bred** B P Walden, L Taylor Et Al **Trained** Lambourn, Berks
■ The first winner for trainer Stef Higgins since she changed her name from Stef Liddiard.

FOCUS
There was a pace strong throughout, courtesy of Doubnov, but that one's stablemate Hindu Kush, who was held up last, couldn't take advantage, ruining his chance by hanging left when produced out wide in the straight. The third has been rated close to his Ffos Las form, and the fourth much in line with his form at this trip.

Duke Of Burgundy(FR) Official explanation: jockey said gelding had a breathing problem

1358 ROBERT SANGSTER MEMORIAL MAIDEN FILLIES' STKS (DIV II) 1m 2f 6y
5:30 (5:30) (Class 4) 3-Y-O £4,857 (£1,445; £722; £360) Stalls Centre

Form				RPR
332-	1		**Gertrude Bell**[175] 6992 3-9-0 81 WilliamBuick 7 (J H M Gosden) *trckd ldrs: drvn to ld over 1f out: styd on strly fnl f* **9/4**[2]	87+
30-	2	2 1/4	**Shimmering Moment (USA)**[186] 6729 3-9-0 0 TomQueally 9 (H R A Cecil) *chsd ldrs: led appr fnl 2f: sn rdn: hdd over 1f out: styd on but no ch w wnr* **12/1**[3]	82
4-	3	nse	**Nouriya**[189] 6628 3-9-0 0 RyanMoore 1 (Sir Michael Stoute) *s.i.s: sn in tch: hdwy 3f out: chsd ldrs fr 2f out: sn rdn: styd on same pce ins fnl f* **10/11**[1]	82
325-	4	7	**Leaving Alone (USA)**[121] 7772 3-9-0 72 RichardHughes 5 (R Hannon) *wnt lft s and sn led: hdd appr fnl 2f: wknd fnl f* **16/1**	68
5-0	5	nse	**Sheila Toss (IRE)**[28] 930 3-9-0 0 JimmyFortune 11 (R Hannon) *chsd ldrs tl wknd ins fnl 2f* **25/1**	68
0-	6	1 1/2	**Peaceful Soul (USA)**[167] 7182 3-9-0 0 TedDurcan 10 (D R Lanigan) *in tch: pushed along fr 3f out: trckd ldrs 2f out: nvr on terms and wknd appr fnl f* **20/1**	65
0	7	2	**Zakeeta (IRE)**[11] 1132 3-9-0 0 (v[1]) SebSanders 2 (J Noseda) *wnt lft at s: t.k.h in rr: hrd rdn ins fnl 3f: hung lft 2f out and nvr any ch* **66/1**	61
	8	nse	**Distant Waters** 3-9-0 0 RobertWinston 3 (A P Jarvis) *hmpd s bhd most of way* **40/1**	61
	9	6	**Lalika** 3-9-0 0 SteveDrowne 4 (C G Cox) *hmpd s: hung violenty rt fr 7f out and no ch after* **40/1**	49
0-3	10	3 1/2	**Double Fortune**[22] 979 3-9-0 0 LiamJones 8 (Jamie Poulton) *chsd ldrs: rdn 3f out: sn wknd* **28/1**	42

2m 11.91s (3.11) **Going Correction** +0.05s/f (Good) 10 Ran SP% **115.2**
Speed ratings (Par 97): **89,87,87,81,81 80,78,78,73,71**
toteswingers:1&2:£5.30, 1&3:£1.10, 2&3:£4.10 CSF £24.85 TOTE £3.30: £1.40, £3.10, £1.10; EX 28.70 Place 6 £36.68, Place 5 £29.44.

Owner Ms Rachel D S Hood **Bred** Ms Rachel Hood **Trained** Newmarket, Suffolk

FOCUS
The likes of Clowance, Folk Opera, Eswarah and Islington have won a division of this in recent seasons. They went a steady pace and the final time, although 0.18 seconds quicker than Pink Symphony managed in the first division, was 2.06 seconds slower than Myplacelater recorded in an earlier conditions race. It has been rated to a similar standard to the first division, with the fourth close to his AW mark.

Lalika Official explanation: jockey said filly hung right throughout

T/Jkpt: Not won. T/Plt: £31.30 to a £1 stake. Pool: £75,647.27. 1,762.97 winning tickets. T/Qpdt: £8.90 to a £1 stake. Pool: £5,065.40. 416.50 winning tickets. ST

THIRSK (L-H)
Friday, April 16
OFFICIAL GOING: Good (good to firm in places; 9.0)
Wind: light 1/2 against Weather: fine and sunny

1359 E B F HABTON NOVICE STKS 5f
2:00 (2:03) (Class 4) 2-Y-O £5,569 (£1,657; £828; £413) Stalls High

Form				RPR
1	1		**Bathwick Bear (IRE)**[10] 1136 2-9-0 0 RichardEvans(5) 6 (P D Evans) *cl up: led 1/2-way: pushed along and hdd over 1f out: rdn and qcknd to ld ins fnl f and edgd lft: kpt on wl towards fin* **2/1**[2]	88+
1	2	nk	**Arctic Feeling (IRE)**[16] 1066 2-9-5 0 PaulHanagan 3 (R A Fahey) *cl up: rdn to ld wl over 1f out: hdd ins fnl f: kpt on* **15/8**[1]	87+
	3	4 1/2	**Coconut Ice** 2-8-4 0 RossAtkinson(5) 1 (Tom Dascombe) *cl up on outer: rdn and ev ch whn hung lft wl over 1f out: hung rt ins fnl f: kpt on* **20/1**	59
	4	1	**Lady Platinum Club** 2-8-9 0 PJMcDonald 10 (G R Oldroyd) *towards rr: switrchd lft and hdwy 2f out: sn rdn and kpt on ins fnl f: nrst fin* **50/1**	55+
	5	1/2	**Boundless Spirit** 2-9-0 0 TomEaves 13 (B Smart) *t.k.h: chsd ldrs: rdn along and hung lft wl over 1f out: sn one pce* **12/1**	58+
	6	3/4	**Another Wise Kid (IRE)** 2-9-0 0 TonyCulhane 11 (P T Midgley) *towards rr: hdwy 2f out: rdn and kpt on ins fnl f: nrst fin* **50/1**	55+
	7	1	**Misty Morn** 2-8-9 0 GrahamGibbons 5 (A D Brown) *chsd ldrs: rdn along and hung lft 2f out: grad wknd* **100/1**	46+
	8	1/2	**Reachtothestars (USA)** 2-9-0 0 PhillipMakin 2 (M Dods) *s.i.s and swtchd rt s: in rr tl hdwy wl over 1f out: swtchd lft ent fnl f and kpt on: nrst fin* **20/1**	53+
	9	5	**Lord Avon** 2-8-11 0 JackDean(3) 9 (W G M Turner) *led: rdn along and hdd 1/2-way: grad wknd* **28/1**	29
	10	2 1/4	**Choose Wisely (IRE)** 2-9-0 0 JohnEgan 12 (K A Ryan) *dwlt and in rr: sme hdwy 2f out: sn edgd lft and wknd* **12/1**	20
	11	1	**Good Faith** 2-8-9 0 PatrickDonaghy(5) 4 (G M Moore) *s.i.s: a in rr* **66/1**	16
1	12	8	**Novabridge**[15] 1073 2-9-5 0 AlanMunro 8 (A B Haynes) *a towards rr* **7/1**[3]	—
	13	3	**Rainbows Son** 2-9-0 0 TonyHamilton 7 (P T Midgley) *s.i.s and wnt lft s: a bhd* **100/1**	—

59.68 secs (0.08) **Going Correction** -0.05s/f (Good) 13 Ran SP% **116.4**
Speed ratings (Par 94): **97,96,89,87,86 85,84,83,75,71 70,57,52**
toteswingers:1&2:£1.50, 1&3:£15.40, 2&3:£7.50 CSF £5.40 TOTE £3.00: £1.30, £1.10, £3.80; EX 7.20.

Owner Bathwick Gold Partnership **Bred** D Veitch & R O'Callaghan **Trained** Pandy, Monmouths

FOCUS
Seven of the past ten winners of this race already had a victory against their name and only two were previously unraced. All three with racecourse experience had won their only previous start, and two of them dominated both the market and the finish. The first two have been rated as useful types.

NOTEBOOK
Bathwick Bear(IRE), winner of a Ffos Las maiden on debut that is working out alright, was one of four disputing the lead from the off and, when it came down to a duel with his main market rival, he kept on finding just enough. He is only small, but does have an engine and now heads for the Lily Agnes at Chester next month. (op 9-4 tchd 5-2)
Arctic Feeling(IRE) justified market confidence on his Fibresand debut and would have found these conditions very different, but having been up there from the start he battled on gamely right to the line and pulled right away from the others. There are more races to be won with him, especially on a slower surface. (tchd 7-4, 2-1 and 85-40 in a place)
Coconut Ice ◆, a £20,000 filly and related to winners at around 1m in France, was another to race handily and did best of the newcomers. She had the worst of the draw, raced very keenly on the wide outside and looked distinctly green under pressure, so it shouldn't be long before she hits the target. (op 16-1)
Lady Platinum Club ◆, out of a half-sister to the smart sprinter Lord Kintyre, did best of those held up and was noted doing some good late work. She is worth keeping an eye on. (op 40-1)
Boundless Spirit ◆, a £30,000 half-brother to three winners including the Listed winner Manston, raced handily from the rails draw but he pulled very hard early and was inclined to hang through greenness in the latter stages. Better can be expected. (op 10-1 tchd 14-1)
Another Wise Kid(IRE) ◆, a 4,500gns half-brother to a couple of winners at up to 7f, stayed on late without being knocked about and is another to note. (op 66-1)
Misty Morn Official explanation: jockey said filly hung left
Novabridge won a heavy-ground Folkestone maiden on his debut, but he never went a yard in these very different conditions. Official explanation: jockey said colt lost its action (op 8-1)

1360 3 YEARS IN A ROW CLAIMING STKS 5f
2:30 (2:33) (Class 4) 2-Y-O £4,274 (£1,271; £635; £317) Stalls High

Form				RPR
25	1		**Lady Brookie**[10] 1136 2-8-3 0 (p) JackDean(3) 8 (W G M Turner) *mde all: edgd lft 1f out: styd on wl* **8/13**[1]	61+
	2	1 1/2	**Belle Royale (IRE)** 2-8-6 0 LukeMorris 4 (W M Brisbourne) *chsd ldrs: swtchd lft over 1f out: styd on to take 2nd towards fin* **25/1**	55
6	3	3/4	**Imperial Waltzer**[15] 1073 2-8-9 0 SamHitchcott 2 (M R Channon) *w ldrs: hung lft over 1f out: kpt on same pce* **8/1**[3]	55
	4	1/2	**Welsh Dresser (IRE)** 2-8-4 0 CathyGannon 9 (P D Evans) *dwlt: sn chsng ldrs: kpt on wl ins fnl f* **15/2**[2]	48
	5	2 1/4	**Look'N'Listen (IRE)** 2-8-12 0 GrahamGibbons 7 (A D Brown) *s.i.s: hdwy over 1f out: nvr nr ldrs* **12/1**	47
	6	2 1/2	**Copex** 2-8-8 0 JohnEgan 3 (K A Ryan) *unruly s: swvd lft s: sn chsng ldrs: hung lft 2f out: carried lft and wknd ins fnl f* **9/1**	35
	7	nk	**Rath Maeve** 2-7-9 0 NoraLooby(7) 10 (A J McCabe) *s.i.s: last whn hung bdly lft over 2f out: nvr a factor* **22/1**	27
0	8	nk	**Soviet Bolt (IRE)**[16] 1066 2-8-7 0 PJMcDonald 5 (P T Midgley) *dwlt: sn chsng ldrs: hung bdly lft and hmpd over 1f out: sn wknd* **33/1**	31

60.54 secs (0.94) **Going Correction** -0.05s/f (Good) 8 Ran SP% **113.6**
Speed ratings (Par 94): **90,87,86,85,82 78,77,77**
toteswingers:1&2:£9.00, 1&3:£1.70, 2&3:£12.00 CSF £22.96 TOTE £1.50: £1.10, £4.40, £1.50; EX 24.20.Lady Brookie was claimed by P. Grayson for £7,000. Imperial Waltzer was claimed by G. M. Moore for £6,000

Owner Mrs M S Teversham **Bred** Mrs Monica Teversham **Trained** Sigwells, Somerset

FOCUS

A modest claimer and the three with racecourse experience had each finished behind the three previous winners in the 2.00 race in their most recent outings. A few of these proved a real handful before the start and several hung all over the place during the race itself. The winning time was 0.86 seconds slower than the opener.

NOTEBOOK

Lady Brookie, runner-up in the Brocklesby on her debut but a disappointing odds-on favourite when well beaten by the winner of the previous race Bathwick Bear at Ffos Las last time, was tried in cheekpieces on this drop in class. She proved much more professional than her rivals, showing good speed against the stands' rail and running straight whilst her nearest challengers took more wayward courses. This gave the yard their fourth victory in the race in the last eight runnings, but the form looks moderate and she will need to improve plenty in order to follow up. She was claimed by Peter Grayson. (op 10-11 tchd Evens and 11-10 in a place)

Belle Royale(IRE), a half-sister to a couple of modest winners at up to 1m, stayed on well and may have given the winner a bit more to think about had she not hung violently away to her left from over a furlong out. The form is hard to gauge, but she cost only £800 so has more than paid her way already. (op 22-1 tchd 20-1)

Imperial Waltzer, who got stuck in the mud when a long way behind the disappointment of the opening race Novabridge on his Folkestone debut, had every chance but he too hung away to his left under pressure inside the last furlong. He was claimed by George Moore. (op 17-2 tchd 7-1)

Welsh Dresser(IRE), a 3,000euros filly, stayed on fairly well in the latter stages and, unlike many of her rivals, ran straight. She is stoutly bred on the dam's side so may need more time and a longer trip. (op 8-1 tchd 17-2)

Look'N'Listen(IRE) cost just 2,000euros as a foal and had little to recommend her on pedigree. She made a little late headway after fluffing the start, but probably achieved little. (tchd 14-1)

Copex, a £12,000 half-sister to three winners including the high-class sprinter Bygone Days, proved very troublesome before the start and dumped her rider on the turf. She showed good early speed once under way, but then hung all over the place entering the last 2f and has plenty of growing up to do. (op 8-1 tchd 7-1)

1361 YORKSHIRE 4X4.CO.UK H'CAP — 7f

3:05 (3:06) (Class 5) (0-75,80) 4-Y-O+ — **£4,274** (£1,271; £635; £317) — **Stalls** Low

Form — RPR

311 **1** **Academy Blues (USA)**[9] 1152 5-9-9 **80** 12ex — AdrianNicholls 3 — 95
(D Nicholls) *t.k.h early: trckd ldrs gng wl: swtchd rt and smooth hdwy 2f out: rdn to ld ins fnl f: kpt on* — **9/2[2]**

56-0 **2** ½ **Captain Dancer (IRE)**[19] 1030 4-9-1 **72** — JoeFanning 9 — 86
(B W Hills) *cl up: led over 2f out and sn rdn: drvn and hdd ins fnl f: kpt on* — **7/1[3]**

60-6 **3** 3¼ **Regeneration (IRE)**[19] 1030 4-9-4 **75** — PaulHanagan 7 — 80
(M L W Bell) *t.k.h: chsd ldng pair: effrt over 2f out: rdn wl over 1f out: sn one pce* — **3/1[1]**

400- **4** 4 **Arabian Pearl (IRE)**[184] 6776 4-9-2 **73** — AlanMunro 12 — 67
(P W Chapple-Hyam) *chsd ldrs: hdwy on outer 3f out: rdn along 2f out: drvn and one pce fr over 1f out* — **10/1**

000- **5** 1 **Glenridding**[160] 7287 6-9-3 **74** — (p) LeeVickers 13 — 66
(J G Given) *midfield: hdwy to chse ldrs wl over 2f out: rdn wl over 1f out and sn one pce* — **25/1**

433- **6** nk **Silver Guest**[133] 7627 5-9-4 **75** — SamHitchcott 5 — 66
(M R Channon) *dwlt and in rr: hdwy wl over 2f out: rdn wl over 1f out: kpt on ins fnl f* — **14/1**

050- **7** 1½ **Burns Night**[179] 6907 4-9-2 **73** — SilvestreDeSousa 8 — 60+
(G A Harker) *in rr: hdwy wl over 2f out: swtchd lft and rdn wl over 1f out: nvr nr ldrs* — **7/1[3]**

520- **8** 1 **Rio Cobolo (IRE)**[143] 7506 4-9-1 **72** — (v) PhillipMakin 1 — 56
(Paul Green) *in tch on inner: rdn along over 2f out: grad wknd* — **18/1**

00-2 **9** 1 **Toledo Gold (IRE)**[12] 1102 4-9-4 **75** — DavidAllan 2 — 56
(E J Alston) *dwlt: rapid hdwy on inner and sn led: rdn and hdd over 2f out: sn drvn and wknd* — **9/1**

00-0 **10** 1 **Violent Velocity (IRE)**[19] 1030 7-8-13 **75** — IanBrennan(5) 11 — 54
(J J Quinn) *chsd ldrs: rdn along wl over 2f out: grad wknd* — **20/1**

030- **11** 1¾ **Cara's Request (AUS)**[167] 7172 5-9-3 **74** — AndrewMullen 10 — 48
(D Nicholls) *a towards rr* — **33/1**

546- **12** shd **Catalan Bay (AUS)**[211] 6020 6-9-2 **73** — LukeMorris 6 — 47
(J R Gask) *a towards rr* — **14/1**

00-0 **13** 10 **Knavesmire (IRE)**[19] 1030 4-9-4 **75** — (b[1]) JimmyQuinn 4 — 22
(M Brittain) *s.i.s: a bhd* — **25/1**

1m 25.92s (-1.28) **Going Correction** -0.05s/f (Good) — **13** Ran SP% **121.3**

Speed ratings (Par 103): **105,104,100,96,95 94,92,91,90,89 87,87,75**

toteswingers:1&2:£10.40, 1&3:£2.80, 2&3:£5.10 CSF £34.86 CT £115.75 TOTE £4.40: £1.10, £2.60, £1.70; EX 39.10.

Owner Bulldog Racing **Bred** Kinghaven Farms Ltd **Trained** Sessay, N Yorks

FOCUS

A modest if competitive handicap and the pace was a decent one. The third is the guide to the level.

Burns Night ◆ Official explanation: jockey said gelding hung right in straight

Cara's Request(AUS) Official explanation: jockey said gelding hung left going into bend and hung right in straight

Knavesmire(IRE) Official explanation: jockey said filly would not face the blinkers

1362 HAMBLETON INN H'CAP — 1m

3:40 (3:43) (Class 5) (0-75,75) 3-Y-O — **£4,274** (£1,271; £635; £317) — **Stalls** Low

Form — RPR

632- **1** **Dolphin Rock**[179] 6901 3-8-10 **67** — PhillipMakin 4 — 79
(T D Barron) *sn w ldr: chal over 2f out: r.o u.p to ld last strides* — **5/2[1]**

616- **2** hd **Jutland**[237] 5265 3-9-3 **74** — JoeFanning 2 — 86
(M Johnston) *dwlt: drvn to sn ld: jnd over 2f out: kpt on wl: hdd nr fin* **4/1[2]**

330- **3** 6 **Diamond Duchess (IRE)**[198] 6391 3-9-3 **74** — AlanMunro 7 — 72
(D R Lanigan) *swtchd lft after s: sn in tch: outpcd over 2f out: kpt on to take modest 3rd wl ins fnl f* — **12/1**

26-0 **4** 1½ **Battle Study (IRE)**[19] 1029 3-8-9 **66** — JamesDoyle 6 — 60
(A J McCabe) *in tch: effrt over 2f out: kpt on same pce* — **20/1**

040- **5** 1¼ **Faithful Duchess (IRE)**[210] 6069 3-8-10 **67** — PaulHanagan 5 — 58
(E A L Dunlop) *trckd ldrs: one pce fnl 2f* — **14/1**

135 **6** 1 **Slikback Jack (IRE)**[16] 1061 3-9-3 **74** — FrederikTylicki 8 — 63
(J A Glover) *mid-div: drvn and outpcd over 4f out: kpt on fnl f* — **5/1[3]**

060- **7** nk **Meetings Man (IRE)**[188] 6679 3-8-5 **62** — PJMcDonald 15 — 50+
(Micky Hammond) *t.k.h in rr: kpt on fnl 2f: nvr nr ldrs* — **100/1**

40-6 **8** 1¼ **Al Dafa (USA)**[42] 815 3-8-3 **67** — IanBurns(7) 3 — 53
(M L W Bell) *towards rr: hdwy and swtchd rt over 2f out: edgd rt: styd on fnl f* — **16/1**

300- **9** 3¾ **Cassidy K**[164] 7218 3-7-13 **61** oh6 — PaulPickard(5) 13 — 38
(D W Thompson) *reminders after s: sn bhd: sme hdwy 2f out: nvr on terms* — **66/1**

402- **10** 1 **Antarctic Desert (IRE)**[204] 6231 3-9-1 **72** — TomEaves 1 — 47
(K A Ryan) *chsd ldrs: lost pl over 1f out* — **10/1**

50-0 **11** 2½ **Tislaam (IRE)**[19] 1029 3-9-4 **75** — TonyHamilton 9 — 44
(J S Wainwright) *led early: trckd ldrs: wknd over 2f out* — **40/1**

0-50 **12** 10 **Bell's Ocean (USA)**[42] 809 3-8-4 **61** — (t) JimmyQuinn 12 — —
(J Ryan) *in rr: bhd and eased fnl f* — **25/1**

000- **13** 16 **Drinking Buddy**[172] 7055 3-8-4 **61** oh9 — DuranFentiman 14 — —
(D W Thompson) *mid-div on outside: lost pl and hmpd over 2f out: sn bhd: virtually p.u* — **100/1**

1m 39.95s (-0.15) **Going Correction** -0.05s/f (Good) — **13** Ran SP% **109.1**

Speed ratings (Par 98): **98,97,91,90,89 88,87,86,82,81 79,69,53**

toteswingers:1&2:£2.00, 1&3:£6.10, 2&3:£8.40 CSF £9.23 CT £72.36 TOTE £3.00: £1.50, £1.30, £3.20; EX 11.00.

Owner Mia Racing **Bred** Mia Racing **Trained** Maunby, N Yorks

FOCUS

An ordinary handicap, but the front pair held those positions throughout and nothing else ever got into it. It has been rated around the third to her turf mark.

1363 NORTHALLERTON SHOOTING & COUNTRY WEAR H'CAP (DIV I) — 5f

4:15 (4:16) (Class 4) (0-80,80) 4-Y-O+ — **£5,245** (£1,560; £780; £389) — **Stalls** High

Form — RPR

214- **1** **Hawkeyethenoo (IRE)**[170] 7119 4-8-7 **72** — GaryBartley(3) 6 — 87+
(J S Goldie) *dwlt and towards rr: swtchd lft to wd outside and hdwy 2f out: rdn over 1f out: str run to ld ins fnl f: kpt on wl* — **3/1[1]**

-646 **2** 2 **Green Park (IRE)**[85] 250 7-8-13 **75** — (b) DavidNolan 1 — 83
(D Carroll) *swtchd rt sn after s and hld up: gd hdwy 2f out: swtchd rt and rdn to chal ins fnl f: ev ch tl nt qckn last 75yds* — **33/1**

20-4 **3** 1¼ **Sirenuse (IRE)**[12] 1099 4-9-4 **80** — TomEaves 2 — 84
(B Smart) *led: rdn along 2f out: drvn over 1f out: hdd & wknd ins fnl f* **6/1[2]**

100- **4** 1¼ **Discanti (IRE)**[189] 6647 5-9-0 **76** — (t) DuranFentiman 11 — 75+
(T D Easterby) *towards rr: hdwy over 2f out: nt clr run over 1f out: styd on ins fnl f: nrst fin* — **7/1[3]**

20-3 **5** shd **Mandarin Spirit (IRE)**[7] 1200 10-8-6 **68** — (b) PaulHanagan 8 — 67
(Miss L A Perratt) *trckd ldrs: hdwy 2f out: rdn to chal over 1f out and ev ch tl wknd ins fnl f* — **11/1**

00-1 **6** 2½ **Dispol Grand (IRE)**[9] 1154 4-8-7 **69** 6ex — JoeFanning 5 — 59
(P T Midgley) *cl up: rdn along 2f out and sn wknd* — **9/1**

060- **7** ½ **Nomoreblondes**[153] 7398 6-8-5 **67** — (p) PJMcDonald 12 — 55
(P T Midgley) *s.i.s: a towards rr* — **16/1**

030- **8** ¾ **La Zamora**[210] 6051 4-9-2 **78** — PhillipMakin 3 — 63
(T D Barron) *hld up: a towards rr* — **10/1**

65-5 **9** 2 **Lucky Leigh**[15] 1074 4-8-10 **72** — SamHitchcott 7 — 50
(M R Channon) *chsd ldrs: rdn along 2f out: drvn over 1f out and sn wknd* — **10/1**

000- **10** 1½ **Speedy Senorita (IRE)**[170] 7122 5-8-4 **66** — SilvestreDeSousa 10 — 39
(J J Quinn) *chsd ldrs: rdn along wl over 1f out: sn wknd* — **12/1**

001- **11** hd **Secret Venue**[198] 6387 4-8-11 **73** — TonyHamilton 9 — 45
(Jedd O'Keeffe) *chsd ldrs: rdn along 1/2-way: sn wknd* — **17/2**

146- **12** 5 **Feelin Foxy**[142] 7511 6-9-4 **80** — LeeVickers 4 — 34
(J G Given) *blind removed late and v s.i.s: a bhd* — **20/1**

58.60 secs (-1.00) **Going Correction** -0.05s/f (Good) — **12** Ran SP% **120.1**

Speed ratings (Par 105): **106,102,100,98,98 94,93,92,89,87 86,78**

toteswingers:1&2:£18.80, 1&3:£4.30, 2&3:£39.80 CSF £121.93 CT £586.11 TOTE £3.20: £1.20, £12.10, £1.10; EX 124.60.

Owner Johnnie Delta Racing **Bred** S Leigh & R Leigh & Islandmore Stud **Trained** Uplawmoor, E Renfrews

FOCUS

A fair but competitive handicap, and solid form rated around the runner-up and third.

Discanti(IRE) ◆ Official explanation: jockey said gelding was denied a clear run

1364 NORTHALLERTON SHOOTING & COUNTRY WEAR H'CAP (DIV II) — 5f

4:45 (4:45) (Class 4) (0-80,80) 4-Y-O+ — **£5,245** (£1,560; £780; £389) — **Stalls** High

Form — RPR

010- **1** **Medici Time**[189] 6647 5-8-11 **73** — (v) GrahamGibbons 3 — 83
(T D Easterby) *w ldrs: led over 1f out: hld on towards fin* — **8/1**

0-21 **2** ½ **Highland Warrior**[7] 1200 11-8-2 **69** 6ex — PaulPickard(5) 8 — 77
(P T Midgley) *rrd s: in rr: gd hdwy over 1f out: tk 2nd ins fnl f: no ex towards fin* — **3/1[1]**

0-34 **3** ½ **Incomparable**[62] 535 5-9-4 **80** — (bt) FrederikTylicki 10 — 86
(J A Glover) *w ldr: kpt on wl ins fnl f* — **7/2[2]**

201- **4** ¾ **Select Committee**[195] 6489 5-8-4 **71** — (v) IanBrennan(5) 11 — 75
(J J Quinn) *hld up in mid-div: nt clr run on inner and swtchd lft 2f out: edgd lft and kpt on same pce fnl f* — **9/1**

366- **5** ¾ **Mullglen**[179] 6902 4-8-11 **73** — (t) DavidAllan 5 — 77+
(T D Easterby) *in rr: hdwy and nt clr run 2f out: hung lft and styd on appr fnl f: eased fnl 75yds: sddle slipped* — **7/1**

050- **6** hd **Sands Crooner (IRE)**[153] 7398 7-8-5 **67** — (v) PaulHanagan 6 — 68+
(J G Given) *swtchd rt after s: hdwy on ins over 1f out: n.m.r on inner and eased fnl 50yds* — **8/1**

046/ **7** shd **Cutting Comments**[552] 6656 4-8-0 **67** — PatrickDonaghy(5) 4 — 67
(M Dods) *in tch: effrt over 1f out: kpt on same pce* — **28/1**

0000 **8** 1¼ **Simple Rhythm**[16] 1064 4-9-0 **76** — AlanMunro 7 — 71
(J Ryan) *led: hdd over 1f out: sn wknd* — **22/1**

405- **9** 2¾ **Time Medicean**[228] 5523 4-9-3 **79** — TonyCulhane 9 — 65
(P T Midgley) *chsd ldrs: lost pl over 1f out* — **5/1[3]**

0060 **10** 1¼ **Tournedos (IRE)**[29] 913 8-8-8 **70** — (b) AndrewElliott 2 — 51
(Mrs R A Carr) *rrd and wnt lft s: sn chsng ldrs: lost pl over 1f out* — **25/1**

59.19 secs (-0.41) **Going Correction** -0.05s/f (Good) — **10** Ran SP% **120.3**

Speed ratings (Par 105): **101,100,99,98,97 96,96,94,90,88**

toteswingers:1&2:£7.20, 1&3:£5.10, 2&3:£2.90 CSF £32.60 CT £104.81 TOTE £9.70: £3.20, £1.10, £2.50; EX 42.70.

Owner Mrs C A Hodgetts **Bred** Mrs Fiona Denniff **Trained** Great Habton, N Yorks

FOCUS

This didn't look quite as competitive as the first division and the winning time was 0.59 seconds slower. The third and fourth have been rated to their marks.

Mullglen ◆ Official explanation: jockey said saddle slipped

1365 PINDER DALE H'CAP (DIV I) — 6f

5:20 (5:21) (Class 5) (0-75,75) 4-Y-O+ — **£3,950** (£1,175; £587; £293) — **Stalls** High

Form — RPR

0-10 **1** **Sir Nod**[38] 832 8-9-2 **73** — PaulHanagan 11 — 83
(Julie Camacho) *cl up on stands' rail: led bef 1/2-way: rdn over 1f out: drvn ins fnl f and hld on wl* — **7/1[2]**

30-0 **2** ½ **Avontuur (FR)**[36] 867 8-8-6 **68** — (b) DeanHeslop(5) 14 — 76
(Mrs R A Carr) *chsd ldrs stands' rail: swtchd lft and hdwy 2f out: rdn to chal over 1f out and ev ch tl drvn and nt qckn last 50yds* — **12/1**

3060 **3** 2¼ **Methaaly (IRE)**[8] 1192 7-9-3 **74** — (be) AlanMunro 7 — 75
(M Mullineaux) *trckd ldrs: hdwy over 1f out: rdn and styd on ins fnl f* **17/2**

020- **4** 2 1/4 **Frisbee**[161] 7273 6-8-8 **65** .... DuranFentiman 13 59
(D W Thompson) *chsd ldrs: rdn along 2f out: drvn over 1f out: kpt on same pce* **16/1**

110- **5** *hd* **Milton Of Campsie**[185] 6764 5-9-0 **71** .... JohnEgan 2 64+
(J Balding) *in tch: hdwy on wd outside wl over 1f out: rdn and ch ent fnl f: sn drvn and btn* **16/1**

360- **6** 2 1/4 **Artsu**[197] 6434 5-9-1 **72** .... PhillipMakin 5 58
(M Dods) *midfield: rdn along 2f out: sn no imp* **8/1**[3]

20-6 **7** *hd* **Caranbola**[28] 935 4-8-7 **64** .... JimmyQuinn 6 49
(M Brittain) *towards rr: rdn along 1/2-way: hdwy to chse ldrs wl over 1f out: sn drvn and btn* **7/1**[2]

000- **8** 1 1/4 **Guertino (IRE)**[171] 7083 5-8-13 **70** .... AndrewElliott 1 51
(C J Teague) *qckly away and led: pushed along and hdd over 3f out: rdn over 2f out and sn wknd* **40/1**

35-2 **9** *shd* **Dispol Kylie (IRE)**[11] 1112 4-8-8 **65** .... JoeFanning 10 46
(P T Midgley) *chsd ldrs: rdn along 2f out: sn wknd* **7/1**[2]

024- **10** 1/2 **Noodles Blue Boy**[171] 7082 4-9-1 **75** .... BarryMcHugh(3) 4 54
(Ollie Pears) *sn outpcd and rdn along: a in rr* **5/1**[1]

1031 **11** 1 3/4 **Raimond Ridge (IRE)**[42] 806 4-8-12 **69** .... LukeMorris 3 43
(J Jay) *dwlt: a in rr* **11/1**

01-0 **U** **Northern Bolt**[7] 1200 5-9-4 **75** .... PJMcDonald 8 —
(I W McInnes) *panicked in stalls and uns rdr* **8/1**[3]

1m 12.23s (-0.47) **Going Correction** -0.05s/f (Good) **12 Ran SP% 117.1**
Speed ratings (Par 103): **101,100,97,94,94 91,90,89,89,88 86,—**
toteswingers:1&2:£20.90, 1&3:£17.40, 2&3:£28.60 CSF £87.13 CT £738.91 TOTE £6.90: £1.80, £4.90, £3.60; EX 84.50.
Owner Brian Nordan **Bred** B Nordan And Mrs S Camacho **Trained** Norton, N Yorks

FOCUS
Another ordinary sprint handicap and another race where it paid to race handily. It has been rated around the runner-up to the best view of last year's form.
Milton Of Campsie ◆ Official explanation: jockey said mare hung left final 1 1/2f

1366 PINDER DALE H'CAP (DIV II) 6f
5:50 (5:51) (Class 5) (0-75,75) 4-Y-0+ **£3,950** (£1,175; £587; £293) **Stalls** High

Form RPR

200- **1** **Leonid Glow**[160] 7287 5-9-2 **73** .... PhillipMakin 5 82
(M Dods) *hld up in mid-div: nt clr run over 1f out: str run to ld ins fnl f: hld on wl* **14/1**

230- **2** 3/4 **Lucky Dan (IRE)**[183] 6798 4-8-12 **69** .... SilvestreDeSousa 11 76
(Paul Green) *dwlt: hld up in rr: hdwy and swtchd outside 2f out: r.o wl fnl f* **16/1**

460- **3** 1/2 **Atlantic Beach**[251] 4783 5-8-8 **65** .... PJMcDonald 13 70
(J Hetherton) *led: hdd ins fnl f: no ex* **8/1**

4402 **4** 1 1/4 **Bo McGinty (IRE)**[6] 1234 9-8-4 **61** oh1 ....(v) PaulHanagan 10 62
(R A Fahey) *chsd ldrs: edgd rt and kpt on same pce fnl f* **5/1**[2]

1634 **5** 1/2 **Bonnie Prince Blue**[30] 905 7-9-4 **75** ....(b) AdrianNicholls 12 74+
(D Nicholls) *in rr: hdwy and nt clr run over 1f out: styd on wl ins fnl f* **15/2**

005- **6** 3/4 **El Dececy (USA)**[273] 4040 6-8-8 **65** .... JohnEgan 6 62
(J Balding) *chsd ldrs: kpt on same pce appr fnl f* **25/1**

2230 **7** 3/4 **Fulford**[3] 1276 5-8-4 **61** oh2 .... JimmyQuinn 7 56
(M Brittain) *in rr-div: hdwy over 2f out: upsides 1f out: wknd ins fnl f* **16/1**

5-15 **8** 2 1/4 **Wyatt Earp (IRE)**[50] 703 9-9-2 **73** ....(p) GregFairley 14 60
(P Salmon) *chsd ldrs: hmpd and fdd fnl f* **7/1**[3]

000- **9** 1/2 **Final Salute**[108] 7870 4-8-10 **67** ....(v) TomEaves 8 53
(B Smart) *chsd ldrs: wkng whn hmpd jst ins fnl f* **28/1**

300- **10** 1/2 **Hazelrigg (IRE)**[167] 7171 5-8-13 **70** ....(p) DavidAllan 9 54+
(T D Easterby) *mid-div: nt clr run over 2f out: nt rcvr* **12/1**

400- **11** 1/2 **Baybshambles (IRE)**[195] 6489 6-8-11 **68** .... TonyHamilton 1 51
(R E Barr) *w ldrs on outer: wknd appr fnl f* **33/1**

0410 **12** 1 1/4 **Kersivay**[42] 808 4-8-12 **69** ....(v) CathyGannon 2 48
(P D Evans) *w ldrs: wkng whn hmpd jst ins fnl f* **14/1**

000- **13** 1 1/4 **Maxwell Hawke (IRE)**[209] 6111 4-9-1 **72** ....(t) AlanMunro 15 47
(P W Chapple-Hyam) *in rr: nt clr run over 2f out: nvr on terms* **3/1**[1]

1m 12.0s (-0.70) **Going Correction** -0.05s/f (Good) **13 Ran SP% 120.1**
Speed ratings (Par 103): **102,101,100,98,98 97,96,93,92,91 91,89,87**
toteswingers:1&2:£30.20, 1&3:£20.10, 2&3:£21.60 CSF £216.75 CT £1983.92 TOTE £17.70: £4.50, £4.70, £3.20; EX 258.70 Place 6 £6.58, Place 5 £4.96.
Owner Mrs G C Stanley **Bred** Mrs G C Stanley **Trained** Denton, Co Durham

FOCUS
Another modest sprint handicap and a few endured trouble in running. The winning time was 0.23 seconds faster than the first division. The first two set the level of the form.
Bonnie Prince Blue ◆ Official explanation: jockey said gelding was denied a clear run
Hazelrigg(IRE) Official explanation: jockey said gelding was denied a clear run
Maxwell Hawke(IRE) Official explanation: jockey said gelding was denied a clear run
T/Plt: £8.00 to a £1 stake. Pool: £53,528.59. 4,853.79 winning tickets. T/Qpdt: £5.90 to a £1 stake. Pool: £3,989.50. 493.68 winning tickets. JR

1367 - 1373a (Foreign Racing) - See Raceform Interactive

1028 DONCASTER (L-H)
Saturday, April 17

OFFICIAL GOING: Good to firm (good in places on round course; 8.8)
Wind: Virtually nil Weather: Fine and dry

1374 AJA LADY RIDERS' H'CAP (LADY AMATEUR RIDERS') 7f
4:40 (4:41) (Class 4) (0-80,79) 4-Y-0+ **£4,059** (£1,259; £629; £314) **Stalls** High

Form RPR

-113 **1** **Camerooney**[86] 248 7-9-0 **65** oh6 .... MissNVorster(7) 10 73
(B Ellison) *a.p: led 1 1/2f out and sn rdn: edgd rt ins fnl f: kpt on gamely towards fin* **20/1**

403- **2** *shd* **Moody Tunes**[168] 7169 7-10-2 **79** .... MissLEBurke(5) 17 87
(J R Weymes) *in tch towards stands' rail: gd hdwy 2f out: rdn over 1f out: styd on to chal ins fnl f and ev ch tl nt qckn nr fin* **20/1**

00-0 **3** 2 1/2 **Game Lad**[20] 1030 8-9-7 **70** ....(t) MissJoannaMason(5) 12 71
(T D Easterby) *in tch towards stands' side: hdwy 2f out: rdn to chal over 1f out and ev ch tl one pce ins fnl f* **12/1**

153- **4** 1 3/4 **Misplaced Fortune**[161] 7287 5-10-7 **79** .... MissEJJones 11 76
(N Tinkler) *chsd ldrs: hdwy 1/2-way: rdn to chal wl over 1f out and ev ch tl wknd ins fnl f* **11/1**

10-0 **5** 2 **Lakeman (IRE)**[12] 1117 4-10-1 **73** .... MissSBrotherton 14 64
(B Ellison) *towards rr: hdwy over 2f out: rdn and styd on appr fnl f: nrst fin* **33/1**

0140 **6** *shd* **Rub Of The Relic (IRE)**[3] 1293 5-9-6 **71** oh7 ow6.(be) MissHDukes(7) 9 62
(P T Midgley) *towards rr: hdwy 2f out: styd on strly appr fnl f: nrst fin* **25/1**

206- **7** *shd* **Sea Salt**[172] 7083 7-9-9 **72** .... MissVBarr(5) 16 63
(R E Barr) *chsd ldrs: hdwy 3f out: rdn and ev ch 2f out: grad wknd appr fnl f* **16/1**

5146 **8** 2 3/4 **General Tufto**[39] 837 5-10-3 **75** ....(b) MissADeniel 8 58
(C Smith) *midfield: rdn along over 2f out: kpt on: nvr nr ldrs* **20/1**

0-52 **9** *shd* **Kingswinford (IRE)**[10] 1149 4-10-3 **75** .... MrsEEvans 6 58
(P D Evans) *chsd ldrs: effrt 2f out: sn rdn and wknd over 1f out* **15/2**[3]

3-12 **10** 3 1/2 **Fol Liam**[7] 1238 4-9-5 **68** ....(p) MissPhillipaTutty(5) 13 41
(A J McCabe) *chsd ldrs towards stands' side: rdn along 2f out: grad wknd* **13/2**[2]

306- **11** 1 **Kilburn**[322] 2495 6-9-6 **67** .... MissZoeLilly(3) 15 38
(A J Lidderdale) *chsd ldrs towards stands' side: rdn along over 2f out: sn wknd* **14/1**

5664 **12** 3/4 **Thunderball**[8] 1202 4-10-7 **79** ....(b) MrsMMorris 3 48
(J A Glover) *racd wd: prom: led 3f out: rdn over 2f out: hdd wl over 1f out and sn wknd* **12/1**

1-02 **13** 6 **Woolfall Sovereign (IRE)**[12] 1129 4-9-4 **69** .... MissKMargarson(7) 1 22
(G G Margarson) *racd towards far side: a towards rr* **8/1**

225- **14** 1 1/4 **French Applause (IRE)**[288] 3566 4-10-2 **79** .... MissKECooper(5) 7 28
(T P Tate) *nvr bttr than midfield* **6/1**[1]

406- **15** 1 1/2 **Bold Marc (IRE)**[165] 7220 8-10-2 **79** .... MissKellyBurke(5) 18 24
(J R Weymes) *racd nr stands' rail: led: rdn along and hdd over 2f out: wknd wl over 1f out* **28/1**

0236 **16** 1 **Kensington (IRE)**[45] 779 9-9-6 **69** ....(p) MissAWallace(5) 4 11
(A J McCabe) *racd towards far side: prom: rdn along 1/2-way: sn wknd* **18/1**

0-00 **17** 16 **Smarty Socks (IRE)**[20] 1030 6-10-2 **79** .... MissWGibson(5) 5 —
(P T Midgley) *virtually ref to r: a t.o* **14/1**

1m 27.19s (0.89) **Going Correction** -0.25s/f (Firm) **17 Ran SP% 123.2**
Speed ratings (Par 105): **84,83,81,79,76 76,76,73,73,69 68,67,60,58,57 56,37**
toteswingers: 1&2 £38.00, 1&3 £74.30, 2&3 £106.40 CSF £350.11 CT £5104.05 TOTE £25.10: £4.50, £5.30, £3.90, £2.80; EX 582.90.
Owner Mrs Jean Stapleton **Bred** Miss Dianne Hill **Trained** Norton, N Yorks

FOCUS
The action took place up the stands' side where the majority of the field raced and a group of four broke clear. The runner-up is the guide to the level.
Thunderball Official explanation: jockey said gelding lost its action closing stages

1375 CROWNHOTEL-BAWTRY.COM MAIDEN FILLIES' STKS 5f
5:10 (5:11) (Class 4) 2-Y-O **£3,885** (£1,156; £577; £288) **Stalls** High

Form RPR

4 **1** **Dingle View (IRE)**[11] 1136 2-9-0 0 .... CathyGannon 8 79+
(P D Evans) *mde most: rdn wl over 1f out: kpt on strly ins fnl f* **7/2**[2]

2 2 **Malpas Missile (IRE)** 2-9-0 0 .... RichardSmith 9 71
(Tom Dascombe) *cl up: effrt to chal 2f out: sn rdn and ev ch tl drvn and one pce ent fnl f* **12/1**

3 *nk* **First Class Favour (IRE)** 2-9-0 0 .... DuranFentiman 13 70+
(T D Easterby) *trckd ldrs: hdwy 2f out: rdn to chse ldng pair ent fnl f: kpt on same pce towards fin* **10/1**

4 2 1/2 **Hortensia (IRE)** 2-9-0 0 .... ChrisCatlin 11 60
(M R Channon) *chsd ldrs: rdn along 2f out: kpt on same pce appr fnl f* **10/3**[1]

5 1 1/2 **Ever Roses** 2-9-0 0 .... TonyCulhane 10 54
(P T Midgley) *in tch: rdn along and outpcd 1/2-way: styd on ins fnl f: nrst fin* **16/1**

6 *shd* **Lady Royale** 2-9-0 0 .... LeeVickers 3 53+
(G R Oldroyd) *dwlt and wnt lft s: hdwy to chse ldrs whn hung lft 2f out: sn rdn and kpt on same pce* **16/1**

7 1/2 **Liberty Green (IRE)** 2-9-0 0 .... JamesDoyle 12 51
(A J McCabe) *chsd ldrs stands' rail: rdn along 2f out: grad wknd* **14/1**

8 3/4 **Merrjanah** 2-8-11 0 .... Louis-PhilippeBeuzelin(3) 7 48
(C E Brittain) *towards rr: sme hdwy over 2f out: sn rdn and n.d* **7/1**[3]

9 1 1/2 **Loves Theme (IRE)** 2-9-0 0 .... StephenCraine 6 42
(A Bailey) *chsd ldrs: rdn along over 2f out: grad wknd* **8/1**

0 **10** 4 1/2 **Danehill Deb**[16] 1073 2-9-0 0 .... RichardMullen 5 24
(B De Haan) *cl up: rdn and ev ch 2f out: sn wknd* **33/1**

11 1 **Dancing Tara** 2-8-9 0 .... AndrewHeffernan(5) 1 20
(P D Evans) *in tch on outer: rdn along 1/2-way: sn wknd* **14/1**

12 6 **Alexs Rainbow (USA)** 2-9-0 0 .... TadhgO'Shea 2 —
(J Gallagher) *wnt lft s: sn chsng ldrs: rdn along 1/2-way: sn lost pl and bhd* **20/1**

60.71 secs (0.21) **Going Correction** -0.25s/f (Firm) **12 Ran SP% 118.5**
Speed ratings (Par 91): **88,84,84,80,77 77,76,75,73,66 64,54**
toteswingers: 1&2 £12.90, 1&3 £11.20, 2&3 £25.00 CSF £45.51 TOTE £3.90: £1.90, £3.60, £2.20; EX 41.80.
Owner Mrs I M Folkes **Bred** Robert Berns **Trained** Pandy, Monmouths
■ Stewards' Enquiry : Stephen Craine two-day ban: careless riding (May 3-4)

FOCUS
Just an ordinary fillies' maiden.

NOTEBOOK
Dingle View(IRE) was one of only two to have seen a racecourse before and that probably made the difference, with David Evans' filly well on top in the final half furlong having been front rank throughout. She is a sister to the stable's decent sprinter Vhujon and, having shaped promisingly at Ffos Las on debut, she showed the benefit of that pipe-opener. She isn't very big but ought to get at least another furlong in time and is likely to win more races, but it's impossible to know how strong this form is at this stage. (op 3-1 tchd 11-4)
Malpas Missile(IRE) ◆ shaped nicely on debut and looks capable of winning races. (op 14-1)
First Class Favour(IRE) ◆ was another to make a pleasing start to her career and she ought to win in similar company before long. (op 11-1 tchd 12-1)
Hortensia(IRE) attracted good support in the market beforehand but she didn't look to have come in her coat beforehand and didn't live up to market billing in the race itself. She kept on from midfield but was never in the hunt and is bred to need further than this in time, so it's likely she'll do better. (op 13-2)
Ever Roses ◆ didn't appear to have much of a clue towards the back of the field through the first half of the race, but the penny seemed to drop in the final furlong and she began to pass horses. She should have learned a lot from this and is one to be interested in next time.

1376 ADVANCED MEDICAL REJUVENATION H'CAP 6f
5:40 (5:41) (Class 3) (0-90,90) 3-Y-O **£6,799** (£2,023; £1,011; £505) **Stalls** High

Form RPR

026- **1** **Victoire De Lyphar (IRE)**[212] 6035 3-8-11 **83** .... PaulQuinn 6 97
(D Nicholls) *trckd ldrs: hdwy over 2f out: rdn to ld 1 1/2f out: drvn and edgd rt ent fnl f: kpt on gamely* **22/1**

4-45 **2** 1 1/2 **Jack My Boy (IRE)**[4] 1281 3-8-6 **78** .... CathyGannon 12 88
(P D Evans) *cl up: rdn along and led briefly 2f out: sn hdd: ev ch tl drvn: edgd lft and one pce ins fnl f* **6/1**[3]

51- **3** ¾ **Deacon Blues**[173] 7058 3-8-6 **78** .... EddieAhern 2 85+
(J R Fanshawe) *trckd ldrs: smooth hdwy over 2f out: chal wl over 1f out and ev ch tl rdn and edgd rt ent fnl f: one pce whn n.m.r towards fin* **5/1**[2]

104- **4** 3¼ **Mon Brav**[280] 3871 3-8-10 **82** .... DavidNolan 13 79
(D Carroll) *hld up towards rr: hdwy 2f out: sn rdn and styd on ent fnl f: nrst fin* **17/2**

01-6 **5** ¾ **Amenable (IRE)**[35] 884 3-8-4 **76** .... AndrewMullen 8 70
(D Nicholls) *led: rdn along and hdd 2f out: drvn and wkng whn n.m.r and hmpd appr fnl f* **18/1**

26-0 **6** 1 **Haadeeth**[28] 945 3-9-4 **90** .... TadhgO'Shea 14 81
(M P Tregoning) *hld up: hdwy over 2f out: swtchd lft and rdn wl over 1f out: no imp appr fnl f* **15/2**

540- **7** 2½ **Crown (IRE)**[197] 6447 3-9-3 **89** .... RichardMullen 15 72
(Miss Jo Crowley) *dwlt and towards rr: hdwy 2f out: sn rdn and n.d* **50/1**

25-4 **8** 1 **Ventura Cove (IRE)**[10] 1153 3-8-3 **78** .... BarryMcHugh(3) 5 58
(R A Fahey) *cl up: rdn along over 2f out: sn wknd* **12/1**

110- **9** 4 **Bossy Kitty**[161] 7290 3-8-5 **77** .... KirstyMilczarek 1 44
(N Tinkler) *towards rr: sme hdwy 2f out: sn rdn and n.d* **33/1**

0-16 **10** 1¼ **Raddy 'Ell Pauline (IRE)**[21] 1019 3-9-1 **87** .... StephenCraine 11 50
(K A Ryan) *in tch: rdn along over 2f out: wkng whn n.m.r wl over 1f out* **20/1**

13-1 **11** 1¾ **Jarrow (IRE)**[31] 901 3-9-4 **90** .... JoeFanning 7 48
(M Johnston) *cl up: rdn along over 2f out: sn wknd* **11/4**[1]

506- **12** *hd* **Toga Tiger (IRE)**[176] 6993 3-8-9 **81** .... TonyCulhane 3 38
(P T Midgley) *a in rr: outpcd fnl 2f* **20/1**

035- **13** 6 **Flaneur**[161] 7290 3-8-4 **76** .... (b) DuranFentiman 4 14
(T D Easterby) *chsd ldrs on outer: rdn along over 1 1/2f out: sn wknd* **12/1**

1m 11.75s (-1.85) **Going Correction** -0.25s/f (Firm) **13** Ran SP% **119.3**
Speed ratings (Par 102): **102,100,99,94,93 92,89,87,82,80 78,78,70**
toteswingers: 1&2 £36.10, 1&3 £27.40, 2&3 £6.60 CSF £141.36 CT £809.78 TOTE £30.70: £7.60, £2.40, £2.30; EX 295.30.

Owner Middleham Park Racing Xviii **Bred** Mrs Monica Hackett **Trained** Sessay, N Yorks

■ Stewards' Enquiry : Cathy Gannon caution: careless riding.

FOCUS
Quite a competitive little handicap featuring and several unexposed and lightly raced sorts.

NOTEBOOK
Victoire De Lyphar(IRE) had more experience than many having raced six times as a juvenile but he had been switched to David Nicholls (from Patrick Haslam) over the winter and his new stable have started the season well. His new trainer decided to dispense with the headgear that was present when disappointing on his final start and it proved a smart move for the gelded son of Bertolini pulled out plenty when Jack My Boy and Deacon Blues closed in, despite displaying a slightly awkward head carriage, and asserted in good style in the final 100 yards. He appears to have wintered well and should have more to offer, while another furlong won't be a problem. (op 28-1 tchd 20-1)

Jack My Boy(IRE) is exposed off this sort of mark, which doesn't help the strength of this form, but he was always going to be suited by the return to this trip and he has run well over this C&D before. (op 15-2 tchd 5-1)

Deacon Blues ◆, making his handicap debut, shaped very encouragingly despite still showing signs of greenness under pressure. He is still learning but he displayed a decent cruising speed through the middle section of the race and there is more to come from him this year. Official explanation: jockey said colt hung right (op 7-1)

Mon Brav stayed on again after getting outpaced mid race and he'll probably be seen to better effect over further. (op 14-1)

Haadeeth was caught in a bit of a pocket up the stands' rail but he didn't really pick up with any great zest when in the clear and has a bit to prove now. (op 5-1)

Jarrow(IRE) was so impressive in a warm event on Polytrack last time, so this was disappointing. It's difficult to pin down exactly what went wrong as he dropped away so tamely, but it may transpire that this quick turf isn't ideal. (tchd 3-1)

1377 UNIVERSAL RECYCLING DONCASTER MILE STKS (LISTED RACE) 1m (R)
6:15 (6:16) (Class 1) 4-Y-0+ £23,704 (£8,964; £4,480; £2,240) **Stalls High**

Form RPR

03-2 **1** **Fanunalter**[35] 885 4-8-12 96 .... DarryllHolland 4 111+
(M Botti) *hld up in rr: hdwy 2f out: squeezed through to chal ent fnl f: rdn and qcknd wl to ld last 75yds* **4/1**

2-26 **2** *hd* **Mia's Boy**[21] 1008 6-8-12 105 .... EddieAhern 5 111
(C A Dwyer) *hld up: hdwy on outer 2f out: rdn to ld ent fnl f: drvn: hdd and nt qckn fnl 75yds* **15/8**[1]

0061 **3** 4 **Dunelight (IRE)**[35] 883 7-9-1 109 .... (v) RyanMoore 2 104
(C G Cox) *led: qcknd over 2f out: and sn rdn: drvn ent fnl f: sn hdd and one pce* **10/3**[3]

16-5 **4** ½ **Light From Mars**[14] 1085 5-8-12 100 .... JamesMillman 1 100+
(B R Millman) *trckd ldr on inner: effrt 2f out: rdn and n.m.r over 1f out: swtchd rt and drvn appr fnl f: kpt on same pce* **3/1**[2]

204- **5** 3 **Cloudy Start**[217] 5855 4-8-12 105 .... JoeFanning 3 93
(J A Osborne) *trckd ldr: effrt over 2f out: sn rdn and wknd over 1f out* **14/1**

1m 38.42s (-1.28) **Going Correction** -0.25s/f (Firm) **5** Ran SP% **109.5**
Speed ratings (Par 111): **96,95,91,91,88**
CSF £11.80 TOTE £4.50: £2.40, £1.20; EX 14.10.

Owner Scuderia Rencati Srl **Bred** Azienda Agricola Francesca **Trained** Newmarket, Suffolk

FOCUS
Only five runners, but a good race. The pace set by Dunelight was just steady. Not strong form for the grade but there looks no fluke about the winner's improvement. The runner-up looks the best guide to the level of the form.

NOTEBOOK
Fanunalter ◆ had to sit and suffer at the back of the field as they grouped up along the far rail, but the son of Falbrav picked up smartly between horses and was always going to get Mia's Boy in the final furlong, indeed Darryll Holland didn't have to resort to the whip at any point. The winner was probably value for a little more than the winning margin and there is no doubt now that this gelding will be able to hold his own at Group level. Marco Botti said afterwards that he might now go for a Group 2 race in Italy, but he is a horse who needs things to drop right.

Mia's Boy swept around the outside to lead going into the final furlong and he doesn't appear to have done much wrong, just losing out to a much more progressive rival. (op 5-2)

Dunelight(IRE) has to go down as a little disappointing given he had the run of the race yet was brushed aside so readily a furlong out. Conceding 3lb all round was never going to be easy but he was entitled to finish much closer to Mia's Boy than this. (op 11-4)

Light From Mars, who had a tough task on these terms, dropped away having held every chance. (tchd 10-3)

1378 SOCIETY LIFESTYLE AND LEISURE MAGAZINE H'CAP 1m 2f 60y
6:50 (6:50) (Class 3) (0-95,90) 4-Y-0+
£6,542 (£1,469; £1,469; £490; £244; £122) **Stalls Low**

Form RPR

31- **1** **Dangerous Midge (USA)**[218] 5828 4-9-2 **88** .... MartinDwyer 2 106+
(B J Meehan) *led 1f: trckd ldr: hdwy to chal 2f out: led 1 1/2f out and sn rdn clr: kpt on strly* **5/1**[3]

060- **2** 5 **Granston (IRE)**[196] 6480 9-8-13 **85** .... DarryllHolland 6 91
(J D Bethell) *led after 1f: rdn over 2f out: hdd and drvn 1 1/2f out: kpt on same pce fnl f* **14/1**

30-2 **2** *dht* **Embsay Crag**[21] 1013 4-8-4 **81** .... IanBrennan(5) 12 87+
(Mrs K Walton) *towards rr: hdwy over 3f out: nt clr run and bmpd wl over 2f out: rdn over 1f out: styd on wl fnl f* **10/1**

04-1 **4** 1½ **Rosbay (IRE)**[21] 1013 6-8-5 **77** .... DuranFentiman 8 80+
(T D Easterby) *dwlt and in rr: hdwy wl over 2f out: swtchd ins and rdn over 1f out: kpt on ins fnl f: nrst fin* **14/1**

6000 **5** *shd* **Reve De Nuit (USA)**[4] 1274 4-9-4 **90** .... (p) JamesDoyle 4 93
(A J McCabe) *hld up towards rr: hdwy whn n.m.r 3f out: swtchd rt and rdn 2f out: kpt on same pce appr fnl f* **28/1**

342- **6** ¾ **The Fonz**[266] 4299 4-8-8 **80** .... RyanMoore 5 82
(Sir Michael Stoute) *trckd ldrs: effrt 3f out: rdn along 2f out: sn drvn and one pce* **11/4**[1]

116- **7** 4 **Tinshu (IRE)**[147] 7489 4-9-1 **87** .... FrederikTylicki 10 81
(D Haydn Jones) *midfield: hdwy on outer over 3f out: rdn to chse ldrs 2f out: sn drvn and wknd over 1f out* **16/1**

1022 **8** 5 **Thunderstruck**[30] 921 5-9-2 **88** .... (p) ChrisCatlin 11 72
(J A Glover) *dwlt: rapid hdwy to chse ldr after 1f: rdn along over 3f out: wknd over 2f out* **12/1**

1210 **9** ½ **Chosen Forever**[44] 790 5-8-12 **84** .... JimmyQuinn 3 68
(G R Oldroyd) *towards rr: hdwy 3f out: rdn along 2f out: sn btn* **25/1**

43-0 **10** 2 **Just Lille (IRE)**[10] 1151 7-9-1 **87** .... StephenCraine 1 67
(Mrs A Duffield) *chsd ldrs on inner: rdn along over 3f out: sn wknd* **25/1**

63-1 **11** 2¼ **Red Jade**[21] 1011 5-9-1 **87** .... PaulHanagan 7 62
(R A Fahey) *chsd ldrs on outer: rdn along 3f out: sn wknd* **7/2**[2]

12-3 **12** ¾ **Desert Vision**[66] 480 6-8-9 **86** .... (vt) JamesSullivan(5) 9 60
(M W Easterby) *t.k.h: in tch: rdn along over 3f out and sn wknd* **20/1**

2m 6.84s (-2.56) **Going Correction** -0.25s/f (Firm) **12** Ran SP% **117.5**
Speed ratings (Par 107): **107,103,103,101,101 101,97,93,93,91 90,89**PL: Granston £4.00, Embsay Crag £3.40; EX: DM-G £39.10, DM-EC £25.40; CSF DM-G £33.94, DM-EC £25.34; TRICAST: DM-G-EC £339.40, DM-EC-G £330.68; toteswingers: 1&2 (Granston) £15.30, 1&2 (Embsay Crag) £13.00, 2&2:£20.40 TOTE £6.30: £2.30 027 Trifecta £Owner Iraj Parvizi Bred.
■ Stewards' Enquiry : James Doyle one-day ban: careless riding (May 3)

FOCUS
What looked a competitive handicap on paper was turned into a rout by Dangerous Midge, who was most progressive as a 3-y-o and he has clearly gone the right way over the winter.

NOTEBOOK
Dangerous Midge(USA) ◆, despite being 9lb higher than when winning over this C&D in September, bolted clear once joining long-time leader Granston over a furlong out and must now be bordering on Listed class. He has done all of his racing over this sort of trip, and on a sound surface, and who knows where he could end up given his rate of progression. (op 4-1 tchd 7-2)
Granston(IRE) was gifted an easy time of things at the head of affairs but has run well nonetheless. (op 18-1)
Embsay Crag came home from a long way back to dead heat with Granston. (op 18-1)
Rosbay(IRE) ◆ had nowhere to go at the back of the field and his rider decided to try and go through horses up the inside rather than come round the outside. He stayed on well once on the rail but could never get in a telling blow. Given he is well served by cut in the ground, this was a promising effort and he is one to keep on side in this sort of event, especially on an easier surface. (tchd 16-1)
Reve De Nuit(USA) kept on well up down the outside from well back and this was much more encouraging than when disappointing in the cheekpieces earlier in the week. (op 33-1)
The Fonz proved disappointing but is sure to benefit from the outing. (op 7-2)

1379 MOSS PROPERTIES FILLIES' H'CAP 1m 2f 60y
7:25 (7:25) (Class 4) (0-85,84) 4-Y-0+ £4,533 (£1,348; £674; £336) **Stalls Low**

Form RPR

5-64 **1** **Aphrodisia**[10] 1156 6-8-10 **76** .... StevieDonohoe 11 86
(Ian Williams) *dwlt and bhd: swtchd wd and gd hdwy over 2f out: rdn over 1f out: styd on to ld ins fnl f: r.o wl* **9/1**

526- **2** ¾ **Lady Artemisia (IRE)**[192] 6594 4-9-4 **84** .... DarryllHolland 8 93
(M Botti) *trckd ldrs: hdwy over 2f out: rdn wl over 1f out: drvn and ev ch ent fnl f: kpt on* **7/2**[1]

550- **3** *nk* **Magic Echo**[176] 6986 6-8-10 **76** .... JamesDoyle 5 84
(M Dods) *s.i.s and bhd: hdwy 3f out: rdn wl over 1f out: swtchd lft and drvn ent fnl f: ev ch tl no ex last 100yds* **16/1**

214- **4** 1 **Bollin Dolly**[164] 7247 7-8-5 **71** .... JimmyQuinn 4 77+
(T D Easterby) *trckd ldr: hdwy and cl up over 2f out: rdn to ld wl over 1f out: drvn and hdd ins fnl f: sn no ex* **8/1**

02-1 **5** 2¼ **Paquerettza (FR)**[20] 1034 4-9-4 **84** .... FrederikTylicki 9 86
(D H Brown) *trckd ldng pair: hdwy 3f out: rdn along 2f out and sn ev ch tl drvn and one pce ins fnl f* **4/1**[2]

-420 **6** 1 **Snow Dancer (IRE)**[44] 790 6-9-0 **80** .... PatrickMathers 6 80
(H A McWilliams) *in tch: hdwy to chse ldrs over 3f out and sn rdn: drvn 2f out: kpt on same pce* **33/1**

211- **7** 3½ **Caster Sugar (USA)**[198] 6420 4-9-1 **81** .... RyanMoore 10 74
(R Hannon) *hld up: effrt and sme hdwy over 3f out: rdn along over 2f out: sn btn* **4/1**[2]

340- **8** 4½ **Antigua Sunrise (IRE)**[209] 6138 4-8-10 **76** .... PaulHanagan 7 61
(R A Fahey) *led: rdn along 3f out: drvn 2f out: hdd wl over 1f out and sn wknd* **7/1**[3]

4106 **9** 8 **Bavarica**[10] 1161 8-8-3 **76** .... AdamBeschizza(7) 1 46
(Miss J Feilden) *chsd ldrs: rdn along 3f out: sn wknd* **33/1**

00-4 **10** 13 **Faldal**[20] 1034 4-9-4 **84** .... AdrianMcCarthy 2 29
(Miss Gay Kelleway) *in tch on inner: pushed along over 3f out: rdn wl over 2f out: sn wknd* **12/1**

2m 7.68s (-1.72) **Going Correction** -0.25s/f (Firm) **10** Ran SP% **115.3**
Speed ratings (Par 102): **104,103,103,102,100 99,96,93,86,76**
toteswingers: 1&2 £8.60, 1&3 £39.30, 2&3 £15.00 CSF £40.10 CT £496.12 TOTE £13.00: £2.90, £1.60, £4.00; EX 58.00.
Owner Ian Williams **Bred** Theobalds Stud **Trained** Portway, Worcs

FOCUS
A decent gallop to this fillies' handicap thanks to Antigua Sunrise, who dropped right away, and the hold-up horses came to the fore in the final two furlongs.

Faldal Official explanation: trainer said filly was unsuited by the good to firm (good in straight) ground

1380 CHIQUE DESIGNER BOUTIQUE OF ARMTHORPE MAIDEN STKS 1m 4f

7:55 (7:57) (Class 4) 3-Y-O+ **£4,533** (£1,348; £674; £336) **Stalls** Low

Form RPR

/45- **1** **Saptapadi (IRE)**[345] 1800 4-9-12 100 .... RyanMoore 4 87+
(Sir Michael Stoute) *trckd ldrs: smooth hdwy over 2f out: led wl over 1f out and sn clr: eased towards fin* **2/7**[1]

42 **2** *5* **Dancing Dude (IRE)**[13] 1103 3-8-7 0 .... JoeFanning 6 72
(M Johnston) *trckd ldrs: hdwy over 3f out: rdn to ld briefly 2f out: sn hdd: drvn and hung rt ins fnl f: one pce* **4/1**[2]

0 **3** *¾* **Najam**[22] 985 3-8-4 0 ow2 .... ChrisCatlin 5 67
(C E Brittain) *led 2f: cl up tl led again wl over 2f out: sn rdn and hdd 2f out: drvn and one pce fr over 1f out* **25/1**

0 **4** *2 ¾* **Enchanting Smile (FR)**[21] 1010 3-7-11 0 .... DeclanCannon(5) 3 61
(A J McCabe) *hld up towards rr: hdwy 3f out: rdn to chse ldrs wl over 1f out: kpt on same pce appr fnl f* **50/1**

5 *2 ¾* **Sleep Over**[68] 5-9-8 0 .... PaulHanagan 7 59
(D Morris) *dwlt: sn in tch: rdn along 3f out: kpt on same pce fnl 2f* **40/1**

0/ **6** *2 ¼* **Daniel Defoe (USA)**[536] 7054 4-9-9 0 .... Louis-PhilippeBeuzelin(3) 9 60
(Sir Michael Stoute) *chsd ldrs on outer: rdn along over 3f out and sn wknd* **16/1**[3]

-63 **7** *1 ¼* **Sir Mark (IRE)**[12] 1116 6-9-13 0 .... DanielTudhope 2 58
(M A Peill) *trckd ldrs: hdwy on inner and cl up 3f out: rdn along over 2f out and sn wknd* **20/1**

8 *2 ¾* **Dream Risk (FR)**[135] 4-9-2 0 .... IanBrennan(5) 10 49
(Mrs K Walton) *a in rr* **50/1**

5-3 **9** *11* **Frankie Falco**[9] 1183 4-9-9 0 .... RussKennemore(3) 8 36
(G Fierro) *towards rr: effrt on outer and hung bdly rt 3f out: sn rdn and bhd* **50/1**

-505 **10** *1* **Penderyn**[21] 1010 3-7-11 50 .... PaulPickard(5) 1 27
(C Smith) *t.k.h: chsd ldr tl led after 2f: rdn along 3f out: sn hdd & wknd* **100/1**

2m 34.9s **Going Correction** -0.25s/f (Firm)
WFA 3 from 4yo 20lb 4 from 5yo+ 1lb **10** Ran SP% **121.6**
Speed ratings (Par 105): **90,86,86,84,82 81,80,78,71,70**
toteswingers: 1&2 £1.10, 1&3 £5.80, 2&3 £8.00 CSF £1.74 TOTE £1.30: £1.02, £1.50, £4.30; EX 2.00 Place 6 £508.32, Place 5 £120.92.
Owner Ballymacoll Stud **Bred** Ballymacoll Stud Farm Ltd **Trained** Newmarket, Suffolk

FOCUS
This looked a straightforward task for Saptapadi on paper and it proved just that as he strode clear of his the field from the 2f pole to win without being extended.
Frankie Falco Official explanation: jockey said colt hung violently right in home straight
T/Plt: £735.10 to a £1 stake. Pool: £46,905.77. 46.58 winning tickets. T/Qpdt: £32.50 to a £1 stake. Pool: £5,594.22. 127.30 winning tickets. JR

1351 NEWBURY (L-H)

Saturday, April 17

OFFICIAL GOING: Good (good to firm in places on straight course) changing to good to firm after race 5 (3.40)
Rail realignment increased distances on the round course by 24 metres.
Wind: Virtually nil Weather: Sunny

1381 DUBAI INTERNATIONAL AIRPORT MAIDEN STKS (DIV I) 1m (S)

1:30 (1:30) (Class 4) 3-Y-O **£4,857** (£1,445; £722; £360) **Stalls** Centre

Form RPR

34- **1** **Colonel Carter (IRE)**[192] 6592 3-9-3 0 .... JimmyFortune 4 84
(B J Meehan) *trckd ldrs: led wl over 1f out: rdn and wnt lft 1f out: sn stened: kpt on strly* **14/1**

2 *¾* **Significant Move** 3-9-3 0 .... SteveDrowne 5 82+
(R Charlton) *hld up towards rr: stdy hdwy fr over 2f out: chsd wnr ins fnl f: no imp fnl 100yds but hld on wl for 2nd* **33/1**

3- **3** *nse* **Latansaa**[175] 7029 3-9-3 0 .... RichardHills 11 82
(M P Tregoning) *stdd in rr: gd hdwy fr 2f out: str run thrght fnl f to press for 2nd last strides but no imp on wnr* **9/4**[2]

53- **4** *½* **Christmas Carnival**[189] 6672 3-9-3 0 .... KierenFallon 1 81
(B J Meehan) *pressed ldr tl narrow advantage ins fnl 3f: styd pressing ldrs tl one pce appr fnl f: styd on wl again fnl 120yds* **16/1**

5 *2 ½* **Osgood** 3-9-3 0 .... AlanMunro 2 75
(M R Channon) *t.k.h: chsd ldrs: rdn over 2f out: wknd ins fnl f* **66/1**

5- **6** *1 ½* **Engulf (IRE)**[245] 5029 3-9-3 0 .... MichaelHills 3 72
(W J Haggas) *t.k.h: in tch: hdwy over 2f out: shkn up and edgd lft over 1f out: one pce ins fnl f* **14/1**

43- **7** *2 ¾* **Advertisement (USA)**[252] 4790 3-9-3 0 .... ShaneKelly 14 65
(J Noseda) *in rr: pushed along 3f out: sme prog fr over 1f out but nvr any threat* **16/1**

3- **8** *nse* **Tenessee**[191] 6620 3-9-3 0 .... AdamKirby 12 65
(C G Cox) *chsd ldrs: drvn along and no imp fr 3f out: btn 2f out* **6/4**[1]

9 *5* **Ritual (IRE)** 3-9-3 0 .... FrankieDettori 10 54
(J Noseda) *slt ld tl hdd ins fnl 3f: wknd qckly over 1f out* **9/1**[3]

10 *2 ¾* **Latent Light (USA)** 3-9-3 0 .... TomQueally 7 48
(E A L Dunlop) *sn towards rr* **100/1**

00- **11** *3 ½* **Helaku (IRE)**[188] 6697 3-9-3 0 .... RichardHughes 6 39
(R Hannon) *chsd ldrs over 5f* **50/1**

5- **12** *71* **Madhaaq (IRE)**[168] 7183 3-8-12 0 .... TadhgO'Shea 13 —
(J L Dunlop) *sltly slow removing blind: v.s.a and lost all ch s: t.o thrght* **25/1**

1m 37.76s (-1.94) **Going Correction** -0.10s/f (Good) **12** Ran SP% **117.1**
Speed ratings (Par 100): **105,104,104,103,101 99,96,96,91,89 85,—**
toteswingers: 1&2 £43.20, 1&3 £9.50, 2&3 £25.70 CSF £407.33 TOTE £11.90: £3.10, £5.30, £1.30; EX 252.70.
Owner Mrs B V Sangster **Bred** Ceka Ireland Limited **Trained** Manton, Wilts

FOCUS
Following a dry morning the ground was changed to good but good to firm in the straight. This maiden has produced some good horses in recent years, Purple Moon, Lucarno and Border Patrol among them, and looks sure to throw up winners, so has been rated positively.

Madhaaq(IRE) Official explanation: jockey said filly missed the break

1382 DUBAI DUTY FREE FINEST SURPRISE STKS (REGISTERED AS THE JOHN PORTER STAKES) (GROUP 3) 1m 4f 5y

2:00 (2:00) (Class 1) 4-Y-O+

£36,900 (£13,988; £7,000; £3,490; £1,748; £877) **Stalls** Low

Form RPR

103- **1** **Harbinger**[175] 7031 4-8-11 112 .... RyanMoore 15 121
(Sir Michael Stoute) *hld up in rr tl stdy hdwy on outside fr 3f out to ld ins fnl 2f: drvn clr fnl f: impressive* **11/2**[2]

213- **2** *3* **Manifest**[198] 6425 4-8-11 103 .... TomQueally 2 116
(H R A Cecil) *chsd ldrs pushed along over 3f out: styd on fnl 2f and ev ch over 1f out: wnt 2nd fnl f and kpt on wl but no ch w wnr* **9/2**[1]

4-46 **3** *2* **Claremont (IRE)**[44] 799 4-8-11 113 .... AhmedAjtebi 8 113
(Mahmood Al Zarooni) *chsd ldrs: led 2f out: sn hdd and edgd lft u.p: stl ev ch over 1f out: readily outpcd ins fnl f* **20/1**

112- **4** *3 ½* **Polly's Mark (IRE)**[204] 6242 4-8-8 102 .... WilliamBuick 10 104
(C G Cox) *in tch: pushed along 3f out: styd on fnl 2f but nvr any ch of rching ldng trio* **25/1**

111 **5** *1 ¼* **Buxted (IRE)**[31] 903 4-8-11 106 .... StevieDonohoe 16 105
(R A Mills) *s.i.s: in rr: pushed along 3f out: styd on fnl 2f but nvr gng pce to get into contention* **17/2**

13- **6** *1* **Blizzard Blues (USA)**[190] 6644 4-8-11 104 .... (b) NeilCallan 9 104
(H R A Cecil) *in rr: pushed along and hdwy over 2f out: styd on fnl f but nvr any threat* **25/1**

/43- **7** *1 ¾* **Purple Moon (IRE)**[385] 1012 7-8-12 115 .... KierenFallon 14 101
(L M Cumani) *trckd ldrs: slt ld 3f out: narrowly hdd 2f out: stl wl there over 1f out: wknd sn after* **8/1**[3]

120- **8** *1 ¾* **Traffic Guard (USA)**[181] 6890 6-8-12 114 .... JamieSpencer 6 98
(P F I Cole) *in rr: pushed along over 2f out: sn swtchd rt: drvn and sme prog fnl f* **9/1**

04-1 **9** *3* **Dansili Dancer**[21] 1015 8-8-12 103 .... AdamKirby 5 93
(C G Cox) *in rr: rdn and hdwy fr 3f out: nvr gng pce to rch ldrs* **16/1**

-21P **10** *1 ¼* **Halicarnassus (IRE)**[44] 799 6-9-3 113 .... AlanMunro 12 96
(M R Channon) *chsd ldrs: rdn over 3f out: wknd over 2f out* **33/1**

24- **11** *½* **Clowance**[174] 7047 5-8-9 111 .... FrankieDettori 11 88
(R Charlton) *led 1f: styd chsng ldr to 3f out: rdn over 2f out: stl rt there over 1f out: eased whn no ch fnl f* **9/2**[1]

320- **12** *1 ¾* **Allied Powers (IRE)**[182] 6873 5-8-12 111 .... MickyFenton 13 88
(M L W Bell) *a towards rr* **16/1**

111- **13** *14* **Akmal**[182] 6854 4-9-0 108 .... RichardHills 4 68
(J L Dunlop) *led after 1f: narrowly hdd 3f out: hd to one side and wknd qckly appr fnl 2f: eased whn no ch* **11/1**

325- **14** *7* **Oasis Knight (IRE)**[182] 6854 4-8-11 104 .... (v) RichardHughes 3 54
(M P Tregoning) *chsd ldrs: rdn over 3f out: wknd qckly over 2f out: eased whn no ch* **25/1**

226/ **15** *14* **Balkan Knight**[546] 6820 10-8-12 107 .... JimmyFortune 7 32
(D R C Elsworth) *a towards rr: eased whn no ch* **66/1**

2m 30.58s (-4.92) **Going Correction** -0.10s/f (Good)
WFA 4 from 5yo+ 1lb **15** Ran SP% **124.2**
Speed ratings (Par 113): **112,110,108,106,105 104,103,102,100,99 99,98,88,84,74**
toteswingers: 1&2 £9.40, 1&3 £24.20, 2&3 £27.10 CSF £28.61 TOTE £5.80: £2.10, £2.60, £6.00; EX 33.80 Trifecta £492.50 Pool: £732.20 - 1.10 winning units..
Owner Highclere Thoroughbred Racing (Adm. Rous) **Bred** Mrs A K H Ooi **Trained** Newmarket, Suffolk

FOCUS
The rails on the top bend were in by three metres, therefore reducing the distance on the round course by 24 metres all told. A big field and a fairly open betting race for this Group 3 prize, but it was good to see an unexposed 4-y-o come out on top. The form looks sound rated around the third and fourth.

NOTEBOOK
Harbinger didn't really fulfil his early promise at three, as he was well beaten in the Great Voltigeur and had to miss the St Leger, for which he was well fancied, as a result. His trainer is known for improving horses from three to four though, and on this evidence he has a horse to go to war with this season. Harbinger was travelling best from some way out and, when asked to quicken, did so in style. He wandered about a bit once in front, but had the race well under control and looks a colt with a bright future. The Ormonde Stakes at Chester, where he won his maiden, was mentioned as his next possible target, with the Coronation Cup likely after that, while one would imagine that the Hardwicke Stakes might fit the bill if he turns up at Royal Ascot. (op 5-1 tchd 6-1)

Manifest, who won his maiden by a country mile last August before disappointing when stepped up to Listed company, was another who promised to improve for another winter on his back. He couldn't live with the winner in the final part of the race but beat off a solid performer in Claremont for second, and can only go forward from this. The Jockey Club Stakes at Newmarket on May 1 looks an ideal race for him. (op 5-1)

Claremont(IRE), who was trained in France by Andre Fabre last season, had the benefit of having raced last month at Meydan, where he finished a close sixth in a Group 2. He hung left under pressure and the ground might have been a little on the fast side for him, but he's probably a fair guide to the level of the form. (tchd 25-1)

Polly's Mark(IRE), who won a fillies' Listed race over C&D last term, looked to have work to do on this step up in class but she ran really well, and will inevitably find things a lot easier back against her own sex.

Buxted(IRE), unbeaten in three starts over this distance earlier this year on Polytrack, had to prove he could be as effective on turf, and he certainly wasn't disgraced. Keeping on at the finish, he did enough to suggest that his trainer might be right in thinking that he'll stay further than this in time. (op 10-1)

Blizzard Blues(USA), who only ran twice last year, was the least-experienced runner in the line-up. He still looked green under pressure, but clearly has plenty of ability and should be able to make it in this grade. (op 33-1)

Purple Moon(IRE) ◆ missed the Dubai Sheema Classic because he had a foot abscess, and he was expected to need this reappearance run, his first since March 2009. He ran as expected, tiring in the closing stages, and this should have put him spot on for the Yorkshire Cup next month.

Traffic Guard(USA), who has a poor strike-rate, took an age to pick up and only ran on past beaten horses. (op 10-1)

Dansili Dancer, who had the benefit of race-fitness following his easy handicap win at Kempton last month, was outclassed, finding little off the bridle.

Clowance ideally needs more cut in the ground than she had here. Official explanation: jockey said mare was unsuited by the good (good to firm in places) ground (op 13-2)

Akmal loves to dominate but probably wants further than this. He dropped right out after taking the field along for much of the way. (op 12-1 tchd 14-1 in places)

1383 BERRY BROS & RUDD MAGNUM SPRING CUP (H'CAP) 1m (S)
2:35 (2:37) (Class 2) 4-Y-0+

£21,808 (£6,531; £3,265; £1,634; £815; £409) Stalls Centre

Form — RPR

104- **1** **Brunston**[287] [3618] 4-8-2 **86** ... HayleyTurner 12 — 94
(R Charlton) *hld up towards rr: gd hdwy 2f out: led 1f out: jnd nr fin: jst prevailed: all out* **40/1**

00-0 **2** *hd* **Marajaa (IRE)**[21] [1006] 8-8-4 **88** ... JamieMackay 11 — 96
(W J Musson) *hld up in midfield: hdwy 2f out: r.o to join wnr nr fin: jst pipped* **50/1**

/00- **3** *2* **Oratory (IRE)**[188] [6702] 4-8-7 **91** ow1 ... SteveDrowne 3 — 94
(R Hannon) *hld up in midfield: hdwy 2f out: drvn to chal 1f out: one pce* **40/1**

/20- **4** *nk* **Cityscape**[350] [1675] 4-9-10 **108** ... JimmyFortune 17 — 111+
(R Charlton) *hld up in midfield: eased lft and r.o fnl 2f: nrst fin* **10/1**

41-3 **5** *shd* **Desert Kiss**[14] [1088] 5-8-1 **85** ... NickyMackay 5 — 87
(W R Swinburn) *led: hrd rdn and hdd 1f out: nt qckn* **16/1**

1-45 **6** *¾* **Extraterrestrial**[21] [1008] 6-8-9 **100** ... LeeTopliss(7) 13 — 101
(R A Fahey) *hld up towards rr: swtchd to far side 2f out: hdwy and hrd rdn over 1f out: one pce* **16/1**

-110 **7** *shd* **Dalradian (IRE)**[28] [946] 4-8-0 **84** ... JimmyQuinn 7 — 85+
(W J Knight) *in tch: n.m.r 2f out tl over 1f out: styd on fnl f* **20/1**

001- **8** *1 ½* **South Cape**[171] [7125] 7-7-5 **82** oh1 ... HarryBentley(7) 9 — 79
(G L Moore) *prom tl wknd over 1f out* **66/1**

110- **9** *¾* **Wannabe King**[196] [6480] 4-9-5 **103** ... (p) TedDurcan 8 — 98+
(D R Lanigan) *hld up in midfield: effrt and n.m.r over 2f out: nowhere to go over 1f out: swtchd lft and styd on fnl f* **25/1**

40-1 **10** *½* **Irish Heartbeat (IRE)**[21] [1006] 5-8-9 **93** ... PaulHanagan 6 — 87+
(R A Fahey) *swtchd rt s: sn last: swtchd to far side again 2f out: rdn and sme hdwy over 1f out: nvr nr to chal* **6/1**[1]

3-10 **11** *½* **Viva Vettori**[21] [1008] 6-8-6 **90** ... WilliamBuick 1 — 83
(D R C Elsworth) *prom tl wknd 1f out* **16/1**

05-2 **12** *2 ¼* **Happy Anniversary (IRE)**[12] [1117] 4-7-11 **86** ow4. DeclanCannon(5) 10 — 74
(Mrs D J Sanderson) *chsd ldr tl wknd 1f out* **33/1**

2200 **13** *¾* **Benandonner (USA)**[14] [1085] 7-7-13 **90** ... JohnFahy(7) 15 — 76
(Mike Murphy) *chsd ldrs over 5f: wkng whn bmpd jst over 2f out* **66/1**

001- **14** *½* **Manassas (IRE)**[217] [5863] 5-9-2 **100** ... DaneO'Neill 14 — 87+
(B J Meehan) *prom: hrd rdn 2f out: squeezed for room on stands' rail and wknd wl over 1f out* **9/1**

123- **15** *½* **Credit Swap**[202] [6307] 5-8-6 **90** ... DavidProbert 16 — 74
(M Wigham) *bhd: drvn along 3f out: nvr trbld ldrs* **18/1**

-110 **16** *½* **Mahadee (IRE)**[35] [883] 5-8-9 **93** ... (b) NeilCallan 4 — 76
(C E Brittain) *chsd ldrs tl hrd rdn and wknd wl over 1f out* **33/1**

00-0 **17** *¾* **Huzzah (IRE)**[21] [1008] 5-8-6 **90** ... AlanMunro 19 — 74+
(B W Hills) *in tch 5f: sn lost pl* **14/1**

04-3 **18** *½* **Lucky Dance (BRZ)**[21] [1006] 8-8-6 **90** ow2 ... RobertHavlin 21 — 76+
(A G Foster) *chsd ldrs: rdn whn hmpd over 2f out: nt rcvr* **33/1**

200- **19** *hd* **Qalahari (IRE)**[262] [4422] 4-8-1 **85** ... AdrianMcCarthy 22 — 64
(D J Coakley) *a bhd* **66/1**

100- **20** *8* **Makaamen**[189] [6675] 4-8-11 **95** ... RichardHills 23 — 56+
(B W Hills) *hld up towards rr: effrt and nt clr run fr 3f out: eased whn no ch of rcvry over 1f out* **16/1**

01-3 **21** *¾* **Mull Of Killough (IRE)**[21] [1008] 4-8-12 **96** ... JamieSpencer 24 — 55+
(J L Spearing) *chsd ldrs on stands' rail: hmpd over 2f out: sn lost pl and nt rcvr* **13/2**[2]

105- **22** *17* **Desert Creek (IRE)**[266] [4296] 4-8-12 **96** ... RyanMoore 20 — 16
(Sir Michael Stoute) *hld up in midfield: wknd 3f out: sn bhd* **8/1**[3]

011- **23** *50* **Big Bay (USA)**[142] [7540] 4-8-8 **92** ... ShaneKelly 18 — —
(Jane Chapple-Hyam) *mid-div: wknd over 3f out: sn bhd: eased fnl 2f* **20/1**

1m 36.98s (-2.72) **Going Correction** -0.10s/f (Good) **23** Ran SP% **126.8**
Speed ratings (Par 109): **109,108,106,106,106 105,105,104,103,102 102,100,99,98,98 97,97,96,96,88 87,70,40**
toteswingers: 1&2 Not won, 1&3 Not won, 2&3 Not won CSF £1381.99 CT £55621.35 TOTE £49.80: £8.70, £13.40, £5.00, £3.00; EX 1590.90 TRIFECTA Not won..
Owner Seasons Holidays **Bred** Seasons Holidays **Trained** Beckhampton, Wilts
■ Stewards' Enquiry : Nicky Mackay three-day ban: careless riding (May 3-5)
Hayley Turner two-day ban: used whip with excessive frequency (May 3-4)

FOCUS
A big competitive field, but they raced in one large group and a rough race produced a number of hard-luck stories. It would be no surprise to see several in the line-up improve greatly on this in the coming weeks. The first three raced wide of the trouble and probably ordinary form for the grade.

NOTEBOOK
Brunston had run over as far as 1m4f last season, but he travelled well enough and the inevitable strong gallop eventually brought his stamina into play. Unlike many others, he enjoyed a clear passage and, just as he looked sure to be done by the runner-up, he found a bit more to prevail. An improver last year, he looks better than ever and connections have a wide variety of trips to choose from.
Marajaa(IRE) is another who looks all the better for a winter under his belt. Though he is on a challenging handicap mark these days, he gave the winner a real scare and can play a part in similar races if maintaining the good work. (tchd 100-1 in a place)
Oratory(IRE) raced only twice last season and had never previously been beyond 7f. However, he got 1m well, albeit not finishing off quite as well as the first two, and should make his mark this season if his trainer can keep him on track.
Cityscape ◆, unraced since finishing sore in last season's 2000 Guineas, made a promising return to action. Despite not getting an ideal run through, he finished best of all and this classy type will be an interesting contender next time out. (tchd 11-1)
Desert Kiss shot up the weights last year and has trained on well. Doing the donkey work at a good gallop in this company cannot have been easy, so she deserves plenty of credit.
Extraterrestrial, winner of this last year, was one of several who switched to the far side of the group in the last 2f in order to find a clear run. Though he managed only a brief effort, it was a creditable attempt from what looks a stiff mark these days. (op 20-1)
Dalradian(IRE) did best of those who suffered serious interference, staying on gamely after being boxed in from the 2f pole. He has never won on turf but this useful Polytrack performer is no slouch on grass. Official explanation: jockey said gelding was denied a clear run (op 16-1)
South Cape has become unreliable in the last two years, but he ended 2009 with a win and this was a decent seasonal debut in a hot race.
Wannabe King is on a much stiffer mark since a purple patch in August last year, and what chance he had was ended when he found himself boxed in for much of the last 3f. In the circumstances, he did well to get as close as he did with a spirited staying-on effort. (op 33-1)
Irish Heartbeat(IRE) had to switch to the far side to make sure of a run, but he was not as seriously hampered as many of his rivals and on the day he simply did not look good enough, though to be fair he did have to make up an immense amount of ground having been dropped out in last place. He should have done better despite his 4lb Spring Mile penalty, and his next race will reveal whether he will build on that win. (op 13-2 tchd 15-2)
Manassas(IRE) was among the worst sufferers in the scrimmaging, from which he was unable to recover. Official explanation: jockey said gelding was denied a clear run (op 8-1)
Qalahari(IRE) Official explanation: jockey said filly was denied a clear run
Makaamen was another who lost any chance he had in the scrimmaging towards the stands' rail. (tchd 18-1 in a place)
Mull Of Killough(IRE) was another hampered near the rail. Official explanation: jockey said gelding was unsuited by the good (good to firm in places) ground (op 7-1 tchd 6-1)
Desert Creek(IRE) Official explanation: jockey said colt ran too free
Big Bay(USA) Official explanation: jockey said colt stopped quickly

1384 DUBAI DUTY FREE STKS (REGISTERED AS THE FRED DARLING STAKES) (GROUP 3) (FILLIES) 7f (S)
3:05 (3:08) (Class 1) 3-Y-0

£36,900 (£13,988; £7,000; £3,490; £1,748; £877) Stalls Centre

Form — RPR

242- **1** **Puff (IRE)**[169] [7147] 3-9-0 107 ... JimCrowley 5 — 109
(R M Beckett) *hld up in tch: hdwy over 1f out: edgd lft ins fnl f: hrd drvn to take narrow ld fnl 100yds: drvn out* **7/1**[3]

120- **2** *nk* **Habaayib**[197] [6449] 3-9-0 107 ... RichardHills 1 — 108
(E A L Dunlop) *in tch: drvn and hdwy over 1f out: qcknd ins fnl f: chal and carried lft sn after: stl upsides fnl 50yds: nt pce of wnr cl home* **8/1**

113- **3** *1* **Lady Of The Desert (USA)**[197] [6449] 3-9-0 113 ... KierenFallon 2 — 105
(B J Meehan) *ponied to s: plld hrd and stdd in rr: pushed along and gd prog fr 2f out to ld over 1f out: edgd lft u.p ins fnl f: hdd fnl 100yds: wknd cl home* **13/8**[1]

102- **4** *½* **Misheer**[197] [6449] 3-9-0 110 ... NeilCallan 7 — 104
(C E Brittain) *plld hrd: led: rdn and hdd appr fnl f f: styd wl there tl wknd nr fin* **5/2**[2]

040- **5** *4* **Mistic Magic (IRE)**[175] [7033] 3-9-0 87 ... JamieSpencer 6 — 93
(P F I Cole) *in rr but in tch: drvn and hdwy to get in bhd ldrs fr 2f out: no ch w ldng quartet fnl f* **16/1**

51- **6** *nk* **Deirdre**[186] [6762] 3-9-0 78 ... WilliamBuick 4 — 93
(J H M Gosden) *chsd ldr: rdn over 2f out: wknd over 1f out* **11/1**

600- **7** *25* **Hairspray**[189] [6660] 3-9-0 91 ... AlanMunro 3 — 25
(M R Channon) *towards rr but in tch tl rdn 3f out: sn wknd* **33/1**

046- **8** *1 ¼* **Bahati (IRE)**[219] [5797] 3-9-0 83 ... TomQueally 8 — 22
(J G Portman) *chsd ldrs: rdn 3f out: hung lft and wknd sn after* **40/1**

1m 23.8s (-1.90) **Going Correction** -0.10s/f (Good) **8** Ran SP% **109.9**
Speed ratings (Par 105): **106,105,104,103,99 99,70,69**
toteswingers: 1&2 £4.90, 1&3 £3.50, 2&3 £3.90 CSF £56.16 TOTE £7.30: £1.80, £2.10, £1.40; EX 51.70 Trifecta £118.20 Pool: £952.36 - 5.96 winning units..
Owner Mr and Mrs David Aykroyd **Bred** Yeomanstown Stud **Trained** Whitsbury, Hants

FOCUS
It's questionable whether this race will have much bearing on the outcome of the 1,000 Guineas, featuring as it did a number of keen-going, sprint-bred fillies. What's more, no winner of this race has gone on to take the Guineas since Wince back in 1999. The winning time was over a second slower than the Greenham later on the card. The Cheveley Park form was well represented, with the second, third, fourth and last from the Newmarket Group 1 taking each other on again, and it was Puff, only fourth that day, who came out on top. The third and fourth here are rated to that form but not a race to rate too positively.

NOTEBOOK
Puff(IRE), representing a trainer who won this race in 2005, pulled too hard in the Cheveley Park and was plenty keen enough through the early part of this race, but Misheer gave her a nice tow through the race and she proved to have the most stamina of this lot at the finish. Her pedigree raises serious doubts about her staying the mile at Newmarket though, which is reflected in the fact that, despite this win, she remains available at 25-1 for the Guineas. (op 8-1)
Habaayib looked good in the first half of last season when successful at Royal Ascot in the Albany Stakes, but was beaten in the Cherry Hinton by Misheer when reportedly in season, and then failed to run her race in the Cheveley Park. She came here with a bit to prove, and connections will no doubt be encouraged by this performance. She was aided by being happier to settle than many of her rivals, but gives little sign that she wants to go further than this, and a drop back to sprinting wouldn't be a surprise. (tchd 9-1)
Lady Of The Desert(USA), whose trainer sent out subsequent Guineas third Super Sleuth to finish second in this race last year, looked the second-best filly in the Cheveley Park last season despite finishing only third, narrowly behind Misheer, and was sent off favourite to emulate her dam Queen's Logic, who won this race in 2002. Just like at Newmarket, though, she once again pulled too hard in the early stages, struggling to get cover. Despite quickening up well to challenge approaching the final furlong, she didn't see her race out, and the conclusion must be drawn that she is a sprinter in the making. She has the makings of a smart performer in that sphere, although connections are clinging to the hope that she might still get a mile and are keeping the French Guineas in mind. (tchd 7-4 and 15-8 in places)
Misheer, who won the Cherry Hinton and was second in the Cheveley Park last term, has a speedy pedigree and wouldn't settle in front. Racing far too keenly, she set the race up for those in behind and is another who will be much more effective when reverting to sprint distances. (op 9-4 tchd 15-8)
Mistic Magic(IRE), proven over this distance at two, settled better than most, which helped her put up a solid effort against much higher-rated opponents. Official explanation: jockey said filly had been struck into (op 28-1)
Deirdre, in contrast to most in the field, is bred to stay further than this; indeed, she could well require middle distances in time. She found these rivals too quick for her but there should be better to come from her as she hails from a family that improves with age. (op 8-1 tchd 12-1)
Hairspray, whose trainer had sent out the winner of this race in four of the previous eight years, was completely outclassed.

1385 BATHWICK TYRES GREENHAM STKS (GROUP 3) (C&G) 7f (S)
3:40 (3:40) (Class 1) 3-Y-0 £36,900 (£13,988; £7,000; £3,490; £1,748) Stalls Centre

Form — RPR

156- **1** **Dick Turpin (IRE)**[182] [6849] 3-9-0 112 ... RyanMoore 4 — 119
(R Hannon) *racd in 2nd: drvn and styd on whn ldr qcknd over 1f out: drvn and r.o strly ins fnl f to ld nr fin* **8/1**[3]

113- **2** *½* **Canford Cliffs (IRE)**[237] [5299] 3-9-0 118 ... RichardHughes 3 — 118
(R Hannon) *led: drvn and qcknd 3 l clr and edgd lft over 1f out: hung lft ins fnl f: hdd and no ex nr fin* **10/11**[1]

111- **3** *7* **Arcano (IRE)**[237] [5299] 3-9-0 118 ... RichardHills 1 — 99
(B J Meehan) *trckd ldrs: rdn along 2f out: sn no ch w ldng duo: kpt on for wl btn 3rd nr fin* **2/1**[2]

U04- **4** *¾* **Rodrigo De Torres**[183] [6811] 3-9-0 91 ... TomQueally 2 — 97
(H R A Cecil) *t.k.h: a in 4th pl: rdn over 2f out and jst in tch: sn btn and styd on same pce to cl on wl btn 3rd nr fin* **25/1**

1 **5** *3 ¾* **Bullwhip (IRE)**[20] 1029 3-9-0 0 .... WilliamBuick 5 87
(J H M Gosden) *s.i.s and a struggling in last pl: sme prog to get in tch 1/2-way: sn rdn and no ch* **10/1**

1m 22.72s (-2.98) **Going Correction** -0.10s/f (Good) **5** Ran SP% **109.8**
Speed ratings (Par 108): **113,112,104,103,99**
CSF £15.97 TOTE £7.30: £2.30, £1.40; EX 10.50.
Owner John Manley **Bred** John McEnery **Trained** East Everleigh, Wilts

FOCUS
No winner of this race has gone on to land the 2,000 Guineas since Wollow in 1976 but it looked a very informative trial on paper as not only did it feature a rematch between Prix Morny winner Arcano and third-placed Canford Cliffs, but the Dewhurst form was also represented by Dick Turpin, who finished sixth at Newmarket. The winning time was 1.08sec quicker than the Fred Darling earlier on the card but the form looks tricky to pin down.

NOTEBOOK
Dick Turpin(IRE) ran up a four-timer before being found out when stepped up both in class and distance on his final two starts last term. Tracking Canford Cliffs for most of this race, he couldn't match his stablemate's initial acceleration, but benefited when that one hung left, and he also showed the greater stamina to get up in the final yards. Although cut from 66-1 to a best price of 16-1 for the Guineas, his trainer, who was recording his fourth success in the race in the last nine years, said that he is more likely to go to the French and/or Irish Guineas, in order to keep him apart from Canford Cliffs. While there are some doubts about him getting a mile on pedigree, he ran through the line here and shapes like he will get the trip. His success gave a boost to supporters of Guineas hopes Beethoven, Fencing Master and Xtension, who all finished in front of him in the Dewhurst. (tchd 13-2)

Canford Cliffs(IRE) is acclaimed by Richard Hannon as the best horse he has ever trained, and that, more than the bare form of his 2-y-o performances, ensured he was sent off an odds-on favourite for this. For all that he was impressive in the Coventry Stakes, when beating subsequent Vintage Stakes winner and Dewhurst third Xtension by 6l, he had been turned over afterwards by Arcano in France, and although the very quick ground was blamed for that defeat, his price here had more to do with tales of brilliant home work with the likes of Paco Boy than anything substantial, especially considering there was a stamina question to answer. He broke well, was soon bowling along in front and set a really solid pace. Asked to quicken up 1½f out, he immediately pulled out a gap on his field but began to edge left, and then further left when hit with the whip. He ended up pretty near the far-side rail and was worn down close home by his stable companion, who raced much straighter. The pair finished well clear of the rest and look smart colts, but on this showing Canford Cliffs will be most effective this season when dropped back to sprint distances. Shunted out from 6-1 to 12-1 for the Guineas, he is still likely to take his chance at Newmarket, but looks an unlikely winner now. (op 4-5 tchd evens in places)

Arcano(IRE) went unbeaten in three starts at two and had 1000 Guineas favourite Special Duty and Canford Cliffs behind him when winning the Prix Morny last summer. His trainer had warned beforehand that the colt would need the run, and he ran like it, being easily seen off by the first two from 1½f out. Were he capable of winning the Guineas one would have expected more from him, though, and he will now miss a trip to Newmarket. It's too early to tell whether he's trained on, but he has a bit to prove now. (op 11-4 tchd 3-1 in places)

Rodrigo De Torres, who probably won't be wanting to go much further this season, has an official mark of 91 and faced a stiff task in this company. He ran about as well as one could expect. (op 22-1)

Bullwhip(IRE), a wide-margin winner of a 7f maiden at Doncaster last month, was taking a big step up in class and had quicker ground to deal with. Slowly away and taken off his feat somewhat, he was the first to be niggled along and eventually finished up well held. He is obviously better than this, but is likely to continue to prove difficult to place. (tchd 8-1)

1386 RACINGUK.COM MAIDEN STKS — 1m 3f 5y
4:15 (4:18) (Class 4) 3-Y-O — **£5,180** (£1,541; £770; £384) Stalls Low

Form — RPR

24- **1** **Tactician**[191] 6617 3-9-3 0 .... HayleyTurner 4 89
(M L W Bell) *plld hrd early: sn chsng ldrs rdn to ld appr fnl f: hung rt u.p ins fnl f: in command fnl 100yds: won gng away* **2/1**[2]

2 *1* **All Action (USA)** 3-9-3 0 .... TomQueally 7 87
(H R A Cecil) *hld up in rr: hdwy on outside over 2f out: styd on wl but immature fnl f: tk 2nd last strides* **7/2**[3]

3 *hd* **Momkinzain (USA)** 3-9-3 0 .... KierenFallon 6 87
(M R Channon) *chsd ldrs: rdn and styd on to chal 1f out: outpcd by wnr ins fnl f: lost 2nd last strides* **18/1**

62- **4** *3 ¼* **Total Command**[175] 7029 3-9-3 0 .... RyanMoore 3 81
(Sir Michael Stoute) *trckd ldr: slt advantage ins fnl 3f: drvn along over 2f out: narrowly hdd appr fnl f: wknd ins fnl f* **13/8**[1]

0- **5** *2 ½* **Idealism**[184] 6792 3-9-3 0 .... WilliamBuick 2 76
(J H M Gosden) *led: narrowly hdd ins fnl 3f: drvn and rallied to chal fr 2f out tl wknd appr fnl f* **16/1**

6- **6** *4* **Aalya (IRE)**[228] 5547 3-8-12 0 .... RichardHills 1 64
(J L Dunlop) *s.i.s: in rr: sme prog fr 3 out but nvr in contention: sn green and wknd* **16/1**

2- **7** *5* **Mighty Mambo**[144] 7502 3-9-3 0 .... ShaneKelly 5 65
(Jane Chapple-Hyam) *reluctant to load: in tch tl rdn and btn 3f out* **16/1**

2m 23.27s (2.07) **Going Correction** -0.10s/f (Good) **7** Ran SP% **116.6**
Speed ratings (Par 100): **88,87,87,84,82 80,76**
toteswingers: 1&2 £2.70, 1&3 £8.90, 2&3 £7.70 CSF £9.90 TOTE £3.40: £1.90, £2.60; EX 10.40.

Owner The Queen **Bred** The Queen **Trained** Newmarket, Suffolk

FOCUS
A maiden that has been won by some smart types over the past ten years, including Millenary, Gamut and Hala Bek, but this renewal didn't produce a winner that looks capable of matching their achievements. The form does not look that solid and is best rated around the winner and fifth.

1387 DUBAI INTERNATIONAL AIRPORT MAIDEN STKS (DIV II) — 1m (S)
4:50 (4:51) (Class 4) 3-Y-O — **£4,857** (£1,445; £722; £360) **Stalls** Centre

Form — RPR

2- **1** **Fair Trade**[183] 6810 3-9-3 .... JimmyFortune 11 89+
(D R C Elsworth) *hld up in tch: led ins fnl f: drvn out and jst hld runner-up* **15/8**[1]

2 *½* **Colour Scheme (IRE)** 3-9-3 .... JamieSpencer 8 86+
(B J Meehan) *hld up in rr: gd hdwy over 1f out: str run to press wnr nr fin: jst hld: promising* **40/1**

22- **3** *1 ¾* **Youm Jamil (USA)**[169] 7146 3-9-3 .... KierenFallon 9 82
(B J Meehan) *trckd ldrs: n.m.r and bmpd 4f out: swtchd lft 3f out: chal and hrd rdn over 1f out: one pce* **5/1**[2]

25- **4** *shd* **William Van Gogh**[183] 6810 3-9-3 .... WilliamBuick 7 82
(J H M Gosden) *led tl over 1f out: no ex fnl f* **13/2**[3]

3- **5** *½* **Udabaa (IRE)**[236] 5312 3-9-3 .... RichardHills 5 83+
(M P Tregoning) *prom: outpcd 2f out: kpt on again fnl f* **7/1**

6 *1 ½* **Eton Forever (IRE)** 3-9-3 .... NeilCallan 12 77
(M A Jarvis) *prom: led over 1f out tl wknd ins fnl f* **9/1**

7 *4* **Point North (IRE)** 3-9-3 .... FrankieDettori 10 69+
(J Noseda) *t.k.h towards rr: effrt over 2f out: no imp* **13/2**[3]

56- **8** *¾* **Primary Colors**[191] 6617 3-9-3 .... AdamKirby 3 66
(C G Cox) *in tch: rdn 3f out: wknd 2f out* **66/1**

9 *3* **Formulation (IRE)** 3-9-3 .... TravisBlock 2 60+
(H Morrison) *dwlt: towards rr: mod effrt over 2f out: n.d* **50/1**

03- **10** *shd* **Knockdolian (IRE)**[175] 7034 3-9-3 .... DaneO'Neill 1 59
(R Charlton) *s.i.s and wnt lft s: bhd: rdn 3f out: nvr nr ldrs* **33/1**

11 *3* **Motirani** 3-9-3 .... HayleyTurner 6 52
(M L W Bell) *dwlt: sn in midfield: wknd over 2f out* **25/1**

24- **12** *8* **Resuscitator (USA)**[219] 5807 3-9-3 .... FergusSweeney 4 34
(Mrs H S Main) *a towards rr: bhd fnl 3f* **33/1**

55 **13** *22* **Heliocentric**[35] 889 3-9-3 .... RichardHughes 13 —
(R Hannon) *racd alone on stands' rail: chsd ldrs: hrd rdn over 3f out: sn wknd* **33/1**

1m 38.01s (-1.69) **Going Correction** -0.10s/f (Good) **13** Ran SP% **119.2**
Speed ratings (Par 100): **104,103,101,101,101 99,95,94,91,91 88,80,58**
toteswingers: 1&2 £13.30, 1&3 £2.70, 2&3 £39.10 CSF £106.28 TOTE £2.70: £1.30, £8.80, £1.80; EX 88.50.
Owner Raymond Tooth **Bred** Highclere Stud **Trained** Newmarket, Suffolk

FOCUS
A decent-looking maiden containing several runners who had shown promise in limited appearances last season, so one can expect a number of future winners to come out of this race. The form looks sound rated around the third and fourth.

1388 DUBAI DUTY FREE MILLENNIUM MILLIONAIRE H'CAP — 1m 2f 6y
5:20 (5:20) (Class 4) (0-85,85) 4-Y-O+ — **£5,180** (£1,541; £770; £384) **Stalls** Low

Form — RPR

/10- **1** **Forte Dei Marmi**[308] 2925 4-9-0 **81** .... KierenFallon 6 96+
(L M Cumani) *in tch: hdwy 3f out: drvn to ld ins fnl 2f: c clr and edgd lft jst ins fnl f: easily* **10/3**[1]

60-0 **2** *3 ½* **Elliptical (USA)**[14] 1088 4-9-3 **84** .... FrankieDettori 1 89
(G A Butler) *led: pushed along ins fnl 3f: hdd ins fnl 2f: no ch w wnner fr over 1f out but hld on wl for 2nd* **6/1**[3]

/12- **3** *1* **Foxhaven**[178] 6936 8-9-1 **82** .... JimCrowley 15 85
(P R Chamings) *mid-div: hdwy over 2f out: rdn: styd on and hung lft fnl f: kpt on cl home* **11/2**[2]

110- **4** *¾* **Potentiale (IRE)**[196] 6470 6-8-11 **81** .... PatrickHills[(3)] 16 83
(J W Hills) *in rr: pushed along and hdwy fr 2f out: styd on fnl f but nvr gng pce to rch ldrs* **16/1**

215- **5** *½* **Feathered Crown (FR)**[181] 6875 4-8-8 **75** .... TomQueally 3 76
(H R A Cecil) *t.k.h: sn trcking ldrs: drvn fr over 2f out: wknd ins fnl f* **9/1**

143- **6** *1 ½* **Putra One (IRE)**[192] 6583 4-8-12 **79** .... NeilCallan 10 77
(M A Jarvis) *chsd ldrs: rdn over 2f out: wknd fnl f* **8/1**

056- **7** *nk* **Resurge (IRE)**[173] 7066 5-8-13 **80** .... FergusSweeney 7 77
(W S Kittow) *chsd ldrs: rdn 3f out: wkd appr fnl f* **10/1**

8 *1 ¾* **Monte Cavallo (SAF)**[342] 5-8-13 **85** .... TobyAtkinson[(5)] 8 78
(M Wigham) *towards rr but in tch: rdn and sme prog fr over 2f out: nvr in contention* **33/1**

10-0 **9** *nk* **Mr Udagawa**[26] 966 4-8-5 **72** .... DavidProbert 13 65
(B J Llewellyn) *in rr: sme prog u.p fr 3f out to get in bhd ldrs 2f out: sn wknd* **40/1**

210- **10** *1* **Silverglas (IRE)**[187] 6740 4-8-9 **76** .... RichardHughes 9 67
(M P Tregoning) *stdd s: in rr: sme hdwy on ins fr 3f out: nvr rchd ldrs and wknd appr fnl f* **7/1**

260- **11** *¾* **Princely Hero (IRE)**[18] 6059 6-8-13 **80** .... HayleyTurner 5 69
(C Gordon) *chsd ldr to 3f out: sn rdn: wknd appr fnl 2f* **20/1**

143- **12** *hd* **North Cape (USA)**[236] 5315 4-8-3 **77** ow3 .... AmyScott[(7)] 12 66
(H Candy) *in rr: sme progres on outside fr 3f out: nvr in contention and sn wknd* **8/1**

2m 6.41s (-2.39) **Going Correction** -0.10s/f (Good) **12** Ran SP% **122.6**
Speed ratings (Par 105): **105,102,101,100,100 99,98,97,97,96 95,95**
toteswingers:1&2:£5.80, 1&3:£2.30, 2&3:£9.70 CSF £23.18 CT £111.22 TOTE £4.10: £1.90, £2.60, £2.40; EX 24.40 Place 6 £268.64, Place 5 £100.99.
Owner Fittocks Stud **Bred** Fittocks Stud **Trained** Newmarket, Suffolk

FOCUS
Probably not the strongest of handicaps, but it was won in impressive fashion by a lightly raced 4-y-o on the up. The level appears sound rated around the placed horses.
Silverglas(IRE) Official explanation: jockey said gelding hung right-handed
T/Plt: £260.70 to a £1 stake. Pool: £95,887.44. 268.47 winning tickets. T/Qpdt: £67.10 to a £1 stake. Pool: £5,297.77. 58.40 winning tickets. ST

1172 NOTTINGHAM (L-H)
Saturday, April 17

OFFICIAL GOING: Good to firm (8.3)
All races on inner course. Rail moved out 2yds from the turn out of the dog leg on the back straight and on the home bend.
Wind: Nil Weather: Fine and sunny

1389 DG TAXIS FIRST PAST POST MAIDEN STKS — 5f 13y
5:00 (5:00) (Class 5) 2-Y-O — **£2,590** (£770; £385; £192) **Stalls** High

Form — RPR

1 **My Son Max** 2-9-3 0 .... PatDobbs 9 86+
(R Hannon) *s.i.s: sn prom: rdn to chse ldr fnl f: r.o to ld nr fin* **5/2**[2]

4 **2** *¾* **Diamond Geezah (IRE)**[21] 1009 2-9-3 0 .... MichaelHills 2 83+
(B W Hills) *chsd ldrs: led over 1f out: sn rdn: hdd nr fin* **1/1**[1]

02 **3** *6* **Sir Lunchalott**[7] 1223 2-9-3 0 .... (p) LiamKeniry 6 59
(J S Moore) *chsd ldrs: rdn and ev ch over 1f out: wknd ins fnl f* **16/1**

4 *nse* **Boundaries** 2-9-3 0 .... GrahamGibbons 1 59
(T D Easterby) *s.i.s and wnt lft s: hdwy over 3f out: rdn and hung rt over 1f out: styd on same pce* **40/1**

20 **5** *½* **Beach Patrol (IRE)**[11] 1136 2-9-3 0 .... EddieCreighton 8 57
(M R Channon) *prom: racd keenly: rdn over 1f out: wknd fnl f* **18/1**

6 *2 ¼* **Rational Act (IRE)** 2-9-0 0 .... KellyHarrison[(3)] 10 48
(T D Easterby) *prom: outpcd over 3f out: hung lft over 1f out: n.d after* **100/1**

7 *1 ½* **Rowan Spirit (IRE)** 2-9-3 0 .... RichardKingscote 7 42
(Tom Dascombe) *w ldr tl led 1/2-way: rdn and hdd over 1f out: wknd fnl f* **16/1**

6 **8** *1 ¾* **Barista (IRE)**[17] 1066 2-9-3 0 .... SebSanders 11 35
(A J McCabe) *led to 1/2-way: rdn and wknd over 1f out* **40/1**

9 *1 ¼* **Colorado Gold** 2-9-3 0 .... StevieDonohoe 5 30
(P F I Cole) *dwlt: sn outpcd: hung lft 1/2-way: eased over 1f out* **7/1**[3]

10 *15* **Capall Dorcha** 2-9-3 0 .... JerryO'Dwyer 3 —
(J R Holt) *s.i.s: sn outpcd* **100/1**

11 *10* **For That Reason (IRE)** 2-9-0 0........................(b[1]) WilliamCarson(3) 4 —
(M G Quinlan) *chsd ldrs tl wknd 2f out* **66/1**

62.15 secs (1.15) **Going Correction** -0.025s/f (Good) **11** Ran SP% **116.5**
Speed ratings (Par 92): **89,87,78,78,77 73,71,68,66,42 26**
toteswingers: 1&2 £1.60, 1&3 £6.50, 2&3 £3.80 CSF £5.16 TOTE £3.90: £1.10, £1.20, £2.90; EX 7.00.
Owner Dougie McKay **Bred** Mrs Fiona Denniff **Trained** East Everleigh, Wilts

FOCUS
An ordinary juvenile maiden. The first pair can rate higher.

NOTEBOOK
My Son Max, from a stable with a remarkable 2-y-o strike-rate this season, was at £31,000 the most expensive sales purchase in the line-up. Not the fastest away, he was nevertheless always travelling sweetly and, asked to make his challenge well inside the final furlong, quickened up nicely. Out of a mare who stayed 7f well, he looks sure to improve when stepped up in trip. (tchd 7-2 in places)
Diamond Geezah(IRE), fourth in the Brocklesby at Doncaster, had been sent off joint-favourite on that occasion and was a well-backed market leader here. That Town Moor form has taken a few knocks, however, and although he showed good pace when asked to go about his business approaching the final furlong, he was never able to establish a decisive advantage and was caught close home. (tchd 11-8 and 6-4 in places)
Sir Lunchalott, inexpensively bought and well behind Diamond Geezah in the Brocklesby, had fared much better when runner-up on his second outing and was not disgraced here, despite finishing a long way adrift of the first two. He showed a fair amount of toe, chasing the pace from the start, but was unable to sustain the gallop all the way to the line. (op 14-1 tchd 12-1)
Boundaries was a late May foal and did not cost a king's ransom but his stable has made a fair start to the season and he showed promise. This form does not entitle him to win a maiden event in the near future, but he seems likely to improve and notch a success somewhere along the line. (op 66-1)
Beach Patrol(IRE), runner-up on his debut at Kempton, then took a marked step backwards when switched to turf for his second start and his run here was more in keeping with that second outing than with the first. He now has something to prove. (op 16-1 tchd 14-1)

1390 DG TAXIS GET YOU HOME SAFELY FILLIES' H'CAP 5f 13y
5:30 (5:30) (Class 5) (0-70,68) 3-Y-O **£2,590** (£770; £385; £192) **Stalls** High

Form RPR
60-2 **1** **Rio Mist**[16] 1075 3-8-13 **63**........................ PatDobbs 1 75
(R Hannon) *chsd ldrs: led over 1f out: sn rdn and edgd rt: r.o wl* **13/2**[3]
000- **2** *3* **Saucy Girl (IRE)**[201] 6345 3-8-3 **56**........................ KellyHarrison(3) 4 57
(T D Easterby) *chsd ldrs: rdn and ev ch over 1f out: styd on same pce* **7/1**
1222 **3** *1 ¾* **Boogie Waltzer**[10] 1175 3-8-8 **65**........................ RyanClark(7) 9 60+
(S C Williams) *s.i.s: hdwy 1/2-way: rdn and n.m.r over 1f out: styd on* **9/2**[2]
26-1 **4** *¾* **Liberty Lady (IRE)**[31] 906 3-9-4 **68**........................ MichaelHills 10 60
(D Donovan) *led: rdn and hdd over 1f out: no ex ins fnl f* **10/3**[1]
5542 **5** *1* **Val C**[29] 936 3-8-12 **62**........................ SebSanders 6 51
(M Botti) *chsd ldrs: rdn and ev ch over 1f out: wknd ins fnl f* **10/3**[1]
504- **6** *3 ¾* **Southwark Newshawk**[157] 7331 3-8-5 **55**........................ SaleemGolam 8 30
(Mrs C A Dunnett) *chsd ldrs: rdn 1/2-way: sn lost pl* **40/1**
2163 **7** *½* **Exceed Power**[11] 1140 3-8-8 **61**........................ AhmedAjtebi(3) 5 34
(D M Simcock) *s.i.s: pushed along thrght: nvr on terms* **7/1**
510- **8** *3* **Existentialist**[194] 6541 3-9-4 **68**........................ StevieDonohoe 7 31
(A E Price) *chsd ldrs tl rdn and wknd over 1f out* **20/1**

60.78 secs (-0.22) **Going Correction** -0.025s/f (Good) **8** Ran SP% **109.9**
Speed ratings (Par 95): **100,95,92,91,89 83,82,78**
toteswingers: 1&2 £10.80, 1&3 £6.60, 2&3 £7.70 CSF £46.84 CT £210.93 TOTE £9.80: £2.20, £2.30, £1.90; EX 48.40.
Owner The Early Bath Partnership **Bred** Mount Coote Stud **Trained** East Everleigh, Wilts

FOCUS
A moderate sprint rated around the runner-up to her 2-y-o form.

1391 DG TAXIS FOR SPEED AND COMFORT H'CAP 5f 13y
6:00 (6:02) (Class 6) (0-65,64) 4-Y-O+ **£2,047** (£604; £302) **Stalls** High

Form RPR
6-10 **1** **Ridley Didley (IRE)**[45] 778 5-8-11 **60**........................ AshleyHamblett(3) 14 72
(N Wilson) *mde all: rdn and hung lft fr over 1f out: styd on* **12/1**
031 **2** *1 ¼* **Wreningham**[12] 1131 5-8-9 **58**........................ WilliamCarson(3) 6 66
(S C Williams) *chsd wnr: rdn and nt clr run over 1f out: hung lft ins fnl f: r.o* **9/2**[1]
5006 **3** *1 ¼* **Meikle Barfil**[7] 1234 8-8-4 **50**........................(bt) LukeMorris 10 53
(J M Bradley) *a.p: rdn over 1f out: styd on* **50/1**
0623 **4** *½* **Fashion Icon (USA)**[10] 1154 4-8-2 **51**........................ AhmedAjtebi(3) 3 52
(J Hetherton) *racd far side tl wnt centre 1/2-way: chsd ldrs: rdn over 1f out: styd on same pce fnl f* **12/1**
050- **5** *nk* **Desert Strike**[157] 7329 4-8-7 **60**........................ DuilioDaSilva(7) 9 60+
(P F I Cole) *hmpd s: hld up: plld hrd: nt clr run 2f out: swtchd rt: r.o ins fnl f: hung lft towards fin: nt rch ldrs* **12/1**
000- **6** *hd* **Braille**[256] 4620 5-9-0 **60**........................ GrahamGibbons 7 59
(T D Walford) *hld up in tch: rdn over 1f out: styd on u.p* **20/1**
414- **7** *½* **Rainy Night**[183] 6825 4-9-4 **64**........................ LiamKeniry 4 62+
(R Hollinshead) *mid-div: swtchd lft and hdwy over 1f out: nt trble ldrs* **16/1**
363- **8** *¾* **First Blade**[172] 7081 4-9-3 **63**........................(b) AmirQuinn 16 58+
(S R Bowring) *s.s: outpcd: hdwy and nt clr run over 1f out: r.o: nt trble ldrs* **15/2**[3]
000- **9** *½* **Divine Spirit**[172] 7081 9-9-2 **62**........................ PaulMulrennan 5 55
(M Dods) *chsd ldrs: rdn over 1f out: wknd fnl f* **28/1**
0-00 **10** *½* **Commander Wish**[37] 866 7-8-5 **51**........................(p) LiamJones 17 42
(Lucinda Featherstone) *stmbld and swvd lft s: bhd: r.o wl towards fin: nvr nrr* **18/1**
24-3 **11** *2* **Comptonspirit**[12] 1112 6-8-13 **59**........................ J-PGuillambert 12 43
(B P J Baugh) *s.i.s: sn prom: rdn over 1f out: wknd fnl f* **17/2**
0145 **12** *1 ½* **Peopleton Brook**[73] 391 8-8-13 **59**........................(t) SteveDrowne 11 38+
(B G Powell) *sn pushed along in rr: no ch whn hmpd 2f out* **22/1**
6063 **13** *1 ½* **Diddums**[12] 1131 4-9-0 **60**........................(b) SebSanders 2 33
(P S McEntee) *racd far side tl moved centre 1/2-way: in tch: rdn 2f out: sn wknd* **16/1**
5-50 **14** *nk* **Exceedingly Good (IRE)**[31] 912 4-8-5 **54**........................ KellyHarrison(3) 8 26
(S R Bowring) *chsd ldrs: rdn and hung lft over 1f out: wknd and eased fnl f* **40/1**
243- **15** *nse* **Mata Hari Blue**[230] 5477 4-9-2 **62**........................ JerryO'Dwyer 13 34
(J R Holt) *prom: rdn 2f out: wknd over 1f out* **16/1**
03-0 **16** *3 ¾* **Russian Rocket (IRE)**[12] 1131 8-9-0 **60**........................ TomMcLaughlin 15 19
(Mrs C A Dunnett) *mid-div: sn pushed along: sme hdwy over 2f out: wknd over 1f out* **13/2**[2]
61-6 **R** **Greek Secret**[95] 132 7-8-10 **56**........................(b) EddieCreighton 1 —
(J O'Reilly) *rrd s and ref to r: tk no part* **25/1**

60.67 secs (-0.33) **Going Correction** -0.025s/f (Good) **17** Ran SP% **120.6**
Speed ratings (Par 101): **101,99,97,96,95 95,94,93,92,91 88,86,83,83,83 77,—**
toteswingers: 1&2 £20.80, 1&3 £199.20, 2&3 £76.60 CSF £58.59 CT £2726.75 TOTE £14.60: £2.80, £1.80, £12.30, £3.80; EX 82.20.
Owner Feenan & Tobin **Bred** Peter Molony **Trained** Sandhutton, N Yorks

FOCUS
An ordinary sprint rated around the runner-up, third and fourth.
Commander Wish Official explanation: jockey said gelding stumbled leaving stalls

1392 DG TAXIS SAFE BET H'CAP 1m 75y
6:35 (6:36) (Class 6) (0-65,65) 3-Y-O **£2,047** (£604; £302) **Stalls** Centre

Form RPR
000- **1** **Our Boy Barrington (IRE)**[248] 4908 3-9-4 **65**........................ PatDobbs 9 70
(R Hannon) *chsd ldrs: rdn over 1f out: r.o to ld wl ins fnl f* **11/1**
066 **2** *2* **Mack's Sister**[29] 930 3-8-13 **60**........................ RobertHavlin 10 60
(D K Ivory) *led 1f: led again over 6f out: hdd over 2f out: rdn and ev ch fr over 1f out tl no ex wl ins fnl f* **14/1**
0562 **3** *nk* **Chateau Zara**[10] 1178 3-8-8 **62**........................ JohnFahy(7) 8 61
(C G Cox) *led over 7f out: hdd over 6f out: led again over 2f out: rdn over 1f out: hdd wl ins fnl f* **11/2**[2]
066- **4** *½* **Goldtrek (USA)**[134] 7622 3-9-1 **62**........................ SteveDrowne 6 60
(R Charlton) *chsd ldrs: rdn and hung lft fr over 1f out: r.o* **8/1**
006- **5** *¾* **Mr Maximas**[201] 6331 3-8-7 **54**........................ LukeMorris 16 50
(B Palling) *hld up: rdn over 3f out: hdwy over 2f out: edgd lft over 1f out: r.o: eased whn nt clr run cl home* **40/1**
023- **6** *1* **Brigadoon**[133] 7637 3-8-10 **64**........................ Mary-AnnParkin(7) 4 58+
(W Jarvis) *dwlt: hld up: r.o ins fnl f: nvr nrr* **7/1**[3]
436- **7** *1* **Green Community (USA)**[215] 5935 3-9-3 **64**........................ LiamKeniry 5 56
(E F Vaughan) *hld up in tch: hmpd over 6f out: rdn over 2f out: styd on same pce fr over 1f out* **17/2**
660- **8** *nk* **Bring Sweets (IRE)**[173] 7055 3-8-4 **51** oh5........................ FranciscoDaSilva 13 42
(B Ellison) *hld up: hdwy over 3f out: outpcd over 2f out: styd on fnl f* **33/1**
055 **9** *1 ¼* **Spirited Lady (IRE)**[30] 922 3-8-13 **60**........................ PaulMulrennan 1 48
(R A Fahey) *mid-div: hdwy 1/2-way: rdn and wknd over 1f out* **12/1**
310- **10** *¾* **Dutiful**[132] 7654 3-9-1 **62**........................ AlanMunro 11 49
(M R Channon) *hld up: rdn over 2f out: nvr trbld ldrs* **12/1**
5-33 **11** *¾* **Tilsworth Glenboy**[10] 1178 3-9-4 **65**........................ TedDurcan 2 50+
(J R Jenkins) *s.i.s and n.m.r sn after s: hld up: nt clr run fr over 3f out: nvr trbld ldrs* **7/2**[1]
000- **12** *6* **Ellies Image**[218] 5839 3-8-4 **51** oh6........................ LiamJones 14 22
(B P J Baugh) *hld up: rdn over 3f out: nvr on terms* **66/1**
060- **13** *4 ½* **Antoella (IRE)**[179] 6912 3-8-2 **56**........................ AlexEdwards(7) 15 17
(Ian Williams) *hld up: rdn over 2f out: a in rr* **40/1**
0-45 **14** *2 ¾* **Cross The Boss (IRE)**[75] 374 3-8-11 **58**........................(t) J-PGuillambert 3 12
(B M R Haslam) *plld hrd and prom: swtchd rt over 6f out: rdn over 2f out: wknd over 1f out* **25/1**

1m 47.83s (-1.77) **Going Correction** -0.30s/f (Firm) **14** Ran SP% **115.3**
Speed ratings (Par 96): **96,94,93,93,92 91,90,90,88,88 87,81,76,74**
toteswingers: 1&2 £24.00, 1&3 £8.50, 2&3 £38.20 CSF £142.77 CT £940.43 TOTE £14.40: £4.40, £6.10, £2.50; EX 247.00.
Owner Mrs J Wood **Bred** Dr Myles Sweeney **Trained** East Everleigh, Wilts

FOCUS
A moderate 3-y-o handicap rated around the front four.
Our Boy Barrington(IRE) Official explanation: trainer's rep said, regarding apparent improvement in form, that the colt was a big weak 2yo who matured over the winter.
Spirited Lady(IRE) Official explanation: jockey said filly jumped right leaving stalls
Tilsworth Glenboy Official explanation: jockey said colt was denied a clear run
Cross The Boss(IRE) Official explanation: jockey said gelding ran too free

1393 DG TAXIS NOTTINGHAM'S MOST RELIABLE MEDIAN AUCTION MAIDEN STKS 1m 2f 50y
7:10 (7:11) (Class 6) 3-Y-O **£2,047** (£604; £302) **Stalls** Low

Form RPR
025- **1** **Flying Destination**[199] 6373 3-9-3 73........................ ShaneKelly 2 72
(W J Knight) *chsd ldr: rdn to ld and edgd rt fr over 1f out: r.o* **3/1**[2]
523- **2** *1 ¼* **Royal Etiquette (IRE)**[154] 7400 3-9-3 76........................ SteveDrowne 5 70
(H J L Dunlop) *chsd ldrs: swtchd rt over 3f out: rdn and hung lft fnl 2f: chsd wnr ins fnl f: styd on* **5/2**[1]
65- **3** *1* **First Fandango**[175] 7034 3-9-3 0........................ SebSanders 8 68+
(J W Hills) *hld up: hdwy over 2f out: rdn over 1f out: r.o* **9/2**[3]
02- **4** *nk* **Tiger Star**[122] 7763 3-9-3 0........................ LukeMorris 6 67
(J M P Eustace) *hld up: hdwy 1/2-way: rdn over 2f out: hung lft over 1f out: r.o* **9/2**[3]
0- **5** *4 ½* **Belgooree**[134] 7630 3-8-12 0........................ PaulMulrennan 12 53
(J G Given) *led: rdn and hdd over 1f out: wknd ins fnl f* **33/1**
000- **6** *1 ¾* **Polebrook**[186] 6754 3-8-10 45........................ DannyBrock(7) 11 54?
(J R Jenkins) *chsd ldrs: rdn over 2f out: wknd over 1f out* **150/1**
0- **7** *½* **Annelko**[178] 6931 3-9-3 0........................ RobertHavlin 3 53
(A B Haynes) *mid-div: hdwy 6f out: rdn and wknd over 2f out* **40/1**
0 **8** *2 ½* **Two Certainties**[12] 1132 3-9-0 0........................ WilliamCarson(3) 4 48
(S C Williams) *hld up: plld hrd: nvr on terms* **33/1**
60- **9** *½* **Free Grain**[168] 7182 3-8-12 0........................ TedDurcan 7 42
(J L Dunlop) *hld up in tch: rdn and wknd over 2f out* **8/1**
00- **10** *2* **Pleasant Way (IRE)**[167] 7199 3-8-12 0........................ SaleemGolam 10 38
(D R Lanigan) *s.i.s: hld up: wknd wl over 2f out* **25/1**
11 *6* **Southwark Newsman** 3-9-3 0........................ TomMcLaughlin 9 31
(Mrs C A Dunnett) *s.s: nvr out of last pl: lost tch fr over 3f out* **125/1**

2m 16.12s (1.82) **Going Correction** -0.30s/f (Firm) **11** Ran SP% **114.7**
Speed ratings (Par 96): **80,79,78,77,74 72,72,70,70,68 63**
toteswingers: 1&2 £3.20, 1&3 £2.30, 2&3 £3.70 CSF £10.13 TOTE £4.00: £1.10, £1.30, £2.10; EX 8.80.
Owner The Pheasant Rew Partnership **Bred** Biddestone Stud **Trained** Patching, W Sussex

FOCUS
A weak maiden and rather dubious form.

1394 DG TAXIS WINNING FORECAST H'CAP 1m 2f 50y
7:40 (7:44) (Class 6) (0-60,60) 3-Y-O **£2,047** (£604; £302) **Stalls** Low

Form RPR
3252 **1** **Captain Cool (IRE)**[5] 1264 3-8-13 **55**........................ PatDobbs 16 59
(R Hannon) *hld up: hdwy to ld over 7f out: rdn over 1f out: styd on* **7/2**[1]
-245 **2** *1 ¼* **Magic Millie (IRE)**[3] 1298 3-8-10 **52**........................ PaulMulrennan 6 54
(J Hetherton) *chsd ldrs: rdn over 1f out: r.o* **11/1**
6-40 **3** *nse* **Spice Fair**[46] 762 3-8-13 **60**........................ LeeNewnes(5) 14 62
(M D I Usher) *hld up: hdwy over 2f out: rdn over 1f out: edgd lft: r.o* **40/1**

0-04 **4** ½ **Nurai**[45] 775 3-8-13 **55** .... TonyCulhane 11 56
(P W D'Arcy) *hld up: hdwy over 2f out: rdn over 1f out: r.o* **7/1**[2]

65-1 **5** 3 ¼ **Destiny's Dancer**[22] 998 3-8-4 **51** .... PatrickDonaghy(5) 5 46
(B M R Haslam) *led: hdd over 7f out: chsd wnr tl rdn over 1f out: no ex ins fnl f* **7/1**[2]

-000 **6** 1 ½ **Tallawalla (IRE)**[10] 1158 3-9-2 **58** .... AlanMunro 10 50
(M R Channon) *mid-div: hdwy over 3f out: rdn over 1f out: wknd ins fnl f* **8/1**[3]

0-22 **7** 1 **Buzz Bird**[60] 574 3-8-9 **51** .... FrannyNorton 1 41
(T D Barron) *prom: rdn over 3f out: wknd over 1f out* **10/1**

046- **8** 4 **French Seventyfive**[255] 4652 3-9-4 **60** .... GrahamGibbons 2 42
(T D Walford) *hld up: pushed along 6f out: hdwy u.p over 2f out: wknd over 1f out* **20/1**

000- **9** 3 ¼ **Albeed**[176] 6992 3-9-4 **60** .... TadhgO'Shea 9 36
(J L Dunlop) *chsd ldrs: rdn over 2f out: wknd over 1f out* **8/1**[3]

50-0 **10** 1 **Princess Lexi (IRE)**[29] 936 3-8-8 **50** .... SteveDrowne 12 24
(K A Ryan) *hld up: rdn over 3f out: nvr on terms* **20/1**

000- **11** 1 ¾ **Mr Mohican (IRE)**[182] 6842 3-8-12 **54** .... JackMitchell 13 25
(Mrs A Duffield) *hld up: a in rr* **14/1**

0324 **12** 2 ¾ **Clayton Flick (IRE)**[53] 670 3-9-0 **56** .... RobertHavlin 3 22
(A B Haynes) *s.i.s: hdwy over 8f out: rdn and wknd over 2f out* **33/1**

000- **13** 7 **Set To Go**[164] 7235 3-9-1 **57** .... SebSanders 7 10
(H J L Dunlop) *mid-div: lost pl 1/2-way: bhd fnl 4f* **40/1**

504- **14** 3 ¼ **Gold Story**[226] 5595 3-8-8 **50** .... RoystonFfrench 8 —
(B Ellison) *chsd ldrs tl rdn and wknd over 2f out* **11/1**

2m 14.31s (0.01) **Going Correction** -0.30s/f (Firm) **14** Ran SP% **119.2**
Speed ratings (Par 96): **87,86,85,85,82 81,80,77,75,74 72,70,65,62**
toteswingers: 1&2 £7.20, 1&3 £40.70, 2&3 £144.40 CSF £39.62 CT £1316.29 TOTE £3.40: £2.00, £3.60, £10.10; EX 28.10 Place 6 £115.21, Place 5 £94.37.
Owner Mrs John Lee **Bred** Jan Revs **Trained** East Everleigh, Wilts

FOCUS
An open handicap. Ordinary but sound form with the first four clear.
Mr Mohican(IRE) Official explanation: jockey said gelding hung left
T/Plt: £65.20 to a £1 stake. Pool: £32,799.03. 367.19 winning tickets. T/Qpdt: £32.90 to a £1 stake. Pool £4,139.52. 93.10 winning tickets. CR

1359 THIRSK (L-H)
Saturday, April 17

OFFICIAL GOING: Good to firm (9.4)
Wind: Light, half behind Weather: Fine and sunny

1395 SALTERSGATE H'CAP (DIV I) 1m
1:55 (1:55) (Class 5) (0-70,72) 4-Y-0+ **£3,950** (£1,175; £587; £293) **Stalls** Low

Form RPR

-203 **1** **Fujin Dancer (FR)**[7] 1241 5-8-7 **64** ....(p) AmyRyan(5) 12 80
(K A Ryan) *swtchd lft s: hld up in rr: hdwy on inner over 3f out: led 2f out: rdn and styd on strly* **9/1**

1221 **2** 3 **Sir George (IRE)**[10] 1149 5-9-3 **72** .... BarryMcHugh(3) 2 84+
(Ollie Pears) *hld up towards rr: hdwy over 3f out: nt clr run over 2f out: swtchd lft: r.o to take 2nd last 75yds* **7/2**[1]

414- **3** 1 ¾ **French Art**[129] 7693 5-9-1 **67** .... AndrewElliott 11 72
(N Tinkler) *in rr-div: hdwy on ins over 2f out: edgd rt and kpt on fnl f* **14/1**

424- **4** 2 **Evening Sunset (GER)**[43] 6784 4-9-0 **66** .... JerryO'Dwyer 1 66
(M G Quinlan) *t.k.h in rr: hdwy on outside over 2f out: kpt on: nt rch ldrs* **10/1**

5-23 **5** 1 ¾ **Ansells Pride (IRE)**[8] 1202 7-9-4 **70** .... TomEaves 8 66
(B Smart) *chsd ldrs: one pce fnl f* **9/2**[2]

-050 **6** 4 ½ **Ninth House (USA)**[26] 966 8-8-12 **64** ....(t) SilvestreDeSousa 10 50
(Mrs R A Carr) *towards rr: hdwy and swtchd rt over 1f out: nvr nr ldrs* **12/1**

5-40 **7** 1 **Dream Win**[74] 378 4-8-0 **57** .... PaulPickard(5) 3 41
(B Ellison) *dwlt: in last: sme hdwy over 2f out: nvr a factor* **25/1**

-004 **8** 2 ½ **Street Devil (USA)**[31] 908 5-8-11 **63** ....(p) GregFairley 15 41
(R Curtis) *w ldrs: led 3f out: hung bdly lft and hdd 2f out: sn wknd* **14/1**

2326 **9** 4 **Seldom (IRE)**[36] 873 4-8-13 **65** .... RobertWinston 5 34
(M Brittain) *prom: effrt over 2f out: sn wknd* **12/1**

223- **10** 1 ¼ **Northside Prince (IRE)**[222] 5731 4-9-2 **68** .... PJMcDonald 13 34
(G A Swinbank) *prom: lost pl over 2f out* **16/1**

3400 **11** 2 ¾ **Maximus Aurelius (IRE)**[37] 868 5-8-9 **61** ....(t) LukeMorris 9 21
(J Jay) *led after 1f: hdd 3f out: edgd rt and lost pl 2f out* **14/1**

444- **12** 1 **Templetuohy Max (IRE)**[196] 6490 5-9-2 **68** ....(v) DarryllHolland 14 25
(J D Bethell) *led 1f: w ldrs: hmpd 2f out: sn wknd* **17/2**[3]

1m 38.18s (-1.92) **Going Correction** -0.15s/f (Firm) **12** Ran SP% **119.8**
Speed ratings (Par 103): **103,100,98,96,94 90,89,86,82,81 78,77**
toteswingers: 1&2 £22.30, 1&3 £33.90, 2&3 £2.50 CSF £40.89 CT £457.41 TOTE £9.10: £2.70, £1.40, £5.80; EX 45.70.
Owner John Duddy **Bred** Loughtown Stud Ltd **Trained** Hambleton, N Yorks

FOCUS
A modest handicap run at a decent early pace, but the leaders may have gone off too quick as the trio who made it dropped right out while the first four home came from well back. The winner is rated back to his best and the form could be worth more than rated.

1396 SALTERSGATE H'CAP (DIV II) 1m
2:25 (2:25) (Class 5) (0-70,71) 4-Y-0+ **£3,950** (£1,175; £587; £293) **Stalls** Low

Form RPR

005- **1** **King Of The Moors (USA)**[121] 7783 7-9-2 **68** ....(p) FrannyNorton 4 76
(R C Guest) *mid-div: swtchd lft over 2f out: hdwy on inner to ld over 1f out: edgd rt: jst hld on* **25/1**

03-5 **2** ½ **Whipma Whopma Gate (IRE)**[3] 1293 5-7-11 **56** oh1..(b) NeilFarley(7) 3 62
(D Carroll) *t.k.h towards rr: gd hdwy on outer over 2f out: upsides and hung lft over 1f out: styd on wl ins fnl f: jst hld* **9/1**

1340 **3** 1 ½ **Ella Woodcock (IRE)**[20] 1028 6-9-2 **68** .... DarryllHolland 14 71+
(E J Alston) *in rr: hdwy and swtchd outside 2f out: fin wl: edgd lft towards fin* **12/1**

201- **4** ½ **Amethyst Dawn (IRE)**[164] 7246 4-9-2 **68** .... DavidAllan 12 70
(T D Easterby) *chsd ldrs: effrt 3f out: kpt on same pce fnl f* **8/1**

135- **5** 1 ¾ **Morocchius (USA)**[180] 6908 5-8-12 **64** .... TomEaves 6 62
(Julie Camacho) *in rr: effrt over 3f out: hung lft and styd on fnl 2f* **6/1**[3]

000- **6** 1 **Fortunate Bid (IRE)**[169] 7153 4-9-0 **66** .... RoystonFfrench 1 62
(Mrs L Stubbs) *in rr: edgd rt and kpt on fnl 2f: nvr nr ldrs* **50/1**

6501 **7** 1 ¼ **Very Well Red**[10] 1172 7-9-2 **71** .... WilliamCarson(3) 13 64
(P W Hiatt) *chsd ldrs: fdd fnl f* **12/1**

0-63 **8** 2 **Wovoka (IRE)**[12] 1117 7-8-13 **70** .... AmyRyan(5) 11 58
(K A Ryan) *swtchd lft s: in rr: hdwy on ins over 2f out: nvr nr ldrs* **11/2**[2]

3022 **9** nse **Laureldeans Best (IRE)**[8] 1204 4-8-8 **60** .... TonyHamilton 5 48
(R A Fahey) *trckd ldrs towards outer: effrt over 2f out: one pce* **10/3**[1]

54-0 **10** 2 **Bere Davis (FR)**[7] 1241 5-8-8 **65** ....(t) AndrewHeffernan(5) 15 48
(M A Barnes) *led 1f: chsd ldrs: wknd over 1f out* **12/1**

120- **11** ½ **Mister Jingles**[156] 7348 7-8-4 **56** .... PaulQuinn 7 38
(R M Whitaker) *wnt rt s: chsd ldrs: one pce whn swtchd rt over 1f out: sn wknd* **25/1**

240- **12** 1 **Go Alone (IRE)**[255] 4664 4-9-2 **68** .... PJMcDonald 2 48
(G A Swinbank) *a towards rr* **20/1**

4200 **13** nse **Mozayada (USA)**[12] 1115 6-8-13 **65** .... RobertWinston 9 45
(M Brittain) *led after 1f: hdd and lost pl over 1f out* **25/1**

45-0 **14** 2 **Northern Flyer (GER)**[12] 1115 4-8-6 **63** .... IanBrennan(5) 8 38
(J J Quinn) *hmpd s: mid-div: effrt 3f out: wknd over 1f out* **10/1**

1m 39.08s (-1.02) **Going Correction** -0.15s/f (Firm) **14** Ran SP% **124.3**
Speed ratings (Par 103): **99,98,97,96,94 93,92,90,90,88 87,86,86,84**
toteswingers: 1&2 £76.70, 1&3 £27.60, 2&3 £39.90 CSF £231.24 CT £2935.83 TOTE £36.40: £10.70, £3.70, £4.00; EX 420.50.
Owner King Treys **Bred** Frank Brown, Hedberg Hall & K Hernandez **Trained** Stainforth, S Yorks
■ Stewards' Enquiry : Paul Quinn three-day ban: careless riding (May 3-5)

FOCUS
Another race where they seemed to go a decent early pace, though the winning time was 0.9 seconds slower than the first division. The form lokks more muddling than the first leg, with the winner the best guide.
Mozayada(USA) Official explanation: jockey said mare was unsuited by the good to firm ground

1397 CONSTANT SECURITY H'CAP 7f
3:00 (3:00) (Class 3) (0-90,90) 4-Y-0+ **£8,159** (£2,428; £1,213; £606) **Stalls** Low

Form RPR

-104 **1** **Snow Bay**[60] 572 4-8-9 **81** .... GregFairley 4 90
(B Smart) *sn w ldr: narrow advtange 2f out: hung lft: hld on wl* **12/1**

254- **2** 1 **Osteopathic Remedy (IRE)**[168] 7169 6-8-12 **84** .... TomEaves 7 91
(M Dods) *chsd ldrs: no ex fnl 75yds* **16/1**

1536 **3** hd **Dubai Dynamo**[12] 1117 5-9-0 **86** .... AndrewElliott 9 92
(Mrs R A Carr) *sn chsng ldrs: edgd rt 1f out: styd on ins fnl f* **9/1**

00-0 **4** 1 ½ **Joseph Henry**[21] 1006 8-9-1 **87** .... AdrianNicholls 14 89
(D Nicholls) *led hdd 2f out: fdd last 100yds* **14/1**

025- **5** hd **Opus Maximus (IRE)**[196] 6485 5-8-13 **85** .... JoeFanning 10 86+
(M Johnston) *trckd ldrs: effrt over 2f out: hung lft: kpt on wl ins fnl f* **8/1**[3]

000- **6** 1 **Glen Molly (IRE)**[161] 7294 4-9-1 **87** .... RobertWinston 8 86+
(B W Hills) *t.k.h towards rr: effrt on outer over 2f out: nvr nr ldrs* **9/2**[2]

35-6 **7** 1 **Lucky Numbers (IRE)**[13] 1099 4-8-11 **83** .... SilvestreDeSousa 5 79
(Paul Green) *trckd ldrs: t.k.h: one pce fnl 2f* **9/1**

00-0 **8** 1 ¾ **Zomerlust**[20] 1030 8-8-7 **84** .... IanBrennan(5) 13 75
(J J Quinn) *in rr: effrt on outside over 2f out: kpt on: nvr a factor* **25/1**

000- **9** shd **Horatio Carter**[210] 6089 5-9-4 **90** ....(p) DarryllHolland 11 81
(K A Ryan) *swtchd lft s: a in rr: nvr a factor* **10/1**

12-1 **10** ½ **She's In The Money**[13] 1102 4-9-0 **86** .... FrederikTylicki 1 76
(R A Fahey) *t.k.h in midfield: effrt on ins over 2f out: sn chsng ldrs: wknd fnl f* **11/4**[1]

00-0 **11** ¾ **The Osteopath (IRE)**[21] 1006 7-9-2 **88** .... PhillipMakin 6 76
(M Dods) *s.i.s: a towards rr* **12/1**

1m 25.27s (-1.93) **Going Correction** -0.15s/f (Firm) **11** Ran SP% **116.8**
Speed ratings (Par 107): **105,103,103,101,101 100,99,97,97,96 95**
toteswingers: 1&2 £23.50, 1&3 £12.80, 2&3 £9.60 CSF £187.31 CT £1841.63 TOTE £19.10: £4.50, £4.80, £2.90; EX 225.50.
Owner Pinnacle Bahamian Bounty Partnership **Bred** West Dereham Abbey Stud **Trained** Hambleton, N Yorks

FOCUS
A decent handicap, but the pace looked ordinary and it was crucial to be handy with the front four at the sharp end throughout. The placed horses are rated to last year's form and set the level.

NOTEBOOK
Snow Bay was 2lb higher than when well beaten in his last two starts on turf, having scored twice on Fibresand in the meantime, and had been gelded since his last outing. He disputed the lead alongside Joseph Henry from the start until shaking off his fellow pace-setter passing the 2f pole and, despite hanging and putting his head in the air, he battled on gamely to hold off his nearest rivals to win with little to spare. He probably doesn't want the ground quite this quick, so this was a good effort. (op 10-1)
Osteopathic Remedy(IRE) ◆, returning from six months off, was also handy from the start and kept on all the way to the line. He is now 3lb lower than for his last win in August 2008 and this should have helped bring him on. (tchd 14-1)
Dubai Dynamo, without a win on turf since the 2007 Redcar Two-Year-Old Trophy, would have been helped by the drying ground and put in a solid effort having raced prominently throughout. This does look to be his best trip. (op 17-2 tchd 8-1)
Joseph Henry, who finished in midfield in the Spring Mile on his return to action, lasted longer this time but couldn't stay with his co-pacemaker over the last 2f. He has become hard to win with as his only success since July 2006 came at Naas a year ago. (tchd 16-1)
Opus Maximus(IRE), returning from six months off and still 3lb above his last winning mark nearly a year ago, made good late progress but, as it turned out, he was at a disadvantage given the way the race was run. The outing should have done him some good in any case.
Glen Molly(IRE), returning from five months off and disappointing after winning off a 6lb lower at Newmarket in August, was very well backed earlier in the day and again on track, but she pulled far too hard early and when her rider eventually got after her there was nothing there. (op 6-1)
She's In The Money was put up 6lb for her successful return to action at Musselburgh earlier this month, though the runner-up did little for the form here the previous day. She found little when asked to pick up on reaching the home straight and, even though the hold-up horses were at a disadvantage, this was still disappointing. Official explanation: trainer had no explanation for the poor form shown

1398 SQUIRE FREDERICK BELL H'CAP 1m 4f
3:35 (3:35) (Class 5) (0-75,75) 4-Y-0+ **£4,274** (£1,271; £635; £317) **Stalls** Low

Form RPR

20-0 **1** **Sir Royal (USA)**[12] 1117 5-9-3 **72** .... TomEaves 9 83
(G A Swinbank) *hld up in rr: hdwy on wd outside over 2f out: led 1f out: hld on towards fin* **12/1**

-220 **2** nk **Kingsdale Orion (IRE)**[13] 1101 6-8-12 **74** .... DaleSwift(7) 8 85
(B Ellison) *hld up in rr: effrt over 2f out: upsides over 1f out: no ex nr fin* **14/1**

0-43 **3** 3 ¼ **Ahmedy (IRE)**[18] 756 7-8-10 **70** .... IanBrennan(5) 16 76
(J J Quinn) *prom: effrt whn nt clr run over 2f out: kpt on to take 3rd nr fin* **6/1**[3]

6-50 **4** nk **Valdan (IRE)**[10] 1169 6-8-8 **68** ....(t) AndrewHeffernan(5) 13 73+
(M A Barnes) *in rr: hdwy 3f out: styd on fnl f* **20/1**

33-5 **5** ½ **Andhaar**[21] 1013 4-9-5 **75** .... DarryllHolland 1 80
(S Gollings) *prom: led 2f out: edgd lft and hdd 1f out: fdd* **4/1**[1]

600- **6** 2 ¾ **Hurlingham**[39] 7271 6-9-1 **70** PaulMulrennan 7 70+
(M W Easterby) *mid-div: hdwy on ins to chse ldrs 2f out: nt clr run: swtchd rt 1f out: styd on nicely* **33/1**

-340 **7** 1 ¾ **Hallstatt (IRE)**[21] 1013 4-9-2 **72** StephenCraine 11 69
(J Mackie) *chsd ldrs: wkng whn n.m.r over 1f out* **14/1**

100- **8** 1 **Umverti**[224] 5671 5-9-2 **71** FrannyNorton 12 67
(N Bycroft) *prom: drvn and nt clr run over 2f out: wknd over 1f out* **16/1**

050- **9** 1 ¼ **Destinys Dream (IRE)**[196] 6490 5-8-13 **68** RoystonFfrench 6 62+
(Miss Tracy Waggott) *mid-div: nt clr run over 2f out: wknd over 1f out* **14/1**

262- **10** 1 **Interdiamonds**[200] 6360 4-9-5 **75** JoeFanning 2 67
(M Johnston) *led 1f: chsd ldrs: wknd over 1f out* **9/2**[2]

1-02 **11** ¾ **Oddsmaker (IRE)**[8] 1199 9-8-11 **66** (t) FrederikTylicki 3 57
(M A Barnes) *led after 1f: hdd 2f out: wknd appr fnl f* **11/1**

-445 **12** 1 ½ **Lava Steps (USA)**[31] 910 4-8-6 **62** PJMcDonald 15 51
(P T Midgley) *mid-div: hdwy 7f out: lost pl 3f out* **28/1**

65-0 **13** nk **Dzesmin (POL)**[70] 220 8-9-2 **74** BarryMcHugh(3) 14 62
(R A Fahey) *mid-div: drvn over 3f out: sn lost pl* **12/1**

23-0 **14** shd **Safebreaker**[47] 756 5-8-10 **70** (p) AmyRyan(5) 5 58
(K A Ryan) *a in rr* **11/1**

1030 **15** 17 **Grey Command (USA)**[29] 941 5-8-9 **64** ow1 RobertWinston 4 25
(M Brittain) *in rr: bhd fnl 2f: eased* **16/1**

2m 34.95s (-1.25) **Going Correction** -0.15s/f (Firm)
WFA 4 from 5yo+ 1lb **15** Ran SP% **127.4**
Speed ratings (Par 103): **98,97,95,95,95 93,92,91,90,89 89,88,88,88,76**
toteswingers: 1&2 £74.90, 1&3 £23.40, 2&3 £37.30 CSF £175.02 CT £1131.72 TOTE £22.60: £7.60, £6.10, £2.80; EX 267.50.
Owner Lennox Ferdinand **Bred** Mrs James Wigan & London TB Services Ltd **Trained** Melsonby, N Yorks

FOCUS
Just a fair middle-distance handicap and the pace looked ordinary. It was significant that the first two home were brought with their efforts widest up the home straight and enjoyed a clear run, while a couple of others met traffic problems towards the inside. The runner-up sets the level rated to last year's best.
Hurlingham ◆ Official explanation: jockey said gelding was denied a clear run
Hallstatt(IRE) Official explanation: jockey said gelding was denied a clear run
Destinys Dream(IRE) ◆ Official explanation: jockey said mare was denied a clear run

1399 THOMAS LORD H'CAP 5f
4:10 (4:12) (Class 3) (0-90,89) 3-Y-O **£8,159** (£2,428; £1,213; £606) **Stalls** High

Form RPR

516- **1** **Whozthecat (IRE)**[245] 5038 3-9-3 **85** DavidNolan 2 90
(D Carroll) *t.k.h in midfield: hdwy over 1f out: edgd lft and styd on wl to ld last 50yds* **10/1**

021- **2** ½ **Confessional**[165] 7217 3-8-12 **80** DavidAllan 4 83
(T D Easterby) *swvd rt s: chsd ldrs: led 1f out: hdd and no ex nr fin* **8/1**[2]

252- **3** 1 ¾ **Tillys Tale**[228] 5552 3-8-7 **80** PaulPickard(5) 10 77
(P T Midgley) *chsd ldrs: kpt on same pce fnl f* **14/1**

164- **4** ½ **Dispol Keasha**[315] 2714 3-8-11 **79** RobertWinston 3 74
(P T Midgley) *led tl hdd 1f out: kpt on same pce* **28/1**

21-1 **5** ½ **Esuvia (IRE)**[13] 1104 3-8-11 **79** TomEaves 13 72+
(B Smart) *s.s: in rr-div: hdwy and nt clr run over 1f out: swtchd ins: kpt on wl ins fnl f: nt rch ldrs* **6/4**[1]

210- **6** nk **Magical Macey (USA)**[171] 7115 3-9-2 **84** (b) PhillipMakin 6 76+
(T D Barron) *wnt lft s: in rr: hdwy whn nt clr run and swtchd lft over 1f out: kpt on ins fnl f* **25/1**

115- **7** nk **Ignatieff (IRE)**[215] 5945 3-8-11 **79** RoystonFfrench 9 70
(Mrs L Stubbs) *chsd ldrs: kpt on same pce appr fnl f* **20/1**

1333 **8** 1 ¼ **Breathless Kiss (USA)**[19] 1052 3-8-12 **80** DarryllHolland 1 67+
(K A Ryan) *hood removed v late: towards rr: kpt on fnl 2f: nvr nr ldrs* **11/1**

210- **9** ½ **Tasmeem (IRE)**[224] 5658 3-9-5 **87** TonyHamilton 5 72
(R A Fahey) *hmpd s: nvr on terms* **9/1**[3]

016- **10** 2 ¼ **Angel Of Fashion (IRE)**[194] 6541 3-8-9 **77** AdrianNicholls 8 54
(D Nicholls) *s.i.s: a in rr* **20/1**

103- **11** 9 **Waveband**[196] 6477 3-9-7 **89** JoeFanning 11 33
(M Johnston) *chsd ldrs: wkng whn hmpd twice over 1f out: lost pl and eased* **8/1**[2]

58.46 secs (-1.14) **Going Correction** -0.15s/f (Firm) **11** Ran SP% **113.1**
Speed ratings (Par 102): **103,102,99,98,97 97,96,94,94,90 76**
toteswingers:1&2:£31.50, 1&3:£11.50, 2&3:£21.20 CSF £75.05 CT £983.60 TOTE £11.30: £2.80, £2.50, £4.30; EX 138.30.
Owner Ninerus **Bred** Liam Queally **Trained** Sledmere, E Yorks

FOCUS
A decent 3-y-o handicap featuring some unexposed and progressive sprinters, but all bar two of these lacked a recent run. As things turned out, this was quite a rough race and the action eventually unfolded down the centre of the track. The form is rated through the third to his final start of last year.

NOTEBOOK
Whozthecat(IRE) ◆, returning from eight months off, was available at 25-1 earlier in the day and he proved the market confidence not to have been misplaced. Having raced in mid-division towards the outside of the field, he was inclined to hang away to his left when delivered with his effort but still found enough to hit the front near to the line. He still has plenty of scope and should be able to win something even better. (op 12-1 tchd 9-1)
Confessional, not seen since winning a soft-ground Catterick maiden in November, was well backed and was handy from the off. He seemed likely to win when leading inside the last furlong and was mugged near the line, but this was still a decent effort as he may prefer the extra furlong now. (op 11-1 tchd 12-1)
Tillys Tale, returning from seven months off, showed good speed against the stands' rail and had every chance. She ran well here and is entitled to come on for it, but she had a busier first season than several of these and doesn't have the same scope for improvement. (tchd 12-1)
Dispol Keasha, making her debut for the yard on this first start since June, led the field a merry dance and wasn't caught until around a furlong from home. She should last longer with this run under her belt.
Esuvia(IRE), 9lb higher than when making all to win in a fast time on her Musselburgh reappearance this month, had the plum draw from which to attack again, but she just missed a beat a the start and had to be content with a stalking role. She didn't enjoy much room over a furlong out, but it would be pushing things to say it made the difference and this has to go down as a disappointment. (tchd 7-4)
Magical Macey(USA) ◆, not seen since a disappointing handicap debut last October, was given a waiting ride but got into all sorts of trouble when trying to make ground and can be rated much closer. (op 28-1)
Ignatieff(IRE), returning from seven months off and 2lb above his last winning mark, was well backed and showed up for a long way, but he is more exposed than most and probably needs to dominate. (op 33-1)
Waveband, who gained her only win to date on Polytrack, was returning from six months off and wasn't totally out of it when getting badly hampered over a furlong out, after which she was eased right off.

1400 MICHAEL FOSTER MEMORIAL EBF CONDITIONS STKS 6f
4:45 (4:45) (Class 2) 4-Y-O+
£11,215 (£3,358; £1,679; £840; £315; £315) **Stalls** High

Form RPR

105- **1** **Markab**[189] 6661 7-9-0 **104** PatCosgrave 5 108
(H Candy) *swtchd rt after s: mde all: edgd lft ins fnl f: hld on wl* **3/1**[2]

30-4 **2** nk **Damien (IRE)**[21] 1007 4-9-0 **99** RobertWinston 6 107
(B W Hills) *in rr: swtchd outside and hdwy over 2f out: almost upsides ins fnl f: no ex* **11/4**[1]

0-40 **3** 1 ¾ **Advanced**[21] 1008 7-9-0 **103** DarryllHolland 4 101
(K A Ryan) *charged gate: chsd ldrs: hung rt jst ins fnl f: styd on wl towards fin* **6/1**[3]

006- **4** ½ **Buachaill Dona (IRE)**[207] 6180 7-9-3 **98** AdrianNicholls 1 103
(D Nicholls) *w wnr: fdd last 150yds* **20/1**

014- **5** 3 **Sea Of Leaves (USA)**[183] 6814 4-8-9 **94** PJMcDonald 3 85
(J S Goldie) *in rr: kpt on ins fnl f: nvr a factor* **12/1**

000- **5** dht **Enderby Spirit (GR)**[189] 6661 4-9-0 **102** TomEaves 7 90
(B Smart) *chsd ldrs: no imp whn n.m.r last 75yds* **12/1**

1-33 **7** 1 **Fitz Flyer (IRE)**[21] 1007 4-9-0 **101** FrederikTylicki 8 87
(D H Brown) *chsd ldrs: outpcd over 2f out: wl hld whn eased nr fin* **3/1**[2]

69.65 secs (-3.05) **Going Correction** -0.15s/f (Firm) **7** Ran SP% **111.1**
Speed ratings (Par 109): **114,113,111,110,106 106,105**
toteswingers: 1&2 £3.50, 1&3 £2.70, 2&3 £3.00 CSF £10.98 TOTE £4.00: £1.70, £2.00; EX 13.30.
Owner Tight Lines Partnership **Bred** Shadwell Estate Company Limited **Trained** Kingston Warren, Oxon
■ Stewards' Enquiry : Darryll Holland one-day ban: careless riding (May 3); caution: used whip down the shoulder in the forehand.

FOCUS
An interesting contest featuring several sprinters bordering on Pattern class. The runner-up is rated back to his best.

NOTEBOOK
Markab, who showed very progressive form last season including winning the Great St Wilfrid, was marginally best in at the weights on this return from six months off. Given a positive ride, despite tending to hang away to his left under pressure, he kept on finding enough to hold the late challenge of the runner-up. He is likely to step back up into Group company now. (op 11-4)
Damien(IRE), far from disgraced when fourth in the Cammidge Trophy considering he was returning from eight months off, seemed to be taken along faster than he cared for early, but he found his stride once switched out wide and finished strongly to give the winner a scare near the line. (op 10-3)
Advanced, back over a more suitable trip after failing to see out 1m in testing conditions in the Lincoln, had a decent chance at the weights. He was always in a good position behind the leaders, but didn't respond immediately when put under pressure and only ran on after hanging over to the stands' rail. (op 13-2 tchd 7-1)
Buachaill Dona(IRE), returning from seven months off, matched strides with the winner until finding it all too much inside the last furlong, though to be fair to him he had a bit to find at these weights. (op 16-1 tchd 14-1)
Sea Of Leaves(USA), the only filly in the field, was returning from six months off but made no impression from the back of the field and may be better off back in sprints confined to her own gender. (op 14-1)
Enderby Spirit(GR), returning from six months off, had a good chance at the weights but, after tracking the leaders early, he found very little when coming under pressure 2f from home. (op 14-1)
Fitz Flyer(IRE) had finished just over a length in front of Damien in the Cammidge Trophy last month, though he had run much more recently than that rival. He was close enough early, but faded tamely under pressure and may just be better over the minimum trip. (op 5-2)

1401 BILSDALE MEDIAN AUCTION MAIDEN STKS (DIV I) 6f
5:15 (5:21) (Class 5) 3-4-Y-O **£3,950** (£1,175; £587; £293) **Stalls** High

Form RPR

256- **1** **Trade Secret**[190] 6646 3-9-0 **70** DavidAllan 12 77
(M Brittain) *w ldr: led over 2f out: hld on ins fnl f* **5/2**[1]

224- **2** ¾ **Powerful Pierre**[180] 6905 3-8-9 **71** PatrickDonaghy(5) 2 75
(Jedd O'Keeffe) *in tch: effrt over 2f out: hung lft and wnt cl 2nd 1f out: kpt on same pce towards fin* **17/2**

2-23 **3** 2 ½ **Hot Spark**[9] 1190 3-9-0 **77** RoystonFfrench 9 67
(K A Ryan) *led tl over 2f out: one pce fnl f* **7/2**[3]

2 **4** 6 **Philosophers Stone (FR)**[31] 911 3-9-0 **0** PhillipMakin 1 48
(T D Barron) *chsd ldrs: edgd rt and wknd over 1f out* **3/1**[2]

5 1 ¾ **Mi Nina Castagna** 3-8-9 **0** SilvestreDeSousa 4 37
(Paul Green) *dwlt: hdwy on outer over 2f out: nvr nr ldrs* **16/1**

403- **6** 1 **Reddy To Star (IRE)**[179] 6911 3-9-0 **68** TomEaves 5 39
(Julie Camacho) *in tch: outpcd 2f out* **5/1**

6- **7** 3 ¼ **Ruler's Honour (IRE)**[147] 7485 3-8-10 **0** ow3 DaleSwift(7) 10 32
(T J Etherington) *dwlt: nvr nr ldrs* **66/1**

000- **8** 1 ¼ **Marchin Star (IRE)**[226] 5595 3-8-7 **45** JohnCavanagh(7) 3 25
(M Brittain) *chsd ldrs: drvn over 2f out: sn lost pl* **50/1**

9 nk **Kings Craic** 3-9-0 **0** DanielTudhope 7 24
(D Carroll) *in rr: hung lft 3f out: nvr a factor* **16/1**

0- **10** ¾ **Velle Est Valere**[161] 7289 3-8-9 **0** AndrewElliott 13 16
(C J Teague) *outpcd and a in rr* **80/1**

00- **11** hd **Monsieur Pontaven**[180] 6896 3-8-7 **0** MatthewLawson(7) 8 21
(R Bastiman) *dwlt: a in rr* **50/1**

1m 11.37s (-1.33) **Going Correction** -0.15s/f (Firm)
WFA 3 from 4yo 11lb **11** Ran SP% **121.4**
Speed ratings (Par 103): **102,101,97,89,87 86,81,80,79,78 78**
toteswingers: 1&2 £5.80, 1&3 £2.90, 2&3 £5.10 CSF £25.78 TOTE £2.90: £1.10, £2.30, £1.90; EX 27.70.
Owner Mel Brittain **Bred** Whitsbury Manor Stud **Trained** Warthill, N Yorks

FOCUS
A moderate sprint maiden, they took a long time to load, and very few ever got into it once under way. The form is rated through the runner-up to last year's nursery form.

1402 BILSDALE MEDIAN AUCTION MAIDEN STKS (DIV II) 6f
5:45 (5:58) (Class 5) 3-4-Y-O **£3,950** (£1,175; £587; £293) **Stalls** High

Form RPR

1 **Steed** 3-9-0 **0** PJMcDonald 7 66+
(K A Ryan) *s.s: sn drvn along: hdwy over 2f out: rn green: styd on to ld nr fin* **10/1**

02-3 **2** ½ **Frequency**[10] 1165 3-9-0 **78** RobertWinston 4 64
(E A L Dunlop) *swtchd rt after 1f: hld up towards stands' side: nt clr run and swtchd lft over 1f out: styd on ins fnl f: no ex nr fin* **11/10**[1]

3223 **3** *shd* **Turning Circle**[30] 915 4-9-4 63 .... JohnCavanagh(7) 6 67
(M Brittain) *w ldrs: led over 1f out: hung lft: hdd and no ex nr fin* **7/1**[3]
444- **4** *nse* **Seven Of Diamonds (IRE)**[183] 6820 3-8-9 62 .... DavidAllan 9 59
(T D Easterby) *w ldrs towards stands' side: rdn over 1f out: kpt on wl clsng stages* **12/1**
0- **5** *nk* **Red Scintilla**[161] 7288 3-8-9 0 .... SilvestreDeSousa 1 58
(N Tinkler) *wnt lft s: w ldrs on outside: edgd rt 2f: hung lft and no ex last 75yds* **33/1**
25- **6** *4 1/2* **Melundy**[215] 5949 3-8-9 0 .... TomEaves 10 44
(Mrs L Stubbs) *mde most stands' side: hdd & wknd over 1f out* **9/2**[2]
0- **7** *3/4* **Arch Walker (IRE)**[353] 1610 3-9-0 0 .... TonyHamilton 11 46
(Jedd O'Keeffe) *hld up: effrt stands' side over 2f out: wknd over 1f out* **66/1**
8 *1* **Stoppers (IRE)** 3-9-0 0 .... DanielTudhope 2 43
(D Carroll) *w ldrs: sltly hmpd 2f out: wknd fnl 150yds* **50/1**
6 **9** *3 1/2* **True Pleasure (IRE)**[22] 997 3-8-9 0 .... GregFairley 3 27
(J D Bethell) *chsd ldrs: lost pl over 1f out* **66/1**
10 *41* **Kaiasedie (IRE)** 3-9-0 0 .... AdrianNicholls 12 —
(D Nicholls) *sed v slow: detached in last: hung bdly lft over 2f out: virtually p.u: hopelessly t.o* **14/1**

1m 12.36s (-0.34) **Going Correction** -0.15s/f (Firm)
WFA 3 from 4yo 11lb **10** Ran SP% **109.6**
Speed ratings (Par 103): **96,95,95,95,94 88,87,86,81,27**
toteswingers:1&2 £3.70, 1&3 £5.00, 2&3 £3.10 CSF £19.16 TOTE £10.10: £1.90, £1.20, £2.10; EX 19.90 Place 6 £4,172.36, Place 5 £1,486.08.
Owner Clipper Logistics **Bred** Rosyground Stud **Trained** Hambleton, N Yorks

FOCUS
This looked more interesting than the first division and it provided a closer finish with five in a line across the track passing the post, though the winning time was almost a second slower. The form is slightly muddling but reasonable rated around the third and fourth.
Turning Circle Official explanation: jockey said colt hung left
T/Plt: £11,205.40 to a £1 stake. Pool: £52,957.44. 3.45 winning tickets. T/Qpdt: £637.20 to a £1 stake. Pool: £3,358.52. 3.90 winning tickets. WG

1403 - 1405a (Foreign Racing) - See Raceform Interactive

NAAS (L-H)
Saturday, April 17
OFFICIAL GOING: Good (good to yielding in places)

1406a WOODLANDS STKS (LISTED RACE) 5f
3:50 (3:51) 3-Y-0+ **£24,446** (£7,146; £3,384; £1,128)

RPR
1 **Velvet Flicker (IRE)**[150] 7446 3-8-10 96 .... CDHayes 2 98+
(Kevin Prendergast, Ire) *settled towards rr: 7th 2f out: hdwy and squeezed through narrow gap under 1f out: qcknd wl to ld cl home* **14/1**
2 *nk* **Luisant**[14] 1091 7-9-9 108 .... FMBerry 1 104
(J A Nash, Ire) *led: drvn along fr over 1f out: kpt on wl: hdd and no ex clsng stages* **10/3**[2]
3 *shd* **Snaefell (IRE)**[188] 6707 6-9-12 108 .... (p) RPCleary 8 107
(M Halford, Ire) *in rr of mid-div on outer: wnt 5th over 1f out: kpt on wl ins fnl f* **9/1**
4 *1/2* **Walk On Bye (IRE)**[202] 6317 3-8-13 102 .... JMurtagh 7 98+
(T Stack, Ire) *a.p: 3rd 1/2-way: ev ch over 1f out: no imp ins fnl f* **7/2**[3]
5 *1 1/4* **Invincible Ash (IRE)**[14] 1091 5-9-6 95 .... (b) GFCarroll 3 94
(M Halford, Ire) *broke wl and settled bhd ldrs: 6th 2f out: nt clr run 1f out: kpt on one pce ins fnl f* **14/1**
6 *1* **Rock Jock (IRE)**[58] 608 3-8-13 98 .... PShanahan 5 90
(Tracey Collins, Ire) *prom: 2nd 2f out: cl 4th but no imp whn hmpd ins fnl f* **20/1**
7 *3/4* **Sir Gerry (USA)**[21] 1021 5-9-9 .... DPMcDonogh 9 91
(J R Best) *t.k.h and settled in rr: drvn along on outer fr 2f out: no imp fr 1f out* **6/1**
8 *1 1/2* **Wi Dud**[10] 1174 6-9-9 .... PJSmullen 6 86
(K A Ryan) *trckd ldrs: 4th 1/2-way: no ex fr over 1f out* **5/2**[1]
9 *1 1/2* **Sioduil (IRE)**[27] 956 4-9-6 95 .... (b1) KJManning 4 77
(J S Bolger, Ire) *a bhd* **14/1**

60.95 secs (-1.05)
WFA 3 from 4yo+ 10lb **9** Ran SP% **122.9**
CSF £64.37 TOTE £22.70: £2.80, £1.90, £1.80; DF 51.40.
Owner Mrs Kevin Prendergast **Bred** Glashare House Stud **Trained** Friarstown, Co Kildare

FOCUS
The runner-up looks a good guide to the level, with the third rated a little off his best on his return.

NOTEBOOK
Velvet Flicker(IRE) came from the back of the field and weaved her way through, challenging between horses inside the final furlong and running on well to snatch the verdict close home. Trainer Kevin Prendergast believes that, although three of the winner's victories have been achieved over the minimum trip, 6f might be a better distance for her. Consequently, the Group 3 Greenlands Stakes at the Curragh next month might be her next start.
Luisant, runner-up over this trip at Dundalk on his previous start but better suited by 6f, attempted to make it all and, after being driven along from almost 2f out, gave best only late on. As he was drawn 1, the tactics used over this trip were understandable, but coming from off the pace suits him better. (op 5/2 tchd 7/2)
Snaefell(IRE), whose seven wins include this race two years ago, showed that he retains plenty of ability. This was his first start of the season and, after making a forward move almost 2f out, he ran on well inside the final furlong.
Walk On Bye(IRE), whose two wins last season were over 6f and included a Group 3 on testing ground at the Curragh, was always prominent and had every chance from 2f out. She could raise no extra inside the final furlong and was eased late when possibly a bit short of room. (op 7/2 tchd 4/1)
Invincible Ash(IRE), a three-time winner, twice over this trip, broke well and was taken back to track the leaders. She was beginning to close when she appeared to encounter some traffic problems about 1f out.
Sir Gerry(USA) raced quite keenly at the back of the field and, after being ridden to try and close 2f out, he was never able to mount a challenge. (op 5/1)
Wi Dud, who started favourite, proved disappointing, weakening over 1f out having chased the leaders. (op 11/4 tchd 9/4)

1408a SUMMER BARBEQUE EVENINGS H'CAP 7f
5:00 (5:03) (60-100,98) 3-Y-0+ **£12,367** (£3,615; £1,712; £570)

RPR
1 **King Jock (USA)**[57] 630 9-9-9 94 .... PShanahan 3 101+
(Tracey Collins, Ire) *mid-div on inner: 6th whn short of room ent st: stdy hdwy tl swtchd rt to chal over 1f out: kpt on wl u.p to ld cl home* **20/1**
2 *hd* **Barack (IRE)**[27] 958 4-9-2 92 .... (p) DEMullins(5) 13 98
(Francis Ennis, Ire) *chsd ldr in 2nd: clsr early st: hdwy to ld over 1f out: kpt on wl u.p: hdd and no ex cl home* **5/1**[2]
3 *1 1/4* **Cobo Bay**[19] 1049 5-9-3 88 .... (b) PJSmullen 11 91
(K A Ryan) *led: sn clr tl 1/2-way: pressed fr 2f out: hdd over 1f out: no ex and kpt on one pce fnl f* **13/2**
4 *3/4* **Six Of Hearts**[8] 1216 6-9-8 98 .... (b) MHarley(5) 6 100+
(Cecil Ross, Ire) *mid-div: 8th 1/2-way: wnt 4th 1f out: kpt on one pce wout threatening ldrs* **7/1**
5 *1/2* **Harriers Call (IRE)**[27] 958 5-9-4 89 .... JMurtagh 2 88
(J C Hayden, Ire) *chsd ldrs: 4th 1/2-way: no imp in 5th fr over 1f out* **4/1**[1]
6 *3/4* **Spirit Of Xaar (IRE)**[169] 7162 4-8-10 81 .... CO'Donoghue 8 78
(David Marnane, Ire) *in rr of mid-div: 11th 1/2-way: sme hdwy on outer fr 2f out: kpt on fnl f* **10/1**
7 *hd* **Good Time Sue (IRE)**[27] 958 6-8-12 88 .... (t) BACurtis(5) 5 85
(Ms M Dowdall Blake, Ire) *chsd ldrs: 5th ent st: 6th and no imp 1f out* **6/1**[3]
8 *shd* **Ohiyesa (IRE)**[27] 956 4-9-8 93 .... (b) KLatham 7 89
(G M Lyons, Ire) *chsd ldrs in 6th: 7th on outer 3f out: no imp fr over 1f out* **16/1**
9 *1 3/4* **Northgate (IRE)**[197] 6467 5-9-5 90 .... DPMcDonogh 4 82
(Joseph G Murphy, Ire) *in rr of mid-div: 10th 1/2-way: nt clr run fr 2f out: hmpd 1f out: kpt on one pce fnl f* **16/1**
10 *1/2* **If Per Chance (IRE)**[173] 7076 5-8-11 82 .... RPCleary 12 72
(M Halford, Ire) *chsd ldrs: 3rd 3f out: no ex fr under 2f out: sn wknd* **12/1**
11 *2 1/2* **Fit The Cove (IRE)**[163] 7262 10-9-5 90 .... (t) WJSupple 15 74
(H Rogers, Ire) *nvr a factor* **25/1**
12 *2 1/2* **Chibcha (IRE)**[229] 5538 4-8-7 78 .... CDHayes 1 55
(Kevin Prendergast, Ire) *mid-div: 9th on inner over 2f out: no imp whn hmpd 1f out* **12/1**
13 *1* **Castle Bar Sling (USA)**[13] 1109 5-9-5 90 .... WMLordan 10 64
(T J O'Mara, Ire) *nvr a factor* **14/1**
14 *1/2* **Star Links (USA)**[8] 1215 4-8-4 75 .... MCHussey 14 48
(S Donohoe, Ire) *s.i.s and a towards rr* **25/1**
15 *3/4* **Toufan Express**[189] 6678 8-9-5 90 .... DJMoran 9 61
(Adrian McGuinness, Ire) *a towards rr* **14/1**

1m 24.19s (-3.31) **15** Ran SP% **138.8**
CSF £130.99 CT £777.53 TOTE £40.20: £5.90, £2.40, £3.80; DF 359.10.
Owner Thistle Bloodstock Limited **Bred** Kenneth Ramsey & Sarah K Ramsey **Trained** The Curragh, Co Kildare
■ Stewards' Enquiry : M Harley one-day ban: careless riding (May 2)

FOCUS
The always-prominent runner-up and third have been rated to their recent best.

NOTEBOOK
King Jock(USA)'s career record includes two Listed wins in Abu Dhabi, a Group 3 success at Leopardstown and victory in a Group 2 in Italy, but had not won since the last of those aforementioned races in June 2008. Now a 9-y-o and back from a couple of runs at Meydan in February, he recorded win number ten of his career, coming through with a well-timed effort from 2f out after appearing to run into a spot of trouble turning for home and running on well after being switched to hit the front close to the finish. His trainer Tracey Collins said: "There is life in the old boy yet and that applies to the jockey too. Pat (Shanahan) gave him a very good ride and, although you have to go back a bit to find his last win, he was a Group 2 winner running in handicap. He loves passing horses." (op 16/1)
Barack(IRE), twice a winner at two and quite consistent without adding to that tally since, was soon racing in second place and got to the front 1 1/2f out, only to be collared close home. (op 5/1 tchd 11/2)
Cobo Bay, a seven-time winner at this trip and over 1m in the UK, was soon clear. His lead was down to one length turning for home and, after being headed 1 1/2f out, he kept on. (op 8/1)
Six Of Hearts, whose six wins include one over this C&D, made progress in the straight and kept on after appearing to hamper both Chibcha and Northgate 1f out. (op 13/2)
Harriers Call(IRE), a three-time winner, once over 6f here and twice over 1m at Leopardstown, was fourth into the straight and closed over 2f out. She kept on but not well enough to get on terms. (op 9/2)

1407 - 1413a (Foreign Racing) - See Raceform Interactive

1035 LEOPARDSTOWN (L-H)
Sunday, April 18
OFFICIAL GOING: Good to firm (good in places)

1414a P.W.MCGRATH MEMORIAL BALLYSAX STKS (GROUP 3) 1m 2f
4:10 (4:12) 3-Y-O **£28,761** (£8,407; £3,982; £1,327)

RPR
1 **Puncher Clynch (IRE)**[9] 1218 3-9-1 93 .... KJManning 7 103
(J S Bolger, Ire) *a.p: led narrowly fr 2f out: strly pressed fnl f: all out cl home* **12/1**
2 *shd* **At First Sight (IRE)**[282] 3886 3-9-1 .... JAHeffernan 2 103
(A P O'Brien, Ire) *led: rdn ent st: hdd narrowly 2f out: kpt on wl fnl f: jst failed* **10/1**
3 *nk* **Mikhail Glinka (IRE)**[155] 7404 3-9-1 110 .... JMurtagh 4 104+
(A P O'Brien, Ire) *reluctant to load: t.k.h chsng ldrs early: 5th 4f out: rdn ent st: kpt on wl fnl f to strly press ldrs cl home* **11/10**[1]
4 *1/2* **Famous Warrior (IRE)**[21] 1038 3-9-1 105 .... DPMcDonogh 1 101
(Kevin Prendergast, Ire) *chsd ldrs: rdn in cl 3rd 2f out: no ex and dropped to 5th ins fnl f* **11/2**[2]
5 *3/4* **Address Unknown**[144] 7529 3-9-1 .... PJSmullen 6 100
(D K Weld, Ire) *hld up on inner: cl 5th ent st: rdn and clsd on heels of ldrs 2f out: blocked and unable to find racing room fr over 1f out* **10/1**
6 *nk* **Icon Dream (IRE)**[220] 5816 3-9-1 .... KLatham 8 99+
(David Wachman, Ire) *dwlt: chsd ldrs: rdn and outpcd 3f out: kpt on on outer fnl f* **8/1**
7 *4 1/2* **Elusive Award (USA)**[176] 7017 3-9-1 100 .... FMBerry 5 90
(Andrew Oliver, Ire) *s.i.s: sn chsd ldrs on outer: rdn in 3rd ent st: sn wknd* **11/1**
8 *3 1/2* **Mister Carter (IRE)**[21] 1039 3-9-1 .... WMLordan 3 83
(T Stack, Ire) *a in rr: rdn and no imp fr 4f out* **13/2**[3]

2m 8.16s (-0.04) **Going Correction** +0.10s/f (Good) **8** Ran SP% **121.7**
Speed ratings: **104,103,103,103,102 102,98,96**
CSF £130.22 TOTE £20.20: £2.10, £3.10, £1.50; DF 142.70.
Owner Ennistown Stud **Bred** Ennistown Stud **Trained** Coolcullen, Co Carlow

FOCUS
Subsequent Derby winners Galileo and High Chaparral won this Group 3 prize in their Classic season, and Sinndar was narrowly beaten in the race before going on to Epsom glory. However, this renewal was a muddling affair with only 1 1/2l covering the first five home, and while one can never be certain about such predictions its impact on the Classics was certainly not obvious. The fourth looks the best early guide to the level of the form.

NOTEBOOK

Puncher Clynch(IRE) confirmed that he is on the upgrade by recording his fourth, and by far his most important victory, with a gutsy performance. After a moderate early pace, he edged ahead under 2f out and battled on bravely for pressure to just hold on.Trainer Jim Bolger believes the winner is not up to coping with what he termed "real Group 1 horses" just yet and indicated that the colt will be campaigned at a slightly lower level in the immediate future.

At First Sight(IRE), not seen since winning a 1m maiden at Gowran Park in July, is Mikhail Glinka's work companion and he acquitted himself well, making the running and rallying in good style inside the final furlong to only just lose out.

Mikhail Glinka(IRE), twice a winner last season when he also ran second in the Group 1 Criterium de Saint-Cloud, had shown all his better form on slow ground and this was easily the quickest ground he has raced on. Slow to load, he raced freely under restraint early on and, after being asked to close off the final bend, eventually strode out well in the closing stages, finishing out the race well without quite getting to the first two. The jury is out for now but Aidan O'Brien obviously expects there will be better to come as he nominated the Derrinstown Stud Derby Trial back at Leopardstown next month as the colt's next likely target. (op 5/4 tchd 11/8)

Famous Warrior(IRE) had beaten Mikhail Glinka in a 1m nursery at Killarney last season and was tackling this trip for the first time having run third in the Group 3 2,000 Guineas Trial at the same track last month. Always close up, he had every chance from 2f out but appeared to hang fire somewhat inside the final furlong, although he wasn't beaten far. (op 6/1)

Address Unknown, a maiden winner over 1m at Dundalk on his second and final start last season, can be considered unlucky not to have gone close as he found himself trapped with no room to manoeuvre from over a furlong out having been held up and made headway early in the straight. (op 7/1)

1415 - 1417a (Foreign Racing) - See Raceform Interactive

CAPANNELLE (R-H)

Sunday, April 18

OFFICIAL GOING: Turf: good

1418a PREMIO PARIOLI (GROUP 3) (COLTS) (3YO) (TURF) 1m

3:30 (3:43) 3-Y-O **£75,221** (£33,097; £18,053; £9,026)

RPR

			RPR
1		**Worthadd (IRE)**[13] 3-9-2 0 ... MircoDemuro 14 (Vittorio Caruso, Italy) *hld up in rr on outer: hdwy 1/2-way: chal ldrs 2f out: sn qcknd 2 l clr: a holding runner-up* **4/6**[1]	106
2	1	**Marshade (ITY)**[21] 3-9-2 0 ... FabioBranca 7 (S Botti, Italy) *broke wl: plld hrd for 2f: lost position on turn: qcknd to trck eventual wnr: ev ch fnl f: a hld* **20/7**[2]	104
3	2 ½	**Back Hunting (USA)**[14] 3-9-2 0 ... GBietolini 8 (Gianluca Bietolini, Italy) *plld hrd for 2f: hld up in rr: trckd eventual runner-up: effrt 2f out: styd on:* **233/10**	98
4	2	**Air Crew (USA)**[21] 3-9-2 0 ... CFiocchi 3 (R Menichetti, Italy) *trckd ldng pair tl 1/2-way: effrt 2 1/2f out: ev ch: styd on* **77/10**	94
5	1 ½	**Twice In Woods (USA)**[21] 3-9-2 0 ...(b) MBelli 6 (R Betti, Italy) *slowly away: hld up in mid-div: effrt 3f out: styd on fnl f* **89/1**	90
6	1	**Collesano (IRE)**[131] 3-9-2 0 ... MEsposito 2 (R Biondi, Italy) *trckd ldng pair for first 3f: ev ch 2f out: hrd rdn: no imp* **13/2**	88
7	1	**Rio Black (IRE)** 3-9-2 0 ... GTemperini 4 (S Bietolini, Italy) *in rr on inner: effrt 3f out: no ex* **125/1**	86
8	¾	**Good For All (IRE)** 3-9-2 0 ... SSulas 9 (I Bugattella, Italy) *in rr: effrt fnl 3f: no imp* **81/1**	84
9	2 ½	**Tauman (IRE)**[168] 7205 3-9-2 0 ... UmbertoRispoli 10 (Vittorio Caruso, Italy) *broke wl: shared ld: led 3f out: hrd rdn and hdd fnl 2f: wknd* **4/6**[1]	78
10	nk	**Golden Stamp (IRE)**[21] 3-9-2 0 ... PBorrelli 11 (A Peraino, Italy) *hld up in mid-dvision: effrt 3f out: sn no ex: eased fnl f* **165/10**	77
11	¾	**Spirit Of Fortune (IRE)**[14] 3-9-2 0 ... DVargiu 5 (B Grizzetti, Italy) *broke wl: mid-div on rail: effrt and ev ch 2f out: wknd* **56/10**[3]	76
12	10	**Super Dubai**[14] 3-9-2 0 ...(b) SDiana 1 (R Biondi, Italy) *broke wl: pushed to chse ldrs: hrd rdn 3f out: no imp: wknd* **13/2**	53
13	5	**Marameo** 3-9-2 0 ... CDemuro 12 (F & L Camici, Italy) *broke wl to be joint ldr: hrd rdn 3f out: sn wknd: t.o* **34/1**	41

1m 38.9s (-0.90) **13** Ran SP% **215.0**

WIN (incl. 1 euro stake): 1.68. (Worthadd coupled with Tauman) PL: 1.37, 1.72, 3.76. DF: 7.02.

Owner Incolinx **Bred** Compagnia Generale S R L **Trained** Italy

1419a PREMIO CARLO CHIESA (GROUP 3) (3YO+) (F&M) (TURF) 6f

4:05 (12:00) 3-Y-O+ **£35,398** (£15,575; £8,495; £4,247)

			RPR
1		**Alta Fedelta**[162] 7303 4-9-2 0 ... FabioBranca 11 (Vittorio Caruso, Italy) *slowly away: hld up in rr: fnd gap 1f out: qcknd impressively ins fnl f: swept to ld fnl half-f* **7/4**[1]	95
2	½	**Madda's Force (ITY)**[315] 4-9-2 0 ... MBelli 14 (R Betti, Italy) *broke wl: among ldrs: hrd rdn to ld ins fnl f: ct cl home* **36/1**	94
3	hd	**Zobenigo (IRE)** 3-8-5 0 ... MEsposito 12 (L Polito, Italy) *slowly away: in rr: effrt on outer fnl 2 fs: ev ch: r.o wl* **15/2**	93
4	nk	**Secret Ridge (ITY)**[63] 4-9-2 0 ... UmbertoRispoli 8 (S Botti, Italy) *slowly away: hld up mid-div: rdn and hdwy 2f out: styd on* **758/100**	92
5	nse	**Rebecca Rolfe**[16] 4-9-2 0 ... MKolmarkaj 6 (M Gasparini, Italy) *broke wl: among ldrs: led 2f out: ct wl ins fnl f* **143/10**	92
6	2	**Lady Marmelade (ITY)**[16] 7-9-2 0 ... SDiana 16 (D Ducci, Italy) *broke wl: trckd ldrs: chal for ld fnl f: wknd* **177/10**	85
7	hd	**Cry Of Liberty (IRE)** 3-8-5 0 ... CDemuro 13 (L Riccardi, Italy) *broke wl: led after quarter m: hrd rdn 1 1/2 fs out: wknd fnl f* **73/20**[2]	85
8	1 ½	**Charming Woman (IRE)**[18] 3-8-5 0 ... MircoDemuro 3 (Vittorio Caruso, Italy) *slowly away: hld up in rr on innder: fnd gap fnl f: hrd rdn: no imp* **7/4**[1]	80
9	nk	**Shellder (IRE)** 3-8-5 0 ... AndreaAtzeni 1 (L Riccardi, Italy) *slowly away: racd in mid-div: effrt 2f out: no imp* **84/10**	79
10	¾	**Ruby Dancer (IRE)**[350] 5-9-2 0 ... SSulas 17 (A Turco, Italy) *broke wl: swift prog on outside to chal ldr: effrt 2f out: hrd rdn: wknd* **197/10**	77
11	½	**Cool Contest (IRE)**[175] 3-8-5 0 ... GBietolini 15 (R Brogi, Italy) *broke wl: chal ldrs on outer at 1/2-way: effrt 2f out: hrd rdn: wknd* **107/10**	75
12	½	**Yajala**[28] 4-9-2 0 ... MMonteriso 10 (E Borromeo, Italy) *mid-div after 2f: hrd rdn: wknd* **181/10**	73
13	3 ½	**Shoshiba (IRE)**[63] 7-9-2 0 ... SGuerrieri 4 (A Turco, Italy) *broke wl: trckd ldrs on inner: effrt 2f out: wknd* **197/10**	62
14	4	**Spirit Mirage (ITY)**[175] 3-8-5 0 ... GMarcelli 9 (L Riccardi, Italy) *slowly away: a in rr* **73/20**[2]	49
15	1	**Aria Di Festa (IRE)**[16] 4-9-2 0 ... DVargiu 7 (B Grizzetti, Italy) *broke wl: w ldrs: rdn and wknd fr 2f out* **69/10**[3]	46
16	7	**Golden Ramon (IRE)**[18] 3-8-5 0 ... PierantonioConvertino 2 (B Grizzetti, Italy) *mid-div: hrd rdn at 1/2-way: hmpd whn already btn* **73/20**[2]	24
17	1	**Purple Kiss (USA)**[16] 4-9-2 0 ... CFiocchi 5 (R Menichetti, Italy) *w ldrs after 2 fs: hrd rdn and wknd fr 1/2-way* **32/1**	21

69.50 secs (-0.80)

WFA 3 from 4yo+ 11lb **17** Ran SP% **225.0**

WIN (incl. 1 euro stake): 2.74 (Alta Fedelta coupled with Charming Woman). PL: 5.82, 13.52, 3.53. DF: 494.25.

Owner Incolinx **Bred** Brinkley Stud Sas **Trained** Italy

COLOGNE (R-H)

Sunday, April 18

OFFICIAL GOING: Turf: good

1420a YOOBET.DE GRAND PRIX PREMIERE (GROUP 3) (TURF) (4YO+) 1m 3f

4:15 (4:22) 4-Y-O+ **£28,318** (£8,849; £4,424; £2,654)

			RPR
1		**Appel Au Maitre (FR)**[217] 5933 6-9-2 0 ... Jan-ErikNeuroth 1 (Wido Neuroth, Norway) *broke wl on ins: led: qcknd decisively in st: hld off all chalrs* **42/10**[3]	106
2	nk	**Touch Of Hawk (FR)**[217] 5933 4-9-2 0 ... LennartHammer-Hansen 2 (Wido Neuroth, Norway) *racd in 3rd bhd ldrs: t.k.h: swtchd to outer on fnl turn: r.o wl to chal wnr to the line* **33/10**[2]	105
3	¾	**Steuben (GER)**[176] 7039 4-9-0 0 ... ADeVries 7 (J Hirschberger, Germany) *s.i.s: racd in rr: swtchd to wd outside in st: r.o wl to fin cl 3rd* **12/5**[1]	102
4	¾	**Il Divo (GER)**[129] 7704 5-9-0 0 ... EPedroza 6 (A Wohler, Germany) *broke wl: racd cl to ldr: cl up on fnl turn: appeared to falter 2f out: r.o* **83/10**	100
5	1 ½	**Panyu (GER)**[197] 6500 4-9-0 0 ... AStarke 3 (P Schiergen, Germany) *racd in 4th: proged and ev ch 2f out: no imp in clsng stages* **87/10**	98
6	nse	**Eminem (GER)**[36] 891 6-8-11 0 ... HenkGrewe 5 (N Sauer, Germany) *racd in 4th: proged early in st: ev ch 2f out: no ex* **43/10**	95
7	1 ¼	**Schiller Danon (GER)**[155] 7406 4-9-0 0 ... APietsch 4 (W Hickst, Germany) *a in rr* **22/5**	96

2m 22.86s (2.06) **7** Ran SP% **130.3**

WIN (incl. 10 euro stake): 52; PL: 20, 19, 15 DF: 125.

Owner Stall Perlen **Bred** Gilles & Aliette Forien **Trained** Norway

1270 PONTEFRACT (L-H)

Monday, April 19

OFFICIAL GOING: Good (good to soft in places; 7.4)

Wind: Virtually nil Weather: Overcast and damp

1421 PREMIER SPORTS CAFE BAR MEDIAN AUCTION MAIDEN FILLIES' STKS 5f

2:10 (2:10) (Class 5) 2-Y-O **£3,238** (£963; £481; £240) **Stalls Low**

Form				RPR
	1		**Geesala (IRE)** 2-9-0 0 ... NeilCallan 5 (K A Ryan) *slt ld on inner: pushed along and qcknd wl over 1f out: rdn and edgd rt appr fnl f: sn clr and kpt on strly* **8/1**	72+
	2	1 ¾	**Abidhabidubai** 2-9-0 0 ... TomEaves 6 (J J Quinn) *chsd ldrs: effrt on inner 2f out: rdn to chse wnr ins fnl f: kpt on* **16/1**	66+
	3	nk	**Little Miss Take** 2-9-0 0 ... RichardKingscote 1 (Tom Dascombe) *chsd ldrs: rdn along 2f out: swtchd rt over 1f out: kpt on u.p ins fnl f* **6/1**[3]	65+
	4	1 ¼	**Silca Conegliano (IRE)** 2-9-0 0 ... KierenFallon 9 (M R Channon) *cl up: rdn 2f out and ev ch tl drvn appr fnl f and grad wknd* **4/1**[1]	61
6	5	3 ¼	**Be A Good Lady**[19] 1065 2-8-9 0 ... PaulPickard(5) 4 (P T Midgley) *s.i.s and bhd: pushed along 1/2-way: hdwy on inner 2f out: sn rdn and kpt on fnl f: nrst fin* **11/1**	49
	6	shd	**Madam Markievicz (IRE)** 2-9-0 0 ... PhillipMakin 7 (M Dods) *dwlt and towards rr: pushed along and hdwy whn edgd lft over 2f out: sn rdn and kpt on same pce* **10/1**	48
	7	hd	**High Kickin** 2-9-0 0 ... JamesDoyle 8 (A J McCabe) *in tch: rdn along and n.m.r and hmpd 2f out: sn swtchd rt and kpt on same pce appr fnl f* **50/1**	48
0	8	hd	**Majestic Style (IRE)**[23] 1009 2-9-0 0 ... FrankieDettori 10 (A P Jarvis) *cl up on outer: rdn along 2f out: grad wknd fr wl over 1f out* **5/1**[2]	47
	9	hd	**Sapphire Girl** 2-9-0 0 ... PaulHanagan 2 (R A Fahey) *in tch: rdn along over 2f out and n.d* **4/1**[1]	46
	10	26	**Lucky Tale** 2-9-0 0 ... DavidAllan 3 (T D Easterby) *sn rdn along in rr: outpcd and bhd fr 1/2-way* **12/1**	—

67.48 secs (4.18) **Going Correction** +0.60s/f (Yiel) **10** Ran SP% **115.0**

Speed ratings (Par 89): **90,87,86,84,79 79,79,78,78,36**

Tote Swingers: 1&2 £15.00, 1&3 £7.90, 2&3 £21.40 CSF £125.29 TOTE £9.20: £2.20, £4.60, £2.50; EX 168.90.

Owner John J Brennan **Bred** Paul & T J Monaghan **Trained** Hambleton, N Yorks

FOCUS

Probably no more than a fair fillies' maiden, and they finished pretty compressed. The form is limited but the winner can rate higher.

NOTEBOOK

Geesala(IRE), a 33,000euros half-sister to useful 5f juvenile winner Tomintoul Singer, showed loads of pace from the off and sustained her challenge right the way to the line. A strong stayer at the trip and for the time of year, she looks quite useful. (op 10-1)

Abidhabidubai, a 8,500gns purchase out of a triple 1m winner, shaped nicely on debut. She lacked the natural speed of the winner, but was never too far away and kept on well. (tchd 20-1)

Little Miss Take, out of a mare who was placed in a bumper, lost her place when outpaced at halfway but she stuck on gradually for pressure, giving the impression she'll be better for the run and improve for a sixth furlong in due course. (op 8-1)

Silca Conegliano(IRE), a £55,000 half-sister to dual 5f winner Nubar Lady, showed plenty of early speed but was outpaced from just before the straight. She's open to improvement, but her trainer is 0-18 with his juveniles so far this year. (op 9-2)

Be A Good Lady, just as on her debut at Southwell, was soon behind after starting slowly before finishing reasonably well. She already needs further, but would give herself more of a chance if she would apply herself better in the opening stages and it's clear she's still got plenty of learning to do. (op 20-1)

Madam Markievicz(IRE) ◆ shaped better than her finishing position suggests. She had to use up plenty of energy to try and recover from a slow start and ran well for a fair way until those exertions told, plus the way she was inclined to edge left in the straight suggests she wants better ground. (tchd 9-1)

High Kickin stayed on well despite not getting the best of runs and has ability.

Majestic Style(IRE) dropped away after showing pace and probably wants more of a speed test. Official explanation: trainer's rep said filly was unsuited by the good (good to soft places) ground (op 11-2 tchd 7-1)

Sapphire Girl was popular in the market, but she was soon behind and showed little. (op 10-3)

1422 CORNMARKET H'CAP — 1m 4f 8y

2:40 (2:41) (Class 5) (0-70,68) 3-Y-O — **£2,914** (£867; £433; £216) **Stalls** Low

Form — RPR

362- **1** **Cornish Beau (IRE)**[164] 7267 3-8-12 **67** .... AshleyMorgan(5) 10 — 76
(M H Tompkins) *t.k.h: led after 1f: pushed along over 2f out: rdn wl over 1f out: kpt on wl fnl f* **8/1**

430- **2** 1 ½ **Iron Condor**[178] 6993 3-9-4 **68** .... LukeMorris 9 — 74
(J M P Eustace) *t.k.h: sn prom: trckd wnr after 3f: effrt over 2f out: swtchd rt and rdn over 1f out: drvn and no imp ins fnl f* **6/1**

06-0 **3** 5 **Ice Viking (IRE)**[5] 1310 3-9-1 **65** .... PaulMulrennan 5 — 63
(J G Given) *led 1f: trckd ldrs on inner: effrt over 2f out: swtchd rt and rdn wl over 1f out: sn drvn and one pce* **4/1**[2]

60-0 **4** nse **Meetings Man (IRE)**[3] 1362 3-8-12 **62** .... PaulHanagan 1 — 60
(Micky Hammond) *t.k.h early: hld up in rr: swtchd outside and hdwy 3f out: rdn along and hung lft over 1f out: drvn and kpt on same pce fnl f* **16/1**

3634 **5** 7 **Red Valerian Two (IRE)**[13] 1145 3-8-4 **54** oh3 .... JimmyQuinn 3 — 41
(P T Midgley) *in tch: rdn along and outpcd over 4f out: plugged on fnl 2f: n.d* **33/1**

60-1 **6** 14 **Il Portico**[21] 1054 3-8-9 **59** ow1 .... KierenFallon 4 — 24
(M R Channon) *in tch: hdwy to trck ldng pair after 4f: effrt 3f out: sn rdn and wknd wl over 1f out* **3/1**[1]

5-04 **7** 2 **Anchorage Boy (USA)**[86] 279 3-8-1 **54** .... (v) MartinLane(3) 6 — 15
(Miss Amy Weaver) *a towards rr* **66/1**

435- **8** 3 ½ **High Rolling**[208] 6215 3-9-0 **64** .... DavidAllan 2 — 20
(T D Easterby) *a in rr: rdn along over 4f out: sn outpcd* **10/1**

330- **9** ¾ **Ting Ting (USA)**[191] 6672 3-8-5 **55** .... AndrewElliott 8 — 10
(T P Tate) *in tch: pushed along over 4f out: rdn over 3f out and sn wknd* **11/2**[3]

0-35 **10** 26 **Mnarani (IRE)**[40] 840 3-9-3 **67** .... LiamKeniry 7 — —
(J S Moore) *chsd ldrs: rdn along over 4f out: sn wknd* **11/1**

2m 47.63s (6.83) **Going Correction** +0.425s/f (Yiel) — **10** Ran SP% **113.5**
Speed ratings (Par 98): **94,93,89,89,84 75,74,71,71,54**
Tote Swingers: 1&2 £10.60, 1&3 £8.50, 2&3 £7.50 CSF £53.86 CT £220.43 TOTE £8.60: £2.00, £4.00, £1.40; EX 72.20.
Owner M Winter **Bred** Thomas Heatrick **Trained** Newmarket, Suffolk

FOCUS
A modest handicap run at a steady pace, resulting in a few of these racing keenly, and it paid to be handy with the front pair nearly always 1-2. Improvement from the first two.

Il Portico Official explanation: trainer said gelding was unsuited by the good (good to soft places) ground

Mnarani(IRE) Official explanation: trainer's rep said gelding was unsuited by the good (good to soft places) ground

1423 RIU PALACE MELONERAS H'CAP — 6f

3:10 (3:10) (Class 2) (0-100,99) 4-Y-O+
£10,592 (£3,172; £1,586; £793; £396; £198) **Stalls** Low

Form — RPR

220- **1** **Castles In The Air**[205] 6270 5-8-13 **94** .... PaulHanagan 4 — 107
(R A Fahey) *in tch: gd hdwy 2f out: chal over 1f out: rdn to ld jst ins fnl f: kpt on strly* **6/1**[2]

0-22 **2** 2 ¾ **Internationaldebut (IRE)**[10] 1202 5-8-8 **89** .... TonyCulhane 13 — 93+
(P T Midgley) *hld up in rr: hdwy 2f out: swtchd lft and rdn to chse ldrs over 1f out: kpt on to chse wnr ins fnl f: no imp* **15/2**

00-0 **3** 1 ¼ **Courageous (IRE)**[22] 1032 4-8-11 **92** .... RichardMullen 10 — 92
(B Smart) *led: rdn along 2f out: drvn over 1f out: hdd jst ins fnl f: kpt on same pce* **16/1**

6120 **4** 1 ½ **Thebes**[32] 916 5-8-12 **93** .... FrankieDettori 3 — 88
(M Johnston) *chsd ldrs: hdwy 2f out: sn rdn and kpt on same pce fnl f* **5/1**[1]

565- **5** 1 ¾ **King's Wonder**[190] 6702 5-8-0 **86** .... BillyCray(5) 14 — 76+
(D Nicholls) *midfield: hdwy on wd outside 1/2-way: rdn and edgd lft wl over 1f out: sn drvn and no imp fnl f* **22/1**

0-45 **6** 1 **Baldemar**[10] 1206 5-8-10 **91** .... TonyHamilton 12 — 77
(R A Fahey) *midfield: hdwy 2f out: rdn to chse ldrs over 1f out: drvn and no imp ins fnl f* **13/2**[3]

410- **7** 2 **Go Go Green (IRE)**[169] 7202 4-8-5 **86** .... PJMcDonald 6 — 66
(D H Brown) *chsd ldrs: effrt on outer 2f out: sn rdn and wknd appr fnl f* **10/1**

1643 **8** 1 ¼ **Bel Cantor**[4] 1332 7-8-1 **85** oh1 .... (p) KellyHarrison(3) 15 — 61
(W J H Ratcliffe) *cl up: rdn along over 2f out: drvn and wkng whn edgd lft over 1f out* **20/1**

50-0 **9** ¾ **Sonny Red (IRE)**[22] 1032 6-9-4 **99** .... KierenFallon 5 — 73
(D Nicholls) *chsd ldrs: rdn along and n.m.r 2f out: sn wknd* **9/1**

14-5 **10** ½ **Hotham**[22] 1032 7-8-5 **89** .... MartinLane(3) 1 — 61
(N Wilson) *chsd ldrs on inner: rdn 2f out: drvn and wknd over 1f out* **10/1**

043- **11** ¾ **Damika (IRE)**[205] 6278 7-8-5 **86** .... PaulQuinn 8 — 56+
(R M Whitaker) *hld up towards rr: hdwy whn nt clr run and swtchd rt over 1f out: nt clr run again ins fnl f: nvr a factor* **16/1**

052- **12** ½ **Marine Boy (IRE)**[171] 7150 4-9-3 **98** .... RichardKingscote 2 — 66+
(Tom Dascombe) *s.i.s: a in rr* **12/1**

2606 **13** 1 ½ **Flowing Cape (IRE)**[52] 722 5-8-7 **88** .... ChrisCatlin 9 — 51
(R Hollinshead) *a in rr* **40/1**

520- **14** 4 **Hamoody (USA)**[221] 5799 6-8-7 **88** .... AdrianNicholls 11 — 38
(D Nicholls) *a in rr* **20/1**

1m 19.06s (2.16) **Going Correction** +0.60s/f (Yiel) — **14** Ran SP% **120.0**
Speed ratings (Par 109): **109,105,103,101,99 98,95,93,92,92 91,90,88,83**
Tote Swingers: 1&2 £8.90, 1&3 £22.20, 2&3 £26.70 CSF £47.65 CT £711.50 TOTE £5.70: £1.50, £3.00, £7.10; EX 84.70 TRIFECTA Not won..
Owner Jim McGrath **Bred** Newgate Stud Company **Trained** Musley Bank, N Yorks
■ Stewards' Enquiry : Tony Hamilton one-day ban: careless riding (May 3)
Frankie Dettori caution: careless riding

FOCUS
A decent, competitive sprint handicap and a smart effort from the winner who produced a clear personal best.

NOTEBOOK

Castles In The Air had sufficient speed to cope with the drop back to 6f and won decisively after 205 days off. This was undoubtedly a career-best performance and he's potentially going to make quite a smart type this season. (op 8-1)

Internationaldebut(IRE), dropped back from 1m, wasn't best away and soon got behind, but he finished his race strongly without ever getting close to the winner. He's now finished second on all three of his runs since joining this yard. (op 9-1)

Courageous(IRE), well held on his reappearance behind Baldemar, Hotham, and Sonny Red, showed good early speed and was able to get across from stall ten, but he simply found a couple too strong in the straight.

Thebes, 3lb higher than when runner-up in this last year, was always handy as usual and he had every chance if good enough. (op 7-1)

King's Wonder ◆, debuting for this stable after 190 days off, shaped nicely. He was stuck wider than ideal throughout, with stall 14 no help, and simply got tired in the straight having briefly looked a threat. (op 28-1)

Baldemar was never really going all that well and only plugged on without threatening. (op 7-1 tchd 6-1)

Sonny Red(IRE) Official explanation: jockey said gelding hung left throughout

1424 PONTEFRACT MARATHON H'CAP — 2m 5f 122y

3:40 (3:41) (Class 5) (0-75,63) 4-Y-O+ — **£3,238** (£963; £481; £240) **Stalls** Low

Form — RPR

040/ **1** **Fair Spin**[164] 3863 10-8-10 **45** .... (v) PaulMulrennan 6 — 53
(Micky Hammond) *hld up in rr: gd hdwy 5f out: led 2f out and sn rdn: drvn ins fnl f: hld on gamely towards fin* **40/1**

5301 **2** nk **Dan Buoy (FR)**[6] 1273 7-9-9 **63** 6ex .... (b) BillyCray(5) 2 — 71
(R C Guest) *led and sn wl clr: pushed along 3f out: rdn and hdd 2f out: rallied u.p ins fnl f and ev ch tl no ex nr line* **7/1**

525- **3** 3 ¾ **King In Waiting (IRE)**[36] 6676 7-9-10 **59** .... (t) TomEaves 5 — 63
(J Hetherton) *in tch: hdwy 1/2-way: effrt 3f out: rdn to chse ldng pair 2f out: sn drvn and kpt on same pce fnl f* **9/2**[3]

50-2 **4** 13 **Born To Perform**[14] 1113 5-9-12 **61** .... KierenFallon 3 — 52
(G A Swinbank) *trckd ldrs: tk clsr order to clr ldr 1/2-way: effrt to chal over 3f out: sn rdn and ev ch tl drvn and wknd wl over 1f out* **5/4**[1]

664/ **5** 5 **Calfraz**[24] 6011 8-8-10 **48** .... (p) KellyHarrison(3) 1 — 34
(Micky Hammond) *chsd clr ldr: pushed along over 7f out: rdn 4f out: grad wknd fnl 3f* **20/1**

/00- **6** 42 **Alloro**[419] 174 6-8-5 **45** .... PaulPickard(5) 4 — —
(A Kirtley) *a bhd* **40/1**

606 **7** 3 ¾ **Pocket Too**[12] 1160 7-9-13 **62** .... (p) KirstyMilczarek 8 — —
(Matthew Salaman) *chsd ldrs: rdn along 4f out: drvn over 3f out and sn wknd* **10/1**

00-3 **8** 42 **Amir Pasha (UAE)**[12] 1150 5-9-7 **56** .... (p) PaulHanagan 7 — —
(Micky Hammond) *hld up towards rr: hdwy 1/2-way: chsd ldrs 5f out: rdn along over 3f out and sn wknd: eased fnl 2f* **4/1**[2]

5m 8.30s (17.30) **Going Correction** +0.425s/f (Yiel) — **8** Ran SP% **113.9**
Speed ratings (Par 103): **85,84,83,78,76 61,60,45**
Tote Swingers: 1&2 £14.30, 1&3 £12.80, 2&3 £3.00 CSF £289.17 CT £1520.16 TOTE £38.40: £8.70, £1.30, £1.50; EX 373.40.
Owner Bendery Properties Holdings Ltd **Bred** A S Reid **Trained** Middleham Moor, N Yorks
■ Stewards' Enquiry : Paul Mulrennan one-day ban: used whip down shoulder in the forehand (May 3)

FOCUS
Very few of these really stay this extreme distance and the form means little. The winner, who was 3lb wrong, showed his first Flat form for nearly four years, and the second produced his best effort since he was a 3yo.

Pocket Too Official explanation: trainer said gelding was unsuited by the good (good to soft places) ground

1425 SUBSCRIBE ONLINE @ RACINGUK.COM MAIDEN STKS — 6f

4:10 (4:14) (Class 5) 3-Y-O+ — **£3,238** (£963; £481; £240) **Stalls** Low

Form — RPR

1 **Bated Breath** 3-9-0 0 .... JimmyFortune 8 — 90+
(R Charlton) *in tch: smooth hdwy 2f out: led 1 1/2f out: sn clr: easily* **5/2**[2]

3- **2** 3 ½ **Tagseed (IRE)**[346] 1840 4-9-11 0 .... RichardHills 3 — 82
(W J Haggas) *trckd ldrs: hdwy 2f out: rdn to chse wnr over 1f out: no imp fnl f* **9/4**[1]

0- **3** 3 **Whitechapel**[268] 4323 3-9-0 0 .... PaulHanagan 10 — 69+
(E J Alston) *towards rr: gd hdwy 2f out: rdn over 1f out: styd on strly fnl f* **20/1**

4 1 **Pelmanism** 3-9-0 0 .... NeilCallan 5 — 66+
(K A Ryan) *s.i.s: hdwy 1/2-way: rdn to chse ldrs 2f out: kpt on same pce appr fnl f* **25/1**

5 3 **Bahamian Jazz (IRE)** 3-8-7 0 .... MatthewLawson(7) 7 — 57
(R Bastiman) *s.i.s and in rr: hdwy on inner 2f out: rdn wl over 1f out: hung rt ins fnl f: kpt on: nrest at fin* **100/1**

5 **6** 3 ¾ **Barnstorm**[12] 1153 3-9-0 0 .... FrankieDettori 6 — 50
(M Johnston) *prom: rdn along 2f out and ev ch: drvn and wknd over 1f out* **11/2**[3]

0-0 **7** 2 ¾ **Bahamian Bolt**[53] 699 3-9-0 0 .... SilvestreDeSousa 16 — 36
(R Bastiman) *qckly away: led 2f: cl up tl rdn along 2f out and sn wknd* **100/1**

00- **8** 1 ¾ **Loss Leader (IRE)**[214] 6018 3-9-0 0 .... DavidAllan 4 — 30
(T D Easterby) *nvr bttr than midfield* **66/1**

9 nk **Gower Diva** 3-8-9 0 .... AndrewMullen 9 — 24
(D Nicholls) *dwlt and towards rr: sme hdwy 2f out: sn rdn and nvr a factor* **66/1**

36- **10** 2 ½ **Gold Crusher (USA)**[238] 5311 3-9-0 70 .... TomEaves 2 — 21
(Julie Camacho) *nvr bttr than midfield* **14/1**

500- **11** 1 1/2 **Scooby Dee**[182] 6895 3-8-6 48 MichaelStainton(3) 13 11
(R M Whitaker) *prom: rdn along 1/2-way: sn wknd* **100/1**
12 3 1/2 **Clare Harrier (IRE)** 3-9-0 0 DanielTudhope 1 5
(A Berry) *s.i.s: a bhd* **150/1**
202- **13** 7 **Itwasonlyakiss (IRE)**[273] 4147 3-8-9 75 KierenFallon 14 —
(J W Hills) *cl up: led after 2f: rdn and hdd 2f out: sn wknd* **11/2**[3]
- **14** 9 **Regal Emperor (IRE)** 3-9-0 0 AdrianNicholls 12 —
(D Nicholls) *midfield: hdwy to join ldrs after 2f and sn cl up: rdn along over 2f out and sn wknd* **20/1**
15 8 **Rabbie Burns** 3-8-11 0 MartinLane(3) 15 —
(N Wilson) *chsd ldrs and sn hanging rt: lost pl and hung bdly rt home turn: sn bhd* **80/1**

1m 20.1s (3.20) **Going Correction** +0.60s/f (Yiel)
WFA 3 from 4yo 11lb 15 Ran SP% **118.0**
Speed ratings (Par 103): **102,97,93,92,88 83,79,77,76,73 71,66,57,45,34**
Tote Swingers: 1&2 £2.90, 1&3 £16.90, 2&3 £15.60 CSF £7.65 TOTE £3.60: £1.60, £1.50, £4.70; EX 9.00.
Owner K Abdulla **Bred** Juddmonte Farms Ltd **Trained** Beckhampton, Wilts

FOCUS
An interesting sprint maiden run at a strong pace. The runners avoided the far rail from the off, with the main action taking place up the middle of the track, meaning comparing the time with the earlier sprint handicap may be misleading. The winner looks well above average with the second the best guide to the form.
Barnstorm Official explanation: jockey said gelding hung right final furlong
Rabbie Burns Official explanation: jockey said gelding hung right throughout

1426 OPEN DAY H'CAP 1m 4y
4:40 (4:42) (Class 5) (0-75,75) 4-Y-0+ **£2,914** (£867; £433; £216) **Stalls** Low

Form RPR
5501 **1** **West End Lad**[12] 1179 7-8-7 67 (b) AshleyHamblett(3) 8 79
(S R Bowring) *t.k.h: cl up: led over 2f out: rdn and qcknd clr over 1f out: kpt on strly fnl f* **18/1**
16-2 **2** 3 **Brushing**[14] 1128 4-8-12 74 AshleyMorgan(5) 13 79+
(M H Tompkins) *hld up: gd hdwy over 2f out: rdn to chse ldrs and edgd lft over 1f out: drvn to chse wnr and hung lft ins fnl f: no imp* **6/1**[2]
3403 **3** 2 1/4 **Ella Woodcock (IRE)**[2] 1396 6-8-11 68 PaulHanagan 3 68
(E J Alston) *in tch: hdwy 3f out: rdn to chse ldrs wl over 1f out: sn drvn and kpt on ins fnl f* **6/1**[2]
4520 **4** 1 **Xpres Maite**[12] 1177 7-8-5 62 (p) ChrisCatlin 4 60
(S R Bowring) *led: rdn along and hdd over 2f out: sn drvn and kpt on same pce fnl f* **11/1**
000- **5** nk **Major Magpie (IRE)**[236] 5333 8-8-8 65 TomEaves 16 62+
(M Dods) *dwlt and in rr: hdwy 2f out: swtchd rt and rdn over 1f out: styd on ins fnl f: nrst fin* **16/1**
/4-0 **6** 1 **Glenmuir (IRE)**[14] 1117 7-8-9 71 IanBrennan(5) 5 66
(J J Quinn) *midfield: hdwy over 2f out: rdn wl over 1f out: kpt on ins fnl f: nrst fin* **14/1**
1-01 **7** 2 3/4 **Cheers For Thea (IRE)**[38] 873 5-8-6 63 (bt) DavidAllan 15 51
(T D Easterby) *midfield: gd hdwy 3f out: chsd ldr 2f out: sn rdn and edgd lft: wknd over 1f out* **5/1**[1]
530- **8** 2 3/4 **Aldaado (IRE)**[191] 6680 4-9-2 73 PhillipMakin 14 58
(M Dods) *midfield: effrt and hdwy to chse ldrs 2f out: sn rdn and one pce* **20/1**
-000 **9** 3/4 **Carlitos Spirit (IRE)**[22] 1030 6-9-4 75 DanielTudhope 1 55
(I W McInnes) *prom: rdn along 3f out: wknd over 2f out* **40/1**
0-26 **10** 9 **Sarwin (USA)**[14] 1115 7-8-10 67 KierenFallon 17 27
(G A Swinbank) *hld up towards rr: sme hdwy on outer 1/2-way: sn rdn along and nvr a factor* **9/1**
01-0 **11** 1 1/2 **Wiseman's Diamond (USA)**[22] 1034 5-8-13 70 NeilCallan 2 26
(P T Midgley) *a towards rr* **8/1**[3]
364- **12** 6 **Sweet Possession (USA)**[249] 4940 4-8-5 62 RichardMullen 7 4
(A P Jarvis) *chsd ldrs: rdn along 3f out: wknd over 2f out* **33/1**
6065 **13** 6 **Classic Descent**[12] 1152 5-8-8 65 AndrewElliott 10 —
(Mrs R A Carr) *v s.i.s and bhd: gd hdwy on inner 2f out: rdn to chse ldrs over 1f out: sn drvn and wknd* **25/1**
651- **14** 2 **Piquante**[179] 6967 4-9-1 72 SilvestreDeSousa 9 —
(N Tinkler) *a towards rr* **14/1**
000- **15** 1/2 **Aussie Blue (IRE)**[166] 7236 6-8-2 64 AmyRyan(5) 6 —
(R M Whitaker) *chsd ldrs: rdn along over 3f out: sn wknd* **25/1**
03-0 **16** 1 3/4 **Prime Circle**[14] 1119 4-8-9 66 (b[1]) JimmyQuinn 11 —
(A D Brown) *dwlt: a bhd* **33/1**

1m 48.54s (2.64) **Going Correction** +0.425s/f (Yiel) 16 Ran SP% **119.9**
Speed ratings (Par 103): **103,100,97,96,96 95,92,89,89,80 78,72,66,64,64 62**
Tote Swingers: 1&2 £16.30, 1&3 £23.50, 2&3 £7.20 CSF £111.00 CT £769.63 TOTE £26.20: £4.40, £2.20, £2.00, £2.80; EX 165.30.
Owner K Nicholls **Bred** Keith Nicholls **Trained** Edwinstowe, Notts

FOCUS
A modest handicap and, not for the first time on this card, it paid to race prominently. The main action took place up the middle of the track. The winner is rated back to his best with the second close to her Yarmouth form.

1427 NRC DAY ON WEDNESDAY 28TH APPRENTICE H'CAP 1m 2f 6y
5:15 (5:16) (Class 5) (0-70,70) 4-Y-0+ **£2,590** (£770; £385; £192) **Stalls** Low

Form RPR
6-30 **1** **Waahej**[22] 1028 4-8-9 63 LauraPike(3) 2 78
(P W Hiatt) *hld up towards rr: stdy hdwy 1/2-way: trckd ldrs 3f out: swtchd rt and effrt to ld 2f out: sn rdn wl clr: easily* **10/1**
32-2 **2** 14 **Patavium (IRE)**[12] 1150 7-8-6 60 AdamCarter(3) 5 47
(E W Tuer) *cl up: rdn along over 2f out and ev ch tl drvn and one pce fr over 1f out* **7/1**
03-2 **3** 2 1/2 **Daredevil Dan**[14] 1133 4-9-1 69 MatthewLawson(3) 4 51
(M H Tompkins) *led: rdn along 3f out: hdd 2f out: kpt on at one pce* **3/1**[1]
0-56 **4** 1 1/2 **Holiday Cocktail**[23] 1012 8-8-5 63 (p) ShaneBKelly(7) 7 42
(J J Quinn) *hld up in rr: hdwy 4f out: chsd ldrs over 2f out: sn rdn and no imp fr wl over 1f out* **10/3**[2]
500- **5** 4 **Heart Of Dubai (USA)**[332] 2237 5-8-0 56 oh5 NeilFarley(5) 3 27
(Micky Hammond) *trckd ldrs on inner: effrt 3f out: rdn along 2f out and sn btn* **50/1**
334- **6** 11 **Simonside**[161] 6767 7-9-1 69 DaleSwift(3) 11 18
(B Ellison) *in rr: effrt and sme hdwy over 3f out: sn rdn and nvr a factor* **13/2**
-000 **7** 2 **Stateside (CAN)**[25] 983 5-8-6 57 LeeTopliss 6 2
(R A Fahey) *prom: effrt to chal 3f out and ev ch tl rdn 2f out and sn wknd* **5/1**[3]
0000 **8** 26 **Pachakutek (USA)**[9] 1239 4-8-5 56 oh2 (p) AmyScott 8 —
(A J Lidderdale) *dwlt: sn rdn along: a in rr* **80/1**
660 **9** 8 **Mojeerr**[22] 1028 4-8-0 56 oh11 (p) NoraLooby(5) 9 —
(A J McCabe) *in tch: rdn along 4f out and sn outpcd* **40/1**
616- **10** 3 1/2 **Andorn (GER)**[135] 6845 6-8-3 59 AlexEdwards(5) 10 —
(P A Kirby) *a in rr* **16/1**
000- **11** 122 **Sri Kuantan (IRE)**[192] 6648 6-9-5 70 (p) CharlesEddery 12 —
(R C Guest) *t.k.h: prom: rdn along over 4f out: wknd qckly and sn bhd* **20/1**

2m 16.81s (3.11) **Going Correction** +0.425s/f (Yiel) 11 Ran SP% **115.9**
Speed ratings (Par 103): **104,92,90,89,86 77,76,55,48,46 —**
Tote Swingers: 1&2 £13.00, 1&3 £5.60, 2&3 £3.70 CSF £74.97 CT £263.75 TOTE £11.00: £4.10, £1.10, £1.80; EX 77.40 Place 6 £384.10, Place 5 £89.91..
Owner P W Hiatt **Bred** David John Brown **Trained** Hook Norton, Oxon
■ Stewards' Enquiry : Dale Swift caution: used whip down shoulder in the forehand.

FOCUS
A weak apprentice handicap and probably form to treat with a bit of caution with the winner's effort way out of line with his profile. The race was strongly run.
Waahej Official explanation: trainer said, regarding apparent improvement in form, that in its last run the gelding was unable to get cover from a wide draw.
T/Jkpt: Not won. T/Plt: £456.40 to a £1 stake. Pool: £61,553.64. 98.45 winning tickets. T/Qpdt: £36.50 to a £1 stake. Pool: £5,004.26. 101.34 winning tickets. JR

1263 WINDSOR (R-H)
Monday, April 19

OFFICIAL GOING: Good to firm (good in places; 9.0)
Straight at full width. Top bend dolled out 2yds from innermost line adding 7yds to races of 1m and over.
Wind: Virtually nil Weather: Bright

1428 SPORTINGBET.COM APPRENTICE H'CAP 6f
5:10 (5:12) (Class 5) (0-75,75) 4-Y-0+ **£2,729** (£806; £403) **Stalls** High

Form RPR
-316 **1** **Beat The Bell**[10] 1206 5-9-3 73 SophieDoyle 3 91
(J A Osborne) *broke wl: trckd ldr and wl clr of 3rd: led appr fnl 2f: sn clr: easily* **4/1**[1]
4100 **2** 4 1/2 **Kersivay**[3] 1366 4-8-8 69 (v) MatthewCosham(5) 13 73
(P D Evans) *chsd ldrs: chsd wnr ins fnl 2f: nvr any ch but kpt on for clr 2nd* **12/1**
-601 **3** 2 3/4 **Alfresco**[55] 672 6-8-12 68 (b) KierenFox 8 63
(J R Best) *slowly away: in rr tl hdwy over 3f out: styd on wl to take 3rd ins fnl f but nvr any ch w ldng duo* **11/2**[2]
-643 **4** 3/4 **Namir (IRE)**[80] 344 8-8-11 70 DavidKenny(3) 12 63
(H J Evans) *s.i.s: drvn and hdwy 1/2-way: styd on u.p towards outside 2f out: kpt on but nvr gng pce to get in to contention* **33/1**
0-22 **5** 3/4 **Ginobili (IRE)**[7] 1267 4-8-12 68 DeclanCannon 6 58
(Andrew Reid) *in tch: rdn and styd on same pce fr over 2f out* **8/1**
5-06 **6** 1/2 **Perfect Friend**[3] 1350 4-9-0 73 TobyAtkinson(3) 15 62
(S Kirk) *s.i.s: in rr tl hdwy over 2f out: kpt on fnl f but nvr a threat* **14/1**
0-36 **7** nk **Todber**[47] 767 5-8-6 67 (v) KatiaScallan(5) 11 55
(M P Tregoning) *trckd ldrs: outpcd fnl 2f* **15/2**[3]
35-5 **8** nk **Poppanan (USA)**[21] 1044 4-8-12 68 SimonPearce 1 55
(S Dow) *s.i.s: in rr: drvn along 1/2-way: sme prog fr over 1f out* **10/1**
655- **9** 1 1/2 **Hustle (IRE)**[127] 7741 5-8-12 75 JulieCumine(7) 2 57
(Miss Gay Kelleway) *s.i.s: outpcd most of way* **12/1**
4045 **10** 1 1/4 **Timeteam (IRE)**[7] 1267 4-9-3 73 RichardEvans 7 60
(P D Evans) *s.i.s: outpcd most of way* **12/1**
03-0 **11** 2 1/4 **Green Lagonda (AUS)**[7] 1266 8-8-13 69 AndrewHeffernan 5 40
(P D Evans) *in tch over 3f* **25/1**
500- **12** 1 1/4 **Summers Target (USA)**[228] 5591 4-8-3 62 RyanClark(3) 9 29
(S C Williams) *s.i.s: in tch over 3f* **16/1**
0130 **13** nk **White Shift (IRE)**[5] 1300 4-8-11 70 JohnFahy(3) 10 41
(P Howling) *chsd ldrs over 3f: eased whn no ch* **16/1**
0-00 **14** 1 1/2 **Brunelleschi**[21] 1044 7-8-12 75 (b) SophieSilvester(7) 4 36
(P L Gilligan) *outpcd* **25/1**
400- **15** 5 **What Katie Did (IRE)**[310] 2911 5-8-11 67 (p) RossAtkinson 14 12
(J M Bradley) *led at str pce: hdd over 2f out: sn btn* **25/1**

1m 11.46s (-1.54) **Going Correction** -0.175s/f (Firm) 15 Ran SP% **123.3**
Speed ratings (Par 103): **103,97,93,92,91 90,90,89,87,86 83,81,81,79,72**
Tote Swingers: 1&2 £29.70, 1&3 £8.10, 2&3 £24.70 CSF £51.17 CT £280.06 TOTE £6.60: £2.20, £7.10, £1.30; EX 131.10 TRIFECTA Not won..
Owner D J P Turner **Bred** D J P Turner **Trained** Upper Lambourn, Berks

FOCUS
A modest handicap but one or two interesting runners from a handicapping perspective including the eventual winner who showed he is just as good on turf as on AW. The runner-up ran just about his best race on turf too. The race was run at a blistering pace and few ever got competitive.
Brunelleschi Official explanation: vet said gelding returned distressed

1429 EBF SPORTINGBET.COM MAIDEN STKS 5f 10y
5:40 (5:41) (Class 5) 2-Y-0 **£3,480** (£1,027; £514) **Stalls** High

Form RPR
5 **1** **Bilko Pak (IRE)**[5] 1309 2-9-3 0 RyanMoore 3 82+
(R Hannon) *chsd ldr: led wl over 1f out: drvn out fnl f* **11/4**[2]
3 **2** 2 1/2 **Littleportnbrandy (IRE)**[7] 1263 2-8-12 0 CathyGannon 1 68
(P D Evans) *led: sn drvn along: hdd wl over 1f out: outpcd by wnr fnl f but kpt on wl for 2nd* **2/1**[1]
3 2 1/2 **Darwin Star** 2-8-12 0 MartinDwyer 6 59
(D K Ivory) *s.i.s and hmpd s: sn pushed along: rn green and hung lft to centre of crse 1/2-way but prog wl over 1f out: stl green but kpt on wl for 3rd ins fnl f* **14/1**[3]
4 hd **Reginald Claude** 2-9-3 0 DavidProbert 5 63
(M D I Usher) *wnt lft s: sn chsng ldrs: rdn: hung lft and rn green 1/2-way: styd on same pce fr over 1f out* **33/1**
5 1 1/2 **Sir Rocky (IRE)** 2-9-3 0 RichardHughes 9 58
(R Hannon) *broke wl: trckd ldrs 2f: rn green and outpcd 1/2-way* **2/1**[1]
6 shd **Tagena (IRE)** 2-8-12 0 TomQueally 7 53
(P D Evans) *s.i.s: rn green: in tch 1/2-way: sn outpcd* **14/1**[3]
7 4 1/2 **Tedious** 2-8-9 0 RussKennemore(3) 4 36
(Andrew Reid) *n.m.r s: sn chsng ldrs: rn green and hung lft fr 2f out: sn wknd* **33/1**

61.23 secs (0.93) **Going Correction** -0.175s/f (Firm) 7 Ran SP% **112.5**
Speed ratings (Par 92): **85,81,77,76,74 74,66**
CSF £8.38 TOTE £3.30: £1.90, £2.60; EX 10.40 Trifecta £142.30 Pool £2,554.83 - 13.28 winning units..
Owner Middleham Park Racing XLIII **Bred** Stuart Weld **Trained** East Everleigh, Wilts

FOCUS
Probably a weak maiden for the track and something of a turn-up with the longer priced of the Hannon pair edging the spoils. The runner-up helped set the level.

NOTEBOOK
Bilko Pak(IRE) had shown some promise on his debut in a better race at Newmarket and proved too sharp for some largely green opponents, always looking likely to run down the leader but edging right when ridden and only workmanlike in victory. By Barathea out of a half-sister to the three top winners, he already looks in need of another furlong. (op 10-3)
Littleportnbrandy(IRE) probably ran to a similar level as she did here last week but is likely to continue to prove vulnerable at this level. (op 3-1 tchd 10-3 and 7-2 in a place)
Darwin Star has a pedigree that suggests she will want a bit further before long but didn't fare too badly considering she was rather isolated wide of the others, keeping on quite well. Official explanation: jockey said filly hung left (op 16-1)
Reginald Claude is from a stable that get few 2yo winners but he showed a bit of promise never far away from the action.
Sir Rocky(IRE) is by a top German 1m4f performer out of a mare that won at 1m2f, so it was rather a surprise to see him out so soon, as well as such a short price. He never gave his supporters much hope, failing to settle and looking too green for his own good, but wasn't given a hard time late and should come on for the experience. (op 11-8 tchd 5-4)
Tagena(IRE), a half-sister to the 7f winner Tri Chara, hinted at ability without looking a 5f perfomer.
Tedious, whose pedigree is a mixture of speed and stamina, was another whom inexperience got the better of, wandering then fading after showing up early. Official explanation: jockey said filly hung left (op 28-1)

1430 19TH ATTHERACES.COM/PUNCHESTOWN H'CAP 1m 67y
6:10 (6:10) (Class 4) (0-85,84) 4-Y-0+ **£4,857** (£1,445; £722; £360) **Stalls** High

Form RPR
510- **1** **Everybody Knows**[296] [3378] 5-9-0 **80** DaneO'Neill 4 96
(Miss Jo Crowley) *mde all: drvn and qcknd clr over 2f out: unchal* **9/1**
26-0 **2** *6* **Laudatory**[23] [1006] 4-9-2 **82** AdamKirby 1 84
(W R Swinburn) *stdd towards rr but in tch: hdwy over 2f out: styd on to go 2nd appr fnl f but nvr any ch w wnr* **4/1**[2]
65/4 **3** *1 ½* **Sacrilege**[86] [191] 5-8-6 **77** ow1 (p) MarkCoumbe(5) 9 76+
(M C Chapman) *s.i.s: in rr: n.m.r and hung lft 2f out: styd on to take wl hld 3rd ins fnl f* **33/1**
221- **4** *2* **Illuminative (USA)**[178] [7004] 4-8-10 **76** TomQueally 3 70
(Stef Higgins) *s.i.s: awkward and hung bdly lft bnd over 5f out: rdn over 2f out: styd on fnl f but nvr a threat* **9/1**
636- **5** *1* **Astrodonna**[157] [7364] 5-8-5 **71** SaleemGolam 11 63
(M H Tompkins) *in tch on rails whn n.m.r over 5f out: hdwy over 2f out to chal for a n.d 2nd wl over 1f out: wknd ins fnl f* **16/1**
06-0 **6** *nse* **Calypso Bay (IRE)**[16] [1088] 4-9-0 **80** HayleyTurner 6 72
(Jonjo O'Neill) *in rr: drvn and detached over 4f out: styd on u.p fnl 2f and gng on cl home but nvr a threat* **25/1**
-045 **7** *1 ½* **L'Hirondelle (IRE)**[61] [580] 6-8-13 **79** LukeMorris 7 67
(M J Attwater) *chsd ldrs: rdn to dispute n.d 2nd ins fnl 2f: wknd fnl f* **8/1**
010- **8** *1 ½* **Uncle Fred**[166] [7233] 5-9-4 **84** JimCrowley 8 69
(P R Chamings) *chsd wnr 5f out: rdn and edgd lft over 2f out: wknd wl over 1f out* **5/2**[1]
-520 **9** *1 ¼* **Councellor (FR)**[47] [769] 8-8-8 **74** (t) WilliamBuick 2 56
(Stef Higgins) *chsd ldrs: rdn to go n.d 2nd 2f out: sn u.p and wknd qckly appr fnl f* **9/2**[3]
10-6 **10** *2 ¾* **Negotiation (IRE)**[24] [990] 4-9-4 **84** FrannyNorton 10 59
(M Quinn) *chsd ldrs tl wknd qckly 2f out: eased whn no ch fnl f* **14/1**
0-00 **11** *4 ½* **Orpen Wide (IRE)**[84] [292] 8-8-7 **76** (b) RobertLButler(3) 5 41
(M C Chapman) *chsd ldrs: awkward bnd over 5f out: mod prog over 3f out: sn rdn: hung lft and wknd qckly* **40/1**

1m 41.53s (-3.17) **Going Correction** -0.225s/f (Firm) **11** Ran SP% **119.6**
Speed ratings (Par 105): **106,100,98,96,95 95,93,92,91,88 83**
Tote Swingers: 1&2 £17.00, 1&3 £90.80, 2&3 £29.00 CSF £45.03 CT £1176.94 TOTE £12.40: £3.60, £1.10, £12.10; EX 73.70 Trifecta £1012.00 Pool £3,692.73 - 2.70 winning units..
Owner Mrs Liz Nelson **Bred** Middle Park Stud Ltd **Trained** Whitcombe, Dorset

FOCUS
A fair handicap turned into something of a procession by the winner who set a fair pace in front then came further clear before winning eased down. There is a slight doubt over the strength of the form, but it has been rated at something like face value.
Sacrilege Official explanation: jockey said gelding was denied a clear run
Illuminative(USA) Official explanation: jockey said gelding failed to handle the bend

1431 GETREADING MAIDEN FILLIES' STKS 1m 67y
6:40 (6:43) (Class 5) 3-Y-O **£2,729** (£806; £403) **Stalls** High

Form RPR
5- **1** **Circus Girl (IRE)**[159] [7325] 3-9-0 0 JimCrowley 1 75
(R M Beckett) *led: rdn and narrowly hdd fnl 100yds: rallied gamely u.p to ld cl home* **16/1**
0- **2** *nk* **Copper Penny**[254] [4792] 3-9-0 0 TedDurcan 7 74+
(D R Lanigan) *in tch: hdwy towards outside over 2f out: drvn to take narrow ld fnl 100yds: rn sltly green u.p and hdd cl home* **16/1**
0-4 **3** *3 ¼* **Easy Terms**[13] [1137] 3-8-11 0 JamesMillman(3) 2 67
(B R Millman) *chsd ldrs: rdn over 2f out: outpcd by ldng duo fnl f* **12/1**
0- **4** *nse* **Half Sister (IRE)**[247] [5021] 3-9-0 0 RichardHughes 14 67
(R Hannon) *chsd ldrs: rdn: rn green: hung lft and lost pl over 2f out: kpt on again fnl f* **14/1**
5 *¾* **Eden Nights (USA)** 3-9-0 0 WilliamBuick 12 65+
(J H M Gosden) *s.i.s: bhd: swtchd lft to outside and hdwy fr 2f out: kpt on ins fnl f* **13/2**[3]
0-4 **6** *3 ½* **Desert Liaison**[14] [1127] 3-9-0 0 ShaneKelly 4 57
(J Noseda) *in tch: drvn to chse ldrs over 2f out: wknd fnl f* **5/2**[1]
7 *2 ¼* **Barberhoney** 3-9-0 0 SimonWhitworth 13 52?
(J R Jenkins) *s.i.s: in rr: styd on steadily fnl 2f but nvr a threat* **100/1**
04- **8** *nse* **Jasmeno**[189] [6727] 3-9-0 0 TravisBlock 3 52
(H Morrison) *s.i.s: in rr: rdn and hdwy 4f out: nvr rchd ldrs: wknd fr 2f out* **28/1**
62- **9** *1 ½* **Akamon**[164] [7276] 3-9-0 0 RyanMoore 6 51
(E A L Dunlop) *chsd wnr tl wknd 2f out* **6/1**[2]
0- **10** *2 ¼* **Main Spring**[156] [7388] 3-9-0 0 HayleyTurner 5 43
(M L W Bell) *bhd most of way* **18/1**
0- **11** *nk* **Princess Seren**[304] [3101] 3-9-0 0 TomMcLaughlin 11 46
(B R Millman) *chsd ldrs over 5f* **100/1**
04- **12** *1 ¾* **Pursestrings**[136] [7624] 3-9-0 0 SteveDrowne 10 38
(R Charlton) *a in rr* **20/1**
13 *4* **Titbit** 3-9-0 0 TomQueally 8 29
(H R A Cecil) *chsd ldrs: rdn over 2f out: sn btn* **10/1**

1m 43.8s (-0.90) **Going Correction** -0.225s/f (Firm) **13** Ran SP% **106.9**
Speed ratings (Par 95): **95,94,91,91,90 87,84,84,83,81 80,79,75**
Tote Swingers: 1&2 £53.10, 1&3 £23.90, 2&3 £57.30 CSF £195.59 TOTE £22.30: £5.60, £7.50, £6.70; EX 223.00 TRIFECTA Not won..
Owner J C Smith **Bred** J Jamgotchian **Trained** Whitsbury, Hants

FOCUS
Historically no more than a fair maiden and little to suggest this renewal is any different. Despite the field getting strung out approaching the top bend, the early pace hadn't been strong and it turned into something of a sprint finish with few getting into it from behind. The winner was another to make all and the form is rated around the third and the time.

1432 JOIN ROYAL WINDSOR RACING CLUB MAIDEN STKS 1m 2f 7y
7:10 (7:14) (Class 5) 3-Y-O+ **£2,729** (£806; £403) **Stalls** Low

Form RPR
1 **Visualize** 3-8-7 0 ow1 RyanMoore 2 67
(Sir Michael Stoute) *led 3f: styd disputing ld tl drvn and qcknd pce fr 5f out: rdn along over 2f out: hld on wl fnl f* **5/2**[1]
0- **2** *½* **Plus Ultra (IRE)**[268] [4314] 3-8-11 0 TomQueally 4 70+
(H R A Cecil) *in tch tl pce increased fr 5f out and sn struggling: rdn fr 3f out: hdd and sltly hmpd ins fnl 2f: continually hanging rt fr over 1f out but kpt on to chse wnr ins fnl f but a hld* **5/2**[1]
00- **3** *1 ½* **Queen Of Wands**[231] [5498] 3-8-7 0 ow1 SteveDrowne 10 63
(H Morrison) *w ldr tl slt advantage after 3f: hdd and briefly outpcd whn wnr qcknd 5f out: styd in 2nd and u.p 2f out: no imp sn after and one pce into 3rd ins fnl f* **11/4**[2]
4 *1* **Hidden** 4-10-0 0 MartinDwyer 7 68+
(B J Meehan) *t.k.h: chsd ldrs: outpcd whn wnr qcknd pce 5f out: chsd ldrs over 2f out: no ex and one pce ins fnl f* **15/2**[3]
3 **5** *3 ¾* **Setter's Princess**[11] [1186] 4-9-9 0 GeorgeBaker 5 56
(R J Hodges) *in tch: rdn 3f out: one pce fnl 2f* **14/1**
00- **6** *nk* **Cuckoo Rock (IRE)**[221] [5787] 3-8-11 0 DaneO'Neill 8 57
(J G Portman) *in tch: rdn to chse ldrs 3f out: one pce and edgd lft ins fnl 2f: sn wknd* **33/1**
50 **7** *10* **Bethlehem (IRE)**[7] [1268] 3-8-11 0 TravisBlock 9 45+
(H Morrison) *a towards rr* **14/1**
8 *2 ¼* **Behest**[44] 5-9-9 0 VinceSlattery 3 31
(D G Bridgwater) *s.i.s: a in rr* **100/1**
0 **9** *2* **Liberty Point (IRE)**[30] [950] 4-10-0 0 RichardThomas 1 32
(I A Wood) *a in rr* **100/1**
0 **10** *6* **Rubbinghouse Com**[25] [980] 3-8-11 0 JackMitchell 11 17
(P M Phelan) *plld hrd: in tch tl hung lft and wknd 3f out* **33/1**

2m 8.20s (-0.50) **Going Correction** -0.225s/f (Firm)
WFA 3 from 4yo+ 17lb **10** Ran SP% **116.8**
Speed ratings (Par 103): **93,92,91,90,87 87,79,77,75,71**
Tote Swingers: 1&2 £2.00, 1&3 £2.70, 2&3 £2.30 CSF £8.85 TOTE £3.90: £1.20, £1.10, £1.80; EX 9.80 Trifecta £36.90 Pool £4,193.26 - 83.95 winning units..
Owner Cheveley Park Stud **Bred** Cheveley Park Stud Ltd **Trained** Newmarket, Suffolk

FOCUS
A weak maiden run at a steady pace, and though one or two are open to improvement, it doesn't appeal as form to get carried away with. The winner was another to make all.
Setter's Princess Official explanation: jockey said filly failed to handle the bend

1433 TRAINERMAGAZINE.COM H'CAP 1m 3f 135y
7:40 (7:40) (Class 5) (0-75,75) 3-Y-O **£2,729** (£806; £403) **Stalls** Low

Form RPR
34-2 **1** **High On A Hill (IRE)**[19] [1059] 3-9-0 **71** RyanMoore 6 77
(S Kirk) *sn in tch: chsd ldr 3f out: rdn to ld over 1f out: styd on strly fnl f* **3/1**[2]
063- **2** *1 ¼* **Dream Spinner**[196] [6533] 3-8-11 **68** EddieAhern 1 72
(J L Dunlop) *led tl hdd 8f out: led again over 3f out: rdn 2f out: hdd over 1f out: sn outpcd* **11/2**[3]
12-0 **3** *1 ¼* **Pullyourfingerout (IRE)**[16] [1086] 3-9-2 **73** FergusSweeney 2 75
(B G Powell) *stdd in rr after 3f: hdwy 3f out: rdn and one pce 2f out: styd on again fnl f* **12/1**
333- **4** *1 ½* **Whiepa Snappa (IRE)**[189] [6735] 3-8-10 **67** ow1 DaneO'Neill 8 66
(P M Phelan) *chsd ldrs: rdn 3f out: wknd appr fnl f* **11/2**[3]
2-12 **5** *¾* **Calypso Star (IRE)**[4] [1317] 3-9-4 **75** RichardHughes 7 73
(R Hannon) *hld up in rr: swtchd lft to outside and hdwy over 2f out: styd on fr over 1f out but nvr rchd ldrs* **15/8**[1]
4433 **6** *6* **Frameit (IRE)**[31] [928] 3-8-8 **65** LiamKeniry 3 53
(J S Moore) *in tch tl wknd qckly fr 3f out* **25/1**
-332 **7** *8* **Septemberintherain**[31] [928] 3-9-1 **72** (v) StevieDonohoe 5 46
(R A Mills) *s.i.s: drvn to ld 8f out: hdd over 3f out: wknd rapidly* **10/1**
404- **8** *83* **Chat De Soie (IRE)**[208] [6200] 3-8-7 **64** LukeMorris 4 —
(J S Moore) *rdn 4f out: a wl bhd: t.o* **40/1**

2m 27.38s (-2.12) **Going Correction** -0.225s/f (Firm) **8** Ran SP% **113.6**
Speed ratings (Par 98): **98,97,96,95,94 90,85,30**
Tote Swingers: 1&2 £4.30, 1&3 £5.60, 2&3 £12.70 CSF £19.63 CT £169.83 TOTE £2.90: £1.90, £1.20, £3.90; EX 22.70 Trifecta £244.20 Part won. Pool £330.05 - 0.60 winning units. Place 6 £197.06, Place 5 £97.38..
Owner Seahorse Five & Tim Pearson **Bred** Dominic Fagan **Trained** Upper Lambourn, Berks

FOCUS
A modest handicap run at something of a stop start gallop, but it was essentially a good test at that trip and the result seemed the right one on the day. Probably decent form for the grade.
T/Plt: £414.60 to a £1 stake. Pool: £62,009.78. 109.17 winning tickets. T/Qpdt: £56.60 to a £1 stake. Pool: £6,577.67. 85.90 winning tickets. ST

SANTA ANITA (L-H)
Monday, April 19

OFFICIAL GOING: Turf: firm

1435a SAN JUAN CAPISTRANO INVITATIONAL H'CAP (GRADE 2) (4YO+) (TURF) 1m 6f
1:08 (1:20) 4-Y-O+ **£55,555** (£18,518; £11,111; £5,555; £1,851)

RPR
1 **Bourbon Bay (USA)**[30] 4-8-10 **0** (b) RBejarano 8 108
(Neil Drysdale, U.S.A) **4/5**[1]
2 *½* **Unusual Suspect (USA)**[23] 6-8-3 **0** (b) AQuinonez 4 98
(Barry Abrams, U.S.A) **211/10**
3 *¾* **Skellytown (USA)** 7-8-1 **0** (b) MGarcia 5 95
(Mike Mitchell, U.S.A) **25/1**

4 1 ½ **Falcon Rock (IRE)**[219] 5865 5-8-2 0 .... JTalamo 3 94
(Simon Callaghan, U.S.A) 5/1[2]
5 ¾ **Romp (ARG)**[30] 6-8-4 0 ow1 .... (b) JRosario 1 95
(Kristin Mulhall, U.S.A) 14/1
6 ½ **Tap It Light (USA)**[23] 6-8-4 0 .... (b) TBaze 7 94
(Mike Mitchell, U.S.A) 9/1
7 5 ½ **Yodelen Dan (USA)**[1717] 7-8-3 0 ow2 .... (b) VEspinoza 2 85
(Kristin Mulhall, U.S.A) 26/1
8 7 **Muhannak (IRE)**[85] 6-8-4 0 .... BBlanc 6 77
(B Cecil, U.S.A) 38/1
9 1 ¼ **Princess Taylor**[53] 712 6-7-13 0 ow1 .... CSantiagoReyes 10 70
(D K Weld, Ire) *hld up: effrt 4f out: sn rdn and wknd fnl 2f* 244/10
10 6 ½ **Stalingrad (USA)**[568] 6-8-5 0 .... DFlores 9 67
(James Cassidy, U.S.A) 13/2[3]

2m 44.52s (164.52)
WFA 4 from 5yo+ 2lb 10 Ran SP% **120.8**
PARI-MUTUEL (all including $2 stake): WIN 3.60; PLACE (1-2) 2.80, 10.60; SHOW (1-2-3) 2.60, 6.20, 7.80; SF 50.60.
Owner David & Jill Heerensperger **Bred** Adena Springs **Trained** USA

BRIGHTON (L-H)

Tuesday, April 20

OFFICIAL GOING: Good to firm (9.1)
Wind: Light, against Weather: Fine, sunny

1436 RADIOREVERB MAIDEN STKS 5f 213y

5:10 (5:10) (Class 5) 3-Y-O+ **£2,590** (£770; £385) **Stalls** Low

Form RPR
154- 1 **Curtains**[297] 3396 3-8-10 93 .... SebSanders 3 71
(S Dow) *mde virtually all: jnd over 2f out: rdn over 1f out: styd on to assert fnl f* 1/5[1]
0- 2 2 **Suzy Alexander**[233] 5478 3-8-10 0 .... ChrisCatlin 1 64
(G G Margarson) *wnt 2nd 1/2-way: sn jnd wnr: rdn and one pce over 1f out* 25/1[3]
2303 3 4 ½ **Blue Zephyr**[20] 1058 3-9-1 64 .... SteveDrowne 2 55
(W R Muir) *chsd wnr to 1/2-way: struggling 2f out: fdd* 9/2[2]

1m 11.29s (1.09) **Going Correction** -0.075s/f (Good) 3 Ran SP% **105.4**
Speed ratings (Par 103): **89,86,80**
CSF £5.30 TOTE £1.10; EX 6.90.
Owner The Pull Yourself Together Partnership **Bred** Sir Eric Parker **Trained** Epsom, Surrey

FOCUS
Due to a drying day the ground was officially described as good to firm. A weak maiden but the odds-on winner had to work and looks some way below his official rating.

1437 RADIOREVERB BRIGHTON CLASSIFIED STKS 7f 214y

5:40 (5:40) (Class 6) 3-Y-O+ **£1,878** (£558; £279; £139) **Stalls** Centre

Form RPR
400- 1 **The Shuffler**[195] 6589 3-8-7 55 .... SamHitchcott 13 66
(G L Moore) *t.k.h: hld up towards rr: stdy prog on outer fr 3f out: led wl over 1f out: rdn clr* 14/1
0-44 2 3 ¼ **Celestial Girl**[77] 381 3-8-7 55 .... SteveDrowne 8 59
(H Morrison) *hld up in midfield gng wl: effrt over 2f out: styd on to chse wnr fnl f: no imp* 13/2[3]
566- 3 ¾ **Firehawk**[200] 6461 3-8-2 55 .... AndrewHeffernan(5) 2 57
(P D Evans) *t.k.h: w ldrs: hrd rdn fr 2f out: one pce* 3/1[1]
0- 4 1 ¼ **Four Kicks (IRE)**[34] 5948 4-9-7 44 .... LiamKeniry 1 58
(J S Moore) *hld up in midfield: effrt on inner over 2f out: nt clr run briefly jst over 1f out: kpt on same pce* 25/1
4323 5 1 ½ **Yakama (IRE)**[26] 984 5-9-7 51 .... (b) AdamKirby 3 55+
(Mrs C A Dunnett) *dwlt: hld up in rr: looking for room on inner fr over 2f out: prog whn hmpd over 1f out: no ch after: kpt on* 4/1[2]
-056 6 ½ **Signora Frasi (IRE)**[48] 780 5-9-7 55 .... TomMcLaughlin 14 53
(A G Newcombe) *trckd ldrs: prog to chal on outer 2f out: wknd jst over 1f out* 13/2[3]
4-60 7 1 ¾ **Haasem (USA)**[73] 442 7-9-7 55 .... PatDobbs 10 49
(J R Jenkins) *hld up towards rr: effrt on outer over 2f out: no imp over 1f out: fdd* 12/1
45-6 8 2 ½ **Chinese Democracy (USA)**[13] 1162 3-8-7 54 .... ChrisCatlin 16 40
(P F I Cole) *w ldrs: led wl over 2f out to wl over 1f out: wknd* 11/1
2005 9 1 ¾ **Kathleen Kennet**[22] 1042 10-9-2 49 .... KierenFox(5) 11 40
(M R Bosley) *mde most to wl over 2f out: wknd* 16/1
000 10 shd **Kalligal**[26] 984 5-9-7 47 .... RichardThomas 5 39
(R Ingram) *taken down early: hld up in rr: effrt on outer 2f out: sn no prog and btn* 40/1
6-00 11 5 **Bahkov (IRE)**[81] 353 4-9-7 50 .... CathyGannon 7 28
(Andrew Turnell) *pressed ldrs: rdn 1/2-way: wknd over 2f out* 16/1
00-0 12 6 **Miss Jabba (IRE)**[97] 146 4-9-0 42 .... AdamBeschizza(7) 12 14
(Miss J Feilden) *cl up: rdn wl over 2f out: sn wknd* 50/1
00-6 13 2 **Court Wing (IRE)**[20] 1062 4-9-7 43 .... StevieDonohoe 4 9
(George Baker) *dropped to last after 3f: nvr a factor: bhd fnl 2f* 50/1
0000 14 2 ½ **One Cool Dream**[6] 1304 4-9-7 48 .... (b) SaleemGolam 9 4
(P W Hiatt) *rel to r: ct up w rest after 3f: wknd over 2f out: eased* 20/1
0-05 15 2 ½ **Amwell House**[19] 1078 5-9-7 42 .... AdrianMcCarthy 6 —
(J R Jenkins) *chsd ldrs to 1/2-way: wknd over 2f out: sn wl bhd* 66/1

1m 35.78s (-0.22) **Going Correction** -0.075s/f (Good)
WFA 3 from 4yo+ 14lb 15 Ran SP% **122.6**
Speed ratings (Par 101): **98,94,94,92,91 90,89,86,84,84 79,73,71,69,66**
toteswingers: 1&2 £30.50, 1&3 £16.20, 2&3 £4.90 CSF £98.16 TOTE £21.20: £6.20, £1.30, £2.20; EX 132.00.
Owner Heart Of The South Racing **Bred** John And Caroline Penny **Trained** Lower Beeding, W Sussex

FOCUS
This was a very weak affair run at an average pace. Three-year-olds dominated and the form seems sound enough.
Yakama(IRE) Official explanation: jockey said gelding was denied a clear run
One Cool Dream Official explanation: jockey said filly was slowly away

1438 BRIGHTON RACECOURSE VE DAY CELEBRATION H'CAP 5f 213y

6:10 (6:10) (Class 4) (0-85,85) 4-Y-O+ **£4,289** (£1,283; £641; £320; £159) **Stalls** Low

Form RPR
063- 1 **Imperial Guest**[274] 4148 4-9-4 85 .... SebSanders 7 94
(G G Margarson) *hld up in last pair: stdy prog on outer over 2f out: wnt 2nd over 1f out: drvn to ld last 100yds* 6/1
20-2 2 1 ¼ **Kerrys Requiem (IRE)**[19] 1076 4-9-3 84 .... CathyGannon 2 89
(M R Channon) *sn in last trio: looking for room 2f out: prog over 1f out: r.o last 100yds to take 2nd post* 8/1
30-1 3 shd **Peter Island (FR)**[5] 1321 7-8-12 79 6ex .... (v) ChrisCatlin 5 84
(J Gallagher) *sn led and clr: drvn over 1f out: hdd & wknd last 100yds: lost 2nd post* 10/3[2]
2120 4 2 ¼ **Sherjawy (IRE)**[5] 1321 6-8-5 72 oh5 ow1 .... SamHitchcott 4 69
(Miss Z C Davison) *mostly chsd clr ldr: rdn over 2f out: no imp: one pce after* 14/1
31-3 5 1 **Daddy's Gift (IRE)**[19] 1076 4-8-9 76 .... PatDobbs 1 79+
(R Hannon) *sn in last trio: rdn and struggling whn short of room on inner over 1f out: one pce* 4/1[3]
046- 6 hd **My Kingdom (IRE)**[190] 6723 4-9-1 82 .... TravisBlock 3 76
(H Morrison) *prom in chsng gp: rdn and no imp 2f out: fdd fnl f* 5/2[1]
0-32 7 4 ½ **Mutamared (USA)**[13] 1167 10-8-8 78 .... (t) RussKennemore(3) 6 57
(Andrew Reid) *prom in chsng gp: rdn over 2f out: wknd over 1f out* 20/1

68.90 secs (-1.30) **Going Correction** -0.075s/f (Good) 7 Ran SP% **108.5**
Speed ratings (Par 105): **105,103,103,100,98 98,92**
toteswingers: 1&2 £4.20, 1&3 £4.10, 2&3 £5.00 CSF £46.27 TOTE £6.80: £2.50, £4.80; EX 41.70.
Owner John Guest **Bred** John Guest Racing Ltd **Trained** Newmarket, Suffolk
■ Stewards' Enquiry : Cathy Gannon one-day ban: careless riding (May 4)

FOCUS
A fair handicap, run at a decent early pace. The winner looked back to his best.

1439 FOOTBALL LEGENDS LUNCH HERE 18TH MAY CLAIMING STKS 1m 3f 196y

6:40 (6:40) (Class 6) 4-Y-O+ **£1,942** (£578; £288; £144) **Stalls** High

Form RPR
0-02 1 **Little Sark (IRE)**[48] 771 5-8-6 56 .... AndrewHeffernan(5) 5 60
(P D Evans) *t.k.h early: hld up in 4th: effrt to chal 3f out: sn rdn and looked in trble: wnt 2nd over 1f out: styd on to ld last 75yds* 13/2[3]
1111 2 ¾ **Sedgwick**[5] 1318 8-8-9 71 .... StevieDonohoe 1 57
(Ian Williams) *hld up in 3rd: smooth effrt to ld jst over 2f out: drvn over 1f out: hdd and no ex last 75yds* 4/5[1]
-404 3 3 **Motarjm (USA)**[15] 1134 6-8-11 62 .... (t) SaleemGolam 4 54
(J Pearce) *hld up last: effrt to chal on inner 3f out: rdn and nt qckn 2f out: hld after* 10/3[2]
65-6 4 1 ¾ **Persian Tomcat (IRE)**[66] 541 4-8-4 43 .... CathyGannon 3 45
(Miss J Feilden) *led to jst over 2f out: fdd jst over 1f out* 25/1
1-40 5 11 **Transvestite (IRE)**[46] 811 8-8-11 72 .... ChrisCatlin 2 34
(Miss Tor Sturgis) *mostly trckd ldr to 3f out: wknd over 1f out* 7/1

2m 34.08s (1.38) **Going Correction** -0.075s/f (Good)
WFA 4 from 5yo+ 1lb 5 Ran SP% **108.3**
Speed ratings (Par 101): **92,91,89,88,81**
CSF £11.99 TOTE £9.10: £2.20, £1.02; EX 16.90.
Owner Trevor Gallienne **Bred** A Pereira **Trained** Pandy, Monmouths

FOCUS
There wasn't much pace on in this ordinary claimer and the first pair dominated inside the final furlong. The favourite was a bit disappointing and the winner didn't have to improve.

1440 CORAL BRIGHTON & HOVE GREYHOUND STADIUM H'CAP 1m 1f 209y

7:10 (7:13) (Class 5) (0-70,70) 4-Y-O+ **£2,331** (£693; £346; £173) **Stalls** High

Form RPR
452- 1 **The Hague**[305] 3099 4-8-9 66 .... AndrewHeffernan(5) 3 74
(P D Evans) *pressed ldr: led 3f out and drvn for home: hrd pressed fnl f: hld on nr fin* 5/1[3]
0-31 2 hd **Blue Tango (IRE)**[10] 1226 4-8-13 65 .... (b) SebSanders 2 73
(Mrs A J Perrett) *led: hdd and outpcd by wnr 3f out: rallied over 1f out: chal fnl f: jst hld* 7/2[1]
560 3 3 ¼ **Granny McPhee**[32] 941 4-8-6 65 .... NatashaEaton(7) 9 67+
(A Bailey) *s.s: hld up in last pair: stdy prog fr 2f out: nudged along and r.o to take 3rd ins fnl f: too much to do* 18/1
5604 4 2 ¼ **Rocky's Pride (IRE)**[4] 1346 4-9-2 68 .... (p) NeilCallan 6 65
(A B Haynes) *trckd ldng pair: rdn over 2f out: no imp over 1f out: one pce and lost 3rd ins fnl f* 7/2[1]
0613 5 1 ¾ **Musashi (IRE)**[10] 1225 5-8-9 61 .... (b) LiamKeniry 8 55
(Mrs L J Mongan) *dwlt: hld up in last pair: outpcd 3f out: drvn on outer over 2f out: sme late prog: no ch* 15/2
000- 6 ½ **Golden Rock (IRE)**[167] 7248 4-9-4 70 .... SteveDrowne 4 63
(R Charlton) *hld up in midfield: stdy prog over 2f out: nt clr run briefly over 1f out: sn folded* 9/2[2]
40-6 7 2 ¾ **Chadwell Spring (IRE)**[23] 1034 4-9-2 68 .... CathyGannon 7 55
(Miss J Feilden) *hld up in midfield: pushed along over 3f out: no prog over 2f out: fdd* 8/1
-256 8 10 **Eastern Gift**[5] 1323 5-8-13 70 .... (b) KylieManser(5) 1 37
(Miss Gay Kelleway) *trckd ldng pair: rdn and fnd nil on inner over 2f out: wknd* 10/1

2m 2.82s (-0.78) **Going Correction** -0.075s/f (Good) 8 Ran SP% **116.5**
Speed ratings (Par 103): **100,99,97,95,94 93,91,83**
toteswingers:1&2 £5.20, 2&3 £10.00, 1&3 £30.70 CSF £23.35 CT £292.59 TOTE £6.00: £1.90, £1.10, £7.90; EX 12.20.
Owner Diamond Racing Ltd **Bred** Darley **Trained** Pandy, Monmouths
■ Penang Cinta (10/1) was withdrawn after proving unruly in the stalls. Deduct 5p in the £ under R4).

FOCUS
An open handicap, run at an uneven pace and the first pair were responsible for setting it. Modest form, rated around the runner-up, with the winner up 4lb on this first start for Evans.

1441 BRIGHTON RACECOURSE H'CAP 6f 209y

7:40 (7:40) (Class 6) (0-60,60) 4-Y-O+ **£2,072** (£616; £308; £153) **Stalls** Low

Form RPR
-323 1 **Eager To Bow (IRE)**[13] 1171 4-8-10 52 .... JimCrowley 16 64
(P R Chamings) *hld up in last pair: stdy prog on wd outside fr 3f out: led jst over 1f out: rdn clr* 9/1
-221 2 2 ¼ **Scruffy Skip (IRE)**[14] 1148 5-9-2 58 .... (p) TomMcLaughlin 8 64
(Mrs C A Dunnett) *pressed ldrs: rdn to chal 2f out: upsides over 1f out: one pce fnl f* 6/1[1]
22-0 3 nk **Sermons Mount (USA)**[13] 1170 4-8-13 55 .... NeilCallan 9 60
(Mouse Hamilton-Fairley) *settled in midfield: prog over 2f out: chal and upsides u.p over 1f out: one pce* 6/1[1]
640- 4 ¾ **Sultans Way (IRE)**[204] 6339 4-8-13 55 .... (p) PatDobbs 6 58
(P F I Cole) *mde most to jst over 1f out: no ex* 8/1
50-2 5 ½ **Namu**[10] 1235 7-8-9 54 .... JackDean(3) 10 56
(Miss T Spearing) *hld up in rr: prog on inner fr 2f out: nvr rchd ldrs* 7/1[3]

34-1 **6** *1 1/2* **Short Cut**[54] 694 4-8-11 **53**.....(t) StevieDonohoe 5 51
(Ian Williams) *trckd ldrs: effrt to chal 2f out: upsides over 1f out: wknd ins fnl f* **13/2**[2]

P-60 **7** *hd* **State General (IRE)**[23] 1028 4-9-2 **58**.....(v[1]) CathyGannon 12 55+
(Miss J Feilden) *hld up in rr: rdn and prog to chse ldrs over 1f out: nt qckn: kpt on nr fin* **25/1**

3240 **8** *3/4* **Top Flight Splash**[29] 961 4-8-3 **50**.....(b[1]) AndrewHeffernan(5) 1 45
(P D Evans) *sn cl up on inner: nt qckn 2f out: no prog over 1f out* **7/1**[3]

4510 **9** *3 1/2* **Jonnie Skull (IRE)**[15] 1130 4-8-6 **55**.....(vt) LeonnaMayor(7) 11 41
(P S McEntee) *chsd ldrs: lost pl over 2f out: n.d fr over 1f out* **25/1**

1046 **10** *2 3/4* **Prince Valentine**[41] 847 9-8-8 **50**.....(p) FergusSweeney 4 28
(G L Moore) *hld up towards rr: no real prog 2f out: n.d after* **16/1**

5065 **10** *dht* **Goodbye Cash (IRE)**[56] 673 6-8-11 **60**..... JohnFahy(7) 2 38
(R J Smith) *restless in stalls: drvn early towards rr: nvr on terms w ldrs* **12/1**

002- **12** *1 3/4* **Talamahana**[142] 7592 5-8-4 **46**.....(v) AdrianMcCarthy 13 20
(A B Haynes) *a towards rr: struggling and no prog over 2f out* **33/1**

-350 **13** *8* **Trading Nation (USA)**[46] 808 4-9-4 **60**..... ChrisCatlin 7 12
(P W Hiatt) *pressed ldr to wl over 2f out: wknd rapidly* **16/1**

0060 **14** *1/2* **Jeannie (IRE)**[50] 753 4-8-4 **46** oh1.....(p) RichardThomas 15 —
(N P Littmoden) *nvr on terms w ldrs: wknd over 2f out: bhd after* **33/1**

000- **15** *6* **Louie's Lad**[220] 5877 4-8-5 **47**.....(p) NeilChalmers 14 —
(J J Bridger) *racd in midfield on outer tl wknd rapidly wl over 2f out* **66/1**

1m 22.24s (-0.86) **Going Correction** -0.075s/f (Good) **15** Ran SP% **122.5**
Speed ratings (Par 101): **101,98,98,97,96 94,94,93,89,86 86,84,75,75,68**
toteswingers:1&2 £10.60, 2&3 £4.80, 1&3 £7.80 CSF £59.84 CT £368.32 TOTE £14.20: £6.30, £3.40, £4.40; EX 84.50 Place 6: £87.63 Place 5: £70.69.
Owner Mrs J E L Wright **Bred** Stone Ridge Farm **Trained** Baughurst, Hants

FOCUS
This was wide-open but the wuinner delivered on his recent promise. There was a sound pace on and the form makes sense, although it is not a race to be positive over in the long term.
Jeannie(IRE) Official explanation: jockey said filly was unsuited by the track
T/Plt: £72.20 to a £1 stake. Pool: £41,927.13. 423.36 winning tickets. T/Qpdt: £22.30 to a £1 stake. Pool: £3,453.50. 114.20 winning tickets. JN

1256 FOLKESTONE (R-H)
Tuesday, April 20

OFFICIAL GOING: Good to firm (firm in places; 8.6)
Wind: light, behind Weather: bright and sunny

1442 TOTEPLACEPOT MAIDEN STKS — 7f (S)
2:00 (2:02) (Class 5) 3-Y-O+ — **£2,729** (£806; £403) **Stalls** Low

Form RPR

042- **1** **The Rectifier (USA)**[194] 6616 3-8-13 80..... MickyFenton 9 78+
(Stef Higgins) *mde all: sn crossed to r on stands' rail: rdn over 1f out: r.o wl to draw clr fnl 100yds: won gng away* **7/4**[1]

02- **2** *2 1/4* **Rolling Hills (IRE)**[176] 7058 3-8-13 0..... DaneO'Neill 10 72
(H Candy) *dwlt: sn rcvrd to press wnr after 1f: ev ch and rdn 2f out: wknd ins fnl f* **5/1**[3]

04-0 **3** *nk* **Yes Chef**[23] 1029 3-8-13 67..... AlanMunro 1 71
(J Gallagher) *taken down early: chsd ldrs: rdn and sltly outpcd wl over 1f out: rallied and styd on wl ins fnl f: pressing for 2nd nr fin* **20/1**

25-0 **4** *6* **Joe Packet**[20] 1061 3-8-13 73..... StephenCraine 7 55
(J G Portman) *chsd ldrs: rdn wl over 1f out: btn ent fnl f: fdd fnl f* **11/2**

020- **5** *3 3/4* **Krymian**[195] 6592 3-8-13 84..... RyanMoore 13 45
(Sir Michael Stoute) *racd off the pce in midfield: pushed along 1/2-way: egded rt wl over 1f out: nvr gng pce to threaten ldrs* **4/1**[2]

00- **6** *3 1/4* **Micky P**[172] 7146 3-8-13 0..... SaleemGolam 11 36
(S C Williams) *dwlt: bhd: pushed along and hdwy into midfield 1/2-way: no hdwy and wl btn fnl 2f* **66/1**

6 **7** *2 1/4* **Majestatic**[13] 1164 3-8-13 0..... DavidProbert 4 30
(S W James) *chsd ldrs tl rdn over 2f out: sn struggling: wl btn over 1f out* **16/1**

0- **8** *hd* **Kinian (USA)**[225] 5722 3-8-13 0..... RobertWinston 6 29
(J R Best) *sn wl bhd: rdn 4f out: swtchd rt over 1f out: modest hdwy fnl f: nvr on terms* **66/1**

0 **9** *2 1/2* **Captain John Nixon**[13] 1165 3-8-13 0..... FrannyNorton 5 23
(Pat Eddery) *a bhd: nvr on terms* **50/1**

0 **10** *1* **Togoaviking**[13] 1165 3-8-13 0..... LiamJones 2 20
(W J Haggas) *racd in midfield tl lost pl and rdn 1/2-way: wl bhd fnl 2f* **14/1**

11 *34* **Paphos** 3-8-10 0..... WilliamCarson(3) 3 —
(S C Williams) *s.i.s: sn wl bhd: t.o fr 1/2-way* **14/1**

1m 23.77s (-3.53) **Going Correction** -0.30s/f (Firm)
WFA 3 from 4yo 13lb **11** Ran SP% **117.3**
Speed ratings (Par 103): **108,105,105,98,93 90,87,87,84,83 44**
toteswingers: 1&2 £3.00, 1&3 £5.50, 2&3 £18.40 CSF £10.21 TOTE £2.40: £1.10, £1.30, £11.10; EX 11.20 Trifecta £134.60 Pool: £312.98 - 1.72 winning units..
Owner Mrs Anne Cowley **Bred** Ceka Ireland Ltd **Trained** Lambourn, Berks

FOCUS
As per usual for Folkestone, the quickest ground looked to be against the stands'-side rail. Probably a fair enough maiden for the track and the time was only 0.01 outside the track record. The form is rated around the third and the winner probably didn't have to match his Newbury run.
Togoaviking Official explanation: trainer's rep said colt was unsuited by the track

1443 TOTESWINGER APPRENTICE H'CAP — 6f
2:30 (2:31) (Class 6) (0-60,59) 4-Y-O+ — **£2,047** (£604; £302) **Stalls** Low

Form RPR

42-5 **1** **Rough Rock (IRE)**[15] 1131 5-8-12 **53**..... MJMurphy 7 62+
(C A Dwyer) *w ldr: stl on bit over 1f out: pushed ahd ins fnl f: pushed clr fnl 100yds: comf* **10/1**

5065 **2** *1 1/4* **Thoughtsofstardom**[27] 972 7-8-5 **54**..... LeonnaMayor(8) 8 59
(P S McEntee) *led and crossed to r on stands' rail: rdn and edgd rt wl over 1f out: hdd ins fnl f: readily brushed aside fnl 100yds but kpt on for clr 2nd* **12/1**

00-0 **3** *2 1/4* **Bahama Baileys**[15] 1129 5-7-13 **45**..... HobieGill(5) 4 43+
(C A Dwyer) *in tch tl lost pl and bhd 4f out: hdwy over 1f out: r.o wl ins fnl f: wnt 3rd last stride: nvr threatened ldrs* **16/1**

0050 **4** *shd* **Bollywood Style**[10] 1224 5-8-12 **58**..... GerardGalligan(5) 1 55
(J R Best) *chsd ldrs: rdn and unable qck over 1f out: edgd rt and one pce fnl f: lost 3rd last stride* **9/2**[1]

5050 **5** *nk* **Whotsit (IRE)**[15] 1129 4-9-0 **55**.....(b) AdamBeschizza 3 52
(Miss Amy Weaver) *towards rr: rdn and effrt 2f out: styd on u.p ins fnl f: nvr gng pce to rch ldrs* **5/1**[2]

5430 **6** *3* **Who's Winning (IRE)**[6] 1304 9-9-0 **55**.....(t) AlexEdwards 11 42
(B G Powell) *chsd ldrs: rdn over 3f out: wknd over 1f out* **13/2**

0040 **7** *1/2* **Dynamo Dave (USA)**[41] 847 5-8-0 **46**.....(b) ThomasBrown(5) 5 31
(M D I Usher) *in rr: rdn and effrt on outer wl over 1f out: no real prog: nvr trbld ldrs* **12/1**

1306 **8** *3/4* **Saddlers Bend (IRE)**[13] 1171 4-9-2 **57**.....(p) BarryAdams 2 40
(George Baker) *a towards rr: rdn and no prog over 2f out: n.d* **8/1**

-535 **9** *hd* **Style Award**[33] 913 5-9-4 **59**..... HarryBentley 6 41
(W J H Ratcliffe) *chsd ldrs: rdn and unable qck wl over 1f out: wknd fnl f* **6/1**[3]

4000 **10** *nk* **Don Pele (IRE)**[13] 1166 8-9-0 **58**.....(b) JakePayne(3) 10 39
(R A Harris) *a towards rr: rdn 2f out: no prog and nvr trbld ldrs* **10/1**

0/0- **11** *nk* **Seven Royals (IRE)**[174] 7105 5-8-6 **52**..... FrancisHayes(5) 9 32
(Miss A M Newton-Smith) *dwlt: sn in tch in midfield: rdn over 3f out: wknd ent fnl 2f* **40/1**

1m 10.66s (-2.04) **Going Correction** -0.30s/f (Firm) **11** Ran SP% **115.5**
Speed ratings (Par 101): **101,99,96,96,95 91,91,90,89,89 89**
toteswingers: 1&2 £7.90, 1&3 £28.00, 2&3 £39.80 CSF £121.61 CT £1897.22 TOTE £11.10: £3.60, £3.50, £5.30; EX 77.00 TRIFECTA Not won..
Owner M M Foulger **Bred** Mrs B Stroomer **Trained** Burrough Green, Cambs

FOCUS
Moderate and questionable form, woth a lot of the runners being best on sand. Most of these apprentices seemed unaware the stands' rail was the place to be.
Saddlers Bend(IRE) Official explanation: trainer said filly was unsuited by the track

1444 TOTEQUADPOT (S) STKS — 5f
3:00 (3:00) (Class 6) 3-Y-O — **£2,047** (£604; £302) **Stalls** Low

Form RPR

1335 **1** **Anjomarba (IRE)**[43] 826 3-8-10 66.....(p) JackDean(3) 1 62
(W G M Turner) *mde all: rdn wl over 1f out: styd on wl to assert ins fnl f* **15/8**[1]

-465 **2** *1 1/2* **Tom Folan**[12] 1181 3-8-13 65.....(p) RobertWinston 3 57
(Andrew Reid) *s.i.s: sn in tch: rdn and effrt on outer over 1f out: chsd wnr ins fnl f: no imp fnl 100yds* **5/2**[2]

0454 **3** *1 1/4* **Annia Galeria (IRE)**[12] 1187 3-8-13 48.....(b[1]) FrannyNorton 2 52
(C A Dwyer) *chsd ldrs: rdn and effrt over 1f out: kpt on same pce ins fnl f* **14/1**[3]

0126 **4** *3/4* **Blue Neptune**[20] 1057 3-9-4 65..... RyanMoore 4 54
(P D Evans) *pressed wnr: ev ch and rdn over 1f out: wknd ins fnl f* **15/8**[1]

59.04 secs (-0.96) **Going Correction** -0.30s/f (Firm) **4** Ran SP% **104.8**
Speed ratings (Par 96): **95,92,90,89**
CSF £6.35 TOTE £4.20; EX 7.60.There was no bid for the winner.
Owner Marbary Partnership **Bred** Tally-Ho Stud **Trained** Sigwells, Somerset

FOCUS
A weak seller which has been rated through the third.

1445 BERNIE WICKS MEMORIAL H'CAP — 5f
3:30 (3:30) (Class 4) (0-80,75) 4-Y-O+ — **£4,857** (£1,445; £722; £360) **Stalls** Low

Form RPR

16 **1** **Absa Lutte (IRE)**[62] 578 7-9-4 **75**.....(t) StephenCraine 1 87+
(Patrick Morris) *taken down early: travelled strly: cl up and maintained position on stands' rail: pushed ahd ins fnl f: pushed clr fnl 100yds: comf* **8/1**

13-4 **2** *1 1/4* **Magical Speedfit (IRE)**[8] 1267 5-9-0 **71**..... DaneO'Neill 7 75
(G G Margarson) *trckd ldrs: rdn and effrt on outer over 1f out: nt pce of wnr fnl 100yds: kpt on to go 2nd nr fin* **3/1**[3]

1211 **3** *hd* **Misaro (GER)**[5] 1320 9-9-4 **75** 6ex.....(b) DavidProbert 5 78
(R A Harris) *disp ld: rdn ent fnl f: hdd ins fnl f: nt pce of wnr fnl 100yds: lost 2nd nr fin* **7/4**[1]

3631 **4** *nk* **Colorus (IRE)**[14] 1146 7-8-11 **73**.....(p) PaulPickard(5) 2 75
(W J H Ratcliffe) *disp ld: rdn over 1f out: hdd ins fnl f: nt pce of wnr fnl 100yds* **15/2**

10-3 **5** *10* **Pocket's Pick (IRE)**[19] 1074 4-8-8 **65**..... RyanMoore 6 31
(G L Moore) *hld up wl in tch: rdn and effrt over 1f out: wknd jst over 1f out: eased whn btn ins fnl f* **5/2**[2]

58.55 secs (-1.45) **Going Correction** -0.30s/f (Firm) course record **5** Ran SP% **112.8**
Speed ratings (Par 105): **99,97,96,96,80**
CSF £32.12 TOTE £11.40: £3.90, £1.70; EX 29.30.
Owner D & D Coatings Ltd **Bred** Ian Amond **Trained** Tarporley, Cheshire

FOCUS
A disappointing turnout numerically and yet again there was a bias towards the stands' rail. It was not that strongly run. The winner carried over her sand improvement.
Pocket's Pick(IRE) Official explanation: jockey said gelding lost its action

1446 TOTEEXACTA H'CAP — 1m 7f 92y
4:05 (4:05) (Class 5) (0-75,72) 4-Y-O+ — **£3,070** (£906; £453) **Stalls** High

Form RPR

000- **1** **Swordsman (GER)**[2] 6692 8-9-8 **66**.....(t) DaneO'Neill 4 74
(C Gordon) *chsd ldr: rdn 3f out: drvn to chal ent fnl 2f: led ins fnl f: styd on wl* **5/2**[2]

342- **2** *3/4* **Wightgold**[181] 6935 4-8-4 **51** oh1..... FrannyNorton 2 58
(H J L Dunlop) *chsd ldng pair: drvn to press ldrs ent fnl f: kpt on one pce fnl 150yds: wnt 2nd last stride* **4/1**[3]

410- **3** *shd* **Benozzo Gozzoli**[166] 7255 4-8-8 **55**..... NickyMackay 6 62+
(H Morrison) *led: rdn and edgd lft ent fnl 2f: hdd ins fnl f: no ex fnl 100yds: lost 2nd last stride* **13/8**[1]

1 **4** *10* **Oscar Close (IRE)**[12] 1183 5-9-7 **70**..... MatthewDavies(5) 1 64
(George Baker) *chsd ldng trio thrght: effrt and rdn ent fnl 2f: hung rt and btn over 1f out* **5/1**

24-0 **5** *5* **Golden Games (IRE)**[15] 120 4-8-10 **62**..... SimonPearce(5) 5 49
(D C O'Brien) *taken down early: a bhd: rdn 3f out: lost tch over 2f out* **16/1**

3m 27.14s (-2.56) **Going Correction** -0.075s/f (Good)
WFA 4 from 5yo+ 3lb **5** Ran SP% **109.2**
Speed ratings (Par 103): **103,102,102,97,94**
CSF £12.32 TOTE £4.30: £3.60, £1.20; EX 10.40.
Owner Mrs Kate Digweed **Bred** M Beining **Trained** Morestead, Hants

FOCUS
A modest staying handicap run at a fair pace. The winner probably did not need to quite match his best.

Benozzo Gozzoli ◆ Official explanation: trainer's rep said gelding was unsuited by the good to firm ground

1447 TOTEPOOL A BETTER WAY TO BET MAIDEN STKS 1m 4f
4:35 (4:35) (Class 5) 3-Y-0+ **£2,729** (£806; £403) **Stalls** High

Form RPR
1 **Submariner (USA)** 4-9-12 0 FrankieDettori 3 87+
(M Johnston) *chsd leader: led over 2f out: rdn wl clr over 1f out: rn green ent fnl f: eased towards fin* **11/8**[1]
6-5 2 8 **Widezain (IRE)**[15] 1132 3-8-7 0 AlanMunro 5 72
(M R Channon) *led: qcknd gallop 4f out: hdd over 2f out: no ch w wnr over 1f out* **15/8**[2]
00-0 3 14 **Sweet Request**[39] 875 6-9-8 45 (v) KevinGhunowa 1 45?
(Dr J R J Naylor) *in tch: chsd ldng pair and rdn 4f out: wl btn over 2f out: no ch fnl 2f* **40/1**
4 15 **All We Know** 3-8-7 0 (b[1]) EddieAhern 2 26
(H R A Cecil) *in tch tl dropped to last 4f out: sn lost tch: t.o* **9/4**[3]

2m 39.64s (-1.26) **Going Correction** -0.075s/f (Good)
WFA 3 from 4yo 20lb 4 from 6yo 1lb **4** Ran SP% **110.1**
Speed ratings (Par 103): **101,95,86,76**
CSF £4.38 TOTE £1.70; EX 4.30.
Owner Sheikh Hamdan Bin Mohammed Al Maktoum **Bred** Darley **Trained** Middleham Moor, N Yorks

FOCUS
A weak maiden but a likeable winner.The form is rated around the runner-up.

1448 HOBBES PARKER TELECOM H'CAP 1m 1f 149y
5:05 (5:06) (Class 5) (0-75,75) 3-Y-O **£3,070** (£906; £453) **Stalls** Centre

Form RPR
653- 1 **Berling (IRE)**[191] 6697 3-9-2 73 EddieAhern 6 83+
(J L Dunlop) *chsd ldrs: rdn and effrt 2f out: drvn and ev ch over 1f out: kpt on wl u.p: led on post* **13/2**
45-1 2 nse **Shelfah (IRE)**[13] 1158 3-8-9 66 FrankieDettori 2 76+
(M A Jarvis) *chsd ldrs: rdn over 2f out: edgd rt u.p wl over 1f out: led but hrd pressed fr over 1f out: kpt on u.p tl hdd on post* **3/1**[2]
1-3 3 shd **Dubai Bounty**[13] 1159 3-9-0 71 RyanMoore 7 80+
(G A Butler) *hld up in tch in last trio: rdn along over 2f out: hdwy to chal ent fnl f: kpt on wl u.p but a jst hld* **5/2**[1]
033- 4 4 ½ **Bonded (IRE)**[125] 7764 3-9-1 72 DaneO'Neill 1 72
(B J Meehan) *hld up in tch towards rr: effrt on outer ent fnl 2f: edgd rt and no imp over 1f out: plugged on same pce ent fnl f* **22/1**
554- 5 hd **Buffett**[209] 6211 3-8-10 67 J-PGuillambert 9 67+
(L M Cumani) *hld up in tch: pushed along 3f out: rdn and no prog on inner over 1f out: styd on same pce ins fnl f* **9/2**[3]
1-0 6 nse **Secretive**[22] 1045 3-9-4 75 GregFairley 8 74
(M Johnston) *broke wl: led: rdn over 2f out: hdd and drvn over 1f out: wknd fnl f: lost 2 pls nr fin* **14/1**
05-5 7 2 **Halyard (IRE)**[14] 1143 3-8-12 69 ShaneKelly 4 64
(W R Swinburn) *hld up in tch: rdn and n.m.r wl over 1f out: no prog u.p and btn over 1f out* **14/1**
3232 8 12 **Lingfield Bound (IRE)**[13] 1168 3-9-1 72 RobertWinston 5 69+
(J R Best) *sn chsng ldr: ev ch and rdn over 2f out: wkng whn bdly hmpd and snatched up wl over 1f out: wl hld after: eased ins fnl f* **8/1**
45-4 9 2 ½ **Leitzu (IRE)**[14] 1138 3-8-9 66 AlanMunro 3 31
(M R Channon) *s.i.s: a bhd: rdn and no prog over 2f out: wl btn and eased ins fnl f* **20/1**

2m 3.91s (-0.99) **Going Correction** -0.075s/f (Good) **9** Ran SP% **118.6**
Speed ratings (Par 98): **100,99,99,96,96 96,94,84,82**
toteswingers: 1&2 £6.80, 1&3 £3.30, 2&3 £3.20 CSF £27.12 CT £63.08 TOTE £8.80: £3.60, £1.10, £1.10; EX 33.20 Trifecta £128.30 Pool: £457.82 - 2.64 winning units. Place 6: £911.20 Place 5: £534.27.
Owner Benny Andersson **Bred** Ballylinch Stud **Trained** Arundel, W Sussex

FOCUS
A relatively interesting 3-y-o handicap featuring some unexposed types from powerful yards. Good form for the grade with the first three finishing clear. The winner improved by 10lb on his 2yo form.
T/Plt: £753.60 to a £1 stake. Pool: £51,932.17. 50.30 winning tickets. T/Qpdt: £86.30 to a £1 stake. Pool: £3,339.16. 28.60 winning tickets. SP

1345 KEMPTON (A.W) (R-H)
Tuesday, April 20

OFFICIAL GOING: Standard
Wind: nil Weather: sunny

1449 POST EVENTS CLAIMING STKS 6f (P)
2:20 (2:22) (Class 6) 3-Y-O **£2,047** (£604; £302) **Stalls** High

Form RPR
5103 1 **Craicattack (IRE)**[32] 932 3-8-11 (p) LiamKeniry 4 67
(J S Moore) *mde all: rdn over 2f out: kpt on wl* **7/4**[1]
20-6 2 1 ¼ **Stef And Stelio**[7] 1280 3-9-5 (p) RichardHughes 3 71
(G A Butler) *w ldr: ev ch over 2f out: sn rdn: kpt on but hld ins fnl f* **9/2**
3144 3 1 **Mrs Boss**[14] 1140 3-8-11 JamesMillman(3) 6 63
(B R Millman) *trckd ldrs: rdn over 2f out: kpt on same pce ins fnl f* **10/3**[3]
000- 4 2 **Musical Delight**[214] 6047 3-8-11 TomQueally 5 53
(A P Jarvis) *chsd ldrs: rdn over 2f out: kpt on same pce* **33/1**
1031 5 2 **Avow (USA)**[10] 1237 3-8-1 (b) RossAtkinson(5) 2 42
(J S Moore) *wnt lft s: racd in 6th: rdn over 2f out: little imp* **3/1**[2]
0-50 6 6 **Back On**[57] 655 3-8-6 MartinDwyer 1 23
(P Leech) *hmpd s: sn trcking ldrs: rdn 3f out: wknd over 1f out* **25/1**

1m 13.75s (0.65) **Going Correction** +0.05s/f (Slow) **6** Ran SP% **109.4**
Speed ratings (Par 96): **97,95,94,91,88 80**
toteswingers: 1&2 £1.90, 2&3 £2.10, 1&3 not won. CSF £9.50 TOTE £3.20: £1.90, £5.30; EX 9.90.
Owner W Adams & J S Moore **Bred** A M F Persse **Trained** Upper Lambourn, Berks

FOCUS
A couple of fair performers in an ordinary claimer which has been rated around the front three. The gallop was only a moderate one and the winner raced centre to far side in the straight.
Avow(USA) Official explanation: jockey said he lost an iron on leaving stalls

1450 IGI INSURANCE MAIDEN STKS 1m (P)
2:50 (2:54) (Class 5) 3-Y-O+ **£2,590** (£770; £385; £192) **Stalls** High

Form RPR
0- 1 **Signor Verdi**[179] 6990 3-8-12 0 KierenFallon 7 78
(B J Meehan) *in tch: rdn 2f out: r.o wl ins fnl f: led nr fin* **16/1**
06- 2 ½ **Aultcharn (FR)**[178] 7029 3-8-12 0 MartinDwyer 4 77
(B J Meehan) *a.p: rdn to ld 2f out: kpt on but no ex whn hdd nr fin* **8/1**[3]
-0 3 ¾ **Bowsers Brave (USA)**[8] 1260 4-9-12 0 KirstyMilczarek 12 79+
(M P Tregoning) *mid-div: outpcd over 2f out: styd on wl fnl f: wnt 3rd towards fin* **66/1**
4 hd **Break Serve (USA)** 3-8-12 0 AdamKirby 2 75+
(W R Swinburn) *hld up towards rr: hdwy over 2f out: sn rdn: styd on wl fnl f: nrst fin* **33/1**
5 nk **Sailorman (IRE)** 3-8-12 0 JoeFanning 1 74
(M Johnston) *led: rdn and hdd 2f out: fdd ins fnl f* **16/1**
33- 6 1 ¾ **Brannagh (USA)**[173] 7130 3-8-12 0 (t) TomQueally 14 70
(J Noseda) *trckd ldrs: rdn over 2f out: kpt on same pce* **9/2**[2]
2-2 7 2 **Clockmaker (IRE)**[15] 1127 4-9-12 0 WilliamBuick 10 69
(J H M Gosden) *t.k.h: trckd ldrs: rdn over 2f out: sn one pce* **4/5**[1]
43 8 ½ **Rock With You**[26] 980 3-8-7 0 LukeMorris 9 59
(J R Gask) *pushed along fr over 4f out: nvr bttr than mid-div* **14/1**
6- 9 hd **Lost In The Moment (IRE)**[192] 6679 3-8-12 0 RichardHughes 13 64
(J Noseda) *mid-div: swtchd lft over 2f out: sn rdn: no imp* **14/1**
05- 10 5 **Apache Kid (IRE)**[209] 6200 3-8-9 0 MartinLane(3) 6 52
(D M Simcock) *mid-div: rdn 3f out: wknd over 1f out* **66/1**
00 11 13 **Collect Art (IRE)**[23] 1029 3-8-12 0 HayleyTurner 5 22
(M L W Bell) *a in rr: hung lft and rn wd 5f out* **66/1**
12 6 **Euroquip Boy (IRE)** 3-8-12 0 JimCrowley 8 9
(M J Scudamore) *mid-div: rdn 3f out: sn wknd* **66/1**
13 3 ½ **Rocky Mood (IRE)** 3-8-12 0 TedDurcan 11 —
(W R Swinburn) *a towards rr* **40/1**
14 5 **Four Quartets (GER)** 4-9-5 0 SeanPalmer(7) 3 —
(D Shaw) *sn struggling in rr: t.o* **66/1**

1m 39.42s (-0.38) **Going Correction** +0.05s/f (Slow)
WFA 3 from 4yo 14lb **14** Ran SP% **122.8**
Speed ratings (Par 103): **103,102,101,101,101 99,97,97,96,91 78,72,69,64**
toteswingers: 1&2 £30.60, 1&3 £179.50, 2&3 £39.10 CSF £138.35 TOTE £29.40: £5.00, £3.10, £26.20; EX 97.60.
Owner Mrs Sheila Tucker **Bred** Newsells Park Stud Limited **Trained** Manton, Wilts
■ Stewards' Enquiry : Sean Palmer one-day ban: used whip when out of contention (May 4)

FOCUS
An interesting maiden on paper, but although this race did not take as much winning as seemed likely, with the favourite disappointing, it should still throw up its share of winners. The gallop was just an ordinary one and the winner came down the centre in the straight.

1451 ASPRAY MAIDEN FILLIES' STKS 1m 4f (P)
3:20 (3:24) (Class 5) 3-Y-O+ **£2,590** (£770; £385; £192) **Stalls** Centre

Form RPR
4 1 **Lady Eclair (IRE)**[33] 922 4-9-13 0 JoeFanning 1 72
(M Johnston) *slowly away: sn trcking ldr: rdn to ld over 1f out: styd on: drvn out* **12/1**
6-5 2 ½ **Gay Mirage (GER)**[7] 1271 3-8-8 0 (b[1]) NeilCallan 9 69
(M A Jarvis) *trckd ldrs: rdn to ld 2f out: sn drifted bdly lft to stands' side rails and hdd: kpt on but nt rcvr* **6/1**
3- 3 nk **Sister Earth (IRE)**[173] 7140 3-8-8 0 WilliamBuick 3 69
(J H M Gosden) *in tch: rdn to chse ldrs 4f out: styd on fnl f* **9/4**[1]
4 nk **Affinity** 3-8-8 0 TomQueally 4 69
(H R A Cecil) *s.i.s: sn in tch: pushed along over 6f out: rdn and hdwy 2f out: styd on fnl f* **5/2**[2]
42 5 5 **Yemeni Princess (IRE)**[46] 803 4-9-13 0 FergusSweeney 8 62
(B G Powell) *led: rdn and hdd 2f out: fdd fnl f* **4/1**[3]
0- 6 ½ **Kleio**[137] 7624 3-8-8 0 HayleyTurner 5 59
(H R A Cecil) *trckd ldrs: rdn over 2f out: fdd fnl f* **12/1**
00 7 7 **Prickles**[6] 1302 5-10-0 0 TomMcLaughlin 7 50?
(Karen George) *a towards rr: nvr gng pce to get on terms* **50/1**
8 16 **Champagne Floozie**[37] 7-10-0 0 LiamKeniry 6 24
(J C Fox) *mid-div tl wknd over 3f out: t.o* **80/1**
000- 9 10 **Tiffany Lady**[134] 7666 4-9-8 38 LeeNewnes(5) 2 8
(M D I Usher) *a towards rr: t.o* **100/1**

2m 35.64s (1.14) **Going Correction** +0.05s/f (Slow)
WFA 3 from 4yo 20lb 4 from 5yo+ 1lb **9** Ran SP% **113.2**
Speed ratings (Par 100): **98,97,97,97,93 93,88,78,71**
toteswingers: 1&2 £7.10, 1&3 £5.60, 2&3 £4.20 CSF £79.92 TOTE £11.10: £3.60, £1.40, £1.70; EX 65.00.
Owner Netherfield House Stud **Bred** Lynch Bages Ltd & Samac Ltd **Trained** Middleham Moor, N Yorks

FOCUS
A weakish maiden and one run at just a modest early gallop. The winner ended up close to the inside rail, whereas the runner-up drifted to the stands' rail late on. The first three showed improvement.
Gay Mirage(GER) Official explanation: jockey said filly hung left-handed
Yemeni Princess(IRE) Official explanation: jockey said filly hung left-handed

1452 ARAG H'CAP 1m 4f (P)
3:55 (3:55) (Class 4) (0-85,81) 3-Y-O **£4,209** (£1,252; £625; £312) **Stalls** Centre

Form RPR
321 1 **Atlantic Tiger (IRE)**[52] 734 3-9-3 77 JoeFanning 3 87+
(M Johnston) *trckd ldr: led over 2f out: rdn and narrowly hdd ent fnl f: rallied wl to ld sn after: styd on strly* **5/2**[2]
33-1 2 2 ¾ **Mawaddah (IRE)**[49] 758 3-9-2 76 RichardHughes 1 83+
(R Hannon) *hld up bhd ldrs: tk clsr order 3f out: rdn over 1f out: led ent fnl f: sn hdd: no ex* **6/1**
110- 3 nk **Wild Rose**[171] 7187 3-9-7 81 HayleyTurner 4 86
(M L W Bell) *trckd ldrs: rdn over 2f out: styd on fnl f* **7/1**
45-1 4 9 **Mercoliano**[57] 664 3-9-5 79 KierenFallon 5 70
(M Botti) *led: rdn and hdd over 2f out: wknd over 1f out* **13/8**[1]
21 5 9 **Goodlukin Lucy**[16] 1103 3-9-1 78 MartinLane(3) 2 54
(Pat Eddery) *trckd ldrs: rdn wl over 2f out: sn btn* **5/1**[3]

2m 33.78s (-0.72) **Going Correction** +0.05s/f (Slow) **5** Ran SP% **110.1**
Speed ratings (Par 100): **104,102,101,95,89**
CSF £16.75 TOTE £2.70: £1.80, £10.20; EX 15.00.
Owner Atlantic Racing Limited **Bred** Darley **Trained** Middleham Moor, N Yorks

FOCUS
Only five runners, but all had won at least once and four had scored on their previous start. However, the gallop was only fair at best and the race took less winning than seemed likely with the market leader disappointing. The first three finished clear and the winner raced in the centre in the straight.

Mercoliano Official explanation: jockey said gelding stopped quickly

1453 SSP H'CAP 7f (P)
4:25 (4:29) (Class 4) (0-80,79) 3-Y-O £4,209 (£1,252; £625; £312) Stalls High

Form				RPR
0-1	1		**Avenuesnalleyways (IRE)**[107] 24 3-8-13 74 ... JimCrowley 5 (R M Beckett) *mde all: stdy on strly: rdn out* 7/1[3]	89
443-	2	2 ½	**Tartan Trip**[181] 6943 3-9-1 76 ... JimmyFortune 11 (A M Balding) *trckd ldrs: rdn to chse wnr wl over 1f out: kpt on but a being hld* 7/2[1]	84
216	3	4	**Dominium (USA)**[17] 1086 3-9-2 77 ... LukeMorris 9 (J R Gask) *in tch: pushed along over 5f out: clsd on ldrs over 1f out: styd on ins fnl f: wnt 3rd nr fin* 5/1[2]	74
00-0	4	1 ½	**Avon River**[24] 1018 3-9-3 78 ... RichardHughes 2 (R Hannon) *prom: rdn over 2f out: no ex ins fnl f: lost 3rd nr fin* 20/1	71
00-4	5	4	**Damietta (USA)**[11] 1210 3-9-0 75 ... JoeFanning 8 (M Johnston) *trckd ldrs: rdn over 2f out: wknd over 1f out* 16/1	62
031-	6	1 ¾	**Scottish Boogie (IRE)**[175] 7097 3-9-2 77 ... WilliamBuick 6 (S Kirk) *nvr bttr than mid-div* 16/1	55
140-	7	hd	**Ice Cool Lady (IRE)**[158] 7363 3-8-11 72 ... TedDurcan 10 (W R Swinburn) *a towards rr* 33/1	49
010-	8	1 ¼	**Running Mate (IRE)**[262] 4525 3-9-2 77 ... FergusSweeney 1 (Miss Jo Crowley) *a towards rr* 40/1	51
00-1	9	½	**Faited To Pretend (IRE)**[25] 985 3-8-12 73 ... MartinDwyer 3 (M Botti) *a towards rr* 16/1	45
540-	10	7	**Farmers Wish (IRE)**[164] 7290 3-9-2 77 ... NeilCallan 4 (J L Spearing) *in tch: rdn over 3f out: wknd over 1f out* 20/1	30

1m 25.94s (-0.06) **Going Correction** +0.05s/f (Slow) 10 Ran SP% 83.9
Speed ratings (Par 100): **102,99,94,92,88 86,86,84,84,76**
toteswingers: 1&2 £3.40, 1&3 £3.50, 2&3 £2.70 CSF £14.65 CT £40.20 TOTE £5.10: £1.40, £1.20, £1.50; EX 19.00.
Owner Tony Perkins & James D Cameron **Bred** P G Lyons **Trained** Whitsbury, Hants

FOCUS
Several previous winners in a fair handicap, but it was weakened by the late defection of market leader Red Gulch, who refused to enter the stalls (7/4F, deduct 35p in the £ under R4). The modest gallop suited the prominent-racers and the winner raced centre to far side in the straight. The form has been rated at something like face value and could be up to 6lb higher.
Avon River Official explanation: jockey said colt hung right-handed in straight
Damietta(USA) Official explanation: jockey said saddle slipped

1454 GROUPAMA HEALTHCARE H'CAP 2m (P)
5:00 (5:00) (Class 4) (0-85,73) 4-Y-O+ £4,209 (£1,252; £625; £312) Stalls High

Form				RPR
122-	1		**Ermyn Lodge**[202] 6388 4-9-8 73 ...(v) JackMitchell 4 (P M Phelan) *mde all: styd on strly fnl f: rdn out* 5/4[1]	82+
422-	2	2 ½	**Gaselee (USA)**[181] 6951 4-9-4 69 ... MartinDwyer 3 (Rae Guest) *trckd wnr: chal 3f out: sn rdn: styd on but no ex fnl f* 5/1[3]	75
35	3	1 ¾	**Prince Charlemagne (IRE)**[25] 989 7-9-7 68 ... FergusSweeney 1 (G L Moore) *hld up: hdwy 3f out: sn rdn: styd on same pce fr over 1f out* 13/2	74
2243	4	3	**Calculating (IRE)**[20] 1069 6-9-6 72 ... LeeNewnes(5) 2 (M D I Usher) *trckd ldrs: chal 4f out: one pce fr over 2f out* 9/2[2]	72
060-	5	9	**Star Of Pompey**[188] 6785 6-8-7 54 ... JoeFanning 5 (M R Hoad) *trckd ldrs: effrt 3f out: wknd over 1f out* 17/2	44
214-	6	23	**Fleur De'Lion (IRE)**[120] 7831 4-8-12 63 ... RichardHughes 7 (S Kirk) *hld up: rdn over 3f out: no imp and sn btn* 12/1	25

3m 32.6s (2.50) **Going Correction** +0.05s/f (Slow)
WFA 4 from 6yo+ 4lb 6 Ran SP% 110.8
Speed ratings (Par 105): **95,93,92,91,86 75**
toteswingers: 1&2 £2.00, 1&3 £2.80, 2&3 £4.40 CSF £7.60 TOTE £2.30: £1.90, £1.90; EX 7.00.
Owner Ermyn Lodge Stud & Heatherwold Stud **Bred** Horizon Bloodstock Limited **Trained** Epsom, Surrey

FOCUS
Exposed performers in just a fair handicap, and a race in which the gallop was a modest one to the straight. The winner, who raced just off the inside rail late on, did not need to improve.

1455 INSURANCE JOBS H'CAP (LONDON MILE QUALIFIER) 1m (P)
5:35 (5:36) (Class 3) (0-95,95) 4-Y-O+ £6,542 (£1,959; £979; £490; £244; £122) Stalls High

Form				RPR
130-	1		**Splendorinthegrass (IRE)**[192] 6675 4-9-4 95 ... TedDurcan 1 (D R Lanigan) *sn trcking ldr: rdn 2f out: str chal thrght fnl f: led fnl strides: all out* 8/1	103
4054	2	hd	**Samarinda (USA)**[31] 947 7-8-9 86 ow1 ... MickyFenton 10 (Mrs P Sly) *led: rdn 2f out: hrd pressed thrght fnl f: battled on gamely: narrowly hdd fnl strides* 9/1	94
50-0	3	¾	**Moynahan (USA)**[24] 1006 5-8-10 87 ...(p) WilliamBuick 2 (P F I Cole) *mid-div: rdn over 2f out: styd on fr over 1f out: little short of room towards fin* 9/2[2]	93
-026	4	1	**Wigram's Turn (USA)**[31] 944 5-8-12 89 ...(v) JimmyFortune 4 (A M Balding) *hld up towards rr: swtchd lft ent st: sn rdn: styd on to chse ldrs ins fnl f: hld fnl 75yds* 13/2	93+
1621	5	nk	**Gaily Noble (IRE)**[31] 943 4-8-8 90 ... AmyBaker(5) 6 (A B Haynes) *trckd ldrs: rdn over 2f out: kpt on but no ex ins fnl f: lost 2 pls nr fin* 5/1[3]	93
-220	6	3 ¼	**Pegasus Again (USA)**[10] 1219 5-8-10 87 ... TomQueally 9 (R A Mills) *s.i.s: towards rr: nt clr run 2f out: sn rdn: sme prog but nvr a danger* 7/2[1]	88+
105-	7	nse	**The Which Doctor**[178] 7035 5-8-11 88 ... HayleyTurner 3 (J Noseda) *a towards rr: sme late prog but nvr gng pce to get on terms* 10/1	84
56-0	8	½	**Grand Vizier (IRE)**[90] 231 6-8-10 87 ... JackMitchell 7 (C F Wall) *hld up towards rr: rdn 4f out: sme prog 3f out: nvr on terms w ldrs* 12/1	82
04-3	9	1 ¼	**Shaws Diamond (USA)**[41] 850 4-8-4 81 oh3 ... LukeMorris 5 (D Shaw) *trckd ldrs: rdn over 2f out: sn wknd* 25/1	73
-510	10	2	**Orchard Supreme**[8] 1265 7-8-12 89 ... RichardHughes 8 (R Hannon) *mid-div: rdn over 2f out: wknd fnl f* 8/1	76

1m 38.81s (-0.99) **Going Correction** +0.05s/f (Slow) 10 Ran SP% 123.3
Speed ratings (Par 107): **106,105,105,104,103 100,100,99,98,96**
CSF £82.32 CT £379.85 TOTE £13.10: £5.60, £4.00, £2.90; EX 106.00 Place 6: £109.30 Place 5: £56.43 .
Owner B E Nielsen **Bred** Ballylinch Stud **Trained** Newmarket, Suffolk

FOCUS
A decent-quality handicap featuring mainly exposed sorts, but a moderate early gallop saw those right up with the pace hold the edge. The first five finished clear of the remainder and the principals came down the centre in the straight. Sound enough form.

NOTEBOOK
Splendorinthegrass(IRE) ◆ reportedly finished sore behind when disappointing on his final start for Roger Charlton last October but ran right up to his best after being ideally positioned on this AW debut and on this first outing since being gelded. Things went his way here but he's a very useful sort and one lightly raced enough to be open to further progress for this yard.
Samarinda(USA) has not won for well over a year, but has slipped to a fair mark and returned to his best dropped a fair way in trip with more forceful tactics adopted. He is capable of breaking that losing run, especially if he's allowed a similarly easy time of it in front. (tchd 17-2)
Moynahan(USA) fared a good deal better returned to Polytrack than he had in the Spring Mile at Doncaster on his reappearance, but although he too has slipped to a fair mark, he's yet to win a handicap and his record since his maiden win in 2007 has been one of inconsistency. He would be no certainty to build on this next time. (op 13-2 tchd 7-1)
Wigram's Turn(USA), having his first run beyond 7f, may be better than the bare form as he fared easily the best of those held up. A stronger end-to-end gallop returned to a shorter distance may be more to his liking and, although he may not be entirely straightforward, he could win again on Polytrack when things drop right. Official explanation: jockey said gelding hung right-handed (op 11-2)
Gaily Noble(IRE) has been running well on Polytrack this year and posted another solid effort, despite racing with the choke out in the first half of the contest. He should continue to give a good account. (op 9-2 tchd 4-1)
Pegasus Again(USA) missed a beat at the start and was below his best after being unable to take his usual position at the head of affairs. He will be worth another chance when it looks as though he will be able to dominate. (op 6-1 tchd 13-2)
Shaws Diamond(USA) Official explanation: jockey said filly hung left-handed
T/Plt: £318.30 to a £1 stake. Pool: £47,577.18. 109.09 winning tickets. T/Qpdt: £8.50 to a £1 stake. Pool: £3,866.12. 335.29 winning tickets. TM

1234 WOLVERHAMPTON (A.W) (L-H)
Tuesday, April 20

OFFICIAL GOING: Standard
Wind: Fresh across Weather: Cloudy

1456 STAY AT THE WOLVERHAMPTON HOLIDAY INN H'CAP 5f 216y(P)
2:10 (2:11) (Class 6) (0-60,60) 3-Y-O £1,774 (£523; £262) Stalls Low

Form				RPR
00-4	1		**Jigajig**[25] 998 3-8-4 46 ... PaulHanagan 12 (K A Ryan) *mde all: rdn over 1f out: r.o* 6/1[2]	55
32-4	2	2 ½	**Dimaire**[11] 1205 3-9-2 58 ... JamieSpencer 13 (D Haydn Jones) *chsd wnr: rdn and hung lft over 1f out: no imp fnl f* 11/2[1]	59
-062	3	2 ¼	**Cheshire Lady (IRE)**[11] 1205 3-8-5 52 ... DeclanCannon(5) 1 (W M Brisbourne) *s.i.s: hld up: hdwy over 1f out: edgd rt and r.o to go 3rd wl ins fnl f: nrst fin* 8/1[3]	46+
4003	4	1	**Lady Brickhouse**[11] 1205 3-8-4 46 ...(b[1]) SilvestreDeSousa 11 (M D Squance) *prom: rdn over 1f out: hung lft ins fnl f: styd on same pce* 12/1	37
4465	5	¾	**Blades Harmony**[25] 991 3-8-10 59 ...(b[1]) DavidKenny(7) 2 (E S McMahon) *s.i.s: hdwy 5f out: rdn over 1f out: kpt on u.p* 12/1	47
000-	6	¾	**Bird On The Wire**[154] 7421 3-8-7 54 ... AshleyMorgan(5) 9 (W G M Turner) *mid-div: hdwy over 2f out: rdn over 1f out: styd on same pce* 33/1	40
60-6	7	½	**Proper Littlemadam**[13] 1175 3-9-4 60 ... FrederikTylicki 3 (C N Kellett) *mid-div: dropped in rr over 3f out: styd on u.p ins fnl f: nt trble ldrs* 40/1	44
-416	8	hd	**Sweet Mirasol (IRE)**[25] 991 3-8-12 54 ...(t) JimmyQuinn 10 (Miss M E Rowland) *s.i.s: sn pushed along in rr: styd on ins fnl f: nvr nrr* 12/1	38+
-560	9	¾	**Caol Ila (IRE)**[15] 1118 3-8-8 50 ... PaulMulrennan 5 (J G Given) *prom: hmpd over 4f out: rdn over 1f out: btn whn hmpd ins fnl f* 10/1	38+
23-3	10	3 ¼	**Sharp Shoes**[13] 1155 3-9-1 57 ... RoystonFfrench 4 (Mrs A Duffield) *chsd ldrs: rdn over 2f out: wknd over 1f out* 6/1[2]	28
00-0	11	2 ¾	**Boga (IRE)**[13] 1168 3-8-11 53 ... RichardKingscote 7 (R J Hodges) *chsd ldrs: rdn and hung lft over 1f out: wknd fnl f* 6/1[2]	15
040-	12	2 ½	**Polly Macho (IRE)**[267] 4384 3-8-11 53 ... PatCosgrave 8 (P D Evans) *sn outpcd: bhd fr 1/2-way* 16/1	7
06-6	13	13	**Crystal Glass**[38] 886 3-8-4 46 oh1 ... DuranFentiman 6 (T D Easterby) *sn pushed along in rr: bhd fr 1/2-way* 33/1	—

1m 14.72s (-0.28) **Going Correction** -0.05s/f (Stan) 13 Ran SP% 115.7
Speed ratings (Par 96): **99,95,92,91,90 89,88,88,87,83 79,76,58**
toteswingers: 1&2 £2.80, 1&3 £7.40, 2&3 £6.10 CSF £37.05 CT £275.07 TOTE £7.20: £2.90, £1.10, £3.40; EX 29.50.
Owner Mrs Maureen Eason **Bred** Miss D Fleming **Trained** Hambleton, N Yorks
■ Stewards' Enquiry : Paul Hanagan one-day ban: careless riding (May 4)

FOCUS
A low-grade 46-60 sprint handicap and the first two home were one-two throughout despite being drawn widest of all. A personal best from the winner on only his second start for Ryan.
Sweet Mirasol(IRE) Official explanation: jockey said filly was denied a clear run
Caol Ila(IRE) Official explanation: jockey said filly suffered interference in running

1457 SPONSOR A RACE BY CALLING 01902 390000 (S) STKS 7f 32y(P)
2:40 (2:41) (Class 6) 3-Y-O+ £1,774 (£523; £262) Stalls High

Form				RPR
4042	1		**Tous Les Deux**[5] 1322 7-9-7 67 ... GeorgeBaker 1 (G L Moore) *trckd ldrs: nt clr run fr over 1f out: hmpd ent fnl f: shkn up and styd on to ld towards fin* 11/8[1]	63+
-455	2	nk	**Libertino (IRE)**[32] 932 3-8-8 67 ...(b[1]) JamieSpencer 2 (B J Meehan) *chsd ldrs: rdn to ld and hung lft fr over 1f out: hdd towards fin* 3/1[2]	57
0004	3	2 ½	**Athaakeel (IRE)**[10] 1239 4-9-2 55 ow2 ... ShaneRyan(7) 8 (R A Harris) *hld up: hdwy 1/2-way: rdn over 1f out: r.o* 25/1	57
40-0	4	shd	**Polemica (IRE)**[13] 1170 4-9-2 56 ... JamesDoyle 4 (F Sheridan) *s.i.s: hld up: hdwy over 2f out: rdn over 1f out: r.o* 16/1	50
00-0	5	1 ¼	**Cordell (IRE)**[15] 1128 5-9-7 85 ...(b[1]) PaulHanagan 6 (P D Evans) *led: rdn and hdd over 1f out: no ex fnl f* 11/2[3]	51
2165	6	1	**Mountain Pass (USA)**[12] 1193 8-9-12 50 ...(p) RobertHavlin 3 (B J Llewellyn) *hld up: r.o ins fnl f: nvr nrr* 22/1	54
/00-	7	4	**Bellomi (IRE)**[336] 2149 5-9-7 70 ... VinceSlattery 5 (A G Juckes) *prom: rdn over 2f out: sn wknd* 33/1	38
4313	8	4 ½	**Tri Chara (IRE)**[10] 1235 6-9-5 57 ...(p) LeeTopliss(7) 7 (R Hollinshead) *sn chsng ldr: rdn over 2f out: wknd over 1f out* 10/1	31

The Form Book, Raceform Ltd, Compton, RG20 6NL

45-0 **9** ½ **Unbelievable Jeff**[13] 1167 4-9-7 46............................(b[1]) PatCosgrave 9 24
(J S Moore) *hld up: rdn and wknd over 2f out* **33/1**
1m 29.36s (-0.24) **Going Correction** -0.05s/f (Stan)
WFA 3 from 4yo+ 13lb **9** Ran SP% **111.5**
Speed ratings (Par 101): **99,98,95,95,94 93,88,83,82**
toteswingers: 1&2 £1.80, 1&3 £5.80, 2&3 £6.60 CSF £4.85 TOTE £2.00: £1.02, £1.70, £6.70; EX 6.60.There was no bid for the winner.
Owner A Grinter **Bred** G And Mrs Middlebrook **Trained** Lower Beeding, W Sussex

FOCUS
A standard selling race. There were doubts over several of them and the winner did not need to match his recent handicap form.

1458 VERSION ONE DOCUMENT MANAGEMENT & IMAGING H'CAP 7f 32y(P)
3:10 (3:10) (Class 4) (0-80,78) 4-Y-0+ **£4,209** (£1,252; £625; £312) **Stalls** High

Form RPR
000- **1** **Malcheek (IRE)**[144] 7558 8-9-4 **78**............................ DavidAllan 3 89
(T D Easterby) *trckd ldrs: led over 1f out: sn edgd rt: shkn up and styd on wl: eased nr fin* **11/2**[2]
-133 **2** 3 **Rubenstar (IRE)**[85] 292 7-8-11 **71**............................ JamieSpencer 8 74
(Patrick Morris) *hld up: hdwy over 1f out: rdn and edgd rt ins fnl f: styd on same pce* **3/1**[1]
353- **3** ½ **Southandwest (IRE)**[111] 7883 6-9-4 **78**............................ JimmyQuinn 7 80
(J S Moore) *prom: rdn over 2f out: r.o ins fnl f* **3/1**[1]
1606 **4** nk **Kipchak (IRE)**[13] 1149 5-9-0 **74**............................(p) PJMcDonald 4 75
(C R Dore) *led: rdn and hdd over 1f out: no ex ins fnl f* **14/1**
265- **5** ½ **Legal Eagle (IRE)**[165] 7269 5-9-3 **77**............................ SilvestreDeSousa 6 77
(Paul Green) *chsd ldr: rdn over 2f out: ev ch wl over 1f out: no ex fnl f* **8/1**
3233 **6** ¾ **Seasider**[6] 1301 5-8-11 **78**............................(b[1]) LauraPike(7) 5 76
(D M Simcock) *s.s: hld up: rdn over 1f out: nt trble ldrs* **6/1**[3]
004- **7** 1 ¼ **Ergo (FR)**[149] 5886 6-8-7 **67**............................(b) PaulHanagan 2 61
(James Moffatt) *hld up: rdn over 2f out: n.d* **16/1**
4241 **8** 9 **Justcallmehandsome**[10] 1238 8-8-8 **73**............................(v) BillyCray(5) 1 43
(D J S Ffrench Davis) *mid-div: sn pushed along: wknd 2f out* **10/1**
1m 27.92s (-1.68) **Going Correction** -0.05s/f (Stan) **8** Ran SP% **112.4**
Speed ratings (Par 105): **107,103,103,102,102 101,99,89**
toteswingers: 1&2 £4.20, 1&3 £4.60, 2&3 £2.10 CSF £21.59 CT £57.88 TOTE £6.10: £1.70, £1.10, £1.60; EX 24.10.
Owner Habton Farms **Bred** Carrigbeg Stud **Trained** Great Habton, N Yorks

FOCUS
An open looking 67-78 handicap, but in the end a most decisive winner in Malcheek, who rates his best effort in two years at face value. The pace was sound.
Justcallmehandsome Official explanation: jockey said gelding never travelled; vet said gelding finished distressed

1459 HOTEL & CONFERENCING AT WOLVERHAMPTON H'CAP 2m 119y(P)
3:45 (3:50) (Class 6) (0-65,63) 4-Y-0+ **£1,774** (£523; £262) **Stalls** Low

Form RPR
0612 **1** **Bold Adventure**[7] 1273 6-9-8 **56**............................ TonyCulhane 9 65+
(W J Musson) *hld up: hdwy over 2f out: rdn and hung rt fr over 1f out: styd on to ld wl ins fnl f* **9/4**[1]
60/5 **2** ¾ **Pearl (IRE)**[21] 121 6-8-12 **46**............................(tp) JimmyQuinn 8 54
(Mrs A M Thorpe) *chsd ldrs: rdn 4f out: ev ch ins fnl f* **20/1**
0-43 **3** ½ **Rare Coincidence**[20] 1071 9-9-2 **50**............................(p) PaulHanagan 3 57
(R F Fisher) *led: rdn over 1f out: edgd rt and hdd wl ins fnl f* **14/1**[3]
4 1 **Salontyre (GER)**[42] 4-9-3 **55**............................ RobertHavlin 4 61+
(B J Llewellyn) *hld up: hdwy over 5f out: rdn over 1f out: styd on same pce ins fnl f* **16/1**
3130 **5** 1 **Delorain (IRE)**[7] 1283 7-9-1 **49**............................(vt) JerryO'Dwyer 1 54
(W B Stone) *chsd ldr: rdn over 2f out: no ex fnl f* **10/1**[2]
3-00 **6** 13 **Dawn Storm (IRE)**[95] 186 5-8-8 **45**............................(v[1]) KellyHarrison(3) 11 34
(J L Spearing) *hld up: hdwy 12f out: rdn and wknd 2f out* **25/1**
6-05 **7** 10 **Telling Stories (IRE)**[20] 1071 4-8-7 **45**............................(bt[1]) SilvestreDeSousa 10 22
(B D Leavy) *mid-div: rdn over 4f out: wknd 3f out* **40/1**
00-4 **8** nk **Uncle Keef (IRE)**[8] 1262 4-9-8 **60**............................ GeorgeBaker 2 43
(M P Tregoning) *chsd ldrs: rdn over 3f out: wknd 2f out: eased* **9/4**[1]
2-04 **9** ½ **Strikemaster (IRE)**[29] 764 4-8-13 **58**............................(p) DaleSwift(7) 5 34
(B Ellison) *hld up: bhd fr 1/2-way* **16/1**
3402 **10** 2 ½ **They All Laughed**[35] 898 7-9-4 **52**............................(p) PJMcDonald 13 25
(Mrs Marjorie Fife) *mid-div: rdn and lost pl over 5f out: sn bhd* **10/1**[2]
156- **11** dist **Harlequinn Danseur (IRE)**[331] 2294 5-9-2 **50**............................ PatCosgrave 12 —
(P D Evans) *hld up: rdn and wknd over 5f out: t.o* **16/1**
12 dist **Catch A Cloud**[9] 5239 4-9-11 **63**............................ FrederikTylicki 6 —
(James Moffatt) *hld up: bhd fnl 7f: t.o* **66/1**
0 **13** 22 **Slayer**[62] 586 5-9-4 **52**............................(vt[1]) VinceSlattery 7 —
(M S Tuck) *chsd ldrs tl rdn and wknd over 5f out: t.o* **100/1**
3m 38.48s (-3.32) **Going Correction** -0.05s/f (Stan)
WFA 4 from 5yo+ 4lb **13** Ran SP% **117.6**
Speed ratings (Par 101): **105,104,104,103,103 97,92,92,92,91 —,—,—**
toteswingers: 1&2 £11.00, 1&3 £5.40, 2&3 £18.00 CSF £57.31 CT £526.34 TOTE £3.00: £1.10, £6.60, £4.60; EX 58.60.
Owner The Adventurers **Bred** Bricklow Ltd **Trained** Newmarket, Suffolk

FOCUS
A modest 45-63 stayers' handicap run at a true gallop and in a fair time for the grade. Solid form.
Uncle Keef(IRE) Official explanation: trainer's rep said gelding had a breathing problem
Catch A Cloud Official explanation: jockey said gelding never travelled

1460 WOLVERHAMPTON HOSPITALITY - A PLEASURE MEDIAN AUCTION MAIDEN STKS 1m 1f 103y(P)
4:15 (4:16) (Class 6) 3-Y-O **£1,774** (£523; £262) **Stalls** Low

Form RPR
44- **1** **Arctic Cosmos (USA)**[186] 6821 3-9-3 0............................ RobertHavlin 5 75+
(J H M Gosden) *s.i.s: hld up: hdwy 2f out: shkn up to ld ins fnl f: edgd lft and r.o: comf* **7/4**[1]
2 4 **Innocuous** 3-9-0 0............................ AhmedAjtebi(3) 6 67+
(D M Simcock) *trckd ldrs: plld hrd: rdn to ld over 1f out: hdd and unable qck ins fnl f: hung lft towards fin* **9/1**
3 1 **Business Bay (USA)** 3-9-3 0............................ JamieSpencer 1 64
(E F Vaughan) *disp ld: rdn and ev ch over 1f out: no ex ins fnl f: hung lft towards fin* **13/2**[3]
0- **4** shd **Lucky Diva**[225] 5714 3-8-12 0............................ JamesDoyle 4 59
(S Kirk) *hld up: rdn over 2f out: r.o ins fnl f: nt rch ldrs* **28/1**
0 **5** ½ **Raktiman (IRE)**[23] 1029 3-9-3 0............................ RichardKingscote 8 63+
(Tom Dascombe) *chsd ldrs: rdn over 3f out: hung lft and no ex fnl f* **16/1**
0- **6** ½ **Home Advantage**[187] 6792 3-9-3 0............................ PaulHanagan 2 64+
(R Charlton) *chsd ldrs: pushed along over 3f out: styng on same pce whn nt clr run towards fin* **9/2**[2]
-323 **7** 1 ½ **Dane Cottage**[40] 858 3-8-12 65............................ JimmyQuinn 7 56
(Miss Gay Kelleway) *hld up: shkn up over 3f out: n.d* **13/2**[3]
53 **8** 1 ¾ **Mark To Market (IRE)**[14] 1143 3-8-12 0............................ SophieDoyle(5) 3 55
(J A Osborne) *disp ld tl over 1f out: wknd ins fnl f* **10/1**
2m 2.74s (1.04) **Going Correction** -0.05s/f (Stan) **8** Ran SP% **109.6**
Speed ratings (Par 96): **93,89,88,88,88 87,86,84**
toteswingers: 1&2 £4.20, 1&3 £3.70, 2&3 £8.80 CSF £16.82 TOTE £3.10: £1.30, £3.60, £2.30; EX 15.80.
Owner Ms Rachel D S Hood **Bred** Sheridan & Iadora Farm **Trained** Newmarket, Suffolk

FOCUS
An ordinary median auction maiden, and muddling form which has been rated around the seventh. The winner is up 6lb on his debut form.

1461 ENJOY THE PARTY PACK GROUP OFFER H'CAP 1m 1f 103y(P)
4:45 (4:46) (Class 6) (0-55,55) 3-Y-O **£1,774** (£523; £262) **Stalls** Low

Form RPR
3406 **1** **Sternian**[15] 1132 3-9-0 **52**............................ JamieMackay 7 52
(M E Rimmer) *a.p: nt clr run over 1f out: rdn to ld and hung lft wl ins fnl f* **20/1**
056- **2** ½ **Man In The Mirror (IRE)**[129] 7722 3-8-11 **52**......(p) AshleyHamblett(3) 8 51
(P L Gilligan) *led over 8f out: rdn over 1f out: hdd wl ins fnl f* **18/1**
030 **3** 1 **Single Lady**[33] 922 3-9-3 **55**............................ JamieSpencer 9 52
(J S Moore) *hld up: hdwy on outer over 4f out: rdn over 1f out: hung lft ins fnl f: r.o* **8/1**
00-5 **4** ½ **Dubara Reef (IRE)**[16] 1100 3-8-8 **46** oh1............................ SilvestreDeSousa 12 42
(Paul Green) *chsd ldrs: rdn over 3f out: ev ch over 1f out: no ex towards fin* **16/1**
2344 **5** 1 **Always De One**[34] 904 3-9-2 **54**............................(p) JimmyQuinn 5 48
(Miss J Feilden) *hld up: hdwy over 3f out: rdn over 1f out: hung lft and no ex ins fnl f* **6/1**[3]
005- **6** 3 **Crushing (IRE)**[124] 7788 3-9-1 **53**............................ TomEaves 4 40
(Julie Camacho) *hld up in tch: plld hrd: nt clr run over 2f out: sn rdn: styd on same pce fnl f* **12/1**
-055 **7** ¾ **Gulf Punch**[8] 1264 3-8-5 **46** oh1............................ Louis-PhilippeBeuzelin(3) 10 32
(M F Harris) *chsd ldrs: rdn over 2f out: ev ch over 1f out: wknd ins fnl f* **16/1**
5-15 **8** 2 ¾ **Destiny's Dancer**[3] 1394 3-8-8 **51**............................ PatrickDonaghy(5) 11 31
(B M R Haslam) *s.i.s: hld up: rdn over 1f out: n.d* **9/2**[2]
550- **9** 1 ¼ **Lucky Traveller**[241] 5253 3-8-8 **46** oh1............................ DavidAllan 2 23
(T D Easterby) *led 1f: chsd ldrs: rdn over 3f out: wknd wl over 2f out* **11/4**[1]
656 **10** ½ **Gems**[39] 872 3-9-3 **55**............................ RobertHavlin 6 31
(H J L Dunlop) *hld up: hdwy 1/2-way: rdn over 2f out: wknd over 1f out* **14/1**
060- **11** 2 **Wavertree Bounty**[175] 7095 3-9-0 **52**............................ PatCosgrave 1 24
(J Ryan) *prom: rdn and wknd over 2f out* **14/1**
000- **12** ¾ **Elie Shore**[138] 7616 3-8-12 **53**............................(v) KellyHarrison(3) 3 24
(B M R Haslam) *sn pushed along in rr: bhd fnl 3f* **66/1**
2m 5.24s (3.54) **Going Correction** -0.05s/f (Stan) **12** Ran SP% **114.6**
Speed ratings (Par 96): **82,81,80,80,79 76,76,73,72,72 70,69**
toteswingers: 1&2 £48.80, 1&3 £13.90, 2&3 £25.60 CSF £328.32 CT £3095.12 TOTE £23.90: £6.40, £7.40, £3.30; EX 366.50.
Owner Clive Dennett **Bred** Clive Dennett **Trained** Newmarket, Suffolk

FOCUS
A rock bottom 46-55 handicap not run at a strong pace, and the first four raced prominently. Weak form.

1462 DINE IN HORIZONS RESTAURANT APPRENTICE H'CAP 1m 4f 50y(P)
5:20 (5:21) (Class 6) (0-65,65) 4-Y-0+ **£1,774** (£523; £262) **Stalls** Low

Form RPR
2-50 **1** **Ghufa (IRE)**[8] 1262 6-8-13 **65**............................ SophieSilvester(7) 5 77
(J Pearce) *hld up: last over 2f out: hdwy on outside over 1f out: led and edgd lft ins fnl f: sn clr* **6/1**
04/4 **2** 3 ½ **Laconicos (IRE)**[10] 1226 8-8-11 **56**............................(t) LauraPike 9 63
(W B Stone) *hld up in tch: pushed along over 2f out: styd on same pce ins fnl f* **16/1**
2124 **3** 1 ¾ **Amical Risks (FR)**[24] 1012 6-8-9 **54**............................(v[1]) JohnCavanagh 4 58
(Joss Saville) *s.i.s: hld up: hdwy over 1f out: rdn and hung lft ins fnl f: styd on same pce* **9/2**[2]
2-10 **4** 1 ¾ **Shandelight (IRE)**[60] 621 6-8-11 **56**............................ DaleSwift 2 57
(Julie Camacho) *chsd ldr: led wl over 2f out: sn rdn and hdd: no ex ins fnl f* **5/1**[3]
6-42 **5** 1 **Lisbon Lion (IRE)**[38] 621 5-8-8 **53**............................ MatthewLawson 3 53
(James Moffatt) *hld up: hdwy over 5f out: rdn to ld over 2f out: hdd & wknd ins fnl f* **9/2**[2]
10-4 **6** 5 **Muncaster Castle (IRE)**[75] 410 6-8-6 **51** oh2............................ AdamCarter 7 43
(R F Fisher) *chsd ldrs: pushed along 3f out: wknd over 1f out* **20/1**
2/50 **7** 2 ½ **Simone Martini (IRE)**[11] 1207 5-8-3 **53**............................(t) NeilFarley(5) 8 41
(M F Harris) *hld up: rdn over 2f out: n.d* **14/1**
5-53 **8** 12 **Ladies Dancing**[83] 309 4-9-3 **63**............................(b) RichardRowe 1 31
(J A Osborne) *led: clr 8f out: hdd & wknd wl over 2f out* **3/1**[1]
460 **9** 1 **Escardo (GER)**[10] 1241 7-8-12 **60**............................ JamesRogers(3) 6 27
(D G Bridgwater) *prom: rdn over 3f out: wknd over 2f out* **40/1**
2m 40.22s (-0.88) **Going Correction** -0.05s/f (Stan)
WFA 4 from 5yo+ 1lb **9** Ran SP% **112.1**
Speed ratings (Par 101): **100,97,96,95,94 91,89,81,81**
toteswingers: 1&2 £11.10, 1&3 £4.90, 2&3 £14.90 CSF £91.58 CT £467.49 TOTE £3.70: £1.10, £4.60, £2.50; EX 84.10 Place 6: £69.79 Place 5: £345.10.
Owner Miss Emma Pearce **Bred** Shadwell Estate Company Limited **Trained** Newmarket, Suffolk
■ Sophie Silvester's first winner.
■ Stewards' Enquiry : Richard Rowe caution: used whip when out of contention.

FOCUS
A modest 51-65 apprentice handicap and the pace increased markedly at the halfway mark. The form is rated at face value with the third a fair guide.

T/Jkpt: Part won. £7,100.00 to a £1 stake. Pool: £10,000.00. 0.50 winning tickets. T/Plt: £45.40 to a £1 stake. Pool: £60,046.35. 964.40 winning tickets. T/Qpdt: £19.60 to a £1 stake. Pool: £3,533.79. 133.11 winning tickets. CR

[1149]CATTERICK (L-H)

Wednesday, April 21

OFFICIAL GOING: Good to firm (firm in places; 9.8)

Wind: Virtually nil Weather: Fine and dry

1463 YORKSHIRE4X4.COM ADVENTURE ACTIVITIES (S) STKS 5f

2:00 (2:01) (Class 6) 2-Y-O **£2,047** (£604; £302) **Stalls** Low

Form RPR

1 **Tanked Up (IRE)** 2-8-11 0 .... AdrianNicholls 4 59+
(D Nicholls) *cl up: led 2f out: rdn ent fnl f: styd on wl* **9/2**

20 2 1 ¼ **Calormen**[13] 1180 2-8-11 0 .... KierenFallon 7 54
(M R Channon) *chsd ldrs: pushed along and sltly outpcd 1/2-way: swtchd rt and rdn 2f out: styd on to chse wnr ins fnl f: kpt on towards fin* **7/2**[2]

4 3 ½ **Welsh Dresser (IRE)**[5] 1360 2-8-6 0 .... CathyGannon 2 47
(P D Evans) *cl up: rdn to ld briefly 1/2-way: hdd 2f out and sn drvn: edgd lft and one pce ins fnl f* **11/4**[1]

4 hd **Mrs Nisbett (IRE)** 2-8-1 0 .... DeclanCannon(5) 5 46
(A J McCabe) *chsd ldrs: rdn along 2f out: swtchd rt and kpt on ins fnl f* **10/1**

00 5 5 **Soviet Bolt (IRE)**[5] 1360 2-8-11 0 ....(p) PJMcDonald 6 31
(P T Midgley) *chsd ldrs: rdn along over 2f out: sn wknd* **33/1**

6 6 nk **Copex**[5] 1360 2-8-6 0 ....(p) SilvestreDeSousa 1 25
(K A Ryan) *led: rdn along 1/2-way: sn hdd & wknd wl over 1f out* **4/1**[3]

7 6 **Little Nuthatch (IRE)** 2-8-6 0 .... GregFairley 3 1
(P D Evans) *s.i.s: a bhd* **7/1**

8 2 **Hannah Cann** 2-8-6 0 .... AdrianMcCarthy 8 —
(Peter Grayson) *dwlt: sn outpcd and bhd* **50/1**

60.91 secs (1.11) **Going Correction** -0.05s/f (Good) 8 Ran SP% **113.6**

Speed ratings (Par 90): **89,87,86,85,77 77,67,64**

.There was no bid for the winner. Calormen was claimed by C. A. Dwyer for £6000. Welsh Dresser was claimed by R Teatum for £6000.\n\x\x

Owner Mrs Love & Mr Barker **Bred** C Farrell **Trained** Sessay, N Yorks

FOCUS

A slightly above average 2-y-o seller in which the first four finished in a heap. The second and third help with the level.

NOTEBOOK

Tanked Up(IRE), a £1,800 half-brother to a couple of winners in the US, certainly knew his job as he travelled strongly up with the pace and battled on well after taking it up 2f from home. He didn't beat much, but is still entitled to improve for the experience. (op 4-1 tchd 5-1)

Calormen, dropped in class after disappointing on his second start, plugged on down the outside to take second and did best of those held up, but this faster ground didn't seem to improve him significantly and he will probably need to stay at this sort of level if he is to win a race. He was claimed by Chris Dwyer. (op 3-1 tchd 4-1)

Welsh Dresser(IRE), in front of two of these in a Thirsk claimer on debut five days earlier, had every chance and kept battling away but she still shapes as though she will appreciate further. She was subsequently claimed. (op 5-2)

Mrs Nisbett(IRE), an 8,000gns foal but only an 800gns yearling, was never far off the pace and kept on going to finish a close-up fourth. A sister to a winning sprinter/hurdler and a half-sister to two other winners, she should be able to repay her purchase price at a modest level based on this debut effort. (op 16-1)

Soviet Bolt(IRE) managed to reverse Thirsk form with Copex, but that is all he achieved.

Copex, who again dumped her rider before the start and looked a real handful, is one to avoid for the time being. (op 11-2)

1464 GO RACING IN YORKSHIRE MAIDEN STKS 7f

2:35 (2:35) (Class 5) 3-Y-O **£2,331** (£693; £346; £173) **Stalls** Low

Form RPR

60-2 1 **Transmit (IRE)**[14] 1153 3-9-3 73 .... DavidAllan 4 71
(T D Easterby) *led 2f: cl up tl rdn to ld again over 2f out: edgd lft and hdd over 1f out: drvn ins fnl f: styd on to ld on line* **10/1**

22 2 nse **Magic Omen (USA)**[42] 843 3-9-3 0 .... GregFairley 1 71
(M Johnston) *cl up: led after 2f: rdn along and hdd over 2f out: led again over 1f out: drvn and edgd lft ins fnl f: hdd on line* **11/8**[1]

3 3 1 ½ **Bajan Flash**[17] 1100 3-9-3 0 .... TomEaves 2 67
(B Smart) *chsd ldng pair: hdwy 2f out: sn rdn: drvn ins fnl f: keeping on whn n.m.r towards fin* **8/1**

634- 4 1 **Mercers Row**[202] 6408 3-9-3 67 .... FrederikTylicki 6 64
(A Dickman) *chsd ldrs on outer: rdn along and sltly outpcd 3f out: styd on fr over 1f out: nrst fin* **20/1**

50- 5 nk **Shayla**[190] 6762 3-8-12 0 .... PJMcDonald 7 59
(G A Swinbank) *dwlt and in rr: pushed along 3f out: rdn and hdwy wl over 1f out: kpt on ins fnl f: nrst fin* **25/1**

0 6 1 **Hong Kong Island (IRE)**[17] 1100 3-9-3 0 .... PhillipMakin 8 60
(J Barclay) *in rr: hung rt home turn and sn rdn: kpt on fnl 2f: nrst fin* **150/1**

42-4 7 ¾ **Danceintothelight**[16] 1119 3-9-3 70 .... SilvestreDeSousa 5 58
(K A Ryan) *in tch: hdwy to chse ldrs wl over 2f out: sn rdn and no imp fr wl over 1f out* **6/1**[3]

05- 8 1 ½ **Hail Bold Chief (USA)**[175] 7121 3-9-3 0 .... KierenFallon 3 54
(G A Swinbank) *dwlt: sn pushed along on inner to chse ldrs: rdn along 3f out: drvn 2f out and sn wknd* **3/1**[2]

1m 25.31s (-1.69) **Going Correction** -0.325s/f (Firm) 8 Ran SP% **110.9**

Speed ratings (Par 98): **96,95,94,93,92 91,90,89**

toteswingers: 1&2 £39.10, 1&3 £57.00, 2&3 £24.10 CSF £22.81 TOTE £8.80: £1.80, £1.20, £2.10; EX 22.30.

Owner Habton Farms **Bred** Rathasker Stud **Trained** Great Habton, N Yorks

FOCUS

Not a great maiden, but a thrilling finish between two horses who dominated the contest from the start. The form has a pretty sound look to it.

Hail Bold Chief(USA) Official explanation: jockey said gelding lost its action

1465 BOOK TICKETS ONLINE AT CATTERICKBRIDGE.CO.UK H'CAP (DIV I) 7f

3:10 (3:10) (Class 6) (0-60,59) 3-Y-O **£1,706** (£503; £252) **Stalls** Low

Form RPR

0406 1 **Sixties Rock**[7] 1298 3-8-13 54 .... FrederikTylicki 5 56
(J A Glover) *in tch: hdwy to chse ldrs over 3f out: rdn to chse ldng pair 2f out: styd on to ld jst ins fnl f sn drvn and jst hld on* **3/1**[1]

403- 2 nk **Elegant Dancer (IRE)**[337] 2161 3-8-11 52 .... SilvestreDeSousa 11 53+
(Paul Green) *hld up: stdy hdwy whn nt clr run and hmpd 1 1/2f out: sn swtchd rt to outer and rdn: styd on strly ins fnl f: jst hld* **11/2**[2]

0352 3 nk **Lord's Seat**[15] 1144 3-8-8 49 .... TomEaves 4 49
(A Berry) *led 3f: cl up: rdn along over 2f out: drvn and ev ch over 1f out: kpt on u.p ins fnl f* **10/1**

400- 4 ½ **No Quarter (IRE)**[214] 6096 3-8-11 57 .... PaulPickard(5) 10 56
(A Dickman) *s.i.s and bhd: gd hdwy wl over 1f out: rdn and styd on strly ins fnl f: fining wl whn nt clr run and swtchd lft nr line* **9/1**

3505 5 hd **Rescent**[26] 993 3-8-4 45 .... AndrewElliott 3 43
(Mrs R A Carr) *cl up on inner: led after 3f: rdn along over 2f out: drvn and hdd ent fnl f: hung lft and sn one pce* **15/2**

0-46 6 1 ¼ **Alphacino**[55] 702 3-9-4 59 ....(p) PhillipMakin 6 57+
(B M R Haslam) *in tch: hdwy 3f out: swtchd lft 1 1/2f out: sn rdn and ch on inner whn hmpd and nt clr run jst ins fnl f: nt rcvr* **14/1**

35-6 7 3 ¼ **Firetrap**[12] 1209 3-9-3 58 .... StephenCraine 8 44
(Mrs A Duffield) *in tch: hdwy on outer 3f out: rdn to chse ldrs over 2f out: sn drvn and wknd* **6/1**[3]

-500 8 10 **Yeah**[16] 1118 3-8-4 50 ....(b) IanBrennan(5) 2 9
(Patrick Morris) *chsd ldrs on inner: effrt whn stmbld 3f out: rdn whn n.m.r wl over 1f out: sn wknd and eased* **10/1**

20-0 9 4 ½ **Blue Avon**[17] 1104 3-8-7 55 .... LeeTopliss(7) 7 2
(R A Fahey) *chsd ldrs: rdn along and lost pl after 3f: sn bhd* **11/1**

36-0 10 9 **Infinity World**[100] 127 3-9-1 56 ....(v[1]) PJMcDonald 9 —
(G R Oldroyd) *prom on wd outside: rdn along 3f out: sn wknd* **12/1**

1m 26.35s (-0.65) **Going Correction** -0.325s/f (Firm) 10 Ran SP% **117.3**

Speed ratings (Par 96): **90,89,89,88,88 87,83,71,66,56**

toteswingers: 1&2 £5.10, 1&3 £7.60, 2&3 £11.20 CSF £19.09 CT £150.37 TOTE £3.70: £1.50, £2.30, £1.40; EX 17.00.

Owner Sexy Six Partnership **Bred** Mrs Yvette Dixon **Trained** Babworth, Notts

■ Stewards' Enquiry : Phillip Makin Two-day ban: careless riding (May 5-6)

Andrew Elliott three-day ban: careless riding (May 5-7)

FOCUS

A very moderate handicap and quite a rough race. The winning time was over a second slower than the maiden. Improvement from the first two, with the form rated around the fifth.

Infinity World Official explanation: jockey said filly lost its action

1466 BETFAIR RICHMOND CONDITIONS STKS 1m 3f 214y

3:45 (3:46) (Class 3) 3-Y-O **£6,542** (£1,959; £979; £490; £244) **Stalls** Low

Form RPR

0-1 1 **Gomrath (IRE)**[32] 949 3-9-4 78 .... KierenFallon 5 85+
(M R Channon) *t.k.h early: trckd ldrs: hdwy wl over 2f out: rdn to ld 1 1/2f out: edgd lft and kpt on wl fnl f* **5/4**[1]

1 2 1 **Tajaarub**[61] 618 3-9-1 0 .... TadhgO'Shea 4 80+
(B W Hills) *trckd ldrs on inner: rdn along 3f out: sn rn green and outpcd: swtchd rt and styd on ent fnl f: gng on wl towards fin* **13/8**[2]

001- 3 2 **Mister Angry (IRE)**[131] 7717 3-9-10 85 .... GregFairley 2 86
(M Johnston) *mde most tl rdn along and hdd over 2f out: drvn over 1f out: kpt on same pce fnl f* **4/1**[3]

0006 4 13 **Tallawalla (IRE)**[4] 1394 3-8-7 58 .... SamHitchcott 3 48
(M R Channon) *cl up: rdn along and led over 2f out: hdd 1 1/2f out and sn wknd* **25/1**

000- 5 8 **Tantsor (FR)**[166] 7266 3-8-7 10 .... PaulPickard(5) 1 40
(P T Midgley) *a in rr: outpcd and bhd fnl 3f* **250/1**

2m 36.15s (-2.75) **Going Correction** -0.325s/f (Firm) 5 Ran SP% **106.8**

Speed ratings (Par 102): **96,95,94,85,80**

CSF £3.30 TOTE £2.20: £1.80, £2.80; EX 3.70.

Owner Jon and Julia Aisbitt **Bred** Kilfrush Stud **Trained** West Ilsley, Berks

FOCUS

Mark Johnston and Mick Channon had won six of the last seven runnings of this race between them and they were strongly represented again this time. The early pace was moderate and it didn't quicken until around 7f from home, which meant that the two rags stayed in touch for longer than might have been expected, though they were ultimately well beaten. The first two can rate better than the bare form.

NOTEBOOK

Gomrath(IRE), whose victory in a 1m2f five-runner Lingfield Polytrack maiden last month is working out well, threatened to spoil his chances by pulling far too hard early, but his stable-companion Tallawalla served it up to Mister Angry starting down the back straight, which resulted in an injection of pace, and he travelled much better after that as a result. Switched out wide to hit the front inside the last 2f, he was soon away and clear and was able to take things easily in the closing stages, thereby giving his trainer his fourth victory in the last five runnings of the race. Described as "still a big baby" by his jockey, he is now likely to head for the Lingfield Derby Trial. (op 6-4 tchd 13-8 in places)

Tajaarub, whose debut victory in a 1m2f Lingfield Polytrack maiden in February has been boosted by the runner-up winning twice since, seemed to travel well enough off the pace but he was caught flat footed when the winner went for home and took too long to gather stride. He finished well, however, and although flattered by the official margin he is entitled to carry on improving. (op 7-4 tchd 2-1 in a place)

Mister Angry(IRE) was trying further than an extended 1m for this first time, but faced a stiff task in conceding weight to a couple of unexposed rivals after four months off. He set out to make all, but the attentions of the winner's stablemate 7f from home meant that he could never dominate this field and he had little left to offer once headed inside the last 2f. He may not be the easiest to place. (op 3-1)

1467 CATTERICKBRIDGE.CO.UK H'CAP 1m 3f 214y

4:15 (4:16) (Class 5) (0-70,70) 4-Y-O+ **£2,331** (£693; £346; £173) **Stalls** Low

Form RPR

000- 1 **That'll Do Nicely (IRE)**[203] 6385 7-8-7 58 .... TomEaves 5 68
(N G Richards) *hld up: smooth hdwy over 3f out: str run on inner to ld wl over 1f out: rdn clr approachng fnl f: kpt on* **11/2**

210- 2 3 ¾ **Park's Prodigy**[173] 7154 6-8-7 58 .... SilvestreDeSousa 4 62
(G A Harker) *in tch on inner: hdwy over 4f out: rdn to chal and ch 2f out: sn drvn and kpt on same pce fnl f* **4/1**[3]

200- 3 ½ **Dimashq**[161] 7336 8-8-5 56 oh6 .... PJMcDonald 2 59
(P T Midgley) *hld up in rr: hdwy on outer 3f out: rdn to chse ldrs whn hung lft over 1f out: kpt on ins fnl f: nrst fin* **16/1**

440- 4 4 ½ **Weetfromthechaff**[143] 1562 5-8-6 57 oh1 ow1 ....(t) GregFairley 9 53
(M A Barnes) *hld up in rr: hdwy on outer 4f out: rdn to chse ldrs wl over 1f out: drvn and no imp ent fnl f* **40/1**

0 5 4 **Spahi (FR)**[25] 1011 4-9-4 70 .... PhillipMakin 3 60
(J Hetherton) *chsd clr ldr: tk clsr order 5f out: rdn to ld over 2f out: drvn and hdd wl over 1f out: grad wknd* **20/1**

-622 6 nse **Nakoma (IRE)**[55] 701 8-8-0 56 oh1 .... PaulPickard(5) 1 46
(B Ellison) *chsd ldrs on inner: rdn along and lost pl 6f out: sn in rr: sme hdwy on inner fnl 2f: n.d* **3/1**[1]

/0-0 7 ¾ **Mt Desert**[16] 1113 8-8-0 56 oh1 ....(b) JamesSullivan(5) 10 44
(E W Tuer) *prom: chsd ldr 1/2-way: rdn along over 3f out and sn wknd* **16/1**

053 **8** *9* **Ferney Boy**[12] 1203 4-8-11 **63** .... KierenFallon 7 37
(G A Swinbank) *hld up: hdwy and in tch on outer 1/2-way: rdn along over 3f out: wknd over 2f out* **7/2**[2]

000- **9** *3 ½* **Avoir Choisi (IRE)**[127] 7762 4-8-5 **57** .... DuranFentiman 12 25
(N Wilson) *t.k.h and sn clr: pushed along over 4f out: rdn 3f out: sn hdd & wknd* **14/1**

060- **10** *8* **Casino Night**[194] 6648 5-9-5 **70** .... TadhgO'Shea 6 26
(R Johnson) *in tch: hdwy to chse ldrs 1/2-way: rdn along over 3f out: sn wknd* **14/1**

2m 33.81s (-5.09) **Going Correction** -0.325s/f (Firm)
WFA 4 from 5yo+ 1lb **10** Ran SP% **114.9**
Speed ratings (Par 103): **103,100,100,97,94 94,93,87,85,80**
toteswingers: 1&2 £4.10, 1&3 £21.70, 2&3 £10.10 CSF £27.34 CT £330.76 TOTE £10.70: £2.70, £1.10, £5.80; EX 25.60.
Owner J D Flood **Bred** J D Flood **Trained** Greystoke, Cumbria

FOCUS
A modest handicap run at a strong pace. The form looks sound enough with the winner close to his best.
Park's Prodigy Official explanation: jockey said gelding was unsuited by the track
Ferney Boy Official explanation: jockey said gelding was unsuited by the track

1468 WHITE MUZZLE H'CAP 5f
4:50 (4:50) (Class 6) (0-60,60) 3-Y-O **£2,047** (£604; £302) **Stalls** Low

Form RPR

200- **1** **Taborcillo**[217] 5977 3-9-4 **60** .... PhillipMakin 10 67+
(T D Barron) *dwlt: sn chsng ldrs on wd outside: hdwy 2f out: rdn to chal over 1f out: edgd lft and led ins fnl f: kpt on wl* **8/1**

-264 **2** *¾* **Dower Glen**[17] 1104 3-8-10 **55** .... GaryBartley[(3)] 7 59
(N Wilson) *chsd ldrs: hdwy 1/2-way: rdn to chal over 1f out and ev ch tl drvn: edgd lft and no ex last 100yds* **15/2**

-346 **3** *2 ½* **Vilnius**[16] 1118 3-9-0 **56** .... KierenFallon 4 51+
(M R Channon) *trckd ldrs: hdwy 2f out: effrt whn n.m.r over 1f out: sn rdn and styd on ins fnl f* **4/1**[2]

000- **4** *nk* **Amoureuse**[323] 2575 3-7-11 **46** oh1 .... NeilFarley[(7)] 9 40
(D Carroll) *prom on outer: effrt 2f out: sn rdn and ev ch tl drvn and one pce ins fnl f* **33/1**

-302 **5** *1 ½* **Drumpellier (IRE)**[16] 1118 3-8-11 **58** .... PaulPickard[(5)] 3 47
(P T Midgley) *cl up on inner: led 1/2-way: rdn wl over 1f out: drvn and hdd jst ins fnl f: wknd* **7/2**[1]

6301 **6** *½* **Your Gifted (IRE)**[14] 1155 3-8-9 **58** ....(b[1]) LeeTopliss[(7)] 1 45
(Patrick Morris) *plld hrd: chsd ldrs: hdwy and ch whn hung bdly lft wl over 1f out: sn rdn and one pce* **7/1**[3]

00-6 **7** *1 ½* **Kirkby's Gem**[14] 1155 3-7-13 **46** oh1 .... JamesSullivan[(5)] 8 28
(A Berry) *dwlt: a towards rr* **33/1**

4-03 **8** *½* **Gower Sophia**[16] 1118 3-8-12 **54** ....(v) DavidAllan 2 39
(M Brittain) *chsd ldrs: hdwy on inner 2f out: rdn over 1f out: sn wknd* **4/1**[2]

400- **9** *11* **Lees Anthem**[176] 7088 3-8-13 **55** .... PJMcDonald 5 —
(C J Teague) *dwlt: a in rr* **9/1**

00-6 **10** *5* **Rightcar Marian**[94] 209 3-8-4 **46** oh1 .... AdrianMcCarthy 6 —
(Peter Grayson) *led: pushed along and hdd 1/2-way: stmbld over 2f out and sn wknd* **100/1**

60.03 secs (0.23) **Going Correction** -0.05s/f (Good) **10** Ran SP% **114.5**
Speed ratings (Par 96): **96,94,90,90,87 87,84,83,66,58**
toteswingers: 1&2 £8.70, 1&3 £6.50, 2&3 £9.70 CSF £64.53 CT £281.42 TOTE £10.50: £3.50, £4.20, £1.70; EX 112.30.
Owner M Dalby **Bred** Brookfield Stud Ltd **Trained** Maunby, N Yorks

FOCUS
A moderate sprint handicap, but quite a competitive one and they went a strong pace. The winner is close to last year's debut form, with the runner-up setting the standard.
Gower Sophia Official explanation: jockey said filly lost its action
Rightcar Marian Official explanation: jockey said filly lost its actione

1469 BOOK TICKETS ONLINE AT CATTERICKBRIDGE.CO.UK H'CAP (DIV II) 7f
5:25 (5:26) (Class 6) (0-60,58) 3-Y-O **£1,706** (£503; £252) **Stalls** Low

Form RPR

6-02 **1** **Take My Hand**[14] 1162 3-9-4 **58** .... KierenFallon 10 60
(M R Channon) *towards rr: hdwy on outer over 2f out: rdn and edgd lft over 1f out: styd on u.p to ld ins fnl f: edgd lft towards fin* **9/4**[1]

00-4 **2** *¾* **Choc'A'Moca (IRE)**[14] 1178 3-8-10 **50** .... DavidNolan 1 50
(D Carroll) *led: rdn along over 2f out: drvn over 1f out: hdd ins fnl f: no ex last 50yds* **3/1**[2]

5253 **3** *½* **Tamarind Hill (IRE)**[15] 1146 3-8-12 **57** ....(b) DeclanCannon[(5)] 5 56
(A J McCabe) *cl up: rdn along over 2f out and ev ch tl drvn and one pce wl ins fnl f: hld whn n.m.r towards fin* **7/1**[3]

3400 **4** *1* **Baby Judge (IRE)**[48] 782 3-8-11 **56** .... MarkCoumbe[(5)] 8 52
(M C Chapman) *chsd ldrs: rdn along over 2f out: drvn wl over 1f out: kpt on same pce* **25/1**

20-5 **5** *hd* **Ochilview Warrior (IRE)**[12] 1201 3-8-12 **52** .... SilvestreDeSousa 9 47
(R Bastiman) *midfield: hdwy to chse ldrs over 2f out: drvn and ch over 1f out: one pce ins fnl f* **7/1**[3]

5235 **6** *3 ¾* **Taper Jean Girl (IRE)**[41] 861 3-8-13 **53** ....(p) PhillipMakin 4 38
(Mrs R A Carr) *chsd ldrs: rdn along over 2f out: drvn over 1f out and sn wknd* **10/1**

03-0 **7** *3 ¼* **Goodison Goal (IRE)**[14] 1163 3-8-11 **51** .... StephenCraine 2 27
(Patrick Morris) *chsd ldrs on inner: rdn along over 2f out: sn wknd* **12/1**

2-04 **8** *8* **Inlovingmemory (IRE)**[12] 1203 3-9-4 **58** .... GregFairley 6 13
(M A Barnes) *a towards rr* **20/1**

500 **9** *13* **Swift Steel**[41] 858 3-8-7 **47** ....(p) TomEaves 3 —
(Mrs A Duffield) *dwlt: a in rr* **25/1**

40-4 **10** *11* **Charmaxjoanne**[26] 993 3-8-3 **46** ....(v) KellyHarrison[(3)] 7 —
(B M R Haslam) *a in rr* **14/1**

1m 26.41s (-0.59) **Going Correction** -0.325s/f (Firm) **10** Ran SP% **116.7**
Speed ratings (Par 96): **90,89,88,87,87 82,79,70,55,42**
toteswingers:1&2 £2.50, 2&3 £7.40, 1&3 £5.50 CSF £8.58 CT £39.03 TOTE £2.30: £1.10, £1.10, £4.30; EX 10.90.
Owner Miss Bridget Coyle **Bred** Mike Channon Bloodstock Ltd **Trained** West Ilsley, Berks
■ Stewards' Enquiry : David Nolan caution: used whip down shoulder in the forehand
Tom Eaves caution: used whip when out of contention.

FOCUS
They went a fair early pace in this and not many ever got into it, though the winning time was fractionally slower than the first division. The winner probably only had to reproduce her previous Kempton run.
Ochilview Warrior(IRE) Official explanation: jockey said colt hung right from halfway
Swift Steel Official explanation: jockey said filly never travelled

Charmaxjoanne Official explanation: jockey said filly lost its action

1470 WE RACE AGAIN 4TH MAY APPRENTICE H'CAP 5f 212y
5:55 (5:55) (Class 6) (0-65,65) 4-Y-0+ **£2,047** (£604; £302) **Stalls** Low

Form RPR

3661 **1** **Cornus**[8] 1276 8-9-2 **62** 6ex........(be) TobyAtkinson 2 71
(A J McCabe) *midfield: on inner: swtchd rt and hdwy 2f out: rdn over 1f out: str run ins fnl f to ld nr fin* **5/1**[3]

30-2 **2** *½* **Mr Wolf**[8] 1276 9-9-5 **65** ....(p) IanBrennan 10 73
(J J Quinn) *led: rdn along 2f out: drvn and edgd rt ins fnl f: hdd and nt qckn towards fin* **5/2**[1]

20-0 **3** *½* **Soto**[14] 1149 7-8-8 **57** .... AdamCarter[(3)] 6 63
(M W Easterby) *chsd ldrs: hdwy on inner to chse ldr ent fnl f: sn rdn and ev ch tl nt qckn towards fin* **16/1**

3123 **4** *½* **Not My Choice (IRE)**[34] 914 5-9-2 **62** ....(t) LeeTopliss 9 66
(D C Griffiths) *chsd ldrs: rdn along 2f out: drvn ent fnl f and kpt on same pce* **13/2**

0-23 **5** *½* **Sea Crest**[6] 1337 4-8-6 **55** .... JohnCavanagh[(3)] 5 58
(M Brittain) *chsd ldrs: rdn along 2f out: drvn ent fnl f and kpt on same pce* **7/2**[2]

000- **6** *½* **Miss Daawe**[188] 6799 6-8-10 **59** ow4 .... DaleSwift[(3)] 8 60
(B Ellison) *bhd: hdwy on inner 2f out: swtchd rt and rdn over 1f out: kpt on ins fnl f: nrst fin* **16/1**

0060 **7** *nk* **Redwater River**[15] 1142 6-8-9 **55** ....(b) RosieJessop 4 55
(Mrs R A Carr) *towards rr: rdn along over 2f out: kpt on u.p ins fnl f: nt rch ldrs* **25/1**

0-00 **8** *nse* **Mandhooma**[68] 532 4-8-6 **52** .... DavidKenny 12 52
(P W Hiatt) *chsd ldr: rdn along over 2f out: drvn over 1f out: wknd ent fnl f* **33/1**

1064 **9** *2 ¼* **Radiator Rooney (IRE)**[14] 1166 7-8-8 **54** ....(v) AmyScott 3 47
(Patrick Morris) *chsd ldrs: hdwy 2f out: rdn wl over 1f out: wknd appr fnl f* **10/1**

02-0 **10** *1* **Neo's Mate (IRE)**[79] 369 4-8-5 **54** .... MatthewLawson[(3)] 1 44
(Paul Green) *a in rr* **16/1**

0000 **11** *1 ¼* **Admirals Way**[14] 1172 5-8-2 **51** oh1 .... NathanAlison[(3)] 7 37
(C N Kellett) *midfield: rdn along 1/2-way: sn wknd* **50/1**

1m 12.38s (-1.22) **Going Correction** -0.325s/f (Firm) **11** Ran SP% **116.3**
Speed ratings (Par 101): **95,94,93,93,92 91,91,91,88,86 85**
toteswingers:1&2 £2.50, 2&3 £9.30, 1&3 £6.40 CSF £17.34 CT £189.93 TOTE £6.80: £2.10, £1.40, £2.50; EX 12.70 Place 6: £34.49 Place 5: £22.66 .
Owner Triple A Partnership **Bred** G Russell **Trained** Averham Park, Notts

FOCUS
A modest apprentice handicap, run at a strong pace thanks to the runner-up. Straightforward form.
Admirals Way Official explanation: jockey said gelding ran too free
T/Plt: £30.00 to a £1 stake. Pool: £40,861.85. 992.27 winning tickets. T/Qpdt: £8.00 to a £1 stake. Pool: £2,509.42. 230.48 winning tickets. JR

EPSOM (L-H)
Wednesday, April 21

OFFICIAL GOING: Derby course - good (good to firm in places); sprint course - good to firm (good in places; derby 8.5; sprint 8.9)
Course dolled out from one mile post to winning post adding about 20yds to distances on round course.
Wind: fresh, half against Weather: bright

1471 INVESTEC CAPITAL MARKETS H'CAP 5f
2:20 (2:20) (Class 3) (0-95,95) 4-Y-0+
£10,904 (£3,265; £1,632; £817; £407; £204) **Stalls** High

Form RPR

530- **1** **Fathom Five (IRE)**[179] 7015 6-9-0 **91** .... AlanMunro 2 102
(C F Wall) *in tch in midfield: hdwy 2f out: rdn to chse ldr jst ins fnl f: led fnl 75yds: r.o wl* **11/2**[3]

-125 **2** *¾* **Rocket Rob (IRE)**[54] 722 4-8-8 **85** .... RyanMoore 1 93
(M Botti) *racd in last trio: hdwy on outer over 1f out: r.o wl u.p fnl 100yds: snatched 2nd on post* **4/1**[1]

43-0 **3** *nse* **Bertoliver**[35] 905 6-8-6 **83** .... PaulHanagan 7 91
(S C Williams) *led: rdn ent fnl f: hdd fnl 75yds: no ex: lost 2nd on post* **14/1**

-034 **4** *hd* **Fol Hollow (IRE)**[7] 1295 5-8-13 **95** .... BillyCray[(5)] 8 102
(D Nicholls) *wnt rt s: chsd ldrs: looking for run over 1f out: swtchd rt ent fnl f: r.o towards fin: unable to rch wnr* **4/1**[1]

62-6 **5** *¾* **Ocean Blaze**[28] 972 6-8-4 **81** .... ChrisCatlin 6 85
(B R Millman) *chsd ldr: rdn over 1f out: lost 2nd jst ins fnl f: one pce fnl 100yds* **16/1**

04-5 **6** *¾* **Indian Trail**[7] 1295 10-8-9 **86** ....(v) FrankieDettori 3 88+
(D Nicholls) *stdd s: hld up in last trio: effrt and looking for run over 1f out: switching lft and rt but denied clr run thrght fnl f: nvr able to chal* **5/1**[2]

60-0 **7** *2* **Rievaulx World**[34] 916 4-9-1 **92** .... NeilCallan 4 87
(K A Ryan) *chsd ldng pair: rdn wl over 1f out: wknd u.p ins fnl f* **14/1**

1/0- **8** *2* **Holbeck Ghyll (IRE)**[369] 1325 8-8-13 **90** .... JimmyFortune 5 77+
(A M Balding) *stdd s: hld up in rr: nt clr run over 1f out: swtchd lft ent fnl f: nvr able to chal* **12/1**

0630 **9** *8* **Hoh Hoh Hoh**[34] 916 8-9-1 **92** .... JamieSpencer 9 51
(R J Price) *bmpd s: in tch: rdn over 1f out: sn btn and eased: dismntd qckly after fin: burst blood vessel* **8/1**

55.31 secs (-0.39) **Going Correction** +0.10s/f (Good) **9** Ran SP% **110.1**
Speed ratings (Par 107): **107,105,105,105,104 103,99,96,83**
toteswingers: 1&2 £6.40, 1&3 £16.00, 2&3 £10.20 CSF £25.66 CT £270.95 TOTE £7.70: £2.20, £2.10, £4.70; EX 33.10.
Owner Hintlesham Thoroughbreds **Bred** Eamonn Connolly **Trained** Newmarket, Suffolk

FOCUS
The sprint course was officially described as good to firm, good in places (GoingStick 8.9), with the Derby course good, good to firm in places (8.5). The rail was dolled out from the 1m point to the finish, adding approximately 20 yards to all Derby course distances. A good sprint handicap and the time was 0.09 seconds under standard. Straightforward form with Fathom Five rated to the same mark as when winning this last year.

NOTEBOOK
Fathom Five(IRE) struggled after winning this race on his reappearance last season, but he was 2lb lower than 12 months ago as a result and confirmed his liking for this track, as well as an ability to go well fresh, with a decisive enough victory after six months off. The one concern beforehand was whether he would handle the quick ground, but it didn't bother him and he benefited from a good ride, getting one clear run out wide. The winner could now go to Chester and/or York, ahead of another tilt at the Dash (sixth off 97 in 2008) back over C&D on Derby day, provided the going is not too quick. (op 6-1 tchd 5-1)

Rocket Rob(IRE), unsuited by a steady pace at Wolverhampton 54 days earlier, was never going to have the same problem this time and he ran creditably, following the winner through out wide without ever looking like getting there. He's yet to win off a mark this high, but he is only a 4-y-o and is with a good yard. (tchd 9-2)
Bertoliver, nicely handicapped on the pick of his form, showed his usual early speed against the stands' rail and kept on well. He'll have to be of interest if turning up at the Chester May meeting (won there off 90 in 2008) with a low draw. (op 16-1)
Fol Hollow(IRE) didn't get the best of runs through but still ran well and gave the impression he's one to keep on side in the coming weeks. He was due to be eased 1lb. (tchd 7-2)
Ocean Blaze, an eyecatcher at Kempton on her reappearance, had every chance this time.
Indian Trail ◆, for by no means the first time in his career, looked desperately unlucky. His hold-up style of racing means he's reliant on getting the gaps and they simply didn't come this time - he was never off the bridle. He was due to be dropped 1lb, but it's clear he retains plenty of ability. Official explanation: jockey said gelding was denied a clear run (op 4-1)
Rievaulx World looked inclined to hang left throughout and did not seem to handle the track.
Holbeck Ghyll(IRE), 5lb higher than when winning the 2008 Dash and having his first run for a year, raced out the back after missing the break and, after losing any chance he might have had when getting stuck in behind the weakening Hoh Hoh Hoh, he was looked after. Official explanation: jockey said gelding suffered interference in running (op 11-1 tchd 10-1)
Hoh Hoh Hoh Official explanation: vet said gelding bled

1472 INVESTEC ASSET MANAGEMENT GREAT METROPOLITAN H'CAP 1m 4f 10y

2:55 (2:55) (Class 3) (0-95,92) 4-Y-O+

£10,904 (£3,265; £1,632; £817; £407; £204) **Stalls** Centre

Form / RPR

100- **1** **Coin Of The Realm (IRE)**[156] 6662 5-9-1 **88** ..... RyanMoore 8 104
(G L Moore) *hld up in midfield: hdwy over 2f out: rdn to ld over 1f out: sn wl clr: r.o strly: easily* **6/1**[2]

030- **2** *8* **Final Victory**[159] 7373 4-8-10 **84** ..... LiamKeniry 4 87
(A M Balding) *chsd ldrs: rdn and effrt over 2f out: nt gng pce of wnr over 1f out: chsd clr wnr ent fnl f: no imp* **9/1**

11-3 **3** *3 ¾* **Mildoura (FR)**[103] 81 5-9-1 **88** ..... DaneO'Neill 3 85
(Mrs L J Mongan) *led for 1f: chsd ldr after: rdn to ld and edgd lft 2f out: hdd over 1f out: sn no ch w wnr: lost 2nd ent fnl f* **8/1**

24-1 **4** *¾* **Trip The Light**[14] 1151 5-9-5 **92** .....(v) PaulHanagan 5 88
(R A Fahey) *chsd ldrs: rdn and unable qck wl over 2f out: no ch w wnr fr over 1f out* **13/2**[3]

02-5 **5** *1* **Yellowstone (IRE)**[25] 1020 6-9-3 **90** ..... JamieSpencer 1 84
(P F I Cole) *dwlt: sn bustled along to rcvr: led after 1f: rdn ent fnl 3f: hdd 2f out: btn whn n.m.r wl over 1f out: no ch fnl f* **8/1**

2210 **6** *4* **Admirable Duque (IRE)**[47] 811 4-7-13 **78** ..... BillyCray(5) 9 66
(D J S Ffrench Davis) *sn niggled along in rr: rdn and no prog 3f out: wl btn and eased ins fnl f* **33/1**

056- **7** *7* **Rajeh (IRE)**[170] 4408 7-9-0 **87** ..... LiamJones 2 64
(J L Spearing) *a in rr: rdn and lost tch over 4f out: wl bhd fnl 3f* **7/1**

111- **8** *1* **Bow To No One (IRE)**[172] 7178 4-8-12 **86** ..... FrankieDettori 6 61
(A P Jarvis) *stdd s: hld up in last trio: rdn and no prog over 2f out: wl btn and eased ins fnl f* **8/1**

020- **9** *66* **Hevelius**[165] 7293 5-9-2 **89** ..... AdamKirby 10 —
(W R Swinburn) *in tch in midfield: rdn and lost pl over 4f out: wl bhd over 3f out: virtually p.u fnl 2f: t.o* **11/4**[1]

2m 37.5s (-1.40) **Going Correction** 0.0s/f (Good)
WFA 4 from 5yo+ 1lb 9 Ran SP% **113.1**
Speed ratings (Par 107): **104,98,96,95,95 92,87,87,43**
toteswingers: 1&2 £14.10, 1&3 £12.80, 2&3 £13.90 CSF £57.21 CT £431.45 TOTE £5.30: £2.00, £3.00, £3.10; EX 68.70.
Owner B Siddle & B D Haynes **Bred** Grangecon Stud **Trained** Lower Beeding, W Sussex

FOCUS

Not that strong a handicap for the class, but at least they seemed to go a fair gallop. The winner runs his best races over C/D but there are doubts over what he achieved here.

NOTEBOOK

Coin Of The Realm(IRE) lost his way after finishing an unlucky fourth off a mark 83 in this race last season and winning at the Derby meeting off 84, but he returned from a five-month break in top form and fairly bolted up. He is now likely to follow the same path as last year, taking in a race over hurdles at Aintree (trainer would like to go for the Swinton but the gelding is rated only 113 in that sphere), before being aimed at that same Derby day handicap, although he'll obviously be much higher in the weights this time, and if goes up more than 12lb he won't even get in. (op 11-2)
Final Victory ◆ ran a pleasing race after over five months off, not least considering Andrew Balding, who is hopeful the gelding can make a decent handicapper this season, said he would prefer a bit of cut in the ground (won his maiden by 7l on good to soft). (op 10-1)
Mildoura(FR), back on turf after 103 days off, was always handily placed but she was one paced under pressure. This ex-French mare is another who will probably prefer easier ground. (tchd 9-1)
Trip The Light was partnered by a 7lb claimer when winning off a mark of 87 on his reappearance and he couldn't defy a 5lb higher rating with a full jockey back aboard. (op 9-2)
Yellowstone(IRE) recovered from a slow start to lead but he didn't offer much under pressure on this drop in trip and return to turf. (op 11-1 tchd 12-1 in places)
Admirable Duque(IRE) was reported to have never been travelling. Official explanation: jockey said gelding never travelled
Rajeh(IRE), third in this last year off a 3lb higher mark, raced out the back after starting slowly on this return from a 170-day break and, bizarrely, didn't seem to handle the downhill run. (op 6-1)
Bow To No One(IRE) had won her last three starts, but she was 10lb higher and never featured after a 172-day break. She was reported to have been unsuited by the track. Official explanation: jockey said filly did not handle the track (op 15-2 tchd 6-1)
Hevelius was strongly supported on his return from 165-days off, but he didn't seem to handle the downhill run into the straight and finished tailed off. Official explanation: jockey said gelding lost its action; vet said gelding finished distressed (op 4-1)

1473 INVESTEC DERBY TRIAL (CONDITIONS STKS) 1m 2f 18y

3:30 (3:30) (Class 2) 3-Y-O **£18,693** (£5,598; £2,799; £1,401) **Stalls** Low

Form / RPR

055- **1** **Dreamspeed (IRE)**[207] 6268 3-8-13 97 ..... JimmyFortune 1 103
(A M Balding) *chsd ldr: rdn to chal 2f out: led ins fnl f: kpt on wl* **3/1**[2]

162- **2** *hd* **Prompter**[193] 6664 3-8-13 106 ..... HayleyTurner 2 103
(M L W Bell) *led: rdn 2f out: drvn ent fnl f: hdd ins fnl f: kpt on but a jst hld after* **4/6**[1]

125- **3** *3 ½* **Togiak (IRE)**[193] 6664 3-8-13 95 ..... RyanMoore 4 96
(E A L Dunlop) *chsd ldng pair: effrt and rdn ent fnl 2f: unable qck over 1f out: one pce fnl f* **9/2**[3]

-216 **4** *6* **Gumnd (IRE)**[18] 1083 3-8-13 77 ..... NeilCallan 3 84
(C E Brittain) *stdd s: hld up in last: rdn and no prog over 2f out: wl btn fnl 2f* **20/1**

2m 9.88s (0.18) **Going Correction** 0.0s/f (Good) 4 Ran SP% **107.9**
Speed ratings (Par 104): **99,98,96,91**
CSF £5.49 TOTE £4.40; EX 8.20.
Owner J C Smith **Bred** Stone Ridge Farm **Trained** Kingsclere, Hants
■ This event was formerly known as the Blue Riband Trial.

FOCUS

Plenty of smart types have contested this race in recent years, indeed Midday was runner-up last season, but the latest running was a Derby Trial in name only as far as the Epsom version is concerned, despite increased prize money. The pace seemed honest enough for the size of field, although the time was 2.89 seconds slower than the Alainmaar recorded in the later 0-105 older-horse handicap. Muddling form, limited by the fourth, with the favourite 7lb off his best.

NOTEBOOK

Dreamspeed(IRE) was held in good company after winning on debut last year, but has done well from two to three and showed a good attitude. Like the runner-up, he gives the impression he'll come on for this, and the Italian Derby has been nominated as his target. (op 11-4 tchd 4-1)
Prompter raced a little freely in front, and his inability to settle better early on probably cost him the race considering the beaten margin. It's true he was slightly leaned on, and certainly intimidated by the winner inside the final furlong, meaning Hayley Turner was not able to use her whip as she would have liked near the finish, but this Motivator colt just looked to be getting the worst of the argument at the time. Michael Bell's runner, who was last seen finishing second in the Autumn Stakes, should come on for this, with the run likely to have taken the freshness out of him. (tchd 4-7)
Togiak(IRE) ran okay without ever looking likely to reverse last year's Autumn Stakes placings with Prompter. (op 5-1)
Gumnd(IRE) had loads to find on the figures and never featured. (op 22-1)

1474 INVESTEC PROPERTY INVESTMENTS CITY AND SUBURBAN STKS (H'CAP) 1m 2f 18y

4:05 (4:07) (Class 2) (0-105,102) 4-Y-O+

£31,155 (£9,330; £4,665; £2,335; £1,165; £585) **Stalls** Low

Form / RPR

211- **1** **Alainmaar (FR)**[201] 6453 4-9-10 **102** ..... RichardHills 12 116+
(M A Jarvis) *chsd ldng trio: hdwy to chse ldr 3f out: rdn to ld over 1f out: r.o strly ins fnl f: comf* **11/8**[1]

011- **2** *2 ¼* **Hanoverian Baron**[191] 6733 5-8-3 **81** ..... DavidProbert 1 90
(A G Newcombe) *hld up in tch in midfield: effrt towards inner ent fnl 2f: hdwy wl over 1f out: chsd wnr jst ins fnl f: no ch w wnr but kpt on for clr 2nd* **14/1**

-663 **3** *1 ¾* **Tartan Gunna**[8] 1272 4-8-12 **90** ..... JoeFanning 5 95+
(M Johnston) *chsd ldrs: effrt on inner when short of room and snatched up jst over 2f out: swtchd rt 2f out: kpt on u.p fnl f: wnt 3rd towards fin* **8/1**[3]

160- **4** *¾* **Cill Rialaig**[165] 7291 5-9-0 **92** ..... SteveDrowne 11 96
(H Morrison) *in tch: hdwy to chse ldrs wl over 2f out: drvn and unable qck over 1f out: kpt on same pce fnl f* **7/1**[2]

330- **5** *nk* **Indian Days**[206] 6303 5-9-10 **102** ..... PaulMulrennan 3 105
(J G Given) *chsd ldr for 2f: chsd ldrs after tl hdwy to ld jst over 2f out: drvn and hdd over 1f out: wknd ins fnl f* **11/1**

200- **6** *½* **Bullet Man (USA)**[235] 5437 5-8-5 **83** .....(p) PaulHanagan 6 85
(R A Fahey) *dwlt: sn bustled along to ld: hdd and edgd lft u.p jst over 2f out: wknd 1f out: btn whn nt clr run: wl ins fnl f* **12/1**

000- **7** *2* **Kavachi (IRE)**[193] 6665 7-8-9 **87** ..... RyanMoore 2 85+
(G L Moore) *t.k.h: hld up towards rr: hdwy towards inner 3f out: carried rt 2f out: no imp after: btn whn nt clr run ins fnl f* **20/1**

0-20 **8** *1* **Bolodenka (IRE)**[43] 837 8-8-7 **85** ..... RobertWinston 7 81
(R A Fahey) *hld up in rr: hdwy wl over 2f out: edgd out rt 2f out: no prog after* **66/1**

0-60 **9** *2* **Porgy**[25] 1015 5-9-1 **93** ..... TonyHamilton 4 85
(R A Fahey) *hld up in midfield: lost pl and towards rr: hdwy u.p 2f out: no prog after* **25/1**

-156 **10** *2 ¼* **Totally Focussed (IRE)**[18] 1088 5-7-12 **76** oh1 ..... JimmyQuinn 8 63
(S Dow) *hld up towards rr: effrt on outer over 3f out: edging lft and no prog 2f out: wl btn after* **28/1**

5500 **11** *4 ½* **Ramona Chase**[28] 974 5-7-13 **77** oh1 ow1 .....(t) LukeMorris 10 55
(M J Attwater) *v.s.a: bhd: hdwy over 4f out: rdn and no prog 3f out: wl btn after* **20/1**

650- **12** *17* **Bazergan (IRE)**[214] 6106 5-8-11 **89** .....(tp) SebSanders 15 33
(C E Brittain) *hld up towards rr: struggling and lost tch over 2f out: eased ins fnl f: t.o* **20/1**

210- **13** *8* **Never Ending Tale**[305] 3154 5-8-7 **85** .....(p) RichardKingscote 13 13
(E F Vaughan) *in tch in midfield on outer: pushed along and lost pl over 4f out: lost tch over 2f out: eased ins fnl f: t.o* **50/1**

050- **14** *2 ¼* **Lord Theo**[188] 6795 6-8-4 **82** ..... ChrisCatlin 14 6
(N P Littmoden) *chsd ldr after 2f tl over 3f out: sn struggling u.p: wl bhd and eased fnl f: t.o* **40/1**

320- **15** *8* **Greylami (IRE)**[200] 6480 5-9-0 **92** ..... JimmyFortune 9 —
(R A Mills) *hld up in midfield: rdn and no rspnse over 2f out: eased fr wl over 1f out: t.o* **12/1**

2m 6.99s (-2.71) **Going Correction** 0.0s/f (Good) 15 Ran SP% **123.6**
Speed ratings (Par 109): **110,108,106,106,105 105,103,103,101,99 96,82,76,74,67**
toteswingers: 1&2 £6.50, 1&3 £4.70, 2&3 £11.80 CSF £20.12 CT £127.90 TOTE £2.20: £1.40, £3.90, £2.30; EX 27.60 Trifecta £146.40 Pool: £886.65 - 4.48 winning units..
Owner Hamdan Al Maktoum **Bred** Fares Stables Ltd **Trained** Newmarket, Suffolk

FOCUS

This looked a good, competitive handicap, if not a strong race for the grade, but the winner totally outclassed his rivals, scoring in a time 2.89 seconds faster than the earlier Derby Trial won by Dreamspeed. The third and fourth were close to their marks.

NOTEBOOK

Alainmaar(FR) ◆ won in the manner of a pattern-class performer. They didn't seem to go that quick, and it paid to race prominently, but the time was quick compared with the earlier Derby Trial. The winner, a progressive type in three runs last year, has done well physically over the winter and readily defied a mark 5lb higher than when successful at Newmarket last October. Richard Hills believes the gelding will get 1m4f, a view the horse's breeding supports, and it will be a surprise if he isn't up to making an impression in Group company. (tchd 6-4)
Hanoverian Baron ◆ ran well considering he had to be switched around 2f out, albeit Alainmaar was going a lot better, and then didn't seem to handle the track when in the clear. The winner of his final two starts last season, he was 5lb higher for this first run in 191 days, but he's evidently still improving, with the promise of more to come back on a galloping track and/or back on easier ground. (op 20-1)
Tartan Gunna was blocked in his run towards the inside around 2f out, but he wasn't unlucky. (op 17-2 tchd 9-1)
Cill Rialaig made a satisfactory return from 165 days off. This likeable mare progressed nicely last term and could have more to offer. (op 8-1)
Indian Days had no easy task under joint-top weight and is entitled to come on for the outing, having been off for 206 days. (op 9-1)
Bullet Man(USA), who had been gelded since leaving Luca Cumani last year, and had cheekpieces fitted, might just have needed this first outing of the season seeing as he's a big, burly horse. He dropped out after setting a modest tempo.
Never Ending Tale Official explanation: jockey said gelding was unsuited by the track

The Form Book, Raceforml Ltd, Compton, RG20 6NL

Greylami(IRE) Official explanation: jockey said gelding lost its action

1475 INVESTEC SPECIALIST PRIVATE BANK MAIDEN STKS 1m 114y
4:40 (4:41) (Class 5) 3-4-Y-O £4,857 (£1,445; £722; £360) **Stalls Low**

Form RPR
050- **1** **Quick Reaction**[203] 6393 3-8-11 77 RichardHughes 6 80
(R Hannon) *chsd ldr: effrt to chal 2f out: rdn to ld over 1f out: kpt on wl fnl f: rdn out* **5/2**[2]
024- **2** 1 3/4 **Tesslam**[170] 7209 3-8-11 78 FrankieDettori 1 76
(M A Jarvis) *wnt rt s: t.k.h: chsd ldng pair: rdn and unable qck 2f out: kpt on fnl 150yds to go 2nd towards fin: nt pce to trble wnr* **7/4**[1]
3-22 **3** hd **Lago Indiano (IRE)**[12] 1211 3-8-11 75 JimCrowley 4 76
(Mrs A J Perrett) *led: rdn and pressed ent fnl 2f: hdd over 1f out: one pce fnl f: lost 2nd towards fin* **4/1**[3]
4 3 1/4 **Bay Willow (IRE)** 3-8-11 0 JoeFanning 2 68
(M Johnston) *s.i.s: sn in tch: pushed along 4f out: rdn and unable qck ent fnl 3f: struggling whn edgd lft over 2f out: one pce after* **5/1**
540- **5** 1/2 **Pebblesonthebeach**[226] 5715 3-8-11 68 MichaelHills 5 67
(J W Hills) *plld hrd: hld up in last pair: outpcd 3f out: one pce and n.d after* **16/1**
560- **6** 22 **Louisiana Gift (IRE)**[183] 6911 3-8-11 66 HayleyTurner 3 16
(J W Hills) *plld hrd: hld up in last pair: racd awkwardly downhill 4f out: sn lost tch: t.o fnl 2f* **33/1**

1m 48.39s (2.29) **Going Correction** 0.0s/f (Good) **6** Ran SP% **110.4**
Speed ratings (Par 103): **89,87,87,84,83 64**
toteswingers: 1&2 £1.80, 2&3 not won, 1&3 not won. CSF £7.03 TOTE £4.20: £3.10, £1.10; EX 7.50.
Owner The Queen **Bred** The Queen **Trained** East Everleigh, Wilts

FOCUS
No more than a fair maiden and the pace was steady. A small personal best from the winner but the favourite was slightly disappointing.
Pebblesonthebeach Official explanation: trainer said gelding was unsuited by the tracki

1476 INVESTEC INVESTMENT BANKING AND SECURITIES H'CAP 1m 114y
5:15 (5:16) (Class 5) (0-75,75) 3-Y-O £4,857 (£1,445; £722; £360) **Stalls Low**

Form RPR
50-3 **1** **Kajima**[14] 1168 3-8-13 **70** RichardHughes 2 76+
(R Hannon) *t.k.h early: trckd ldrs: chsd ldr 3f out: rdn to ld over 1f out: r.o wl fnl f* **3/1**[1]
325- **2** 3/4 **Logos Astra (USA)**[228] 5682 3-9-4 **75** TedDurcan 9 79+
(D R Lanigan) *hld up in last trio: hdwy on outer wl over 1f out: str run ins fnl f: wnt 2nd fnl 100yds: nt rch wnr* **8/1**
405- **3** 3/4 **Candleshoe (IRE)**[247] 5096 3-8-8 **65** RyanMoore 3 68+
(R Hannon) *hld up wl bhd: swtchd ins and hdwy over 1f out: drvn ent fnl f: kpt on wl to go 3rd towards fin* **7/1**[3]
-430 **4** 1/2 **Rain On The Wind (IRE)**[21] 1058 3-8-5 **65** (t) WilliamCarson(3) 8 66
(S C Williams) *sn led: rdn wl over 2f out: hdd over 1f out: kpt on wl u.p tl no ex ins fnl f: lost 2 pls fnl 100yds* **22/1**
-400 **5** 1 3/4 **Lou Bear (IRE)**[21] 1058 3-8-4 **61** oh1 JimmyQuinn 11 58
(J Akehurst) *hld up towards rr: hdwy on inner wl over 2f out: chsd ldrs and swtchd rt over 1f out: drvn ent fnl f: wknd fnl 150yds* **40/1**
41 **6** 2 1/2 **Buona Sarah (IRE)**[12] 1209 3-8-6 **63** JoeFanning 7 60+
(J R Boyle) *hld up towards rr: effrt whn nt clr run and hmpd over 2f out: edging lft after: hdwy on inner ent fnl f: nvr able to chal* **14/1**
640- **7** 1 **Mr Harmoosh (IRE)**[177] 7056 3-8-5 **62** ChrisCatlin 1 51
(E F Vaughan) *t.k.h: hld up in midfield: swtchd rt and effrt wl over 1f out: no prog ent fnl f* **33/1**
2121 **8** 1 1/2 **Tuscan King**[27] 977 3-8-12 **69** (b) JimmyFortune 5 55
(P D Evans) *in tch in midfield: rdn and unable qck wl over 2f out: no threat to ldrs fnl 2f* **14/1**
003- **9** 4 1/2 **Imperial Warrior**[182] 6948 3-8-8 **65** SteveDrowne 13 41
(H Morrison) *in tch on outer: rdn and edgd lft 3f out: no prog 2f out: wl btn fnl f* **16/1**
-113 **10** 2 3/4 **Ostentation**[61] 617 3-9-4 **75** LiamKeniry 12 44
(R A Teal) *hld up wl in tch: n.m.r and shuffled bk over 2f out: drvn and no hdwy 2f out* **18/1**
031- **11** 7 **Christopher Wren (USA)**[191] 6736 3-9-4 **75** RobertWinston 10 28
(J R Best) *chsd ldrs: rdn 3f out: wkng whn short of room over 2f out: wl bhd and eased ins fnl f* **7/1**[3]
01 **12** 10 **Skyfire**[17] 1100 3-9-4 **75** FrankieDettori 6 5
(M Johnston) *chsd ldr over 6f out tl 3f out: sn struggling: wl bhd and eased ins fnl f* **10/3**[2]

1m 46.44s (0.34) **Going Correction** 0.0s/f (Good) **12** Ran SP% **118.4**
Speed ratings (Par 98): **98,97,96,96,94 92,91,90,86,83 77,68**
toteswingers: 1&2 £7.00, 1&3 £4.40, 2&3 £9.70 CSF £26.85 CT £160.11 TOTE £3.90: £2.00, £3.30, £3.30; EX 34.30 Place 6: £131.80 Place 5: £50.96 .
Owner Miss Yvonne Jacques **Bred** F J O' Connor **Trained** East Everleigh, Wilts

FOCUS
A reasonable race for the grade that should produce some winners. Sound form, judged around the fourth.
Buona Sarah(IRE) Official explanation: jockey said filly was denied a clear run
Skyfire Official explanation: jockey said colt lost its action
T/Jkpt: Part won. £7,100.00 to a £1 stake. Pool: £10,000.00. 0.50 winning tickets. T/Plt: £158.20 to a £1 stake. Pool: £68,329.53. 315.20 winning tickets. T/Qpdt: £13.00 to a £1 stake. Pool: £4,253.72. 240.94 winning tickets. SP

1449 KEMPTON (A.W) (R-H)
Wednesday, April 21

OFFICIAL GOING: Standard
Wind: Moderate ahead Weather: Bright getting chilly

1477 CHAMPAGNE LANSON "EXTRA AGE" BRUT CLASSIFIED STKS 6f (P)
6:50 (6:50) (Class 6) 3-Y-O+ £2,047 (£604; £302) **Stalls High**

Form RPR
-060 **1** **West Leake (IRE)**[30] 961 4-9-9 52 LiamKeniry 12 61
(P Burgoyne) *in tch: hdwy fr 2f out: chal 1f out: drvn to ld fnl 120yds and pushed rt: hld on wl* **12/1**
0-41 **2** nk **Cavitie**[21] 1072 4-9-9 55 DarryllHolland 1 60
(Andrew Reid) *in tch: drvn and hdwy fr 2f out: rdn to take slt ld appr fnl f: wnt rt ins fnl f and narrowly hdd fnl 120yds: edgd lft u.p and no ex nr fin* **4/1**[1]
50-0 **3** 1 1/4 **Desert Pride**[14] 1171 5-9-9 53 (b[1]) PaulMulrennan 8 56
(W S Kittow) *t.k.h: chsd ldrs: drvn to chal appr fnl f outpcd by ldng duo fnl 75yds* **7/1**
0000 **4** nk **Shawkantango**[8] 1280 3-8-12 50 (v[1]) NeilCallan 5 52
(D Shaw) *bmpd s: in rr: gd hdwy fr 2f out: styd on fnl f and gng on whn carried lft cl home* **25/1**
0-05 **5** 3 1/4 **Soul Murmur (IRE)**[14] 1167 5-9-9 55 (bt) JamesDoyle 3 45
(F Sheridan) *bmpd s and wnt rt: led after 1f: rdn 2f out: hdd appr fnl f: wknd ins fnl f* **14/1**
2354 **6** 1/2 **Turf Time**[14] 1163 3-8-12 54 ChrisCatlin 2 40+
(J A Glover) *stmbld s and bhd: racd on outside and wd into st: kpt on fr over 1f out but nvr a threat* **11/2**[2]
0-05 **7** 2 1/4 **Monte Cassino (IRE)**[96] 195 5-9-9 55 JamieSpencer 10 41+
(J O'Reilly) *t.k.h in rr: n.m.r after 2f: sme late prog* **8/1**
303- **8** 1/2 **Sorrel Point**[159] 7371 7-9-9 54 (vt) JimmyQuinn 11 34
(H J Collingridge) *towards rr tl rapid hdwy to chse ldrs wl over 2f out: wknd appr fnl f* **6/1**[3]
00-0 **9** 1/2 **Blushing Maid**[11] 1234 4-9-9 52 DaneO'Neill 6 33
(H S Howe) *chsd ldrs tl wknd qckly over 1f out* **33/1**
10 1 **Marjustar (IRE)**[196] 6600 3-8-12 53 PatCosgrave 4 26
(J R Boyle) *s.i.s: a in rr* **12/1**
263/ **11** 3 **Ganache (IRE)**[889] 6809 8-9-9 50 JimCrowley 9 20
(P R Chamings) *led 1f: styd chsng ldrs tl wknd ins fnl 2f* **6/1**[3]
6006 **12** 55 **Lunaticus**[5] 1345 4-9-9 29 (v[1]) LukeMorris 7 —
(M J Attwater) *plld hrd: bhd fr 1/2-way: t.o* **100/1**

1m 13.36s (0.26) **Going Correction** -0.025s/f (Stan)
WFA 3 from 4yo+ 11lb **12** Ran SP% **117.4**
Speed ratings (Par 101): **97,96,94,94,90 89,86,85,85,83 79,—**
toteswingers: 1&2 £13.40, 1&3 £11.30, 2&3 £5.70 CSF £58.27 TOTE £28.10: £8.70, £1.10, £1.70; EX 89.40.
Owner L Tomlin **Bred** Rathbarry Stud **Trained** Shepton Montague, Somerset

FOCUS
An ordinary handicap. The field had managed just four wins between them in a total of 161 starts. The pace was decent and the first four pulled clear of the rest. The form is rated around the runner-up.
Soul Murmur(IRE) Official explanation: jockey said gelding hung left
Turf Time Official explanation: jockey said gelding stumbled leaving stalls

1478 CHAMPAGNE LANSON 250TH ANNIVERSARY H'CAP 1m 4f (P)
7:20 (7:21) (Class 6) (0-55,55) 4-Y-O+ £2,047 (£604; £302) **Stalls Centre**

Form RPR
2262 **1** **On Terms (USA)**[27] 982 4-9-3 **55** HayleyTurner 6 70
(S Dow) *trckd ldrs: led over 4f out: drvn 3 l clr 3f out: rdn along over 2f out: styd on wl u.p and in n.d fnl 2f* **7/2**[1]
31-0 **2** 3 3/4 **Through The Forest (USA)**[76] 411 4-9-1 **53** AdamKirby 11 62
(W R Swinburn) *chsd ldrs: drvn to dispute 2nd fr 2f out: wnt 2nd ins fnl f but nvr any ch w wnr* **11/1**
05-1 **3** 3/4 **Peintre D'Argent (IRE)**[13] 1194 4-9-1 **53** JimCrowley 12 61
(W J Knight) *in tch: rdn and hdwy fr 3f out to chse wnr over 2f out: nvr any ch and sn one pce: lost 2nd ins fnl f* **6/1**[3]
0-00 **4** nk **Iceman George**[16] 720 6-8-12 **52** (p) WilliamCarson(3) 13 59
(G C Bravery) *in rr: drvn and hdwy over 2f out: styd on fnl f and clsng nr fin but nvr any ch w wnr* **20/1**
004- **5** 1 3/4 **Flying Squad (UAE)**[132] 7354 6-9-1 **52** (t) SteveDrowne 2 57
(M F Harris) *in tch: drvn and hdwy over 3f out: styd on appr fnl f: no imp on wnr: wknd ins fnl f* **4/1**[2]
1-04 **6** nk **Champagne Fizz (IRE)**[49] 771 4-9-3 **55** DaneO'Neill 1 59
(Miss Jo Crowley) *in rr: pushed along and hdwy over 3f out: styd on fnl 2f but nvr gng pce to get into contention* **12/1**
-005 **7** 3 **Comrade Cotton**[9] 1262 6-8-13 **53** Louis-PhilippeBeuzelin(3) 10 52
(J Ryan) *in rr: stl plenty to do over 2f out: styd on fr over 1f out but nvr a threat* **14/1**
5-00 **8** 1/2 **Broughtons Paradis (IRE)**[14] 1177 4-9-3 **55** StevieDonohoe 14 53
(W J Musson) *in rr tl sme hdwy fnl 2f* **14/1**
1020 **9** nk **Playful Asset (IRE)**[6] 1318 4-9-1 **53** KirstyMilczarek 3 51
(P Howling) *chsd ldrs: rdn on outside over 3f out: wknd 2f out* **20/1**
43-4 **10** 9 **Bussell Along (IRE)**[47] 803 4-9-3 **55** TomQueally 8 39
(Stef Higgins) *in tch: rdn 4f out: sme prog over 2f out: sn wknd* **20/1**
0000 **11** 1 1/2 **Pachakutek (USA)**[2] 1427 4-8-11 **54** (p) JemmaMarshall(5) 4 35
(A J Lidderdale) *s.i.s: a towards rr* **40/1**
0434 **12** 8 **Mullitovermaurice**[13] 1194 4-9-2 **54** (p) PaulMulrennan 7 22
(J G Given) *sn led: hdd over 4f out: wknd ins fnl 3f* **16/1**
04-0 **13** 1 3/4 **Good Buy Dubai (USA)**[9] 1262 4-9-2 **54** ChrisCatlin 5 20
(C Gordon) *sn bhd* **12/1**

2m 33.41s (-1.09) **Going Correction** -0.025s/f (Stan)
WFA 4 from 5yo+ 1lb **13** Ran SP% **116.2**
Speed ratings (Par 101): **102,99,99,98,97 97,95,95,94,88 87,82,81**
toteswingers: 1&2 £11.80, 1&3 £11.70, 2&3 £2.80 CSF £38.55 CT £225.10 TOTE £2.30: £1.10, £5.60, £1.40; EX 43.20.
Owner S Dow **Bred** Juddmonte Farms Inc **Trained** Epsom, Surrey

FOCUS
A modest handicap run at a reasonable pace but nothing got into it from behind. The form makes sense.
Mullitovermaurice Official explanation: jockey said gelding had a breathing problem and made a noise
Good Buy Dubai(USA) Official explanation: jockey said gelding never travelled

1479 DIGIBET MEDIAN AUCTION MAIDEN STKS 1m 3f (P)
7:50 (7:53) (Class 5) 3-5-Y-O £2,590 (£770; £385; £192) **Stalls High**

Form RPR
5- **1** **Huff And Puff**[173] 7146 3-8-9 0 NeilCallan 6 75+
(Mrs A J Perrett) *trckd ldrs in 3rd: pushed along and hdwy over 2f out: led wl over 1f out: drvn fnl f and a jst doing enough* **4/5**[1]
2 3/4 **Eshtyaaq** 3-8-9 0 RichardHills 1 74+
(M P Tregoning) *s.i.s: in rr and wd bnd after 2f: hld up: shkn up and green over 2f out: qckhd appr fnl f and styd on wl to chse wnr fnl 120yds but a hld* **15/8**[2]
3 6 **Status Symbol (IRE)**[35] 5-9-11 0 WilliamCarson(3) 4 71+
(G C Bravery) *hld up towards rr but wl in tch: hdwy 3f out: slt ld appr fnl 2f: sn drvn: hdd wl over 1f out: nt gng pce of wnr and lost 2nd fnl 120yds: sn heavily eased* **7/1**[3]
06-4 **4** 8 **Suhailah**[14] 1157 4-9-4 45 JemmaMarshall(5) 7 48
(M J Attwater) *sn chsng ldr: rdn 3f out: wknd over 2f out* **50/1**
0-5 **5** 19 **Platinum Bounty**[14] 1157 4-9-9 0 JerryO'Dwyer 2 16
(N P Mulholland) *led: rdn over 3f out: hdd and btn over 2f out* **66/1**

2m 21.04s (-0.86) **Going Correction** -0.025s/f (Stan)
WFA 3 from 4yo+ 19lb **5** Ran SP% **106.3**
Speed ratings (Par 103): **102,101,97,91,77**
CSF £2.29 TOTE £1.90: £1.10, £1.30; EX 2.50.
Owner A D Spence **Bred** Sir Eric Parker **Trained** Pulborough, W Sussex

FOCUS
An interesting maiden. The pace was solid and the form pick fought out the finish with a very well-bred debutant. The form is rated slightly positively but the winner may not have needed to improve on last year's debut. The front pair look sure to do better.

1480 DIGIBET SPORTS BETTING H'CAP (LONDON MILE QUALIFIER) 1m (P)
8:20 (8:20) (Class 4) (0-85,82) 3-Y-O **£4,209** (£1,252; £625; £312) **Stalls** High

Form RPR

551- **1** **Hypnotized (USA)**[154] 7430 3-9-0 **78**........................ JamieSpencer 6 88+
(M L W Bell) *hld up in tch: hdwy and n.m.r over 1f out: squeezed through to ld ins fnl f: hrd drvn to assert: readily* **15/8**[1]

21 **2** *1* **Bohemian Melody**[27] 980 3-9-1 **79**........................ JerryO'Dwyer 5 84
(M Botti) *chsd ldrs: drvn to chal 2f out: sn slt ld: hdd ins fnl f: one pce whn edgd lft nr fin* **2/1**[2]

662- **3** *1* **Walcot Square (IRE)**[231] 5564 3-8-12 **76**........................ SteveDrowne 2 78
(R Charlton) *t.k.h: hld up in rr: hdwy over 1f out: styng on whn crossed: swtchd rt and tk 3rd cl home* **8/1**

530- **4** *shd* **Dark Eyes (IRE)**[172] 7187 3-9-3 **81**........................ RobertWinston 1 83
(D J Coakley) *s.i.s: sn rcvrd and in tch: hdwy over 2f out: drvn to chal over 1f out: kpt on same pce ins fnl f and lost 3rd cl home* **8/1**

3314 **5** *1 1/4* **Novay Essjay (IRE)**[23] 1052 3-8-7 **71**........................ HayleyTurner 3 70
(C R Dore) *led: rdn and narrowly hdd ins fnl 2f: stl ev ch appr fnl f: wknd fnl 120yds* **20/1**

010- **6** *8* **Admire The View (IRE)**[256] 4795 3-9-4 **82**........................ TedDurcan 4 62
(D R Lanigan) *in rr but in tch: rdn on outside and sme prog fr 3f out: nvr rchd ldrs and sn wknd* **15/2**[3]

3415 **7** *1 1/4* **Lockantanks**[23] 1045 3-9-0 **78**........................ SebSanders 7 55
(A B Haynes) *chsd ldrs: rdn over 2f out: wknd qckly wl over 1f out* **20/1**

1m 40.36s (0.56) **Going Correction** -0.025s/f (Stan) 7 Ran SP% **111.6**
Speed ratings (Par 100): **96,95,94,93,92 84,83**
toteswingers: 1&2 £2.00, 1&3 £3.50, 2&3 £4.60 CSF £5.58 TOTE £3.30: £3.10, £1.20; EX 5.90.
Owner Ali Saeed **Bred** Rabbah Bloodstock Llc **Trained** Newmarket, Suffolk
■ Stewards' Enquiry : Jamie Spencer caution: used whip down shoulder in the forehand

FOCUS
A decent handicap. It was won by highly progressive Mirrored in 2009, and there were several interesting types and potential improvers in this line-up. The form could be worth following, although the race was not truly run. The winner in particular can do better.
Admire The View(IRE) Official explanation: jockey said filly had no more to give

1481 DIGIBET.COM H'CAP 7f (P)
8:50 (8:51) (Class 3) (0-95,91) 4-Y-0+
£6,542 (£1,959; £979; £490; £244; £122) **Stalls** High

Form RPR

00-2 **1** **Crown Choice**[11] 1219 5-9-4 **91**........................ AdamKirby 2 104+
(W R Swinburn) *trckd ldrs in 3rd: travelling smoothly upsides fr 2f out: led 1f out: strly chal fnl 140yds: hrd rdn to assert fnl 50yds* **1/1**[1]

-141 **2** *nk* **New Leyf (IRE)**[35] 905 4-8-9 **82**........................ SteveDrowne 4 94+
(J R Gask) *hld up in rr but in tch: hdwy on ins fr 2f out: str chal fr 1f out and upsides fnl 120yds: jst outpcd fnl 50yds* **3/1**[2]

312- **3** *3 1/4* **Belle Des Airs (IRE)**[220] 5918 4-9-1 **88**........................ JimCrowley 3 91
(R M Beckett) *led: rdn 2f out: hdd 1f out: wknd ins fnl f* **9/2**[3]

3205 **4** *1/2* **Ilie Nastase (FR)**[11] 1219 6-8-10 **83**........................ LiamKeniry 6 85
(C R Dore) *hld up in rr: sme prog fr over 1f out but nvr a threat* **14/1**

5656 **5** *2 1/2* **Carcinetto (IRE)**[18] 1084 8-8-11 **89** ow1........................ RichardEvans(5) 5 84
(P D Evans) *in rr: rdn and sme prog to get in bhd ldrs over 2f out: wknd over 1f out* **12/1**

020- **6** *2 1/4* **Mut'Ab (USA)**[328] 2402 5-8-5 **78**........................(b) ChrisCatlin 1 67
(C E Brittain) *t.k.h and sn chsng ldr: rdn ins fnl 3f: wknd 2f out* **14/1**

1m 24.13s (-1.87) **Going Correction** -0.025s/f (Stan) 6 Ran SP% **114.2**
Speed ratings (Par 107): **109,108,104,104,101 98**
toteswingers:1&2 £1.80, 2&3 £2.40, 1&3 £1.50 CSF £4.34 TOTE £2.00: £1.40, £2.00; EX 6.20.
Owner P W Harris **Bred** Howard Barton Stud **Trained** Aldbury, Herts

FOCUS
There were not many runners for this decent handicap but the pace was fair and the first two pulled clear. The form is rated around the third, with personal bests from the first two.

NOTEBOOK
Crown Choice was just overhauled by a faster finisher when well-backed on his reappearance over 7f at Lingfield last time. He was 2lb higher here but travelled smoothly just behind the pace and showed a gutsy attitude to fight off a persistent challenger and maintain his unbeaten record of 3-3 at this track. He will face another rise after this win but is still relatively lightly raced and should have some more room to successfully manoeuvre. (op 6-4 tchd 13-8 in a place)
New Leyf(IRE) ran a big race stepped back up to 7f and now has a record of 2112 round here. His mark is upwardly mobile but he has raised his form several notches since switched to Polytrack and should be able to gain compensation for this close call. (tchd 11-4 tchd 10-3 in a place)
Belle Des Airs(IRE) dictated the pace on her Polytrack debut and return from 220 days off but could not respond when the first two kicked on. The reliable and uncomplicated front-runner should last longer next time but she looks high enough in the weights at present. (op 7-2)
Ilie Nastase(FR) got caught flat-footed at a crucial stage before staying on when it was all over. A return to 1m or a bit further will suit. (op 12-1)
Carcinetto(IRE) was pushed along some way out and could never get involved. She is a tough mare but age seems to have blunted her tactical speed and her losing run has now stretched to 25. (tchd 11-1)
Mut'Ab(USA) was a bit keen and faded on his return from 328 days off. He is entitled to benefit from the run but there are some wild swings in his profile and his sole win in 14 starts was in a 7f Yarmouth maiden in July 2008. (op 22-1)

1482 KEMPTON FOR CONFERENCES H'CAP 6f (P)
9:20 (9:21) (Class 5) (0-70,70) 4-Y-0+ **£2,590** (£770; £385; £192) **Stalls** High

Form RPR

152/ **1** **Tubby Isaacs**[523] 7315 6-9-4 **70**........................ NeilCallan 8 81+
(D K Ivory) *t.k.h: hld up in rr: hdwy: hung rt anf nt clr run ins fnl 2f: swtchd lft over 1f out: str run fnl f: qcknd to ld cl home* **11/2**[2]

0331 **2** *1/2* **Riflessione**[30] 967 4-9-3 **69**........................(b) LiamJones 12 79
(R A Harris) *chsd ldrs: styd on wl fr 2f out to ld ins fnl f: kpt on u.p: hdd and no ex cl home* **7/1**[3]

0343 **3** *1/2* **Gone Hunting**[49] 767 4-8-13 **70**........................(t) SimonPearce(5) 11 78
(J Pearce) *in rr: hdwy on ins fr 2f out: chsd ldrs fnl f and wnt 2nd briefly fnl 50yds: one pce cl home* **11/2**[2]

-125 **4** *2 1/2* **Boho Chic**[7] 1300 4-8-11 **63**........................(p) ChrisCatlin 10 63
(George Baker) *led: rdn 2f out: hdd ins fnl f: sn wknd* **10/1**

104 **5** *shd* **Valentino Swing (IRE)**[5] 1350 7-8-13 **68**........................ JackDean(3) 6 68
(Miss T Spearing) *in rr tl hdwy over 1f out: kpt on fnl f but nvr a threat* **12/1**

5451 **6** *1 3/4* **Chjimes (IRE)**[14] 1167 6-9-2 **68**........................ LiamKeniry 5 62
(C R Dore) *chsd ldrs: rdn over 2f out: sn outpcd* **14/1**

6410 **7** *nk* **Lady Kent (IRE)**[33] 931 4-9-4 **70**........................ PatCosgrave 2 63
(J R Boyle) *chsd ldrs on outside tl outpcd over 2f out* **14/1**

4050 **8** *1/2* **Figaro Flyer (IRE)**[34] 913 7-8-11 **63**........................ J-PGuillambert 3 55
(P Howling) *s.i.s: outpcd* **33/1**

F-11 **9** *1/2* **Replicator**[34] 924 5-8-11 **66**........................(e) AshleyHamblett(3) 7 56
(P L Gilligan) *chsd ldrs tl wknd qckly over 1f out* **2/1**[1]

0-14 **10** *1* **Prince Namid**[23] 1044 8-9-2 **68**........................ LukeMorris 4 55
(J A T De Giles) *outpcd most of way* **12/1**

3222 **11** *2* **Romantic Queen**[44] 828 4-8-5 **62**........................(t) MatthewDavies(5) 9 42
(George Baker) *chsd ldrs 4f* **14/1**

1m 11.81s (-1.29) **Going Correction** -0.025s/f (Stan) 11 Ran SP% **124.0**
Speed ratings (Par 103): **107,106,105,102,102 99,99,98,98,96 94**
toteswingers: 1&2 £7.30, 1&3 £4.70, 2&3 £11.50 CSF £46.48 CT £229.29 TOTE £3.70: £1.10, £7.40, £5.00; EX 51.30 Place 6: £10.81 Place 5: £4.06.
Owner John Khan **Bred** J W Ford **Trained** Radlett, Herts

FOCUS
A competitive handicap, involving three last-time-out winners and five others who finished in the frame on their latest start, and the form looks solid. They seemed to go quite hard up front.
Replicator Official explanation: jockey said gelding ran too free
T/Plt: £12.80 to a £1 stake. Pool: £66,488.19. 3,787.35 winning tickets. T/Qpdt: £5.10 to a £1 stake. Pool: £5,801.40. 830.20 winning tickets. ST

1292 BEVERLEY (R-H)
Thursday, April 22

OFFICIAL GOING: Good to firm (9.1)
Wind: light 1/2 behind Weather: fine and sunny

1483 BEVERLEY MINSTER CLAIMING STKS 5f
2:00 (2:00) (Class 5) 3-Y-O **£2,428** (£722; £361; £180) **Stalls** High

Form RPR

252 **1** **Micky's Knock Off (IRE)**[22] 1057 3-8-9 72........................(e) FrannyNorton 3 72
(R C Guest) *mde all: hung rt and wnt clr 1f out: eased towards fin* **11/8**[1]

420- **2** *5* **Final Ovation (IRE)**[198] 6556 3-8-6 67........................ IanBrennan(5) 1 56
(J J Quinn) *t.k.h: trckd ldrs: wnt 2nd over 2f out: hung rt over 1f out: no ch w wnr* **9/4**[2]

1633 **3** *3 1/4* **Magenta Strait**[14] 1187 3-8-3 61........................ DavidProbert 5 36
(R Hollinshead) *t.k.h: trckd ldrs: hmpd after 1f: fdd fnl f* **3/1**[3]

00-0 **4** *3* **Media Jury**[25] 1029 3-8-11 46........................(p) DavidNolan 2 34
(J S Wainwright) *chsd ldrs: edgd lft and wknd over 1f out* **40/1**

060- **5** *1 1/2* **Camacho Flyer (IRE)**[187] 6841 3-8-6 65........................ PaulPickard(5) 4 28
(P T Midgley) *trckd ldrs: swtchd outside after 1f: drvn over 2f out: wknd over 1f out* **14/1**

64.16 secs (0.66) **Going Correction** +0.10s/f (Good) 5 Ran SP% **107.0**
Speed ratings (Par 98): **98,90,84,80,77**
CSF £4.42 TOTE £2.00: £1.10, £1.30; EX 4.70.
Owner Miss Alison Ibbotson **Bred** J Cullinan **Trained** Stainforth, S Yorks

FOCUS
A very weak 3-y-o claimer. The winner is rated in line with a best view of his sand form.

1484 GET MARRIED AT BEVERLEY RACECOURSE H'CAP 1m 4f 16y
2:30 (2:30) (Class 4) (0-85,80) 4-Y-0+ **£4,857** (£1,445; £722; £360) **Stalls** High

Form RPR

5615 **1** **Kames Park (IRE)**[6] 1348 8-9-1 **76**........................ JimmyQuinn 7 86+
(R C Guest) *s.s: hld up in last: hdwy and nt clr run over 2f out: str burst to ld jst ins fnl f: styd on wl* **25/1**

2/62 **2** *2 1/4* **Southern Regent (IND)**[37] 897 9-8-8 **74**........................ IanBrennan(5) 9 79
(J J Quinn) *chsd ldrs: t.k.h: styd on to take 2nd towards fin* **16/1**

5415 **3** *3/4* **Taaresh (IRE)**[15] 1156 5-8-10 **71**........................ JoeFanning 3 75
(K A Morgan) *trckd ldr: led over 1f out: hdd and no ex jst ins fnl f* **16/1**

112 **4** *shd* **Sworn Tigress (GER)**[34] 941 5-9-2 **77**........................ TedDurcan 6 81
(George Baker) *trckd ldrs: effrt over 2f out: styd on same pce fnl f* **5/2**[1]

123- **5** *1 1/2* **Deauville Flyer**[181] 6995 4-9-4 **80**........................ DavidAllan 10 83+
(T D Easterby) *in tch: effrt 4f out: nt clr run over 2f out: hmpd over 1f out: kpt on ins fnl f* **3/1**[2]

541/ **6** *1* **The Oil Magnate**[582] 6012 5-9-5 **80**........................ PhillipMakin 4 80
(M Dods) *hld up in rr: hdwy on ins whn nt clr run over 1f out: swtchd lft and kpt on* **11/1**

160/ **7** *shd* **Dalhaan (USA)**[580] 6079 5-9-0 **75**........................(t) StevieDonohoe 8 75+
(Ian Williams) *in rr: effrt on ins over 3f out: nt clr run and hmpd over 1f out: styd on ins fnl f* **9/1**

500- **8** *1/2* **Haljaferia (UAE)**[271] 4319 4-8-9 **71**........................ DaneO'Neill 2 70
(D R C Elsworth) *t.k.h in midfield: hdwy on outside over 2f out: nvr threatened ldrs* **11/2**[3]

1344 **9** *1* **Eseej (USA)**[9] 1277 5-8-9 **73**........................ WilliamCarson(3) 1 70
(P W Hiatt) *led: t.k.h: qcknd over 3f out: hung rt and hdd over 1f out: hdd over 1f out: wknd fnl 150yds* **12/1**

1-00 **10** *nk* **Amazing Blue Sky**[26] 1013 4-8-12 **74**........................ SilvestreDeSousa 5 71
(Mrs R A Carr) *in tch: effrt on outer over 2f out: n.m.r over 1f out: nvr a threat* **28/1**

2m 40.45s (0.65) **Going Correction** -0.15s/f (Firm)
WFA 4 from 5yo+ 1lb 10 Ran SP% **114.0**
Speed ratings (Par 105): **95,93,93,92,91 91,91,90,90,90**
toteswingers: 1&2 £25.90, 1&3 £28.20, 2&3 £21.40 CSF £364.27 CT £6431.00 TOTE £23.40: £5.10, £5.00, £5.00; EX 150.50.
Owner Future Racing (Notts) Limited **Bred** Pat Beirne **Trained** Stainforth, S Yorks

FOCUS
A competitive handicap whioch was run at a fairly steady pace. The first four were all returning from the AW and the winner stepped up on his sand form.
Deauville Flyer ◆ Official explanation: jockey said gelding was denied a clear run
Eseej(USA) Official explanation: jockey said gelding hung right

1485 CONSTANT SECURITY MAIDEN STKS 1m 100y
3:00 (3:02) (Class 5) 3-Y-0+ **£2,590** (£770; £385; £192) **Stalls** High

Form RPR

0-4 **1** **Bin Shamardal (IRE)**[33] 950 3-8-11 0........................ MichaelHills 4 74+
(B W Hills) *wnt lft s: chsd ldrs: hdwy to ld over 1f out: readily* **2/1**[2]

04- **2** *1 1/2* **Wulfrida (IRE)**[184] 6921 3-8-6 0........................ HayleyTurner 3 65+
(J R Fanshawe) *hmpd s: in rr: hdwy and swtchd outside over 2f out: r.o to take 2nd 1f out: edgd rt: no imp* **6/4**[1]

3 *1 1/4* **Law To Himself (IRE)** 3-8-11 0........................ KierenFallon 7 67
(G A Swinbank) *chsd ldrs: wnt 2nd over 1f out: edgd rt: kpt on same pce* **11/1**

6 **4** *1 1/4* **I'm Frank**[18] 1100 4-9-11 0........................ PJMcDonald 5 68
(G A Swinbank) *in rr: hdwy over 2f out: styd on ins fnl f* **33/1**

5 *2* **Tamarillo Grove (IRE)** 3-8-11 0........................ RichardMullen 6 59+
(B Smart) *s.s: bhd: sme hdwy on outside over 2f out: kpt on wl fnl f* **10/1**[3]

	6	3/4	**Wolf Rock** 3-8-11 0 .... PhillipMakin 11	57+
			(T D Barron) *s.s: in rr: hdwy over 2f out: kpt on: nvr nr ldrs* **22/1**	
250-	7	1	**Red China Blues (USA)**[229] 5672 4-9-11 57 .... TomEaves 8	59
			(R E Barr) *led tl 6f out: chsd ldrs: wkng whn sltly hmpd jst ins fnl f* **33/1**	
	8	1/2	**Defence Of Realm (GER)** 3-8-11 0 .... TedDurcan 10	54
			(George Baker) *unruly s: in tch: hdwy 3f out: one pce fnl 2f* **25/1**	
	9	3/4	**Lucky Belle (IRE)** 3-8-1 0 .... PatrickDonaghy(5) 1	47
			(M Dods) *dwlt: t.k.h in rr: sme hdwy over 1f out: nvr a factor* **40/1**	
	10	1/2	**Accamelia**[48] 4-9-3 0 .... KellyHarrison(3) 2	50
			(C W Fairhurst) *swvd lft s: sn trcking ldrs: t.k.h: hdwy to ld 6f out: hdd over 1f out: sn wknd* **100/1**	
	11	1 3/4	**Switched Off**[37] 5-9-6 0 .... JamesSullivan(5) 9	51
			(M W Easterby) *s.i.s: sn wl bhd: kpt on fnl 2f: nvr on terms* **50/1**	
	12	23	**One More Tico** 3-8-11 0 .... JoeFanning 12	—
			(M Johnston) *prom: drvn over 2f out: wknd 2f out: bhd whn eased ins fnl f* **10/1**[3]	

1m 46.57s (-1.03) **Going Correction** -0.15s/f (Firm)
WFA 3 from 4yo+ 14lb **12** Ran SP% **119.3**
Speed ratings (Par 103): **99,97,96,95,93 92,91,90,90,89 87,64**
toteswingers: 1&2 £1.90, 1&3 £4.90, 2&3 £6.20 CSF £4.99 TOTE £2.80: £1.20, £1.10, £3.60; EX 5.30.
Owner Mohamed Obaida **Bred** Rabbah Bloodstock Limited **Trained** Lambourn, Berks

FOCUS
Not a bad maiden, but it was a messy race. The exposed seventh looks a suitable guide to the form.
Accamelia Official explanation: jockey said filly ran too free

1486 MOORENDS HOTEL H'CAP 1m 1f 207y

3:30 (3:31) (Class 5) (0-70,70) 3-Y-O **£2,590** (£770; £385; £192) **Stalls** High

Form				RPR
040-	1		**Sparkling Smile (IRE)**[195] 6628 3-9-0 66 .... TedDurcan 6	77+
			(D R Lanigan) *trckd ldrs: effrt and swtchd lft over 2f out: qcknd to ld appr fnl f: styd on strly: eased nr fin: v readily* **10/11**[1]	
36-6	2	2 3/4	**Monkton Vale (IRE)**[25] 1029 3-9-4 70 .... TonyHamilton 3	73
			(R A Fahey) *s.s: rcvrd after 1f: hld up in rr: hdwy over 2f out: styd on to take 2nd jst ins fnl f: no imp* **5/1**[2]	
-422	3	3	**Christmas Coming**[54] 734 3-9-4 70 .... DaneO'Neill 2	67
			(D R C Elsworth) *chsd ldrs: hung rt and outpcd over 2f out: kpt on fnl f: tk 3rd last 50yds* **5/1**[2]	
420-	4	1 1/2	**Storm Command (IRE)**[204] 6391 3-8-10 62 .... TomEaves 4	58
			(B Smart) *led: hdd 2f out: sn hmpd: edgd lft and one pce* **10/1**	
35-6	5	nk	**Interakt**[15] 1178 3-9-1 67 .... KierenFallon 1	60
			(M R Channon) *trckd ldr: led 2f out: hung rt: hdd appr fnl f: wknd fnl 150yds* **8/1**[3]	
604	6	2 1/2	**Major Pop (USA)**[18] 1103 3-8-13 65 .... FrederikTylicki 5	53
			(R A Fahey) *s.s: rcvrd after 2f: hld up in rr: effrt over 2f out: wknd 1f out: eased nr fin* **16/1**	

2m 6.35s (-0.65) **Going Correction** -0.15s/f (Firm) **6** Ran SP% **111.8**
Speed ratings (Par 98): **96,93,91,90,89 87**
toteswingers: 1&2 £2.60, 1&3 £2.10, 2&3 £2.20 CSF £5.78 TOTE £2.10: £1.20, £1.80; EX 6.30.
Owner Saif Ali & Saeed H Altayer **Bred** Georgestown Stud **Trained** Newmarket, Suffolk

FOCUS
A tight-looking 3-y-o handicap, but the unexposed winner bolted up.The form is rated around the third's AW form.

1487 RACING UK STKS (H'CAP) 7f 100y

4:05 (4:05) (Class 3) (0-90,87) 3-Y-O **£7,447** (£2,216; £1,107; £553) **Stalls** High

Form				RPR
1	1		**Hacienda (IRE)**[80] 374 3-9-4 87 .... FrankieDettori 1	94+
			(M Johnston) *wnt lft s: sn w ldr: chal over 2f out: sn led: rdn and styd on strly: eased nr fin* **10/11**[1]	
201-	2	1 3/4	**Elusive Sue (USA)**[219] 5958 3-8-8 77 .... FrederikTylicki 2	78
			(R A Fahey) *trckd ldrs: effrt 3f out: wnt 2nd over 1f out: kpt on same pce* **12/1**[3]	
102-	3	shd	**Bonfire Knight**[234] 5515 3-8-4 78 .... IanBrennan(5) 4	79+
			(J J Quinn) *led early: chsd ldrs: effrt and outpcd over 2f out: styd on strly ins fnl f* **15/8**[2]	
200-	4	4	**Avonrose**[201] 6486 3-9-0 83 .... GregFairley 5	74
			(M Johnston) *chsd ldrs: pushed along over 3f out: wknd over 1f out* **16/1**	
130-	5	3 1/2	**Silver Symphony (IRE)**[224] 5797 3-8-13 82 .... JoeFanning 6	64
			(P F I Cole) *trckd ldrs: stdd into rr after 2f: effrt on outer over 2f out: wknd over 1f out* **18/1**	
021-	6	7	**Excellent Day (IRE)**[259] 4711 3-8-7 76 .... SamHitchcott 3	41
			(M R Channon) *sn led: stmbld bdly over 5f out: hdd 2f out: wknd rapidly fnl f: eased nr fin* **16/1**	

1m 32.51s (-1.29) **Going Correction** -0.15s/f (Firm) **6** Ran SP% **111.9**
Speed ratings (Par 102): **101,99,98,94,90 82**
toteswingers: 1&2 £2.50, 1&3 £1.30, 2&3 £2.20 CSF £13.21 TOTE £1.70: £1.10, £4.60; EX 8.40.
Owner Sheikh Hamdan Bin Mohammed Al Maktoum **Bred** Yeomanstown Stud **Trained** Middleham Moor, N Yorks

FOCUS
A very interesting handicap that should work out. The form is rated around the runner-up and there is more to come from the winner..

NOTEBOOK
Hacienda(IRE) ◆ came into this under the "could be anything" category having won easily on his belated debut at Wolverhampton in February. That maiden hasn't worked out well, but there was always a chance he could be better than an opening mark of 87 and so it proved. He soon settled matters when asked to go clear and obviously had no trouble with the quick ground. It may be that he turns out to be a Pattern performer by the season's end, but it would be surprising were connections not eyeing a decent 3-y-o handicap for him during the summer, most probably the Britannia Stakes at Royal Ascot. He would need one more run beforehand to get a run in that, however, and there is a valuable handicap at York's Dante meeting next month that could be for him. (tchd evens in places)
Elusive Sue(USA), off the mark at the fifth attempt on her final outing at two, posted a respectable return to the track yet left the impression this test was stiff enough for her at this stage. She ought to benefit a deal for the run. (op 17-2)
Bonfire Knight ◆ had some decent nursery form to his name last year and, looking fit for this seasonal debut, was well backed. He came under pressure 3f out and looked one-paced, but was fairly motoring home inside the closing stages. There can be little doubt after this run that he now needs further. (op 11-4)
Avonrose kept on as though this first run back was needed, but has little room for manoeuvre from her current handicap mark. (tchd 20-1)
Silver Symphony(IRE) was ridden to get the longer distance on this 3-y-o debut and shaped as though she would improve for the outing. (op 12-1)
Excellent Day(IRE) was taking a big step up in trip for this return from her winter break and her stamina was badly found out under such positive tactics. (tchd 18-1)

1488 NEXT RACEDAY HERE MONDAY 3RD MAY H'CAP 7f 100y

4:40 (4:40) (Class 5) (0-70,70) 3-Y-O **£2,428** (£722; £361; £180) **Stalls** High

Form				RPR
40-2	1		**Fibs And Flannel**[8] 1298 3-8-12 64 .... DavidAllan 4	72+
			(T D Easterby) *w ldrs: led 6f out: styd on strly fnl 2f: readily* **13/8**[1]	
-145	2	1 1/4	**Ginger Grey (IRE)**[15] 1168 3-9-0 66 ....(p) DaneO'Neill 5	69
			(D R C Elsworth) *hld up: hdwy 3f out: wnt 2nd appr fnl f: kpt on: no imp* **8/1**	
44-2	3	3 1/4	**Chushka**[18] 1100 3-9-1 67 .... TomEaves 3	62
			(B Smart) *chsd ldr: edgd rt over 1f out: one pce* **4/1**[2]	
10-6	4	nk	**Saxby (IRE)**[8] 1297 3-9-4 70 .... SilvestreDeSousa 2	64
			(G A Harker) *hmpd s: in rr: drvn over 3f out: hdwy over 1f out: hung rt and kpt on ins fnl f* **25/1**	
-414	5	hd	**Honest Broker (IRE)**[15] 1168 3-8-13 65 .... JoeFanning 7	60
			(M Johnston) *led: hdd 6f out: one pce whn hmpd on ins over 1f out* **13/2**	
444-	6	10	**Tia Juana (IRE)**[219] 5969 3-8-13 65 .... KierenFallon 6	34
			(B M R Haslam) *t.k.h: chsd ldrs: lost pl 6f out: hrd drvn over 3f out: hung rt and wknd 2f out* **10/1**	
26-1	7	7	**Orpen Arms (IRE)**[13] 1201 3-8-11 63 .... TonyHamilton 1	14
			(R A Fahey) *wnt rt s: in rr: sn drvn along: sme hdwy over 3f out: lost pl 2f out* **9/2**[3]	

1m 32.45s (-1.35) **Going Correction** -0.15s/f (Firm) **7** Ran SP% **113.7**
Speed ratings (Par 98): **101,99,95,95,95 83,75**
toteswingers: 1&2 £3.60, 1&3 £2.60, 2&3 £6.40 CSF £15.44 TOTE £2.60: £3.50, £6.60; EX 14.70.
Owner Jim McGrath **Bred** J A And M A Knox **Trained** Great Habton, N Yorks

FOCUS
A modest handicap, run at a fair pace. The runner-up limits the form to some effect but the winner looks sure to do better.
Saxby(IRE) Official explanation: jockey said gelding hung right
Orpen Arms(IRE) Official explanation: trainer had no explanation for the poor form shown

1489 CELEBRATE YOUR BIRTHDAY AT BEVERLEY FILLIES' H'CAP 1m 1f 207y

5:15 (5:16) (Class 5) (0-70,65) 4-Y-0+ **£2,590** (£770; £385; £192) **Stalls** High

Form				RPR
-061	1		**Sudden Impulse**[13] 1199 9-8-13 60 .... SilvestreDeSousa 1	70
			(A D Brown) *in rr: nt clr run over 2f out: swtchd rt over 1f out: r.o wl to ld ins fnl f* **17/2**	
0306	2	1 1/4	**Boa**[8] 1296 5-8-11 58 .... DavidProbert 6	66
			(R Hollinshead) *mid-div: pushed along 5f out: styd on to ld over 1f out: hdd and no ex ins fnl f* **13/2**[3]	
530-	3	3 3/4	**Love In The West (IRE)**[220] 5947 4-8-13 60 .... KierenFallon 5	60+
			(G A Swinbank) *chsd ldrs on outer: styd on same pce fnl 2f* **17/2**	
540-	4	3/4	**Chichen Daawe**[171] 7214 4-7-13 51 oh3 .... PaulPickard(5) 7	50
			(B Ellison) *chsd ldrs on outer: effrt 3f out: edgd rt over 1f out: kpt on one pce* **20/1**	
4	5	1 1/4	**Kataragama**[17] 1116 4-9-1 65 .... KellyHarrison(3) 2	61
			(Mrs K Walton) *hld up in rr: effrt on outer over 2f out: kpt on: nvr rchd ldrs* **10/1**	
116-	6	5	**Sceilin (IRE)**[164] 6760 6-9-3 64 ....(t) StephenCraine 3	50
			(J Mackie) *s.i.s: in rr: kpt on fnl 2f: nvr a factor* **16/1**	
44-3	7	2	**Light Dubai (IRE)**[16] 1141 4-9-4 65 .... TonyCulhane 12	47
			(M R Channon) *w ldr: led 3f out: hdd over 1f out: sn wknd* **10/3**[1]	
010-	8	shd	**Tres Froide (FR)**[176] 7127 5-9-0 61 .... HayleyTurner 10	43
			(N Tinkler) *led tl 3f out: wknd over 1f out* **10/1**	
-232	9	1 1/4	**Tomintoul Star**[50] 776 4-8-8 55 .... AndrewElliott 4	34
			(Mrs R A Carr) *t.k.h towards rr: effrt 3f out: nt clr run over 1f out: nvr a factor* **9/1**	
005	10	3/4	**Gheed (IRE)**[12] 1226 5-8-3 57 ....(t) RyanClark(7) 9	35
			(K A Morgan) *chsd ldrs: drvn over 3f out: lost pl over 1f out* **20/1**	
5-00	11	3/4	**Dispol Diva**[26] 1012 4-8-8 55 ....(v) JoeFanning 8	31
			(P T Midgley) *chsd ldrs: lost pl over 1f out* **5/1**[2]	

2m 4.55s (-2.45) **Going Correction** -0.15s/f (Firm) **11** Ran SP% **117.7**
Speed ratings (Par 100): **103,102,99,98,97 93,91,91,90,90 89**
toteswingers: 1&2 £15.10, 1&3 £16.20, 2&3 £13.10 CSF £62.93 CT £483.23 TOTE £13.90: £4.70, £3.30, £1.60; EX 80.00 Place 6: £123.00 Place 5: £94.42 .
Owner A D Brown **Bred** Sagittarius Bloodstock Associates Ltd **Trained** Yedingham, N Yorks

FOCUS
A moderate fillies' handicap, run at a reasonable pace, and the form looks sound. The winner's best effort for two years.
Light Dubai(IRE) Official explanation: trainer had no explanation for the poor form shown
T/Plt: £96.60 to a £1 stake. Pool: £49,585.96. 374.69 winning tickets. T/Qpdt: £7.20 to a £1 stake. Pool: £3,645.78. 370.02 winning tickets. WG

1142 SOUTHWELL (L-H)

Thursday, April 22

OFFICIAL GOING: Standard
Wind: Virtually nil Weather: Fine and dry

1490 LADBROKES.COM MEDIAN AUCTION MAIDEN STKS 7f (F)

5:25 (5:26) (Class 6) 3-4-Y-O **£2,047** (£604; £302) **Stalls** Low

Form				RPR
22-5	1		**Flouncing (IRE)**[10] 1257 3-8-8 78 .... LiamJones 9	68
			(W J Haggas) *trckd ldrs: hdwy 3f out: chal 1 1/2f out: rdn to take slt ld over 1f out: drvn towards fin and jst hld on* **2/1**[1]	
32-0	2	shd	**Primo De Vida (IRE)**[15] 1178 3-8-13 68 .... JimCrowley 8	73
			(R M Beckett) *cl up: led 1/2-way: rdn along over 2f out: hdd over 1f out: drvn and rallied ins fnl f: jst failed* **5/2**[2]	
6	3	5	**Wadi Wanderer (IRE)**[13] 1211 3-8-13 0 .... LiamKeniry 6	59
			(E F Vaughan) *led to 1/2-way: cl up tl rdn along over 2f out and grad wknd appr fnl f* **12/1**	
6	4	2 3/4	**British Sea Power (IRE)**[16] 1137 3-8-6 0 .... JohnFahy(7) 4	52+
			(J R Gask) *towards rr: hdwy on inner over 2f out: sn rdn and kpt on appr fnl f: nvr nr ldrs* **20/1**	
005-	5	1/2	**George Adamson (IRE)**[297] 3449 4-9-12 54 .... RobertWinston 3	55
			(G A Swinbank) *towards rr and reminders after s: hdwy to trck ldrs 1/2-way: rdn along wl over 2f out: drvn: hung bdly rt over 1f out and sn wknd* **14/1**	
544	6	1 1/2	**Zephyron (IRE)**[35] 915 3-8-13 64 ....(p) JerryO'Dwyer 11	46
			(J R Holt) *chsd ldrs on inner: rdn along wl over 2f out and grad wknd* **11/1**	

20-4 **7** *7* **Marafong**[10] 1257 3-8-6 70 AdamBeschizza(7) 1 28
(Miss J Feilden) *a towards rr* **6/1**[3]
-540 **8** *1 ½* **Montego Breeze**[49] 794 4-9-7 45 (p) MickyFenton 2 23
(John A Harris) *a towards rr* **50/1**
9 *3 ½* **Fuego Dreamer** 3-8-13 0 JimmyQuinn 10 14
(J R Holt) *s.i.s: sn rdn along and a bhd* **33/1**
0-50 **10** *6* **Pinewood Polly**[7] 1336 3-8-8 0 KevinGhunowa 5 —
(S A Harris) *chsd ldrs on inner: rdn along 1/2-way: sn wknd* **250/1**
50-0 **11** *2 ¾* **Singin' The Blues**[9] 1280 3-8-13 65 LukeMorris 7 —
(J M P Eustace) *sn rdn along in rr: hdwy and in tch whn rdn 1/2-way and sn wknd* **20/1**

1m 29.76s (-0.54) **Going Correction** -0.075s/f (Stan)
WFA 3 from 4yo 13lb 11 Ran SP% **113.7**
Speed ratings (Par 101): **100,99,94,91,90 88,80,79,75,68 65**
toteswingers: 1&2 £2.00, 1&3 £6.40, 2&3 £7.20 CSF £6.24 TOTE £3.40: £1.80, £1.10, £4.20; EX 6.30.
Owner Goddard, Hamer & Hawkes **Bred** Mrs Noelle Walsh **Trained** Newmarket, Suffolk

FOCUS
A modest maiden, but it was well run and the form looks pretty sound. The winner didn't match her 2yo best.
Montego Breeze Official explanation: jockey said filly did not face the kickback

1491 WATCH LIVE SPORT AT LADBROKES.COM CLAIMING STKS 6f (F)
5:55 (5:55) (Class 6) 3-Y-0+ £2,047 (£604; £302) Stalls Low

Form RPR
0605 **1** **Ingleby Arch (USA)**[7] 1332 7-9-11 88 PhillipMakin 5 81
(T D Barron) *chsd ldng pair: rdn along 1/2-way and wd st: hdwy wl over 1f out: sn drvn and styd on ins fnl f to ld last 50yds* **7/4**[1]
4302 **2** *¾* **Clear Ice (IRE)**[12] 1237 3-8-4 68 (b) AdrianNicholls 2 65
(D Nicholls) *chsd ldr: hdwy to ld over 2f out: rdn wl over 1f out: drvn and hung lft ins fnl f: hdd and no ex last 50yds* **9/2**[2]
3050 **3** *¾* **Cape Of Storms**[31] 961 7-9-1 55 (b) PaulMulrennan 6 66
(R Brotherton) *led and set str pce: rdn along and hdd over 2f out: sn drvn and one pce appr fnl f* **22/1**
6625 **4** *7* **Calmdownmate (IRE)**[16] 1147 5-9-1 60 PJMcDonald 4 44
(Mrs R A Carr) *rdn along and outpcd towards rr: sme hdwy over 2f out: sn drvn and no imp* **11/1**[3]
-300 **5** *2 ¾* **Confuchias (IRE)**[25] 1032 6-9-11 85 (b) LukeMorris 3 45
(J R Gask) *sn rdn along and a bhd* **7/4**[1]
4602 **6** *¾* **Captain Bluebird (IRE)**[15] 1155 3-8-9 62 ShaneKelly 1 34
(D Donovan) *in tch: rdn along bef 1/2-way and sn wknd* **14/1**

1m 15.59s (-0.91) **Going Correction** -0.075s/f (Stan)
WFA 3 from 5yo+ 11lb 6 Ran SP% **110.3**
Speed ratings (Par 101): **103,102,101,91,88 87**
toteswingers: 1&2 £1.20, 1&3 £9.20, 2&3 £8.70 CSF £9.78 TOTE £2.30: £1.10, £6.70; EX 8.40.Clear Ice was claimed by Shaun Taylor for £5,000.
Owner Dave Scott **Bred** Alexander-Groves Thoroughbreds **Trained** Maunby, N Yorks

FOCUS
A fair claimer run at a strong pace. The form is rated around the third.
Confuchias(IRE) Official explanation: jockey said horse never travelled

1492 PLAY POKER AT LADBROKES.COM H'CAP 7f (F)
6:25 (6:25) (Class 5) (0-70,71) 4-Y-0+ £2,729 (£806; £403) Stalls Low

Form RPR
3303 **1** **Flores Sea (USA)**[17] 1115 6-9-2 67 (b) PhillipMakin 7 78
(Mrs R A Carr) *in tch: wd st and hdwy 2f out: rdn to chse ldrs over 1f out: styd on to chal ent fnl f: sn led and kpt on wl* **6/1**
1524 **2** *2* **Young Gladiator (IRE)**[17] 1115 5-9-1 66 (b) FrederikTylicki 6 72
(Julie Camacho) *led: rdn 2f out: drvn over 1f out: hdd ins fnl f: kpt on same pce* **10/3**[1]
1/ **3** *nk* **Fadhb Ar Bith (IRE)**[624] 4756 5-8-13 69 MarkCoumbe(5) 4 74
(John A Harris) *hld up in rr: hdwy on outer and shkn up 2f out: chsd ldrs over 1f out: kpt on under hand riding ins fnl f: nrst fin* **40/1**
4434 **4** *½* **Kladester (USA)**[35] 925 4-8-6 57 (p) PJMcDonald 5 61
(M Herrington) *towards rr: hdwy wl over 2f out: sn rdn and styd on appr fnl f: nrst fin* **9/1**
2505 **5** *nk* **Elusive Warrior (USA)**[36] 907 7-9-4 69 (p) JamesDoyle 3 72
(A J McCabe) *cl up: rdn along over 2f out: drvn over 1f out: wknd fnl f* **16/1**
40-5 **6** *9* **Crocodile Bay (IRE)**[16] 1148 7-8-4 55 oh1 (b) FrannyNorton 8 34
(R C Guest) *v.s.a and lost many l s: sme hdwy over 2f out: sn rdn and nvr nr ldrs* **9/2**[3]
6304 **7** *1 ¾* **Owed**[16] 1148 8-7-11 55 oh8 (tp) MatthewLawson(7) 1 29
(R Bastiman) *chsd ldng pair on inner: rdn along wl over 2f out: sn wknd* **40/1**
5321 **8** *1 ¼* **Army Of Stars (IRE)**[8] 1304 4-9-6 71 6ex (p) ShaneKelly 11 42
(J A Osborne) *chsd ldrs: rdn along 3f out: cl over 2f out: sn drvn and wknd* **7/2**[2]
0 **9** *3 ¼* **Running Flame (IRE)**[9] 1270 4-8-10 68 ConorQuish(7) 9 30
(A J McCabe) *dwlt: a towards rr* **50/1**
00-0 **10** *2 ¾* **Illicit**[21] 1078 5-8-4 55 (bt¹) JimmyQuinn 2 9
(J R Holt) *s.i.s: a bhd* **50/1**
112- **11** *1* **Blue Noodles**[189] 6790 4-8-12 68 AndrewHeffernan(5) 10 20
(P D Evans) *chsd ldrs: rdn along 1/2-way: sn wknd* **8/1**

1m 29.47s (-0.83) **Going Correction** -0.075s/f (Stan) 11 Ran SP% **113.6**
Speed ratings (Par 103): **101,98,98,97,97 87,85,83,80,76 75**
toteswingers: 1&2 £4.70, 1&3 £50.20, 2&3 £20.40 CSF £24.84 CT £721.19 TOTE £5.00: £1.40, £1.20, £25.00; EX 26.20.
Owner C W Racing Club 2 **Bred** Beckie McLay-Irons **Trained** Huby, N Yorks

FOCUS
Several of these missed the break quite badly and, with the pace strong, the field were soon strung out. The runner-up is a sound guide to the form.
Fadhb Ar Bith(IRE) Official explanation: jockey said, regarding running and riding, that his orders were to sit handy, keep the gelding out of the kickback and pick up in the straight, adding that it stayed on in straight through beaten horses, plugging on one pace; trainer confirmed adding that the gelding had run better than expected having had a wind operation and only been in training for ten weeks.
Crocodile Bay(IRE) Official explanation: jockey said gelding was slowly away
Illicit Official explanation: jockey said gelding was slowly away and hung right

1493 DIARYWORLD LTD H'CAP 1m 4f (F)
6:55 (6:55) (Class 5) (0-75,74) 4-Y-0+ £2,729 (£806; £403) Stalls Low

Form RPR
00-1 **1** **Bivouac (UAE)**[47] 720 6-8-7 62 PJMcDonald 5 73
(G A Swinbank) *trckd ldng pair: hdwy 3f out: chal 2f out and sn rdn: drvn over 1f out: kpt on u.p to ld wl ins fnl f* **11/4**[1]
3160 **2** *½* **Daaweitza**[9] 1272 7-8-12 74 (b) DaleSwift(7) 3 84
(B Ellison) *t.k.h: trckd ldr tl led after 4f and sn clr: rdn along and jnd 2f out: drvn over 1f out: hdd and no ex wl ins fnl f* **11/4**[1]
2200 **3** *3* **Mustajed**[8] 1303 9-8-11 69 ow1 (b) JamesMillman(3) 1 74
(B R Millman) *trckd ldrs: hdwy on inner 4f out: rdn along 3f out: drvn and kpt on same pce fnl 2f* **8/1**
3-30 **4** *14* **Onemoreandstay**[12] 1028 5-8-10 65 (v¹) RobertWinston 6 48
(H J Collingridge) *hld up in rr: hdwy on outer 5f out: rdn along to chse ldrs 3f out: drvn and btn 2f out* **11/2**[3]
00-2 **5** *7* **Group Leader (IRE)**[17] 1134 4-8-4 60 oh2 AdrianMcCarthy 4 32
(J R Jenkins) *hld up in rr: effrt 5f out: sn rdn along and outpcd fnl 3f* **5/1**[2]
050/ **6** *3 ¼* **Zabeel Palace**[61] 5725 8-8-13 68 TomQueally 2 34
(B J Curley) *led 4f: prom tl rdn along over 4f out and sn wknd* **13/2**

2m 40.38s (-0.62) **Going Correction** -0.075s/f (Stan)
WFA 4 from 5yo+ 1lb 6 Ran SP% **109.8**
Speed ratings (Par 103): **99,98,96,87,82 80**
toteswingers: 1&2 £2.60, 1&3 £3.20, 2&3 £3.40 CSF £9.79 TOTE £2.90: £1.80, £5.90; EX 11.20.

Owner Mrs J M Penney **Bred** Darley **Trained** Melsonby, N Yorks

FOCUS
They finished strung out behind the front two and this was a weak race. The winner is rated back to his best form.

1494 FRANK BRADLEY MEMORIAL H'CAP 1m (F)
7:25 (7:25) (Class 5) (0-75,75) 4-Y-0+ £2,729 (£806; £403) Stalls Low

Form RPR
10-3 **1** **Just Five (IRE)**[36] 908 4-9-4 75 PhillipMakin 5 85
(M Dods) *t.k.h: trckd ldrs: hdwy over 2f out: rdn to ld wl over 1f out: drvn and edgd rt ins fnl f: kpt on wl* **5/2**[1]
4251 **2** *2* **Miss Bootylishes**[16] 1141 5-8-12 74 AmyBaker(5) 2 79
(A B Haynes) *a cl up: effrt 3f out: rdn 2f out and sn ev ch tl drvn and one pce ins fnl f* **17/2**
1460 **3** *2* **General Tufto**[5] 1374 5-9-1 75 (b) MartinLane(3) 3 75
(C Smith) *in rr: rdn along and outpcd 3f out: styd on fr over 1f out: nrst fin* **11/2**[3]
/50- **4** *1* **Liteup My World (USA)**[267] 4436 4-8-4 61 oh2 RoystonFfrench 1 59
(B Ellison) *led: rdn along 3f out: hdd wl over 1f out: sn drvn and wknd appr fnl f* **5/2**[1]
65-6 **5** *2 ¼* **Green Agenda**[17] 1128 4-8-11 68 JoeFanning 4 61
(M Johnston) *chsd ldrs: effrt on inner and cl up 3f out: sn rdn and wknd over 2f out* **7/2**[2]
450- **6** *5* **Rising Kheleyf (IRE)**[217] 6015 4-9-0 71 PJMcDonald 6 52
(G A Swinbank) *cl up on outer: rdn along 3f out: wknd over 2f out* **8/1**

1m 42.66s (-1.04) **Going Correction** -0.075s/f (Stan) 6 Ran SP% **116.4**
Speed ratings (Par 103): **102,100,98,97,94 89**
toteswingers: 1&2 £1.70, 1&3 £2.80, 2&3 £4.20 CSF £24.97 TOTE £3.10: £1.20, £2.40; EX 11.10.
Owner Just Five Racing Partners **Bred** Rathbarry Stud **Trained** Denton, Co Durham

FOCUS
An ordinary, uneventful handicap. Straightforward form with the progressive winner up 6lb.

1495 BET IN PLAY AT LADBROKES.COM H'CAP 1m (F)
7:55 (7:55) (Class 6) (0-60,60) 3-Y-0 £2,047 (£604; £302) Stalls Low

Form RPR
-220 **1** **Buzz Bird**[5] 1394 3-8-9 51 PhillipMakin 11 65
(T D Barron) *in tch: rdn along and hdwy over 3f out: chal wl over 1f out: styd on u.p to ld ent fnl f: r.o* **5/2**[1]
-326 **2** *2* **D'Urberville**[74] 455 3-9-1 57 JimCrowley 3 66
(J R Jenkins) *cl up on inner: led 1/2-way: pushed clr 3f out: rdn 2f out: drvn and hdd ent fnl f: kpt on same pce* **7/2**[2]
254 **3** *6* **Market Puzzle (IRE)**[63] 597 3-9-2 58 (b¹) TomMcLaughlin 5 53
(W M Brisbourne) *bhd and sn rdn along swtchd wd to stands' rail st and hdwy 2f out: sn drvn and styd on strly ins fnl f: nrst fin* **16/1**
000- **4** *1* **Shercon (IRE)**[188] 6819 3-8-4 46 oh1 SilvestreDeSousa 1 39
(N Tinkler) *towards rr: hdwy wl over 2f out: sn rdn and styd on to chse ldng pair over 1f out: sn one pce* **33/1**
665- **5** *10* **Emeralds Spirit (IRE)**[210] 6232 3-8-7 49 LukeMorris 8 19
(J R Weymes) *chsd ldrs: rdn along 3f out: outpcd fnl 2f* **14/1**
3-55 **6** *1* **Prince Yarraman (IRE)**[88] 283 3-9-4 60 ShaneKelly 12 28
(J A Osborne) *prom: effrt to chse ldr 3f out: rdn along over 2f out and sn wknd* **7/2**[2]
330- **7** *1* **Labretella (IRE)**[125] 7792 3-8-12 54 MickyFenton 13 19
(S A Harris) *a towards rr* **33/1**
00-0 **8** *2* **Securitisation (IRE)**[64] 583 3-8-13 55 TomQueally 2 16
(B J Curley) *s.i.s: a bhd* **12/1**
00-0 **9** *¾* **Catawollow**[27] 993 3-8-4 46 oh1 PaulEddery 7 —
(R C Guest) *led to 1/2-way: rdn along over 3f out and sn wknd* **20/1**
0600 **10** *3 ½* **Just Say Please**[15] 1162 3-8-12 54 JimmyQuinn 6 —
(D K Ivory) *chsd ldrs: rdn along over 3f out: sn wknd* **20/1**
0-60 **11** *1 ¼* **Zambuka (FR)**[10] 1261 3-8-10 52 KevinGhunowa 10 —
(R Curtis) *prom: rdn along over 3f out: sn wknd* **8/1**[3]

1m 43.5s (-0.20) **Going Correction** -0.075s/f (Stan) 11 Ran SP% **119.8**
Speed ratings (Par 96): **98,96,90,89,79 78,77,75,74,70 69**
toteswingers: 1&2 £3.10, 1&3 £9.10, 2&3 £3.90 CSF £10.71 CT £115.81 TOTE £2.50: £1.02, £3.20, £7.60; EX 13.70 Place 6: £19.23, Place 5: £14.26..
Owner Twinacre Nurseries Ltd **Bred** Twinacre Nurseries Ltd **Trained** Maunby, N Yorks

FOCUS
A moderate handicap, although the front two pulled nicely clear. The race is rated around the runner-up but there are doubts over the form.
T/Plt: £20.00 to a £1 stake. Pool: £56,227.14. 2,051.13 winning tickets. T/Qpdt: £9.20 to a £1 stake. Pool: £4,755.00. 381.70 winning tickets. JR

1291 SAINT-CLOUD (L-H)
Thursday, April 22

OFFICIAL GOING: Turf: good to soft

1496a PRIX PENELOPE (FILLIES) (GROUP 3) (3YO) (TURF) 1m 2f 110y
1:35 (12:00) 3-Y-0 £35,398 (£12,389; £12,389; £7,079; £3,539)

RPR
1 **Dariole (FR)**[13] 3-9-0 0 GregoryBenoist 10 102
(P Bary, France) *racd in 2nd fr s: qckned to ld 1 1/2f out: r.o: jst hld on* **87/10**

The Form Book, Raceform Ltd, Compton, RG20 6NL

2 *nk* **Middle Club**[29] 973 3-9-0 0 .... RichardHughes 3 101
(R Hannon) *racd in midfield fr s: qckd 2f out: r.o strly to share 2nd on line* **5/2**[1]

2 *dht* **A Media Luz (FR)**[43] 3-9-0 0 .... ThierryThulliez 8 101
(Y Fouin, France) *led fr s: hdd 1 1/2f out: c again cl home: ct on line for 2nd* **17/2**

4 *1 1/2* **Seeking Solace**[24] 3-9-0 0 .... MickaelBarzalona 9 98
(A Fabre, France) *racd in 4th: proged to 3rd early in st: no ex: styd on ins fnl f* **9/2**[3]

5 *1* **Plume Rose**[33] 952 3-9-0 0 .... StephanePasquier 6 96
(Y De Nicolay, France) *racd in rr fr s: qcknd wl 2f out: no ex* **12/1**

6 *1/2* **Ginger Bazouka (FR)**[21] 3-9-0 0 .... (p) MaximeGuyon 4 95
(P Demercastel, France) *wl in rr fr s: racd wd into st: hrd rdn 2f out: styd on* **29/1**

7 *shd* **Sinndarina (FR)**[13] 3-9-0 0 .... AnthonyCrastus 1 95
(P Demercastel, France) *racd in 3rd fr s: prom early in st: fdd fr 2f out* **13/1**

8 *1* **Sound Of Summer (USA)**[33] 952 3-9-0 0 .... ChristopheSoumillon 7 93
(J-C Rouget, France) *racd in midfield: failed to qckn in st: fdd* **4/1**[2]

9 *2 1/2* **Scandola (USA)**[33] 952 3-9-0 0 .... OlivierPeslier 2 88
(S Wattel, France) *racd towards rr on rail: n.m.r early in st: fdd* **10/1**

10 *nk* **Terra Nova (FR)**[9] 3-9-0 0 .... SebastienMaillot 5 88
(Robert Collet, France) *prom early: no ex in st* **58/1**

2m 19.9s (0.30) **10** Ran SP% **116.5**
WIN (Incl. 1 euro stake); 9.70. PLACES: 2.50, 2.80 (A Media Luz), 1.80 (Middle Club). DF 15.20 (D/AML); 8.20 (D/MC). SF 20.80 (D/MC); 37.80 (D/AML).
Owner Mme Patrick Barbe **Bred** Rene Wattinne **Trained** Chantilly, France

NOTEBOOK
Middle Club, a Group 3 winner at Chantilly last autumn and fit from a recent success on Polytrack, was encountering cut in the ground for the first time and finished strongly from off the pace to share second in a close finish. She will now step up in trip with races like the Prix de Royaumont, Prix de Malleret and the Oaks d'Italia on the agenda.

SANDOWN (R-H)

Friday, April 23

OFFICIAL GOING: Good (good to firm in places)

Rail at outermost configuration in back straight and around home bend adding circa 8yds to races on round course.

Wind: virtually nil Weather: sunny,quite warm

1497 BET365.COM ESHER CUP (H'CAP) 1m 14y

1:10 (1:10) (Class 2) (0-100,95) 3-Y-O

£12,462 (£3,732; £1,866; £934; £466; £234) **Stalls** High

Form RPR

1- **1** **Fallen Idol**[225] 5807 3-8-12 **89** .... WilliamBuick 1 101+
(J H M Gosden) *hld up in tch in last trio: rdn 2f out: qcknd to ld 1f out: r.o strly to go clr ins fnl f: eased towards fin: impressive* **4/1**[2]

11-0 **2** *2 1/4* **Karaka Jack**[9] 1310 3-8-13 **90** .... JoeFanning 6 93
(M Johnston) *bmpd s: sn rcvrd to ld: rdn 2f out: drvn and hdd 1f out: nt pce of wnr after: kpt on* **9/1**

13-1 **3** *1/2* **Huygens**[27] 1018 3-9-2 **93** .... EddieAhern 5 95
(D J Coakley) *stdd and wnt rt s: t.k.h: hld up in last pair: rdn and effrt 2f out: styd on u.p fnl f: wnt 3rd fnl 100yds: no threat to wnr* **9/2**[3]

610- **4** *1 1/2* **Red Badge (IRE)**[181] 7030 3-9-1 **92** .... RichardHughes 8 94+
(R Hannon) *t.k.h: trckd ldrs: rdn 3f out: drvn over 1f out: keeping on u.p but no ch w wnr whn nt clr run ins fnl f* **7/1**

5231 **5** *1 1/4* **Duellist**[20] 1086 3-8-10 **87** .... FrankieDettori 3 83
(M Johnston) *t.k.h: trckd ldrs: rdn and effrt ent fnl 2f: unable qck over 1f out: wknd fnl 100yds* **11/1**

031- **6** *1/2* **Invincible Soul (IRE)**[189] 6810 3-8-7 **84** .... RyanMoore 2 79
(R Hannon) *dwlt: t.k.h: sn pressing ldr: ev ch and rdn 2f out: drvn over 1f out: wknd ins fnl f* **5/2**[1]

130- **7** *nk* **Blakey's Boy**[195] 6664 3-8-12 **89** .... TedDurcan 7 83
(J L Dunlop) *hmpd s: t.k.h: hld up in rr: rdn and hanging rt over 2f out: no hdwy and wl btn over 1f out: plugged on ins fnl f: n.d* **22/1**

412- **8** *10* **Raine's Cross**[202] 6472 3-9-4 **95** .... JimCrowley 4 66
(P Winkworth) *t.k.h: hld up in midfield: rdn and btn 2f out: wl bhd fnl f* **10/1**

1m 44.6s (1.30) **Going Correction** +0.075s/f (Good) **8** Ran SP% **111.0**
Speed ratings (Par 104): **96,93,93,91,90 90,89,79**
Tote Swingers: 1&2 £7.50, 1&3 £4.40, 2&3 £7.20 CSF £36.87 CT £161.45 TOTE £5.40: £1.70, £2.80, £1.80; EX 44.90 Trifecta £229.20 Pool: £483.38 - 1.56 winning units..
Owner Normandie Stud Ltd **Bred** Normandie Stud Ltd **Trained** Newmarket, Suffolk

FOCUS
Traditionally a strong handicap, and John Gosden, who last year sent out Racketeer to win by 6l, followed that up with another easy winner in the shape of Fallen Idol. He looks up to Listed class at least, and this looks good form.

NOTEBOOK
Fallen Idol looked a promising sort last term when beating a couple of more experienced Godolphin horses on his debut, and a St James's Palace entry hinted that connections expect him to make his mark outside of handicap company this term. Running off a mark of 89, he showed himself to be extremely well handicapped, quickening up smartly when given a crack with the whip, and his rider was able to take things easy close home. His trainer nominated the Heron Stakes as his next target, and presumably if things go well there then Royal Ascot will be on his agenda. (tchd 9-2 in places)
Karaka Jack, like the winner a son of Pivotal, made most of the running and kept battling away when challenged inside the final 2f. The drop back to a mile suited him, as it promised to on pedigree, but he did also have the benefit of a recent outing, which no doubt helped. (op 12-1 tchd 17-2)
Huygens ◆, ridden patiently just behind the winner, was left for dead when that rival quickened away but he stayed on nicely down the outside to take the minor placing, and gave the impression that his new mark following his Kempton success is not beyond him. (op 4-1)
Red Badge(IRE), who had a progressive profile last term before getting stuck in the mud when stepped up to Group company on his final start, had conditions back in his favour here. He found his path blocked next to the far-side rail from a furlong out and his rider was pretty easy on him afterwards. He would have probably finished placed with a clear run. (op 8-1)
Duellist may have found this too stiff a test. He shouldn't mind a drop back to 7f. (op 8-1)
Invincible Soul(IRE)'s trainer had warned beforehand that the colt would probably need the run and, having kept the leader company to a furlong out, he got tired and dropped out. He should be straighter next time. (op 11-4 tchd 3-1 in places)
Blakey's Boy didn't look comfortable on the ground and will be happier when he can get his toe in. (op 20-1)
Raine's Cross was too keen through the early stages and failed to land a blow. Official explanation: vet said colt returned lame behind (op 12-1 tchd 14-1)

1498 BET365 CLASSIC TRIAL (GROUP 3) 1m 2f 7y

1:45 (1:45) (Class 1) 3-Y-O **£37,076** (£14,163; £7,176; £3,666; £1,924) **Stalls** High

Form RPR

110- **1** *2 1/4* **Azmeel**[208] 6319 3-9-0 100 .... WilliamBuick 4 109
(J H M Gosden) *t.k.h: hld up in tch: n.m.r over 2f out: hdwy between horses 2f out: sn chsng wnr and rdn: btn ins fnl f: no ch w wnr after but kpt on for clr 2nd: awrdd r* **11/2**[3]

513- **2** *5* **Simenon (IRE)**[195] 6664 3-9-0 101 .... LiamKeniry 7 99+
(A M Balding) *t.k.h: chsd ldr for 2f: styd handy: rdn and outpcd over 2f out: edging lft u.p over 1f out: wnt modest 3rd ins fnl f: no ch w ldng pair* **10/1**

2-52 **3** *3/4* **Bikini Babe (IRE)**[57] 709 3-8-11 105 .... JoeFanning 5 95
(M Johnston) *chsd ldr after 2f: led wl over 2f out: rdn and hdd wl over 1f out: outpcd and no ch w ldng pair over 1f out: lost 3rd ins fnl f* **8/1**

041- **4** *4 1/2* **Take It To The Max**[174] 7184 3-9-0 97 .... JimmyFortune 1 89
(G M Moore) *led: hdd and pushed along wl over 2f out: rdn and wknd 2f out: wl btn fnl f* **28/1**

312- **5** *16* **Waseet**[209] 6268 3-9-0 110 .... RichardHills 2 71
(J L Dunlop) *t.k.h: trckd ldrs: rdn and effrt over 2f out: unable qck and struggling whn sltly hmpd 2f out: sn wl btn: eased ins fnl f* **2/1**[2]

20- **D** **Chabal (IRE)**[188] 6849 3-9-0 115 .... (t) FrankieDettori 6 114
(Saeed Bin Suroor) *stdd s: t.k.h: hld up in rr: pushed along 3f out: gd hdwy 2f out: led wl over 1f out: drew clr fnl 150yds: comf; fin 1st, disq (prohibited subs.)* **7/4**[1]

2m 10.94s (0.44) **Going Correction** +0.075s/f (Good) **6** Ran SP% **108.7**
Speed ratings (Par 108): **99,95,94,91,78 101**
Tote Swingers: 1&2 £2.30, 1&3 £4.30, 2&3 £5.90 CSF £10.96 TOTE £2.40: £1.40, £3.00; EX 11.50.
Owner M Al-Qatami & K M Al-Mudhaf **Bred** Elsdon Farms **Trained** Newmarket, Suffolk
■ Stewards' Enquiry : William Buick two-day ban: careless riding (May 7-8)

FOCUS
It's a while since this race was a significant Derby trial, with nothing of note winning it since Sakhee in 2000, and the last winner to go on to win at Epsom was Shahrastani in 1986. The pace was not strong and it is doubtful the winner had to match his 2yo best.

NOTEBOOK
Azmeel, a winner of his first two races last year before being sent off favourite but finishing down the field in the Goffs Million Mile, had something to prove up in class and trip on his reappearance. His trainer dominated this race in the 1990s though, and with the stable in form a good run was not a surprise. The winner proved different class but it was a sound effort, and Gosden is now keen to give him another go in a trial at Chester or Lingfield. (op 4-1 tchd 3-1)
Simenon(IRE) was gelded over the winter and his trainer had warned that he had been slow to come to hand and would improve for the run. In the circumstances this was about as much as one could expect, especially considering the steady early pace wouldn't have been in his favour. (op 14-1)
Bikini Babe(IRE), who didn't run badly out an Meydan in February, was well placed throughout in a steadily run race and it's difficult to make many excuses for her, even allowing for the fact that she was the only filly in the line-up. (tchd 15-2)
Take It To The Max, winner of the Zetland Stakes on his final start at two, was taking on tougher opposition here, and enjoying the run of things out in front didn't help him much. (op 33-1 tchd 40-1 in places)
Waseet, runner-up in the Royal Lodge last season, looked the main danger to the favourite on that piece of form, but he found nothing when his rider asked him to pick up 2 1/2f out and dropped out very tamely, hanging left as he did so. This was clearly not a true reflection of his ability and perhaps he didn't handle the watered ground. Official explanation: jockey said colt ran too free early (tchd 7-4)
Chabal(IRE) put up quite an impressive performance in victory, was cut to a best price of 20-1 for the Derby, and is now likely to have his credentials tested further in the Dante. He raced far too keenly in the Dewhurst on his final start at two, but settled much better here, despite the modest early pace, and once switched to the outside to challenge 2f out he quickened up smartly, with only Azmeel able to stay in touch. He won very cosily in the end, but with the second-favourite running no sort of race and his stamina for 1m4f still in some question, he has a bit to prove still, and if he turns up at York we should learn a lot more. (op 9-4 tchd 11-4)

1499 BET365 H'CAP 5f 6y

2:20 (2:20) (Class 2) (0-100,100) 3-Y-O

£9,969 (£2,985; £1,492; £747; £372; £187) **Stalls** High

Form RPR

156- **1** **Duchess Dora (IRE)**[195] 6677 3-8-12 **94** .... IanBrennan(5) 4 99+
(J J Quinn) *travelled strly: chsd ldr: pushed ahd over 1f out: rdn ent fnl f: hld on cl home* **14/1**

0-56 **2** *shd* **Fratellino**[9] 1315 3-9-5 **96** .... JamesDoyle 8 101
(A J McCabe) *broke wl: led: rdn ent fnl 2f: hdd over 1f out: rallied u.p ins fnl f: kpt on gamely* **5/2**[2]

205- **3** *1 1/4* **Dorback**[175] 7150 3-9-3 **94** .... DaneO'Neill 3 95
(H Candy) *t.k.h: in tch: hdwy to chse ldng pair 1/2-way: drvn over 1f out: kpt on same pce u.p ins fnl f* **11/2**[3]

523- **4** *1 1/2* **Take Ten**[202] 6478 3-9-1 **92** .... FrankieDettori 7 87
(M Johnston) *chsd ldrs: rdn and edging off rail wl over 1f out: no imp ins fnl f: btn and eased towards fin* **9/4**[1]

553- **5** *1 3/4* **Nosedive**[202] 6486 3-9-6 **97** .... LiamJones 2 86+
(W J Haggas) *dropped in bhd after s: hld up in rr: effrt and rdn 1/2-way: no prog fr over 1f out* **11/1**

20-3 **6** *6* **Yurituni**[10] 1281 3-8-7 **84** .... TonyCulhane 1 51
(Eve Johnson Houghton) *chsd ldrs: rdn over 2f out: wknd wl over 1f out: wl btn fnl f* **8/1**

305- **7** *2 1/4* **Di Stefano**[205] 6398 3-9-4 **95** .... KierenFallon 5 54
(M R Channon) *chsd ldrs: pushed along and lost pl 3f out: bhd fr 1/2-way* **8/1**

60.46 secs (-1.14) **Going Correction** -0.125s/f (Firm) **7** Ran SP% **111.9**
Speed ratings (Par 104): **104,103,101,99,96 87,83**
Tote Swingers: 1&2 £8.60, 1&3 £11.70, 2&3 £4.20 CSF £47.09 CT £219.45 TOTE £18.30: £4.20, £2.10; EX 61.90.
Owner The Clay Family **Bred** Glending Bloodstock **Trained** Settrington, N Yorks

FOCUS
Very few got into this, with the pace holding up well. It was not as strong as this race can be, but there wer some positives to take from it. The winner is rated up 6lb.

NOTEBOOK
Duchess Dora(IRE) is especially suited to racing over a stiff 5f, as she showed when successful both here and at Beverley last term. Sent to the front 1 1/2f out, she idled, allowing the runner-up to rally next to the rail and make it a tight call at the line. In hindsight her rider wished he'd delayed his challenge longer, but on the plus side his mount won by a slim margin and should not be hammered by the handicapper. There should be more to come from her. (op 16-1)

Fratellino, who is race-fit, had the rails draw and showed bright early speed to take them along. He rallied after being headed and ran a sound race in defeat, but he could remain vulnerable to better handicapped rivals. Having said that, granted a favourable draw, he could take some catching round Chester. (op 10-3 tchd 7-2)

Dorback, whose trainer has sent out Kyllachy and Corrybrough to win this, had to be of some interest, despite his more exposed profile. He ran a sound race on his reappearance, is just as effective over 6f and is fully entitled to come on for the outing. (op 9-2 tchd 6-1 in places)

Take Ten, who finished third in the Tatersalls Timeform Million over 7f on his final start at two, threatened to find this trip on the short side. He ran really well in the circumstances, tracking the leader on the rail for a long way, but he can surely only benefit from a return to 6f. (op 5-2 tchd 11-4)

Nosedive won his maiden first time up over this C&D last term and was then highly tried, running in Pattern company on each of his next six starts. He struggled to get into this race and it remains to be seen if he's trained on. (op 13-2 tchd 6-1)

Yurituni, who was bred to be a speedy 2-y-o, had the worst of the draw but did have a run under her belt, so this was disappointing.

Di Stefano, gelded over the winter, never threatened to get involved on this drop back in distance. (op 10-1 tchd 15-2)

1500 CASINO AT BET365.COM CONDITIONS STKS — 1m 14y

2:55 (2:55) (Class 3) 3-Y-O — £6,542 (£1,959; £979; £490; £244) Stalls High

Form — RPR

16- **1** **No Hubris (USA)**[311] 2993 3-9-2 98 ... JamieSpencer 3 — 99
(P F I Cole) *chsd ldr: rdn to chal 2f out: drvn to ld over 1f out: kpt on gamely u.p: hld on cl home* **3/1**[3]

1- **2** *shd* **Sowaylm**[173] 7199 3-8-12 88 ... (t) FrankieDettori 4 — 95
(Saeed Bin Suroor) *wnt rt s: t.k.h: chsd ldng pair: rdn and effrt 2f out: hld hd awkwardly and edging lft u.p 1f out: chsd wnr ins fnl f: kpt on towards fin: nvr quite getting to wnr* **15/8**[1]

31- **3** *2* **Below Zero (IRE)**[322] 2649 3-9-2 99 ... JoeFanning 2 — 94
(M Johnston) *t.k.h: led tl hdd over 1f out: rdn ent fnl f: no ex and btn fnl 100yds* **11/2**

1- **4** *3¼* **Commissionaire**[178] 7095 3-9-2 0 ... WilliamBuick 1 — 87+
(J H M Gosden) *stdd s and dropped in bhd: t.k.h: rdn and unable qck ent fnl 2f: no hdwy and wl btn over 1f out* **9/4**[2]

5 *12* **Red Flash (IRE)** 3-8-9 0 ... RichardKingscote 5 — 52?
(P Leech) *bmpd s and s.i.s: in tch in last pair: rdn 3f out: drvn ent fnl 2f: wknd wl over 1f out* **100/1**

1m 46.14s (2.84) **Going Correction** +0.075s/f (Good) — **5** Ran SP% **106.9**

Speed ratings (Par 102): **88,87,85,82,70**

CSF £8.49 TOTE £4.00: £2.20, £1.20; EX 8.90.

Owner Mrs Fitri Hay **Bred** Brereton C Jones **Trained** Whatcombe, Oxon

FOCUS

Quite an interesting little conditions race. It was run at a steady pace, but the form can be taken at face value with the winner up a length on her 2yo form.

NOTEBOOK

No Hubris(USA) had been off the track since finishing sixth in the Coventry on his second start at two. He had been due to run in the Superlative Stakes at Newmarket's July meeting, but injured a tibia. He holds a Derby entry, but his pedigree doesn't really support that, and it's more likely that he remains at around this distance, with a Listed or Group 3 race the natural next step. (tchd 7-2)

Sowaylm, who won a Polytrack maiden last autumn, confirmed the good form of his stable with a fine effort in defeat on his reappearance, especially considering he looked far from happy in the straight, carrying his head high and changing his legs on several occasions. Perhaps this watered ground didn't suit him. (op 2-1 tchd 11-5 in a place)

Below Zero(IRE), who was able to win over 5½f at two but is bred to stay middle distances, enjoyed the run of things out in front but was done for toe in the closing stages. He should be sharper for this run. (op 4-1)

Commissionaire, whose sire Medicean won this race in 2000, struggled to get cover in this small field and raced a bit keenly. He can do better than this held up off the pace in a bigger field. (op 5-2)

Red Flash(IRE), who cost just 1,000gns, faced a very stiff task on his racecourse debut and was predictably outclassed. (op 150-1)

1501 POKER AT BET365.COM MAIDEN FILLIES' STKS — 1m 2f 7y

3:25 (3:26) (Class 4) 3-Y-O — £4,533 (£1,348; £674; £336) Stalls High

Form — RPR

02- **1** **Fatanah (IRE)**[160] 7390 3-9-0 0 ... RichardHills 10 — 88
(M P Tregoning) *mde all: rdn over 2f out: forged clr over 1f out: styd on wl to draw wl clr ins fnl f: eased towards fin* **15/8**[1]

0- **2** *4* **Issabella Gem (IRE)**[193] 6729 3-9-0 0 ... RichardHughes 4 — 79+
(C G Cox) *hld up towards rr: effrt and hanging rt 3f out: plld to outer over 2f out: edging rt but styd on wl u.p fnl f: wnt 2nd towards fin: no ch w wnr* **12/1**

5- **3** *½* **Ship's Biscuit**[155] 7450 3-9-0 0 ... RyanMoore 3 — 78
(Sir Michael Stoute) *chsd wnr: rdn to press wnr over 2f out: edging rt and unable qck over 1f out: one pce fnl f: lost 2nd towards fin* **7/2**[2]

4 *2½* **Fascination (IRE)** 3-9-0 0 ... FrankieDettori 8 — 73
(Sir Michael Stoute) *chsd ldng pair: rdn over 2f out: drvn and unable qck over 1f out: plugged on same pce fnl f* **12/1**

5- **5** *nk* **Golden Waters**[205] 6393 3-9-0 0 ... NeilCallan 7 — 72
(Eve Johnson Houghton) *chsd ldng trio: rdn and unable qck wl over 1f out: styd on same pce but no ch w wnr fnl f* **10/1**

5- **6** *1* **Effervesce (IRE)**[160] 7396 3-9-0 0 ... RichardMullen 1 — 70
(Sir Michael Stoute) *in tch in midfield: effrt over 2f out: racd awkwardly and outpcd over 1f out: no prog and wl hld fnl f* **10/1**

0- **7** *6* **Happy Mood**[174] 7182 3-9-1 0 ow1 ... GeorgeBaker 11 — 59
(G L Moore) *stdd after s: hld up in rr: rdn and outpcd 3f out: nvr trbld ldrs* **100/1**

5 **8** *4* **Sonnellino**[7] 1355 3-9-0 0 ... WilliamBuick 9 — 50
(J H M Gosden) *s.i.s: rn green in rr: rdn and struggling 3f out: wl btn after* **12/1**

0 **9** *6* **Princess Of Troy (IRE)**[8] 1335 3-9-0 0 ... JamesDoyle 6 — 38
(P D Evans) *t.k.h: chsd ldrs: hmpd and dropped to midfield after 1f: in tch tl wknd qckly over 2f out: wl bhd fnl f* **100/1**

04- **10** *2¼* **Fantastic Cuix (FR)**[155] 7450 3-9-0 0 ... KierenFallon 5 — 34
(L M Cumani) *dwlt: sn rcvrd and chsng ldrs whn sltly hmpd after 1f: in tch in midfield after: rdn and btn 3f out: wl bhd fnl 2f* **7/1**[3]

422- **11** *1* **Rare Malt (IRE)**[231] 5643 3-9-0 77 ... HayleyTurner 2 — 32
(Miss Amy Weaver) *stdd after s: t.k.h: hld up in last pair: rdn 3f out: lost tch over 2f out* **14/1**

2m 10.32s (-0.18) **Going Correction** +0.075s/f (Good) — **11** Ran SP% **119.4**

Speed ratings (Par 97): **103,99,99,97,97 96,91,88,83,81 80**

Tote Swingers: 1&2 £7.20, 1&3 £2.90, 2&3 £12.30 CSF £27.38 TOTE £2.70: £1.20, £3.30, £1.90; EX 28.60.

Owner Hamdan Al Maktoum **Bred** Shadwell Estate Company Limited **Trained** Lambourn, Berks

FOCUS

An interesting maiden, won two years ago by Dar Re Mi. This didn't look quite as hot a renewal, but the time was the quickest of the three races run over the distance and this is still good maiden form.

Rare Malt(IRE) Official explanation: vet said filly lost a hind shoe

1502 BET365.COM H'CAP — 1m 2f 7y

3:55 (3:57) (Class 3) (0-90,86) 3-Y-O

£7,477 (£2,239; £1,119; £560; £279; £140) Stalls High

Form — RPR

21- **1** **Verdant**[196] 6627 3-8-12 80 ... RyanMoore 8 — 96+
(Sir Michael Stoute) *dwlt: sn rcvrd: to chse ldrs: lost pl and towards rr 7f out: plld out and rdn over 2f out: hdwy over 1f out: drvn to ld fnl 75yds: r.o wl* **9/2**[1]

1113 **2** *½* **Rock A Doodle Doo (IRE)**[26] 1033 3-8-9 77 ... FrankieDettori 9 — 86
(W Jarvis) *t.k.h: hld up wl in tch: rdn ent fnl 2f: chal and edgd rt ent fnl f: led fnl 100yds: sn hdd and no ex towards fin* **14/1**

415- **3** *½* **Averroes (IRE)**[216] 6133 3-8-10 85 ... JohnFahy[(7)] 10 — 93
(C G Cox) *led for 1f: chsd ldrs after: wnt 2nd wl over 2f out: rdn to ld over 1f out: hrd pressed ent fnl f: hdd fnl 100yds: one pce after* **11/1**

51- **4** *1¾* **Soul Station (FR)**[193] 6728 3-9-0 82 ... RichardKingscote 1 — 86
(R Charlton) *t.k.h: trckd ldrs: rdn to chse ldng pair over 2f out: pressing ldrs but u.p whn short of room 1f out: one pce and btn after* **20/1**

531- **5** *1¼* **Zahoo (IRE)**[209] 6284 3-8-7 75 ... RichardHills 13 — 82+
(J L Dunlop) *hld up bhd: nt clr run jst over 2f out: hdwy on inner wl over 1f out: nt clr run and swtchd lft 1f out: nt clr run again and swtchd lft ins fnl f: kpt on towards fin: unable to rch ldrs* **12/1**

16-2 **6** *nse* **Jutland**[7] 1362 3-8-6 74 ... JoeFanning 2 — 75
(M Johnston) *chsd ldr tl led after 1f: rdn ent fnl 2f: hdd and drvn over 1f out: wknd ins fnl f* **5/1**[2]

321- **7** *½* **Start Right**[195] 6672 3-9-1 83 ... KierenFallon 6 — 83+
(L M Cumani) *t.k.h: hld up in tch: effrt and hanging rt over 2f out: plld out lft and hdwy wl over 1f out: styng on whn hung lft jst ins fnl f: kpt on but nvr gng pce to rch ldrs* **15/2**[3]

24-1 **8** *nk* **Street Entertainer (IRE)**[25] 1046 3-8-12 80 ... JimCrowley 14 — 80
(Mrs A J Perrett) *in tch in midfield: effrt to chse ldrs and rdn over 2f out: drvn and no ex ent fnl f: wknd fnl 150yds* **12/1**

100- **9** *3½* **Meglio Ancora**[264] 4565 3-9-1 83 ... DaneO'Neill 5 — 76
(J G Portman) *hld up in rr: rdn wl over 3f out: sme hdwy fnl f: nvr trbld ldrs* **50/1**

51- **10** *2* **Higgy's Ragazzo (FR)**[225] 5787 3-8-12 80 ... RichardHughes 4 — 69
(R Hannon) *in tch in midfield: effrt and rdn on outer 3f out: sn struggling: no ch fnl 2f* **10/1**

1232 **11** *1¾* **Thundering Home**[23] 1060 3-8-10 78 ... HayleyTurner 12 — 63
(M J Attwater) *s.i.s: a bhd: nvr on terms* **40/1**

0-1 **12** *5* **Senate**[27] 1010 3-9-4 86 ... WilliamBuick 3 — 61
(J H M Gosden) *in tch: sn chsng ldrs: wnt 2nd over 7f out tl over 2f out: wkng whn hmpd jst over 2f out: wl btn after* **5/1**[2]

132- **13** *nk* **First Cat**[217] 6067 3-9-0 82 ... PatDobbs 11 — 57
(R Hannon) *chsd ldrs: rdn and losing pl whn hmpd jst over 2f out: wl btn after* **25/1**

014- **14** *13* **Fontley**[181] 7033 3-9-0 82 ... NeilCallan 7 — 31
(Eve Johnson Houghton) *chsd ldrs: n.m.r and shuffled bk to midfield after 2f: rdn and struggling 3f out: wl bhd and eased ins fnl f* **28/1**

2m 10.54s (0.04) **Going Correction** +0.075s/f (Good) — **14** Ran SP% **119.2**

Speed ratings (Par 102): **102,101,101,99,98 98,98,98,95,93 92,88,88,77**

Tote Swingers: 1&2 £15.80, 1&3 £26.60, 2&3 £13.00 CSF £63.15 CT £662.23 TOTE £5.00: £2.00, £4.20, £4.40; EX 95.90 Place 6: £62.69 Place 5: £23.66 .

Owner K Abdulla **Bred** Juddmonte Farms Ltd **Trained** Newmarket, Suffolk

FOCUS

This looked a very hot handicap, featuring several unexposed and potentially well-handicapped horses from big yards. The previous five winners of this race include two subsequent King George V Handicap winners and a Ribblesdale winner, and it'll be a big surprise if this race doesn't throw up many winners in the coming months. Form to rate positively.

NOTEBOOK

Verdant ◆ is a half-brother to three pattern-race winners, and it wouldn't be a surprise if he joins them in picking up black type at some stage, despite the fact that he only won here off a mark of 80. A Dante entry, he did well to come from behind considering the pace held up quite well, and the way he finished his race suggests he'll get further in time. He showed his inexperience by hanging right under pressure but he was comfortably the best horse in the race, is an exciting prospect, and can only go on from this. There are plenty of possible targets, including the London Gold Cup at Newbury on Lockinge Day next month, the 1m2f handicap at Epsom on Derby day that Conduit won for the stable after finishing third in this race back in 2008, not to mention the King George V Handicap at Royal Ascot, or even the King Edward VII if he's thought up to it. (op 7-2)

Rock A Doodle Doo(IRE) ◆ couldn't cope with the softish ground at Doncaster last time out but he'd been progressive on Polytrack before that and showed here that he remains on an upward curve. He can win again in the coming weeks. (op 16-1)

Averroes(IRE) ◆, who was backed at prices in the morning, is held in some regard by connections and ran really well on his reappearance, travelling strongly to 2f out. He didn't quite see it out as strongly as the first two but is fully entitled to come on for the run, and he'll make plenty of appeal in similar company, perhaps in the London Gold Cup. (op 10-1 tchd 12-1)

Soul Station(FR) ◆ had a bit of use made of him early to overcome his poor draw in stall one and get over to race prominently. He ended up racing a touch keenly and was trapped wider than ideal, so in the circumstances he ran with plenty of credit. (op 22-1 tchd 25-1)

Zahoo(IRE) ◆ didn't get much daylight as she looked to make a run up the inside rail and was also short of room when challenging between horses inside the last. She was not given a hard time at all to finish where she did and is clearly handicapped to win off her current mark. Another 2f won't cause her any concern as the season goes on. (op 10-1)

Jutland is already due to be raised 6lb following his fine effort in defeat at Thirsk a week earlier. It's possible that he didn't stay the trip, but more likely that he simply bumped into rivals who were even better handicapped than him, so connections should not despair that he'll be weighted out of things off his new mark. (op 11-2 tchd 6-1)

Start Right, who took six starts to get off the mark last term, was a bit keen and hung right in the closing stages. He got the trip all right though, and is entitled to come on for the run. (op 10-1)

Street Entertainer(IRE), a winner of his maiden over this trip on the Polytrack on his reappearance, enjoyed a nice trip but wasn't good enough. He'll be of interest again in less-competitive company. (op 10-1)

Meglio Ancora didn't build on the promise of his debut victory in two subsequent starts last season, and he's going to need some help from the handicapper to be competitive in a race like this.

Higgy's Ragazzo(FR) failed to land a blow but he's still unexposed, bred to appreciate this sort of trip and it's entirely possible that he simply needed the run. (op 11-1)

Senate, a Dante entry who didn't beat much when successful in a soft-ground maiden on his reappearance at Doncaster, was saddled with top-weight, had different ground to cope with and had plenty of use made of him from his low draw. He was a beaten horse early in the straight. (op 11-2 tchd 9-2 and 6-1 in places)

T/Plt: £148.80 to a £1 stake. Pool: £76,515.02. 375.29 winning tickets. T/Qpdt: £31.10 to a £1 stake. Pool: £5,586.76. 132.90 winning tickets. SP

[1456]WOLVERHAMPTON (A.W) (L-H)

Friday, April 23

OFFICIAL GOING: Standard

Wind: Light behind Weather: Fine and sunny

1503 WOLVERHAMPTON RACECOURSE APPRENTICE H'CAP (DIV I) 1m 1f 103y(P)

1:25 (1:26) (Class 6) (0-55,58) 4-Y-O+ £1,433 (£423; £211) Stalls Low

Form RPR

00-0 1 **Portrush Storm**[51] 780 5-8-6 **47** .... JohnCavanagh 7 53
(R E Peacock) *hld up in tch: plld hrd: hmpd over 7f out: rdn over 2f out: chsd ldr over 1f out: led ins fnl f: styd on u.p* **40/1**

02-0 2 ½ **Major Promise**[30] 969 5-8-9 **55** .... LewisWalsh(5) 4 60
(Jane Chapple-Hyam) *edgd rt s: hld up: hdwy over 2f out: rdn and edgd lft ins fnl f: r.o* **7/1**[2]

300- 3 ¾ **Strike Force**[153] 7495 6-8-12 **53** ....(t) MatthewLawson 6 56
(M E Rimmer) *led after 1f: hdd over 5f out: led again 3f out: rdn and hdd ins fnl f: styd on same pce* **7/1**[2]

504- 4 1¾ **Feet Of Fury**[202] 6497 4-9-3 **58** ow4 .... ShaneRyan 11 58
(W M Brisbourne) *prom: rdn over 1f out: edgd lft ins fnl f: styd on* **12/1**

0/0- 5 hd **Quadrifolio**[177] 7126 4-7-12 **46** oh1 .... JordanDodd(7) 13 45
(Paul Green) *s.i.s: hld up: hdwy over 4f out: rdn over 1f out: hung lft ins fnl f: styd on same pce* **40/1**

0616 6 2¼ **Naledi**[28] 995 6-8-6 **50** .... AlexEdwards(3) 10 45
(R J Price) *chsd ldrs: rdn over 1f out: no ex fnl f* **18/1**

01-0 7 ¾ **Hint Of Honey**[57] 705 4-8-11 **52** .... RichardRowe 1 45
(A G Newcombe) *hld up: rdn over 1f out: r.o ins fnl f: nvr nrr* **16/1**

-434 8 hd **John Potts**[63] 622 5-8-5 **46** oh1 .... RyanPowell 8 39
(B P J Baugh) *s.i.s: hld up: hdwy over 1f out: sn rdn: no ex ins fnl f* **10/1**[3]

3330 9 ½ **Turkish Sultan (IRE)**[35] 940 7-8-1 **49** ....(b) LeonnaMayor(7) 5 41
(J M Bradley) *s.i.s: hld up: rdn over 2f out: n.d* **16/1**

060/ 10 ½ **Contradiktive (IRE)**[503] 7574 4-8-0 **46** oh1 .... HarryBentley(5) 9 37
(Tim Vaughan) *prom: pushed along and lost pl wl over 3f out: rallied over 1f out: no ex ins fnl f* **5/4**[1]

-603 11 6 **Mr Chocolate Drop (IRE)**[15] 1193 6-8-12 **56** ow1 ....(b) MJMurphy(3) 12 34
(Miss M E Rowland) *plld hrd and sn prom: led over 5f out: hdd 3f out: rdn 2f out: wknd fnl f* **12/1**

30-3 12 5 **Kingaroo (IRE)**[17] 1148 4-8-6 **50** .... JakePayne(3) 2 17
(G Woodward) *prom: rdn over 3f out: sn wknd* **12/1**

23-6 13 ¾ **Bold Indian (IRE)**[14] 1208 6-9-0 **55** .... AdamCarter 3 21
(M E Sowersby) *led 1f: chsd ldrs: rdn over 3f out: wknd over 2f out* **25/1**

2m 3.82s (2.12) **Going Correction** +0.175s/f (Slow) **13 Ran SP% 127.4**

Speed ratings (Par 101): **97,96,95,94,94 92,91,91,90,90 85,80,79**

Tote Swingers: 1&2 £75.30, 1&3 £8.10, 2&3 £18.60 CSF £316.70 CT £2240.37 TOTE £77.40: £14.50, £2.20, £2.60; EX 290.50 TRIFECTA Not won..

Owner John P Evitt **Bred** Northmore Stud **Trained** Kyre Park, Worcs

■ Stewards' Enquiry : Shane Ryan four-day ban: used whip with excessive force and frequency (May 7-8, 10-11)

FOCUS

A modest handicap for apprentice riders, run at a steady pace initially, with the gamble on the well-backed favourite going astray. Weak form.

Hint Of Honey Official explanation: jockey said filly reared leaving stalls

1504 HOTEL & CONFERENCING AT WOLVERHAMPTON MAIDEN FILLIES' STKS 7f 32y(P)

1:55 (1:59) (Class 5) 3-Y-O £2,456 (£725; £362) Stalls High

Form RPR

3 1 **Flighty Frances (IRE)**[11] 1257 3-9-0 0 .... RobertWinston 2 74+
(D R C Elsworth) *chsd ldrs: pushed along over 4f out: rdn to ld over 1f out: edgd lft: r.o* **7/1**[3]

2- 2 2¼ **Wishformore (IRE)**[154] 7463 3-9-0 0 .... LukeMorris 5 67
(J S Moore) *chsd ldrs: rdn and ev ch over 1f out: styd on same pce ins fnl f* **14/1**

0- 3 ¾ **Alice Cullen**[174] 7182 3-9-0 0 .... AdamKirby 11 65+
(W R Swinburn) *s.i.s: hld up: hdwy over 1f out: r.o: nvr nr to chal* **11/1**

02- 4 2 **Vaultage (USA)**[156] 7430 3-9-0 0 .... TomQueally 8 60
(E A L Dunlop) *prom: chsd ldr 4f out: led over 2f out: rdn: hung lft and hdd over 1f out: wknd ins fnl f* **5/2**[2]

5 1 **Confrontation** 3-9-0 0 .... FergusSweeney 7 57+
(D M Simcock) *s.i.s: hld up: hdwy over 1f out: r.o: nrst fin* **28/1**

34 6 ¾ **Fillibeg (IRE)**[50] 793 3-9-0 0 .... TonyHamilton 6 55
(R A Fahey) *mid-div: hdwy over 1f out: wknd ins fnl f* **25/1**

6-3 7 2¾ **Dizziness (USA)**[16] 1164 3-9-0 0 .... SteveDrowne 3 48
(R Charlton) *chsd ldrs: rdn over 2f out: wknd fnl f* **11/8**[1]

00- 8 hd **Dance With Chance (IRE)**[174] 7183 3-9-0 0 .... ShaneKelly 1 47
(W R Swinburn) *s.i.s: hld up: rdn over 1f out: n.d* **66/1**

0- 9 ½ **Hanbelation (USA)**[145] 7585 3-9-0 0 .... PatCosgrave 9 46
(E F Vaughan) *hld up: hdwy 1/2-way: sn rdn: wknd 2f out* **66/1**

00 10 2 **Adoyen Spice**[34] 950 3-9-0 0 .... CathyGannon 4 41
(Mike Murphy) *sn led: hdd over 5f out: n.m.r 1/2-way: rdn and wknd 2f out* **100/1**

6 11 17 **Roxy Spirit (IRE)**[53] 755 3-9-0 0 .... TomEaves 12 —
(M Mullineaux) *sn pushed along and a in rr: lost tch fnl 3f* **200/1**

12 3¼ **Rockie Bright**[260] 4723 3-9-0 0 .... PaulMulrennan 10 —
(J G Given) *w ldr tl led over 5f out: hdd over 2f out: wknd over 1f out* **16/1**

1m 31.28s (1.68) **Going Correction** +0.175s/f (Slow) **12 Ran SP% 115.8**

Speed ratings (Par 95): **97,94,93,91,90 89,86,85,85,83 63,59**

Tote Swingers: 1&2 £12.40, 1&3 £5.80, 2&3 £18.20 CSF £92.02 TOTE £5.40: £1.50, £2.60, £2.70; EX 54.30 TRIFECTA Not won..

Owner D R C Elsworth **Bred** Yeomanstown Stud **Trained** Newmarket, Suffolk

FOCUS

No more than a fair maiden and one run at something of a stop-start pace leading to a bit of bunching on the home turn. The winner was up a stone on her debut and can still do better.

Vaultage(USA) Official explanation: jockey said filly hung left

Dizziness(USA) Official explanation: jockey said filly never travelled

Adoyen Spice Official explanation: jockey said filly hung right

Rockie Bright Official explanation: jockey said filly hung right

1505 GREAT OFFERS AT WOLVERHAMPTON-RACECOURSE.CO.UK (S) STKS 7f 32y(P)

2:30 (2:30) (Class 6) 3-Y-O £1,774 (£523; £262) Stalls High

Form RPR

6-1 1 **Catherines Call (IRE)**[11] 1259 3-8-12 0 .... ShaneKelly 6 66+
(D Donovan) *s.i.s: hld up: hdwy over 1f out: r.o to ld wl ins fnl f* **7/2**[3]

60-0 2 1¼ **A Pocketful Of Rye (IRE)**[10] 1275 3-8-7 68 .... AdrianNicholls 10 58
(D Nicholls) *hld up: hdwy 1/2-way: chsd ldr over 2f out: rdn: ev ch and hung lft fr over 1f out: styd on same pce ins fnl f* **11/4**[1]

013 3 nk **Moors Gorse**[13] 1237 3-8-12 62 ....(p) FergusSweeney 5 62
(R Hollinshead) *led over 6f out: rdn over 1f out: hdd and unable qck wl ins fnl f* **13/2**

-362 4 1½ **Kenswick**[9] 1293 3-8-7 58 ....(b) JimmyQuinn 2 53
(Pat Eddery) *a.p: rdn and hung lft over 1f out: no ex wl ins fnl f* **3/1**[2]

0524 5 2½ **Tealing**[43] 856 3-8-12 62 ....(e) FrannyNorton 1 51
(R C Guest) *prom: nt clr run over 1f out: sn rdn: styd on* **10/1**

3315 6 3½ **Tiger Hawk (USA)**[11] 1259 3-9-0 65 ....(b) AndrewHeffernan(3) 7 47
(P D Evans) *prom: rdn 1/2-way: wknd over 1f out* **14/1**

00 7 12 **Higenius**[28] 997 3-8-12 0 .... VinceSlattery 4 9
(D Burchell) *s.i.s: sn prom: hmpd 6f out: lost pl over 4f out: wknd over 3f out* **100/1**

000- 8 7 **Reel Credit Crunch**[198] 6586 3-8-4 53 .... KellyHarrison(3) 3 —
(I W McInnes) *led early: chsd ldrs: rdn 3f out: wknd over 2f out* **66/1**

4-0 9 19 **Little Weed (IRE)**[70] 527 3-8-12 0 .... DavidProbert 9 —
(B Palling) *chsd ldrs: rdn 1/2-way: wknd wl over 1f out* **20/1**

1m 31.65s (2.05) **Going Correction** +0.175s/f (Slow) **9 Ran SP% 110.2**

Speed ratings (Par 96): **95,93,93,91,88 84,70,62,41**

Tote Swingers: 1&2 £8.20, 1&3 £7.40, 2&3 £3.40 CSF £12.45 TOTE £6.20: £1.80, £1.50, £3.10; EX 14.60 Trifecta £37.40 Pool: £291.52 - 5.76 winning units..The winner was bought in for 10,500gns. A Pocketful Of Rye was claimed by Paul Howling for £6,500.

Owner Philip Mclaughlin **Bred** K Maginn **Trained** Newmarket, Suffolk

FOCUS

Marginally better than the average seller and an impressive winner at the conclusion of what was a well-run race. The third is the best guide and the winner looks a bit better than the bare form.

1506 SPONSOR A RACE BY CALLING 01902 390000 H'CAP 5f 20y(P)

3:05 (3:05) (Class 4) (0-85,85) 4-Y-O+ £4,209 (£1,252; £625; £312) Stalls Low

Form RPR

15-4 1 **Captain Carey**[36] 916 4-9-0 **81** .... TomMcLaughlin 8 93
(M S Saunders) *hld up: hdwy over 1f out: rdn and hung lft ins fnl f: r.o to ld towards fin* **4/1**[1]

2141 2 ¾ **Grudge**[17] 1147 5-8-5 **72** ....(be) JimmyQuinn 5 81
(C R Dore) *t.k.h: led over 3f out: rdn and hdd towards fin* **5/1**[2]

3211 3 2¼ **Master Lightfoot**[11] 1267 4-9-2 **83** 6ex .... ShaneKelly 6 84
(W R Swinburn) *hld up in tch: rdn over 1f out: hung lft and no ex ins fnl f* **4/1**[1]

2120 4 hd **Onceaponatime (IRE)**[11] 1266 5-9-1 **85** .... WilliamCarson(3) 3 85+
(M D Squance) *hmpd sn after s: hld up: r.o ins fnl f: nvr nrr* **8/1**

3232 5 1¼ **Wotashirtfull (IRE)**[28] 986 5-9-2 **83** ....(v) PatCosgrave 7 79
(J R Boyle) *sn pushed along to chse ldrs: rdn over 1f out: styd on* **4/1**[1]

0-45 6 ½ **The Jobber (IRE)**[11] 1266 9-8-10 **77** .... TomQueally 2 71
(M Blanshard) *chsd ldrs: rdn over 1f out: no ex fnl f* **6/1**[3]

155- 7 2¼ **Red Rosanna**[280] 4043 4-8-10 **77** .... FergusSweeney 1 63
(R Hollinshead) *led: hdd over 3f out: rdn over 1f out: wknd fnl f* **16/1**

065- 8 13 **Stoneacre Lad (IRE)**[243] 5293 7-8-6 **73** ....(b) AdrianMcCarthy 4 12
(Peter Grayson) *prom to 1/2-way* **18/1**

62.32 secs (0.02) **Going Correction** +0.175s/f (Slow) **8 Ran SP% 113.2**

Speed ratings (Par 105): **106,104,101,100,98 98,94,73**

Tote Swingers: 1&2 £6.90, 1&3 £5.80, 2&3 £3.30 CSF £23.55 CT £83.48 TOTE £6.20: £1.60, £1.70, £1.80; EX 28.40 Trifecta £251.40 Part won. Pool: £339.81 - 0.73 winning units..

Owner M S Saunders **Bred** B Walters **Trained** Green Ore, Somerset

FOCUS

A tight handicap perhaps not run at as strong a pace as might have been expected, but the result seemed the right one on the day, though the eventual fourth would have finished third with a better run. The winner looked well in and the second posted a personal best.

1507 WOLVERHAMPTON RACECOURSE APPRENTICE H'CAP (DIV II) 1m 1f 103y(P)

3:35 (3:36) (Class 6) (0-55,56) 4-Y-O+ £1,433 (£423; £211) Stalls Low

Form RPR

0002 1 **Bajan Pride**[17] 1148 6-9-0 **55** .... AdamCarter 13 61
(R A Fahey) *led early: prom: chsd ldr 5f out: led over 2f out: rdn over 1f out: jst hld on* **8/1**

46-6 2 shd **Al Rayanah**[15] 1193 7-8-5 **53** ow3 ....(p) RichardOld(7) 4 59
(G Prodromou) *s.s: hld up: hdwy over 1f out: r.o wl towards fin: jst failed* **14/1**

/00 3 ¾ **King Zeal (IRE)**[15] 1193 6-8-8 **52** .... JamesRogers(3) 9 56
(B D Leavy) *hld up: hdwy over 2f out: rdn and hung lft over 1f out: r.o* **16/1**

4204 4 shd **Kielty's Folly**[15] 1193 6-8-8 **54** .... DannyBrock(5) 12 58
(B P J Baugh) *hld up: hdwy over 2f out: rdn over 1f out: r.o* **7/2**[1]

/056 5 1½ **Border Fox**[36] 918 7-8-5 **46** oh1 ....(t) MatthewLawson 10 47
(P Salmon) *s.i.s: plld hrd and hdwy over 7f out: led over 6f out: rdn and hdd over 2f out: styd on same pce fnl f* **14/1**

5406 6 ¾ **Hatch A Plan (IRE)**[8] 1318 9-8-9 **50** .... NathanAlison 8 49
(Mouse Hamilton-Fairley) *mid-div: hdwy over 2f out: rdn over 1f out: styd on same pce fnl f* **9/2**[2]

6600 7 2¼ **Mojeerr**[4] 1427 4-8-0 **46** oh1 ....(p) NoraLooby(5) 7 41
(A J McCabe) *mid-div: hdwy over 3f out: sn rdn: hmpd over 1f out: wknd ins fnl f* **12/1**

640- 8 3¾ **Extracurricular (USA)**[242] 5316 4-8-7 **53** .... AdamBeschizza(5) 11 40
(S Gollings) *prom: t.k.h: pushed along over 2f out: n.m.r over 1f out: wknd fnl f* **16/1**

0026 9 3¼ **Corrib (IRE)**[44] 854 7-8-4 **50** ....(p) MatthewCosham(5) 5 30
(B Palling) *hld up: rdn over 2f out: sn wknd* **12/1**

006- 10 1¼ **Bluebird Chariot**[149] 7520 7-7-12 **46** oh1 ....(b[1]) HobieGill(7) 2 23
(J M Bradley) *prom: rdn over 3f out: wknd over 2f out* **25/1**

5430 11 nk **Kings Topic (USA)**[13] 1226 10-9-1 **56** ow1 ....(b) ShaneRyan 3 33
(A B Haynes) *dwlt: rdn along and looked reluctant in rr: hdwy over 2f out: hung lft and wknd over 1f out: eased* **12/1**

0-35 12 3½ **Deportista**[15] 1188 4-8-2 **46** .... AlexEdwards(3) 1 15
(J A Pickering) *chsd ldrs: rdn over 3f out: hung rt and wknd over 2f out* **13/2**[3]

0320 **13** *10* **Libre**[78] 407 10-8-3 **47**.. JakePayne(3) 6 —
(F Jordan) *hld up: a in rr: rdn over 3f out: sn lost tch* **12/1**

2m 3.32s (1.62) **Going Correction** +0.175s/f (Slow) **13** Ran SP% **124.6**
Speed ratings (Par 101): **99,98,98,98,96 96,94,90,87,86 86,83,74**
Tote Swingers: 1&2 £25.10, 1&3 £21.60, 2&3 £59.60 CSF £120.10 CT £1775.90 TOTE £4.30: £2.70, £5.30, £6.20; EX 137.20 TRIFECTA Not won..

Owner R A Fahey **Bred** Plantation Stud **Trained** Musley Bank, N Yorks

■ Stewards' Enquiry : Adam Carter one-day ban: failed to ride to draw (May 7)

James Rogers two-day ban: careless riding (May 7-8)

FOCUS
The faster division of the apprentice handicap despite a steady early pace, but still just modest form. The winner was close to the level of his January Southwell win.

Kings Topic(USA) Official explanation: jockey said gelding was reluctant to race

1508 DINE IN THE HORIZONS RESTAURANT H'CAP — 1m 141y(P)
4:05 (4:05) (Class 6) (0-65,65) 4-Y-O+ — **£1,774** (£523; £262) **Stalls** Low

Form — RPR

6-61 **1** **Bernix**[13] 1239 8-8-13 **60**..(p) J-PGuillambert 9 68
(N Tinkler) *chsd ldrs: led over 1f out: sn rdn: jst hld on* **20/1**

3332 **2** *hd* **Tevez**[7] 1350 5-8-12 **59**.. DavidProbert 7 67
(D Donovan) *s.i.s: hld up: hdwy over 2f out: rdn and ev ch ins fnl f: styd on* **9/2**[3]

560- **3** *2 ¼* **Flying Silks (IRE)**[170] 7246 4-9-4 **65**.. RobertHavlin 10 68
(J R Gask) *prom: rdn to chse ldr over 2f out: ev ch over 1f out: no ex ins fnl f* **14/1**

53- **4** *½* **Aegean King**[293] 3611 4-8-10 **62**.. TobyAtkinson(5) 1 64
(M Wigham) *hld up in tch: nt clr run over 2f out: rdn over 1f out: sn edgd lft: styd on same pce fnl f* **6/4**[1]

45-0 **5** *1 ¼* **The Grey One (IRE)**[13] 1225 7-9-2 **63**..(p) LukeMorris 3 62
(J M Bradley) *mid-div: hdwy over 2f out: rdn and edgd lft over 1f out: styd on same pce fnl f* **12/1**

3-52 **6** *1 ¼* **Land Hawk (IRE)**[8] 1323 4-8-13 **65**.. SimonPearce(5) 12 61
(J Pearce) *hld up: hdwy over 1f out: nvr nrr* **4/1**[2]

-510 **7** *1 ¼* **Border Owl (IRE)**[37] 908 5-9-3 **64**.. GregFairley 11 57
(P Salmon) *chsd ldr tl led over 2f out: rdn and hdd over 1f out: edgd lft and wknd ins fnl f* **33/1**

5005 **8** *2* **Blue Charm**[9] 1305 6-9-4 **65**.. TomEaves 13 53
(I W McInnes) *hld up: rdn over 2f out: nvr on terms* **20/1**

0506 **9** *1* **Ninth House (USA)**[6] 1395 8-8-12 **64**..(t) DeanHeslop(5) 5 50
(Mrs R A Carr) *hld up: a in rr* **20/1**

50-5 **10** *17* **Goose Green (IRE)**[13] 1225 6-8-10 **60**.. WilliamCarson(3) 2 7
(R J Hodges) *chsd ldrs: rdn 3f out: wknd 2f out* **10/1**

000- **11** *20* **Echo Dancer**[141] 7615 4-9-2 **63**.. RobertWinston 6 —
(T Wall) *led: rdn and hdd over 2f out: wknd over 1f out* **100/1**

1m 51.31s (0.81) **Going Correction** +0.175s/f (Slow) **11** Ran SP% **119.8**
Speed ratings (Par 101): **103,102,100,100,99 98,97,95,94,79 61**
Tote Swingers: 1&2 £9.20, 1&3 £31.40, 2&3 £14.20 CSF £104.51 CT £1337.06 TOTE £25.00: £4.80, £1.70, £3.50; EX 116.70 TRIFECTA Not won..

Owner Danum Racing **Bred** M Lagardere **Trained** Langton, N Yorks

FOCUS
Standard fare for the grade, though the steady pace meant that very few got into contention and the performances of some of those dropped right out are best overlooked. The race is best judged around the second.

1509 WOLVERHAMPTON-RACECOURSE.CO.UK H'CAP — 7f 32y(P)
4:35 (4:35) (Class 5) (0-75,75) 4-Y-O+ — **£2,456** (£725; £362) **Stalls** High

Form — RPR

3-11 **1** **Global Village (IRE)**[7] 1350 5-9-1 **75** 6ex.. WilliamCarson(3) 5 89
(G C Bravery) *led early: chsd ldrs: pushed along to ld again 2f out: rdn over 1f out: r.o* **7/4**[1]

1141 **2** *1 ¼* **Copperwood**[13] 1224 5-8-9 **66**.. TomQueally 6 77
(M Blanshard) *s.i.s: hld up: hdwy over 1f out: r.o wl: wnt 2nd post* **4/1**[2]

60-6 **3** *hd* **Standpoint**[25] 1051 4-9-4 **75**.. FergusSweeney 9 85
(R Hollinshead) *a.p: rdn to chse wnr over 1f out: styd on* **12/1**

2360 **4** *5* **Kensington (IRE)**[6] 1374 9-8-12 **69**..(p) RobertWinston 3 66
(A J McCabe) *mid-div: rdn over 2f out: wknd fnl f* **16/1**

33-0 **5** *nk* **Emeebee**[15] 1185 4-9-3 **74**.. StevieDonohoe 1 70
(W J Musson) *hld up: rdn over 1f out: r.o ins fnl f: nvr nrr* **5/1**[3]

5431 **6** *nk* **Imperial Djay (IRE)**[13] 1236 5-8-5 **62**.. JimmyQuinn 10 57
(Mrs R A Carr) *dwlt: hld up: r.o ins fnl f: nrst fin* **9/1**

1146 **7** *1 ¾* **Whatyouwoodwishfor (USA)**[16] 1152 4-8-8 **65**..(b) TonyHamilton 7 56
(R A Fahey) *led over 6f out: hdd over 5f out: chsd ldr tl rdn over 2f out: wknd over 1f out* **16/1**

0-02 **8** *1* **Avontuur (FR)**[7] 1365 8-8-4 **66**..(b) DeanHeslop(5) 11 54
(Mrs R A Carr) *chsd ldrs: led over 5f out: rdn and hdd 2f out: wknd fnl f* **20/1**

/21- **9** *1 ¾* **Kyleene**[256] 4859 4-8-11 **73**.. LeeNewnes(5) 2 56
(M D I Usher) *hld up: n.d* **16/1**

0- **10** *6* **Cheveyo (IRE)**[123] 7829 4-9-0 **71**..(p) StephenCraine 8 38
(Patrick Morris) *mid-div: hdwy over 2f out: rdn and wknd over 1f out* **50/1**

1m 29.48s (-0.12) **Going Correction** +0.175s/f (Slow) **10** Ran SP% **115.1**
Speed ratings (Par 103): **107,105,105,99,99 98,96,95,93,86**
Tote Swingers: 1&2 £2.70, 1&3 £6.00, 2&3 £9.20 CSF £8.23 CT £62.38 TOTE £2.80: £1.70, £1.10, £4.00; EX 8.70 Trifecta £51.50 Pool: £367 - 5.28 winning units. Place 6: £1153.97 Place 5: £298.00.

Owner Mrs Janice Jones **Bred** Kilfrush Stud **Trained** Cowlinge, Suffolk

FOCUS
A fair handicap run at a good pace, though few ever got into it and the finish was fought out by the two most progressive horses in the line up. The first three finished clear and this is good form for the grade.

Imperial Djay(IRE) Official explanation: jockey said gelding jumped awkwardly leaving stalls

T/Jkpt: Not won. T/Plt: £521.80 to a £1 stake. Pool: £55,225.56. 77.25 winning tickets. T/Qpdt: £25.30 to a £1 stake. Pool: £5,357.72. 156.38 winning tickets. CR

HAYDOCK (L-H)
Saturday, April 24

OFFICIAL GOING: Good to firm (7.8)
All races run on old standside course and advertised distances on round course increased by 10yds.
Wind: Light across Weather: Sunny and dry

1510 EBF BUCKLEY FAMILY MAIDEN FILLIES' STKS — 5f
5:30 (5:30) (Class 5) 2-Y-O — **£3,432** (£1,021; £510; £254) **Stalls** High

Form — RPR

1 **Turn The Tide** 2-9-0 0.. MickyFenton 9 74+
(A Bailey) *trckd ldrs: hdwy 1/2-way: led wl over 1f out: rdn and edgd lft ins fnl f: kpt on wl* **7/2**[2]

2 *1 ½* **Magic Stella** 2-8-9 0.. MatthewDavies(5) 2 69+
(A P Jarvis) *in tch: hdwy wl over 1f out: sn rdn and styd on wl fnl f* **28/1**

0 **3** *1 ¼* **Hoppy's Flyer (FR)**[9] 1331 2-9-0 0.. RichardSmith 11 64
(Tom Dascombe) *a.p: effrt 2f out and ev ch: rdn and n.m.r over 1f out: edgd lft and kpt on same pce ins fnl f* **9/1**

4 *1 ¼* **Alensgrove (IRE)** 2-9-0 0.. TonyCulhane 1 60+
(P T Midgley) *dwlt and towards rr: hdwy wl over 1f out: kpt on ins fnl f: nrst fin* **25/1**

5 *2* **Dolly Parton (IRE)** 2-9-0 0.. AdrianNicholls 8 52
(D Nicholls) *cl up: effrt 2f out and ev ch tl rdn: edgd lft and wknd ent fnl f: n.m.r and swtchd rt towards fin* **5/1**[3]

04 **6** *1 ¾* **Roodee Queen**[10] 1294 2-9-0 0.. JamieSpencer 10 48
(Patrick Morris) *led: rdn along 2f out: sn hdd and wkng whn n.m.r appr fnl f* **11/1**

7 *½* **Bon Appetit** 2-9-0 0.. TomEaves 5 44
(N Tinkler) *prom: rdn along 1/2-way: sn wknd* **16/1**

8 *2* **Inagh River** 2-9-0 0.. PatDobbs 6 37+
(R Hannon) *a outpcd in rr* **2/1**[1]

9 *1* **Sarojini** 2-9-0 0.. FrederikTylicki 3 34
(J A Glover) *a towards rr* **16/1**

10 *9* **My Mate Al** 2-9-0 0.. PhillipMakin 4 1
(Tom Dascombe) *wnt lft s: midfield: rdn along 1/2-way: sn wknd and bhd* **16/1**

11 *5* **Dark Times (IRE)** 2-9-0 0.. AndrewElliott 7 —
(J R Weymes) *s.i.s: a bhd* **50/1**

60.51 secs (-0.49) **Going Correction** -0.275s/f (Firm) **11** Ran SP% **117.5**
Speed ratings (Par 89): **93,90,88,86,83 80,79,76,75,60 52**
Tote Swingers: 1&2 £26.30, 1&3 £6.70, 2&3 £25.10 CSF £101.21 TOTE £4.70: £1.80, £5.60, £3.30; EX 133.50.

Owner P T Tellwright **Bred** P T Tellwright **Trained** Newmarket, Suffolk

FOCUS
Little experience on show, with many of the runners looking and sounding green in the paddock, but a few of them should be winning in the next few months. Not easy to pin down the level of the form but the winner did it quite well.

NOTEBOOK
Turn The Tide, a Footstepsinthesand newcomer, had been well backed from 16-1 earlier in the day, and she was ready to do the business even though she edged left after taking the lead. A leggy sort, she should progress as she strengthens, and on breeding she will stay further in due course. (tchd 4-1)
Magic Stella ◆, a Danbird half-sister to the speedy Little Perisher, made a most encouraging debut. Though taking a while to pick up, she flew home once she got the idea, and she looks a good bet to take a similar event next time. (tchd 33-1)
Hoppy's Flyer(FR), who showed minor promise on her debut, stepped up on that with a solid effort. She looks more likely to find a race now, with nurseries available after one more run. (op 8-1 tchd 10-1 in places)
Alensgrove(IRE) ◆, a Byron filly from a decent family, was outpaced and green for much of the race, but caught the eye with a good finish. She should come on a lot for this and must be considered next time.
Dolly Parton(IRE) had done plenty of work, with trainer Dandy Nicholls reporting that this Tagula filly "travels well at home", where she had been working with the stable's juvenile winner Tanked Up. She has plenty of early speed, and connections won't be afraid to drop her in grade if she isn't up to winning a maiden. (op 9-2)
Roodee Queen, with two previous races to her name, had more experience than her rivals but on this evidence will be hard pushed to win a maiden. However, she would have finished closer but for being squeezed out and will be more at home in nurseries when the time comes. (op 12-1 tchd 10-1)
Bon Appetit, described beforehand by her jockey as "sharp and quick", did indeed show early pace on this debut, and can last longer with experience.
Inagh River, a well bred Fasliyev debutante, did not live up to her market position after being slowly into her stride and lacking the experience to recover. She can be given another chance to show what she can do, and 6f should suit her when she gets the chance. (tchd 9-4 and 11-4 in places)

1511 RRF AND DOW SCHOFIELD WATTS H'CAP — 5f
6:00 (6:00) (Class 5) (0-75,74) 3-Y-O — **£2,914** (£867; £433; £216) **Stalls** High

Form — RPR

06-2 **1** **Diman Waters (IRE)**[20] 1104 3-8-12 **68**.. PatCosgrave 6 83+
(E J Alston) *prom: hdwy 2f out: rdn to ld ent fnl f: kpt on wl towards fin* **4/1**[2]

0-21 **2** *1 ¼* **Rio Mist**[7] 1390 3-8-13 **72**.. PatrickHills(3) 7 82+
(R Hannon) *in tch: hdwy 2f out: rdn to chal ent fnl f: sn edgd lft and ev ch tl no ex towards fin* **11/4**[1]

1420 **3** *2 ½* **Il Forno**[24] 1058 3-8-13 **69**..(v[1]) JamieSpencer 4 70
(Ian Williams) *qckly away and sn clr: pushed along wl over 1f out: sn rdn: drvn and hdd ent fnl f: wknd* **7/1**[3]

1011 **4** *½* **Athwaab**[16] 1187 3-9-1 **74**.. WilliamCarson(3) 2 73
(M G Quinlan) *wnt lft s: sn chsng ldr: rdn and ch wl over 1f out: edgd lft and drvn appr fnl f: sn wknd* **14/1**

10-3 **5** *1* **Tell Me A Story**[17] 1175 3-8-11 **67**.. GregFairley 12 63
(M Brittain) *chsd ldrs: rdn along 2f out: drvn over 1f out: sn no imp* **14/1**

210- **6** *2 ¾* **Patch Patch**[256] 4875 3-9-0 **70**.. PhillipMakin 3 56+
(M Dods) *rrd s and bhd: hdwy 1/2-way: styd on appr fnl f: nvr nr ldrs* **20/1**

1640 **7** *1* **Little Perisher**[21] 1086 3-8-11 **72**.. MatthewDavies(5) 11 54+
(A P Jarvis) *in rr: rdn along 1/2-way: sme late hdwy* **16/1**

045- **8** *1* **Lieu Day Louie (IRE)**[178] 7115 3-8-4 **63**.. MartinLane(3) 1 42
(N Wilson) *awkward and sltly hmpd s: towards rr: hdwy on outer 1/2-way: rdn and in tch wl over 1f out: sn wknd* **50/1**

-053 **9** *1 ½* **Dazeen**[20] 1104 3-8-11 **67**.. TonyCulhane 9 40
(P T Midgley) *a towards rr* **20/1**

406- **10** *hd* **Lady Lube Rye (IRE)**[240] 5358 3-8-4 **60** .... DuranFentiman 10 32
(N Wilson) *chsd ldrs: rdn along bef 1/2-way: sn wknd* **25/1**

554- **11** *hd* **Key Breeze**[266] 4537 3-8-11 **67** .... PatDobbs 8 39
(K A Ryan) *hld up: a in rr* **7/1**[3]

10-6 **12** *1 1/2* **Royal Holiday (IRE)**[20] 1104 3-8-9 **68** .... BarryMcHugh(3) 14 34
(B Ellison) *a in rr* **33/1**

000- **13** *2* **Monalini (IRE)**[201] 6534 3-9-2 **72** .... TomEaves 5 31
(B Smart) *a in rr* **20/1**

500- **14** *2 1/2* **Bilash**[219] 6018 3-9-0 **70** .... MickyFenton 13 20
(R Hollinshead) *midfield: rdn along bef 1/2-way: sn wknd* **40/1**

59.24 secs (-1.76) **Going Correction** -0.275s/f (Firm) **14** Ran SP% **116.4**
Speed ratings (Par 98): **103,101,97,96,94 90,88,87,84,84 83,81,78,74**
Tote Swingers: 1&2 £4.00, 1&3 £5.40, 2&3 £5.30 CSF £13.19 CT £74.38 TOTE £4.20: £1.30, £1.20, £2.40; EX 15.70.
Owner Con Harrington **Bred** Mrs Chris Harrington **Trained** Longton, Lancs

FOCUS
A scorching gallop soon had them stretched out, and the winner did particularly well since he was chasing the pace throughout. The time was decent and the first two were clear, so this is probably form to view positively.
Bilash Official explanation: jockey said colt lost its action

1512 DEBRA MILLAR'S 40TH H'CAP — 1m 2f 95y
6:35 (6:36) (Class 4) (0-80,80) 4-Y-0+ **£5,180** (£1,541; £770; £384) **Stalls** Low

Form RPR

200- **1** **Russian George (IRE)**[196] 6680 4-9-2 **78** .... JamieSpencer 4 89
(S Gollings) *dwlt and hld up in rr: hdwy on wd outside over 2f out: rdn to chse ldrs over 1f out: drvn and edgd lft ins fnl f: kpt on to ld post* **11/1**

1114 **2** *shd* **Pendragon (USA)**[19] 1117 7-8-7 **72** .... BarryMcHugh(3) 5 83
(B Ellison) *trckd ldrs: hdwy over 2f out: rdn to ld ent fnl f: sn drvn: hdd and no ex post* **6/1**[2]

6211 **3** *2 1/4* **Danderek**[14] 1241 4-9-2 **78** .... FrederikTylicki 10 84
(R A Fahey) *cl up: led after 2f: rdn along 2f out: drvn over 1f out: hdd ent fnl f: kpt on u.p* **3/1**[1]

4-14 **4** *1* **Rosbay (IRE)**[7] 1378 6-9-1 **77** .... DuranFentiman 12 81
(T D Easterby) *dwlt and in rr: hdwy on outer 3f out: rdn along wl over 1f out: drvn and kpt on ins fnl f* **13/2**[3]

44-4 **5** *1 1/4* **Oriental Cavalier**[14] 1241 4-8-9 **71** .... (v[1]) MickyFenton 3 73
(R Hollinshead) *trckd ldrs on inner: hdwy 4f out: rdn along over 2f out: drvn over 1f out and kpt on same pce* **11/1**

2222 **6** *3* **Tropical Blue**[16] 1186 4-8-10 **72** .... (p) StephenCraine 6 68
(Jennie Candlish) *trckd ldrs: hdwy 4f out and sn cl up: rdn to chal 2f out and ev ch tl drvn and wknd appr fnl f* **12/1**

036- **7** *1* **King's Head (IRE)**[183] 6986 7-8-12 **74** .... PhillipMakin 8 68
(Miss L A Perratt) *hld up: hdwy 3f out: rdn along and n.m.r 2f out: sn no imp* **28/1**

34-0 **8** *2 3/4* **Una Pelota (IRE)**[26] 1051 4-8-13 **75** .... RichardSmith 11 64
(Tom Dascombe) *hld up in midfield: swtchd rt and hdwy 3f out: rdn to chse ldrs 2f out: sn drvn and wknd* **8/1**

-405 **9** *1 1/4* **Cry Alot Boy**[59] 676 7-8-10 **72** .... PatCosgrave 13 59
(K A Morgan) *dwlt: a in rr* **15/2**

4206 **10** *3* **Snow Dancer (IRE)**[7] 1379 6-9-0 **76** .... PatrickMathers 2 57
(H A McWilliams) *chsd ldrs on inner: rdn along over 3f out: grad wknd* **16/1**

6-02 **11** *1* **River Ardeche**[49] 405 5-8-11 **78** .... PatrickDonaghy(5) 7 57
(B M R Haslam) *cl up: rdn along 3f out: sn wknd* **33/1**

3-00 **12** *2* **Iron Out (USA)**[92] 266 4-8-13 **80** .... PaulPickard(5) 1 55
(R Hollinshead) *trckd ldrs: rdn along over 3f out: wknd wl over 2f out* **25/1**

2m 10.92s (-5.08) **Going Correction** -0.075s/f (Good) **12** Ran SP% **116.0**
Speed ratings (Par 105): **105,104,103,102,101 98,98,95,94,92 91,90**
Tote Swingers: 1&2 £17.40, 1&3 £8.30, 2&3 £5.40 CSF £72.51 CT £250.82 TOTE £14.40: £4.10, £2.60, £1.70; EX 118.00.
Owner P J Martin **Bred** Martin Walsh **Trained** Scamblesby, Lincs

FOCUS
A testing gallop set things up for the hold-up performers. Solid form, with improvement from the first two.

1513 HAYDOCK PARK RAILS AND RING BOOKMAKERS H'CAP — 1m 30y
7:05 (7:05) (Class 4) (0-85,85) 4-Y-0+ **£5,180** (£1,541; £770; £384) **Stalls** Low

Form RPR

3460 **1** **Just Bond (IRE)**[44] 863 8-8-10 **80** .... BarryMcHugh(3) 8 88
(G R Oldroyd) *hld up and bhd: smooth hdwy 3f out: effrt and nt clr run 2f out: swtchd rt and qcknd to ld ent fnl f: sn rdn and kpt on wl towards fin* **12/1**

6611 **2** *1/2* **Kidlat**[17] 1156 5-8-13 **80** .... MickyFenton 7 87
(A Bailey) *hld up: hdwy over 3f out: rdn and sltly outpcd wl over 1f out: drvn and styd on ins fnl f: ev ch tl no ex towards fin* **10/1**

113- **3** *nk* **Off Chance**[231] 5670 4-9-4 **85** .... DuranFentiman 17 91
(T D Easterby) *hld up towards rr: hdwy over 2f out: rdn over 1f out: styd on wl fnl f* **8/1**[2]

35-0 **4** *3/4* **Ezdeyaad (USA)**[11] 1272 6-8-12 **79** .... JamieSpencer 5 83
(G A Swinbank) *prom: effrt to ld 1 1/2f out: rdn: hung rt and hdd ent fnl f: sn drvn and ch tl one pce last 100yds* **9/2**[1]

200- **5** *3 1/4* **Celtic Change (IRE)**[203] 6485 6-8-13 **80** .... (bt) PhillipMakin 2 77
(M Dods) *led: rdn along wl over 2f out: drvn and hdd 1 1/2f out: grad wknd* **10/1**

020- **6** *1/2* **Come And Go (UAE)**[241] 5340 4-8-9 **76** .... PJMcDonald 15 72+
(G A Swinbank) *hld up in rr: hdwy wl over 2f out: kpt on ins fnl f: nrst fin* **25/1**

35-0 **7** *nk* **Charlie Tipple**[19] 1117 6-8-13 **80** .... (p) FrederikTylicki 14 75
(T D Easterby) *towards rr: hdwy on outer wl over 2f out: sn rdn and kpt on ins fnl f: nt rch ldrs* **14/1**

211- **8** *1 1/4* **Espero (IRE)**[177] 7141 4-9-1 **82** .... TomEaves 12 74
(Miss L A Perratt) *midfield: smooth hdwy 1/2-way: trckd ldrs 3f out: effrt 2f out and ch tl rdn and wknd appr fnl f* **20/1**

006- **9** *3/4* **Willow Dancer (IRE)**[197] 6633 6-9-3 **84** .... ShaneKelly 4 75
(W R Swinburn) *trckd ldrs on inner: hdwy 1/2-way: rdn along over 2f out: wknd over 1f out* **12/1**

000- **10** *1 3/4* **Visions Of Johanna (USA)**[239] 5409 5-8-4 **71** oh1 ..... (p) LukeMorris 13 57
(Ian Williams) *chsd ldrs: hdwy 3f out: cl up and rdn 2f out: drvn and wknd appr fnl f* **12/1**

4033 **11** *1 3/4* **Ella Woodcock (IRE)**[5] 1426 6-8-4 **71** oh3 .... FrannyNorton 3 56
(E J Alston) *nvr nr ldrs* **17/2**[3]

0205 **12** *3/4* **Johnmanderville**[15] 1202 4-8-8 **78** .... (tp) MartinLane(3) 11 59
(N Wilson) *chsd ldrs: rdn along wl over 2f out: drvn wl over 1f out and grad wknd* **12/1**

654- **13** *2* **Arizona John (IRE)**[141] 7633 5-8-10 **77** .... StephenCraine 10 53
(J Mackie) *chsd ldrs: rdn along 3f out: wknd over 2f out* **12/1**

20-0 **14** *2* **Rio Cobolo (IRE)**[8] 1361 4-8-1 **71** .... (v) AndrewHeffernan(3) 9 43
(Paul Green) *in tch on inner: rdn along wl over 2f out: sn wknd* **33/1**

126- **15** *5* **Muftarres (IRE)**[171] 7233 5-8-13 **80** .... (t) TonyCulhane 16 40
(P T Midgley) *a bhd* **20/1**

06-0 **16** *1 1/2* **Bold Marc (IRE)**[7] 1374 8-8-11 **78** .... AndrewElliott 6 35
(J R Weymes) *chsd ldrs to 1/2-way: sn rdn along and wknd* **33/1**

1m 42.16s (-2.54) **Going Correction** -0.075s/f (Good) **16** Ran SP% **122.4**
Speed ratings (Par 105): **105,104,104,103,100 99,99,98,97,95 93,93,91,89,84 82**
Tote Swingers: 1&2 £9.30, 1&3 £8.70, 2&3 £17.70 CSF £118.45 CT £1068.73 TOTE £11.70: £2.70, £2.60, £2.70, £1.10; EX 131.60.
Owner R C Bond **Bred** Schwindibode Ag **Trained** Brawby, N Yorks
■ Stewards' Enquiry : Barry McHugh one-day ban: used whip with excessive frequency (May 8)

FOCUS
Another race run at a good pace, ideal for the hold-up types in this competitive event. Sound form with the winner rated back to his best.
Ella Woodcock(IRE) Official explanation: jockey said the gelding lost its action

1514 WARRINGTON GUARDIAN H'CAP — 1m 30y
7:35 (7:35) (Class 5) (0-75,78) 3-Y-O **£2,914** (£867; £433; £216) **Stalls** Low

Form RPR

30-2 **1** **Layla's Lexi**[39] 894 3-8-6 **63** .... PJMcDonald 1 69
(Ian Williams) *chsd ldrs: hdwy on inner over 2f out: rdn wl over 1f out: drvn to chal ent fnl f: led last 100yds and kpt on wl* **20/1**

0-10 **2** *1 1/2* **Tafawut**[17] 1159 3-9-4 **75** .... LukeMorris 8 79+
(C G Cox) *hld up towards rr: hdwy whn nt clr run 2f out: rdn and hdwy over 1f out: styd on strly ins fnl f* **14/1**

54-5 **3** *shd* **Deely Plaza**[24] 1070 3-8-9 **66** .... FrederikTylicki 3 68
(J A Glover) *mde most: rdn along over 2f out: drvn over 1f out: hdd and one pce last 100yds* **14/1**

341 **4** *1/2* **Understory (USA)**[50] 815 3-9-4 **75** .... GregFairley 6 76
(M Johnston) *cl up: rdn along wl over 2f out: drvn over 1f out and ev ch tl one pce ins fnl f* **4/1**[2]

41- **5** *1/2* **Think Its All Over (USA)**[216] 6136 3-9-4 **75** .... JamieSpencer 7 75+
(T P Tate) *trckd ldng pair on outer: pushed along 3f out: rdn and sltly outpcd 2f out: kpt on ins fnl f* **13/8**[1]

00-5 **6** *2 1/2* **Tammela**[30] 978 3-8-3 **65** .... MatthewDavies(5) 2 59
(A P Jarvis) *in rr tl sme late hdwy* **40/1**

2302 **7** *shd* **Adam De Beaulieu (USA)**[24] 1070 3-8-11 **68** .... (t) PhillipMakin 10 61
(B M R Haslam) *hld up: hdwy 1/2-way and sn in tch: effrt to chse ldrs 2f out: rdn wl over 1f out: wknd ins fnl f* **22/1**

001- **8** *1 3/4* **Gypsy Jazz (IRE)**[199] 6589 3-8-10 **67** .... StephenCraine 4 56
(Jennie Candlish) *chsd ldrs: rdn along over 2f out: drvn and wknd over 1f out* **20/1**

25-4 **9** *1 1/4* **Leaving Alone (USA)**[8] 1358 3-8-13 **70** .... PatDobbs 9 56
(R Hannon) *in tch: rdn along over 3f out: rdn over 2f out and sn btn* **11/2**[3]

2202 **10** *nk* **Lisahane Bog**[10] 1307 3-9-7 **78** .... (b[1]) DaneO'Neill 5 63
(P R Hedger) *a in rr* **7/1**

1m 43.97s (-0.73) **Going Correction** -0.075s/f (Good) **10** Ran SP% **115.6**
Speed ratings (Par 98): **96,94,94,93,93 90,90,89,87,87**
Tote Swingers: 1&2 £27.80, 1&3 £53.50, 2&3 £27.60 CSF £255.34 CT £4106.83 TOTE £10.10: £3.20, £4.50, £4.50; EX 322.30.
Owner Dr Marwan Koukash **Bred** Plantation Stud **Trained** Portway, Worcs
■ Stewards' Enquiry : Frederik Tylicki one day ban: careless riding (May 8)

FOCUS
A fair gallop, but not as fast as previous races, gave the prominent runners more of a chance. Improvement from the winner, with the third the best guide.

1515 ST HELENS STAR MAIDEN STKS — 1m 3f 200y
8:05 (8:07) (Class 5) 3-Y-O **£2,914** (£867; £433; £216) **Stalls** High

Form RPR

3-22 **1** **Deauville Post (FR)**[10] 1314 3-9-3 83 .... PatDobbs 1 80+
(R Hannon) *trckd ldr: hdwy 3f out: led 2f out: sn rdn and kpt on strly fnl f* **4/9**[1]

3-03 **2** *10* **Layla's Boy**[24] 1059 3-9-3 70 .... JamieSpencer 3 68
(Ian Williams) *led: pushed along over 3f out: rdn and hdd 2f out: drvn and no imp ent fnl f: eased towards fin* **4/1**[2]

6 **3** *4* **Thingathong (FR)**[28] 1010 3-8-12 0 .... RichardKingscote 4 53
(Tom Dascombe) *s.i.s: sn chsng ldng pair: rdn along and hung rt 2f out: sn outpcd* **7/1**[3]

4 *1/2* **Ruby Dazzler** 3-8-12 0 .... TonyCulhane 5 52
(S Lycett) *in tch: rdn along over 3f out: drvn over 2f out: n.d* **25/1**

5 *13* **Susie** 3-8-12 0 .... TomEaves 2 31
(K A Ryan) *s.i.s: a bhd* **14/1**

2m 34.71s (0.71) **Going Correction** -0.075s/f (Good) **5** Ran SP% **112.3**
Speed ratings (Par 98): **91,84,81,81,72**
CSF £2.70 TOTE £1.40: £1.10, £1.10; EX 2.00 Place 6: £195.21 Place 5: £46.89 .
Owner Jaber Abdullah **Bred** Haras D'Etreham **Trained** East Everleigh, Wilts

FOCUS
The slackest tempo of the evening, but they finished more or less in the right order. The form is rated around the runner-up and the easy winner did not need to match his previous form.
T/Plt: £223.20 to a £1 stake. Pool: £5,0015.18. 163.55 winning tickets. T/Qpdt: £76.20 to a £1 stake. Pool: £5,399.76. 52.40 winning tickets. JR

1180 LEICESTER (R-H)
Saturday, April 24

OFFICIAL GOING: Good to firm (good in places; 8.5)
Wind: virtually nil Weather: bright and sunny

1516 BEST ODDS GUARANTEED AT TOTESPORT.COM H'CAP — 5f 218y
1:55 (1:55) (Class 4) (0-85,85) 4-Y-O+ **£4,533** (£1,348; £674; £336) **Stalls** Low

Form RPR

060- **1** **Sunrise Safari (IRE)**[161] 7395 7-9-3 **84** .... (v) TonyHamilton 9 93
(R A Fahey) *bhd: rdn over 2f out: hdwy and swtchd rt ent fnl f: styd on strly to ld nr fin* **20/1**

00 **2** *hd* **Indian Skipper (IRE)**[38] 902 5-8-3 **75** .... (v) BillyCray(5) 5 83
(R C Guest) *dwlt: sn rcvrd and chsng ldrs: rdn over 2f out: drvn over 1f out: kpt on u.p to ld wl ins fnl f: hdd nr fin* **20/1**

546- **3** *1/2* **Rowayton**[264] 4601 4-9-1 **82** .... FrankieDettori 4 89
(J D Bethell) *w ldr: rdn ent fnl 2f: drvn to ld over 1f out: hdd and no ex wl ins fnl f* **14/1**

60-4 **4** ½ **Dancing Maite**[16] 1185 5-8-6 **73** .... JimmyQuinn 12 78
(S R Bowring) *racd alone towards centre tl 1/2-way: in midfield: rdn over 2f out: hdwy to chse ldrs and drvn jst over 1f out: kpt on same pce fnl 100yds* **9/1**[3]

-134 **5** 1½ **Lucky Redback (IRE)**[30] 981 4-9-4 **85** .... PatDobbs 10 85
(R Hannon) *bhd: pushed along 4f out: rdn over 2f out: hdwy and switching lft 1f out: styd on wl ins fnl f: nvr gng pce to rch ldrs* **8/1**[2]

3161 **6** *hd* **Beat The Bell**[5] 1428 5-8-7 **74** ow1 .... ShaneKelly 6 74
(J A Osborne) *led: rdn 2f out: hdd over 1f out: wknd ins fnl f* **4/6**[1]

0-44 **7** *nse* **Ra Junior (USA)**[20] 1102 4-9-2 **83** .... AdrianNicholls 11 83
(D Nicholls) *dropped in bhd after s: hld up in rr: hdwy on stands' rail 2f out: drvn and kpt on same pce ent fnl f* **10/1**

-600 **8** ½ **Frognal (IRE)**[9] 1332 4-9-1 **82** .... AndrewElliott 2 80
(Mrs R A Carr) *stdd s: hld up in tch in midfield: edging rt and hdwy over 2f out: rdn over 1f out: keeping on same pce and hld whn short of room fnl 100yds* **50/1**

60-0 **9** ½ **Coleorton Choice**[27] 1032 4-9-4 **85** .... RobertWinston 7 83
(R Hollinshead) *chsd ldrs: rdn over 3f out: drvn and unable qck wl over 1f out: wknd jst ins fnl f* **33/1**

00-0 **10** 2 **Aroundthebay**[30] 981 4-9-1 **82** .... DavidProbert 3 72
(H J L Dunlop) *in tch in midfield: lost pl and towards rr whn rdn over 2f out: no prog* **40/1**

250- **11** 4½ **Hi Shinko**[194] 6731 4-8-10 **77** .... TomMcLaughlin 1 53
(B R Millman) *broke wl: w ldrs tl over 2f out: sn drvn and struggling: wl bhd fnl f* **25/1**

1m 10.91s (-2.09) **Going Correction** -0.20s/f (Firm) **11** Ran SP% **117.6**
Speed ratings (Par 105): **105,104,104,103,101 101,101,100,99,97 91**
toteswingers: 1&2 £24.80, 1&3 £17.60, 2&3 £26.90 CSF £334.85 CT £5665.46 TOTE £23.10: £5.50, £4.90, £3.30; EX 377.00.
Owner Timeform Betfair Racing Club Ltd **Bred** Mervyn Stewkesbury **Trained** Musley Bank, N Yorks

FOCUS
A fair, competitive sprint handicap. The favourite disappointed, but straightforward form amongst the principals.
Beat The Bell Official explanation: trainer was unable to offer any explanation for the poor performance shown

1517 FREE RACING POST AT TOTESPORT.COM MEDIAN AUCTION MAIDEN STKS 5f 2y
2:25 (2:31) (Class 5) 2-Y-O **£2,914** (£867; £433; £216) **Stalls** Low

Form RPR

1 **Drawing Board** 2-9-3 0 .... RichardMullen 8 81+
(K A Ryan) *racd in centre: chsd ldng trio: rdn and hdwy over 1f out: chsd ldr fnl 100yds: kpt on wl to ld nr fin* **13/2**[3]

222 **2** *hd* **Scarlet Rocks (IRE)**[12] 1263 2-8-12 0 .... RobertWinston 12 76
(P D Evans) *led and racd on far side: rdn over 1f out: hrd drvn and hung rt ins fnl f: hdd nr fin* **3/1**[2]

43 **3** 1¼ **Master Macho (IRE)**[10] 1294 2-9-3 0 .... AlanMunro 15 76
(M R Channon) *chsd ldrs on far side: clsd over 1f out: rdn ent fnl f: keeping on same pce whn nt clr run nr fin* **8/1**

4 ½ **Bunce (IRE)** 2-9-3 0 .... PatDobbs 4 74
(R Hannon) *racd in centre: chsd ldr: rdn over 1f out: no ex ins fnl f* **9/4**[1]

2 **5** 8 **Mica Mika (IRE)**[15] 1198 2-9-3 0 .... TonyHamilton 16 45
(R A Fahey) *racd far side: s.i.s: midfield but nvr on terms w ldrs: rdn and no prog 2f out* **16/1**

6 1¼ **Royal Opera** 2-9-0 0 .... JamesMillman(3) 11 41
(B R Millman) *racd in centre: wl off the pce in midfield: rdn and no hdwy 1/2-way* **33/1**

7 1¾ **May Be Some Time** 2-9-3 0 .... ShaneKelly 6 35
(W S Kittow) *racd in centre: dwlt: sn bustled along in midfield: nvr on terms w ldrs* **33/1**

8 1¾ **Addock And Egg** 2-9-3 0 .... JimCrowley 13 28
(Tom Dascombe) *racd in centre: v.s.a: a outpcd in midfield: rdn and no prog 1/2-way* **12/1**

9 1 **Press Release** 2-9-3 0 .... RichardSmith 3 25
(Tom Dascombe) *racd in centre: v.s.a: bhd: sme hdwy 1/2-way: no prog after and wl btn fnl 2f* **25/1**

10 *nk* **Fred Willetts (IRE)** 2-9-3 0 .... CathyGannon 7 24
(P D Evans) *racd in centre: wnt rt s and v.s.a: sn rdn: a outpcd in rr* **40/1**

11 2 **Nalany** 2-8-12 0 .... DaneO'Neill 5 11
(D Haydn Jones) *racd in centre: s.i.s: a outpcd in rr* **100/1**

12 1 **Henrys Air** 2-9-0 0 .... MichaelGeran(3) 2 13
(D G Bridgwater) *racd in centre: a wl outpcd in rr* **100/1**

13 2 **Guinea Seeker** 2-9-3 0 .... DavidNolan 1 —
(T D Easterby) *racd in centre: wl off the pce in midfield: nvr trbld ldrs: struggling and rdn 1/2-way: wl bhd over 1f out* **40/1**

59.91 secs (-0.09) **Going Correction** -0.20s/f (Firm) **13** Ran SP% **110.4**
Speed ratings (Par 92): **92,91,89,88,76 74,71,68,66,66 63,61,58**
toteswingers: 1&2 £4.20, 1&3 £10.90, 2&3 £4.90 CSF £22.90 TOTE £7.00: £2.50, £1.20, £2.50; EX 32.20.
Owner J C Fretwell **Bred** Peter Webb **Trained** Hambleton, N Yorks

FOCUS
There was a delay of around seven minutes, and with a few of these young horses forced to wait in the stalls for longer than ideal, several of them missed the break. They were soon strung out and the first four finished well clear in what was probably just a fair juvenile maiden. The main action took place middle to far side. The form should work out well.

NOTEBOOK
Drawing Board, a £20,000 purchase, showed some speed to chase the pace up the centre of the track early on and gradually responded to pressure to get on top late on. He's open to improvement and looks a useful type in the making. (op 15-2)
Scarlet Rocks(IRE) displayed loads of natural speed up towards the far-side rail but was picked off near the line, finding one too good, just as on her three previous starts. It's clear she's up to winning a similar event, but is vulnerable to something potentially useful. (op 11-4 tchd 5-2)
Master Macho(IRE) was not beaten far and looked to improve slightly on his first two efforts. A modest race should come his way. (op 9-1)
Bunce(IRE), a 65,000gns out of a mare who was placed over 6f, looked well educated, showing bright pace from the off up the middle of the track. He was a long way ahead of the remainder and should soon be winning. (tchd 5-2)
Mica Mika(IRE) probably ran to just a moderate level when runner-up in a three-runner race on his debut and this was tougher. (op 14-1)

1518 TOTESPORT 0800 221 221 H'CAP 1m 3f 183y
3:00 (3:00) (Class 3) (0-95,85) 3-Y-O **£6,854** (£2,052; £1,026; £513; £256) **Stalls** High

Form RPR

1-23 **1** **Exemplary**[18] 1138 3-9-2 **80** .... FrankieDettori 3 87+
(M Johnston) *mde all: rdn and qcknd ent fnl 2f: clr over 1f out: r.o wl: comf* **15/8**[1]

10-5 **2** 1¾ **Sharaayeen**[27] 1033 3-9-0 **78** .... TadhgO'Shea 5 82
(B W Hills) *trckd wnr: rdn and nt pce of wnr ent fnl 2f: wl hld by wnr fnl f but kpt on for clr 2nd* **11/4**[2]

61-4 **3** 3 **Green Lightning (IRE)**[27] 1033 3-9-3 **81** .... RoystonFfrench 4 80
(M Johnston) *racd in tch in last pair: rdn and unable qck over 2f out: hld hd high u.p after: wnt 3rd ins fnl f: no ch w ldng pair* **4/1**[3]

232- **4** 1½ **Aquarian Spirit**[217] 6088 3-9-4 **82** .... TonyHamilton 2 79
(R A Fahey) *t.k.h: hld up in last pair: hdwy on outer 3f out: pressed ldrs and rdn over 2f out: btn wl over 1f out* **4/1**[3]

105- **5** 13 **Ishtar Gate (USA)**[203] 6472 3-9-7 **85** .... AlanMunro 1 61
(P F I Cole) *chsd ldng pair: pushed along and hdwy to press ldrs 3f out: wknd ent fnl 2f: eased ins fnl f* **14/1**

2m 34.61s (0.71) **Going Correction** -0.20s/f (Firm) **5** Ran SP% **108.1**
Speed ratings (Par 102): **89,87,85,84,76**
CSF £6.98 TOTE £2.50: £1.20, £1.80; EX 8.80.
Owner Sheikh Hamdan Bin Mohammed Al Maktoum **Bred** Darley **Trained** Middleham Moor, N Yorks

FOCUS
A disappointing turnout numerically and the pace was modest. The form is still rated on the positive side, with improvement from the first two.

NOTEBOOK
Exemplary was allowed a soft lead and, having set no more than a modest pace, it was no surprise he kept on so well. This ground seemed to suit him better than the soft surface he encountered at Ffos Las last time. (op 5-2 tchd 7-4)
Sharaayeen, trying 1m4f for the first time, reversed recent Doncaster placings with Green Lightning but couldn't get to the winner, who had been allowed too much rope in front. (tchd 5-2 and 3-1)
Green Lightning(IRE), coltish in the paddock, missed the break and didn't seem to travel all that well. He ran on past beaten horses in the straight but was never a threat. It would be no surprise to see him do better back on easier ground. (tchd 11-2)
Aquarian Spirit, upped half a mile in trip, seemed to travel okay but he ultimately looked a non-stayer. (op 3-1 tchd 9-2)
Ishtar Gate(USA), reappearing after a break of 203 days, ran poorly. (op 11-1)

1519 TOTESPORT.COM LEICESTERSHIRE STKS (LISTED RACE) 7f 9y
3:35 (3:36) (Class 1) 4-Y-O+
£22,708 (£8,608; £4,308; £2,148; £1,076; £540) **Stalls** Low

Form RPR

24-1 **1** **Spirit Of Sharjah (IRE)**[14] 1219 5-9-2 94 .... FrankieDettori 5 104+
(Miss J Feilden) *stdd s: hld up in rr: smooth hdwy to trck ldrs over 1f out: rdn and effrt between horses ent fnl f: led ins fnl f: r.o wl* **7/2**[3]

6565 **2** ½ **Carcinetto (IRE)**[3] 1481 8-8-11 88 .... CathyGannon 4 98
(P D Evans) *chsd ldrs: rdn 3f out: drvn and ev ch 2f out: unable qck fnl 100yds: kpt on* **14/1**

6-54 **3** ½ **Light From Mars**[7] 1377 5-9-2 100 .... JamesMillman 2 102
(B R Millman) *in tch: hdwy to join ldr over 2f out: pushed into ld wl over 1f out: rdn ent fnl f: hdd and no ex ins fnl f* **2/1**[1]

1520 **4** 8 **Ishiadancer**[27] 1030 5-8-11 82 .... DavidProbert 1 75
(E J Alston) *led tl 4f out: chsd ldrs after: drvn 2f out: wknd qckly ent fnl f* **18/1**

/41- **5** 2¾ **Alyarf (USA)**[336] 2278 4-9-2 109 .... TadhgO'Shea 3 73
(B W Hills) *t.k.h: chsd ldr tl led 4f out: hdd wl over 1f out: sn wknd: wl btn fnl f* **11/4**[2]

0000 **6** 1¼ **Ocean's Minstrel**[35] 946 4-9-2 99 .... AlanMunro 6 69
(J Ryan) *in tch: rdn over 2f out: wknd u.p wl over 1f out: wl btn fnl f* **13/2**

U **7** 12 **Bagutta Sun**[9] 1333 4-8-11 0 .... JimCrowley 7 32
(Tom Dascombe) *chsd ldrs: rdn and btn ent fnl 2f: eased whn no ch ins fnl f* **20/1**

1m 22.99s (-3.21) **Going Correction** -0.20s/f (Firm) **7** Ran SP% **112.2**
Speed ratings (Par 111): **110,109,108,99,96 95,81**
toteswingers: 1&2 £6.20, 1&3 £3.30, 2&3 £7.70 CSF £46.61 TOTE £4.90: £2.70, £7.20; EX 39.40.
Owner A Dee **Bred** Mrs Kathleen Reynolds **Trained** Exning, Suffolk
■ Stewards' Enquiry : Cathy Gannon one-day ban: used whip with excessive frequency (May 8)

FOCUS
A weakish Listed race, but the pace was good and the time was 0.81 seconds under standard. The winner looks back to his best and the form is rated around the runner-up.

NOTEBOOK
Spirit Of Sharjah(IRE) lost his way somewhat after showing smart form as a juvenile, but he's firmly on the up again now and he coped with the return to pattern company (won at this level as a juvenile) to follow up his recent Polytrack handicap success. He was always cruising under an ultra-confident Frankie Dettori and, although ultimately having to work for it when off the bridle, he always looked like winning. A horse who seems to be on really good terms with himself, there could be more to come. (tchd 11-4)
Carcinetto(IRE), already having her 15th start of the year, ran a game race in defeat to pick up some more black type, improving on her third placing in this last year. (op 18-1 tchd 12-1)
Light From Mars seemed to have every chance but he didn't look to run up to his official mark of 100 considering he had something in hand over the front two at the weights. (op 11-4)
Ishiadancer, rated only 82, ran creditably considering she was worst off at the weights (of those with official ratings), although she was still beaten a long way. (op 25-1)
Alyarf(USA), off the track since winning in this grade at Newmarket last May, looked to be carrying plenty of condition and was weak in the market. He finished well held and seemed badly in need of the run. Official explanation: jockey said the colt ran too freely (op 6-4)
Ocean's Minstrel ran nowhere near his best form. (op 10-1 tchd 6-1)
Bagutta Sun, who unseated her rider leaving the stalls when returning from a long absence on her British debut nine days earlier, showed nothing. (op 28-1)

1520 MORE LIVE FOOTBALL BETTING AT TOTESPORT.COM H'CAP 1m 1f 218y
4:05 (4:05) (Class 5) (0-70,70) 4-Y-O+ **£3,238** (£963; £481; £240) **Stalls** High

Form RPR

446- **1** **Arashi**[128] 7790 4-8-8 **60** .... (p) JimmyQuinn 5 69
(Lucinda Featherstone) *hld in tch in midfield: hdwy over 2f out: rdn to chse ldr over 1f out: str chal u.p 1f out: kpt on wl to ld on post* **10/1**

130- **2** *nse* **Baltimore Jack (IRE)**[182] 7014 6-9-4 **70** .... JimCrowley 4 79
(T D Walford) *led: rdn 2f out: hrd drvn and kpt on fnl f: hdd on post* **85/40**[1]

-210 **3** 2 **Carr Hall (IRE)**[14] 1225 7-8-1 **60** ow4 .... JohnFahy(7) 8 65
(A W Carroll) *stdd s: t.k.h: hld up in midfield: switching lft to outer over 2f out: rdn to chse ldng pair jst ins fnl f: no ex and btn fnl 100yds* **4/1**[2]

55-0 **4** 4½ **Kyle Of Bute**[17] 1177 4-8-8 **60** .... J-PGuillambert 7 56
(B P J Baugh) *t.k.h: hld up in tch: hdwy 3f out: chsd ldr 2f out tl over 1f out: drvn and wknd 1f out* **12/1**

5-05 **5** 5 **Divinatore**[79] 400 4-8-6 **58** .... HayleyTurner 6 44
(D Haydn Jones) *hld up in rr: hdwy on inner over 2f out: no prog u.p over 1f out: nvr threatened ldrs* **7/1**

60-0 **6** 3 1/4 **Green Passion (USA)**[10] 1296 4-8-10 **62**.................. RoystonFfrench 3 41
(M Johnston) *chsd ldrs: rdn over 3f out: wknd and edgd rt u.p jst over 2f out* **16/1**

00-0 **7** 3/4 **Pitbull**[17] 1177 7-8-1 **58** oh4 ow2..(p) BillyCray(5) 1 36
(A Berry) *v.s.a: rcvrd and in tch in rr after 2f: rdn and struggling 3f out: wl btn fnl 2f* **40/1**

3506 **8** 2 **El Libertador (USA)**[26] 1047 4-8-12 **64**........................... SteveCarson 2 38
(E A Wheeler) *chsd ldr: rdn over 2f out: lost 2nd 2f out: sn wknd: wl bhd fnl f* **8/1**

503- **9** 3 1/4 **Marju King (IRE)**[246] 5223 4-9-3 **69**.............................. RobertWinston 9 36
(W S Kittow) *t.k.h: chsd ldrs: rdn over 3f out: wknd qckly ent fnl 2f: wl bhd and eased ins fnl f* **5/1**[3]

5-30 **10** 1 1/4 **Frankie Falco**[7] 1380 4-7-13 **56** oh2........................... SimonPearce(5) 10 21
(G Fierro) *stdd after s: hld up in rr: rdn and lost tch over 2f out* **40/1**

2m 5.19s (-2.71) **Going Correction** -0.20s/f (Firm) **10** Ran SP% **119.8**
Speed ratings (Par 103): **102,101,100,96,92 90,89,87,85,84**
toteswingers: 1&2 £8.10, 1&3 £10.20, 2&3 £3.10 CSF £32.46 CT £103.03 TOTE £10.50: £3.90, £1.10, £2.00; EX 42.40.

Owner Stuart Barnett **Bred** Wyck Hall Stud Ltd **Trained** Atlow, Derbyshire

FOCUS
A well run handicap and sound if modest form, with the first three clear. The winner is rated back to his best.

1521 BET IN-PLAY ON FOOTBALL AT TOTESPORT.COM MAIDEN STKS 1m 1f 218y
4:40 (4:41) (Class 5) 3-Y-O+ **£2,590** (£770; £385; £192) **Stalls** High

Form RPR

04- **1** **Green Moon (IRE)**[182] 7029 3-8-10 0............................ FrankieDettori 5 90+
(H J L Dunlop) *mde all: jnd and rdn 3f out: drew clr over 1f out: wl clr ins fnl f: eased towards fin* **5/4**[1]

0- **2** 5 **Mataaleb**[193] 6759 3-8-10 0.. TadhgO'Shea 1 75
(M A Jarvis) *t.k.h: chsd wnr thrght: upsides and rdn 3f out: btn over 1f out: no ch w wnr fnl f* **15/8**[2]

\- **3** 5 **Langen Voraus (GER)** 4-9-8 0....................................... JimmyQuinn 4 63
(H R A Cecil) *chsd ldng trio: rdn 3f out: outpcd by ldng pair ent 2f out: 3rd and wl btn over 1f out* **4/1**[3]

00- **4** 4 **Almutaham (USA)**[236] 5499 3-8-10 0.......................... RichardMullen 7 57
(J L Dunlop) *chsd ldng pair: rdn and btn wl over 2f out: no ch fnl 2f* **16/1**

5 9 **Ionaguru**[19] 5-9-1 0.. DavidKenny(7) 6 37
(B D Leavy) *dwlt: hld up in last trio: lost tch and hung lft over 2f out* **150/1**

0 **6** 1 3/4 **Playground**[12] 1268 3-8-10 0.. HayleyTurner 3 36
(M L W Bell) *plld hrd: hld up in last trio: rdn and lost tch over 3f out* **16/1**

7 1 3/4 **Anis Etoile**[225] 5-9-8 0.. IvaMilickova 2 30
(John Berry) *s.i.s: a bhd: lost tch 3f out* **40/1**

2m 6.93s (-0.97) **Going Correction** -0.20s/f (Firm)
WFA 3 from 4yo+ 17lb **7** Ran SP% **114.1**
Speed ratings (Par 103): **95,91,87,83,76 75,73**
toteswingers: 1&2 £2.20, 1&3 £1.80, 2&3 £2.80 CSF £3.79 TOTE £1.80: £1.10, £2.60; EX 4.70.

Owner Mrs Ben Goldsmith **Bred** Goldsmith Bloodstock Partnership **Trained** Lambourn, Berks

FOCUS
An uncompetitive maiden and a modest pace resulted in a time 1.74secs slower than the earlier 56-70 handicap. The winner set a good standard and was value for a bit extra.

1522 TOTESPORTCASINO.COM H'CAP 7f 9y
5:15 (5:15) (Class 5) (0-70,70) 3-Y-O **£2,590** (£770; £385; £192) **Stalls** Low

Form RPR

005- **1** **Haatheq (USA)**[213] 6199 3-9-4 **70**.................................... TadhgO'Shea 4 81+
(J L Dunlop) *in tch: rdn to ld ent fnl 2f: r.o wl and forged ahd ins fnl f: gng away at fin* **7/2**[2]

300- **2** 1 3/4 **Jimmy The Poacher (IRE)**[190] 6829 3-9-0 **66**................. DavidNolan 5 72
(T D Easterby) *chsd ldr: ev ch and rdn over 2f out: no ex and btn jst ins fnl f* **10/1**

60-1 **3** 1 3/4 **Tribal Myth (IRE)**[10] 1298 3-8-9 **61**.............................. FrankieDettori 7 62
(K A Ryan) *wnt rt s: sn rcvrd and led: rdn wl over 2f out: hdd ent fnl 2f: no ex and btn ent fnl f* **5/4**[1]

140- **4** 1 1/4 **Truly Magic**[187] 6895 3-8-7 **59**... DavidProbert 2 57
(H J L Dunlop) *hld up in tch in rr: rdn and effrt wl over 2f out: no imp and btn over 1f out* **10/1**

6U3- **5** 1 **Sarahthecarer (IRE)**[8] 1368 3-8-7 **66**................................. DEEgan(7) 1 61
(P M Mooney, Ire) *sn nudged along towards rr: rdn 3f out: hung rt and no prog u.p over 1f out* **11/1**

-330 **6** 3 **Tilsworth Glenboy**[7] 1392 3-8-13 **65**................................ SebSanders 3 52
(J R Jenkins) *t.k.h: hld up in tch in rr: rdn and effrt wl over 2f out: wknd wl over 1f out* **6/1**[3]

00-0 **7** 2 **High Holborn (IRE)**[17] 1178 3-8-10 **62**........................(v1) PaulFitzsimons 6 47
(Miss J R Tooth) *dwlt: t.k.h: hdwy to press ldrs after 2f: rdn over 2f out: wknd and edgd rt 2f out* **33/1**

00-0 **8** 6 **Dovedon Diva**[27] 1029 3-8-5 **57** oh1 ow1....................... SaleemGolam 8 26
(T Keddy) *in tch on outer: rdn over 2f out: hung rt and btn wl over 1f out: eased ins fnl f* **33/1**

1m 24.53s (-1.67) **Going Correction** -0.20s/f (Firm) **8** Ran SP% **113.3**
Speed ratings (Par 98): **101,99,97,95,94 91,88,81**
toteswingers: 1&2 £4.60, 1&3 £1.90, 2&3 £5.10 CSF £37.07 CT £64.31 TOTE £5.00: £1.60, £3.00, £1.10; EX 36.80 Place 6: £246.94 Place 5: £19.17.

Owner Hamdan Al Maktoum **Bred** Shadwell Farm LLC **Trained** Arundel, W Sussex

FOCUS
A modest three-year-old handicap but probably reasonable form for the grade.

Haatheq(USA) Official explanation: trainer's rep said, regarding apparent improvement in form, that the colt had matured and developed over the winter.

T/Plt: £265.90 to a £1 stake. Pool: £51,297.71. 140.81 winning tickets. T/Qpdt: £11.40 to a £1 stake. Pool: £3,441.88. 221.90 winning tickets. SP

[1331] RIPON (R-H)
Saturday, April 24

OFFICIAL GOING: Good to firm (good in places; 8.6)
Rail on bend into straight moved out 6metres increasing distances on round course by 12yds.
Wind: Slight, behind Weather: Overcast

1523 TOTESCOOP6 H'CAP 6f
2:15 (2:16) (Class 3) (0-95,95) 3-Y-O
£7,788 (£2,332; £1,166; £583; £291; £146) **Stalls** Low

Form RPR

-452 **1** **Jack My Boy (IRE)**[7] 1376 3-8-1 **81** oh1..........(b1) AndrewHeffernan(3) 2 89
(P D Evans) *led after 1f: mde rest: drvn 2f out: hrd pressed fnl f: styd on wl* **4/1**[2]

112- **2** 1 **Midnight Martini**[217] 6090 3-9-1 **92**.................................... DavidAllan 1 97
(T D Easterby) *led 1f: chsd wnr: effrt 2f out: ev ch fnl f: hld towards fin* **4/1**[2]

000- **3** 4 **Ballodair (IRE)**[211] 6247 3-8-4 **81** oh3.............................. PaulHanagan 4 73
(R A Fahey) *trckd ldrs: effrt over 1f out: outpcd fnl f* **8/1**

511- **4** 2 1/4 **The Only Boss (IRE)**[189] 6841 3-8-13 **90**..................... JamieSpencer 5 75
(W J Haggas) *dwlt: t.k.h: hld up in tch: effrt 1/2-way: edgd rt and outpcd 2f out: n.d after* **15/8**[1]

01-0 **5** hd **Comedy Hall (USA)**[10] 1315 3-9-0 **91**.............................. JoeFanning 7 75
(M Johnston) *prom: rdn over 2f out: wknd over 1f out* **11/2**[3]

1121 **6** 30 **Lewyn**[16] 1191 3-8-9 **86**... WilliamBuick 8 —
(K A Ryan) *bhd on outside: hung rt and struggling 1/2-way: sn btn: eased whn no ch fnl f* **8/1**

1m 10.79s (-2.21) **Going Correction** -0.40s/f (Firm) **6** Ran SP% **112.4**
Speed ratings (Par 102): **98,96,91,88,88 48**
Tote Swingers: 1&2 £2.70, 1&3 £6.70, 2&3 £6.20 CSF £20.11 CT £119.09 TOTE £5.10: £2.20, £2.00; EX 18.70 Trifecta £118.00 Pool: £432.32 - 2.71 winning units..
Owner Terry Earle **Bred** Mrs Sheila Walker **Trained** Pandy, Monmouths

FOCUS
The rail on the bottom bend into the straight was moved out by 6m, increasing distances on the round course by 12 yards. The ground had been watered in the straight only and one of the jockeys in the first reported it to be riding just on the fast side of good. A decent handicap for three-year-olds in which the field raced on the stands' side. It was dominated throughout by the first pair nearest the rail. With a couple running moderately, the form does not look that strong for the grade but the time was quick, 0.31 seconds faster than the RP standard. The winner produced a personal best.

NOTEBOOK
Jack My Boy(IRE), for whom there was support, had posted a career best when runner-up at Doncaster the previous Saturday and was effectively 3lb higher here. Fitted with first-time blinkers, he was pushed along from the stalls to grab the lead after a furlong and got over to the stands' rail just past halfway. The runner-up looked a big threat but he saw her off in willing fashion. He takes his racing well and may have more to offer. (op 13-2)
Midnight Martini had a fine first season, bagging a big pot in a sales race at York before finishing second in an Ayr Group 3. She travelled well on this reappearance, always up with the speed, but could not quite force her way past the winner, who had inconvenienced her slightly when crossing to the rail over two furlongs out. While this was an encouraging effort, she may not prove that easy to place this year. (op 7-2 tchd 9-2)
Ballodair(IRE), another for whom there was money, was on his toes in the paddock. Chasing the first two in vain all the way, he stuck on for third. He has been gelded since his last appearance at two and this was a satisfactory return from 3lb out of the handicap. (op 12-1 tchd 15-2)
The Only Boss(IRE) bolted to post when winning at Catterick on his last start as a juvenile and connections took precautions here, assigning two handlers to him in the paddock before Spencer took him very steadily to post. Slowest to leave the gate, the favourite never looked happy on this undulating track and was in trouble by halfway. Official explanation: jockey said colt was unsuited by the track (op 13-8)
Comedy Hall(USA) did not show a great deal on his return at Newmarket and he could never make his presence felt from a wide draw here, disputing third for much of the way before fading. He is not a straightforward ride and is one to have doubts about. (op 13-2)
Lewyn has been in terrific form on the Wolverhampton Polytrack but this represented a totally different test. Even so, she should have run better than she did and presumably something was amiss. Official explanation: jockey said filly was unsuited by the track (op 15-2 tchd 7-1)

1524 STOWE FAMILY LAW LLP H'CAP 5f
2:50 (2:50) (Class 5) (0-75,71) 4-Y-O+ **£2,914** (£867; £433; £216) **Stalls** Low

Form RPR

3216 **1** **Sir Geoffrey (IRE)**[15] 1200 4-9-1 **68**...........................(b) FrederikTylicki 3 79
(J A Glover) *cl up stands' side: led that gp 2f out: drvn and hld on wl fnl f: 1st of 7 in gp* **11/1**

50-6 **2** nk **Sands Crooner (IRE)**[8] 1364 7-8-13 **66**....................(v) PaulMulrennan 4 76
(J G Given) *in tch stands' side: effrt over 1f out: swtchd rt ins fnl f: r.o wl: jst hld: 2nd of 7 in gp* **8/1**

-050 **3** 1 **Lucky Art (USA)**[15] 1200 4-9-1 **68**.......................... SilvestreDeSousa 12 74
(Mrs R A Carr) *chsd far side ldr: effrt over 1f out: kpt on to ld that gp nr fin: hld by stands' side pair: 1st of 6 in gp* **16/1**

214- **4** hd **Lost In Paris (IRE)**[161] 7398 4-8-12 **65**..........................(b) DavidAllan 13 71+
(T D Easterby) *led and set decent gallop far side: rdn 2f out: kpt on: ct cl home: 2nd of 6 in gp* **9/2**[2]

05-2 **5** 3/4 **Kyzer Chief**[9] 1337 5-8-8 **61**... PaulHanagan 2 64
(R E Barr) *led stands' side gp to 2f out: kpt on same pce ins fnl f: 3rd of 7 in gp* **3/1**[1]

11-2 **6** hd **Diamond Blade**[18] 1147 4-8-13 **66**..................................(p) TedDurcan 6 68
(T D Easterby) *chsd stands' side ldrs: effrt 2f out: one pce fnl f: 4th of 7 in gp* **15/2**[3]

60-0 **7** 1 **Nomoreblondes**[8] 1363 6-8-13 **66**..............................(p) TonyCulhane 11 65
(P T Midgley) *in tch far side: drvn over 3f out: plugged on fnl f: no imp: 3rd of 6 in gp* **14/1**

01-4 **8** 1/2 **Select Committee**[8] 1364 5-8-13 **71**.........................(v) IanBrennan(5) 8 68
(J J Quinn) *trckd far side ldrs: effrt over 2f out: one pce fnl f: 4th of 6 in gp* **15/2**[3]

60-0 **9** 3/4 **King Of Swords (IRE)**[9] 1337 6-9-2 **69**.........................(p) EddieAhern 9 63
(N Tinkler) *hld up in tch far side: rdn 2f out: swtchd lft ins fnl f: no imp: 5th of 6 in gp* **20/1**

00-0 **10** 1 1/4 **Guertino (IRE)**[8] 1365 5-8-11 **67**............................ AndrewHeffernan(3) 7 57
(C J Teague) *dwlt: bhd stands' side: drvn 1/2-way: nvr rchd ldrs: 5th of 7 in gp* **40/1**

0-16 **11** 1/2 **Dispol Grand (IRE)**[8] 1363 4-9-2 **69**................................. PhillipMakin 5 57
(P T Midgley) *prom stands' side: rdn over 2f out: sn no ex: 6th of 7 in gp* **18/1**

600- **12** *2* **Captain Scooby**[191] 6798 4-9-1 **71**.......................... MichaelStainton(3) 1 52
(R M Whitaker) *bhd stands' side: rdn and hung rt 1/2-way: sn wknd: last of 7 in gp* **20/1**

20-0 **13** *11* **Future Gem**[11] 1276 4-8-12 **65**..................................(p) WilliamBuick 10 6
(A Dickman) *hmpd sn after s: sn wl bhd far side: nvr on terms: last of 6 in gp* **28/1**

58.24 secs (-2.46) **Going Correction** -0.40s/f (Firm) **13** Ran SP% **119.4**
Speed ratings (Par 103): **103,102,100,100,99 99,97,96,95,93 92,89,71**
Tote Swingers: 1&2 £22.90, 1&3 £39.20, 2&3 £38.10 CSF £91.64 CT £1464.60 TOTE £13.80: £3.20, £3.10, £4.10; EX 148.10 TRIFECTA Not won..
Owner Dixon, Howlett & The Chrystal Maze Ptn **Bred** P Rabbitte **Trained** Babworth, Notts
■ Stewards' Enquiry : David Allan one-day ban: used whip with excessive frequency (May 8)

FOCUS
A moderate sprint handicap. They split into two groups from the stalls, with half a dozen tacking over to the far rail and the other seven remaining on the stands' side. The first two home came from the near-side group but there was little or no advantage in racing there. Again they beat the RP standard, confirming that the ground was riding pretty fast, and the form has been rated pretty positively with the winner back to his best.
Future Gem Official explanation: jockey said filly was unsuited by the good to firm ground

1525 TOTETENTOFOLLOW.CO.UK H'CAP — 2m
3:25 (3:29) (Class 2) (0-100,97) 4-Y-0+
£14,019 (£4,198; £2,099; £1,050; £524; £263) **Stalls** High

Form RPR

310- **1** **Dazinski**[176] 7151 4-8-7 **83**.................................. TedDurcan 6 93+
(M H Tompkins) *prom: effrt over 2f out: edgd rt and led over 1f out: styd on wl u.p fnl f* **7/2**[2]

/0-1 **2** *2* **My Arch**[20] 1101 8-8-5 **80**.............................. BarryMcHugh(3) 7 85
(Ollie Pears) *hld up on ins: drvn and outpcd over 3f out: rallied over 1f out: swtchd lft and styd on fnl f: wnt 2nd nr fin: nt pce of wnr* **6/1**

30-3 **3** *hd* **Halla San**[17] 1176 8-9-11 **97**.............................. PaulHanagan 5 102
(R A Fahey) *prom: effrt and ev ch over 2f out to ins fnl f: edgd rt: kpt on same pce* **9/2**[3]

66-4 **4** *½* **Swiss Act**[24] 1069 6-9-1 **87**.............................. JoeFanning 4 91
(M Johnston) *chsd ldr: rdn and led over 2f out: hdd over 1f out: kpt on same pce fnl f* **14/1**

61-0 **5** *1¼* **Gordonsville**[20] 1101 7-8-12 **84**.......................... WilliamBuick 3 87
(J S Goldie) *hld up: rdn and outpcd 4f out: rallied over 1f out: no imp fnl f* **5/1**

04-3 **6** *10* **Bogside Theatre (IRE)**[20] 1101 6-8-6 **78** oh1............ PJMcDonald 1 69
(G M Moore) *led: rdn over 3f out: wknd fr 2f out* **5/2**[1]

0/0 **7** *8* **Track Record**[11] 1274 5-9-2 **88**.......................... GeorgeBaker 9 69
(Jonjo O'Neill) *trckd ldrs: drvn 2f out: sn wknd: eased whn no ch ins fnl f* **25/1**

321- **8** *2½* **Mudawin (IRE)**[8] 4332 9-8-3 **78**................... AndrewHeffernan(3) 2 56
(James Moffatt) *hld up: struggling and hung rt over 4f out: sn lost tch* **20/1**

3m 29.43s (-2.37) **Going Correction** -0.075s/f (Good)
WFA 4 from 5yo+ 4lb **8** Ran SP% **115.2**
Speed ratings (Par 109): **102,101,100,100,100 95,91,89**
Tote Swingers: 1&2 £6.20, 1&3 £4.70, 2&3 £5.70 CSF £24.97 CT £95.49 TOTE £4.80: £1.80, £2.10, £1.90; EX 30.40 Trifecta £106.20 Pool: £5904.04 - 4.11 winning units..
Owner Mrs Beryl Lockey **Bred** Darley **Trained** Newmarket, Suffolk

FOCUS
A valuable staying handicap but not a great race for the money. The leader slowed the pace down the far side before quickening things up on the home turn. The form is rated around the third with another personal best from the winner.

NOTEBOOK
Dazinski had a progressive profile last year until disappointing on his final start when he had probably had enough for the season. Looking fit for this reappearance, he got to the front inside the last and was driven out to score. He holds an entry in the Chester Cup and would be suited by some fast ground there, but the penalty he picks up for this may not be enough to get him in the race. (op 9-2)
My Arch was caught out when the tempo quickened in the straight and even after being switched out for a run he took time to pick up. After looking set to finish fourth he found his stride late on and finished well. Successful at Musselburgh from a 3lb lower mark last time, he handled the extra quarter mile and faster surface well and confirmed his superiority over Bogside Theatre and Gordonsville. (op 9-2)
Halla San had every chance but appeared to hang a little and could not quicken. This was a reasonable effort but he continues to prove difficult to win with. (tchd 4-1 and 5-1)
Swiss Act was sharper for his return to action last month and briefly reached the front, but could not hold on over this longer trip. (op 9-1 tchd 17-2)
Gordonsville was never able to reach a challenging position in a race not run to suit him. (op 6-1)
Bogside Theatre(IRE), runner-up in this race two years ago, adopted her usual front-running role and dictated the pace but could not hold on when tackled. (op 7-2 tchd 4-1)
Track Record has yet to show a great deal since arriving in this country from Andre Fabre's yard. He travelled quite well but did not find much when pulled out and appeared not to stay. (op 18-1 tchd 16-1)
Mudawin(IRE) was a winner on his last Flat start back in July but he has not been in much form over hurdles and was the first beaten here. (op 16-1)

1526 TOTEEXACTA (S) STKS — 1m 1f 170y
4:00 (4:00) (Class 5) 3-4-Y-0
£2,590 (£770; £385; £192) **Stalls** High

Form RPR

236 **1** **Wrongwayround (IRE)**[33] 963 4-9-10 **70**.................. PJMcDonald 9 71
(G A Swinbank) *hld up in tch: smooth hdwy over 3f out: led 2f out: edgd rt and drvn clr fnl f* **5/2**[1]

5-40 **2** *5* **Sultan's Choice**[26] 1048 3-7-13 **55**.................. AndrewHeffernan(3) 3 52
(P D Evans) *hld up: rdn over 3f out: hdwy and chsd wnr appr fnl f: kpt on same pce fnl f* **11/2**

220- **3** *2¾* **Tropical Bachelor (IRE)**[18] 6845 4-9-10 **56**...............(b) PaulHanagan 5 54
(T J Pitt) *led: rdn 4f out: hdd 2f out: sn outpcd* **9/1**

360- **4** *6* **Moggy (IRE)**[63] 7324 4-9-5 **44**...........................(p) SilvestreDeSousa 8 37
(G A Harker) *bhd: struggling 4f out: rallied appr fnl f: nvr able to chal* **16/1**

00/5 **5** *2¼* **Without Equal**[44] 858 4-9-0 **30**.............................. IanBrennan(5) 6 32
(A Dickman) *s.i.s: hld up: rdn over 3f out: nvr able to chal* **50/1**

4420 **6** *hd* **Heathyards Junior**[28] 1012 4-9-9 **66**.....................(p) DeclanCannon(5) 1 40
(A J McCabe) *hld up in midfield: outpcd 3f out: hung rt: sn no ex* **9/2**[3]

2464 **7** *25* **Monaco Dream (IRE)**[9] 1318 4-9-5 **63**.....................(p) JoeFanning 4 —
(W Jarvis) *chsd ldr tl rdn and wknd 3f out: eased whn no ch fnl f* **3/1**[2]

00-0 **8** *2½* **Cassidy K**[8] 1362 3-8-2 **53**.............................. FrannyNorton 2 —
(D W Thompson) *chsd ldrs: drvn over 2f out: sn wknd: eased whn no ch fnl f* **20/1**

4400 **9** *dist* **Mydy Easy (USA)**[10] 1293 4-9-5 **58**..........................(t) PaulPickard(5) 7 —
(P T Midgley) *bhd: struggling over 6f out: lost tch 4f out: virtually p.u* **16/1**

2m 4.32s (-1.08) **Going Correction** -0.075s/f (Good)
WFA 3 from 4yo 17lb **9** Ran SP% **115.6**
Speed ratings (Par 103): **101,97,94,90,88 88,68,66,—**
Tote Swingers: 1&2 £4.60, 1&3 £6.10, 2&3 £5.60 CSF £16.73 TOTE £3.90: £1.70, £2.20, £2.40; EX 21.50 Trifecta £115.50 Pool: £438.94 - 2.81 winning units..There was no bid for the winner.
Owner Brian Harker **Bred** Denis McDonnell **Trained** Melsonby, N Yorks

FOCUS
There were doubts over most of these in this very ordinary seller but the winner is a bit better than this grade. Three of the runners disputed a frantic pace through the early stages.
Monaco Dream(IRE) Official explanation: trainer's rep had no explanation for the poor form shown
Mydy Easy(USA) Official explanation: jockey said gelding finished lame behind

1527 TOTESWINGER MAIDEN AUCTION FILLIES' STKS — 5f
4:35 (4:38) (Class 5) 2-Y-O
£2,914 (£867; £433; £216) **Stalls** Low

Form RPR

2 **1** **Meandmyshadow**[9] 1331 2-8-4 0.................................. FrannyNorton 3 67
(A D Brown) *trckd ldrs: effrt: edgd rt and led ins fnl f: drvn out* **4/1**[2]

3 **2** *½* **Coconut Ice**[8] 1359 2-8-5 0.............................. RossAtkinson(5) 5 71
(Tom Dascombe) *led tl edgd rt and hdd ins fnl f: kpt on towards fin* **6/5**[1]

4 **3** *nk* **Glenns Princess**[10] 1292 2-8-4 0.............................. PaulHanagan 2 64
(R A Fahey) *trckd ldrs: drvn over 2f out: edgd rt and styd on ins fnl f: nrst fin* **8/1**

4 *1* **Vienna Woods (IRE)** 2-8-1 0.............................. KellyHarrison(3) 4 61+
(B M R Haslam) *dwlt: bhd tl hdwy on outside 2f out: kpt on fnl f: no imp fnl 100yds* **33/1**

32 **5** *½* **Molly Mylenis**[16] 1180 2-8-3 0..........................(v[1]) AndrewHeffernan(3) 7 61
(P D Evans) *pressed ldr: rdn 1/2-way: no ex ins fnl f* **9/2**[3]

6 *2* **Nellie Ellis (IRE)** 2-8-4 0.............................. SilvestreDeSousa 9 54+
(K A Ryan) *s.s: outpcd: hdwy 2f out: no imp fnl f* **16/1**

0 **7** *2* **Losing Draw (IRE)**[9] 1331 2-7-13 0.............................. PaulPickard(5) 1 44
(P T Midgley) *prom tl rdn and wknd fr 2f out* **12/1**

0 **8** *2½* **Reel Amber**[10] 1294 2-7-13 0.............................. JamesSullivan(5) 6 35
(T D Easterby) *towards rr: hung rt thrght: struggling fr 1/2-way* **40/1**

59.97 secs (-0.73) **Going Correction** -0.40s/f (Firm) **8** Ran SP% **113.7**
Speed ratings (Par 89): **89,88,87,86,85 82,78,74**
Tote Swingers: 1&2 £2.40, 1&3 £3.70, 2&3 £3.40 CSF £9.05 TOTE £4.20: £1.10, £1.10, £2.50; EX 10.10 Trifecta £34.60 Pool: £ 502.18 - 10.73 winning units..
Owner G Morrill **Bred** M J Dawson **Trained** Yedingham, N Yorks
■ Stewards' Enquiry : Ross Atkinson one-day ban: used whip with excessive frequency (tbn, remedial training)
Franny Norton five-day ban: used whip with excessive frequency without giving filly time to respond (May 8-12)

FOCUS
Ordinary early-season maiden form. The winner is rated to a similar level to her debut, with improvement from the second. .

NOTEBOOK
Meandmyshadow went one better than on her recent debut over course and distance. She appeared to trap her nose in the stalls and her participation briefly looked in doubt, but she showed no ill effects and ran on to strike the front inside the last. There is further improvement to come from her when she is given the chance to tackle a sixth furlong. (op 10-3)
Coconut Ice, third at Thirsk first time, was conceding weight all round. Setting the pace but again wandering and looking green, she was run down inside the last. This was an improvement on her debut form. (op 2-1)
Glenns Princess found her stride late on and finished with a flourish to grab third. This was an improvement on her debut effort and she is another who will appreciate an extra furlong. (op 13-2)
Vienna Woods(IRE), a £5,000 half-sister to the fair perfomer Outside Edge, showed promise on this debut. Outpaced early on, she improved to look a threat approaching the furlong pole and was not given a hard time when held. (op 25-1)
Molly Mylenis, visired for the first time, was tackling very different ground than when placed on her first two starts. She knew her job and raced up with the pace but faded in the final furlong. (tchd 4-1)
Nellie Ellis(IRE), the first foal of a winning half-sister to smart sprinter Godfrey Street, was a cheap buy but showed a hint of promise. She missed the break and raced in rear before making late progress. (op 10-1 tchd 9-1)

1528 BET TOTEPOOL AT TOTESPORT.COM MAIDEN STKS — 1m 1f 170y
5:10 (5:11) (Class 5) 3-Y-O
£2,914 (£867; £433; £216) **Stalls** High

Form RPR

05- **1** **Harris Tweed**[169] 7276 3-9-3 0.............................. EddieAhern 4 81
(W J Haggas) *trckd ldr: led over 3f out: drvn clr fnl f* **4/5**[1]

3 **2** *3¾* **Laverre (IRE)**[9] 1336 3-8-12 0.............................. DavidAllan 6 69
(T D Easterby) *prom: hdwy and ev ch over 3f out: one pce ins fnl f* **2/1**[2]

6 **3** *12* **Trojan Gift (USA)**[19] 1119 3-9-3 0.............................. PaulMulrennan 5 50
(Julie Camacho) *hld up: drvn over 4f out: hdwy over 2f out: plugged on fnl f: no ch w first two* **16/1**

4 *1* **Sheiling (IRE)** 3-8-12 0.............................. PaulHanagan 2 43
(R A Fahey) *hld up in tch: drvn and green 1/2-way: hdwy on outside over 2f out: no imp wl over 1f out* **8/1**[3]

4-5 **5** *1* **Brootommitty (IRE)**[15] 1203 3-8-12 0.............................. SilvestreDeSousa 1 41
(N Wilson) *t.k.h: in tch: rdn and hung rt 3f out: sn outpcd* **33/1**

005- **6** *14* **Dead Womans Pass (IRE)**[178] 7114 3-8-9 **42**.............. AshleyHamblett(3) 7 13
(N Wilson) *plld hrd: hld up: struggling 4f out: sn btn: t.o* **50/1**

0-0 **7** *4* **One Cat Diesel (IRE)**[20] 1100 3-9-0 0.............................. GaryBartley(3) 3 10
(N Wilson) *t.k.h: led to over 3f out: wknd over 2f out: t.o* **66/1**

2m 3.83s (-1.57) **Going Correction** -0.075s/f (Good) **7** Ran SP% **112.3**
Speed ratings (Par 98): **103,100,90,89,88 77,74**
Tote Swingers: 1&2 £1.20, 1&3 £3.00, 2&3 £3.20 CSF £2.44 TOTE £1.70: £1.40, £1.70; EX 2.70.
Owner B Haggas **Bred** J B Haggas **Trained** Newmarket, Suffolk

FOCUS
Not much in depth to this maiden, which was run at a moderate pace. The first two finished well clear and the winner showed big improvement.
Dead Womans Pass(IRE) Official explanation: jockey said filly hung left throughout
One Cat Diesel(IRE) Official explanation: jockeyb said gelding hung left throughout

1529 BET TOTEPOOL ON 0800 221 221 CONDITIONS STKS — 1m 4f 10y
5:45 (5:46) (Class 3) 4-Y-O+
£6,542 (£1,959; £979; £490; £244) **Stalls** High

Form RPR

115- **1** **King Of Wands**[238] 5425 4-8-8 **98**.............................. WilliamBuick 4 112+
(J H M Gosden) *t.k.h early: trckd ldrs: effrt 3f out: led wl over 1f out: edgd rt and styd on wl fnl f: eased cl home* **6/4**[1]

454- **2** *1* **Tactic**[180] 7059 4-8-12 **103**.............................. EddieAhern 2 112
(J L Dunlop) *trckd ldrs: smooth hdwy to ld over 2f out: sn rdn: hdd wl over 1f out: kpt on ins fnl f* **9/2**[3]

The Form Book, Raceform Ltd, Compton, RG20 6NL

25-0 **3** 3½ **Drill Sergeant**[17] 1176 5-8-9 105 JoeFanning 3 102
(M Johnston) *pressed ldr: led over 3f out to over 2f out: sn rdn: one pce over 1f out* **3/1**[2]
1152 **4** 7 **Spruce (USA)**[27] 1031 4-8-8 100 TedDurcan 1 95
(Miss J Feilden) *hld up: effrt on outside 3f out: edgd rt and outpcd fr 2f out* **9/2**[3]
234- **5** 19 **Classic Punch (IRE)**[204] 6452 7-9-4 102 PaulMulrennan 5 85
(D R C Elsworth) *led to over 3f out: rdn and wknd over 2f out: eased whn no ch fnl f* **11/1**
2m 33.45s (-3.25) **Going Correction** -0.075s/f (Good)
WFA 4 from 5yo+ 1lb **5** Ran SP% **109.7**
Speed ratings (Par 107): **107,106,104,99,86**
CSF £8.48 TOTE £2.10: £1.10, £1.90; EX 8.50 Place 6: £66.27 Place 5: £31.04.
Owner Normandie Stud Ltd **Bred** Normandie Stud Ltd **Trained** Newmarket, Suffolk

FOCUS
The classiest race of the day, this good conditions event was run at just an ordinary gallop. The five runners are all essentially "twilight" horses who may not prove too easy to place. Typically muddling conditions race form which could be a few pounds out either way.

NOTEBOOK
King Of Wands has the lowest BHA rating of these but progressed well for John Dunlop last year before coming up short on his first run in Listed company on his final start. After sweeping past the runner-up to lead, he was eased close home and was value for a slightly greater margin of victory. Another crack at a Listed race would be the obvious way forward with him. (op 7-4 tchd 15-8)
Tactic made the frame in three Group 3 races last term and has been gelded since his last appearance six months ago. He travelled well into the race but his stint in the lead did not last long and he was readily held by the winner. He beat the rest well enough and was going on at the finish, which augurs well for his prospects when he moves back up in trip. On the negative side he did carry his head a shade awkwardly. (op 4-1 tchd 11-2)
Drill Sergeant had 5lb in hand on these terms but was unable to make the running as he likes. Although he briefly showed in front in the straight he was soon left behind by the first two. (op 9-4)
Spruce(USA), running on fast ground for the first time, settled at the back of the field and tried without success to get into it in the straight. He has made remarkable progress since coming over from France but may find winning opportunities hard to come by in the near future, although he is still 10lb lower on sand than he is on turf. (op 5-1)
Classic Punch(IRE) won this race a year ago but was comfortably the worst in at the weights this time. He won the early skirmish for the lead with Drill Sergeant but did not offer much resistance when tackled in the straight and finished well adrift. (op 12-1 tchd 14-1)
T/Plt: £58.70 to a £1 stake. Pool: £74,362.18. 924.50 winning tickets. T/Qpdt: £4.30 to a £1 stake. Pool: £4,305.91. 732.35 winning tickets. RY

1497 SANDOWN (R-H)
Saturday, April 24

OFFICIAL GOING: Good (good to firm in back straight on flat course; good to firm in places on jumps courses; 8.6)
Rails in back straight and around home bend at outermost configuration adding circa 8yds to distances on round course. Other races under Rules of Jump Racing.
Wind: Light, half behind Weather: Sunny, warm

1530 CASINO AT BET365.COM FLAT V JUMP JOCKEYS H'CAP 1m 14y
1:00 (1:00) (Class 4) (0-80,78) 4-Y-O+ **£6,476** (£1,927; £963; £481) **Stalls** High

Form RPR
4524 **1** **Halsion Chancer**[12] 1258 6-10-12 **72** AdamKirby 9 80
(J R Best) *hld up in 8th: prog over 2f out: rdn and decisive move to ld over 1f out: sn over a l clr and in command: drvn out* **8/1**
16-6 **2** 1¾ **Black N Brew (USA)**[73] 485 4-10-12 **72** APMcCoy 7 76+
(J R Best) *trckd ldrs: looking for room and lost pl sltly 2f out: swtchd ins and prog over 1f out: drvn and styd on to take 2nd nr fin* **12/1**
660- **3** nk **Directorship**[194] 6740 4-11-3 **77** TimmyMurphy 13 80
(P R Chamings) *hld up in last pair: plenty to do 3f out: gd prog fr 2f out: chsd wnr 1f out: no imp: lost 2nd nr fin* **7/1**
5351 **4** 1½ **Millfields Dreams**[9] 1323 11-10-10 **70** (p) NeilCallan 4 73+
(P Leech) *hld up in 10th: rdn whn nt clr run 3f out: effrt whn nowhere to go and snatched up 2f out: prog over 1f out: styd on: nrst fin* **16/1**
104- **5** 1½ **Kiss A Prince**[176] 7149 4-10-10 **70** RichardHughes 11 66
(D K Ivory) *hld up in last: prog on wd outside over 2f out: kpt on fr over 1f out: no threat* **11/2**[3]
0-00 **6** ¾ **Mr Udagawa**[7] 1388 4-10-9 **69** (p) TomQueally 10 64+
(B J Llewellyn) *settled in 7th: rdn over 3f out: prog but nt clrest of passages fr 2f out: no hdwy fnl f* **14/1**
505- **7** 2½ **Aurora Sky (IRE)**[233] 5591 4-10-10 **70** AidanColeman 6 59
(J Akehurst) *hld up in 6th: prog over 2f out: led briefly wl over 1f out: wknd fnl f* **14/1**
4-15 **8** 9 **Striding Edge (IRE)**[12] 1265 4-11-4 **78** SamThomas 3 46
(W R Muir) *hld up in 9th: rdn and effrt on outer over 2f out: no prog and btn over 1f out: wknd* **7/2**[1]
0000 **9** 1¼ **Carlitos Spirit (IRE)**[5] 1426 6-11-1 **75** RichardJohnson 8 40
(I W McInnes) *pressed ldr to over 2f out: wknd qckly* **16/1**
603- **10** 12 **Twilight Star (IRE)**[208] 6336 6-11-0 **74** KierenFallon 5 12
(R A Teal) *led at str pce: hdd & wknd wl over 1f out: eased* **5/1**[2]
3100 **11** nse **Sapphire Prince (USA)**[9] 1322 4-10-9 **69** SteveDrowne 2 7
(J R Best) *trckd ldng pair: rdn over 2f out: sn wknd rapidly* **40/1**
-000 **12** 12 **Best In Class**[31] 975 4-10-11 **71** (v) PaddyBrennan 14 —
(S C Williams) *trckd ldng pair: rdn and stl cl up 2f out: wkng whn n.m.r over 1f out: eased: t.o* **25/1**
1m 45.03s (1.73) **Going Correction** +0.10s/f (Good) **12** Ran SP% **117.0**
Speed ratings (Par 105): **95,93,92,91,89 89,86,77,76,64 64,52**
toteswingers: 1&2 £30.70, 1&3 £19.50, 2&3 £13.70 CSF £98.92 CT £717.59 TOTE £10.10: £2.70, £3.60, £2.50; EX 70.30 TRIFECTA Not won..
Owner Halsion Ltd **Bred** Mrs S Hansford **Trained** Hucking, Kent

FOCUS
A competitive novelty event, as is often the case, though probably not form to put much faith in due to the nature of the race, though it was run at a good gallop. The first four came from the rear. Trainer John Best was responsible for the one-two.
Striding Edge(IRE) Official explanation: vet said gelding finished distressed

1531 BET365 MILE (GROUP 2) 1m 14y
3:40 (3:44) (Class 1) 4-Y-O+
£56,770 (£21,520; £10,770; £5,370; £2,690; £1,350) **Stalls** High

Form RPR
142- **1** **Paco Boy (IRE)**[269] 4419 5-9-0 124 RichardHughes 3 123+
(R Hannon) *t.k.h: hld up in 5th: smooth prog to trck ldrs 2f out: led jst ins fnl f: qcknd away impressively* **11/10**[1]
130- **2** 3¼ **Pressing (IRE)**[132] 7746 7-9-4 117 NeilCallan 1 120
(M A Jarvis) *t.k.h: trckd ldng pair: led jst over 2f out: rdn and hdd jst ins fnl f: kpt on but no match for wnr* **16/1**
2/1- **3** 1½ **The Cheka (IRE)**[281] 4052 4-9-0 108 KierenFallon 8 113+
(Eve Johnson Houghton) *hld up in 6th: shkn up over 2f out: sn outpcd: styd on fr over 1f out: tk 3rd last strides* **14/1**
5510 **4** nk **Cat Junior (USA)**[28] 1022 5-9-0 115 (bt) MartinDwyer 4 112
(B J Meehan) *led at decent pce: hdd and rdn jst over 2f out: outpcd over 1f out: lost 3rd last strides* **11/1**
645- **5** 1¾ **Beacon Lodge (IRE)**[203] 6505 5-9-0 113 AdamKirby 5 108
(C G Cox) *t.k.h: hld up last: pushed along over 2f out and limited prog: shkn up and kpt on fnl f: no threat* **25/1**
16-0 **6** hd **Confront**[28] 1025 5-9-0 115 RyanMoore 7 107
(Sir Michael Stoute) *chsd ldng trio: first one u.p 3f out: sn struggling: plugged on fr over 1f out* **4/1**[2]
102- **7** ¾ **Border Patrol**[174] 7208 4-9-0 114 SteveDrowne 9 106
(R Charlton) *trckd ldr: chal and upsides jst over 2f out: wknd over 1f out* **14/1**
151- **8** 1¼ **Fareer**[310] 3049 4-9-0 100 RichardHills 2 103
(E A L Dunlop) *t.k.h: hld up in 7th: shkn up on outer over 2f out: no prog wl over 1f out: fdd* **16/1**
111- **9** 1 **Prince Of Dance**[175] 7186 4-9-0 108 RichardKingscote 6 100
(Tom Dascombe) *hld up in last pair: shkn up and no prog over 2f out* **8/1**[3]
1m 41.65s (-1.65) **Going Correction** +0.10s/f (Good) **9** Ran SP% **116.0**
Speed ratings (Par 115): **112,108,107,106,105 105,104,103,102**
toteswingers: 1&2 £6.90, 1&3 £3.70, 2&3 £10.00 CSF £22.17 TOTE £2.10: £1.20, £4.70, £2.30; EX 27.00 Trifecta £140.00 Pool: £1326.53 - 7.01 winning units..
Owner The Calvera Partnership No 2 **Bred** Mrs Joan Browne **Trained** East Everleigh, Wilts

FOCUS
The match between the front two in the market didn't develop, and Richard Hannon's record in the race now reads five wins in the last seven years. Unsurprisingly, it was the quickest of the three races run at the distance. Paco Boy had plenty in hand on pre-race figures and the form is rated around the runner-up.

NOTEBOOK
Paco Boy(IRE), not having to shoulder the penalty he did when winning the race a year ago, his first win at 1m, went on to capture the Group 1 Queen Anne, and arguably bettered that form when chasing home Rip Van Winkle in the Sussex Stakes. Although connections were concerned over the ground being too quick, his class really shone through and, having been asked to change gear over 1f out, he readily did so, and was soon clear. This win suggests he is as good, if not better, than last season, and he looks sure to be a major force in all the major 1m Group 1 races once again, with the Lockinge the next target before attempting to win a second straight Queen Anne. (op 11-8)
Pressing(IRE) ◆, who wasn't fancied in the market on this first run since finishing last in the Hong Kong Mile, ran a cracker under the penalty. He looked to be going powerfully when sent to the front over 2f out, but had no answer when the winner produced his burst. Amazingly, he has still to win a race in Britain, and it's once again likely that he will ply his trade in Europe this summer, with a return to Italy next on the agenda.
The Cheka(IRE), who has only made the racecourse three times up until now - winning twice, including a decent conditions race at Newbury last season - was up to 1m for the first time, but clearly goes well fresh and there were plenty of positives to be taken from his performance. He was a little outpaced when initially asked for his effort, but Kieren Fallon, with the future in mind, was keen not to beat him up, and the pair came home in taking fashion for third. The rider reported that he will be better suited by a straight mile, so it would come as no surprise were he to give the winner more of a race in the Lockinge. (op 12-1 tchd 11-1)
Cat Junior(USA), winner of a Group 3 on Tapeta at Meydan in March, took them along at a decent clip, but was always going to struggle to hold on and he was overtaken by the classier ones at the business end. (op 10-1 tchd 12-1)
Beacon Lodge(IRE) stayed on without threatening, and he will find easier opportunities. His rider reported that he ran too free. Official explanation: jockey said horse ran too free (op 18-1)
Confront was a major disappointment. He progressed well last season, winning a Group 3, and could be forgiven his down-the-field run in the Dubai Duty Free on account of meeting interference. Like so many from this yard, he was expected to have progressed again from four to five, but was made to look woefully one-paced, and it must be wondered whether he now needs 1m2f, a distance his sire excelled at. (op 9-2)
Border Patrol showed himself to be very smart on his favoured soft surface last season, winning a Group 3 at the Curragh, and is certainly the type to have progressed again from three to four. He wouldn't have been at his best here, possibly feeling the ground late on, and he certainly deserves another chance. (op 11-1)
Fareer was keen and didn't get home on this first run since winning last season's Britannia. (op 12-1)
Prince Of Dance, who made the step up from handicaps when winning a Listed race at Newmarket last October, was backed beforehand, but his stable aren't in top form yet, and he could make no impression having been held up at the back. It's likely a slower surface would suit, too. (op 11-1 tchd 15-2)

1532 BET365 GORDON RICHARDS STKS (GROUP 3) 1m 2f 7y
4:15 (4:15) (Class 1) 4-Y-O+
£36,900 (£13,988; £7,000; £3,490; £1,748; £877) **Stalls** High

Form RPR
142- **1** **Glass Harmonium (IRE)**[190] 6812 4-9-0 112 RyanMoore 3 116
(Sir Michael Stoute) *hld up in 6th: gd prog on outer 2f out: led wl over 1f out: edgd rt after: drvn and jnd last 100yds: battled on wl* **5/1**[2]
/10- **2** hd **Redwood**[345] 2014 4-9-0 107 MichaelHills 4 116
(B W Hills) *nudged along in last: effrt on outer over 2f out: gd prog to go 2nd 1f out: jnd wnr last 100yds and looked likely to go by: jst denied nr fin* **11/1**
211- **3** 4½ **Laaheb**[175] 7188 4-9-0 112 RichardHills 2 107
(M A Jarvis) *led: rdn and jnd over 2f out: hdd and outpcd wl over 1f out* **9/4**[1]
-220 **4** 1¼ **Crowded House**[28] 1027 4-9-0 117 KierenFallon 5 107+
(B J Meehan) *trckd ldng trio: rdn and nt qckn whn hmpd wl over 1f out: hmpd again jst over 1f out: kpt on fnl f but no ch* **9/4**[1]
30-0 **5** ¾ **Soul City (IRE)**[35] 946 4-9-0 110 RichardHughes 6 103
(R Hannon) *trckd ldr 4f: drvn over 3f out: tried to keep in tch u.p 2f out: steadily fdd* **25/1**
01-4 **6** 1¾ **Steele Tango (USA)**[9] 1328 5-9-3 112 LiamKeniry 7 102
(R A Teal) *hld up in 5th: rdn 3f out and sn outpcd in last: n.d after* **12/1**
1-12 **7** 1 **Tranquil Tiger**[9] 1328 6-9-3 112 (b) TomQueally 1 100
(H R A Cecil) *sn prom: trckd ldr 6f out: poised to chal over 2f out gng easily: rdn 2f out and fnd nil: wknd rapidly over 1f out* **6/1**[3]
2m 8.03s (-2.47) **Going Correction** +0.10s/f (Good) **7** Ran SP% **112.4**
Speed ratings (Par 113): **113,112,109,108,107 106,105**
toteswingers: 1&2 £8.70, 1&3 £2.30, 2&3 £10.90 CSF £53.85 TOTE £5.50: £3.20, £5.10; EX 51.70.
Owner Ballymacoll Stud **Bred** Ballymacoll Stud Farm Ltd **Trained** Newmarket, Suffolk

FOCUS
Some good horses have won this, Sir Michael Stoute taking the last two runnings with Ask and Tartan Bearer, but this year's renewal didn't look the strongest, for all that it was competitive. The first two finished clear and the winner is rated to the level of last year's Royal Ascot win.

NOTEBOOK
Glass Harmonium(IRE), though winless in three previous tries at Group level, came close when just denied by Steele Tango at Newmarket on his final start at three. As is often the case with horses from the stable, he looks to have done really well from three to four and, not for the first time, showed a particularly pleasing attitude to hold on. The way in which he made his ground was impressive, Ryan Moore driving him to the front over 1f out, and both the way he stayed on and his breeding suggest that he will stay 1m4f. Expected to make plenty of improvement on this by his trainer, he has work to do to become a Group 1 performer, but is clearly heading the right way, and the Tattersalls Gold Cup was mentioned as his next possible target. (op 9-2)

Redwood hadn't been seen since beating only one home in the Dante last May, and had very much become a forgotten horse. A fine-looking son of High Chaparral, he looked a bit rusty, and had to be nudged along early, but came with a strong-looking challenge inside the final 2f, and looked set to claim the winner close home, but his lack of experience may still have been telling a bit and he failed to get past. He should learn a lot from this, has always been highly regarded, and is expected to improve for 1m4f, so looks a horse to keep on side. Official explanation: jockey said colt hung right-handed (op 12-1 tchd 9-1)

Laaheb was a most progressive 3-y-o last season, winning four times, including a Listed contest at Newmarket on his final start and, though this represented another step forward, his yard has made a very good start to the season. Soon in front, it was clear from over 2f out that he wasn't going to win, but he kept on well enough, despite getting a bit squeezed for room. Considering he had things his own way in front, this could go down as a little disappointing, but it would come as no surprise were he to improve again for a step up to 1m4f. (op 2-1)

Crowded House, who finished ninth - beaten 3l - in the Dubai World Cup, needs things to fall right for him, and they certainly didn't here as he was twice hampered, but he was already under pressure and looking held at the time. He's not going to be an easy horse to win with in these small-field Group races, for all that he has plenty of natural ability. (op 5-2 tchd 11-4)

Soul City(IRE), well held in the Winter Derby on his reappearance, was well placed just in behind the leader, but couldn't quicken and was ultimately well held. He was reported to have hung right, and will find more winnable opportunities back down in grade. Official explanation: jockey said colt hung right-handed (op 20-1)

Steele Tango(USA), a satisfactory fourth in the Earl Of Sefton on his reappearance, looked vulnerable under his 3lb penalty, and couldn't muster the speed to mount a challenge. (op 16-1)

Tranquil Tiger gained a first success at this level when winning the Winter Derby, and has since run well in defeat in the Earl Of Sefton. He looked vulnerable here under a 3lb penalty, though, and found very little, having travelled strongly. (op 7-1 tchd 11-2)

1533 POKER AT BET365.COM H'CAP — 1m 14y
4:50 (4:50) (Class 2) (0-100,100) 4-Y-0+
£9,969 (£2,985; £1,492; £747; £372; £187) Stalls High

Form / RPR

111- **1** **Mabait**[180] 7060 4-8-12 94 ... KierenFallon 4 — 112+
(L M Cumani) *hld up in 5th and off the pce: stdy prog over 2f out: led over 1f out gng easily: romped clr* 9/4[2]

5206 **2** 3 ¼ **Tartan Gigha (IRE)**[11] 1274 5-8-13 95 ... RichardHills 2 — 104
(M Johnston) *hld up in last pair and wl off the pce early: stdy prog fr 2f out: styd on to take 2nd last 100yds: no ch w wnr* 6/1[3]

30-2 **3** 2 **Dunn'o (IRE)**[21] 1085 5-8-12 94 ... AdamKirby 3 — 98
(C G Cox) *taken down early: led at str pce but pressed: jnd over 2f out: hdd and outpcd over 1f out: one pce and lost 2nd last 100yds* 2/1[1]

04-0 **4** 2 ¼ **Mount Hadley (USA)**[17] 1156 6-8-5 87 ...(b) NickyMackay 7 — 86
(G A Butler) *pressed ldr: upsides over 2f out to over 1f out: wknd fnl f* 16/1

303- **5** nse **General Eliott (IRE)**[49] 7810 5-9-4 100 ... NeilCallan 5 — 99
(P F I Cole) *chsd ldng trio: rdn over 2f out: sn outpcd: plugged on fnl f: nrly snatched 4th* 20/1

22-2 **6** 1 **Chapter And Verse (IRE)**[21] 1088 4-8-2 87 Louis-PhilippeBeuzelin(3) 6 — 83
(Mike Murphy) *hld up in last pair and wl off the pce early: rdn 3f out: no prog: plugged on* 8/1

120- **7** shd **Swift Chap**[175] 7189 4-8-4 86 ... KirstyMilczarek 1 — 82
(B R Millman) *chsd ldng pair to over 2f out: steadily wknd u.p* 11/1

100- **8** 2 ¾ **Mujood**[195] 6694 7-8-8 90 ... TomQueally 8 — 80
(Eve Johnson Houghton) *nvr gng wl: rdn and struggling towards rr 1/2-way: sn no ch* 20/1

1m 42.19s (-1.11) **Going Correction** +0.10s/f (Good) 8 Ran SP% **113.2**
Speed ratings (Par 109): **109,105,103,101,101 100,100,97**
toteswingers: 1&2 £4.10, 1&3 £1.30, 2&3 £3.20 CSF £15.93 CT £29.59 TOTE £3.00: £1.40, £2.10, £1.10; EX 18.30 Trifecta £27.50 Pool: £1120.82 - 30.07 winning units. Place 6: £491.82 Place 5: £113.59.
Owner Sheikh Mohammed Obaid Al Maktoum **Bred** L A C Ashby Newhall Estate Farm **Trained** Newmarket, Suffolk

FOCUS
A decent handicap, nothing more, but it was hard not to be taken with Mabait's performance. He could be headed for Listed classs at least. The second is rated to the best view pof his previous form.

NOTEBOOK
Mabait readily disposed of his rivals. Ridden by Kieren Fallon, who was bidding to maintain his 100 per cent record with the son of Kyllachy (previously 3-3), he was 7lb higher than when winning at this trip for the first at Leicester on his final outing at three (Swift Chap second), but it made no difference whatsoever as, having readily closed 2f out - with Fallon looking round - he just had to be nudged out to score a most emphatic victory, one that marks him down as a possible pattern performer in the making. He can expect a stiff rise off the back of this, but can be rated as a far easier winner than the official margin suggests, and would already have to be considered a major Royal Hunt Cup contender. (tchd 2-1 and 11-4)

Tartan Gigha(IRE) ran his best race since returning from Dubai, but was no match for the winner, and is going to remain vulnerable to less exposed types off his current rating. (tchd 11-2)

Dunn'o(IRE), 8lb higher than when the race last year, had run really well on his reappearance at Kempton, but raced keenly in setting a fast enough gallop, and it took its toll late on. (op 11-4)

Mount Hadley(USA) isn't the strongest of finishers, and the drop back to 1m from 1m2f didn't really help. (op 12-1)

General Eliott(IRE), well beaten on last month's hurdling debut, was never going to win this off 100, and he stayed on in a manner to suggest a step back up in trip will suit. (op 14-1)

Chapter And Verse(IRE) was entitled to reverse Leicester form with the winner strictly at the weights, but evidently isn't as progressive, and may just have needed this. (op 15-2 tchd 9-1)

Swift Chap never got into the race on this return to turf. (op 10-1 tchd 12-1)

Mujood wasn't on a going day. (op 16-1)

T/Jkpt: Not won. T/Plt: £590.40 to a £1 stake. Pool: £142,120.70. 175.71 winning tickets. T/Qpdt: £37.50 to a £1 stake. Pool: £13,329.77. 262.82 winning tickets. JN

1503 WOLVERHAMPTON (A.W) (L-H)
Saturday, April 24

OFFICIAL GOING: Standard
Wind: Light behind Weather: Hazy sunshine

1534 CE PROPERTY SERVICES GROUP AMATEUR RIDERS' H'CAP — 5f 216y(P)
6:50 (6:52) (Class 6) (0-60,60) 4-Y-0+
£1,714 (£527; £263) Stalls Low

Form / RPR

0101 **1** **Ride A White Swan**[14] 1235 5-11-0 60 ...(p) MrSWalker 5 — 69
(D Shaw) *stdd s: hld up: hdwy over 1f out: swtchd rt sn after: led ins fnl f: hung rt: rdn out* 2/1[1]

-213 **2** hd **Miss Firefly**[71] 532 5-10-6 57 ... MrPPrince(5) 2 — 65
(R J Hodges) *trckd ldrs: gng wl over 1f out and looked the likely wnr: delayed chal: ev ch whn hmpd 1f out: r.o* 17/2[3]

55 **3** 1 ¼ **Sir Mozart (IRE)**[19] 1129 7-10-7 58 ... MrDLQueally(5) 3 — 62
(B J Curley) *hld up: nt clr run over 2f out: hdwy over 1f out: edgd rt: r.o: nt rch ldrs* 14/1

0313 **4** 1 **Captain Kallis (IRE)**[24] 1072 4-10-6 57 ...(be) MrCMartin(5) 4 — 58
(D J S Ffrench Davis) *sn chsng ldr: led over 2f out: rdn over 1f out: hdd and unable qck ins fnl f* 11/2[2]

1026 **5** ¾ **Guildenstern (IRE)**[10] 1305 8-10-8 59 ... MrJPFeatherstone(5) 11 — 57
(P Howling) *hld up: swtchd lft over 1f out: r.o wl ins fnl f: nt rch ldrs* 20/1

5650 **6** hd **Loyal Royal (IRE)**[33] 961 7-10-3 56 ...(bt) MissHDavies(7) 12 — 54
(J M Bradley) *s.i.s: hld up: r.o wl ins fnl f: nvr nrr* 25/1

4015 **7** 1 **Muktasb (USA)**[17] 1166 9-10-12 58 ...(v) MrsMMorris 8 — 53
(D Shaw) *mid-div: plld hrd: hmpd 4f out: hdwy over 2f out: rdn over 1f out: no ex ins fnl f* 14/1

455- **8** 1 ¼ **Two Turtle Doves (IRE)**[179] 7082 4-10-6 57 ... MissMMullineaux(5) 9 — 48
(M Mullineaux) *chsd ldrs: rdn over 1f out: sn wknd* 33/1

624- **9** 1 ½ **If Only**[208] 6340 4-10-7 58 ... MrBMMorris(5) 1 — 44
(J Jay) *s.i.s: sn pushed along in rr: nvr nrr* 17/2[3]

30-0 **10** nk **Blessed Place**[17] 1166 10-10-7 56 ... MrStephenHarrison(3) 13 — 41
(D J S Ffrench Davis) *led: hdd over 2f out: sn rdn: wknd ins fnl f* 40/1

156 **11** ½ **Albero Di Giuda (IRE)**[46] 836 5-10-6 57 ...(t) MrMOwen(5) 10 — 40
(F Sheridan) *plld hrd and prom: hmpd 4f out: rdn and wknd over 1f out* 14/1

450- **12** ½ **Silvanus (IRE)**[188] 6877 5-10-6 57 ... MissWGibson(5) 7 — 39
(P T Midgley) *hld up: plld hrd: hdwy and rn into the bk of rivals 4f out: rdn: edgd lft and wknd over 1f out* 20/1

3320 **13** hd **Sir Edwin Landseer (USA)**[17] 1167 10-11-0 60 ..(be) MrJoshuaMoore 6 — 41
(G L Moore) *chsd ldrs: rdn over 2f out: wknd over 1f out* 12/1

1m 16.78s (1.78) **Going Correction** +0.125s/f (Slow) 13 Ran SP% **116.2**
Speed ratings (Par 101): **93,92,91,89,88 88,87,85,83,83 82,81,81**
Tote Swingers: 1&2 £5.00, 1&3 £9.40, 2&3 £16.30 CSF £16.56 CT £172.45 TOTE £3.00: £1.40, £1.10, £4.80; EX 19.80.
Owner N Morgan **Bred** Michael John Williamson **Trained** Sproxton, Leics

FOCUS
A modest amateur riders' handicap. It was strongly run and the winner ran a small personal best, with the second running her best race since she was a 3yo.

1535 CLEANEVENT H'CAP — 5f 20y(P)
7:20 (7:22) (Class 6) (0-65,72) 3-Y-0
£1,774 (£523; £262) Stalls Low

Form / RPR

5425 **1** **Val C**[7] 1390 3-8-13 60 ...(b) SebSanders 7 — 65
(M Botti) *a.p: chsd ldr 2f out: rdn to ld and edgd lft ins fnl f: jst hld on* 3/1[2]

2340 **2** ¾ **Duke Of Rainford**[19] 1118 3-8-10 57 ... TonyHamilton 3 — 59
(M Herrington) *s.i.s: hld up: hdwy over 1f out: fin wl: nt quite get up* 12/1

50-5 **3** 2 ½ **Ishipink**[16] 1187 3-7-13 51 oh5 ... AmyBaker(5) 2 — 44
(R J Hodges) *led: rdn over 1f out: hdd and no ex ins fnl f*

4422 **4** 1 ¼ **Papageno**[9] 1316 3-9-2 63 ... JimCrowley 4 — 52
(J R Jenkins) *hld up: hdwy 2f out: sn rdn: styd on same pce* 9/2[3]

2054 **5** 2 **Tulip Explosion**[9] 1316 3-8-4 51 oh3 ... JimmyQuinn 1 — 32
(D Shaw) *hld up: hung rt 1/2-way: nvr trbld ldrs* 14/1

34-5 **6** ¾ **Madam Isshe**[33] 962 3-8-11 58 ... TomMcLaughlin 5 — 37
(M S Saunders) *chsd ldrs: rdn 1/2-way: wknd over 1f out* 20/1

00-0 **7** 4 ½ **Greenore Gordon**[45] 849 3-8-5 52 oh3 ow1 ... AdrianNicholls 6 — 14
(M S Saunders) *chsd ldr 3f: sn rdn: wknd fnl f* 20/1

3-01 **8** 4 ½ **Vanilla Loan (IRE)**[11] 1280 3-9-11 72 ... MartinDwyer 9 — 18
(M Botti) *s.i.s: sn pushed along in rr: bhd fr 1/2-way* 11/8[1]

0420 **9** 10 **Lets Move It**[9] 1316 3-8-4 51 oh4 ...(v) DavidProbert 8 — —
(D Shaw) *sn outpcd: bhd fr 1/2-way* 20/1

62.98 secs (0.68) **Going Correction** +0.125s/f (Slow) 9 Ran SP% **116.4**
Speed ratings (Par 96): **99,97,93,91,88 87,80,73,57**
Tote Swingers: 1&2 £5.70, 1&3 £24.30, 2&3 £32.50 CSF £35.33 CT £1204.85 TOTE £2.90: £1.10, £2.20, £16.50; EX 34.10.
Owner Franconson Partners **Bred** Black Horse Farm **Trained** Newmarket, Suffolk

FOCUS
This was run at a blistering gallop and very few got anywhere near landing a blow. Four of these were out of the weights and this is weak form, but the winner deserves credit.
Papageno Official explanation: jockey said colt hung right-handed
Vanilla Loan(IRE) Official explanation: jockey said filly never travelled

1536 RINGSIDE CONFERENCE SUITE (S) STKS — 1m 141y(P)
7:50 (7:50) (Class 6) 3-Y-0+
£1,774 (£523; £262) Stalls Low

Form / RPR

0133 **1** **Royal Dignitary (USA)**[10] 1293 10-10-0 70 ... AdrianNicholls 5 — 75
(D Nicholls) *mde all: rdn over 1f out: styd on gamely* 6/1[3]

0421 **2** ½ **Tous Les Deux**[4] 1457 7-10-0 67 ... GeorgeBaker 7 — 74
(G L Moore) *hld up in tch: rdn to chse wnr ins fnl f: styd on u.p* 9/4[2]

64-2 **3** 4 ½ **Wind Star**[20] 1098 7-9-9 85 ... RobertWinston 1 — 59
(G A Swinbank) *a.p: trckd wnr gng wl 3f out: rdn over 1f out: wknd towards fin* 5/4[1]

55-5 **4** 1 ½ **Swiss Art (IRE)**[14] 1239 4-9-7 65 ... LeeTopliss(7) 3 — 60
(R Hollinshead) *prom: rdn over 2f out: no ex ins fnl f* 16/1

0030 **5** 6 **Bansha (IRE)**[61] 661 4-9-9 46 ...(v[1]) JamieMackay 9 — 41
(A Bailey) *prom: rdn over 2f out: wknd over 1f out* 66/1

4030 **6** 7 **City Gossip (IRE)**[67] 574 3-8-3 56 ...(v[1]) JimmyQuinn 10 — 20
(Miss M E Rowland) *hld up: nt clr run over 2f out: sn rdn: and wknd* 33/1

46-1 **7** 2 ¾ **The Mumbo**[26] 1042 4-9-9 62 ...(b) AlanMunro 6 — 19
(W Jarvis) *hld up: pushed along over 3f out: a in rr* 8/1

6 **8** 6 **Orpenia (IRE)**[15] 1203 4-9-4 0 ... TomMcLaughlin 2 — —
(Miss L A Perratt) *hld up in tch: rdn over 2f out: wknd over 1f out* 50/1

9 9 **Starway To Heaven**[144] 5-9-4 0 LiamKeniry 11 —
(J Jay) *sn pushed along and a in rr: lost tch fnl 3f* **66/1**

00 10 3 ½ **Idol Deputy (FR)**[42] 889 4-9-4 0 LeeNewnes(5) 8 —
(M D I Usher) *chsd wnr tl rdn 3f out: sn wknd* **100/1**

1m 50.55s (0.05) **Going Correction** +0.125s/f (Slow)
WFA 3 from 4yo+ 15lb 10 Ran SP% **115.4**
Speed ratings (Par 101): **104,103,99,98,92 86,84,78,70,67**
Tote Swingers: 1&2 £3.40, 1&3 £2.10, 2&3 £1.20. CSF £19.50 TOTE £3.80: £1.10, £1.10, £1.50; EX 18.90.There was no bid for the winner. Wind Star was claimed by M. F. Harris for £6,000.
Owner Middleham Park Racing XXXVI **Bred** Bentley Smith, J Michael O'Farrell Jr , Joan Thor **Trained** Sessay, N Yorks

FOCUS
A poor race dominated by the market principals although the favourite disappointed in third and the form is best rated around the front pair.

1537 CE RISK, SAFETY & SECURITY FILLIES' H'CAP 1m 141y(P)
8:20 (8:21) (Class 5) (0-70,70) 3-Y-O £3,238 (£963; £481; £240) Stalls Low

Form RPR
031- 1 **Hulcote Rose (IRE)**[185] 6942 3-9-4 70 GeorgeBaker 7 79+
(S Kirk) *hld up: hdwy over 2f out: rdn to ld wl ins fnl f: r.o* **7/2**[2]

00-5 2 hd **Babycakes (IRE)**[30] 979 3-9-0 66 HayleyTurner 6 75+
(M L W Bell) *chsd ldr tl led over 2f out: rdn and hdd wl ins fnl f: r.o* **7/1**

30-4 3 3 **Thereafter (USA)**[45] 843 3-9-2 68 SteveDrowne 4 70
(R Charlton) *a.p: wnt 3rd over 3f out: pushed along over 2f out: rdn over 1f out: edgd lft: no ex ins fnl f* **3/1**[1]

335- 4 1 **Crystal Gale (IRE)**[232] 5627 3-9-4 70 JimCrowley 9 70
(W J Knight) *hld up: rdn over 1f out: hung lft and r.o ins fnl f: nrst fin* **11/2**

04-0 5 2 **Mini Max**[17] 1158 3-8-5 57 KevinGhunowa 3 52
(B W Duke) *prom: hmpd over 7f out: rdn over 3f out: nvr trbld ldrs* **20/1**

630- 6 nse **Charpoy Cobra**[186] 6923 3-8-8 60 KirstyMilczarek 1 55
(J A R Toller) *trckd ldrs: racd keenly: rdn over 2f out: wknd ins fnl f* **14/1**

36-0 7 2 ¾ **Green Community (USA)**[7] 1392 3-8-10 62 LiamKeniry 2 51
(E F Vaughan) *led over 5f: rdn over 1f out: wknd ins fnl f* **9/2**[3]

01-0 8 3 ¾ **Ravens Rose**[17] 1159 3-8-10 62 SaleemGolam 5 42
(J G Portman) *hld up: rdn and wknd over 2f out* **28/1**

430- 9 32 **Daniella De Bruijn (IRE)**[177] 7139 3-9-4 70 SebSanders 8 —
(A B Haynes) *chsd ldrs: rdn 4f out: wknd wl over 2f out: eased: t.o* **16/1**

1m 51.58s (1.08) **Going Correction** +0.125s/f (Slow) 9 Ran SP% **114.0**
Speed ratings (Par 95): **100,99,97,96,94 94,92,88,60**
Tote Swingers: 1&2 £2.60, 1&3 £2.60, 2&3 £6.60 CSF £27.85 CT £80.63 TOTE £2.90: £1.10, £4.00, £3.80; EX 12.80.
Owner The Kathryn Stud **Bred** Ecurie Des Monceaux **Trained** Upper Lambourn, Berks

FOCUS
Some unexposed fillies on show here and the front two, especially, are ones to keep on the right side of next time. The winner is rated up 10lb.

1538 STAY AT THE WOLVERHAMPTON HOLIDAY INN MAIDEN FILLIES' STKS 1m 1f 103y(P)
8:50 (8:51) (Class 5) 3-Y-O+ £2,456 (£725; £362) Stalls Low

Form RPR
4 1 **Bakongo (IRE)**[8] 1356 3-8-10 0 HayleyTurner 4 78+
(M L W Bell) *stdd s: hld up: hdwy over 2f out: led ins fnl f: readily* **11/10**[1]

220- 2 1 ¼ **Indian Valley (USA)**[182] 7033 3-8-10 71 MartinDwyer 1 70
(Rae Guest) *led: rdn and hdd ins fnl f: styd on same pce* **9/2**[3]

426 3 1 ¾ **Nadinska**[11] 1278 3-8-10 70 AlanMunro 2 66
(M R Channon) *a.p: racd keenly: chsd ldr 2f out: rdn ins fnl f: styd on same pce* **7/1**

4 4 2 ¼ **White Finch (USA)**[30] 979 3-8-10 0 DavidProbert 5 62
(A M Balding) *chsd ldr tl rdn 2f out: edgd rt over 1f out: no ex* **4/1**[2]

00- 5 ½ **Seattle Speight (USA)**[228] 5752 3-8-10 0 JimCrowley 3 61
(W J Knight) *prom: rdn over 2f out: sn outpcd* **33/1**

02- 6 ¾ **Al Shababiya (IRE)**[126] 7816 3-8-7 0 MartinLane(3) 6 59
(D M Simcock) *chsd ldrs: rdn over 2f out: hung lft and wknd over 1f out* **12/1**

7 1 ½ **Marju's Reward (IRE)** 3-8-10 0 RobertWinston 8 56
(G A Swinbank) *hld up: rdn over 3f out: nvr on terms* **20/1**

8 ½ **Jasmin Rai** 3-8-10 0 ShaneKelly 7 55
(D Donovan) *s.i.s: sn pushed along and a in rr: bhd whn hung lft over 1f out* **50/1**

2m 4.62s (2.92) **Going Correction** +0.125s/f (Slow) 8 Ran SP% **115.7**
Speed ratings (Par 100): **92,90,89,87,86 86,84,84**
Tote Swingers: 1&2 £5.20, 1&3 £1.70, 2&3 £2.60 CSF £6.30 TOTE £1.90: £1.30, £1.10, £1.30; EX 6.90.
Owner Sheikh Marwan Al Maktoum **Bred** Darley **Trained** Newmarket, Suffolk

FOCUS
A modest fillies' maiden which was steadily run. The winner is rated better than the bare form with the runner-up the best guide.

1539 CLEANWASTESOLUTIONS H'CAP 1m 4f 50y(P)
9:20 (9:21) (Class 6) (0-60,60) 4-Y-O+ £1,774 (£523; £262) Stalls Low

Form RPR
0012 1 **Nayessence**[15] 1207 4-8-11 58 (t) JamesSullivan(5) 12 65
(M W Easterby) *mde all: rdn and edgd lft ins fnl f: all out* **13/8**[1]

662- 2 ½ **Carter**[180] 7049 4-9-3 59 ShaneKelly 6 65
(W M Brisbourne) *a.p: chsd wnr 3f out tl rdn over 2f out: r.o again to go 2nd nr fin* **8/1**

6-43 3 ¾ **Birkside**[15] 1199 7-8-12 60 LeeTopliss(7) 1 65
(Miss L A Perratt) *hld up in tch: chsd wnr over 2f out: rdn and n.m.r ins fnl f: lost 2nd nr fin* **8/1**

5543 4 4 **Naheell**[16] 1194 4-9-3 59 (p) SaleemGolam 5 57
(G Prodromou) *pushed along early to chse ldrs: rdn over 2f out: no ex fnl f* **6/1**[2]

0-60 5 10 **National Monument (IRE)**[93] 244 4-9-1 57 GeorgeBaker 3 39
(J A Osborne) *hld up: hdwy 3f out: sn rdn: wkng whn hung lft over 1f out* **13/2**[3]

100- 6 1 ¾ **Looks The Business (IRE)**[173] 7214 9-8-11 52 SebSanders 7 32
(A B Haynes) *chsd ldr tl rdn 3f out: wknd over 2f out* **16/1**

100- 7 shd **Mystic Touch**[150] 7517 4-8-13 55 (p) RobertHavlin 4 34
(A B Haynes) *hld up: rdn and wknd over 2f out* **25/1**

1114 8 16 **Lyrical Intent**[70] 540 4-9-4 60 JimmyQuinn 9 14
(P Howling) *chsd ldrs tl rdn and wknd over 2f out: t.o* **8/1**

6306 9 11 **Look Officer (USA)**[15] 1207 4-9-4 60 AdamKirby 10 —
(Miss M E Rowland) *s.i.s: hld up: drvn along 7f out: hung rt and wknd 6f out: t.o* **20/1**

2m 41.39s (0.29) **Going Correction** +0.125s/f (Slow)
WFA 4 from 6yo+ 1lb 9 Ran SP% **113.5**
Speed ratings (Par 101): **104,103,103,100,93 92,92,81,74**
Tote Swingers: 1&2 £4.00, 1&3 £7.40, 2&3 £19.70 CSF £14.90 CT £80.04 TOTE £1.50: £1.02, £4.20, £3.90; EX 27.90 Place 6: £14.35 Place 5: £7.76.
Owner Steve Hull **Bred** Gainsborough Stud Management Ltd **Trained** Sheriff Hutton, N Yorks

FOCUS
A weak handicap in which nothing got in a blow from off the sound pace and the first three, who all raced prominently, finished clear. Length personal bests from the first two.
Look Officer(USA) Official explanation: jockey said filly hung right-handed
T/Plt: £17.20 to a £1 stake. Pool: £62,073.41. 2,630.52 winning tickets. T/Qpdt: £1.80 to a £1 stake. Pool: £6,030.93. 2,431.34 winning tickets. CR

1252 SAN SIRO (R-H)
Saturday, April 24

OFFICIAL GOING: Turf: soft

1540a PREMIO AMBROSIANO (GROUP 3) (4YO+) (TURF) 1m 2f
4:05 (12:00) 4-Y-O+ £35,398 (£15,575; £8,495; £4,247)

RPR
1 **Jakkalberry (IRE)**[32] 4-8-11 0 FabioBranca 3 107
(E Botti, Italy) *broke wl: hld up in in rr of ldng gp: hdwy 2f out: shkn up to chal ldr 1 1/2f out: rdn and r.o wl ins fnl f: comf* **27/10**[3]

2 2 ½ **Estejo (GER)**[167] 7313 6-9-6 0 MircoDemuro 4 111
(R Rohne, Germany) *broke wl: settled in 2nd for three-quarters of a m: swtchd to centre of trck: rdn 2f out: passed by wnr 1 1/2f out: styd on to take 2nd fnl strides* **7/3**[2]

3 nse **Johannes Mozart (IRE)**[167] 7312 4-8-11 0 SBasile 1 102
(F & L Camici, Italy) *broke wl and led after 1f: set gd pce: styd on inner rail ent st as pack swtchd wd: rdn to go clr 3f out: hrd rdn 2f out: ct by ldr 1 1/2f out: styd on: ct on line for 2nd* **17/2**

4 3 ¼ **Cima De Triomphe (IRE)**[175] 7196 5-9-6 0 DVargiu 6 104
(B Grizzetti, Italy) *broke wl: stdd and then rdn to go 3rd after 3f: rdn and ev ch fnl 3f: hrd rdn: no imp fnl 1 1/2f* **27/20**[1]

5 5 **Night Of Magic (IRE)**[181] 7046 4-8-8 0 DPorcu 2 82
(H Steinmetz, Germany) *settled in rr: shkn up 4f out: no rspnse: styd on fnl 2f* **128/10**

6 2 ¼ **Seul Blue (ITY)**[13] 4-8-11 0 LManiezzi 5 81
(R Menichetti, Italy) *trckd ldng pair for 2f: 4th ent st: rdn and no imp fr 3f out: wknd fnl quarter* **34/1**

7 2 **Apprimus (IRE)**[13] 4-8-11 0 SMulas 7 77
(S Botti, Italy) *s.i.s: prog on outer to move 3rd after 2f: plld hrd: hrd rdn 3f out: no imp* **92/10**

2m 3.50s (-3.20) 7 Ran SP% **130.0**
WIN (Incl. 1 euro stake): 3.71. PLACES: 1.85, 1.89. DF: 6.15. SF: 69.21.
Owner Effevi **Bred** Azienda Agricola Allevamento Deni **Trained** Italy

BATH (L-H)
Sunday, April 25

OFFICIAL GOING: Firm (good to firm in places; 10.2)
Wind: Moderate across Weather: Dull

1541 EBF AND VENETIA ELIZABETH BELL MAIDEN STKS 5f 11y
2:10 (2:10) (Class 5) 2-Y-O £3,885 (£1,156; £577; £288) Stalls Centre

Form RPR
0 1 **Rosina Grey**[19] 1136 2-8-10 0 ow1 JamesMillman(3) 4 68
(B R Millman) *trckd ldrs: shkn up: green and qcknd over 1f out: led ins fnl f: drvn out* **14/1**

2 1 ¼ **Alfraamsey** 2-9-3 0 AlanMunro 10 67+
(M R Channon) *s.i.s: outpcd and bhd tl hdwy over 1f out: styd on strly fnl f to take 2nd nr fin but no imp on wnr* **9/1**[3]

00 3 1 ¾ **The Best Mode (IRE)**[17] 1180 2-9-3 0 TomQueally 1 60
(P D Evans) *slt advantage: drvn along fr 1/2-way: hdd ins fnl f: wknd and lost 2nd nr fin* **8/1**[2]

5 4 nk **Lady Excellentia (IRE)**[13] 1256 2-8-12 0 SebSanders 5 54
(A B Haynes) *chsd ldrs: drvn along 1/2-way: styd on to chal over 1f out: wknd fnl 120yds* **12/1**

5 1 **Scatty (IRE)** 2-9-3 0 LiamKeniry 2 55
(S Kirk) *s.i.s: sn rcvrd and in tch: pushed along 2f out: kpt on same pce fr over 1f out* **22/1**

6 6 nk **Ruby Alexander (IRE)**[10] 1319 2-8-12 0 JackMitchell 9 49
(R M Beckett) *in tch: pushed along to chse ldrs 1/2-way: wknd ins fnl f* **9/1**[3]

7 1 ¼ **Barking (IRE)** 2-9-3 0 RichardHughes 6 49
(R Hannon) *w ldr: rdn 1/2-way: wknd qckly 1f out* **1/1**[1]

8 13 **Crystal Set (IRE)** 2-9-3 0 NeilCallan 7 —
(A B Haynes) *s.i.s: a outpcd* **25/1**

9 ¾ **Classic Gem (IRE)** 2-8-12 0 RichardKingscote 8 —
(Tom Dascombe) *early spd: rdn and bhd fr 1/2-way* **8/1**[2]

63.07 secs (0.57) **Going Correction** 0.0s/f (Good) 9 Ran SP% **114.8**
Speed ratings (Par 92): **95,93,90,89,88 87,85,64,63**
Tote Swingers: 1&2 £24.10, 1&3 £9.90, 2&3 £9.10 CSF £131.80 TOTE £17.00: £5.10, £3.50, £3.60; EX 189.90 TRIFECTA Not won..
Owner P Gibbins M Daly **Bred** The Three Point Partnership **Trained** Kentisbeare, Devon

FOCUS
A modest juvenile maiden with the field compressed, but the time was fair.

NOTEBOOK
Rosina Grey badly needed her debut outing at Ffos Las 19 days earlier, but that is a race working out well and she became the fourth winner to emerge from it. She still showed signs of greenness when put under pressure here, so is entitled to go forward for the experience and clearly likes quick ground. Connections believe she will be better over another furlong, but if she improves with racing also added they will aim her at the Super Sprint at Newbury later in the season. This was also a first winner for her first-season sire. (tchd 12-1)
Alfraamsey ◆, whose dam scored at two, proved far too green to do himself full justice and this was a promising effort all considered. He took an age to get going, but was getting the hang of things turning for home and stayed on nicely towards the finish for an unlikely looking second. Granted the normal improvement for this initial experience he ought to prove hard to beat next time out. (op 10-1 tchd 12-1)

The Best Mode(IRE) was making her third appearance on the track and rates the best guide for this form. She seemed to enjoy the quicker surface and has now steadily improved with each run. (tchd 7-1)
Lady Excellentia(IRE) broke better a lot from the gates and showed the clear benefit of her debut experience at Folkestone 13 days earlier. The quicker ground was also in her favour. (tchd 10-1)
Scatty(IRE) was very green in the preliminaries and shaped in the race as though the experience was much needed. He will know more next time. (op 20-1 tchd 25-1)
Ruby Alexander(IRE) looked a threat on the outer of the pack inside the final furlong, but couldn't sustain her effort when it mattered most. The ground may have been quicker than she really cares for. (tchd 10-1)
Barking(IRE) was all the rage here for his racecourse debut. He was keen to post, though, and in the race itself, eventually fading tamely at the furlong marker. Better was clearly expected and it is likely he will leave this behind when consenting to settle. (op 11-10 tchd 5-4 in a place)

1542 CATERPLUSLTD.COM - COMMERCIAL CATERING ENGINEERS MEDIAN AUCTION MAIDEN STKS — 1m 5y

2:40 (2:44) (Class 6) 3-4-Y-O — **£2,493** (£741; £370; £185) **Stalls** Low

Form				RPR
	1		**Seafarer (IRE)** 3-8-12 0 ... MartinDwyer 4 (B J Meehan) *ponied to s: trckd ldrs: t.k.h: awkward bnd 5f out: str run fr 2f out to chal 1f out: led fnl 120yds and hld on wl* **9/1**[3]	78+
43-3	2	nk	**High Importance (USA)**[15] 1240 3-8-12 74 ... TomQueally 6 (J Noseda) *trckd ldrs: drvn and qcknd 2f out: chal 1f out: styd on to press wnr ins fnl f but a jst hld* **9/2**[2]	77
4	3	2 ¼	**Belgique (IRE)**[9] 1355 3-8-8 0 ow1 ... RichardHughes 1 (R Hannon) *led: awkward bnd 5f out: drvn and jnd fr over 4f out: narrowly hdd over 2f out: drvn to retake slt ld again appr fnl f: hdd & wknd fnl 120yds* **11/8**[1]	68
220-	4	hd	**Yarra River**[204] 6478 3-8-12 80 ... DavidProbert 7 (A M Balding) *trckd ldr: upsides fr over 4f out tl drvn into slt ld over 2f out: hdd u.p appr fnl f: fnd little and sn btn* **11/8**[1]	71
6	5	13	**Shades Of Grey**[31] 979 3-8-7 0 ... LukeMorris 9 (C G Cox) *s.i.s: sn in tch: rdn and bhd over 4f out: no ch after* **33/1**	36
0-0	6	hd	**Sparkle Park**[65] 624 3-8-7 0 ... (b[1]) TadhgO'Shea 5 (B J Meehan) *s.i.s: bhd most of way* **66/1**	36
2-50	7	16	**Angelena Ballerina (IRE)**[31] 978 3-8-7 63 ... (p) ChrisCatlin 3 (Karen George) *a in rr* **25/1**	—
0-00	8	shd	**Devon Diva**[11] 1303 4-9-2 40 ... MarkCoumbe(5) 8 (J F Panvert) *s.i.s: t.k.h: a bhd* **150/1**	—

1m 41.61s (0.81) **Going Correction** 0.0s/f (Good)
WFA 3 from 4yo 14lb — **8** Ran SP% **121.3**
Speed ratings (Par 101): **95,94,92,92,79 79,63,62**
Tote Swingers: 1&2 £5.90, 1&3 £2.20, 2&3 £2.50 CSF £50.32 TOTE £9.20: £2.70, £1.10, £1.10; EX 39.90 Trifecta £62.60 Pool: £410.06 - 4.84 winning units..
Owner M Tabor & Mrs John Magnier **Bred** Mrs Emily Henry **Trained** Manton, Wilts

FOCUS
The first four dominated this maiden and the form should work out, although it is only modest. The runner-up looks the best guide.

1543 ACADEMYEYEWEAR.CO.UK H'CAP — 1m 5y

3:15 (3:15) (Class 5) (0-70,70) 4-Y-O+ — **£3,238** (£963; £481; £240) **Stalls** Low

Form				RPR
5043	1		**Fault**[10] 1322 4-8-13 **65** ... (t) TomQueally 6 (Stef Higgins) *mde all: awkward bnd 5f out: hrd rdn and hld on gamely thrght fnl f: all out* **11/4**[1]	71
0222	2	½	**Spinning Ridge (IRE)**[34] 965 5-9-0 **66** ... LukeMorris 4 (R A Harris) *t.k.h: chsd ldrs: awkward bnd 5f out: drvn and styd on to chse wnr ins fnl f: edgd lft u.p: a jst hld* **5/1**[3]	71
444-	3	shd	**Magroom**[177] 7153 6-9-3 **69** ... GeorgeBaker 3 (R J Hodges) *s.i.s: in rr: hdwy 2f out: n.m.r 1f out and swtchd rt ins fnl f: str run fnl 100yds to press for 2nd cl home but nt rch wnr* **9/2**[2]	74
430-	4	nk	**Sunny Future (IRE)**[181] 7065 4-8-12 **64** ... TomMcLaughlin 9 (M S Saunders) *in rr: awkward bnd 5f out: hdwy on outside fr 2f out: str run ins fnl f: kpt on cl home but nt rch wnr* **14/1**	68
156-	5	½	**Hobson**[201] 6562 5-9-4 **70** ... NeilCallan 10 (Eve Johnson Houghton) *t.k.h: in rr and awkward bnd 5f out: rdn and hdwy on outside over 1f out: str run thrght fnl f but nt rch ldrs* **9/2**[2]	73
0-00	6	1 ¼	**Prince Rossi (IRE)**[46] 855 6-8-6 **58** ... (v) PaulHanagan 5 (A E Price) *chsd ldrs: t.k.h and awkward bnd 5f out: wnt 2nd over 3f out: drvn to chal 2 out: btn off 1f out: hld whn n.m.r ins fnl f and eased* **10/1**	58
500-	7	nk	**Apex**[208] 6365 9-9-2 **68** ... FergusSweeney 1 (M Hill) *s.i.s: in rr tl hdwy 4f out: effrt on ins fr over 1f out: n.m.r and one pce ins fnl f* **8/1**	67
2065	8	¾	**Straight Face (IRE)**[11] 1301 6-8-5 **64** ... (b) KevinLundie(7) 8 (P D Evans) *chsd wnr: awkward bnd 5f out: lost 2nd over 3f out: wknd over 1f out* **20/1**	62
00/0	9	48	**Definite Honey**[60] 682 4-7-13 **56** oh11 ... (b[1]) AmyBaker(5) 2 (J M Bradley) *slowly away: a bhd: rdn 1/2-way: sn lost tch: t.o fnl 3f* **66/1**	—

1m 40.33s (-0.47) **Going Correction** 0.0s/f (Good) — **9** Ran SP% **112.8**
Speed ratings (Par 103): **102,101,101,101,100 99,99,98,50**
Tote Swingers: 1&2 £2.80, 1&3 £1.80, 2&3 £1.50 CSF £16.03 CT £58.19 TOTE £3.80: £1.80, £1.30, £1.30; EX 12.60 Trifecta £35.70 Pool: £106.68 - 2.21 winning units..
Owner David Gilbert **Bred** Mrs A M Vestey **Trained** Lambourn, Berks
■ Stewards' Enquiry : Luke Morris caution: careless riding; one-day ban: used whip with excessive frequency (May 10)

FOCUS
An open and tricky looking handicap. There were a host of chances inside the final furlong and something of a bunched finish. Muddling form which should not be taken too literally.
Magroom Official explanation: jockey said gelding was denied a clear run

1544 STRADA AND CAFE ROUGE H'CAP — 1m 5f 22y

3:50 (3:50) (Class 3) (0-90,88) 4-Y-O+ — **£8,418** (£2,505; £1,251; £625) **Stalls** High

Form				RPR
34-1	1		**Sherman McCoy**[18] 1161 4-8-11 **83** ... JamesMillman(3) 7 (B R Millman) *racd in 3rd and 8 l off ldng duo 1/2-way: styd on fr 3f out: wnt 2nd wl over 1f out: kpt on to ld ins fnl f: styd on wl* **10/3**[2]	94
315-	2	2	**Cool Strike (UAE)**[271] 4408 4-9-5 **88** ... (v) LiamKeniry 3 (A M Balding) *led after 1f and sn j. path: 1 l clr of 2nd and 8 l ahd of 3rd 1/2-way: rdn and styd on wl whn chal over 2f out: hdd and no ex ins fnl f* **2/1**[1]	96
442-	3	2 ¼	**Hawridge King**[177] 7151 8-8-8 **76** ... AlanMunro 1 (W S Kittow) *towards rr and wl bhd clr ldng duo 1/2-way: hdwy fr 4f out: styd on wl fr over 2f out and tk 3rd ins fnl f but a hld* **5/1**	81
110-	4	4	**Callisto Moon**[9] 7117 6-9-3 **85** ... (p) NeilCallan 2 (R Curtis) *chsd wnr and 8 l clr of 3rd 1/2-way: drvn and effrt over 2f out but nvr quite upsides: lost 2nd over 1f out: wknd ins fnl f* **4/1**[3]	84
131-	5	13	**Crocus Rose**[184] 6995 4-8-8 **77** ... JimmyQuinn 4 (H J L Dunlop) *in rr whn hung bdly rt and lost grnd bnd after 4f: rcvrd and in tch whn hung bdly rt off trck bnd 5f out and lost any ch* **9/1**	57
213-	6	11	**Brett Vale (IRE)**[127] 7811 4-9-3 **86** ... DaneO'Neill 5 (P R Hedger) *a in rr* **12/1**	49
500-	7	63	**War Party**[17] 3587 6-8-10 **78** ... SteveDrowne 6 (Dr R D P Newland) *a in rr: t.o* **25/1**	—

2m 48.07s (-3.93) **Going Correction** 0.0s/f (Good)
WFA 4 from 6yo+ 1lb — **7** Ran SP% **114.6**
Speed ratings (Par 107): **112,110,109,106,98 92,53**
Tote Swingers: 1&2 £2.80, 1&3 £1.80, 2&3 £1.50 CSF £10.50 TOTE £5.50: £3.10, £1.10; EX 11.70.
Owner Mustajed Partnership **Bred** Horizon Bloodstock Limited **Trained** Kentisbeare, Devon

FOCUS
This was a fair staying handicap. The two early leaders went off at a frantic early pace and ensured the field was well strung out on the back straight. The form is rated slightly positively around the third.

NOTEBOOK
Sherman McCoy was content to allow the leaders to take each other on and was ideally placed when they began to wilt inside the final furlong. He went for everything at the furlong marker and was always going to get there at the business end. He was 4lb higher than when winning at Kempton 16 days earlier and is clearly progressive, though the race rather fell into his lap here. (op 6-1)
Cool Strike(UAE) ◆ was popular on his return from a nine-month absence and had won at the track on his only previous visit last year. He was asked to race on the pace early on and proved free in winning the battle for the lead. He was unsurprisingly mown down inside the final furlong, considering he did too much early on, and really did well to finish second. There could be a nice pot in him this season. (op 5-2 tchd 11-4)
Hawridge King's one win last year came on firm ground and he didn't go unbacked for this seasonal debut, despite being a horse that usually needs a few runs to hit peak form each term. He ran an encouraging enough race and will enjoy returning to a stiffer test. (op 7-1)
Callisto Moon hinted at a return to winning ways over hurdles last time out and his previous form figures here read 21. He wasn't suited by being taken on for the lead, however, and like the runner-up also did plenty through the early parts. (op 3-1)
Crocus Rose was never seriously in the hunt on her first run of the year, but would have been closer had she not hung badly off the bends. She will come on for it and appreciate getting back on an easier surface, but it would not be surprising to see her going the other way round after this. Official explanation: jockey said filly finished lame (op 7-1)
Brett Vale(IRE) found himself well out of his ground due to being restrained early on here and ultimately shaped as though the run was needed. (op 8-1)
War Party Official explanation: jockey said gelding bled from the nose

1545 EUROPEAN BREEDERS' FUND LANSDOWN FILLIES' STKS (LISTED RACE) — 5f 11y

4:25 (4:25) (Class 1) 3-Y-O+
£22,708 (£8,608; £4,308; £2,148; £1,076; £540) **Stalls** Centre

Form				RPR
31-2	1		**Gilt Edge Girl**[30] 992 4-9-0 95 ... LukeMorris 4 (C G Cox) *stdd towards rr but wl in tch: hdwy towards outside over 1f out: str run and rdn to ld ins fnl f: kpt on wl cl home* **13/2**	108
111-	2	¾	**Golden Destiny (IRE)**[224] 5902 4-9-0 101 ... (p) SebSanders 6 (P J Makin) *chsd ldrs tl drvn to ld over 1f out: hdd ins fnl f: styd on but nt pce of wnr* **9/2**[3]	105
236-	3	1 ½	**Anglezarke (IRE)**[295] 3638 4-9-0 104 ... PaulHanagan 1 (R A Fahey) *s.i.s: sn rcvrd: pushed along 1/2-way: hdwy 2f out: chsd ldrs over 1f out: no imp and outpcd ins fnl f* **6/4**[1]	100
213-	4	4 ½	**Tomintoul Singer (IRE)**[177] 7147 3-8-4 96 ... JimmyQuinn 2 (H R A Cecil) *crossed s and s.i.s: in rr: hdwy 2f out: n.m.r over 1f out: kpt on same pce ins fnl f* **11/4**[2]	79
0	5	nk	**Atlantic Cycle (IRE)**[22] 1091 3-8-4 95 ... TadhgO'Shea 7 (K J Condon, Ire) *drvn to ld after 1f: rdn over 2f out: hdd over 1f out: wknd ins fnl f* **25/1**	78
60-4	6	2	**Angus Newz**[18] 1174 7-9-0 82 ... FrannyNorton 5 (M Quinn) *led 1f: styd chsng ldrs tl wknd 1f out* **28/1**	75
2560	7	2	**Ramamara (IRE)**[36] 945 3-8-4 71 ... CathyGannon 8 (P D Evans) *wnt lft s: chsd ldrs tl wknd over 1f out* **100/1**	64
052-	8	3	**Impressible**[211] 6283 4-9-0 87 ... NeilCallan 3 (S C Williams) *plunged s: sn rdn: outpcd most of way* **16/1**	57

61.07 secs (-1.43) **Going Correction** 0.0s/f (Good)
WFA 3 from 4yo+ 10lb — **8** Ran SP% **112.3**
Speed ratings (Par 108): **111,109,107,100,99 96,93,88**
Tote Swingers: 1&2 £5.30, 1&3 £3.20, 2&3 £2.30 CSF £34.17 TOTE £7.60: £2.60, £1.50, £1.60; EX 21.30 Trifecta £54.40 Pool: £388.47 - 5.28 winning units..
Owner Wood Street Syndicate V & C J Harper **Bred** Whitsbury Manor Stud **Trained** Lambourn, Berks

FOCUS
This Listed sprint for fillies was run at a decent pace and the first three came nicely clear. The winner is progressive and the form is rated around the runner-up.

NOTEBOOK
Gilt Edge Girl stepped up on her previous form and ran out a determined winner on this step up in class. She posted a career-best in defeat when mugged on the AW on her return last month and, ridden with more restraint here, showed a typically game attitude when it mattered. The ground was obviously to her liking and this win nicely enhances her future paddock value. She will now have to stick to this sort of level and her consistency should continue to hold her in good stead. (op 15-2)
Golden Destiny(IRE) was a big improver last season, winning her last four races, two of which came at this track over a little further on firm ground. She posted a very pleasing return to the track with a game effort under a positive ride and could well nick one of these this year. (tchd 4-1)
Anglezarke(IRE), whose finest hour last term came when placed in the King's Stand, was having her first outing for Richard Fahey. She had also been successful first time out in both her previous seasons and proved solid in the market. Having made an awkward start, though, she failed to pick up as might have been expected when pulled out with her challenge and was held inside the final furlong. It may be this track was not for her and ground may also have been a little too quick, so she is not one to be writing off. (op 15-8)
Tomintoul Singer(IRE) was placed at this level on her final outing last year and attracted support earlier in the day. She was another that didn't get a good start and really looked as though this first run back was needed. There will be other days for her. (op 9-4)
Atlantic Cycle(IRE) improved on her disappointing return at Dundalk, but set the race up for the principals and is likely to be hard to place this season. (op 20-1)

1546 HEIDI TOYNBEE SECRETARIAL SERVICES H'CAP — 5f 11y

4:55 (4:55) (Class 4) (0-80,76) 3-Y-O — **£5,828** (£1,734; £866; £432) **Stalls** Centre

Form				RPR
123-	1		**Felsham**[169] 7290 3-9-2 74 ... DaneO'Neill 5 (H Candy) *chsd ldrs: rdn over 2f out: led 1f out: rdn out* **11/10**[1]	80+

216- **2** *1 ¼* **Nepotism**[233] 5650 3-9-0 **72**.......... FergusSweeney 3 73
(M S Saunders) *chsd ldrs: rdn to ld ins fnl 2f: hdd 1f out: sn outpcd by wnr and jst hld on for 2nd* **22/1**

301- **3** *nse* **Hot Pursuits**[188] 6903 3-9-3 **75**.......... SteveDrowne 8 76
(H Morrison) *s.i.s: in rr but in tch: hdwy on outside fr 2f out: styd on u.p fnl f to press for 2nd last strides but no ch w wnr* **15/2**[3]

0-22 **4** *2 ½* **Dusty Spirit**[27] 1052 3-9-1 **76**..........(tp) JackDean(3) 9 68
(W G M Turner) *chsd ldr to 1/2-way: outpcd fnl f* **5/1**[2]

462- **5** *½* **Feeling Fragile (IRE)**[136] 7700 3-9-0 **72**.......... SebSanders 4 62
(Pat Eddery) *t.k.h: hld up towards rr: hdwy over 1f out: kpt on fnl f but nvr gng pce to get into contention* **8/1**

04-5 **6** *1* **Avonvalley**[19] 1140 3-9-3 **75**.......... TomMcLaughlin 7 62
(M S Saunders) *in rr tl styd on fr over 1f out: kpt on u.p ins fnl f wout ever looking a threat* **16/1**

6-24 **7** *1* **Leleyf (IRE)**[12] 1281 3-9-2 **74**.......... ChrisCatlin 2 57
(M R Channon) *chsd ldrs: rdn 1/2-way: wknd fnl f* **8/1**

3216 **8** *8* **Wanchai Whisper**[17] 1187 3-8-8 **66**.......... JimmyQuinn 1 20
(P R Hedger) *broke wl: stdd after s: outpcd* **33/1**

310- **9** *¾* **Morgans Choice**[191] 6827 3-9-1 **73**.......... NeilCallan 6 25
(J L Spearing) *led tl hdd ins fnl 2f: wknd sn after* **25/1**

62.39 secs (-0.11) **Going Correction** 0.0s/f (Good) **9** Ran SP% **115.3**
Speed ratings (Par 100): **100,98,97,93,93 91,89,77,75**
Tote Swingers: 1&2 £10.50, 1&3 £3.60, 2&3 £26.90 CSF £32.86 CT £133.52 TOTE £1.80: £1.10, £5.00, £2.30; EX 31.70 Trifecta £159.20 Pool: £215.26 - 1 winning unit..
Owner Six Too Many **Bred** Mrs R D Peacock **Trained** Kingston Warren, Oxon

FOCUS
Not a bad sprint handicap for the class. The winner is better than the bare form, which has been rated around the second and third.

1547 RIVERSIDE CAFE AND RESTAURANT - 01225 480532 H'CAP 5f 161y
5:25 (5:25) (Class 5) (0-70,70) 3-Y-O+ **£3,238** (£963; £481; £240) **Stalls** Centre

Form RPR
046- **1** **Kakapuka**[202] 6534 3-8-11 **68**.......... RussKennemore(3) 4 79+
(Mrs A L M King) *trckd ldrs on ins tl hmpd and lost pl ins fnl 2f: checked bk: swtchd rt to wd outside and plenty to do over 1f out: rapid hdwy fnl f to ld cl home* **40/1**

0-13 **2** *¾* **Cwmni**[53] 773 4-8-13 **56** oh1.......... DavidProbert 2 61
(B Palling) *s.i.s: bhd: hdwy over 1f out: str run fnl f to ld fnl 100yds: hdd cl home* **11/1**

4024 **3** *1 ¼* **Bo McGinty (IRE)**[9] 1366 9-9-5 **62**..........(v) PaulHanagan 8 63
(R A Fahey) *in tch: drvn to press ldrs fr 2f out and stl ev ch ins fnl f outpcd fnl 75yds* **7/1**[3]

3312 **4** *½* **Riflessione**[4] 1482 4-9-12 **69**..........(b) ChrisCatlin 3 69+
(R A Harris) *hld up in rr: nt clr run ins fnl 2f and hmpd over 1f out: str run to chse ldrs fnl 100yds: one pce nr fin* **9/2**[1]

52-3 **5** *1 ¾* **Green Velvet**[18] 1166 5-9-5 **62**.......... SebSanders 7 56
(P J Makin) *in tch: chsd ldrs 2f out: led 1f out: hdd and outpcd fnl 100yds* **6/1**[2]

500- **6** *1* **Bateleur**[223] 5955 6-9-3 **60**.......... EddieCreighton 10 50
(M R Channon) *s.i.s: in rr tl hdwy on outside over 1f out: kpt on fnl f but nvr a threat* **20/1**

323- **7** *1 ¼* **Mazzola**[179] 7122 4-9-5 **62**.......... LiamKeniry 13 48
(J M Bradley) *s.i.s: sn rcvrd: chsd ldrs 1/2-way: led ins fnl 2f: hdd 1f out: wknd ins fnl f* **14/1**

02-0 **8** *shd* **Talamahana**[5] 1441 5-8-8 **56** oh10..........(v) AmyBaker(5) 6 42
(A B Haynes) *s.i.s: pushed along 1/2-way: sme hdwy fnl f* **40/1**

0-41 **9** *1 ¾* **Kyllachy Storm**[11] 1300 6-9-13 **70**.......... GeorgeBaker 14 50
(R J Hodges) *chsd ldrs: led over 2f out: hdd ins fnl 2f: wknd fnl f* **9/2**[1]

026- **10** *½* **Piazza San Pietro**[150] 7534 4-9-11 **68**.......... NeilCallan 5 47+
(A B Haynes) *in tch: hdwy on ins whn bdly hmpd over 1f out: nt rcvr* **6/1**[2]

1254 **11** *9* **Boho Chic**[4] 1482 4-9-3 **65**..........(p) MatthewDavies(5) 9 14
(George Baker) *chsd ldrs: rdn: n.m.r and edgd lft over 1f out: wknd fnl f* **8/1**

630- **12** *4* **Ghost Dancer**[175] 7203 6-9-10 **67**..........(p) LukeMorris 11 3
(J M Bradley) *outpcd* **20/1**

00-0 **13** *6* **What Katie Did (IRE)**[6] 1428 5-9-10 **67**..........(p) SteveDrowne 12 —
(J M Bradley) *sn led: hdd over 2f out: sn btn* **20/1**

1m 12.01s (0.81) **Going Correction** 0.0s/f (Good)
WFA 3 from 4yo+ 11lb **13** Ran SP% **122.7**
Speed ratings (Par 103): **94,93,91,90,88 87,85,85,82,82 70,64,56**
Tote Swingers: 1&2 £112.50, 1&3 £76.30, 2&3 £12.40 CSF £420.02 CT £3568.87 TOTE £65.70: £14.10, £3.80, £2.90; EX 423.90 TRIFECTA Not won. Place 6: £23.29 Place 5: £3.66.
Owner Mrs E Mills & A Murphy **Bred** Paradime Ltd **Trained** Wilmcote, Warwicks

FOCUS
A moderate sprint. The winner is value for a deal further and better than the bare form.
Riflessione Official explanation: jockey said gelding was denied a clear run
Piazza San Pietro Official explanation: jockey said gelding suffered interference in running
What Katie Did(IRE) Official explanation: jockey said gelding suffered interference in runing
T/Plt: £67.90 to a £1 stake. Pool: £74,596.51. 800.82 winning tickets. T/Qpdt: £5.20 to a £1 stake. Pool: £6,319.35. 895.15 winning tickets. ST

1556 - 1559a (Foreign Racing) - See Raceform Interactive

NAVAN (L-H)
Sunday, April 25

OFFICIAL GOING: Good (good to firm in places)

1560a VINTAGE CROP STKS (LISTED RACE) 1m 5f
4:05 (4:05) 4-Y-O+ **£24,446** (£7,146; £3,384; £1,128)

RPR
1 **Roses For The Lady (IRE)**[287] 3896 4-8-12 110.......... FMBerry 7 109+
(John M Oxx, Ire) *mde all and set str pce: rdn fr 2f out: strly pressed 1f out: styd on wl fnl f: comf* **6/4**[1]

2 *3* **Merchant Of Dubai**[28] 1031 5-9-2.......... RobertWinston 3 107
(G A Swinbank) *chsd ldr in cl 2nd: rdn along ent st: strly pressed wnr 1f out: no imp on wnr ins fnl f* **15/8**[2]

3 *5 ½* **Grace O'Malley (IRE)**[181] 7077 4-9-3 101.......... PJSmullen 4 101
(D K Weld, Ire) *trckd ldrs in mod 4th: wnt mod 3rd after 1/2-way: clsr in 3rd and rdn 2f out: no imp on ldrs over 1f out* **10/1**

4 *6* **Mid Mon Lady (IRE)**[44] 881 5-8-13 98..........(b) DCByrne 2 87+
(H Rogers, Ire) *s.i.s and sn off pce in rr: no imp and rdn fr 3f out: wnt mod 4th 2f out: no ex* **16/1**

5 *11* **Zaralabad (IRE)**[171] 7261 6-9-2 95.......... WJLee 1 73
(C F Swan, Ire) *hld up in rr: rdn and no imp fr 4f out* **14/1**

6 *nk* **Celtic Soprano (IRE)**[14] 1245 5-8-13 89.......... WJSupple 6 70
(P D Deegan, Ire) *chsd ldrs in mod 3rd: 4th after 1/2-way: rdn and wknd fr 4f out* **9/2**[3]

7 *9* **End Of The Affair (IRE)**[215] 6197 6-8-13 90.......... CDHayes 5 56
(V C Ward, Ire) *dwlt sltly: hld up in rr: no imp fr 5f out: rdn in mod 6th ent st: no imp* **20/1**

2m 46.82s (-13.18)
WFA 4 from 5yo+ 1lb **7** Ran SP% **119.4**
CSF £4.90 TOTE £2.90: £1.10, £1.60; DF 3.20.
Owner Neil Jones **Bred** Abergwaun Farm **Trained** Currabeg, Co Kildare
■ Stewards' Enquiry : F M Berry severe caution: excessive use of the whip

FOCUS
A race that had been won in recent years by Kastoria (2006), Yeats (2007 and 2008) and Alandi (2009), all of them Group 1 winners after or before landing this 1m5f event. It was run at a strong pace throughout and the third looks the best guide to the level.

NOTEBOOK
Roses For The Lady(IRE), last year's Irish Oaks runner-up, made all and stuck well to her task, having been harried for the lead by the runner-up for much of the journey. The winner was well on top inside the final furlong and may head next for the Yorkshire Cup, although trainer John Oxx indicated that a trip to the Knavesmire would depend on the ground conditions. "She has now won two races, both of them on fast ground, but she needs if soft to be seen at her best and we'll see what the forecast is like for York. She won't go there unless there is a good chance of soft ground. She does stay well." (op 11/8)
Merchant Of Dubai, a tough and consistent performer, ran second throughout and was putting it up to the winner from early in the back straight. He came under strong pressure over 2f out and it was only inside the final furlong that his efforts took their toll. It was a game effort on his part and, like the winner, he would probably have been happier on easier ground. (op 2/1)
Grace O'Malley(IRE), over 8l behind Roses For The Lady when fourth in the Irish Oaks, had run poorly on her only subsequent start. She made an encouraging return here and, after being almost 8l off the leading pair into the straight, she closed gradually before her effort petered out in the final furlong. (op 10/1 tchd 9/1)
Mid Mon Lady(IRE) had run up a hat-trick of wins over shorter trips in October and was stepping up to this trip for the first time. She raced in rear and made some late headway without ever being in contention.
Zaralabad(IRE), a three-time winner from 1m4f to 2m and on extremes of ground, was unable to make any impression from 5f out.

1561 - 1563a (Foreign Racing) - See Raceform Interactive

KREFELD (R-H)
Sunday, April 25

OFFICIAL GOING: Turf: good

1564a GROSSER PREIS DER KREFELDER WIRTSCHAFT DR BUSCH MEMORIAL (GROUP 3) (3YO) (TURF) 1m 110y
4:10 (4:26) 3-Y-O **£28,318** (£8,849; £4,424; £2,654)

RPR
1 **Zazou (GER)**[162] 7404 3-9-2 0.......... THellier 2 106
(Mario Hofer, Germany) *racd in 3rd on rail fr s: swtchd to outer in st: cruised to ld 2f out: wnt clr: comf* **1/2**[1]

2 *3* **Kite Hunter (IRE)**[28] 3-9-2 0.......... EPedroza 6 99
(Mario Hofer, Germany) *broke wl: racd in 2nd: r.o wl in st: n.d to wnr* **74/10**

3 *2 ½* **Wuhan (GER)** 3-9-2 0.......... HenkGrewe 1 94
(S Smrczek, Germany) *difficult to load: sweated up: racd in 5th on ins: hrd rdn in st: no imp* **22/5**[2]

4 *1 ½* **Go Country (FR)**[217] 6151 3-9-2 0.......... AStarke 7 91
(P Schiergen, Germany) *broke through stalls at s: settled in 4th: flattered briefly in st: no ex* **49/10**[3]

5 *5* **Opera Moon (GER)** 3-9-2 0.......... APietsch 5 80
(W Hickst, Germany) *led fr s at mod pce: qcknd early in st: effrt short-lived and hdd 2f out: fdd* **67/10**

6 *20* **Touchmeifyoucan (GER)** 3-9-2 0.......... AHelfenbein 3 36
(P Vovcenko, Germany) *difficult to load: sweated up bdly: a last and struggling: nvr figured: wl btn* **165/10**

1m 44.09s (-2.51) **6** Ran SP% **132.7**
WIN (including 10 euro stake): 15; PLACES 11, 17; SF 49.
Owner WH Sport International **Bred** Gestut Fahrhof **Trained** Germany

1253 LONGCHAMP (R-H)
Sunday, April 25

OFFICIAL GOING: Turf: good

1565a PRIX DE FONTAINEBLEAU (GROUP 3) (3YO COLTS) (TURF) 1m
1:35 (12:00) 3-Y-O **£35,398** (£14,159; £10,619; £7,079; £3,539)

RPR
1 **Rajsaman (FR)**[198] 6656 3-9-2 0.......... ThierryJarnet 7 113
(A De Royer-Dupre, France) *led fr s: wnt clr: stl wl clr in st: rdn 2f out: r.o wl: jst hld on* **25/1**

2 *½* **Siyouni (FR)**[203] 6524 3-9-2 0.......... GeraldMosse 5 112
(A De Royer-Dupre, France) *racd in 4th fr s: rdn 2f out: no immediate rspnse but qcknd wl ins fnl f: fin strly to claim 2nd in fnl strides* **8/13**[1]

3 *shd* **Lope De Vega (IRE)**[203] 6524 3-9-2 0.......... MaximeGuyon 1 112
(A Fabre, France) *racd in 3rd fr s: rdn early in st to chse ldr: r.o wl: ct in fnl strides for 2nd* **5/1**[2]

4 *4* **Makani (GER)**[12] 3-9-2 0..........(p) Christophe-PatriceLemaire 3 103
(J E Pease, France) *followed ldr fr s: rdn early in st to chse ldr but mde no imp: styd on wl for 4th* **6/1**[3]

5 *hd* **Too Nice Name (FR)**[17] 1195 3-9-2 0.......... OlivierPeslier 6 102
(Robert Collet, France) *settled in 4th: rdn early in st: styd on wl* **25/1**

6 *snk* **Shamalgan (FR)**[24] 1079 3-9-2 0.......... StephanePasquier 2 102
(A Savujev, Czech Republic) *racd in rr: rdn early in st: no imp* **40/1**

7 *nk* **Arasin (IRE)**[175] 7207 3-9-2 0.......... ThierryThulliez 4 101
(P Bary, France) *racd in 6th: rdn early in st: r.o* **10/1**

1m 39.36s (0.96) **Going Correction** +0.325s/f (Good) **7** Ran SP% **112.1**
Speed ratings: **108,107,107,103,103 103,102**
WIN (incl. 1 euro stake): 1.80 (Rajsaman coupled with Siyouni). PLACES: 4.90, 1.40. SF: 40.90..
Owner H H Aga Khan **Bred** Haras De Son Altesse L'Aga Khan Scea **Trained** Chantilly, France

NOTEBOOK
Rajsaman(FR), a Listed winner last season, was in as pacemaker for the favourite but established such an advantage that he was able to hold on to the line. He will go for the Poulains and will be employed in the same manner, but is unlikely to be allowed such an advantage there.
Siyouni(FR), who beat subsequent Breeders' Cup Juvenile Turf winner Pounced in the Jean Luc Lagardere last season, was sent off at odds on. However, he did not pick up at once when asked to go in pursuit of his stable companion and, although he finished strongly, it was too late. His trainer was pleased with the effort though, and he will go to the Poulains next.
Lope De Vega(IRE) finished fourth in the Lagardere and closed the gap with Siyouni this time. However, he made his effort before that rival and was run down late, so is not sure to confirm this in the Poulains.

1566a PRIX DE LA GROTTE (GROUP 3) (3YO FILLIES) (TURF) 1m
2:40 (12:00) 3-Y-O £35,398 (£14,159; £10,619; £7,079; £3,539)

RPR
1 **Anna Salai (USA)**[20] 3-9-0 0 MaximeGuyon 12 107
(A Fabre, France) *racd in rr: rdn 2f out: split horses: qcknd brilliantly: led ins fnl 110yds: comf* **11/1**
2 1 ½ **Gotlandia (FR)**[24] 1080 3-9-0 0 Pierre-CharlesBoudot 2 103
(Y De Nicolay, France) *w.w in 5th on rail: swtchd: qcknd wl: split horses: r.o wl: led briefly fnl 110yds: ct cl home* **50/1**
3 ¾ **Rosanara (FR)**[175] 7207 3-9-0 0 GeraldMosse 3 101
(A De Royer-Dupre, France) *racd in 4th on rail: qcknd wl early in st: r.o wl to ld ins fnl f: hdd and no ex fnl 110yds* **1/1**[1]
4 1 **Aruna (USA)**[205] 3-9-0 0 Christophe-PatriceLemaire 4 99
(J E Pease, France) *racd in midfield: swtchd and qcknd in st: evewry ch: no ex ins fnl f* **18/1**
5 snk **Via Medici (IRE)**[42] 3-9-0 0 Francois-XavierBertras 11 98
(F Rohaut, France) *prom early: chsd ldr early in st: hrd rdn: no ex fnl f* **10/1**
6 hd **Kartica**[24] 1080 3-9-0 0 StephanePasquier 6 98
(P Demercastel, France) *racd towards rr: proged on outer early in st: r.o wl* **66/1**
7 snk **Barouda (FR)**[187] 6929 3-9-0 0 KierenFallon 9 98
(J-M Beguigne, France) *racd in seventh: clsd on ldrs in st: fnd no room to chal: styd on wl* **6/1**[2]
8 1 ½ **Irish Cat (IRE)**[160] 7441 3-9-0 0 GregoryBenoist 7 94
(Robert Collet, France) *a towards the rr: no imp in fnl 2f* **66/1**
9 snk **Dolled Up (IRE)**[173] 7231 3-9-0 0 IoritzMendizabal 1 94
(Robert Collet, France) *prom early: rdn early in st: no ex fnl 2f* **12/1**
10 nk **Evaporation (FR)**[34] 3-9-0 0 OlivierPeslier 8 93
(C Laffon-Parias, France) *a in rr: no prog in st* **7/1**[3]
11 **Givine (FR)**[30] 3-9-0 0 JimmyMartin 5 93
(B De Montzey, France) *led fr s: rdn 2f out: hdd fnl f: dropped away* **20/1**

1m 38.33s (-0.07) **Going Correction** +0.325s/f (Good) 11 Ran SP% **116.9**
Speed ratings: **113,111,110,109,109 109,109,107,107,107 107**
WIN (incl. 1 euro stake): 9.60. PLACES: 2.20, 7.00, 1.20. DF: 224.20. SF: 338.00.
Owner Godolphin SNC **Bred** Darley **Trained** Chantilly, France

NOTEBOOK
Anna Salai(USA) was a maiden coming into the race but she quickened up really well to take this Guineas trial and eventually won quite comfortably. The Poule d'Essai des Pouliches will clearly now come into consideration.
Gotlandia(FR), beaten in Listed company in her last two starts, was an outsider here and looked to face a stiff task, but she picked up well between horses to get the better of the favourite, only to find the winner finishing even stronger on her outside.
Rosanara(FR), last year's Marcel Boussac winner, couldn't match the winner's turn of foot but kept on well enough, and her trainer expects her to come on plenty for the run. She's likely to reoppose the winner in the Poule d'Essai des Pouliches.

1567a PRIX LA FORCE (GROUP 3) (3YO) (TURF) 1m 2f
3:10 (12:00) 3-Y-O £35,398 (£14,159; £10,619; £7,079; £3,539)

RPR
1 **Simon De Montfort (IRE)**[21] 1110 3-9-2 0 MickaelBarzalona 8 105
(A Fabre, France) *in rr fr s and stl last 1 1/2f out: split horses: qcknd brilliantly: ct ldr fnl strides* **10/3**[1]
2 nk **Pain Perdu (FR)**[21] 1110 3-9-2 0 OlivierPeslier 2 105
(N Clement, France) *led fr s: set slow pce: qcknd wl in st: stl led ins fnl f: ct fnl strides* **10/1**
3 ¾ **Circumvent**[189] 6889 3-9-2 0 IoritzMendizabal 3 103
(P F I Cole) *prom fr s: qcknd wl in st: r.o wl* **11/2**
4 hd **Celtic Celeb (IRE)**[36] 951 3-9-2 0 ThierryThulliez 5 103
(F Doumen, France) *a.p: chal ldr fr 2f out: no ex fnl f* **7/1**
5 ½ **War Monger (IRE)**[36] 951 3-9-2 0 AnthonyCrastus 6 102
(E Lellouche, France) *racd towards rr: swtchd to outer early in st: hrd rdn 1 1/2f out: no ex fnl f* **4/1**[2]
6 ½ **Darizi (FR)**[33] 3-9-2 0 GeraldMosse 1 101
(J-C Rouget, France) *racd in 2nd: rdn early in st: r.o* **7/1**
7 ¾ **Gomez Adams (IRE)**[20] 3-9-2 0 StephanePasquier 7 99?
(P Demercastel, France) *racd in 5th tl st: effrt early in st: no ex clsng stages* **33/1**
8 ½ **Speartooth**[16] 3-9-2 0 Christophe-PatriceLemaire 4 98
(P Bary, France) *prom tl st: no ex fnl 2f* **5/1**[3]

2m 7.12s (3.12) **Going Correction** +0.325s/f (Good) 8 Ran SP% **112.2**
Speed ratings: **100,99,99,99,98 98,97,97**
WIN (incl. 1 euro stake): 5.20. PLACES: 1.60, 2.40, 2.10. DF: 19.60. SF: 25.50.
Owner Godolphin SNC **Bred** Darley **Trained** Chantilly, France

NOTEBOOK
Simon De Montfort(IRE) did not make his debut until October and followed up his recent Listed success by taking this Group 3. He showed good acceleration on his first try on anything other than soft ground and looks set to take his chance in the Prix du Jockey-Club.
Pain Perdu(FR) had finished three quarters of a length behind today's winner at Saint-Cloud earlier in the month, and finished closer having dictated a steady gallop before quickening. He is another who could go to Chantilly.
Circumvent, a winner on fast ground in Britain, had done well on two previous visits to France and ran his race on this first start since October against race-fit rivals. Connections believe he will be better with a stronger gallop and he will return to France for similar events.

SHA TIN (R-H)
Sunday, April 25

OFFICIAL GOING: Turf: good

1568a AUDEMARS PIGUET QE II CUP (GROUP 1) (3YO+) (TURF) 1m 2f
9:35 (12:00) 3-Y-O+
£636,435 (£238,663; £119,331; £63,643; £35,799; £19,888)

RPR
1 **Viva Pataca**[21] 8-9-0 0 WCMarwing 7 120
(J Moore, Hong Kong) *racd in 4th: rdn and str run fr 1 1/2f out: led ins fnl 110yds: hld on wl* **154/10**
2 nk **Lizard's Desire (SAF)**[29] 1027 5-9-0 0 ChristopheSoumillon 2 120
(M F De Kock, South Africa) *racd in 5th: rdn and r.o ins fnl 2f: disp 2nd fr 1f out: r.o wl* **11/1**
3 nk **Super Satin (NZ)**[42] 5-9-0 0 DouglasWhyte 4 119
(C Fownes, Hong Kong) *racd in 6th: rdn and outpcd 2f out: styd on strly fnl f* **12/1**
4 1 **Never Bouchon (JPN)**[29] 7-9-0 0 HirokiGoto 1 117
(Masanori Ito, Japan) *sn led: qcknd 2f out: hdd 110yds out: one pce* **44/1**
5 shd **Presvis**[29] 1025 6-9-0 0 RyanMoore 6 117
(L M Cumani) *last: hdwy ins fnl 2f: fin wl* **41/10**[2]
6 shd **Collection (IRE)**[21] 5-9-0 0 (t) DarrenBeadman 8 117
(J Moore, Hong Kong) *hld up and plld hrd early: r.o fnl 1 1/2f: n.d* **7/10**[1]
7 ½ **Super Pistachio (IRE)**[42] 4-9-0 0 (t) FCoetzee 5 116
(A S Cruz, Hong Kong) *chsd ldr: ev ch fr 2f out: one pce fnl f* **66/10**[3]
8 ¾ **Mr Medici (IRE)**[21] 5-9-0 0 HWLai 3 114
(L Ho, Hong Kong) *racd 3rd: rdn and nt qckn fnl 110yds* **15/1**
9 1 ½ **Unique Jewellery (NZ)**[21] 6-9-0 0 BrettPrebble 9 111
(J Size, Hong Kong) *a bhd* **63/1**

2m 4.97s (3.57) 9 Ran SP% **123.7**
PARI-MUTUEL (all including HK$10 stake): WIN 163.50; PLACE 29.50, 31.50, 29.00; DF 833.50.
Owner Stanley Ho Hung Sun **Bred** Floors Farming And Side Hill Stud **Trained** Hong Kong

NOTEBOOK
Presvis, held up at the back of the field, failed to get competitive in a race where the gallop slowed right down before they sprinted up the straight. They finished in a heap and clearly a stronger all-round pace would have suited him much better.

NEWCASTLE (L-H)
Monday, April 26

OFFICIAL GOING: Good to firm (good in places from 1m to 3.5f on round course; 7.5)
Wind: Fresh, half against Weather: Cloudy, fine

1569 COMPLETE FOOTBALL H'CAP 5f
2:10 (2:10) (Class 6) (0-55,55) 4-Y-O+ £2,719 (£809; £404; £202) Stalls High

Form RPR
050- 1 **King Of Eden (IRE)**[181] 7082 4-8-10 50 DavidAllan 14 63+
(E J Alston) *cl up stands' side: led over 1f out: clr of that gp ins fnl f: kpt on wl to collar far side ldr nr fin: 1st of 8 in gp* **9/1**[3]
00-6 2 nse **Miss Daawe**[5] 1470 6-8-8 55 DaleSwift(7) 5 68
(B Ellison) *in tch far side: led 2f out and sn clr of that gp: r.o wl fnl f: jst ct by stands' side wnr: 1st of 7 in gp* **5/1**[1]
-052 3 5 **Fasliyanne (IRE)**[19] 1154 4-9-1 55 (b) NeilCallan 9 50
(K A Ryan) *led stands' side gp to over 1f out: kpt on same pce fnl f: 2nd of 8 in gp* **5/1**[1]
0/ 4 3 **Socceroo**[684] 2928 5-9-1 55 PhillipMakin 15 39+
(D C Griffiths) *s.i.s: hld up in tch stands' side: effrt over 2f out: drvn and no imp fnl f: 3rd of 8 in gp* **14/1**
6234 5 nse **Fashion Icon (USA)**[9] 1391 4-8-11 51 JamieSpencer 1 35
(J Hetherton) *cl up far side: led that gp after 2f: hdd 2f out: one pce fnl f: 2nd of 7 in gp* **5/1**[1]
-064 6 ½ **Monsieur Harvey**[20] 1146 4-8-6 46 oh1 JoeFanning 4 28
(B Smart) *led 2f: cl up far side: drvn 1/2-way: one pce over 1f out: 3rd of 7 in gp* **20/1**
1300 7 ½ **Lujiana**[19] 1154 5-8-8 55 JohnCavanagh(7) 2 35
(M Brittain) *hld up far side: hdwy u.p over 1f out: kpt on: nvr able to chal: 4th of 7 in gp* **20/1**
004- 8 1 **Clanachy**[211] 6308 4-8-6 46 oh1 AndrewMullen 7 23
(A G Foster) *in tch far side: rdn over 2f out: one pce wl over 1f out: 5th of 7 in gp* **50/1**
30-0 9 hd **Darcy's Pride (IRE)**[21] 1112 6-9-0 54 (t) TonyHamilton 6 30
(P T Midgley) *chsd far side ldrs: drvn and outpcd 2f out: no imp after: 6th of 7 in gp* **10/1**
0260 10 ½ **Angle Of Attack (IRE)**[13] 1270 5-9-1 55 (v) GrahamGibbons 16 29
(A D Brown) *chsd stands' side ldrs: rdn 1/2-way: wknd appr fnl f: 4th of 8 in gp* **6/1**[2]
3650 11 ½ **Bertbrand**[16] 1235 5-8-8 48 (p) RoystonFfrench 12 21
(I W McInnes) *chsd stands' side ldrs tl rdn and wknd over 1f out: 5th of 8 in gp* **25/1**
-050 12 hd **Monte Cassino (IRE)**[5] 1477 5-9-1 55 TomEaves 10 27
(J O'Reilly) *prom on outside of stands' side gp: outpcd over 2f out: sn wknd: 6th of 8 in gp* **33/1**
000- 13 1 **Sleepy Valley (IRE)**[192] 6823 4-8-1 46 oh1 (p) PaulPickard(5) 3 14
(A Dickman) *t.k.h: chsd far side ldrs tl wknd over 1f out: last of 7 in gp* **66/1**
02-0 14 1 ¼ **Hosanna**[17] 1200 4-8-7 47 PaulHanagan 11 11
(J Barclay) *in tch stands' side: drvn over 2f out: sn btn: 7th of 8 in gp* **16/1**
0-00 15 ½ **Red Cell (IRE)**[19] 1154 4-8-4 47 (b) KellyHarrison(3) 8 9
(I W McInnes) *hld up stands' side: effrt over 2f out: wknd wl over 1f out: last of 8 in gp* **66/1**

61.56 secs (0.46) **Going Correction** +0.35s/f (Good) 15 Ran SP% **117.2**
Speed ratings (Par 101): **107,106,98,94,94 93,92,90,90,89 88,88,87,85,84**
toteswingers: 1&2 £13.70, 1&3 £11.90, 2&3 £6.50 CSF £48.03 CT £257.90 TOTE £10.40: £2.60, £3.10, £1.60; EX 72.40 Trifecta £133.00 Part won. Pool: £179.73 - 0.20 winning units..
Owner The Grumpy Old Geezers **Bred** Gainsborough Stud Management Ltd **Trained** Longton, Lancs
■ Stewards' Enquiry : David Allan caution: used whip with excessive frequency

FOCUS
The meeting here on Grand National day almost three weeks ago had to be abandoned and only the 5f track could be used on the straight course. The going was reckoned on the quick side of good. A low-grade sprint started proceedings. Eight raced on the far side, the other seven on the stands' side and at the line the first home on each side were split by a whisker. Both finished clear of their respective groups.

1570 LA TAXIS CONDITIONS STKS 1m (R)
2:40 (2:40) (Class 3) 3-Y-0+ **£6,854** (£2,052; £1,026; £513; £256) **Stalls** Centre

Form RPR

5503 **1** **Lovelace**[44] 883 6-9-5 105 .... AdrianNicholls 4 104
(D Nicholls) *t.k.h: hld up in tch: hdwy whn nt clr run briefly 2f out: rdn to ld ins fnl f: hrd pressed: jst hld on* **1/1**[1]

254- **2** *nse* **Dream Lodge (IRE)**[205] 6485 6-9-9 108 .... PaulHanagan 3 108
(R A Fahey) *pressed ldr 2f: cl up: rdn to ld appr 2f out to ins fnl f: styd upsides: jst failed* **7/4**[2]

3/30 **3** *4 ½* **Souter's Sister (IRE)**[44] 883 4-9-0 104 .... JerryO'Dwyer 5 88
(M Botti) *prom: effrt and chsd ldr over 1f out: sn rdn: outpcd ins fnl f* **13/2**[3]

4-30 **4** *2 ¼* **Lucky Dance (BRZ)**[9] 1383 8-9-5 88 .... RobertHavlin 6 88
(A G Foster) *t.k.h: chsd ldr after 2f: effrt wd of remainder 2f out: btn ins fnl f* **10/1**

/5-0 **5** *4* **Back To Paris (IRE)**[114] 19 8-9-5 62 .... DavidNolan 1 78?
(Paul Murphy) *set ordinary gallop to appr 2f out: sn rdn and wknd* **100/1**

1m 42.94s (-2.36) **Going Correction** -0.20s/f (Firm) **5 Ran SP% 109.8**
Speed ratings (Par 107): **103,102,98,96,92**
CSF £2.97 TOTE £2.10: £1.20, £1.90; EX 3.30.
Owner Dab Hand Racing **Bred** Mrs Mary Taylor **Trained** Sessay, N Yorks

FOCUS
A fair conditions event and the pace was sound. The form is rated around the runer-up,. but the fifth is flattered and this form is far from solid.

NOTEBOOK
Lovelace, 1lb ahead of Dream Lodge on official figures, without a win since 2008 and as usual highly tried including at Meydan this winter, was bought out of Mark Johnston's stable for £34,000. Now in the same ownership as top sprinter Regal Parade, he was given a patient ride. Denied a clear run at one stage, after going head-to-head he poked his nose in front on the line. This was his 32nd career start and, rated 105, opportunities will be thin on the ground, but a trip to Royal Ascot is likely according to connections with either a similar race at Haydock or a handicap at York likely beforehand. (op 11-8)
Dream Lodge(IRE), much improved at five for Richard Fahey, is happiest when allowed to dominate. That was not the case here and after hitting the front he was piped right on the line battling back bravely. Rated 108, he too will need careful placing with the John Smith's Cup at York a likely handicap target. He would not want the ground any quicker. (op 13-8 tchd 6-4 and 15-8 and 2-1 in a place)
Souter's Sister(IRE), a Group 3 winner at two for another yard, missed all of last year. A dozen lengths behind Lovelace on her second start back at Wolverhampton last month, she shaped better here but her current rating of 104 flatters her. (op 6-1 tchd 9-2)
Lucky Dance(BRZ), who had over a stone to find with the first pair, tended to race wide. He ran one of his better races and connections will be hoping his rating of 88 is not changed. (tchd 12-1)
Back To Paris(IRE), well beaten in two starts in all-weather claimers, was a smart three-year-old defying a mark of 95 at Leopardstown on his final start. Now rated just 62, he raced keenly and took them along until falling in a hole. How much of the old ability is still there remains to be seen.

1571 IPCSECURITY.CO.UK FILLIES' H'CAP 1m (R)
3:10 (3:12) (Class 4) (0-80,80) 3-Y-0 **£4,415** (£1,321; £660; £330; £164) **Stalls** Centre

Form RPR

226- **1** **Battlemaiden (IRE)**[207] 6418 3-8-13 75 .... JoeFanning 7 83+
(M Johnston) *dictated ordinary gallop: shkn up and qcknd over 1f out: kpt on wl fnl f: unchal* **9/2**[3]

00-3 **2** *1 ½* **Nimue (USA)**[11] 1329 3-9-4 80 .... JamieSpencer 1 84+
(P F I Cole) *t.k.h: hld up in tch: smooth hdwy to chse wnr over 1f out: rdn and hung lft ins fnl f: rdr looked over wrong shoulder and eased briefly cl home: jst hld on for 2nd* **6/4**[1]

-213 **3** *shd* **Sweet Child O'Mine**[17] 1210 3-9-1 77 .... FrannyNorton 3 80
(R C Guest) *t.k.h: trckd ldrs: rdn and outpcd 2f out: kpt on strly fnl f* **7/2**[2]

16-0 **4** *3 ¼* **Dance For Julie (IRE)**[38] 934 3-8-10 72 .... PhillipMakin 6 67
(B M R Haslam) *s.s: sn rcvrd and hld up: shkn up and hdwy 2f out: no imp fnl f* **16/1**

0-1 **5** *3* **Bear Tobouggie**[21] 1119 3-8-10 72 .... PJMcDonald 2 60
(G A Swinbank) *trckd ldrs: drvn and outpcd over 2f out: no imp over 1f out* **8/1**

456- **6** *1 ½* **Ananda Kanda (USA)**[221] 6011 3-9-3 79 .... TomEaves 4 63
(B Ellison) *hld up in tch: outpcd over 2f out: sn n.d* **33/1**

532- **7** *½* **Brink**[180] 7114 3-8-4 69 ow1 .... BarryMcHugh(3) 5 52
(T J Pitt) *t.k.h: sn trcking wnr: rdn and lost 2nd over 1f out: wknd* **7/1**

1m 44.65s (-0.65) **Going Correction** -0.20s/f (Firm) **7 Ran SP% 112.8**
Speed ratings (Par 97): **95,93,93,90,87 85,85**
toteswingers: 1&2 £2.20, 1&3 £2.50, 2&3 £2.10 CSF £11.37 TOTE £4.60: £1.60, £1.30; EX 10.60.
Owner Sheikh Hamdan Bin Mohammed Al Maktoum **Bred** Woodcote Stud Ltd **Trained** Middleham Moor, N Yorks

FOCUS
A 68-80 fillies' only three-year-old handicap. It was much the slowest of the four C/D races. The winner had the run of the race and is rated up 6lb in a race rated around the third.

1572 PARKLANDS GOLF CLUB MAIDEN STKS 1m 4f 93y
3:40 (3:41) (Class 5) 3-4-Y-0 **£3,280** (£981; £490; £245; £122) **Stalls** Low

Form RPR

422 **1** **Dancing Dude (IRE)**[9] 1380 3-8-9 80 .... JoeFanning 3 63+
(M Johnston) *pressed ldr: led after 3f: jnd over 2f out: kpt on gamely fnl f* **5/6**[1]

2 *1* **Stetson**[40] 4-10-0 0 .... PJMcDonald 7 63
(G A Swinbank) *hld up: smooth hdwy and ev ch 2f out: sn drvn: edgd lft and rt u.p ins fnl f: r.o* **5/2**[2]

0- **3** *½* **Across The Sea (USA)**[208] 6382 3-8-10 0 ow1 .... MickyFenton 5 61
(T P Tate) *cl up: wnt 2nd 1/2-way: effrt and disp ld over 2f out to over 1f out: one pce ins fnl f* **7/1**[3]

4 *1 ¼* **Captain Cornelius (IRE)** 3-8-9 0 .... DuranFentiman 2 58
(Joss Saville) *hld up: hdwy and in tch over 2f out: rdn and kpt on same pce ins fnl f* **33/1**

600- **5** *¾* **Henry Havelock**[180] 7116 3-8-9 44 .... TonyHamilton 9 57
(C Grant) *prom: effrt and ch 2f out: rdn and one pce appr fnl f* **100/1**

6 **6** *6* **On The Right Path**[13] 1271 3-8-6 0 .... KellyHarrison(3) 6 47
(Paul Murphy) *prom tl hung lft and wknd over 2f out* **66/1**

00 **7** *6* **I Got Music**[13] 1271 3-7-13 0 .... PaulPickard(5) 10 35
(K G Reveley) *hld up: outpcd 4f out: sn no imp* **80/1**

8 *nk* **Tinseltown**[291] 3838 4-10-0 0 .... RoystonFfrench 4 39
(B S Rothwell) *t.k.h: in tch: rdn and outpcd over 4f out: sn btn* **10/1**

650- **9** *44* **Dinkys Diamond (IRE)**[220] 6046 3-8-9 54 .... TomEaves 1 —
(B Ellison) *led 4f: cl up tl wknd over 4f out: t.o* **33/1**

2m 46.49s (0.89) **Going Correction** -0.20s/f (Firm)
WFA 3 from 4yo 20lb **9 Ran SP% 114.3**
Speed ratings (Par 103): **89,88,88,87,86 82,78,78,49**
toteswingers: 1&2 £1.30, 1&3 £2.60, 2&3 £2.70 CSF £2.90 TOTE £1.90: £1.02, £1.40, £2.40; EX 3.30 Trifecta £9.40 Pool: £574.87 - 45.21 winning units..
Owner A D Spence **Bred** Wadud Syndicate **Trained** Middleham Moor, N Yorks

FOCUS
Just an ordinary maiden with little to choose between the first five home in the end. It was slowly run and the winner probably didn't need to get near his previous form.

1573 IPC SECURITY H'CAP 5f
4:10 (4:10) (Class 2) (0-105,104) 4-Y-0+
£9,969 (£2,985; £1,492; £747; £372; £187) **Stalls** High

Form RPR

06-4 **1** **Buachaill Dona (IRE)**[9] 1400 7-9-1 98 .... AdrianNicholls 4 106
(D Nicholls) *in tch: effrt on outside and led appr 1f out: edgd rt: drvn out* **7/2**[1]

310- **2** *½* **Captain Dunne (IRE)**[198] 6678 5-8-13 96 .... DavidAllan 10 106+
(T D Easterby) *t.k.h: hld up: nt clr run fr 2f out: effrt whn hmpd appr fnl f: gd hdwy whn clr last 150yds: styd on strly to take 2nd cl home: unlucky* **13/2**

41-5 **3** *hd* **Quest For Success (IRE)**[19] 1174 5-9-2 99 .... PaulHanagan 9 104
(R A Fahey) *in tch: rdn over 2f out: chsd wnr and edgd rt ins fnl f: one pce and lost 2nd cl home* **4/1**[2]

440- **4** *1 ¾* **Masta Plasta (IRE)**[240] 5420 7-9-2 104 .... BillyCray(5) 2 103
(D Nicholls) *cl up outside: led 1/2-way: edgd rt and hdd 1f out: kpt on same pce* **14/1**

10-0 **5** *nse* **The Nifty Fox**[12] 1295 6-8-4 87 .... DuranFentiman 7 86
(T D Easterby) *w ldrs tl rdn and nt qckn over 1f out* **20/1**

03-0 **6** *3 ½* **Master Rooney (IRE)**[12] 1295 4-8-4 87 .... RoystonFfrench 6 73
(B Smart) *slt ld to 1/2-way: rdn and outpcd over 1f out* **5/1**[3]

030- **7** *¾* **Red Cape (FR)**[185] 6994 7-8-5 88 .... AndrewElliott 5 71
(Mrs R A Carr) *w ldrs tl edgd lft and no ex fr 2f out* **33/1**

300- **8** *3 ¼* **Roker Park (IRE)**[212] 6270 5-8-12 95 ....(p) NeilCallan 8 67
(K A Ryan) *in tch: rdn whn checked over 1f out: edgd lft and sn outpcd* **4/1**[2]

304- **9** *½* **Strike Up The Band**[181] 7090 7-8-12 100 .... MichaelO'Connell(5) 11 70
(D Nicholls) *prom: n.m.r and lost pl 2f out: n.d after* **12/1**

61.23 secs (0.13) **Going Correction** +0.35s/f (Good) **9 Ran SP% 114.3**
Speed ratings (Par 109): **109,108,107,105,105 99,98,93,92**
toteswingers: 1&2 £6.30, 1&3 £3.90, 2&3 £5.40 CSF £26.29 CT £94.22 TOTE £4.90: £1.80, £2.70, £1.90; EX 26.20 Trifecta £70.50 Pool: £447.81 - 4.70 winning units..
Owner Mike Browne **Bred** John O Browne **Trained** Sessay, N Yorks
■ Stewards' Enquiry : Paul Hanagan two-day ban: careless riding (May 10-11)

FOCUS
A good, competitive 87-104 sprint handicap. It was originally intended to be run over six but with the track's problems it had to be reduced by a furlong. They raced in one group towards the stands' side but the rail itself did not look the place to be. The race is rated around the third.

NOTEBOOK
Buachaill Dona(IRE), who had shaped well over six on his return at Thirsk, missed a beat at the start. It may have aided his cause because he was able to get cover against the strong headwind. He is equally effective over five and six but would not want the ground any quicker. His season will no doubt revolve another crack at the Gosforth Cup back here later on. (op 11-4 tchd 5-2)
Captain Dunne(IRE), who achieved a RPR of 105 when winning on his penultimate start at four at Beveley, reappeared here rated just 96. He looked in need of the outing but was a most unlucky loser. He met serious traffic problems when making his way to the outside from his number 10 stall and would have got there with a bit further to go. He looks an ideal candidate for the 0-100 handicap at York in two weeks' time. (tchd 15-2)
Quest For Success(IRE), a winner three times last year, showed the benefit of his reappearance. He threw down a strong challenge to the winner and is another who would not have appreciated this quick ground. It was later reported that the gelding had been struck into on his near hind. Official explanation: jockey said gelding was struck into left-hind (op 6-1)
Masta Plasta(IRE), who has had a tie-forward operation since last year when he did not reappear after August, was drawn widest of all. After taking charge he drifted towards the stands' side. He is all speed and a less testing track plays more to his strengths. He is definitely on a winning mark now. (op 8-1)
The Nifty Fox, 5lb higher than his last winning mark, is better suited by a much sharper track. (op 16-1)
Master Rooney(IRE) was far from disgraced but is better suited by six. (op 11-2)
Red Cape(FR), another returning to action, gained all his four wins last year over the extra furlong. (op 40-1)
Strike Up The Band Official explanation: jockey said gelding was unsuited by the good to firm (good in places) ground

1574 GOSFORTH DECORATING & BUILDING SERVICES H'CAP (DIV I) 1m (R)
4:40 (4:41) (Class 6) (0-65,65) 4-Y-0+ **£2,266** (£674; £337; £168) **Stalls** Centre

Form RPR

4641 **1** **Quiet Mountain (IRE)**[18] 1193 5-8-10 **60** .... BarryMcHugh(3) 11 68+
(Ollie Pears) *hld up: hdwy over 2f out: led over 1f out: pushed out fnl f* **6/1**

50-0 **2** *¾* **Film Festival (USA)**[21] 1115 7-8-11 **65** .... DaleSwift(7) 4 71
(B Ellison) *bhd tl hdwy 2f out: chsd wnr ins fnl f: kpt on fin* **11/1**

465- **3** *¾* **Fathey (IRE)**[195] 6755 4-8-11 **58** .... JoeFanning 3 62
(C Smith) *cl up: rdn over 2f out: rallied and ev ch over 1f out: one pce ins fnl f* **11/1**

/00- **4** *1 ¼* **Polish World (USA)**[350] 1924 6-8-4 **51** oh1 .... DuranFentiman 2 52
(P T Midgley) *t.k.h: led tl edgd rt and hdd over 1f out: one pce fnl f* **25/1**

2-22 **5** *9* **Silken Promise (USA)**[95] 244 4-8-13 **60** ....(p) HayleyTurner 5 41
(T B P Coles) *in tch: effrt over 2f out: sn outpcd: no imp fnl f* **3/1**[1]

35-5 **6** *½* **Morocchius (USA)**[9] 1396 5-9-2 **63** ....(p) TomEaves 7 43
(Julie Camacho) *midfield: pushed along and outpcd over 2f out: n.d after* **7/2**[2]

030/ **7** *¾* **Emirate Isle**[140] 6950 6-9-4 **65** ....(p) PJMcDonald 10 43
(B Storey) *midfield on outside: outpcd 3f out: nvr able to chal* **25/1**

100- **8** *1 ¼* **Phantom Serenade (IRE)**[192] 6817 5-8-11 **58** .... PhillipMakin 6 33
(M Dods) *cl up: effrt 3f out: wknd over 1f out* **11/1**

00-0 **9** *1 ¼* **Silly Gilly (IRE)**[21] 1115 6-8-8 **55** .... PaulHanagan 8 27
(R E Barr) *in tch: outpcd over 2f out: btn over 1f out* **5/1**[3]

244- **10** ½ **Hettie Hubble**[234] 5621 4-7-13 **51** oh3 PaulPickard(5) 1 22
(D W Thompson) *sn pushed along towards rr: shortlived effrt on ins wl over 2f out: nvr on terms* **28/1**

1m 43.34s (-1.96) **Going Correction** -0.20s/f (Firm) **10** Ran SP% **114.3**
Speed ratings (Par 101): **101,100,99,98,89 88,88,86,85,85**
toteswingers: 1&2 £14.50, 1&3 £10.80, 2&3 £24.90 CSF £66.37 CT £724.24 TOTE £7.50: £2.70, £3.60, £3.30; EX 87.20 TRIFECTA Not won..
Owner O'Brien, Moll, Spencer, Vaux, Davies **Bred** Mrs P Grubb **Trained** Norton, N Yorks

FOCUS
Part one of a divided 51-65 handicap. It was slightly slower than division two but the form seems sound and the winner can do better still.
Polish World(USA) Official explanation: jockey said gelding hung right-handed throughout
Silken Promise(USA) Official explanation: trainer said filly was in season

1575 GOSFORTH DECORATING & BUILDING SERVICES H'CAP (DIV II) 1m (R)
5:15 (5:15) (Class 6) (0-65,65) 4-Y-0+ **£2,266** (£674; £337; £168) **Stalls** Centre

Form			Horse	RPR
5020	**1**		**Saving Grace**[19] 1172 4-8-4 **51** oh3 DuranFentiman 6 — (E J Alston) *cl up: led over 2f out: rdn and edgd lft over 1f out: styd on wl fnl f* **14/1**	60
30-6	**2**	1 ¾	**Mohawk Ridge**[19] 1172 4-9-3 **64** PhillipMakin 2 — (M Dods) *hld up towards rr: rdn over 2f out: hdwy over 1f out: chsd wnr ins fnl f: r.o* **3/1**[1]	71+
3630	**3**	1 ½	**Louisiade (IRE)**[19] 1171 9-8-4 **51** oh4 (p) FrannyNorton 7 — (R C Guest) *prom: effrt over 2f out: chsd wnr briefly ins fnl f: kpt on same pce* **11/1**	53
400-	**4**	nk	**Hansomis (IRE)**[195] 6765 6-8-13 **60** PaulHanagan 3 — (B Mactaggart) *led to over 2f out: rallied: kpt on same pce u.p fnl f* **14/1**	61
1406	**5**	½	**Rub Of The Relic (IRE)**[9] 1374 5-8-6 **58** (be) PaulPickard(5) 4 — (P T Midgley) *hld up: rdn 3f out: no imp tl hdwy fnl f: nrst fin* **17/2**	58
00-6	**6**	nse	**Fortunate Bid (IRE)**[9] 1396 4-9-2 **63** RoystonFfrench 5 — (Mrs L Stubbs) *hld up in midfield: effrt and chsd ldrs over 2f out: edgd rt over 1f out: one pce fnl f* **6/1**[2]	63
50-0	**7**	1	**Carragold**[104] 139 4-8-7 **54** DavidAllan 11 — (M Brittain) *chsd ldrs: drvn over 4f out: rallied 3f out: one pce fr 2f out* **8/1**[3]	51
00-3	**8**	¾	**Cigalas**[17] 1204 5-8-6 **58** PatrickDonaghy(5) 9 — (Mrs J C McGregor) *s.i.s: bhd tl styd on fnl f: nvr rchd ldrs* **11/1**	54
405-	**9**	2 ¼	**Indian Violet (IRE)**[210] 6333 4-8-11 **65** DuilioDaSilva(7) 8 — (D W Thompson) *prom: chsd wnr over 2f out tl ins fnl f: wknd* **12/1**	55
326	**10**	hd	**Fitzolini**[46] 857 4-8-9 **56** (p) GrahamGibbons 1 — (A D Brown) *prom tl drvn and wknd fr 2f out* **8/1**[3]	46
1036	**11**	7	**Positivity**[20] 1142 4-8-7 **54** (p) TomEaves 10 — (B Smart) *hld up: rdn over 4f out: hung lft over 2f out: sn wknd* **14/1**	28

1m 43.02s (-2.28) **Going Correction** -0.20s/f (Firm) **11** Ran SP% **116.4**
Speed ratings (Par 101): **103,101,99,99,98 98,97,97,94,94 87**
toteswingers: 1&2 £10.20, 1&3 £18.60, 2&3 £10.30 CSF £55.26 CT £501.50 TOTE £19.00: £6.30, £1.40, £3.50; EX 71.10 TRIFECTA Not won..
Owner Liam & Tony Ferguson **Bred** Liam & Tony Ferguson **Trained** Longton, Lancs

FOCUS
Part two and another low-grade affair. It was the quicker division and although the winner and third were out of the weights the form has been rated fairly positively.
Fitzolini Official explanation: trainer had no explanation for the poor form shown

1576 LA TAXIS APPRENTICE H'CAP 1m 2f 32y
5:45 (5:45) (Class 6) (0-60,59) 4-Y-0+ **£1,683** (£501; £250; £125) **Stalls** Centre

Form			Horse	RPR
625-	**1**		**Shekan Star**[211] 6310 8-8-13 **53** MatthewLawson 2 — (K G Reveley) *hld up: hdwy on outside over 2f out: styd on wl fnl f: led nr fin* **8/1**	61+
0021	**2**	hd	**Bajan Pride**[3] 1507 6-9-0 **59** 6ex MarzenaJeziorek(5) 9 — (R A Fahey) *in tch: smooth hdwy over 1f out: led over 1f out: rdn and kpt on fnl f: hdd nr fin* **5/1**[2]	67
040-	**3**	1 ¼	**Sharp Sovereign (USA)**[185] 6987 4-8-0 **45** NoelGarbutt(5) 3 — (T D Barron) *prom: rdn over 2f out: effrt and ev ch over 1f out: kpt on same pce wl ins fnl f* **9/2**[1]	50
-464	**4**	nk	**Piverina (IRE)**[41] 898 5-8-5 **45** (p) RichardRowe 1 — (Julie Camacho) *midfield: effrt and hdwy over 2f out: kpt on ins fnl f* **10/1**	50
00/0	**5**	2	**Gulf Coast**[12] 1296 5-8-9 **56** LukeStrong(7) 13 — (T D Walford) *midfield: effrt over 2f out: plugged on fnl f* **7/1**[3]	57
0300	**6**	1	**Grey Command (USA)**[9] 1398 5-9-5 **59** JohnCavanagh 8 — (M Brittain) *in tch: drvn and outpcd over 3f out: rallied over 1f out: kpt on fnl f* **9/1**	58
04-4	**7**	nse	**Red Skipper (IRE)**[17] 1204 5-8-7 **54** (p) ShirleyTeasdale(7) 10 — (N Wilson) *led to over 1f out: sn one pce* **10/1**	52
01-0	**8**	2 ½	**Bollin Freddie**[12] 1296 6-8-8 **55** ShaneBKelly(7) 11 — (A J Lockwood) *cl up: ev ch over 2f out: one pce over 1f out* **16/1**	48
0-06	**9**	5	**Agricultural**[22] 1103 4-8-11 **54** MJMurphy(3) 12 — (Mrs L B Normile) *hld up: rdn over 2f out: nvr able to chal* **100/1**	37
1400	**10**	3	**Mehendi (IRE)**[13] 1277 4-9-1 **55** DaleSwift 4 — (B Ellison) *chsd ldrs: drvn and outpcd over 3f out: n.d after* **10/1**	32
035-	**11**	shd	**Cecina Marina**[163] 7080 7-8-1 **46** NeilFarley(5) 14 — (Mrs K Walton) *in tch: hdwy over 3f out: wknd fr 2f out* **16/1**	23
400-	**12**	1 ¼	**Rain Stops Play (IRE)**[192] 6818 8-8-5 **48** JakePayne(3) 16 — (N G Richards) *t.k.h: hld up: effrt over 2f out: sn btn* **16/1**	23
00-0	**13**	6	**Firsaan (IRE)**[108] 90 4-8-3 **46** JamesRogers(3) 15 — (J R Norton) *hld up: rdn 1/2-way: nvr on terms* **40/1**	9
366-	**14**	31	**Le Petit Vigier**[391] 1054 4-8-8 **48** (t) AdamCarter 6 — (P F Holmes) *s.s: a bhd: lost tch fnl 3f* **25/1**	—

2m 11.22s (-0.68) **Going Correction** -0.20s/f (Firm) **14** Ran SP% **120.7**
Speed ratings (Par 101): **94,93,92,92,91 90,90,88,84,81 81,80,75,51**
toteswingers: 1&2 £7.70, 1&3 £9.60, 2&3 £7.00 CSF £47.27 CT £207.41 TOTE £8.80: £3.00, £1.50, £2.70; EX 40.20 Trifecta £35.10 Part won. Pool: £47.48 - 0.30 winning units. Place 6: £18.03 Place 5: £9.18 .
Owner D Young **Bred** The Welcome Alliance **Trained** Lingdale, Redcar & Cleveland

FOCUS
A low-grade 45-59 apprentice handicap. Straightforward but limited form with the winner rated back to her best.
T/Plt: £14.80 to a £1 stake. Pool: £59,389.02. 2,921.29 winning tickets. T/Qpdt: £8.10 to a £1 stake. Pool: £3,178.97. 289.34 winning tickets. RY

1428 WINDSOR (R-H)
Monday, April 26

OFFICIAL GOING: Good to firm (good in places; 8.5)
Stands rail between 6f and 3.5f dolled out 4yds. Top bend dolled out 2yds from innermost line adding 9yds to races of a mile and over.
Wind: Light, behind Weather: Fine

1577 SPORTINGBET.COM MAIDEN AUCTION FILLIES' STKS 5f 10y
5:10 (5:13) (Class 5) 2-Y-O **£2,729** (£806; £403) **Stalls** High

Form			Horse	RPR
	1		**The Sydney Arms (IRE)** 2-8-13 0 RichardHughes 13 — (R Hannon) *wnt lft s: chsd ldng pair: pushed along 1/2-way: squeezed between rivals 1f out: shkn up to ld last 50yds: shade cleverly* **11/10**[1]	84+
	2	nk	**Dress Up (IRE)** 2-8-4 0 DavidProbert 14 — (S Kirk) *led: rdn over 1f out: waved tail u.p: kpt on but hdd and hld last 50yds* **25/1**	74
23	**3**	1 ¼	**Style And Panache (IRE)**[19] 1173 2-8-5 0 AndrewHeffernan(3) 4 — (P D Evans) *pressed ldr: rdn and no imp 2f out: lost 2nd and one pce fnl f* **4/1**[2]	73+
	4	1 ¾	**Electric Waves (IRE)** 2-8-6 0 RichardMullen 8 — (E S McMahon) *chsd ldrs but nt on terms: kpt on to take 4th jst over 1f out: nvr able to chal* **7/1**[3]	65+
	5	3	**Melodize** 2-8-6 0 MartinDwyer 7 — (W R Muir) *chsd ldrs: rdn 2f out: steadily outpcd fr over 1f out* **16/1**	54+
	6	1 ½	**Fifth Ave** 2-8-6 0 FergusSweeney 16 — (J A Osborne) *dwlt: cl up bhd ldrs and racd against nr side rail: outpcd wl over 1f out: rn green after* **50/1**	49+
	7	1	**Eucharist (IRE)** 2-8-13 0 RyanMoore 5 — (R Hannon) *chsd ldrs 3f: nvr on terms: fdd fr over 1f out* **8/1**	52
	8	hd	**Ventose** 2-8-4 0 SamHitchcott 15 — (M R Channon) *dwlt: chsd ldrs but sn pushed along: wl outpcd fr 1/2-way: nvr on terms after* **25/1**	43
	9	nk	**Two Feet Of Snow (IRE)** 2-8-4 0 FrankieMcDonald 3 — (R Hannon) *dwlt: nvr beyond midfield and nvr on terms w ldrs: no real prog over 1f out* **33/1**	42
	10	4 ½	**Kissing Clara (IRE)** 2-8-4 0 LukeMorris 9 — (J S Moore) *dwlt: rn green and sn pushed along: nvr on terms: drvn and no prog 2f out* **66/1**	25
	11	1	**Bathwick Freeze** 2-7-11 0 KevinLundie(7) 12 — (P D Evans) *s.s: rn green and wl bhd: nvr a factor* **33/1**	22
	12	2 ½	**Lucky Tricks** 2-8-4 0 TadhgO'Shea 6 — (S Kirk) *s.s: sn wl bhd* **66/1**	13
	13	¾	**Atia** 2-8-13 0 PatCosgrave 1 — (J G Portman) *racd on her own in centre: chsd ldrs to 1/2-way: sn bhd* **33/1**	19
	14	4 ½	**Bendigedig** 2-8-6 0 RichardSmith 11 — (S Kirk) *dwlt: outpcd and a struggling in rr* **66/1**	—
	15	1 ½	**Stacey** 2-8-4 0 NeilChalmers 10 — (Jean-Rene Auvray) *dwlt: rn green and sn wl bhd* **100/1**	—
	16	13	**Shesanindian (IRE)** 2-8-8 0 JamieMackay 2 — (A W Carroll) *s.s: outpcd and a wl in rr: wknd 1/2-way: t.o* **100/1**	—

60.89 secs (0.59) **Going Correction** +0.10s/f (Good) **16** Ran SP% **122.0**
Speed ratings (Par 89): **99,98,96,93,88 86,84,84,84,76 75,71,70,62,60 39**
toteswingers: 1&2 £13.20, 1&3 £23.20, 2&3 £22.40 CSF £41.15 TOTE £2.60: £1.40, £4.90, £1.40; EX 50.30 Trifecta £559.60 Pool: £4068.57 - 5.38 winning units..
Owner R Morecombe, J Reus & D Anderson **Bred** Fergus Cousins **Trained** East Everleigh, Wilts

FOCUS
After a dry night the going was changed to good, good to firm in places. There was a strong tailwind down the straight.\n\x\x A juvenile fillies' maiden auction in which only one of the runners had racecourse experience. The pace was strong and the first four finished clear of the rest. The race averages and the third set the level.

NOTEBOOK
The Sydney Arms(IRE) was always well positioned just behind the leaders and fought her way through a gap in the closing stages to land a gamble and win with a bit more in hand than the margin suggests on debut. Out of an unraced daughter of good sprinter Dafayna, she seems to have plenty of natural pace and represents a yard that has been in scintillating form with its juveniles. She may be turned out quickly for a fillies' conditions event at Salisbury on Sunday. (op 6-4 tchd 13-8 in places)
Dress Up(IRE) attracted no interest at the sales but she is from a decent sprinting family and made an audacious bid against the stands' rail on her debut. She will have learned a lot from the experience and should be able to win a similar race. (op 22-1)
Style And Panache(IRE) chased home a nice prospect at Southwell on debut and was reportedly unsuited by soft ground when odds-on third of five behind a pair of stable companions at Nottingham earlier in the month. She had a low draw to contend with this time but put in a highly creditable effort and adds some solidity to the form. (op 7-2 tchd 9-2)
Electric Waves(IRE) was slowly away but stayed on steadily to post a very encouraging debut effort. Her sire gets plenty of speedy types, and her half-sister Tut was a 7f winner at two. She could prove a bargain at £8,500. (op 8-1)
Melodize shaped with some promise and was not given a hard time when the front four got away. She is the first foal of an unraced half-sister to Hypnotic, who was a prolific 7f-1m winner. (tchd 18-1)
Fifth Ave, a February foaled half-sister to a 5f 2-y-o winner, didn't get the best of runs against the near rail and rates a bit better than her finishing position. (op 66-1)
Eucharist(IRE) showed some ability from a tough draw on debut. Her pedigree is an interesting mixture of speed and stamina, being by a good sprinter and out of a 1m4f winner. (op 6-1)

1578 SPORTINGBET.COM H'CAP 1m 3f 135y
5:40 (5:40) (Class 5) (0-70,68) 3-Y-O **£2,729** (£806; £403) **Stalls** Low

Form			Horse	RPR
6-1	**1**		**Bebopalula (IRE)**[75] 484 3-9-4 **68** FrankieDettori 4 — (B W Hills) *mde virtually all: rdn and pressed over 2f out: hd at awkward angle but drew clr fr over 1f out* **5/6**[1]	79+
2521	**2**	5	**Captain Cool (IRE)**[9] 1394 3-8-12 **62** PatDobbs 8 — (R Hannon) *cl up: rdn over 3f out: clsd over 2f out: sn outpcd: kpt on to take 2nd fnl f* **7/1**[2]	62
4336	**3**	¾	**Frameit (IRE)**[7] 1433 3-8-8 **65** (b[1]) RyanPowell(7) 3 — (J S Moore) *trckd ldrs: rdn to go 2nd 4f out: chal u.p over 2f out: btn off over 1f out: sn lost 2nd* **33/1**	64
60-0	**4**	3	**Specialising**[14] 1260 3-8-8 **58** EddieCreighton 11 — (M R Channon) *hld up in last trio: rdn 5f out: prog u.p after: wnt 4th 2f out: no real imp after* **20/1**	52
06-2	**5**	1 ¾	**One Cool Poppy (IRE)**[14] 1261 3-8-6 **56** LukeMorris 1 — (H J L Dunlop) *trckd ldng pair tl rdn 4f out: steadily fdd* **8/1**[3]	47

3050 **6** *7* **Orsett Lad (USA)**[14] 1261 3-8-7 **60** .... MarcHalford(3) 2 40
(J R Best) *dwlt: hld up in last trio: pushed along and sme prog fr over 3f out: nvr nr ldrs* **50/1**

06-5 **7** *6* **Sansili**[87] 340 3-8-13 **63** .... RichardHughes 5 33
(P Bowen) *hld up wl in rr: nvr on terms: lft bhd by ldrs fr 4f out* **16/1**

65-6 **8** *4* **Varachi**[14] 1261 3-9-1 **65** ....(b[1]) RyanMoore 10 28
(E A L Dunlop) *chsd wnr: drvn 4f out: sn lost pl: grad wknd* **9/1**

00-3 **9** *15* **Lauberhorn**[19] 1157 3-9-1 **65** .... EddieAhern 9 3
(Eve Johnson Houghton) *chsd ldrs but nt on terms: wknd over 3f out: t.o* **20/1**

050 **10** *10* **The Wonga Coup (IRE)**[14] 1268 3-8-13 **63** .... FergusSweeney 6 —
(P M Phelan) *hld up in last trio: prog into 6th 4f out but nt on terms w ldrs: pushed along and wknd 3f out: eased and sn bhd* **33/1**

544 **11** *56* **Mister Pleau (USA)**[28] 1046 3-8-10 **60** .... SteveDrowne 7 —
(J R Best) *in tch tl wknd rapidly over 4f out: wl t.o* **33/1**

2m 31.0s (1.50) **Going Correction** +0.10s/f (Good) **11** Ran SP% **114.4**
Speed ratings (Par 98): **99,95,95,93,92 87,83,80,70,64 26**
toteswingers: 1&2 £1.70, 1&3 £17.80, 2&3 £27.00 CSF £5.59 CT £107.86 TOTE £1.70: £1.02, £1.50, £14.30; EX 7.00 Trifecta £93.30 Pool: £6441.29 - 51.07 winning units..
Owner Phil Cunningham **Bred** William Flynn **Trained** Lambourn, Berks

FOCUS
This did not a look a particularly strong handicap but the runaway winner ran her rivals into gradual submission and they finished well strung out behind. The form is rated around the second and third.
Mister Pleau(USA) Official explanation: jockey said colt had a breathing problem

1579 JOIN THE ROYAL WINDSOR RACING CLUB H'CAP — 1m 3f 135y
6:10 (6:11) (Class 4) (0-80,80) 4-Y-O+ **£4,857** (£1,445; £722; £360) **Stalls** Low

Form RPR

541- **1** **Aurorian (IRE)**[143] 7628 4-9-5 **80** .... RichardHughes 12 91
(R Hannon) *hld up wl in rr: stdy prog on inner fr over 3f out: wnt 2nd jst over 1f out: sn rdn to chal: styd on to ld last 75yds* **8/1**

14-0 **2** *nk* **King's Song (IRE)**[19] 1161 4-8-12 **73** .... RyanMoore 6 84
(Sir Michael Stoute) *hld up in midfield: swift move on outer to ld 3f out: veered in front over 2f out but drvn 2 l clr: hdd and nt qckn last 75yds* **11/4**[1]

1422 **3** *5* **Oxford City (IRE)**[7] 1087 6-8-10 **70** ....(t) LukeMorris 4 72
(P M Phelan) *mostly trckd ldr to jst over 3f out: sn rdn: kpt on to dispute 2nd again over 1f out: sn outpcd* **12/1**

516- **4** *nk* **Rockfella**[164] 7373 4-9-1 **76** .... EddieAhern 5 78
(D J Coakley) *trckd ldrs: rdn and nt qckn over 2f out: short of room briefly after: kpt on again fnl f* **10/1**

100- **5** *¾* **Brooklyn Spirit**[207] 6420 4-8-4 **72** .... JohnFahy(7) 10 73
(C G Cox) *settled in midfield: rdn over 3f out: sn outpcd: kpt on u.p fnl 2f: n.d* **25/1**

04-1 **6** *3¼* **Penchesco (IRE)**[10] 1346 5-8-13 **73** .... JimCrowley 1 68
(Mrs A J Perrett) *prom: rdn over 3f out: chsd ldr wl over 2f out to jst over 1f out: wknd* **6/1**[2]

210- **7** *3¼* **Dove Cottage (IRE)**[187] 6936 8-8-12 **72** .... FergusSweeney 11 62
(W S Kittow) *led to 3f out: sn outpcd: wknd 2f out* **25/1**

30-3 **8** *hd* **Epsom Salts**[23] 1087 5-9-3 **77** .... JackMitchell 7 66+
(P M Phelan) *s.s: hld up in detached last: sme prog 3f out but nowhere nr ldrs: swtchd to inner and hmpd over 1f out: pushed out fnl 50yds: nvr involved* **25/1**

131- **9** *1¾* **Parc Des Princes (USA)**[278] 4206 4-8-11 **72** .... DavidProbert 2 59
(A M Balding) *hld up wl in rr: prog on outer 3f out: clsd on ldrs jst over 2f out: sn wknd* **15/2**[3]

21-4 **10** *hd* **Illuminative (USA)**[7] 1430 4-9-1 **76** .... TomQueally 9 62
(Stef Higgins) *dwlt: hld up in last pair: u.p and struggling 4f out: plugging on but no ch whn short of room over 1f out* **50/1**

5-11 **11** *¾* **Turjuman (USA)**[33] 974 5-9-1 **75** .... StevieDonohoe 13 60
(W J Musson) *trckd ldrs: rdn over 3f out: wknd over 2f out* **8/1**

5/43 **12** *3½* **Sacrilege**[7] 1430 5-8-11 **76** ....(p) MarkCoumbe(5) 3 55
(M C Chapman) *taken down early: prom tl wknd u.p 3f out* **20/1**

020- **13** *4½* **Gross Prophet**[20] 7204 5-8-12 **72** ....(p) SteveDrowne 14 44
(A J Lidderdale) *chsd ldrs: u.p 4f out: sn lost pl: grad wknd* **50/1**

042/ **14** *28* **Northumberland**[633] 4589 4-8-0 **66** .... SophieDoyle(5) 8 —
(M C Chapman) *dwlt: t.k.h: hld up towards rr: wknd over 4f out: t.o* **100/1**

2m 29.02s (-0.48) **Going Correction** +0.10s/f (Good)
WFA 4 from 5yo+ 1lb **14** Ran SP% **118.7**
Speed ratings (Par 105): **105,104,101,101,100 98,96,96,95,95 94,92,89,70**
toteswingers: 1&2 £4.80, 1&3 £21.10, 2&3 £9.00 CSF £27.51 CT £270.80 TOTE £7.50: £4.30, £1.50, £5.20; EX 27.30 Trifecta £1130.90 Pool: £2139.65 - 1.40 winning units..
Owner Martin Mitchell **Bred** Richard Moses Bloodstock **Trained** East Everleigh, Wilts
■ Stewards' Enquiry : Stevie Donohoe three-day ban: careless riding (May 10-12)

FOCUS
A decent handicap, involving several improvers. The first two finished a long way clear and the form looks pretty sound.
King's Song(IRE) Official explanation: jockey said colt hung badly right-handed and lost a right-hind shoe

1580 REED & MACKAY H'CAP — 6f
6:40 (6:41) (Class 4) (0-80,80) 4-Y-O+ **£4,533** (£1,348; £674; £336) **Stalls** High

Form RPR

10-0 **1** **Getcarter**[23] 1088 4-9-4 **80** .... RichardHughes 8 91
(R Hannon) *hld up in rr: stdy prog on outer fr over 2f out: drvn to ld ins fnl f: r.o wl* **3/1**[1]

355- **2** *1* **Zero Money (IRE)**[186] 6976 4-8-12 **74** .... SteveDrowne 2 82
(R Charlton) *trckd ldrs: prog on outer to ld 1f out: sn hdd: r.o but a hld* **8/1**[3]

54-2 **3** *2¼* **Thunderous Mood (USA)**[11] 1321 4-9-3 **79** .... JamieSpencer 7 80
(P F I Cole) *dwlt: hld up in last: prog on outer over 2f out: threatened to cl on ldrs 1f out: tk 3rd but nt qckn fnl f* **13/2**[2]

1-51 **4** *½* **Sarah's Art (IRE)**[82] 393 7-9-4 **80** ....(t) TomQueally 16 79
(Stef Higgins) *trckd ldrs: effrt against nr side rail 2f out: upsides jst over 1f out: fdd ins fnl f* **12/1**

50-0 **5** *½* **Phantom Whisper**[31] 987 7-8-11 **76** .... JamesMillman(3) 14 74
(B R Millman) *chsd ldrs: pushed along 1/2-way: struggling to hold pl over 1f out: styd on again ins fnl f* **16/1**

005- **6** *shd* **C'Mon You Irons (IRE)**[202] 6564 5-8-12 **74** .... JackMitchell 9 71
(M R Hoad) *mde most to 1f out: wknd* **16/1**

5342 **7** *½* **Anne Of Kiev (IRE)**[18] 1192 5-8-13 **75** ....(t) LukeMorris 10 71+
(J R Gask) *hld up in rr: nt clr run 2f out and swtchd rt: trying to make prog whn nt clr run 1f out and swtchd lft: kpt on but no ch* **12/1**

424- **8** *1¼* **Lodi (IRE)**[196] 6726 5-8-13 **75** ....(t) AdamKirby 15 67
(J Akehurst) *chsd ldrs: drvn 2f out: wknd fnl f* **14/1**

4030 **9** *½* **Ebraam (USA)**[17] 1206 7-9-1 **77** .... LiamKeniry 4 67
(S Curran) *cl up bhd ldrs: rdn and nt qckn 2f out: fdd* **16/1**

600- **10** *1* **Desert Icon (IRE)**[213] 6240 4-9-4 **80** .... JimCrowley 13 67
(W J Knight) *stdd s: hld up in rr: last whn one reminder over 1f out: passed a few rivals fnl f: nvr nr ldrs* **9/1**

260- **11** *¾* **George Thisby**[193] 6798 4-8-12 **74** .... DavidProbert 11 59
(B R Millman) *w ldr to over 1f out: wknd* **14/1**

4300 **12** *nk* **Divine Force**[18] 1192 4-9-0 **76** ....(p) SimonWhitworth 6 60
(M Wigham) *dwlt: hld up towards rr: cl enough 2f out: shkn up and fnd nil* **50/1**

2006 **13** *1¼* **Lujeanie**[11] 1321 4-9-3 **79** ....(p) FergusSweeney 12 59
(D K Ivory) *hld up in midfield against nr side rail: rdn 2f out: no prog: wknd fnl f* **25/1**

1-35 **14** *¾* **Daddy's Gift (IRE)**[6] 1438 4-9-0 **76** .... RyanMoore 3 53
(R Hannon) *a in rr: struggling in last trio 2f out* **11/1**

111- **15** *18* **Ziggy Lee**[339] 2219 4-9-1 **80** .... WilliamCarson(3) 1 —
(S C Williams) *hld up in midfield: prog on wd outside to press ldrs 2f out: wknd rapidly over 1f out: eased: t.o* **20/1**

1m 13.34s (0.34) **Going Correction** +0.10s/f (Good) **15** Ran SP% **124.7**
Speed ratings (Par 105): **101,99,96,96,95 95,94,92,92,90 89,89,87,86,62**
toteswingers: 1&2 £8.40, 1&3 £5.80, 2&3 £15.10 CSF £25.87 CT £153.28 TOTE £3.80: £1.50, £4.80, £1.40; EX 40.60 Trifecta £359.60 Pool: £2940.19 - 6.05 winning units..
Owner Mrs J K Powell **Bred** C R Mason **Trained** East Everleigh, Wilts

FOCUS
A competitive sprint handicap. The first three were surprisingly drawn in single figures and raced towards the centre of the track. This still looks form to rate positively.
Phantom Whisper Official explanation: jockey said gelding was denied a clear run
Anne Of Kiev(IRE) Official explanation: jockey said mare was denied a clear run

1581 NEIL SLOAN WELCOME ALONG MAIDEN STKS — 1m 2f 7y
7:10 (7:11) (Class 5) 3-Y-O **£2,729** (£806; £403) **Stalls** Low

Form RPR

0 **1** **Sunny Game**[14] 1268 3-9-3 0 .... JamieSpencer 2 79
(M L W Bell) *trckd ldrs: prog 3f out to ld 2f out: rdn and wl in command fnl f* **9/2**[3]

64- **2** *2* **Grey Bunting**[182] 7050 3-9-3 0 .... FrankieDettori 13 75
(B W Hills) *trckd ldng pair: effrt to chse wnr wl over 1f out: hld whn rdr dropped whip 150yds out* **12/1**

6- **3** *nk* **Pekan Three (IRE)**[192] 6810 3-9-3 0 .... KierenFallon 15 75
(P F I Cole) *s.i.s: sn in midfield: rousted along 4f out: prog on outer 2f out: styd on to take 3rd nr fin* **9/4**[1]

334- **4** *nk* **Weekend Millionair (IRE)**[215] 6214 3-8-12 74 .... RichardEvans(5) 11 74
(P D Evans) *mde most after 1f to 2f out: wandered and nt qckn* **25/1**

0-3 **5** *½* **Alfonso The Wise (IRE)**[14] 1268 3-9-3 0 .... ShaneKelly 10 73+
(J Noseda) *hld up in midfield: gng wl in 7th 3f out: shkn up 2f out: kpt on but nvr able to chal* **6/1**

6 *1½* **Whitby Jack** 3-9-3 0 .... GeorgeBaker 3 70
(G L Moore) *hld up in rr of midfield: prog over 3f out: pushed along and clsd on ldrs over 1f out: no imp fnl f: fair effrt* **100/1**

5- **7** *1½* **Hierarch (IRE)**[274] 4336 3-9-3 0 .... RichardHughes 5 67
(R Hannon) *led 1f: trckd ldng pair: rdn over 2f out: nt qckn over 1f out: fdd ins fnl f* **3/1**[2]

8 *1¼* **Lamps** 3-9-3 0 .... MartinDwyer 16 65
(B J Meehan) *a in midfield: shkn up over 2f out: no imp on ldrs after* **20/1**

9 *¾* **Court Circle** 3-9-3 0 .... RyanMoore 9 63+
(Sir Michael Stoute) *hld up wl in rr: stl there over 2f out: swtchd to r alone against nr side rail: shkn up and styd on fnl f: nrst fin* **12/1**

0 **10** *3¼* **Gifted Lady (IRE)**[32] 978 3-8-12 0 .... FergusSweeney 14 52
(P M Phelan) *stdd s: t.k.h: hld up in last: modest prog over 2f out: nvr involved* **150/1**

00- **11** *1½* **Spring Heather (IRE)**[209] 6363 3-8-12 0 .... RichardMullen 8 49+
(J L Dunlop) *hld up wl in rr: nudged along and sme prog 3f out: nvr nr ldrs: eased over 1f out* **100/1**

45- **12** *2* **Boston Blue**[163] 7388 3-9-3 0 .... JimCrowley 1 50+
(W J Knight) *hld up wl in rr: pushed along and no real prog over 2f out* **40/1**

0-4 **13** *1* **Half Sister (IRE)**[7] 1431 3-8-12 0 .... PatDobbs 6 43
(R Hannon) *w ldr after 1f to jst over 2f out: wknd rapidly* **25/1**

0 **14** *3½* **Best Of Broadway (IRE)**[11] 1325 3-9-3 0 .... TedDurcan 4 41
(D R Lanigan) *hld up wl in rr: nvr a factor* **50/1**

15 *½* **Massachusetts** 3-9-3 0 .... EddieAhern 7 40
(B J Meehan) *chsd ldrs to 4f out: steadily wknd* **66/1**

6 **16** *11* **Oh Two**[32] 978 3-8-9 0 .... WilliamCarson(3) 12 13
(S C Williams) *hld up in rr: no prog over 3f out: t.o* **150/1**

2m 10.45s (1.75) **Going Correction** +0.10s/f (Good) **16** Ran SP% **125.3**
Speed ratings (Par 98): **97,95,95,94,94 93,92,91,90,87 86,85,84,81,81 72**
toteswingers: 1&2 £10.70, 1&3 £3.90, 2&3 £7.30 CSF £55.68 TOTE £7.50: £2.00, £3.80, £1.50; EX 81.70 Trifecta £1840.40 Pool: £3183.48 - 1.28 winning units..
Owner Tsega Horses **Bred** Tsega Breeding Limited **Trained** Newmarket, Suffolk

FOCUS
An intriguing maiden, featuring several well-bred types representing powerful yards. Rather muddling form rated around the fourth.

1582 FOLLOW WINDSOR & ETON F.C. @ WEFC.CO.UK H'CAP — 1m 67y
7:40 (7:41) (Class 5) (0-75,75) 3-Y-O **£2,729** (£806; £403) **Stalls** High

Form RPR

003- **1** **Contredanse (IRE)**[158] 7450 3-9-4 75 .... KierenFallon 1 88+
(L M Cumani) *t.k.h early: a ldng trio: chal over 2f out: upsides after tl drvn ahd ins fnl f* **11/4**[1]

00-1 **2** *hd* **Our Boy Barrington (IRE)**[9] 1392 3-8-12 69 .... RichardHughes 8 81+
(R Hannon) *a ldng trio: effrt to ld narrowly over 2f out: hrd pressed after: hdd ins fnl f* **11/2**[3]

523- **3** *4* **Right Rave (IRE)**[215] 6215 3-8-9 66 .... EddieCreighton 7 69
(P J McBride) *t.k.h: trckd ldrs: effrt to chal 2f out: upsides over 1f out: nt qckn and outpcd fnl f* **12/1**

114 **4** *1½* **Dream On Buddy (IRE)**[19] 1159 3-9-3 74 .... FrankieDettori 10 74
(B W Hills) *s.i.s: sn rushed up to ld: hdd over 2f out: grad fdd but stl clr of chsng pack* **4/1**[2]

630- **5** *3* **Catchanova (IRE)**[173] 7235 3-8-7 64 .... EddieAhern 9 57
(Eve Johnson Houghton) *hld up in midfield: gng wl enough over 3f out: sn outpcd by ldrs: styd on fnl f: no ch* **33/1**

63-0 **6** *2¼* **Katehari (IRE)**[14] 1269 3-9-4 75 .... DavidProbert 11 62
(A M Balding) *hld up in midfield: rdn and lft bhd fr over 3f out: plugged on but no ch after* **14/1**

6432 **7** *¾* **Ant Music (IRE)**[32] 977 3-8-8 65 ....(b) LiamKeniry 14 51
(J S Moore) *chsd ldrs: outpcd fr 3f out: steadily fdd* **33/1**

330- **8** 1 1/4 **One Good Emperor (IRE)**[192] 6826 3-9-4 75................ SteveDrowne 5 58
(J R Best) *hld up towards rr: rdn 3f out but already wl off the pce: no ch after* **66/1**

421- **9** 1/2 **Essexbridge**[186] 6962 3-9-3 74.. RyanMoore 6 56
(R Hannon) *hld up in last pair: pushed along 4f out: wl off the pce after: styd on wl fnl f* **8/1**

-140 **10** 1/2 **Ana Moutabahi**[12] 1307 3-8-8 68......................... AndrewHeffernan(3) 4 49
(P D Evans) *chsd ldrs: rdn and outpcd over 2f out: wknd* **66/1**

310- **11** 1 1/4 **Rezwaan**[141] 7654 3-9-1 72.. ShaneKelly 3 50
(Jane Chapple-Hyam) *hld up wl in rr: lft bhd whn pce lifted over 3f out: nvr in the hunt after* **16/1**

1-36 **12** 4 **Crunched**[18] 1189 3-9-0 71.. JamieSpencer 2 45
(M L W Bell) *hld up in last pair: gng wl enough over 3f out: taken to wd outside sn after and nowhere nr ldrs: eased fnl f* **11/1**

2-24 **13** 1 3/4 **Katchmore (IRE)**[26] 698 3-8-9 66.............................. JimCrowley 13 30
(Jean-Rene Auvray) *rdn in midfield 1/2-way: struggling after: no ch over 2f out* **25/1**

034- **14** nse **Ermyn Express**[127] 7825 3-8-7 64........................... FergusSweeney 12 32
(P M Phelan) *a towards rr: wknd over 2f out* **80/1**

1m 45.76s (1.06) **Going Correction** +0.10s/f (Good) **14** Ran SP% **115.7**
Speed ratings (Par 98): **98,97,93,92,89 87,86,85,84,84 82,78,77,77**
toteswingers: 1&2 £3.50, 1&3 £13.30, 2&3 £14.60 CSF £15.79 CT £159.32 TOTE £3.80: £1.60, £2.10, £4.80; EX 20.70 Trifecta £230.80 Part won. Pool: £311.95 - 0.63 winning Place 6: £8.44 Place 5: £6.37 .
Owner S Stuckey **Bred** Ahdaab Syndicate **Trained** Newmarket, Suffolk

FOCUS
A fair handicap. The pace was steady and nothing got into it from behind. However, the first two were both prominent in the market and pulled clear of the rest, so the form looks solid enough, rated around the third. The front pair are unexposed.
Ermyn Express Official explanation: jockey said filly hung left-handed
T/Jkpt: £4,018.30 to a £1 stake. Pool: £33,958.24. 6.00 winning tickets. T/Plt: £14.80 to a £1 stake. Pool: £81,835.23. 4,016.46 winning tickets. T/Qpdt: £14.50 to a £1 stake. Pool: £6,708.60. 341.69 winning tickets. JN

1534 WOLVERHAMPTON (A.W) (L-H)

Monday, April 26

OFFICIAL GOING: Standard

Wind: Light across, becoming fresher half-behind from race 2 onwards Weather: Cloudy with sunny spells

1583 WOLVERHAMPTON HOSPITALITY - A PLEASURE CLAIMING STKS 5f 20y(P)

2:30 (2:30) (Class 6) 3-Y-O+ **£1,774** (£523; £262) **Stalls Low**

Form RPR

050- **1** **Little Edward**[331] 2474 12-9-9 92.................................... GeorgeBaker 1 68+
(R J Hodges) *a.p: chsd ldr over 1f out: r.o to ld wl ins fnl f* **5/6**[1]

0520 **2** 1/2 **Ten Down**[35] 967 5-9-3 54... SebSanders 3 60
(M Quinn) *led: rdn and hdd wl ins fnl f* **11/1**

001- **3** 1/2 **Hinton Admiral**[332] 2456 6-9-5 77.................................. VinceSlattery 4 60
(M S Tuck) *prom: rdn and edgd lft ins fnl f: r.o* **8/1**[3]

052 **4** 1 1/2 **Best One**[20] 1146 6-9-1 52...(b) ChrisCatlin 2 51+
(R A Harris) *dwlt: sn pushed along in rr: hdwy u.p over 1f out: nt rch ldrs* **12/1**

0236 **5** nk **Bluebok**[35] 967 9-9-1 55..(bt) StevieDonohoe 7 50
(J M Bradley) *chsd ldr: rdn 1/2-way: no ex fnl f* **20/1**

-215 **6** 1/2 **Desperate Dan**[52] 810 9-8-12 73...................................(v) AmyBaker(5) 6 50
(A B Haynes) *dwlt: hdwy over 3f out: styd on same pce fnl f* **3/1**[2]

0-00 **7** 1 **Michael Collins (IRE)**[20] 1148 4-8-13 43.................... KevinGhunowa 5 42
(G J Smith) *dwlt: hung lft thrght: rdn over 1f out: no ex* **200/1**

61.70 secs (-0.60) **Going Correction** 0.0s/f (Stan) **7** Ran SP% **112.0**
Speed ratings (Par 101): **104,103,102,100,99 98,97**
toteswingers: 1&2 £3.00, 1&3 £3.60, 2&3 £6.10 CSF £11.19 TOTE £1.50: £1.10, £5.70; EX 9.00.
Owner J W Mursell **Bred** J W Mursell **Trained** Charlton Mackrell, Somerset

FOCUS
The likes of the 54-rated runner-up and the 52-rated fourth look the best guide to this form. The winner didn't have to be anywhere near his best.
Desperate Dan Official explanation: jockey said gelding was slowly away
Michael Collins(IRE) Official explanation: vet said gelding finished lame

1584 ENJOY THE PARTY PACK GROUP OFFER H'CAP 5f 216y(P)

3:00 (3:00) (Class 4) (0-80,79) 3-Y-O **£4,209** (£1,252; £625; £312) **Stalls Low**

Form RPR

2615 **1** **Knightfire (IRE)**[13] 1280 3-8-9 70.......................................(t) ShaneKelly 3 78
(W R Swinburn) *broke wl: settled to chse ldrs: rdn and r.o to ld last strides* **9/1**

15 **2** hd **Solstice**[44] 884 3-9-3 78.. FrederikTylicki 10 86
(Julie Camacho) *chsd ldrs: led 4f out: rdn ins fnl f: hdd last strides* **9/2**[2]

215- **3** 1 1/2 **Cape Kimberley**[158] 7453 3-8-13 74............................ PaulMulrennan 6 77
(J G Given) *chsd ldrs: rdn over 1f out: r.o* **28/1**

134- **4** 1/2 **Night Trade (IRE)**[178] 7156 3-8-12 73.......................... SilvestreDeSousa 8 74
(Mrs D J Sanderson) *sn pushed along in rr: hdwy u.p fr over 1f out: edgd lft: r.o* **6/1**

1-46 **5** 1 **Thrust Control (IRE)**[12] 1307 3-9-4 79................................ AlanMunro 1 77
(M R Channon) *hld up: swtchd lft over 1f out: r.o ins fnl f: nvr nr to chal* **25/1**

231- **6** nk **Admin (IRE)**[197] 6700 3-9-4 79.. JimCrowley 5 76
(R M Beckett) *hld up in tch: racd keenly: chsd ldr 2f out: sn rdn: wknd ins fnl f* **5/1**[3]

13-0 **7** 3 1/2 **Newbury Street**[19] 1168 3-8-3 71 ow2............................. LeeTopliss(7) 2 57
(R A Fahey) *hld up: rdn 1/2-way: nvr on terms* **9/1**

6- **8** nse **Pilgrim Dancer (IRE)**[257] 4920 3-9-3 78........................ StephenCraine 4 64
(Patrick Morris) *s.i.s: hld up: n.d* **50/1**

00-0 **9** 1 1/4 **Avongate**[20] 1140 3-8-12 73.. ChrisCatlin 7 55
(R A Harris) *chsd ldr: led 5f out to 4f out: rdn over 1f out: wknd fnl f* **66/1**

2506 **10** 1 1/4 **Italian Tom (IRE)**[20] 1140 3-9-0 75.................................. LiamJones 12 53
(R A Harris) *sn outpcd: hdwy on outside over 2f out: sn wknd* **40/1**

0-16 **11** 1 1/4 **Eight Hours**[53] 782 3-8-6 67...(b) JimmyQuinn 9 41
(R A Fahey) *chsd ldrs: rdn over 2f out: sn wknd* **25/1**

32-1 **P** **Call To Arms (IRE)**[63] 655 3-9-4 79............................. FrankieDettori 11 —
(M Johnston) *led 1f: chsd ldrs: rdn over 3f out: wknd qckly over 2f out: wl bhd whn p.u and dismntd over 1f out: b.b.v* **13/8**[1]

1m 14.68s (-0.32) **Going Correction** 0.0s/f (Stan) **12** Ran SP% **124.3**
Speed ratings (Par 100): **102,101,99,99,97 97,92,92,90,89 87,—**
toteswingers: 1&2 £8.90, 1&3 £26.70, 2&3 £18.40 CSF £48.91 CT £1141.67 TOTE £12.10: £2.10, £2.30, £9.20; EX 57.30.
Owner The Castle Guards **Bred** J Owens **Trained** Aldbury, Herts

FOCUS
A fair sprint handicap. Improvement from the first two, with the form rated around the third and fourth.
Call To Arms(IRE) Official explanation: jockey said gelding bled from the nose

1585 WOLVERHAMPTON-RACECOURSE.CO.UK H'CAP 7f 32y(P)

3:30 (3:30) (Class 6) (0-65,65) 4-Y-O+ **£1,774** (£523; £262) **Stalls High**

Form RPR

50-0 **1** **Chief Red Cloud (USA)**[19] 1152 4-9-1 62.................... FrederikTylicki 5 76
(J R Weymes) *mid-div: hdwy over 2f out: led ins fnl f: r.o wl: hung rt towards fin* **14/1**

341- **2** 2 3/4 **Landucci**[249] 5179 9-9-4 65...(p) JamesDoyle 2 72
(S Curran) *a.p: chsd ldr over 2f out: led 1f out: sn rdn and hdd: styd on same pce* **16/1**

-053 **3** 1 1/2 **December**[12] 1305 4-8-10 57...(vt) DarryllHolland 1 60
(Mrs C A Dunnett) *led: rdn and hdd 1f out: no ex* **9/2**[2]

301 **4** 1 1/2 **Gracie's Gift (IRE)**[48] 839 8-8-13 60................................. DaneO'Neill 6 59
(R C Guest) *chsd ldrs: rdn over 2f out: styd on same pce fnl f* **12/1**

4-00 **5** nk **Foreign Investment (IRE)**[46] 868 4-9-1 62.................. CathyGannon 3 60
(P D Evans) *mid-div: hdwy over 2f out: rdn and edgd rt fnl f: no ex* **9/2**[2]

262- **6** 1 1/2 **Lord Of The Dance (IRE)**[145] 7610 4-9-4 65................ ShaneKelly 7 59
(W M Brisbourne) *s.i.s: hld up: hdwy over 1f out: sn rdn: no ex ins fnl f* **14/1**

2241 **7** 1/2 **Lopinot (IRE)**[19] 1170 7-9-3 64..(v) GeorgeBaker 11 58
(M R Bosley) *hld up: hdwy over 1f out: rdn whn hmpd ins fnl f: no further prog* **12/1**

140- **8** 3 **Location**[172] 7250 4-8-10 57... StevieDonohoe 9 42
(Ian Williams) *hld up: rdn over 1f out: nvr on terms* **28/1**

0233 **9** 6 **Bentley**[35] 968 6-8-13 60..(v) PaulMulrennan 12 28
(J G Given) *hld up: rdn 3f out: sn wknd* **16/1**

0351 **10** 1 1/4 **Woolston Ferry (IRE)**[47] 845 4-9-0 61.........................(p) ChrisCatlin 8 26
(David Pinder) *prom tl wknd 2f out* **7/2**[1]

22-5 **11** hd **Many Welcomes**[21] 1115 5-8-5 57........................... JemmaMarshall(5) 4 22
(B P J Baugh) *chsd ldr tl rdn over 2f out: wknd over 1f out* **6/1**[3]

0401 **12** 3/4 **Zeffirelli**[35] 965 5-8-12 59... SebSanders 10 22
(M Quinn) *chsd ldrs: rdn 3f out: wknd 2f out* **11/1**

1m 29.01s (-0.59) **Going Correction** 0.0s/f (Stan) **12** Ran SP% **125.1**
Speed ratings (Par 101): **103,99,98,96,96 94,93,90,83,82 81,81**
toteswingers: 1&2 £27.00, 1&3 £16.90, 2&3 £15.50 CSF £230.99 CT £1187.93 TOTE £16.90: £3.80, £3.80, £1.60; EX 196.50.
Owner Mrs Elaine M Burke **Bred** Lochlow Farm **Trained** Middleham Moor, N Yorks

FOCUS
A moderate handicap. The form is rated around the third and the winner has a progressive profile on the AW.
Woolston Ferry(IRE) Official explanation: jockey said, regarding running, that the gelding was inconvenienced by having to run wide throughout

1586 HOTEL & CONFERENCING AT WOLVERHAMPTON MEDIAN AUCTION MAIDEN STKS 1m 141y(P)

4:00 (4:02) (Class 5) 3-5-Y-O **£2,456** (£725; £362) **Stalls Low**

Form RPR

324- **1** **Party Doctor**[251] 5133 3-8-11 109.............................. RichardKingscote 5 71+
(Tom Dascombe) *trckd ldrs: shkn up to chse ldr over 2f out: rdn to ld over 1f out: styd on wl* **1/5**[1]

36- **2** 3 1/2 **Search For The Key (USA)**[229] 5778 3-8-11 0................ AlanMunro 7 63
(P F I Cole) *s.i.s: hld up: rdn over 1f out: r.o to go 2nd nr fin: no ch w wnr* **12/1**[2]

00- **3** 3/4 **Batgirl**[177] 7182 3-8-6 0... IvaMilickova 4 56
(John Berry) *hld up in tch: rdn over 1f out: styd on same pce ins fnl f* **150/1**

05 **4** hd **Raktiman (IRE)**[6] 1460 3-8-6 0................................. RossAtkinson(5) 2 61
(Tom Dascombe) *s.i.s: sn drvn along to chse ldr: rdn over 2f out: no ex fnl f* **28/1**

56 **5** 1 1/2 **Barnstorm**[7] 1425 3-8-11 0... GregFairley 6 57
(M Johnston) *led: rdn and hung rt fr over 2f out: hdd over 1f out: wknd ins fnl f* **14/1**[3]

1m 50.6s (0.10) **Going Correction** 0.0s/f (Stan) **5** Ran SP% **101.8**
Speed ratings (Par 103): **99,95,95,95,93**
CSF £2.33 TOTE £1.10: £1.10, £2.10; EX 2.20.
Owner Sir Robert Ogden **Bred** Cheveley Park Stud Ltd **Trained** Malpas, Cheshire
■ Sunley Spinalonga was withdrawn (14/1, refused to ent stalls). R4 applies, deduct 5p in the £.

FOCUS
A slowly run and weak maiden in which the winner Party Doctor ran nowhere near his official mark of 109. The form is rated around the second and fourth.
Barnstorm ◆ Official explanation: jockey said gelding hung right-handed

1587 CELEBRATE YOUR BIRTHDAY AT WOLVERHAMPTON RACECOURSE CLAIMING STKS 1m 1f 103y(P)

4:30 (4:30) (Class 6) 4-Y-O+ **£1,774** (£523; £262) **Stalls Low**

Form RPR

3-11 **1** **Fremen (USA)**[22] 1098 10-9-0 82........................... MichaelGeran(3) 5 78
(D Nicholls) *s.i.s: plld hrd and rcvrd to ld over 8f out: hdd 7f out: remained handy: chsd ldr over 2f out: shkn up to ld over 1f out: rdn and hung lft ins fnl f: r.o* **9/4**[2]

4121 **2** 1 3/4 **Plush**[17] 1208 7-9-6 81....................................... RossAtkinson(5) 2 82
(Tom Dascombe) *s.i.s: hld up: hdwy over 2f out: rdn over 1f out: r.o* **2/1**[1]

2344 **3** 1/2 **New Star (UAE)**[39] 920 6-8-2 69.................................. KierenFox(5) 1 63+
(W M Brisbourne) *stmbld s and led: hdd over 8f out: chsd ldrs: outpcd over 2f out: rallied over 1f out: r.o* **5/1**[3]

/20- **4** 1 1/4 **Mataram (USA)**[436] 550 7-8-11 74.................................. AlanMunro 4 64
(W Jarvis) *hld up: hdwy over 1f out: r.o: nt rch ldrs* **13/2**

1-52 **5** nse **Pyrus Time (IRE)**[38] 929 4-9-7 71................................ LiamJones 6 74
(R A Harris) *plld hrd and prom: led 7f out: rdn and hung rt wl over 1f out: sn hdd: no ex ins fnl f* **18/1**

5-54 **6** 3 **Swiss Art (IRE)**[2] 1536 4-8-7 65..................................... ChrisCatlin 3 54
(R Hollinshead) *plld hrd and prom: trckd ldr over 6f out tl rdn over 2f out: wknd fnl f* **12/1**

645- **7** *6* **Cantabilly (IRE)**25 [835] 7-9-3 63 RichardKingscote 8 51
(R J Hodges) *chsd ldrs: rdn over 3f out: wknd over 2f out* **40/1**

2m 3.63s (1.93) **Going Correction** 0.0s/f (Stan) 7 Ran SP% **109.5**
Speed ratings (Par 101): **91,89,89,87,87 85,79**
toteswingers: 1&2 £1.60, 1&3 £2.90, 2&3 £3.00 CSF £6.49 TOTE £3.20: £3.40, £1.20; EX 4.20.
Owner Middleham Park Racing XXXV C King A Seed **Bred** Flaxman Holdings Ltd **Trained** Sessay, N Yorks

FOCUS
A good claimer but the pace was steady, resulting in a time 5.63 seconds outside standard. The form is rated around the second and fifth and the principals were all below their best.

1588 GREAT OFFERS AT WOLVERHAMPTON-RACECOURSE.CO.UK FILLIES' H'CAP 5f 216y(P)
5:05 (5:06) (Class 4) (0-80,75) 4-Y-0+ **£4,209** (£1,252; £625; £312) **Stalls** Low

Form RPR
640- **1** **Dametime (IRE)**15 [1248] 4-9-7 **75** AndreaAtzeni 4 81
(Daniel Mark Loughnane, Ire) *chsd ldr tl led over 1f out: r.o: eased nr fin* **11/4**[1]

5-50 **2** *1 1/4* **Lucky Leigh**10 [1363] 4-9-6 **74** (v) AlanMunro 7 75
(M R Channon) *hld up: hdwy 1/2-way: rdn to chse wnr fnl f: styd on same pce towards fin* **11/2**

5404 **3** *3/4* **Kheley (IRE)**16 [1234] 4-8-1 **60** ow4 KierenFox(5) 1 59
(W M Brisbourne) *broke wl: prom: rdn over 2f out: hung lft 1f out: no imp wl ins fnl f* **7/2**[3]

00- **4** *1 1/4* **Suzie Quw**190 [6879] 4-9-0 **75** LeeTopliss(7) 2 70
(J R Weymes) *s.i.s: rdn over 1f out: styd on ins fnl f: nvr nrr* **10/1**

002- **5** *3 1/4* **Real Diamond**181 [7082] 4-9-0 **68** SilvestreDeSousa 5 52
(Ollie Pears) *trckd ldrs: racd keenly: rdn over 1f out: wknd ins fnl f* **3/1**[2]

/0-0 **6** *6* **Ajara (IRE)**16 [1238] 4-9-0 **68** RichardKingscote 3 33
(Tom Dascombe) *sn led: rdn and hdd over 1f out: wknd fnl f* **7/1**

1m 14.49s (-0.51) **Going Correction** 0.0s/f (Stan) 6 Ran SP% **110.9**
Speed ratings (Par 102): **103,101,100,98,94 86**
toteswingers: 1&2 £3.50, 1&3 £2.30, 2&3 £2.70 CSF £17.46 TOTE £4.30: £2.40, £3.90; EX 17.30 Place 6: £60.67 Place 5: £44.21.
Owner Brian Forkan **Bred** Tally-Ho Stud **Trained** Trim, Co Meath

FOCUS
An ordinary sprint handicap for the grade.
T/Plt: £110.90 to a £1 stake. Pool: £51,833.36. 341.05 winning tickets. T/Qpdt: £16.80 to a £1 stake. Pool: £3,346.39. 146.55 winning tickets. CR

1219 LINGFIELD (L-H)
Tuesday, April 27

OFFICIAL GOING: Standard
Wind: light, half behind Weather: light cloud

1589 BLUESQUARE.COM IPHONE APP MEDIAN AUCTION MAIDEN STKS (DIV I) 1m (P)
2:00 (2:02) (Class 5) 3-Y-0 **£2,388** (£705; £352) **Stalls** High

Form RPR
2- **1** **Bintalwaadi**271 [4468] 3-8-12 0 RichardHills 10 83+
(E A L Dunlop) *leggy: athletic: mde all: jnd over 2f out: rdn over 1f out: asserted ent fnl f: styd on strly to go clr fnl 100yds: readily* **6/5**[1]

606- **2** *2 3/4* **Fireback**220 [6108] 3-9-3 73 DavidProbert 2 76
(A M Balding) *chsd wnr: upsides wnr over 2f out: rdn wl over 1f out: btn ins fnl f: kpt on for clr 2nd* **9/2**[2]

3 *8* **Conceptual Art** 3-9-3 0 HayleyTurner 6 58
(M L W Bell) *w'like: scope: bit bkwd: chsd ldng pair: rdn and wl outpcd over 2f out: plugged on but no ch w ldng pair fnl 2f* **13/2**[3]

4 *1/2* **Star Prospect (IRE)** 3-8-12 0 TobyAtkinson(5) 8 57
(Luke Comer, Ire) *w'like: bit bkwd: s.i.s: bhd: gd hdwy on outer over 3f out: rdn and outpcd by ldng pair over 2f out: no ch fnl 2f* **66/1**

06- **5** *3/4* **Fever Tree**141 [7663] 3-8-12 0 SebSanders 1 50
(P J Makin) *leggy: dwlt: bhd: nt clr run on inner over 2f out: hdwy over 1f out: kpt on fnl f: nvr trbld ldrs* **40/1**

0-6 **6** *3 1/2* **Home Advantage**7 [1460] 3-9-3 0 SteveDrowne 5 47
(R Charlton) *w'like: strong: s.i.s: sn pushed along in midfield: rdn and wl btn over 2f out* **12/1**

004- **7** *2 1/4* **Cereal Killer (IRE)**198 [6696] 3-9-3 75 PatDobbs 7 42
(R Hannon) *lw: chsd ldrs: rdn and lost pl wl over 2f out: no ch fnl 2f* **7/1**

00- **8** *1* **Silk Runner (IRE)**223 [5984] 3-8-9 0 PatrickHills(3) 9 34
(J W Hills) *s.i.s: a in rr: short lived effrt 3f out: wl bhd fnl 2f* **66/1**

35- **9** *4 1/2* **Lady Valiant**300 [3507] 3-8-12 0 JimCrowley 3 24
(R M Beckett) *w'like: sn pushed along in midfield: rdn and dropped to in rr 3f out: wl bhd fnl 2f* **10/1**

1m 39.02s (0.82) **Going Correction** +0.175s/f (Slow) 9 Ran SP% **111.7**
Speed ratings (Par 98): **102,99,91,90,90 86,84,83,78**
toteswingers: 1&2 £2.30, 1&3 £3.30, 2&3 £6.30 CSF £6.22 TOTE £1.90: £1.10, £2.10, £2.20; EX 7.80.
Owner Hamdan Al Maktoum **Bred** Shadwell Estate Company Limited **Trained** Newmarket, Suffolk

FOCUS
A weak and uncompetitive maiden and the two market leaders dominated throughout. The form is rated around the best view of the runner-up's Newbury form.

1590 BLUESQUARE.COM IPHONE APP MEDIAN AUCTION MAIDEN STKS (DIV II) 1m (P)
2:30 (2:34) (Class 5) 3-Y-0 **£2,388** (£705; £352) **Stalls** High

Form RPR
1 **Beachfire** 3-9-3 0 WilliamBuick 6 76+
(J H M Gosden) *strong: bit bkwd: dwlt: rn green: in tch towards rr on outer: pushed along 5f out: rdn 3f out: stl plenty to do over 1f out: str burst to press ldr ins fnl f: led nr fin* **7/1**[3]

424- **2** *shd* **Suited And Booted (IRE)**221 [6061] 3-9-3 78 PatDobbs 7 76
(R Hannon) *lw: hld up wl in tch: gng wl and poised to chal 2f out: rdn and qcknd to ld ent fnl f: pressed and drvn ins fnl f: hdd nr fin* **13/8**[1]

-424 **3** *5* **Larkrise Star**27 [1061] 3-8-7 66 MarkCoumbe(5) 2 59
(D K Ivory) *t.k.h: hld up wl in tch: n.m.r over 1f out: drvn and kpt on ins fnl f: nvr gng pce to rch ldng pair* **8/1**

4 *1* **Craicajack (IRE)** 3-9-3 0 EddieCreighton 10 62
(E J Creighton) *w'like: strong: dwlt: t.k.h: chsd ldr after 2f: rdn to ld 2f out: hdd ent fnl f: nt pce of ldng pair after: lost 3rd wl ins fnl f* **33/1**

5 *3/4* **Grand Piano (IRE)** 3-9-3 0 DavidProbert 4 60
(A M Balding) *unf: dwlt: in tch towards rr: rdn and effrt ent fnl 2f: hdwy over 1f out: one pce ins fnl f* **14/1**

0 **6** *1/2* **Ramble On Love**80 [443] 3-8-12 0 FrankieMcDonald 9 54
(P Winkworth) *w'like: dwlt: t.k.h: hdwy to chse ldrs over 5f out: rdn and unable qck ent fnl 2f: outpcd fnl f* **25/1**

6-42 **7** *1 1/4* **Gra Adhmhar (IRE)**47 [864] 3-9-3 74 JamieSpencer 1 56+
(D J Coakley) *stdd after s: t.k.h: hld up in tch towards rr on inner: nt clr run over 2f out tl swtchd rt 1f out: no imp and hung lft ins fnl f: nvr able to chal* **15/8**[2]

00 **8** *2 3/4* **Yehonala (USA)**14 [1278] 3-8-12 0 SteveDrowne 8 44
(J R Best) *led: rdn and hdd 2f out: wknd qckly 1f out* **100/1**

00- **9** *1 1/4* **Federal Reserve**252 [5119] 3-9-3 0 LiamKeniry 3 46
(M Madgwick) *s.i.s: a in rr: struggling u.p over 2f out: no ch fnl 2f* **100/1**

1m 40.65s (2.45) **Going Correction** +0.175s/f (Slow) 9 Ran SP% **111.9**
Speed ratings (Par 98): **94,93,88,87,87 86,85,82,81**
toteswingers: 1&2 £2.80, 1&3 £5.90, 2&3 £2.90 CSF £17.98 TOTE £5.80: £1.40, £1.40, £2.70; EX 14.70.
Owner H R H Princess Haya Of Jordan **Bred** Bridgewater Equine Ltd **Trained** Newmarket, Suffolk

FOCUS
As in the first division the front two pulled a long way clear of the others, but the winning time was 1.63 seconds slower. The form is rated around the second and third.
Gra Adhmhar(IRE) Official explanation: jockey said gelding ran too freely and was denied a clear run

1591 £66 FREE BET AT BLUESQUARE.COM H'CAP 1m 2f (P)
3:00 (3:02) (Class 6) (0-60,60) 4-Y-0+ **£2,388** (£705; £352) **Stalls** Low

Form RPR
0150 **1** **Binnion Bay (IRE)**34 [970] 9-8-10 **52** (b) NeilChalmers 3 61
(J J Bridger) *s.i.s: hld up towards rr: hdwy into midfield gng wl 3f out: rdn and qcknd to ld jst over 1f out: drvn fnl f: kpt on wl* **25/1**

5452 **2** *3/4* **Where's Susie**33 [983] 5-9-0 **56** RobertHavlin 4 64
(M Madgwick) *in tch: rdn to chse ldr ent fnl 2f: chsd wnr ent fnl f: kpt on u.p* **6/1**[3]

600- **3** *2 1/4* **Generous Lad (IRE)**227 [5872] 7-8-4 **51** (p) AmyBaker(5) 12 54
(A B Haynes) *stdd s: hld up in rr: nt clr run briefly on inner ent fnl 2f: gd hdwy over 1f out: chsd ldng pair ins fnl f: no imp fnl 100yds* **25/1**

00-0 **4** *1 1/2* **Straight And Level (CAN)**95 [262] 5-9-1 **57** DaneO'Neill 8 57
(Miss Jo Crowley) *hld up towards rr: effrt and short of room jst over 2f out: gd hdwy to chse ldrs over 1f out: styd on same pce u.p fnl f* **14/1**

6-05 **5** *hd* **La Columbina**42 [897] 5-9-3 **59** (v) FrankieMcDonald 7 59
(H J Evans) *in tch in midfield: rdn and effrt on outer bnd 2f out: kpt on u.p fnl f: nvr gng pce to rch ldrs* **10/1**

00-4 **6** *shd* **Douchkette (FR)**13 [1301] 4-9-3 **59** GeorgeBaker 6 58+
(John Berry) *lw: hld up in midfield: switching rt bnd 2f out: sn rdn and unable qck: kpt on steadily fnl f: nvr gng pce to rch ldrs* **15/2**

2-53 **7** *2 1/2* **Felicia**26 [1078] 5-8-7 **49** SamHitchcott 1 43
(J E Long) *chsd ldrs: rdn and unable qck wl over 1f out: hrd drvn and no prog ent fnl f* **14/1**

2224 **8** *1 1/4* **Alfredtheordinary**17 [1225] 5-9-4 **60** ChrisCatlin 11 52
(M R Channon) *hld up towards rr: rdn and effrt on outer bnd jst over 2f out: no real prog: nvr trbld ldrs* **5/1**[2]

004- **9** *1* **Big Sur**150 [7576] 4-9-4 **60** LiamKeniry 9 50
(T Keddy) *lw: t.k.h: in tch towards rr: rdn and no prog ent fnl 2f: no ch fnl f* **4/1**[1]

6004 **10** *nk* **Bookiebasher Babe (IRE)**20 [1179] 5-9-4 **60** FrannyNorton 2 49
(M Quinn) *sn bustled up to ld: rdn ent fnl 2f: hdd jst over 1f out: sn wknd* **40/1**

0-00 **11** *7* **Navene (IRE)**12 [1322] 6-8-13 **55** FergusSweeney 5 30
(M R Bosley) *t.k.h: chsd ldr tl 3f out: wl btn over 1f out* **40/1**

4000 **12** *6* **Maximus Aurelius (IRE)**10 [1395] 5-9-3 **59** (t) SebSanders 14 22
(J Jay) *hld up in midfield: hdwy on outer to chse ldrs over 7f out: wnt 2nd 3f out tl jst over 2f out: sn wknd* **12/1**

/0-5 **13** *8* **Kilkenny Bay**40 [925] 4-9-0 **56** WilliamBuick 10 3
(W Jarvis) *lw: t.k.h: in tch: rdn wl over 3f out: lost pl u.p wl over 2f out: wl btn fnl 2f* **8/1**

000- **14** *14* **Mumtaz Begum**231 [5747] 5-8-1 **46** oh1 (v1) NataliaGemelova(3) 13 —
(J E Long) *dwlt: towards rr on outer: hdwy into midfield 6f out: struggling and rdn 4f out: lost tch over 2f out: eased fr over 1f out: t.o* **100/1**

2m 7.39s (0.79) **Going Correction** +0.175s/f (Slow) 14 Ran SP% **117.5**
Speed ratings (Par 101): **103,102,100,99,99 99,97,96,95,95 89,84,78,67**
toteswingers: 1&2 £27.30, 1&3 £94.20, 2&3 £35.20 CSF £160.61 CT £3800.56 TOTE £29.20: £6.50, £1.50, £11.20; EX 132.30.
Owner J J Bridger **Bred** Fieldspring Ltd **Trained** Liphook, Hants
■ Stewards' Enquiry : William Buick caution: used whip without giving filly time to respond.

FOCUS
A typically competitive Lingfield handicap in which the pace didn't appear that strong but the winner, third and fourth came from the rear. The winner is rated to his best and the form is sound enough.
Binnion Bay(IRE) Official explanation: trainer said, regarding apparent improvement in form, that on its previous run the gelding had been unable to be covered up.
Mumtaz Begum Official explanation: trainer said mare was unable to handle the bend

1592 PICK A WINNER WITH BLUE SQUARE ICARD (S) STKS 1m 4f (P)
3:30 (3:30) (Class 6) 4-Y-0+ **£2,047** (£604; £302) **Stalls** Low

Form RPR
030- **1** **Timocracy**15 [5334] 5-8-13 77 JamieSpencer 3 54+
(A B Haynes) *t.k.h early: chsd ldr: rdn and clsd 2f out: drvn over 1f out: led ins fnl f: kpt on wl* **6/1**[3]

3360 **2** *3/4* **Mister Frosty (IRE)**47 [865] 4-8-5 46 CharlotteKerton(7) 1 53
(G Prodromou) *dwlt: t.k.h: sn rcvrd and led: wl clr 9f out: rdn enteing fnl 2f: hdd ins fnl f: kpt on same pce after* **25/1**

1112 **3** *2* **Sedgwick**7 [1439] 8-9-5 75 StevieDonohoe 7 56+
(Ian Williams) *hld up in last trio: hdwy over 3f out: rdn and clsd on ldr 2f out: no ex u.p ins fnl f* **1/1**[1]

2144 **4** *1* **Zero Cool (USA)**39 [941] 6-9-5 64 (p) GeorgeBaker 6 54+
(G L Moore) *lw: hld up in main gp: clsd on ldr 2f out: rdn over 1f out: no ex u.p ins fnl f* **11/4**[2]

1400 **5** *6* **Sunset Boulevard (IRE)**19 [1188] 7-9-5 57 ChrisCatlin 4 45
(Miss Tor Sturgis) *hld up in main gp: rdn and effrt 3f out: nvr trbld ldrs* **14/1**

3352 **6** *1 1/4* **Quince (IRE)**40 [923] 7-8-13 62 (v) SaleemGolam 5 37
(J Pearce) *racd in main gp: rdn and no real prog 3f out: n.d* **7/1**

6-00 **7** *8* **Shouldntbethere (IRE)**34 [969] 6-8-8 44 AmyBaker(5) 2 24
(Mrs P N Dutfield) *stdd and v awkward leaving stalls: a wl bhd* **50/1**

/00- **8** *nse* **Charlie Be (IRE)**[252] 5120 5-8-13 40 .... FergusSweeney 8 24
(Mrs P N Dutfield) *stdd s: t.k.h: a wl bhd* **100/1**

2m 37.57s (4.57) **Going Correction** +0.175s/f (Slow)
WFA 4 from 5yo+ 1lb 8 Ran SP% **116.9**
Speed ratings (Par 101): **91,90,89,88,84 83,78,78**
.The winner was bought in for 4,400gns. Sedgwick was claimed by S A Harris for £6000. \n\x\x
Owner Ms J Loylert **Bred** Gainsborough Stud Management Ltd **Trained** Limpley Stoke, Bath

FOCUS
A mess of a race and several of these riders must have had red faces as they allowed the freely-running Mister Frosty far too much rope. Only the winner was able to get to him, and then only just. Limited form.

1593 BET AT BLUESQUARE.COM FILLIES' H'CAP 7f (P)
4:00 (4:00) (Class 5) (0-70,70) 3-Y-O **£3,238** (£963; £481; £240) **Stalls** Low

Form RPR

602- **1** **Kingston Acacia**[164] 7389 3-8-10 **62** .... (v) DavidProbert 2 70
(A M Balding) *b.hind: lw: mde all: pushed clr over 1f out: kpt on wl and in command fnl f* **5/1[3]**

405- **2** *3 ¼* **Madame Roulin (IRE)**[172] 7277 3-8-12 **64** .... HayleyTurner 1 63
(M L W Bell) *bit bkwd: chsd ldrs: rdn ent fnl 2f: drvn and one pce over 1f out: chsd wnr ins fnl f: no imp* **16/1**

5051 **3** *nk* **Mary's Pet**[18] 1205 3-8-12 **64** .... SebSanders 5 62+
(J Akehurst) *lw: in tch in midfield: rdn and hdwy jst over 2f out: outpcd over 1f out: rallied ins fnl f: kpt on but nvr a threat to wnr* **4/1[2]**

45-2 **4** *½* **Giulietta Da Vinci**[39] 932 3-8-12 **64** .... JimCrowley 4 61
(S Woodman) *stdd after s: t.k.h: hld up in last pair: rdn and hdwy on inner over 1f out: styng on but no ch w wnr whn nt clr run ins fnl f: kpt on fnl 50yds* **16/1**

02-1 **5** *shd* **Mount Juliet (IRE)**[39] 933 3-9-4 **70** .... MartinDwyer 3 67
(M Botti) *hld up towards rr: effrt on inner 2f out: styd on same pce and no threat to wnr ins fnl f* **11/8[1]**

0-35 **6** *½* **Slasi**[39] 934 3-8-8 **60** .... ChrisCatlin 7 55
(C E Brittain) *chsd ldr: rdn ent fnl 2f: drvn and unable qck over 1f out: lost 2nd ins fnl f* **17/2**

245- **7** *hd* **Brinscall**[145] 7618 3-9-0 **69** .... BarryMcHugh(3) 8 64
(Julie Camacho) *in tch towards rr: effrt on outer and rdn over 2f out: lost pl bnd 2f out: kpt on fnl f but nvr any threat to wnr* **50/1**

10-0 **8** *nk* **Dream Number (IRE)**[20] 1168 3-9-1 **67** .... WilliamBuick 9 61
(W R Muir) *stdd s: t.k.h: hld up in last pair: rdn and effrt wl over 1f out: keeping on but no ch w wnr whn nt clr run ins fnl f: n.d* **20/1**

300- **9** *hd* **Dixi Heights**[202] 6589 3-8-5 **57** .... NickyMackay 6 50
(J R Boyle) *chsd ldng trio: lost pl u.p bnd wl over 1f out: one pce after* **25/1**

1m 25.79s (0.99) **Going Correction** +0.175s/f (Slow) 9 Ran SP% **111.6**
Speed ratings (Par 95): **101,97,96,96,96 95,95,95,94**
toteswingers: 1&2 £12.00, 1&3 £3.90, 2&3 £13.80 CSF £74.00 CT £344.39 TOTE £4.40: £1.10, £6.20, £1.30; EX 60.90.
Owner Richard Hains **Bred** Kingston Park Studs Pty Ltd **Trained** Kingsclere, Hants

FOCUS
An ordinary fillies' handicap. The winner improved but the rest finished bunched and this is not form to be positive about.

1594 £66 FREE BET AT BLUESQUARE.COM CLAIMING STKS 7f (P)
4:30 (4:30) (Class 6) 3-Y-O **£2,047** (£604; £302) **Stalls** Low

Form RPR

3145 **1** **Novay Essjay (IRE)**[6] 1480 3-9-0 71 .... HayleyTurner 2 68
(C R Dore) *mde all: set stdy gallop tl rdn and qcknd clr w rival wl over 1f out: battled on wl fnl f* **5/2[2]**

1031 **2** *½* **Craicattack (IRE)**[7] 1449 3-9-3 73 .... (p) LiamKeniry 5 70
(J S Moore) *lw: t.k.h: chsd wnr: rdn to chal 2f out: ev ch after: no ex fnl 100yds* **6/1**

1452 **3** *1 ½* **Ginger Grey (IRE)**[5] 1488 3-9-3 66 .... (p) DaneO'Neill 6 66+
(D R C Elsworth) *stdd s: hld up in last pair: effrt and rdn to chse clr ldng pair jst over 1f out: drvn 1f out: no imp fnl 100yds* **15/8[1]**

66- **4** *3 ¾* **Trewarthenick**[246] 5312 3-9-3 0 .... DavidProbert 3 56
(A M Balding) *in tch: rdn to chse ldrs over 2f out: unable qck ent fnl 2f: wl btn fnl f* **3/1[3]**

-560 **5** *2* **Chandrayaan**[27] 1058 3-8-11 61 .... (v) SamHitchcott 4 44
(J E Long) *dwlt: hld up in last pair: struggling whn sltly hmpd bnd jst over 2f out: no ch w ldrs after: swtchd lft ins fnl f* **25/1**

3033 **6** *nk* **Blue Zephyr**[7] 1436 3-8-13 64 .... MartinDwyer 7 46
(W R Muir) *in tch: hdwy to chse ldrs over 2f out: wknd u.p wl over 1f out* **12/1**

00-0 **7** *7* **Impressioniste (IRE)**[27] 1057 3-8-8 0 .... TobyAtkinson(5) 1 27
(Luke Comer, Ire) *chsd ldrs: rdn and struggling over 2f out: wl btn over 1f out* **66/1**

1m 27.03s (2.23) **Going Correction** +0.175s/f (Slow) 7 Ran SP% **115.7**
Speed ratings (Par 96): **94,93,91,87,85 84,76**
toteswingers: 1&2 £2.90, 1&3 £2.20, 2&3 £3.00 CSF £18.30 TOTE £3.20: £1.50, £2.00; EX 13.80.Novay Essjay was claimed by Nigel I. P. Brown for £10,500.
Owner Patrick Wilmott **Bred** Camogue Stud Ltd **Trained** Cowbit, Lincs

FOCUS
A weak and uncompetitive claimer in which the front pair dominated throughout. The winning time was 1.24 seconds slower than the fillies' handicap. The runner-up is rated to his winter best.

1595 BLUE SQUARE SUPPORTING MARIE CURIE CANCER CARE H'CAP (DIV I) 6f (P)
5:00 (5:00) (Class 6) (0-65,65) 4-Y-O+ **£2,047** (£604; £302) **Stalls** Low

Form RPR

0-20 **1** **Charles Darwin (IRE)**[13] 1300 7-9-1 **62** .... FrannyNorton 1 70
(M Blanshard) *chsd ldng trio: swtchd rt and hdwy to press ldrs over 1f out: ev ch fnl f: drvn ahd towards fin* **16/1**

530- **2** *hd* **Amosite**[257] 4952 4-8-11 **65** .... DannyBrock(7) 5 72
(J R Jenkins) *chsd ldr: pushed along to ld jst over 1f out: sn hrd pressed: kpt on fnl f tl hdd towards fin* **25/1**

1006 **3** *¾* **Imperial House**[61] 695 4-9-4 **65** .... (b) DavidProbert 2 70
(R A Harris) *lw: wnt rt s and s.i.s: towards rr: hdwy 3f out: swtchd rt and rdn to chse ldrs jst over 1f out: hanging lft u.p after: no imp fnl 100yds* **12/1**

415- **4** *¾* **Plumage**[284] 4051 5-9-0 **61** .... LiamKeniry 8 63
(Miss Tor Sturgis) *chsd ldrs: rdn and effrt ent fnl 2f: styd on same pce u.p ins fnl f* **12/1**

140- **5** *nse* **Mr Skipiton (IRE)**[237] 5576 5-9-0 **61** .... JackMitchell 12 63+
(B J McMath) *swtg: dropped in bhd after s: hdwy on outer 1/2-way: rdn wl over 1f out: kpt on u.p ins fnl f: nt rch ldrs* **7/1**

-062 **6** *1 ½* **Musical Script (USA)**[13] 1300 7-9-3 **64** .... (b) DaneO'Neill 4 61
(Mouse Hamilton-Fairley) *lw: in tch in midfield: drvn and effrt wl over 1f out: kpt on same pce u.p fnl f* **15/2**

6551 **7** *½* **Teen Ager (FR)**[13] 1305 6-9-1 **62** .... GeorgeBaker 11 58
(P Burgoyne) *hld up in tch midfield: rdn and unable qck wl over 1f out: kpt on ins fnl f but nvr gng pce to rch ldrs* **9/1**

0-56 **8** *½* **Learo Dochais (USA)**[17] 1224 4-9-3 **64** .... (p) PhilipRobinson 6 58
(M A Jarvis) *hld up towards rr: effrt on inner over 1f out: no imp u.p ins fnl f* **5/1[2]**

6023 **9** *2* **Bobs Dreamflight**[13] 1300 4-8-11 **63** .... (b) MarkCoumbe(5) 3 51
(D K Ivory) *restless in stalls: led: clr 1/2-way: rdn and hdd jst over 1f out: wknd qckly fnl f* **6/1[3]**

55-6 **10** *3 ½* **Ask Jenny (IRE)**[20] 1166 8-8-12 **59** .... JamieSpencer 7 35
(Patrick Morris) *stdd s: hld up in rr: n.d* **9/2[1]**

1450 **11** *1 ¾* **Peopleton Brook**[10] 1391 8-9-4 **65** .... (t) SteveDrowne 9 36
(B G Powell) *a bhd: nvr on terms* **20/1**

650- **12** *7* **Kheylide (IRE)**[22] 6857 4-8-13 **60** .... ChrisCatlin 10 8
(D C O'Brien) *in tch tl lost pl and rdn 4f out: wl bhd fnl 2f* **33/1**

1m 12.76s (0.86) **Going Correction** +0.175s/f (Slow) 12 Ran SP% **116.2**
Speed ratings (Par 101): **101,100,99,98,98 96,96,95,92,88 85,76**
toteswingers: 1&2 £57.10, 1&3 £38.00, 2&3 £28.70 CSF £362.57 CT £4878.05 TOTE £17.90: £5.00, £11.60, £4.10; EX 318.10.
Owner The Breeze-In Partnership **Bred** M And P Associates **Trained** Upper Lambourn, Berks

FOCUS
A moderate sprint handicap run at a strong pace but a length slower than the second division. Straightforward form.
Imperial House Official explanation: jockey said colt jumped right

1596 BLUE SQUARE SUPPORTING MARIE CURIE CANCER CARE H'CAP (DIV II) 6f (P)
5:30 (5:30) (Class 6) (0-65,65) 4-Y-O+ **£2,047** (£604; £302) **Stalls** Low

Form RPR

4106 **1** **Titus Gent**[13] 1300 5-9-0 **61** .... DavidProbert 4 71
(R A Harris) *mde all: rdn clr over 1f out: kpt on wl fnl f* **9/2[2]**

1234 **2** *½* **Not My Choice (IRE)**[6] 1470 5-9-1 **62** .... (t) JamieSpencer 10 70
(D C Griffiths) *chsd wnr: rdn and nt pce of wnr over 1f out: rallied towards fin but a hld* **13/2[3]**

0640 **3** *1 ½* **Radiator Rooney (IRE)**[6] 1470 7-8-6 **60** ow2 .... MJMurphy(7) 1 63
(Patrick Morris) *t.k.h: trckd ldrs: hmpd after 1f: rdn and nt qckn over 1f out: kpt on same pce fnl f* **14/1**

135- **4** *1* **Cativo Cavallino**[160] 7432 7-9-0 **64** .... NataliaGemelova(3) 2 64+
(J E Long) *bustled along in midfield whn hmpd and lost pl 5f out: bhd 1/2-way: rdn and gd hdwy on inner over 1f out: styd on wl: nt rch ldrs* **12/1**

4155 **5** *¾* **Sweet Applause (IRE)**[11] 1350 4-8-7 **61** .... CharlotteKerton(7) 6 59
(G Prodromou) *midfield whn hmpd 5f out: pushed along and effrt over 1f out: kpt on fnl f: nvr trbld ldrs* **20/1**

000- **6** *½* **Requisite**[167] 7337 5-9-4 **65** .... (v) RichardThomas 3 61
(I A Wood) *hld up in rr: gd hdwy towards inner ent fnl f: no imp u.p fnl 100yds* **33/1**

660/ **7** *1 ¾* **Blue Aura (IRE)**[939] 5874 7-9-4 **65** .... FergusSweeney 12 55
(B G Powell) *chsd ldrs: rdn ent fnl 2f: wknd jst over 1f out* **25/1**

5211 **8** *½* **Waterloo Dock**[20] 1166 5-9-3 **64** .... (v) MartinDwyer 9 53
(M Quinn) *t.k.h: trckd ldrs: rdn ent fnl 2f: nt qckn u.p over 1f out: wknd ent fnl f* **9/4[1]**

3200 **9** *nk* **Sir Edwin Landseer (USA)**[3] 1534 10-8-10 **60** .... MichaelStainton(3) 8 48
(G L Moore) *dwlt: midfield: rdn and no prog 1/2-way: nvr trbld ldrs* **20/1**

626- **10** *1 ¼* **Louphole**[177] 7203 8-9-2 **63** .... SimonWhitworth 5 47
(J R Jenkins) *stdd s: hld up in rr: c wd bnd wl over 1f out: nvr on terms* **9/1**

6306 **11** *½* **Kyle (IRE)**[21] 1147 6-9-1 **62** .... LiamKeniry 11 44
(C R Dore) *dropped in bhd after s: effrt on outer 1/2-way: n.d* **10/1**

050- **12** *nse* **Song Of Praise**[189] 6915 4-9-4 **65** .... DaneO'Neill 7 47
(M Blanshard) *midfield whn hmpd 5f out: rdn and nt qckning whn rdr dropped reins over 1f out: no ch ins fnl f* **16/1**

1m 12.51s (0.61) **Going Correction** +0.175s/f (Slow) 12 Ran SP% **117.9**
Speed ratings (Par 101): **102,101,99,98,97 96,94,93,92,91 90,90**
toteswingers: 1&2 £5.80, 1&3 £16.50, 2&3 £11.60 CSF £31.76 CT £387.24 TOTE £5.30: £2.60, £2.60, £5.60; EX 27.50 Place 6: £82.75 Place 5: £68.89.
Owner Alan & Adam Darlow, A Darlow Productions **Bred** Heather Raw **Trained** Earlswood, Monmouths

FOCUS
The early pace seemed honest enough with three disputing the advantage, including the first two home, and few got into it from behind. The winning time was 0.25 seconds faster than the first division. Straightforward form.
T/Plt: £39.90 to a £1 stake. Pool: £65,955.67. 1,206.07 winning tickets. T/Qpdt: £21.30 to a £1 stake. Pool: £4,003.14. 138.47 winning tickets. SP

1389 NOTTINGHAM (L-H)
Tuesday, April 27

OFFICIAL GOING: Good to firm changing to firm after race 1 (5.35)
All races run on inner course.
Wind: Light half-against Weather: Cloudy with sunny spells

1597 E B F TOTEPLACEPOT MAIDEN STKS 5f 13y
5:35 (5:36) (Class 5) 2-Y-O **£3,561** (£1,059; £529; £264) **Stalls** High

Form RPR

1 **Orientalist** 2-9-3 0 .... TedDurcan 2 72+
(Eve Johnson Houghton) *s.i.s: sn mid-div: swtchd rt and hdwy over 1f out: r.o to ld nr fin* **12/1**

2 *1* **Leiba Leiba** 2-9-3 0 .... DarryllHolland 10 69+
(M Botti) *a.p: led and hung lft fr over 1f out: shkn up ins fnl f: hdd nr fin* **11/2**

4 **3** *hd* **Just For Leo (IRE)**[12] 1331 2-9-0 0 .... AndrewHeffernan(3) 1 68
(P D Evans) *w ldrs: led 3f out: rdn and hdd over 1f out: edgd lft: r.o* **3/1[1]**

6 **4** *4 ½* **Surely This Time (IRE)**[13] 1294 2-9-3 0 .... NeilCallan 9 52
(K A Ryan) *led 2f: remained handy: hung lft fr over 1f out: wknd ins fnl f* **5/1[3]**

5 *1 ½* **Angle Knight (USA)** 2-9-3 0 .... EddieAhern 4 46
(B J Meehan) *s.i.s: outpcd: r.o ins fnl f: nvr nrr* **12/1**

6 *1 ¼* **Evening Dress** 2-8-12 0 .... JoeFanning 8 37+
(M Johnston) *w ldrs tl pushed along 1/2-way: wknd wl over 1f out* **13/2**

7 *½* **Key To The Motion (IRE)** 2-8-12 0 .... PJMcDonald 6 35
(P T Midgley) *s.i.s: sn pushed along in rr: nvr on terms* **66/1**

8 *nk* **Torteval (IRE)** 2-9-3 0........................ CathyGannon 5 39
(P D Evans) *s.i.s: outpcd: swvd lft 4f out: n.d* **25/1**

9 *13* **Roche Des Vents** 2-9-3 0........................ RichardHughes 3 —
(R Hannon) *w ldrs: rdn 1/2-way: sn hung lft and wknd* **9/2**[2]

61.90 secs (0.90) **Going Correction** -0.025s/f (Good) **9** Ran SP% **109.3**
Speed ratings (Par 92): **91,89,89,81,79 77,76,76,55**
toteswingers: 1&2 £4.70, 1&3 £11.30, 2&3 £8.90 CSF £69.97 TOTE £17.70: £6.00, £3.00, £1.02; EX 64.70.
Owner Eden Racing IV **Bred** Whitsbury Manor Stud **Trained** Blewbury, Oxon

FOCUS
Following this opener, the ground, which had been watered, was changed from good to firm to just 'firm'. Ted Durcan felt it was lively but safe. This was no more than a fair juvenile maiden, run at a strong pace. The main action took place middle to stands' side, with the winner racing close to the rail. The third helps with the level.

NOTEBOOK
Orientalist ◆, a 14,000gns half-brother to 7f winner Hucking Heist, out of a 6f scorer in Germany, overcame greenness to make a successful introduction. He was off the bridle soon enough but responded well to pressure, displaying a likeable attitude, and was also helped by the leaders tiring late on. There should be plenty more to come, including over a little further in due course. (op 8-1 tchd 7-1)
Leiba Leiba, a half-brother to, among others, 5f 2yo winner Tia Mia, looked set to take this when getting to the front over 1f out but didn't see the race out as expected. Darryll Holland was not at his most vigorous near the line, giving the impression he thought the race was safe, although the colt may well have been caught anyway. Marco Botti's runner obviously has ability, but he lacks size and is probably not open to much improvement. (op 7-1 tchd 15-2)
Just For Leo(IRE) shaped well when fourth on his debut at Ripon, but he failed to find sufficient improvement from that run. He showed speed towards the middle of the track but simply wasn't good enough. (op 4-1)
Surely This Time(IRE) compromised his chance by hanging left, possibly feeling this quick ground. Official explanation: jockey said colt hung both ways (op 6-1 tchd 9-2)
Angle Knight(USA) is a half-brother to 2m hurdle winner Alhaque, but there is speed in his pedigree as well and he should be all the better for this experience. He was very green for the most part but made some encouraging late headway. (tchd 9-1)
Evening Dress, a 190,000gns purchase, is quite a big filly for the time of year. (op 7-1 tchd 6-1)
Key To The Motion(IRE) shaped as though she will come on a good deal for this experience.
Roche Des Vents hung badly left in the closing stages without being given a hard time and perhaps something was amiss. Official explanation: jockey said colt hung left (op 3-1 tchd 5-1)

1598 TOTESWINGER H'CAP 5f 13y
6:05 (6:05) (Class 6) (0-60,60) 4-Y-O+ **£2,047** (£604; £302) **Stalls** High

Form RPR

020- **1** **Micky Mac (IRE)**[151] 7555 6-9-2 **58**........................ KierenFallon 8 69
(C J Teague) *w ldr: led 3f out: rdn and hung lft ins fnl f: r.o* **10/1**

50-5 **2** *1 ¼* **Desert Strike**[10] 1391 4-9-4 **60**........................ RichardHughes 5 67
(P F I Cole) *dwlt: in rr and pushed along 1/2-way: hdwy over 1f out: sn rdn and carried hd high: no imp wl ins fnl f* **11/4**[1]

0652 **3** *½* **Thoughtsofstardom**[7] 1443 7-8-5 **54**........................ LeonnaMayor(7) 7 59
(P S McEntee) *chsd ldrs: rdn 1/2-way: styd on same pce ins fnl f* **5/1**[2]

14-0 **4** *¾* **The History Man (IRE)**[14] 1276 7-9-1 **57**........................(b) KirstyMilczarek 14 59
(B D Leavy) *led 2f: remained handy: rdn and hung lft over 1f out: styd on same pce ins fnl f* **15/2**[3]

3-00 **5** *nk* **You'relikemefrank**[17] 1234 4-8-4 **46** oh1........................(p) TadhgO'Shea 13 47
(J Balding) *hld up: r.o ins fnl f: nt rch ldrs* **20/1**

1-6R **6** *nk* **Greek Secret**[10] 1391 7-9-0 **56**........................(b) DavidNolan 3 56
(J O'Reilly) *s.i.s: hld up: pushed along 2f out: r.o ins fnl f: nt trble ldrs* **25/1**

0063 **7** *hd* **Meikle Barfil**[10] 1391 8-8-8 **50**........................(bt) LukeMorris 9 49
(J M Bradley) *prom: rdn over 1f out: no ex ins fnl f* **12/1**

00-0 **8** *¾* **City For Conquest (IRE)**[22] 1112 7-8-4 **46** oh1........(b) CathyGannon 4 43
(John A Harris) *sn pushed along in rr: r.o wl ins fnl f: nvr nrr* **25/1**

0600 **9** *½* **Tournedos (IRE)**[11] 1364 8-9-4 **60**........................(b) PhillipMakin 16 55
(Mrs R A Carr) *s.i.s: hdwy 1/2-way: rdn over 1f out: styd on same pce* **8/1**

5350 **10** *hd* **Style Award**[7] 1443 5-9-0 **59**........................(p) KellyHarrison(3) 1 53
(W J H Ratcliffe) *mid-div: hdwy over 1f out: wknd ins fnl f* **10/1**

0240 **11** *¾* **Taboor (IRE)**[22] 1131 12-8-4 **46** oh1........................ RoystonFfrench 11 38
(R M H Cowell) *mid-div: lost pl 1/2-way: n.d after* **33/1**

5000 **12** *¾* **Miacarla**[27] 1068 7-8-4 **46** oh1........................ PatrickMathers 15 35
(H A McWilliams) *hld up in tch: plld hrd: rdn over 1f out: wknd ins fnl f* **66/1**

4450 **13** *3* **Mister Incredible**[60] 721 7-8-4 **46** oh1........................(b) JoeFanning 10 24
(J M Bradley) *chsd ldrs: rdn over 1f out: wknd ins fnl f* **25/1**

-000 **14** *2 ¼* **Town House**[60] 727 8-7-13 **46** oh1........................ SophieDoyle(5) 17 16
(B P J Baugh) *chsd ldrs: rdn 1/2-way: wknd over 1f out* **25/1**

60.75 secs (-0.25) **Going Correction** -0.025s/f (Good) **14** Ran SP% **116.7**
Speed ratings (Par 101): **101,99,98,97,96 96,95,94,93,93 92,91,86,82**
toteswingers: 1&2 £7.60, 1&3 £10.50, 2&3 £3.80 CSF £33.24 CT £158.19 TOTE £12.10: £6.40, £1.02, £2.50; EX 43.50.
Owner A M McArdle **Bred** Stephen O'Rourke **Trained** Station Town, Co Durham

FOCUS
A moderate sprint handicap in which it paid to race prominently. The main action took place up the centre of the track. The form is best judged around the third.

1599 TOTEQUADPOT MAIDEN STKS 5f 13y
6:35 (6:35) (Class 5) 3-4-Y-O **£2,729** (£806; £403) **Stalls** High

Form RPR

3- **1** **Kanaf (IRE)**[320] 2853 3-9-3 0........................ TadhgO'Shea 6 77+
(E A L Dunlop) *s.i.s: swtchd lft: pushed along and hdwy 1/2-way: led over 1f out: edgd rt ins fnl f: r.o* **1/1**[1]

2462 **2** *2 ¼* **Diamond Johnny G (USA)**[11] 1345 3-9-0 75........(t) AlanCreighton(3) 1 69
(E J Creighton) *dwlt: sn prom: rdn and ev ch over 1f out: styd on same pce ins fnl f* **7/1**[3]

42 **3** *2 ½* **Sulis Minerva (IRE)**[15] 1257 3-8-12 0........................(t) LukeMorris 4 55
(J R Gask) *hld up in tch: led wl over 1f out: sn hdd: no ex ins fnl f* **15/8**[2]

-0 **4** *1* **Regal Emperor (IRE)**[8] 1425 3-9-0 0........................ MichaelGeran(3) 5 56+
(D Nicholls) *sn outpcd: styd on ins fnl f: nvr nrr* **22/1**

-40 **5** *1 ¾* **Slap And Tickle (IRE)**[83] 392 4-9-8 0........................(t) RoystonFfrench 2 45
(S C Williams) *led: rdn: hung lft and hdd wl over 1f out: wknd fnl f* **25/1**

6 **6** *¾* **Wirral Way**[96] 253 4-9-13 0........................(t) JamesDoyle 3 47
(F Sheridan) *chsd ldrs: rdn 1/2-way: wknd over 1f out* **100/1**

61.25 secs (0.25) **Going Correction** -0.025s/f (Good)
WFA 3 from 4yo 10lb **6** Ran SP% **106.5**
Speed ratings (Par 103): **97,93,89,87,85 83**
toteswingers: 1&2 £1.60, 1&3 £1.10, 2&3 £1.50 CSF £7.49 TOTE £1.50: £1.10, £5.70; EX 5.40.
Owner Hamdan Al Maktoum **Bred** Catcher Equine Ltd **Trained** Newmarket, Suffolk
■ Stewards' Enquiry : Alan Creighton one-day ban: used whip continually slapping down shoulder (May 11)

FOCUS
The 75-rated runner-up may be the best guide to the form, but this was an uncompetitive contest and the time was poor, being 0.50 seconds slower than the 58-rated 4-y-o Micky Mac recorded in an earlier handicap. It is doubtful if the winner had to improve on last year's debut.
Sulis Minerva(IRE) ◆ Official explanation: trainer said filly was unsuited by the firm ground
Slap And Tickle(IRE) Official explanation: jockey said filly ran too free
Wirral Way Official explanation: jockey said gelding jumped awkwardly from stalls

1600 TOTEEXACTA H'CAP 1m 2f 50y
7:05 (7:06) (Class 3) (0-90,90) 4-Y-O **£7,569** (£2,265; £1,132; £566; £282) **Stalls** Low

Form RPR

550- **1** **Shavansky**[178] 7194 6-8-13 **88**........................ JamesMillman(3) 1 95
(B R Millman) *stdd s: hld up and plld v hrd: swtchd lft and hdwy over 1f out: rdn to ld ins fnl f: jst hld on* **16/1**

524- **2** *nse* **Sam Sharp (USA)**[199] 6680 4-8-7 **79**........................ EddieAhern 2 86
(H R A Cecil) *hld up: hdwy 3f out: led ins fnl f: sn rdn: hung lft and hdd: r.o* **9/2**[3]

-000 **3** *1 ¾* **Iron Out (USA)**[3] 1512 4-8-3 **80**........................ PaulPickard(5) 9 84
(R Hollinshead) *chsd ldr tl led over 1f out: rdn and hdd ins fnl f: edgd rt: styd on same pce* **66/1**

205- **4** *2* **Veroon (IRE)**[174] 7233 4-8-5 **77**........................(p) PaulHanagan 7 77
(J G Given) *led: rdn over 2f out: sn hung rt: hdd over 1f out: no ex wl ins fnl f* **12/1**

1-35 **5** *hd* **Perpetually (IRE)**[40] 921 4-9-4 **90**........................ JoeFanning 4 90
(M Johnston) *prom: rdn over 2f out: sn styd on same pce appr fnl f* **4/1**[2]

05-2 **6** *1 ¼* **Sohcahtoa (IRE)**[31] 1006 4-9-0 **86**........................(b[1]) RichardHughes 5 83
(R Hannon) *chsd ldrs: rdn over 2f out: wknd ins fnl f* **9/2**[3]

105- **7** *2 ¼* **Prince Of Johanne (IRE)**[220] 6114 4-8-12 **84**........ MickyFenton 10 77
(T P Tate) *hld up: hdwy 1/2-way: rdn and hung lft over 1f out: sn wknd* **25/1**

/0-5 **8** *2 ¾* **Sirgarfieldsobers (IRE)**[14] 1274 4-9-2 **88**........ RoystonFfrench 11 76
(B S Rothwell) *s.i.s: hld up: pushed along over 3f out: a in rr* **12/1**

1/2- **9** *7* **Cygnet**[223] 6002 4-8-13 **85**........................ KierenFallon 3 66
(L M Cumani) *hld up in tch: racd keenly: pushed along 4f out: wknd 2f out* **7/4**[1]

2m 10.61s (-3.69) **Going Correction** -0.50s/f (Hard) **9** Ran SP% **119.3**
Speed ratings (Par 107): **94,93,92,90,90 89,88,85,80**
toteswingers: 1&2 £12.90, 1&3 £25.50, 2&3 £37.00 CSF £89.38 CT £4651.01 TOTE £26.20: £5.60, £2.30, £17.60; EX 106.40.
Owner John Southway & Andrew Hughes **Bred** George Strawbridge **Trained** Kentisbeare, Devon

FOCUS
Probably an ordinary handicap for the grade and the pace didn't seem that strong.

NOTEBOOK
Shavansky was slow to get going, probably by design, and then pulled hard under restraint, so he deserves credit for this narrow success. He was 6lb above his highest winning mark, but he dead-heated first time out last season so a six-month absence wasn't a concern and these are his conditions. (op 20-1 tchd 22-1)
Sam Sharp(USA), who had travelled well, just failed to get up with his rider, Eddie Ahern, appearing to use his whip only sparingly. However, Ahern pointed out afterwards that the idea was to make sure the gelding didn't have an overly hard race, with it being his first outing for 199 days. This horse's only win to date came on soft ground, but the jockey felt these conditions suited fine. (op 7-1 tchd 4-1)
Iron Out(USA) ran much better than he had at Haydock on his return from a break just three days earlier.
Veroon(IRE) had been off for around six months but according to trainer James Given, he had done a lot of work and was quite well forward. (op 18-1 tchd 20-1)
Perpetually(IRE) found only the one pace for pressure, not improving as one might have hoped for the return to turf. (op 11-2)
Sohcahtoa(IRE), 3lb higher than when runner-up in the Spring Mile on his reappearance, had blinkers fitted for the first time and was returned to quick ground, but he ran disappointingly. He remains unproven over this trip. (op 4-1)
Prince Of Johanne(IRE) Official explanation: trainer said gelding was unsuited by the firm ground
Cygnet ◆, who managed only one run last year, finishing a close second under similar conditions off a 3lb lower mark, was a bit keen early on and, after being slightly squeezed for room around the turn into the straight, he came off the bridle and failed to pick up. This was a rather unsatisfactory contest, though, and the impression was that Luca Cumani's gelding could be a different proposition next time. Official explanation: jockey said, regarding running, that the gelding appeared to lose its action (op 13-8 tchd 2-1)

1601 TOTEPOOL BEAT THE BOOKIES H'CAP 1m 2f 50y
7:35 (7:38) (Class 6) (0-65,65) 3-Y-O **£2,047** (£604; £302) **Stalls** Low

Form RPR

2-30 **1** **Until The Man (IRE)**[81] 425 3-9-2 **63**........................(p) DarryllHolland 5 67
(Mrs L J Mongan) *plld hrd: led over 8f out: rdn over 1f out: styd on wl* **10/1**

40-4 **2** *1 ¼* **Aegean Destiny**[105] 133 3-8-13 **60**........................ StephenCraine 11 62
(J Mackie) *s.i.s: hld up: rdn over 3f out: hdwy over 2f out: r.o u.p to go 2nd wl ins fnl f: nt rch wnr* **22/1**

10 **3** *1 ¼* **Rubi Dia**[20] 1178 3-9-4 **65**........................ JoeFanning 7 64
(M Johnston) *racd keenly: led: hdd over 8f out: chsd wnr: rdn and ev ch over 1f out: no ex and lost 2nd wl ins fnl f* **9/1**

004- **4** *2* **Leader Of The Land (IRE)**[136] 7721 3-8-13 **60**........(b[1]) TedDurcan 9 55
(D R Lanigan) *hld up in tch: rdn over 2f out: hung lft over 1f out: styd on same pce* **10/3**[1]

-403 **5** *3 ¾* **Spice Fair**[10] 1394 3-9-0 **61**........................ LukeMorris 1 49
(M D I Usher) *hld up in tch: racd keenly: rdn over 2f out: sn outpcd* **6/1**[3]

0-30 **6** *1 ¼* **Stratton Banker (IRE)**[20] 1178 3-9-1 **62**........................(t) SaleemGolam 2 48
(S C Williams) *hld up: plld hrd: hdwy 4f out: rdn and wknd over 1f out* **40/1**

06-4 **7** *34* **Lady Willa (IRE)**[55] 768 3-9-3 **64**........................ KierenFallon 3 —
(B W Hills) *s.i.s: hdwy over 7f out: rdn and wknd over 2f out: t.o* **4/1**[2]

5335 **8** *4* **Pascalina**[15] 1261 3-8-13 **60**........................ RichardHughes 12 —
(J Akehurst) *trckd ldrs: plld hrd: j. path 8f out: sn lost pl: rdn over 4f out: wknd 3f out: t.o* **4/1**[2]

405- **9** *4 ½* **Romeos Girl**[225] 5934 3-8-13 **60**........................ TadhgO'Shea 8 —
(Jennie Candlish) *hld up: detached 1/2-way: t.o* **28/1**

05-4 **10** *4* **Brave Enough (USA)**[108] 106 3-9-3 **64**........................(p) PaulHanagan 4 —
(M A Magnusson) *hld up: rdn 4f out: wknd 3f out: eased fnl 2f: t.o* **8/1**

2m 13.7s (-0.60) **Going Correction** -0.50s/f (Hard) **10** Ran SP% **117.8**
Speed ratings (Par 96): **82,81,80,78,75 74,47,44,40,37**
toteswingers: 1&2 £31.80, 2&3 £9.30, 1&3 not won. CSF £194.58 CT £1778.11 TOTE £12.10: £3.80, £8.40, £2.60; EX 179.20.
Owner S. G. M. **Bred** Tally-Ho Stud **Trained** Epsom, Surrey
■ Kahfre was withdrawn after losing a shoe (11/1, deduct 5p in the £ under R4).

FOCUS
They went a slow pace (time 4.80 seconds outside standard), resulting in most of these racing keenly, and the form doesn't look worth a great deal. The winner is rated close to his best AW form.
Pascalina Official explanation: trainer's rep said filly was unsuited by the firm ground and also stumbled at the road crossing

1602 TOTEPOOL A BETTER WAY TO BET CLASSIFIED STKS — 1m 75y
8:05 (8:06) (Class 5) 3-Y-O — £3,238 (£963; £481; £240) Stalls Centre

Form — RPR
525- 1 **Oriental Scot**[136] 7721 3-9-0 70 ... JoeFanning 3 — 84
(W Jarvis) *sn led: shkn up over 1f out: r.o strly* **4/1**[2]
56-0 2 6 **Primary Colors**[10] 1387 3-9-0 70 ... (p) AdamKirby 1 — 70+
(C G Cox) *led early: settled to trckd ldrs: rdn over 3f out: styd on u.p to chse wnr over 1f out: no ex fnl f* **11/8**[1]
200- 3 6 **Decree Absolute (USA)**[210] 6367 3-9-0 68 ... PaulFitzsimons 2 — 56
(Miss J R Tooth) *hld up: rdn over 3f out: wknd over 1f out: wnt mod 3rd wl ins fnl f* **33/1**
355- 4 1 1/4 **Irish Jugger (USA)**[255] 5038 3-8-11 70 ... JamesMillman(3) 4 — 54
(B R Millman) *sn chsng wnr: rdn over 2f out: wknd over 1f out: lost 3rd wl ins fnl f* **9/2**[3]
003- 5 3 1/4 **Sandy Shaw**[226] 5906 3-9-0 69 ... KierenFallon 6 — 46+
(J W Hills) *hld up: hdwy 3f out: rdn and wknd over 1f out* **4/1**[2]
4-30 6 1 **Rainbow Six**[27] 1061 3-9-0 68 ... JerryO'Dwyer 5 — 44
(M Botti) *prom: racd keenly: rdn over 2f out: wknd over 1f out* **12/1**
1-00 7 1 1/4 **Chocolate Cookie (IRE)**[53] 809 3-9-0 66 ... TomMcLaughlin 7 — 41
(Miss M E Rowland) *hld up: rdn over 3f out: sn wknd* **20/1**

1m 45.97s (-3.63) **Going Correction** -0.50s/f (Hard) — 7 Ran SP% **115.7**
Speed ratings (Par 98): **98,92,86,84,81 80,79**
toteswingers:1&2 £1.40, 2&3 £10.90, 1&3 £19.40 CSF £10.18 TOTE £6.50: £2.80, £1.70; EX 12.00 Place 6: £378.54 Place 5: £169.41.
Owner Dr J Walker **Bred** Miss K Rausing **Trained** Newmarket, Suffolk

FOCUS
The winner set only a steady pace, recording a slow time, but he has plenty of scope and pulled away from the well-backed favourite, who was in turn nicely clear of the remainder, suggesting this is fair form for the grade. At the weights there was only 4lb between the field but the winner scored easily.
Irish Jugger(USA) Official explanation: trainer's rep said gelding lost its front shoe
T/Plt: £529.50 to a £1 stake. Pool: £62057.11. 85.54 winning tickets. T/Qpdt: £171.20 to a £1 stake. Pool: £4993.15. 21.58 winning tickets. CR

1278 YARMOUTH (L-H)
Tuesday, April 27

OFFICIAL GOING: Good to firm
Wind: nil Weather: hot and sunny, becoming chilly

1603 CRABBIE'S ALCOHOLIC GINGER BEER MAIDEN AUCTION STKS — 5f 43y
2:10 (2:11) (Class 6) 2-Y-O — £2,072 (£616; £308; £153) Stalls High

Form — RPR
1 **Child Bride** 2-8-1 0 ... IanBrennan(5) 7 — 72+
(P F I Cole) *in rr div early: sustained prog over 1f out: urged ahd fnl 75yds: cosily* **20/1**
2 2 1 1/4 **Belle Royale (IRE)**[11] 1360 2-8-0 0 ow1 ... KierenFox(5) 1 — 66
(W M Brisbourne) *sn led: rdn and hdd 75yds out: nt qckn* **20/1**
4 3 1 **Emma's Gift (IRE)**[12] 1324 2-8-11 0 ... JimmyQuinn 4 — 68
(Miss J Feilden) *prom: rdn and ev ch ins fnl f: kpt on same pce last 100yds* **6/4**[1]
4 5 **Comrade Bond** 2-8-6 0 ... AshleyMorgan(5) 6 — 50+
(M H Tompkins) *rn green in rr: rdn 1/2-way: styd on fnl f: snatched 4th but nvr nr ldrs* **40/1**
0 5 nk **Rowan Spirit (IRE)**[10] 1389 2-8-13 0 ... RichardKingscote 5 — 51
(Tom Dascombe) *chsd ldrs: rdn over 2f out: 4th and wl outpcd by ldng trio over 1f out* **20/1**
433 6 1 3/4 **Master Macho (IRE)**[3] 1517 2-8-11 0 ... AlanMunro 8 — 43
(M R Channon) *cl up on stands' rails tl rdn and wknd 2f out* **7/4**[2]
4 7 1 **Reginald Claude**[8] 1429 2-8-13 0 ... TomQueally 9 — 41
(M D I Usher) *chsd ldrs: rdn 2f out: edgd lft after: btn wl over 1f out* **33/1**
8 1 3/4 **Battenberg** 2-8-6 0 ... JerryO'Dwyer 2 — 28
(Miss Amy Weaver) *s.i.s: rdn 1/2-way: nvr on terms* **100/1**
9 4 1/2 **Little Hazel** 2-8-1 0 ... MartinLane(3) 3 — 9
(Pat Eddery) *rdn and labouring in rr after 1/2-way* **14/1**
10 21 **Blade Pirate** 2-8-11 0 ... MichaelHills 10 — —
(J Ryan) *sn struggling: t.o fr 1/2-way* **10/1**[3]

64.20 secs (1.50) **Going Correction** 0.0s/f (Good) — 10 Ran SP% **112.8**
Speed ratings (Par 90): **84,82,80,72,71 69,67,64,57,23**
toteswingers: 1&2 £25.50, 1&3 £5.80, 2&3 £4.40 CSF £314.77 TOTE £33.30: £6.30, £4.70, £1.10; EX 195.60 TRIFECTA Not won..
Owner Mr & Mrs C Wright & P F I Cole **Bred** Stratford Place Stud **Trained** Whatcombe, Oxon

FOCUS
A moderate juvenile maiden where three came clear. The winner did it nicely and the third helps with the form.

NOTEBOOK
Child Bride arguably had the best pedigree on show, being a half-sister by Invincible Spirit to four winners that had shown at least fair form, for all she had been bought back cheaply as a yearling. She made quite an impressive debut, picking up the leaders with a good turn of foot before being ridden clear to win with a bit in hand. In the Super Sprint at Newbury, she will be suited by 6f in time but clearly isn't short of speed. (op 16-1)
Belle Royale(IRE) stepped up on her debut effort with a solid front-running display, battling back well to regain second well inside the last and showing little sign of hanging this time. She'll continue to get a good weight concession in these types of races and might be able to pinch one before the better horses come out.
Emma's Gift(IRE) took the eye in the preliminaries but didn't really see her race out after travelling easily, and this effort wasn't a great advertisement for the form of the fillies' maiden that she ran in at Newmarket. (op 13-8 tchd 15-8)
Comrade Bond is out of a mare that hasn't had much success so far but he showed promise, looking very inexperienced throughout the first half of the race but getting the message well late on. His yard rarely has their newcomers wound up first time out, and he can be expected to be a fair bit sharper next time. (op 50-1)
Rowan Spirit(IRE), from a yard still looking for their first 2-y-o winner of the year, showed up well to past halfway before having his limitations exposed. He wants dropping in grade. (op 14-1)
Master Macho(IRE) might have found this coming too quickly after his apparently improved effort at Leicester on Saturday. (op 9-4)
Blade Pirate Official explanation: jockey said colt suffered interference shortly after start

1604 GREAT YARMOUTH MERCURY H'CAP — 5f 43y
2:40 (2:40) (Class 5) (0-70,69) 3-Y-O — £2,460 (£732; £365; £182) Stalls High

Form — RPR
4203 1 **Il Forno**[3] 1511 3-9-4 69 ... (p) RyanMoore 2 — 77
(Ian Williams) *led and a gng best: rdn and firmly in command fnl f* **11/10**[1]
50-2 2 2 **Danzoe (IRE)**[14] 1280 3-9-3 68 ... TomMcLaughlin 4 — 69
(Mrs C A Dunnett) *pushed along to chse wnr 2f out: carried hd high and n.g.t wr effrt: wl hld fnl f* **10/3**[2]
606- 3 4 **Watch Chain (IRE)**[172] 7268 3-8-6 57 ... JimmyQuinn 3 — 43
(M H Tompkins) *plld hrd early: chsd ldrs over 3f: 3rd and faltering 1f out* **11/1**
05-4 4 1 1/2 **Young Simon**[14] 1280 3-9-0 65 ... TomQueally 6 — 46
(G G Margarson) *towards rr: rdn and no rspnse over 2f out: n.d after* **6/1**[3]
04-6 5 1 1/4 **Southwark Newshawk**[10] 1390 3-7-13 55 oh3 ... KierenFox(5) 1 — 32
(Mrs C A Dunnett) *racd in centre and chsd wnr 4f: drvn and sn dropped out* **25/1**
3520 6 hd **Arken Lad**[11] 1347 3-9-0 65 ... (v) JerryO'Dwyer 5 — 41
(D Donovan) *bhd: put hd in air whn rdn over 2f out: fnd nil after* **8/1**

63.92 secs (1.22) **Going Correction** 0.0s/f (Good) — 6 Ran SP% **108.3**
Speed ratings (Par 98): **86,82,76,74,72 71**
toteswingers: 1&2 £1.60, 1&3 £3.60, 2&3 £4.50 CSF £4.47 TOTE £1.70: £1.60, £1.90; EX 3.60.
Owner Dr Marwan Koukash **Bred** C J Murfitt **Trained** Portway, Worcs

FOCUS
A prety weak handicap. The winner dictated and is rated back to his 2yo best.
Southwark Newshawk Official explanation: jockey said filly hung right

1605 NORFOLK NELSON MUSEUM H'CAP — 6f 3y
3:10 (3:11) (Class 6) (0-60,60) 3-Y-O — £1,942 (£578; £288; £144) Stalls High

Form — RPR
00-6 1 **Scarcity (IRE)**[15] 1260 3-9-2 58 ... RyanMoore 4 — 67+
(E A L Dunlop) *trckd ldrs gng wl towards far side: led over 1f out: rdn and in command after* **6/4**[1]
3063 2 1 1/4 **Miss Polly Plum**[20] 1163 3-8-4 46 ... JimmyQuinn 2 — 51
(C A Dwyer) *plld hrd and hld up: hdwy far side over 2f out: styd on to go 2nd ins fnl f: drvn and a hld fnl 100yds* **16/1**
000- 3 3/4 **Speedyfix**[159] 7453 3-8-4 46 ... (tp) AdrianMcCarthy 1 — 49
(Mrs C A Dunnett) *bhd on far side: rdn and effrt 2f out: wnt 3rd ins fnl f: one pce after* **33/1**
5-50 4 1 1/2 **Aqua Vitae (IRE)**[14] 1275 3-9-4 60 ... FrankieDettori 6 — 58
(M Johnston) *led: rdn and hdd over 1f out: lost two pls ins fnl f: eased cl home* **7/1**[3]
6023 5 3 3/4 **Rathbawn Girl (IRE)**[12] 1316 3-8-11 60 ... AdamBeschizza(7) 7 — 46
(Miss J Feilden) *t.k.h and sn cl up: rdn 2f out: wknd over 1f out* **11/1**
-500 6 1 **Bell's Ocean (USA)**[11] 1362 3-9-1 57 ... MichaelHills 8 — 40
(J Ryan) *prom tl rdn and wknd over 1f out* **16/1**
0646 7 hd **Reach For The Sky (IRE)**[20] 1168 3-9-4 60 ... TomQueally 5 — 42
(G Prodromou) *s.i.s: brief effrt 1/2-way: sn btn* **16/1**
4004 8 1/2 **Baby Judge (IRE)**[6] 1469 3-8-11 56 ... AshleyHamblett(3) 12 — 36
(M C Chapman) *midfield: racing awkwardly fr 1/2-way: n.d after* **16/1**
354- 9 1 **Avec Moi**[153] 7514 3-7-13 46 oh1 ... KierenFox(5) 11 — 23
(Mrs C A Dunnett) *a towards rr: no ch fnl 2f* **33/1**
3-16 10 4 1/2 **Cookie Galore**[20] 1163 3-9-2 58 ... FrederikTylicki 10 — 21
(J A Glover) *s.s: sme prog 1/2-way: drvn and sn struggling* **9/2**[2]
0623 11 1 3/4 **Cheshire Lady (IRE)**[7] 1456 3-8-10 52 ... LiamJones 3 — 9
(W M Brisbourne) *chsd ldrs: wknd qckly 2f out: racd awkwardly after* **10/1**

1m 15.23s (0.83) **Going Correction** 0.0s/f (Good) — 11 Ran SP% **117.5**
Speed ratings (Par 96): **94,92,91,89,84 83,82,82,80,74 72**
toteswingers: 1&2 £9.70, 1&3 £19.80, 2&3 £37.20 CSF £29.47 CT £504.98 TOTE £2.60: £1.80, £5.70, £11.10; EX 30.90 TRIFECTA Not won..
Owner Highclere Thoroughbred Racing (Buchan) **Bred** Buttinelli Mariangela **Trained** Newmarket, Suffolk

FOCUS
A poor 3-y-o handicap won by a progressive filly from some exposed and moderate types.
Scarcity(IRE) ◆ Official explanation: trainer said, regarding apparent improvement in form, that the filly benefited from a drop back in distance in what he considered a lesser race.
Speedyfix Official explanation: jockey said gelding was denied a clear run

1606 INJURED JOCKEYS FUND (S) STKS — 1m 2f 21y
3:40 (3:40) (Class 6) 3-4-Y-O — £1,683 (£501; £250; £125) Stalls Low

Form — RPR
2335 1 **Atacama Sunrise**[12] 1318 4-8-13 63 ... SimonPearce(5) 6 — 48+
(J Pearce) *confidently rdn in rr: nt a lot of room 2f out: sn impr and wormed through whn swtchd lft to ld over 1f out: pushed along and a gng best after* **8/13**[1]
0100 2 1/2 **Jiggalong**[15] 1262 4-9-9 50 ... RyanMoore 7 — 52
(Jim Best) *hld up in last pair tl prog 4f out: led 2f out tl over 1f out: hrd drvn and kpt on but no match for wnr* **9/2**[2]
000- 3 1/2 **Captain Clint (IRE)**[167] 7335 3-8-6 45 ... JimmyQuinn 3 — 48
(M H Tompkins) *cl up: chal for ld 2f out: drvn and ev ch 200yds out: kpt on same pce* **10/1**
0200 4 1 1/2 **Playful Asset (IRE)**[6] 1478 4-9-9 53 ... J-PGuillambert 1 — 48
(P Howling) *cl up: rdn whn n.m.r over 1f out: nt pushed whn hld fnl f* **8/1**[3]
-605 5 3 **Bubses Boy**[35] 622 4-9-9 45 ... TomQueally 8 — 42
(P Howling) *racd keenly: jnd ldr after 2f: rdn and lost pl over 2f out: plugged on after* **20/1**
00-6 6 7 **Joe Rua (USA)**[106] 118 3-8-3 45 ... (p) MarcHalford(3) 2 — 31
(J Ryan) *set modest pce: rdn and hdd 2f out: sn lost pl: eased fnl f* **25/1**
7 11 **Johanna Dee (USA)**[136] 4-9-1 0 ... Louis-PhilippeBeuzelin(3) 5 — —
(Dr J D Scargill) *last away and immediately rdn: struggling 4f out: t.o* **33/1**
0-00 8 15 **Rivitivo**[18] 1209 3-8-0 39 ow4 ... KierenFox(5) 4 — —
(W M Brisbourne) *t.k.h early: chsd ldrs: rdn over 3f out: sn lost pl: t.o* **66/1**

2m 11.58s (1.08) **Going Correction** 0.0s/f (Good)
WFA 3 from 4yo 17lb — 8 Ran SP% **113.3**
Speed ratings (Par 101): **95,94,94,93,90 85,76,64**
toteswingers: 1&2 £1.90, 1&3 £2.90, 2&3 £4.30 CSF £3.33 TOTE £1.50: £1.02, £1.20, £4.70; EX 3.80 Trifecta £14.10 Pool: £525.71 - 27.59 winning units..The winner was bought by G Prodromou for 5,800gns.
Owner Ian Bishop **Bred** J R Furlong **Trained** Newmarket, Suffolk

FOCUS
A weak seller, run at an ordinary pace. The winner had a straightforward task against inferior rivals.

1607 GREAT YARMOUTH TOURISM MEDIAN AUCTION MAIDEN STKS 1m 2f 21y
4:10 (4:13) (Class 5) 3-Y-O £2,590 (£770; £385; £192) **Stalls** Low

Form RPR

0- **1** **On Her Way**[178] 7183 3-8-12 0 PatCosgrave 1 76
(H R A Cecil) *v mulish s and stalls handlers did a fine job to eventually load her: cl up tl led wl over 3f out: rapidly shot clr: unchal after but ears bk and rdn tl rdr eased up cl home* **7/2**[3]

0- **2** *10* **Doyenne Dream**[182] 7095 3-8-12 0 StephenCraine 7 56
(J M P Eustace) *handy: wnt 2nd over 3f out: rdn and almost immediately outpcd by wnr: plugged on in vain pursuit* **20/1**

3 *½* **Loyalty** 3-9-3 0 RyanMoore 4 60+
(Sir Michael Stoute) *squealing in paddock: drvn along and clueless in last: hanging lft and sme prog over 3f out: nvr seriously involved* **4/5**[1]

06- **4** *1 ½* **Astromoon**[182] 7095 3-8-7 0 AshleyMorgan(5) 3 52
(M H Tompkins) *chsd ldrs: rdn over 3f out: little rspnse and n.d after* **3/1**[2]

0 **5** *22* **Rumballina**[31] 1010 3-8-12 0 JerryO'Dwyer 2 8
(Miss Amy Weaver) *set stdy pce: hdd wl over 3f out: fdd bdly: t.o and eased wl over 1f out* **16/1**

0 **6** *½* **Silver Astralis**[22] 1127 3-8-12 0 TomMcLaughlin 5 7
(Mrs C A Dunnett) *t.k.h early: chsd ldr tl checked and lost pl rapidly 4f out: t.o fnl 2f* **100/1**

2m 11.13s (0.63) **Going Correction** 0.0s/f (Good) **6** Ran SP% **114.4**
Speed ratings (Par 98): **97,89,88,87,69 69**
toteswingers: 1&2 £6.50, 1&3 £1.30, 2&3 £4.50 CSF £60.30 TOTE £4.30: £1.70, £6.10; EX 48.70.
Owner Malih L Al Basti **Bred** Whatton Manor Stud **Trained** Newmarket, Suffolk

FOCUS
A weak maiden and the winner looks flattered, with the favourite very green.
Astromoon Official explanation: jockey said saddle slipped
Rumballina Official explanation: jockey said filly hung right

1608 SCROBY SANDS WINDFARM H'CAP 1m 2f 21y
4:40 (4:41) (Class 5) (0-75,75) 3-Y-O £2,460 (£732; £365; £182) **Stalls** Low

Form RPR

61- **1** **Agent Archie (USA)**[216] 6200 3-8-13 **75** KierenFox(5) 5 85+
(J R Best) *pressed ldr: led 3f out: tending to edge rt after: rdn fnl f: hld on gamely: all out* **16/1**

52-6 **2** *shd* **Ice Diva**[20] 1159 3-8-12 **69** TonyCulhane 9 79+
(P W D'Arcy) *plld v hrd early and towards rr: drvn 3f out: gd prog over 1f out: sustained run fnl f: jst hld cl home: looked difficult ride* **4/1**[2]

4322 **3** *2* **Mejd (IRE)**[17] 1240 3-9-4 **75** AlanMunro 3 81
(M R Channon) *prom and t.k.h: rdn and carried rt whn ev ch 1f out: one pce fnl 200yds* **6/1**[3]

-424 **4** *¾* **Heading To First**[27] 1059 3-8-8 **68** (p) AhmedAjtebi(3) 7 73
(C E Brittain) *prom and t.k.h: chal on outside 2f out: hmpd over 1f out: ev ch tl hung lft and nt run on ins fnl f* **9/1**

566- **5** *nk* **Bondage (IRE)**[132] 7763 3-8-9 **66** [1] PatCosgrave 2 70
(J R Fanshawe) *midfield: rdn 3f out: effrt 2f out: sn stalled: kpt on again ins fnl f but no ch* **12/1**

050- **6** *2* **Amno Dancer (IRE)**[167] 7333 3-8-8 **65** JimmyQuinn 8 65+
(M H Tompkins) *bhd: effrt over 2f out: rdn and btn over 1f out* **25/1**

50-6 **7** *5* **Silent Majority (IRE)**[22] 1127 3-8-11 **68** RyanMoore 1 60
(E A L Dunlop) *chsd ldrs: drvn 3f out: lost pl 2f out: fading ins fnl f* **15/8**[1]

3-33 **8** *6* **Epic (IRE)**[48] 840 3-9-2 **73** GregFairley 10 51
(M Johnston) *t.k.h in ld: rdn and hdd 3f out: wknd 2f out: eased whn btn* **9/1**

1365 **9** *¾* **Yorksters Prince (IRE)**[41] 904 3-8-4 **64** ow1 AshleyHamblett(3) 4 40
(G Prodromou) *last trio: struggling over 3f out: sn wl bhd* **20/1**

13-0 **10** *3 ½* **Miss Whippy**[20] 1158 3-7-11 **61** oh7 JulieCumine(7) 6 30
(P Howling) *last trio: struggling over 3f out: t.o* **33/1**

2m 10.78s (0.28) **Going Correction** 0.0s/f (Good) **10** Ran SP% **114.2**
Speed ratings (Par 98): **98,97,96,95,95 93,89,85,84,81**
toteswingers: 1&2 £10.50, 1&3 £5.00, 2&3 £5.90 CSF £75.73 CT £435.73 TOTE £15.80: £4.00, £1.30, £2.40; EX 103.70 Trifecta £304.30 Part won. Pool of £411.34 - 0.40 winning units..
Owner D Gorton **Bred** Earle I Mack **Trained** Hucking, Kent
■ Stewards' Enquiry : Kieren Fox three-day ban: careless riding (May 11-13)

FOCUS
A modest 3-y-o handicap, run at an uneven pace. The third is the best guide to the form.
Amno Dancer(IRE) Official explanation: jockey said gelding stumbled

1609 BBC RADIO NORFOLK H'CAP 1m 3f 101y
5:10 (5:10) (Class 5) (0-75,72) 4-Y-O+ £2,460 (£732; £365; £182) **Stalls** Low

Form RPR

440- **1** **Locum**[206] 6473 5-8-9 **63** RyanMoore 4 72
(M H Tompkins) *settled 3rd and gng wl: wnt 2nd wl over 1f out: led over 1f out: sn rdn clr: comf* **85/40**[2]

221- **2** *2 ½* **Kazbow (IRE)**[149] 7590 4-9-4 **72** J-PGuillambert 2 77
(L M Cumani) *led at modest pce: drvn over 2f out: hdd over 1f out: sn outpcd* **4/5**[1]

3300 **3** *5* **Moscow Oznick**[20] 1150 5-8-5 **64** (p) DeclanCannon(5) 3 60
(D Donovan) *chsd ldr tl rdn wl over 1f out: wl btn fnl f* **18/1**

-616 **4** *11* **Paint The Town Red**[32] 996 5-8-4 **58** JimmyQuinn 5 36
(H J Collingridge) *dropped out last: rdn 3f out: struggling bdly fnl 2f* **11/1**[3]

0050 **5** *4* **Valmari (IRE)**[11] 1346 7-8-11 **72** RichardOld(7) 1 43
(G Prodromou) *t.k.h in last pair: plld v wd and flapped along over 3f out: sn floundering bdly: t.o* **14/1**

2m 35.04s (6.34) **Going Correction** 0.0s/f (Good) **5** Ran SP% **107.8**
Speed ratings (Par 103): **76,74,70,62,59**
CSF £3.99 TOTE £3.10: £2.60, £1.02; EX 4.40 Place 6: £91.81 Place 5: £47.83.
Owner Ray Smith and Partners **Bred** Cheveley Park Stud Ltd **Trained** Newmarket, Suffolk

FOCUS
A modest handicap that was a very tactical race. The winner is rated back to his best.
T/Plt: £170.40 to a £1 stake. Pool: £56,713.52. 242.96 winning tickets. T/Qpdt: £61.60 to a £1 stake. Pool: £3,688.56. 44.30 winning tickets. IM

CHANTILLY (R-H)
Tuesday, April 27

OFFICIAL GOING: Turf: good

1610a PRIX SIGY (LISTED RACE) (3YO) (TURF) 6f
2:05 (12:00) 3-Y-O £24,336 (£9,734; £7,300; £4,867; £2,433)

RPR

1 **Mister Manannan (IRE)**[221] 6049 3-9-4 0 AdrianNicholls 11 110
(D Nicholls) *swvd rt at s on wd outside but sn led: rdn 2f out: drifted to lft: stened and r.o wl: wnt clr: won comf* **53/10**[3]

2 *2* **Yosolito (FR)**[25] 3-8-11 0 ChristopheSoumillon 5 97
(L A Urbano-Grajales, France) **58/10**

3 *¾* **Top Music**[34] 3-8-11 0 OlivierPeslier 8 95
(A Fabre, France) **21/1**

4 *snk* **Ufologue (IRE)**[25] 3-8-11 0 Pierre-CharlesBoudot 10 94
(A Fabre, France) **9/1**

5 *hd* **Forum Magnum (USA)**[197] 6752 3-8-11 0 MaximeGuyon 3 93
(A Fabre, France) **20/1**

6 *shd* **Head Of Steam (USA)**[25] 3-8-11 0 StephanePasquier 6 93
(Mme C Head-Maarek, France) **23/10**[1]

7 *snk* **Orife (IRE)**[8] 3-8-11 0 SylvainRuis 4 93
(G Botti, Italy) **19/5**[2]

8 *snk* **Okapina (FR)**[40] 926 3-8-8 0 ThierryJarnet 1 89
(Mlle S-V Tarrou, France) **20/1**

9 *1* **Otou (GER)**[139] 3-8-11 0 HenkGrewe 9 89
(S Smrczek, Germany) **29/1**

10 *1 ½* **Kolokol (IRE)**[180] 7144 3-9-1 0 GeraldMosse 2 88
(D Prod'Homme, France) **17/1**

11 **Kelty In Love (FR)**[40] 926 3-8-11 0 FranckBlondel 7 —
(T Larriviere, France) **50/1**

1m 10.1s (-1.30) **11** Ran SP% **116.6**
WIN (incl. 1 euro stake): 6.30. PLACES: 2.70, 2.30, 5.10. DF: 24.40. SF: 49.50.
Owner Mrs Maureen Quayle **Bred** Mull Enterprises Ltd **Trained** Sessay, N Yorks

NOTEBOOK
Mister Manannan(IRE), trying 6f for the first time and carrying a 7lb penalty for this seasonal reappearance, made just about all the running and never looked in much danger of defeat. There are no firm plans for him at present, but a return to France is a possibility.

ASCOT (R-H)
Wednesday, April 28

OFFICIAL GOING: Good (straight: 8.1, round 8.4)
Stands str. rail moved in about 10yds, round course rail moved in 4yds moved in from 12f start to home str. adding 4yds to Old Mile and 20yds to 2m race.
Wind: Moderate across Weather: Bright, hazy

1612 ALDERMORE CONDITIONS STKS 5f
2:10 (2:10) (Class 3) 2-Y-O
£7,477 (£2,239; £1,119; £560; £279; £140) **Stalls** Low

Form RPR

1 **1** **Zebedee**[16] 1263 2-9-1 0 RichardHughes 2 90+
(R Hannon) *w'like: t.k.h: stdd in rr and hld up bhd ldrs: swtchd lft to stands' rail and qcknd over 1f out: led jst ins fnl f: shkn up: comf* **2/7**[1]

63 **2** *2 ¼* **Saucy Buck (IRE)**[16] 1256 2-8-11 0 TonyCulhane 3 76
(M R Channon) *w'like: disp ld: slt advantage over 1f out: hdd jst ins fnl f and sn outpcd by wnr but hld on wl for 2nd* **16/1**[3]

4 **3** *shd* **Straight Line (IRE)**[16] 1263 2-8-11 0 KierenFallon 5 76
(A P Jarvis) *leggy: chsd ldrs: drvn to dispute ld over 1f out: outpcd by wnr jst ins fnl f but styd on wl to dispute 2nd* **12/1**[2]

4 *2 ¾* **Reposer (IRE)** 2-8-11 0 SteveDrowne 4 66
(J R Best) *unf: tall: scope: slowly intto stride: t.k.h: sn trcking ldrs: drvn and qcknd to chal over 1f out: wknd ins fnl f* **25/1**

51 **5** *2 ½* **Pick A Little**[13] 1319 2-8-11 0 DaneO'Neill 6 57
(B W Duke) *w'like: disp ld tl slt advantage fr 1/2-way: hdd over 1f out and wknd qckly* **20/1**

6 *4* **Ocean's Glacier** 2-8-8 0 MarcHalford(3) 7 42
(J Ryan) *w'like: bit bkwd: wnt rt s and slowly away: sn rcvrd to chse ldrs: wknd ins fnl 2f* **40/1**

7 *6* **Joe Junior** 2-8-11 0 (b[1]) FrankieDettori 1 21
(Miss Gay Kelleway) *unf: in tch: hdwy to trck ldrs 1/2-way: wknd ins fnl 2f* **12/1**[2]

62.33 secs (1.83) **Going Correction** +0.25s/f (Good) **7** Ran SP% **110.1**
Speed ratings (Par 96): **95,91,91,86,82 76,66**
toteswingers:1&2:£2.70, 1&3:£2.10, 2&3:£5.20 CSF £5.32 TOTE £1.20: £1.10, £5.00; EX 5.70.
Owner Mrs J Wood **Bred** Hascombe & Valiant Studs **Trained** East Everleigh, Wilts

FOCUS
Not a terribly competitive event on paper and perhaps not as good a race as it can be, but the winner is a decent early 2yo.

NOTEBOOK
Zebedee set a pretty high standard, and he had little trouble in following up under a 4lb penalty. Always travelling strongly off the pace, he picked up in good style next to the stands' side, and won without being given too hard a race, but he didn't beat the third as easily as he did at Windsor and he wouldn't appear to be the strongest Norfolk Stakes candidate at the moment. He could go straight to the Royal meeting now, though might take in the National Stakes at Sandown first. (op 1-3 tchd 2-5 in a places and 4-11 in places)
Saucy Buck(IRE) looks to be improving with racing and perhaps this quicker ground was also in his favour, as this was a nice step up on his maiden form. He should be capable of winning a maiden.
Straight Line(IRE), all the better for his debut outing behind Zebedee at Windsor, got a lot closer to that rival, and considering his pedigree it's encouraging he can show this sort of speed, as he's bred to come into his own over 1m plus. (tchd 10-1)
Reposer(IRE) did best of the newcomers, keeping on quite well out wider. He should come on for this experience and find a maiden.
Pick A Little tried to put his experience to good use and was given a positive ride, but his limitations were exposed.
Ocean's Glacier, awkward out of the stalls, may not have been helped by racing widest of all on his debut. (tchd 50-1 in places)

Joe Junior had the rail to help, but this newcomer, who wore blinkers and was coltish in the prelims, failed to get involved, and looked to need this. (tchd 14-1in a place)

1613 X FACTOR STKS (CONDITIONS RACE) (FILLIES) 1m (R)
2:45 (2:45) (Class 3) 3-Y-O **£6,542** (£1,959; £979; £490; £244) **Stalls** High

Form RPR

1- **1** **Aviate**[160] 7450 3-9-1 0 TomQueally 2 103+
(H R A Cecil) *w'like: lw: trckd ldr: upsides fr 4f out tl ld over 2f out: drvn and styd on strly fr over 1f out: readily* **6/4**[1]

046- **2** *1¾* **Blue Angel (IRE)**[214] 6269 3-9-1 102 RichardHughes 5 99
(R Hannon) *chsd ldrs: rdn and one pce 2f out: styd on again fnl f to take 2nd cl home but no ch w wnr* **10/3**[2]

54-2 **3** *nk* **Bella Swan**[25] 1082 3-9-1 93 AdamKirby 1 98
(W R Swinburn) *hld up in rr: drvn and hdwy on outside fr over 2f out: chsd wnr wl over 1f out but no imp: lost 2nd cl home* **10/3**[2]

51-6 **4** *4* **Deirdre**[11] 1384 3-9-1 94 WilliamBuick 4 91
(J H M Gosden) *lw: led: jnd fr 4f out: drvn along fr 3f out: hdd over 2f out: sn outpcd by wnr: lost 2nd wl over 1f out: wknd fnl f* **5/1**[3]

-411 **5** *7* **Yawary**[28] 1070 3-8-12 86 (t) NeilCallan 3 69
(C E Brittain) *lw: plld hrd early: chsd ldrs: rdn ins fnl 3f: wknd ins fnl 2f* **20/1**

1m 43.61s (2.91) **Going Correction** +0.25s/f (Good) **5** Ran SP% **107.6**
Speed ratings (Par 99): **95,93,92,88,81**
CSF £6.39 TOTE £2.30: £1.30, £1.80; EX 4.80.
Owner K Abdulla **Bred** Juddmonte Farms Ltd **Trained** Newmarket, Suffolk

FOCUS
There wasn't much pace on here and it developed into a bit of a sprint up the straight. Decent conditions form, the winner confirming the good impression of her maiden win.

NOTEBOOK
Aviate, who came into this race on the back of a single win in a backend 2-y-o maiden, came here with a similar profile to that of Apple Charlotte, who won it for Henry Cecil last year. She quickened up well from 2f out, taking a couple of lengths out of the field in the process, and held on to that advantage to the line. It was a very pleasing performance, and the question now is whether she has the potential to make up into an Oaks-type filly or will she be happier at around this trip? Both this performance and her pedigree suggest her Coronation Stakes entry looks more realistic than her Oaks/Ribblesdale entries, although she has the potential to get 1m2f, and the plan is to run in the Musidora next to find out which way to go with her. (op 13-8 tchd 11-8 and 7-4 in places)
Blue Angel(IRE), last seen finishing sixth in the Fillies' Mile, had to be switched to come around the tiring Deirdre and then took a while to pick up. She could have done with a stronger all-round pace and looks a natural candidate for the Sandringham Handicap back here at the Royal meeting. (op 3-1 tchd 7-2)
Bella Swan stayed on well to take second behind Pipette at Kempton on her reappearance, and given her pedigree, which points to her improving when stepped up to 1m2f plus, a steadily run race over 1m was never really going to suit. She still had her winter coat, and there should be better to come from her as the season progresses. (tchd 7-2)
Deirdre, bred to appreciate further, was handed a tactical advantage in being allowed to set an ordinary gallop, but she raced keenly and proved one-paced in the straight.
Yawary only won a handicap at Southwell off 74 last time out and this proved a much tougher assignment. (op 18-1 tchd 25-1 in a place)

1614 BRITAIN'S GOT TALENT PARADISE STKS (LISTED RACE) 1m (S)
3:20 (3:20) (Class 1) 4-Y-O+ **£22,708** (£8,608; £4,308; £2,148) **Stalls** Low

Form RPR

515- **1** **King Of Dixie (USA)**[333] 2476 6-9-0 105 JimCrowley 1 112
(W J Knight) *trckd ldr tl led ins fnl 3f: rdn and edgd rt u.p fnl f: wnt lft nr fin: a jst doing enough* **4/1**[2]

20-4 **2** *nk* **Cityscape**[11] 1383 4-9-0 108 RyanMoore 3 111
(R Charlton) *lw: trckd ldr tl wnt 2nd and rdn over 2f out: effrt and carried rt fnl f: styd on wl and edgd lft nr fin: a hld* **4/9**[1]

230- **3** *13* **Nasri**[315] 3011 4-9-0 103 JamieSpencer 5 86
(D M Simcock) *bit bkwd: led tl hdd ins fnl 3f: wknd fr 2f out* **8/1**[3]

131/ **4** *23* **Minor Vamp (IRE)**[577] 6319 4-8-9 101 RichardHughes 2 47
(R Hannon) *a in last pl: dropped away fr over 2f out: eased fr over 1f out* **10/1**

1m 40.23s (-0.37) **Going Correction** +0.25s/f (Good) **4** Ran SP% **109.5**
Speed ratings (Par 111): **111,110,97,74**
CSF £6.47 TOTE £5.80; EX 8.80.
Owner Bluehills Racing Limited **Bred** Bee Zee LLC **Trained** Patching, W Sussex

FOCUS
This threatened to be run at a muddling pace, but in the event Nasri took them along at a good gallop. The first two finished clear and the form is rated around them.

NOTEBOOK
King Of Dixie(USA), a winner on his seasonal debut the previous two years, clearly goes well fresh and, being very effective, indeed unbeaten in four starts, on Polytrack (horses who go well on that surface have a good record here), and third in the Victoria Cup on his only previous start at this track, he looked to have plenty in his favour. The good pace suited him, as he can race a bit keenly and, having travelled best of all, he was always holding the favourite's challenge in the closing stages. He wouldn't be a sure thing to build on this next time out, however. (op 9-2)
Cityscape, unlike his rivals, had the benefit of having had a run already this season, when fourth in the Newbury Spring Cup off a mark of 108. That was a fine effort and, back at the track where he recorded his best effort to date (second in the Royal Lodge), he looked to hold sound claims. He was well backed, but was the first to be niggled along and, although he responded and kept on well to challenge the winner, he was always just about coming off second-best. It's possible that he doesn't want the ground as quick as this - his only previous below-par effort was when returning sore after the Guineas, which was run on good to firm. (op 8-13 tchd 4-6 in places)
Nasri, debuting for a new stable, dropped out having set a good gallop. He'd never run as far as this before and he'll be suited by a drop back to sprinting in due course. (op 13-2 tchd 17-2)
Minor Vamp(IRE), who fractured her pelvis after winning the Goffs Fillies Million in September 2008, raced in last place throughout and wasn't knocked about at any stage. She'd never run on ground as quick as this before and was fully entitled to need this return to action. Official explanation: jockey said filly did not stride out (op 8-1 tchd 11-1)

1615 MOSS BROS SAGARO STKS (GROUP 3) 2m
3:55 (3:55) (Class 1) 4-Y-O+
£36,900 (£13,988; £7,000; £3,490; £1,748; £877) **Stalls** High

Form RPR

0043 **1** **Illustrious Blue**[18] 1220 7-9-1 106 JimCrowley 10 111
(W J Knight) *lw: hld up in rr tl swtchd to outside and str run fr over 2f out: chsd ldr fnl f: led u.p fnl 100yds: styd on gamely* **16/1**

1/1- **2** *½* **Aajel (USA)**[241] 5481 6-9-1 100 MartinDwyer 7 110
(M P Tregoning) *led: pushed along and qcknd pce fr 6f out: hrd rdn fr 2f out: styd on wl u.p fnl f tl hdd and one pce fnl 100yds* **13/2**[3]

510- **3** *1* **Electrolyser (IRE)**[193] 6851 5-9-1 98 AdamKirby 3 109
(C G Cox) *bit bkwd: chsd ldrs: rdn over 3f out: chsd ldr ins fnl 2f: no imp and styd on same pce into 3rd fnl f* **15/2**

-002 **4** *3* **Montaff**[21] 1176 4-8-11 102 AlanMunro 8 106
(M R Channon) *swtg: in tch mid-div: pushed along 3f out: hdwy to chse ldrs ins fnl 2f: no imp and one pce fr over 1f out* **14/1**

10-1 **5** *4½* **Yes Mr President (IRE)**[22] 1139 5-9-1 108 JoeFanning 2 100
(M Johnston) *swtg: chsd ldrs: rdn over 3f out: wknd ins fnl 2f* **5/1**[2]

25-0 **6** *4* **Oasis Knight (IRE)**[11] 1382 4-8-11 104 (v) RichardHughes 6 95
(M P Tregoning) *swtg: chsd ldrs: rdn 3f out: wknd fr 2f out* **12/1**

11-0 **7** *1¼* **Akmal**[11] 1382 4-9-0 106 RichardHills 4 97+
(J L Dunlop) *plld hrd: in tch: plld way into 2nd 10f out: rdn ins fnl 3f: nt rch ldr and wknd qckly ins fnl 2f* **9/2**[1]

156- **8** *10* **Askar Tau (FR)**[185] 7047 5-9-6 110 (v) RyanMoore 1 87
(M P Tregoning) *in rr and rdn 4f out: sme prog into mid-div u.p 3f out: nvr any threat and wknd fr 2f out* **5/1**[2]

26/0 **9** *4* **Balkan Knight**[11] 1382 10-9-1 101 DaneO'Neill 5 77
(D R C Elsworth) *bit bkwd: b.hind: rdn 4f out: bhd most of way* **28/1**

6-30 **10** *17* **Mojave Moon**[62] 712 4-8-11 108 (v) AhmedAjtebi 9 57
(Mahmood Al Zarooni) *str: swtg: plld hrd towards rr: shkn up 4f out: and little rspnse: sn dropped away* **15/2**

3m 29.08s (0.08) **Going Correction** +0.25s/f (Good)
WFA 4 from 5yo+ 4lb **10** Ran SP% **112.1**
Speed ratings (Par 113): **109,108,108,106,104 102,101,96,94,86**
toteswingers:1&2:£13.10, 1&3:£17.00, 2&3:£10.30 CSF £111.85 TOTE £20.00: £4.10, £2.70, £2.60; EX 120.20 Trifecta £848.60 Part won. Pool: £1,146.87 - 0.10 winning units..
Owner Mr & Mrs I H Bendelow **Bred** B J And Mrs Crangle **Trained** Patching, W Sussex
■ Stewards' Enquiry : Jim Crowley one-day ban: used whip with excessive frequency in the forehand (May 12)

FOCUS
The round course rail had been moved in approx 4yds from the 1m4f start to the home straight, resulting in this race being run over a distance approximately 20yds further than advertised. Patkai won this last year and went on to finish second to the now retired Yeats in the Gold Cup back here at the Royal meeting, but it's doubtful this year's renewal will have much bearing on the big race. The early pace was modest. This was not a strong race for the grade but the form seems sound enough.

NOTEBOOK
Illustrious Blue was stepping up 4f in distance but he came into this race-fit, and the modest early gallop arguably played to his strengths. Having been ridden patiently out the back, he used his speed to mow down his rivals in the closing stages. He isn't bred to stay this far, but his style of running has always hinted that he might get a trip, and he saw this race out well in good fashion. The Goodwood Cup looks the obvious mid-season target for him as he's won six of his 13 starts at that track, but before that he's likely to take his chance in the Yorkshire Cup next month. (op 14-1)
Aajel(USA), an unexposed 6-y-o, having been off the track for almost two years with leg problems prior to winning on his only start last season, went off in front and didn't set a mad gallop. Having enjoyed the run of things, he took a bit of passing in the straight, and this was a good effort on his reappearance. He looks progressive. (op 8-1 tchd 6-1)
Electrolyser(IRE), whose Cesarewitch run can be forgiven as he was hampered, was the only previous C&D winner in the line-up. He ran a sound race in defeat and, as his trainer had stated that he's need this, improvement can be expected. (op 8-1 tchd 17-2)
Montaff, who had the benefit of race-fitness, prefers softer ground, so conditions were probably not ideal for him.
Yes Mr President(IRE) was another to arrive here with a recent run under his belt. He too has a preference for give in the ground, and this was a step up in class for him as well having won a handicap at Ffos Las off 100 last time. (op 9-2)
Oasis Knight(IRE), second to Electrolyser over this C&D last autumn, had the benefit of a recent outing in the John Porter, but was a bit disappointing, failing to find much at all in the straight. (op 16-1 tchd 20-1 in a place)
Akmal loves to make the running, but on this occasion his owner's second-string, who also likes to lead, was sent on, and an attempt was made to drop him in and get him settled. He would not consent to that, though, pulled too hard and eventually Richard Hills let him pull himself up to second place. He'd run his race by the time they got to 2f out, and he'll presumably revert to front-running next time. Official explanation: jockey said gelding ran too free (op 5-1)
Askar Tau(FR) was burdened with a 5lb penalty but he had ground conditions to suit. He hasn't run well on his seasonal reappearance in previous years, though, and after drifting in the betting he ran as though he needed this outing. (op 7-2)
Mojave Moon could have done with them going quicker as he pulled much too hard through the early stages and gave himself little chance of getting home. (op 7-1 tchd 13-2)

1616 CLEANEVENT PAVILION STKS (LISTED RACE) 6f
4:30 (4:30) (Class 1) 3-Y-O
£22,708 (£8,608; £4,308; £2,148; £1,076; £540) **Stalls** Low

Form RPR

110- **1** **Society Rock (IRE)**[207] 6478 3-8-11 93 PatCosgrave 9 109+
(J R Fanshawe) *lw: hld up in rr: hdwy and nt clr run 2f out: stl travelling wl whn nt clr run ins fnl f and swtchd lft: str burst fnl 100yds to ld nr fin: won gng away* **9/2**[3]

616- **2** *¾* **Corporal Maddox**[186] 7016 3-9-0 104 TomQueally 4 105
(H R A Cecil) *trckd ldrs: pushed between horses 2f out: chal over 1f out: slt ld ins fnl f: edgd lft: hdd nr fin* **5/1**

101- **3** *¾* **Mon Cadeaux**[210] 6398 3-8-11 100 WilliamBuick 8 100
(A M Balding) *lw: awkward s: t.k.h: sn trcking ldrs: bmpd 2f out: drvn to take slt ld over 1f out: hdd ins fnl f: styd on same pce u.p* **7/2**[2]

246- **4** *1½* **Reignier**[274] 4407 3-8-11 98 AndrewElliott 7 95
(J R Weymes) *wnt rt s: chsd ldrs: rdn to chal over 1f out: styd on same pce ins fnl f and hld whn bmpd fnl 100yds* **18/1**

34-6 **5** *1¾* **Iver Bridge Lad**[14] 1311 3-9-0 106 AlanMunro 6 92
(J Ryan) *lw: led tl hdd over 1f out: wknd ins fnl f* **10/1**

011- **6** *¾* **Our Jonathan**[176] 7231 3-9-4 111 JamieSpencer 5 94
(K A Ryan) *swtg: s.i.s: hld up in rr: stdy hdwy over 2f out: to trck ldrs over 1f out: wknd ins fnl f* **2/1**[1]

-110 **7** *3½* **Edinburgh Knight (IRE)**[13] 1327 3-8-11 90 TonyCulhane 2 76
(P W D'Arcy) *lw: chsd ldr: pushed along 2f out: wknd ins fnl f* **14/1**

1 **8** *19* **Shearman (IRE)**[58] 751 3-8-11 0 RichardMullen 1 15
(E S McMahon) *unf: in tch to 1/2-way: sn rdn: wknd fnl 2f* **10/1**

1m 14.12s (-0.28) **Going Correction** +0.25s/f (Good) **8** Ran SP% **120.5**
Speed ratings (Par 106): **111,110,109,107,104 103,99,73**
toteswingers:1&2:£5.60, 1&3:£3.80, 2&3:£3.70 CSF £28.85 TOTE £6.00: £1.60, £1.90, £1.70; EX 28.90 Trifecta £253.40 Pool: £945.41 - 2.76 winning units..
Owner Simon Gibson **Bred** San Gabriel Investments **Trained** Newmarket, Suffolk
■ Stewards' Enquiry : Tom Queally two-day ban: careless riding (May 12-13)

FOCUS
This looked a really interesting 3-y-o sprint on paper and the form is rated slightly positively. The winner looked a fair bit better than the bare form.

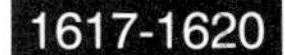

NOTEBOOK

Society Rock(IRE) ◆ was last seen running over 7f in the Tatersalls Timeform Million, when second on his side in a race that has thrown up countless winners. That trip stretched his stamina - he only ran in the race because of the big money on offer - and he was fully expected to appreciate a return to sprinting. The impressive manner of this victory marks him out as one to keep on side in the division as he overcame a troubled passage and showed an ability to quicken well inside the last that will hold him in good stead in better company. His stable won this race two years ago with Sir Gerry, who went on to finish third in the Golden Jubilee that season, and it wouldn't be a surprise if this fellow was able to make the leap to the top table as well. He's available at 33-1 with Victor Chandler for the Royal Ascot race. (tchd 5-1 and 11-2 in a place)

Corporal Maddox, a winner over 7f here last season, battled on strongly but had no answer when the winner quickened up past him well inside the last. He was unlucky to bump into a horse destined for greater things, but he's a solid performer at this sort of level and will have other opportunities. (op 7-1 tchd 8-1 in places)

Mon Cadeaux, twice a winner over this trip at Salisbury last term, kept on well towards the outside and ran a perfectly good race on his reappearance. He's entitled to come on for it and, despite being out of a mare who won over 1m4f, looks as if he'll be perfectly happy sticking to sprinting. (op 9-2)

Reignier, who finished second in the Norfolk last year, was debuting for a new stable. He didn't get home and, while he's entitled to have needed the run, this isn't the first time he's appeared to not stay 6f, so a return to the minimum looks in order. (tchd 14-1)

Iver Bridge Lad, race-fit following an outing in the Free Handicap, promised to be suited by the drop back to sprinting. He set too strong a gallop out in front, though, and somewhat set things up for a closer. (tchd 12-1 in a place)

Our Jonathan, winner of the Cornwallis and a French Group 2 last term, had a 7lb penalty to carry and, after threatening on the outside approaching the final furlong, failed to pick up. He didn't shape at all badly and will be fitter for this reappearance. Official explanation: jockey said colt banged its head on leaving stalls (op 9-4 tchd 5-2)

Edinburgh Knight(IRE) raced far too freely in the Craven and didn't pick up here having travelled well enough. The ground might have been plenty quick enough for him. (op 8-1)

Shearman(IRE), winner of a Wolverhampton maiden on his debut not so long ago, found this rise in class far too tough at this stage of his career. Official explanation: vet said gelding finished lame (op 12-1)

1617 BETINTERNET.COM H'CAP (DIV I) 1m (S)

5:05 (5:07) (Class 4) (0-85,85) 4-Y-O+ £4,857 (£1,445; £722; £360) **Stalls** Low

Form				RPR
252-	1		**Play It Sam**[209] 6421 4-8-10 **73** EddieAhern 6	84
			(W R Swinburn) *lw: led: rdn whn strly chal thrght fnl f: hld on gamely* **8/1**	
21-5	2	¾	**Jordaura**[20] 1185 4-9-4 **81** JerryO'Dwyer 11	91+
			(J R Holt) *towards rr: clsd up 1/2-way: rdn and hdwy over 1f out: swtchd lft and str run ins fnl f: fin wl to take 2nd nr fin but a hld by wnr* **8/1**	
2110	3	nk	**Ocean Legend (IRE)**[18] 1219 5-9-1 **78** SebSanders 12	87
			(A W Carroll) *chsd ldrs: wnt 2nd u.p over 1f out and str effrt thrght fnl f but a hld: lost 2nd nr fin* **16/1**	
600-	4	1 ¾	**Habshan (USA)**[278] 4262 10-9-5 **82** AlanMunro 5	87
			(C F Wall) *in tch: pushed along over 2f out: styd on fr over 1f out but nvr gng pce to rch ldrs* **25/1**	
1030	5	nk	**Audemar (IRE)**[32] 1006 4-9-8 **85** RichardHughes 8	89+
			(E F Vaughan) *stdd s: hld up in rr: hdwy fr 2f out: drvn and kpt on fnl f but nvr a threat* **8/1**	
06-6	6	½	**Ellemujie**[16] 1265 5-9-3 **80** FrankieDettori 9	83
			(D K Ivory) *towards rr: drvn and rapid hdwy over 2f out to chse ldrs over 1f out: no imp and wknd fnl f* **5/1**[2]	
303-	7	½	**Barliffey (IRE)**[167] 7360 5-8-8 **71** oh1 (v) JamieSpencer 4	73
			(D J Coakley) *swtg: in rr tl pushed along and hdwy 2f out: hung rt u.p fr over 1f out but kpt on fnl f* **6/1**[3]	
3-00	8	2 ¼	**Rainbow Mirage (IRE)**[15] 1272 6-9-8 **85** RichardMullen 7	82
			(E S McMahon) *in rr tl mod prog fnl f* **14/1**	
20-2	9	2 ¼	**Hail Promenader (IRE)**[16] 1265 4-9-7 **84** MichaelHills 2	76
			(B W Hills) *lw: chsd wnr: rdn over 2f out: wknd qckly over 1f out* **9/2**[1]	
-144	10	½	**Erinjay (IRE)**[77] 487 4-8-13 **76** StephenCraine 3	66
			(M Wigham) *lw: chsd ldrs tl wknd ins fnl 2f* **7/1**	
/1-5	11	12	**One Slick Chick (IRE)**[69] 593 4-9-3 **80** WilliamBuick 10	43
			(M Botti) *in tch: rdn to chse ldrs 3f out: wknd wl over 1f out: eased whn no ch fnl f* **20/1**	

1m 42.8s (2.20) **Going Correction** +0.25s/f (Good) **11** Ran SP% **116.1**

Speed ratings (Par 105): **99,98,97,96,95 95,94,92,90,89 77**

toteswingers:1&2:£13.70, 1&3:£24.80, 2&3:£29.50 CSF £69.65 CT £1019.42 TOTE £8.70: £2.80, £2.80, £4.10; EX 82.50 Trifecta £554.30 Pool: £749.14 - 1.00 winning units..

Owner P W Harris **Bred** Shortgrove Manor Stud **Trained** Aldbury, Herts

FOCUS

They went a steady pace here and little got into it from behind with the winner making all in a time 0.54sec slower than division two. A personal best from the winner.

One Slick Chick(IRE) Official explanation: jockey said filly had no more to give

1618 BETINTERNET.COM H'CAP (DIV II) 1m (S)

5:40 (5:41) (Class 4) (0-85,85) 4-Y-O+ £4,857 (£1,445; £722; £360) **Stalls** Low

Form				RPR
01-0	1		**South Cape**[11] 1383 7-9-4 **81** RyanMoore 11	89
			(G L Moore) *hld up in rr: gd hdwy fr 2f out: qcknd to ld jst ins fnl f: styd on strly* **5/1**[2]	
0-30	2	1	**Wise Dennis**[25] 1088 8-9-5 **82** AlanMunro 3	88
			(A P Jarvis) *hld up towards rr: gd hdwy fr 2f out: str run fnl f to take 2nd cl home but a hld by wnr* **7/1**	
50-1	3	½	**Highly Regal (IRE)**[25] 1088 5-9-3 **80** (b) LiamKeniry 5	85+
			(R A Teal) *in tch: hdwy over 2f out: led over 1f out: hung bdly lft and hdd jst ins fnl f: sn fnd no ex and lost 2nd cl home* **11/1**	
06-4	4	1 ¼	**Edgeworth (IRE)**[16] 1265 4-8-13 **76** KierenFallon 6	78
			(B G Powell) *in tch: pushed along 3f out: qcknd to chal u.p appr fnl f: styd on same pce* **9/2**[1]	
20-0	5	1 ½	**Satwa Laird**[18] 1219 4-9-5 **85** AshleyHamblett(3) 12	83
			(E A L Dunlop) *hld up in rr: hdwy fr 2f out to press ldrs over 1f out: wknd ins fnl f* **6/1**[3]	
060-	6	½	**Bomber Command (USA)**[166] 7375 7-8-3 **71** oh4 KierenFox(5) 10	68
			(J W Hills) *pressed ldrs tl slt ld 2f out: hdd wl over 1f out: wknd ins fnl f* **25/1**	
624-	7	1 ½	**Greensward**[292] 3801 4-9-3 **80** EddieAhern 9	74
			(B J Meehan) *stdd s: hdwy 2f out: slt ld wl over 1f out: sn hdd: wknd fnl f* **7/1**	
0542	8	1 ¼	**Samarinda (USA)**[8] 1455 7-8-12 **75** MickyFenton 2	66
			(Mrs P Sly) *mde most tl hdd 2f out: wknd wl over 1f out* **8/1**	
40-0	9	3	**Smart Endeavour (USA)**[16] 1265 4-9-1 **78** ShaneKelly 1	—
			(W R Swinburn) *pressed ldr tl wknd wl over 2f out* **10/1**	
410-	10	3 ½	**Netta (IRE)**[224] 5996 4-9-3 **80** SebSanders 4	—
			(P J Makin) *in tch: chsd ldrs 1/2-way: wknd over 2f out* **9/1**	

1m 42.26s (1.66) **Going Correction** +0.25s/f (Good) **10** Ran SP% **116.5**

Speed ratings (Par 105): **101,100,99,98,96 96,94,93,90,87**

toteswingers:1&2:£8.50, 1&3:£10.00, 2&3:£18.20 CSF £39.91 CT £378.24 TOTE £6.00: £1.70, £3.00, £4.10; EX 39.70 TRIFECTA Not won. Place 6 £352.01; Place 5 £293.19.

Owner Heart Of The South Racing **Bred** John And Mrs Caroline Penny **Trained** Lower Beeding, W Sussex

FOCUS

They went a stronger early pace in this division, which suited those held up, and the final time was 0.54sec quicker than the earlier heat. The winner is rated close to his best old form.

Highly Regal(IRE) Official explanation: jockey said gelding hung left

Greensward Official explanation: jockey said gelding lost its action

T/Jkpt: Part won. £9,557.40 to a £1 stake. Pool: £13,461.24. 0.50 winning tickets. T/Plt: £583.90 to a £1 stake. Pool: £95731.54. 119.68 winning tickets. T/Qpdt: £188.20 to a £1 stake. Pool: £5049.69. 19.85 winning tickets. ST

1477 KEMPTON (A.W) (R-H)

Wednesday, April 28

OFFICIAL GOING: Standard

Wind: Light, half behind Weather: Fine but cloudy, warm

1619 WATCH RACING UK ON SKY 432 CLASSIFIED STKS 7f (P)

6:05 (6:06) (Class 5) 3-Y-O £2,590 (£770; £385; £192) **Stalls** High

Form				RPR
605-	1		**He's Invincible**[292] 3792 3-9-0 69 (b[1]) MartinDwyer 4	73
			(B J Meehan) *sn trckd ldng pair: effrt over 2f out: drvn to ld narrowly over 1f out: edgd rt and a holding on* **9/1**	
15-3	2	nk	**Kilt Rock (IRE)**[12] 1347 3-9-0 70 JimCrowley 6	72
			(R A Mills) *trckd ldr: led over 2f out: hdd over 1f out: edgd rt but rallied wl: jst hld* **6/1**[3]	
36-0	3	1 ¾	**Gobama**[21] 1159 3-9-0 70 RichardHills 2	67
			(J W Hills) *racd wd in midfield: rdn 3f out: prog fr 2f out to take 3rd 1f out: no imp after* **20/1**	
44-0	4	½	**Kings 'n Dreams**[16] 1269 3-9-0 70 SteveDrowne 5	66
			(D K Ivory) *dwlt: hld up in rr: prog to chse ldrs 2f out: rdn and nt qckn over 1f out: styd on ins fnl f* **33/1**	
-100	5	nk	**Highland Bridge**[16] 1261 3-9-0 65 DaneO'Neill 9	65
			(D R C Elsworth) *mde most to over 2f out: nt qckn wl over 1f out: one pce* **16/1**	
64-4	6	3 ½	**Athenian Garden (USA)**[15] 1278 3-9-0 70 TomQueally 8	56
			(H R A Cecil) *trckd ldrs: cl enough wl over 1f out: sn rdn and nt qckn: wknd fnl f* **10/11**[1]	
20-2	7	2 ¼	**Kilmanseck**[12] 1347 3-9-0 70 HayleyTurner 1	50
			(Eve Johnson Houghton) *hld up in last: effrt on inner over 2f out: no prog and wl btn over 1f out* **12/1**	
105-	8	3 ¼	**So Surreal (IRE)**[152] 7551 3-9-0 70 FergusSweeney 7	41
			(G L Moore) *dropped to rr by 1/2-way: sn rdn and struggling* **25/1**	
3-24	9	3	**Welsh Artist**[22] 1143 3-9-0 70 (p) NeilCallan 3	41
			(Mrs A J Perrett) *stmbld s: hld up in rr: effrt over 2f out: no prog whn n.m.r wl over 1f out: wknd and eased* **11/2**[2]	
40-0	10	4 ½	**Classical Piece (USA)**[14] 1298 3-9-0 67 EddieCreighton 10	21
			(Mrs D J Sanderson) *trckd ldrs on inner tl wknd over 2f out* **66/1**	

1m 26.33s (0.33) **Going Correction** +0.025s/f (Slow) **10** Ran SP% **118.7**

Speed ratings (Par 98): **99,98,96,96,95 91,89,85,82,76**

toteswingers:1&2:£7.00, 1&3:£27.60, 2&3:£13.20 CSF £60.64 TOTE £12.00: £4.40, £1.40, £2.10; EX 52.00.

Owner Brimacombe,McNally,Vinciguerra,Sangster **Bred** Aiden Murphy **Trained** Manton, Wilts

FOCUS

Seven of the runners had a rating on the ceiling for this 0-70 classified event. The pace was steady and the hot favourite was disappointing. Ordinary form.

He's Invincible Official explanation: trainer's rep said, regarding apparent improvement in form, that the gelding had a knee operation last year, and has benefited from time off.

Welsh Artist Official explanation: vet said gelding was struck into and lost an off-fore shoe

1620 WATCH RACING UK ON VIRGIN MEDIA 536 MAIDEN FILLIES' STKS (DIV I) 1m (P)

6:35 (6:39) (Class 5) 3-Y-O+ £2,590 (£770; £385; £192) **Stalls** High

Form				RPR
00-	1		**Sweet Clementine (IRE)**[181] 7135 3-8-12 0 JimCrowley 4	78+
			(W J Knight) *hld up in last trio: sweeping prog on wd outside fr 3f out: led over 1f out: rdn clr: decisively* **12/1**	
00-	2	2	**Song To The Moon (IRE)**[187] 6992 3-8-12 0 DavidProbert 3	73
			(A M Balding) *racd freely: led: rdn and hdd over 1f out: no ch w wnr fnl f: hld on for 2nd* **8/1**	
053-	3	nse	**Hill Tribe**[248] 5284 3-8-12 74 SteveDrowne 11	73
			(J R Gask) *trckd ldng pair to 2f out: sn rdn: racd on inner and styd on fnl f: jst failed to snatch 2nd* **13/2**	
2-	4	nse	**Skyrider (IRE)**[203] 6591 3-8-12 0 NeilCallan 13	73+
			(R Charlton) *t.k.h: trckd ldng quartet: sltly awkward and nt qckn 2f out: styd on fnl f: nrly grabbed a pl* **10/3**[2]	
3-	5	hd	**Chelsea Morning (USA)**[292] 3810 3-8-12 0 MichaelHills 5	72
			(B W Hills) *trckd ldr: rdn 2f out: nt qckn and sn lost 2nd: kpt on but lost 2 pls nr fin* **5/2**[1]	
00-	6	2 ¾	**Fame Is The Spur**[215] 6241 3-8-12 0 LiamJones 12	66
			(J W Hills) *trckd ldng quartet: rdn and no prog over 2f out: one pce after* **20/1**	
0	7	nk	**Nahab**[12] 1355 3-8-12 0 RichardMullen 8	65+
			(D R Lanigan) *hld up in 7th: nt pce to make prog over 2f out: one pce after* **25/1**	
0-0	8	½	**Main Spring**[9] 1431 3-8-12 0 HayleyTurner 10	64+
			(M L W Bell) *a in same pl: pushed along fr over 2f out: kpt on but no prog* **40/1**	
00-	9	7	**Fiancee (IRE)**[285] 4057 4-9-12 0 JackMitchell 14	47
			(R Brotherton) *dwlt: a in rr: lft bhd fnl 2f* **100/1**	
0	10	½	**Asterales**[15] 1278 3-8-12 0 TonyCulhane 2	46
			(W J Musson) *stdd s: hld up in last pair: nvr a factor* **100/1**	
	11	2	**Just My Girl** 3-8-12 0 EddieCreighton 9	41
			(P Leech) *s.s: a in last pair: nvr a factor* **100/1**	

4- **12** 2 ¾ **Wajanaat**[236] 5643 3-8-12 0 RichardHills 7 34
(M P Tregoning) *plld hrd: trckd ldng trio to over 2f out: wknd and eased* **4/1**[3]

1m 41.32s (1.52) **Going Correction** +0.025s/f (Slow)
WFA 3 from 4yo 14lb **12** Ran SP% **117.8**
Speed ratings (Par 100): **93,91,90,90,90 87,87,87,80,79 77,74**
toteswingers:1&2:£13.40, 1&3:£14.50, 2&3:£10.30 CSF £98.53 TOTE £19.30: £8.10, £6.30, £2.30; EX 85.20.
Owner D G Hardisty Bloodstock **Bred** D G Hardisty Bloodstock **Trained** Patching, W Sussex

FOCUS
This looked a fairly decent fillies' maiden. The pace was pretty modest and there was a surprise winner, but the two market leaders finished in the lead group which pulled clear of the rest. The winner can do better and the form seems sound. Chief Wren (66/1) had a nasty experience when falling down in the stalls and was withdrawn.
Wajanaat Official explanation: jockey said filly ran too free

1621 WATCH RACING UK ON VIRGIN MEDIA 536 MAIDEN FILLIES' STKS (DIV II) 1m (P)
7:05 (7:09) (Class 5) 3-Y-0+ **£2,590** (£770; £385; £192) **Stalls** High

Form RPR
0-2 **1** **Towbaat**[15] 1278 3-8-12 0 FrankieDettori 7 76
(M A Jarvis) *trckd ldr: pushed up to chal 3f out drvn and edgd ahd 2f out: asserted fnl f* **5/4**[1]
0- **2** 2 **Mavalenta (IRE)**[222] 6055 3-8-12 0 MichaelHills 10 71+
(J W Hills) *t.k.h early: trckd ldrs: green and hanging wl over 2f out: picked up fr over 1f out: styd on wl to take 2nd ins fnl f* **40/1**
3 1 ¼ **Derecho** 3-8-12 0 AdamKirby 13 68
(C G Cox) *mostly trckd ldng pair: shkn up 2f out: kpt on but no real imp: disp 2nd ins fnl f: kpt on* **25/1**
36 **4** ½ **Spicewood (USA)**[13] 1329 3-8-12 0 WilliamBuick 11 67
(J H M Gosden) *led at decent pce: pressed 3f out: rdn and hdd 2f out: tried to rally but fdd ins fnl f* **4/1**[2]
5 shd **Hyperspace** 3-8-12 0 TomQueally 2 67+
(H R A Cecil) *hld up in midfield on outer: pushed along firmly over 2f out: kpt on steadily: n.d* **15/2**[3]
6 ½ **Medici Palace** 3-8-12 0 PatCosgrave 3 66+
(J R Fanshawe) *stdd s: hld up in rr: pushed along and prog fr 2f out: nvr rchd ldrs but kpt on steadily* **16/1**
7 ½ **Ishraaqat** 3-8-12 0 RichardHills 8 64+
(M P Tregoning) *hld up in rr: shuffled along on outer fr 2f out: kpt on encouragingly: nrst fin* **9/1**
0 **8** 10 **Dolphin's Dream**[13] 1329 3-8-12 0 KierenFallon 5 41
(B J Meehan) *trckd ldrs tl rdn and wknd over 2f out* **16/1**
9 1 ¼ **Razzina (IRE)** 3-8-12 0 TedDurcan 12 39
(D R Lanigan) *s.i.s: sn in midfield but rn green: hit rail wl over 2f out: wknd* **16/1**
10 3 **Candotoo (IRE)** 3-8-12 0 RichardHughes 4 32
(J Noseda) *hld up in last pair: rdn and rn green 3f out: wknd and sn bhd* **16/1**
0-0 **11** 3 ¾ **Star Of Soho (IRE)**[16] 1260 3-8-12 0 (b[1]) EddieCreighton 6 23
(E J Creighton) *chsd ldrs to 1/2-way: sn wknd and bhd* **100/1**
12 5 **Bellini Surprise** 3-8-12 0 RichardMullen 9 12
(A P Jarvis) *sn last pair: rdn and wknd 1/2-way: t.o* **66/1**

1m 39.61s (-0.19) **Going Correction** +0.025s/f (Slow) **12** Ran SP% **118.5**
Speed ratings (Par 100): **101,99,97,97,97 96,96,86,84,81 78,73**
toteswingers:1&2:£30.50, 1&3:£9.40, 2&3:£105.50 CSF £77.03 TOTE £2.10: £1.30, £12.10, £7.50; EX 84.30.
Owner Sheikh Ahmed Al Maktoum **Bred** Darley **Trained** Newmarket, Suffolk

FOCUS
This second division of the fillies' maiden looked another interesting contest, and it was run a lot quicker than division one. The market leaders filled the first two positions for most of the way and nothing got into it from behind. The form is rated a round the fourth. Queenie's Star (100/1) refused to enter the stalls and was withdrawn.
Razzina(IRE) Official explanation: jockey said filly ran green and shied away

1622 DIGIBET MAIDEN STKS 6f (P)
7:35 (7:35) (Class 5) 3-Y-0 **£2,590** (£770; £385; £192) **Stalls** High

Form RPR
4 **1** **Island Rhapsody**[34] 980 3-8-12 0 DavidProbert 12 73+
(A M Balding) *mde all: edgd lft fr 2f out: sn drew clr: readily* **9/4**[2]
03- **2** 2 ½ **Law Of Attraction (IRE)**[285] 4062 3-9-3 0 LukeMorris 8 68
(J R Gask) *chsd ldng pair: rdn over 2f out: kpt on to take 2nd 1f out: no ch w wnr* **25/1**
64- **3** ½ **Vanilla Rum**[184] 7058 3-9-3 0 DaneO'Neill 1 66
(H Candy) *s.v.s: rcvrd and sn in 8th: pushed along firmly and prog over 2f out: styd on wl to take 3rd nr fin* **8/1**
- **4** ¾ **Greeley Bright (USA)** 3-8-12 0 LeeVickers 7 59
(J G Given) *chsd ldrs: effrt over 2f out: kpt on same pce fnl f: n.d* **33/1**
2 **5** 2 ¼ **Fairy Shoes**[15] 1275 3-8-12 0 FrederikTylicki 5 51
(R A Fahey) *pressed wnr: edgd lft fr over 2f out: nt qckn and hld wl over 1f out: wknd fnl f* **15/8**[1]
6 ½ **Music Lover** 3-9-3 0 LiamJones 6 55
(R A Harris) *chsd ldrs: pushed along 1/2-way: nt pce to make prog: plugged on u.p* **66/1**
7 2 **Visual Element (USA)** 3-8-12 0 SteveDrowne 4 43
(R Charlton) *stdd s: plld hrd and hld up: struggling fr over 2f out* **12/1**
8 ¾ **Major Eradicator (USA)** 3-9-3 0 EddieAhern 11 46
(R M H Cowell) *dwlt: hld up in rr: styd alone against ins rail fnl 2f: no ch* **5/1**[3]
0 **9** 3 ¼ **Paphos**[8] 1442 3-9-3 0 SaleemGolam 3 36
(S C Williams) *dwlt: chsd ldrs to 1/2-way: wknd u.p* **50/1**
10 8 **Lordsbury Pride (USA)** 3-9-3 0 TonyCulhane 10 10
(J R Best) *dwlt: sn detached in last: t.o* **16/1**

1m 12.93s (-0.17) **Going Correction** +0.025s/f (Slow) **10** Ran SP% **117.1**
Speed ratings (Par 98): **102,98,98,97,94 93,90,89,85,74**
toteswingers:1&2:£9.80, 1&3:£5.70, 2&3:£12.90 CSF £62.47 TOTE £3.40: £1.10, £6.70, £4.20; EX 53.80.
Owner DH Caslon R McCreery Mildmay Bloodstock **Bred** Stowell Hill Ltd **Trained** Kingsclere, Hants

FOCUS
A modest maiden, weakened by the poor run of the drifting favourite. The form is hard to weigh up, but the winner was impressive.
Vanilla Rum Official explanation: jockey said gelding was slowly away
Visual Element(USA) Official explanation: jockey said filly ran too free

1623 DIGIBET SPORTS BETTING H'CAP 1m 3f (P)
8:10 (8:12) (Class 5) (0-70,70) 4-Y-0+ **£2,590** (£770; £385; £192) **Stalls** High

Form RPR
1136 **1** **Lytham (IRE)**[18] 1226 9-8-10 **62** SebSanders 10 68
(A W Carroll) *sn trckd ldng trio: wnt 2nd 2f out and sn chalng: drvn ahd jst ins fnl f: styd on wl* **8/1**[3]
24-6 **2** ½ **Seventh Hill**[48] 868 5-8-7 **59** FergusSweeney 9 64
(M Blanshard) *trckd ldng quartet: rdn and effrt on inner 2f out: styd on to take 2nd wl ins fnl f: nt rch wnr* **14/1**
-100 **3** ½ **Zerzura**[23] 1128 4-9-3 **69** KierenFallon 3 73
(P Howling) *racd freely: led: kicked on 3f out: hrd rdn whn pressed 2f out: hdd jst ins fnl f: kpt on* **16/1**
66-6 **4** nk **Love In The Park**[12] 1346 5-8-12 **64** PatCosgrave 1 67
(R Brotherton) *trckd ldrs in 6th: drvn and nt qckn on outer over 2f out: styd on fr over 1f out: nvr able to chal* **16/1**
660- **5** ¾ **Straight Laced**[320] 2877 4-8-4 **56** oh1 (p) HayleyTurner 6 58
(W J Knight) *sn chsd ldr: rdn over 3f out: lost 2nd 2f out: one pce u.p after* **16/1**
-501 **6** nk **Ghufa (IRE)**[8] 1462 6-8-8 **65** SimonPearce(5) 11 67+
(J Pearce) *sweating: hld up in last trio: plenty to do whn prog 2f out: chsd ldrs 1f out: keeping on but no ch whn short of room ins fnl f* **5/2**[1]
6-00 **7** 1 ½ **Wabbraan (USA)**[75] 529 5-8-4 **56** oh4 LukeMorris 7 55
(M Hill) *trckd ldng pair to 2f out: lost pl and wl btn over 1f out: plugged on* **66/1**
314/ **8** shd **Sumner (IRE)**[546] 5979 6-9-4 **70** JimCrowley 13 69+
(F Sheridan) *stdd s: hld up in last: swtchd to inner and sme prog over 1f out: one reminder and kpt on: nrst fin* **16/1**
25-1 **9** ¾ **Beaubrav**[18] 1225 4-9-2 **68** (t) LiamKeniry 2 66
(M Madgwick) *hld up in 9th: rdn and effrt on outer over 2f out: hanging and no prog over 1f out: plugged on* **7/2**[2]
4400 **10** 2 ¾ **Resplendent Ace (IRE)**[14] 1303 6-9-0 **66** J-PGuillambert 8 61
(P Howling) *hld up in last trio: pushed along 2f out: no imp on ldng gp but lost no grnd: eased ins fnl f: rdr nvr picked up whip* **33/1**
14-6 **11** 1 **Fleur De'Lion (IRE)**[8] 1454 4-8-11 **63** DavidProbert 4 54
(S Kirk) *hld up in 8th: lost pl on outer over 2f out: steadily fdd* **25/1**
0-00 **12** 6 **Mixing**[56] 770 8-7-13 **56** oh11 KierenFox(5) 12 37
(M J Attwater) *settled in midfield: rdn and wknd 2f out* **50/1**

2m 22.54s (0.64) **Going Correction** +0.025s/f (Slow) **12** Ran SP% **102.3**
Speed ratings (Par 103): **98,97,97,97,96 96,95,95,94,92 91,87**
toteswingers:1&2:£6.40, 1&3:£10.10, 2&3:£13.70 CSF £75.97 CT £909.47 TOTE £10.30: £2.80, £4.60, £6.70; EX 58.40.
Owner Morgan, Clarke & Parris **Bred** Mrs A S O'Brien And Lars Pearson **Trained** Cropthorne, Worcs
■ Blue Eyed Eloise was withdrawn (refused to enter stalls, 100/30, deduct 20p in the £ under R4).

FOCUS
A fair handicap run at a stop-start pace. The winner looked better than ever with the next two to form.
Ghufa(IRE) Official explanation: jockey was denied a clear run
Beaubrav Official explanation: jockey ran too free

1624 DIGIBET.COM H'CAP 1m 3f (P)
8:40 (8:40) (Class 4) (0-80,79) 3-Y-0 **£4,209** (£1,252; £625; £312) **Stalls** High

Form RPR
062- **1** **Activate**[188] 6965 3-8-12 **73** HayleyTurner 3 79+
(M L W Bell) *hld up in last: clsd on ldrs as pce lifted over 2f out: drvn to chal fnl f: led nr fin* **9/4**[1]
00-1 **2** hd **Dromore (IRE)**[13] 1317 3-9-3 **78** DavidProbert 2 84
(A M Balding) *hld up in last pair: moved up to chal 2f out: drvn to ld narrowly 1f out: styd on wl but hdd nr fin* **11/2**[3]
21 **3** shd **Zuider Zee (GER)**[15] 1271 3-9-0 **75** WilliamBuick 5 81
(J H M Gosden) *trckd ldng pair: quick move to ld over 2f out but sn pressed: narrowly hdd 1f out: battled on wl but jst hld* **9/4**[1]
31- **4** 3 ½ **Valid Reason**[133] 7764 3-9-4 **79** JimCrowley 1 79
(Mrs A J Perrett) *mostly trckd ldr to over 2f out: nt qckn in dash fnl 2f* **3/1**[2]
225- **5** 1 ½ **Baltimore Clipper (USA)**[198] 6728 3-9-1 **76** RichardHughes 4 73
(P F I Cole) *led: hdd and nt qckn over 2f out: kpt wanting to hang lft fr over 1f out* **7/1**

2m 20.75s (-1.15) **Going Correction** +0.025s/f (Slow) **5** Ran SP% **114.4**
Speed ratings (Par 100): **105,104,104,102,101**
CSF £15.22 TOTE £3.40: £1.50, £2.70; EX 22.90.
Owner Highclere Thoroughbred Racing Tudor Min **Bred** Card Bloodstock **Trained** Newmarket, Suffolk

FOCUS
A fascinating handicap involving some unexposed improvers. It turned into a bit of a sprint and there was a tight three-way finish. The first three all seemed to improve.
Baltimore Clipper(USA) Official explanation: jockey said colt hung left throughout

1625 FAMILY FUN DAY ON MONDAY H'CAP 7f (P)
9:10 (9:13) (Class 4) (0-85,85) 4-Y-0+ **£4,209** (£1,252; £625; £312) **Stalls** High

Form RPR
231- **1** **Primaeval**[194] 6823 4-8-12 **79** HayleyTurner 2 87+
(J R Fanshawe) *hld up in last pair: gd prog fr 2f out to cl on ldrs 1f out: led last 150yds: drvn out* **8/1**
5024 **2** ¾ **Gazboolou**[18] 1238 6-8-0 **71** ow1 KierenFox(5) 12 78
(David Pinder) *chsd ldr: clsd to ld narrowly wl over 1f out: hdd last 150yds: kpt on to keep 2nd* **14/1**
640- **3** shd **Sakhee's Pearl**[186] 7032 4-9-1 **82** MickyFenton 11 88
(Miss Gay Kelleway) *hld up in 6th: effrt fr 2f out: styng on over 1f out but wnr gng past: maintained effrt to take 3rd nr fin* **16/1**
233- **4** nse **Cape Rock**[251] 5182 5-8-11 **78** JimCrowley 7 84
(W J Knight) *t.k.h: trckd ldng trio: effrt 2f out: chal and upsides 1f out: nt qckn after* **5/2**[1]
20- **5** ¾ **Dukes Art**[186] 7027 4-8-13 **80** LiamKeniry 3 84
(J A R Toller) *hld up in 5th: rdn jst over 2f out and nt qckn: styd on fnl f: unable to chal* **20/1**
114- **6** ½ **Arrivederla (IRE)**[326] 2696 4-9-2 **83** RichardHughes 4 86
(H J L Dunlop) *trckd ldng pair: appeared to be gng wl 2f out: qcknd over 1f out: wl hld whn short of room nr fin* **8/1**
14-0 **7** ¾ **Cheam Forever (USA)**[16] 1265 4-8-10 **77** RichardKingscote 1 77
(R Charlton) *led at str pce: narrowly hdd wl over 1f out: wknd fnl f* **20/1**
2511 **8** ½ **Jake The Snake (IRE)**[14] 1306 9-9-4 **85** SebSanders 8 84
(A W Carroll) *hld up in 10th: rdn on outer over 2f out: no prog over 1f out: kpt on* **4/1**[2]

/05-	9	nk	**Hurricane Hymnbook (USA)**[304] 3431 5-9-4 **85**.......... TomQueally 10	83
			(Stef Higgins) *hld up in 9th: u.p 3f out and no prog: kpt on ins fnl f* **11/2**[3]	
3123	10	½	**Caprio (IRE)**[34] 981 5-9-3 **84**.. NickyMackay 9	89+
			(J R Boyle) *dwlt: hld up in last pair: prog on inner 2f out: cl up bhd ldrs and keeping on whn hmpd and snatched up 150yds out* **9/1**	
0450	11	1	**L'Hirondelle (IRE)**[9] 1430 6-9-2 **83**.................................... LukeMorris 5	77
			(M J Attwater) *blindfold off sltly late and dwlt: hld up in 7th: u.p and no prog over 2f out: sn btn* **16/1**	
2000	12	6	**Hereford Boy**[25] 1088 6-8-11 **78**.....................................(b) RobertHavlin 6	56
			(D K Ivory) *t.k.h: hld up in abt 8th and racd wd: wknd 2f out* **33/1**	

1m 24.94s (-1.06) **Going Correction** +0.025s/f (Slow) **12** Ran SP% **127.1**
Speed ratings (Par 105): **107,106,106,105,105 104,103,103,102,102 101,94**
toteswingers:1&2:£19.50, 1&3:£12.30, 2&3:£47.80 CSF £119.65 CT £1811.77 TOTE £16.90: £3.80, £6.40, £6.10; EX 112.70 Place 6 £938.39; Place 5 £213.01.
Owner Lord Vestey **Bred** Stowell Park Stud **Trained** Newmarket, Suffolk
■ Stewards' Enquiry : Jim Crowley two-day ban: careless riding (May 13-14)

FOCUS
A decent handicap run at a strong pace. They finished in a bit of bunch but the winner did the job in good style from an unpromising position. The form seems pretty sound.
T/Plt: £1739.80 to a £1 stake. Pool: £57557.89. 24.15 winning tickets. T/Qpdt: £48.10 to a £1 stake. Pool: £7241.51. 111.24 winning tickets. JN

1421 PONTEFRACT (L-H)
Wednesday, April 28

OFFICIAL GOING: Good to firm (watered; 8.3)
Wind: Light across Weather: Cloudy with sunny periods

1626 EUROPEAN BREEDERS' FUND NORTHERN RACING COLLEGE MAIDEN STKS — 5f
2:20 (2:22) (Class 4) 2-Y-O — **£4,533** (£1,348; £674; £336) **Stalls** Low

Form				RPR
	1		**Bahceli (IRE)** 2-9-3 0.. PatDobbs 2	80+
			(R Hannon) *dwlt: trckd ldrs on inner: hdwy 2f out: swtchd rt over 1f out: rdn and qcknd to ld ins fnl f: sn hung lft and kpt on wl* **4/1**[2]	
4	2	1½	**Hortensia (IRE)**[11] 1375 2-8-12 0.................................... ChrisCatlin 1	70
			(M R Channon) *led 2f: cl up: pushed along 2f out: sn rdn and ev ch ins fnl f: kpt on* **4/1**[2]	
	3	1¾	**Lenjawi Pride** 2-8-12 0... RichardKingscote 8	64
			(Tom Dascombe) *chsd ldrs on outer: hdwy to ld after 2f: rdn along over 1f out: hdd ins fnl f: one pce* **12/1**	
	4	4½	**Mr Optimistic** 2-9-3 0.. PaulHanagan 5	53
			(R A Fahey) *t.k.h: prom: pushed along over 2f out: rdn wl over 1f out: grad wknd* **2/1**[1]	
3	5	½	**Little Miss Take**[9] 1421 2-8-7 0................................. RossAtkinson(5) 6	46
			(Tom Dascombe) *chsd ldrs: effrt and hdwy on outer 2f out: sn rdn and no imp appr fnl f* **4/1**[2]	
	6	6	**George Woolf** 2-9-3 0... JamesDoyle 4	29
			(A J McCabe) *cl up: rdn along 2f out: sn wknd* **10/1**[3]	
0	7	11	**Dispol Snapper (IRE)**[14] 1294 2-9-3 0............................ PhillipMakin 7	—
			(P T Midgley) *s.i.s: a bhd* **100/1**	

65.52 secs (2.22) **Going Correction** +0.15s/f (Good) **7** Ran SP% **111.1**
Speed ratings (Par 94): **88,85,82,75,74 65,47**
toteswingers:1&2:£2.70, 1&3:£6.70, 2&3:£9.60 CSF £19.08 TOTE £5.20: £2.70, £2.50; EX 15.60.
Owner Middleham Park Racing II **Bred** Dr Mariann And Richard Klay **Trained** East Everleigh, Wilts

FOCUS
This looked a fair maiden and winners should emerge from it. The winner made a nice start and the runner-up improved on her debut effort.

NOTEBOOK
Bahceli(IRE), from a stable that can do little wrong with its juveniles at present, put up a nice winning debut. Travelling well off the pace early, he moved smoothly into contention rounding the bend and hit the front well inside the last furlong despite hanging away to his left. A £48,000 half-brother to three winning juveniles including the useful Damien, he should go on from here. (tchd 9-2)
Hortensia(IRE), a fair fourth on her Doncaster debut, came off the bridle at halfway but plugged on up the rail in the last furlong to snatch second. Out of a 1m4f winner, she appreciated this stiffer track and should benefit from an even greater test of stamina in due course. (op 5-1 tchd 7-2)
Lenjawi Pride, a £16,000 half-sister to five winners at up to 1m including the useful Johnny Jumpup, had to do a bit of running to gain the early advantage from the outside stall, but stayed there until well inside the last furlong. Normal improvement should see her win a race before long. (op 14-1 tchd 16-1)
Mr Optimistic, a £38,000 half-brother to two winners at up to 1m, pulled too hard in a prominent position early and as a result didn't have much left for the business end. He should have learnt from this. (op 7-4)
Little Miss Take, a stable-companion of the third, looked the yard's second string on jockey bookings despite having finished a fair third over C&D on debut nine days earlier, but not according to the market. She was forced to race very wide around the home bend, but even so she never got involved and this wasn't an improvement. (tchd 9-2)

1627 CORAL TV MAIDEN STKS — 1m 2f 6y
2:55 (2:57) (Class 5) 3-Y-O — **£3,238** (£963; £481; £240) **Stalls** Low

Form				RPR
2-	1		**Lion Mountain**[183] 7099 3-9-3 0...................................... TedDurcan 3	91+
			(Mahmood Al Zarooni) *wnt rt and green s: hdwy to ld after 1f: rdn clr wl over 1f out: kpt on strly* **5/6**[1]	
0-	2	6	**Raqeeb (USA)**[165] 7390 3-9-3 0...................................... TadhgO'Shea 1	79+
			(Sir Michael Stoute) *s.i.s: hdwy and in tch after 2f: effrt to chse ldng pair 3f out: sn rdn and chsd wnr fr wl over 1f out: no imp* **11/2**[3]	
03	3	4	**Najam**[11] 1380 3-8-12 0.. ChrisCatlin 4	66
			(C E Brittain) *cl up: rdn along 3f out: drvn 2f out and sn one pce* **14/1**	
52-0	4	2	**Plato (JPN)**[16] 1268 3-9-3 80.. JimmyQuinn 6	67+
			(H R A Cecil) *hld up: hdwy 3f out: rdn along and in tch 2f out: sn btn* **9/2**[2]	
	5	1¾	**Suyoof (USA)** 3-9-3 0.. RoystonFfrench 8	64+
			(M Johnston) *in tch: pushed along over 4f out: rdn 3f out: outpcd and hung bdly lft over 1f out* **10/1**	
0	6	¾	**Fantastic Favour**[23] 1116 3-8-12 0.......................... PatrickDonaghy(5) 2	62?
			(Jedd O'Keeffe) *led 1f: prom: rdn along and outpcd over 3f out: n.m.r on inner 2f out: wl hld whn n.m.r again 1f out: sn swtchd rt and kpt on* **150/1**	
0-6	7	hd	**Peaceful Soul (USA)**[12] 1358 3-8-12 0......................... SaleemGolam 5	57+
			(D R Lanigan) *dwlt: hld up and bhd tl sme late hdwy* **10/1**	
	8	18	**Admiral Rodney** 3-9-3 0... JamieMackay 7	26
			(Mrs P Sly) *s.i.s: t.k.h: a in rr* **100/1**	

2m 14.5s (0.80) **Going Correction** +0.15s/f (Good) **8** Ran SP% **114.6**
Speed ratings (Par 98): **102,97,94,92,91 90,90,75**
toteswingers:1&2:£2.30, 1&3:£2.80, 2&3:£6.40 CSF £5.94 TOTE £1.60: £1.10, £1.30, £2.50; EX 4.80.
Owner Godolphin **Bred** James Thom And Sons **Trained** Newmarket, Suffolk
■ The first winner in Britain for Godolphin's new second trainer, Mahmood Al Zarooni.

FOCUS
A modest maiden, run at an ordinary pace, and the winner is the only one to take from the race. The form is rated around the third.

1628 BETFRED.COM H'CAP — 1m 4y
3:30 (3:30) (Class 5) (0-70,70) 4-Y-O+ — **£2,914** (£867; £433; £216) **Stalls** Low

Form				RPR
14-3	1		**French Art**[11] 1395 5-9-1 **67**...(p) PhillipMakin 1	75
			(N Tinkler) *trckd ldrs: hdwy 2f out: rdn to ld over 1f out: drvn and kpt on wl fnl f* **9/4**[1]	
1323	2	1½	**Hits Only Jude (IRE)**[15] 1270 7-8-4 **63**............................ NeilFarley(7) 11	68
			(D Carroll) *trckd ldng pair: hdwy 2f out: rdn over 1f out: drvn and ev ch ins fnl f: no ex fnl 75yds* **7/1**	
0050	3	¾	**Blue Charm**[5] 1508 6-8-10 **65**... GaryBartley(3) 4	68
			(I W McInnes) *midfield: hdwy 3f out: rdn 2f out: styd on u.p ins fnl f* **11/1**	
00-0	4	½	**Aussie Blue (IRE)**[9] 1426 6-8-7 **64**.................................. AmyRyan(5) 10	66
			(R M Whitaker) *hld up and bhd: hdwy 2f out: swtchd rt and rdn over 1f out: kpt on ins fnl f: nrst fin* **25/1**	
51-5	5	shd	**Daniel Thomas (IRE)**[89] 348 8-9-1 **70**..............(v) RussKennemore(3) 5	71
			(Mrs A L M King) *dwlt and in rr: hdwy 3f out: swtchd outside and rdn wl over 1f out: kpt on ins fnl f: nrst fin* **16/1**	
5204	6	hd	**Xpres Maite**[9] 1426 7-8-11 **63** ow1......................................(p) AmirQuinn 8	64
			(S R Bowring) *cl up: effrt 2f out: sn rdn and ev ch tl drvn and sltly outpcd over 1f out: kpt on u.p ins fnl f* **6/1**[3]	
-235	7	2¼	**Ansells Pride (IRE)**[11] 1395 7-9-2 **68**................................. TomEaves 3	64
			(B Smart) *led: rdn along over 2f out: drvn and hdd over 1f out: wknd fnl f* **9/2**[2]	
0-00	8	2¼	**Fiefdom (IRE)**[21] 1171 8-8-4 **56**.................................... RoystonFfrench 2	47
			(I W McInnes) *chsd ldrs: rdn along over 2f out: grad wknd* **14/1**	
1-00	9	11	**Wiseman's Diamond (USA)**[9] 1426 5-8-13 **70**............ PaulPickard(5) 7	35
			(P T Midgley) *chsd ldrs: rdn along 3f out: sn wknd* **12/1**	
50-0	10	7	**Cherri Fosfate**[15] 1276 6-9-0 **66**................................... DanielTudhope 6	15
			(D Carroll) *a in rr* **16/1**	

1m 46.72s (0.82) **Going Correction** +0.15s/f (Good) **10** Ran SP% **114.0**
Speed ratings (Par 103): **101,99,98,98,98 97,95,93,82,75**
toteswingers:1&2:£3.90, 1&3:£8.60, 2&3:£10.80 CSF £17.66 CT £144.07 TOTE £3.00: £1.20, £1.80, £4.10; EX 16.20.
Owner N Patsalides & M Patel **Bred** Newsells Park Stud Limited **Trained** Langton, N Yorks

FOCUS
A modest handicap, but quite a competitive one. The winner is rated in line with the best view of last year's form. The pace looked fair.

1629 LADBROKES.COM FILLIES' H'CAP — 1m 2f 6y
4:05 (4:06) (Class 3) (0-90,80) 3-Y-O+ — **£9,346** (£2,799; £1,399; £700; £349; £175) **Stalls** Low

Form				RPR
40-0	1		**Antigua Sunrise (IRE)**[11] 1379 4-9-8 **74**......................... PaulHanagan 1	83
			(R A Fahey) *trckd ldng pair on inner: hdwy 2f out: rdn to ld jst ins fnl f: sn drvn and kpt on gamely* **6/1**	
45-5	2	1¼	**Dazzling Light (UAE)**[24] 1101 5-9-6 **75**......................... GaryBartley(3) 2	82
			(J S Goldie) *hld up in rr: hdwy on inner 2f out: swtchd rt and rdn over 1f out: chsd wnr ins fnl f: sn edgd lft and no imp towards fin* **11/4**[2]	
14-4	3	1	**Bollin Dolly**[11] 1379 7-9-5 **71**.. DavidAllan 3	76+
			(T D Easterby) *trckd ldrs: t.k.h and n.m.r 1/2-way: hmpd on inner over 3f out: hdwy and swtchd rt 2f out: carried wd after home turn and sn rdn: drvn whn rdr dropped whip jst ins fnl f: kpt on* **9/4**[1]	
00-0	4	2¾	**Umverti**[11] 1398 5-9-2 **68**... GrahamGibbons 6	67
			(N Bycroft) *set stdy pce: qcknd 3f out: rdn along 2f out: drvn and hdd jst ins fnl f: grad wknd* **11/1**	
153-	5	shd	**Some Sunny Day**[181] 7134 4-9-8 **74**................................... TravisBlock 7	73
			(H Morrison) *sn trcking ldr: effrt and cl up 3f out: rdn and hung rt home turn: sn ev ch: drvn over 1f out and wknd ins fnl f: eased cl home* **8/1**	
-641	6	9	**Aphrodisia**[11] 1379 6-10-0 **80**.. StevieDonohoe 4	61
			(Ian Williams) *hld up in rr: hdwy 3f out: rdn to chse ldrs on outer 2f out: sn drvn and btn* **5/1**[3]	
4-30	7	3½	**Shaws Diamond (USA)**[8] 1455 4-9-12 **78**........................ JimmyQuinn 5	52
			(D Shaw) *trckd ldrs: rdn along 3f out: sn wknd* **22/1**	

2m 13.73s (0.03) **Going Correction** +0.15s/f (Good) **7** Ran SP% **112.2**
Speed ratings (Par 104): **105,104,103,101,100 93,90**
toteswingers:1&2:£3.80, 1&3:£2.80, 2&3:£1.90 CSF £21.97 TOTE £6.20: £4.30, £1.50; EX 23.40.
Owner David And Jackie Knaggs **Bred** Michael Morrin **Trained** Musley Bank, N Yorks
■ Stewards' Enquiry : Travis Block three-day ban: failed to ride out for 4th (May 12-14)

FOCUS
A decent fillies' handicap, but spoiled by a pedestrian gallop which didn't help a few. The winning time was still 0.77 seconds faster than the maiden. Straightforward form.

NOTEBOOK
Antigua Sunrise(IRE), well beaten behind a couple of these on her Doncaster reappearance, was just 2lb higher than when completing a hat-trick in May/June last year, but the key to this victory was that she was always in a good position in a steadily run affair. She quickened up well to hit the front a furlong from home and this progressive filly, who seems oblivious to ground conditions, looks the type to carry on improving.
Dazzling Light(UAE), racing over a trip this short for the first time in over a year, has been tried over as far as 2m in the meantime so a slowly run race over this distance wasn't ideal, but under the circumstances she did very well to stay on and finish where she did. She is worth noting if returned to a more suitable trip. (op 9-2)
Bollin Dolly raced far too keenly in the middle of the field and ran into the back of rivals on a couple of occasions, losing her action as she did so. She still looked a possible danger when switched wide for her effort after turning in, but the leaders were quickening too and her rider then lost his whip inside the last furlong. She is 4lb higher than when winning over C&D in October, but doesn't look handicapped out of things just yet. (op 5-2 tchd 2-1)
Umverti, disappointing in three starts since the second of two victories off 3lb lower here last season, performed better this time but she had the run of the race out in front until collared at the furlong pole. (op 14-1)
Some Sunny Day, 2lb above her last winning mark and having her first start since October, had every chance until inside the last furlong and should come on for it. Her rider received a three-day ban for dropping his hands near the line and just failing to hold on for fourth. (op 5-1)

Aphrodisia, raised 4lb for her Doncaster success, seemed disappointing, but being held up in a slowly run race wasn't ideal and she is worth another chance. (tchd 6-1)

1630 SPORTINGBET.COM H'CAP — 1m 4f 8y
4:40 (4:40) (Class 5) (0-75,75) 3-Y-O — £2,914 (£867; £433; £216) Stalls Low

Form — RPR

61-2 **1** **Beat The Rush**[14] 1299 3-9-4 **75** .... TomEaves 4 — 86+
(Julie Camacho) *t.k.h: trckd ldng pair on inner: nt clr run 3f out: swtchd rt and hdwy to chal 2f out: sn led: pushed clr ent fnl f: easily* **1/1**[1]

000- **2** 4 ½ **Red Barcelona (IRE)**[216] 6235 3-8-6 **63** .... JimmyQuinn 1 — 63
(M H Tompkins) *hld up in rr: hdwy over 2f out: rdn to chse ldng pair and hung rt ins fnl f: kpt on to take 2nd nr fin* **8/1**

062- **3** nk **Molon Labe (IRE)**[175] 7243 3-9-2 **73** .... RobertWinston 2 — 73
(T P Tate) *led: rdn along 3f out: drvn 2f out: sn hdd and kpt on same pce: lost 2nd towards fin* **3/1**[2]

525- **4** 12 **Pena Dorada (IRE)**[205] 6533 3-9-1 **72** .... PhillipMakin 5 — 53
(J R Weymes) *trckd ldrs: hdwy on outer to chal 3f out: rdn 2f out and sn btn* **4/1**[3]

66-0 **5** 16 **All Moving Parts (USA)**[21] 1178 3-8-5 **62** .... RoystonFfrench 3 — 17
(J S Wainwright) *clsd up: rdn along 3f out: drvn 2f out and wknd qckly* **33/1**

2m 40.66s (-0.14) **Going Correction** +0.15s/f (Good) — **5** Ran SP% **109.1**
Speed ratings (Par 98): **106,103,102,94,84**
CSF £9.48 TOTE £1.80: £1.10, £4.40; EX 7.70.
Owner Axom (XX) **Bred** David Brown & G B Turnbull Ltd **Trained** Norton, N Yorks

FOCUS
A modest pace for this ordinary handicap, but an impressive winner. The first three finished clear and the form is rated at something like face value.

1631 BET IN PLAY FOOTBALL AT TOTESPORT.COM H'CAP — 1m 2f 6y
5:15 (5:15) (Class 5) (0-75,74) 4-Y-O+ — £3,238 (£963; £481; £240) Stalls Low

Form — RPR

323- **1** **Mr Freddy (IRE)**[270] 4518 4-9-2 **72** .... PaulHanagan 3 — 86+
(R A Fahey) *trckd ldrs: hdwy over 2f out: rdn to ld jst ins fnl f: styd on strly* **3/1**[3]

1-11 **2** 2 ¾ **Zaplamation (IRE)**[14] 1296 5-8-6 **67** .... IanBrennan(5) 8 — 75
(J J Quinn) *hld up: hdwy on outer over 3f out: rdn to chse wnr ins fnl f: sn drvn and no imp* **11/4**[2]

424 **3** 1 **Ahlawy (IRE)**[72] 565 7-9-4 **74** ....(t) JamesDoyle 4 — 80
(F Sheridan) *s.i.s: hld up and bhd: hdwy on outer over 2f out: rdn to chse ldng pair over 1f out: kpt on same pce ins fnl f* **18/1**

42-6 **4** ¾ **Inspirina (IRE)**[21] 1177 6-8-11 **67** .... TonyHamilton 7 — 72
(R Ford) *t.k.h: chsd ldng pair: hdwy to chal 3f out: rdn to ld 2f out: drvn and hdd jst ins fnl f: kpt on same pce* **10/1**

0-02 **5** 10 **Pedasus (USA)**[18] 1226 4-8-8 **64** ....(b) RobertWinston 2 — 49
(T Keddy) *trckd ldr: hdwy 3f out: rdn along over 2f out: wknd wl over 1f out* **14/1**

3-00 **6** 3 ¼ **Prime Circle**[9] 1426 4-8-10 **66** .... JimmyQuinn 1 — 44
(A D Brown) *led and sn clr: rdn along and jnd 3f out: hdd 2f out and wknd qckly* **100/1**

-301 **7** ½ **Waahej**[9] 1427 4-8-7 **63** .... ChrisCatlin 5 — 40
(P W Hiatt) *trckd ldrs: n.m.r over 2f out and sn rdn along: lost pl and btn wl over 1f out* **13/8**[1]

2m 14.3s (0.60) **Going Correction** +0.15s/f (Good) — **7** Ran SP% **111.8**
Speed ratings (Par 103): **103,100,100,99,91 88,88**
toteswingers:1&2:£1.90, 1&3:£8.80, 2&3:£8.90 CSF £11.13 CT £118.22 TOTE £3.20: £1.60, £2.30; EX 11.50 Place 6 £50.65; Place 5 £18.85.
Owner R F White **Bred** Spratstown Stud Gm **Trained** Musley Bank, N Yorks

FOCUS
Another ordinary handicap and the pace was modest as the bulk of the field were inclined to ignore the clear leader. The winning time was 0.2 seconds faster than the maiden, but 0.57 seconds slower than the fillies' handicap. The form is rated around the second and third, with more to come from the winner.
Waahej Official explanation: trainer said, regarding running, that the gelding was unsuited by the good to firm ground
T/Plt: £59.50 to a £1 stake. Pool: £55464.54. 679.69 winning tickets. T/Qpdt: £10.80 to a £1 stake. Pool: £3162.41. 215.24 winning tickets. JR

1436 BRIGHTON (L-H)
Thursday, April 29

OFFICIAL GOING: Good to firm
Wind: Almost nil Weather: Light rain

1632 TARPAN VODKA E B F MAIDEN STKS — 5f 59y
5:00 (5:01) (Class 5) 2-Y-O — £3,238 (£963; £481; £240) Stalls Low

Form — RPR

0 **1** **Prophet In A Dream**[13] 1351 2-9-3 0 .... AlanMunro 1 — 66
(M R Channon) *chsd ldrs: effrt 2f out: edgd rt over 1f out: led ins fnl f: rdn out* **11/4**[2]

3 **2** nk **Stunning In Purple (IRE)**[19] 1223 2-8-12 0 .... NeilCallan 6 — 60
(A B Haynes) *chsd ldrs: nt clr run and swtchd lft over 1f out: drvn to chal ins fnl f: r.o* **3/1**[3]

6 **3** 1 ½ **Johnny Hancocks (IRE)**[33] 1017 2-9-3 0 .... DavidProbert 2 — 60
(P D Evans) *disp ld: led 2f out: edgd lft over 1f out: hdd and one pce ins fnl f* **11/8**[1]

4 5 **Vivre La Secret** 2-8-7 0 .... AshleyMorgan(5) 3 — 37
(W G M Turner) *s.i.s: outpcd in last tl hdwy to press ldrs 2f out: wandered and wknd over 1f out* **11/1**

000 **5** 15 **Bold Deceiver**[14] 1324 2-8-12 0 .... ChrisCatlin 5 — —
(P S McEntee) *disp ld tl wknd rapidly and veered rt 2f out* **14/1**

63.76 secs (1.46) **Going Correction** -0.025s/f (Good) — **5** Ran SP% **108.8**
Speed ratings (Par 92): **87,86,84,76,52**
CSF £10.96 TOTE £3.40: £1.20, £1.10; EX 12.20.
Owner Lord Ilsley Racing (Stokes Syndicate) **Bred** Mike Channon Bloodstock Ltd **Trained** West Ilsley, Berks

FOCUS
This is probably just modest juvenile form. The main action took place up the centre of the track.

NOTEBOOK
Prophet In A Dream showed little on debut at Newbury, but this was a much weaker race and he had clearly learnt plenty from that initial experience. He showed a good attitude and is probably one for ordinary nurseries in due course. (op 5-2)
Stunning In Purple(IRE) was beaten only 1/2l on the Polytrack first time up, but that was a moderate race that's not working out. She had her chance after being switched towards the inside in the closing stages, showing enough to suggest she might be able to make her mark in similarly weak company. (op 11-4 tchd 5-2)
Johnny Hancocks(IRE), who ran to just a moderate level on debut, was taken on up front by Bold Deceiver and couldn't find extra late on. (op 7-4 tchd 15-8)
Vivre La Secret, the first foal of a mare who was placed over 1m-1m4f, shaped a little better than the beaten margin suggests. Having missed the break and been niggled along early, she made encouraging headway to move into contention early in the straight, before simply getting tired. (tchd 9-1)

1633 CROWN DRINKS LTD NEWHAVEN H'CAP — 6f 209y
5:30 (5:30) (Class 6) (0-55,55) 4-Y-O+ — £2,201 (£655; £327; £163) Stalls Centre

Form — RPR

6060 **1** **Yourgolftravel Com**[22] 1170 5-8-12 **52** .... StephenCraine 14 — 65+
(M Wigham) *stdd s: hld up in rr: nt clr run and swtchd wd 2f out: gd hdwy over 1f out: styd on to ld nr fin* **16/1**

0-4 **2** nk **Four Kicks (IRE)**[9] 1437 4-8-6 **46** oh1 .... LiamKeniry 2 — 58
(J S Moore) *prom: drvn to ld ins fnl f: kpt on u.p: hdd nr fin* **8/1**

2-03 **3** 2 ¾ **Sermons Mount (USA)**[9] 1441 4-9-1 **55** ....(p) NeilCallan 10 — 60
(Mouse Hamilton-Fairley) *chsd ldrs: drvn to chal on far rail over 1f out: one pce fnl 100yds* **7/2**[1]

4306 **4** nk **Who's Winning (IRE)**[9] 1443 9-9-1 **55** ....(tp) KirstyMilczarek 13 — 59
(B G Powell) *chsd ldrs: hrd rdn over 1f out: n.m.r ins fnl f: kpt on nr fin* **18/1**

40-4 **5** nk **Sultans Way (IRE)**[9] 1441 4-9-1 **55** ....(b) TomQueally 1 — 58
(P F I Cole) *led: hrd rdn and hdd ins fnl f: no ex* **4/1**[2]

6056 **6** 1 ½ **Djalalabad (FR)**[15] 1301 6-8-6 **46** oh1 .... SaleemGolam 9 — 45
(J Pearce) *mid-div: effrt over 2f out: rdn to chse ldrs over 1f out: one pce* **20/1**

2-51 **7** ¾ **Rough Rock (IRE)**[9] 1443 5-8-6 **53** .... MJMurphy(7) 16 — 50
(C A Dwyer) *chsd ldrs on outer tl edgd lft and outpcd fnl 2f* **13/2**

5100 **8** 1 ½ **Jonnie Skull (IRE)**[9] 1441 4-9-1 **55** ....(vt) ChrisCatlin 5 — 48
(P S McEntee) *w ldrs: lost pl over 2f out: sn btn* **25/1**

0400 **9** 2 ¼ **Dynamo Dave (USA)**[9] 1443 5-8-6 **46** ....(p) HayleyTurner 7 — 33
(M D I Usher) *bhd: rdn over 3f out: sme late hdwy* **25/1**

3235 **10** 1 ¼ **Yakama (IRE)**[9] 1437 5-8-11 **51** ....(b) AdamKirby 6 — 34
(Mrs C A Dunnett) *s.s: bhd tl sme hdwy on outer 1/2-way: wknd and hung lft wl over 1f out* **6/1**[3]

6530 **11** 1 **Shadow Bay (IRE)**[15] 1305 4-8-8 **53** .... RossAtkinson(5) 12 — 34
(Miss Z C Davison) *in tch tl wknd over 2f out* **25/1**

000 **12** 2 **Kalligal**[9] 1437 5-8-7 **47** .... RichardThomas 3 — 22
(R Ingram) *in tch on rail tl wknd over 2f out* **66/1**

-600 **13** 7 **Haasem (USA)**[9] 1437 7-9-1 **55** ....(b[1]) JimCrowley 11 — 11
(J R Jenkins) *mid-div on outer: hung lft and wknd 2f out* **14/1**

50-0 **P** **Torquemada (IRE)**[92] 318 9-8-1 **46** ....(p) KierenFox(5) 8 — —
(M J Attwater) *bhd: rdn 3f out: no ch whn p.u ins fnl f* **66/1**

1m 22.6s (-0.50) **Going Correction** -0.025s/f (Good) — **14** Ran SP% **118.0**
Speed ratings (Par 101): **101,100,97,97,96 95,94,92,89,88 87,85,77,—**
toteswingers: 1&2 £42.90, 1&3 £22.40, 2&3 £8.40 CSF £126.11 CT £571.42 TOTE £35.00: £14.00, £6.20, £1.10; EX 267.90.
Owner Your Golf Travel Ltd **Bred** Gainsborough Stud Management Ltd **Trained** Newmarket, Suffolk

FOCUS
A moderate handicap run at an even pace, and the time was 1.02 seconds slower than the following Class 5 event won by Ocean Countess. They raced middle to far side in the straight. The form makes a fair bit of sense.
Yourgolftravel Com Official explanation: trainer said, regarding apparent improvement in form, that in its last race the gelding had been keen from a wide draw, beaten 3 lengths, and had benefited from a change of tactics.
Who's Winning(IRE) Official explanation: starter said tongue strap had come adrift shortly before gates opened
Torquemada(IRE) Official explanation: jockey said gelding had a breathing problem

1634 TARPAN VODKA H'CAP — 6f 209y
6:00 (6:00) (Class 5) (0-75,75) 4-Y-O+ — £2,901 (£868; £434; £217; £108) Stalls Centre

Form — RPR

156- **1** **Ocean Countess (IRE)**[137] 7742 4-8-10 **67** .... CathyGannon 4 — 79
(Miss J Feilden) *off the pce in 6th: hdwy 2f out: hrd rdn and led 1f out: styd on wl* **15/2**

60-0 **2** 1 ½ **My Learned Friend (IRE)**[19] 1224 6-8-10 **74** .... ThomasBrown(7) 5 — 82
(A M Balding) *prom: disp ld 2f out: led over 1f out: sn hdd and edgd rt: one pce fnl 100yds* **5/1**[2]

00-0 **3** ½ **Purus (IRE)**[22] 1170 8-8-5 **62** .... LukeMorris 9 — 69
(R A Teal) *outpcd towards rr: drvn and hdwy over 1f out: styd on fnl f* **10/1**

0-05 **4** 1 ¼ **Cordell (IRE)**[9] 1457 5-8-6 **63** ....(t) DavidProbert 3 — 67
(P D Evans) *chsd ldrs: hrd rdn and one pce fnl 2f* **16/1**

3263 **5** ¾ **Billberry**[19] 1224 5-8-5 **62** ....(t) SaleemGolam 8 — 64
(S C Williams) *outpcd and bhd: rdn 3f out: styd on appr fnl f: nt rch ldrs* **6/1**[3]

10-0 **6** shd **Avertis**[51] 837 5-9-4 **75** ....(tp) TomQueally 6 — 76
(Stef Higgins) *prom: disp ld 2f out tl hrd rdn and wknd over 1f out* **16/1**

6064 **7** 1 ¾ **Kipchak (IRE)**[9] 1458 5-8-13 **70** ....(p) LiamKeniry 1 — 67
(C R Dore) *led and set gd pce tl 2f out: hrd rdn: wknd fnl f* **15/2**

060 **8** 5 **Noble Jack (IRE)**[17] 1265 4-9-4 **75** .... GeorgeBaker 7 — 58
(G L Moore) *s.s: a bhd and nvr gng wl* **4/1**[1]

6030 **9** 1 ¼ **Ivory Lace**[19] 1224 9-9-1 **72** .... JackMitchell 10 — 52
(S Woodman) *outpcd towards rr: rdn 4f out: nvr nr ldrs* **12/1**

00-1 **10** 3 ½ **Print (IRE)**[29] 1064 4-9-0 **71** .... AlanMunro 2 — 54
(M R Channon) *in tch in 5th: hrd rdn over 2f out: sn btn: hung bdly lft over 1f out: eased* **5/1**[2]

1m 21.58s (-1.52) **Going Correction** -0.025s/f (Good) — **10** Ran SP% **119.7**
Speed ratings (Par 103): **107,105,104,103,102 102,100,94,93,89**
toteswingers: 1&2 £10.90, 1&3 £38.60, 2&3 £23.10 CSF £46.12 CT £393.26 TOTE £4.00: £1.10, £1.10, £10.60; EX 64.00.
Owner Ocean Trailers Ltd **Bred** Don Commins **Trained** Exning, Suffolk

FOCUS
A tight handicap in which those with previous course form came to the fore. They went a decent pace, with plenty of competition for the lead, and the time was 1.02 seconds quicker than the earlier Class 6 contest. The runners were positioned middle to far side late on. Pretty solid form, with a clear personal best from the winner.
Noble Jack(IRE) Official explanation: jockey said gelding was slowly away
Print(IRE) Official explanation: jockey said colt lost its action

1635 DRINKS & FOOD UK LTD H'CAP — 1m 3f 196y
6:30 (6:31) (Class 6) (0-60,57) 4-Y-O+ — £2,201 (£655; £327; £163) Stalls High

Form — RPR

253- **1** **Galiotto (IRE)**[209] 6457 4-9-0 **52** .... GeorgeBaker 11 — 67+
(C F Wall) *hld up in midfield: hdwy to ld 4f out: hrd rdn over 1f out: styd on wl* **9/2**[3]

2555 **2** *3 ¼* **Stanley Rigby**[34] 995 4-8-9 **47** JackMitchell 5 55
(C F Wall) *sn towards rr: rdn 1/2-way: drvn and hdwy 3f out: edgd lft and chal 1f out: one pce* **17/2**

0603 **3** *1* **Barbirolli**[17] 1262 8-8-9 **46** JerryO'Dwyer 10 52
(W B Stone) *bhd: sme hdwy on outer 4f out: styd on u.p fnl 2f: nvr nrr* **14/1**

5-13 **4** *hd* **Peintre D'Argent (IRE)**[8] 1478 4-9-1 **53** JimCrowley 3 59
(W J Knight) *chsd ldrs: wnt 2nd and hrd rdn 3f out: no ex fnl f* **7/2**[1]

0500 **5** *1* **Dazzling Begum**[21] 1194 5-8-4 **46** SimonPearce(5) 8 50
(J Pearce) *hld up in rr: swtchd wd and hdwy 3f out: edgd lft and kpt on fnl 2f: nt pce to chal* **10/1**

56-0 **6** *2 ¼* **Minder**[11] 983 4-9-5 **57** (tp) TomQueally 4 58
(J G Portman) *s.s: bhd tl hdwy into midfield after 5f: rdn 4f out: drvn to chse ldrs 2f out: wknd 1f out* **28/1**

00-1 **7** *20* **Gamesters Lady**[35] 622 7-9-5 **56** (b) AlanMunro 14 25
(Jim Best) *prom on outer: rdn over 4f out: wknd over 3f out* **4/1**[2]

-202 **8** *7* **Turner's Touch**[70] 590 8-8-5 **49** (b) HarryBentley(7) 1 6
(G L Moore) *hld up in midfield: kidded along 3f out: no rspnse* **18/1**

56-0 **9** *11* **Harlequinn Danseur (IRE)**[9] 1459 5-8-13 **50** (v) CathyGannon 2 —
(P D Evans) *mid-div: rdn 1/2-way: sn wknd: bhd fnl 4f: eased fnl 2f* **12/1**

-400 **10** *6* **Achromatic**[17] 1262 4-8-13 **51** AdamKirby 13 —
(W R Swinburn) *towards rr: drvn along 4f out: n.d* **16/1**

000 **11** *12* **Hopefull Blue (IRE)**[55] 803 4-8-7 **45** LiamKeniry 12 —
(J W Mullins) *in tch: rdn and wknd 1/2-way: t.o fnl 4f* **66/1**

6-10 **12** *9* **Dulce Domum**[29] 1071 4-8-12 **50** NeilCallan 6 —
(A B Haynes) *prom: hrd rdn 4f out: wknd 3f out: eased whn no ch fnl 2f* **16/1**

5536 **13** *5* **Six Of Clubs**[17] 1262 4-8-7 **45** (b) HayleyTurner 7 —
(W G M Turner) *led tl wknd qckly 4f out: sn bhd: eased whn no ch fnl 2f* **25/1**

2m 32.88s (0.18) **Going Correction** -0.025s/f (Good)
WFA 4 from 5yo+ 1lb **13** Ran SP% **120.2**
Speed ratings (Par 101): **98,95,95,95,94 92,79,74,67,63 55,49,46**
toteswingers: 1&2 £8.70, 1&3 £10.10, 2&3 £19.50 CSF £42.29 CT £505.23 TOTE £4.20: £1.20, £5.10, £5.90; EX 39.20.
Owner Archangels 2 **Bred** Ballintaggart Syndicate **Trained** Newmarket, Suffolk

FOCUS
Just a moderate handicap, but it was well run. Again, the main action was middle to far side in the closing stages. Pretty solid form, with the winner looking a class above and better than the bare form.
Dulce Domum Official explanation: jockey said filly was unsuited by the track

1636 TARPAN VODKA H'CAP 1m 1f 209y
7:00 (7:02) (Class 6) (0-65,65) 4-Y-O+ **£2,201** (£655; £327; £163) **Stalls** High

Form RPR

603 **1** **Granny McPhee**[9] 1440 4-9-4 **65** RobertWinston 7 73
(A Bailey) *towards rr: rdn and hdwy over 2f out: hung lft and styd on wl fnl 2f: drvn to ld post* **11/4**[2]

-312 **2** *shd* **Blue Tango (IRE)**[9] 1440 4-9-4 **65** (b) JimCrowley 6 72
(Mrs A J Perrett) *prom in chsng gp: wnt 2nd 4f out: led over 2f out: hrd rdn over 1f out: kpt on u.p: ct post* **5/2**[1]

0-50 **3** *hd* **Goose Green (IRE)**[6] 1508 6-9-1 **62** GeorgeBaker 8 69
(R J Hodges) *hld up in rr: hdwy over 2f out: drvn to chal fnl f: r.o* **13/2**

0610 **4** *6* **Golden Prospect**[22] 1179 6-9-2 **63** PaulFitzsimons 9 58
(Miss J R Tooth) *mid-div: edgd lft and drvn to dispute 3rd 2f out: one pce* **25/1**

050- **5** *1 ½* **Kashmina**[120] 7873 5-8-12 **62** RobertLButler(3) 4 54
(Miss Sheena West) *towards rr: effrt on outer 3f out: hung lft and wknd 2f out* **16/1**

0-30 **6** *5* **Rosy Dawn**[28] 1078 5-8-4 **51** oh6 DavidProbert 10 33
(J J Bridger) *chsd clr ldr: hrd rdn 3f out: wknd 2f out* **18/1**

534- **7** *3* **Dancer's Legacy**[205] 6565 5-8-7 **54** HayleyTurner 2 30
(J R Boyle) *chsd ldrs in main gp: drvn along over 3f out: n.m.r on rail 2f out: sn wknd* **17/2**

00/0 **8** *1 ¾* **Mamichor**[28] 1078 7-7-11 **51** oh6 RichardRowe(7) 1 24
(Mrs L J Mongan) *difficult on way to post: led and racd freely: sn 15 l clr: hdd over 2f out: sn wknd* **100/1**

000- **9** *11* **Sularno**[194] 6862 6-8-0 **52** SimonPearce(5) 3 3
(J Pearce) *chsd ldrs in main gp: wknd 4f out: sn bhd* **50/1**

46-4 **10** *1 ¼* **Altimatum (USA)**[14] 1323 4-9-1 **62** (t) AlanMunro 5 10
(P F I Cole) *bhd: rdn 5f out: no ch fnl 4f* **5/1**[3]

2m 3.06s (-0.54) **Going Correction** -0.025s/f (Good) **10** Ran SP% **113.7**
Speed ratings (Par 101): **101,100,100,95,94 90,88,86,78,77**
toteswingers: 1&2 £2.00, 1&3 £4.90, 2&3 £3.60 CSF £9.63 CT £38.74 TOTE £2.70: £1.10, £3.10, £1.30; EX 10.90.
Owner Middleham Park Racing XXVI & Alan Bailey **Bred** Sugar Puss Corporation **Trained** Newmarket, Suffolk
■ Stewards' Enquiry : Jim Crowley two-day ban: used whip with excessive frequency (May 16-17)

FOCUS
A modest handicap. Tearaway leader Mamichor, who soon shot well clear, was ignored by his rivals for much of the way, but the main group still went a decent pace. Once more, the action was middle to far side. The form makes sense, rated around the third.

1637 IMPERIAL WHOLESALE LONDON H'CAP 7f 214y
7:30 (7:30) (Class 5) (0-70,71) 4-Y-O+ **£2,901** (£868; £434; £217; £108) **Stalls** Low

Form RPR

44-3 **1** **Magroom**[4] 1543 6-9-4 **69** GeorgeBaker 10 76
(R J Hodges) *hld up in 2nd last: swtchd outside and hdwy over 2f out: edgd lft and led jst ins fnl f: pushed out* **11/4**[2]

5442 **2** *1 ½* **War And Peace (IRE)**[19] 1224 6-9-1 **66** DavidProbert 7 70
(P D Evans) *chsd ldr: led 2f out tl jst ins fnl f: nt qckn* **3/1**[3]

600- **3** *¾* **Jeremiah (IRE)**[45] 7479 4-9-1 **66** (p) StephenCraine 9 68
(J G Portman) *in tch: rdn whn bmpd over 2f out: hung bdly lft and struggling after tl styd on wl fnl f* **40/1**

265- **4** *½* **Rosco Flyer (IRE)**[200] 6698 4-8-12 **63** LiamKeniry 1 64
(R A Teal) *hld up in rr: rdn and r.o fnl 2f: hung lft: nrst fin* **20/1**

100- **5** *1* **Choreography**[205] 6562 7-9-4 **69** (p) SteveDrowne 3 68
(Jim Best) *chsd ldrs: rdn and one pce fnl 2f* **10/1**

0431 **6** *3* **Fault**[4] 1543 4-9-6 **71** 6ex (t) TomQueally 2 63
(Stef Higgins) *led tl 2f out: hrd rdn and wknd 1f out* **5/2**[1]

-600 **7** *5* **State General (IRE)**[9] 1441 4-8-7 **58** (v) CathyGannon 4 38
(Miss J Feilden) *prom tl wknd over 2f out* **16/1**

00-0 **8** *9* **Pab Special (IRE)**[19] 1226 7-8-10 **61** PatCosgrave 5 20
(B R Johnson) *mid-div on rail: rdn over 3f out: sn struggling* **14/1**

460- **9** *7* **Admiral Sandhoe (USA)**[243] 5429 4-8-13 **64** NeilCallan 6 7
(Mrs A J Perrett) *mid-div: hrd rdn over 2f out: sn btn* **18/1**

02-6 **10** *5* **Beauchamp Wizard**[14] 1322 5-9-2 **67** JerryO'Dwyer 8 —
(G A Butler) *t.k.h: prom on outer: c alone centre st: wknd over 2f out: hung lft and sn bhd: eased* **25/1**

1m 35.79s (-0.21) **Going Correction** -0.025s/f (Good) **10** Ran SP% **118.2**
Speed ratings (Par 103): **100,98,97,97,96 93,88,79,72,67**
toteswingers: 1&2 £1.80, 1&3 £13.70, 2&3 £22.40 CSF £11.37 CT £253.61 TOTE £2.70: £1.10, £1.20, £24.40; EX 13.30.
Owner Mrs A Hart Mrs A Hodges Mrs C Penny **Bred** Mrs M Chaworth-Musters **Trained** Charlton Mackrell, Somerset
■ Stewards' Enquiry : George Baker one-day ban: careless riding (May 13)

FOCUS
An ordinary handicap run at a decent pace. The principals raced far side in the straight. An improved effort from the winner.
Rosco Flyer(IRE) Official explanation: jockey said gelding hung left

1638 TARPAN VODKA H'CAP 5f 59y
8:00 (8:00) (Class 5) (0-70,66) 4-Y-O+ **£2,775** (£830; £415; £207; £103) **Stalls** Low

Form RPR

1204 **1** **Sherjawy (IRE)**[9] 1438 6-8-13 **66** RossAtkinson(5) 5 75
(Miss Z C Davison) *chsd ldrs: outpcd over 2f out: rallied and hung lft over 1f out: drvn to ld fnl 50yds* **9/2**[2]

024- **2** *½* **Tiger Trail (GER)**[210] 6422 6-8-7 **55** LukeMorris 3 62
(Mrs N Smith) *s.i.s: bhd tl gd hdwy 1/2-way: slt ld ins fnl f: hrd rdn: hdd fnl 50yds* **9/1**

312 **3** *1 ¼* **Wreningham**[12] 1391 5-8-9 **60** WilliamCarson(3) 2 63
(S C Williams) *led over 1f: disp ld after tl led again over 1f out: hdd and one pce ins fnl f* **6/4**[1]

-000 **4** *1 ½* **Mandhooma**[8] 1470 4-8-4 **52** ChrisCatlin 1 49
(P W Hiatt) *chsd ldrs: rdn and outpcd fnl 2f* **10/1**

6523 **5** *nk* **Thoughtsofstardom**[2] 1598 7-7-13 **54** LeonnaMayor(7) 7 50
(P S McEntee) *chsd ldr: disp ld over 3f out tl over 1f out: hung lft: no ex* **5/1**[3]

000- **6** *1 ¼* **Thumberlina**[213] 6335 4-7-13 **52** oh7 (p) KierenFox(5) 6 44?
(Mrs C A Dunnett) *in tch: outpcd and hrd rdn over 2f out: hung lft over 1f out: no imp* **66/1**

000- **7** *4* **Joss Stick**[176] 7240 5-8-4 **52** DavidProbert 4 29
(B R Johnson) *in tch: rdn over 2f out: wknd over 1f out* **11/2**

62.42 secs (0.12) **Going Correction** -0.025s/f (Good) **7** Ran SP% **110.8**
Speed ratings (Par 103): **98,97,95,92,92 90,83**
toteswingers: 1&2 £3.10, 1&3 £2.90, 2&3 £3.10 CSF £40.30 TOTE £4.00: £1.60, £3.30; EX 41.20 Place 6: £107.22, Place 5: £52.12..
Owner Charlie's Starrs **Bred** Darley **Trained** Hammerwood, E Sussex

FOCUS
A modest sprint handicap and ordinary form. They raced up the middle of the track in the closing stages.
T/Jkpt: Not won. T/Plt: £82.40 to a £1 stake. Pool: £62,544.77. 553.80 winning tickets. T/Qpdt: £13.90 to a £1 stake. Pool: £7,127.67. 378.10 winning tickets. LM

1442 FOLKESTONE (R-H)
Thursday, April 29

OFFICIAL GOING: Good to firm (8.8)
Wind: Virtually nil Weather: Light cloud

1639 HYTHE MAIDEN STKS 5f
2:10 (2:10) (Class 5) 3-Y-O+ **£2,729** (£806; £403) **Stalls** Low

Form RPR

4622 **1** **Diamond Johnny G (USA)**[2] 1599 3-9-0 75 (t) EddieCreighton 1 71
(E J Creighton) *chsd ldng trio: rdn and effrt over 1f out: chal ins fnl f: led wl ins fnl f: pushed out* **5/2**[1]

6365 **2** *hd* **Fine Silk (USA)**[52] 828 4-9-5 65 (p) JerryO'Dwyer 3 69
(M G Quinlan) *led: rdn 2f out: edgd lft u.p over 1f out: kpt on u.p tl hdd and no ex wl ins fnl f* **10/1**

6 **3** *3 ½* **Crazy Parachute**[19] 1222 3-9-0 0 GeorgeBaker 4 58+
(G L Moore) *stdd s: hld up in last pair: shkn up and effrt 2f out: nt clr run on stands' rail over 1f out: hdwy 1f out: styd on to go 3rd nr fin: nvr trbld ldrs* **5/2**[1]

02-0 **4** *nk* **Itwasonlyakiss (IRE)**[10] 1425 3-8-9 75 MichaelHills 7 52
(J W Hills) *chsd ldrs on outer: ev ch but wanting to hang rt fnl 2f: wknd fnl 100yds* **7/2**[2]

0- **5** *1 ½* **Lady Of Garmoran (USA)**[199] 6730 3-8-9 0 RichardHughes 6 46
(P F I Cole) *s.i.s: racd in last pair: rdn and unable qck 2f out: plugged on same pce after* **8/1**

4224 **6** *nk* **Papageno**[5] 1535 3-9-0 63 KierenFallon 2 50
(J R Jenkins) *racd keenly: pressed ldr: shkn up and edgd rt wl over 1f out: hmpd over 1f out: rdn and wknd ent fnl f* **7/1**[3]

60.21 secs (0.21) **Going Correction** -0.025s/f (Good)
WFA 3 from 4yo 10lb **6** Ran SP% **112.1**
Speed ratings (Par 103): **97,96,91,90,88 87**
toteswingers: 1&2 £4.30, 1&3 £2.50, 2&3 £7.70 CSF £27.08 TOTE £3.90: £2.20, £4.90; EX 26.20.
Owner John Griffin Owen Mullen **Bred** B & B Thoroughbreds Llc **Trained** Wormshill, Kent

FOCUS
The going was described as good to firm for this modest maiden, with the ceiling of those that have earned a mark being a questionable 75, but the pace was a brisk one. There were doubts over most of these and the form is rated around the runner-up.
Papageno Official explanation: jockey said colt lost its action

1640 FREE RACING POST FORM AT TOTESPORT.COM FILLIES' H'CAP 6f
2:40 (2:43) (Class 5) (0-70,71) 3-Y-O **£3,070** (£906; £453) **Stalls** Low

Form RPR

6-11 **1** **Catherines Call (IRE)**[6] 1505 3-9-6 **71** 6ex ShaneKelly 2 75+
(D Donovan) *hld up in last pair: trckd rival through on stands' rail over 1f out: chsd ldr and swtchd rt 1f out: pushed along and qcknd to ld wl ins fnl f: comf* **9/2**[2]

3310 **2** *¾* **Caramelita**[13] 1347 3-9-3 **68** KierenFallon 1 70
(J R Jenkins) *awkward leaving stalls: t.k.h: hld up in tch: hdwy on stands' rail 2f out: rdn to ld 2f over 1f out: hdd and one pce wl ins fnl f* **9/2**[2]

60-5 **3** *2 ½* **Mellifera**[29] 1058 3-9-4 **69** AdamKirby 6 63
(W R Swinburn) *chsd ldrs: rdn and outpcd and n.m.r wl over 1f out: rallied u.p into 3rd fnl 75yds: nt pce to trble ldrs* **5/1**[3]

20-3 **4** *1 ¾* **Katy's Secret**[19] 1222 3-9-2 **67** FrankieDettori 3 55+
(W Jarvis) *stdd s: t.k.h: hld up in tch: rdn and hdwy ent fnl 2f: rdn to chse ldrs over 1f out: wknd ins fnl f* **5/2**[1]

236- **5** ¾ **Gundaroo**[246] 5344 3-9-4 **69** EddieAhern 9 55+
(J L Dunlop) *bhd: effrt whn short of room over 1f out: sn rdn: no prog and wl hld fnl f* **9/1**

-331 **6** 3 **Posy Fossil (USA)**[60] 745 3-8-11 **65** (t) WilliamCarson(3) 5 41
(S C Williams) *w ldr: led after 2f: edging rt off of stands' rail 2f out: sn rdn: hdd over 1f out: sn wknd* **9/1**

005- **7** 2 **Rosiliant (IRE)**[185] 7056 3-8-4 **55** (b) LukeMorris 8 25
(C G Cox) *s.i.s: t.k.h: sn rcvrd and chsd ldrs after 1f: wknd qckly u.p wl over 1f out* **14/1**

55-3 **8** 5 **Show Willing (IRE)**[22] 1162 3-8-4 **60** MatthewDavies(5) 7 14
(A P Jarvis) *got loose and galloped solo to s: racd freely: led for 2f: styd prom tl wknd qckly 2f out: wl bhd fnl f* **16/1**

1m 13.28s (0.58) **Going Correction** -0.025s/f (Good) **8** Ran SP% **114.2**
Speed ratings (Par 95): **95,94,90,88,87 83,80,74**
toteswingers: 1&2 £4.40, 1&3 £4.60, 2&3 £4.90 CSF £24.93 CT £104.79 TOTE £4.70: £1.50, £1.90, £1.50; EX 27.90 Trifecta £181.30 Pool: £448.41 - 1.83 winning units..
Owner Philip Mclaughlin **Bred** K Maginn **Trained** Newmarket, Suffolk

FOCUS
A competitive fillies' handicap run at a decent pace. Modest form, but another improved effort from the winner.
Gundaroo Official explanation: jockey said filly was unsuited by the good to firm ground

1641 BEST ODDS GUARANTEED AT TOTESPORT.COM H'CAP 6f
3:10 (3:11) (Class 5) (0-75,73) 4-Y-0+ **£3,070** (£906; £453) **Stalls** Low

Form RPR
1616 **1** **Beat The Bell**[5] 1516 5-8-13 **73** SophieDoyle(5) 3 85
(J A Osborne) *racd keenly: chsd ldr for 2f: styd handy: nt clr run 2f out: hdwy between horses over 1f out: pushed into ld 1f out: r.o wl* **5/4**[1]

6611 **2** 1 ¼ **Cornus**[8] 1470 8-8-4 **64** (be) DeclanCannon(5) 5 72+
(A J McCabe) *taken down early: hmpd s: hld up in tch: n.m.r wl over 1f out: rdn and hdwy to chse ldng pair 1f out: wnt 2nd u.p fnl 100yds: kpt on but nvr gng pce to rch wnr* **6/1**[3]

00-2 **3** 1 ¾ **For Life (IRE)**[31] 1044 8-9-0 **72** NataliaGemelova(3) 2 74
(J E Long) *taken down early: led: hdd over 1f out: rdn and nt pce of wnr 1f out: one pce fnl f* **7/1**

-435 **4** 2 ¾ **Another Try (IRE)**[57] 767 5-8-5 **65** MatthewDavies(5) 1 58+
(A P Jarvis) *in tch on stands' rail: nt clr run over 1f out: swtchd rt and rdn 1f out: no imp after* **4/1**[2]

300- **5** 2 ¼ **Darcey**[181] 7149 4-9-3 **72** JerryO'Dwyer 7 58
(Miss Amy Weaver) *bhd: hdwy and nt clr run wl over 1f out: sn swtchd rt and rdn: wknd 1f out* **33/1**

3120 **6** 3 **Fazbee (IRE)**[52] 828 4-9-1 **70** DarryllHolland 4 46
(P W D'Arcy) *wnt rt s: sn bustled along and chsd ldr after 2f: rdn wl over 1f out: wknd qckly ent fnl f* **8/1**

1300 **7** 12 **White Shift (IRE)**[10] 1428 4-9-1 **70** KierenFallon 6 37
(P Howling) *in tch: rdn and effrt to press ldrs wl over 1f out: btn ent fnl f: heavily eased fnl 150yds* **20/1**

1m 12.09s (-0.61) **Going Correction** -0.025s/f (Good) **7** Ran SP% **110.0**
Speed ratings (Par 103): **103,101,99,95,92 88,72**
toteswingers: 1&2 £2.30, 1&3 £2.90, 2&3 £3.50 CSF £8.43 TOTE £1.70: £1.10, £2.30; EX 7.40.
Owner D J P Turner **Bred** D J P Turner **Trained** Upper Lambourn, Berks
■ Stewards' Enquiry : Natalia Gemelova caution: careless riding.

FOCUS
An interesting 61-75 handicap run at a fair pace with a couple looking ahead of the handicapper, and they duly filled the first two places. The form is rated around the third.
Another Try(IRE) Official explanation: jockey said gelding was denied a clear run
White Shift(IRE) Official explanation: trainer said filly finished distressed

1642 MORE LIVE FOOTBALL BETTING AT TOTESPORT.COM (S) STKS 6f
3:40 (3:42) (Class 6) 3-Y-0+ **£2,047** (£604; £302) **Stalls** Low

Form RPR
4125 **1** **Lastkingofscotland (IRE)**[19] 1224 4-9-12 69 (b) RichardHughes 4 76
(Jim Best) *racd in midfield: hdwy over 2f out: rdn to ld over 1f out: r.o strly and wl clr fnl 150yds: eased towards fin* **5/4**[1]

-360 **2** 3 ¾ **Bold Ring**[38] 961 4-9-1 55 EddieCreighton 2 52
(E J Creighton) *towards rr: pushed along 1/2-way: hdwy on outer over 2f out: chsd wnr over 1f out: wl btn ins fnl f: kpt on* **15/2**[3]

3351 **3** 1 **Anjomarba (IRE)**[9] 1444 3-8-7 66 (p) JackDean(3) 6 52
(W G M Turner) *led: rdn ent fnl 2f: hdd over 1f out: no ch w wnr ins fnl f* **4/1**[2]

0023 **4** ¾ **Dream Express (IRE)**[38] 961 5-9-6 56 DarryllHolland 8 51
(P Howling) *wnt rt s: bhd: pushed along and racd awkwardly fr 1/2-way: hdwy into modest 4th ent fnl f: n.d* **15/2**[3]

4010 **5** 3 ¼ **Equinity**[22] 1166 4-9-2 58 (t) SimonPearce(5) 3 42
(J Pearce) *taken down early: racd keenly: chsd ldrs tl edgd rt and wknd qckly u.p over 1f out* **10/1**

0-00 **6** ½ **Crystal B Good (USA)**[65] 674 4-9-1 54 SebSanders 1 34
(J R Best) *chsd ldrs: pushed along 1/2-way: struggling over 2f: out: wl btn fnl 2f* **33/1**

-336 **7** 11 **Irish Music (IRE)**[42] 914 5-9-1 55 (v[1]) MatthewDavies(5) 7 4
(A P Jarvis) *chsd ldr tl 2f out: wknd rapidly wl over 1f out: wl bhd fnl f* **12/1**

/000 **8** 24 **Savanna's Gold**[34] 986 6-8-8 34 RichardRowe(7) 5 —
(R Rowe) *v.s.a: a detached in last: t.o and heavily eased fnl f* **100/1**

1m 13.1s (0.40) **Going Correction** -0.025s/f (Good)
WFA 3 from 4yo+ 11lb **8** Ran SP% **108.7**
Speed ratings (Par 101): **96,91,89,88,84 83,69,37**
toteswingers: 1&2 £3.10, 1&3 £2.30, 2&3 £4.00 CSF £10.03 TOTE £2.20: £1.90, £2.90, £1.10; EX 11.10 Trifecta £108.50 Pool: £435.79 - 2.97 winning units..The winner was bought in for £8,000.
Owner M & R Refurbishments Ltd **Bred** Baronrath Stud **Trained** Lewes, E Sussex

FOCUS
A modest seller run at just a fair pace. There were doubts over most but the winner showed improved form.
Dream Express(IRE) Official explanation: jockey said gelding hung right throughout

1643 BET LIVE IN-PLAY AT TOTESPORT.COM H'CAP 7f (S)
4:10 (4:12) (Class 6) (0-60,60) 3-Y-0 **£2,047** (£604; £302) **Stalls** Low

Form RPR
006- **1** **Cool Kitten (IRE)**[196] 6786 3-8-11 **53** WilliamBuick 5 58+
(W J Knight) *racd stands' side: chsd ldrs tl rdn and lost pl 1/2-way: rallied u.p over 1f out: drvn and r.o wl fnl 100yds: led on post* **9/2**[2]

00-1 **2** shd **Decency (IRE)**[22] 1163 3-9-2 **58** KierenFallon 1 63
(E A L Dunlop) *taken down early: racd stands' side: chsd ldrs: ev ch and rdn over 2f out: led narrowly over 1f out: kpt on u.p tl hdd on post: 2nd of 7 in gp* **9/4**[1]

5-60 **3** hd **Chinese Democracy (USA)**[9] 1437 3-8-12 **54** RichardHughes 8 58
(P F I Cole) *racd stands' side: chsd ldr: rdn to ld narrowly over 2f out: hdd over 1f out: ev ch after: no ex nr fin: 3rd of 7 in gp* **10/1**

0-61 **4** ¾ **Motty's Gift**[22] 1162 3-8-13 **55** (v) ShaneKelly 7 57
(W R Swinburn) *racd stands' side: sltly hmpd s: in tch: rdn over 2f out: hdwy and swtchd rt 1f out: pressed ldrs ins fnl f: no ex fnl 75yds: 4th of 7 in gp* **12/1**

000- **5** 2 ¼ **Azaday (IRE)**[188] 6992 3-9-2 **58** EddieAhern 3 54+
(C F Wall) *racd stands' side: hld up towards rr: hdwy over 2f out: chsng ldrs but drvn whn carried rt 1f out: no imp ins fnl f: 5th of 7 in gp* **13/2**

-205 **6** 2 ¼ **Singingintherain (IRE)**[76] 519 3-9-4 **60** MichaelHills 11 50
(R A Mills) *swtchd to r far side: led that gp and prom overall: rdn 2f out: wknd 1f out and wl btn fnl 100yds: 1st of 3 in gp* **14/1**

0-00 **7** ¾ **Denton Ryal**[24] 1127 3-8-13 **55** (t) JamieMackay 2 43
(M E Rimmer) *racd stands' side: bhd: hung rt and no prog ent fnl 2f: nvr trbld ldrs: 6th of 7 in gp* **25/1**

2533 **8** 1 ¼ **Tamarind Hill (IRE)**[8] 1469 3-8-10 **57** (b) DeclanCannon(5) 6 42
(A J McCabe) *racd stands' side: led: rdn and hdd over 2f out: sn wknd: wl btn over 1f out: 7th of 7 in gp* **12/1**

0-54 **9** ¾ **Tregony Bridge**[22] 1162 3-8-8 **50** FergusSweeney 9 33
(M Blanshard) *swtchd to r far side: t.k.h: chsd far side ldr: rdn and hung lft ent fnl 2f: no ch fr over 1f out: 2nd of 3 in gp* **6/1**[3]

0-60 **10** 5 **Stay On Track (IRE)**[22] 1165 3-9-2 **58** SebSanders 10 27
(E F Vaughan) *swtchd to r far side: hld up in last of that gp: rdn and no prog 2f out: wl btn over 1f out: 3rd of 3 in gp* **33/1**

1m 27.2s (-0.10) **Going Correction** -0.025s/f (Good) **10** Ran SP% **114.5**
Speed ratings (Par 96): **99,98,98,97,95 92,91,90,89,83**
toteswingers: 1&2 £4.20, 1&3 £9.60, 2&3 £8.10 CSF £14.68 CT £96.63 TOTE £5.90: £2.00, £1.50, £3.50; EX 15.50 Trifecta £244.60 Pool: £386.88 - 1.17 winning units..
Owner G Roddick **Bred** David Jamison Bloodstock **Trained** Patching, W Sussex

FOCUS
Three tacked over to the far rail (Tregony Bridge, Singingintherain and Stay On Track), while the majority raced up the favoured stands' side, and it was that group who came to the fore well over a furlong out. The race was run at a good pace and it was a battle of heads inside the final furlong. The form looks sound rated around the fourth, with the first two improvers.
Cool Kitten(IRE) Official explanation: trainer said, regarding apparent improvement in form, that the filly had matured and strenghtened over the winter.
Tamarind Hill(IRE) Official explanation: jockey said gelding hung badly right throughout

1644 BET TOTEPOOL AT TOTESPORT.COM MEDIAN AUCTION MAIDEN STKS 1m 1f 149y
4:40 (4:40) (Class 6) 3-4-Y-0 **£2,729** (£806; £403) **Stalls** Centre

Form RPR
003- **1** **Round Won (USA)**[202] 6629 3-8-10 73 ShaneKelly 3 74
(W J Knight) *mde all: rdn ent fnl 2f: in command over 1f out: styd on wl: comf* **5/2**[2]

2 3 ½ **Storming Redd** 3-8-10 0 SebSanders 4 67
(J M P Eustace) *dwlt: chsd ldng pair: rdn over 2f out: chsd wnr over 1f out: no imp and readily hld fnl f* **11/1**[3]

00-3 **3** 2 ¾ **Swish Dish (CAN)**[13] 1356 3-8-6 73 ow1 RichardHughes 2 57
(R Hannon) *chsd wnr: rdn and fnd little bnd jst over 2f out: nt look happy after and lost 2nd wl over 1f out: no ch fnl f* **8/15**[1]

4 nk **Well Overdue (IRE)** 4-9-8 0 SophieDoyle(5) 1 63?
(J A Osborne) *stdd s: t.k.h: hld up in last: sltly outpcd 4f out: clsd again over 2f out: no prog whn rdn 2f out* **25/1**

2m 9.74s (4.84) **Going Correction** +0.575s/f (Yiel)
WFA 3 from 4yo 17lb **4** Ran SP% **106.0**
Speed ratings (Par 101): **103,100,98,97**
CSF £20.71 TOTE £5.90; EX 17.80.
Owner Bluehills Racing Limited **Bred** Dr & Mrs Thomas Bowman & Rebecca Davis **Trained** Patching, W Sussex

FOCUS
Only a small field for this modest auction maiden with two of the four making their racecourse debuts. It was run at a steady pace until things quickened up entering the final bend. The winner didn't run her race and it's hard to know how much the winner improved.
Swish Dish(CAN) Official explanation: jockey said filly moved poorly

1645 BET TOTEPOOL ON 0800 221221 H'CAP 1m 1f 149y
5:10 (5:10) (Class 4) (0-80,79) 4-Y-0+ **£4,857** (£1,445; £722; £360) **Stalls** Centre

Form RPR
250- **1** **Addwaitya**[141] 7684 5-9-3 **78** FergusSweeney 5 86
(Mrs L J Mongan) *chsd ldr: chal over 2f out: rdn to ld wl over 1f out: clr ent fnl f: kpt on wl: eased towards fin* **7/2**[2]

5-02 **2** 1 ½ **Diamond Twister (USA)**[19] 1225 4-8-4 **65** (t) TadhgO'Shea 3 69
(J R Best) *led: jnd and rdn over 2f out: hdd wl over 1f out: one pce and a hld by wnr after* **7/2**[2]

5643 **3** 1 ½ **Follow The Flag (IRE)**[40] 943 6-8-12 **78** (p) DeclanCannon(5) 1 79
(A J McCabe) *hld up in tch: rdn wl over 2f out: one pce and btn over 1f out* **9/2**[3]

2141 **4** 10 **Charlie Smirke (USA)**[31] 1047 4-8-9 **70** RichardHughes 4 67
(G L Moore) *hld up in tch: effrt and rdn 2f out: no real prog and btn 1f out: eased ins fnl f* **11/10**[1]

2m 9.28s (4.38) **Going Correction** +0.575s/f (Yiel) **4** Ran SP% **110.2**
Speed ratings (Par 105): **105,103,102,94**
CSF £15.00 TOTE £4.90; EX 10.70 Place 6: £48.47, Place 5: £18.80..
Owner Mrs P J Sheen **Bred** L McLaughlin **Trained** Epsom, Surrey

FOCUS
Another small field for this modest 66-80 handicap and another upset with the well-fancied Charlie Smirke being well beaten. Muddling form, rated a round the runner-up.
Charlie Smirke(USA) Official explanation: trainer said gelding had a breathing problem

T/Plt: £78.30 to a £1 stake. Pool: £57,297.12. 533.97 winning tickets. T/Qpdt: £16.80 to a £1 stake. Pool: £4,063.80. 178.78 winning tickets. SP

1112 REDCAR (L-H)

Thursday, April 29

OFFICIAL GOING: Good to firm (firm in places; 9.4)

Wind: Light across Weather: Cloudy with sunny periods

1646 WIN A VIP DAY OUT @ REDCARRACING.CO.UK MAIDEN AUCTION STKS 5f

2:00 (2:02) (Class 5) 2-Y-O **£2,396** (£712; £356; £177) **Stalls** Centre

Form RPR

0 **1** **Misty Morn**[13] 1359 2-8-4 0 GrahamGibbons 1 64
(A D Brown) *mde all: rdn along wl over 1f out: kpt on ins fnl f: hld on wl towards fin* **9/2**[2]

3 **2** *hd* **Saltergate**[15] 1292 2-8-9 0 AndrewElliott 2 68
(N Tinkler) *prom: hmpd 1/2-way and sn swtchd rt: rdn over 1f out: drvn to chse wnr ins fnl f: styd on: jst failed* **5/1**[3]

3 **3** *1 3/4* **Bachelor Knight (IRE)**[14] 1331 2-8-9 0 PaulHanagan 3 62
(R A Fahey) *wnt rt s: cl up: hung lft 1/2-way: rdn and ev ch over 1f out: sn edgd lft and one pce fnl f* **1/1**[1]

4 *2 1/4* **Puddle Duck** 2-8-12 0 JamieSpencer 5 59+
(K A Ryan) *sltly hmpd s and sn swtchd lft: trckd ldrs: hdwy 1/2-way: rdn and ch wl over 1f out: sn edgd lft and wknd* **7/1**

5 **5** *4 1/2* **Ever Roses**[12] 1375 2-7-13 0 PaulPickard(5) 6 32
(P T Midgley) *in tch: swtchd lft 2f out and sn rdn along: no imp* **7/1**

6 *9* **Upark Flyer** 2-8-0 0 ow1 BillyCray(5) 4 —
(Patrick Morris) *s.i.s and a bhd* **40/1**

59.01 secs (0.41) **Going Correction** -0.075s/f (Good) 6 Ran SP% **112.3**

Speed ratings (Par 92): **93,92,89,86,79 64**

toteswingers: 1&2 £3.00, 1&3 £1.40, 2&3 £1.70 CSF £26.51 TOTE £5.60: £2.30, £2.30; EX 26.10.

Owner B Selective Partnership **Bred** P A Mason **Trained** Yedingham, N Yorks

FOCUS

An ordinary maiden auction event. The time was slower than the seller and this is limited form.

NOTEBOOK

Misty Morn, who showed speed on her debut in a novice event at Thirsk, was well supported. She trapped smartly and had her rivals at full stretch throughout. In the end she did just enough, and is clearly all speed. (op 8-1)

Saltergate, third first time at Beverley, had to be checked after a couple of furlongs. Staying on under the stands' rail, he needed two more strides. Less firm ground and a slightly stiffer track will aid his cause.

Bachelor Knight(IRE), who is not very big, finished third first time in what looked a better race than this at Ripon. He was awkward to load and swerved leaving the stalls. Soon flat out, he lacked the pace to make a sustained challenge in the final furlong. An extra furlong and less quick ground will be in his favour. (op 5-4 tchd 11-8 in a place)

Puddle Duck, very inexperienced beforehand, went well for much of the trip and was given as easy a time as possible in the closing stages. This will have taught him plenty. (op 10-3)

Ever Roses hung badly left and dropped away as if feeling the ground. (op 17-2 tchd 9-1)

Upark Flyer lost many lengths at the start and could never go the pace. (op 66-1 tchd 33-1)

1647 RACING UK CHANNEL 432 (S) STKS 5f

2:30 (2:30) (Class 6) 2-Y-O **£1,842** (£544; £272) **Stalls** Centre

Form RPR

10 **1** **Novabridge**[13] 1359 2-9-3 0 JamieSpencer 6 70
(A B Haynes) *cl up: pushed along 1/2-way: rdn to ld wl over 1f out and sn edgd lft: clr whn hung lft ins fnl f: kpt on* **11/4**[2]

1 **2** *4* **Tanked Up (IRE)**[8] 1463 2-9-3 0 AdrianNicholls 4 56
(D Nicholls) *led: rdn along over 2f out: hdd and drvn wl over 1f out: kpt on same pce fnl f* **4/7**[1]

5 **3** *1 3/4* **Look'N'Listen (IRE)**[13] 1360 2-8-7 0 GrahamGibbons 2 39
(A D Brown) *cl up: rdn along 1/2-way: sn edgd lft: drvn over 1f out: rdr dropped whip and sn one pce* **11/2**[3]

0 **4** *3* **Rath Maeve**[13] 1360 2-8-7 0 JamesDoyle 3 29
(A J McCabe) *sn rdn along in rr: outpcd fr 1/2-way* **40/1**

58.55 secs (-0.05) **Going Correction** -0.075s/f (Good) 4 Ran SP% **108.1**

Speed ratings (Par 90): **97,90,87,83**

CSF £4.80 TOTE £2.70; EX 4.80.The winner was bought in for £16,500.

Owner Dajam Ltd **Bred** Bishopswood Bloodstock & Trickledown Stud **Trained** Limpley Stoke, Bath

FOCUS

Only a selling race but the time was nearly half a second quicker than the opener and the winner was carrying nearly a stone more. Agood standard for the grade with the first two better than average platers.

NOTEBOOK

Novabridge, a decent sort, had made all when a clear-cut winner on heavy ground at Folkestone first time. He never figured and finished tailed off on fast ground in a novice event at Thirsk next time. Dropped markedly in class, Jamie Spencer was at his most determined, giving him a couple of sharp reminders at the halfway mark. In the end he readily mastered the pacesetter Tanked Up and not surprisingly he attracted plenty of interest at the auction, but he was eventually retained. (op 9-4 tchd 3-1)

Tanked Up(IRE), who took a seller on his debut at Catterick, took them along but in the end was completely overpowered by the winner. (op 8-13)

Look'N'Listen(IRE), slowly away in a claimer first time, was very keen. She hung left and her rider dropped his stick soon after the halfway mark. She does not look entirely straightforward but may need less quick ground. (op 7-1 tchd 5-1)

Rath Maeve, a couple of lengths and two places behind Look'N'Listen on her debut at Thirsk, was soon flat out in last and could never take a hand.

1648 BECOME AN ANNUAL BADGE HOLDER TODAY MEDIAN AUCTION MAIDEN STKS 7f

3:00 (3:01) (Class 5) 3-Y-O **£2,396** (£712; £356; £177) **Stalls** Centre

Form RPR

2- **1** **Always Dazzling**[290] 3910 3-8-12 0 JoeFanning 8 66+
(M Johnston) *led early: cl up tl led again over 4f out: pushed along over 2f out: rdn wl over 1f out: kpt on fnl f* **15/8**[2]

0-5 **2** *1 3/4* **Red Scintilla**[12] 1402 3-8-12 0 AndrewElliott 9 61
(N Tinkler) *wnt lft s: towards rr: hdwy 3f out: rdn to chse ldng pair over 1f out: hung lft ins fnl f: tk 2nd nr fin* **8/1**[3]

0 **3** *nse* **Forks**[14] 1335 3-9-3 0 TomEaves 1 66
(B Smart) *in tch: hdwy 3f out: rdn to chse wnr over 1f out: drvn and one pce fnl f* **16/1**

0 **4** *7* **Director General (USA)**[14] 1336 3-9-0 0 BarryMcHugh(3) 6 47
(Julie Camacho) *in tch: hdwy to chse ldrs over 2f out: sn rdn: edgd lft and no imp over 1f out* **14/1**

5 *3/4* **Where's Denton** 3-9-3 0 PhillipMakin 7 45
(M Dods) *s.i.s: a towards rr* **9/1**

605- **6** *6* **Mr Prize Fighter**[216] 6246 3-9-3 50 DanielTudhope 2 29
(I W McInnes) *cl up on outer: effrt over 2f out: sn rdn and wknd wl over 1f out* **20/1**

4 **7** *8* **Elle Est**[14] 1335 3-8-12 0 DavidAllan 3 —
(E J Alston) *cl up: effrt 1/2-way: rdn along wl over 2f out and sn wknd* **13/8**[1]

0-0 **8** *11* **Velle Est Valere**[12] 1401 3-8-9 0 ow2 LanceBetts(5) 5 —
(C J Teague) *sn led: pushed along and hdd over 4f out: sn rdn and lost pl: bhd fnl 3f* **100/1**

1m 24.63s (0.13) **Going Correction** -0.075s/f (Good) 8 Ran SP% **112.3**

Speed ratings (Par 98): **96,94,93,85,85 78,69,56**

toteswingers: 1&2 £2.30, 1&3 £7.20, 2&3 £13.60 CSF £16.74 TOTE £2.90: £1.20, £1.20, £4.90; EX 8.70.

Owner Always Trying Partnership VII **Bred** Aston Mullins Stud & Knockainey Stud **Trained** Middleham Moor, N Yorks

FOCUS

A very ordinary median auction maiden race. With the favourite disappointing the winner had little to beat on paper. The form is rated around the front pair.

Elle Est Official explanation: jockey said filly was unsuited by the good to firm (firm in places) ground

Velle Est Valere Official explanation: trainer said filly was in season

1649 JOHN SMITH'S REDCAR STRAIGHT-MILE CHAMPIONSHIP STKS (H'CAP) (QUALIFIER) 1m

3:30 (3:30) (Class 5) (0-75,75) 3-Y-O **£2,396** (£712; £356; £177) **Stalls** Centre

Form RPR

003- **1** **Caldercruix (USA)**[188] 6990 3-9-0 **71** JamieSpencer 1 84+
(T P Tate) *mde all: pushed along 1/2-way: rdn 3f out: styd on strly appr fnl f* **11/4**[2]

1 **2** *2* **Don't Call Me (IRE)**[42] 915 3-9-3 **74** (t) RichardMullen 2 82
(B Smart) *trckd ldrs: hdwy 3f out: rdn to chse wnr wl over 1f out: drvn and no imp fnl f* **9/2**[3]

4-0 **3** *4* **Refuse To Wait (IRE)**[15] 1298 3-8-7 **64** DavidAllan 4 63
(T D Easterby) *hld up: hdwy 1/2-way: chsd wnr 3f out: rdn over 2f out: drvn wl over 1f out and sn one pce* **12/1**

25-2 **4** *nk* **Logos Astra (USA)**[8] 1476 3-9-4 **75** TedDurcan 3 73
(D R Lanigan) *trckd ldrs: effrt 3f out: rdn along over 2f out: sn drvn and btn wl over 1f out* **1/1**[1]

6-04 **5** *11* **Battle Study (IRE)**[13] 1362 3-8-7 **64** JamesDoyle 5 37
(A J McCabe) *cl up: pushed along over 4f out: rdn over 3f out and sn wknd* **9/1**

1m 36.92s (-1.08) **Going Correction** -0.075s/f (Good) 5 Ran SP% **112.5**

Speed ratings (Par 98): **102,100,96,95,84**

CSF £15.27 TOTE £3.00: £1.10, £1.80; EX 15.90.

Owner Mrs Fitri Hay **Bred** Bjorn Nielsen **Trained** Tadcaster, N Yorks

FOCUS

An interesting 64-75 3-y-o handicap. Considering the pace was very steady to the halfway mark the winning time was surprisingly quick, and this was a decent little race for the grade. A positive view has been taken of the first pair.

1650 BOOK TICKETS ONLINE @ REDCARRACING.CO.UK H'CAP 6f

4:00 (4:00) (Class 4) (0-85,80) 3-Y-O+ **£4,209** (£1,252; £625; £312) **Stalls** Centre

Form RPR

30-1 **1** **Tangerine Trees**[16] 1270 5-9-6 74 TomEaves 1 82+
(B Smart) *prom: hdwy 1/2-way: led 2f out: rdn ent fnl f: kpt on wl towards fin* **6/1**[2]

6345 **2** *nk* **Bonnie Prince Blue**[13] 1366 7-9-7 75 (b) AdrianNicholls 6 82
(D Nicholls) *towards rr: hdwy over 2f out: swtchd lft and rdn over 1f out: drvn and ch ins fnl f: kpt on* **7/1**[3]

00-5 **3** *nk* **Floor Show**[25] 1102 4-9-9 80 GaryBartley(3) 10 86
(N Wilson) *towards rr: hdwy 2f out: swtchd lft and rdn over 1f out: kpt on wl fnl f* **7/1**[3]

00-0 **4** *3 1/4* **Maze (IRE)**[14] 1332 5-9-2 75 MichaelO'Connell(5) 4 71
(D Nicholls) *prom: rdn along over 2f out: kpt on same pce appr fnl f* **10/1**

00-4 **5** *1/2* **Favourite Girl (IRE)**[14] 1332 4-9-10 78 DavidAllan 9 72
(T D Easterby) *trckd ldrs: effrt over 2f out: sn rdn and kpt on same pce* **4/1**[1]

5/-0 **6** *3/4* **Haigh Hall**[25] 1099 4-9-10 78 PaulHanagan 3 70
(R A Fahey) *cl up: effrt 2f out and ev ch: sn rdn and wknd ent fnl f* **6/1**[2]

65-0 **7** *1* **Solar Spirit (IRE)**[25] 1099 5-9-6 79 IanBrennan(5) 8 67
(J J Quinn) *cl up: rdn along 1/2-way: grad wknd* **7/1**[3]

150- **8** *1 3/4* **Who's Shirl**[214] 6309 4-8-11 68 KellyHarrison(3) 5 51
(C W Fairhurst) *in tch: rdn along over 2f out and sn wknd* **16/1**

0603 **9** *nk* **Methaaly (IRE)**[13] 1365 7-9-6 74 (be) TedDurcan 11 56
(M Mullineaux) *s.i.s: a in rr* **10/1**

-630 **10** *2 3/4* **Klynch**[21] 1192 4-9-7 75 (b) AndrewElliott 2 48
(Mrs R A Carr) *s.i.s: a in rr* **12/1**

020- **11** *1 1/2* **Bravely (IRE)**[183] 7123 6-9-7 75 DuranFentiman 7 43
(T D Easterby) *led: rdn along 1/2-way: drvn and hdd 2f out: sn wknd* **33/1**

1m 10.59s (-1.21) **Going Correction** -0.075s/f (Good) 11 Ran SP% **116.0**

Speed ratings (Par 105): **105,104,104,99,99 98,96,94,94,90 88**

toteswingers: 1&2 £4.70, 1&3 £9.60, 2&3 £9.40 CSF £47.00 CT £302.88 TOTE £5.90: £2.10, £2.90, £3.50; EX 42.00.

Owner Tangerine Trees Partnership **Bred** Mrs B A Matthews **Trained** Hambleton, N Yorks

FOCUS

A highly competitive 68-80 sprint handicap. The winner built on his Pontefract win with the next two to form and the first three clear.

Haigh Hall Official explanation: jockey said filly finished distressed

1651 REDCAR CONFERENCE AND EXHIBITION CENTRE APPRENTICE CLAIMING STKS 6f

4:30 (4:31) (Class 6) 3-4-Y-O **£1,842** (£544; £272) **Stalls** Centre

Form RPR

00-4 **1** **Whispered Times (USA)**[24] 1118 3-8-13 58 KellyHarrison 2 69
(Miss Tracy Waggott) *led: rdn along and hdd over 1f out: rallied u.p to ld again ins fnl f: edgd lft and kpt on gamely* **12/1**[3]

0126 **2** *1* **Lord Fidelio (IRE)**[50] 851 4-9-6 75 LeeTopliss(4) 1 69
(Ollie Pears) *trckd ldrs: hdwy 1/2-way: rdn to ld over 1f out: drvn and hdd ins fnl f: one pce* **7/4**[1]

16-0 **3** *2 1/4* **Angel Of Fashion (IRE)**[12] 1399 3-8-12 75 MichaelGeran 8 58
(D Nicholls) *sltly hmpd s: sn prom: effrt over 2f out: sn rdn and ev ch tl drvn and one pce ent fnl f* **7/4**[1]

4150 **4** *hd* **Lockantanks**[8] 1480 3-8-9 78 JohnFahy(4) 9 58
(A B Haynes) *trckd ldrs on outer: hdwy over 2f out: rdn and ch wl over 1f out: wknd ent fnl f* **4/1**[2]

400- 5 8 **Cool Art (IRE)**[188] 6989 4-9-6 55 .... AmyRyan(2) 5 34
(J S Wainwright) *t.k.h early: trckd ldrs: effrt over 2f out: sn rdn and btn* **25/1**

00-0 6 1 3/4 **Star Cruiser (USA)**[14] 1335 3-8-11 55 .... (b1) LanceBetts(2) 7 27
(T D Easterby) *sltly hmpd s: in tch: rdn along over 2f out and sn wknd* **25/1**

060- 7 1 1/2 **Cygnet Committee (IRE)**[184] 7098 3-8-2 52 .... (v1) JamesSullivan(2) 6 13
(J S Wainwright) *wnt rt s: a in rr* **25/1**

000- 8 shd **Dispol Kabira**[185] 7056 3-8-2 47 ow4 .... DuilioDaSilva(4) 3 15
(D W Thompson) *a in rr* **40/1**

1m 11.44s (-0.36) **Going Correction** -0.075s/f (Good)
WFA 3 from 4yo 11lb 8 Ran SP% **114.4**
Speed ratings (Par 101): **99,97,94,94,83 81,79,79**
toteswingers: 1&2 £3.90, 1&3 £3.90, 2&3 £1.50 CSF £32.50 TOTE £11.50: £2.60, £2.20, £1.10; EX 30.30.
Owner Michael Howarth **Bred** Hetrich-McCarthy Livestock **Trained** Spennymoor, Co Durham

FOCUS
A claimer with three 75-rated horses rated at least 17lb ahead of the remainder, but it was one of the lower-rated horses who came out on top in a tight finish. A tricky race tio assess and it has not been rated too positively.

1652 FOLLOW REDCAR RACING ON FACEBOOK H'CAP 1m 2f
5:05 (5:05) (Class 5) (0-75,72) 3-Y-O **£2,396** (£712; £356; £177) **Stalls** Low

Form RPR

40-1 1 **Sparkling Smile (IRE)**[7] 1486 3-9-5 72 6ex .... TedDurcan 1 83+
(D R Lanigan) *hld up in rr: hdwy on inner over 3f out: effrt to chal 2f out and sn rdn: drvn and edgd rt ins fnl f: styd on to ld last 100yds* **8/15**[1]

40-3 2 3/4 **Gritstone**[24] 1119 3-9-4 71 .... PaulHanagan 6 80+
(R A Fahey) *set gd pce: pushed along 3f out: jnd 2f out: sn rdn and edgd rt: drvn and hung rt ent fnl f: hdd and no ex last 100yds* **11/4**[2]

35-0 3 5 **High Rolling**[10] 1422 3-8-11 64 .... DavidAllan 5 63
(T D Easterby) *trckd ldr: effrt 3f out: rdn 2f out and ev ch tl drvn and one pce appr fnl f* **20/1**

0-04 4 4 1/2 **Sharakti (IRE)**[16] 1271 3-9-1 68 .... JamesDoyle 4 58
(A J McCabe) *hld up in rr: hdwy on outer 3f out: rdn to chse ldrs over 2f out: sn drvn and wknd wl over 1f out* **16/1**[3]

20-4 5 16 **Storm Command (IRE)**[7] 1486 3-8-9 62 .... TomEaves 3 20
(B Smart) *chsd ldng pair: rdn along over 3f out: wknd over 2f out* **16/1**[3]

2m 6.71s (-0.39) **Going Correction** -0.075s/f (Good) 5 Ran SP% **108.4**
Speed ratings (Par 98): **98,97,93,89,77**
CSF £2.12 TOTE £1.80: £1.80, £1.10; EX 2.50 Place 6: £188.21, Place 5: £58.04..
Owner Saif Ali & Saeed H Altayer **Bred** Georgestown Stud **Trained** Newmarket, Suffolk

FOCUS
A tactical affair after a strong early pace. The first pair finished clear and have been rated positively.
T/Plt: £115.10 to a £1 stake. Pool: £47,353.12. 300.10 winning tickets. T/Qpdt: £9.10 to a £1 stake. Pool: £3,867.64. 312.08 winning tickets. JR

1374 DONCASTER (L-H)
Friday, April 30

OFFICIAL GOING: Good (good to firm in places; 8.4)
Wind: fresh 1/2 against Weather: overcast, light rain

1653 CROWNHOTEL-BAWTRY.CO.UK H'CAP 7f
2:30 (2:31) (Class 5) (0-70,70) 4-Y-O+ **£2,729** (£806; £403) **Stalls** High

Form RPR

21-4 1 **Watch Amigo (IRE)**[17] 1276 4-9-3 69 .... ShaneKelly 7 91+
(W R Swinburn) *hld up in mid-div: nt clr run over 2f out tl swtchd lft over 1f out: qcknd to ld jst ins fnl f: r.o strly: v readily* **7/4**[1]

521- 2 3 3/4 **Night Lily (IRE)**[218] 6223 4-9-0 66 .... (t) TonyCulhane 8 74
(P W D'Arcy) *trckd ldrs: led over 2f out: hdd jst ins fnl f: no ex* **10/1**

-050 3 hd **Apache Ridge (IRE)**[78] 508 4-9-2 68 .... NeilCallan 4 75
(K A Ryan) *w ldr: upsides 1f out: kpt on same pce* **14/1**

-002 4 2 1/4 **Toby Tyler**[25] 1115 4-8-12 64 .... (p) PaulMulrennan 15 65
(P T Midgley) *racd stands' side: hdwy to chse ldrs 4f out: edgd lft 2f out: one pce appr fnl f* **13/2**[2]

-466 5 hd **Sairaam (IRE)**[94] 297 4-8-4 56 oh11 .... KirstyMilczarek 12 57
(C Smith) *chsd ldrs: hung lft and nit much room 2f out: and one pce* **100/1**

4-50 6 1 3/4 **Bahamian Lad**[22] 1192 5-9-4 70 .... JerryO'Dwyer 10 66
(R Hollinshead) *hld up in mid-div: hdwy over 3f out: kpt on same pce appr fnl f* **20/1**

11-4 7 nk **Final Drive (IRE)**[15] 1322 4-8-9 61 .... EddieCreighton 2 56
(E J Creighton) *mid-div: hdwy over 2f out: kpt on same pce* **9/1**[3]

062- 8 2 1/4 **Jimwil (IRE)**[196] 6824 4-9-1 67 .... (p) PhillipMakin 5 60+
(M Dods) *t.k.h towards rr: hdwy and nt clr run over 1f out: nvr nr to chal* **14/1**

00-0 9 3/4 **Maxwell Hawke (IRE)**[14] 1366 4-9-4 70 .... (p) TomQueally 11 57
(P W Chapple-Hyam) *t.k.h towards rr: hdwy to chse ldrs 3f out: wknd over 1f out* **9/1**[3]

05-6 10 1 3/4 **El Dececy (USA)**[14] 1366 6-8-12 64 .... (p) RobertWinston 13 46
(J Balding) *racd stands' side: sn trcking ldrs: wknd over 1f out* **14/1**

0-64 11 1 1/4 **He's A Humbug (IRE)**[17] 1270 6-8-12 64 .... (v) KierenFallon 14 43
(J O'Reilly) *in rr stands' side: drvn and sme hdwy over 2f out: nvr a factor* **12/1**

5000 12 2 **Resplendent Alpha**[15] 1321 6-8-8 60 .... JimmyQuinn 9 39
(P Howling) *swvd bdly lft s: bhd: hdwy and in tch over 3f out: wknd fnl f* **33/1**

00-0 13 1 **Barataria**[25] 1115 8-8-7 66 .... MatthewLawson(7) 3 40
(R Bastiman) *hood removed v late: dwlt: hdwy 4f out: sn chsng ldrs: lost pl over 1f out* **66/1**

-605 14 3 1/2 **Kheskianto (IRE)**[106] 171 4-7-11 56 oh1 .... RyanPowell(7) 6 18
(M C Chapman) *led tl over 2f out: lost pl over 1f out* **66/1**

5055 15 2 3/4 **Elusive Warrior (USA)**[8] 1492 7-8-0 59 ow1 .... (p) JohnFahy(7) 1 13
(A J McCabe) *w ldrs: wknd 2f out* **20/1**

1m 26.44s (0.14) **Going Correction** +0.10s/f (Good) 15 Ran SP% **122.9**
Speed ratings (Par 103): **103,98,98,95,95 93,93,90,89,87 86,84,83,79,75**
toteswingers:1&2:£6.80, 1&3:£10.60, 2&3:£28.40 CSF £18.75 CT £201.22 TOTE £2.60: £1.60, £3.00, £4.70; EX 21.90 Trifecta £204.30 Part won. Pool: £276.12 - 0.20 winning units..
Owner Ian Harris & Tim Halpin **Bred** Thurso Limited **Trained** Aldbury, Herts

FOCUS
This opening handicap looked very competitive for the class. The field merged to the middle of the track and went off at an average sort of pace. The winner was value for further and the second ran to her 3yo form.
He's A Humbug(IRE) Official explanation: jockey said gelding lost its action
Barataria Official explanation: jockey said gelding had no more to give

1654 ATTEYS SOLICITORS MAIDEN FILLES' STKS 1m (S)
3:00 (3:03) (Class 4) 3-Y-O+ **£4,533** (£1,348; £674; £336) **Stalls** High

Form RPR

2- 1 **Mainstay**[162] 7452 4-9-12 0 .... NeilCallan 6 81
(J H M Gosden) *w ldrs: racd keenly: led 5f out: hld on towards fin* **9/1**

2 nk **Cookie Crumbles (IRE)** 3-8-12 0 .... JackMitchell 7 76+
(C F Wall) *in rr: gd hdwy over 1f out: tk 2nd last 75yds: fin wl* **33/1**

3 2 1/4 **Najoom Zaman (IRE)** 3-8-12 0 .... KierenFallon 13 71
(L M Cumani) *chsd ldrs: kpt on same pce fnl f* **9/2**[2]

4 1/2 **Heavenly Dawn** 3-8-12 0 .... RichardMullen 1 70
(Sir Michael Stoute) *swvd lft s: hdwy to trck ldrs over 3f out: chsd wnr over 1f out: kpt on same pce* **10/1**

5 2 1/2 **Red Skies (IRE)** 3-8-12 0 .... DuranFentiman 4 64
(Mrs L Stubbs) *mid-div: hdwy over 2f out: wknd over 1f out* **125/1**

6 1/2 **Strawberry Rose** 3-8-12 0 .... KirstyMilczarek 11 63+
(M P Tregoning) *dwlt: in rr: edgd lft and kpt on fnl 2f: nvr nr ldrs* **14/1**

4-2 7 1 1/2 **Goolagong (IRE)**[36] 979 3-8-12 0 .... JimCrowley 9 60
(R M Beckett) *led tl 5f out: wknd appr fnl f* **5/1**[3]

8 1 3/4 **Najlaa** 3-8-12 0 .... MichaelHills 5 56
(W J Haggas) *chsd ldrs: hung lft and wknd over 1f out* **16/1**

5- 9 nk **Ajool (USA)**[181] 7182 3-8-12 0 .... TadhgO'Shea 2 55
(B W Hills) *hld up in mid-div: hdwy to chse ldrs 3f out: wknd over 1f out* **11/2**

3 10 3 3/4 **Law Of The Range**[17] 1278 3-8-12 0 .... DarryllHolland 10 46
(M Botti) *hld up towards rr: hdwy and swtchd lft over 2f out: lost pl over 1f out* **11/4**[1]

11 4 **Fantastic Sam (IRE)** 3-8-12 0 .... PaulMulrennan 8 37
(Mrs K Walton) *chsd ldrs: hung lft and wknd over 2f out* **100/1**

0 12 5 **Western Eyes (IRE)**[14] 1355 3-8-12 0 .... JimmyFortune 12 46
(B J Meehan) *prom: lost pl over 1f out* **25/1**

1m 39.93s (0.63) **Going Correction** +0.10s/f (Good)
WFA 3 from 4yo 14lb 12 Ran SP% **117.1**
Speed ratings (Par 105): **100,99,97,96,94 93,92,90,90,86 82,77**
toteswingers:1&2:£44.10, 1&3:£6.40, 2&3:£37.60 CSF £275.09 TOTE £11.80: £3.30, £4.60, £1.90; EX 262.70 TRIFECTA Not won..
Owner Ms Rachel D S Hood **Bred** Juddmonte Farms Ltd **Trained** Newmarket, Suffolk

FOCUS
This looked an interesting fillies' maiden beforehand and the form looks worth following in the coming weeks, although it is not an easy race to rate. There wasn't much of a pace on through the early parts and the field came over more towards the nearside this time.
Law Of The Range Official explanation: jockey said filly lost its action
Western Eyes(IRE) Official explanation: jockey said filly had lost its action

1655 TOTEPOOL FREE BET GIVEAWAY H'CAP 1m 4f
3:35 (3:36) (Class 4) (0-80,79) 4-Y-O+ **£4,776** (£1,410; £705) **Stalls** Low

Form RPR

214 1 **Carlton Scroop (FR)**[16] 1303 7-8-7 66 .... (b) JimmyQuinn 7 72
(J Jay) *hld up in last: effrt 3f out: sn nt clr run: styd on wl u.str.p fnl f: led last strides* **7/1**

62-0 2 hd **Interdiamonds**[13] 1398 4-8-13 73 .... JoeFanning 2 79
(M Johnston) *led: kpt on gamely fnl 2f: hdd fnl strides* **7/2**[2]

50-0 3 hd **Destinys Dream (IRE)**[13] 1398 5-8-9 68 ow1 .... PhillipMakin 8 74
(Miss Tracy Waggott) *hld up in rr: hdwy 7f out: nt clr run over 3f out tl over 2f out: chal jst ins fnl f: no ex nr fin* **6/1**

3400 4 1 **Hallstatt (IRE)**[13] 1398 4-8-10 70 .... GrahamGibbons 6 74
(J Mackie) *trckd ldrs: effrt 4f out: hung lft over 2f out: kpt on same pce* **12/1**

531- 5 1 **Bollin Greta**[301] 3563 5-8-13 72 .... TonyHamilton 1 74
(T D Easterby) *trckd ldrs: effrt and nt clr run over 2f out: one pce fnl f* **4/1**[3]

1-4 6 nse **Abayaan**[34] 1013 4-9-5 79 .... ShaneKelly 3 81
(Jane Chapple-Hyam) *trckd ldrs: kpt on same pce fnl f* **2/1**[1]

0 7 21 **Carnac (IRE)**[23] 1176 4-9-4 78 .... PaulMulrennan 4 57
(J S Wainwright) *mid-div: hdwy to chse ldrs: wknd 2f out: sn bhd and eased* **33/1**

2m 32.84s (-2.06) **Going Correction** -0.05s/f (Good)
WFA 4 from 5yo+ 1lb 7 Ran SP% **113.0**
Speed ratings (Par 105): **105,104,104,104,103 103,89**
toteswingers:1&2:£4.70, 1&3:£8.60, 2&3:£5.00 CSF £30.80 CT £155.16 TOTE £7.50: £2.40, £2.50; EX 22.40 Trifecta £84.40 Pool: £292.14 - 2.56 winning units..
Owner S Hussain **Bred** Jonathan Jay **Trained**
■ Stewards' Enquiry : Phillip Makin one-day ban: careless riding (May 14)

FOCUS
A modest handicap. It was run at an ordinary pace and the first five finished in something of a heap, so the form is muddling. It is rated through the second and third.

1656 TOTEPOOL BEAT THE BOOKIES H'CAP 5f
4:10 (4:10) (Class 3) (0-90,83) 3-Y-O **£7,165** (£2,115; £1,058) **Stalls** High

Form RPR

10-6 1 **Magical Macey (USA)**[13] 1399 3-9-4 83 .... (b) PhillipMakin 3 88
(T D Barron) *trckd ldrs: led over 1f out: rdn and r.o strly: readily* **4/1**[2]

011 2 2 1/2 **Murura (IRE)**[14] 1347 3-8-8 73 .... PaulMulrennan 1 69+
(J G Given) *s.s: last tl hdwy on outside appr fnl f: styd on wl to take 2nd last stride* **15/8**[1]

10-0 3 shd **Bossy Kitty**[13] 1376 3-8-11 76 .... KirstyMilczarek 4 72
(N Tinkler) *chsd ldrs: wnt 2nd 1f out: styd on same pce* **16/1**

15-0 4 2 1/4 **Ignatieff (IRE)**[13] 1399 3-8-13 78 .... DuranFentiman 7 66
(Mrs L Stubbs) *charged gate and wl away: led: hung lft and hdd over 1f out: kpt on same pce* **7/1**

320- 5 nse **Dancing Freddy (IRE)**[174] 7290 3-9-1 80 .... TomQueally 6 67
(J G Given) *chsd ldrs: kpt on same pce appr fnl f* **7/1**

00-0 6 6 **The Hermitage (IRE)**[24] 1140 3-8-12 77 .... JoeFanning 5 43
(M Johnston) *sltly hmpd s: outpcd and in rr: sme hdwy over 2f out: sn wknd* **12/1**

64-4 7 3 1/2 **Dispol Keasha**[13] 1399 3-8-13 78 .... RobertWinston 2 31
(P T Midgley) *sn w ldr: wknd appr fnl f* **9/2**[3]

60.43 secs (-0.07) **Going Correction** +0.10s/f (Good) 7 Ran SP% **111.5**
Speed ratings (Par 102): **104,100,99,96,96 86,80**
toteswingers:1&2:£2.20, 1&3:£13.00, 2&3:£8.20 CSF £11.32 TOTE £4.50: £2.20, £1.40; EX 14.00 Trifecta £278.20 Pool: £488.73 - 1.30 winning units..
Owner K J Alderson **Bred** Silver Springs Stud Farm Inc & Mrs J Costelloe **Trained** Maunby, N Yorks

FOCUS
This was fast and furious thanks to the fourth and seventh. The winner is rated up 5lb.

NOTEBOOK

Magical Macey(USA) shaped better than the bare form when finding trouble on his return at Thirsk 13 days earlier and was bidding to reverse that form with Dispol Keasha. He was helped by that one tearing off in the lead and travelled nicely to her nearing the final furlong. He soon had matters under control when pushed to the front and can be rated value for a little further as he was idling late on. (op 9-2)

Murura(IRE) was having his first run on turf and dropping back from 6f. He was expected to enjoy the decent pace, but blew his chance by falling out of the gates. He was fighting a losing battle thereafter and remains one to be interested in when reverting to another furlong. (op 9-4)

Bossy Kitty, behind the winner at Thirsk on her seasonal debut, stepped up nicely on that effort and reversed form with Dispol Keasha and Ignatieff. She can go forward again for the run. (op 12-1)

Ignatieff(IRE) seems to be the sort that needs to dominate his races and that was never going to the case here. (op 8-1)

The Hermitage(IRE) has now looked out of sorts in two runs since resuming and has to prove she has trained on. (op 10-1)

1657 TOTEPOOL A BETTER WAY TO BET H'CAP — 1m 2f 60y

4:45 (4:46) (Class 4) (0-85,82) 3-Y-O — **£4,776** (£1,410; £705) **Stalls** Low

Form — RPR

02-1 **1** **Dandino**[25] 1116 3-8-13 **77** PaulMulrennan 3 — 85+
(J G Given) *trckd ldrs: effrt on inner over 3f out: swtchd ins 2f out: led over 1f out: styd on wl* **12/1**

21- **2** *1 ¼* **Rigidity**[225] 6033 3-8-13 **77** TomQueally 4 — 82
(H R A Cecil) *sn trcking ldrs: effrt over 2f out: styd on same pce fnl f* **4/5**[1]

034- **3** *nk* **Ingleby Spirit**[223] 6088 3-9-4 **82** TonyHamilton 7 — 86
(R A Fahey) *hld up in rr: effrt 4f out: styd on wl appr fnl f: tk 3rd clsng stages* **28/1**

421- **4** *1 ¼* **Hidden Glory**[144] 7663 3-9-0 **78** RobertWinston 5 — 80
(Pat Eddery) *hld up: nt clr run over 2f out: rdr lost whip appr fnl f: styd on same pce* **4/1**[2]

312- **5** *¾* **Realisation (USA)**[206] 6569 3-9-2 **80** JoeFanning 2 — 80
(M Johnston) *led: racd keenly: hdd over 1f out: fdd fnl 150yds* **9/1**[3]

-610 **6** *¾* **Muwalla**[15] 1330 3-9-4 **82** (t) NeilCallan 6 — 81
(C E Brittain) *hld up in rr: hdwy 6f out: sn chsng ldrs: styd on same pce fnl 2f* **20/1**

31-0 **7** *1 ¼* **First In The Queue (IRE)**[15] 1330 3-8-12 **76** PatDobbs 1 — 73
(S Kirk) *dwlt: sn chsng ldrs: dropped bk after 2f: hdwy on inner over 3f out: one pce fnl 2f* **10/1**

0-12 **8** *7* **First Post (IRE)**[57] 781 3-8-9 **73** ow1 DarryllHolland 8 — 56
(D Haydn Jones) *racd keenly: sn trcking ldrs: wknd over 1f out: eased* **20/1**

2m 9.17s (-0.23) **Going Correction** -0.05s/f (Good) — 8 Ran SP% **115.3**

Speed ratings (Par 100): **106,105,104,103,103 102,101,95**

toteswingers:1&2:£4.10, 1&3:£13.10, 2&3:£6.20 CSF £21.94 CT £285.75 TOTE £12.30: £2.30, £1.10, £4.40; EX 26.60 Trifecta £278.20 Pool: £198.90 - 1.40 winning units..

Owner Elite Racing Club **Bred** Elite Racing Club **Trained** Willoughton, Lincs

FOCUS

A handicap featuring some potentially very useful 3-y-os, run at an average pace. Pretty sound form, and the winner can improve further.

First Post(IRE) Official explanation: jockey said gelding ran too free

1658 PEGLER YORKSHIRE H'CAP — 1m (R)

5:15 (5:17) (Class 4) (0-85,81) 3-Y-O — **£4,776** (£1,410; £705) **Stalls** High

Form — RPR

101- **1** **Ransom Note**[201] 6693 3-9-0 **77** MichaelHills 6 — 96+
(B W Hills) *in rr: nt clr run over 3f out tl swtchd outside over 1f out: str run to ld jst ins fnl f: styd on strly: v readily* **3/1**[1]

11-0 **2** *2 ¼* **New Christmas (USA)**[15] 1334 3-9-3 **80** TomQueally 7 — 89
(B J Meehan) *hld up in rr: effrt over 3f out: led over 1f out: hdd jst ins fnl f: no ex* **12/1**

22-2 **3** *5* **Finest Reserve (IRE)**[15] 1335 3-8-13 **76** NeilCallan 1 — 73
(M R Channon) *dwlt: hdwy to chse ldrs after 3f: edgd rt over 1f out: one pce* **5/1**[3]

14-3 **4** *2 ½* **Layla's Dancer**[16] 1297 3-9-1 **78** TonyHamilton 3 — 70
(R A Fahey) *in rr: hdwy 4f out: effrt over 2f out: kpt on fnl f* **3/1**[1]

0-11 **5** *3* **Avenuesnalleyways (IRE)**[10] 1453 3-9-3 **80** 6ex JimCrowley 2 — 65
(R M Beckett) *trckd ldrs: t.k.h: wknd fnl f* **4/1**[2]

140- **6** *10* **Fairy Promises (USA)**[210] 6447 3-9-4 **81** RobertWinston 4 — 43
(Pat Eddery) *w ldrs: drvn 3f out: wknd over 1f out: eased ins fnl f* **28/1**

0-1 **7** *9* **Falakee**[23] 1165 3-9-2 **79** JimmyFortune 8 — 20
(P W Chapple-Hyam) *led tl hdd over 1f out: sn wknd: eased ins fnl f* **16/1**

61-3 **8** *14* **Jupiter Fidius**[15] 1334 3-8-13 **76** PaulMulrennan 5 — —
(Mrs K Walton) *chsd ldrs: edgd lft and lost pl 2f out: eased whn bhd ins fnl f* **9/1**

1m 38.2s (-1.50) **Going Correction** -0.05s/f (Good) — 8 Ran SP% **113.7**

Speed ratings (Par 100): **105,102,97,95,92 82,73,59**

toteswingers:1&2:£6.20, 1&3:£4.40, 2&3:£5.70 CSF £39.68 CT £174.10 TOTE £3.90: £1.70, £3.00, £1.40; EX 42.00 Trifecta £198.90 Place 6 £104.48; Place 5 £51.64.

Owner H R Mould **Bred** Rabbah Bloodstock Limited **Trained** Lambourn, Berks

FOCUS

A fair 3-y-o handicap that had an open look about it. They went a solid early pace and so it was no real surprise to see the closers dominate. The winner was value for twice the actual margin.

Falakee Official explanation: jockey said colt lost its action

Jupiter Fidius Official explanation: jockey said gelding never tra velled

T/Jkpt: Not won. T/Plt: £232.20 to a £1 stake. Pool: £98,824.14. 310.60 winning tickets. T/Qpdt: £31.40 to a £1 stake. Pool: £6,161.90. 145.21 winning tickets. WG

1589 LINGFIELD (L-H)

Friday, April 30

OFFICIAL GOING: Standard

Wind: fresh, half behind Weather: overcast

1659 £66 FREE BET AT BLUESQUARE.COM MAIDEN STKS (DIV I) — 7f (P)

1:40 (1:41) (Class 5) 3-4-Y-O — **£3,561** (£1,059; £529; £264) **Stalls** Low

Form — RPR

20-4 **1** **Faithful One (IRE)**[15] 1329 3-8-7 **80** TedDurcan 7 — 73+
(D R Lanigan) *chsd ldng trio: rdn ent fnl 2f: r.o to chal fnl 150yds: led wl ins fnl f* **11/4**[2]

02-3 **2** *1* **Count Of Anjou (USA)**[16] 1308 3-8-12 **78** RichardHughes 2 — 76
(R Hannon) *sn led: rdn ent fnl 2f: edgd rt but kpt on wl u.p tl hdd and nt pce of wnr wl ins fnl f* **4/1**[3]

0-4 **3** *1* **Compton Park**[23] 1164 3-8-12 0 WilliamBuick 1 — 73
(W J Knight) *chsd ldng pair: rdn and effrt between horses over 1f out: pressed ldrs u.p 1f out: edgd rt and one pce fnl 150yds* **20/1**

4 *1* **Zakiy** 3-8-12 0 (t) JamieSpencer 5 — 70+
(W J Haggas) *in tch in midfield: edging out rt and no imp whn rdn over 1f out: styd on wl fnl 100yds: gng on fin* **20/1**

04 **5** *¾* **Hatta Stream (IRE)**[18] 1260 4-9-6 0 SimonPearce(5) 3 — 73?
(J Pearce) *chsd ldr: rdn jst over 2f out: ev ch ent fnl f: keeping on same pce and btn whn edgd rt: clipped heels and stmbld ins fnl f* **33/1**

262- **6** *2 ½* **Robinson Cruso**[189] 6991 3-8-12 **84** PhilipRobinson 10 — 62
(M A Jarvis) *in tch in midfield: rdn and unable qck 2f out: styd on same pce after* **7/4**[1]

5-5 **7** *4 ½* **Khajaaly (IRE)**[25] 1127 3-8-12 0 RichardHills 12 — 49+
(E A L Dunlop) *stdd and dropped in bhd s: hld up wl in rr: edging out rt wl over 1f out: kpt on fnl f: n.d* **9/1**

0 **8** *nk* **Resolute Road**[15] 1325 3-8-12 0 DavidProbert 14 — 49+
(B W Hills) *stdd and dropped in bhd after s: t.k.h early: hld up in rr: wd bnd 2f out: sme late hdwy: n.d* **80/1**

55- **9** *1* **Qaraqum (USA)**[147] 7624 3-8-7 0 EddieAhern 13 — 41+
(D J Coakley) *hld up towards rr: rdn ent fnl 2f: nvr trbld ldrs* **125/1**

10 *1 ½* **Serious Matters (IRE)** 3-8-12 0 AdamKirby 9 — 42+
(W R Swinburn) *hld up in last trio: nvr trbld ldrs* **50/1**

11 *3 ½* **But Beautiful (IRE)** 3-8-8 0 ow1 StevieDonohoe 11 — 28
(R A Mills) *racd in midfield: pushed along 3f out: struggling ent fnl 2f: wl bhd fnl f* **50/1**

12 *1* **Vertumnus** 3-8-12 0 J-PGuillambert 4 — 30
(N P Littmoden) *s.i.s: t.k.h: sn in midfield: struggling and rdn over 2f out: sn bhd* **100/1**

00 **13** *10* **Faraday's Fancy (IRE)**[18] 1260 4-9-6 0 TravisBlock 8 — —
(Miss A M Newton-Smith) *a towards rr: lost tch ent fnl 2f: eased ins fnl f* **250/1**

1m 25.78s (0.98) **Going Correction** +0.10s/f (Slow)

WFA 3 from 4yo 13lb — 13 Ran SP% **112.8**

Speed ratings (Par 103): **98,96,95,94,93 90,85,85,84,82 78,77,65**

toteswingers:1&2:£2.90, 1&3:£8.90, 2&3:£9.30 CSF £12.23 TOTE £2.60: £1.10, £2.20, £3.30; EX 10.40.

Owner Saif Ali **Bred** Darley **Trained** Newmarket, Suffolk

■ Stewards' Enquiry : William Buick caution: used whip without giving colt time to respond.

FOCUS

An ordinary maiden. The time was 0.05secs slower than the second division. Muddling form, rated around the runner-up.

Hatta Stream(IRE) Official explanation: jockey said gelding stumbled

Khajaaly(IRE) Official explanation: jockey said colt was slowly away

Resolute Road Official explanation: jockey said colt ran too freely

Vertumnus Official explanation: jockey said gelding ran too freely

1660 E B F BLUESQUARE.COM MAIDEN FILLIES' STKS — 5f (P)

2:10 (2:11) (Class 5) 2-Y-O — **£3,885** (£1,156; £577; £288) **Stalls** High

Form — RPR

5 **1** **Phoebs**[15] 1324 2-9-0 0 StevieDonohoe 9 — 72
(R A Mills) *sn bustled along: in tch in rr of main gp: rdn ent fnl 2f: stl plenty do over 1f out: str run ins fnl f to ld towards fin* **5/2**[2]

2 *½* **Jambo Bibi (IRE)** 2-9-0 0 RichardHughes 6 — 70
(R Hannon) *chsd ldr: flashed tail on bnd 2f out: jnd ldr over 1f out: led wl ins fnl f: immediately hdd and no ex* **2/1**[1]

3 *½* **Breedj (IRE)** 2-9-0 0 ChrisCatlin 2 — 68
(C E Brittain) *led: jnd and rdn over 1f out: hdd wl ins fnl f: one pce towards fin* **11/4**[3]

4 *¾* **Fifth Commandment (IRE)** 2-9-0 0 EddieAhern 1 — 66+
(J A Osborne) *dwlt: in tch: effrt u.p towards inner over 1f out: kpt on u.p fnl f: nt rch ldrs* **12/1**

6 **5** *¾* **Russian Ice**[18] 1263 2-9-0 0 AdamKirby 7 — 63
(D K Ivory) *chsd ldrs: rdn and unable qck ent fnl 2f: kpt on same pce fnl f* **20/1**

6 *¾* **Danube Dancer (IRE)** 2-9-0 0 LiamKeniry 3 — 60
(J S Moore) *chsd ldrs: rdn and unable qck 2f out: one pce and no threat to ldrs after* **16/1**

7 *7* **Three Scoops** 2-9-0 0 FrankieMcDonald 8 — 35
(D J S Ffrench Davis) *s.i.s: in tch in rr of main gp: rdn and lost tch ent fnl 2f* **150/1**

8 *¾* **Disco Doll** 2-9-0 0 SaleemGolam 10 — 32
(G D Blake) *v.s.a: a wl bhd* **200/1**

50 **9** *4 ½* **Helen Of Toy**[15] 1324 2-9-0 0 FergusSweeney 5 — 16
(B G Powell) *in tch tl wknd qckly u.p wl over 1f out* **33/1**

60.13 secs (1.33) **Going Correction** +0.10s/f (Slow) — 9 Ran SP% **111.0**

Speed ratings (Par 89): **93,92,91,90,89 87,76,75,68**

toteswingers:1&2:£1.50, 1&3:£1.50, 2&3:£2.00 CSF £7.32 TOTE £3.30: £1.10, £1.20, £1.10; EX 8.40.

Owner R A Mills N Clement **Bred** Sherwoods Transport Ltd **Trained** Headley, Surrey

FOCUS

This juvenile maiden should produce winners although the form looks only ordinary.

NOTEBOOK

Phoebs, a promising fifth at Newmarket on debut, found herself a bit outpaced early and still had plenty of ground to make up turning in, but she came with a strong run down the outside and always looked likely to get up in the final 100 yards. She is clearly in need of 6f, and should improve again. A conditions/novice event could be next. (op 11-4 tchd 3-1 in places)

Jambo Bibi(IRE), whose dam won over 1m, comes from a yard that has made a tremendous start with their juveniles and she looked the likely winner over 1f out, but didn't pick up as expected when asked for her effort by Hughes. (op 9-4)

Breedj(IRE), a highly regarded daughter of Acclamation, has still to come in her coat but she showed good early speed and stuck on once headed. She seemed to know her job, but should still improve and can win an ordinary maiden. (op 9-4)

Fifth Commandment(IRE), an April-foaled daughter of Holy Roman Emperor, wasn't the best away and showed signs of inexperience, but was closing at the line and will prove well suited by an extra furlong. (op 14-1)

Russian Ice had clearly learnt a bit from her first run and wasn't beaten far. (tchd 16-1)

Danube Dancer(IRE), a daughter of Balmont, showed enough to suggest she will win races. (op 20-1)

Three Scoops was reported to have run green. Official explanation: jockey said filly ran green throughout (op 100-1)

1661 £66 FREE BET AT BLUESQUARE.COM MAIDEN STKS (DIV II) 7f (P)
2:40 (2:41) (Class 5) 3-4-Y-O **£3,561** (£1,059; £529; £264) **Stalls** Low

Form RPR

0- **1** **Hidden Fire**[200] 6730 3-8-7 0 .... WilliamBuick 11 74
(D R C Elsworth) *t.k.h: hld up in midfield: rdn and effrt wl over 1f out: drvn to chse ldng pair 1f out: str run to ld nr fin* **25/1**

6-4 **2** *hd* **Streets Of War (USA)**[42] 930 3-8-12 0 .... RobertHavlin 3 78
(P W Chapple-Hyam) *chsd clr ldr: clsd over 2f out: led wl over 1f out: drvn fnl f: kpt on wl tl hdd nr fin* **2/1**[1]

0-0 **3** *1* **Blue Again**[17] 1278 3-8-7 0 .... TedDurcan 4 70
(W R Swinburn) *prom in main gp: rdn to chse ldr over 1f out: styd on same pce u.p fnl f* **33/1**

4 **4** *2 ¾* **Seyaaq (USA)**[15] 1325 3-8-12 0 .... RichardHills 10 68
(B W Hills) *sltly hmpd s: hld up towards rr: pushed along and wd bnd 2f out: styd on steadily fnl f: nvr trbld ldrs* **9/2**[3]

5 *1 ¼* **Perfect Point (IRE)** 3-8-12 0 .... AdamKirby 12 65+
(W R Swinburn) *dropped in bhd after s: pushed along wl over 1f out: nt clr run and swtchd rt ent fnl f: kpt on fnl f: nvr trbld ldrs* **14/1**

50- **6** *hd* **Caldermud (IRE)**[233] 5778 3-8-12 0 .... SebSanders 9 64+
(J R Best) *fly-jmpd leaving stalls and rdr lost iron: sn led and clr: taken wd 4f out: c bk to field over 2f out: hdd wl over 1f out: wknd ent fnl f* **20/1**

00- **7** *1 ¾* **Tudor Princess**[206] 6563 3-8-7 0 .... HayleyTurner 6 54
(W R Muir) *chsd ldrs in main gp: rdn and wknd wl over 1f out* **33/1**

8 *hd* **Divine Call** 3-8-12 0 .... LiamJones 5 59+
(W J Haggas) *hld up towards rr: effrt on inner over 1f out: nvr trbld ldrs* **9/4**[2]

40- **9** *shd* **Hounds Ditch**[213] 6356 3-8-13 0 ow1 .... SteveCarson 8 60
(Eve Johnson Houghton) *chsd ldrs in main gp: rdn and struggling 2f out: wl btn over 1f out* **100/1**

0- **10** *5* **Rowan Light**[381] 1269 4-9-6 0 .... PatCosgrave 1 45
(J R Boyle) *s.i.s: in midfield of main gp: struggling over 2f out: wl bhd fnl 2f* **66/1**

0- **11** *4* **Miss California**[206] 6567 3-8-2 0 .... RossAtkinson(5) 7 29
(Miss Tor Sturgis) *t.k.h: hld up in rr: lost tch 2f out* **100/1**

12 *11* **Bit Of Bling** 3-8-8 0 ow1 .... RyanMoore 13 1
(J Noseda) *s.i.s: sn rdn along and nvr gng pce: a wl bhd: eased fr over 1f out* **9/1**

1m 25.73s (0.93) **Going Correction** +0.10s/f (Slow)
WFA 3 from 4yo 13lb **12** Ran SP% **116.9**
Speed ratings (Par 103): **98,97,96,93,92 91,89,89,89,83 79,66**
toteswingers:1&2:£16.90, 1&3:£74.40, 2&3:£22.20 CSF £72.00 TOTE £27.70: £4.60, £1.60, £7.90; EX 117.20.
Owner J C Smith **Bred** Littleton Stud **Trained** Newmarket, Suffolk

FOCUS
As with the first division, this race should produce winners although this is just ordinary maiden form. The time was 0.05secs quicker than division one.
Seyaaq(USA) Official explanation: jockey said gelding never travelled
Caldermud(IRE) Official explanation: jockey said he lost an iron leaving stalls

1662 BLUESQUARE.COM IPHONE APP H'CAP 7f (P)
3:15 (3:16) (Class 2) (0-105,104) 4-Y-0+ **£12,952** (£3,854; £1,926; £962) **Stalls** Low

Form RPR

1204 **1** **Thebes**[11] 1423 5-8-10 **96** .... FrankieDettori 2 104
(M Johnston) *chsd ldrs: effrt to chse ldr and swtchd rt wl over 1f out: rdn to ld ins fnl f: hld on wl whn chal fnl 100yds* **5/1**[2]

-106 **2** *½* **Vitznau (IRE)**[27] 1085 6-8-11 **97** .... RichardHughes 1 103
(R Hannon) *hld up in last trio: gd hdwy on inner over 1f out: chsd ldng pair and swtchd rt jst ins fnl f: chal fnl 100yds: no ex and hld towards fin* **11/4**[1]

65 **3** *nse* **Noble Citizen (USA)**[48] 885 5-8-7 **93** .... (be) WilliamBuick 9 99+
(D M Simcock) *hld up in last trio: n.m.r bnd 2f out: swtchd out rt over 1f out: str run u.p fnl f: nt quite rch ldrs* **11/1**

00-0 **4** *1 ½* **Al Muheer (IRE)**[56] 818 5-9-1 **104** .... (v[1]) AhmedAjtebi(3) 4 106
(Mahmood Al Zarooni) *sn led: rdn over 1f out: hdd ins fnl f: one pce fnl 100yds* **10/1**

0620 **5** *¾* **Autumn Blades (IRE)**[27] 1085 5-8-11 **97** .... (v) DavidProbert 7 97
(A Bailey) *t.k.h: hld up wl in tch: rdn and nt qckn over 1f out: styd on same pce fnl f* **11/2**[3]

3100 **6** *nk* **The Scorching Wind (IRE)**[27] 1085 4-8-3 **92** .... (t) WilliamCarson(3) 8 91
(S C Williams) *t.k.h early: chsd ldrs: rdn to press ldrs 2f out: wknd ent fnl f* **8/1**

2000 **7** *2 ½* **Imprimis Tagula (IRE)**[21] 1206 6-8-6 **95** .... (v) MarcHalford(3) 10 87
(A Bailey) *hld up in midfield on outer: rdn and effrt bnd 2f out: no prog and wl hld after* **33/1**

4-04 **8** *1 ¾* **Eisteddfod**[104] 204 9-8-12 **98** .... (p) JamieSpencer 6 86
(P F I Cole) *sn chsng ldr: lost 2nd wl over 1f out: sn wknd* **16/1**

306- **9** *hd* **Icelandic**[174] 7292 8-9-0 **100** .... (t) JamesDoyle 5 87
(F Sheridan) *stdd s: hld up in rr: short of room and hmpd bnd wl over 1f out: n.d* **20/1**

006- **10** *nse* **Titan Triumph**[364] 1640 6-8-9 **95** .... LukeMorris 3 82
(W J Knight) *taken down early: stdd after s: hld up in last pair: no prog whn rdn wl over 1f out* **7/1**

1m 24.01s (-0.79) **Going Correction** +0.10s/f (Slow) **10** Ran SP% **113.3**
Speed ratings (Par 109): **108,107,107,105,104 104,101,99,99,99**
toteswingers:1&2:£2.20, 1&3:£10.40, 2&3:£9.90 CSF £18.51 CT £144.93 TOTE £4.50: £2.00, £1.10, £3.20; EX 16.00.
Owner Sheikh Hamdan Bin Mohammed Al Maktoum **Bred** Whitsbury Manor Stud And Mrs M E Slade **Trained** Middleham Moor, N Yorks

FOCUS
A competitive and valuable handicap. The early pace was only fair, but even so the winning time was much faster than both divisions of the maiden, as would be expected. A personal best from the winner.

NOTEBOOK
Thebes had won just once over this trip before and his other six successes had all come over 6f, but he was always in a great position behind the leaders against the inside rail here. Angled out to challenge over a furlong from home, he got first run on his main rivals and quickly established enough of an advantage to just last home. This was a good effort from 6lb above his previous highest winning mark. (tchd 7-2)
Vitznau(IRE), still 4lb higher than when winning a steadily run Lincoln Trial at Wolverhampton last month, was given a patient ride but got a nice run through on the inside turning for home and was close enough if good enough a furlong out. He ran on well once switched right, but could never quite get there. (op 7-2)
Noble Citizen(USA) ◆, nearly 3l behind Vitznau in the Lincoln Trial and 5lb better off, was given plenty to do and had to wait to get a clear run rounding the home bend. He flew down the wide outside once in the clear, but the line was always going to beat him. He hasn't scored since October 2008, but now looks ready to put that right. (op 9-1 tchd 12-1)
Al Muheer(IRE), a winner here over a year ago, was making his debut for Godolphin after failing to beat a rival on his Meydan reappearance. Although often blinkered in the past, this was his first try in a visor and he was soon bowling in front. It looked at one stage turning in as though he might take some catching, but he had little left when the winner got to him a furlong out and may still have just needed it. (op 16-1)
Autumn Blades(IRE), still 4lb higher than for the last of four wins on Polytrack during the winter, needs everything to fall right but he held a good position throughout here and just wasn't good enough on the day. (op 8-1 tchd 9-1 and 5-1)
The Scorching Wind(IRE), who didn't enjoy the rub of the green in either start since winning off 3lb lower over C&D in January, raced keenly enough in the early stages and then didn't find much when coming off the bridle 2f from home. The stable are just struggling a bit for winners at present. (op 6-1)
Imprimis Tagula(IRE), below form in his recent starts, didn't have much go right here as he saw plenty of daylight on the outside of the field, was too keen as a result, and was then forced very wide on the home turn. He has won twice on Polytrack, but his other eight wins have come on Fibresand and he is worth keeping an eye on back on that surface, especially when the money is down.

1663 BET AT BLUESQUARE.COM H'CAP 6f (P)
3:50 (3:50) (Class 3) (0-90,87) 3-Y-O **£7,771** (£2,312; £1,155; £577) **Stalls** Low

Form RPR

01-4 **1** **Little Garcon (USA)**[22] 1191 3-9-3 **83** .... WilliamBuick 1 91
(M Botti) *hld up in last pair: hdwy and swtchd rt over 1f out: sn rdn: chsd ldr ins fnl f: r.o strly to ld cl home* **11/2**

21- **2** *shd* **Summerinthecity (IRE)**[288] 4000 3-9-5 **85** .... RyanMoore 8 93+
(J Noseda) *carried rt strart: stdd and dropped in bhd: hld up in last: rdn 2f out: stl 7th 1f out: storming run ins fnl f: wnt 2nd on post: nt quite get up* **3/1**[2]

004- **3** *shd* **Lowdown (IRE)**[209] 6478 3-9-7 **87** .... FrankieDettori 2 95
(M Johnston) *led: rdn and forged clr ent fnl f: drvn ins fnl f: hdd and lost 2 pls cl home* **11/4**[1]

12-5 **4** *3 ½* **Fly Silca Fly (IRE)**[17] 1279 3-9-1 **81** .... AlanMunro 3 77
(M R Channon) *chsd ldrs: rdn and unable qck over 1f out: one pce and wl hld fnl f* **16/1**

40-0 **5** *shd* **Wisecraic**[14] 1352 3-9-4 **84** .... (b[1]) RichardKingscote 7 80
(Tom Dascombe) *wnt bdly rt s and s.i.s: sn rdn along to press ldr: ev ch and rdn over 2f out: wknd u.p 1f out* **12/1**

-116 **6** *1* **Sir Frank Wappat**[22] 1191 3-8-7 **73** .... GregFairley 4 66
(M Johnston) *in tch in midfield: rdn and effrt jst over 2f out: wkng whn hmpd over 1f out: no ch after* **10/1**

430- **7** *4* **Imperial Delight**[182] 7145 3-8-11 **77** .... DaneO'Neill 6 57
(H Candy) *pressed ldrs tl wknd u.p 2f out: wl btn fnl f* **4/1**[3]

6-10 **8** *13* **Amary (IRE)**[41] 945 3-9-7 **87** .... (p) SebSanders 5 25
(C E Brittain) *in tch in midfield on outer: rdn 4f out: wknd qckly 2f out: wl bhd fnl f* **25/1**

1m 11.42s (-0.48) **Going Correction** +0.10s/f (Slow) **8** Ran SP% **113.6**
Speed ratings (Par 102): **107,106,106,102,101 100,95,77**
toteswingers:1&2:£4.30, 1&3:£5.50, 2&3:£3.40 CSF £22.06 CT £54.54 TOTE £5.90: £2.00, £1.10, £1.50; EX 21.90.
Owner Joseph Barton **Bred** Castleton Lyons **Trained** Newmarket, Suffolk

FOCUS
A good, competitive 3-y-o sprint handicap that produced a cracking three-way finish. The first three are all progressive.

NOTEBOOK
Little Garcon(USA), too keen when fourth off this mark at Wolverhampton on his reappearance, settled nicely off the pace and readily made his ground. He took a while to hit top gear, but just got up, and there wasn't enough time for the fast-finishing second to get past. He shouldn't go up much for this and remains capable of better. (op 15-2 tchd 5-1)
Summerinthecity(IRE) ◆, not seen after winning a 6f novice stakes at Doncaster last summer, looked to be on a fair mark for this handicap debut, but he soon found himself further behind than ideal and still only had one behind over 1f out. He fairly flew home, and would have got up in another stride or two, but it wasn't to be. Clearly the horse to take from the race, he can be expected to make an impact in some of the better 3-y-o sprints on turf this season. (op 7-2 tchd 9-4)
Lowdown(IRE), a fine fourth in the Tattersalls Timeform Million on his final outing at two, was soon in front on this drop in trip and looked the winner when surging clear 1f out, but he was unable to fend off the front pair. This was a promising reappearance from a horse that will be suited by a return to turf. (tchd 3-1)
Fly Silca Fly(IRE) improved on her Yarmouth effort and is one to watch out for in a slightly lesser race. (op 12-1)
Wisecraic, who went sharply right out of the gate, was ridden to take up a prominent position in the first-time blinkers, but in doing so left himself vulnerable in the straight, and he emptied from 1f out.
Sir Frank Wappat has been exposed since going up in grade and this mark looks beyond him. He was already beaten when hampered over 1f out. (tchd 12-1)
Imperial Delight dropped right away having been up disputing the early running. He deserves another chance, as he looks to have done well from two to three, but this does leave him with a bit to prove. (tchd 5-1)

1664 £66 FREE BET AT BLUESQUARE.COM CONDITIONS STKS 1m (P)
4:25 (4:27) (Class 2) 3-Y-O+
£14,331 (£4,291; £2,145; £1,074; £535; £269) **Stalls** High

Form RPR

1 **Storm Ultralight (ARG)**[383] 4-9-1 100 .... AhmedAjtebi 1 112+
(Mahmood Al Zarooni) *chsd ldrs: wnt 2nd over 5f out: pushed ahd ent fnl 2f: rdn clr over 1f out: wl clr fnl f: eased towards fin* **8/1**

056- **2** *3 ¾* **Tazeez (USA)**[279] 4329 6-9-4 113 .... RichardHills 7 103
(J H M Gosden) *t.k.h: hld up in tch: rdn and effrt towards outer 2f out: pressing for 2nd but no ch w wnr 1f out: wnt 2nd wl ins fnl f* **1/1**[1]

04-5 **3** *½* **Cloudy Start**[13] 1377 4-9-8 108 .... (p) RichardHughes 4 106
(J A Osborne) *broke wl: w ldr tl stdd into midfield after 1f: rdn and effrt 2f out: no ch w wnr 1f out: kpt on* **16/1**

2225 **4** *¾* **Suits Me**[34] 1016 7-9-4 106 .... MickyFenton 3 100
(T P Tate) *dwlt: sn bustled up to chse ldrs: wnt 2nd but nt pce of wnr over 1f out: no ch w wnr 1f out: lost 2 pls wl ins fnl f* **7/2**[2]

12/ **5** *2* **Abbeyside**[635] 4673 4-9-4 0 .... (t) FrankieDettori 5 96
(P F I Cole) *v.s.a: styd wd: wl bhd: clsd and in tch 3f out: rdn and btn 2f out* **9/2**[3]

52-0 **6** 3 1/4 **Marine Boy (IRE)**[11] 1423 4-9-4 98........................(p) RichardKingscote 6 88
(Tom Dascombe) *led tl ent fnl 2f: wknd qckly u.p over 1f out* **33/1**

1m 37.28s (-0.92) **Going Correction** +0.10s/f (Slow) **6** Ran SP% **110.3**
Speed ratings (Par 109): **108,104,103,103,101 97**
toteswingers:1&2:£2.70, 1&3:£5.20, 2&3:£3.20 CSF £16.07 TOTE £9.90: £3.90, £1.10; EX 20.60.
Owner Godolphin **Bred** La Biznaga **Trained** Newmarket, Suffolk

FOCUS
An interesting conditions event that could have unearthed a smart performer in Storm Ultralight, although there are doubts over what he beat.

NOTEBOOK
Storm Ultralight(ARG), ex-Uruguayan, made an impressive debut for Godolphin. Off since winning a Listed race by 12 3/4l in his homeland 383 ago, he had stamina to prove over this trip, but had to be respected as a complete unknown, and showed a bright change of pace to race into a clear lead inside the final quarter-mile. Whether he can reproduce this sort of form on turf remains to be seen, and it would be unwise to get carried away with the favourite running below par, but there's no doubting his potential, and it will be fascinating to see where he goes next. (op 10-1)
Tazeez(USA) set a high standard and had won first time out for each of the last two seasons. He had never run on Polytrack before, though, and didn't look overly happy on the track, only getting going once in the straight. He will appreciate the return to a galloping track on turf, but isn't going to be the easiest to win with this season. (op 10-11)
Cloudy Start, last of five in the Doncaster Mile on his recent return/debut for connections, improved on that and was clearly helped by the cheekpieces. He too isn't going to be easy to place with an official rating of 108. (tchd 20-1)
Suits Me was always likely to struggle on this drop in trip. (op 9-2)
Abbeyside, returning from a 635-day absence, blew any chance he had at the start and soon found himself well behind. He did close before the straight, but had expended too much energy in doing so, and ended up well beaten. He deserves another chance. (tchd 4-1 and 5-1)
Marine Boy(IRE) stopped quickly, having made the early running, and finished well adrift. (op 25-1)

1665 BLUESQUARE.COM 0-0 LIVE FOOTBALL CASHBACK H'CAP 1m 2f (P)
4:55 (4:56) (Class 2) (0-105,105) 4-Y-O+ **£12,952** (£3,854; £1,926; £962) **Stalls** Low

Form RPR

420- **1** **Kings Destiny**[174] 7293 4-8-13 **100**................................ PhilipRobinson 8 111+
(M A Jarvis) *mde all: pushed clr ent fnl 2f: in n.d fnl f: comf* **9/2**[3]

30-2 **2** 2 1/4 **Safari Sunup (IRE)**[34] 1016 5-8-13 **100**................................ LukeMorris 4 104
(P Winkworth) *in tch in midfield: rdn and effrt over 2f out: no ch w wnr but pressing for 2nd ent fnl f: chsd wnr fnl 100yds: kpt on* **8/1**

24-5 **3** 1/2 **Pachattack (USA)**[15] 1328 4-9-0 **101**........................(b) RichardHughes 5 104
(G A Butler) *stdd s: t.k.h: hld up in last trio: effrt on inner ent fnl 2f: rdn and chalng for 2nd over 1f out: no ch w wnr but kpt on fnl f* **16/1**

-114 **4** 2 3/4 **Island Sunset (IRE)**[27] 1084 4-8-5 **92**................................ AlanMunro 1 90
(W R Muir) *t.k.h: chsd ldrs: rdn and nt pce of wnr ent fnl 2f: wnt 2nd over 1f out: no imp: lost 2nd and wknd fnl 100yds* **4/1**[2]

1213 **5** 1 **December Draw (IRE)**[34] 1016 4-8-12 **99**........................ HayleyTurner 7 97
(W J Knight) *t.k.h: chsd ldrs: rdn and unable qck over 2f out: wl btn fr over 1f out* **7/2**[1]

05-0 **6** 1 1/2 **Desert Creek (IRE)**[13] 1383 4-8-7 **94**................................ RyanMoore 2 87
(Sir Michael Stoute) *t.k.h: chsd wnr: rdn and nt pce of wnr ent fnl 2f: lost 2nd over 1f out: wknd 1f out* **8/1**

214- **7** 7 **Eastern Aria (UAE)**[195] 6872 4-9-4 **105**........................ FrankieDettori 3 84
(M Johnston) *hld up in last trio: rdn 3f out: struggling over 2f out: wl btn fnl 2f* **9/2**[3]

2130 **8** 2 **Mafeking (UAE)**[20] 1220 6-8-5 **92**................................ ChrisCatlin 6 67
(M R Hoad) *dwlt: hld up towards rr: rdn and struggling wl over 2f out: wl btn whn wd bnd 2f out* **11/1**

4/0- **9** 1/2 **Racecar Rhapsody (USA)**[421] 771 5-9-4 **105**............. GeorgeBaker 9 79
(G L Moore) *stdd s: hld up in last: rdn and short lived effrt on outer over 2f out: wl btn fnl 2f* **66/1**

2m 5.02s (-1.58) **Going Correction** +0.10s/f (Slow) **9** Ran SP% **116.5**
Speed ratings (Par 109): **110,108,107,105,104 103,98,96,96**
toteswingers:1&2:£5.10, 1&3:£6.00, 2&3:£12.60 CSF £40.60 CT £530.50 TOTE £5.50: £1.60, £3.50, £9.50; EX 45.80.
Owner Dennis Yardy **Bred** D A Yardy **Trained** Newmarket, Suffolk

FOCUS
A good handicap. The winner seems to have improved again and the form is rated around the third and fourth.

NOTEBOOK
Kings Destiny received a well-judged ride and showed a good change of pace to go clear rounding the final bend. A generally progressive sort last season, when tried up to 1m6f, he has reportedly got quicker as he's strengthened from three to four, and though very much having the run of things, he could yet improve again back on turf. He was winning off 100, so may find himself contesting pattern races before long. (tchd 7-2 and 5-1 in places)
Safari Sunup(IRE), second in the Magnolia Stakes on his reappearance, was racing from a career-high mark on this return to handicaps and stayed on best of the remainder, but was never in with a chance of getting near the winner. (op 7-1)
Pachattack(USA), well held in the Earl Of Sefton latest, was a bit keen towards rear, but did make good ground to have every chance for second. She isn't the easiest to place. (op 12-1)
Island Sunset(IRE) was 7lb higher than when winning over C&D in March and she failed to see her race out having been a bit keen early. She needs to make further progress if she is to win off this sort of mark. (op 5-1)
December Draw(IRE), representing the red-hot William Knight stable, has been in fine form and again looked a big player, but he was yet another that failed to settle early, and he had nothing left from over 1f out. (op 5-1)
Desert Creek(IRE), who having been caught flat-footed by the winner, faded in the straight. The drop back to 1m may help, but he has it all to prove at present. (op 7-1 tchd 12-1)
Eastern Aria(UAE) won seven times last year, shooting up 29lb in the handicap, and finished a good fourth in the Grade 1 E P Taylor Stakes on her final outing. A Coronation Cup entry suggests she has progressed again from three to four, and this run can safely be ignored, as not only did she fail to get a prominent position, but she was later reported to have struck into herself. Official explanation: trainer said filly was struck into (tchd 5-1)

1666 £66 FREE BET AT BLUESQUARE.COM H'CAP 1m 4f (P)
5:25 (5:25) (Class 4) (0-80,79) 3-Y-O **£5,180** (£1,541; £770; £384) **Stalls** Low

Form RPR

51-1 **1** **Corsica (IRE)**[16] 1299 3-9-7 **79**................................ FrankieDettori 3 89+
(M Johnston) *mde all: cocked jaw and hung rt bnd over 9f out: sn rcvrd: pushed clr 2f out: r.o strly: easily* **4/7**[1]

51- **2** 4 1/2 **Fairy Flight (USA)**[147] 7622 3-9-1 **73**................................ WilliamBuick 1 75
(W J Knight) *trckd ldng pair: effrt to chse wnr wl over 1f out: edgd rt u.p over 1f out: no prog and wl hld fnl f* **7/2**[2]

-032 **3** 1 1/2 **Layla's Boy**[6] 1515 3-8-12 **70**................................ JamieSpencer 4 70
(Ian Williams) *stdd s: hld up in last: rdn and effrt on inner wl over 1f out: no ch w wnr fnl f* **9/1**[3]

350- **4** 1/2 **Aattash (IRE)**[193] 6901 3-9-0 **72**................................ AlanMunro 5 71
(M R Channon) *t.k.h: chsd wnr: carried wd bnd over 9f out: rdn and nt pce of wnr 2f out: wl hld fnl f* **20/1**

2563 **5** 13 **Bubbly Braveheart (IRE)**[18] 1261 3-8-12 **70**.................... RyanMoore 2 48
(A Bailey) *t.k.h: hld up in tch: rdn and btn 2f out: eased fnl f* **9/1**[3]

2m 32.66s (-0.34) **Going Correction** +0.10s/f (Slow) **5** Ran SP% **110.6**
Speed ratings (Par 100): **105,102,101,100,92**
CSF £2.88 TOTE £1.50: £1.10, £1.20; EX 3.80 Place 6 £14.27; Place 5 £5.33.
Owner Sheikh Hamdan Bin Mohammed Al Maktoum **Bred** Epona Bloodstock Ltd And P A Byrne **Trained** Middleham Moor, N Yorks

FOCUS
An uncompetitive handicap, run at a reasonable gallop, and only one horse counted up the home straight, Corsica stepping up on his previous form. The form is rated around the third.
T/Plt: £15.70 to a £1 stake. Pool: £64,772.81. 2,994.41 winning tickets. T/Qpdt: £7.10 to a £1 stake. Pool: £4,271.53. 441.58 winning tickets. SP

1198 MUSSELBURGH (R-H)
Friday, April 30

OFFICIAL GOING: Round course - good (good to firm in places); straight course - good to firm (good in places)
Wind: Light against Weather: Cloudy with sunny periods

1667 SEMICHEM.CO.UK FRAGRANCE H'CAP 5f
2:20 (2:22) (Class 6) (0-65,65) 3-Y-O **£2,266** (£674; £337; £168) **Stalls** Low

Form RPR

00-0 **1** **Lees Anthem**[9] 1468 3-8-11 **55**................................ PatrickMathers 8 62
(C J Teague) *chsd ldrs: hdwy 2f out: effrt and edgd lft over 1f out: sn rdn and styd on to chal ins fnl f: kpt on to ld last 50yds* **33/1**

0-41 **2** hd **Jigajig**[10] 1456 3-8-1 **52** 6ex................................ MarkPower(7) 9 58
(K A Ryan) *cl up: led 2f out: rdn over 1f out: drvn ins fnl f: hdd and no ex last 50yds* **5/1**[3]

2642 **3** 1 3/4 **Dower Glen**[9] 1468 3-8-8 **55**................................ GaryBartley(3) 4 59+
(N Wilson) *trckd ldrs: whn nt clr run and hmpd over 1f out and again jst ins fnl f: rdn and styd on wl towards fin* **11/4**[1]

44-4 **4** 1 **Seven Of Diamonds (IRE)**[13] 1402 3-9-4 **62**................(t) DavidAllan 10 58
(T D Easterby) *chsd ldrs: hdwy and cl up 2f out: sn rdn and ev ch tl drvn and one pce ent fnl f* **3/1**[2]

00-0 **5** 2 1/4 **Kristen Jane (USA)**[21] 1201 3-8-4 **48** oh1 ow2......... RoystonFfrench 12 36
(Miss L A Perratt) *hld up towards rr: hdwy on outer wl over 1f out: sn rdn and kpt on ins fnl f: nt rch ldrs* **40/1**

3016 **6** 1 1/4 **Your Gifted (IRE)**[9] 1468 3-9-0 **58**................................ StephenCraine 1 42
(Patrick Morris) *cl up on stands' rails: rdn wl over 1f out and sn wknd* **10/1**

02-0 **7** 2 1/4 **Ya Boy Sir (IRE)**[106] 167 3-8-6 **53**................................ MartinLane(3) 3 28
(N Wilson) *dwlt and in rr: hdwy 2f out: swtchd rt and rdn over 1f out: sn no imp* **12/1**

600- **8** 1 **Stanley Bridge**[181] 7168 3-8-2 **46** oh1.......................... AndrewMullen 11 18
(A Berry) *sn outpcd and a towards rr* **100/1**

500- **9** 3/4 **Classlin**[211] 6409 3-8-8 **52**................................ FrederikTylicki 7 21
(J S Goldie) *a towards rr* **6/1**

1264 **10** 1 3/4 **Blue Neptune**[10] 1444 3-9-4 **65**................................ AndrewHeffernan(3) 6 28
(P D Evans) *led: rdn along and hdd 2f out: sn wknd* **16/1**

00-0 **11** 2 1/4 **Sydney Bridge**[21] 1201 3-8-9 **53**................................ TomEaves 2 8
(J Barclay) *prom: rdn along bef 1/2-way: sn wknd* **28/1**

60.70 secs (0.30) **Going Correction** -0.10s/f (Good) **11** Ran SP% **115.1**
Speed ratings (Par 96): **93,92,89,88,84 82,79,77,76,73 69**
toteswingers:1&2:£41.00, 1&3:£26.30, 2&3:£3.60 CSF £184.80 CT £617.15 TOTE £32.50: £8.20, £1.80, £1.50; EX 287.40.
Owner A Rice **Bred** Silvano Scanu **Trained** Station Town, Co Durham
■ The first winner since 2008 for Patrick Mathers, who has recently returned to the saddle after a break from riding.

FOCUS
The round course was described as good, good to firm in places, with the straight track good to firm, good in places, and the GoingStick was 7.2. A moderate sprint handicap. The winner produced his best form since his early 2yo days.
Lees Anthem Official explanation: trainer had no explanation for the apparent improvement in form
Your Gifted(IRE) Official explanation: jockey said saddle slipped

1668 EUROPEAN BREEDERS' FUND MAIDEN STKS 5f
2:50 (2:51) (Class 4) 2-Y-O **£5,828** (£1,734; £866; £432) **Stalls** Low

Form RPR

1 **Majestic Myles (IRE)** 2-9-3 0................................ PaulHanagan 6 80+
(R A Fahey) *cl up: effrt over 1f out: shkn up to ld ent fnl f: rdn and kpt on wl towards fin* **11/4**[2]

5 **2** 2 **Dolly Parton (IRE)**[6] 1510 2-8-12 0................................ AdrianNicholls 1 66
(D Nicholls) *led: rdn along wl over 1f out: drvn and hdd ent fnl f: kpt on u.p towards fin* **5/1**[3]

3 1 **Kassaab** 2-9-0 0................................ MartinLane(3) 8 67+
(N Wilson) *prom: effrt 2f out: rdn to chal over 1f out: sn drvn and one pce ins fnl f* **11/2**

4 **4** hd **Trading**[30] 1065 2-9-3 0................................ DavidAllan 5 66
(T D Easterby) *prom: rdn along and sltly outpcd 2f out: kpt on u.p ins fnl f* **16/1**

5 1 3/4 **Crimson Knot (IRE)** 2-8-7 0................................ MarkCoumbe(5) 4 55
(A Berry) *in tch: hdwy on outer 2f out: rdn to chse ldrs over 1f out: wknd ins fnl f* **40/1**

6 **6** 7 **Mother Jones**[15] 1324 2-8-12 0................................ FrederikTylicki 7 30
(D H Brown) *awkward and wnt rt s: towards rr: hdwy after 2f: rdn and hung rt 2f out: sn btn* **13/8**[1]

7 16 **Whipperoo (IRE)** 2-8-12 0................................ StephenCraine 2 —
(Patrick Morris) *v s.i.s: a bhd* **40/1**

61.06 secs (0.66) **Going Correction** -0.10s/f (Good) **7** Ran SP% **107.6**
Speed ratings (Par 94): **90,86,85,84,82 70,45**
toteswingers:1&2:£2.10, 1&3:£3.70, 2&3:£5.10 CSF £14.72 TOTE £3.40: £1.80, £2.60; EX 11.50.
Owner James Gaffney **Bred** Arctic Tack Stud **Trained** Musley Bank, N Yorks

FOCUS
A non-bonus maiden and probably no more than fair form. The race has ben rated around the time and the race averages.

NOTEBOOK
Majestic Myles(IRE), an £11,500 purchase, showed plenty of speed, racing enthusiastically close to the pace, and did not need maximum pressure to draw clear. He gave the impression he'll improve for the experience and looks quite a nice type. (op 10-3 tchd 9-4 and 4-1 in a place)

Dolly Parton(IRE), just as on her debut at Haydock, showed bright speed. She was no match for the winner late on, but she showed enough to suggest she can win a similar race and be competitive in ordinary nurseries in due course. (op 7-2)
Kassaab, a £60,000 half-brother to sprint winner Kurtanella, raced close up for much of the way but was onepaced under pressure. He's entitled to entitled to come on for this. (op 5-1 tchd 15-2)
Trading improved on the form he showed on Fibresand first time up, but was still well held. He might be more of a nursery type. (op 12-1)
Crimson Knot(IRE) ran green and is open to improvement.
Mother Jones, who had shaped nicely on debut in a fair Newmarket maiden (fifth won at Lingfield on same day as this meeting), disappointed badly. She looked a speedy type on debut, but after missing the break this time she was never really going and seemed inclined to hang out to her right. Official explanation: trainer said filly was in season (op 15-8 tchd 2-1)
Whipperoo(IRE) Official explanation: jockey said filly missed the break

1669 HART BUILDERS (EDINBURGH) LTD H'CAP — 1m 1f
3:25 (3:25) (Class 4) (0-80,79) 4-Y-O+ **£5,180** (£1,541; £770; £384) **Stalls** High

Form — RPR
0-05 **1** **Sand Tiger (IRE)**63 725 4-9-4 **79** PaulHanagan 4 — 89
(R A Fahey) *trckd ldrs: hdwy over 2f out: rdn over 1f out: edgd rt ent fnl f: sn led and drvn out* **10/1**
2031 **2** *hd* **Fujin Dancer (FR)**13 1395 5-8-4 **70** (p) AmyRyan(5) 11 — 81+
(K A Ryan) *in rr: pushed along 3f out: nt clr run and swtchd ins 2f out: rdn and styng on whn nt clr run over 1f out and again ins fnl f: kpt on wl: jst hld* **10/3**1
330- **3** *1 3/4* **Grand Diamond (IRE)**154 7113 6-8-1 **65** KellyHarrison(3) 5 — 71
(J S Goldie) *hld up: stdy hdwy on outer over 2f out: rdn over 1f out: styd on ins fnl f: tk 3rd nr fin* **25/1**
06-4 **4** *3/4* **Charlie Cool**34 1011 7-9-3 **78** (b) PJMcDonald 1 — 82
(Mrs R A Carr) *cl up: led over 3f out: rdn along 2f out: drvn and hdd jst ins fnl f: wknd last 100yds* **11/2**2
050- **5** *1/2* **Danehillsundance (IRE)**193 6900 6-8-11 **72** (t) FrederikTylicki 7 — 77+
(D H Brown) *hld up: hdwy wl over 2f out: rdn and n.m.r over 1f out: sn swtchd lft and kpt on ins fnl f* **14/1**
50-0 **6** *5* **Burns Night**14 1361 4-8-11 **72** SilvestreDeSousa 8 — 64
(G A Harker) *hld up in rr: pushed along 3f out: rdn 2f out: n.d* **9/1**
400- **7** *1* **Northern Acres**224 6052 4-8-5 **66** AdrianNicholls 2 — 56
(D Nicholls) *led: pushed along and hdd over 3f out: rdn over 2f out and grad wknd* **10/1**
-404 **8** *1 3/4* **United Nations**43 923 9-8-1 **65** (p) MartinLane(3) 10 — 51
(N Wilson) *towards rr: hdwy wl over 2f out: rdn whn n.m.r wl over 1f out: sn no imp* **80/1**
600- **9** *3 1/4* **Jewelled Dagger (IRE)**76 5522 6-8-13 **77** GaryBartley(3) 3 — 56
(J S Goldie) *chsd ldrs: rdn along wl over 2f out: sn wknd* **7/1**3
126- **10** *3/4* **Ogre (USA)**203 6657 5-9-1 **79** (t) AndrewHeffernan(3) 6 — 56
(P D Evans) *cl up: n.m.r on inner over 3f out: swtchd lft over 2f out and sn rdn: ch tl drvn and hld whn n.m.r appr fnl f: sn wknd* **10/3**1

1m 53.89s (-0.01) **Going Correction** +0.15s/f (Good) **10** Ran SP% **114.0**
Speed ratings (Par 105): **109,108,107,106,106 101,100,99,96,95**
toteswingers:1&2:£6.60, 1&3:£21.40, 2&3:£10.20 CSF £42.36 CT £836.06 TOTE £10.70: £2.70, £1.60, £5.20; EX 48.70.
Owner Wildcard Racing Syndicate **Bred** Irish National Stud **Trained** Musley Bank, N Yorks

FOCUS
A fair handicap run at a good pace. The winner was back to his early French form, with the second arguably unlucky and the third the best guide.
Danehillsundance(IRE) Official explanation: jockey said gelding was denied a clear run
Burns Night Official explanation: jockey said gelding never travelled
United Nations Official explanation: jockey said gelding hung right throughout
Jewelled Dagger(IRE) Official explanation: jockey said gelding stumbled leaving stalls

1670 CORE OIL AND GAS LOWBALL BOOTH CONDITIONS STKS — 5f
4:00 (4:01) (Class 2) 3-Y-O+ **£12,462** (£3,732; £1,866; £934; £466) **Stalls** Low

Form — RPR
0-02 **1** **Moorhouse Lad**23 1174 7-8-12 98 TomEaves 2 — 99
(B Smart) *mde all: rdn over 1f out: drvn ins fnl f: hld on gamely towards fin* **11/8**1
000- **2** *hd* **Striking Spirit**223 6091 5-8-12 95 AndrewMullen 3 — 99+
(D Nicholls) *chsd ldrs: rdn along and hdwy over 1f out: drvn and styd on strly ins fnl f: jst hld* **10/1**
163 **3** *hd* **Rebel Duke (IRE)**23 1174 6-8-12 94 BarryMcHugh 4 — 98
(Ollie Pears) *hld up and bhd: gd hdwy on outer wl over 1f out: rdn to chal ent fnl f and ev ch tl drvn and nt qckn nr fin* **9/1**
006- **4** *7* **City Dancer (IRE)**222 6135 4-8-7 90 AdrianNicholls 6 — 68
(D Nicholls) *chsd ldrs: rdn and hdwy to chse wnr 2f out: drvn and btn over 1f out* **9/4**2
32-0 **5** *2 1/2* **Jargelle (IRE)**14 1353 4-8-7 97 PaulHanagan 1 — 59
(K A Ryan) *cl up: rdn along 2f out: sn drvn and wknd over 1f out* **9/2**3

58.69 secs (-1.71) **Going Correction** -0.10s/f (Good) **5** Ran SP% **110.1**
Speed ratings (Par 109): **109,108,108,97,93**
CSF £14.99 TOTE £2.10: £1.10, £6.10; EX 18.10.
Owner Ron Hull **Bred** Peter Onslow **Trained** Hambleton, N Yorks

FOCUS
A good conditions race in which the five runners were separated by only 8lb at the weights. The third is the key to the form.

NOTEBOOK
Moorhouse Lad confirmed recent soft-ground Nottingham placings with Rebel Duke, travelling well on the lead for much of the way before finding just enough for pressure. This was his first success since landing a Group 3 in 2008, so his confidence might have been boosted, and presumably he'll step back up in grade now. (op 7-4)
Striking Spirit has done well over the winter according to his trainer, and has won when fresh in the past, and he duly ran a fine race after 223 days off. He probably ideally wants 6f, making this fast-finishing second all the more creditable. (op 8-1)
Rebel Duke(IRE) took a while to get into his stride, but he eventually had his chance out wide and ran close to form. (op 8-1 tchd 15-2)
City Dancer(IRE), who has apparently been with David Nicholls for about eight weeks (formerly with Alan Berry), was walked to the start. She never really looked like winning and finished well adrift of the front three, suggesting she needed this quite badly. (op 11-4)
Jargelle(IRE) had upwards of 4lb in hand of these at the weights, but she ran disappointingly, failing to improve on a lacklustre effort at Newbury on her reappearance. (op 7-2 tchd 11-2)

1671 BOOGIE IN THE MORNING H'CAP — 1m 6f
4:35 (4:35) (Class 5) (0-70,69) 4-Y-O+ **£3,238** (£963; £481; £240) **Stalls** High

Form — RPR
10-2 **1** **Park's Prodigy**9 1467 6-9-2 **58** SilvestreDeSousa 5 — 66
(G A Harker) *hld up in tch: hdwy 5f out: chsd ldng pair 4f out: rdn and sltly outpcd over 2f out: styd on u.p to chal over 1f out: drvn to ld ins fnl f: kpt on* **3/1**2
-020 **2** *3/4* **Oddsmaker (IRE)**13 1398 9-9-5 **64** (t) AndrewHeffernan(3) 8 — 71
(M A Barnes) *t.k.h: trckd ldrs on inner: hdwy to ld over 6f out: rdn clr 3f out: drvn wl over 1f out: hdd ins fnl f: no ex towards fin* **7/2**3
020- **3** *1 3/4* **Petella**184 7124 4-8-1 **48** KellyHarrison(3) 3 — 53+
(C W Thornton) *hld up and bhd: hdwy 3f out: rdn to chse ldrs over 1f out: hung rt ins fnl f: swtchd lft and kpt on wl towards fin* **20/1**
605- **4** *4* **Los Nadis (GER)**8 2044 6-9-3 **59** PaulHanagan 1 — 58
(P Monteith) *prom: effrt to chse ldr over 5f out: rdn 3f out: drvn 2f out and grad wknd* **6/1**
006- **5** *nk* **Silent Lucidity (IRE)**139 7733 6-8-6 **48** oh3 (p) RoystonFfrench 7 — 47
(P D Niven) *hld up towards rr: sme hdwy on outer wl over 2f out: sn rdn and n.d* **20/1**
5225 **6** *1* **Smarties Party**17 1273 7-9-1 **57** PJMcDonald 6 — 54
(C W Thornton) *towards rr: sme hdwy on outer wl over 2f out: sn rdn and no imp appr fnl f* **12/1**
44-6 **7** *12* **Classic Contours (USA)**23 1150 4-9-6 **69** IanBrennan(5) 4 — 56
(J J Quinn) *t.k.h: chsd ldrs: pushed along over 3f out: rdn over 2f out: sn drvn and wknd* **5/2**1
544- **8** *30* **Kyber**219 4873 9-8-8 **50** FrederikTylicki 2 — —
(J S Goldie) *led: rdn along and hdd over 6f out: wknd 4f out and sn bhd* **14/1**

3m 6.26s (0.96) **Going Correction** +0.15s/f (Good)
WFA 4 from 6yo+ 2lb **8** Ran SP% **114.0**
Speed ratings (Par 103): **103,102,101,99,99 98,91,74**
toteswingers:1&2:£3.90, 1&3:£8.90, 2&3:£16.90 CSF £13.87 CT £169.74 TOTE £3.60: £1.50, £1.70, £4.20; EX 11.00.
Owner John J Maguire **Bred** P D And Mrs Player **Trained** Thirkleby, N Yorks

FOCUS
A moderate staying handicap and the early pace was ordinary. The form is rated around the runner-up.
Classic Contours(USA) Official explanation: trainer had no explanation for the poor form shown

1672 CENTRAL TAXIS H'CAP — 7f 30y
5:05 (5:07) (Class 3) (0-90,88) 4-Y-O+
£7,477 (£2,239; £840; £840; £279; £140) **Stalls** High

Form — RPR
5-04 **1** **Ezdeyaad (USA)**6 1513 6-8-12 **79** PJMcDonald 1 — 88
(G A Swinbank) *trckd ldrs: hdwy over 2f out: swtchd rt and rdn over 1f out: led ent fnl f: kpt on wl* **4/1**1
1131 **2** *1/2* **Camerooney**13 1374 7-7-11 **69** DeclanCannon(5) 10 — 77
(B Ellison) *cl up: effrt over 2f out: sn rdn to chal and ev ch whn carried lft over 1f out: drvn and rallied ins fnl f: styd on wl towards fin* **14/1**
0-50 **3** *shd* **Beckermet (IRE)**20 1219 8-9-4 **85** RoystonFfrench 3 — 92
(R F Fisher) *chsd ldrs: hdwy over 2f out: swtchd rt and rdn over 1f out: drvn and styd on wl fnl f* **22/1**
5363 **3** *dht* **Dubai Dynamo**13 1397 5-9-7 **88** AndrewElliott 5 — 95+
(Mrs R A Carr) *hld up and bhd: hdwy on outer wl over 2f out: swtchd rt and rdn over 1f out: styd on strly ins fnl f: nrst fin* **12/1**
1041 **5** *1* **Snow Bay**13 1397 4-8-11 **85** AdamCarter(7) 13 — 90
(B Smart) *led: rdn along over 2f out: drvn and edgd lft over 1f out: hdd jst ins fnl f and one pce* **7/1**
43-0 **6** *1 1/2* **Damika (IRE)**11 1423 7-9-2 **86** MichaelStainton(3) 2 — 87
(R M Whitaker) *midfield: hdwy 3f out: rdn to chse ldrs wl over 1f out: sn drvn and no imp fnl f* **16/1**
064- **7** *1 1/2* **Northern Fling**181 7171 6-8-7 **77** GaryBartley(3) 6 — 74+
(J S Goldie) *in rr tl styd on fnl 2f: nrst fin* **20/1**
23-6 **8** *3* **Stellite**26 1102 10-7-13 **69** KellyHarrison(3) 4 — 57
(J S Goldie) *towards rr tl sme late hdwy* **33/1**
44-1 **9** *1/2* **Deadly Encounter (IRE)**33 1030 4-9-3 **84** (p) PaulHanagan 9 — 71
(R A Fahey) *midfield: effrt 3f out: sn rdn along and no imp fnl 2f* **9/2**2
5652 **10** *1* **Carcinetto (IRE)**6 1519 8-9-4 **88** AndrewHeffernan(3) 14 — 72
(P D Evans) *chsd ldrs on inner: rdn along 3f out: grad wknd* **13/2**
3-04 **11** *1 1/4* **Desert Dreamer (IRE)**102 214 9-9-4 **85** TomEaves 8 — 66
(P D Evans) *s.i.s: a in rr* **40/1**
00-1 **12** *2 1/4* **Malcheek (IRE)**10 1458 8-9-3 **84** 6ex DavidAllan 12 — 59
(T D Easterby) *t.k.h: chsd ldrs: rdn along wl over 2f out: sn drvn and wknd* **11/2**3
3020 **13** *1 3/4* **Sendreni (FR)**26 1102 6-8-4 **71** AndrewMullen 7 — 41
(Mrs J C McGregor) *a towards rr* **100/1**
006- **14** *1 3/4* **Liberty Trail (IRE)**160 7496 4-8-2 **72** MartinLane(3) 11 — 38
(N Wilson) *s.i.s: a in rr* **33/1**

1m 29.58s (0.58) **Going Correction** +0.15s/f (Good) **14** Ran SP% **118.1**
Speed ratings (Par 107): **102,101,101,101,100 98,96,93,92,91 90,87,85,83**PL: Dubai Dynamo £2.00; Beckermet £4.50. T/C - Ezdeyaad, Camerooney, Dubai Dynamo £320.18; Ezdeyaad, Camerooney, Beckermet £565.23. toteswingers:EZ&CM:£11.90, EZ&DD:£6.10, CM&DD:£6.10, EZ&BK:£13.40, CM&BK:£32.10 CSF £54.99 TOTE £3.80: £1.50, £5.40; EX 74.50 Trifecta £27 Owner B Boanson & M Wane.
■ Stewards' Enquiry : Declan Cannon two-day ban: careless riding (May 14,16)

FOCUS
A good handicap run at a decent pace, although the time was only 0.25 seconds quicker than the later Class 6 contest. The form appears sound at face value.

NOTEBOOK
Ezdeyaad(USA) landed a gamble and deserves extra credit considering he was forced to race out wide for much of the way from the least favourable draw. He had run well against a pace bias when fourth over 1m at Haydock six days earlier and coped with the drop in distance to gain his first success over 7f. In this form, he's a handicapper to keep onside and he may now go to Chester next Friday for a race last year's winner of this contest, Opus Maximus, went on to finish second in 12 months ago. (op 6-1)
Camerooney, 4lb higher than when winning an amateur riders' event over this trip at Doncaster on his previous start, was always handily placed and fared best of the prominent racers.
Dubai Dynamo raced well out the back for much of the way and simply got going too late. (op 18-1)
Beckermet(IRE) wasn't asked to dominate but he ran on quite well from off the pace. He's well treated these days and looks ready to win in due course. (op 18-1)
Snow Bay, 4lb higher than when winning under a non-claiming jockey at Thirsk on his previous start, went off plenty quick enough and edged left when beaten late on, failing to confirm recent placings with Dubai Dynamo. (tchd 15-2)
Deadly Encounter(IRE), tried in cheekpieces for the first time, was below the form he showed when winning on easier ground off a 5lb lower mark on his reappearance. (op 7-2)

Malcheek(IRE), carrying a penalty for his reappearance success at Wolverhampton, was well enough placed but he had been a bit keen and dropped out tamely, suggesting this second run back came too soon. (op 15-2)

1673 RACING UK H'CAP — 7f 30y

5:35 (5:37) (Class 6) (0-65,65) 4-Y-0+ — **£2,266** (£674; £337; £168) **Stalls** High

Form				RPR
22-0	1		**Nufoudh (IRE)**[23] 1152 6-8-11 **58** .... FrederikTylicki 8	72

(Miss Tracy Waggott) *mde all: rdn and qcknd clr 3f out: drvn ent fnl f and kpt on wl* **8/1**

025- **2** *2* **Jonny Lesters Hair (IRE)**[181] 7172 5-9-4 **65** .... DavidAllan 13 — 74
(T D Easterby) *chsd ldng pair: hdwy 3f out: rdn to chse wnr 2f out: sn drvn and no imp ins fnl f* **5/2**[1]

20-0 **3** *3/4* **Mister Jingles**[13] 1396 7-8-6 **56** ow1 .... MichaelStainton(3) 10 — 63
(R M Whitaker) *chsd ldrs: rdn along over 2f out: drvn wl over 1f out: kpt on ins fnl f* **16/1**

160- **4** *1 3/4* **Finsbury**[181] 7172 7-8-13 **60** .... AdrianNicholls 6 — 62+
(D Nicholls) *s.i.s and bhd: hdwy on inner wl over 2f out: swtchd lft and rdn over 1f out: styd on ins fnl f: nrst fin* **8/1**

00-4 **5** *3/4* **Nuit Sombre (IRE)**[23] 1149 10-9-1 **62** .... SilvestreDeSousa 14 — 62
(G A Harker) *chsd wnr: rdn along 3f out: drvn over 2f out and grad wknd* **8/1**

406- **6** *1/2* **Daring Dream (GER)**[189] 6984 5-8-13 **63** .... GaryBartley(3) 11 — 63
(J S Goldie) *chsd ldrs on inner: rdn along 3f out: drvn 2f out: sn one pce* **13/2**[3]

0600 **7** *1 1/4* **Redwater River**[9] 1470 6-8-3 **55** .... (b) JamesSullivan(5) 9 — 50
(Mrs R A Carr) *midfield: effrt over 2f out: sn rdn no hdwy fr over 1f out* **16/1**

4-00 **8** *1 1/4* **Bere Davis (FR)**[13] 1396 5-8-12 **62** .... (t) AndrewHeffernan(3) 4 — 54
(M A Barnes) *nvr bttr than midfield* **16/1**

2-45 **9** *hd* **Lilly Grove**[43] 918 5-8-8 **55** .... PJMcDonald 5 — 46
(G A Swinbank) *chsd ldrs: rdn along wl over 2f out: drvn and wknd wl over 1f out* **6/1**[2]

-054 **10** *hd* **Stoic Leader (IRE)**[42] 940 10-8-10 **57** .... RoystonFfrench 12 — 48
(R F Fisher) *a in rr* **18/1**

650- **11** *7* **Woodsley House (IRE)**[184] 7113 8-8-9 **59** .... BarryMcHugh(3) 1 — 31
(A G Foster) *dwlt: a in rr* **20/1**

320- **12** *7* **Shunkawakhan (IRE)**[203] 6637 7-8-8 **55** .... PaulHanagan 2 — 8
(Miss L A Perratt) *midfield on outer: rdn along over 3f out and sn wknd* **18/1**

1m 29.83s (0.83) **Going Correction** +0.15s/f (Good) — **12** Ran SP% **122.5**
Speed ratings (Par 101): **101,98,97,95,95 94,93,91,91,91 83,75**
toteswingers:1&2:£6.20, 1&3:£4.40, 2&3:£5.70 CSF £29.15 CT £332.66 TOTE £9.30: £2.80, £1.40, £5.20; EX 39.60 Place 6 £115.90; Place 5 £58.36.
Owner H Conlon **Bred** Swordlestown Stud **Trained** Spennymoor, Co Durham

FOCUS
A moderate handicap and few were ever involved. The time was only 0.25 seconds slower than the earlier Class 3 handicap. The winner looks better thna ever and the form is rated around the third.
Daring Dream(GER) Official explanation: jockey said bit slipped through gelding's mouth
T/Plt: £111.30 to a £1 stake. Pool: £64,029.63. 419.76 winning tickets. T/Qpdt: £38.90 to a £1 stake. Pool: £3,991.84. 75.84 winning tickets. JR

1674 - 1675a (Foreign Racing) - See Raceform Interactive

1105 CORK (R-H)

Friday, April 30

OFFICIAL GOING: Good to yielding

1676a CORK STKS (LISTED RACE) — 6f

6:00 (6:02) 3-Y-0+ — **£24,446** (£7,146; £3,384; £1,128)

RPR

1 **Rain Delayed (IRE)**[189] 7007 4-9-7 103 .... KLatham 15 — 110
(G M Lyons, Ire) *cl 2nd on far side: rdn to dispute ld 1 1/2f out: led under 1f out: styd on wl and all out to hold on cl home* **11/1**

2 *hd* **Miss Gorica (IRE)**[5] 1557 6-9-4 107 .... PJSmullen 9 — 106
(Ms Joanna Morgan, Ire) *attempted to make all: rdn and jnd 1 1/2f out: hdd under 1f out: rallied to strly press wnr to line* **4/1**[1]

3 *1 1/4* **Rock Jock (IRE)**[13] 1406 3-8-10 98 .... PShanahan 7 — 102
(Tracey Collins, Ire) *prom: rdn in 3rd 2f out: kpt on wl wout threatening ldrs ins fnl f* **25/1**

4 *2 1/2* **Wrong Answer**[33] 1036 3-8-10 101 .... CDHayes 12 — 94
(Kevin Prendergast, Ire) *towards rr: prog 1/2-way: rdn in 4th 2f out: kpt on same pce fnl f* **20/1**

5 *1 3/4* **Snaefell (IRE)**[13] 1406 6-9-12 108 .... (p) FMBerry 14 — 97+
(M Halford, Ire) *towards rr: clsr 1/2-way: rdn in 5th 1 1/2f out: no ex fnl f* **8/1**

6 *1/2* **Moonreach (IRE)**[19] 1244 3-8-10 94 .... WJSupple 13 — 87
(P D Deegan, Ire) *chsd ldrs: rdn in 6th under 2f out: kpt on same pce* **16/1**

7 *4 1/2* **Invincible Ash (IRE)**[13] 1406 5-9-4 95 .... (b) GFCarroll 5 — 73
(M Halford, Ire) *mid-div: rdn and kpt on one pce fr 2f out* **16/1**

8 *hd* **Sir Gerry (USA)**[13] 1406 5-9-7 .... GerardGalligan 8 — 75
(J R Best) *mid-div: rdn 1/2-way: kpt on same pce fr 1 1/2f out* **16/1**

9 *nk* **Six Of Hearts**[13] 1408 6-9-7 98 .... (b) KJManning 2 — 74
(Cecil Ross, Ire) *in tch on stands' side: rdn fr 2 1/2f out: no imp over 1f out* **7/1**[3]

10 *2* **The Tooth Fairy (IRE)**[13] 1407 4-9-7 94 .... ShaneFoley 11 — 68
(Michael Mulvany, Ire) *nvr bttr than mid-div* **20/1**

11 *1 1/2* **Senor Benny (USA)**[13] 1407 11-9-7 96 .... (b) DPMcDonogh 1 — 63
(M McDonagh, Ire) *in tch on stands' side: rdn and wknd fr 2f out* **33/1**

12 *shd* **Santo Padre (IRE)**[27] 1091 6-9-7 102 .... CO'Donoghue 10 — 63
(David Marnane, Ire) *dwlt sltly: a towards rr* **7/1**[3]

13 *2 1/2* **Daffodil Walk (IRE)**[19] 1248 4-9-4 87 .... JAHeffernan 4 — 52
(P D Deegan, Ire) *nvr bttr than mid-div: wknd fr 2f out* **20/1**

14 *1 1/2* **Zorija Rose (IRE)**[15] 1341 5-9-4 99 .... WJLee 3 — 47
(T Stack, Ire) *prom: rdn after 1/2-way: no imp fr 2f out* **10/1**

15 *5* **Walk On Bye (IRE)**[13] 1406 3-8-12 102 .... JMurtagh 6 — 33
(T Stack, Ire) *chsd ldrs: rdn after 1/2-way: wknd fr 2f out: bhd and eased ins fnl f* **9/2**[2]

69.75 secs (-2.85)
WFA 3 from 4yo+ 11lb — **15** Ran SP% **130.4**
CSF £54.58 TOTE £15.40: £5.10, £2.20, £5.70; DF 92.50.
Owner Anamoine Limited **Bred** Anamoine Ltd **Trained** Dunsany, Co. Meath

FOCUS
The first three were prominent throughout and have been rated to their marks.

NOTEBOOK
Rain Delayed(IRE) ploughed something of a lone furrow on the far side of the track to win. A horse with plenty of speed, he led more or less the whole way and, although he may have briefly been headed over a furlong out, he quickened again and managed to hold on to his advantage on the run to the line. He's speedy, tough and consistent and should continue to hold his form and maybe even improve. (op 8/1)
Miss Gorica(IRE) was coming off her weight-carrying exploits at Navan last weekend and ran as well in defeat here. Showing plenty of speed, she was at least disputing from halfway and, although she couldn't immediately match the winner's turn of foot, she picked up and stayed on again inside the last but just couldn't get there. There's every reason to think that she has improved this year and she may just be good enough to pick up a race like this. (op 5/1)
Rock Jock(IRE) was race-fit from his few runs in Dubai during the winter, but even so showed improved form from his run at Naas a couple of weeks ago. He appreciated the extra furlong, coming with a run over a furlong out and then keeping on very well close home to be on the heels of the front two.
Wrong Answer was dropping back in trip after running in a Guineas trial at Leopardstown last month. She got outpaced and came home well, but certainly found the trip on the short side for her.
Snaefell(IRE) had the right trip but would have preferred more rain as he kept on inside the last.
Santo Padre(IRE) Official explanation: trainer said gelding was lame post race
Walk On Bye(IRE) was prominent early but was in trouble at halfway and was one of the first horses beaten.` Official explanation: jockey said filly never travelled (op 7/2)

1677 - 1683a (Foreign Racing) - See Raceform Interactive

1653 DONCASTER (L-H)

Saturday, May 1

OFFICIAL GOING: Good to firm (good in places; 8.7)
Wind: Moderate half behind Weather: Overcast

1684 CROWNHOTEL-BAWTRY.CO.UK APPRENTICE H'CAP — 1m 2f 60y

5:35 (5:35) (Class 4) (0-85,85) 4-Y-0+ — **£4,533** (£1,348; £674; £336) **Stalls** Low

Form				RPR
6433	1		**Follow The Flag (IRE)**[2] 1645 6-8-5 **78** .... (p) ConorQuish(7) 4	84

(A J McCabe) *t.k.h: chsd ldr: cl up over 2f out: rdn to chal over 1f out: led jst ins fnl f: kpt on wl* **6/1**[3]

0220 **2** *2* **Thunderstruck**[14] 1378 5-8-9 **82** .... (p) JonathanHinch(7) 3 — 84
(J A Glover) *t.k.h: led: pushed along over 2f out: rdn wl over 1f out: hdd jst ins fnl f: kpt on same pce* **6/1**[3]

00-1 **3** *hd* **Russian George (IRE)**[7] 1512 4-9-2 **82** .... RosieJessop 1 — 84+
(S Gollings) *rrd s and s.i.s: in rr tl hdwy on wd outside over 3f out: chsd ldrs over 2f out: sn rdn and hung lft over 1f out: kpt on u.p ins fnl f* **7/2**[1]

1156 **4** *3/4* **Benedict Spirit (IRE)**[6] 1069 5-8-11 **82** .... (v) MatthewCosham(5) 6 — 82
(P D Evans) *trckd ldng pair: hdwy 3f out: rdn 2f out: drvn over 1f out: no ex wl ins fnl f* **12/1**

40-0 **5** *3 3/4* **Camps Bay (USA)**[18] 1274 6-9-5 **85** .... JohnCavanagh 5 — 78
(D Nicholls) *dwlt: sn in tch: rdn along over 3f out: drvn 2f out and n.d* **6/1**[3]

2100 **6** *shd* **Chosen Forever**[14] 1378 5-8-4 **77** .... GarethEdwards(7) 9 — 70
(G R Oldroyd) *in tch: hung rt home turn: chsd ldrs 3f out: rdn along whn n.m.r 2f out: swtchd rt and drvn: sn no imp* **12/1**

200 **7** *1 1/2* **Bolodenka (IRE)**[10] 1474 8-9-2 **82** .... LeeTopliss 8 — 72
(R A Fahey) *hld up in tch: hdwy 4f out: pushed along 3f out: rdn 2f out: sn edgd rt and btn* **9/2**[2]

1-35 **8** *3 1/2* **Dream Of Fortune (IRE)**[73] 586 6-8-0 **73** .... KevinLundie(7) 2 — 56
(P D Evans) *dwlt and in rr: sme hdwy on inner over 3f out: sn rdn and nvr a factor* **11/1**

51-0 **9** *1 1/2* **Piquante**[12] 1426 4-8-0 **71** oh1 .... NoraLooby(5) 7 — 52
(N Tinkler) *in tch: hdwy to chse ldrs 4f out: rdn along 3f out: wknd fnl 2f* **22/1**

2m 8.40s (-1.00) **Going Correction** -0.15s/f (Firm) — **9** Ran SP% **111.3**
Speed ratings (Par 105): **105,103,103,102,99 99,98,95,94**
toteswingers:1&2:£6.20, 1&3:£4.00, 2&3:£4.60 CSF £39.56 CT £140.26 TOTE £7.70: £2.20, £2.00, £1.70; EX 41.70.
Owner S Gillen **Bred** Martin Francis **Trained** Averham Park, Notts
■ Conor Quish's first winner.

FOCUS
A fair handicap but it was not strong run and a few of these are better on the AW.

1685 ZESTBARANDGRILL.COM MEDIAN AUCTION MAIDEN STKS — 6f

6:10 (6:13) (Class 5) 3-4-Y-O — **£2,590** (£770; £385; £192) **Stalls** High

Form				RPR
3-	1		**Victory Ide Say (IRE)**[139] 7736 3-9-2 0 .... AlanMunro 12	87+

(P W Chapple-Hyam) *trckd ldrs: hdwy 1/2-way: led 2f out: rdn clr ent fnl f and kpt on strly* **1/1**[1]

0- **2** *3 1/4* **Burning Thread (IRE)**[149] 7618 3-8-9 0 .... DaleSwift(7) 8 — 76
(T J Etherington) *led 2f: cl up: rdn along 2f out and ch tl drvn and one pce ent fnl f* **150/1**

4-4 **3** *shd* **Song Of Parkes**[18] 1275 3-8-11 0 .... SebSanders 15 — 71
(E J Alston) *trckd ldrs: hdwy over 2f out: rdn to chse wnr over 1f out: drvn and one pce ins fnl f* **4/1**[2]

0- **4** *2 1/2* **Mighty Aphrodite**[198] 6797 3-8-11 0 .... SaleemGolam 14 — 63
(Rae Guest) *towards rr: hdwy over 2f out: sn rdn and kpt on appr fnl f: nrst fin* **100/1**

6242 **5** *4 1/2* **Starlight Muse (IRE)**[19] 1269 3-8-11 76 .... GrahamGibbons 2 — 49
(E S McMahon) *chsd ldrs on outer: rdn along 2f out: sn one pce* **5/1**[3]

0- **6** *1 1/2* **Rafiki (IRE)**[198] 6802 3-9-2 0 .... NickyMackay 11 — 49+
(W R Swinburn) *s.i.s and towards rr tl styd on fnl 2f: nvr nr ldrs* **50/1**

52- **7** *1/2* **Dandarrell**[165] 7420 3-8-13 0 .... BarryMcHugh(3) 7 — 47
(Julie Camacho) *dwlt: wnt lft s and towards rr: pushed along 1/2-way: rdn and sme hdwy 2f out: nvr nr ldrs* **20/1**

8 *3/4* **Avaricious** 3-8-11 0 .... MickyFenton 9 — 40+
(C F Wall) *midfield: rdn along 1/2-way: sn wknd* **40/1**

9 *3/4* **Lady Vyrnwy (IRE)**[209] 6514 3-8-4 0 .... LeeTopliss(7) 3 — 37
(R A Fahey) *cl up: rdn along over 2f out: sn drvn and wknd* **33/1**

0 **10** *3/4* **Gower Diva**[12] 1425 3-8-11 0 ow3 .... MichaelGeran(3) 4 — 38
(D Nicholls) *dwlt: rapid hdwy to chse ldrs after 1f: led after 2f: rdn along and hdd 2f out: sn wknd* **33/1**

0 **11** *3/4* **Stoppers (IRE)**[14] 1402 3-9-2 0 .... RobertHavlin 10 — 38
(D Carroll) *a towards rr* **40/1**

12 *3/4* **Zamid (FR)** 3-8-11 0 .... TonyHamilton 5 — 30
(R A Fahey) *s.i.s: a in rr* **11/1**

13 *32* **Whispering Ridge** 3-9-2 0 .... JamesDoyle 13 — —
(M Wellings) *wnt rt s: a in rr: bhd fr 1/2-way* **66/1**

1m 10.75s (-2.85) **Going Correction** -0.35s/f (Firm) — **13** Ran SP% **115.6**
Speed ratings (Par 103): **105,100,100,97,91 89,88,87,86,85 84,83,43**
toteswingers:1&2:£43.20, 1&3:£1.60, 2&3:£80.00 CSF £304.82 TOTE £2.40: £1.10, £31.10, £1.20; EX 279.50.

Owner P W Chapple-Hyam **Bred** Rathasker Stud **Trained** Newmarket, Suffolk

FOCUS

A modest maiden. The big-priced second and fourth lend doubts to the form but the winner looks an above-average maiden winner. The form is rated slightly on the positive side.

1686 SOCIETY LIFESTYLE AND LEISURE MAGAZINE MAIDEN STKS 5f

6:45 (6:47) (Class 5) 2-Y-O £2,590 (£770; £385; £192) Stalls High

Form RPR

1 **Zaidan (USA)** 2-9-3 0 SebSanders 12 87+
(C E Brittain) *midfield: pushed along 1/2-way: hdwy 2f out: swtchd rt and qcknd ent fnl f: sn led and styd on wl* **10/1**

4 2 *2 1/4* **Bunce (IRE)**[7] 1517 2-9-3 0 PaulHanagan 9 79
(R Hannon) *trckd ldrs: hdwy over 2f out: rdn to ld over 1f out: edgd rt and drvn ent fnl f: sn hdd and kpt on same pce* **85/40**[1]

3 *1/2* **Foghorn Leghorn** 2-9-3 0 AlanMunro 7 77+
(P W Chapple-Hyam) *cl up: rdn along 2f out and ev ch tl drvn and one pce ent fnl f* **9/2**[3]

4 *1 1/2* **Tarantella Lady** 2-8-12 0 PJMcDonald 11 67+
(G M Moore) *dwlt and towards rr: hdwy 1/2-way: swtchd lft over 2f out and sn rdn: kpt on ins fnl f: nrst fin* **66/1**

5 *nse* **Breathless Storm (USA)** 2-9-3 0 JamieSpencer 8 72+
(T P Tate) *led: rdn along and hdd over 1f out: sn rn green and hung rt: drvn and wandered ent fnl f: sn lost action and wknd* **11/4**[2]

6 *3* **Roman Dancer (IRE)** 2-9-3 0 TadhgO'Shea 5 61
(J Gallagher) *prom: rdn along over 2f out: grad wknd over 1f out* **66/1**

7 *1/2* **Lizzie (IRE)** 2-8-12 0 GrahamGibbons 13 54
(T D Easterby) *in tch towards stands' rail: effrt 2f out: sn rdn and no imp* **9/1**

4 8 *shd* **Lady Platinum Club**[15] 1359 2-8-9 0 BarryMcHugh(3) 3 54
(G R Oldroyd) *towards rr: hdwy whn nt clr run wl over 2f out: nvr a factor* **10/1**

9 *shd* **Jossy Johnston (IRE)** 2-9-3 0 TomQueally 1 58
(E J Alston) *prom on wd outside: rdn along over 2f out and sn wknd* **66/1**

10 *3/4* **First Pressing** 2-8-12 0 MickyFenton 6 51
(John Berry) *chsd ldrs: rdn along bef 1/2-way and sn lost pl* **50/1**

11 *1 3/4* **Hi Ho Ron** 2-9-3 0 RoystonFfrench 4 49
(D H Brown) *dwlt: a in rr* **33/1**

12 *4 1/2* **Bonjour Bongee** 2-9-3 0 JamesDoyle 2 33
(A J McCabe) *s.i.s: a in rr* **66/1**

58.76 secs (-1.74) **Going Correction** -0.35s/f (Firm) **12** Ran SP% **115.9**

Speed ratings (Par 93): **99,95,94,92,92 87,86,86,86,85 82,75**

toteswingers:1&2:£4.50, 1&3:£32.00, 2&3:£5.00 CSF £30.37 TOTE £9.20: £3.10, £1.60, £1.50; EX 24.90.

Owner Saeed Manana **Bred** Stratford Place Stud **Trained** Newmarket, Suffolk

FOCUS

An interesting juvenile maiden and the form looks strong. A race likely to produce a good few winners.

NOTEBOOK

Zaidan(USA) ◆, a $200,000 yearling out of a half-sister to the smart 7f/1m performer Ramooz, made quite an impressive debut, taking some time to get organised but picking up the leaders in good fashion and then after looking green in front, running on strongly to pull clear. He'll be well suited by 6f and being a May foal, ought to improve significantly for this. His trainer considers him potential Coventry Stakes material. (op 12-1)

Bunce(IRE) built on his debut with an effort that suggests he won't be long in opening his account, tracking the leaders travelling well but having no answer to the winner. (op 2-1 tchd 9-4)

Foghorn Leghorn is another that can win a similar event. A half-brother to the 2yo 5f winner Azif out of a mare that won at 5f, he showed plenty of speed and fought on well despite drifting slightly right, not given a hard time. (op 11-4 tchd 5-2 in places)

Tarantella Lady has a bit of a mixed pedigree but none of her siblings have won as 2yos and she looked in need of a stiffer test, keeping in after being ridden along soon after halfway.

Breathless Storm(USA) who cost $300,000 at the sales and is closely related to the smart 2yo Frost Giant, showed plenty of speed and was still in front inside the last 2f when cocking his jaw and losing his place. He again looked quirky inside the last, edging left, and though he is clearly well thought of, it remains to be seen how he progresses. Official explanation: jockey said colt cocked its jaw and hung badly right (op 11-2)

Roman Dancer(IRE) is a brother to the fair 2yo 6f winner Ailsa Carmel and showed up well for a long way until leaving the impression the race was needed.

Lizzie(IRE), a filly by Acclamation, was another that left the impression she should be better for the race. (op 17-2 tchd 12-1)

Lady Platinum Club hinted again that she has more to give, perhaps at 6f. (op 12-1)

1687 VICTORCHANDLER.COM CONDITIONS STKS 7f

7:15 (7:16) (Class 3) 3-Y-O £6,542 (£1,959; £979; £490; £244) Stalls High

Form RPR

04-4 1 **Rodrigo De Torres**[14] 1385 3-9-0 100 TomQueally 3 107
(H R A Cecil) *cl up: led over 2f out: rdn over 1f out: kpt on wl u.p fnl f* **9/2**[3]

01-1 2 *1 1/4* **Meezaan (IRE)**[15] 1352 3-9-0 97 TadhgO'Shea 2 104
(J H M Gosden) *dwlt: sn trcking ldrs: hdwy over 2f out: rdn to chse wnr wl over 1f out: sn edgd lft: kpt on ins fnl f* **4/6**[1]

113- 3 *5* **Citrus Star (USA)**[189] 7016 3-8-12 99 AlanMunro 4 89
(C F Wall) *trckd ldng pair: effrt and ch over 1f out: sn rdn and hung lft: drvn and one pce appr fnl f* **4/1**[2]

31-3 4 *1 1/4* **Below Zero (IRE)**[8] 1500 3-9-0 99 RoystonFfrench 5 87
(M Johnston) *led: rdn along 3f out: drvn and hdd over 2f out: sn wknd* **12/1**

310- 5 *1 1/4* **Exceedingly Bold**[189] 7030 3-9-0 92 MickyFenton 1 84
(Miss Gay Kelleway) *t.k.h: hld up: a in rr* **33/1**

1m 22.78s (-3.52) **Going Correction** -0.35s/f (Firm) **5** Ran SP% **108.8**

Speed ratings (Par 103): **106,104,98,97,96**

CSF £7.85 TOTE £5.10: £1.90, £1.70; EX 7.30.

Owner Mogeely Stud & Mrs Maura Gittins **Bred** Worksop Manor Stud **Trained** Newmarket, Suffolk

FOCUS

A decent conditions event in which the first two looked potentially smart in pulling clear of some useful opponents at the end of a well run race. A step up from the winner but the favourite was a bit disappointing.

NOTEBOOK

Rodrigo De Torres had had his Greenham form franked by both Dick Turpin and Canford Cliffs in the 2000 Guineas and, down in grade, he showed that he has a future at Listed level at least with an authoritative defeat of one thought good enough to still hold a St James's Palace entry, only needing one crack after travelling strongly to assert readily. Value for a bit more than the winning margin, this looks his trip for now and something like the King Charles II Stakes at Newmarket later this month looks the ideal objective to test his Royal Ascot aspirations (most likely the Jersey Stakes) more thoroughly. (op 5-1)

Meezaan(IRE) is still in the St James's Palace Stakes and though that looks a little out of his league, the step up to a mile will suit him and he looks good enough to win a Listed prize. Never travelling quite as easily as the winner after a sluggish start, he nevertheless pulled clear of the rest without being not knocked about once it was clear the winner had his measure, and he remains open to more improvement. (op 4-5 tchd 8-13 and 5-6 in places)

Citrus Star(USA) promised to finish closer for a long way than he did ultimately conceding race fitness to the first two and didn't help his chances by hanging left when coming off the bridle. He's bred to stay this far but had no trouble with 5f after making his debut at 6f and perhaps a return to the latter trip might suit him ideally for now. (op 7-2 tchd 5-1)

Below Zero(IRE) ran more encouragingly than he had at Sandown but was still put in his place readily. His ideal trip isn't easy to establish and his official rating of 99 promises to make him hard to place. (op 11-1 tchd 10-1)

Exceedingly Bold had a bit to find on ratings and couldn't have been expected to have done any better, ruining any chance he had by failing to settle.

1688 VICTOR CHANDLER H'CAP 6f

7:50 (7:50) (Class 3) (0-90,90) 4-Y-O+ £6,799 (£2,023; £1,011; £505) Stalls High

Form RPR

400- 1 **Tabaret**[166] 7414 7-8-11 86 MichaelStainton(3) 8 95
(R M Whitaker) *prom: hdwy 1/2-way: led 2f out: rdn over 1f out: kpt on wl fnl f* **33/1**

3323 2 *1* **Brierty (IRE)**[23] 1192 4-7-12 77 NeilFarley(7) 16 83
(D Carroll) *chsd ldrs towards stands' rail: hdwy and cl up over 2f out: rdn over 1f out: hung lft ins fnl f: kpt on* **11/1**

5-60 3 *1/2* **Lucky Numbers (IRE)**[14] 1397 4-8-10 82 PaulMulrennan 14 86
(Paul Green) *cl up: effrt 2f out: sn rdn and ev ch: drvn ins fnl f: hld whn n.m.r towards fin* **14/1**

6640 4 *hd* **Five Star Junior (USA)**[22] 1206 4-9-4 90 TomEaves 4 94
(Mrs L Stubbs) *dwlt: gd hdwy 1/2-way: chsd ldrs wl over 1f out: sn rdn and kpt on ins fnl f: no ex towards fin* **10/1**

3-50 5 *3/4* **Shifting Star (IRE)**[78] 528 5-9-4 90 NickyMackay 15 91
(W R Swinburn) *a.p: rdn along 2f out: drvn over 1f out: kpt on same pce ins fnl f* **8/1**[3]

53-4 6 *nk* **Misplaced Fortune**[14] 1374 5-8-3 78 Louis-PhilippeBeuzelin(3) 18 78+
(N Tinkler) *dwlt and towards rr: gd hdwy over 2f out: rdn to chse ldrs over 1f out: one pce ins fnl f* **9/2**[1]

6000 7 *1/2* **Frognal (IRE)**[7] 1516 4-8-8 80 AndrewElliott 12 79
(Mrs R A Carr) *n.m.r s and towards rr: hdwy 2f out: sn rdn and keeping on whn n.m.r ins fnl f* **28/1**

00-6 8 *2 1/4* **Celtic Sultan (IRE)**[21] 1219 6-9-1 87 MickyFenton 13 79
(T P Tate) *n.m.r s and sn in rr: hdwy wl over 1f out: kpt on ins fnl f: nrst fin* **5/1**[2]

00-0 9 *nk* **Protector (SAF)**[34] 1032 9-8-11 83 (t) AndrewMullen 9 74
(A G Foster) *nvr bttr than midfield* **25/1**

466- 10 *1/2* **Barons Spy (IRE)**[208] 6540 9-8-11 83 JamesDoyle 10 72
(R J Price) *wnt rt s: led: rdn along 1/2-way: hdd 2f out and grad wknd* **25/1**

4-50 11 *1/2* **Hotham**[12] 1423 7-8-13 88 GaryBartley(3) 19 75
(N Wilson) *a towards rr* **10/1**

6060 12 *2* **Flowing Cape (IRE)**[12] 1423 5-8-9 86 PaulPickard(5) 17 67
(R Hollinshead) *nvr nr ldrs* **25/1**

600- 13 *2* **Galpin Junior (USA)**[192] 6949 4-8-13 88 MichaelGeran(3) 2 63
(D Nicholls) *prom on outer: rdn along 1/2-way: sn wknd* **25/1**

00-6 14 *3/4* **Silver Wind**[33] 1049 5-8-8 83 (v) AndrewHeffernan(3) 1 55
(P D Evans) *cl up on wd outside: rdn along wl over 2f out and sn wknd* **25/1**

0-05 15 *87* **Pusey Street Lady**[15] 1349 6-9-3 89 JamieSpencer 7 —
(J Gallagher) *rrd s: s.i.s: sn eased and t.o* **5/1**[2]

1m 10.43s (-3.17) **Going Correction** -0.35s/f (Firm) **15** Ran SP% **121.4**

Speed ratings (Par 107): **107,105,105,104,103 103,102,99,99,98 97,95,92,91,51**

toteswingers:1&2:£35.60, 1&3:£96.20, 2&3:£18.10 CSF £340.94 CT £5373.18 TOTE £50.70: £10.20, £4.40, £5.60; EX 707.90.

Owner T L Adams **Bred** The P B T Group And G F Pemberton **Trained** Scarcroft, W Yorks

FOCUS

A fair sprint handicap that lost much of its interest after three of the likely market leaders were withdrawn because of the fast ground. The action unfolded towards the centre. Ordinary form.

NOTEBOOK

Tabaret, who'd run well first time out as a 2yo but hadn't done much on his reappearance since, emerged the winner on merit and ended a losing run stretching back to June 2008, always close up in the centre, travelling best 2f out and then holding on gamely. He was probably helped to a degree by the tailwind, and is clearly as effective at 6f as 5f, but given his overall profile doesn't appeal as one to follow up. (tchd 40-1)

Brierty(IRE) is on a good mark (lower here than when winning at York last summer) and continued her good recent AW form with a solid effort, doing best of those that raced on the stands rail. (op 14-1)

Lucky Numbers(IRE) has now been placed on all three C&D starts and ran well, always close up in the centre. His form figures on soft or heavy read 1132 and he'd be interesting off his current mark if getting those conditions sometime soon. (op 16-1)

Five Star Junior(USA) ran right up to his recent best switched back to turf but had no excuses after getting a good tow behind the pace in the centre. (op 17-2)

Shifting Star(IRE) seemed to appreciate the return to turf and drop in grade and shaped as if he isn't a lost cause. (op 11-1)

Misplaced Fortune was sent off favourite but got rather detached early before making good headway to threaten briefly. This was a second promising effort of the season from a mare still on a good mark. (op 6-1 tchd 13-2 in places)

Frognal(IRE) ◆ looks to have been running himself into form for his new yard and left the impression his turn might not be far away especially if dropped into lower grade. (op 25-1)

Celtic Sultan(IRE) promised to be an interesting participant dropped in trip but was squeezed out soon after the start and never threatened. This run is best ignored. Official explanation: jockey said gelding missed the break (op 6-1 tchd 9-2)

Protector(SAF) Official explanation: jockey said gelding hung right

Barons Spy(IRE) showed up well for a long way on his reappearance and left the impression he retains all his ability. He's best ridden a bit more patiently on a turning track and would be interesting if getting that scenario next time. (tchd 28-1 tchd 33-1 in places)

Pusey Street Lady Official explanation: jockey said, regarding running and riding, that the mare became restive immediately before gates opened and consequently fly-leapt, losing considerable ground and also resulted in the saddle slipping and therefore felt it prudent for it to get home in its own time.

1689 VANILLA ROOMS HAIR AND HOLISTICS BAWTRY H'CAP 1m 6f 132y

8:20 (8:20) (Class 4) (0-85,84) 4-Y-O+ £4,533 (£1,348; £674; £336) Stalls Low

Form RPR

610- 1 **Lady Hestia (USA)**[197] 6822 5-8-8 65 TadhgO'Shea 4 75+
(M P Tregoning) *trckd ldng pair: effrt on inner over 2f out and nt clr run: swtchd rt and rdn over 1f out: drvn and styd on strly ins fnl f to ld nr fin* **7/2**[2]

161- **2** *nk* **Twist Again (IRE)**[213] 6384 4-9-1 **74**.......... KierenFallon 8 80+
(P Howling) *hld up in tch: tk clsr order 4f out: rdn to chal 2f out: sn led: drvn ins fnl f: wknd and hdd nr fin* **2/1**[1]

51-4 **3** *1* **Royal Trooper (IRE)**[24] 1150 4-8-12 **71**.......... PaulMulrennan 6 76
(J G Given) *led: pushed along 3f out: jnd and rdn 2f out: sn hdd: drvn and rallied ent fnl f: kpt on same pce fnl 100yds* **4/1**[3]

-230 **4** *3 1/2* **Chocolate Caramel (USA)**[31] 1069 8-9-1 **72**.......... PaulHanagan 5 72
(R A Fahey) *t.k.h: hld up in rr: hdwy 3f out: rdn to chse ldrs 2f out: sn drvn and no imp appr fnl f* **6/1**

10-0 **5** *11* **Kimberley Downs (USA)**[24] 1151 4-9-8 **84**.......... GaryBartley(3) 7 69
(N Wilson) *trckd ldr: rdn along 3f out: drvn over 2f out and sn wknd* **14/1**

02-4 **6** *17* **Maraased**[76] 554 5-9-3 **74**.......... JamieSpencer 2 35
(S Gollings) *hld up in rr: hdwy over 3f out: rdn to chse ldrs over 2f out: sn hung lft and n.m.r: lost action and eased over 1f out* **13/2**

00-0 **7** *dist* **Sri Kuantan (IRE)**[12] 1427 6-8-10 **67**..........(t[1]) AlanMunro 1 —
(R C Guest) *chsd ldrs: rdn along 4f out: sn wknd and bhd: eased fnl 2f* **25/1**

3m 8.05s (0.65) **Going Correction** -0.15s/f (Firm)
WFA 4 from 5yo+ 2lb **7** Ran SP% **113.7**
Speed ratings (Par 105): **90,89,89,87,81 72,56**
toteswingers:1&2:£3.80, 1&3:£3.00, 2&3:£3.30 CSF £10.81 CT £27.77 TOTE £4.40: £1.70, £2.20; EX 16.20.
Owner Mr And Mrs A E Pakenham **Bred** Shadwell Farm LLC **Trained** Lambourn, Berks

FOCUS
A modest handicap which proved a tactical affair. It has been rated around the winner and third and the front pair look progressive.
Maraased Official explanation: jockey said gelding lost its action
T/Plt: £146.70 to a £1 stake. Pool: £62,258.81. 309.75 winning tickets. T/Qpdt: £26.10 to a £1 stake. Pool: £5,462.24. 154.50 winning tickets. JR

GOODWOOD (R-H)
Saturday, May 1

OFFICIAL GOING: Good
First 2f of 1m crse dolled out abt 5yds, top bend dolled out abt 3yds, rail from 6f on lower bend to 2f in str dolled out circa 6yds. Dist increased abt 15yds.
Wind: Brisk across Weather: Overcast, showers

1690 HAVEAGO@STANJAMES.COM STKS (H'CAP) 1m 6f
2:15 (2:15) (Class 4) (0-85,83) 4-Y-0+ **£6,476** (£1,927; £963; £481) **Stalls** High

Form RPR

21/4 **1** **Just Rob**[15] 224 5-9-9 82.......... MartinDwyer 11 90
(Ian Williams) *pushed along to chse ldr after 3f: led ins fnl 3f: drvn out fnl f* **20/1**

43-3 **2** *1* **Curacao**[24] 1161 4-9-3 77.......... EddieCreighton 3 84
(Mrs A J Perrett) *chsd ldrs tl drvn and outpcd over 3f out: rdn and styd on again fr over 2f out: r.o to take 2nd wl ins fnl f but nt rch wnr* **9/2**[2]

00-2 **3** *3/4* **Devil To Pay**[15] 1357 4-9-3 77.......... FergusSweeney 6 83
(A King) *in rr: pushed along and stdy prog on outside fr over 2f out: styd on wl to go 3rd wl ins fnl f but nt rch ldng duo* **2/1**[1]

35-6 **4** *nk* **Relative Strength (IRE)**[15] 1348 5-8-11 70..........(v) NeilChalmers 13 76
(A M Balding) *prom: chsd wnr and rdn over 2f out: no imp over 1f out and outpcd into 4th wl ins fnl f* **8/1**

210- **5** *1 3/4* **Mykingdomforahorse**[203] 6676 4-9-1 75.......... TedDurcan 7 80+
(M R Channon) *in rr tl hdwy and nt clr run over 2f out: swtchd lft to outside wl over 1f out and kpt on wl fnl f but nt rch ldrs* **5/1**[3]

2106 **6** *hd* **Admirable Duque (IRE)**[10] 1472 4-8-11 74..........(p) AshleyHamblett(3) 8 77
(D J S Ffrench Davis) *in tch: pushed along and hdwy fr over 2f out: styd on ins fnl f but nvr a threat* **20/1**

6200 **7** *2* **Gargano (IRE)**[27] 1101 5-8-13 72.......... GregFairley 10 72
(M Johnston) *led tl hdd ins fnl 3f: styd wl there tl wknd ins fnl f* **12/1**

6655 **8** *14* **Uncle Eli (IRE)**[17] 1303 8-7-12 64 oh3.......... RichardRowe(7) 12 44
(R Rowe) *stdd s: in rr tl rapid progres to chse ldrs 6f out: wknd u.p fr 2f out* **50/1**

20/3 **9** *5* **Rock 'N' Roller (FR)**[56] 224 6-8-12 71.......... LukeMorris 9 44
(G L Moore) *chsd ldrs: edgd lft over 6f out: rdn 3f out and sn wknd* **33/1**

11-4 **10** *2 3/4* **Rowan Tiger**[24] 1161 4-9-0 74.......... PatCosgrave 2 44
(J R Boyle) *plld hrd: chsd ldrs and stl t.k.h whn n.m.r on rails over 6f out: rdn 3f out: hung rt and wknd over 2f out* **11/1**

-222 **11** *8* **Red Hot Desert**[17] 1303 4-8-11 71.......... ShaneKelly 4 29
(W R Swinburn) *hld up in rr: shkn up ins fnl 3f: little rspnse and eased 2f out* **11/1**

3m 8.75s (5.15) **Going Correction** +0.275s/f (Good)
WFA 4 from 5yo+ 1lb **11** Ran SP% **118.1**
Speed ratings (Par 105): **96,95,95,94,93 93,92,84,81,80 75**
toteswingers:1&2:£3.50, 1&3:£10.80, 2&3:£2.10 CSF £104.82 CT £267.69 TOTE £13.90: £3.50, £1.80, £1.30; EX 58.50 Trifecta £250.60 Part won. Pool: £338.75 - 0.70 winning units..
Owner Favourites Racing XXV **Bred** S L Edwards **Trained** Portway, Worcs

FOCUS
A fair staying handicap where the gallop appeared decent, but it proved difficult to come from off the pace. A Flat best from the winner with the level set around the second and third.
Red Hot Desert Official explanation: jockey said gelding stumbled on first bend

1691 ROYAL SUSSEX REGIMENT STKS (H'CAP) 5f
2:50 (2:50) (Class 3) (0-90,84) 4-Y-0+ **£6,799** (£2,023; £1,011; £505) **Stalls** Low

Form RPR

500- **1** **Osiris Way**[202] 6694 8-9-2 **82**.......... GeorgeBaker 1 91
(P R Chamings) *chsd ldr tl led ins fnl 2f: drvn and styd on strly fnl f* **7/2**[2]

4100 **2** *1* **Even Bolder**[63] 736 7-8-5 **76**.......... KierenFox(5) 3 81
(E A Wheeler) *trckd ldrs: shkn up 2f out: drvn and styng on whn rdr dropped reins ins fnl f: kpt on wl to take 2nd last stride but a hld by wnr* **14/1**

2-65 **3** *nse* **Ocean Blaze**[10] 1471 6-9-0 **80**.......... DarryllHolland 7 85
(B R Millman) *led tl hdd ins fnl 2f: styd chsng wnr but no imp fnl f: ct for 2nd last stride* **2/1**[1]

61 **4** *1 3/4* **Absa Lutte (IRE)**[11] 1445 7-9-1 **81**..........(t) StephenCraine 4 80
(Patrick Morris) *restless in stalls: slowly away: in rr: sme hdwy and in tch 1/2-way: rdn and one pce fr over 1f out* **9/2**[3]

420- **5** *1 3/4* **Our Piccadilly (IRE)**[191] 6972 5-8-11 **77**.......... FergusSweeney 6 69
(W S Kittow) *s.i.s: sn in tch and chsd ldrs 1/2-way: outpcd fnl f* **15/2**

60-5 **6** *1/2* **Cerito**[36] 992 4-8-13 **79**.......... PatCosgrave 5 69
(J R Boyle) *chsd ldrs: rdn over 2f out: outpcd fnl f* **14/1**

000- **7** *2 1/2* **Piscean (USA)**[217] 6283 5-9-4 **84**..........(b) TedDurcan 2 65
(T Keddy) *slowly away: rdn and effrt 1/2-way: a outpcd* **6/1**

58.84 secs (0.44) **Going Correction** +0.275s/f (Good) **7** Ran SP% **113.1**
Speed ratings (Par 107): **107,105,105,102,99 98,94**
toteswingers:1&2:£10.10, 1&3:£1.50, 2&3:£6.80 CSF £47.36 TOTE £4.60: £2.60, £4.20; EX 68.40.
Owner Mrs Alexandra J Chandris **Bred** Whitsbury Manor Stud **Trained** Baughurst, Hants

FOCUS
A relatively small field for this decent sprint, but after several made tardy starts they were soon strung out. The second and third set the standard.

NOTEBOOK
Osiris Way has raced mainly at 6f of late but is capable at this trip and has gone well fresh in the past. He was always up with the pace and, when he took the advantage well over a furlong out, always looked like holding on. This rather surprised connections but he has won off 90 in the past, so might still be well handicapped after reassessment. (op 9-2)
Even Bolder was held up early before making his effort towards the stands' side. His rider rather got his reins tangled entering the final furlong but he still managed to get up to take second. (op 11-1)
Ocean Blaze has a good record on this track and tried to make all the running. However, she tended to drift right when headed by the winner and could not respond. (op 11-4)
Absa Lutte(IRE) has been steadily progressive in the last six months, although mainly on sand. She ran on late but compromised her chance by dwelling in the stalls. Official explanation: jockey said mare missed the break (op 4-1)
Our Piccadilly(IRE) was another to miss the break, but made up her ground fairly quickly and had nothing in reserve for the last furlong. (op 7-1)
Piscean(USA) was the worst starter of all and never got out of last place. Official explanation: jockey said gelding missed the break (tchd 11-2 and 13-2 and 7-1 in a place)

1692 BELUCKY@STANJAMES.COM STKS (H'CAP) 6f
3:25 (3:25) (Class 4) (0-85,85) 4-Y-0+ **£4,857** (£1,445; £722; £360) **Stalls** Low

Form RPR

060- **1** **Definightly**[322] 2934 4-9-4 85.......... FergusSweeney 3 94+
(R Charlton) *stdd s: hld up in rr: stdy hdwy and grad swtchd rt to outside fr wl over 1f out: str run ins fnl f to ld cl home: won gng away* **9/1**

60-3 **2** *nk* **Make My Dream**[19] 1266 7-8-4 71.......... MartinDwyer 9 79
(J Gallagher) *in rr: rdn along 1/2-way and hdwy fr 2f out: led jst ins fnl f tl hdd and outpcd cl home* **5/1**[2]

310- **3** *2 1/2* **Russian Spirit**[190] 6994 4-9-3 84.......... PhilipRobinson 5 84
(M A Jarvis) *chsd ldr tl led 2f out: sn rdn: hdd jst ins fnl f: outpcd by ldng duo fnl 100yds* **13/8**[1]

0-22 **4** *hd* **Kerrys Requiem (IRE)**[11] 1438 4-9-4 85.......... CathyGannon 6 84
(M R Channon) *in tch: rdn to chse ldrs and nt clr run ins fnl 2f: got through to chse ldrs again 1f out: styd on same pce ins fnl f* **7/1**

3-42 **5** *2* **Magical Speedfit (IRE)**[11] 1445 5-7-11 71.......... RyanPowell(7) 2 64
(G G Margarson) *chsd ldrs: rdn over 2f out: outpcd fnl f* **14/1**

00-1 **6** *3/4* **King's Caprice**[19] 1258 9-8-7 74.......... RichardThomas 7 65
(J C Fox) *chsd ldrs: rdn over 2f out: outpcd ins fnl f* **10/1**

0-34 **7** *5* **Viking Spirit**[23] 1192 8-9-4 85..........(p) ShaneKelly 8 60
(W R Swinburn) *hld up in rr: swtchd rt to outside and sme prog 2f out: nvr in contention and wknd fnl f* **6/1**[3]

060- **8** *1 3/4* **Perfect Flight**[202] 6694 5-9-3 84.......... TedDurcan 1 53
(M Blanshard) *sn outpcd* **14/1**

-320 **9** *2 3/4* **Mutamared (USA)**[11] 1438 10-8-9 76..........(t) DarryllHolland 4 36
(Andrew Reid) *led tl hdd 2f out: sn btn* **25/1**

1m 13.0s (0.80) **Going Correction** +0.275s/f (Good) **9** Ran SP% **117.8**
Speed ratings (Par 105): **105,104,101,101,98 97,90,88,84**
toteswingers:1&2:£9.70, 1&3:£3.30, 2&3:£3.40 CSF £54.62 CT £112.33 TOTE £12.30: £2.70, £2.10, £1.30; EX 71.50 Trifecta £238.00 Pool: 579.09 - 1.80 winning units..
Owner S Emmet And Miss R Emmet **Bred** S Emmet And Miss R Emmet **Trained** Beckhampton, Wilts

FOCUS
Another good sprint in which several were returning from long breaks. The runner-up looks a reliable guide.

1693 EBF CONQUEROR STKS (LISTED RACE) (F&M) 1m
4:00 (4:00) (Class 1) 3-Y-0+
£22,708 (£8,608; £4,308; £2,148; £1,076; £540) **Stalls** High

Form RPR

50-1 **1** **Shamwari Lodge (IRE)**[28] 1084 4-9-9 105.......... PatDobbs 10 113+
(R Hannon) *hld up in tch on ins: edgd lft to outside fr 2f out and str run fr over 1f out to ld fnl 100yds: readily* **5/2**[1]

21-5 **2** *1* **Hafawa (IRE)**[17] 1312 3-8-7 96.......... GregFairley 1 102
(M Johnston) *t.k.h: trckd ldr: chal 3f out: led over 2f out: sn rdn: qcknd over 1f out: hdd and outpcd by wnr fnl 100yds but kpt on wl for clr 2nd* **5/1**[3]

230- **3** *2* **Super Sleuth (IRE)**[342] 2304 4-9-6 107.......... MartinDwyer 9 100
(B J Meehan) *chsd ldrs: n.m.r on ins bnd 4f out: rdn and kpt on fr 2f out tl outpcd ins fnl f* **5/2**[1]

0-22 **4** *nk* **Aspectoflove (IRE)**[65] 711 4-9-9 105.......... TedDurcan 7 102
(Saeed Bin Suroor) *t.k.h: chsd ldrs: rdn over 2f out: sn chsng wnr and rdn: outpcd fnl f* **4/1**[2]

054- **5** *1* **First City**[200] 6757 4-9-6 93.......... ShaneKelly 4 97+
(D M Simcock) *in rr: hdwy over 2f out: shkn up and sn hanging rt: kpt on fnl f but nvr in contention* **33/1**

210- **6** *2 1/2* **Tropical Paradise (IRE)**[217] 6272 4-9-6 100.......... LukeMorris 6 91
(P Winkworth) *t.k.h: towards rr but in tch: rdn over 2f out: kpt on same pce and nvr in contention* **20/1**

2-06 **7** *3 1/4* **Ahla Wasahl**[65] 711 4-9-9 102.......... FergusSweeney 11 87
(D M Simcock) *chsd ldrs: rdn over 2f out: wknd wl over 1f out* **18/1**

00-5 **8** *3/4* **Please Sing**[28] 1084 4-9-6 95.......... EddieCreighton 5 82
(M R Channon) *awkward stalls and s.i.s: t.k.h: rdn over 2f out but a towards rr* **16/1**

060- **9** *17* **All Annalena (IRE)**[143] 7697 4-9-6 99.......... DarryllHolland 8 43
(Mrs L Wadham) *led tl hdd & wknd over 2f out* **33/1**

1m 40.8s (0.90) **Going Correction** +0.275s/f (Good)
WFA 3 from 4yo+ 13lb **9** Ran SP% **115.6**
Speed ratings (Par 111): **106,105,103,102,101 99,95,95,78**
toteswingers:1&2:£2.90, 1&3:£2.40, 2&3:£5.40 CSF £15.11 TOTE £3.30: £1.40, £2.00, £1.60; EX 17.70.
Owner Andrew Russell **Bred** Pier House Stud **Trained** East Everleigh, Wilts

FOCUS
This fillies' Listed race has been dominated by three and four-year-olds and they were the only age groups represented this time, with only one representative the younger category. It looked a decent race of its type on paper but the form may not prove as strong as it might have done. The form is rated through the runner-up with the fifth holding things down.

NOTEBOOK

Shamwari Lodge(IRE) ◆ has progressed really well with racing and gained her second Listed success by producing a turn of foot once getting out of a pocket with 2f to go. She is a really likeable, reliable type and looks capable of picking up a Group race against her own sex this season. (op 11-4 tchd 3-1)

Hafawa(IRE), who had built on her decent juvenile season when a close fifth in the Nell Gwyn last time. She was always up with the pace and then picked up well when asked to take the lead. She beat off all challengers apart from the winner and there was no disgrace in finishing second to a progressive older filly. (op 13-2)

Super Sleuth(IRE) finished third in last season's 1000 Guineas, but had not been seen since finishing well beaten on heavy ground in the Irish version just over 11 months previously. She ran pretty well and had her chance but could not find a change of gear late on. She is still a maiden, so might benefit from picking up a small race before reverting to this sort of company. (op 3-1)

Aspectoflove(IRE), narrowly beaten in a couple of Group 3s at Meydan in February, put up a fair performance and is another consistent sort who should win her share at this level. (op 3-1 tchd 11-4 in a place)

First City was third in last year's Nell Gwyn but has been held in all subsequent tries and only ran on when the race was over.

Tropical Paradise(IRE) might prefer more cut in the ground but did not help her chance by running too keenly early on. (op 16-1)

1694 GARDEN PARTY MEDIAN AUCTION MAIDEN STKS — 7f

4:35 (4:36) (Class 5) 3-Y-O — **£3,238** (£963; £481; £240) **Stalls** High

Form			Horse	Jockey	RPR
00-	1		**Sard**[207] 6563 3-8-12 0 (M A Jarvis) *t.k.h: sn trcking ldr: led jst ins fnl 2f: drvn and asserted readily fnl f* **7/1**	PhilipRobinson 11	79+
343-	2	2 1/2	**King Of Reason**[282] 4233 3-9-3 79 (D M Simcock) *trckd ldrs: shkn up and impr to chse wnr over 1f out: kpt on fnl f but a readily hld* **9/4**[1]	FergusSweeney 9	77
	3	3 1/2	**Jay's Treaty (USA)** 3-9-3 0 (M Johnston) *rn green and drvn in rr after 1f: rdn and stl green 3f out: hdwy fr 2f out: styd on wl fr over 1f out to take 3rd wl ins fnl f but nt trble ldng duo* **11/2**[3]	GregFairley 4	68+
	4	1/2	**Whisper Wind** 3-9-3 0 (G L Moore) *stdd s: hld up in rr: stdy hdwy on ins over 2f out: nvr rchd ldrs and one pce fnl f* **16/1**	GeorgeBaker 6	66
	5	3/4	**Chilli Green** 3-8-12 0 (J Akehurst) *wnt lft s: t.k.h in rr: stdy hdwy fr 2f out: kpt on fnl f but nvr any threat* **25/1**	PatDobbs 1	59
-	6	2	**Frances Stuart (IRE)** 3-8-12 0 (A M Balding) *chsd ldrs: green and drvn over 4f out: styd front rnk tl wknd over 1f out* **16/1**	NeilChalmers 2	54
524-	7	3 1/4	**Sophie's Beau (USA)**[190] 7001 3-9-3 78 (B J Meehan) *led: sn clr: hdd jst ins fnl 2f: btn over 1f out: eased whn no ch ins fnl f* **5/2**[2]	MartinDwyer 5	55
5-46	8	2 1/4	**Silvee**[19] 1257 3-8-12 52 (J J Bridger) *t.k.h early: a towards rr* **66/1**	TravisBlock 8	39
0	9	1/2	**Baxter (IRE)**[22] 1211 3-8-12 0 (J W Hills) *chsd ldrs: rdn 3f out: wknd ins fnl 2f* **33/1**	KierenFox(5) 3	43
06-	10	7	**Cunning Plan (IRE)**[193] 6922 3-9-3 0 (P W Chapple-Hyam) *a in rr* **14/1**	TedDurcan 7	24
-0	11	1 1/4	**Thalia Grace**[21] 1222 3-8-12 0 (L Montague Hall) *t.k.h early: sn in tch: wknd fr 3f out* **33/1**	DarryllHolland 10	15

1m 29.66s (2.76) **Going Correction** +0.275s/f (Good) 11 Ran SP% **116.9**
Speed ratings (Par 99): **98,95,91,90,89 87,83,81,80,72 71**
toteswingers:1&2:£4.60, 1&3:£7.60, 2&3:£4.40 CSF £22.30 TOTE £8.50: £2.50, £1.50, £2.10; EX 31.10.
Owner Tony Bloom **Bred** Jeremy Green And Sons **Trained** Newmarket, Suffolk

FOCUS

A fair median auction maiden but only minor encouragement in the pedigrees of the newcomers. The form is rated around the runner-up, who set a fair standard.

Sophie's Beau(USA) Official explanation: jockey said gelding ran too free

1695 EUROPEAN BREEDERS' FUND GOODWOOD HOTEL MAIDEN STKS — 5f

5:10 (5:10) (Class 5) 2-Y-O — **£3,238** (£963; £481; £240) **Stalls** Low

Form			Horse	Jockey	RPR
	1		**Casual Glimpse** 2-9-3 0 (R Hannon) *wnt lft over 3f out: racd in 2nd tl drvn ahd as ldr hung bdly rt fr over 1f out: styd on strly cl home* **1/1**[1]	PatDobbs 6	80+
	2	2	**Chilworth Lad** 2-9-3 0 (M R Channon) *slowly away: rcvrd and in tch 1/2-way: styng on whn carried bdly rt fr over 1f out: kpt on for 2nd wl ins fnl f but nt rch unhindered wnr on stands' side* **11/4**[2]	EddieCreighton 7	73+
	3	hd	**Remotelinx (IRE)** 2-9-3 0 (J W Hills) *s.i.s: in tch whn sltly hmpd over 3f out: drvn and hdwy appr fnl f: fin wl to press for 2nd cl home but no ch w wnr* **7/1**	MartinDwyer 4	72
0	4	2	**Terrys Flutter**[30] 1073 2-8-12 0 (M A Allen) *sn led: rdn: hung bdly rt and hdd fr over 1f out: wknd fnl 100yds* **40/1**	FergusSweeney 3	60?
	5	5	**Milldown Magic** 2-9-0 0 (B R Millman) *s.i.s: in tch whn hmpd over 3f out: sn bhd* **13/2**[3]	JamesMillman(3) 2	47+
	6	13	**Miss Maudie (IRE)** 2-8-12 0 (J J Bridger) *s.i.s: in tch 1/2-way: hung lft and sn wknd* **22/1**	NeilChalmers 5	—

61.33 secs (2.93) **Going Correction** +0.275s/f (Good) 6 Ran SP% **109.3**
Speed ratings (Par 93): **87,83,83,80,72 51**
toteswingers:1&2:£1.50, 1&3:£2.00, 2&3:£2.40 CSF £3.65 TOTE £2.10: £1.30, £2.00; EX 4.30.
Owner N A Woodcock & John Manley **Bred** Wickfield Farm Partnership **Trained** East Everleigh, Wilts

■ Stewards' Enquiry : Pat Dobbs one-day ban: careless riding (May 16)

FOCUS

This looked an uncompetitive race with only four appearing to have a chance according to the betting. The time was nearly 2.5sec slower than the earlier handicap for older horses. Not an easy race to put a figure on.

NOTEBOOK

Casual Glimpse, a 40,000gns half-brother to five winners, knew his job and kept straight while his nearest rivals wandered across the track in the closing stages. He has a sales-race entry later in the season but could make up into an Ascot juvenile if going on from this. (op 4-5 tchd 5-4 in a place and 6-5 in places)

Chilworth Lad is out of a mare who was quite speedy but has produced nothing of note so far. He overcame a tardy start to challenge entering the final furlong, but was then carried wide by the fourth before running on when eventually getting past that rival. He can win a race before long. (op 9-2)

Remotelinx(IRE), another with a couple of sales-race entries, is bred to be speedy and ran quite well despite looking in need of the race experience-wise, as he followed a couple of his rivals when they drifted across the course. (op 15-2 tchd 8-1)

Terrys Flutter, the only one with previous experience, had been tailed off on his debut but that was on heavy ground and the conditions here were clearly much more suitable. He showed good pace from the start but went right as he saw the crowd in the closing stages, carrying the runner-up with him. He can win a small race on a sharp track on this evidence. Official explanation: jockey said filly hung right

Milldown Magic was a market drifter and missed the break on this debut. He was also done no favours by the winner after a couple of furlongs and can be expected to do better in time. Official explanation: jockey said colt missed the break (op 5-1 tchd 7-1)

Miss Maudie(IRE) was another to miss the break before showing bright speed to join the leaders at around halfway, but her exertions told in the closing stages. (op 20-1)

1696 FAMILY FUN ON 31 MAY STKS (H'CAP) — 1m 1f 192y

5:40 (5:41) (Class 5) (0-70,70) 3-Y-O — **£3,238** (£963; £481; £240) **Stalls** High

Form			Horse	Jockey	RPR
003-	1		**Eltheeb**[191] 6965 3-9-2 68 (J L Dunlop) *trckd ldrs: drvn to ld appr fnl 2f: edgd lft ins fnl f and styd on strly* **5/2**[1]	TedDurcan 1	76+
416	2	2 1/2	**Buona Sarah (IRE)**[10] 1476 3-8-11 63 (J R Boyle) *s.i.s: sn in tch: drvn to cl on ldrs fr 3f out: styd on u.p to take 2nd ins fnl f but no ch w wnr* **15/2**	PatCosgrave 5	66
46-0	3	1 1/4	**Milnagavie**[17] 1302 3-9-4 70 (R Hannon) *led: hmpd by loose horse after 2f: t.k.h: rdn and hdd appr fnl 2f: hld whn crossed by wnr ins fnl f: sn wknd and lost 2nd* **12/1**	PatDobbs 8	70
000-	4	4	**Flyinflyout**[215] 6345 3-8-8 63 ow3 (Miss Sheena West) *trckd ldr: rdn over 2f out: wknd over 1f out* **33/1**	RobertLButler(3) 4	55
600-	5	6	**Miniyamba (IRE)**[190] 6993 3-9-2 68 (J L Dunlop) *in rr: pushed along 4f out: in tch whn shkn up over 2f out: sn btn* **4/1**[3]	MartinDwyer 3	48
-214	6	2	**Pastello**[43] 934 3-9-0 69 (R Hannon) *in rr: in tch 1/2-way: rdn 3f out: wknd fr 2f out* **9/1**	PatrickHills(3) 2	45
040-	7	4	**Rigid**[197] 6829 3-8-3 62 (A W Carroll) *s.i.s: t.k.h: hld up in rr: a bhd* **10/1**	JohnFahy(7) 6	30
301	U		**Until The Man (IRE)**[4] 1601 3-9-3 69 6ex (Mrs L J Mongan) *uns rdr s* **3/1**[2]	(p) DarryllHolland 7	—

2m 10.41s (2.41) **Going Correction** +0.275s/f (Good) 8 Ran SP% **115.1**
Speed ratings (Par 99): **101,99,98,94,90 88,85,—**
toteswingers:1&2:£6.40, 1&3:£8.00, 2&3:£17.50 CSF £22.10 CT £188.68 TOTE £3.30: £1.90, £2.10, £2.80; EX 19.10 Place 6: £12.82, Place 5: £7.79..
Owner Hamdan Al Maktoum **Bred** Bricklow Ltd **Trained** Arundel, W Sussex

FOCUS

A modest handicap and last year's successful trainer was doubly represented. The early pace was strong before settling after half a mile and nothing got into contention from off the pace. The form is rated around the second and third.

T/Plt: £53.40 to a £1 stake. Pool: £89,589.00. 1,223.12 winning tickets. T/Qpdt: £5.00 to a £1 stake. Pool: £4,909.71. 717.05 winning tickets. ST

1324 NEWMARKET (Rowley Mile) (R-H)

Saturday, May 1

OFFICIAL GOING: Good to firm

Stands' side track used.

Wind: Fresh behind Weather: Cloudy with sunny spells

1697 STANJAMES.COM SUFFOLK STKS (H'CAP) — 1m 1f

1:55 (1:55) (Class 2) 3-Y-O+ — **£31,155** (£9,330; £4,665; £2,335; £1,165; £585) **Stalls** Low

Form			Horse	Jockey	RPR
2062	1		**Tartan Gigha (IRE)**[7] 1533 5-9-0 95 (M Johnston) *mid-div: hdwy over 3f out: led over 1f out: drvn out* **12/1**	KierenFallon 15	105
0-02	2	hd	**Elliptical (USA)**[14] 1388 4-8-4 85 (G A Butler) *lw: chsd ldrs: led 3f out: hdd over 2f out: rdn and ev ch fr over 1f out: r.o* **14/1**	Christophe-PatriceLemaire 7	95
010-	3	nk	**Riggins (IRE)**[294] 3873 6-9-1 96 (A M Balding) *hld up: hdwy and hung rt over 1f out: r.o* **12/1**	JimmyFortune 4	105
-100	4	1	**Viva Vettori**[14] 1383 6-8-7 88 (D R C Elsworth) *hld up in tch: rdn over 1f out: styd on* **16/1**	WilliamBuick 11	95
6633	5	3	**Tartan Gunna**[10] 1474 4-8-9 90 (M Johnston) *chsd ldrs: led over 2f out: rdn and hdd over 1f out: styd on same pce fnl f* **11/1**[3]	JoeFanning 12	90
311-	6	hd	**Shamali**[279] 4339 5-9-5 100 (W J Haggas) *bit bkwd: hld up: hdwy over 2f out: rdn and edgd lft over 1f out: wknd wl ins fnl f* **5/1**[1]	RichardHills 16	100+
150-	7	1	**Sandor**[253] 5209 4-8-9 90 (P J Makin) *prom: rdn and n.m.r over 2f out: hung rt and outpcd over 1f out: styd on towards fin* **20/1**	NeilCallan 9	88
-301	8	nk	**Albaqaa**[18] 1274 5-9-5 100 (R A Fahey) *swtg: s.s: hdwy over 3f out: rdn and swtchd rt over 1f out: wknd ins fnl f* **11/1**[3]	TonyHamilton 10	97
04-1	9	2 3/4	**Brunston**[14] 1383 4-8-10 91 (R Charlton) *lw: hld up: hdwy over 4f out: rdn over 2f out: sn hung rt: wknd over 1f out* **7/1**[2]	HayleyTurner 6	82
50-2	10	9	**Marvo**[18] 1272 6-7-10 82 (M H Tompkins) *hld up: rdn over 2f out: a in rr* **20/1**	SimonPearce(5) 2	53
1100	11	1 1/2	**Dalradian (IRE)**[14] 1383 4-8-3 84 (W J Knight) *hld up in tch: rdn over 2f out: sn wknd* **5/1**[1]	DavidProbert 3	52
311-	12	2 3/4	**Ithinkbest**[197] 6830 4-8-7 88 ow2 (Sir Michael Stoute) *swtg: chsd ldrs: ev ch over 2f out: wknd wl over 1f out* **7/1**[2]	RyanMoore 13	50
5000	13	12	**Kaolak (USA)**[35] 1008 4-8-8 92 (J Ryan) *led 1f: chsd ldr tl led again 5f out: hdd 3f out: n.m.r and wknd 2f out* **40/1**	(v) MarcHalford(3) 14	28
50-0	14	6	**Lord Theo**[10] 1474 6-7-13 80 (N P Littmoden) *hld up: hdwy 1/2-way: sn rdn: wknd over 2f out* **100/1**	NickyMackay 1	2
0-60	15	nk	**Negotiation (IRE)**[12] 1430 4-7-11 81 (M Quinn) *led 8f out: rdn and hdd 5f out: wknd 3f out* **66/1**	Louis-PhilippeBeuzelin(3) 5	3
11-0	16	9	**Big Bay (USA)**[14] 1383 4-8-11 92 (Jane Chapple-Hyam) *lw: awkward leaving stalls: sn pushed along in rr: bhd fnl 4f* **40/1**	IvaMilickova 8	—

1m 50.15s (-1.55) **Going Correction** +0.075s/f (Good) 16 Ran SP% **119.8**
Speed ratings (Par 109): **109,108,108,107,105 104,103,103,101,93 91,89,78,73,73 65**
toteswingers:1&2:£24.50, 1&3:£22.30, 2&3:£34.70 CSF £156.81 CT £2143.83 TOTE £14.80: £3.20, £4.30, £2.30, £3.60; EX 242.50 TRIFECTA Not won..
Owner Exors of the Late Mrs I Bird **Bred** Gainsborough Stud Management Ltd **Trained** Middleham Moor, N Yorks

FOCUS

A good-quality, competitive handicap run at a solid gallop, and the whole field came up the centre of the track. Very solid form with slight step ups from the first three.

NOTEBOOK

Tartan Gigha(IRE) was beaten by a handicap good thing in the shape of Mabait at Sandown last time, but he beat the rest handily enough and RPRs rated it a career-best effort. Up a furlong in distance, and back over the same course and distance as when beaten a nose in the Cambridgeshire last term, he proved gutsy under pressure and saw the trip out strongly. A tough sort who takes his racing well, he's a winner at Epsom in the past and perhaps the 1m2f handicap on Derby day will suit him.

Elliptical(USA), like the winner, was unlucky to bump into a very well-handicapped Luca Cumani-trained rival at Newbury last time, but he too ran a fine race in defeat that day, especially considering the track bias towards those held up. Prominent but happy to take a lead, he travelled well through this race, was given every chance by Lemaire, and simply found one too good. He remains relatively lightly raced and open to improvement. (op 16-1 tchd 20-1 in a place and 18-1 in a place)

Riggins(IRE) ◆ is a talented horse but he's clearly been difficult to train. Now a six-year-old and having just his sixth start, he was debuting for a new stable having been sold out of Luca Cumani's yard for 18,000gns in the autumn, and gelded in the interim. He ran a blinder in defeat, especially considering how keenly he raced through the early stages, and providing he can be kept sound he looks sure to pick up a decent prize this season. The Hunt Cup would be an obvious target. (tchd 16-1 in a place and 14-1 in places)

Viva Vettori, who finished second in this race last year, appreciated the return to a sound surface and, by rating his performance similar to last year's, provides a good anchor for the level of the form. He remains a better horse on Polytrack. (tchd 20-1 in place)

Tartan Gunna, like his stablemate, a tough performer who can be relied upon to run his race, travelled better than the winner into the Dip but failed to see his race out as well. It wouldn't be a surprise to see him join his stablmate at Epsom for the 1m2f handicap on Derby day, and at the revised weights there will not be a lot to choose between them. (op 12-1)

Shamali ◆ looked a smart performer in the making when recording back-to-back victories at Ascot last summer, but he was off the track afterwards with a minor injury. He looked to be returning on a fair mark, but after travelling well and coming to challenge on the outer, faded in the manner of a horse who needed his reappearance. He'll come on for this and will be one to be on next time. (tchd 11-2)

Sandor, off the track since August, looked to find this trip on the short side and is likely to appreciate 1m2f plus this season.

Albaqaa, who missed the break, faced a stiffer task under a 5lb higher mark than when successful at Pontefract last time. (op 14-1)

Brunston, shock winner of a messy Newbury Spring Cup a fortnight earlier, was in a similar position on the weights front and may have found this race coming too soon. (tchd 15-2)

Marvo Official explanation: jockey said gelding was unsuited by the good to firm ground

Dalradian(IRE) was unlucky in running at Newbury last time, but his place in the market had more to do with the incredible form his yard has been in rather than his efforts to date on this surface. His best form is undoubtedly on Polytrack. (op 11-2)

Ithinkbest took a while to get off the mark last term, but then followed up in a handicap on his Polytrack debut. Bred to be decent, out of a Group 2 winner, but weak in the market on this return, he had every chance approaching the two-furlong marker, but then weakened right out. He might well have needed this quite badly. Official explanation: jockey said gelding had no more to give (op 11-2 tchd 8-1)

1698 STANJAMES.COM JOCKEY CLUB STKS (GROUP 2) 1m 4f

2:25 (2:27) (Class 1) 4-Y-O+ **£56,770** (£21,520; £10,770; £5,370; £2,690) **Stalls** Centre

Form					RPR
12-0	**1**		**Jukebox Jury (IRE)**^{35} 1026 4-9-3 118 (M Johnston) *chsd ldr tl led 4f out: clr over 1f out: rdn and styd on wl*	(v^{1}) RoystonFfrench 3 **7/4**^{1}	120
304-	**2**	*3¾*	**Nanton (USA)**^{141} 7720 8-8-12 107 (J S Goldie) *hld up: hdwy over 2f out: rdn to chse wnr and hung rt over 1f out: no imp ins fnl f*	RyanMoore 1 **9/2**^{3}	109
-463	**3**	*3¾*	**Claremont (IRE)**^{14} 1382 4-8-12 112 (Mahmood Al Zarooni) *lw: prom: racd keenly: chsd wnr over 3f out: sn rdn: hung lft over 1f out: nt run on*	AhmedAjtebi 2 **15/8**^{2}	103
5-03	**4**	*1*	**Drill Sergeant**^{7} 1529 5-8-12 104 (M Johnston) *led 8f: rdn over 2f out: sn outpcd*	JoeFanning 5 **9/1**	101
21P0	**5**	*18*	**Halicarnassus (IRE)**^{14} 1382 6-9-1 112 (M R Channon) *lw: prom: pushed along 4f out: wknd over 2f out*	AlanMunro 4 **11/1**	76

2m 32.34s (-1.16) **Going Correction** +0.075s/f (Good) **5** Ran SP% **107.7**
Speed ratings (Par 115): **106,103,101,100,88**
CSF £9.35 TOTE £1.90: £1.10, £3.20; EX 9.30.

Owner A D Spence **Bred** Paul Nataf **Trained** Middleham Moor, N Yorks

FOCUS

The Jockey Club Stakes has been won by some high-class performers in recent years with the likes of Millenary, Marienbard, Shirocco, Sixties Icon and Getaway all successful since 2000. This looked a weakish renewal on paper, but the Mark Johnston pair made sure it was run at a proper gallop and class eventually shone through. Jukebox Jury only needed to run to form.

NOTEBOOK

Jukebox Jury(IRE) was conceding weight all round on account of winning the Group 1 Preis Von Europa at Cologne last September and had a visor on for the first time following his moderate effort in the Dubai Sheema Classic on his return. However, he needed his first run last season, so there was every chance that he would step up from his Meydan effort and he duly did so. Always travelling powerfully behind his stable companion, he made his move half a mile from home before taking over in front before the three-furlong pole. Soon in a clear lead, he only needed to be kept up to his work from thereon in and had plenty in reserve to hold off the runner-up, despite a certain amount of stargazing. Connections are now thinking in terms of the Coronation Cup and Eclipse. (tchd 13-8 and 15-8)

Nanton(USA), a versatile and tough handicapper returning from a five-month break, has only ever tried Pattern company once before and that was when fourth in a Listed race. Switched off out the back in the early stages, he stayed on under pressure over the last two furlongs to take the runner-up spot, and although he managed to get within a couple of lengths of the winner inside the last furlong, he never looked like catching him. This was a very commendable effort, but his proximity rather underlines what a modest Group 2 this was. (op 11-2)

Claremont(IRE), beaten by Halicarnassus at Meydan in February but well ahead of him in the John Porter last time, did his chances no good by taking a strong hold on the outside of the field in the first-half of the contest, and although he was challenging for the lead passing the half-mile pole, he then started to hang about all over the track and looked very uncomfortable. His best form for Andre Fabre last year came on softer ground and he is worth another chance when those conditions prevail. (op 13-8 tchd 2-1 in places)

Drill Sergeant, the lowest-rated horse in the field and a well-beaten last of three in this race last year, tried to make every yard once again and at least made sure the pace was honest, but he was done with as soon as his stablemate headed him over 3f from home. He tries hard, but isn't the easiest to win with and isn't proving easy to place. (op 10-1)

Halicarnassus(IRE), carrying a 3lb penalty for winning the Group 2 Bosphorus Cup at Veliefendi last September, started the year off well in Dubai but his last two efforts had been poor. Keen through the early stages, he found nothing once off the bridle 4f from home and this sort of level has proved beyond him domestically in recent years. (op 14-1)

1699 STANJAMES.COM 2000 GUINEAS STKS (202ND RUNNING) (GROUP 1) (ENTIRE COLTS & FILLIES) 1m

3:05 (3:07) (Class 1) 3-Y-O

£227,080 (£86,080; £43,080; £21,480; £10,760; £5,400) **Stalls** Centre

Form					RPR
1	**1**		**Makfi**^{23} 1195 3-9-0 0 (M Delzangles, France) *w'like: str: lengthy: lw: hld up: hdwy over 2f out: led wl ins fnl f: r.o wl*	Christophe-PatriceLemaire 15 **33/1**	123+
56-1	**2**	*1¼*	**Dick Turpin (IRE)**^{14} 1385 3-9-0 117 (R Hannon) *w ldrs: led over 3f out: rdn and hung rt fr over 1f out: hdd wl ins fnl f:*	RyanMoore 11 **16/1**	120
13-2	**3**	*½*	**Canford Cliffs (IRE)**^{14} 1385 3-9-0 118 (R Hannon) *lw: hld up: plld hrd: hdwy over 1f out: rdn and hung rt ins fnl f: no ex towards fin*	RichardHughes 4 **12/1**	119+
213-	**4**	*1*	**Xtension (IRE)**^{196} 6849 3-9-0 116 (C G Cox) *hld up: hdwy over 3f out: rdn over 1f out: styd on same pce ins fnl f*	AdamKirby 17 **25/1**	117
12-1	**5**	*½*	**Elusive Pimpernel (USA)**^{16} 1327 3-9-0 117 (J L Dunlop) *lw: hld up: rdn over 3f out: hdwy and hung rt fr over 1f out: r.o: nt rch ldrs*	EddieAhern 1 **9/2**^{2}	115+
11-	**6**	*nk*	**St Nicholas Abbey (IRE)**^{189} 7017 3-9-0 124 (A P O'Brien, Ire) *prom: rdn over 2f out: outpcd over 1f out: styd on again wl ins fnl f*	JMurtagh 12 **1/1**^{1}	115+
2-	**7**	*½*	**Fencing Master**^{196} 6849 3-9-0 0 (A P O'Brien, Ire) *bit bkwd: chsd ldrs: rdn and hung rt over 1f out: styd on same pce ins fnl f*	CO'Donoghue 9 **14/1**	114+
03-1	**8**	*nse*	**Red Jazz (USA)**^{17} 1311 3-9-0 112 (B W Hills) *lw: prom: rdn over 2f out: edgd rt and styd on same pce ins fnl f*	MichaelHills 3 **66/1**	113
113-	**9**	*2¼*	**Al Zir (USA)**^{189} 7017 3-9-0 110 (Saeed Bin Suroor) *awkward leaving stalls: hdwy over 5f out: rdn and hung rt over 1f out: no ex ins fnl f*	FrankieDettori 10 **16/1**	110
2-1	**10**	*2½*	**Fair Trade**^{14} 1387 3-9-0 86 (D R C Elsworth) *lw: w ldrs: rdn over 2f out: wknd over 1f out*	JimmyFortune 16 **50/1**	103
20-2	**11**	*½*	**Viscount Nelson (USA)**^{34} 1038 3-9-0 110 (A P O'Brien, Ire) *hld up: rdn over 3f out: r.o ins fnl f: nrst fin*	KierenFallon 14 **40/1**	101+
15-1	**12**	*1*	**Lord Zenith**^{21} 1221 3-9-0 102 (A M Balding) *prom: rdn over 2f out: wkng whn hung rt over 1f out*	WilliamBuick 5 **100/1**	99
111-	**13**	*1*	**Hearts Of Fire**^{202} 6716 3-9-0 116 (Pat Eddery) *prom: rdn over 2f out: sn wknd*	StephanePasquier 6 **40/1**	97
355-	**14**	*1½*	**Buzzword**^{175} 7304 3-9-0 114 (Mahmood Al Zarooni) *chsd ldrs: rdn and hung lft fr over 2f out: wknd over 1f out*	AhmedAjtebi 19 **80/1**	93
111-	**15**	*1*	**Awzaan**^{211} 6450 3-9-0 117 (M Johnston) *nt grwn: mid-div: rdn over 3f out: wkng whn hung rt over 1f out*	RichardHills 2 **8/1**^{3}	91
1-	**16**	*½*	**Inler (IRE)**^{197} 6809 3-9-0 0 (J R Best) *hld up: plld hrd: hdwy over 3f out: wknd over 2f out*	TonyCulhane 18 **33/1**	90
43-4	**17**	*nk*	**Audacity Of Hope**^{17} 1311 3-9-0 104 (P J McBride) *lw: s.i.s: hld up: rdn over 3f out: a in rr: no ch whn hung rt over 2f out*	(t) JamieSpencer 8 **125/1**	89
1112	**18**	*5*	**Greyfriarschorista**^{42} 945 3-9-0 99 (M Johnston) *led over 4f: rdn and wknd over 2f out*	JoeFanning 13 **200/1**	78
1-	**19**	*1½*	**Elspeth's Boy (USA)**^{180} 7209 3-9-0 87 (J R Best) *medium-sized: free to post: hld up: rdn and wknd 3f out*	SteveDrowne 7 **100/1**	74

1m 36.35s (-2.25) **Going Correction** +0.075s/f (Good) **19** Ran SP% **128.0**
Speed ratings (Par 113): **114,112,112,111,110 110,109,109,107,105 104,103,102,101,100 99,99,94,92**
toteswingers:1&2:£97.30, 1&3:£52.80, 2&3:£26.50 CSF £491.42 CT £6753.50 TOTE £12.80: £2.80, £6.10, £3.60; EX 470.60 Trifecta £6520.70 Pool: £30,400.60 - 3.45 winning units..
Owner Mathieu Offenstadt **Bred** Shadwell Estate Company Limited **Trained** France

■ The first Classic winner for Mikel Delzangles, and the longest priced 2000 Guineas winner since Bolkonski in 1975.

FOCUS

A Guineas that promised much, for on paper it looked a quality renewal, featuring as it did not only the Champion two-year-old and Racing Post Trophy winner St Nicholas Abbey, whose impressive Doncaster form had been advertised by Elusive Pimpernel's runaway success in the Craven, but also the unbeaten Group 1 winner Awzaan, and the placed horses from the Dewhurst. In addition, there were a number of talking horses in opposition. However, they raced pretty spread out, the early pace wasn't great, a number of horses raced keenly, and the race developed into more of a test of speed than stamina. The form might not be the most reliable for that reason but it does make a fair deal of sense with the second, third, fifth, eighth and ninth all within a pound of their pre-race marks. The unbeaten Makfi is rated an up-to-scratch Guineas winner.

NOTEBOOK

Makfi, in retaining his unbeaten record, showed himself to be the top-class miler he was bred to be. By Dubawi out of a half-sister to Alhaarth, he was bred to win this race, but was sold by Hamdan Al Maktoum at Tattersalls last October for 26,000gns before setting foot on a racecourse. His new connections promptly won a minor race in the French provinces with him, but the colt stepped up hugely on that when an easy winner of the Prix Djebel on his return. He still had plenty to prove in this top company, not least his ability to handle quicker ground, but clearly his trainer, far from having no fears on that score, expected him to improve for a better surface, as he could always have gone to Longchamp for the French Guineas instead. Held up in the centre of the track, tracking the favourite for much of the race, he quickened up well inside the last and was quite comfortably on top close home. The French Guineas remains a possible target, but it's likely that he'll skip that and wait for the St James's Palace Stakes at Royal Ascot. (tchd 40-1)

Dick Turpin(IRE)'s trainer wanted to send him for the French Guineas after he won the Greenham, to avoid clashing with Canford Cliffs again, but his owner wanted to run here, and the decision was justified as the colt ran a blinder from the front. His stamina wasn't guaranteed for this trip, but in a race where the early pace wasn't overly strong, he was able to conserve his energy and it was only well inside the last that he was overhauled. He confirmed Greenham form with Canford Cliffs and, while the French Guineas could come too soon for him, there's always the Irish Guineas or Royal Ascot, although he might not get things so much his own way there. (op 25-1)

Canford Cliffs(IRE), in contrast with Newbury, where he pinged the gates and set out to make every yard, was buried in the pack this time. On the one hand the fairly steady early pace was against him in that he proved very hard to settle, but on the other, it resulted in something of a sprint finish, which undoubtedly suited him. He travelled best into contention, but simply didn't have enough left in the tank to get past the first two on the run to the line, hanging right rather than left as he tired this time. It's quite clear that he's a very talented colt with a fine turn of foot and the ability to win in Group 1 company, but whether it's over this distance remains in question. Connections plan to persist at the trip for the time being, with the St James's Palace Stakes his likely next stop, but he'll surely prove himself a top-class sprinter later in the season, when he'll be a fascinating contender for races like the July Cup. (tchd 14-1 in places)

Xtension(IRE), third in the Dewhurst on his final start at two, has a profile of steady progress, and he ran a sound race in fourth. He might just prove short of the very best at the top level, but he's a consistent sort and looks a miler through and through.

Elusive Pimpernel(USA) was one of those who could have done with a stronger all-round gallop, for he demonstrated in the Craven that he stays a mile really well, and will probably want further as the season goes on. He was always going to be vulnerable in a steadily run affair, and in the circumstances he wasn't disgraced, especially given how big an effort he must have put in to win so well over the course and distance just 16 days earlier. He might be one for the Irish Guineas, but the French Derby might be a more suitable target. (op 13-2 tchd 7-1 in a place)

St Nicholas Abbey(IRE), who proved himself the best of his generation last season with a scintillating display in the Racing Post Trophy, was the subject of high expectation. There was talk of the Triple Crown being on his agenda if all went well, and he was a heavily backed market leader, but he's a son of Montjeu, who's better known for siring middle-distance horses, and having been campaigned like a Derby prospect last term, he still had it to prove that he had the pace to live with the speedier types he never had to meet last year. The way the race was run didn't help matters, as clearly a stronger all-round gallop would have helped, but he was ultimately done for toe. While on the face of it disappointing, he ran a perfectly good Derby trial, a race he is far more suited to running in on pedigree, but he was shunted out to as big as 4-1 by some bookmakers for Epsom on the back of this. (op 11-10 tchd 6-5 and 5-4 in places)

Fencing Master, second in the Dewhurst on only his second start last term, was ridden positively and kept battling away once he came under pressure. A likeable sort who's likely to keep improving as the season progresses, he'll have no trouble getting 1m2f later on.

Red Jazz(USA), the Free Handicap winner, had big stamina questions to answer and, although he ultimately failed to stay, he ran a perfectly good race, and looks just the type to run well in the Jersey Stakes. (op 80-1)

Al Zir(USA), third in the Racing Post Trophy on his last start at two, always looked the type to make up into a better three-year-old, and his connections have never hidden the regard in which they hold him. Awkward from the stalls, he raced alongside the favourite for much of the way and, like him, got outpaced when the speedier types stepped it up. A lengthener rather than a quickener, he'll be suited by a longer trip, and probably easier ground, too. (tchd 20-1 in places)

Fair Trade showed up well for a long way towards the far side and posted a decent effort on this huge step up in grade. (op 66-1)

Viscount Nelson(USA), the stable's third string, had the benefit of having had an outing this term, but he looked more exposed than most in the field beforehand and was simply not good enough. (op 50-1)

Lord Zenith, who didn't look happy running down into the Dip, remains capable of better and will be of more interest in a more realistic grade.

Hearts Of Fire's improvement last autumn, including a win in an Italian Group 1, came in soft ground, and he found conditions very different here. He looks the type more likely to find success abroad again this year. (tchd 33-1)

Buzzword, who was heavily campaigned at two and looked to have his limitations exposed at the top level, was under pressure some way out here. As a son of Pivotal, he probably won't mind getting his toe in in future - his Group 3 win in France last term came with give. (op 66-1)

Awzaan came into the race with a taking profile, being unbeaten in four starts at two, including the Middle Park Stakes, but despite his pedigree suggesting the trip should be within his compass, he still had his stamina to prove. He was beaten a long way out, and while it's sometimes foolish to jump to conclusions, he hasn't grown from two to three, and there has to be a suspicion that he simply hasn't trained on. (op 9-1)

Inler(IRE), the subject of bullish reports from connections in the run-up to the race, is bred to stay this trip but the way he races suggests he's a sprinter. He didn't settle at all through the early stages and gave himself no chance. It wouldn't be a surprise if his connections switch his attentions to valuable handicaps now. Official explanation: jockey said colt ran too free (op 28-1)

Audacity Of Hope Official explanation: trainer said colt lost a near-fore shoe

1700 STANJAMES.COM PALACE HOUSE STKS (GROUP 3) 5f

3:40 (3:42) (Class 1) 3-Y-O+

£36,900 (£13,988; £7,000; £3,490; £1,748; £877) **Stalls** Low

Form					RPR
50-1	**1**		**Equiano (FR)**^{16} [1326] 5-8-13 108 MichaelHills 9 (B W Hills) *mde all: rdn and edgd lft over 1f out: styd on gamely* **$5/1^{2}$**		117
160-	**2**	¾	**Borderlescott**^{139} [7745] 8-8-13 116 NeilCallan 10 (R Bastiman) *prom: pushed along 1/2-way: rdn and edgd lft over 1f out: chsd wnr ins fnl f: styd on* **8/1**		114
00-1	**3**	½	**Blue Jack**^{15} [1353] 5-8-13 105 RichardKingscote 1 (Tom Dascombe) *lw: hld up: hdwy over 1f out: r.o: nt rch ldrs* **8/1**		113+
30-1	**4**	1¼	**Sole Power**^{28} [1091] 3-8-4 103 WMLordan 11 (Edward Lynam, Ire) *trckd ldrs: rdn over 1f out: styd on same pce ins fnl f* **14/1**		104
5-22	**5**	¾	**Elnawin**^{15} [1353] 4-8-13 104 RichardHughes 4 (R Hannon) *prom: rdn and hung lft over 1f out: styd on same pce* **10/1**		105
216-	**6**	*shd*	**Total Gallery (IRE)**^{139} [7745] 4-9-7 118 JMurtagh 6 (J S Moore) *hld up: hdwy 2f out: n.m.r over 1f out: no ex ins fnl f* **$13/2^{3}$**		113+
261-	**7**	1¼	**Spin Cycle (IRE)**^{212} [6427] 4-8-13 107 RichardMullen 3 (B Smart) *lw: chsd ldrs: rdn 1/2-way: no ex fnl f* **16/1**		100
442-	**8**	¾	**Bonnie Charlie**^{197} [6815] 4-8-13 104 RyanMoore 2 (W J Haggas) *in rr: rdn and r.o wl ins fnl f: nvr nrr* **12/1**		98
105-	**9**	¾	**Amour Propre**^{253} [5233] 4-8-13 112 DaneO'Neill 8 (H Candy) *lw: trckd ldrs: racd keenly: rdn over 1f out: wknd ins fnl f* **$5/2^{1}$**		95
00-0	**10**	½	**Star Rover (IRE)**^{35} [1007] 3-8-4 100 DavidProbert 12 (P D Evans) *chsd ldrs: rdn 1/2-way: wknd over 1f out* **40/1**		89
-141	**11**	½	**Arganil (USA)**^{42} [948] 5-8-13 100 (b) JamieSpencer 5 (K A Ryan) *sn pushed along in rr: rdn over 1f out: nvr on terms* **25/1**		91
0-54	**12**	1¼	**Rowe Park**^{15} [1353] 7-8-13 102 TomQueally 7 (Mrs L C Jewell) *dwlt: hld up: rdn and wknd wl over 1f out* **50/1**		87

58.40 secs (-0.70) **Going Correction** +0.075s/f (Good)
WFA 3 from 4yo+ 9lb **12** Ran SP% **118.4**
Speed ratings (Par 113): **108,106,106,104,102 102,100,99,98,97 96,94**
toteswingers:1&2:£9.40, 1&3:£9.00, 2&3:£13.50 CSF £44.07 TOTE £5.20: £2.10, £2.60, £3.50; EX 42.50 Trifecta £216.20 Pool: £2,651.05 - 9.07 winning units..

Owner J Acheson **Bred** Ecurie Skymarc Farm **Trained** Lambourn, Berks

FOCUS

This first Group sprint of the domestic season has been won by some high-class speedsters in recent years, including the likes of Kyllachy and Dandy Man, and three-year-olds had taken this in three of the past four seasons. As would be expected for a race of this class, there was no hanging about and the form looks rock-solid. The winner was close to his old form.

NOTEBOOK

Equiano(FR) was winning his first race since the 2008 King's Stand when just holding on over a furlong further in the Abernant here last month, but he relished this return to the minimum trip. Sustained market support beforehand suggested that he was expected to run a big race, and he did just that. Quick from the stalls, he set a decent tempo and when the challengers arrived running into the Dip, he kept on pulling out more and was well on top at the line. He has clearly returned to top form following a modest 2009 and will head for the King's Stand again, possibly taking in another race en-route. (op 7-1)

Borderlescott, winner of the Nunthorpe for the last two years, just missed out on having to carry an 8lb penalty here by a matter of days, but that was also true when firmly put in his place by Amour Propre in this event last year. Behind Total Gallery in his last two outings, he had been given a recent racecourse gallop in an attempt to get him fit and this performance suggests that the piece of work did him good. Off the bridle at halfway, he stayed on well up the hill and although never quite able to get to the winner, this was still a most encouraging return. No-one would back against him winning his third Nunthorpe following this effort, but in the meantime he will head for the Temple Stakes at Haydock before clashing again with the winner in the King's Stand. (op 13-2)

Blue Jack ◆, stepping up in class after beating Elnawin in a handicap at Newbury on his seasonal reappearance, was given plenty to do but he finished with a real rattle in the final furlong and on this evidence can pick up a Group sprint at some stage. (tchd 7-1)

Sole Power, one of two three-year-olds in the field whose two wins so far have come on the Dundalk Polytrack, ran a blinder especially here as he raced very freely in a prominent position in the early stages, but he didn't drop away as might have been expected. He can win a Listed sprint at the very least. (tchd 16-1 in a place)

Elnawin, over two lengths behind Blue Jack at Newbury and 7lb better off, attracted market support but he could only plug on after coming off the bridle at halfway and probably needs to go back up in trip. (op 14-1 tchd 16-1 in a place)

Total Gallery(IRE), not seen since finishing unplaced at Sha Tin in December, was successful first time out last year but he had an 8lb penalty to carry for his success under Murtagh in the Prix de l'Abbaye. He travelled well off the pace, but didn't have a lot of room to play with between Borderlescott and Amour Propre over a furlong out and could only make limited progress once through. This was a pleasing enough return and there will be other days.

Spin Cycle(IRE), last seen winning a Listed event over course and distance last October, gradually hung over towards the stands' rail and couldn't get involved. He won first time out last season, so it remains to be seen how much he comes on for it. (op 14-1 tchd 12-1)

Bonnie Charlie ◆, making his debut for the yard on this first start since October, hadn't raced over the minimum trip since his second start as a juvenile and he performed better here than his finishing position might suggest. Held up early, he was still in last place a furlong out but he passed a few horses up the final climb and was still going forward at the line. His new yard is still learning about him, so it would be no surprise to see him leave this effort well behind in due course. (op 14-1 tchd 16-1)

Amour Propre finished unplaced in both starts after winning this race on his reappearance last year, but he was only two lengths behind Borderlescott when fifth in the Nunthorpe in August when last seen and came out of that race with sore feet. Keen enough in a handy position early, the way he eventually dropped away was disappointing and he was reported to have finished distressed. Official explanation: vet said colt finished distressed (op 11-4 tchd 3-1 in places)

1701 BELUCKY@STANJAMES.COM H'CAP 6f

4:15 (4:16) (Class 2) (0-100,100) 3-Y-O **£12,952** (£3,854; £1,926; £962) **Stalls** Low

Form					RPR
4521	**1**		**Jack My Boy (IRE)**^{7} [1523] 3-8-4 86 (b) MartinLane(3) 2 (P D Evans) *lw: chsd ldrs: led over 3f out: rdn over 1f out: r.o* **16/1**		97
322-	**2**	1½	**Bagamoyo**^{206} [6585] 3-9-0 93 EddieAhern 15 (J R Fanshawe) *hld up: hdwy: nt clr run and swtchd rt over 1f out: rdn and hung lft ins fnl f: r.o* **20/1**		99+
21-1	**3**	*shd*	**Horseradish**^{18} [1279] 3-8-3 82 HayleyTurner 16 (M L W Bell) *swtg: hld up in tch: pushed along over 2f out: rdn over 1f out: hung lft ins fnl f: r.o* **$3/1^{1}$**		88
13-4	**4**	*1*	**Racy**^{17} [1315] 3-8-8 87 RyanMoore 10 (Sir Michael Stoute) *swtg: prom: chsd wnr over 3f out: rdn and ev ch over 1f out: styd on same pce ins fnl f* **$10/3^{2}$**		90
50-1	**5**	½	**Monsieur Joe (IRE)**^{18} [1281] 3-8-12 91 AdamKirby 1 (W R Swinburn) *trckd ldrs: racd keenly: rdn whn stmbld over 1f out: styd on u.p* **12/1**		92
00-5	**6**	*nk*	**Swilly Ferry (USA)**^{17} [1315] 3-9-3 96 MichaelHills 4 (B W Hills) *hld up: rdn over 2f out: hdwy over 1f out: edgd rt: no imp wl ins fnl f* **$9/2^{3}$**		96
42-2	**7**	½	**Singeur (IRE)**^{23} [1184] 3-9-7 100 DanielTudhope 8 (R Bastiman) *s.i.s: hld up: hdwy over 1f out: nt clr run ins fnl f: nvr trbld ldrs* **18/1**		99
1150	**8**	2¾	**Love Delta (USA)**^{17} [1315] 3-9-1 94 JoeFanning 11 (M Johnston) *led: hdd over 3f out: rdn over 1f out: wknd ins fnl f* **25/1**		84
2-00	**9**	1¾	**Ongoodform (IRE)**^{17} [1315] 3-8-9 88 NeilCallan 13 (P W D'Arcy) *prom: rdn over 1f out: wknd and eased ins fnl f* **33/1**		72
00-0	**10**	¾	**Hairspray**^{14} [1384] 3-8-10 89 KierenFallon 12 (M R Channon) *s.i.s: hld up: hdwy over 2f out: rdn over 1f out: wknd ins fnl f* **25/1**		71
411-	**11**	1¼	**Freeforaday (USA)**^{185} [7108] 3-8-12 91 SteveDrowne 14 (J R Best) *chsd ldrs: rdn over 1f out: wknd fnl f* **14/1**		69
53-5	**12**	3¼	**Nosedive**^{8} [1499] 3-9-2 95 LiamJones 5 (W J Haggas) *hld up: pushed along 1/2-way: sn outpcd* **20/1**		62
466-	**13**	*5*	**Footstepsofspring (FR)**^{213} [6398] 3-8-11 90 TonyCulhane 7 (W J Musson) *lw: hld up: rdn over 2f out: a in rr* **66/1**		41
16-1	**14**	3¼	**Whozthecat (IRE)**^{14} [1399] 3-8-11 90 DavidNolan 9 (D Carroll) *prom: plld hrd: rdn and wknd over 1f out* **9/1**		31

1m 11.54s (-0.66) **Going Correction** +0.075s/f (Good) **14** Ran SP% **123.4**
Speed ratings (Par 105): **107,105,104,103,102 102,101,98,95,94 93,88,82,77**
toteswingers:1&2:£26.20, 1&3:£11.60, 2&3:£14.20 CSF £312.79 CT £1268.60 TOTE £22.50: £4.50, £5.30, £1.70; EX 286.80 Trifecta £902.00 Part won. Pool: £1,218.93 - 0.40 winning units..

Owner Terry Earle **Bred** Mrs Sheila Walker **Trained** Pandy, Monmouths

■ Stewards' Enquiry : Eddie Ahern one-day ban: careless riding (May 16)

FOCUS

A competitive sprint handicap run at a true pace and the form looks sound, with another clear step up from the winner.

NOTEBOOK

Jack My Boy(IRE) was 5lb higher than when winning in first-time blinkers at Ripon seven days earlier and was more exposed than most, but the yard's runners thrive on hard work and he is yet another example. In front before halfway, he looked sure to be swallowed up as he hung away to his left over a furlong from home, but he found more on reaching the rising ground and simply wasn't for catching. Another rise is inevitable, but he is obviously tough and it would be a brave person who backs against him completing the hat-trick. (op 18-1)

Bagamoyo ◆, reappearing after seven month off, was the unlucky horse of the race as he travelled particularly well behind the leaders, but had a wall of horses in front of him just when he needed a gap and had to be switched very wide in order to see daylight. He ran on strongly once in the clear, but the damage had been done and it is surely only a matter of time before he gains compensation. (op 25-1)

Horseradish, raised 6lb after winning narrowly over 7f on his Yarmouth reappearance, was always close up on the far side of the field and stayed on all the way to the line. He remains unexposed and on this evidence a return to further may be in order. (tchd 4-1 in places)

Racy, just in front of Swilly Ferry when fourth on his reappearance over course and distance last month, was sent off very well backed and had every chance having been handy from the off. He still has a bit of scope and there are more races to be won with him. (tchd 5-1 in a place)

Monsieur Joe(IRE), up 3lb after scraping home on his Yarmouth reappearance, was trying this extra furlong for the first time and though he broke well, his rider was keen to get some cover and tucked him in behind the leaders. He stayed on well up the hill and on this evidence it wasn't lack of stamina that beat him.

Swilly Ferry(USA) was possibly unlucky when just behind Racy (who raced on the opposite flank) here last month, but there seemed no excuses this time. He ran on towards the nearside of the track after coming off the bridle at halfway, but was never getting there in time. (tchd 11-2 in a place and 7-2 in places)

Singeur(IRE), beaten at odds-on in a soft-ground three-runner condition event at Leicester on his reappearance, should have found these quicker conditions much more to his liking, but he raced keenly after missing the break and although he stayed on up the hill, it was far too late. He looks to be on an awkward mark now. (op 16-1)

Love Delta(USA) showed good speed for much of the way, but didn't get up the hill and looks held off this sort of mark now. (tchd 22-1)

Whozthecat(IRE), who landed a gamble on his Thirsk reappearance, ran poorly in his only previous try over 6f but he pulled far too hard here and this was too bad to be true. (tchd 12-1 in places)

1702 HAVEAGO@STANJAMES.COM NEWMARKET STKS (LISTED RACE) (C&G) 1m 2f

4:50 (4:51) (Class 1) 3-Y-O **£28,385** (£10,760; £5,385; £2,685; £1,345) **Stalls** Low

Form				RPR
16-5	**1**		**Gardening Leave**[15] 1354 3-8-12 94 ... JimmyFortune 4 (A M Balding) *lw: chsd ldr: rdn to ld over 1f out: styd on gamely* **16/1**	104
15-1	**2**	*nk*	**Wigmore Hall (IRE)**[16] 1330 3-8-12 101 ... JamieSpencer 2 (M L W Bell) *stdd s: hld up: hdwy over 1f out: chsd wnr and hrd rdn ins fnl f: r.o* **4/6**[1]	103
1-	**3**	*1 ½*	**Rashaad (USA)**[190] 6991 3-8-12 87 ... RichardHills 3 (B W Hills) *lw: s.i.s: sn rcvrd and set stdy pce: qcknd 3f out: rdn and hdd over 1f out: edgd rt: styd on same pce ins fnl f* **4/1**[2]	100
313-	**4**	*1*	**Namecheck (GER)**[194] 6898 3-8-12 97 ... AhmedAjtebi 1 (Mahmood Al Zarooni) *chsd ldrs: rdn over 2f out: edgd lft over 1f out: styd on* **12/1**	98
12-	**5**	*1*	**Anhar (USA)**[182] 7184 3-8-12 96 ... FrankieDettori 5 (Saeed Bin Suroor) *hld up in tch: rdn over 2f out: sn outpcd: styd on ins fnl f* **9/2**[3]	96

2m 5.69s (-0.11) **Going Correction** +0.075s/f (Good) **5** Ran SP% **111.7**
Speed ratings: **103,102,101,100,99**
CSF £28.50 TOTE £15.30: £3.30, £1.30; EX 39.60.
Owner Another Bottle Racing 2 **Bred** Darley **Trained** Kingsclere, Hants

FOCUS
A small turnout for this Listed contest and it was run at a rather muddling early pace. It may be that the form will not prove too reliable.

NOTEBOOK
Gardening Leave got a nice lead from Rashaad and came out on top in a driving finish with the favourite. Thought good enough to take his chance in the Group 1 Criterium de Saint-Cloud on his final start last season, he ran as though in need of the outing at Newbury on his reappearance, but he put up a career-best effort here, fighting off the favourite in game fashion inside the last. Although he carries his head rather awkwardly he's perfectly genuine, and the plan now is to go to Royal Ascot for the Hampton Court Stakes. (op 14-1)

Wigmore Hall(IRE), impressive winner of a competitive handicap over the course and distance at the Craven meeting, looked well up to contesting this class of race that day, and was ridden very confidently by Jamie Spencer out the back. Keen to get cover as long as possible, he was brought to challenge the winner well inside the last and had plenty of time to get by if good enough, but he came up short. There's more to come from him, and a bigger field, coupled with being delivered with a late challenge will suit him much better, so he could well reverse form with the winner at Royal Ascot. (op 8-11 tchd 4-5 in places)

Rashaad(USA), winner of a 7f Doncaster maiden on his only start at two, enjoyed the run of things out in front but couldn't take advantage. He edged right under pressure, but this was a sound effort on this step up in class and he can only improve for the experience. (op 5-1)

Namecheck(GER) ran around a bit under pressure and was unable to land a blow. He could be the type who is difficult to place this season off his mark in the high 90s. (op 9-1)

Anhar(USA), who looked to throw away his race through greenness when runner-up over this course and distance in the Zetland Stakes on his second start last term, could have done with a stronger all-round gallop. While unlikely to live up to his pedigree, a sterner test of stamina should suit him. (op 5-1)

1703 LASTCHANCETOWIN@STANJAMES.COM H'CAP 1m

5:25 (5:25) (Class 2) (0-105,100) 3-Y-O **£12,952** (£3,854; £1,926; £962) **Stalls** Low

Form				RPR
21-5	**1**		**Oasis Dancer**[15] 1352 3-9-2 93 ... JimCrowley 10 (R M Beckett) *plld hrd: led 7f out: rdn and hung lft over 1f out: r.o* **4/1**[2]	102+
2-31	**2**	*2*	**Balducci**[17] 1308 3-8-4 81 ... DavidProbert 4 (A M Balding) *lw: a.p: rdn to chse wnr over 1f out: r.o* **8/1**[3]	86+
-000	**3**	*1 ¼*	**Kona Coast**[17] 1310 3-8-9 86 ... (p) WilliamBuick 7 (J H M Gosden) *led 1f: chsd ldr: rdn over 2f out: hung rt ins fnl f: styd on same pce* **20/1**	88
51-1	**4**	*1*	**Hypnotized (USA)**[10] 1480 3-8-7 84 ... JamieSpencer 8 (M L W Bell) *lw: hld up: plld hrd: hdwy over 2f out: sn rdn and hung lft: no imp ins fnl f* **7/2**[1]	85+
51-3	**5**	*1*	**Rumool**[38] 973 3-8-13 90 ... RyanMoore 1 (C E Brittain) *hld up: plld hrd: rdn over 1f out: r.o ins fnl f: nvr nrr* **8/1**[3]	87+
10-4	**6**	*¾*	**Musaafer (IRE)**[21] 1221 3-9-7 98 ... NeilCallan 5 (M A Jarvis) *hld up in tch: rdn over 2f out: wknd ins fnl f* **11/1**	94
1-02	**7**	*1*	**Karaka Jack**[8] 1497 3-9-0 91 ... JoeFanning 9 (M Johnston) *chsd ldrs: rdn over 2f out: wknd fnl f* **8/1**[3]	84
415-	**8**	*shd*	**Flip Flop (IRE)**[182] 7187 3-8-8 85 ... MichaelHills 2 (B W Hills) *swtg: hld up: hdwy over 1f out: edgd rt: no imp fnl f* **20/1**	78
41-5	**9**	*9*	**Fremont (IRE)**[17] 1311 3-9-9 100 ... RichardHughes 3 (R Hannon) *mid-div: rdn over 3f out: sn wknd* **20/1**	72
140-	**10**	*½*	**Black Spirit (USA)**[217] 6268 3-9-8 99 ... AdamKirby 11 (C G Cox) *hld up: rdn over 3f out: sn wknd* **8/1**[3]	70
160-	**11**	*10*	**The Human League**[274] 4488 3-8-9 86 ... SamHitchcott 12 (M R Channon) *hld up: a in rr: wknd 3f out* **33/1**	34
14-2	**12**	*10*	**Azizi**[28] 1083 3-9-7 98 ... (b) RichardHills 6 (W J Haggas) *chsd ldrs: rdn and wknd 3f out* **8/1**[3]	23

1m 37.94s (-0.66) **Going Correction** +0.075s/f (Good) **12** Ran SP% **123.3**
Speed ratings (Par 105): **106,104,102,101,100 100,99,98,89,89 79,69**
toteswingers:1&2:£6.90, 1&3:£15.50, 2&3:£22.00 CSF £35.55 CT £598.75 TOTE £4.70: £1.80, £3.40, £4.70; EX 42.20 Trifecta £813.00 Part won. Pool: £1,098.72 - 0.10 winning units. Place 6: £912.56, Place 5: £207.40..
Owner Mrs M E Slade **Bred** Whitsbury Manor Stud And Mrs M E Slade **Trained** Whitsbury, Hants
■ Stewards' Enquiry : Adam Kirby two-day ban: careless riding (May 16-17)

FOCUS
The pace was decent and they finished well spread out, so the form should work out, whilst the winning time was 1.59secs slower than the Guineas. The runners certainly used the full width of the track and there were almost three distinct groups at one stage. The form of the principals has been taken at face value and the winner is rated up 10lb.

NOTEBOOK
Oasis Dancer ◆, winner of the Tattersalls Timeform Million here last October, was all the better for his Newbury reappearance and much of the credit for this victory must go to Jim Crowley, who took him to race alone out in the centre of the track and let him bowl along in front. It was obvious from some way out that his rivals weren't going to catch him and, despite hanging away to his left over a furlong out, he maintained his advantage all the way to the line. The Britannia would seem the obvious target for him after this. (op 6-1)

Balducci ◆, making his handicap debut after winning a 7f maiden here last month, ran on towards the nearside of the track to finish a clear second-best and he still has scope for further improvement at the trip. (op 9-1)

Kona Coast, another making his handicap debut, was weighted to reverse Tattersalls Timeform Million form with Oasis Dancer, but he had run poorly in three outings since. However, he took the nearside group along for most of the way and kept staying on, so this was certainly an improvement on recent efforts. (tchd 25-1 in a place)

Hypnotized(USA), winner of his last two starts on Polytrack, was up 6lb for this return to turf but despite the solid gallop he raced far too keenly off the pace. Although he stayed on late his earlier exertions can't have helped, but he remains unexposed on grass and is worth another chance. Official explanation: jockey said colt hung left (tchd 10-3 and 4-1 in places)

Rumool, dropping back in trip for this handicap debut, hasn't looked straightforward in his last two starts but on this occasion he didn't find his stride until it was too late. A step back up in distance looks required.

Musaafer(IRE), making his handicap debut, didn't have the race run to suit when a disappointing favourite in a Listed event on Polytrack last month. He got the strong pace he needs this time and raced prominently for a long way, but didn't find much off the bridle. (op 9-1 tchd 17-2)

Karaka Jack is effective from the front and led the centre group, but he came off the bridle three furlongs from home and gradually dropped away. (tchd 15-2)

Flip Flop(IRE) ◆, making her handicap debut and not disgraced when fifth behind Timepiece in a course and distance Listed event when last seen in October, was entitled to need this and looks capable of better with the run under her belt. (op 16-1)

Azizi, who probably came up against a nice prospect when a beaten favourite on his Kempton reappearance, showed up prominently in the centre group until past halfway but then stopped as though something were amiss. (tchd 15-2)

T/Jkpt: Not won. T/Plt: £1,885.10 to a £1 stake. Pool: £189,931.38. 73.55 winning tickets. T/Qpdt: £146.40 to a £1 stake. Pool: £11,301.42. 57.10 winning tickets. CR

[1395]THIRSK (L-H)

Saturday, May 1

OFFICIAL GOING: Good (9.1)
Wind: light 1/2 against Weather: overcast

1704 BEST ODDS GUARANTEED AT TOTESPORT.COM MAIDEN AUCTION STKS 5f

1:45 (1:45) (Class 5) 2-Y-O **£4,209** (£1,252; £625; £312) **Stalls** High

Form				RPR
023	**1**		**Sir Lunchalott**[14] 1389 2-9-0 0 ... (p) RussKennemore(3) 3 (J S Moore) *chsd ldrs: reminders after 1f: edgd lft and styd on to ld towards fin* **3/1**[2]	71
	2	*nk*	**Tilliemint (IRE)** 2-8-12 0 ... DavidAllan 5 (T D Easterby) *dwlt: hdwy to chse ldrs over 2f out: led 100yds out: edgd lft and hdd nr fin: will improve* **5/2**[1]	65+
6	**3**	*3 ½*	**Madam Markievicz (IRE)**[12] 1421 2-8-12 0 ... PhillipMakin 7 (M Dods) *w ldr: hung lft thrght: led over 3f out: hdd 100yds out: sn wknd* **7/2**[3]	52
0	**4**	*8*	**Capall Dorcha**[14] 1389 2-9-3 0 ... JerryO'Dwyer 2 (J R Holt) *s.i.s: sn chsng ldrs: rdn 2f out: sn wknd* **66/1**	29
	5	*nk*	**Celtic Anu** 2-9-3 0 ... PaulMulrennan 1 (Patrick Morris) *swvd lft s: in rr: hung bdly rt over 1f out* **10/1**	27
	6	*8*	**Sacrosanctus** 2-9-3 0 ... FrederikTylicki 6 (J A Glover) *led over 1f: w ldrs: wkng whn sltly checked over 1f out* **7/1**	—
	7	*9*	**Kodibelle (IRE)** 2-8-12 0 ... DuranFentiman 4 (T D Easterby) *s.i.s: sn wl outpcd and detached in last* **8/1**	—

61.94 secs (2.34) **Going Correction** +0.275s/f (Good) **7** Ran SP% **110.0**
Speed ratings (Par 93): **92,91,85,73,72 59,45**
toteswingers:1&2:£1.70, 1&3:£1.10, 2&3:£2.80 CSF £10.05 TOTE £3.40: £2.40, £1.10; EX 11.90.
Owner Richard J Lilley & A J Speyer **Bred** The National Stud Blakeney Club **Trained** Upper Lambourn, Berks

FOCUS
An ordinary juvenile sprint maiden run at a generous early pace. The form is limited with the winner running marginally his best race to date.

NOTEBOOK
Sir Lunchalott, the most experienced in the line-up with three previous tries, had looked in need of a stiffer test when a one-paced second at Lingfield on his second outing. That remains the overriding impression despite victory here. Outpaced and in receipt of reminders immediately, the Pastoral Pursuits colt had to respond well to driving to force his way to the front inside the furlong marker and stay there. This was a first juvenile winner of the new campaign at the tenth attempt for his yard.

Tilliemint(IRE) ◆, who was somewhat edgy down at the start, travelled well off the pace after being slowly away. Produced in the final third of the race, she kept the winner up to his work and possesses the raw material to land a similarly modest contest. (op 7-2)

Madam Markievicz(IRE)'s rider had to angle her to the stands' rail from an early stage to prevent her from hanging left, a trait she had also displayed late on her Pontefract debut. She headed towards the centre of the course once Sacrosanctus's fading cleared the way to do so, eventually forfeiting her lead 1f out. It wouldn't surprise to see connections reaching for some form of headgear next time. Official explanation: jockey said filly hung left throughout (op 3-1)

Sacrosanctus decanted Freddie Tylicki in the preliminaries and was another to prove edgy before loading, but broke well and showed good early speed. He may yet be capable of a bit better around an even sharper 5f. (op 6-1)

1705 FREE RACING POST FORM AT TOTESPORT.COM MAIDEN STKS 1m 4f

2:20 (2:27) (Class 5) 3-Y-O+ **£4,274** (£1,271; £635; £317) **Stalls** Low

Form				RPR
0-	**1**		**Park View**[182] 7183 3-8-3 0 ... PaulHanagan 1 (B W Hills) *led: shkn up and qcknd over 3f out: styd on strly to forge clr ins fnl f* **15/8**[1]	66+
	2	*3 ¼*	**Royal Swain (IRE)**[21] 4-9-13 0 ... RobertWinston 8 (G A Swinbank) *trckd ldrs: wnt 2nd 3f out: chal and hung lft over 1f out: styd on same pce* **2/1**[2]	68+

4 **3** *6* **Hidden**[12] 1432 4-9-13 0 TadhgO'Shea 4 58
(B J Meehan) *chsd ldrs: drvn and outpcd over 3f out: kpt on fnl f: tk modest 3rd nr fin* **13/2**

000- **4** *nse* **Kendalewood**[351] 2042 4-9-13 50 GrahamGibbons 5 58?
(T D Walford) *chsd wnr: drvn over 4f out: one pce fnl 3f* **100/1**

0 **5** *nk* **Switched Off**[9] 1485 5-9-8 0 JamesSullivan(5) 7 55
(M W Easterby) *s.i.s: bhd and sn pushed along: sme hdwy over 4f out: styd on fnl 2f* **33/1**

6 *1* **Barra Raider** 3-8-8 0 TomEaves 6 54?
(R F Fisher) *s.i.s: hdwy and in tch 8f out: kpt on fnl f* **100/1**

5- **7** *hd* **Danube (IRE)**[242] 5547 3-8-3 0 JimmyQuinn 9 49
(H R A Cecil) *swtchd lft after s: mid-div: outpcd over 3f out: styd on fnl f* **7/2**[3]

8 *80* **Kirkum (IRE)**[26] 5-9-13 0 PhillipMakin 3 —
(Miss Diana Weeden) *s.s: sn wl bhd: reminders 6f out: t.o 3f out: virtually p.u* **100/1**

9 *22* **Quitao (GER)** 3-8-8 0 PaulMulrennan 10 —
(M Johnston) *s.i.s: sn prom: lost pl over 4f out: t.o 3f out: virtually p.u* **12/1**

2m 39.51s (3.31) **Going Correction** +0.35s/f (Good)
WFA 3 from 4yo+ 19lb **9** Ran SP% **117.3**
Speed ratings (Par 103): **102,99,95,95,95 94,94,42,28**
toteswingers:1&2:£2.20, 1&3:£3.60, 2&3:£4.10 CSF £6.04 TOTE £3.20: £1.50, £1.40, £2.20; EX 6.10.
Owner K Abdulla **Bred** Juddmonte Farms Ltd **Trained** Lambourn, Berks

FOCUS
A modest maiden. The front pair finished clear and the form makes some sense without looking totally reliable.
Kirkum(IRE) Official explanation: trainer said gelding was coughing post-race

1706 MORE LIVE FOOTBALL BETTING AT TOTESPORT.COM MAIDEN STKS 7f
2:55 (2:57) (Class 4) 3-Y-O **£5,569** (£1,657; £828; £413) **Stalls** Low

Form RPR

1 **Rainfall (IRE)** 3-8-12 0 PaulMulrennan 4 85+
(M Johnston) *trckd ldrs: edgd lft and led over 1f out: sn clr: v readily* **10/3**[2]

0-3 **2** *6* **Fifty Moore**[34] 1029 3-9-3 0 AndrewElliott 9 73
(Jedd O'Keeffe) *in tch: hdwy and swtchd outside 2f out: kpt on to take 2nd ins fnl f* **12/1**

33- **3** *½* **Cockney Class (USA)**[274] 4499 3-9-3 0 SebSanders 12 72+
(B J Meehan) *w ldrs on outer: hung rt bnd over 4f out: chal over 2f out: styd on same pce appr fnl f* **7/4**[1]

3-4 **4** *3 ¼* **Jack O'Lantern**[27] 1100 3-9-3 0 PaulHanagan 14 63
(R A Fahey) *mid-div: hdwy over 2f out: styd on fnl f* **9/2**[3]

55- **5** *¾* **Boss's Destination**[264] 4847 3-9-3 0 PJMcDonald 3 61+
(G A Swinbank) *mid-div: edgd lft 2f out: styd on: nvr nr ldrs* **20/1**

00- **6** *½* **Irish Eyes**[238] 5669 3-8-12 0 PatrickDonaghy(5) 8 60
(Jedd O'Keeffe) *in tch: outpcd over 2f out: kpt on fnl f* **150/1**

7 *shd* **Viking Warrior (IRE)** 3-9-3 0 PhillipMakin 7 60
(M Dods) *s.i.s: in rr: styd on wl fnl f: nt rch ldrs* **33/1**

0- **8** *1 ½* **Royal Patriot (IRE)**[246] 5401 3-9-3 0 SilvestreDeSousa 6 56+
(Paul Green) *in rr: nt clr run over 1f out: nvr nr ldrs* **100/1**

9 *nk* **Piddie's Power** 3-8-12 0 GrahamGibbons 11 50
(E S McMahon) *w ldrs: wknd over 1f out* **20/1**

33 **10** *hd* **Bajan Flash**[10] 1464 3-9-3 0 TomEaves 13 54
(B Smart) *chsd ldrs on outside: carried wd bnd over 4f out: hung lft and wknd 2f out* **12/1**

0-0 **11** *1* **Arch Walker (IRE)**[14] 1402 3-9-3 0 FrederikTylicki 10 51
(Jedd O'Keeffe) *led: hdd & wknd over 1f out* **100/1**

4 **12** *nk* **Pelmanism**[12] 1425 3-9-3 0 FrannyNorton 1 51
(K A Ryan) *drvn to chse ldrs after 2f: drvn over 3f out: wknd over 1f out* **8/1**

60 **13** *4* **True Pleasure (IRE)**[14] 1402 3-8-12 0 JimmyQuinn 5 35
(J D Bethell) *s.i.s: a towards rr* **100/1**

0 **14** *¾* **Marsh's Gift**[16] 1336 3-9-0 0 BarryMcHugh(3) 2 38
(R E Barr) *s.i.s: a in rr* **150/1**

1m 28.81s (1.61) **Going Correction** +0.35s/f (Good) **14** Ran SP% **120.9**
Speed ratings (Par 101): **104,97,96,92,92 91,91,89,89,89 87,87,82,82**
toteswingers:1&2:£23.10, 1&3:£7.90, 2&3:£12.20 CSF £40.95 TOTE £4.20: £2.00, £3.30, £1.30; EX 92.40.
Owner Sheikh Hamdan Bin Mohammed Al Maktoum **Bred** Barouche Stud Ireland Ltd **Trained** Middleham Moor, N Yorks

FOCUS
A fair maiden and an impressive winner who looks potentially smart. The time was quicker than the following handicap.
Royal Patriot(IRE) Official explanation: jockey said gelding ran green
Pelmanism Official explanation: jockey said gelding had no more to give

1707 TOTEPOOL H'CAP 7f
3:30 (3:30) (Class 4) (0-85,82) 4-Y-O+ **£5,569** (£1,657; £828; £413) **Stalls** Low

Form RPR

401- **1** **Keys Of Cyprus**[182] 7171 8-8-13 77 PaulQuinn 13 88
(D Nicholls) *hld up towards rr: hdwy on outer 3f out: r.o to ld ins fnl f: kpt on wl* **14/1**

-235 **2** *dht* **Nightjar (USA)**[74] 573 5-9-3 81 PaulHanagan 3 89+
(K A Ryan) *trckd ldrs: nt clr run and hmpd over 1f out: r.o ins fnl f: fin dead-heat 2nd plcd 2nd* **6/1**[2]

224- **3** *1 ¾* **Sunnyside Tom (IRE)**[192] 6946 6-9-1 82 BarryMcHugh(3) 10 88
(R A Fahey) *trckd ldrs: hung lft and led over 1f out: hdd and no ex ins fnl f: fin dead-heat 2nd plcd 3rd* **8/1**

0-50 **4** *1 ¼* **Legal Legacy**[16] 1332 4-8-13 77 PhillipMakin 11 80
(M Dods) *in rr: swtchd lft after 1f: drvn bnd over 4f out: hdwy on outer over 1f out: styd on ins fnl f* **9/1**

601- **5** *½* **Mujaadel (USA)**[196] 6847 5-8-13 77 (p) AndrewMullen 12 78+
(D Nicholls) *mid-div: hdwy and hung lft over 2f out: nt clr run appr fnl f: kpt on ins fnl f* **14/1**

-440 **6** *1 ½* **Ra Junior (USA)**[7] 1516 4-9-4 82 AdrianNicholls 7 79
(D Nicholls) *in rr: hdwy and swtchd outside over 2f out: hung lft and kpt on: nvr nr ldrs* **7/1**[3]

340- **7** *nse* **Reel Buddy Star**[210] 6485 5-9-3 81 TomEaves 6 78
(G M Moore) *chsd ldrs: one pce appr fnl f* **11/1**

6-00 **8** *1 ¼* **Bold Marc (IRE)**[7] 1513 8-8-11 75 AndrewElliott 8 69
(J R Weymes) *chsd ldrs: chal 2f out: wknd fnl 150yds* **40/1**

200- **9** *hd* **Desert Falls**[170] 7356 4-8-9 76 MichaelStainton(3) 5 69
(R M Whitaker) *s.i.s: hdwy in inner over 2f out: sn chsng ldrs: wknd fnl f* **18/1**

16-0 **10** *nk* **Euston Square**[27] 1099 4-8-12 81 BillyCray(5) 1 73
(D Nicholls) *s.v.s: hdwy 2f out: nvr on terms* **25/1**

0-03 **11** *1 ¾* **Game Lad**[14] 1374 8-8-5 69 (t) DuranFentiman 4 63
(T D Easterby) *mid-div: effrt over 2f out: wknd over 1f out: nt clr run whn eased towards fin* **6/1**[2]

00-5 **12** *2 ¾* **Glenridding**[15] 1361 6-8-8 72 (p) PaulMulrennan 2 52
(J G Given) *led tl hdd over 1f out: sn wknd* **7/2**[1]

50-6 **13** *¾* **Rising Kheleyf (IRE)**[9] 1494 4-8-7 71 PJMcDonald 9 49
(G A Swinbank) *mid-div: swtchd lft over 1f out: sn wknd* **33/1**

010- **14** *2 ¼* **Ishe Mac**[243] 5523 4-9-0 78 FrannyNorton 14 50
(N Bycroft) *hld up towards rr: sme hdwy on outside over 2f out: hung rt and sn wknd* **14/1**

1m 28.92s (1.72) **Going Correction** +0.35s/f (Good) **14** Ran SP% **127.2**
Speed ratings (Par 105): **104,101,101,100,99 98,98,96,96,96 94,90,90,87**
toteswingers:1&2:£51.30, 1&3:£11.30, 2&3:£17.00 CSF £49.90 CT £380.90 TOTE £16.80: £7.10, £2.80, £2.00; EX 231.90 TRIFECTA Not won..
Owner The Beasley Gees **Bred** Juddmonte Farms **Trained** Sessay, N Yorks
■ Stewards' Enquiry : Barry McHugh one-day ban: careless riding (May 16)

FOCUS
A fair handicap won in a time one tenth of a second slower than the preceding maiden. The form has been taken at face value.
Ra Junior(USA) Official explanation: jockey said gelding hung left
Desert Falls Official explanation: trainer said gelding missed the break
Euston Square Official explanation: jockey said gelding missed the break
Ishe Mac Official explanation: jockey said filly hung right in straight

1708 TOTESPORT.COM THIRSK HUNT CUP (H'CAP) 1m
4:05 (4:09) (Class 2) (0-100,100) 4-Y-O+ **£12,045** (£3,584; £1,791; £894) **Stalls** Low

Form RPR

54-2 **1** **Osteopathic Remedy (IRE)**[14] 1397 6-8-4 86 PJMcDonald 7 93
(M Dods) *chsd ldrs: wnt 2nd 2f out: styd on to ld narrowly appr fnl f: hld on towards fin* **8/1**[3]

20-0 **2** *¾* **Billy Dane (IRE)**[35] 1006 6-8-5 87 (p) PaulHanagan 12 92
(F P Murtagh) *led: narrowly hdd appr fnl f: stuck on gamely: no ex towards fin* **11/1**

3536 **3** *nk* **Balcarce Nov (ARG)**[57] 818 5-9-4 100 MickyFenton 9 104
(T P Tate) *s.i.s: hdwy on outer over 2f out: styd on wl ins fnl f* **7/1**[2]

060- **4** *shd* **Invincible Force (IRE)**[203] 6675 6-8-11 93 (b) SilvestreDeSousa 16 97
(Paul Green) *chsd ldrs: kpt on same pce fnl f* **40/1**

3633 **5** *nk* **Dubai Dynamo**[1] 1672 5-8-6 88 AndrewElliott 5 93+
(Mrs R A Carr) *in rr-div: hdwy on outer over 2f out: nt clr run and swtchd outside ins fnl f: fin wl* **8/1**[3]

3113 **6** *½* **Cobo Bay**[14] 1408 5-8-6 88 (b) FrannyNorton 17 90
(K A Ryan) *trckd ldrs on outer: effrt over 2f out: carried hd high: one pce appr fnl f* **11/1**

11-0 **7** *nk* **Collateral Damage (IRE)**[35] 1008 7-9-0 96 (t) DavidAllan 8 98
(T D Easterby) *chsd ldrs: kpt on same pce appr fnl f* **8/1**[3]

500- **8** *½* **Docofthebay (IRE)**[210] 6480 6-8-13 95 FrederikTylicki 14 95
(J A Glover) *s.i.s: hdwy over 2f out: swtchd lft over 1f out: kpt on wl* **8/1**[3]

-014 **9** *½* **Exit Smiling**[16] 1333 8-8-4 86 JimmyQuinn 11 85
(P T Midgley) *chsd ldrs: one pce fnl 2f* **25/1**

360- **10** *2 ½* **Wildcat Wizard (USA)**[210] 6482 4-8-12 94 (t) TomEaves 10 88
(P F I Cole) *hld up in rr: kpt on fnl 2f: nvr nr ldrs* **28/1**

00-0 **11** *2 ¾* **Medici Pearl**[18] 1272 6-8-6 88 DuranFentiman 2 75
(T D Easterby) *dwlt: mid-div and drvn 4f out: nvr a factor* **16/1**

401- **12** *3 ¾* **Esoterica (IRE)**[197] 6815 7-8-7 92 (v) GaryBartley(3) 13 71
(J S Goldie) *a in rr* **20/1**

040- **13** *4* **Majuro (IRE)**[357] 1861 6-8-11 93 JackMitchell 4 62
(C F Wall) *hld up in rr: nvr on terms* **5/1**[1]

/00- **14** *2 ½* **Peter Tchaikovsky**[196] 6867 4-8-9 98 TimothyAyres(7) 6 62
(B S Rothwell) *s.i.s: effrt on outside over 2f out: sn wknd* **50/1**

304- **15** *¾* **Mirrored**[217] 6277 4-8-12 99 MichaelO'Connell(5) 3 61
(D Nicholls) *chsd ldrs: wknd over 2f out* **14/1**

1m 40.96s (0.86) **Going Correction** +0.35s/f (Good) **15** Ran SP% **119.3**
Speed ratings (Par 109): **109,108,107,107,107 107,106,106,105,103 100,96,92,90,89**
toteswingers:1&2:£15.50, 1&3:£4.40, 2&3:£7.60 CSF £82.15 CT £570.30 TOTE £6.50: £2.30, £4.30, £2.60; EX 73.60.
Owner Kevin Kirkup **Bred** Airlie Stud **Trained** Denton, Co Durham

FOCUS
One of the course's highlights of the season, and as usual a very competitive affair. The early pace was strong. Straightforward form.

NOTEBOOK
Osteopathic Remedy(IRE) beat only one home when racing off 2lb higher in last year's contest, though early trouble in running out of stall one effectively cost him any chance. He got himself into the prominent position he prefers this time, while not straying too close to the pace, and had plenty left to push on with once the front-runners started to come off the bridle. Winless in 2009 and back below his last winning mark, connections were quick to point out his fondness for Thirsk (two wins and five places from ten visits), but fear he may be vulnerable again if raised for this victory.
Billy Dane(IRE) soon wrested the lead he prefers from Invincible Force and didn't fold once the winner had sailed by. He was still holding on for one of these, but a mark 6lb above his highest winning one doesn't make life easy. (op 14-1)
Balcarce Nov(ARG)'s forward move was wound up gradually from the top of the home straight and he was still gaining close home. That wasn't a dissimilar effort to those he produced over 7f-1m at Meydan over the winter, and it may be time to step him back up to 1m1f. (op 8-1)
Invincible Force(IRE) has never won before late June in his four previous seasons of racing but posted a fair effort considering he couldn't dominate. There should be more to come later in the summer, especially if slipping a few pounds.
Dubai Dynamo had to be delivered wide to produce his effort, and although that probably didn't cost him victory he can still be comfortably regarded as having done better than the bare form. (op 10-1)
Collateral Damage(IRE), a six-time winner last autumn, remains 4lb above his highest winning mark and is likely to find winning tough this term.
Docofthebay(IRE) always had a bit too much to do after being slowest away. (op 12-1)
Majuro(IRE), a strong-staying fourth in this last year off 1lb higher having slipped leaving the stalls, had no such excuses this time and has obliged in just one of his last 27 starts. (op 13-2 tchd 7-1)

1709 BET TOTEPOOL AT TOTESPORT.COM CLASSIFIED STKS 6f
4:40 (4:47) (Class 5) 3-Y-O **£4,274** (£1,271; £635; £317) **Stalls** High

Form RPR

5-40 **1** **Ventura Cove (IRE)**[14] 1376 3-9-0 75 PaulHanagan 4 83
(R A Fahey) *chsd ldrs: swtchd rt after 1f: led over 1f out: hrd rdn: hld on towards fin* **8/1**

35-0 **2** *nk* **Flaneur**[14] 1376 3-9-0 75 ....(p) DavidAllan 6 82
(T D Easterby) *sn chsng ldrs: chal appr fnl f: no ex nr fin* **9/1**

531- **3** *4* **Mark Anthony (IRE)**[259] 5036 3-9-0 72 .... FrannyNorton 9 69
(K A Ryan) *w ldr: led over 3f out: hdd over 1f out: kpt on same pce* **3/1**[1]

56-1 **4** *nk* **Trade Secret**[14] 1401 3-9-0 75 .... RobertWinston 7 68
(M Brittain) *led tl over 3f out: kpt on same pce appr fnl f* **7/2**[2]

341- **5** *6* **Belinsky (IRE)**[241] 5583 3-9-0 72 .... J-PGuillambert 5 49
(N Tinkler) *sn chsng ldrs: wknd over 1f out* **25/1**

100- **6** *½* **Emirates Hills**[222] 6169 3-9-0 75 ....(p) FrederikTylicki 10 47
(E F Vaughan) *in tch: effrt over 2f out: wknd over 1f out* **12/1**

40-1 **7** *hd* **Loveinthesand (IRE)**[81] 473 3-9-0 75 .... PaulMulrennan 1 47
(M Johnston) *chsd ldrs on outer: sn drvn along: edgd lft and lost pl over 1f out* **10/1**

10-3 **8** *3 ¼* **Ferris Wheel (IRE)**[19] 1269 3-9-0 75 .... TomEaves 8 36
(P F I Cole) *s.i.s: a outpcd: hung lft over 1f out* **11/2**[3]

00-0 **9** *31* **Scarboro Warning (IRE)**[17] 1298 3-9-0 68 .... AdrianNicholls 2 —
(J O'Reilly) *chsd ldrs on outside: lost pl over 1f out: eased and sn wl bhd: t.o* **40/1**

1m 14.18s (1.48) **Going Correction** +0.275s/f (Good) **9** Ran SP% **106.8**
Speed ratings (Par 99): **101,100,95,94,86 86,85,81,41**
toteswingers:1&2:£7.70, 1&3:£6.60, 2&3:£7.80 CSF £64.48 TOTE £7.40: £2.00, £2.20, £1.80; EX 67.00.
Owner Keith Denham **Bred** Hyde Park Stud & Paddy Conney **Trained** Musley Bank, N Yorks
■ Stewards' Enquiry : David Allan one-day ban: used whip with excessive frequency (May 16)

FOCUS
A tight event, with all bar the outside rated within 3lb of the ceiling of 75. However, the first two finished some way clear. This is probably not form to get carried away with.

1710 BET TOTEPOOL ON 0800 221 221 H'CAP (DIV I) 5f
5:15 (5:19) (Class 4) (0-80,80) 4-Y-0+ **£5,245** (£1,560; £780; £389) **Stalls** High

Form RPR

521- **1** **Igoyougo**[185] 7119 4-8-12 **74** .... SilvestreDeSousa 4 84
(G A Harker) *chsd ldrs: led jst ins fnl f: jst hld on* **9/2**[2]

00-4 **2** *shd* **Discanti (IRE)**[15] 1363 5-9-0 **76** ....(t) DavidAllan 8 86
(T D Easterby) *mid-div: swtchd lft over 2f out: chsd wnr appr fnl f: r.o: jst failed* **7/2**[1]

30-2 **3** *1 ¾* **Lucky Dan (IRE)**[15] 1366 4-8-8 **70** .... TomEaves 3 74
(Paul Green) *mid-div: hdwy and edgd lft over 1f out: wandered: styd on ins fnl f* **9/1**

6314 **4** *nk* **Colorus (IRE)**[11] 1445 7-8-6 **73** ....(p) PaulPickard(5) 5 76
(W J H Ratcliffe) *chsd ldr: led over 1f out: hdd and no ex jst ins fnl f* **20/1**

46-0 **5** *½* **Feelin Foxy**[15] 1363 6-9-4 **80** .... PaulMulrennan 2 81
(J G Given) *led: crossed to stands' side rail over 2f out: hdd over 1f out: kpt on same pce* **33/1**

0-00 **6** *nk* **King Of Swords (IRE)**[7] 1524 6-8-5 **67** ....(p) AndrewElliott 6 67+
(N Tinkler) *hld up towards rr: nt clr run over 2f out: nt clr run ins fnl f: swtchd rt and styd on wl* **12/1**

-343 **7** *¾* **Incomparable**[15] 1364 5-9-4 **80** ....(b) FrederikTylicki 10 77
(J A Glover) *chsd ldrs: edgd rt after 1f: wknd over 1f out* **6/1**[3]

55-0 **8** *hd* **Red Rosanna**[8] 1506 4-8-13 **75** .... JerryO'Dwyer 7 71
(R Hollinshead) *s.i.s: in rr: swtchd lft over 1f out: styd on wl ins fnl f* **20/1**

1412 **9** *1 ½* **Grudge**[8] 1506 5-8-11 **73** ....(be) RobertWinston 9 64
(C R Dore) *exited stalls w blindfold stl on: s.s: swtchd outside over 2f out: nvr on terms* **6/1**[3]

00-0 **10** *1* **Van Bossed (CAN)**[16] 1332 5-8-13 **75** ....(v[1]) AdrianNicholls 11 69+
(D Nicholls) *chsd ldrs: n.m.r on ins over 2f out: nt clr run over 1f out: eased ins fnl f* **15/2**

30-0 **11** *9* **La Zamora**[15] 1363 4-9-1 **77** .... PhillipMakin 1 32
(T D Barron) *dwlt: sn chsng ldrs on outer: wknd appr fnl f: eased and sn bhd* **14/1**

60.31 secs (0.71) **Going Correction** +0.275s/f (Good) **11** Ran SP% **117.6**
Speed ratings (Par 105): **105,104,102,101,100 100,99,98,96,94 80**
toteswingers:1&2:£4.40, 1&3:£4.90, 2&3:£8.30 CSF £20.02 CT £139.15 TOTE £5.90: £3.00, £1.90, £1.50; EX 18.70.
Owner Miss K Watson **Bred** Karen Watson **Trained** Thirkleby, N Yorks

FOCUS
Just an ordinary handicap run in a similar time to division one. Straightforward form.
Red Rosanna Official explanation: jockey said filly was slowly away
Grudge Official explanation: jockey said gelding missed break as blindfold became caught in eye shield

1711 BET TOTEPOOL ON 0800 221 221 H'CAP (DIV II) 5f
5:45 (5:47) (Class 4) (0-80,80) 4-Y-0+ **£5,245** (£1,560; £780; £389) **Stalls** High

Form RPR

66-5 **1** **Mullglen**[15] 1364 4-8-11 **73** ....(tp) DavidAllan 2 81
(T D Easterby) *chsd ldr on outer: led ins fnl f: hld on wl* **9/2**[2]

0503 **2** *nk* **Lucky Art (USA)**[7] 1524 4-8-6 **68** .... AndrewElliott 8 75
(Mrs R A Carr) *led: hdd ins fnl f: kpt on wl: a jst hld* **7/2**[1]

6462 **3** *2* **Green Park (IRE)**[15] 1363 7-9-0 **76** ....(b) RobertWinston 3 76
(D Carroll) *rrd s: swtchd rt after s: hdwy over 2f out: styd on ins fnl f* **15/2**

421 **4** *nse* **Ryan Style (IRE)**[23] 1190 4-8-13 **75** .... SilvestreDeSousa 5 75
(Mrs L Williamson) *prom: sn drvn along: styd on fnl f* **5/1**[3]

0-04 **5** *1 ¼* **Bosun Breese**[16] 1320 5-8-10 **77** .... DeanHeslop(5) 7 72
(T D Barron) *w ldr on outer: edgd rt over 1f out: fdd ins fnl f* **10/1**

550- **6** *½* **Inter Vision (USA)**[179] 7220 10-8-7 **74** .... IanBrennan(5) 6 67
(A Dickman) *mid-div: kpt on fnl 2f: nvr trbld ldrs* **22/1**

50-0 **7** *½* **Rothesay Dancer**[27] 1099 7-9-0 **79** .... KellyHarrison(3) 9 71+
(J S Goldie) *in rr: hdwy and swtchd lft ins fnl f: nvr on terms* **28/1**

04-0 **8** *¾* **Mandurah (IRE)**[16] 1332 6-9-4 **80** .... J-PGuillambert 1 72
(B P J Baugh) *chsd ldrs on outer: wknd over 1f out* **12/1**

4-16 **9** *¾* **After The Show**[46] 896 9-7-11 **66** oh3 .... NoelGarbutt(7) 10 52
(Rae Guest) *rrd s: in rr: swtchd outside over 2f out: nvr on terms* **25/1**

01-0 **10** *1 ¼* **Secret Venue**[15] 1363 4-8-11 **73** .... TomEaves 11 55
(Jedd O'Keeffe) *chsd ldrs stands' side: wknd over 1f out* **7/1**

222- **11** *7* **Liberty Ship**[301] 3607 5-8-8 **70** ....(bt) JimmyQuinn 4 26
(J D Bethell) *swtchd rt after s: in rr-div: sme hdwy over 2f out: lost pl and eased over 1f out* **8/1**

60.26 secs (0.66) **Going Correction** +0.275s/f (Good) **11** Ran SP% **120.9**
Speed ratings (Par 105): **105,104,101,101,99 98,97,96,95,93 82**
toteswingers:1&2:£3.80, 1&3:£8.80, 2&3:£6.80 CSF £20.76 CT £120.85 TOTE £4.90: £2.00, £1.20, £3.20 Place 6: £62.31, Place 5: £40.90..
Owner Richard Taylor & Philip Hebdon **Bred** Rosyground Stud **Trained** Great Habton, N Yorks

FOCUS
By a whisker the fastest of the three races run over 5f. Straightforward form with the runner-up back to his 2yo best.
T/Plt: £77.30 to a £1 stake. Pool: £53,903.47. 508.60 winning tickets. T/Qpdt: £25.80 to a £1 stake. Pool: £3,209.46. 92.00 winning tickets. WG

1418 CAPANNELLE (R-H)
Saturday, May 1

OFFICIAL GOING: Turf: good

1712a PREMIO SIGNORINO (LISTED RACE) (4YO+) (TURF) 1m 1f
1:30 (12:00) 4-Y-0+ **£24,778** (£10,902; £5,946; £2,973)

RPR

1 **Fratazz** 5-8-10 0 .... NPinna 8 99
(S Botti, Italy) **26/5**

2 *1* **Diocleziano (USA)**[13] 5-8-10 0 ....(b) CFiocchi 7 97
(R Menichetti, Italy) **177/10**

3 *1 ½* **Pepper Popper (IRE)**[13] 4-8-10 0 .... MEsposito 6 94
(L Polito, Italy) **5/2**[3]

4 *1 ¾* **Falchargue**[357] 1904 4-8-10 0 .... DVargiu 4 90
(B Grizzetti, Italy) **73/10**

5 *1* **Elleno (IRE)**[34] 6-8-10 0 ....(b) CDemuro 3 88
(F & L Camici, Italy) **109/10**

6 *1* **Mibar (USA)**[104] 4-8-10 0 .... UmbertoRispoli 1 86
(F De Sanctis, Italy) **29/1**

7 *½* **Salisburgo (ITY)**[13] 7-8-10 0 .... SDiana 5 85
(A Cascio, Italy) **59/1**

8 *1* **Yahrab (IRE)**[16] 1328 5-8-10 0 .... ChrisCatlin 2 83
(C E Brittain) *pushed to ld after 1f: stdd pce for 4f: led ent st: u.p 3 1/2f out: hrd rdn: no imp fr 2 1/2f out* **49/20**[2]

9 *4* **Piterino (IRE)**[20] 5-8-10 0 .... MMonteriso 9 74
(L Polito, Italy) **5/2**[3]

10 *7* **Selmis**[349] 2115 6-9-6 0 .... MircoDemuro 10 70
(Vittorio Caruso, Italy) **7/4**[1]

1m 53.4s (-1.30) **10** Ran SP% **169.4**
WIN (incl. 1 euro stake): 6.19. PLACES: 1.90, 3.07, 1.59. DF: 97.12.
Owner Scuderia Rencati Srl **Bred** Azienda Agricola Francesca **Trained** Italy

1713a PREMIO REGINA ELENA (GROUP 3) (3YO FILLIES) (TURF) 1m
3:10 (12:00) 3-Y-0 **£75,221** (£33,097; £18,053; £9,026)

RPR

1 **Evading Tempete**[23] 1196 3-8-11 0 ....(p) Jean-BernardEyquem 5 103
(F Rohaut, France) *broke wl: settled 3rd: hdwy after 4f: chal to ld 3f marker: rdn and pushed 2 l 2f: kpt on: a holding runner-up* **6/5**[1]

2 *1 ¼* **Cronsa (GER)**[20] 1252 3-8-11 0 .... NPinna 7 100
(S Botti, Italy) *broke wl: trckd ldrs: 4th bhd eventual wnr ent st: lened to go 2nd whn pce qckned at 3f marker: styd on fnl 2f* **705/100**

3 *¾* **Zobenigo (IRE)**[13] 1419 3-8-11 0 .... MEsposito 18 98
(L Polito, Italy) *stdd at break: moved to rail in rr: last on rail ent st: rdn and hdwy fr 3f out: a clsng fnl f* **122/10**

4 *1 ½* **Kadabra (IRE)**[174] 3-8-11 0 .... CDemuro 10 95
(F & L Camici, Italy) *stdd mid-div for first 4f: rdn and hdwy to go 4th ent fnl 2f: hrd rdn ins fnl f: no imp on ldrs* **145/10**

5 *2* **Jira**[17] 1310 3-8-11 0 .... ChrisCatlin 4 90
(C E Brittain) *broke wl: hld in in 2nd for 4f: rdn to ld briefly at 3f marker: hrd rdn fnl 2f: no ex* **69/20**[2]

6 *¾* **Jet Set Woman (IRE)**[27] 3-8-11 0 .... CDiStasio 3 89
(R Menichetti, Italy) *broke wl: steaded in 6th bhd ldrs: effrt at 3f marker to move 4th: hrd rdn 2f out: wknd ent fnl f* **138/1**

7 *nse* **Mabura (IRE)**[146] 3-8-11 0 .... UmbertoRispoli 14 88
(S Botti, Italy) *settled mid-div: hdwy on outer ent st: moved to win 4 l of ldng gp: hrd rdn and no ex fnl 2f* **705/100**

8 *2* **Paloma Varga (IRE)**[20] 1252 3-8-11 0 .... ASanna 11 84
(Gabriele Miliani, Italy) *stdd at s: hld up in rr: effrt on outer entering st: hrd rdn fnl 2f: styd on* **217/10**

9 *2 ½* **Giulia Vis (IRE)** 3-8-11 0 .... CFiocchi 9 78
(F Santella, Italy) *hld up in rr: hrd rdn fnl 3f: styd on fnl f* **34/1**

10 *2 ½* **Spinning Yarn** 3-8-11 0 .... MircoDemuro 13 72
(A Renzoni, Italy) *hld up nr rr: effrt and no imp fnl 3f* **107/20**[3]

11 *½* **Misano Lasen (IRE)**[27] 3-8-11 0 .... SBasile 6 71
(M Massimi Jr, Italy) *hld up mid-div: hrd rdn in st: no impressioin fnl 3f* **122/10**

12 *½* **Wedding Fair** 3-8-11 0 .... FabioBranca 17 70
(E Botti, Italy) *hld up nr rr: effrt 3f out: wknd ent fnl f* **132/10**

13 *1 ½* **Sadowa Destination** 3-8-11 0 .... DVargiu 15 67
(B Grizzetti, Italy) *settled mid-div on outer: hdwy in st to go 5th: hrd rdn fnl 3f: no ex fnl 2f: sn wknd* **135/10**

14 *1 ½* **Golden Ramon (IRE)**[13] 1419 3-8-11 0 .... SMulas 2 63
(B Grizzetti, Italy) *hld up in mid-div on inner: rdn ent st: hdwy fnl 3f: hmpd whn already btn 2f out* **145/10**

15 *¾* **Camilla Grey (IRE)** 3-8-11 0 .... GMarcelli 19 61
(Camilla Trapassi, Italy) *in rr: effrt and no imp fnl 3f* **96/1**

16 *½* **Hard Life (IRE)**[174] 3-8-11 0 .... SDiana 1 60
(M Oppo, Italy) *hld-up mid-div: hrd rdn and no imp fnl 2f: sn wknd* **55/1**

17 *1* **Train Deal (IRE)**[146] 3-8-11 0 .... MMonteriso 16 58
(F De Sanctis, Italy) *slowly away: hld in rr: no hdwy whn rdn fnl 3f* **63/1**

18 *½* **Lovisa Beat**[20] 1252 3-8-11 0 .... SUrru 8 57
(B Grizzetti, Italy) *slowly away: hrd rdn to ld after a f: 4 l clr ent st: rdn and sn btn at 3f marker* **135/10**

19 *15* **Snooze (USA)** 3-8-11 0 .... GBietolini 12 22
(B Grizzetti, Italy) *a in rr: eased up fnl 2f* **122/1**

1m 38.3s (-1.50) **19** Ran SP% **170.6**
WIN (incl. 1 euro stake): 2.18. PLACES: 1.50, 4.02, 3.45. DF: 22.44.
Owner A Mouknass & A Forde **Bred** Wentworth Racing (pty) Ltd **Trained** Sauvagnon, France

NOTEBOOK
Evading Tempete, just ahead of Special Duty when runner-up in the Imprudence last time, travelled well until taking over 3f from home and from then on was always doing enough to see her race out. She may head for the Coronation Stakes next.
Jira showed up in a prominent position until past halfway and hit the front for a few strides, but was made to look one-paced after losing the lead.

CHURCHILL DOWNS (L-H)

Saturday, May 1

OFFICIAL GOING: Dirt: sloppy; turf: yielding

1714a KENTUCKY DERBY PRESENTED BY YUM! BRANDS (GRADE 1) (3YO) (DIRT) 1m 2f (D)

11:24 (11:32) 3-Y-O £879,753 (£246,913; £123,456; £61,728; £37,037)

RPR

1 **Super Saver (USA)**21 3-9-0 0 CHBorel 4 124
(Todd Pletcher, U.S.A) **8/1**2

2 2 ½ **Ice Box (USA)**42 3-9-0 0 JLezcano 2 119+
(Nicholas Zito, U.S.A) **117/10**

3 nk **Paddy O'Prado (USA)**21 3-9-0 0 KDesormeaux 10 118
(Dale Romans, U.S.A) **123/10**

4 2 **Make Music For Me (USA)**21 3-9-0 0 (b) JRosario 9 114+
(Alexis Barba, U.S.A) **30/1**

5 1 ¼ **Noble's Promise (USA)**21 3-9-0 0 WMartinez 3 112
(Kenneth McPeek, U.S.A) **249/10**

6 1 **Lookin At Lucky (USA)**28 3-9-0 0 GKGomez 1 113+
(Bob Baffert, U.S.A) **63/10**1

7 ½ **Dublin (USA)**21 3-9-0 0 (b) TJThompson 17 109
(D Wayne Lukas, U.S.A) **20/1**

8 1 ¼ **Stately Victor (USA)**21 3-9-0 0 AGarcia 6 106
(Michael J Maker, U.S.A) **202/10**

9 2 **Mission Impazible (USA)**35 3-9-0 0 RMaragh 14 102
(Todd Pletcher, U.S.A) **167/10**

10 1 ¼ **Devil May Care (USA)**42 3-8-9 0 (b1) JRVelazquez 11 95
(Todd Pletcher, U.S.A) **109/10**

11 6 ¾ **American Lion (USA)**28 3-9-0 0 DFlores 7 86
(Eoin Harty, U.S.A) **232/10**

12 nk **Jackson Bend (USA)**28 1097 3-9-0 0 MESmith 13 85
(Nicholas Zito, U.S.A) **23/1**

13 6 ½ **Discreetly Mine (USA)**35 3-9-0 0 JJCastellano 15 72
(Todd Pletcher, U.S.A) **32/1**

14 3 ¼ **Dean's Kitten (USA)**35 3-9-0 0 (b) RAlbarado 8 66
(Michael J Maker, U.S.A) **26/1**

15 14 ½ **Conveyance (USA)**34 3-9-0 0 MGarcia 12 37
(Bob Baffert, U.S.A) **27/1**

16 10 ½ **Homeboykris (USA)**63 3-9-0 0 (b) RADominguez 19 16
(Richard Dutrow Jr, U.S.A) **27/1**

17 ½ **Sidney's Candy (USA)**28 3-9-0 0 JTalamo 20 15
(John W Sadler, U.S.A) **19/2**3

18 6 ¼ **Line Of David (USA)**21 3-9-0 0 (b) RBejarano 5 2
(John W Sadler, U.S.A) **199/10**

19 nk **Awesome Act (USA)**28 1097 3-9-0 0 JRLeparoux 16 2
(J Noseda) **116/10**

20 9 ½ **Backtalk (USA)**28 3-9-0 0 MMena 18 —
(Thomas Amoss, U.S.A) **231/10**

2m 4.45s (3.26) **20** Ran SP% **119.4**

PARI-MUTUEL (all including $2 stake): WIN 18.00; PLACE (1-2) 8.80, 11.20; SHOW (1-2-3) 6.00, 8.00, 7.40; SF 152.40.

Owner WinStar Farm LLC **Bred** Winstar Farm **Trained** USA

■ A third Kentucky Derby success in the space of four years for jockey Calvin Borel, and a first ever for trainer Todd Pletcher.

FOCUS

The absence of long-term ante-post favourite Eskendereya, and to a lesser extent the quietly fancied Endorsement, as well as a sloppy track, made for a wide-open Kentucky Derby. The pace was predictably strong.

NOTEBOOK

Super Saver(USA) proved well suited by the conditions and received a tremendous ride from Calvin Borel, who judged the pace correctly and kept the colt tight against the rail for nearly the entire journey, only having to come around one rival on the final bend. While Super Saver certainly had the run of things, while some of his rivals did not, there was still plenty to like about this success and it would probably be unwise to underestimate him. The Preakness Stakes is now the plan.

Ice Box(USA), the Florida Derby winner, was as expected held up well out the back, so the strong pace was in his favour, but he didn't get much of a run through. He still had around 8l to find on the winner when denied a clear trip early in the straight and he did well to stay on for second. The return to 1m1f for the Preakness is unlikely to suit, but the Belmont distance of 1m4f could bring out the best in him, provided he has a decent gallop to chase.

Paddy O'Prado(USA) produced a career best on his dirt debut. He enjoyed a similar trip to the winner but that rival was simply too good. He's a possible for the Preakness.

Make Music For Me(USA), hard to fancy beforehand, stayed on past mainly beaten horses from last place out wide in the straight. He's another possible for the Preakness.

Noble's Promise(USA)'s chance was compromised by racing close to the overly quick pace, and he simply didn't stay, but he still finished close up and is clearly a pretty talented colt. If he takes this race okay he's got to be worth a shot at the Preakness.

Lookin At Lucky(USA) lost any chance he might have had when sluggish away from the unfavourable inside stall, ending up a mile off the pace after soon being squeezed out. He did well to stay on and finish as close as he did, although according to his jockey his run was flattening out near the line. He's a possible for the Preakness.

Awesome Act(USA) was quite well fancied to provide Britain with their first winner in the race, but according to Jeremy Noseda, he picked up an injury. He's apparently going to continue his career in the US with Steve Asmussen.

1250 DUSSELDORF (R-H)

Saturday, May 1

OFFICIAL GOING: Turf: good

1715a GERMAN 1000 GUINEAS (GROUP 2) (3YO FILLIES) (TURF) 1m

3:30 (3:34) 3-Y-O £67,256 (£24,778; £12,389; £6,194)

RPR

1 **Kali (GER)**20 3-9-2 0 ADeVries 10 103
(W Hickst, Germany) *broke wl: trckd ldr: moved to mid-trck to avoid tiring ldr: led under 2f out: r.o wl to see off all chals decisively* **104/10**

2 1 ¼ **Reine Heureuse (GER)**20 1250 3-9-2 0 YannLerner 7 100
(Uwe Ostmann, Germany) *broke wl: racd in 4th: fnd a gap 1/2-way down st: qcknd wl to chse ldr: r.o strly* **51/10**3

3 nk **Neon Light (GER)**188 7045 3-9-2 0 EPedroza 8 100
(A Wohler, Germany) *racd in 5th: swtchd to middle of trck: encountered traffic problems: only fnd room ins fnl f: fin strly* **37/10**1

4 nk **Prakasa (FR)**20 1250 3-9-2 0 KClijmans 3 99
(W Hickst, Germany) *broke slowly and towards rr: had to work hrd to overcome traffic problems in st: fin wl* **41/1**

5 nk **Kinky Afro (IRE)**20 1250 3-9-2 0 LiamKeniry 11 98
(J S Moore) *broke smartly: racd in 6th on outside: mde move early in st: r.o: no ex fnl f* **7/1**

6 ½ **Devilish Lips (GER)**20 1250 3-9-2 0 (b) THellier 4 97
(Andreas Lowe, Germany) *racd in 7th: hit traffic problems in st: stdd: r.o wl in clsng stages* **98/10**

7 nk **Vanjura (GER)**190 3-9-2 0 WilliamMongil 12 96
(R Dzubasz, Germany) *broke bdly: qckly mde grnd down bk stretch: had to be stdd in st: fin strly* **61/10**

8 1 ¼ **Mi Rubina (IRE)** 3-9-2 0 JBojko 6 94
(A Wohler, Germany) *broke fast: settled in 3rd: briefly mde move on inner rail in st: no ex* **13/1**

9 ½ **Aslana (IRE)**34 3-9-2 0 AStarke 1 92
(P Schiergen, Germany) *racd in rr: c through tired horses in st* **51/10**3

10 ½ **Genovesa (GER)**20 1250 3-9-2 0 AHelfenbein 9 91
(C Von Der Recke, Germany) *led fr s: set gd pce: hdd under 2f out: fdd* **47/1**

11 1 ¾ **Diatribe**216 3-9-2 0 FilipMinarik 13 87
(H Blume, Germany) *broke slowly: settled in midfield: briefly threatened early in st: no imp* **27/1**

12 2 ½ **Ronja (USA)**20 1250 3-9-2 0 APietsch 14 82
(W Hickst, Germany) *broke slowly: racd towards rr: wd into st: qcknd wl then fdd qckly* **43/10**2

1m 38.04s (-3.12) **12** Ran SP% **132.7**

WIN (incl. 10 euro stake): 114. PLACES: 42, 24, 22. DF: 943. SF: 7,481.

Owner Gestut Park Wiedingen **Bred** Gestut Park Wiedingen **Trained** Germany

NOTEBOOK

Kali(GER) was always in the first two and held on well once striking the front. She is unlikely to get more than a mile.

Kinky Afro(IRE) ran well and was still in with a chance of a place with 50 yards to run.

1496 SAINT-CLOUD (L-H)

Saturday, May 1

OFFICIAL GOING: Turf: good to soft

1716a PRIX DU MUGUET (GROUP 2) (4YO+) (TURF) 1m

2:40 (12:00) 4-Y-O+ £65,575 (£25,309; £12,079; £8,053; £4,026)

RPR

1 **Byword**23 1197 4-8-11 0 MaximeGuyon 6 118
(A Fabre, France) *cl up bhd ldrs: qcknd wl in st to chal ldr 1 1/2f out: r.o wl to gain verdict on line* **16/5**2

2 shd **Gris De Gris (IRE)**27 1111 6-8-11 0 GeraldMosse 7 117
(A De Royer-Dupre, France) *sn led and hld ld tl chal 1 1/2f out: hrd rdn and battled to the line: jst failed* **9/5**1

3 1 ½ **Sehrezad (IRE)**20 1251 5-8-11 0 IoritzMendizabal 1 114
(Andreas Lowe, Germany) *racd in midfield: qcknd early in st and r.o wl for 3rd* **18/1**

4 1 **Vertigineux (FR)**27 1111 6-9-1 0 PhilippeSogorb 3 116
(Mme C Dufreche, France) *followed ldr fr s: r.o wl in st: lost 3rd ins fnl f* **13/1**

5 2 **Elusive Wave (IRE)**237 5710 4-9-1 0 ChristopheSoumillon 8 111
(J-C Rouget, France) *racd in rr fr s: mde move along rail early in st: short of room: swtchd and fin wl wout threatening ldrs* **7/2**3

6 nk **Polytechnicien (USA)**30 4-8-11 0 OlivierPeslier 5 106
(A Fabre, France) *w.w fr s: failed to prog in st* **13/1**

7 2 **Silver Frost (IRE)**258 5086 4-9-4 0 Pierre-CharlesBoudot 4 109
(Y De Nicolay, France) *a towards the rr: rdn early in st: no imp* **12/1**

8 2 **Enzio (GER)**20 1251 4-8-11 0 DominiqueBoeuf 2 97
(N Milliere, France) *racd in midfield fr s: rdn hrd early in st: no ex: fdd* **16/1**

1m 39.5s (-8.00) **8** Ran SP% **114.9**

WIN (incl. 1 euro stake: 4.20. PLACES: 1.40, 1.20, 2.30. DF: 4.00. SF: 7.10.

Owner K Abdulla **Bred** Juddmonte Farms Ltd **Trained** Chantilly, France

NOTEBOOK

Byword just got the better of the favourite following a dour battle. He holds an entry in the Prince of Wales's Stakes, but is likely to run in the Prix d'Ispahan next.

HAMILTON (R-H)

Sunday, May 2

OFFICIAL GOING: Good (good to firm in places) changing to good after race 5 (4:50)

Dolling out around loop increased advertised distances on round course by about 8yds.

Wind: Light, half against Weather: Overcast

1717 HAMILTON-PARK.CO.UK H'CAP (QUALIFIER FOR THE COSMIC CASES SCOTTISH TROPHY HANDICAP SERIES FINAL) 1m 65y

2:30 (2:30) (Class 5) (0-70,70) 4-Y-O+ £3,238 (£963; £481; £240) Stalls High

Form RPR

0312 1 **Fujin Dancer (FR)**2 1669 5-9-2 70 (p) AmyRyan(5) 6 86
(K A Ryan) *hld up: n.m.r and swtchd lft over 2f out: hdwy in centre to ld 1f out: pushed clr ins fnl f* **13/8**1

05-5 2 4 ½ **George Adamson (IRE)**10 1490 4-8-7 56 oh2 PJMcDonald 8 62
(G A Swinbank) *in tch: effrt and ch over 1f out: kpt on fnl f: nt pce of wnr* **16/1**

0201 3 2 ¼ **Saving Grace**6 1575 4-8-7 56 6ex DuranFentiman 4 56
(E J Alston) *led 1f: cl up: led over 3f out: rdn and edgd rt 2f out: hdd 1f out: kpt on same pce* **5/1**2

010- 4 3 **Botham (USA)**183 7172 6-9-2 65 DanielTudhope 12 59
(J S Goldie) *hld up towards rr: effrt over 2f out: kpt on fnl f: no imp* **8/1**3

000- 5 3 **Champain Sands (IRE)**246 5418 11-8-10 59 DavidAllan 5 46
(E J Alston) *hld up: effrt over 2f out: styd on fnl f: nvr able to chal* **18/1**

The Form Book, Raceform Ltd, Compton, RG20 6NL

00-0 **6** *2 1/4* **Call Of Duty (IRE)**[25] 1150 5-8-2 **56** oh4........................ IanBrennan(5) 9 38
(Mrs Dianne Sayer) *midfield: pushed along 3f out: no imp fr 2f out* **10/1**

00-0 **7** *3/4* **Primo Way**[28] 1098 9-8-2 **56** oh4............................... JamesSullivan(5) 13 36
(D A Nolan) *midfield: drvn over 3f out: wknd over 1f out* **66/1**

0-30 **8** *3/4* **Cigalas**[6] 1575 5-8-4 **58**.................................... PatrickDonaghy(5) 3 36
(Mrs J C McGregor) *s.i.s: hld up on outside: rdn over 3f out: hung rt and wknd over 1f out* **16/1**

00-0 **9** *3 1/2* **Avoir Choisi (IRE)**[11] 1467 4-8-4 **56** oh3........................ MartinLane(3) 1 26
(N Wilson) *led after 1f and set decent gallop: hdd over 3f out: wknd wl over 1f out* **20/1**

60-0 **10** *1* **Casino Night**[11] 1467 5-9-6 **69**.................................... GrahamGibbons 10 37
(R Johnson) *hld up: drvn over 3f out: nvr on terms* **16/1**

0-00 **11** *2 3/4* **Pitbull**[8] 1520 7-8-2 **56** oh6...(p) BillyCray(5) 7 17
(A Berry) *missed break: bhd: rdn over 4f out: hung lft u.p over 2f out: nvr on terms* **66/1**

50-0 **12** *16* **Red China Blues (USA)**[10] 1485 4-8-8 **57**...................... PaulHanagan 2 —
(R E Barr) *prom tl rdn and wknd over 2f out* **12/1**

0- **13** *3 3/4* **Catcher Of Dreams (IRE)**[183] 7173 4-8-7 **56** oh2...... AndrewMullen 11 —
(A G Foster) *cl up tl rdn and wknd fr 3f out* **100/1**

1m 49.58s (1.18) **Going Correction** +0.225s/f (Good) **13** Ran SP% **114.3**
Speed ratings (Par 103): **103,98,96,93,90 88,87,86,83,82 79,63,59**
toteswingers:1&2:£7.60, 1&3:£1.60, 2&3:£15.80 CSF £28.91 CT £109.80 TOTE £2.30: £1.10, £4.10, £2.80; EX 22.70.
Owner John Duddy **Bred** Loughtown Stud Ltd **Trained** Hambleton, N Yorks

FOCUS
This proved a modest 56-70 handicap run at a sound pace. There was little depth to the race with over half of the field out of the weights.

1718 TOTEPOOL H'CAP — 1m 65y
3:05 (3:05) (Class 4) (0-85,85) 3-Y-O **£6,476** (£1,927; £963; £481) **Stalls** High

Form RPR

0-21 **1** **Fibs And Flannel**[10] 1488 3-8-6 **70**....................................... DavidAllan 7 81+
(T D Easterby) *prom: cruised up to chal over 1f out: shkn up to ld ins fnl f: readily* **11/4**[3]

32-1 **2** *3/4* **Dolphin Rock**[16] 1362 3-8-10 **74**...................................... GrahamGibbons 6 78+
(T D Barron) *trckd ldrs: rdn over 3f out: n.m.r and swtchd lft appr fnl f: kpt on fnl f: flattered by proximity to wnr* **85/40**[1]

10-4 **3** *1/2* **William Morgan (IRE)**[17] 1334 3-9-0 **78**......................... PaulHanagan 4 81
(R A Fahey) *plld hrd early: cl up: led over 1f out to ins fnl f: kpt on same pce u.p* **9/4**[2]

154- **4** *3 1/2* **Sunnandaeg**[190] 7013 3-9-4 **85**....................................... MartinLane(3) 1 80
(N Wilson) *hld up last: effrt over 2f out: no imp fnl f* **10/1**

00-4 **5** *3/4* **Avonrose**[10] 1487 3-9-4 **82**... GregFairley 2 75
(M Johnston) *sn led: set stdy pce: rdn over 2f out: hdd over 1f out: sn outpcd* **12/1**

200- **6** *1 1/2* **High Resolution**[191] 6983 3-7-11 **66** oh9..................... JamesSullivan(5) 3 56
(Miss L A Perratt) *plld hrd: hld up in tch on outside: outpcd over 2f out: rallied ins fnl f: no imp* **100/1**

130- **7** *8* **Pycian**[288] 4086 3-9-3 **81**.. TonyHamilton 5 52
(Mrs L Stubbs) *prom tl rdn and wknd over 2f out* **25/1**

1m 51.65s (3.25) **Going Correction** +0.225s/f (Good) **7** Ran SP% **111.1**
Speed ratings (Par 101): **92,91,90,87,86 85,77**
toteswingers:1&2:£1.10, 1&3:£1.40, 2&3:£1.80 CSF £8.46 TOTE £3.70: £2.30, £1.10; EX 6.80.
Owner Jim McGrath **Bred** J A And M A Knox **Trained** Great Habton, N Yorks

FOCUS
An interesting 66-85 three-year-old handicap but the leader dropped anchor and the pace was very steady until halfway up the home straight. Muddling form, limited to an extent by the sixth, but the winner is improving fast.

1719 DAILY RECORD H'CAP — 6f 5y
3:40 (3:41) (Class 5) (0-70,70) 4-Y-O+ **£3,238** (£963; £481; £240) **Stalls** Low

Form RPR

604- **1** **Top Bid**[186] 7122 6-8-6 **58**..(b) GrahamGibbons 2 77+
(T D Easterby) *racd w one other stands' side: in tch: hdwy to ld 1f out: drew clr ins fnl f* **13/2**[3]

1150 **2** *4* **Where's Reiley (USA)**[28] 1099 4-8-13 **70**...................... DeanHeslop(5) 4 73
(T D Barron) *chsd ldrs: drvn and outpcd over 2f out: rallied and ev ch 1f out: nt pce of wnr fnl f* **9/2**[1]

0-35 **3** *1 1/4* **Mandarin Spirit (IRE)**[16] 1363 10-9-0 **66**..................(b) TonyHamilton 5 65
(Miss L A Perratt) *t.k.h: led to 1f out: sn one pce* **7/1**

3-0 **4** *1* **Spavento (IRE)**[25] 1152 4-9-0 **66**.......................................(b) DavidAllan 1 62
(E J Alston) *racd w wnr stands' side: spd to over 1f out: kpt on same pce fnl f* **10/1**

20-4 **5** *1 1/2* **Frisbee**[16] 1365 6-8-13 **65**.. DuranFentiman 10 56+
(D W Thompson) *chsd ldrs: rdn over 2f out: edgd rt and no ex over 1f out* **11/1**

0-00 **6** *hd* **Guertino (IRE)**[8] 1524 5-8-11 **63**...................................... AndrewElliott 7 53
(C J Teague) *prom: outpcd over 2f out: n.d after* **10/1**

1011 **7** *2* **Ride A White Swan**[8] 1534 5-8-9 **64**.............................(p) GaryBartley(3) 3 48
(D Shaw) *hld up: rdn over 2f out: no imp over 1f out* **5/1**[2]

06-0 **8** *9* **Sea Salt**[15] 1374 7-9-4 **70**.. PaulHanagan 9 25+
(R E Barr) *dwlt and bmpd s: bhd and outpcd: no ch fr 1/2-way* **9/2**[1]

00-5 **9** *9* **The Bear**[23] 1200 7-8-6 **61**.. AndrewHeffernan(3) 8 —
(Miss L A Perratt) *blindfold removed late and wnt rt s: chsd ldrs tl wknd over 2f out* **8/1**

000- **10** *10* **Defi (IRE)**[248] 5364 8-7-13 **56** oh11.............................(bt) JamesSullivan(5) 6 —
(D A Nolan) *in tch: struggling 1/2-way: sn wknd: t.o* **100/1**

1m 13.92s (1.72) **Going Correction** +0.40s/f (Good) **10** Ran SP% **117.5**
Speed ratings (Par 103): **104,98,97,95,93 93,90,78,66,53**
toteswingers:1&2:£22.80, 1&3:£16.10, 2&3:£7.90 CSF £36.16 CT £213.90 TOTE £8.00: £3.20, £2.10, £3.30; EX 55.10.
Owner John & Marilyn Williams **Bred** Southill Stud **Trained** Great Habton, N Yorks

FOCUS
A modest 56-70 sprint handicap run at a breakneck pace. The winner was value for 5l with his best effort since he was a 3yo on face value.
Sea Salt Official explanation: jockey said gelding was slowly away
The Bear Official explanation: jockey said, regarding why he appeared to be late removing blindfold, that it was tucked tightly under the bridle and his first attempt he was unable to remove it, making a second, at which point the runners had left the stalls.

1720 TOTEPOOL BUTTONHOOK H'CAP — 1m 5f 9y
4:15 (4:15) (Class 3) (0-90,89) 4-Y-O+ **£10,361** (£3,083; £1,540; £769) **Stalls** High

Form RPR

0410 **1** **Prince Picasso**[28] 1101 7-8-6 **74**..(b) PaulHanagan 1 85
(R A Fahey) *prom: rdn to ld over 2f out: styd on strly fnl f* **8/1**

1-05 **2** *3 1/4* **Gordonsville**[8] 1525 7-9-1 **83**.. DanielTudhope 11 91+
(J S Goldie) *in tch: effrt over 2f out: styng on whn nt clr run over 1f out: rcvrd and chsd wnr ins fnl f: no imp* **7/2**[2]

-504 **3** *1 1/4* **Valdan (IRE)**[15] 1398 6-7-13 **70** oh2.....................(t) AndrewHeffernan(3) 2 74
(M A Barnes) *t.k.h: hld up: hdwy over 1f out: rdn and one pce fnl f* **14/1**

625- **4** *hd* **Proud Times (USA)**[282] 4280 4-8-8 **76**............................ PJMcDonald 7 80
(G A Swinbank) *prom: rdn over 2f out: kpt on same pce fnl f* **15/2**

245- **5** *hd* **Hawk Mountain (UAE)**[233] 5823 5-8-11 **84**.................. IanBrennan(5) 5 88
(J J Quinn) *hld up in midfield: effrt and hung rt over 2f out: rdn and kpt on fnl f: no imp* **3/1**[1]

-110 **6** *1 1/2* **Wicked Daze (IRE)**[28] 1101 7-8-9 **77**................................ TonyHamilton 9 78
(Miss L A Perratt) *led to over 2f out: wknd ent fnl f* **16/1**

0/3- **7** *2 1/4* **Black Jacari (IRE)**[255] 4212 5-8-10 **81**.................. RussKennemore(3) 3 79
(P A Kirby) *hld up: drvn and outpcd over 3f out: plugged on fnl f: no imp* **20/1**

63-3 **8** *1* **Alcalde**[19] 1282 4-9-7 **89**.. GregFairley 6 86
(M Johnston) *cl up: rdn and ev ch over 2f out: btn fnl f* **4/1**[3]

6151 **9** *3 1/2* **Kames Park (IRE)**[10] 1484 8-8-8 **81**................................... BillyCray(5) 4 72
(R C Guest) *hld up: effrt and rdn over 2f out: wknd over 1f out* **12/1**

30/0 **10** *19* **Planetarium**[28] 1101 5-7-13 **72**.................................. JamesSullivan(5) 10 35
(P Monteith) *in tch: drvn and outpcd over 3f out: sn lost tch* **50/1**

2m 53.96s (0.06) **Going Correction** +0.225s/f (Good) **10** Ran SP% **117.1**
Speed ratings (Par 107): **108,106,105,105,104 104,102,102,99,88**
toteswingers:1&2:£6.70, 1&3:£18.50, 2&3:£19.00 CSF £36.30 CT £392.68 TOTE £11.20: £2.60, £1.50, £4.80; EX 44.40.
Owner Aidan J Ryan **Bred** Cheveley Park Stud Ltd **Trained** Musley Bank, N Yorks

FOCUS
Quite a valuable 70-89 handicap and the pace was just steady. The winner is rated back to something like his best form.

NOTEBOOK
Prince Picasso, a decisive all-the-way winner at Wolverhampton two outings ago from a 6lb lower mark, had run poorly when unable to get in front at Musselburgh next time. Happy to accept a lead on this occasion he was given a fine tactical ride and went for home at just the right time. He never looked like being overhauled but definitely had luck on his side. Consistency is hardly his strong suit, however. Official explanation: trainer had no explanation for the apparent improvement in form (op 10-1)
Gordonsville, twice a winner last year from just a 1lb lower mark, should have given the winner more to do. He was full of running but shut in against the far side rail from the intersection. When he eventually saw daylight he stayed on in willing fashion, but the winner had flown. A versatile type, he thoroughly deserves compensation. (op 9-2 tchd 5-1 in a place)
Valdan(IRE), 2lb out of the handicap, was keen towards the rear. He was putting in some solid late work and looks right back to his best. (op 16-1)
Proud Times(USA), runner-up in four of his six starts, was another to take time to find full stride. He was staying on at the finish and will surely break his duck this time. (op 7-1)
Hawk Mountain(UAE), highly progressive at three, kept on without ever threatening to take a hand. More galloping tracks suit him a lot better and he should add to his record this year. (op 7-2)
Wicked Daze(IRE), having his second outing for this yard, cut out the running. His two wins on the all-weather in January were in claiming company and he is no where near as good as he was in his prime two years ago when he defied a mark of 92. (op 12-1)
Alcalde, inclined to sweat up, did not look at his best beforehand. He was far too keen and was some way below his best. (op 7-2 tchd 10-3)

1721 GARRY OWEN MAIDEN STKS — 1m 3f 16y
4:50 (4:50) (Class 5) 3-5-Y-O **£3,238** (£963; £481; £240) **Stalls** High

Form RPR

4- **1** **Rawnaq (IRE)**[234] 5801 3-8-11 0... GregFairley 5 79+
(M Johnston) *prom: hdwy to ld over 2f out: shkn up over 1f out: kpt on strly: readily* **1/1**[1]

33-5 **2** *5* **Palawi (IRE)**[27] 1116 3-8-11 70...................................... GrahamGibbons 4 70+
(J J Quinn) *plld hrd: hld up in tch: hdwy to chse wnr over 2f out: sn rdn: one pce appr fnl f* **2/1**[2]

64 **3** *9* **I'm Frank**[10] 1485 4-10-0 0... PJMcDonald 2 56
(G A Swinbank) *prom: rdn and outpcd over 3f out: rallied 2f out: no imp* **9/2**[3]

4 **4** *20* **Le Volcan D'Or (USA)**[104] 219 3-8-11 0.......................... PaulMulrennan 3 21
(M Johnston) *chsd clr ldr: led over 3f out tl over 2f out: sn wknd* **14/1**

00- **5** *5* **Haunting**[201] 6766 4-9-9 0.. TonyHamilton 1 8
(Miss L A Perratt) *led: clr after 4f to over 4f out: hdd over 3f out: sn struggling* **80/1**

2m 28.74s (3.14) **Going Correction** +0.225s/f (Good)
WFA 3 from 4yo 17lb **5** Ran SP% **109.4**
Speed ratings (Par 103): **97,93,86,72,68**
CSF £3.20 TOTE £1.90: £1.30, £1.10; EX 4.00.
Owner Hamdan Al Maktoum **Bred** Jim Monaghan **Trained** Middleham Moor, N Yorks

FOCUS
The rain had arrived by now. A weak-looking maiden but in the end a very ready winner of some potential. The runner-up looks the best guide.

1722 CANCER RESEARCH UK CLAIMING STKS — 6f 5y
5:25 (5:26) (Class 6) 4-6-Y-O **£2,388** (£705; £352) **Stalls** Low

Form RPR

01-6 **1** **Cawdor (IRE)**[119] 26 4-9-0 79... TonyHamilton 2 74
(Mrs L Stubbs) *prom: rdn to ld over 1f out: styd on wl fnl f* **5/2**[2]

1202 **2** *2 1/2* **Ingleby Star (IRE)**[23] 1200 5-8-9 71............................(p) GaryBartley(3) 4 64
(N Wilson) *t.k.h: cl up: drvn and outpcd over 1f out: rallied to chse wnr ins fnl f: r.o* **2/1**[1]

00/ **3** *3/4* **Dolly Royal (IRE)**[615] 5361 5-7-11 0.............................. PaulPickard(5) 3 51
(R Johnson) *dwlt: bhd and outpcd: hdwy on outside over 1f out: r.o fnl f: nrst fin* **80/1**

3005 **4** *3/4* **Carnival Dream**[22] 1235 5-8-5 51...................................... PatrickMathers 7 52
(H A McWilliams) *prom: drvn over 2f out: kpt on same pce fnl f* **20/1**

0-0 **5** *2 1/4* **Cheveyo (IRE)**[9] 1509 4-8-7 69...(t) PaulHanagan 1 47
(Patrick Morris) *in tch: rdn and edgd rt over 2f out: no imp fnl f* **8/1**

40-0 **6** *1 1/2* **Go Alone (IRE)**[15] 1396 4-8-10 65.. PJMcDonald 8 45
(G A Swinbank) *dwlt: sn prom: drvn over 2f out: no ex over 1f out* **7/2**[3]

00-0 **7** *1/2* **Royal Premium**[87] 407 4-8-2 53...(v) IanBrennan(5) 9 40
(James Moffatt) *set decent gallop to over 1f out: sn wknd* **12/1**

60 **8** *8* **Orpenia (IRE)**[8] 1536 4-7-13 0..................................... AndrewHeffernan(3) 5 10
(Miss L A Perratt) *prom tl drvn and wknd fr 2f out* **33/1**

1m 15.35s (3.15) **Going Correction** +0.40s/f (Good) **8** Ran SP% **111.9**
Speed ratings: **95,91,90,89,86 84,84,73**
toteswingers:1&2:£2.10, 2&3:£13.10, 1&3:£5.80 CSF £7.48 TOTE £3.30: £1.50, £1.20, £4.50; EX 5.20.
Owner Mrs L Stubbs **Bred** Mrs D J Hughes **Trained** Norton, N Yorks

FOCUS
After an hour's persistent rain, the ground was changed to good all round but it was again reported to be slower than the official version. A low-grade sprint claimer and the first two did not need to be at their best.
Royal Premium Official explanation: jockey said colt hung left-handed final 2f

1723 JOHN QUIGLEY MEMORIAL H'CAP — 5f 4y
5:55 (5:58) (Class 6) (0-60,58) 4-Y-0+ — £2,388 (£705; £352) Stalls Low

Form — RPR

505- **1** **Ace Of Spies (IRE)**[221] 6221 5-9-1 **55** SilvestreDeSousa 11 — 66+
(G A Harker) *prom: rdn to ld over 1f out: edgd lft: hld on wl fnl f* — 7/2[2]

5423 **2** ½ **Welcome Approach**[45] 924 7-8-9 **49** PaulMulrennan 4 — 58
(J R Weymes) *in tch: drvn over 2f out: hdwy over 1f out: chsd wnr ins fnl f: kpt on fin* — 6/1[3]

4032 **3** 2 **Megalo Maniac**[26] 1142 7-8-6 **46** (v) PaulHanagan 12 — 48+
(R A Fahey) *bhd and outpcd: hdwy on outside appr fnl f: kpt on fnl f: nt pce of first two* — 6/1[3]

410- **4** ¾ **Tongalooma**[153] 7595 4-9-0 **54** PJMcDonald 9 — 53
(James Moffatt) *prom: effrt and ev ch over 1f out: one pce ins fnl f* — 16/1

214 **5** shd **Fuzzy Cat**[18] 1300 4-9-1 **55** GrahamGibbons 8 — 54
(T D Barron) *dwlt: bhd and pushed along: hdwy 2f out: kpt on same pce ins fnl f* — 3/1[1]

00-0 **6** 1 ¼ **Officer Mor (USA)**[25] 1154 4-8-2 **47** IanBrennan(5) 6 — 41
(Mrs Dianne Sayer) *prom: effrt and ev ch over 1f out: outpcd ins fnl f* — 10/1

500- **7** ¾ **Thunder Bay**[148] 7645 5-8-13 **53** TonyHamilton 2 — 44
(R E Barr) *in tch: rdn and ev ch over 1f out: no ex ins fnl f* — 16/1

0000 **8** ½ **Admirals Way**[11] 1470 5-7-12 **45** NathanAlison(7) 5 — 35
(C N Kellett) *in tch: effrt and edgd rt 2f out: sn no imp* — 33/1

000- **9** ¾ **Ryedane (IRE)**[221] 6216 8-9-4 **58** (b) DuranFentiman 3 — 45
(T D Easterby) *bhd: drvn over 2f out: styd on ins fnl f: nvr able to chal* — 12/1

066/ **10** 4 ½ **Chambers (IRE)**[502] 7693 4-8-9 **49** DavidAllan 13 — 20
(E J Alston) *cl up tl rdn and wknd wl over 1f out* — 14/1

600- **11** 4 **Howards Prince**[223] 6161 7-8-0 **45** (p) JamesSullivan(5) 10 — 1
(D A Nolan) *t.k.h: led to over 1f out: sn btn* — 100/1

0200 **12** 2 ¾ **Sonhador**[25] 1154 4-8-2 **49** (p) CharlotteKerton(7) 7 — —
(A Berry) *sn outpcd and drvn along: nvr on terms* — 40/1

0000 **13** 6 **Miacarla**[5] 1598 7-8-5 **45** (t) PatrickMathers 1 — —
(H A McWilliams) *s.s: a wl bhd* — 40/1

61.87 secs (1.87) **Going Correction** +0.40s/f (Good) — 13 Ran SP% **119.8**
Speed ratings (Par 101): **101,100,97,95,95 93,92,91,90,83 76,72,62**
toteswingers:1&2:£8.30, 1&3:£8.50, 2&3:£4.40 CSF £24.50 CT £129.11 TOTE £5.20: £2.10, £1.80, £2.10; EX 33.70 Place 6 £18.71; Place 5 £12.18.
Owner A S Ward **Bred** Gainsborough Stud Management Ltd **Trained** Thirkleby, N Yorks

FOCUS
A low-grade sprint handicap. The winner is rated back to last year's best.
Miacarla Official explanation: jockey said, regarding appearing to be late removing blindfold, that it and his gloves were wet from the rain and his hand slipped as he attempted to remove it.
T/Plt: £35.60 to a £1 stake. Pool: £50,577.44. 1,036.96 winning tickets. T/Qpdt: £15.40 to a £1 stake. Pool: £3677.74. 176.54 winning tickets. RY

1697 NEWMARKET (Rowley Mile) (R-H)
Sunday, May 2

OFFICIAL GOING: Good to soft
Stands' side track used.
Wind: Fresh across Weather: Overcast

1724 STANJAMES.COM STKS (H'CAP) — 1m 4f
2:05 (2:06) (Class 2) (0-105,105) 4-Y-0+
£31,155 (£9,330; £4,665; £2,335; £1,165; £585) Stalls Centre

Form — RPR

32-2 **1** **Tinaar (USA)**[22] 1220 4-8-9 **90** FrankieDettori 17 — 103+
(G A Butler) *hld up in tch: led over 1f out: sn rdn and hung lft: styd on* — 8/1[3]

220- **2** 1 ½ **Chiberta King**[217] 6302 4-8-9 **90** WilliamBuick 18 — 99
(A M Balding) *lw: led: hdd over 6f out: led again 5f out: rdn and hdd over 1f out: sn hung lft: styd on* — 12/1

4-36 **3** 1 **Heliodor (USA)**[36] 1016 4-9-8 **103** JimmyFortune 21 — 110
(R Hannon) *hld up: hdwy over 3f out: rdn over 1f out: rdn and edgd lft ins fnl f: styd on u.p* — 40/1

322- **4** 1 ½ **Hillview Boy (IRE)**[176] 7293 6-8-13 **94** TomQueally 12 — 99+
(J S Goldie) *s.i.s: hld up: hdwy over 3f out: rdn over 1f out: styd on* — 9/1

00-6 **5** ½ **Topolski (IRE)**[22] 1220 4-8-4 **85** DavidProbert 15 — 89
(A M Balding) *a.p: rdn over 2f out: kpt on* — 18/1

40-4 **6** hd **Classic Vintage (USA)**[19] 1274 4-9-1 **96** JimCrowley 19 — 99
(Mrs A J Perrett) *lw: hld up in tch: rdn to join ldrs 3f out: styng on same pce whn hung lft ins fnl f* — 13/2[2]

240- **7** 5 **Class Is Class (IRE)**[204] 6662 4-9-2 **97** RyanMoore 2 — 92
(Sir Michael Stoute) *lw: hld up: hdwy u.p and hung rt fr 2f out: nvr rchd ldrs* — 9/2[1]

000- **8** ½ **Macarthur**[217] 6303 6-9-10 **105** ShaneKelly 11 — 100
(Jane Chapple-Hyam) *prom: outpcd over 3f out: swtchd lft and rallied over 1f out: styd on* — 25/1

111- **9** 1 **Royal Diamond (IRE)**[204] 6671 4-9-4 **99** PhillipMakin 6 — 92
(M Dods) *s.i.s: hld up: hdwy over 2f out: nvr trbld ldrs* — 25/1

-253 **10** 9 **Becausewecan (USA)**[25] 1151 4-9-0 **95** JoeFanning 1 — 74
(M Johnston) *chsd ldrs: rdn over 3f out: wknd over 2f out* — 14/1

30-6 **11** ½ **Martyr**[36] 1015 5-8-8 **89** RichardHughes 8 — 67
(R Hannon) *hld up: hdwy over 3f out: rdn over 2f out: sn hung rt and wknd* — 11/1

0005 **12** 3 **Reve De Nuit (USA)**[15] 1378 4-8-7 **88** (p) JamesDoyle 10 — 61
(A J McCabe) *chsd ldr tl led over 6f out: hdd 5f out: wkng whn n.m.r and swvd lft over 3f out* — 25/1

440- **13** 12 **Far From Old (IRE)**[418] 7-9-2 **97** JamieSpencer 4 — 51
(M L W Bell) *hld up: rdn over 2f out: bhd whn hung rt over 1f out: t.o* — 11/1

0415 **14** 6 **Raptor (GER)**[19] 1282 7-8-0 **81** NickyMackay 7 — 25
(M E Rimmer) *chsd ldrs tl rdn and wknd 3f out: t.o* — 33/1

40-0 **15** 2 ¾ **Pevensey (IRE)**[36] 1015 8-8-9 **90** (p) TomEaves 16 — 30
(J J Quinn) *hld up: plld hrd: hmpd after 2f: hdwy 5f out: rdn and wknd wl over 2f out: t.o* — 40/1

6245 **16** 20 **Record Breaker (IRE)**[22] 1220 6-9-0 **95** (b) RichardHills 5 — —
(M Johnston) *hld up: rdn: hung rt and wknd 3f out: t.o* — 12/1

/4-0 **17** 19 **Ouster (GER)**[19] 1274 4-8-5 **86** TadhgO'Shea 9 — —
(D R C Elsworth) *hld up: plld hrd: hdwy over 6f out: wknd over 3f out: t.o* — 20/1

2m 36.98s (3.48) **Going Correction** +0.40s/f (Good) — 17 Ran SP% **120.7**
Speed ratings (Par 109): **104,103,102,101,101 100,97,97,96,90 90,88,80,76,74 61,48**
toteswingers:1&2:£13.20, 1&3:£112.40, 2&3:£154.10 CSF £90.32 CT £3591.78 TOTE £6.80: £2.00, £4.40, £10.30, £2.50; EX 90.10 Trifecta £1074.40 Part won. Pool: £1,451.95 - 0.10 winning units..
Owner Fawzi Abdulla Nass **Bred** Robert S Evans **Trained** Newmarket, Suffolk

FOCUS
After a total of 8mm of overnight rain and showers in the morning the ground description was changed to good to soft. This high-class handicap has been won by horses at both ends of the weights in the last ten years, four and five-year-olds share the best record in that period and it was the former age group that dominated the finish. The first two are improvers with the winner looking better than the bare form. The fourth helps set the standard.

NOTEBOOK
Tinaar(USA), the only filly in the field, had good form on the all-weather and, although progressive, was a stone above her previous winning mark. She was always travelling well just off the pace and, once she went on 2f from home, always looked like holding on. She can be expected to go on again from this and connections have the Lancashire Oaks in mind for her. (op 7-1 tchd 17-2 in places)
Chiberta King ◆, a C&D winner on fast ground last May, goes well fresh and ran a big race from the front. Although unable to respond when the winner first took the advantage, he kept finding for pressure and rallied up the hill. He looks set for a good season and is the sort who could make up into an Ebor horse later on. (op 11-1)
Heliodor(USA), a winner of the Zetland Stakes over 1m2f here on easy ground as a juvenile, had shown his best form since on Polytrack. He had not contested a handicap since running in nurseries as a two-year-old but ran pretty well from off the pace, and his future may now lie at this trip.
Hillview Boy(IRE) had gained his wins over shorter but was well suited by soft ground and finished runner-up in the November Handicap on his last start in November 2009. Racing off a 4lb higher mark, he was held up in the rear before making good headway 3f out travelling well. However, he could not make any further impression up the hill. (op 17-2 tchd 8-1)
Topolski(IRE), a dual 1m2f winner on fast ground was never far away but looked in trouble some way from home before staying on again. He is 11lb above his last winning mark but still appears to be progressing. (op 20-1)
Classic Vintage(USA), a dual winner over 1m4f on fast going last season, has also handled soft ground in the past. He ran his race but could not pick up in the closing stages, and might be held by the Handicapper off 6lb higher than his last winning mark. (op 11-2 tchd 7-1)
Class Is Class(IRE) had won first time out last season and was once again well backed. He was held up in the rear but was only able to make late headway without ever figuring. Although he has handled soft ground before, he might be happier back on a faster surface. (op 6-1)
Macarthur, the 2008 winner of the Group 2 Hardwicke Stakes, was having his first run for a new trainer, having formerly been with both Aidan O'Brien and Mike de Kock. He was running off a mark a stone below his highest rating and ran a fairly encouraging race having been held up.
Royal Diamond(IRE) ◆, a progressive performer for Sir Mark Prescott who had won his four previous starts, all at around 1m6f, before being sold for 400,000gns, was making his seasonal debut for a new trainer. Raised 14lb for his last success, he ran on from the rear despite being side-swiped by the weakening Reve De Nuit, and should do better back over further with this run under his belt. (tchd 33-1 in places)
Reve De Nuit(USA) Official explanation: jockey said colt dived quickly right 3f out
Ouster(GER) Official explanation: jockey said colt ran too free

1725 STANJAMES.COM DAHLIA STKS (GROUP 3) (F&M) — 1m 1f
2:40 (2:43) (Class 1) 4-Y-0+
£36,900 (£13,988; £7,000; £3,490; £1,748; £877) Stalls Low

Form — RPR

114- **1** **Strawberrydaiquiri**[211] 6479 4-8-12 **113** RyanMoore 9 — 103+
(Sir Michael Stoute) *racd centre: chsd ldr tl led that gp 3f out: pushed along and edgd lft 2f out: rdn to ld overall over 1f out: drvn out* — 11/8[1]

10-4 **2** hd **Honimiere (IRE)**[36] 1016 4-8-12 **94** NeilCallan 1 — 103?
(G A Swinbank) *lw: racd alone on stands' side rail: overall ldr: clr 3f out: rdn: edgd rt and hdd over 1f out: rallied ins fnl f: r.o* — 16/1

303- **3** 4 **Spacious**[211] 6479 5-8-12 **113** JMurtagh 6 — 94
(J R Fanshawe) *swtg: racd centre: chsd ldrs: rdn over 2f out: styd on same pce fnl f* — 11/4[2]

/12- **4** 5 **Three Moons (IRE)**[364] 1701 4-8-12 **104** FrankieDettori 3 — 85
(H J L Dunlop) *edgd rt s: led gp in centre 6f: sn rdn: wknd over 1f out* — 17/2

020- **5** 3 ½ **Annabelle's Charm (IRE)**[172] 7347 5-8-12 **104** KierenFallon 7 — 76
(L M Cumani) *bit bkwd: racd centre: hld up: sme hdwy over 2f out: wknd wl over 1f out* — 16/1

260- **6** ¾ **Plaisterer**[176] 7291 5-8-12 **96** JackMitchell 4 — 74
(C F Wall) *hmpd s: hld up in centre gp: a in rr* — 16/1

011- **7** nk **Moonlife (IRE)**[185] 7132 4-8-12 **107** (t) AhmedAjtebi 10 — 73
(Mahmood Al Zarooni) *lw: racd centre: plld hrd and prom: rdn and wknd over 2f out* — 13/2[3]

562- **8** 3 **Badiat Alzaman (IRE)**[170] 7366 4-8-12 **91** JimCrowley 8 — 67
(E A L Dunlop) *racd centre: hld up: rdn and wknd over 3f out* — 33/1

1m 54.03s (2.33) **Going Correction** +0.40s/f (Good) — 8 Ran SP% **113.2**
Speed ratings (Par 113): **105,104,101,96,93 93,92,90**
toteswingers:1&2:£5.20, 1&3:£1.50, 2&3:£8.30 CSF £25.73 TOTE £2.20: £1.30, £3.10, £1.40; EX 29.20 Trifecta £139.90 Pool: £1,433.87 - 7.58 winning units..
Owner Mrs R J Jacobs **Bred** Newsells Park Stud Limited **Trained** Newmarket, Suffolk
■ Stewards' Enquiry : Neil Callan three-day ban: used whip with excessive frequency (May 16-18)
Kieren Fallon caution: used whip down the shoulder int he forehand.

FOCUS
The absence of last season's dual Oaks winner Sariska due to a foot injury appeared to give Sir Michael Stoute an excellent chance of taking this race for the fourth year in succession. The form is muddling, although the winner looks to have improved again from last season.

NOTEBOOK
Strawberrydaiquiri, progressive throughout her three-year-old campaign, had finished behind Spacious in the Group 1 Sun Chariot Stakes last October (getting 3lb) but reversed that form on both of their first starts of the season. Ryan Moore had his mount fairly handy in the chasing bunch throughout and his filly fought on well in the final furlong to deny a brave runner-up. Connections will be delighted to get a first Group-race success into their horse and one would imagine that she will be a force in similar events during the summer. The Windsor Forest Stakes or the Pretty Polly at the Curragh is next on the agenda. (op 13-8, tchd 7-4 in places)
Honimiere(IRE)'s performance was interesting in so much that she followed her own path up the home straight close to the stands' rail (one that proved to be a big advantage on the day), and then responded to her jockey's urgings to make the winner fight for victory. She did have the advantage of race fitness on her side, but is 19lb inferior to Strawberrydaiquiri on official figures, so had no right to go so close, tough though she is. However, it was a fine piece of placement by her connections and they should be delighted with what she has achieved. (op 12-1)

Spacious, runner-up in the 1000 Guineas over this course two years previously, took the Group 2 Windsor Forest Stakes last summer and finished ahead of Strawberrydaiquiri when they met at the end of last season. She took a good grip here in the chasing bunch before getting outpaced for a few strides when the tempo lifted over 3f out. The lengths she lost at that stage were enough to end her challenge for victory. (op 3-1)

Three Moons(IRE), having her first start since finishing second on this day last season in the Pretty Polly Stakes, took the group along in the middle but tired about 2f out. She was fully entitled to need the run and one would imagine connections will be pleased. (op 10-1)

Annabelle's Charm(IRE), the winner of a Listed event in 2009, was never seen with any chance once the gallop increased and is probably not quite up to this grade. (op 12-1 tchd 18-1)

Moonlife(IRE) won her final two starts of last season, the last of which was a Listed contest on the all-weather at Lingfield. The improved form coincided with the fitting of a tongue-tie, which was on here, but she looked an awkward ride here under restraint and out of her depth when off the bridle. (op 6-1)

1726 STANJAMES.COM 1000 GUINEAS STKS (GROUP 1) (FILLIES) 1m

3:20 (3:23) (Class 1) 3-Y-O

£227,080 (£86,080; £43,080; £21,480; £10,760; £5,400) **Stalls** Centre

Form				RPR
21-3	**1**		**Special Duty**[24] 1196 3-9-0 117 .... StephanePasquier 1 *(Mme C Head-Maarek, France) racd stands' side: hld up: hdwy 2f out: sn rdn and edgd rt: ev ch whn bmpd ins fnl f: sn carried rt: r.o: fin 2nd, nse: plcd 1st* **9/2**[1]	111
10-0	**2**	*nse*	**Jacqueline Quest (IRE)**[18] 1312 3-9-0 97 .... TomQueally 4 *(H R A Cecil) lw: racd stands' side: hld up: hdwy 3f out: rdn to ld overall over 1f out: hung rt thrght fnl f: jst hld on: fin 1st, nse: plcd 2nd* **66/1**	111
5-	**3**	*hd*	**Gile Na Greine (IRE)**[23] 1214 3-9-0 88 .... KJManning 2 *(J S Bolger, Ire) str: racd stands' side: chsd ldr: rdn and ev ch over 1f out: r.o: 3rd of 7 in group* **25/1**	110
314-	**4**	*1/2*	**Sent From Heaven (IRE)**[218] 6269 3-9-0 105 .... MichaelHills 6 *(B W Hills) overall ldr on stands' side: rdn and hdd over 1f out: r.o: 4th of 7 in group* **33/1**	109
10-6	**5**	*5*	**Distinctive**[18] 1312 3-9-0 102 .... TomEaves 7 *(B Smart) lw: racd stands' side: prom: rdn over 2f out: hung lft over 1f out: wknd fnl f: 5th of 7 in group* **66/1**	98
01-1	**6**	*3/4*	**Music Show (IRE)**[18] 1312 3-9-0 110 .... RyanMoore 15 *(M R Channon) lw: racd centre: prom: led that gp over 2f out: sn rdn: kpt on: no ch w stands' side: 1st of 10 in group* **7/1**[3]	96+
1-1	**7**	*3/4*	**Rumoush (USA)**[18] 1313 3-9-0 107 .... RichardHills 18 *(M P Tregoning) lw: racd centre: chsd ldrs: rdn over 1f out: styd on: 2nd of 10 in group* **7/1**[3]	94+
20-2	**8**	*4*	**Habaayib**[15] 1384 3-9-0 107 .... TadhgO'Shea 3 *(E A L Dunlop) racd stands' side: chsd ldrs: rdn over 2f out: hung lft and wknd over 1f out: 6th of 7 in group* **40/1**	85
25-2	**9**	*1 3/4*	**Blue Maiden**[18] 1312 3-9-0 105 .... JamieSpencer 14 *(P J McBride) racd centre side: hld up in tch: rdn over 2f out: wknd over 1f out: 3rd of 10 in group* **12/1**	81+
132-	**10**	*2 1/4*	**Lady Darshaan (IRE)**[218] 6269 3-9-0 108 .... WilliamBuick 8 *(J S Moore) lw: ponied down to the s: racd centre: prom: rdn over 2f out: sn hung lft and wknd: 4th of 10 in group* **25/1**	76+
211-	**11**	*5*	**Pollenator (IRE)**[233] 5825 3-9-0 105 .... RichardHughes 16 *(R Hannon) lw: racd centre: chsd ldr tl lft in ld of that gp over 6f out: hdd over 2f out: rdn and wknd over 1f out: 5th of 10 in group* **8/1**	64+
13-	**12**	*1*	**Seta**[233] 5825 3-9-0 102 .... KierenFallon 9 *(L M Cumani) racd centre: hld up: hdwy over 2f out: hung lft and wknd over 1f out: 6th of 10 in group* **13/2**[2]	62+
13-1	**13**	*2 1/2*	**Pipette**[29] 1082 3-9-0 97 .... JimmyFortune 10 *(A M Balding) racd centre: hld up: hdwy over 2f out: rdn over 1f out: sn wknd: 7th of 10 in group* **12/1**	56+
232-	**14**	*3 1/4*	**Nurture (IRE)**[183] 7187 3-9-0 99 .... JimCrowley 12 *(R M Beckett) racd centre: with ldrs until rdn and wknd over 2f out: 8th of 10 in group* **40/1**	49+
2-2	**15**	*3 1/2*	**Devoted To You (IRE)**[42] 957 3-9-0 104 .... JMurtagh 5 *(A P O'Brien, Ire) racd stands' side: chsd ldrs: rdn and wknd over 2f out: last of 7 in group* **11/1**	41
221-	**16**	*shd*	**Hibaayeb**[218] 6269 3-9-0 110 .... FrankieDettori 13 *(Saeed Bin Suroor) lw: racd centre: prom: rdn 2f out: wknd and eased over 1f out: 9th of 10 in group* **12/1**	41+
02-4	**17**	*11*	**Misheer**[15] 1384 3-9-0 110 .... NeilCallan 17 *(C E Brittain) plld hrd and led centre gp tl wnt far side over 6f out: rejnd centre gp over 5f out: chsd ldr tl wknd over 2f out: last of 10 in group* **28/1**	15+

1m 39.66s (1.06) **Going Correction** +0.40s/f (Good) **17 Ran SP% 121.0**
Speed ratings (Par 110): **109,110,109,109,104 103,102,98,97,94 89,88,86,83,79 79,68**
toteswingers:1&2:£68.20, 1&3:£36.90, 2&3:£124.80 CSF £348.74 CT £4078.45 TOTE £3.50: £1.30, £18.30, £9.90; EX 338.70 Trifecta £3663.20 Pool: £8,415.49 - 1.70 winning units..
Owner K Abdulla **Bred** Juddmonte Farms Ltd **Trained** Chantilly, France

■ The first Classic 'winner' to be thrown out on the day by the stewards since Nureyev in the 2000 Guineas of 1980.

■ Stewards' Enquiry : Tom Queally three-day ban: careless riding (May 16-18)

FOCUS

This fillies' Classic has produced its fair share of surprise winners in recent seasons and but for the stewards' intervention would have done so again. This year's running produced an average-sized field and they raced in two groups, with the stands' side group having a considerable advantage, and five of the seven that raced in that group coming home ahead of the runners that raced mainly centre to far side. It produced a tremendous and controversial finish. The form looks substandard for the race with the bias ending the chance of many and the placed horses running well above previous marks. The fifth is the best guide for now.

NOTEBOOK

Special Duty was Europe's champion juvenile filly last season, having been touched off by a colt in the Prix Morny and then won the Cheveley Park. However, she was beaten into third in the Prix Imprudence over 7f on very soft ground on her seasonal reappearance, and there was clearly a question over her stamina for the mile. The Maisons-Laffitte form did receive a boost of sorts when the runner-up there won the Italian 1000 Guineas earlier in the weekend though, and she proved that the very soft ground there had been against her by picking up well to challenge having been held up. She would have got the better of her rival but for the bumping and justice was ultimately done. She could reappear in the Pouliches in a fortnight but the Coronation Stakes at Ascot looks more likely for her next start. (op 5-1)

Jacqueline Quest(IRE), a winner over 7f on fast ground but held in Listed and Group company since, stepped up on all her previous form and prevailed by the narrowest of margins but in the process carried the favourite across the course and bumped her at least twice, as her rider switched his whip to his left hand and persisted in using it despite his filly drifting. A stewards' inquiry was inevitable and they came to the correct conclusion that the placings ought to be reversed, and it also cost her rider a three-day ban. Connections might look for compensation in the Coronation Stakes.

Gile Na Greine(IRE) ◆, representing a trainer with a fine recent record in Newmarket Classics, was a 7f winner on soft and fifth in the Moyglare last season. She had finished runner-up over 1m on Polytrack on her return though, and the winner had been beaten since. She ran a fine race back on turf, being close up throughout and then rallying well up the hill to be beaten only narrowly by the principals. She looked as though she would have won in another 100 yards and appeals as a possible Oaks filly, although her pedigree does not necessarily suggest she will stay that far. She might run in the Irish version next, with the alternative the Musidora. (op 50-1)

Sent From Heaven(IRE) set the pace near the stands' rail and did not weaken out of things until late on. She had finished fourth behind a couple of today's rivals in the Fillies' Mile, which suggests that the draw had a great deal to do with this result. (tchd 40-1)

Distinctive, a dual winner at 6f, was held behind Music Show in both the Rockfel and Nell Gwyn. She was able to reverse those placings with the aid of a favourable draw. (op 80-1)

Music Show(IRE) ◆ came out best of those that raced centre to far side, and a line through the fifth suggests that she would have gone very close without the track bias, as she had beaten that rival by five lengths in the Nell Gwyn and was beaten just under a length here. She will be fancied if she takes on those ahead of her in either the Irish 1000 Guineas or the Coronation Stakes. (op 8-1)

Rumoush(USA), a half-sister to last year's winner Ghanaati, had beaten colts in a Listed race over 1m1f here last month. She ran really well from the outside draw and is another who can be expected to improve on this next time. (tchd 8-1)

Habaayib, a 6f Group 3 winner and runner-up in the Newbury trial for this on her return, raced on the favoured stands' side but appeared to not last the trip, and a drop back to 7f for something like the Jersey Stakes seems possible. (op 50-1 tchd 66-1)

Blue Maiden, runner-up to Music Show in Nell Gwyn, could not run up to that form this time but may have been unsuited by the ease in the ground. (op 16-1)

Lady Darshaan(IRE), a surprise runner-up in the Fillies' Mile, probably lost her chance when her rider decided to join the bigger group racing in the centre rather than those on the stands' side. However, she drifted left again under pressure and is another who may have not liked the ground.

Pollenator(IRE) was drawn high and raced up the centre. She confirmed May Hill form with Seta but is yet another who can do better back on fast ground. She may go for the Prix de Diane. (op 15-2)

Seta also went to join the group up the centre and was held up but failed to make much headway on ground that should have come in her favour, and then hung late on. She now has something to prove. (op 9-2)

Pipette had form on soft ground but was stepping up in grade and appeared to find this too much for her at this stage of her career. (tchd 11-1)

Nurture(IRE) is still a maiden but ran reasonably before tiring and can win races at a lower level. (op 33-1)

Devoted To You(IRE), all of whose runs had been on soft, showed up well on the stands' side but faded to finish some way last of that group. (op 12-1)

Hibaayeb split Pollenator and Seta in the May Hill then won Group 1 Fillies' Mile at Ascot from Lady Darshaan. She joined Godolphin over the winter but was untried on ground softer than good and it may not have suited, as she was eased late on when beaten. (op 16-1)

Misheer finished runner-up to Special Duty in the Cheveley Park, but had looked a suspect stayer behind Habaayib at Newbury and did not help her chance by running far too freely early on. (op 33-1)

1727 BETTINGMADEEASY@STANJAMES.COM STKS (H'CAP) 6f

3:55 (3:56) (Class 2) 4-Y-O+

£31,155 (£9,330; £4,665; £2,335; £1,165; £585) **Stalls** Low

Form				RPR
14-1	**1**		**Hawkeyethenoo (IRE)**[16] 1363 4-8-1 81 .... AndreaAtzeni 5 *(J S Goldie) hld up in tch: nt clr run: swtchd lft and stmbld over 1f out: r.o to ld wl ins fnl f* **10/1**[3]	97+
223-	**2**	*1 1/4*	**Enact**[198] 6814 4-9-1 95 .... RyanMoore 8 *(Sir Michael Stoute) lw: chsd ldrs: rdn to ld 1f out: hdd wl ins fnl f* **15/2**[1]	104
0-46	**3**	*3/4*	**Angus Newz**[7] 1545 7-8-3 83 ow1 ....(v) ChrisCatlin 4 *(M Quinn) led over 3f: rallied to ld over 1f out: sn rdn and hdd: edgd rt ins fnl f: styd on same pce towards fin* **33/1**	90
103-	**4**	*1/2*	**Genki (IRE)**[203] 6707 6-9-9 103 .... WilliamBuick 25 *(R Charlton) s.s: hld up: hdwy on outer over 1f out: r.o wl: nt rch ldrs* **16/1**	108+
05-6	**5**	*hd*	**Parisian Pyramid (IRE)**[18] 1295 4-8-9 89 .... NeilCallan 7 *(K A Ryan) a.p: rdn and ev ch over 1f out: styd on same pce ins fnl f* **8/1**[2]	94
0/-1	**6**	*1/2*	**Secret Asset (IRE)**[23] 1206 5-8-7 94 .... LewisWalsh(7) 10 *(Jane Chapple-Hyam) chsd ldrs: rdn over 2f out: styd on same pce fnl f* **25/1**	97
00-1	**7**	*1*	**Mo Mhuirnin (IRE)**[24] 1192 4-8-8 88 .... FrederikTylicki 6 *(R A Fahey) s.i.s: hdwy over 3f out: rdn over 1f out: styd on* **18/1**	88
-102	**8**	*shd*	**Flipando (IRE)**[23] 1206 9-9-4 98 .... TomEaves 9 *(T D Barron) hld up: r.o ins fnl f: nrst fin* **14/1**	98
4-10	**9**	*1/2*	**Medicean Man**[18] 1295 4-8-9 89 ....(p) FrankieDettori 11 *(J R Gask) hld up: hdwy over 1f out: r.o: nt rch ldrs* **12/1**	87
401	**10**	*3/4*	**Prohibit**[36] 1014 5-9-5 99 .... PatCosgrave 19 *(R M H Cowell) hld up: hdwy over 2f out: rdn over 1f out: no ex ins fnl f* **25/1**	95+
00-0	**11**	*2 1/2*	**Zidane**[35] 1032 8-9-1 95 .... JMurtagh 12 *(J R Fanshawe) hld up: pushed along over 2f out: rdn over 1f out: nvr on terms* **8/1**[2]	83
0430	**12**	*3/4*	**Rileyskeepingfaith**[29] 1085 4-9-6 100 ....(v) KierenFallon 20 *(M R Channon) hld up: hdwy over 2f out: rdn: hung lft and wknd over 1f out* **25/1**	85+
0-03	**13**	*shd*	**Courageous (IRE)**[13] 1423 4-8-12 92 .... RichardMullen 13 *(B Smart) prom: rdn over 2f out: wknd over 1f out* **16/1**	77
514-	**14**	*1 1/2*	**Rapid Water**[261] 4990 4-8-0 80 .... DavidProbert 3 *(A M Balding) chsd ldr tl led over 2f out: rdn and hdd over 1f out: wknd ins fnl f* **12/1**	60
001-	**15**	*shd*	**Doric Lady**[169] 7395 5-8-1 81 .... KirstyMilczarek 17 *(J A R Toller) prom: rdn over 1f out: wknd fnl f* **40/1**	61
5-02	**16**	*3/4*	**Saucy Brown (IRE)**[35] 1032 4-8-12 92 .... AdrianNicholls 18 *(D Nicholls) prom: rdn 1/2-way: wknd over 1f out* **14/1**	69
30	**17**	*1/2*	**Orpsie Boy (IRE)**[37] 987 7-8-2 82 .... LukeMorris 1 *(N P Littmoden) pushed along in rr: nvr on terms* **28/1**	58
000-	**18**	*1*	**Golden Desert (IRE)**[190] 7019 6-9-9 103 .... JimmyFortune 21 *(R A Mills) hld up: rdn over 2f out: n.d* **50/1**	76
2-00	**19**	*1/2*	**Fantasy Explorer**[23] 1206 7-8-5 85 .... JoeFanning 15 *(J J Quinn) hld up in tch: rdn over 1f out: sn wknd* **33/1**	56
2	**20**	*nk*	**Indian Skipper (IRE)**[8] 1516 5-7-13 79 oh1 ow1 ....(v) JimmyQuinn 2 *(R C Guest) s.i.s: hld up: rdn and wknd wl over 1f out* **33/1**	49
12-6	**21**	*1 3/4*	**Jonny Mudball**[35] 1032 4-8-10 90 .... RichardKingscote 23 *(Tom Dascombe) chsd ldrs: rdn over 2f out: hung lft and wknd over 1f out* **12/1**	54
03-0	**22**	*2 1/2*	**Abraham Lincoln (IRE)**[18] 1295 6-8-10 90 .... LiamJones 14 *(R A Harris) hld up: hdwy over 2f out: wknd over 1f out* **33/1**	46

0055 **23** 2 **Barney McGrew (IRE)**[17] 1326 7-9-10 104.................... PhillipMakin 24 54
(M Dods) *hld up: rdn over 2f out: a in rr* **25/1**

1m 12.5s (0.30) **Going Correction** +0.40s/f (Good) **23** Ran SP% **131.5**
Speed ratings (Par 109): **114,112,111,110,110 109,108,108,107,106 103,102,102,100,100 99,98,97,96,95 93,90,87**
toteswingers:1&2:£19.00, 1&3:£151.90, 2&3:£182.30 CSF £75.11 CT £2457.02 TOTE £11.40: £2.50, £2.00, £7.30, £4.70; EX 89.90 Trifecta £930.50 Pool: £1,886.32 - 1.50 winning units..
Owner Johnnie Delta Racing **Bred** S Leigh & R Leigh & Islandmore Stud **Trained** Uplawmoor, E Renfrews

FOCUS
With 23 runners sprinters hurtling down the track, this was never going to be an easy puzzle for punters to solve, although the assistance of what looked a draw bias towards the stands' rail looked to make things a little easier. The form looks a little fluid and is best rated around the first two.

NOTEBOOK
Hawkeyethenoo(IRE)'s backers were probably praying as much as the jockey that a gap would appear up the rail when it was desperately needed. Fortunately for everyone involved, the space appeared and he raced clear once hitting top gear. His last three victories had come over 5f, but he was a mile winner last July when with Mick Easterby, so the sixth furlong was not going to be an issue. Jim Goldie has done an excellent job with the horse and the winner's long-term aim is the Ayr Gold Cup. Connections may possibly take in the Wokingham Handicap at Royal Ascot. (op 12-1)
Enact, having her first outing since October, was well placed towards the head of affairs and ran all the way to the line. This was arguably a career-best performance and comes from a stable renowned for improving horses with age. (op 9-1)
Angus Newz, who only ran because sufficient rain fell, had a great draw considering her racing style and ran a blinder. She hasn't won for a while but is obviously fairly handicapped as a result. (op 40-1 tchd 50-1 in places)
Genki(IRE) ran a blinder from stall 25. The winner of last year's Stewards' Cup, he is lightly raced and evidently still improving. His chances in handicap company will probably be limited off his current mark, so conditions events or a step back into Listed company could be his best chance of winning this season.
Parisian Pyramid(IRE) has not won since winning on his handicap debut as a two-year-old and is his own worst enemy, as he continues to run solid races, which means he never gets much respite from the Handicapper. (op 10-1)
Secret Asset(IRE) was always to the fore and had every chance. His young rider Lewis Walsh was mainly tidy in the latter stages and did not panic under pressure. One would imagine a few trainers will be interested in using him and his 7lb claim.
Mo Mhuirnin(IRE) made ground at the end of the race, but found trouble on the way. She found her way blocked a couple of times when trying to get through as the pace increased. However, neither would have won with a clear passage. (op 16-1)
Flipando(IRE) also made ground at the end of the race, having found trouble on the way but would not have won, even with a clear passage. (op 16-1)
Medicean Man, in cheekpieces for the first time, carried his head high and ran on without being a danger. (tchd 14-1)
Zidane was well backed during the morning but looked an awkward ride while trying to make ground from the rear. His head was very high under pressure. Official explanation: jockey said gelding never travelled (op 7-1)
Rapid Water ◆, a son of the great Lochsong, was far too free on his return to action and gave the impression a drop to 5f is what he wants, even though he is a dual winner at 6f. He is lightly raced so capable of plenty of improvement still. (op 16-1)
Orpsie Boy(IRE) Official explanation: jockey said gelding never travelled

1728 BELUCKY@STANJAMES.COM MAIDEN STKS 5f
4:30 (4:30) (Class 2) 2-Y-O **£9,714** (£2,890; £1,444; £721) **Stalls** Low

Form RPR

1 **Temple Meads** 2-9-3 0.. RichardMullen 1 87+
(E S McMahon) *str: lw: hld up: hdwy 1/2-way: swtchd rt over 1f out: shkn up to ld ins fnl f: r.o wl* **4/1**[2]

2 1 ¾ **Oracle (IRE)**[21] 1243 2-9-3 0.. JMurtagh 11 81
(A P O'Brien, Ire) *str: lw: chsd ldr tl led over 1f out: rdn and hdd ins fnl f: styd on same pce* **7/2**[1]

3 1 ½ **Al Aasifh (IRE)** 2-9-3 0.. FrankieDettori 8 76+
(Saeed Bin Suroor) *athletic: lw: s.i.s and hmpd s: hld up: hdwy 1/2-way: rdn over 1f out: edgd lft and styd on same pce ins fnl f* **11/2**

2 **4** hd **Yarooh (USA)**[17] 1324 2-8-12 0.. ChrisCatlin 6 70
(C E Brittain) *led: rdn and hdd over 1f out: edgd rt and no ex ins fnl f* **4/1**[2]

5 nk **Sheer Courage (IRE)** 2-9-3 0.. RyanMoore 10 74+
(R Hannon) *angular: unf: scope: bit bkwd: edgd lft s: chsd ldrs: rdn over 1f out: hung lft and no ex ins fnl f* **10/1**

0 **6** ¾ **On Wings Of Love (IRE)**[17] 1324 2-8-12 0.................... DavidProbert 3 66+
(A Bailey) *chsd ldrs: outpcd 2f out: running on whn n.m.r wl ins fnl f* **12/1**

7 ½ **Numeral (IRE)** 2-9-3 0.. RichardHughes 2 70+
(R Hannon) *lengthy: lw: s.i.s: hld up: rdn and hung rt over 1f out: running on wl whn nt clr run and eased wl ins fnl f* **5/1**[3]

8 2 **Pretium Sceleris** 2-9-3 0.. AndreaAtzeni 5 62
(M Botti) *cmpt: prom: lost pl 3f out: n.d after* **20/1**

61.21 secs (2.11) **Going Correction** +0.40s/f (Good) 8 Ran SP% **115.8**
Speed ratings (Par 99): **99,96,93,93,93 91,91,87**
toteswingers:1&2:£5.00, 1&3:£6.00, 2&3:£5.00 CSF £18.70 TOTE £5.40: £2.00, £1.80, £1.90; EX 26.50 Trifecta £360.90 Pool: £1,043.87 - 2.14 winning units..
Owner J C Fretwell **Bred** Whitsbury Manor Stud **Trained** Lichfield, Staffs

FOCUS
This usually goes to decent sort and one making its debut (Aidan O'Brien's Achilles Of Troy was the only recent exception), but the also rans are worth keeping for the notebook, as last year Radiohead finished second in this and went on to take the Norfolk Stakes at Royal Ascot, while a certain George Washington found the 5f too sharp for him in 2005 when only finishing third. The form makes sense and the race should produce winners.

NOTEBOOK
Temple Meads ◆, a half-brother to stable´s very useful 6f 2yo Sneak Preview, looked a horse with a future by taking this in good style. Well backed late on, he's a fine, big sort with an engine, and the way he quickly put the result beyond doubt once surging to the front suggests he can make his mark at Royal Ascot if heading in that direction (the Coventry was mentioned as a target). He should be difficult to beat in the early part of this season. (op 5-1 after 11-2 and 6-1 in places)
Oracle(IRE) represented connections to be respected and had the advantage of a previous run. Ridden prominently, as one would have expected with experience on his side and being out of a Rainbow Quest mare, he has every chance but could not contain Temple Meads as he flew past. His effort pays a compliment to stablemate Samuel Morse, who was a few lengths better than him at the Curragh when winning. (tchd 4-1)
Al Aasifh(IRE), a 90,000 euros half-brother to useful miler Cordell, was the first two-year-old runner of the season for Saeed Bin Suroor. He does not look the biggest but shaped with plenty of promise after a slow start and being hampered. (op 5-1 tchd 6-1)
Yarooh(USA) finished in front of On Wings Of Love over the C&D in April when showing good speed, and confirmed those positions in this. She was smartly into her stride but outpaced inside the final furlong. (op 5-1 tchd 7-2 and 6-1 in places)
Sheer Courage(IRE), a 120,000gns half-brother to some talented sorts, notably Al Khaleej, Grand Ducal and Hurricane Floyd, who were all successful at two, knew his job and made a satisfactory debut despite running a little green. His pedigree suggests further will be required. (op 15-2)
Numeral(IRE) ◆, whose dam's sire is Sadler's Wells, found his sales price rise markedly to 85,000gns as a yearling from 38,000 euros as a foal. Representing a stable with a fine record in this maiden, he caught the eye and is much better than his final position suggests - he had nowhere to go inside the final furlong when finishing strongly. 6f will be easily within his range. (op 9-2)
Pretium Sceleris, the first foal of a 1m Canadian Listed winner, was unsold for £38,000 at breeze-ups at Kempton in March (his third time of going to the sales) and was green out the back.

1729 HAVEAGO@STANJAMES.COM PRETTY POLLY STKS (LISTED RACE) (FILLIES) 1m 2f
5:05 (5:05) (Class 1) 3-Y-O
£28,385 (£10,760; £5,385; £2,685; £1,345; £675) **Stalls** Low

Form RPR

4-43 **1** **Marie De Medici (USA)**[18] 1313 3-8-12 102.................. FrankieDettori 8 101
(M Johnston) *set stdy pce tl qcknd over 2f out: styd on wl* **7/2**[2]

45- **2** ¾ **Red Fantasy (IRE)**[215] 6363 3-8-12 0.................................. MichaelHills 6 100
(B W Hills) *lw: chsd wnr: rdn over 1f out: styd on* **20/1**

-321 **3** ¾ **Miss Starlight**[24] 1182 3-8-12 83.................................. EddieCreighton 2 98+
(P J McBride) *lw: hld up: shkn up 3f out: rdn and swtchd lft over 1f out: r.o wl ins fnl f: nt rch ldrs* **11/1**

1-3 **4** nk **Principal Role (USA)**[18] 1312 3-8-12 100.......................... TomQueally 3 97
(H R A Cecil) *plld hrd and hung rt s: trckd ldrs: swtchd rt 2f out: rdn over 1f out: styd on same pce ins fnl f* **11/8**[1]

120- **5** 4 ½ **Mudaaraah**[218] 6269 3-9-3 102.. RichardHills 7 93
(J L Dunlop) *prom: rdn over 1f out: wknd fnl f* **6/1**[3]

41-0 **6** hd **Gallic Star (IRE)**[18] 1313 3-9-3 96.................................. KierenFallon 5 93
(M R Channon) *hld up: rdn over 2f out: wknd over 1f out* **12/1**

32-1 **7** 2 **Serafina's Flight**[22] 1240 3-8-12 74.................................. RyanMoore 4 84?
(W R Muir) *hld up in tch: rdn 2f out: nt handle the dip and wknd over 1f out* **25/1**

01-1 **8** 1 **Totally Ours**[25] 1159 3-8-12 81.. MartinDwyer 1 82
(W R Muir) *hld up: rdn: hung rt and wknd over 1f out* **12/1**

2m 9.42s (3.62) **Going Correction** +0.40s/f (Good) 8 Ran SP% **110.9**
Speed ratings: **101,100,99,99,95 95,94,93**
toteswingers:1&2:£12.10, 1&3:£5.70, 2&3:£16.30 CSF £63.27 TOTE £4.20: £1.70, £2.90, £3.30; EX 80.20 Trifecta £933.50 Part won. Pool: £1,261.56 - 0.10 winning units..
Owner Sheikh Hamdan Bin Mohammed Al Maktoum **Bred** Flaxman Holdings Ltd **Trained** Middleham Moor, N Yorks

FOCUS
This Listed race and Oaks Trial has not often thrown up a star, although the great Ouija Board proved a rare exception. Four of the last ten winners had won their only previous start but two winners came into the race as maidens and one was a debutante. The race was run at a steady gallop until the last couple of furlongs and that was confirmed by the time, which was nearly two seconds slower than the following handicap. The form does not look that solid as a result and the winner is probably the best guide.

NOTEBOOK
Marie De Medici(USA) finished third behind subsequent 1000 Guineas seventh Rumoush on her seasonal return over a furlong shorter here at the Craven meeting and came into this with the highest adjusted official rating. She soon got over to the favoured stands' rail from her outside draw and Frankie Dettori dictated a steady pace until asking her to pick up just over 2f from home, from which point she ran on stoutly to gain her first success at this level. She is in the Oaks but her pedigree does not suggest she is totally sure to get that far, although her dam stayed it, and she may go for the Italian Oaks over 1m3f instead. (op 3-1 tchd 4-1 in places)
Red Fantasy(IRE) had shown only modest ability in a couple of fast-ground maidens last season but had clearly improved over the winter and picked up black type here. She was never far away and stuck on to the line without ever looking like getting past the winner. She is in the Ribblesdale but the Swettenham Stud Fillies' Trial could be next on the agenda. (op 22-1)
Miss Starlight had been progressive in handicaps this season at around this trip and handled the step up in grade to earn valuable black type. She finished well from the rear in a race where the others in the frame were ridden close to the pace, and looks as if she will get further. (op 16-1)
Principal Role(USA) had won on her debut prior to finishing third in the Nell Gwyn. However, she was stepping up in trip and encountering softer ground this time, and did not help her chances by being keen under restraint early on. As a result, she did not pick up when switched out to get an opening, just keeping on at the one pace. Her pedigree suggests she should stay and she can be given another chance to prove it. (op 5-4 tchd 6-4 in places)
Mudaaraah was another drawn out wide but she was held up and stayed out there, which was probably not the place to be on the day. She is another who can be expected to do better, possibly back on a sounder surface. (op 11-2 tchd 13-2 and 7-1 in places)
Gallic Star(IRE) was also held up in a race where it paid to race closer to the pace and she also finished up more towards the centre of the track. (op 16-1)

1730 COMEONENGLAND@STANJAMES.COM H'CAP 1m 2f
5:40 (5:40) (Class 2) (0-100,88) 3-Y-O
£12,462 (£3,732; £1,866; £934; £466; £234) **Stalls** Low

Form RPR

51- **1** **London Stripe (IRE)**[187] 7096 3-9-2 83.............................. RyanMoore 4 91+
(Sir Michael Stoute) *a.p: racd keenly: swtchd rt over 2f out: led sn after: rdn over 1f out: styd on wl* **5/2**[1]

1 **2** 1 ¼ **Heddwyn (IRE)**[20] 1268 3-9-4 85.................................. MartinDwyer 3 90+
(M P Tregoning) *athletic: str: lw: hld up: swtchd rt over 2f out: hdwy over 1f out: rdn and ev ch ins fnl f: unable qck towards fin* **7/1**

0-12 **3** ½ **Power Series (USA)**[23] 1210 3-9-6 87.............................. WilliamBuick 7 91
(J H M Gosden) *s.i.s: hld up: hdwy over 2f out: rdn and ev ch over 1f out: styd on same pce ins fnl f* **10/1**

4 ¾ **September Morn (IRE)**[14] 1416 3-9-5 86.............................. JMurtagh 2 89
(A P O'Brien, Ire) *w'like: str: lw: hld up and bhd: swtchd rt and hdwy over 2f out: rdn and hung rt over 1f out: styd on towards fin* **9/2**[3]

631- **5** nk **Red Courtier**[144] 7683 3-8-13 80.................................. FrankieDettori 1 82
(P F I Cole) *bit bkwd: chsd ldrs: rdn over 3f out: hung rt and outpcd over 1f out: styd on towards fin* **12/1**

12 **6** 9 **Tajaarub**[11] 1466 3-8-13 80.. RichardHills 5 64
(B W Hills) *chsd ldr: rdn and ev ch over 2f out: wknd over 1f out* **4/1**[2]

5-1 **7** 1 ½ **Shernando**[75] 570 3-9-6 87.. JoeFanning 8 68
(M Johnston) *chsd ldrs: rdn over 3f out: wkng whn n.m.r over 2f out* **14/1**

26-1 **8** ¾ **Much Acclaimed (IRE)**[17] 1335 3-9-7 88.............................. MickyFenton 6 67
(T P Tate) *leggy: led: rdn and hdd 2f out: sn wknd* **8/1**

2m 7.71s (1.91) **Going Correction** +0.40s/f (Good) 8 Ran SP% **113.8**
Speed ratings (Par 105): **108,107,106,106,105 98,97,96**
toteswingers:1&2:£5.50, 1&3:£4.20, 2&3:£6.90 CSF £20.32 CT £147.37 TOTE £3.10: £1.60, £2.50, £2.90; EX 26.00 Trifecta £178.90 Pool: £1,170.22 - 4.84 winning units. Place 6 £271.77; Place 5 £53.88.
Owner Takashi Watanabe **Bred** Takashi Watanabe **Trained** Newmarket, Suffolk
■ Stewards' Enquiry : Ryan Moore one-day ban: careless riding (May 16)

FOCUS
Only one of these had not won a race, so this looked a strong contest and the form ought to be worth following. It also provided all of the runners except for the John Gosden-trained horse with their handicap debut. The form is a little messy but looks worth treating positively.

NOTEBOOK
London Stripe(IRE), who holds a number of top-class entries, won a maiden as a two-year-old that has worked out fairly well, as the runner-up won both of his subsequent races. A fine looker, he found plenty for pressure and got to the front when asked to quicken. The trainer had won with his only other previous runner in this contest (Dr Faustus), who went on to run with credit behind Collection in the Hampton Court Stakes at Royal Ascot on his next start. It will be interesting to see whether London Stripe heads down the handicap route or is tried at a higher level. (tchd 11-4)
Heddwyn(IRE) was a shock winner on his racecourse debut this season judged on his starting price, but proved that success was no fluke with a great performance. He appeared to struggle with the undulations and would have given the winner a bigger challenge on a more level surface. It would be a surprise if he doesn't find another race this year. (op 8-1)
Power Series(USA), back on turf after a couple of efforts on the all-weather, came through to have every chance but failed to quicken once there. (op 9-1)
September Morn(IRE) became detached at one point but seemed a big danger as he started to catch up. A half-brother to both Purple Moon and the smart Vespone among others, he has the look of a horse who could win a good handicap later in the year, possibly the Ebor, although his attitude needs to improve somewhat under pressure. (op 4-1)
Red Courtier is quite a big sort and may have been in need of the run. The way he stayed on inside the final furlong suggested he is one to be with next time if given a realistic target.
Tajaarub ran poorly after starting his career so well. Ridden prominently dropped in trip, this was disappointing as he was beaten before the distance became a factor. (op 5-1)
Shernando, whose stable had taken two of the previous three renewals of this race, was hampered by the winner while weakening but that made little difference to his final position. (op 10-1)
Much Acclaimed(IRE), up in trip, got to the lead up the favoured rail but looked legless once joined and passed. (op 9-1 tchd 15-2)
T/Jkpt: Not won. T/Plt: £324.60 to a £1 stake. Pool: £200,238.57. 450.24 winning tickets. T/Qpdt: £107.90 to a £1 stake. Pool: £9,968.82. 68.33 winning tickets. CR

SALISBURY (R-H)
Sunday, May 2

OFFICIAL GOING: Good to soft
Rail up straight positioned 20ft off far side rail.
Wind: moderate breeze against Weather: overcast with rain at times

1731 TOTEPLACEPOT MAIDEN STKS — 6f
1:50 (1:51) (Class 5) 3-Y-O+ — **£3,885** (£1,156; £577; £288) **Stalls** High

Form				RPR
033-	1		**The Confessor**[195] 6896 3-9-0 75 ... DaneO'Neill 1 (H Candy) *led stands' side gp: prom overall: rdn to chal fr over 2f out: led ent fnl f: drifted rt: r.o* **13/2**	78
	2	1	**Blackdown Boy** 3-8-11 0 ... JamesMillman(3) 8 (B R Millman) *racd alone in centre tl jnd stands' side gp over 3f out: led over 2f out: sn rdn: hung rt and hdd ent fnl f: kpt on* **33/1**	75
4-	3	3 ½	**Poppy Seed**[289] 4047 3-8-9 0 ... PatDobbs 10 (R Hannon) *racd far side: chsd ldrs: led far side gp and ev ch fr 2f out: kpt on same pce fnl f* **5/2**[2]	59+
0-	4	4 ½	**Alkhataaf (USA)**[226] 6054 3-9-0 0 ... TedDurcan 3 (J L Dunlop) *racd stands' side: chsd ldrs: rdn 3f out: sn one pce* **9/1**	49
5-	5	nk	**Dungannon**[314] 3218 3-9-0 0 ... LiamKeniry 14 (A M Balding) *racd far side: hld up: hdwy to chse ldrs 3f out: sn rdn: one pce fnl 2f* **9/4**[1]	48+
023-	6	hd	**Humidor (IRE)**[188] 7058 3-9-0 77 ... SteveDrowne 12 (R Charlton) *overall ldr on far side tl rdn over 2f out: one pce after* **5/1**[3]	48+
	7	8	**Poppy Golightly** 3-8-9 0 ... AlanMunro 13 (R J Hodges) *racd far side: s.i.s: a towards rr* **50/1**	17
50-	8	7	**Fire Raiser**[195] 6903 3-9-0 0 ... NeilChalmers 5 (A M Balding) *racd stands' side: chsd ldrs: rdn 3f out: wknd 2f out* **25/1**	—
	9	1	**Tigers Charm** 3-9-0 0 ... RoystonFfrench 4 (J M Bradley) *racd stands' side: s.i.s: a towards rr* **150/1**	—
65	10	8	**My Meteor**[37] 997 3-9-0 0 ... RichardThomas 9 (A G Newcombe) *racd far side: chsd ldrs tl wknd over 2f out* **40/1**	—
00-	11	2 ½	**Steeple Caster**[349] 2122 4-9-10 0 ... FergusSweeney 6 (J M Bradley) *racd stands' side: stdd s: mid-div tl wknd over 2f out* **200/1**	—
	12	2 ¼	**Trader Way (GR)** 3-9-0 0 ... SebSanders 7 (P R Chamings) *racd far side: s.i.s: a towards rr* **25/1**	—
	13	14	**Pappas Fc** 3-9-0 0 ... RobertHavlin 2 (J M Bradley) *racd stands' side: s.i.s: a towards rr* **100/1**	—

1m 14.98s (0.18) **Going Correction** +0.075s/f (Good) — **13** Ran SP% **116.5**
WFA 3 from 4yo 10lb
Speed ratings (Par 103): **101,99,95,89,88 88,77,68,67,56 53,50,31**
toteswingers:1&2:£50.00, 1&3:£3.10, 2&3: Not won CSF £201.25 TOTE £8.10: £2.20, £6.60, £1.30; EX 270.20.
Owner Six Too Many **Bred** Mrs C R D Wilson **Trained** Kingston Warren, Oxon

FOCUS
Rail up straight positioned 20ft off far side rail. Following 8mm of rain, the ground was changed from good to firm to good to soft. The far rail was out by 18ft. This looked no more than a fair maiden, and there was a split in the field, with half of them staying on the far side and the rest tacking over to race stands' side, which is normally the place to be at this course when the ground is on the soft side. The winner probably didn't have to improve much on his 2yo form.

1732 TOTEPOOL H'CAP — 6f 212y
2:20 (2:21) (Class 2) (0-100,95) 3-Y-O
£11,215 (£3,358; £1,679; £840; £419; £210) **Stalls** Centre

Form				RPR
21-	1		**Dafeef**[246] 5431 3-9-2 90 ... TedDurcan 9 (Saeed Bin Suroor) *veered lft s: travelled wl: hld up: smooth hdwy to ld wl over 1f out: sn wl in command: pushed out: readily* **7/4**[1]	104+
250-	2	2 ½	**Gunner Lindley (IRE)**[232] 5864 3-8-11 85 ... RobertWinston 1 (B W Hills) *mid-div: nt clr run whn lost pl over 2f out: swtchd to stands' side rail: sn rdn: r.o to go 2nd ins fnl f: no ch w wnr* **11/1**	91+
515-	3	1 ¾	**Treadwell (IRE)**[188] 7063 3-9-5 93 ... FergusSweeney 2 (J A Osborne) *hld up: hdwy 3f out: sn rdn: chsd wnr over 1f out tl ins fnl f: no ex* **28/1**	92
12-	4	1	**Side Glance**[214] 6397 3-9-2 90 ... LiamKeniry 4 (A M Balding) *plld hrd: mid-div: nt clrest of runs fr over 2f out: hdwy over 1f out: sn rdn: kpt on same pce* **9/1**	87+
131-	5	½	**Dubai Set**[176] 7290 3-8-13 87 ... PatDobbs 7 (R Hannon) *trckd ldrs: rdn over 2f out: kpt on same pce* **11/2**[3]	82
10-	6	3	**Hunting Tartan**[213] 6426 3-9-7 95 ... RobertHavlin 10 (J H M Gosden) *s.i.s: hld up: hmpd after 2f: hdwy 3f out: sn rdn: unable to chal: fdd ins fnl f* **16/1**	82
51-3	7	3 ¼	**Gramercy (IRE)**[16] 1352 3-8-11 85 ... HayleyTurner 6 (M L W Bell) *t.k.h: in tch: trckd ldrs 3f out: sn rdn: wknd fnl f* **11/4**[2]	63
345-	8	9	**Kurtanella**[211] 6471 3-8-2 83 ... CharlesEddery(7) 5 (R Hannon) *mid-div: squeezed up whn swtchd rt after 2f: effrt wl over 1f out: wknd fnl f* **50/1**	37
03-0	9	nk	**Waveband**[15] 1399 3-9-1 89 ... RoystonFfrench 8 (M Johnston) *led: rdn and hdd wl over 1f out: wknd fnl f* **33/1**	42
416-	10	1	**Secret Queen**[211] 6486 3-8-11 85 ... EddieAhern 3 (B J Meehan) *trckd ldrs: rdn over 2f out: wknd over 1f out* **20/1**	36

1m 28.6s (-0.40) **Going Correction** +0.075s/f (Good) — **10** Ran SP% **115.7**
Speed ratings (Par 105): **105,102,100,99,98 95,91,81,80,79**
toteswingers:1&2:£6.10, 1&3:£24.00, 2&3:£26.00 CSF £21.43 CT £412.22 TOTE £2.40: £1.10, £3.60, £8.30; EX 22.90.
Owner Godolphin **Bred** Shadwell Estate Company **Trained** Newmarket, Suffolk

FOCUS
A decent handicap in which the whole field gradually tacked over to race middle to stands' side. The first three raced nearest the favoured stands' rail but the winner impressed all the same.

NOTEBOOK
Dafeef has done well in Dubai over the winter and was always cruising at the back of this pack. Getting a nice gap up the stands' rail, he quickened up well to hit the front and, although he carried his head awkwardly, he won with any amount in hand, his jockey looking over his shoulder for dangers from just inside the last, to minimise the winning distance. He looks up to tackling much better company and can defy a rise in the handicap in the short term. (op 2-1)
Gunner Lindley(IRE) benefited from being switched to race behind the winner on the favoured stands' side around 2f out, and finished his race well. His best runs at two came on good ground or softer and clearly this surface suited him. (op 12-1 tchd 14-1)
Treadwell(IRE), who was drawn low and raced more towards the favoured stands' side throughout, posted a respectable effort on his reappearance, although he might be a touch flattered by the bare result. (op 33-1)
Side Glance ◆ raced keenly through the early stages and could have done with a stronger pace. His performance should be upgraded as he challenged away from the stands' side, and he looks one to be interested in off his current mark, especially on quicker ground. (tchd 10-1)
Dubai Set, who showed he acts with plenty of cut when successful in a soft-ground nursery last November, only began to make progress once he edged over towards the stands' side with 1½f to run. He's worth another go at this distance. (tchd 5-1)
Hunting Tartan didn't have much go right. He had the worst of the draw, was slowly away, then hampered after 2f and forced to race on the outside of the pack, getting no cover. Widest throughout, he had no chance given the stands' side bias, and this run can be safely ignored. (op 14-1)
Gramercy(IRE) looked to have conditions to suit and got to race off the same mark as when a good third at Newbury on his reappearance. He didn't settle through the early stages of the race, though, and just didn't see his race out. (op 3-1)

1733 TOTEQUADPOT FILLIES' CONDITIONS STKS — 5f
2:55 (2:55) (Class 3) 2-Y-O — **£6,476** (£1,927; £963; £481) **Stalls** High

Form				RPR
41	1		**Dingle View (IRE)**[15] 1375 2-8-12 0 ... CathyGannon 6 (P D Evans) *mde all: rdn ent fnl f: r.o strly: comf* **6/1**[2]	85+
1	2	2 ¾	**Shewalksinbeauty (IRE)**[22] 1223 2-8-9 0 ... PatDobbs 2 (R Hannon) *trckd ldrs: rdn over 2f out: kpt on ins fnl f: wnt 2nd nr fin* **13/2**[3]	72
01	3	½	**Rosina Grey**[7] 1541 2-8-9 0 ... JamesMillman(3) 3 (B R Millman) *racd keenly: trckd ldrs: chal wnr 2f out: sn rdn: no ex ins fnl f: lost 2nd nr fin* **12/1**	73
4	4	3 ½	**Silca Conegliano (IRE)**[13] 1421 2-8-9 0 ... AlanMunro 1 (M R Channon) *hld up last but in tch: hdwy 2f out: sn rdn: kpt on same pce fnl f* **8/1**	58
51	5	1	**Little Libretto (IRE)**[25] 1173 2-8-12 0 ... SteveDrowne 5 (P D Evans) *prom: rdn over 2f out: fading whn squeezed up on rails over 1f out* **8/1**	58+
1	6	1 ¾	**The Sydney Arms (IRE)**[6] 1577 2-8-9 0 ... DaneO'Neill 4 (R Hannon) *trckd ldrs: rdn over 2f out: wknd jst over 1f out* **5/6**[1]	48+

62.01 secs (1.01) **Going Correction** +0.075s/f (Good) — **6** Ran SP% **112.1**
Speed ratings (Par 94): **94,89,88,83,81 78**
toteswingers:1&2:£3.30, 1&3:£3.10, 2&3:£12.70 CSF £42.36 TOTE £5.90: £2.40, £2.00; EX 46.00.
Owner Mrs I M Folkes **Bred** Robert Berns **Trained** Pandy, Monmouths

FOCUS
Confirmation that the stands' rail was a significant advantage, with the winner and runner-up both using it to their advantage. Slightly muddling form but the winner built on her Doncaster win.

NOTEBOOK
Dingle View(IRE) showed good speed from the gate and gradually made her way over to the stands' rail. Little Libretto denied her the luxury of being right on it until the latter part of the race, but it proved a huge help to the winner in fighting off the attentions of Rosina Grey, and in the end she won quite comfortably. Her trainer had been worried about the ground but she coped with it fine. She's in the Lily Agnes on Wednesday and, providing she comes out of this okay, the plan will be to run. (op 15-2 tchd 11-2)
Shewalksinbeauty(IRE), a winner on the Polytrack first time up, looked the stable's second string, but she ran well, benefiting from getting to the stands' rail and edging out Rosina Grey for second as a result. Quicker ground will probably suit her ideally. (op 6-1 tchd 7-1)
Rosina Grey, a winner on firm ground at Bath last time, had different conditions to deal with here and wasn't disgraced, especially as she never had the advantage of the rail, like the first two. (op 9-1 tchd 17-2)
Silca Conegliano(IRE), who ran only modestly on her debut but holds an entry in the Group 1 Phoenix Stakes, still looked in need of the experience, but stayed on out wider. (op 17-2 tchd 9-1)
Little Libretto(IRE) was beating a retreat when squeezed for room next to the stands' rail. Proven in soft ground, this was a little disappointing. (op 10-1 tchd 11-1)
The Sydney Arms(IRE) was sent off a hot favourite. It didn't help that she couldn't get cover widest of all and, as had been seen in earlier races, she was probably racing on slower ground away from the stands' rail. It was later reported that she choked during the race. Official explanation: trainer said filly choked post-race (op 10-11 tchd Evens)

1734 TOTESWINGER H'CAP — 1m 1f 198y
3:30 (3:30) (Class 4) (0-85,83) 3-Y-O — **£4,857** (£1,445; £722; £360) **Stalls** High

Form				RPR
11-0	1		**Spanish Duke (IRE)**[17] 1330 3-9-7 83 ... EddieAhern 6 (J L Dunlop) *trckd ldrs: nt clr run 2f out: sn rdn: led jst ins fnl f: styd on wl* **17/2**	92+
4413	2	1 ½	**Paintball (IRE)**[24] 1182 3-9-1 77 ... DaneO'Neill 9 (W R Muir) *trckd ldr: led over 2f out: sn rdn: hdd jst ins fnl f: styd on* **5/1**[2]	83
526-	3	nk	**Kensei (IRE)**[191] 7003 3-8-13 75 ... SebSanders 7 (R M Beckett) *hld up towards rr: rdn 3f out: weaved way through field fr over 1f out: styd on: nrst fin* **10/1**	80+

21 **4** *1 ¼* **Beneath**[45] 922 3-9-4 **80** RobertWinston 10 83
(Pat Eddery) *trckd ldrs: rdn to chal 3f out: ev ch 2f out: styd on same pce fnl f* **10/1**

1- **5** *2 ½* **Sierra Alpha**[244] 5528 3-9-3 **79** TedDurcan 1 77
(Mrs A J Perrett) *hld up towards rr: rdn and sme prog into midfield over 2f out: styd on same pce: nvr rchd ldrs* **7/1**[3]

41- **6** *nk* **Spoken**[214] 6393 3-9-3 **79** SteveDrowne 2 76+
(R Charlton) *travelled wl in tch: tk clsr order over 4f out: rdn whn ev ch 2f out: no ex fnl f* **5/2**[1]

32-0 **7** *3* **First Cat**[9] 1502 3-9-4 **80** PatDobbs 8 71
(R Hannon) *hld up towards rr: rdn and prog into midfield over 2f out: no further imp: fdd ins fnl f* **11/1**

3-12 **8** *2 ½* **Mawaddah (IRE)**[12] 1452 3-8-12 **77** PatrickHills(3) 4 63+
(R Hannon) *mid-div: hdwy 3f out: sn rdn: wknd over 1f out* **7/1**[3]

21-4 **9** *8* **White Dart**[24] 1189 3-9-1 **77** AlanMunro 12 47
(M R Channon) *led tl rdn over 2f out: sn wknd* **12/1**

00-5 **10** *5* **The Starboard Bow**[26] 1138 3-9-2 **78** LiamKeniry 3 38
(S Kirk) *hld up towards rr: hdwy over 4f out: rdn over 2f out: sn wknd* **40/1**

346- **11** *9* **Universal Circus**[199] 6805 3-9-3 **79** SamHitchcott 11 21
(M R Channon) *mid-div tl wknd 3f out* **33/1**

2m 11.3s (1.40) **Going Correction** +0.15s/f (Good) **11** Ran SP% **120.4**
Speed ratings (Par 101): **100,98,98,97,95 95,92,90,84,80 73**
toteswingers:1&2:£7.80, 1&3:£19.50, 2&3:£14.30 CSF £51.93 CT £442.06 TOTE £10.70: £2.70, £2.50, £3.70; EX 58.80.
Owner Windflower Overseas Holdings Inc **Bred** Windflower Overseas Holdings Inc **Trained** Arundel, W Sussex

FOCUS
They came towards the stands' side in the straight. The winner got back on track with the runner-up a fairly sound guide to the form.

1735 TOTEEXACTA MAIDEN STKS 1m 4f
4:05 (4:08) (Class 5) 3-Y-O **£3,885** (£1,156; £577; £288) **Stalls** High

Form RPR

0-3 **1** **Awsaal**[18] 1314 3-9-3 0 TedDurcan 7 90
(J L Dunlop) *trckd ldrs: rdn to ld over 1f out: hrd pressed ins fnl f: styd on: jst hld on: all out* **5/4**[1]

3- **2** *hd* **Ashbrittle**[179] 7243 3-9-3 0 SebSanders 10 90
(R M Beckett) *sn w ldr: rdn to ld over 2f out: hdd over 1f out: rallied thrght fnl f: styd on: jst hld* **7/2**[2]

23-2 **3** *11* **Ebony Boom (IRE)**[18] 1302 3-9-3 76 EddieAhern 11 72
(H R A Cecil) *in tch: cl 3rd and effrt 3f out: wknd ent fnl f* **4/1**[3]

4- **4** *3* **Dynamic Idol (USA)**[148] 7638 3-9-3 0 SteveDrowne 8 67+
(M A Magnusson) *led: rdn 3f out: sn hdd: wknd ent fnl f* **11/1**

5 *2 ¼* **Pilote Celebre** 3-9-3 0 LiamKeniry 5 64
(A M Balding) *mid-div: rdn 3f out: no imp* **12/1**

6 *4* **Joseph Lister** 3-9-3 0 RobertHavlin 9 57+
(J H M Gosden) *s.i.s: towards rr: sme modest late hdwy* **12/1**

7 *nse* **Never Can Tell (IRE)** 3-8-12 0 FergusSweeney 3 52
(J A Osborne) *hld up towards rr: prog into midfield over 3f out: no further imp fnl 2f* **40/1**

8 *4 ½* **Now What** 3-8-12 0 StephenCraine 2 45
(J G Portman) *mid-div: effrt over 3f out: wknd over 1f out* **66/1**

0 **9** *6* **Five Bells (IRE)**[16] 1356 3-8-12 0 AlanMunro 1 35
(M R Channon) *a towards rr* **40/1**

6 **10** *12* **Pennfield Pirate**[32] 1067 3-9-3 0 TravisBlock 4 21
(H Morrison) *trckd ldrs: awkward on bnd over 6f out: rdn and wknd over 3f out* **100/1**

3240 **11** *31* **Brave Talk**[51] 872 3-9-3 0 PatDobbs 6 —
(S Kirk) *a bhd: t.o* **33/1**

2m 38.6s (0.60) **Going Correction** +0.15s/f (Good) **11** Ran SP% **120.7**
Speed ratings (Par 99): **104,103,96,94,93 90,90,87,83,75 46**
toteswingers:1&2:£2.00, 1&3:£2.30, 2&3:£3.10 CSF £5.63 TOTE £2.30: £1.30, £1.60, £1.30; EX 7.60.
Owner Hamdan Al Maktoum **Bred** Meon Valley Stud **Trained** Arundel, W Sussex

FOCUS
A couple of useful performers came clear in this maiden, and the winner is rated close to his Newmarket form.
Brave Talk Official explanation: jockey said gelding hung left-handed from 1 1/2f out

1736 BET TOTEPOOL AT TOTESPORT.COM H'CAP 1m 6f 21y
4:40 (4:41) (Class 3) (0-95,91) 4-Y-O+ **£7,123** (£2,119; £1,059; £529)

Form RPR

10-0 **1** **It's A Date**[25] 1161 5-9-3 **83** FergusSweeney 9 91
(A King) *mde all: styd on gamely whn hrd pressed fr 2f out: all out* **16/1**

00-4 **2** *½* **Highland Legacy**[28] 1101 6-9-3 **83** HayleyTurner 7 90+
(M L W Bell) *hld up in last pair: rdn and stdy hdwy fr over 2f out: styd on wl fnl f: wnt 2nd and clsng on wnr nring fin* **10/3**[1]

103- **3** *1* **Penang Princess**[199] 6803 4-8-13 **80** SebSanders 3 86
(R M Beckett) *trckd ldrs: rdn and ev ch fr 2f out tl ins fnl f: no ex: lost 2nd towards fin* **9/2**[2]

220- **4** *¾* **Woolfall Treasure**[23] 6851 5-9-9 **89** (b) LiamKeniry 2 94
(G L Moore) *in tch: tk clsr order 4f out: rdn 3f out: styd on same pce fnl 2f* **9/1**

142- **5** *2 ¼* **Dayia (IRE)**[186] 7117 6-9-6 **86** SaleemGolam 1 88
(J Pearce) *mid-div: rdn 3f out: styd on same pce fnl 2f* **11/2**

6-44 **6** *2 ½* **Swiss Act**[8] 1525 6-9-7 **87** RoystonFfrench 4 85
(M Johnston) *mid-div: rdn 3f out: one pce fnl 2f* **11/1**

005- **7** *4 ½* **Lethal Glaze (IRE)**[184] 7151 4-9-10 **91** PatDobbs 8 83
(R Hannon) *trckd ldrs: rdn 3f out: wknd over 1f out* **5/1**[3]

313- **8** *11* **Art Man**[19] 3273 7-9-1 **81** DaneO'Neill 5 58
(J D Frost) *mid-div tl lost pl over 4f out: nvr bk on terms* **28/1**

50-0 **9** *1 ½* **Puzzlemaster**[18] 205 4-9-1 **82** (t) TravisBlock 6 57
(H Morrison) *hld up in last pair: hdwy to trck ldrs 4f out: rdn 3f out: sn hld: wknd over 1f out* **13/2**

3m 6.95s (-0.45) **Going Correction** +0.15s/f (Good)
WFA 4 from 5yo+ 1lb **9** Ran SP% **114.3**
Speed ratings (Par 107): **107,106,106,105,104 103,100,94,93**
toteswingers:1&2:£13.40, 1&3:£6.80, 2&3:£3.00 CSF £68.24 CT £286.68 TOTE £22.90: £3.80, £1.30, £1.90; EX 85.80.
Owner Horace 5 **Bred** Mrs F M Gordon **Trained** Barbury Castle, Wilts

FOCUS
As usual there were no stalls for this staying handicap. The third and fourth set the level.

NOTEBOOK
It's A Date only knows one way of running and, although he had yet to prove he could stay this far, this proved that he could. He made every yard and fought off the challenge of Penang Princess, albeit with the benefit of racing next to the stands' rail, before holding off the late charge of Highland Legacy. Versatile with regard to ground conditions, he can't go up too much for this success and will remain of interest when likely to get his own way in front. (op 14-1)
Highland Legacy, who had conditions to suit, stays further than this and could have done with a contested lead and a stronger gallop. Running without the visor he's had on in his four most recent starts, he finished well but was never quite getting there. (op 7-2 tchd 11-4 and 4-1 in a place)
Penang Princess, who has won over 2m, may well be at her best on a fast surface, but she had every chance here. She tracked the leader for much of the race and simply found him unwilling to be headed in the closing stages. (op 4-1 tchd 5-1)
Woolfall Treasure, who won this race last year off a 2lb lower mark, was last seen finishing tailed off over hurdles at Aintree. He came to challenge in the straight, but three of four horse widths off the favoured stands' rail where the winner raced. (op 17-2)
Dayia(IRE), running off a career-high mark, was entitled to need her seasonal reappearance. (op 17-2)
Swiss Act was a little disappointing as he promised to be suited by the drop back from 2m. (op 7-1)
Lethal Glaze(IRE) also failed to live up to expectations. He won first time up last year so lack of a recent outing didn't look a concern beforehand, but he ran as though it was needed. (op 15-2)

1737 BET TOTEPOOL ON 0800 221 221 LADY RIDERS' H'CAP 6f 212y
5:15 (5:17) (Class 6) (0-65,65) 4-Y-O+ **£2,810** (£871; £435; £217) **Stalls** Centre

Form RPR

0650 **1** **Straight Face (IRE)**[7] 1543 6-10-6 **64** (b) MrsEEvans 3 71
(P D Evans) *chsd ldrs: rdn to ld narrowly over 1f out: kpt on gamely but looked to be fighting a losing battle: hld on* **11/1**

404- **2** *nse* **Advertise**[199] 6790 4-10-0 **65** MissLProbert(7) 4 73
(A M Balding) *mid-div: smooth hdwy to draw upsides wnr 2f out: remained upsides travelling bttr than wnr: rdr nvr moved: btn line* **3/1**[1]

-650 **3** *2 ½* **Takitwo**[25] 1171 7-9-10 **54** MissSBrotherton 9 54+
(P D Cundell) *mid-div: drifted to far side rail over 2f out: hdwy u.p to hold ev ch ent fnl f: edgd lft: no ex* **4/1**[2]

5304 **4** *2* **Cruise Control**[18] 1305 4-9-4 **51** oh1 MissZoeLilly(3) 7 46
(R J Price) *mid-div: hdwy 2f out: sn rdn: styd on same pce fnl f* **20/1**

00-0 **5** *nse* **Louie's Lad**[12] 1441 4-9-7 **51** oh6 (p) MissGAndrews 13 46
(J J Bridger) *led: rdn and hdd over 1f out: no ex* **40/1**

4534 **6** *1* **Mocha Java**[47] 893 7-9-7 **51** (p) MissLHorner 10 43
(Matthew Salaman) *prom: rdn and ev ch 2f out: wknd fnl f* **8/1**

4001 **7** *1* **Batchworth Blaise**[25] 1171 7-9-2 **53** MissCNosworthy(7) 6 42
(E A Wheeler) *s.i.s: towards rr: drifted rt and hdwy fr 3f out: no further imp ins fnl f* **7/1**[3]

4200 **8** *3 ¾* **Towy Boy (IRE)**[18] 1304 5-9-9 **53** (bt) MissEJJones 2 32
(I A Wood) *t.k.h: in tch: rdn and ch whn sltly squeezed up over 1f out: wknd fnl f* **8/1**

1-52 **9** *6* **Ede's Dot Com (IRE)**[18] 1305 6-9-11 **62** MissLWilliams(7) 1 25
(P M Phelan) *s.i.s: a towards rr* **7/1**[3]

0000 **10** *9* **One Cool Dream**[12] 1437 4-9-2 **51** oh6 MissAWallace(5) 12 —
(P W Hiatt) *prom tl wknd over 2f out* **33/1**

60-0 **11** *7* **Catchmeifyoucan (FR)**[25] 1172 4-9-8 **57** (t) MissRKneller(5) 11 —
(Andrew Turnell) *a bhd* **25/1**

650/ **12** *1 ¾* **Operachy**[40] 1897 5-9-6 **57** MissDaisySharp(7) 5 —
(J D Frost) *prom for over 3f* **20/1**

1m 31.4s (2.40) **Going Correction** +0.075s/f (Good) **12** Ran SP% **119.3**
Speed ratings (Par 101): **89,88,86,83,83 82,81,77,70,60 52,50**
toteswingers:1&2:£8.40, 1&3:£12.50, 2&3:£4.00 CSF £41.46 CT £163.01 TOTE £11.40: £3.40, £1.60, £2.00; EX 53.50 Place 6 £132.80; Place 5 £50.00.
Owner Mrs I M Folkes **Bred** P J Towell **Trained** Pandy, Monmouths
■ Stewards' Enquiry : Miss L Probert 28-day ban: failed to ride out for first (tbn)

FOCUS
A modest handicap confined to lady riders which featured a controversial finish. The runner-up should have won and is rated back to his best.
Ede's Dot Com(IRE) Official explanation: jockey said gelding was slowly away
T/Plt: £184.50 to a £1 stake. Pool: £54,036.47. 213.70 winning tickets. T/Qpdt: £36.90 to a £1 stake. Pool: £3646.02. 73.04 winning tickets. TM

1738 - 1744a (Foreign Racing) - See Raceform Interactive

1251

FRANKFURT (L-H)
Sunday, May 2

OFFICIAL GOING: Turf: good

1745a FRUHJAHRSPREIS DES BANKHAUSES METZLER (GROUP 3) (3YO) (TURF) 1m 2f
4:10 (4:32) 3-Y-O **£28,318** (£8,849; £4,424; £2,654)

RPR

1 **Scalo** 3-9-2 0 EPedroza 4 99
(A Wohler, Germany) *hld up in midfield: a travelling smoothly: qcknd wl arnd fnl turn: effrt on ins: led 2f out: saw off all chalrs: won comf* **13/10**[1]

2 *2 ½* **Keep Cool**[175] 7314 3-9-2 0 THellier 1 94
(Andreas Lowe, Germany) *settled as bkmarker: swung wd on fnl turn: qcknd wl in st: fin strly ins fnl f to take 2nd* **51/10**

3 *1* **Nightdance Paolo (GER)**[175] 7314 3-9-2 0 FilipMinarik 3 92
(P Schiergen, Germany) *racd on 2nd on rail: clsd on ldr arnd fnl turn: first to chal in st: r.o wl: lost 2nd cl home* **6/1**

4 *nk* **Montparnasse (GER)** 3-9-2 0 DPorcu 7 91
(M Rulec, Germany) *led fr s: racd two l clr: shortened stride arnd fnl turn: hdd 2f out: r.o gamely for 4th* **161/10**

5 *¾* **Lamool (GER)**[182] 3-9-2 0 FrannyNorton 6 90
(Mario Hofer, Germany) *settled in 4th: qcknd wl in st but mde no imp* **2/1**[2]

6 *hd* **Langley**[140] 7743 3-9-2 0 GaetanMasure 5 90
(A Wohler, Germany) *(broke through stalls at s: qckly ct: but r delayed) settled in midfield: followed wnr in st: fdd qckly* **41/10**[3]

2m 7.85s (-0.72) **6** Ran SP% **132.9**
WIN (incl. 10 euro stake): 23. PLACES: 15, 19. DF: 128..
Owner Gestut Ittlingen **Bred** Gestut Hof Ittlingen **Trained** Germany

The Form Book, Raceform Ltd, Compton, RG20 6NL

[1565]LONGCHAMP (R-H)
Sunday, May 2

OFFICIAL GOING: Turf: good

1746a PRIX VANTEAUX - BEACHCOMBER HOTELS LE ROYAL PALM *****LUXE (GROUP 3) (3YO FILLIES) (TURF) 1m 1f 55y
1:35 (12:00) 3-Y-0 £35,398 (£14,159; £10,619; £7,079; £3,539)

RPR

1 **Zagora (FR)**[31] 1080 3-9-0 0 ChristopheSoumillon 1 105+
(J-C Rouget, France) *followed ldr fr s: qcknd wl 2f out: grabbed ld 1 1/2f: sn clr: won comf* **5/4**[1]

2 2 1/2 **On Verra (IRE)**[21] 1253 3-9-0 0 ThierryThulliez 3 100
(F Doumen, France) *racd in 3rd fr s: tk a while to hit stride in st but ins fnl f fin wl: grabbed 2nd on line* **11/4**[2]

3 hd **Gold Harvest (FR)**[21] 1253 3-9-0 0 Pierre-CharlesBoudot 2 100
(Y De Nicolay, France) *led: rdn 2f out: hdd 1 1/2f out: r.o wl: lost 2nd on line* **7/1**

4 1/2 **Plain Vanilla (FR)**[19] 3-9-0 0 RonanThomas 5 99
(P Van De Poele, France) *in rr fr s: rdn early in st: r.o wl along rail wout threatening ldrs* **8/1**

5 1 1/2 **American Nizzy (FR)**[21] 1253 3-9-0 0 MaximeGuyon 4 96
(Y De Nicolay, France) *racd in 4th fr s: rdn early in st: no imp* **4/1**[3]

1m 55.5s (0.20) **5** Ran SP% **114.7**
WIN (incl. 1 euro stake): 1.80. PLACES: 1.30, 1.50. SF: 4.50..
Owner Martin S Schwartz **Bred** E Puerari & Oceanic Bloodstock **Trained** Pau, France

NOTEBOOK
Zagora(FR), making her debut for the yard, showed a decent turn of foot to pull clear of her rivals in the closing stages and will now go for the Prix de Diane.

1747a PRIX GANAY "PRIX AIR MAURITIUS" (GROUP 1) (4YO+) (TURF) 1m 2f 110y
2:40 (12:00) 4-Y-0+ £151,699 (£60,690; £30,345; £15,159; £7,592)

RPR

1 **Cutlass Bay (UAE)**[21] 1255 4-9-2 0 MaximeGuyon 6 119
(A Fabre, France) *settled in 4th after 2f: maintained position after Shalanaya shot to ld after 4f: qcknd early in st to chse ldr: hung in towards ldr ins fnl f but r.o wl to gain control* **1/1**[1]

2 3/4 **Shalanaya (IRE)**[168] 4-8-13 0 Christophe-PatriceLemaire 5 115
(M Delzangles, France) *racd in midfield fr s: sent on to ld after 2f to qckn pce: led into st: qcknd wl and only ct ins fnl f: r.o* **9/2**[2]

3 1 1/2 **Pallodio (IRE)**[43] 946 5-9-2 0 DavyBonilla 2 115
(J E Hammond, France) *smartly away but sn settled towards rr: gd prog in st and r.o wl to hold 3rd on line* **25/1**

4 hd **Celimene (IRE)**[21] 1255 4-8-13 0 YannLerner 3 112
(C Lerner, France) *racd towards rr: rdn early in st: r.o wl: fin strly to jst miss 3rd* **9/1**[3]

5 3/4 **Starlish (IRE)**[21] 1255 5-9-2 0 AnthonyCrastus 4 113
(E Lellouche, France) *reluctantly led after 1f: dropped bk to 3rd after 2f: rdn early in st: no ex in clsng stages* **16/1**

6 3 **Chinchon (IRE)**[43] 953 5-9-2 0 (p) OlivierPeslier 8 108
(C Laffon-Parias, France) *prom early: wnt 2nd after 2f: rdn early in st: failed to qckn: styd on* **9/2**[2]

7 5 **King Of Sydney (USA)**[21] 1251 4-9-2 0 ThierryThulliez 7 98
(Mario Hofer, Germany) *racd towards rr: no prog in st: n.d* **33/1**

8 1 1/2 **Court Canibal**[21] 1255 5-9-2 0 GeraldMosse 1 95
(M Delzangles, France) *a towards rr: no imp in st* **11/1**

9 hd **The Bogberry (USA)**[21] 1255 5-9-2 0 IoritzMendizabal 9 95
(A Savujev, Czech Republic) *racd in midfield: hrd rdn early in st: no ex: dropped away* **33/1**

2m 11.8s (1.60) **9** Ran SP% **120.3**
WIN (incl. 1 euro stake): 2.20. PLACES: 1.20, 2.00, 2.00. DF: 7.40. SF: 9.20.
Owner Godolphin SNC **Bred** Darley **Trained** Chantilly, France

NOTEBOOK
Cutlass Bay(UAE) maintained his unbeaten record despite hanging into the runner-up inside the last furlong. His rider believed that he still won with a bit in hand and he currently holds entries in both the Coronation Cup and Prince of Wales's Stakes.
Shalanaya(IRE) ran with plenty of credit on this return to action as she was forced to make her own running and her rider dropped his whip a furlong out. She may go for the Prix Corrida next and then either the Grand Prix de Saint-Cloud or the Prince of Wales's.

1748a PRIX DE BARBEVILLE - M.T.P.A. "OFFICE DE TOURISME DE L'ILE MAURICE" (GROUP 3) (4YO+) (TURF) 1m 7f 110y
3:10 (12:00) 4-Y-0+ £35,398 (£14,159; £10,619; £7,079; £3,539)

RPR

1 **Blek (FR)**[19] 1291 5-9-0 0 AnthonyCrastus 5 106
(E Lellouche, France) *racd in 3rd fr s: qcknd to ld early in st: hung in towards the rail in clsng stages but hld on wl* **5/2**[2]

2 nk **Kasbah Bliss (FR)**[140] 7744 8-9-2 0 ThierryThulliez 6 108
(F Doumen, France) *racd in 5th fr s: qcknd wl on the outside early in st: hmpd but r.o strly in fnl f* **10/11**[1]

3 3/4 **Green Tango (FR)**[19] 1291 7-8-10 0 RonanThomas 3 101
(P Van De Poele, France) *racd bhd the ldrs: qcknd wl in st and swtchd to rail: r.o wl: fnd no room in clsng stages: r.o strly: unlucky* **10/1**

4 hd **Tres Rock Danon (FR)**[19] 1291 4-8-10 0 DominiqueBoeuf 1 104
(W Hickst, Germany) *led fr s: rdn early in st: r.o wl* **12/1**

5 3/4 **Terre Du Vent (FR)**[19] 1291 4-8-11 0 ow1 ChristopheSoumillon 4 104
(Y De Nicolay, France) *racd in 4th: mde gd prog early in st: hrd rdn: no ex clsng stages* **8/1**[3]

6 10 **Serious Impact (USA)**[21] 5-8-10 0 MaximeGuyon 2 89
(F Vermeulen, France) *racd at the bk of the field: effrt early in st: no imp: dropped away* **25/1**

3m 22.5s (1.00)
WFA 4 from 5yo+ 2lb **6** Ran SP% **112.7**
WIN (incl. 1 euro stake): 2.50. PLACES: 1.20, 1.20. SF: 4.40..
Owner Alain Maubert **Bred** Alain Maubert **Trained** Lamorlaye, France

NOTEBOOK
Blek(FR) was sent for home once into the straight, but caused problems by hanging towards the inside rail in the closing stages and it took 20 minutes for the stewards to let him keep the prize. The Gold Cup is a possibility.
Kasbah Bliss(FR) ran a blinder on this return to action and was closing down the race-fit winner all the way to the line. His trainer confirmed that he would have needed this and is likely to head for the Gold Cup.

[1483]BEVERLEY (R-H)
Monday, May 3

OFFICIAL GOING: Good (good to firm in places; 9.0)
Wind: Moderate across Weather: Overcast and blustery

1749 TURFTV MEDIAN AUCTION MAIDEN STKS 5f
2:20 (2:21) (Class 6) 2-Y-0 £1,942 (£578; £288; £144) Stalls High

Form RPR

1 **Dads Amigo** 2-9-3 0 PhillipMakin 12 71+
(D H Brown) *dwlt and pushed along towards rr: hdwy 2f out: swtchd lft and rdn over 1f out: styd on strly ins fnl f to ld last 50yds* **8/1**[3]

2 hd **Last Destination (IRE)** 2-9-3 0 SilvestreDeSousa 13 70+
(N Tinkler) *chsd ldrs: effrt whn n.m.r and swtchd lft wl over 1f out: rdn to ld appr fnl f: hdd and no ex last 50yds* **18/1**

3 1 1/4 **Azzurra Du Caprio (IRE)** 2-8-12 0 TomEaves 9 61+
(B M R Haslam) *in rr: hdwy over 1f out: sn swtchd lft and rdn: styd on strly ins fnl f: nrst fin* **25/1**

0 4 2 1/4 **Galtymore Lad**[21] 1263 2-9-3 0 RobertWinston 4 58+
(M R Channon) *hld up in rr: hdwy wl over 1f out: rdn and kpt on ins fnl f: nrst fin* **17/2**

5 1/2 **Chadford** 2-9-3 0 DuranFentiman 1 56
(T D Walford) *in tch on outer: hdwy 1/2-way: rdn to chse ldrs and ch over 1f out: one pce ins fnl f* **50/1**

6 1 **West Stand** 2-8-12 0 FrederikTylicki 11 47
(Mrs K Walton) *dwlt and in rr: hdwy wl over 1f out: sn rdn along and kpt on ins fnl f: nrst fin* **8/1**[3]

7 1/2 **Bellemere** 2-8-12 0 GrahamGibbons 2 45
(M W Easterby) *cln up: rdn along 2f out: grad wknd appr fnl f* **25/1**

8 2 1/2 **Key Impeller** 2-9-0 0 BarryMcHugh[(3)] 10 41
(Ollie Pears) *green: a towards rr* **9/1**

5 9 3/4 **Blind Stag (IRE)**[18] 1331 2-9-3 0 TonyCulhane 6 39
(P T Midgley) *cl up: led 1/2-way: rdn along wl over 1f out: hdd & wknd appr fnl f* **11/4**[1]

10 3 **Gunalt Penny Sweet** 2-8-12 0 DavidAllan 8 23
(M W Easterby) *chsd ldrs: rdn along 2f out: grad wknd* **14/1**

11 5 **Tufty** 2-8-12 0 JamesSullivan[(5)] 5 10
(M W Easterby) *midfield: pushed along over 2f out: sn wknd* **28/1**

12 10 **Music News (USA)** 2-9-3 0 JoeFanning 7 —
(M Johnston) *led to 1/2-way: sn rdn along on inner and wknd qckly* **4/1**[2]

64.50 secs (1.00) **Going Correction** -0.30s/f (Firm) **12** Ran SP% **114.4**
Speed ratings (Par 91): **80,79,77,74,73 71,70,66,65,60 52,36**
toteswingers:1&2:£25.00, 1&3:£17.50, 2&3:£50.10 CSF £130.58 TOTE £10.70: £3.50, £7.40, £8.60; EX 70.70.
Owner Ron Hull **Bred** Grove Farm Stud **Trained** Maltby, S Yorks

FOCUS
Probably just a modest maiden, in which the newcomers came to the fore, but it is hard to set the level with confidence. The pace seemed a decent one and the picture changed significantly inside the last furlong. The principals were drawn high.

NOTEBOOK
Dads Amigo, a February foal out of a mare who won at 6f on her debut as a 2yo, made a winning start, taking time to get the hang of things but finding the penny dropping inside the last and staying on strongly. A scopey sort and a likely improver, he already looks as though he will benefit from a step up in trip.
Last Destination(IRE), from a stable in form, gave some trouble in the paddock but shaped well once the race was under way, soon tracking the pace travelling well but not quite able to fend off the winner. Out of a mare who won at middle distances, he will also be suited by further and ought to improve enough to win a similar event. (tchd 20-1)
Azzurra Du Caprio(IRE) is by a sprinter out of a mare who has produced a 1m2f winner in France. She was in rear going nowhere passing halfway but really got the message approaching the last, staying on strongly, and ought to improve.
Galtymore Lad stepped up on his Windsor debut but never threatened to finish any nearer than his final position and already looks in need of another furlong. Official explanation: jockey said colt hung left-handed (op 11-1)
Chadford is from a speedy family and shaped well considering he had the worst of the draw, making eyecatching headway in the middle of the race widest of all. He should improve. (op 40-1)
West Stand, another with plenty of speed in her pedigree, made some progress from a poor position at halfway and ought to be sharper next time. (op 9-1)
Bellemere also ran better than her finishing position after coming across from a wide draw to dispute the lead and will do better. (op 20-1)
Blind Stag(IRE) couldn't build on his effort at Ripon but might have helped do too much too soon and would be of interest at this trip if dropped in grade. (op 7-2)
Music News(USA) is from a yard in great form but looked extremely green, running around despite having the rail to help him, and dropped right away after being headed passing halfway. (tchd 7-2)

1750 MAYDAY RACEDAY H'CAP 5f
2:50 (2:51) (Class 5) (0-75,75) 3-Y-0 £2,396 (£712; £356; £177) Stalls High

Form RPR

41-0 1 **Hoof It**[19] 1298 3-8-9 **66** GrahamGibbons 5 83+
(M W Easterby) *prom on outer: effrt 2f out: rdn to ld and edgd lft over 1f out: styd on strly ins fnl f* **6/1**[3]

425- 2 2 3/4 **Kellys Eye (IRE)**[196] 6896 3-9-1 **72** RobertWinston 8 79+
(D H Brown) *trckd ldrs: hdwy 2f out: rdn over 1f out: styng on whn hung bdly lft ins fnl f: kpt on towards fin* **13/2**

46-1 3 1/2 **Kakapuka**[8] 1547 3-9-0 **74** 6ex RussKennemore[(3)] 2 79
(Mrs A L M King) *cl up: led 1/2-way: rdn and hung lft wl over 1f out: drvn and hdd appr fnl f: kpt on same pce* **9/2**[2]

3022 4 1 1/4 **Clear Ice (IRE)**[11] 1491 3-8-6 **63** (v[1]) FrannyNorton 6 64
(R C Guest) *towards rr: hdwy 2f out: sn swtchd rt: rdn over 1f out: kpt on ins fnl f* **12/1**

1124 5 nk **Texas Queen**[75] 577 3-9-4 **75** JoeFanning 7 75
(M R Channon) *chsd ldrs: rdn along wl over 1f out: drvn and no imp appr fnl f* **9/1**

10-6 6 hd **Patch Patch**[9] 1511 3-8-11 **68** PhillipMakin 3 67
(M Dods) *led: rdn along 1/2-way: sn hung lft and hdd wl over 1f out: drvn and wknd appr fnl f* **17/2**

534- 7 1 1/4 **Kalahari Desert (IRE)**[188] 7088 3-8-1 **63** PaulPickard[(5)] 4 57
(R M Whitaker) *hld up towards rr: hdwy over 2f out: rdn to chse ldrs whn n.m.r and swtchd rt over 1f out: no imp fnl f* **16/1**

301- 8 1 **Besty**[187] 7115 3-9-2 **73** TomEaves 9 64
(B Smart) *chsd ldrs: rdn along 2f out: sn drvn and grad wknd* **7/2**[1]

0530 **9** 4 1/2 **Dazeen**[9] 1511 3-8-8 **65**.................... TonyCulhane 10 40
(P T Midgley) *n.m.r s: sn outpcd and a in rr* **10/1**
515- **10** nk **Tartufo Dolce (IRE)**[149] 7636 3-9-1 **72**.................... PaulHanagan 1 46
(J G Given) *in tch: rdn along 1/2-way: sn wknd* **22/1**
62.08 secs (-1.42) **Going Correction** -0.30s/f (Firm) **10** Ran SP% **115.6**
Speed ratings (Par 99): **99,94,93,91,91 91,89,87,80,79**
toteswingers:1&2:£6.80, 1&3:£5.60, 2&3:£6.60 CSF £44.33 CT £196.76 TOTE £8.80: £3.10, £1.90, £2.50; EX 49.90.
Owner A Chandler & L Westwood **Bred** Bond Thoroughbred Corporation **Trained** Sheriff Hutton, N Yorks

FOCUS

A modest handicap in which the majority of the field drifted over towards the traditionally unfavoured stands' rail, with the winner racing nearest to it. The form is not rated too positively.
Kakapuka Official explanation: vet said colt had been struck into
Patch Patch Official explanation: jockey said gelding hung left-handed

1751 BEVERLEY ROTARY CLUB H'CAP 1m 1f 207y
3:20 (3:21) (Class 4) (0-80,79) 4-Y-0+ **£4,759** (£1,416; £707; £353) **Stalls** High

Form RPR
50-2 **1** **King Fingal (IRE)**[20] 1277 5-8-9 **75**.................... IanBrennan(5) 10 85
(J J Quinn) *midfield: rdn along 3f out: hdwy 2f out: effrt and n.m.r over 1f out: rdn and styd on ins fnl f to ld nr fin* **4/1**[1]
4603 **2** 1/2 **General Tufto**[11] 1494 5-8-4 **68**....................(b) BarryMcHugh(3) 7 77
(C Smith) *trckd ldrs: hdwy on outer 3f out: rdn over 1f out: styd on to ld ent fnl f: hdd and no ex nr fin* **16/1**
22-3 **3** 2 3/4 **Mannlichen**[71] 653 4-9-4 **79**.................... JoeFanning 3 83
(M Johnston) *chsd ldrs: hdwy over 2f out: rdn wl over 1f out and ch tl drvn and one pce ins fnl f* **9/1**
3-55 **4** 1/2 **Andhaar**[16] 1398 4-8-12 **73**.................... PhillipMakin 12 76+
(S Gollings) *hld up in rr: hdwy 2f out: rdn and n.m.r over 1f out: swtchd lft jst ins fnl f and kpt on wl towards fin* **6/1**[3]
-321 **5** 1/2 **Hydrant**[66] 718 4-8-4 **70**.................... BillyCray(5) 2 72
(P Salmon) *prom: chsd ldr 1/2-way: cl up over 2f out and ev ch tl rdn and one pce ent fnl f* **20/1**
310/ **6** 1 3/4 **Ubi Ace**[573] 6549 4-8-10 **71**.................... TomEaves 13 69
(T D Walford) *hld up towards rr: hdwy over 2f out: rdn over 1f out: no imp ent fnl f* **50/1**
140- **7** 1/2 **Herrera (IRE)**[192] 6995 5-8-6 **67**.................... PaulHanagan 11 64+
(R A Fahey) *hld up: towards rr tl sme late hdwy* **9/1**
01-4 **8** nk **Amethyst Dawn (IRE)**[16] 1396 4-8-7 **68**.................... DavidAllan 9 64
(T D Easterby) *t.k.h: trckd ldng pair: hdwy 3f out: led 2f out: sn rdn: hdd & wknd ent fnl f* **7/1**
30-2 **9** hd **Baltimore Jack (IRE)**[9] 1520 6-8-12 **73**.................... GrahamGibbons 6 69
(T D Walford) *trckd ldrs on inner: rdn along over 2f out: grad wknd* **11/2**[2]
-020 **10** nk **River Ardeche**[9] 1512 5-8-11 **77**.................... PatrickDonaghy(5) 1 72
(B M R Haslam) *led: rdn along 3f out: hdd 2f out and sn wknd* **40/1**
2361 **11** nk **Wrongwayround (IRE)**[9] 1526 4-8-9 **70**.................... PJMcDonald 8 65
(G A Swinbank) *nvr bttr than midfield* **11/2**[2]
456- **12** 1 3/4 **Maybeme**[191] 7014 4-8-4 **65**.................... DuranFentiman 4 56
(N Bycroft) *dwlt: a in rr* **25/1**
110- **13** 1 **Nevada Desert (IRE)**[184] 7194 10-9-0 **78**.................... MichaelStainton(3) 5 67
(R M Whitaker) *in tch: effrt 3f out: sn rdn along and wknd over 2f out* **25/1**
2m 5.36s (-1.64) **Going Correction** -0.125s/f (Firm) **13** Ran SP% **120.3**
Speed ratings (Par 105): **101,100,98,98,97 96,95,95,95,95 94,93,92**
toteswingers:1&2:£19.90, 1&3:£6.90, 2&3:£21.00 CSF £67.49 CT £554.89 TOTE £5.90: £2.40, £5.60, £3.10; EX 107.60.
Owner King Fingal Partnership **Bred** The Lavington Stud **Trained** Settrington, N Yorks

FOCUS

A fair handicap run at a steady pace initially, and though it increased approaching the home bend it still proved difficult to come from off it. Once again, the action unfolded away from the far rail. The winner is rated back to his best.
Amethyst Dawn(IRE) Official explanation: jockey said filly ran too free

1752 GARDEN FETE IN THE COURSE ENCLOSURE H'CAP 1m 100y
3:50 (3:50) (Class 4) (0-85,85) 4-Y-0+ **£4,759** (£1,416; £707; £353) **Stalls** High

Form RPR
50-5 **1** **Danehillsundance (IRE)**[3] 1669 6-8-5 **72**....................(t) PJMcDonald 2 84
(D H Brown) *trckd ldrs: hdwy over 2f out: nt clr run and swtchd lft over 1f out: rdn and qcknd wl to ld ins fnl f: edgd rt and sn clr* **9/2**
05-0 **2** 3 1/4 **Handsome Falcon**[20] 1272 6-9-0 **81**.................... PaulHanagan 5 86
(R A Fahey) *set stdy pce: qcknd 3f out: rdn and qcknd again 2f out: drvn over 1f out: hdd ins fnl f: kpt on* **7/2**[2]
05-1 **3** 2 1/4 **King Of The Moors (USA)**[16] 1396 7-8-4 **71**.............(p) FrannyNorton 4 70
(R C Guest) *trckd ldr: effrt and cl up over 2f out: rdn wl over 1f out: ev ch tl drvn and one pce ent fnl f* **8/1**
3-00 **4** 1 1/4 **Just Lille (IRE)**[16] 1378 7-9-0 **84**....................(p) BarryMcHugh(3) 7 80
(Mrs A Duffield) *hld up towards rr: hdwy over 3f out: rdn along and sltly outpcd 2f out: kpt on u.p fnl f* **8/1**
330- **5** 1 1/4 **Observatory Star (IRE)**[177] 7287 7-8-12 **79**............(tp) FrederikTylicki 6 73
(T D Easterby) *trckd ldng pair on inner: hdwy over 2f out: rdn over 1f out and ev ch tl drvn and wknd ent fnl f* **4/1**[3]
-000 **6** 1/2 **Rainbow Mirage (IRE)**[5] 1617 6-9-4 **85**.................... GrahamGibbons 8 77+
(E S McMahon) *hld up: effrt over 2f out: sn rdn along and n.d* **10/3**[1]
00-0 **7** 2 1/2 **Summer Dancer (IRE)**[29] 1102 6-8-13 **80**.................... PhillipMakin 1 67
(P T Midgley) *t.k.h: chsd ldrs on outer: effrt over 2f out: sn rdn and wknd wl over 1f out* **22/1**
1m 45.55s (-2.05) **Going Correction** -0.125s/f (Firm) **7** Ran SP% **110.1**
Speed ratings (Par 105): **105,101,99,98,97 96,94**
toteswingers:1&2:£4.00, 1&3:£8.00, 2&3:£3.90 CSF £18.96 CT £111.61 TOTE £7.80: £4.50, £1.50; EX 19.90.
Owner J P Hardiman **Bred** J P Hardiman **Trained** Maltby, S Yorks

FOCUS

A muddling affair, with the early pace only steady. The winner made his effort widest of all, but there's little doubt he was the best horse on the day. The runner-up sets the standard.

1753 WHITE RABBIT H'CAP 7f 100y
4:20 (4:21) (Class 6) (0-65,64) 3-Y-0 **£1,942** (£578; £288; £144) **Stalls** High

Form RPR
0-13 **1** **Tribal Myth (IRE)**[9] 1522 3-9-1 **61**.................... PaulHanagan 2 68
(K A Ryan) *a.p: trckd ldr 1/2-way: cl up over 2f out: rdn to ld appr fnl f: sn drvn and kpt on wl* **7/2**[1]
005 **2** 3/4 **Killing Moon (USA)**[18] 1336 3-8-13 **64**.................... MichaelO'Connell(5) 1 69
(K A Ryan) *hld up in midfield: hdwy 2f out: rdn over 1f out: styd on strly ins fnl f* **28/1**
5-13 **3** nk **Dazakhee**[19] 1298 3-9-1 **61**.................... TonyCulhane 8 65
(P T Midgley) *hld up: hdwy 2f out: rdn to chse ldrs over 1f out: drvn ins fnl f and kpt on* **8/1**
0-54 **4** nk **Eeny Mac (IRE)**[19] 1298 3-8-5 **51**.................... FrannyNorton 4 55
(N Bycroft) *ld: rdn along and jnd 2f out: drvn and hdd appr fnl f: kpt on* **17/2**
4061 **5** 2 1/2 **Sixties Rock**[12] 1465 3-8-10 **56**.................... FrederikTylicki 3 53
(J A Glover) *trckd ldrs: hdwy 3f out: chal 2f out: sn rdn and ev ch tl drvn and wknd ent fnl f* **11/1**
55-0 **6** 1/2 **Alsufooh (USA)**[20] 1278 3-9-4 **64**.................... JoeFanning 6 60
(M Johnston) *cl up: rdn along 2f out: drvn over 1f out: wknd fnl f* **15/2**[3]
0-02 **7** 1/2 **A Pocketful Of Rye (IRE)**[10] 1505 3-9-0 **63**......... MichaelStainton(3) 12 58
(P Howling) *hld up towards rr: hdwy wl over 1f out: kpt on ins fnl f: nrst fin* **12/1**
-466 **8** hd **Alphacino**[12] 1465 3-8-13 **59**....................(p) PhillipMakin 10 53
(B M R Haslam) *chsd ldrs: effrt 2f out: sn rdn and one pce appr fnl f* **16/1**
03-2 **9** 3/4 **Elegant Dancer (IRE)**[12] 1465 3-8-7 **53**.................... SilvestreDeSousa 9 47
(Paul Green) *hld up: a towards rr* **5/1**[2]
0-42 **10** 4 1/2 **Choc'A'Moca (IRE)**[12] 1469 3-8-5 **51**.................... DuranFentiman 7 32
(D Carroll) *chsd ldrs: rdn along over 2f out: dfriven over 1f out: n.m.r and wknd appr fnl f* **15/2**[3]
300- **11** 4 **Forshour**[196] 6901 3-9-2 **62**.................... GrahamGibbons 11 33
(E S McMahon) *a in rr* **16/1**
000- **12** 3 **William Arnold**[209] 6557 3-8-4 **50**.................... AndrewElliott 5 14
(C W Fairhurst) *a towards rr* **40/1**
1m 33.39s (-0.41) **Going Correction** -0.125s/f (Firm) **12** Ran SP% **117.7**
Speed ratings (Par 97): **97,96,95,95,92 92,91,91,90,85 80,77**
toteswingers:1&2:£34.60, 1&3:£6.50, 2&3:£26.30 CSF £109.42 CT £752.72 TOTE £4.70: £1.70, £11.70, £1.40; EX 134.60.
Owner Mr & Mrs K Hughes and Dr J Gozzard **Bred** Norelands Stallions **Trained** Hambleton, N Yorks

FOCUS

A modest handicap run at just a fair pace and fought out largely by exposed horses. Sound form. The action again unfolded towards the centre of the track.

1754 GO RACING IN YORKSHIRE SUMMER FESTIVAL H'CAP 7f 100y
4:50 (4:50) (Class 5) (0-75,73) 4-Y-0+ **£2,396** (£712; £356; £177) **Stalls** High

Form RPR
0-01 **1** **Dabbers Ridge (IRE)**[19] 1293 8-8-11 **69**.................... GaryBartley(3) 5 78
(I W McInnes) *bhd: hdwy on wd outside 2f out: rdn over 1f out: styd on strly ins fnl f to ld nr line* **14/1**
2212 **2** shd **Sir George (IRE)**[16] 1395 5-9-1 **73**.................... BarryMcHugh(3) 9 82
(Ollie Pears) *hld up in tch: hdwy over 2f out: rdn to chse ldr over 1f out: drvn to ld wl ins fnl f: hdd and no ex nr line* **13/8**[1]
210- **3** 1 1/2 **Just Sam (IRE)**[202] 6765 5-8-13 **68**.................... PhillipMakin 6 73
(R E Barr) *led: rdn clr 2f out: drvn ins fnl f: hdd and no ex last 100yds* **12/1**[3]
00-4 **4** 1 3/4 **Arabian Pearl (IRE)**[17] 1361 4-9-3 **72**.................... RobertWinston 10 73
(P W Chapple-Hyam) *trckd ldrs: hdwy to chse ldr over 2f out: rdn wl over 1f out: drvn and one pce ent fnl f* **85/40**[2]
000- **5** hd **Boy Blue**[177] 7287 5-8-13 **73**.................... BillyCray(5) 1 73
(P Salmon) *in tch: hdwy 3f out: rdn to chse ldrs 2f out: drvn and no imp fnl f* **18/1**
5-00 **6** 3 3/4 **Northern Flyer (GER)**[16] 1396 4-8-0 **60**.................... IanBrennan(5) 4 51
(J J Quinn) *a in midfield* **16/1**
-000 **7** 1 3/4 **Orpen Wide (IRE)**[14] 1430 8-8-12 **70**.................... MichaelGeran(3) 3 57
(M C Chapman) *nvr nr ldrs* **33/1**
00-0 **8** 1 3/4 **Mey Blossom**[20] 1270 5-8-4 **59** oh1.................... FrannyNorton 2 41
(R M Whitaker) *a towards rr* **16/1**
0-00 **9** hd **Violent Velocity (IRE)**[17] 1361 7-8-11 **73**.................... ShaneBKelly(7) 7 55
(J J Quinn) *prom: rdn along wl over 2f out: sn wknd* **22/1**
42/0 **10** 7 **Northumberland**[7] 1579 4-8-6 **66**.................... MarkCoumbe(5) 8 30
(M C Chapman) *chsd ldr: rdn along 3f out: sn wknd* **66/1**
0000 **11** 3 1/2 **Carlitos Spirit (IRE)**[9] 1530 6-9-1 **70**....................(p) TomEaves 11 26
(I W McInnes) *midfield: rdn along 1/2-way: sn wknd* **25/1**
1m 32.36s (-1.44) **Going Correction** -0.125s/f (Firm) **11** Ran SP% **114.1**
Speed ratings (Par 103): **103,102,101,99,98 94,92,90,90,82 78**
toteswingers:1&2:£7.40, 1&3:£10.50, 2&3:£5.90 CSF £34.84 CT £292.64 TOTE £13.20: £3.40, £1.40, £1.80; EX 31.90 Place 6 £363.85; Place 5 £55.18.
Owner G Parkinson **Bred** Franco Castelfranci **Trained** Catwick, E Yorks
■ Stewards' Enquiry : Barry McHugh caution: used whip with excessive frequency.

FOCUS

A fair handicap in which the field were soon well strung out and the winner once again stayed off the far rail. He is rated close to last year's best.
T/Plt: £1,039.60 to a £1 stake. Pool: £45,718.09, 32.10 winning tickets. T/Qpdt: £34.40 to a £1 stake. Pool: £4,526.92, 97.18 winning tickets. JR

CHEPSTOW (L-H)
Monday, May 3

OFFICIAL GOING: Good (good to soft in places; 7.5)
Wind: Quite strong behind Weather: Cloudy with sunny periods

1755 WYVERN ICES H'CAP (DIV I) 1m 4f 23y
2:35 (2:35) (Class 6) (0-65,65) 4-Y-0+ **£1,942** (£578; £288; £144) **Stalls** Low

Form RPR
-325 **1** **Jezza**[24] 1207 4-8-4 **51** oh2.................... JamieMackay 8 59
(Karen George) *mid-div: hdwy over 4f out: rdn over 2f out: styd on wl: led fnl 100yds: rdn out* **7/1**[3]
425 **2** 1 1/2 **Yemeni Princess (IRE)**[13] 1451 4-9-4 **65**.................... StevieDonohoe 2 71
(B G Powell) *prom: led over 3f out: rdn over 2f out: styd on but no ex whn hdd fnl 100yds* **17/2**
032- **3** 3 **Meirig's Dream (IRE)**[124] 7873 4-8-12 **59**.................... PaulFitzsimons 1 60
(Miss N A Lloyd-Beavis) *mid-div: hdwy 4f out: rdn to chse ldrs over 2f out: styd on same pce* **16/1**
00-3 **4** 3 1/4 **Fulfilment (IRE)**[25] 1188 4-8-6 **53**.................... ChrisCatlin 11 49
(W J Musson) *mid-div: hdwy 5f out: led briefly 4f out: sn rdn to chse ldr: styd on same pce fnl f* **3/1**[1]
-512 **5** 1 **Jackie Kiely**[66] 720 9-8-10 **57**....................(tp) JackMitchell 4 51
(R Brotherton) *hld up towards rr: effrt into midfield over 3f out: styd on same pce fnl 2f* **9/1**
220- **6** 1 1/2 **Outland (IRE)**[187] 7124 4-8-11 **58**.................... WilliamBuick 3 50
(M G Rimell) *hld up towards rr: hdwy 4f out: sn rdn: one pce fnl 2f* **6/1**[2]

00-0 **7** ½ **St Savarin (FR)**[75] 588 9-8-12 **59** ... JimCrowley 5 50
(M S Tuck) *hld up towards rr: rdn over 3f out: sme late prog: nvr a factor* **9/1**

610- **8** ½ **Lucy's Perfect**[196] 6910 4-8-7 **57** ow1 ... (b) JamesMillman(3) 12 47
(B R Millman) *mid-div: hdwy over 4f out: ev ch 3f out: sn rdn: wknd 2f out* **8/1**

034- **9** 1¼ **Aspirational (IRE)**[142] 7733 4-8-7 **54** ... DavidProbert 7 42
(B Palling) *trckd ldrs: rdn 4f out: sn wknd* **12/1**

0-00 **10** 13 **Polish Power (GER)**[23] 1226 10-8-12 **59** ... FrankieMcDonald 6 27
(P G Murphy) *s.i.s: towards rr: hdwy into midfield over 3f out: sn rdn: wknd 2f out* **16/1**

115- **11** 6 **Phoenix Enforcer**[152] 5128 4-8-13 **65** ... (p) MatthewDavies(5) 10 23
(George Baker) *led for 4f: chsd ldrs tl wknd 3f out* **25/1**

660- **12** 2 **Heart Of Tuscany**[271] 4640 4-8-4 **51** ... JimmyQuinn 9 6
(J A T De Giles) *racd keenly: sn prom: led 8f out: hdd 4f out: sn wknd* **25/1**

2m 40.48s (1.48) **Going Correction** +0.15s/f (Good) **12** Ran SP% **120.6**
Speed ratings (Par 101): **101,100,98,95,95 94,93,93,92,84 80,78**
toteswingers:1&2:£6.70, 1&3:£53.00, 2&3:£15.30 CSF £66.58 CT £922.32 TOTE £9.10: £2.30, £2.30, £3.40; EX 104.00.
Owner Mrs Clare E Smith **Bred** C P Ranson **Trained** Higher Eastington, Devon

FOCUS
The ground was reported to be riding on the slow side of good and the time was six seconds outside the Racing Post standard. A modest handicap run at a fair pace. The first two pulled clear of the third who was some way ahead of the rest. The form is rated around the front pair.

1756 WYVERN ICES H'CAP (DIV II) 1m 4f 23y
3:05 (3:07) (Class 6) (0-65,65) 4-Y-O+ **£1,942** (£578; £288; £144) **Stalls** Low

Form RPR

2103 **1** **Carr Hall (IRE)**[9] 1520 7-8-12 **59** ... SebSanders 12 73+
(A W Carroll) *hld up towards rr: smooth hdwy fr 4f out: led 2f out: pushed clr ent fnl f: comf* **5/2**[1]

500- **2** 4 **Amroth**[185] 7154 4-8-2 **52** ... AndrewHeffernan(3) 1 56
(P D Evans) *mid-div: rdn 4f out: no imp tl styd on fr over 1f out: wnt 2nd fnl 100yds: no ch w wnr* **9/1**

43-0 **3** 1 **Party Palace**[24] 1207 6-8-4 **51** oh1 ... GregFairley 3 54
(H S Howe) *disp ld: rdn 4f out: hdd 2f out: styd on same pce* **9/1**

042- **4** ½ **Cote D'Argent**[17] 3095 7-9-4 **65** ... (t) ChrisCatlin 4 67
(C J Down) *disp ld: rdn 3f out: hdd 2f out: styd on same pce* **25/1**

500- **5** ¾ **Mae Cigan (FR)**[56] 6936 7-8-11 **58** ... JimmyQuinn 8 62+
(M Blanshard) *squeezed up s: towards rr: pushed along fr 3f out: sme prog whn nt clr run ent fnl f: swtchd rt: r.o* **9/2**[2]

-600 **6** 1½ **Sparkaway**[28] 1134 4-8-8 **55** ... JamieMackay 7 53
(W J Musson) *s.i.s: towards rr: rdn 4f out: no imp tl styd on ins fnl f: nrst fin* **8/1**[3]

5435 **7** ½ **Choral Festival**[32] 1077 4-8-13 **60** ... (p) NeilChalmers 5 58
(J J Bridger) *mid-div: hdwy over 3f out: rdn and ev ch 2f out: fdd fnl f* **12/1**

45-0 **8** hd **Cantabilly (IRE)**[7] 1587 7-8-11 **58** ... JimCrowley 9 55
(R J Hodges) *mid-div: hdwy over 4f out: sn rdn to chse ldrs: edgd lft and fdd ins fnl f* **8/1**[3]

6166 **9** 2 **Naledi**[10] 1503 6-8-4 **51** oh3 ... DavidProbert 10 45
(R J Price) *rdn over 3f out: nvr bttr than mid-div* **14/1**

605- **10** ½ **Herecomethegirls**[171] 7374 4-8-4 **54** ow1 ... WilliamCarson(3) 11 47
(W G M Turner) *a towards rr* **16/1**

606- **11** 22 **Pallaton**[324] 2922 4-8-10 **57** ... (v[1]) StevieDonohoe 6 15
(B G Powell) *racd keenly: trckd ldrs tl wknd over 3f out: t.o* **25/1**

125- **12** 20 **Guga (IRE)**[219] 4719 4-8-12 **59** ... FrankieMcDonald 2 —
(Dr R D P Newland) *trckd ldrs tl wknd over 4f out: t.o* **22/1**

2m 39.53s (0.53) **Going Correction** +0.15s/f (Good) **12** Ran SP% **121.3**
Speed ratings (Par 101): **104,101,100,100,99 98,98,98,97,96 82,68**
toteswingers:1&2:£11.60, 1&3:£8.00, 2&3:£36.80 CSF £25.61 CT £177.72 TOTE £2.50: £1.10, £5.50, £2.30; EX 34.00.
Owner A W Carroll **Bred** R Cody **Trained** Cropthorne, Worcs

FOCUS
The quicker and stronger division of an ordinary handicap. It was run at a fair pace and the in-form winner was impressive.

1757 LINDLEY CATERING MAIDEN STKS 1m 2f 36y
3:35 (3:36) (Class 5) 3-Y-O+ **£2,590** (£770; £385; £192) **Stalls** Low

Form RPR

5- **1** **Hayzoom**[188] 7099 3-8-12 0 ... JackMitchell 5 81+
(P W Chapple-Hyam) *mid-div: pudhed along briefly over 5f out: hdwy over 3f out: sn rdn: styd on wl fnl f: led fnl 75yds* **8/1**

4 **2** ¾ **Bay Willow (IRE)**[12] 1475 3-8-12 0 ... GregFairley 8 76+
(M Johnston) *prom: rdn to ld 3f out: rallied gamely whn hrd pressed fr over 2f out: drew 2 l clr briefly ent fnl f: no ex whn hdd fnl 75yds* **7/2**[1]

3 2¼ **Weathervane** 3-8-12 0 ... WilliamBuick 12 72+
(J H M Gosden) *hld up towards rr of midfield: hdwy 3f out: rdn to chal 2f out: edgd lft: no ex fnl f* **5/1**[3]

4 nk **Montparnasse (IRE)** 3-8-12 0 ... JamieMackay 1 71+
(B J Meehan) *mid-div: rdn 3f out: styd on fr over 1f out: improve* **20/1**

5 1¾ **Sirdave** 4-9-10 0 ... WilliamCarson(3) 11 69
(P W Hiatt) *hld up towards rr: rdn and stdy prog fr 3f out: styd on fnl f: improve* **100/1**

524- **6** 1 **Cotillion**[181] 7221 4-9-13 75 ... StevieDonohoe 2 67
(Ian Williams) *t.k.h: trckd ldrs: rdn over 3f out: one pce fnl f* **11/2**

65-3 **7** 3¼ **First Fandango**[16] 1393 3-8-12 77 ... SebSanders 3 59
(J W Hills) *trckd ldrs: rdn 3f out: wknd fnl f* **8/1**

550 **8** 4½ **Heliocentric**[16] 1387 3-8-12 68 ... JimCrowley 6 50
(R Hannon) *led tl 3f out: sn rdn: grad fdd* **25/1**

35 **9** 2 **Setter's Princess**[14] 1432 4-9-8 0 ... J-PGuillambert 13 42
(R J Hodges) *a towards rr* **50/1**

0 **10** nk **Behest**[14] 1432 5-9-5 0 ... AndrewHeffernan(3) 4 41
(D G Bridgwater) *trckd ldrs: rdn 4f out: sn wknd* **200/1**

3- **11** 2 **Retrato (USA)**[208] 6593 3-8-7 0 ... ChrisCatlin 10 36
(Rae Guest) *t.k.h in mid-div: hdwy over 3f out: rdn over 2f out: sn wknd* **10/1**

0- **12** 1 **Istidlaal**[214] 6423 3-8-12 0 ... TadhgO'Shea 9 39
(Sir Michael Stoute) *trckd ldrs: rdn over 3f out: wknd over 2f out* **9/2**[2]

0- **13** 16 **Fidler Bay**[340] 2395 4-9-13 0 ... FrankieMcDonald 7 8
(H Candy) *a towards rr* **66/1**

14 55 **Mullsdword (IRE)** 3-8-12 0 ... KevinGhunowa 14 —
(P G Murphy) *s.i.s: a bhd* **100/1**

2m 13.8s (3.20) **Going Correction** +0.15s/f (Good)
WFA 3 from 4yo+ 15lb **14** Ran SP% **118.3**
Speed ratings (Par 103): **93,92,90,90,88 88,85,81,80,80 78,77,64,20**
toteswingers:1&2 £16.10, 1&3 £6.50, 2&3 £15.20 CSF £34.32 TOTE £12.90: £4.00, £1.80, £2.30; EX 52.10.
Owner Ziad A Galadari **Bred** Newsells Park Stud **Trained** Newmarket, Suffolk

FOCUS
There was an open market for this fairly interesting maiden which could throw up several future winners. The form horses were a bit disappointing and the first three are capable of rating higher than the bare form.

1758 LINDLEY CATERING FIRST CHOICE FOR EVENTS H'CAP (DIV I) 2m 49y
4:05 (4:06) (Class 6) (0-60,60) 4-Y-O+ **£1,942** (£578; £288; £144) **Stalls** Low

Form RPR

310- **1** **Picot De Say**[149] 5790 8-8-11 **50** ... RichardThomas 6 64+
(B J Llewellyn) *stdd s: last: smooth hdwy on bit fr 4f out: led over 1f out: pushed clr: eased nr fin* **8/1**

2003 **2** 5 **Mustajed**[11] 1493 9-9-4 **60** ... JamesMillman(3) 3 68
(B R Millman) *mid-div: rdn 3f out: little imp tl styd on fr over 1f out: wnt 2nd nr fin: no ch w wnr* **7/2**[2]

4-3 **3** ½ **Hassadin**[87] 90 4-8-4 **46** oh1 ... NeilChalmers 11 53
(A B Haynes) *prom: rdn over 3f out: stl w ev ch over 1f out: sn no ch w wnr: lost 2nd nr fin* **10/1**

050- **4** 3¼ **Eastwell Smiles**[41] 2760 6-9-2 **55** ... (t) JimCrowley 7 58
(R T Phillips) *led tl rdn 4f out: kpt pressing ldrs: no ex fnl f* **14/1**

6/6- **5** ½ **Intersky Music (USA)**[176] 4263 7-8-10 **49** ... GregFairley 5 52
(Jonjo O'Neill) *hld up towards rr: hdwy over 4f out: effrt over 3f out: one pce fnl 2f* **8/1**

0511 **6** 2½ **Mountain Forest (GER)**[26] 1160 4-9-1 **57** ... JimmyQuinn 1 57
(H Morrison) *racd keenly: trckd ldr: led 4f out: rdn and hdd over 1f out: fdd fnl f* **2/1**[1]

36-0 **7** 2 **Whitcombe Spirit**[36] 982 5-8-13 **55** ... MarcHalford(3) 4 52
(Jamie Poulton) *trckd ldrs: rdn 4f out: sn btn* **14/1**

305- **8** 1½ **Googoobarabajagal (IRE)**[49] 6188 4-8-4 **46** ... ChrisCatlin 2 41
(W S Kittow) *trckd ldrs tl rdn 4f out: nvr a threat after* **9/2**[3]

0-03 **9** 19 **Sweet Request**[13] 1447 6-8-7 **46** oh1 ... (v) KevinGhunowa 10 19
(Dr J R J Naylor) *mid-div: rdn 4f out: wknd over 2f out* **66/1**

00-0 **10** 21 **Tiffany Lady**[13] 1451 4-8-4 **46** oh1 ... DavidProbert 8 —
(M D I Usher) *mid-div: rdn over 3f out: wknd over 2f out* **66/1**

3m 43.3s (4.40) **Going Correction** +0.15s/f (Good)
WFA 4 from 5yo+ 3lb **10** Ran SP% **121.4**
Speed ratings (Par 101): **95,92,92,90,90 89,88,87,77,67**
toteswingers:1&2 £3.20, 1&3 £3.90, 2&3 £2.70 CSF £37.73 CT £291.48 TOTE £11.60: £4.30, £1.90, £4.10; EX 46.40.
Owner Irish Legend Racing Team **Bred** Henry And Mrs Rosemary Moszkowicz **Trained** Fochriw, Caerphilly

FOCUS
A low-grade staying handicap, nearly four seconds quicker than division one. The winner was potentially well in on his jumps form and the second has been given a chance by the handicapper.

1759 LINDLEY CATERING FIRST CHOICE FOR EVENTS H'CAP (DIV II) 2m 49y
4:35 (4:36) (Class 6) (0-60,59) 4-Y-O+ **£1,942** (£578; £288; £144) **Stalls** Low

Form RPR

30-2 **1** **Any Given Moment (IRE)**[20] 1283 4-8-12 **53** ... ChrisCatlin 4 65+
(D M Simcock) *led tl over 6f out: rdn to press ldr fr 4f out: tk narrow advantage 2f out: styd on u.p: hld on gamely* **9/4**[2]

100/ **2** hd **Sangfroid**[9] 5899 6-9-2 **54** ... WilliamBuick 9 66+
(Nick Williams) *trckd ldrs: rdn whn ct sltly flat-footed 3f out: styd on to chal jst ins fnl f: jst hld* **6/5**[1]

4 **3** nk **Salontyre (GER)**[13] 1459 4-9-0 **55** ... (p) StevieDonohoe 6 67
(B J Llewellyn) *in tch: outpcd 3f out: swtchd rt and str run ins fnl f: clsng wl at fin* **15/2**[3]

4 4 **Ocean Bright (USA)**[38] 1005 4-8-4 **45** ... (b) JimmyQuinn 10 52
(J G Given) *s.i.s: sn rcvrd to join ldr: led over 6f out: rdn 3f out: narrowly hdd 2f out: no ex fnl f* **20/1**

60-2 **5** 3½ **Act Three**[21] 1262 6-9-3 **55** ... (t) SebSanders 7 58+
(Mouse Hamilton-Fairley) *hld up last: gd hdwy 4f out: to join ldrs: rdn 3f out: wknd ent fnl f* **8/1**

000 **6** 1¾ **Prickles**[13] 1451 5-8-10 **48** ... J-PGuillambert 5 49
(Karen George) *hld up: rdn and hdwy to chse ldrs over 3f out: wknd fnl f* **40/1**

-050 **7** ½ **Telling Stories (IRE)**[13] 1459 4-8-1 **45** ... (t) AndrewHeffernan(3) 2 45
(B D Leavy) *hld up: rdn 3f out: unable to get on terms* **40/1**

5514 **8** 13 **Zaffeu**[33] 1071 9-9-7 **59** ... (p) JimCrowley 8 44
(A G Juckes) *mid-div tl wknd over 3f out* **16/1**

405- **9** 1¾ **Robbmaa (FR)**[37] 3259 5-8-0 **45** ... JakePayne(7) 3 27
(A W Carroll) *trckd ldrs tl rdn 4f out: sn btn* **50/1**

3m 47.03s (8.13) **Going Correction** +0.15s/f (Good)
WFA 4 from 5yo+ 3lb **9** Ran SP% **116.6**
Speed ratings (Par 101): **85,84,84,82,81 80,79,73,72**
toteswingers:1&2 £1.30, 1&3 £6.60, 2&3 £4.40 CSF £5.17 CT £15.49 TOTE £3.70: £1.30, £1.20, £2.90; EX 5.70.
Owner Malcolm Caine **Bred** W Lazy T Ranch **Trained** Newmarket, Suffolk
■ Stewards' Enquiry : William Buick five-day ban: excessive use of whip (May 17-21)
Chris Catlin three-day ban: excessive use of whip (May 17-19)

FOCUS
The second division of a minor 2m handicap, and nearly four seconds slower than division one. There was a tight three-way-finish and a big gap back to the rest. Perhaps not as strong form as the first division, it has been rated around the fourth.
Prickles Official explanation: jockey said mare ran too free

1760 LINDLEY CATERING H'CAP 6f 16y
5:05 (5:06) (Class 6) (0-65,64) 3-Y-O **£2,266** (£674; £337; £168) **Stalls** High

Form RPR

-231 **1** **Thaliwarru**[25] 1181 3-9-3 **63** ... SebSanders 1 69
(J R Gask) *prom: rdn 2f out: led over 1f out: sn edgd lft: r.o wl: drvn out* **4/1**[2]

000- **2** ¾ **French Fantasy**[175] 7317 3-8-4 **50** oh2 ... JimmyQuinn 3 54
(H Morrison) *led: rdn and hdd over 1f out: sltly hmpd ent fnl f: kpt on* **12/1**

006- **3** 1½ **Erebus (IRE)**[126] 7859 3-9-4 **64** ... WilliamBuick 5 63
(S Kirk) *prom: rdn and ev ch 3f out: kpt on same pce ent fnl f* **6/1**[3]

4033 **4** nk **Hill Of Miller (IRE)**[21] 1259 3-9-1 **61** ... (t) ChrisCatlin 2 59
(Rae Guest) *mid-div: rdn 3f out: stdy prog fr 2f out: kpt on fnl f* **10/1**

020- **5** 5 **Dragonessa (IRE)**[180] 7242 3-8-13 **59**............ NeilChalmers 9 41
(B Palling) *prom: rdn 3f out: one pce fnl 2f* **12/1**

500- **6** 2 ½ **Ridgeway Sapphire**[216] 6355 3-8-4 **50**............ DavidProbert 10 24
(M D I Usher) *mid-div: hdwy 3f out: sn rdn: wknd ent fnl f* **20/1**

2-42 **7** 1 ¼ **Dimaire**[13] 1456 3-8-12 **58**............ JimCrowley 7 28
(D Haydn Jones) *prom: rdn and ev ch 2f out: wknd jst over 1f out* **7/2**[1]

604- **8** nk **Macroy**[215] 6386 3-8-11 **60**............ JamesMillman(3) 11 29
(B R Millman) *mid-div: hdwy 3f out: sn rdn: wknd ent fnl f* **14/1**

54-0 **9** 3 ¾ **First Term**[18] 1329 3-9-3 **63**............ FrankieMcDonald 8 20
(R Hannon) *prom tl 2f out: sn wknd* **13/2**

10-0 **10** 3 **Existentialist**[16] 1390 3-9-4 **64**............ StevieDonohoe 13 11
(A E Price) *in tch: rdn over 3f out: wknd over 2f out* **20/1**

00-0 **11** 1 ¼ **Reel Love**[18] 1336 3-8-5 **51** oh5 ow1............ GregFairley 4 —
(J R Holt) *in tch: rdn 3f out: wknd 2f out* **50/1**

40-0 **12** 2 **Polly Macho (IRE)**[13] 1456 3-8-1 **50** oh1.........(b[1]) AndrewHeffernan(3) 6 —
(P D Evans) *in tch: rdn 4f out: sn btn* **25/1**

0-00 **13** 32 **Dunfishin (IRE)**[39] 980 3-8-4 **50** oh5............ JamieMackay 14 —
(M S Tuck) *sn outpcd: a detached in last: t.o* **80/1**

1m 12.51s (0.51) **Going Correction** +0.05s/f (Good) **13** Ran SP% **117.5**
Speed ratings (Par 97): **98,97,95,94,87 84,82,82,77,73 71,69,26**
toteswingers:1&2:£15.40, 1&3:£2.80, 2&3:£11.40 CSF £47.01 CT £238.44 TOTE £3.60: £1.10, £4.60, £1.70; EX 75.60.
Owner Tony Bloom **Bred** Mr & Mrs Kevan Watts **Trained** Sutton Veny, Wilts

FOCUS
A modest sprint handicap for 3-y-os. Modest form, the fourth the best guide. The first four pulled a long way clear of the rest.
Macroy Official explanation: jockey said gelding was unsuited by the track
First Term Official explanation: jockey said filly hung left-handed
Dunfishin(IRE) Official explanation: jockey said gelding never travelled

1761 WINEAUX.CO.UK H'CAP 1m 14y
5:35 (5:36) (Class 4) (0-80,80) 3-Y-O **£4,857** (£1,445; £722; £360) **Stalls** High

Form RPR

513- **1** **Agony And Ecstasy**[178] 7267 3-9-3 **79**............(p) JimCrowley 1 88
(R M Beckett) *sn swtchd to stands' side rail: mde all: kpt on wl: comf* **11/2**[3]

1-20 **2** 3 **Gallant Eagle (IRE)**[17] 1352 3-9-3 **79**............ ChrisCatlin 6 81+
(S Kirk) *hld up towards rr: hdwy 3f out: sn rdn: chsd ldrs 2f out: wnt 2nd ent fnl f but a being hld* **12/1**

0-04 **3** ¾ **Avon River**[13] 1453 3-9-0 **76**............ SebSanders 2 76
(R Hannon) *chsd ldrs: rdn 3f out: kpt on same pce* **14/1**

154- **4** ½ **Missionaire (USA)**[248] 5399 3-9-4 **80**............ JimmyQuinn 3 79+
(W J Knight) *s.i.s: sn pushed along towards rr: hdwy fr 3f out: sn rdn: chsd ldrs 2f out: kpt on same pce fnl f* **7/2**[1]

1210 **5** ½ **Tuscan King**[12] 1476 3-8-1 **66**............(b) AndrewHeffernan(3) 11 64
(P D Evans) *mid-div: rdn 3f out: kpt on ins fnl f* **16/1**

343- **6** 1 ¼ **Sir Bruno (FR)**[216] 6366 3-8-11 **73**............ NeilChalmers 9 68
(B Palling) *trckd ldrs: rdn 3f out: kpt on same pce fnl 2f* **12/1**

222 **7** 1 **Magic Omen (USA)**[12] 1464 3-9-0 **76**............ GregFairley 12 69
(M Johnston) *trckd ldrs: rdn 4f out: one pce fr 2f out* **9/2**[2]

025- **8** 1 ½ **Shabak Hom (IRE)**[226] 6125 3-8-10 **72**............ StevieDonohoe 8 61+
(D M Simcock) *bhd: rdn over 3f out: hdwy over 1f out: running on whn snatched up short of room on stands' side rails jst ins fnl f: nt rcvr* **25/1**

42-4 **9** 1 ¾ **White Devil**[19] 1307 3-9-3 **79**............ DavidProbert 4 64
(A M Balding) *racd freely: trckd ldrs: rdn 3f out: wknd over 1f out* **9/2**[2]

003- **10** 3 ¾ **La Pantera**[175] 7320 3-9-1 **77**............ FrankieMcDonald 10 53
(R Hannon) *t.k.h in mid-div: rdn 4f out: sn btn* **14/1**

0-40 **11** 17 **Texan Star (IRE)**[20] 1279 3-9-1 **77**............(p) WilliamBuick 5 14
(J H M Gosden) *hld up towards rr: rdn 4f out: no imp: eased fr over 1f out* **16/1**

1m 35.52s (-0.68) **Going Correction** +0.05s/f (Good) **11** Ran SP% **118.3**
Speed ratings (Par 101): **105,102,101,100,100 99,98,96,94,91 74**
toteswingers:1&2 £15.40, 1&3 £2.80, 2&3 £11.40. CSF £70.23 CT £896.21 TOTE £7.00: £2.40, £6.80, £5.70; EX 82.20.
Owner Miss Rachel Tregaskes **Bred** Downfield Cottage Stud **Trained** Whitsbury, Hants

FOCUS
This looked quite competitive but there was a runaway winner. The form is rated through the third.

1762 LINDLEY CATERING FIRST CHOICE FOR CONFERENCES H'CAP 7f 16y
6:05 (6:08) (Class 5) (0-70,70) 4-Y-O+ **£2,914** (£867; £433; £216) **Stalls** High

Form RPR

56-5 **1** **Hobson**[8] 1543 5-8-11 **70**............ AmyScott(7) 4 79
(Eve Johnson Houghton) *mid-div: rdn and hdwy over 2f out: led over 1f out: kpt on: pushed out* **10/1**

25-0 **2** ½ **Space Station**[21] 1258 4-9-3 **69**............ JimCrowley 7 77
(S Dow) *mid-div: hdwy 3f out: sn rdn: pressed wnr ins fnl f: hld nr fin* **8/1**

-064 **3** 1 ¼ **Dr Wintringham (IRE)**[27] 1141 4-8-7 **59**............ ChrisCatlin 3 66+
(Karen George) *hld up: rdn: swtchd lft and hdwy fr 2f out: styd on fnl f* **12/1**

2222 **4** 2 ¼ **Spinning Ridge (IRE)**[8] 1543 5-9-0 **66**............(b) GregFairley 12 64
(R A Harris) *led: rdn and hdd over 1f out: no ex* **9/2**[2]

15-6 **5** 1 ¼ **Cadeaux Fax**[19] 1304 5-8-8 **63**............ JamesMillman(3) 10 58
(B R Millman) *chsd ldr: rdn over 2f out: kpt on same pce* **9/4**[1]

120 **6** ½ **Unlimited**[23] 1224 8-8-11 **63**............ SebSanders 2 56
(A W Carroll) *hld up: rdn and hdwy over 2f out: kpt on same pce fnl f* **7/1**[3]

-005 **7** 1 ½ **Foreign Investment (IRE)**[7] 1585 4-8-7 **62**.....(v[1]) AndrewHeffernan(3) 5 51
(P D Evans) *chsd ldrs: rdn over 2f out: fdd fnl f* **9/1**

0205 **8** nse **Harare**[23] 1238 9-8-8 **63**............(v) WilliamCarson(3) 6 52
(R J Price) *s.i.s: towards rr: sme late prog: nvr a factor* **25/1**

3650 **9** 1 ¼ **Commandingpresence (USA)**[45] 931 4-8-4 **56** oh10 NeilChalmers 14 42
(J J Bridger) *nvr bttr than mid-div* **80/1**

00-0 **10** ½ **Memphis Man**[21] 1267 7-8-11 **70**............ KevinLundie(7) 9 55
(P D Evans) *(led to s by groom) s.i.s: a towards rr* **33/1**

011- **11** 3 ¾ **Abhainn (IRE)**[216] 6362 4-8-6 **58**............ DavidProbert 8 32
(B Palling) *chsd ldrs tl wknd over 2f out* **8/1**

000- **12** 26 **Miskin Spirit**[164] 7459 4-8-4 **56** oh11............ JimmyQuinn 11 —
(B Palling) *s.i.s: a outpcd in rr* **80/1**

1m 22.94s (-0.26) **Going Correction** +0.05s/f (Good) **12** Ran SP% **119.7**
Speed ratings (Par 103): **103,102,101,98,97 96,94,94,93,92 88,58**
toteswingers:1&2 £20.50, 1&3 £12.40, 2&3 £34.10 CSF £86.69 CT £981.26 TOTE £19.30: £4.90, £3.50, £4.50; EX 110.20 Place 6 £92.14; Place 5 £24.45.
Owner Anthony Pye-Jeary And Mel Smith **Bred** Hunscote House Farm Stud **Trained** Blewbury, Oxon

FOCUS
A fair handicap run at a sound pace.

T/Jkpt: Not won. T/Plt: £211.40 to a £1 stake. Pool: £72,155.21, 249.16 winning tickets. T/Qpdt: £23.40 to a £1 stake. Pool: £5,375.15, 169.46 winning tickets. TM

1619 KEMPTON (A.W) (R-H)
Monday, May 3

OFFICIAL GOING: Standard
Wind: Fresh 1/2 against Weather: Mostly fine, couple of heavy showers

1763 SUMMER SERIES STARTS 2ND JUNE H'CAP 1m 2f (P)
2:00 (2:01) (Class 6) (0-65,65) 4-Y-O+ **£2,047** (£604; £302) **Stalls** High

Form RPR

443- **1** **Inch Lodge**[138] 7767 8-9-0 **61**............(t) SaleemGolam 11 73
(Miss D Mountain) *chsd ldrs: led over 2f out: styd on wl fnl f* **14/1**

2140 **2** 2 ½ **Freedom Fire (IRE)**[61] 770 4-9-1 **62**............ LiamKeniry 5 69
(G L Moore) *chsd ldrs: wnt handy 2nd over 1f out: styd on same pce* **13/2**[1]

6-40 **3** 8 **Altimatum (USA)**[4] 1636 4-9-1 **62**............ JamieSpencer 13 53
(P F I Cole) *towards rr: reminders over 6f out: hdwy u.p over 2f out: kpt on to take modest 3rd nr fin* **8/1**[3]

0022 **4** hd **Ermine Grey**[25] 1193 9-8-11 **58**............ NeilCallan 2 49
(A W Carroll) *swtchd rt after s: prom: effrt 3f out: kpt on same pce fnl 2f* **7/1**[2]

40-6 **5** nk **Lunar River (FR)**[23] 1241 7-9-4 **65**............(t) FergusSweeney 14 55
(David Pinder) *led early: chsd ldrs: one pce fnl 2f* **7/1**[2]

6135 **6** 2 **Musashi (IRE)**[13] 1440 5-8-13 **60**............(b) IanMongan 9 46
(Mrs L J Mongan) *t.k.h: led after 1f: hdd over 2f out: wknd fnl f* **13/2**[1]

0465 **7** 1 ¼ **See Elsie Play**[18] 1322 4-8-10 **57** ow2............ SamHitchcott 1 41
(Miss Z C Davison) *swtchd rt s: hld up in rr: hdwy u.p over 2f out: nvr nr ldrs* **12/1**

-130 **8** 1 ¾ **Wrighty Almighty (IRE)**[35] 1047 8-9-3 **64**............ RichardKingscote 7 44
(P R Chamings) *hld up in rr: kpt on fnl 2f: nvr nr ldrs* **20/1**

-225 **9** 2 ½ **Silken Promise (USA)**[7] 1574 4-8-13 **60**............(p) TomMcLaughlin 6 35
(T B P Coles) *hld up in rr: sme hdwy 2f out: nvr a factor* **9/1**

650- **10** 8 **Magic Warrior**[255] 5211 10-8-8 **55**............ LukeMorris 8 14
(J C Fox) *t.k.h towards rr: effrt 3f out: sn btn* **66/1**

-530 **11** 9 **Ladies Dancing**[13] 1462 4-9-1 **62**............(p) FrankieDettori 12 3
(J A Osborne) *sn led: hdd after 1f: drvn over 3f out: wknd over 1f out: eased ins fnl f* **13/2**[1]

05-0 **12** ¾ **Starlight Gazer**[26] 1172 7-8-10 **57**............(p) TravisBlock 3 —
(J C Fox) *midfield: lost pl 3f out: eased whn bhd* **33/1**

056/ **13** 6 **Cool The Heels (IRE)**[623] 5146 5-8-12 **59**............ MickyFenton 4 —
(Miss E C Lavelle) *t.k.h: mid-div: rdn and lost pl over 2f out: eased whn bhd* **25/1**

5000 **14** 1 ½ **Efficiency**[23] 1225 4-8-10 **57**............ SteveDrowne 10 —
(M Blanshard) *prom: sn drvn along: lost pl over 4f out: sn bhd: eased* **40/1**

2m 6.10s (-1.90) **Going Correction** -0.05s/f (Stan) **14** Ran SP% **116.0**
Speed ratings (Par 101): **105,103,96,96,96 94,93,92,90,83 76,76,71,70**
toteswingers:1&2:£11.20, 1&3:£16.20, 2&3:£10.60 CSF £93.50 CT £787.05 TOTE £14.50: £4.00, £2.80, £2.60; EX 105.70.
Owner Ahmad Kobeissi **Bred** Gainsborough Stud Management Ltd **Trained** Newmarket, Suffolk

FOCUS
Mainly exposed performers in a modest opener. A moderate gallop saw those up with the pace hold a big advantage and the winner, who pulled clear with the runner-up, raced centre to far side in the straight. Probably not form to take at face value.
Cool The Heels(IRE) Official explanation: jockey said gelding lost its action; trainer said gelding subsequently showed traces of blood and mucus following scope

1764 EUROPEAN BREEDERS' FUND MAIDEN STKS 5f (P)
2:30 (2:33) (Class 4) 2-Y-O **£4,533** (£1,348; £674; £336) **Stalls** High

Form RPR

0 **1** **Lord Avon**[17] 1359 2-9-0 **0**............ JackDean(3) 5 79
(W G M Turner) *mde all: rdn over 1f out: hld on towards fin* **12/1**

2 **2** 1 **Jambo Bibi (IRE)**[3] 1660 2-8-12 **0**............ SteveDrowne 8 70
(R Hannon) *drvn to sn chse wnr: drvn over 1f out: kpt on same pce ins fnl f* **4/6**[1]

3 nse **Avonmore Star** 2-9-0 **0**............ PatrickHills(3) 4 75+
(R Hannon) *awkward to load: dwlt: hdwy over 3f out: styd on fnl f* **9/1**[3]

205 **4** 9 **Beach Patrol (IRE)**[16] 1389 2-9-3 **0**............ KierenFallon 1 42
(M R Channon) *chsd ldrs: wknd over 1f out: eased ins fnl f* **5/1**[2]

5 1 ¼ **Dancing With Fire** 2-8-12 **0**............ AndreaAtzeni 3 33
(D Donovan) *trckd ldrs: effrt over 2f out: wknd fnl f* **11/1**

6 ¾ **Ree's Rascal (IRE)** 2-9-3 **0**............ PatCosgrave 6 35
(J R Boyle) *dwlt: outpcd and sn bhd: kpt on fnl f: nvr on terms* **12/1**

7 6 **Volturi (IRE)** 2-9-3 **0**............ AdrianMcCarthy 7 14
(Peter Grayson) *s.i.s: sn drvn along: hdwy over 3f out: lost pl 2f out* **50/1**

61.34 secs (0.84) **Going Correction** -0.05s/f (Stan) **7** Ran SP% **112.3**
Speed ratings (Par 95): **91,89,89,74,72 71,62**
toteswingers:1&2:£3.10, 1&3:£9.00, 2&3:£2.20. CSF £19.93 TOTE £12.90: £4.20, £1.10; EX 22.60.
Owner Mrs M S Teversham **Bred** Mrs Monica Teversham **Trained** Sigwells, Somerset

FOCUS
No more than a fair maiden in which the gallop was only an ordinary one and the first three pulled clear. The winner raced centre to far side in the straight. The second is not one of the stable's lesser lights.

NOTEBOOK
Lord Avon had been well beaten on his debut at Thirsk but attracted support and duly turned in a much improved display, showing both plenty of foot and a good attitude. This course seemed to suit him better than either of the placed horses and it will be interesting to see if he can step up again on this. (op 20-1)
Jambo Bibi(IRE) posted an encouraging effort on her debut at Lingfield only three days earlier but failed to build on that after taking a good hold and after racing wide turning for home. She's capable of picking up a small race but she lacks much in the way of physical scope. (tchd 4-5)
Avonmore Star ◆ noticeably green both before and during the race on this debut outing, is the one to take from the race. He should come on a good deal for this initial experience, is in very good hands and is sure to make his mark in similar company at the very least in the coming weeks. (op 15-2 tchd 7-1)
Beach Patrol(IRE) again failed by a long chalk to confirm the promise shown over this course and distance on his debut run. He will have to show a fair bit more before he is a solid betting proposition. (op 13-2)
Dancing With Fire, the third foal of a dual 6f winner, was too green to do herself justice on this racecourse debut but may do better with time and over a bit further. (op 16-1)

The Form Book, Raceform Ltd, Compton, RG20 6NL

Ree's Rascal(IRE), who has winners over a variety of distances in his pedigree, is the type to do better in time and over a bit further. (op 10-1)

1765 SILVER BLAZE WESSEX CUP H'CAP 5f (P)
3:00 (3:01) (Class 4) (0-85,83) 3-Y-O **£4,209** (£1,252; £625; £312) **Stalls** High

Form RPR

2451 **1** **Kylladdie**[26] [1175] 3-7-13 **71** ow1 .... JohnFahy(7) 2 76
(S Gollings) *sn drvn along towards rr: hdwy over 2f out: styd on wl over 1f out: carried lft and led post* **7/2**[1]

521 **2** *nse* **Micky's Knock Off (IRE)**[11] [1483] 3-8-4 **69** oh2......(e) AdrianMcCarthy 5 74
(R C Guest) *hdwy to trck ldrs over 3f out: led over 2f out: edgd lft ins fnl f: hdd fnl stride* **12/1**

6-14 **3** *hd* **Liberty Lady (IRE)**[16] [1390] 3-8-4 **69** oh1 .... LukeMorris 4 73
(D Donovan) *sn drvn along in rr: hdwy over 2f out: styd on on ins ins fnl f: r.o* **6/1**

16-2 **4** *2 1/4* **Nepotism**[8] [1546] 3-8-7 **72** .... FergusSweeney 1 73
(M S Saunders) *chsd ldrs: drvn over 2f out: upsides jst ins fnl f: 4th and hld whn squeezed out nr fin* **7/2**[1]

202- **5** *4 1/2* **Grand Zafeen**[304] [3559] 3-9-4 **83** .... KierenFallon 3 63
(M R Channon) *s.i.s: outpcd in rr: nvr on terms* **11/2**[3]

3116 **6** *1 1/2* **Silver Linnet (IRE)**[20] [1281] 3-7-13 **69** oh2.............(b) DeclanCannon(5) 6 43
(M G Quinlan) *w ldrs: hung rt and rn wd bnd over 3f out: lost pl over 1f out* **7/1**

134- **7** *1/2* **Six Diamonds**[231] [5945] 3-9-1 **80** .... SteveDrowne 7 53
(H Morrison) *led: hdd over 2f out: wknd over 1f out* **4/1**[2]

60.08 secs (-0.42) **Going Correction** -0.05s/f (Stan) 7 Ran SP% **114.3**
Speed ratings (Par 101): **101,100,100,97,89 87,86**
toteswingers:1&2:£5.60, 1&3:£6.00, 2&3:£4.90 CSF £44.21 TOTE £5.00: £2.90, £3.50; EX 37.10.
Owner P S Walter **Bred** Horizon Bloodstock Limited **Trained** Scamblesby, Lincs
■ Stewards' Enquiry : Adrian McCarthy three-day ban: careless riding (May 17-19)

FOCUS
A fair handicap run at a strong gallop and a time that was a second quicker than the previous juvenile maiden. The winner came down the centre in the straight and did not need to match his Nottingham win.
Micky's Knock Off(IRE) Official explanation: vet said gelding finished lame
Silver Linnet(IRE) Official explanation: jockey said filly hung left on bend
Six Diamonds Official explanation: jockey said filly hung left on bend

1766 VICTOR CHANDLER MAIDEN STKS (DIV I) 1m (P)
3:30 (3:32) (Class 4) 3-Y-O **£3,885** (£1,156; £577; £288) **Stalls** High

Form RPR

3-5 **1** **Udabaa (IRE)**[16] [1387] 3-9-3 0 .... RichardHills 7 80
(M P Tregoning) *chsd ldr: hrd drvn over 4f out: styd on fnl f: led nr fin* **8/13**[1]

43-0 **2** *1/2* **Advertisement (USA)**[16] [1381] 3-9-3 77 .... FrankieDettori 13 79
(J Noseda) *led: 2 l ahd appr fnl f: worn down nr fin* **4/1**[2]

43- **3** *3 3/4* **Plutocraft**[191] [7024] 3-9-3 0 .... PatCosgrave 14 70
(J R Fanshawe) *awkward to load: trckd ldrs: t.k.h: styd on same pce appr fnl f* **14/1**

4 *shd* **Valeur** 3-8-12 0 .... RichardMullen 3 65+
(Sir Michael Stoute) *mid-div: hdwy over 2f out: r.o fnl f: will improve* **11/1**[3]

03 **5** *1 1/2* **Edition**[21] [1260] 3-9-3 0 .... LiamKeniry 5 66
(J R Gask) *trckd ldrs: effrt over 2f out: kpt on same pce over 1f out* **33/1**

0 **6** *1/2* **Formulation (IRE)**[16] [1387] 3-9-3 0 .... TravisBlock 12 65+
(H Morrison) *s.i.s: hdwy and hung rt over 2f out: kpt on: nt rch ldrs* **20/1**

0- **7** *2 1/2* **Two Minds (FR)**[160] [7507] 3-9-3 0 .... IanMongan 4 59
(Eugene Stanford) *mid-div: effrt over 2f out: nvr trbld ldrs* **100/1**

6 **8** *shd* **Amends (USA)**[54] [843] 3-9-3 0 .... AndreaAtzeni 9 59
(J R Best) *chsd ldrs: one pce fnl 2f* **66/1**

00- **9** *2* **Donair**[187] [7121] 3-9-3 0 ....(t) KierenFallon 8 54
(P F I Cole) *chsd ldrs: wknd appr fnl f* **66/1**

405- **10** *3 1/4* **Lutine Charlie (IRE)**[180] [7243] 3-9-3 78 .... MickyFenton 10 46
(P Winkworth) *s.i.s: hld up in rr: kpt on fnl 2f: nvr a factor* **20/1**

0 **11** *hd* **Motirani**[16] [1387] 3-9-3 0 .... JamieSpencer 11 46
(M L W Bell) *in rr: bhd fnl 3f* **25/1**

12 *2 1/4* **Norse Dame** 3-8-7 0 .... DeclanCannon(5) 1 35
(D R C Elsworth) *s.s: in rr: drvn over 4f out: bhd fnl 3f* **50/1**

13 *1 3/4* **Farmer Palmer** 3-9-3 0 .... SamHitchcott 2 36
(Louise Best) *in rr: drvn over 4f out: nvr on terms* **100/1**

1m 39.09s (-0.71) **Going Correction** -0.05s/f (Stan) 13 Ran SP% **120.2**
Speed ratings (Par 101): **101,100,96,96,95 94,92,92,90,86 86,84,82**
toteswingers:1&2:£1.90, 1&3:£5.50, 2&3:£7.60 CSF £2.67 TOTE £1.60: £1.20, £1.20, £2.80; EX 4.30.
Owner Hamdan Al Maktoum **Bred** Philip Brady **Trained** Lambourn, Berks

FOCUS
An ordinary gallop but useful form from the two market leaders, who pulled clear of the remainder. The winner raced down the centre in the straight.
Lutine Charlie(IRE) Official explanation: jockey said gelding hung left in straight

1767 KEMPTON.CO.UK JUBILEE H'CAP (LONDON MILE QUALIFIER) 1m (P)
4:00 (4:02) (Class 3) (0-90,89) 4-Y-O+
£7,477 (£2,239; £1,119; £560; £279; £140) **Stalls** High

Form RPR

6350 **1** **Den's Gift (IRE)**[30] [1088] 6-8-5 **83** ....(b) JohnFahy(7) 11 96
(C G Cox) *sn led: mde rest: styd on strly fnl 2f: unchal* **10/1**

0426 **2** *2 1/4* **The Kyllachy Kid**[25] [1185] 4-8-13 **84** ....(p) IanMongan 6 92
(S Gollings) *led early: chsd ldrs: wnt 2nd over 1f out: kpt on: no imp* **28/1**

1-35 **3** *3/4* **Desert Kiss**[16] [1383] 5-9-0 **85** .... AdamKirby 14 91
(W R Swinburn) *chsd ldrs: styd on same pce fnl 2f* **7/2**[1]

0-03 **4** *nk* **Moynahan (USA)**[13] [1455] 5-9-2 **87** ....(p) KierenFallon 9 92+
(P F I Cole) *hld up towards rr: swtchd lft over 2f out: kpt on wl fnl f* **5/1**[2]

14-5 **5** *shd* **Hurricane Spirit (IRE)**[19] [1306] 6-8-12 **83** .... JamieSpencer 13 88
(J R Best) *trckd ldrs: effrt on ins over 2f out: styd on same pce appr fnl f* **7/1**

6013 **6** *1 3/4* **Alfresco**[14] [1428] 6-8-7 **78** ....(b) LukeMorris 7 79
(J R Best) *trckd ldrs: effrt over 2f out: kpt on same pce* **16/1**

2054 **7** *1* **Ilie Nastase (FR)**[12] [1481] 6-8-11 **82** .... LiamKeniry 3 81
(C R Dore) *hld up in rr: kpt on fnl 2f: nvr nr ldrs* **20/1**

05-0 **8** *1/2* **The Which Doctor**[13] [1455] 5-9-2 **87** .... NeilCallan 8 85
(J Noseda) *s.i.s: kpt on fnl 2f: nvr nr ldrs* **14/1**

214- **9** *1 1/4* **Mac's Power (IRE)**[221] [6229] 4-9-0 **85** ....(t) PatCosgrave 4 80
(J R Fanshawe) *stdd sn after s: hld up towards rr: hdwy over 2f out: nvr nr ldrs* **6/1**[3]

-410 **10** *1 1/4* **Arachnophobia (IRE)**[23] [1219] 4-9-2 **87** .... FrankieDettori 2 79
(Pat Eddery) *mid-div: effrt over 3f out: one pce fnl 2f* **15/2**

5100 **11** *nse* **Orchard Supreme**[13] [1455] 7-9-0 **88** .... PatrickHills(3) 10 80
(R Hannon) *mid-div: hdwy on ins over 2f out: wknd fnl f* **33/1**

220- **12** *3 1/4* **Woodcote Place**[279] [4409] 7-9-4 **89** .... RichardKingscote 12 73
(P R Chamings) *dwlt: sn chsng ldrs: wknd over 1f out* **25/1**

6-00 **13** *6* **Grand Vizier (IRE)**[13] [1455] 6-9-0 **85** .... LiamJones 5 56
(C F Wall) *s.i.s: in rr and sn given reminders: bhd fnl 3f* **25/1**

01/ **14** *6* **Phoenix Ice (IRE)**[167] [6795] 6-9-2 **87** .... MickyFenton 1 44
(Jonjo O'Neill) *s.i.s: racd wd: in rr: bhd fnl 3f* **66/1**

1m 37.77s (-2.03) **Going Correction** -0.05s/f (Stan) 14 Ran SP% **119.4**
Speed ratings (Par 107): **108,105,105,104,104 102,101,101,100,98 98,95,89,83**
toteswingers:1&2:£39.20, 1&3:£7.00, 2&3:£21.60 CSF £273.33 CT £1210.81 TOTE £13.20: £3.90, £10.80, £1.90; EX 531.10.
Owner Mrs Olive Shaw **Bred** Mrs J A Dene **Trained** Lambourn, Berks

FOCUS
Mainly exposed types in a useful handicap. The gallop was an ordinary one and those held up were at a disadvantage. The winner raced centre to far side in the straight and ran a length personal best, with the next four close to their marks.

NOTEBOOK
Den's Gift(IRE) had chased too strong a pace on his previous start but was allowed to adopt his customary front-running role this time, and he returned to his best after again displaying a gritty attitude. Life will he harder after reassessment but he will remain of interest against exposed types when it looks as though he will be able to do his own thing in front. (op 11-1 tchd 12-1)
The Kyllachy Kid had been well beaten on his only previous start over 1m but, although he was well placed in a race run at an ordinary gallop, he showed himself fully effective over it. He has won from a slightly higher rating in the past but he has have little margin for error from his current mark. (op 20-1)
Desert Kiss came here on the back of two solid runs and posted another creditable effort from her decent draw after racing up with the pace. This was only her third run on Polytrack and she may well be able add to her tally on either turf or sand this summer. (op 4-1)
Moynahan(USA) has shown patchy form since his maiden win in 2007, but he's slipped a fair way in the weights and looks better than the bare form after faring the best of those to come from off the pace. A more truly run race would have suited better but, although he's on a fair mark, he looks the type that needs things to drop right, and it remains to be seen whether this will be built on next time. (op 9-2 tchd 11-2)
Hurricane Spirit(IRE) extended his run of creditable efforts after racing close to the ordinary gallop but he'll have to raise his game to win from his current mark. (op 8-1 tchd 9-1)
Alfresco wasn't disgraced after racing with the choke out but will have to improve to win a competitive race from this mark. (op 20-1)
Ilie Nastase(FR), returned to 1m, looks a bit better than the bare form after being dropped out and he's the type to win races at some stage for current connections. (op 16-1)

1768 VICTORCHANDLER.COM H'CAP 2m (P)
4:30 (4:31) (Class 5) (0-75,70) 4-Y-O+ **£2,590** (£770; £385; £192) **Stalls** High

Form RPR

-410 **1** **Coda Agency**[26] [1160] 7-9-3 **63** .... NeilCallan 7 69
(D W P Arbuthnot) *mde all: hld on gamely: in command at line* **9/2**

041- **2** *1 1/4* **Babilu**[47] [4264] 5-8-11 **60** ....(p) JackDean(3) 3 65
(D Burchell) *rrd s: t.k.h in last: hdwy over 2f out: chal 1f out: styd on same pce fnl 100yds: wl hld at line* **16/1**

0/52 **3** *1 1/2* **Pearl (IRE)**[13] [1459] 6-7-12 **51** oh3........(tp) RichardRowe(7) 2 54
(Mrs A M Thorpe) *chsd ldrs: drvn over 3f out: one pce fnl 2f* **4/1**[3]

-310 **4** *7* **Soundbyte**[17] [1357] 5-9-10 **70** .... FergusSweeney 4 64
(J Gallagher) *chsd ldrs: drvn to chal over 3f out: wknd fnl f* **5/2**[1]

0-15 **5** *8* **Mr Plod**[26] [1169] 5-9-1 **61** .... FrankieDettori 5 46
(Andrew Reid) *hld up: hdwy over 3f out: sn chsng ldrs: wknd over 1f out* **11/4**[2]

300- **6** *9* **Haldibari (IRE)**[194] [6021] 6-8-6 **52** .... RichardKingscote 8 26
(S Lycett) *trckd ldrs: drvn 5f out: wknd 2f out* **8/1**

/ **7** *12* **Annie The Doc**[11] [6349] 5-8-11 **57** ....(t) TravisBlock 1 17
(Miss A M Newton-Smith) *dwlt: pushed along towards rr over 7f out: hung lft bnd over 4f out: sn lost pl and bhd: t.o 3f out* **66/1**

3m 30.26s (0.16) **Going Correction** -0.05s/f (Stan) 7 Ran SP% **111.9**
Speed ratings (Par 103): **97,96,95,92,88 83,77**
toteswingers:1&2:£7.30, 1&3:£4.80, 2&3:£8.20 CSF £65.10 CT £306.25 TOTE £5.50: £1.90, £9.90; EX 112.10.
Owner Banfield, Thompson **Bred** Baydon House Stud **Trained** Compton, Berks

FOCUS
A modest handicap but, with the two market leaders disappointing, it was one that took less winning than seemed likely beforehand. A steady gallop only increased turning for home and the winner raced in the centre in the straight. He did not need to match his best form.
Haldibari(IRE) Official explanation: jockey said gelding had no more to give
Annie The Doc Official explanation: jockey said mare hung right throughout

1769 VICTOR CHANDLER MAIDEN STKS (DIV II) 1m (P)
5:00 (5:01) (Class 4) 3-Y-O **£3,885** (£1,156; £577; £288) **Stalls** High

Form RPR

6 **1** **Eton Forever (IRE)**[16] [1387] 3-9-3 0 .... NeilCallan 12 96+
(M A Jarvis) *trckd ldrs: smooth hdwy to ld 1f out: pushed out: readily* **2/1**[1]

2 *3/4* **Afsare** 3-9-3 0 .... KierenFallon 9 91+
(L M Cumani) *s.i.s: hdwy 4f out: str run to go 2nd jst ins fnl f: hld nr line: promising* **7/2**[3]

- **3** *3 3/4* **Azimuth (USA)** 3-9-3 0 .... FrankieDettori 1 82
(J Noseda) *trckd ldrs: effrt over 2f out: styd on fnl f: tk 3rd nr line* **20/1**

3-3 **4** *shd* **Latansaa**[16] [1381] 3-9-3 0 .... RichardHills 4 82
(M P Tregoning) *trckd ldr: led over 2f out: hdd 1f out: fdd* **9/4**[2]

0 **5** *3 1/4* **Glacial**[18] [1325] 3-9-3 0 .... FergusSweeney 11 78+
(E F Vaughan) *in rr: effrt over 2f out: kpt on fnl f: nvr nr ldrs* **66/1**

6 *3 1/4* **Fancy Vivid (IRE)** 3-8-12 0 .... RichardMullen 3 62+
(Sir Michael Stoute) *in rr: hmpd over 5f out: hdwy 2f out: styd on ins fnl f* **33/1**

7 *1* **Green Destiny (IRE)** 3-9-3 0 .... LiamJones 6 65+
(W J Haggas) *mid-div: sn drvn along: one pce fnl 3f* **33/1**

4-2 **8** *3 1/4* **Strong Vigilance (IRE)**[18] [1336] 3-9-3 0 .... JamieSpencer 2 58
(M L W Bell) *mid-div: rdn and outpcd over 2f out: sn wknd* **8/1**

304- **9** *3/4* **Verity Lane (USA)**[178] [7277] 3-8-12 73 .... RichardKingscote 14 51
(R M H Cowell) *led tl hdd over 2f out: wknd over 1f out* **33/1**

10 *1* **Stoical (IRE)** 3-9-3 0 .... IanMongan 8 54+
(W Jarvis) *a towards rr: nvr a factor* **80/1**

64 **11** *3/4* **British Sea Power (IRE)**[11] [1490] 3-9-3 0 .... LiamKeniry 7 52
(J R Gask) *mid-div: sn pushed along: lost pl over 2f out* **100/1**

56- **12** *hd* **One Hit Wonder**[327] [2825] 3-9-3 0 .... TravisBlock 10 51
(Mouse Hamilton-Fairley) *s.s: in rr: drvn over 4f out: bhd fnl 3f* **100/1**

13 *8* **Embarkation** 3-9-3 0 .... PatCosgrave 5 33
(J R Fanshawe) *s.i.s: in rr: bhd fnl 2f* **100/1**

30-2 **14** *23* **Soho Theatre**[26] [1165] 3-9-3 77.................................(p) MickyFenton 13 —
(D R C Elsworth) *chsd ldrs: lost pl 2f out: sn bhd and eased: t.o* **20/1**
1m 37.87s (-1.93) **Going Correction** -0.05s/f (Stan) 14 Ran SP% **121.5**
Speed ratings (Par 101): **107,106,102,102,99 95,94,91,90,89 89,88,80,57**
toteswingers:1&2:£3.00, 1&3:£10.30, 2&3:£15.00 CSF £8.66 TOTE £3.20: £1.90, £1.10, £5.80; EX 12.30.
Owner H R H Sultan Ahmad Shah **Bred** Mrs Brid Cosgrove **Trained** Newmarket, Suffolk
FOCUS
An interesting maiden and, although the gallop was an ordinary one, the time was over a second quicker than the first division. The first two pulled clear and this looks a strong maiden that should throw up plenty of winners. Winner and runner-up, both potentially very useful sorts, raced to the far side in the closing stages.
Soho Theatre Official explanation: jockey said gelding lost its action in straight

1770 FAMILY FUN DAY FILLIES' H'CAP 6f (P)
5:30 (5:31) (Class 4) (0-85,82) 4-Y-O+ **£4,209** (£1,252; £625; £312) **Stalls** High

Form RPR
4625 **1** **Ray Of Joy**[18] [1321] 4-8-12 **76**.................................. FergusSweeney 6 86
(J R Jenkins) *trckd ldrs: led over 1f out: r.o strly* **6/1**
600- **2** *2* **All The Nines (IRE)**[276] [4507] 4-8-10 **79**................ DeclanCannon(5) 5 82
(Mrs D J Sanderson) *led: hung lft bnd over 3f out: hdd over 1f out: kpt on same pce* **20/1**
104- **3** *shd* **Evelyn May (IRE)**[179] [7253] 4-8-11 **78**.......................... PatrickHills(3) 2 81
(B W Hills) *trckd ldrs: effrt over 1f out: kpt on same pce* **9/2**[3]
40-3 **4** *nk* **Sakhee's Pearl**[5] [1625] 4-9-4 **82**.................................. MickyFenton 7 84
(Miss Gay Kelleway) *chsd ldrs: effrt over 2f out: hung rt: kpt on fnl f* **3/1**[2]
255- **5** *hd* **Cut The Cackle (IRE)**[179] [7253] 4-8-12 **76**...................... IanMongan 3 77+
(P Winkworth) *hld up: effrt 3f out: hdwy over 1f out: styd on wl ins fnl f* **7/1**
01-2 **6** *1 3/4* **Perfect Act**[120] [26] 5-9-0 **78**.. LukeMorris 4 74
(C G Cox) *dwlt: hld up: effrt on ins over 2f: sn chsng ldrs: wknd fnl 150yds* **5/2**[1]
-502 **7** *2 1/2* **Lucky Leigh**[7] [1588] 4-8-10 **74**.......................................(v) KierenFallon 1 62
(M R Channon) *chsd ldrs: drvn over 2f out: lost pl over 1f out* **10/1**
1m 12.28s (-0.82) **Going Correction** -0.05s/f (Stan) 7 Ran SP% **112.4**
Speed ratings (Par 102): **103,100,100,99,99 97,93**
toteswingers:1&2:£9.50, 1&3:£5.20, 2&3:£14.70 CSF £101.89 TOTE £5.50: £1.60, £12.40; EX 164.60 Place 6 £211.30; Place 5 £60.55.
Owner Robin Stevens **Bred** D R Tucker **Trained** Royston, Herts
FOCUS
Few progressive sorts but a fair fillies' handicap run at just a reasonable gallop, and another race on the card that saw those up with the pace hold the edge. The winner edged from the centre towards the far rail in the closing stages. The form is rated around the third.
Lucky Leigh Official explanation: jockey said filly banged its head on the gate and never travelled
T/Plt: £347.80 to a £1 stake. Pool: £55,876.42, 117.25 winning tickets. T/Qpdt: £102.90 to a £1 stake. Pool: £3,276.04, 23.55 winning tickets. WG

WARWICK (L-H)
Monday, May 3

OFFICIAL GOING: Soft (6.9)
Wind: Strong against Weather: Sunshine and showers

1771 KNOWLE APPRENTICE H'CAP (DIV I) 1m 22y
2:10 (2:12) (Class 6) (0-60,60) 4-Y-O+ **£1,706** (£503; £252) **Stalls** Low

Form RPR
0-00 **1** **Shared Moment (IRE)**[27] [1141] 4-9-0 **55**..........................(p) AmyRyan 9 65
(J Gallagher) *hld up: hdwy and c stands' side 2f out: rdn to ld and edgd lft ins fnl f: r.o* **13/2**[3]
60-4 **2** *nk* **Moon Lightning (IRE)**[28] [1129] 4-9-4 **59**..................... AshleyMorgan 12 68
(M H Tompkins) *hld up in tch: racd keenly: c stands' side over 2f out: led over 1f out: rdn and hdd ins fnl f: r.o* **9/2**[2]
000- **3** *1 1/2* **Touch Of Style (IRE)**[201] [6770] 6-8-5 **46** oh1................ RossAtkinson 8 52
(Matthew Salaman) *hld up: hdwy and swtchd rt to stands' side over 2f out: rdn over 1f out: r.o* **11/1**
-000 **4** *2 3/4* **Bahkov (IRE)**[13] [1437] 4-8-5 **46** oh1................................(t) SimonPearce 1 46
(Andrew Turnell) *chsd ldrs: rdn over 1f out: styd on same pce fnl f* **9/1**
2026 **5** *hd* **Castle Myth (USA)**[19] [1293] 4-8-11 **57**........................... DaleSwift(5) 3 56
(B Ellison) *hld up: rdn over 2f out: hdwy over 1f out: no imp fnl f* **7/2**[1]
4600 **6** *1* **Escardo (GER)**[13] [1462] 7-8-8 **54**.............................(b[1]) JamesRogers(5) 4 51
(D G Bridgwater) *sn pushed along in rr: rdn over 3f out: styd on ins fnl f: nvr nrr* **33/1**
4330 **7** *1* **Black Draft**[23] [1235] 8-8-5 **46** oh1.................................... SophieDoyle 7 41
(B Forsey) *chsd ldrs: rdn and edgd rt 2f out: wknd fnl f* **14/1**
2-00 **8** *hd* **Under Fire (IRE)**[70] [661] 7-8-9 **50**................................... KierenFox 10 44
(A W Carroll) *chsd ldr: rdn and ev ch over 1f out: wknd ins fnl f* **9/2**[2]
505- **9** *nk* **Abu Dubai (IRE)**[311] [2681] 4-8-12 **60**.................... JonathanHinch(7) 6 53
(J A Glover) *led: plld hrd: rdn and hdd over 1f out: wknd fnl f* **17/2**
5000 **10** *3 1/4* **Easy Wonder (GER)**[54] [847] 5-8-3 **47** oh1 ow1.....(b) TobyAtkinson(3) 2 33
(I A Wood) *plld hrd and prom: rdn over 3f out: wknd over 1f out* **25/1**
1m 42.28s (1.28) **Going Correction** +0.125s/f (Good) 10 Ran SP% **114.2**
Speed ratings (Par 101): **98,97,96,93,93 92,91,91,90,87**
toteswingers:1&2:£7.00, 1&3:£18.10, 2&3:£12.80 CSF £35.07 CT £258.88 TOTE £8.70: £2.60, £2.10, £4.30; EX 42.00.
Owner Mark Benton **Bred** Mrs E R Cantillon **Trained** Chastleton, Oxon
FOCUS
A moderate handicap for apprentice riders, run at a fair pace. There was a divided opinion between the jockeys from the turn into the home straight. The far side was shunned as most wanted to come more towards the stands' side and that proved the best place to be. This was the weaker and slower of the two divisions. The winner was seemingly back to her best.

1772 KNOWLE APPRENTICE H'CAP (DIV II) 1m 22y
2:40 (2:41) (Class 6) (0-60,60) 4-Y-O+ **£1,706** (£503; £252) **Stalls** Low

Form RPR
3-52 **1** **Whipma Whopma Gate (IRE)**[16] [1396] 5-8-12 **58**......(v[1]) NeilFarley(5) 8 70
(D Carroll) *a.p: swtchd rt wl over 1f out: led 1f out: rdn and hung lft ins fnl f: r.o wl* **5/2**[1]
6005 **2** *4* **Grey Boy (GER)**[86] [442] 9-8-4 **52**........................... GeorgeDowning(7) 1 55
(A W Carroll) *chsd ldrs: rdn and ev ch over 1f out: styd on same pce ins fnl f* **10/1**
-000 **3** *1/2* **My Jeanie (IRE)**[45] [940] 6-8-5 **46** oh1........................... SophieDoyle 11 48
(J C Fox) *hld up: rdn over 2f out: hdwy over 1f out: styd on u.p* **40/1**
3200 **4** *nk* **Libre**[10] [1507] 10-8-5 **46** oh1.. AshleyMorgan 6 48
(F Jordan) *hld up: hdwy and c stands' side over 2f out: hmpd wl over 1f out: rdn and hung lft ent fnl f: styd on* **18/1**
105- **5** *2* **Fitz**[200] [6787] 4-9-2 **57**...(p) RossAtkinson 9 54
(Matthew Salaman) *hld up: hdwy and c stands' side over 2f out: hmpd wl over 1f out: styd on same pce* **9/1**
0203 **6** *nse* **Having A Ball**[18] [1323] 6-8-10 **51**................................... AmyRyan 12 48
(P D Cundell) *hld up: rdn: swtchd lft and hdwy over 1f out: no ex ins fnl f* **8/1**[3]
0-10 **7** *hd* **Lady Lam**[25] [1193] 4-8-10 **54**.. TobyAtkinson(3) 4 50
(S Kirk) *chsd ldr tl led over 6f out: c towards stands' side: over 2f out: rdn and hdd 1f out: wknd ins fnl f* **8/1**[3]
6-00 **8** *1 1/4* **Ymir**[26] [1170] 4-8-13 **54**...(p) KierenFox 7 47
(M J Attwater) *led: hdd over 6f out: chsd ldrs: rdn over 1f out: wknd ins fnl f* **9/1**
6042 **9** *1/2* **Count Ceprano (IRE)**[26] [1171] 6-9-1 **56**......................... SimonPearce 3 48
(J Pearce) *hld up: hdwy u.p over 1f out: wknd ins fnl f* **9/2**[2]
66-0 **10** *1/2* **Komreyev Star**[81] [503] 8-8-3 **47** oh1 ow1 .... JohnCavanagh(3) 2 38
(R E Peacock) *chsd ldr: rdn and ev ch over 2f out: wknd over 1f out* **16/1**
4000 **11** *3/4* **Machinate (USA)**[25] [1193] 8-8-0 **46** oh1................. MatthewLawson(5) 5 35
(W M Brisbourne) *s.s: hld up: rdn over 2f out: n.d* **28/1**
1m 41.76s (0.76) **Going Correction** +0.125s/f (Good) 11 Ran SP% **115.1**
Speed ratings (Par 101): **101,97,96,96,94 94,93,92,92,91 90**
toteswingers:1&2:£6.00, 1&3:£22.40, 2&3:£65.00 CSF £27.84 CT £807.73 TOTE £2.80: £1.30, £2.70, £13.30; EX 30.60.
Owner John Seed & Mrs Angela Seed **Bred** Pat Roche **Trained** Sledmere, E Yorks
FOCUS
This was run at a stronger pace than the first division and the winner was far too strong, although he did not have much to beat.
Count Ceprano(IRE) Official explanation: jockey said gelding was unsuited by the soft ground

1773 EUROPEAN BREEDERS' FUND PRIMROSE MAIDEN FILLIES' STKS 5f
3:10 (3:10) (Class 5) 2-Y-O **£3,626** (£1,079; £539) **Stalls** Low

Form RPR
3 **1** **Golden Shine**[18] [1324] 2-9-0 0.. AlanMunro 3 67+
(M R Channon) *led: hdd over 3f out: led again over 1f out: hung rt: shkn up and r.o* **1/8**[1]
0 **2** *2 1/4* **Dancing Tara**[16] [1375] 2-9-0 0.. PaulDoe 4 59
(P D Evans) *w wnr tl led over 3f out: rdn and hdd over 1f out: nt clr run sn after: no ex ins fnl f* **17/2**[2]
0 **3** *nk* **Alexs Rainbow (USA)**[16] [1375] 2-8-11 0....................... MartinLane(3) 5 58
(J Gallagher) *dwlt: sn pushed along in rr: hdwy and in tch 3f out: stmbld over 2f out: sn edgd rt: rdn over 1f out: styd on same pce ins fnl f* **12/1**[3]
63.32 secs (3.72) **Going Correction** +0.525s/f (Yiel) 3 Ran SP% **107.1**
Speed ratings (Par 90): **91,87,86**
CSF £1.77 TOTE £1.10; EX 1.90.
Owner Jaber Abdullah **Bred** Mickley Stud & Mr & Mrs D Leggate **Trained** West Ilsley, Berks
FOCUS
A simple task for the winner, but she was still green and only workmanlike. Very hard to rate her performance.
NOTEBOOK
Golden Shine looked nigh on impossible to oppose here and she duly shed her maiden tag, but was workmanlike in doing so. She ran a deal better than her final placing suggested on debut at Newmarket and, granted the normal improvement from that experience, a simple task awaited her here. She ran freely in a share of the lead and looked set to win nicely when shaking off the runner-up 2f out. She had to be given a smack entering the final furlong, though, and still showed distinct signs of greenness. This was just her second outing and there could be a good deal more to come as she learns about racing, with a return to quicker ground sure to be more to her liking. (op 1-7 tchd 1-6 in places)
Dancing Tara put it up to Golden Shine through the early parts and proved game once that one went on. This was a nice improvement on the level of her debut outing and she should go forward again for the run. (tchd 9-1)
Alexs Rainbow(USA) made a messy start and proved free when recovering to track her two rivals. She just looked to find the ground easy enough and it was also an improved effort from her. (op 11-1 tchd 14-1)

1774 WARWICK FOR WEDDINGS H'CAP 5f
3:40 (3:41) (Class 6) (0-60,60) 3-Y-O **£2,047** (£604; £302) **Stalls** Low

Form RPR
3463 **1** **Vilnius**[12] [1468] 3-9-0 **56**.. AlanMunro 4 59
(M R Channon) *mid-div: hdwy over 1f out: r.o to ld post* **7/2**[1]
0166 **2** *hd* **Your Gifted (IRE)**[3] [1667] 3-9-1 **57**.......................... DanielTudhope 11 59
(Patrick Morris) *prom: rdn to ld and hung lft fr over 1f out: hdd post* **7/1**[3]
4543 **3** *1/2* **Annia Galeria (IRE)**[13] [1444] 3-8-8 **50**......................(b) EddieAhern 10 50
(C A Dwyer) *chsd ldr tl led 3f out: rdn and hung rt wl over 1f out: sn hdd and hung lft: r.o* **9/1**
3-30 **4** *nk* **Sharp Shoes**[13] [1456] 3-9-0 **56**.. MartinDwyer 7 55+
(Mrs A Duffield) *hmpd s: hld up: hdwy u.p fr over 1f out: edgd lft ins fnl f: r.o* **8/1**
4200 **5** *1/2* **Sandy Toes**[26] [1162] 3-7-13 **46** oh1.............................. SimonPearce(5) 6 44
(J A Glover) *wnt rt s: hld up: rdn over 1f out: r.o ins fnl f: nt rch ldrs* **12/1**
500 **6** *nk* **Gemma's Delight (IRE)**[24] [1205] 3-8-9 **51** ow1.................. ShaneKelly 8 48
(J W Unett) *hmpd s: chsd ldrs: outpcd over 1f out: r.o ins fnl f* **16/1**
0-53 **7** *3/4* **Ishipink**[9] [1535] 3-7-13 **46**.. AmyBaker(5) 12 40
(R J Hodges) *led 2f: chsd ldrs: rdn whn hmpd over 1f out: no ex wl ins fnl f* **12/1**
1630 **8** *nse* **Exceed Power**[16] [1390] 3-8-11 **60**.................................... LauraPike(7) 9 54
(D M Simcock) *s.s: bhd: r.o ins fnl f: nrst fin* **10/1**
4200 **9** *2 1/4* **Lets Move It**[9] [1535] 3-8-2 **47**...(v) MartinLane(3) 2 33
(D Shaw) *prom: drvn along over 3f out: wknd fnl f* **11/2**[2]
62.60 secs (3.00) **Going Correction** +0.525s/f (Yiel) 9 Ran SP% **101.6**
Speed ratings (Par 97): **97,96,95,95,94 94,92,92,89**
toteswingers:1&2:£4.50, 1&3:£4.90, 2&3:£9.90 CSF £20.99 CT £124.51 TOTE £3.70: £1.50, £1.50, £2.30; EX 23.30.
Owner P Trant **Bred** P Trant & Mike Channon Bloodstock Limited **Trained** West Ilsley, Berks
■ Saucy Girl was withdrawn (9/2, unruly in the stalls). R4 applies, deduct 15p in the £.
■ Stewards' Enquiry : Eddie Ahern caution: careless riding
FOCUS
A weak handicap and some dubious types. The form is rated around the winner

1775 QUANTUM MANUFACTURING FILLIES' H'CAP 7f 26y
4:10 (4:13) (Class 5) (0-70,70) 3-Y-O+ **£2,590** (£770; £385; £192) **Stalls** Low

Form RPR
05-3 **1** **Candleshoe (IRE)**[12] [1476] 3-8-13 **67**................................... PatDobbs 1 72
(R Hannon) *sn pushed along to chsd ldr: rdn over 2f out: r.o to ld nr fin* **6/4**[1]
4-30 **2** *hd* **Light Dubai (IRE)**[11] [1489] 4-9-6 **62**............................... AlanMunro 5 70
(M R Channon) *chsd ldrs: led over 1f out: sn rdn: hdd nr fin* **4/1**[3]

11- **3** *hd* **Ela Gorrie Mou**[233] 5869 4-9-13 **69**.............................. EddieCreighton 3 76+
(P Charalambous) *s.i.s: sn pushed along in rr: hdwy over 1f out: rdn and ev ch ins fnl f: r.o* **11/2**

10-3 **4** *2 3/4* **Simla Sunset (IRE)**[21] 1258 4-10-0 **70**.......................(t) EddieAhern 10 70
(J R Gask) *hld up: hdwy 2f out: rdn 1f out: no ex wl ins fnl f* **7/2**[2]

001- **5** *1 3/4* **Empress Leizu (IRE)**[147] 7669 3-8-1 **60**.......................... AmyBaker(5) 8 51
(A W Carroll) *chsd ldrs: rdn over 2f out: styd on same pce fr over 1f out* **25/1**

00-0 **6** *1 1/4* **Miss Hollybell**[21] 1258 4-9-9 **68**....................................... MartinLane(3) 9 60
(J Gallagher) *hld up in tch: plld hrd: outpcd over 2f out: rdn and nt clr run over 1f out: kpt on ins fnl f* **20/1**

60-0 **7** *1 3/4* **Ken's Girl**[21] 1258 6-9-9 **65**.. ShaneKelly 6 52
(W S Kittow) *led: shkn up 3f out: rdn: hdd and edgd rt over 1f out: wknd ins fnl f* **9/1**

0000 **8** *3 1/4* **Affirmatively**[23] 1235 5-8-9 **56** oh11............................... TobyAtkinson(5) 4 34
(A W Carroll) *hld up: effrt over 2f out: wknd over 1f out* **40/1**

1m 25.7s (1.10) **Going Correction** +0.125s/f (Good)
WFA 3 from 4yo+ 12lb 8 Ran SP% **117.3**
Speed ratings (Par 100): **98,97,97,94,92 90,88,85**
toteswingers:1&2:£2.40, 1&3:£2.90, 2&3:£3.30 CSF £7.87 CT £26.17 TOTE £2.10: £1.60, £1.10, £1.30; EX 9.60.
Owner Mrs J Wood **Bred** Tullamaine Castle Stud **Trained** East Everleigh, Wilts
■ Stewards' Enquiry : Alan Munro two-day ban: used whip with excessive frequency without giving filly time to respond (May 17-18)

FOCUS
A modest fillies' handicap which saw a tight three-way finish. The winner built on her Epsom run with the second rated to her handicap best.

1776 RACING UK H'CAP (FOR THE COVENTRY CUP) 7f 26y
4:40 (4:41) (Class 4) (0-80,80) 3-Y-O **£5,828** (£1,734; £866; £432) **Stalls** Low

Form RPR

152- **1** **Masked Dance (IRE)**[184] 7168 3-9-2 **78**..........................(p) AlanMunro 8 89
(K A Ryan) *mde all: rdn and hung rt over 1f out: styd on gamely* **8/1**

441- **2** *hd* **Gene Autry (USA)**[266] 4851 3-9-0 **76**.................................... PatDobbs 4 87
(R Hannon) *hld up in tch: chsd wnr over 2f out: rdn and ev ch fr over 1f out: r.o* **9/4**[1]

4-03 **3** *3 1/2* **Yes Chef**[13] 1442 3-8-11 **73**.. JerryO'Dwyer 2 74
(J Gallagher) *sowly into stride: hld up: hdwy 2f out: sn rdn and edgd rt: styd on same pce fnl f* **12/1**

04-4 **4** *2* **Mon Brav**[16] 1376 3-9-4 **80**.. DavidNolan 7 76
(D Carroll) *prom: rdn over 2f out: wknd fnl f* **9/2**[2]

240- **5** *1 1/4* **Onyx Of Arabia (IRE)**[198] 6842 3-8-10 **72**....................... MartinDwyer 6 65
(B J Meehan) *chsd ldrs: rdn over 3f out: wknd over 1f out* **8/1**

5-1 **6** *1 1/4* **Maid In Heaven (IRE)**[20] 1275 3-9-0 **76**........................... ShaneKelly 14 65
(W R Swinburn) *hld up: hdwy over 2f out: wknd fnl f* **7/1**[3]

-466 **7** *5* **Kumbeshwar**[18] 1334 3-8-12 **79**.................................. RichardEvans(5) 3 55
(P D Evans) *sn chsng wnr: rdn over 2f out: wknd over 1f out* **10/1**

30-5 **8** *2* **Silver Symphony (IRE)**[11] 1487 3-8-11 **80**.............. DuilioDaSilva(7) 13 50
(P F I Cole) *chsd ldrs: rdn over 2f out: wknd over 1f out* **33/1**

4-53 **9** *6* **Deely Plaza**[9] 1514 3-8-0 **67**.. SimonPearce(5) 1 21
(J A Glover) *mid-div: lost pl 1/2-way: sn bhd* **12/1**

415- **10** *1 1/2* **Many A Slip**[248] 5399 3-8-8 **73**.. MartinLane(3) 11 23
(J L Dunlop) *s.i.s: hld up: hdwy 1/2-way: rdn and wknd 2f out* **16/1**

1m 24.54s (-0.06) **Going Correction** +0.125s/f (Good) 10 Ran SP% **117.0**
Speed ratings (Par 101): **105,104,100,98,97 95,89,87,80,79**
toteswingers:1&2:£4.90, 1&3:£10.00, 2&3:£8.90 CSF £26.40 CT £226.14 TOTE £9.50: £2.40, £1.20, £3.70; EX 37.60.
Owner Mrs L D Edwards **Bred** Canice Farrell Jnr **Trained** Hambleton, N Yorks

FOCUS
A good handicap for the class.
Maid In Heaven(IRE) Official explanation: jockey said, regarding running and riding, he was able to settle the filly in behind early and was tracking leaders as they turned for home, however when asked to quicken it found little, changed its legs and would not have finished closer for more vigorous riding approaching line.

1777 MAY CONTRACTORS ANNIVERSARY SUPPORTING NSPCC MEDIAN AUCTION MAIDEN FILLIES' STKS 1m 22y
5:10 (5:13) (Class 5) 3-5-Y-O **£2,590** (£770; £385; £192) **Stalls** Low

Form RPR

020- **1** **Lost Horizon (IRE)**[203] 6730 3-8-12 77.................................. PatDobbs 4 62+
(R Hannon) *chsd ldr: rdn over 2f out: led over 1f out: r.o wl* **7/4**[2]

2-2 **2** *1 1/4* **Cabal**[26] 1164 3-8-9 0.......................... Louis-PhilippeBeuzelin(3) 5 59+
(Sir Michael Stoute) *nrly wnt down as the stalls opened and lost several l: hdwy into 4th pl over 6f out: rdn to go 3rd over 1f out: r.o to go 2nd post: nt trble wnr* **4/6**[1]

3560 **3** *shd* **Hathaway (IRE)**[83] 475 3-8-12 48.. ShaneKelly 1 59
(W M Brisbourne) *led at stdy pce: rdn to qckn over 2f out: hdd over 1f out: styd on: lost 2nd post* **50/1**

00- **4** *6* **Astrovenus**[188] 7096 3-8-7 0..................................... AshleyMorgan(5) 2 45
(M H Tompkins) *chsd ldrs: hung rt over 3f out: sn rdn: wknd over 1f out* **11/1**[3]

0/ **5** *8* **Born To Frill**[399] 3452 5-9-4 0.. DaleSwift(7) 3 27
(Miss L C Siddall) *hld up: rdn and wknd over 2f out* **66/1**

1m 48.01s (7.01) **Going Correction** +0.125s/f (Good)
WFA 3 from 5yo 13lb 5 Ran SP% **108.1**
Speed ratings (Par 100): **69,67,67,61,53**
CSF £3.10 TOTE £2.60: £1.40, £1.10; EX 2.90.
Owner Mrs J Wood **Bred** Seminole Horse Trader Inc **Trained** East Everleigh, Wilts

FOCUS
This was run at a crawl and the third limits the form, but she was able to dictate and is flattered. The first pair were unable to show their form.

1778 BETFAIR H'CAP 1m 4f 134y
5:40 (5:40) (Class 5) (0-70,70) 3-Y-O **£2,590** (£770; £385; £192) **Stalls** Low

Form RPR

05-3 **1** **Blinka Me**[27] 1145 3-7-13 **56** oh1.................................. SimonPearce(5) 3 60
(M H Tompkins) *led: hdd 2f out: rallied to ld 1f out: hung rt wl ins fnl f: jst hld on* **17/2**

535- **2** *nk* **Gordon Flash**[227] 6067 3-8-13 **65**.. PatDobbs 5 69+
(R Hannon) *chsd wnr over 2f: remained handy: rdn and swtchd rt over 1f out: r.o wl towards fin: nt quite get up* **4/1**[2]

20-4 **3** *2* **Rose Alba (IRE)**[21] 1261 3-8-12 **64**...................................... EddieAhern 1 65
(J L Dunlop) *chsd wnr 10f out: led 2f out: sn rdn: hdd 1f out: styd on same pce* **7/4**[1]

4-66 **4** *2 3/4* **Head Hunted**[46] 922 3-8-8 **63**.. MartinLane(3) 2 59
(D M Simcock) *hld up: rdn over 2f out: styd on: nt trble ldrs* **11/2**[3]

41-0 **5** *1 1/2* **Sounds Of Thunder**[25] 1189 3-9-4 **70**................................ ShaneKelly 6 64
(H J L Dunlop) *prom: rdn 3f out: wknd over 1f out* **11/1**

00-3 **6** *1 1/4* **Queen Of Wands**[14] 1432 3-9-1 **67**................................. RobertHavlin 4 59
(H Morrison) *hld up: rdn over 2f out: wknd over 1f out* **4/1**[2]

2m 49.94s (5.34) **Going Correction** +0.125s/f (Good) 6 Ran SP% **110.6**
Speed ratings (Par 99): **88,87,86,84,83 83**
toteswingers:1&2:£4.90, 1&3:£3.10, 2&3:£2.50 CSF £40.35 TOTE £13.00: £6.10, £1.20; EX 47.90 Place 6 £27.50; Place 5 £7.15.
Owner Trevor Benton **Bred** Lordship Stud **Trained** Newmarket, Suffolk

FOCUS
A moderate handicap, run at an uneven pace set by the winner. This is not form to take too positively or literally.
T/Plt: £18.60 to a £1 stake. Pool: £39,881.24, 1,564.41 winning tickets. T/Qpdt: £3.10 to a £1 stake. Pool: £2,139.29, 495.02 winning tickets. CR

1577 WINDSOR (R-H)
Monday, May 3

OFFICIAL GOING: Soft (good to soft in places) changing to good to soft after race 2 (2.55)
Stands rail dolled out 7yds at 6f down to 3yds at winning post. Top end dolled out 6yards from innermost line adding 22yds to races of 1m and over.
Wind: Brisk ahead Weather: Sunny intervals

1779 BETFAIR RACING EXCELLENCE APPRENTICE TRAINING SERIES H'CAP 6f
2:25 (2:25) (Class 5) (0-75,75) 4-Y-O+ **£2,729** (£806; £403) **Stalls** High

Form RPR

5-50 **1** **Poppanan (USA)**[14] 1428 4-8-5 **66**........................... AdamBeschizza(5) 3 78
(S Dow) *s.i.s: sn rcvrd and racd centre crse: chal 2f out: led sn after: drvn and edgd lft wl ins fnl f: readily* **4/1**[2]

-520 **2** *1 1/4* **Kingswinford (IRE)**[16] 1374 4-8-13 **74**.................. MatthewCosham(5) 2 82
(P D Evans) *chsd ldrs towards centre crse: slt ld 2f out: sn hdd: styd chsng wnr and edgd rt 1f out: readily hld whn wnt lft wl ins fnl f* **7/2**[1]

44 **3** *3 1/4* **Ejeed (USA)**[19] 1304 5-8-2 **61**.....................................(p) RichardRowe(3) 6 59
(Miss Z C Davison) *chsd ldrs: towards centre crse: rdn 1/2-way: styd on same pce fr over 1f out* **11/1**

2310 **4** *3/4* **Hip Hip Hooray**[19] 1304 4-8-9 **65**.. CharlesEddery 8 60
(L A Dace) *towards rr: pushed along 1/2-way: styd on fnl 2f but nvr a threat* **11/1**

540- **5** *2* **Cape Melody**[193] 6964 4-8-13 **72**.. RyanPowell(3) 14 61
(H Morrison) *wnt lft s: chsd ldrs towards centre crse: wknd ins fnl f* **10/1**

0000 **6** *1 1/4* **Simple Rhythm**[17] 1364 4-8-10 **73**.................................... JoshCrane(7) 1 58
(J Ryan) *w ldr: upsides and u.p 2f out: wknd fnl f* **14/1**

55-0 **7** *nk* **Hustle (IRE)**[14] 1428 5-8-10 **73**.................................. JulieCumine(7) 13 57
(Miss Gay Kelleway) *bmpd s and in rr: racd towards stands' side: sme prog and edgd lft ins fnl f* **14/1**

0262 **8** *1* **Westwood**[21] 1258 5-8-13 **69**.. RyanClark 7 50
(D Haydn Jones) *slt ld in centre crse: narrowly hdd 2f out: styd wl there tl wknd fnl f* **9/2**[3]

206- **9** *1/2* **Gallego**[215] 6392 8-8-5 **68**... LeonnaMayor(7) 5 47
(R J Price) *s.i.s: outpcd* **33/1**

230- **10** *1 1/4* **Sometsuke**[200] 6798 4-9-0 **70**... RosieJessop 12 45
(P J Makin) *bmpd s: racd stands' side: outpcd most of way* **12/1**

110- **11** *23* **Mythical Blue (IRE)**[206] 6647 4-9-2 **75**........................... ShaneRyan(3) 15 —
(J M Bradley) *wnt lft s: racd stands' side and spd 3f: wknd qckly fr 2f out: eased whn no ch fnl f* **13/2**

1m 14.93s (1.93) **Going Correction** +0.40s/f (Good) 11 Ran SP% **123.5**
Speed ratings (Par 103): **103,101,97,96,93 91,91,89,89,87 56**
toteswingers:1&2:£38.70, 1&3:£26.20, 2&3:£40.30 CSF £19.47 CT £148.80 TOTE £7.10: £2.00, £1.50, £4.10; EX 30.00 TRIFECTA Not won..
Owner Joe Cole **Bred** Liberation Farm And Brandywine Farm Llc **Trained** Epsom, Surrey
■ Stewards' Enquiry : Adam Beschizza one-day ban: careless riding (May 17)

FOCUS
A low-grade sprint handicap and the majority of runners came down the centre of the course. The runner-up is a pretty solid guide to the form.
Hustle(IRE) Official explanation: jockey said gelding suffered interference at start

1780 IT DOESN'T GET BETTER THAN BARBADOS H'CAP 1m 2f 7y
2:55 (2:56) (Class 4) (0-85,85) 4-Y-O+ **£3,151** (£3,151; £722; £360) **Stalls** Low

Form RPR

43-6 **1** **Putra One (IRE)**[16] 1388 4-8-11 **78**.............................. PhilipRobinson 3 86
(M A Jarvis) *chsd ldrs and t.k.h early: wnt 2nd 2f out: drvn and upsides thrght fnl f to force dead-heat* **9/2**[2]

16-0 **1** *dht* **Tinshu (IRE)**[16] 1378 4-9-1 **82**.. DarryllHolland 1 90
(D Haydn Jones) *chsd ldrs: wnt 2nd 5f out: led over 4f out: hrd rdn fr 2f out: jnd thrght fnl f: hld on all out for dead-heat* **14/1**

5000 **3** *1/2* **Ramona Chase**[12] 1474 5-8-3 **75**.......................(t) JemmaMarshall(5) 7 82
(M J Attwater) *chsd ldr tl 4f out: outpcd over 2f out: styd on again fnl f to cl on ldng duo nr fin but a hld* **33/1**

441- **4** *1* **At Wits End**[205] 6673 4-8-8 **75**.. KirstyMilczarek 8 80
(J A R Toller) *in tch: chsd ldrs fr 5f out: styd on fnl 2f and gng on cl home but nt rch ldng trio* **14/1**

6-31 **5** *3/4* **Aspro Mavro (IRE)**[28] 1132 4-8-11 **78**................................ RobertHavlin 2 82
(J H M Gosden) *in tch: awkward bnd 6f out: drvn to chse ldrs fr 4f out: styd on same pce fnl 2f* **4/1**[1]

650- **6** *2* **Dubai Crest**[196] 6907 4-9-2 **83**... JimmyFortune 6 83
(Mrs A J Perrett) *in rr but in tch: pushed along and hdwy fr over 2f out but nvr in contention* **9/1**

11-0 **7** *2 1/2* **Caster Sugar (USA)**[16] 1379 4-9-0 **81**........................ RichardHughes 11 76
(R Hannon) *in rr: pushed along and sme prog 3f out: nvr rchd ldrs and btn fnl 2f* **10/1**

1115 **8** *1* **Franco Is My Name**[26] 1161 4-9-4 **85**............................. RyanMoore 10 78
(P R Hedger) *in rr: rdn and plld to outside over 2f out: hung lft sn after and wknd qckly* **7/1**

343- **9** *1* **Wiggy Smith**[261] 5028 11-8-13 **80**...................................... DaneO'Neill 9 71
(H Candy) *in rr: rdn and hdwy to get in bhd ldrs 3f out: wknd fr 2f out* **12/1**

6112 **10** *2* **Kidlat**[9] 1513 5-9-1 **82**.. AdamKirby 4 69
(A Bailey) *sn led: hdd over 4f out: wknd ins fnl 2f* **17/2**

2/0- **11** *14* **Nizhoni Dancer**[325] 2890 4-8-10 **77** ..... TedDurcan 5 36
(C F Wall) *in rr: rdn and dropped away 3f out* **5/1**[3]

2m 9.52s (0.82) **Going Correction** +0.225s/f (Good) **11** Ran SP% **120.9**
Speed ratings (Par 105): **105,105,104,103,103 101,99,98,98,96 85**WIN: Putra One £3.10 Tinshu £8.50 PL: Putra One £3.10, Tinshu £3.80, Ramona Chase £7.50 EX: PO/TS £54.40 TS/PO £73.20 CSF: PO/TS £34.02 TS/PO £39.09 Tricast: PO/TS/RC £938.51 TS/PO/RC £1,042.67. toteswingers:PO&TS:£30.60, TS&RC:Not won, PO&RC:£43.70 CT £27 TOTE £Owner: £H R H Sultan Ahmad Shah, £Bred, £Airlie Stud, £TrainedNewmarket, Suffolk.

Owner Llewelyn, Runeckles **Bred** Mrs M L Parry & P M Steele-Mortimer **Trained** Efail Isaf, Rhondda C Taff

FOCUS
The whole field went far side in what was a tight handicap, and the front pair were unable to be separated at the line. The pace was just a steady one. Putra One posted a small personal best with Tinshu rated to her AW form.

Nizhoni Dancer Official explanation: trainer had no explanation for the poor form shown

1781 VIRGIN HOLIDAYS H'CAP — 1m 67y
3:25 (3:25) (Class 3) (0-90,90) 3-Y-O **£7,771** (£2,312; £1,155; £577) **Stalls** High

Form RPR

512- **1** **Constant Contact**[212] 6471 3-9-1 **87** ..... JimmyFortune 2 93
(A M Balding) *sn led: rdn and hdd over 2f out: styd chsng ldr and rallied u.p to chal fnl 120yds: led last stride* **7/2**[3]

31-6 **2** *nse* **Invincible Soul (IRE)**[10] 1497 3-8-12 **84** ..... RichardHughes 4 90
(R Hannon) *stdd s: in rr but wl in tch: drvn and qcknd to ld over 2f out: rdn over 1f out: jnd fnl 120yds: hdd last stride* **11/4**[2]

210 **3** *3 1/4* **Al Farahidi (USA)**[20] 1279 3-8-13 **85** ..... AdrianNicholls 7 84
(M Johnston) *t.k.h: trckd wnr tl wl over 2f out: rdn and hld whn hung bdly lft thrght fnl f* **8/1**

16- **4** *3/4* **Aerodynamic (IRE)**[317] 3138 3-9-4 **90** ..... DaneO'Neill 6 87
(Pat Eddery) *stdd s: hld up in rr but in tch: drvn and hdwy 2f out: nvr quite on terms and wknd appr fnl f* **4/1**

411- **5** *9* **Centigrade (IRE)**[226] 6088 3-9-3 **89** ..... MichaelHills 5 65
(W J Haggas) *hld up: trckd ldrs in 3rd: shkn up over 2f out: no imp and sn btn: collapsed fatally after line* **9/4**[1]

1m 47.11s (2.41) **Going Correction** +0.225s/f (Good) **5** Ran SP% **110.8**
Speed ratings (Par 103): **96,95,92,91,82**
CSF £13.45 TOTE £5.40: £1.60, £2.30; EX 12.40.

Owner Kingsclere Racing CLub **Bred** Kingsclere Stud **Trained** Kingsclere, Hants

FOCUS
This had the look of a decent 3-y-o handicap. The time was slower than the following maiden but the form is rated on the positive side.

NOTEBOOK
Constant Contact, narrowly denied off 2lb lower on his handicap debut last October, always seemed likely to improve for 1m this season, and he showed excellent battling qualities to get back past the runner-up, Jimmy Fortune being seen at his absolute best. He very much had the run of things, but the front pair were over 3l clear at the line, and he remains open to further progress. (op 5-1)

Invincible Soul(IRE), in need of the run when only sixth in the Esher Cup on his reappearance, moved up nicely and went on over 2f out, but he couldn't get away from the persistent winner, and just lost out in the final stride. This effort showed him to be a useful handicapper and it's not hard to see him making further progress back on better ground, with him looking likely to stay 1m2f at some stage. (op 5-2 tchd 9-4 and 3-1 in a place)

Al Farahidi(USA) ran too badly to be true on his recent handicap debut at Yarmouth, but he had earlier looked good in winning his maiden, and this was more in keeping with that earlier promise. He did hang under pressure, but faster ground is going to suit in future, and he remains capable of better. (op 13-2 tchd 9-1 in a place)

Aerodynamic(IRE), off since finishing sixth in the Chesham at Royal Ascot, came in for good late support, but he never got into it having been held up in last and found an opening mark of 90 beyond him. It's possible he will improve for this, but he needs to. (op 13-2 tchd 7-1)

Centigrade(IRE), who had won his last two starts at two and was expected to make into a smart handicapper this season, tragically collapsed and died of a heart attack. (op 15-8 tchd 13-8)

1782 ALMOND RESORTS PREMIER ALL INCLUSIVE MEDIAN AUCTION MAIDEN STKS — 1m 67y
3:55 (3:55) (Class 5) 3-4-Y-O **£2,729** (£806; £403) **Stalls** High

Form RPR

24-2 **1** **Suited And Booted (IRE)**[6] 1590 3-9-1 78 ..... RichardHughes 4 79+
(R Hannon) *trckd ldrs: chal 2f out: sn led: drvn and asserted ins fnl f: readily* **6/4**[1]

0 **2** *5* **Distant Waters**[17] 1358 3-8-10 0 ..... DaneO'Neill 7 61
(A P Jarvis) *s.i.s: in rr: hdwy over 3f out: styd on fnl 2f to take wl hld 3rd cl home: fin 3rd, plcd 2nd*

6 **3** *1/2* **New Code**[18] 1325 3-9-1 0 ..... DarryllHolland 9 65
(W R Muir) *chsd ldrs: drvn and upsides 3f out: outpcd 2f out: wknd over 1f out: lost wl hld 3rd cl home: fin 4th, plcd 3rd* **14/1**[3]

20-4 **4** *6* **Yarra River**[8] 1542 3-9-1 80 ..... (v[1]) JimmyFortune 6 51
(A M Balding) *sn led: hung lft bnd over 5f out: jnd over 2f out: hdd & wknd sn after: fin 5th, plcd 4th* **11/4**[2]

403- **5** *1 1/2* **Cheers Big Ears (IRE)**[189] 7069 4-10-0 53 ..... GeorgeBaker 11 51
(R J Price) *in rr: sme hdwy fr 2f out: edgd lft fnl f: nvr in contention* **16/1**

0-00 **6** *3 1/4* **Bibiana Bay**[75] 583 3-8-10 45 ..... KirstyMilczarek 3 35
(B I Case) *chsd ldrs: ever ch 3f out: wknd over 2f out* **100/1**

0 **7** *3 3/4* **Barberhoney**[14] 1431 3-8-10 0 ..... SimonWhitworth 1 27
(J R Jenkins) *t.k.h: in tch to 1/2-way* **25/1**

00- **8** *1/2* **Calm And Serene (USA)**[200] 6786 3-8-10 0 ..... TedDurcan 12 26
(Rae Guest) *a in rr* **33/1**

22- **D** *1/2* **Peponi**[133] 7829 4-10-0 0 ..... RyanMoore 10 81
(P J Makin) *hld up in rr: stdy hdwy 3f out: chal fr 2f out and stl w wnr 1f out: styd on to tl outpcd fnl 120yds: fin 2nd, disq. (prohibited substance)* **11/4**[2]

1m 46.72s (2.02) **Going Correction** +0.225s/f (Good)
WFA 3 from 4yo 13lb **9** Ran SP% **118.4**
Speed ratings (Par 103): **98,92,92,86,84 81,77,77,97**
toteswingers:1&2:£1.20, 1&3:£13.30, 2&3:£17.30 CSF £5.74 TOTE £2.80: £1.40, £1.10, £5.80; EX 7.00 Trifecta £178.70 Pool £386.43 - 1.60 winning units..

Owner R Morecombe and D Anderson **Bred** Carpet Lady Partnership **Trained** East Everleigh, Wilts

FOCUS
The front pair drew clear in what was a weak maiden overall. The form seems sound enough and the winner did not need to match his previous best.

Yarra River Official explanation: jockey said gelding ran too free

Bibiana Bay Official explanation: jockey said filly was unsuited by the good to soft ground

1783 GARRISON SAVANNAH CLASSIC H'CAP — 1m 3f 135y
4:25 (4:25) (Class 4) (0-85,86) 4-Y-0+ **£4,857** (£1,445; £722; £360) **Stalls** Low

Form RPR

-424 **1** **Hollow Green (IRE)**[20] 1282 4-8-10 **77** ..... CathyGannon 8 85
(P D Evans) *s.i.s: in rr tl hdwy fr 2f out: drvn to take slt ld over 1f out: styd on gamely whn strly chal thrght fnl f* **8/1**

41-1 **2** *1/2* **Aurorian (IRE)**[7] 1579 4-9-5 **86** 6ex ..... RichardHughes 4 93
(R Hannon) *s.i.s: in rr: gd hdwy over 2f out: edgd lft over 1f out: sn drvn to press wnr and upsides ins fnl f tl jst hld nr fin* **11/2**[2]

633- **3** *3/4* **Strathcal**[163] 7476 4-8-8 **75** ..... SteveDrowne 7 81
(H Morrison) *chsd ldrs: drvn and hung lft over 2f out: ev ch sn after and pressed ldrs: kpt on same pce ins fnl f* **20/1**

/51- **4** *1 1/2* **Grey Granite (IRE)**[347] 2199 4-8-11 **78** ..... JimmyFortune 5 81
(W Jarvis) *led: rdn over 2f out: kpt slt advantage tl hdd over 1f out: wknd ins fnl f* **8/1**

166- **5** *shd* **Norman The Great**[169] 5649 6-8-10 **77** ..... TomQueally 11 80
(A King) *in rr: effrt and edgd lft over 2f out: drvn and styd on fr over 1f out: kpt on fnl f but nvr gng to rch ldrs* **28/1**

4-02 **6** *1/2* **King's Song (IRE)**[7] 1579 4-8-7 **74** ow1 ..... RyanMoore 10 76
(Sir Michael Stoute) *towards rr tl hdwy on outside and rdn over 2f out: nvr gng pce to get into contention and wknd fnl f* **5/4**[1]

12-3 **7** *3/4* **Foxhaven**[16] 1388 8-9-1 **82** ..... DarryllHolland 9 83
(P R Chamings) *in tch: rdn to chse ldrs fr 3f out: wknd over 1f out* **7/1**[3]

142- **8** *1 1/4* **Featherweight (IRE)**[185] 7148 4-9-0 **81** ..... MichaelHills 2 80
(B W Hills) *chsd ldrs: pushed along over 3f out: ev ch ins fnl 2f: wknd qckly appr fnl f* **14/1**

260- **9** *3 1/2* **El Diego (IRE)**[206] 6634 6-8-8 **75** ..... TedDurcan 1 68
(J R Gask) *s.i.s: sn in tch: rdn ins fnl 3f: wknd ins fnl 2f* **25/1**

0/1- **10** *2 1/4* **Shimoni**[364] 1753 6-9-4 **85** ..... GeorgeBaker 3 74
(G L Moore) *chsd ldrs: rdn over 2f out: wknd qckly wl over 1f out* **16/1**

3/2- **11** *6* **Pass The Port**[422] 787 9-8-13 **80** ..... DaneO'Neill 6 59
(D Haydn Jones) *bhd most of way* **40/1**

2m 31.1s (1.60) **Going Correction** +0.225s/f (Good) **11** Ran SP% **121.6**
Speed ratings (Par 105): **103,102,102,101,101 100,100,99,97,95 91**
toteswingers:1&2:£3.60, 1&3:£42.30, 2&3:£21.50 CSF £51.15 CT £869.58 TOTE £10.90: £1.80, £2.40, £6.10; EX 60.80 Trifecta £345.40 Part won. Pool £466.77 - 0.10 winning units..

Owner Raymond N R Auld **Bred** R N Auld **Trained** Pandy, Monmouths

■ Stewards' Enquiry : Jimmy Fortune one-day ban: careless riding (May 17)

FOCUS
A fair handicap that was run at just a modest gallop. The favourite disappointed but the form makes sense at face value.

Norman The Great Official explanation: jockey said gelding hung left

Foxhaven Official explanation: jockey said gelding was denied a clear run

1784 MANGO BAY BARBADOS CLASSIC H'CAP — 5f 10y
4:55 (4:56) (Class 5) (0-70,70) 3-Y-O **£2,729** (£806; £403) **Stalls** High

Form RPR

2223 **1** **Boogie Waltzer**[16] 1390 3-8-4 **63** ..... (t) RyanClark(7) 3 71
(S C Williams) *sn trcking ldrs: led over 1f out: pushed out fnl f* **4/1**[3]

4652 **2** *1 1/4* **Tom Folan**[13] 1444 3-8-10 **62** ..... (p) DarryllHolland 5 65
(Andrew Reid) *in tch: chsd ldrs 1/2-way: wnt 2nd 1f out: styd on u.p fnl f but a hld by wnr* **6/1**

0-35 **3** *nk* **Pherousa**[18] 1316 3-8-8 **60** ..... SteveDrowne 7 62+
(M Blanshard) *in rr: drvn and hdwy over 1f out: styd on wl to take 3rd ins fnl f but nt rch ldng duo* **14/1**

-525 **4** *2 1/2* **Master Mylo (IRE)**[17] 1347 3-9-4 **70** ..... RichardHughes 10 63
(D K Ivory) *in rr: pushed along and hdwy over 1f out: styd on ins fnl f but nvr gng pce to rch ldng trio* **7/2**[2]

33-0 **5** *1* **Autocracy**[17] 1347 3-9-1 **67** ..... (b[1]) RyanMoore 2 56
(W J Haggas) *led tl hdd over 1f out: wknd ins fnl f* **9/4**[1]

4206 **6** *3/4* **Miss Kitty Grey (IRE)**[24] 1205 3-8-0 **57** ..... JemmaMarshall(5) 6 44
(J R Boyle) *in tch: hdwy and hung lft insde fnl 2f: nvr a threat after* **28/1**

-251 **7** *shd* **Flaxen Lake**[42] 962 3-9-2 **68** ..... (p) DaneO'Neill 9 54
(J M Bradley) *pressed ldrs to 1/2-way: sn btn* **12/1**

2640 **8** *nk* **Blue Neptune**[3] 1667 3-8-8 **60** ..... CathyGannon 8 45
(P D Evans) *chsd ldrs tl wknd appr fnl f* **16/1**

406- **9** *15* **Bush Master**[148] 7655 3-9-2 **68** ..... TomQueally 1 —
(J R Boyle) *easy spd: sn bhd* **20/1**

62.78 secs (2.48) **Going Correction** +0.40s/f (Good) **9** Ran SP% **115.7**
Speed ratings (Par 99): **96,94,93,89,87 86,86,86,62**
toteswingers:1&2:£7.60, 1&3:£18.40, 2&3:£6.90 CSF £28.33 CT £305.26 TOTE £5.10: £1.30, £2.80, £3.90; EX 34.50 Trifecta £231.60 Part won. Pool £312.98 - 0.74 winning units. Place 6 £208.78; Place 5 £113.23.

Owner Michael Edwards and John Parsons **Bred** Michael Edwards And John Parsons **Trained** Newmarket, Suffolk

FOCUS
Just a modest 3-y-o sprint, with the favourite disappointing. The winner looks the best guide. After an initial split, the field merged in the straight.
T/Plt: £296.00 to a £1 stake. Pool: £75,881.37, 187.10 winning tickets. T/Qpdt: £21.10 to a £1 stake. Pool: £4,865.42, 170.48 winning tickets. ST

1785 - (Foreign Racing) - See Raceform Interactive

[1243]CURRAGH (R-H)
Monday, May 3

OFFICIAL GOING: Straight course - yielding; round course - good

1786a DYLAN THOMAS EUROPEAN BREEDERS FUND TETRARCH STKS (GROUP 3) (ENTIRE COLTS & FILLIES) — 7f
2:45 (2:45) 3-Y-O **£34,513** (£10,088; £4,778; £1,592)

RPR

1 **Free Judgement (USA)**[36] 1038 3-9-1 110 ..... KJManning 5 103
(J S Bolger, Ire) *a.p: niggled along 3f out: chal and disp ld fr 1 1/2f out: gained narrow ld u.p ins fnl f: styd on wl: all out* **10/3**[2]

2 *shd* **Dynasty**[185] 7159 3-9-1 93 ..... JMurtagh 3 103+
(A P O'Brien, Ire) *sn settled towards rr: rdn to chse ldrs in 3rd 1f out: styd on wl fnl f: nt quite get to wnr* **9/2**

3 *3/4* **Zayaan**[16] 1403 3-9-1 92 ..... DPMcDonogh 7 100
(Kevin Prendergast, Ire) *in tch towards rr: 5th and prog fr 3f out: chal and disp ld 1 1/2f out: narrowly hdd ins fnl f and kpt on one pce cl home* **10/1**

4 *2* **Hacienda (IRE)**[11] 1487 3-9-1 ..... RoystonFfrench 4 95
(M Johnston) *sn towards rr: rdn in last 3f out: kpt on wout threatening fr over 1f out* **4/1**[3]

5 1 ¾ **Foolish Ambition (GER)**[22] 1244 3-8-12 97 .... WMLordan 1 87
(David Wachman, Ire) *prom: 2nd for much: no ex u.p 1 1/2f out* **7/1**

6 1 ¾ **Aznavour (IRE)**[8] 1550 3-9-1 .... FMBerry 2 86
(John M Oxx, Ire) *sn led: strly pressed and hdd 2f out: sn no ex* **3/1**[1]

7 1 ¼ **Elusive Award (USA)**[15] 1414 3-9-1 100 .... PJSmullen 6 82
(Andrew Oliver, Ire) *v.s.a: sn in tch due to slow pce: 3rd 3f out: chal and led fr 2f out: hdd 1 1/2f out: wknd* **11/1**

1m 28.88s (-1.92) **Going Correction** -0.375s/f (Firm) 7 Ran SP% **116.2**
Speed ratings: **95,94,94,91,89 87,86**
CSF £19.26 TOTE £4.30: £2.60, £2.30; DF 20.40.
Owner Mrs June Judd **Bred** Twin Hopes Farm Inc **Trained** Coolcullen, Co Carlow

FOCUS
Jim Bolger and Kevin Manning continued their decent strike rate in this Group 3 race. The sixth has been rated to his maiden form and the second, third and fourth to reasonable personal bests.

NOTEBOOK
Free Judgement(USA) provided Bolger and Manning with their third win in four years. Last season's mid-division finisher in the Dewhurst had landed a similar contest over this trip at Leopardstown but his seasonal debut effort in the 2,000 Guineas Trial at the Dublin track was disappointing. The benefit of that run and more so this better ground played to his strengths. Helped by a good ride, he did enough to just hold the staying-on Dynasty. The winner will come back for the Abu Dhabi 2,000 Guineas on May 22 according to his trainer who said "hopefully he'll get a nice bit of ground". (op 3/1 tchd 7/2)
Dynasty needed four runs before he opened his account last term and looks sure to come on a fair bit from this. Once he got going, he stayed on best of all inside the final furlong and he looks another who'll appreciate a sounder surface over this trip and longer. (op 6/1)
Zayaan had put up a decent performance at Naas last month over a furlong longer. The recent maiden winner arrived on the outer with every chance but when his rider pressed the button he was unable to make his presence felt on this step up in class. The easier ground probably did him no favours when the race unfolded. (op 10/1 tchd 12/1)
Hacienda(IRE) was fancied to keep his unbeaten record intact stepping up in class following wins at Wolverhampton and Beverley over this trip earlier in the year. Despite staying on under pressure from the rear in the closing stages, he never looked like getting in a blow. This was the first time he'd had to encounter easier underfoot conditions, and it probably didn't do him any favours. (op 3/1)
Foolish Ambition(GER) was backed at fancy prices beforehand but she dropped away after racing close to the pace for a long way. (op 8/1)
Aznavour(IRE) broke smartly to lead but, when asked to raise his game, was found wanting. Official explanation: jockey said colt ran too free early on and that today's race may have come too soon after his last run
Elusive Award(USA) had the benefit of a recent run but he lost plenty of ground at the start. He was soon back in the mix and took over up front passing the 2f pole before dropping away tamely inside the final furlong. (op 10/1)

1787a ORATORIO EUROPEAN BREEDERS FUND ATHASI STKS (GROUP 3) (F&M) 7f
3:15 (3:15) 3-Y-0+ **£43,141** (£12,610; £5,973; £1,991)

RPR

1 **Lolly For Dolly (IRE)**[29] 1106 3-8-11 .... WMLordan 9 104+
(T Stack, Ire) *sn mid-div: rdn to chal between horses 1f out: led ins fnl f and styd on wl to sn draw clr* **3/1**[1]

2 2 **Famous (IRE)**[36] 1036 3-8-11 105 .... JMurtagh 7 98+
(A P O'Brien, Ire) *sn trckd ldrs: rdn 1/2-way: chal and on terms 1f out: hdd and kpt on same pce ins fnl f* **9/2**[2]

3 1 ¼ **Duchess Of Foxland (IRE)**[36] 1036 3-8-11 100 .... EJMcNamara 5 95
(Mark L Fagan, Ire) *sn chsd ldrs: 6th 1/2-way: chal u.p and almost on terms 1f out: no imp and kpt on same pce ins fnl f* **5/1**[3]

4 shd **Miss Laa Di Da**[36] 1036 3-8-11 87 .... PJSmullen 10 94
(Noel Meade, Ire) *sn trckd ldrs: 4th 1/2-way: chal and almost on terms u.p 1f out: no imp and kpt on same pce ins fnl f* **20/1**

5 hd **Latin Love (IRE)**[43] 957 4-9-9 102 .... FMBerry 4 98
(David Wachman, Ire) *sn led: attempted to assert u.p fr 2f out: strly pressed and hdd fr 1f out: sn no imp and kpt on same pce* **7/1**

6 ½ **Jamaayel**[22] 1244 3-8-11 94 ....(t) DPMcDonogh 11 92
(Kevin Prendergast, Ire) *sn mid-div: 7th 1/2-way: rdn to chal and ev ch 1f out: no imp and kpt on same pce ins fnl f* **10/1**

7 1 ¼ **Pollen (IRE)**[43] 957 5-9-12 100 .... WJLee 6 96
(T Stack, Ire) *hld up: rdn into mod 8th over 1f out: sn no imp and kpt on* **7/1**

8 ½ **Full Of Hope (IRE)**[18] 1342 3-8-11 77 .... CO'Donoghue 12 88?
(A P O'Brien, Ire) *sn mid-div: 8th 1/2-way: rdn to cl and chal 1f out: no imp ins fnl f* **20/1**

9 1 ¼ **Harriers Call (IRE)**[16] 1408 5-9-9 89 .... KLatham 1 88
(J C Hayden, Ire) *sn trckd ldrs: lost pl and no imp fr after 1/2-way* **20/1**

10 ¾ **Monivea (IRE)**[218] 6320 4-9-9 92 ....(p) CDHayes 8 86
(Brian Nolan, Ire) *prom: 2nd 1/2-way: lost pl and no ex fr 2f out* **50/1**

11 ¾ **Gold Bubbles (USA)**[246] 5488 3-8-11 102 .... KJManning 2 80
(J S Bolger, Ire) *chsd ldrs: t.k.h early: wknd 2f out* **8/1**

12 1 **Queen Of Troy (IRE)**[24] 1214 3-8-11 92 .... JAHeffernan 3 78
(A P O'Brien, Ire) *chsd ldrs early: no ex fr over 2f out* **25/1**

1m 25.89s (-4.91) **Going Correction** -0.375s/f (Firm)
WFA 3 from 4yo+ 12lb 12 Ran SP% **125.1**
Speed ratings: **113,110,109,109,108 108,106,106,104,104 103,102**
CSF £15.80 TOTE £3.10: £1.50, £2.70, £2.50; DF 16.60.
Owner David Keoghan **Bred** J Jamgotchian **Trained** Golden, Co Tipperary

FOCUS
This looked a decent Group 3 contest and it produced a worthy winner. The front-running fifth helps set the standard, with the third to a small personal best.

NOTEBOOK
Lolly For Dolly(IRE) ◆ looks a filly with a bright future. The impressive Cork maiden winner in heavy ground didn't enjoy the clearest of passages when the race began to take shape, but once she got through a tight gap she picked up in admirable fashion to win going away in the style of a decent filly. (op 5/2)
Famous(IRE), a sister to Mastercraftsman and runner-up in last season's Moyglare Stakes, had a run behind her coming into this when she disappointed at Leopardstown. This was better from the Ballydoyle filly as she plugged on inside the final furlong after coming under pressure over 2f from home. She appreciated this sounder surface and will be more effective when the ground dries out more. (op 5/1)
Duchess Of Foxland(IRE) had form good enough to make her presence felt. The Leopardstown Group 3 runner-up in soft ground ran creditably after holding every chance entering the final furlong. (op 6/1)
Miss Laa Di Da wasn't helped when the winner came through a tight gap but she was under pressure at the time. She looks another who should be more at home on some nicer ground.
Latin Love(IRE) made a bold attempt to make the running. Her rider poached a couple of lengths after halfway but they were forming a line in behind before the furlong pole and she was soon fighting a losing battle.
Gold Bubbles(USA) had run well around this time last year but she never settled and dropped out after halfway. (op 7/1)

1789a HIGH CHAPARRAL EUROPEAN BREEDERS FUND MOORESBRIDGE STKS (GROUP 3) 1m 2f
4:15 (4:18) 4-Y-0+ **£43,141** (£12,610; £5,973; £1,991)

RPR

1 **Fame And Glory**[22] 1247 4-9-6 128 .... JMurtagh 4 123+
(A P O'Brien, Ire) *racd in mod 4th: str hdwy travelling wl fr 3f out: led 2f out: styd on wl to draw clr fnl f: comf* **30/100**[1]

2 5 **Recharge (IRE)**[15] 1413 4-9-1 109 .... CDHayes 2 108
(Kevin Prendergast, Ire) *racd in mod 3rd: clsd and chal fr 2f out: no imp u.p and kpt on same pce fnl f* **13/2**[2]

3 2 ½ **Galileo's Choice (IRE)**[208] 6603 4-9-1 102 .... PJSmullen 1 103
(D K Weld, Ire) *racd wl off pce in rr: no imp u.p st: kpt on wout threatening fr over 1f out: wnt 3rd nr fin* **12/1**

4 ½ **Dixie Music (IRE)**[22] 1247 4-9-1 100 .... JAHeffernan 5 102
(A P O'Brien, Ire) *led and clr: reduced ld fr under 3f out: hdd 2f out: sn no ex* **14/1**

5 ½ **Popmurphy**[22] 1247 4-9-1 102 ....(b) WJSupple 3 101
(P D Deegan, Ire) *chsd ldr in mod 2nd: clsd under 3f out: no ex fr under 2f out* **10/1**[3]

2m 13.92s (1.32) **Going Correction** +0.25s/f (Good) 5 Ran SP% **113.7**
Speed ratings: **114,110,108,107,107**
CSF £3.11 TOTE £1.10: £1.02, £1.60; DF 2.70.
Owner Derrick Smith **Bred** Ptarmigan Bloodstock And Miss K Rausing **Trained** Ballydoyle, Co Tipperary
■ Stewards' Enquiry : J A Heffernan severe caution: used whip with excessive frequency

FOCUS
The better ground and pace compared with his Listed race defeat here on his previous start was a definite plus for the winner. The runner-up is the best guide to the level of the form.

NOTEBOOK
Fame And Glory won easily after being held up in a race run at a decent pace set by the winner's stablemate Dixie Music, who soon had the small field well strung out. Fourth of the five runners into the straight, Fame And Glory, last year's Irish Derby winner, was soon asked to close and he did so quite smoothly, arriving on the outside to lead well over a furlong out. Soon pushed clear, he was in no danger inside the final furlong and will probably return to the Curragh for the Tattersalls Gold Cup on May 23 in search of a third Group 1 win. (op 1/3)
Recharge(IRE), 25 lengths behind Fame And Glory in the Irish Derby last year and second to Famous Name in a 1m Listed event at Leopardstown on his reappearance, raced in third place and closed ahead of the winner, briefly touching the front before being put in his place. (op 11/2 tchd 7/1)
Galileo's Choice(IRE), twice a winner from five attempts last year, was racing in his first Pattern race. Held up in rear, he stayed on past beaten horses from 1½f out to snatch third spot close home. (op 14/1)
Dixie Music(IRE) dropped away having done his job. (op 12/1)
Popmurphy, 2l in front of Fame And Glory when second here last month, followed the pacemaker but was done with almost 2f out. (op 10/1 tchd 9/1)

1790 - 1791a (Foreign Racing) - See Raceform Interactive

1610 CHANTILLY (R-H)
Monday, May 3

OFFICIAL GOING: Turf: soft

1792a PRIX ALLEZ FRANCE (GROUP 3) (4YO+ FILLIES & MARES) (TURF) 1m 2f
3:10 (12:00) 4-Y-0+ **£35,398** (£14,159; £10,619; £7,079; £3,539)

RPR

1 **Shemiyla (FR)**[187] 7128 4-8-9 0 .... Christophe-PatriceLemaire 6 104
(A De Royer-Dupre, France) *racd freely fr s towards the rr: mde gd prog early in st in mid-trck: qcknd wl 1f out: fin strly: got up on line* **14/5**[1]

2 nk **Superstition (FR)**[24] 4-8-7 0 .... GeraldMosse 12 102
(A De Royer-Dupre, France) *racd in 4th fr s: grabbed ld after 4f: led into st: looked to be fading and hdd 1f out but c again to ld ins fnl f: fin strly: ct in fnl strides* **7/2**[2]

3 shd **La Boum (GER)**[22] 1255 7-8-9 0 .... ThierryJarnet 5 104
(Robert Collet, France) *a.p on the outside: front rnk 1/2-way down st: r.o wl: grabbed ld 1f out: ct wl ins fnl f* **44/5**

4 ¾ **Plumania**[24] 4-8-9 0 .... OlivierPeslier 10 102
(A Fabre, France) *restrained fr s: followed eventual wnr in st: r.o wl* **63/10**[3]

5 ¾ **Fleur Enchantee (FR)**[24] 6-8-7 0 ....(p) DavyBonilla 8 99
(P Van De Poele, France) *broke wl: a.p: shared ld early in st: r.o wl but fdd in clsng stages* **21/1**

6 ¾ **Biased**[24] 4-8-7 0 .... MaximeGuyon 7 97
(M Delzangles, France) *w.w in rr: gd prog early in st: r.o* **39/1**

7 1 ½ **Soberania (GER)**[232] 5929 4-8-9 0 .... JohanVictoire 11 96
(J De Roualle, France) *broke wl: prom: amongst ldrs early in st: hmpd 1f out and dropped away* **17/1**

8 ¾ **Peinture Rare (IRE)**[24] 4-8-9 0 .... AnthonyCrastus 4 95
(E Lellouche, France) *w.w towards rr on rail: rdn early in st: swtchd to mid-trck and briefly threatened: no imp: dropped away* **13/2**

8 dht **Cavaliere (FR)**[38] 4-8-9 0 .... IoritzMendizabal 2 95
(M Cesandri, France) *prom tl 1/2-way down st: r.o* **16/1**

10 ¾ **Eire**[44] 953 6-8-7 0 .... LaurentHuart 9 91
(M Nigge, France) *in rr fr s: threatened briefly on outside early in st: no ex* **24/1**

0 **Sans Chichi (FR)**[45] 6-8-9 0 .... MaximeFoulon 3 —
(Y Barberot, France) *smartly away: racd in 2nd: failed to qckn in st: fdd* **26/1**

0 **Wilside (IRE)**[204] 6718 4-9-0 0 .... ChristopheSoumillon 1 —
(M Delzangles, France) *led fr s: hdd 4f out and grad lost pl: no ex in st* **16/1**

2m 7.50s (2.70) 12 Ran SP% **117.8**
WIN (incl. 1 euro stake): 3.80. PLACES: 1.70, 1.80, 2.40. DF: 5.80. SF: 12.10.
Owner H H Aga Khan **Bred** H H The Aga Khan's Studs S C **Trained** Chantilly, France

NOTEBOOK
Shemiyla(FR), runner-up in a Group 3 at Saint-Cloud on her final start last year, showed a nice turn of foot to get up near the line and deny her stable companion. She has clearly progressed from three to four.
Superstition(FR) won nicely on her reappearance but was taking a step up in class. She had a difficult draw to overcome and a stronger early gallop would surely have suited her better, but she kept on strongly and was only denied by her stablemate close home.

[1541] BATH (L-H)

Tuesday, May 4

OFFICIAL GOING: Good (good to firm in places; 7.9)

Wind: Brisk across Weather: Sunny Intervals

1793 WILLIAMS AUTOMOBILES BRISTOL - LOTUS SPORTS CAR MAIDEN AUCTION STKS 5f 11y

2:30 (2:33) (Class 5) 2-Y-O **£2,590** (£770; £385; £192) **Stalls** Centre

Form RPR

6 1 **Fifth Ave**[8] 1577 2-8-8 0 FergusSweeney 4 77+
(J A Osborne) *trckd ldrs: led ins fnl 2f: drvn clr fnl f: readily* **5/1**[1]

0 2 3 1/4 **Colorado Gold**[17] 1389 2-9-3 0 TomQueally 12 74
(P F I Cole) *pressed ldrs tl slt ld 1/2-way: hdd ins fnl 2f: styd chsng wnr but no ch fnl f* **8/1**

0 3 2 1/2 **Honourable Knight (IRE)**[18] 1351 2-8-11 0 MartinDwyer 9 59
(M D I Usher) *in tch: hdwy fr 2f out: drvn and styd on to take 3rd ins fnl f but no ch w ldng duo* **16/1**

4 1 3/4 **Basilica** 2-8-10 0 JamesMillman(3) 5 55+
(B R Millman) *in rr: sme hdwy on ins whn hung bdly rt over 1f out: stl green but kpt on wl fnl f: nt rch ldrs* **15/2**[3]

5 3/4 **King Of Cassis** 2-8-8 0 JackDean(3) 2 50
(W G M Turner) *slt ld 1f: styd pressing ldrs to 1/2-way: wknd appr fnl f* **28/1**

6 6 shd **Tagena (IRE)**[15] 1429 2-8-5 0 AndrewHeffernan(3) 3 47
(P D Evans) *chsd ldrs: rdn 1/2-way: wknd over 1f out* **10/1**

7 1 1/2 **Shes Rosie** 2-8-6 0 LukeMorris 15 41+
(J G M O'Shea) *s.i.s: in rr: sn drvn along: hdwy and nt clr run wl over 1f out: swtchd rt and r.o fnl f but nvr a threat* **33/1**

8 3/4 **He's The Star (IRE)** 2-8-11 0 PaulDoe 14 43+
(P D Evans) *in rr: hdwy, rn green and n.m.r over 1f out: kpt on fnl f* **10/1**

032 9 3/4 **Ivan's A Star (IRE)**[19] 1319 2-8-11 0 (b[1]) LiamKeniry 1 39
(J S Moore) *led after 1f tl hdd 1/2-way: wknd fnl f* **5/1**[1]

10 2 **Magical Star** 2-8-6 0 RichardHughes 10 31
(R Hannon) *chsd ldrs: rdn 2f out: wknd appr fnl f* **11/2**[2]

0 11 1/2 **Lady On Top (IRE)**[19] 1319 2-8-3 0 AmyBaker(5) 8 27
(Mrs P N Dutfield) *chsd ldrs 3f* **33/1**

12 hd **Bathwick Nero** 2-8-7 0 MartinLane(3) 13 30
(P D Evans) *outpcd most of way* **20/1**

6 13 4 **Enrichment**[22] 1256 2-8-8 0 DavidProbert 6 12
(H J L Dunlop) *in tch 3f* **20/1**

14 1/2 **Our Folly** 2-8-13 0 SteveDrowne 7 15
(W S Kittow) *s.i.s: a outpcd* **25/1**

15 7 **Amicolini** 2-8-6 0 ChrisCatlin 11 —
(Karen George) *s.i.s: outpcd most of way* **50/1**

62.27 secs (-0.23) **Going Correction** -0.125s/f (Firm) **15** Ran SP% **120.3**

Speed ratings (Par 93): **96,90,86,84,82 82,80,79,77,74 73,73,67,66,55**

toteswingers: 1&2 £15.10, 1&3 £28.80, 2&3 £30.90 CSF £40.09 TOTE £5.70: £1.60, £2.50, £6.50; EX 67.00.

Owner M Pennick **Bred** Llety Stud **Trained** Upper Lambourn, Berks

■ Stewards' Enquiry : James Millman one-day ban: careless riding (May 18)

FOCUS

An ordinary-looking maiden auction where those drawn low figured prominently. The winner impressed and the time and averages set the level.

NOTEBOOK

Fifth Ave had shown promise despite not getting the best of runs on her debut and came on considerably for that. She was never far away and, when asked to go to the front inside the last quarter-mile, she soon went clear and won with a fair amount in hand. She looks capable of winning better races and the Hilary Needler will be considered as there are not many options for her now. (op 11-1)

Colorado Gold also built considerably on his debut and did well to race prominently from his double-figure draw. He beat the rest well enough and should pick up a similar contest. (op 9-1)

Honourable Knight(IRE) lost his race when hampered at the start on his debut, and his trainer indicated then that he is well thought-of. He ran on pretty well in the closing stages and can build on this again next time. (op 20-1)

Basilica came from well back despite being switched twice (doing a couple of his rivals few favours and earning his rider a one-day ban in the process), and finished best of all. The rider reported he ran green, and he should not be long in winning races at this trip. Official explanation: jockey said colt ran green (op 10-1 tchd 7-1)

King Of Cassis showed ability on this debut but is bred to get further and should improve over a more suitable trip. His rider reported the colt hung left. Official explanation: jockey said colt hung right (op 66-1)

Shes Rosie reportedly hung right.

He's The Star(IRE) set the standard on a couple efforts, especially his only turf start at Ffos Las in a race that has worked out well. He was in the front rank from the start but could not respond when the winner went for home. Official explanation: jockey said colt hung left (op 14-1)

Ivan's A Star(IRE) opened up as favourite but drifted. She was switched in behind the leaders from her high draw and looked close enough at halfway, but failed to pick up and was not given a hard time once beaten. She should be better for the experience. (op 7-2 tchd 11-2)

1794 MOBIL 1 (S) STKS 5f 11y

3:00 (3:00) (Class 6) 2-Y-O **£1,683** (£501; £250; £125) **Stalls** Centre

Form RPR

0 1 **Joyously**[22] 1263 2-8-7 0 ow1 RichardHughes 7 62+
(P D Evans) *s.i.s: reminders sn after s and drvn: in tch 1/2-way: rdn and hdwy over 1f out: styd on to ld fnl 120yds: kpt on wl* **7/2**[3]

66 2 2 1/4 **Crazy In Love**[24] 1223 2-8-3 0 (b[1]) JackDean(3) 6 52
(W G M Turner) *led: rdn appr fnl f: hdd and outpcd fnl 120yds* **8/1**

05 3 3 1/4 **Bobby Smith (IRE)**[19] 1319 2-8-8 0 WilliamCarson(3) 3 45
(M G Quinlan) *wnt rt s: chsd ldrs: rdn over 2f out: wknd ins fnl f* **9/4**[1]

0 4 1 **Nalany**[10] 1517 2-8-6 0 FrankieMcDonald 8 37
(D Haydn Jones) *chsd ldrs: rdn 1/2-way: wknd over 1f out* **16/1**

5 nk **Capa Cruz (IRE)** 2-8-11 0 DavidProbert 2 41
(R A Harris) *chsd ldr: rdn 2f out: wknd ins fnl f* **11/4**[2]

6 3 3/4 **Coolree Pearl (IRE)** 2-8-1 0 AmyBaker(5) 1 22
(A B Haynes) *s.i.s: a outpcd* **6/1**

0 7 45 **Wotitis**[34] 1065 2-8-6 0 (p) MatthewDavies(5) 5 —
(W G M Turner) *pushed rt s: sn bhd: t.o fnl 2f* **25/1**

63.41 secs (0.91) **Going Correction** -0.125s/f (Firm) **7** Ran SP% **114.8**

Speed ratings (Par 91): **87,83,78,76,76 70,—**

toteswingers: 1&2 £5.90, 1&3 £3.30, 2&3 £1.90 CSF £31.08 TOTE £7.90: £4.80, £4.30; EX 30.90.The winner was bought in for £6,000.

Owner Nick Shutts **Bred** N Shutts **Trained** Pandy, Monmouths

FOCUS

A typical early-season juvenile seller and the time was 1.14secs slower than the opening race. The winner may turn out to be a bit better than rated.

NOTEBOOK

Joyously had been well beaten behind subsequent winner Zebedee on her debut at Windsor but the experience gained there and this drop in class made the difference. A rare ride for Richard Hughes (who put up a pound overweight) for the trainer, she was given a r[illegible]inder to get her racing in the first furlong but picked up well to take the lead inside the last furlo[illegible] and ultimately score comfortably. She was bought in for 6,000gns and connections thi[illegible] she might be better than this grade. (tchd 10-3 and 3-1 in places)

Crazy In Love, wearing blinkers for the first time on this third start and turf debut, broke quickly and made the running, then stuck on well although no match for the winner. She could win a race at this level. (op 9-1)

Bobby Smith(IRE), whose form was not particularly boosted by the eighth in the opening race, was an easy-to-back favourite. He had every chance on this turf debut but failed to find another gear in the closing stages. (op 13-8 tchd 5-2)

Nalany had been outpaced on her debut and still looked in need of the experience, tending to wander about before running on as if she will appreciate a little further. (op 22-1)

Capa Cruz(IRE) is quite well bred but this first foal is not that big, which is presumably why Darley sold him cheaply. He showed speed early on this debut but tended to wander and faded under pressure. He will know more next time but whether he can improve on this remains to be seen. (op 6-1)

1795 BATH ABBEY H'CAP (DIV I) 1m 5y

3:30 (3:30) (Class 6) (0-60,60) 3-Y-O **£1,619** (£481; £240; £120) **Stalls** Low

Form RPR

006- 1 **It's A Deal (IRE)**[238] 5748 3-8-8 **50** LukeMorris 9 58
(P Winkworth) *chsd ldr: chal fr 2f out: hrd rdn to take slt ld ins fnl f: all out* **25/1**

0-03 2 hd **Kingsdine (IRE)**[25] 1209 3-8-12 **54** TomMcLaughlin 14 61
(M S Saunders) *chsd ldrs: slt ld and rdn over 2f out: hdd ins fnl f: kpt on u.p: a jst hld* **14/1**

3230 3 3 1/2 **Sunrise Lyric (IRE)**[27] 1163 3-9-4 **60** RichardHughes 7 59+
(P F I Cole) *plld hrd: hld up in rr: moved rt off rail 2f out: sn hmpd and swtchd rt to outside: rapid hdwy appr fnl f: fin wl to take 3rd last strides but no ch w ldng duo* **6/1**[3]

3624 4 hd **Kenswick**[11] 1505 3-9-1 **57** (b) DarryllHolland 5 56
(Pat Eddery) *led tl hdd over 2f out: styd chsng ldng duo but no ch fr over 1f out: lost 3rd last strides* **13/2**

000- 5 1 1/4 **Baoli**[171] 7389 3-9-0 **56** AndreaAtzeni 10 52
(L M Cumani) *chsd ldrs: rdn over 2f out: styd on same pce fnl f* **11/2**[2]

-402 6 2 **Sultan's Choice**[10] 1526 3-8-10 **55** (v[1]) AndrewHeffernan(3) 15 46
(P D Evans) *in rr: hrd rdn and hdwy on outside fr 2f out: nvr gng pce to rch ldrs* **4/1**[1]

0-06 7 2 3/4 **Annacaboe (IRE)**[27] 1165 3-9-3 **59** AdrianMcCarthy 16 44
(D K Ivory) *chsd ldrs: awkward bnd 5f out: rdn 3f out: wknd fr 2f out* **66/1**

3330 8 1/2 **Roybuoy**[25] 1205 3-8-10 **52** (b) JimmyQuinn 12 36
(H J L Dunlop) *s.i.s: in rr: rdn over 3f out: sme hdwy on outside fr 2f out but nvr in contention* **14/1**

000- 9 shd **Naseby (USA)**[202] 6774 3-9-2 **58** FergusSweeney 4 41
(Miss S L Davison) *chsd ldrs: rdn 3f out: wknd wl over 1f out* **40/1**

0-60 10 hd **Proper Littlemadam**[14] 1456 3-9-1 **57** TomQueally 13 40
(C N Kellett) *in tch: rdn and wkng whn hmpd ins fnl 2f* **33/1**

2532 11 1/2 **Novillero**[27] 1163 3-8-7 **49** SamHitchcott 3 31
(J C Fox) *s.i.s: in rr: hdwy into mid-div 4f out: sn rdn: wknd 2f out* **7/1**

00-0 12 1 1/4 **Vert Chapeau**[27] 1164 3-9-3 **59** LiamKeniry 6 38
(E F Vaughan) *chsd ldrs: rdn 3f out: wknd over 2f out* **16/1**

600- 13 1 3/4 **Red Eddie**[197] 6895 3-9-1 **57** JackMitchell 8 32
(S Dow) *a in rr* **16/1**

030 14 3 **Better Be Blue (IRE)**[27] 1158 3-8-5 **47** DavidProbert 11 15
(A W Carroll) *nvr bttr than mid-div: rdn 3f out: wknd sn after* **12/1**

1m 41.38s (0.58) **Going Correction** -0.025s/f (Good) **14** Ran SP% **119.0**

Speed ratings (Par 97): **96,95,92,92,90 88,86,85,85,85 84,83,81,78**

toteswingers: 1&2 £71.30, 1&3 £36.80, 2&3 £12.60 CSF £331.15 CT £2441.76 TOTE £35.40: £11.70, £4.70, £1.50; EX 511.90.

Owner Badger's Set **Bred** Waterford Stud **Trained** Chiddingfold, Surrey

FOCUS

A big field for this first division of a competitive-looking low-grade handicap, and an open betting heat. However, it paid to race close to the pace and it produced a surprise winner, who ran a stone personal best.

It's A Deal(IRE) Official explanation: trainer said regarding apparent improvement in form, that the filly had strengthened up and matured over the winter,

Sunrise Lyric(IRE) Official explanation: jockey said filly was denied a clear run

Annacaboe(IRE) Official explanation: jockey said filly was unsuited by the good (good to firm places) ground

Vert Chapeau Official explanation: jockey said filly was unsuited by the good (good to firm places) ground

1796 BATH ABBEY H'CAP (DIV II) 1m 5y

4:00 (4:02) (Class 6) (0-60,60) 3-Y-O **£1,619** (£481; £240; £120) **Stalls** Low

Form RPR

060- 1 **Flag Of Glory**[189] 7099 3-9-1 **57** GeorgeBaker 9 72+
(C F Wall) *unruly s: trckd ldr: led appr fnl 2f: pushed clar over 1f out: eased fnl 50yds* **7/1**[3]

00-2 2 2 3/4 **Celtic Ransom**[25] 1209 3-9-3 **59** MichaelHills 6 62
(J W Hills) *sn led: rdn and hdd appr fnl 2f: no ch w easy wnr ins fnl f but hld on wl for 2nd* **7/1**[3]

000- 3 nk **Kanace**[218] 6347 3-8-5 **47** oh1 ow1 StevieDonohoe 10 50
(Ian Williams) *plld hrd: chsd ldrs: rdn to take 3rd over 1f out: styd on to press for wl hld to go 2nd cl home* **9/2**[1]

000- 4 3/4 **Optimistic Duke (IRE)**[174] 7325 3-9-1 **57** RichardHughes 14 58
(W R Muir) *chsd ldrs: rdn 3f out: no imp on ldrs ins fnl 2f: styd on same pce fnl f* **28/1**

-442 5 2 1/4 **Celestial Girl**[14] 1437 3-8-13 **55** SteveDrowne 12 51
(H Morrison) *sn in tch: chsd ldrs and rdn fr 3f out: nvr on terms: wknd fnl f* **5/1**[2]

060- 6 3/4 **My Grand Duke (USA)**[126] 7865 3-8-3 **50** SophieDoyle(5) 15 44
(J A Osborne) *chsd ldrs and racd wd: outpcd over 2f out: styd on again ins fnl f* **33/1**

55-3 7 1/2 **Red Amy**[27] 1158 3-9-1 **57** TomQueally 13 50
(M L W Bell) *in rr: rdn and hdwy on outside fr 3f out: nvr rchd ldrs and styd on same pce fnl 2f* **5/1**[2]

006- 8 1 **Finch Flyer (IRE)**[194] 6965 3-8-11 **53** FergusSweeney 3 44
(G L Moore) *in tch: pushed along on ins and outpcd 3f out: mod prog again ins fnl f* **18/1**

0662 9 nse **Mack's Sister**[17] 1392 3-9-4 **60** RobertHavlin 1 51
(D K Ivory) *t.k.h: chsd ldrs tl wknd over 1f out: btn whn stmbld ins fnl f* **9/1**

0303 10 hd **Single Lady**[14] 1461 3-8-13 **55** LukeMorris 8 45
(J S Moore) *in rr and rdn over 3f out: mod prog fnl f* **16/1**

000- **11** *1* **Philippa Jane**[145] 7700 3-8-10 **52** FrankieMcDonald 5 40
(P Winkworth) *in rr: pushed along anf flashed tail bnd over 4f out: plld to outside and mod prog fnl f* **66/1**

402- **12** *1 ¼* **Looks Like Slim**[232] 5935 3-9-0 **56** MartinDwyer 7 41
(P F I Cole) *in tch early: rdn and dropped in rr over 3f out: nvr a factor after* **12/1**

40-6 **13** *5* **Aldorable**[33] 1075 3-8-10 **59** JohnFahy(7) 2 32
(R A Teal) *a towards rr* **66/1**

02-5 **14** *nk* **Pie Poudre**[106] 216 3-9-1 **57** JackMitchell 11 37
(R Brotherton) *s.i.s: in rr tl rapid hdwy on outside fr 4f out to chse ldrs over 2f out: wknd over 1f out* **33/1**

000- **15** *5* **Acting Elegant**[209] 6589 3-8-1 **46** oh1 AndrewHeffernan(3) 16 7
(P D Evans) *rdn and bhd fr 1/2-way* **40/1**

00-0 **16** *hd* **Lady Christie**[34] 1059 3-8-6 **48** JimmyQuinn 4 9
(M Blanshard) *t.k.h: early: a in rr* **40/1**

1m 41.14s (0.34) **Going Correction** -0.025s/f (Good) **16** Ran SP% **122.5**
Speed ratings (Par 97): **97,94,93,93,90 90,89,88,88,88 87,86,81,80,75 75**
toteswingers: 1&2 £13.40, 1&3 £19.70, 2&3 £11.80 CSF £53.00 CT £250.22 TOTE £10.00: £2.50, £2.30, £2.20, £8.00; EX 77.90.

Owner Follow The Flag Partnership **Bred** Follow The Flag Partnership **Trained** Newmarket, Suffolk

FOCUS
The pace in this second division was solid and the time was just under a quarter of a second faster that the first leg. Again it paid to race handily. Stronger form than the first division, rated around the runner-up.

Flag Of Glory Official explanation: trainer said, regarding apparent improvement in form, that it had improved as a result of being gelded over the winter.

Pie Poudre Official explanation: jockey said gelding stumbled inside final furlong

1797 CRABBIES ALCOHOLIC GINGER BEER FILLIES' H'CAP 1m 5y

4:30 (4:30) (Class 5) (0-75,73) 4-Y-0+ **£2,590** (£770; £385; £192) **Stalls** Low

Form RPR

5010 **1** **Very Well Red**[17] 1396 7-8-13 **71** WilliamCarson(3) 7 80
(P W Hiatt) *trckd ldr: led appr fnl 2f: drvn and styd on wl whn strly chal thrght ins fnl f: a jst doing enough* **8/1**

5360 **2** *shd* **My Best Bet**[53] 873 4-9-4 **73** TomQueally 6 82
(Stef Higgins) *in tch: chsd ldrs 3f out: rdn and edgd rt over 1f out: pressed wnr u.p thrght fnl f but a jst hld* **11/2**[2]

1146 **3** *2 ¾* **Make Amends (IRE)**[33] 1077 5-8-7 **67** AmyBaker(5) 5 70
(R J Hodges) *s.i.s: in rr: hdwy on outside over 1f out: str run fnl f to take 3rd cl home but nvr any threat to ldng duo* **8/1**

300- **4** *½* **Foxtrot Alpha (IRE)**[181] 7236 4-8-6 **61** FrankieMcDonald 3 63
(P Winkworth) *in rr: sme hdwy on ins 3f out: grad swtchd rt and hdwy over 1f out: kpt on ins fnl f* **16/1**

24-4 **5** *nk* **Evening Sunset (GER)**[17] 1395 4-8-9 **64** DavidProbert 9 65
(M G Quinlan) *chsd ldrs: rdn 3f out: one pce 2f out: kpt on again fnl f* **9/2**[1]

-653 **6** *1* **Perfect Class**[80] 544 4-8-13 **68** LukeMorris 4 67
(C G Cox) *in rr tl hdwy 3f out to chse ldrs over 2f out: rdn and one pce u.p whn bmpd over 1f out: no ex fnl f* **6/1**[3]

46-0 **7** *¾* **Catalan Bay (AUS)**[18] 1361 6-9-1 **70** (t) SteveDrowne 1 67
(J R Gask) *led tl hdd over 2f out: styd pressing ldrs tl wknd ins fnl f* **14/1**

45-3 **8** *6* **Steel Free (IRE)**[34] 1064 4-9-2 **71** RobertHavlin 2 54
(M Madgwick) *chsd ldrs tl wknd over 2f out* **9/1**

-206 **9** *hd* **Jewelled**[28] 1141 4-8-13 **68** MichaelHills 8 51
(J W Hills) *in rr tl hdwy on outside to chse ldrs briefly over 2f out: sn wknd* **10/1**

520- **10** *2 ½* **Welsh Anthem**[277] 4498 4-9-1 **70** MartinDwyer 10 47
(W R Muir) *chsd ldrs 5f* **11/2**[2]

-000 **11** *9* **Devon Diva**[9] 1542 4-8-4 **59** oh14 (p) JimmyQuinn 11 15
(J F Panvert) *bhd most of way* **100/1**

1m 38.85s (-1.95) **Going Correction** -0.025s/f (Good) **11** Ran SP% **118.1**
Speed ratings (Par 100): **108,107,105,104,104 103,102,96,96,93 84**
toteswingers: 1&2 £10.60, 1&3 £22.70, 2&3 £14.70 CSF £51.84 CT £369.40 TOTE £8.60: £2.80, £3.30, £3.80; EX 65.40.

Owner Phil Kelly **Bred** Butts Enterprises Limited **Trained** Hook Norton, Oxon

FOCUS
This fillies' handicap was a better race than the two divisions of the earlier handicap over the trip and the time was 2.29secs faster than the quickest of them. Pretty solid form, rated around the fifth.

1798 BATH ORGANICS H'CAP 2m 1f 34y

5:00 (5:00) (Class 4) (0-85,85) 4-Y-0+ **£4,533** (£1,348; £674; £336) **Stalls** Centre

Form RPR

10-4 **1** **Callisto Moon**[9] 1544 6-9-12 **85** (p) DarryllHolland 3 87+
(R Curtis) *racd in 3rd tl qcknd to go 2nd 9f out: led 1m out: drvn and asserted fr 3f out: in command fnl 2f* **9/4**[1]

2434 **2** *3* **Calculating (IRE)**[14] 1454 6-8-7 **66** oh5 DavidProbert 1 63
(M D I Usher) *chsd ldr to 9f out: dropped in rr 5f out: lost and drvn fr ins fnl 3f: swtchd to outside and styd on wl fr over 1f out to take wl hld 2nd last strides* **8/1**

630- **3** *hd* **Rare Ruby (IRE)**[189] 7084 6-8-8 **67** TomQueally 2 64
(Jennie Candlish) *in last pl tl hdd ins fnl 3f: styd on u.p to dispute 2nd ins fnl f: no ch w wnr: lost 3rd last strides* **3/1**[2]

42-2 **4** *¾* **Wightgold**[14] 1446 4-8-4 **66** oh14 JimmyQuinn 6 62
(H J L Dunlop) *in tch: hdwy 9f out: chsd wnr 5f out: hrd drvn and one pce fr 3f out: outstyd in 4th nr fin* **10/1**

420- **5** *nk* **Baddam**[25] 6115 8-9-10 **83** SaleemGolam 5 79
(Ian Williams) *led tl hdd after 9f: rdn and lost pl over 3f out: rallied on rails fnl 2f and styd on to press for 2nd ins fnl f: sn one pce* **4/1**[3]

1564 **6** *2 ¼* **Benedict Spirit (IRE)**[3] 1684 5-9-6 **82** (v) AndrewHeffernan(3) 4 75
(P D Evans) *in rr tl hdwy 3f out: styd on to press for wl hld 2nd 1f out: wknd ins fnl f* **5/1**

3m 51.02s (-0.88) **Going Correction** -0.025s/f (Good)
WFA 4 from 5yo+ 3lb **6** Ran SP% **112.6**
Speed ratings (Par 105): **101,99,99,99,99 97**
toteswingers: 1&2 £3.60, 1&3 £2.70, 2&3 £5.30 CSF £20.52 TOTE £2.80: £1.80, £3.30; EX 15.80.

Owner B Bedford & Mrs Gill White **Bred** Barton Stud **Trained** Lambourn, Berks

FOCUS
A fair staying handicap full of mainly exposed stayers. The winner is rated up 5lb, but this is muddling form.

1799 ELITE TELECOM H'CAP 5f 11y

5:30 (5:30) (Class 6) (0-65,67) 4-Y-0+ **£1,942** (£578; £288; £144) **Stalls** High

Form RPR

0601 **1** **West Leake (IRE)**[13] 1477 4-8-9 **56** LiamKeniry 11 66
(P Burgoyne) *hld up in rr: hdwy on outside over 1f out: squeezed between horses and qcknd ins fnl f: drvn to ld nr fin* **16/1**

3134 **2** *¾* **Captain Kallis (IRE)**[10] 1534 4-8-5 **57** BillyCray(5) 6 64
(D J S Ffrench Davis) *hld up towards rr tl rapid hdwy to chal wl ins fnl f: nt gng pce of wnr cl home* **18/1**

200- **3** *½* **Avrilo**[172] 7370 4-8-6 **53** FergusSweeney 16 58
(M S Saunders) *chsd ldrs: chal 1f out: led fnl 120yds: hdd and outpcd nr fin* **25/1**

23-0 **4** *½* **Mazzola**[9] 1547 4-9-1 **62** LukeMorris 7 65
(J M Bradley) *chsd ldrs: slt ld appr fnl f sn hdd: fdd cl home* **8/1**[3]

000- **5** *nk* **Stamford Blue**[239] 5719 9-8-5 **59** (b) JakePayne(7) 4 61
(R A Harris) *in tch: chsd ldrs and hmpd 1f out: styd on ins fnl f but nt gng pce to chal* **33/1**

0-52 **6** *nk* **Desert Strike**[7] 1598 4-8-13 **60** RichardHughes 10 61
(P F I Cole) *hld up in rr: hdwy and swtchd lft over 1f out: styd on ins fnl f: n.m.r fnl 100yds: kpt on* **7/2**[1]

-053 **7** *1 ¼* **Tune Up The Band**[46] 936 6-8-5 **52** JimmyQuinn 17 49
(R J Hodges) *chsd ldrs: chal 2f out to 1f out: edgd lft and wknd ins fnl f* **14/1**

1061 **8** *hd* **Titus Gent**[7] 1596 5-9-6 **67** 6ex DavidProbert 15 63
(R A Harris) *chsd ldrs on outside: rdn 2f out: styd on same pce fnl f* **10/1**

30-0 **9** *½* **Musical Bridge**[25] 1200 4-9-3 **64** DarryllHolland 5 58
(Mrs L Williamson) *slt ld tl hdd over 3f out: sn rdn: styd chssing ldrs tl wknd ins fnl f* **17/2**

0600 **10** *nk* **Financial Times (USA)**[19] 1321 8-9-2 **63** (t) TomQueally 3 63+
(Stef Higgins) *in rr tl hdwy over 1f out sn nt clr run and again ins fnl f: nt rcvr* **8/1**[3]

4-16 **11** *hd* **Short Cut**[14] 1441 4-8-6 **53** (t) StevieDonohoe 1 45
(Ian Williams) *in rr tl hdwy on ins over 1f out: kpt on fnl f but nvr a threat* **7/1**[2]

0-00 **12** *¾* **Blessed Place**[10] 1534 10-8-7 **54** FrankieMcDonald 9 44
(D J S Ffrench Davis) *w ldr tl led over 3f out: hdd appr fnl f: btn whn n.m.r wl ins fnl f* **25/1**

0-03 **13** *½* **Desert Pride**[13] 1477 5-8-7 **54** ow1 (b) SteveDrowne 13 42
(W S Kittow) *in rr tl sme hdwy on outside over 2f out: sn btn* **11/1**

0-35 **14** *1 ¾* **Pocket's Pick (IRE)**[14] 1445 4-9-3 **64** GeorgeBaker 2 45
(G L Moore) *chsd ldrs: hanging lft whn hmpd 1f out* **22/1**

0-00 **15** *2 ¾* **What Katie Did (IRE)**[9] 1547 5-9-4 **65** (p) ChrisCatlin 8 37
(J M Bradley) *s.i.s: outpcd* **33/1**

61.74 secs (-0.76) **Going Correction** -0.125s/f (Firm) **15** Ran SP% **120.6**
Speed ratings (Par 101): **101,99,99,98,97 97,95,94,94,93 93,92,91,88,84**
toteswingers: 1&2 £22.80, 1&3 £67.30, 2&3 £60.50 CSF £258.30 TOTE £23.00: £6.40, £6.90, £6.60; EX 262.00 Place 6: £653.32 Place 5: £216.13.

Owner L Tomlin **Bred** Rathbarry Stud **Trained** Shepton Montague, Somerset

FOCUS
A big-field sprint and they went pretty quick, as the first two came from well off the pace. Straightforward form.

Stamford Blue Official explanation: jockey said gelding was denied a clear run
Titus Gent Official explanation: jockey said gelding never travelled
Financial Times(USA) Official explanation: jockey said gelding was denied a clear run
Desert Pride Official explanation: jockey said gelding hung right throughout
Pocket's Pick(IRE) Official explanation: jockey said gelding hung right throughout

T/Jkpt: Not won. T/Plt: £795.80 to a £1 stake. Pool: £66733.51, 61.21 winning tickets. T/Qpdt: £54.70 to a £1 stake. Pool: £5800.78, 78.44 winning tickets. ST

1463 CATTERICK (L-H)

Tuesday, May 4

OFFICIAL GOING: Firm (good to firm in places)

Wind: Virtually nil Weather: Overcast

1800 YORKSHIRE4X4.COM ADVENTURE ACTIVITIES MAIDEN AUCTION STKS 5f

6:00 (6:01) (Class 6) 2-Y-O **£2,047** (£604; £302) **Stalls** Low

Form RPR

3 **1** **First Class Favour (IRE)**[17] 1375 2-8-6 0 DavidAllan 1 72
(T D Easterby) *cl up on inner: led wl over 1f out: rdn ins fnl f: kpt on* **4/5**[1]

5 **2** *¾* **Melodize**[8] 1577 2-8-8 0 SilvestreDeSousa 2 71
(W R Muir) *chsd ldrs: hdwy 2f out: sn rdn and hung lft ins fnl f: kpt on* **10/3**[2]

0 **3** *hd* **Choose Wisely (IRE)**[18] 1359 2-8-11 0 JamieSpencer 4 74+
(K A Ryan) *trckd ldrs: hdwy 2f out: rdn to chse ldng pair whn n.m.r ins fnl f: sn nt clr run: kpt on towards fin* **11/2**[3]

4 *3 ½* **Novalist** 2-8-4 0 MatthewLawson(7) 5 59
(R Bastiman) *s.i.s and bhd: gd hdwy on wd outside 1/2-way: chsd ldrs over 1f out: edgd lft and kpt on ins fnl f* **100/1**

40 **5** *¾* **Mini Bon Bon**[20] 1294 2-8-4 0 JamieMackay 7 50
(A Bailey) *led: rdn along over 2f out: hdd wl over 1f out: hld whn hmpd and wknd ins fnl f* **40/1**

6 *2 ¼* **Wild Hysteria (IRE)** 2-8-11 0 MickyFenton 6 47
(T P Tate) *chsd ldrs: pushed along 1/2-way: sn rdn and outpcd fr wl over 1f out* **10/1**

7 *13* **Golda Go** 2-7-13 0 PaulPickard(5) 3 —
(P T Midgley) *s.i.s: a in rr* **50/1**

60.49 secs (0.69) **Going Correction** -0.15s/f (Firm) **7** Ran SP% **108.5**
Speed ratings (Par 91): **88,86,86,80,79 76,55**
Tote Swingers: 1&2 £1.20, 1&3 £1.30, 2&3 £2.00 CSF £3.18 TOTE £2.20: £2.50, £1.10; EX 3.10.

Owner S A Heley **Bred** Oghill House Stud **Trained** Great Habton, N Yorks

■ Stewards' Enquiry : Silvestre De Sousa three-day ban: careless riding (May 18-20)

FOCUS
After a dry, breezy day the ground was changed to firm, good to firm in places. This was an ordinary auction maiden which has been rated around the winner and averages.

NOTEBOOK
First Class Favour(IRE), third behind a subsequent winner on her debut at Doncaster, had the plum number one draw. With the rail on her inside she mastered the pacesetter and was always doing more than enough. In the longer term nurseries beckon. (op 5-6 tchd 8-11)

Melodize, fifth first time at Windsor in a race that had thrown up a ready Bath winner earlier in the day, was under pressure at halfway. She persisted in hanging left interfering with two opponents but in the end the winner was always holding her challenge. A flatter, more orthodox track will suit her better. (op 11-4)
Choose Wisely(IRE), very inexperienced first time, shaped better and looked second best on merit. He should improve again and find a similar event. (op 8-1)
Novalist, full of himself beforehand, stayed on nicely late on down the outside. This should have taught him plenty.
Mini Bon Bon, having her third start, is well named. After taking them along she was on the retreat when hampered by the second. She looks something of a short runner. (op 33-1)
Wild Hysteria(IRE), on his toes beforehand, ran as if both the outing and the experience was needed. There should be a fair bit better to come. Official explanation: jockey said gelding was unsuited by the track (tchd 9-1 and 12-1)

1801 BOOK RACEDAY HOSPITALITY ON 01748 810165 CLAIMING STKS 1m 3f 214y
6:30 (6:30) (Class 6) 4-Y-0+ **£2,047** (£604; £302) **Stalls** Low

Form RPR
45-3 **1** **Slip**[57] 565 5-8-13 72 .... JamieSpencer 2 72
(Tim Vaughan) *trckd ldrs: hdwy over 2f out: led wl over 1f out: rdn and edgd lft ent fnl f: sn drvn and hld on wl towards fin* **7/4**[1]
300- **2** *hd* **Eijaaz (IRE)**[182] 7222 9-8-7 60 ....(p) SilvestreDeSousa 13 66
(G A Harker) *hld up in rr: stdy hdwy on inner over 3f out: swtchd rt and effrt wl over 1f out: rdn to chse wnr ent fnl f: sn drvn to chal and ev ch tl no ex nr fin* **3/1**[2]
3 *7* **Authentic Act (IRE)**[53] 6-8-11 67 .... PhillipMakin 8 59
(M Todhunter) *in tch: hdwy on outer over 2f out: rdn wl over 1f out: kpt on ins fnl f: tk 3rd nr line* **20/1**
5-05 **4** *nk* **Back To Paris (IRE)**[8] 1570 8-8-7 62 .... AndrewElliott 3 54
(Paul Murphy) *led: rdn along 3f out: drvn 2f out: sn hdd and kpt on same pce* **8/1**[3]
20-3 **5** *1 ¾* **Tropical Bachelor (IRE)**[10] 1526 4-8-7 56 ....(b) TomEaves 12 52
(T J Pitt) *trckd ldng pair: hdwy and cl up 1/2-way: rdn along over 2f out: drvn wl over 1f out and grad wknd* **8/1**[3]
6 *6* **Flockton Tobouggie**[6] 4-8-8 0 .... JamesSullivan(5) 6 48
(M W Easterby) *midfield: hdwy to chse ldrs over 4f out: rdn along 3f out and sn wknd* **20/1**
003- **7** *1 ¾* **Lady Norlela**[253] 5306 4-7-9 42 .... TimothyAyres(7) 7 34
(B S Rothwell) *chsd ldr: pushed along over 4f out: rdn along over 3f out: wknd over 2f out* **33/1**
-564 **8** *nk* **Anduril**[13] 521 9-8-0 44 .... NeilFarley(7) 11 39
(D Carroll) *chsd ldrs: rdn along over 3f out: drvn over 2f out and sn wknd* **20/1**
35-0 **9** *nse* **Cecina Marina**[8] 1576 7-7-13 46 .... KellyHarrison(3) 9 34
(Mrs K Walton) *chsd ldrs: rdn along 4f out: sn wknd* **12/1**
0/60 **10** *½* **I Feel Fine**[21] 1273 7-7-13 42 .... PaulPickard(5) 10 35
(A Kirtley) *s.i.s: a in rr* **100/1**
0-0 **11** *16* **Its Beyond Me**[27] 1149 6-8-2 0 .... IanBrennan(5) 15 12
(F P Murtagh) *midfield: pushed along 1/2-way: lost pl over 4f out and sn bhd* **100/1**
000- **12** *129* **Rain And Shade**[353] 2068 6-8-13 57 .... DavidAllan 14 —
(E W Tuer) *a in rr: pushed along 1/2-way: sn bhd and lost tch 4f out: eased fnl 2f* **33/1**

2m 36.15s (-2.75) **Going Correction** -0.15s/f (Firm) **12** Ran SP% **113.4**
Speed ratings (Par 101): **103,102,98,98,96 92,91,91,91,91 80,—**
Tote Swingers: 1&2 £1.60, 1&3 £13.90, 2&3 £12.60 CSF £5.66 TOTE £3.00: £1.80, £2.60, £6.90; EX 8.00.Slip was claimed by C. R. Dore for £8,000.
Owner M Khan X2 **Bred** Mrs H T Jones **Trained** Aberthin, Vale of Glamorgan
■ Stewards' Enquiry : Paul Pickard two-day ban: used whip when out of contention (May 18-19)

FOCUS
Plenty of dead wood in this claimer. The form is rated around the runner-up.

1802 DURHAM SCHOOL H'CAP 7f
7:00 (7:00) (Class 4) (0-80,85) 4-Y-0+ **£4,209** (£1,252; £625; £312) **Stalls** Low

Form RPR
600- **1** **Turn Me On (IRE)**[189] 7083 7-8-11 **80** .... LukeStrong(7) 2 88
(T D Walford) *a.p: effrt 2f out: rdn over 1f out: chal ent fnl f and sn n.m.r: styd on to ld last 100yds* **15/2**
-020 **2** *½* **Avontuur (FR)**[11] 1509 8-8-3 **70** ....(b) DeanHeslop(5) 5 76
(Mrs R A Carr) *chsd ldr: hdwy and cl up 2f out: rdn to chal over 1f out: drvn: edgd rt and led briefly wl ins fnl f: hdd and no ex last 100yds* **18/1**
1144 **3** *hd* **Smalljohn**[54] 867 4-8-7 **69** ....(v) TomEaves 4 75
(B Smart) *led: rdn along and edgd lft bnd 2f out: drvn wl over 1f out: hdd wl ins fnl f: no ex last 75yds* **7/1**
150- **4** *nk* **Poppet's Lovein**[204] 6731 4-9-2 **78** .... JamieSpencer 6 83
(A B Haynes) *hld up in rr: swtchd outside and hdwy wl over 1f out: rdn to chse ldrs ent fnl f: sn drvn and edgd lft: ev ch tl no ex last 75yds* **9/2**[2]
4-06 **5** *½* **Glenmuir (IRE)**[15] 1426 7-8-2 **69** .... IanBrennan(5) 7 73
(J J Quinn) *cl up on the outer: pushed along and lost pl 1/2-way: rdn and hdwy 2f out: drvn over 1f out: short of room ins fnl f: kpt on* **8/1**
-041 **6** *1 ¼* **Ezdeyaad (USA)**[4] 1672 6-9-9 **85** 6ex .... PJMcDonald 1 85
(G A Swinbank) *trckd ldng pair on inner: effrt whn nt clr run and hmpd bnd over 2f out: swtchd rt and rdn wl over 1f out: sn drvn and one pce* **13/8**[1]
6112 **7** *½* **Cornus**[5] 1641 8-7-13 **66** ....(be) DeclanCannon(5) 3 65
(A J McCabe) *dwlt: sn in tch: hdwy 2f out: rdn wl over 1f out: drvn and no imp appr fnl f* **6/1**[3]

1m 24.96s (-2.04) **Going Correction** -0.15s/f (Firm) **7** Ran SP% **111.2**
Speed ratings (Par 105): **105,104,104,103,103 101,101**
Tote Swingers: 1&2 £8.60, 1&3 £5.90, 2&3 £17.50 CSF £113.72 TOTE £8.00: £4.30, £9.20; EX 60.70.
Owner David Dickson **Bred** Brendan Lavery **Trained** Sheriff Hutton, N Yorks
■ Stewards' Enquiry : Tom Eaves one-day ban: careless riding (May 18)

FOCUS
A tight 66-85 handicap which resulted in a bunch finish. The form is sound.

1803 WE RACE AGAIN FRIDAY 21ST MAY H'CAP 1m 7f 177y
7:30 (7:32) (Class 6) (0-65,64) 4-Y-0+ **£2,047** (£604; £302) **Stalls** Low

Form RPR
4020 **1** **They All Laughed**[14] 1459 7-8-12 **50** ....(p) PhillipMakin 13 60
(Mrs Marjorie Fife) *hld up in rr: stdy hdwy on outer over 3f out: rdn wl over 1f out: str run to ld wl ins fnl f: sn clr* **12/1**
00-0 **2** *3 ¼* **Drop The Hammer**[29] 1113 4-8-9 **50** .... PaulMulrennan 3 56
(J Hetherton) *led: pushed along wl over 2f out: rdn and qcknd clr over 1f out: sn drvn: hdd and one pce wl ins fnl f* **33/1**
0-30 **3** *¾* **Amir Pasha (UAE)**[15] 1424 5-9-3 **55** ....(p) FrederikTylicki 12 60
(Micky Hammond) *chsd ldrs: rdn along wl over 2f out: drvn over 1f out: kpt on u.p fnl f* **12/1**
/1-1 **4** *1 ¾* **Sendali (FR)**[29] 1113 6-9-2 **54** .... JamieSpencer 9 59+
(J D Bethell) *dwlt: sn in tch in midfield: hdwy to trck ldrs 6f out: hdwy 3f out: rdn to chse ldrs 2f out: drvn and hld whn n.m.r ins fnl f* **4/1**[2]
000- **5** *¾* **Royal Flynn**[39] 6822 8-8-11 **52** ....(p) KellyHarrison(3) 10 54
(Mrs K Walton) *dwlt and towards rr: hdwy over 3f out: rdn along 2f out: kpt on appr fnl f: nrest at fin* **22/1**
0-24 **6** *¾* **Born To Perform**[15] 1424 5-9-8 **60** .... KierenFallon 15 61
(G A Swinbank) *dwlt: sn trcking ldrs: hdwy and cl up after 6f: effrt 3f out: rdn along 2f out: drvn over 1f out and sn wknd* **13/8**[1]
60-3 **7** *6* **Luna Landing**[21] 1273 7-9-12 **64** ....(b) TonyHamilton 2 58
(Jedd O'Keeffe) *dwlt and reminders s: sn in tch: rdn along over 3f out: drvn 2f out and sn wknd* **12/1**
160- **8** *2 ¼* **Harcas (IRE)**[227] 6102 8-9-3 **55** .... PJMcDonald 14 46
(M Todhunter) *a towards rr* **22/1**
363- **9** *2 ¾* **Obara D'Avril (FR)**[203] 6769 8-8-7 **50** .... PaulPickard(5) 11 38
(S G West) *s.i.s: a bhd* **11/1**
0121 **10** *½* **Nayessence**[10] 1539 4-9-3 **63** ....(t) JamesSullivan(5) 7 50
(M W Easterby) *chsd ldr: pushed along over 4f out: rdn over 3f out and sn wknd* **9/1**[3]
006- **11** *3* **Daltaban (FR)**[45] 7712 6-8-12 **50** .... AndrewMullen 8 34
(P Salmon) *midfield: rdn along 5f out: sn wknd* **100/1**
40-4 **12** *6* **Weetfromthechaff**[13] 1467 5-9-1 **53** ....(t) GregFairley 4 30
(M A Barnes) *chsd ldrs: rdn along 4f out: drvn and wknd wl over 2f out* **28/1**

3m 27.84s (-4.16) **Going Correction** -0.15s/f (Firm)
WFA 4 from 5yo+ 3lb **12** Ran SP% **115.6**
Speed ratings (Par 101): **104,102,102,101,100 100,97,96,94,94 93,90**
Tote Swingers: 1&2 £87.50, 1&3 £17.00, 2&3 £92.90 CSF £359.10 CT £4757.46 TOTE £22.10: £5.80, £15.60, £5.90; EX 392.30.
Owner Green Lane **Bred** T G And B B Mills **Trained** Stillington, N Yorks

FOCUS
A 50-64 stayers' handicap run at a sound pace and not without incident. Pretty solid form for the grade with the winner rated close to AW best.
Sendali(FR) Official explanation: jockey said gelding was denied a clear run

1804 CATTERICKBRIDGE.CO.UK MAIDEN STKS 7f
8:00 (8:04) (Class 5) 3-Y-0+ **£2,331** (£693; £346; £173) **Stalls** Low

Form RPR
02-2 **1** **Dherghaam (IRE)**[24] 1222 3-9-0 77 .... TadhgO'Shea 11 90
(E A L Dunlop) *prom: chsd ldr after 2f: effrt to ld over 2f out: rdn clr over 1f out: kpt on strly* **10/3**[2]
24-2 **2** *3 ¾* **Tesslam**[13] 1475 3-9-0 76 .... PhilipRobinson 2 80
(M A Jarvis) *chsd ldr 2f: prom: effrt to chse wnr wl over 1f out: sn rdn and no imp fnl f* **1/1**[1]
3 *7* **Kathlatino** 3-8-9 0 .... FrederikTylicki 4 56
(Micky Hammond) *uns rdr and rn loose bef s: towards rr: hdwy 2f out: swtchd lft and rdn over 1f out: styd on fnl f: nrest at fin* **100/1**
50- **4** *1 ½* **Baraconti (IRE)**[206] 6672 3-9-0 0 .... TonyHamilton 5 57
(R A Fahey) *in rr: hdwy 2f out: sn rdn and styd on ins fnl f* **16/1**
5 *nse* **Roose Blox (IRE)** 3-9-0 0 .... TomEaves 6 57+
(R F Fisher) *s.i.s and bhd: hdwy on outer wl over 1f out: sn rdn and kpt on ins fnl f* **100/1**
0 **6** *1 ½* **Concurrence (USA)**[27] 1164 3-9-0 0 .... GregFairley 1 53+
(M Johnston) *chsd ldrs: rdn along 1/2-way: sn rn green and lost pl: one pce fnl 2f* **11/2**[3]
44-0 **7** *½* **Hettie Hubble**[8] 1574 4-9-0 48 .... DuilioDaSilva(7) 7 50
(D W Thompson) *chsd ldrs: rdn along over 2f out: sn drvn and wknd wl over 1f out* **66/1**
0 **8** *1 ½* **Accamelia**[12] 1485 4-9-4 0 .... KellyHarrison(3) 8 46
(C W Fairhurst) *s.i.s: a in rr* **100/1**
/0-3 **9** *1 ¾* **Grand Stitch (USA)**[27] 1153 4-9-12 75 .... DavidNolan 10 47
(D Carroll) *set str pce: rdn and hdd wl over 2f out: sn wknd* **12/1**
05-0 **10** *1 ¾* **Hail Bold Chief (USA)**[13] 1464 3-9-0 0 .... PJMcDonald 3 38
(G A Swinbank) *in tch: pushed along and bhd fr 1/2-way* **14/1**

1m 24.62s (-2.38) **Going Correction** -0.15s/f (Firm)
WFA 3 from 4yo+ 12lb **10** Ran SP% **113.2**
Speed ratings (Par 103): **107,102,94,93,92 91,90,88,86,84**
Tote Swingers: 1&2 £1.80, 1&3 £42.60, 2&3 £26.10 CSF £6.77 TOTE £3.50: £1.10, £1.40, £24.60; EX 7.70.
Owner Hamdan Al Maktoum **Bred** Shadwell Estate Company Limited **Trained** Newmarket, Suffolk

FOCUS
A modest maiden with plenty of dead wood, but the time was quicker than the preceding handicap over the same distance won by an 80-rated horse. Improvement from the winner.

1805 DON'T MISS TOTESPORT SATURDAY 29TH MAY H'CAP 5f
8:30 (8:31) (Class 5) (0-70,68) 4-Y-0+ **£2,456** (£725; £362) **Stalls** Low

Form RPR
14-4 **1** **Lost In Paris (IRE)**[10] 1524 4-9-1 **65** ....(b) DavidAllan 5 85+
(T D Easterby) *qckly away and set str pce: rdn and qcknd clr wl over 1f out: eased towards fin* **7/4**[1]
436- **2** *3 ½* **Caribbean Coral**[218] 6341 11-8-12 **62** .... PhillipMakin 4 62
(A B Haynes) *chsd ldrs: rdn along 2f out: styd on wl fnl f: nrest at fin* **25/1**
000- **3** *hd* **Angelo Poliziano**[173] 7355 4-9-3 **67** .... TadhgO'Shea 8 66
(Mrs A Duffield) *dwlt and towards rr: hdwy on outer ovver 2f out: rdn wl over 1f out: kpt on wl fnl f* **50/1**
5032 **4** *½* **Lucky Art (USA)**[3] 1711 4-9-4 **68** .... SilvestreDeSousa 10 65
(Mrs R A Carr) *chsd wnr: rdn along 2f out: drvn over 1f out: no imp ins fnl f: wknd and lost 2nd nr fin* **2/1**[2]
00-0 **5** *2 ½* **Baybshambles (IRE)**[18] 1366 6-9-3 **67** .... TonyHamilton 6 55
(R E Barr) *in tch: rdn along 2f out: sn no imp* **10/1**[3]
00-0 **6** *1 ¼* **Speedy Senorita (IRE)**[18] 1363 5-8-10 **65** .... IanBrennan(5) 7 49
(J J Quinn) *chsd ldng pair: rdn along 2f out: sn drvn and wknd* **16/1**
0-46 **7** *6* **Spirit Of Coniston**[27] 1154 7-8-11 **61** .... TonyCulhane 1 23
(P T Midgley) *chsd ldrs: rdn along over 2f out: grad wknd* **12/1**
10-0 **8** *7* **Hitches Dubai (BRZ)**[47] 913 5-8-13 **63** .... AdrianNicholls 2 —
(D Nicholls) *a towards rr* **16/1**
20-1 **9** *11* **Micky Mac (IRE)**[7] 1598 6-9-0 **64** 6ex .... KierenFallon 9 —
(C J Teague) *s.i.s: a in rr* **10/1**[3]

58.87 secs (-0.93) **Going Correction** -0.15s/f (Firm) **9** Ran SP% **113.1**
Speed ratings (Par 103): **101,95,95,94,90 88,78,67,49**
Tote Swingers: 1&2 £13.50, 1&3 £6.80, 2&3 £19.40 CSF £46.42 CT £1598.62 TOTE £1.70: £1.02, £9.60, £14.50; EX 52.60 Place 6 £987.30, Place 5 £864.95..
Owner W H Ponsonby **Bred** Yeomanstown Stud **Trained** Great Habton, N Yorks

FOCUS
A modest 61-68 sprint handicap but a hugely impressive all-the-way winner wo was value fior nearer 6l. The form is rated around the second and third.
Micky Mac(IRE) Official explanation: jockey said gelding never travelled
T/Plt: £301.60 to a £1 stake. Pool: £52,760.03. 127.70 winning tickets. T/Qpdt: £264.70 to a £1 stake. Pool: £3,793.06. 10.60 winning tickets. JR

1569 NEWCASTLE (L-H)

Tuesday, May 4

OFFICIAL GOING: Good to firm (firm in places; 8.0)
Wind: Almost nil Weather: Cloudy

1806 EUROPEAN BREEDERS' FUND MEDIAN AUCTION MAIDEN STKS — 5f
2:10 (2:10) (Class 5) 2-Y-O — **£3,626** (£1,079; £539; £269) **Stalls** High

Form — RPR
1 **On The High Tops (IRE)** 2-9-3 0 .... MickyFenton 7 — 83+
(T P Tate) *prom: effrt over 1f out: styd on wl to ld towards fin* **5/1[3]**
2 *nk* **Premier Clarets (IRE)** 2-9-3 0 .... TonyHamilton 4 — 82
(R A Fahey) *led: rdn over 1f out: edgd lft ins fnl f: kpt on: hdd towards fin* **4/1[2]**
3 *3 ¾* **Its You Again** 2-9-3 0 .... JerryO'Dwyer 3 — 68
(M G Quinlan) *w ldrs tl rdn and no ex ins fnl f* **20/1**
4 *2* **Mysterious Bounty (IRE)** 2-9-3 0 .... PhillipMakin 6 — 61+
(M Dods) *s.i.s: hld up in tch: effrt 2f out: edgd lft: styd on fnl f: no imp* **7/2[1]**
04 5 *2 ¾* **Unknown Rebel (IRE)**[26] [1180] 2-8-12 0 .... MichaelO'Connell(5) 9 — 51
(K A Ryan) *w ldrs tl rdn and wknd appr fnl f* **10/1**
6 *1 ½* **Fast Shot** 2-9-3 0 .... DavidAllan 1 — 46
(T D Easterby) *hld up in tch: rdn and wnt rt 2f out: sn outpcd* **9/1**
7 *2 ¼* **Red Snapper (IRE)** 2-9-3 0 .... PaulMulrennan 8 — 38
(J R Weymes) *s.i.s: bhd and outpcd: sme late hdwy: nvr on terms* **25/1**
8 *2 ¾* **Waking Warrior** 2-9-3 0 .... NeilCallan 5 — 39+
(K A Ryan) *dwlt: hld up: rdn whn checked 2f out: hung lft and sn btn: eased whn no ch ins fnl f* **13/2**
63 9 *¾* **Imperial Waltzer**[18] [1360] 2-9-3 0 .... PJMcDonald 2 — 25
(G M Moore) *in tch: drvn after 2f: wknd fr 2f out* **9/1**

61.04 secs (-0.06) **Going Correction** -0.275s/f (Firm) — **9** Ran SP% **109.9**
Speed ratings (Par 93): **86,85,79,76,71 69,65,61,60**
toteswingers: 1&2 £8.50, 1&3 £35.70, 2&3 £7.80 CSF £23.30 CT £204.50 TOTE £5.80: £1.60, £3.90, £10.90; EX 27.90 Trifecta £204.50 Part won. Pool of £276.46 - 0.97 winning units..
Owner The Ivy Syndicate **Bred** Mrs Clodagh McStay **Trained** Tadcaster, N Yorks

FOCUS
They finished strung out behind the front two, but this was probably a fair maiden for the track and time of year. The winner can build on the bare form.

NOTEBOOK
On The High Tops(IRE), a £34,000 already gelded half-brother to Greek 7f-1m winner Elusive Boy, out of 1m2f winner, justified market confidence with a narrow success on debut. He'll be suited by further in due course and looks useful. (op 7-1)
Premier Clarets(IRE), a £25,000 half-brother to a number of winners, showed good speed throughout but was caught in the final strides. He should be hard to beat next time. (op 5-2)
Its You Again, a £5,500 half-brother to a couple of modest winners out of a fair sprinter, showed speed but didn't see his race out. He should come on for this. (op 16-1)
Mysterious Bounty(IRE), a 35,000euros half-brother to French 7.5f-1m winner Aldo L'Argentin, had to be niggled along soon after leaving the stalls and never looked like winning. He apparently had a racecourse gallop, yet still seemed badly in need of this experience. (op 9-2 tchd 5-1)
Unknown Rebel(IRE) showed speed against the rail but didn't see his race out. (op 11-1)
Fast Shot, who cost only 1,000gns, was not helped by the wide draw and ran green from about halfway. He's open to a deal of improvement. (op 16-1)
Red Snapper(IRE) ran green.
Waking Warrior was never competitive after starting slowly. (tchd 6-1)

1807 BORDER MINSTREL RE-OPENING 14TH MAY H'CAP — 1m 4f 93y
2:40 (2:40) (Class 5) (0-70,70) 4-Y-0+ — **£2,719** (£809; £404; £202) **Stalls** Low

Form — RPR
4-0 1 **Monreale (GER)**[26] [294] 6-9-1 67 .... (t) GregFairley 11 — 76+
(D E Pipe) *hld up in midfield on outside: hdwy to ld appr fnl f: pushed out* **7/1[3]**
0-03 2 *½* **Destinys Dream (IRE)**[4] [1655] 5-9-1 67 .... PhillipMakin 2 — 78+
(Miss Tracy Waggott) *t.k.h: prom whn nt clr run over 2f out to over 1f out: sn rdn: hdwy to chse wnr ins fnl f: r.o* **2/1[1]**
2-22 3 *1 ¾* **Patavium (IRE)**[15] [1427] 7-8-8 60 .... TonyHamilton 12 — 66
(E W Tuer) *t.k.h: prom: led over 2f out to appr fnl f: lost 2nd and one pce ins fnl f* **9/1**
226- 4 *3* **Madamlily (IRE)**[219] [6313] 4-9-2 68 .... GrahamGibbons 7 — 69
(J J Quinn) *in tch: effrt 2f out: kpt on same pce appr fnl f* **16/1**
-213 5 *1 ¼* **Brockfield**[20] [1296] 4-9-1 67 .... AlanMunro 8 — 66
(M Brittain) *plld hrd early: cl up: ev ch and rdn over 2f out: outpcd fnl f* **9/2[2]**
25-1 6 *2* **Shekan Star**[8] [1576] 8-7-11 56 oh3 .... MatthewLawson(7) 5 — 52
(K G Reveley) *missed break: bhd: hdwy on outside over 2f out: edgd lft: no imp appr fnl f* **10/1**
/00- 7 *½* **Duty Free (IRE)**[246] [1581] 6-9-4 70 .... FrederikTylicki 10 — 65
(James Moffatt) *trckd ldrs: drvn over 2f out: waekened wl over 1f out* **16/1**
220- 8 *1 ¾* **Amazing King (IRE)**[163] [6768] 6-8-13 65 .... LeeVickers 9 — 57
(P A Kirby) *hld up: nt clr run over 2f out: shkn up and no imp over 1f out* **25/1**
6226 9 *hd* **Nakoma (IRE)**[13] [1467] 8-8-4 56 oh1 .... RoystonFfrench 6 — 48
(B Ellison) *cl up: rdn and lost pl whn hmpd wl over 1f out: n.d after* **9/1**
4450 10 *2 ¼* **Lava Steps (USA)**[17] [1398] 4-8-8 60 ow1 .... (p) TonyCulhane 13 — 48
(P T Midgley) *t.k.h: hld up: drvn over 2f out: nvr on terms* **20/1**
5/0- 11 *4 ½* **Starbougg**[108] [7084] 6-8-1 56 oh11 .... KellyHarrison(3) 4 — 37
(K G Reveley) *set stdy pce: rdn and hdd over 2f out: sn wknd* **100/1**

2m 43.73s (-1.87) **Going Correction** -0.075s/f (Good) — **11** Ran SP% **114.5**
Speed ratings (Par 103): **103,102,101,99,98 97,97,95,95,94 91**
toteswingers: 1&2 £5.80, 1&3 £11.90, 2&3 £3.30 CSF £20.31 CT £128.14 TOTE £9.20: £3.70, £1.60, £1.10; EX 13.60 Trifecta £175.80 Part won. Pool of £237.70 - 0.60 winning units..
Owner Inglethorpe **Bred** Stall Le Premier **Trained** Nicholashayne, Devon

FOCUS
A modest handicap and the early pace was steady, resulting in a time 5.03 seconds over standard. Ordinary form but the winner can do better.
Shekan Star Official explanation: jockey said mare missed the break
Nakoma(IRE) Official explanation: jockey said mare was denied a clear run

1808 NORTHERN GRILL ONE H'CAP — 7f
3:10 (3:10) (Class 5) (0-75,74) 4-Y-0+ — **£2,719** (£809; £404; £202) **Stalls** High

Form — RPR
-030 1 **Game Lad**[3] [1707] 8-8-13 69 .... (tp) DavidAllan 8 — 82
(T D Easterby) *hld up in tch: smooth hdwy 2f out: shkn up to ld over 1f out: pushed clr ins fnl f: eased nr fin* **3/1[2]**
360- 2 *3 ¾* **Celtic Lynn (IRE)**[240] [5697] 5-9-3 73 .... PhillipMakin 6 — 75
(M Dods) *stdd s: hld up: hdwy over 1f out: rdn to chse wnr ins fnl f: one pce* **2/1[1]**
05-0 3 *2 ¾* **Big Whitfield**[27] [1179] 4-8-1 62 .... PatrickDonaghy(5) 2 — 57
(M Dods) *dictated modest gallop: rdn and hdd over 1f out: sn one pce* **16/1**
2000 4 *2* **Mozayada (USA)**[17] [1396] 6-8-6 62 .... AlanMunro 4 — 52
(M Brittain) *trckd ldrs: drvn and outpcd 2f out: no imp fnl f* **16/1**
0650 5 *1 ¾* **Classic Descent**[15] [1426] 5-8-4 60 .... AndrewElliott 3 — 45
(Mrs R A Carr) *s.v.s: rcvrd to join gp after 2f: effrt over 2f out: sn outpcd* **8/1**
5-65 6 *1 ¼* **Green Agenda**[12] [1494] 4-8-9 65 .... (b[1]) JoeFanning 5 — 47
(M Johnston) *trckd ldrs: drvn and outpcd 2f out: sn n.d* **4/1[3]**
1460 7 *6* **Whatyouwoodwishfor (USA)**[11] [1509] 4-8-6 62 .... RoystonFfrench 1 — 27
(R A Fahey) *cl up tl rdn and wknd fr 2f out* **7/1**

1m 26.24s (-2.46) **Going Correction** -0.275s/f (Firm) — **7** Ran SP% **113.7**
Speed ratings (Par 103): **103,98,95,93,91 89,83**
toteswingers: 1&2 £1.40, 1&3 £18.70, 2&3 £16.00 CSF £9.33 CT £77.49 TOTE £3.30: £1.50, £1.10; EX 11.20 Trifecta £138.20 Pool of £422.35 - 2.26 winning units..
Owner T D Easterby **Bred** M H Easterby **Trained** Great Habton, N Yorks
■ Stewards' Enquiry : David Allan caution: careless riding
Patrick Donaghy one-day ban: careless riding (May 18)

FOCUS
An ordinary handicap and the pace was fair, setting this up for a couple of the hold-up performers. The first three raced on the rail and this was not the most competitive event.
Classic Descent Official explanation: jockey said gelding missed the break
Whatyouwoodwishfor(USA) Official explanation: jockey said gelding hung right throughout

1809 PFS AND DIRECT TECHNOLOGY MAIDEN FILLIES' STKS — 1m 2f 32y
3:40 (3:42) (Class 5) 3-Y-0+ — **£2,719** (£809; £404; £202) **Stalls** Centre

Form — RPR
3-4 1 **Kronful**[22] [1268] 3-8-8 0 .... FrankieDettori 1 — 73+
(M A Jarvis) *set stdy pce: rdn over 1f out: styd on strly to go clr ins fnl f* **30/100[1]**
2 *2 ¼* **Tartaria** 4-9-9 0 .... KierenFallon 5 — 66
(D M Simcock) *t.k.h: in tch: hdwy to press wnr over 1f out: sn rdn: kpt on same pce ins fnl f* **5/1[2]**
4 3 *½* **Sheiling (IRE)**[10] [1528] 3-8-8 0 .... TonyHamilton 2 — 64
(R A Fahey) *t.k.h: trckd ldrs: effrt and rdn over 2f out: kpt on ins fnl f* **20/1**
4 *4 ½* **Cat O' Nine Tails** 3-8-8 0 .... JoeFanning 4 — 55
(M Johnston) *pressed wnr tl rdn and wknd over 1f out* **12/1[3]**
0 5 *6* **Lucky Belle (IRE)**[12] [1485] 3-8-3 0 .... PatrickDonaghy(5) 3 — 43
(M Dods) *dwlt: plld hrd in tch: struggling over 2f out: sn wknd: eased whn no ch fnl f* **40/1**

2m 13.3s (1.40) **Going Correction** -0.075s/f (Good)
WFA 3 from 4yo 15lb — **5** Ran SP% **108.5**
Speed ratings (Par 100): **91,89,88,85,80**
CSF £2.08 TOTE £1.20: £1.10, £1.90.
Owner Sheikh Ahmed Al Maktoum **Bred** Darley **Trained** Newmarket, Suffolk

FOCUS
A weak fillies' maiden and not easy form to assess.

1810 IPC SECURITY H'CAP — 1m (R)
4:10 (4:11) (Class 5) (0-70,68) 3-Y-O — **£2,719** (£809; £404; £202) **Stalls** Centre

Form — RPR
343- 1 **Mighty Clarets (IRE)**[197] [6895] 3-8-10 67 .... LeeTopliss(7) 2 — 69
(R A Fahey) *led 1f: cl up: led over 2f out: rdn and hung rt over 1f out: hung lft ins fnl f: r.o* **3/1[2]**
005- 2 *½* **Emerald Glade (IRE)**[230] [5980] 3-8-6 56 .... DuranFentiman 9 — 57
(T D Easterby) *trckd ldrs: effrt 2f out: pressed wnr ins fnl f: kpt on: hld towards fin* **12/1**
00-0 3 *1 ¼* **On The Cusp (IRE)**[27] [1178] 3-9-3 67 .... FrankieDettori 8 — 65
(M A Jarvis) *hld up: effrt on outside 2f out: edgd lft and kpt on u.p ins fnl f* **13/2**
2133 4 *1 ¼* **Miami Gator (IRE)**[60] [812] 3-9-2 66 .... AndrewElliott 6 — 61
(J R Weymes) *hld up in tch: drvn and outpcd over 2f out: rallied appr fnl f: kpt on* **8/1**
-020 5 *½* **Always Dixie (IRE)**[20] [1298] 3-8-5 55 .... JoeFanning 5 — 49
(M Johnston) *s.i.s: rcvrd and led after 1f: hdd over 2f out: rallied: one pce fnl f* **14/1**
-021 6 *1 ¾* **Take My Hand**[13] [1469] 3-8-13 63 .... KierenFallon 4 — 62+
(M R Channon) *prom: drvn over 2f out: rallied over 1f out: 4th and styng on steadily whn hmpd and snatched up ins fnl f: nt rcvr* **9/4[1]**
2-40 7 *½* **Danceintothelight**[13] [1464] 3-9-4 68 .... NeilCallan 5 — 57
(K A Ryan) *prom on outside tl rdn and wknd over 1f out* **11/2[3]**
6-00 8 *2 ¼* **Electric City (IRE)**[34] [1061] 3-9-1 65 .... AlanMunro 7 — 49
(M G Quinlan) *hld up on ins: struggling over 2f out: sn btn* **40/1**
50-0 9 *29* **Dinkys Diamond (IRE)**[8] [1572] 3-8-4 54 .... RoystonFfrench 3 — —
(B Ellison) *hld up: struggling 3f out: lost tch fnl 2f: t.o* **80/1**

1m 44.74s (-0.56) **Going Correction** -0.075s/f (Good) — **9** Ran SP% **113.6**
Speed ratings (Par 99): **99,98,97,96,95 93,93,91,62**
toteswingers: 1&2 £10.00, 1&3 £6.10, 2&3 £14.80 CSF £37.95 CT £218.38 TOTE £3.00: £1.10, £6.20, £1.30; EX 37.90 Trifecta £354.50 Part won. Pool of £497.06 - 0.83 winning units..
Owner Dale Scaffolding Co Ltd **Bred** Ellesmere Bloodstock Ltd **Trained** Musley Bank, N Yorks
■ Stewards' Enquiry : Lee Topliss four-day ban: careless riding (May 18-21)

FOCUS
A modest handicap and the early pace was not particularly strong. The form makes a fair bit of sense.

1811 JOHN BURDON MEMORIAL "EACH WAY" H'CAP — 6f
4:40 (4:40) (Class 5) (0-70,70) 3-Y-O — **£2,719** (£809; £404; £202) **Stalls** High

Form — RPR
0-41 1 **Whispered Times (USA)**[5] [1651] 3-8-3 58 .... KellyHarrison(3) 9 — 69
(Miss Tracy Waggott) *mde all: rdn and edgd lft over 1f out: kpt on strly fnl f* **9/4[1]**
530- 2 *1 ¼* **Sharp Eclipse**[352] [2099] 3-8-10 62 .... NeilCallan 10 — 69
(K A Ryan) *trckd ldrs: swtchd lft and chsd wnr over 1f out: kpt on ins fnl f* **7/2[2]**

250- **3** *2* **Rio Caribe (IRE)**[276] 4515 3-9-1 **67**.......................... GrahamGibbons 11 68
(T D Walford) *hld up on ins: hdwy over 1f out: kpt on fnl f: nt rch first two* **11/1**

0-00 **4** *4 ½* **Tislaam (IRE)**[18] 1362 3-9-3 **69**..................................(p) PaulMulrennan 4 56
(J S Wainwright) *t.k.h: hld up: rdn 2f out: styd on fnl f: nvr able to chal* **33/1**

03-6 **5** *2* **Reddy To Star (IRE)**[17] 1401 3-8-12 **67**..................... BarryMcHugh(3) 1 47
(Julie Camacho) *cl up on outside tl rdn and wknd appr fnl f* **22/1**

00-1 **6** *¾* **Taborcillo**[13] 1468 3-9-0 **66**... PhillipMakin 3 44
(T D Barron) *t.k.h early: cl up: rdn over 2f out: wknd over 1f out* **5/1**[3]

34-4 **7** *1 ¾* **Mercers Row**[13] 1464 3-9-4 **70**..................................... DanielTudhope 2 42
(A Dickman) *dwlt: midfield on outside: effrt over 2f out: wknd over 1f out* **16/1**

346 **8** *¾* **Fillibeg (IRE)**[11] 1504 3-8-12 **64**...................................... TonyHamilton 8 34
(R A Fahey) *midfield: drvn over 2f out: wknd over 1f out* **14/1**

0-35 **9** *½* **Tell Me A Story**[10] 1511 3-8-13 **65**....................................... AlanMunro 7 33
(M Brittain) *dwlt: bhd: drvn 1/2-way: nvr rchd ldrs* **9/1**

4005 **10** *2 ½* **Pavement Games**[27] 1162 3-8-4 **56** oh11..................... FrannyNorton 6 16
(R C Guest) *plld hrd: prom tl rdn and wknd over 2f out* **33/1**

1-5 **11** *2 ½* **Midget**[27] 1175 3-8-11 **63**... DavidNolan 5 15
(D Carroll) *rrd s: hld up: pushed along over 2f out: sn btn* **16/1**

1m 13.74s (-0.86) **Going Correction** -0.275s/f (Firm) **11** Ran SP% **116.7**
Speed ratings (Par 99): **98,96,93,87,85 84,81,80,80,76 73**
toteswingers: 1&2 £2.40, 1&3 £9.60, 2&3 £9.90 CSF £9.40 CT £68.34 TOTE £3.90: £1.90, £1.10, £3.70; EX 12.20 Trifecta £132.70 Pool of £310.44 - 1.73 winning units..
Owner Michael Howarth **Bred** Hetrich-McCarthy Livestock **Trained** Spennymoor, Co Durham

FOCUS
A weak sprint handicap in which it paid to race prominently and on the rail. The winner is rated similarly to his Redcar win.
Tislaam(IRE) Official explanation: jockey said colt ran too free

1812 LA TAXIS H'CAP (DIV I) 7f
5:10 (5:10) (Class 6) (0-60,59) 4-Y-0+ **£1,878** (£558; £279; £139) **Stalls** High

Form RPR

4316 **1** **Imperial Djay (IRE)**[11] 1509 5-9-1 **56**........................... RobertWinston 6 63+
(Mrs R A Carr) *stdd s: hld up: nt clr run over 2f out to 1f out: qcknd to ld ins fnl f: r.o* **9/2**[3]

0066 **2** *½* **King's Sabre**[27] 1170 4-8-6 **47**.......................................(e) FrannyNorton 1 53+
(R C Guest) *t.k.h: hld up: hdwy over 1f out: ev ch ins fnl f: kpt on* **7/1**

65-3 **3** *1 ¾* **Fathey (IRE)**[8] 1574 4-9-3 **58**... JoeFanning 2 59
(C Smith) *w ldr on outside: led over 2f out: rdn and edgd rt over 1f out: hdd and no ex ins fnl f* **3/1**[1]

00-5 **4** *2 ¾* **Cool Art (IRE)**[5] 1651 4-9-0 **55**...................................... PaulMulrennan 4 49
(J S Wainwright) *prom: effrt 2f out: kpt on same pce fnl f* **25/1**

0/00 **5** *¾* **Loyal Knight (IRE)**[25] 1204 5-8-6 **47**..........................(t) DuranFentiman 9 39
(P T Midgley) *hld up: effrt on outside wl over 1f out: no imp fnl f* **16/1**

005- **6** *2 ¼* **Papa's Princess**[232] 5944 6-8-9 **50**.............................. RoystonFfrench 7 35
(James Moffatt) *rdr slow to remove blindfold but sn cl up: rdn over 2f out: wknd over 1f out* **20/1**

1065 **7** *shd* **Pipers Piping (IRE)**[19] 1320 4-9-1 **59**.................... MichaelStainton(3) 5 44
(P Howling) *t.k.h: w ldrs tl wknd over 1f out* **9/2**[3]

-300 **8** *5* **Northgate Lodge (USA)**[64] 753 5-8-6 **47** ow2................ AlanMunro 8 19
(M Brittain) *slt ld to over 2f out: wknd over 1f out* **16/1**

30-2 **9** *1* **Eye For The Girls**[29] 1130 4-9-0 **55**.............................. KierenFallon 10 24+
(M R Channon) *prom: nt clr run over 2f out: no room over 1f out: no imp whn short of room ins fnl f* **4/1**[2]

1m 27.76s (-0.94) **Going Correction** -0.275s/f (Firm) **9** Ran SP% **114.2**
Speed ratings (Par 101): **94,93,91,88,87 84,84,79,77**
toteswingers: 1&2 £4.40, 1&3 £3.40, 2&3 £4.60 CSF £35.51 CT £108.89 TOTE £6.70: £2.40, £3.60, £1.90; EX 39.90 Trifecta £68.10 Pool of £306.70 - 3.33 winning units..
Owner Hollinbridge Partnership **Bred** D Veitch And Musagd Abo Salim **Trained** Huby, N Yorks
■ Stewards' Enquiry : Michael Stainton three-day ban: careless riding (May 18-20)

FOCUS
A moderate but competitive handicap run in a time 0.93 seconds slower than the second division. The winner got the rail but this is potentially weak form.
Eye For The Girls Official explanation: jockey said gelding was denied a clear run

1813 LA TAXIS H'CAP (DIV II) 7f
5:40 (5:40) (Class 6) (0-60,58) 4-Y-0+ **£1,878** (£558; £279; £139) **Stalls** High

Form RPR

1532 **1** **Dhhamaan (IRE)**[20] 1304 5-8-6 **46**...........................(b) RobertWinston 10 61
(Mrs R A Carr) *mde all: set mod gallop: qcknd over 2f out: clr over 1f out: kpt on strly: eased nr fin* **11/4**[1]

004- **2** *3 ¾* **Cross Of Lorraine (IRE)**[247] 5465 7-8-12 **52**.............(b) TonyHamilton 9 57
(J Wade) *prom: effrt over 2f out: chsd wnr over 1f out: no imp ins fnl f* **15/2**

250- **3** *1 ¼* **Desert Hunter (IRE)**[254] 5289 7-8-13 **53**....................... FrederikTylicki 3 55+
(Micky Hammond) *in tch on outside: rdn and effrt 2f out: kpt on u.p ins fnl f* **8/1**

060- **4** *shd* **Fyodorovich (USA)**[217] 5730 5-8-5 **48** ow3.............(v) BarryMcHugh(3) 1 49
(J S Wainwright) *dwlt: hld up: hdwy over 1f out: kpt on fnl f: no imp* **20/1**

2300 **5** *6* **Fulford**[18] 1366 5-9-3 **57**.. AlanMunro 4 42
(M Brittain) *hld up: drvn over 2f out: nvr able to chal* **13/2**[3]

40-0 **6** *hd* **Eyes Like A Hawk (IRE)**[27] 1179 4-8-10 **55**.......... PatrickDonaghy(5) 7 39
(Jedd O'Keeffe) *stdd in rr: shkn up 2f out: nvr rchd ldrs* **33/1**

6303 **7** *hd* **Louisiade (IRE)**[8] 1575 9-8-7 **47**...................................(p) FrannyNorton 5 31
(R C Guest) *prom tl drvn and outpcd fr 2f out* **4/1**[2]

2600 **8** *8* **Angle Of Attack (IRE)**[8] 1569 5-9-1 **55**.....................(p) GrahamGibbons 6 17
(A D Brown) *pressed wnr to over 1f out: wknd* **10/1**

0265 **9** *11* **Guildenstern (IRE)**[10] 1534 8-9-4 **58**........................... KierenFallon 2 —
(P Howling) *hld up: effrt on outside over 2f out: sn wknd* **8/1**

004- **10** *10* **Aquapark**[39] 7725 4-8-5 **45**...(b[1]) RoystonFfrench 8 —
(R Craggs) *prom: lost pl 1/2-way: sn struggling* **100/1**

1m 26.83s (-1.87) **Going Correction** -0.275s/f (Firm) **10** Ran SP% **111.8**
Speed ratings (Par 101): **99,94,93,93,86 86,85,76,64,52**
toteswingers: 1&2 £4.10, 2&3 £13.70, 1&3 not won. CSF £22.25 CT £146.10 TOTE £3.10: £1.50, £1.60, £3.40; EX 27.00 Trifecta £156.50 Pool of £289.92 - 1.37 winning units. Place 6: £18.00 Place 5: £5.49.
Owner S B Clark **Bred** D Veitch And Musagd Abo Salim **Trained** Huby, N Yorks

FOCUS
The time was 0.93 seconds quicker than the first division. The first two and fourth raced on the favoured rail and the form is not rock solid.
Guildenstern(IRE) Official explanation: jockey said gelding was unsuited by the good to firm (firm in places) ground
T/Plt: £50.50 to a £1 stake. Pool: £49581.90, 716.11 winning tickets. T/Qpdt: £15.60 to a £1 stake. Pool: £3800.62, 179.30 winning tickets. RY

CHESTER (L-H)
Wednesday, May 5

OFFICIAL GOING: Good (7.8)
Course at normal configuration and distances as advertised.
Wind: light, against Weather: Overcast and drizzle

1819 MANOR HOUSE STABLES LILY AGNES CONDITIONS STKS 5f 16y
1:45 (1:48) (Class 2) 2-Y-0
£13,085 (£3,918; £1,959; £980; £489; £245) **Stalls** Low

Form RPR

04 **1** **Julius Geezer (IRE)**[21] 1309 2-8-12 0...................... RichardKingscote 5 92
(Tom Dascombe) *mde all: shkn up over 1f out: rdn ins fnl f and r.o wl: a in command* **12/1**

11 **2** *2 ¾* **Bathwick Bear (IRE)**[19] 1359 2-9-4 0........................... JimmyFortune 3 88
(P D Evans) *neat: chsd ldrs: wnt 2f out: rdn over 1f out: nt gng pce of wnr fnl f: jst hld on for 2nd cl home* **8/11**[1]

1 **3** *nse* **Primo Lady**[37] 1043 2-8-7 0...(v) LukeMorris 1 77
(Miss Gay Kelleway) *w'like: str: b.hind: lw: missed break: towards rr: hdwy over 2f out: r.o ins fnl f: jst failed to get 2nd cl home* **3/1**[2]

4 *1 ¼* **So Is She (IRE)** 2-8-7 0... JamieMackay 2 72+
(A Bailey) *unf: tall: bit bkwd: missed break: outpcd and bhd: plld out and hdwy over 1f out: rn green: styd on ins fnl f: nt gng pce to chal* **16/1**

32 **5** *½* **Coconut Ice**[11] 1527 2-8-7 0.. RichardSmith 7 73+
(Tom Dascombe) *athletic: racd keenly in tch: rdn and outpcd over 1f out: wanted to lugg lft fnl f: kpt on towards fin* **10/1**[3]

0 **6** *6* **Love Club**[20] 1331 2-8-12 0... DavidProbert 6 54
(B P J Baugh) *neat: chsd wnr to 2f out: rdn and wknd over 1f out* **150/1**

515 **7** *2 ½* **Little Libretto (IRE)**[3] 1733 2-8-10 0............................. CathyGannon 8 43
(P D Evans) *leggy: chsd ldrs: rdn over 2f out: sn wknd* **14/1**

61.64 secs (0.64) **Going Correction** -0.025s/f (Good) **7** Ran SP% **112.9**
Speed ratings (Par 99): **93,88,88,86,85 76,72**
toteswingers: 1&2 £2.00, 1&3 £4.70, 2&3 £1.10 CSF £20.85 TOTE £12.10: £3.90, £1.10; EX 29.10 Trifecta £58.30 Pool: £1050.82 - 13.33 winning units..
Owner Basing Bellman Newton Stroud **Bred** Ballyhane Stud **Trained** Malpas, Cheshire

FOCUS
This looked a weaker than average running of the Lily Agnes, and as usual for a sprint race at Chester, close up against the rail was the place to be. The form has been rated at face value with the second a good guide.

NOTEBOOK
Julius Geezer(IRE) made just about all of the running after showing sufficient speed from stall five. A buzzy, free-going type who didn't see his race out when fourth in a red-hot conditions race at Newmarket last time, this speed-favouring track proved ideal. He was again keen, despite the fitting of a cross noseband, but still ran on really strongly, taking this for a yard which sponsored the race, and he's clearly a pretty talented colt. However, he if is to progress in the long term, he will need to mature mentally and learn to settle, as right now he looks as though he could either way. (op 10-1)

Bathwick Bear(IRE), the winner of a Ffos Las maiden and a Thirsk novice event, was on his toes beforehand and broke well, but couldn't match the winner's early speed and had to settle for a stalking position. He was then one-paced in the straight and found the task of conceding weight all round too much. (op Evens tchd 11-10 in places)

Primo Lady, who had the visor fitted when winning a Polytrack maiden in nice style on debut (form has not worked out), ruined her chance this time by missing the break, having proved reluctant to load. She ran on okay in the straight, but never threatened the winner. (op 9-4)

So Is She(IRE) ◆, a £10,000 purchase, shaped really nicely. She was never seen in with a chance after missing the break, but kept on gradually in the straight and showed plenty of ability. (op 25-1)

Coconut Ice had been going better than the winner at home according to Tom Dascombe. However, she simply pulled much too hard when tracking the leaders from her wide draw. (op 11-1)

Little Libretto(IRE), slightly on her toes beforehand, was caught wide from the outside stall and never featured. (op 20-1)

1820 WEATHERBYS BANK CHESHIRE OAKS (FOR THE ROBERT SANGSTER MEMORIAL CUP) (LISTED RACE) 1m 3f 79y
2:15 (2:15) (Class 1) 3-Y-0
£22,708 (£8,608; £4,308; £2,148; £1,076; £540) **Stalls** Low

Form RPR

32-1 **1** **Gertrude Bell**[19] 1358 3-8-12 86....................................... WilliamBuick 6 98+
(J H M Gosden) *lw: racd keenly: chsd ldr: rdn to ld over 1f out: r.o gamely whn pressed ins fnl f: a doing enough* **5/2**[1]

0- **2** *¾* **Acquainted**[186] 7183 3-8-12 0... RichardHughes 4 96
(B W Hills) *led: rdn and hdd over 1f out: r.o u.p and continued to chal ins fnl f: hld cl home* **8/1**

10- **3** *hd* **Champagnelifestyle**[200] 6852 3-8-12 88........................... MichaelHills 3 96
(B W Hills) *lw: racd keenly: trckd ldrs: rdn and nt qckn 2f out: r.o to chal ins fnl f: run flattened out and no ex cl home* **11/2**

1251 **4** *hd* **Myplacelater**[19] 1354 3-8-12 97... DaneO'Neill 1 96+
(D R C Elsworth) *midfield: effrt and hdwy 1f out: swtchd lft fnl 150yds: r.o cl home: nt quite gng pce to get there* **4/1**[2]

3213 **5** *2* **Miss Starlight**[3] 1729 3-8-12 83.................................... EddieCreighton 2 92
(P J McBride) *hld up: hdwy on outside to chse ldrs over 2f out: outpcd over 1f out: sn hung lft: kpt on same pce ins fnl f* **6/1**

6 *1 ½* **Dance On By (IRE)**[38] 1035 3-8-12 0.................................. JMurtagh 7 89+
(A P O'Brien, Ire) *str: lw: swtchd lft s: hld up in last pl: rdn over 1f out: no hdwy and stl looked green* **5/1**[3]

45-2 **7** *4* **Miss Miracle**[41] 978 3-8-12 71....................................... LukeMorris 5 82?
(C G Cox) *racd ldrs: effrt over 2f out: wknd over 1f out* **18/1**

2m 26.98s (0.38) **Going Correction** -0.025s/f (Good) **7** Ran SP% **111.3**
Speed ratings (Par 107): **97,96,96,96,94 93,90**
toteswingers: 1&2 £18.60, 1&3 £2.40, 2&3 £12.10 CSF £21.76 TOTE £3.50: £2.00, £5.00; EX 42.20.
Owner Ms Rachel D S Hood **Bred** Ms Rachel Hood **Trained** Newmarket, Suffolk

FOCUS
Not always that strong a race, but Light Shift won it in 2007 before landing the Oaks, and Shadow Dancing was successful in 2002 before placing at Epsom, while in 2006 Mont Etoile was runner-up ahead of landing the Ribblesdale. This year's race didn't look much of an Oaks Trial, and a steady pace meant those who raced prominently were at an advantage. Not easy form to rate with the first three all improvers.

NOTEBOOK

Gertrude Bell won a maiden on her reappearance at Newbury that has gone to some smart types over the years (the likes of Clowance, Folk Opera, Eswarah and Islington) and she showed herself to be pretty decent in her own right. However, she was always well placed considering the way the race unfolded, and the bare form is ordinary for the level. So while she has a good attitude, and is entitled to improve when upped in trip (half-sister to 2m winner), it will be a surprise if she's good enough to win the Oaks. She's now around a 20-1 shot for Epsom. (op 3-1 tchd 10-3)

Acquainted showed little in a hot 7f maiden in one run for Michael Bell last year, but there's plenty of stamina on the dam's side of her pedigree and she produced a greatly improved effort over this longer trip on her return. She's entitled to progress again, but enjoyed the run of the race in front and this is not a performance to get carried away with. (op 16-1)

Champagnelifestyle, a winner on the July course on soft ground first time out last year, but well beaten in the Rockfel, has been a bit backward in her coat according to Barry Hills, and would have preferred a stronger pace, so this was a creditable effort. (op 5-1 tchd 9-2)

Myplacelater, who defeated some promising colts in what is often a hot conditions race at Newbury on her previous start, is better than she showed this time. She fared best of those held up, but had little hope of making a telling impression and would have preferred a stronger pace. (op 3-1)

Miss Starlight, third in the Pretty Polly at Newmarket three days earlier, is another better than she showed as she raced out the back in a slowly run race and made her move out wide. Plus, she prefers easier ground. (op 13-2 tchd 7-1)

Dance On By(IRE), a beaten favourite over 7f on her sole start at two, and shunned by Johnny Murtagh when well held over 1m2f on her return, refused to settle after being dropped out from her wide draw and was never involved. This sister to High Chaparral may mature into a nice type, but has plenty to prove for now. (op 9-2)

1821 TOTESPORT.COM CHESTER CUP (HERITAGE H'CAP) 2m 2f 147y

2:45 (2:46) (Class 2) 4-Y-O+

£74,772 (£22,392; £11,196; £5,604; £2,796; £1,404) **Stalls** High

Form				RPR
3/2-	**1**		**Mamlook (IRE)**[27] 6851 6-8-12 **96** ... RichardHughes 5 *(D E Pipe) lw: trckd ldrs: effrt over 2f out: wnt 2nd over 1f out: led narrowly ins fnl f: r.o gamely: prevailed in driving fin* **7/1**[1]	102
20-0	**2**	*hd*	**Tastahil (IRE)**[28] 1176 6-9-10 **108** ... RichardHills 16 *(B W Hills) lw: chsd ldr: led over 2f out: rdn and edgd lft over 1f out: hdd narrowly ins fnl f: r.o gamely w wnr and jst denied on the nod* **22/1**	114
0-33	**3**	*3/4*	**Halla San**[11] 1525 8-8-13 **97** ... PaulHanagan 6 *(R A Fahey) lw: chsd ldrs: pushed along 4f out: rdn 2f out: edgd lft over 1f out: r.o ins fnl f: nt quite pce of front pair* **9/1**[2]	102
201/	**4**	*shd*	**Majestic Concorde (IRE)**[216] 6321 7-9-1 **99** ... PJSmullen 1 *(D K Weld, Ire) lw: in tch: pushed along 4f out: rdn to chse ldrs and nt qckn 2f out: swtchd rt over 1f out: r.o ins fnl f: nt quite pce of ldrs* **14/1**	104
30-0	**5**	*3/4*	**Swingkeel (IRE)**[28] 1176 5-8-11 **95** ... (p) JimmyFortune 4 *(J L Dunlop) midfield: pushed along 2f out: swtchd lft and hdwy 1f out: styd on to chse ldrs ins fnl f: one pce cl home* **10/1**[3]	99+
100-	**6**	*2 1/4*	**Desert Sea (IRE)**[236] 5823 7-8-11 **95** ... MartinDwyer 3 *(D W P Arbuthnot) midfield: hdwy over 2f out: rdn and swtchd rt over 1f out: sn bmpd sltly: styd on same pce ins fnl f* **10/1**[3]	97
006-	**7**	*1/2*	**Som Tala**[189] 7117 7-8-3 **87** ... (v[1]) LukeMorris 2 *(M R Channon) in tch: rdn over 2f out: sn outpcd: edgd lft and styd on ins fnl f: nt pce of ldrs* **12/1**	88
5-01	**8**	*2 3/4*	**Red Cadeaux**[25] 1220 4-8-7 **95** ow1 ... KierenFallon 7 *(E A L Dunlop) n.m.r and hmpd after 1f: hld up: hdwy whn nt clr run 2f out: rdn and styng on whn n.m.r and hmpd jst ins fnl f: unable to rcvr* **10/1**[3]	93+
00-4	**9**	*hd*	**Rangefinder**[28] 1151 6-8-4 **88** ... JoeFanning 14 *(Jane Chapple-Hyam) hld up: rdn over 1f out and sme hdwy: no imp on ldrs* **33/1**	86
06-0	**10**	*2 1/2*	**Liszt (IRE)**[39] 1015 4-8-7 **96** ... (p) JamieSpencer 12 *(Ian Williams) led: rdn 3f out: hdd over 2f out: hmpd over 1f out and again whn btn sn after* **20/1**	90
50/5	**11**	*5*	**Raincoat**[28] 1176 6-8-10 **94** ... TedDurcan 18 *(F J Brennan) lw: swtchd lft s: hld up in rr: pushed along over 1f out: nvr able to chal* **25/1**	84
620-	**12**	*nk*	**Spring Jim**[20] 7018 9-8-3 **87** ... HayleyTurner 11 *(J R Fanshawe) lw: in tch: effrt to chse ldrs 3f out: wknd over 1f out* **20/1**	76
131-	**13**	*hd*	**Bernie The Bolt (IRE)**[228] 6115 4-8-7 **95** ... DavidProbert 15 *(A M Balding) bit bkwd: midfield: rdn over 2f out: wknd over 1f out* **9/1**[2]	84
560-	**14**	*11*	**Fiulin**[50] 5823 5-9-1 **99** ... JMurtagh 17 *(Evan Williams) chsd ldrs: rdn fr 6f out: wknd over 2f out* **22/1**	76
053/	**15**	*23*	**La Vecchia Scuola (IRE)**[600] 5853 6-8-4 **88** ... AndreaAtzeni 9 *(J S Goldie) midfield: rdn 6f out: wknd 5f out: sn wl bhd* **16/1**	40
045-	**16**	*39*	**Ajaan**[200] 6851 6-9-4 **102** ... (b) TomQueally 13 *(H R A Cecil) midfield: niggled along and lost pl after 5f: bhd fnl 6f: t.o* **11/1**	12
020-	**17**	*dist*	**Nemo Spirit (IRE)**[200] 6851 5-8-6 **90** ... RichardKingscote 10 *(Tom Dascombe) hld up: rdn and struggling 7f out: t.o* **12/1**	—

4m 3.74s (-1.06) **Going Correction** -0.025s/f (Good) **17** Ran SP% **121.0**

WFA 4 from 5yo+ 4lb

Speed ratings (Par 109): **101,100,100,100,100 99,99,97,97,96 94,94,94,89,80 64,—**

CSF £165.29 CT £1410.90 TOTE £7.10: £1.90, £6.70, £2.90, £3.10; EX 318.90 Trifecta £2698.10 Part won. Pool: £3646.11- 0.80 winning units..

Owner P A Deal & G Lowe **Bred** Peter Jones And G G Jones **Trained** Nicholashayne, Devon

■ Stewards' Enquiry : Richard Hills one-day ban: careless riding

Jimmy Fortune two-day ban: careless riding (May 19-20)

FOCUS

A typically competitive Chester Cup, but one lacking in unexposed, progressive types. The pace was just ordinary, meaning those who raced prominently were at an advantage, and the seven lowest drawn runners accounted for seven of the first eight finishers. The bare form is sound but nothing special.

NOTEBOOK

Mamlook(IRE), back on the Flat after a good season over hurdles, was beautifully ridden and narrowly defied a mark 7lb higher than when runner-up in the Cesarewitch on his last Flat start. He's a very useful stayer, but everything went his way and he'll appeal as one to take on next time. In the long term, Richard Hughes apparently thinks he could be a Melbourne Cup horse. (op 9-1 tchd 10-1 in places)

Tastahil(IRE) was given a fine ride in defeat by Richard Hills, soon sitting in second, only one off the rail, having started in stall 16. The top weight had run no sort of a race on soft ground (plenty of form on that sort of going) in a Nottingham Listed race on his reappearance, but he returned to form with a fine effort over the furthest trip he has tried to date. He didn't seem to use up that much energy in getting across from his wide draw, but even so, looking at the stalls positions of the other principals, it's clear this was a tremendous effort. It's possible he'll now go for the Henry II Stakes, a race he was third in last year.

Halla San, 2lb higher than when third in this last year, was always close up and, although hitting a bit of a flat spot before the straight, he stayed on for pressure to post another fine effort. He is likely to be aimed at the Northumberland Plate, and the Melbourne Cup was even mentioned as a possible target. (op 10-1)

Majestic Concorde(IRE), a winner over fences when last seen in October, had the inside stall and was never far away. (op 12-1 tchd 16-1)

Swingkeel(IRE), unsuited by soft ground on his reappearance, tried cheekpieces for the first time on this return to more suitable conditions, but he didn't take advantage of his good draw, ending up well back after finding trouble soon after the start. He found further trouble when trying to stay on and should have finished closer. (tchd 11-1)

Desert Sea(IRE), fourth off the same mark 12 months ago, raced further back than ideal after starting slower than some of those around him, and then proceeded to race keenly. He briefly looked as though he might get involved when the race got serious, but those ridden more positively simply didn't come back to him.

Som Tala is a dour galloper who has run some of his best races from the front, including when landing last year's Northumberland Plate off a 5lb lower mark, and he was drawn only one from the rail with a visor fitted for the first time, so it was a real surprise he wasn't ridden more positively, not least considering the modest pace.

Red Cadeaux ◆ was only 5lb higher (including 1lb overweight) than when winning a 1m4f Polytrack handicap on his previous start, a race that's worked out really well, but he endured a nightmare trip. Out the back for much of the way after being badly hampered soon after leaving the stalls, he was squeezed for room when trying to make a move against the inside rail around the final turn, and was again baulked when plugging on inside the final furlong.

Rangefinder, racing beyond 1m4f for the first time, stayed on from well back past beaten horses but was never competitive.

Liszt(IRE) couldn't take advantage of enjoying the run of the race in front, although being hampered when on the retreat exaggerated the beaten margin. Official explanation: jockey said gelding hung left-handed (op 18-1)

Bernie The Bolt(IRE), 8lb higher than when winning over this trip at Newmarket on his final start last season, was poorly drawn and has been a bit behind some of his stablemates in his work according to Andrew Balding, so he can be given another chance.

Ajaan, having only his fourth run since finishing second on his reappearance in this off a 7lb lower mark last year, raced wide without cover for much of the way, leaving him with little hope. (tchd 12-1 in places)

Nemo Spirit(IRE) was bought out of William Muir's yard for 100,000gns, with this race in mind according to Tom Dascombe, but he prefers easier ground and was never going. Official explanation: vet said gelding had a fibrillating heart (op 16-1 tchd 11-1)

1822 CLATTERBRIDGE CANCER RESEARCH H'CAP 5f 16y

3:15 (3:19) (Class 2) (0-105,105) 4-Y-O+ **£13,877** (£4,153; £2,076; £1,038; £517) **Stalls** Low

Form				RPR
002-	**1**		**Masamah (IRE)**[208] 6631 4-8-6 **90** ... WilliamBuick 3 *(K A Ryan) mde all: rdn and hung lft fr over 1f out: r.o wl and in command fnl f* **9/1**	106
00-3	**2**	*2 1/4*	**Hamish McGonagall**[21] 1295 5-8-8 **92** ... DavidAllan 7 *(T D Easterby) lw: chsd ldrs: rdn and hung lft whn tk 2nd ins fnl f: kpt on: could nt trble wnr* **7/2**[1]	100+
0344	**3**	*1 3/4*	**Fol Hollow (IRE)**[14] 1471 5-8-5 **94** ... BillyCray[(5)] 5 *(D Nicholls) chsd ldrs: rdn over 1f out: rdr dropped rein jst ins fnl f: styd on: no imp on front pair after* **11/2**[3]	96
052-	**4**	*nse*	**Look Busy (IRE)**[214] 6499 5-9-2 **105** ... MarkCoumbe[(5)] 2 *(A Berry) missed break: sn in midfield: hdwy over 1f out: styd on ins fnl f: nt gng pce of ldrs* **8/1**	106
00-5	**5**	*1/2*	**Sohraab**[19] 1353 6-8-13 **97** ... TravisBlock 8 *(H Morrison) in tch: rdn over 1f out: styd on ins fnl f: gng on at fin* **9/1**	97+
00-0	**6**	*3/4*	**Pavershooz**[38] 1032 5-8-8 **92** ... DuranFentiman 6 *(N Wilson) lw: chsd ldr: rdn over 1f out: lost 2nd ins fnl f: sn wknd* **20/1**	89
11-6	**7**	*nk*	**Royal Intruder**[10] 1557 5-8-6 **90** ... RichardHughes 1 *(S Donohoe, Ire) in tch: effrt over 1f out: nt qckning whn n.m.r jst ins fnl f: sn eased* **7/1**	89+
410-	**8**	*nk*	**Doctor Parkes**[221] 6283 4-8-2 **86** oh1 ... DavidProbert 13 *(E J Alston) swtchd lft s: hld up: rdn over 1f out: no imp on ldrs* **33/1**	81
04-0	**9**	*shd*	**Strike Up The Band**[9] 1573 7-8-13 **100** ... MichaelGeran[(3)] 9 *(D Nicholls) midfield: rdn over 1f out: swtchd lft whn nt clr run ins fnl f: nt pce to trble ldrs* **33/1**	94+
6-41	**10**	*1*	**Buachaill Dona (IRE)**[9] 1573 7-9-6 **104** 6ex ... AdrianNicholls 10 *(D Nicholls) squeezed out s: a bhd: nvr on terms* **20/1**	95
5-65	**11**	*1/2*	**Parisian Pyramid (IRE)**[3] 1727 4-8-5 **89** ... (p) JohnEgan 11 *(K A Ryan) bhd: rdn over 1f out: nt clr run ins fnl f: eased fnl 75yds* **20/1**	81
0-20	**12**	*3 1/2*	**Green Manalishi**[32] 1091 9-8-11 **95** ... (p) NeilCallan 4 *(K A Ryan) chsd ldrs: rdn over 1f out: wknd ins fnl f: b.b.v* **9/2**[2]	71
40-4	**13**	*2*	**Masta Plasta (IRE)**[9] 1573 7-9-6 **104** ... KierenFallon 12 *(D Nicholls) a bhd* **20/1**	73

59.69 secs (-1.31) **Going Correction** -0.025s/f (Good) **13** Ran SP% **124.3**

Speed ratings (Par 109): **109,105,102,102,101 100,100,99,99,97 97,91,88**

toteswingers: 1&2 £8.60, 1&3 £12.20, 2&3 £6.60 CSF £38.02 CT £197.01 TOTE £9.70: £3.10, £1.80, £2.30; EX 48.10 Trifecta £995.70 Pool: £2085.79 - 1.55 winning units..

Owner Dr Marwan Koukash **Bred** Stanley Estate & Stud Co & Mount Coote Stud **Trained** Hambleton, N Yorks

FOCUS

No horse drawn higher than stall eight had placed in this sprint handicap for the last 11 years, and that was the case once more. A personal best from the winner, but everything went his way.

NOTEBOOK

Masamah(IRE) outsprinted his rivals to grab the early lead from a favourable stall and kept on well in the straight. Sold out of Ed Dunlop's yard for 30,000gns since he last seen in October, he's clearly a very useful recruit for his new yard. He's in the Dash, but his connections believe Epsom won't suit, so it's unlikely he'll go there. (op 10-1 tchd 11-1)

Hamish McGonagall, 3lb below his last winning mark, and successful on his only previous start at the track, came very wide into the straight and couldn't reel in the winner. (op 9-2)

Fol Hollow(IRE), on his toes beforehand, is holding his form well, and this was another good effort, but he looks weighted up to his best. (tchd 6-1)

Look Busy(IRE) was well drawn but she ruined her chance with a slow start. Still, she ran on quite well and looks set for another good season. (tchd 7-1 and 9-1)

Sohraab, only 1lb higher than when winning this race last year, never really travelled that well, getting reminders a fair way out, and although he eventually ran on, it's possible he now needs headgear. (op 8-1 tchd 10-1 in places)

Pavershooz, reported to have bled from his nose on his reappearance at Doncaster, fared better this time, although he was well drawn.

Royal Intruder's style of running is probably not suited to this track and he was held when short of room late on. (op 9-1 tchd 10-1 in places)

Doctor Parkes was edgy beforehand.

Green Manalishi proved disappointing from a favourable draw. Official explanation: trainer said gelding bled from th nose (op 5-1 tchd 6-1)

1823 BENTLEY MOTORS H'CAP — 1m 4f 66y
4:00 (4:00) (Class 3) (0-95,94) 3-Y-O **£10,037** (£2,986; £1,492; £745) **Stalls** Low

Form RPR

02-2 **1** **Alrasm (IRE)**[27] [1182] 3-9-9 **94**.......... RichardHills 3 105
(M A Jarvis) *sn led: rdn over 1f out: r.o wl and in command fnl f: comf* **5/2**[1]

15-3 **2** *2 ½* **Averroes (IRE)**[12] [1502] 3-8-10 **88**.......... JohnFahy(7) 8 95+
(C G Cox) *hld up: hdwy to chse ldrs over 4f out: swtchd rt over 1f out: styd on take 2nd ins fnl f: could nt trble wnr* **7/2**[2]

1 **3** *1 ¼* **Maxim Gorky (IRE)**[27] [1186] 3-8-12 **83**.......... RyanMoore 1 88
(Sir Michael Stoute) *w'like: athletic: lw: midfield: hdwy over 5f out: chsd wnr over 2f out: lost 2nd ins fnl f: one pce after* **5/2**[1]

0-52 **4** *3 ¼* **Sharaayeen**[11] [1518] 3-8-7 **78**.......... TadhgO'Shea 4 78
(B W Hills) *lw: trckd ldrs: wnt 2nd after 4f: rdn over 4f out: lost 2nd over 2f out: wknd over 1f out* **10/1**[3]

33-1 **5** *29* **Ipswich Lad**[21] [1302] 3-8-9 **80**..........(v) DavidProbert 7 33
(A M Balding) *lw: midfield: rdn over 5f out: wknd over 3f out* **12/1**

25-0 **6** *20* **Mark Twain (IRE)**[21] [1310] 3-9-5 **90**.......... JamieSpencer 2 11
(D M Simcock) *a bhd: struggling 4f out: nvr on terms* **14/1**

01-3 **7** *7* **Mister Angry (IRE)**[14] [1466] 3-9-0 **85**.......... JoeFanning 6 —
(M Johnston) *lw: led early: remained prom: rdn over 5f out: wknd over 4f out* **14/1**

2m 35.56s (-4.34) **Going Correction** -0.025s/f (Good) 7 Ran SP% **109.5**
Speed ratings (Par 103): **113,111,110,108,89 75,71**
toteswingers: 1&2 £2.00, 1&3 £1.70, 2&3 £1.80 CSF £10.38 CT £20.40 TOTE £3.30: £1.80, £2.20; EX 8.00 Trifecta £16.30 Pool: £1025.46 - 46.31 winning units..
Owner Hamdan Al Maktoum **Bred** New Deal Partnership **Trained** Newmarket, Suffolk

FOCUS
There was a heavy shower before the off, but the winning time was under standard, suggesting the rain had not got into the ground. This is often a hot 3-y-o handicap, but this year's race lacked strength in depth. The pace seemed reasonable. The first three came clear and the form is rated positively.

NOTEBOOK
Alrasm(IRE), soon in front, was able to get a breather in before the straight and had enough left to defy a 4lb higher mark than when second to the improving Miss Starlight over 1m2f on his reappearance. He was far from sure to get this trip judged on his breeding, but he stayed well and is progressing nicely. (tchd 9-4, 11-4 in places)
Averroes(IRE), 3lb higher than when third in a decent 1m2f handicap at Sandown on his reappearance, ran well without suggesting he's up to justifying his Group-race entries. He might have finished a little closer had he been ridden more positively, as he didn't get the best of runs through into the straight, and had too much ground to make up on the winner by the time he was in the clear, but that said, he hardly looked an unlucky loser. (tchd 4-1 in places)
Maxim Gorky(IRE) didn't beat much on debut at Leicester and has no big-race entries. Well held on this switch to handicap company, he probably needs more time. (tchd 11-4)
Sharaayeen is not progressing. (op 11-1)
Ipswich Lad Official explanation: trainer said gelding failed to handle the track

1824 RESIDENCE AT HQ MAIDEN STKS — 1m 2f 75y
4:35 (4:35) (Class 4) 3-Y-O **£7,123** (£2,119; £1,059; £529) **Stalls** High

Form RPR

5- **1** **Thaahira (USA)**[205] [6729] 3-8-12 0.......... RichardHills 2 94+
(M A Jarvis) *attractive: athletic: hld up: hdwy 2f out: wnt 2nd over 1f out: qcknd to ld ins fnl f: pushed out: readily: nice prospect* **5/1**[3]

36-4 **2** *3 ¾* **Cultivar**[38] [1029] 3-9-3 82.......... MichaelHills 8 86
(B W Hills) *lengthy: lw: led: drew 5 l clr over 2f out: rdn over 1f out: hdd ins fnl f: no ch w wnr after* **9/1**

32-0 **3** *2* **Longliner**[21] [1310] 3-9-3 89.......... RyanMoore 5 82
(Sir Michael Stoute) *racd keenly: chsd ldrs: wnt 2nd 7f out: rdn and outpcd by ldr over 2f out: lost 2nd over 1f out: kpt on same fnl f* **5/2**[2]

00- **4** *1 ½* **Veni Vedi Veci (IRE)**[209] [6620] 3-8-12 0.......... DavidProbert 7 74
(A M Balding) *chsd ldr to 7f out: remained prom: rdn 2f out: one pce fnl f* **33/1**

5 *10* **Abu Wathab** 3-9-3 0.......... JimmyFortune 6 59
(P W Chapple-Hyam) *str: tall: dwlt: a bhd: pushed along 4f out: nvr on terms* **25/1**

6-3 **6** *3 ¼* **Pekan Three (IRE)**[9] [1581] 3-9-3 0.......... JamieSpencer 1 53
(P F I Cole) *lw: hld up: hdwy on outside 7f out: rdn over 4f out: wknd 2f out* **13/2**

22-3 **7** *2 ½* **Youm Jamil (USA)**[18] [1387] 3-9-3 80.......... KierenFallon 4 48
(B J Meehan) *lw: chsd ldrs tl rdn and wknd wl over 1f out* **13/8**[1]

2m 11.05s (-1.15) **Going Correction** -0.025s/f (Good) 7 Ran SP% **113.5**
Speed ratings (Par 101): **103,100,98,97,89 86,84**
toteswingers: 1&2 £5.70, 1&3 £2.70, 2&3 £4.40 CSF £46.76 TOTE £5.60: £3.00, £4.00; EX 43.50 Trifecta £134.40 Pool: £1057.61 - 5.82 winning units. Place 6: £129.09 Place 5: £85.47.
Owner Hamdan Al Maktoum **Bred** Shadwell Farm LLC **Trained** Newmarket, Suffolk
■ Stewards' Enquiry : Kieren Fallon two-day ban: careless riding (May 19-20)

FOCUS
The race time suggests that the rain had not got into the ground that much, but the runners were kicking up the turf a bit. Some really smart types have contested this maiden in recent years, and this season's race looked a good contest. They seemed to go a good, even gallop. The winner impressed and was value for more than the bare form.
T/Jkpt: Not won. T/Plt: £202.60 to a £1 stake. Pool: £174068.98, 626.98 winning tickets. T/Qpdt: £50.70 to a £1 stake. Pool: £9021.21, 131.55 winning tickets. DO

1490 SOUTHWELL (L-H)
Wednesday, May 5

OFFICIAL GOING: Standard
Wind: Virtually nil Weather: Overcast

1825 BEST ODDS GUARANTEED AT LADBROKES.COM MAIDEN STKS — 5f (F)
1:55 (1:57) (Class 5) 3-Y-O+ **£2,593** (£765; £383) **Stalls** High

Form RPR

53 **1** **Special Quality (USA)**[40] [997] 3-9-1 0.......... GrahamGibbons 6 73
(R M H Cowell) *mde all: rdn clr over 1f out: comf* **6/1**[3]

6- **2** *1 ¼* **Ravenfield (IRE)**[231] [5977] 3-9-1 0.......... FrederikTylicki 11 69+
(D H Brown) *towards rr and pushed along after 2f: hdwy wl over 1f out: rdn and n.m.r whn swtchd rt ent fnl f: styd on wl towards fin* **15/8**[1]

36-0 **3** *1 ¼* **Bronze Beau**[31] [1104] 3-9-1 70.......... TomEaves 10 64
(Mrs L Stubbs) *prom: chsd wnr 1/2-way: rdn wl over 1f out: edge lft and one pce fnl f* **18/1**

4 *hd* **Gold Gleam (USA)** 3-9-1 0.......... ShaneKelly 4 63
(J Noseda) *chsd ldrs: rdn along 2f out: kpt on same pce ent fnl f* **7/1**

50 **5** *1 ½* **Bird Call (IRE)**[53] [886] 3-8-5 0.......... DeanHeslop(5) 3 53
(T D Barron) *chsd ldrs: rdn along wl over 1f out: drvn: edgd lft and wknd ins fnl f* **33/1**

05-2 **6** *nse* **Superior Edge**[29] [1137] 3-8-10 73.......... NeilChalmers 7 53
(B Palling) *towards rr: hdwy over 2f out: sn rdn and kpt on ins fnl f: nrst fin* **7/2**[2]

0-0 **7** *5* **Miracle Wish (IRE)**[40] [997] 3-8-10 0.......... JimCrowley 1 35
(R M Beckett) *in tch on wd outside: hdwasy to chse ldrs 1/2-way: rdn wl over 1f out and sn wknd* **16/1**

00/0 **8** *shd* **Marron Flore**[56] [849] 7-9-5 35..........(t) SteveDrowne 9 38
(A J Lidderdale) *chsd ldrs: rdn along over 2f out: sn wknd* **150/1**

0 **9** *½* **Marju's Reward (IRE)**[11] [1538] 3-8-10 0.......... RobertWinston 8 33
(G A Swinbank) *a in rr* **25/1**

3 **10** *2 ½* **Force To Spend**[70] [683] 3-8-10 0.......... J-PGuillambert 5 24
(N P Littmoden) *a towards rr* **14/1**

11 *½* **Somethin' Stupid** 3-9-1 0.......... SebSanders 13 27
(Sir Mark Prescott) *s.i.s: a bhd* **25/1**

12 *7* **Rodrigo Fontana** 3-9-1 0.......... StevieDonohoe 2 —
(Sir Mark Prescott) *s.i.s: a bhd* **16/1**

59.10 secs (-0.60) **Going Correction** -0.025s/f (Stan)
WFA 3 from 7yo 9lb 12 Ran SP% **118.8**
Speed ratings (Par 103): **103,101,99,98,96 96,88,88,87,83 82,71**
toteswingers: 1&2 £3.30, 1&3 £14.40, 2&3 £12.30 CSF £17.08 TOTE £7.90: £1.90, £1.70, £5.60; EX 20.00 TRIFECTA Not won..
Owner Yvonne Jacques Julia Morley Mr & Mrs R Foulkes **Bred** Cliveden Stud Ltd **Trained** Six Mile Bottom, Cambs

FOCUS
A moderate maiden and it seems unlikely it will produce many winners, although it was relatively quicker than the later handicap. The front pair stepped forward.
Superior Edge Official explanation: jockey said filly did not face the kickback

1826 BET IN PLAY AT LADBROKES.COM H'CAP — 7f (F)
2:25 (2:26) (Class 3) (0-90,87) 4-Y-O- **£6,938** (£2,076; £1,038; £519; £258) **Stalls** Low

Form RPR

1110 **1** **Trans Sonic**[39] [1013] 7-8-8 **82**.......... JamesSullivan(5) 12 95
(J Hetherton) *cl up: led after 1f: rdn wl over 1f out: drvn ent fnl f: sn edgd lft and styd on strly* **10/1**

3111 **2** *1 ½* **Academy Blues (USA)**[19] [1361] 5-9-3 **86**.......... PaulQuinn 6 95
(D Nicholls) *trckd ldrs: hdwy 3f out: rdn wl over 1f out: drvn to chse wnr ins fnl f: swtchd rt and one pce towards fin* **13/2**[3]

2020 **3** *nk* **Elusive Fame (USA)**[21] [1306] 4-8-7 **76**..........(b) RoystonFfrench 7 84
(M Johnston) *a.p: chsd wnr 1/2-way: rdn 2f out and ch tl drvn ent fnl f and kpt on same pce*

3031 **4** *1* **Flores Sea (USA)**[13] [1492] 6-7-13 **73** oh1..........(b) PaulPickard(5) 4 78+
(Mrs R A Carr) *s.i.s and bhd: swtchd wd home turn: rdn and hdwy on stands' rails wl over 1f out: styd on wl fnl f: nrst fin* **14/1**

35-0 **5** *½* **Masai Moon**[25] [1219] 6-8-13 **85**.......... JamesMillman(3) 10 89
(B R Millman) *hld up towards rr: hdwy over 2f out: rdn and styng on whn edgd lft over 1f out: kpt on ins fnl f* **7/1**

0-31 **6** *1* **Just Five (IRE)**[13] [1494] 4-8-6 **80**.......... PatrickDonaghy(5) 2 81
(M Dods) *towards rr: hdwy 3f out: rdn over 2f out: sn drvn and no imp appr fnl f* **14/1**

4-04 **7** *2 ¼* **Mount Hadley (USA)**[11] [1533] 6-8-9 **78**..........(v) PaulMulrennan 3 73
(G A Butler) *chsd ldrs: rdn along wl over 2f out: sn drvn and btn wl over 1f out* **11/2**[1]

1136 **8** *¾* **Cobo Bay**[4] [1708] 5-8-11 **85**..........(b) AmyRyan(5) 9 78
(K A Ryan) *chsd ldrs: rdn along over 2f out: grad wknd* **11/2**[1]

300- **9** *nk* **Pravda Street**[214] [6482] 5-9-4 **87**.......... TomEaves 13 79
(P F I Cole) *dwlt: a towards rr* **33/1**

1204 **10** *2 ¼* **Onceaponatime (IRE)**[12] [1506] 5-8-13 **85**.......... WilliamCarson(3) 8 71
(M D Squance) *swtchd lft s and hld up in rr: sme hdwy over 2f out: sn rdn and btn* **25/1**

6430 **11** *5* **Bel Cantor**[16] [1423] 7-8-12 **84**..........(p) KellyHarrison(3) 5 57
(W J H Ratcliffe) *led 1f: prom tl rdn along wl over 2f out and sn wknd* **16/1**

23-2 **12** *31* **Lochan Mor**[27] [1185] 4-8-11 **80**.......... SteveDrowne 1 —
(M L W Bell) *in tch on inner: rdn along 1/2-way: wknd qckly: bhd and eased fnl 2f* **6/1**[2]

1m 27.1s (-3.20) **Going Correction** -0.225s/f (Stan) 12 Ran SP% **111.9**
Speed ratings (Par 107): **109,107,106,105,105 104,101,100,100,97 92,56**
toteswingers: 1&2 £10.70, 1&3 £34.90, 2&3 £20.90 CSF £69.37 CT £1035.33 TOTE £13.60: £5.40, £2.90, £5.10; EX 76.90 TRIFECTA Not won..
Owner Mrs Lynne Lumley **Bred** I A Balding **Trained** Norton, N Yorks

FOCUS
A decent handicap for the track and, with so many established front-runners in the field, a strong pace was always likely. Sound form.

NOTEBOOK
Trans Sonic, back on Fibresand off an 8lb higher mark after completing a hat-trick of wins over 1m here in March, was one of those that normally likes to make it and he did well to soon get across and establish the early advantage from his wide draw. He faced some serious challenges starting up the home straight, but with proven stamina on his side, he was never going to be caught and saw it out in game fashion. Connections will look for something similar. (op 12-1 tchd 9-1)
Academy Blues(USA), bidding for a four-timer off a 6lb higher mark following three successes on turf, was travelling every bit as well as the winner turning in, but as hard as he tried he could never get to him. He had run well in his only previous try here, so the surface wasn't a problem. (op 6-1)
Elusive Fame(USA) is effective under these conditions and ran another decent race, having been handy from the off, but he isn't the easiest to win with remains 8lb higher than for his last success here in November. (op 14-1)
Flores Sea(USA), 1lb wrong and therefore 6lb higher than when successful over C&D last month, ran a remarkable race as he completely blew the start and gave away plenty of ground, but once switched over to the stands' rail in the straight he flew home. He would have done even better with a clean break. (op 12-1)
Masai Moon ◆, successful on his only previous try over C&D, was all the better for his Lingfield reappearance last month and was running on well at the death. He hasn't won for nearly two years, but is handicapped to put that right. (op 8-1)
Just Five(IRE), a three-time winner on Fibresand, had his chance but is 5lb higher than when successful here last month and looks held now. (tchd 12-1)
Mount Hadley(USA) has gained his four career wins over similar trips to this, even though he has been running over further lately. Able to race off a 7lb lower mark than on turf, he showed up for a long way but had run his race entering the final furlong. (op 6-1 tchd 5-1)
Cobo Bay is most effective when able to dominate, so wasn't helped by being unable to lead. (op 17-2)
Bel Cantor is another most effective when able to dominate. (op 20-1)

Lochan Mor, never out of the frame in eight previous starts and making his Fibresand debut after a narrow defeat on his Leicester reappearance, is another that usually likes to force it but the way he dropped right out suggests that something was amiss. Official explanation: trainer's rep had no explanation for the poor form shown (op 9-2)

1827 WATCH LIVE SPORT AT LADBROKES.COM FILLIES' H'CAP 5f (F)
2:55 (2:55) (Class 4) (0-80,80) 4-Y-0+ **£4,533** (£1,348; £674; £336) **Stalls** High

Form RPR

4115 **1** **La Capriosa**[20] [1337] 4-8-8 **70** ow1 RobertWinston 4 77
(J A Glover) *qckly away: mde all: rdn over 1f out: kpt on fnl f* **11/4**[2]

6-05 **2** ½ **Feelin Foxy**[4] [1710] 6-9-4 **80** PaulMulrennan 2 85
(J G Given) *trckd ldng pair: hdwy 2f out: rdn to chal over 1f: sn drvn and ev ch tl nt qckn wl ins fnl f* **3/1**[3]

440- **3** ¾ **Spring Green**[208] [6647] 4-8-13 **75** SteveDrowne 1 77
(H Morrison) *wnt lft s: chsd ldrs: hdwy 2f out: rdn and ev ch over 1f out: drvn and one pce wl ins fnl f* **5/2**[1]

0-00 **4** 5 **La Zamora**[4] [1710] 4-9-1 **77** (b[1]) ShaneKelly 3 61
(T D Barron) *cl up: rdn along over 2f out: drvn wl over 1f out and sn wknd* **7/1**

30-0 **5** 2½ **Sharpened Edge**[23] [1267] 4-9-0 **76** (p) NeilChalmers 5 51
(B Palling) *racd on stands' rail: rdn along: outpcd and bhd fr 1/2-way* **9/2**

58.90 secs (-0.80) **Going Correction** -0.025s/f (Stan) **5** Ran SP% **110.9**
Speed ratings (Par 102): **105,104,103,95,91**
CSF £11.63 TOTE £3.80: £3.40, £1.40; EX 7.50.
Owner Paul J Dixon **Bred** Slatch Farm Stud **Trained** Babworth, Notts

FOCUS
A modest fillies' handicap in which the quintet used the full width of the track. The winning time was 0.2 seconds faster than the earlier maiden and the winner posted a small personal best.
Sharpened Edge Official explanation: jockey said filly did not handle the surface

1828 PLAY POKER AT LADBROKES.COM H'CAP 1m 6f (F)
3:30 (3:30) (Class 5) (0-75,71) 4-Y-0+ **£2,590** (£770; £385; £192) **Stalls** Low

Form RPR

0-11 **1** **Bivouac (UAE)**[13] [1493] 6-9-4 **65** PJMcDonald 5 79
(G A Swinbank) *trckd ldrs: smooth hdwy over 3f out: led wl over 1f out: sn clr: easily* **10/3**[1]

4000 **2** 8 **Mehendi (IRE)**[9] [1576] 4-9-0 **62** (p) TomEaves 7 64
(B Ellison) *hld up in rr: hdwy 1/2-way: jnd ldrs 4f out: rdn and cl up over 2f out: drvn to chse wnr over 1f out: kpt on ins fnl f but no ch w wnr* **14/1**

/012 **3** 2¼ **Sarah's Boy**[78] [575] 5-8-6 **53** GregFairley 4 52
(D E Pipe) *trckd ldng pair: hdwy to ld over 4f out: rdn along 3f out: drvn and hdd over 2f out: kpt on same pce* **10/3**[1]

06-1 **4** ½ **Three Boars**[57] [833] 8-8-13 **60** (b) IanMongan 2 58
(S Gollings) *trckd ldrs: hdwy 1/2-way: cl up 4f out: rdn along to ld briefly over 2f out: sn hdd and drvn: kpt on same pce* **7/1**

0 **5** 1¼ **Tifoso (FR)**[41] [983] 5-8-5 **52** oh2 (e) FrannyNorton 3 48
(R C Guest) *hld up in rr: sme hdwy over 3f out: sn rdn and plugged on fnl 2f: nvr nr ldrs* **16/1**

42-0 **6** ¾ **Saloon (USA)**[28] [1150] 6-9-10 **71** (p) ShaneKelly 9 66
(Jane Chapple-Hyam) *hld up in rr: hdwy and in tch over 4f out: rdn along over 3f out and nvr a factor* **5/1**[3]

420/ **7** 10 **Snow's Ride**[318] [785] 10-9-4 **65** TonyHamilton 1 46
(M Herrington) *chsd ldrs: rdn along 4f out: sn btn* **66/1**

3440 **8** 2½ **Eseej (USA)**[13] [1484] 5-9-9 **70** ChrisCatlin 8 48
(P W Hiatt) *led: rn wd bnd after 5f: hung bdly rt to wd outside rail 1m out: rdn and hdd over 4f out: sn wknd and eased* **9/2**[2]

-006 **9** 5 **Dawn Storm (IRE)**[15] [1459] 5-8-5 **52** oh7 (v) FrankieMcDonald 10 23
(J L Spearing) *trckd ldr: rdn along 5f out: wknd wl over 3f out* **22/1**

3m 6.87s (-1.43) **Going Correction** -0.225s/f (Stan)
WFA 4 from 5yo+ 1lb **9** Ran SP% **111.9**
Speed ratings (Par 103): **95,90,89,88,88 87,82,80,77**
toteswingers: 1&2 £13.20, 1&3 £2.30, 2&3 £6.90 CSF £49.78 CT £163.59 TOTE £3.70: £1.20, £7.00, £1.10; EX 48.60 Trifecta £154.50 Pool: £378.06 - 1.81 winning units..
Owner Mrs J M Penney **Bred** Darley **Trained** Melsonby, N Yorks

FOCUS
An ordinary staying handicap run at just a fair pace, but a very impressive winner. There are doubts over what he beat, though.

1829 MEMBERSHIP OF SOUTHWELL GOLF CLUB H'CAP 1m 4f (F)
4:10 (4:10) (Class 3) (0-95,95) 4-Y-0+
£6,854 (£2,052; £1,026; £513; £256; £128) **Stalls** Low

Form RPR

/112 **1** **Veloso (FR)**[31] [1101] 8-8-1 **81** oh4 KellyHarrison(3) 7 87
(J A Glover) *cl up: rdn to ld 3f out: drvn wl over 1f out: edgd rt and kpt on gamely fnl f* **5/1**[3]

33-2 **2** ½ **Ella**[28] [1151] 6-9-0 **91** RobertWinston 6 96
(G A Swinbank) *trckd ldng pair on inner: hdwy 3f out: rdn along wl over 1f out: swtchd rt and drvn to chal ins fnl f: ev ch tl no ex nr fin* **3/1**[2]

11-2 **3** 1 **Lucky Punt**[35] [1069] 4-8-13 **90** FergusSweeney 8 93
(B G Powell) *led: pushed along and jnd 4f out: rdn and hdd 3f out: drvn and ev ch tl no ex wl ins fnl f* **5/2**[1]

0050 **4** 1½ **Reve De Nuit (USA)**[3] [1724] 4-8-11 **93** DeclanCannon(5) 3 94
(A J McCabe) *hld up: hdwy over 4f out: effrt on outer to chse ldrs over 2f out: sn rdn and kpt on same pce appr fnl f* **12/1**

1123 **5** nk **Sedgwick**[8] [1592] 8-8-4 **81** oh6 ChrisCatlin 4 82?
(S A Harris) *trckd ldrs: hdwy 3f out: rdn and ch over 2f out: sn drvn and one pce appr fnl f* **33/1**

6 2½ **Silver Point (FR)**[179] [463] 7-9-4 **95** NeilChalmers 9 92
(B Palling) *trckd ldrs: hdwy and cl up 4f out: rdn along wl over 2f out and ev ch tl edgd rt and wknd over 1f out* **33/1**

164- **7** 2½ **Bothy**[49] [6795] 4-8-11 **88** TomEaves 5 81
(B Ellison) *hld up in tch: rdn along over 4f out: drvn 3f out and sn btn* **11/2**

0-00 **8** 2¾ **Lang Shining (IRE)**[22] [1282] 6-8-13 **90** JimCrowley 2 78
(J A Osborne) *hld up in rr: effrt and sme hdwy on outer over 2f out: sn rdn: edgd lft and nvr a factor* **9/1**

14-0 **9** 13 **Mull Of Dubai**[22] [1274] 7-9-0 **91** PaulQuinn 1 58
(D Nicholls) *hld up: a in rr: bhd and eased fnl 2f* **25/1**

2m 37.0s (-4.00) **Going Correction** -0.225s/f (Stan) **9** Ran SP% **113.0**
Speed ratings (Par 107): **104,103,103,102,101 100,98,96,87**
toteswingers: 1&2 £3.00, 1&3 £3.30, 2&3 £2.60 CSF £19.53 CT £44.90 TOTE £5.40: £1.30, £2.20, £1.10; EX 23.90 Trifecta £26.70 Pool: £431.83 - 11.96 winning units..
Owner Brian Morton **Bred** Jean Louis Pariente **Trained** Babworth, Notts

FOCUS
A decent handicap and the form looks sound enough among the principals despite the winner being 4lb wrong. This was a race where it paid to race handily, as the first three passing the winning post on the first circuit were also the first three home, though not in the same order.

NOTEBOOK
Veloso(FR), 4lb 'wrong', was therefore 10lb higher than for the second of two wins here in March, but it made little difference. Well handled by his replacement rider, he served it up to the favourite rounding the home turn and showed real grit and determination to see his race out from that point. He has now either won or finished second in his last eight starts and is still lightly raced for an 8-y-o. Connections believe that he needs cut in the ground on turf, so he could be worth another try in a decent staying handicap when those conditions prevail. (tchd 11-2)
Ella, an encouraging second on her Catterick reappearance last month, raced a bit too keen in a handy position early and then took too long to get into gear once under pressure in the home straight, but she stayed on all the way to the line and proved that this surface is no problem to her. (op 7-2)
Lucky Punt, successful five times and second twice from seven outings here within the past year, tried to make all and looked as though he would drop right away when the winner headed him 4f from home, but he battled back in ultra-game fashion and went down with all guns blazing. However, the feeling is that the handicapper may have him now. (op 9-4 tchd 2-1 and 11-4 in a place)
Reve De Nuit(USA), disappointing since making a winning British debut for connections over 1m here in January, was well beaten when stepped up to this trip for the first time at Newmarket three days earlier, but the way he flew home up the stands' rail here suggested he needs this trip and more. More evidence is needed relating to his distance requirements.
Sedgwick, very consistent for Ian Williams at a modest level so far this year, had every chance turning in but couldn't take advantage and he was inclined to carry his head a little high. He was 6lb 'wrong', however, and is already due to drop another 2lb on sand so may be worth another chance off his proper mark. (op 20-1)
Silver Point(FR), a Listed winner on the AW in France, became disappointing over hurdles after showing early ability for Evan Williams. Making his debut for his new yard after six months off, he had every chance turning in but then seemed to blow up and should strip fitter next time.
Bothy, making his AW debut after winning three times on soft ground over hurdles during the winter, was sent off well backed but his supporters knew their fate as soon as he came seriously off the bridle fully 5f from home. (op 9-1)

1830 DINE IN THE QUEEN MOTHER RESTAURANT H'CAP 1m 3f (F)
4:45 (4:45) (Class 5) (0-70,68) 3-Y-O £2,331 (£693; £346; £173) **Stalls** Low

Form RPR

0-15 **1** **Sir Pitt**[21] [1299] 3-9-4 **68** RobertHavlin 7 80+
(J H M Gosden) *wnt rt s: hld up in rr: hdwy to take clsr order 1/2-way: cl up 4f out: chal over 2f out: rdn to ld wl over 1f out and sn hung rt: clr ent fnl f* **10/3**[2]

04-1 **2** 4 **On Khee**[23] [1261] 3-9-3 **67** SteveDrowne 6 69
(H Morrison) *hld up in rr: hdwy to trck ldrs 4f out: effrt over 2f out: rdn: edgd lft and sltly outpcd 2f out: drvn to chse wnr and swtchd lft ent fnl f: sn no imp* **4/5**[1]

6-03 **3** 2 **Ice Viking (IRE)**[16] [1422] 3-9-1 **65** PaulMulrennan 1 64
(J G Given) *led: rdn along 3f out: drvn 2f out: sn hdd and kpt on same pce appr fnl f* **8/1**

6-65 **4** 2¾ **As Brave As You (IRE)**[49] [909] 3-8-4 **54** oh2 (p) RoystonFfrench 4 48
(B Ellison) *chsd ldng pair: rdn along over 3f out: drvn over 2f out and sn btn* **25/1**

053- **5** ½ **Dubai Phantom (USA)**[200] [6858] 3-9-1 **68** MartinLane(3) 3 61
(D M Simcock) *trckd ldrs: pushed along over 3f out: rdn wl over 2f out: sn drvn and btn* **6/1**[3]

660- **6** 21 **Young Firth**[208] [6639] 3-8-5 **55** oh1 ow1 PJMcDonald 2 12
(J R Norton) *chsd ldr to 1/2-way: sn lost pl and bhd fnl 3f* **66/1**

2m 25.23s (-2.77) **Going Correction** -0.225s/f (Stan) **6** Ran SP% **109.4**
Speed ratings (Par 99): **101,98,96,94,94 79**
toteswingers: 1&2 £1.70, 1&3 £2.20, 2&3 £2.10 CSF £6.03 TOTE £3.40: £1.20, £1.60; EX 6.50 Place 6: £38.38 Place 5: £21.05 .
Owner A E Oppenheimer **Bred** Hascombe And Valiant Studs **Trained** Newmarket, Suffolk

FOCUS
A weak and uncompetitive 3-y-o handicap and the pace was ordinary. The form is rated around the fourth.
T/Plt: £30.80 to a £1 stake. Pool: £40964.97, 969.64 winning tickets. T/Qpdt: £2.70 to a £1 stake. Pool: £3560.90, 974.90 winning tickets. JR

1819 CHESTER (L-H)
Thursday, May 6

OFFICIAL GOING: Good (good to soft in places) changing to good to soft after race 1 (1.45)
False rail in place increasing distances by 8yds
Wind: Light, across Weather: Overcast

1831 CORDJIA RENAISSANCE H'CAP 1m 2f 75y
1:45 (1:45) (Class 2) (0-100,100) 4-Y-0+ **£14,193** (£4,248; £2,124; £1,062; £528) **Stalls** High

Form RPR

203- **1** **Sweet Lightning**[229] [6106] 5-8-8 **90** TomEaves 2 98+
(M Dods) *hld up: hdwy 2f out: nt clr run briefly over 1f out: qcknd between horses to ld ins fnl f: r.o willingly and kpt finding more towards fin* **13/2**

366- **2** ½ **Last Three Minutes (IRE)**[286] [4261] 5-8-7 **87** ow2 RyanMoore 8 96
(Sir Michael Stoute) *on toes: chsd ldr: rdn to ld over 1f out: hdd ins fnl f: r.o u.p but looked hld cl home* **10/3**[2]

-600 **3** ½ **Porgy**[15] [1474] 5-8-8 **90** PaulHanagan 3 96
(R A Fahey) *t.k.h: in tch: effrt 2f out: carried hd high whn chsd ldrs after: kpt on* **8/1**

100 **4** hd **Cairnsmore**[40] [1015] 4-8-11 **93** JoeFanning 1 99
(M Johnston) *broke wl: led v early: prom: rdn to chal fr over 1f out: nt qckn cl home* **16/1**

10-2 **5** 6 **Almiqdaad**[21] [1333] 4-9-4 **100** RichardHills 7 94
(M A Jarvis) *hld up: effrt to chse ldrs 2f out but no real imp: edgd lft and wknd ins fnl f* **6/4**[1]

1 **6** nk **Submariner (USA)**[16] [1447] 4-8-5 **87** RoystonFfrench 4 80
(M Johnston) *lengthy: lw: hld up: pushed along fr over 4f out: nvr on terms w ldrs* **20/1**

112- **7** 3¼ **Leceile (USA)**[249] [5472] 4-8-8 **90** HayleyTurner 5 77
(W J Haggas) *sn led: rdn and hdd over 1f out: wknd ent fnl f* **6/1**[3]

0003 **8** 14 **Iron Out (USA)**[9] [1600] 4-7-13 **86** oh10 PaulPickard(5) 6 45
(R Hollinshead) *in tch on outside: pushed along to chse ldrs over 3f out: rdn and wknd over 2f out* **50/1**

2m 14.92s (2.72) **Going Correction** +0.35s/f (Good) **8** Ran SP% **114.4**
Speed ratings (Par 109): **103,102,102,102,97 97,94,83**
toteswingers: 1&2 £6.00, 1&3 £8.70, 2&3 £9.80 CSF £28.48 CT £176.07 TOTE £7.70: £1.90, £1.60, £2.50; EX 36.60 Trifecta £201.00 Pool: £663.49 - 3.30 winning units..
Owner Andrew Tinkler **Bred** Mrs M Lavell **Trained** Denton, Co Durham

FOCUS

After 2mm of rain overnight and a further 5mm during the morning, the ground was changed to good, good to soft in places. The rail was moved out four yards from the 4f marker to the top of the home straight in order to provide fresh ground. This was a decent handicap, but they only went a modest pace and a few were keen as a result. Probably ordinary form for the grade, but sound enough.

NOTEBOOK

Sweet Lightning, making his debut for the yard having not been seen since finishing nearly 2l behind Almiqdaad in a hot Newbury handicap last September, had a 5lb pull here and looked fit enough. Settled off the pace, he travelled particularly well and the only question was whether he would get the gap when he needed it. Fortunately one appeared inside the last furlong and he made no mistake. The change of stables has obviously done him no harm and he should be able to build on this. He may now head for the Zetland Gold Cup and then possibly the John Smith's Cup. (op 7-1)

Last Three Minutes(IRE), another making his debut for the yard following a ten-month absence, travelled well in the middle of the pack and looked likely to win when taking over in front over a furlong out, but the winner proved too strong in the run to the line. The 2lb overweight wouldn't have helped, but he is entitled to step forward from this and should be winning before long. (op 4-1 tchd 9-2)

Porgy, disappointing in three starts for his current yard so far this year, is edging down the weights as a result and ran much better here. He was forced to make his effort wide after turning in and ran on well, but one negative was that he was inclined to show a rather high head-carriage. (op 12-1)

Cairnsmore, disappointing in a couple of hot Polytrack handicaps since making a successful debut for the yard in an uncompetitive Kempton maiden in January, travelled well just behind the leaders and had his chance when a gap appeared over a furlong from home, but he lacked the finishing speed to make it count. (op 14-1)

Almiqdaad, who split a couple of much higher-rated opponents when runner-up in a Ripon conditions event on his reappearance, was disappointing as he found little when asked to make an effort off the final bend. Official explanation: the trainer unable to offer any explanation for the poor performance shown (op 7-4)

Submariner(USA), easy winner of a weak four-runner 1m4f Folkestone maiden on debut last month, was never travelling well at any stage at the back of the field before making a little late headway. He probably needs more time and a return to a stiffer test. (op 12-1)

Leceile(USA), who has had problems with the stalls in the past, hadn't been seen since just failing to complete a hat-trick in a Goodwood fillies' Listed handicap last August. She would have appreciated the rain, but having enjoyed the run of the race out in front she appeared to blow up when headed over a furlong from home. (op 11-2)

1832 BETFAIR HUXLEY STKS (FOR THE TRADESMAN'S CUP) (GROUP 3) 1m 2f 75y

2:15 (2:15) (Class 1) 4-Y-O+

£36,900 (£13,988; £7,000; £3,490; £1,748; £877) **Stalls** High

Form				RPR
5-00	**1**		**Debussy (IRE)**[63] [800] 4-9-0 113 .... WilliamBuick 1 (J H M Gosden) *led for abt 1f: chsd ldr after: r.o to ld fnl 150yds and sn edgd lft: wl on top at fin* **11/1**	118
341-	**2**	*2*	**Les Fazzani (IRE)**[158] [7589] 6-8-11 111 .... PaulHanagan 7 (K A Ryan) *led after abt 1f: pushed along over 2f out: rdn over 1f out: hdd fnl 150yds: no answer to wnr after* **10/1**	111
16-1	**3**	*3*	**South Easter (IRE)**[40] [1016] 4-9-0 105 .... (t) JMurtagh 2 (W J Haggas) *chsd ldrs: rdn and outpcd over 2f out: styd on fnl 100yds: nt trble front 2* **3/1**[1]	108+
45-1	**4**	*hd*	**Kings Gambit (SAF)**[21] [1333] 6-9-0 110 .... JamieSpencer 4 (T P Tate) *chsd ldrs: pushed along over 3f out: rdn and outpcd by front pair over 1f out: kpt on same pce ins fnl f* **17/2**	108
33-0	**5**	*½*	**Kingdom Of Fife**[21] [1328] 5-9-0 111 .... (v) RyanMoore 5 (Sir Michael Stoute) *lw: hld up: pushed along 2f out: sme hdwy over 1f out: kpt on ins fnl f: nt gng pce to chal ldrs* **15/2**	107
23-6	**6**	*3*	**Sans Frontieres (IRE)**[21] [1328] 4-9-0 110 .... JimmyFortune 6 (J Noseda) *midfield: pushed along 3f out: outpcd 2f out: no imp on ldrs* **10/1**	101
10-2	**7**	*2 ¼*	**Redwood**[12] [1532] 4-9-0 113 .... RichardHills 8 (B W Hills) *lw: s.i.s: in rr: nvr looked happy: pushed along over 2f out: nvr able to get on terms* **7/2**[2]	96
46-4	**8**	*19*	**Stotsfold**[47] [946] 7-9-0 114 .... AdamKirby 3 (W R Swinburn) *in rr: niggled along over 4f out: nvr on terms: eased ins fnl f whn wl btn* **4/1**[3]	80

2m 12.38s (0.18) **Going Correction** +0.35s/f (Good) **8** Ran SP% **116.0**

Speed ratings (Par 113): **113,111,109,108,108 106,104,89**

toteswingers: 1&2 £19.40, 1&3 £7.10, 2&3 £7.00 CSF £114.57 TOTE £12.80: £2.60, £3.10, £1.60; EX 97.90 Trifecta £281.00 Pool: £1260.89 - 3.32 winning units..

Owner H R H Princess Haya Of Jordan **Bred** Darley **Trained** Newmarket, Suffolk

FOCUS

A good race for favourites in the past with the market leader having won seven of the last ten runnings and this year's renewal was run at a strong pace, but despite that the front pair held those positions throughout. The winning time was 2.54 seconds faster than the opener and the form is rated around the runner-up.

NOTEBOOK

Debussy(IRE), third in the Chester Vase on this day last year, ran moderately in two starts at Meydan earlier this year but was a different proposition this time. He was always travelling best of the rest in the slipstream of the leader and quickened up well after the intersection to hit the front well inside the last furlong. Already a Group 2 winner in France last year, he holds an entry in the Prince Of Wales's Stakes at Royal Ascot.

Les Fazzani(IRE), not seen since winning a Kempton Listed event in November, needs soft ground so the rain would have been a help and she was joint best-in at the weights. Given a positive ride, she got her rivals off the bridle one by one but the winner was the exception and she had no answer to him when he ranged alongside. This was an excellent return and she deserves to go one better before long. (op 9-1 tchd 8-1)

South Easter(IRE), narrow winner from Gitano Hernando in the Dee Stakes over C&D a year ago, had a bit to find on official ratings but he proved his wellbeing with a successful return from 11 months off in a Kempton Listed event in March. Never far away, he became outpaced inside the last half-mile but due to his rider's persistence he ran on again to snatch third place near the line. A step back up to 1m4f looks to be in order. (op 7-2)

Kings Gambit(SAF), back in Group company after beating the disappointing favourite (Almiqdaad) in the first race in a Ripon conditions event on his reappearance, raced handily throughout but became outpaced on the turn for home and had little more to offer. (op 8-1 tchd 9-1 and 10-1 in places)

Kingdom Of Fife, narrowly beaten in the opening handicap on this card last year, represented the stable that had won this race four times in the past five years. A bit disappointing in the Earl Of Sefton at Newmarket on his reappearance, he made little impression from off the pace and may need to drop into Listed company. (tchd 7-1 and 8-1)

Sans Frontieres(IRE) was having his first start since finishing third in last year's Dante when just in front of Kingdom Of Fife in the Earl of Sefton at Newmarket last month, but was off the bridle a fair way out here and still has plenty of questions to answer. (op 11-1 tchd 12-1)

Redwood, narrowly beaten in the Gordon Richards Stakes at Sandown 12 says earlier when returning from 11 months off, never made any impression from off the pace and may not have liked the track, but he remains unexposed. Official explanation: jockey said that the colt was never travelling (op 4-1)

Stotsfold, a dual winner over C&D in handicap company, didn't find the race panning out as he would have liked when a close fourth in the Winter Derby on his return to action. He was the other best in at these weights along with the runner-up, but the easing of the ground wouldn't have been in his favour and he was struggling in last place passing the 4f pole. Official explanation: trainer said that the gelding was unsuited by the good to soft ground (op 9-2 tchd 11-2 and 6-1 in places)

1833 MBNA CHESTER VASE (GROUP 3) (C&G) 1m 4f 66y

2:45 (2:45) (Class 1) 3-Y-O

£39,739 (£15,064; £7,539; £3,759; £1,883; £945) **Stalls** Low

Form				RPR
013-	**1**		**Ted Spread**[187] [7184] 3-8-12 94 .... DarrylHolland 1 (M H Tompkins) *racd keenly: chsd ldrs: chalng upsides over 3f out: rdn to ld 2f out: hdd narrowly over 1f out: rallied to regain ld fnl 100yds: r.o gamely* **8/1**	106
6	**2**	*hd*	**Icon Dream (IRE)**[18] [1414] 3-8-12 0 .... JamieSpencer 7 (David Wachman, Ire) *sluggish s: hld up: hdwy over 2f out: rdn to ld narrowly over 1f out: hdd fnl 100yds: r.o u.p but looked hld after* **15/2**[3]	105
-122	**3**	*3 ¾*	**Chink Of Light**[30] [1138] 3-8-12 84 .... (v[1]) JimmyFortune 5 (A M Balding) *lw: led after 1f: rdn and hdd 2f out: sn n.m.r: kpt on same pce fnl f and no ch w front pair* **16/1**	99
15-5	**4**	*6*	**Morana (IRE)**[21] [1327] 3-8-12 107 .... AlanMunro 3 (P W Chapple-Hyam) *racd keenly: chsd ldrs: pushed along 3f out: wknd ins fnl f* **7/2**[2]	89
612-	**5**	*½*	**Tominator**[199] [6898] 3-8-12 97 .... GrahamGibbons 6 (R Hollinshead) *bit bkwd: hld up: outpcd over 3f out: nvr able to get on terms* **20/1**	89
	6	*½*	**Rocket Man (IRE)**[25] [1249] 3-8-12 0 .... JMurtagh 4 (A P O'Brien, Ire) *str: good bodied: coltish in paddock: hld up: pushed along 4f out: outpcd sn after: nvr able to get on terms* **9/4**[1]	88
15-3	**7**	*nk*	**Critical Moment (USA)**[21] [1327] 3-8-12 105 .... RichardHills 2 (B W Hills) *led for 1f: chsd ldr: chal 3 wd fr over 3f out: wknd over 1f out* **7/2**[2]	87

2m 43.32s (3.42) **Going Correction** +0.55s/f (Yiel) **7** Ran SP% **108.7**

Speed ratings (Par 109): **110,109,107,103,103 102,102**

toteswingers: 1&2 £6.50, 1&3 £5.50, 2&3 £6.60 CSF £58.36 TOTE £10.00: £2.90, £4.20; EX 52.50.

Owner False Nose 'N Glasses Partnership **Bred** Pollards Stables **Trained** Newmarket, Suffolk

FOCUS

The Chester Vase is usually won by a smart performer, though no Epsom Derby winner had been successful since Shergar in 1981. This was run at something of a stop-start gallop and it seems unlikely it will have much bearing on the Epsom Classic. The winner was a big improver but this was not a strong renewal and is a long way below Derby form.

NOTEBOOK

Ted Spread, not seen since finishing third in the Zetland Stakes last October, was always close up but took a furious hold and had to be angled out to see daylight passing the half-mile pole. In front over a furlong from home, he looked sure to be swallowed up by the runner-up after the intersection but he pulled out extra from somewhere under strong pressure and forced his head back in front where it mattered. He is currently a top-priced 50-1 for the Derby with Victor Chandler and Hills, which looks realistic, but his trainer thinks he may be more of a St Leger horse.

Icon Dream(IRE), who shaped as though this extra 2f would suit when sixth in the Ballysax, could have done without fluffing the start and handing his rivals an advantage. Despite that, he still looked the likely winner when swooping around the outside of the leaders on the turn for home and hitting the front a furlong out, but his rivals refused to lie down and he was worried out of it. He should be able to win a race at this level. (tchd 6-1)

Chink Of Light, visored for the first time on this step up from handicap company, had plenty to find on official ratings but was given a positive ride. Gradually stepping up the pace from the front, he battled on well when joined but had run his race when hampered against the inside rail approaching the cutaway. Connections think he needs further so the Queen's Vase could be just the race for him. (op 12-1)

Morana(IRE), racing beyond 1m for the first time after finishing nearly 4l behind Critical Moment in the Craven, raced handily throughout but came seriously off the bridle passing the 3f pole and was soon left behind. He has won at this level, but his stamina for the trip remains questionable. (op 4-1 tchd 9-2 in places)

Tominator, the most experienced in the field and last seen getting caught on the line in a Pontefract Listed event last October, was another trying beyond 1m for the first time. Weak in the market, he was keen enough at the back of the field and made no impression but connections had warned that softening ground would be a problem. (op 14-1)

Rocket Man(IRE), workmanlike rather than impressive when winning a 1m2f Curragh maiden on very testing ground last month, is from a yard that had won this twice in the past three years, but he was very disappointing. He travelled well enough off the pace, but once off the bridle found nothing. The trainer's representative reported that the colt ran green on the tight track. Official explanation: trainer'srepresentative said that the colt ran green on the tight track (op 11-4 tchd 3-1 in places)

Critical Moment(USA), stepping up 4f in trip after finishing third in the Craven on his return to action, was battling for the lead starting the turn for home but then dropped out as though stamina was an issue. (op 3-1)

1834 BOODLES DIAMOND ETERNITY H'CAP 7f 122y

3:15 (3:16) (Class 2) (0-100,98) 3-Y-O **£14,193** (£4,248; £2,124; £1,062; £528) **Stalls** Low

Form				RPR
242-	**1**		**Yaa Wayl (IRE)**[194] [7013] 3-8-8 **88** .... PhilipRobinson 6 (M A Jarvis) *racd keenly: chsd ldrs: plld out over 1f out: led 1f out: all out towards fin: jst hld on* **7/2**[1]	97+
315-	**2**	*nse*	**Our Joe Mac (IRE)**[229] [6088] 3-8-8 **88** .... PaulHanagan 12 (R A Fahey) *hld up: hdwy over 2f out: forced sltly wd over 1f out: r.o strly ins fnl f: jst failed* **7/1**[3]	97+
10	**3**	*2 ¾*	**Burghley**[54] [884] 3-8-4 **84** oh2 .... HayleyTurner 10 (M L W Bell) *lw: chsd ldr: rdn over 1f out whn chalng: nt qckn ins fnl f* **16/1**	86
3-10	**4**	*1*	**Jarrow (IRE)**[19] [1376] 3-8-10 **90** .... JoeFanning 4 (M Johnston) *led: rdn and hdd 1f out: styd on same pce ins fnl f* **8/1**	89
020-	**5**	*1 ¾*	**Sea Lord (IRE)**[194] [7013] 3-8-8 **88** .... RoystonFfrench 2 (M Johnston) *chsd ldrs: pushed along 4f out: nt qckn over 1f out: one pce ins fnl f* **12/1**	83
15	**6**	*½*	**Bullwhip (IRE)**[19] [1385] 3-9-4 **98** .... WilliamBuick 3 (J H M Gosden) *hld up: n.m.r over 4f out: hdwy 2f out: styd on steadily ins fnl f: nt pce to chal ldrs* **5/1**[2]	92+
53-0	**7**	*2 ½*	**Syrian**[21] [1334] 3-8-12 **92** .... JamieSpencer 7 (M L W Bell) *swtg: edgy: s.s: hld up in rr: forced wd over 4f out: sme hdwy on wd outside over 1f out: no imp on ldrs* **16/1**	80+
145-	**8**	*nk*	**Transvaal Sky**[215] [6481] 3-8-8 **88** .... RichardKingscote 8 (Tom Dascombe) *in tch: pushed along over 2f out: wknd fnl f* **16/1**	75

221- **9** 2 3/4 **Fine Sight**[189] 7130 3-8-4 **84** oh3 .... FrannyNorton 11 64
(R Hannon) *in tch: pushed along over 4f out: wknd over 1f out* **16/1**

0-1 **10** nk **Signor Verdi**[16] 1450 3-8-4 **84** oh2 .... EddieAhern 5 63+
(B J Meehan) *s.i.s: hld up: hmpd over 4f out: nvr on terms* **7/1**[3]

5-00 **11** 1 1/2 **Kingdom Of Munster (IRE)**[22] 1315 3-8-7 **87** .... TomEaves 9 62
(Ian Williams) *midfield: pushed along over 4f out: wknd over 2f out* **33/1**

-101 **12** 25 **Niran (IRE)**[38] 1052 3-8-7 **87** .... ChrisCatlin 1 —
(C E Brittain) *b.hind: midfield: wknd over 2f out* **8/1**

1m 37.01s (3.21) **Going Correction** +0.55s/f (Yiel) **12** Ran SP% **120.3**
Speed ratings (Par 105): **105,104,102,101,99 98,96,96,93,93 91,66**
toteswingers: 1&2 £8.00, 1&3 £20.80, 2&3 £32.20 CSF £28.08 CT £359.52 TOTE £4.00: £1.60, £2.90, £6.60; EX 30.40 Trifecta £960.30 Part won. Pool: £1297.77 - 0.52 winning units..
Owner Sheikh Ahmed Al Maktoum **Bred** Ballylinch Stud **Trained** Newmarket, Suffolk

FOCUS
A decent 3-y-o handicap, but a race in which it was crucial to race handily and very few got into it from off the pace. Given the nature of the track the form is not rated too positively.

NOTEBOOK
Yaa Wayl(IRE), last seen getting narrowly beaten off 5lb lower in first-time blinkers in a Doncaster nursery last October, would have been suited by the easing of the ground. Keen enough in a handy position, he was ridden to the front a furlong from home and got first run on the runner-up, which was just as well as he held on by the skin of his teeth. (op 4-1 tchd 9-2)
Our Joe Mac(IRE), last seen enjoying little luck in running in an Ayr nursery last September, was well backed and is the one to take from the race as he started from the outside stall and was the only one to make any significant progress from off the pace. He came from well back too, yet only just failed to get up and he will surely go one better before too long. (op 11-1)
Burghley, making his turf debut from 2lb wrong, was always handy and had every chance a furlong from home. This was a lot better than on his handicap debut at Wolverhampton last time and he still has plenty of scope. (tchd 20-1)
Jarrow(IRE), a big disappointment on fast ground at Doncaster last time having shown decent form on Polytrack during the winter, tried to make all and travelled well in front until inside the last furlong. He may have been suited by being at the front end given the way the race was run, but this was still better. (op 9-1)
Sea Lord(IRE), who blew rather hot and cold in six outings at two, was another to be suited by racing handily and it will be interesting to see if he can build on this with the outing under his belt. (op 11-1)
Bullwhip(IRE), making his handicap debut after finishing a well-beaten last of five behind Dick Turpin and Canford Cliffs in the Greenham, didn't look at all happy on the track but was noted making some late progress from well off the pace. This was only his third start so he still has some scope for improvement. (op 9-2 tchd 4-1)
Syrian, beaten a very long way after pulling his chance away on his Ripon reappearance, can be rated as having run better as he blew the start and was then forced to make his effort extremely wide off the final bend.
Signor Verdi, making his handicap debut from 2lb wrong after just getting up to win a 1m Kempton maiden last month, was badly hampered against the inside rail half a mile from home so can be given another chance, but he may need further in any case. (op 8-1)

1835 ABODE HOTEL E B F MAIDEN STKS 5f 16y
3:55 (3:56) (Class 3) 2-Y-O **£8,418** (£2,505; £1,251; £625) **Stalls** Low

Form RPR

2 **1** **Dress Up (IRE)**[10] 1577 2-8-12 0 .... WilliamBuick 7 77
(S Kirk) *leggy: led: hdd over 4f out: remained w ldrs and racd 3 wd: led over 2f out: kicked over 1f out: kpt up to work towards fin: hld on wl* **9/2**

43 **2** 3/4 **Shafgaan**[20] 1351 2-9-3 0 .... ChrisCatlin 2 80+
(C E Brittain) *lw: hmpd s: sn lost pl and bhd: hdwy over 1f out: r.o strly ins fnl f: gng on at fin* **7/2**[2]

2 **3** nk **Malpas Missile (IRE)**[19] 1375 2-8-12 0 .... RichardKingscote 12 73+
(Tom Dascombe) *w'like: in tch: ouptpced over 2f out: prog ins fnl f: r.o towards fin* **11/1**

42 **4** 2 1/2 **Diamond Geezah (IRE)**[19] 1389 2-9-3 0 .... RichardHills 9 69+
(B W Hills) *w'like: on toes: hmpd sltly s: chsd ldrs after 1f: rdn to take 2nd over 1f out: nt qckn w wnr: lost 2nd fnl 100yds: sn edgd lft: no ex towards fin* **5/2**[1]

5 3 **Safe Haven (IRE)** 2-8-12 0 .... FrannyNorton 5 53+
(A Bailey) *leggy: sn pushed along and bhd: kpt on ins fnl f: nt gng pce to get competitive* **16/1**

0 **6** hd **Press Release**[12] 1517 2-9-3 0 .... RichardSmith 6 57+
(Tom Dascombe) *wnt rt s: racd keenly: hdwy to chse ldrs over 3f out: hung rt sn after and looked ill at ease on trck: wknd 1f out* **33/1**

5 **7** 2 1/4 **Mandy's Princess (IRE)**[38] 1043 2-8-12 0 .... PaulHanagan 4 44
(R A Fahey) *w'like: tall: gd spd: led over 4f out: hdd over 2f out: wknd ins fnl f* **12/1**

43 **8** 2 1/4 **Just For Leo (IRE)**[9] 1597 2-9-3 0 .... JimmyFortune 3 41+
(P D Evans) *w'like: athletic: w ldrs: rdn over 1f out: wknd ins fnl f: eased whn btn fnl 100yds* **4/1**[3]

0 **9** 3 1/2 **Chester Deelyte (IRE)**[22] 1292 2-8-12 0 .... TomEaves 8 24
(Mrs L Williamson) *str: midfield early: bhd and outpcd fnl 3f* **40/1**

0 **10** 9 **Volturi (IRE)**[3] 1764 2-9-3 0 .... AdrianMcCarthy 1 —
(Peter Grayson) *cl cpld: on toes: wnt rt s: midfield: outpcd and bhd fnl 3f* **40/1**

64.72 secs (3.72) **Going Correction** +0.65s/f (Yiel) **10** Ran SP% **118.7**
Speed ratings (Par 97): **96,94,94,90,85 85,81,78,72,58**
toteswingers: 1&2 £3.80, 1&3 £7.50, 2&3 £8.20 CSF £20.82 TOTE £5.40: £1.60, £2.00, £2.90; EX 26.40 Trifecta £187.20 Pool: £979.50 - 3.87 winning units..
Owner Mrs Ciara Murphy **Bred** Redpender Stud Ltd **Trained** Upper Lambourn, Berks

FOCUS
No horse drawn higher than stall five had won this race since 2003. The four non-runners would have started from stalls 10, 11, 13 and 14. This looked an ordinary maiden, but the pace was decent and a handful of winners should emerge from it. Sound form, rated around the principals and race averages.

NOTEBOOK
Dress Up(IRE), who was only just caught after trying to make all on her Windsor debut ten days earlier, was one of three vying for the early lead until gaining the advantage on her own 2f from home. She saw it out in game fashion from then on and there should be more races to be won with her. (op 5-1)
Shafgaan, who showed early speed in each of his first two starts, was the unlucky horse of the race as he was cannoned into by Volturi exiting the stalls and lost plenty of ground as a result. He finished strongly down the outside, but the damage had been done and he could never quite get there. He deserves compensation. (tchd 4-1)
Malpas Missile(IRE), who split a couple of subsequent winners when runner-up on her Doncaster debut last month, found herself starting from the outside stall and gave herself a bit to do but was another doing her best work late. She should get off the mark before too long. (op 12-1 tchd 10-1)
Diamond Geezah(IRE), whose stable won this race three years in a row between 2005 and 2007, finished clear of a subsequent winner when narrowly beaten at Nottingham last time. Well backed, he was always in a great position but failed to pick up when asked and there seemed no real excuses. (op 7-2)
Safe Haven(IRE), a 17,000gns filly out of an unraced half-sister to Tiger Hill, took a walk in the market but was noted staying on steadily under hands-and-heels riding late on and she should come on plenty for this. (op 10-1)
Press Release, who looked badly in need of the experience when ninth of 13 on his Leicester debut, was all over the place on the track but did show something and looks capable of better back on a more conventional track. (op 25-1)
Just For Leo(IRE) Official explanation: jockey said that the colt hung right.

1836 STELLAR GROUP H'CAP 6f 18y
4:30 (4:33) (Class 3) (0-90,88) 3-Y-O **£10,361** (£3,083; £1,540; £769) **Stalls** Low

Form RPR

1-13 **1** **Horseradish**[5] 1701 3-8-12 **82** .... HayleyTurner 6 99
(M L W Bell) *broke wl: trckd ldrs: led jst over 1f out: r.o wl: pushed out* **11/4**[2]

21-2 **2** 2 1/2 **Rule Of Nature**[23] 1279 3-8-10 **80** .... RyanMoore 2 89
(Sir Michael Stoute) *lw: trckd ldrs: led wl over 1f out: sn hdd u.p: nt gng pce of wnr fnl 100yds* **2/1**[1]

110 **3** 3 3/4 **Srda (USA)**[22] 1312 3-9-2 **86** .... ChrisCatlin 11 83+
(C E Brittain) *lw: in rr: plld out and hdwy over 1f out: r.o ins fnl f: nt rch front 2: nrst fin* **25/1**

20-5 **4** 1/2 **Dancing Freddy (IRE)**[6] 1656 3-8-10 **80** .... PaulMulrennan 4 75
(J G Given) *lw: sn led: hdd after 100yds: chsd ldr: led 2f out: sn hdd: one pce ins fnl f* **25/1**

10-0 **5** 1 **Tasmeem (IRE)**[19] 1399 3-9-1 **85** .... PaulHanagan 1 77+
(R A Fahey) *broke wl: hld up: rdn and r.o ins fnl f: nt rch ldrs* **8/1**

6-0 **6** 1 **Pilgrim Dancer (IRE)**[10] 1584 3-8-8 **78** .... EddieAhern 7 67
(Patrick Morris) *midfield: rdn 2f out: hdwy to chse ldrs over 1f out: one pce fnl 75yds* **66/1**

04-3 **7** 4 1/2 **Lowdown (IRE)**[6] 1663 3-9-3 **87** .... JoeFanning 9 61
(M Johnston) *lw: chsd ldrs: n.m.r and hmpd over 3f out: pushed along over 2f out: tried to rally over 1f out: wknd ins fnl f* **11/2**[3]

0-40 **8** 4 **Ghostwing**[22] 1315 3-9-4 **88** .... WilliamBuick 8 49
(J Gallagher) *on toes: racd on outside: hld up in midfield: outpcd fnl 2f* **22/1**

06-0 **9** 3 3/4 **Toga Tiger (IRE)**[19] 1376 3-8-9 **79** .... TonyCulhane 10 28
(P T Midgley) *a bhd* **50/1**

2-1 **10** 6 **Johannesgray (IRE)**[29] 1153 3-8-8 **78** .... KierenFallon 3 —+
(D Nicholls) *squeezed out: racd in midfield: effrt over 2f out: nt clr run over 1f out: sn btn: eased ins fnl f* **6/1**

-160 **11** 1 1/2 **Raddy 'Ell Pauline (IRE)**[19] 1376 3-9-1 **85** ....(b[1]) JamieSpencer 12 10
(K A Ryan) *on toes: led after 100yds: hdd 2f out: got unbalanced sn after and wknd* **33/1**

1m 17.33s (3.53) **Going Correction** +0.65s/f (Yiel) **11** Ran SP% **119.2**
Speed ratings (Par 103): **102,98,93,93,91 90,84,79,74,66 64**
toteswingers: 1&2 £2.10, 1&3 £15.00, 2&3 £12.20 CSF £8.14 CT £114.67 TOTE £3.80: £1.50, £1.10, £6.00; EX 8.10 Trifecta £154.60 Pool: £1725.89 - 8.26 winning units..
Owner Mrs G Rowland-Clark **Bred** Mrs F A Veasey **Trained** Newmarket, Suffolk

FOCUS
A hot 3-y-o sprint handicap and the form should work out. The form has been rated fairly positively.

NOTEBOOK
Horseradish, closely matched with Rule Of Nature on last month's Yarmouth running over 7f, is already due to go up 3lb following his decent effort over this trip at Newmarket on Saturday, so he was well in here. He travelled beautifully behind the leaders throughout and, once quickening to the front a furlong out, was always finding enough to see off his old rival. He won't mind a return to further and there are more decent prizes to be won with him. (op 10-3 tchd 7-2 in places)
Rule Of Nature, well backed to reverse Yarmouth form with the winner on 1lb better terms. She raced prominently throughout and the gaps opened up for her just when she needed them, but although she quickened up well her old rival made his effort at the same time and he saw his race out just the better. (op 11-4 tchd 3-1 in places)
Srda(USA), tailed-off last of 11 in the Nell Gwyn last time after winning her first two starts on Polytrack, reportedly pulled up stiff at Newmarket and this was better, especially as she came from a mile back but was finishing in great style. A return to further should see her winning again. (op 18-1)
Dancing Freddy(IRE), without a win in a year, was all the better for his Doncaster reappearance and, having raced handily, hit the front over a furlong from home but he was soon swamped. He is already due to drop 2lb, so is worth keeping an eye on. (op 28-1)
Tasmeem(IRE), never in the race after getting hampered at the start over 5f on his Thirsk reappearance last month, was another to finish in good style from well off the pace and is another to watch out for back on a fast surface. (op 7-1 tchd 6-1)
Pilgrim Dancer(IRE), disappointing since beating Alfred Nobel in a Naas maiden 13 months ago including on his debut for the yard/seasonal reappearance last month, wasn't totally disgraced from 3lb wrong.
Johannesgray(IRE), making his handicap debut after narrowly winning a Catterick maiden last month from which the second and fourth have won since, looked relaxed beforehand but took an age to find his stride after breaking from the stalls and never looked happy thereafter. He is worth another chance to show this running to be all wrong. (op 9-2)
Raddy 'Ell Pauline(IRE), twice disappointing since winning off 2lb lower on the Lingfield Polytrack in February, did far too much too early in the first-time blinkers from the outside stall.

1837 CVAM H'CAP 1m 2f 75y
5:05 (5:07) (Class 3) (0-90,90) 4-Y-O+ **£8,095** (£2,408; £1,203; £601) **Stalls** High

Form RPR

001- **1** **Thin Red Line (IRE)**[206] 6724 4-9-1 **87** .... TomEaves 12 99
(M Dods) *trckd ldrs: rdn to ld over 1f out: r.o wl to draw clr fnl 100 yds* **25/1**

054- **2** 3 1/2 **Norwegian Dancer (UAE)**[174] 7373 4-8-10 **82** .... GrahamGibbons 9 87
(E S McMahon) *on toes: prom: led over 3f out: hdd over 1f out: one pce and wl hld by wnr fnl 100 yds* **8/1**

4241 **3** 1 1/4 **Hollow Green (IRE)**[3] 1783 4-8-11 **83** 6ex .... JimmyFortune 11 86
(P D Evans) *lw: midfield: hdwy over 2f out: chsd front 2 over 1f out: styd on tl one pce fnl 75 yds* **8/1**

6-02 **4** 1 **Laudatory**[17] 1430 4-8-10 **82** .... EddieAhern 5 83
(W R Swinburn) *lw: squeezed out s: hld up: hdwy over 1f out: styd on ins fnl f: nt trble ldrs* **14/1**

2-15 **5** nk **Paquerettza (FR)**[19] 1379 4-8-12 **84** .... FrederikTylicki 3 84+
(D H Brown) *hmpd s: hld up: n.m.r and hmpd after 1 1/2 f: rdn and hdwy over 1f out: styd on towards fin: nvr nrr* **17/2**

111- **6** 1/2 **Luc Jordan**[195] 6996 4-9-1 **87** .... KierenFallon 2 86+
(L M Cumani) *midfield: pushed along over 2f out: outpcd over 1f out: nvr able to chal* **5/1**[2]

00-1 **7** nk **Bugaku**[23] 1282 5-8-13 **85** .... RyanMoore 1 83
(Sir Michael Stoute) *in tch: pushed along 4f out: outpcd over 2f out: n.d after* **7/2**[1]

23-0 **8** ½ **Credit Swap**[19] 1383 5-8-13 **90**.................................... TobyAtkinson(5) 8 87
(M Wigham) *on toes: hld up: pushed along over 1f out: styd on ins fnl f: nt trble ldrs* **14/1**

13-0 **9** 7 **Fastnet Storm (IRE)**[23] 1272 4-9-4 **90**.............................. MickyFenton 4 73
(T P Tate) *fractious s: bustled along to go prom: rdn over 1f out: wknd fnl f* **5/1**[2]

50-4 **10** 3 **Ben Chorley**[40] 1006 6-9-2 **88**.. JohnEgan 10 65
(P D Evans) *sn led: hdd over 3f out: rdn and wknd over 1f out* **13/2**[3]

1212 **11** 3 ¾ **Plush**[10] 1587 7-8-4 **81**... RossAtkinson(5) 13 51
(Tom Dascombe) *s.s: a bhd* **33/1**

0-50 **12** 5 **Moheebb (IRE)**[23] 1272 6-9-2 **88**...............................(b) PaulMulrennan 7 48
(Mrs R A Carr) *in tch: rdn and wknd 2f out* **28/1**

2m 16.66s (4.46) **Going Correction** +0.65s/f (Yiel) **12** Ran SP% **125.2**
Speed ratings (Par 107): **108,105,104,103,103 102,102,102,96,94 91,87**
toteswingers: 1&2 £35.70, 1&3 £24.60, 2&3 £16.60 CSF £221.48 CT £1781.58 TOTE £19.90: £4.40, £3.00, £3.10; EX 251.60 TRIFECTA Not won. Place 6: £487.84 Place 5: £177.38 .
Owner William Stobart **Bred** Peter Jones And G G Jones **Trained** Denton, Co Durham

FOCUS
A decent handicap run at just a fair pace in which it again paid to race handily, but ultimately this was a one-horse race. The winning time was 1.74 seconds slower than the opening Class 2 handicap and 4.28 seconds slower than the Huxley Stakes. The winner impressed but again this is not form to take too literally.

NOTEBOOK
Thin Red Line(IRE) was making his debut for Michael Dods after seven months off having been bought out of Ed Dunlop's stable for 80,000gns. He travelled powerfully behind the leaders and was still on the bridle when hitting the front over a furlong from home before powering clear. He stays further than this, so has plenty of options open to him and looks set for a good season. (op 16-1)
Norwegian Dancer(UAE), having his first start since November but 2-4 over C&D and 1lb below his last winning mark, travelled well on the shoulder of the leader before taking over in front over 2f from home, but he was soon swept aside by a progressive rival. This was still a decent return and he should be winning again before too long. (op 10-1)
Hollow Green(IRE), carrying a 6lb penalty for her narrow win over further at Windsor three days earlier, was 1lb worse off with Bugaku having finished almost 2l behind him at Yarmouth last month, but she still managed to turn that form around. She stayed on well from off the pace over the last couple of furlongs, but could never get on terms with the front pair. (tchd 16-1 in places)
Laudatory, without a win in over a year and trying this trip for the first time, made good late progress against the inside rail and the distance didn't seem to be a problem. (op 12-1)
Paquerettza(FR), disappointing off this mark over this trip at Doncaster last month, has gained all three of her wins over 1m but she does stay this far and just clicked into gear much too late. (op 9-1 tchd 10-1)
Luc Jordan, who ended last season with a hat-trick, was 6lb higher for this return to action but he was being niggled along to stay in touch 3f from home and made no impression from that point. He may have needed it. Official explanation: jockey said the colt suffered interference at the start (op 7-2)
Bugaku, raised 5lb for his Yarmouth success, was having to be ridden along a fair way out but found nothing at all off the bridle. (tchd 5-1 in places)
Fastnet Storm(IRE), an established front-runner and back up to his best trip, got upset in the stalls and missed the break. Soon ridden into a handy position but unable to lead, he pulled like a train and gave himself little chance. It may be best to ignore this. Official explanation: jockey said the gelding suffered interference at the start (op 13-2)
T/Jkpt: Not won. T/Plt: £583.60 to a £1 stake. Pool: £167407.16, 209.40 winning tickets. T/Qpdt: £76.40 to a £1 stake. Pool: ££9,903.90, 95.90 winning tickets. DO

1136 FFOS LAS (L-H)
Thursday, May 6

OFFICIAL GOING: Good changing to good (good to soft in places) after race 3 (7:00)
Wind: Light against Weather: Raining

1838 EUROPEAN BREEDERS' FUND MAIDEN FILLIES' STKS 5f
5:55 (5:56) (Class 5) 2-Y-O **£3,561** (£1,059; £529; £264) **Stalls** High

Form RPR

233 **1** **Style And Panache (IRE)**[10] 1577 2-9-0 0.................. CathyGannon 2 74
(P D Evans) *mde all: rdn over 1f out: r.o: edgd lft nr fin* **8/13**[1]

2 1 ¾ **Indian Narjes** 2-9-0 0.. EddieCreighton 4 67
(M R Channon) *chsd ldrs: sn pushed along: wnt 2nd 2f out: rdn over 1f out: styd on same pce ins fnl f* **9/2**[2]

54 **3** 2 ½ **Lady Excellentia (IRE)**[11] 1541 2-9-0 0........................... SebSanders 5 58
(A B Haynes) *chsd wnr 3f: sn rdn: styd on same pce fnl f* **5/1**[3]

4 nk **Veil Of Night** 2-9-0 0.. DaneO'Neill 3 57
(D Haydn Jones) *dwlt: outpcd: hdwy 1/2-way: rdn over 1f out: no ex ins fnl f* **14/1**

5 11 **Molly Piccles** 2-9-0 0.. DavidProbert 1 17+
(M S Tuck) *s.s: outpcd: sme hdwy 1/2-way: hung lft and wknd over 1f out* **16/1**

58.77 secs (1.37) **Going Correction** -0.025s/f (Good) **5** Ran SP% **109.3**
Speed ratings (Par 90): **88,85,81,80,63**
CSF £3.67 TOTE £1.50: £1.20, £1.20; EX 3.90.
Owner Roger Ambrose,Sean Ambrose & Bill Reilly **Bred** Rathasker Stud **Trained** Pandy, Monmouths

FOCUS
There was 10mm of rain during the day and a torrential downpour half an hour before the first race. The winner is rated to her previous level in this modest maiden.

NOTEBOOK
Style And Panache(IRE) set a fair standard on her three placed efforts, the latest when a close third from a low draw behind a very well-backed Richard Hannon-trained rival in a decent Windsor maiden. She was a hot favourite for this fillies' maiden and did the job in professional, rather than flashy style under a positive ride. It is hard to know what the form amounts to but she seems a consistent and reliable type who should be competitive in nurseries off a mark likely to be in the mid 70s. (tchd 4-7 and 4-6 in a place)
Indian Narjes stuck to her task quite well on debut. The 13,000gns filly is by a high-class multiple 7f-1m winner and is out of an unraced half-sister to Campsie Fells, a 1m winner at two and a Group 3 1m1f winner in France at three. She should have learned something from this experience and should improve with time and distance. (op 7-1)
Lady Excellentia(IRE) kept plugging away after being driven along some way out on her third start. The half-sister to an Italian sprint winner seems to be quietly progressing with practice and should do better in nursery events over 6f. (op 4-1)
Veil Of Night attracted little interest at the sales and was all over the place in the preliminaries but she seemed to gradually get the hang of things during the race and showed some ability on debut.
Molly Piccles ran very green and was always detached after a slow start on debut. Official explanation: jockey said that the filly missed the break

1839 DESIGN OFFICE CLAIMING STKS 1m (R)
6:25 (6:26) (Class 6) 3-Y-O+ **£2,388** (£705; £352) **Stalls** Low

Form RPR

-111 **1** **Fremen (USA)**[10] 1587 10-9-7 82.................................... AdrianNicholls 3 63
(D Nicholls) *led: hdd over 6f out: chsd ldr tl led again over 2f out: rdn over 1f out: styd on gamely* **4/6**[1]

41-2 **2** nk **Landucci**[10] 1585 9-9-5 65...(p) JamesDoyle 9 60
(S Curran) *hld up in tch: rdn to chse wnr over 1f out: sn ev ch: styd on* **7/1**[3]

2105 **3** 1 ½ **Tuscan King**[3] 1761 3-8-8 66...(b) CathyGannon 2 55
(P D Evans) *chsd ldrs: rdn over 3f out: nt clr run fr over 1f out: nvr able to chal* **7/2**[2]

-525 **4** 1 **Pyrus Time (IRE)**[10] 1587 4-9-7 71.................................. LiamJones 7 56
(R A Harris) *chsd ldr tl led over 6f out: rdn and hdd over 2f out: styd on same pce fnl f* **8/1**

1656 **5** ¾ **Mountain Pass (USA)**[16] 1457 8-9-4 52.......................(p) DavidProbert 4 51
(B J Llewellyn) *chsd ldrs: rdn over 2f out: styd on same pce fr over 1f out* **25/1**

6000 **6** shd **James Pollard (IRE)**[26] 1239 5-9-1 44.............(p) AndrewHeffernan(3) 6 51?
(B J Llewellyn) *hld up: rdn over 2f out: no imp fr over 1f out* **50/1**

1m 43.32s (2.82) **Going Correction** +0.25s/f (Good)
WFA 3 from 4yo+ 13lb **6** Ran SP% **111.6**
Speed ratings (Par 101): **95,94,93,92,91 91**
toteswingers:1&2:£1.10, 1&3:£3.60, 2&3:£3.50 CSF £6.06 TOTE £1.60: £1.30, £1.40; EX 5.00.
Owner Middleham Park Racing XXXV C King A Seed **Bred** Flaxman Holdings Ltd **Trained** Sessay, N Yorks

■ Stewards' Enquiry : James Doyle two-day ban: careless riding (May20-21)

FOCUS
A fair claimer but the pace was steady and they finished in a bit of a bunch. The winner stood out beforehand and this is not solid form.
James Pollard(IRE) Official explanation: jockey said that the gelding finished distressed.

1840 BURDENS AND TY HAFAN CHARITY H'CAP 1m 2f (R)
7:00 (7:00) (Class 4) (0-80,80) 4-Y-O+ **£4,857** (£1,445; £722; £360) **Stalls** Low

Form RPR

-512 **1** **King's Masque**[26] 1241 4-8-1 **66** oh5..................... AndrewHeffernan(3) 1 72
(B J Llewellyn) *sn chsng ldr: led over 1f out: rdn out* **9/2**[3]

003- **2** ½ **Mabuya (UAE)**[225] 6203 4-9-4 **80**.. SebSanders 4 88+
(P J Makin) *hld up: racd keenly: nt clr run fr over 2f out tl swtchd rt ins fnl f: r.o wl* **7/2**[1]

150- **3** ½ **Lyra's Daemon**[138] 7811 4-8-12 **74**...................................... DaneO'Neill 8 78
(W R Muir) *led: rdn over 2f out: hdd over 1f out: styd on* **9/1**

00-0 **4** 1 ¼ **Visions Of Johanna (USA)**[12] 1513 5-8-5 **67**............... TadhgO'Shea 3 69
(Ian Williams) *hld up: hdwy over 2f out: rdn over 1f out: edgd lft and styd on same pce ins fnl f* **6/1**

4-23 **5** nse **Wind Star**[12] 1536 7-9-4 **80**...(p) SteveDrowne 2 81
(M F Harris) *hld up in tch: rdn over 1f out: styd on same pce ins fnl f* **10/1**

10-4 **6** ½ **Potentiale (IRE)**[19] 1388 6-9-1 **80**.................................... PatrickHills(3) 7 80
(J W Hills) *s.i.s: sn prom: rdn over 2f out: no ex ins fnl f* **4/1**[2]

-350 **7** 2 ½ **Dream Of Fortune (IRE)**[5] 1684 6-8-11 **73**..............(v[1]) CathyGannon 5 68
(P D Evans) *hld up: plld hrd: rdn over 2f out: nvr trbld ldrs* **10/1**

100- **8** 1 ½ **Pelham Crescent (IRE)**[197] 6936 7-9-2 **78**.................... DavidProbert 6 70
(B Palling) *chsd ldrs: rdn over 3f out: wknd fnl f* **8/1**

2m 11.7s (3.30) **Going Correction** +0.25s/f (Good) **8** Ran SP% **114.0**
Speed ratings (Par 105): **96,95,95,94,94 93,91,90**
toteswingers:1&2:£3.40, 1&3:£5.50, 2&3:£5.90 CSF £20.50 CT £134.22 TOTE £5.40: £1.80, £1.90, £3.90; EX 21.60.
Owner B J Llewellyn **Bred** Deerfield Farm **Trained** Fochriw, Caerphilly

FOCUS
They went a stop-start gallop for this fair handicap. It was an advantage to race prominently and the runner-up was unlucky. Muddling form, with the winner 5lb wrong. It was reported that the ground was riding very slow.
Potentiale(IRE) Official explanation: jockey said the gelding was unsuited by the ground (good – good to soft in places).
Pelham Crescent(IRE) Official explanation: jockey said that the gelding was unsuited by the ground (good – good to soft in places).

1841 CPM GROUP H'CAP 1m (R)
7:30 (7:31) (Class 4) (0-85,85) 4-Y-O+ **£4,857** (£1,445; £722; £360) **Stalls** Low

Form RPR

1133 **1** **Mr Hichens**[24] 1265 5-8-12 **79**... TadhgO'Shea 6 84+
(Karen George) *hld up: hdwy over 3f out: led over 2f out: shkn up over 1f out: r.o wl* **11/2**

20-0 **2** 3 ½ **Swift Chap**[12] 1533 4-9-4 **85**... SebSanders 4 82
(B R Millman) *chsd ldr tl led 3f out: sn hdd: rdn over 1f out: styd on same pce* **9/2**

-006 **3** ½ **Mr Udagawa**[12] 1530 4-8-4 **71** oh4.................................(p) DavidProbert 3 67
(B J Llewellyn) *hld up: hdwy over 2f out: sn hung lft: rdn over 1f out: styd on same pce fnl f* **11/1**

226- **4** nk **Effigy**[207] 6695 6-8-12 **79**.. DaneO'Neill 2 74
(H Candy) *chsd ldrs: rdn over 2f out: styd on same pce fnl f* **4/1**[3]

25-5 **5** ¾ **Opus Maximus (IRE)**[19] 1397 5-9-4 **85**........................... GregFairley 7 78
(M Johnston) *trckd ldrs: racd keenly: rdn over 2f out: styd on same pce appr fnl f* **3/1**[1]

3514 **6** 2 ½ **Millfields Dreams**[12] 1530 11-8-4 **71** oh1.......................(p) PaulEddery 5 59
(P Leech) *s.i.s: hld up: rdn over 3f out: nvr trbld ldrs* **16/1**

4-55 **7** 12 **Jesse James (IRE)**[23] 1272 4-9-4 **85**................................. SteveDrowne 1 45
(J R Gask) *sn led: rdn and hdd 3f out: wknd over 1f out* **7/2**[2]

1m 41.39s (0.89) **Going Correction** +0.25s/f (Good) **7** Ran SP% **115.0**
Speed ratings (Par 105): **105,101,101,100,99 97,85**
toteswingers:1&2:£5.50, 1&3:£8.60, 2&3:£10.20 CSF £30.52 CT £262.90 TOTE £8.10: £3.20, £6.80; EX 39.10.
Owner Eastington Racing Club **Bred** C A Green **Trained** Higher Eastington, Devon

The Form Book, Raceform Ltd, Compton, RG20 6NL

FOCUS
A decent grade handicap, but several of the runners had been below-par on their latest start and this is not strong form. The pace was decent and the ground was cutting up quite a bit. The going was changed to good, good to soft in places.

1842 SAINT GOBAIN H'CAP 6f
8:05 (8:06) (Class 5) (0-75,75) 3-Y-O **£2,752** (£818; £409; £204) **Stalls** High

Form RPR
21-5 **1** **Basle**[24] 1269 3-9-2 **73**.......... DavidProbert 6 79
(Miss Gay Kelleway) *w ldrs: rdn and ev ch fr over 1f out: styd on u.p to ld wl ins fnl f* **11/4**[1]
440- **2** *shd* **Fawley Green**[207] 6693 3-9-1 **72**.......... DaneO'Neill 1 77
(W R Muir) *chsd ldr tl led over 3f out: rdn over 1f out: hdd wl ins fnl f* **5/1**[3]
530- **3** *2 ¼* **Could It Be Magic**[151] 7654 3-8-11 **71**..........(p) JackDean(3) 4 69
(W G M Turner) *prom: rdn over 2f out: edgd rt ins fnl f: styd on* **15/2**
0-1 **4** *2 ¾* **Fayre Bella**[30] 1137 3-9-4 **75**.......... TadhgO'Shea 5 64
(J Gallagher) *dwlt: hld up: plld hrd: hdwy over 2f out: rdn over 1f out: no ex fnl f* **13/2**
-511 **5** *3* **Kirsty's Boy (IRE)**[75] 633 3-8-11 **75**.......... RyanPowell(7) 9 55
(J S Moore) *chsd ldrs: rdn over 2f out: wknd over 1f out* **9/2**[2]
5600 **6** *½* **Ramamara (IRE)**[11] 1545 3-9-0 **71**.......... CathyGannon 3 49
(P D Evans) *rrd s: plld hrd and sn prom: rdn over 2f out: wknd over 1f out* **6/1**
066- **7** *2 ¾* **King's Approach (IRE)**[211] 6585 3-9-1 **72**.......... LiamJones 7 41
(R A Harris) *prom tl rdn and wknd over 2f out* **20/1**
56-0 **8** *¾* **Strike Shot**[24] 1269 3-8-12 **69**.......... SebSanders 2 36
(W R Muir) *led: hdd over 3f out: wknd over 1f out* **10/1**

69.62 secs (-0.08) **Going Correction** -0.025s/f (Good) **8 Ran SP% 114.8**
Speed ratings (Par 99): **99,98,95,92,88 87,83,82**
toteswingers:1&2:£3.30, 1&3:£6.80, 2&3:£5.80 CSF £16.66 CT £91.94 TOTE £3.90: £3.20, £2.60, £5.70; EX 12.60.
Owner Raymond Tooth **Bred** W H R John And Partners **Trained** Exning, Suffolk

FOCUS
A fair handicap run at a good pace. The first two were clear of the third and there was a gap back to the rest. The form is rated through the third and looks pretty limited.
Ramamara(IRE) Official explanation: jockey the filly reared as the gates opened

1843 POLYPIPE CIVIL FILLIES' H'CAP 6f
8:35 (8:36) (Class 5) (0-70,69) 4-Y-O+ **£2,752** (£818; £409; £204) **Stalls** High

Form RPR
0-06 **1** **Miss Hollybell**[3] 1775 4-9-3 **68**.......... TadhgO'Shea 1 77
(J Gallagher) *s.i.s: sn chsng ldrs: led over 4f out: rdn over 1f out: r.o wl: edgd lft towards fin* **7/1**
3652 **2** *2 ¼* **Fine Silk (USA)**[7] 1639 4-9-0 **65**..........(p) JerryO'Dwyer 6 67
(M G Quinlan) *led: hdd over 4f out: chsd wnr: rdn over 2f out: hung lft and styd on same pce ins fnl f* **8/1**
-132 **3** *hd* **Cwmni**[11] 1547 4-8-4 **55**.......... DavidProbert 3 56
(B Palling) *sn pushed along in rr: hdwy 1/2-way: rdn and hung lft fr over 2f out: no ex ins fnl f* **11/8**[1]
3602 **4** *1 ½* **Bold Ring**[7] 1642 4-8-1 **55**.......... AndrewHeffernan(3) 7 51
(E J Creighton) *prom: rdn over 2f out: hung lft and no ex fnl f* **10/1**
15-4 **5** *1 ¾* **Plumage**[9] 1595 5-8-10 **61**.......... DaneO'Neill 8 52
(Miss Tor Sturgis) *hld up: hdwy over 2f out: rdn and wknd over 1f out* **3/1**[2]
105- **6** *½* **Quiquillo (USA)**[203] 6798 4-9-3 **68**.......... CathyGannon 4 57
(P D Evans) *chsd ldrs: rdn 4f out: lost pl over 2f out: wknd wl over 1f out* **4/1**[3]

69.43 secs (-0.27) **Going Correction** -0.025s/f (Good) **6 Ran SP% 119.8**
Speed ratings (Par 100): **100,97,96,94,92 91**
toteswingers:1&2:£3.60, 1&3:£3.70, 2&3:£1.10 CSF £61.58 CT £122.93 TOTE £12.30: £7.10, £7.10; EX 61.10 Place 6 £310.96; Place 5 £271.72.
Owner Gallagher Partnership **Bred** Mrs R J Gallagher **Trained** Chastleton, Oxon

FOCUS
A fairly competitive fillies' handicap.
T/Plt: £97.60 to a £1 stake. Pool £46,763.07 - 349.73 winning tickets. T/Qpdt: £73.10 to a £1 stake. Pool £4,221.01 - 42.72 winning tickets. CR

1690 GOODWOOD (R-H)
Thursday, May 6

OFFICIAL GOING: Good (good to firm in places; 8.6)
Rail realignment increased distances on round course by 15yards
Wind: airly modest, half behind Weather: overcast

1844 FAMILY FUN ON 31ST MAY MAIDEN STKS 1m
1:55 (1:56) (Class 5) 3-Y-O+ **£3,238** (£963; £481; £240) **Stalls** High

Form RPR
4-2 **1** **Harvest Dancer (IRE)**[22] 1308 3-9-0 0.......... MartinDwyer 14 84+
(B J Meehan) *chsd ldr tl 1/2-way: rdn ent fnl 2f: led ent fnl f: hung lft but r.o wl fnl f* **6/5**[1]
23-2 **2** *1 ¼* **Spa's Dancer (IRE)**[24] 1260 3-9-0 81.......... RichardHughes 10 81
(J W Hills) *racd keenly: led: rdn and hung bdly lft fr 2f out: hdd ent fnl f: kpt on u.p* **6/1**[3]
5-0 **3** *nk* **Madhaaq (IRE)**[19] 1381 3-8-9 0.......... TadhgO'Shea 12 75+
(J L Dunlop) *t.k.h: hld up wl in tch: pushed along ent fnl 2f: kpt on ins fnl f: nt gng pce to rch wnr* **12/1**
4 *¾* **Give Your Verdict (USA)** 3-9-0 0.......... RichardMullen 1 78+
(Sir Michael Stoute) *in tch: pushed along ent fnl 2f: kpt on same pce under hands and heels riding fnl f* **20/1**
3 **5** *1 ½* **Squall**[21] 1325 3-9-0 0.......... FrankieDettori 2 75
(J Noseda) *chsd ldng pair tl wnt 2n 1/2-way: rdn and unable qck 2f out: one pce fr over 1f out* **9/2**[2]
22-5 **6** *1 ¼* **Mountrath**[24] 1260 3-9-0 77.......... LiamKeniry 6 72
(B R Johnson) *t.k.h: hld up in tch in midfield on outer: rdn and hung lft jst over 2f out: styd on same pce fr over 1f out* **25/1**
6-0 **7** *nse* **Lost In The Moment (IRE)**[16] 1450 3-9-0 0.......... ShaneKelly 4 74+
(J Noseda) *hld up in tch in midfield: pushed along and unable qck wl over 1f out: hung rt u.p and hmpd jst ins fnl f: nvr gng pce to threaten ldrs* **33/1**
5 **8** *nse* **Osgood**[19] 1381 3-9-0 0.......... NeilCallan 7 72
(M R Channon) *chsd ldng trio: rdn and unable qck jst over 2f out: wknd ent fnl f* **11/1**
0 **9** *2* **Rocky Mood (IRE)**[16] 1450 3-9-0 0.......... TomQueally 11 67
(W R Swinburn) *dwlt: a in rr: rdn and no prog 3f out: kpt on steadily fnl f: nvr trbld ldrs* **100/1**
-03 **10** *nk* **Bowsers Brave (USA)**[16] 1450 4-9-13 0.......... PatDobbs 8 66
(M P Tregoning) *in tch whn clipped heels and stmbld after 1f: sn towards rr: pushed along over 2f out: plugged on: nvr gng pce to rch ldrs* **14/1**
11 *1* **Our Drama Queen (IRE)** 3-8-9 0.......... FrankieMcDonald 15 59
(R Hannon) *s.i.s: sn rcvrd and in midfield: rdn and effrt towards inner 2f out: sn btn* **50/1**
12 *1 ½* **Affordable (IRE)** 3-9-0 0.......... SamHitchcott 5 61
(M R Channon) *stdd s: t.k.h: hld up towards rr: rdn and effrt jst over 2f out: wknd wl over 1f out* **100/1**
30- **13** *6* **Forget (IRE)**[359] 1968 3-8-9 0.......... LukeMorris 13 42
(Jamie Poulton) *dwlt: a in rr: rdn and toiling wl over 2f out* **100/1**
14 *6* **Medici Brave** 3-9-0 0.......... JimCrowley 9 33
(Mrs A J Perrett) *dwlt: sn last and niggled along: rdn and lost tch 3f out* **66/1**

1m 39.72s (-0.18) **Going Correction** 0.0s/f (Good)
WFA 3 from 4yo 13lb **14 Ran SP% 118.6**
Speed ratings (Par 103): **100,98,98,97,96 94,94,94,92,92 91,90,84,78**
toteswingers:1&2 £2.50, 2&3 £26.00, 1&3 £4.80 CSF £7.66 TOTE £2.60: £1.30, £1.20, £3.00; EX 8.10.
Owner Paul & Jenny Green **Bred** Paul Green **Trained** Manton, Wilts

FOCUS
This looked a good maiden that should produce winners. Sound form, judged around the runner-up and sixth. The runners were well spread out in the closing stages, racing middle to stands' side.
Mountrath Official explanation: jockey the gelding hung badly left throughout
Bowsers Brave(USA) Official explanation: jockey said that the colt clipped heels

1845 EUROPEAN BREEDERS' FUND GOODWOOD.COM MAIDEN STKS 6f
2:30 (2:30) (Class 5) 2-Y-O **£3,561** (£1,059; £529; £264) **Stalls** Low

Form RPR
2 **1** **Sikeeb (IRE)**[22] 1309 2-9-3 0.......... NeilCallan 1 84
(C E Brittain) *w ldr: pushed and hdd ent fnl 2f: r.o strly u.p fnl f* **9/4**[2]
2 *1* **Dr Green (IRE)** 2-9-3 0.......... RichardHughes 10 81+
(R Hannon) *wnt lft s: in tch in midfield: rdn jst over 2f out: drvn and hdwy over 1f out: chsd wnr ins fnl f: r.o wl but a hld* **7/1**[3]
6 **3** *5* **Royal Opera**[12] 1517 2-9-0 0.......... JamesMillman(3) 7 66
(B R Millman) *led tl rdn and hdd ent fnl 2f: lost 2nd ins fnl f: fdd fnl 100yds* **25/1**
4 *2 ¾* **Trade Storm** 2-9-3 0.......... TadhgO'Shea 5 58+
(J Gallagher) *v.s.a: bhd: hdwy on outer 2f out: kpt on to go modest 4th ins fnl f: nvr trbld ldrs* **66/1**
5 *1 ¼* **Sarandjam** 2-9-3 0.......... SamHitchcott 9 54
(M R Channon) *wnt lft s: t.k.h: chsd ldrs: rdn over 2f out: wknd over 1f out and wl btn fnl f* **33/1**
6 *½* **Pasquino (USA)** 2-9-0 0.......... AhmedAjtebi(3) 3 53
(Mahmood Al Zarooni) *chsd ldng trio: rdn and fnd little over 2f out: wknd wl over 1f out* **14/1**
7 *3* **Watered Silk** 2-9-3 0.......... PatDobbs 8 44
(M P Tregoning) *s.i.s: sn niggled along in rr: struggling fr 1/2-way: n.d* **12/1**
5 **8** *shd* **Angle Knight (USA)**[9] 1597 2-9-3 0.......... MartinDwyer 2 43
(B J Meehan) *stdd s: a bhd: struggling fr 1/2-way: nvr on terms* **16/1**
9 *nse* **Signs In The Sand** 2-9-3 0.......... FrankieDettori 6 43+
(Saeed Bin Suroor) *in tch in midfield: hdwy on outer over 2f out: chsd ldrs and rdn over 1f out: btn 1f out: wknd qckly and eased whn no ch fnl 75yds* **13/8**[1]
10 *4 ½* **Commercial (IRE)** 2-9-3 0.......... FergusSweeney 11 30
(J A Osborne) *stdd and dropped in bhd after s: hld up towards rr: rdn and struggling over 2f out: wl bhd fnl f* **40/1**
11 *4 ½* **Amore Et Labore** 2-9-3 0.......... LiamKeniry 4 16
(S Kirk) *dwlt: sn pushed along and struggling in rr: lost tch 1/2-way* **66/1**

1m 12.39s (0.19) **Going Correction** 0.0s/f (Good) **11 Ran SP% 113.8**
Speed ratings (Par 93): **95,93,87,83,81 81,77,76,76,70 64**
toteswingers: 1&2 £2.00, 1&3 £14.00, 2&3 £12.10 CSF £16.95 TOTE £2.70: £1.20, £1.30, £6.10; EX 13.60.
Owner Saeed Manana **Bred** Ms Dolores Jones **Trained** Newmarket, Suffolk

FOCUS
This looked a good juvenile maiden. The front pair pulled clear and the form has been rated on the positive side.

NOTEBOOK
Sikeeb(IRE) became the third winner from just three runners to come out of the 2-y-o conditions race at the Newmarket Craven meeting, following on from Bilko Pak's Windsor success and Julius Geezer's Lily Agnes triumph. It's clear Richard Hannon's Retainer, the decisive victor that day, is smart and should be followed wherever he goes next. This time Clive Brittain's colt put his experience to good use to take advantage of stall one, showing good speed against the rail from the off, and he ran on strongly for pressure. He seemed to jink slightly soon after the line and unseated Neil Callan, but it appeared there was no real harm done. A rise in class awaits. (op 11-4 tchd 2-1 and 3-1 in a place)
Dr Green(IRE) ◆, drawn ten, was pitched a bit wide early on and was soon being niggled along, but he ran on nicely, pulling well clear of all bar the experienced winner. This £24,000 purchase looks likely to progress into a very useful type. (op 4-1)
Royal Opera was beaten 11l on debut at Leicester, but he clearly benefited form that experience and proved suited by the extra furlong this time.
Trade Storm ◆ raced out the back for much of the way after starting slowly, before running on well when switched out wide in the second half of the contest. He should improve significantly. (op 50-1)
Sarandjam, a half-brother to, among others, 1m winner Edge Fund, showed ability and should improve for the run. (op 40-1)
Pasquino(USA), the first foal of a top-class sprinter in the US, was easy to back and made no impression. (op 12-1)
Watered Silk, out of an unraced half-sister to Seta, was never seen with a chance after missing the break. He should be a lot better for the run. (op 9-1)
Signs In The Sand, the first foal of a high-class multiple 6f-1m1f winner, travelled well until about halfway, but he found disappointingly little, not convincing that he handled the track. (op 2-1 tchd 6-4)

1846 TOTEPOOL A BETTER WAY TO BET CLASSIFIED STKS 1m 1f
3:00 (3:00) (Class 4) 3-Y-O+ **£6,799** (£2,023; £1,011; £505) **Stalls** High

Form RPR
033- **1** **Cumulus Nimbus**[205] 6756 3-8-12 **85**.......... RichardHughes 3 92+
(R Hannon) *stdd s: hld up in last: plld out and rdn wl over 1f out: chsd clr wnr 1f out: r.o wl to ld nr fin* **15/2**
2164 **2** *nk* **Gumnd (IRE)**[15] 1473 3-8-12 **85**..........(p) NeilCallan 1 86
(C E Brittain) *led: stdd gallop 1/2-way: qcknd over 2f out and sn clr drvn ent fnl f: kpt on wl tl worn down and hdd nr fin* **28/1**

63-1 **3** 2 ¾ **Tudor Key (IRE)**[24] 1265 4-9-12 84 JimCrowley 5 82
(Mrs A J Perrett) *chsd ldr: rdn and unable qck over 2f out: drvn 2f out: lost 2nd 1f out: plugged on same pce after* **6/1**[3]

-022 **4** nk **Elliptical (USA)**[5] 1697 4-9-12 85 FrankieDettori 6 81
(G A Butler) *chsd ldng pair: rdn and unable qck over 2f out: drvn and styd on same pce fr over 1f out* **5/6**[1]

00-0 **5** shd **Kavachi (IRE)**[15] 1474 7-9-12 85 GeorgeBaker 2 81
(G L Moore) *in tch in midfield: rdn and unable qck ent fnl 2f: wanting to hang rt ent fnl f: plugged on same pce* **5/1**[2]

10-0 **6** 6 **Uncle Fred**[17] 1430 5-9-12 84 LiamKeniry 4 68
(P R Chamings) *stdd s: hld up in last pair: effrt on inner 2f out: unable qck u.p: wknd fnl f* **11/1**

1m 56.07s (-0.23) **Going Correction** 0.0s/f (Good)
WFA 3 from 4yo+ 14lb 6 Ran SP% **109.1**
Speed ratings (Par 105): **101,100,98,98,97 92**
toteswingers: 1&2 £7.70, 1&3 £3.10, 2&3 £14.20 CSF £138.94 TOTE £7.60: £2.60, £8.70; EX 69.00.
Owner Mrs John Lee **Bred** Chantilly Bloodstock Agency **Trained** East Everleigh, Wilts

FOCUS
Only 5lb separated this lot at the weights and it was a tactical affair, with the pace steady. The winner is rated better than the bare form in coming from behind.

1847 JUNE 4TH EVENING RACING MAIDEN STKS (DIV I) 1m 4f
3:35 (3:35) (Class 5) 3-Y-0+ **£2,914** (£867; £433; £216) **Stalls** Low

Form RPR

62-4 **1** **Total Command**[19] 1386 3-8-9 80 RichardMullen 6 81+
(Sir Michael Stoute) *t.k.h early: handy in main gp: clsd on ldr 3f out: rdn over 2f out: led ent fnl f: edgd rt jst ins fnl f: styd on wl* **6/5**[1]

04-6 **2** ½ **Bombadero (IRE)**[24] 1268 3-8-9 78 TedDurcan 2 80+
(J L Dunlop) *prom in main gp: clsd on ldr 3f out: rdn to ld 2f out: drvn and hdd ent fnl f: kpt on same pce fnl 150yds* **9/2**[3]

0 **3** 5 **Indian Ghyll (IRE)**[22] 1302 4-10-0 0 LiamKeniry 9 67
(R A Teal) *sn led: allowed to go wl clr after 2f: c bk to field 3f out: hdd and rdn 2f out: drvn over 1f out: nt pce of ldng pair fnl f* **50/1**

5-0 **4** 2 ¾ **Regal Park (IRE)**[24] 1268 3-8-9 0 ShaneKelly 11 61
(J Noseda) *s.i.s: hld up off the pce in midfield: clsd on ldr 3f out: rdn and no prog 2f out: wl hld fnl f* **9/4**[2]

0-0 **5** ½ **Swain's Quest (USA)**[42] 978 3-8-4 0 AndreaAtzeni 7 55
(Eve Johnson Houghton) *racd wl off the pce in midfield: rdn and clsd over 3f out: outpcd u.p and swtchd rt over 1f out: n.d fnl f* **100/1**

/34- **6** 1 **Coiled Spring**[355] 2090 4-10-0 76 PatCosgrave 10 60
(Mrs A J Perrett) *t.k.h early: chsd clr ldr: clsd 3f out: rdn and nt qckn 2f out: hung lft and btn over 1f out: wknd fnl f* **14/1**

44- **7** 4 **Lovely Eyes (IRE)**[220] 6331 3-8-4 0 MartinDwyer 8 47
(D M Simcock) *stdd s: hld up in rr: effrt over 2f out: rdn and no prog 2f out: wl btn after* **12/1**

0 **8** 12 **Anis Etoile**[12] 1521 5-9-9 0 IvaMilickova 1 30
(John Berry) *stdd s: hld up in rr: rdn and struggling over 3f out: hung rt and lost tch over 2f out* **100/1**

9 hd **Rio Prince** 3-8-9 0 NeilChalmers 4 32
(J J Bridger) *s.i.s: a bhd: rdn and lost tch 3f out* **125/1**

2m 39.72s (1.32) **Going Correction** 0.0s/f (Good)
WFA 3 from 4yo+ 19lb 9 Ran SP% **113.5**
Speed ratings (Par 103): **98,97,94,92,92 91,88,80,80**
toteswingers: 1&2 £1.60, 1&3 £15.10, 2&3 £16.90 CSF £7.00 TOTE £2.20: £1.20, £1.50, £12.10; EX 5.50.
Owner K Abdulla **Bred** Juddmonte Farms Ltd **Trained** Newmarket, Suffolk

FOCUS
An ordinary maiden in which the pace gradually increased, with Indian Ghyll opening up a lead of around 15l by halfway. The time was 1.84 seconds slower than the second division, which was won by Theology. The first two are rated better than the bare form.
Rio Prince Official explanation: jockey said the gelding ran green

1848 FRANKIE FILLIES AND FROCKS JUNE 11TH STKS (H'CAP) 6f
4:10 (4:11) (Class 4) (0-80,80) 4-Y-0+ **£4,209** (£1,252; £625; £156; £156) **Stalls** Low

Form RPR

6-10 **1** **Quasi Congaree (GER)**[24] 1258 4-8-8 70 (t) RichardHughes 5 81
(I A Wood) *led for 1f: chsd ldr tl over 3f out: gng wl waiting for clr run over 1f out: pushed along and qcknd to ld ins fnl f: rdn and r.o strly fnl 150yds* **12/1**

46-6 **2** 1 ½ **My Kingdom (IRE)**[16] 1438 4-9-4 80 (t) GeorgeBaker 8 86
(H Morrison) *hld up in rr: hdwy on outer ent fnl 2f: rdn to chal ent fnl f: edgd lft and nt gng pce of wnr fnl 100yds: kpt on* **7/2**[3]

4543 **3** 2 ¼ **Rondeau (GR)**[38] 1044 5-8-10 72 JimCrowley 1 71
(P R Chamings) *dwlt: sn bustled along and rcvrd to ld after 1f: rdn ent fnl 2f: drvn and hdd over 1f out: wknd fnl 150yds* **6/1**

4-23 **4** nk **Thunderous Mood (USA)**[10] 1580 4-9-3 79 (t) MartinDwyer 4 77
(P F I Cole) *chsd ldrs: wnt 2nd over 3f out: drvn to ld over 1f out: hdd ins fnl f: wknd fnl 100yds* **5/2**[1]

2041 **4** dht **Sherjawy (IRE)**[7] 1638 6-8-10 72 6ex SamHitchcott 7 70
(Miss Z C Davison) *chsd ldrs: rdn 1/2-way: drvn to press ldrs ent fnl 2f: wknd jst ins fnl f* **8/1**

0-05 **6** 1 ¾ **Phantom Whisper**[10] 1580 7-8-11 76 JamesMillman(3) 6 79+
(B R Millman) *sn pushed along in last pair: rdn over 3f out: nvr gng pce to chal ldrs: wl hld whn nt clr run ins fnl f* **11/4**[2]

1m 11.38s (-0.82) **Going Correction** 0.0s/f (Good) 6 Ran SP% **110.5**
Speed ratings (Par 105): **105,103,100,99,99 97**
toteswingers: 1&2 £6.20, 1&3 £6.30, 2&3 £3.90 CSF £51.34 CT £267.01 TOTE £19.70: £8.10, £1.30; EX 59.00.
Owner M Forbes & C R Lamborne **Bred** Graf And Grafin Von Stauffenberg **Trained** Upper Lambourn, Berks

FOCUS
A fair sprint handicap. The time was ordinary.
Quasi Congaree(GER) Official explanation: trainer said, regarding the apparent improvement of form, that the gelding was better suited by today's course and the faster conditions
Phantom Whisper Official explanation: jockey said the gelding was denied a clear run

1849 JUNE 18TH EVENING RACING STKS (H'CAP) 2m
4:45 (4:45) (Class 5) (0-70,70) 4-Y-0+ **£3,238** (£963; £481; £240) **Stalls** High

Form RPR

2621 **1** **On Terms (USA)**[15] 1478 4-9-2 62 TomQueally 8 70
(S Dow) *dwlt and sn bustled along in rr: pushed along and hdwy to ld after 3f: rdn 3f out: hdd 2f out: stl ev ch: drvn ahd again ins fnl f: forged clr and idling fnl 100yds: rdn out* **5/1**[1]

22-2 **2** 2 ¼ **Gaselee (USA)**[16] 1454 4-9-10 70 MartinDwyer 2 75
(Rae Guest) *led for 3f: chsd wnr after: upsides and rdn over 2f out: led 2f out: hdd over 1f out: stl ev ch tl no ex and btn fnl 150yds* **5/1**[1]

0-06 **3** ¾ **Ned Ludd (IRE)**[20] 1357 7-9-3 60 (v[1]) StephenCraine 9 64
(J G Portman) *hld up in tch: hdwy to chse ldrs gng wl 3f out: upsides 2f out: shkn up to ld over 1f out: sn rdn and nt run on: hdd ins fnl f: fdd tamely fnl 150yds* **16/1**

1331 **4** 2 ¾ **Broughtons Point**[23] 1283 4-8-11 57 JamieMackay 3 58+
(W J Musson) *stdd after s: hld up in rr: stl plenty to do 3f out: hdwy ent fnl 2f: chsd ldng trio jst over 1f out: kpt on: nvr threatened ldrs* **11/2**[2]

50-2 **5** ¾ **Honorable Endeavor**[112] 164 4-8-8 54 LiamKeniry 4 54+
(E F Vaughan) *hmpd sn after s: hld up in last trio: rdn and effrt 3f out: no real prog tl styd on u.p fnl f: nvr trbld ldrs* **22/1**

010/ **6** 1 ¾ **Commemoration Day (IRE)**[27] 4056 9-9-9 66 (b) GeorgeBaker 6 64
(G L Moore) *chsd ldrs: rdn and unable qck over 2f out: wknd over 1f out: no ch fnl f* **14/1**

60-5 **7** ½ **Star Of Pompey**[16] 1454 6-8-10 53 JackMitchell 7 50
(M R Hoad) *hld up towards rr: hdwy 1/2-way: rdn and edging lft off of rail 3f out: no hdwy and wl hld fnl 2f* **33/1**

5-00 **8** 19 **Dubai Gem**[29] 1177 4-9-1 61 NeilCallan 10 35
(Jamie Poulton) *t.k.h: chsd ldrs: rdn and struggling 4f out: lost tch over 2f out: eased whn wl btn ins fnl f* **6/1**[3]

00-1 **9** 1 ¼ **Swordsman (GER)**[16] 1446 8-9-12 69 (t) FrankieDettori 11 42
(C Gordon) *t.k.h: chsd ldrs: rdn over 4f out: struggling 3f out: sn wl btn: eased fnl f* **6/1**[3]

641- **10** 6 **Perception (IRE)**[14] 5990 4-9-7 67 RichardHughes 5 33
(A King) *hld up in last trio: rdn and no prog over 3f out: wl bhd and eased ins fnl f: t.o* **9/1**

1305 **11** 1 ½ **Delorain (IRE)**[16] 1459 7-8-8 51 oh2 ow1 (vt) TedDurcan 1 15
(W B Stone) *in tch tl lost pl 5f out: rdn and wl btn 4f out: wl bhd and eased ins fnl f: t.o* **12/1**

3m 29.91s (0.91) **Going Correction** 0.0s/f (Good)
WFA 4 from 6yo+ 3lb 11 Ran SP% **114.8**
Speed ratings (Par 103): **97,95,95,94,93 92,92,83,82,79 78**
toteswingers: 1&2 £6.10, 1&3 £16.90, 2&3 £19.60 CSF £28.74 CT £370.76 TOTE £5.20: £1.40, £1.60, £3.40; EX 27.70.
Owner S Dow **Bred** Juddmonte Farms Inc **Trained** Epsom, Surrey

FOCUS
A modest staying handicap in which those held up struggled to get involved. The first pair are progressing.
Swordsman(GER) Official explanation: jockey said that the gelding was unsuited by the track

1850 FREEPHONE 08000 188191 FILLIES' STKS (H'CAP) 1m
5:20 (5:20) (Class 4) (0-85,85) 3-Y-0 **£4,209** (£1,252; £625; £312) **Stalls** High

Form RPR

1 **1** **I'm A Dreamer (IRE)**[23] 1278 3-8-10 77 PatCosgrave 4 89+
(D M Simcock) *plld hrd: hld up towards rr: plld out and hdwy ent fnl 2f: rdn and gd hdwy over 1f out: led 1f out: drvn fnl 100yds: hld on cl home* **13/2**

341- **2** nk **Forest Crown**[183] 7234 3-8-13 80 JimCrowley 2 88
(R M Beckett) *dropped in bhd after s: t.k.h: hld up in tch towards rr: swtchd lft and gd hdwy wl over 1f out: chsd wnr wl ins fnl f: r.o strly:: nt quite rch wnr* **12/1**

32-1 **3** 1 ½ **Whirly Dancer**[24] 1260 3-9-1 82 TomQueally 3 86
(H R A Cecil) *chsd ldrs: rdn to chal ent fnl 2f: led over 1f out: sn hung rt: hdd ins fnl f: no ex fnl 75yds* **7/2**[2]

011- **4** ½ **Nafura**[175] 7359 3-9-4 85 (p) FrankieDettori 8 89
(Saeed Bin Suroor) *led at stdy gallop: rdn over 2f out: hdd over 1f out: hmpd and carried rt ent fnl f: styd on same pce fnl 150yds* **3/1**[1]

-102 **5** hd **Tafawut**[12] 1514 3-8-9 76 LukeMorris 9 79+
(C G Cox) *taken down early: plld hrd: hld up in tch in rr: n.m.r and edging out lft wl over 1f out: hung lft but r.o wl ins fnl f: nt rch ldrs* **16/1**

31 **6** ¾ **Flighty Frances (IRE)**[13] 1504 3-8-7 79 DeclanCannon(5) 6 80
(D R C Elsworth) *in tch in last trio: rdn and effrt jst over 2f out: drvn and hdwy over 1f out: kpt on btu nvr pce to threaten ldrs* **16/1**

30-4 **7** ¾ **Dark Eyes (IRE)**[15] 1480 3-9-0 81 RobertWinston 10 81
(D J Coakley) *plld hrd: trckd ldrs: rdn and effrt on inner 2f out: unable qck ent fnl f: eased wl ins fnl f* **14/1**

1-66 **8** 1 ½ **Al Khimiya (IRE)**[36] 1061 3-8-5 72 RichardMullen 7 68
(S Woodman) *t.k.h: hld up wl in tch: n.m.r ent fnl 2f: rdn and styd on same pce fr over 1f out* **33/1**

431- **9** 13 **Golden Aria (IRE)**[230] 6062 3-8-13 80 PatDobbs 5 44
(R Hannon) *restless stalls: v awkward leaving stalls and v.s.a: t.k.h in last pair: hdwy on outer 3f out: hung lft and btn 2f out: virtually p.u ins fnl f* **5/1**[3]

021- **10** 22 **Mirabella (IRE)**[174] 7363 3-9-1 82 RichardHughes 1 —
(R Hannon) *chsd ldr tl rdn 2f out: btn jst over 1f out: heavily eased fnl f: t.o* **10/1**

1m 41.38s (1.48) **Going Correction** 0.0s/f (Good) 10 Ran SP% **115.4**
Speed ratings (Par 98): **92,91,90,89,89 88,88,86,73,51**
toteswingers: 1&2 £13.80, 1&3 £6.60, 2&3 £9.80 CSF £80.52 CT £269.18 TOTE £9.10: £2.30, £3.10, £1.40; EX 93.10.
Owner Tick Tock Partnership **Bred** Sean Murphy **Trained** Newmarket, Suffolk

FOCUS
This looked a decent fillies' handicap, but they went a steady pace, resulting in a time 1.66 seconds slower than the earlier maiden, and the bare form needs treating with caution. That said the first pair did well to come from the rear.
Tafawut Official explanation: jockey said filly was lame on the right hind leg
Mirabella(IRE) Official explanation: jokcey said that the filly stopped quickly, was lame on the right hind leg

1851 JUNE 4TH EVENING RACING MAIDEN STKS (DIV II) 1m 4f
5:50 (5:52) (Class 5) 3-Y-0+ **£2,914** (£867; £433; £216) **Stalls** Low

Form RPR

30-4 **1** **Theology**[22] 1314 3-8-9 80 FrankieDettori 10 88+
(J Noseda) *hld up towards rr: hdwy 4f out: trckd ldng pair gng wl 2f out: pushed ahd ent fnl f: flashed tail whn rdn but drew wl clr ins fnl f: comf* **2/1**[1]

2 4 ½ **Kid Charlemagne (IRE)**[816] 7-10-0 0 MartinDwyer 3 81
(W J Greatrex) *s.i.s: sn bustled along and rcvrd to chse ldrs after 1f: led 3f out: sn rdn: hdd ent fnl f: no ch w wnr fnl 150yds* **33/1**

3 **3** ¾ **Sophies Trophy (IRE)**[12] 1302 5-10-0 0 IanMongan 7 79
(P M Phelan) *towards rr: hdwy over 4f out: drvn 3f out: chsd ldrs 2f out: plugged on u.p fnl f but no ch w wnr* **12/1**

2- **4** *4* **Prince Of Dreams**194 7034 3-8-9 0 JimCrowley 4 71
(W J Knight) *t.k.h early: hld up off the pce in midfield: hdwy over 4f out: drvn 3f out: wknd over 1f out* **2/1**1

0-2 **5** *5* **Plus Ultra (IRE)**17 1432 3-8-9 0 (b) TomQueally 5 63
(H R A Cecil) *chsd ldr: pushed along and ev ch over 3f out: drvn and hung rt wl over 1f out: sn wknd* **7/1**3

6 *6* **Businessmoney Judi**27 4-9-6 0 JamesMillman(3) 1 50
(B R Millman) *v s.i.s: wl bhd: sme prog 5f out: no hdwy u.p and wl btn fnl 3f* **66/1**

7 *3 1/4* **Tzora**18 5-10-0 0 PatDobbs 9 50
(P J Hobbs) *s.i.s: racd wl off the pce in midfield: rdn and wl btn 3f out: eased ins fnl f* **16/1**

00 **8** *10* **Best Of Broadway (IRE)**10 1581 3-8-9 0 TedDurcan 2 32
(D R Lanigan) *a wl bhd: lost tch over 3f out: t.o and eased ins fnl f* **100/1**

23-2 **9** *3* **Royal Etiquette (IRE)**19 1393 3-8-9 79 (v1) RichardHughes 8 27
(H J L Dunlop) *racd keenly: led tl 3f out: sn btn: t.o and eased ins fnl f* **5/1**2

10 *19* **Refuse To Give Up (IRE)** 3-8-4 0 AndreaAtzeni 6 —
(D M Simcock) *dwlt: a bhd: lost tch wl over 3f out: t.o and eased fr over 1f out* **33/1**

2m 37.88s (-0.52) **Going Correction** 0.0s/f (Good)
WFA 3 from 4yo+ 19lb **10** Ran SP% **117.8**
Speed ratings (Par 103): **101,98,97,94,91 87,85,78,76,64**
toteswingers:1&2 £17.80, 2&3 £30.10, 1&3 £7.90 CSF £83.96 TOTE £3.60: £1.70, £9.60, £3.50; EX 85.30 Place 6: £698.57 Place 5: £490.90 .
Owner Highclere Thoroughbred Racing Touchstone **Bred** Giacinto Guglielmi **Trained** Newmarket, Suffolk

FOCUS
They seemed to go a good pace and the time was 1.84 seconds quicker than the first division, which was won by Total Command. There is a bit of doubt over the merit of the form but the winner posted a clear personal best.
Royal Etiquette(IRE) Official explanation: jockey said the gelding ran too free
T/Plt: £453.70 to a £1 stake. Pool: ££47,172.85, 75.90 winning tickets. T/Qpdt: £101.30 to a £1 stake. Pool £3,493.62, 25.50 winnign tickets. SP

1852 - 1855a (Foreign Racing) - See Raceform Interactive

1746 LONGCHAMP (R-H)
Thursday, May 6

OFFICIAL GOING: Turf: good

1856a PRIX D'HEDOUVILLE (GROUP 3) (4YO+) (TURF) 1m 4f
2:05 (12:00) 4-Y-O+ **£35,398** (£14,159; £10,619; £7,079; £3,539)

RPR

1 **Allied Powers (IRE)**19 1382 5-8-11 0 IoritzMendizabal 1 113
(M L W Bell) *w.w in rr: rdn early in st: swtchd to rail 1 1/2f out: qcknd wl: fnd room ins long-time ldr: grabbed ld 50yds out: rdn to hold slender advantage over runner-up cl home* **12/1**

2 *hd* **Mores Wells**23 6-8-9 0 (p) StephanePasquier 3 111
(R Gibson, France) *racd in 3rd on rail: rdn early in st: rdn to chal ldr 1 1/2f out: grabbed ld ins fnl f: lost ld 50yds out: c again: failed narrowly* **48/10**3

3 *2 1/2* **Aizavoski (IRE)**47 4-8-11 0 AnthonyCrastus 4 109
(E Lellouche, France) *tk ld sn after s and led tl f marker: r.o: no ex clsng stages: jst hld 3rd* **1/1**1

4 *nse* **Telluride**196 6978 4-8-11 0 GeraldMosse 2 109
(J E Hammond, France) *in rr fr s: rdn early in st: styd on wl to gain 4th on line* **11/2**

5 *nk* **Timos (GER)**32 5-8-9 0 OlivierPeslier 6 106
(T Doumen, France) *racd in 4th fr s: rdn 2f out: styd on wl: lost 4th cl home* **9/2**2

6 *4* **Steuben (GER)**18 1420 4-8-11 0 ChristopheSoumillon 5 102
(J Hirschberger, Germany) *racd in 2nd fr s: hrd rdn early in st: r.o but fnd no ex fr f marker: eased clsng stages* **73/10**

2m 28.3s (-2.10) **Going Correction** +0.15s/f (Good) **6** Ran SP% **120.5**
Speed ratings: **113,112,111,111,110 108**
WIN (incl. 1 euro stake): 13.80. PLACES: 4.90, 3.30. SF: 68.50.
Owner David Fish And Edward Ware **Bred** Saad Bin Mishrif **Trained** Newmarket, Suffolk

NOTEBOOK
Allied Powers(IRE), settled at the rear of the field, quickened in style once a gap appeared on the rail. He swept past his rivals to lead inside the final furlong and then he held off the determined challenge of Mores Wells to secure his first win in Group company. Softer ground would have suited him even better, and the Hardwicke will now be considered, provided the ground is suitable.

1831 CHESTER (L-H)
Friday, May 7

OFFICIAL GOING: Good to soft (7.0)
False rail in use - rail stepped out 7yds from the 6f marker to the top of the home straight to provide fresh ground, adding 12yds to the overall distance
Wind: Almost nil Weather: Fine

1857 SL INVESTMENT MANAGEMENT EARL GROSVENOR H'CAP 7f 122y
1:45 (1:48) (Class 2) (0-105,99) 4-Y-O+ **£25,232** (£7,552; £3,776; £1,888; £940) **Stalls** Low

Form RPR

6205 **1** **Autumn Blades (IRE)**7 1662 5-9-6 95 (v) FrannyNorton 7 103
(A Bailey) *lw: hld up: hdwy 2f out: chsd ldr over 1f out: r.o ins fnl f to ld towards fin* **25/1**

1112 **2** *hd* **Academy Blues (USA)**2 1826 5-8-11 86 AdrianNicholls 12 93
(D Nicholls) *hld up: hdwy into midfield 5f out: rapid prog on outside 2f out: led over 1f out: hdd towards fin* **8/1**3

210- **3** *1/2* **Suruor (IRE)**237 5874 4-9-9 98 JamieSpencer 13 104
(D M Simcock) *fit: hld up bhd: hdwy wl over 1f out: sn rdn: r.o ins fnl f: gng on at fin* **9/1**

002- **4** *1 3/4* **Brae Hill (IRE)**223 6278 4-9-5 94 PaulHanagan 2 103+
(R A Fahey) *lw: trckd ldrs: n.m.r and hmpd wl over 1f out: sn lost pl: swtchd lft sn after: styd on wl and edgd rt ins fnl f: no imp on ldng trio* **4/1**1

0-04 **5** *4 1/2* **Joseph Henry**20 1397 8-8-12 87 AndrewMullen 6 77
(D Nicholls) *trckd ldrs: pushed along over 3f out: rdn over 1f out: one pce fnl f* **14/1**

6520 **6** *3/4* **Carcinetto (IRE)**7 1672 8-9-1 95 RichardEvans(5) 3 84
(P D Evans) *towards rr: rdn and outpcd 2f out: styd on u.p fr over 1f out: nt rch ldrs* **20/1**

60-4 **7** *1 3/4* **Invincible Force (IRE)**6 1708 6-9-4 93 (b) SilvestreDeSousa 9 77
(Paul Green) *led: hdd narrowly over 4f out: continued to r w ldr tl rdn over 1f out: wknd ins fnl f* **9/1**

0-23 **8** *nk* **Dunn'o (IRE)**13 1533 5-9-0 94 JohnFahy(5) 8 77+
(C G Cox) *racd keenly in midfield: rdn and outpcd over 1f out: n.d* **7/1**2

035- **9** *1/2* **Webbow (IRE)**181 7294 8-9-1 90 JimmyFortune 1 72+
(N Tinkler) *lw: midfield: nt clr run 2f out: hmpd wl over 1f out: swtchd rt whn nt clr run 1f out: denied a run again shortly after: eased* **7/1**2

-456 **10** *3* **Extraterrestrial**20 1383 6-9-7 99 BarryMcHugh(3) 5 74
(R A Fahey) *lw: hld up: rdn over 1f out: nvr able to trble ldrs* **4/1**1

00-1 **11** *3 1/2* **Guilded Warrior**29 1185 7-8-12 87 FergusSweeney 11 53
(W S Kittow) *w ldr: led narrowly over 4f out: rdn and hdd over 1f out: sn wknd* **12/1**

1m 35.42s (1.62) **Going Correction** +0.45s/f (Yiel) **11** Ran SP% **119.1**
Speed ratings (Par 109): **109,108,108,106,102 101,99,99,98,95 92**
Tote Swingers: 1&2 £34.70, 1&3 £39.20, 2&3 £11.30 CSF £215.58 CT £1990.80 TOTE £30.60: £5.80, £3.00, £3.40; EX 124.80 Trifecta £672.40 Part won. Pool: £908.75 - 0.10 winning units..
Owner John Stocker **Bred** Dr D Crone & P Lafarge & P Johnston **Trained** Newmarket, Suffolk

FOCUS
Following a dry night the going was described as good to soft. The false rail in use with the rail stepped out 7yds from the 6f marker to the top of the home straight to provide fresh ground, adding 12yds to the overall distance. A competitive handicap in which the top-weight was rated 6lb below the ceiling. They went a decent gallop up front and when the leaders tired rounding the turn into the straight there was plenty of trouble in behind towards the inside. All this played into the hands of those held up off the pace, who swept around the outside turning in. A small personal best p

NOTEBOOK
Autumn Blades(IRE), who was last seen on turf getting beaten in a claimer at Yarmouth last autumn, but went on to have a fantastic winter on the AW, winning four times and rising over 20lb in the handicap. He has clearly transferred that improvement back to turf, likes a tight track, and his rider did well in timing his challenge so that he wasn't in front too long. (old market op 25-1)
Academy Blues(USA), poorly drawn and so held up, was the first to commit around the outside entering the straight and got first run on his rivals, but he just couldn't hold off the winner, who tracked him through. He remains progressive. (new market)
Suruor(IRE), who was held up in last place from his bad draw, was another to benefit when the pace collapsed up front. He stayed on well down the outside in the straight and put up a sound effort off a 5lb higher mark than when last successful. (new market op 10-1)
Brae Hill(IRE) ◆ had a good draw and travelled well next to the rail chasing the pace, but when the two leaders hit the wall turning in he found his path blocked, just as the first three were sweeping around the outside full of momentum. He then got into a bad barging match with Webbow and in the circumstances it was some effort to run on for fourth. Needless to say he shaped a lot better than his finishing position suggests. (new market)
Joseph Henry raced one off the rail and was always being niggled along in pursuit of the leaders. He is not a horse who finds winning easy. (old market op 12-1)
Carcinetto(IRE) remains plenty high enough in the weights. (old market tchd 22-1)
Invincible Force(IRE) did too much in front and was cooked on the turn in. (old market op 10-1)
Dunn'o(IRE) couldn't lead from stall eight and pulled too hard as a result. (old market tchd 9-1 new market op 15-2)
Webbow(IRE) ◆ was the other horse in the race who got murdered on the inside turning in. He'd travelled smoothly throughout but was held up in his run and hampered at the point where the false rail came to an end, and was then constantly denied a clear run up the straight. His finishing position is no reflection on how he ran. Official explanation: jockey said gelding was denied a clear run (old market op 8-1)
Extraterrestrial didn't enjoy the clearest of runs when trying to make up ground from the top of the straight but remains high in the weights. (old market op 13-2 new market op 9-2)

1858 ADDLESHAW GODDARD DEE STKS (GROUP 3) (C&G) 1m 2f 75y
2:15 (2:15) (Class 1) 3-Y-O
£39,739 (£15,064; £7,539; £3,759; £1,883; £945) **Stalls** High

Form RPR

10-2 **1** **Azmeel**14 1498 3-8-12 109 FrankieDettori 6 111+
(J H M Gosden) *lw: hld up: rdn and hdwy over 1f out: r.o to ld fnl 150yds: kpt on wl cl home* **7/2**2

14-2 **2** *1/2* **Dancing David (IRE)**22 1327 3-8-12 110 MartinDwyer 2 108
(B J Meehan) *trckd ldr: moved upsides over 4f out: led 2f out: rdn and hrd pressed over 1f out: hdd fnl 150yds: kpt on u.p but a hld after* **5/2**1

51-4 **3** *nse* **Rasmy**21 1354 3-8-12 96 TadhgO'Shea 1 108
(M P Tregoning) *trckd ldrs: rdn to chal ins fnl f: nt qckn cl home* **12/1**

21-3 **4** *2 1/2* **Tamaathul**22 1330 3-8-12 89 RichardHills 4 103
(B W Hills) *lw: trckd ldrs: effrt to chal over 1f out: sn hung lft: no ex fnl 150yds* **4/1**3

5 *1 3/4* **Encompassing (IRE)**24 1287 3-8-12 96 JMurtagh 7 99
(A P O'Brien, Ire) *w'like: hld up in rr: rdn and swtchd lft over 1f out: failed to pick-up: no imp* **10/1**

24-1 **6** *14* **Party Doctor**11 1586 3-8-12 109 RichardKingscote 8 71
(Tom Dascombe) *led: pushed along and hdd 2f out: rdn and wknd over 1f out* **9/1**

62-2 **7** *dist* **Prompter**16 1473 3-8-12 106 HayleyTurner 5 —
(M L W Bell) *hld up: pushed along over 4f out: sn lft wl bhd: virtually p.u fnl f* **13/2**

2m 14.75s (2.55) **Going Correction** +0.45s/f (Yiel) **7** Ran SP% **110.9**
Speed ratings (Par 109): **107,106,106,104,103 91,—**
Tote Swingers: 1&2 £2.00, 1&3 £7.70, 2&3 £7.10 CSF £11.88 TOTE £3.90: £2.30, £1.90; EX 6.70 Trifecta £139.20 Pool: £871.49 - 4.63 winning units..
Owner M Al-Qatami & K M Al-Mudhaf **Bred** Elsdon Farms **Trained** Newmarket, Suffolk

FOCUS
Something of a bunch finish to this Derby trial, and it was not a great renewal. The form is rated around the runner-up, with a small personal best from the winner.

NOTEBOOK
Azmeel won more cosily than the margin of victory would suggest. Runner-up in the Sandown Classic Trial on his reappearance, he had clearly come on plenty for that outing and, having been held up off the pace, picked up in good style to edge out a couple of rivals who'd got first run on him. The bare form might not be the hottest, but he paid a handsome compliment to Chabal, who beat him comfortably at Sandown and is scheduled to run in the Dante next week, and perhaps the Prix du Jockey Club rather than the Epsom Derby will prove a more attractive option for connections of Azmeel, who remains 33-1 for Epsom with Hills and Totesport.
Dancing David(IRE) promised to be suited by the step up to this trip when second in the Craven Stakes on his reappearance, but despite leading into the final furlong, he didn't quite see it out as well as the winner. Chantilly was supposed to be the target after this, and it's possible connections will still go that way with him, but on this evidence he'll find a few too good. He was later reported to have lost an off-fore shoe. (op 3-1)

Rasmy, who ran as though needing the race when fourth behind Myplacelater (close fourth in Cheshire Oaks since) in a conditions event at Newbury last month, is out of a mare who won the Cheshire Oaks. He improved on his Newbury form, enjoying the run of the race tracking the leader on the inside, and there's probably more to come from him, especially, as his trainer noted, he's a very late May foal. (op 11-1)
Tamaathul, third in a hot Newmarket handicap on his reappearance, crossed swords with Dancing David last year when making his racecourse debut, and coincidentally finished a similar distance behind him again. He hung left under pressure and this course probably wasn't ideal for him, but he'll be of interest again when reverting to a more galloping track. (op 9-2)
Encompassing(IRE) got off the mark at the fourth time of asking when taking a Limerick maiden last month was warm beforehand. By Montjeu out of a Coronation Stakes winner, he's bred to be decent, but he struggled to get competitive here after being held up in last place. (op 9-1)
Party Doctor, who didn't have to run anywhere near his best to get off the mark at Wolverhampton on his reappearance, made the running on this return to Group company but his stamina ran out over this longer trip. (op 8-1)
Prompter, with whom something went amiss, was virtually pulled up. Michael Bell later reported that the colt finished sore. Official explanation: trainer said colt finished sore (op 7-1)

1859 BOODLES DIAMOND ORMONDE STKS (GROUP 3) — 1m 5f 89y
2:45 (2:45) (Class 1) 4-Y-O+
£42,577 (£16,140; £8,077; £4,027; £2,017; £1,012) **Stalls** Low

Form | RPR
03-1 **1** **Harbinger**^{20} [1382] 4-9-3 116 ... RyanMoore 2 126+
(Sir Michael Stoute) *lw: trckd ldrs: wnt 2nd over 5f out: led over 1f out: r.o ins fnl f: pushed out and in command towards fin* **8/13**^{1}
102- **2** *1 ½* **Age Of Aquarius (IRE)**^{297} [3970] 4-9-0 117 ... JMurtagh 1 120+
(A P O'Brien, Ire) *lw: trckd ldrs: rdn to chal and wnt 2nd over 1f out: edgd ins fnl f: nt gckn fnl 100yds: shaped wl* **7/2**^{2}
120- **3** *5* **Munsef**^{185} [7215] 8-9-0 111 ... JamieSpencer 6 112
(Ian Williams) *trckd ldr: led over 5f out: rdn and hdd over 1f out: outpcd by front 2 fnl 150yds* **12/1**
1-51 **4** *9* **Once More Dubai (USA)**^{63} [820] 5-9-0 111 ...(bt) FrankieDettori 5 99
(Saeed Bin Suroor) *s.s: hld up: rdn and unable to go pce of ldng trio fnl 2f* **9/1**^{3}
600- **5** *2* **Snoqualmie Girl (IRE)**^{190} [7131] 4-8-11 105 ... HayleyTurner 3 93
(D R C Elsworth) *lw: racd keenly: hld up: pushed along and outpcd over 2f out: nvr a danger* **28/1**
320- **6** *4* **Victoria Montoya**^{239} [5796] 5-8-11 96 ... JimmyFortune 4 87
(A M Balding) *lw: led: flashed tail and tried to down tools and hdd over 5f out: rdn 3f out: sn wknd* **18/1**

2m 56.73s (3.53) **Going Correction** +0.45s/f (Yiel) **6** Ran SP% **110.5**
Speed ratings (Par 113): **107,106,103,97,96 93**
Tote Swingers: 1&2 £1.10, 1&3 £2.80, 2&3 £4.10 CSF £2.88 TOTE £1.60: £1.10, £2.00; EX 2.70.
Owner Highclere Thoroughbred Racing (Adm. Rous) **Bred** Mrs A K H Ooi **Trained** Newmarket, Suffolk

FOCUS
The winner further enhanced his reputation and is rated up 4lb, with the third looking the best guide.
NOTEBOOK
Harbinger, the support for whom suggested his edge in fitness would prove decisive against the 1lb higher-rated Age Of Aquarius, to whom he was conceding 3lb. Impressive winner of the John Porter at Newbury on his reappearance, he was up a furlong in trip, but he showed his liking for the track when winning his maiden at this meeting last year and travelled comfortably before quickening well once in line for home. He displayed a bit of a knee action and probably wouldn't want the ground too quick, but he's now likely to head to Royal Ascot for the Hardwicke, after which, providing all goes well, he'll be stepped up to Group 1 company. He looks just the sort to keep improving. (op 8-11 tchd 4-5 in places)
Age Of Aquarius(IRE) was strongly fancied to win the St Leger last term but missed the race because of a pulled muscle. He always looked to have the makings of a smart older horse though, and in receipt of 3lb from Harbinger, he looked to hold sound claims. The market told the story though, as he drifted right out, suggesting he was far from cherry ripe first time up. This should not have come as a surprise as his stable's inmates have tended to need a run, and in that context he ran a perfectly good race, although his head carriage in the closing stages raised some questions. (tchd 4-1 in places)
Munsef, whose last run was in the Melbourne Cup, where he wasn't beaten far despite finishing only 12th, had won on his previous two starts at this track. He ran an honest race on ground easier than ideal and clearly retains plenty of ability. He should be found a Listed race somewhere. (op 10-1)
Once More Dubai(USA), winner of three of his last four starts, including last time when defying a mark of 107 in a handicap at Meydan, faced tougher competition here, but was still a little disappointing. Perhaps a combination of a longer trip on softish ground proved too much of a test. (tchd 8-1)
Snoqualmie Girl(IRE) won a Listed race here last September but her season tailed off after that. Taking on tougher opposition on her seasonal reappearance, she raced a bit keenly early and struggled to land a blow. She'll be of more interest back down in grade against her own sex. (op 20-1)
Victoria Montoya, who is in-foal to Mount Nelson, set out to make all, but she flashed her tail and looked very unco-operative. (op 16-1 tchd 20-1)

1860 SPORTINGBET.COM H'CAP — 5f 16y
3:15 (3:17) (Class 2) (0-100,100) 3-Y-O **£14,193** (£4,248; £2,124; £1,062; £528) **Stalls** Low

Form | RPR
404- **1** **Archers Road (IRE)**^{195} [7016] 3-9-4 95 ... JamieSpencer 5 99
(T D Barron) *chsd ldrs: rdn to ld 1f out: r.o ins fnl f: a doing enough cl home* **15/2**
6-21 **2** *nk* **Diman Waters (IRE)**^{13} [1511] 3-8-4 81 oh6 ... RoystonFfrench 3 84
(E J Alston) *lw: chsd ldrs: nt qckn over 2f out: rdn and swtchd rt over 1f out: r.o ins fnl f: nt quite get there* **4/1**^{3}
21-2 **3** *¾* **Confessional**^{20} [1399] 3-8-6 83 ...(b) DavidAllan 7 83+
(T D Easterby) *bhd: effrt and hung lft over 1f out: styd on ins fnl f: nt quite pce of front 2* **5/1**
56-1 **4** *shd* **Duchess Dora (IRE)**^{14} [1499] 3-9-1 97 ... IanBrennan$^{(5)}$ 1 97
(J J Quinn) *lw: led: lugged off rail most of way: rdn and hdd 1f out: styd on same pce cl home* **3/1**^{2}
0-00 **5** *¾* **Star Rover (IRE)**^{6} [1700] 3-9-9 100 ... JohnEgan 6 97
(P D Evans) *towards rr: pushed along over 3f out: rdn over 1f out: kpt on ins fnl f: nt pce to chal* **12/1**
41-1 **6** *nk* **Falasteen (IRE)**^{29} [1184] 3-9-3 94 ... PaulHanagan 2 90
(R A Fahey) *lw: pressed ldr tl rdn over 1f out: no ex wl ins fnl f* **2/1**^{1}

63.00 secs (2.00) **Going Correction** +0.45s/f (Yiel) **6** Ran SP% **114.5**
Speed ratings (Par 105): **102,101,100,100,98 98**
Tote Swingers: 1&2 £5.60, 1&3 £3.90, 2&3 £4.00 CSF £37.78 TOTE £9.40: £3.90, £2.30; EX 48.60.
Owner Connect 4 **Bred** John Fielding **Trained** Maunby, N Yorks
■ Stewards' Enquiry : Jamie Spencer caution: used whip with excessive frequency.

FOCUS
The two leaders went off too quick here and it played into the hands of those ridden more patiently. The winner produced a small step up, with the second running well from out of the weights and the next three close to their marks.
NOTEBOOK
Archers Road(IRE), who was beaten narrowly in the Lily Agnes at this meeting last year, ran 16 times and proved very consistent at two. Making his seasonal reappearance and handicap debut for a new yard, he chased the pace set by the duelling leaders and was well placed to strike for home once they straightened up. He battled on gamely under pressure, but things fell kindly this time and he might well struggle off a higher mark. (op 8-1 tchd 7-1)
Diman Waters(IRE) was nicely backed before running out an impressive winner at Haydock on his reappearance. As a result of being 6lb out of the handicap, he was effectively 13lb higher here, but his trainer had won this race twice in the previous nine years, and he was solid in the market. He came home really well from off the pace and, while it looks like a chance to win off his correct mark was sacrificed here, he's an improving sort and could well be up to defying an even higher rating. (op 9-2 tchd 7-2)
Confessional struggled to go the early pace but finished with purpose. He won his maiden last year over 6f on soft ground, and perhaps a return to that trip will suit him. (op 7-1)
Duchess Dora(IRE), a cosy winner at Sandown on her reappearance and only 3lb higher, tried to make use of her good draw but got into a speed duel with Falasteen and the pair cut each others' throats. She never looked that happy on the track and a return to a more conventional course can see her return to winning ways. (op 11-4 tchd 7-2)
Star Rover(IRE) made all to beat Archers Road in the Lily Agnes here last year, but he didn't have the early pace to overcome his draw and lead this time. (op 9-1)
Falasteen(IRE), a winner over this C&D last September, made a successful reappearance over 6f in a three-runner affair at Leicester last month. Back over the minimum trip, he was unable to gain an uncontested lead and paid the price for duelling with Duchess Dora up front. (op 5-2 tchd 11-4 in places)

1861 HIGHSTREETVOUCHERS.COM MAIDEN FILLIES' STKS — 7f 2y
3:55 (3:56) (Class 4) 3-Y-O **£7,123** (£2,119; £1,059; £529) **Stalls** Low

Form | RPR
3-4 **1** **Safina**^{23} [1312] 3-9-0 0 ... RyanMoore 3 89
(Sir Michael Stoute) *in tch: effrt 2f out: chsd ldr over 1f out: r.o to ld fnl 150yds: edgd rt and in command towards fin* **8/13**^{1}
52- **2** *1* **Strictly Dancing (IRE)**^{211} [6615] 3-9-0 0 ... JimmyFortune 9 86
(A M Balding) *hld up in midfield: hdwy over 1f out: sn plld wde: r.o ins fnl f: gng on at fin: nt quite rch wnr* **10/1**
0-32 **3** *1 ¼* **Nimue (USA)**^{11} [1571] 3-9-0 80 ... JamieSpencer 8 83
(P F I Cole) *lw: rrd s: chsd ldr: led over 5f out: rdn ins fnl f: hdd fnl 150yds: no ex cl home* **8/1**^{3}
6-0 **4** *1 ¾* **Fetching**^{22} [1329] 3-9-0 0 ... MichaelHills 6 78
(B W Hills) *lw: racd keenly: hld up: rdn and hdwy over 1f out: styd on ins fnl f: no imp on front trio* **16/1**
60- **5** *5* **Path Of Peace**^{196} [6990] 3-9-0 0 ... FrankieDettori 2 65
(J D Bethell) *bhd: rdn over 1f out: nvr rchd chalng position* **20/1**
2 **6** *nk* **Qudwah (IRE)**^{21} [1355] 3-9-0 0 ... RichardHills 7 64
(M A Jarvis) *in tch: chsd ldrs over 5f out: wnt 2nd over 4f out: rdn and wknd over 1f out* **4/1**^{2}
0-46 **7** *1 ½* **Catbells (IRE)**^{24} [1275] 3-9-0 65 ... JamieMackay 5 60
(A Bailey) *rrd s: bhd: pushed along over 2f out: nvr on terms* **50/1**
6- **8** *3 ¼* **Mrs Mogg**^{307} [3633] 3-9-0 0 ... RichardKingscote 4 51
(Tom Dascombe) *w'like: led: hdd over 5f out: remained prom: wknd over 1f out* **25/1**
00 **9** *3 ½* **Princess Of Troy (IRE)**^{14} [1501] 3-9-0 0 ... JohnEgan 1 42
(P D Evans) *in tch: wknd over 2f out: eased whn wl btn over 1f out* **50/1**

1m 30.17s (3.67) **Going Correction** +0.45s/f (Yiel) **9** Ran SP% **120.5**
Speed ratings (Par 98): **97,95,94,92,86 86,84,80,76**
Tote Swingers: 1&2 £3.30, 1&3 £2.20, 2&3 £6.80 CSF £8.35 TOTE £1.50: £1.02, £2.90, £2.30; EX 7.50 Trifecta £31.30 Pool: £1022.29 - 24.12 winning units..
Owner Cheveley Park Stud **Bred** Cheveley Park Stud Ltd **Trained** Newmarket, Suffolk

FOCUS
One or two interesting fillies lined up for this maiden, but the market only wanted to know about the winner. She did not need to get close to her Nell Gwyn form, with the level set around the third.
Qudwah(IRE) Official explanation: vet said filly exhibited nasal discharge

1862 BOXES AND PACKAGING H'CAP — 7f 2y
4:30 (4:31) (Class 4) (0-85,85) 4-Y-O+ **£7,123** (£2,119; £1,059; £529) **Stalls** Low

Form | RPR
203- **1** **Dance And Dance (IRE)**^{163} [7523] 4-9-4 85 ... JamieSpencer 2 95
(E F Vaughan) *racd keenly: in tch: effrt over 1f out: led ent fnl f: sn edgd rt: r.o wl* **10/1**
060- **2** *1 ½* **Viva Ronaldo (IRE)**^{251} [5432] 4-8-12 82 ... BarryMcHugh$^{(3)}$ 14 88+
(R A Fahey) *hld up: hdwy 2f out: rdn 1f out: styd on to take 2nd fnl 100yds: nt rch wnr* **14/1**
-603 **3** *½* **Lucky Numbers (IRE)**^{6} [1688] 4-9-1 82 ... RyanMoore 1 87
(Paul Green) *chsd ldrs: lost pl over 4f out: rallied over 1f out: prog ins fnl f: styd on towards fin* **9/2**^{2}
4054 **4** *½* **Fathsta (IRE)**^{21} [1349] 5-9-4 85 ... MartinDwyer 8 89+
(D M Simcock) *racd keenly in midfield: hdwy to go prom over 4f out: led 2f out: hdd ent fnl f: styd on same pce fnl 100yds* **7/1**^{3}
-215 **5** *nk* **Last Sovereign**^{34} [1088] 6-9-0 81 ... FrankieDettori 3 85
(Jane Chapple-Hyam) *led: hdd over 5f out: continued to chse ldrs: rdn over 1f out: n.m.r and bmpd whn stl in cl contention ins fnl f: no ex cl home* **4/1**^{1}
0-00 **6** *¾* **Zomerlust**^{20} [1397] 8-8-10 82 ... IanBrennan$^{(5)}$ 5 83
(J J Quinn) *in tch: rdn and nt qckn over 1f out: kpt on ins fnl f: nt pce of ldrs*
040- **7** *nk* **Mr Macattack**^{322} [3091] 5-9-4 85 ...(t) RichardKingscote 6 85+
(Tom Dascombe) *stdd s: hld up: rdn and sme hdwy 1f out: kpt on ins fnl f: nt trble ldrs* **9/2**^{2}
-224 **8** *¾* **Kerrys Requiem (IRE)**^{6} [1692] 4-9-4 85 ... JimmyFortune 11 83
(M R Channon) *midfield: rdn over 1f out: no imp* **16/1**
0-60 **9** *¾* **Silver Wind**^{6} [1688] 5-9-2 83 ...(b) JohnEgan 7 79
(P D Evans) *w ldr: led over 5f out: hdd 2f out: rdn and wknd ins fnl f* **33/1**
-040 **10** *2 ¾* **Desert Dreamer (IRE)**^{7} [1672] 9-8-13 85 ... RichardEvans$^{(5)}$ 10 74
(P D Evans) *missed break: a bhd: nvr able to get on terms* **25/1**
-502 **11** *nk* **Abbondanza (IRE)**^{39} [1042] 7-9-1 85 ... MichaelGeran$^{(3)}$ 13 73
(D Nicholls) *restless in stalls: chsd ldrs: rdn over 1f out: wknd ins fnl f* **25/1**
204- **12** *2 ¾* **Leverage (IRE)**^{195} [7027] 4-9-0 81 ... NickyMackay 4 61
(M Wigham) *racd keenly in midfield tl lost pl over 4f out: n.d after* **10/1**

1m 29.51s (3.01) **Going Correction** +0.45s/f (Yiel) **12** Ran SP% **118.6**
Speed ratings (Par 105): **100,98,97,97,96 95,95,94,93,90 90,87**
Tote Swingers: 1&2 £41.80, 1&3 £5.90, 2&3 £19.10 CSF £138.62 CT £734.46 TOTE £11.50: £2.70, £4.70, £1.90; EX 192.30 Trifecta £781.40 Part won. Pool: £1056 - 0.10 winning units..
Owner Mohammed Rashid **Bred** Darley **Trained** Newmarket, Suffolk

The Form Book, Raceform Ltd, Compton, RG20 6NL

FOCUS
An open handicap run in a time 0.66sec quicker than fillies' maiden earlier on the card. A 5lb personal best from the winner, and fairly sound form.

1863 CRUISE NIGHTSPOT H'CAP — 1m 4f 66y
5:05 (5:05) (Class 4) (0-85,83) 4-Y-0+ £7,771 (£2,312; £1,155; £577) Stalls Low

Form				RPR
30-4	1		**Jedi**[27] 1220 4-9-4 **83** RyanMoore 12 *(Sir Michael Stoute) lw: midfield: hdwy over 3f out: led over 2f out: rdn over 1f out: r.o wl and wl in command towards fin* **5/2**[1]	91
-543	2	1 3/4	**I'm In The Pink (FR)**[6] 1077 6-8-7 **72** JohnEgan 2 *(P D Evans) hld up: hdwy 2f out: sn rdn: wnt 2nd 1f out: styd on: nt pce of wnr towards fin* **11/1**	77
0-22	3	1/2	**Embsay Crag**[20] 1378 4-8-11 **81** IanBrennan(5) 5 *(Mrs K Walton) chsd ldrs: rdn over 2f out: styd on u.p ins fnl f: nt quite pce of ldrs* **11/4**[2]	85
2154	4	shd	**Paktolos (FR)**[77] 620 7-9-1 **80** (p) FergusSweeney 4 *(John A Harris) lw: in rr: hdwy over 1f out: hung lft and prog ins fnl f: styd on towards fin* **25/1**	84
6-33	5	1/2	**Hindu Kush (IRE)**[21] 1357 5-8-13 **78** JamieSpencer 11 *(Ian Williams) chsd ldrs: dropped to midfield after 2f: hdwy 4f out: rdn to chse wnr over 2f out: lost 2nd over 1f out: kpt on u.p and nt pce of ldrs ins fnl f: no ex cl home* **6/1**[3]	81
02-0	6	6	**Manshoor (IRE)**[24] 1282 5-8-11 **76** HayleyTurner 7 *(Mrs L Wadham) hld up: niggled along 6f out: hdwy over 3f out: rdn to chse ldrs 2f out: fdd fnl f* **25/1**	70
12-6	7	3/4	**Starla Dancer (GER)**[41] 1013 4-8-11 **79** BarryMcHugh(3) 10 *(R A Fahey) midfield: snatched up whn n.m.r 4f out: effrt 2f out: no real imp on ldrs: wknd fnl f* **10/1**	71
50-0	8	16	**Phoenix Flight (IRE)**[21] 1348 5-8-12 **77** (b[1]) FrankieDettori 8 *(H J Evans) racd keenly: chsd ldrs: wnt 2nd after 3f: lost 2nd and wknd qckly over 2f out* **20/1**	44
4-00	9	12	**Una Pelota (IRE)**[13] 1512 4-8-7 **72** RichardKingscote 1 *(Tom Dascombe) led: rdn and hdd over 2f out: wknd over 1f out* **14/1**	20
2-02	10	10	**Interdiamonds**[7] 1655 4-8-8 **73** JoeFanning 3 *(M Johnston) chsd ldr after 1f tl after 3f: remained handy: pushed along over 4f out: wknd qckly wl over 3f out* **6/1**[3]	5

2m 42.77s (2.87) **Going Correction** +0.45s/f (Yiel) **10 Ran SP% 120.4**
Speed ratings (Par 105): **108,106,106,106,106 102,101,90,82,76**
Tote Swingers: 1&2 £8.70, 1&3 £2.80, 2&3 £12.10 CSF £31.27 CT £81.20 TOTE £3.30: £1.30, £2.40, £1.60; EX 43.00 Trifecta £313.50 Pool: £1012.77 - 2.39 winning units. Place 6: £216.07 Place 5: £28.85 .
Owner Philip Newton **Bred** Philip Newton **Trained** Newmarket, Suffolk

FOCUS
A decent handicap and a smooth success for Jedi. The third is a solid guide to the form.
Phoenix Flight(IRE) Official explanation: jockey said gelding had no more to give
Una Pelota(IRE) Official explanation: jockey said gelding hung right-handed
Interdiamonds Official explanation: jockey said, regarding running, that he ahd no explanation for the poor form shown
T/Jkpt: £124,595.70. Pool: £877,428.09 - 5 winning units. T/Plt: £285.90. Pool: £182,279.40 - 465.30 winning units. T/Qpdt: £28.40. Pool: £10,267.53 - 266.85 winning units. DO

[1717]HAMILTON (R-H)
Friday, May 7

OFFICIAL GOING: Good (9.0)
Races on round course run over 8yards further than advertised due to dolling out around the loop.
Wind: Fresh, across Weather: Fine

1864 EUROPEAN BREEDERS' FUND MAIDEN STKS — 5f 4y
6:15 (6:16) (Class 5) 2-Y-0 £3,561 (£1,059; £529; £264) Stalls Low

Form				RPR
632	1		**Saucy Buck (IRE)**[9] 1612 2-9-3 0 KierenFallon 1 *(M R Channon) mde all: rdn and drifted rt over 1f out: styd on strly fnl f* **1/9**[1]	74+
046	2	3 3/4	**Roodee Queen**[13] 1510 2-8-12 0 StephenCraine 5 *(Patrick Morris) trckd ldrs: effrt and wnt 2nd over 1f out: edgd rt and no imp fnl f* **20/1**[3]	55
	3	1 3/4	**Mr Khan** 2-9-3 0 FrederikTylicki 2 *(James Moffatt) dwlt: sn prom: rdn and outpcd after 2f: styd on fnl f: no ch w first two* **22/1**	53+
	4	1/2	**Hollyhocks (IRE)** 2-8-9 0 MartinLane(3) 4 *(N Wilson) t.k.h: sn w ldr: edgd rt and outpcd over 1f out: sn no ex* **14/1**[2]	46
0	5	1 1/2	**Whipperoo (IRE)**[7] 1668 2-8-9 0 AndrewHeffernan(3) 3 *(Patrick Morris) trckd ldrs tl rdn and outpcd fr 1/2-way: n.d after* **66/1**	41

62.20 secs (2.20) **Going Correction** +0.20s/f (Good) **5 Ran SP% 107.3**
Speed ratings (Par 93): **90,84,81,80,78**
CSF £3.97 TOTE £1.10: £1.02, £3.30; EX 2.40.
Owner Mrs M Findlay **Bred** T Sherman **Trained** West Ilsley, Berks

FOCUS
The winner duly accomplished a simple task and the level of the form will be dictated by the other four.

NOTEBOOK
Saucy Buck(IRE) was very hard to oppose on the strength of his previous second to the Royal-Ascot bound Zebedee and he completed the task from the front, making it four wins from as many runners in the race for the stable. He had the advantage of the stands' rail, but he drifted out to the centre of the track after 2f and had to be kept up to his work. He could be best off leaving alone until the nurseries start. (op 1-8 tchd 1-7 in a place)
Roodee Queen took time to settle and was predictably no match for the winner. She was still a clear second-best, though, and this was her most encouraging effort yet. (op 18-1)
Mr Khan is already gelded but showed ability on this debut. He ran green from the start and got well behind, but stayed on fairly well once the penny dropped. Better should be expected next time. (op 20-1)
Hollyhocks(IRE) is a cheap purchase who needs more time and will learn for the experience. (tchd 16-1)
Whipperoo(IRE) evidently still has plenty to learn about racing.

1865 HAMILTON-PARK.CO.UK CONDITIONS STKS — 6f 5y
6:45 (6:45) (Class 3) 3-Y-0 £8,418 (£2,505; £1,251) Stalls Low

Form				RPR
120-	1		**Bow Beaver (USA)**[229] 6134 3-8-9 **80** FrederikTylicki 1 *(J Howard Johnson) w ldr: rdn over 1f out: styd on to ld wl ins fnl f: r.o* **14/1**[3]	93
15-1	2	2	**Mister Hughie (IRE)**[23] 1315 3-8-9 **99** KierenFallon 4 *(M R Channon) trckd ldrs: pushed along after 2f: hdwy on outside to ld over 1f out: rdn and edgd lft: hdd wl ins fnl f: r.o same pce* **1/2**[1]	87
1-34	3	4 1/2	**Below Zero (IRE)**[6] 1687 3-8-12 **99** GregFairley 3 *(M Johnston) t.k.h: led to over 1f out: sn btn* **2/1**[2]	76

1m 12.79s (0.59) **Going Correction** +0.20s/f (Good) **3 Ran SP% 106.7**
Speed ratings (Par 103): **104,101,95**
CSF £22.17 TOTE £12.40; EX 23.10.
Owner W M G Black & J Howard Johnson **Bred** Hertrich-McCarthy Livestock **Trained** Billy Row, Co Durham

FOCUS
A decent conditions stakes despite the small field. Guessy form, the time not backing up the apparent improvement from the winner.

NOTEBOOK
Bow Beaver(USA) did the job in game fashion on his return to action. Trainer Howard Johnson has been sending out winners over jumps recently, but his 3-y-o here looked to face a tough task at the weights. The way he went about his business suggests it was no fluke and, as a big horse, he was always likely to progress this year. He was going away at the finish and is entitled to improve a deal for the run, but does now have to prove he is not best caught fresh. (op 10-1 tchd 16-1)
Mister Hughie(IRE) won a competitive handicap on his return at Newmarket 23 days earlier and, best in at the weights here, looked to have been found an ideal conditions race in which to follow up. He got a little bump at the start and had to be niggled along before the halfway stage. Things looked good when he angled out with his run nearing the 2f pole as he came back onto the bridle, but the winner found more. He was well held at the finish and this can only rate as a missed opportunity. Perhaps coming from behind again in a big field will see him back in a better light. (op 4-11 tchd 1-3 in a place)
Below Zero(IRE) attracted support on this drop back a furlong, but was unable to get an easy lead and could have settled better. He did have something to find at the weights and this was probably too sharp for him. (op 3-1)

1866 RACING UK H'CAP — 1m 4f 17y
7:20 (7:20) (Class 5) (0-70,65) 3-Y-O £2,590 (£770; £385; £192) Stalls Low

Form				RPR
0-04	1		**Meetings Man (IRE)**[18] 1422 3-9-0 **58** TomEaves 1 *(Micky Hammond) in tch: stdy hdwy over 3f out: rdn to ld over 1f out: styd on wl fnl f* **2/1**[1]	66
0-16	2	2 1/4	**Il Portico**[18] 1422 3-9-0 **58** KierenFallon 5 *(M R Channon) t.k.h: trckd ldrs: effrt and chal over 1f out: hung lft: one pce u.p ins fnl f* **11/4**[2]	62
65-5	3	4	**Emeralds Spirit (IRE)**[15] 1495 3-8-0 **47** AndrewHeffernan(3) 3 *(J R Weymes) tk fierce hold: sn cl up: led 1/2-way: rdn over 3f out: hung lft and hdd over 1f out: no ex* **16/1**	45
060-	4	4 1/2	**Lady Pacha**[223] 6274 3-8-0 **47** oh1 ow1 MartinLane(3) 4 *(T J Pitt) t.k.h early: hld up: effrt and rdn over 3f out: no imp fnl 2f* **12/1**	37
300-	5	50	**Decimus Meridius (IRE)**[229] 6136 3-9-5 **63** FrederikTylicki 2 *(J Howard Johnson) t.k.h: prom to 1/2-way: lost tch fnl 4f: t.o* **10/3**[3]	—
6046	6	4	**Major Pop (USA)**[15] 1486 3-9-7 **65** (p) TonyHamilton 6 *(R A Fahey) led to 1/2-way: sn rdn: struggling fr over 3f out: t.o* **13/2**	—

2m 41.03s (2.43) **Going Correction** +0.05s/f (Good) **6 Ran SP% 110.0**
Speed ratings (Par 99): **93,91,88,85,52 49**
toteswingers:1&2:£1.80, 1&3:£5.50, 2&3:£6.70 CSF £7.38 TOTE £2.40: £1.10, £1.20; EX 7.60.
Owner Paul R Snook **Bred** Hakan Keles **Trained** Middleham Moor, N Yorks

FOCUS
This was a poor 3-y-o handicap on paper, in which stamina looked a serious query for the majority. It was run at a sound pace and the pair that had proven stamina that eventually dominated. The form makes sense among the front pair.

1867 JFM ELECTRICAL H'CAP — 1m 1f 36y
7:50 (7:50) (Class 4) (0-80,78) 4-Y-0+ £5,180 (£1,541; £770; £384) Stalls High

Form				RPR
4153	1		**Taaresh (IRE)**[15] 1484 5-8-6 **71** AmyRyan(5) 4 *(K A Morgan) trckd ldrs: hdwy to ld over 2f out: sn hrd pressed: hld on wl fnl f* **15/2**	81
2113	2	1	**Danderek**[13] 1512 4-9-4 **78** FrederikTylicki 9 *(R A Fahey) led 1f: pressed ldr: led over 4f to 2f out: rallied and ev ch ins fnl f: no ex nr fin* **9/4**[1]	86
-112	3	hd	**Zaplamation (IRE)**[9] 1631 5-8-7 **67** TomEaves 2 *(J J Quinn) hld up: hdwy on outside over 2f out: sn pushed along: no imp tl styd on wl fnl f: nrst fin* **11/4**[2]	74
04-0	4	9	**Ergo (FR)**[17] 1458 6-8-4 **67** (b) AndrewHeffernan(3) 1 *(James Moffatt) s.i.s: hld up: rdn and outpcd over 3f out: rallied 2f out: no imp fnl 2f* **18/1**	55
30-0	5	3	**Aldaado (IRE)**[18] 1426 4-8-11 **71** TonyHamilton 5 *(M Dods) prom: rdn over 3f out: wknd fnl 2f* **17/2**	52
344-	6	23	**The Galloping Shoe**[181] 7287 5-9-2 **76** GregFairley 7 *(A C Whillans) hld up in tch: effrt over 4f out: wknd fr 3f out: t.o* **8/1**	6
0-00	7	16	**Wind Shuffle (GER)**[15] 1202 7-8-12 **72** (p) KierenFallon 8 *(J S Goldie) led after 1f to over 4f out: hung lft and wknd 3f out: eased whn no ch* **5/1**[3]	—

1m 58.94s (-0.76) **Going Correction** +0.05s/f (Good) **7 Ran SP% 112.8**
Speed ratings (Par 105): **105,104,103,95,93 72,58**
toteswingers:1&2:£4.60, 1&3:£3.50, 2&3:£2.90 CSF £24.09 CT £57.78 TOTE £11.10: £3.90, £1.20; EX 25.90.
Owner P Doughty **Bred** Shadwell Estate Company Limited **Trained** Newmarket, Suffolk

FOCUS
A modest handicap, run at a brisk pace and the first three came clear. The form looks sound with the winner back to his former best.
Wind Shuffle(GER) Official explanation: jockey said gelding hung left-handed in straight

1868 BRAVEHEART NIGHT NEXT WEEK MAIDEN STKS — 6f 5y
8:20 (8:28) (Class 5) 3-5-Y-O £2,590 (£770; £385; £192) Stalls Low

Form				RPR
00-	1		**Beat Baby (IRE)**[259] 5234 3-9-0 0 FrederikTylicki 10 *(J Howard Johnson) mde all: sn crossed to stands' rail: pushed clr fr 2f out* **9/2**	87
02-0	2	5	**Antarctic Desert (IRE)**[21] 1362 3-9-0 72 KierenFallon 5 *(K A Ryan) chsd wnr: pushed along over 2f out: sn one pce* **4/1**[3]	71
24-2	3	3 3/4	**Powerful Pierre**[20] 1401 3-8-9 73 (v) PatrickDonaghy(5) 1 *(Jedd O'Keeffe) prom: rdn over 2f out: sn outpcd: n.d after* **85/40**[1]	59
/	4	7	**Rosbertini** 4-9-5 0 AmyRyan(5) 2 *(Miss L A Perratt) s.s: bhd and outpcd: sme late hdwy: nvr rchd ldrs* **22/1**	37
	5	3/4	**Tabiet** 3-8-9 0 TonyHamilton 7 *(James Moffatt) bhd and sn outpcd: sme hdwy 2f out: nvr on terms* **25/1**	29
06	6	2	**Hong Kong Island (IRE)**[16] 1464 3-9-0 0 TomEaves 8 *(J Barclay) in tch on outside: outpcd 1/2-way: nvr on terms* **20/1**	28

7 14 **Opera Cat (USA)** 3-9-0 0 .... GregFairley 3 —
(M Johnston) *wnt rt s: rn green and sn outpcd: no ch fr 1/2-way* **5/2**[2]

0 8 7 **Rabbie Burns**[18] 1425 3-8-11 0 .... MartinLane(3) 4 —
(N Wilson) *bmpd s: t.k.h and sn cl up: drifted rt to far rail 1/2-way: eased: sddle slipped* **100/1**

9 6 **Prince Of Fife (IRE)** 3-9-0 0 .... StephenCraine 9 —
(Miss L A Perratt) *s.v.s: t.o thrght* **20/1**

1m 12.46s (0.26) **Going Correction** +0.20s/f (Good)
WFA 3 from 4yo 10lb 9 Ran SP% **117.5**
Speed ratings (Par 103): **106,99,94,85,84 81,62,53,45**
toteswingers:1&2:£1.20, 1&3:£3.30, 2&3:£3.10 CSF £21.40 TOTE £6.70: £2.80, £2.20, £1.10; EX 22.30.
Owner J Howard Johnson **Bred** Paget Bloodstock **Trained** Billy Row, Co Durham

FOCUS

A decidedly weak maiden that saw them finish well strung out. The time was decent though and the winner was much improved on his 2yo form.

Rabbie Burns Official explanation: jockey said saddle slipped

Prince Of Fife(IRE) Official explanation: jockey said gelding missed the break

1869 TURFTV H'CAP 6f 5y

8:50 (8:55) (Class 5) (0-75,75) 3-Y-0+ **£2,729** (£806; £403) **Stalls** Low

Form RPR

003- **1** **Tadalavil**[286] 4311 5-9-2 **65** .... TomEaves 8 74
(Miss L A Perratt) *cl up: led wl over 1f out: sn rdn: hld on wl fnl f* **25/1**

0-04 **2** ¾ **Guest Connections**[24] 1270 7-8-12 **61** oh2 .... (v) AndrewMullen 4 67
(D Nicholls) *sn outpcd and bhd: gd hdwy over 1f out: styd on wl to take 2nd cl home: nrst fin* **4/1**[2]

1-0U **3** nse **Northern Bolt**[21] 1365 5-9-9 **75** .... (v) MartinLane(3) 6 81
(I W McInnes) *hld up: hdwy over 1f out: chsd wnr ins fnl f: kpt on: hld and lost 2nd cl home* **12/1**

0503 **4** nk **Apache Ridge (IRE)**[7] 1653 4-9-0 **68** .... (p) AmyRyan(5) 3 73
(K A Ryan) *sn bhd and outpcd: hdwy over 1f out: styd on wl fnl f: hld towards fin* **7/2**[1]

412- **5** 2 ¾ **Cheyenne Red (IRE)**[204] 6798 4-9-2 **70** .... PatrickDonaghy(5) 5 66+
(M Dods) *prom: effrt and cl up over 1f out: wknd ins fnl f* **9/2**[3]

0-00 **6** 3 ¼ **Bid For Gold**[24] 1276 6-9-5 **68** .... TonyHamilton 7 54
(Jedd O'Keeffe) *midfield: outpcd over 2f out: kpt on fnl f: no imp* **13/2**

0-50 **7** nk **The Bear**[5] 1719 7-8-9 **61** .... AndrewHeffernan(3) 2 46
(Miss L A Perratt) *led to wl over 1f out: sn drvn and outpcd* **18/1**

00-6 **8** 1 ¼ **Bateleur**[12] 1547 6-8-12 **61** oh1 .... KierenFallon 13 42
(M R Channon) *dwlt: bhd: hdwy and prom over 1f out: wknd ins fnl f* **8/1**

/00- **9** 5 **Geojimali**[206] 6764 8-9-5 **71** .... GaryBartley(3) 1 36
(J S Goldie) *dwlt: sn outpcd: plenty to do 1/2-way: nvr on terms* **16/1**

2-00 **10** 4 **Hosanna**[11] 1569 4-8-9 **63** oh14 ow2 .... MichaelO'Connell(5) 11 15
(J Barclay) *midfield: drvn and outpcd over 2f out: sn btn* **66/1**

510- **11** 2 ¾ **Stonehaugh (IRE)**[276] 4621 7-9-11 **74** .... FrederikTylicki 9 17
(J Howard Johnson) *prom: drvn and outpcd over 2f out: n.d after* **14/1**

156- **12** 4 **Military Call**[273] 4739 3-8-13 **72** .... GregFairley 10 2
(A C Whillans) *in tch tl edgd rt and wknd fr 1/2-way* **16/1**

56-5 **13** 2 **Hold On Tiger (IRE)**[33] 1104 3-8-13 **72** .... StephenCraine 14 —
(J Barclay) *midfield on outside: struggling 1/2-way: sn btn* **33/1**

1m 12.92s (0.72) **Going Correction** +0.20s/f (Good)
WFA 3 from 4yo+ 10lb 13 Ran SP% **124.5**
Speed ratings (Par 103): **103,102,101,101,97 93,93,91,84,79 75,70,67**
toteswingers:1&2:£41.30, 1&3:£83.40, 2&3:£14.70 CSF £126.47 CT £1316.04 TOTE £33.20: £8.90, £1.90, £6.70; EX 190.30 Place 6 £245.12, Place 5 £225.24.
Owner Ayrshire Racing **Bred** Theakston Stud **Trained** East Kilbride, South Lanarks

FOCUS

The field surprisingly shunned the near-side rail in this moderate sprint and emerged down the centre of the track. The form looks straightforward with the winner taking advantage of a lowly mark.

T/Plt: £238.40. Pool: £35,578.00 - 108.90 winning units. T/Qpdt: £18.50. Pool: £4,039.94 - 161.40 winning units. RY

1659 LINGFIELD (L-H)

Friday, May 7

OFFICIAL GOING: Turf course - good to firm (good in places) changing to good to firm after race 2 (2.05); all weather - standard

Wind: fresh, half against Weather: bright, light cloud

1870 DERBY TRIAL HERE TOMORROW MAIDEN STKS (DIV I) 7f

1:35 (1:36) (Class 5) 3-Y-0 **£2,388** (£705; £352) **Stalls** High

Form RPR

532- **1** **Mutafajer**[184] 7234 3-9-3 82 .... (v[1]) TedDurcan 7 79+
(Saeed Bin Suroor) *led and grabbed stands' rail: overall ldr tl hdd over 5f out: led again over 1f out: drew clr fnl f: comf* **6/5**[1]

0- **2** 3 **Ocean Rosie (IRE)**[228] 6164 3-8-12 0 .... CathyGannon 9 66
(Miss J Feilden) *chsd wnr: rdn and unable qck ent fnl 2f: no ch w wnr ins fnl f: wnt overall 2nd fnl 100yds* **33/1**

4 **3** 2 **Danehill Sunset (IRE)**[60] 825 3-9-3 0 .... RichardHughes 2 66+
(B W Hills) *taken down early: hmpd and pushed lft s: hung lft thrght: racd alone in centre but hung across to r on far rail fr 1/2-way: prom: overall ldr over 5f out tl over 1f out: wknd ins fnl f* **9/4**[2]

00- **4** 1 ½ **Sweet Pilgrim**[175] 7365 3-8-12 0 .... DavidProbert 6 56
(M D I Usher) *wnt bdly lft s: t.k.h and sn in tch: rdn and unable qck ent fnl 2f: no threat to wnr fnl f* **66/1**

0 **5** 1 ¼ **Hope She Does (USA)**[42] 985 3-8-12 0 .... TomQueally 12 53
(Mrs L C Jewell) *chsd ldrs: rdn and unable qck over 2f out: one pce and wl hld fr over 1f out* **100/1**

02 **6** 3 ¼ **Avonside (IRE)**[25] 1259 3-9-3 0 .... SebSanders 5 49
(J J Bridger) *hmpd s and s.i.s: sn swtchd rt: wl bhd: styd on past btn horses fnl f: nvr trbld ldrs* **20/1**

7 1 **Rileys Crane** 3-9-3 0 .... TomMcLaughlin 10 47
(Mrs C A Dunnett) *t.k.h: hld up in tch in midfield: rdn and struggling 1/2-way: no ch fnl 2f* **150/1**

4 **8** nk **Craicajack (IRE)**[10] 1590 3-9-3 0 .... EddieCreighton 8 46
(E J Creighton) *chsd ldrs: rdn and struggling 1/2-way: no ch fr wl over 1f out* **18/1**

9 ½ **Shut Up Shapiro (IRE)** 3-9-3 0 .... TonyCulhane 3 44
(George Baker) *hmpd s: sn swtchd rt: bhd and sn rdn along: nvr on terms* **50/1**

230- **10** 1 **Aalsmeer**[209] 6660 3-8-12 92 .... DarryllHolland 4 37
(Karen George) *hmpd s: sn swtchd rt: in tch: rdn and btn over 2f out* **6/1**[3]

00 **11** ¾ **Baxter (IRE)**[6] 1694 3-9-3 0 .... SimonWhitworth 11 40
(J W Hills) *stdd s: hld up in rr: struggling bdly fr 1/2-way: nvr on terms* **66/1**

4- **12** 1 ½ **Freedom Pass (USA)**[170] 7429 3-8-12 0 .... AlanMunro 1 31
(J A R Toller) *hmpd s: sn swtchd rt: chsd ldrs tl wknd 2f out: eased wl ins fnl f* **20/1**

1m 24.34s (1.04) **Going Correction** +0.05s/f (Good) 12 Ran SP% **114.8**
Speed ratings (Par 99): **96,92,90,88,87 83,82,81,81,80 79,77**
Tote Swingers: 1&2 £16.70, 1&3 £1.10, 2&3 £21.30 CSF £56.07 TOTE £1.80: £1.02, £8.30, £1.70; EX 61.10 Trifecta £118.20 Part won. Pool: 159.86 - 0.43 winning units..
Owner Godolphin **Bred** Shadwell Estate Company Limited **Trained** Newmarket, Suffolk

FOCUS

The first and slower division of what was an uncompetitive maiden was won with ease by the 82-rated Mutafajer. The winner did not need to improve on last season's maiden form.

Danehill Sunset(IRE) Official explanation: jockey said colt hung left

Sweet Pilgrim Official explanation: jockey said filly jumped left

Baxter(IRE) Official explanation: jockey said gelding ran too free

1871 EUROPEAN BREEDERS' FUND MAIDEN STKS 5f

2:05 (2:05) (Class 5) 2-Y-0 **£3,302** (£982; £491; £245) **Stalls** High

Form RPR

0 **1** **Roche Des Vents**[10] 1597 2-9-3 0 .... RichardHughes 5 79
(R Hannon) *broke wl and sn grabbed stands' rail: mde all: sn clr: rdn over 1f out: jnd ins fnl f: fnd ex and asserted towards fin* **11/2**[3]

2 **2** ¾ **Leiba Leiba**[10] 1597 2-9-3 0 .... DarryllHolland 2 76+
(M Botti) *t.k.h: hld up in midfield: chsd ldr 3f out: clsd over 1f out: plld out and rdn to chal jst ins fnl f: nt qckn u.p and btn towards fin* **5/4**[1]

2 **3** nk **Alfraamsey**[12] 1541 2-9-3 0 .... AlanMunro 3 75+
(M R Channon) *chsd clr ldr tl 3f out: sn bustled along and wl outpcd: rallied u.p ent fnl f: styd on wl fnl 150yds: gng on fin* **15/8**[2]

4 11 **Maggie's Treasure (IRE)** 2-9-3 0 .... SebSanders 7 35+
(J Gallagher) *restless in stalls: awkward s and slowly away: sn bustled along and struggling to go pce: rn green and edgd lft 1/2-way: nvr on terms* **10/1**

5 2 **Ridgeway Hawk** 2-8-12 0 .... LeeNewnes(5) 6 28
(M D I Usher) *sn rdn along and outpcd in last pair* **66/1**

6 7 **Whitby Jet (IRE)** 2-9-3 0 .... LiamKeniry 4 —
(E F Vaughan) *sn outpcd in rr: t.o* **16/1**

58.83 secs (0.63) **Going Correction** +0.05s/f (Good) 6 Ran SP% **111.1**
Speed ratings (Par 93): **96,94,94,76,73 62**
Tote Swingers: 1&2 £6.70, 1&3 £2.50, 2&3 £1.10 CSF £12.62 TOTE £5.90: £1.50, £1.20; EX 13.30.
Owner Robin Blunt **Bred** G Howard-Spink **Trained** East Everleigh, Wilts

FOCUS

An ordinary juvenile maiden and the stands' rail played a big part in the outcome. It was still a good start from the winner to see off a pair with experience.

NOTEBOOK

Roche Des Vents shot out of the gates and soon found himself clear. He began to look vulnerable from over 1f out and was joined by the favourite 100 yards out, but pluckily pulled out more and began to assert again in the final strides. He had finished well behind the runner-up on debut, when failing to meet with market expectation, but this was clearly a truer reflection of his ability. (op 8-1)

Leiba Leiba, who would probably have made a winning debut at Nottingham had Holland been more vigorous close home (seemed to think he was going to win a shade comfortably), closed up on the winner and it looked a case of when he wanted to pick him off, but having been switched left to challenge, he didn't find as much as expected and was outstayed close home. (op 11-8 tchd 6-4)

Alfraamsey, a promising second at Bath on debut, couldn't go the early pace, but did come home well and nearly grabbed second. He will be suited by 6f and can win an ordinary maiden. (op 6-4 tchd 9-4)

Maggie's Treasure(IRE), reportedly a precocious type, wasn't the best away and will be sharper next time. (op 12-1 tchd 15-2)

Ridgeway Hawk, a half-brother to a couple of modest winning sprinters for the yard, was quickly in trouble. (op 100-1)

Whitby Jet(IRE), who is related to a 7f winner, was soon in toruble. (tchd 12-1)

1872 DERBY TRIAL HERE TOMORROW MAIDEN STKS (DIV II) 7f

2:35 (2:36) (Class 5) 3-Y-0 **£2,388** (£705; £352) **Stalls** High

Form RPR

524- **1** **Cansili Star**[213] 6561 3-9-3 82 .... PhilipRobinson 10 88+
(M A Jarvis) *mde all against stands' rail: pushed clr over 1f out: v easily* **1/1**[1]

3-35 **2** 3 **Sheer Force (IRE)**[23] 1307 3-9-3 74 .... ShaneKelly 9 77
(W J Knight) *chsd ldrs: hdwy to trck wnr over 2f out: rdn and effrt wl over 1f out: btn ent fnl f: plugged on for clr 2nd* **13/2**[3]

0- **3** 2 ½ **Tap Dance Way (IRE)**[228] 6164 3-8-12 0 .... LiamKeniry 4 65+
(P R Chamings) *stdd s: t.k.h: hld up in rr: hdwy over 1f out: kpt on to go 3rd ins fnl f: nvr trbld ldrs* **20/1**

242- **4** 1 ½ **Music Maestro (IRE)**[186] 7209 3-9-3 81 .... SebSanders 3 66+
(B W Hills) *chsd ldrs: rdn ent fnl 2f: wl btn ent fnl f* **5/2**[2]

5 3 ½ **Macie (IRE)** 3-8-12 0 .... RichardHughes 11 52
(J Noseda) *sn chsng ldrs: rdn and unable qck ent fnl 2f: wknd over 1f out: wl btn fnl f* **9/1**

00 **6** hd **Togoaviking**[17] 1442 3-9-3 0 .... LiamJones 5 56
(W J Haggas) *t.k.h: wl in tch: rdn wl over 2f out: wknd 2f out: no ch fnl f* **50/1**

04- **7** hd **Explorator (IRE)**[127] 7886 3-9-3 0 .... TonyCulhane 7 56
(George Baker) *stdd s: hld up wl in rr: pushed along and no prog ent fnl 2f: kpt on ins fnl f: nvr on terms* **33/1**

8 ¾ **Dilys Maud** 3-8-12 0 .... AndreaAtzeni 6 49
(R Ingram) *s.i.s: hld up towards rr: hdwy 1/2-way: rdn and sltly hmpd 2f out: sn wknd* **100/1**

00- **9** 5 **Acquaviva**[307] 3633 3-8-12 0 .... TomQueally 2 35
(Eve Johnson Houghton) *racd in midfield: rdn and edgd lft 2f out: sn wknd: wl bhd fnl f* **66/1**

0 **10** 12 **Bravo Tango**[27] 1222 3-9-3 0 .... AlanMunro 8 8
(D W P Arbuthnot) *chsd ldrs: rdn and lost pl wl over 2f out: t.o and eased wl ins fnl f* **150/1**

0-0 **11** ½ **Miss California**[7] 1661 3-8-12 0 .... DavidProbert 1 —
(Miss Tor Sturgis) *chsd wnr tl over 2f out: sn edgd lft u.p and wknd qckly: t.o and eased wl ins fnl f* **150/1**

1m 23.07s (-0.23) **Going Correction** +0.05s/f (Good) 11 Ran SP% **115.4**
Speed ratings (Par 99): **103,99,96,95,91 90,90,89,83,70 69**
Tote Swingers: 1&2 £11.30, 2&3 £3.40 CSF £7.91 TOTE £2.10: £1.10, £1.50, £5.50; EX 8.20 Trifecta £80.60 Pool: £346.64 - 3.10 winning units..
Owner A D Spence **Bred** Hascombe And Valiant Studs **Trained** Newmarket, Suffolk

FOCUS
The time of this second division was 1.27secs quicker than the first and this looked the stronger and more solid race with the runner-up a pretty sound guide. .

1873 TOTESWINGER H'CAP 7f
3:05 (3:08) (Class 5) (0-70,70) 3-Y-O **£3,885** (£1,156; £577; £288) **Stalls** High

Form RPR

6-45 **1** **Tell Halaf**[30] 1178 3-8-11 **63** RichardHughes 14 72+
(M L W Bell) *in tch: rdn and effrt ent fnl 2f: str chal and drvn 1f out: led wl ins fnl f: r.o wl* **11/4**[1]

250- **2** ½ **Duster**[200] 6905 3-9-4 **70** GeorgeBaker 12 78
(H Morrison) *broke wl: sn crossed to r on stands' rail and led: rdn wl over 1f out: jnd and edgd lft u.p 1f out: hdd and no ex wl ins fnl f* **6/1**[2]

5-32 **3** 3¾ **Kilt Rock (IRE)**[9] 1619 3-9-4 **70** TomQueally 3 68
(R A Mills) *broke wl and sn crossed rt over to chse ldr towards stands' rail: rdn and unable qck over 1f out: one pce and no threat to ldng pair fnl f* **9/1**

03-0 **4** 1¾ **Imperial Warrior**[16] 1476 3-8-10 **62** TravisBlock 15 55
(H Morrison) *trckd ldrs on stands ' rail swtchd off rail and rdn 2f out: btn ent fnl f: wl hld after* **7/1**[3]

05-1 **5** 1 **Sonny G (IRE)**[30] 1168 3-8-9 **61** AndreaAtzeni 2 51+
(J R Best) *stdd and swtchd sharply rt after s: hld up bhd on stands' rail: pushed along and hdwy over 1f out: nt clr run and switching lft fnl f: kpt on: nvr able to chal* **16/1**

4005 **6** nk **Lou Bear (IRE)**[16] 1476 3-8-7 **59** JimmyQuinn 7 49
(J Akehurst) *hld up in rr: rdn over 2f out: no prog tl kpt on fnl f: nvr gng pce to trble ldrs* **8/1**

350- **7** 2¼ **Yabtree (IRE)**[177] 7326 3-9-4 **70** SteveDrowne 9 54+
(R Charlton) *t.k.h: hld up wl in tch: rdn 2f out: sn struggling: wl btn fnl f* **8/1**

2010 **8** 1 **Premium Charge**[49] 933 3-8-11 **70** MJMurphy(7) 13 51
(C A Dwyer) *hld up in rr: pushed along and hdwy over 1f out: nvr trbld ldrs* **12/1**

521- **9** 2 **Tucker's Law**[186] 7210 3-8-10 **65** JamesMillman(3) 10 40
(B R Millman) *in tch in midfield: rdn 1/2-way: no ch fnl 2f* **14/1**

6-01 **10** nse **Do More Business (IRE)**[22] 1316 3-8-4 **63** RichardRowe(7) 8 38
(P M Phelan) *chsd ldrs tl rdn and edgd lft ent fnl 2f: sn wknd* **25/1**

5-24 **11** ¾ **Giulietta Da Vinci**[10] 1593 3-9-2 **68** DavidProbert 1 41
(S Woodman) *swtchd rt after s: hld up towards rr: rdn and btn ent fnl 2f* **25/1**

04-0 **12** 8 **Arnie Guru**[43] 980 3-8-8 **65** KierenFox(5) 4 17
(M J Attwater) *chsd ldrs on outer: rdn over 2f out: sn struggling: no ch fnl 2f* **66/1**

550- **13** 3¼ **Brave Ghurka**[138] 7824 3-8-13 **65** LiamKeniry 6 8
(S Kirk) *s.i.s: sn swtchd rt: bhd: struggling fr 1/2-way: wl bhd fnl 2f* **50/1**

1m 23.44s (0.14) **Going Correction** +0.05s/f (Good) **13** Ran SP% **117.1**
Speed ratings (Par 99): **101,100,96,94,93 92,90,88,86,86 85,76,72**
Tote Swingers: 1&2 £5.60, 1&3 £5.00, 2&3 £5.10 CSF £17.07 CT £135.95 TOTE £3.40: £1.10, £3.60, £2.50; EX 28.10 Trifecta £166.40 Part won. Pool: £128.24 - 0.43 winning units..
Owner Baron F C Oppenheim **Bred** Baron F Von Oppenheim **Trained** Newmarket, Suffolk

FOCUS
Few got into this 3-y-o handicap but the right horses were involved and the form looks sound.
Imperial Warrior Official explanation: jockey said gelding hung left throughout

1874 TOTEEXACTA FLEXI BETTING H'CAP 5f
3:45 (3:46) (Class 4) (0-85,85) 4-Y-O+ **£5,180** (£1,541; £770; £384) **Stalls** High

Form RPR

5-62 **1** **Rocker**[25] 1266 6-8-7 **74** ShaneKelly 6 80
(G L Moore) *racd in midfield: swtchd off of rail and hdwy over 1f out: rdn to chal 1f out: pushed ahd ins fnl f: kpt on* **3/1**[1]

10-6 **2** ½ **Taurus Twins**[25] 1267 4-8-9 **76** (b) TomQueally 2 80
(R J Price) *broke wl and crossed to ld on stands' rail: rdn over 1f out: drvn and hdd ins fnl f: kpt on towards fin but a hld* **11/2**

2413 **3** 1¾ **Love You Louis**[25] 1267 4-8-8 **75** RichardHughes 3 73
(J R Jenkins) *chsd ldr on stands' rail: plld off of rail and rdn to press ldr over 1f out: keeping on same pce whn short of room ins fnl f: wl hld after* **10/3**[2]

00-0 **4** 1½ **Piscean (USA)**[6] 1691 5-9-3 **84** JimmyQuinn 8 77
(T Keddy) *s.i.s: bhd: swtchd lft and hdwy wl over 1f out: kpt on but nvr gng pce to rch ldrs* **8/1**

20-0 **5** 4½ **Just For Mary**[20] 1407 6-9-3 **84** SebSanders 5 60
(Daniel Mark Loughnane, Ire) *a in last pair: rdn and no prog over 2f out: wl btn fnl f* **8/1**

2113 **6** 1 **Misaro (GER)**[17] 1445 9-8-8 **75** (b) DavidProbert 1 48
(R A Harris) *chsd ldrs: rdn 1/2-way: wknd wl over 1f out* **7/2**[3]

57.79 secs (-0.41) **Going Correction** +0.05s/f (Good) **6** Ran SP% **107.9**
Speed ratings (Par 105): **105,104,101,99,91 90**
Tote Swingers: 1&2 £1.70, 1&3 £6.00, 2&3 £1.10 CSF £17.87 CT £48.44 TOTE £4.30: £2.70, £3.60; EX 20.30 Trifecta £111.00 Pool: £422.23 - 2.81 winning units..
Owner Sir Eric Parker **Bred** Sir Eric Parker **Trained** Lower Beeding, W Sussex

FOCUS
A fair sprint handicap. Straightforward form with the winner to his best.
Misaro(GER) Official explanation: jockey said gelding was unsuited by the good to firm ground

1875 TOTETRIFECTA H'CAP (DIV I) 1m (P)
4:20 (4:20) (Class 5) (0-70,70) 4-Y-O+ **£2,729** (£806; £403) **Stalls** High

Form RPR

1505 **1** **Expensive Problem**[22] 1323 7-9-2 **68** GeorgeBaker 5 77
(R J Smith) *hld up in tch in last trio: hdwy over 2f out: rdn to chse ldng pair jst over 1f out: drvn to ld wl ins fnl f: r.o wl* **10/1**

00-6 **2** 1¼ **Golden Rock (IRE)**[17] 1440 4-9-1 **67** SteveDrowne 10 73
(R Charlton) *dwlt: sn bustled along: chsd ldrs 5f out: drvn to chse ldr wl over 1f out: led ent fnl f: hdd and nt pce of wnr wl ins fnl f* **7/1**[3]

2224 **3** ½ **Spinning Ridge (IRE)**[4] 1762 5-9-0 **66** (b) DavidProbert 12 71+
(R A Harris) *in tch in rr: wd bnd 2f out: str run u.p on outer ent fnl f: wnt 3rd wl ins fnl f: nvr gng pce to rch ldrs* **9/2**[2]

253- **4** nk **Piccolo Mondo**[169] 7452 4-9-4 **70** IanMongan 4 74
(P Winkworth) *w ldr tl led over 4f out: rdn ent fnl 2f: hdd ent fnl f: edgd rt and no ex fnl 150yds* **8/1**

4422 **5** ¾ **War And Peace (IRE)**[8] 1637 6-9-0 **66** RichardHughes 11 69
(P D Evans) *in tch: niggled along 5f out: n.m.r jst over 2f out: drvn to chse ldrs jst ins fnl f: no imp fnl 100yds* **7/2**[1]

5146 **6** ¾ **Millfields Dreams**[1] 1841 11-9-4 **70** (p) SaleemGolam 8 71
(P Leech) *s.i.s: sn dropped in bhd: n.m.r and effrt over 1f out: r.o fnl f: nvr able to chal* **25/1**

1040 **7** ¾ **Stanley Goodspeed**[48] 943 7-8-11 **68** (t) KierenFox(5) 9 67
(J W Hills) *in tch on outer: wd and lost pl bnd 2f out: drvn and edging lft wl over 1f out: styd on same pce fnl f* **10/1**

6460 **8** ¾ **Trafalgar Square**[21] 1346 8-9-4 **70** AlanMunro 1 67
(M J Attwater) *dwlt: in tch in rr: n.m.r on inner bnd 2f out: nvr trbld ldrs* **14/1**

5510 **9** 3¾ **Teen Ager (FR)**[10] 1595 6-8-10 **62** TomMcLaughlin 6 51
(P Burgoyne) *plld hrd: led tl over 4f out: styd w ldr tl rdn and wknd over 1f out* **12/1**

0-60 **10** ½ **Chadwell Spring (IRE)**[17] 1440 4-9-0 **66** JimmyQuinn 3 54
(Miss J Feilden) *in tch: rdn and lost pl over 2f out: no ch fnl f* **25/1**

332- **11** ¾ **Fernando Torres**[128] 7876 4-9-1 **67** (p) DarryllHolland 7 53
(Matthew Salaman) *chsd ldrs: rdn and unable qck over 2f out: wknd and bhd whn nt clr run and swtchd rt ins fnl f* **7/1**[3]

1m 38.2s **Going Correction** +0.075s/f (Slow) **11** Ran SP% **116.7**
Speed ratings (Par 103): **103,101,101,100,100 99,98,97,94,93 92**
Tote Swingers: 1&2 £29.80, 1&3 £9.90, 2&3 £3.60 CSF £77.76 CT £365.06 TOTE £15.80: £5.30, £2.60, £1.10; EX 140.40 TRIFECTA Not won..
Owner F Willson **Bred** T J Cooper **Trained** Epsom, Surrey

FOCUS
A modest handicap. The early pace was very steady indeed, though the time was still 1.20secs quicker than the second division.

1876 LINGFIELDPARK.CO.UK CLASSIFIED STKS 1m 2f (P)
4:55 (4:55) (Class 5) 3-Y-O **£3,070** (£906; £453) **Stalls** Low

Form RPR

022- **1** **Life And Soul (IRE)**[193] 7064 3-9-0 75 PhilipRobinson 6 80
(Mrs A J Perrett) *awkward leaving stalls and s.i.s: hld up in last pair: hdwy to chse ldr over 5f out: rdn to ld wl over 1f out: styd on wl fnl f* **10/3**[3]

542- **2** 1¼ **Opera Gal (IRE)**[207] 6729 3-9-0 72 DavidProbert 4 77
(A M Balding) *chsd ldr tl over 5f out: stl in tch after: rdn ent fnl 2f: chsd wnr ins fnl f: no ex and btn fnl 75yds* **5/2**[2]

363- **3** 2¼ **Another Magic Man (USA)**[189] 7157 3-9-0 74 SteveDrowne 5 72
(J R Best) *hld up in tch: rdn along 3f out: effrt on outer 2f out: styd on one pce after: wnt 3rd nr line* **14/1**

01-4 **4** nse **Gifted Apakay (USA)**[22] 1317 3-9-0 74 TomQueally 1 72
(E A L Dunlop) *chsd ldng pair: rdn and effrt ent fnl 2f: styd on same pce u.p fnl f* **8/1**

22-1 **5** 1¾ **Fonterutoli (IRE)**[28] 1210 3-9-0 74 AndreaAtzeni 2 68
(M Botti) *led tl rdn and hdd 2f out: wknd jst ins fnl f* **11/8**[1]

2m 7.44s (0.84) **Going Correction** +0.075s/f (Slow) **5** Ran SP% **111.5**
Speed ratings (Par 99): **99,98,96,96,94**
CSF £12.16 TOTE £2.80: £1.10, £2.90; EX 11.40 TRIFECTA Not won..
Owner A D Spence **Bred** Kildaragh Stud **Trained** Pulborough, W Sussex

FOCUS
A really interesting classified stakes that may have been won by a useful prospect.

1877 TOTETRIFECTA H'CAP (DIV II) 1m (P)
5:25 (5:26) (Class 5) (0-70,70) 4-Y-O+ **£2,729** (£806; £403) **Stalls** High

Form RPR

21-2 **1** **Night Lily (IRE)**[7] 1653 4-9-0 **66** TonyCulhane 5 74
(P W D'Arcy) *t.k.h: hld up in tch: pushed along to chal ent fnl f: led ins fnl f: drvn towards fin: jst lasted* **9/4**[1]

004- **2** shd **Saturn Way (GR)**[267] 4956 4-9-2 **68** LiamKeniry 11 76+
(P R Chamings) *stdd after s: t.k.h: hld up in tch in rr: effrt on outer and n.m.r over 1f out: squeezed between horses and str run ins fnl f: chsd wnr fnl 75yds: jst failed* **14/1**

0346 **3** 1¼ **Trade Centre**[27] 1238 5-9-1 **67** LiamJones 1 72
(R A Harris) *led: rdn and qcknd ent fnl 2f: hdd ins fnl f: one pce after* **12/1**

5533 **4** hd **Sotik Star (IRE)**[27] 1239 7-8-8 **60** (p) JimmyQuinn 4 64
(K A Morgan) *hld up in tch towards rr: hmpd 5f out: rdn and hdwy towards inner over 1f out: chsd ldrs and drvn ins fnl f: no imp fnl 100yds* **8/1**

1412 **5** nse **Copperwood**[14] 1509 5-9-3 **69** TomQueally 8 73+
(M Blanshard) *t.k.h: hld up towards rr on outer: rdn and hdwy but edging lft ent fnl f: r.o fnl 100yds but nvr able to chal* **9/2**[2]

6332 **6** 1½ **I Confess**[79] 587 5-9-4 **70** (v) PaulDoe 10 71
(Jim Best) *t.k.h: chsd ldr tl 5f out: rdn 3f out: unable qck u.p ent fnl f: eased whn btn fnl 75yds* **5/1**[3]

0-00 **7** 1¼ **Pab Special (IRE)**[8] 1637 7-8-9 **61** FrankieMcDonald 7 59
(B R Johnson) *stdd and dropped in bhd after s: hld up in tch in rr: rdn wl over 1f out: nt clr run and sltly hmpd 1f out: nvr able to chal* **40/1**

300/ **8** 1 **Beat Up**[553] 7105 4-8-13 **65** SaleemGolam 12 61
(G D Blake) *stdd and dropped in bhd after s: hld up in last: rdn 3f out: plugged on fnl f but nvr trbld ldrs* **20/1**

00-0 **9** ¾ **Head Down**[111] 200 4-9-4 **70** GeorgeBaker 3 64
(M R Bosley) *in tch in midfield on inner: rdn and unable qck ent fnl 2f: no ch w ldrs fnl f* **12/1**

050- **10** hd **Buxton**[211] 6614 6-9-1 **67** (t) AndreaAtzeni 2 61
(R Ingram) *chsd ldrs: rdn to chse ldr wl over 1f out: pressing ldr and drvn ent fnl f: wknd qckly fnl 100yds* **12/1**

6000 **11** ½ **State General (IRE)**[8] 1637 4-9-0 **66** CathyGannon 9 58
(Miss J Feilden) *in tch: hdwy on outer to chse ldr 5f out: rdn and lost 2nd wl over 1f out: sn wknd* **25/1**

1m 39.4s (1.20) **Going Correction** +0.075s/f (Slow) **11** Ran SP% **117.5**
Speed ratings (Par 103): **97,96,95,95,95 93,92,91,90,90 90**
Tote Swingers: 1&2 £25.50, 1&3 £9.50, 2&3 £13.60 CSF £36.08 CT £325.36 TOTE £4.30: £2.40, £8.60, £5.60; EX 47.40 Place 6: £20.57 Place 5: £15.99.
Owner K Snell **Bred** Keith Wills **Trained** Newmarket, Suffolk

FOCUS
This looked the stronger of the two divisions, although the time of this was 1.20secs slower than the first division.
I Confess Official explanation: jockey said gelding lost a shoe

T/Plt: £41.90. Pool: £52,179.91 - 907.47 winning units. T/Qpdt: £25.80. Pool: £3,643.94 - 104.26 winning units. SP

[1597]NOTTINGHAM (L-H)

Friday, May 7

OFFICIAL GOING: Good (good to firm in places; 8.4)

All races run on outer track.

Wind: Light half behind Weather: Cloudy with sunny periods

1878 IT'S LADIES' DAY TOMORROW MEDIAN AUCTION MAIDEN STKS 6f 15y

1:25 (1:27) (Class 5) 3-Y-O **£2,590** (£770; £385; £192) **Stalls** Centre

Form				RPR
5	1		**Timeless Stride (IRE)**[23] 1308 3-9-0 0......... Louis-PhilippeBeuzelin[(3)] 7 (Sir Michael Stoute) *cl up: led wl over 2f out: rdn over 1f out: kpt on* **11/10**[1]	73+
00-0	2	*1*	**Bilash**[13] 1511 3-9-3 65......... JerryO'Dwyer 5 (R Hollinshead) *led: pushed along 1/2-way: rdn and hdd wl over 2f out: drvn over 1f out: kpt on same pce fnl f* **28/1**	70
0	3	*1 ¾*	**Excellent Aim**[23] 1308 3-9-3 0......... EddieAhern 11 (Jane Chapple-Hyam) *sn trcking ldrs: effrt over 2df out: rdn along wl over 1f out: no imp fnl f* **10/3**[2]	64
56-	4	*nse*	**Final Turn**[132] 7843 3-9-3 0......... DaneO'Neill 2 (H Candy) *in tch: hdwy to chse ldrs 1/2-way: rdn along 2f out: no imp appr fnl f* **20/1**	64
5	5	*1 ¾*	**Mush Mir (IRE)**[30] 1165 3-9-3 0......... PatCosgrave 14 (J R Boyle) *midfield: pushed along towards outer over 2f out: rdn and kpt on ins fnl f: nrst fin* **40/1**	59
0	6	*¾*	**Vertumnus**[7] 1659 3-9-3 0......... J-PGuillambert 12 (N P Littmoden) *towards rr: hdwy 2f out: rdn and styd on ins fnl f: nrst fin* **100/1**	56
0-40	7	*½*	**Marafong**[15] 1490 3-8-10 75......... AdamBeschizza[(7)] 8 (Miss J Feilden) *midfield: effrt over 2f out: sn rdn and no hdwy* **25/1**	55
0	8	*1*	**Major Eradicator (USA)**[9] 1622 3-9-3 0......... GrahamGibbons 13 (R M H Cowell) *s.i.s and bhd tl sme late hdwy* **16/1**	51+
	9	*hd*	**Twice As Nice** 3-9-3 0......... PatDobbs 6 (R Hannon) *towards rr: hdwy over 2f out: rdn and n.m.r over 1f out: no imp after* **8/1**[3]	51+
0	10	*2 ¾*	**Saigon Kitty (IRE)**[21] 1355 3-8-12 0......... LukeMorris 10 (J R Best) *chsd ldrs: rdn along over 2f out: grad wknd* **14/1**	37
	11	*¾*	**Du Plessis** 3-8-10 0......... DaleSwift[(7)] 9 (B Ellison) *a towards rr* **18/1**	40
0	12	*7*	**Aim'Ees Star**[58] 849 3-8-7 0......... MarkCoumbe[(5)] 3 (John A Harris) *chsd ldrs to 1/2-way: sn wknd* **100/1**	12
	13	*shd*	**Noisy Noverre (IRE)** 3-8-7 0......... MatthewDavies[(5)] 1 (George Baker) *s.i.s: a in rr* **100/1**	12
-	14	*5*	**Battleship Grey** 3-9-3 0......... RobertHavlin 4 (D K Ivory) *in tch: swtchd to r alone on far rail: rdn along over 2f out and sn wknd* **66/1**	—

1m 12.78s (-2.12) **Going Correction** -0.525s/f (Hard) 14 Ran SP% **118.6**

Speed ratings (Par 99): **93,91,89,89,86 85,85,83,83,80 79,69,69,62**

Tote Swingers: 1&2 £16.20, 1&3 £1.30, 2&3 £18.30 CSF £47.87 TOTE £2.00: £1.10, £10.80, £1.40; EX 48.00.

Owner Saeed Suhail **Bred** Diomed Bloodstock Ltd **Trained** Newmarket, Suffolk

FOCUS

The ground had dried out to Good to Firm, Good in places, with a GoingStick reading of 8.4. A modest maiden in which they raced up the middle of the track.

Aim'Ees Star Official explanation: jockey said filly hung left

Battleship Grey Official explanation: jockey said gelding hung left

1879 MORE THAN JUST RACING MEDIAN AUCTION MAIDEN FILLIES' STKS 5f 13y

1:55 (1:56) (Class 5) 2-Y-O **£2,590** (£770; £385; £192) **Stalls** Centre

Form				RPR
0	1		**Inagh River**[13] 1510 2-9-0 0......... PatDobbs 7 (R Hannon) *mde most: rdn clr over 1f out: kpt on ins fnl f: comf* **4/1**[2]	72+
	2	*1 ¼*	**Never Can Stop** 2-9-0 0......... PatCosgrave 10 (J G Portman) *prom on outer: effrt 1/2-way: rdn to chse wnr over 1f out: no imp ins fnl f* **7/2**[1]	68+
	3	*¾*	**Diablo Dancer** 2-9-0 0......... GrahamGibbons 1 (T D Walford) *wnt lft s: sn chsng ldrs on outer: hdwy 1/2-way: rdn over 1f out: kpt on ins fnl f* **9/1**	65
	4	*3*	**Box Of Frogs (IRE)** 2-9-0 0......... JamesDoyle 8 (A J McCabe) *in tch: pushed along and outpcd 1/2-way: rdn wl over 1f out: kpt on ins fnl f: nrst fin* **22/1**	54+
	5	*½*	**Empress Royal** 2-9-0 0......... PhillipMakin 5 (M Dods) *prom: pushed along over 2f out: rdn wl over 1f out and sn wknd* **4/1**[2]	52
	6	*2*	**Blue Ivy** 2-8-11 0......... KellyHarrison[(3)] 6 (C W Fairhurst) *s.i.s and bhd: hdwy 2f out: rdn and hung bdly lft over 1f out: kpt on ins fnl f* **25/1**	45
	7	*1 ¼*	**Liberty Ess (IRE)** 2-9-0 0......... NeilCallan 4 (K A Ryan) *in tch: rdn along over 2f out: sn wknd* **10/1**	41
	8	*nk*	**Allegrissimo (IRE)** 2-9-0 0......... AdamKirby 2 (C G Cox) *a in rr: outpcd fnl 2f* **9/2**[3]	39
	9	*7*	**Jam Maker** 2-9-0 0......... JimCrowley 3 (J R Jenkins) *cl up: rdn along 1/2-way: sn wknd* **16/1**	14

59.98 secs (-1.02) **Going Correction** -0.525s/f (Hard) 9 Ran SP% **113.6**

Speed ratings (Par 90): **87,85,83,79,78 75,73,72,61**

Tote Swingers: 1&2 £5.60, 1&3 £7.50, 2&3 £11.50 CSF £18.07 TOTE £4.10: £1.90, £2.20, £4.20; EX 21.10.

Owner Denis J Barry **Bred** David J Brown, Slatch Farm Stud & J Berry **Trained** East Everleigh, Wilts

FOCUS

Probably just an ordinary fillies' maiden with the race averages helping to set the level. They raced middle to stands' side.

NOTEBOOK

Inagh River ran no sort of race when 2-1 for her debut at Haydock, but she proved a different proposition this time. Although having to be niggled along on leaving the stalls, she was soon showing bright speed and ultimately won with her ears pricked, suggesting she had a bit in hand. Presumably her connections will look for something better now. (op 3-1 tchd 11-4)

Never Can Stop, an £800 half-sister to a dual winner in Japan, was sent off favourite for her debut, having been available at bigger prices in the morning, but her trainer reported beforehand that the filly was going to come "plenty for the run." Racing towards the stands' side, she had to be niggled along from a fair way out to maintain her position close to the pace and simply found the more experienced winner too strong. (op 5-1)

Diablo Dancer, a 3,500gns half-sister to six winners, showed good speed and looks a filly with plenty of ability, but she compromised her chance by wanting to hang left for much of the way.

Box Of Frogs(IRE), not sold at 900gns, lacked the knowhow of some of these but made encouraging late headway. (op 25-1 tchd 20-1)

Empress Royal, a half-sister to a couple of sprint winners, out of a 7f scorer, showed good speed but found disappointingly little. (op 9-2)

Allegrissimo(IRE) was solid in the market for her debut but she never featured. (op 5-1 tchd 11-2)

1880 FINDARACEHORSE.COM THE WEBSITE FOR BUYING RACEHORSES H'CAP 1m 6f 15y

2:25 (2:25) (Class 5) (0-75,75) 3-Y-O **£3,238** (£963; £481; £240) **Stalls** Low

Form				RPR
5212	1		**Captain Cool (IRE)**[11] 1578 3-8-8 **62**......... PatDobbs 9 (R Hannon) *hld up in rr: tk clsr order over 5f out: chsd ldrs 3f out: rdn to chal ent fnl f: styd on to ld fnl 50yds* **7/1**	66
63-2	2	*½*	**Dream Spinner**[18] 1433 3-9-1 **69**......... EddieAhern 5 (J L Dunlop) *trckd ldrs: hdwy over 4f out: effrt 2f out and sn rdn: styd on to ld jst ins fnl f: sn drvn: hdd and no ex fnl 50yds* **9/4**[1]	72+
1113	3	*1 ¼*	**Desert Recluse (IRE)**[23] 1299 3-9-7 **75**......... NeilCallan 4 (Pat Eddery) *cl up: led 3f out: rdn 2f out: drvn over 1f out: hdd jst ins fnl f and kpt on same pce* **9/2**[3]	76
3-44	4	*1 ¼*	**Dr Finley (IRE)**[29] 1182 3-8-11 **72**......... IanBurns[(7)] 3 (M L W Bell) *chsd ldrs: pushed along and lost pl over 5f out: rdn and hdwy over 2f out: drvn to chse ldrs over 1f out: kpt on same pce* **12/1**	72
30-2	5	*3 ½*	**Iron Condor**[18] 1422 3-9-3 **71**......... LukeMorris 2 (J M P Eustace) *led: rdn along and hdd 3f out: drvn 2f out and ev ch tl wknd appr fnl f* **4/1**[2]	66
0052	6	*12*	**Rosewood Lad**[31] 1145 3-7-11 **58** oh7 ow2......... RyanPowell[(7)] 1 (J S Moore) *trckd ldrs on inner: rdn along over 4f out: wknd 3f out* **33/1**	36
-044	7	*½*	**Nurai**[20] 1394 3-7-11 **56** oh1......... DeclanCannon[(5)] 7 (P W D'Arcy) *hld up in rr: hdwy 1/2-way: chsd ldrs 4f out: rdn along 3f out: drvn over 2f out and sn wknd* **8/1**	33
000-	8	*46*	**Lis Pendens**[174] 7400 3-8-5 **59**......... RichardMullen 8 (W R Muir) *chsd ldrs: hdwy and cl up over 4f out: rdn along over 3f out and wknd qckly* **8/1**	—

3m 1.85s (-5.45) **Going Correction** -0.30s/f (Firm) 8 Ran SP% **114.3**

Speed ratings (Par 99): **103,102,102,101,99 92,92,65**

Tote Swingers: 1&2 £5.10, 1&3 £3.30, 2&3 £2.80 CSF £23.15 CT £79.13 TOTE £5.50: £2.20, £1.10, £1.20; EX 15.50.

Owner Mrs John Lee **Bred** Jan Revs **Trained** East Everleigh, Wilts

FOCUS

A modest staying handicap run at an ordinary pace.

Nurai Official explanation: jockey said filly lost action in home straight

Lis Pendens Official explanation: trainer said gelding was unsuited by the good to firm (good in places) ground

1881 CONCEPT CABINS 10TH ANNIVERSARY MAIDEN FILLIES' STKS (DIV I) 1m 75y

2:55 (2:56) (Class 5) 3-Y-O **£2,266** (£674; £337; £168) **Stalls** Centre

Form				RPR
-	1		**Marie De Guise (IRE)** 3-9-0 0......... RichardMullen 8 (Sir Michael Stoute) *hld up: stdy hdwy over 3f out: chsd ldrs 2f out: rdn to chse ldr ent fnl f: styd on wl to ld on line* **9/2**[2]	82+
0-2	2	*shd*	**Copper Penny**[18] 1431 3-9-0 0......... ChrisCatlin 10 (D R Lanigan) *t.k.h: trckd ldrs: hdwy over 3f out: led over 2f out: rdn clr and edgd lft ent fnl f: drvn fnl 50yds: hdd on line* **7/2**[1]	79
	3	*1 ¾*	**Viewing** 3-9-0 0......... RobertHavlin 9 (J H M Gosden) *dwlt and towards rr: hdwy wl over 2f out: styd on ins fnl f: nrst fin* **13/2**	75+
	4	*1 ¾*	**Akinoshirabe (JPN)** 3-9-0 0......... J-PGuillambert 7 (L M Cumani) *t.k.h: cl up: rdn to ld briefly 3f out: hdd and drvn over 2f out: grad wknd appr fnl f* **18/1**	71+
5-	5	*¾*	**Al Jaadi**[213] 6567 3-9-0 0......... DaneO'Neill 12 (W Jarvis) *hld up in midfield: hdwy on outer 3f out: rdn to chse wnr wl over 1f out: drvn appr fnl f and sn one pce* **5/1**[3]	69
00-	6	*4*	**Lily Rio (IRE)**[207] 6729 3-9-0 0......... JimCrowley 5 (W R Muir) *cl up on inner: led over 5f out: rdn and hdd 3f out: drvn over 2f out and sn wknd* **50/1**	59?
3-	7	*nk*	**Infanta (IRE)**[191] 7114 3-8-11 0......... AhmedAjtebi[(3)] 6 (Mahmood Al Zarooni) *s.i.s and a in rr* **7/2**[1]	58
	8	*1 ¼*	**Blue Zealot (IRE)** 3-9-0 0......... EddieAhern 1 (M L W Bell) *a towards rr* **9/1**	55
	9	*7*	**Shesells Seashells** 3-9-0 0......... JackMitchell 4 (C F Wall) *s.i.s: a in rr* **22/1**	39
0-0	10	*3*	**Princess Seren**[18] 1431 3-9-0 0......... KirstyMilczarek 11 (B R Millman) *plld hrd: led: hdd over 5f out: rdn along 4f out and sn wknd* **66/1**	31

1m 46.72s (1.12) **Going Correction** -0.30s/f (Firm) 10 Ran SP% **115.7**

Speed ratings (Par 96): **82,81,80,78,77 73,73,72,65,62**

Tote Swingers: 1&2 £6.60, 1&3 £4.20, 2&3 £9.80 CSF £20.20 TOTE £6.40: £2.20, £1.20, £1.50; EX 21.30.

Owner Ballymacoll Stud **Bred** Ballymacoll Stud Farm Ltd **Trained** Newmarket, Suffolk

FOCUS

An interesting fillies' maiden, with plenty of powerful connections represented, and the race should produce a few winners. However, the pace was steady and the time was 0.75 seconds slower than the second division.

1882 CONCEPT CABINS 10TH ANNIVERSARY MAIDEN FILLIES' STKS (DIV II) 1m 75y

3:30 (3:31) (Class 5) 3-Y-O **£2,266** (£674; £337; £168) **Stalls** Centre

Form				RPR
03-	1		**Miss Mittagong (USA)**[188] 7182 3-9-0 0......... JimCrowley 2 (R M Beckett) *hld up in rr: hdwy over 3f out: swtchd outside and effrt 2f out: rdn and qcknd to ld appr fnl f: sn edgd lft and kpt on wl* **7/2**[2]	85+
44-	2	*1 ½*	**Woodford Belle (USA)**[206] 6762 3-9-0 0......... DaneO'Neill 9 (B J Meehan) *chsd ldrs: hdwy 4f out: rdn to chal over 2f out: sn ev ch: drvn ent fnl f and sn edgd lft: kpt on same pce* **20/1**	78
3	3	*¾*	**Titivation**[21] 1355 3-9-0 0......... EddieAhern 3 (M L W Bell) *hld up towards rr: hdwy towards inner whn nt clr run 2f out: chsd ldrs and n.m.r over 1f out: swtchd rt ins fnl f and kpt on wl: nrst fin* **6/4**[1]	76+
0-	4	*nk*	**Best Intent**[188] 7182 3-9-0 0......... NeilCallan 6 (M A Jarvis) *towards rr: hdwy to trck ldrs 1/2-way: pushed along 3f out: outpcd wl over 1f out: styd on under hand riding ins fnl f: nrst fin* **14/1**	75
30	5	*shd*	**Law Of The Range**[7] 1654 3-9-0 0......... KirstyMilczarek 5 (M Botti) *trckd ldrs: hdwy 4f out: chal over 2f out: sn rdn and ev ch tl drvn and one pce ent fnl f* **20/1**	75

0-0 **6** 2¼ **That's My Style**[22] 1329 3-9-0 0 .... RobertHavlin 11 70
(J H M Gosden) *t.k.h: cl up: led 3f out: rdn over 2f out: hdd appr fnl f: sn wknd* **12/1**

7 ¾ **Free As A Lark** 3-9-0 0 .... JackMitchell 1 68
(C F Wall) *s.i.s and in rr tl styd on fnl 2f* **100/1**

3 **8** 1¼ **Derecho**[9] 1621 3-9-0 0 .... AdamKirby 7 65
(C G Cox) *led: rdn along and hdd 3f out: drvn over 2f out and grad wknd* **11/1**

-3 **9** 4 **Heaven Forbid**[32] 1127 3-9-0 0 .... PatCosgrave 10 55
(J R Fanshawe) *in rr: hdwy on outer to chse ldrs 3f out: rdn along over 2f out: sn wknd* **9/2**[3]

0 **10** 8 **Floating Angel (USA)**[21] 1355 3-9-0 0 .... LukeMorris 4 36
(J R Best) *prom: rdn along on inner over 3f out: sn wknd* **100/1**

1m 45.97s (0.37) **Going Correction** -0.30s/f (Firm) 10 Ran SP% **114.6**
Speed ratings (Par 96): **86,84,83,83,83 81,80,79,75,67**
Tote Swingers: 1&2 £7.70, 1&3 £2.40, 2&3 £7.40 CSF £72.78 TOTE £3.80: £1.80, £3.50, £1.20; EX 77.10.
Owner R A Pegum **Bred** St George Farm LLC **Trained** Whitsbury, Hants

FOCUS
This looked a good fillies' maiden and the time was 0.75 seconds quicker than the steadily run first division.

1883 RACING UK H'CAP 1m 2f 50y

4:10 (4:10) (Class 5) (0-75,74) 4-Y-0+ **£3,238** (£963; £481; £240) **Stalls** Low

Form RPR

44- **1** **Bourne**[211] 6613 4-9-2 72 .... J-PGuillambert 1 82+
(L M Cumani) *dwlt: hld up towards rr: hdwy on inner into midfield 1/2-way: pushed along and n.m.r over 3f out: swtchd rt and gd hdwy 2f out: rdn to chse ldrs over 1f out: styd on strly ins fnl f: led nr fin* **11/2**[2]

4-45 **2** hd **Oriental Cavalier**[13] 1512 4-9-0 70 ....(v) GrahamGibbons 3 80
(R Hollinshead) *trckd ldrs: hdwy over 4f out: cl up 3f out: led 2f out: rdn over 1f out: drvn and edgd lft ins fnl f: hdd and no ex nr fin* **8/1**

3405 **3** 1 **Hawaana (IRE)**[39] 1051 5-8-12 71 .... KellyHarrison(3) 9 79
(Miss Gay Kelleway) *dwlt: hld up and bhd: hdwy over 2f out: swtchd rt and rdn wl over 1f out: styd on ins fnl f: nrst fin* **12/1**

43-0 **4** 1 **North Cape (USA)**[20] 1388 4-9-4 74 .... DaneO'Neill 10 80
(H Candy) *trckd ldrs: hdwy to ld 3f out: rdn 2f out and sn hdd: drvn and one pce ent fnl f* **6/1**[3]

420- **5** 2½ **Chantilly Pearl (USA)**[163] 7512 4-8-9 65 .... PaulMulrennan 5 66
(J G Given) *towards rr: hdwy over 3f out: swtchd ins 2f out and sn rdn: styd on ins fnl f: nrst fin* **25/1**

00-6 **6** ½ **Hurlingham**[20] 1398 6-9-0 70 .... NeilCallan 6 70
(M W Easterby) *trckd ldrs: hdwy 4f out: rdn along 2f out: drvn over 1f out and sn one pce* **9/2**[1]

-022 **7** 5 **Diamond Twister (USA)**[8] 1645 4-8-9 65 ....(t) LukeMorris 11 56
(J R Best) *chsd ldrs: rdn along 3f out: drvn over 2f out and grad wknd* **12/1**

0-02 **8** 1¾ **Film Festival (USA)**[11] 1574 7-8-9 65 .... ChrisCatlin 15 53
(B Ellison) *towards rr: hdwy over 4f out: rdn along 3f out: no hdwy fnl 2f* **10/1**

040- **9** 2¼ **Uncle Brit**[239] 5806 4-8-9 65 .... RobertHavlin 7 48
(J M Jefferson) *t.k.h: rdn along 4f out: n.d* **40/1**

2222 **10** 3 **West Emirates (USA)**[21] 1346 4-9-3 73 .... AdamKirby 4 51
(C G Cox) *chsd ldr: rdn along 4f out: wknd 3f out* **15/2**

105- **11** ¾ **Mons Calpe (IRE)**[316] 3321 4-9-2 72 .... PatDobbs 14 48
(P F I Cole) *towards rr: hdwy into midfield 1/2-way: in tch 4f out: sn rdn and wknd* **18/1**

41-0 **12** 1 **Calahonda**[25] 1265 4-9-3 73 .... EddieAhern 8 47
(P W D'Arcy) *a towards rr* **16/1**

451- **13** hd **Dragon Slayer (IRE)**[191] 7127 8-8-8 69 .... MarkCoumbe(5) 12 43
(John A Harris) *v s.i.s: a bhd* **25/1**

2040 **14** 41 **Whodunit (UAE)**[21] 1346 6-8-6 65 ....(b) WilliamCarson(3) 13 —
(P W Hiatt) *led: rdn along 4f out: hdd 3f out and sn wknd* **28/1**

2m 9.83s (-1.87) **Going Correction** -0.30s/f (Firm) 14 Ran SP% **119.9**
Speed ratings (Par 103): **95,94,94,93,91 90,86,85,83,81 80,79,79,46**
Tote Swingers: 1&2 £8.30, 1&3 £12.90, 2&3 £24.30 CSF £46.88 CT £515.34 TOTE £6.20: £2.30, £2.60, £4.30; EX 57.90.
Owner Aston House Stud **Bred** Aston House Stud **Trained** Newmarket, Suffolk

FOCUS
An ordinary handicap. The winner is capable of better.
Mons Calpe(IRE) Official explanation: jockey said gelding hung left in home straight

1884 COME TO "LADIES' NIGHT" 3RD JULY APPRENTICE H'CAP (DIV I) 6f 15y

4:45 (4:48) (Class 6) (0-60,60) 4-Y-0+ **£1,706** (£503; £252) **Stalls** Centre

Form RPR

050- **1** **Secret City (IRE)**[199] 6926 4-8-10 56 ....(b) MatthewLawson(5) 6 67
(R Bastiman) *a.p: effrt to chal over 2f out: sn carried rt: rdn whn sltly hmpd ent fnl f: sn led and drvn out* **20/1**

2604 **2** 1½ **Divertimenti (IRE)**[27] 1236 6-8-11 52 ....(b) AshleyMorgan 4 58
(S R Bowring) *led: rdn over 2f out: rdn and edgd rt over 1f out: drvn and hung rt ent fnl f: sn hdd and kpt on same pce* **12/1**

1235 **3** hd **Punching**[24] 1276 6-9-0 60 .... DaleSwift(5) 13 65
(C R Dore) *chsd ldrs: gd hdwy 2f out: effrt whn nt clr run and swtchd lft jst ins fnl f: sn rdn and styd on wl towards fin* **5/2**[1]

0-00 **4** ¾ **Fortezza**[85] 499 4-8-10 51 .... DeclanCannon 14 54+
(A J McCabe) *hmpd s and bhd: hdwy over 2f out: rdn and styng on whn n.m.r jst ins fnl f: kpt on wl towards fin* **12/1**

5235 **5** nk **Thoughtsofstardom**[8] 1638 7-8-7 55 .... LeonnaMayor(7) 2 57
(P S McEntee) *prom: hdwy to chal over 2f out and ev ch tl rdn over 1f out and kpt on same pce ins fnl f* **14/1**

4-04 **6** 2¼ **The History Man (IRE)**[10] 1598 7-8-13 57 ....(b) DavidKenny(3) 9 52
(B D Leavy) *chsd ldrs: rdn along whn swtchd lft wl over 1f out: drvn ins fnl f and sn one pce* **7/1**[3]

0-03 **7** ¾ **Bahama Baileys**[17] 1443 5-8-5 49 oh1 ow3 .... AmyScott(3) 11 41+
(C A Dwyer) *towards rr: hdwy on wd outside wl over 1f out: sn rdn and kpt on ins fnl f: nt rch ldrs* **10/1**

000 **8** 2 **Brazilian Brush (IRE)**[27] 1236 5-8-4 48 ....(bt) RyanClark(3) 5 34
(J M Bradley) *chsd ldrs: rdn along and n.m.r wl over 1f out: kpt on same pce* **28/1**

0-00 **9** hd **Kingsmaite**[27] 1239 9-8-0 46 ....(b) RyanPowell(5) 15 31
(S R Bowring) *wnt lft s: a towards rr* **14/1**

265- **10** ½ **Cheap Street**[245] 5634 6-9-1 56 .... MatthewDavies 17 40
(J G Portman) *nvr nr ldrs* **11/2**[2]

150- **11** 2 **Bermondsey Bob (IRE)**[207] 6739 4-8-9 50 .... SimonPearce 16 27
(J L Spearing) *nvr bttr than midfield* **8/1**

560 **12** 1½ **Albero Di Giuda (IRE)**[13] 1534 5-8-13 54 ....(t) AmyBaker 3 27
(F Sheridan) *prom: rdn along over 2f out: wknd over 1f out* **25/1**

0-00 **13** 4½ **Boundless Applause**[95] 369 4-8-8 49 ....(b[1]) JamesSullivan 1 7
(I A Wood) *a towards rr* **40/1**

-000 **14** 3¾ **Red Cell (IRE)**[11] 1569 4-8-1 47 ....(b) AdamBeschizza(5) 7 —
(I W McInnes) *wnt rt s: a in rr* **100/1**

0500 **15** 7 **Jessica Wigmo**[44] 976 7-8-3 47 oh1 ow1 .... TobyAtkinson(3) 8 —
(A W Carroll) *hmpd s: a in rr* **28/1**

0060 **16** ¾ **Place The Duchess**[60] 829 4-8-2 46 oh1 ....(tp) CharlesEddery(3) 10 —
(A J Lidderdale) *a in rr* **40/1**

1m 12.29s (-2.61) **Going Correction** -0.525s/f (Hard) 16 Ran SP% **126.7**
Speed ratings (Par 101): **96,94,93,92,92 89,88,85,85,84 82,80,74,69,59 58**
Tote Swingers: 1&2 £43.50, 1&3 £16.50, 2&3 £7.40 CSF £239.73 CT £854.97 TOTE £30.60: £4.90, £2.40, £1.10, £3.90; EX 323.60.
Owner Ms M Austerfield **Bred** Miss Karen Theobald **Trained** Cowthorpe, N Yorks

FOCUS
A moderate sprint handicap run in a time 0.78 seconds slower than the second division. They raced middle to stands' side.
Place The Duchess Official explanation: trainer said filly was unsuited by the good to firm (good in places) ground

1885 COME TO "LADIES' NIGHT" 3RD JULY APPRENTICE H'CAP (DIV II) 6f 15y

5:15 (5:15) (Class 6) (0-60,58) 4-Y-0+ **£1,706** (£503; £252) **Stalls** Centre

Form RPR

2145 **1** **Fuzzy Cat**[5] 1723 4-9-2 55 .... DeanHeslop 14 68
(T D Barron) *cl up towards stands' rail: effrt 2f out: rdn over 1f out: led jst ins fnl f* **5/1**[2]

55-0 **2** 1 **Two Turtle Doves (IRE)**[13] 1534 4-8-10 56 .... JosephYoung(7) 16 66
(M Mullineaux) *racd towards stands' rail: led: rdn along over 1f out: hdd jst ins fnl f: sn edgd lft and kpt on wl* **25/1**

0662 **3** 3½ **King's Sabre**[3] 1812 4-8-5 47 ....(e) CharlesEddery(3) 8 46
(R C Guest) *dwlt and towards rr: hdwy 2f out: swtchd rt and rdn over 1f out: kpt on ins fnl f: nrst fin* **6/1**[3]

600- **4** 1 **Westport**[164] 7499 7-8-6 50 .... MatthewLawson(5) 2 46
(R Bastiman) *in tch: hdwy on wd outside over 2f out: rdn to chse ldng pair over 1f out: drvn and no imp ins fnl f* **28/1**

0-62 **5** 1¾ **Miss Daawe**[11] 1569 6-8-13 57 .... DaleSwift(5) 12 47
(B Ellison) *chsd ldrs: effrt and ev ch over 2f out: sn rdn and one pce fr wl over 1f out* **5/2**[1]

1235 **6** 2¾ **Bold Diva**[23] 1304 5-8-9 51 ....(v) TobyAtkinson(3) 3 32
(A W Carroll) *towards rr: hdwy 2f out: rdn and kpt on ins fnl f: nt rch ldrs* **14/1**

0-45 **7** 1½ **Sultans Way (IRE)**[8] 1633 4-8-13 55 ....(v[1]) DuilioDaSilva(3) 11 32
(P F I Cole) *prom: rdn along 2f out: edgd lft over 1f out and kpt on same pce* **13/2**

0-00 **8** ¾ **City For Conquest (IRE)**[10] 1598 7-8-6 45 ....(b) AmyBaker 6 19
(John A Harris) *towards rr: rdn along and hdwy wl over 1f out: kpt on ins fnl f: nvr a factor* **40/1**

633- **9** 1¼ **Elkhorn**[199] 6926 8-8-13 52 ....(v) MatthewDavies 10 22
(Julie Camacho) *towards rr: rdn along 2f out: no hdwy* **10/1**

0150 **10** ½ **Muktasb (USA)**[13] 1534 9-8-3 47 ....(v) SeanPalmer(5) 9 16
(D Shaw) *dwlt: a towards rr* **25/1**

0-03 **11** 1 **Soto**[16] 1470 7-9-5 58 .... JamesSullivan 13 23
(M W Easterby) *a towards rr* **12/1**

356- **12** 3¼ **Port Ronan (USA)**[230] 6101 4-8-6 45 ....(p) SimonPearce 4 —
(J S Wainwright) *racd towards centre: chsd ldrs: rdn along over 2f out and sn wknd* **50/1**

0456 **13** hd **Shannon Golden**[27] 1235 4-8-6 45 .... AshleyMorgan 17 —
(S R Bowring) *wnt rt s: a in rr* **16/1**

4500 **14** 5 **Mister Incredible**[10] 1598 7-8-3 45 ....(b) RyanClark(3) 7 —
(J M Bradley) *cl up: rdn along 1/2-way: sn wknd* **50/1**

6500 **15** 7 **Bertbrand**[11] 1569 5-8-4 48 ....(v) AdamBeschizza(5) 1 —
(I W McInnes) *racd centre and cl up: rdn along 1/2-way: sn wknd* **66/1**

1m 11.51s (-3.39) **Going Correction** -0.525s/f (Hard) 15 Ran SP% **121.2**
Speed ratings (Par 101): **101,99,95,93,91 87,85,84,83,82 81,76,76,69,60**
Tote Swingers: 1&2 £26.00, 1&3 £6.00, 2&3 £24.80 CSF £132.07 TOTE £4.60: £1.10, £4.40, £3.30; EX 115.80 Place 6: £17.19 Place 5: £13.28.
Owner Richard Barnes, Colin Aitken **Bred** Baroness Bloodstock **Trained** Maunby, N Yorks

FOCUS
The time was 0.78 seconds quicker than the first division. The main action was around centre field.
Shannon Golden Official explanation: trainer said gelding lost a shoe
T/Plt: £11.00. Pool: £41,616.39 - 2,753.95 winning units. T/Qpdt: £7.50. Pool: £2,764.14 - 271.08 winning units. JR

1523 RIPON (R-H)

Friday, May 7

OFFICIAL GOING: Good to firm (good in places; 9.0)
Rail on bend from from back straight moved out 7yards adding 12yards to distances on round course.
Wind: Moderate 1/2 against Weather: Overcast, breezy and cold

1886 ISIS MAIDEN AUCTION STKS 5f

5:55 (5:56) (Class 5) 2-Y-0 **£2,914** (£867; £433; £216) **Stalls** Low

Form RPR

4 **1** **Puddle Duck**[8] 1646 2-8-12 0 .... PhillipMakin 7 71+
(K A Ryan) *w ldrs: rdn: hung lft and led 1f out: drvn out* **3/1**[1]

00 **2** 1¼ **Reel Amber**[13] 1527 2-8-6 0 ....(b[1]) DuranFentiman 6 60
(T D Easterby) *led after 1f: crowded and hdd 1f out: no ex* **50/1**

63 **3** 4½ **Johnny Hancocks (IRE)**[8] 1632 2-8-6 0 ....(v[1]) PaulPickard(5) 3 49
(P D Evans) *led 1f: chsd ldrs: rdn and hung lft 2f out: wknd fnl 100yds* **4/1**[2]

4 1¾ **Dark Dune (IRE)** 2-9-1 0 .... DavidNolan 4 47
(T D Easterby) *dwlt: sn chsng ldrs: sn pushed along: wknd fnl 150yds* **7/1**[3]

5 2½ **Bradbury (IRE)** 2-8-12 0 .... RobertWinston 2 38+
(J D Bethell) *s.s: detached in last: sme hdwy 2f out: hung lft and wknd fnl f: eased nr fin* **14/1**

62.78 secs (2.08) **Going Correction** +0.225s/f (Good) 5 Ran SP% **66.1**
Speed ratings (Par 93): **92,90,82,80,76**
CSF £31.65 TOTE £2.70: £1.60, £8.70; EX 38.60.
Owner Mrs S J Barker **Bred** Cecil And Miss Alison Wiggins **Trained** Hambleton, N Yorks

FOCUS
Rail on bend from back straight moved out 7yds adding 12yds to distances on Round course. A modest maiden weakened by the removal of the favourite Saltergate, who was withdrawn after trying to break out from under the stalls (5/4F, deduct 40p in the £ under R4). A fair effort from the winner with the third the best guide.

NOTEBOOK
Puddle Duck perhaps wasn't left with much to beat with the favourite out of the way and though he did all that was required, he wasn't overly impressive bearing in mind that the runner-up had shown little in two previous outings. He'll struggle to follow up in novice company, and his future looks in modest nurseries. (op 9-4 tchd 7-2)
Reel Amber was clearly lit up by the blinkers and though always looking likely to be reeled in by the winner from halfway, kept on well enough to beat the rest convincingly. She appeals more as one to win a claimer or seller than a maiden, always assuming the headgear works as well next time.
Johnny Hancocks(IRE) didn't find any improvement for the headgear, looking third best from some way out His yard aren't averse to dropping their youngster quickly in grade, and sellers/claimers look more his level. (tchd 7-2)
Dark Dune(IRE) hails from a yard in great form but was weak in the market and never really threatened. He has a bit more scope than these and should improve, but his Listed entry later in the year already looks a tad optimistic. (op 10-1 tchd 6-1)
Bradbury(IRE), from a yard whose newcomers are seldom wound up, was green in the preliminaries and even more so when the race was under way. He never threatened but looked to be getting the hang of things late and ought to do better next time. Official explanation: jockey said colt ran green and hung left (op 20-1)

1887 HARROGATE AUDI Q POWER (S) STKS — 1m 1f 170y
6:25 (6:26) (Class 6) 3-4-Y-O — £2,590 (£770; £385; £192) Stalls High

Form — RPR
55-3 **1** **So Bazaar (IRE)**[28] 1201 3-8-9 61 ... PJMcDonald 6 — 61
(G A Swinbank) *mid-div: effrt over 3f out: chal over 1f out: edgd rt: kpt on to ld nr fin* **4/1**[1]
0-35 **2** *hd* **Tropical Bachelor (IRE)**[3] 1801 4-9-5 56 ... JohnFahy(5) 2 — 62
(T J Pitt) *mid-div: hdwy 4f out: sn chsng ldrs: led appr fnl f: edgd lft: hdd nr fin* **11/2**[3]
0525 **3** *3 ¾* **Blues Forever (IRE)**[65] 775 3-8-9 67 ... DavidAllan 12 — 53
(P D Evans) *chsd ldrs: effrt 4f out: styng on same pce whn n.m.r and swtchd rt jst ins fnl f* **5/1**[2]
00-4 **4** *2* **Shercon (IRE)**[15] 1495 3-8-9 44 ... SilvestreDeSousa 9 — 49
(N Tinkler) *prom: drvn over 4f out: one pce fnl 2f* **9/1**
43-0 **5** *¾* **Dean Iarracht (IRE)**[33] 1103 4-9-10 54 ...(p) RobertWinston 10 — 48
(Miss Tracy Waggott) *trckd ldrs: chal over 3f out: wknd fnl 100yds* **8/1**
22-0 **6** *½* **Musigny (USA)**[32] 1114 4-9-3 59 ... LeeTopliss(7) 5 — 47
(Miss S E Hall) *in rr: hdwy and hung rt over 2f out: kpt on: nvr nr ldrs* **20/1**
40-0 **7** *2 ¼* **Ask Dan (IRE)**[24] 1270 4-9-10 54 ...(p) PhillipMakin 1 — 43
(M Dods) *swtchd rt after s: led: hdd appr fnl f: sn wknd* **10/1**
60-4 **8** *¾* **Moggy (IRE)**[13] 1526 4-9-5 44 ...(p) DanielTudhope 13 — 36
(G A Harker) *s.i.s: reminders after s: hdwy on ins 3f out: wknd jst ins fnl f: eased nr fin* **20/1**
0-50 **9** *½* **Meml**[71] 705 4-9-2 44 ...(b[1]) AshleyHamblett(3) 3 — 35
(J D Bethell) *s.i.s: drvn over 3f out: nvr a factor* **22/1**
000- **10** *8* **Gadobout Dancer**[219] 6389 3-8-1 31 ... KellyHarrison(3) 7 — 17
(D Carroll) *t.k.h: trckd ldr: chal over 3f out: edgd rt and wknd over 1f out: eased nr fin* **80/1**
5050 **11** *2* **Penderyn**[20] 1380 3-7-13 45 ... PaulPickard(5) 11 — 13
(C Smith) *trckd ldr: t.k.h: lost pl over 1f out: eased nr fin* **40/1**
00 **12** *41* **Egorr Redfeer**[73] 670 3-8-9 0 ... DuranFentiman 8 — —
(P T Midgley) *s.i.s: in rr: drvn over 4f out: sn lost tch: t.o 2f out: virtually p.u* **66/1**

2m 6.32s (0.92) **Going Correction** 0.0s/f (Good)
WFA 3 from 4yo 15lb — 12 Ran SP% **101.3**
Speed ratings (Par 101): **96,95,92,91,90 90,88,87,87,81 79,46**
toteswingers: 1&2 £4.10, 1&3 £2.70, 2&3 £5.50 CSF £16.74 TOTE £4.00: £2.40, £2.40, £1.20; EX 23.40.There was no bid for the winner.
Owner Chris Tremewan **Bred** Mrs Virginia Moeran And Mount Coote Stud **Trained** Melsonby, N Yorks

FOCUS
A weak seller in which the early leaders seemed to set things up for those ridden with a bit more patience. Original second favourite Dr Mathias was withdrawn on veterinary advice at the start (5/1, deduct 15p in the £ under R4).
Egorr Redfeer Official explanation: jockey said gelding lost its action

1888 SIS PICTURE SERVICES H'CAP — 6f
6:55 (6:55) (Class 4) (0-85,83) 4-Y-O+ — £5,504 (£1,637; £818; £408) Stalls Low

Form — RPR
0-42 **1** **Discanti (IRE)**[6] 1710 5-8-11 76 ...(t) DavidAllan 8 — 87
(T D Easterby) *hld up: gd hdwy on outside 2f out: qckned to ld appr fnl f: edgd lft: readily* **5/2**[1]
00-0 **2** *3 ¼* **Pearly Wey**[22] 1332 7-9-1 80 ... DanielTudhope 3 — 81
(I W McInnes) *s.i.s: in rr: swtchd outside over 1f out: styd on to take 2nd jst ins fnl f:* **10/1**
3232 **3** *nk* **Brierty (IRE)**[6] 1688 4-8-12 77 ... DavidNolan 1 — 77+
(D Carroll) *rr-div: effrt and nt clr run over 2f out: n.m.r over 1f out: styd on fnl f* **3/1**[2]
65-5 **4** *1* **Legal Eagle (IRE)**[17] 1458 5-8-11 76 ... SilvestreDeSousa 2 — 72
(Paul Green) *rrd s: sn w ldrs: led over 2f out: hdd appr fnl f: kpt on same pce* **4/1**[3]
0-00 **5** *1 ½* **Coleorton Choice**[13] 1516 4-9-4 83 ...(p) RobertWinston 6 — 75
(R Hollinshead) *chsd ldrs: wknd fnl 75yds* **14/1**
0-00 **6** *1 ½* **Haajes**[22] 1332 6-9-4 83 ...(t) PJMcDonald 4 — 70
(P T Midgley) *chsd ldrs: n.m.r over 1f out: fdd jst ins fnl f* **11/1**
140- **7** *nk* **Shotley Mac**[286] 4310 6-9-4 83 ...(b) PhillipMakin 7 — 69
(N Bycroft) *w ldrs: wknd fnl f* **18/1**
0-00 **8** *15* **Van Bossed (CAN)**[6] 1710 5-8-10 75 ...(v) AdrianNicholls 5 — 13
(D Nicholls) *led: swtchd rt to r stands' side rail over 4f out: hdd over 2f out: wkng whn hmpd over 1f out: hung rt jst ins fnl f: sn eased and bhd* **11/1**

1m 13.47s (0.47) **Going Correction** +0.225s/f (Good) — 8 Ran SP% **111.3**
Speed ratings (Par 105): **105,100,100,98,96 94,94,74**
toteswingers: 1&2 £6.40, 1&3 £3.10, 2&3 £6.90 CSF £26.58 CT £74.61 TOTE £2.50: £1.10, £3.90, £1.20; EX 26.10.
Owner The Lapin Blanc Racing Partnership **Bred** Glending Bloodstock **Trained** Great Habton, N Yorks

FOCUS
A fair sprint run at a good pace. The winner and third came here in good form and the second has dropped to a decent mark, so this looks form to be positive about.
Haajes Official explanation: jockey said gelding was denied a clear run

1889 SIS OB SERVICES H'CAP — 1m 1f 170y
7:30 (7:30) (Class 3) (0-90,89) 4-Y-O+ — £9,066 (£2,697; £1,348; £673) Stalls High

Form — RPR
521- **1** **Oneofapear (IRE)**[228] 6158 4-8-11 82 ... PJMcDonald 5 — 92
(G A Swinbank) *hld up in mid-div: effrt over 4f out: styd on to ld appr fnl f: jst hld on* **9/1**
-144 **2** *shd* **Rosbay (IRE)**[13] 1512 6-8-5 76 ... DuranFentiman 3 — 86
(T D Easterby) *in rr: drvn over 4f out: n.m.r over 1f out: wnt 2nd 150yds out: styd on wl: jst failed* **10/1**
60-2 **3** *2 ¼* **Granston (IRE)**[20] 1378 9-9-0 85 ... RobertWinston 6 — 91
(J D Bethell) *chsd ldrs: wnt 2nd over 3f out: led over 1f out: sn hdd: kpt on same pce* **4/1**[1]
0-13 **4** *½* **Russian George (IRE)**[6] 1684 4-8-6 82 ... JohnFahy(5) 7 — 87
(S Gollings) *dwlt: swtchd outside and hdwy 3f out: sn rdn: hung rt and styd on same pce fnl f* **9/2**[2]
00-6 **5** *½* **Bullet Man (USA)**[16] 1474 5-8-10 81 ...(p) PaulHanagan 4 — 85
(R A Fahey) *hld up in mid-div: hdwy over 5f out: drvn 3f out: n.m.r over 1f out: hung rt and kpt on* **5/1**[3]
0-02 **6** *5* **Billy Dane (IRE)**[6] 1708 6-9-2 87 ...(p) PhillipMakin 2 — 81
(F P Murtagh) *chsd clr ldr tl over 3f out: wknd fnl 150yds* **7/1**
000- **7** *1 ¾* **City Of The Kings (IRE)**[193] 7060 5-9-4 89 ... SilvestreDeSousa 1 — 79
(G A Harker) *stdd and swtchd rt s: hdwy 3f out: one pce whn hmpd over 1f out* **12/1**
6-44 **8** *6* **Charlie Cool**[7] 1669 7-8-7 78 ...(b) PaulMulrennan 8 — 56
(Mrs R A Carr) *set str pce and sn clr: hung rt and hdd over 1f out: sn wknd: eased nr fin* **4/1**[1]

2m 3.51s (-1.89) **Going Correction** 0.0s/f (Good) — 8 Ran SP% **114.1**
Speed ratings (Par 107): **107,106,105,104,104 100,98,94**
toteswingers: 1&2 £9.00, 1&3 £7.00, 2&3 £7.80 CSF £92.76 CT £417.22 TOTE £11.50: £3.70, £4.10, £1.10; EX 100.90.
Owner Mrs I Gibson & Dr C Emmerson **Bred** Tyrone Molloy **Trained** Melsonby, N Yorks

FOCUS
A fair handicap run at a strong pace that soon had the field well strung out. The placed horses came into this race in decent heart and the form promises to work out.

NOTEBOOK
Oneofapear(IRE) hadn't been seen since winning a maiden at Hamilton last autumn and looked to face a stiffish task on his handicap debut, but he has very few miles on the clock and has clearly improved over the winter. A combination of idling in front and lack of a recent run meant his winning margin was less than it looked it would be passing the furlong pole, and he strikes as the type that will find enough to offset a small rise in the weights. (tchd 10-1)
Rosbay(IRE) finished with a rattle from the rear to nearly steal it on the line, reversing recent form in the process with Russian George and Granston. The good gallop at the trip suited, and more of the same and easier underfoot conditions can see him get his head in front again. (op 11-1 tchd 9-1)
Granston(IRE) ran well in his attempt to win the race for the second year running and briefly looked full of running when leading 2f out. This run extended his good course record, but he is as high in the weights as he wants to be and will remain vulnerable to less exposed types. (op 5-1)
Russian George(IRE) fared well enough given he was set a bit to do, but he tended to carry his head a bit awkwardly and might be in need of a break after three hard races in fairly quick succession. (op 11-2 tchd 7-1)
Bullet Man(USA)'s new yard might yet find the key to him, but this in-and-out performer was something of an enigma when with Luca Cumani. He should be eligible for 0-80s after this, though, and will be of more interest back in that grade, not least back on Polytrack. (op 4-1 tchd 100-30)
Billy Dane(IRE) wasn't able to get to the front but didn't convince with his stamina anyway. (tchd 15-2)
City Of The Kings(IRE) would have finished a fair bit closer had he not been badly squeezed passing the furlong pole. He was all or nothing last year but won second time out and, back below his last winning mark, is worth close consideration next time. (op 10-1)

1890 SIS LIVE MAIDEN STKS — 6f
8:00 (8:01) (Class 5) 3-Y-O — £2,914 (£867; £433; £216) Stalls Low

Form — RPR
52-3 **1** **Bonheurs Art (IRE)**[31] 1137 3-8-12 72 ... RobertWinston 6 — 67
(B W Hills) *trckd ldrs: shkn up to ld over 1f out: drvn rt out: hld on towards fin* **5/4**[1]
2 *¾* **Kielder (IRE)** 3-9-3 0 ... PhillipMakin 1 — 70
(T D Barron) *s.s: hdwy over 2f out: n.m.r jst ins fnl f: styd on wl towards fin: will improve* **14/1**
0-3 **3** *1 ½* **Whitechapel**[18] 1425 3-9-3 0 ... DavidAllan 4 — 65
(E J Alston) *led: hdd over 1f out: kpt on same pce* **13/8**[2]
0- **4** *1 ¾* **Interest Free**[235] 5949 3-8-12 0 ... PaulHanagan 3 — 54
(T D Easterby) *trckd ldrs: one pce whn sltly hmpd jst ins fnl f* **12/1**
0-0 **5** *6* **Royal Patriot (IRE)**[6] 1706 3-9-3 0 ... SilvestreDeSousa 8 — 40
(Paul Green) *chsd ldrs: wknd appr fnl f* **20/1**
0 **6** *8* **Clare Harrier (IRE)**[18] 1425 3-8-12 0 ... MarkCoumbe(5) 5 — 14
(A Berry) *chsd ldrs: outpcd over 3f out: lost pl over 1f out* **100/1**
7 *13* **Jack Bell (IRE)** 3-9-3 0 ... PJMcDonald 2 — —
(G A Swinbank) *chsd ldrs: drvn and outpcd over 3f out: sn lost pl: eased whn bhd ins fnl f* **11/1**[3]
-04 **8** *shd* **Regal Emperor (IRE)**[10] 1599 3-9-3 0 ... AdrianNicholls 7 — —
(D Nicholls) *w ldrs: drvn 3f out: lost pl over 1f out: eased whn bhd towards fin* **20/1**

1m 14.82s (1.82) **Going Correction** +0.225s/f (Good) — 8 Ran SP% **115.7**
Speed ratings (Par 99): **96,95,93,90,82 72,54,54**
toteswingers: 1&2 £4.00, 1&3 £1.10, 2&3 £6.60 CSF £20.19 TOTE £2.30: £1.20, £3.40, £1.10; EX 22.00.
Owner D Powell,D & J Clee,R Dollar,D Harrison **Bred** Catridge Farm Stud Ltd **Trained** Lambourn, Berks

FOCUS
A modest maiden. The pace wasn't strong and the runners were well bunched for a long way.
Regal Emperor(IRE) Official explanation: jockey said gelding lost its action

1891 SIS FIRST FOR FOOTBALL DATA H'CAP — 2m
8:30 (8:30) (Class 5) (0-70,70) 4-Y-O+ — £2,914 (£867; £433; £216) Stalls Low

Form — RPR
000- **1** **Spruzzo**[10] 7750 4-8-2 51 oh5 ... DuranFentiman 6 — 56
(C W Thornton) *chsd clr ldr after 3f: sn niggled along: led over 3f out: strly chal ins fnl f: hld on wl nr fin* **66/1**
414- **2** *nk* **Jackday (IRE)**[90] 7084 5-8-13 62 ... BarryMcHugh(3) 10 — 67
(T D Easterby) *hld up: smooth hdwy 4f out: trcking ldrs whn n.m.r 2f out: shkn up to chal jst ins fnl f: no ex nr fin* **2/1**[1]
11-6 **3** *3 ¾* **Unawatuna**[32] 1113 5-8-9 58 ... KellyHarrison(3) 9 — 59
(Mrs K Walton) *led 1f: chsd ldrs: chal over 3f out: one pce fnl f* **3/1**[2]

010- **4** 4 ½ **Terenzium (IRE)**[15] 6899 8-8-9 **55**.............................(p) PaulMulrennan 8 50
(Micky Hammond) *chsd ldrs: n.m.r on inner 2f out: wknd appr fnl f* **14/1**

460- **5** ½ **Knock Three Times (IRE)**[47] 5734 4-7-11 **51** oh6... JamesSullivan(5) 7 46
(W Storey) *hld up towards rr: hdwy over 3f out: sn chsng ldrs: wknd over 1f out* **40/1**

210- **6** hd **Spiders Star**[243] 5696 7-9-0 **65**.. PaulPickard(5) 3 59
(S G West) *hld up in rr: effrt 4f out: rdn and outpcd over 2f out: styd on fnl f* **11/2**[3]

/54- **7** 13 **San Deng**[344] 1242 8-8-5 **51** oh2.. PaulHanagan 5 30
(Micky Hammond) *chsd ldrs: chal over 3f out: lost pl wl over 1f out* **14/1**

00-3 **8** 8 **Dimashq**[16] 1467 8-8-9 **55**.. PJMcDonald 1 24
(P T Midgley) *s.s: swtchd rt after s: hdwy on outer 4f out: edgd rt and wknd 2f out* **12/1**

0-04 **9** 10 **Coole Dodger (IRE)**[23] 1296 5-8-11 **57** ow3..................... PhillipMakin 2 14
(B Ellison) *s.s: t.k.h: hdwy to ld after 1f: sn clr tl 8f out: hdd and hung rt over 3f out: lost pl over 2f out: bhd whn eased ins fnl f* **13/2**

3m 34.67s (2.87) **Going Correction** 0.0s/f (Good)
WFA 4 from 5yo+ 3lb **9** Ran SP% **112.0**
Speed ratings (Par 103): **92,91,89,87,87 87,80,76,71**
toteswingers: 1&2 £5.80, 1&3 £109.30, 2&3 £2.10 CSF £189.89 CT £545.86 TOTE £84.40: £10.50, £1.10, £1.30; EX 406.90 Place 6 £11.77, Place 5 £5.54.
Owner 980 Racing **Bred** C And Mrs Wilson **Trained** Middleham Moor, N Yorks

FOCUS
A modest handicap and a shock result. With the runaway leader ignored, the pace in the chasing bunch was only fair and apart from the runner-up, nothing improved its position in the straight from off the pace.
Spruzzo Official explanation: trainer said, regarding apparent improvement in form, that the gelding benefitted from stepping up to race over 2m on turf.
Coole Dodger(IRE) Official explanation: jockey said gelding ran too free and hung right
T/Plt: £5.50 to a £1 stake. Pool: £54,815.43 - 7,253.71 winning tickets. T/Qpdt: £3.40 to a £1 stake. Pool: £4,477.24 - 952.68 winning tickets. WG

1892 - 1897a (Foreign Racing) - See Raceform Interactive

1612 ASCOT (R-H)
Saturday, May 8

OFFICIAL GOING: Good to firm changing to good after race 2 (2:50)
False rail increased distances on round course by nine yards.
Wind: Moderate across Weather: Overcast/drizzle

1898 JOHN DOYLE BUCKHOUNDS STKS (LISTED RACE) 1m 4f
2:20 (2:20) (Class 1) 4-Y-O+ **£22,708** (£8,608; £4,308; £2,148; £1,076) **Stalls** High

Form RPR

440- **1** **Barshiba (IRE)**[203] 6850 6-8-7 111...................... HayleyTurner 3 106
(D R C Elsworth) *t.k.h: trckd ldr tl led and stl keen after 4f: drvn and hdd appr fnl 2f: slt ld again over 1f out: edgd lft u.p whn strly chal ins fnl f: r.o gamely fnl 120yds* **11/4**[2]

403- **2** ½ **Duncan**[273] 4780 5-8-12 117.. RichardHughes 4 110
(J H M Gosden) *hld up in 3rd: stdy hdwy over 3f out: shkn up to chse ldng duo and edgd rt over 2f out: rdn to chal and upsides fr over 1f out: chal but hung rt ins fnl f: outbattled cl home* **4/5**[1]

026- **3** 1 **Starfala**[203] 6854 5-8-7 103.. JoeFanning 2 103
(P F I Cole) *disp 4th tl rdn over 4f out: kpt on fr over 2f out and str run on ins fnl f to take 3rd cl home but nt rch ldng duo* **20/1**

20-0 **4** 1 ½ **Traffic Guard (USA)**[21] 1382 6-8-12 114..................... JamieSpencer 6 110+
(P F I Cole) *led 4f: styd chsng wnr: rdn to take slt ld again appr fnl 2f: narrowly hdd again over 1f out: styng on same pce whn hmpd and squeezed out fnl 120yds: lost 3rd cl home* **5/1**[3]

U05- **5** 48 **Hatton Flight**[238] 5854 6-8-12 99..................................(b) MartinDwyer 1 29
(A M Balding) *disp 4th tl rdn and dropped out fnl 4f* **20/1**

2m 32.03s (-0.47) **Going Correction** +0.25s/f (Good) **5** Ran SP% **108.4**
Speed ratings (Par 111): **111,110,110,109,77**
CSF £5.19 TOTE £3.20: £1.70, £1.10; EX 4.60.
Owner J C Smith **Bred** Littleton Stud **Trained** Newmarket, Suffolk

FOCUS
There was only light rain overnight and the ground was still riding on the fast side, with the GoingStick measurement suggesting the ground on the straight track was fastest down the centre. There was a false rail on the round course which added nine yards to the races over 1m4f and 2m. This Listed race again produced a single-figure field, but looked a better than average contest for the grade although this is not easy form to assess.

NOTEBOOK
Barshiba(IRE) is well suited by a fast surface and had every chance to give up once headed, but refused to be denied. This was all the more creditable considering she pulled hard for the first half-mile before her rider let her go on, and then she was headed by not only the runner-up but also the fourth before renewing her effort. She tended to hang left but her rider always had the whip in the correct hand. A return here for the Royal meeting looks likely after this, with the Hardwicke the obvious target. (op 10-3 tchd 5-2)
Duncan was bidding to follow up last year's success. He had the highest official rating and was sent off at odds-on, got a good lead into the race and looked the winner when cruising onto the heels of the leaders 2f out. However, he found less than looked likely under pressure, tending to lean slightly to the right, and in the end was outbattled. He did have an excuse, though, as one of his shoes came loose in the race. Official explanation: jockey said horse hung right (op 8-11 tchd 10-11 and evens in places)
Starfala finished runner-up to Duncan in this race last year and got closer to her old rival this time. She was held up out the back before staying on steadily up the straight, and looks as though a return to further is in order after this. (op 16-1 tchd 11-1)
Traffic Guard(USA) made the early running but was taken on for the lead in Swinley Bottom. He got back to the lead briefly at around the 2f pole but was soon headed and was weakening when squeezed out between the front two, which probably cost him third place. (op 13-2 tchd 7-1)
Hatton Flight had a lot to find judged on official ratings and was in trouble before the home turn. (op 16-1 tchd 14-1)

1899 BOVIS HOMES FILLIES' H'CAP 1m (S)
2:50 (2:54) (Class 2) 3-Y-O+ **£29,142** (£8,671; £4,333; £2,164) **Stalls** Centre

Form RPR

142- **1** **Alsace Lorraine (IRE)**[224] 6267 5-9-7 **92**.................... JamieSpencer 15 105+
(J R Fanshawe) *stdd and swtchd lft s: hld up in rr: nt clr run over 2f out: shkn up and qcknd wl over 1f out: drvn and str run fnl f to ld fnl 100yds: won gng away* **6/1**[2]

54-5 **2** 1 **First City**[7] 1693 4-9-8 **93**.. ShaneKelly 11 104
(D M Simcock) *stdd s: hld up in rr: nt clr run over 2f out: qcknd over 1f out and drvn to ld ins fnl f: hdd and outpcd fnl 100yds* **12/1**

13-3 **3** 1 ¼ **Off Chance**[14] 1513 4-9-1 **86**.. DuranFentiman 8 94
(T D Easterby) *in tch: hdwy over 2f out: drvn to chal fnl f: outpcd by ldng duo fnl 110yds* **13/2**[3]

120- **4** 1 **Flora Trevelyan**[204] 6813 4-9-2 **87**.................................... AdamKirby 13 93+
(W R Swinburn) *in rr: hdwy fr 2f out: rdn: nt clr run: swtchd lft and styd on thrght fnl f: nvr a threat but kpt on wl to take 4th nr fin* **5/1**[1]

2-14 **5** 1 **Clairvoyance (IRE)**[35] 1082 3-8-6 **90**........................ NickyMackay 9 90
(J H M Gosden) *chsd ldrs: wnt 2nd over 3f out: led ins fnl 2f: hdd ins fnl f: wknd fnl 100yds* **12/1**

-060 **6** 5 **Victoria Sponge (IRE)**[35] 1084 4-9-1 **89**.................. WilliamCarson(3) 6 81
(S C Williams) *in tch: rdn over 3f out: outpcd over 2f out: styd on again fnl f but nvr a threat* **25/1**

205- **7** 3 **Sarah Park (IRE)**[160] 7588 5-9-7 **92**................................ MartinDwyer 4 77
(B J Meehan) *w ldr 2f: styd front rnk tl wknd qckly wl over 1f out* **20/1**

46-2 **8** 1 **Blue Angel (IRE)**[10] 1613 3-9-4 **102**.......................... RichardHughes 12 82
(R Hannon) *in tch: rdn along and outpcd 3f out: n.d after* **6/1**[2]

64-0 **9** ½ **Seradim**[35] 1084 4-9-4 **89**.. DaneO'Neill 14 71
(P F I Cole) *s.i.s: in rr: sme prog 3f out: nvr rchd ldrs and sn btn* **33/1**

01-0 **10** ¾ **Good Again**[100] 334 4-9-5 **95**.. JohnFahy(5) 16 75
(G A Butler) *chsd ldrs: rdn over 2f out and sn btn* **13/2**[3]

400- **11** ½ **Arabian Mirage**[304] 3746 4-9-4 **89**.............................. TadhgO'Shea 3 68
(B J Meehan) *sn led: hdd ins fnl 2f: sn btn* **66/1**

254- **12** 7 **Rafiqa (IRE)**[225] 6239 4-9-5 **90**.. EddieAhern 5 53
(C F Wall) *chsd ldrs: wkng whn hmpd over 2f out* **12/1**

62-0 **13** 9 **Badiat Alzaman (IRE)**[6] 1725 4-9-6 **91**........................ KierenFallon 1 33
(E A L Dunlop) *chsd ldrs 5f* **16/1**

0-00 **14** 2 **Charlotte Point (USA)**[26] 1265 4-8-6 **77**........................ JoeFanning 7 14
(P F I Cole) *rrd and s.i.s: sn in tch: wknd 1/2-way* **20/1**

1m 40.05s (-0.55) **Going Correction** +0.075s/f (Good)
WFA 3 from 4yo+ 13lb **14** Ran SP% **118.7**
Speed ratings (Par 96): **105,104,102,101,100 95,92,91,91,90 90,83,74,72**
toteswingers:1&2:£18.20, 1&3:£3.20, 2&3:£13.90 CSF £69.62 CT £500.64 TOTE £4.80: £1.80, £6.40, £2.00; EX 106.70 Trifecta £229.20 Pool: £1,062.77 - 3.43 winning units..
Owner Merry Fox Stud Limited **Bred** 6c Stallions Ltd **Trained** Newmarket, Suffolk

FOCUS
A good fillies' handicap in which the pace did not appear that strong early but quickened up soon after halfway, and the first four came from well back. The form is rated on the positive side. The ground was changed to Good all round after this race.

NOTEBOOK
Alsace Lorraine(IRE) is a really likeable mare and she came through from last place over 3f out to win cosily. A consistent and progressive sort last season, she is clearly still on the upgrade and is likely to return here for the Group 2 Windsor Forest at the Royal meeting. (op 9-2 tchd 13-2)
First City had arguably run her best previous race in a Listed race on fast ground here last autumn and put up a creditable effort, only to find the winner too strong in the closing stages. She could renew rivalry with the winner on better terms here next month. (op 14-1)
Off Chance is another progressive sort, having gone up 19lb since this time last year. This was a good effort on this step up in grade and she would not be inconvenienced by a return to further. (op 6-1)
Flora Trevelyan is relatively inexperienced but ran a decent race after briefly getting outpaced and then having to be switched in the closing stages. She should be better for the outing and is another who is likely to appreciate a return to further. (op 15-2 tchd 8-1)
Clairvoyance(IRE) was a market drifter on this first start on turf but ran with plenty of credit. She was the only one to race up with the pace that was still involved in the last furlong and might appreciate a slightly easier surface on turf. (op 8-1 tchd 14-1 in places)
Victoria Sponge(IRE) missed the break and ran on late to be best of the rest, but was a fair way behind the leading quintet.
Good Again, last year's winner, was quite keen early and was beaten some way from home. (op 8-1)

1900 TOTESPORT VICTORIA CUP (HERITAGE H'CAP) 7f
3:25 (3:28) (Class 2) 4-Y-O+
£52,963 (£15,861; £7,930; £3,969; £1,980; £994) **Stalls** Centre

Form RPR

0- **1** **Dandy Boy (ITY)**[29] 1216 4-8-13 **95**.................................... CO'Donoghue 9 107
(David Marnane, Ire) *mid-div: hdwy jst over 2f out: rdn over 1f out: sn drifted lft: r.o wl whn stened fnl f: led towards fin* **16/1**

11-1 **2** nk **Mabait**[14] 1533 4-9-8 **104**.. KierenFallon 16 115
(L M Cumani) *towards rr of midfield: hdwy over 2f out: rdn whn swtchd rt over 1f out: r.o wl to ld ins fnl f: ct towards fin* **4/1**[1]

0-02 **3** ½ **Marajaa (IRE)**[21] 1383 8-8-10 **92**.................................... JamieMackay 21 101
(W J Musson) *towards rr of midfield: outpcd 3f out: hdwy over 1f out: r.o strly fr jst ins fnl f* **40/1**

653 **4** ½ **Noble Citizen (USA)**[8] 1662 5-8-5 **90**......................(be) MartinLane(3) 25 98
(D M Simcock) *mid-div: rdn over 2f out: hdwy over 1f out: kpt on fnl f* **33/1**

500- **5** 1 ½ **Big Noise**[204] 6815 6-8-5 **90**........................... Louis-PhilippeBeuzelin(3) 7 94
(Dr J D Scargill) *hld up towards rr: hdwy 3f out: sn rdn: chsd wnr on nr side ent fnl f: sltly impeded sn after: kpt on* **33/1**

0-00 **6** ¾ **Huzzah (IRE)**[21] 1383 5-8-5 **87**.. JimmyQuinn 2 89
(B W Hills) *hld up towards rr: rdn over 2f out: no imp tl r.o fnl f: nrst fin* **25/1**

2041 **7** nk **Thebes**[8] 1662 5-8-12 **94**.. JoeFanning 23 95
(M Johnston) *chsd ldrs: rdn over 2f out: ch over 1f out: egded lft and no ex fnl f* **33/1**

1020 **8** nk **Flipando (IRE)**[6] 1727 9-9-2 **98**.................................... JamieSpencer 1 98+
(T D Barron) *hld up last: nt clr run w wall of horses 2f out: swtchd rt and rt again but gd hdwy fr over 1f out: kpt on wl but fin on far side fr draw 1* **25/1**

00-0 **9** ¾ **Golden Desert (IRE)**[6] 1727 6-9-7 **103**........................ StevieDonohoe 20 101
(R A Mills) *mid-div: rdn over 1f out: kpt on fnl f* **66/1**

0-21 **10** shd **Crown Choice**[17] 1481 5-8-8 **90**.. EddieAhern 26 88
(W R Swinburn) *prom: rdn to ld 2f out: hdd jst over 1f out: fdd fnl 100yds* **20/1**

40-0 **11** shd **Dhaular Dhar (IRE)**[42] 1006 8-8-6 **88**........................ DavidProbert 18 86
(J S Goldie) *rdn over 2f out: kpt on same pce* **16/1**

-403 **12** hd **Advanced**[21] 1400 7-9-1 **102**.. AmyRyan(5) 27 99
(K A Ryan) *chsd ldrs: rdn over 2f out: one pce fnl f* **33/1**

01-0 **13** 1 **Manassas (IRE)**[21] 1383 5-9-4 **100**.............................. MartinDwyer 11 95
(B J Meehan) *chsd ldrs: rdn 2f out: one pce fnl f* **22/1**

60-3 **14** ½ **Kay Gee Be (IRE)**[35] 1085 6-8-9 **91**.............................. HayleyTurner 15 84+
(W Jarvis) *mid-div: effrt 2f out: squeezed out ent fnl f: kpt on but no ch after* **25/1**

00-3 **15** hd **Oratory (IRE)**[21] 1383 4-8-9 **91**.................................... RichardHughes 10 84+
(R Hannon) *mid-div: rdn over 2f out: nt clr run and swtchd rt jst ins fnl f: no further imp* **10/1**[3]

2214 **16** ¾ **Bravo Echo**[35] 1085 4-8-12 **94**.. LukeMorris 5 85
(M J Attwater) *chsd ldrs: rdn over 2f out: wknd ins fnl f* **40/1**

4300 **17** ½ **Rileyskeepingfaith**[6] 1727 4-9-4 **100**........................(v) ChrisCatlin 17 89
(M R Channon) *led: rdn and hdd 2f out: wknd jst over 1f out* **50/1**

-222 **18** *hd* **Internationaldebut (IRE)**[19] 1423 5-8-7 **89**.................. TonyCulhane 6 78+
(P T Midgley) *hld up towards rr: sme hdwy over 2f out: nt clr run and sltly hmpd jst over 1f out: sn rdn: no further imp* **25/1**

00-0 **19** *½* **Makaamen**[21] 1383 4-8-11 **93**.. TadhgO'Shea 13 80+
(B W Hills) *hld up towards rr: nt best of runs fr 2f out: rdn fnl f: nt pce to find gaps* **16/1**

20-1 **20** *hd* **Castles In The Air**[19] 1423 5-8-13 **102**........................... LeeTopliss(7) 8 89
(R A Fahey) *mid-div: hdwy u.p 2f out: fdd ins fnl f* **9/1[2]**

0613 **21** *¾* **Dunelight (IRE)**[21] 1377 7-9-5 **106**...............................(v) JohnFahy(5) 19 91
(C G Cox) *prom: rdn over 2f out: remained chalng tl wknd ent fnl f* **25/1**

2-62 **22** *½* **Prime Exhibit**[42] 1008 5-8-11 **96**................................ WilliamCarson(3) 4 79
(R A Fahey) *chsd ldrs: rdn over 2f out: wknd over 1f out* **12/1**

20-1 **23** *2 ¼* **Street Power (USA)**[22] 1349 5-8-6 **88** ow1.................. SteveDrowne 24 65
(J R Gask) *mid-div: rdn and prog over 2f out: wknd fnl f* **16/1**

006- **24** *1 ¼* **Signor Peltro**[208] 6732 7-9-2 **98**.. DaneO'Neill 29 72
(H Candy) *towards rr of midfield: sme hdwy over 2f out: sn rdn: swtchd nrly to far side: nvr gng pce to get on terms: wknd fnl f* **25/1**

30-1 **25** *nse* **Splendorinthegrass (IRE)**[18] 1455 4-9-2 **98**.................. LiamKeniry 22 72
(D R Lanigan) *trckd ldrs: rdn 2f out: edgd lft: wknd over 1f out* **33/1**

04-3 **26** *1 ¼* **One Way Or Another (AUS)**[41] 1032 7-8-5 **92**........ SimonPearce(5) 28 62
(J R Gask) *in tch: rdn over 2f out: wknd over 1f out* **14/1**

01-0 **27** *7* **Captain Macarry (IRE)**[42] 1006 5-8-7 **89**.............(v) FergusSweeney 12 41
(J J Quinn) *prom: rdn wl over 2f out: wknd over 1f out* **66/1**

04-0 **28** *11* **Mirrored**[7] 1708 4-9-2 **98**... SamHitchcott 3 20
(D Nicholls) *mid-div for 3f: sn struggling in rr* **66/1**

06-0 **29** *12* **Titan Triumph**[8] 1662 6-8-8 **90**... ShaneKelly 14 —
(W J Knight) *struggling bef 1/2-way: eased whn btn fr 2f out* **100/1**

1m 26.73s (-1.27) **Going Correction** +0.075s/f (Good) **29** Ran SP% **136.2**
Speed ratings (Par 109): **110,109,109,108,106 105,105,105,104,104 104,103,102,102,102 101,100,100,99,99 98,98,95,94,94**
toteswingers:1&2:£38.50, 1&3:£400.30, 2&3:£224.80 CSF £64.89 CT £2678.22 TOTE £20.20: £3.80, £1.70, £13.30, £8.10; EX 69.10 Trifecta £17115.30 Pool: £23822.64 - 1.03 winning units..

Owner Malih L Al Basti **Bred** Az Ag Rz Emiliana Srl **Trained** Bansha, Co Tipperary

FOCUS
A long established handicap which, with the big field, looked as competitive as usual. In recent seasons, a double-figure draw has proven ideal as they have tended to race up the centre of the track. Four and five-year-olds have dominated in recent seasons and that was the case again. The field raced in one group up the centre of the track, but the winner ended up drifting towards the stands' side. The form makes sense and is backed up by a good time.

NOTEBOOK
Dandy Boy(ITY) was well suited by 7f but his form in Ireland was on Polytrack or soft ground, and he was 5lb above his last winning mark. However, he settled well in behind the leaders before coming to make his challenge entering the final furlong. He then responded well to vigorous riding, despite drifting, to get the upper hand late on. He has a Group 3 entry in Ireland but the Royal Hunt Cup could be on the agenda now. (tchd 20-1 in a place)
Mabait, the well-backed favourite, came into this a really progressive performer, having impressed when beating subsequent winner Tartan Gigha at Sandown. Although 10lb higher, he was a well-backed favourite and when he hit the front, the market support looked justified. However, his stride began to shorten inside the last furlong and he lost out to the challenger on the other side of the track. This was still a step up and he could re-oppose the winner in the Royal Hunt Cup, but it is worth noting that all his wins at 7f and 1m have been on turning tracks. (tchd 5-1 in places)
Marajaa(IRE), whose last three wins have been at 1m, finished runner-up in the Newbury Spring Cup last time and ran another fine race, coming with his customary strong finish. He is another who could be back here for the Royal Hunt Cup, with the extra furlong sure to be in his favour.
Noble Citizen(USA) ◆ has not won since October 2008 but the eyeshield and blinkers combination has made him more consistent. He was under pressure some way out but kept responding and was reeling in the placed horses at the finish. This is his optimum trip and the Buckingham Palace Handicap back here looks a feasible target. (tchd 40-1 in a place)
Big Noise has run well in similar handicaps before and has gone well fresh. He did so again, running home well in the wake of the winner towards the stands' side. (tchd 40-1 in a place)
Huzzah(IRE) ◆ is a regular in this type of race, having finished runner-up in Hunt Cup here last season. Dropped 9lb since that run, he finished strongly and can be expected to be back here next month attempting to go one better.
Thebes has been running well on Polytrack but handles fast ground and was 2lb below his last winning Polytrack mark, when he beat today's fourth. He ran his race but could not pick up in the final furlong. (tchd 50-1 in a place)
Flipando(IRE) ◆ is capable from 6f-1m but his last three wins have been on Polytrack and he had not won on turf for nearly three years. However, he followed up a decent effort at Newmarket the previous week with another strong-finishing effort, after having to be switched, and his turn does not look far away. (op 33-1)
Golden Desert(IRE) is very effective at around this trip and was a C&D winner last season. He ran his race but is 3lb above his last winning mark and might need a slight ease in the weights.
Crown Choice, all of whose wins have been at 7f on Polytrack, has not looked as effective on turf or at this level but ran with plenty of credit having been close up throughout. (op 16-1)
Dhaular Dhar(IRE) has not won for two years but has gone well in similar races here and was third in this last season. He has dropped 11lb in the handicap since this time last year and ran well for a long way. (op 20-1)
Advanced won a big handicap over C&D last season and was another who showed up for a long way.
Oratory(IRE), third in Newbury Spring Cup and 4lb better of with today's third this time, did not get the clearest of runs when trying to make ground and can be given another chance. (op 11-1)
Castles In The Air, up 8lb for winning a decent race at Pontefract on his return, made some headway to reach the heels of the leaders around the 2f pole but could make no further headway thereafter. It might be he is best suited by good or easy ground. (op 12-1 tchd 14-1)
One Way Or Another(AUS) was soon prominent from his outside draw but probably saw too much daylight and did too much early. (op 16-1)
Titan Triumph reportedly finished lame. Official explanation: trainer said gelding returned lame

1901 MCGEE GROUP MAIDEN STKS 5f
4:00 (4:04) (Class 3) 2-Y-O **£6,476** (£1,927; £963; £481) **Stalls** Centre

Form RPR

2 **1** **Chilworth Lad**[7] 1695 2-9-3 0... ChrisCatlin 10 83
(M R Channon) *pressed ldrs: slt ld 1/2-way: drvn and styd on strly fnl f* **13/2[3]**

2 *¾* **Old Master Expert** 2-9-3 0.. HayleyTurner 9 80+
(M L W Bell) *stdd towards rr: gd prog over 1f out: styd on wl fnl f to chse wnr fnl 100yds but a jst hld* **4/1[1]**

3 *nk* **Approve (IRE)** 2-9-3 0.. EddieAhern 8 79+
(W J Haggas) *t.k.h: chsd ldrs: chal fr 1/2-way and stl ev ch 1f out: styd on same pce fnl 120yds and lost 2nd fnl 100yds* **14/1**

4 *nk* **Welsh Dancer** 2-9-3 0... DaneO'Neill 5 79+
(R Hannon) *in rr: styng on whn hmpd appr fnl f: sn rcvrd: fin wl* **20/1**

5 *1 ¼* **West Leake Bridge (IRE)** 2-9-3 0.............................. SteveDrowne 6 74
(B W Hills) *in tch: pushed along to chse ldrs 1/2-way: kpt on same pce fnl f* **25/1**

2 **6** *½* **Magic Stella**[14] 1510 2-8-12 0.. KierenFallon 3 67+
(A P Jarvis) *pressed ldrs to 1/2-way: outpcd whn hmpd over 1f out: rallied and r.o again ins fnl f* **4/1[1]**

7 *1 ¼* **Al Sharood** 2-8-12 0.. TadhgO'Shea 11 63
(Mahmood Al Zarooni) *wnt rt s: sn rcvrd: hdwy 2f out: chsd ldrs over 1f out but no imp: wknd ins fnl f* **10/1**

8 *¾* **Partout Le Magasin** 2-9-3 0.. LiamKeniry 7 65
(J S Moore) *pressed ldrs: rdn and ev ch 2f out: wknd 1f out* **66/1**

9 *1* **Velvet Underground (IRE)** 2-9-3 0............................. MartinDwyer 4 61+
(B J Meehan) *crossed s and sn outpcd: rallied and sme hdwy fr 2f out: nvr in contention: wknd nfl f* **10/1**

10 *3 ½* **Planet Waves (IRE)** 2-9-3 0.. JamieSpencer 1 49+
(C E Brittain) *in tch: pushed along and green 1/2-way: btn whn hmpd over 1f out: eased fnl 100yds* **10/1**

U **Kojak (IRE)** 2-9-3 0.. RichardHughes 2 63+
(R Hannon) *fly-jmpd to s: led to 1/2-way: rdn and stl pressing ldrs whn veered bdly lft and uns rdr over 1f out* **9/2[2]**

62.46 secs (1.96) **Going Correction** +0.075s/f (Good) **11** Ran SP% **115.6**
Speed ratings (Par 97): **87,85,85,84,82 82,80,78,77,71** —
toteswingers:1&2:£7.80, 1&3:£20.40, 2&3:£17.20 CSF £31.41 TOTE £7.70: £2.00, £1.90, £5.50; EX 37.10 Trifecta £397.30 Pool: £767.81 - 1.43 winning units..
Owner 7Rus **Bred** Phil Jen Racing **Trained** West Ilsley, Berks

FOCUS
Plenty of major yards were represented but it was a race in which only two had previously seen the racecourse, and those were trained by handlers who had both been successful in the race's short history. Probably decent form.

NOTEBOOK
Chilworth Lad, who had been unlucky when runner-up at Goodwood the previous weekend, and put that experience to good use with a game effort. He has clearly gone the right way from that debut and can win again. (op 7-1 tchd 15-2)
Old Master Expert, a £50,000 half-brother to the useful juvenile Rodrigo De Torres, was a well-backed favourite and put up a decent show on this debut, but the winner's experience proved the deciding factor. (op 7-2 tchd 9-2)
Approve(IRE) ◆ is pretty speedily bred and ran a pleasing race on this debut. He had his chance and his rider was not unduly hard on him in the closing stages, so he can be expected to benefit considerably for the experience. (tchd 12-1 and 16-1 in a place)
Welsh Dancer also caught the eye, coming from last at halfway to reach the frame despite having to avoid the fallen Richard Hughes. (op 25-1 tchd 16-1)
West Leake Bridge(IRE) is also well bred and ran with promise despite looking as if the experience was needed. (tchd 20-1 and 28-1)
Magic Stella, a half-sister to last year's winner of this race Little Perisher, showed up for most of the way but the colts proved too strong. (tchd 7-2 and 9-2)
Planet Waves(IRE) was reportedly eased to avoid the loose horse. Official explanation: jockey said he eased colt down closing stages to avoid being impeded by loose horse (op 9-1)
Kojak(IRE) looks one to watch in the short term after this display on his debut. He performed a rodeo act on the way to post but showed plenty of pace and was still in the firing line when deciding to jink sharply left at around the 2f pole and giving his rider a fall. He might be in danger of a visit to the vet if he repeats these antics. (op 5-1 tchd 6-1)

1902 EUROPA EVENTS DIVA BEACH CHELSEA H'CAP 2m
4:35 (4:35) (Class 3) (0-90,90) 4-Y-O+
£6,854 (£2,052; £1,026; £513; £256; £128) **Stalls** High

Form RPR

22-1 **1** **Ermyn Lodge**[18] 1454 4-8-10 **77**..................................(v) TadhgO'Shea 12 86
(P M Phelan) *led: rdn 3f out: hdd over 1f out: rallied gamely to ld again ins fnl f: styd on gamely* **17/2**

11-0 **2** *1 ¼* **Bow To No One (IRE)**[17] 1472 4-9-5 **86**........................ KierenFallon 2 93
(A P Jarvis) *hld up in rr: hdwy and egged lft bnd 3f out: str run fr 2f out to ld over 1f out: hdd and no ex ins fnl f* **16/1**

301- **3** *nk* **Aaim To Prosper (IRE)**[190] 7151 6-9-8 **86**................. MartinDwyer 8 93
(B J Meehan) *chsd ldrs: rdn and styd on to chal over 1f out: kpt on fnl f to press for 2nd but outstyd by wnr* **13/2[2]**

3241 **4** *1 ¼* **Satwa Gold (USA)**[22] 1357 4-9-0 **81**.............................. JamieSpencer 1 87
(Stef Higgins) *hld up in rr: hdwy: nt clr run and swtchd rt over 2f out: n.m.r on ins 2f out: swtchd lft 1f out and styd on but nvr gng pce to rch ldrs* **8/1**

660- **5** *¾* **Perfect Shot (IRE)**[190] 7151 4-9-1 **82**............................ EddieAhern 13 87
(J L Dunlop) *mid-div: hdwy over 2f out: styng on same pce whn carried lft 1f out* **11/1**

211- **6** *1 ¼* **Theola (IRE)**[210] 6676 4-8-9 **81**................................ AshleyMorgan(5) 11 84+
(M H Tompkins) *in rr: hdwy on outside fr 4f out: styng on whn pushed lft bnd wl over 2f out: kpt on fnl f: gng on cl home* **7/1[3]**

42-3 **7** *1 ¼* **Hawridge King**[13] 1544 8-8-9 **76**............................ JamesMillman(3) 10 78
(W S Kittow) *in rr tl hdwy fr 3f out: kpt on fnl 2f but nvr rchd ldrs* **12/1**

230/ **8** *2 ¾* **Colloquial**[597] 6061 9-9-12 **90**.................................(v) FergusSweeney 6 88
(H Candy) *chsd wnr after 4th to 10f out: wknd over 1f out* **40/1**

0-04 **9** *1 ½* **Sweetheart**[22] 1357 6-8-9 **73**.. SteveDrowne 15 70
(Jamie Poulton) *chsd ldrs: pushed along fr 4f out: fading whn hmpd on ins 2f out* **7/1[3]**

4- **10** *½* **Nampour (FR)**[7] 5912 5-9-4 **82**.. ChrisCatlin 4 78
(P J Hobbs) *in tch: rdn 4f out: styd on same pce fnl 3f* **20/1**

541- **11** *1 ¼* **Lombok**[301] 3861 4-8-5 **72**.. HayleyTurner 7 66
(M L W Bell) *t.k.h: chsd wnr 10f out: rdn 3f out: wknd ins fnl 2f* **10/1**

0 **12** *4* **Morar**[73] 688 4-8-13 **80**... PaulDoe 5 70
(Mrs L J Mongan) *in rr: pushed along 5f out: nvr rchd ldrs* **66/1**

000- **13** *3 ¾* **Judgethemoment (USA)**[190] 7151 5-9-8 **86**.............. CO'Donoghue 3 71
(Jane Chapple-Hyam) *chsd ldrs: rdn over 3f out: wknd over 2f out* **5/1[1]**

/00- **14** *23* **Missoula (IRE)**[326] 2994 7-9-2 **80**............................. SamHitchcott 9 38
(Miss Suzy Smith) *chsd ldrs: rdn 5f out: wknd fr 3f out: no ch whn hmpd on ins fnl 2f* **40/1**

13-6 **15** *8* **Brett Vale (IRE)**[13] 1544 4-9-5 **86**.................................. DaneO'Neill 14 34
(P R Hedger) *in rr: sme prog 5f out: sn wknd* **40/1**

3m 32.09s (3.09) **Going Correction** +0.25s/f (Good)
WFA 4 from 5yo+ 3lb **15** Ran SP% **121.2**
Speed ratings (Par 107): **102,101,101,100,100 99,98,97,96,96 95,93,92,80,76**
toteswingers:1&2:£38.80, 1&3:£13.20, 2&3:£23.90 CSF £131.20 CT £952.16 TOTE £9.90: £3.00, £3.60, £2.30; EX 158.10 Trifecta £619.40 Part won. Pool: £837.10 - 0.60 winning units..
Owner Ermyn Lodge Stud & Heatherwold Stud **Bred** Horizon Bloodstock Limited **Trained** Epsom, Surrey

■ Stewards' Enquiry : C O'Donoghue three-day ban: careless riding (May 22-24)
Jamie Spencer two-day ban: careless riding (May 22-23)

FOCUS
A decent staying handicap and something of a dress rehearsal for the Ascot Stakes at the Royal meeting. Straightforward and sound form, with the progressive winner up 3lb.

NOTEBOOK

Ermyn Lodge has developed into a resolute stayer since being fitted with the visor and, after making most of the running, battled back to deny the runner-up and win going away. He seems likely to come back here for the Ascot Stakes, although his trainer seemed more in favour of waiting for the Goodwood equivalent. While the longer trip is an unknown, his attitude is a valuable asset. (op 10-1)

Bow To No One(IRE) was held up off the pace before making good progress to take a narrow lead over a furlong out. However, once there she had nothing more to give and the winner proved too strong for her. Nevertheless, she remains progressive. (tchd 14-1)

Aaim To Prosper(IRE) ◆ won on his only previous visit here and, making his seasonal debut, ran a race full of promise. This should put him right for the Ascot Stakes and he looks a leading contender, especially as the visor could be back on then. (op 8-1)

Satwa Gold(USA), whose improvement on the AW has been transferred to turf, helped by the step up in trip, ran pretty well from off the pace, although his rider got two days for his part in the scrimmaging, which principally affected Sweetheart, near the home turn. He was staying on well at the finish, and looks as if he will get the longer trip if connections decide to come back for the Royal meeting. (op 15-2)

Perfect Shot(IRE) ◆ was noted running a creditable race on this reappearance and is one to bear in mind, especially as he is now just a pound above his last winning mark. (op 14-1)

Theola(IRE) ran better than her finishing position suggests, especially as she had to race quite wide in order to make ground from the approach to the straight. She will relish a return to further. (op 8-1 tchd 17-2)

Hawridge King was closely matched with today's third on last autumn's form and ran a reasonable race. (tchd 14-1 in a place)

Colloquial, who was reappearing after missing last season, ran with promise and was not given a hard time when beaten. (op 50-1)

Sweetheart, who needs further than this nowadays, was ridden close to the pace but was on the retreat when hampered coming off the home turn. (op 15-2 tchd 8-1)

Lombok pulled too hard in the first mile and paid for it later on. (op 6-1)

Judgethemoment(USA) won this in 2009 and was able to race off a 2lb lower mark this time, but was under pressure before the home turn on this seasonal debut, and his replacement rider got a three-day ban for interference on the bend. He should come on a fair amount for the outing. (op 11-2 tchd 6-1 in a place)

1903 ALFRED FRANKS & BARTLETT SUNGLASSES H'CAP — 6f

5:10 (5:11) (Class 3) (0-95,95) 4-Y-0+ **£7,123** (£2,119; £1,059; £529) **Stalls** Centre

Form — RPR

-100 **1** **Medicean Man**[6] 1727 4-8-12 **89**.....(p) JimmyQuinn 10 — 101+
(J R Gask) stdd s: sn in tch: hdwy 2f out: led over 1f out and edgd lft: rdn and asserted ins fnl f and in command whn veered rt fnl 50yds **8/1**[3]

60-0 **2** 1 ½ **Wildcat Wizard (USA)**[7] 1708 4-8-13 **90**.....(t) JamieSpencer 7 — 97
(P F I Cole) stdd s: in rr tl rapid hdwy fr over 1f out: styd on u.p to chse wnr fnl 100yds but no imp **18/1**

00-4 **3** ¾ **Noverre To Go (IRE)**[43] 992 4-9-2 **93**.....(t) RichardKingscote 5 — 98
(Tom Dascombe) chsd ldrs: rdn over 2f out: kpt on fnl f but nvr gng pce to chal **12/1**

-16 **4** shd **Secret Asset (IRE)**[6] 1727 5-8-10 **94**..... LewisWalsh(7) 8 — 99
(Jane Chapple-Hyam) chsd ldrs: led ins fnl 2f: hdd over 1f out: kpt on same pce **9/2**[1]

0-01 **5** 2 **Getcarter**[12] 1580 4-8-11 **88**..... LiamKeniry 4 — 86
(R Hannon) towards rr: pushed along over 2f out: styd on thrght fnl f: nt rch ldrs **9/2**[1]

-050 **6** nk **Pusey Street Lady**[7] 1688 6-8-9 **89**..... MartinLane(3) 2 — 86
(J Gallagher) slt advantage tl hdd ins fnl 2f: wknd fnl f **33/1**

040- **7** hd **Seamus Shindig**[197] 6994 8-8-5 **89** ow2..... AmyScott(7) 3 — 86
(H Candy) towards rr tl shkn up and styd on fr over 1f out: gng on cl home **33/1**

000- **8** ¾ **Safari Mischief**[286] 4341 7-8-13 **90**..... LukeMorris 14 — 84
(P Winkworth) in tch on outside: rdn and haeday to chse ldrs 1f out: styd on same pce **50/1**

40-1 **9** 5 **Dametime (IRE)**[12] 1588 4-8-4 **81** oh1..... HayleyTurner 6 — 59
(Daniel Mark Loughnane, Ire) pressed ldrs: rdn 2f out: wknd qckly fnl f **33/1**

105- **10** ¾ **Tagula Night (IRE)**[211] 6631 4-8-6 **83**.....(vt) ChrisCatlin 1 — 59
(W R Swinburn) pressed ldr 4f: wknd over 1f out **20/1**

1412 **11** 3 ½ **New Leyf (IRE)**[17] 1481 4-8-10 **87**..... SteveDrowne 15 — 52
(J R Gask) s.i.s: outpcd most of way **8/1**[3]

0-54 **12** 2 ¾ **Rulesn'regulations**[28] 1219 4-9-0 **91**..... CO'Donoghue 11 — 47
(Matthew Salaman) pressed ldrs over 3f **15/2**[2]

0-00 **13** hd **Zidane**[6] 1727 8-9-4 **95**.....(p) EddieAhern 13 — 50
(J R Fanshawe) outpcd **8/1**[3]

02-2 **14** 4 **We Have A Dream**[22] 1349 5-8-10 **87**..... MartinDwyer 12 — 29
(W R Muir) pressed ldrs over 3f **8/1**[3]

030- **15** 9 **Aye Aye Digby (IRE)**[197] 6994 5-9-0 **91**..... StephenCraine 9 — 5
(J R Boyle) chsd ldrs 3f **20/1**

1m 13.38s (-1.02) **Going Correction** +0.075s/f (Good) **15** Ran SP% **125.8**
Speed ratings (Par 107): **109,107,106,105,103 102,102,101,94,93 89,85,85,79,67**
toteswingers:1&2:£31.10, 1&3:£26.00, 2&3:£46.50 CSF £136.68 CT £1747.32 TOTE £11.00: £3.70, £7.40, £4.50; EX 310.90 Trifecta £739.50 Part won. Pool: £999.35 - 0.08 winning units. Place 6: £694.77 Place 5: £609.21..
Owner Stuart Dobb & Miss Kate Dobb **Bred** Barry Taylor **Trained** Sutton Veny, Wilts

FOCUS

A good sprint handicap. The form is rated at face value around the third.

NOTEBOOK

Medicean Man ◆ ran creditably behind Secret Asset in a good handicap at Newmarket the previous week but had a bit to find with that rival on the same terms. However, he travelled really well here, so much so that his rider was able to sit still inside the last 2f to prevent his mount hitting the front too soon. Once there, it was clear why he wanted to delay taking the lead, as his mount wandered around, but he always had enough in hand to score comfortably. He looks progressive and it would be no surprise to see him follow up. (op 12-1)

Wildcat Wizard(USA) ◆ put up a fine effort, especially considering he missed the break and was still last after halfway. He finished well and, considering he was Listed placed as a juvenile, is reasonably handicapped now if this effort signals a revival. (op 16-1 tchd 20-1)

Noverre To Go(IRE) finished behind today's winner on his reappearance on Polytrack in March and was 6lb better off this time. He ran on well over a course he clearly likes and got a little closer, giving the impression he is coming to hand. (op 11-1)

Secret Asset(IRE) finished ahead of today's winner at Newmarket last week and ran his race. He has held his form well since returning from a long absence. (op 6-1)

Getcarter was held up off the pace by his replacement rider but found himself with too much ground to make up. He is better than his finishing position indicates. (tchd 11-2 and 6-1 in places)

Pusey Street Lady disputed the lead early but, after showing in front entering the last 2f, was run down by the stronger finishers. She is generally happier on a softer surface.

Seamus Shindig was another to stay on late, and this was a reasonable seasonal debut.

Safari Mischief also put up a reasonable seasonal debut, having not run since July.

Zidane, the 2007 winner, was looking for a revival in fortune, having seemingly lost his way of late, but the cheekpieces failed to spark a revival and he was subsequently reported as having been retired. (op 13-2 tchd 10-1 in a place)

T/Jkpt: Not won. T/Plt: £709.80 to a £1 stake. Pool: £165,695.16 - 170.40 winning tickets. T/Qpdt: £168.30 to a £1 stake. Pool: £6,801.07 - 29.90 winning tickets. ST

1510 HAYDOCK (L-H)

Saturday, May 8

OFFICIAL GOING: Jumps course - good changing to good (good to firm in places) after race 3 (3.00); flat couse - good to firm

Rail realignment increased distances on round course by 10yds. All races run on inside chase course and hurdle races run over shorter than advertised.

Wind: Moderate, half-behind Weather: Fine

1904 TOTESCOOP6 SPRING TROPHY STKS (LISTED RACE) — 7f 30y

2:00 (2:00) (Class 1) 3-Y-0+

£22,708 (£8,608; £4,308; £2,148; £1,076; £540) **Stalls** Low

Form — RPR

5031 **1** **Lovelace**[12] 1570 6-9-7 105..... AdrianNicholls 3 — 114
(D Nicholls) in tch: impr to ld over 1f out: sn edgd lft: r.o ins fnl f: hld on wl cl home **3/1**[2]

-262 **2** ½ **Mia's Boy**[21] 1377 6-9-7 105..... DarryllHolland 5 — 113
(C A Dwyer) hld up: rdn over 1f out: hdwy ent fnl f: r.o: gng on at fin **7/4**[1]

40 **3** 1 ¾ **Marching (AUS)**[64] 818 6-9-7 107..... TedDurcan 1 — 108+
(Mahmood Al Zarooni) chsd ldr: rdn and chalng over 1f out: u.p whn n.m.r and hmpd jst ins fnl f: styd on same pce after **15/2**

024- **4** 2 ½ **Georgebernardshaw (IRE)**[263] 5135 5-9-7 105..... NeilCallan 7 — 105+
(D M Simcock) stdd s: hld up: effrt w work to do whn nt clr run jst over 1f out: plld to outside sn after: styd on ins fnl f but unable to rch ldrs **12/1**

10P- **5** 1 ½ **Welsh Emperor (IRE)**[196] 7019 11-9-7 105..... MickyFenton 6 — 97
(T P Tate) bustled along to ld: rdn and hdd over 1f out: sn sltly checked whn u.p: wknd ins fnl f **20/1**

100- **6** 1 ¼ **Ordnance Row**[218] 6448 7-9-7 112..... PatDobbs 2 — 94
(R Hannon) handy: rdn to chal over 1f out: wknd ins fnl f **6/1**[3]

060- **7** 3 ¾ **Tombi (USA)**[217] 6487 6-9-7 103..... TonyHamilton 4 — 84
(J Howard Johnson) racd keenly in tch: rdn 2f out: wknd over 1f out **8/1**

1m 29.35s (-3.35) **Going Correction** +0.175s/f (Good) **7** Ran SP% **111.0**
Speed ratings (Par 111): **111,110,108,105,103 102,98**
Tote Swingers: 1&2 £1.10, 1&3 £3.70, 2&3 £4.50 CSF £8.11 TOTE £3.50: £1.90, £1.50; EX 6.90.
Owner Dab Hand Racing **Bred** Mrs Mary Taylor **Trained** Sessay, N Yorks
■ Stewards' Enquiry : Adrian Nicholls three-day ban: careless riding (May 22-24)

FOCUS

They went a good gallop for this Listed prize, thanks to the veteran Welsh Emperor.

NOTEBOOK

Lovelace produced a decisive burst over 1f out (badly hampering Marching in the process), that put him in an unassailable lead. Formerly with Mark Johnston, he made a winning debut for the yard when taking a 1m conditions race at Nottingham last month, and this represented a stiffer task, but he is a dual Group winner, and always looked to be holding on from the fast-finishing runner-up. Connections did extremely well with another ex-Johnston inmate Regal Parade, who went on to win the Group 1 Haydock Sprint Cup, and this fellow looks surely to win again at some stage. He's in a handicap at York on Thursday and may well take his chance there under a 5lb penalty. (op 4-1 tchd 11-4)

Mia's Boy, narrowly denied in the Doncaster Mile latest, is always a threat in this type of race and he was well supported at the head of the market, but struggled a little to go the early pace, finding himself last and having to be niggled. He eventually got going, coming with a strong run inside the last, but the winner wasn't for catching. (op 9-4 tchd 5-2 in a place)

Marching(AUS), twice not beaten far in handicaps in Dubai earlier in the year, travelled strongly in behind the speed and picked up well against the rail to challenge, but he was hampered when the winner cut across him and couldn't recover. He wouldn't have been beaten far, probably be rated a length or two better than the bare form, and can win a Listed/conditions race at some stage. (op 13-2)

Georgebernardshaw(IRE), a formerly smart performer with Aidan O'Brien, was another who should have been a bit closer, travelling well but then being denied a clear run before keeping on late. He should pay his way in similar events. (op 10-1)

Welsh Emperor(IRE) gave his all on this first start in 196 days, but was always going to prove vulnerable. (op 18-1)

Ordnance Row, runner-up in the race a year ago, often takes a run to set him straight and he got a little tired late. (op 9-2)

Tombi(USA) was one of the first in trouble. (op 9-1)

1905 TOTESWINGER MAIDEN STKS — 6f

2:30 (2:33) (Class 5) 2-Y-0 **£2,914** (£867; £433; £216) **Stalls** High

Form — RPR

1 **Clarke Lane (USA)** 2-9-3 0..... NeilCallan 8 — 78+
(M A Jarvis) pressed ldrs: rdn and str chal thrght fnl f: nosed ahd fnl strides **11/4**[2]

2 shd **Ahtoug** 2-9-3 0..... TedDurcan 7 — 78+
(Mahmood Al Zarooni) hld up: hdwy over 2f out: led 1f out: r.o u.p but pressed thrght fnl f: hdd narrowly fnl strides **7/4**[1]

0 **3** 3 ½ **Loves Theme (IRE)**[21] 1375 2-8-9 0..... MarcHalford(3) 2 — 62+
(A Bailey) w ldr: led 2f out: rdn and hdd 1f out: no ex fnl 100yds **33/1**

4 ¾ **Indian Ballad (IRE)** 2-9-3 0..... AdrianNicholls 6 — 65+
(E S McMahon) trckd ldrs: rdn to chal over 1f out: kpt on same pce ins fnl f **12/1**

5 shd **My Single Malt (IRE)** 2-9-3 0..... MickyFenton 3 — 65
(T P Tate) dwlt: rn green: in tch: pushed along 1/2-way: kpt on same pce ins fnl f: nt pce to chal **6/1**[3]

6 2 **King Of Aquitaine (IRE)** 2-9-3 0..... DarryllHolland 1 — 59
(K A Ryan) wnt lft s: towards rr: pushed along over 2f out: outpcd over 1f out **8/1**

0 **7** nk **Jossy Johnston (IRE)**[7] 1686 2-9-3 0..... TonyHamilton 5 — 58
(E J Alston) led: hdd 2f out: sn rdn: wknd 1f out **20/1**

8 23 **Plea** 2-9-3 0..... RobertHavlin 4 — —
(J H M Gosden) green to post and in r: dwlt: a bhd: lost tch fnl f **8/1**

1m 14.85s (1.35) **Going Correction** -0.10s/f (Good) **8** Ran SP% **114.9**
Speed ratings (Par 93): **90,89,85,84,84 81,81,50**
Tote Swingers: 1&2 £2.70, 1&3 £16.50, 2&3 £19.20 CSF £8.01 TOTE £3.30: £1.10, £1.80, £5.00; EX 9.60.
Owner Stephen Dartnell **Bred** Ieah Stables & Ashford Stud **Trained** Newmarket, Suffolk

FOCUS

The first 6f 2-y-o maiden of the season in Britain. The front pair drew clear and can do better, and the race should produce winners.

NOTEBOOK
Clarke Lane(USA), whose dam won the American Oaks on dirt, holds a Derby entry, as well as engagements in a couple of good juvenile races, and he proved strong in the market. Reportedly a precocious sort, he isn't the biggest, but clearly has more speed than his pedigree suggests and, having looked set to come off second best, he dug deep and just managed to deny the favourite. This was a pleasing start and he will have one more run before going to Royal Ascot for the Chesham Stakes. (op 7-2 tchd 4-1)
Ahtoug, a half-brother to high-class miler Bowman, is a tall sort with a nice action and he certainly travelled like a decent colt. He looked the winner when quickening up to lead 1f out, but ran green and lost out in the final stride. This was a very promising effort and he should have no trouble winning a maiden. (op 2-1 tchd 9-4)
Loves Theme(IRE), well beaten on her debut at Doncaster, has clearly improved for the outing and showed enough to suggest she can win a maiden, possibly back at 5f. (op 25-1)
Indian Ballad(IRE), whose dam was placed at up to 1m1f, comes from a yard that can ready a newcomer, but he was found wanting for pace. This was still a promising start, though, and he looks another likely future winner. (op 10-1 tchd 9-1)
My Single Malt(IRE), whose dam was a smart 5-8f winner, is said to need more time, so should improve on this at some stage. His inexperience showed. (op 8-1 tchd 5-1)
King Of Aquitaine(IRE), whose dam was a 6f winner at two, was soon under pressure and never got into it. (op 9-1)
Jossy Johnston(IRE) knew her job and showed speed, but stopped very quickly. (op 14-1)
Plea, a half-brother to high-class middle-distance/staying performer Ask, was very green in the preliminaries and looked clueless in the race itself. He should improve, but clearly needs to. (op 7-1)

1906 TOTEEXACTA CONDITIONS STKS 6f
4:45 (4:46) (Class 2) 3-Y-O+

£12,462 (£3,732; £1,866; £934; £466; £234) **Stalls** High

Form				RPR
0024	1		**Prime Defender**[29] 1206 6-9-0 105 ... DarryllHolland 4 (B W Hills) *chsd ldrs: rdn and nt qckn over 1f out: r.o ins fnl f: led towards fin* **3/1**[2]	110
0-40	2	1	**Redford (IRE)**[42] 1007 5-9-0 102 ... NeilCallan 3 (K A Ryan) *chsd ldrs: led over 1f out: edgd lft ins fnl f: hdd towards fin* **8/1**	107
-225	3	1 ¼	**Elnawin**[7] 1700 4-9-0 104 ... PatDobbs 5 (R Hannon) *w ldr: rdn over 1f out: ev ch and chalng ins fnl f: nt qckn fnl 50yds* **15/8**[1]	103
000	4	1 ¼	**Mac Gille Eoin**[49] 948 6-9-0 97 ... IanMongan 7 (J Gallagher) *led: rdn and hdd over 1f out: hung lft and styd on same pce ins fnl f* **20/1**	99
600-	5	½	**Valery Borzov (IRE)**[231] 6091 6-9-0 99 ... TonyHamilton 1 (R A Fahey) *in rr: rdn over 2f out: styd on ins fnl f: nt pce to chal* **16/1**	97
063-	6	¾	**Run For The Hills**[219] 6427 4-9-0 101 ... RobertHavlin 2 (J H M Gosden) *hld up: rdn over 1f out: kpt on ins fnl f: nvr able to chal* **13/2**	95
4-04	7	½	**Evens And Odds (IRE)**[23] 1326 6-9-0 102 ... AdrianNicholls 6 (D Nicholls) *chsd ldrs: rdn over 2f out: outpcd over 1f out* **4/1**[3]	93

1m 12.03s (-1.47) **Going Correction** -0.10s/f (Good) **7** Ran SP% **114.9**
Speed ratings (Par 109): **109,107,106,104,103 102,102**
Tote Swingers: 1&2 £5.10, 1&3 £2.00, 2&3 £2.30 CSF £26.94 TOTE £3.50: £2.80, £4.40; EX 21.00.
Owner S Falle, M Franklin, J Sumsion **Bred** Christopher J Mason **Trained** Lambourn, Berks
■ Stewards' Enquiry : Ian Mongan caution: used whip down shoulder in the forehand position
FOCUS
This didn't take much winning in the end.
NOTEBOOK
Prime Defender proved too determined for his rivals in the finish. Officially, the highest-rated of these, albeit only by 1lb, he hadn't won for over a year coming into the race, but fully deserved a win, and he stayed on strongly from a couple of horses who find it tricky to get their head in front. He can expect things to get tougher as he goes back up in grade, however. (op 11-4)
Redford(IRE), a talented but difficult-to-win-with performer, got to the front inside the final furlong, but not for the first time was found wanting in a finish.
Elnawin, who hasn't won since 2-y-o days, has twice run well over 5f this term, without suggesting he has the speed for it, and this trip was always likely to suit better. He had his chance and simply couldn't stay on as strongly as the winner. (op 10-3)
Mac Gille Eoin, the lowest-rated of these, was soon in front and kept on to hold fourth, but was no doubt flattered. His rider reported he hung left. (tchd 25-1)
Valery Borzov(IRE) appeared to have a bit to find on this debut for the yard, and wasn't ridden as positively as usual, so there was plenty to like about his effort. He isn't easy to place, but has a win in him. (op 14-1)
Run For The Hills, having only his eighth start, refused to settle early and then emptied out late on having made a brief forward move. (op 5-1)
Evens And Odds(IRE), a decent fourth in the Abernant Stakes, was one of the first beaten. (op 7-2 tchd 3-1)

1907 TOTETRIFECTA H'CAP 1m 2f 95y
5:20 (5:21) (Class 4) (0-85,83) 4-Y-O+ **£5,180** (£1,541; £770; £384) **Stalls** Centre

Form				RPR
243	1		**Ahlawy (IRE)**[10] 1631 7-8-8 **73** ... (t) DarryllHolland 2 (F Sheridan) *trckd ldrs: pushed along over 2f out: rdn to ld over 1f out: styd on and a doing enough cl home* **10/1**	79
05-0	2	¾	**Prince Of Johanne (IRE)**[11] 1600 4-9-4 **83** ... MickyFenton 3 (T P Tate) *hld up in rr: rdn 2f out: hdwy over 1f out: sn hung lft: chsd wnr ins fnl f: chal fnl 100yds: hld fnl strides* **10/1**	88
136-	3	2	**Lady Luachmhar (IRE)**[210] 6681 4-9-3 **82** ... TonyHamilton 8 (R A Fahey) *hld up: rdn 2f out: effrt whn nt clr run 1f out: kpt on ins fnl f: nt pce to get to front pair* **3/1**[2]	86+
615-	4	¾	**Jawaab (IRE)**[196] 7020 6-8-12 **77** ... AdrianMcCarthy 6 (Mark Buckley) *in tch: chal 2f out: rdn and upsides over 1f out: no ex fnl 75yds* **16/1**	77
56-0	5	1 ¼	**Resurge (IRE)**[21] 1388 5-8-13 **78** ... PatDobbs 1 (W S Kittow) *midfield: effrt over 2f out: nt qckn over 1f out: eased whn no imp fnl 75yds* **10/3**[3]	77
	6	nk	**Bucephalus (IRE)**[13] 5559 6-8-0 **72** ... (t) RosieJessop(7) 4 (M A Barnes) *hld up: rdn over 3f out: drifted rt 1f out: nvr a danger* **33/1**	69
24-2	7	5	**Sam Sharp (USA)**[11] 1600 4-9-3 **82** ... IanMongan 7 (H R A Cecil) *prom: led over 2f out: rdn and hdd over 1f out: wknd ent fnl f* **2/1**[1]	69
2226	8	1	**Tropical Blue**[14] 1512 4-8-4 **70** ow2 ... (p) MarcHalford(3) 5 (Jennie Candlish) *led: rdn and hdd over 2f out: n.m.r over 1f out: sn eased whn btn* **10/1**	57

2m 15.04s (-0.96) **Going Correction** +0.175s/f (Good) **8** Ran SP% **117.5**
Speed ratings (Par 105): **98,97,95,95,94 93,89,89**
Tote Swingers: 1&2 £11.90, 1&3 £5.20, 2&3 £5.50 CSF £105.83 CT £376.93 TOTE £13.70: £2.90, £2.80, £1.40; EX 91.00 Trifecta £107.50 Pool: £145.38 - 1.00 winning units. Place 6: £57.18 Place 5: £47.90..

Owner Frank Sheridan **Bred** Castlemartin Stud And Skymarc Farm **Trained** Averham Park, Notts
FOCUS
A fair handicap.
Resurge(IRE) Official explanation: jockey said gelding was denied a clear run
Sam Sharp(USA) Official explanation: trainer's rep had no explanation for the poor form shown
Tropical Blue Official explanation: jockey said gelding was denied a clear run
T/Plt: £76.30. Pool: £90,733.76 - 867.39 winning units. T/Qpdt: £38.00. Pool: £4,634 - 90.22 winning units. DO

1870 LINGFIELD (L-H)
Saturday, May 8
OFFICIAL GOING: Good to firm (round 8.0; straight 8.3)
Wind: modest, half against Weather: overcast, light rain at times

1908 TOTESPORT 0800 221 221 CHARTWELL FILLIES' STKS (GROUP 3) 7f
2:10 (2:10) (Class 1) 3-Y-O+

£36,900 (£13,988; £7,000; £3,490; £1,748; £877) **Stalls** High

Form				RPR
411-	1		**Pyrrha**[267] 5005 4-9-3 100 ... AlanMunro 8 (C F Wall) *h.d.w: mde all: rdn over 1f out: styd on wl u.p fnl f* **10/3**[2]	111
10-6	2	¾	**Golden Stream (IRE)**[23] 1326 4-9-3 103 ... RyanMoore 3 (Sir Michael Stoute) *lw: stdd s: hld up in rr: grad crossed to stands' rail: hdwy wl over 1f out: swtchd lft and drvn over 1f out: chsd wnr ent fnl f: kpt on wl but a hld* **7/2**[3]	109
266-	3	3 ½	**Reggane**[217] 6505 4-9-3 113 ... (t) GeraldMosse 1 (A De Royer-Dupre, France) *stdd s: in rr and niggled along after 1f: swtchd lft and rdn over 2f out: sme hdwy 2f out: no imp on ldrs and edgd rt over 1f out: wnt 3rd wl ins fnl f* **5/4**[1]	100
31-0	4	2 ½	**Queen's Grace**[24] 1312 3-8-6 100 ow1 ... SteveDrowne 4 (H Morrison) *on toes: chsd wnr: rdn ent fnl 2f: drvn and wknd 1f out* **16/1**	90
500-	5	3 ¼	**Penny's Gift**[224] 6272 4-9-3 106 ... MichaelHills 6 (R Hannon) *chsd ldrs: rdn and effrt to dispute 2nd ent fnl 2f: wknd over 1f out: wl btn fnl f* **8/1**	84
-060	6	1 ½	**Ahla Wasahl**[7] 1693 4-9-3 99 ... AhmedAjtebi 2 (D M Simcock) *t.k.h early: in tch on outer: rdn and struggling over 2f out: wl btn fr over 1f out* **25/1**	80
-135	7	1	**Areeda (IRE)**[42] 1018 3-8-5 75 ... EddieCreighton 7 (C E Brittain) *chsd ldrs: struggling u.p wl over 2f out: wl bhd fr over 1f out* **66/1**	73

1m 22.16s (-1.14) **Going Correction** +0.075s/f (Good)
WFA 3 from 4yo+ 12lb **7** Ran SP% **112.1**
Speed ratings (Par 110): **109,108,104,101,97 95,94**
Tote Swingers: 1&2 £3.60, 1&3 £1.30, 2&3 £1.40 CSF £14.76 TOTE £4.40: £2.00, £1.80; EX 16.50 Trifecta £29.10 Pool: £438.38 - 11.02 winning units..
Owner Lady Juliet Tadgell **Bred** Hong Kong Breeders Club **Trained** Newmarket, Suffolk
FOCUS
A strong-looking line-up for the level even after a couple were withdrawn in the morning, but the form might be a little suspect because of a possible draw bias and the proximity of the seventh. The race has been rated around the front pair.
NOTEBOOK
Pyrrha got on a roll last season, winning her final two starts in handicaps, so was worthy of her place at this grade for the first time. She was given an intelligent ride by Alan Munro, who bagged the seemingly favoured stands'-side rail and won cosily despite taking a pull during the race. She is undoubtedly up to this grade but may have been flattered by the draw. The Windsor Forest Stakes at Royal Ascot seems the likely target for her, although the 1m trip will be the unknown. (op 7-2 tchd 3-1)
Golden Stream(IRE) had a record of three wins from four starts over 7f before this, so her effort in the Abernant Stakes over 6f was a good one. Back up to what looked a more suitable distance, she weaved her way through rivals heading to the two-furlong pole but could not get out when it looked like her rider wanted to go. When she did get out, the winner had quickened away and could not be caught.
Reggane, representing the stable that took this race in 2008, looked far from exposed and had more than enough in her form to suggest she would be difficult to beat here. Her second to Guineas winner Ghanaati in the Group 1 Coronation Stakes at Royal Ascot stood out against her rivals but she had looked a tricky ride on occasions and, to some extent, did so again here from a poor draw. A return to 1m may help. (op 13-8)
Queen's Grace, one of two three-year-olds taking on their elders, was disappointing in the Nell Gwyn on her reappearance but had great form as a juvenile over 6f, as she beat both Puff and 1,000 Guineas first past the post Jacqueline Quest. Her dam Palace Affair won this race as a three-year-old in 2001 and much like her, sprinting trips will probably suit the Hughie Morrison filly best in due course, considering the way she found one pace from about a furlong out here. (op 12-1)
Penny's Gift was tried at a good level last season and won the German 1,000 Guineas. Behind Golden Stream on her final start of 2009, her trainer felt she would improve for the run and that looked the case, as she never got into contention.
Ahla Wasahl was disappointing in a similar Listed contest the previous weekend and connections stated before this race that there was a slight worry she only comes right in the autumn despite working well at home. She again never got competitive. (op 16-1 tchd 28-1)

1909 TOTESPORTCASINO.COM OAKS TRIAL STKS (LISTED RACE) (FILLIES) 1m 3f 106y
2:40 (2:40) (Class 1) 3-Y-O **£28,385** (£10,760; £5,385; £2,685; £1,345) **Stalls** High

Form				RPR
15-0	1		**Dyna Waltz**[24] 1312 3-8-12 102 ... RyanMoore 1 (J H M Gosden) *led for 1f: in tch after: pushed along and struggling 4f out: modest 4th over 3f out: wnt 3rd u.p 2f out: no imp tl styd on dourly ins fnl f: led fnl 75yds* **7/1**[3]	105
11-4	2	1	**Timepiece**[24] 1313 3-9-1 105 ... TomQueally 4 (H R A Cecil) *lw: hld up in tch: wnt 3rd 1/2-way: chsd ldr ent fnl 3f: rdn to ld over 2f out: hanging lft and racd awkwardly after: hdd fnl 75yds* **4/7**[1]	106
1-	3	2 ½	**Ceilidh House**[213] 6593 3-8-12 0 ... JimCrowley 5 (R M Beckett) *lw: chsd ldr after 2f: led 3f out: sn hdd and rdn: kpt battling on: drvn and stl pressing ldr 1f out: wknd fnl 100yds* **4/1**[2]	99
6-11	4	18	**Bebopalula (IRE)**[12] 1578 3-8-12 ... MichaelHills 3 (B W Hills) *lengthy: athletic: dwlt: sn rdn along to ld after 1f: clr after 2f tl over 5f out: rdn and hdd 3f out: sn wl btn: t.o* **9/1**	68
5-5	5	15	**Golden Waters**[15] 1501 3-8-12 0 ... AlanMunro 6 (Eve Johnson Houghton) *a last: pushed along 8f out: lost tch 5f out: t.o fnl 3f* **40/1**	43

2m 32.46s (0.96) **Going Correction** +0.30s/f (Good) **5** Ran SP% **108.6**
Speed ratings (Par 104): **108,107,105,92,81**
CSF £11.40 TOTE £7.60: £2.20, £1.10; EX 12.00.
Owner George Strawbridge **Bred** George Strawbridge **Trained** Newmarket, Suffolk

FOCUS
Most of the recent winners have made their way to Epsom for the Oaks and, of course, the 2008 runner-up of this trial Look Here went on to land the fillies' Classic. However, not many have gone on to win both races. Lady Carla, Ramruma and User Friendly did it in the 1990s, while the later-disqualified Aliysa did the double in 1989. This race was run at a decent pace, so there will be no stamina worries about the three who dominated the finish. The form looks some way shy of Oaks standard.

NOTEBOOK
Dyna Waltz was taking a big step up in trip after starting her season behind Music Show in the Nell Gwyn. She is bred to stay, so the move up in distance was not a concern, and some of her form as a juvenile was good enough to make her a live contender in any case. Outpaced on the home bend, her chance still looked remote passing the three-furlong marker, but galvanised by a strong ride, she kept finding more and got to the two weakening fillies in front of her close to the winning line. No matter what race she runs in during the season, she will need a strong gallop to chase. There was no decision about whether she goes to Epsom immediately after the race. (op 15-2 tchd 6-1)
Timepiece, representing last year's winning connections, was at the head of some bookmakers' lists for the Oaks before this run but was predictably eased after this. Slightly unlucky in running behind Rumoush in the Feilden Stakes on her reappearance, the half-sister to Father Time and Group 1 winner Passage Of Time travelled nicely just in behind but tended to wander under pressure once in the lead, and started to hang to her left. It's difficult to argue she doesn't stay this trip considering how well she ran, but it would not be the biggest surprise to see her hold her own at 1m2f later in the year. Official explanation: jockey said filly hung left (op 8-11)
Ceilidh House ◆ looked the most interesting runner, as she represented the connections who took the 2008 Oaks with Look Here (runner-up in this race) and the 2007 winner of this trial Kayah. Successful at Nottingham in her only start as a two-year-old (form that has proved to be ordinary), Ralph Beckett reported before the race that she would come on for this outing, so one would imagine they were delighted with her effort. After holding every chance, Jim Crowley was far from hard on her and she is entitled to run well at Epsom if taking her chance. (op 3-1)
Bebopalula(IRE), raised significantly in class, was chasing a hat-trick and set a good pace. On her toes in the paddock, she ensured it was a proper test, so this effort can probably be forgotten. (op 17-2 tchd 8-1)
Golden Waters is a Dubai Destination half-sister to 2005 Oaks runner-up Something Exciting, so connections were obviously going to be hopeful that this trip was within her compass. Noted as flashing her tail under pressure last time, she lost touch early and never featured. (op 33-1)

1910 TOTESPORT.COM DERBY TRIAL STKS (GROUP 3) (C&G) 1m 3f 106y
3:10 (3:13) (Class 1) 3-Y-O
£36,900 (£13,988; £7,000; £3,490; £1,748; £877) **Stalls** High

Form				RPR
1-2	1		**Bullet Train**[22] [1354] 3-8-12 99 ... TomQueally 3 (H R A Cecil) *lw: mde all: lft clr over 3f out: rdn and drew wl clr wl over 1f out: in command after: comf* **11/4**[2]	111+
60-4	2	2 ¼	**Dubawi Phantom**[23] [1327] 3-8-12 104 ... AhmedAjtebi 5 (D M Simcock) *swtg: stdd after s: hld up in last: effrt on inner 2f out: rdn and styd on to chse clr wnr fnl 100yds: kpt on but nvr a threat to wnr* **8/1**	105
16-3	3	1 ½	**Hot Prospect**[24] [1310] 3-8-12 95 ... PhilipRobinson 7 (M A Jarvis) *in tch: lft 3rd over 3f out: rdn and effrt over fnl 2f: unable qck and drvn wl over 1f out: chsd clr wnr 1f out: no imp and lost 2nd fnl 100yds* **8/1**	102
25-3	4	3 ½	**Togiak (IRE)**[17] [1473] 3-8-12 95 ... GeraldMosse 4 (E A L Dunlop) *lw: hld up in tch: lft 5th and hmpd bnd over 3f out: sn rdn: unable qck ent fnl 2f: wl btn fnl f* **40/1**	96+
1	5	¾	**Desert Myth (USA)**[24] [1314] 3-8-12 0 ... RyanMoore 1 (Sir Michael Stoute) *lw: t.k.h: chsd ldng pair: lft 2nd over 3f out: drvn and unable qck 2f out: lost 2nd 1f out: wknd* **6/4**[1]	95
4-0	6	2 ¼	**Don Carlos (GER)**[24] [1310] 3-8-12 105 ... RichardHills 6 (A P O'Brien, Ire) *w'like: str: s.i.s: in tch: lft 4th and rdn over 3f out: wknd u.p 2f out: wl bhd fnl f* **16/1**	91
	P		**Captain James Cook**[22] [1373] 3-8-12 0 ... JMurtagh 2 (A P O'Brien, Ire) *sn chsng ldr: pushed along to press wnr 4f out: lost action bnd over 3f out: sn p.u: fatally injured* **7/1**[3]	—

2m 32.48s (0.98) **Going Correction** +0.30s/f (Good) 7 Ran SP% **109.7**
Speed ratings (Par 109): **108,106,105,102,102 100,—**
Tote Swingers: 1&2 £5.00, 1&3 £4.00, 2&3 £18.40 CSF £22.45 TOTE £3.50: £1.40, £5.50; EX 26.80.
Owner K Abdulla **Bred** Juddmonte Farms Ltd **Trained** Newmarket, Suffolk

FOCUS
It's fair to say this trial has produced plenty of decent horses down the years, although none of them since 2000 went on to win a Group 1 (Percussionist, Franklin Gardens and Bandari won at Group 2 level). Since the turn of the millennium, only Percussionist and Aqaleem have gone on to be placed in the Derby and the last horse to complete the Lingfield/Epsom double was High-Rise back in 1998. Unlike the fillies' trial on the card, this was run at a modest early gallop (although the winner's time was only fractionally slower than Dyna Waltz) and it's not too difficult to argue that the winner stole it from the front under a fine tactical ride.

NOTEBOOK
Bullet Train is not bred to stay middle distances on the dam's side (Kind was a Listed-class sprinter for Roger Charlton, despite being out of a Rainbow Quest mare) but he did run well in a 1m2f conditions race at Newbury on his reappearance last month. Sent straight to the front, Tom Queally dictated things and quickened the tempo at the right time to gain an advantage. There can be little doubt the winner is up to at least this level, possibly higher, but it seems unlikely that he will be handed such an easy lead in the future. One would imagine Khalid Abdullah will wait to see how Workforce performs in the Dante before committing Bullet Train to any engagement, as they also have the option of the King Edward VII Stakes at Royal Ascot, a race won by the owner\trainer in 2009, if they need to separate them. He is a general 12/1 shot for Classic success next month. (tchd 3-1)
Dubawi Phantom arguably had the best bit of form, as he was not beaten far by Elusive Pimpernel in the Craven Stakes. Held up in the rear, he stayed on strongly after becoming outpaced and was closing inside the final furlong. The trainer suggested afterwards that his horse may be aimed towards the King Edwards VII Stakes and in the long-term the St Leger. (op 17-2 tchd 9-1 and 7-1)
Hot Prospect, by a Derby winner, showed decent form at two and was not disgraced in the Tattersalls Timeform 3-y-o Trophy on his first run of the year. A horse who had tended to take a strong hold under restraint, he settled much better here and appeared to have no excuses. One would imagine his trainer will find him the right opportunities. (op 15-2 tchd 17-2)
Togiak(IRE) started his season in the Investec Derby Trial at Epsom and was a readily held third of four. Towards the rear here, he was starting to make a move when meeting the injured Captain James Cook on the home bend, which meant Gerald Mosse was forced to take evasive action for a few strides. That incident obviously did not help his chances, but it's also unlikely that it cost him too many positions. Official explanation: jockey said colt suffered interference in running (op 25-1)
Desert Myth(USA), who missed an engagement in the Dee Stakes the previous day because there was ease in the ground at Chester, did not make the course at two but got his season off to a flyer last month in a Newmarket maiden that is working out nicely. He sat just off the leader but, after being given every chance, could not go with him as he quickened. It was a steep rise in class for him and he should be given another chance. (op 13-8 tchd 11-8)
Don Carlos(GER) was the second string of the O'Brien pair on riding arrangements, although he was good enough to finish fourth in a Group 1 as a two-year-old in France. Slowly away, he never made much impression and was easily held, continuing the modest start to the season for his trainer. (op 14-1)
Captain James Cook, winner of a Dundalk maiden, was virtually upsides Bullet Train turning in before sustaining a fatal injury. (op 13-2 tchd 11-2 and 15-2)

1911 WEATHERBYS BLOODSTOCK INSURANCE CONDITIONS STKS 1m 2f
3:45 (3:45) (Class 2) 4-Y-O+ **£12,462** (£3,732; £1,866; £934; £466) **Stalls** Low

Form				RPR
11-1	1		**Alainmaar (FR)**[17] [1474] 4-8-12 110 ... RichardHills 2 (M A Jarvis) *swtg: chsd ldr: rdn along 3f out: chal u.p ent fnl f: led ins fnl f: forged ahd fnl 75yds* **1/3**[1]	115
631-	2	2	**Peligroso (FR)**[211] [6644] 4-8-12 109 ... AlanMunro 5 (Saeed Bin Suroor) *lw: led: clr after 2f: clr w wnr over 2f out: hrd pressed and rdn ent fnl f: kpt on gamely tl hdd ins fnl f: btn fnl 75yds* **11/2**[2]	111
500-	3	7	**Via Galilei (IRE)**[19] [6867] 5-8-12 104 ... RyanMoore 3 (G L Moore) *hld up in last: rdn and outpcd by ldng pair 3f out: no ch w ldrs fnl 2f: swtchd rt over 1f out: kpt on fnl f to go 3rd nr fin* **50/1**	97
6/30	4	hd	**Burdlaz (IRE)**[64] [820] 5-9-2 105 ... AhmedAjtebi 4 (Mahmood Al Zarooni) *leggy: stdd after s: hld up in tch: rdn and nt qckn w ldng pair wl over 2f out: wl hld fnl 2f: lost 3rd nr fin* **25/1**	101
-120	5	2 ¼	**Tranquil Tiger**[14] [1532] 6-9-12 112 ... (b) TomQueally 1 (H R A Cecil) *lw: hld up in tch: rdn and nt qckn over 2f out: btn and edgd lft u.p 2f out: no ch after* **7/1**[3]	106

2m 10.61s (0.11) **Going Correction** +0.30s/f (Good) **5** Ran SP% **108.7**
Speed ratings (Par 109): **111,109,103,103,101**
CSF £2.52 TOTE £1.30: £1.02, £2.40; EX 2.70.
Owner Hamdan Al Maktoum **Bred** Fares Stables Ltd **Trained** Newmarket, Suffolk

FOCUS
A tight conditions event in which all the runners had at least one question to answer with regards to form, surface or class. The progressive winner probably didn't need to match his impressive Epsom reappearance win.

NOTEBOOK
Alainmaar(FR) is a horse on the up and deserved his chance against this calibre of opposition after blitzing his rivals under a big weight in the City and Suburban Handicap at Epsom. Heavily punted during the morning, he made desperately hard work of claiming the runner-up in the final stages but, in all fairness, the small field may not have played to his strengths. The Hardwicke Stakes at Royal Ascot was nominated as a likely target. (op 2-5, tchd 4-9 in a place)
Peligroso(FR) had four runs for Godolphin after joining them from Mario Hofer in Germany, and finally paid back some of his purchase price on his final start at three. His participation was in doubt due to the ground, but under an excellent ride from Alan Munro, he almost stole victory. One would imagine he might be campaigned abroad in search of easier ground. (tchd 6-1)
Via Galilei(IRE) won a maiden hurdle on his previous start after taking a while to get the hang of that discipline, and was up to a good standard on the Flat when with Jim Bolger. However, he failed to make any impression in this after being held up. (op 40-1)
Burdlaz(IRE), a Listed winner when trained in France, did well for his new connections at Meydan but showed little here. (op 16-1)
Tranquil Tiger enjoyed a good time on the all-weather at this course in three races from November to March (which included the Group 3 Winter Derby) and ran a solid race in the Group 3 Earl of Sefton back on turf, but finished last of seven in the Gordon Richards Stakes on his most recent start. Under a 14lb penalty, he gave the impression he needs a break. (op 13-2)

1912 TOTESPORTGAMES.COM MAIDEN STKS 1m 2f
4:20 (4:21) (Class 5) 3-Y-O+ **£4,857** (£1,445; £722; £360) **Stalls** Low

Form				RPR
	1		**Eavesdropper** 3-8-8 0 ... AhmedAjtebi(3) 6 (Mahmood Al Zarooni) *w'like: str: dwlt: sn in tch in midfield: rn wd bnd over 3f out: rdn to chal over 2f out: led 2f out: sn edging lft: continued to edge lft and bmpd rival jst ins fnl f: kpt on u.p* **6/1**[3]	83+
	2	nk	**Direct Answer (USA)** 3-8-11 0 ... RyanMoore 8 (Sir Michael Stoute) *lengthy: unf: s.i.s: t.k.h: hld up in last trio: hdwy on inner 3f out: pressing ldrs whn nt clr run and hmpd over 1f out: swtchd rt 1f out: rallied and r.o strly fnl 100yds: nt quite rch wnr* **6/1**[3]	84+
623-	3	¾	**Super Collider**[224] [6285] 3-8-11 81 ... PhilipRobinson 5 (M A Jarvis) *t.k.h: led at stdy gallop: hrd pressed and rdn over 2f out: narrowly hdd 2f out: edgd lft over 1f out: stl ev ch and bmpd ins fnl f: no ex and btn fnl 75yds* **11/10**[1]	79
6-5	4	1 ½	**Dynamic Drive (IRE)**[26] [1268] 3-8-11 0 ... AdamKirby 3 (W R Swinburn) *w'like: broke wl: led early: sn trcking ldng pair: effrt between horses 3f out: ev ch but unable qck whn hmpd wl over 1f out: plugged on same pce after* **4/1**[2]	76
6	5	¾	**Whitby Jack**[12] [1581] 3-8-11 0 ... AmirQuinn 7 (G L Moore) *str: lw: t.k.h: chsd ldr: ev ch and rdn over 3f out: keeping on same pce whn hmpd 2f out: one pce and btn after* **14/1**	74
00-	6	8	**Green Energy**[199] [6930] 3-8-11 0 ... GregFairley 1 (Mrs A J Perrett) *w'like: in tch in midfield: rdn and struggling 3f out: lost tch 2f out* **100/1**	58
4-	7	1 ¼	**Destiny Blue (IRE)**[175] [7388] 3-8-11 0 ... JimCrowley 2 (J A Osborne) *str: stdd s: t.k.h: hld up in last pair: rdn and effrt 3f out: hanging lft and wl btn 2f out* **10/1**	56
00-	8	21	**Baltic Ben (USA)**[208] [6728] 3-8-11 0 ... AlanMunro 4 (Eve Johnson Houghton) *w'like: leggy: a towards rr: dropped to last over 5f out: lost tch 4f out: t.o* **66/1**	14

2m 15.87s (5.37) **Going Correction** +0.30s/f (Good) **8** Ran SP% **114.4**
Speed ratings (Par 103): **90,89,89,87,87 80,79,63**
Tote Swingers: 1&2 £2.30, 1&3 £2.60, 2&3 £1.30 CSF £41.58 TOTE £6.70: £1.40, £2.80, £1.10; EX 16.80.
Owner Godolphin **Bred** Darley **Trained** Newmarket, Suffolk
■ Stewards' Enquiry : Ahmed Ajtebi three-day ban: careless riding (May 22-24)

FOCUS
The only runner with an official mark was rated 81, but it is extremely doubtful that he ran to that mark. The outcome was far from satisfactory.

1913 BET IN-PLAY ON LIVE FOOTBALL AT TOTESPORT.COM H'CAP 7f
4:55 (4:58) (Class 3) (0-90,90) 3-Y-O **£9,714** (£2,890; £1,444; £721) **Stalls** High

Form				RPR
06-2	1		**Fireback**[11] [1589] 3-8-6 78 ... DavidProbert 18 (A M Balding) *lw: mde all: clr of field w rival after 2f: pushed clr 2f out: in n.d after: easily* **8/1**[3]	84+
201-	2	3	**Rakaan (IRE)**[222] [6328] 3-8-13 90 ... SophieDoyle(5) 12 (J A Osborne) *in tch in midfield: swtchd lft and rdn 2f out: chalng for placings 1f out: kpt on to go 2nd towards fin: no ch w wnr* **33/1**	88

0660 **3** ½ **Transfixed (IRE)**[35] 1086 3-7-11 **76** oh4........................ KevinLundie(7) 6 73
(P D Evans) *chsd wnr and crossed over towards stands' rail: clr w wnr 5f out: rdn and nt pce of wnr 2f out: stl 2nd but wl hld 1f out: lost 2nd wl ins fnl f* **66/1**

34-1 **4** ¾ **Fivefold (USA)**[113] 180 3-8-6 **78**.. AlanMunro 13 73
(J Akehurst) *chsd ldrs: rdn and unable qck ent fnl 2f: plugged on same pce fr over 1f out: no ch w wnr* **33/1**

1-20 **5** ½ **Edgewater (IRE)**[24] 1315 3-9-1 **87**.. MichaelHills 14 80
(J Akehurst) *sn niggled along towards rr: switching lft off of stands' rail and hdwy 2f out: kpt on fnl f: nvr threatened wnr* **7/1**[2]

16-0 **6** 2 ¾ **Swiss Cross**[24] 1315 3-8-2 **79**.. JohnFahy(5) 11 65
(G A Butler) *chsd ldrs: swtchd lft and rdn ent fnl 2f: no ch w wnr over 1f out* **5/1**[1]

565- **7** 2 ½ **Desert Auction (IRE)**[196] 7013 3-8-13 **88**.................... PatrickHills(3) 16 67
(R Hannon) *hld up towards rr: rdn and effrt over 2f out: hanging lft but hdwy wl 1f out: no prog 1f out: nvr trbld ldrs* **20/1**

150- **8** 5 **Goodwood Maestro**[196] 7013 3-8-5 **77**........................ PaulEddery 15 43
(J L Dunlop) *bit bkwd: swtg: stdd s: hld up bhd: rdn and sme hdwy 2f out: no prog over 1f out: wl btn fnl f* **16/1**

322- **9** 1 ¼ **Be A Devil**[141] 7804 3-8-1 **76**........................ Louis-PhilippeBeuzelin(3) 5 38
(W R Muir) *chsd ldrs: rdn and unable qck ent fnl 2f: plugged on same pce and no ch w wnr after* **33/1**

13- **10** 11 **San Cassiano (IRE)**[220] 6398 3-9-4 **90**........................ JimCrowley 9 23
(R M Beckett) *lw: in tch: rdn over 2f out: sn struggling: wl btn and eased ins fnl f* **9/1**

523- **11** ½ **Warning Song (USA)**[178] 7325 3-8-5 **77**.................... EddieCreighton 10 8
(Mrs A J Perrett) *a towards rr: strugglung and rdn 1/2-way: no ch fnl 2f* **66/1**

10-0 **12** 1 ¾ **Russian Rock (IRE)**[22] 1352 3-8-13 **85**........................ NickyMackay 8 11
(R A Teal) *stdd towards rr: rdn and no prog over 2f out: nvr a factor: eased ins fnl f* **33/1**

2102 **13** 3 ¾ **Candyfloss Girl**[30] 1191 3-8-5 **77**........................ SaleemGolam 2 —
(H J L Dunlop) *a towards rr: rdn and wl btn over 2f out: wl bhd and eased ins fnl f: t.o* **50/1**

3-1 **14** 5 **Prince Of Vasa (IRE)**[29] 1211 3-8-8 **80**........................ GregFairley 4 —
(M Johnston) *tall: unf: racd out towards centre: midfield tl rdn and wknd qckly 3f out: wl bhd fnl 2f: eased ins fnl f: t.o* **25/1**

241- **15** *hd* **Atlaal (USA)**[225] 6246 3-8-13 **85**........................ RichardHills 1 —
(M A Jarvis) *swtg: awkward leaving stalls: styd out in centre: midfield tl btn over 2f out: eased fr over 1f out: t.o* **12/1**

1m 23.15s (-0.15) **Going Correction** +0.075s/f (Good) 15 Ran SP% 89.2
Speed ratings (Par 103): **103,99,99,98,97 94,91,85,84,71 71,69,65,59,59**
Tote Swingers:1&2:£56.60, 1&3:£56.60, 2&3:£56.60 CSF £133.82 CT £5480.27 TOTE £5.80: £1.70, £9.00, £24.10; EX 197.70.
Owner Kennet Valley Thoroughbreds VII **Bred** M Pennell **Trained** Kingsclere, Hants

FOCUS
When considering the evidence of the first race to be run over 7f, punters appeared to only want to know about horses drawn high. They piled into Alice Alleyne (drawn 17), who in all fairness looked to have an obvious chance for leading connections any way, but after appearing to play up in the stalls, she was withdrawn on the vet's advice (2/1F, deduct 30p in the £ under R4). There is a bit of doubt over the form but the winner has been rated up 20lb on his reappearance effort.

NOTEBOOK
Fireback got to the rail quickly and won in convincing style. His first effort of the season on the all-weather at this course entitled him to take this, but one should remember he had the advantage of what seemed to be a golden highway up the stands'-side rail. Hopefully the handicapper will not take the manner of his victory literally given his stalls position, and there is a chance he could head to the Britannia Stakes at Royal Ascot. (op 9-1 tchd 10-1)
Rakaan(IRE) shaped nicely on his first outing since leaving Brian Meehan and is the sort who ought to be thereabouts in similar contests. (op 28-1)
Transfixed(IRE), returning to turf and 4lb out of the handicap, did well to get across from stall six, and in some ways showed what an advantage it was to be close to the rail, as her recent form had looked modest. (op 50-1)
Fivefold(USA) ◆, having his first start on turf, was kept close to the rail but didn't have the acceleration to get near the winner. He may want 1m. (op 28-1)
Edgewater(IRE) tracked Fivefold and stayed on nicely without being a threat. Official explanation: jockey said gelding was denied a clear run (op 6-1)
Swiss Cross was always thereabouts and kept on. (op 11-2)
Desert Auction(IRE) got going late from a good draw and should be straighter for the run. (op 16-1)
Prince Of Vasa(IRE), having his first start on turf, was not well drawn but ran disappointingly. He has quite a bit to prove next time. (op 16-1)
Atlaal(USA) will be better judged after his next outing. (op 6-1)

1914 TOTESPORTBINGO.COM H'CAP (LADY AMATEUR RIDERS) 7f
5:30 (5:30) (Class 5) (0-75,75) 4-Y-0+ £3,123 (£968; £484; £242) Stalls High

Form RPR

010- **1** **Realt Na Mara (IRE)**[182] 7287 7-9-13 **72**.................... MissRKneller(5) 6 83
(H Morrison) *chsd ldrs and grad crossed towards stands' rail: wnt 2nd over 2f out: chal over 1f out: led jst ins fnl f: styd on wl and asserted towards fin* **14/1**

6060 **2** 1 ½ **Hazzard County (USA)**[66] 769 6-10-5 **73**.................... MissEJJones 12 80
(D M Simcock) *sn crossed to r on stands' rail: chsd ldrs: effrt over 1f out: chal ins fnl f: hung lft u.p and nt qckn fnl 100yds: btn towards fin* **4/1**[2]

2-25 **3** 1 ½ **Shaded Edge**[106] 259 6-10-4 **72**........................ MissSBrotherton 9 75
(D W P Arbuthnot) *sn crossed over to stands' rail: towards rr: shkn up over 2f out: styd on ent fnl f: snatched 3rd nr fin but nvr gng pce to rch ldrs* **7/1**[3]

350 **4** *nk* **Headache**[23] 1323 5-9-4 **65**..(bt) MissCEReid(7) 4 67
(B W Duke) *led: rdn over 1f out: hdd jst ins fnl f: btn fnl 75yds: nt rdn and lost 3rd nr fin* **16/1**

660- **5** 1 ¼ **Oh So Saucy**[244] 5697 6-10-4 **72**........................ MissGAndrews 1 71+
(C F Wall) *stdd s: grad switching rt to r nrr to stands' rail: in tch towards rr: hdwy into midfield 3f out: rdn and no prog over 1f out: kpt on same pce fnl f* **12/1**

0506 **6** 2 ¾ **Carmenero (GER)**[25] 1270 7-9-6 **67**........................ MissBAndrews(7) 7 58+
(C R Dore) *in tch: hdwy to chse ldrs and rdn ent fnl 2f: wknd over 1f out* **33/1**

1543 **7** ¾ **Ravi River (IRE)**[40] 1042 6-9-9 **70**........................(v) MissHJones(7) 14 59
(P D Evans) *restless in stalls: s.i.s: bhd: carried bdly rt over 4f out: wl bhd but edging bk towards stands' rail after: u.p wl over 1f out: styd on past btn horses ins fnl f: n.d* **16/1**

654/ **8** 2 ¼ **Oi Vay Joe (IRE)**[564] 6890 6-9-2 **61** oh9........................ MissLAllan(5) 11 44
(W Jarvis) *t.k.h: hld up in tch: sltly hmpd over 5f out: rdn ent fnl 2f: wknd wl over 1f out* **16/1**

0-02 **9** 1 **My Learned Friend (IRE)**[9] 1634 6-10-0 **75**.................... MissLProbert(7) 15 56
(A M Balding) *sn towards rr: switching lft and taking rival w him over 4f out: n.d* **7/4**[1]

1451 **10** 3 ¼ **Alqaahir (USA)**[23] 1322 8-10-2 **73**........................ MissZoeLilly(3) 5 45
(P Butler) *stdd s: hld up towards rr: hdwy 5f out: chsd ldrs and rdn ent 2f out: sn wknd: wl bhd fnl f* **16/1**

6501 **11** 8 **Straight Face (IRE)**[6] 1737 6-10-2 **70** 6ex........................(b) MrsEEvans 10 20
(P D Evans) *in tch tl wknd u.p ent fnl 2f: wl btn fnl f and eased towards fin* **10/1**

-006 **12** 1 ¾ **Crystal B Good (USA)**[9] 1642 4-9-2 **61** oh13........ MissJFerguson(5) 3 6
(J R Best) *chsd ldr tl over 2f out: sn wknd: wl bhd and wandering lft and rt over 1f out* **80/1**

1m 24.96s (1.66) **Going Correction** +0.075s/f (Good) 12 Ran SP% 120.0
Speed ratings (Par 103): **93,91,89,89,87 84,83,81,80,76 67,65**
Tote Swingers: 1&2 £34.30, 1&3 £70.70, 2&3 £4.10 CSF £70.13 CT £445.35 TOTE £18.20: £3.70, £2.40, £2.00; EX 96.70 Place 6: £60.27 Place 5: £22.36..
Owner H Morrison **Bred** J C Condon **Trained** East Ilsley, Berks
■ Stewards' Enquiry : Miss H Jones two-day ban: careless riding (tbn); one-day ban; used whip when out of contention (tbn)

FOCUS
A modest contest. The form is straightforward, judged around the third.
T/Plt: £122.90. Pool: £76,148.68 - 452.12 winning units. T/Qpdt: £35.40. Pool: £4,099.28 - 85.50 winning units. SP

1878 NOTTINGHAM (L-H)
Saturday, May 8

OFFICIAL GOING: Good (good to firm in places)
All races run on outer track.
Wind: Virtually nil Weather: Dull and raining

1915 CHAMPAGNE LANSON BLACK LABEL N.V. H'CAP 5f 13y
1:55 (1:56) (Class 5) (0-70,70) 4-Y-0+ £2,590 (£770; £385; £192) Stalls High

Form RPR

04-1 **1** **Top Bid**[6] 1719 6-8-12 **64** 6ex........................(b) GrahamGibbons 14 75
(T D Easterby) *dwlt and sltly hmpd s: bhd: hdwy 1/2-way: rdn to chse ldrs stands' side wl over 1f out: drvn ins fnl f: sn hung lft: led last 75yds* **3/1**[1]

-101 **2** ½ **Ridley Didley (IRE)**[21] 1391 5-8-11 **66**........................ AshleyHamblett(3) 4 75
(N Wilson) *trckd ldr far side: hdwy to ld that gp and overall ldr 2f out: rdn over 1f out: drvn ins fnl f: hdd and no ex last 75yds: 1st of 3 in gp* **13/2**[3]

3330 **3** ½ **Cape Royal**[47] 967 10-9-4 **70**........................(bt) PatCosgrave 10 77
(J M Bradley) *overall ldr stands' side: rdn and hdd 2f out: drvn and kpt on same pce ins fnl f: 3rd of 12 in gp* **22/1**

50-1 **4** *nk* **King Of Eden (IRE)**[12] 1569 4-8-4 **56**........................ PaulHanagan 12 64+
(E J Alston) *towards rr stands' side: hdwy 2f out: rdn wl over 1f out: styng on whn nt clr run ins fnl f: kpt on: 3rd of 12 in gp* **4/1**[2]

5231 **5** *nk* **Verinco**[23] 1337 4-8-5 **64**........................(v) AdamCarter(7) 1 69
(B Smart) *led far side gp: rdn along and hdd 2f out: sn drvn and kpt on: 2nd of 3 in gp* **10/1**

500- **6** 1 ¼ **Revue Princess (IRE)**[183] 7269 5-8-11 **63**........................ SebSanders 2 63
(T D Easterby) *chsd ldng pair far side: rdn along and sltly outpcd over 2f out: styd on u.p fnl f: 3rd of 3 in gp* **18/1**

5006 **7** 2 ½ **Steel City Boy (IRE)**[23] 1320 7-8-8 **60**........................ RobertWinston 15 51
(D Shaw) *chsd ldrs stands' side: rdn along 2f out: sn one pce: 4th of 12 in gp* **28/1**

406- **8** ½ **Island Legend (IRE)**[211] 6635 4-8-10 **65** ow1........... MichaelGeran(3) 8 55
(J M Bradley) *prom stands' side: rdn along 2f out: grad wknd over 1f out: 5th of 12 in gp* **33/1**

00- **9** *nk* **The Lord**[355] 2130 10-8-11 **66**........................ JackDean(3) 9 55
(W G M Turner) *chsd ldrs towards stands' side: rdn along wl over 1f out: sn wknd: 6th of 12 in gp* **66/1**

6434 **10** ½ **Namir (IRE)**[19] 1428 8-8-9 **68**........................ DavidKenny(7) 5 55
(H J Evans) *chsd ldrs towards stands' side: rdn along 1/2-way: sn wknd: 7th of 12 in gp* **16/1**

1042 **11** ¾ **Mr Funshine**[33] 1131 5-8-4 **56**........................ RoystonFfrench 16 40
(D Shaw) *racd stands' side: rdn along 1/2-way: nvr nr ldrs: 8th of 12 in gp* **14/1**

0-62 **12** 1 ¼ **Sands Crooner (IRE)**[14] 1524 7-9-3 **69**........................(v) PaulMulrennan 6 49
(J G Given) *dwlt: a in rr: 9th of 12 in gp* **15/2**

2006 **13** 5 **Guto**[23] 1337 7-8-12 **67**........................ KellyHarrison(3) 17 29
(W J H Ratcliffe) *a in rr stands' side: 10th of 12 in gp* **25/1**

0310 **14** 12 **Raimond Ridge (IRE)**[22] 1365 4-9-2 **68**........................ AndreaAtzeni 13 —
(J Jay) *stmbld s: a bhd: 11th of 12 in gp* **20/1**

3-00 **15** *nk* **Russian Rocket (IRE)**[21] 1391 8-8-6 **58**........................ RichardMullen 7 —
(Mrs C A Dunnett) *a in rr stands' side: 12th of 12 in gp* **28/1**

59.29 secs (-1.71) **Going Correction** -0.225s/f (Firm) 15 Ran SP% 121.3
Speed ratings (Par 103): **104,103,102,101,101 99,95,94,94,93 92,90,82,62,62**
Tote Swingers: 1&2 £5.80, 1&3 £21.70, 2&3 £31.30 CSF £20.04 CT £381.32 TOTE £4.00: £1.80, £3.40, £10.90; EX 26.50.
Owner John & Marilyn Williams **Bred** Southill Stud **Trained** Great Habton, N Yorks
■ Stewards' Enquiry : Graham Gibbons one-day ban; careless riding (22nd May)

FOCUS
A competitive handicap in which the three lowest drawn runners all went far side and filled three of the first six positions, though the overall result suggested there appeared to be little between either group.

1916 WEATHERBYS BLOODSTOCK INSURANCE H'CAP 1m 6f 15y
2:25 (2:25) (Class 4) (0-80,77) 4-Y-0+ £4,533 (£1,348; £674; £336) Stalls Low

Form RPR

4004 **1** **Hallstatt (IRE)**[8] 1655 4-9-2 **70**........................ SebSanders 4 76
(J Mackie) *led 2f: trckd ldrs tl hdwy 3f out: led over 2f out: rdn clr ent fnl f: styd on wl* **5/1**[3]

2201 **2** 2 ¾ **Red Wine**[31] 1150 11-8-6 **62**........................ KellyHarrison(3) 6 64
(J A Glover) *hld up in rr: hdwy on outer 3f out: rdn wl over 1f out: chsd wnr ins fnl f: sn no imp* **7/1**

63-6 **3** ¾ **Puy D'Arnac (FR)**[34] 1101 7-9-5 **72**........................ RobertWinston 1 73
(G A Swinbank) *trckd ldrs: hdwy 6f out: effrt over 3f out: rdn wl over 2f out: sn drvn and one pce appr fnl f* **11/4**[1]

-040 **4** 1 **Strikemaster (IRE)**[18] 1459 4-8-11 **65**........................(b[1]) TomEaves 3 65
(B Ellison) *hld up in rr: pushed along and hdwy 3f out: rdn wl over 1f out: kpt on u.p fnl f* **9/1**

1124 **5** 2 ½ **Sworn Tigress (GER)**[16] 1484 5-9-5 **77**........................ MatthewDavies(5) 7 73
(George Baker) *prom: led 1/2-way: rdn along over 3f out: hdd over 2f out: drvn wl over 1f out and grad wknd* **7/2**[2]

The Form Book, Raceform Ltd, Compton, RG20 6NL

2141 **6** *8* **Carlton Scroop (FR)**[8] 1655 7-9-2 **69**..........................(b) AndreaAtzeni 2 54
(J Jay) *hld up: hdwy over 4f out: swtchd ins and rdn to chse ldrs over 2f out: drvn wl over 1f out and sn wknd* **5/1**[3]

420/ **7** *27* **Motarid (USA)**[73] 6948 5-9-5 **72**..............................(b) GrahamGibbons 5 19
(T D Walford) *cl up: led after 2f: hdd 1/2-way: rdn along 4f out: wknd 3f out and sn bhd* **8/1**

3m 6.08s (-1.22) **Going Correction** +0.05s/f (Good)
WFA 4 from 5yo+ 1lb **7** Ran SP% **115.8**
Speed ratings (Par 105): **105,103,103,102,101 96,81**
Tote Swingers: 1&2 £4.80, 1&3 £6.70, 2&3 £4.20 CSF £39.92 TOTE £8.20: £2.50, £5.00; EX 51.30.
Owner A B Hill **Bred** Darley **Trained** Church Broughton , Derbys

FOCUS
A fair handicap run at a much better pace than expected seeing there was no obvious front-runner in the field, and ultimately a good test at the trip.

1917 WEATHERBYS BETTRENDS.CO.UK H'CAP 6f 15y
2:55 (2:55) (Class 3) (0-95,92) 3-Y-O **£7,123** (£2,119; £1,059; £529) **Stalls** High

Form RPR

13-0 **1** **Folly Bridge**[24] 1315 3-8-6 **80**.......................... RichardMullen 11 90
(R Charlton) *trckd ldrs: pushed along 2f out: rdn over 1f out: qcknd to ld ins fnl f: edgd lft and kpt on wl towards fin* **13/2**

51-3 **2** *1 1/4* **Deacon Blues**[21] 1376 3-8-4 **78**.......................... AndreaAtzeni 6 84+
(J R Fanshawe) *hld up in rr: hdwy over 2f out: rdn and squeezed through to ld briefly ins fnl f: sn hdd and nt qckn towards fin* **2/1**[1]

10-3 **3** *1 1/4* **Sunraider (IRE)**[24] 1315 3-9-1 **89**.......................... RobertWinston 2 91
(B W Hills) *a cl up: effrt wl over 1f out: sn rdn and ev ch tl drvn and nt able to qckn ins fnl f* **3/1**[2]

65-0 **4** *hd* **Colonel Mak**[24] 1315 3-9-2 **90**.......................... PhillipMakin 7 91
(T D Barron) *trckd ldrs: rdn along and outpcd over 1f out: drvn and hdwy whn nt clr run and sxwitched lft ins fnl f: kpt on towards fin* **6/1**[3]

3-50 **5** *shd* **Nosedive**[7] 1701 3-9-4 **92**.......................... LiamJones 12 93
(W J Haggas) *stdd s and hld up in rr: swtchd rt and hdwy 2f out: rdn over 1f out: styd on ins fnl f: nrst fin* **16/1**

1-05 **6** *1/2* **Comedy Hall (USA)**[14] 1523 3-9-1 **89**.......................... RoystonFfrench 4 88
(M Johnston) *led: rdn along and hdd over 2f out: drvn and wknd over 1f out* **20/1**

310- **7** *1 1/2* **Coin From Heaven (IRE)**[190] 7147 3-8-11 **85**.............. PaulHanagan 9 79
(R A Fahey) *trckd ldrs: rdn along 2f out: drvn and wknd over 1f out* **16/1**

421- **8** *nk* **London Gold**[182] 7289 3-8-4 **78**.......................... FrankieMcDonald 8 71
(H Candy) *cl up: led over 2f out: rdn over 1f out: drvn and hdd ins fnl f: wknd* **14/1**

0-36 **9** *17* **Yurituni**[15] 1499 3-8-9 **83**.......................... SilvestreDeSousa 5 22
(Eve Johnson Houghton) *trckd ldrs: rdn along over 2f out: sn wknd* **20/1**

631- **10** *1* **Wishbone (IRE)**[220] 6378 3-8-9 **83**.......................... PatCosgrave 3 19
(M G Quinlan) *dwlt and in rr: sme hdwy on outer 1/2-way: sn rdn along and outpcd fr over 2f out* **33/1**

1m 12.9s (-2.00) **Going Correction** -0.225s/f (Firm) **10** Ran SP% **116.8**
Speed ratings (Par 103): **104,102,100,100,100 99,97,97,74,73**
Tote Swingers: 1&2 £4.70, 1&3 £5.40, 2&3 £2.70 CSF £19.39 CT £49.35 TOTE £9.60: £2.20, £1.30, £1.50.
Owner D J Deer **Bred** The National Stud Never Say Die Club Ltd **Trained** Beckhampton, Wilts

FOCUS
A useful handicap though one that lost some of its interest after a couple of withdrawals in the morning. The field all came down the centre and the pace didn't really begin to pick up until after halfway, so the result promises to be a bit muddling.

NOTEBOOK
Folly Bridge reversed Newmarket form with Sunraider with an authoritative performance, taking a while to pick up but then pulling away in good style late on. She was a bit disappointing tried at 7f on her final run last year, but left the impression here that that the trip will prove within reach now. (op 17-2)
Deacon Blues ran well in defeat and though he was briefly short of room when making his challenge and seemed to lose his action for a few strides it didn't affect the result. Once again, he impressed with the way he travelled and he can win something a bit less competitive at this trip. (tchd 15-8 and 9-4)
Sunraider(IRE) was never far away and held every chance from some way out. There's some stamina on the female side of his pedigree and he should prove better at 7f. (op 4-1)
Colonel Mak hails from a yard in great form but never managed to land a blow. His current mark leaves him with little room for error but a stronger pace would have seen him in a better light and he might even be worth a try at 7f. (op 7-1 tchd 11-2)
Nosedive ran better than he had in handicaps in either of his previous starts this season without ever promising to finish any closer. He still retains a touch of class but the way this race panned out would have been in his favour.
Comedy Hall(USA) ran his best race this year, but very much had the run of things from the front and might have been a touch flattered. (op 16-1)
Coin From Heaven(IRE) was out of her depth in Listed company when last seen, but she left the impression here she hasn't come to herself yet and shouldn't be written off from what still looks a potentially good mark. (op 18-1)
London Gold ◆ was very weak in the market but travelled noticeably well for a long way before leaving the impression the race was badly needed. Second to a subsequent Group 3 winner on his second start, he's also on a potentially lenient mark and is just the type his trainer does well with. (op 9-1)
Wishbone(IRE) ran here in preference to the following Listed race but was another that was very weak in the market and that's seldom a good sign from her yard. The handicapper looks to have taken few chances with her mark. (op 20-1)

1918 WEATHERBYS BANK KILVINGTON FILLIES' STKS (LISTED RACE) 6f 15y
3:30 (3:31) (Class 1) 3-Y-O+
£22,708 (£8,608; £4,308; £2,148; £1,076; £540) **Stalls** High

Form RPR

346- **1** **Prescription**[168] 7488 5-9-3 95.......................... SebSanders 11 97+
(Sir Mark Prescott) *in rr whn hmpd and swtchd rt after 1f: hdwy on stands' rail 2f out: rdn over 1f out and qcknd wl to ld ins fnl f: kpt on wl* **8/1**[3]

010- **2** *1/2* **Serious Attitude (IRE)**[272] 4837 4-9-3 109.............. RobertWinston 12 95
(Rae Guest) *hld up in tch: hdwy to trck ldrs 1/2-way: rdn along and sltly outpcd whn n.m.r wl over 1f out: styd on u.p ins fnl f* **6/4**[1]

10- **3** *hd* **Tropical Treat**[196] 7016 3-8-7 87.......................... JackMitchell 6 92
(R M Beckett) *dwlt and wnt lft s: in rr tl hdwy over 2f out: chsd ldrs and swtchd lft wl over 1f out: rdn to chal and ev ch ent fnl f: drvn and nt qckn fnl 100yds* **16/1**

5204 **4** *1/2* **Ishiadancer**[14] 1519 5-9-3 80.......................... SilvestreDeSousa 10 93?
(E J Alston) *led: rdn along 2f out: drvn wl over 1f out: edgd lft and hdd ins fnl f* **50/1**

126- **5** *2 3/4* **Bounty Box**[204] 6814 4-9-3 95.......................... GeorgeBaker 4 84
(C F Wall) *trckd ldrs: effrt 2f out: sn rdn and edgd lft ent fnl f: kpt on same pce* **12/1**

350- **6** *nk* **Pretty Bonnie**[224] 6282 5-9-3 85.......................... NataliaGemelova 16 83
(A E Price) *in tch on stands' rail: effrt 2f out: sn rdn along and kpt on ins fnl f: nvr rchd ldrs* **50/1**

135- **7** *3/4* **Astrophysical Jet**[203] 6852 3-8-7 94.......................... GrahamGibbons 7 78
(E S McMahon) *prom: rdn along 2f out and ev ch tl drvn: edgd lft and wknd appr fnl f* **11/1**

52-0 **8** *1 1/2* **Impressible**[13] 1545 4-9-3 87.......................... RichardMullen 15 76
(S C Williams) *cl up on stands' rail: rdn along 2f out and ev ch tl drvn and wknd appr fnl f* **33/1**

14-5 **9** *1* **Sea Of Leaves (USA)**[21] 1400 4-9-3 94.......................... PhillipMakin 3 73
(J S Goldie) *hld up: a towards rr* **12/1**

/303 **10** *hd* **Souter's Sister (IRE)**[12] 1570 4-9-3 95..................(b[1]) KirstyMilczarek 2 72
(M Botti) *chsd ldrs towards outer: rdn along over 2f out and sn wknd* **25/1**

11-2 **11** *1 3/4* **Golden Destiny (IRE)**[13] 1545 4-9-3 100..................(p) PatCosgrave 14 67
(P J Makin) *chsd ldrs to 1/2-way: sn wknd* **8/1**[3]

140- **12** *2 1/4* **Seeking Dubai**[190] 7147 3-8-7 92.......................... RoystonFfrench 13 57
(E F Vaughan) *kkeen: midfield whn sltly hmpd after 1f: rdn along 1/2-way and sn in rr* **40/1**

104- **13** *3/4* **Rose Blossom**[239] 5822 3-8-7 99.......................... PaulHanagan 1 54
(R A Fahey) *in tch: hdwy to chse ldrs on wd outside 1/2-way: rdn along over 2f out and sn wknd* **5/1**[2]

1m 12.34s (-2.56) **Going Correction** -0.225s/f (Firm)
WFA 3 from 4yo+ 10lb **13** Ran SP% **121.6**
Speed ratings (Par 108): **108,107,107,106,102 102,101,99,98,97 95,92,91**
Tote Swingers: 1&2 £4.20, 1&3 £36.10, 2&3 £15.30 CSF £19.93 TOTE £6.80: £1.60, £2.10, £8.20; EX 29.00.
Owner Cheveley Park Stud **Bred** Cheveley Park Stud Ltd **Trained** Newmarket, Suffolk
■ Stewards' Enquiry : Jack Mitchell one-day ban; used whip with excessive frequency (22nd May)

FOCUS
A useful contest that once again went the way of the older contingent. The field stayed stand side this time and the pace again wasn't strong, with the runners well bunched at halfway and one of the outsiders still there at the finish.

NOTEBOOK
Prescription had been a steady improver last year and it looked significant that her connections had persevered with her as a 5yo. Knocked back to the rear at halfway, she picked up really well when a gap appeared next to the rail and won a touch cosily. This rates a career-best performance and, as she is only lightly raced, she can become an even better performer later this season, either at 6f or 7f.
Serious Attitude(IRE) was easy to back on her first run since last August and ran a creditable race, albeit below her best. She had to wait for a run just as the winner was getting the gaps and might have been closer otherwise, but appeared to lack race sharpnes. She might meet the winner again in the Cecil Frail Stakes at Haydock later in the month. (tchd 7-4)
Tropical Treat ◆ ran an excellent first race of the season, working her way towards the outside and possibly showing ahead briefly inside the last. Well regarded, she looks up to winning something similar at this trip back against her own age group. (op 18-1 tchd 14-1)
Ishiadancer is clearly better at this trip than 7f on the turf, but she was flattered by being up with the gallop and won't be easy to place now that her handicap mark on both surfaces will increase.
Bounty Box threatened briefly but didn't see her race out and probably needed this reappearance. She's twice come up short at this level now, but she's still only lightly raced and did enough last year to suggest she'll get there before long. (op 11-1)
Pretty Bonnie isn't usually at her best first time out but she didn't run too badly and will be of more interest next time, particularly in a handicap, given her record second time out as she won at 9-1 last year and was beaten a neck at 25-1 in 2008. (op 80-1)
Astrophysical Jet was another that left the impression she needed the race, but she showed up for a long way. (tchd 9-1)
Seeking Dubai Official explanation: jockey said filly ran to free
Rose Blossom more often than not failed to live up to her home reputation last year and was well held again here after seeing too much daylight and pulling too hard. Official explanation: jockey said filly hung left (op 7-1)

1919 CHAMPAGNE LANSON BLACK LABEL ROSE N.V. H'CAP (DIV I) 1m 2f 50y
4:05 (4:05) (Class 6) (0-60,60) 4-Y-O+ **£1,706** (£503; £252) **Stalls** Low

Form RPR

0-23 **1** **Royal Straight**[31] 1177 5-9-4 **60**.......................... PaulHanagan 11 76
(R A Fahey) *trckd ldrs: smooth hdwy 3f out: led 2f out: rdn clr over 1f out: comf* **2/1**[1]

2-02 **2** *6* **Major Promise**[15] 1503 5-9-0 **56**.......................... PatCosgrave 8 61
(Jane Chapple-Hyam) *hld up in midfield: hdwy over 3f out: rdn over 2f out: drvn to chse wnr ins fnl f: sn no imp* **8/1**

6221 **3** *1/2* **Colonel Sherman (USA)**[24] 1303 5-8-5 **50**........ AndrewHeffernan(3) 10 54
(P A Kirby) *sn led: clr over 4f out: rdn 3f out: hdd 2f out and sn drvn: kpt on same pce* **4/1**[2]

-134 **4** *1 1/2* **Magic Haze**[41] 1028 4-9-1 **57**.......................... SebSanders 4 58
(Miss S E Hall) *hld up in tch: hdwy on outer to chse ldrs 3f out: rdn along 2f out: sn drvn and one pce* **13/2**[3]

020- **5** *1/2* **What A Day**[251] 5470 4-9-0 **56**.......................... GrahamGibbons 7 56
(J J Quinn) *prom: rdn along over 3f out: drvn over 2f out and sn wknd* **16/1**

10-0 **6** *shd* **Tres Froide (FR)**[16] 1489 5-9-3 **59**.......................... AndrewElliott 12 59
(N Tinkler) *in tch: hdwy to chse ldrs 3f out: rdn along over 2f out: sn drvn and kpt on same pce* **16/1**

5-04 **7** *2 1/4* **Kyle Of Bute**[14] 1520 4-9-2 **58**.......................... J-PGuillambert 14 54
(B P J Baugh) *hld up in midfield: hdwy on inner over 3f out: rdn 2f out and sn no imp* **10/1**

3060 **8** *1 3/4* **Look Officer (USA)**[14] 1539 4-9-1 **57**.......................... TomMcLaughlin 3 49
(Miss M E Rowland) *s.i.s: a in rr* **40/1**

3630 **9** *11* **Sea Land (FR)**[15] 1204 6-8-13 **55**.......................... KirstyMilczarek 9 27
(B Ellison) *a in rr* **16/1**

020- **10** *nk* **Rascal In The Mix (USA)**[188] 7197 4-8-8 **53**........ MichaelStainton(3) 16 24
(R M Whitaker) *in tch: rdn along 3f out: drvn over 2f out and sn wknd* **33/1**

6320 **11** *1 3/4* **Desert Fairy**[64] 816 4-8-8 **50** ow2.......................... RobertWinston 1 18
(J W Unett) *chsd ldr: rdn along over 3f out: wknd over 2f out* **25/1**

0/ **12** *6* **Celtic Warrior (IRE)**[584] 2266 7-8-8 **55**.......................... MarkCoumbe(5) 2 11
(John A Harris) *a bhd* **40/1**

000- **13** *1 1/2* **Applaude**[132] 7851 5-8-13 **60**..........................(p) BillyCray(5) 6 13
(R C Guest) *a in rr* **33/1**

1-00 **14** *2 3/4* **Hint Of Honey**[15] 1503 4-8-8 **50**.......................... RoystonFfrench 5 —
(A G Newcombe) *dwlt: hdwy and in tch after 2f: rdn along over 3f out: sn wknd* **28/1**

2m 13.21s (1.51) **Going Correction** +0.05s/f (Good) **14** Ran SP% **122.6**
Speed ratings (Par 101): **95,90,89,88,88 88,86,84,76,75 74,69,68,66**
Tote Swingers: 1&2 £4.80, 1&3 £3.50, 2&3 £6.60 CSF £17.41 CT £61.44 TOTE £2.50: £1.10, £4.10, £2.00; EX 20.00.
Owner McAndrew Utilities Limited **Bred** Brook Stud Bloodstock & Leydens Farm Stud **Trained** Mulsey Bank, N Yorks

FOCUS
A modest handicap run at a steady pace initially in which the form horses came to the fore. The result makes sense.
Hint Of Honey Official explanation: jockey said filly ran free and hung right

1920 CHAMPAGNE LANSON BLACK LABEL ROSE N.V. H'CAP (DIV II) 1m 2f 50y
4:40 (4:41) (Class 6) (0-60,60) 4-Y-0+ £1,706 (£503; £252) Stalls Low

Form RPR
6554 **1** **Noah Jameel**[43] 995 8-8-5 **47** RoystonFfrench 5 54
(A G Newcombe) *in tch: hdwy over 2f out: rdn wl over 1f out: drvn and styd on ins fnl f to ld nr line* **16/1**
03-5 **2** *hd* **Highkingofireland**[31] 1177 4-9-3 **59** AndrewElliott 3 66
(J R Weymes) *trckd ldrs: hdwy 3f out: rdn along 2f out: drvn over 1f out: styd on to ld wl ins fnl f: hdd nr line* **6/1**[2]
-640 **3** *shd* **Singbella**[30] 1188 4-9-2 **58** (p) GeorgeBaker 6 64
(C G Cox) *a.p: effrt to chse clr ldr wl over 2f out: drvn over 1f out: ev ch ent fnl f tl no ex towards fin* **10/1**
00-6 **4** *¾* **Nesno (USA)**[44] 814 7-8-13 **55** (p) PhillipMakin 4 60
(M Dods) *led: clr wl over 2f out: rdn and hung bdly rt 2f out: drvn along on stands' rail over 1f out: hdd and no ex wl ins fnl f* **10/1**
/00- **5** *2¼* **Christophers Quest**[201] 6908 5-8-11 **53** (t) PaulFitzsimons 12 54
(Miss N A Lloyd-Beavis) *bhd: hdwy over 2f out: sn rdn and styd on ins fnl f: nrst fin* **33/1**
002- **6** *3* **Avitus**[206] 6236 4-8-10 **57** PaulPickard(5) 13 52
(Micky Hammond) *in rr tl styd on fnl 3f: n.d* **16/1**
000- **7** *2½* **Paddy Partridge**[316] 3336 4-8-10 **57** RossAtkinson(5) 14 47
(Tom Dascombe) *towards rr and rdn along after 4f: sme hdwy on outer over 2f out: n.d* **12/1**
340- **8** *nk* **Tivers Song (USA)**[159] 7594 6-8-3 **50** (b) AmyBaker(5) 11 40
(John A Harris) *dwlt and towards rr: hdwy on wd outside 3f out: rdn along 2f out: sn no imp* **14/1**
5500 **9** *1¼* **Shame The Devil (IRE)**[28] 1226 5-9-0 **56** FrankieMcDonald 9 43
(H J Evans) *a towards rr* **33/1**
3062 **10** *1½* **Boa**[16] 1489 5-9-4 **60** RobertWinston 7 44
(R Hollinshead) *towards rr: effrt and sme hdwy over 3f out: rdn along over 2f out and nvr a factor* **3/1**[1]
20-3 **11** *½* **Maybe I Wont**[25] 1277 5-8-11 **60** (p) DavidKenny(7) 16 44
(Lucinda Featherstone) *in tch on outer: rdn along over 3f out: sn wknd* **15/2**[3]
350- **12** *3¾* **Highland Love**[147] 6126 5-8-10 **57** PatrickDonaghy(5) 10 33
(Jedd O'Keeffe) *chsd ldrs: rdn along 3f out: drvn over 2f out and sn wknd* **20/1**
40-4 **13** *1¼* **Chichen Daawe**[16] 1489 4-8-6 **48** KirstyMilczarek 15 22
(B Ellison) *chsd ldrs: rdn along over 3f out and sn wknd* **10/1**
4340 **14** *1* **Mullitovermaurice**[17] 1478 4-8-12 **54** (b[1]) LeeVickers 1 26
(J G Given) *prom on inner: rdn along 3f out: drvn and wknd 2f out* **33/1**
600- **15** *45* **Short Supply (USA)**[177] 7353 4-8-8 **50** GrahamGibbons 8 —
(T D Walford) *midfield whn mot much room and hmpd after 2f: towards rr fr 1/2-way: bhd and virtually p.u fnl 2f* **10/1**

2m 13.44s (1.74) **Going Correction** +0.05s/f (Good) **15 Ran SP% 127.1**
Speed ratings (Par 101): **95,94,94,94,92 89,87,87,86,85 85,82,81,80,44**
Tote Swingers: 1&2 £23.10, 1&3 £36.10, 2&3 £12.70 CSF £110.52 CT £1033.37 TOTE £25.10: £4.70, £2.40, £3.60; EX 311.20.
Owner A G Newcombe **Bred** Michael Ng **Trained** Yarnscombe, Devon

FOCUS
The second and weaker division and run in a slightly slower time than the opening contest, largely on account of a steadier earlier pace.
Chichen Daawe Official explanation: jockey said filly never picked up
Mullitovermaurice Official explanation: jockey said gelding hung left
Short Supply(USA) Official explanation: trainers representative said suffered interference im back straight and never travelled after

1921 BEST DRESSED LADY H'CAP 1m 75y
5:15 (5:15) (Class 5) (0-75,74) 3-Y-0 £3,238 (£963; £481; £240) Stalls Centre

Form RPR
42-0 **1** **Count Bertoni (IRE)**[78] 625 3-9-4 **74** (p) GeorgeBaker 3 76
(S Gollings) *trckd ldrs: effrt 2f out and sn rdn: drvn ins fnl f: styd on to ld nr fin* **9/1**
1-06 **2** *shd* **Secretive**[18] 1448 3-9-3 **73** RoystonFfrench 7 75
(M Johnston) *towards rr and remindetrs after 3f: hdwy on outer 3f out: rdn along to chse ldrs 2f out: drvn ins fnl f and kpt on wl towards fin* **4/1**[3]
00-1 **3** *shd* **Lord Raglan (IRE)**[31] 1178 3-8-11 **67** AndrewElliott 5 69
(J R Weymes) *cl up: effrt over 2f out: rdn over 1f out: drvn ins fnl f: kpt on wl towards fin* **7/2**[2]
5-40 **4** *½* **Leitzu (IRE)**[18] 1448 3-8-6 **62** KirstyMilczarek 4 62
(M R Channon) *led: rdn clr ent fnl f: sn drvn: hdd & wknd nr fin* **12/1**
451- **5** *1¼* **Starry Mount**[189] 7168 3-9-3 **73** PhillipMakin 8 71
(A B Haynes) *hld up: effrt 3f out: rdn along 2f out: drvn over 1f out: kpt on same pce fnl f* **4/1**[3]
00-2 **6** *2¾* **Jimmy The Poacher (IRE)**[14] 1522 3-8-12 **68** J-PGuillambert 6 59
(T D Easterby) *trckd ldng pair: effrt and hdwy 3f out: rdn 2f out: drvn over 1f out: wknd ins fnl f* **15/8**[1]

1m 47.41s (1.81) **Going Correction** +0.05s/f (Good) **6 Ran SP% 114.7**
Speed ratings (Par 99): **92,91,91,91,90 87**
Tote Swingers: 1&2 £5.20, 1&3 £6.30, 2&3 £2.10 CSF £45.19 CT £151.59 TOTE £17.30: £6.80, £2.80; EX 49.30.
Owner Richard Swift **Bred** Le Thenney S A **Trained** Scamblesby, Lincs
■ Shayla (9/2) was withdrawn on vet's advice. Deduct 15p in the £ under R4.

FOCUS
Five withdrawals rendered what promised to be an informative event run of the mill. It was run at just a fair gallop, the pace only really picking up 3f out and the form promises to be unreliable.

1922 HEART106 APPRENTICE H'CAP 1m 75y
5:45 (5:45) (Class 6) (0-60,64) 4-Y-0+ £1,942 (£578; £288; £144) Stalls Centre

Form RPR
0-42 **1** **Four Kicks (IRE)**[9] 1633 4-8-5 **51** RyanPowell(5) 5 63
(J S Moore) *trckd ldng pair: hdwy over 2f out: rdn to ld wl over 1f out: edgd rt ins fnl f: kpt on* **7/1**[3]
-521 **2** *1* **Whipma Whopma Gate (IRE)**[5] 1772 5-9-6 **64** 6ex(v) RichardEvans(3) 13 74
(D Carroll) *trckd ldrs: hdwy over 2f out: sn rdn: drvn to chse wnr ins fnl f: no imp towards fin* **13/8**[1]
050- **3** *1¾* **One Scoop Or Two**[192] 7105 4-8-2 **50** NicolaJackson(7) 14 56
(R Hollinshead) *led: rdn along over 2f out: hdd wl over 1f out and kpt on same pce fnl f* **28/1**
0212 **4** *1½* **Bajan Pride**[12] 1576 6-8-13 **61** MarzenaJeziorek(7) 16 64
(R A Fahey) *cl up: rdn along over 2f out: sn one pce* **6/1**[2]
2240 **5** *2¼* **Alfredtheordinary**[11] 1591 5-9-1 **59** MatthewDavies(3) 11 56
(M R Channon) *midfield: effrt 3f out: rdn over 2f out: plugged on same pce* **6/1**[2]
2310 **5** *dht* **Royal Acclamation (IRE)**[31] 1170 5-8-8 **54** DavidKenny(5) 2 51
(H J Evans) *midfield: hdwy 3f out: rdn along 2f out: sn drvn and one pce* **14/1**
006- **7** *3½* **Wotatomboy**[173] 7417 4-8-3 **49** ow3 DuilioDaSilva(5) 9 38
(R M Whitaker) *in tch: rdn along 3f out: drvn over 2f out and sn btn* **33/1**
060- **8** *½* **Some Time Good (IRE)**[170] 2380 4-9-5 **60** (p) RussKennemore 4 48
(Miss J S Davis) *a towards rr* **40/1**
00-5 **9** *2* **Heart Of Dubai (USA)**[19] 1427 5-8-7 **51** DeclanCannon(3) 1 35
(Micky Hammond) *chsd ldrs: rdn along 3f out: wknd 2f out* **16/1**
0-01 **10** *6* **Portrush Storm**[15] 1503 5-8-3 **49** JohnCavanagh(5) 8 19
(R E Peacock) *t.k.h: chsd ldrs: rdn along 3f out: wknd over 2f out* **12/1**
3350 **11** *2¼* **Special Cuvee**[51] 918 4-9-0 **58** AmyBaker(3) 3 23
(A B Haynes) *s.i.s: a in rr* **14/1**
66-0 **12** *36* **Le Petit Vigier**[12] 1576 4-8-0 **46** (t) NathanAlison(5) 10 —
(P F Holmes) *v s.i.s: a bhd* **50/1**

1m 46.37s (0.77) **Going Correction** +0.05s/f (Good) **12 Ran SP% 116.9**
Speed ratings (Par 101): **98,97,95,93,91 91,88,87,85,79 77,41**
Tote Swingers: 1&2 £4.90, 1&3 £20.70, 2&3 £13.90 CSF £17.88 CT £311.75 TOTE £8.40: £3.00, £1.40, £5.90; EX 19.90 Place 6: £110.61 Place 5: £52.20.
Owner James Clements **Bred** Fortview Stud **Trained** Upper Lambourn, Berks

FOCUS
A modest finale weakened by several withdrawals. It was run at a good pace but those ridden prominently, essentially the form horses, still dominated.
T/Plt: £127.30. Pool: £48,964.50 - 280.70 winning units. T/Qpdt: £29.20. Pool: £2,539.98 - 64.30 winning units. JR

1704 THIRSK (L-H)
Saturday, May 8

OFFICIAL GOING: Good (good to firm in places; 9.7)
Wind: overcast, breezy and cold Weather: moderate 1/2 against

1923 TURFTV.CO.UK (S) STKS 6f
6:05 (6:05) (Class 5) 3-Y-0+ £4,274 (£1,271; £635; £317) Stalls High

Form RPR
4006 **1** **Chosen One (IRE)**[38] 1072 5-9-1 56 JamesSullivan(5) 10 76
(J Hetherton) *w ldrs: led 2f out: edgd rt ins fnl f: jst hld on* **20/1**
5-00 **2** *hd* **Solar Spirit (IRE)**[9] 1650 5-9-1 77 IanBrennan(5) 1 75
(J J Quinn) *led tl 2f out: styd on and upsides ins fnl f: no ex nr fin* **4/1**[2]
3452 **3** *nse* **Bonnie Prince Blue**[9] 1650 7-9-11 77 (b) PaulQuinn 7 80+
(D Nicholls) *s.i.s: hdwy over 2f out: swtchd rt to stands' side rail ins fnl f: chalng whn squeezed for room last 50yds: jst hld* **15/8**[1]
0-00 **4** *6* **Rothesay Dancer**[7] 1711 7-8-12 77 KellyHarrison(3) 12 51
(J S Goldie) *hld up in rr stands' rail: nt clr run over 2f out and over 1f out: styd on fnl f* **9/2**[3]
5330 **5** *3¼* **Tamarind Hill (IRE)**[9] 1643 3-8-10 57 (b) JohnEgan 14 43
(A J McCabe) *chsd ldrs: hung rt and wknd over 1f out* **25/1**
00-0 **6** *2* **Divine Spirit**[21] 1391 9-9-6 60 TomEaves 11 39
(M Dods) *in rr: hdwy stands' side 2f out: styd on fnl f* **11/1**
0-00 **7** *¾* **Cherri Fosfate**[10] 1628 6-9-6 64 (t) DanielTudhope 4 37
(D Carroll) *s.i.s: kpt on f inal 2f: nvr nr ldrs* **25/1**
40-4 **8** *2* **Springwell Giant (IRE)**[86] 507 3-8-3 58 NoraLooby(7) 5 27
(A J McCabe) *chsd ldrs on wd outside: hung lft and one pce fnl 2f* **66/1**
0-05 **9** *nk* **Cheveyo (IRE)**[6] 1722 4-9-6 69 (b[1]) PaulMulrennan 6 29
(Patrick Morris) *mid-div: effrt over 2f out: sn wknd* **25/1**
0-60 **10** *½* **Reprieved**[32] 1142 5-9-6 43 PJMcDonald 9 28
(J J Quinn) *chsd ldrs: lost pl over 2f out* **33/1**
-060 **11** *4½* **Avonlini**[72] 693 4-8-10 39 JemmaMarshall(5) 13 —
(B P J Baugh) *chsd ldrs: wknd over 2f out* **150/1**
60-0 **12** *3½* **Maison Dieu**[23] 1337 7-9-6 59 PatrickMathers 8 —
(A Berry) *chsd ldrs: rdn and lost pl over 2f out* **100/1**
1262 **13** *7* **Lord Fidelio (IRE)**[9] 1651 4-9-6 70 (b[1]) MichaelO'Connell(5) 3 —
(Ollie Pears) *s.i.s: mid-div: effrt over 2f out: sn lost pl* **8/1**
0063 **14** *6* **Imperial House**[11] 1595 4-9-11 65 (b) LiamJones 2 —
(R A Harris) *chsd ldrs on outer: hung lft and lost pl over 2f out: sn bhd* **20/1**

1m 13.09s (0.39) **Going Correction** +0.10s/f (Good)
WFA 3 from 4yo+ 10lb **14 Ran SP% 119.6**
Speed ratings (Par 103): **101,100,100,92,88 85,84,82,81,80 74,70,60,52**
Tote Swingers: 1&2 £17.60, 1&3 £10.10, 2&3 £3.50 CSF £91.48 TOTE £39.20: £13.90, £1.20, £1.10; EX 183.90.There was no bid for the winner.
Owner R G Fell **Bred** Carl Holt **Trained** Norton, N Yorks
■ Stewards' Enquiry : James Sullivan one-day ban: careless riding (May 22)

FOCUS
The jockeys reported it to be riding fast. Run at an even tempo, the race developed down the stands' side and it helped to race with the pace. Not many landed any sort of blow.
Imperial House Official explanation: jockey said colt was unsuited by the good (good to firm places) grou7nd

1924 DICK PEACOCK SPRINT H'CAP 6f
6:35 (6:35) (Class 5) (0-75,75) 4-Y-0+ £4,274 (£1,271; £635; £317) Stalls High

Form RPR
140- **1** **Averoo**[194] 7062 5-8-4 **61** (p) PaulQuinn 14 73+
(M D Squance) *in rr: gd hdwy and nt clr run over 1f out: swtchd lft: r.o strly to ld last 100yds: readily* **22/1**
0-45 **2** *1¼* **Frisbee**[6] 1719 6-8-5 **65** AshleyHamblett(3) 15 72
(D W Thompson) *mid-div: hdwy over 2f out: swtchd lft: styd on to take 2nd nr fin* **8/1**
260- **3** *½* **Mandalay King (IRE)**[246] 5623 5-8-8 **70** DeanHeslop(5) 5 75
(Mrs Marjorie Fife) *s.i.s: in rr: hdwy over 2f out: led over 1f out: hdd ins fnl f: no ex* **12/1**
2644 **4** *nse* **Secret Witness**[23] 1321 4-9-4 **75** (b) LiamJones 7 80
(R A Harris) *chsd ldrs: edgd rt and kpt on wl fnl f* **18/1**
6300 **5** *2¼* **Klynch**[9] 1650 4-8-8 **70** (b) JamesSullivan(5) 2 68
(Mrs R A Carr) *chsd ldrs on outside: one pce appr fnl f* **40/1**
00 **6** *1½* **Running Flame (IRE)**[16] 1492 4-8-5 **65** KellyHarrison(3) 9 58
(A J McCabe) *s.i.s: in rr: hdwy and hung lft 2f out: kpt on fnl f* **100/1**
00-0 **7** *½* **Hazelrigg (IRE)**[22] 1366 5-8-12 **69** (p) PaulMulrennan 10 61
(T D Easterby) *chsd ldrs: edgd lft 2f out: edgd rt 1f out: kpt on same pce* **12/1**

10-5 **8** 1 ½ **Milton Of Campsie**[22] 1365 5-9-0 **71** .... JohnEgan 1 58
(J Balding) *w ldrs: edgd rt over 3f out: led over 2f out: hdd over 1f out: sn wknd* **11/1**
2233 **9** 2 **Turning Circle**[21] 1402 4-8-8 **65** .... AndrewMullen 12 45
(M Brittain) *in rr stands' side: nt clr run and swtchd lft 2f out: nvr a factor* **14/1**
50-6 **10** 1 **Inter Vision (USA)**[7] 1711 10-9-1 **72** .... DanielTudhope 4 49
(A Dickman) *in rr: sme hdwy over 2f out: nvr nr ldrs* **14/1**
60-3 **11** hd **Atlantic Beach**[22] 1366 5-8-8 **65** .... PJMcDonald 13 67+
(J Hetherton) *chsd ldrs: keeping on whn bdly hmpd 1f out: eased* **3/1**[1]
-150 **12** nk **Wyatt Earp (IRE)**[22] 1366 9-8-10 **72** ....(p) TobyAtkinson(5) 3 48
(P Salmon) *in tch: effrt on outside 2f out: sn wknd* **18/1**
0-04 **13** 2 ¾ **Maze (IRE)**[9] 1650 5-8-11 **73** .... MichaelO'Connell(5) 6 40
(D Nicholls) *w ldrs: led over 3f out: hdd over 2f out: sn wknd* **7/1**[3]
0-22 **14** 1 ½ **Mr Wolf**[17] 1470 9-8-7 **69** ....(p) IanBrennan(5) 11 31
(J J Quinn) *led tl over 3f out: wkng whn n.m.r on ins over 1f out* **6/1**[2]
00-0 **15** 1 **Final Salute**[22] 1366 4-8-8 **65** ....(v) TomEaves 8 24
(B Smart) *chsd ldrs: wknd 2f out* **22/1**

1m 12.84s (0.14) **Going Correction** +0.10s/f (Good) **15** Ran SP% **122.6**
Speed ratings (Par 103): **103,101,100,100,97 95,94,92,90,88 88,88,84,82,81**
Tote Swingers: 1&2 £27.60, 1&3 £92.10, 2&3 £78.10 CSF £186.70 CT £2285.19 TOTE £33.40: £8.00, £3.40, £4.90; EX 160.50.
Owner Miss K Squance **Bred** Mrs H Johnson Houghton & Mrs R F Johnson Hought **Trained** Newmarket, Suffolk
■ Stewards' Enquiry : Ian Brennan one-day ban: failed to ride to draw (May 22)
John Egan one-day ban: failed to ride to draw (May 22)

FOCUS
An open 61-75 handicap, run at a furious pace and the first three home had nothing to do with the early gallop. The race developed down the stands' side.
Frisbee Official explanation: jockey said mare finished lame
Hazelrigg(IRE) Official explanation: jockey said gelding hung right
Milton Of Campsie Official explanation: jockey said mare was unsuited by the good (good to firm places) ground
Atlantic Beach Official explanation: jockey said gelding was denied a clear run
Mr Wolf Official explanation: jockey said gelding hung left throughout

1925 GT GROUP H'CAP 1m 4f
7:05 (7:05) (Class 4) (0-80,82) 4-Y-0+ **£5,569** (£1,657; £828; £413) **Stalls Low**

Form RPR
-032 **1** **Destinys Dream (IRE)**[4] 1807 5-8-5 **70** .... KellyHarrison(3) 13 81+
(Miss Tracy Waggott) *hld up in rr: smooth hdwy over 2f out: led on bit over 1f out: shkn up and qcknd clr: v readily* **5/2**[1]
46-0 **2** 3 **Red Kestrel (USA)**[42] 1011 5-8-10 **77** .... MichaelO'Connell(5) 5 80
(K A Ryan) *hld up in rr: hdwy over 3f out: swtchd rt over 2f out: styd on to go 2nd 1f out: no ch w wnr* **20/1**
0-04 **3** 1 ¾ **Umverti**[10] 1629 5-8-4 **66** .... PaulQuinn 12 66
(N Bycroft) *rr-div: drvn over 4f out: hdwy and nt clr run over 2f out: kpt on fnl f* **12/1**
00 **4** nk **Carnac (IRE)**[8] 1655 4-8-6 **73** ow1 .... LanceBetts(5) 9 73
(J S Wainwright) *chsd ldrs: led over 2f out: hdd over 1f out: one pce* **100/1**
4331 **5** 4 ½ **Follow The Flag (IRE)**[7] 1684 6-8-13 **82** ....(p) ConorQuish(7) 8 74
(A J McCabe) *sn chsng ldrs: led 3f out: sn hdd: wknd fnl f* **9/1**
05 **6** ¾ **Spahi (FR)**[17] 1467 4-7-13 **66** .... JamesSullivan(5) 2 57
(J Hetherton) *chsd ldrs: nt clr run over 2f out: wknd jst ins fnl f* **28/1**
31-5 **7** 3 **Bollin Greta**[8] 1655 5-8-9 **71** .... TomEaves 7 57
(T D Easterby) *t.k.h in midfield: effrt over 4f out: lost pl over 1f out* **4/1**[2]
423- **8** 3 ¼ **Regal Lyric (IRE)**[80] 6538 4-8-4 **66** oh1 .... AndrewMullen 3 47
(T P Tate) *in rr: effrt over 3f out: nvr on terms* **16/1**
05-4 **9** 1 ¾ **Veroon (IRE)**[11] 1600 4-9-0 **76** ....(p) PaulMulrennan 6 54
(J G Given) *chsd ldrs: upsides over 2f out: wknd over 1f out* **13/2**
-000 **10** 15 **Amazing Blue Sky**[16] 1484 4-8-11 **73** .... LiamJones 4 27
(Mrs R A Carr) *led: hdd 8f out: wknd over 2f out: bhd whn eased ins last* **25/1**
2135 **11** 7 **Brockfield**[4] 1807 4-8-5 **67** .... AdrianNicholls 10 10
(M Brittain) *chsd ldr: led 8f out tl 3f out: lost pl 2f out: eased whn bhd* **9/2**[3]

2m 37.44s (1.24) **Going Correction** +0.25s/f (Good) **11** Ran SP% **116.7**
Speed ratings (Par 105): **105,103,101,101,98 98,96,93,92,82 78**
Tote Swingers: 1&2 £8.50, 1&3 £6.00, 2&3 £53.10 CSF £59.99 CT £514.48 TOTE £4.40: £1.90, £6.50, £2.90; EX 98.10.
Owner H Conlon **Bred** Sean Burke **Trained** Spennymoor, Co Durham

FOCUS
Run at an even pace and there's no reason to think the form won't work out and throw up a few winners.
Brockfield Official explanation: jockey said colt was unsuited by the good (good to firm places) ground

1926 CALVERTS CARPETS H'CAP 1m
7:35 (7:36) (Class 5) (0-75,75) 4-Y-0+ **£4,274** (£1,271; £635; £317) **Stalls Low**

Form RPR
20-6 **1** **Come And Go (UAE)**[14] 1513 4-9-4 **75** .... PJMcDonald 10 86
(G A Swinbank) *w ldrs: led over 1f out: edgd lft and kpt on wl* **10/1**
404- **2** 1 ¼ **Shadowtime**[220] 6383 5-8-7 **64** .... AndrewMullen 13 72
(Miss Tracy Waggott) *led: hdd over 1f out: styd on same pce ins fnl f* **16/1**
44-0 **3** nk **Templetuohy Max (IRE)**[21] 1395 5-8-11 **68** ....(v) RoystonFfrench 7 76
(J D Bethell) *chsd ldrs: styd on same pce fnl f* **25/1**
2122 **4** nk **Sir George (IRE)**[5] 1754 5-8-13 **75** .... IanBrennan(5) 14 82
(Ollie Pears) *in tch: effrt over 2f out: kpt on same pce fnl f* **4/1**[1]
5060 **5** 6 **Ninth House (USA)**[15] 1508 8-8-0 **62** ....(t) JamesSullivan(5) 18 55
(Mrs R A Carr) *s.i.s: swtchd lft after s: hdwy over 2f out: styd on ins fnl f* **25/1**
4-31 **6** nk **French Art**[10] 1628 5-9-2 **73** ....(p) PhillipMakin 6 66
(N Tinkler) *in tch: effrt: nt clr run and swtchd rt over 2f out: nvr threatened* **9/2**[2]
634- **7** nk **Steel Trade**[228] 6182 4-8-10 **67** .... TomEaves 8 59
(M Brittain) *s.i.s: effrt on outside over 2f out: kpt on: nvr nr ldrs* **33/1**
0-50 **8** nse **Glenridding**[7] 1707 6-8-13 **70** ....(p) PaulMulrennan 16 62
(J G Given) *mid-div: effrt on outer over 2f out: nvr threatened ldrs* **14/1**
332- **9** hd **Celtic Step**[147] 7723 6-8-4 **61** oh1 .... PatrickMathers 9 52
(P D Niven) *chsd ldrs: edgd lft and one pce fnl 2f* **25/1**
-630 **10** ½ **Wovoka (IRE)**[21] 1396 7-8-8 **70** .... MichaelO'Connell(5) 17 60
(K A Ryan) *s.i.s: kpt on fnl 2f: nvr a factor* **20/1**
306- **11** 1 ½ **Ailsa Craig (IRE)**[172] 7423 4-8-9 **66** .... DuranFentiman 5 53
(E W Tuer) *t.k.h in rr: hmpd over 2f out: swtchd rt: nvr a factor* **33/1**
02/- **12** ¾ **Frontline Girl (IRE)**[597] 6037 4-8-5 **62** .... AndrewElliott 11 47
(J R Weymes) *chsd ldrs: wknd over 1f out* **33/1**
/04- **13** 1 ¼ **Ubenkor (IRE)**[350] 2257 5-8-12 **69** .... DanielTudhope 15 51
(M Herrington) *towards rr: nvr on terms* **50/1**
66-0 **14** ¾ **Tanforan**[31] 1172 8-8-1 **63** .... BillyCray(5) 4 43
(B P J Baugh) *in rr: nvr on terms* **33/1**
3232 **15** 1 ½ **Hits Only Jude (IRE)**[10] 1628 7-8-8 **65** .... J-PGuillambert 3 42
(D Carroll) *chsd ldrs: wknd appr fnl f* **8/1**[3]
5011 **16** nk **West End Lad**[19] 1426 7-9-0 **74** ....(b) AshleyHamblett(3) 2 50
(S R Bowring) *in rr: rdn and edgd rt over 2f out: nvr on terms* **8/1**[3]
2631 **17** 1 ¼ **By Command**[33] 1129 5-8-12 **69** ....(p) JohnEgan 12 42
(K A Ryan) *s.i.s: swtchd lft after s: nvr on terms* **12/1**
0-04 **18** 20 **Aussie Blue (IRE)**[10] 1628 6-8-6 **63** .... PaulQuinn 1 —
(R M Whitaker) *mid-div: lost pl over 2f out: sn bhd and eased: virtually p.u* **22/1**

1m 40.97s (0.87) **Going Correction** +0.25s/f (Good) **18** Ran SP% **124.1**
Speed ratings (Par 103): **105,103,103,103,97 96,96,96,96,95 94,93,92,91,90 89,88,68**
Tote Swingers: 1&2 £35.70, 1&3 £15.20, 2&3 £37.80 CSF £141.20 CT £3881.29 TOTE £16.20: £3.20, £6.90, £6.50, £1.10; EX 290.50.
Owner B Valentine **Bred** Darley **Trained** Melsonby, N Yorks
■ Stewards' Enquiry : Ashley Hamblett two-day ban: careless riding (May 22-23)

FOCUS
A good gallop and yet again it paid to race up with the pace.
Aussie Blue(IRE) Official explanation: jockey said gelding lost its action

1927 ARMY BENEVOLENT FUND MAIDEN STKS 1m
8:05 (8:10) (Class 5) 3-Y-0+ **£4,274** (£1,271; £635; £317) **Stalls Low**

Form RPR
22- **1** **Huntingfortreasure**[203] 6842 3-8-13 0 .... PhillipMakin 9 77
(M Dods) *reluctant to leave paddock: walked to post: v unruly: trckd ldrs: hung lft and led jst ins fnl f: hdd last strides: fin 2nd, nk: awrdd r* **7/1**[3]
22- **2** 1 **Taste The Victory (USA)**[192] 7116 3-8-13 0 .... PJMcDonald 4 74
(G A Swinbank) *chsd ldrs: upsides over 1f out: no ex fnl 50yds: fin 3rd: nk & 3/4l: plcd 2nd* **9/4**[2]
0 **3** 2 **Khandaq (USA)**[23] 1336 3-8-13 0 .... AdrianNicholls 7 70
(M Johnston) *led 1f: chsd ldrs: ev ch over 1f out: edgd lft and kpt on same pce ins fnl f: fin 4th: plcd 3rd* **16/1**
5 **4** 1 ¾ **Hail Tiberius**[33] 1119 3-8-13 0 .... DanielTudhope 1 66
(T D Walford) *chsd ldrs: led over 2f out: hdd jst ins fnl f: sltly hmpd and fdd: fin 5th: plcd 4th* **33/1**
30- **5** ½ **Princess Emma**[211] 6638 3-8-8 0 .... TonyHamilton 3 59+
(R A Fahey) *mid-div: outpcd over 3f out: kpt on fnl f: fin 6th: plcd 5th* **20/1**
32 **6** hd **Laverre (IRE)**[14] 1528 3-8-8 0 .... DuranFentiman 2 59
(T D Easterby) *led after 1f: hdd jst ins fnl f: wknd: fin 7th: plcd 6th* **8/1**
6-0 **7** hd **Ruler's Honour (IRE)**[21] 1401 3-8-7 0 ow1 .... DaleSwift(7) 14 64
(T J Etherington) *t.k.h: trckd ldrs: lost pl over 3f out: kpt on fnl f: fin 8th: plcd 7th* **100/1**
0 **8** 3 ¼ **Frontline Phantom (IRE)**[23] 1336 3-8-13 0 ....(t) AndrewElliott 18 56
(J R Weymes) *in rr: sme hdwy over 2f out: kpt on fnl f: fin 9th: plcd 8th* **100/1**
0-6 **9** 4 ½ **Myraid**[23] 1336 3-8-13 0 .... LeeVickers 5 45
(Ollie Pears) *t.k.h in midfield: lost pl 4f out: fin 10th: plcd 9th* **50/1**
10 ½ **Siberian Sunset (IRE)** 4-9-9 0 .... GaryBartley(3) 10 44
(G A Swinbank) *s.i.s: a towards rr: fin 11th: plcd 10th* **33/1**
05 **11** ½ **Switched Off**[7] 1705 5-9-7 0 .... JamesSullivan(5) 6 42
(M W Easterby) *s.i.s: a in rr: fin 12th: plcd 11th* **40/1**
0 **12** 1 ¼ **One More Tico**[16] 1485 3-8-13 0 .... RoystonFfrench 13 39
(M Johnston) *in rr: sn drvn along: fin 13th: plcd 12th* **40/1**
-432 **13** ½ **Minortransgression (USA)**[92] 424 3-8-13 80 .... J-PGuillambert 17 38
(T J Pitt) *a in rr: fin 14th: plcd 13th* **16/1**
14 16 **Cayo** 3-8-13 0 .... PaulMulrennan 16 —
(M Johnston) *rr-div: sme hdwy over 3f out: sn lost pl and bhd: t.o: fin 15th: plcd 14th* **33/1**
D **Sunbow (USA)** 3-8-10 0 .... AhmedAjtebi(3) 11 81+
(Mahmood Al Zarooni) *s.i.s: poor 11th 2f out: hung lft and rt: wandered bdly: rapid hdwy fnl f: fin fast to ld nr fin: fin 1st: disq: jockey weighed in light* **2/1**[1]

1m 43.76s (3.66) **Going Correction** +0.25s/f (Good)
WFA 3 from 4yo+ 13lb **15** Ran SP% **121.9**
Speed ratings (Par 103): **90,89,87,86,85 85,85,82,77,77 76,75,74,58,91**
Tote Swingers: 1&2 £5.40, 1&3 £19.70, 2&3 £11.70 CSF £21.56 TOTE £9.70: £7.10, £1.10, £7.10; EX 21.40.
Owner Les Waugh **Bred** Serpentine Bloodstock Et Al **Trained** Denton, Co Durham
■ Stewards' Enquiry : Adrian Nicholls two-day ban: careless riding (May 25-26)
Ahmed Ajtebi three-day ban: weighing in more than 1lb light (May 25-27)

FOCUS
An ordinary maiden run at a sound pace and a controversial outcome with the first past the post Sunbow being disqualified for his rider weighing in a pound and a half light.

1928 KEITH SANDERSON MEMORIAL H'CAP 7f
8:35 (8:38) (Class 6) (0-55,56) 4-Y-0+ **£2,914** (£867; £433; £216) **Stalls Low**

Form RPR
4665 **1** **Sairaam (IRE)**[8] 1653 4-8-12 **53** .... KirstyMilczarek 9 65
(C Smith) *hld up in rr: hdwy on outer over 2f out: r.o down wd outside to ld jst ins fnl f: kpt on wl* **7/1**
61U- **2** 1 ¼ **Mr Lu**[197] 6984 5-9-0 **55** .... DanielTudhope 7 64
(J S Goldie) *hld up towards rr: hdwy on wd outside 2f out: r.o to take 2nd ins fnl f: no imp* **17/2**
601- **3** 2 ¾ **Clumber Place**[236] 5941 4-8-9 **55** .... BillyCray(5) 3 57
(R C Guest) *chsd ldrs: upsides over 1f out: edgd rt: styd on same pce ins fnl f* **11/1**
0-00 **4** hd **Ask Dan (IRE)**[1] 1887 4-8-13 **54** ....(p) PhillipMakin 1 55
(M Dods) *drvn to improve on ins and led after 1f: hdd jst ins fnl f: no ex* **3/1**[1]
0-06 **5** 1 **Dancing Wave**[79] 603 4-8-6 **54** .... KaseyLoftus(7) 14 52
(M C Chapman) *led 1f: trckd ldrs: effrt on outer 2f out: one pce* **28/1**
6050 **6** shd **Kheskianto (IRE)**[8] 1653 4-8-10 **54** .... RussKennemore(3) 4 52
(M C Chapman) *chsd ldrs: one pce appr fnl f* **25/1**
3050 **7** ½ **Only A Game (IRE)**[28] 1236 5-8-11 **55** ....(tp) GaryBartley(3) 11 52
(I W McInnes) *mid-div: effrt over 2f out: kpt on: nvr trbld ldrs* **14/1**
6000 **8** hd **Redwater River**[8] 1673 6-8-7 **53** ....(b) DeanHeslop(5) 2 49
(Mrs R A Carr) *s.i.s: hdwy on ins over 3f out: chsng ldrs over 1f out: sn fdd* **5/1**[2]
0-00 **9** 1 ¾ **Silly Gilly (IRE)**[12] 1574 6-8-9 **53** .... KellyHarrison(3) 12 44
(R E Barr) *chsd ldrs: wknd over 1f out* **13/2**[3]

0043 **10** *1* **Athaakeel (IRE)**[18] 1457 4-9-0 **55** ..... LiamJones 13 44
(R A Harris) *chsd ldr: chal 3f out: edgd rt: wknd over 1f out* **16/1**

200- **11** *8* **Prince Andjo (USA)**[209] 6705 4-9-0 **55** ..... DavidNolan 6 22
(D Carroll) *chsd ldrs: lost pl over 2f out* **8/1**

3000 **12** *3 3/4* **Lujiana**[12] 1569 5-8-5 **53** ..... JohnCavanagh[(7)] 5 10
(M Brittain) *a in rr* **28/1**

00-0 **13** *4 1/2* **Fortina's Boy (USA)**[28] 1235 4-8-7 **53** .....(t) IanBrennan[(5)] 8 —
(W R Swinburn) *s.i.s: in rr and drvn along: bhd fnl 2f* **12/1**

1m 29.45s (2.25) **Going Correction** +0.25s/f (Good) **13** Ran SP% **128.5**
Speed ratings (Par 101): **97,95,92,92,91 90,90,90,88,87 77,73,68**
Tote Swingers: 1&2 £8.10, 1&3 £23.60, 2&3 £21.20 CSF £69.23 CT £687.31 TOTE £5.60: £1.40, £8.20, £5.90; EX 64.20 Place 6: £566.26 Place 5: £361.99 .
Owner Phil Martin & Trev Sleath **Bred** Shadwell Estate Company Limited **Trained** Temple Bruer, Lincs

FOCUS
A run-of-the-mill handicap run at a good pace, with the first two coming from a long way back.
Only A Game(IRE) Official explanation: jockey said gelding lost a front right shoe
T/Plt: £876.90. Pool: £54,574.18 - 45.43 winning units. T/Qpdt: £39.70. Pool: £5,392.98 - 100.38 winning units. WG

1771 WARWICK (L-H)
Saturday, May 8

OFFICIAL GOING: Good (8.2)
Wind: Light against Weather: Showery

1929 RACING UK H'CAP 6f
5:50 (5:54) (Class 6) (0-65,65) 4-Y-0+ **£1,942** (£578; £288; £144) **Stalls** Low

Form RPR

10-0 **1** **Mayoman (IRE)**[31] 1154 5-8-11 **58** .....(b) DavidNolan 7 67
(D Carroll) *w ldrs: led over 2f out: rdn and hung rt over 1f out: hung lft towards fin: jst hld on* **7/1**[2]

4043 **2** *1/2* **Kheley (IRE)**[12] 1588 4-8-13 **65** ..... KierenFox[(5)] 8 72
(W M Brisbourne) *led 2f: chsd ldrs: rdn over 1f out: hung lft ins fnl f: kpt on* **20/1**

6250 **3** *1/2* **Spoof Master (IRE)**[33] 1131 6-8-8 **55** .....(t) JamesDoyle 4 61
(C R Dore) *w ldr tl led 4f out: hdd over 2f out: sn rdn: styd on* **20/1**

0504 **4** *3/4* **Bollywood Style**[18] 1443 5-8-11 **58** ..... TedDurcan 6 61
(J R Best) *a.p: rdn over 1f out: kpt on* **11/1**

0-25 **5** *1/2* **Namu**[18] 1441 7-8-4 **54** ..... JackDean[(3)] 1 56
(Miss T Spearing) *hld up: hdwy u.p over 1f out: nt rch ldrs* **15/2**[3]

0626 **6** *nk* **Musical Script (USA)**[11] 1595 7-8-10 **57** .....(b) TravisBlock 13 58
(Mouse Hamilton-Fairley) *hld up in tch: lost pl 1/2-way: rallied over 1f out: r.o* **22/1**

40-5 **7** *3* **Mr Skipiton (IRE)**[11] 1595 5-9-0 **61** ..... TomMcLaughlin 9 52
(B J McMath) *prom: rdn and edgd rt over 1f out: no ex ins fnl f* **4/1**[1]

1555 **8** *1 1/2* **Sweet Applause (IRE)**[11] 1596 4-8-6 **60** ..... CharlotteKerton[(7)] 3 46
(G Prodromou) *chsd ldrs: rdn over 1f out: no ex fnl f* **22/1**

0000 **9** *hd* **Bishopbriggs (USA)**[24] 1300 5-8-13 **60** ..... JamieMackay 2 46
(M G Quinlan) *s.s: nvr nrr* **25/1**

60/0 **10** *3/4* **Blue Aura (IRE)**[11] 1596 7-9-2 **63** ..... StevieDonohoe 15 46
(B G Powell) *hmpd s: sn pushed along in rr: n.d* **25/1**

43-0 **11** *nk* **Mata Hari Blue**[21] 1391 4-8-13 **60** ..... JerryO'Dwyer 10 42
(J R Holt) *chsd ldrs: rdn over 2f out: wknd over 1f out* **28/1**

030- **12** *2 1/2* **Yankee Storm**[146] 7738 5-8-11 **58** ..... JackMitchell 11 32
(H J Collingridge) *sn pushed along and a in rr* **14/1**

2342 **13** *1/2* **Not My Choice (IRE)**[11] 1596 5-9-3 **64** ..... RichardMullen 17 37
(D C Griffiths) *edgd lft s: sn chsng ldrs: rdn over 2f out: sn wknd* **10/1**

0230 **14** *3/4* **Bobs Dreamflight**[11] 1595 4-8-10 **62** .....(b) MarkCoumbe[(5)] 5 32
(D K Ivory) *unruly in stalls: s.s: a in rr* **12/1**

22-2 **15** *1/2* **South African (USA)**[30] 1190 4-9-4 **65** ..... PaulHanagan 14 34
(M A Magnusson) *plld hrd and prom: lost pl wl over 2f out: sn bhd* **7/1**[2]

0503 **16** *3/4* **Cape Of Storms**[16] 1491 7-8-11 **58** .....(b) PatCosgrave 16 24
(R Brotherton) *chsd ldrs: rdn 1/2-way: wknd over 2f out* **22/1**

1m 14.3s (2.50) **Going Correction** +0.45s/f (Yiel) **16** Ran SP% **122.3**
Speed ratings (Par 101): **101,100,99,98,98 97,93,91,91,90 89,86,85,84,84 83**
toteswingers:1&2:£42.30, 1&3:£47.80, 2&3:£82.10 CSF £143.58 CT £2683.50 TOTE £6.60: £1.30, £4.20, £7.00, £3.40; EX 151.70.
Owner Tom Tuohy **Bred** James Cosgrove **Trained** Sledmere, E Yorks

FOCUS
A modest handicap, with the top weight rated 65, but it looked competitive. They went a decent gallop and it paid to be up with the pace.
Not My Choice(IRE) Official explanation: jockey said gelding never travelled

1930 PSA PEUGEOT CITROEN LONG SERVICE MAIDEN AUCTION STKS 5f 110y
6:20 (6:26) (Class 5) 2-Y-O **£2,729** (£806; £403) **Stalls** Low

Form RPR

1 **Ladyanne (IRE)** 2-8-6 0 ..... RichardSmith 5 74
(S Kirk) *s.s: outpcd and green in rr: hdwy and hung rt fr over 1f out: led ins fnl f: r.o* **40/1**

2 *1 3/4* **Where's Romeo (IRE)** 2-9-2 0 ..... RichardMullen 2 79+
(D H Brown) *chsd ldrs: led over 3f out: hung rt fr over 2f out: rdn and hdd ins fnl f: hld whn hmpd nr fin* **3/1**[2]

0 **3** *2 3/4* **Two Feet Of Snow (IRE)**[12] 1577 2-8-6 0 ..... FrankieMcDonald 10 59
(R Hannon) *chsd ldrs: rdn over 1f out: no ex ins fnl f* **14/1**

3 **4** *1/2* **Darwin Star**[19] 1429 2-8-11 0 ..... PatCosgrave 11 63+
(D K Ivory) *s.i.s: hdwy 4f out: hung lft wl over 1f out: sn swtchd rt: styd on u.p* **12/1**

5 *1* **Da Ponte** 2-9-2 0 ..... AndreaAtzeni 12 64
(Pat Eddery) *sn pushed along in rr: hdwy over 1f out: r.o: nt trble ldrs* **25/1**

6 *1 3/4* **Temptingfaith (IRE)** 2-8-6 0 ..... JerryO'Dwyer 4 48
(M G Quinlan) *sn led: hdd over 3f out: rdn over 1f out: no ex ins fnl f* **66/1**

0 **7** *1 1/2* **Henrys Air**[14] 1517 2-8-11 0 ..... TomMcLaughlin 8 48
(D G Bridgwater) *chsd ldrs: pushed along 1/2-way: wknd fnl f* **150/1**

2 **8** *nse* **Lovat Lane**[24] 1292 2-8-4 0 ..... SilvestreDeSousa 6 41
(Eve Johnson Houghton) *chsd ldrs: rdn over 1f out: wknd ins fnl f* **11/4**[1]

4 **9** *1 1/2* **Boundaries**[21] 1389 2-8-13 0 ..... GrahamGibbons 17 45
(T D Easterby) *s.i.s: sn chsng ldrs: rdn and hung rt over 1f out: wknd fnl f* **7/1**

10 *hd* **Justbookie Dot Com (IRE)** 2-8-13 0 ..... SebSanders 14 44
(Louise Best) *prom: rdn over 2f out: wknd over 1f out* **28/1**

0 **11** *nse* **Three Scoops**[8] 1660 2-8-4 0 ..... JamieMackay 3 35
(D J S Ffrench Davis) *prom: rdn over 2f out: wknd fnl f* **66/1**

0 **12** *1* **Bendigedig**[12] 1577 2-8-7 0 ow1 ..... JamesDoyle 13 35
(S Kirk) *sn pushed along in rr: n.d* **100/1**

0 **13** *1* **Fred Willetts (IRE)**[14] 1517 2-8-10 0 ..... AndrewHeffernan[(3)] 1 37
(P D Evans) *hld up: hdwy and hung lft fr over 1f out: wknd ins fnl f* **50/1**

4 **14** *2 1/2* **Reposer (IRE)**[10] 1612 2-8-11 0 ..... TedDurcan 16 27
(J R Best) *hld up: hdwy over 2f out: sn wknd* **11/2**[3]

15 *1 1/4* **Prison Cat (IRE)** 2-8-3 0 ..... WilliamCarson[(3)] 9 18
(E F Vaughan) *sn outpcd* **33/1**

16 *nk* **Layla's Princess** 2-8-6 0 ..... PaulHanagan 15 17
(K A Ryan) *s.i.s: hdwy over 2f out: sn wknd* **12/1**

69.38 secs (3.48) **Going Correction** +0.45s/f (Yiel) **16** Ran SP% **120.9**
Speed ratings (Par 93): **94,91,88,87,86 83,81,81,79,79 79,77,76,73,71 71**
Tote Swingers: 1&2 £54.40, 1&3 £59.20, 2&3 £13.30 CSF £151.97 TOTE £80.30: £19.50, £2.40, £4.70; EX 434.60.
Owner Miss E Power & The Creevies Cronies **Bred** Tally-Ho Stud **Trained** Upper Lambourn, Berks
■ Stewards' Enquiry : Richard Smith two-day ban: careless riding (May 22-23)

FOCUS
An ordinary juvenile maiden. The race averages and the fourth help set the level of the form.

NOTEBOOK
Ladyanne(IRE), out of a 7f juvenile winner, was slowly away and apparently struggling in the early stages. She began to make rapid progress at halfway, though, and, making her initial challenge in the middle of the course before edging right inside the final furlong, she won with something in hand. She seems certain to stay longer trips.
Where's Romeo(IRE) ◆, a £14,000 half-sister to juvenile winner Hold On Tiger, was backed as if he had been showing plenty at home. Quickly away, travelling nicely, he hit the front before the 2f pole, but was outpointed - and slightly impeded - by the faster-finishing winner. He should come on for this run and ought to win soon. (op 4-1)
Two Feet Of Snow(IRE), from a stable whose juveniles can improve vastly from their debut run, did precisely that, stepping up considerably on her ninth at Windsor 12 days earlier. Always prominent, she has the speed to notch a success in ordinary company. (op 16-1)
Darwin Star met trouble in running on her debut, but still managed to make third, and she again did enough to suggest she can find a small race. (op 10-1 tchd 9-1)
Lovat Lane was never seriously in the hunt and ran miles below his debut form. Official explanation: jockey said filly was unsuited by the good ground (op 10-3 tchd 7-2)
Fred Willetts(IRE) Official explanation: jockey said gelding hung right
Prison Cat(IRE) Official explanation: jockey said filly was slowly away
Layla's Princess Official explanation: jockey said filly lost its action

1931 OFFICIAL AFTERPARTY AT KOKO'S NIGHTCLUB LEAMINGTON H'CAP 1m 6f 213y
6:50 (6:52) (Class 5) (0-75,71) 4-Y-0+ **£2,590** (£770; £385; £192) **Stalls** Low

Form RPR

314- **1** **My Mate Max**[190] 7151 5-9-11 **69** .....(p) GrahamGibbons 5 77
(R Hollinshead) *led after 1f: set stdy pce tl qcknd over 2f out: rdn: edgd rt and bmpd sn after: styd on wl* **11/10**[1]

100/ **2** *1/2* **Moon Star (GER)**[502] 1609 9-9-4 **62** ..... PaulHanagan 6 69
(R Curtis) *hld up in tch: rdn over 3f out: swtchd lft over 1f out: chsd wnr ins fnl f: styd on* **9/1**

40-3 **3** *2 1/2* **Bell Island**[31] 1169 6-9-8 **66** .....(v) SebSanders 3 70
(Lady Herries) *hld up: hdwy 2f out: sn rdn: styd on same pce ins fnl f* **3/1**[2]

005/ **4** *1 1/2* **Corredor Sun (USA)**[20] 6330 4-9-5 **65** .....(v) NeilCallan 2 67
(N A Twiston-Davies) *led 1f: trckd wnr: ev ch whn bmpd over 2f out: rdn and swtchd lft over 1f out: no ex ins fnl f* **20/1**

61 **5** *5* **Two Oclock John**[80] 585 4-9-9 **69** ..... JackMitchell 7 65
(H J Collingridge) *hld up: hdwy 5f out: rdn over 3f out: wknd over 1f out* **11/2**[3]

4/6- **6** *4* **Edgefour (IRE)**[172] 6225 6-8-7 **51** ow1 ..... TedDurcan 1 41
(B I Case) *chsd ldrs: rdn over 3f out: wknd over 1f out* **12/1**

3m 25.61s (6.61) **Going Correction** +0.25s/f (Good)
WFA 4 from 5yo+ 2lb **6** Ran SP% **110.5**
Speed ratings (Par 103): **92,91,90,89,86 84**
Tote Swingers: 1&2 £3.60, 1&3 £1.50, 2&3 £4.20 CSF £11.57 TOTE £1.30: £1.02, £15.20; EX 12.60.
Owner Tim Leadbeater **Bred** Tim Leadbeater **Trained** Upper Longdon, Staffs
■ Stewards' Enquiry : Graham Gibbons two-day ban: careless riding (May 23-24)

FOCUS
A moderate staying handicap, run at an uneven pace.

1932 EUROPEAN BREEDERS' FUND MAIDEN FILLIES' STKS 1m 2f 188y
7:20 (7:23) (Class 5) 3-Y-O+ **£3,561** (£1,059; £529; £264) **Stalls** Low

Form RPR

0-2 **1** **Warling (IRE)**[33] 1119 3-8-11 0 ..... ShaneKelly 7 76
(J Noseda) *trckd ldrs: shkn up to ld ins fnl f: hung rt: r.o* **4/1**[2]

0- **2** *1 1/2* **Ellbeedee (IRE)**[197] 6992 3-8-11 0 ..... NeilCallan 3 73
(M A Jarvis) *prom: racd keenly: rdn to ld and hung rt over 1f out: hdd ins fnl f: styd on same pce* **10/3**[1]

3 *shd* **Mascarene (USA)** 3-8-11 0 ..... RyanMoore 8 73
(Sir Michael Stoute) *sn chsng ldr: shkn up and ev ch over 1f out: styd on* **9/2**[3]

4 *1 1/2* **Marywell** 3-8-11 0 ..... RobertHavlin 11 71+
(J H M Gosden) *s.i.s: hld up: swtchd lft and hdwy over 1f out: r.o wl: eased nr fin: promising* **14/1**

5- **5** *4 1/2* **Rahaala (IRE)**[242] 5752 3-8-11 0 ..... TadhgO'Shea 6 63
(Sir Michael Stoute) *sn led: rdn: hdd and hmpd over 1f out: wknd ins fnl f* **5/1**

0- **6** *2 1/4* **Craighall**[197] 6992 3-8-11 0 ..... StevieDonohoe 13 59
(D M Simcock) *prom: racd keenly: rdn over 2f out: wknd over 1f out* **9/1**

44 **7** *1 1/4* **Marrimeclaire (IRE)**[24] 1302 3-8-11 0 ..... JackMitchell 5 57
(B J McMath) *hld up: hdwy u.p over 1f out: n.d* **20/1**

0- **8** *1/2* **Sunshine Buddy**[297] 3979 3-8-11 0 ..... VinceSlattery 2 56
(C J Down) *mid-div: rdn over 3f out: n.d* **200/1**

9 *1/2* **Jewellery (IRE)** 3-8-11 0 ..... PatCosgrave 10 55
(J R Fanshawe) *hld up: rdn over 2f out: n.d* **25/1**

5 **10** *5* **Sleep Over**[21] 1380 5-10-0 0 ..... AndreaAtzeni 15 48
(D Morris) *mid-div: hdwy over 3f out: wknd over 2f out* **50/1**

0 **11** *2* **Tymora (USA)**[22] 1356 3-8-11 0 ..... TomQueally 1 44
(H R A Cecil) *hld up in tch: effrt over 2f out: sn wknd* **10/1**

00 **12** *1/2* **Behest**[5] 1757 5-9-11 0 ..... AndrewHeffernan[(3)] 9 44
(D G Bridgwater) *s.s: a bhd* **200/1**

5 **13** *9* **Ionaguru**[14] 1521 5-9-7 0 ..... DavidKenny[(7)] 16 28
(B D Leavy) *chsd ldrs: rdn over 3f out: sn wknd* **200/1**

14 *12* **Le Muguet (IRE)** 3-8-11 0 ..... PaulHanagan 17 7
(E A L Dunlop) *hld up: rdn over 4f out: sn wknd* **40/1**

4 **15** *1* **Ruby Dazzler**[14] 1515 3-8-11 0 ..... SebSanders 14 5
(S Lycett) *chsd ldrs tl rdn and wknd over 2f out* **50/1**

16 53 **Kamphora (IRE)** 5-10-0 0 (b[1]) JerryO'Dwyer 4 —
(T T Clement) *s.s: a wl bhd: t.o* **125/1**

2m 22.48s (1.38) **Going Correction** +0.25s/f (Good)
WFA 3 from 4yo+ 17lb **16** Ran SP% **120.9**
Speed ratings (Par 100): **104,102,102,101,98 96,95,95,95,91 90,89,83,74,73 35**
Tote Swingers: 1&2 £4.80, 1&3 £8.90, 2&3 £6.20 CSF £16.70 TOTE £4.70: £1.40, £1.10, £2.60; EX 22.10.
Owner Ballygallon Stud Limited **Bred** Ballygallon Stud Limited **Trained** Newmarket, Suffolk

FOCUS
An interesting fillies' maiden. The first three dominated.

1933 BAM CONSTRUCTION H'CAP 7f 26y
7:50 (7:53) (Class 4) (0-85,84) 4-Y-O+ **£5,180** (£1,541; £770; £384) **Stalls** Low

Form RPR
0-63 **1** **Regeneration (IRE)**[22] 1361 4-8-8 **74** JamieSpencer 9 85
(M L W Bell) *led 1f: chsd ldr: rdn to ld ins fnl f: edgd rt: r.o* **11/2**[3]
1103 **2** 1 **Ocean Legend (IRE)**[10] 1617 5-9-0 **80** SebSanders 4 88
(A W Carroll) *a.p: rdn over 1f out: r.o* **9/1**
01-2 **3** ¾ **Brother Cha (IRE)**[24] 1306 4-9-1 **81** KierenFallon 5 88
(L M Cumani) *plld hrd: led 6f out: rdn over 1f out: hdd ins fnl f: styng on same pce whn n.m.r sn after* **15/8**[1]
5202 **4** ¾ **Kingswinford (IRE)**[5] 1779 4-8-5 **74** AndrewHeffernan(3) 13 78
(P D Evans) *mid-div: hdwy on outer 1/2-way: rdn over 1f out: r.o* **20/1**
0-63 **5** hd **Standpoint**[15] 1509 4-8-12 **78** GrahamGibbons 14 82
(R Hollinshead) *chsd ldrs: rdn over 1f out: styd on* **28/1**
0-05 **6** hd **Satwa Laird**[10] 1618 4-9-3 **83** RyanMoore 7 86+
(E A L Dunlop) *hld up: hdwy over 1f out: sn rdn and edgd rt: r.o* **9/2**[2]
40-5 **7** hd **Ocean Transit (IRE)**[8] 191 5-8-9 **75** PaulHanagan 1 78
(R J Price) *chsd ldrs: rdn over 1f out: kpt on* **16/1**
5-20 **8** 1 **Happy Anniversary (IRE)**[21] 1383 4-9-2 **82** SilvestreDeSousa 12 86+
(Mrs D J Sanderson) *mid-div: lost pl over 2f out: rallied and nt clr run over 1f out: swtchd lft and r.o ins fnl f* **11/1**
00-2 **9** hd **Salient**[98] 359 6-8-12 **78** PaulDoe 10 77
(M J Attwater) *hld up: nt clr run 1/2-way: hdwy u.p over 1f out: one pce ins fnl f* **33/1**
1-26 **10** 3 **Defector (IRE)**[106] 259 4-8-9 **75** MartinDwyer 2 66
(W R Muir) *hld up in tch: rdn over 1f out: wknd ins fnl f* **33/1**
122- **11** ½ **Kindest**[273] 4799 4-8-10 **76** RichardMullen 11 66
(C F Wall) *hld up: rdn over 2f out: nvr trbld ldrs* **25/1**
1345 **12** 1 ½ **Lucky Redback (IRE)**[14] 1516 4-9-4 **84** TedDurcan 3 70
(R Hannon) *s.s: hld up: rdn over 2f out: nvr on terms* **14/1**
21-0 **13** shd **Kyleene**[15] 1509 4-8-8 **74** ow1 RobertHavlin 8 60
(M D I Usher) *s.i.s: hld up: a in rr* **50/1**

1m 25.41s (0.81) **Going Correction** +0.25s/f (Good) **13** Ran SP% **119.1**
Speed ratings (Par 105): **105,103,103,102,101 101,101,100,100,96 96,94,94**
Tote Swingers: 1&2 £12.40, 1&3 £3.20, 2&3 £5.90 CSF £49.36 CT £128.02 TOTE £6.60: £1.90, £3.50, £1.70; EX 75.40.
Owner Tamdown Group Limited **Bred** Tally-Ho Stud **Trained** Newmarket, Suffolk
■ Stewards' Enquiry : Jamie Spencer caution: careless riding

FOCUS
A fair handicap.
Kingswinford(IRE) Official explanation: jockey said gelding was denied a clear run
Happy Anniversary(IRE) Official explanation: jockey said filly was unable to handle bend

1934 CHAMPAGNE LANSON H'CAP 7f 26y
8:20 (8:22) (Class 5) (0-75,75) 3-Y-O **£2,590** (£770; £385; £192) **Stalls** Low

Form RPR
0-31 **1** **Kajima**[17] 1476 3-9-4 **75** RichardMullen 10 86+
(R Hannon) *hld up: hdwy over 1f out: rdn and r.o to ld post* **15/8**[1]
34-4 **2** nse **Night Trade (IRE)**[12] 1584 3-9-2 **73** SilvestreDeSousa 4 83
(Mrs D J Sanderson) *led 1f: chsd ldrs: rdn to ld and edgd rt over 1f out: hdd post* **15/2**
3-32 **3** 2 ¾ **High Importance (USA)**[13] 1542 3-9-3 **74** RyanMoore 1 77
(J Noseda) *hld up: hdwy over 1f out: sn rdn: no ex ins fnl f* **9/4**[2]
430- **4** 3 ¼ **Merchant Of Medici**[177] 7359 3-9-1 **72** MartinDwyer 2 66
(W R Muir) *trckd ldrs: racd keenly: led 5f out: rdn and hdd over 1f out: wknd fnl f* **20/1**
40-0 **5** 1 ¼ **Ice Cool Lady (IRE)**[18] 1453 3-9-4 **75** (v[1]) ShaneKelly 12 66
(W R Swinburn) *led 6f out: hdd 5f out: chsd ldr: rdn and wknd over 1f out* **33/1**
62-0 **6** ¾ **Akamon**[19] 1431 3-8-10 **67** PaulHanagan 5 56
(E A L Dunlop) *prom: rdn over 2f out: wknd over 1f out* **25/1**
61-3 **7** 1 **Two Kisses (IRE)**[116] 141 3-8-9 **66** ow1 StevieDonohoe 7 52
(B G Powell) *hld up: hdwy over 1f out: nvr trbld ldrs* **25/1**
10-0 **8** 5 **Pintura**[31] 1168 3-8-12 **69** JamieSpencer 8 42
(D M Simcock) *s.i.s: hld up: a in rr* **7/1**[3]
4204 **9** 8 **Marjolly (IRE)**[22] 1347 3-8-10 **67** (p) TadhgO'Shea 9 18
(J Gallagher) *prom: rdn over 2f out: wknd wl over 1f out* **33/1**
2020 **10** 19 **Lisahane Bog**[14] 1514 3-9-2 **73** (p) SebSanders 3 —
(P R Hedger) *s.i.s: a in rr: wknd over 2f out* **16/1**

1m 25.52s (0.92) **Going Correction** +0.25s/f (Good) **10** Ran SP% **114.0**
Speed ratings (Par 99): **104,103,100,97,95 94,93,87,78,57**
Tote Swingers: 1&2 £4.10, 1&3 £1.10, 2&3 £4.50 CSF £14.73 CT £32.58 TOTE £4.10: £2.50, £1.70, £1.02; EX 19.40 Place 6: £41.49 Place 5: £7.55 .
Owner Miss Yvonne Jacques **Bred** F J O' Connor **Trained** East Everleigh, Wilts

FOCUS
A modest handicap. The first pair came clear in a bobbing finish.
Pintura Official explanation: jockey said gelding was slowly away
T/Plt: £77.70. Pool: £52,451.77 - 492.70 winning units. T/Qpdt: £3.20. Pool: £5,085.28 - 1,169.66 winning units. CR

1935 - 1942a (Foreign Racing) - See Raceform Interactive

1712 CAPANNELLE (R-H)
Saturday, May 8

OFFICIAL GOING: Turf: heavy

1943a PREMIO CARLO D'ALESSIO (GROUP 3) (4YO+) (TURF) 1m 4f
2:50 (12:00) 4-Y-O+ **£35,398** (£15,575; £8,495; £4,247)

RPR
1 **Il Fenomeno (ITY)**[42] 4-8-9 0 DVargiu 5 100
(B Grizzetti, Italy) *broke wl and led: set decent pce: shkn up and lened 4f out: 3 l clr ent fnl 2f: drifted rt ent fnl f: styd on* **71/20**[2]
2 1 **Sant'Antonio (ITY)**[181] 7313 5-8-9 0 UmbertoRispoli 8 98
(S Botti, Italy) *slowly away on outer: settled nr rr first 5f: shkn up 4f out: rdn and proged between horses 3f out: ev ch 2f out: styd on for 2nd* **7/10**[1]
3 3 **Permesso**[27] 5-8-9 0 MircoDemuro 1 93
(G Pucciatti, Italy) *slowly away on inner: settled in mid-div after 2f: swtchd to outer after 3f: lost grnd and dropped bk to rr ent fnl bnd: rn wd and racd on own ent st: rdn and proged to chal fnl 2f* **71/20**[2]
4 snk **Piterino (IRE)**[7] 1712 5-8-9 0 MEsposito 7 93
(L Polito, Italy) *broke wl: 2nd after 1f: settled in 3rd down bk stretch: 4th ent st: hrd rdn 3f out and no imp* **33/4**[3]
5 1 ¼ **Gibraltar Applied (IRE)**[42] 5-8-9 0 ASanna 4 91
(F & L Camici, Italy) *broke wl: trckd ldrs tl 4f out: hrd rdn 3f out: no imp: wknd fnl 2f* **105/10**
6 1 **Dar Said**[41] 4-8-9 0 NPinna 3 89
(D Camuffo, Italy) *slowly away: hld up in rr: plld hrd for first 4f: hdwy on inner ent st: chal ldrs 3f out: wknd fnl 2f* **42/1**
7 1 ½ **Ponticelli (IRE)**[151] 4-8-9 0 FabioBranca 6 87
(S Cannavo', Italy) *settled in mid-div after 2f: hdwy ent st to go 3rd: rdn 3f out: sn wknd* **187/10**

2m 35.2s (8.00) **7** Ran SP% **129.7**
WIN (incl. 1 euro stake): 4.55. PLACES: 1.61, 1.32. DF: 3.34.
Owner Scuderia Blueberry **Bred** Razza Del Sole S R L **Trained** Italy

1944a PREMIO TUDINI (GROUP 3) (3YO+) (TURF) 6f
3:25 (12:00) 3-Y-O+ **£35,398** (£15,575; £8,495; £4,247)

RPR
1 **Charming Woman (IRE)**[20] 1419 3-8-5 0 MircoDemuro 5 103
(Vittorio Caruso, Italy) *slowly away: hld up in rr for 4f: shkn up and mde gd prog to ld ent fnl f: a holding 2nd fnl 110yds* **9/2**[3]
2 1 **Alta Fedelta**[20] 1419 4-9-1 0 FabioBranca 6 103
(Vittorio Caruso, Italy) *slowly away: hld up in rr: shkn up to chal ldrs 2f out: led briefly: no ex fnl 110yds* **9/2**[3]
3 1 ¾ **Titus Shadow (IRE)**[21] 6-9-4 0 DVargiu 12 100
(B Grizzetti, Italy) *broke wl on outer: prom 3f: hrd rdn and prog 2f out: styd on fnl f* **42/10**[2]
4 1 **Thinking Robins (IRE)**[188] 7206 7-9-4 0 (b) SSulas 17 97
(A Turco, Italy) *broke wl: hld up to trck ldrs on outer: prog under hrd ride on outer to chal ent fnl f: no ex ins fnl 110yds* **73/10**
5 nk **Ekin**[21] 5-9-4 0 GMarcelli 14 96
(P Riccioni, Italy) *broke wl: settled to trck ldrs for 3f: led briefly 2f out: hrd rdn and no ex fnl f* **93/10**
6 nse **Grenso (ITY)**[146] 7743 3-8-8 0 UmbertoRispoli 2 93
(S Botti, Italy) *broke wl on inner: travelling wl and ev ch fnl 2f: hrd rdn and sn no ex* **51/10**
7 1 ½ **Morgan Drive (IRE)**[64] 817 5-9-4 0 FrankieDettori 1 91
(M Gasparini, Italy) *slowly away: hld up in rr: last 2f ouut: fnd gap fnl f: proged under hrd ride clsng stages* **12/5**[1]
8 ½ **Radler (FR)** 4-9-4 0 SLandi 3 90
(E Galli, Italy) *settled in mid-div on inner: rdn and no imp 3f out: styd on* **208/10**
9 3 **Tony Douglas (IRE)**[21] 6-9-4 0 ACorniani 11 80
(A Di Dio, Italy) *broke wl and led 4f: hrd rdn ent st: hdd 2f out: sn wknd* **139/10**
10 ½ **Madda's Force (ITY)**[20] 1419 4-9-1 0 MBelli 16 75
(R Betti, Italy) *slowly away: plld hrd early: moved to trck ldrs on outer: hrd rdn 3f out: no rspnse and eased fnl f* **26/1**
11 2 **Lady Marmelade (ITY)**[20] 1419 7-9-1 0 SDiana 13 69
(D Ducci, Italy) *hld up mid-div: effrt 2 1/2f out: no imp fnl f* **75/1**
12 1 **El Suacillo (IRE)**[29] 3-8-8 0 MEsposito 9 66
(D Camuffo, Italy) *hld up in midfield: effrt 2f out: no imp and eased fnl f* **195/10**
13 6 **Remarque (IRE)**[182] 7303 5-9-4 0 (b) CDemuro 8 50
(L Riccardi, Italy) *broke wl: w ldrs for 3f: led briefly ent fnl 2f: hrd rdn: sn wknd* **39/1**
14 ½ **Reykon (IRE)**[21] 6-9-4 0 PBorrelli 10 48
(D Grilli, Italy) *broke wl: w ldrs 3f: grabbed ld 2f out: wknd ent fnl f: eased* **155/10**
15 7 **Xenes**[83] 6-9-4 0 LManiezzi 4 26
(R Menichetti, Italy) *broke wl and amongst ldrs for 2f: hrd rdn 3f out: wknd* **44/1**

1m 10.7s (0.40)
WFA 3 from 4yo+ 10lb **15** Ran SP% **155.1**
WIN (incl. 1 euro stake): 5.52 (Charming Woman coupled with Alta Fedelta). PLACES: 3.52, 3.23, 2.08. DF: 32.80.
Owner Incolinx **Bred** Societa Allevamento Razza Latina Srl **Trained** Italy

1945a 127TH DERBY ITALIANO BETTER (GROUP 2) (3YO COLTS & FILLIES) (TURF) 1m 3f
4:35 (12:00) 3-Y-O **£327,433** (£144,070; £78,584; £39,292)

RPR
1 **Worthadd (IRE)**[20] 1418 3-9-2 0 MircoDemuro 10 107
(Vittorio Caruso, Italy) *broke wl: trckd ldr in 2nd for 6f: chal to ld ent fnl 3f: hung off rail ent fnl 2f: hrd rdn fnl f: jst hld 2nd and 3rd on line* **57/20**[2]
2 shd **Ansiei (ITY)**[20] 3-9-2 0 MEsposito 8 107
(L Polito, Italy) *slowly away: hld up in rr: hdwy ent st on inner: shkn up 3f out: hrd rdn and picked up fnl f to chal fnl strides* **155/10**
3 hd **Saratoga Black (IRE)**[20] 3-9-2 0 GBietolini 5 107
(Gianluca Bietolini, Italy) *settled mid-div on inner: rdn and no room 3f out: swtchd and proged ent fnl 2f on outer: hrd rdn: ct for 2nd cl home* **35/1**
4 2 **Lord Chaparral (IRE)**[20] 3-9-2 0 UmbertoRispoli 2 103
(R Brogi, Italy) *broke wl: steaded to trck ldrs on inner: rdn to chal for ld fnl 2f: hrd rdn and no ex fnl f* **40/1**
5 2 **Dreamspeed (IRE)**[17] 1473 3-9-2 0 JimmyFortune 7 100
(A M Balding) *settled mid-div: asked for effrt ent st: hrd rdn 3f out: styd on fnl f* **69/10**[3]
6 2 **Kidnapping (IRE)**[21] 3-9-2 0 FabioBranca 4 96
(S Botti, Italy) *broke wl and settled in 3rd: chal ldrs ent fnl 3f: hrd rdn and no ex fnl 2f* **81/10**
7 1 ½ **Air Crew (USA)**[20] 1418 3-9-2 0 (b) LManiezzi 3 94
(R Menichetti, Italy) *slowly away in rr: hdwy on inner ent st: hmpd bdly 3f out: v hrd rdn to stay in tch fnl 2f: styd on* **164/10**

8 *4* **Big Creek (IRE)**21 3-9-2 0 .... DVargiu 16 87
(B Grizzetti, Italy) *settled mid-div on outer: 5th ent st: no imp whn asked for effrt 3f out* **213/10**

9 *2* **Italian Wizard (ITY)**20 3-9-2 0 .... ASanna 12 84
(P A Picchi, Italy) *hld up nr rr: prog ent st: effrt and no ex fnl 3f* **101/1**

10 *shd* **Ameer (IRE)**24 [1310] 3-9-2 0 .... FrankieDettori 11 84
(Saeed Bin Suroor) *pushed to ld after 1f: set stdy pce for 6f: kicked for home ent st: hdd 3f out: hrd rdn ent fnl 2f: wknd fnl 1 1/2f* **94/100**1

11 *nk* **Blow Up (IRE)**20 3-9-2 0 .... CFiocchi 1 83
(R Menichetti, Italy) *slowly away in rr: rdn and no imp fnl 4f* **164/10**

12 *6* **Christian Love (ITY)**21 3-9-2 0 .... GMarcelli 9 73
(R Menichetti, Italy) *broke wl: trckd ldrs: 3rd ent st: hrd rdn: no imp: sn wknd* **164/10**

13 *5* **Ladiesandgentlemen (IRE)**21 3-9-2 0 .... SLandi 15 64
(R Feligioni, Italy) *hld up mid-div: effrt 4f out: no imp* **57/1**

14 *2* **Titus Awarded (IRE)**20 3-9-2 0 .... GTemperini 6 61
(Giuseppe Ligas, Italy) *slowly away in rr: effrt and no imp 4f out* **201/10**

15 *1 ½* **Cima De Pluie**20 3-9-2 0 .... CColombi 14 58
(B Grizzetti, Italy) *slowly away: settled mid-divsion on outer: hrd rdn 4f out: no imp: sn wknd* **67/1**

16 *15* **Paladino Di Sabbia (IRE)**20 3-9-2 0 .... CDemuro 13 33
(F & L Camici, Italy) *broke wl: lost position after 1f: hld up in rr: no imp whn asked 4f out* **62/1**

2m 22.1s (142.10) **16** Ran SP% **144.7**
WIN (incl. 1 euro stake): 3.85. PLACES: 1.86, 3.31, 5.31. DF: 64.64.
Owner Incolinx **Bred** Compagnia Generale S R L **Trained** Italy

NOTEBOOK
Worthadd(IRE), whose stamina was in doubt, was given a brilliant waiting-in-front ride and was nursed home with his jockey only going for the stick in the last 100 yards. The colt is likely to be put away until the autumn now.
Dreamspeed(IRE), winner of the Derby Trial at Epsom last time out, was niggled along over half a mile from home but plugged on resolutely to finish fifth, beaten just over four lengths. The chances are he'll get further than this.
Ameer(IRE), runner-up to Coordinated Cut in the Tattersalls Timeform 3-y-o Trophy on his reappearance, was very disappointing, running well below that form. Dettori reported that his mount "never felt himself", and the trainer was inclined to blame the heavy ground.

1716 SAINT-CLOUD (L-H)
Saturday, May 8

OFFICIAL GOING: Turf: good to soft

1946a PRIX CLEOPATRE (GROUP 3) (3YO FILLIES) (TURF) 1m 2f 110y
4:25 (12:00) 3-Y-O **£35,398** (£14,159; £10,619; £7,079; £3,539)

RPR

1 **Sandbar**49 [952] 3-8-9 0 .... Francois-XavierBertras 1 96+
(F Rohaut, France) *racd bhd ldrs on rail: swtchd early in st to mid-trck: qcknd wl to ld ent fnl f: r.o strly* **23/5**

2 *¾* **Pearl Away (FR)**27 3-8-9 0 .... StephanePasquier 2 94
(Y De Nicolay, France) *prom early: qcknd wl early in st in mid-trck: r.o wl: only succumbed wl ins fnl f* **4/1**3

3 *½* **Heaven's Vault (IRE)**7 3-8-9 0 .... IoritzMendizabal 5 93
(Robert Collet, France) *racd towards rr: mde gd prog on rail early in st: r.o wl clsng stages* **30/1**

4 *¾* **Baahama (IRE)**18 3-8-9 0 .... OlivierPeslier 7 92
(A Fabre, France) *broek wl and prom: outpcd early in st: hmpd 2f out whn qckning wl: r.o wl ins f* **6/4**1

5 *1 ½* **Sesimbra (IRE)**46 3-8-9 0 .... AnthonyCrastus 4 89
(E Lellouche, France) *led fr s at modest pce: rdn early in st: no ex fr 2f out* **13/1**

6 *snk* **A Media Luz (FR)**16 [1496] 3-8-9 0 .... ThierryThulliez 3 89
(Y Fouin, France) *racd towards the rr and last ent fnl turn: rdn but no imp* **19/5**2

7 *2 ½* **Classic Angel (GER)**45 3-8-9 0 .... ChristopheSoumillon 6 84
(Y De Nicolay, France) *a towards the rr: no imp in st* **9/1**

2m 14.3s (-5.30) **Going Correction** -0.525s/f (Hard) **7** Ran SP% **119.1**
Speed ratings: **98,97,97,96,95 95,93**
WIN (incl. 1 euro stake): 5.60. PLACES: 3.10, 2.50. SF: 22.40..
Owner Lady O'Reilly **Bred** Petra Bloodstock Agency **Trained** Sauvagnon, France

NOTEBOOK
Sandbar, whose trainer's fillies are in terrific form, landed a hat-trick and confirmed her ability to handle better ground. The Italian Oaks could now be on her agenda.
Pearl Away(FR) could probably have done with a stronger pace, but it was still a good effort on just her second ever start.

1947a PRIX GREFFULHE (GROUP 2) (3YO COLTS & FILLIES) (TURF) 1m 2f
4:55 (12:00) 3-Y-O **£65,575** (£25,309; £12,079; £8,053; £4,026)

RPR

1 **Ice Blue**27 3-9-2 0 .... StephanePasquier 1 104
(P Bary, France) *racd in 4th: mde gd prog in st: qcknd wl ins 2f out: grabbed ld ins fnl f: r.o strly* **13/10**1

2 *¾* **Handsome Devil**27 3-9-2 0 .... AnthonyCrastus 7 102
(E Lellouche, France) *racd towards rr on rail: mde gd prog early in st: qcknd wl f marker: r.o wl clsng stages* **78/10**3

3 *1* **Green Rock (FR)**49 [951] 3-9-2 0 .... AlexisBadel 2 100
(Mme M Bollack-Badel, France) *led fr s: r.o wl whn chal in st: hdd and fnd no ex ins fnl f* **23/1**

4 *2 ½* **Royal Revival**231 [6131] 3-9-2 0 .... MaximeGuyon 4 95
(A Fabre, France) *prom fr the s: rdn 2f out: no ex fnl f* **9/5**2

5 *1 ½* **Waldhorn (FR)**18 3-9-2 0 .... OlivierPeslier 6 92
(T Doumen, France) *settled at bk of field: mde move 2f out: styd on* **23/1**

6 *½* **Paris Vegas (USA)**27 [1254] 3-9-2 0 .... ThierryThulliez 5 91
(F Chappet, France) *broke wl: prom: rdn early in st: no ex fnl 2f* **29/1**

7 *¾* **Tenacious Spring (FR)**27 [1254] 3-9-2 0 .... Christophe-PatriceLemaire 8 90
(T Lemer, France) *w.w towards rr: rdn early in st: no imp* **11/1**

8 *hd* **Dara Tango (FR)**27 [1254] 3-9-2 0 .... ThierryJarnet 3 89
(Mlle S-V Tarrou, France) *prom tl st: fnd no ex* **13/1**

2m 7.80s (-8.20) **Going Correction** -0.525s/f (Hard) **8** Ran SP% **117.7**
Speed ratings: **111,110,109,107,106 106,105,105**
WIN (incl. 1 euro stake): 2.30. PLACES: 1.30, 1.80, 3.30. DF: 8.20. SF: 8.90.
Owner K Abdulla **Bred** Juddmonte Farms Ltd **Trained** Chantilly, France

NOTEBOOK
Ice Blue had nowhere to go early in the straight but, once extracted 1½f out, he quickened like a class act. The son of Dansili passed the post going away, confirming Longchamp form with Handsome Devil in the process. His trainer suggested that he's now likely to go for the Prix du Jockey Club, and he will have no problem staying the extra half furlong.
Handsome Devil was another to run on in the final stages but couldn't reverse last-time-out form with the winner. The Grand Prix de Paris might be on his agenda now.
Royal Revival hadn't been out since last September and was entitled to need the race. He should come on a lot for it.

1948 - 1950a (Foreign Racing) - See Raceform Interactive

1410 LEOPARDSTOWN (L-H)
Sunday, May 9

OFFICIAL GOING: Good to firm

1951a DERRINSTOWN STUD DERBY TRIAL STKS (GROUP 2) 1m 2f
4:05 (4:07) 3-Y-O **£57,522** (£16,814; £7,964; £2,654)

RPR

1 **Midas Touch**189 [7207] 3-9-1 110 .... JMurtagh 2 112+
(A P O'Brien, Ire) *hld up in rr: mod 4th 1/2-way: tk clsr order 3f out: 3rd st: rdn to ld over 100yds out: r.o wl* **2/1**1

2 *2* **Address Unknown**21 [1414] 3-9-1 .... PJSmullen 3 106
(D K Weld, Ire) *reluctant to enter stalls: racd in mod 3rd: prog into 2nd and rdn appr st: chal 1 1/2f out: led over 1f out: hdd 100yds out: no ex whn jinked rt cl home* **2/1**1

3 *4* **At First Sight (IRE)**21 [1414] 3-9-1 104 .... JAHeffernan 4 99
(A P O'Brien, Ire) *sn led: set str pce: 3 l clr appr st: strly pressed 1 1/2f out: hdd over 1f out: no ex* **11/4**2

4 *dist* **Reiteration (USA)**7 [1742] 3-9-1 97 .... (b1) KJManning 1 —
(J S Bolger, Ire) *cl up in 2nd: drvn along over 3f out: wknd appr st: eased fr under 2f out: t.o* **11/2**3

2m 2.54s (-5.66) **Going Correction** -0.15s/f (Firm) **4** Ran SP% **108.7**
Speed ratings: **116,114,111,—**
CSF £6.27 TOTE £2.20; DF 3.90.
Owner Mrs John Magnier **Bred** Belgrave Bloodstock Ltd **Trained** Ballydoyle, Co Tipperary

FOCUS
Previous winners of this Group 2 include Sinndar, Galileo and High Chaparral, all of whom went on to Derby glory at Epsom before landing the Irish Derby. Alamshar, Dylan Thomas and Fame And Glory also won this trial and the Irish Derby, and while it is debatable what impact this renewal will have on the upcoming Classics, it was a strongly run race - the time was the fastest recorded for over 20 years - with the winner coming from the back of the four-runner field to lead well inside the final furlong. It has been rated close to an average renewal.

NOTEBOOK
Midas Touch had twice been beaten by stablemate Jan Vermeer and was almost 6l behind that colt when fourth in the Group 1 Criterium International at Saint-Cloud in November. The winner is now generally 12-1 and 14-1 for the Investec Derby and will take his chance at Epsom with improvement from this first run of the season both likely and needed for the task he will face next time. (op 13/8)
Address Unknown had enjoyed no luck in running when a close-up fifth in the Ballysax Stakes over this course and trip last month. Reluctant to load - he had to be hooded before eventually going in - he raced in third place before being ridden to go second into the straight. Soon under pressure, he went to the front over a furlong out but was no match for Midas Touch in the closing stages. He edged right when beaten. He is not entered for the Derby or the Irish Derby but holds an entry for the King Edward VII Stakes at Royal Ascot. Trainer Dermot Weld believes the colt will appreciate some ease in the ground. (op 2/1 tchd 7/4)
At First Sight(IRE), work companion of stablemate Mikhail Glinka, had finished second in the Ballysax Stakes on his first start of the season. He set a stronger gallop here and led until over a furlong out before his exertions took their toll. (op 3/1 tchd 7/2)
Reiteration(USA) was on a hat-trick after wins at a lower level and over shorter trips. First-time blinkers replaced the cheekpieces he wore for his two wins and this was the fastest ground he has raced on. After running second, he dropped out quickly turning for home and was soon eased, finishing tailed off. (op 11/2 tchd 5/1)

1952a DERRINSTOWN STUD 1,000 GUINEAS TRIAL (GROUP 3) (FILLIES) 1m
4:35 (4:35) 3-Y-O **£37,389** (£10,929; £5,176; £1,725)

RPR

1 **Bethrah (IRE)**26 [1285] 3-9-0 .... PJSmullen 6 103+
(D K Weld, Ire) *trckd ldrs in 4th: smooth prog into 3rd ent st: sn rdn: 2nd and chal fr 1f out: kpt on wl to ld cl home* **5/1**2

2 *nk* **Atasari (IRE)**25 [1312] 3-9-0 109 .... KJManning 3 102
(J S Bolger, Ire) *racd in 2nd: rdn to chal early st: led 1 1/2f out: strly pressed whn edgd rt u.p wl ins fnl f: hdd cl home* **2/1**1

3 *1 ¼* **Hen Night (IRE)**14 [1561] 3-9-0 94 .... WMLordan 4 99
(David Wachman, Ire) *trckd ldrs in 3rd: 4th into st: sn rdn: 3rd and chal under 1f out: no ex cl home* **8/1**3

4 *1* **Cornakill (USA)**210 [6708] 3-9-0 89 .... DPMcDonogh 5 97
(Kevin Prendergast, Ire) *hld up in 6th: 5th st: kpt on fr over 1f out* **22/1**

5 *¾* **Picture Perfect (IRE)**22 [1409] 3-9-0 94 .... JMurtagh 1 95
(David Wachman, Ire) *led: strly pressed st: hdd 1 1/2f out: wknd ins fnl f* **2/1**1

6 *1 ¼* **Queen Of Troy (IRE)**6 [1787] 3-9-0 90 .... CO'Donoghue 8 92
(A P O'Brien, Ire) *hld up in rr: sme prog into 6th over 1f out: kpt on same pce* **14/1**

7 *10* **Full Of Hope (IRE)**6 [1787] 3-9-0 92 .... JAHeffernan 7 69
(A P O'Brien, Ire) *hld up in 5th: no ex early st* **9/1**

1m 38.2s (-3.00) **Going Correction** -0.15s/f (Firm) **7** Ran SP% **115.5**
Speed ratings: **109,108,107,106,105 104,94**
CSF £15.78 TOTE £5.00: £2.80, £1.50; DF 14.20.
Owner Hamdan Al Maktoum **Bred** Tullpark Limited **Trained** The Curragh, Co Kildare

FOCUS
The front-running fifth and the sixth have been rated to their marks, while the winner looked to score a shade cosily after showing a quick burst of speed to lead inside the final half furlong.

NOTEBOOK
Bethrah(IRE) will attempt to buck the trend of previous winners of this Group 3, none of whom went on to win the Irish 1,000 Guineas. This was only her third start and, having won a 7f maiden very easily at Limerick, she showed that she is going the right way by scoring here. Travelling well in fourth place into the straight, she went second 1½f out and appeared to be struggling for a time before getting the hang of things to lead well inside the final furlong. She won a shade cleverly, and trainer Dermot Weld said: "She was a bit excitable last year but a lot of work went into her over the winter and it has paid off. She is improving and will represent us well in the Irish Guineas." (op 7/2)
Atasari(IRE), disappointing in the Nell Gwyn Stakes on her previous start, had run her best race when beaten a neck in the Rockfel Stakes last season. She raced in second place, closing on the leader over 3f out and going to the front a 1½f out. She kept on for pressure, but the winner had her measure towards the finish before she edged right. (op 2/1 tchd 9/4)

The Form Book, Raceform Ltd, Compton, RG20 6NL

Hen Night(IRE), well beaten when tackling 1m2f for the first time at Navan on her previous start, had beaten subsequent 1,000 Guineas third Gile Na Greine by three lengths over this trip at Dundalk on her reappearance last month. She ran a solid race and, after tracking the leaders, had every chance entering the final furlong before finding no extra in the closing stages. (op 7/1 tchd 9/1)
Cornakill(USA), the lowest rated of those with an official mark, ran quite well on what was her first start of the season. Twice a winner over 7f last year, she kept on steadily from 2f out and was nearest at the finish.
Picture Perfect(IRE), who made all to win a 7f maiden at Naas last month, again set off in front and led until 1½f out. She kept on when headed. (op 9/4)

1954a WWW.TOTEGORACINGCLUB.COM AMETHYST STKS (GROUP 3) 1m
5:35 (5:35) 3-Y-O+ **£34,513** (£10,088; £4,778; £1,592)

RPR

1 **Famous Name**[21] 1413 5-9-12 117 PJSmullen 5 110+
(D K Weld, Ire) *settled in 2nd: led fr bef 1/2-way: rdn and strly pressed fnl f: styd on wl: all out* **1/3**[1]
2 shd **King Jock (USA)**[22] 1408 9-9-9 100 PShanahan 3 107
(Tracey Collins, Ire) *trckd ldrs in 3rd: tk clsr order appr st: 2nd and rdn to chal fnl f: styd on wl: jst failed* **16/1**[3]
3 4½ **Rose Hip (IRE)**[7] 1741 6-9-6 99 CDHayes 1 94
(Joseph G Murphy, Ire) *racd in 4th: rdn and outpcd ent st: kpt on u.p fnl f* **16/1**[3]
4 hd **Duff (IRE)**[147] 7746 7-10-0 115 FMBerry 4 101
(Edward Lynam, Ire) *led: hdd bef 1/2-way: 2nd and rdn ent st: 3rd 1f out: sn no ex* **7/2**[2]
5 7 **Big Robert**[28] 1247 6-9-9 93 (p) WJSupple 2 80
(P D Deegan, Ire) *slowly away and hld up in rr: sme prog 3f out: no ex early st* **25/1**

1m 37.33s (-3.87) **Going Correction** -0.15s/f (Firm) 5 Ran SP% **112.9**
Speed ratings: **113,112,108,108,101**
CSF £7.91 TOTE £1.30: £1.10, £4.40; DF 6.70.
Owner K Abdulla **Bred** Juddmonte Farms Ltd **Trained** The Curragh, Co Kildare

FOCUS
The winner probably went a bit too hard in front and weakened inside the final furlong. The runner-up has been rated to the best of last year's form.

NOTEBOOK
Famous Name was scoring for the third time at this level. Successful in a Listed event over this C&D on his reappearance last month, he made all on this occasion and only just held on. This ground, similar to what it was for his previous victory, is quicker than ideal for him, with most of his wins having been achieved on going ranging from yielding to heavy. (op 2/7)
King Jock(USA), rated 17lb below the winner on official figures, was getting 5lb from him here and this ten-time victor, who won for the first time in two and a half years when landing a handicap over this trip at Naas last month, threw down a strong challenge from over a furlong out and only just failed to get up.
Rose Hip(IRE), a four-time winner who had been placed once at this level, kept on from 2f out without ever holding a winning chance.
Duff(IRE), an eight-time winner, including twice at this level and once in a Group 2, has won at this trip but is most effective at 7f. This was his first run of the year and, after racing in second place, he came under pressure under 2f out and was soon beaten. (op 7/2 tchd 4/1)
Big Robert, winner of the Irish Lincolnshire in March, was up against it at the weights and, after being slowly into his stride, never posed any sort of threat. (op 20/1)
T/Jkpt: @7,500.00. Pool of @10,000.00 - 1 winning unit. T/Plt: @218.10. Pool of @17,782.00 - 61 winning units. II

1953 - 1954a (Foreign Racing) - See Raceform Interactive

1420 COLOGNE (R-H)
Sunday, May 9

OFFICIAL GOING: Turf: soft

1955a SILBERNE PEITSCHE DES GERLING QUARTIERS (GROUP 3) (3YO+) (TURF) 6f 110y
2:40 (2:47) 3-Y-O+
£28,318 (£9,734; £4,867; £2,654; £1,769; £1,327)

RPR

1 **Contat (GER)**[196] 7044 7-9-6 0 RJuracek 11 113
(P Vovcenko, Germany) *racd in 3rd fr s: trckd pce: tk command on fnl turn: led into st: drew clr: easily* **154/10**
2 2 **Smooth Operator (GER)**[28] 1251 4-9-6 0 StefanieHofer 1 107
(Mario Hofer, Germany) *broke fast: settled in 2nd: trckd pce: gd move ent st: chsd wnr home but nvr threatened* **113/10**
3 nse **Amico Fritz (GER)**[37] 1081 4-9-6 0 MaximeGuyon 5 107
(H-A Pantall, France) *racd in midfield after slow s: moved through on ins fnl f: r.o wl for 3rd* **4/1**[2]
4 1¾ **Varenar (FR)**[218] 6503 4-9-6 0 Christophe-PatriceLemaire 9 102+
(A De Royer-Dupre, France) *broke slowly: racd in midfield: slow to pick up in st and r.o past tired horses* **1/2**[1]
5 ½ **Walero (GER)**[37] 4-9-6 0 PJWerning 8 100
(Uwe Ostmann, Germany) *racd in midfield: proged arnd fnl turn: threatened briefly: tired ins fnl f* **81/10**[3]
6 nse **Glad Sky**[229] 4-9-6 0 FilipMinarik 3 100
(W Gulcher, Germany) *towards rr fr s: nvr figured* **57/1**
7 nk **Nareion (GER)**[196] 7044 4-9-6 0 HenkGrewe 4 99
(W Baltromei, Germany) *racd towards rr: nvr figured* **37/1**
8 1 **Earl Of Fire (GER)**[218] 6505 5-9-6 0 DominiqueBoeuf 7 97
(W Baltromei, Germany) *broke wl: prom: proged early in st but then fdd* **14/1**
9 3½ **Able Master (IRE)**[24] 1326 4-9-6 0 SteveDrowne 10 86
(J R Gask) *bkmarker fr s and only passed tiring horses in st* **213/10**
10 1 **Shinko's Best (IRE)**[238] 9-9-6 0 APietsch 6 84
(A Kleinkorres, Germany) *a in rr and nvr figured* **52/1**
11 1½ **Golden Tirol (GER)**[28] 1251 4-9-6 0 LASorrentino 2 79
(T Kluczynski, Poland) *led fr s: passed arnd fnl turn: wknd qckly in st* **42/1**

1m 17.27s (77.27) 11 Ran SP% **131.6**
WIN (incl. 10 euro stake): 164. PLACES: 34, 31, 17. SF: 2,767..
Owner Stall Sunny **Bred** Klaus Laakman **Trained** Germany

1956a GERLING-PREIS (GROUP 2) (4YO+) (TURF) 1m 4f
4:25 (4:33) 4-Y-O+ **£35,398** (£13,716; £5,752; £3,539; £2,212)

RPR

1 **Eye Of The Tiger (GER)**[344] 5-9-0 0 THellier 4 113
(J Hirschberger, Germany) *led fr s: set gd pce: led into st: r.o wl to beat off ev chal and win comf* **51/10**[3]
2 shd **Getaway (GER)**[217] 6526 7-9-6 0 ADeVries 1 119
(J Hirschberger, Germany) *bkmarker fr s: swung wd ent st: r.o wl but no imp on wnr* **3/5**[1]
3 4½ **Norderney (GER)**[210] 6714 4-8-10 0 FilipMinarik 3 102
(P Schiergen, Germany) *racd in 3rd: r.o wl in st to hold pl comf* **83/10**
4 2½ **Eastern Aria (UAE)**[9] 1665 4-8-10 0 GregFairley 5 98
(M Johnston) *racd in 2nd fr s: pulling freely: first to chal in st: r.o wl but wknd ins fnl f* **32/5**
5 3 **Flamingo Fantasy (GER)**[266] 5082 5-9-3 0 APietsch 2 100
(W Hickst, Germany) *racd in 4th fr s: threatened ent st but no ex: r.o one pce* **27/10**[2]

2m 31.95s (-0.95) 5 Ran SP% **130.2**
WIN (incl. 10 euro stake): 61. PLACES: 16, 13. SF: 97..
Owner Baron G Von Ullmann **Bred** Baron G Von Ullmann **Trained** Germany

1632 BRIGHTON (L-H)
Monday, May 10

OFFICIAL GOING: Good to firm (good in places) changing to good to firm after race 1 (2:10)
Wind: Fresh, half behind Weather: Sunny

1957 BRIGHTON RACECOURSE MAIDEN AUCTION STKS 5f 59y
2:10 (2:10) (Class 5) 2-Y-O **£3,154** (£944; £472; £236; £117) **Stalls** Low

Form RPR

2222 1 **Scarlet Rocks (IRE)**[16] 1517 2-8-12 0 RichardHughes 3 72+
(P D Evans) *mde all: rdn and kpt on wl fnl f: a holding runner-up* **1/2**[1]
4336 2 ¾ **Master Macho (IRE)**[13] 1603 2-8-12 0 AlanMunro 5 69
(M R Channon) *pressed wnr: hrd rdn over 1f out: kpt on: a hld* **10/3**[2]
3 1¼ **Singapore Lilly (IRE)** 2-8-10 0 EddieCreighton 4 63
(M R Channon) *dwlt: hdwy to trck ldng pair after 2f: one pce fnl f* **14/1**[3]
5 4 hd **King Of Cassis**[6] 1793 2-8-8 0 JackDean[(3)] 2 63
(W G M Turner) *in tch: green and unbalanced 1/2-way: rdn 2f out: styd on same pce* **22/1**
5 8 **Kodiac Star (IRE)** 2-8-8 0 FergusSweeney 1 31
(J A Osborne) *dwlt: outpcd: a detached in last* **20/1**

61.70 secs (-0.60) **Going Correction** -0.275s/f (Firm) 5 Ran SP% **105.5**
Speed ratings (Par 93): **93,91,89,89,76**
CSF £2.09 TOTE £1.40: £1.10, £1.40; EX 2.20.
Owner Nick Shutts **Bred** Mountarmstrong Stud **Trained** Pandy, Monmouths

FOCUS
A modest maiden and the winner didn't need to improve.

NOTEBOOK
Scarlet Rocks(IRE), runner-up on each of her four previous starts, set a high standard and was soon in front, but made hard work of putting her rivals away. This win suggests she isn't going to find it easy to follow up, and she may take her chance in a conditions race at Newbury on Friday. (op 4-7 tchd 8-13 in a place)
Master Macho(IRE), one place behind the winner at Leicester last month, bounced back from a disappointing effort at Yarmouth, but never looked like getting the better of the winner. (op 11-4 tchd 7-2)
Singapore Lilly(IRE), whose dam is a half-sister to Wovoka, wasn't the best away, but she quickly recovered and showed good speed to challenge. The lack of an outing told, but she should improve. (op 16-1)
King Of Cassis showed speed when fifth at Bath on his debut six days earlier, but he didn't look overly happy on the track, and can no doubt win a race once dropped in grade. Official explanation: jockey said colt hung right (op 25-1)
Kodiac Star(IRE), who has a bit of speed in her pedigree, was slowly away and looked clueless on the track. (op 16-1)

1958 BRIGHTON RACECOURSE CLASSIFIED STKS 6f 209y
2:40 (2:40) (Class 6) 3-Y-O+ **£2,590** (£770; £385; £192) **Stalls** Centre

Form RPR

005- 1 **My Flame**[159] 7614 5-9-8 52 DarryllHolland 8 57
(J R Jenkins) *chsd ldr: led after 2f: edgd lft over 1f out: drvn to hold on fnl f* **4/1**[3]
-100 2 ½ **Lady Lam**[7] 1772 4-9-8 54 RichardHughes 4 56
(S Kirk) *hld up in 6th: rdn and hdwy 2f out: pressed wnr fnl f: nt qckn nr fin* **5/2**[1]
-030 3 2¼ **Bahama Baileys**[3] 1884 5-9-8 44 PatCosgrave 6 50
(C A Dwyer) *pushed along in rr: drvn and hdwy over 1f out: wnt 3rd ent fnl f: one pce* **5/1**
/00- 4 1¼ **Raise All In (IRE)**[349] 2361 4-9-8 49 (b[1]) TomQueally 2 47
(I W McInnes) *dwlt: bhd: rdn 3f out: sme hdwy on rail over 1f out: nvr able to chal* **18/1**
020- 5 1¾ **Contemplate**[202] 6925 4-9-5 52 (b) Louis-PhilippeBeuzelin[(3)] 3 42
(Dr J D Scargill) *trckd ldrs: rdn 3f out: carried lft over 1f out: sn wknd* **12/1**
5-00 6 2¾ **Pacific Bay (IRE)**[33] 1149 4-9-8 55 J-PGuillambert 7 34
(R Ford) *hld up in 5th on outer: outpcd fnl 2f* **12/1**
0-00 7 nk **Miss Jabba (IRE)**[20] 1437 4-9-8 42 CathyGannon 5 34
(Miss J Feilden) *rdn thrght: chsd ldrs tl wknd over 1f out* **33/1**
-400 8 33 **Gold Rock (FR)**[33] 1171 5-9-8 52 (v[1]) SebSanders 1 —
(A W Carroll) *led 2f: wknd 2f out: eased whn btn* **7/2**[2]

1m 21.65s (-1.45) **Going Correction** -0.275s/f (Firm) 8 Ran SP% **111.0**
Speed ratings (Par 101): **97,96,93,92,90 87,86,49**
toteswingers:1&2:£3.30, 1&3:£3.90, 2&3:£3.40 CSF £13.54 TOTE £5.00: £1.20, £1.10, £2.20; EX 14.90 Trifecta £52.30 Pool: £320.89 - 4.54 winning units..
Owner Smart K Syndicate **Bred** Mrs S Cavenagh **Trained** Royston, Herts

FOCUS
A weak 0-55 classified stakes and the winner did not need to be at his best.

1959 JUICE FM MAIDEN STKS 7f 214y
3:10 (3:11) (Class 5) 3-Y-O+ **£3,784** (£1,132; £566; £283; £141) **Stalls** Low

Form RPR

33-6 1 **Brannagh (USA)**[20] 1450 3-9-0 77 (t) RyanMoore 5 78+
(J Noseda) *chsd ldr: rdn over 2f out: led over 1f out: drew clr fnl 100yds: readily* **5/4**[1]
3 2 3 **Jay's Treaty (USA)**[9] 1694 3-9-0 0 GregFairley 2 71+
(M Johnston) *led tl over 1f out: nt pce of wnr ins fnl f* **15/8**[2]
50 3 1 **Yashrid (USA)**[35] 1127 3-9-0 0 PhilipRobinson 1 69+
(M A Jarvis) *in tch in 4th: rdn over 2f out: styd on to take 3rd fnl f* **13/2**[3]
02-0 4 3¾ **Bonnie Brae**[27] 1278 3-8-9 65 SebSanders 4 55
(G G Margarson) *t.k.h in rr: rdn over 2f out: n.d* **9/1**
0-4 5 ¾ **Lucky Diva**[20] 1460 3-8-9 0 RichardHughes 3 53
(S Kirk) *hdwy to chse ldrs after 2f: wknd wl over 1f out* **20/1**

050- 6 ½ **Red Willow**[244] 5747 4-9-8 45 .... SamHitchcott 6 55?
(J E Long) *in tch in 5th: rdn 3f out: wknd 2f out* 100/1

1m 34.34s (-1.66) **Going Correction** -0.275s/f (Firm)
WFA 3 from 4yo 13lb 6 Ran SP% **108.3**
Speed ratings (Par 103): **97,94,93,89,88 88**
toteswingers:1&2:£1.40, 1&3:£1.70, 2&3:£2.20 CSF £3.47 TOTE £1.50: £1.10, £1.60; EX 3.90.
Owner Ms Gillian Khosla **Bred** Vimal Khosla, Gillian Khosla Et Al **Trained** Newmarket, Suffolk

FOCUS

An uncompetitive maiden. The sixth finished close enough and the winner is the best guide.

1960 VE DAY CELEBRATION H'CAP 1m 3f 196y

3:40 (3:41) (Class 3) (0-90,88) 4-Y-0+

£6,854 (£2,052; £1,026; £513; £256; £128) **Stalls** High

Form RPR

1120 1 **King Olav (UAE)**[30] 1220 5-9-4 88 .... SebSanders 1 93
(A W Carroll) *chsd ldr: led 4f out: drvn and hld on wl fnl f* 4/1[2]

-235 2 ½ **Wind Star**[4] 1840 7-8-10 80 .... (p) LiamKeniry 4 84
(M F Harris) *hld up in 5th: nt clr run over 2f out: wnt 3rd ins fnl 2f: drvn to chal ins fnl f: kpt on* 11/1

-355 3 ½ **Perpetually (IRE)**[13] 1600 4-9-4 88 .... GregFairley 5 91
(M Johnston) *in tch in 4th: rdn to chse wnr over 2f out: nt qckn fnl 75yds* 7/4[1]

032- 4 18 **Resplendent Light**[219] 6483 5-9-4 88 .... NeilCallan 3 62
(W R Muir) *trckd ldrs tl rdn and wknd 2f out* 4/1[2]

2011 5 1 **Chalice Welcome**[24] 1348 7-9-0 84 .... JackMitchell 6 57
(N B King) *hld up in rr: pushed along 5f out: hrd rdn and wknd over 2f out* 8/1

012- 6 4½ **Eton Fable (IRE)**[267] 5067 5-8-10 80 .... (p) TravisBlock 2 46
(W J H Ratcliffe) *led: rdn and hdd 4f out: wknd over 2f out* 13/2[3]

2m 29.25s (-3.45) **Going Correction** -0.275s/f (Firm) 6 Ran SP% **109.1**
Speed ratings (Par 107): **100,99,99,87,86 83**
toteswingers:1&2:£5.50, 1&3:£1.60, 2&3:£5.20 CSF £40.73 TOTE £6.20: £3.70, £6.70; EX 42.80 TRIFECTA Pool: £195.19 - 1.80 winning units..
Owner Cover Point Racing **Bred** Darley **Trained** Cropthorne, Worcs

FOCUS

The front three drew clear in what was a fair handicap. The winner ran much his best turf race at face value.

NOTEBOOK

King Olav(UAE), in great form on the AW earlier in the year, looked very fairly weighted for this return to turf and a decisive move by Seb Sanders to send to gelding up to lead over 4f out won him the race. He proved most determined when challenged on both sides inside the final 2f, and may well win again. (op 3-1)
Wind Star, back to form when not beaten far at Ffos Las four days earlier, is on a good mark these days and he travelled well in behind runners, but the winner proved too determined in the finish. He should score again before long. (op 12-1 tchd 10-1)
Perpetually(IRE) has looked paceless on occasions this season, and was expected to be suited by the step up in trip, but he couldn't quicken having come to hold every chance and clearly hasn't progressed as connections had hoped. (op 5-2)
Resplendent Light ended up well held and looked in need of this first start in 219 days. (op 5-1 tchd 7-2)
Chalice Welcome, a winner on his only previous start here, has been in good form on the AW, but never got out of the rear on this return to turf. (tchd 10-1)
Eton Fable(IRE), an improver towards the end of last season, dropped right out in the end, having made the early running, and should improve on this first outing in 267 days. (op 4-1)

1961 WHOOPSADAISY CHARITY H'CAP 1m 1f 209y

4:10 (4:10) (Class 5) (0-70,69) 4-Y-0+ **£3,238** (£963; £481; £240) **Stalls** High

Form RPR

006- 1 **Agapanthus (GER)**[112] 7248 5-8-12 63 .... TomQueally 5 75
(B J Curley) *towards rr: last and pushed along 5f out: hdwy over 2f out: styd on to ld ins fnl f* 2/1[1]

2-64 2 2 **Inspirina (IRE)**[12] 1631 6-9-1 66 .... J-PGuillambert 1 74
(R Ford) *plld hrd: chsd ldr: led over 4f out tl ins fnl f: one pce* 5/1

-503 3 2½ **Goose Green (IRE)**[11] 1636 6-9-1 66 .... DarryllHolland 4 69
(R J Hodges) *t.k.h: sn in tch: outpcd 3f out: rallied and carried lft over 1f out: styd on to take 3rd ins fnl f* 8/1

1402 4 3 **Freedom Fire (IRE)**[7] 1763 4-8-11 62 .... LiamKeniry 3 59
(G L Moore) *in tch: hrd rdn 2f out: btn whn edgd lft over 1f out* 6/1

-612 5 1¼ **What's Up Doc (IRE)**[6] 1239 9-9-2 67 .... IanMongan 2 62
(Mrs Lawney Hill) *led and set modest pce: hdd over 4f out: edgd lft and wknd 1f out* 7/2[2]

3122 6 11 **Blue Tango (IRE)**[11] 1636 4-9-4 69 .... (b) NeilCallan 6 48
(Mrs A J Perrett) *plld hrd: prom: outpcd over 2f out: btn whn hmpd just over 1f out* 4/1[3]

2m 1.75s (-1.85) **Going Correction** -0.275s/f (Firm) 6 Ran SP% **117.6**
Speed ratings (Par 103): **96,94,92,90,89 80**
toteswingers:1&2:£3.30, 1&3:£3.40, 2&3:£7.50 CSF £13.25 TOTE £3.90: £2.70, £4.60; EX 20.60.
Owner Curley Leisure **Bred** Gestut Schlenderhan **Trained** Newmarket, Suffolk

FOCUS

A modest handicap but sound enough form.
What's Up Doc(IRE) Official explanation: jockey said gelding hung left

1962 6TH JUNE ALICE IN RACELAND FUNDAY H'CAP 7f 214y

4:40 (4:40) (Class 3) (0-90,89) 4-Y-0+

£6,854 (£2,052; £1,026; £513; £256; £128) **Stalls** Low

Form RPR

00-0 1 **Mujood**[16] 1533 7-9-4 89 .... (v) TomQueally 2 97
(Eve Johnson Houghton) *prom: pushed along 5f out: led 1f out: rdn clr* 13/2

32-6 2 3¼ **Cheviot (USA)**[61] 850 4-9-3 88 .... (b[1]) PhilipRobinson 8 89
(M A Jarvis) *led: hung bdly lft fnl 2f: hdd 1f out: no ex ins fnl f* 11/4[1]

-050 3 1¼ **My Gacho (IRE)**[95] 405 8-8-13 84 .... (v) J-PGuillambert 4 82
(M Johnston) *chsd ldr: rdn 3f out: one pce appr fnl f* 10/1

53-3 4 2 **Southandwest (IRE)**[20] 1458 6-8-7 78 .... LiamKeniry 6 71
(J S Moore) *in tch in 4th: hrd rdn over 2f out: one pce* 9/2[2]

/50 5 11 **Mesa Marauder**[72] 738 6-9-2 87 .... NeilCallan 7 55
(M Botti) *towards rr: hrd rdn and modest effrt over 2f out: sn wknd* 6/1

1560 6 13 **Totally Focussed (IRE)**[19] 1474 5-8-4 75 .... KirstyMilczarek 3 13
(S Dow) *s.s: drvn along 3f out: a bhd* 11/2[3]

114- 7 64 **Royal Defence (IRE)**[247] 5670 4-8-13 84 .... (p) DarryllHolland 5 —
(Matthew Salaman) *a towards rr: last and struggling 5f out: t.o* 13/2

1m 32.4s (-3.60) **Going Correction** -0.275s/f (Firm) 7 Ran SP% **110.3**
Speed ratings (Par 107): **107,103,102,100,89 76,12**
toteswingers:1&2:£4.20, 1&3:£7.90, 2&3:£6.70 CSF £22.92 CT £165.35 TOTE £11.30: £7.00, £1.10; EX 17.20 Trifecta £80.20.
Owner Eden Racing **Bred** Bloomsbury Stud & The Hon Sir David Sieff **Trained** Blewbury, Oxon

FOCUS

A fair handicap that appeared to be run at a good pace. It is doubtful if this form can be taken at face value.

NOTEBOOK

Mujood, never going a yard on his reappearance in a good race at Sandown, has a course win to his name, and he looked a different proposition with the visor back on. He seemed to really relish the stiff test, chasing the early leader before taking over inside the final furlong, but won't always have things go his way. (tchd 11-2)
Cheviot(USA), a major flop at Wolverhampton in March, went charging off in the first-time blinkers and looked the winner until hanging into the rail, making life very difficult for Philip Robinson. He did keep on for second, but is clearly a tricky customer, and certainly not one to be putting much faith in. Official explanation: jockey said gelding hung left (op 2-1 tchd 3-1)
My Gacho(IRE) was soon chasing the pace and kept plugging away for third. (op 17-2)
Southandwest(IRE) never got close enough to throw down a serious challenge. (op 5-1)
Mesa Marauder never looked happy on the ground. (op 7-1 tchd 9-2)
Totally Focussed(IRE) never recovered from a slow start. Official explanation: jockey said gelding was slowly away (op 8-1)
Royal Defence(IRE), a progressive sort last year, had cheekpieces on for this debut for the yard, but he stopped quickly and was virtually pulled up. Something was evidently amiss. Official explanation: jockey said gelding hung left and moved poorly throughout (op 8-1)

1963 FOOTBALL LEGENDS LUNCH HERE 18TH MAY H'CAP 5f 213y

5:10 (5:10) (Class 4) (0-80,80) 4-Y-0+ **£4,415** (£1,321; £660; £330; £164) **Stalls** Low

Form RPR

0-13 1 **Peter Island (FR)**[20] 1438 7-9-3 79 .... (v) DarryllHolland 6 87
(J Gallagher) *sn led: mde virtually all: hrd drvn and hld on gamely fnl f* 10/3[2]

254- 2 ½ **Johnstown Lad (IRE)**[15] 1557 6-8-11 73 .... (t) NeilCallan 3 79
(Daniel Mark Loughnane, Ire) *prom: effrt and n.m.r on rail over 1f out tl ins fnl f: r.o: jst hld* 4/1[3]

-303 3 ¾ **Whiskey Junction**[25] 1321 6-8-13 75 .... SebSanders 7 79
(M Quinn) *broke wl: chsd wnr: rdn 2f out: kpt on* 13/2

6-62 4 ½ **My Kingdom (IRE)**[4] 1848 4-9-4 80 .... (t) TravisBlock 1 82
(H Morrison) *towards rr: hdwy and hrd rdn over 1f out: one pce ins fnl f* 11/4[1]

0414 5 1¾ **Sherjawy (IRE)**[4] 1848 6-8-2 69 .... RossAtkinson(5) 4 65
(Miss Z C Davison) *sn outpcd towards rr: styd on fnl f* 11/1

0-23 6 6 **For Life (IRE)**[11] 1641 8-8-7 72 .... NataliaGemelova(3) 5 49
(J E Long) *s.i.s: sn in midfield: wknd 2f out* 10/1

24-0 7 1¼ **Lodi (IRE)**[14] 1580 5-8-13 75 .... (t) TomQueally 8 48
(J Akehurst) *dwlt: outpcd: a bhd* 7/1

67.41 secs (-2.79) **Going Correction** -0.275s/f (Firm) 7 Ran SP% **113.0**
Speed ratings (Par 105): **107,106,105,104,102 94,92**
toteswingers:1&2:£2.80, 1&3:£4.50, 2&3:£6.30 CSF £16.61 CT £80.00 TOTE £4.50: £3.40, £2.40; EX 25.40 Trifecta £176.40 Part won. Pool: £218.39 - 0.43 winning units. Place 6 £20.64; Place 5 £18.75.
Owner C R Marks (banbury) **Bred** Earl Elevage De La Source **Trained** Chastleton, Oxon
■ Stewards' Enquiry : Ross Atkinson caution: careless riding

FOCUS

Another race in which it was hard to make ground, although the pace was good. The form reads sound enough.
Lodi(IRE) Official explanation: jockey said gelding was slowly away
T/Plt: £29.20. Pool: £53,862.61 - 1,344.33 winning units. T/Qpdt: £27.10. Pool: £2,939.03 - 80.00 winning units. LM

1646 REDCAR (L-H)

Monday, May 10

OFFICIAL GOING: Good to firm (8.5)

Wind: Light half against Weather: Sunny periods

1964 BUY YOUR TICKETS ON-LINE @ REDCARRACING.CO.UK MEDIAN AUCTION MAIDEN STKS 5f

2:20 (2:20) (Class 6) 2-Y-O **£1,842** (£544; £272) **Stalls** Centre

Form RPR

3 1 **Azzurra Du Caprio (IRE)**[7] 1749 2-8-12 0 .... TomEaves 4 68+
(B M R Haslam) *cl up: effrt over 2f out: rdn to ld wl over 1f out: kpt on ins fnl f* 6/4[1]

2 1¾ **Lady Del Sol** 2-8-12 0 .... PJMcDonald 3 61
(G R Oldroyd) *dwlt and towards rr: hdwy over 2f out: sn rdn: green and edgd lft ent fnl f: kpt on towards fin* 5/1[3]

25 3 1½ **Mica Mika (IRE)**[16] 1517 2-9-3 0 .... TonyHamilton 1 61
(R A Fahey) *chsd ldng pair: rdn along and outpcd 1/2-way: styd on u.p fnl f* 13/2

4 ¾ **Miserere (IRE)** 2-8-12 0 .... PaulMulrennan 2 53+
(J S Wainwright) *wnt lft s: sn led: shkn up over 2f out: rdn and hdd wl over 1f out: wknd fnl f* 10/1

5 18 **Nobutjust** 2-8-12 0 .... DavidAllan 6 —
(T D Easterby) *wnt bdly rt s and in rr: rdn: green and edgd lft over 2f out: sn outpcd and eased* 9/4[2]

60.81 secs (2.21) **Going Correction** +0.20s/f (Good) 5 Ran SP% **109.9**
Speed ratings (Par 91): **90,87,84,83,54**
CSF £9.26 TOTE £2.20: £2.30, £2.80; EX 8.30.
Owner Blue Lion Racing VIII **Bred** Glending Bloodstock **Trained** Middleham Moor, N Yorks

FOCUS

On a cool, breezy day the ground was described as 'good'. A very modest median auction maiden race featuring three newcomers. Weak form, although the winner scored in fair style.

NOTEBOOK

Azzurra Du Caprio(IRE), much more settled beforehand than when a staying-on third on her debut at Redcar, knew her job this time. She always looked in command and ran out a cosy winner. Her action suggests she would not want the ground any firmer. (op 7-4)
Lady Del Sol, bred purely for speed, is not very big. She showed plenty of toe but was always tending to hang left. In the end she was very much second best. (op 15-2 tchd 8-1)
Mica Mika(IRE), having his third start, was very weak beforehand. Blanketed for stalls entry, he kept on after being outpaced at the halfway mark and 6f nurseries beckon later on. (op 7-2)
Miserere(IRE), who ducked left leaving the stalls, was soon matching strides with the winner but tired noticeably late on. The outing will not be lost on her. (op 12-1)

Nobutjust, a cheaply bought half-sister to the stable's Hilary Needler winner Miss Meggy, dropped out of contention soon after halfway and may well have needed this debut. (op 5-2 tchd 11-4)

1965 ENJOY HOSPITALITY AT REDCAR RACECOURSE (S) STKS 5f

2:50 (2:50) (Class 6) 3-Y-O+ **£1,842** (£544; £272) **Stalls** Centre

Form RPR

2156 **1** **Desperate Dan**[14] 1583 9-9-7 72 (v) JamieSpencer 3 65
(A B Haynes) *hld up: hdwy to trck ldrs 1/2-way: swtchd rt and effrt over 1f out: rdn to ld ins fnl f: kpt on* **2/1**[1]

660- **2** *1* **Foreign Rhythm (IRE)**[195] 7081 5-9-2 46 PhillipMakin 1 57
(R E Barr) *prom on outer: rdn along 2f out: drvn ent fnl f: kpt on towards fin* **9/1**[3]

100- **3** *¾* **Raccoon (IRE)**[243] 5767 10-9-7 74 PJMcDonald 6 59
(Mrs R A Carr) *led: rdn along over 1f out: drvn ent fnl f: sn hdd and one pce* **2/1**[1]

-042 **4** *½* **Guest Connections**[3] 1869 7-9-7 59 (v) AdrianNicholls 2 57
(D Nicholls) *dwlt and wnt rt s: sn outpcd and pushed along in rr: hdwy 1/2-way: rdn to chse ldrs over 1f out: sn drvn and no imp* **10/3**[2]

0000 **5** *5* **Miacarla**[8] 1723 7-9-2 37 (b) PatrickMathers 5 34
(H A McWilliams) *cl up: rdn along 2f out: drvn and wknd ent fnl f* **66/1**

0-06 **6** *5* **Mr Rooney (IRE)**[34] 1146 7-9-2 37 IanBrennan(5) 4 21
(A Berry) *chsd ldrs to 1/2-way: sn wknd* **100/1**

000- **7** *5* **Princess Charlmane (IRE)**[216] 6553 7-9-2 51 (p) DanielTudhope 8 —
(C J Teague) *chsd ldrs to 1/2-way: sn wknd* **14/1**

2000 **8** *2¼* **Sonhador**[8] 1723 4-9-2 49 MarkCoumbe(5) 7 —
(A Berry) *a in rr: outpcd and bhd fr 1/2-way* **100/1**

59.91 secs (1.31) **Going Correction** +0.20s/f (Good) **8 Ran SP% 109.9**
Speed ratings (Par 101): **97,95,94,93,85 77,69,65**
toteswingers:1&2:£3.00, 1&3:£1.80, 2&3:£4.40 CSF £19.79 TOTE £2.90: £1.20, £2.40, £1.02; EX 19.40.There was no bid for the winner
Owner Joe McCarthy **Bred** Sheikh Amin Dahlawi **Trained** Limpley Stoke, Bath

FOCUS
A selling race with two prolific winners heading the market, but there were doubts over them. The second sets the level.

1966 VOLTIGEUR 2 COURSE SPECIAL MENU £10.95 MAIDEN FILLIES' STKS 6f

3:20 (3:23) (Class 5) 3-Y-O+ **£2,396** (£712; £356; £177) **Stalls** Centre

Form RPR

63 **1** **Carrie's Magic**[27] 1275 3-8-12 0 PhillipMakin 3 70+
(T D Barron) *cl up: led over 2f out: rdn over 1f out: drvn and edgd lft ins fnl f: kpt on wl* **3/1**[2]

0-0 **2** *¾* **Hanbelation (USA)**[17] 1504 3-8-12 0 AndreaAtzeni 1 68
(E F Vaughan) *trckd ldrs: hdwy 2f out: rdn to chal over 1f out and ev ch ins fnl f: drvn and no ex last 100yds* **33/1**

3 *2¼* **Beauty Pageant (IRE)** 3-8-12 0 RichardMullen 12 60+
(E S McMahon) *trckd ldrs: hdwy over 2f out: rdn over 1f out: kpt on same pce ins fnl f* **7/4**[1]

-4 **4** *¾* **Greeley Bright (USA)**[12] 1622 3-8-12 0 LeeVickers 10 58
(J G Given) *s.i.s: hdwy into midfield after 2f out: rdn to chse ldrs 2f out: kpt on ins fnl f: nrst fin* **8/1**

4-44 **5** *3* **Seven Of Diamonds (IRE)**[10] 1667 3-8-12 60 (p) DavidAllan 13 48
(T D Easterby) *towards rr: hdwy 2f out: sn rdn and kpt on ins fnl f: nt rch ldrs* **9/2**[3]

6 *2* **Haafhd Sharp** 3-8-12 0 JerryO'Dwyer 8 42
(M G Quinlan) *chsd ldrs: rdn along over 2f out: drvn wl over 1f out and grad wknd* **11/1**

0 **7** *1¼* **Lady Vyrnwy (IRE)**[9] 1685 3-8-5 0 LeeTopliss(7) 4 38+
(R A Fahey) *midfield on outer: rdn along 1/2-way: n.d* **33/1**

0- **8** *nk* **Aleqa**[214] 6615 3-8-12 0 TedDurcan 11 37+
(C F Wall) *dwlt and towards rr whn sltly hmpd after 1f: bhd tl sme late hdwy* **14/1**

050- **9** *3½* **Kookie**[249] 5595 3-8-12 48 TonyHamilton 6 26
(R E Barr) *a in rr* **100/1**

060- **10** *½* **Balzarine**[231] 6170 4-9-8 45 (p) JimmyQuinn 5 27
(C J Teague) *chsd ldrs: rdn along over 2f out: sn wknd* **125/1**

505- **11** *hd* **Miss Lauz**[310] 3626 3-8-7 0 MarkCoumbe(5) 2 24
(A Berry) *dwlt: a in rr* **200/1**

0- **12** *2¾* **Rio's Girl**[327] 3032 3-8-9 0 MichaelStainton(3) 7 15
(R M Whitaker) *led: rdn and hdd over 2f out: hung rt over 1f out and wknd qckly ent fnl f* **100/1**

1m 13.03s (1.23) **Going Correction** +0.20s/f (Good)
WFA 3 from 4yo 10lb **12 Ran SP% 114.8**
Speed ratings (Par 100): **99,98,95,94,90 87,85,85,80,79 79,76**
toteswingers:1&2:£14.30, 1&3:£3.70, 2&3:£13.40 CSF £104.23 TOTE £3.20: £1.20, £13.20, £1.10; EX 114.10.
Owner J Starbuck **Bred** John Starbuck **Trained** Maunby, N Yorks

FOCUS
A very modest fillies' sprint maiden but the form looks pretty sound.

1967 REDCAR RACECOURSE WEDDING AND CONFERENCE VENUE H'CAP 7f

3:50 (3:56) (Class 5) (0-70,69) 3-Y-O+ **£2,396** (£712; £356; £177) **Stalls** Centre

Form RPR

-400 **1** **Dream Win**[23] 1395 4-9-0 55 TomEaves 11 62
(B Ellison) *mde all: pushed along over 2f out: rdn wl over 1f out: drvn ins fnl f and hld on wl* **17/2**

50-3 **2** *nk* **Rio Caribe (IRE)**[6] 1811 3-9-0 67 GrahamGibbons 4 69
(T D Walford) *in tch: hdwy to chse ldrs 2f out: rdn over 1f out: drvn ins fnl f and ev ch tl no ex towards fin* **5/1**[2]

31-0 **3** *1¼* **Orangeleg**[77] 668 4-9-2 60 WilliamCarson(3) 2 63
(S C Williams) *cl up: effrt to chal over 2f out: rdn wl over 1f out: drvn and ev ch ent fnl f: kpt on same pce towards fin* **5/2**[1]

0-00 **4** *½* **Rio Cobolo (IRE)**[16] 1513 4-10-0 69 (v) PaulMulrennan 10 72+
(Paul Green) *midfield: hdwy 2f out: sn rdn and kpt on same pce ins fnl f* **25/1**

0615 **5** *1* **Sixties Rock**[7] 1753 3-8-3 56 AndreaAtzeni 9 51
(J A Glover) *trckd ldrs: hdwy 1/2-way: chal 2f out: sn rdn and ev ch tl wknd ent fnl f* **9/1**

05-0 **6** *1¼* **Indian Violet (IRE)**[14] 1575 4-9-8 63 JimmyQuinn 5 58
(D W Thompson) *towards rr: hdwy 2f out: sn rdn and kpt on ins fnl f: nrst fin* **25/1**

60-4 **7** *½* **Finsbury**[10] 1673 7-9-2 60 (v) GaryBartley(3) 7 54+
(D Nicholls) *towards rr: hdwy over 2f out: sn rdn and no imp fnl f* **10/1**

62-0 **8** *1¾* **Jimwil (IRE)**[10] 1653 4-9-12 67 (p) PhillipMakin 6 56
(M Dods) *hld up in rr: effrt and sme hdwy 2f out: sn rdn and no imp appr fnl f* **8/1**

6450 **9** *½* **Peter's Gift (IRE)**[33] 1152 4-9-2 62 AmyRyan(5) 8 50
(K A Ryan) *chsd ldrs: rdn along 2f out: sn edgd rt and wknd* **16/1**

040/ **10** *2¼* **Custard Cream Kid (IRE)**[591] 6247 4-8-9 57 LeeTopliss(7) 12 39
(R A Fahey) *a towards rr* **16/1**

26-0 **11** *2¼* **Piazza San Pietro**[15] 1547 4-9-12 67 JamieSpencer 13 43
(A B Haynes) *hld up: a towards rr* **6/1**[3]

000- **12** *4½* **Woldgate**[212] 6679 3-8-9 62 PJMcDonald 3 22
(G R Oldroyd) *cl up: rdn along 3f out: sn wknd* **100/1**

1m 26.56s (2.06) **Going Correction** +0.20s/f (Good)
WFA 3 from 4yo+ 12lb **12 Ran SP% 120.7**
Speed ratings (Par 103): **96,95,94,93,92 91,90,88,87,85 82,77**
toteswingers:1&2:£9.90, 1&3:£9.50, 2&3:£3.10 CSF £50.89 CT £142.79 TOTE £13.00: £3.30, £2.60, £1.10; EX 59.30.
Owner Koo's Racing Club **Bred** Juddmonte Farms Ltd **Trained** Norton, N Yorks

FOCUS
A modest 56-69 seven furlong handicap and the initial pace was very steady. The winner matched his best form since his 2yo debut.
Dream Win Official explanation: trainer said, regarding apparent improvement in form, that the colt was better suited by being able to dictate the race.
Piazza San Pietro Official explanation: jockey said gelding hung right final 2f

1968 WIN A VIP DAY @ REDCARRACING.CO.UK CLAIMING STKS 6f

4:20 (4:20) (Class 6) 3-Y-O+ **£1,842** (£544; £272) **Stalls** Centre

Form RPR

5020 **1** **Abbondanza (IRE)**[3] 1862 7-9-8 85 AdrianNicholls 7 80
(D Nicholls) *trckd ldr: hdwy and cl up 1/2-way: led over 2f out: rdn over 1f out: clr ent fnl f: rdn out* **6/5**[1]

5000 **2** *7* **Bertbrand**[3] 1885 5-8-12 45 (v) GaryBartley(3) 1 51
(I W McInnes) *trckd ldrs: hdwy 1/2-way: rdn to chal wl over 1f out and ev ch tl drvn and one pce ent fnl f* **50/1**

-030 **3** *1¾* **Soto**[3] 1885 7-9-5 58 (v) GrahamGibbons 10 49
(M W Easterby) *led: rdn along and hdd over 2f out: sn drvn and kpt on same pce* **8/1**

1-61 **4** *½* **Cawdor (IRE)**[8] 1722 4-9-10 79 TonyHamilton 6 53
(Mrs L Stubbs) *chsd ldrs: rdn over 2f out: sn drvn and one pce* **5/2**[2]

065- **5** *¾* **Timber Treasure (USA)**[185] 7275 6-9-10 67 (b) SilvestreDeSousa 9 50
(Paul Green) *chsd ldrs: hdwy 1/2-way: rdn over 2f out: drvn wl over 1f out and kpt on same pce* **10/1**

0000 **6** *1¾* **Red Cell (IRE)**[3] 1884 4-8-10 43 AmyRyan(5) 8 36
(I W McInnes) *a in rr* **100/1**

-160 **7** *5* **Eight Hours**[14] 1584 3-8-10 66 (b) FrederikTylicki 2 22
(R A Fahey) *a in rr* **6/1**[3]

1m 13.35s (1.55) **Going Correction** +0.20s/f (Good)
WFA 3 from 4yo+ 10lb **7 Ran SP% 111.5**
Speed ratings (Par 101): **97,87,85,84,83 81,74**
toteswingers:1&2:£12.40, 1&3:£2.70, 2&3:£15.70 CSF £58.37 TOTE £3.10: £2.50, £10.70; EX 48.30.
Owner Middleham Park Racing XXXI **Bred** M Nolan **Trained** Sessay, N Yorks

FOCUS
A sprint claimer with 35lb between the highest and lowest rated on official figures. Muddling form, rated around the runner-up.
Cawdor(IRE) Official explanation: jockey said gelding stumbled leaving stalls and never travelled

1969 RACING UK ON CHANNEL 432 H'CAP 1m 1f

4:50 (4:50) (Class 4) (0-85,82) 3-Y-O **£4,209** (£1,252; £625; £312) **Stalls** Low

Form RPR

03-1 **1** **Caldercruix (USA)**[11] 1649 3-9-1 79 JamieSpencer 6 93+
(T P Tate) *mde all: pushed along after 3f and again 4f out: rdn wl over 2f out: edgd rt over 1f out: clr ent fnl f: kpt on* **13/8**[1]

25-2 **2** *1¼* **I'm Super Too (IRE)**[26] 1297 3-8-8 72 PJMcDonald 4 80
(G A Swinbank) *t.k.h: trckd ldrs: hdwy over 3f out: rdn to chse wnr wl over 1f out: sn drvn and kpt on fnl f* **5/1**[3]

3414 **3** *3½* **Understory (USA)**[16] 1514 3-8-11 75 JoeFanning 1 75
(M Johnston) *chsd wnr: rdn along 3f out: drvn 2f out: edgd lft over 1f out and kpt on same pce* **8/1**

0-41 **4** *2¼* **Bin Shamardal (IRE)**[18] 1485 3-9-1 79 MichaelHills 2 74
(B W Hills) *trckd ldrs: hdwy 4f out: rdn along 3f out: drvn 2f out and sn one pce* **3/1**[2]

5-14 **5** *3¾* **Mercoliano**[20] 1452 3-9-1 79 (t) AndreaAtzeni 5 66
(M Botti) *in tch: hdwy 4f out: rdn along wl over 2f out: sn drvn and btn* **8/1**

2323 **6** *4½* **Green Earth (IRE)**[25] 1317 3-8-13 77 JimmyQuinn 3 54
(Mrs A J Perrett) *dwlt: a in rr* **12/1**

10- **7** *1* **Cono Zur (FR)**[188] 7218 3-9-4 82 PaulMulrennan 7 57
(M Johnston) *chsd ldrs tl edgd rt and lost pl bnd after 3f: rdn along over 3f out and sn btn* **22/1**

1m 55.05s (2.05) **Going Correction** +0.275s/f (Good) **7 Ran SP% 114.0**
Speed ratings (Par 101): **101,99,96,94,91 87,86**
toteswingers:1&2:£2.40, 1&3:£3.20, 2&3:£6.20 CSF £10.14 TOTE £2.30: £1.20, £1.90; EX 11.00.
Owner Mrs Fitri Hay **Bred** Bjorn Nielsen **Trained** Tadcaster, N Yorks

FOCUS
An interesting 72-82 3-y-os only handicap and a highly progressive winner who was value for extra. Decent form for the grade.

1970 JOHN SMITH'S REDCAR STRAIGHT-MILE CHAMPIONSHIP (H'CAP) (QUALIFIER) (DIV I) 1m

5:20 (5:20) (Class 6) (0-60,59) 3-Y-O **£1,501** (£443; £221) **Stalls** Centre

Form RPR

40-0 **1** **Mr Harmoosh (IRE)**[19] 1476 3-9-4 59 AndreaAtzeni 8 64
(E F Vaughan) *hld up: hdwy to chse ldrs over 2f out: effrt and hmpd over 1f out: swtchd rt and rdn ent fnl f: styd on and squeezed through to ld nr fin* **11/2**

6-05 **2** *½* **All Moving Parts (USA)**[12] 1630 3-8-12 56 BarryMcHugh(3) 14 60
(J S Wainwright) *in tch on outer: hdwy over 2f out and sn rdn along: styd on to chal over 1f out: drvn: hung lft and led briefly wl ins fnl f: hdd and nt qckn last 50yds* **33/1**

00-5 **3** *nk* **Azaday (IRE)**[11] 1643 3-9-2 57 TedDurcan 6 60+
(C F Wall) *hld up: hdwy 3f out: n.m.r 2f out: sn rdn: drvn and styd on ins fnl f: ev ch tl nt qckn nr fin* **10/3**[1]

30-0 **4** *¾* **Ting Ting (USA)**[21] 1422 3-8-12 53 JamieSpencer 4 61+
(T P Tate) *stdd and sltly hmpd s: hld up and bhd: stdy hdwy 2f out: effrt whn nt clr run over 1f out and jst ins fnl f: sn swtchd rt and kpt on towards fin* **8/1**

-150 **5** *nse* **Destiny's Dancer**[20] 1461 3-8-4 **50** PatrickDonaghy(5) 12 51
(B M R Haslam) *trckd ldrs: hdwy to ld wl over 2f out: rdn and hung lft over 1f out and again ins fnl f: hdd & wknd last 100yds* **25/1**

005- **6** *1* **Inshaallah**[174] 7420 3-8-9 **50** PaulMulrennan 11 49+
(J G Given) *hld up in tch: hdwy on wd outside 2f out: rdn over 1f out: kpt on ins fnl f* **16/1**

00-0 **7** *1 1/4* **Scooby Dee**[21] 1425 3-8-2 **48** AmyRyan(5) 2 44
(R M Whitaker) *in tch: hdwy 3f out: chsd ldrs whn hmpd 2f out: kpt on ins fnl f* **80/1**

60-0 **8** *1 1/2* **Bring Sweets (IRE)**[23] 1392 3-8-5 **46** PJMcDonald 9 39
(B Ellison) *led 2f: cl up: rdn along over 2f out: drvn and edgd lft over 1f out: hld whn n.m.r and snatched up ins fnl f* **5/1**[3]

00-0 **9** *1* **Dispol Kabira**[11] 1651 3-8-6 **47** PatrickMathers 7 37
(D W Thompson) *prom: pushed along 3f out: rdn and hung lft 2f out: drvn and kpt on same pce appr fnl f* **100/1**

-544 **10** *2* **Eeny Mac (IRE)**[7] 1753 3-8-10 **51** JimmyQuinn 13 37
(N Bycroft) *cl up: led after 2f: hdd and rdn wl over 2f out: drvn over 1f out and n.m.r: grad wknd* **9/2**[2]

2201 **11** *9* **Buzz Bird**[18] 1495 3-9-1 **56** PhillipMakin 1 21
(T D Barron) *hld up: effrt and hdwy on wd outside whn hmpd 2f out and nt rcvr* **15/2**

50-0 **12** *4 1/2* **Lucky Traveller**[20] 1461 3-8-4 **45** DuranFentiman 5 —
(T D Easterby) *cl up: rdn along 3f out: hmpd 2f out and sn wknd* **25/1**

05-6 **13** *9* **Crushing (IRE)**[20] 1461 3-8-11 **52** TomEaves 3 —
(Julie Camacho) *t.k.h: prom: rdn along 3f out: wkng whn n.m.r 2f out: sn bhd* **14/1**

1m 40.01s (2.01) **Going Correction** +0.20s/f (Good) 13 Ran SP% **121.6**
Speed ratings (Par 97): **97,96,96,95,95 94,93,91,90,88 79,75,66**
toteswingers:1&2:£34.10, 1&3:£6.70, 2&3:£33.00 CSF £187.38 CT £732.94 TOTE £7.50: £2.50, £11.30, £2.20; EX 263.00.

Owner Salem Rashid **Bred** Thomas G Cooke **Trained** Newmarket, Suffolk

■ Stewards' Enquiry : Patrick Donaghy two-day ban: careless riding (May 24-25)

Barry McHugh three-day ban: careless riding (May 24-26)

FOCUS
The first division of a low-grade 45-59 three-year-olds only 1m handicap and first prize a paltry £1,501. Last year the final of this series here in September had a bottom rating of 82, so these two qualifiers are rendered meaningless. The pace was sound but they tendered to end up in a bunch towards the far side, and altogether it was a most unsatisfactory affair. The winner got back to his debut promise.

Ting Ting(USA) Official explanation: jockey said filly was denied a clear run

1971 JOHN SMITH'S REDCAR STRAIGHT-MILE CHAMPIONSHIP (H'CAP) (QUALIFIER) (DIV II) 1m

5:50 (5:51) (Class 6) (0-60,59) 3-Y-O **£1,501** (£443; £221) **Stalls** Centre

Form RPR

0-00 **1** **Princess Lexi (IRE)**[23] 1394 3-8-5 **46** PJMcDonald 14 58
(Ian Williams) *mde all: rdn over 2f out: drvn over 1f out: edgd lft and kpt on gamely ins fnl f* **8/1**

0-00 **2** *1 1/4* **Broctune Papa Gio**[27] 1271 3-7-13 **45** PaulPickard(5) 2 54
(K G Reveley) *prom: effrt to chse wnr over 2f out: rdn to chal over 1f out and ev ch tl drvn and one pce wl ins fnl f* **25/1**

-450 **3** *1 1/4* **Cross The Boss (IRE)**[23] 1392 3-9-1 **56** (t) PhillipMakin 8 62
(B M R Haslam) *dwlt: t.k.h in rr: stdy hdwy 3f out: rdn wl over 1f out: kpt on ins fnl f: nrst fin* **12/1**

60-0 **4** *4* **Cygnet Committee (IRE)**[11] 1651 3-8-9 **50** (b) PaulMulrennan 7 47
(J S Wainwright) *hld up in rr: hdwy over 2f out: rdn wl over 1f out: kpt on ins fnl f: nrst fin* **22/1**

46-0 **5** *nk* **French Seventyfive**[23] 1394 3-9-2 **57** GrahamGibbons 5 53
(T D Walford) *prom: rdn along 2f out: drvn and ev ch over 1f out: kpt on same pce ent fnl f* **9/2**[1]

-504 **6** *2 3/4* **Aqua Vitae (IRE)**[13] 1605 3-9-4 **59** JoeFanning 9 49
(M Johnston) *chsd ldrs: hdwy 3f out: rdn and ev ch over 1f out: drvn and wknd ent fnl f* **7/1**[3]

00-0 **7** *1 1/2* **Mr Mohican (IRE)**[23] 1394 3-8-11 **52** PaulQuinn 1 39
(Mrs A Duffield) *racd wd: in tch: hdwy and cl up after 3f: rdn along wl over 2f out and grad wknd* **12/1**

3-20 **8** *shd* **Elegant Dancer (IRE)**[7] 1753 3-8-12 **53** SilvestreDeSousa 13 39
(Paul Green) *chsd ldrs: hdwy over 2f out: rdn and ev ch over 1f out: drvn and wknd ent fnl f* **9/2**[1]

000- **9** *4 1/2* **Woodhouse Mill (IRE)**[236] 5981 3-8-4 **45** JimmyQuinn 10 21
(N Tinkler) *a towards rr* **80/1**

504- **10** *1/2* **Hedgerow (IRE)**[222] 6378 3-9-1 **56** DanielTudhope 12 31
(A Dickman) *hld up in rr: effrt over 2f out: sn rdn: edgd lft and nvr a factor* **13/2**[2]

00-0 **11** *1 1/4* **Loss Leader (IRE)**[21] 1425 3-8-5 **46** DuranFentiman 6 18
(T D Easterby) *t.k.h early: hld up in midfield: pushed along over 3f out: sn wknd* **9/2**[1]

00-0 **12** *6* **Hotgrove Boy**[34] 1145 3-8-7 **48** AndrewMullen 11 6
(A G Foster) *cl up: rdn along over 3f out: sn wknd* **33/1**

044- **13** *8* **Charity Fair**[191] 7168 3-8-9 **50** ow1 TomEaves 4 —
(A Berry) *a in rr* **20/1**

1m 39.76s (1.76) **Going Correction** +0.20s/f (Good) 13 Ran SP% **124.0**
Speed ratings (Par 97): **99,97,96,92,92 89,87,87,83,82 81,75,67**
toteswingers:1&2:£55.00, 1&3:£20.60, 2&3:£41.40 CSF £204.38 CT £2476.78 TOTE £20.00: £2.60, £14.50, £7.80; EX 187.40 Place 6 £8.21; Place 5 £4.81.

Owner Dr Marwan Koukash **Bred** Epona Bloodstock Ltd And P A Byrne **Trained** Portway, Worcs

FOCUS
The 13 runners went into this without a previous success between them. The first three finished clear and the form could be rated a bit higher.

Princess Lexi(IRE) Official explanation: trainer said, regarding apparent improvement in form, that he could offer no explanation as this was the filly's first run for the stable.

T/Plt: £15.10. Pool: £49,515.70 - 2,387.18 winning units. T/Qpdt: £10.60. Pool: £3111.64 - 215.98 winning units. JR

1779 WINDSOR (R-H)

Monday, May 10

OFFICIAL GOING: Good to firm (good in places)
Wind: Light, across Weather: Overcast becoming fine, cold

1972 ATTHERACES.COM MAIDEN FILLES' STKS 5f 10y

5:40 (5:41) (Class 4) 2-Y-O **£4,209** (£1,252; £625; £312) **Stalls** High

Form RPR

1 **Rimth** 2-9-0 0 TadhgO'Shea 15 80+
(P F I Cole) *nt that wl away: wl in rr against nr side rail: swtchd lft 1/2-way and sn on outer: gd prog over 1f out: led jst ins fnl f: sn clr* **6/1**[3]

4 **2** *3 1/2* **Fifth Commandment (IRE)**[10] 1660 2-9-0 0 FergusSweeney 9 67
(J A Osborne) *trckd ldrs: effrt and cl up over 1f out: styd on fnl f to take 2nd nr fin* **5/1**[2]

3 *3/4* **The Thrill Is Gone** 2-9-0 0 AlanMunro 4 64
(M R Channon) *wl plcd bhd ldrs: effrt on outer to chal over 1f out: kpt on same pce* **50/1**

4 *hd* **Good Morning Dubai (IRE)** 2-9-0 0 KierenFallon 8 64
(B J Meehan) *pressed ldrs: chal fr 2f out: upsides and hanging lft over 1f out: nt qckn fnl f* **12/1**

5 *shd* **Swiss Dream** 2-9-0 0 RyanMoore 1 63
(D R C Elsworth) *dwlt: gd spd and sn pressed ldr: led 1/2-way: grabbed nr side rail sn after: hdd and fdd jst ins fnl f* **3/1**[1]

6 *3* **Byrony (IRE)** 2-9-0 0 PatDobbs 3 52
(R Hannon) *gd spd on outer to chse ldrs: rdn to chal over 1f out: wknd fnl f* **22/1**

7 *6* **Rum Sun N Sand (USA)** 2-9-0 0 FrankieDettori 10 31
(J W Hills) *dwlt: rcvrd and sn chsd ldrs: shkn up 2f out: sn wknd and eased* **16/1**

8 *1/2* **Rafella (IRE)** 2-9-0 0 JimCrowley 7 29
(R M Beckett) *dwlt: wl in rr: pushed along and sme prog on outer fr over 1f out* **12/1**

9 *1* **My Ruby (IRE)** 2-9-0 0 PaulDoe 6 25
(Jim Best) *dwlt: off the pce in midfield: pushed along over 1f out: n.d* **33/1**

10 *1/2* **Time For Applause** 2-9-0 0 WilliamBuick 13 24
(E A L Dunlop) *sn wl off the pce: no prog and btn whn bmpd over 1f out* **12/1**

11 *3/4* **Chilworth Lass (IRE)** 2-9-0 0 SamHitchcott 2 21
(M R Channon) *dwlt: off the pce towards rr: rdn and jst in tch 2f out: sn wknd* **66/1**

12 *2* **Aurivorous** 2-9-0 0 SteveDrowne 14 14
(Jonjo O'Neill) *wl plcd bhd ldrs against nr side rail: wkng whn swtchd lft over 1f out* **66/1**

13 *5* **Brandy Snap (IRE)** 2-9-0 0 RichardHughes 16 —
(R Hannon) *s.s: outpcd and a wl in rr* **5/1**[2]

04 **14** *3 1/2* **Terrys Flutter**[9] 1695 2-9-0 0 StephenCraine 5 —
(M A Allen) *led to 1/2-way: wknd rapidly over 1f out* **33/1**

15 *3/4* **Shutterbug** 2-9-0 0 SaleemGolam 11 —
(S C Williams) *outpcd and a in last trio* **100/1**

16 *shd* **I Scream (IRE)** 2-9-0 0 PatCosgrave 12 —
(D R C Elsworth) *dwlt: outpcd and a bhd* **40/1**

61.56 secs (1.26) **Going Correction** +0.075s/f (Good) 16 Ran SP% **120.2**
Speed ratings (Par 95): **92,86,85,84,84 79,70,69,67,67 65,62,54,49,47 47**
toteswingers:1&2:£5.80, 1&3:£56.60, 2&3:£76.20 CSF £33.43 TOTE £6.80: £1.80, £3.00, £8.30; EX 44.20 TRIFECTA Not won..

Owner Denford Stud **Bred** Belgrave Bloodstock Ltd **Trained** Whatcombe, Oxon

FOCUS
Just two of the runners had experience in this fillies' maiden. The time was not great but the impressive winner shot clear of the next four and they were well strung out behind.

NOTEBOOK
Rimth was in an unpromising position turning for home but found a power-packed finish switched out wide to win in good style. Her dam was a 1m AW winner but is from a speedy family and is a half-sister to King's Stand winner Dominica, who is out of a 5f 2-y-o Listed winning half-sister to Nunthorpe winner Ya Malak. This form is hard to evaluate but the style of the win was impressive and she looks a good prospect who could go on to much better things. The Queen Mary could be her next assignment. (tchd 11-2 and 13-2)
Fifth Commandment(IRE) kept on nicely in the closing stages when close-up fourth of nine in a 5f AW maiden at Lingfield on her recent debut. She put in another very encouraging staying-on effort and adds some substance to the form. A half-sister to useful French 1m-1m1f winner Via Medici, she shapes like she is ready for an extra furlong. (op 6-1 tchd 7-1)
The Thrill Is Gone showed quite a bit of natural speed and ability on debut. A half-sister to useful 5f winners Group Therapy and Classic Encounter, she is bred to sprint and should be wiser for her first run. (op 66-1)
Good Morning Dubai(IRE) ran a big race on debut, hitting the front at the furlong pole before fading in the closing stages. She should have learned a lot from the experience and is a well-bred type, being out of a half-sister to high-class 2-y-o/miler Zafeen. (op 16-1)
Swiss Dream had to use up a lot of energy to cut over to the stands' rail but showed plenty of promise from a horror draw on debut. A half-sister to useful sprinters Swiss Franc and Swiss Diva, she has a very fast pedigree and could make a big impact in a similar race next time. She was reported to have been struck into quite badly. (op 10-3 tchd 11-4)

1973 SPORTINGBET.COM H'CAP 1m 2f 7y

6:10 (6:10) (Class 5) (0-75,75) 3-Y-O **£2,729** (£806; £403) **Stalls** Centre

Form RPR

54-5 **1** **Buffett**[20] 1448 3-8-9 **66** KierenFallon 1 75+
(L M Cumani) *t.k.h: trckd ldng pair: lft 2nd 3f out: rdn to chal 2f out: narrow ld ins fnl f: a doing enough after* **4/1**[2]

21-0 **2** *1/2* **Essexbridge**[14] 1582 3-9-3 **74** RichardHughes 2 82+
(R Hannon) *pressed ldr: lft in ld 3f out: drvn 2f out: narrowly hdd ins fnl f: r.o but a hld* **7/1**[3]

0-25 **3** *4 1/2* **Banks And Braes**[79] 634 3-9-1 **72** RyanMoore 6 71
(R Hannon) *trckd ldrs: cl 3rd over 2f out: rdn and nt qckn wl over 1f out: steadily outpcd* **4/1**[2]

2320 **4** *2 3/4* **Thundering Home**[17] 1502 3-9-1 **72** AlanMunro 4 65
(M J Attwater) *rn in snatches: effrt and rdn over 3f out: wl hld in 4th fr over 1f out* **15/2**

35-0 **5** *4 1/2* **Inpursuitoffreedom**[35] 1132 3-8-13 **70** EddieCreighton 8 54
(P J McBride) *hld up in last pair: keen bnd over 5f out: effrt 4f out: outpcd fr over 2f out* **20/1**

1-00 **6** *1* **First In The Queue (IRE)**[10] 1657 3-9-2 **73** StephenCraine 10 55
(S Kirk) *hld up in 5th: rdn over 2f out: wandering u.p and nt qckn: wl btn after* **9/1**

23-6 **7** *hd* **Brigadoon**[23] 1392 3-8-7 **64** WilliamBuick 9 46
(W Jarvis) *hld up in last pair: shkn up over 2f out: no rspnse and wl btn after* **7/2**[1]

34-4 **8** *13* **Weekend Millionair (IRE)**[14] 1581 3-8-12 **74** RichardEvans(5) 5 30
(P D Evans) *racd freely: led: rdn whn jinked rt 3f out and nrly uns: dropped to last and no ch after* **15/2**

2m 8.50s (-0.20) **Going Correction** -0.025s/f (Good) **8** Ran SP% **113.0**
Speed ratings (Par 99): **99,98,95,92,89 88,88,77**
toteswingers:1&2:£6.60, 1&3:£3.60, 2&3:£5.20 CSF £31.09 CT £117.23 TOTE £3.40: £1.10, £1.40, £1.70; EX 13.80 Trifecta £28.30 Pool: £4295.32 - 112.23 winning units.
Owner Aston House Stud **Bred** Aston House Stud **Trained** Newmarket, Suffolk

FOCUS
A fair handicap for the grade. It was run at a stop-start pace. The first two pulled clear and nothing got into it from behind. The winner should progress.
Inpursuitoffreedom Official explanation: jockey said filly ran to free

1974 SPORTINGBET.COM ROYAL WINDSOR STKS (LISTED RACE) (C&G) 1m 67y

6:40 (6:40) (Class 1) 3-Y-O+ **£22,708** (£8,608; £4,308; £2,148; £1,076) **Stalls** High

Form RPR

203- **1** **Bushman**[191] 7186 6-9-2 106 KierenFallon 4 113
(D M Simcock) *trckd ldr: pushed into ld over 2f out: rdn and readily asserted fnl f* **10/3**[3]

00-6 **2** *2 3/4* **Ordnance Row**[2] 1904 7-9-2 112 RichardHughes 5 107
(R Hannon) *fast away but dictated mod pce: hdd and shkn up over 2f out: one pce fnl f* **5/2**[2]

1062 **3** *1 1/2* **Vitznau (IRE)**[10] 1662 6-9-2 99 RyanMoore 2 103
(R Hannon) *trckd ldng pair to 1/2-way: seemed gng wl enough but nt on terms over 2f out: wnt 3rd again 1f out: no ch to chal* **5/1**

45-5 **4** *1* **Beacon Lodge (IRE)**[16] 1531 5-9-2 113 AdamKirby 1 101
(C G Cox) *t.k.h: hld up in 4th: quick move to press ldng pair over 3f out: rdn and fnd nil 2f out: wknd and lost 3rd 1f out* **15/8**[1]

2336 **5** *8* **Mister Green (FR)**[51] 946 4-9-2 96 (b) StephenCraine 3 83
(K McAuliffe) *stdd s: hld up in last: in tch over 2f out: sn wknd* **20/1**

1m 46.96s (2.26) **Going Correction** -0.025s/f (Good) **5** Ran SP% **107.9**
Speed ratings (Par 111): **87,84,82,81,73**
CSF £11.46 TOTE £5.40: £3.50, £2.30; EX 16.50.
Owner Khalifa Dasmal **Bred** Darley **Trained** Newmarket, Suffolk

FOCUS
A strong Listed race on paper but it was steadily run and the form is muddling. The two market leaders had both been successful in Group 3 company but it became quite tactical and went to a well-backed 106-rated performer. Probably not form to take at face value.

NOTEBOOK
Bushman had come up a bit short in this grade in the past and is usually a non-participant when the ground is on the fast side but he took his chance this time and put in a feisty display to justify support and comfortably get the better of a rival with a 6lb higher official rating. (op 9-2)
Ordnance Row was a bit below-par on his comeback in a Haydock Listed race on Saturday but quite a bit of the spark was back 48 hours later and he put in a respectable front-running effort in a bid to land a hat-trick in this race. The likeable 7-y-o can throw in the odd modest effort these days but most of his ability seems intact and a switch back to more patient tactics will suit. (op 9-4 tchd 11-4 and 2-1 in a place)
Vitznau(IRE) had some work to do on these terms but ran a creditable race without ever really posing a threat. He has not had the cards fall his way since producing a good turn of foot off a steady pace to win the Lincoln Trial on his return in March but could be a handful off 99 back in a handicap if getting some luck. (op 6-1)
Beacon Lodge(IRE), a Group 3 winner at Chantilly last June, had the highest BHA rating (113) of these and looked a major player in this grade. The fast ground was a potential problem but it was the tactical nature of this race that probably caused his downfall. He was very free early on, as he was in the Sandown Mile on his return, and went out quite quickly at the two furlong pole. This was a disappointing effort but the 5-y-o has had just 14 starts and could easily bounce back in a more strongly run race on good or slower ground. (op 6-4 tchd 2-1)
Mister Green(FR), a much improved performer in blinkers on Polytrack over the winter, could make no impression before fading in this hot contest back on turf. (op 16-1)

1975 JOIN ROYAL WINDSOR RACING CLUB H'CAP 1m 3f 135y

7:10 (7:11) (Class 5) (0-75,74) 3-Y-O **£2,729** (£806; £403) **Stalls** Centre

Form RPR

406- **1** **Love Action (IRE)**[172] 7450 3-9-0 **73** PatrickHills(3) 5 79+
(R Hannon) *hld up in last pair: gng strly but plenty to do 3f out: prog 2f out: swtchd to outer and only 8th jst over 1f out: r.o wl to ld post* **20/1**

4-21 **2** *nse* **High On A Hill (IRE)**[21] 1433 3-9-4 **74** WilliamBuick 11 80
(S Kirk) *trckd ldng pair: rdn over 2f out: clsd to go 2nd ent fnl f: drvn ahd nr fin: hdd last stride* **5/1**[2]

35-2 **3** *nse* **Gordon Flash**[7] 1778 3-8-9 **65** PatDobbs 6 71
(R Hannon) *pressed ldr: led jst over 2f out: hrd rdn over 1f out: narrowly hdd nr fin: jst hld* **12/1**

5-12 **4** *1 3/4* **Shelfah (IRE)**[20] 1448 3-9-0 **70** FrankieDettori 9 75+
(M A Jarvis) *trckd ldrs in 6th: drvn over 2f out: sme imp over 1f out: keeping on but hld whn short of room briefly ins fnl f* **7/4**[1]

5-50 **5** *1 1/2* **Halyard (IRE)**[20] 1448 3-8-10 **66** ShaneKelly 8 66
(W R Swinburn) *led to jst over 2f out: pressed ldr tl fdd ent fnl f* **14/1**

2-03 **6** *1 3/4* **Pullyourfingerout (IRE)**[21] 1433 3-9-2 **72** KierenFallon 2 70
(B G Powell) *t.k.h: hld up in 7th: effrt 3f out: drvn to try to cl on ldrs over 1f out: hld and eased last 100yds* **7/1**[3]

-125 **7** *1 1/4* **Calypso Star (IRE)**[21] 1433 3-9-4 **74** RichardHughes 4 69
(R Hannon) *hld up in last pair: effrt 3f out: drvn to chse ldrs 2f out: no imp over 1f out: fdd* **7/1**[3]

3363 **8** *2* **Frameit (IRE)**[14] 1578 3-8-8 **64** (b) LiamKeniry 7 56
(J S Moore) *trckd ldrs: cl up and rdn over 2f out: hld over 1f out: wknd* **20/1**

045- **9** *7* **Fochabers**[132] 7865 3-8-8 **64** SteveDrowne 3 44
(R Charlton) *trckd ldrs: pushed along 4f out: wknd over 2f out* **40/1**

1 **10** *5* **Visualize**[21] 1432 3-9-3 **73** RyanMoore 10 44
(Sir Michael Stoute) *s.i.s: hld up towards rr: rdn and no prog 3f out: wl btn fnl 2f* **9/1**

3350 **11** *6* **Pascalina**[13] 1601 3-8-4 **60** oh2 NickyMackay 1 21
(J Akehurst) *awkward s: hld up towards rr: wknd 3f out* **28/1**

2m 29.53s (0.03) **Going Correction** -0.025s/f (Good) **11** Ran SP% **117.8**
Speed ratings (Par 99): **98,97,97,96,95 94,93,92,87,84 80**
toteswingers:1&2:£3.70, 1&3:£14.30, 2&3:£11.40 CSF £113.15 CT £1278.58 TOTE £22.70: £13.50, £4.00, £8.20; EX 266.70 TRIFECTA Not won..
Owner Mrs R Ablett **Bred** Lodge Park Stud **Trained** East Everleigh, Wilts

FOCUS
An interesting handicap, involving some potential improvers. The pace was fair and there was an exciting three-way-finish. The winner can do better still and the form is sound rated around the next four.

Visualize Official explanation: jockey said filly never travelled

1976 BEST OF BRITISH SAUSAGE FESTIVAL 24TH MAY MEDIAN AUCTION MAIDEN STKS 1m 2f 7y

7:40 (7:42) (Class 5) 3-5-Y-O **£2,729** (£806; £403) **Stalls** Centre

Form RPR

200- **1** **Valiant Knight (FR)**[229] 6199 3-8-13 76 RichardHughes 11 80+
(R Hannon) *trckd ldrs: gng bttr than rest 2f out: plld out over 1f out: rdn to ld ins fnl f: readily* **5/1**[2]

2 **2** *1 1/2* **Soviet Secret**[25] 1325 3-8-13 0 RyanMoore 10 74+
(P J McBride) *t.k.h: trckd ldrs: effrt to ld 2f out: drvn and hdd ins fnl f: one pce* **11/10**[1]

25-5 **3** *nk* **Baltimore Clipper (USA)**[12] 1624 3-8-13 74 WilliamBuick 7 73
(P F I Cole) *t.k.h: hld up bhd ldrs: prog and prom 1/2-way: rdn to chal over 2f out: upsides over 1f out: fnd nil* **5/1**[2]

4 *4 1/2* **Roanstar** 3-8-13 0 LiamKeniry 12 64
(A M Balding) *hld up in midfield: effrt 3f out: n.m.r over 1f out and swtchd lft: sn outpcd* **33/1**

3-40 **5** *1 3/4* **Bussell Along (IRE)**[19] 1478 4-9-9 52 (vt[1]) PatCosgrave 9 57?
(Stef Higgins) *awkward s and rousted along early: in tch: effrt 3f out: plugged on one pce fnl 2f: n.d* **66/1**

6 *2* **Technophobe (IRE)** 3-8-13 0 ShaneKelly 6 57+
(W J Knight) *hld up in rr: pushed along over 3f out: sn outpcd: kpt on steadily fnl 2f* **40/1**

6 **7** *1 3/4* **Strawberry Rose**[10] 1654 3-8-8 0 MartinDwyer 1 48
(M P Tregoning) *led 2f: led again over 3f out: drvn and hdd 2f out: wknd over 1f out* **5/1**[2]

5 **8** *6* **Sirdave**[7] 1757 4-10-0 0 JimCrowley 5 42
(P W Hiatt) *dwlt: nvr bttr than midfield: rdn and no prog 3f out: wknd 2f out* **14/1**[3]

00- **9** *5* **Keep Silent**[196] 7061 3-8-8 0 KirstyMilczarek 8 26
(John Berry) *mostly in last: nvr a factor* **100/1**

0 **10** *7* **Latent Light (USA)**[23] 1381 3-8-13 0 KierenFallon 2 43
(E A L Dunlop) *led after 2f to over 3f out: wknd rapidly over 2f out: eased* **25/1**

2m 11.47s (2.77) **Going Correction** -0.025s/f (Good)
WFA 3 from 4yo 15lb **10** Ran SP% **116.0**
Speed ratings (Par 103): **87,85,85,81,80 78,77,72,68,63**
toteswingers:1&2:£1.70, 1&3:£4.50, 2&3:£2.60 CSF £10.56 TOTE £4.90: £1.80, £1.10, £1.10; EX 14.00 Trifecta £50.90 Pool: £418.44 - 6.08 winning units.
Owner Mrs Sue Brendish **Bred** Fullarton Lodge Stud Ltd **Trained** East Everleigh, Wilts

FOCUS
A maiden which was run at a very steady pace. A 76-rated performer beat the well-backed favourite but the form looks muddling. The winner is better than the bare figure.
Latent Light(USA) Official explanation: jockey said colt lost his action

1977 HEROS GIVE EX-RACEHORSES A FUTURE H'CAP 1m 67y

8:10 (8:12) (Class 5) (0-70,70) 3-Y-O **£2,729** (£806; £403) **Stalls** High

Form RPR

23-3 **1** **Right Rave (IRE)**[14] 1582 3-9-0 **66** RichardHughes 2 78
(P J McBride) *trckd ldrs in 5th: gng easily over 2f out: rdn to ld jst over 1f out: sn hrd pressed: r.o wl to hold on* **7/1**

00-1 **2** *nk* **The Shuffler**[20] 1437 3-8-10 **62** RyanMoore 14 73
(G L Moore) *hld up in 8th and off the pce: prog over 2f out: drvn to chal 1f out: r.o but jst hld* **3/1**[1]

2412 **3** *3 3/4* **Volatilis (IRE)**[66] 809 3-8-8 **65** KierenFox(5) 8 67
(J W Hills) *trckd ldng pair after 1f: rdn over 2f out: kpt on same pce: outpcd fnl f* **16/1**

5623 **4** *2 3/4* **Chateau Zara**[23] 1392 3-8-5 **62** JohnFahy(5) 4 58
(C G Cox) *t.k.h: hld up bhd ldrs in 6th: effrt against nr side rail over 2f out: one pce over 1f out* **14/1**

301U **5** *1/2* **Until The Man (IRE)**[9] 1696 3-9-1 **67** (p) PaulDoe 13 62
(Mrs L J Mongan) *led after 1f and set gd pce: hung lft over 1f out: sn hdd & wknd* **13/2**

66-4 **6** *2 1/4* **Goldtrek (USA)**[23] 1392 3-8-10 **62** SteveDrowne 5 52+
(R Charlton) *hld up in aobut 10th and wl off the pce: rdn over 2f out: plugged on but n.d* **6/1**[3]

000- **7** *2* **Super Duplex**[203] 6906 3-8-7 **59** LiamKeniry 3 49+
(P M Phelan) *hld up wl in rr and wl off the pce: limited prog over 2f out: rdn and keeping on whn nt clr run 1f out: nrst fin* **18/1**

00-6 **8** *1* **Cuckoo Rock (IRE)**[21] 1432 3-8-10 **62** PatCosgrave 1 45
(J G Portman) *led 1f: restrained: awkward bnd over 5f out: stl chsng ldrs but wandering bdly over 1f out: wknd* **33/1**

500- **9** *2 3/4* **Tom Wade (IRE)**[190] 7199 3-8-13 **65** PhilipRobinson 12 42
(M A Jarvis) *hld up wl in rr and wl off the pce: shkn up over 2f out: nvr on terms* **7/2**[2]

300- **10** *1 1/2* **Rockweiller**[206] 6829 3-8-7 **59** WilliamBuick 11 37
(C R Egerton) *hld up in 7th and off the pce: effrt on otuer 3f out: no prog 2f out: wknd and eased* **33/1**

006- **11** *nk* **Dauntsey Park (IRE)**[177] 7389 3-8-7 **59** FergusSweeney 9 31
(Miss Tor Sturgis) *dwlt: hld up wl in rr and wl off the pce: sme prog 3f out: no hdwy 2f out: fdd* **33/1**

000- **12** *2* **Othello (IRE)**[173] 7430 3-8-7 **59** EddieAhern 7 27
(E F Vaughan) *dwlt: last and nt gng wl: nvr a factor* **22/1**

13 *shd* **Boragh Jamal (IRE)**[205] 6865 3-9-4 **70** MartinDwyer 10 42
(B J Meehan) *trckd ldr after 1f: losing pl whn bmpd over 1f out: wknd rapidly and eased* **25/1**

030- **14** *nk* **Killusty Fancy (IRE)**[234] 6071 3-8-13 **65** KierenFallon 6 37
(D J S Ffrench Davis) *hld up towards rr: brief effrt on wd outside 3f out: no prog 2f out: wknd and eased* **50/1**

1m 44.46s (-0.24) **Going Correction** -0.025s/f (Good) **14** Ran SP% **124.1**
Speed ratings (Par 99): **100,99,95,93,92 90,88,87,84,83 82,80,80,80**
toteswingers:1&2:£4.70, 1&3:£19.20, 2&3:£12.70 CSF £27.16 CT £347.87 TOTE £5.50: £1.80, £2.90, £5.20; EX 16.10 Trifecta £81.20 Pool: £431.26 - 3.93 winning units. Place 6 £123.73; Place 5 £45.23.
Owner Jason Anderson **Bred** Garry Chong **Trained** Newmarket, Suffolk

FOCUS
They went a fair pace and the first two pulled clear in this handicap for 3yos. The form looks solid with a small personal best from the winner.
Until The Man(IRE) Official explanation: jockey said gelding hung both ways
Killusty Fancy(IRE) Official explanation: jockey said colt lost its action
T/Jkpt: Not won. T/Plt: £83.70. Pool: £91,074.71 - 793.75 winning units. T/Qpdt: £11.60. Pool: £6,472.50 - 410.04 winning units. JN

1583 WOLVERHAMPTON (A.W) (L-H)
Monday, May 10

OFFICIAL GOING: Standard
Wind: Fresh against Weather: Overcast

1978 SPORTINGBET STEVE BULL CLAIMING STKS 5f 20y(P)
2:30 (2:31) (Class 6) 2-Y-O £1,774 (£523; £262) Stalls Low

Form RPR
0 1 **Tedious**[21] 1429 2-8-8 0 ow1 RussKennemore(3) 2 70
(Andrew Reid) *chsd ldr tl led 2f out: rdn out* 40/1
515 2 2 ½ **Pick A Little**[12] 1612 2-8-13 0 DaneO'Neill 9 63
(B W Duke) *chsd ldrs: hung rt over 3f out: rdn over 1f out: r.o* 4/1[2]
65 3 hd **Russian Ice**[10] 1660 2-8-2 0 SimonPearce(5) 6 56
(D K Ivory) *broke wl: sn outpcd: hdwy over 1f out: r.o* 7/2[1]
633 4 2 **Johnny Hancocks (IRE)**[3] 1886 2-8-9 0 AndrewHeffernan(3) 3 54
(P D Evans) *chsd ldrs: sn pushed along: rdn over 1f out: styd on same pce: fnl f* 7/2[1]
0 5 1 ½ **Tufty**[7] 1749 2-8-7 0 JamesSullivan(5) 7 49
(M W Easterby) *sn outpcd: hdwy over 1f out: nt trble ldrs* 40/1
0 6 ½ **Little Hazel**[13] 1603 2-8-0 0 ow1 MartinLane(3) 4 38
(Pat Eddery) *mid-div: sn pushed along: outpcd 1/2-way: styd on ins fnl f* 16/1
53 7 3 ½ **Look'N'Listen (IRE)**[11] 1647 2-8-4 0 ow2 ChrisCatlin 1 26
(A D Brown) *sn led: rdn and hdd 2f out: wknd fnl f* 7/1
4 8 5 **Mrs Nisbett (IRE)**[19] 1463 2-7-11 0 DeclanCannon(5) 8 —
(A J McCabe) *chsd ldrs: sn pushed along: rdn and hung rt 1/2-way: wknd over 1f out* 6/1[3]
5 9 9 **Capa Cruz (IRE)**[6] 1794 2-8-10 0 LiamJones 5 —
(R A Harris) *s.i.s: outpcd* 12/1
10 7 **Lasercutter (IRE)** 2-9-0 0 AdrianMcCarthy 10 —
(Peter Grayson) *s.i.s: outpcd* 125/1

63.60 secs (1.30) **Going Correction** +0.10s/f (Slow) 10 Ran SP% 110.5
Speed ratings (Par 91): **93,89,88,85,83 82,76,68,54,43**
toteswingers:1&2:£16.40, 1&3:£37.00, 2&3:£2.60 CSF £183.23 TOTE £47.90: £13.80, £1.60, £1.40; EX 303.30.Tedious was claimed by Sylvester Kirk for £13,000
Owner A S Reid **Bred** A S Reid **Trained** Mill Hill, London NW7

FOCUS
A juvenile claimer run at a strong pace. The form is rated around the second to the fourth with the winner showing big improvement.

NOTEBOOK
Tedious was always front rank and settled the issue when lengthening clear off the home turn. The result was in no real danger thereafter and this was a big step up on the level of her debut run at Windsor last month, when she finished last. The drop in class obviously helped, but she deserves credit as she was partly responsible for the frantic early pace. She was later claimed to go to Sylvester Kirk. (op 50-1)
Pick A Little was the only previous winner in attendance and was quickly dropped in class having been exposed at Ascot 12 days previously. He never seriously looked like getting to the winner, but rates the benchmark and has found his level. (op 3-1)
Russian Ice kept on steadily inside the final furlong after struggling to go the early pace. She ought to be capable of winning in this class. (op 5-2)
Johnny Hancocks(IRE), without the visor, raced handily but faded from the furlong marker and probably found the race coming too soon. (op 4-1 tchd 3-1)
Tufty, quickly dropped in grade, looked a possible threat when travelling into contention round the home turn and his jockey could have been harder on him at that stage. However, his effort petered out and he looks to need more time. (op 80-1 tchd 100-1)

1979 SPORTINGBET KEVIN DOYLE CLAIMING STKS 5f 20y(P)
3:00 (3:01) (Class 6) 3-Y-0+ £1,774 (£523; £262) Stalls Low

Form RPR
00-4 1 **Monte Mayor One**[32] 1181 3-8-1 55 (p) FrankieMcDonald 2 62
(D Haydn Jones) *chsd ldr: rdn to ld wl ins fnl f: r.o* 25/1
4516 2 hd **Chjimes (IRE)**[19] 1482 6-9-2 67 HayleyTurner 9 72
(C R Dore) *hld up: hdwy over 1f out: rdn and ev ch ins fnl f: r.o* 12/1
2220 3 1 ¼ **Romantic Queen**[19] 1482 4-8-6 62 (t) MatthewDavies(5) 3 62
(George Baker) *s.i.s: hld up: r.o ins fnl f: nt rch ldrs* 13/2[3]
0300 4 hd **Ebraam (USA)**[14] 1580 7-9-12 92 JamesDoyle 8 76
(S Curran) *trckd ldrs: rdn and hung lft over 1f out: r.o* 7/4[1]
500- 5 nk **Harry Up**[156] 7646 9-9-1 74 RussKennemore(3) 7 67
(Andrew Reid) *sn led: rdn over 1f out: edgd rt and hdd wl ins fnl f* 10/1
50-1 6 ½ **Little Edward**[14] 1583 12-9-10 89 GeorgeBaker 1 71
(R J Hodges) *chsd ldrs: rdn over 1f out: edgd rt and styd on same pce ins fnl f* 11/4[2]
0000 7 ¾ **Don Pele (IRE)**[20] 1443 8-9-1 58 (b) LiamJones 6 60
(R A Harris) *prom: rdn over 1f out: nt clr run ins fnl f: one pce* 25/1
01-3 8 1 **Hinton Admiral**[14] 1583 6-9-5 72 VinceSlattery 5 64
(M S Tuck) *s.i.s: sn pushed along into mid-div: rdn 1/2-way: styng on same pce whn hmpd ins fnl f* 14/1
524 9 3 ¼ **Best One**[14] 1583 6-9-2 52 (b) ChrisCatlin 4 45
(R A Harris) *s.i.s: sn pushed along in rr: n.d* 40/1
-60 10 17 **Madame Bonaparte (IRE)**[82] 583 3-8-2 0 JamieMackay 10 —
(P L Gilligan) *sn outpcd* 100/1

62.36 secs (0.06) **Going Correction** +0.10s/f (Slow)
WFA 3 from 4yo+ 9lb 10 Ran SP% 110.9
Speed ratings (Par 101): **103,102,100,100,99 99,97,96,91,63**
toteswingers:1&2:£49.40, 1&3:£39.80, 2&3:£7.00 CSF £273.75 TOTE £37.80: £10.70, £4.10, £1.30; EX 193.90.Ebraam was claimed by M. Murphy for £16,000. Monte Mayor One was claimed by P. Monteith for £5,000.
Owner R Phillips **Bred** Mrs D J Hughes **Trained** Efail Isaf, Rhondda C Taff

FOCUS
A modest claimer and muddling form with the obvious horses not at their best.

1980 SPORTINGBET MICK MCCARTHY H'CAP 1m 5f 194y(P)
3:30 (3:34) (Class 6) (0-65,64) 4-Y-0+ £1,774 (£523; £262) Stalls Low

Form RPR
-213 1 **Cozy Tiger (USA)**[62] 835 5-9-7 63 TonyCulhane 11 72+
(W J Musson) *hld up: plld hrd: hdwy over 1f out: rdn to ld wl ins fnl f* 11/2[3]
4/42 2 ½ **Laconicos (IRE)**[20] 1462 8-8-7 56 (t) LauraPike(7) 3 64
(W B Stone) *hld up: plld hrd: hdwy over 3f out: rdn to ld ins fnl f: sn hdd: styd on* 12/1
5005 3 1 ¾ **Dazzling Begum**[11] 1635 5-8-4 46 LiamJones 2 52
(J Pearce) *hld up: hdwy over 2f out: rdn over 1f out: styd on* 14/1
645- 4 ¾ **Lapina (IRE)**[263] 3593 6-9-3 59 DaneO'Neill 8 64
(A Middleton) *led after 1f: hdd 12f out: chsd ldr tl led over 3f out: rdn over 1f out: hdd and unable qck ins fnl f* 33/1
002- 5 1 ¾ **Brad's Luck (IRE)**[11] 6859 4-8-8 51 RobertHavlin 7 55
(M Blanshard) *hld up in tch: rdn and lost pl over 3f out: nt clr run over 2f out: last turning for home: r.o ins fnl f* 20/1
-551 6 hd **Kickahead (USA)**[115] 198 8-9-1 57 (t) EddieAhern 6 59
(Ian Williams) *hld up in tch: racd keenly: rdn over 1f out: edgd lft: no ex ins fnl f* 3/1[1]
4000 7 1 ½ **Resplendent Ace (IRE)**[12] 1623 6-9-8 64 RobertWinston 5 64
(P Howling) *hld up: hdwy 6f out: rdn over 1f out: wknd ins fnl f: b.b.v* 7/1
4320 8 ½ **Barodine**[39] 1078 7-9-1 57 GeorgeBaker 9 56
(R J Hodges) *s.i.s: hld up: hdwy over 1f out: styd on same pce ins fnl f* 14/1
6164 9 shd **Paint The Town Red**[13] 1609 5-9-2 58 ChrisCatlin 12 57
(H J Collingridge) *hld up: hdwy 7f out: rdn over 1f out: wknd ins fnl f* 16/1
600- 10 1 ¾ **Spume (IRE)**[368] 790 6-8-5 47 AndrewElliott 13 43
(J Balding) *led 1f: chsd ldrs: rdn over 3f out: wknd fnl f* 40/1
62-2 11 1 ½ **Carter**[16] 1539 4-9-4 61 ShaneKelly 4 55
(W M Brisbourne) *s.i.s: hdwy to ld 12f out: set stdy pce tl hdd over 3f out: sn rdn: wknd fnl f* 4/1[2]
06-0 12 nk **Zalkani (IRE)**[32] 1188 10-8-3 50 SimonPearce(5) 1 44
(J Pearce) *chsd ldrs: rdn over 2f out: wknd over 1f out* 16/1

3m 8.82s (2.82) **Going Correction** +0.10s/f (Slow)
WFA 4 from 5yo+ 1lb 12 Ran SP% 115.8
Speed ratings (Par 101): **95,94,93,93,92 92,91,91,90,89 89,88**
toteswingers:1&2:£13.40, 1&3:£26.70, 2&3:£22.10 CSF £66.60 CT £876.80 TOTE £4.70: £1.50, £4.60, £6.20; EX 88.80.
Owner McHugh & Partners **Bred** Alan S Kline Et Al **Trained** Newmarket, Suffolk

FOCUS
A poor staying handicap, run at an uneven pace and the overall form is somewhat suspect. The winner may be better than the bare form.
Resplendent Ace(IRE) Official explanation: trainer's rep said gelding bled from the nose

1981 SPORTINGBET JACK HARRIS MAIDEN AUCTION FILLIES' STKS 5f 20y(P)
4:00 (4:00) (Class 4) 2-Y-O £4,209 (£1,252; £625; £312) Stalls Low

Form RPR
3 1 **Lenjawi Pride**[12] 1626 2-8-12 0 RichardKingscote 9 82
(Tom Dascombe) *mde all: shkn up and r.o wl ins fnl f* 15/8[1]
22 2 3 ½ **Belle Royale (IRE)**[13] 1603 2-8-4 0 LiamJones 5 61
(W M Brisbourne) *prom: racd keenly: trckd wnr over 3f out: rdn over 1f out: edgd lft: styd on same pce fnl f* 11/4[2]
32 3 1 ½ **Stunning In Purple (IRE)**[11] 1632 2-8-0 0 AmyBaker(5) 1 59
(A B Haynes) *prom: hmpd and lost pl over 3f out: hdwy and hung lft over 1f out: styd on to go 3rd wl ins fnl f* 9/2[3]
6 4 ½ **Nellie Ellis (IRE)**[16] 1527 2-8-6 0 ChrisCatlin 2 56
(K A Ryan) *s.s: hdwy over 3f out: rdn over 1f out: styd on same pce: lost 3rd wl ins fnl f* 8/1
5 10 **Renesmee (IRE)** 2-8-6 0 AdrianMcCarthy 3 20
(Peter Grayson) *s.s: outpcd* 100/1
5 6 1 ½ **Dancing With Fire**[7] 1764 2-8-3 0 MartinLane(3) 4 15
(D Donovan) *chsd ldrs: edgd lft over 3f out: rdn and wknd wl over 1f out* 25/1
4 7 6 **Vienna Woods (IRE)**[16] 1527 2-8-3 0 KellyHarrison(3) 7 —
(B M R Haslam) *chsd wnr to over 3f out: remained handy tl rdn and wknd wl over 1f out: fin lame* 5/1

62.88 secs (0.58) **Going Correction** +0.10s/f (Slow) 7 Ran SP% 112.2
Speed ratings (Par 92): **99,93,91,90,74 71,62**
toteswingers:1&2:£1.70, 1&3:£2.20, 2&3:£1.60 CSF £6.93 TOTE £3.50: £1.90, £1.10; EX 8.10.
Owner A G D Lenjawi **Bred** Mill House Stud **Trained** Malpas, Cheshire

FOCUS
An above average winner for the track, showing big improvement from her debut.

NOTEBOOK
Lenjawi Pride showed speed on her debut from a wide draw at Pontefract when third so being housed in stall nine, especially after the non-runners, was of no real concern on this switch to Polytrack. She made all for a convincing success and is entitled to go forward again for the outing, but will not be simple to place successfully again in the short term. (op 5-2 tchd 7-4)
Belle Royale(IRE), another AW debutante, has now finished second on her three outings to date so obviously sets the level of the form. A drop back into claiming company could see her deservedly off the mark. (tchd 3-1)
Stunning In Purple(IRE) didn't get the best of passages through the first half, but came there with what looked a promising challenge at the furlong pole. She rather hung fire when it mattered, though, and may not be the most resolute. (op 5-1)
Nellie Ellis(IRE) was bidding to give her stable a third win from as many runners in this race. She lost out with a sluggish start, but was coming back at them late on and this was a step in the right direction. (op 11-2 tchd 10-1)
Vienna Woods(IRE) was in front of Nellie Ellis on debut at Ripon, and she clearly failed to run her race. Official explanation: jockey said filly lost its action; vet said filly finished lame (op 6-1)

1982 SPORTINGBET BILLY WRIGHT FILLIES' H'CAP 1m 141y(P)
4:30 (4:30) (Class 5) (0-70,70) 3-Y-O £2,456 (£725; £362) Stalls Low

Form RPR
0-52 1 **Babycakes (IRE)**[16] 1537 3-9-4 70 HayleyTurner 5 84+
(M L W Bell) *trckd ldrs: led over 1f out: edgd rt: styd on wl* 10/11[1]
02-4 2 4 **Vaultage (USA)**[17] 1504 3-9-2 68 (t) GeorgeBaker 6 71+
(E A L Dunlop) *hld up: hdwy and nt clr run over 1f out: sn rdn and hung lft: styd on to go 2nd ins fnl f: no ch w wnr* 9/4[2]
4220 3 1 ¾ **Mary Helen**[109] 254 3-8-8 60 ShaneKelly 1 58
(W M Brisbourne) *chsd ldrs: rdn over 1f out: styd on same pce fnl f* 16/1[3]
44-6 4 3 ¾ **Tia Juana (IRE)**[18] 1488 3-8-10 65 KellyHarrison(3) 2 54
(B M R Haslam) *hld up: rdn over 2f out: nvr trbld ldrs* 28/1
6-40 5 1 ¼ **Lady Willa (IRE)**[13] 1601 3-8-10 62 RobertWinston 8 49
(B W Hills) *s.i.s: sn chsng ldrs: led over 2f out: rdn and hdd over 1f out: wknd fnl f* 22/1
-000 6 1 ½ **Chocolate Cookie (IRE)**[13] 1602 3-8-10 62 TomMcLaughlin 4 45
(Miss M E Rowland) *hld up: hdwy over 3f out: wknd wl over 1f out* 50/1
3445 7 ¾ **Always De One**[20] 1461 3-8-4 56 oh4 LiamJones 3 37
(Miss J Feilden) *s.i.s: sn pushed along in rr: hdwy over 4f out: rdn and ev ch over 2f out: hmpd over 1f out: wknd fnl f* 22/1
4243 8 3 ¼ **Larkrise Star**[13] 1590 3-8-13 65 ChrisCatlin 7 39
(D K Ivory) *sn led: hdd over 2f out: wknd fnl f* 16/1[3]
30-0 9 13 **Daniella De Bruijn (IRE)**[16] 1537 3-9-2 68 (b[1]) DaneO'Neill 9 12
(A B Haynes) *sn w ldrs: rdn over 2f out: wknd over 1f out* 50/1

1m 50.56s (0.06) **Going Correction** +0.10s/f (Slow) 9 Ran SP% 111.0
Speed ratings (Par 96): **103,99,97,94,93 92,91,88,77**
toteswingers:1&2:£1.70, 1&3:£4.20, 2&3:£5.00 CSF £2.54 CT £13.76 TOTE £1.90: £1.10, £1.10, £2.50; EX 3.10.

Owner J Acheson **Bred** Alan Dargan **Trained** Newmarket, Suffolk
FOCUS
A modest handicap. The first pair were unexposed and should rate higher.

1983 SPORTINGBET STAN CULLIS AMATEUR RIDERS' H'CAP (DIV I) 1m 4f 50y(P)
5:00 (5:00) (Class 6) (0-55,55) 4-Y-0+ £1,384 (£425; £212) Stalls Low

Form RPR
/50- 1 **Savaronola (USA)**[64] 1568 5-10-9 **55** MrDLQueally(5) 8 69
(B J Curley) *hld up in tch: led over 2f out: clr over 1f out: comf* **11/10**[1]
2 6 **If I Had Him (IRE)**[96] 5738 6-10-9 **50** MrSWalker 10 55
(George Baker) *hld up in tch: pushed along over 2f out: rdn to chse wnr over 1f out: edgd lft and no imp* **2/1**[2]
003- 3 ½ **Bedarra Boy**[150] 6188 4-10-2 **48** MrPTFinn(5) 2 52
(D W P Arbuthnot) *chsd ldrs: rdn over 2f out: styd on same pce appr fnl f* **12/1**
66-0 4 ¾ **Darfour**[119] 124 6-10-3 **49** MrJPMcGrath(5) 5 52
(M Hill) *chsd ldrs: rdn over 1f out: styd on same pce* **40/1**
0-06 5 1¾ **Call Of Duty (IRE)**[8] 1717 5-10-6 **52** MissECSayer(5) 12 52+
(Mrs Dianne Sayer) *s.s: hld up and bhd: plld hrd: hdwy over 2f out: rdn over 1f out: no ex fnl f* **25/1**
4646 6 1 **Haka Dancer (USA)**[95] 411 7-10-3 **51** MrATBrook(7) 9 49
(P A Kirby) *s.s: hld up: hdwy over 6f out: led over 5f out: hdd over 2f out: wknd over 1f out* **20/1**
600- 7 5 **Laura Land**[211] 6705 4-10-8 **52** MrBenBrisbourne(3) 4 42
(W M Brisbourne) *chsd ldr: rdn over 2f out: wknd over 1f out* **40/1**
50-0 8 1¼ **Magic Warrior**[7] 1763 10-10-9 **55** MrsSarah-JaneFox(5) 3 43
(J C Fox) *s.i.s: hld up: racd keenly: a in rr* **100/1**
314- 9 *hd* **Snowberry Hill (USA)**[235] 6025 7-10-7 **53** MrJPFeatherstone(5) 6 41
(Lucinda Featherstone) *prom: rdn over 3f out: wknd 2f out* **10/1**[3]
000- 10 4½ **Anasy (USA)**[206] 6831 4-10-4 **48** MrRBirkett(3) 7 29
(Miss Gay Kelleway) *hld up: rdn and wknd 2f out* **80/1**
100/ 11 22 **Cemgraft**[500] 4929 9-10-3 **47** (p) MissZoeLilly(3) 11 —
(P Butler) *hld up: bhd fnl 5f: t.o* **66/1**
2304 12 1 **Highland River**[15] 1053 4-10-11 **52** MissEJJones 1 —
(A Sadik) *led: hdd over 5f out: sn rdn: wknd over 3f out: t.o* **20/1**

2m 44.11s (3.01) **Going Correction** +0.10s/f (Slow) 12 Ran SP% 119.7
Speed ratings (Par 101): **93,89,88,88,87 86,83,82,82,79 64,63**
toteswingers:1&2:£2.10, 1&3:£7.30, 2&3:£6.10 CSF £3.01 CT £15.96 TOTE £3.10: £2.50, £1.10, £3.50; EX 6.30.
Owner Curley Leisure **Bred** Stonestreet Mares Llc **Trained** Newmarket, Suffolk
FOCUS
This first division of the handicap for amateur riders was run at an ordinary pace and the winner did it comfortably. The gambled winner is rated back to something like his 3yo form.

1984 SPORTINGBET STAN CULLIS AMATEUR RIDERS' H'CAP (DIV II) 1m 4f 50y(P)
5:30 (5:33) (Class 6) (0-55,55) 4-Y-0+ £1,384 (£425; £212) Stalls Low

Form RPR
0522 1 **Blackstone Vegas**[60] 865 4-10-11 **52** (v) MrSWalker 1 61
(D Shaw) *chsd ldrs: rdn over 1f out: led ins fnl f: styd on* **5/1**[2]
-425 2 1 **Lisbon Lion (IRE)**[20] 1462 5-10-5 **53** MissRebeccaSparkes(7) 4 60
(James Moffatt) *hld up: hdwy over 2f out: ev ch ins fnl f: styd on same pce* **11/1**[3]
0006 3 *nk* **Prickles**[7] 1759 5-10-2 **48** MrCDThompson(5) 12 54
(Karen George) *chsd ldrs: led over 3f out: rdn over 1f out: hdd and unable qck ins fnl f* **25/1**
-421 4 ¼ **Bright Sparky (GER)**[12] 661 7-10-9 **50** (bt) MrOGreenall 8 56
(M W Easterby) *hld up: hdwy over 2f out: rdn over 1f out: styd on* **12/1**
500- 5 2¼ **Sommersturm (GER)**[64] 4373 6-10-9 **55** MrDLQueally(5) 6 57+
(B J Curley) *hld up: rdn over 2f out: hdwy and swtchd lft over 1f out: r.o: nt rch ldrs* **1/3**[1]
6033 6 ½ **Barbirolli**[11] 1635 8-9-12 **46** MissCScott(7) 2 48
(W B Stone) *s.s: hld up: hdwy over 4f out: styd on same pce appr fnl f* **33/1**
1660 7 1½ **Naledi**[7] 1756 6-10-4 **48** MrMPrice(3) 5 47
(R J Price) *hld up: racd keenly: nvr trbld ldrs* **50/1**
3040 8 1¼ **Wee Ziggy**[11] 1188 7-10-6 **52** (be) MissMMullineaux(5) 9 49
(M Mullineaux) *plld hrd and prom: rdn over 2f out: wknd over 1f out* **80/1**
-000 9 5 **Wabbraan (USA)**[12] 1623 5-10-10 **51** MissEJJones 7 40
(M Hill) *chsd ldrs: rdn over 3f out: wknd over 1f out* **20/1**
45-0 10 9 **Schinken Otto (IRE)**[24] 541 9-10-4 **48** MissRJefferson(3) 3 23
(J M Jefferson) *prom tl wknd wl over 2f out* **40/1**
041- 11 8 **Kristopher James (IRE)**[193] 7143 4-10-11 **55** MrBenBrisbourne(3) 10 17
(W M Brisbourne) *led: hdd over 3f out: wknd sn after* **20/1**

2m 43.4s (2.30) **Going Correction** +0.10s/f (Slow) 11 Ran SP% 129.7
Speed ratings (Par 101): **96,95,95,94,93 93,92,91,87,81 76**
toteswingers:1&2:£5.10, 1&3:£27.50, 2&3:£29.10 CSF £58.29 CT £1308.06 TOTE £4.20: £1.10, £1.50, £8.40; EX 40.20 Place 6 £56.90; Place 5 £28.03.Key to Love was withdrawn. Price at time of withdrawal 125/1. Rule 4 does not apply
Owner Mrs V Franklin **Bred** Elms Stud Co Ltd **Trained** Sproxton, Leics
FOCUS
The second division of the handicap for amatuer riders, run at an average pace.
T/Plt: £305.60. Pool: £55,888.72 - 133.50 winning units. T/Qpdt: £8.00. Pool: £5061.57 - 465.26 winning units. CR

1792 CHANTILLY (R-H)
Monday, May 10

OFFICIAL GOING: Turf: good

1985a PRIX DE GUICHE (GROUP 3) (3YO COLTS) (TURF) 1m 1f
2:40 (12:00) 3-Y-0 £35,398 (£14,159; £10,619; £7,079; £3,539)

RPR
1 **Behkabad (FR)**[39] 1079 3-9-2 0 Christophe-PatriceLemaire 3 114
(J-C Rouget, France) *broke wl: sent to ld after 1f and in front ent st: qcknd wl and wnt clr: c u.p at 1f out: r.o wl* **2/1**[1]
2 *nk* **No Risk At All (FR)**[39] 1079 3-9-2 0 ChristopheSoumillon 4 113
(J-P Gallorini, France) *towards rr tl st: swtchd wd: qcknd wl 1f out: jockey lost whip: r.o strly fnl f to threaten ldr: narrowly failed* **7/2**[2]
3 2 **Tip Toe (FR)**[39] 1079 3-9-2 0 ThierryThulliez 8 109
(F Doumen, France) *racd in 4th fr s: moved to 2nd after 4f: r.o wl in st to briefly threaten ldr: no ex fnl f* **10/1**
4 ¾ **Foreteller**[21] 1434 3-9-2 0 StephanePasquier 6 107
(D Smaga, France) *in rr fr s: rdn early in st: mde gd prog and fin wl wout threatening ldrs* **43/10**[3]
5 ½ **Russian Dream (FR)**[27] 3-9-2 0 FredericSpanu 7 106
(T Castanheira, France) *dwlt at s: moved up to 5th: rdn early in st: r.o wl towards fin* **43/1**
6 *snk* **Memory Cloth**[31] 3-9-2 0 MaximeGuyon 5 106
(A Fabre, France) *racd in 3rd early: dropped bk to 4th: rdn early in st: r.o but fnd no ex fnl f* **48/10**
7 2½ **Carnaby Street (IRE)**[30] 1221 3-9-2 0 JimmyFortune 2 101
(R Hannon) *smartly away: settled in 3rd: rdn early in st: no prog fr 1f out: grad fdd* **17/2**
8 4 **Bottega (USA)**[180] 7346 3-9-2 0 DominiqueBoeuf 9 92
(M Delcher-Sanchez, Spain) *a in rr: nvr figured* **36/1**

1m 51.0s (-0.10) 8 Ran SP% 116.3
WIN (incl. 1 euro stake): 3.00. PLACES: 1.30, 1.50, 2.00. DF: 6.30. SF: 15.30.
Owner H H Aga Khan **Bred** H H The Aga Khan's Studs S C **Trained** Pau, France

NOTEBOOK
Behkabad(FR) made every yard of the running. He coasted into the straight and was only shaken up by Lemaire 1½f out. The colt responded well and ran on to hold off the late challenge of No Risk At All. The better ground helped him, he's entitled to come on for his reappearance, and he is now likely to go for the Prix du Jockey Club. He should stay the extra 1½f without any problems as his dam Behkara was a Group 2 winner and runner-up to Westerner in the Prix Royal-Oak.
No Risk At All(FR) ran well considering his rider lost his whip. His trainer thought that he would have gone even closer if the colt had started his run earlier, and the plan is now to go for the Jockey Club.
Carnaby Street(IRE) didn't let himself down on the quick ground according to his rider. He could go for the German Guineas next.

1749 BEVERLEY (R-H)
Tuesday, May 11

OFFICIAL GOING: Good to firm (9.3)
Wind: Light behind Weather: Overcast

1986 TURFTV BETTING SHOP SERVICE MAIDEN STKS 5f
2:00 (2:01) (Class 5) 2-Y-0 £2,729 (£806; £403) Stalls High

Form RPR
04 1 **Galtymore Lad**[8] 1749 2-9-3 0 TonyCulhane 8 85+
(M R Channon) *trckd ldrs: hdwy 2f out: rdn to chal over 1f out: kpt on u.p to ld wl ins fnl f* **10/11**[1]
6 2 1½ **Lady Royale**[24] 1375 2-8-12 0 PJMcDonald 4 75
(G R Oldroyd) *led 1f: cl up tl led again 2f out: rdn over 1f out: hdd and no ex wl ins fnl f* **5/1**[2]
64 3 5 **Surely This Time (IRE)**[14] 1597 2-9-3 0 PhillipMakin 3 62
(K A Ryan) *cl up: led after 1f: rdn along and hdd 2f out: wknd appr fnl f* **7/1**[3]
4 3 **Ice Trooper** 2-9-3 0 TomEaves 1 51
(Mrs L Stubbs) *wnt lft s: sn chsng ldrs: rdn along wl over 1f out: sn edgd rt and wknd* **11/1**
0 5 ¾ **Bon Appetit**[17] 1510 2-8-12 0 JimCrowley 7 44
(N Tinkler) *in tch: rdn along 2f out: sn no imp* **17/2**
6 7 **Cinderkamp** 2-9-3 0 AndreaAtzeni 5 23
(E F Vaughan) *dwlt: sn pushed along and a in rr* **8/1**
7 1¼ **Jealousy Defined (IRE)** 2-8-12 0 SilvestreDeSousa 6 14
(N Tinkler) *sn outpcd and a in rr* **25/1**
0 8 9 **Gunalt Penny Sweet**[8] 1749 2-8-7 0 JamesSullivan(5) 2 —
(M W Easterby) *a in rr* **50/1**

62.19 secs (-1.31) **Going Correction** -0.275s/f (Firm) 8 Ran SP% 117.3
Speed ratings (Par 93): **99,96,88,83,82 71,69,55**
toteswingers: 1&2 £3.00, 1&3 £2.50, 2&3 £3.80 CSF £6.01 TOTE £1.90: £1.10, £1.30, £1.40; EX 6.10.
Owner Mrs M Findlay **Bred** Bearstone Stud **Trained** West Ilsley, Berks
FOCUS
The ground was praised by the jockeys riding in the first but the times were probably improved by the fact there was quite a fresh tail wind. An ordinary looking juvenile maiden.
NOTEBOOK
Galtymore Lad was well supported. He had stepped up on his debut run here the previous week and was clearly expected to get off the mark, which he did in the end. However, he took a long time to wear down the runner-up before eventually outstaying her, and is likely to be seen racing over further before long. (op 9-4)
Lady Royale made a fair debut in a fillies' maiden that has since produced two winners, and built on that here. She showed plenty of speed before the favourite got her measure inside the last and can win races, especially against her own sex. (op 9-2 tchd 4-1)
Surely This Time(IRE) was easy in the market but appeared to run his race and is another who will appreciate further in time. (op 4-1)
Ice Trooper is bred to be pretty speedy and did well to get into the firing line considering he was drawn in the lowest stall, and then dwelt slightly and went left as the gates opened. He can be expected to come on a fair amount for this. (op 10-1)
Bon Appetit was free to post, and chased the principals for most of the way without every looking likely to take a hand. (op 8-1 tchd 15-2)

1987 FANTASTIC PRIZES AT LUCKY IN LOVE (S) STKS 5f
2:30 (2:30) (Class 6) 3-Y-0 £2,266 (£674; £337; £168) Stalls High

Form RPR
0-65 1 **Petrocelli**[31] 1237 3-8-11 **72** (b) JamesDoyle 3 59
(A J McCabe) *trckd ldng pair: effrt over 1f out and sn rdn: styd on u.p ins fnl f to ld last 50yds* **5/2**[2]
20-2 2 ¾ **Final Ovation (IRE)**[19] 1483 3-8-6 **67** IanBrennan(5) 5 56
(J J Quinn) *led: rdn along over 1f out: drvn ins fnl f: hdd and no ex last 50yds* **4/6**[1]
0-04 3 4½ **Media Jury**[19] 1483 3-8-11 **46** (p) DavidNolan 6 40
(J S Wainwright) *cl up on inner: effrt 2f out: sn rdn and ev ch tl drvn and wknd ent fnl f* **25/1**
0-06 4 5 **Star Cruiser (USA)**[12] 1651 3-8-11 **51** (b) DuranFentiman 4 22
(T D Easterby) *in rr and rdn along 1/2-way: nvr a factor* **10/1**[3]
0-60 5 3 **Kirkby's Gem**[20] 1468 3-8-1 **43** JamesSullivan(5) 2 6
(A Berry) *chsd ldrs: rdn along over 2f out and sn outpcd* **25/1**
00-0 6 14 **Reel Credit Crunch**[18] 1505 3-8-6 **50** (b) PJMcDonald 1 —
(I W McInnes) *chsd ldrs: rdn along 2f out: sn wknd* **33/1**

62.75 secs (-0.75) **Going Correction** -0.275s/f (Firm) 6 Ran SP% 108.3
Speed ratings (Par 97): **95,93,86,78,73 51**
toteswingers: 1&2 £1.50, 1&3 £4.40, 2&3 £2.90 CSF £4.17 TOTE £2.30: £1.10, £2.10; EX 4.80.There was no bid for the winner.
Owner Raymond Tooth **Bred** Raymond Clive Tooth **Trained** Averham Park, Notts
■ Stewards' Enquiry : David Nolan six-day ban: weighed-in 2lb heavy (May 25-30)

FOCUS
A very uncompetitive seller and the market suggested it was a two-horse race. However, they did not come home in the order the betting suggested. The form is rated around the runner-up.
Media Jury Official explanation: five-day ban; weighed in light (25th-30th May)

1988 ANNIE OXTOBY MEMORIAL H'CAP 5f
3:00 (3:01) (Class 5) (0-75,75) 4-Y-0+ **£2,914** (£867; £433; £216) **Stalls** High

Form RPR

24-0 **1** **Noodles Blue Boy**[25] 1365 4-9-3 **74**............................ TonyHamilton 10 85
(Ollie Pears) *chsd ldng pair: hdwy and swtchd lft over 1f out: sn rdn and edgd rt ent fnl f: drvn and styd on wl to ld last 50yds* **15/2**

2161 **2** *1* **Sir Geoffrey (IRE)**[17] 1524 4-9-1 **72**..............................(b) FrederikTylicki 7 79
(J A Glover) *led: clr 2f out: rdn over 1f out: drvn ent fnl f: hdd and nt qckn last 50yds* **13/2**[2]

212- **3** *1* **Solemn**[186] 7269 5-9-1 **72**..(b) NickyMackay 6 75
(J M Bradley) *chsd ldr: rdn 2f out: drvn and ev ch over 1f out: kpt on same pce ins fnl f* **14/1**

0-05 **4** *1 ¼* **Baybshambles (IRE)**[7] 1805 6-8-7 **67**...................... KellyHarrison(3) 9 66
(R E Barr) *chsd ldrs: hdwy 2f out: rdn over 1f out: drvn and kpt on ins fnl f: nrst fin* **11/1**

0-23 **5** *¾* **Lucky Dan (IRE)**[10] 1710 4-8-13 **70**.................... SilvestreDeSousa 8 66+
(Paul Green) *midfield: rdn along 2f out: styd on ins fnl f: nrst fin* **7/1**[3]

1-40 **6** *1 ½* **Select Committee**[17] 1524 5-8-13 **70**....................(v) GrahamGibbons 12 61
(J J Quinn) *in tch on inner: effrt 2f out: sn rdn and no imp appr fnl f* **7/1**[3]

-006 **7** *1* **King Of Swords (IRE)**[10] 1710 6-8-10 **67**....................(p) AndrewElliott 13 54
(N Tinkler) *towards rr: hdwy 1/2-way: swtchd lft and rdn wl over 1f out: sn no imp* **5/1**[1]

3005 **8** *1 ½* **The Tatling (IRE)**[76] 678 13-8-13 **73**............................ JackDean(3) 5 55
(J M Bradley) *in rr tl sme late hdwy* **33/1**

100- **9** *nk* **Rio Sands**[210] 6765 5-8-4 **61** oh2................................... PaulQuinn 2 42
(R M Whitaker) *chsd ldrs: rdn along over 2f out: grad wknd* **66/1**

0243 **10** *2* **Bo McGinty (IRE)**[16] 1547 9-8-5 **62**................................(v) PJMcDonald 1 36
(R A Fahey) *midfield: rdn along over 2f out: n.d* **25/1**

445- **11** *½* **Joyeaux**[165] 7555 8-8-4 **61** oh1................................ DuranFentiman 15 33
(Ollie Pears) *a towards rr* **33/1**

6110 **12** *½* **Lord Of The Reins (IRE)**[27] 1295 6-8-13 **75**.......... DeclanCannon(5) 16 45
(J G Given) *a in rr* **15/2**

060- **13** *3 ¼* **Pacific Pride**[220] 6489 7-7-13 **61** oh3.......................(p) JamesSullivan(5) 4 19
(J J Quinn) *plld hrd: chsd ldrs 2f: sn rdn along and lost pl: sn bhd* **22/1**

5-00 **14** *1 ¼* **Red Rosanna**[10] 1710 4-8-12 **74**...................................... IanBrennan(5) 14 28
(R Hollinshead) *s.i.s: a in rr* **12/1**

026- **15** *2 ½* **Avertuoso**[195] 7119 6-8-7 **64**.. TomEaves 3 9
(B Smart) *s.i.s: a bhd* **28/1**

61.69 secs (-1.81) **Going Correction** -0.275s/f (Firm) **15** Ran SP% **120.2**
Speed ratings (Par 103): **103,101,99,97,96 94,92,90,89,86 85,84,79,77,73**
toteswingers: 1&2 £12.40, 1&3 £15.20, 2&3 £10.40 CSF £51.04 CT £680.56 TOTE £8.10: £4.50, £1.60, £4.40; EX 84.00.
Owner Keith Taylor & Keith West **Bred** Fifehead Farms M C Denning **Trained** Norton, N Yorks
■ Stewards' Enquiry : Declan Cannon caution: used whip when out of contention

FOCUS
A modest but competitive sprint handicap in which the last two winners took their chance again. Very few got into the race. The runner-up is the best guide to the form.
Bo McGinty(IRE) Official explanation: jockey said gelding hung right throughout

1989 LUCKY IN LOVE NIGHT 17 JUNE H'CAP 1m 4f 16y
3:30 (3:31) (Class 6) (0-60,60) 3-Y-0 **£2,460** (£732; £365; £182) **Stalls** High

Form RPR

04-4 **1** **Leader Of The Land (IRE)**[14] 1601 3-9-3 **59**.................... TedDurcan 8 66
(D R Lanigan) *trckd ldrs: hdwy to trck ldr 1/2-way: effrt 2f out: rdn to ld jst ins fnl f: styd on strly and sn clr* **11/4**[1]

5-03 **2** *3* **High Rolling**[12] 1652 3-9-4 **60**................................ GrahamGibbons 2 62
(T D Easterby) *t.k.h: sn led: rdn along over 2f out: drvn wl over 1f out: hdd jst ins fnl f and wknd* **9/1**

0-54 **3** *nse* **Dubara Reef (IRE)**[21] 1461 3-8-4 **46** oh1............. SilvestreDeSousa 11 48+
(Paul Green) *hld up towards rr: swtchd outside and hdwy wl over 2f out: rdn wl over 1f out: styd on strly ins fnl f* **10/1**

3-00 **4** *1 ½* **Miss Whippy**[14] 1608 3-8-12 **54**................................ RobertWinston 9 54
(P Howling) *prom: effrt to chse ldr over 2f out: rdn and ev ch over 1f out: sn drvn and grad wknd* **22/1**

00-3 **5** *1 ¾* **Captain Clint (IRE)**[14] 1606 3-8-6 **48**.......................... NickyMackay 5 45
(M H Tompkins) *chsd ldrs: rdn along over 2f out: drvn over 1f out: hld whn n.m.r ent fnl f* **11/2**[3]

00-0 **6** *1* **Torran Sound**[29] 1257 3-8-8 **50**.. LukeMorris 3 45
(J M P Eustace) *midfield: hdwy on outer wl over 2f out: rdn to chse ldrs wl over 1f out: sn drvn and kpt on same pce* **12/1**

60-0 **7** *½* **Antoella (IRE)**[24] 1392 3-8-11 **53**.................................. PJMcDonald 6 47
(Ian Williams) *in tch: hdwy on inner to chse ldrs over 2f out: rdn wl over 1f out: wknd appr fnl f* **40/1**

00-5 **8** *2 ½* **Seattle Speight (USA)**[17] 1538 3-9-4 **60**........................ JimCrowley 12 52
(W J Knight) *in rr: rdn along 3f out: nvr a factor* **15/2**

00-6 **9** *½* **Polebrook**[24] 1393 3-8-6 **55**....................................... DannyBrock(7) 10 45
(J R Jenkins) *nvr nr ldrs* **33/1**

-654 **10** *4* **As Brave As You (IRE)**[6] 1830 3-8-10 **52**.......................... TomEaves 7 35
(B Ellison) *s.i.s: a bhd* **20/1**

0-04 **11** *2 ¼* **Specialising**[15] 1578 3-9-0 **56**..................................... EddieCreighton 1 36
(M R Channon) *chsd ldrs: rdn along over 2f out and sn wknd* **3/1**[2]

2m 42.58s (2.78) **Going Correction** +0.05s/f (Good) **11** Ran SP% **120.1**
Speed ratings (Par 97): **96,94,93,92,91 91,90,89,88,86 84**
toteswingers: 1&2 £4.60, 1&3 £8.70, 2&3 £10.30 CSF £27.51 CT £222.74 TOTE £3.90: £1.20, £4.00, £4.80; EX 26.20.
Owner Saeed H Altayer **Bred** Rabbah Bloodstock Limited **Trained** Newmarket, Suffolk

FOCUS
A very moderate 3-y-o handicap in which the early pace was steady and did not pick up until turning for home. A considerable step up from the winner with the second the best guide.
Specialising Official explanation: trainer had no explanation for the poor form shown

1990 BRIAN AND BARBARA'S GOLDEN WEDDING ANNIVERSARY H'CAP 1m 100y
4:00 (4:01) (Class 4) (0-85,85) 4-Y-0+ **£5,180** (£1,541; £770; £384) **Stalls** High

Form RPR

00-5 **1** **Celtic Change (IRE)**[17] 1513 6-8-12 **79**.........................(bt) PhillipMakin 6 90
(M Dods) *led and set stdy pce: qcknd clr over 2f out: edgd lft and rdn over 1f out: styd on wl fnl f* **11/4**[1]

4601 **2** *3* **Just Bond (IRE)**[17] 1513 8-9-0 **84**............................ BarryMcHugh(3) 4 88
(G R Oldroyd) *trckd ldrs: hdwy on inner over 2f out: rdn to chse wnr over 1f out: no imp ins fnl f* **9/1**

050- **3** *1 ¼* **Deadly Secret (USA)**[268] 5070 4-9-4 **85**......................... TonyHamilton 8 86
(R A Fahey) *chsd wnr: rdn along 2f out: drvn over 1f out: kpt on same pce ent fnl f* **14/1**

3121 **4** *nk* **Fujin Dancer (FR)**[9] 1717 5-8-8 **80** 6ex..........................(p) AmyRyan(5) 5 81
(K A Ryan) *in rr: effrt and pushed along over 2f out: swtchd outside and rdn wl over 1f out: styd on ent fnl f: nrst fin* **9/2**[3]

000 **5** *shd* **Bolodenka (IRE)**[10] 1684 8-8-5 **79**............................... LeeTopliss(7) 3 79
(R A Fahey) *in tch: effrt over 2f out and sn pushed along: rdn wl over 1f out: kpt on same pce* **10/1**

0-51 **6** *1 ½* **Danehillsundance (IRE)**[8] 1752 6-8-11 **78** 6ex.............. PJMcDonald 2 75
(D H Brown) *trckd ldng pair: effrt over 2f out: rdn along wl over 1f out: drvn and wknd appr fnl f* **3/1**[2]

-330 **7** *13* **Tamasou (IRE)**[107] 286 5-8-9 **76**.............................. FrankieMcDonald 7 43
(R Curtis) *a in rr: bhd fr 1/2-way* **20/1**

0-05 **8** *¾* **Lakeman (IRE)**[24] 1374 4-8-4 **71**................................... AndreaAtzeni 9 36
(B Ellison) *a towards rr* **33/1**

5420 **U** **Samarinda (USA)**[13] 1618 7-8-6 **73**............................ JamieMackay 10 —
(Mrs P Sly) *unruly and uns rdr as stalls opened* **15/2**

1m 46.96s (-0.64) **Going Correction** +0.05s/f (Good) **9** Ran SP% **115.1**
Speed ratings (Par 105): **105,102,100,100,100 98,85,85,—**
toteswingers: 1&2 £5.80, 1&3 £8.70, 2&3 £14.90 CSF £28.08 CT £296.31 TOTE £2.20: £1.10, £4.10, £4.30; EX 29.80.
Owner P Taylor **Bred** Wardstown Stud Ltd **Trained** Denton, Co Durham

FOCUS
A fair handicap but again it proved best to be close to the pace. The winner may not have had to improve.

1991 NEW MINSTER GRANDSTAND MAIDEN STKS 7f 100y
4:30 (4:32) (Class 5) 3-Y-0 **£2,590** (£770; £385; £192) **Stalls** High

Form RPR

0-2 **1** **Dance East**[26] 1329 3-8-12 0...................................... FrankieDettori 2 84+
(J Noseda) *trckd ldrs: hdwy 3f out: effrt 2f out and sn rdn along: styd on u.p to ld appr fnl f: sn clr* **1/5**[1]

4 **2** *4 ½* **Ezra Church (IRE)**[26] 1336 3-9-3 0............................. GrahamGibbons 6 78
(T D Barron) *led: rdn along over 2f out: drvn and hdd appr fnl f: kpt on same pce* **11/1**[2]

3 *nk* **Rule Breaker (IRE)** 3-9-3 0.. GregFairley 1 77
(M Johnston) *cl up: rdn along over 2f out: sltly outpcd over 1f out: kpt on u.p ins fnl f* **12/1**[3]

-233 **4** *2 ½* **Hot Spark**[24] 1401 3-9-3 71.. PhillipMakin 4 71
(K A Ryan) *t.k.h: chsd ldng pair: rdn along over 2f out: drvn wl over 1f out and sn one pce* **11/1**[2]

6 **5** *8* **Robbie Burnett**[36] 1116 3-9-3 0.. PJMcDonald 3 51
(G A Swinbank) *v.s.a: a bhd* **80/1**

6 *2* **Farmers Glory** 3-9-3 0.. RobertWinston 7 46
(G A Swinbank) *s.i.s: a in rr* **33/1**

5 **7** *7* **Bahamian Jazz (IRE)**[22] 1425 3-8-10 0................. MatthewLawson(7) 5 29
(R Bastiman) *a towards rr: outpcd and bhd fnl 2f* **50/1**

1m 32.58s (-1.22) **Going Correction** +0.05s/f (Good) **7** Ran SP% **113.8**
Speed ratings (Par 99): **108,102,102,99,90 88,80**
toteswingers: 1&2 £1.60, 1&3 £3.00, 2&3 £3.20 CSF £3.47 TOTE £1.30: £1.10, £2.20; EX 3.70.
Owner Cheveley Park Stud **Bred** Cheveley Park Stud Ltd **Trained** Newmarket, Suffolk

FOCUS
One or two interesting performers in this maiden but a one-horse race according to the betting, and that is how it worked out. The form is rated around the runner-up and the winner didnt need to match his reappearance form.
Bahamian Jazz(IRE) Official explanation: jockey said colt ran too free early stages

1992 BEST UK RACECOURSES ON TURFTV H'CAP 1m 1f 207y
5:00 (5:01) (Class 5) (0-70,70) 3-Y-0 **£3,238** (£963; £481; £240) **Stalls** High

Form RPR

022- **1** **Saint Thomas (IRE)**[171] 7474 3-8-13 **65**..................... GrahamGibbons 1 70
(J Mackie) *trckd ldr: hdwy to ld wl over 2f out: rdn wl over 1f out: drvn ins fnl f and kpt on wl* **5/1**[3]

-045 **2** *¾* **Battle Study (IRE)**[12] 1649 3-8-5 **62**........................ DeclanCannon(5) 9 65
(A J McCabe) *hld up in rr: gd hdwy on inner over 2f out: rdn to chal over 1f out: drvn and edgd lft ins fnl f: ev ch tl no ex towards fin* **10/1**

35-4 **3** *3 ½* **Crystal Gale (IRE)**[17] 1537 3-9-2 **68**................................ JimCrowley 8 64
(W J Knight) *trckd ldng pair: effrt over 2f out and sn pushed along: rdn wl over 1f out and sn one pce* **2/1**[1]

020- **4** *½* **Power Of Dreams (IRE)**[181] 7335 3-9-2 **68**........................ TedDurcan 5 63
(M H Tompkins) *wnt lft s: trckd ldrs: hdwy wl over 2f out: rdn to chse ldng pair wl over 1f out: drvn and one pce appr fnl f* **10/3**[2]

630- **5** *5* **Green For Luck (IRE)**[218] 6533 3-8-10 **62**...................... RobertWinston 7 50
(S Gollings) *sn led: rdn along 3f out: sn hdd: drvn 2f out and wknd wl over 1f out* **12/1**

206- **6** *nk* **Jamarjo (IRE)**[171] 7491 3-8-5 **57**........................... SilvestreDeSousa 4 41
(S Gollings) *t.k.h: a towards rr* **5/1**[3]

00-5 **7** *2 ½* **Henry Havelock**[15] 1572 3-8-13 **65**................................ TonyHamilton 6 44
(C Grant) *a towards rr* **14/1**

2m 8.42s (1.42) **Going Correction** +0.05s/f (Good) **7** Ran SP% **113.2**
Speed ratings (Par 99): **96,95,92,92,88 87,85**
toteswingers: 1&2 £6.80, 1&3 £3.30, 2&3 £5.80 CSF £50.64 CT £130.38 TOTE £5.40: £2.20, £3.50; EX 58.90 Place 6: £18.04 Place 5: £14.97.
Owner P Riley **Bred** S Coughlan **Trained** Church Broughton , Derbys

FOCUS
The two top weights were withdrawn from this moderate handicap. The early pace did not look that strong but in the end two came clear of the rest.
Green For Luck(IRE) Official explanation: jockey said bit slipped through colt's mouth
T/Plt: £31.20. Pool £46,455.87 - 1,085.09 winning tickets. T/Qpdt: £20.30. Pool £2,966.60 - 107.80 winning tickets. JR

1825 SOUTHWELL (L-H)
Tuesday, May 11

OFFICIAL GOING: Standard
Wind: light 1/2 against Weather: fine but cold

1993 SOUTHWELL GOLF CLUB MEDIAN AUCTION MAIDEN STKS 1m (F)
5:50 (5:51) (Class 5) 3-5-Y-0 **£2,456** (£725; £362) **Stalls** Low

Form RPR

2 **1** **Innocuous**[21] 1460 3-9-0 0.. LiamKeniry 7 82+
(D M Simcock) *trckd ldrs: chal over 2f out: led over 1f out: edgd lft and rt: styd on strly* **7/2**[2]

The Form Book, Raceform Ltd, Compton, RG20 6NL

222- **2** 2 ¾ **George Benjamin**[214] 6646 3-9-0 75 AdrianNicholls 3 75
(D Nicholls) *led: hdd and hung rt over 1f out: kpt on same pce* **4/1**[3]
36-2 **3** 5 **Search For The Key (USA)**[15] 1586 3-9-0 70 KierenFallon 5 63
(P F I Cole) *hld up wl in tch: drvn over 4f out: outpcd over 2f out: kpt on to take modest 3rd over 1f out* **7/2**[2]
64 **4** 5 **New Code**[8] 1782 3-9-0 0 TomEaves 1 52
(W R Muir) *trckd ldrs: effrt over 2f out: wknd over 1f out* **16/1**
5 ¾ **Nezhenka** 3-8-9 0 SebSanders 4 45
(Sir Mark Prescott) *s.i.s: hld up in rr: effrt on ins over 2f out: wknd over 1f out* **20/1**
2 **6** 9 **Widow Bird (IRE)**[35] 1143 3-8-9 0 SteveDrowne 6 24
(H Morrison) *hld up in tch: effrt over 4f out: lost pl over 2f out* **15/8**[1]
000- **7** 7 **Moonlight Babe (USA)**[255] 5417 3-8-11 43 ow2 DavidNolan 2 10
(D Carroll) *chsd ldrs: bucked and lost pl afterr 75yds: swtchd outside and hdwy on outside to chse ldrs after 2f: drvn over 4f out: lost pl 3f out* **100/1**

1m 40.66s (-3.04) **Going Correction** -0.30s/f (Stan) 7 Ran SP% **110.9**
Speed ratings (Par 103): **103,100,95,90,89 80,73**
toteswingers: 1&2 £2.50, 1&3 £2.70, 2&3 £1.50 CSF £16.69 TOTE £3.40: £2.10, £1.50; EX 16.50.
Owner Saeed Misleh **Bred** Darley **Trained** Newmarket, Suffolk

FOCUS
A fair maiden in which the gallop was only reasonable but the first two pulled clear. The winner came down the centre in the straight and the consistent runner-up and the third look the best guide to the form.
Widow Bird(IRE) Official explanation: trainer had no explanatioon for the poor form shown

1994 HOSPITALITY AT SOUTHWELL RACECOURSE (S) STKS 6f (F)
6:20 (6:20) (Class 6) 3-Y-O **£1,748** (£520; £260; £129) **Stalls** Low

Form RPR
0-34 **1** **Katy's Secret**[12] 1640 3-8-7 65 TomEaves 2 64
(W Jarvis) *trckd ldrs: wnt 2nd over 2f out: styd on u.p fnl f: led nr fin* **9/4**[1]
0224 **2** *hd* **Clear Ice (IRE)**[8] 1750 3-9-3 68 (v) KierenFallon 5 73
(R C Guest) *led: rdn over 1f out: hdd nr fin* **9/4**[1]
0336 **3** 8 **Blue Zephyr**[14] 1594 3-8-12 62 (b[1]) SebSanders 7 42
(W R Muir) *w ldrs: one pce fnl 2f* **9/2**[3]
3513 **4** 8 **Anjomarba (IRE)**[12] 1642 3-8-9 65 (p) JackDean(3) 1 17
(W G M Turner) *w ldrs: drvn 3f out: lost pl 2f out* **7/2**[2]
00-6 **5** *nse* **Special Betty**[33] 1181 3-8-7 45 (p) FrankieMcDonald 6 12
(D Haydn Jones) *chsd ldrs: wknd over 1f out* **50/1**
4160 **6** 1 **Sweet Mirasol (IRE)**[21] 1456 3-8-13 53 ow1 (t) AdamKirby 3 14
(Miss M E Rowland) *chsd ldrs: drvn and outpcd over 3f out: brought wd and sn lost pl* **20/1**

1m 15.68s (-0.82) **Going Correction** -0.30s/f (Stan) 6 Ran SP% **108.7**
Speed ratings (Par 97): **93,92,82,71,71 70**
toteswingers: 1&2 £1.40, 1&3 £2.80, 2&3 £1.60 CSF £6.96 TOTE £3.90: £5.50, £1.10; EX 6.50.There was no bid for the winner.
Owner Miss S E Hall **Bred** Miss S E Hall **Trained** Newmarket, Suffolk

FOCUS
A weak seller in which the pace was reasonable and the first two pulled clear. The winner raced in the centre in the straight and is rated to her maiden form.

1995 SOUTHWELL-RACECOURSE.CO.UK CLAIMING STKS 1m (F)
6:50 (6:50) (Class 6) 3-Y-O+ **£1,842** (£544; £272) **Stalls** Low

Form RPR
1331 **1** **Royal Dignitary (USA)**[17] 1536 10-9-5 70 AdrianNicholls 2 83
(D Nicholls) *led: qcknd 3f out: rdn wl clr 1f out: unchal* **6/4**[1]
0640 **2** 11 **Kipchak (IRE)**[12] 1634 5-9-6 73 (p) LiamKeniry 6 59
(C R Dore) *w wnr: kpt on same pce fnl 2f* **8/1**[3]
0265 **3** 1 ½ **Castle Myth (USA)**[8] 1771 4-9-0 60 BarryMcHugh(3) 8 52
(B Ellison) *chsd ldrs: outpcd and lost pl over 3f out: hdwy over 2f out: kpt on to take 3rd over 1f out* **10/1**
3-60 **4** 3 ¾ **Brave Decision**[97] 385 3-8-4 65 LukeMorris 3 44
(R M H Cowell) *chsd ldrs: sn pushed along: one pce fnl 3f* **12/1**
3156 **5** 6 **Tiger Hawk (USA)**[18] 1505 3-8-0 63 (b) AndrewHeffernan(3) 4 29
(P D Evans) *sn outpcd and drvn along in rr: sme hdwy over 2f out: nvr on terms* **8/1**[3]
-546 **6** 9 **Swiss Art (IRE)**[15] 1587 4-9-3 62 KierenFallon 5 9
(R Hollinshead) *sn chsng ldrs: outpcd over 3f out: sn lost pl: bhd whn eased ins fnl f* **3/1**[2]
2350 **7** 2 ¼ **Island Chief**[27] 1293 4-8-13 63 (p) AmyRyan(5) 1 5
(K A Ryan) *s.s: hdwy to chse ldrs after 2f: reminders over 4f out: lost pl over 2f out* **16/1**
0040 **8** 7 **Bookiebasher Babe (IRE)**[14] 1591 5-8-12 55 SebSanders 7 —
(M Quinn) *chsd ldrs: reminders after 1f: outpcd and lost pl over 3f out: sn bhd* **28/1**

1m 39.96s (-3.74) **Going Correction** -0.30s/f (Stan)
WFA 3 from 4yo+ 13lb 8 Ran SP% **113.3**
Speed ratings (Par 101): **106,95,93,89,83 74,72,65**
toteswingers: 1&2 £4.00, 1&3 £5.20, 2&3 £12.70 CSF £14.17 TOTE £1.60: £1.02, £4.80, £1.40; EX 12.70.
Owner Middleham Park Racing XXXVI **Bred** Bentley Smith, J Michael O'Farrell Jr , Joan Thor **Trained** Sessay, N Yorks

FOCUS
Several course specialists in a moderately run claimer but a very one-sided event. The winner came down the centre in the straight and probably didn't need to improve on his recent efforts.
Swiss Art(IRE) Official explanation: jockey said gelding never travelled

1996 SOUTHWELL-RACECOURSE.CO.UK H'CAP 1m 3f (F)
7:20 (7:20) (Class 4) (0-80,76) 4-Y-O+ **£4,209** (£1,252; £625; £312) **Stalls** Low

Form RPR
/622 **1** **Southern Regent (IND)**[19] 1484 9-8-11 74 IanBrennan(5) 4 83
(J J Quinn) *chsd ldrs: c wd and chal over 2f out: styd on to ld jst ins fnl f: hld on wl* **15/2**
42- **2** ¾ **Speed Dating**[253] 5524 4-8-9 67 SebSanders 6 75
(Sir Mark Prescott) *hld up in tch: hdwy over 4f out: c wd 3f out: narrow ld over 1f out: hdd jst ins fnl f: edgd lft: kpt on same pce* **3/1**[2]
1602 **3** 2 ¼ **Daaweitza**[19] 1493 7-9-3 75 TomEaves 8 79
(B Ellison) *hld up in tch: effrt on ins 3f out: one pce fnl 2f* **9/2**[3]
-630 **4** 2 ½ **Sir Mark (IRE)**[24] 1380 6-8-9 67 ow1 KierenFallon 1 66
(M A Peill) *chsd ldrs: one pce fnl 2f* **18/1**
-111 **5** 2 **Bivouac (UAE)**[6] 1828 6-8-13 71 6ex PJMcDonald 2 67
(G A Swinbank) *trckd ldrs: narrow ld and hung rt over 2f out: hdd over 1f out: sn wknd* **15/8**[1]
4400 **6** 7 **Eseej (USA)**[6] 1828 5-8-9 70 WilliamCarson(3) 3 53
(P W Hiatt) *led: t.k.h: c wd and hdd over 2f out: wknd over 1f out: eased ins fnl f* **11/1**
1235 **7** 3 **Sedgwick**[6] 1829 8-9-1 73 PhillipMakin 7 51
(S A Harris) *hld up in tch: hdwy 7f out: c wd 3f out: sn hung lft and wknd: eased ins fnl f* **11/1**
420- **8** 77 **Bavarian Nordic (USA)**[214] 6648 5-9-4 76 TonyCulhane 5 —
(Mrs A Duffield) *chsd ldrs: rdn and wd over 3f out: sn lost pl and bhd: t.o whn virtually p.u 1f out* **20/1**

2m 24.92s (-3.08) **Going Correction** -0.30s/f (Stan) 8 Ran SP% **116.4**
Speed ratings (Par 105): **99,98,96,95,93 88,86,31**
toteswingers: 1&2 £6.90, 1&3 £3.80, 2&3 £4.80 CSF £30.90 CT £114.98 TOTE £20.20: £7.20, £4.70, £1.10; EX 32.50.
Owner Allan Stennett **Bred** Usha Stud Et Al **Trained** Settrington, N Yorks

FOCUS
The market leader was disappointing but this was still a fair handicap in which the winner raced centre to stands side in the closing stages. He ran his best race since 2007. The pace was an ordinary one.

1997 PLAY GOLF AT SOUTHWELL GOLF CLUB H'CAP 1m (F)
7:50 (7:51) (Class 4) (0-80,79) 4-Y-O+ **£4,209** (£1,252; £625; £312) **Stalls** Low

Form RPR
0203 **1** **Elusive Fame (USA)**[6] 1826 4-9-1 76 (b) JoeFanning 7 89
(M Johnston) *trckd ldrs: wnt 2nd over 2f out: led appr fnl f: rdn clr* **9/2**[2]
2320 **2** 5 **Hits Only Jude (IRE)**[3] 1926 7-9-4 79 DavidNolan 4 81
(D Carroll) *led hdd appr fnl f: kpt on same pce* **10/1**
015- **3** 1 ¼ **Major Phil (IRE)**[299] 3996 4-9-3 78 KierenFallon 6 77
(L M Cumani) *chsd ldrs on outer: rdn and outpcd over 2f out: wnt mod 3rd appr fnl f: kpt on* **7/2**[1]
1/3 **4** 8 **Fadhb Ar Bith (IRE)**[19] 1492 5-8-8 69 RobertWinston 3 49
(John A Harris) *trckd ldrs: t.k.h: hrd drvn over 3f out: sn outpcd: wknd over 1f out* **7/2**[1]
0314 **5** ¾ **Flores Sea (USA)**[6] 1826 6-8-11 72 (b) PhillipMakin 5 51
(Mrs R A Carr) *sn drvn along in rr: lost pl over 4f out: nvr on terms* **11/2**[3]
2512 **6** *hd* **Miss Bootylishes**[19] 1494 5-8-8 74 AmyBaker(5) 2 52
(A B Haynes) *chsd ldrs: styd far side in home st: wknd rapidly over 1f out* **16/1**
211- **7** 2 ½ **Salerosa (IRE)**[151] 7711 5-9-4 79 JimmyQuinn 8 51
(Mrs A Duffield) *t.k.h: stdd and dropped to in rr after 1f: effoert over 3f out: wknd over 1f out* **9/2**[2]
/430 **8** 3 ¾ **Sacrilege**[15] 1579 5-8-8 74 (p) MarkCoumbe(5) 1 38
(M C Chapman) *s.s: sn in tch: outpcd and lost pl 4f out: bhd fnl 3f* **33/1**

1m 39.58s (-4.12) **Going Correction** -0.30s/f (Stan) 8 Ran SP% **114.1**
Speed ratings (Par 105): **108,103,101,93,93 92,90,86**
toteswingers: 1&2 £9.10, 1&3 £3.60, 2&3 £8.20 CSF £47.72 CT £174.07 TOTE £7.30: £3.20, £6.50, £1.10; EX 43.50.
Owner Mark Johnston Racing Ltd **Bred** Summer Wind Farm **Trained** Middleham Moor, N Yorks

FOCUS
Another fair handicap but one in which a couple of the market leaders weren't at their best. The gallop was a moderate one and the winner was another to come down the centre in the straight. It is probably unwise to take this form at face value.
Miss Bootylishes Official explanation: jockey said mare ran flat

1998 SOUTHWELL GOLF CLUB H'CAP 7f (F)
8:20 (8:21) (Class 6) (0-60,60) 4-Y-O+ **£1,774** (£523; £262) **Stalls** Low

Form RPR
2212 **1** **Scruffy Skip (IRE)**[21] 1441 5-9-3 59 (p) TomMcLaughlin 4 69
(Mrs C A Dunnett) *trckd ldrs: led over 1f out: styd on strly: readily* **7/2**[1]
5-56 **2** 1 ¾ **Tenancy (IRE)**[121] 112 6-8-4 46 oh1 ChrisCatlin 7 51
(S A Harris) *led: hdd over 1f out: kpt on same pce* **40/1**
2044 **3** ¾ **Kielty's Folly**[18] 1507 6-8-13 55 TonyCulhane 5 58+
(B P J Baugh) *in rr: effrt and swtchd rt over 2f out: wnt 3rd 1f out: kpt on same pce* **12/1**
0004 **4** 1 **Vogarth**[7] 1142 6-8-2 49 SophieDoyle(5) 6 49
(M C Chapman) *in tch: outpcd over 3f out: kpt on fnl 2f* **25/1**
000- **5** *nk* **Sparky Vixen**[168] 7500 6-8-6 48 oh1 ow2 KirstyMilczarek 12 47
(C J Teague) *chsd ldrs: kpt on one pce fnl 2f* **50/1**
0-56 **6** 5 **Crocodile Bay (IRE)**[19] 1492 7-8-12 54 (b) KierenFallon 14 40
(R C Guest) *trckd ldrs on outside: t.k.h: wknd over 1f out: eased towards fin* **5/1**[3]
0323 **7** 2 **Megalo Maniac**[9] 1723 7-8-8 50 TonyHamilton 9 31
(R A Fahey) *in rr: kpt on fnl 2f: nvr a factor* **9/2**[2]
4002 **8** 4 **Royal Envoy (IRE)**[34] 1170 7-8-10 55 MichaelStainton(3) 13 25
(P Howling) *s.i.s: nvr a factor* **20/1**
2356 **9** *nk* **Bold Diva**[4] 1885 5-9-0 56 (v) LukeMorris 3 25
(A W Carroll) *s.i.s: sn in midfield: effrt 3f out: wknd over 1f out* **6/1**
10 11 **Smart Spark (IRE)**[206] 6864 4-9-4 60 MartinDwyer 1 —
(B J Meehan) *trckd ldrs on ins: styd far side in home st: lost pl over 1f out: eased* **10/1**
4-4 **11** ½ **Big Boom**[36] 1130 5-9-4 60 SebSanders 8 —
(M Quinn) *chsd ldrs: reminders over 3f out: lost pl 2f out* **17/2**
6030 **12** 1 **Mr Chocolate Drop (IRE)**[18] 1503 6-8-13 55 (b) JimmyQuinn 11 —
(Miss M E Rowland) *in rr: bhd and eased over 1f out* **18/1**

1m 29.11s (-1.19) **Going Correction** -0.30s/f (Stan) 12 Ran SP% **116.9**
Speed ratings (Par 101): **94,92,91,90,89 83,81,77,76,64 63,62**
toteswingers: 1&2 £47.00, 1&3 £6.70, 2&3 £48.20 CSF £162.16 CT £1523.12 TOTE £4.50: £1.20, £15.40, £3.20; EX 194.70 Place 6: £69.48 Place 5: £18.83 .
Owner C Dunnett, D Cooper, R Clarke & J Power **Bred** Darley **Trained** Hingham, Norfolk

■ Stewards' Enquiry : Sophie Doyle seven-day ban: breach of Rule A32.2.1 (May 25-31)

FOCUS
A moderate handicap but, although the gallop was a decent one, those held up were at a disadvantage. The winner raced centre to stands side in the straight. The winner is rated up 5lb.
Royal Envoy(IRE) Official explanation: jockey said he had mistimed removing blindfold and gelding missed the break
Big Boom Official explanation: jockey said gelding had no more to give
T/Plt: £68.90. Pool:£69,186.13 732.64 winning tickets. T/Qpdt: £19.50. Pool:£5,648.54 214.00 winning tickets . WG

1929 WARWICK (L-H)

Tuesday, May 11

OFFICIAL GOING: Good (good to firm in places; 8.5)

Wind: Light against Weather: Overcast

1999 EUROPEAN BREEDERS' FUND MAIDEN FILLIES' STKS — 5f 110y

2:10 (2:11) (Class 5) 2-Y-O — **£3,626** (£1,079; £539; £269) Stalls Low

Form — RPR

6 **1** **Danube Dancer (IRE)**[11] 1660 2-9-0 0 .... LiamKeniry 3 — 69
(J S Moore) *chsd ldrs: rdn and hung rt fr over 1f out: r.o to ld nr fin* **9/2**[2]

2 *hd* **Marlinka** 2-9-0 0 .... SteveDrowne 12 — 68
(R Charlton) *prom: led 3f out: rdn ins fnl f: hdd nr fin* **7/1**

3 *2 ½* **Freckenham (IRE)** 2-9-0 0 .... HayleyTurner 9 — 60
(M L W Bell) *chsd ldrs: drvn along and hung rt thrght: kpt on u.p* **5/2**[1]

3 **4** *hd* **Mollyow (IRE)**[33] 1180 2-9-0 0 .... DavidProbert 2 — 59
(B Palling) *chsd ldrs: rdn over 3f out: hung rt fr over 1f out: styd on* **11/2**[3]

0 **5** *2 ¼* **Bathwick Freeze**[15] 1577 2-8-11 0 .... MartinLane(3) 11 — 52
(P D Evans) *sn outpcd: styd on u.p fr over 1f out: nt trble ldrs* **22/1**

6 *1* **Veeb (IRE)** 2-9-0 0 .... ChrisCatlin 7 — 49
(M R Channon) *w ldrs: effrt and n.m.r over 1f out: wknd ins fnl f* **10/1**

02 **7** *6* **Dancing Tara**[8] 1773 2-9-0 0 .... CathyGannon 8 — 29
(P D Evans) *sn led: hdd 3f out: rdn and wknd over 1f out* **8/1**

0 **8** *¾* **Indian Dip**[43] 1043 2-9-0 0 .... FergusSweeney 5 — 26
(R Curtis) *prom: rdn 1/2-way: wknd over 1f out* **50/1**

9 *5* **Symphony Of Love** 2-9-0 0 .... VinceSlattery 10 — 10
(D Burchell) *s.i.s: outpcd* **100/1**

0 **10** *5* **Prison Cat (IRE)**[3] 1930 2-9-0 0 .... TomQueally 1 — —
(E F Vaughan) *s.i.s: outpcd* **28/1**

00 **11** *16* **Majestic Style (IRE)**[22] 1421 2-9-0 0 .... KierenFallon 6 — —
(A P Jarvis) *s.i.s: outpcd: t.o* **12/1**

68.85 secs (2.95) **Going Correction** +0.275s/f (Good) — 11 Ran SP% **113.3**

Speed ratings (Par 90): **91,90,87,87,84 82,74,73,67,60 39**

toteswingers: 1&2 £8.80, 1&3 £4.20, 2&3 £4.70 CSF £33.42 TOTE £3.80: £1.10, £3.50, £1.80; EX 37.10.

Owner Ron Smith Recycling Ltd **Bred** 547 Bloodstock **Trained** Upper Lambourn, Berks

■ Stewards' Enquiry : Liam Keniry three-day ban: used whip with excessive force (May 25-27)

FOCUS

Continuing the recent trend at the track, runners came centre-to-stands' side in the straight. This was just an ordinary fillies' maiden.

NOTEBOOK

Danube Dancer(IRE), a promising sixth at Lingfield on debut, had clearly learnt from that experience and was soon on the speed. She had to really dig in to beat the winner, needing every yard of the trip, and may progress again as she goes up to 6f. (op 5-1 tchd 4-1)

Marlinka, a first 2-y-o runner of the season for the yard, is out of a half-sister to Soviet Song and she clearly knew her job. She looked the winner over 1f out, but her lack of previous experience may have told in the finish. This was a promising start and she can win a standard maiden. (op 8-1 tchd 17-2)

Freckenham(IRE), made favourite on this racecourse debut, was soon outpaced in behind the leaders and couldn't quicken to challenge in the straight. She looked green under pressure and should improve. (op 7-4)

Mollyow(IRE) improved on her debut effort and kept on in the manner of a horse that will benefit from a stiffer test. She will be a nursery horse further down the line. (op 5-1 tchd 9-2)

Bathwick Freeze was quickly in trouble, but she ran on nicely close home and will very much be one to watch out for in nurseries. (op 33-1)

Veeb(IRE), related to a winner in France, comes from a yard whose juveniles have been needing a run and that very much looked the case with her. She showed good speed and should improve. (op 16-1)

Dancing Tara, second to a hot-pot in a three-runner race at the course last week, was well held in this more competitive event. She is another nursery prospect. (op 10-1)

Majestic Style(IRE) Official explanation: jockey said filly never travelled

2000 WARWICK FOR WEDDINGS H'CAP — 6f

2:40 (2:40) (Class 6) (0-65,65) 3-Y-O — **£2,047** (£604; £302) Stalls Low

Form — RPR

50-5 **1** **Super Yellow**[104] 313 3-9-2 **63** .... FergusSweeney 16 — 71
(J A Osborne) *chsd ldrs: led over 1f out: hung rt ins fnl f: rdn out* **10/1**[3]

04-0 **2** *1 ½* **Macroy**[8] 1760 3-8-11 **61** ow1 .... JamesMillman(3) 5 — 64
(B R Millman) *sn pushed along in rr: hdwy over 2f out: rdn and hung rt ins fnl f: kpt on* **18/1**

5006 **3** *nk* **Gemma's Delight (IRE)**[8] 1774 3-8-4 **51** oh1 .... (p) HayleyTurner 6 — 53
(J W Unett) *chsd ldrs: rdn and ev ch over 1f out: styd on* **50/1**

4-00 **4** *1 ¾* **First Term**[8] 1760 3-9-2 **63** .... RichardHughes 10 — 59+
(R Hannon) *hmpd s: in rr: hdwy over 1f out: r.o* **14/1**

06-3 **5** *1* **Watch Chain (IRE)**[14] 1604 3-8-3 **55** .... AshleyMorgan(5) 7 — 48
(M H Tompkins) *prom: rdn and swtchd rt over 1f out: styd on* **8/1**[2]

6333 **6** *¾* **Magenta Strait**[19] 1483 3-8-11 **58** .... ChrisCatlin 4 — 49
(R Hollinshead) *hmpd s: hdwy 2f out: sn rdn: styd on same pce ins fnl f* **25/1**

05-0 **7** *¾* **Rosiliant (IRE)**[12] 1640 3-8-1 **53** .... (b) JohnFahy(5) 13 — 41
(C G Cox) *prom: lost pl 4f out: rdn and hung lft over 1f out: n.d after* **25/1**

030- **8** *¾* **Spinning Spirit (IRE)**[167] 7514 3-9-4 **65** .... PaulMulrennan 2 — 51
(J G Given) *chsd ldrs: rdn over 1f out: wknd fnl f* **18/1**

30-2 **9** *¾* **Sharp Eclipse**[7] 1811 3-9-1 **62** .... KierenFallon 11 — 46
(K A Ryan) *hmpd s: sn in mid-div: shkn up over 2f out: no imp fr over 1f out* **5/4**[1]

500- **10** *hd* **Bramshill Lady (IRE)**[197] 7055 3-8-12 **62** .... MartinLane(3) 14 — 45
(Pat Eddery) *sn outpcd: hung rt and styd on ins fnl f: n.d* **66/1**

-002 **11** *1 ½* **Boga (IRE)**[8] 1814 3-8-4 **51** oh1 .... RichardKingscote 9 — 29
(R J Hodges) *wnt rt s: led: hdd over 3f out: sn rdn: wknd fnl f* **28/1**

20-5 **12** *1 ½* **Dragonessa (IRE)**[8] 1760 3-8-12 **59** .... NeilChalmers 3 — 32
(B Palling) *chsd ldrs: rdn over 1f out: wknd fnl f* **12/1**

040- **13** *hd* **Oasis Jade**[204] 6905 3-9-3 **64** .... GeorgeBaker 8 — 37
(G L Moore) *mid-div: rdn over 2f out: wknd over 1f out* **16/1**

00-6 **14** *2 ½* **Bird On The Wire**[21] 1456 3-8-5 **52** .... (p) KirstyMilczarek 1 — 17
(W G M Turner) *w ldrs: led over 3f out: rdn and hdd over 1f out: wknd fnl f* **33/1**

4655 **15** *8* **Blades Harmony**[21] 1456 3-8-10 **57** .... (p) TadhgO'Shea 17 — —
(E S McMahon) *s.i.s: hdwy 4f out: wknd over 2f out* **22/1**

1m 13.37s (1.57) **Going Correction** +0.275s/f (Good) — 15 Ran SP% **117.3**

Speed ratings (Par 97): **100,98,97,95,93 92,91,90,89,89 87,85,85,82,71**

toteswingers: 1&2 £24.50, 1&3 £49.70, 2&3 £125.70 CSF £158.18 CT £8430.04 TOTE £13.70: £4.60, £9.10, £11.60; EX 284.90.

Owner A Taylor & K Conlan **Bred** S J Mear **Trained** Upper Lambourn, Berks

FOCUS

A modest 3-y-o sprint handicap. The winner is rated up 10lb with the third rated to the best view of his handicap form. .

Super Yellow Official explanation: trainer said, regarding apparent improvement in form, that the gelding was better suited by running on turf.

Sharp Eclipse Official explanation: trainer said gelding ran flat

Bramshill Lady(IRE) Official explanation: jockey said, regarding running and riding, that his orders were to jump the filly out and do his best, but it was outpaced throughout, found the ground to be a little bit quick, and had a high head carriage, therefore feeling it prudent to ride out hands and heels.

2001 RACING UK HORSERACING IN YOUR HOME H'CAP — 5f

3:10 (3:10) (Class 5) (0-70,71) 4-Y-O+ — **£2,729** (£806; £403) Stalls Low

Form — RPR

4456 **1** **Step It Up (IRE)**[29] 1258 6-9-2 **68** .... JoeFanning 6 — 77
(J R Boyle) *chsd ldrs: pushed along 1/2-way: rdn to ld wl ins fnl f: r.o* **16/1**

4120 **2** *hd* **Grudge**[10] 1710 5-9-4 **70** .... (be) JimmyQuinn 4 — 78
(C R Dore) *led early: chsd ldrs: rdn over 1f out: r.o* **9/1**[3]

4-41 **3** *nk* **Lost In Paris (IRE)**[7] 1805 4-9-5 **71** 6ex .... (b) DavidAllan 1 — 78
(T D Easterby) *prom: racd keenly: trckd ldr over 3f out: led over 1f out: sn rdn and edgd rt: hdd wl ins fnl f* **1/2**[1]

3303 **4** *1 ¾* **Cape Royal**[3] 1915 10-9-4 **70** .... (bt) DavidProbert 2 — 71
(J M Bradley) *sn led: rdn and hdd over 1f out: n.m.r ins fnl f: styd on same pce* **8/1**[2]

6000 **5** *hd* **Financial Times (USA)**[7] 1799 8-8-11 **63** .... (t) TomQueally 5 — 63
(Stef Higgins) *sn pushed along in rr: r.o ins fnl f: nt trble ldrs* **16/1**

3124 **6** *¾* **Riflessione**[16] 1547 4-9-4 **70** .... (b) LiamJones 7 — 67
(R A Harris) *chsd ldrs: outpcd 1/2-way: r.o ins fnl f* **8/1**[2]

60.58 secs (0.98) **Going Correction** +0.275s/f (Good) — 6 Ran SP% **110.7**

Speed ratings (Par 103): **103,102,102,99,99 97**

toteswingers: 1&2 £8.80, 1&3 £2.80, 2&3 £1.80 CSF £135.03 TOTE £16.70: £5.30, £2.70; EX 117.10.

Owner The Vine Associates **Bred** David Fitzgerald **Trained** Epsom, Surrey

■ Stewards' Enquiry : David Allan one-day ban: used whip without giving gelding time to respond (May 25)

FOCUS

This was all about whether Lost In Paris could repeat the form of his blitzing all-the-way win at Catterick last week, but with fellow trail-blazer Cape Royal opposition, he couldn't. Lost In Paris is rated 7lb off with turf bests from the first two.

2002 TURFTV.CO.UK H'CAP — 1m 22y

3:40 (3:40) (Class 4) (0-85,85) 3-Y-O — **£6,476** (£1,927; £963; £481) Stalls Low

Form — RPR

10-3 **1** **Subtefuge**[28] 1279 3-8-11 **78** .... TomQueally 7 — 89
(H R A Cecil) *trckd ldr: racd keenly: led over 1f out: r.o wl* **7/2**[1]

1-62 **2** *2 ¾* **Invincible Soul (IRE)**[8] 1781 3-9-3 **84** .... RichardHughes 6 — 89+
(R Hannon) *s.i.s: hld up: hdwy over 1f out: rdn to chse wnr ins fnl f: no imp: eased whn hld nr fin* **4/1**[2]

02-1 **3** *¾* **Gold Rules**[27] 1307 3-9-4 **85** .... KierenFallon 5 — 88
(L M Cumani) *prom: rdn over 2f out: styd on same pce ins fnl f* **9/2**[3]

2315 **4** *½* **Duellist**[18] 1497 3-9-4 **85** .... JoeFanning 4 — 87
(M Johnston) *a.p: racd keenly: rdn to chse wnr over 1f out tl ins fnl f: styd on same pce* **12/1**

055- **5** *3* **Invincible Prince (IRE)**[207] 6811 3-8-11 **78** .... (b) RichardKingscote 3 — 73?
(R M Beckett) *led: rdn and hdd over 1f out: edgd rt: no ex fnl f* **33/1**

21-4 **6** *1 ¼* **Hidden Glory**[11] 1657 3-8-8 **78** .... MartinLane(3) 9 — 70
(Pat Eddery) *hld up: pushed along over 3f out: rdn and nt clr run over 1f out: nvr trbld ldrs* **9/1**

-211 **7** *hd* **Fibs And Flannel**[9] 1718 3-8-9 **76** 6ex .... DavidAllan 1 — 68
(T D Easterby) *hld up: hdwy over 1f out: wknd ins fnl f* **7/2**[1]

6603 **8** *1 ¼* **Transfixed (IRE)**[3] 1913 3-8-5 **72** .... CathyGannon 8 — 61
(P D Evans) *trckd ldrs: plld hrd: rdn over 2f out: wknd over 1f out* **20/1**

-244 **9** *2 ½* **Robust Wish (USA)**[68] 792 3-8-12 **79** .... (b) EddieAhern 2 — 62
(B J Meehan) *hld up: rdn over 2f out: wknd over 1f out* **33/1**

1m 39.39s (-1.61) **Going Correction** -0.15s/f (Firm) — 9 Ran SP% **111.0**

Speed ratings (Par 101): **102,99,98,98,95 93,93,92,89**

toteswingers: 1&2 £4.60, 1&3 £4.40, 2&3 £4.20 CSF £16.37 CT £59.61 TOTE £4.10: £2.00, £1.10, £1.60; EX 18.60.

Owner Dr Catherine Wills **Bred** St Clare Hall Stud **Trained** Newmarket, Suffolk

FOCUS

A good 3-y-o handicap that should produce winners. Front runners were again favoured and the form is rated around the third and fourth.

2003 WARWICK RACECOURSE MAIDEN STKS (DIV I) — 7f 26y

4:10 (4:13) (Class 5) 3-Y-O+ — **£2,729** (£806; £403) Stalls Low

Form — RPR

30-0 **1** **Lenkiewicz**[34] 1159 3-8-9 74 .... TadhgO'Shea 10 — 79
(B R Millman) *a.p: chsd ldr 3f out: led over 1f out: edgd lft ins fnl f: r.o wl* **9/1**

65- **2** *2 ½* **Touch Tone**[256] 5397 3-8-9 0 .... MichaelHills 6 — 72+
(B W Hills) *unruly in stalls: s.s: hdwy over 4f out: rdn to chse wnr fnl f: no imp* **5/4**[1]

0 **3** *6* **Sula Two**[34] 1165 3-8-9 0 .... RichardKingscote 9 — 56
(R J Hodges) *hld up: hdwy over 1f out: r.o to go 3rd nr fin: nvr nrr* **125/1**

4 *¾* **Liel** 4-9-7 0 .... MartinDwyer 5 — 58+
(B J Meehan) *led: hdd and hung lft over 1f out: wknd fnl f* **6/1**

0 **5** *hd* **Twice As Nice**[4] 1878 3-9-0 0 .... RichardHughes 4 — 58
(R Hannon) *chsd ldrs: rdn over 2f out: wknd fnl f* **9/2**[2]

0-0 **6** *1 ¼* **Kinian (USA)**[21] 1442 3-9-0 0 .... PaulMulrennan 8 — 55+
(J R Best) *prom: lost pl over 4f out: n.d after* **50/1**

0- **7** *hd* **House Point**[207] 6809 3-8-6 0 .... WilliamCarson(3) 11 — 50
(S C Williams) *s.s: hld up: nvr nrr* **11/2**[3]

0 **8** *½* **Euroquip Boy (IRE)**[21] 1450 3-9-0 0 .... HayleyTurner 14 — 53
(M J Scudamore) *plld hrd and sn prom: rdn over 2f out: sn wknd* **66/1**

9 *13* **Pound Lane (IRE)** 4-9-12 0 .... VinceSlattery 1 — 22
(Miss T Spearing) *sn outpcd: t.o* **66/1**

0 **10** *13* **Pappas Fc**[9] 1731 3-9-0 0 .... (p) DavidProbert 2 — —
(J M Bradley) *chsd ldr 5f: sn rdn and wknd: t.o* **100/1**

6 **11** *4* **Tehente Son**[22] 669 5-9-12 0 .... ChrisCatlin 3 — —
(Andrew Turnell) *s.s: outpcd: t.o* **50/1**

The Form Book, Raceform Ltd, Compton, RG20 6NL

12 1 3/4 **Annie Moyles**[38] 4-9-7 0 TomMcLaughlin 13 —
(C N Kellett) *s.s: outpcd: t.o* **100/1**

1m 24.83s (0.23) **Going Correction** -0.15s/f (Firm)
WFA 3 from 4yo+ 12lb **12** Ran SP% **112.0**
Speed ratings (Par 103): **92,89,82,81,81 79,79,78,64,49 44,42**
toteswingers: 1&2 £2.50, 1&3 £55.90, 2&3 £38.10 CSF £19.44 TOTE £7.00: £1.80, £1.20, £27.00; EX 17.60.
Owner The Lenkiewicz Partnership **Bred** T E Pocock **Trained** Kentisbeare, Devon

FOCUS
The first and quicker division of what was a modest maiden. The winner showed she wasn't flattered by last year's Ascot form.
Touch Tone Official explanation: jockey said filly missed the break
Liel Official explanation: jockey said filly hung left

2004 WARWICK RACECOURSE MAIDEN STKS (DIV II) 7f 26y
4:40 (4:42) (Class 5) 3-Y-O+ **£2,729** (£806; £403) **Stalls** Low

Form RPR
3-2 **1** **Tagseed (IRE)**[22] 1425 4-9-12 0 TadhgO'Shea 11 84+
(W J Haggas) *mde all: shkn up over 1f out: r.o: edgd lft nr fin* **5/4**[1]
6-42 **2** 1 **Streets Of War (USA)**[11] 1661 3-9-0 78 RobertHavlin 12 77+
(P W Chapple-Hyam) *hld up: hdwy over 1f out: rdn to chse wnr ins fnl f: r.o: carried lft nr fin* **3/1**[2]
035- **3** 4 **Pirate's Song**[221] 6443 3-9-0 66 (t) JimmyFortune 1 66
(J A R Toller) *prom: racd keenly: rdn over 1f out: no ex ins fnl f* **10/1**
2-25 **4** nk **Picnic Party**[28] 1275 3-8-9 70 DaneO'Neill 6 60
(D R C Elsworth) *plld hrd: trckd wnr: rdn over 1f out: no ex fnl f* **12/1**
0-3 **5** 1 3/4 **Alice Cullen**[18] 1504 3-8-9 0 EddieAhern 8 55
(W R Swinburn) *trckd ldrs: shkn up over 1f out: styd on same pce* **9/2**[3]
50- **6** 4 1/2 **Rose Aurora**[188] 7234 3-8-9 0 PatDobbs 2 43+
(M P Tregoning) *hld up: shkn up over 1f out: nvr nr to chal* **33/1**
554- **7** 2 3/4 **Ettrick Mill**[232] 6158 4-9-12 63 JoeFanning 9 45
(J M Bradley) *prom: rdn over 2f out: wknd over 1f out* **80/1**
0 **8** nk **Tigers Charm**[9] 1731 3-9-0 0 DavidProbert 5 40
(J M Bradley) *s.s: pushed along into mid-div 5f out: rdn and wknd 2f out* **150/1**
0- **9** 2 **Zelos Spirit**[208] 6796 3-8-9 0 ChrisCatlin 13 30
(Rae Guest) *hld up: plld hrd: shkn up over 2f out: nvr on terms* **50/1**
10 1 1/2 **Billys Flyer (IRE)** 5-9-12 0 FergusSweeney 7 35
(Evan Williams) *s.i.s: hld up and a in rr* **66/1**
0 **11** 17 **Lordsbury Pride (USA)**[13] 1622 3-9-0 0 PaulMulrennan 3 —
(J R Best) *s.i.s: a in rr: bhd fnl 4f: t.o* **100/1**

1m 25.96s (1.36) **Going Correction** -0.15s/f (Firm)
WFA 3 from 4yo+ 12lb **11** Ran SP% **113.7**
Speed ratings (Par 103): **86,84,80,79,77 72,69,69,67,65 45**
toteswingers: 1&2 £1.90, 1&3 £3.80, 2&3 £5.30 CSF £4.66 TOTE £2.80: £1.40, £1.70, £3.40; EX 5.70.
Owner Hamdan Al Maktoum **Bred** Miss A R Byrne **Trained** Newmarket, Suffolk

FOCUS
Probably the stronger of the two divisions, although it was slower. Sound form among the principals with the winner progressive.
Rose Aurora Official explanation: vet said filly lost a shoe

2005 WARWICK FOR CONFERENCES FILLIES' H'CAP 7f 26y
5:10 (5:12) (Class 5) (0-70,69) 3-Y-O **£3,238** (£963; £481; £240) **Stalls** Low

Form RPR
02-1 **1** **Kingston Acacia**[14] 1593 3-9-4 **69** (v) DavidProbert 14 79
(A M Balding) *mde all: rdn ins fnl f: styd on wl* **11/2**[2]
24-6 **2** 2 1/2 **Love Match**[25] 1347 3-9-3 **68** JimmyFortune 10 71+
(R Charlton) *hld up: hdwy 2f out: rdn to chse wnr over 1f out: hung rt ins fnl f: styd on same pce* **6/1**[3]
000 **3** 2 **Eywa**[36] 1127 3-8-8 **59** FergusSweeney 7 57+
(W Jarvis) *chsd ldrs: rdn over 2f out: hmpd over 1f out: styd on* **12/1**
05-0 **4** shd **So Surreal (IRE)**[13] 1619 3-9-4 **69** (b) GeorgeBaker 13 66
(G L Moore) *hld up: hdwy and swtchd rt over 1f out: stayqed on u.p* **33/1**
05-2 **5** 2 3/4 **Madame Roulin (IRE)**[14] 1593 3-8-13 **64** HayleyTurner 8 54
(M L W Bell) *prom: rdn over 2f out: hung rt and wknd ins fnl f* **9/1**
0-50 **6** 2 **Weeping Willow (IRE)**[28] 1278 3-8-13 **64** RobertHavlin 5 55+
(J H M Gosden) *hld up: swtchd lft and running on whn nt clr run ins fnl f: eased: nvr trbld ldrs* **8/1**
523 **7** 1 3/4 **Golden Ratio (IRE)**[32] 1211 3-8-10 **61** (b[1]) JimmyQuinn 1 41
(J R Gask) *s.s: hdwy over 5f out: rdn and wknd over 1f out* **17/2**
4263 **8** nse **Nadinska**[17] 1538 3-9-4 **69** ChrisCatlin 4 49
(M R Channon) *prom: chsd wnr 3f out: rdn 2f out: wknd ins fnl f* **16/1**
2056 **9** 1/2 **Singingintherain (IRE)**[12] 1643 3-8-2 **58** JohnFahy(5) 3 36
(R A Mills) *s.i.s: hld up: nvr on terms* **8/1**
0133 **10** 3/4 **Moors Gorse**[18] 1505 3-8-4 **62** NicolaJackson(7) 9 38
(R Hollinshead) *unruly on the way to post: stdd s: hld up and a in rr* **20/1**
2-1 **11** 1 3/4 **Always Dazzling**[12] 1648 3-9-2 **67** JoeFanning 2 39
(M Johnston) *chsd wnr 4f: rdn and wknd over 1f out* **3/1**[1]
245- **12** 4 1/2 **Anaya**[142] 7825 3-8-9 **65** RossAtkinson(5) 11 24
(Tom Dascombe) *s.s: a bhd* **14/1**

1m 24.95s (0.35) **Going Correction** -0.15s/f (Firm) **12** Ran SP% **125.4**
Speed ratings (Par 96): **92,89,86,86,83 81,79,79,78,77 75,70**
toteswingers: 1&2 £7.60, 1&3 £14.30, 2&3 £21.90 CSF £40.97 CT £399.94 TOTE £6.20: £2.10, £1.20, £4.70; EX 38.00.
Owner Richard Hains **Bred** Kingston Park Studs Pty Ltd **Trained** Kingsclere, Hants

FOCUS
A modest fillies' handicap but another race where the winner made all. The form is rated slightly positively.
Weeping Willow(IRE) Official explanation: jockey said filly was denied a clear run

2006 BEST HORSE RACING ON SKY CHANNEL 432 H'CAP 1m 2f 188y
5:40 (5:40) (Class 6) (0-55,55) 4-Y-O+ **£2,047** (£604; £302) **Stalls** Low

Form RPR
-004 **1** **Iceman George**[20] 1478 6-8-13 **52** (v) LiamJones 7 62
(G C Bravery) *s.i.s: pushed along in rr early: hdwy 6f out: led over 3f out: drvn out* **9/1**
00-5 **2** 1/2 **City Stable (IRE)**[109] 261 5-9-0 **53** RichardHughes 15 62
(M Wigham) *hld up: hdwy over 3f out: rdn over 1f out: r.o* **2/1**[1]
6-06 **3** hd **Minder**[12] 1635 4-9-1 **54** (p) RichardKingscote 10 63+
(J G Portman) *hld up: hdwy 2f out: rdn and edgd rt fr over 1f out: r.o* **6/1**[2]
/003 **4** 1 3/4 **King Zeal (IRE)**[18] 1507 6-9-0 **53** JimmyFortune 11 59
(B D Leavy) *chsd ldrs: rdn over 1f out: styd on* **11/1**
4436 **5** 1 3/4 **New England**[33] 1194 8-9-1 **54** GeorgeBaker 6 57
(N J Vaughan) *prom: rdn over 1f out: no ex ins fnl f* **17/2**
4005 **6** 5 **Sunset Boulevard (IRE)**[14] 1592 7-9-0 **53** DavidProbert 17 47
(Miss Tor Sturgis) *prom: rdn over 2f out: wknd over 1f out* **33/1**
00- **7** 3/4 **Berriedale**[219] 4755 4-8-8 **52** JohnFahy(5) 12 44
(Mrs A Duffield) *hld up: hdwy 2f out: sn rdn: wknd ins fnl f* **33/1**
006 **8** 4 1/2 **Siena Star (IRE)**[31] 1225 12-9-2 **55** TomQueally 16 39
(Stef Higgins) *hld up: hdwy 6f out: rdn over 2f out: sn wknd* **10/1**
04-4 **9** nse **Feet Of Fury**[18] 1503 4-9-2 **55** EddieAhern 5 39
(W M Brisbourne) *s.i.s: hld up: hdwy 2f out: rdn and nt clr run over 1f out: sn wknd* **8/1**[3]
0/0 **10** 3 **Celtic Warrior (IRE)**[3] 1919 7-8-13 **55** MartinLane(3) 3 34
(John A Harris) *sn pushed along and prom: lost pl 1/2-way: sn bhd* **28/1**
6006 **11** 1/2 **Escardo (GER)**[8] 1771 7-9-1 **54** (b) TomMcLaughlin 8 32
(D G Bridgwater) *prom: rdn over 2f out: sn wknd* **50/1**
05-0 **12** 1/2 **Herecomethegirls**[8] 1756 4-8-9 **53** MatthewDavies(5) 2 30
(W G M Turner) *hld up in tch: rdn over 2f out: wknd over 1f out* **20/1**
-605 **13** 3/4 **National Monument (IRE)**[17] 1539 4-9-1 **54** FergusSweeney 13 30
(J A Osborne) *chsd ldrs tl rdn and wknd over 1f out* **33/1**
-100 **14** 2 **Litenup (IRE)**[31] 1225 4-9-1 **54** (t) WandersonD'Avila 14 26
(A J Lidderdale) *led: clr 7f out: hdd over 3f out: wknd over 1f out* **25/1**

2m 19.06s (-2.04) **Going Correction** -0.15s/f (Firm) **14** Ran SP% **119.5**
Speed ratings (Par 101): **101,100,100,99,97 94,93,90,90,88 87,87,87,85**
toteswingers: 1&2 £8.70, 1&3 £12.70, 2&3 £5.70 CSF £25.01 CT £122.62 TOTE £12.00: £3.00, £1.20, £1.40; EX 29.20 Place 6: £606.91 Place 5: £396.93.
Owner John Mangan **Bred** T J And J Wells **Trained** Cowlinge, Suffolk

FOCUS
This looked an open handicap and it was run at a sound pace. Once again the stands' rail proved the place to be. The form is solid for the grade.
Minder Official explanation: jockey said gelding missed the break
T/Plt: £326.70. Pool £57,946.11 - 129.45 winning tickets. T/Qpdt: £28.80. Pool £4,097.46 - 105.20 winning tickets. CR

1603 YARMOUTH (L-H)
Tuesday, May 11

OFFICIAL GOING: Good to firm (7.9)
Wind: fresh, half behind Weather: dry, breezy

2007 EUROPEAN BREEDERS' FUND MAIDEN STKS 6f 3y
1:50 (1:52) (Class 5) 2-Y-O **£3,154** (£944; £472; £236; £117) **Stalls** High

Form RPR
0 **1** **Mayhab**[45] 1009 2-9-3 0 NeilCallan 3 78
(C E Brittain) *mde all: rdn ent fnl 2f: edgd lft u.p 1f out: kpt on wl fnl f* **3/1**[2]
324 **2** 3/4 **Bajan Bullet**[29] 1256 2-8-12 0 RichardMullen 6 71
(P D Evans) *t.k.h: chsd wnr tl over 2f out: outpcd u.p wl over 1f out: rallied u.p to chse wnr fnl 100yds: kpt on* **10/1**
3 2 **Battle Of Britain** 2-9-0 0 AhmedAjtebi(3) 7 70+
(Mahmood Al Zarooni) *t.k.h: hld up in tch: rdn and effrt ent fnl 2f: hld hd awkwardly u.p and styd on one pce fnl f* **7/4**[1]
4 3/4 **Tamareen (IRE)** 2-9-3 0 RichardHills 2 69+
(E A L Dunlop) *t.k.h: chsd ldrs: wnt 2nd over 2f out: pressed wnr and rdn 2f out: ev ch tl wknd fnl 100yds* **6/1**
5 4 1/2 **Tokum (IRE)** 2-9-3 0 RyanMoore 4 54
(J Noseda) *dwlt: rn green and pushed along in rr: struggling and rdn 1/2-way: wl btn over 1f out* **10/3**[3]
0 **6** 1 1/4 **Lady Morganna (IRE)**[26] 1324 2-8-12 0 MickyFenton 1 46
(Miss Gay Kelleway) *dwlt: t.k.h: hld up wl in tch: rdn ent fnl 2f: sn btn: wl bhd fnl f* **14/1**

1m 15.2s (0.80) **Going Correction** -0.25s/f (Firm) **6** Ran SP% **114.5**
Speed ratings (Par 93): **84,83,80,79,73 71**
toteswingers: 1&2 £3.70, 1&3 £2.60, 2&3 £2.10 CSF £31.57 TOTE £3.30: £1.80, £6.10; EX 36.70.
Owner Saeed Manana **Bred** Whitsbury Manor Stud & Pigeon House Stud **Trained** Newmarket, Suffolk

FOCUS
The back straight and bottom bend were dolled out by three metres. Several well-connected juveniles were making their debuts, but it was the two with experience who carried the day.

NOTEBOOK
Mayhab clearly benefited from a rest since finishing seventh in the Brocklesby 45 days earlier and enjoyed an extra furlong. That Doncaster form looked decent with two subsequent winners finishing behind Mayhab, Sir Lunchalott and Las Verglas Star. Once again he showed good early pace and a good attitude when asked to assert from over a furlong out. There are good winners in his pedigree including the smart two-year-old Dazed And Amazed who reached a mark of 101 in 2006. He has three valuable Tattersalls Million options later in the season and while those are a long way off, he should improve again for this. (op 9-2)
Bajan Bullet was having her fourth run and was a touch fractious at the stalls. She is bred to want further than the 5f she had been running over and although under pressure plenty soon enough, responded well and got going throughout the final furlong to take second. It will be a surprise if she doesn't win something quite soon. (op 8-1)
Battle Of Britain was the most expensive of these, costing 180,000gns, and will leave this behind. As could be expected of a brother to the Prix Du Jockey Club and Prix Jean Prat winner Lawman, he found the early stages a bit on the sharp side but picked up nicely as the tumblers clicked into place from over a furlong out. He'll be very interesting next time, possibly when the 7f maidens start. (op 2-1)
Tamareen(IRE) tried to match the winner for pace and lack of fitness and experience told. However he was given a sensible ride and can only have enjoyed this experience over a trip that should be ideal next time when he will be hard to beat in any normal maiden. (op 5-1)
Tokum(IRE) found everything happening too quickly and never got into the action. He'll be more aware next time, but it could still take another run before we see him at his best. (op 4-1 tchd 3-1)

2008 NORFOLK NELSON MUSEUM H'CAP (DIV I) 6f 3y
2:20 (2:21) (Class 6) (0-60,60) 4-Y-O+ **£1,619** (£481; £240; £120) **Stalls** High

Form RPR
4530 **1** **Sirjosh**[50] 838 4-8-0 **47** BillyCray(5) 6 58
(D Donovan) *s.i.s: sn outpcd in rr and rdn along: stl last 2f out: gd hdwy towards stands' side over 1f out: edgd lft u.p but r.o strly to ld wl ins fnl f* **12/1**
000- **2** 1 1/4 **Maryolini**[202] 6939 5-8-10 **52** RichardHills 7 59
(T Keddy) *stdd after s: hld up in tch: hdwy 2f out: squeezed between horses and rdn to ld 1f out: drvn ins fnl f: hdd and no ex wl ins fnl f* **25/1**
1451 **3** 1 3/4 **Fuzzy Cat**[4] 1885 4-8-8 **55** DeanHeslop(5) 2 56
(T D Barron) *dwlt: sn chsng ldrs: niggled and along and carried hd high fr 4f out: ev ch and rdn wl over 1f out: nt qckn fnl f: wknd fnl 75yds* **5/6**[1]
0-60 **4** 3 **Briannsta (IRE)**[34] 1167 8-8-4 **49** (b) NataliaGemelova(3) 5 41
(J E Long) *chsd ldr: rdn to ld over 1f out: edgd lft u.p ent fnl f: hdd 1f out: wknd ins fnl f* **33/1**

20-0 **5** *nk* **Come On Buckers (IRE)**[64] 829 4-9-1 **57**.............(v) JamieSpencer 11 48
(E J Creighton) *led: rdn and hdd over 1f out: racd v awkwardly and wandering arnd u.p ent fnl f: sn fdd* **14/1**

0566 **6** *½* **Djalalabad (FR)**[12] 1633 6-8-5 **47** oh1 ow1..................(t) SaleemGolam 4 36
(J Pearce) *in tch towards rr: rdn and no real prog over 2f out: nvr gng pce to threaten ldrs* **16/1**

2355 **7** *1 ½* **Thoughtsofstardom**[4] 1884 7-8-13 **55**........................ RyanMoore 1 44+
(P S McEntee) *chsd ldrs: ev ch and drvn wl over 1f out: stl pressing ldrs but nt qckning whn squeezed out and hmpd ent fnl f: no ch after* **4/1**[2]

00-6 **8** *3 ¾* **Thumberlina**[12] 1638 4-8-4 **46** oh1........................(p) AdrianMcCarthy 10 18
(Mrs C A Dunnett) *in tch in last trio: rdn and no prog ent fnl 2f: wknd u.p wl over 1f out* **66/1**

2000 **9** *7* **Towy Boy (IRE)**[9] 1737 5-8-11 **53**..............................(bt) NeilCallan 8 3
(I A Wood) *chsd ldrs: lost pl u.p ent fnl 2f: wl btn 1f out: eased towards fin* **8/1**[3]

1m 13.0s (-1.40) **Going Correction** -0.25s/f (Firm) **9** Ran SP% **114.2**
Speed ratings (Par 101): **99,97,95,91,90 89,87,82,73**
toteswingers: 1&2 £24.20, 2&3 £3.50, 1&3 not won. CSF £255.03 CT £521.73 TOTE £19.60: £4.20, £6.60, £1.10; EX 164.20 TRIFECTA Not won..
Owner River Racing **Bred** Mrs Clair Murphy **Trained** Newmarket, Suffolk
■ Stewards' Enquiry : Natalia Gemelova two-day ban: careless riding (May 25-26); three-day ban: used whip with excessive frequency down shoulder in the forehand (May 27-29)

FOCUS
A weak race which on paper.

2009 WEATHERBYS BETTRENDS.CO.UK H'CAP 7f 3y
2:50 (2:50) (Class 5) (0-75,74) 4-Y-O+ **£2,590** (£770; £385; £192) **Stalls** High

Form RPR

2024 **1** **Kingswinford (IRE)**[3] 1933 4-9-4 **74**........................ RyanMoore 6 85
(P D Evans) *a.p: chsd wnr after 1f: rdn 2f out: drvn and ev ch over 1f out: led fnl 100yds: r.o wl to assert towards fin* **5/2**[1]

00-3 **2** *¾* **Mishrif (USA)**[36] 1128 4-9-2 **72**..........................(b[1]) DarryllHolland 2 81
(J R Jenkins) *dwlt: rcvrd to ld after 1f: rdn over 1f out: hdd fnl 100yds: kpt on tl no ex and btn towards fin* **7/2**[2]

1251 **3** *1 ½* **Lastkingofscotland (IRE)**[12] 1642 4-9-3 **73**...................(b) PaulDoe 10 78
(Jim Best) *in tch: hdwy to chse ldng pair 2f out: sn rdn: hrd drvn fnl f: no ex and btn fnl 75yds* **8/1**[3]

35-4 **4** *6* **Cativo Cavallino**[14] 1596 7-8-5 **64**..................... NataliaGemelova(3) 4 53
(J E Long) *in tch in midfield: pushed along and hdwy over 2f out: chsd ldng trio over 1f out: no prog and wl hld fnl f* **16/1**

3322 **5** *1* **Tevez**[18] 1508 5-8-7 **63** ow1.. ShaneKelly 11 49+
(D Donovan) *v.s.a: bhd: clsd and in tch after 2f: rdn and no prog over 2f out: styd on past btn horses fnl f: nvr trbld ldrs* **8/1**[3]

443 **6** *1 ¼* **Ejeed (USA)**[8] 1779 5-8-6 **62** ow1..............................(b[1]) SamHitchcott 8 45
(Miss Z C Davison) *in tch: rdn wl over 2f out: wl outpcd 2f out: no ch w ldrs after: plugged on past btn horses ins fnl f* **16/1**

1653 **7** *2 ¼* **Harting Hill**[27] 1304 5-8-6 **62**............................ WilliamBuick 12 39
(M P Tregoning) *hld up in last trio: rdn and effrt jst over 2f out: no prog and wl btn over 1f out* **14/1**

4-30 **8** *shd* **Mudhish (IRE)**[75] 696 5-8-11 **67**..........................(b) NeilCallan 5 43
(C E Brittain) *in tch in midfield: rdn and nt qckn ent fnl 2f: no ch w ldrs fr over 1f out* **14/1**

6-00 **9** *¾* **Seneschal**[41] 1063 9-9-2 **72**.............................. JamieSpencer 9 46
(A B Haynes) *led for 1f: styd prom tl rdn ent fnl 2f: sn btn* **16/1**

00-0 **10** *½* **King Columbo (IRE)**[36] 1128 5-8-6 **69**.............. AdamBeschizza(7) 3 42
(Miss J Feilden) *chsd ldrs: rdn and outpcd by ldng trio wl over 1f out: wknd and wl btn 1f out* **25/1**

0-10 **11** *1 ½* **Print (IRE)**[12] 1634 4-9-1 **71**................................ AlanMunro 7 40
(M R Channon) *in tch in midfield: pushed along 1/2-way: rdn and lost pl ent fnl 2f: wl btn over 1f out* **20/1**

00-5 **12** *nk* **Darcey**[12] 1641 4-9-0 **70**.. MickyFenton 1 38
(Miss Amy Weaver) *stdd after s: hld up in last trio: shkn up and effrt ent fnl 2f: rdn and wl btn wl over 1f out* **14/1**

1m 24.69s (-1.91) **Going Correction** -0.25s/f (Firm) **12** Ran SP% **119.3**
Speed ratings (Par 103): **100,99,97,90,89 88,85,85,84,83 82,81**
toteswingers: 1&2 £3.20, 1&3 £7.00, 2&3 £8.80 CSF £10.70 CT £62.78 TOTE £2.60: £1.10, £2.20, £4.00; EX 13.60 Trifecta £53.40 Pool: £226.05 - 3.13 winning units..
Owner Nick Shutts **Bred** J Costello **Trained** Pandy, Monmouths
■ Stewards' Enquiry : Shane Kelly one-day ban: careless riding (May 25)

FOCUS
An ordinary handicap.
Tevez Official explanation: jockey said gelding was slowly away
Darcey Official explanation: trainer said filly was unsuited by the good to firm ground

2010 NORFOLK NELSON MUSEUM H'CAP (DIV II) 6f 3y
3:20 (3:20) (Class 6) (0-60,59) 4-Y-O+ **£1,619** (£481; £240; £120) **Stalls** High

Form RPR

-510 **1** **Rough Rock (IRE)**[12] 1633 5-8-11 **59**................... MJMurphy(7) 3 67+
(C A Dwyer) *in tch: jnd ldrs gng wl 2f out: led 1f out: sn pushed along: a doing enough: kpt on* **4/1**[3]

6024 **2** *¾* **Bold Ring**[5] 1843 4-8-12 **53**.............................. JamieSpencer 1 59
(E J Creighton) *in tch in midfield: swtchd lft and effrt 2f out: pressed wnr and drvn 1f out: unable qck and hld fnl 75yds* **10/3**[2]

0-54 **3** *1 ¼* **Cool Art (IRE)**[7] 1812 4-8-11 **52**........................... RyanMoore 9 54
(J S Wainwright) *in tch: rdn and effrt and rdn ent fnl 2f: hrd drvn and styd on same pce fr over 1f out* **11/2**

60-4 **4** *nk* **Fyodorovich (USA)**[7] 1813 5-8-1 **45**........(v) Louis-PhilippeBeuzelin(3) 10 46
(J S Wainwright) *stdd s: hld up in last trio: rdn and effrt ent fnl 2f: no real prog tl kpt on fnl 100yds: nvr gng pce to rch ldrs* **7/1**

5300 **5** *hd* **Shadow Bay (IRE)**[12] 1633 4-8-10 **51**..................... SamHitchcott 6 51
(Miss Z C Davison) *chsd ldrs: rdn to press ldrs 2f out: hrd drvn and unable qck ent fnl f: styd on same pce after* **20/1**

0105 **6** *1 ¼* **Equinity**[12] 1642 4-8-9 **55**......................................(t) SimonPearce(5) 5 51
(J Pearce) *taken down early: led: rdn 2f out: hdd 1f out: wknd ins fnl f* **14/1**

0000 **7** *nk* **Easy Wonder (GER)**[8] 1771 5-8-0 **46** ow1.....................(v) BillyCray(5) 7 41
(I A Wood) *s.i.s and short of room s: a in rr but in tch: u.p over 3f out: kpt on fnl f but nvr gng pce to trble ldrs* **50/1**

0533 **8** *nk* **December**[15] 1585 4-9-2 **57**..................................(vt) DarryllHolland 2 51
(Mrs C A Dunnett) *chsd ldr: ev ch and rdn ent fnl 2f: wknd qckly 1f out* **3/1**[1]

000- **9** *25* **Bold Hawk**[307] 3743 4-8-4 **45**..............................(b) AdrianMcCarthy 4 —
(Mrs C A Dunnett) *a in rr: rdn and toiling over 3f out: lost tch 2f out: t.o and eased ins fnl f* **40/1**

1m 12.62s (-1.78) **Going Correction** -0.25s/f (Firm) **9** Ran SP% **111.8**
Speed ratings (Par 101): **101,100,98,97,97 96,95,95,61**
toteswingers: 1&2 £3.30, 1&3 £4.50, 2&3 £4.10 CSF £16.78 CT £70.95 TOTE £9.40: £3.20, £1.10, £1.80; EX 18.40 Trifecta £80.70 Pool: £231.25 - 2.12 winning units..
Owner M M Foulger **Bred** Mrs B Stroomer **Trained** Burrough Green, Cambs

FOCUS
Another moderate handicap.
December Official explanation: jockey said gelding hung right-handed throughout

2011 WEATHERBYS BLOODSTOCK INSURANCE MEDIAN AUCTION MAIDEN STKS 1m 2f 21y
3:50 (3:52) (Class 6) 3-Y-O **£2,331** (£693; £346; £173) **Stalls** Low

Form RPR

0- **1** **Lucky Breeze (IRE)**[155] 7663 3-8-12 0........................ ShaneKelly 6 79+
(W J Knight) *taken down early: stdd s: hld up towards rr: hdwy 4f out: led 2f out: clr and rdn ent fnl f: r.o wl: comf* **66/1**

54- **2** *5* **Astral Flower**[178] 7400 3-8-12 0.............................. RyanMoore 1 69+
(Sir Michael Stoute) *dwlt: sn bustled up and in tch: t.k.h after 1f: effrt to chse ldrs and nt clr run ent fnl 2f: swtchd rt and outpcd by wnr over 1f out: styd on to go 2nd nr fin: no threat to wnr* **11/4**[2]

2 **3** *½* **Eshtyaaq**[20] 1479 3-9-3 0.................................. RichardHills 4 73
(M P Tregoning) *led at stdy gallop: rdn 3f out: hdd 2f out: sn nt qckn w wnr: wl hld fnl f: lost 2nd nr fin* **11/10**[1]

04-0 **4** *1 ½* **Fantastic Cuix (FR)**[18] 1501 3-8-12 77........................ J-PGuillambert 9 65
(L M Cumani) *stdd s: t.k.h: hld up in last trio: nudged along and hdwy over 3f out: keeping on steadily and sltly hmpd over 1f out: nvr trbld ldrs* **14/1**

3 **5** *8* **Business Bay (USA)**[21] 1460 3-9-3 0....................... JamieSpencer 3 54
(E F Vaughan) *chsd ldr: rdn over 3f out: ev ch and drvn 2f out: sn outpcd by wnr: wl btn 1f out: wknd fnl f* **10/1**[3]

0- **6** *1 ½* **That's Showbiz**[155] 7663 3-9-3 0............................ NeilCallan 2 51
(W J Knight) *t.k.h: chsd ldng pair: n.m.r on inner ent fnl 3f: rdn and wknd qckly 2f out* **66/1**

7 *¾* **Sposalizio (IRE)** 3-9-3 0.................................. RichardMullen 11 50+
(Sir Michael Stoute) *s.i.s: in tch towards rr: rdn and rn green over 4f out: sn struggling: wl btn 2f out: plugged on ins fnl f: n.d* **25/1**

2 **8** *1 ¾* **Storming Redd**[12] 1644 3-9-3 0............................. StephenCraine 7 46
(J M P Eustace) *chsd ldng trio: rdn over 3f out: wkng u.p whn sltly hmpd over 1f out: tired fnl f* **25/1**

54- **9** *14* **Tahseen**[201] 6962 3-9-3 0..................................... WilliamBuick 5 18
(M P Tregoning) *t.k.h: hld up in tch in midfield: rdn and lost pl over 4f out: wl bhd fnl 3f: t.o* **10/1**[3]

03- **10** *4 ½* **Miss Wendy**[249] 5637 3-8-12 0............................... DarryllHolland 10 4
(M H Tompkins) *a in rr: toiling bdly 4f out: t.o fnl 2f* **25/1**

11 *8* **Cromwellian** 3-9-3 0... AlanMunro 8 —
(M R Channon) *s.i.s: rn green and a in rr: lost tch over 4f out: t.o fnl 3f* **80/1**

0 **12** *24* **Just My Girl**[13] 1620 3-8-12 0.............................. SaleemGolam 12 —
(P Leech) *t.k.h: chsd ldrs on outer: wknd rapidly 4f out: t.o fnl 3f* **200/1**

2m 10.87s (0.37) **Going Correction** -0.05s/f (Good) **12** Ran SP% **115.4**
Speed ratings (Par 97): **96,92,91,90,84 82,82,80,69,66 59,40**
toteswingers: 1&2 £39.60, 1&3 £24.70, 2&3 £1.40 CSF £231.82 TOTE £137.90: £20.60, £1.10, £1.10; EX 428.60 TRIFECTA Not won..
Owner Mrs Sheila Mitchell **Bred** P D Savill **Trained** Patching, W Sussex

FOCUS
Precious little public form to go on here
Storming Redd Official explanation: trainer said gelding was unsuited by the good to firm ground
Tahseen Official explanation: trainer said colt was unsuited by the good to firm ground

2012 SIS LIVE H'CAP 1m 2f 21y
4:20 (4:22) (Class 6) (0-60,60) 4-Y-O+ **£1,942** (£578; £288; £144) **Stalls** Low

Form RPR

40-3 **1** **Sharp Sovereign (USA)**[15] 1576 4-8-1 **46** oh1
Louis-PhilippeBeuzelin(3) 4 58+
(T D Barron) *dwlt: sn bustled up to ld after 1f: mde rest: clr 5f out: drvn ent fnl 2f: kpt on wl* **7/2**[1]

-025 **2** *3* **Pedasus (USA)**[13] 1631 4-9-4 **60**.............................(b) RichardHills 7 66
(T Keddy) *awkward leaving stalls and s.i.s: hld up towards rr: plld out and hdwy over 2f out: chalng for placings and drvn wl over 1f out: kpt on to go 2nd ins fnl f: nvr gng pce to rch wnr* **9/1**

0000 **3** *nk* **Maximus Aurelius (IRE)**[14] 1591 5-9-0 **56**...................(t) NeilCallan 1 61
(J Jay) *hld up in tch in midfield: hdwy over 3f out: disputing 2nd and drvn over 1f out: chsd wnr 1f out tl ins fnl f: kpt on but nvr a threat to wnr* **14/1**

00-3 **4** *2 ½* **Strike Force**[18] 1503 6-8-11 **53**..........................(tp) JackMitchell 3 53
(P Leech) *hld up in tch towards rr: hdwy over 3f out: drvn and unable qck 2f out: plugged on same pce fnl f* **7/1**

4644 **5** *½* **Piverina (IRE)**[15] 1576 5-7-13 **46** oh1........................(p) SimonPearce(5) 2 45
(Julie Camacho) *chsd ldrs: chsd clr wnr 3f out: rdn and no imp over 2f out: lost 2nd over 1f out: one pce after* **11/2**[3]

00-0 **6** *½* **Molly The Witch (IRE)**[53] 939 4-8-11 **53**..................... RyanMoore 9 51
(W J Musson) *in tch in midfield: effrt over 3f out: chsd clr wnr and racd awkwardly u.p over 1f out tl 1f out: one pce and wl hld fnl f* **13/2**

00-3 **7** *7* **Generous Lad (IRE)**[14] 1591 7-7-13 **46** oh1................(p) AmyBaker(5) 8 30
(A B Haynes) *stdd s: hld up in rr: short-lived effrt on inner 3f out: wl btn fnl 2f* **12/1**

2/00 **8** *3* **Sensible**[36] 1134 5-8-12 **54**.............................. DarryllHolland 11 32
(H J Collingridge) *hld up towards rr: rdn and short-lived effrt wl over 2f out: sn btn and wl bhd* **33/1**

466/ **9** *2* **Ernmoor**[764] 1246 8-8-4 **46** oh1.............................. AdrianMcCarthy 10 20
(A E Price) *chsd ldrs tl over 3f out: sn lost pl u.p: no ch fnl 2f* **28/1**

00-0 **10** *11* **Sularno**[12] 1636 6-8-7 **49**...................................... SaleemGolam 6 1
(J Pearce) *t.k.h early: chsd ldrs tl lost pl u.p 3f out: sn wl bhd: t.o fnl f* **50/1**

-403 **11** *31* **Altimatum (USA)**[8] 1763 4-9-4 **60**.......................... JamieSpencer 5 —
(P F I Cole) *led for 1f: chsd wnr after: rdn and no rspnse over 4f out: lost 2nd 3f out: sn dropped out and eased: wl t.o fnl f* **4/1**[2]

2m 9.47s (-1.03) **Going Correction** -0.05s/f (Good) **11** Ran SP% **116.1**
Speed ratings (Par 101): **102,99,99,97,96 96,90,88,86,78 52**
toteswingers: 1&2 £7.10, 1&3 £11.50, 2&3 £18.00 CSF £34.51 CT £393.82 TOTE £3.40: £1.10, £5.90, £6.90; EX 36.00 Trifecta £132.20 Part won. Pool of £178.75 - 0.30 winning units..
Owner Raymond Miquel **Bred** James Sumter Carter **Trained** Maunby, N Yorks

FOCUS
Another moderate handicap.

Altimatum(USA) Official explanation: jockey said gelding hung badly left

2013 RACING WELFARE H'CAP — 1m 3f 101y
4:50 (4:50) (Class 5) (0-70,67) 4-Y-O+ — **£2,590** (£770; £385; £192) **Stalls** Low

Form — RPR

325- **1** **Capable Guest (IRE)**[180] 7357 8-9-1 **64** ... AlanMunro 7 — 71
(M R Channon) *chsd ldr: rdn and ev ch fr over 2f out: drvn and led wl ins fnl f* **13/2**[3]

-000 **2** *nk* **Broughtons Paradis (IRE)**[20] 1478 4-8-10 **59** ... SaleemGolam 3 — 65
(W J Musson) *hld up in tch: hdwy to join ldrs gng wl jst over 2f out: led wl over 1f out: sn rdn: drvn ins fnl f: hdd and no ex wl ins fnl f* **11/4**[2]

3003 **3** *nk* **Moscow Oznick**[14] 1609 5-8-12 **61** ... ShaneKelly 6 — 67
(D Donovan) *t.k.h: hld up in last pair: hdwy to ld 7f out: hrd pressed and rdn ent fnl 2f: hdd wl over 1f out: drvn and unable qck wl ins fnl f* **25/1**

40-1 **4** *nk* **Locum**[14] 1609 5-9-4 **67** ... RyanMoore 4 — 72
(M H Tompkins) *hld up in tch: effrt and swtchd to inner over 2f out: rdn and ev ch ent fnl f tl unable qck fnl 100yds* **13/8**[1]

3351 **5** *10* **Atacama Sunrise**[14] 1606 4-9-0 **63** ... JamieSpencer 2 — 51
(G Prodromou) *hld up wl in tch in last pair: rdn and unable qck ent fnl 2f: sn wl btn* **9/1**

201- **6** *½* **Annambo**[229] 6226 10-8-11 **63** ... RussKennemore(3) 1 — 51
(Andrew Reid) *hld up in last pair: rdn and unable qck jst over 2f out: sn outpcd and wl btn* **8/1**

0000 **7** *52* **Best In Class**[17] 1530 4-9-2 **65** ...(t) WilliamBuick 5 — —
(S C Williams) *led tl 7f out: rdn and wknd qckly jst over 2f out: virtually p.u fnl f: t.o* **20/1**

2m 32.3s (3.60) **Going Correction** -0.05s/f (Good) — **7** Ran SP% **107.8**
Speed ratings (Par 103): **84,83,83,83,76 75,37**
toteswingers: 1&2 £7.10, 1&3 £11.50, 2&3 £18.00 CSF £21.86 TOTE £8.60: £4.00, £1.10; EX 28.30.
Owner M Channon **Bred** Mountarmstrong Stud **Trained** West Ilsley, Berks
■ Stewards' Enquiry : Alan Munro three-day ban: used whip with excessive frequency without giving gelding time to respond (May 25-27)

FOCUS
A tight handicap on paper and so it proved with four of the seven runners having a claim to success in the final 100yds.
Best In Class Official explanation: trainer's rep said gelding was unsuited by the good to firm ground

2014 FIRST FURNISHING SUPERSTORE 01493 445454 H'CAP — 1m 6f 17y
5:20 (5:20) (Class 5) (0-75,72) 4-Y-O+ — **£2,590** (£770; £385; £192) **Stalls** High

Form — RPR

-060 **1** **Royal Premier (IRE)**[28] 1283 7-7-12 **52** oh7 ... SimonPearce(5) 3 — 59
(H J Collingridge) *in tch: chsd ldng pair 4f out: rdn to chse ldr ent fnl 2f: chal over 1f out: pushed ahd ins fnl f: kpt on wl* **33/1**

21-2 **2** *¾* **Kazbow (IRE)**[14] 1609 4-9-8 **72** ... J-PGuillambert 5 — 78
(L M Cumani) *led: clr 10f out: rdn wl over 2f out: hrd pressed and drvn over 1f out: hdd and no ex ins fnl f* **15/8**[1]

402/ **3** *2* **Ultimate Quest (IRE)**[665] 4067 5-8-8 **57** ... WilliamBuick 2 — 60
(Sir Mark Prescott) *chsd ldrs: wnt 2nd 5f out: rdn ent fnl 2f: drvn and unable qck over 1f out: btn jst ins fnl f* **10/3**[3]

41 **4** *13* **Lady Eclair (IRE)**[21] 1451 4-9-4 **68** ... RichardHills 1 — 60
(M Johnston) *hld up in last pair: rdn and effrt over 2f out: edgd lft and btn 2f out: eased ins fnl f* **2/1**[2]

-155 **5** *23* **Mr Plod**[8] 1768 5-8-11 **60** ... DarryllHolland 4 — 13
(Andrew Reid) *t.k.h: chsd wnr tl 5f out: lost pl u.p 4f out: t.o fnl 2f* **7/1**

3m 5.64s (-1.96) **Going Correction** -0.05s/f (Good)
WFA 4 from 5yo+ 1lb — **5** Ran SP% **106.6**
Speed ratings (Par 103): **103,102,101,94,80**
CSF £88.75 TOTE £38.30: £15.00, £1.10; EX 92.90 Place 6: £43.36 Place 5: £9.14.
Owner Maynard Durrant Partnership I **Bred** Mrs Anne Hughes **Trained** Exning, Suffolk

FOCUS
A small but tricky race.
Royal Premier(IRE) Official explanation: trainer said, regarding apparent improvement in form, that the gelding benefited from the removal of the visor.
Mr Plod Official explanation: trainer's rep said gelding was unsuited by the good to firm ground
T/Jkpt: Not won. T/Plt: £29.10 Pool £67,937.80 - 1,7037.80 winning tickets. T/Qpdt: £5.60. Pool £4,644.84 - 609.10 winning tickets. SP

JAGERSRO (R-H)
Tuesday, May 11
OFFICIAL GOING: Dirt: standard

2019a LANWADES STUD JAGERSRO SPRINT (LISTED RACE) (3YO+) (DIRT) — 6f (D)
6:29 (12:00) 3-Y-O+ — **£25,974** (£8,658; £4,329; £2,597; £1,731)

RPR

1 **Tertio Bloom (SWE)**[23] 5-9-6 0 ... ManuelMartinez 4 — 105
(Fredrik Reuterskiold, Sweden) **7/10**[1]

2 *1* **Alcohuaz (CHI)**[23] 5-9-6 0 ...(b) LennartHammer-Hansen 3 — 102
(Lennart Reuterskiold Jr, Sweden) **3/1**[2]

3 *4* **Exhibition (IRE)**[23] 5-9-6 0 ... RafaelSchistl 5 — 89
(Francisco Castro, Sweden) **93/10**

4 *¾* **Prohibit**[9] 1727 5-9-6 0 ... PatCosgrave 7 — 87
(R M H Cowell) *dwlt s: sn rdn to go prom: wnt 2nd 1/2-way: ev ch st: wknd wl ins fnl f* **63/10**[3]

5 *3* **Simian (SWE)**[19] 5-9-6 0 ... Jan-ErikNeuroth 6 — 77
(Wido Neuroth, Norway) **153/10**

6 *nk* **Ancient Egypt**[723] 2233 8-9-6 0 ... DinaDanekilde 2 — 76
(Annelie Larsson, Sweden) **173/10**

7 *nse* **Master Chef (IRE)**[240] 5-9-6 0 ...(b) JacobJohansen 8 — 76
(Bent Olsen, Denmark) **27/1**

8 *2½* **Buen Rumbero (USA)** 4-9-6 0 ... ElioneChaves 1 — 68
(Francisco Castro, Sweden) **33/1**

1m 11.6s (71.60) — **8** Ran SP% **125.3**
PARI-MUTUEL (all including 1sek stake): WIN 1.70; PLACE 1.07, 1.17, 1.39; SF 4.09.
Owner Stall In Bloom **Bred** Triple Crown Bloomers A B & P Frisk **Trained** Sweden

2020a PRAMMS MEMORIAL (LISTED RACE) (4YO+) (DIRT) — 1m 143y(D)
8:04 (12:00) 4-Y-O+ — **£51,948** (£17,316; £8,658; £5,194; £3,463)

RPR

1 **Luca Brasi (FR)**[212] 6-9-4 0 ... RafaelSchistl 3 — 97
(Francisco Castro, Sweden) **13/10**[1]

2 *2½* **Quick Release (IRE)**[116] 197 5-9-4 0 ... KimAndersen 6 — 91
(Sven Christensen, Denmark) **156/10**

3 *1¼* **Highway (IRE)**[228] 7-9-4 0 ...(b) ManuelSantos 8 — 88
(Francisco Castro, Sweden) **35/1**

4 *1* **Entangle**[212] 4-9-0 0 ... LennartHammer-Hansen 4 — 82
(Arnfinn Lund, Norway) **17/5**[2]

5 *nse* **Prince Fasliyev**[89] 511 6-9-4 0 ... Per-AndersGraberg 2 — 86
(Niels Petersen, Norway) **239/10**

6 *1½* **Quilboquet (BRZ)**[10] 7-9-4 0 ... EspenSki 7 — 83
(Lennart Reuterskiold Jr, Sweden) **33/1**

7 *9* **Erroll (SWE)** 4-9-4 0 ...(b) JacobJohansen 5 — 63
(Patrick Wahl, Sweden) **145/10**

8 *1¾* **Handsome Hawk (IRE)**[30] 1251 4-9-4 0 ... Jan-ErikNeuroth 1 — 59
(Wido Neuroth, Norway) **111/10**

9 *9* **Cloudy Start**[11] 1664 4-9-4 0 ...(b[1]) ManuelMartinez 10 — 39
(J A Osborne) *4th early: sn rdn to hold position: grad lost pl fr 1/2-way: sn bhd* **54/10**[3]

10 *dist* **Theatrical Award (NOR)**[19] 5-9-0 0 ... CarlosLopez 9 — —
(Michael Taylor, Norway) **32/5**

1m 46.2s (106.20) — **10** Ran SP% **125.8**
PARI-MUTUEL (all including 1sek stake): WIN 2.30; PLACE 1.38, 3.41, 3.08; SF 23.11.
Owner Mac Racing & Stall Chicken **Bred** T Ryan **Trained** Sweden

1793 BATH (L-H)
Wednesday, May 12
OFFICIAL GOING: Good to firm (firm in places; 9.6)
Wind: Moderate, across Weather: Dull, chilly

2021 FARPOINT BATH'S APPLE PREMIUM RESELLER H'CAP — 5f 11y
6:00 (6:00) (Class 6) (0-60,60) 4-Y-O+ — **£1,942** (£578; £288; £144) **Stalls** Centre

Form — RPR

6403 **1** **Radiator Rooney (IRE)**[15] 1596 7-8-10 **52** ... RichardHughes 11 — 58
(Patrick Morris) *hld up in rr: nt clr run and swtchd rt wl over 1f out: str run on outside fnl f to ld nr fin* **7/1**[3]

5240 **2** *¾* **Best One**[2] 1979 6-8-10 **52** ...(b) ChrisCatlin 13 — 55
(R A Harris) *s.i.s: sn rcvrd to chse ldrs: led and wnt lft over 1f out: styd on u.p ins fnl f: hdd and outpcd nr fin* **16/1**

00-5 **3** *shd* **Stamford Blue**[8] 1799 9-8-10 **59** ...(b) JakePayne(7) 12 — 62
(R A Harris) *in tch: chsd ldrs 2f out: edgd lft 1f out and styd on to press for 2nd fnl 100yds: nt pce of wnr nr fin* **14/1**

0454 **4** *1* **Hart Of Gold**[32] 1235 6-8-10 **52** ...(b) LiamJones 4 — 51+
(R A Harris) *chsd ldrs: rdn and hapered fr over 1f out: styd on fnl 100yds: nt rcvr* **14/1**

2-00 **5** *½* **Talamahana**[17] 1547 5-7-13 **46** oh1 ...(v) AmyBaker(5) 3 — 43+
(A B Haynes) *in rr: hdwy whn bdly hmpd appr fnl f: rallied fnl 100yds: kpt on: nt rcvr* **33/1**

1342 **6** *nk* **Captain Kallis (IRE)**[8] 1799 4-8-10 **57** ... BillyCray(5) 6 — 53+
(D J S Ffrench Davis) *in tch: hdwy fr 2f out: styng on whn bdly hmpd fr over 1f out: kpt on fnl 100yds: nt rcvr* **10/1**

4232 **7** *¾* **Welcome Approach**[10] 1723 7-8-7 **49** ... JimmyQuinn 10 — 42+
(J R Weymes) *s.i.s: in rr tl hdwy 2f out: nt clr run on ins sn after: styng on whn bdly hmpd 1f out and ins fnl f: kpt on cl home but nt rcvr* **9/2**[2]

00-3 **8** *nk* **Avrilo**[8] 1799 4-8-11 **53** ... DaneO'Neill 5 — 45+
(M S Saunders) *chsd ldrs: rdn and ev ch whn bdly hmpd 1f out: nt rcvr* **4/1**[1]

0530 **9** *1½* **Tune Up The Band**[8] 1799 6-8-10 **52** ... RichardKingscote 2 — 39+
(R J Hodges) *sn led: hdd over 1f out: sn bdly hmpd and no ch after* **9/2**[2]

3-04 **10** *1* **Mazzola**[8] 1799 4-9-4 **60** ... LukeMorris 14 — 43+
(J M Bradley) *trckd ldrs tl v bdly hmpd over 1f out: nt rcvr* **7/1**[3]

0/00 **11** *¾* **Marron Flore**[7] 1825 7-8-4 **46** oh1 ...(tp) WandersonD'Avila 9 — 27
(A J Lidderdale) *pressed ldrs: ev ch fr 2f out: wknd 1f out* **100/1**

050- **12** *1* **Mr Loire**[302] 3947 6-8-1 **46** oh1 ...(b) Louis-PhilippeBeuzelin(3) 8 — 23
(M F Harris) *outpcd fr 1/2-way* **40/1**

-405 **13** *2½* **Slap And Tickle (IRE)**[15] 1599 4-8-13 **55** ...(e[1]) TomMcLaughlin 1 — 23
(M D Squance) *s.i.s: outpcd* **25/1**

2365 **14** *½* **Bluebok**[16] 1583 9-8-7 **52** ...(bt) JackDean(3) 7 — 18+
(J M Bradley) *chsd ldrs tl bdly hmpd over 1f out: nt rcvr and eased* **16/1**

62.14 secs (-0.36) **Going Correction** -0.025s/f (Good) — **14** Ran SP% **125.8**
Speed ratings (Par 101): **101,99,99,98,97 96,95,95,92,91 89,88,84,83**
toteswingers: 1&2 £40.40, 1&3 £14.00, 2&3 £66.60 CSF £116.16 CT £1023.32 TOTE £13.40: £5.10, £5.60, £3.80; EX 181.70.
Owner Vincent Gleeson **Bred** Barry Lyons **Trained** Tarporley, Cheshire
■ Stewards' Enquiry : Jake Payne six-day ban: carless riding (May 26-31)
Chris Catlin six-day ban: careless riding (May 26-31)

FOCUS
Almost a re-run of the course and distance handicap last week, but plenty of trouble in running on this occasion and not a result to take at face value given the problems nearly half the field encountered. The rider of the runner-up received a six-day ban and the rider of the third a four-day ban. The form is rated fairly negatively, around the runner-up.
Hart Of Gold Official explanation: jockey said gelding was denied a clear run
Captain Kallis(IRE) Official explanation: jockey said gelding was struck into
Welcome Approach Official explanation: jockey said gelding suffered interference in running
Avrilo Official explanation: jockey said filly was struck into
Tune Up The Band Official explanation: jockey said gelding suffered interference in running
Slap And Tickle(IRE) Official explanation: jockey said filly was slowly away

2022 E B F AND RG KELLY WINDOWS MEDIAN AUCTION MAIDEN STKS — 5f 11y
6:30 (6:30) (Class 5) 2-Y-O — **£3,238** (£963; £481; £240) **Stalls** Centre

Form — RPR

43 **1** **Emma's Gift (IRE)**[15] 1603 2-8-12 0 ... JimmyQuinn 3 — 72
(Miss J Feilden) *trckd ldrs: drvn and styd on wl to chse ldr ins fnl f: outbattled faltering rival cl home* **7/2**[2]

U **2** *nk* **Kojak (IRE)**[4] 1901 2-9-3 0 ... RichardHughes 6 — 76
(R Hannon) *w ldr led on bit appr fnl f: flashed tail under hand driving sn after: coaxed along but stl hung lft: fnd little and hdd cl home* **6/5**[1]

0 **3** 4 ½ **He's The Star (IRE)**[8] 1793 2-9-0 0 .... AndrewHeffernan(3) 9 60
(P D Evans) *chsd ldrs: rdn and styd on to take n.d 3rd wl ins fnl f* **25/1**

0 **4** ¾ **Silly Billy (IRE)**[30] 1263 2-9-3 0 .... DavidProbert 10 57
(S Kirk) *slt ld tl hdd appr fnl f: wknd fnl 100yds* **8/1**

5 *hd* **Kyncraighe (IRE)** 2-9-3 0 .... TedDurcan 5 56+
(Eve Johnson Houghton) *s.i.s: bhd tl gd hdwy over 1f out: styd on wl fnl 120yds: gng on cl home* **11/1**

6 ¾ **Swendab (IRE)** 2-9-3 0 .... LukeMorris 1 54+
(J G M O'Shea) *green: sn rdn and wl off pce tl swtchd rt to outside fr 2f out: str run appr fnl f: fin wl* **33/1**

7 *1* **Uncle Dermot (IRE)** 2-9-3 0 .... FergusSweeney 11 50
(B G Powell) *sn pressing ldrs: ev ch 2f out tl wknd jst ins fnl f* **6/1**[3]

6 **8** *1* **Coolree Pearl (IRE)**[8] 1794 2-8-7 0 .... AmyBaker(5) 2 41
(A B Haynes) *sn in tch: pushed along 2f out: wknd fnl f* **100/1**

0 **9** *nse* **Bathwick Nero**[8] 1793 2-8-12 0 .... CathyGannon 4 41
(P D Evans) *s.i.s: outpcd: rdn over 2f out: styd on fnl f but nvr a threat* **40/1**

0 **10** 2 ¼ **First Pressing**[11] 1686 2-8-12 0 .... AlanMunro 8 33
(John Berry) *outpcd fr 1/2-way* **14/1**

0 **11** 3 ½ **Crystal Set (IRE)**[17] 1541 2-9-3 0 .... DaneO'Neill 7 26
(A B Haynes) *s.i.s: sn rdn: a outpcd* **100/1**

62.58 secs (0.08) **Going Correction** -0.025s/f (Good) **11** Ran SP% **119.3**
Speed ratings (Par 93): **98,97,90,89,88 87,86,84,84,80 75**
toteswingers: 1&2 £1.50, 1&3 £9.80, 2&3 £7.60 CSF £7.95 TOTE £3.70: £1.10, £1.50, £7.40; EX 12.50.
Owner Mrs Emma Raffan **Bred** Mark Commins **Trained** Exning, Suffolk

FOCUS
Nothing of the calibre of 2009 winner Don't Tell Mary (who went on to win the Listed Hilary Needler at Beverley) in this field but the two form horses came to the fore in a race few got into from behind.

NOTEBOOK
Emma's Gift(IRE) had been a bit disappointing conceding weight at Yarmouth last time but showed more like her debut form here, becoming the third winner from that race, getting a good tow in behind and then pouncing late to deny the runner-up. She's probably going to struggle unless she progresses further, and the Albany Stakes, which connections mentioned afterwards as a possibility, looks a step too far. (tchd 9-2)
Kojak(IRE) was given every chance to amend for his wayward display at Ascot but again looked far from straightforward. Jinking around on the rail with a furlong to go when seemingly in command, he then flashed his tail and surrendered rather tamely when tackled late by the eventual winner. It was noticeable that his rider didn't go for his whip, but whether he'd have found much anyway has to be doubtful. Official explanation: jockey said colt was reluctant in final furlong (op 13-8)
He's The Star(IRE) had clearly benefited from his debut but always looked tapped for toe even on this stiff track until staying on late and looks to be ready for 6f. (tchd 20-1)
Silly Billy(IRE) showed plenty of speed for a long way and no repeat of his antics at Windsor where he hung left from halfway. He might well be up to winning a claimer and would be of interest on Fibresand given his pedigree. (op 9-1)
Kyncraighe(IRE), a 20,000gns yearling, shaped well for his in-form stable, travelling comfortably before running green then finding the penny dropping late. He looks a sure improver and, having some stamina in his pedigree, will be suited by a step up to 6f before long. (op 10-1 tchd 9-1)
Swendab(IRE) was very green beforehand and was clueless once the race was under way, only making late headway when it was all over. He's likely to improve a fair amount next time. (op 20-1)
Uncle Dermot(IRE), a half-brother to the useful Jewelled Dagger, was well backed but left the impression the race was just needed to put him spot-on. He looked at least fourth best for much of the way, and will improve. (tchd 15-2)
Coolree Pearl(IRE) needs a drop back into selling company. (op 125-1 tchd 150-1)

2023 OAKLEY GREEN CONSERVATORIES H'CAP — 1m 5f 22y
7:00 (7:00) (Class 6) (0-65,65) 4-Y-0+ **£1,942** (£578; £288; £144) **Stalls** High

Form RPR

42-4 **1** **Cote D'Argent**[9] 1756 7-9-4 **65** .... (t) ChrisCatlin 4 73
(C J Down) *mde all: hrd rdn fr over 2f out: styd on wl: unchal* **10/1**

3-00 **2** *3* **Graylyn Ruby (FR)**[49] 282 5-8-12 **59** .... JimmyQuinn 8 63
(R Dickin) *in tch: chsd ldrs 5f out: rdn to chse wnr ins fnl 2f but no imp fr over 1f out* **8/1**

5164 **3** *1* **War Of The Roses (IRE)**[35] 1169 7-9-2 **63** .... J-PGuillambert 12 65
(R Brotherton) *in rr tl hdwy over 3f out: rdn to dispute 2nd over 2f out tl over 1f out: no imp on wnr and styd on same pce* **10/1**

121- **4** *2* **Saute**[158] 7642 4-9-4 **65** .... TedDurcan 13 64
(W R Swinburn) *chsd ldrs tl lost position over 6f out: rdn and struggling over 3f out: styd on again fr 2f out but nvr a threat* **10/3**[2]

34-0 **5** *1* **Aspirational (IRE)**[9] 1755 4-8-7 **54** .... LukeMorris 10 52
(B Palling) *chsd ldrs: rdn 3f out: wknd over 1f out* **12/1**

564- **6** 1 ¼ **Spinning Waters**[226] 6330 4-8-10 **57** .... RichardHughes 11 53
(Eve Johnson Houghton) *in tch: hdwy 7f out: trckd wnr over 5f out: rdn and no imp over 3f out: wknd fr 2f out* **3/1**[1]

3-03 **7** 1 ¾ **Party Palace**[9] 1756 6-8-4 **51** oh1 .... CathyGannon 1 44
(H S Howe) *chsd wnr tl over 5f out: wknd ins fnl 3f* **6/1**[3]

5/0- **8** 2 ¾ **Olivino (GER)**[178] 342 9-8-1 **51** oh6 .... AndrewHeffernan(3) 3 40
(B J Llewellyn) *in tch: rdn over 3f out: wknd over 2f out* **11/1**

000/ **9** *6* **Alright Chuck**[539] 7387 6-8-1 **51** oh6 .... KellyHarrison(3) 5 31
(P W Hiatt) *a towards rr* **66/1**

0-00 **10** *22* **Warrior Nation (FR)**[28] 1305 4-8-4 **51** oh4 .... NeilChalmers 2 —
(A J Chamberlain) *t.k.h: a in rr* **66/1**

06-0 **11** *41* **Bluebird Chariot**[19] 1507 7-8-4 **51** oh6 .... (b) DavidProbert 9 —
(J M Bradley) *rdn 7f out: a bhd: t.o* **50/1**

3-04 **U** **Bertie Smalls**[82] 611 4-7-13 **51** oh6 .... SimonPearce(5) 14 —
(M H Tompkins) *mid-div whn slipped and uns rdr bnd after 2 1/2f* **18/1**

2m 51.23s (-0.77) **Going Correction** -0.025s/f (Good) **12** Ran SP% **117.9**
Speed ratings (Par 101): **101,99,98,97,96 95,94,93,89,75 25,—**
toteswingers: 1&2 £16.50, 1&3 £8.30, 2&3 £18.10 CSF £86.85 CT £826.71 TOTE £7.50: £1.60, £5.90, £5.70; EX 152.80.
Owner Culm Valley Racing **Bred** Darley **Trained** Mutterton, Devon

FOCUS
A modest handicap run at an uneven pace. The winner dictated but was the best horse at the weights on the day. This was his best run since he was a 2yo.
Saute Official explanation: jockey said gelding slipped about 10f out
Aspirational(IRE) Official explanation: jockey said gelding slipped 10f out

2024 PREMIER CONSERVATORY ROOFS 10TH ANNIVERSARY BE HOPEFUL H'CAP — 1m 5y
7:30 (7:30) (Class 5) (0-75,75) 4-Y-0+ **£3,885** (£1,156; £577; £288) **Stalls** Low

Form RPR

021- **1** **Compton Blue**[205] 6908 4-9-3 **74** .... (b) RichardHughes 3 81
(R Hannon) *disp ld 1f: styd trcking ldrs: squeezed through to ld jst ins fnl f: drvn out* **15/2**

36-3 **2** *nk* **Full Victory (IRE)**[35] 1179 8-8-7 **64** .... LiamKeniry 6 71
(R A Farrant) *hld up in rr: swtchd to outside and str run fr 2f out: styd on wl to chse wnr ins fnl f: nt quite get up* **12/1**

30-4 **3** 1 ¾ **Sunny Future (IRE)**[17] 1543 4-8-7 **64** .... JimmyQuinn 1 67+
(M S Saunders) *trckd ldrs tl nt clr run and lost position over 2f out: hdwy and stl n.m.r over 1f out tl styd on ins fnl f: gng on cl home but nt rcvr* **16/1**

4-31 **4** *nk* **Magroom**[13] 1637 6-9-1 **72** .... GeorgeBaker 11 74
(R J Hodges) *in rr tl hdwy 4f out: chsd ldrs over 2f out: chal appr fnl f: sn no ex: wknd fnl 100yds* **7/1**

00-0 **5** *shd* **Apex**[17] 1543 9-8-10 **67** .... FergusSweeney 13 69
(M Hill) *chsd ldrs: chal and upsides fr over 2f out tl 1f out: wknd fnl 100yds* **14/1**

424- **6** 1 ¼ **Wilfred Pickles (IRE)**[208] 6823 4-9-4 **75** .... DaneO'Neill 2 76+
(Miss Jo Crowley) *in rr: nt clr run on ins fr 3f out tl 2f out: hdwy again: hung lft and nt clr run over 1f out tl ins fnl f: kpt on fnl 50yds: nt rcvr* **10/1**

50-0 **7** ½ **Hi Shinko**[18] 1516 4-9-4 **75** .... TomMcLaughlin 4 73
(B R Millman) *t.k.h: trckd ldrs: awkward bnd 5f out: rdn 3f out: rdn 2f out: styd on same pce fnl f* **33/1**

4-00 **8** *shd* **Cheam Forever (USA)**[14] 1625 4-9-4 **75** .... RichardKingscote 8 73
(R Charlton) *chsd ldrs: rdn over 2f out: wknd fnl 120yds* **9/2**[1]

4316 **9** *shd* **Fault**[13] 1637 4-8-11 **68** .... (t) SebSanders 9 65
(Stef Higgins) *t.k.h: led after 1f: jnd and rdn over 2f out: kpt slt advantage tl bmpd and hdd jst ins fnl f: sn wknd* **6/1**[3]

36-5 **10** *4* **Astrodonna**[23] 1430 5-8-12 **69** .... TedDurcan 7 57
(M H Tompkins) *in rr: nt clr run ins fnl 3f and 2f out: nvr in contention after* **12/1**

120- **11** 2 ¾ **Spring Secret**[189] 7247 4-8-11 **68** .... LukeMorris 5 50
(B Palling) *chsd ldrs tl wknd over 3f out* **22/1**

0063 **12** 3 ¼ **Mr Udagawa**[6] 1841 4-8-7 **67** .... AndrewHeffernan(3) 10 41
(B J Llewellyn) *in rr: awkward bnd over 5f out: rdn and effrt on outside 3f out: nvr in contention and sn wknd* **5/1**[2]

1m 40.27s (-0.53) **Going Correction** -0.025s/f (Good) **12** Ran SP% **117.7**
Speed ratings (Par 103): **101,100,98,98,98 97,96,96,96,92 89,86**
toteswingers: 1&2 £28.00, 1&3 £21.30, 2&3 £10.00 CSF £93.58 CT £1421.02 TOTE £7.60: £4.00, £4.90, £5.50; EX 145.00.
Owner Godfrey Wilson **Bred** Caroline Wilson **Trained** East Everleigh, Wilts

FOCUS
A fair handicap run at a solid pace in which neither those held up nor prominent were favoured. The winner is rated close to his Windsor win.
Sunny Future(IRE) Official explanation: jockey said gelding was denied a clear run
Wilfred Pickles(IRE) Official explanation: jockey said gelding was denied a clear run

2025 KENT PLASTICS CLASSIFIED STKS — 1m 5y
8:00 (8:01) (Class 5) 3-Y-O **£2,590** (£770; £385; £192) **Stalls** Low

Form RPR

3223 **1** **Mejd (IRE)**[15] 1608 3-9-0 75 .... AlanMunro 1 77
(M R Channon) *trckd ldrs tl lost pl 3f out: rallied and styd on wl fr 2f out to ld jst ins fnl f: hld on wl cl home* **5/1**

410- **2** ½ **Tarita (IRE)**[244] 5797 3-9-0 75 .... RichardHughes 6 76
(R Hannon) *hld up in rr: hdwy over 2f out: drvn and qcknd to chse wnr fnl 120yds but a jst hld* **4/1**[2]

03-1 **3** *1* **Round Won (USA)**[13] 1644 3-9-0 75 .... ShaneKelly 5 74+
(W J Knight) *in tch: awkward bnd 5f out: rdn and one pce 2f out: tended to edge lft over 1f out: styd on u.p fnl f to take 3rd fnl 100yds but nt rch ldng duo* **5/2**[1]

-223 **4** 1 ¾ **Lago Indiano (IRE)**[21] 1475 3-9-0 75 .... JimmyQuinn 2 70
(Mrs A J Perrett) *led: rdn over 2f out: hdd jst ins fnl f: wknd fnl 120yds* **7/1**

36-4 **5** *hd* **Kerchak (USA)**[30] 1269 3-9-0 74 .... DavidProbert 3 69
(W Jarvis) *s.i.s: in rr: rdn and struggling over 3f out: swtchd to outside and r.o wl fnl f: gng on cl home* **9/2**[3]

-312 **6** 1 ¾ **Purple Gallery (IRE)**[89] 522 3-9-0 75 .... LiamKeniry 8 65
(J S Moore) *chsd ldrs: awkward bnd 5f out: stl wl there towards outside tl wknd fnl f* **16/1**

-420 **7** *hd* **Gra Adhmhar (IRE)**[15] 1590 3-9-0 74 .... SebSanders 7 65
(D J Coakley) *chsd ldr: awkward bnd 5f out: str chal 2f out: wknd ins fnl f* **11/1**

246- **8** *24* **Bradford (IRE)**[296] 4152 3-9-0 72 .... TedDurcan 4 9
(Eve Johnson Houghton) *in rr: rdn over 4f out: wknd 3f out: eased whn no ch* **25/1**

1m 41.0s (0.20) **Going Correction** -0.025s/f (Good) **8** Ran SP% **114.0**
Speed ratings (Par 99): **98,97,96,94,94 92,92,68**
toteswingers: 1&2 £5.10, 1&3 £2.90, 2&3 £3.50 CSF £25.12 TOTE £3.10: £1.10, £2.40, £1.80; EX 30.30.
Owner M Al-Qatami & K M Al-Mudhaf **Bred** Michael Dalton **Trained** West Ilsley, Berks
■ Stewards' Enquiry : Alan Munro caution: used whip without giving colt time to respond

FOCUS
A fair minor event that was not really a test of stamina at the trip. There was only 3lb between the runners on official ratings. The winner is rated to the best view of his maiden form.
Purple Gallery(IRE) Official explanation: jockey said gelding hung right

2026 COAL IT SERVICES FILLIES' H'CAP — 5f 161y
8:30 (8:30) (Class 5) (0-70,67) 3-Y-0+ **£2,590** (£770; £385; £192) **Stalls** Centre

Form RPR

3000 **1** **White Shift (IRE)**[13] 1641 4-9-12 **67** .... J-PGuillambert 7 72
(P Howling) *chsd ldrs: rdn 3f out: led ins fnl 2f: kpt on strly cl home* **20/1**

2132 **2** ¾ **Miss Firefly**[18] 1534 5-9-5 **60** .... GeorgeBaker 9 63
(R J Hodges) *chsd ldrs: rdn to go 2nd ins fnl f and kpt on tl no imp on wnr fnl 75yds* **4/1**[2]

2-35 **3** *1* **Green Velvet**[17] 1547 5-9-5 **60** .... SebSanders 4 60
(P J Makin) *chsd ldrs: rdn over 2f out: styng on whn nt clr run over 1f out: kpt on ins fnl f but nvr gng pce of ldng duo* **9/4**[1]

263- **4** *2* **Matterofact (IRE)**[226] 6329 7-9-12 **67** .... TomMcLaughlin 3 60
(M S Saunders) *in tch: rdn 2f out: styd on same pce u.p fnl f* **9/1**

-603 **5** ½ **Dualagi**[32] 1236 6-8-12 **53** oh1 .... FergusSweeney 6 44
(M R Bosley) *in rr: rdn and sme hdwy over 1f out: one pce ins fnl f* **5/1**[3]

-552 **6** 1 ¼ **True Red (IRE)**[34] 1187 3-8-2 **53** .... (b) DavidProbert 8 37
(Mrs N S Evans) *led after 1f: hdd ins fnl 2f: wknd ins fnl f* **14/1**

50-0 **7** 1 ¼ **Song Of Praise**[15] 1596 4-8-12 **53** oh3 .... JimmyQuinn 1 36
(M Blanshard) *sn chsng ldrs: rdn over 2f out: wknd fnl f* **11/1**

0004 **8** 2 ¼ **Mandhooma**[13] 1638 4-8-12 **53** oh3 .... ChrisCatlin 2 28
(P W Hiatt) *led 1f: styd wl there tl wknd 1f out* **9/1**

1662 **9** 3 1/2 **Your Gifted (IRE)**[9] [1774] 3-8-1 **57** .... JohnFahy(5) 5 18
(Patrick Morris) *t.k.h: in tch: rdn and sme hdwy over 2f out: sn btn* **8/1**
1m 11.71s (0.51) **Going Correction** -0.025s/f (Good)
WFA 3 from 4yo+ 10lb **9** Ran SP% **118.3**
Speed ratings (Par 100): **95,94,92,90,89 87,86,83,78**
toteswingers: 1&2 £28.20, 1&3 £22.70, 2&3 £1.90 CSF £100.80 CT £260.87 TOTE £19.40: £3.50, £1.80, £1.40; EX 163.10 Place 6 £517.14, Place 5 £79.52.
Owner Paul Terry **Bred** Grange Stud **Trained** Newmarket, Suffolk
FOCUS
A tightly knit handicap that was run at a good clip with none of the trouble in running that blighted the opener. Modest fillies' form.
Dualagi Official explanation: jockey said mare hung right
T/Plt: £362.80 to a £1 stake. Pool: £83,589.56. 168.16 winning tickets. T/Qpdt: £47.10 to a £1 stake. Pool: £6,409.38. 100.52 winning tickets. ST

YORK (L-H)
Wednesday, May 12

OFFICIAL GOING: Good (good to firm in places) changing to good to firm after race 4 (3.10)
Wind: Moderate, half against Weather: Overcast, breezy, showers

2027 £66 OF FREE BETS AT BLUESQUARE.COM H'CAP 1m 2f 88y
1:40 (1:43) (Class 2) (0-100,100) 4-Y-O+ **£12,952** (£3,854; £1,926; £962) **Stalls** Low

Form RPR
0/2- **1** **Imposing**[391] [1303] 4-8-12 **91** .... RyanMoore 12 105+
(Sir Michael Stoute) *hld up: pushed along and hdwy on outer 4f out: rdn over 1f out: styd on to ld ins fnl f* **7/2**[2]
30-5 **2** 1 1/4 **Indian Days**[21] [1474] 5-9-7 **100** .... PaulMulrennan 4 111
(J G Given) *sn led: rdn and qckn over 2f out: drvn over 1f out: hdd and one pce ins fnl f* **7/1**[3]
6335 **3** 5 **Tartan Gunna**[11] [1697] 4-8-10 **89** .... JoeFanning 5 93+
(M Johnston) *trckd ldrs: effrt 3f out: nt clr run 2f out: sn swtchd rt and rdn wl over 1f out: styd on ins fnl f: tk 3rd nr line* **15/2**
10-1 **4** hd **Forte Dei Marmi**[25] [1388] 4-9-0 **93** .... KierenFallon 9 94
(L M Cumani) *hld up: stdy hdwy over 4f out: chsd ldr 2f out: sn rdn and edgd lft: drvn and edgd rt ins fnl f: sn one pce* **9/4**[1]
215- **5** 4 **Recession Proof (FR)**[242] [5870] 4-8-7 **91** .... IanBrennan(5) 2 84
(J J Quinn) *hld up: effrt and pushed along over 3f out: swtchd rt over 2f out: kpt on appr fnl f: nrst fin* **12/1**
150- **6** 3/4 **Changing The Guard**[286] [4455] 4-8-8 **87** .... FrederikTylicki 7 78
(R A Fahey) *chsd ldrs: effrt to chse ldng pair 4f out: rdn along 3f out: n.m.r 2f out: sn drvn and wknd* **9/1**
210- **7** 2 **Saga De Tercey (FR)**[235] [6115] 5-8-7 **86** .... RobertWinston 8 73
(G A Swinbank) *chsd ldr: rdn along 4f out: wknd wl over 2f out* **14/1**
-051 **8** 14 **Sand Tiger (IRE)**[12] [1669] 4-8-7 **86** oh3 .... PaulHanagan 6 45
(R A Fahey) *chsd ldng pair: rdn along over 4f out: sn wknd* **14/1**
402- **9** 15 **Spectait**[285] [4486] 8-9-2 **95** .... GeorgeBaker 3 24
(Jonjo O'Neill) *a towards rr* **20/1**
00-0 **10** 1 3/4 **Peter Tchaikovsky**[11] [1708] 4-9-0 **93** .... MickyFenton 1 19
(B S Rothwell) *in tch: effrt 4f out: sn rdn along and wknd 3f out* **100/1**
630- **11** hd **Call It On (IRE)**[24] [6996] 4-8-8 **87** .... DarryllHolland 13 12
(M H Tompkins) *s.i.s: a bhd* **33/1**
2m 7.41s (-5.09) **Going Correction** -0.275s/f (Firm) **11** Ran SP% **117.0**
Speed ratings (Par 109): **109,108,104,103,100 100,98,87,75,73 73**
toteswingers: 1&2 £5.60, 1&3 £5.80, 2&3 £7.60 CSF £27.70 CT £174.19 TOTE £4.30: £1.50, £2.30, £2.20; EX 26.20 Trifecta £147.90 Pool: £760.18 - 3.80 winning units..
Owner D Smith, Mrs J Magnier, M Tabor **Bred** N P Bloodstock And Morton Bloodstock **Trained** Newmarket, Suffolk
FOCUS
The official going was described as good, good to firm in places, with the straight predominantly on the fast side. They went a good clip here with Indian Days setting a strong pace up front, and with the first two finishing clear of a pair of in-form rivals, it looks very solid form. The winner is rated up 10lb on his sole 3yo run.
NOTEBOOK
Imposing had been off the track with a fracture since making his one and only start last year at the Craven meeting. It looked significant that his high-profile connections had decided to keep him in training, and this performance gives an indication as to why. Held up off the pace, he was towards the rear and being nudged along entering the straight, but he stayed on strongly down the outside and picked up again when his rider went for the whip, and in the end he won with a bit up his sleeve. He should come on for the run, and a step up to 1m4f looks like it might suit him, so the Duke Of Edinburgh Handicap at Royal Ascot might fit the bill. (op 9-2 tchd 5-1)
Indian Days is a consistent sort but the handicapper has been in charge for some time now. Given a very positive ride on a track that often suits that style of running, he set out to make every yard, and ran a stormer in defeat. He simply bumped into an unexposed and well-handicapped rival, but then that has been his problem for some time. Another rise in the weights for this won't help matters, but he's likely to go for a Listed race over this trip at Goodwood next. (tchd 8-1)
Tartan Gunna is a similar sort to the runner-up and can always be relied upon to run his race. He didn't get the clearest of runs this time but lacked the winner's finishing burst once in the clear. He's another who is likely to remain vulnerable to less-exposed rivals. (op 8-1)
Forte Dei Marmi, put up 12lb for his impressive success at Newbury on his return, travelled strongly into contention and was last off the bridle, but he didn't find as much as expected under pressure. This strongly run extended 1m2f seemed to find him out, and given the way he travels through his races he'll be interesting dropped back to a mile. (tchd 2-1 and 5-2)
Recession Proof(FR), debuting for a new stable, stays much further than this so the good gallop will have suited him. He's entitled to come on for the run, and will be interesting when reverting to a longer trip. (op 14-1)
Changing The Guard, a C&D winner last year, had conditions to suit but his trainer had warned that he might need his reappearance. He ran as such, weakening in the closing stages, and this should put him spot on. (op 11-1)
Saga De Tercey(FR) is a winner over 2m. He kept the winner company for a long way, but lacked the pace to remain competitive in the latter part of the race. (op 20-1)

2028 YORK CITY AT WEMBLEY WITH BLUE SQUARE H'CAP 7f
2:10 (2:11) (Class 2) (0-100,98) 3-Y-O **£12,952** (£3,854; £1,926; £962) **Stalls** Low

Form RPR
62-0 **1** **Kaptain Kirkup (IRE)**[28] [1315] 3-9-3 **94** .... TomEaves 10 107
(M Dods) *hld up: hdwy on outside over 2f out: shkn up to ld over 1f out: r.o wl* **6/1**[3]
15-3 **2** 3 1/4 **Treadwell (IRE)**[10] [1732] 3-9-2 **93** .... FergusSweeney 9 97
(J A Osborne) *hld up towards rr: hdwy over 2f out: nt clr run: swtchd outside over 1f out: styd on to take 2nd ins fnl f* **8/1**
-230 **3** nk **Navajo Chief**[26] [1354] 3-9-2 **93** .... KierenFallon 1 98+
(A P Jarvis) *t.k.h: trckd ldrs on inner: n.m.r 2f out: nt clr run on ins fnl f: styd on wl* **16/1**
12- **4** 1 3/4 **Business As Usual**[210] [6779] 3-8-11 **88** .... PhilipRobinson 2 87
(M A Jarvis) *led tl over 2f out: kpt on same pce* **5/1**[2]
21-2 **5** 1 **Summerinthecity (IRE)**[12] [1663] 3-8-11 **88** .... RyanMoore 11 84
(J Noseda) *chsd ldrs on outer: led over 2f out: hdd over 1f out: fdd ins fnl f* **11/4**[1]
10-6 **6** 2 **Hunting Tartan**[10] [1732] 3-9-4 **95** .... WilliamBuick 3 86
(J H M Gosden) *trckd ldrs: effrt over 2f out: one pce* **8/1**
125- **7** 1 **Bond Fastrac**[245] [5763] 3-9-1 **92** .... PJMcDonald 7 80
(G R Oldroyd) *s.i.s: styd on fnl 2f: nvr nr ldrs* **16/1**
600- **8** 4 1/2 **She's A Character**[235] [6090] 3-8-13 **90** .... TonyHamilton 4 66
(R A Fahey) *w ldrs: wkng whn n.m.r 2f out* **28/1**
10-5 **9** 1/2 **Exceedingly Bold**[11] [1687] 3-8-13 **90** .... MickyFenton 12 64
(Miss Gay Kelleway) *swtchd lft s: in rr: hdwy on ins over 2f out: n.m.r: wknd over 1f out* **33/1**
1- **10** 1/2 **Rock 'N' Royal**[205] [6896] 3-8-7 **84** oh2 .... PaulHanagan 6 57
(R A Fahey) *chsd ldrs: edgd lft and wknd 2f out* **7/1**
1m 25.61s (0.31) **Going Correction** +0.175s/f (Good) **10** Ran SP% **110.5**
Speed ratings (Par 105): **105,101,100,98,97 95,94,89,88,88**
toteswingers: 1&2 £9.10, 1&3 £15.50, 2&3 £11.10 CSF £49.80 CT £703.49 TOTE £7.30: £2.30, £2.10, £3.60; EX 54.90 Trifecta £705.60 Part won. Pool: £953.63 - 0.62 winning units..
Owner Kevin Kirkup **Bred** David Barry **Trained** Denton, Co Durham
FOCUS
A race featuring a number of unexposed 3-y-os, several of whom have the potential to rate higher as the season progresses. The early gallop wasn't breakneck and they were well bunched passing the 2f pole. The form is rated around the second and third.
NOTEBOOK
Kaptain Kirkup(IRE) could only finish in mid-division at Newmarket on his reappearance, but he didn't get the clearest of runs that day, whereas on this occasion he enjoyed a trouble-free run down the outside and saw out this longer trip in fine style to win by a clear margin. He will face a stiff rise in the weights now, but he looks the sort who will soon be tackling Listed-class opposition anyway, and he could even be worth sending to the Jersey Stakes in the hope of a good draw. His trainer, who thinks he'll get a mile eventually, said he wouldn't want the ground any quicker than this. (op 15-2)
Treadwell(IRE) looked like he might have been flattered by racing on the best ground at Salisbury on his reappearance, but he confirmed form with Hunting Tartan from that race, and probably preferred the return to quicker ground. He got the trip well and can probably find a similar race. (tchd 15-2 and 17-2)
Navajo Chief, who pulled too hard and didn't get home over 1m2f last time out, appreciated the drop back in trip and ran well, especially considering he was momentarily stopped in his run 1 1/2f out. He remains on a mark that can be exploited.
Business As Usual made the running, just as he did in his two starts at two, but was overhauled by race-fit rivals in the closing stages. He's fully entitled to come on for this and will be dangerous if allowed the run of things. (op 4-1)
Summerinthecity(IRE) made a very promising return to action at Lingfield and, despite being 3lb higher, looked to hold sound claims. Despite having shaped as though this trip would suit though, he very much ran like a non-stayer, weakening badly inside the last. A return to sprinting can see him bounce back to winning form. (op 5-2)
Hunting Tartan could be excused his run at Salisbury when little went right, and he promised to be suited by the return to fast ground. He was disappointing though, and now has something to prove. (op 9-1)
Rock 'N' Royal won a Pontefract maiden last year that has worked out pretty well and, although racing from 2lb out of the weights, looked interesting on his reappearance. He ran as though he needed the outing, though. (op 8-1)

2029 TATTERSALLS MUSIDORA STKS (GROUP 3) 1m 2f 88y
2:40 (2:41) (Class 1) 3-Y-O
£36,900 (£13,988; £7,000; £3,490; £1,748; £877) **Stalls** Low

Form RPR
1-1 **1** **Aviate**[14] [1613] 3-8-12 106 .... EddieAhern 8 111+
(H R A Cecil) *hld up: nt clr run fr over 3f out: hdwy on ins jst ins fnl f: fin fast to ld fnl strides* **11/4**[2]
66-0 **2** hd **Gold Bubbles (USA)**[9] [1787] 3-8-12 102 .... KJManning 6 106
(J S Bolger, Ire) *stdd s: hdwy over 4f out: led over 1f out: hung lft ins fnl f: hdd last strides* **20/1**
01-2 **3** 3/4 **Eleanora Duse (IRE)**[27] [1334] 3-8-12 81 .... RyanMoore 5 105
(Sir Michael Stoute) *trckd ldrs: chal over 1f out: styng on same pce whn hmpd nr fin* **15/2**
24-1 **4** 1 1/2 **Pink Symphony**[26] [1356] 3-8-12 87 .... JamieSpencer 3 101
(P F I Cole) *mid-div: effrt over 4f out: kpt on same pce appr fnl f* **9/1**
-524 **5** 1 1/2 **Bikini Babe (IRE)**[19] [1498] 3-8-12 100 .... JoeFanning 7 98
(M Johnston) *led: hdd over 1f out: edgd rt: one pce* **7/1**[3]
50-5 **6** 3/4 **Cracking Lass (IRE)**[28] [1310] 3-8-12 87 .... PaulHanagan 2 97
(R A Fahey) *in rr: drvn over 5f out: kpt on fnl 3f: nvr a threat* **33/1**
10- **7** 1 1/4 **Cabaret (IRE)**[220] [6523] 3-8-12 107 .... JMurtagh 4 94
(A P O'Brien, Ire) *chsd ldrs: rdn over 2f out: wknd over 1f out* **2/1**[1]
45-2 **8** 3 1/2 **Red Fantasy (IRE)**[10] [1729] 3-8-12 101 .... MichaelHills 1 87
(B W Hills) *chsd ldrs: wkng whn hmpd on ins 2f out* **10/1**
2m 9.14s (-3.36) **Going Correction** -0.275s/f (Firm) **8** Ran SP% **111.1**
Speed ratings (Par 109): **102,101,101,100,98 98,97,94**
toteswingers: 1&2 £12.90, 1&3 £4.60, 2&3 £16.10 CSF £50.72 TOTE £3.70: £1.40, £3.70, £2.20; EX 69.20 Trifecta £792.30 Pool: £1,466.91 - 1.37 winning units..
Owner K Abdulla **Bred** Juddmonte Farms Ltd **Trained** Newmarket, Suffolk
■ Stewards' Enquiry : K J Manning three-day ban: careless riding (May 26-28)
FOCUS
Traditionally an informative Oaks trial - Sariska doubled up last year, while Alexandrova finished runner-up in 2006 before going one better at Epsom. There were questions over the quality of this year's field beforehand, and they remain, despite the favourable impression left by the winner who looks better than the bare form. The second is up 7lb on her 2yo best. The time was 1.32 sec slower than the closing 3yo handicap.
NOTEBOOK
Aviate overcame a troubled passage to score. Chopped for room on the turn out of the back straight and denied a clear run 2f out to inside the last, it was only once she got to the rail well inside the final furlong that the winner saw daylight, and the response under pressure was impressive, as she quickened up really well to retain her unbeaten record. The winning margin was narrow and the form looks ordinary for the grade (winning time was 1.73sec slower than the opening older horse handicap and 1.32sec slower than the closing 3-y-o handicap), but she clearly has plenty of class, was far better than these, and her strong finish suggested that she'll probably stay further. Her pedigree wouldn't guarantee she'll get 1m4f, but her grand-dam won the Cheshire Oaks and there's enough there to offer encouragement. Her connections wouldn't confirm her for the Oaks - she has the option of going to France for the Prix de Diane instead - but it would be a bit of a surprise if she didn't go for the race now, and she's generally 8-1 across the boards for Epsom. (op 5-2 tchd 3-1)
Gold Bubbles(USA) was comfortably held in good company last summer and on her reappearance, but she was stepping up 3f in distance and showed improved form. Plenty was done at 1.01 when the winner impressively pegged her back on the line, but she picked up valuable black type in defeat and might have more to offer now that her correct distance has been found. The Group 1 Pretty Polly at the Curragh next month is likely to be her next race. (op 16-1)

Eleanora Duse(IRE), who holds no big-race entries, had been beaten in a handicap off 78 on her reappearance and looked to have plenty to find at this level, but she's well bred, being a half-sister to Irish Oaks runner-up Scottish Stage, and with her stable in such good form it wasn't a surprise to see her run well. Her connections will no doubt be thrilled to have picked up some black type with her. (op 8-1 tchd 9-1)
Pink Symphony, who cost a lot of money at the sales, won a division of a Newbury maiden on her reappearance that has thrown up some classy winners in the past. This was a step up in class for her, but she ran well, staying on down the outside in the manner of a filly who will appreciate another 2f. Her pedigree also suggests she'll appreciate 1m4f. (op 11-1)
Bikini Babe(IRE) took on the colts in the Sandown Classic Trial last time out, and that form had been given a boost when the runner-up won the Dee Stakes next time out. She was unable to take advantage of a tactical advantage in being allowed an uncontested lead, though, and didn't look to run up to her best. (tchd 13-2)
Cracking Lass(IRE), who was running on at the end of the Tattersalls Timeform 3-y-o Trophy on her reappearance, could only stay on past beaten horses here and was never a threat. There's a handicap to be won with her off her current mark, though. (op 25-1)
Cabaret(IRE) had an excuse when tailed off in the Marcel Boussac on her final start at two as her saddle slipped, but she'd looked progressive before that, and her pedigree suggested she would relish the step up to this sort of trip on her reappearance. Solid in the market despite her stable's iffy form so far this season, she was beaten before they reached the 2f pole, so judgement on her ability will have to be reserved until there is a sign her yard has turned the corner. (op 5-2 tchd 9-4 in a place)
Red Fantasy(IRE), runner-up in the Pretty Polly on her reappearance, was already beaten when tightened up for room next to the rail 2f out. It's possible she needs easier ground to be seen at her best. (op 9-1 tchd 8-1)

2030 DUKE OF YORK BLUE SQUARE STKS (GROUP 2) 6f
3:10 (3:12) (Class 1) 3-Y-O+

£56,770 (£21,520; £10,770; £5,370; £2,690; £1,350) **Stalls** Low

Form				RPR
0241	**1**		**Prime Defender**[4] 1906 6-9-7 105 .... RobertWinston 1 (B W Hills) *w ldrs: led over 1f out: edgd rt ins fnl f: hld on wl* **20/1**	116
113-	**2**	½	**Showcasing**[222] 6450 3-8-11 114 .... WilliamBuick 11 (J H M Gosden) *in rr: gd hdwy over 1f out: r.o wl ins fnl f* **4/1**[1]	111+
004-	**3**	*hd*	**Main Aim**[207] 6848 5-9-7 117 .... RyanMoore 6 (Sir Michael Stoute) *chsd ldrs: effrt over 2f out: swtchd lft appr fnl f: r.o wl* **5/1**[2]	114
10-3	**4**	*shd*	**Doncaster Rover (USA)**[27] 1326 4-9-7 104 .... FrankieDettori 10 (D H Brown) *racd towards stands' side: in rr: hdwy over 2f out: kpt on wl fnl f* **14/1**	113
	5	1 ¼	**Starspangledbanner (AUS)**[67] 4-9-12 117 .... JMurtagh 3 (A P O'Brien, Ire) *w ldrs: wknd last 100yds* **4/1**[1]	114
5-41	**6**	1 ½	**Inxile (IRE)**[46] 1007 5-9-7 108 .... AdrianNicholls 4 (D Nicholls) *led: hdd over 1f out: fdd fnl 150yds* **9/1**	105
0-42	**7**	*shd*	**Damien (IRE)**[25] 1400 4-9-7 103 .... MichaelHills 7 (B W Hills) *in rr: effrt over 2f out: kpt on fnl f: nvr nr ldrs* **20/1**	104
036-	**8**	*shd*	**Edge Closer**[298] 4087 6-9-7 103 .... JimmyFortune 9 (R Hannon) *chsd ldrs: kpt on same pce fnl 2f* **66/1**	104
541-	**9**	½	**Sayif (IRE)**[227] 6304 4-9-10 115 .... RichardHills 8 (P W Chapple-Hyam) *chsd ldrs: effrt over 2f out: kpt on one pce* **13/2**[3]	105
36-3	**10**	½	**Anglezarke (IRE)**[17] 1545 4-9-4 102 .... PaulHanagan 2 (R A Fahey) *sn chsng ldrs: one pce fnl 2f* **16/1**	98
3/32	**11**	5	**Mullionmileanhour (IRE)**[27] 1326 4-9-7 107 .... SteveDrowne 12 (J R Best) *in rr towards stands' side: sme hdwy over 2f out: sn wknd* **15/2**	85
0016	**12**	9	**Judd Street**[46] 1021 8-9-7 109 ....(v) KierenFallon 5 (Eve Johnson Houghton) *dwlt: racd keenly and sn trcking ldrs: lost pl over 2f out* **33/1**	56

1m 11.19s (-0.71) **Going Correction** +0.175s/f (Good)
WFA 3 from 4yo+ 10lb **12** Ran SP% **118.3**
Speed ratings (Par 115): **111,110,110,109,108 106,106,106,105,104 98,86**
toteswingers: 1&2 £17.60, 1&3 £20.60, 2&3 £2.80 CSF £95.26 TOTE £24.80: £6.20, £1.50, £2.20; EX 152.10 Trifecta £1150.40 Pool: £1,771.77 - 1.13 winning units..
Owner S Falle, M Franklin, J Sumsion **Bred** Christopher J Mason **Trained** Lambourn, Berks

FOCUS
Not for the first time this sprint threw up a shock result, but there's every reason to believe that the race-fit winner will struggle to confirm form with the second and third, who were both making their seasonal returns, if they clash again at Royal Ascot. Inxile ensured it was run at a good gallop, and there didn't appear to be any draw advantage. Prime Defender seems back to his very best, with a clear personal best from the fourth.

NOTEBOOK
Prime Defender, making a quick reappearance after going in at Haydock at the weekend, is a three-time winner at Listed level but has always come up short in better company. He's a reliable campaigner who goes on any ground, though, and he made the most of his fitness advantage to notch his first Group race win at the 20th attempt. (tchd 25-1)
Showcasing, the only 3-y-o in the field, ran a race full of promise. Impressive winner of the Gimcrack over this C&D last year, reports suggested that he was very much in need of this reappearance run, so in the circumstances this has to rate a very promising effort. He ran on really well from off the pace, should appreciate the stiffer test he'll get at Ascot, and now looks like he'll be a big player in the Golden Jubilee, for which he was cut to a best price of 12-1. This was only his fifth ever start so one would imagine there's plenty of improvement to come. (op 7-2)
Main Aim, runner-up in the July Cup last year, looked to hold solid claims at the weights, but he lacked a recent run and that might have been the difference. He stays 7f so this speed-favouring 6f would not have been ideal. An uphill finish, which he'll get at Ascot and Newmarket, will suit him much better and he was another who had his price trimmed for the Golden Jubilee, in his case to a general 16-1. (op 9-2)
Doncaster Rover(USA) didn't handle the Dip at Newmarket but his trainer expected him to appreciate this flatter track, and he was spot on, as the gelding ran a personal best in defeat, challenging, like the runner-up, on the stands' side from off the pace. He clearly has the ability to win at Listed level. (op 16-1)
Starspangledbanner(AUS), who is already scheduled to retire to stud later this year, is a winner of two Group 1 races in Australia, over 6f and 1m. He had to give weight all round on his debut for his new stable, but still looked to hold strong claims. He had no trouble going the early pace as he was up there the whole way until weakening inside the last. Although he could have been expected to have been fit enough, having run as recently as two months ago, the way he finished his race suggests he needed it. He'll have every chance of reversing the form at Ascot, where he'll be better off at the weights, and the bookmakers now make him a best price of 12-1 for the Golden Jubilee. (op 11-2 tchd 6-1)
Inxile(IRE), four times a winner at Listed level, including last time out in the Cammidge Trophy when he had Prime Defender back in second, tried to repeat the trick he pulled off at Doncaster in making every yard of the running. This is a good track on which to employ such tactics, but he was up in class and running on quicker ground, and he didn't see it out. He's probably happiest over 5f. (op 10-1)
Damien(IRE) is a difficult horse to place off his current rating and, although he ran all right here, is likely to remain so. (op 18-1)
Edge Closer, off the track since last July, is a dual Listed winner. Fully entitled to have needed this, he'll be of more interest when dropped in grade. (op 50-1)
Sayif(IRE), a consistent sort who won the Group 2 Diadem on his final start last year, had a 3lb penalty to carry as a result. He was another entitled to need his seasonal return, stays further/appreciates a stiffer track, and can do better with this run under his belt. (op 8-1)
Anglezarke(IRE) faced a stiff task on this step up from the minimum trip and didn't see her race out. She will be more effective when dropped back to 5f.
Mullionmileanhour(IRE) was drawn on the outside and couldn't get cover. The way the race unfolded didn't suit him but his Abernant run showed he's capable of better than this. Official explanation: jockey said colt never travelled (tchd 7-1 and 8-1)
Judd Street won out in Dubai during the carnival but was up against it in this class.

2031 BET AT BLUESQUARE.COM SP GUARANTEE H'CAP 1m 4f
3:45 (3:46) (Class 4) (0-85,85) 4-Y-O+ **£7,123** (£2,119; £1,059; £529) **Stalls** Centre

Form				RPR
23-5	**1**		**Deauville Flyer**[20] 1484 4-9-2 **80** .... KierenFallon 17 (T D Easterby) *mid-div: hdwy 4f out: styd on wl appr fnl f: led post* **8/1**[2]	89+
42-6	**2**	*shd*	**The Fonz**[25] 1378 4-9-1 **79** .... RyanMoore 1 (Sir Michael Stoute) *trckd ldr: led over 2f out: r.o: ct fnl stride* **4/1**[1]	88+
30-6	**3**	2 ½	**Persian Peril**[29] 1272 6-9-4 **82** .... PJMcDonald 8 (G A Swinbank) *chsd ldrs: edgd lft and styd on same pce fnl f* **10/1**[3]	87
0-50	**4**	*nk*	**Sirgarfieldsobers (IRE)**[15] 1600 4-9-7 **85** .... RobertWinston 6 (B S Rothwell) *s.i.s: sn chsng ldrs: kpt on same pce fnl 2f* **33/1**	89
1510	**5**	3	**Kames Park (IRE)**[10] 1720 8-9-3 **81** .... PhillipMakin 9 (R C Guest) *t.k.h towards rr: stdy hdwy on outside over 2f out: carried hd high: wknd appr fnl f* **33/1**	81
2-33	**6**	*hd*	**Mannlichen**[9] 1751 4-9-1 **79** .... JoeFanning 5 (M Johnston) *chsd ldrs: kpt on same pce fnl 2f* **14/1**	78
2202	**7**	1	**Kingsdale Orion (IRE)**[25] 1398 6-8-11 **78** .... BarryMcHugh[(3)] 16 (B Ellison) *in rr: hdwy 3f out: styd on fnl f: nvr nr ldrs* **28/1**	76
11-6	**8**	*hd*	**Blue Nymph**[54] 252 4-9-0 **83** .... IanBrennan[(5)] 2 (J J Quinn) *chsd ldrs: drvn over 3f out: one pce* **18/1**	80
22-6	**9**	*nk*	**Omokoroa (IRE)**[29] 1282 4-9-3 **81** .... DarryllHolland 11 (M H Tompkins) *prom: effrt on ins 3f out: nvr a threat* **8/1**[2]	78
430-	**10**	2 ¼	**Aleatricis**[235] 6115 5-9-3 **81** .... GrahamGibbons 19 (J J Quinn) *mid-div: effrt 3f out: one pce* **50/1**	74
50	**11**	1 ¾	**Cluain Alainn (IRE)**[35] 1156 4-9-2 **80** .... EddieAhern 10 (Ian Williams) *mid-div: effrt on ins 3f out: wknd 1f out* **8/1**[2]	70
6-33	**12**	*nk*	**Silk Hall (UAE)**[56] 811 5-9-4 **82** ....(b[1]) JimmyFortune 12 (A King) *in rr: drvn 4f out: nvr on terms* **16/1**	72
-004	**13**	¾	**Just Lille (IRE)**[9] 1752 7-9-6 **84** ....(p) PaulMulrennan 13 (Mrs A Duffield) *led: qcknd over 4f out: hdd over 2f out: wknd over 1f out* **12/1**	73
21-3	**14**	*nse*	**Incendo**[26] 1348 4-9-1 **79** ....(t) HayleyTurner 20 (J R Fanshawe) *swtchd lft s: hld up in rr: nvr a factor* **10/1**[3]	68
0/00	**15**	9	**Track Record**[18] 1525 5-9-5 **83** .... JamieSpencer 14 (Jonjo O'Neill) *mid-div: effrt on outer 3f out: wknd and eased over 1f out* **25/1**	65
20P-	**16**	9	**Geneva Geyser (GER)**[207] 6855 4-9-7 **85** .... MickyFenton 7 (J M P Eustace) *in rr: drvn over 4f out: lost pl over 2f out: eased 1f out and sn bhd* **33/1**	45
0-05	**17**	44	**Camps Bay (USA)**[11] 1684 6-9-4 **82** .... AdrianNicholls 4 (D Nicholls) *s.v.s: a bhd: virtually p.u 2f out: t.o* **11/1**	—

2m 32.03s (-1.17) **Going Correction** -0.275s/f (Firm) **17** Ran SP% **123.4**
Speed ratings (Par 105): **92,91,90,90,88 87,87,87,86,85 84,84,83,83,77 71,42**
toteswingers: 1&2 £6.30, 1&3 £22.40, 2&3 £10.50 CSF £37.34 CT £336.44 TOTE £7.40: £2.10, £1.30, £2.70, £8.20; EX 33.80 Trifecta £777.40 Pool: £1,281.68 - 1.22 winning units..
Owner Mr And Mrs J D Cotton **Bred** Harts Farm And Stud **Trained** Great Habton, N Yorks
■ Stewards' Enquiry : Kieren Fallon caution: used whip down shoulder in the forehand.

FOCUS
The ground was drying out all the time and the official description was changed to good to firm all round. This was a competitive handicap and a difficult race to solve, but the early tempo was nothing special and a few were inclined to pull as a result. The form is rated around the third and fourth and the first two may do better.
Camps Bay(USA) Official explanation: jockey said gelding missed the break

2032 BLUE SQUARE SUPPORTING MARIE CURIE E B F NOVICE STKS 5f
4:20 (4:21) (Class 3) 2-Y-O **£7,771** (£2,312; £1,155; £577) **Stalls** Low

Form				RPR
1	**1**		**Bahceli (IRE)**[14] 1626 2-9-5 0 .... RyanMoore 5 (R Hannon) *sson trcking ldrs: chsd wnr over 1f out: hung lft ins fnl f: styd on to ld last strides* **15/8**[1]	88+
1	**2**	*hd*	**Cocktail Charlie**[27] 1331 2-9-5 0 .... DavidAllan 3 (T D Easterby) *trckd ldr: qcknd to ld over 1f out: rdn ins fnl f: hdd last stride* **9/4**[2]	88+
6321	**3**	3 ¾	**Saucy Buck (IRE)**[5] 1864 2-9-5 0 .... TonyCulhane 4 (M R Channon) *hld up: effrt 2f out: kpt on same pce* **8/1**	74
1	**4**	*hd*	**Majestic Myles (IRE)**[12] 1668 2-9-5 0 .... PaulHanagan 1 (R A Fahey) *trckd ldrs: keeping on same pce whn hmpd over 1f out: kpt on ins fnl f* **3/1**[3]	75+
01	**5**	3 ¼	**Misty Morn**[13] 1646 2-8-11 0 .... GrahamGibbons 2 (A D Brown) *led: hung rt throught: hdd and edgd lft over 1f out: sn wknd* **12/1**	54

60.75 secs (1.45) **Going Correction** +0.175s/f (Good) **5** Ran SP% **109.4**
Speed ratings (Par 97): **95,94,88,88,83**
CSF £6.30 TOTE £2.80: £1.20, £2.20; EX 6.10.
Owner Middleham Park Racing II **Bred** Dr Mariann And Richard Klay **Trained** East Everleigh, Wilts

FOCUS
Each of these 2-y-os had won last time out but the market called it right.

NOTEBOOK
Bahceli(IRE) won despite finding the track putting too much emphasis on speed for his liking. He still looked green under pressure, hanging left behind the leader until his rider changed his whip through to the other hand, but he then stayed on strongly to get up close home. Clearly a stiffer track and/or another furlong is going to suit him, and he looks to have the ability to cope with a step up in grade. (op 2-1 tchd 9-4)
Cocktail Charlie travelled liked the winner through the race and quickened up well to lead with over a furlong to run, but in the end he was just outstayed by the winner. He looks perfectly capable of winning a race of this nature on a sharp track. (op 5-2)
Saucy Buck(IRE), the most experienced of these, had nothing to beat at Hamilton last time and faced stiffer competition and quicker ground here. He was simply outclassed. (op 17-2 tchd 9-1)
Majestic Myles(IRE), a winner at Musselburgh on his debut, didn't get the clearest of runs, but he would only have been third had everything gone right. This was disappointing but his stable, which was in such cracking form in March and April, has hit the wall this month, notching only four winners from 57 runners so far this month. (tchd 5-2)

Misty Morn won an ordinary race at Redcar last time and found this much tougher. She hung right throughout and perhaps this second start on quick ground wasn't to her liking. (op 11-1)

2033 THERIPLEYCOLLECTION.COM H'CAP 1m 2f 88y
4:55 (4:59) (Class 4) (0-85,85) 3-Y-O **£6,540** (£1,946; £972; £485) **Stalls** Low

Form RPR

-166 **1** **Arlequin**[27] 1330 3-9-0 **78** PhilipRobinson 17 95+
(J D Bethell) *towards rr: hdwy over 5f out: nt clr run and swtchd rt over 2f out: wnt 2nd over 1f out: styd on wl to ld post* **20/1**

21-2 **2** *nse* **Rigidity**[12] 1657 3-9-1 **79** EddieAhern 14 96+
(H R A Cecil) *mid-div: hdwy over 3f out: led over 2f out: 3 l clr 1f out: jst ct* **7/1**[2]

41-4 **3** *2 ¾* **Contract Caterer (IRE)**[27] 1330 3-9-7 **85** FrankieDettori 10 99+
(Pat Eddery) *wl chsd ldrs: hmpd over 2f out: nt clr run and swtchd rt 2f out: styd on fnl f* **7/1**[2]

001- **4** *8* **Forgotten Army (IRE)**[236] 6065 3-8-7 **71** oh1 WilliamBuick 6 66
(M H Tompkins) *s.i.s: hdwy 3f out: kpt on fnl f: nvr nr ldrs* **20/1**

55-5 **5** *nk* **Boss's Destination**[11] 1706 3-8-12 **76** PJMcDonald 9 70
(G A Swinbank) *mid-div: hdwy over 3f out: one pce fnl 2f* **20/1**

214- **6** *3* **Venutius**[201] 7003 3-8-13 **77** GrahamGibbons 13 65
(E S McMahon) *chsd ldrs: one pce fnl 2f* **33/1**

1-02 **7** *2 ¾* **New Christmas (USA)**[12] 1658 3-9-5 **83** MartinDwyer 15 66
(B J Meehan) *in rr: hdwy 3f out: nvr nr ldrs* **16/1**

1-24 **8** *2 ½* **Brooklands Bay (IRE)**[96] 428 3-9-1 **79** DarryllHolland 16 57
(J R Weymes) *s.s: sme hdwy over 2f out: nvr a factor* **66/1**

031- **9** *1 ¾* **Tres Coronas (IRE)**[187] 7267 3-9-4 **82** (b) PhillipMakin 5 56
(T D Barron) *led: hdd over 2f out: wknd over 1f out* **14/1**[3]

41-5 **10** *hd* **Think Its All Over (USA)**[18] 1514 3-8-11 **75** JamieSpencer 3 49
(T P Tate) *chsd ldrs: drvn over 3f out: lost pl 2f out* **7/1**[2]

32-5 **11** *7* **Official Style**[27] 1330 3-9-3 **81** RyanMoore 4 57+
(Sir Michael Stoute) *trckd ldrs: effrt over 2f out: wknd over 1f out: sn eased* **5/2**[1]

-130 **12** *4 ½* **Whippers Love (IRE)**[27] 1330 3-9-2 **80** JoeFanning 8 31
(M Johnston) *chsd ldrs: lost pl over 2f out* **33/1**

543- **13** *1 ¾* **City Vaults Girl (IRE)**[204] 6923 3-8-7 **71** oh1 PaulHanagan 1 19
(R A Fahey) *mid-div: sme hdwy 3f out: nvr on terms* **20/1**

-320 **14** *½* **Tenacestream (CAN)**[29] 1279 3-8-12 **76** RobertWinston 11 23
(J R Best) *mid-div: sme hdwy on outside 3f out: sn wknd* **66/1**

56-6 **15** *2 ½* **Ananda Kanda (USA)**[16] 1571 3-8-13 **77** TomEaves 7 19
(B Ellison) *in rr: hdwy over 3f out: sn lost pl: eased ins fnl f* **100/1**

2m 7.82s (-4.68) **Going Correction** -0.275s/f (Firm) **15** Ran SP% **107.5**
Speed ratings (Par 101): **107,106,104,98,98 95,93,91,90,89 84,80,79,78,76**
toteswingers: 1&2 £18.20, 1&3 £23.80, 2&3 £4.90 CSF £111.94 CT £808.60 TOTE £20.80: £4.70, £2.30, £2.20; EX 168.10 Trifecta £457.90 Pool: £928.25 - 1.50 winning units. Place 6 £133.53, Place 5 £59.11.
Owner J Carrick **Bred** Dr A J F Gillespie **Trained** Middleham Moor, N Yorks

FOCUS
They went a solid gallop here and the winning time was 0.41sec slower than the opening handicap for older horses but quicker than the Musidora. The first three finished clear and the form is rated positively.
Official Style Official explanation: trainer had no explanation for the poor form shown
Tenacestream(CAN) Official explanation: jockey said colt was unsuited by good to firm ground
T/Jkpt: Not won. T/Plt: £176.00 to a £1 stake. Pool: £187,990.06. 779.31 winning tickets. T/Qpdt: £7.40 to a £1 stake. Pool: £10,373.06. 1,024.06 winning tickets. WG

2034 - (Foreign Racing) - See Raceform Interactive

1403 NAAS (L-H)
Wednesday, May 12

OFFICIAL GOING: Good

2035a FISHERY LANE RACE 6f
6:10 (6:12) 2-Y-O **£10,075** (£2,336; £1,022; £584)

RPR

1 **Zoffany (IRE)**[24] 1410 2-9-6 JMurtagh 1 94+
(A P O'Brien, Ire) *trckd ldrs in 3rd racing keenly: swtchd rt 2f out: qcknd impressively to ld 1f out: stretched clr fnl f: v easily* **1/5**[1]

2 *3 ½* **Scriobhai (IRE)**[24] 1410 2-9-0 DJMoran 3 75
(J S Bolger, Ire) *led: pushed along fr 1 1/2f out: hdd 1f out: no ch w wnr and kpt on one pce* **33/1**

3 *3* **Suntan (IRE)**[52] 954 2-9-0 KJManning 4 66
(J S Bolger, Ire) *trckd ldr in 2nd: rdn fr 2f out: 3rd and no ex fr 1f out: kpt on one pce* **7/2**[2]

4 *3 ½* **Mrs Happy (IRE)**[17] 1558 2-8-9 PShanahan 2 50
(P J Prendergast, Ire) *hld up in 4th: plld hrd early: rdn on outer over 2f out: sn no imp* **14/1**[3]

1m 14.02s (0.82) **4** Ran SP% **115.2**
CSF £10.72 TOTE £1.10; DF 9.00.
Owner Michael Tabor **Bred** Epona Bloodstock Ltd **Trained** Ballydoyle, Co Tipperary

FOCUS
This race was run in a time 1.35 seconds slower that the opening fillies' maiden.

NOTEBOOK
Zoffany(IRE) comfortably kept his unbeaten record intact, accounting for his three rivals with little fuss. Not surprisingly, it was a tactical race with stable companions' Scriobhai and Suntan leading the charge with the 1-5 shot, who was keen from the outset, sitting in behind before the tempo increased after halfway. The only anxious moment for his long odds-on backers came when the winning rider had to manoeuvre his way out to mount his challenge before the furlong pole. Once out, though, he quickened with the minimum of fuss and won as he liked. He looks a nice prospect and surely Royal Ascot will now figure in future plans. (op 2/7)
Scriobhai(IRE), the rank outsider of the quartet, had finished over 7l behind the winner when they clashed at Leopardstown. This was a better display on his third start to record a career-best finish, and he again appreciated some decent ground.
Suntan(IRE) had shaped well over 5f in testing ground at the Curragh back in March and, according to the market, was expected to play a prominent role. However, he was unable to raise his game when the race unfolded from the 2f pole. (op 10/3 tchd 4/1)
Mrs Happy(IRE) was held up at the rear before she closed on the favourite's outer, but she was soon struggling to maintain that momentum, which allowed the Ballydoyle runner enough room to switch out and go about his business. (op 12/1)

2037a BLUE WIND STKS (GROUP 3) (F&M) 1m 2f
7:10 (7:10) 3-Y-O+ **£46,017** (£13,451; £6,371; £2,123)

RPR

1 **Akdarena**[17] 1561 3-8-9 **104** (bt) KJManning 4 111+
(J S Bolger, Ire) *mde all: sent clr fr 3f out: styd on strly: v easily* **7/2**[2]

2 *7* **Indiana Gal (IRE)**[10] 1741 5-9-9 **96** (p) FMBerry 6 97
(Patrick Martin, Ire) *towards rr: 6th 1/2-way: mod 5th u.p 2f out: swtchd lft and sme hdwy on far rail into 2nd under 1f out: kpt on* **14/1**

3 *¾* **Grace O'Malley (IRE)**[17] 1560 4-9-12 **101** PJSmullen 3 98
(D K Weld, Ire) *trckd ldrs in 4th: wnt 3rd 3f out: 2nd and no imp on wnr 2f out: dropped to mod 3rd under 1f out* **10/3**[1]

4 *hd* **She's Our Mark**[10] 1741 6-9-12 **106** DPMcDonogh 1 98
(Patrick J Flynn, Ire) *chsd ldrs in 5th: pushed along ent st: mod 4th fr 2f out: kpt on one pce* **4/1**[3]

5 *4 ½* **Lady Lupus (IRE)**[17] 1561 3-8-9 **96** JPO'Brien 2 86
(A P O'Brien, Ire) *trckd ldrs in 3rd: drvn along appr st: mod 6th over 2f out: kpt on one pce* **20/1**

6 *2* **Unity (IRE)**[17] 1561 3-8-9 **99** (p) JMurtagh 8 82
(David Wachman, Ire) *trckd ldr in 2nd: rdn ent st: no imp in 3rd 2f out: no ex* **9/2**

7 *28* **Dazzling Day**[17] 1561 3-8-9 **98** CDHayes 10 26
(Kevin Prendergast, Ire) *a towards rr: 7th 1/2-way: wknd fr 3f out* **7/1**

8 *½* **Dance On By (IRE)**[7] 1820 3-8-9 **97** CO'Donoghue 5 25
(A P O'Brien, Ire) *mid-div: dropped towards rr 1/2-way: drvn along and no ex 4f out: wknd* **12/1**

9 *hd* **Mid Mon Lady (IRE)**[10] 1741 5-9-9 **94** (b) WJSupple 9 24
(H Rogers, Ire) *a bhd: trailing fr early st* **25/1**

2m 11.21s (-4.39)
WFA 3 from 4yo+ 15lb **9** Ran SP% **118.9**
CSF £52.79 TOTE £4.20: £2.30, £3.50, £1.80; DF 75.10.
Owner Miss K Rausing **Bred** Miss K Rausing **Trained** Coolcullen, Co Carlow
■ Stewards' Enquiry : D P McDonogh severe caution: used whip with excessive frequency

FOCUS
This looked a decent Group 3 event and it was won in emphatic style. The trip was on the short side for the third and the fourth prefers softer ground, but the time compares well with the maiden over the same distance and so the race has been rated at face value for the time being.

NOTEBOOK
Akdarena made every yard a winning one. She had shown plenty of improvement on quick ground when she landed the Salsabil Stakes over this trip last time and, with the tongue-strap and blinkers fitted again, she was different class to her eight rivals. Her next race will be either the Epsom or Curragh Oaks according to her trainer, who will wait before making any decision, but she is going the right way and clearly relishes a decent surface. She had her chasing rivals in trouble turning for home and she galloped all the way to the line to suggest another 2f should be well within her compass. (op 5/2)
Indiana Gal(IRE) proved best of the rest and she put a disappointing effort at Gowran Park 11 days ago behind her. She ran on well inside the final furlong when she got to the far rail, and she coped well with this sounder surface.
Grace O'Malley(IRE) had a seasonal debut run behind her coming into this, having finished third over 1m5f in a Listed event at Navan. She had finished a well-beaten fourth in the Irish Oaks last term and there was a question mark about how she'd cope with this shorter trip. Despite every call from the saddle after closing rounding the home turn, she was unable to make inroads on the leader after they straightened for home. (op 4/1 tchd 3/1)
She's Our Mark travelled better than most leaving the back straight but was another to struggle when asked to go about her business as the leader kept up the relentless gallop at the head of affairs. She had chased home Chinese White in similar ground at Gowran Park last time but she seems to be more effective with more ease in the ground. She may also prefer a slightly longer journey as she showed when winning the Alleged Stakes at the Curragh last time.
Lady Lupus(IRE), well behind the winner when they clashed at Navan, raced in the leading group until she weakened.
Dazzling Day dropped right out in the straight. Official explanation: jockey said gelding never travelled
Dance On By(IRE) was done no favours when hampered in the early stages. (op 10/1)
Mid Mon Lady(IRE) looked up against it on figures and she ran accordingly.

2038 - 2040a (Foreign Racing) - See Raceform Interactive

1724 NEWMARKET (Rowley Mile) (R-H)
Thursday, May 13

OFFICIAL GOING: Good to firm (8.5)
Wind: Light, behind. Weather: Overcast

2041 GUARDIAN DIRECT MARKETING PRINT PACK & POST MEDIAN AUCTION MAIDEN STKS 5f
5:45 (5:45) (Class 5) 2-Y-O **£3,238** (£963; £481) **Stalls** Low

Form RPR

1 **Twist Of Silver (USA)** 2-8-12 0 RyanMoore 4 80+
(J Noseda) *mde all: pushed clr fr over 1f out: r.o wl* **1/3**[1]

2 *13* **Alantina** 2-9-3 0 SebSanders 1 38
(J R Jenkins) *chsd wnr: rdn 2f out: wknd over 1f out* **9/2**[2]

3 *2 ¼* **Annalika** 2-8-9 0 KellyHarrison(3) 3 25
(W J H Ratcliffe) *s.i.s: sn chsng ldrs: rdn and wknd over 1f out* **13/2**[3]

62.03 secs (2.93) **Going Correction** +0.25s/f (Good) **3** Ran SP% **106.5**
Speed ratings (Par 93): **86,65,61**
CSF £2.13 TOTE £1.20; EX 1.40.
Owner S E Construction (Kent) Ltd **Bred** G David Shashura & Diane Shashura **Trained** Newmarket, Suffolk

FOCUS
Probably an ordinary juvenile maiden, and it is difficult to pin down the merit of the winner's wide margin win.

NOTEBOOK
Twist Of Silver(USA) was sent off odds-on favourite and won accordingly, albeit in a time that was over four seconds outside of standard. That said, she did everything that was required, enjoying the quick surface as her low action suggested she would and running all the way to the line in a style that indicated that she'll get further. (op 1-4 tchd 4-11 in places)
Alantina, a half-brother to the stable's fair 2yo 5f winner/sprinter Love You Louis, looked as if he still has some furnishing to do as could be anticipated from a May foal. His stride shortened significantly as he tired late on and he should progress as he matures. (op 6-1)
Annalika, a cheap purchase whose half-sister won at 7f at two before going on to score over hurdles, was awkward when leaving the stalls. Like the other two, the experience won't have been lost on her, but she probably requires time to strengthen and - judged on pedigree - will want further than the minimum distance to be seen to best effect. (op 7-1 tchd 8-1)

2042 HOMESTORE AND SAFEPAC H'CAP 1m
6:15 (6:17) (Class 5) (0-75,75) 3-Y-O **£3,238** (£963; £481; £240) **Stalls** Low

Form RPR

6-03 **1** **Gobama**[15] 1619 3-8-13 **70** SebSanders 15 79
(J W Hills) *s.i.s: hld up: hdwy over 2f out: led over 1f out: rdn out* **16/1**

0-21 **2** *3 ½* **Layla's Lexi**[19] 1514 3-8-10 **67** NeilCallan 2 68
(Ian Williams) *mid-div: hdwy 3f out: rdn over 1f out: chsd wnr ins fnl f: styd on* **9/1**

30-3 **3** ½ **Diamond Duchess (IRE)**[27] 1362 3-9-2 **73**..................(b[1]) TedDurcan 1 73
(D R Lanigan) *dwlt: hld up: swtchd rt and hdwy over 1f out: sn rdn: r.o: nt rch ldrs* **15/2**

20-2 **4** ¾ **Indian Valley (USA)**[19] 1538 3-9-0 **71**.............................. ChrisCatlin 11 69
(Rae Guest) *led: rdn and hdd over 1f out: no ex ins fnl f* **14/1**

36-5 **5** 1 **Granite Girl**[30] 1278 3-8-12 **69**...................................... EddieCreighton 14 65
(P J McBride) *hld up: hdwy over 3f out: rdn 2f out: no ex ins fnl f* **13/2**[2]

31-1 **6** 1 ¾ **Hulcote Rose (IRE)**[19] 1537 3-9-4 **75**.............................. RyanMoore 13 67
(S Kirk) *hld up in tch: rdn and ev ch over 1f out: wknd ins fnl f* **9/2**[1]

550- **6** dht **Snoqualmie Star**[198] 7099 3-8-13 **70**.............................. HayleyTurner 3 62
(D R C Elsworth) *chsd ldrs: rdn over 2f out: styd on same pce appr fnl f* **8/1**

024- **8** ¾ **Wild Rockette**[176] 7434 3-9-3 **74**.................................... NickyMackay 12 64
(B J Meehan) *chsd ldrs: rdn and ev ch over 1f out: wknd ins fnl f* **16/1**

4061 **9** nse **Sternian**[23] 1461 3-8-7 **64**.. JamieMackay 8 54
(M E Rimmer) *hld up: styd on ins fnl f: nvr nrr* **80/1**

0-53 **10** 1 **Mellifera**[14] 1640 3-8-11 **68**.. WilliamBuick 9 56
(W R Swinburn) *broke wl: stdd and sn lost pl: hdwy over 3f out: rdn: edgd lft and wknd over 1f out* **7/1**[3]

40-0 **11** 3 ½ **Baileys Vision**[45] 1048 3-8-1 **61** oh3.......................... KellyHarrison(3) 7 41
(C A Dwyer) *hld up: a in rr* **50/1**

00-0 **12** 4 ½ **Consider Yourself (USA)**[31] 1260 3-8-10 **67**................ MickyFenton 5 36
(M L W Bell) *dwlt: hld up: hdwy over 3f out: wknd over 2f out* **9/1**

310- **13** nse **Cat Hunter**[194] 7187 3-8-12 **69**...................................... EddieAhern 6 38
(Mrs A J Perrett) *chsd ldrs: rdn over 2f out: wknd and eased over 1f out* **16/1**

0-40 **14** 3 ½ **Half Sister (IRE)**[17] 1581 3-9-1 **72**.............................. J-PGuillambert 10 33
(R Hannon) *prom: rdn over 3f out: wknd over 2f out* **25/1**

00-3 **15** 1 **Batgirl**[17] 1586 3-8-4 **61** oh1.. IvaMilickova 4 20
(John Berry) *prom: lost pl over 3f out: bhd whn hung rt over 1f out* **66/1**

1m 39.75s (1.15) **Going Correction** +0.25s/f (Good) 15 Ran SP% **119.7**
Speed ratings (Par 99): **104,100,100,99,98 96,96,95,95,94 91,86,86,83,82**
Tote Swingers: 1&2 £14.30, 1&3 £71.50, 2&3 £8.90 CSF £149.14 CT £1207.04 TOTE £30.20: £8.30, £1.90, £2.40; EX 175.40.
Owner W Y Chen **Bred** Newsells Park Stud Limited **Trained** Upper Lambourn, Berks
■ Stewards' Enquiry : J-P Guillambert two-day ban: careless riding (May 27-28)

FOCUS
A modest fillies' handicap, but competitive. It was quicker than the later conditions race and the form looks sound judged around the second and third.
Consider Yourself(USA) Official explanation: jockey said filly lost its action
Half Sister(IRE) Official explanation: jockey said filly was unsuited by the good to firm ground

2043 TAXFREEMONEY.COM MAIDEN STKS 1m 2f
6:50 (6:50) (Class 4) 3-Y-O **£5,180** (£1,541; £770; £384) **Stalls** Low

Form RPR

0- **1** **Sour Mash (IRE)**[209] 6810 3-9-3 0.............................. J-PGuillambert 11 93+
(L M Cumani) *hld up: racd keenly: hdwy over 3f out: rdn to ld and edgd lft wl ins fnl f: r.o* **25/1**

20- **2** ½ **Sing Sweetly**[222] 6477 3-8-12 0.............................. NickyMackay 1 87
(G A Butler) *a.p: chsd ldr 2f out: rdn to ld ins fnl f: edgd lft and sn hdd: styd on* **16/1**

3 1 ¾ **Sharedah (IRE)** 3-8-12 0.. TadhgO'Shea 4 87+
(Sir Michael Stoute) *s.i.s: hdwy over 8f out: swtchd rt and nt clr run over 1f out: r.o to go 3rd post* **20/1**

2 **4** nse **All Action (USA)**[26] 1386 3-9-3 0.............................. EddieAhern 2 88
(H R A Cecil) *led: rdn and edgd rt fr over 1f out: hdd ins fnl f: n.m.r sn after: lost 3rd post* **4/6**[1]

5 2 ¼ **Reality Show (IRE)** 3-9-3 0.. TedDurcan 5 84+
(Mahmood Al Zarooni) *s.s: hld up: rdn over 3f out: sn outpcd: r.o ins fnl f: nt trble ldrs* **25/1**

25-4 **6** 1 ¼ **William Van Gogh**[26] 1387 3-9-3 80.............................. WilliamBuick 3 81
(J H M Gosden) *chsd ldr tl rdn over 2f out: n.m.r over 1f out: wknd ins fnl f* **3/1**[2]

7 7 **Starshine** 3-8-12 0.. RyanMoore 7 62
(Sir Michael Stoute) *prom: rdn over 3f out: wknd over 2f out* **14/1**[3]

8 4 **La Concorde (FR)** 3-8-12 0.. RichardMullen 9 54
(Sir Michael Stoute) *hld up: bhd fnl 4f* **66/1**

\- **9** 1 ¼ **Old Hundred (IRE)** 3-9-3 0.. PatCosgrave 10 57
(J R Fanshawe) *s.s: sn drvn along and a in rr* **66/1**

10 4 **Cape Dutch (IRE)** 3-9-0 0.. AhmedAjtebi(3) 8 49
(Mahmood Al Zarooni) *s.s: a bhd* **20/1**

11 31 **Tigranes The Great (IRE)** 3-9-3 0.............................. SebSanders 6 —
(M Botti) *hld up: rdn 1/2-way: wknd 4f out: t.o* **40/1**

2m 6.22s (0.42) **Going Correction** +0.25s/f (Good) 11 Ran SP% **120.2**
Speed ratings (Par 101): **108,107,106,106,104 103,97,94,93,90 65**
Tote Swingers: 1&2 £28.10, 1&3 £28.50, 2&3 £46.30 CSF £347.00 TOTE £50.00: £8.10, £5.10, £6.10; EX 353.10.
Owner The Honorable Earle I Mack **Bred** Epona Bloodstock Ltd **Trained** Newmarket, Suffolk

FOCUS
There should be winners coming from this maiden, which is often a good race. The form is rated around the fourth.
Sharedah(IRE) Official explanation: jockey said filly was denied a clear run
All Action(USA) Official explanation: jockey said, regarding appearing to ease approaching line, that the colt was hanging right and he was concerned that it may clip the heels of the third.

2044 SIMON GIBSON H'CAP 1m 2f
7:25 (7:25) (Class 3) (0-90,89) 4-Y-O+ **£7,771** (£2,312; £1,155; £577) **Stalls** Low

Form RPR

3315 **1** **Follow The Flag (IRE)**[5] 1925 6-8-6 **82**................(p) DeclanCannon(5) 1 90
(A J McCabe) *hld up: hdwy and swtchd rt over 2f out: rdn and r.o to ld wl ins fnl f* **16/1**

5-26 **2** ¾ **Sohcahtoa (IRE)**[16] 1600 4-9-1 **86**.............................. RichardHughes 3 92
(R Hannon) *prom: swtchd lft and rdn over 1f out: r.o to go 2nd nr fin* **8/1**[3]

50-0 **3** hd **Sandor**[12] 1697 4-9-4 **89**.. RyanMoore 7 95
(P J Makin) *chsd ldrs: led over 1f out: sn hung lft: rdn and hdd wl ins fnl f* **9/4**[1]

4440 **4** 2 ½ **Baylini**[33] 1220 6-8-6 **77**.. HayleyTurner 2 78
(Ms J S Doyle) *hld up: hdwy over 2f out: rdn and no ex ins fnl f* **11/1**

255- **5** 1 **Jo'Burg (USA)**[222] 6470 6-8-3 **77**.............................. MartinLane(3) 6 76
(Lady Herries) *s.s: hld up: hdwy over 3f out: rdn: hung lft and no ex ins fnl f* **12/1**

215- **6** 4 ½ **Anice Stellato (IRE)**[224] 6419 4-9-4 **89**.............................. NeilCallan 8 79
(R M Beckett) *prom: chsd ldr 1/2-way: rdn: edgd rt and ev ch 2f out: wknd ins fnl f* **6/1**[2]

222- **7** 4 ½ **Rumble Of Thunder (IRE)**[223] 6453 4-8-12 **83**.............. MartinDwyer 9 64
(D W P Arbuthnot) *led: rdn and hdd over 1f out: wknd fnl f* **6/1**[2]

0 **8** 23 **Monte Cavallo (SAF)**[26] 1388 5-8-7 **83**.............................. TobyAtkinson(5) 4 18
(M Wigham) *hld up: rdn over 3f out: wknd over 2f out* **20/1**

/2-0 **9** 5 **Cygnet**[16] 1600 4-9-0 **85**.. J-PGuillambert 5 10
(L M Cumani) *hld up: racd keenly: rdn and wknd over 2f out* **8/1**[3]

0603 **10** 67 **Donaldson (GER)**[43] 1062 8-9-1 **86**.............................. SebSanders 10 —
(Jonjo O'Neill) *chsd ldr tl rdn 1/2-way: sn lost pl: wknd 3f out: t.o* **16/1**

2m 6.42s (0.62) **Going Correction** +0.25s/f (Good) 10 Ran SP% **114.1**
Speed ratings (Par 107): **107,106,106,104,103 99,96,77,73,20**
Tote Swingers: 1&2 £6.90, 1&3 £9.80, 2&3 £23.70 CSF £135.03 CT £400.85 TOTE £21.50: £5.60, £3.20, £1.50; EX 152.60.
Owner S Gillen **Bred** Martin Francis **Trained** Averham Park, Notts

FOCUS
A fair handicap, and ordinary but sound form for the grade.

NOTEBOOK
Follow The Flag(IRE) was 4lb higher than his previous best winning mark but produced a cracking finishing kick despite having to tack around all his rivals to get a run on the outer. He had only two rivals behind him as he was angled out from the inner rail approaching three furlongs out, and with the splits failing to come, was forced widest of all. That didn't stop him and he rattled home, skimming over the decent ground to score.
Sohcahtoa(IRE), with the blinkers off here, must frustrate connections as he is definitely capable of winning off this sort of mark. He hasn't scored since 2008 and just needs things to fall right for him. To be fair to him, he may just not have seen the winner challenging wide on the track after collaring the favourite. (tchd 15-2)
Sandor, tightened up for space when finishing seventh in a hot 1m1f handicap at Newmarket at the Guineas meeting, had every chance as he led over a furlong out. He hung left in the closing stages but that had no bearing on the final outcome as he was made to look a little one-paced. It will probably prove wise to give him another chance although he may be best served by being produced late, based on the fact he edged left after hitting the front. (op 11-4 tchd 3-1 and 10-3 in places)
Baylini, having her first start on turf in ten races, gave a decent account of herself. But it is hard to make a case for her on grass as all her winning has been done on the AW. (tchd 10-1)
Anice Stellato(IRE) travelled well but found little for pressure. (tchd 5-1)
Rumble Of Thunder(IRE), making his seasonal bow, was unable to replicate the respectable form of each of his last three starts of 2009 in which he finished second on each occasion. Official explanation: jockey said gelding ran too free (op 7-1)
Monte Cavallo(SAF) Official explanation: jockey said gelding ran too free

2045 ORBITAL FOODS MACHINERY CONDITIONS STKS 1m
8:00 (8:00) (Class 3) 3-Y-O **£9,066** (£2,697; £1,348; £673) **Stalls** Low

Form RPR

12-2 **1** **Quadrille**[29] 1311 3-9-2 105.. RichardHughes 5 111
(R Hannon) *chsd ldr: shkn up over 2f out: led over 1f out: r.o wl* **9/4**[1]

40-4 **2** 5 **High Twelve (IRE)**[29] 1310 3-8-12 100.............................. WilliamBuick 6 95
(J H M Gosden) *a.p: rdn to chse wnr fnl f: styd on same pce* **3/1**[2]

21-5 **3** 1 **Mufarrh (IRE)**[29] 1313 3-8-12 96.. RichardHills 2 93
(J L Dunlop) *led: rdn and hdd over 1f out: no ex ins fnl f* **5/1**

1 **4** ½ **Diescentric (USA)**[28] 1325 3-8-12 0.............................. EddieAhern 4 92
(H R A Cecil) *hld up: racd keenly: hdwy over 3f out: rdn over 1f out: no ex ins fnl f* **4/1**[3]

0- **5** 1 ¾ **Field Of Dream**[247] 5743 3-9-6 0.............................. J-PGuillambert 1 96
(L M Cumani) *hld up: plld hrd: rdn over 1f out: wknd wl ins fnl f* **20/1**

212- **6** 4 ½ **Pleasant Day (IRE)**[201] 7030 3-8-12 104......................(b) MartinDwyer 3 77
(B J Meehan) *chsd ldrs: rdn and wknd over 1f out* **6/1**

1m 39.93s (1.33) **Going Correction** +0.25s/f (Good) 6 Ran SP% **111.5**
Speed ratings (Par 103): **103,98,97,96,94 90**
Tote swingers:1&2:£2.50, 1&3:£2.90, 2&3:£5.10 CSF £9.09 TOTE £2.60: £1.30, £1.30; EX 9.30.
Owner The Queen **Bred** The Queen **Trained** East Everleigh, Wilts

FOCUS
The progressive winner was far too good in this conditions event. Slightly muddling form, rated around the third.

NOTEBOOK
Quadrille ◆ looked really well beforehand in the paddock and got a nice tow into the race from Mufarrh. He settled it in a matter of strides approaching the final furlong and drew right away from his rivals in a manner that indicated he'll stay a little further. Indeed, connections reported that they will now consider the 1m2f Listed Hampton Court Stakes at Royal Ascot. (op 2-1 tchd 5-2)
High Twelve(IRE) was another to catch the eye in the paddock and ran respectably, dropped back in trip after finishing a well-beaten fourth in a valuable sales race at Newmarket last month. He has the profile of a horse who may be difficult to place. (tchd 11-4 and 10-3 and 7-2 in places)
Mufarrh(IRE), fifth in the Feilden Stakes a month ago, enjoyed the ground, but he didn't have the speed to go on with Quadrille and, again, it may be tricky to find suitable opportunities for him to add to his tally of one win.\ (op 11-2 tchd 9-2 and 6-1 in places)
Diescentric(USA) last month won the Wood Ditton, a race that hasn't had the greatest of records in recent times. He was unable to get a meaningful blow in here and his future is likely to depend on the mark that the handicapper gives him. (op 5-1 tchd 11-2)
Field Of Dream Soft ground Listed winner in Italy as a 2yo (used to race prominently in that country), may be best suited by some underfoot ease. (op 16-1)
Pleasant Day(IRE), just touched off in the Horris Hill on his final start last year, might have found the ground too fast. (op 7-1 tchd 15-2 in places)

2046 ST NICHOLAS HOSPICE CARE H'CAP 5f
8:30 (8:30) (Class 5) (0-75,75) 3-Y-O **£3,238** (£963; £481; £240) **Stalls** Low

Form RPR

6522 **1** **Tom Folan**[10] 1784 3-8-5 **62**..(p) MartinDwyer 1 67
(Andrew Reid) *racd stands' side: chsd ldrs: swtchd rt over 1f out: rdn and r.o to ld post* **8/1**

3-10 **2** shd **The Strig**[30] 1281 3-9-1 **75**.. WilliamCarson(3) 7 79
(S C Williams) *racd alone in centre and overall ldr: rdn and hung lft over 1f out: r.o: hdd post* **14/1**

-332 **3** 1 ½ **Maldon Prom (IRE)**[30] 1281 3-9-4 **75**..............................(v) EddieAhern 3 74
(C A Dwyer) *racd stands' side: hld up: rdn over 1f out: r.o ins fnl f* **7/2**[2]

522- **4** 2 ½ **Drift And Dream**[239] 5992 3-9-1 **72**.............................. TedDurcan 4 62
(C F Wall) *dwlt: racd stands' side: hld up: rdn and hung rt over 1f out: nvr trbld ldrs* **11/10**[1]

1- **5** 6 **Black Baccara**[408] 1044 3-9-3 **74**.............................. ChrisCatlin 2 42
(P S McEntee) *s.i.s: sn chsng ldr on stands' side: rdn over 1f out: wknd ins fnl f* **14/1**

0114 **6** 3 ¼ **Athwaab**[19] 1511 3-9-1 **72**.. NeilCallan 6 29
(M G Quinlan) *led stands' side: rdn over 1f out: wknd fnl f* **9/2**[3]

60.80 secs (1.70) **Going Correction** +0.25s/f (Good) 6 Ran SP% **112.5**
Speed ratings (Par 99): **96,95,93,89,79 74**
Tote swingers:1&2:£8.40, 1&3:£4.60, 2&3:£4.00 CSF £98.63 TOTE £4.70: £1.20, £7.70; EX 81.90 Place 6 £4,565.82, Place 5 £3,322.52..
Owner Dave Clayton **Bred** Chippenham Lodge Stud Ltd **Trained** Mill Hill, London NW7

FOCUS
A modest affair, rated around the third.
T/Plt: £7,625.10 to a £1 stake. Pool: £62,672.49. 6.00 winning tickets. T/Qpdt: £2,107.20 to a £1 stake. Pool: £4,556.27. 1.60 winning tickets. CR

1731 SALISBURY (R-H)

Thursday, May 13

OFFICIAL GOING: Good to firm (9.2)

Wind: Moderate across Weather: sunny intervals

2047 EUROPEAN BREEDERS' FUND FILLIES' H'CAP 1m 1f 198y

1:55 (1:55) (Class 4) (0-85,84) 3-Y-O **£7,123** (£2,119; £1,059; £529) **Stalls** High

Form RPR

03-1 **1** **Contredanse (IRE)**[17] 1582 3-9-7 **84** KirstyMilczarek 2 100+
(L M Cumani) *mde all: shkn up and c clr fr 2f out: unchal* **4/1**[2]

1- **2** *6* **Namaskar**[247] 5741 3-9-5 **82** DaneO'Neill 8 86+
(J H M Gosden) *plld hrd: hld up in rr and stl keen 5f out: swtchd to outside over 3f out and sn green: pushed along: carried hd awkwardly but styd on fr 2f out: chsd wnr fnl f but nvr any ch* **11/4**[1]

10-3 **3** *½* **Wild Rose**[23] 1452 3-9-3 **80** HayleyTurner 4 83
(M L W Bell) *chsd wnr tl over 3f out: styd disputing 2nd but nvr any ch: styd on same pce into 3rd fnl f* **14/1**

5-05 **4** *½* **Sheila Toss (IRE)**[27] 1358 3-8-9 **72** PatDobbs 6 74
(R Hannon) *chsd ldrs: rdn and styd on same pce fnl 2f* **28/1**

31-5 **5** *¾* **Zahoo (IRE)**[20] 1502 3-8-12 **75** TadhgO'Shea 9 76+
(J L Dunlop) *in rr tl swtchd lft to outside over 2f out: styd on fr over 1f out and clsng on plcd horses ins fnl f but nvr any ch w wnr* **11/4**[1]

51- **6** *2 ¾* **Addahab (USA)**[196] 7140 3-8-10 **76** (t) AhmedAjtebi(3) 1 71
(Saeed Bin Suroor) *chsd ldrs: wnt 2nd over 3f out: rdn 2f out: wknd appr fnl f* **7/1**[3]

2-10 **7** *3* **Serafina's Flight**[11] 1729 3-8-11 **74** MartinDwyer 5 63
(W R Muir) *flashed tail after s: chsd ldrs tl wknd wl over 1f out* **16/1**

10-0 **8** *1 ½* **Sunarise (IRE)**[29] 1310 3-9-7 **84** RichardHughes 3 70
(R Hannon) *stdd in rr: swtchd to outside over 2f out: sn rdn and no prog* **8/1**

156- **9** *12* **Moonline Dancer (FR)**[217] 6619 3-8-11 **77** PatrickHills(3) 10 39
(R Hannon) *a in rr* **20/1**

2m 6.95s (-2.95) **Going Correction** -0.225s/f (Firm) 9 Ran SP% **117.7**
Speed ratings (Par 98): **102,97,96,96,95 93,91,90,80**
toteswingers:1&2:£3.90, 1&3:£8.50, 2&3:£6.30 CSF £15.77 CT £140.84 TOTE £4.20: £1.20, £1.30, £2.90; EX 22.00.
Owner S Stuckey **Bred** Ahdaab Syndicate **Trained** Newmarket, Suffolk

FOCUS

A good fillies' handicap and, despite there being no hanging about, few landed a blow from off the pace. It was a particularly decent winning time and the winner was much improved again.

Sunarise(IRE) Official explanation: jockey said filly hung left-handed

2048 TURFTV MAIDEN STKS 5f

2:30 (2:30) (Class 4) 2-Y-O **£3,885** (£1,156; £577; £288) **Stalls** High

Form RPR

1 **Dinkum Diamond (IRE)** 2-9-3 0 DaneO'Neill 6 85+
(H Candy) *t.k.h: hld up toward rr tl plld to outside and qcknd smartly to ld appr fnl f: sn in command: comf* **11/4**[2]

3 **2** *1 ½* **Foghorn Leghorn**[12] 1686 2-9-3 0 JackMitchell 4 80
(P W Chapple-Hyam) *in tch: hdwy over 1f out: styd on to chsd wnr jst ins fnl f but readily hld* **2/1**[1]

3 *1 ¾* **Button Moon (IRE)** 2-8-12 0 RichardThomas 7 68
(I A Wood) *chsd ldrs: drvn to chal over 1f out: sn edgd lft and green: styd on same pce* **16/1**

5 **4** *¾* **Milldown Magic**[12] 1695 2-9-0 0 JamesMillman(3) 11 71
(B R Millman) *led tl hdd over 1f out: wknd ins fnl f* **25/1**

5 *1 ¾* **Emilio Largo** 2-9-3 0 RichardKingscote 10 64
(R M Beckett) *chsd ldrs: rdn 2f out: wknd fnl f* **12/1**

6 *1* **Reckless Reward (IRE)** 2-9-3 0 RichardHughes 2 65+
(R Hannon) *wnt lft s: in rr whn faltered and bdly lost action over 3f out and bhd tl styd on fnl f* **10/3**[3]

7 *3 ½* **Valdaw** 2-9-3 0 LiamKeniry 3 48
(J S Moore) *chsd ldrs: hung rt and wknd ins fnl 2f* **66/1**

8 *1* **Bussa** 2-8-12 0 RichardEvans(5) 5 45
(P D Evans) *s.i.s: outpcd* **25/1**

9 *½* **Mi Regalo** 2-9-3 0 DavidProbert 8 43
(A M Balding) *chsd ldrs to 1/2-way* **9/1**

10 *19* **Impulse Dancer** 2-8-12 0 NeilChalmers 1 —
(J J Bridger) *carried lft s: sn wl bhd* **100/1**

60.66 secs (-0.34) **Going Correction** -0.225s/f (Firm) 10 Ran SP% **116.8**
Speed ratings (Par 95): **93,90,87,86,83 82,76,75,74,43**
toteswingers:1&2:£3.10, 1&3:£13.40, 2&3:£8.70 CSF £8.45 TOTE £4.70: £2.00, £1.10, £5.20; EX 10.90.
Owner Eight Star Syndicate **Bred** Ms H W Topping **Trained** Kingston Warren, Oxon

FOCUS

A fair juvenile maiden and the winner looks useful. The form is well up to scratch for the track.

NOTEBOOK

Dinkum Diamond(IRE) ◆, who attracted support, is related to winning sprinters and he ran out a taking debut winner. He took time to get the hang of things, but once getting organised he quickened nicely and was well on top at the finish. He looks potentially very useful, this will have no doubt delighted connections as it was the stable's first juvenile runner of the season, and it wouldn't be surprising to see him highly tried in due course, but his trainer later said it is likely to be a novice event next time. (op 3-1 tchd 9-4 and 7-2 in a place)

Foghorn Leghorn, third at Doncaster on debut 12 days earlier, was ridden with a little more restraint this time and probably posted a slightly improved effort. It should be remembered his previous experience counted for plenty here, but he rates a good benchmark and can be found an opening before long. (tchd 5-2)

Button Moon(IRE) ◆ is related to winners from 5f to 1m. She showed early speed despite running green and connections look to have a nice juvenile on their hands. (op 14-1 tchd 18-1)

Milldown Magic showed the benefit of his debut experience at Goodwood and much more early speed. He was a sitting duck, but is going the right way and has a future. Official explanation: jockey said colt hung left throughout (tchd 22-1)

Emilio Largo cost 65,000euros and has plenty of speed in his pedigree. He was green to post and through the race, but left the clear impression he would prove a deal sharper next time. (op 16-1)

Reckless Reward(IRE)'s stable's juveniles have once again hit the ground running this year. He went out to his left at the start and lost ground, looking distinctly green. He also appeared to lose his action around halfway and seemed likely to be a back number, but caught the eye running on when the race was effectively over. There is a strong chance he will go a lot closer now he has a run under his belt. Official explanation: jockey said colt lost its action (op 3-1 tchd 7-2)

Valdaw Official explanation: jockey said colt hung right final 2f

Impulse Dancer Official explanation: jockey said filly felt wrong behind; vet said filly had sore ashins

2049 CHIPMUNK EQUINE DUST EXTRACTED HORSE BEDDING CLAIMING STKS 6f 212y

3:00 (3:00) (Class 5) 3-Y-O **£3,238** (£963; £481; £240) **Stalls** Centre

Form RPR

-465 **1** **Thrust Control (IRE)**[17] 1584 3-8-13 78 CathyGannon 10 66
(M R Channon) *chsd ldrs: rdn over 2f out: hung lft u.p over 1f out and sn chsng ldr: styd on u.p to ld fnl 30yds* **9/4**[1]

-603 **2** *nk* **Chinese Democracy (USA)**[14] 1643 3-8-6 55 MartinDwyer 4 58
(P F I Cole) *led tl hdd ins fnl 5f: led again 3f out: hrd drvn fr over 1f out: hdd and no ex fnl 30yds* **4/1**[2]

5605 **3** *2 ¾* **Chandrayaan**[16] 1594 3-8-13 59 (v) SamHitchcott 12 58
(J E Long) *in tch: rdn and outpcd 3f out: styd on again fr over 1f out to take 3rd ins fnl f but no ch w ldng duo* **50/1**

5115 **4** *2* **Kirsty's Boy (IRE)**[7] 1842 3-9-1 75 LiamKeniry 1 58
(J S Moore) *chsd ldrs: rdn over 2f out: styng on to dispute 2nd whn bmpd over 1f out: styd on same pce fnl f* **6/1**

5-40 **5** *¾* **Leaving Alone (USA)**[19] 1514 3-8-7 67 CharlesEddery(7) 9 52
(R Hannon) *s.i.s: in rr and rdn along thrght tl sme hdwy fnl f* **9/1**

1443 **6** *½* **Mrs Boss**[23] 1449 3-8-11 68 JamesMillman(3) 3 50
(B R Millman) *chsd ldr: led ins fnl 5f tl hdd 3f out: wknd over 1f out* **10/1**

4320 **7** *1 ¼* **Ant Music (IRE)**[17] 1582 3-8-4 63 (b) RyanPowell(7) 6 44
(J S Moore) *s.i.s: impr and in tch whn bmpd over 3f out: no ch fr ins fnl 2f* **16/1**

0-50 **8** *8* **Silver Symphony (IRE)**[10] 1776 3-9-0 80 TadhgO'Shea 5 25
(P F I Cole) *t.k.h: bhd fr 1/2-way* **9/2**[3]

1m 27.51s (-1.49) **Going Correction** -0.225s/f (Firm) 8 Ran SP% **110.2**
Speed ratings (Par 99): **99,98,95,93,92 91,90,81**
toteswingers:1&2:£2.90, 1&3:£12.30, 2&3:£11.10 CSF £10.30 TOTE £2.50: £1.10, £1.70, £6.00; EX 13.20.Chinese Democracy was claimed by P. D. Evans for £8,000. Thrust Control was claimed by Brian Ellison for £9,000
Owner Mrs T Burns **Bred** Rathasker Stud **Trained** West Ilsley, Berks
■ Stewards' Enquiry : Cathy Gannon two-day ban: careless riding (May 27-28)

FOCUS

A moderate claimer.

Chinese Democracy(USA) Official explanation: jockey said filly hung left-handed

Mrs Boss Official explanation: jockey said saddle slipped

2050 SUBSCRIBE NOW TO RACING UK MAIDEN FILLIES' STKS (DIV I) 1m 1f 198y

3:35 (3:38) (Class 5) 3-Y-O+ **£3,561** (£1,059; £529; £264) **Stalls** High

Form RPR

42- **1** **Shimmering Surf (IRE)**[216] 6628 3-8-12 0 LukeMorris 6 84
(P Winkworth) *trckd ldr: drvn to take slt ld ins fnl 2f: pushed out fnl f* **7/2**[3]

42- **2** *2 ¾* **Scorn (USA)**[194] 7183 3-8-12 0 RichardHughes 10 79
(J H M Gosden) *led: shkn up and hdd ins fnl 2f: nt pce of wnr fnl f but hld on wl for 2nd* **6/5**[1]

24- **3** *¾* **Giants Play (USA)**[202] 6992 3-8-12 0 RichardMullen 1 77
(Sir Michael Stoute) *in tch: hdwy to go 3rd appr fnl 2f: kpt on same pce fnl f* **3/1**[2]

4 *2 ¾* **Island Dreams (USA)** 3-8-9 0 Louis-PhilippeBeuzelin(3) 5 72+
(Sir Michael Stoute) *in tch: outpcd and pushed along 3f out: styd on again fr over 1f out: gng on cl home* **12/1**

5 *nk* **Nabari (JPN)** 3-8-12 0 KirstyMilczarek 4 71
(L M Cumani) *chsd ldrs: pushed along over 2f out: outpcd appr fnl f* **25/1**

0 **6** *½* **Balatoma (IRE)**[27] 1355 3-8-12 0 PatDobbs 8 70
(M P Tregoning) *chsd ldrs: pushed along over 3f out: styd in tch tl wknd ins fnl f* **20/1**

0 **7** *3 ¾* **Never Can Tell (IRE)**[11] 1735 3-8-7 0 SophieDoyle(5) 7 62
(J A Osborne) *in rr tl sme prog fnl 2f* **66/1**

6-6 **8** *2 ¾* **Aalya (IRE)**[26] 1386 3-8-12 0 TadhgO'Shea 9 57
(J L Dunlop) *rdn along over 4f out: a towards rr* **20/1**

00- **9** *23* **Banco Busto (IRE)**[219] 6567 3-8-12 0 DaneO'Neill 3 11
(H S Howe) *s.i.s: sn bhd* **200/1**

2m 9.82s (-0.08) **Going Correction** -0.225s/f (Firm) 9 Ran SP% **115.7**
Speed ratings (Par 100): **91,88,88,86,85 85,82,80,61**
toteswingers:1&2:£3.10, 1&3:£2.80, 2&3:£1.90 CSF £7.73 TOTE £4.90: £1.60, £1.10, £1.10; EX 9.40.
Owner Butterfield, Strong & Williams **Bred** Cathal Ryan **Trained** Chiddingfold, Surrey

FOCUS

A decent fillies' maiden, as it often is, although it was slowly run. The form is rated around the second and third.

Never Can Tell(IRE) Official explanation: jockey said, regarding running and riding, that her orders were to pop out, get a posiition, take it easy round the bend as it is quite sharp, get the filly running and do her best, adding that it ran in snatches, hung left up the straight and ran green.

Banco Busto(IRE) Official explanation: jockey said filly hung left-handed

2051 SUBSCRIBE NOW TO RACING UK MAIDEN FILLIES' STKS (DIV II) 1m 1f 198y

4:10 (4:13) (Class 5) 3-Y-O+ **£3,561** (£1,059; £529; £264) **Stalls** High

Form RPR

30-2 **1** **Shimmering Moment (USA)**[27] 1358 3-8-12 79 IanMongan 4 84+
(H R A Cecil) *trckd ldr: led 6f out: pushed clr fr over 1f out: comf* **9/4**[2]

46- **2** *3* **Roxy Flyer (IRE)**[196] 7135 3-8-12 0 JimmyQuinn 2 78
(Mrs A J Perrett) *in rr but in tch: hdwy over 3f out to chse wnr over 2f out: nvr any ch but kpt on wl for clr 2nd* **14/1**

3 *2 ¼* **Pink Palace (USA)** 3-8-12 0 RichardMullen 9 74+
(Sir Michael Stoute) *hld up in rr: hdwy fr 3f out: hdwy fr 2f out: shkn up and green over 1f out: styd on ins fnl f: gng on cl home* **10/1**[3]

65 **4** *3* **Shades Of Grey**[18] 1542 3-8-12 0 LukeMorris 5 68
(C G Cox) *led 4f: styd chsng ldrs: rdn over 2f out: sn outpcd: wknd over 1f out* **125/1**

5-2 **5** *1 ½* **Mujdeya**[27] 1356 3-8-12 0 TadhgO'Shea 1 65
(J H M Gosden) *s.i.s: sn chsng ldrs: wnt 2nd 5f out: rdn 3f out: wknd 2f out* **1/1**[1]

6 *1* **Tulle (IRE)** 3-8-12 0 MartinDwyer 3 63+
(B J Meehan) *s.i.s: in rr tl styd on fr over 1f out* **25/1**

7 *1 ¼* **Polly Floyer** 3-8-12 0 AdamKirby 6 60+
(W R Swinburn) *fractious bef s: in tch tl bmpd 3f out: green: hung rt and sn fdd* **25/1**

0- **8** *1 ¼* **Juwireya**[247] 5741 3-8-12 0 PatDobbs 8 58
(M P Tregoning) *s.i.s: a towards rr* **20/1**

9 *shd* **Gale Green** 3-8-12 0 DaneO'Neill 7 57
(H Candy) *a towards rr* **25/1**

60-0 **10** *7* **Free Grain**26 1393 3-8-12 0 .... RichardHughes 10 50
(J L Dunlop) *chsd ldrs: shkn up 3f out: sn wknd* **33/1**

2m 8.29s (-1.61) **Going Correction** -0.225s/f (Firm) **10** Ran SP% **116.6**
Speed ratings (Par 100): **97,94,92,90,89 88,87,86,86,80**
toteswingers:1&2:£6.90, 1&3:£2.80, 2&3:£6.00 CSF £28.13 TOTE £3.40: £1.10, £2.20, £1.80; EX 45.30.
Owner Mogeely Stud & Mrs Maura Gittins **Bred** Dapple Bloodstock Et Al **Trained** Newmarket, Suffolk

FOCUS
The second division of the fillies' maiden and probably the weaker of the two, despite being run in a quicker winning time. The favourite disappointed and there was little depth, and the form is rated around the winner.
Mujdeya Official explanation: jockey said filly was unsuited by the good to firm ground

2052 BET AT VICTORCHANDLER.COM H'CAP 6f
4:45 (4:46) (Class 5) (0-75,75) 3-Y-O **£3,238** (£963; £481; £240) **Stalls** High

Form RPR
-212 **1** **Rio Mist**19 1511 3-9-4 **75** .... RichardHughes 6 85+
(R Hannon) *trckd ldrs: qcknd to ld appr fnl f: styd on strly* **10/3**1
0-1 **2** *1 ½* **Addictive Dream (IRE)**55 936 3-9-4 **75** .... ShaneKelly 7 81+
(W R Swinburn) *hld up in rr: stdy hdwy over 2f out: rdn and styd on to chse wnr fnl 100yds but a hld* **7/1**
5-04 **3** *½* **Joe Packet**23 1442 3-8-13 **70** .... DavidProbert 11 74
(J G Portman) *mde most tl hdd appr fnl f: styd chsng wnr tl outpcd into 3rd fnl 100yds* **15/2**
-460 **4** *1 ¼* **Silvee**12 1694 3-7-13 **61** oh9 .... AmyBaker(5) 9 61?
(J J Bridger) *mid-div and drvn along fr 1/2-way: hdwy over 1f out: styd on but nvr a threat to ldng trio* **200/1**
231- **5** *1* **Elusive Trader (USA)**239 5977 3-9-4 **75** .... RichardKingscote 5 74+
(R M Beckett) *in rr tl hdwy on ins fr 2f out: styng on whn hmpd over 1f out: kpt on again ins fnl f* **9/1**
1400 **6** *2 ¾* **Nubar Boy**40 1086 3-8-12 **74** ow1 .... RichardEvans(5) 13 62
(P D Evans) *chsd ldrs: rdn and fading whn wnt rt over 1f out* **18/1**
02-2 **7** *4* **Rolling Hills (IRE)**23 1442 3-9-3 **74** .... DaneO'Neill 2 49
(H Candy) *in rr: pushed along 3f out: sme prog fr over 1f out* **9/2**2
4-56 **8** *½* **Avonvalley**18 1546 3-9-1 **72** .... TomMcLaughlin 12 46
(M S Saunders) *chsd ldrs: rdn over 2f out: wknd over 1f out* **28/1**
40-2 **9** *hd* **Fawley Green**7 1842 3-9-1 **72** .... MartinDwyer 8 45
(W R Muir) *pressed ldrs: upsides fr over 3f out tl ins fnl 2f: wknd and wnt rt over 1f out* **13/2**3
62-5 **10** *2* **Feeling Fragile (IRE)**18 1546 3-9-0 **71** .... AndreaAtzeni 1 38
(Pat Eddery) *in rr: sme hdwy u.p whn wnt rt and bmpd 2f out: hung rt over 1f out: nvr in contention* **16/1**
31- **11** *1 ½* **Kingsgate Choice (IRE)**167 7556 3-9-4 **75** .... RobertWinston 10 37+
(J R Best) *t.k.h: stdd towards rr: sme prog whn bmpd 2f out: sn btn* **8/1**
122- **12** *10* **Valmina**153 7707 3-9-3 **74** ....(t) LiamKeniry 14 4
(Andrew Turnell) *pressed ldrs over 3f* **40/1**
-222 **13** *3* **Torres Del Paine**74 744 3-9-2 **73** .... JimmyQuinn 3 —
(J C Fox) *s.i.s: a in rr* **28/1**

1m 13.47s (-1.33) **Going Correction** -0.225s/f (Firm) **13** Ran SP% **120.9**
Speed ratings (Par 99): **99,97,96,94,93 89,84,83,83,80 78,65,61**
toteswingers:1&2:£7.10, 1&3:£6.00, 2&3:£9.60 CSF £26.39 CT £168.20 TOTE £3.10: £1.20, £3.20, £3.10; EX 30.10.
Owner The Early Bath Partnership **Bred** Mount Coote Stud **Trained** East Everleigh, Wilts
■ Stewards' Enquiry : Martin Dwyer two-day ban: careless riding (Jun 3, 6)

FOCUS
A competitive handicap for the class. The fourth is a bit of a concern but overall the form looks sound.

2053 AXMINSTER CARPETS RACING EXCELLENCE APPRENTICE H'CAP (WHIPS SHALL BE CARRIED BUT NOT USED) 6f 212y
5:15 (5:18) (Class 5) (0-70,68) 4-Y-O+ **£3,238** (£963; £481; £240) **Stalls** Centre

Form RPR
4225 **1** **War And Peace (IRE)**6 1875 6-8-12 **66** .... MatthewCosham(5) 10 75
(P D Evans) *trckd ldrs: pushed along to ld fnl 100yds: hld on wl* **4/1**2
0242 **2** *¾* **Gazboolou**15 1625 6-9-2 **65** .... DavidKenny 11 72
(David Pinder) *chsd ldrs: drvn to chal 1f out: kpt on for 2nd cl home but no imp on wnr* **15/2**3
0400 **3** *hd* **Stanley Goodspeed**6 1875 7-9-2 **68** ....(t) HollyHall(3) 13 74
(J W Hills) *hld up towards rr but in tch: stdy hdwy over 1f out: styd on to press for 2nd fnl 100yds but nt rch wnr* **12/1**
000- **4** *½* **Super Frank (IRE)**219 6562 7-8-8 **60** .... NathanAlison(3) 9 65
(J Akehurst) *led: pushed along 2f out: kpt slt ld tl hdd and no ex fnl 100yds* **14/1**
04-2 **5** *1 ½* **Advertise**11 1737 4-8-9 **65** .... HobieGill(7) 4 66+
(A M Balding) *rrd stalls and slowly away: in rr tl hdwy fr 2f out: styd on wl fnl f gng on cl home* **11/4**1
10-0 **6** *¾* **Annes Rocket (IRE)**27 1350 5-8-9 **58** .... RyanClark 12 57
(J C Fox) *slowly away: rcvrd to chse ldrs over 3f out: pressed ldrs 2f out: wknd fnl 120yds* **16/1**
620- **7** *1 ½* **The Name Is Frank**143 7835 5-8-4 **58** ....(t) LewisWalsh(5) 7 53
(Mark Gillard) *t.k.h: pressed ldr: pushed along 2f out: wknd ins fnl f* **22/1**
0010 **8** *hd* **Batchworth Blaise**11 1737 7-8-2 **54** oh1 .... RichardRowe(3) 6 48+
(E A Wheeler) *bdly hmpd s and wl bhd: stl last 2f out: rapid hdwy appr fnl f: fin strly* **25/1**
0-20 **9** *2 ¼* **Eye For The Girls**9 1812 4-8-6 **55** .... CharlesEddery 14 46
(M R Channon) *chsd ldrs: drvn over 2f out: wknd appr fnl f* **20/1**
300- **10** *1 ½* **Frank Street**353 2336 4-9-0 **68** .... BarryAdams(5) 3 52
(Eve Johnson Houghton) *chsd ldrs tl wknd appr fnl f* **20/1**
6503 **11** *1* **Takitwo**11 1737 7-8-0 **54** ....(v) AdamBeschizza(5) 8 35
(P D Cundell) *chsd ldrs: drvn over 2f out: wknd wl over 1f out* **8/1**
213- **12** *5* **It's A Mans World**258 5391 4-8-5 **61** .... KevinLundie(7) 1 29
(P D Evans) *slowly away: a in rr* **10/1**
2410 **13** *2 ¾* **Lopinot (IRE)**17 1585 7-8-10 **64** ....(v) AlexEdwards(5) 2 24
(M R Bosley) *s.i.s: a towards rr* **33/1**
0055 **14** *22* **Tan Bonita (USA)**10 1814 5-8-0 **54** oh9 .... JakePayne(5) 5 —
(R J Smith) *rrd: wnt rt stalls and slowly away: sn plld hrd and chsd ldrs: wknd* **100/1**

1m 27.96s (-1.04) **Going Correction** -0.225s/f (Firm) **14** Ran SP% **120.5**
Speed ratings (Par 103): **96,95,94,94,92 91,90,89,87,85 84,78,75,50**
toteswingers:1&2:£5.00, 1&3:£7.20, 2&3:£14.50 CSF £30.83 CT £270.67 TOTE £4.70: £1.30, £2.00, £2.50; EX 41.60 Place 6 £15.61; Place 5 £8.30.
Owner Shropshire Wolves 3 **Bred** Tower Bloodstock **Trained** Pandy, Monmouths

FOCUS
A handicap for apprentice riders where whips were carried but were not permitted to be used. With something of a blanket finish between the first four the form is worth treating with a degree of caution, although it does appear sound enough.

T/Plt: £22.20 to a £1 stake. Pool: £48,640.59. 1,595.60 winning tickets. T/Qpdt: £6.30 to a £1 stake. Pool: £3,177.72. 373.16 winning tickets. ST

2027 YORK (L-H)
Thursday, May 13

OFFICIAL GOING: Good to firm (8.5)
Wind: Breezy half bhd Weather: Fine and dry

2054 TOTEPOOL FLEXI BETTING H'CAP 5f
1:40 (1:42) (Class 2) (0-100,99) 4-Y-O+ **£12,952** (£3,854; £1,926; £962) **Stalls** Low

Form RPR
003- **1** **Johannes (IRE)**202 6994 7-9-3 **95** .... PaulHanagan 4 106
(R A Fahey) *in tch: pushed along and hdwy 2f out: swtchd rt and rdn over 1f out: chsd ldr ent fnl f: styd on strly to ld last 75yds* **11/1**
1-13 **2** *1* **Jaconet (USA)**54 948 5-9-0 **92** ....(b) PhillipMakin 8 99
(T D Barron) *sn led: rdn clr 2f out: drvn ins fnl f: hdd and nt qckn last 75yds* **11/2**1
00-1 **3** *1 ¼* **Tabaret**12 1688 7-8-9 **90** .... MichaelStainton(3) 16 93
(R M Whitaker) *midfield: hdwy to chse ldrs 2f out: sn rdn and kpt on ins fnl f* **16/1**
00-5 **4** *¾* **River Falcon**39 1099 10-8-7 **85** .... KierenFallon 1 85
(J S Goldie) *towards rr: hdwy wl over 1f out: sn rdn and styd on ins fnl f: nrst fin* **10/1**
00-3 **5** *½* **Judge 'n Jury**27 1353 6-9-7 **99** ....(t) LiamJones 15 97
(R A Harris) *chsd ldrs: rdn along wl over 1f out: drvn and one pce ent fnl f* **14/1**
5424 **6** *½* **Peak District (IRE)**72 761 6-8-2 **85** oh2 .... AmyRyan(5) 2 82
(K A Ryan) *prom on wd outside: rdn over 2f out: sn hung bdly rt: drvn ent fnl f and sn one pce* **14/1**
0-05 **7** *1 ¼* **The Nifty Fox**17 1573 6-8-8 **86** .... DavidAllan 5 78
(T D Easterby) *midfield: rdn along over 2f out: kpt on u.p ins fnl f: nrst fin* **25/1**
33 **8** *nse* **Rebel Duke (IRE)**13 1670 6-8-13 **94** .... BarryMcHugh(3) 14 86
(Ollie Pears) *hld up: hdwy over 1f out: sn rdn and kpt on ins fnl f: neaerest fin* **14/1**
20-0 **9** *1 ¼* **Hamoody (USA)**24 1423 6-8-5 **88** .... BillyCray(5) 9 75+
(D Nicholls) *in tch: rdn along 2f out: hmpd wl over 1f out and one pce after* **25/1**
4-00 **10** *hd* **Swiss Franc**34 1206 5-9-3 **95** .... JamieSpencer 11 82
(D R C Elsworth) *dwlt and hmpd s: bhd: swtchd lft and rdn 1/2-way: hdwy over 1f out: kpt on fnl f: nrst fin* **14/1**
0-00 **11** *1* **Ishetoo**29 1295 6-8-7 **90** .... IanBrennan(5) 10 73
(Ollie Pears) *sn riddn along in rr: sme hdwy u.p over 1f out: n.d* **8/1**3
0-13 **12** *hd* **Le Toreador**48 992 5-9-3 **95** ....(tp) NeilCallan 7 77
(K A Ryan) *prom: rdn along over 2f out: sn hung rt and wknd* **16/1**
3-03 **13** *shd* **Bertoliver**22 1471 6-8-4 **85** oh2 .... WilliamCarson(3) 17 67
(S C Williams) *chsd ldrs on wd outside: hdwy 2f out: sn rdn and edgd lft ent fnl f: sn wknd* **20/1**
3443 **14** *2* **Fol Hollow (IRE)**8 1822 5-9-2 **94** .... AdrianNicholls 6 69
(D Nicholls) *prom: rdn along over 2f out: sn drvn and wknd wl over 1f out* **8/1**3
10-3 **15** *1 ¼* **Russian Spirit**12 1692 4-8-7 **85** oh1 .... PhilipRobinson 13 55+
(M A Jarvis) *wnt lft s: in tch: rdn along whn hmpd wl over 1f out: nt rcvr* **13/2**2
0-00 **16** *1 ¼* **Rievaulx World**22 1471 4-8-11 **89** ....(b1) DarryllHolland 12 55
(K A Ryan) *hmpd s: a bhd* **20/1**

57.85 secs (-1.45) **Going Correction** -0.05s/f (Good) **16** Ran SP% **124.0**
Speed ratings (Par 109): **109,107,105,104,103 102,100,100,98,98 96,96,96,92,90 88**
toteswingers:1&2:£11.00, 1&3:£68.50, 2&3:£40.90 CSF £67.60 CT £1025.51 TOTE £11.30: £2.60, £1.80, £5.40, £3.00; EX 76.10 TRIFECTA Not won..
Owner John Nicholls Ltd/David Kilburn **Bred** Blue Bloodstock Limited **Trained** Musley Bank, N Yorks

FOCUS
Following a dry night the ground remained good to firm. Rail movement meant that the distances of races of over 1m1f were reduced by 27yds. A typically competitive York sprint handicap and they went a furious pace thanks to the runner-up. The winner looks better than ever and the form is rated around the third.

NOTEBOOK
Johannes(IRE), having his first start since October but successful on his reappearance last year, was racing over the minimum trip for the first time in 18 months and the strong pace played right into his hands. He travelled well behind the leaders and produced a decent turn of foot to catch the pace-setter well inside the last furlong. He was 6lb above his last winning mark, so seems to be as good as ever, and the Wokingham and Stewards' Cup (he won the consolation race last year) are now possibilities. (op 12-1)
Jaconet(USA) was a revelation over 6f on Polytrack last summer, but her previous turf successes have come at a much lower level than this. Given her usual attacking ride, she was soon in a clear lead and had most of her rivals in trouble, but the winner cut her down late. Given her blinding speed, the Dash on Derby Day could be an interesting option. (op 8-1)
Tabaret, 4lb higher than when ending a long losing run at Doncaster on his reappearance earlier this month, ran another solid race and was staying on well at the line. (op 14-1)
River Falcon, a three-time winner over C&D and appearing at the track for the 22nd time, hasn't been at his best for a while but he ran his usual sort of race, getting outpaced earlier before finishing in great style. That is often the way with him these days. (op 11-1 tchd 12-1 in a place)
Judge 'n Jury, all the better for his encouraging Newbury return, likes to be up there and, having raced prominently, kept on trying all the way to the line. (op 12-1)
Peak District(IRE), kept busy on sand during the winter, was drawn towards the far side but hung right as he stayed on under pressure in the closing stages. This was a good effort back on turf, but he isn't easy to win with. (op 16-1)
The Nifty Fox stayed on in the latter stages, but has gained all seven of his wins on good or softer ground.
Rebel Duke(IRE), who has gained five of his six wins on the AW, was well backed but he didn't get into gear until it was too late. He remains 8lb above his last winning mark.
Swiss Franc Official explanation: jockey said gelding suffered interference leaving stalls
Russian Spirit, together with Hamoody, tried to go for the same gap as the winner over a furlong out, but they both lost out and suffered serious interference as they did so. Russian Spirit was eased right off and this is best ignored. Official explanation: jockey said filly was unsuited by the good to firm ground (op 5-1)

Rievaulx World Official explanation: jockey said gelding suffered interference leaving stalls

2055 TOTESPORT.COM MIDDLETON STKS (GROUP 2) (F&M) 1m 2f 88y
2:10 (2:10) (Class 1) 4-Y-O+ **£56,770** (£21,520; £10,770; £5,370) **Stalls** Low

Form RPR

123- **1** **Sariska**[208] 6850 4-8-12 118 JamieSpencer 4 118+
(M L W Bell) *mde all: qcknd 3f out: pushed clr 2f out: shkn up ins fnl f and kpt on* **10/11**[1]

131- **2** *1 ¾* **Midday**[188] 7284 4-9-3 120 EddieAhern 1 119
(H R A Cecil) *hld up in tch: hdwy on inner 1/2-way: pushed along wl over 3f out: rdn and outpcd over 2f out: styd on wl u.p ent fnl f:* **15/8**[2]

116- **3** *2 ¼* **Flying Cloud (IRE)**[200] 7046 4-8-12 109 (t) FrankieDettori 3 110
(Saeed Bin Suroor) *trckd ldng pair: hdwy to chser wnr over 3f out: rdn along 2f out: drvn and one pce ent fnl f* **6/1**[3]

0-42 **4** *21* **Honimiere (IRE)**[11] 1725 4-8-12 94 NeilCallan 5 70
(G A Swinbank) *trckd wnr: rdn along 4f out: wknd 3f out: bhd and eased fnl 2f* **16/1**

2m 6.20s (-6.30) **Going Correction** -0.275s/f (Firm) course record **4** Ran SP% **107.3**
Speed ratings (Par 115): **114,112,110,94**
CSF £2.82 TOTE £1.80; EX 2.30.

Owner Lady Bamford **Bred** Lady Bamford **Trained** Newmarket, Suffolk

■ Stewards' Enquiry : Eddie Ahern two-day ban: used whip with excessive frequency without giving filly time to respond (May 27-28)

FOCUS
Last year's running of this race provided a thrilling finish between Crystal Capella and Dar Re Mi and this also promised to be a real feast, with the contest promoted to Group 2 status for the first time. Despite the small field, this was a race for the connoisseur, featuring as it did the winners of last year's English and Irish Oaks, Nassau, Breeders' Cup Filly & Mare Turf, Ribblesdale and Musidora. Sariska made all at a good pace and her form is rated in line with her fast-ground efforts.

NOTEBOOK
Sariska was the star 3-y-o middle-distance filly of last season with wins in the English and Irish Oaks and Musidora, and then lost little in defeat when subsequently placed in the Yorkshire Oaks and Champion Stakes. She missed her intended comeback in the Dahlia Stakes due to a pricked foot, but the conditions of this race meant she avoided a penalty and the only real question was how she would cope with this quick ground. In fact her participation was in doubt until the last minute after her trainer had walked the track, but she was allowed to take her chance. Soon sent into the lead by Jamie Spencer, she set a good pace and, having gradually wound up the tempo, was kicked into a clear lead coming to the last 2f. She looked likely to win easily at that stage, but then got tired and she didn't have that much to spare at the line, though she never looked like getting caught. This outing should have done her the power of good and she will now head for the Coronation Cup. All being well, her long-term target is the Arc. (op Evens tchd 11-10)

Midday, behind Sariska in both the English and Irish Oaks, went on to gain success at the highest level at Goodwood and Santa Anita, but the conditions of this race meant that she had to carry a 5lb penalty for those victories whilst her old rival didn't. She had apparently proved that she can cope with any ground, but this performance raised a few questions. Held up in last, she didn't look very happy in the early stages as she held her head high, and then started to carry it to one side when coming off the bridle turning into the straight. She looked sure to be well beaten, but to her credit her class kicked in and she stayed on strongly up the inside rail over the last furlong or so and wasn't beaten far at the line. Technically, because of her penalty she comes out almost the same filly as Sariska, but connections believed that she hated the ground, so it will be interesting to see how she performs in her next outing. (tchd 7-4 and 2-1)

Flying Cloud(IRE), an ex-Andre Fabre inmate who made a successful debut for Godolphin in last season's Ribblesdale, was rather disappointing in a Group 1 at Capannelle in her only subsequent start. Sporting a first-time tongue tie here, her connections had warned that she might need the race having had a setback in Dubai, so they must have been pleased with this effort as she looked the one most likely to finish closest to Sariska when she made an effort passing the 3f pole. There should be plenty of opportunities for her to win another Group race at home or abroad this season. (tchd 11-2)

Honimiere(IRE), whose improved effort in the Dahlia Stakes at Newmarket 11 days earlier appeared to be mainly down to a track bias, was totally outclassed over the last half-mile. (tchd 20-1)

2056 TOTESPORT DANTE STKS (GROUP 2) 1m 2f 88y
2:40 (2:41) (Class 1) 3-Y-O **£85,155** (£32,280; £16,155; £8,055; £4,035) **Stalls** Low

Form RPR

11- **1** **Cape Blanco (IRE)**[264] 5275 3-9-0 110 JMurtagh 1 120+
(A P O'Brien, Ire) *trckd ldng pair: hdwy over 3f out: chal 2f out and sn led: rdn clr ent fnl f: styd on* **9/2**

1- **2** *3 ¼* **Workforce**[232] 6199 3-9-0 0 RyanMoore 5 114+
(Sir Michael Stoute) *hld up towards rr: effrt over 4f out: pushed along: hanging lft over 3f out and bit wnt through mouth: rdn and hdwy whn hung lft 2f out: sn drvn and kpt on ins fnl f to take 2nd last 100yds* **2/1**[2]

10-1 **3** *¾* **Coordinated Cut (IRE)**[29] 1310 3-9-0 107 JamieSpencer 2 112
(M L W Bell) *trckd ldr: hdwy over 4f out: led over 3f out: rdn and jnd 2f out: sn hdd and drvn: one pce ent fnl f* **4/1**[3]

20-1 **4** *16* **Chabal (IRE)**[20] 1498 3-9-0 115 (t) FrankieDettori 4 80
(Saeed Bin Suroor) *hld up in rr: hdwy over 4f out: rdn along over 3f out: wknd wl over 2f out: and sn eased* **7/4**[1]

12-3 **5** *11* **Circumvent**[18] 1567 3-9-0 103 PaulHanagan 3 58
(P F I Cole) *set even gallop: rdn along 4f out: hdd over 3f out: wkng whn hmpd 2f out* **22/1**

2m 6.70s (-5.80) **Going Correction** -0.275s/f (Firm) **5** Ran SP% **112.2**
Speed ratings (Par 111): **112,109,108,96,87**
CSF £14.20 TOTE £5.10: £1.80, £1.90; EX 16.40.

Owner D Smith, Mrs J Magnier, M Tabor **Bred** Jack Ronan & Des Vere Hunt Far **Trained** Ballydoyle, Co Tipperary

FOCUS
Named after the 1945 Derby winner, the Dante has been run since 1958 and in that time nine winners have gone on to win the Derby, the most recent being Authorized in 2007. All bar Circumvent in this field are entered for Epsom and, while this was the smallest field for the race since Sakhee also beat four rivals in the 2000 running, the class of the field looked well up to par with three of the five runners having already been successful at Group level. Thankfully, despite the small field the pace set by the outsider Circumvent was solid and the winning time was only half a second slower than Sariska in the preceding contest, which suggests the form is strong. The form is rated around the third and Cape Blanco rates the main form challenger to stablemate St Nicholas Abbey in the Derby.

NOTEBOOK
Cape Blanco(IRE), unbeaten in three starts at two including in the Group 2 Futurity Stakes at Fairyhouse on his final start, was unproven on ground faster than good though his connections believed he wouldn't have a problem with these conditions. This extra 3f wasn't expected to be a problem for the son of Galileo either, even though he is out of a mare who only ran once beyond 5f in 25 starts. A slight setback at the weekend wasn't thought to be of any significance and he put up a performance of real class. Settled in third early, he was brought to make his effort out in the centre of the track once into the straight and produced a smart turn of foot to hit the front over a furlong out and win going away. He did appear to be lame after the race, but connections played down any problems and the assumption was that he may have banged himself on the same spot on his heel that he had nicked at the weekend. He was immediately cut to a top-priced 6-1 for the Derby and his rider believes that he has all the right attributes for Epsom, though the stable still have other possibilities for that race, not least the favourite St Nicholas Abbey and Midas Touch, but provided he remains in one piece he has earned his place in the line up, even though the dam's side of his pedigree will still give some cause for concern over his stamina. (op 4-1 tchd 5-1)

Workforce came into this as second-favourite for the Derby on account of his hugely impressive 6l win in a Goodwood maiden in his only previous start last September, a race that has since worked out extremely well. There is plenty in the dam's side of his pedigree which suggested this extra 3f would be well within his compass and though he has been slow to come to hand, his recent homework had been better. However, things didn't seem too bright when he came under pressure at the back of the field turning in and he showed a very awkward head-carriage, but he eventually ran on and was staying on well at the line. It transpired that he had pulled the bit through his mouth, which explains him hanging, and connections had made no secret of the fact that they didn't want the ground too quick, so all in all this wasn't a bad effort at all. Described as "still a big baby" by connections, he remains a colt of real potential for later on when he gets his conditions. His Derby odds lengthened to a top-priced 10-1 and of course if he turns up he will have to overturn the old chestnut that no horse beaten in the Dante has ever won the Derby. (op 5-2 tchd 11-4 in a place)

Coordinated Cut(IRE) was a narrow winner of the Tattersalls Timeform 3-y-o Trophy at Newmarket last month on his debut for the yard, but no winners have yet come out of that race. Having tracked the leader early, he took over passing the 3f pole and hung in there until headed by the winner over a furlong from home. He doesn't look a Derby contender on this performance and the King Edward VII may be an option. (tchd 9-2)

Chabal(IRE) was the big disappointment of the race, especially as his victory in the Sandown Classic Trial on his debut for Godolphin was given a boost when the runner-up Azmeel went on to take the Dee Stakes at Chester last Friday. Held up last in the early stages, his rider was at him fully half a mile from home and he found absolutely nothing. This was too bad to be true and his rider was at a loss to explain it, but it may be that he is at his best when caught fresh. Official explanation: trainer had no explanation for the poor form shown (op 15-8 tchd 2-1 in places)

Circumvent was having his first run in Britain since winning a four-runner novice event at Leicester last September, having run with plenty of credit in three French Group 3s in the meantime. He set the early fractions, but had nothing left when losing the advantage 3f from home and was allowed to come home in his own time. (op 20-1)

2057 TOTESPORT 0800 221 221 HAMBLETON H'CAP (LISTED RACE) 1m
3:10 (3:10) (Class 1) (0-110,108) 4-Y-O+ **£23,704** (£8,964; £4,480; £2,240) **Stalls** Low

Form RPR

51-0 **1** **Fareer**[19] 1531 4-9-1 102 RichardHills 4 112
(E A L Dunlop) *mde all: rdn 2f out: drvn ins fnl f: kpt on gamely towards fin* **11/2**[2]

111- **2** *hd* **Rainbow Peak (IRE)**[201] 7035 4-9-2 103 NeilCallan 13 112+
(M A Jarvis) *hld up towards rr: hdwy on outer 3f out: rdn to chse ldrs over 1f out: drvn and kpt on ins fnl f:* **7/2**[1]

5363 **3** *hd* **Balcarce Nov (ARG)**[12] 1708 5-8-13 100 JamieSpencer 12 109
(T P Tate) *trckd wnr: hdwy 3f out: rdn over 1f out: chal ent fnl f and ev ch tl drvn and nt qckn last 50yds* **13/2**[3]

163- **4** *3* **Acrostic**[266] 5200 5-9-2 103 KierenFallon 1 105
(L M Cumani) *trckd ldrs on inner: effrt 3f out: rdn 2f out: sn drvn and kpt on same pce ent fnl f* **7/2**[1]

00-0 **5** *hd* **Docofthebay (IRE)**[12] 1708 6-8-7 94 FrederikTylicki 6 96
(J A Glover) *towards rr: pushed along over 3f out: rdn 2f out: kpt on ins fnl f: nrst fin* **12/1**

1-00 **6** *1 ¼* **Collateral Damage (IRE)**[12] 1708 7-8-8 95 (t) DavidAllan 9 94
(T D Easterby) *trckd ldrs: hdwy 3f out: rdn wl over 1f out: edgd lft and wknd ent fnl f* **16/1**

4-11 **7** *1 ¼* **Spirit Of Sharjah (IRE)**[19] 1519 5-9-1 102 MichaelHills 3 98
(Miss J Feilden) *hld up in tch: hdwy over 2f out: rdn and n.m.r wl over 1f out: sn no imp* **14/1**

4-53 **8** *nse* **Pachattack (USA)**[13] 1665 4-9-0 101 (b) RyanMoore 5 97
(G A Butler) *a in midfield* **14/1**

10-0 **9** *1* **Wannabe King**[26] 1383 4-9-2 103 (p) TedDurcan 7 96
(D R Lanigan) *trckd ldng pair: effrt over 3f out: rdn over 2f out: drvn and wkng whn hmpd ent fnl f* **11/2**[2]

00-0 **10** *31* **Isabella Grey**[41] 1081 4-8-7 94 oh2 AdrianNicholls 11 16
(K A Ryan) *a in rr: outpcd and bhd fnl 3f* **66/1**

1m 36.42s (-2.38) **Going Correction** -0.05s/f (Good) **10** Ran SP% **116.9**
Speed ratings (Par 111): **109,108,108,105,105 104,102,102,101,70**
toteswingers:1&2:£5.20, 1&3:£7.00, 2&3:£5.70 CSF £25.16 CT £132.08 TOTE £6.60: £2.10, £1.70, £2.30; EX 22.50 Trifecta £113.50 Pool: £1,297.34 - 8.45 winning units..

Owner Hamdan Al Maktoum **Bred** Bishopswood Bloodstock & Trickledown Stud **Trained** Newmarket, Suffolk

FOCUS
A high-quality handicap but the early pace was modest and it paid to be up there. Still form to be positive about with the third a solid guide.

NOTEBOOK
Fareer raced too keenly when in need of the outing on his reappearance in a Group 2 at Sandown, and this represented a drop in class for him. He bounced out of the gates, found himself in front and was allowed to dictate an ordinary pace to suit himself. Winding things up in the straight, he always had things under control, and got home without being subjected to a hard race. The Hunt Cup will be considered, but another option is to step him back up to Group company for the Diomed at Epsom on Derby day. (op 6-1)

Rainbow Peak(IRE) ran a cracker in defeat considering the way the race unfolded. Held up off the pace in a race dominated by those who raced prominently, he stayed on really well to be beaten only narrowly, and clearly he remains a very progressive gelding. Easier ground will no doubt suit him better, and connections clearly hold him in some regard as they are now thinking about stepping him into Group company, with the Brigadier Gerard Stakes being seriously considered. (op 3-1 tchd 4-1)

Balcarce Nov(ARG), third off the same mark in the Thirsk Hunt Cup last time out, got away on terms and chased the leader throughout, so was well positioned in a race lacking pace. He had every chance and no excuse.

Acrostic is a confirmed hold-up performer but raced closer to the pace than normal. Given the way the race was run that was a good thing, but he was still a bit keen, would have appreciated a stronger gallop, and is entitled to come on for this seasonal reappearance. (op 5-1)

Docofthebay(IRE) is another who needs the leaders to set a good gallop for him as he likes to stay on past horses. He finished quite well once switched, but this race didn't play to his strengths. He's on a decent mark, though, and is one to bear in mind for the big summer cavalry charges, especially the Hunt Cup, in which he was second in 2008 off a mark of 103. (op 14-1)

Collateral Damage(IRE) enjoyed a successful time of it last season but now looks held by the handicapper. Official explanation: jockey said gelding hung left

Spirit Of Sharjah(IRE) is most effective over shorter than this, having recorded his last three wins over 7f. Official explanation: jockey said gelding was unsuited by the good to firm ground

Pachattack(USA) is not an easy filly to place. Dropping back in distance from 1m2f, it goes without saying that a stronger pace would have suited her better. (tchd 16-1)

Wannabe King, who didn't enjoy much luck in running in the Spring Cup at Newbury, was a bit disappointing considering he raced in behind the speed. He's another who now faces a challenge off a three-figure mark, though. (tchd 6-1 in a place)

2058 EUROPEAN BREEDERS' FUND CONDITIONS STKS — 5f

3:45 (3:48) (Class 2) 3-Y-O — **£12,952** (£3,854; £1,926; £962) Stalls Low

Form — RPR

04-0 **1** **Rose Blossom**[5] 1918 3-8-11 99 .... PaulHanagan 3 — 98
(R A Fahey) *mde all: rdn and qcknd ent fnl f: r.o strly* **8/1**

12-2 **2** *1 1/4* **Midnight Martini**[19] 1523 3-9-0 94 .... DavidAllan 4 — 97
(T D Easterby) *cl up: effrt wl over 1f out: sn rdn and ev ch tl nt qckn wl ins fnl f* **3/1**[1]

6-14 **3** *1/2* **Duchess Dora (IRE)**[6] 1860 3-8-11 97 .... JMurtagh 6 — 92+
(J J Quinn) *trckd ldrs: effrt and nt clr run wl over 1f out: swtchd rt and rdn ent fnl f: kpt on* **9/2**[3]

13-4 **4** *3/4* **Tomintoul Singer (IRE)**[18] 1545 3-8-11 96 .... FrankieDettori 7 — 89
(H R A Cecil) *dwlt: sn chsng ldrs: rdn over 1f out: kpt on same pce fnl f* **4/1**[2]

114- **5** *nk* **Living It Large (FR)**[168] 7536 3-9-2 89 .... TonyHamilton 2 — 93
(R F Fisher) *cl up: rdn 2f out and ev ch: drvn over 1f out and kpt on same pce* **33/1**

0- **6** *2 3/4* **Secret Millionaire (IRE)**[222] 6486 3-9-2 90 .... StephenCraine 8 — 83
(Patrick Morris) *cl up on outer: effrt 2f out: ev ch tl rdn and wknd ent fnl f* **28/1**

-562 **7** *3* **Fratellino**[20] 1499 3-9-2 98 .... JamesDoyle 1 — 72
(A J McCabe) *chsd ldrs: rdn along after 2f: sn lost pl and bhd* **11/2**

055- **8** *1 1/4* **Tawaabb**[215] 6660 3-9-2 101 .... KierenFallon 9 — 68
(M R Channon) *wnt rt s: in tch: rdn along 1/2-way and sn outpcd* **11/2**

9 *3* **Ejteyaaz**[299] 4106 3-9-2 0 .... BarryMcHugh 5 — 57
(R A Fahey) *sn outpcd and a bhd* **22/1**

57.98 secs (-1.32) **Going Correction** -0.05s/f (Good) — 9 Ran SP% **115.8**
Speed ratings (Par 105): **108,106,105,104,103 99,94,92,87**
toteswingers:1&2:£7.10, 1&3:£9.20, 2&3:£3.10 CSF £31.72 TOTE £10.30: £2.50, £1.40, £2.10; EX 36.30 Trifecta £168.10 Pool: £1,118.13 - 4.92 winning units..
Owner Highclere Thoroughbred Racing (Blossom) **Bred** J R Mitchell **Trained** Musley Bank, N Yorks

FOCUS

A decent conditions' sprint and there was no hanging about. This was one for the girls as the four fillies filled the first four places. The winner looks better than ever.

NOTEBOOK

Rose Blossom, joint best-in at the weights but disappointing when last of 13 in a 6f Listed event at Nottingham on her reappearance five days earlier, was a totally different proposition back on this quicker ground. Quick from the stalls, she made all the running and refused to give in when challenged. She looks well worth another try in Pattern company and will head for the Ballyhogan Stakes at Leopardstown on June 10th. (op 7-1)

Midnight Martini, winner of the ultra-valuable sales race at the Ebor meeting, chased home a subsequent winner in a Ripon handicap on her return to action. Always in about the same place, she tried her hardest but could never quite get to the pace-setter. She was 6lb badly in with the winner, so has at least run up to her mark. (op 7-2)

Duchess Dora(IRE), the other joint best-in at the weights alongside the winner and just ahead of Fratellino on her Sandown reappearance, didn't seem suited to Chester six days earlier but seemed happier here. Having tracked the leaders, she was staying on at the line and probably prefers a stiffer track. (op 4-1)

Tomintoul Singer(IRE), who didn't get the best of runs when fourth in a Bath Listed race on her reappearance, had her ideal conditions but could only plug on under pressure and there seemed no real excuses. (op 11-2)

Living It Large(FR) had plenty to find on these terms but he showed good speed for a long way and is entitled to come on for this first start since November. (op 28-1)

Secret Millionaire(IRE), having his first start since October, also had plenty to find at the weights but, having travelled well, he didn't find an awful lot off the bridle. (tchd 33-1)

Fratellino never looked happy and was hanging all over the place after halfway. Official explanation: jockey said colt missed the break (op 7-1)

Tawaabb, another having his first start since October, proved awkward to load and didn't show a lot of enthusiasm once under way. Official explanation: jockey said colt was unsuited by the good to firm ground (tchd 5-1)

2059 STRATFORD PLACE STUD FOR ROYAL ASCOT 2YOS EBF MAIDEN STKS — 6f

4:20 (4:20) (Class 3) 2-Y-O — **£7,123** (£2,119; £1,059; £529) Stalls Low

Form — RPR

1 **Elzaam (AUS)** 2-9-3 0 .... RichardHills 6 — 92+
(M A Jarvis) *mde all: styd on strly fnl 2f: pushed out: readily* **2/1**[1]

2 *1 1/4* **Sir Reginald** 2-9-3 0 .... PaulHanagan 12 — 88+
(R A Fahey) *hmpd s: trckd ldrs: wnt cl 2nd over 2f out: kpt on wl ins fnl f* **9/1**

3 *2* **Rerouted (USA)** 2-9-3 0 .... MichaelHills 1 — 82+
(B W Hills) *dwlt: sn chsng ldrs: kpt on same pce appr fnl f* **6/1**[3]

6 **4** *2 1/4* **Rojo Boy**[27] 1351 2-9-3 0 .... JimmyFortune 17 — 76
(A M Balding) *chsd ldrs towards stands' side: styd on same pce fnl 2f* **20/1**

5 *5* **Jibaal (IRE)** 2-9-3 0 .... JoeFanning 8 — 61
(M Johnston) *chsd ldrs: drvn and outpcd 3f out: kpt on fnl f* **18/1**

6 *3 1/2* **Tinkertown (IRE)** 2-9-3 0 .... JamieSpencer 2 — 50+
(P F I Cole) *chsd ldrs far side: hung bdly rt and lost pl over 2f out: kpt on fnl f* **12/1**

7 *1/2* **Juliet Capulet (IRE)**[26] 1405 2-8-12 0 .... JMurtagh 14 — 44
(A P O'Brien, Ire) *chsd ldrs: wknd over 1f out* **5/1**[2]

8 *1/2* **Mariachi Man** 2-9-3 0 .... DavidAllan 9 — 48+
(T D Easterby) *s.v.s: green and hung lft over 2f out: styd on over 1f out: will improve* **50/1**

0 **9** *1/2* **Bonjour Bongee**[12] 1686 2-9-3 0 .... JamesDoyle 11 — 46
(A J McCabe) *in rr: kpt on fnl 2f: nvr nr ldrs* **100/1**

4 **10** *1* **Comrade Bond**[16] 1603 2-9-3 0 .... DarryllHolland 15 — 43
(M H Tompkins) *chsd ldrs: wknd 2f out* **18/1**

11 *3/4* **Move In Time** 2-9-3 0 .... TomEaves 7 — 40
(B Smart) *s.i.s: hdwy and hung lft over 2f out: nvr on terms* **33/1**

12 *1* **Market Maker (IRE)** 2-9-3 0 .... GrahamGibbons 3 — 37
(T D Easterby) *dwlt: mid-div: lost pl over 2f out* **66/1**

6 **13** *1/2* **Dreamweaving (IRE)**[28] 1331 2-8-12 0 .... SilvestreDeSousa 4 — 31
(N Tinkler) *chsd ldrs: lost pl over 2f out* **25/1**

14 *4* **Windward Islands** 2-9-3 0 .... FrankieDettori 5 — 24
(Mahmood Al Zarooni) *chsd ldrs: lost pl over 1f out* **9/1**

5 **15** *9* **Scatty (IRE)**[18] 1541 2-9-3 0 .... StephenCraine 10 — —
(S Kirk) *sn drvn along in rr: bhd fnl 3f* **28/1**

16 *18* **Little Oddy (IRE)** 2-9-0 0 .... AndrewHeffernan(3) 13 — —
(M A Barnes) *s.i.s: reminders after s: sn wl bhd: t.o* **100/1**

1m 11.43s (-0.47) **Going Correction** -0.05s/f (Good) — 16 Ran SP% **122.9**
Speed ratings (Par 97): **101,99,96,93,87 82,81,81,80,79 78,76,76,70,58 34**
toteswingers:1&2:£8.60, 1&3:£4.40, 2&3:£13.20 CSF £19.18 TOTE £3.10: £1.40, £3.20, £2.60; EX 27.50 Trifecta £121.20 Pool: £556.93 - 3.40 winning units..
Owner Hamdan Al Maktoum **Bred** Kia Ora Stud **Trained** Newmarket, Suffolk

FOCUS

This was one of the best juvenile maidens of the year so far and the front four came right away. The winner made all on a day front runners were favoured but this was still a very nice start.

NOTEBOOK

Elzaam(AUS), a 280,000euros half-brother to two winners in Australia, was all the rage in the market and the vibes were proved right. Quickly away, he proved very professional and kept on finding more than enough to stay in front when challenged. He looks a very nice prospect and the Coventry Stakes is now on the agenda. (tchd 5-1 in places)

Sir Reginald, a 75,000gns half-brother to four winners including the smart Henrik, raced keenly enough in a handy position but he never stopped trying and just ran into a nice prospect. He will be hard to beat next time. (tchd 12-1 in a place)

Rerouted(USA) took a while to realise what was required but finished his race off in pleasing style and this half-brother to three winners including the smart Critical Moment will win races. (tchd 8-1 in a place)

Rojo Boy, too green to do himself justice on his Newbury debut, again came off the bridle a fair way out but he kept on well to pull clear of the rest. Admittedly he had the benefit of a previous run compared to the front trio, but he still looked to need it and shouldn't take long in getting off the mark. (op 18-1)

Jibaal(IRE), a £62,000 half-brother to a winning juvenile sprinter and in the same ownership as the winner, showed enough on this debut to suggest he has a future. (op 20-1)

Tinkertown(IRE), a 55,000euros colt whose dam is from the family of the Irish 1,000 Guineas winner Arctique Royale, represented last year's winning stable and ran a strange debut. Prominent early, he looked likely to drop out at halfway but, despite hanging all over the track, he stayed on again to finish fifth at a respectful distance. Plenty of improvement can be expected.

Juliet Capulet(IRE), fourth of seven in a decent Naas maiden on debut, is bred to appreciate this extra furlong and travelled like a good horse before fading. She still looks capable of better. (tchd 9-2)

Mariachi Man, a 7,500gns half-brother to three winners at up to 1m2f, made an eyecatching debut. Very slow from the stalls, he gave his rivals a start but was noted staying on late in the day without being knocked about. He seems sure to step up a good deal from this in due course. (op 66-1)

2060 INVESTEC H'CAP — 2m 2f

4:55 (4:55) (Class 4) (0-80,79) 4-Y-O+ — **£6,540** (£1,946; £972; £485) Stalls Low

Form — RPR

400- **1** **Hollins**[28] 6681 6-9-4 70 .... FrederikTylicki 11 — 85+
(Micky Hammond) *hld up in midfield: stdy hdwy over 5f out: chsd ldrs over 3f out: led 2f out: rdn clr ent fnl f: styd on strly* **9/1**

500- **2** *6* **Smugglers Bay (IRE)**[12] 2315 6-8-11 63 .... (b) DarryllHolland 18 — 69
(T D Easterby) *hld up and bhd: stdy hdwy 4f out: swtchd rt and rdn along 2f out: styd on strly ins fnl f* **20/1**

25-3 **3** *nse* **King In Waiting (IRE)**[24] 1424 7-8-8 60 oh1 .... (t) JamieSpencer 5 — 67+
(J Hetherton) *trckd ldrs: hdwy 4f out: rdn along over 2f out: styng on whn nt clr run and hmpd ins fnl f: sn swtchd lft and drvn: kpt on: fin 4th, 6l, nk, nse: plcd 3rd* **15/2**[3]

1-43 **4** *nk* **Royal Trooper (IRE)**[12] 1689 4-9-2 72 .... PaulMulrennan 14 — 78
(J G Given) *chsd ldrs: hdwy 5f out: cl up 3f out: rdn 2f out: drvn and one pce whn swtchd rt ins fnl f: kpt on: fin 3rd, 6l, nk: disq and plcd 4th* **10/1**

1511 **5** *3/4* **Jeer (IRE)**[43] 1062 6-9-13 79 .... (b) GrahamGibbons 6 — 84
(M W Easterby) *hld up in tch: hdwy 5f out: led 3f out: rdn and hdd 2f out: drvn and edgd lft ins fnl f: wknd* **12/1**

0404 **6** *2* **Strikemaster (IRE)**[5] 1916 4-8-9 65 .... (b) TomEaves 4 — 68
(B Ellison) *towards rr and sn pushed along: hdwy 5f out: chsd ldrs over 2f out: sn drvn and one pce* **14/1**

61-2 **7** *nk* **Twist Again (IRE)**[12] 1689 4-9-6 76 .... KierenFallon 9 — 79
(P Howling) *hld up in midfield: swtchd outside and hdwy over 3f out: rdn wl over 2f out: drvn and wknd fnl f* **3/1**[1]

15-6 **8** *1* **Hi Dancer**[7] 910 7-8-8 65 .... AmyRyan(5) 13 — 67
(B M R Haslam) *towards rr: effrt on inner 3f out and sn rdn along: kpt on appr fnl f: nvr nr ldrs* **10/1**

25-4 **9** *4 1/2* **Proud Times (USA)**[11] 1720 4-9-6 76 .... PJMcDonald 16 — 73
(G A Swinbank) *trckd ldrs: hdwy 6f out: led briefly over 3f out: sn rdn and hdd 3f out: grad wknd fnl 2f* **6/1**[2]

21-0 **10** *2* **Mudawin (IRE)**[19] 1525 9-9-11 77 .... PhillipMakin 12 — 71
(James Moffatt) *hld up: a in rr* **16/1**

3012 **11** *14* **Dan Buoy (FR)**[24] 1424 7-8-9 66 .... (b) BillyCray(5) 15 — 45
(R C Guest) *sn led and clr: rdn along over 5f out: hdd wl over 3f out and sn wknd* **9/1**

100/ **12** *7* **Strobe**[85] 2135 6-9-4 73 .... BarryMcHugh(3) 1 — 44
(Mrs L B Normile) *chsd ldng pair: rdn along 5f out and sn wknd* **33/1**

0202 **13** *8* **Oddsmaker (IRE)**[13] 1671 9-8-12 67 .... (t) AndrewHeffernan(3) 3 — 30
(M A Barnes) *plld hrd: chsd clr ldr: hdwy and cl up 6f out: rdn along 4f out: sn wknd* **16/1**

3m 53.94s (-4.46) **Going Correction** -0.275s/f (Firm)
WFA 4 from 6yo+ 4lb — 13 Ran SP% **123.1**
Speed ratings (Par 105): **98,95,95,95,94 93,93,93,91,90 84,81,77**
toteswingers:1&2:£43.90, 1&4:£11.70, 2&4:£36.90 CSF £181.25 CT £1433.24 TOTE £11.40: £3.70, £6.50, £6.50; EX 280.60 Trifecta £525.40 Part won. Pool: £710.05 - 0.20 winning units. Place 6 £39.48; Place 5 £13.65.
Owner R D Bickenson **Bred** Bricklow Ltd And Hyperion Stud Ltd **Trained** Middleham Moor, N Yorks

■ Stewards' Enquiry : Paul Mulrennan four-day ban: careless riding (May 27-30)

FOCUS

Despite the five non-runners this was still a decent staying handicap. The bulk of the field were inclined to ignore the suicidal early pace set by Dan Buoy and Oddsmaker and it was no surprise that both eventually dropped right out. Improvement from the winner but the form seems sound.

Twist Again(IRE) Official explanation: jockey said filly was unsuited by the good to firm ground

T/Jkpt: £75,460.10 to a £1 stake. Pool: £106,281.96. 1 winning ticket. T/Plt: £86.80 to a £1 stake. Pool: £200,5293.45. 1,684.88 winning tickets. T/Qpdt: £15.40 to a £1 stake. Pool: £8,009.89. 383.58 winning tickets. JR

2061 - 2067a (Foreign Racing) - See Raceform Interactive

1864 HAMILTON (R-H)

Friday, May 14

OFFICIAL GOING: Good (good to firm in places on loop; 9.4)

Wind: Almost nil Weather: Overcast

2068 EUROPEAN BREEDERS' FUND MAIDEN STKS 5f 4y

6:20 (6:20) (Class 5) 2-Y-O **£3,885** (£1,156; £577; £288) **Stalls** Low

Form RPR

5 **1** **Boundless Spirit**[28] 1359 2-9-3 0 PaulMulrennan 1 81+
(B Smart) *t.k.h: mde all: rdn and edgd rt 2f out: kpt on strly fnl f* **11/10**[1]

2 *1 ¾* **Lexi's Hero (IRE)** 2-9-0 0 TonyHamilton 4 72+
(K A Ryan) *s.i.s: rn green in rr: hdwy and drifted rt over 1f out: chsd wnr ins fnl f: r.o* **7/2**[3]

0 **3** *2 ½* **Hi Ho Ron**[13] 1686 2-9-3 0 RobertWinston 3 64
(D H Brown) *t.k.h: prom: effrt over 2f out: one pce fnl f* **14/1**

4 *¾* **Night Singer** 2-9-0 0 FrederikTylicki 2 58
(J Howard Johnson) *chsd ldrs: effrt over 2f out: edgd rt over 1f out: no ex fnl f* **9/1**

3 **5** *5* **Kassaab**[14] 1668 2-9-0 0 MartinLane(3) 5 43
(N Wilson) *trckd wnr: rdn 2f out: wknd ins fnl f* **3/1**[2]

61.54 secs (1.54) **Going Correction** +0.225s/f (Good) 5 Ran SP% 111.5
Speed ratings (Par 93): **96,93,89,88,80**
CSF £5.37 TOTE £2.30: £1.10, £1.50; EX 5.90.

Owner Pinnacle Invincible Spirit Partnership **Bred** Silfield Bloodstock **Trained** Hambleton, N Yorks

FOCUS

Rail realignment around the loop reduced advertised distances on the Round course by 8yds. Fair form from the winner in an uncompetitive maiden in which the benefit of previous experience was clear to see. The runner-up made a promising debut.

NOTEBOOK

Boundless Spirit had shaped quite encouragingly on his debut in a better race than this at Thirsk and made all to give his yard their third winner in this race in four years. For all he looked in command from halfway, he still left the impression he was in need of the experience and, not fully extended, he ought to improve further as well as stay another furlong. (op 7-4 tchd 15-8)

Lexi's Hero(IRE), a son of Invincible Spirit was colty beforehand and ran an encouraging first race after being slow to stride and not finding the penny dropping until halfway. He can't really be considered unlucky, as he wasn't making any impression late on, but he ought to improve enough to win a modest race. (tchd 3-1)

Hi Ho Ron stepped up on his debut while leaving the impression he still has some learning to do. He wasn't knocked about late on and, while probably no better than modest, can make a bit more progress next time. (op 12-1)

Night Singer has a pedigree that suggests he will probably need further and that's how he ran, making some headway at halfway and then sticking on without threatening to challenge. (op 8-1 tchd 7-1)

Kassaab's Musselburgh third arguably set the standard but that form looks no better than modest and he went backwards from that run, beaten 2f out. (op 9-4)

2069 WILLIAM WALLACE H'CAP 6f 5y

6:50 (6:53) (Class 4) (0-80,78) 3-Y-O **£5,180** (£1,541; £770; £384) **Stalls** Centre

Form RPR

10-3 **1** **Ginger Ted (IRE)**[36] 1184 3-9-5 **77** (p) AndrewHeffernan(3) 7 87
(R C Guest) *cl up: rdn over 2f out: ev ch over 1f out: led wl ins fnl f: all out* **40/1**

5-02 **2** *shd* **Flaneur**[13] 1709 3-9-8 **77** (b) FrederikTylicki 2 87
(T D Easterby) *mde most tl hdd wl ins fnl f: kpt on wl: jst hld* **10/1**

25-2 **3** *nk* **Kellys Eye (IRE)**[11] 1750 3-9-3 **72** RobertWinston 10 81
(D H Brown) *dwlt: outpcd in centre: swtchd lft over 2f out: gd hdwy over 1f out: kpt on wl fnl f: jst hld* **7/1**[3]

-411 **4** *7* **Whispered Times (USA)**[10] 1811 3-8-13 **71** 6ex KellyHarrison(3) 4 58
(Miss Tracy Waggott) *cl up: effrt and ev ch 2f out: sn rdn and edgd rt: outpcd fnl f* **12/1**

00-3 **5** *nk* **Ballodair (IRE)**[20] 1523 3-9-2 **78** LeeTopliss(7) 12 64
(R A Fahey) *prom: effrt and ev ch over 1f out: edgd lft: sn no ex* **11/1**

621- **6** *1 ½* **Glen Shiel (USA)**[244] 5867 3-9-8 **77** JoeFanning 3 58
(M Johnston) *in tch: rdn and outpcd over 2f out: no imp fnl f* **16/1**

6-06 **7** *1 ¼* **Pilgrim Dancer (IRE)**[8] 1836 3-9-6 **75** DanielTudhope 5 52
(Patrick Morris) *midfield: outpcd and hung rt 1/2-way: sme late hdwy: nvr rchd ldrs* **40/1**

0112 **8** *½* **Murura (IRE)**[14] 1656 3-9-4 **73** PaulMulrennan 1 48
(J G Given) *hld up: drvn over 2f out: wknd over 1f out* **11/4**[1]

41- **9** *½* **Commanche Raider (IRE)**[220] 6556 3-9-7 **76** TonyHamilton 6 50
(M Dods) *dwlt: hld up: hdwy over 2f out: wknd over 1f out* **7/2**[2]

45-0 **10** *2 ½* **Lieu Day Louie (IRE)**[20] 1511 3-8-2 **60** MartinLane(3) 8 26
(N Wilson) *cl up tl rdn and wknd fr 2f out* **100/1**

1 **11** *¾* **Steed**[27] 1402 3-9-1 **70** RobertHavlin 9 33
(K A Ryan) *wnt lft s: sn in tch: effrt over 2f out: wknd wl over 1f out* **9/1**

51-3 **12** *13* **Tres Amigos**[36] 1191 3-9-7 **76** FrankieDettori 11 —
(D Nicholls) *disp ld to 1/2-way: wknd 2f out: eased whn no ch* **8/1**

1m 13.31s (1.11) **Going Correction** +0.225s/f (Good) 12 Ran SP% 119.4
Speed ratings (Par 101): **101,100,100,91,90 88,87,86,85,82 81,64**
toteswingers: 1&2 £102.00, 1&3 £40.90, 2&3 £7.60 CSF £401.77 CT £3181.31 TOTE £27.80: £9.20, £3.80, £1.10; EX 255.20.

Owner Showhouse Furniture Ltd **Bred** T Counihan **Trained** Stainforth, S Yorks

■ Stewards' Enquiry : Andrew Heffernan eight-day ban, including five deferred: used whip with excessive frequency (May 28-Jun 4)

FOCUS

A fair handicap in which the runners spread right across the track with no apparent advantage either side. The first three improved and finished clear, but this is probably not form to take too literally.

Tres Amigos Official explanation: jockey said gelding ran flat

2070 TOTEPOOL GLASGOW STKS (LISTED RACE) (C&G) 1m 3f 16y

7:25 (7:25) (Class 1) 3-Y-O **£26,667** (£10,084; £5,040; £2,520) **Stalls** Centre

Form RPR

1-11 **1** **Corsica (IRE)**[14] 1666 3-9-0 88 JoeFanning 4 109
(M Johnston) *t.k.h: mde all: rdn and edgd lft over 2f out: hrd pressed ins fnl f: hld on gamely fnl f* **11/2**[3]

13 **2** *1 ½* **Admission**[28] 1354 3-9-0 96 HayleyTurner 5 106
(M L W Bell) *hld up in tch: stdy hdwy over 3f out: effrt and rn green over 2f out: ev ch ins fnl f: hld last 50yds* **11/4**[2]

41-5 **3** *7* **Take It To The Max**[21] 1498 3-9-0 97 RobertWinston 1 93
(G M Moore) *chsd wnr: effrt and ev ch over 2f out: no ex appr fnl f* **16/1**

520- **4** *12* **Layali Al Andalus**[181] 7404 3-9-0 110 (t) FrankieDettori 3 72
(Saeed Bin Suroor) *trckd ldrs: effrt on outside over 2f out: wknd wl over 1f out* **4/6**[1]

2m 24.77s (-0.83) **Going Correction** +0.10s/f (Good) 4 Ran SP% 107.9
Speed ratings (Par 107): **107,105,100,92**
CSF £19.53 TOTE £5.70; EX 12.20.

Owner Sheikh Hamdan Bin Mohammed Al Maktoum **Bred** Epona Bloodstock Ltd And P A Byrne **Trained** Middleham Moor, N Yorks

FOCUS

An interesting Listed race that developed into a tactical affair and produced something of a surprise result. A clear personal best from Corsica, but only ordinary form for the grade.

NOTEBOOK

Corsica(IRE)'s form had taken off since being upped to 1m4f but, even allowing for the official handicapper probably underestimating his last win, he still looked to face a stiff task. His yard know what it takes to win this race, though, having won the last three renewals, and after being allowed to set his own gallop and then steadying things coming down the hill, he found plenty when asked to win in the style of a very useful middle-distance stayer in the making. The King George V Handicap might still be a possible after this if his new rating allows, but he was pulling away at the end and might be the sort that relish the 2m of the Queen's Vase. (op 9-2)

Admission's last piece of form had been franked by Group wins for two of the horses around him that day, but despite this being his third race he still seemed found out by inexperience, looking uncoordinated when asked to improve and then making no impression close home after getting to within half a length of the winner. This was still a good effort, and he's well up to winning something similar. (tchd 3-1)

Take It To The Max is usually a front runner but wasn't asked to make it on this occasion. He was close enough if good enough starting the final climb, but was readily outpaced and would have preferred more emphasis on stamina.

Layali Al Andalus, wearing a tongue strap for the first time, was a disappointment on his first run for Godolphin and has something to prove after this, only able to respond briefly when the eventual winner stepped up the tempo on the climb for home then hanging right and fading. Stamina ought not to have been an issue. Official explanation: trainer had no explanation for the poor form shown (op 8-11)

2071 BELSTANE RACING STABLES BRAVEHEART H'CAP (LISTED RACE) 1m 4f 17y

8:00 (8:01) (Class 1) (0-110,107) 4-Y-O+ **£23,704** (£8,964; £4,480; £2,240) **Stalls** Centre

Form RPR

22-4 **1** **Hillview Boy (IRE)**[12] 1724 6-8-11 **94** DanielTudhope 3 102+
(J S Goldie) *t.k.h: hld up: hdwy on outside over 2f out: led over 1f out: hung rt ins fnl f: readily* **11/4**[2]

0-15 **2** *2* **Yes Mr President (IRE)**[16] 1615 5-9-9 **106** JoeFanning 2 111+
(M Johnston) *cl up: led over 2f out to over 1f out: kpt on ins fnl f: nt gng pce of wnr* **8/1**

2-21 **3** *2* **Tinaar (USA)**[12] 1724 4-8-10 **93** 3ex FrankieDettori 6 95
(G A Butler) *prom: effrt and rdn over 2f out: kpt on ins fnl f: no imp* **11/8**[1]

16-1 **4** *nk* **Stanstill (IRE)**[44] 1069 4-8-12 **95** RobertWinston 8 96
(G A Swinbank) *plld hrd: set stdy pce to over 2f out: sn one pce* **7/1**[3]

311- **5** *nk* **Lady Jane Digby**[264] 5296 5-9-10 **107** GregFairley 4 108
(M Johnston) *trckd ldrs: effrt and ev ch 2f out: one pce fnl f* **14/1**

4-14 **6** *3 ¾* **Trip The Light**[23] 1472 5-8-10 **93** oh2 (v) TonyHamilton 5 88
(R A Fahey) *hld up: drvn and outpcd over 3f out: nvr able to chal* **12/1**

050- **7** *3 ½* **Uvinza**[197] 7131 4-9-0 **97** HayleyTurner 7 86
(W J Knight) *trckd ldrs: drvn over 3f out: wknd over 2f out* **12/1**

2m 38.95s (0.35) **Going Correction** +0.10s/f (Good) 7 Ran SP% 114.4
Speed ratings (Par 111): **102,100,99,99,98 96,94**
toteswingers: 1&2 £4.50, 1&3 £1.20, 2&3 £2.90 CSF £24.63 CT £41.18 TOTE £5.00: £2.70, £6.90; EX 21.10.

Owner Connor & Dunne **Bred** John Coleman **Trained** Uplawmoor, E Renfrews

FOCUS

A very useful handicap spoilt by a steady early gallop, turning what should have been a test of stamina into a test of finishing speed. The result looks potentially muddling but the form has been taken at face value.

NOTEBOOK

Hillview Boy(IRE) had looked as good as ever at Newmarket on his reappearance and, with the benefit of that run behind him, turned in a career best to reverse form readily with Tinaar, always going well and showing an impressive turn of foot to bound clear. His action suggests he's always going to need some give in the ground, but, a big sort who looks just to be coming to himself, he could make up into something better than a handicapper before long. This trip seems ideal for now. (op 9-2)

Yes Mr President(IRE) ran well, not least considering that this trip would have been plenty sharp enough for him in view of the steady early gallop. He's not going to be the easiest to place, but he will be suited by a return to 2m and presumably connections have one eye on the Northumberland Plate.

Tinaar(USA) wasn't discredited but couldn't continue her recent good form and was never travelling with the same fluency as on her last two starts, staying on only when the race was over. Only up 3lb for her Newmarket win over a large field, she still looks on a good mark and is worth another chance with much of her form working out well. (tchd 6-4)

Stanstill(IRE) had won impressively on Fibresand last time but had got a good lead then and didn't seem suited by having to make his own running, tapped for toe at the bottom of the hill before staying on again. He's another that will be suited by a return to further, with the Ebor still a feasible target. (op 5-1)

Lady Jane Digby was second in this race last year off a mark 13lb lower. She's plenty of form fresh but left the impression she just needed this, having fractured a hip over the winter. Her current mark makes her vulnerable in handicaps, and she'll be of more interest back in Listed races against her own sex. (op 10-1 tchd 9-1)

Trip The Light never promised to get involved having been dropped out taking on better rivals than usual.

Uvinza, who was third in the Ribblesdale last year, didn't really progress after and made an inauspicious reappearance in her first handicap, beaten a long way out. (tchd 10-1)

2072 LUDDON CONSTRUCTION MAIDEN STKS 1m 1f 36y

8:35 (8:37) (Class 5) 3-Y-O+ **£2,590** (£770; £385; £192) **Stalls** High

Form RPR

6- **1** **Oriental Cat**[203] 6990 3-8-13 0 RobertHavlin 8 85+
(J H M Gosden) *t.k.h: in tch: effrt and swtchd lft over 2f out: led over 1f out: sn clr: eased wl ins fnl f* **6/4**[1]

-44 **2** *5* **Omaruru (IRE)**[62] 889 3-8-13 0 JoeFanning 2 71
(M Johnston) *cl up: effrt over 2f out: ev ch and rdn over 1f out: kpt on fnl f: no ch w wnr* **5/1**[3]

624- **3** *½* **Elmfield Giant (USA)**[260] 5371 3-8-13 77 TonyHamilton 9 70
(R A Fahey) *trckd ldrs: drvn along over 2f out: sn outpcd: kpt on fnl f: no imp* **13/8**[2]

6 **4** *3 ½* **Smarty Sam (USA)**[29] 1335 3-8-13 0 RobertWinston 10 62+
(G A Swinbank) *hld up: n.m.r 3f out: sn shkn up: kpt on fnl f: nt gng pce to chal* **10/1**

00- **5** 2 ¾ **Newtons Cradle (IRE)**[284] 4595 3-8-13 0 .... FrederikTylicki 4 56
(J Howard Johnson) *led to over 1f out: sn rdn and btn* **33/1**

0- **6** ¾ **Silkenveil (IRE)**[146] 7816 3-8-3 0 ow2 .... LeeTopliss(7) 5 52
(R A Fahey) *in tch: rdn and outpcd over 2f out: n.d after* **25/1**

7 6 **Sinatramania** 3-8-10 0 .... KellyHarrison(3) 7 41
(Miss Tracy Waggott) *missed break: hld up: effrt over 2f out: sn btn* **25/1**

00- **8** ½ **Suburbia (USA)**[226] 6390 4-9-8 0 .... PatrickDonaghy(5) 1 42
(J Barclay) *prom tl rdn and wknd over 2f out* **100/1**

000- **9** 9 **Acol**[195] 7167 3-8-13 40 .... PaulMulrennan 3 20
(A G Foster) *hld up in midfield on outside: rdn over 3f out: wknd fnl 2f* **100/1**

000- **10** 7 **Just Call Me Dave (USA)**[171] 7500 4-9-8 43 .... AmyRyan(5) 6 7
(Mrs L Williamson) *hld up: struggling over 3f out: sn wknd* **66/1**

1m 59.78s (0.08) **Going Correction** +0.10s/f (Good)
WFA 3 from 4yo 14lb **10** Ran SP% **118.0**
Speed ratings (Par 103): **103,98,98,95,92 91,86,86,78,71**
toteswingers: 1&2 £4.30, 1&3 £1.10, 2&3 £4.00 CSF £9.24 TOTE £2.70: £1.10, £1.20, £1.10; EX 11.40.
Owner H R H Princess Haya Of Jordan **Bred** Whitley Stud **Trained** Newmarket, Suffolk

FOCUS
A modest maiden lacking strength in depth but the form looks reasonable for the track. The winner looks smart.

2073 CASH FOR KIDS RACENIGHT IN JUNE H'CAP 5f 4y
9:05 (9:07) (Class 5) (0-75,75) 4-Y-0+ **£3,238** (£963; £481; £240) **Stalls** Centre

Form RPR

2022 **1** **Ingleby Star (IRE)**[12] 1722 5-9-2 71 ....(p) MartinLane(3) 3 79
(N Wilson) *w ldrs: led 2f out: hrd pressed and hung rt ins fnl f: hld on wl* **9/1**

0-50 **2** *hd* **Milton Of Campsie**[6] 1924 5-9-5 71 .... RobertWinston 5 78
(J Balding) *prom: rdn over 2f out: hdwy to chal ins fnl f: carried rt: kpt on: jst hld* **5/1**[3]

-000 **3** 4 **Commander Wish**[27] 1391 7-8-4 56 oh6 ....(p) JoeFanning 8 49
(Lucinda Featherstone) *sn drvn bhd ldrs: hdwy over 1f out: no imp fnl f* **20/1**

-500 **4** 1 ¼ **The Bear**[7] 1869 7-8-6 61 .... AndrewHeffernan(3) 9 49
(Miss L A Perratt) *disp ld to 2f out: kpt on same pce fnl f* **9/2**[2]

2430 **5** 1 ¼ **Bo McGinty (IRE)**[3] 1988 9-8-10 62 ....(b) FrederikTylicki 6 46
(R A Fahey) *prom: sn drvn along: one pce fr over 1f out* **5/1**[3]

-353 **6** 2 ½ **Mandarin Spirit (IRE)**[12] 1719 10-9-0 66 ....(b) TonyHamilton 10 41
(Miss L A Perratt) *slt ld tl hung rt and hdd 2f out: sn outpcd* **8/1**

005- **7** ½ **Sandwith**[198] 7119 7-8-13 65 .... PaulMulrennan 2 38
(A G Foster) *prom: drvn along over 2f out: sn no ex* **16/1**

4214 **8** 7 **Ryan Style (IRE)**[13] 1711 4-9-2 75 .... LeeTopliss(7) 1 23
(Mrs L Williamson) *in tch: rdn and hung rt over 2f out: sn btn* **5/2**[1]

-212 **9** 2 ½ **Highland Warrior**[28] 1364 11-9-1 72 .... PaulPickard(5) 7 11
(P T Midgley) *s.i.s: bhd and sn drvn along: nvr on terms* **10/1**

61.29 secs (1.29) **Going Correction** +0.225s/f (Good) **9** Ran SP% **120.9**
Speed ratings (Par 103): **98,97,91,89,87 83,82,71,67**
toteswingers: 1&2 £9.90, 1&3 £34.00, 2&3 £47.40 CSF £56.11 CT £902.37 TOTE £7.90: £1.20, £3.30, £11.10; EX 60.60 Place 6: £573.64 Place 5: £381.48.
Owner The Crown Partnership **Bred** Pat Cosgrove **Trained** Sandhutton, N Yorks
■ Stewards' Enquiry : Martin Lane careless riding; five-day ban: used whip with excessive frequency in incorrect place (May 28-Jun 1)
Robert Winston caution: used whip with excessive frequency

FOCUS
A modest handicap in which the runners came down the centre of the track, those racing in the group nearer the stand rail coming out on top.
Highland Warrior Official explanation: jockey said gelding finished distressed
T/Plt: £736.10. Pool of £55,652.98 - 55.19 winning units. T/Qpdt: £54.10. Pool £4,462.02 - 61.00 winning tickets. RY

1381 NEWBURY (L-H)
Friday, May 14

OFFICIAL GOING: Good to firm (8.1)
Wind: Brisk ahead Weather: Cloudy

2074 DUKE OF WESTMINSTER V INLAND REVENUE HL 1935 FILLIES' CONDITIONS STKS 5f 34y
1:50 (1:51) (Class 3) 2-Y-0
£5,919 (£1,772; £886; £443; £221; £111) **Stalls** Centre

Form RPR

16 **1** **The Sydney Arms (IRE)**[12] 1733 2-8-10 0 .... RyanMoore 6 81+
(R Hannon) *trckd ldrs: nt clr run over 1f out: drvn and qcknd between horses ins fnl f: styd on wl to ld cl home* **2/1**[1]

01 **2** *hd* **Inagh River**[7] 1879 2-8-10 0 .... RichardHughes 4 79
(R Hannon) *led: grad c to stands' side: rdn and styd in ins fnl f: hdd cl home* **4/1**

51 **3** ¾ **Phoebs**[14] 1660 2-8-13 0 .... StevieDonohoe 1 81+
(R A Mills) *in tch: rdn and hdwy on stands' side fnl f: sn n.m.r: squeezed through and styd on wl cl on ldng duo nr fin but a jst hld* **7/2**[3]

4 1 ¼ **Serena's Pride** 2-8-7 0 .... RichardKingscote 2 69
(A P Jarvis) *pressed ldrs: rdn over 1f out: kpt on same pce ins fnl f* **25/1**

31 **5** 1 **Golden Shine**[11] 1773 2-8-13 0 .... AlanMunro 3 71
(M R Channon) *chsd ldr: ev ch 1f out: wknd fnl 120yds* **3/1**[2]

6 ¾ **Paris Is Burning** 2-8-7 0 .... LukeMorris 5 63
(J S Moore) *prom early: sn drvn along and struggling to go pce but kpt in tch: kpt on wl fnl f but nt gng pce to rch ldrs* **40/1**

7 1 **Silent Fright (USA)** 2-8-7 0 .... JamieSpencer 7 59
(P F I Cole) *wnt rt s: sn in tch: hdwy 2f out to chse ldrs over 1f out: wknd fnl 120yds* **12/1**

62.58 secs (1.18) **Going Correction** +0.05s/f (Good) **7** Ran SP% **114.5**
Speed ratings (Par 94): **92,91,90,88,86 85,84**
toteswingers: 1&2 £3.30, 2&3 £2.10, 1&3 not won. CSF £10.46 TOTE £2.50: £1.60, £2.80; EX 9.60.
Owner R Morecombe, J Reus & D Anderson **Bred** Fergus Cousins **Trained** East Everleigh, Wilts

FOCUS
Mick Channon and Richard Hannon have dominated this race in recent years, sending out seven of the previous ten winners between them, and the latter had the first two home this time around. The runners started up the centre of the track before drifting over towards the stands' rail. The winner was back to her debut level but the time was not great and it remains to be seen if the race works out.

NOTEBOOK
The Sydney Arms(IRE) had a valid excuse for getting beaten at odds-on at Salisbury last time as it turned out she got a clod of mud stuck in her throat, but she'd looked good at Windsor previously, and this was a return to form. The quicker ground no doubt suited this daughter of Elusive City and, although she carried her head slightly to one side, she picked up well between horses to edge ahead close home. The Albany might be a tall order on this evidence, but she'll still probably take her chance. (op 9-4 tchd 11-4)
Inagh River, who won nicely at Nottingham a week earlier, tried to make every yard and showed a good attitude. She looks to be improving and there are more races to be won with her. (op 7-2 tchd 10-3)
Phoebs comes out as the best horse in the race at the weights as she was giving 3lb to the first two. She got outpaced approaching the furlong pole and then found things getting very tight as she tried to make her run up the inside rail, but she finished well. The stronger the pace the better it will be for her. (op 6-1)
Serena's Pride, whose dam won over 6f at two, did best of the newcomers and will have easier opportunities than this. (tchd 20-1)
Golden Shine, whose trainer sent out his star fillies Queen's Logic and Flashy Wings to win this race, showed up well for a long way but she was a bit keen and didn't see her race out. (op 10-3 tchd 11-4)
Paris Is Burning ran as though the experience was needed. (op 66-1)
Silent Fright(USA), who was a $400,000 breeze-up buy, shaped with encouragement but was noticeably green in the closing stages. She should improve a bundle for this debut. (op 7-1)

2075 BERKSHIRE COUNTY BLIND SOCIETY CARNARVON STKS (LISTED RACE) 6f 8y
2:20 (2:22) (Class 1) 3-Y-O
£22,708 (£8,608; £4,308; £2,148; £1,076; £540) **Stalls** Centre

Form RPR

120- **1** **Angel's Pursuit (IRE)**[223] 6486 3-9-0 111 .... RichardHughes 5 109
(R Hannon) *hreld up rr: stdy hdwy fr 2f out: drvn and qcknd fnl f: edgd lft and led fnl 120yds: pushed out* **11/1**[3]

10-1 **2** ½ **Society Rock (IRE)**[16] 1616 3-9-3 107 .... GeorgeBaker 4 111
(J R Fanshawe) *trckd ldrs: led travelling smoothly ins fnl 2f: rdn and hdd 1f out: one pce u.p but rallied fnl 100yds to take 2nd cl home* **8/11**[1]

5-12 **3** *nk* **Mister Hughie (IRE)**[7] 1865 3-9-0 99 .... AlanMunro 6 107?
(M R Channon) *hld up in rr: gd hdwy fr 2f out to take slt ld 1f out: hdd fnl 120yds: lost 2nd cl home* **28/1**

0063 **4** 1 ¾ **Rock Jock (IRE)**[14] 1676 3-9-0 106 .... PShanahan 2 102
(Tracey Collins, Ire) *pressed ldr tl led 3f out: rdn and hdd 1f out: fading whn hmpd fnl 120yds* **25/1**

1-0 **5** 8 **Inler (IRE)**[13] 1699 3-9-0 100 .... TonyCulhane 1 75
(J R Best) *t.k.h: led until narrowly hdd 3f out: rdn 2f out: wknd qckly over 1f out* **9/2**[2]

16-2 **6** 8 **Corporal Maddox**[16] 1616 3-9-3 105 .... EddieAhern 7 53
(H R A Cecil) *chsd ldrs: rdn over 2f out: sn btn* **9/2**[2]

1m 12.16s (-0.84) **Going Correction** +0.05s/f (Good) **6** Ran SP% **109.9**
Speed ratings (Par 107): **107,106,105,103,92 82**
toteswingers: 1&2 £2.20, 1&3 £6.20, 2&3 £5.00 CSF £18.96 TOTE £11.30: £3.30, £1.30; EX 20.90.
Owner Malih L Al Basti **Bred** Hong Kong Breeders Club **Trained** East Everleigh, Wilts
■ Stewards' Enquiry : Richard Hughes one-day ban: careless riding (May 28)
Alan Munro one-day ban: used whip without giving colt time to respond (May 28)

FOCUS
July Cup winner Sakhee's Secret won this race three years ago but it'll be a surprise if anything from this race hits those heights. The pace was good, though, and the form looks solid enough for the grade. The winner is rated to his Mill Reef form.

NOTEBOOK
Angel's Pursuit(IRE) was seemingly at a disadvantage in being the only one of this field not to have had a run this season, but he won first time out last year, ran his best race over this C&D when runner-up in the Mill Reef and came into this race the highest rated of the field. He travelled well in behind the speed, quickened up well once switched towards the stands' side, and saw his race out strongly. He deserves another go in a Group race now, but opportunities against his own age group over this trip are thin on the ground, so he might be stepped up to 7f for the Jersey Stakes next. (op 10-1 tchd 12-1 and 8-1 in places)
Society Rock(IRE), so impressive in overcoming a troubled passage to win with a sharp turn of foot at Ascot on his reappearance, was very well backed to follow up. It's possible he saw daylight plenty soon enough but in reality there was probably no disgrace in finishing second to a rival rated 4lb higher while giving him 3lb. He remains on an upward curve, just not as steep as some believed. (op 4-5 tchd 4-6)
Mister Hughie(IRE) didn't have things go his way when turned over at odds-on last time, but this was much more like it thanks to a stronger pace for him to chase. He's a reliable yardstick and could yet win at this level at some point this term. (op 16-1)
Rock Jock(IRE) ran well considering he was up there throughout. His fellow pacesetter Inler dropped right out but he battled on well and will be dangerous if getting into a race where he's likely to get an easy lead. (op 11-1)
Inler(IRE) was a talking horse before the Guineas but pulled much too hard at Newmarket and gave himself little chance of seeing the trip out. Despite his pedigree, he's always threatened to be more effective over sprint distances, but having made much of the running he dropped out very tamely once things got serious. Handicaps remain the best option for him, despite the previous hype. (op 5-1 tchd 11-2)
Corporal Maddox was 3lb better off with Society Rock compared to Ascot, but he never looked like reversing the form. He has a few questions to answer now. Official explanation: jockey said colt was unsuited by the good to firm ground (op 7-1)

2076 SWETTENHAM STUD FILLIES' TRIAL STKS (LISTED RACE) 1m 2f 6y
2:55 (2:55) (Class 1) 3-Y-O
£22,708 (£8,608; £4,308; £2,148; £1,076; £540) **Stalls** Centre

Form RPR

1-34 **1** **Principal Role (USA)**[12] 1729 3-8-12 100 .... EddieAhern 8 104+
(H R A Cecil) *trckd ldrs: wnt 2nd 3f out: hrd drvn and styd on wl fr over 1f out: sustained chal fnl f to ld last strides* **3/1**[2]

02-1 **2** *shd* **Fatanah (IRE)**[21] 1501 3-8-12 87 .... RichardHills 3 103+
(M P Tregoning) *sn led at modest pce and t.k.h: pushed along and qcknd fr 3f out: styd on wl fnl f: ct last strides* **11/4**[1]

11-0 **3** 4 ½ **Pollenator (IRE)**[12] 1726 3-9-4 105 .... RichardHughes 2 100
(R Hannon) *hld up in rr but in tch: hdwy 3f out: rdn to chse ldrs 2f out but nvr on terms: wknd fnl f* **9/2**[3]

2- **4** 2 ½ **Desert Sage**[219] 6592 3-8-12 0 .... RichardKingscote 1 89
(R M Beckett) *chsd ldrs: rdn along fr 4f out: styd in tch but easily outpcd fnl 2f* **12/1**

1- **5** 1 ¼ **Hymnsheet**[206] 6920 3-8-12 0 .... RyanMoore 4 86
(Sir Michael Stoute) *in rr but in tch: hdwy on outside fr 3f out: nvr gng pce to get into contention* **6/1**

0-2 **6** 2 ¼ **Issabella Gem (IRE)**[21] 1501 3-8-12 0 .... AdamKirby 5 82
(C G Cox) *rdn along 3f out: a towards rr* **22/1**

2514 **7** *6* **Myplacelater**[9] 1820 3-8-12 97 .... DaneO'Neill 7 70
(D R C Elsworth) *sn chsng ldr: rdn fr 4f out: wknd 3f out* **6/1**

2m 6.08s (-2.72) **Going Correction** -0.075s/f (Good) **7** Ran SP% **110.5**
Speed ratings (Par 104): **107,106,103,101,100 98,93**
toteswingers: 1&2 £3.10, 1&3 £2.50, 2&3 £3.40 CSF £10.84 TOTE £3.70: £2.20, £2.00; EX 11.00.
Owner K Abdulla **Bred** Juddmonte Farms Inc **Trained** Newmarket, Suffolk

FOCUS
Eswarah won this race in 2005 before going on to win the Oaks but other than that it hasn't been a great guide to Epsom in recent years. Although the form is only ordinary for the grade this looked a decent renewal, with several strands of form coming together, and while its immediate impact on the Oaks betting was slight, it was another boost for Henry Cecil, who already stables the current second and third favourites for Epsom. The early pace was modest.

NOTEBOOK
Principal Role(USA) travelled well in behind and drew alongside the favourite with over 2f to run. The leader took some passing but strength from the saddle got the Cecil filly home, and the pair finished nicely clear. She'd run well in the Nell Gwyn on her reappearance and then pulled too hard when only fourth on softish ground in the Pretty Polly, but conditions were more suitable here and she bounced back to form. Although cut to a best price of 20-1 for the Oaks, she looks the type more likely to head for the Ribblesdale, especially as her trainer has stronger cards to play for Epsom in the shape of Timepiece and Aviate. (op 7-2)
Fatanah(IRE) benefited from a good front-running ride when winning at Sandown on her reappearance, and she was again handed an uncontested lead. Although a little keen, she wasn't the only one, and all in all she had no excuses given the way the race unfolded. On pedigree it's questionable whether she'll want to go much further than this, but she wouldn't be out of place in the Ribblesdale. (op 4-1)
Pollenator(IRE) didn't have things go her way in the Guineas where the ground had gone against her, she was drawn on the wrong side and she ended up racing freely in front. Held up with plenty of cover this time, the turn of foot she showed in the May Hill wasn't present, but she kept on quite nicely and in the circumstances it wasn't a bad effort under her 6lb penalty. A stronger pace might have seen her to better effect, but it has to be questionable whether she'll get that in the Prix de Diane, her intended target. (op 4-1)
Desert Sage ◆ looked a filly to follow when, despite running very green, she stayed on to finish second on her debut at Nottingham last autumn. A big filly who was never considered for Epsom, this flat, galloping track promised to suit her well. The steady early gallop and sprint to the line against race-fit rivals wasn't ever likely to play to her strengths, though, especially as she's a daughter of Selkirk and the ground would have been plenty quick enough. She ran a perfectly good race on her comeback and is entitled to come on plenty.
Hymnsheet, winner of her only start at two over 1m at Yarmouth, struggled to make up ground from off the pace in what was something of a tactical affair. A daughter of Pivotal, perhaps this ground was on the fast side for her. (op 5-1 tchd 9-2)
Issabella Gem(IRE), who did best of the hold-up horses when running on to be second behind Fatanah at Sandown on her return, could have gone for easy pickings in a maiden so it was interesting to see connections happy to take on the winner again. However, the way the race was run gave her little chance to get involved from the back of the field. (op 25-1)
Myplacelater beat the Lingfield Derby Trial winner Bullet Train into second over this C&D two starts back and could be excused her effort in the Cheshire Oaks where little went right for her, but having been well placed into the straight she weakened badly from 3f out, and this was a shocker. (op 9-2 tchd 13-2)

2077 BERKSHIRE COUNTY BLIND SOCIETY MAIDEN STKS (DIV I) 6f 8y
3:25 (3:29) (Class 4) 2-Y-O **£4,209** (£1,252; £625; £312) **Stalls** Centre

Form RPR
4 **1** **Memen (IRE)**[28] 1351 2-9-3 0 .... JamieSpencer 9 84+
(P F I Cole) *trckd ldrs: led jst ins fnl 2f: drvn to assert ins fnl f: readily* **11/4**[1]
2 *1 ¾* **King Of Jazz (IRE)** 2-9-3 0 .... RichardHughes 1 79
(R Hannon) *chsd ldrs: rdn to chal 1f out: kpt on ins fnl f but nt pce of wnr fnl 50yds* **7/2**[2]
3 *¾* **Sylas Ings** 2-9-3 0 .... DaneO'Neill 11 77+
(P M Phelan) *chsd ldrs: drvn and styd on to chal 1f out: kpt on wl but nt gng pce of wnr* **66/1**
4 *1 ¼* **Face The Problem (IRE)** 2-9-3 0 .... MichaelHills 13 73+
(B W Hills) *s.i.s: in rr: gd prog over 2f out: styd on press ldrs appr fnl f: kpt on same pce* **9/2**[3]
5 *nse* **Extra Power (IRE)** 2-9-3 0 .... AlanMunro 12 73+
(M R Channon) *in tch: pushed along and hdwy 2f out: styd on ins fnl f: gng on cl home* **12/1**
6 *nse* **Blue Dazzler (IRE)** 2-9-3 0 .... AdamKirby 10 72+
(Mrs A J Perrett) *s.i.s: in rr: hdwy 1/2-way: styd on fr 2f out: r.o ins fnl f: gng on cl home* **25/1**
7 *3 ¼* **Talk Talk (IRE)** 2-9-3 0 .... RyanMoore 7 63
(B J Meehan) *slt ld tl hdd jst ins fnl 2f: wknd fnl f* **13/2**
8 *2 ½* **Seas Of Sorrow (IRE)** 2-8-7 0 .... SophieDoyle(5) 5 50
(B W Duke) *pressed ldrs: ev ch 2f out: wknd: hung rt and green over 1f out* **100/1**
9 *1 ¾* **Aramid (IRE)** 2-9-3 0 .... RichardHills 8 50+
(B W Hills) *s.i.s: in rr: sme hdwy and nt clr run over 2f out: n.d after* **14/1**
10 *½* **Mrs Neat (IRE)** 2-8-12 0 .... RichardSmith 14 43
(S Kirk) *wnt rt s: in rr: sme prog 2f out: sn wknd* **100/1**
11 *1* **Bankroller** 2-9-3 0 .... PatCosgrave 6 45
(J G Portman) *slowly away: in rr: sme hdwy 1/2-way and in tch over 2f out: sn wknd* **20/1**
12 *½* **King Bling (IRE)** 2-9-3 0 .... GeorgeBaker 2 44
(S Kirk) *in rr: hdwy 1/2-way: chsd ldrs over 2f out: wknd over 1f out* **25/1**
13 *hd* **Salvationist** 2-9-3 0 .... EddieAhern 3 43
(J L Dunlop) *wnt bdly rt s: in rr: sme prog to cl on main gp 1/2-way: sn bhd* **16/1**
14 *1 ¼* **Irie Ute** 2-9-3 0 .... SteveDrowne 4 40
(S Kirk) *in tch: drvn to chse ldrs over 2f out: wknd wl over 1f out* **40/1**

1m 14.94s (1.94) **Going Correction** +0.05s/f (Good) **14** Ran SP% **119.0**
Speed ratings (Par 95): **89,86,85,84,83 83,79,76,73,73 71,71,70,69**
toteswingers: 1&2 £2.10, 1&3 £62.40, 2&3 £42.40 CSF £11.09 TOTE £3.90: £1.30, £2.60, £22.80; EX 15.30.
Owner Jared Sullivan **Bred** Keatly Overseas Ltd **Trained** Whatcombe, Oxon

FOCUS
Always an informative maiden, and one that has been won by a subsequent Group race winner six times in the previous seven years (there were two divisions in 2005 and 2008). The winning time was poor compared to the second division, and previous experience made the difference. The time was slower than division two but this still looks decent maiden form.

NOTEBOOK
Memen(IRE), the only runner to have raced previously, having run over 5f here on his debut, stepped up on that form to hold off some interesting newcomers. His trainer thinks another furlong will suit him in time, but he won't qualify for the Chesham so is unlikely to go to Royal Ascot. In the meantime he could be the sort for the Woodcote at Epsom. (op 4-1)
King Of Jazz(IRE) ◆, a £48,000 son of Acclamation, ran with plenty of promise on his debut. He knew his job but will still come on for the experience and be difficult to beat next time. (op 5-2 tchd 9-4)
Sylas Ings, a half-brother to four-time 6f winner China Cherub, is from a stable not known for sending out 2-y-o winners, but he ran well and certainly looks to have the ability to win a maiden.
Face The Problem(IRE), a brother to Thomas Baines, who won over 7f at two, cost 75,000euros. Up there for a long way on the stands' side, he lacked a bit late on but should benefit from the outing. (tchd 4-1 and 5-1 in places)
Extra Power(IRE) is another by Acclamation, but there's stamina on the dam's side of his pedigree. He showed plenty of ability. (op 20-1)
Blue Dazzler(IRE) stayed on nicely under hands and heels. He looks the type to derive plenty from this debut effort. (op 20-1)
Talk Talk(IRE) showed speed for a long way, but he hails from a yard whose juveniles invariably need their debuts. (op 6-1 tchd 5-1)
Aramid(IRE) shaped better than his finishing position suggests and is bred to improve over further in time. (op 16-1)

2078 BERKSHIRE COUNTY BLIND SOCIETY MAIDEN STKS (DIV II) 6f 8y
4:00 (4:01) (Class 4) 2-Y-O **£4,209** (£1,252; £625; £312) **Stalls** Centre

Form RPR
1 **Strong Suit (USA)** 2-9-3 0 .... RichardHughes 10 99+
(R Hannon) *trckd ldr: shkn up and qcknd to chal whn carried lft fr ins fnl 2f: led wl over 1f out: shkn up and r.o strly fnl 100yds: won gng away* **6/4**[1]
2 *1 ¼* **Neebras (IRE)** 2-9-3 0 .... DaneO'Neill 5 94+
(D R Lanigan) *s.i.s: sn rcvrd: gd hdwy 2f out to chse wnr jst ins fnl f: r.o wl but a readily hld* **25/1**
3 *6* **Formosina (IRE)** 2-9-3 0 .... RyanMoore 13 76
(J Noseda) *chsd ldrs: rdn and kpt on for wl hld 3rd ins fnl f* **5/1**[3]
43 **4** *2* **Straight Line (IRE)**[16] 1612 2-9-3 0 .... RichardKingscote 12 70
(A P Jarvis) *led: rdn and hung lft fr ins fnl 2f: hdd wl over 1f out: wknd fnl f* **4/1**[2]
5 *6* **Major Conquest (IRE)** 2-9-3 0 .... SteveDrowne 9 52+
(J W Hills) *in rr: pushed along 1/2-way: kpt on fnl f but nvr anywhere nr ldrs* **25/1**
6 *1 ¾* **Presto Volante (IRE)** 2-9-3 0 .... AdamKirby 1 47
(Mrs A J Perrett) *s.i.s: bhd: pushed along over 2f out: mod prog fnl f* **33/1**
7 *½* **Indigo Way** 2-9-3 0 .... EddieAhern 4 46
(B J Meehan) *chsd ldrs: rdn over 2f out: wknd wl over 1f out* **16/1**
6 **8** *1 ½* **Ree's Rascal (IRE)**[11] 1764 2-9-3 0 .... PatCosgrave 2 41
(J R Boyle) *pressed ldrs tl over 2f out* **66/1**
9 *½* **Silken Thoughts** 2-8-12 0 .... IvaMilickova 6 35
(John Berry) *slowly away: a in rr* **100/1**
10 *2* **Tarjeyh (IRE)** 2-9-3 0 .... RichardHills 7 34+
(M P Tregoning) *chsd ldrs tl wknd over 2f out* **7/1**
11 *6* **Shostakovich (IRE)** 2-9-3 0 .... GeorgeBaker 8 16
(S Kirk) *s.i.s: outpcd* **10/1**
12 *32* **Bournefree (IRE)** 2-8-9 0 .... PatrickHills(3) 11 —
(S Kirk) *slowly away: a wl bhd* **100/1**

1m 12.73s (-0.27) **Going Correction** +0.05s/f (Good) **12** Ran SP% **118.2**
Speed ratings (Par 95): **103,101,93,90,82 80,79,77,77,74 66,23**
toteswingers: 1&2 £11.60, 1&3 £3.80, 2&3 £19.30 CSF £52.28 TOTE £2.70: £1.40, £7.40, £1.80; EX 62.60.
Owner Mrs J Wood **Bred** Mcdowell Farm, Gainsborough Farm Et Al **Trained** East Everleigh, Wilts

FOCUS
The second division of a maiden which invariably throws up some decent juveniles, and it was run in a time much quicker than the first division. The form looks very strong indeed with the first two finishing clear, and the winner looks a Coventry candidate.

NOTEBOOK
Strong Suit(USA) ◆, representing the all-conquering Hannon yard, was sent off a short price to make a winning debut, and he justified the support in impressive style. He travelled comfortably in behind the pace and, if anything got to the front too soon, but he was going so well that his rider had no option but to go on, and the response when shaken up was taking, as he quickened up smartly. The winning time was 2.21sec quicker than the first division of this maiden and only 0.57sec slower than that recorded by the 111-rated Angel's Pursuit in winning the 3-y-o Listed race earlier on the card, so it's clear he's put up a very smart performance. He's a brother to Naseehah, who won over 1m1½f as a 3-y-o, but he clearly has a good deal more speed than him, and on this evidence he looks a leading candidate for the Coventry Stakes at Royal Ascot. Canford Cliffs won a division of this race for Hannon last year before winning the Coventry. Coral make Strong Suit an 8-1 shot for the Ascot race, which looks a fair price. (op 7-4 tchd 15-8 and 2-1 in places)
Neebras(IRE) ◆, who cost 75,000gns, is out of a sister to the Listed-class Foodbroker Fancy. He bumped into a Hannon hotpot here but ran a cracker in defeat, finishing well clear of the rest, and clearly possesses plenty of ability. Another who looks up to running at the Royal meeting, he shouldn't find winning a maiden too difficult if reproducing this form.
Formosina(IRE) ◆, whose price rose from 50,000gns as a foal to 105,000gns as a yearling, is out of a half-sister to Tumbleweed Ridge. Well placed throughout, he ran a perfectly satisfactory race, good enough to win most maidens, but on this occasion he ran into a couple of above-average types. He can soon go two places better. (op 6-1)
Straight Line(IRE) had the advantage of previous experience and promised to be very much suited by the step up from 5f as he's bred to stay a good deal further in time, but having shown his pace he dropped out inside the last. A drop back to the minimum looks in order. (tchd 9-2 in a place)
Major Conquest(IRE), a half-brother to winners over distances ranging from 5f to 1m7f, was running on nicely at the finish and is entitled to do better in time. (op 66-1)
Presto Volante(IRE) was slowly away but showed enough to think he has a future.
Indigo Way, who is already gelded, should improve for the run, as most juveniles from his yard do. (tchd 14-1)
Tarjeyh(IRE), whose sales price shot up from 16,000gns as a foal to 220,000gns as a yearling, is a half-brother to Navajo Chief, who won his debut over the minimum trip. His stable is 1-37 with 2-y-os at this track over the last five seasons though, and he looks sure to come on for this debut effort. (op 15-2 tchd 8-1)
Shostakovich(IRE), who has plenty of speed in his pedigree, might well appreciate dropping back to the minimum trip. (op 17-2 tchd 12-1)

2079 BERKSHIRE COUNTY BLIND SOCIETY H'CAP 1m 3f 5y
4:35 (4:35) (Class 4) (0-80,80) 3-Y-O **£4,533** (£1,348; £674; £336) **Stalls** Centre

Form RPR
53-1 **1** **Berling (IRE)**[24] 1448 3-9-2 78 .... EddieAhern 13 96+
(J L Dunlop) *hld up in rr: stdy hdwy on outside fr 3f out: led appr fnl 2f: gng readily clr whn veered bdly rt across trck ins fnl quarter m: sn rcvrd and styd on strly fnl f* **9/2**[1]
62-1 **2** *2 ¾* **Activate**[16] 1624 3-9-1 77 .... JamieSpencer 4 89+
(M L W Bell) *hld up in rr: stdy hdwy on outside over 2f out: styd on to go 2nd as wnr veered bdly rt across trck: nvr any ch and styd on same pce* **9/2**[1]

44-1 **3** 2 1/4 **Arctic Cosmos (USA)**[24] 1460 3-9-2 78 WilliamBuick 8 88+
(J H M Gosden) *in rr: nt clr run fr 3f out tl swtchd rt to outside and hdwy ins fnl 2f: styd on to take readily hld 3rd ins fnl f* **5/1**[2]

0333 **4** 4 **Corres (IRE)**[39] 1132 3-8-10 72 MichaelHills 6 73
(D R C Elsworth) *chsd ldrs: slt ld 3f out tl hdd appr fnl 2f: wknd appr fnl f* **20/1**

5-1 **5** shd **Huff And Puff**[23] 1479 3-9-2 78 AlanMunro 9 79
(Mrs A J Perrett) *in tch tl nt clr run: lost pl and swtchd rt ins fnl 3f: styd on fr over 1f out but nvr gng pce to get into contention* **10/1**

4-10 **6** shd **Street Entertainer (IRE)**[21] 1502 3-9-3 79 PatCosgrave 11 80
(Mrs A J Perrett) *hanpered sn after s: t.k.h: chsd ldrs on outside and rt there fr 4f out to 2f out: wknd appr fnl f* **16/1**

31-5 **7** nse **Red Courtier**[12] 1730 3-9-4 80 AdamKirby 3 81
(P F I Cole) *led after 2f: hdd 3f out: wknd appr fnl f* **8/1**[3]

1-02 **8** 1/2 **Essexbridge**[4] 1973 3-8-12 74 RichardHughes 12 75
(R Hannon) *chsd ldrs: rdn over 2f out: wknd u.p wl over 1f out* **9/2**[1]

51-0 **9** 2 1/2 **Higgy's Ragazzo (FR)**[21] 1502 3-8-13 78 PatrickHills(3) 7 73
(R Hannon) *in rr: rdn: hdwy and squeezed through on ins wl over 2f out: nvr rchd ldrs* **16/1**

35-6 **10** 1 **King's Parade**[36] 1182 3-8-10 72 (v[1]) RyanMoore 5 65
(Sir Michael Stoute) *led 2f: styd chsng ldrs tl wknd qckly fr 2f out* **14/1**

51-3 **11** 3 3/4 **If I Were A Boy (IRE)**[130] 33 3-8-11 73 FrankieMcDonald 2 60
(D J S Ffrench Davis) *s.i.s: chsd ldrs: tl wknd and n.m.r on ins wl over 2f out* **66/1**

00-0 **12** 5 **Meglio Ancora**[21] 1502 3-9-2 78 DaneO'Neill 10 56
(J G Portman) *sn chsng ldrs on outside: rdn 3f out: sn btn* **28/1**

2m 19.99s (-1.21) **Going Correction** -0.075s/f (Good) **12** Ran SP% **119.5**
Speed ratings (Par 101): **101,99,97,94,94 94,94,93,92,91 88,85**
toteswingers: 1&2 £4.90, 2&3 £5.40, 1&3 £8.40 CSF £24.10 CT £107.05 TOTE £4.40: £1.10, £2.70, £2.70; EX 27.10.
Owner Benny Andersson **Bred** Ballylinch Stud **Trained** Arundel, W Sussex

FOCUS
A decent middle-distance handicap and strong form for the grade, with the first three all looking ahead of the handicapper. . The principals came from the back of the field.
Higgy's Ragazzo(FR) Official explanation: jockey said colt suffered interference in running

2080 BERKSHIRE COUNTY BLIND SOCIETY H'CAP — 1m 2f 6y
5:10 (5:11) (Class 5) (0-70,70) 4-Y-O+ **£2,590** (£770; £385; £192) **Stalls** Centre

Form RPR

1463 **1** **Make Amends (IRE)**[10] 1797 5-9-1 67 GeorgeBaker 12 79+
(R J Hodges) *in tch: hdwy on outside over 2f out to ld over 1f out: pushed out* **11/2**[2]

65-4 **2** 2 1/4 **Rosco Flyer (IRE)**[15] 1637 4-8-11 63 DaneO'Neill 1 71
(R A Teal) *in tch: n.m.r ins fnl 3f: hdwy fr 2f out: styd on to chse wnr ins fnl f but a readily hld* **15/2**[3]

1-40 **3** hd **Rowan Tiger**[13] 1690 4-9-4 70 PatCosgrave 7 77
(J R Boyle) *in tch: hdwy 3f out: chsd ldrs 2f out: wnt 2nd over 1f out but no imp on wnr: lost 2nd ins fnl f* **10/1**

20-0 **4** 2 1/4 **Gross Prophet**[18] 1579 5-9-3 69 (b[1]) SteveDrowne 13 72
(A J Lidderdale) *led: t.k.h: rdn over 2f out: hdd over 1f out: wknd ins fnl f* **33/1**

1414 **5** nk **Charlie Smirke (USA)**[15] 1645 4-9-4 70 RyanMoore 9 73
(G L Moore) *in rr tl hdwy on ins over 2f out: no imp on ldrs fnl f* **9/1**

461- **6** nk **Jenny Potts**[17] 3019 6-9-1 70 RobertLButler(3) 16 71
(C J Down) *in rr: hdwy fr 3f out: styd on fr over 1f out but nt rch ldrs* **12/1**

200- **7** 2 1/2 **Shy**[293] 4301 5-8-11 66 JamesMillman(3) 15 62
(B R Millman) *stdd s: in rr tl plld sharply rt to outside 3f out: sn rdn: styd on fr over 1f out: nt rch ldrs* **14/1**

242- **8** 1 1/4 **Seventh Cavalry (IRE)**[222] 5802 5-9-1 67 RichardHughes 10 61
(A King) *hld up in rr: stdy hdwy fr 3f out: in tch whn rdn ins fnl 2f: sn btn* **5/1**[1]

6502 **9** 2 3/4 **Scamperdale**[28] 1348 8-8-13 65 TonyCulhane 4 53
(B P J Baugh) *t.k.h: chsd ldrs: rdn over 2f out: wknd wl over 1f out* **11/1**

06-0 **10** 1 **Folio (IRE)**[100] 383 10-8-10 62 StevieDonohoe 5 48
(W J Musson) *nvr rchd ldrs* **22/1**

41-0 **11** 4 1/2 **Aine's Delight (IRE)**[38] 1141 4-8-6 63 SimonPearce(5) 8 40
(Andrew Turnell) *chsd ldrs tl wknd ins fnl 3f* **16/1**

4066 **12** 2 1/4 **Hatch A Plan (IRE)**[21] 1507 9-7-11 56 oh4 CharlesEddery(7) 3 29
(Mouse Hamilton-Fairley) *nt clr run on ins over 3f out: sn rdn: a in rr* **33/1**

62-6 **13** 1 **Lord Of The Dance (IRE)**[18] 1585 4-8-11 63 EddieAhern 14 34
(W M Brisbourne) *chsd ldrs tl wknd over 2f out: eased whn btn* **22/1**

60-6 **14** 2 **Bomber Command (USA)**[16] 1618 7-9-1 67 MichaelHills 6 34
(J W Hills) *chsd ldrs tl wknd qckly ins fnl 2f* **14/1**

000- **15** 8 **Shooting Party (IRE)**[214] 6733 4-9-1 70 PatrickHills(3) 11 21
(R Hannon) *chsd ldrs tl wknd qckly 3f out* **14/1**

010- **16** 33 **Foxtrot Charlie**[39] 6289 4-9-2 68 (b) LukeMorris 2 —
(P Winkworth) *chsd ldrs tl rdn, rdn lost whip and wknd 4f out: t.o* **33/1**

2m 6.78s (-2.02) **Going Correction** -0.075s/f (Good) **16** Ran SP% **122.3**
Speed ratings (Par 103): **105,103,103,101,101 100,98,97,95,94 91,89,88,86,80 54**
toteswingers: 1&2 £8.50, 1&3 £15.20, 2&3 £16.50 CSF £43.48 CT £403.83 TOTE £6.00: £1.70, £2.50, £3.20, £8.50; EX 60.00.
Owner Miss R Dobson **Bred** Moyglare Stud Farm Ltd **Trained** Charlton Mackrell, Somerset

FOCUS
An ordinary handicap. The winner built on his Bath effort, with the runner-up to form.
Lord Of The Dance(IRE) Official explanation: jockey said gelding was unsuited by the good to firm ground
Shooting Party(IRE) Official explanation: jockey said gelding hung left-handed
Foxtrot Charlie Official explanation: jockey said gelding was unsuited by the good to firm ground

2081 INKERMAN LONDON APPRENTICE H'CAP — 1m 4f 5y
5:40 (5:40) (Class 5) (0-75,74) 4-Y-O+ **£2,590** (£770; £385; £192) **Stalls** Centre

Form RPR

2-00 **1** **Maslak (IRE)**[90] 546 6-8-10 66 RyanClark 5 75
(P W Hiatt) *mde all: shkn up over 2f out: styd on gamely fnl f* **6/1**[3]

4223 **2** 1 **Oxford City (IRE)**[18] 1579 6-8-10 69 (t) RichardRowe(3) 4 76+
(P M Phelan) *hld up in rr and wl off pce over 4f out: hdwy over 2f out: styd on wl to chse wnr ins fnl f: kpt on but a hld* **9/2**[2]

1060 **3** 2 **Bavarica**[27] 1379 8-8-11 72 AdamBeschizza(5) 8 76
(Miss J Feilden) *chsd ldrs: rdn and styd on same pce fr over 1f out* **14/1**

420- **4** 3/4 **Beauchamp Xiara**[215] 6698 4-8-12 68 AmyScott 7 71
(H Candy) *chsd wnr 6f out: rdn along over 2f out: no imp and wknd ins fnl f* **9/2**[2]

121- **5** 3 1/4 **Saborido (USA)**[205] 6935 4-9-0 70 CharlesEddery 3 68
(Mrs A J Perrett) *chsd wnr 6f: styd chsng ldrs tl wknd over 1f out* **8/1**

50-0 **6** nk **Sgt Schultz (IRE)**[31] 1277 7-8-11 70 RyanPowell(3) 6 67
(J S Moore) *towards rr: hdwy on outside fr 3f out: chsd ldrs 2f out: sn wknd* **9/1**

1031 **7** 2 1/4 **Carr Hall (IRE)**[11] 1756 7-8-2 65 6ex GeorgeDowning(7) 2 59
(A W Carroll) *towards rr: rdn 3f out: nvr rchd ldrs and sn wknd* **10/3**[1]

1-40 **8** 5 **Illuminative (USA)**[18] 1579 4-9-4 74 DuilioDaSilva 1 60
(Stef Higgins) *a towards rr* **15/2**

2m 36.37s (0.87) **Going Correction** -0.075s/f (Good) **8** Ran SP% **113.3**
Speed ratings (Par 103): **94,93,92,91,89 89,87,84**
toteswingers: 1&2 £7.60, 1&3 £18.90, 2&3 £12.00 CSF £32.41 CT £359.53 TOTE £10.70: £2.30, £1.80, £4.40; EX 60.00 Place 6: £10.32 Place 5: £5.31.
Owner Alan Swinburne **Bred** Shadwell Estate Company Limited **Trained** Hook Norton, Oxon

FOCUS
The early pace wasn't hectic here and it paid to race handily. The winner did not need to match last year's best, with the second the guide to the form.
Carr Hall(IRE) Official explanation: trainer had no explanation for the poor form shown
T/Plt: £18.00. Pool of £72,015.32 - 2,906.36 winning tickets T/Qpdt: £8.60. Pool £3,511.47 - 299.28 winning tickets. ST

1806 NEWCASTLE (L-H)
Friday, May 14

OFFICIAL GOING: Good to firm (7.5)
Wind: almost nil Weather: overcast, rain 1st 2

2082 LA TAXIS NOVICE STKS — 6f
6:10 (6:10) (Class 4) 2-Y-O **£3,784** (£1,132; £566; £283) **Stalls** Centre

Form RPR

1 **1** **Drawing Board**[20] 1517 2-9-2 0 RichardMullen 4 83+
(K A Ryan) *stdd s: hld up: effrt and swtchd lft over 2f out: rdn to ld jst ins fnl f: edgd rt: kpt on* **4/6**[1]

01 **2** 3/4 **Joyously**[10] 1794 2-8-9 0 JamesDoyle 3 72
(P D Evans) *chsd ldrs: drvn over 3f out: rdn to chal 1f out: styd on same pce ins fnl f* **14/1**

21 **3** 1 1/4 **Meandmyshadow**[20] 1527 2-8-11 0 FrannyNorton 2 70
(A D Brown) *led: shkn up and qcknd over 3f out: hdd jst ins fnl f: wl hld whn hmpd towards fin* **9/4**[2]

01 **4** 2 **Prophet In A Dream**[15] 1632 2-9-0 0 IanBrennan(5) 1 72
(M R Channon) *w ldr: drvn over 3f out: lost pl 1f out* **9/1**[3]

1m 17.12s (2.52) **Going Correction** +0.05s/f (Good) **4** Ran SP% **107.4**
Speed ratings (Par 95): **89,88,86,83**
CSF £9.67 TOTE £1.40; EX 10.20.
Owner J C Fretwell **Bred** Peter Webb **Trained** Hambleton, N Yorks

FOCUS
After a dry day the ground was described as good to firm, although it did start to drizzle before this race. All four were previous winners in this novice stakes; it was run at an even pace and all of them had a chance with a furlong to run. Straightforward form with the winer value for a bit extra.

NOTEBOOK
Drawing Board, a winner over 5f on his debut, relished the step up in trip here and won going away in the end. Despite his pedigree, it looks like he might even stay further in due course. A big horse, connections aren't in a rush with him. (tchd 8-11)
Joyously, a winner of a seller last time out, also ran well up in trip. Her respected trainer is sure to keep her busy and there is little reason why she shouldn't continue to pay her way. (op 11-1)
Meandmyshadow, also stepping up in trip, showed plenty of early pace and on the evidence of this could still mix it back at the minimum trip. She appeared to have a good attitude. (op 11-4)
Prophet In A Dream was readily brushed aside inside the final furlong. It was no easy task trying to give weight away all round, however he did carry his head high close home, which was slightly concerning. (tchd 10-1)

2083 IPC SECURITY MEDIAN AUCTION MAIDEN STKS — 1m 2f 32y
6:40 (6:45) (Class 5) 3-Y-O **£3,497** (£1,040; £520; £259) **Stalls** Centre

Form RPR

1 **Pass Muster** 3-9-3 0 TedDurcan 1 86+
(Mahmood Al Zarooni) *dwlt: sn trcking ldrs: wnt 2nd 2f out: styd on fnl f: led nr fin* **11/10**[1]

2 nk **Rule Maker** 3-9-3 0 SebSanders 2 85+
(J Noseda) *led: kpt on fnl 2f: hdd and no ex cl home* **7/2**[3]

52 **3** 7 **Forsyth**[31] 1271 3-9-3 0 PJMcDonald 3 71
(G A Swinbank) *trckd ldr: drvn 4f out: wknd fnl f* **11/4**[2]

63 **4** 9 **Trojan Gift (USA)**[20] 1528 3-9-3 0 TomEaves 4 53+
(Julie Camacho) *sn pushed along in rr: wl outpcd over 4f out: kpt on to take modest 4th 2f out* **28/1**

4 **5** 12 **Captain Cornelius (IRE)**[18] 1572 3-9-3 0 MickyFenton 6 29
(Joss Saville) *t.k.h in rr: hdwy over 5f out: wnt 4th over 4f out: chsng ldrs 3f out: sn wknd* **14/1**

0 **6** 23 **Cayo**[6] 1927 3-9-3 0 AndrewMullen 7 —
(M Johnston) *chsd ldrs: drvn over 7f out: lost pl over 4f out: t.o 3f out* **40/1**

2m 14.38s (2.48) **Going Correction** +0.275s/f (Good) **6** Ran SP% **109.1**
Speed ratings (Par 99): **101,100,95,87,78 59**
toteswingers: 1&2 £1.90, 1&3 £1.70, 2&3 £1.10 CSF £4.92 TOTE £1.80: £1.02, £3.90; EX 5.80.
Owner Godolphin **Bred** Darley **Trained** Newmarket, Suffolk

FOCUS
Probably just an ordinary maiden which was run at an even pace and the two newcomers dominated the finish.

2084 DUNES, SOUTH SHIELDS HEART OF ENTERTAINMENT H'CAP — 1m 2f 32y
7:15 (7:15) (Class 4) (0-80,81) 4-Y-O+ **£4,533** (£1,348; £674; £336) **Stalls** Centre

Form RPR

50-3 **1** **Magic Echo**[27] 1379 6-9-2 78 JamesDoyle 5 87
(M Dods) *hld up: smooth hdwy to ld 2f out: hld on wl towards fin* **7/2**[3]

1442 **2** nk **Rosbay (IRE)**[7] 1889 6-9-0 76 DuranFentiman 4 84
(T D Easterby) *s.i.s: sn trcking ldrs: hdwy on ins to chal over 1f out: no ex towards fin* **5/2**[1]

0-21 **3** 2 **King Fingal (IRE)**[11] 1751 5-9-0 81 6ex IanBrennan(5) 6 85
(J J Quinn) *hld up: hdwy 4f out: styd on to take 3rd over 1f out: kpt on same pce* **11/4**[2]

2-30 **4** 4 1/2 **Desert Vision**[27] 1378 6-8-13 80 (vt) JamesSullivan(5) 3 75
(M W Easterby) *t.k.h: trckd ldrs: outpcd over 2f out: kpt on one pce* **14/1**

0611 **5** 1 **Sudden Impulse**[22] 1489 9-8-4 66 oh1 SilvestreDeSousa 7 59
(A D Brown) *hld up in rr: effrt over 3f out: one pce fnl 2f* **8/1**

0-00 **6** 3 1/2 **Casino Night**[12] 1717 5-8-7 69 GrahamGibbons 1 55
(R Johnson) *led: hdd over 2f out: wkng whn hmpd over 1f out* **33/1**

23-0 **7** 1 1/4 **Northside Prince (IRE)**[27] 1395 4-8-6 **68** .... PJMcDonald 2 52
(G A Swinbank) *trckd ldrs: led briefly over 2f out: edgd lft and wknd over 1f out* **6/1**

2m 13.22s (1.32) **Going Correction** +0.275s/f (Good) **7** Ran SP% **112.5**
Speed ratings (Par 105): **105,104,103,99,98 95,94**
CSF £12.25 TOTE £7.10: £4.00, £1.50.
Owner D C Batey **Bred** D C Batey **Trained** Denton, Co Durham
■ Stewards' Enquiry : James Doyle caution: used whip with excessive frequency.

FOCUS
Only seven runners, but an interesting little handicap, with four of them already winners at this track. It was run at an even pace.

2085 CRABBIE'S ALCOHOLIC GINGER BEER H'CAP 2m 19y
7:50 (7:50) (Class 5) (0-70,62) 4-Y-0+ **£3,626** (£1,079; £539; £269) **Stalls** Low

Form RPR

00-6 **1** **Alloro**[6] 1424 6-8-8 **45** .... FrannyNorton 1 51
(A Kirtley) *mde all: styd on wl fnl 2f: unchal* **80/1**

-224 **2** 3 1/4 **Spring Breeze**[55] 506 9-8-8 **50** .... IanBrennan(5) 6 52
(J J Quinn) *prom: drvn and lost pl 5f out: styd on wl fnl 2f: tk 2nd towards fin* **4/1**[2]

06-5 **3** 1/2 **Silent Lucidity (IRE)**[14] 1671 6-8-8 **45** ....(p) PaulHanagan 7 47
(P D Niven) *chsd ldrs: drvn over 5f out: wnt 2nd over 2f out: edgd lft: kpt on same pce fnl f* **9/2**[3]

0-21 **4** 4 1/2 **Park's Prodigy**[14] 1671 6-9-11 **62** .... SilvestreDeSousa 2 58
(G A Harker) *dwlt: hld up in rr: hdwy 3f out: nvr nr ldrs* **5/2**[1]

0 **5** 1 3/4 **Dream Risk (FR)**[27] 1380 4-9-3 **57** .... PJMcDonald 4 51
(Mrs K Walton) *chsd ldrs: one pce fnl 2f* **12/1**

00-1 **6** 6 **Spruzzo**[7] 1891 4-8-12 **52** 6ex .... DuranFentiman 3 39
(C W Thornton) *chsd wnr: reminders over 6f out: wknd over 2f out* **8/1**

/600 **7** 7 **I Feel Fine**[10] 1801 7-8-8 **45** .... AndrewElliott 10 23
(A Kirtley) *stdd s: in rr: bhd fnl 3f* **50/1**

2260 **8** 2 3/4 **Nakoma (IRE)**[10] 1807 8-9-4 **55** .... TomEaves 5 30
(B Ellison) *chsd ldrs: chal over 3f out: lost pl over 2f out* **9/2**[3]

404- **9** 10 **Dechiper (IRE)**[207] 6899 8-9-10 **61** .... GrahamGibbons 8 24
(R Johnson) *hld up: hdwy and in tch after 3f: drvn over 4f out: lost pl over 2f out: sn bhd: eased* **12/1**

160/ **P** **Treason Trial**[944] 6186 9-9-2 **53** .... MickyFenton 9 —
(Joss Saville) *unruly in stalls and banged hd: tk fierce hold in rr: hung bdly rt, eased and lost pl over 4f out: sn p.u* **20/1**

3m 40.4s (1.00) **Going Correction** +0.275s/f (Good)
WFA 4 from 6yo+ 3lb **10** Ran SP% **119.4**
Speed ratings (Par 103): **108,106,106,103,103 100,96,95,90,—**
toteswingers: 1&2 £33.30, 1&3 £55.10, 2&3 £4.40 CSF £385.77 CT £1799.34 TOTE £124.40: £16.50, £1.10, £2.00; EX 341.60.
Owner A Kirtley **Bred** E Dafydd **Trained** West Auckland, Co Durham

FOCUS
A handicap for horses rated 51-70, but the top-weight was 8lb below the ceiling rating. This isn't strong form and it proved hard to make ground from the rear.
Alloro Official explanation: trainer said, regarding apparent improvement in form, that the gelding was better suited by being ridden more positively and therefore able to dominate.
Treason Trial Official explanation: jockey said gelding banged its head in the stalls and hung badly right

2086 NEW DEBENHAMS NEWCASTLE STORE H'CAP 7f
8:25 (8:25) (Class 3) (0-90,89) 4-Y-0 **£6,938** (£2,076; £1,038; £519; £258) **Stalls** Centre

Form RPR

6335 **1** **Dubai Dynamo**[13] 1708 5-9-4 **89** .... AndrewElliott 5 101
(Mrs R A Carr) *hrd rdn: w ldrs: led 3f out: edgd lft and rt ins fnl f: jst hld on* **4/1**[2]

0-00 **2** shd **The Osteopath (IRE)**[27] 1397 7-9-1 **86** .... DavidAllan 3 98
(M Dods) *trckd ldrs: effrt on outside 2f out: chsd wnr jst ins fnl f: hrd rdn and r.o wl towards fin: jst hld* **8/1**

503 **3** 4 1/2 **Beckermet (IRE)**[14] 1672 8-9-1 **86** .... FrannyNorton 7 86
(R F Fisher) *w ldrs: t.k.h: outpcd over 1f out: rallied ins fnl f: tk mod 3rd nr fin* **6/1**[3]

2-10 **4** 1/2 **She's In The Money**[27] 1397 4-9-1 **86** .... PaulHanagan 1 84
(R A Fahey) *swvd lft at s: sn chsng ldrs: wnt 2nd over 1f out: kpt on same pce* **15/2**

0-53 **5** 2 1/4 **Floor Show**[15] 1650 4-8-10 **81** .... SebSanders 8 73
(N Wilson) *trckd ldrs: t.k.h: effrt over 2f out: wknd over 1f out* **7/1**

40-0 **6** shd **Reel Buddy Star**[13] 1707 5-8-9 **80** .... PJMcDonald 10 72
(G M Moore) *led tl 3f out: wknd over 1f out* **9/1**

2-54 **7** 4 **Kiwi Bay**[31] 1272 5-9-2 **87** .... TomEaves 4 68
(M Dods) *hld up in rr: drvn over 2f out: nvr on terms* **7/2**[1]

0301 **8** 3/4 **Game Lad**[10] 1808 8-8-4 **75** 6ex ....(tp) DuranFentiman 6 54
(T D Easterby) *in rr: rdn over 2f out: no rspnse* **9/1**

00-0 **9** 18 **Desert Falls**[13] 1707 4-8-4 **75** .... PaulQuinn 9 5
(R M Whitaker) *t.k.h: trckd ldrs: hung lft: lost pl 3f out: sn bhd: eased ins fnl f* **20/1**

1m 27.78s (-0.92) **Going Correction** +0.05s/f (Good) **9** Ran SP% **116.6**
Speed ratings (Par 107): **107,106,101,101,98 98,93,93,72**
toteswingers: 1&2 £33.30, 1&3 £55.10, 2&3 £4.40 CSF £36.33 CT £192.48 TOTE £3.90: £1.10, £3.20, £3.10; EX 48.20.
Owner The Bottom Liners **Bred** T K & Mrs P A Knox **Trained** Huby, N Yorks
■ Stewards' Enquiry : David Allan one-day ban: used whip with excessive freauency (May 28)
Andrew Elliott caution: used whip with excessive frequency

FOCUS
Six course and distance winners in this line-up made it a competitive 76-90 handicap. Once again it paid to race up with the pace.

NOTEBOOK
Dubai Dynamo had dropped to his last winning mark and a positive ride did the job here. However, it will require a career best to follow up next time, that said, his trainer does well with these types. (op 5-1)
The Osteopath(IRE) again ran with credit and, coming from an in-form yard, he should remain competitive.
Beckermet(IRE) was again placed, but remains hard to win with. (op 9-1)
She's In The Money went left as the stalls opened and, off her current mark, has no margin for error. (op 13-2 tchd 8-1)
Floor Show ran okay to a point but he is also in the grip of the handicapper. (op 6-1)
Kiwi Bay would appear badly handicapped and never got into it. (op 3-1)
Game Lad was very easy to back and never looked like taking a hand in the finish. (op 8-1 tchd 10-1)

2087 METRO RADIO MORE MUSIC VARIETY FILLIES' H'CAP 5f
8:55 (8:55) (Class 5) (0-70,69) 3-Y-0+ **£3,238** (£963; £481; £240) **Stalls** Centre

Form RPR

0-00 **1** **Mey Blossom**[11] 1754 5-8-12 **58** .... MichaelStainton(3) 5 69
(R M Whitaker) *chsd ldrs: led 2f out: hld on wl towards fin* **17/2**

343- **2** 1 **Poppy's Rose**[266] 5225 6-9-0 **57** .... AndrewElliott 6 64
(T J Etherington) *stdd s: hld up in rr: gd hdwy to chal over 1f out: no extra ins fnl f* **9/1**

5-20 **3** hd **Dispol Kylie (IRE)**[28] 1365 4-9-8 **65** .... PaulHanagan 4 71
(P T Midgley) *chsd ldrs: styd on same pce ins fnl f* **8/1**

-625 **4** 4 1/2 **Miss Daawe**[7] 1885 6-8-10 **60** .... DaleSwift(7) 2 50
(B Ellison) *swtchd lft and racd alone far side: w ldrs: edgd rt and wknd fnl f* **11/4**[2]

02-5 **5** 2 **Real Diamond**[18] 1588 4-9-10 **67** .... SilvestreDeSousa 3 50
(Ollie Pears) *led: hdd 2f out: wknd fnl f* **14/1**

00-6 **6** 2 1/2 **Revue Princess (IRE)**[6] 1915 5-9-6 **63** ....(b) DavidAllan 1 37
(T D Easterby) *chsd ldrs: rdn 2f out: wknd appr fnl f* **9/4**[1]

5020 **7** 3 **Lucky Leigh**[11] 1770 4-9-7 **69** ....(v) IanBrennan(5) 7 32
(M R Channon) *in rr div: hdwy u.p to chse ldrs 2f out: sn wknd* **15/2**[3]

600- **8** 8 **Keep Dancing (IRE)**[207] 6904 4-9-7 **64** .... TomEaves 8 —
(R E Barr) *in tch: lost pl 2f out: sn bhd* **20/1**

0/4- **9** 27 **She Who Dares Wins**[409] 1055 10-8-12 **55** oh10...(b[1]) DuranFentiman 9 —
(L R James) *s.i.s: a outpcd and in rr: bhd fnl 2f: t.o* **33/1**

60.94 secs (-0.16) **Going Correction** +0.05s/f (Good) **9** Ran SP% **115.2**
Speed ratings (Par 100): **100,98,98,90,87 83,78,66,22**
toteswingers:1&2 £10.40, 2&3 £13.70, 1&3 £8.00 CSF £81.67 CT £636.77 TOTE £13.40: £4.10, £4.40, £3.80; EX 99.70 Place 6: £108.93 Place 5: £64.05.
Owner Waz Developments Ltd **Bred** Hellwood Stud Farm **Trained** Scarcroft, W Yorks

FOCUS
A run of the mill fillies' handicap run at a very generous pace. The race developed down the centre of the track.
T/Plt: £209.00. Pool of £65,134.78 - 227.50 winning tickets. T/Qpdt: £35.50. Pool of £5,838.09 - 121.40 winning tickets. WG

2041 NEWMARKET (Rowley Mile) (R-H)
Friday, May 14

OFFICIAL GOING: Good to firm (9.1)
Wind: Light half-behind Weather: Overcast

2088 32RED E B F MAIDEN FILLIES' STKS 6f
2:00 (2:01) (Class 4) 2-Y-0 **£5,180** (£1,541; £770; £384) **Stalls** High

Form RPR

42 **1** **Hortensia (IRE)**[16] 1626 2-9-0 0 .... ChrisCatlin 6 77
(M R Channon) *broke wl: mde all: rdn and hung lft fr over 1f out: r.o* **5/2**[1]

2 2 1/4 **Madany (IRE)** 2-9-0 0 .... JimmyQuinn 3 70+
(B W Hills) *hld up: hdwy 1/2-way: nt clr run and swtchd rt 1f out: r.o to go 2nd post* **5/1**[2]

3 nse **Looksmart** 2-9-0 0 .... PatDobbs 8 70
(R Hannon) *a.p: rdn to chse wnr over 1f out: lost 2nd post* **7/1**

4 2 3/4 **Idiom (IRE)** 2-9-0 0 .... NeilCallan 4 62
(Mahmood Al Zarooni) *chsd wnr tl rdn and hung lft over 1f out: no ex fnl f* **13/2**

5 2 **Al Janadeirya** 2-9-0 0 .... IanMongan 2 56+
(D R Lanigan) *s.s: hld up: shkn up and hdwy over 1f out: nt trble ldrs* **11/2**[3]

6 3 1/4 **Qanateer (IRE)** 2-9-0 0 .... NickyMackay 5 46
(G A Butler) *dwlt: hld up: effrt over 2f out: hung rt and wknd over 1f out* **20/1**

7 5 **Sweetie Time** 2-9-0 0 .... HayleyTurner 1 31
(M L W Bell) *chsd ldrs: pushed along over 3f out: wknd 2f out* **6/1**

8 14 **Sixty Roses (IRE)** 2-9-0 0 .... ShaneKelly 7 —
(J L Dunlop) *hld up: pushed along over 3f out: wknd and eased sn after* **25/1**

1m 14.85s (2.65) **Going Correction** +0.05s/f (Good) **8** Ran SP% **109.3**
Speed ratings (Par 92): **84,81,80,77,74 70,63,44**
toteswingers: 1&2 £4.20, 1&3 £2.00, 2&3 £5.50 CSF £13.51 TOTE £3.10: £1.10, £2.30, £2.50; EX 15.00.
Owner Box 41 **Bred** River Downs Stud **Trained** West Ilsley, Berks

FOCUS
This was a field almost exclusively comprised of newcomers and there should be plenty of winners to come from it. The time was slow, though.

NOTEBOOK
Hortensia(IRE) was the only one with previous racetrack experience and she put it to good use, successfully stepping up to 6f. She showed that she was more streetwise than her rivals by bursting from the stalls to assume pole position and was never headed, digging deep in the closing stages.. If there was a slight negative it was that she hung left under pressure late on but it's fair to assume she'll continue to improve and can build on this first career win. (tchd 9-4 and 11-4 in places)
Madany(IRE) cost 130,000gns and is half-sister to six siblings that scored at two. She looks sure to further enhance the family record based on this very promising first run and there should be plenty more to come with this experience under her belt. It will take a good one to beat her next time. (op 7-1 tchd 15-2)
Looksmart had the benefit of the far rail. She was a relatively cheap purchase and is related to a bunch of winners over a variety of trips. This distance appeals for the time being and she'll know more for her next engagement when she'll likely take the beating. (op 13-2)
Idiom(IRE) impressed on paddock inspection and is entitled to have a fitness edge, as well as being more mentally prepared, next time. She did hang in the closing stages but this could be put down to green-ness or maybe it was because the surface was as quick as she has encountered so far. (tchd 6-1)
Al Janadeirya was very slowly away but finished her race well when the penny dropped. She is another who should be more clued up next time and her speedy pedigree - she is by a top-class sprinter out of a dam who won at 6f - suggests this is the right trip for her to make her mark over the coming months. (tchd 5-1)
Qanateer(IRE) also missed the break. She has an interesting pedigree with winners over middle-distance and staying trips, even though the dam won over 6f at two. This April foal is best watched for the time being and may prove better over further as she matures. Official explanation: jockey said filly ran green (op 12-1)

Sixty Roses(IRE) has a pedigree that suggests she'll come into her own over considerably further and the ground may have been a little on the fast side for her on her debut. Official explanation: jockey said filly ran green and was unsuited by the good to firm ground (op 16-1)

2089 32RED.COM H'CAP — 1m

2:30 (2:30) (Class 5) (0-75,75) 3-Y-O — **£3,885** (£1,156; £577; £288) **Stalls** High

Form — RPR

30-0 **1** — **One Good Emperor (IRE)**[18] 1582 3-8-11 **73** .... KierenFox(5) 1 — 85
(J R Best) *hld up: hdwy over 2f out: led over 1f out: styd on wl* — **25/1**

-062 **2** *3/4* **Secretive**[6] 1921 3-9-2 **73** ....(b[1]) NeilCallan 8 — 83
(M Johnston) *sn chsng ldrs: rdn over 3f out: ev ch 1f out: styd on* — **6/1**[3]

4304 **3** *2 3/4* **Rain On The Wind (IRE)**[23] 1476 3-8-5 **65** ....(t) WilliamCarson(3) 11 — 69
(S C Williams) *led: rdn and hdd over 1f out: edgd lft: no ex ins fnl f* — **8/1**

40-5 **4** *4 1/2* **Onyx Of Arabia (IRE)**[11] 1776 3-9-1 **72** ....(b[1]) ShaneKelly 7 — 65
(B J Meehan) *chsd ldr tl rdn over 1f out: wknd fnl f* — **12/1**

60-1 **5** *nk* **Flag Of Glory**[10] 1796 3-8-6 **63** 6ex .... JackMitchell 9 — 55
(C F Wall) *prom: racd keenly: rdn over 2f out: wknd fnl f* — **13/8**[1]

26-3 **6** *2 3/4* **Kensei (IRE)**[12] 1734 3-9-4 **75** .... StephenCraine 4 — 60
(R M Beckett) *hld up: hdwy and nt clr run 3f out: sn swtchd lft: rdn and wknd over 1f out* — **4/1**[2]

401- **7** *3 1/4* **Sidney Melbourne (USA)**[175] 7463 3-9-0 **71** .... JimmyQuinn 10 — 49
(J R Best) *hld up: a in rr: wknd over 2f out* — **16/1**

2310 **8** *2* **Juicy Pear (IRE)**[48] 1018 3-9-4 **75** .... ChrisCatlin 6 — 48
(M L W Bell) *hld up: hdwy over 3f out: wkng whn hung rt over 1f out* — **28/1**

661- **9** *nk* **Number One Guy**[206] 6923 3-9-1 **72** .... SaleemGolam 3 — 44
(M H Tompkins) *hld up: hdwy over 3f out: wknd over 2f out* — **11/1**

04-0 **10** *3* **Cereal Killer (IRE)**[17] 1589 3-9-4 **75** .... PatDobbs 2 — 40
(R Hannon) *chsd ldrs tl wknd over 2f out* — **50/1**

1m 37.58s (-1.02) **Going Correction** +0.05s/f (Good) — **10** Ran SP% **114.7**
Speed ratings (Par 99): **107,106,103,99,98 95,92,90,90,87**
toteswingers: 1&2 £26.70, 2&3:£11.90, 1&3 £63.30 CSF £163.60 CT £1350.95 TOTE £40.50: £8.60, £1.10, £3.30; EX 283.60.

Owner S Malcolm M Winwright P Tindall **Bred** Jerry O'Sullivan **Trained** Hucking, Kent

FOCUS
Very few got into this but the form looks pretty sound. The favourite was way off his Bath level.
One Good Emperor(IRE) Official explanation: trainer said, regarding apparent improvement in form, that the colt may have benefited from a more consistently run contest.

2090 BET AT 32RED.COM H'CAP — 6f

3:00 (3:00) (Class 3) (0-95,94) 3-Y-O — **£9,066** (£2,697; £1,348; £673) **Stalls** High

Form — RPR

33-3 **1** — **Cockney Class (USA)**[13] 1706 3-8-9 **85** .... LiamJones 2 — 93
(B J Meehan) *sn chsng ldr: rdn over 1f out: r.o to ld wl ins fnl f* — **9/2**[3]

-104 **2** *1 1/2* **Jarrow (IRE)**[8] 1834 3-9-0 **90** .... NeilCallan 6 — 93
(M Johnston) *led: rdn over 1f out: edgd lft and hdd wl ins fnl f* — **7/2**[2]

3-1 **3** *3/4* **Kanaf (IRE)**[17] 1599 3-8-5 **81** .... AdrianMcCarthy 5 — 82
(E A L Dunlop) *s.i.s: plld hrd and sn trcking ldrs: rdn over 1f out: styd on* — **7/2**[2]

103 **4** *2 1/2* **Burghley**[8] 1834 3-8-6 **82** .... SaleemGolam 1 — 75
(M L W Bell) *broke wl: stdd and dropped in rr after 1f: hdwy over 3f out: shkn up over 2f out: styd on same pce fr over 1f out* — **11/4**[1]

-431 **5** *1* **Yer Woman (IRE)**[48] 1019 3-9-4 **94** .... PatDobbs 4 — 83
(R Hannon) *hld up: pushed along over 2f out: nvr trbld ldrs* — **6/1**

05-0 **6** *6* **Di Stefano**[21] 1499 3-9-2 **92** .... ChrisCatlin 3 — 62
(M R Channon) *chsd ldrs tl rdn and wknd over 1f out* — **16/1**

1m 12.05s (-0.15) **Going Correction** +0.05s/f (Good) — **6** Ran SP% **109.5**
Speed ratings (Par 103): **103,101,100,96,95 87**
toteswingers:1&2 £6.50, 2&3 £4.10, 1&3 £2.70 CSF £19.34 TOTE £5.60: £2.60, £2.30; EX 18.30.

Owner Roldvale Limited **Bred** Fox Hill Farms Inc **Trained** Manton, Wilts

FOCUS
A decent sprint handicap and the winner was up a stone on his 2yo form.

NOTEBOOK
Cockney Class(USA)'s initial handicap mark of 85 looked high enough for what he'd achieved, but he vindicated connections' decision to run him here with a taking display. He really quickened up smartly to settle this inside the final furlong and may be a bright sprinting prospect if kept to his own age group for the time being. The ground was the quickest he'd encountered and probably played a part in bringing about his best career performance to date. He will be significantly raised in the handicap after this but should certainly pay to follow with this confidence-boosting win under his belt and further improvement likely. (op 11-2)
Jarrow(IRE) ran a brave race as so many from his stable do, trying to make all. He was brought back to 6f after finishing fourth over further at Chester last week and sprinting looks his game. There are likely to be further wins in this willing performer, who seems to handle quick conditions which bodes well for the summer. (op 4-1 tchd 9-2)
Kanaf(IRE) may not have appreciated the lively surface, judging by the way he changed his lead leg on more than one occasion. Stepped back up to 6f after his Nottingham win last month, he wanted to over-race early which may just have cost him a place. (op 9-2 tchd 5-1 in places)
Burghley was having his first crack at a sprint trip, having proved effective over further. It seemed a little strange then that after breaking well his jockey chose to take him back and drop in towards the rear. Perhaps if he had been allowed to go on he would have gone closer and is certainly worth giving another chance to next time. (op 5-2 tchd 3-1)
Yer Woman(IRE) never threatened and may be in the grip of the handicapper. (op 4-1)
Di Stefano has questions to answer now after finishing last for the second successive race. (tchd 14-1)

2091 32REDPOKER.COM H'CAP — 7f

3:35 (3:35) (Class 3) (0-95,90) 4-Y-O+ — **£9,066** (£2,697; £1,348; £673) **Stalls** High

Form — RPR

010/ **1** — **Coasting**[1007] 4372 5-9-4 **90** .... PatDobbs 2 — 99+
(Mrs A J Perrett) *s.i.s: hld up: hdwy over 1f out: hmpd sn after: r.o to ld nr fin* — **15/2**

1032 **2** *1/2* **Ocean Legend (IRE)**[6] 1933 5-8-3 **80** .... KierenFox(5) 6 — 88
(A W Carroll) *trckd ldr: plld hrd: shkn up to ld 1f out: hdd nr fin* — **11/4**[1]

33-4 **3** *hd* **Cape Rock**[16] 1625 5-8-7 **79** .... ShaneKelly 8 — 86
(W J Knight) *led: rdn: edgd lft and hdd 1f out: r.o* — **4/1**[2]

311- **4** *1* **Santefisio**[237] 6111 4-8-11 **83** .... NeilCallan 1 — 88+
(P J Makin) *s.i.s: hld up: plld hrd: hdwy over 3f out: nt clr run and hmpd 1f out: r.o* — **5/1**[3]

006- **5** *3* **Without Prejudice (USA)**[210] 6815 5-9-2 **88** .... GeraldMosse 5 — 85
(J Noseda) *s.i.s: racd keenly and sn prom: stdd and lost pl 5f out: rdn over 1f out: no imp ins fnl f* — **4/1**[2]

66-0 **6** *1 3/4* **Barons Spy (IRE)**[13] 1688 9-8-7 **82** .... WilliamCarson(3) 3 — 74
(R J Price) *chsd ldrs: rdn over 2f out: wknd fnl f* — **16/1**

203 **7** *3/4* **Orpenindeed (IRE)**[28] 1349 7-9-1 **87** ....(p) KirstyMilczarek 4 — 77
(M Botti) *hld up in tch: plld hrd: shkn up 2f out: wknd fnl f* — **10/1**

0-34 **8** *5* **Lindoro**[37] 1167 5-9-1 **87** ....(t) JerryO'Dwyer 9 — 63
(T T Clement) *prom: rdn over 2f out: wknd over 1f out* — **40/1**

1m 26.06s (0.66) **Going Correction** +0.05s/f (Good) — **8** Ran SP% **112.5**
Speed ratings (Par 107): **98,97,97,96,92 90,89,84**
toteswingers: 1&2 £5.80, 1&3 £13.40, 2&3 £3.80 CSF £27.53 CT £94.68 TOTE £10.90: £2.90, £2.00, £2.10; EX 29.70.

Owner Sir John Ritblat,David & Jennifer Sieff **Bred** Mrs Dare Wigan **Trained** Pulborough, W Sussex

FOCUS
Arguably one of the training performances of the season, with the winner as good as ever after a long absence. The form is a bit muddling but makes sense around the placed horses.

NOTEBOOK
Coasting defied an absence since August 2007 to come from last to first under top weight in fine fashion. He was a promising juvenile, winning twice before his long spell on the sidelines. While the trainer wasn't present, it was informative that his jockey feels Coasting could be Listed class. The five-year-old gelding looked fit enough and overcame a little trouble in running over 1f out as Cape Rock edged left, causing Santefisio to slightly bump hi, but it didn't have a significant effect on the outcome as he posted his third career victory from five starts. As long as he remains sound, he should be competitive in good handicaps and maybe in an even higher class. The fact that connections have persisted with him all this time speaks volumes for the high regard he must be held in at home. (op 14-1)
Ocean Legend(IRE) ran very well to finish second at Warwick last Saturday and off the same mark here had to be of interest. Once again he performed with credit, showing that he is just as effective on a fast surface as he is on the all-weather where all his winning has been done. His consistency is admirable but he was due to go up 3lb before this, another solid showing. (op 10-3 tchd 5-2)
Cape Rock caused the interference going into the Dip and may have been a little uncomfortable on the ground at that point before picking up again upon meeting the rising ground. He is a horse who can add to his solitary career success, especially on ground with a little underfoot ease. (op 7-2)
Santefisio enjoyed a fine three-year-old campaign, winning three times in seven starts. Still off what appears a workable mark, this was a most satisfactory return to action and he will be worth serious consideration next time. Official explanation: jockey said gelding ran too free (op 4-1 tchd 11-2)
Without Prejudice(USA) is 9lb higher than his best winning mark of 79 and could be in the grip of the handicapper although he is entitled to come on for his first start of the year. (op 5-1)
Barons Spy(IRE) is returning to a realistic mark, he is best watched for the time being. (tchd 14-1)
Orpenindeed(IRE) did his cause no favours at all early on by running keen early on. Official explanation: jockey said gelding ran too free (op 8-1)
Lindoro, back on turf, offered little encouragement after running unsuccessfully in sellers on the AW. (op 33-1)

2092 32RED CASINO MAIDEN FILLIES' STKS — 1m 4f

4:10 (4:11) (Class 4) 3-Y-O — **£5,180** (£1,541; £770; £384) **Stalls** Centre

Form — RPR

33- **1** — **Meeznah (USA)**[206] 6921 3-9-0 0 .... ChrisCatlin 6 — 86
(D R Lanigan) *led 1f: chsd ldr tl led again over 2f out: sn clr: styd on strly* — **6/5**[1]

3- **2** *9* **Radio Wave**[206] 6920 3-9-0 0 .... NickyMackay 1 — 72
(J H M Gosden) *s.i.s: rcvrd to ld after 1f: hdd over 2f out: sn rdn and edgd lft: styng on same pce whn hung rt over 1f out* — **13/8**[2]

4 **3** *1/2* **Affinity**[24] 1451 3-9-0 0 .... IanMongan 3 — 71
(H R A Cecil) *hld up in tch: rdn over 2f out: sn outpcd: no ch whn swtchd rt over 1f out* — **5/1**[3]

0-6 **4** *33* **Kleio**[24] 1451 3-9-0 0 .... JimmyQuinn 4 — 18
(H R A Cecil) *chsd ldrs tl wknd over 3f out: t.o* — **16/1**

2m 34.14s (0.64) **Going Correction** +0.05s/f (Good) — **4** Ran SP% **106.1**
Speed ratings (Par 98): **99,93,92,70**
CSF £3.30 TOTE £2.10; EX 3.10.

Owner Saif Ali & Saeed H Altayer **Bred** Swettenham Stud **Trained** Newmarket, Suffolk

FOCUS
An uncompetitive maiden but the winner impressed. The second and third were close to their initial efforts.

2093 32RED H'CAP — 1m 2f

4:45 (4:46) (Class 5) (0-75,75) 4-Y-O+ — **£3,885** (£1,156; £577; £288) **Stalls** High

Form — RPR

0625 **1** — **Buddy Holly**[48] 1011 5-9-3 **74** .... StephenCraine 1 — 85
(Pat Eddery) *a.p: chsd ldr over 1f out: shkn up to ld ins fnl f: r.o wl* — **8/1**[3]

4-16 **2** *2* **Penchesco (IRE)**[18] 1579 5-9-2 **73** .... PatDobbs 4 — 80
(Mrs A J Perrett) *led: rdn over 1f out: hdd and unable qck ins fnl f* — **11/4**[1]

0-00 **3** *3/4* **Archie Rice (USA)**[30] 1306 4-9-1 **72** .... SaleemGolam 12 — 78
(T Keddy) *stdd s: hld up: plld hrd: hdwy over 2f out: rdn over 1f out: styd on* — **20/1**

000- **4** *3* **Petsas Pleasure**[193] 7212 4-8-6 **63** .... ChrisCatlin 10 — 63
(Ollie Pears) *hld up: swtchd lft and hdwy over 1f out: r.o: nt trble ldrs* — **16/1**

6032 **5** *1/2* **General Tufto**[11] 1751 5-8-11 **68** ....(b) KirstyMilczarek 8 — 67
(C Smith) *prom: chsd ldr 2f out tl rdn over 1f out: styd on same pce* — **7/1**[2]

2-03 **6** *nk* **Basra (IRE)**[83] 637 7-9-3 **74** .... IanMongan 5 — 72
(Miss Jo Crowley) *trckd ldrs: rdn over 1f out: styd on same pce* — **9/1**

1006 **7** *3/4* **Chosen Forever**[13] 1684 5-9-3 **74** .... JimmyQuinn 9 — 70
(G R Oldroyd) *mid-div: rdn over 3f out: outpcd over 2f out: styd on ins fnl f* — **10/1**

333 **8** *1* **Gordon Road (IRE)**[53] 963 4-8-13 **70** ....(p) NeilCallan 2 — 64
(M G Quinlan) *s.i.s: hld up: hdwy over 6f out: rdn and wknd over 1f out* — **12/1**

-020 **9** *1 3/4* **Woolfall Sovereign (IRE)**[27] 1374 4-8-12 **69** .... GeraldMosse 3 — 60
(G G Margarson) *plld hrd and prom: stdd and lost pl over 7f out: rdn over 2f out: n.d after* — **8/1**[3]

100- **10** *nk* **Hits Only Cash**[209] 6860 8-8-4 **61** .... LiamJones 11 — 51
(J Pearce) *hld up in tch: rdn over 3f out: wknd fnl f* — **33/1**

-003 **11** *1/2* **It's Dubai Dolly**[39] 1133 4-9-2 **73** .... NickyMackay 6 — 62
(A J Lidderdale) *racd keenly: trckd ldr tl rdn over 2f out: wknd over 1f out* — **14/1**

0003 **12** *2 3/4* **Ramona Chase**[11] 1780 5-8-13 **75** ....(t) JemmaMarshall(5) 7 — 59
(M J Attwater) *s.s: hld up: a in rr* — **8/1**[3]

2m 7.38s (1.58) **Going Correction** +0.05s/f (Good) — **12** Ran SP% **119.5**
Speed ratings (Par 103): **95,93,92,90,90 89,89,88,86,86 86,84**
toteswingers: 1&2 £6.60, 1&3 £41.90, 2&3 £17.40 CSF £30.40 CT £438.96 TOTE £13.90: £4.10, £1.10, £7.60; EX 41.10.

Owner EDS Roofing Supplies Ltd **Bred** R J & S A Carter **Trained** Nether Winchendon, Bucks

FOCUS
They only went a steady pace in this and it favoured those who raced close to the pace. Ordinary but sound form.

It's Dubai Dolly Official explanation: jockey said filly had no more to give and was unsuited by the good to firm ground

2094 32RED CASINO H'CAP 5f

5:20 (5:20) (Class 4) (0-80,80) 4-Y-0+ **£4,856** (£1,445; £722; £180; £180) **Stalls** High

Form RPR

11-0 **1** **Ziggy Lee**[18] 1580 4-8-13 **78** WilliamCarson(3) 1 89+
(S C Williams) *hld up: hdwy over 1f out: shkn up to ld ins fnl f: r.o* **8/1**

-124 **2** ½ **Brynfa Boy**[32] 1266 4-8-9 **71** LiamJones 3 80+
(P W D'Arcy) *hld up: hdwy over 1f out: r.o wl: nt rch wnr* **5/1**[2]

20-5 **3** 1¾ **Our Piccadilly (IRE)**[13] 1691 5-9-0 **76** IanMongan 10 79
(W S Kittow) *a.p: nt clr run over 1f out: sn rdn: hung lft ins fnl f: r.o* **16/1**

-456 **4** ½ **The Jobber (IRE)**[21] 1506 9-8-12 **74** NeilCallan 4 75
(M Blanshard) *chsd ldrs: led over 1f out: sn rdn: hdd and unable qck ins fnl f* **12/1**

04-3 **4** *dht* **Evelyn May (IRE)**[11] 1770 4-8-5 **72** AshleyMorgan(5) 9 73+
(B W Hills) *awkward leaving stalls: hld up: hmpd over 1f out: swtchd rt: nt clr run sn after tl r.o wl ins fnl f: nrst fin* **9/2**[1]

3430 **6** 1½ **Incomparable**[13] 1710 5-9-4 **80** (bt) EddieCreighton 6 76
(J A Glover) *hld up in tch: plld hrd: rdn and edgd rt over 1f out: styd on same pce fnl f* **16/1**

0-62 **7** *hd* **Taurus Twins**[7] 1874 4-9-0 **76** (b) GeraldMosse 2 71
(R J Price) *chsd ldrs: rdn over 1f out: styd on same pce fnl f* **9/2**[1]

0-32 **8** *nk* **Make My Dream**[13] 1692 7-8-11 **73** PatDobbs 5 67
(J Gallagher) *sn pushed along in mid-div: rdn and nt clr run ins fnl f: n.d* **6/1**[3]

-653 **9** ¾ **Ocean Blaze**[13] 1691 6-9-4 **80** ChrisCatlin 7 71
(B R Millman) *led: rdn and hdd over 1f out: wknd ins fnl f* **7/1**

00-0 **10** ¾ **Zowington**[32] 1267 8-9-2 **78** (v) SaleemGolam 12 66
(S C Williams) *hmpd s: hld up: nvr on terms* **40/1**

6522 **11** ¾ **Fine Silk (USA)**[8] 1843 4-8-4 **66** (p) JimmyQuinn 11 52
(M G Quinlan) *chsd ldr: rdn over 1f out: wknd ins fnl f* **18/1**

155- **12** ¾ **Corton Charlemagne (IRE)**[226] 6387 4-8-2 **71** NoelGarbutt(7) 13 54
(Rae Guest) *a in rr* **12/1**

59.38 secs (0.28) **Going Correction** +0.05s/f (Good) **12** Ran SP% **117.6**
Speed ratings (Par 105): **99,98,95,94,94 92,91,91,90,89 87,86**
toteswingers: 1&2 £4.90, 1&3 £20.70, 2&3 £15.00 CSF £47.32 CT £642.26 TOTE £12.70: £3.60, £1.50, £4.80; EX 79.60 Place 6: £112.17 Place 5: £66.76.
Owner Rothmere Racing Limited **Bred** Ian Allan **Trained** Newmarket, Suffolk

FOCUS

They went quick early on and it favoured those who were held up for a finish. The first two are relatively unexposed as sprinters.
T/Plt: £222.70. Pool of £56,500.11- 185.20 winning tickets. T/Qpdt: £31.20. Pool of £3,463.41- 82.08 winning tickets. CR

2054 YORK (L-H)

Friday, May 14

OFFICIAL GOING: Good to firm (8.5)

Wind: moderate half behind Weather: Fine and breezy

2095 LANGLEYS SOLICITORS E B F MARYGATE FILLIES' STKS (LISTED RACE) 5f

1:40 (1:40) (Class 1) 2-Y-O **£17,778** (£6,723; £3,360; £1,680) **Stalls** Low

Form RPR

13 **1** **Primo Lady**[9] 1819 2-8-12 0 (v) DavidProbert 9 91
(Miss Gay Kelleway) *qckly away: mde most: rdn over 1f out: kpt on wl fnl f* **7/1**

3 **2** 1¾ **Breedj (IRE)**[14] 1660 2-8-12 0 SebSanders 6 86+
(C E Brittain) *athletic: chsd ldrs: hdwy 2f out: rdn and styd on to chse wnr ins fnl f: sn hung lft and kpt on* **4/1**[3]

61 **3** 2¼ **Fifth Ave**[10] 1793 2-8-12 0 FergusSweeney 4 77
(J A Osborne) *cl cpld: cl up: rdn along wl over 1f out and ev ch tl drvn and one pce ins fnl f* **9/4**[1]

1 **4** 1 **Geesala (IRE)**[25] 1421 2-8-12 0 DarryllHolland 5 73
(K A Ryan) *w'like: lengthy: chsd ldng pair: rdn along and edgd lft over 1f out: drvn and edgd rt ins fnl f: one pce* **7/1**

40 **5** 1¼ **Lady Platinum Club**[13] 1686 2-8-12 0 PJMcDonald 8 69
(G R Oldroyd) *in tch on outer: rdn along and hdwy 2f out: sn drvn and no imp* **25/1**

251 **6** ½ **Lady Brookie**[28] 1360 2-8-12 0 LiamKeniry 1 67
(Peter Grayson) *chsd ldrs 2f: rdn along 1/2-way: sn outpcd* **18/1**

1 **7** 2¾ **Turn The Tide**[20] 1510 2-8-12 0 MickyFenton 3 58+
(A Bailey) *tall: scope: lw: dwlt and hmpd shortly after s: sn rdn along and a towards rr: hung lft and eased ent fnl f* **11/4**[2]

59.42 secs (0.12) **Going Correction** -0.05s/f (Good) **7** Ran SP% **111.5**
Speed ratings (Par 98): **97,94,90,89,87 86,81**
toteswingers: 1&2 £5.90, 1&3 £6.20, 2&3 £3.10 CSF £33.13 TOTE £7.00: £2.80, £2.20; EX 33.80 Trifecta £107.70 Pool: £861.30 - 5.91 winning units..
Owner K Jarvis, G Hodson, P Moule **Bred** Mr And Mrs L Baker **Trained** Exning, Suffolk

FOCUS

The track had been watered on Thursday evening, with 3mm applied to the straight and 5mm to the bends. There were still more than 20 non-runners on the card because of the fast ground. The sixth running of this event, the first Listed race of the season for juveniles, lacked strength in depth and looked a below-par renewal on paper. The winner did it well and showed improvement, but there have to be doubts over the strength of the form. The time was around 1.5 slower than the RP standard.

NOTEBOOK

Primo Lady had become upset at the stalls and started slowly on both her previous outings, especially in the Lily Agnes at Chester last week where she came home strongly for third. Her trainer had taken precautions here and the filly was hooded to keep her calm while walking around down at the start. She broke very smartly and she and the third were clear of the rest approaching the final furlong. After burning off that rival, her lead was being reduced late on as the runner-up closed but she was never in any danger of being caught. The Queen Mary at Ascot is the obvious target for this speedy filly but she will need to improve again there. (op 9-2)

Breedj(IRE) represented the connections of last year's winner Misheer, who went on to prove herself one of the best of her generation. This filly had only been third on her debut on Polytrack but stepped up markedly on that form, running on well inside the final furlong but too late to get to the winner. She may benefit from a sixth furlong and the Albany Stakes at Ascot could be the race for her. (op 9-2)

Fifth Ave only won a maiden auction at Bath but she ran with plenty of credit in this much stronger grade, showing bright pace to shadow the winner and only missing out on second after her stride started to shorten inside the last. (op 10-3)

Geesala(IRE), another maiden auction winner last time, on easy ground at Pontefract, lacked the pace to trouble the principals but didn't stop trying. She has more long-term scope than some of these and will be ready for an extra furlong before long. (op 6-1)

Lady Platinum Club was slightly impeded soon after the start and she could never get into the race down the outside. She has the ability to win in lesser company (op 28-1)

Lady Brookie has not really gone on from her second in the Brocklesby in March but the ground was against her on her first run for a new yard. (op 20-1)

Turn The Tide was squeezed out leaving the start and although she quickly recovered to race in touch, she was on the retreat again entering the final quarter mile. Her rider reported that she had been struck into. (op 3-1)

2096 SPORTINGBET.COM JORVIK STKS (H'CAP) 1m 4f

2:10 (2:10) (Class 2) (0-105,104) 4-Y-O+**£25,904** (£7,708; £3,852; £1,924) **Stalls** Centre

Form RPR

11-2 **1** **Hanoverian Baron**[23] 1474 5-8-3 **83** DavidProbert 9 94
(A G Newcombe) *trckd ldrs: hdwy 4f out: led over 2f out: rdn clr and edgd lft ent fnl f: drvn out* **7/1**[2]

02-0 **2** 2¼ **Crackentorp**[37] 1151 5-8-11 **91** DavidAllan 1 98
(T D Easterby) *lw: hld up in rr: swtchd outside and hdwy 3f out: rdn wl over 1f out: styd on ins fnl f: nt rch wnr* **12/1**

30-0 **3** *hd* **Mystery Star (IRE)**[31] 1274 5-9-3 **97** TedDurcan 17 104
(M H Tompkins) *hld up towards rr: hdwy 3f out: rdn along wl over 1f out: styd on ins fnl f: nrst fin* **16/1**

0-01 **4** 1 **Antigua Sunrise (IRE)**[16] 1629 4-7-13 **79** ow1 PaulHanagan 14 84
(R A Fahey) *hld up towards rr: hdwy over 3f out: rdn to chse wnr ent fnl f: sn drvn and one pce* **10/1**

5-52 **5** 3¾ **Dazzling Light (UAE)**[16] 1629 5-7-12 **78** oh2 SilvestreDeSousa 8 77
(J S Goldie) *hld up in rr: hdwy on outer wl over 2f out: rdn to chse ldrs over 1f out: drvn and no imp ins fnl f* **16/1**

1-1 **6** 7 **Dangerous Midge (USA)**[27] 1378 4-9-5 **99** MartinDwyer 4 87
(B J Meehan) *lw: trckd ldrs on inner: effrt over 3f out and sn pushed along: rdn over 2f out and no imp* **4/1**[1]

4-10 **7** 1¼ **Dansili Dancer**[27] 1382 8-9-2 **101** JohnFahy(5) 10 87
(C G Cox) *trckd ldrs: hdwy over 4f out: chsd ldr 3f out: rdn and ch 2f out: drvn and wknd over 1f out* **14/1**

-133 **8** 8 **Shadows Lengthen**[31] 1274 4-8-13 **93** (b) GrahamGibbons 19 66
(M W Easterby) *a in rr* **22/1**

110- **9** ¾ **Lochiel**[202] 7018 6-8-13 **93** PJMcDonald 2 65
(Mrs L B Normile) *hld up in rr: sme hdwy on inner over 3f out: rdn over 2f out and nvr a factor* **50/1**

4-00 **10** 1¾ **Mull Of Dubai**[9] 1829 7-8-11 **91** AdrianNicholls 13 60
(D Nicholls) *a towards rr* **40/1**

-034 **11** 6 **Drill Sergeant**[13] 1698 5-9-10 **104** JoeFanning 3 63
(M Johnston) *lw: led: 1f: chsd clr ldr: hdwy over 4f out: rdn along over 3f out: grad wknd* **16/1**

15-2 **12** 5 **Cool Strike (UAE)**[19] 1544 4-8-10 **90** (v) LiamKeniry 15 41
(A M Balding) *lw: prom: rdn along 4f out: wknd qckly over 3f out: sn bhd* **8/1**

40-0 **13** 3½ **Class Is Class (IRE)**[12] 1724 4-9-0 **97**...(v[1]) Louis-PhilippeBeuzelin(3) 12 43
(Sir Michael Stoute) *lw: dwlt: rapid hdwy to ld after 1f and sn clr: rdn along over 3f out: hdd over 2f out and wknd qckly* **8/1**

/14- **14** 2½ **Fortuni (IRE)**[300] 4103 4-8-9 **89** SebSanders 5 31
(Sir Mark Prescott) *t.k.h: chsd ldrs: rdn along over 3f out: sn wknd* **15/2**[3]

34-5 **15** ½ **Classic Punch (IRE)**[20] 1529 7-9-2 **96** JimmyFortune 18 37
(D R C Elsworth) *lw: racd wd in midfield: rdn along 3f over 3f out and sn wknd* **40/1**

2m 28.98s (-4.22) **Going Correction** -0.125s/f (Firm) **15** Ran SP% **118.8**
Speed ratings (Par 109): **109,107,107,106,104 99,98,93,92,91 87,84,82,80,80**
toteswingers: 1&2 £21.20, 1&3 £44.10, 2&3 £38.20 CSF £83.88 CT £1305.04 TOTE £8.40: £3.00, £4.80, £6.30; EX 118.40 TRIFECTA Not won..
Owner Paul Moulton **Bred** S Coughlan **Trained** Yarnscombe, Devon

FOCUS

A valuable and competitive handicap, run at a strong pace thanks to Class Is Class who was soon in a clear lead. The form looks rock solid with a personal best from the winner.

NOTEBOOK

Hanoverian Baron ◆ travelled really well on his first try at the trip and and ran out a comfortable winner. If anything he appeared to be idling in front, and there is surely more to come from him. Paying a real compliment to Alainmaar, who beat him in the City and Suburban at Epsom, he may drop back in trip for the John Smith's Cup here in July. He ought to get into that race after a rise in the weights for this victory. (op 8-1)

Crackentorp was just about last turning in but he made rapid headway down the outside once into the straight. He could never trouble the winner, but he loses nothing in defeat and this lightly raced 5yo looks sure to win a nice handicap for his new yard this term. (op 10-1)

Mystery Star(IRE) had ground conditions to suit and he ran a sound race, coming from off the pace after briefly having to wait for a run and just missing out on second. The handicapper remains in control, though.

Antigua Sunrise(IRE), a winner on this card a year ago, beat members of her own sex at Pontefract last time and was effectively 5lb higher here. She ran a brave race back over this longer trip, improving from the rear and keeping on willingly for pressure. (op 12-1)

Dazzling Light(UAE), runner-up to Antiguan Star at Pontefract, was another to run on from the rear divsion and this was a solid effort from 2lb out of the weights.

Dangerous Midge(USA) was raised a hefty 11lb for his impressive Doncaster win last month. After racing prominently in the chasing pack he was being pushed along shortly after halfway. He failed to threaten the principals and his rider gave up persevering inside the last. Whether or not he stayed is hard to say, but he is probably worth another try at this trip. (op 9-2)

Dansili Dancerwas the first to go out after the clear leader in the straight but was on the retreat with just under a quarter of a mile left. He is high enough in the weights.\n (op 16-1)

Drill Sergeant has yet to recapture his form this term.

Cool Strike(UAE) was another to pay for his early exertions.

Class Is Class(IRE) wore a visor for the first time but it had the wrong effect as he went off too quickly. He soon compiled a lengthy lead but came right back to his field in the straight. He is talented but looks one to be wary of.

Fortuni(IRE) is capable of better but will need to settle. (tchd 8-1)

2097 EMIRATES AIRLINE YORKSHIRE CUP (GROUP 2) 1m 6f

2:40 (2:40) (Class 1) 4-Y-O+ **£79,478** (£30,128; £15,078; £7,518; £3,766) **Stalls** Low

Form RPR

13-2 **1** **Manifest**[27] 1382 4-8-12 110 TomQueally 7 121+
(H R A Cecil) *trckd ldr: hdwy 4f out: qcknd to ld 3f out: rdn and edgd lft 2f out: sn clr: eased nr fin: impressive* **13/8**[1]

43-0 **2** 8 **Purple Moon (IRE)**[27] 1382 7-8-13 115 KierenFallon 8 110
(L M Cumani) *lw: hld up in tch: hdwy over 3f out: rdn over 2f out: drvn and kpt on ent fnl f: no ch w wnr* **9/4**[2]

051- **3** 3¾ **Wajir (FR)**[250] 5711 4-8-12 117 FrankieDettori 6 105
(Saeed Bin Suroor) *lengthy: lw: trckd ldng pair: hdwy over 4f out: cl up 3f out: rdn to chal over 2f out and ev ch tl drvn and one pce wl over 1f out* **7/2**[3]

5-06 **4** *3* **Oasis Knight (IRE)**[16] 1615 4-8-12 102......................(p) JimmyFortune 4 101
(M P Tregoning) *set stdy pce: qcknd over 4f out and sn rdn: hdd 3f out: sn drvn and wknd* **25/1**

04-2 **5** *nk* **Nanton (USA)**[13] 1698 8-8-13 107................................ DanielTudhope 2 100
(J S Goldie) *hld up in rr: effrt and sme hdwy 3f out: rdn over 2f out: sn drvn and no imp* **8/1**

2m 58.99s (-1.21) **Going Correction** -0.125s/f (Firm)
WFA 4 from 5yo+ 1lb **5** Ran SP% **106.0**
Speed ratings (Par 115): **98,93,91,89,89**
CSF £5.07 TOTE £2.40: £1.50, £1.40; EX 4.80 Trifecta £5.80 Pool: £567.79 - 72.41 winning units..
Owner K Abdulla **Bred** Juddmonte Farms Ltd **Trained** Newmarket, Suffolk

FOCUS
Not a strong renewal of the Yorkshire Cup, the race losing a lot of its interest with the defection of likely favourite Kite Wood, but it still saw a highly impressive winning performance. The form is not rated too positively, with the fourth perhaps the best guide. It was run at a stop-start pace with the tempo lifting again once they were into the home straight, but the time was decent, just a second outside the RP standard.

NOTEBOOK
Manifest ◆, runner-up to Harbinger in the John Porter on his reappearance, was the least experienced runner in this line-up. After tracking the pacesetter from the off he headed for the centre of the track once into the straight, the three behind following him there, and soon took over in front. He briefly had to work to see off his nearest pursuers, but found a fine turn of foot from the two pole and really lengthened his stride to pull well clear. This was impressive, and he surely has further improvement in him. He looks a leading contender for the Gold Cup at Ascot, and although that race is over an extra three-quarters of a mile his trainer thinks he will stay. Cecil did add that the colt would not want the ground any firmer than this. (op 15-8)
Purple Moon(IRE) was sharper for his run at Newbury and finished a shade closer to Manifest this time but was still no match for the younger horse. Racing keenly and turning into the straight in third, he battled on to get the better of a duel for second but was well held by his old opponent. He is without a win since taking the Ebor over course and distance in 2007 but his cause may be helped by a step up in trip now, and he will renew rivalry in the Gold Cup. (op 2-1)
Wajir(FR) became the sole Godolphin runner once Kite Wood was taken out. Successful at this level in the Prix Hocquart, and later in the Prix de Lutece for Elie Lellouche last year, he ran respectably on his debut for new connections and momentarily posed a threat to the winner before he was left trailing by him in the final quarter mile. He is another with a Gold Cup entry. (op 10-3)
Oasis Knight(IRE), on whom cheekpieces replaced a visor, set the pace and tried to wind things up once into the straight, but he was quickly put in his place. He looked set to finish last when dropping away but did rally to claim a remote fourth. (op 20-1)
Nanton(USA) was outpaced when the tempo lifted once in line for home and could never get into the action.

2098 SPORTINGBET.COM FILLIES' STKS (REGISTERED AS THE MICHAEL SEELY MEMORIAL STAKES) (LISTED RACE) 1m
3:10 (3:13) (Class 1) 3-Y-O **£22,708** (£8,608; £4,308; £2,148; £1,076) **Stalls** Low

Form RPR

365- **1** **Chachamaidee (IRE)**[267] 5199 3-8-12 95........................ TomQueally 3 106
(H R A Cecil) *s.i.s: t.k.h early: hld up in rr: hdwy on inner wl over 2f out: rdn to chse ldr over 1f out: styd on u.p ins fnl f to ld last 100yds* **5/1**

6-11 **2** *¾* **Carioca (IRE)**[33] 1252 3-9-1 98... KierenFallon 1 107
(M Botti) *lw: unruly bef s: led: qcknd over 2f out: rdn wl over 1f out: drvn and edgd lft ins fnl f: hdd and no ex last 100yds* **7/2**[2]

102- **3** *3 ¼* **Sweet Sonnet (USA)**[253] 5606 3-8-12 100.................... FrankieDettori 2 97
(Saeed Bin Suroor) *trckd ldr: hdwy 3f out: rdn 2f out: drvn and one pce appr fnl f* **7/2**[2]

1-52 **4** *2 ¾* **Hafawa (IRE)**[13] 1693 3-8-12 100..................................... TadhgO'Shea 6 90
(M Johnston) *lw: chsd ldng pair: hdwy 3f out: rdn along over 2f out: sn drvn and btn* **2/1**[1]

1- **5** *10* **Muwakaba (USA)**[235] 6163 3-8-12 0............................ RichardMullen 7 67
(Sir Michael Stoute) *t.k.h: hld up: a towards rr* **9/2**[3]

1m 37.68s (-1.12) **Going Correction** -0.05s/f (Good) **5** Ran SP% **112.6**
Speed ratings (Par 104): **103,102,99,96,86**
CSF £22.58 TOTE £6.20: £2.60, £2.10; EX 29.10 Trifecta £101.70 Pool: £884.11 - 6.43 winning units..
Owner R A H Evans **Bred** Cheval Court Stud **Trained** Newmarket, Suffolk

FOCUS
A decent fillies' Listed race although another event hit by withdrawals. The runner-up set a brisk pace and the time was inside the standard. The form has been rated on the positive side.

NOTEBOOK
Chachamaidee(IRE) was found wanting in Group company after her winning debut last term. A lot of work has been done with this free and headstrong filly to settle her and although she missed the break on this reappearance, it was partly by design. Last into the straight, she came with her run nearest to the inside rail and wore down the long-time leader to win in game style. A likeable filly, she holds entries at the top level in the Irish 1,000 Guineas and the Coronation Stakes, but the former may come too soon and her trainer has other options in the Ascot race, not least Jacqueline Quest. She got the mile well and can add to this if she doesn't fly too high. (op 6-1)
Carioca(IRE)'s trainer won this event with Raymi Coya two years ago. A winner in this grade from the subsequent Italian Guineas runner-up at San Siro last time, when she enjoyed the run of the race, she took a great deal of persuading to go into the stalls here before making the running. She had most of her rivals in trouble in the straight but could not fend off the winner late on. (tchd 10-3)
Sweet Sonnet(USA), making her seasonal debut, became warm in the preliminaries but had cooled down a little before the start. After tracking the leader she was unable to quicken up in the straight and she could prove a little difficult to place successfully, with her Coronation Stakes entry looking unrealistic on this evidence. (op 4-1)
Hafawa(IRE) ran well against older fillies when runner-up at Goodwood latest but she did not build on that, appearing to hang on the fast ground and never within striking distance. (op 5-2)
Muwakaba(USA), a Kempton maiden winner in September on her sole start, is another with Group 1 entries. Failing to settle and always towards the rear on this turf debut, she will need to prove she has trained on. (op 4-1)

2099 RALPH RAPER MEMORIAL STKS (H'CAP) 5f
3:45 (3:47) (Class 4) (0-80,79) 3-Y-O **£6,540** (£1,946; £972; £485) **Stalls** Low

Form RPR

1-01 **1** **Hoof It**[11] 1750 3-8-11 72 6ex... GrahamGibbons 1 87
(M W Easterby) *chsd ldrs on outer: hdwy 1/2-way: rdn to ld wl over 1f out: clr and edgd lft ins fnl f: kpt on strly* **5/2**[2]

-212 **2** *2 ½* **Diman Waters (IRE)**[7] 1860 3-9-0 75................................ DavidAllan 12 81
(E J Alston) *lw: cl up on wd outside: effrt to chal 2f out: sn rdn and ev ch tl drvn and one pce ins fnl f* **7/4**[1]

13-0 **3** *¾* **Imjin River (IRE)**[31] 1279 3-8-11 72.............................. DarryllHolland 6 75+
(M H Tompkins) *towards rr: hdwy whn n.m.r and swtchd lft over 1f out: sn rdn and styd on wl fnl f* **14/1**

6-14 **4** *1* **Trade Secret**[13] 1709 3-9-0 75.. JimmyFortune 5 75
(M Brittain) *lw: sn rdn along towards rr: hdwy 1/2-way: n.m.r and swtchd rt over 1f out: drvn and kpt on same pce ins fnl f* **17/2**[3]

635- **5** *nk* **Fear Nothing**[220] 6556 3-9-0 75..................................... RichardMullen 10 74
(E S McMahon) *lw: in tch: hdwy to chse ldrs 2f out: rdn wl over 1f out: one pce ent fnl f* **12/1**

523- **6** *2 ¼* **We'll Deal Again**[195] 7168 3-8-0 66.......................... JamesSullivan(5) 11 57
(M W Easterby) *dwlt and in rr: hdwy on outer 2f out: sn chsng ldrs: edgd lft and no imp ins fnl f* **28/1**

52-3 **7** *4 ½* **Tillys Tale**[27] 1399 3-8-13 79.. PaulPickard(5) 7 53
(P T Midgley) *prom: rdn along over 2f out: sn drvn and wknd* **18/1**

0-01 **8** *shd* **Lucky Flyer**[28] 1345 3-8-9 70.. LiamKeniry 2 44
(S Kirk) *chsd ldrs: rdn along 1/2-way: sn wknd* **25/1**

0-16 **9** *nk* **Taborcillo**[10] 1811 3-8-5 66.. DavidProbert 13 39
(T D Barron) *in tch: rdn along 2f out: wkng whn hmpd over 1f out* **18/1**

01-0 **10** *11* **Besty**[11] 1750 3-8-12 73... TomEaves 8 6
(B Smart) *chsd ldrs: rdn along 1/2-way: sn wknd* **16/1**

4-40 **11** *12* **Dispol Keasha**[14] 1656 3-9-1 76.. KierenFallon 4 —
(P T Midgley) *led: rdn along over 2f out: drvn and hdd wl over 1f out: sn wknd and bhd whn eased ins fnl f* **18/1**

58.91 secs (-0.39) **Going Correction** -0.05s/f (Good) **11** Ran SP% **118.8**
Speed ratings (Par 101): **101,97,95,94,93 90,82,82,82,64 45**
toteswingers: 1&2 £1.90, 1&3 £12.60, 2&3 £7.90 CSF £7.32 CT £50.38 TOTE £3.60: £1.70, £1.10, £3.80; EX 7.50 Trifecta £101.60 Pool: £ 1112.90 - 8.10 winning units..
Owner A Chandler & L Westwood **Bred** Bond Thoroughbred Corporation **Trained** Sheriff Hutton, N Yorks

FOCUS
This is often a decent sprint handicap and with the first two home this year both ahead of the handicapper, the form looks strong. It could be 2-3lb better than rated.

2100 SPORTINGBET.COM STKS (H'CAP) 6f
4:20 (4:21) (Class 2) (0-105,105) 4-Y-O+ **£10,361** (£3,083; £1,540; £769) **Stalls** Low

Form RPR

102- **1** **Ingleby Lady**[238] 6050 4-8-8 92...................................... GrahamGibbons 11 102+
(T D Barron) *dwlt: smooth hdwy to trck ldrs after 2f: effrt and edgd rt over 2f out: led wl over 1f out: rdn and hung rt ent fnl f: hld on wl* **6/1**[1]

-456 **2** *¾* **Baldemar**[25] 1423 5-8-4 91 ow1.................................... BarryMcHugh(3) 8 99
(R A Fahey) *chsd ldrs: rdn along whn sltly hmpd over 2f out: drvn to chse wnr ent fnl f: kpt on u.p towards fin* **6/1**[1]

01-0 **3** *1* **Esoterica (IRE)**[13] 1708 7-8-8 92..................................(v) KierenFallon 17 97
(J S Goldie) *in tch: rdn along and outpcd over 2f out: hdwy over 1f out: kpt on wl u.p ins fnl f* **18/1**

60-0 **4** *¾* **Oldjoesaid**[30] 1295 6-8-9 93... DarryllHolland 9 95
(K A Ryan) *in rr: hdwy wl over 1f out: sn rdn and styd on strly ins fnl f* **12/1**

30-0 **5** *3* **Red Cape (FR)**[18] 1573 7-8-2 86.................................... AndrewElliott 3 79
(Mrs R A Carr) *slt ld: rdn along over 2f out: drvn and hdd wl over 1f out: grad wknd ent fnl f* **12/1**

60-1 **6** *1* **Sunrise Safari (IRE)**[20] 1516 7-8-3 87..........................(v) PaulHanagan 6 77
(R A Fahey) *chsd ldrs: rdn 2f out: swtchd lft and drvn ent fnl f and sn one pce* **13/2**[2]

103- **7** *¾* **Brave Prospector**[216] 6661 5-9-7 105........................(t) JimmyFortune 14 92
(P W Chapple-Hyam) *chsd ldrs: hdwy on outer over 2f out: ev ch tl rdn and wknd appr fnl f* **7/1**[3]

334- **8** *½* **Himalya (IRE)**[149] 7768 4-9-4 102.................................... TomQueally 4 88
(J Noseda) *prom: effrt over 2f out: sn rdn and ev ch tl drvn and wknd ent fnl f* **13/2**[2]

100- **9** *hd* **Magaling (IRE)**[330] 3049 4-7-13 88.......................... JamesSullivan(5) 12 73
(M W Easterby) *a towards rr* **33/1**

-410 **10** *½* **Buachaill Dona (IRE)**[9] 1822 7-9-4 102......................... AdrianNicholls 1 85
(D Nicholls) *disp ld: rdn along 2f out: ev ch tl drvn and wknd appr fnl f* **9/1**

0-04 **11** *2 ¾* **Al Muheer (IRE)**[14] 1662 5-9-6 104............................(b) SebSanders 13 79
(C E Brittain) *a towards rr* **14/1**

001- **12** *14* **Nota Bene**[301] 4059 8-9-5 103... LiamKeniry 2 33
(D R C Elsworth) *chsd ldrs on wd outside: rdn along 2f out: sn wknd* **16/1**

200- **13** *2* **Whistledownwind**[391] 1352 5-8-9 93................................... PaulQuinn 15 16
(D Nicholls) *in rr: rdn along bef 1/2-way: sn outpcd and bhd* **20/1**

1m 11.09s (-0.81) **Going Correction** -0.05s/f (Good) **13** Ran SP% **118.6**
Speed ratings (Par 109): **103,102,100,99,95 94,93,92,92,91 88,69,66**
toteswingers: 1&2 £6.60, 1&3 £24.10, 2&3 £25.10 CSF £40.52 CT £641.48 TOTE £7.30: £2.30, £2.30, £4.90; EX 39.10 Trifecta £959.40 Part won. Pool of £1296.56 - 0.73 winng units..
Owner Dave Scott **Bred** Hellwood Stud Farm **Trained** Maunby, N Yorks

FOCUS
A competitive sprint handicap, but the early pace didn't look strong. The first three home all made the frame in last September's Ayr Bronze Cup. Straightforward form.

NOTEBOOK
Ingleby Lady, having her first run since finishing second to Baldemar in the Ayr Bronze Cup in the autumn, didn't break on terms, but she was soon travelling well in touch and she quickly asserted once in front despite drifting over to the stands' rail. She looks to have thrived physically from three to four, and unlike a lot of her sire's progeny is thoroughly at home on fast ground. She is well capable of winning again. (op 13-2)
Baldemar, the inaugural Ayr Bronze Cup winner, has been held off higher marks since but had run creditably on his first two starts this spring. He was below par last time, but bounced back with a solid effort. But for meeting a little trouble, and his rider putting up a pound overweight, he would have finished closer to the filly. (op 13-2)
Esoterica(IRE) back down at this trip for the first time since his Bronze Cup fourth, stayed on well from towards the rear without quite reaching the leaders. (op 16-1)
Oldjoesaid ◆ shaped with plenty of promise, having to be switched right before running on strongly. He is well handicapped these days and his new yard should soon be winning races with him. (op 11-1)
Red Cape(FR) showed bags of pace on this return to 6f but could not hold on when headed. (op 16-1)
Sunrise Safari(IRE), 3lb higher than when winning at Leicester, hit a flat spot before keeping on again and would have preferred a truer gallop. (tchd 6-1)
Brave Prospector was third in an Ascot Group 3 when last seen in the autumn and is now 8lb higher than when winning at the St Leger meeting. He showed up prominently on this return but it remains to be seen if he can build on it. (op 8-1)
Himalya(IRE) was not disgraced on this handicap debut but may not prove an easy horse to place again. (op 7-1 tchd 15-2)

2101 GRAND HOTEL & SPA YORK STKS (H'CAP) 1m 4f
4:55 (4:56) (Class 4) (0-80,80) 3-Y-O **£6,540** (£1,946; £972; £485) **Stalls** Centre

Form RPR

201- **1** **Judiciary (IRE)**[189] 7266 3-9-2 78.............................. AhmedAjtebi(3) 3 82+
(Mahmood Al Zarooni) *lw: led 1f: prom: hdwy over 4f out: chal 3f out: rdn and slt ld wl over 1f out: drvn and edgd lft ins fnl f: hld on wl* **15/8**[1]

6-62 **2** *nk* **Monkton Vale (IRE)**[22] 1486 3-8-13 72............................ PaulHanagan 4 76+
(R A Fahey) *cl up: led after 1f: pushed along over 3f out: rdn 2f out and sn hdd: rallied gamely u.p ent fnl f and ev ch tl no ex nr fin* **5/2**[2]

100 **3** 2 ½ **Munaawer (USA)**36 1189 3-9-5 78 (p) TomQueally 2 78
(J D Bethell) *hld up in tch: hdwy to chse ldng pair 3f out: rdn wl over 1f out: drvn and one pce ins fnl f* **8/1**

532 **4** 25 **Musical Mark**37 1157 3-9-2 75 (b) AndreaAtzeni 6 35
(M Botti) *chsd ldng pair: pushed along over 4f out: rdn and outpcd over 3f out: bhd fnl 2f* **7/1**

4221 **5** 1 ¾ **Dancing Dude (IRE)**18 1572 3-9-7 80 KierenFallon 7 37
(M Johnston) *lw: wnt rt s and in rr: rapid hdwy to trck ldr ldr over 7f out: rdn along 4f out: sn wknd and bhd fnl 2f* **10/3**3

2m 33.82s (0.62) **Going Correction** -0.125s/f (Firm) **5** Ran SP% **110.0**
Speed ratings (Par 101): **92,91,90,73,72**
CSF £6.82 TOTE £2.70: £1.70, £1.80; EX 7.20 Trifecta £61.50 Pool: £394.66 - 4.74 winning units. Place 6: £217.99 Place 5: £48.77.
Owner Godolphin **Bred** Irish National Stud **Trained** Newmarket, Suffolk

FOCUS
There were four withdrawals from this handicap, and unsurprisingly it was not as strong a race as it can be. Only three of them gave their running but the time was decent and a fairly positive view has been taken of the front pair.
T/Jkpt: Not won. T/Plt: £251.60. Pool of £207,303.92 - 601.41 winning tickets. T/Qpdt: £9.90. Pool of £9,121.56 - 678.23 winning tickets. JR

2102 - 2108a (Foreign Racing) - See Raceform Interactive

1684DONCASTER (L-H)
Saturday, May 15

OFFICIAL GOING: Good to firm (8.7)
Wind: Light across Weather: Fine and dry

2109 PTL OCCUPATIONAL HYGIENE ASBESTOS SURVEYS APPRENTICE H'CAP 1m 4f
6:00 (6:00) (Class 5) (0-70,70) 4-Y-O+ **£2,590** (£770; £385; £192) **Stalls** Low

Form RPR

005/ **1** **Silk Drum (IRE)**70 4077 5-8-10 66 LeeTopliss(5) 9 72
(J Howard Johnson) *trckd ldng pair: trckd ldr fr 1/2-way: led wl over 2f out: rdn wl over 1f out: drvn ins fnl f and sn hung rt: kpt on wl towards fin* **6/1**2

-352 **2** ½ **Tropical Bachelor (IRE)**8 1887 4-8-3 59 JohnFahy(5) 7 64
(T J Pitt) *hld up: hdwy over 3f out: effrt wl over 1f out: swtchd lft and rdn ent fnl f: fin wl* **9/1**

45 **3** shd **Kataragama**23 1489 4-8-11 62 KellyHarrison 5 67
(Mrs K Walton) *hld up: hdwy 4f out: chsd ldrs over 2f out: nt clr run wl over 1f: rdn to chse wnr ent fnl f: kpt on* **9/1**

0-20 **4** 1 ¾ **Orkney (IRE)**20 1071 5-8-4 58 (b1) PatrickDonaghy(3) 4 62+
(Julie Camacho) *in rr and reminders after s: hdwy and rdn over 2f out: swtchd ins over 1f out: sn nt clr run and hmpd: swtchd rt and drvn ins fnl f: styd on strly* **25/1**

00-0 **5** ½ **Haljaferia (UAE)**23 1484 4-9-0 68 DeclanCannon(3) 6 69
(D R C Elsworth) *trckd ldrs: effrt 4f out: rdn along and ch over 2f out: drvn and one pce ent fnl f* **4/1**1

6000 **6** nk **Mojeerr**22 1507 4-8-1 57 oh11 ow1 (be) TobyAtkinson(5) 14 58
(A J McCabe) *hld up and bhd: hdwy on outer 3f out: rdn to chse ldrs over 1f out: drvn and one pce ins fnl f* **66/1**

-000 **7** 4 **Bere Davis (FR)**15 1673 5-8-8 59 (t) AndrewHeffernan 1 53
(M A Barnes) *hld up in midfield: hdwy and in tch 1/2-way: rdn to chse ldrs over 3f out: drvn over 1f out: wknd ins fnl f* **16/1**

065- **8** 1 **Mistoffelees**231 6287 4-8-8 66 TalibHussain(7) 11 59
(L M Cumani) *trckd ldrs: effrt on outer over 3f out: rdn 2f out and grad wknd* **13/2**3

1210 **9** 2 **Nayessence**11 1803 4-8-7 61 (t) JamesSullivan(3) 15 51
(M W Easterby) *led: pushed along over 3f out: rdn and hdd wl over 2f out: drvn and wknd over 1f out* **8/1**

16-0 **10** hd **Andorn (GER)**26 1427 6-8-1 57 RichardRowe(5) 13 46
(P A Kirby) *cl up: effrt 3f out: sn rdn and ev ch tl drvn and wknd over 1f out* **40/1**

000- **11** 4 **Fantino**208 6910 4-8-9 63 BillyCray(3) 3 46
(J Mackie) *chsd ldrs: rdn along on outer wl over 2f out: drvn wl over 1f out and sn wknd* **14/1**

14/0 **12** 10 **Sumner (IRE)**17 1623 6-9-1 69 PaulPickard(3) 12 36
(F Sheridan) *a towards rr* **10/1**

500- **13** 3 ½ **Scarab (IRE)**217 6681 5-8-12 70 LukeStrong(7) 2 31
(T D Walford) *a towards rr* **14/1**

362- **14** 14 **Miss Ferney**234 6218 6-8-1 57 oh1 ow1 CharlesEddery(5) 10 —
(A Kirtley) *a towards rr* **16/1**

2m 32.58s (-2.32) **Going Correction** -0.125s/f (Firm) **14** Ran SP% **120.7**
Speed ratings (Par 103): **103,102,102,101,101 100,98,97,96,96 93,86,84,75**
Tote Swingers: 1&2 £16.10, 1&3 £14.50, 2&3 £11.20 CSF £58.63 CT £491.92 TOTE £5.60: £1.60, £3.70, £3.60; EX 67.60.
Owner Andrea & Graham Wylie **Bred** Mrs Cherry Faeste **Trained** Billy Row, Co Durham
■ Stewards' Enquiry : Lee Topliss two-day ban: careless riding (May 29-30)

FOCUS
Not the strongest gallop on this ordinary apprentice riders' handicap and a few ran quite freely through the early stages.

2110 MULTIFAB METALS ENGINEERING & FABRICATION H'CAP 1m (R)
6:30 (6:32) (Class 4) (0-85,83) 3-Y-O **£4,533** (£1,348; £674; £336) **Stalls** High

Form RPR

34-1 **1** **Colonel Carter (IRE)**28 1381 3-9-4 83 JimmyFortune 4 89
(B J Meehan) *trckd ldng pair: hdwy and cl up 2f out: rdn to ld ins fnl f: kpt on* **11/4**1

6-06 **2** nk **Swiss Cross**7 1913 3-8-12 77 (b1) PhillipMakin 9 82
(G A Butler) *t.k.h: led and sn clr: rdn along and jnd 2f out: drvn and edgd lft ent fnl f: sn hdd kpt on wl u.p towards fin* **8/1**

244- **3** 1 ½ **Lay Claim (USA)**198 7130 3-8-10 78 Louis-PhilippeBeuzelin(3) 3 80
(Sir Michael Stoute) *hld up: stdy hdwy over 4f out: trckd ldrs 3f out: swtchd ins and ev ch wl over 1f out: sn rdn and n.m.r ent fnl f: kpt on same pce* **7/2**2

0-45 **4** 2 ½ **Avonrose**13 1718 3-9-0 79 JoeFanning 6 75
(M Johnston) *hld up: hdwy over 3f out: rdn 2f out: styd on ins fnl f: nrst fin* **25/1**

1-40 **5** 3 ½ **White Dart**13 1734 3-8-9 74 ChrisCatlin 7 62
(M R Channon) *hld up: hdwy 3f out: rdn to chse ldrs 2f out: sn no imp* **20/1**

12 **6** 9 **Don't Call Me (IRE)**16 1649 3-8-10 75 (t) RichardMullen 5 42
(B Smart) *chsd ldrs: rdn along and edgd lft wl over 2f out: sn btn* **5/1**

31-5 **7** ½ **Antoniola (IRE)**30 1334 3-9-2 81 PaulMulrennan 2 47
(T D Easterby) *trckd ldrs on inner: hdwy over 3f out: rdn along over 2f out: sn drvn and wknd* **4/1**3

140- **8** 8 **Bahamian Music (IRE)**230 6305 3-9-4 83 PaulHanagan 1 31
(R A Fahey) *chsd ldr: rdn along wl over 2f out: sn wknd* **14/1**

0- **9** 9 **Les Yeux Bleus (IRE)**200 7103 3-8-8 80 TalibHussain(7) 8 7
(L M Cumani) *bhd: hdwy on wd outside and in tch over 3f out: sn rdn along and wknd wl over 2f out* **33/1**

1m 38.16s (-1.54) **Going Correction** -0.125s/f (Firm) **9** Ran SP% **114.9**
Speed ratings (Par 101): **102,101,100,97,94 85,84,76,67**
Tote Swingers: 1&2 £4.70, 1&3 £3.60, 2&3 £7.40 CSF £24.65 CT £78.81 TOTE £3.10: £1.10, £2.90, £1.90; EX 22.90.
Owner Mrs B V Sangster **Bred** Ceka Ireland Limited **Trained** Manton, Wilts

FOCUS
Some improving three-year-olds on show.
Don't Call Me(IRE) Official explanation: trainer said colt had a breathing problem

2111 BELL & WEBSTER PRECAST CONCRETE MAIDEN AUCTION STKS 5f
7:05 (7:05) (Class 5) 2-Y-O **£2,590** (£770; £385; £192) **Stalls** High

Form RPR

1 **Oneladyowner** 2-8-11 0 PhillipMakin 2 70+
(D H Brown) *hmpd s: sn swtchd rt to stands' rail: trckd ldrs: swtchd lft and hdwy over 1f out: rdn and qcknd wl to ld ins fnl f: edgd lft and kpt on* **7/2**2

00 **2** hd **Fred Willetts (IRE)**7 1930 2-8-8 0 AndrewHeffernan(3) 6 69
(P D Evans) *slt ld: rdn along 2f out: drvn ent fnl f: sn hdd: kpt on wl towards fin* **20/1**

3 shd **Mandy's Hero** 2-8-13 0 PaulHanagan 5 71
(R A Fahey) *cl up: effrt 2f out: sn rdn and ev ch: drvn ins fnl f: nt qckn towards fin* **2/1**1

4 7 **Crown Ridge (IRE)** 2-8-11 0 AlanMunro 1 44
(M R Channon) *trckd ldrs on outer: hdwy over 2f out: rdn wl over 1f out and wknd appr fnl f* **7/1**

00 **5** shd **Dispol Snapper (IRE)**17 1626 2-8-9 0 JoeFanning 7 41+
(P T Midgley) *dwlt: swtchd lft after s and t.k.h: chsd ldrs: rdn over 2f out and sn one pce* **50/1**

6 3 ¼ **Go Maggie Go (IRE)** 2-8-7 0 ow1 JamieSpencer 4 28
(K A Ryan) *cl up: rdn and edgd lft over 2f out: sn wknd* **7/2**2

7 ½ **Sky Booster** 2-8-11 0 LiamJones 3 30
(W J Haggas) *wnt bdly lft s: keen and sn chsng ldrs: green and lost pl over 2f out:* **5/1**3

61.34 secs (0.84) **Going Correction** -0.125s/f (Firm) **7** Ran SP% **113.7**
Speed ratings (Par 93): **88,87,87,76,76 70,70**
Tote Swingers: 1&2 £20.60, 1&3 £2.70, 2&3 £6.90 CSF £63.32 TOTE £4.40: £1.60, £9.60; EX 75.10.
Owner Bolland, Watson, Gregory, Lloyd & Oades **Bred** Barry Minty **Trained** Maltby, S Yorks
■ Stewards' Enquiry : Andrew Heffernan one-day ban: used whip with excessive frequency (Jun 10)

FOCUS
Not easy to pitch the level, but hard to see this turning out to be anything other than modest maiden form. The first three finished clear, racing nearer the stands' side than the next three.

NOTEBOOK
Oneladyowner looked thoroughly professional on debut, travelling smoothly in behind the pace before showing a nice turn of foot to pick up when switched out. He was made to work harder than initially looked likely when brought out to challenge, but was all out to score. This half-brother to Jimmy Styles looks a nice type for connections to go to war with in nurseries later in the season. (op 11-4 tchd 4-1)
Fred Willetts(IRE) had been beaten 16l and 13l on his first two starts, so the fact he went so close here doesn't bode well for the strength of the form. However, he looks to be improving with experience and the way he kept on suggests another furlong wouldn't go amiss. (op 16-1)
Mandy's Hero is bred to make a sprinting juvenile and there was plenty to like about this debut. He is entitled to improve for this and it will be a surprise if he doesn't go on to win races. (op 3-1)
Go Maggie Go(IRE) didn't show enough to be of interest next time. Official explanation: jockey said filly ran green (op 5-1)
Sky Booster was too green to do himself justice and he should improve for the experience. (op 4-1 tchd 7-2 and 6-1)

2112 GILKS FENCING CONTRACTORS H'CAP 7f
7:35 (7:35) (Class 4) (0-85,82) 3-Y-O **£4,533** (£1,348; £674; £336) **Stalls** High

Form RPR

2334 **1** **Hot Spark**4 1991 3-8-7 71 (t) AlanMunro 5 80
(K A Ryan) *cl up: led 2f out: rdn and edgd lft ent fnl f: drvn out* **10/1**

120- **2** 1 ¼ **Unshakable Will (IRE)**203 7013 3-9-3 81 TomEaves 8 87
(B Smart) *t.k.h early: trckd ldrs: swtchd lft and hdwy 2f out: rdn and ch whn n.m.r and swtchd rt ins fnl f: drvn and styd on wl towards fin* **10/1**

4-42 **3** nk **Night Trade (IRE)**7 1934 3-9-0 78 SilvestreDeSousa 10 83
(Mrs D J Sanderson) *in rr: swtchd lft to wd outside and hdwy 1/2-way: rdn to chal wl over 1f out: ev ch tl drvn: edgd rt and one pce ins fnl f* **7/2**1

01- **4** nk **Saharia (IRE)**161 7644 3-9-4 82 ShaneKelly 7 86
(J Noseda) *hld up towards rr: gd hdwy wl over 2f out: rdn to chse ldrs over 1f out: n.m.r and kpt on same pce ins fnl f* **5/1**2

1-65 **5** 1 ½ **Amenable (IRE)**28 1376 3-8-10 74 AdrianNicholls 9 74
(D Nicholls) *led: rdn along and hdd 2f out: sn drvn and grad wknd appr fnl f* **15/2**

311- **6** 4 **Jeannie Galloway (IRE)**218 6643 3-9-0 78 PaulHanagan 6 67
(R A Fahey) *t.k.h: chsd ldrs: rdn along wl over 2f out: sn wknd* **7/2**1

0-21 **7** 1 **Transmit (IRE)**24 1464 3-8-12 76 DavidAllan 3 63
(T D Easterby) *wnt rt s: trckd ldrs: hdwy 3f out: rdn along 2f out: sn drvn and wknd* **7/1**3

6-00 **8** 7 **Toga Tiger (IRE)**9 1836 3-8-11 75 TonyCulhane 4 43
(P T Midgley) *hmpd s: a in rr* **25/1**

02-5 **9** ¾ **Grand Zafeen**12 1765 3-9-1 79 ChrisCatlin 1 45
(M R Channon) *hld up towards rr: effrt and sme hdwy 3f out: rdn along over 2f out and sn wknd* **16/1**

6030 **10** 2 ¼ **Transfixed (IRE)**4 2002 3-8-4 75 KevinLundie(7) 2 35
(P D Evans) *wnt rt s: prom: rdn along 1/2-way: sn wknd* **25/1**

1m 25.14s (-1.16) **Going Correction** -0.125s/f (Firm) **10** Ran SP% **117.1**
Speed ratings (Par 101): **101,99,99,98,97 92,91,83,82,80**
Tote Swingers: 1&2 £21.00, 1&3 £8.90, 2&3 £5.00 CSF £105.94 CT £430.30 TOTE £15.50: £4.60, £3.80, £1.10; EX 140.70.
Owner T G & Mrs M E Holdcroft **Bred** Bearstone Stud **Trained** Hambleton, N Yorks

FOCUS
Just a fair handicap.

2113 REPLAS CONCRETE REPAIR & REFURBISHMENT H'CAP 6f
8:10 (8:12) (Class 4) (0-80,79) 4-Y-O+ **£4,533** (£1,348; £674; £336) **Stalls** High

Form RPR
52/1 **1** **Tubby Isaacs**[24] 1482 6-8-9 **70**........................ NeilCallan 11 81
(D K Ivory) *dwlt and towards rr: stdy hdwy fr 1/2-way: chsd ldrs 2f out: rdn and qckmd to ld 1f out: drvn and edgd rt ins fnl fulong: kpt on wl* **8/1**
00-1 **2** *1 ¼* **Leonid Glow**[29] 1366 5-9-1 **76**........................ PhillipMakin 18 83+
(M Dods) *racd nr stands' rail: hld up in rr: hdwy and n.m.r over 1f out: swtchd lft and rdn ent fnl f: sn chsng wnr: no imp towards fin* **15/2**
0-44 **3** *1* **Dancing Maite**[21] 1516 5-8-9 **73**........................ RussKennemore(3) 16 77
(S R Bowring) *prom towards stands' rail: effrt 2f out and sn ev ch: rdn and edgd rt ent fnl f: sn drvn and one pce* **10/1**
3420 **4** *nse* **Anne Of Kiev (IRE)**[19] 1580 5-9-0 **75**........................(t) JamieSpencer 2 79+
(J R Gask) *heavily stdd s: bhd and swtchd rt towards stands' rail: hdwy 2f out: swtchd rt to inner over 1f out and sn nt clr run: swtchd lft and n.m.r ent fnl f: fin strly* **5/1**[2]
0-00 **5** *1 ¾* **Hazelrigg (IRE)**[7] 1924 5-8-7 **68** ow1........................(p) DavidAllan 7 66
(T D Easterby) *racd towards centre: prom: rdn along and edgd rt 2f out: drvn and wandered over 1f out: kpt on same pce fnl f* **14/1**
-506 **6** *nse* **Bahamian Lad**[15] 1653 5-8-7 **68**........................ JerryO'Dwyer 14 66
(R Hollinshead) *chsd ldrs towards stands' rail: hdwy 2f out: sn rdn and kpt on same pce ent fnl f* **16/1**
0-00 **7** *1* **Memphis Man**[12] 1762 7-8-0 **68**........................ KevinLundie(7) 15 63+
(P D Evans) *in tch: hdwy to chse ldrs over 2f out: rdn and hung lft over 1f out: sn drvn and one pce* **50/1**
1120 **8** *2 ¼* **Cornus**[11] 1802 8-8-6 **67**........................(be) JamesDoyle 1 54
(A J McCabe) *in tch: hdwy 2f out: sn rdn and n.m.r over 1f out: kpt on same pce* **25/1**
0-11 **9** *nk* **Tangerine Trees**[16] 1650 5-9-2 **77**........................ TomEaves 6 64
(B Smart) *racd towards centre: chsd ldrs: rdn 2f out: drvn and wknd over 1f out* **7/1**[3]
343- **10** *1 ¼* **Tyfos**[266] 5247 5-9-2 **77**........................ TomMcLaughlin 13 60
(B P J Baugh) *overall ldr stands' rail: rdn along 2f out: drvn and hdd over 1f out: wknd ins fnl f* **25/1**
55-2 **11** *3 ¼* **Zero Money (IRE)**[19] 1580 4-9-3 **78**........................ SteveDrowne 5 50
(R Charlton) *chsd ldrs towards centre: rdn and hdwy 2f out: chsd ldrs over 1f out: wknd ins fnl f* **9/2**[1]
00-2 **12** *1 ½* **All The Nines (IRE)**[12] 1770 4-9-4 **79**........................ SilvestreDeSousa 3 46
(Mrs D J Sanderson) *racd wd: prom: rdn along 2f out: drvn and wknd over 1f out* **20/1**
004- **13** *nk* **Devil You Know (IRE)**[242] 5974 4-8-12 **78**........................ JamesSullivan(5) 12 44
(M W Easterby) *in tch towards stands' rail: rdn to chse ldrs 2f out: drvn whn hmpd and wknd over 1f out* **25/1**
00/6 **14** *nk* **Tawzeea (IRE)**[95] 474 5-8-13 **74**........................ PaulHanagan 10 39
(J D Bethell) *chsd ldrs: rdn along over 2f out: wkng whn hmpd over 1f out* **40/1**
3420 **15** *2 ¾* **Not My Choice (IRE)**[7] 1929 5-7-13 **65** oh2........................(t) DeclanCannon(5) 9 22
(D C Griffiths) *towards rr fr 1/2-way* **33/1**
1400 **16** *1 ¼* **Ponting (IRE)**[32] 1270 4-8-1 **67**........................ PaulPickard(5) 4 20
(P T Midgley) *racd centre: prom: rdn along over 2f out and grad wknd* **40/1**
3005 **17** *1 ½* **Klynch**[7] 1924 4-8-8 **69**........................(b) AndrewElliott 17 17
(Mrs R A Carr) *rrd s and a in rr* **20/1**
560- **18** *nk* **Errigal Lad**[257] 5516 5-9-3 **78**........................ ShaneKelly 8 25+
(J Balding) *a towards rr* **33/1**

1m 11.35s (-2.25) **Going Correction** -0.125s/f (Firm) **18** Ran SP% **125.6**
Speed ratings (Par 105): **110,108,107,106,104 104,103,100,99,98 93,91,91,91,87 85,83,83**
Tote Swingers: 1&2 £18.70, 1&3 £17.30, 2&3 £18.00 CSF £59.79 CT £641.12 TOTE £8.90: £2.30, £2.50, £3.20, £1.60; EX 67.10.
Owner John Khan **Bred** J W Ford **Trained** Radlett, Herts
■ Stewards' Enquiry : Phillip Makin three-day ban: careless riding (May 29-31)

FOCUS
Mainly exposed sprinters here.
Anne Of Kiev(IRE) ◆ Official explanation: jockey said mare was denied a clear run
Hazelrigg(IRE) ◆ Official explanation: jockey said gelding hung right throughout
Not My Choice(IRE) Official explanation: jockey said gelding missed the break
Errigal Lad Official explanation: jockey said gelding hung right

2114 AUTEC CONSTRUCTION & INDUSTRIAL TRAINING MEDIAN AUCTION MAIDEN STKS 6f
8:40 (8:42) (Class 5) 3-4-Y-O **£2,590** (£770; £385; £192) **Stalls** High

Form RPR
23-6 **1** **Humidor (IRE)**[13] 1731 3-9-3 **75**........................ SteveDrowne 8 66
(R Charlton) *t.k.h: cl up: led wl over 2f out: rdn and jnd over 1f out: drvn ins fnl f: edgd lft and hld on gamely towards fin* **5/2**[2]
0-02 **2** *shd* **Bilash**[8] 1878 3-9-3 **70**........................ JerryO'Dwyer 6 66
(R Hollinshead) *a cl up: effrt 2f out: rdn to chal over 1f out and ev ch tl drvn ins fnl f and no ex nr line* **11/2**[3]
3 *nk* **Feel The Heat** 3-9-3 0........................ TomEaves 3 65
(B Smart) *in tch on wd outside: hdwy 2f out: rdn and ev ch over 1f out: drvn and edgd rt ins fnl f: no ex towards fin* **22/1**
00-5 **4** *1 ½* **Erfaan (USA)**[100] 399 3-9-0 **72**........................ BarryMcHugh(3) 11 60
(Julie Camacho) *chsd ldrs on inner: hdwy 2f out: swtchd lft and rdn over 1f out: kpt on u.p ins fnl f* **25/1**
6-2 **5** *shd* **Ravenfield (IRE)**[10] 1825 3-9-3 0........................ JamieSpencer 4 60
(D H Brown) *trckd ldrs: hdwy 2f out: rdn wl over 1f out and ch tl drvn ent fnl f and sn wknd* **11/10**[1]
6 *hd* **Ingleby King (USA)** 4-9-8 0........................ DeanHeslop(5) 10 62+
(T D Barron) *rrd s and s.i.s: bhd: swtchd lft to wd outside 2f out: rdn over 1f out: styd on ins fnl f: nrst fin* **25/1**
40 **7** *3* **Pelmanism**[14] 1706 3-9-3 0........................ NeilCallan 5 49
(K A Ryan) *chsd ldrs: rdn along over 2f out: grad wknd* **25/1**
8 *2 ¼* **Verluga (IRE)** 3-9-3 0........................ DavidAllan 1 42
(T D Easterby) *dwlt: sn trcking ldrs: pushed along wl over 2f out: sn rdn and wknd* **33/1**
9 *8* **Mottley Crewe** 3-9-3 0........................ PhillipMakin 9 17
(M Dods) *led: rdn along and hdd wl over 2f out: sn wknd* **14/1**
66 **10** *4 ½* **Wirral Way**[18] 1599 4-9-13 0........................(t) JamesDoyle 7 5
(F Sheridan) *a in rr* **50/1**

1m 12.92s (-0.68) **Going Correction** -0.125s/f (Firm)
WFA 3 from 4yo 10lb **10** Ran SP% **119.0**
Speed ratings (Par 103): **99,98,98,96,96 96,92,89,78,72**
Tote Swingers: 1&2 £2.60, 1&3 £11.10, 2&3 £18.50 CSF £15.27 TOTE £3.90: £1.40, £1.80, £3.10; EX 14.20 Place 6: £203.67 Place 5: £68.86.

Owner Beckhampton Stables Ltd 1 **Bred** Yeomanstown Stud **Trained** Beckhampton, Wilts
■ Stewards' Enquiry : Steve Drowne two-day ban: used whip with excessive frequency (May 29-30)

FOCUS
Only around two lengths separated the first six home, so it's probably best not to get carried away with the form.
T/Plt: £219.30. Pool: £88,114.33 - 293.24 winning units. T/Qpdt: £49.90. Pool: £6,270.43 - 92.90 winning units. JR

2074 NEWBURY (L-H)
Saturday, May 15

OFFICIAL GOING: Good to firm (8.5)
Wind: Moderate behind Weather: Bright

2115 BATHWICK TYRES MAIDEN STKS 1m 2f 6y
1:25 (1:25) (Class 4) 3-Y-O **£5,180** (£1,541; £770; £384) **Stalls** Centre

Form RPR
5-3 **1** **Moose Moran (USA)**[32] 1271 3-9-3 0........................ TomQueally 2 87+
(H R A Cecil) *led 2f: styd trcking ldrs: squeezed through on ins to ld wl over 1f out: shkn up and c clr ins fnl f: comf* **5/1**[3]
2 *3* **Abrasive (IRE)** 3-9-3 0........................ JMurtagh 7 81
(W J Haggas) *t.k.h: trckd ldrs: drvn and qckmd over 2f out to chal wl over 1f out: nt pce on wnr ins fnl f but kpt on wl for 2nd: encouraging* **5/2**[1]
42 **3** *½* **Bay Willow (IRE)**[12] 1757 3-9-3 0........................ FrankieDettori 6 80
(M Johnston) *led aftre 2f: drvn and styd on wl fr 3f out: hdd wl over 1f out: kpt on ins fnl f: jst outpcd for 2nd sn after* **3/1**[2]
020- **4** *5* **Banana Republic (IRE)**[222] 6548 3-9-3 **74**........................ JamieSpencer 8 70
(P F I Cole) *chsd ldrs: rdn 3f out: wknd 2f out* **25/1**
50 **5** *2* **Osgood**[9] 1844 3-9-3 0........................ EddieCreighton 10 66
(M R Channon) *in rr: swtchd rt 3f out: sme prog on outer over 2f out: nvr rchd ldrs and sn wknd* **10/1**
6 *1 ¾* **Surface Tension (IRE)** 3-9-3 0........................ KierenFallon 3 63+
(L M Cumani) *chsd ldrs: rdn and effrt 3f out: nvr quite on terms and wknd fr 2f out* **12/1**
4 **7** *2 ¼* **Montparnasse (IRE)**[12] 1757 3-9-3 0........................ RichardHughes 1 58
(B J Meehan) *stdd s: in rr but in tch: pushed along 4f out: rdn whn bmpd 3f out: styd in tch tl wknd fr 2f out* **6/1**
8 *1 ½* **In Your Time** 3-8-12 0........................ RyanMoore 9 50
(Sir Michael Stoute) *towards rr: pushed along 3f out: nvr on terms and sn dropped away* **11/1**
000- **9** *42* **Daryainur (IRE)**[201] 7064 3-8-9 **45**........................ PatrickHills(3) 5 —
(W De Best-Turner) *chsd ldrs: rdn 4f out: sn btn: t.o* **200/1**

2m 6.86s (-1.94) **Going Correction** -0.20s/f (Firm) **9** Ran SP% **114.0**
Speed ratings (Par 101): **99,96,96,92,90 89,87,86,52**
toteswingers: 1&2 £4.10, 1&3 £3.00, 2&3 £2.40 CSF £17.63 TOTE £5.70: £1.90, £1.40, £1.60; EX 19.20.
Owner Raymond Tooth **Bred** Liberty Road Stables **Trained** Newmarket, Suffolk

FOCUS
A fair maiden, run at an uneven pace. Sound form, with big improvement from the winner.

2116 TOTEPOOL ASTON PARK STKS (LISTED RACE) 1m 5f 61y
2:00 (2:00) (Class 1) 4-Y-O+
£22,708 (£8,608; £4,308; £2,148; £1,076; £540) **Stalls** Centre

Form RPR
4633 **1** **Claremont (IRE)**[14] 1698 4-8-12 **109**........................(v[1]) WilliamBuick 4 113
(Mahmood Al Zarooni) *t.k.h: trckd ldrs: upsides 3f out and sn led: drvn and styd on strly fr over 1f out* **11/2**[3]
3-41 **2** *1 ¼* **Sabotage (UAE)**[79] 712 4-8-12 **111**........................ FrankieDettori 10 111
(Saeed Bin Suroor) *trckd ldrs: swtchd rt to outside 3f out and r.o to chse wnr 2f out: kpt on u.p but no imp fnl f* **5/2**[1]
626/ **3** *nk* **Petara Bay (IRE)**[594] 6306 6-8-12 **102**........................ StevieDonohoe 9 111
(R A Mills) *in rr: swtchd rt to outside 3f out: drvn and styd on to take 3rd over 1f out and kpt on wl to press for 2nd cl home but no imp on wnr* **20/1**
-363 **4** *2 ¼* **Heliodor (USA)**[13] 1724 4-8-12 **105**........................ RichardHughes 5 107
(R Hannon) *in tch: rdn to chse ldrs fr 3f out: one pce fnl 2f* **6/1**
2/ **5** *¾* **Bergo (GER)**[35] 1689 7-8-12 **105**........................ RyanMoore 1 106
(G L Moore) *led: narrowly hdd over 4f out: styd on same pce fr over 1f out* **11/1**
000- **6** *3 ½* **Centennial (IRE)**[244] 5932 5-8-12 **100**........................ JMurtagh 7 101
(Jonjo O'Neill) *chsd ldr tl slt ld over 4f out: hdd jst ins fnl 3f: wknd over 2f out* **16/1**
6/00 **7** *nk* **Balkan Knight**[17] 1615 10-8-12 **97**........................ DaneO'Neill 2 100
(D R C Elsworth) *s.i.s: in rr: rdn along 3f out: nvr gng pce to get into contention* **40/1**
110- **8** *2 ¼* **Red Merlin (IRE)**[269] 5173 5-8-12 **103**........................(v) PhilipRobinson 6 97
(C G Cox) *hld up in rr: shkn up and hung lft 2f out: no rspnse* **13/2**
13-6 **9** *4 ½* **Blizzard Blues (USA)**[28] 1382 4-8-12 **102**........................(b) TomQueally 8 90
(H R A Cecil) *chsd ldrs: drvn to chal over 3f out: chsd wnr sn after tl over 2f out: sn wknd* **4/1**[2]

2m 50.9s (-1.10) **Going Correction** -0.20s/f (Firm) **9** Ran SP% **113.0**
Speed ratings (Par 111): **95,94,94,92,92 90,89,88,85**
Tote Swingers: 1&2 £2.80, 1&3 £20.40, 2&3 £7.70 CSF £19.16 TOTE £6.20: £2.10, £1.60, £4.60; EX 14.70 Trifecta £266.80 Part won. Pool of £775.33 - 2.15 winning units..
Owner Godolphin **Bred** Darley **Trained** Newmarket, Suffolk

FOCUS
A good Listed race for stayers, run at an ordinary early pace. The winner ran his best race for current connections and paid another compliment to his John Porter conqueror Harbinger. The form has been rated around the Godolphin 1-2, but may not procve sound.

NOTEBOOK
Claremont(IRE) was friendless in the betting ring as he sweated up and looked out of sorts in the paddock. He also got lit up by the first-time visor through the early parts, but the further he went, the better he looked and he is clearly talented on his day. He could have been called the winner shortly after the two-furlong pole and it's not hard to see why he was tried over 1m7f on his final outing for Andre Fabre last year. The headgear has to go down as having held the desired effect, but William Buick thought it was more of a hindrance, so it will be interesting to see if it is retained. This also proves he is effective on a quick surface, which was a worry after he hung all over the track at Newmarket last time. A return to Group company is on the cards and the Henry II Stakes over 2m at Sandown this month could be next for him. (op 4-1)
Sabotage(UAE) made it a one-two for Godolphin with a solid effort on this first run since winning over 2m at Meydan 79 days previously. He was well backed and looked on good terms with himself in the preliminaries, but never seriously looked like getting on top. A return to a stiffer test should suit and he could reoppose Claremont at Sandown. (op 10-3 tchd 7-2 in places)

Petara Bay(IRE) was having his first outing since running in this grade at Ascot in 2008. He was doing his best work towards the finish and the engine clearly remains intact, but one will have to be mindful of the potential bounce factor next time. (op 25-1)

Heliodor(USA) was again ridden with restraint and was staying on well enough late on to suggest he got the trip. He is not easy to place successfully. (op 15-2)

Bergo(GER) was having his first outing on the Flat since coming over from Germany, where his best effort was a second over 2m in a Group 3. He was a sitting duck in the home straight, but kept on gamely in the style of a horse who will appreciate stepping back up in distance. (tchd 10-1)

Centennial(IRE) lost his way last year and was running for a new yard after a 244-day absence. He would have found the ground plenty quick enough and shaped as though the run was needed. (tchd 14-1)

Balkan Knight would have found this sharp enough but continues to look on the downgrade. (op 50-1)

Red Merlin(IRE) was another who ran as though this seasonal debut was needed, but he is another who has become difficult to place. He was later reported to have run too free. Official explanation: jockey said gelding ran too free (op 11-2)

Blizzard Blues(USA) dropped disappointingly out under maximum pressure and something may well have gone amiss with him. (op 9-2 tchd 5-1)

2117 TOTESCOOP6 LONDON GOLD CUP (H'CAP) 1m 2f 6y

2:30 (2:30) (Class 2) (0-105,92) 3-Y-O

£21,808 (£6,531; £3,265; £1,634; £815; £409) **Stalls** Centre

Form				RPR
04-1	**1**		**Green Moon (IRE)**[21] 1521 3-8-11 **82** ..... JamieSpencer 11 (H J L Dunlop) *mde all: drvn along fr 2f out: drvn clr fr over 1f out: unchal* **11/1**	104
2111	**2**	*4*	**Monterosso**[30] 1334 3-9-3 **88** ..... FrankieDettori 1 (M Johnston) *drvn to chse ldrs fr s: styd cl 3rd tl chsd wnr over 2f out: styd on u.p: nvr any imp but r.o strly for clr 2nd* **11/2**[2]	102
1-10	**3**	*3 ½*	**Doctor Zhivago**[31] 1310 3-9-1 **86** ..... GregFairley 3 (M Johnston) *chsd ldrs: rdn over 2f out: wnt 3rd wl over 1f out and kpt on but nvr any ch w ldng duo* **25/1**	93
02-3	**4**	*½*	**Bonfire Knight**[23] 1487 3-8-4 **80** ..... IanBrennan(5) 6 (J J Quinn) *chsd ldrs: rdn and one pce 3f out: rallied and kpt on fr over 1f out but nvr any threat* **9/1**	86
04-6	**5**	*nse*	**Private Story (USA)**[29] 1354 3-9-6 **91** ..... RichardHughes 13 (R Hannon) *in rr: swtchd rt towards outside fr 3f out: styd on fnl 2f and gng on ins fnl f but nvr a danger* **18/1**	97+
15-2	**6**	*1 ½*	**Right Step**[30] 1330 3-9-2 **87** ..... KierenFallon 9 (A P Jarvis) *s.i.s: in rr: grad moved rt towards outside fr 3f out: drvn and styd on fnl 2f but nvr anywhere nr ldrs* **13/2**[3]	90+
21-1	**7**	*shd*	**Verdant**[22] 1502 3-9-4 **89** ..... RyanMoore 10 (Sir Michael Stoute) *sn towards rr: nt clr run over 3f out: grad moved rt towards outside sn after: drvn and styd on fnl 2f but nvr in contention* **2/1**[1]	92+
32-4	**8**	*¾*	**Aquarian Spirit**[21] 1518 3-8-10 **81** ..... TonyHamilton 12 (R A Fahey) *chsd ldrs: rdn over 2f out: wknd appr fnl f* **33/1**	82
34-3	**9**	*1 ¼*	**Ingleby Spirit**[15] 1657 3-8-12 **83** ..... PaulHanagan 14 (R A Fahey) *towards rr and racing on outside: rdn 3f out and nvr gng pce to get on terms: wknd wl over 1f out* **14/1**	82
30-0	**10**	*nk*	**Blakey's Boy**[22] 1497 3-9-2 **87** ..... WilliamBuick 2 (J L Dunlop) *mid-div: rdn 3f out and no imp* **25/1**	85
6106	**11**	*½*	**Muwalla**[15] 1657 3-8-9 **80** ..... DarryllHolland 7 (C E Brittain) *in rr: nt clr run over 3f out: sn rdn and no improvement* **50/1**	77
0-12	**12**	*4 ½*	**Dromore (IRE)**[17] 1624 3-8-9 **80** ..... DavidProbert 15 (A M Balding) *t.k.h: chsd ldrs on outside: rdn over 3f out: sn btn* **20/1**	68
1216	**13**	*1*	**Exceedthewildman**[52] 973 3-9-1 **86** ..... (p) JMurtagh 8 (J S Moore) *s.i.s: in rr: sme hdwy on ins 3f out: nvr in contention and sn wknd* **33/1**	72
231-	**14**	*1 ½*	**Whistleinthewind (IRE)**[171] 7522 3-9-3 **88** ..... GeorgeBaker 5 (G L Moore) *chsd wnr tl over 2f out: sn wknd* **20/1**	71
146-	**15**	*1 ¾*	**Mingun Bell (USA)**[196] 7184 3-9-7 **92** ..... TomQueally 4 (H R A Cecil) *t.k.h: chsd ldrs 5f out: rdn 3f out: wknd 2f out* **33/1**	72

2m 5.45s (-3.35) **Going Correction** -0.20s/f (Firm) **15** Ran SP% **120.3**
Speed ratings (Par 105): **105,101,99,98,98 97,97,96,95,95 95,91,90,89,88**
Tote Swingers: 1&2 £11.80, 1&3 £54.80, 2&3 £28.20 CSF £62.60 CT £1504.86 TOTE £11.00: £3.00, £1.70, £7.10; EX 68.80 Trifecta £2106.60 Pool: £31600.04 - 11.10 winning units..

Owner Mrs Ben Goldsmith **Bred** Goldsmith Bloodstock Partnership **Trained** Lambourn, Berks

FOCUS

This is a traditionally strong and informative handicap. It appeared to be run at an uneven pace, with few managing to get into contention from out the back, and it paid to race handily. The form has been rated at face value with big improvement from the first two.

NOTEBOOK

Green Moon(IRE) ◆, coltish in the paddock and easy to back, made all to win in great style on this handicap debut. He no doubt got very much the run of the race, but it would be dangerous to assume he was not a worthy winner, as there was plenty to like about the manner in which he went about his business. He did look a horse with a big future when winning his maiden at Leicester on his return last month and this was only his fourth outing. The son of Montjeu holds an entry in the Group 2 King George VII Stakes at Royal Ascot and the extra two furlongs should be within his compass, but the Listed Hampton Court Stakes at the same meeting is likely to come into consideration for him too. His trainer said he would not risk him on very quick ground there, though. (op 9-1)

Monterosso did amazingly well to land the hat-trick on his turf debut at Ripon last month and was 5lb higher here. He had something to prove over the extra distance, but was ridden as though it wouldn't be a problem and stayed the trip well enough. He was helped by racing handily and was the only one to look a serious threat to the winner, but again showed his inexperience when put under maximum pressure. There should be more races to be won with him. (op 13-2)

Doctor Zhivago, the stable's second string, was another who raced handily and showed he handles turf with a much more encouraging effort. An easier surface should suit the lightly raced colt ideally, though. (op 28-1)

Bonfire Knight ◆ looked to be crying out for this trip on his return at Beverley and ran a solid race. There should be something for him in the coming weeks. (op 10-1 tchd 11-1)

Private Story(USA) ◆ did best of those coming from way off the pace and is better than the bare form. He has begun handicaps on a workable mark and looks as though he will get further. (op 22-1)

Right Step, 4lb higher, was ridden right out the back and had far too much to do in the home straight. It was a good effort in the circumstances and he can be given another chance. (tchd 15-2)

Verdant got up late on to win a good handicap at Sandown on his comeback 22 days earlier and there was a good chance he was still ahead of the handicapper off this 9lb higher mark. The repeated patient tactics failed to work out because of the way the race unfolded and it is way too soon to be writing him off. (op 9-4 tchd 5-2 in places)

2118 TOTESPORT.COM LOCKINGE STKS (GROUP 1) 1m (S)

3:05 (3:06) (Class 1) 4-Y-O+

£113,540 (£43,040; £21,540; £10,740; £5,380; £2,700) **Stalls** Centre

Form				RPR
42-1	**1**		**Paco Boy (IRE)**[21] 1531 5-9-0 124 ..... RichardHughes 3 (R Hannon) *hld up in tch: eased rt and smooth prog on bit to chal 1f out: sn led: drvn and qcknd to assert fnl 120yds: styd on strly* **8/11**[1]	125+
642-	**2**	*¾*	**Ouqba**[210] 6848 4-9-0 114 ..... RichardHills 1 (B W Hills) *hld up towards rr but wl in tch: stdy hdwy and swtchd lft fr 2f out: drvn and qckd 1f out to press wnr ins fnl f: outpcd fnl 120yds but clrly 2nd best* **16/1**	121
150-	**3**	*3 ½*	**Lord Shanakill (USA)**[189] 7305 4-9-0 118 ..... TomQueally 7 (H R A Cecil) *chsd ldrs: rdn to take slt ld wl over 1f out: hdd jst ins fnl f: sn outpcd by ldng duo* **9/1**[3]	113
514-	**4**	*1*	**Pipedreamer**[210] 6850 6-9-0 118 ..... JamieSpencer 4 (K A Ryan) *in tch: hdwy to chse ldrs 2f out: ev ch wl over 1f out tl jst ins fnl f: wknd fnl 120yds* **14/1**	111
/1-3	**5**	*hd*	**The Cheka (IRE)**[21] 1531 4-9-0 110 ..... KierenFallon 9 (Eve Johnson Houghton) *s.i.s: in rr but in tch: pushed along 3f out: sme hdwy over 2f out: nvr quite rchd ldrs and wknd fnl f* **14/1**	110
/54-	**6**	*2 ½*	**Stimulation (IRE)**[239] 6058 5-9-0 114 ..... DarryllHolland 5 (H Morrison) *s.i.s but sn led tl hdd wl over 1f out: sn btn* **25/1**	104
04-1	**7**	*hd*	**Kargali (IRE)**[34] 1246 5-9-0 108 ..... (t) JMurtagh 6 (Luke Comer, Ire) *s.i.s: in rr but in tch: pushed along and sme prog over 2f out but nvr in contention: sn wknd* **66/1**	104
11-0	**8**	*2 ¼*	**Prince Of Dance**[21] 1531 4-9-0 108 ..... RichardKingscote 2 (Tom Dascombe) *chsd ldr: rdn and ev ch over 2f out: wknd qckly over 1f out* **40/1**	99
220-	**9**	*28*	**Zacinto**[189] 7308 4-9-0 122 ..... RyanMoore 8 (Sir Michael Stoute) *chsd ldrs: rdn 2f out: sn btn eased appr fnl f* **7/2**[2]	34

1m 37.31s (-2.39) **Going Correction** 0.0s/f (Good) **9** Ran SP% **117.1**
Speed ratings (Par 117): **111,110,106,105,105 103,102,100,72**
Tote Swingers: 1&2 £5.70, 1&3 £2.70, 2&3 £12.40 CSF £15.56 TOTE £1.60: £1.10, £4.90, £2.90; EX 17.00 Trifecta £90.90 Pool: £30056.92 - 244.66 winning units..

Owner The Calvera Partnership No 2 **Bred** Mrs Joan Browne **Trained** East Everleigh, Wilts

FOCUS

Another uninspiring Lockinge, but Paco Boy rates a very worthy winner. He did not have to run to his best with doubts over some of these and his main rival Zacinto running poorly. There was a sound pace on and the first pair came clear.

NOTEBOOK

Paco Boy(IRE) was the clear form pick and had looked better than ever when successfully defending his title in the Sandown Bet365 Mile last month. In contrast to last season, when connections weren't happy with him and later found he had an infected hoof, his preparation this year had gone smoothly and he was sent off at a short price. He ultimately outclassed his rivals, cantering over them before having to work to fend off the runner-up, and landed his second win at the highest level. It looked for a moment as though Ouqba may cause an upset, but Paco Boy's response when asked to dig deep was immediate and he was comfortably on top at the line. His two races this year suggests he wants all of this distance and he will head for his defence of the Queen Anne at Royal Ascot full of confidence. While he will rightly be popular there, he will have to step up again on this form to succeed, as he is likely to face much classier rivals in Rip Van Winkle, his Sussex Stakes conqueror, and the brilliant Goldikova. It will be a clash to savour. (op 4-5 tchd 10-11 in a place and 5-6 in places)

Ouqba was making his comeback and having his first run over the distance since fading in the 2,000 Guineas. His final outing last year was a career-best, though, and this represents another step forward. He was ultimately outstayed, but made the winner work for his prize and beat the rest comfortably. His short-term options are not clear and it would be hard to see him reversing form if taking on the winner again at Royal Ascot, but connections intend the Queen Anne to be his nest assignment. He deserves to get his head back in front.

Lord Shanakill(USA), the only other Group 1 winner in the race, was having his first run back since being trained in the US and running well below par in the Breeders' Cup Turf Sprint. His new stable is having a great time and he ran a pleasing race. The suspicion remains that 7f is his optimum trip and he should improve for the run, but his best chance of further success this term may again be on foreign shores. (op 12-1)

Pipedreamer, fourth in the Champion Stakes on his final start last year, was making his debut for connections. He ran a big race, having every chance, and looks to have resumed in great heart. It was the first time he had run over 1m since winning his maiden and the trip looked sharp enough for him, so he will probably need 1m1f before proving successful again.

The Cheka(IRE) finished third to Paco Boy on his comeback and was expected to improve a good deal. He never looked like reversing form, but again ran with promise and looks worth a more positive ride over this trip. This was just his fifth outing and he should relish some cut underfoot again. (op 12-1)

Stimulation(IRE), restricted to just two outings last year, took them along at a fair gallop and faded shortly after being headed. The run should bring him on a bundle, though, and dropping back to 7f should be much to his liking.

Kargali(IRE) was ridden to get the trip and ran respectably on ground he would have found plenty fast enough. He does look out of his depth in this class, however.

Prince Of Dance, who won his maiden on this card last season, showed more than on his seasonal return behind Paco Boy at Sandown but needs his sights lowering.

Zacinto was the big danger to Paco Boy on official ratings and always looked as though he could improve with age. This was his first run since failing to shine in the Breeders' Cup Mile, where there had been excuses, and his trainer's record in the race entitled him to respect. The signs were not good beforehand, however, as he was edgy and sweated up. The manner in which he folded suggested something was amiss and he has plenty to prove. It is too soon to write him off, though, and it is worth remembering that Aqlaam flopped in this race last year before finishing third in the Queen Anne and then landing a Group 1. He was later reported to have run flat. Official explanation: jockey said colt ran flat

2119 TOTESPORT 0800 221 221 H'CAP 6f 8y

3:40 (3:40) (Class 2) (0-100,100) 4-Y-O+

£9,969 (£2,985; £1,492; £747; £372; £187) **Stalls** Centre

Form				RPR
3000	**1**		**Rileyskeepingfaith**[7] 1900 4-9-1 **97** ..... (v) RyanMoore 9 (M R Channon) *in rr tl gd hdwy wl over 1f out: str run u.p fnl f: edgd rt: led fnl 50yds* **6/1**[2]	108
-505	**2**	*½*	**Shifting Star (IRE)**[14] 1688 5-8-7 **89** ..... WilliamBuick 6 (W R Swinburn) *trckd ldrs: led appr fnl f: sn hrd drvn and strly chal: hdd and outpcd fnl 50yds* **8/1**[3]	98
0-02	**3**	*½*	**Wildcat Wizard (USA)**[7] 1903 4-8-10 **92** ..... (t) JamieSpencer 4 (P F I Cole) *in tch: gd hdwy over 1f out to chal ins fnl f: no ex and one pce fnl 50yds* **5/1**[1]	99

00-2 **4** *3* **Striking Spirit**[15] 1670 5-8-13 **95**.................................. AndrewMullen 10 93
(D Nicholls) *chsd ldrs: rdn and hung lft fr over 1f out: styd on same pce ins fnl f* **5/1**[1]

6404 **5** *nse* **Five Star Junior (USA)**[14] 1688 4-8-8 **90**................. KirstyMilczarek 12 88
(Mrs L Stubbs) *bumper s: in rr: drvn and styd on fr 2f out: kpt on fnl f but nvr gng pce to get into contention* **12/1**

000- **6** *½* **Spanish Bounty**[224] 6482 5-8-8 **90**.................................... TomQueally 8 86
(J G Portman) *disp ld tl def advantage over 2f out: rdn and hdd appr fnl f: sn btn* **16/1**

06-0 **7** *2 ½* **Icelandic**[15] 1662 8-9-1 **97**...(t) DarryllHolland 13 85
(F Sheridan) *slowly ito stride: in rr: sme prog fr over 1f out but nvr in contention* **20/1**

0506 **8** *1* **Pusey Street Lady**[7] 1903 6-8-6 **88**.......................... RichardKingscote 1 73
(J Gallagher) *racd alone far side and disupted ld to 2f out: wknd over 1f out* **14/1**

2-16 **9** *2* **Arthur's Edge**[49] 1007 6-9-4 **100**...................................... DavidProbert 15 78
(B Palling) *sn rdn: outpcd most of way* **12/1**

/0-5 **10** *shd* **Desert Phantom (USA)**[29] 1353 4-8-12 **94**.............. RichardHughes 11 72
(D M Simcock) *bmpd s: outpcd most of way* **8/1**[3]

000- **11** *nse* **Beaver Patrol (IRE)**[245] 5874 8-8-7 **89** ow1............(b) StevieDonohoe 16 67
(Eve Johnson Houghton) *chsd ldrs to 1/2-way: sn wknd* **12/1**

65-0 **12** *1 ¼* **Macdillon**[29] 1349 4-7-13 **86** oh1........................... SimonPearce(5) 2 60
(W S Kittow) *chsd ldr in centre of crse over 3f* **16/1**

036- **13** *¾* **Baunagain (IRE)**[135] 7891 5-8-4 **86** oh1...................... AdrianMcCarthy 3 58
(P W Chapple-Hyam) *racd in centre crse and narrow overall ldr tl hdd over 2f out: wknd qckly wl over 1f out* **40/1**

1m 11.57s (-1.43) **Going Correction** 0.0s/f (Good) **13** Ran SP% **118.6**
Speed ratings (Par 109): **109,108,107,103,103 102,99,98,95,95 95,93,92**
Tote Swingers: 1&2 £12.70, 1&3 £3.30, 2&3 £10.70 CSF £53.04 CT £260.97 TOTE £6.80: £2.10, £2.80, £2.00; EX 51.90 Trifecta £581.80 Pool: £1478.10 - 1.88 winning units..
Owner Jolly Roger Racing **Bred** M Barrett **Trained** West Ilsley, Berks

FOCUS
A typically competitive sprint handicap for the class. The main action developed down the centre of the track and the first three fought it out late on. Sound form overall with a personal best from the winner.

NOTEBOOK
Rileyskeepingfaith got up late on, enjoying the decent pace under a strong ride. He had looked to be struggling with the handicapper and was 3lb lower for this drop back in trip, but had shown enough in Dubai earlier in the year to suggest his turn would come before long. It was his first success since his juvenile campaign and the Wokingham at Royal Ascot could be on his agenda (op 9-1 tchd 10-1 in places)
Shifting Star(IRE) took another step in the right direction and ran a big race. He is clearly back in good heart and has fallen to a decent mark, so will still look nicely treated despite going back up for this. (op 9-1)
Wildcat Wizard(USA) ◆ returned to form when staying on strongly at Ascot a week previously and was 2lb higher. He travelled strongly and held every chance, but was not done any favours when the runner-up drifted right over to him inside the final furlong. He may well have been second except for that and deserves to get his head back in front. (op 11-2 tchd 6-1 in a place)
Striking Spirit had just been held on his return at Musselburgh 15 days earlier. He had his chance and ran a sound race on this return to handicap company, helping to set the level. (op 9-2)
Five Star Junior(USA), who wasn't the best away after getting bumped, stayed on from off the pace and gave his all over a test he would have found sharp enough. He looks held by the handicapper, though.
Spanish Bounty showed early pace and helped set the tempo. He eventually faded out of it, but should be all the sharper for this seasonal return and is on a fair mark. (op 25-1)
Pusey Street Lady ploughed a lone furrow on the far side and wasn't disgraced, but remains on a long losing run. (op 9-1)

2120 BET LIVE IN PLAY AT TOTESPORT.COM FILLIES' H'CAP 7f (S)
4:15 (4:15) (Class 4) (0-85,85) 3-Y-O **£5,180** (£1,541; £770; £384) **Stalls** Centre

Form RPR

561- **1** **Miss Zooter (IRE)**[201] 7061 3-9-0 **81**.................................. JimCrowley 10 92+
(R M Beckett) *s.i.s: in rr tl gd hdwy fr 2f out: rdn to ld fnl 120yds: kpt on strly* **16/1**

04-5 **2** *¾* **Dubai Media (CAN)**[30] 1329 3-8-7 **74**.......................... WilliamBuick 14 83
(D M Simcock) *in tch: hdwy 2f out: rdn to ld jst ins fnl f: hdd and nt qckn fnl 120yds* **7/1**

01- **3** *1 ¼* **Plume**[232] 6245 3-8-13 **80**... RichardHughes 11 86
(R Hannon) *trckd ldr tl led 2f out: sn rdn: hdd jst ins fnl f: sn outpcd by ldng duo fnl 120yds* **6/4**[1]

335- **4** *1 ¼* **Lady Pattern (IRE)**[213] 6774 3-8-4 **71**............................ DavidProbert 9 73
(P W D'Arcy) *chsd ldrs: rdn over 2f out: styd on fnl f but nvr gng pce to chal* **25/1**

46-0 **5** *shd* **Bahati (IRE)**[28] 1384 3-9-2 **83**.. PatCosgrave 13 85
(J G Portman) *in rr: n.m.r over 2f out: rdn and hdwy over 1f out: edgd lft and r.o ins fnl f but nvr a thrr* **50/1**

316 **6** *hd* **Flighty Frances (IRE)**[9] 1850 3-8-11 **78**........................ DaneO'Neill 8 79
(D R C Elsworth) *in rr tl hdwy fr 2f out: kpt on fnl f but nvr in contention* **16/1**

21-6 **7** *3* **Excellent Day (IRE)**[23] 1487 3-8-9 **76**......................... EddieCreighton 5 69
(M R Channon) *s.i.s: t.k.h: kpt on fr 2f out and styd on fnl f but nvr gng pce to be competitive* **50/1**

00-1 **8** *¾* **Sard**[14] 1694 3-8-12 **79**.. PhilipRobinson 3 70
(M A Jarvis) *t.k.h: chsd ldrs tl wknd appr fnl f* **11/2**[3]

450- **9** *½* **Perfect Ch'l (IRE)**[187] 7320 3-8-7 **74**............................ CathyGannon 6 64
(I A Wood) *sn led: hdd 2f out: styd wl there tl wknd fnl f* **66/1**

46-0 **10** *4* **Universal Circus**[13] 1734 3-8-9 **76**............................... SamHitchcott 12 55
(M R Channon) *chsd ldrs: rdn 3f out: sn btn* **20/1**

40-0 **11** *¾* **Crown (IRE)**[28] 1376 3-9-4 **85**.. IanMongan 1 62
(Miss Jo Crowley) *mid-div: sme hdwy on outside 3f out: rdn and wknd 2f out* **66/1**

221- **12** *2* **Alice Alleyne (IRE)**[226] 6436 3-8-10 **77**............................ RyanMoore 2 49
(Sir Michael Stoute) *t.k.h and stdd towards rr sn after s: hdwy to chse ldrs 3f: upsides 2f out: sn rdn: wknd qckly over 1f out* **9/2**[2]

41-1 **13** *3* **Key Light (IRE)**[33] 1269 3-8-10 **77**.............................. MichaelHills 4 41
(J W Hills) *in tch over 4f* **22/1**

-111 **14** *1* **Catherines Call (IRE)**[16] 1640 3-8-11 **78** ow1...................... JMurtagh 7 39
(D Donovan) *a in rr* **12/1**

142- **15** *7* **Shibhan**[222] 6534 3-8-8 **75**.. DarryllHolland 15 17
(C E Brittain) *chsd ldrs tl wknd qckly over 2f out* **40/1**

1m 25.43s (-0.27) **Going Correction** 0.0s/f (Good) **15** Ran SP% **124.3**
Speed ratings (Par 98): **101,100,98,97,97 96,93,92,92,87 86,84,80,79,71**
Tote Swingers: 1&2 £23.00, 1&3 £17.60, 2&3 £4.80 CSF £121.20 CT £275.76 TOTE £14.80: £3.20, £2.80, £1.10; EX 157.00.
Owner Timeform Betfair Racing Club Ltd **Bred** Rathyork Stud **Trained** Whitsbury, Hants

FOCUS
A strong three-year-old handicap for fillies. They raced in two groups in the middle of the track early on before merging and coming towards the stands' side from halfway. A double-figure draw was an advantage and the first three all look decent types, though the form does seem to have limitations.
Sard Official explanation: vet said filly had been struck into right hind leg
Perfect Ch'l(IRE) Official explanation: jockey said filly hung left-handed

2121 FEDERATION OF BLOODSTOCK AGENTS MAIDEN STKS (DIV I) 7f (S)
4:50 (4:52) (Class 4) 3-Y-O **£4,857** (£1,445; £722; £360) **Stalls** Centre

Form RPR

1 **Moretta Blanche** 3-8-12 0.. JimCrowley 5 81+
(R M Beckett) *s.i.s: t.k.h and stl plld whn hdwy over 3f out: drvn to chse ldr wl over 1f out: styd on wl fnl f to ld fnl 120yds: in command cl home* **7/1**[3]

5-6 **2** *½* **Engulf (IRE)**[28] 1381 3-9-3 0.. JMurtagh 1 82
(W J Haggas) *wnt lft s: racd alone on far side and overall ldr: jnd by main gp over 3f out: rdn and kpt on whn chal ins fnl f: hdd and nt qcknd fial 120yds but wl clr of 3rd* **13/8**[2]

3 *6* **Startle** 3-9-3 0.. RichardHughes 2 66+
(R Hannon) *in tch: rdn 3f out: styd on to take wl hld 3rd fnl f* **8/1**

00 **4** *3* **Lordsbury Pride (USA)**[4] 2004 3-9-3 0............................ GeorgeBaker 8 58
(J R Best) *sn chsng ldrs: rdn 3f out and tried to cl on ldrs 2f out: nvr on term and no ch fr over 1f out* **66/1**

0 **5** *nk* **Medici Brave**[9] 1844 3-9-3 0.. PatCosgrave 9 57
(Mrs A J Perrett) *in rr: rdn 3f out: mod prog fr over 1f out* **33/1**

00 **6** *1 ¼* **Resolute Road**[15] 1659 3-9-3 0...................................... MichaelHills 10 54
(B W Hills) *in rr: pushed along over 2f out: mod prog fnl f* **20/1**

7 *3* **Ertikaan** 3-9-3 0.. RichardHills 4 45
(M A Jarvis) *trckd ldrs and wnt 2nd over 3f out: lost 2nd wl over 1f out: sn dropped away* **6/4**[1]

00 **8** *6* **Captain John Nixon**[25] 1442 3-9-3 0............................ DarryllHolland 7 29
(Pat Eddery) *a towards rr* **33/1**

00 **9** *3* **Floating Angel (USA)**[8] 1882 3-8-7 0........................... KierenFox(5) 6 16
(J R Best) *chsd ldrs: rdn 4f out: wknd over 3f out* **50/1**

10 *1 ¼* **Proud Tuscan** 3-9-0 0.. RussKennemore(3) 11 18
(J S Moore) *s.i.s: bhd most of way* **33/1**

00- **11** *18* **Billyonair**[182] 7388 3-9-0 0.. PatrickHills(3) 3 —
(W De Best-Turner) *unruly stalls: pressed ldr to 1/2-way* **150/1**

1m 26.97s (1.27) **Going Correction** 0.0s/f (Good) **11** Ran SP% **119.4**
Speed ratings (Par 101): **92,91,84,81,80 79,75,69,65,64 43**
Tote Swingers: 1&2 £3.20, 1&3 £3.80, 2&3 £3.30 CSF £18.37 TOTE £8.40: £2.30, £1.10, £2.20; EX 20.80.
Owner P K Gardner **Bred** Springcombe Park Stud **Trained** Whitsbury, Hants

FOCUS
The first pair came clear, but it was a very ordinary winning time, 2.46sec slower than the second division, and the form is only ordinary. It has been rated around the runner-up.

2122 FEDERATION OF BLOODSTOCK AGENTS MAIDEN STKS (DIV II) 7f (S)
5:25 (5:26) (Class 4) 3-Y-O **£4,857** (£1,445; £722; £360) **Stalls** Centre

Form RPR

5- **1** **Flambeau**[215] 6730 3-8-12 0.. DaneO'Neill 2 85
(H Candy) *trckd ldrs: wnt 2nd appr fnl f: rdn to ld sn after: pushed out: readily* **5/2**[1]

0- **2** *¾* **Kakatosi**[197] 7146 3-9-3 0... DavidProbert 4 88
(A M Balding) *chsd ldrs: rdn to ld appr fnl f: hdd sn after: styd on but nt pce of wnr* **7/2**[3]

0-4 **3** *2 ½* **Alkhataaf (USA)**[13] 1731 3-9-3 0.................................. RichardHills 8 81
(J L Dunlop) *led tl rdn and hdd appr fnl f: styd on same pce* **11/1**

224- **4** *5* **Lean Machine**[245] 5867 3-9-3 82.................................. RichardHughes 6 68
(R Hannon) *hld up in rr: hdwy to cl on ldrs over 2f out: nvr on terms and wknd over 1f out* **11/4**[2]

0- **5** *1 ¼* **Starclass**[215] 6730 3-8-12 0.. WilliamBuick 9 59
(W R Swinburn) *awkward stalls: towards rr tl drvn and hdwy cl on ldrs ins fnl 2f: nvr on terms and sn btn* **14/1**

00 **6** *1 ¾* **Michael's Nook**[33] 1260 3-9-3 0.. IanMongan 3 60
(W S Kittow) *s.i.s: in rr: rdn over 3f out: mod prog fnl 2f* **66/1**

03- **7** *11* **Panpiper**[314] 3658 3-9-3 0... GeorgeBaker 7 30
(G L Moore) *shkn up and wnt rt over 2f out: nvr a factor* **22/1**

00 **8** *1 ½* **Saigon Kitty (IRE)**[8] 1878 3-8-7 0................................. KierenFox(5) 1 21
(J R Best) *chsd ldrs tl rdn and wknd 3f out* **40/1**

5 **9** *6* **Crinan Classic**[36] 1211 3-9-3 0...................................... PhilipRobinson 11 10
(C G Cox) *chsd ldrs tl wknd and hmpd over 2f out* **33/1**

05- **10** *nk* **Rosie's Magic**[214] 6756 3-8-9 0................................. PatrickHills(3) 10 4
(W De Best-Turner) *chsd ldrs over 4f* **100/1**

03- **P** **En Fuego**[200] 7096 3-9-3 0... TomQueally 5 —
(P W Chapple-Hyam) *in rr: eased over 3f out: p.u ins fnl f* **6/1**

1m 24.51s (-1.19) **Going Correction** 0.0s/f (Good) **11** Ran SP% **119.0**
Speed ratings (Par 101): **106,105,102,96,95 93,80,78,72,71** —
Tote Swingers: 1&2 £3.50, 1&3 £8.80, 2&3 £10.00 CSF £11.25 TOTE £3.50: £1.60, £1.90, £2.90; EX 11.40 Place 6: £29.19 Place 5: £23.20 .
Owner Major M G Wyatt **Bred** Dunchurch Lodge Stud Co **Trained** Kingston Warren, Oxon

FOCUS
The second division of the 7f maiden and the first three dominated. The winning time was over two seconds quicker than the first division. Big improvement on their debut efforts from the first two, with the form rated fairly positively.
Lean Machine Official explanation: jockey said colt was unsuited by the good to firm ground
En Fuego Official explanation: jockey said colt lost its action
T/Jkpt: Not won. T/Plt: £52.20. Pool £158,859.20 - 2,219.83 winning tickets. T/Qpdt: £27.70. Pool £7,434.12 - 198.26 winning tickets. ST

2088 NEWMARKET (Rowley Mile) (R-H)
Saturday, May 15

OFFICIAL GOING: Good to firm (8.7)
Wind: Light, half behind Weather: Fine but cloudy

2123 RACING EXCELLENCE "HANDS AND HEELS" APPRENTICE SERIES H'CAP (SPONSORED BY CAREERSINRACING) 6f
1:45 (1:46) (Class 5) (0-75,72) 4-Y-O+ **£3,885** (£1,156; £577; £288) **Stalls** High

Form RPR

0000 **1** **Imprimis Tagula (IRE)**[15] 1662 6-9-1 **71**................(v) NatashaEaton(3) 2 78
(A Bailey) *trckd ldrs: wnt 2nd jst over 1f out: pushed along and styd on wl to ld last 100yds* **4/1**[1]

4500 **2** ¾ **Peopleton Brook**[18] 1595 8-8-2 **58** oh3..............(t) MatthewCosham[(3)] 1 63
(B G Powell) *hld up in last trio: gd prog on outer over 1f out: styd on wl to take 2nd last strides* **28/1**

3550 **3** *hd* **Thoughtsofstardom**[4] 2008 7-8-0 **58** oh4.................. LeonnaMayor[(5)] 4 62
(P S McEntee) *racd centre: mde most: pushed along over 1f out: hdd and one pce last 100yds: lost 2nd fnl strides* **14/1**

6030 **4** *2* **Methaaly (IRE)**[16] 1650 7-9-0 **72**..........................(be) JosephYoung[(5)] 6 70
(M Mullineaux) *chsd ldrs: outpcd jst over 2f out: urged along furiously and styd on wl fnl f* **11/2**[2]

30-2 **5** *1 ¾* **Amosite**[18] 1595 4-9-1 **71**.. DannyBrock[(3)] 3 63
(J R Jenkins) *plld hrd: w ldr to 2f out: fdd fnl f* **12/1**

00-6 **6** ½ **Requisite**[18] 1596 5-8-10 **63**..................................(v) MatthewLawson 9 54
(I A Wood) *racd against far rail: pressed ldrs: wnt 2nd 2f out and chalng: fdd fnl f* **8/1**

5-00 **7** *shd* **Hustle (IRE)**[12] 1779 5-9-0 **70**.......................... StephanieBancroft[(3)] 8 60
(Miss Gay Kelleway) *sn outpcd: wl bhd in last 1/2-way: r.o wl fnl f: nrst fin* **6/1**[3]

-425 **8** *1 ¼* **Magical Speedfit (IRE)**[14] 1692 5-9-4 **71**........................ RyanPowell 7 57
(G G Margarson) *pressed ldrs: nt qckn 2f out: wknd fnl f* **6/1**[3]

1332 **9** *1 ¼* **Rubenstar (IRE)**[25] 1458 7-9-1 **71**...............................[1] MJMurphy[(3)] 11 53
(Patrick Morris) *v s.i.s: rcvrd to chse ldrs: wknd jst over 1f out* **7/1**

3100 **10** *4 ½* **Raimond Ridge (IRE)**[7] 1915 4-8-9 **65**.................. AdamBeschizza[(3)] 5 33
(J Jay) *a in last trio: struggling fr 1/2-way* **20/1**

-000 **11** *4* **Brunelleschi**[26] 1428 7-9-2 **72**............................(b) SophieSilvester[(3)] 10 27
(P L Gilligan) *pressed ldrs: hanging and wknd rapidly over 1f out* **14/1**

1m 12.46s (0.26) **Going Correction** 0.0s/f (Good) 11 Ran SP% **116.8**
Speed ratings (Par 103): **98,97,96,94,91 91,90,89,87,81 76**
toteswingers: 1&2 £31.60, 1&3 £14.50, 2&3 £43.90 CSF £121.57 CT £1038.11 TOTE £4.50: £1.40, £8.60, £4.80; EX 113.50 TRIFECTA Not won..
Owner Middleham Park Racing XLI & Alan Bailey **Bred** Glashare House Stud **Trained** Newmarket, Suffolk

FOCUS
An ordinary "hands and heels" apprentice handicap run at a solid pace.

2124 32RED.COM H'CAP 1m
2:15 (2:15) (Class 3) (0-95,95) 4-Y-0+ **£9,066** (£2,697; £1,348; £673) **Stalls** High

Form RPR

1404 **1** **Vainglory (USA)**[73] 769 6-8-7 **87**................................. MartinLane[(3)] 2 97
(D M Simcock) *pressed ldng pair on outer: inclined to hang but led wl over 1f out: styd on wl and in command after* **10/1**

0305 **2** *2* **Audemar (IRE)**[17] 1617 4-8-8 **85**..................................... MartinDwyer 3 90
(E F Vaughan) *trckd ldrs: rdn 3f out: effrt over 1f out to press for 2nd: kpt on same pce fnl f* **4/1**[2]

115- **3** *hd* **St Moritz (IRE)**[391] 1395 4-9-2 **93**.................................... JoeFanning 7 98
(M Johnston) *w ldr: upsides wl over 1f out: sn outpcd by wnr: lost 2nd fnl strides* **5/1**[3]

110- **4** *nse* **Invisible Man**[245] 5880 4-9-4 **95**.. TedDurcan 5 99+
(Saeed Bin Suroor) *hld up bhd ldrs: rdn and nt qckn 2f out: bmpd and rdr lost iron briefly jst over 1f out: kpt on to press for 2nd nr fin* **7/4**[1]

0-13 **5** *1* **Highly Regal (IRE)**[17] 1618 5-8-6 **83** ow1......................(b) LiamKeniry 4 85
(R A Teal) *stdd s: hld up in last: rdn 2f out and no rspnse: swtchd lft jst over 1f out: kpt on: no ch* **7/1**

0540 **6** *1 ¼* **Ilie Nastase (FR)**[12] 1767 6-8-4 **81**................................ HayleyTurner 8 80
(C R Dore) *in tch: pushed along over 3f out: struggling and no prog 2f out* **16/1**

06-0 **7** *2* **Willow Dancer (IRE)**[21] 1513 6-8-4 **81** oh1................(p) NickyMackay 6 76
(W R Swinburn) *mde most to wl over 1f out: wknd rapidly fnl f* **6/1**

1m 37.47s (-1.13) **Going Correction** 0.0s/f (Good) 7 Ran SP% **114.8**
Speed ratings (Par 107): **105,103,102,102,101 100,98**
toteswingers: 1&2 £6.30, 1&3 £3.80, 2&3 £4.40 CSF £49.74 CT £226.68 TOTE £11.80: £4.30, £2.00; EX 46.20 Trifecta £367.10 Part won. Pool £496.16 - 0.60 winning units..
Owner DXB Bloodstock Ltd **Bred** Darley **Trained** Newmarket, Suffolk

FOCUS
A decent handicap, but they didn't go much of a pace and it paid to be handy.

NOTEBOOK
Vainglory(USA), a tough and reliable handicapper, raced on the outside of the leading trio from the start and there was a danger he would see too much daylight, but as it turned out he was in the ideal spot. Set alight coming to the last furlong, he stays further than this so stamina was never going to desert him and he saw it out well. He was 4lb above his previous highest winning mark here, so seems better than ever and connections may try and find a race for him at the Epsom Derby meeting.
Audemar(IRE), a four-time winner on Polytrack having only his fifth start on turf, ran very well considering the way the race was run as he was off the bridle a fair way out, but kept staying on to just snatch the runner-up spot. (op 11-2)
St Moritz(IRE), having only his fourth start and his first since finishing unplaced in a German Group 3 more than a year ago, disputed the advantage against the far rail and stayed there until the winner swept past over a furlong out. Gelded since last seen, he was entitled to need this.
Invisible Man, a progressive handicapper for John Gosden last season before finishing lame on his final start at Goodwood in September, was making his debut for Godolphin. Never far away, he didn't have a lot of room to play with between Audemar and Willow Dancer over a furlong from home, but wasn't going anywhere at the time so he still has a few questions to answer. (tchd 15-8 and 2-1 in places)
Highly Regal(IRE), who might have done even better than third had he kept straight at Ascot last time, was restrained in last place early but when asked to make an effort he didn't find much and looked to be hating the ground. He has gained all seven of his wins on sand and probably needs an easier surface than this on turf. (op 13-2 tchd 6-1)
Ilie Nastase(FR), having his first start on turf since October but busy on the AW since, became outpaced at halfway and doesn't look an easy ride. (tchd 20-1)
Willow Dancer(IRE), lightly raced and disappointing since winning off 4lb higher over C&D in October 2008, helped force the pace until dropping away tamely over a furlong from home and continues to under-perform. Official explanation: jockey said gelding stopped very quickly (op 15-2)

2125 32RED CASINO H'CAP 1m 4f
2:45 (2:48) (Class 3) (0-95,88) 3-Y-0 **£9,066** (£2,697; £1,348; £673) **Stalls** Centre

Form RPR

1-43 **1** **Green Lightning (IRE)**[21] 1518 3-8-13 **78**..................(b[1]) JoeFanning 5 90
(M Johnston) *racd freely: mde all: cajoled along w little use of whip fr over 2f out: hd high but styd on wl* **12/1**

05-1 **2** *1 ¾* **Harris Tweed**[21] 1528 3-9-6 **85**..................................... EddieAhern 3 96+
(W J Haggas) *hld up in 4th: chsd wnr 3f out: rdn over 2f out: nt qckn and a abt a l down after* **9/4**[1]

214 **3** *4 ½* **Beneath**[13] 1734 3-9-1 **80**.. GeraldMosse 2 82
(Pat Eddery) *hld up in 5th: pushed along 4f out: wnt 3rd over 2f out: no imp on ldng pair u.p* **11/2**

2111 **4** *8* **Into Wain (USA)**[39] 1138 3-9-4 **83**................................ MartinDwyer 1 72
(D M Simcock) *thld up in last: reminder wl over 3f out: sn struggling: tk modest 4th over 1f out* **5/2**[2]

215- **5** *3 ¾* **Navy List (FR)**[204] 6993 3-9-6 **88**.............................. AhmedAjtebi[(3)] 4 71
(Mahmood Al Zarooni) *t.k.h: pressed wnr to 3f out: dropped out rapidly* **5/1**[3]

1-0 **6** *3* **Next Move (IRE)**[31] 1310 3-9-9 **88**...................................... TedDurcan 6 66
(Saeed Bin Suroor) *trckd ldng pair: rdn over 3f out: sn btn and bhd* **8/1**

2m 30.84s (-2.66) **Going Correction** 0.0s/f (Good) 6 Ran SP% **110.2**
Speed ratings (Par 103): **108,106,103,98,96 94**
toteswingers: 1&2 £7.70, 1&3 £8.70, 2&3 £3.90 CSF £37.83 TOTE £10.30: £3.30, £2.10; EX 36.00.
Owner The Green Dot Partnership **Bred** Western Bloodstock **Trained** Middleham Moor, N Yorks

FOCUS
The pace appeared ordinary but they still finished well spread out which suggests the form is reliable.

NOTEBOOK
Green Lightning(IRE) was blinkered for the first time after looking awkward on occasions, but there was no doubting his application here. Soon setting the pace, he faced some serious challenges over the last 3f but he kept on pulling out more and refused to be passed. Despite the blinkers he again held his head high over the last furlong or so, but that may have been more on account of the ground as his previous win came on a much softer surface. The headgear may well have made the difference and much will depend on whether it works again. (op 15-2)
Harris Tweed looked as though he would relish this longer trip when winning a maiden at Ripon on his reappearance last month and, having travelled well behind the leaders, seemed to be running all over his rivals entering the last 3f. Despite giving his all he couldn't get the better of the winner and it was noticeable that he looked awkward running into the Dip. This was only his fourth start and the best of him is yet to be seen. (op 3-1 tchd 2-1 and 7-2 in places)
Beneath saw plenty of daylight on the outside of the field and could only plug on at the one pace to finish a remote third, albeit well clear of the other three. He didn't see the racecourse until March, so is entitled to find a bit more improvement. (tchd 5-1)
Into Wain(USA), the only one in the field to have already won over the trip and bidding for a four-timer, was in trouble at the back of the field passing the half-mile pole and never got into the race. He was off a 10lb higher mark here but the quick ground may have been an even bigger problem. Official explanation: jockey said colt was unsuited by the good to firm ground (tchd 11-4 and 3-1 in places)
Navy List(FR), having his first start since October, is bred to be suited by this sort of trip but he pulled much too hard early and, after holding every chance, fell apart inside the last 3f. (op 13-2)
Next Move(IRE), having only his third start and making his handicap debut after finishing well beaten in the Tattersalls Timeform 3-y-o Trophy here on his return, is also bred to appreciate this sort of trip but he too dropped out very tamely and has plenty of questions to answer. (op 7-1)

2126 32RED H'CAP 1m 6f
3:25 (3:25) (Class 2) (0-105,96) 4-Y-0+
£21,808 (£6,531; £3,265; £1,634; £815; £409) **Stalls** Centre

Form RPR

20-2 **1** **Chiberta King**[13] 1724 4-9-8 **94**...................................... JimmyFortune 7 104+
(A M Balding) *mde all: shkn up to draw clr 2f out: in full command after: readily* **11/4**[1]

4-12 **2** *2* **Gala Evening**[29] 1139 8-9-10 **95**.. AdamKirby 5 101+
(J A B Old) *settled in last trio: reminder 8f out: looking for room over 3f out: prog over 2f out: styd on dourly to take 2nd last stride* **25/1**

-446 **3** *shd* **Swiss Act**[13] 1736 6-9-0 **85**... JoeFanning 10 91
(M Johnston) *prom: lost pl 4f out: effrt again on inner over 2f out: styd on to chse wnr ins fnl f: no imp: lost 2nd last stride* **16/1**

-052 **4** *1 ½* **Gordonsville**[13] 1720 7-8-13 **84**...................................... SebSanders 1 88
(J S Goldie) *chsd wnr: drvn 3f out: no imp and wl hld 2f out: lost 2 pls ins fnl f* **9/2**[2]

33-3 **5** ¾ **Strathcal**[12] 1783 4-8-3 **75**.. JimmyQuinn 8 78
(H Morrison) *settled in midfield: looking for room over 3f out: rdn and prog over 2f out: one pce fr over 1f out* **8/1**

10-5 **6** *4 ½* **Mykingdomforahorse**[14] 1690 4-8-3 **75**........................ NickyMackay 4 71
(M R Channon) *settled in last trio: pushed along over 7f out: effrt on outer 4f out: no imp 2f out: fdd* **13/2**[3]

12-3 **7** ¾ **Moonbeam Dancer (USA)**[115] 232 4-7-13 **71**............... LukeMorris 11 66
(D M Simcock) *s.s: sn in midfield: u.p 3f out: fdd wl over 1f out* **20/1**

11-0 **8** *7* **Royal Diamond (IRE)**[13] 1724 4-9-10 **96**........................ PhillipMakin 2 82
(M Dods) *t.k.h: hld up towards rr: effrt on outer 4f out: sn rdn and no prog: wknd over 2f out* **15/2**

40-0 **9** *9* **Far From Old (IRE)**[13] 1724 7-9-7 **92**............................ HayleyTurner 9 65
(M L W Bell) *chsd ldrs: rdn in 3rd 3f out: wknd rapidly over 2f out: eased fnl f* **12/1**

440- **10** *10* **Keenes Day (FR)**[210] 6851 5-9-9 **94**............................ J-PGuillambert 3 53
(M Johnston) *nvr gng wl: mostly last: lost tch u.p 4f out: t.o and eased fnl f* **16/1**

00-0 **11** *3 ½* **Judgethemoment (USA)**[7] 1902 5-9-0 **85**....................... ShaneKelly 6 39
(Jane Chapple-Hyam) *prom: rdn over 3f out: wknd rapidly over 2f out: t.o and eased fnl f* **16/1**

2m 55.23s (-3.27) **Going Correction** 0.0s/f (Good)
WFA 4 from 5yo+ 1lb 11 Ran SP% **115.0**
Speed ratings (Par 109): **109,107,107,106,106 103,103,99,94,88 86**
toteswingers: 1&2 £6.70, 1&3 £13.10, 2&3 £52.30 CSF £77.19 CT £931.95 TOTE £2.60: £1.10, £6.90, £6.70; EX 75.30 Trifecta £598.70 Pool: £1011.41 - 1.25 winning units..
Owner The Pink Hat Racing Partnership **Bred** Watership Down Stud **Trained** Kingsclere, Hants

FOCUS
A very decent staying handicap, but very few got into it.

NOTEBOOK
Chiberta King, soon in front, his rider brought him down the centre of the track for half a mile or so after turning for home before edging back to the far rail over 5f out. He gradually wound things up entering the last 3f and it was soon clear that he had all of his rivals stone cold. Now that he has proven his stamina, he could be just the type for the Ebor. (op 7-2)
Gala Evening, a consistent sort on the Flat and over hurdles in recent years, needs further than this so it was no great surprise his rider was having to give him reminders to keep him in touch a mile from home, but his stamina eventually kicked in and he passed several tiring rivals to snatch the runner-up spot close home. There are more nice prizes to be won with him under either code, granted a sufficient test. (tchd 20-1)
Swiss Act was never far away and kept staying on after coming off the bridle 3f from home. This was better after three indifferent efforts since returning from a layoff in March. (op 12-1)
Gordonsville, raised 1lb after enjoying no luck at all at Hamilton in his most recent start, had to do a bit of running early in order to get across and take a handy position from the outside stall, so he did well to stay in the thick of the action for as long as he did. There will be other days for him. (op 5-1)
Strathcal ◆, who should have appreciated this quicker surface after his encouraging Windsor reappearance, didn't always see a great deal of daylight over the last 3f but kept staying on and he should be cherry-ripe after this. (tchd 9-1)

Mykingdomforahorse, well backed for this following his encouraging Goodwood reappearance at the start of the month, wasn't travelling that well off the pace from some way out and, though he tried to stay on down the outside, was never doing enough. (op 6-1)

Moonbeam Dancer(USA), only once out of the frame in 12 previous outings, was having her third try on turf on this first start since January. She had every chance passing the 3f pole before getting outpaced and might be worth another chance on an easier surface. (op 16-1)

2127 32REDPOKER.COM NOVICE STKS 6f

4:00 (4:01) (Class 4) 2-Y-O £6,476 (£1,927; £963; £481) Stalls High

Form RPR

1 **1** **Klammer**[29] 1351 2-9-5 0 ShaneKelly 3 90+
(Jane Chapple-Hyam) *dwlt: trckd ldng pair over 3f out gng easily: narrow ld on outer 2f out: jnd fnl f: rdn and asserted last 75yds* 6/4[1]

1 **2** *nk* **My Son Max**[28] 1389 2-9-5 0 PatDobbs 5 89+
(R Hannon) *disp ld to 2f out: shkn up and pressed wnr after: upsides ins fnl f: jst hld nr fin* 9/4[2]

23 **3** *4* **Alfraamsey**[8] 1871 2-9-0 0 AlanMunro 1 72
(M R Channon) *disp ld to 2f out: shkn up and steadily outpcd fr over 1f out* 11/1

1 **4** *6* **Orientalist**[18] 1597 2-9-5 0 TedDurcan 4 63
(Eve Johnson Houghton) *cl up: pushed along 1/2-way: lft bhd fr over 2f out* 5/1[3]

4 **5** *5* **So Is She (IRE)**[10] 1819 2-8-6 0 MarcHalford(3) 2 34
(A Bailey) *reluctant to enter stalls: t.k.h: hld up: in tch to 1/2-way: sn wknd* 6/1

1m 12.83s (0.63) **Going Correction** 0.0s/f (Good) 5 Ran SP% **110.1**
Speed ratings (Par 95): **95,94,89,81,74**
CSF £5.12 TOTE £2.50: £1.20, £1.10; EX 5.20.
Owner Yan Wah Wu **Bred** Ermyn Lodge Stud Limited **Trained** Dalham, Suffolk

FOCUS
A fascinating race with all five runners having shown ability, including three who had been successful in their only previous starts, and there seems little doubt that the first two home this year are colts of real potential. They pulled clear of the slightly improved third. The winning time was only 0.37 seconds slower than the opening older-horse handicap.

NOTEBOOK
Klammer ◆, winner of an eight-runner Newbury maiden on debut last month from which the fourth and seventh horses have both since won, is bred to have appreciated this extra furlong on the dam's side of his pedigree. His rider was keen to restrain him at the start but he moved up stylishly on the outside of the field and looked likely to win comfortably when poking his head in front over a furlong out. However, he looked uncomfortable in the Dip and, with the runner-up rallying, had to dig deep to keep him at bay. He will now head for the Coventry Stakes. (op 13-8 tchd 7-4)
My Son Max ◆, winner of a Nottingham maiden on debut last month that has since worked out quite well, is also bred to have appreciated this extra furlong and set out to make all. He rallied in splendid fashion when the favourite ranged alongside and it's only a matter of time before he is winning again. (tchd 2-1 and 5-2)
Alfraamsey, who has been shaping as though this extra furlong would suit in his two previous starts, proved weak in the market. He showed good speed for a long way but had to give best to two progressive rivals from over a furlong out and lacks their scope for improvement. He should still be able to win an ordinary maiden. (op 7-1)
Orientalist shaped as though this extra furlong would suit when overcoming greenness to make a winning debut at Nottingham last month and the form has worked out reasonably well, but he was struggling to keep up from over 2f out and needs his sights lowered if he is to win again. (op 13-2)
So Is She(IRE), who faced a stiff task on debut in the Lily Agnes, showed a lot of ability in finishing a staying-on fourth at Chester but she pulled far too hard here and also ran green. This quicker surface may not have been ideal either and she probably needs more time. (op 13-2)

2128 32RED.COM MAIDEN STKS 1m

4:35 (4:35) (Class 4) 3-Y-O £5,180 (£1,541; £770; £384) Stalls High

Form RPR

2 **1** **Afsare**[12] 1769 3-9-3 0 KierenFallon 7 85+
(L M Cumani) *awkward s: sn trckd ldr: led 5f out: hung bdly lft fnl 2f and ended against nr side rail: styd on* 4/11[1]

0- **2** *1 1/4* **Battle Honour**[197] 7146 3-9-3 0 FergusSweeney 8 82
(H Candy) *in tch: effrt to go 3rd 2f out: hung lft following ldrs fr over 1f out: wnt 2nd ins fnl f: kpt on* 25/1

3 *1 1/2* **Linnens Star (IRE)** 3-9-3 0 JackMitchell 1 78
(R M Beckett) *t.k.h early: cl up: wnt 2nd over 2f out and sn chalng: carried lft fr wl over 1f out but nt seriously impeded: one pce and lost 2nd ins fnl f* 25/1

35 **4** *8* **Squall**[9] 1844 3-9-3 0 GeraldMosse 4 59
(J Noseda) *led 3f: chsd wnr to 2f out: wknd* 11/2[2]

5 *8* **Dhaafer** 3-9-3 0 TadhgO'Shea 6 40
(W J Haggas) *mostly last: pushed along 1/2-way: sn lost tch* 10/1[3]

6 *5* **Sir Sandford (IRE)** 3-9-3 0 LiamKeniry 9 28
(D M Simcock) *stdd s: hld up in tch: wknd 3f out: t.o* 20/1

1m 37.81s (-0.79) **Going Correction** 0.0s/f (Good) 6 Ran SP% **110.2**
Speed ratings (Par 101): **103,101,100,92,84 79**
toteswingers: 1&2 £3.90, 1&3 £4.00, 2&3 £9.50 CSF £14.00 TOTE £1.40: £1.10, £4.60; EX 9.90 Trifecta £127.10 Pool: £635.57 - 3.70 winning units..
Owner Sheikh Mohammed Obaid Al Maktoum **Bred** Darley **Trained** Newmarket, Suffolk

FOCUS
A weak and uncompetitive maiden and though the long odds-on favourite won he was hardly impressive.

2129 32REDPOKER.COM H'CAP 7f

5:10 (5:11) (Class 4) (0-80,79) 4-Y-O+ £4,857 (£1,445; £722; £360) Stalls High

Form RPR

531- **1** **Day Of The Eagle (IRE)**[197] 7149 4-9-1 76 KierenFallon 2 92+
(L M Cumani) *dwlt: sn trckd ldrs: prog on outer to ld over 1f out: pushed out: v readily* 10/3[1]

2336 **2** *1* **Seasider**[25] 1458 5-8-8 76 LauraPike(7) 1 84
(D M Simcock) *dwlt: hld up in last trio: prog on outer over 1f out: chsd wnr ins fnl f: r.o but no ch* 16/1

14-0 **3** *1 1/4* **Mac's Power (IRE)**[12] 1767 4-9-4 79 (t) AdamKirby 3 84
(J R Fanshawe) *hld up in last trio: nt clr run over 2f out: prog over 1f out: wnt 3rd ins fnl f: styd on same pce* 9/2[2]

-635 **4** *1/2* **Standpoint**[7] 1933 4-9-3 78 FergusSweeney 11 82+
(R Hollinshead) *trckd ldrs on inner: gng wl 2f out: outpcd and pushed along 1f out: shkn up and styd on nr fin* 5/1[3]

0-44 **5** *1/2* **Arabian Pearl (IRE)**[12] 1754 4-8-9 70 (b[1]) JackMitchell 5 74+
(P W Chapple-Hyam) *stdd s: hld up in last trio: nt clr run over 2f out to over 1f out: kpt on fnl f: no ch* 10/1

5241 **6** *hd* **Halsion Chancer**[21] 1530 6-9-1 76 LukeMorris 8 78+
(J R Best) *t.k.h early: trckd ldrs: lost pl 1/2-way: struggling in last pair over 1f out: kpt on again last 150yds* 11/1

-600 **7** *hd* **Negotiation (IRE)**[14] 1697 4-9-2 77 MartinDwyer 9 78
(M Quinn) *led: stdy pce to 1/2-way: hdd over 1f out: wknd ins fnl f* 33/1

60-0 **8** *nk* **George Thisby**[19] 1580 4-8-9 73 JamesMillman(3) 6 73
(B R Millman) *t.k.h: chsd ldr to 3f out: rdn and stl disputing 2nd 2f out: wknd fnl f* 9/1

5110 **9** *1* **Jake The Snake (IRE)**[17] 1625 9-9-4 79 SebSanders 10 77
(A W Carroll) *hld up towards rr: nt qckn over 2f out: one pce and no prog after* 11/2

0-03 **10** *3/4* **Purus (IRE)**[16] 1634 8-7-13 65 oh3 SophieDoyle(5) 4 61
(R A Teal) *t.k.h: prom: chsd ldr 3f out to 2f out: wknd* 14/1

1m 25.05s (-0.35) **Going Correction** 0.0s/f (Good) 10 Ran SP% **116.2**
Speed ratings (Par 105): **102,100,99,98,98 98,97,97,96,95**
toteswingers: 1&2 £15.10, 1&3 £3.60, 2&3 £11.70 CSF £59.10 CT £215.41 TOTE £4.20: £2.40, £3.30, £1.30; EX 85.60 Trifecta £291.70 Pool: £701.76 - 1.78 winning units. Place 6: £78.34 Place 5: £23.74.
Owner Chris Wright & Andy MacDonald **Bred** Swersky & Associates **Trained** Newmarket, Suffolk

FOCUS
A fair handicap, but they went at no pace at all early and a few were inclined to pull too hard, with Halsion Chancer and Purus the main culprits. However, the principals all came from well off the pace.
Standpoint Official explanation: jockey said gelding was denied a clear run
T/Plt: £259.20. Pool £112,904.33 - 317.96 winning units. T/Qpdt: £6.40. Pool £5,510.89 - 634.37 winning units. JN

1923 THIRSK (L-H)

Saturday, May 15

OFFICIAL GOING: Good to firm (9.9)
Wind: Fresh, half behind Weather: Fine

2130 E B F MARION GIBSON BROWN MEMORIAL MAIDEN FILLIES' STKS 5f

2:05 (2:07) (Class 4) 2-Y-O £5,569 (£1,657; £828; £413) Stalls High

Form RPR

52 **1** **Dolly Parton (IRE)**[15] 1668 2-9-0 0 AdrianNicholls 9 79
(D Nicholls) *cl up: rdn and flashed tail over 1f out: led ins fnl f: kpt on strly* 8/1[3]

2 *1 1/4* **Orchid Street (USA)** 2-9-0 0 PaulMulrennan 2 75+
(Mrs A Duffield) *led and crossed over to stands' rail over 3f out: rdn over 1f out: hdd ins fnl f: r.o* 28/1

24 **3** *2 3/4* **Yarooh (USA)**[13] 1728 2-9-0 0 ChrisCatlin 11 65
(C E Brittain) *cl up: rdn over 2f out: kpt on same pce fnl f* 10/11[1]

4 *1/2* **Ingleby Exceed (IRE)** 2-9-0 0 GrahamGibbons 8 63+
(T D Barron) *t.k.h: in tch: shkn up 2f out: kpt on fnl f: no imp* 11/1

5 *1 3/4* **Lady Kildare (IRE)** 2-9-0 0 AndrewElliott 5 57
(Jedd O'Keeffe) *trckd ldrs: effrt over 2f out: outpcd fnl f* 100/1

222 **6** *2* **Belle Royale (IRE)**[5] 1981 2-9-0 0 LiamJones 1 49
(W M Brisbourne) *prom: drvn over 2f out: wknd ent fnl f* 12/1

7 *1 1/2* **Royal Hush** 2-9-0 0 NeilCallan 10 44+
(K A Ryan) *reluctant to enter stalls: in tch: rdn and rn green over 2f out: btn appr fnl f* 11/4[2]

8 *2 1/4* **Vintage Grape (IRE)** 2-9-0 0 DavidAllan 4 36
(E J Alston) *sn bhd and drvn along: sme late hdwy: nvr on terms* 28/1

6 **9** *3* **West Stand**[12] 1749 2-9-0 0 FrederikTylicki 3 25
(Mrs K Walton) *s.i.s: bhd and outpcd: nvr on terms* 22/1

10 *4 1/2* **Whats For Pudding (IRE)** 2-9-0 0 DavidNolan 7 9
(D Carroll) *bhd and sn outpcd: no ch fr 1/2-way* 80/1

55 **11** *12* **Ever Roses**[16] 1646 2-9-0 0 TonyCulhane 6 —
(P T Midgley) *bhd: rdn and no imp whn hung bdly lft 2f out: eased* 66/1

59.47 secs (-0.13) **Going Correction** -0.15s/f (Firm) 11 Ran SP% **121.1**
Speed ratings (Par 92): **95,93,88,87,85 81,79,75,71,63 44**
toteswingers: 1&2 £69.50, 1&3 £1.50, 2&3 £14.30 CSF £209.51 TOTE £5.40: £1.40, £7.10, £1.80; EX 183.90.
Owner Mrs Love and Mrs Barker **Bred** I W Glenton **Trained** Sessay, N Yorks

FOCUS
The ground had been watered and one of the jockeys in the first felt it was riding good. The opener was just a fair fillies' maiden, but winners should come out of it. Improved form from Dolly Parton. The time was 1.47 seconds above standard.

NOTEBOOK
Dolly Parton(IRE) had tried to make all when runner-up at Musselburgh on her second start, but despite breaking well here she had to be content with chasing the pace. She came under pressure at halfway but, despite giving a flash of the tail, came home strongly to get on top inside the last. She was not stopping at the end and should get 6f. (tchd 15-2)
Orchid Street(USA) ◆ showed considerable promise on this debut, showing bright pace to get across from her low draw and lead. She could not hold on inside the last but this 48,000gns breeze-up buy should be up to winning a maiden. (op 33-1)
Yarooh(USA) was unable to take advantage of what looked an ideal opportunity after two good efforts at Newmarket. She was best drawn adjacent to the stands' rail and was always up with the pace, but found a couple too strong for her late on. This was disappointing. (op 5-4)
Ingleby Exceed(IRE), a leggy debutante, kept on pleasingly for fourth. An extra furlong should suit this filly, whose dam did her winning at 1m-1m2f. (op 12-1)
Lady Kildare(IRE) is a half-sister to four winners, notably decent sprinter Duchess Dora, out of a 6f juvenile winner. She made a satisfactory debut and normal improvement should see her competitive in a similar event.
Belle Royale(IRE) had been runner-up on each of her three previous starts but her limitations were apparent here, albeit she was drawn on the wide outside. (tchd 10-1)
Royal Hush, whose price rose to £78,000 at the breeze-ups, moved well to post but was reluctant to load into the stalls. Chasing the leading bunch without being able to mount a real challenge, she should come on for the run. (tchd 5-2 and 7-2)
Ever Roses Official explanation: jockey said filly hung left throughout

2131 WHITBY MAIDEN STKS 1m 4f

2:40 (2:46) (Class 5) 3-Y-O+ £4,274 (£1,271; £635; £317) Stalls Low

Form RPR

2 **1** **Royal Swain (IRE)**[14] 1705 4-10-0 0 RobertWinston 12 60+
(G A Swinbank) *t.k.h: trckd ldr: rdn to ld appr 2f out: kpt on wl: eased towards fin* 2/5[1]

0-40 **2** *1 1/2* **Weetfromthechaff**[11] 1803 5-10-0 50 (t) ChrisCatlin 2 54
(M A Barnes) *t.k.h early: prom: drvn 3f out: chsd wnr over 1f out: edgd lft: kpt on: nrst fin* 28/1

00-0 **3** *1* **Baltic Ben (USA)**[7] 1912 3-8-9 59 SilvestreDeSousa 8 49
(Eve Johnson Houghton) *chsd ldrs: drvn and outpcd over 2f out: rallied over 1f out: kpt on ins fnl f* 25/1

6 **4** *3* **Flockton Tobouggie**[11] 1801 4-9-9 0 JamesSullivan(5) 5 47
(M W Easterby) *t.k.h: in tch: drvn over 2f out: kpt on fnl f: no imp* 40/1

/65 **5** *3* **Decibel**[78] 718 6-10-0 0 NeilCallan 10 42
(K A Ryan) *unruly bef s: set stdy pce: rdn and hdd appr 2f out: sn one pce* **16/1**[2]

00- **6** *4* **Dubawi King**[199] 7121 3-8-9 0 TonyCulhane 6 33
(N Tinkler) *dwlt: t.k.h: midfield: outpcd over 2f out: sn n.d* **50/1**

0 **7** *3/4* **Siberian Sunset (IRE)**[7] 1927 4-10-0 0 PJMcDonald 4 34
(G A Swinbank) *hld up: shkn up and outpcd 3f out: n.d after* **18/1**[3]

6 **8** *8* **Barra Raider**[14] 1705 3-8-9 0 TomEaves 3 19
(R F Fisher) *hld up towards rr: struggling over 3f out: sn btn* **16/1**[2]

66 **U** **On The Right Path**[19] 1572 3-8-6 0 KellyHarrison(3) 11 —
(Paul Murphy) *stmbld s: bhd: drvn and outpcd whn jinked rt and uns rdr 4f out* **40/1**

2m 38.18s (1.98) **Going Correction** -0.075s/f (Good)
WFA 3 from 4yo+ 19lb **9** Ran SP% **102.6**
Speed ratings (Par 103): **90,89,88,86,84 81,81,75,—**
toteswingers: 1&2 £3.50, 1&3 £2.90, 2&3 £38.00 CSF £14.46 TOTE £1.20: £1.02, £2.50, £4.20; EX 13.70.
Owner Andrew Sparks **Bred** Patrick Cummins **Trained** Melsonby, N Yorks

FOCUS
A very weak and uncompetitive maiden, which was only steadily run. Two of the likelier types were taken out in the morning, and second favourite Bollin Alan, one of several to play up behind the stalls, was withdrawn.

2132 SANDS END H'CAP 1m
3:15 (3:15) (Class 6) (0-65,65) 3-Y-O **£2,914** (£867; £433; £216) **Stalls** Low

Form RPR

5603 **1** **Hathaway (IRE)**[12] 1777 3-8-8 **55** GrahamGibbons 1 59
(W M Brisbourne) *mde all: rdn over 2f out: hld on wl u.p fnl f* **28/1**

0052 **2** *hd* **Killing Moon (USA)**[12] 1753 3-9-4 **65** NeilCallan 5 69
(K A Ryan) *dwlt: sn midfield: hdwy over 3f out: effrt and hdwy over 1f out: hung bdly rt 1f out: kpt on: jst hld* **7/2**[1]

-03 **3** *1 1/4* **Refuse To Wait (IRE)**[16] 1649 3-9-1 **62** (p) DavidAllan 3 63
(T D Easterby) *prom on ins: effrt over 2f out: keeping on whn carried bdly rt ent fnl f: one pce last 100yds* **11/2**[2]

1505 **4** *nk* **Destiny's Dancer**[5] 1970 3-7-13 **51** oh1 PatrickDonaghy(5) 9 51
(B M R Haslam) *hld up: effrt and hdwy over 2f out: edgd rt over 1f out: kpt on u.p ins fnl f: nrst fin* **10/1**

2452 **5** *2* **Magic Millie (IRE)**[28] 1394 3-8-6 **53** SilvestreDeSousa 4 48
(J Hetherton) *in tch: effrt over 2f out: one pce whn carried sltly rt ins fnl f* **7/2**[1]

0216 **6** *hd* **Take My Hand**[11] 1810 3-9-2 **63** ChrisCatlin 7 60
(M R Channon) *hld up: hdwy and prom 2f out: drvn and one pce whn checked ent fnl f: no ex* **15/2**[3]

00-4 **7** *6* **No Quarter (IRE)**[24] 1465 3-8-10 **57** DanielTudhope 13 37
(A Dickman) *hld up: rdn and edgd lft over 2f out: nvr able to chal* **8/1**

640- **8** *nk* **Bubber (IRE)**[148] 7799 3-8-4 **54** ow1 BarryMcHugh(3) 10 34
(R A Fahey) *t.k.h: prom tl hung lft and wknd fr over 2f out* **15/2**[3]

0-00 **9** *7* **Blue Avon**[24] 1465 3-8-6 **53** FranciscoDaSilva 8 16
(R A Fahey) *t.k.h early: prom: lost pl after 3f: n.d after* **33/1**

5-00 **10** *6* **Barastar**[79] 698 3-8-6 **56** KellyHarrison(3) 6 4
(N Tinkler) *t.k.h: cl up tl wknd over 2f out* **40/1**

0040 **11** *hd* **Baby Judge (IRE)**[18] 1605 3-8-2 **54** BillyCray(5) 11 2
(M C Chapman) *chsd ldrs on outside tl rdn and wknd over 3f out* **33/1**

1m 40.05s (-0.05) **Going Correction** -0.075s/f (Good) **11** Ran SP% **115.3**
Speed ratings (Par 97): **97,96,95,95,93 93,87,86,79,73 73**
toteswingers: 1&2 £22.90, 1&3 £36.40, 2&3 £4.40 CSF £119.19 CT £526.98 TOTE £37.20: £6.50, £2.20, £2.00; EX 114.80.
Owner W M Clare **Bred** Tally-Ho Stud **Trained** Great Ness, Shropshire

FOCUS
A moderate handicap. The pace was sound, but it was something of a messy race with the runner-up causing problems late on.

2133 STONEACRE FORD H'CAP 1m
3:50 (3:50) (Class 4) (0-85,85) 4-Y-O+ **£5,569** (£1,657; £828; £413) **Stalls** Low

Form RPR

-440 **1** **Charlie Cool**[8] 1889 7-8-10 **77** (b) RobertWinston 3 89
(Mrs R A Carr) *in tch: hdwy to ld over 1f out: styd on strly fnl f* **5/1**[3]

54-0 **2** *2* **Arizona John (IRE)**[21] 1513 5-8-9 **76** GrahamGibbons 4 83
(J Mackie) *chsd ldrs: effrt and ev ch over 1f out: kpt on fnl f: nt rch wnr* **6/1**

0-61 **3** *1 1/2* **Come And Go (UAE)**[7] 1926 4-8-13 **80** PJMcDonald 6 84
(G A Swinbank) *cl up: effrt over 2f out: chal and edgd lft over 1f out: kpt on same pce ins fnl f* **10/3**[2]

0415 **4** *2 1/2* **Snow Bay**[15] 1672 4-9-4 **85** TomEaves 7 83
(B Smart) *led: rdn: edgd rt and hdd over 1f out: kpt on same pce* **9/1**

5/1- **5** *2* **Cape Quarter (USA)**[184] 7353 4-8-5 **72** LiamJones 2 65
(W J Haggas) *dwlt: hld up: hdwy and prom over 2f out: rdn and no ex over 1f out* **11/4**[1]

2050 **6** *hd* **Johnmanderville**[21] 1513 4-8-5 **75** AshleyHamblett(3) 1 68
(N Wilson) *hld up: drvn over 2f out: kpt on fnl f: nvr able to chal* **16/1**

6 **7** *2* **Bucephalus (IRE)**[7] 1907 6-8-4 **71** oh2 (t) ChrisCatlin 9 59
(M A Barnes) *s.i.s: bhd: outpcd 1/2-way: hdwy over 1f out: nvr rchd ldrs* **33/1**

5-02 **8** *10* **Handsome Falcon**[12] 1752 6-9-0 **81** FrederikTylicki 8 46
(R A Fahey) *prom tl hung lft and wknd over 2f out* **17/2**

4300 **9** *8* **Sacrilege**[4] 1997 5-8-5 **77** ow3 (p) MarkCoumbe(5) 5 24
(M C Chapman) *cl up tl hung lft and wknd fr 3f out* **40/1**

1m 38.33s (-1.77) **Going Correction** -0.075s/f (Good) **9** Ran SP% **112.5**
Speed ratings (Par 105): **105,103,101,99,97 96,94,84,76**
toteswingers: 1&2 £11.30, 1&3 £3.40, 2&3 £6.50 CSF £33.86 CT £112.34 TOTE £6.10: £1.70, £2.10, £2.00; EX 28.40.
Owner Middleham Park Racing Xxiv **Bred** Middle Park Stud Ltd **Trained** Huby, N Yorks

FOCUS
A fair handicap, run in a time around 1.7 seconds quicker than the earlier 51-65 event.
Johnmanderville Official explanation: jockey said gelding missed the break

2134 ROBIN HOODS BAY H'CAP 6f
4:25 (4:25) (Class 3) (0-90,87) 4-Y-O+ **£8,159** (£2,428; £1,213; £606) **Stalls** High

Form RPR

3-06 **1** **Damika (IRE)**[15] 1672 7-9-0 **86** MichaelStainton(3) 10 96
(R M Whitaker) *cl up stands' side: led over 1f out: drvn out fnl f* **11/2**[2]

10-0 **2** *1/2* **Doctor Parkes**[10] 1822 4-9-1 **84** RobertWinston 6 93
(E J Alston) *plld hrd early: prom: nt clr run fr 1/2-way to wl over 1f out: effrt and chsd wnr ins fnl f: r.o* **6/1**[3]

-421 **3** *1 1/4* **Discanti (IRE)**[8] 1888 5-9-1 **84** (t) DavidAllan 1 89
(T D Easterby) *in tch: hdwy on outside and ev ch over 1f out: sn rdn: kpt on same pce ins fnl f* **9/4**[1]

46-3 **4** *1 3/4* **Rowayton**[21] 1516 4-9-0 **83** GrahamGibbons 2 82
(J D Bethell) *cl up: rdn and ev ch over 1f out: edgd lft: no ex fnl f* **7/1**

0-05 **5** *1 1/4* **Red Cape (FR)**[1] 2100 7-9-3 **86** AndrewElliott 5 81
(Mrs R A Carr) *led to over 1f out: rdn and kpt on same pce* **17/2**

005- **6** *1 1/4* **Filligree (IRE)**[193] 7227 5-8-13 **85** WilliamCarson(3) 9 76
(Rae Guest) *hld up: pushed along 1/2-way: hdwy appr fnl f: n.d* **14/1**

20 **7** *3/4* **Indian Skipper (IRE)**[13] 1727 5-8-3 **77** (v) BillyCray(5) 4 66
(R C Guest) *dwlt: hld up: hdwy and ev ch on outside 2f out: edgd lft and wknd appr fnl f* **14/1**

0-02 **8** *1 1/2* **Pearly Wey**[8] 1888 7-8-11 **80** DanielTudhope 3 64
(I W McInnes) *hld up: rdn along 2f out: sn outpcd* **14/1**

4623 **9** *11* **Green Park (IRE)**[14] 1711 7-8-7 **76** (b) DuranFentiman 8 25
(D Carroll) *trckd ldrs tl rdn and wknd fr 2f out* **12/1**

00-0 **10** *61* **Jobe (USA)**[48] 1032 4-9-3 **86** NeilCallan 7 —
(K A Ryan) *sn drvn along towards rr: struggling fr 1/2-way: eased whn no ch over 1f out: lame* **12/1**

1m 10.71s (-1.99) **Going Correction** -0.15s/f (Firm) **10** Ran SP% **118.9**
Speed ratings (Par 107): **107,106,104,102,100 99,98,96,81,—**
toteswingers: 1&2 £6.50, 1&3 £5.10, 2&3 £4.60 CSF £39.33 CT £98.72 TOTE £7.10: £2.40, £2.30, £1.60; EX 43.70.
Owner G B Bedford **Bred** Patrick J Monahan **Trained** Scarcroft, W Yorks

FOCUS
A decent sprint handicap run in a time below standard.

NOTEBOOK
Damika(IRE) had not shown much in two previous starts this spring, but had fallen a stone in the weights in the past year. Drawn closest to the stands' rail and always towards the fore, he struck the front going to the furlong pole and went on to score gamely. He would ideally prefer easier conditions underfoot. (op 8-1)
Doctor Parkes, badly drawn at Chester last week, had to wait for a run and looked to be hanging a little, but came home well for second. This was his first run over 6f since his juvenile days and he got it well enough. (op 7-1 tchd 11-2)
Discanti(IRE) won well at Ripon last time and he ran a thoroughly creditable race here, but an 8lb rise and a low draw combined to scupper his chance. (tchd 15-8)
Rowayton has run well on both her starts this spring, not helped by her draw here, but her consistency has been noted by the handicapper and she remains without a win since her racecourse debut. (op 8-1 tchd 17-2)
Red Cape(FR) had run with credit at York the previous day and ran a similar race, showing his customary bright pace but unable to hold off the challengers. (op 12-1)
Filligree(IRE) could never get into the race, but made late headway and this was a pleasing return after an absence since November. (op 11-1)
Indian Skipper(IRE) Official explanation: jockey said gelding hung left
Jobe(USA) Official explanation: vet said gelding finished lame behind

2135 SCARBOROUGH H'CAP 5f
5:00 (5:01) (Class 2) (0-100,99) 4-Y-O+ **£12,045** (£3,584; £1,791; £894) **Stalls** High

Form RPR

4430 **1** **Fol Hollow (IRE)**[2] 2054 5-8-12 **93** AdrianNicholls 4 102
(D Nicholls) *cl up: rdn to ld over 1f out: edgd rt ent fnl f: hld on wl* **8/1**[3]

10-2 **2** *3/4* **Captain Dunne (IRE)**[19] 1573 5-9-4 **99** DavidAllan 6 105
(T D Easterby) *t.k.h: cl up: effrt and pressed wnr ins fnl f: r.o: hld nr fin* **2/1**[1]

2-05 **3** *1 1/4* **Jargelle (IRE)**[15] 1670 4-8-11 **92** (t) TomEaves 1 94
(K A Ryan) *led: crossed over towards stands' rail over 3f out: hdd over 1f out: checked ent fnl f: kpt on same pce* **33/1**

0-13 **4** *nk* **Tabaret**[2] 2054 7-8-6 **90** MichaelStainton(3) 3 91
(R M Whitaker) *in tch: pushed along 1/2-way: hdwy over 1f out: kpt on same fnl f* **10/1**

-132 **5** *1 1/4* **Jaconet (USA)**[2] 2054 5-8-11 **92** (b) GrahamGibbons 2 88
(T D Barron) *prom on outside: drvn 1/2-way: kpt on same pce fr over 1f out* **2/1**[1]

1410 **6** *hd* **Arganil (USA)**[14] 1700 5-9-4 **99** (p) NeilCallan 7 95
(K A Ryan) *dwlt: bhd and drvn along: hdwy whn nt clr run briefly over 1f out: no imp whn n.m.r ins fnl f: one pce* **5/1**[2]

0-06 **7** *nk* **Pavershooz**[10] 1822 5-8-8 **89** DuranFentiman 5 83
(N Wilson) *chsd ldrs: rdn over 2f out: n.m.r briefly over 1f out: sn no ex* **16/1**

58.11 secs (-1.49) **Going Correction** -0.15s/f (Firm) **7** Ran SP% **112.4**
Speed ratings (Par 109): **105,103,101,101,99 99,98**
toteswingers: 1&2 £2.90, 1&3 £12.40, 2&3 £10.40 CSF £23.60 TOTE £10.90: £4.70, £2.70; EX 26.80.
Owner Middleham Park Racing Iii **Bred** Dan O'Brien **Trained** Sessay, N Yorks

FOCUS
A good sprint handicap. The time was marginally slower than the lesser handicap half an hour later. Three of these ran in the race won by Johannes at York on Thursday.

NOTEBOOK
Fol Hollow(IRE) had finished behind two of these rivals when down the field at York two days earlier. Always prominent but under pressure by halfway, he edged to his left in front but held on to end a losing run extending back to last June. This consistent sort will go for the 6f handicap at Epsom on Derby day, a race in which his trainer has a good record. Official explanation: trainer had no explanation for the apparent improvement in form (op 17-2 tchd 15-2)
Captain Dunne(IRE), in the same ownership as the winner and carrying the first colours, had gone up 3lb for his unlucky defeat at Newcastle. Travelling well against the rail but slightly trapped there for a time, he ran on well enough when in the clear but was always just being held. He has a good record at this venue. (op 7-4)
Jargelle(IRE) ◆, fitted with a tongue tie for the first time, was the longer priced of the Kevin Ryan pair. Despite not getting the best of breaks, she showed fine pace to get over to the rail to lead from stall one, and although she could not repel the winner, this was still a better effort. (op 20-1)
Tabaret, ahead of today's winner at York two days earlier, was outpaced through the early parts, then veered left and appeared to bump Jaconet when attempting to improve over a furlong out. (op 8-1 tchd 15-2)
Jaconet(USA) blazed the trail at York two days earlier before eventually finishing second, but she was not well away from a troublesome draw here and lacked the same spark. (op 5-2)
Arganil(USA), out of his depth in the Group 3 Palace House Stakes on his return to turf, was another to miss the kick and he could never get into it, although he wasn't beaten too far in the end. (op 13-2 tchd 7-1)
Pavershooz, dropped 3lb since Chester, was briefly short of room behind the leaders before fading in the last half furlong. He is now only 1lb higher than when winning at Ayr last summe (op 14-1)

2136 FILEY H'CAP 5f
5:30 (5:31) (Class 4) (0-85,85) 4-Y-O+ **£5,569** (£1,657; £828; £413) **Stalls** High

Form RPR

0-43 **1** **Sirenuse (IRE)**[29] 1363 4-8-12 **79** TomEaves 9 91
(B Smart) *mde all: drvn 2f out: styd on strly fnl f* **9/1**

2323 **2** *1 ¼* **Brierty (IRE)**[8] 1888 4-8-11 **78** DavidNolan 7 85
(D Carroll) *midfield: rdn 1/2-way: styd on wl fnl f: tk 2nd towards fin: nt rch wnr* **16/1**

4-56 **3** *hd* **Indian Trail**[24] 1471 10-9-4 **85** (v) AdrianNicholls 11 91
(D Nicholls) *towards rr: rdn 1/2-way: hdwy appr fnl f: styd on wl towards fin* **7/1**

4246 **4** *¾* **Peak District (IRE)**[2] 2054 6-8-11 **83** AmyRyan(5) 8 87
(K A Ryan) *cl up: chsd wnr appr fnl f: one pce ins fnl f: lost 2nd towards fin* **5/1**[2]

614 **5** *½* **Absa Lutte (IRE)**[14] 1691 7-9-0 **81** (t) StephenCraine 6 83
(Patrick Morris) *hld up in tch: effrt over 1f out: kpt on same pce fnl f* **20/1**

21-1 **6** *1 ¼* **Igoyougo**[14] 1710 4-8-12 **79** SilvestreDeSousa 13 76
(G A Harker) *dwlt: bhd tl hdwy over 1f out: kpt on fnl f: nrst fin* **3/1**[1]

0324 **7** *1 ½* **Lucky Art (USA)**[11] 1805 4-8-5 **72** AndrewElliott 1 64
(Mrs R A Carr) *racd alone towards far side: rdn and edgd lft fr 2f out: no imp w stands' side ldrs* **20/1**

10-3 **8** *shd* **Rasaman (IRE)**[41] 1099 6-8-12 **82** GaryBartley(3) 14 74
(J S Goldie) *hld up: rdn 2f out: kpt on fnl f: nvr able to chal* **11/2**[3]

-033 **9** *¾* **Stolt (IRE)**[57] 935 6-8-12 **82** AshleyHamblett(3) 5 71
(N Wilson) *chsd wnr to appr fnl f: sn rdn: wknd ins fnl f* **25/1**

10-1 **10** *½* **Medici Time**[29] 1364 5-8-10 **77** (v) GrahamGibbons 2 64
(T D Easterby) *midfield on outside: outpcd over 2f out: n.d after* **10/1**

20-0 **11** *½* **Bravely (IRE)**[16] 1650 6-8-7 **74** DuranFentiman 3 59
(T D Easterby) *bhd and sn pushed along: nvr on terms* **40/1**

-030 **12** *½* **Bertoliver**[2] 2054 6-8-13 **83** WilliamCarson(3) 10 66
(S C Williams) *chsd ldrs: drvn 1/2-way: hung lft and wknd over 1f out* **9/1**

05-0 **13** *14* **Time Medicean**[29] 1364 4-8-10 **77** TonyCulhane 12 10
(P T Midgley) *towards rr: struggling 1/2-way: sn lost tch* **20/1**

57.98 secs (-1.62) **Going Correction** -0.15s/f (Firm) 13 Ran SP% **125.1**
Speed ratings (Par 105): **106,104,103,102,101 99,97,97,95,95 94,93,71**
toteswingers: 1&2 £27.60, 1&3 £15.30, 2&3 £22.00 CSF £138.27 CT £1086.68 TOTE £13.60: £3.90, £6.00, £3.40; EX 162.40 Place 6: £13.23 Place 5: £8.39.
Owner M Barber **Bred** David Jamison Bloodstock And G Roddick **Trained** Hambleton, N Yorks
■ Stewards' Enquiry : William Carson one-day ban: failed to ride to draw (May 29)

FOCUS
This was fast and furious and the time was slightly quicker than the preceding Class 2 handicap. Not many got into it.
T/Plt: 21.50. Pool £60,476.95 - 2,049.65 winning tickets. T/Qpdt: £11.10.Pool £3,188.32 - 210.80 winning tickets. RY

PIMLICO (L-H)
Saturday, May 15
OFFICIAL GOING: Turf couse: firm; dirt: fast

2137a PREAKNESS STKS (GRADE 1) (3YO) (DIRT) 1m 1f 110y(D)
11:12 (11:19) 3-Y-O **£370,370** (£123,456; £67,901; £37,037; £18,518)

RPR

1 **Lookin At Lucky (USA)**[14] 1714 3-9-0 0 MGarcia 7 121+
(Bob Baffert, U.S.A) **12/5**[2]

2 *¾* **First Dude (USA)**[35] 3-9-0 0 RADominguez 11 118
(Dale Romans, U.S.A) **238/10**

3 *hd* **Jackson Bend (USA)**[14] 1714 3-9-0 0 MESmith 6 118
(Nicholas Zito, U.S.A) **116/10**

4 *1* **Yawanna Twist (USA)**[42] 3-9-0 0 EPrado 5 116
(Richard Dutrow Jr, U.S.A) **166/10**

5 *4* **Dublin (USA)**[14] 1714 3-9-0 0 (b) GKGomez 12 108
(D Wayne Lukas, U.S.A) **98/10**

6 *4 ¾* **Paddy O'Prado (USA)**[14] 1714 3-9-0 0 KDesormeaux 10 99
(Dale Romans, U.S.A) **15/2**[3]

7 *nse* **Caracortado (USA)**[42] 3-9-0 0 PAtkinson 9 98
(Michael Machowsky, U.S.A) **188/10**

8 *1* **Super Saver (USA)**[14] 1714 3-9-0 0 CHBorel 8 96
(Todd Pletcher, U.S.A) **19/10**[1]

9 *¾* **Schoolyard Dreams (USA)**[42] 1097 3-9-0 0 (b) ECoa 2 95
(Derek S Ryan, U.S.A) **154/10**

10 *2 ½* **Aikenite (USA)**[21] 3-9-0 0 JJCastellano 1 90
(Todd Pletcher, U.S.A) **30/1**

11 *3 ½* **Pleasant Prince (USA)**[21] 3-9-0 0 JRLeparoux 3 83
(Wesley A Ward, U.S.A) **235/10**

12 *3 ½* **Northern Giant (USA)**[35] 3-9-0 0 (b) TJThompson 4 76
(D Wayne Lukas, U.S.A) **31/1**

1m 55.47s (-0.12) 12 Ran SP% **124.1**
PARI-MUTUEL (all including $2 stake): WIN 6.80; PLACE (1-2) 4.60, 16.60; SHOW (1-2-3) 3.80, 9.20, 6.60; SF 188.60.
Owner Karl Watson, Michael E Pegram & Paul Weitman **Bred** Gulf Coast Farms LLC **Trained** USA

NOTEBOOK
Lookin At Lucky(USA) has endured some tough trips, including in the Kentucky Derby, but it all went right here. Suited by the strong pace, he had to come four-wide off the home bend but battled on very gamely to win.
Super Saver(USA) had no real excuses except that this may have come too soon after his hard race in the Kentucky Derby. He will be given a break now and be brought back later in the summer.

1886 RIPON (R-H)
Sunday, May 16
OFFICIAL GOING: Good to firm (8.5)
Wind: Slight, half against Weather: Cloudy

2138 SIS LIVE MAIDEN STKS 6f
2:10 (2:12) (Class 5) 2-Y-O **£2,914** (£867; £433; £216) **Stalls** Low

Form RPR

5 **1** **Breathless Storm (USA)**[15] 1686 2-9-3 0 MickyFenton 2 76
(T P Tate) *hld up: hung rt thrght: effrt over 2f out: hdwy over 1f out: led ins fnl f: styd on wl* **1/1**[1]

2 *nk* **Defence Council (IRE)** 2-9-3 0 FrederikTylicki 6 75
(J Howard Johnson) *led: rdn over 2f out: edgd rt and hdd ins fnl f: r.o* **10/1**

0 **3** *nk* **Anddante (IRE)**[32] 1294 2-9-3 0 DuranFentiman 7 74
(T D Easterby) *trckd ldrs: drvn and ev ch over 1f out: kpt on ins fnl f: hld cl home* **25/1**

5 **4** *7* **Sarandjam**[10] 1845 2-9-3 0 AlanMunro 3 54+
(M R Channon) *trckd ldrs: drvn over 2f out: edging rt and one pce whn carried rt over 1f out: sn wknd* **6/1**[3]

5 *2 ½* **Greek Islands (IRE)** 2-9-3 0 TadhgO'Shea 1 47+
(Mahmood Al Zarooni) *missed break: hdwy on outside and in tch over 3f out: rdn and wknd over 1f out* **11/4**[2]

6 *6* **Captain Loui (IRE)** 2-9-3 0 TomEaves 8 28+
(K A Ryan) *dwlt: sn in tch on outside: rdn over 2f out: sn wknd* **12/1**

0 **7** *¾* **Rainbows Son**[30] 1359 2-9-3 0 TonyCulhane 5 25
(P T Midgley) *s.i.s: towards rr: hung rt and outpcd 1/2-way: sn btn* **100/1**

8 *38* **Santorino** 2-9-3 0 TonyHamilton 4 —
(P T Midgley) *dwlt: bhd: lost tch 1/2-way: t.o* **33/1**

1m 15.51s (2.51) **Going Correction** +0.20s/f (Good) 8 Ran SP% **115.5**
Speed ratings (Par 93): **91,90,90,80,77 69,68,17**
toteswingers: 1&2 £2.90, 1&3 £6.20, 2&3 £23.10 CSF £12.71 TOTE £2.20: £1.10, £3.70, £5.80; EX 14.20 Trifecta £151.50 Part won. Pool of £204.84 - 0.43 winning units..
Owner Mrs Fitri Hay **Bred** Manganaro Llc **Trained** Tadcaster, N Yorks
■ Stewards' Enquiry : Micky Fenton one-day ban: careless riding (May 30)

FOCUS
Rail on bottom bend into home straight moved out 6metres, adding 12yds to advertised distances on Round course. Possibly a below-par renewal as none of those with experience had shown form good enough to have won this in most previous years yet they still filled two of the first three places. The first three finished clear and the winner looks talented but quirky.

NOTEBOOK
Breathless Storm(USA) stepped forward from his Doncaster debut but made hard work of things and once again looked anything but straightforward, repeatedly on and off the bridle and looking quirky before hanging badly right late on when pulled out for his challenge. Reported by his trainer to be one of the fastest horses he has trained, he might have been unsuited by the undulations here and is probably a fair bit better than this but has some growing up to do if he is to progress. (op 7-4 tchd 15-8)
Defence Council(IRE), a costly yearling by Kheleyf, ran a promising first race for all that he had the benefit of the rail, soon disputing the lead and keeping on well. He might be able to progress enough to win a similar race.
Anddante(IRE) had been given a break since his debut and left that form well behind, seeing his race out much better on this occasion. (tchd 22-1)
Sarandjam improved for his debut and might have finished a bit closer but for being hampered by the winner, but he really only looked fifth best on the day anyway. (op 11-2 tchd 4-1)
Greek Islands(IRE), an expensive son of Oasis Dream, looked inexperienced, losing many lengths at the start, but he made good mid-race progress until being eased after getting hampered when the winner hung right. A close-up fourth would have been a better reflection of how he ran, and he'll step up a good deal on this next time. (op 9-4)
Captain Loui(IRE) looked to be carrying condition and dropped right out as if needing the race. He's bred to come into his own over further and on softer ground. (op 9-1)

2139 WOODEN SPOON STIRRING CHILDREN'S SMILES CHARITY (S) STKS 6f
2:40 (2:41) (Class 6) 2-Y-O **£2,590** (£770; £385; £192) **Stalls** Low

Form RPR

33 **1** **Bachelor Knight (IRE)**[17] 1646 2-9-0 0 PaulHanagan 4 56+
(R A Fahey) *hld up: hdwy and swtchd rt over 1f out: led ins fnl f: kpt on strly* **5/4**[1]

2 *½* **Muse To Use** 2-8-4 0 PatrickDonaghy(5) 1 50
(M Dods) *trckd ldrs: rdn to ld over 1f out: hdd ins fnl f: r.o* **8/1**

0 **3** *1 ¾* **Kodibelle (IRE)**[15] 1704 2-8-6 0 ow2 (b[1]) LanceBetts(5) 5 46
(T D Easterby) *dwlt: sn in tch: drvn over 3f out: rallied over 1f out: no ex wl ins fnl f* **25/1**

2054 **4** *3 ¼* **Beach Patrol (IRE)**[13] 1764 2-9-0 0 AlanMunro 8 40
(M R Channon) *plld hrd early: cl up: ev ch and rdn over 2f out: no ex over 1f out* **4/1**[2]

56 **5** *1 ½* **Dancing With Fire**[6] 1981 2-8-9 0 JoeFanning 2 30
(D Donovan) *in tch: effrt whn n.m.r briefly over 1f out: sn outpcd* **28/1**

662 **6** *5* **Crazy In Love**[12] 1794 2-8-6 0 (b) JackDean(3) 9 15
(W G M Turner) *cl up: ev ch and rdn over 2f out: wknd appr fnl f* **13/2**[3]

002 **7** *4 ½* **Reel Amber**[9] 1886 2-8-9 0 (b) DuranFentiman 10 2
(T D Easterby) *led to over 1f out: sn rdn and btn* **7/1**

00 **8** *½* **Sailor Boy (IRE)**[38] 1180 2-8-11 0 MartinLane(3) 7 5
(D Donovan) *dwlt and wnt rt s: bhd and pushed along: struggling 1/2-way: nvr on terms* **80/1**

04 **9** *3* **Rath Maeve**[17] 1647 2-8-9 0 RobertWinston 3 —
(A J McCabe) *bhd: hung rt and struggling over 2f out: nvr on terms* **28/1**

1m 16.4s (3.40) **Going Correction** +0.20s/f (Good) 9 Ran SP% **113.4**
Speed ratings (Par 91): **85,84,82,77,75 69,63,62,58**
toteswingers: 1&2 £3.40, 1&3 £19.60, 2&3 £33.60 CSF £11.34 TOTE £1.90: £1.10, £2.40, £8.30; EX 13.60 Trifecta £231.90 Pool: £479.65 - 1.53 winning units..The winner was bought in for 5,500gns. Beach Patrol was claimed by E. J. Creighton for £6000. Muse To Use was claimed by I. W. McInnes for £6000.
Owner Lets Go Racing 1 **Bred** Angelo Robiati **Trained** Musley Bank, N Yorks

FOCUS
A modest seller that went the way of the form pick, who didn't need to improve dropped in grade.

NOTEBOOK
Bachelor Knight(IRE), down in grade, made much harder work of winning than his outstanding chance on form suggested, only getting on top late after starting to be pushed at halfway. He had proved difficult to load and it remains to be seen whether he goes the right way, though he'll have no problem staying 7f. He was retained at the subsequent auction. (op Evens tchd 5-6)
Muse To Use showed enough to suggest she can win a similar event next time. Never far away on the rail, she pushed the winner hard inside the last and also left the impression she'll prove just as effective at 7f. (op 10-1 tchd 12-1)
Kodibelle(IRE) shaped much better dropped in class and tried in headgear but she looked a bit quirky, hanging left and right. She showed a pronounced round action, and might be best with more give in the ground. (op 22-1)
Beach Patrol(IRE), for much of the way, looked likely to finish a bit closer than he did. This is clearly his level now and, tending to carry his head a little high, might be worth a try in headgear. (op 13-2 tchd 7-1)
Dancing With Fire was down in grade but never threatened. Her pedigree suggests that she'll be suited by another furlong before long. (tchd 33-1)
Crazy In Love was unable to repeat her form of the first time she was tried in headgear, but showed early pace and promises to be suited by a drop back to 5f. (op 6-1 tchd 7-1)
Reel Amber looks by being suited by a drop back to the minimum trip. (op 15-2 tchd 13-2)

2140 C. B. HUTCHINSON MEMORIAL CHALLENGE CUP (FILLIES' H'CAP) 6f
3:10 (3:11) (Class 3) (0-95,84) 3-Y-O **£7,885** (£2,360; £1,180; £590; £293) **Stalls** Low

Form RPR

3-46 **1** **Misplaced Fortune**[15] 1688 5-9-7 **77** (v) JoeFanning 3 86
(N Tinkler) *trckd ldrs: effrt 2f out: edgd rt and led appr fnl f: hld on wl* **13/2**

1-15 **2** *nk* **Esuvia (IRE)**[29] 1399 3-9-0 79 TomEaves 6 84
(B Smart) *t.k.h: led after 2f to appr fnl f: kpt on ins fnl f* **5/2**[1]
152 **3** *3/4* **Solstice**[20] 1584 3-9-3 82 PhillipMakin 7 85
(Julie Camacho) *hld up in tch: effrt over 1f out: rdn and kpt on same pce wl ins fnl f* **9/2**
2240 **4** *1 1/4* **Kerrys Requiem (IRE)**[9] 1862 4-10-0 84 TonyCulhane 4 86
(M R Channon) *hld up: nt clr run over 2f out: hdwy appr fnl f: kpt on: no imp* **15/2**
0-45 **5** *nk* **Favourite Girl (IRE)**[17] 1650 4-9-6 76 (p) GrahamGibbons 5 77
(T D Easterby) *led 2f: rdn over 2f out: edgd rt: no ex appr fnl f* **7/2**[2]
01-2 **6** *nse* **Elusive Sue (USA)**[24] 1487 3-9-0 79 PaulHanagan 1 77
(R A Fahey) *trckd ldrs: sn pushed along: effrt u.p over 2f out: sn outpcd: kpt on u.p ins fnl f: no imp* **4/1**[3]
0-14 **7** *3 1/4* **Fayre Bella**[10] 1842 3-8-10 75 TadhgO'Shea 2 62
(J Gallagher) *dwlt: hld up: outpcd over 2f out: n.d after* **25/1**

1m 13.58s (0.58) **Going Correction** +0.20s/f (Good)
WFA 3 from 4yo+ 9lb **7** Ran SP% **117.9**
Speed ratings (Par 104): **104,103,102,100,100 100,96**
toteswingers: 1&2 £6.50, 1&3 £3.20, 2&3 £6.10 CSF £24.24 CT £82.53 TOTE £10.40: £4.70, £2.40; EX 32.40 Trifecta £181.70 Pool: £351.28 - 1.43 winning units..
Owner W F Burton **Bred** Adrian Smith **Trained** Langton, N Yorks

FOCUS
Effectively a 0-85 rather than the 0-95 suggested in the race title and, as in recent years, it went to one of the older contingent. The pace was a good one.

NOTEBOOK
Misplaced Fortune had run well at Doncaster last time in a race working out well, by and large, and she benefited from a better position closer to a good gallop on this occasion to edge ahead inside the last. Things dropped right for her here, but she was progressive in 2009 and looks at least as good if not better this year. (op 9-2)
Esuvia(IRE) ◆ trapped much better than she had last time and ran a much better race as a result, giving best only inside the last. This was a good effort considering that three-year-olds generally face a stiff task against their elders at this time of year, and she'll be of ample interest next time back against her own age group either at 5f or 6f. (op 7-2 tchd 4-1 in places)
Solstice, second home of the younger generation, also ran well considering that it was her first run on turf. She doesn't possess the basic speed of the runner-up but was closing steadily late and in view of her running style and pedigree, might improve further for a step up to 7f.
Kerrys Requiem(IRE) has the ability to get back to winning ways but isn't easy to catch right and didn't help herself here by tending to carry her head awkwardly. (op 9-1)
Favourite Girl(IRE) is a shadow of her former self and even with her yard in cracking form and the benefit of the rail she couldn't take advantage. (op 5-1)
Elusive Sue(USA) was a bit troublesome in the stalls and then missed the break. She's probably flying a bit high at this level. (op 7-2)
Fayre Bella Official explanation: jockey said filly was slowly away

2141 RIPON, YORKSHIRE'S GARDEN RACECOURSE H'CAP 1m
3:40 (3:40) (Class 2) (0-100,95) 4-Y-O+ **£10,092** (£3,020; £1,510; £755; £376) **Stalls** High

Form RPR
14-0 **1** **Tiger Reigns**[50] 1008 4-9-4 93 PhillipMakin 2 103
(M Dods) *prom: hdwy and ev ch 2f out: sn drvn: styd on wl u.p fnl f: led towards fin* **4/1**[3]
3351 **2** *nk* **Dubai Dynamo**[2] 2086 5-9-6 95 6ex AndrewElliott 5 104
(Mrs R A Carr) *hld up in tch: swtchd lft 4f out: hdwy to ld 2f out: sn rdn and edgd rt: kpt on fnl f: hdd towards fin* **3/1**[1]
1360 **3** *3 1/4* **Cobo Bay**[11] 1826 5-8-13 88 (p) PaulMulrennan 1 89
(K A Ryan) *dwlt: sn prom on outside: hdwy and ev ch over 3f out: edgd rt and kpt on same pce over 1f out* **6/1**
0140 **4** *1 1/4* **Exit Smiling**[15] 1708 8-8-10 85 TonyCulhane 4 83+
(P T Midgley) *t.k.h: chsd ldrs: drvn and outpcd over 2f out: rallied ins fnl f: no imp* **14/1**
24-2 **5** *1* **Sunnyside Tom (IRE)**[15] 1707 6-8-10 85 PaulHanagan 6 81
(R A Fahey) *set stdy pce: jnd and rdn over 3f out: hdd 2f out: sn no ex* **7/2**[2]
0-03 **6** *3/4* **Mountain Cat (IRE)**[42] 1102 6-8-9 84 RobertWinston 3 78
(G A Swinbank) *t.k.h: trckd ldrs: outpcd over 2f out: n.d after* **7/2**[2]

1m 43.3s (1.90) **Going Correction** +0.25s/f (Good) **6** Ran SP% **110.4**
Speed ratings (Par 109): **100,99,96,95,94 93**
toteswingers: 1&2 £3.50, 1&3 £5.90, 2&3 £4.20 CSF £15.75 TOTE £4.10: £2.70, £2.60; EX 16.30.
Owner Joe Buzzeo **Bred** Richard Green And New England Stud **Trained** Denton, Co Durham

FOCUS
The rails on the bottom bend into the home straight had been moved out adding 12 yards to distances of races on the round course. A disappointing turnout for the money, and a potentially muddling piece of form as well after the race developed into something of a sprint finish.

NOTEBOOK
Tiger Reigns hadn't come to himself according to his trainer when down the field in the Lincoln on his reappearance but with the yard's horses going much better now, continued the progress he made throughout most of 2009 with a hard-earned success, albeit probably benefiting by running his race in a more efficient manner than the runner-up after looking held running into the last. He looks set to take higher rank as a handicapper this year, though the Hunt Cup looks out as he is thought to be better on a turning track and the ground at Ascot may well be too lively for him. (op 11-4)
Dubai Dynamo was a tad unfortunate not to add to his win at Newcastle two days earlier. Ridden from the front then, he was held up some way back here but his rider seemed to make his move too early and after quickening impressively from last to first, was a sitting duck for the winner late on. He wasn't beaten by the trip though 7f might well be his ideal distance. (tchd 11-4 and 7-2)
Cobo Bay ran respectably with the cheekpieces replacing blinkers but looked quirky, carrying his head awkwardly and running wide on the bend. He's capable in this grade but isn't always inclined to show his full ability. (op 11-2)
Exit Smiling left the impression he was better than his finishing position, only really beginning to stay on well, and then without being knocked about, when the race was all but over. (tchd 16-1)
Sunnyside Tom(IRE) had the benefit of an uncontested lead and it was a bit disappointing that he couldn't do any better. (op 4-1 tchd 10-3)
Mountain Cat(IRE) was progressive last year and had shaped as if on the way back last time but wasn't ridden with as much enterprise on this occasion and never threatened. That said, the undulations might have caught him out and it might be that he'll fare better next time back on a flatter track. Official explanation: jockey said gelding ran too free (op 11-2)

2142 MIDDLEHAM TRAINERS ASSOCIATION H'CAP 1m 1f 170y
4:10 (4:10) (Class 4) (0-85,81) 4-Y-O+ **£4,857** (£1,445; £722; £360) **Stalls** High

Form RPR
4-43 **1** **Bollin Dolly**[18] 1629 7-8-8 71 GrahamGibbons 3 80+
(T D Easterby) *pressed ldr: led over 3f out: clr and rdn over 1f out: styd on strly* **5/4**[1]
0000 **2** *2 3/4* **Orpen Wide (IRE)**[13] 1754 8-8-1 67 (b) KellyHarrison(3) 6 68
(M C Chapman) *prom: effrt and chsd wnr 3f out: kpt on fnl f: nt gng pce of wnr* **28/1**
060- **3** *2 1/2* **Arabian Spirit**[212] 6830 5-9-2 79 PaulHanagan 4 75
(R A Fahey) *hld up: hdwy and prom wl over 1f out: edgd rt and sn no ex* **3/1**[2]
25-0 **4** *8* **French Applause (IRE)**[29] 1374 4-9-0 77 MickyFenton 8 57
(T P Tate) *trckd ldrs tl rdn and wknd fr 2f out* **9/2**[3]
3610 **5** *4 1/2* **Wrongwayround (IRE)**[13] 1751 4-8-6 69 PJMcDonald 2 40
(G A Swinbank) *dwlt: hld up: struggling over 2f out: nvr on terms* **9/2**[3]
-054 **6** *9* **Back To Paris (IRE)**[12] 1801 8-8-5 68 oh9 ow1 AndrewElliott 7 20
(Paul Murphy) *led to over 3f out: sn rdn and lost pl* **33/1**

2m 6.53s (1.13) **Going Correction** +0.25s/f (Good) **6** Ran SP% **112.2**
Speed ratings (Par 105): **105,102,100,94,90 83**
toteswingers: 1&2 £10.10, 1&3 £1.10, 2&3 £7.10 CSF £36.27 CT £90.32 TOTE £2.00: £1.20, £6.30; EX 22.00 Trifecta £143.30 Pool: £275.31 - 1.42 winning units..
Owner Sir Neil Westbrook **Bred** Sir Neil And Lady Westbrook **Trained** Great Habton, N Yorks

FOCUS
An uncompetitive handicap run at a fair pace. The winner probably didn't have to improve much on recent efforts.

2143 ATTHERACES.COM WITH FREE TIMEFORM MAIDEN STKS 1m 1f
4:40 (4:40) (Class 5) 3-Y-O **£2,914** (£867; £433; £216) **Stalls** High

Form RPR
6-3 **1** **Florentine Ruler (USA)**[31] 1335 3-9-3 0 IanMongan 8 83+
(H R A Cecil) *in tch: smooth hdwy 4f out: led over 2f out: edgd rt and drew clr over 1f out: readily* **13/8**[1]
400- **2** *8* **Rasselas (IRE)**[212] 6810 3-9-3 79 MichaelHills 5 65
(B W Hills) *t.k.h: cl up: led after 3f to over 2f out: no ch w wnr* **7/4**[2]
0- **3** *1 1/2* **Ticket To Paradise**[193] 7243 3-9-3 0 RobertWinston 10 62+
(D R Lanigan) *prom: drvn and outpcd 3f out: plugged on fnl f: no imp* **9/1**
0 **4** *3/4* **Affordable (IRE)**[10] 1844 3-9-3 0 AlanMunro 3 60
(M R Channon) *t.k.h: trckd ldrs: drvn and edgd rt over 2f out: sn outpcd* **16/1**
0 **5** *6* **Fantastic Sam (IRE)**[16] 1654 3-8-12 0 PaulMulrennan 4 42
(Mrs K Walton) *bhd: rdn along and c wd bnd over 4f out: hdwy over 1f out: kpt onf fnl f: nvr on terms* **100/1**
3-44 **6** *12* **Jack O'Lantern**[15] 1706 3-9-3 78 PaulHanagan 7 20
(R A Fahey) *led 3f: cl up tl rdn and wknd over 2f out* **5/1**[3]
0-00 **7** *1 3/4* **Isle Of Ellis (IRE)**[73] 782 3-9-0 40 KellyHarrison(3) 1 17
(R E Barr) *dwlt: bhd: hdwy on outside over 4f out: wknd fr 3f out* **150/1**
000- **8** *hd* **Naughty Norris**[193] 7244 3-8-10 35 MatthewLawson(7) 6 16
(R Bastiman) *trckd ldrs tl wknd fr 4f out* **150/1**
4-0 **9** *4* **Golden Gates (IRE)**[50] 1010 3-9-3 0 TonyCulhane 2 7
(Mrs A Duffield) *hld up: drvn over 4f out: nvr on terms* **33/1**
00 **10** *12* **One More Tico**[8] 1927 3-9-3 0 JoeFanning 9 —
(M Johnston) *hld up: struggling fr 4f out: t.o* **50/1**

1m 57.71s (3.01) **Going Correction** +0.25s/f (Good) **10** Ran SP% **114.2**
Speed ratings (Par 99): **96,88,87,86,81 70,69,69,65,54**
toteswingers: 1&2 £1.80, 1&3 £4.00, 2&3 £4.40 CSF £4.55 TOTE £2.50: £1.10, £2.10, £3.90; EX 5.90 Trifecta £72.00 Pool: £426.28 - 4.38 winning units..
Owner Malih L Al Basti **Bred** Darley **Trained** Newmarket, Suffolk

FOCUS
An uncompetitive maiden run at an uneven pace and a facile winner.
Golden Gates(IRE) Official explanation: jockey said gelding was denied a clear run

2144 TOTESWINGER H'CAP 5f
5:10 (5:12) (Class 5) (0-70,69) 4-Y-O+ **£2,914** (£867; £433; £216) **Stalls** Low

Form RPR
0-00 **1** **Musical Bridge**[12] 1799 4-8-11 62 (b[1]) TomEaves 2 73
(Mrs L Williamson) *in tch: effrt over 1f out: drvn to ld wl ins fnl f: r.o* **20/1**
0-30 **2** *nk* **Atlantic Beach**[8] 1924 5-9-0 65 SilvestreDeSousa 3 75
(J Hetherton) *chsd ldrs: effrt and rdn over 1f out: led briefly ins fnl f: kpt on* **11/4**[1]
1012 **3** *1 1/2* **Ridley Didley (IRE)**[8] 1915 5-8-13 67 AshleyHamblett(3) 5 72
(N Wilson) *t.k.h: led to ins fnl f: kpt on same pce* **11/4**[1]
-620 **4** *2 1/4* **Sands Crooner (IRE)**[8] 1915 7-9-4 69 (v) PaulMulrennan 4 65
(J G Given) *hld up in tch: hdwy and edgd rt over 1f out: kpt on fnl f: no imp* **15/2**[3]
400- **5** *nk* **Piste**[227] 6413 4-8-9 60 FrederikTylicki 10 55
(Miss T Jackson) *dwlt: bhd on outside: hdwy over 1f out: kpt on same pce ins fnl f* **33/1**
46/0 **6** *1 3/4* **Cutting Comments**[30] 1364 4-9-0 65 PhillipMakin 6 54+
(M Dods) *hld up: nt clr run fr 2f out to 1f out: sn shkn up: nvr nr to chal* **10/1**
00-0 **7** *3/4* **Ryedane (IRE)**[14] 1723 8-8-4 55 (b) DuranFentiman 8 41
(T D Easterby) *midfield on outside: drvn and outpcd 1/2-way: no imp over 1f out* **22/1**
-460 **8** *1 3/4* **Spirit Of Coniston**[12] 1805 7-8-8 59 PJMcDonald 1 39
(P T Midgley) *bhd and sn pushed along: nvr able to chal* **33/1**
0-00 **9** *1 1/4* **Nomoreblondes**[22] 1524 6-9-0 65 (p) TonyCulhane 9 41
(P T Midgley) *cl up tl rdn and wknd fr 2f out* **16/1**
5-25 **10** *nk* **Kyzer Chief**[22] 1524 5-8-7 61 KellyHarrison(3) 7 35
(R E Barr) *cl up: drvn over 2f out: sn lost pl* **4/1**[2]

59.83 secs (-0.87) **Going Correction** -0.075s/f (Good) **10** Ran SP% **115.1**
Speed ratings (Par 103): **103,102,100,96,96 93,92,89,87,86**
toteswingers: 1&2 £20.30, 1&3 £11.90, 2&3 £2.40 CSF £71.29 CT £203.40 TOTE £25.80: £4.10, £1.70, £1.40; EX 91.20 TRIFECTA Not won. Place 6: £20.88, Place 5: £11.79..
Owner John Conway **Bred** John Starbuck **Trained** Saighton, Cheshire

FOCUS
A modest handicap run at a strong pace.
Cutting Comments ◆ Official explanation: jockey said gelding was denied a clear run
Kyzer Chief Official explanation: jockey said gelding lost its action
T/Plt: £16.50. Pool of £93,877.94 - 4,129.11 winning tickets T/Qpdt: 8.90 Pool of £4,651.97 - 386.10 winning tickets RY

2145 - 2151a (Foreign Racing) - See Raceform Interactive

[1943]CAPANNELLE (R-H)
Sunday, May 16

OFFICIAL GOING: Heavy

2152a PREMIO PRESIDENTE REPUBBLICA GBI RACING (GROUP 1) (4YO+) (TURF) 1m 2f
4:40 (12:00) 4-Y-O+ **£119,469** (£52,566; £28,672; £14,336)

RPR

1 **Querari (GER)**[35] 1251 4-9-2 0 EPedroza 4 121
(A Wohler, Germany) *settled midfield: asked for effrt 3f out: hdwy on inner 2f out: swtchd lft and hrd rdn fnl f: tk ld fnl 110yds* **178/10**

2 ¾ **Voila Ici (IRE)**[189] 7313 5-9-2 0 MircoDemuro 6 119
(Vittorio Caruso, Italy) *rdn to share ld after 1f: then settled 3rd for 6f: sent to ld ent fnl 3f and comf holding chal on his inner: shkn up and hrd rdn whn chal on outer ent fnl f: hdd fnl 110yds: styd on for 2nd* **9/10**[1]

3 1 ½ **Pressing (IRE)**[22] 1531 7-9-2 0 NeilCallan 3 116
(M A Jarvis) *hld up in midfield on inner: effrt 3f out: hdwy on rail to chal and ld 2f out: hrd rdn ent fnl f: no ex clsng stages* **67/20**[2]

4 3 **Campanologist (USA)**[50] 1026 5-9-2 0 TedDurcan 9 110
(Saeed Bin Suroor) *settled midfield on outer: rdn to go 3rd ent fnl 3f: hrd rdn and no imp fnl 2f: styd on one pce* **5/1**

5 ½ **Johannes Mozart (IRE)**[22] 1540 4-9-2 0 SBasile 2 109
(F & L Camici, Italy) *broke wl on inner: disp ld 1f: sole ldr after 1f tl 3f out whn rdn and outpcd: styd on fnl 2f* **34/1**

6 12 **Jakkalberry (IRE)**[22] 1540 4-9-2 0 FabioBranca 7 85
(E Botti, Italy) *slowly away and settled nr rr: outpcd ent fnl 4f: sme hdwy 3f out: wandered lft and rt under hrd ride: styd on* **4/1**[3]

7 7 **Night Magic (GER)**[203] 7046 4-8-13 0 KKerekes 5 68
(W Figge, Germany) *broke wl and trckd ldr for 6f: asked for effrt 3f out: sn wknd and eased fnl 2f* **96/10**

8 7 **Silver Arrow (ITY)**[189] 7312 5-9-2 0 LManiezzi 8 57
(R Menichetti, Italy) *broke wl: stdd to r in rr: prog on outer ent st: hrd rdn and no ex fnl 2f: wknd* **25/1**

2m 6.00s (2.70) **8** Ran SP% **133.7**
WIN (incl. 1 euro stake): 18.83. PLACES: 2.83, 1.29, 1.47. DF: 56.52.
Owner Stiftung Gestut Fahrhof **Bred** Stiftung Gestut Fahrhof **Trained** Germany

NOTEBOOK
Querari(GER), having his first try at this level, picked up really well once switched out to challenge and wore down the favourite in the final half furlong. He is clearly improving.
Voila Ici(IRE), who is ideally suited by 1m4f, had the ground in his favour and he held evry chance having gone on, but was just done for a chance of pace late on. This was a very encouraging reappearance and he looks likely to win another good prize or two this season.
Pressing(IRE), run down late on in the race two years ago, may well have won had the ground not turned soft, as his stamina was stretched over this distance. His reappearance run at Sandown suggested he was as good, if not better, as ever (gave 4lb to Paco Boy), and he looks sure to add to his tally at some stage his year.
Campanologist(USA), another ideally suited by better ground, had won a Group 2 in Dubai earlier this year, but he couldn't quicken out of testing surface.
Jakkalberry(IRE) has been progressing well and he looked a big player, but never recovered from a slow start.

KRANJI (L-H)
Sunday, May 16

OFFICIAL GOING: Turf: yielding

2154a SINGAPORE AIRLINES INTERNATIONAL CUP (GROUP 1) (3YO+) (TURF) 1m 2f
1:40 (12:00) 3-Y-O+
£753,303 (£267,621; £135,462; £66,079; £26,431; £13,215)

RPR

1 **Lizard's Desire (SAF)**[21] 1568 5-9-0 0 KShea 9 123+
(M F De Kock, South Africa) *hld up: 7th st (2f out): styd on strly on outside to ld ins fnl 50yds* **3/1**[2]

2 ½ **Gloria De Campeao (BRZ)**[50] 1027 7-9-0 0 BReis 6 122
(P Bary, France) *chsd clr ldr: moved clsr 1/2-way: chal u.p 2f out: led 1 1/2f out: hdd ins fnl 50yds* **17/5**[3]

3 1 ¾ **Al Shemali**[50] 1025 6-9-0 0 (t) RoystonFfrench 7 119
(A Al Raihe, UAE) *racd in midfield: 6th and rdn st: r.o fnl 1 1/2f: n.m.r fnl 50yds* **7/1**

4 2 ½ **Waikato (NZ)**[14] 7-9-0 0 (b) JMoreira 8 114
(L Laxon, Singapore) *a.p: 3rd st: kpt on wout qckning* **30/1**

5 1 ¼ **Presvis**[21] 1568 6-9-0 0 RyanMoore 10 111
(L M Cumani) *hld up: 8th st: sme late hdwy but no real imp* **12/5**[1]

6 nk **Jolie's Shinju (JPN)**[49] 5-8-10 0 RonnieStewart 2 106
(H Takaoka, Singapore) *broke wl and set clr ld tl hdd 1 1/2f out and wknd* **122/10**

7 1 ¼ **Lahaleeb (IRE)**[50] 1025 4-8-10 0 JohnEgan 4 104
(F Nass, Bahrain) *racd in midfield: clsd 2f out: sn rdn and btn* **27/1**

8 1 **El Dorado (JPN)**[23] 6-9-0 0 JSaimee 11 106
(H Takaoka, Singapore) *a bhd* **29/1**

9 ½ **Drovetti (AUS)**[23] 6-9-0 0 (bt) JohnPowell 12 105
(S Burridge, Singapore) *nvr plcd to chal* **67/1**

10 2 **Goldschatz (NZ)**[23] 7-9-0 0 (b) VladDuric 3 101
(S Gray, Singapore) *racd in 4th tl rdn and wknd ins fnl 2f* **106/10**

11 11 ¾ **Yamanin Kingly (JPN)**[42] 5-9-0 0 YuichiShibayama 5 77
(Hiroshi Kawachi, Japan) *nvr a factor* **108/10**

2m 2.12s (122.12) **11** Ran SP% **125.9**
PARI-MUTUEL (all including 5 sgd stakes): WIN 20.00; PLACE 6.00, 11.00, 13.00; DF 25.00.
Owner Sheikh Mohammed Bin Khalifa Al Maktoum **Bred** A J Boshoff **Trained** South Africa

NOTEBOOK
Lizard's Desire(SAF), so narrowly beaten by Gloria De Campeao in the Dubai World Cup, gained his revenge in a race where the strong pace was very much in his favour. His rider described him as a real stayer and he could even become a Melbourne Cup horse.
Presvis lost a near-fore shoe on the first bend and although he met trouble in running on occasions, his finishing effort was tame. His rider was inclined to blame the loose ground.

[1564]KREFELD (R-H)
Sunday, May 16

OFFICIAL GOING: Turf: good

2155a PREIS DER SWK - KREFELDER STUTENPREIS (LISTED RACE) (4YO+ FILLIES & MARES) (TURF) 1m 3f
3:35 (12:00) 4-Y-O+ **£10,619** (£3,893; £2,123; £1,061)

RPR

1 **Miss Europa (IRE)**[317] 3604 4-9-4 0 AStarke 7 95
(P Schiergen, Germany) **2/5**[1]

2 nk **Doggerbank (IRE)**[276] 4948 4-9-2 0 EFrank 3 93
(T Mundry, Germany) **99/10**

3 1 ¼ **Terre Neuve (IRE)**[181] 4-9-4 0 StefanieHofer 1 93
(A Wohler, Germany) **206/10**

4 ½ **Lunduv (IRE)**[41] 5-9-4 0 AHelfenbein 2 92
(C Von Der Recke, Germany) **25/1**

5 nk **Night Of Magic (IRE)**[22] 1540 4-9-4 0 HenkGrewe 4 91
(H Steinmetz, Germany) **54/10**[3]

6 2 ½ **Near Galante (GER)**[217] 6715 4-9-4 0 THellier 8 87
(A Wohler, Germany) **13/2**

7 6 **Deportment**[39] 1176 4-9-0 0 WilliamCarson 6 73
(S C Williams) *broke wl: sent to the ld on outer: set gd pce: began to tire at end of bkstretch: fdd to rr in st* **22/5**[2]

2m 15.93s (135.93) **7** Ran SP% **136.6**
WIN (incl. 10 euro stake): 14. PLACES: 11, 15, 19. SF: 78.
Owner Gestut Hony-Hof **Bred** Gestut Hony-Hof **Trained** Germany

[1855]LONGCHAMP (R-H)
Sunday, May 16

OFFICIAL GOING: Turf: good

2157a PRIX DE SAINT-GEORGES (GROUP 3) (3YO+) (TURF) 5f (S)
1:05 (12:00) 3-Y-O+ **£35,398** (£14,159; £10,619; £7,079; £3,539)

RPR

1 **Marchand D'Or (FR)**[350] 2523 7-9-0 0 DavyBonilla 1 110
(M Delzangles, France) *w.w in rr on rail: mde gd prog 2f out: swtchd away fr rail to make move between horses: qcknd brilliantly to snatch victory on line* **7/1**

2 hd **Benbaun (IRE)**[50] 1024 9-9-6 0 (b) JamieSpencer 9 115
(K A Ryan) *led fr s: clr ent fnl f: ct on line* **15/2**

3 1 **Kolokol (IRE)**[19] 1610 3-8-6 0 Christophe-PatriceLemaire 4 102
(D Prod'Homme, France) *broke wl along rail: qcknd 1 1/2f out: r.o wl but no answer to first two* **25/1**

4 nse **Black Mambazo (IRE)**[37] 5-9-0 0 FrankieDettori 2 106
(L Riccardi, Italy) *settled in gd position travelling wl: rdn 1 1/2f out: no ex in clsng stages* **4/1**[2]

5 ½ **Bluster (FR)**[19] 1611 4-9-2 0 ChristopheSoumillon 6 106
(Robert Collet, France) *bhd ldrs fr s: rdn 1 1/2f out: no ex clsng stages* **8/1**

6 1 ½ **Mood Music**[308] 3908 6-9-0 0 (b) MaximeGuyon 7 98
(Mario Hofer, Germany) *broke wl: racd bhd ldrs: qcknd wl 1 1/2f out but no ex in clsng stages* **16/1**

7 2 ½ **Mister Manannan (IRE)**[19] 1610 3-8-8 0 AdrianNicholls 8 87
(D Nicholls) *broke wl and racd alongside ldr: fnd no ex fr dist and fdd* **11/4**[1]

8 nk **Sorciere (IRE)**[241] 6044 3-8-9 0 GeraldMosse 10 87
(C Lerner, France) *racd promly tl 1/2-way: fdd* **13/2**[3]

9 ¾ **Manzila (FR)**[19] 1611 7-8-10 0 (b) RonanThomas 11 82
(Mme C Barande-Barbe, France) *smartly away on outside: dropped away 2f out* **25/1**

10 2 **Best Joking (GER)**[44] 1081 5-8-10 0 IoritzMendizabal 5 74
(W Hefter, Germany) *nvr figured* **20/1**

55.90 secs (-0.40) **Going Correction** +0.25s/f (Good)
WFA 3 from 4yo+ 8lb **10** Ran SP% **113.7**
Speed ratings: 113,112,111,111,110 107,103,103,102,98
PARI-MUTUEL (all including 1 euro stakes): WIN: 11.00. PLACES: 3.80, 3.80, 9.00. DF: 42.10. SF: 78.50.
Owner Mme Jean-Louis Giral **Bred** Mme C Giral **Trained** France

NOTEBOOK
Marchand D'Or(FR), having his first start for his new yard, returned to something like the from that saw him so dominant in the sprinting division a couple of years ago. Potential targets are the Prix du Gros-Chene, King's Stand and Golden Jubilee, before attempting to win the Prix Maurice de Gheest for a fourth time.
Benbaun(IRE) did his best to make all and was only mugged on the line. This was another cracking effort from him.
Mister Manannan(IRE) paid for trying to match strides with Benbaun early.

2158a POULE D'ESSAI DES POULICHES (GROUP 1) (3YO FILLIES) (TURF) 1m
1:35 (12:00) 3-Y-O **£227,548** (£91,035; £45,517; £22,738; £11,389)

RPR

1 **Special Duty**[14] 1726 3-9-0 0 StephanePasquier 10 115+
(Mme C Head-Maarek, France) *settled in rr: short of room 2f out: in clr 1f out: r.o wl: jst failed: fin in 2nd, hd: awrdd r* **6/4**[1]

2 ½ **Baine (FR)**[35] 1253 3-9-0 0 (p) Francois-XavierBertras 5 114
(F Rohaut, France) *broke wl and led: sn settled in 2nd: short of room on rail 2f out: kpt on wl ins fnl f: fin 3rd: hd & nk: plcd 2nd* **20/1**

3 hd **Joanna (IRE)**[38] 1196 3-9-0 0 ChristopheSoumillon 4 113
(J-C Rouget, France) *disp 2nd: led over 2f out: hdd and nt qckn fnl 50yds: fin 4th: plcd 3rd* **7/2**[2]

4 hd **Rosanara (FR)**[21] 1566 3-9-0 0 Christophe-PatriceLemaire 8 113+
(A De Royer-Dupre, France) *hld up: bmpd and faltered 2f out: r.o wl fnl f: nvr nrr: fin 5th: plcd 4th* **9/2**[3]

5 nk **Lady Of The Desert (USA)**[29] 1384 3-9-0 0 KierenFallon 1 112
(B J Meehan) *racd in midfield: 5th on rail 2 1/2f out: plld out but gap clsd: fnd room to run on 1f out tl no room and snatched up fnl 50yds: fin 6th: plcd 5th* **10/1**

6 Liliside (FR)[45] 1080 3-9-0 0................................ Jean-BernardEyquem 3 115
(F Rohaut, France) *7th on rail: plld wd for non-existent gap 2f out: r.o u.p fnl f to ld fnl 50yds: fin 1st: disqualified and plcd 6th* **16/1**

7 ¾ Barouda (FR)[21] 1566 3-9-0 0.. OlivierPeslier 9 111
(J-M Beguigne, France) *bhd: sme hdwy fnl 300yds: nvr threatened* **16/1**

8 2½ Ayun Tara (FR)[94] 514 3-9-0 0................................(p) GregoryBenoist 7 105
(X Nakkachdji, France) *sn led: hdd over 2f out: rdn and fdd* **33/1**

9 ½ Dolled Up (IRE)[21] 1566 3-9-0 0................................ IoritzMendizabal 2 106+
(Robert Collet, France) *chsd ldrs: 4th and ev ch 2f out: sn rdn: squeezed for room and nt rcvr fnl f* **33/1**

10 4 Full Steam[19] 3-9-0 0.. MaximeGuyon 6 94
(A Fabre, France) *racd in midfield: hmpd 2 1/2f out: sn rdn and btn* **11/1**

1m 37.4s (-1.00) **Going Correction** +0.05s/f (Good) **10** Ran SP% **120.2**
Speed ratings: **106,106,106,106,105 107,105,102,102,98**
PARI-MUTUEL (all including 1 euro stakes): WIN 2.80 (coupled with Full Steam); PLACE 1.70, 4.80, 1.70; DF 39.20; SF 47.40.
Owner K Abdulla **Bred** Juddmonte Farms Ltd **Trained** Chantilly, France
■ The last filly to land the English/French 1000 Guineas double was Ravinella, also trained by Criquette Head, in 1988.

NOTEBOOK
Special Duty gained a second Classic in the stewards' room, having been awarded the 1,000 Guineas at Newmarket a fortnight earlier. She was only the second filly to run from the Newmarket Classic, before which some had questioned whether she would stay a truly run mile given her defeat over 61/2f on her reappearance. She silenced the doubters at Newmarket, where she was slightly fortunate perhaps to be awarded the race on the disqualification of Jacqueline Quest, who carried her right in the final furlong, though her jockey never had to stop riding. She was also the lucky recipient here, running on well to finish runner-up to first-past-the-post Liliside. She is no Zarkava, but the fact that she was able to 'win' just a fortnight after her exertions at Newmarket is commendable, and after a promised summer break she should take a lot of beating at Deauville on August 1, when the target is the Prix Rothschild.
Baine(FR) was also a Listed-race winner producing her best effort yet and kept on well to edge out Joanna for what turned out to be third place.
Joanna(IRE) had every chance, but again didn't quite get home and she may need to be ridden with a bit more patience in order to help her see out the 1m trip.
Rosanara(FR), like Special Duty, came from the rear off the back of the slow pace, and she would have finished even closer but for being knocked about as Liliside edged left. She has perhaps been a trifle disappointing in the wake of her impressive triumph in the Prix Marcel Boussac last October, since when she has finished third twice, in the Criterium International and Prix de la Grotte, and now technically fourth here. She is in the Coronation Stakes, and, perhaps more significantly also the Irish Oaks, for she ran here as though she can stay further than 1m.
Lady Of The Desert(USA) was the sole British challenger, and running over 1m for the first time. She was quite free early on, so it was encouraging that she finished her race well and her connections reckoned she might even have won had she not been impeded a couple of times. The worst bit of interference happened too late in the day to have made the difference between winning and losing on its own, but the cumulative effect was significant. As she clearly gets 1m, her connections can now look forward to next month's Coronation Stakes at Royal Ascot.
Liliside(FR)'s manoeuvre early in the straight knocked Full Steam - in the same ownership as Special Duty - askew, who in turn impeded Rosanara and Barouda. The decision to disqualify her and place her sixth took 75 minutes to be announced. She still produced a career-best on ground significantly quicker than she had won her two Listed races on, and apparently will also be prepared for the Rothschild. There is, of course, no reason why she would not give Special Duty and Goldikova a race there on this evidence.
Full Steam finished last of ten but, given the interference, as well as the fact this was only her third start - she was much the least experienced in the line-up - she can be given another chance.

2159a POULE D'ESSAI DES POULAINS (GROUP 1) (3YO COLTS) (TURF) 1m
2:50 (12:00) 3-Y-O **£227,548** (£91,035; £45,517; £22,738; £11,389)

RPR

1 Lope De Vega (IRE)[21] 1565 3-9-2 0.......................... MaximeGuyon 15 121
(A Fabre, France) *hld up: plld wd st: hdwy on outside 2f out to ld fnl f: r.o wl* **10/1**[3]

2 ½ Dick Turpin (IRE)[15] 1699 3-9-2 0................................ RichardHughes 1 120
(R Hannon) *chsd ldrs: 4th 2f out: 2nd and ev ch fnl f: r.o* **3/1**[2]

3 1½ Shamalgan (FR)[21] 1565 3-9-2 0................................ ThierryJarnet 12 116
(A Savujev, Czech Republic) *in rr: hdwy over 2f out: swtchd and r.o fr 1 1/2f out: no ex fnl 100yds* **100/1**

4 2½ Buzzword[15] 1699 3-9-2 0.. AhmedAjtebi 7 111
(Mahmood Al Zarooni) *racd in midfield: rdn 2 1/2f out: styd on u.p fnl f: n.d* **33/1**

5 hd Meezaan (IRE)[15] 1687 3-9-2 0.. RichardHills 3 110
(J H M Gosden) *racd in midfield: hdwy on rail st: rdn and ev ch 1f out: sn wknd* **20/1**

6 nse Zazou (GER)[21] 1564 3-9-2 0.. OlivierPeslier 14 110
(Mario Hofer, Germany) *hld up: last tl r.o ins fnl 2f: nvr nrr* **11/1**

7 3 Boltcity (FR)[38] 1195 3-9-2 0............................ ChristopheSoumillon 9 103
(J-C Rouget, France) *hld up: n.m.r and swtchd 1 1/2f out: kpt on same pce* **16/1**

8 2 Poet's Voice[226] 6450 3-9-2 0.. FrankieDettori 11 99
(Saeed Bin Suroor) *chsd ldrs: rdn and btn fnl 2f* **10/1**[3]

9 snk Siyouni (FR)[21] 1565 3-9-2 0.................... Christophe-PatriceLemaire 6 98
(A De Royer-Dupre, France) *hld up: n.m.r 2f out: swtchd and sme late hdwy: n.d* **2/1**[1]

10 hd Rajsaman (FR)[21] 1565 3-9-2 0.. GeraldMosse 2 98
(A De Royer-Dupre, France) *disp ld: grad wknd ins fnl 1 1/2f* **14/1**

11 1½ Mon Cadeaux[18] 1616 3-9-2 0.. JimmyFortune 4 94
(A M Balding) *chsd ldng trio: rdn and fdd fnl 1 1/2f* **33/1**

12 snk Forum Magnum (USA)[19] 1610 3-9-2 0.................... MickaelBarzalona 5 94
(A Fabre, France) *disp ld: rdn and hdd fnl 300yds* **50/1**

13 ¾ Mata Keranjang (USA)[32] 1311 3-9-2 0.......................... JamieSpencer 16 92
(P F I Cole) *a bhd* **25/1**

14 2 Aldovrandi (IRE)[43] 1083 3-9-2 0.............................. StephanePasquier 10 88
(M Botti) *n.d* **16/1**

15 1½ Classic Colori (IRE)[43] 1083 3-9-2 0.......................... RichardKingscote 13 84
(Tom Dascombe) *prom: 3rd st: rdn and dropped out ins fnl 2f* **50/1**

1m 36.1s (-2.30) **Going Correction** +0.05s/f (Good) **15** Ran SP% **122.7**
Speed ratings: **113,112,111,108,108 108,105,103,103,102 101,101,100,98,97**
PARI-MUTUEL (all including 1 euro stakes): WIN 9.70; PLACE 3.60, 2.80, 20.30; DF 21.80; SF 69.60.
Owner Gestut Ammerland **Bred** Gestut Ammerland **Trained** Chantilly, France

NOTEBOOK
Lope De Vega(IRE) was settled in rear early, his draw in 15 being far from favourable, and was still second last entering the straight. Lope De Vega made relentless progress down the outside from then on. Grabbing the lead at the furlong pole, he kept on well to fend off Dick Turpin. The Prix du Jockey-Club could be next and although his jockey voiced some concern over whether an extra two and a half furlongs would be within his range, it is the most obvious next step for him.
Dick Turpin(IRE) gave the form of the English 2000 Guineas a boost. He did not buckle when Lope De Vega grabbed the lead at the furlong pole, and his consistency is commendable. He may go for the St James's Palace Stakes, but the impression is that even though he has beaten stablemate Canford Cliffs twice this season, the yard still reckons Canford Cliffs to be the better horse.
Shamalgan(FR) ran his best race to date to defy his huge odds and, like the winner, could now be aimed at the French Derby, where he would be tackling 1m21/2f for the first time.
Buzzword, like Dick Turpin, gave the form of the 2,000 Guineas a frank with a good effort to be fourth - he had finished 14th at Newmarket - but whether the St James's Palace is the right next race for him remains to be seen; perhaps the King Edward VII might be a better bet, although he is unproven beyond 1m and connections may view such a leap in distance as too risky.
Meezaan(IRE), having just his fifth start and also his first over this distance, travelled well and, though he is in the July Cup, his connections can surely hope he can win over this trip, or perhaps over 7f so the Jersey might be the race for him.
Zazou(GER) had already won over 1m1f but may struggle to win at the top level, certainly in as strong a race as this.
Boltcity(FR) ran quite well on his first try at Group 1 level, but may also struggle to win a race at this class.
Poet's Voice was eighth, but as the only runner having his first start of the season, and his first run over this trip, that was not a bad outcome.
Siyouni(FR) was not given a hard time at all once his chance had gone after he was interfered with early on in the straight. It was the first time he had finished worse than second and he should improve dramatically on this bare finishing position next time, even if that next time comes in the St James's Palace Stakes.
Mon Cadeaux found this level beyond him.
Mata Keranjang(USA) never got into it and remains a maiden.
Aldovrandi(IRE) never figured but remains capable of better.
Classic Colori(IRE) was completely outclassed.

2160a PRIX HOCQUART (GROUP 2) (3YO COLTS & FILLIES) (TURF) 1m 3f
3:25 (12:00) 3-Y-O **£65,575** (£25,309; £12,079; £8,053; £4,026)

RPR

1 Silver Pond (FR)[18] 3-9-2 0.. OlivierPeslier 5 114+
(C Laffon-Parias, France) *settled in 6th fr s: qcknd wl early in st: briefly hmpd but c again to chal for ld 1f out: qcknd wl to win comf* **7/2**[1]

2 1 Celtic Celeb (IRE)[21] 1567 3-9-2 0.............................. ThierryThulliez 3 112
(F Doumen, France) *racd in 2nd fr s: rdn early in st: grabbed ld 1 1/2f out but sn chal and passed by wnr: r.o wl* **9/2**[3]

3 2 Ivory Land (FR)[35] 1254 3-9-2 0...................................... GeraldMosse 4 109+
(A De Royer-Dupre, France) *racd in 5th: dropped in rr of field bef st: swtchd to outer and r.o wl to go 3rd ins fnl half-f* **5/1**

4 1 Dansico[14] 3-9-2 0.. Jean-BernardEyquem 2 107
(Y Durepaire, Spain) *racd in 3rd: rdn early in st: styd on wl: losing 3rd in clsng stages* **20/1**

5 4 Tenacious Spring (FR)[8] 1947 3-9-2 0...................... IoritzMendizabal 1 100
(C Boutin, France) *led fr s: failed to qckn in st and sn passed: no imp fnl f* **18/1**

6 2 Makani (GER)[21] 1565 3-9-2 0................(p) Christophe-PatriceLemaire 8 97
(J E Pease, France) *towards rr fr s: forced wd in st and mde no imp* **4/1**[2]

7 ¾ Emirates Dream (USA)[212] 6811 3-9-2 0...................... FrankieDettori 7 95
(Saeed Bin Suroor) *racd in 4th: rdn early in st: failed to qckn and fdd* **5/1**

8 4 Lion Mountain[18] 1627 3-9-2 0.. AhmedAjtebi 6 89
(Mahmood Al Zarooni) *a towards rr: fnd nthing in st* **11/2**

2m 17.0s (-2.90) **Going Correction** +0.05s/f (Good) **8** Ran SP% **119.1**
Speed ratings: **112,111,109,109,106 104,104,101**
PARI-MUTUEL (all including 1 euro stakes): WIN: 2.90. PLACES: 1.30, 1.60, 1.40. DF: 7.90. SF:13.40.
Owner Haras Du Quesnay **Bred** Haras Du Quesnay **Trained** Chantilly, France

NOTEBOOK
Silver Pond(FR) has looked good in a couple of lesser races this spring and he took the step up to Group 2 company in his stride, quickening well to score despite having been a bit interfered with. It will be the Jockey Club next and he shouldn't be underestimated.
Celtic Celeb(IRE) ran another fine race, but was put in his place by the winner close home.
Emirates Dream(USA) had stamina doubts on this rise in trip and failed to get home. He isn't up to this level.
Lion Mountain, impressive winner of a Pontefract maiden, didn't pick up at all when asked for his effort and was disappointing.

LES LANDES
Sunday, May 16
OFFICIAL GOING: Firm (good to firm in places)

2161a HEMMINGS FAMILY H'CAP SPRINT 5f 100y
3:05 (3:12) (0-60,) 3-Y-O+ **£1,460** (£525; £315)

RPR

1 Fast Freddie[13] 1814 6-10-11 .... VinceSlattery 4 —
(Mrs A Malzard, Jersey) **13/8**[1]

2 shd Nordic Light (USA)[158] 7689 6-10-5 .... MattieBatchelor 1 —
(Mrs A Malzard, Jersey) **9/1**

3 shd Top Level (IRE)[13] 7-10-2 .... MarkLawson 5 —
(Mrs A Corson, Jersey) **7/2**

4 ½ Majestical (IRE)[258] 5541 8-10-11 ....(p) AntonyProcter 8 —
(J S O Arthur, Jersey) **2/1**[2]

5 ½ Top Pursuit[41] 8-10-3 .... MrPCollington 6 —
(Ms V S Lucas, Jersey) **5/1**

6 5 Sandy Toes[13] 1774 3-10-3 .... J-PGuillambert 7 —
(J A Glover) **9/4**[3]

7 4 Joli Haven (IRE)[356] 4-10-9 .... DCuthbert 2 —
(Ms H McVittie, Jersey) **20/1**

69.00 secs
WFA 3 from 4yo+ 8lb **7** Ran SP% **155.8**
Owner Gordon Crawford **Bred** New Hall Stud **Trained** St Ouen, Jersey

2162a ANIMAL HEALTH TRUST 2010 JERSEY GUINEAS 1m 100y
3:40 (3:43) 3-Y-O+ **£1,790** (£662; £398)

RPR

1 Danehill Dazzler (IRE)[41] 8-10-2 ....(p) MrPCollington 5 —
(J S O Arthur, Jersey) **7/4**[2]

2 1 King Kenny[41] 5-10-5 .... KylieManser 4 —
(Mrs A Malzard, Jersey) **5/1**

3 2 1/2 **Buckie Massa**[41] 6-10-5 .... AntonyProcter 7 —
(J S O Arthur, Jersey) **6/4**[1]
4 1/2 **Hold The Bucks (USA)**[13] 1815 4-10-5 ....(p) MattieBatchelor 3 —
(Mrs A Malzard, Jersey) **7/2**[3]
5 2 **Deely Plaza**[13] 1776 3-8-11 .... J-PGuillambert 2 —
(J A Glover) **7/2**[3]
6 3 1/2 **Superduper**[13] 1814 5-10-2 .... VinceSlattery 6 —
(Mrs A Malzard, Jersey) **13/2**
7 10 **River Du Nord (FR)** 3-8-8 .... PFleming 7 —
(Mrs A Malzard, Jersey) **20/1**

1m 53.0s (113.00)
WFA 3 from 4yo+ 12lb **7 Ran SP% 155.6**

Owner John Poynton & B Morton **Bred** Sean Finnegan **Trained** Jersey

2021 BATH (L-H)

Monday, May 17

OFFICIAL GOING: Firm (good to firm in places; 9.5)
Wind: Virtually nil Weather: Bright

2163 E.B.F./SPONSORSHIP OPPORTUNITY WITH HIGH FIVE RACING MAIDEN STKS 5f 161y
2:00 (2:01) (Class 5) 2-Y-O **£3,238** (£963; £481; £240) **Stalls** Centre

Form RPR
1 **Jollywood (IRE)** 2-8-12 0 .... PatDobbs 5 73+
(R Hannon) *hld up in tch: swtchd rt and qcknd between horses ins fnl 2f: rdn fnl f and styd on to ld cl home* **8/1**
44 2 nk **Silca Conegliano (IRE)**[15] 1733 2-8-12 0 .... KierenFallon 4 72+
(M R Channon) *w ldr: led and edgd rt 2f out: shkn up and rdr lost whip 1f out: stl hld narrow ld tl hdd cl home* **9/2**[3]
3 3/4 **With Hindsight (IRE)** 2-9-3 0 .... LukeMorris 1 75+
(C G Cox) *sn chsng ldrs: rdn 2f out: styd on to chal ins fnl f: outpcd fnl 50yds* **15/2**
4 3 1/4 **Diamond Vine (IRE)** 2-9-3 0 .... LiamJones 10 64
(R A Harris) *sn pushed along in rr: sme hdwy whn pushed rt ins fnl 2f: styd on fnl f but nvr a threat* **50/1**
5 hd **Mullins Way (USA)** 2-9-3 0 .... TonyCulhane 7 63
(R Curtis) *s.i.s: sn rcvrd: hdwy to press ldrs whn pushed rt 2f out: sn drvn and lost position: rallied 1f out: wknd fnl 120yds* **3/1**[2]
6 6 2 1/4 **Byrony (IRE)**[7] 1972 2-8-12 0 .... RichardHughes 8 51
(R Hannon) *in tch: hdwy 2f out: sn chsng ldrs: wknd fnl f* **9/4**[1]
543 7 1/2 **Lady Excellentia (IRE)**[11] 1838 2-8-7 0 .... AmyBaker(5) 9 49
(A B Haynes) *slt ld tl hdd 2f out: wknd over 1f out* **18/1**
8 shd **Captain Dimitrios** 2-9-3 0 .... CathyGannon 11 54
(P D Evans) *in tch: styng on whn pushed rt ins fnl 2f: sn one pce* **16/1**
9 11 **Gower Rules (IRE)** 2-9-3 0 .... RobertHavlin 2 17
(M D I Usher) *slowly away: a in rr* **66/1**
10 22 **Titian Queen** 2-8-12 0 .... AmirQuinn 6 —
(Mrs P N Dutfield) *v.s.a and a wl bhd* **100/1**

1m 12.16s (0.96) **Going Correction** -0.05s/f (Good) **10 Ran SP% 112.4**
Speed ratings (Par 93): **91,90,89,85,85 82,81,81,66,37**
toteswingers: 1&2 £5.90, 1&3 £9.30, 2&3 £8.30 CSF £42.16 TOTE £10.90: £3.30, £2.20, £3.70; EX 47.80 Trifecta £236.70 Pool: £409.45 - 1.28 winning units..
Owner Mrs J Wood **Bred** Tony O'Dwyer **Trained** East Everleigh, Wilts
■ Stewards' Enquiry : Pat Dobbs two-day ban: careless riding (May 31-Jun 1)

FOCUS
This was probably a fair maiden, and it should produce winners. The time and averages set the level.

NOTEBOOK
Jollywood(IRE), the supposed Hannon second-string, comes from a powerful 2-y-o yard and she stayed on well to edge ahead close home. Having initially picked up well when switched right to challenge, she took a while to get on top, her lack of experience possibly telling, but she's bred to appreciate a bit further than this and definitely appeals as the type to improve. She had reportedly been going well at home, and it would come as no surprise to see her end up in the Super Sprint. (op 12-1)
Silca Conegliano(IRE) had shown enough to win an ordinary maiden in two previous starts, and she battled on well when challenged, but just got beaten by a better filly. She should be helped by a stiffer test. (op 7-2)
With Hindsight(IRE), related to several winners, settled nicely just in behind the speed and briefly looked the winner when coming to challenge, but couldn't quicken late on. This was a very promising start and he should win a maiden with this experience under his belt. (op 8-1)
Diamond Vine(IRE), whose dam was placed over 5f as a juvenile, found himself outpaced early on, but did make headway over 2f out and he too should learn a great deal.
Mullins Way(USA), a half-brother to Al Jadeed, raced a bit freely in behind the pace and could quicken under pressure inside the final furlong. Better was clearly expected, so don't be surprised if he improves next time. (op 5-2 tchd 9-4)
Byrony(IRE), a promising sixth from a bad draw at Windsor a week earlier, was strong in the market, but lacked the pace to challenge and faded disappointingly late on. She is clearly more of a nursery type. Official explanation: jockey said filly jumped left leaving stalls (op 11-4)
Lady Excellentia(IRE) is another likely to fare better in handicaps. (op 16-1 tchd 20-1)
Captain Dimitrios, whose dam was a 5f winner, has more stamina on his sire's side and he showed enough to suggest he has a future over a bit further. (op 18-1)

2164 LINDLEY CATERING MEDIAN AUCTION MAIDEN STKS 5f 11y
2:30 (2:30) (Class 6) 3-4-Y-O **£1,942** (£578; £288; £144) **Stalls** Centre

Form RPR
5-5 1 **Dungannon**[15] 1731 3-9-0 0 .... LiamKeniry 3 72
(A M Balding) *trckd ldrs: rdn to ld 1f out: styd on strly* **11/4**[2]
- 2 2 **Nollaig Shona (IRE)**[218] 6706 3-8-9 0 .... JimmyQuinn 6 60
(J W Mullins) *disp ld tl slt advantage ins fnl 2f: hdd 1f out: sn nt gng pce of wnr but hld on wl for 2nd* **10/1**
2 3 nk **Blackdown Boy**[15] 1731 3-8-11 0 .... JamesMillman(3) 2 64
(B R Millman) *disp ld tl ins fnl 2f: stl ev ch whn rdn 1f out: sn no ex and one pce* **10/11**[1]
40-0 4 1 **Hounds Ditch**[17] 1661 3-9-0 65 ....(b¹) ShaneKelly 1 60
(Eve Johnson Houghton) *rdn fr stalls to stay in tch: rdn again 2f out: mod prog u.p fnl 100yds* **10/1**
0 5 10 **Visual Element (USA)**[19] 1622 3-8-9 0 .... SteveDrowne 5 19
(R Charlton) *plunged s: plld hrd: chsd ldrs tl rdn and wknd qckly 2f out* **13/2**[3]

62.16 secs (-0.34) **Going Correction** -0.05s/f (Good) **5 Ran SP% 110.6**
Speed ratings (Par 101): **100,96,96,94,78**
CSF £26.31 TOTE £2.80: £1.10, £7.50; EX 44.30.
Owner I G Burbidge **Bred** J A E Hobby **Trained** Kingsclere, Hants

FOCUS
A weak sprint maiden. The winner reversed Salisbury form with the favoutite and it is not hard to have doubts over the form.
Blackdown Boy Official explanation: jockey said gelding was unsuited by the firm (good to firm places) ground

2165 LINDLEY CATERING FILLIES' H'CAP 1m 5f 22y
3:00 (3:02) (Class 5) (0-70,70) 4-Y-O+ **£2,590** (£770; £385; £192) **Stalls** High

Form RPR
10-1 1 **Lady Hestia (USA)**[16] 1689 5-9-3 69 .... MartinDwyer 6 75+
(M P Tregoning) *mde all: styd on strly under hand driving fnl f: unchal* **11/10**[1]
055- 2 1 1/4 **Ragdollianna**[197] 7201 6-9-4 70 .... LiamKeniry 4 74
(M J McGrath) *in rr but in tch: hdwy 6f out: disp 2nd 3f out tl chsd wnr over 2f out: kpt on but a comf hld* **28/1**
-030 3 4 1/2 **Party Palace**[5] 2023 6-7-11 56 oh6 .... RichardRowe(7) 5 53
(H S Howe) *chsd wnr: jnd for 2nd 3f out and rdr dropped reins sn after: outpcd into 3rd 2f out and sn no ch w ldng duo* **28/1**
4522 4 nk **Where's Susie**[20] 1591 5-8-13 65 .... RobertHavlin 2 62
(M Madgwick) *chsd ldrs: rdn to dispute 2nd over 2f out: sn outpcd but styd pressing for wl hld 3rd fnl f* **5/1**[2]
4-60 5 12 **Fleur De'Lion (IRE)**[19] 1623 4-8-8 60 .... SteveDrowne 7 39
(S Kirk) *a last: rdn over 3f out: sn lost tch* **25/1**[3]

2m 52.34s (0.34) **Going Correction** -0.05s/f (Good) **5 Ran SP% 75.0**
Speed ratings (Par 100): **96,95,92,92,84**
CSF £11.67 TOTE £1.20: £1.10, £6.50; EX 9.90.
Owner Mr And Mrs A E Pakenham **Bred** Shadwell Farm LLC **Trained** Lambourn, Berks

FOCUS
A moderate fillies' handicap. The third limits the form and the winner does not need to improve.

2166 M.J. CHURCH H'CAP 5f 161y
3:30 (3:30) (Class 5) (0-70,70) 4-Y-O+ **£2,590** (£770; £385; £192) **Stalls** Centre

Form RPR
30-0 1 **Sometsuke**[14] 1779 4-9-2 68 .... FergusSweeney 4 85+
(P J Makin) *in tch: drvn and hdwy 2f out: led wl over 1f out: rdn clr fnl f* **13/2**
1246 2 5 **Riflessione**[6] 2001 4-9-4 70 ....(b) LiamJones 9 71
(R A Harris) *w ldrs: racd wd fr 3f out: sn upsides and led wl over 2f out: sn rdn: hdd wl over 1f out: no ch w wnr fnl f but kpt on for clr 2nd* **3/1**[1]
-410 3 2 1/2 **Kyllachy Storm**[22] 1547 6-9-4 70 .... GeorgeBaker 8 62
(R J Hodges) *chsd ldrs: kpt on for wl-hld 3rd ins fnl f* **9/2**[3]
010- 4 2 1/4 **Brandywell Boy (IRE)**[147] 7832 7-8-13 65 .... RichardThomas 3 50
(D J S Ffrench Davis) *disp ldr tl wl over 2f out: sn rdn: wknd appr fnl f* **10/1**
450- 5 11 **Francis Walsingham (IRE)**[229] 6396 4-9-4 70 .... SteveDrowne 5 19
(H Morrison) *disp ld tl wl over 2f out: wknd qckly u.p wl over 1f out* **7/1**
0040 6 3/4 **Mandhooma**[5] 2026 4-8-4 56 oh6 .... HayleyTurner 7 2
(P W Hiatt) *disp ldr 3f: wknd over 2f out* **20/1**
36-2 7 1 1/4 **Caribbean Coral**[13] 1805 11-8-10 62 .... RobertHavlin 2 4
(A B Haynes) *disp ld tl wl over 2f out: sn btn* **9/1**
-040 8 3 1/4 **Mazzola**[5] 2021 4-8-9 61 .... LukeMorris 6 —
(J M Bradley) *in tch: sme hdwy whn n.m.r over 2f out: wknd qckly* **7/2**[2]

1m 10.36s (-0.84) **Going Correction** -0.05s/f (Good) **8 Ran SP% 115.1**
Speed ratings (Par 103): **103,96,93,90,75 74,72,68**
toteswingers: 1&2 £5.00, 1&3 £6.30, 2&3 £4.30 CSF £26.54 CT £98.10 TOTE £6.20: £1.80, £1.10, £2.00; EX 38.00 Trifecta £190.00 Pool: £269.64 - 1.05 winning units..
Owner M H Holland R P Marchant T W Wellard **Bred** Aston Mullins Stud **Trained** Ogbourne Maisey, Wilts

FOCUS
A modest sprint handicap. The form is rated around the second with the back with a bang after some below-par runs.

2167 FMW CONSULTANCY H'CAP 1m 5y
4:00 (4:01) (Class 5) (0-70,69) 4-Y-O+ **£2,590** (£770; £385; £192) **Stalls** Low

Form RPR
0-62 1 **Golden Rock (IRE)**[10] 1875 4-9-3 68 .... SteveDrowne 7 75
(R Charlton) *mde all: drvn and styd on fnl 2f: hld on wl cl home* **4/1**[3]
6-32 2 3/4 **Full Victory (IRE)**[5] 2024 8-8-13 64 .... LiamKeniry 6 69
(R A Farrant) *trckd ldrs: rdn to chse wnr over 1f out: styd on ins fnl f and kpt on cl home but a hld* **13/8**[1]
6536 3 1 3/4 **Perfect Class**[13] 1797 4-9-1 66 .... LukeMorris 1 67
(C G Cox) *in rr and in tch: hdwy and swtchd rt wl over 2f out: styd on u.p to dispute in 2nd wl over 1f out: styd on same pce ins fnl f* **7/2**[2]
3200 4 2 **Barodine**[7] 1980 7-8-6 57 .... JimmyQuinn 2 54
(R J Hodges) *chsd ldrs: rdn over 2f out: wknd appr fnl f* **16/1**
1-55 5 hd **Daniel Thomas (IRE)**[19] 1628 8-8-11 69 ....(v) RyanClark(7) 5 65
(Mrs A L M King) *s.i.s: in rr and pushed along 4f out: styd on towards outside u.p fr over 1f out: kpt on cl home: nvr any threat* **9/1**
5060 6 1/2 **El Libertador (USA)**[23] 1520 4-8-11 62 ....(b¹) LiamJones 8 57
(E A Wheeler) *chsd ldrs: disp 2nd u.p over 2f out: wknd over 1f out* **6/1**
550- 7 2 1/4 **Lilly Blue (IRE)**[196] 7211 4-8-4 55 ....(t) CathyGannon 3 45
(R Brotherton) *rdn 4f out: a towards rr* **40/1**
2302 8 1/2 **Dichoh**[33] 1301 7-8-12 63 ....(v) RobertHavlin 4 52
(M Madgwick) *chsd ldrs tl hmpd wl over 2f out and sn btn* **12/1**

1m 40.37s (-0.43) **Going Correction** -0.05s/f (Good) **8 Ran SP% 120.6**
Speed ratings (Par 103): **100,99,97,95,95 94,92,92**
toteswingers: 1&2 £2.90, 2&3 £3.50, 1&3 not won. CSF £11.61 CT £25.70 TOTE £5.40: £2.20, £1.10, £1.30; EX 12.60 Trifecta £28.60 £370.12 - 9.55 winning units..
Owner H R H Sultan Ahmad Shah **Bred** Dr Peter Harms **Trained** Beckhampton, Wilts
■ Stewards' Enquiry : Luke Morris two-day ban: careless riding (May 31-Jun 1)

FOCUS
Little got into this. Straightforward form with the winner back to his maiden best.

2168 IMPERIAL WINDOWS & CONSERVATORIES LTD H'CAP 1m 2f
4:30 (4:30) (Class 5) (0-75,75) 3-Y-O **£2,590** (£770; £385; £192) **Stalls** Low

Form RPR
0-66 1 **Home Advantage**[20] 1589 3-8-5 62 .... LiamJones 7 67
(R Charlton) *trckd ldrs: drvn to chal ins fnl 2f: led appr fnl f: rdn out* **15/2**
5-30 2 1 1/2 **First Fandango**[14] 1757 3-9-4 75 .... GeorgeBaker 3 77
(J W Hills) *trckd ldr: drvn to chal 2f out and stl upsides 1f out: styd on same pce* **11/2**[3]
2146 3 2 **Pastello**[16] 1696 3-8-11 68 .... PatDobbs 5 66
(R Hannon) *hld up in rr: hdwy on ins over 1f out: styd on to take 3rd ins fnl f but no imp on ldng duo* **8/1**

30-5 **4** 3½ **Catchanova (IRE)**[21] 1582 3-8-7 **64** ow1 ShaneKelly 1 55
(Eve Johnson Houghton) *led: rdn and jnd 2f out: hdd appr fnl f: hung lft and btn sn after* **4/1**[2]

33-4 **5** 1 **Whiepa Snappa (IRE)**[28] 1433 3-8-1 **65** RichardRowe(7) 6 54
(P M Phelan) *in rr: hdwy on outside 4f out to chse ldrs 3f out: sn rdn: btn 2f out* **10/3**[1]

1053 **6** 3 **Tuscan King**[11] 1839 3-8-6 **66** (b) WilliamCarson(3) 2 49
(P D Evans) *chsd ldrs tl wknd appr fnl 2f* **4/1**[2]

40-4 **7** 7 **Truly Magic**[23] 1522 3-8-4 **61** oh3 JimmyQuinn 4 30
(H J L Dunlop) *a bhd* **8/1**

2m 5.56s (-2.74) 7 Ran SP% **112.5**
toteswingers: 1&2 £8.50, 1&3 £11.30, 2&3 £5.80 CSF £45.95 TOTE £10.00: £6.70, £2.30; EX 50.70.
Owner K Abdulla **Bred** Juddmonte Farms Ltd **Trained** Beckhampton, Wilts

FOCUS
This was a modest 3-y-o handicap. The race has been rated around the second and there are one or two doubts over the form.
Home Advantage Official explanation: trainer said, regarding apparent improvement in form, that the colt was suited by the step up in trip and the firmer ground

2169 SIS LIVE H'CAP 2m 1f 34y
5:00 (5:00) (Class 6) (0-65,58) 4-Y-0+ **£1,942** (£578; £288; £144) **Stalls** Centre

Form RPR

0040 **1** **Spiritonthemount (USA)**[21] 982 5-8-11 **47** (b) WilliamCarson(3) 4 54
(P W Hiatt) *trckd ldr 10f out: rdn: one pce and c wd 3f out: rallied u.p fr over 2f out: led fnl 120yds: all out* **10/1**

54-0 **2** ½ **Brandy Butter**[11] 140 4-9-1 **50** (bt) GregFairley 7 56
(D E Pipe) *in tch: pushed along and chsd ldrs fr 3f out: led u.p appr fnl f: hdd and no ex fnl 120yds* **5/1**

2-24 **3** 2 **Wightgold**[13] 1798 4-9-9 **58** JimmyQuinn 5 62
(H J L Dunlop) *trckd ldrs: wnt 2nd 3f out: led over 2f out: sn rdn: hdd appr fnl f: wknd fnl 120yds* **7/2**[2]

2365 **4** 3¼ **Poppy Gregg**[18] 982 5-8-7 **45** (v) AmyBaker(5) 2 45
(Dr J R J Naylor) *in rr: hdwy 4f out: nvr rchd ldrs and styd on same pce fr over 2f out* **13/2**

261- **5** 2 **Brave Bugsy (IRE)**[274] 3997 7-9-8 **55** (v) LiamKeniry 1 53
(A M Balding) *led tl hdd over 2f out: btn sn after* **9/4**[1]

00/- **6** 12 **Irish Legend (IRE)**[21] 5367 10-8-13 **46** RichardThomas 6 31
(B J Llewellyn) *a towards rr: mod prog 3f out: sn dropped away* **9/2**[3]

0-04 **7** 110 **Bristol Delauriere (FR)**[39] 1183 6-8-12 **45** (p) SteveDrowne 3 —
(Miss N A Lloyd-Beavis) *chsd ldr 7f: wknd 10f out and t.o fr 1/2-way* **50/1**

3m 50.97s (-0.93) **Going Correction** -0.05s/f (Good)
WFA 4 from 5yo+ 2lb 7 Ran SP% **112.2**
Speed ratings (Par 101): **100,99,98,97,96 90,67**
toteswingers: 1&2 £9.60, 1&3 £8.90, 2&3 £4.60 CSF £56.27 TOTE £14.80: £8.40, £3.30 Place 6: £165.99 Place 5: £53.42.
Owner Bob Coles **Bred** Ivy Dell Stud, Llc **Trained** Hook Norton, Oxon

FOCUS
A weak staying handicap. Sound enough form at face value.
T/Plt: £72.90. Pool £64,309.62 - 643.87 winning tickets T/Qpdt: £15.50.Pool £5,362.52 - 255.48 winning tickets . ST

1516 LEICESTER (R-H)
Monday, May 17

OFFICIAL GOING: Good to firm (good in places)
Wind: Light behind Weather: Cloudy with sunny spells

2170 JOHN FERNELEY H'CAP 7f 9y
6:00 (6:00) (Class 4) (0-80,80) 3-Y-O **£4,209** (£1,252; £625; £312) **Stalls** Low

Form RPR

05-1 **1** **Haatheq (USA)**[23] 1522 3-9-0 **76** RichardHills 8 91+
(J L Dunlop) *chsd ldrs: led over 1f out: shkn up and r.o wl: eased nr fin* **7/4**[1]

0-41 **2** 3 **Faithful One (IRE)**[17] 1659 3-9-4 **80** TedDurcan 5 84
(D R Lanigan) *a.p: rdn over 1f out: styd on same pce fnl f: wnt 2nd nr fin* **7/1**

-115 **3** nk **Avenuesnalleyways (IRE)**[17] 1658 3-9-3 **79** JackMitchell 3 82
(R M Beckett) *trckd ldr tl led over 2f out: rdn and hdd over 1f out: no ex ins fnl f: lost 2nd nr fin* **4/1**[2]

43-6 **4** 2½ **Sir Bruno (FR)**[14] 1761 3-8-10 **72** NeilChalmers 6 68
(B Palling) *hld up: rdn over 2f out: hdwy over 1f out: nt trble ldrs* **20/1**

00-4 **5** 2¼ **State Gathering**[33] 1308 3-9-1 **77** DaneO'Neill 7 67
(H Candy) *s.i.s: hld up: hdwy u.p over 2f out: wknd ins fnl f* **9/2**[3]

0-30 **6** 4½ **Ferris Wheel (IRE)**[16] 1709 3-8-12 **74** JamieSpencer 1 52
(P F I Cole) *sn bhd: mod late prog* **20/1**

2-1P **7** 1¾ **Call To Arms (IRE)**[21] 1584 3-9-3 **79** JoeFanning 2 52
(M Johnston) *hld up in tch: plld hrd: rdn over 2f out: hung rt and wknd over 1f out* **8/1**

-130 **8** 8 **Best Trip (IRE)**[74] 783 3-9-1 **77** FrannyNorton 9 28
(R C Guest) *plld hrd: led: rdn and hdd over 2f out: wknd wl over 1f out* **33/1**

1m 23.75s (-2.45) **Going Correction** -0.325s/f (Firm) 8 Ran SP% **110.6**
Speed ratings (Par 101): **101,97,97,94,91 86,84,75**
toteswingers: 1&2 £3.00, 1&3 £2.30, 2&3 £5.70 CSF £13.39 CT £39.94 TOTE £1.70: £1.10, £1.70, £2.80; EX 14.40.
Owner Hamdan Al Maktoum **Bred** Shadwell Farm LLC **Trained** Arundel, W Sussex

FOCUS
This had an open feel to it on paper but there was an easy winner in Haatheq who looks a fair bit better than his current mark. The form looks pretty solid.

2171 E B F EMIL ADAM MAIDEN STKS 5f 2y
6:30 (6:30) (Class 4) 2-Y-O **£4,857** (£1,445; £722; £360) **Stalls** Low

Form RPR

1 **Nasharra (IRE)** 2-9-3 0 JamieSpencer 4 82+
(K A Ryan) *led: hdd over 3f out: chsd ldr: shkn up to ld and hung lft wl ins fnl f: r.o* **7/2**[2]

2 1 **Mujrayaat (IRE)** 2-9-3 0 RichardHills 3 78
(M A Jarvis) *trckd ldr: led over 3f out: rdn and hdd whn bmpd wl ins fnl f: styd on* **8/13**[1]

3 1¾ **Rossetti** 2-9-3 0 FrankieMcDonald 5 72+
(R Hannon) *s.i.s: plld hrd and sn prom: rdn over 1f out: rn green: styd on* **13/2**[3]

4 7 **Silver Shine (IRE)** 2-9-3 0 MichaelHills 1 47
(W J Haggas) *prom and sn pushed along: rdn and wknd over 1f out* **9/1**

62.56 secs (2.56) **Going Correction** -0.325s/f (Firm) 4 Ran SP% **107.5**
Speed ratings (Par 95): **66,64,61,50**
CSF £6.16 TOTE £3.00; EX 7.80.
Owner Mr & Mrs Julian And Rosie Richer **Bred** P McCutcheon **Trained** Hambleton, N Yorks

FOCUS
The race comprised of four newcomers and the ratings are very guessy, but there were some decent pedigrees on show and the winner looks a nice recruit.

NOTEBOOK
Nasharra(IRE), a half-brother to triple 5f juvenile winner Give Me The Night, broke well and was always close to the hot favourite before proving too strong in the closing stages. He edged across his rival slightly close home but the result was clear-cut in the end and he could well turn out to be above average. (op 4-1)
Mujrayaat(IRE), who was well supported, travelled well out in front but he was a bit green when coming under pressure, wandering off a straight line, and he could never shake off the attentions of the winner. This was an encouraging debut and although he didn't look very big, it'll be a surprise if he doesn't get off the mark very soon. (op 8-13 after early 4-6 and 8-11 in places)
Rossetti was far too keen through the first half of the race yet caught the eye back in third, finishing well without being knocked about and, with this under his belt, he could be capable of significant improvement next time. (op 15-2 tchd 8-1)
Silver Shine(IRE) was the first one beat, coming under pressure over 2f out before dropping away but he looked badly in need of this (unruly beforehand, got loose in parade ring) so is another who should fare better in time. (op 6-1)

2172 JAMES WARD (S) STKS 1m 60y
7:00 (7:00) (Class 6) 3-Y-O+ **£1,942** (£578; £288; £144) **Stalls** Low

Form RPR

2236 **1** **Rapid City**[75] 765 7-9-7 68 PaulDoe 5 66
(Jim Best) *hld up in tch: outpcd over 2f out: rallied over 1f out: styd on u.p to ld wl ins fnl f* **11/1**

6244 **2** ½ **Kenswick**[13] 1795 3-8-4 55 (b) FrannyNorton 9 57
(Pat Eddery) *chsd ldrs: led over 1f out: rdn and hdd wl ins fnl f* **17/2**

0-40 **3** ½ **Finsbury**[7] 1967 7-9-4 60 GaryBartley(3) 13 63
(D Nicholls) *hld up: hdwy over 1f out: edgd rt ins fnl f: r.o* **12/1**

0600 **4** ¾ **Flowing Cape (IRE)**[16] 1688 5-9-7 82 JamieSpencer 12 64
(R Hollinshead) *hld up: swtchd lft 2f out: swtchd rt and hdwy wl over 1f out: sn rdn: nt clr run ent fnl f tl r.o wl towards fin: nt rch ldrs* **15/8**[1]

00-0 **5** ¾ **Set To Go**[30] 1394 3-8-9 55 (b[1]) TedDurcan 11 57
(H J L Dunlop) *sn led: hdd over 6f out: chsd ldr tl led again over 2f out: rdn and hdd over 1f out: styng on same pce whn edgd lft wl ins fnl f* **33/1**

-340 **6** nk **Lindoro**[3] 2091 5-9-7 87 (t) DavidProbert 7 59
(T T Clement) *hld up: slipped 6f out: hdwy 3f out: rdn over 1f out: styd on same pce* **7/2**[2]

1-22 **7** 1½ **Landucci**[11] 1839 9-9-7 66 (p) JamesDoyle 6 56
(S Curran) *hld up in tch: hmpd 6f out: rdn over 1f out: no ex fnl f* **6/1**[3]

0400 **8** 1½ **Bookiebasher Babe (IRE)**[6] 1995 5-9-2 50 (v) JerryO'Dwyer 10 47
(M Quinn) *s.i.s and stmbld s: hld up: slipped 6f out: rdn over 2f out: n.d* **40/1**

424- **9** 2¾ **San Silvestro (IRE)**[236] 4876 5-9-4 61 (p) BarryMcHugh(3) 3 46
(Mrs A Duffield) *chsd ldrs: rdn over 2f out: wknd over 1f out* **9/1**

0-00 **10** 29 **Sularno**[6] 2012 6-9-7 49 SaleemGolam 4 —
(J Pearce) *led over 6f out: rdn and hdd over 2f out: sn wknd* **100/1**

1m 45.05s (-0.05) **Going Correction** 0.0s/f (Good)
WFA 3 from 4yo+ 12lb 10 Ran SP% **114.2**
Speed ratings (Par 101): **100,99,99,98,97 97,95,94,91,62**
toteswingers: 1&2 £9.80, 1&3 £17.90, 2&3 £12.70 CSF £97.52 TOTE £14.40: £4.30, £2.10, £6.40.
Owner M & R Refurbishments Ltd **Bred** Juddmonte Farms Ltd **Trained** Lewes, E Sussex
■ Stewards' Enquiry : Paul Doe seven-day ban: used whip with excessive frequency down shoulder in the forehand (May 31-Jun 6)

FOCUS
Hard to know what to make of this form with the two 80+ rated performers out of the frame and the runner-up having a mark of just 55, so it is probably best to take it with a pinch of salt. The second, third and fifth look the best guides.
Lindoro Official explanation: jockey said gelding slipped rounding bend into straight
Bookiebasher Babe(IRE) Official explanation: jockey said mare slipped rounding bend into straight and was unsuited by the good to firm (good in patches) ground

2173 G.D. GILES H'CAP 1m 1f 218y
7:30 (7:30) (Class 4) (0-80,80) 4-Y-O+ **£4,209** (£1,252; £625; £312) **Stalls** High

Form RPR

15-5 **1** **Feathered Crown (FR)**[30] 1388 4-8-12 **74** EddieAhern 9 83+
(H R A Cecil) *trckd ldrs: led over 1f out: styd on wl* **15/8**[1]

40- **2** 2¼ **Silent Oasis**[221] 6621 4-8-10 **72** LukeMorris 2 74
(J S Moore) *hld up: racd keenly: pushed along 1/2-way: hdwy over 3f out: rdn to chse wnr fnl f: no imp* **28/1**

6251 **3** 1 **Buddy Holly**[3] 2093 5-9-4 **80** 6ex StephenCraine 4 80
(Pat Eddery) *hld up in tch: rdn over 1f out: no ex ins fnl f* **11/4**[2]

43-0 **4** ¾ **Wiggy Smith**[14] 1780 11-9-3 **79** DaneO'Neill 7 78
(H Candy) *hld up: hdwy over 3f out: sn rdn: r.o* **17/2**

16-6 **5** shd **Sceilin (IRE)**[25] 1489 6-8-4 **66** oh3 (t) JoeFanning 10 64
(J Mackie) *hld up: hdwy over 1f out: nt clr run and swtchd rt ins fnl f: r.o: nt rch ldrs* **28/1**

0-00 **6** 5 **Brouhaha**[96] 480 6-8-9 **78** SoniaEaton(7) 1 66
(Tom Dascombe) *s.i.s: sn chsng ldrs: rdn and wknd fnl f* **33/1**

5-31 **7** 1 **Slip**[13] 1801 5-8-9 **71** PhilipRobinson 3 57
(C R Dore) *hld up: rdn over 3f out: nvr nrr* **13/2**[3]

030- **8** ¾ **Snowed Under**[292] 4426 9-9-3 **79** DarryllHolland 8 64
(J D Bethell) *led: rdn and hdd over 1f out: wknd fnl f* **20/1**

0030 **9** ½ **Iron Out (USA)**[11] 1831 4-8-13 **80** PaulPickard(5) 11 64
(R Hollinshead) *hld up in tch: rdn over 3f out: wknd over 1f out* **20/1**

00-0 **10** 4½ **Pelham Crescent (IRE)**[11] 1840 7-9-1 **77** DavidProbert 6 52
(B Palling) *s.i.s: hld up: rdn over 3f out: wknd sn after* **16/1**

0-00 **11** 1½ **Lord Theo**[16] 1697 6-9-1 **77** J-PGuillambert 5 49
(N P Littmoden) *trckd ldr: racd keenly: rdn 2f out: wknd over 1f out* **33/1**

2m 6.58s (-1.32) **Going Correction** 0.0s/f (Good) 11 Ran SP% **113.5**
Speed ratings (Par 105): **105,103,102,101,101 97,96,96,95,92 91**
toteswingers: 1&2 £16.00, 1&3 £2.20, 2&3 £43.60 CSF £66.61 TOTE £2.60: £1.50, £9.30, £1.10; EX 50.80.
Owner H E Sheikh Sultan Bin Khalifa Al Nahyan **Bred** Sheikh Sultan Bin Khalifa Al Nayan **Trained** Newmarket, Suffolk

FOCUS
There was not much depth to this handicap. The winner built on his promising reappearance and can do better.

Snowed Under Official explanation: jockey said gelding had no more to give

2174 SARTORIUS MAIDEN STKS 5f 218y

8:00 (8:01) (Class 5) 3-Y-0 **£2,590** (£770; £385; £192) **Stalls** Low

Form				RPR
5-	**1**		**Dever Dream**[241] 6061 3-8-12 0 ... MichaelHills 8	76+
			(W J Haggas) *hld up in tch: rdn to ld ins fnl f: r.o: readily* **7/4**[1]	
64-3	**2**	½	**Vanilla Rum**[19] 1622 3-9-3 73 ... DaneO'Neill 3	79
			(H Candy) *chsd ldrs: rdn to ld over 1f out: edgd lft ins fnl f: sn edgd rt and hdd: r.o* **5/2**[2]	
0-2	**3**	1½	**Suzy Alexander**[27] 1436 3-8-12 0 ... SebSanders 1	69
			(G G Margarson) *hld up: hdwy over 1f out: sn rdn: styd on same pce wl ins fnl f* **8/1**	
4	**4**	2¾	**Gold Gleam (USA)**[12] 1825 3-9-3 0 ... EddieAhern 13	65
			(J Noseda) *chsd ldrs: rdn and ev ch over 1f out: no ex ins fnl f* **7/2**[3]	
0-6	**5**	2¼	**Rafiki (IRE)**[16] 1685 3-9-3 0 ... NickyMackay 12	58
			(W R Swinburn) *s.i.s: hdwy over 4f out: rdn over 1f out: wknd fnl f* **16/1**	
30	**6**	1	**Force To Spend**[12] 1825 3-8-12 0 ... LukeMorris 7	50
			(N P Littmoden) *led: rdn and hdd over 1f out: wknd fnl f* **66/1**	
00	**7**	8	**Major Eradicator (USA)**[10] 1878 3-9-3 0 ... GrahamGibbons 4	29
			(R M H Cowell) *sn outpcd: styd on ins fnl f: nvr nrr* **28/1**	
06	**8**	shd	**Vertumnus**[10] 1878 3-9-3 0 ... J-PGuillambert 10	29+
			(N P Littmoden) *hld up: pushed along 1/2-way: nvr on terms* **28/1**	
00	**9**	½	**Aim'Ees Star**[10] 1878 3-8-7 0 ... MarkCoumbe(5) 9	22
			(John A Harris) *chsd ldrs: rdn over 2f out: wkng whn hung lft over 1f out* **200/1**	
00	**10**	1¼	**Paphos**[19] 1622 3-9-3 0 ... SaleemGolam 11	23
			(S C Williams) *sn outpcd* **66/1**	
	11	7	**Correlandie (USA)** 3-8-12 0 ... PatCosgrave 6	—
			(J R Gask) *s.s: a wl bhd* **25/1**	
0	**12**	3¼	**Whispering Ridge**[16] 1685 3-9-3 0 ... JamesDoyle 2	—
			(M Wellings) *chsd ldrs: rdn over 2f out: hung rt and wknd sn after* **200/1**	

1m 12.03s (-0.97) **Going Correction** -0.325s/f (Firm) **12** Ran SP% **118.9**

Speed ratings (Par 99): **93,92,90,86,83 82,71,71,70,69 59,55**

toteswingers: 1&2 £1.40, 1&3 £3.10, 2&3 £7.70 CSF £5.93 TOTE £2.30: £1.10, £1.30, £7.40.

Owner Options O Syndicate **Bred** F C T Wilson **Trained** Newmarket, Suffolk

FOCUS

There was a good finish to this ordinary maiden. The form is rated around the runner-up.

2175 HENRY ALKEN H'CAP 1m 3f 183y

8:30 (8:31) (Class 5) (0-70,69) 3-Y-0 **£2,590** (£770; £385; £192) **Stalls** High

Form				RPR
000-	**1**		**Corr Point (IRE)**[172] 7538 3-8-4 **55** oh2 ... (t) GrahamGibbons 2	61
			(J A Osborne) *plld hrd: sn trcking ldr: led over 3f out: rdn over 1f out: styd on* **9/1**	
6-52	**2**	1¾	**Gay Mirage (GER)**[27] 1451 3-9-3 **68** ... (b) PhilipRobinson 5	71
			(M A Jarvis) *led 1f: chsd ldrs: rdn over 3f out: styd on to go 2nd on line* **11/4**[2]	
5-31	**3**	nse	**Blinka Me**[14] 1778 3-8-4 **60** ... SimonPearce(5) 7	63
			(M H Tompkins) *led after 1f: rdn and hdd over 3f out: styd on same pce ins fnl f: lost 2nd on line* **9/2**[3]	
66-5	**4**	1	**Bondage (IRE)**[20] 1608 3-9-0 **65** ... PatCosgrave 6	66
			(J R Fanshawe) *hld up: hmpd over 6f out: rdn over 3f out: styd on ins fnl f: edgd rt: nt rch ldrs* **9/4**[1]	
25-4	**5**	1¼	**Pena Dorada (IRE)**[19] 1630 3-9-4 **69** ... AndrewElliott 3	68
			(J R Weymes) *hld up: hdwy 1/2-way: rdn over 2f out: styd on same pce fnl f* **13/2**	
3230	**6**	2½	**Dane Cottage**[27] 1460 3-8-12 **63** ... DavidProbert 4	58
			(Miss Gay Kelleway) *hld up: hdwy 3f out: rdn over 1f out: wknd ins fnl f* **12/1**	
-044	**7**	2½	**Sharakti (IRE)**[18] 1652 3-8-7 **63** ... DeclanCannon(5) 8	54
			(A J McCabe) *prom: hmpd over 6f out: rdn over 3f out: wknd and eased fnl f* **16/1**	

2m 34.77s (0.87) **Going Correction** 0.0s/f (Good) **7** Ran SP% **112.5**

Speed ratings (Par 99): **97,95,95,95,94 92,90**

toteswingers:1&2 £11.20, 2&3 £4.20, 1&3 £11.20 CSF £32.88 CT £126.64 TOTE £17.30: £9.60, £2.60; EX 48.20 Place 6: £223.13 Place 5: £154.65.

Owner J Duddy & R A Pegum **Bred** T J Pabst And Newtown Stud **Trained** Upper Lambourn, Berks

FOCUS

Just an ordinary handicap and Blinka Me was allowed to dictate at pretty modest fractions. Muddling and weakish form.

T/Plt: £162.90. Pool £74,662.82- 334.52 winning tickets. T/Qpdt: £21.00. Pool £5,431.26 - 190.50 winning tickets. CR

1972 WINDSOR (R-H)

Monday, May 17

OFFICIAL GOING: Good (good to soft in places) changing to good after race 2 (6.40)

Wind: Light, half behind Weather: Fine

2176 EUROPEAN BREEDERS' FUND RIPPLEFFECT MAIDEN FILLIES' STKS 5f 10y

6:10 (6:12) (Class 5) 2-Y-0 **£3,367** (£1,002; £500; £250) **Stalls** High

Form				RPR
	1		**Masaya** 2-8-11 0 ... AhmedAjtebi(3) 11	71
			(C E Brittain) *mde virtually all: rdn over 1f out: kpt on fnl f: jst hld on* **9/2**[3]	
	2	nse	**Millyluvstobougie** 2-9-0 0 ... RichardHughes 8	71+
			(C G Cox) *towards rr tl prog 1/2-way: chsd wnr 1f out and swtchd to rail: r.o nr fin: jst failed* **11/1**	
	3	1½	**Kokojo (IRE)** 2-9-0 0 ... FergusSweeney 1	65+
			(B G Powell) *wnt lft s: towards rr: effrt on wd outside 2f out: rdn and styd on fnl f* **40/1**	
	4	1¼	**Overwhelm** 2-8-11 0 ... RussKennemore(3) 3	61
			(Andrew Reid) *free to post: racd keenly: in tch: effrt on outer to press ldrs 2f out and rn green: one pce fnl f* **14/1**	
	5	½	**Koha (USA)** 2-9-0 0 ... HayleyTurner 10	59+
			(D K Ivory) *chsd ldrs: rdn 2f out: fdd fnl f* **16/1**	
2	**6**	½	**Indian Narjes**[11] 1838 2-9-0 0 ... KierenFallon 5	57
			(M R Channon) *chsd ldrs: rdn and nt qckn 2f out: sn struggling* **11/8**[1]	
	7	shd	**Freedom Trail** 2-9-0 0 ... RobertHavlin 6	57+
			(D R C Elsworth) *trckd ldrs 2f: lost pl and n.m.r on inner sn after: nudged along and styd on again fnl f* **20/1**	
52	**8**	shd	**Melodize**[13] 1800 2-9-0 0 ... MartinDwyer 4	57
			(W R Muir) *mostly chsd wnr to 1f out: wknd* **7/2**[2]	
	9	1¾	**Excello** 2-9-0 0 ... IanMongan 9	55+
			(M S Saunders) *s.s: rn green in last pair: nudged along and began to run on over 1f out: no ch and eased last 100yds* **20/1**	
	10	6	**Laugia** 2-9-0 0 ... SimonWhitworth 7	29
			(J R Jenkins) *free to post: s.s: a last and struggling* **100/1**	

61.98 secs (1.68) **Going Correction** +0.175s/f (Good) **10** Ran SP% **116.3**

Speed ratings (Par 90): **93,92,90,88,87 86,86,86,83,74**

toteswingers: 1&2 £3.20, 1&3 £70.00, 2&3 £20.70 CSF £49.90 TOTE £6.60: £1.70, £2.20, £10.00; EX 45.30 Trifecta £938.20.

Owner Saeed Manana **Bred** S P Tindall **Trained** Newmarket, Suffolk

FOCUS

An average fillies' maiden.

NOTEBOOK

Masaya was by some way the most expensive of these purchased at sales, selling for 140,000gns, and had the benefit of the highest draw for this debut. She made it count by pinging out early on and showed a very willing attitude when put under pressure from 2f out. There is plenty of speed in her pedigree, but another furlong will not bother her and it is fair to expect a nice bit of improvement for the experience. (op 6-1 tchd 13-2)

Millyluvstobougie ◆, in total contrast to the winner, cost connections just £1,000 and she so nearly went in at the first time of asking. She had to wait for her challenge before switching to the stands' rail from the furlong pole, which probably made the difference and this rates a very pleasing initial effort. She can be considered a winner without a penalty next time. (op 9-1)

Kokojo(IRE) had to make her effort more towards the centre of the track thanks to her outside stall and left the impression she would learn a deal for the outing.

Overwhelm showed ability and is another expected to show the benefit of this experience on her next assignment. A stiffer test may suit ideally, though. (op 12-1)

Koha(USA), who cost 85,000gns, was doing some fair work late on against the rail and, in keeping with her pedigree, shaped as though this test was plenty sharp enough.

Indian Narjes was a popular choice to go one better than her debut second at Ffos Las, but her fate was apparent from halfway as she posted a laboured effort. The signs were not good beforehand, though, as she was edgy and played up down at the start. (tchd 6-5 and 6-4 in places)

Freedom Trail lacked the pace to land a serious blow yet certainly wasn't disgraced. (op 14-1)

Melodize dropped out disappointingly after showing early pace. Getting warm beforehand cannot have aided her cause. (op 9-2)

2177 WEATHERBYS BANK CONDITIONS STKS 5f 10y

6:40 (6:40) (Class 2) 2-Y-0 **£11,039** (£3,304; £1,652; £826; £411) **Stalls** High

Form				RPR
1	**1**		**Cape To Rio (IRE)**[35] 1256 2-8-11 0 ... RichardHughes 1	88+
			(R Hannon) *hld up in 5th: prog wl over 1f out: pushed firmly into ld ins fnl f: readily* **1/4**[1]	
2221	**2**	1	**Scarlet Rocks (IRE)**[7] 1957 2-8-6 0 ... HayleyTurner 6	78
			(P D Evans) *trckd ldng pair: pushed along 2f out: styd on to take 2nd last 100yds: no imp on wnr* **15/2**[2]	
14	**3**	¾	**Takeaway**[40] 1173 2-9-0 0 ... PatrickHills 3	84
			(R Hannon) *trckd ldng trio: effrt on outer over 1f out: outpcd as wnr wnt by 1f out: styd on* **16/1**[3]	
01	**4**	hd	**Lord Avon**[14] 1764 2-9-0 0 ... JackDean 5	83
			(W G M Turner) *mde most against nr side rail: hdd and fdd ins fnl f* **20/1**	
2331	**5**	3¾	**Style And Panache (IRE)**[11] 1838 2-8-9 0 ... CathyGannon 2	64
			(P D Evans) *w ldr to over 1f out: wknd* **16/1**[3]	
014	**6**	6	**Prophet In A Dream**[3] 2082 2-9-0 0 ... SamHitchcott 4	48
			(M R Channon) *a last: urged along to stay in tch after 2f: wknd over 1f out* **66/1**	

60.99 secs (0.69) **Going Correction** +0.175s/f (Good) **6** Ran SP% **109.8**

Speed ratings (Par 99): **101,99,98,97,91 82**

toteswingers: 1&2 £1.10, 1&3 £1.40, 2&3 £2.70 CSF £2.55 TOTE £1.20: £1.10, £2.30; EX 2.60.

Owner Kennet Valley Thoroughbreds I **Bred** Paul Hensey **Trained** East Everleigh, Wilts

FOCUS

A warm conditions event, run at a solid pace. The winner backed up the good impression from his debut and scored in a fast time, but there are doubts over the strength of the opposition.

NOTEBOOK

Cape To Rio(IRE) had won the same maiden that stablemate Monsieur Chevalier landed on his debut last year, at Folkestone in April, and was said to rank highly in the pecking order of Richard Hannon's juveniles. He has different ground to content with here and being by Captain Rio the quicker surface was a definite question mark, but it wasn't enough to stop him from eventually running out a decisive winner. He made up his ground smoothly around 2f out, but his response when asked to win the race wasn't immediate. That may have been due to the ground, but also still down to inexperience and he probably wasn't helped by having to make his challenge more towards the centre. It could also prove that he would now appreciate a stiffer test, and he is certainly bred to enjoy further down the line. His trainer also later added he believed this colt will be happier when tacking another furlong, but that he is still likely to follow the same route as Monsieur Chevalier and head to the National Stakes en-route to the Norfolk, where the more demanding track ought to suit better. (op 4-11 tchd 2-5 in places)

Scarlet Rocks(IRE) deservedly opened her account at Brighton a week earlier and her previous second to the winner's stablemate Zebedee over C&D last month is a race working out well enough. She again gave her all and rates a solid benchmark. (op 11-2)

Takeaway was the second string from his winning stable on jockey bookings and was expected to enjoy returning to a sounder surface. He did just that, reversing last-time-out form with Style And Panache, and shaping as though he could now improve for another furlong. (op 11-1)

Lord Avon made all to beat a Hannon juvenile, Jambo Bibi, at Kempton a fortnight earlier and set out for a repeat bid on his return to turf. He was aided by the stands' rail, but wasn't helped by being taken on for the lead and ran a solid race in defeat. (op 25-1 tchd 28-1 and 33-1 in a place)

Style And Panache(IRE) had also finished placed behind a Hannon juvenile, this time The Sydney Arms, on her only previous run over C&D and that form has worked out nicely. She didn't help her cause by refusing to settle in a share of the early lead here (also keen to post and ran below her previous level. (op 12-1)

Prophet In A Dream was beaten a long way out, never looking that happy on this drop back a furlong, and surely found it coming too soon.

2178 SPORTINGBET.COM CLAIMING STKS 6f

7:10 (7:10) (Class 5) 3-Y-0+ **£2,456** (£725; £362) **Stalls** High

Form				RPR
0450	**1**		**Timeteam (IRE)**[28] 1428 4-9-0 70 ... CathyGannon 7	71
			(P D Evans) *taken down early: hld up: prog to trck ldrs 1/2-way: rdn 2f out: led u.p ins fnl f: hld on* **15/2**[3]	
-600	**2**	nk	**Silver Wind**[10] 1862 5-9-8 81 ... (v) RichardHughes 8	78
			(P D Evans) *trckd ldrs: rdn 2f out: fnlly styd on to take 2nd wl ins fnl f: clsd on wnr fin* **1/1**[1]	
2-51	**3**	¾	**Flouncing (IRE)**[25] 1490 3-8-8 72 ... LiamJones 5	69
			(W J Haggas) *dwlt: t.k.h: hld up in rr: prog on outer 2f out: drvn to chal ins fnl f: no ex last 100yds* **9/2**[2]	
130-	**4**	nk	**Rioliina (IRE)**[161] 7662 4-8-13 69 ... HayleyTurner 1	66
			(J G Portman) *pressed ldr: led over 1f out: hrd rdn and hdd ins fnl f: fnd nil* **8/1**	

The Form Book, Raceform Ltd, Compton, RG20 6NL

6-34 **5** *2* **Lethal**[41] 1147 7-8-11 63 RussKennemore(3) 4 60
(Andrew Reid) *taken down early: led: sn crossed to nr side rail: hdd over 1f out: fdd u.p* **8/1**

150 **6** *nk* **Doctor Hilary**[35] 1258 8-8-9 61 (vt) JohnFahy(5) 9 59
(M R Hoad) *dwlt: hld up last: effrt on outer over 2f out: no imp on ldrs over 1f out* **20/1**

3005 **7** *½* **Shadow Bay (IRE)**[6] 2010 4-9-0 51 SamHitchcott 10 58
(Miss Z C Davison) *in tch in rr: rdn fr 1/2-way: no prog and struggling fnl 2f* **25/1**

00-0 **8** *27* **Joss Stick**[18] 1638 5-9-6 49 IanMongan 3 —
(B R Johnson) *taken down early: chsd ldrs to 1/2-way: wknd rapidly sn after: t.o* **100/1**

1m 13.88s (0.88) **Going Correction** +0.175s/f (Good)
WFA 3 from 4yo+ 9lb **8** Ran SP% **111.8**
Speed ratings (Par 103): **101,100,99,99,96 96,95,59**
toteswingers: 1&2 £3.70, 1&3 £6.50, 2&3 £1.30 CSF £14.76 TOTE £10.90: £2.20, £1.10, £1.50; EX 19.40 Trifecta £77.50.
Owner Roger Ambrose & William Reilly **Bred** R N Auld **Trained** Pandy, Monmouths
■ Stewards' Enquiry : Richard Hughes one-day ban: used whip with excessive frequency (May 31)
Cathy Gannon one-day ban: used whip with excessive frequency (May 31)

FOCUS
A modest claimer and muddling form. The winner only needed to run near his recent turf form.

2179 SPORTINGBET.COM H'CAP 5f 10y

7:40 (7:44) (Class 4) (0-85,83) 3-Y-O **£4,857** (£1,445; £722; £360) **Stalls** High

Form RPR

0-00 **1** **Russian Rock (IRE)**[9] 1913 3-9-4 **83** LiamKeniry 2 94
(R A Teal) *settled in last trio: prog on outer 1/2-way: wnt 2nd over 1f out: drvn to ld ins fnl f: styd on* **15/2**

5-04 **2** *1* **Ignatieff (IRE)**[17] 1656 3-8-12 **77** DuranFentiman 1 84
(Mrs L Stubbs) *pushed up to ld and swtchd to nr side rail: rdn over 2f out: hanging over 1f out: hdd and no qckn ins fnl f* **8/1**

-240 **3** *2½* **Leleyf (IRE)**[22] 1546 3-8-2 **72** MatthewDavies(5) 9 70
(M R Channon) *chsd ldrs: rdn and nt qckn wl over 1f out: plugged on to take 3rd nr fin* **11/2**[3]

020- **4** *hd* **Schoolboy Champ**[206] 6983 3-8-3 **71** Louis-PhilippeBeuzelin(3) 8 68
(Patrick Morris) *chsd ldrs: u.p and struggling 2f out: kpt on fnl f: n.d* **15/2**

6-24 **5** *1* **Nepotism**[14] 1765 3-8-8 **73** FergusSweeney 3 67
(M S Saunders) *chsd ldrs: wnt 2nd 2f out to over 1f out: fdd fnl f* **7/2**[2]

31-6 **6** *1¾* **Admin (IRE)**[21] 1584 3-8-13 **78** RichardHughes 5 65
(R M Beckett) *stdd s: t.k.h and hld up in last pair: gng easily 2f out: effrt over 1f out: shkn up ent fnl f: no rspnse and sn eased* **10/3**[1]

43-5 **7** *13* **Kings Of Leo**[128] 111 3-8-10 **75** MartinDwyer 4 16
(J R Boyle) *reluctant to go nr stalls: chsd ldr to 2f out: wknd rapidly and eased* **20/1**

10-0 **8** *5* **Morgans Choice**[22] 1546 3-8-5 **70** LiamJones 6 —
(J L Spearing) *stdd s: t.k.h: hld up in last pair: rdn 1/2-way: wknd over 1f out: eased* **33/1**

60.97 secs (0.67) **Going Correction** +0.175s/f (Good) **8** Ran SP% **103.0**
Speed ratings (Par 101): **101,99,95,95,93 90,69,61**
toteswingers: 1&2 £9.40, 1&3 £3.70, 2&3 £4.40 CSF £52.11 CT £261.87 TOTE £8.50: £3.30, £2.80, £2.80; EX 44.30 Trifecta £181.30.
Owner M Vickers **Bred** Barronstown Stud And Mrs T Stack **Trained** Ashtead, Surrey
■ Diamond Jonny G was withdrawn (7/1, broke out of stalls). R4 applies, deduct 10p in the £.

FOCUS
A modest sprint, run at a decent pace, but pretty ordinary form.
Admin(IRE) Official explanation: jockey said gelding ran too free early and found nothing under pressure

2180 TALKSPORT MAIDEN FILLIES' STKS 1m 67y

8:10 (8:18) (Class 5) 3-Y-O+ **£2,729** (£806; £403) **Stalls** High

Form RPR

4 **1** **Heavenly Dawn**[17] 1654 3-8-12 0 RichardMullen 2 77
(Sir Michael Stoute) *mde virtually all: rdn over 1f out: hrd pressed fnl f: hld on* **5/2**[1]

43 **2** *nk* **Belgique (IRE)**[22] 1542 3-8-12 0 RichardHughes 7 76
(R Hannon) *prom: effrt over 2f out: rdn to take 2nd fnl f: str chal nr last 100yds: jst hld* **10/1**[3]

3 *¾* **Madonna Dell'Orto** 3-8-12 0 ShaneKelly 3 74
(W R Swinburn) *prom: chsd wnr 1/2-way: rdn to chal 2f out: lost 2nd fnl f: styd on* **50/1**

2-4 **4** *1¾* **Skyrider (IRE)**[19] 1620 3-8-12 0 FergusSweeney 8 70
(R Charlton) *trckd ldrs: rdn over 2f out: one pce and no imp fr over 1f out* **7/2**[2]

0- **5** *2* **Treasure Way**[251] 5741 3-8-12 0 LiamKeniry 9 66
(P R Chamings) *t.k.h: hld up in rr: stdy prog on outer fr 3f out: chsd ldrs over 1f out: fdd fnl f* **10/1**[3]

5 **6** *2¼* **Eden Nights (USA)**[28] 1431 3-8-12 0 RobertHavlin 6 62
(J H M Gosden) *hld up in abt 8th: rdn over 2f out: rchd 6th but nt on terms 1f out: eased last 75yds* **7/2**[2]

6- **7** *shd* **Affirmable**[276] 5000 3-8-12 0 HayleyTurner 12 60+
(J W Hills) *uns rdr and cantered off bef s: hld up last: shkn up 4f out: stl in last trio over 2f out: pushed along and styd on wl after: nrst fin* **40/1**

0 **8** *½* **Blue Zealot (IRE)**[10] 1881 3-8-5 0 IanBurns(7) 4 59+
(M L W Bell) *hld up in rr: sme prog 3f out: pushed along and steadily outpcd fnl 2f* **100/1**

0 **9** *2¼* **Our Drama Queen (IRE)**[11] 1844 3-8-12 0 PatDobbs 1 54
(R Hannon) *trckd ldrs: outpcd fr over 2f out: keeping on whn n.m.r jst over 1f out* **12/1**

0 **10** *1¾* **Ayam Zainah**[31] 1355 3-8-12 0 KierenFallon 14 50
(M R Channon) *pressed wnr to 1/2-way: rdn and lost pl 3f out: struggling after* **33/1**

11 *nk* **Neptune's Girl (IRE)** 3-8-9 0 Louis-PhilippeBeuzelin(3) 5 49
(Sir Michael Stoute) *hld up in last trio: limited prog on outer over 2f out: sn no hdwy* **25/1**

33 **12** *¾* **Jumeirah Palm (USA)**[54] 971 3-8-9 0 AhmedAjtebi(3) 11 47
(D M Simcock) *hld up towards rr: pushed along and steadily lost pl fr over 2f out* **25/1**

13 *7* **Greeley's Qik Chic (USA)** 3-8-7 0 MatthewDavies(5) 10 31
(George Baker) *a in last trio: struggling 3f out* **100/1**

60 **14** *36* **Strawberry Rose**[7] 1976 3-8-12 0 MartinDwyer 13 —
(M P Tregoning) *prom: lost pl 1/2-way: sn wknd: t.o* **20/1**

1m 47.42s (2.72) **Going Correction** +0.175s/f (Good) **14** Ran SP% **120.7**
Speed ratings (Par 100): **93,92,91,90,88 85,85,85,83,81 81,80,73,37**
toteswingers: 1&2 £8.00, 1&3 £17.40, 2&3 £80.00 CSF £26.90 TOTE £4.40: £1.80, £3.90, £13.60; EX 23.00 Trifecta £322.10.
Owner Cheveley Park Stud **Bred** Cheveley Park Stud Ltd **Trained** Newmarket, Suffolk

FOCUS
An interesting maiden for 3yo fillies' that ought to produce plenty of future winners. The form looks sound with the fourth setting a fair standard.
Eden Nights(USA) Official explanation: jockey said filly had no more to give
Jumeirah Palm(USA) Official explanation: vet said filly returned lame

2181 A C BECK H'CAP 1m 3f 135y

8:40 (8:44) (Class 4) (0-80,80) 4-Y-O+ **£4,533** (£1,348; £674; £336) **Stalls** Centre

Form RPR

53-5 **1** **Some Sunny Day**[19] 1629 4-8-11 **73** HayleyTurner 7 82+
(H Morrison) *trckd ldrs: lost pl on inner bnd 6f out: rousted along to take bttr position against rail over 3f out: rdn to ld over 1f out: styd on wl* **13/2**

420- **2** *1¼* **Run For Ede's**[208] 6936 6-9-0 **76** IanMongan 8 83
(P M Phelan) *stdd s: hld up in last pair: prog on outer fr 3f out: rdn to chal over 1f out: kpt on same pce fnl f* **5/1**[3]

40-2 **3** *1* **Goodwood Starlight (IRE)**[46] 1077 5-8-12 **77** RobertLButler(3) 6 82
(Miss Sheena West) *t.k.h: prog to go 2nd 7f out: led wl over 2f out: hdd and one pce over 1f out* **10/1**

-110 **4** *nse* **Turjuman (USA)**[21] 1579 5-8-10 **72** StevieDonohoe 5 77+
(W J Musson) *hld up in rr: last 4f out: stl in last pair and shkn up over 2f out: prog wl over 1f out: styd on wl fnl f: nrst fin* **5/1**[3]

430- **5** *3* **Sequillo**[206] 6996 4-9-4 **80** RichardHughes 9 80
(R Hannon) *hld up in rr: effrt 3f out: rdn and limited prog over 2f out: wl hld in 5th whn n.m.r ins fnl f: eased* **4/1**[2]

245- **6** *2½* **Etruscan (IRE)**[48] 7780 5-8-13 **75** LiamKeniry 1 71
(C Gordon) *trckd ldrs: disp 3rd wl over 2f out: shkn up and fnd nil sn after* **40/1**

00 **7** *8* **Morar**[9] 1902 4-8-13 **75** PatDobbs 2 57
(Mrs L J Mongan) *hld up in tch: shkn up 3f out: wknd tamely over 2f out* **16/1**

66-5 **8** *½* **Norman The Great**[14] 1783 6-9-1 **77** FergusSweeney 4 58
(A King) *sn hld up in midfield: effrt 3f out: rdn and nt qckn over 2f out: steadily wknd* **7/2**[1]

9 *3* **Rebel Dancer (FR)**[4] 5-9-4 **80** (t) MartinDwyer 3 56
(P J Hobbs) *led to wl over 2f out: wknd* **16/1**

1 **10** *24* **Shut The Bar**[29] 963 5-8-13 **80** MatthewDavies(5) 10 16
(George Baker) *nt wl away but chsd ldr to 7f out: rdn and wknd 5f out: t.o* **25/1**

2m 33.4s (3.90) **Going Correction** +0.175s/f (Good) **10** Ran SP% **116.0**
Speed ratings (Par 105): **94,93,92,92,90 88,83,83,81,65**
toteswingers: 1&2 £9.40, 1&3 £23.40, 2&3 £9.10 CSF £38.81 CT £324.44 TOTE £7.90: £3.90, £1.30, £5.30; EX 47.90 Trifecta £287.60 Place 6: £101.63 Place 5: £26.23 .
Owner Mrs Julia Scott & J F Dean **Bred** Miss B Swire **Trained** East Ilsley, Berks

FOCUS
A fair handicap, run at an ordinary early pace. Muddling form, best judged around the third.
T/Plt: £132.90. Pool: £97,893.07 - 537.49 winning tickets T/Qpdt: £12.00 Pool: £8,754.45 - 537.96 winning tickets JN

1978 WOLVERHAMPTON (A.W) (L-H)

Monday, May 17

OFFICIAL GOING: Standard
Wind: Light, across Weather: Dry and sunny

2182 FREE HORSE RACING TIPS AT BIGTIPS.CO.UK AMATEUR RIDERS' CLAIMING STKS 1m 4f 50y(P)

2:10 (2:10) (Class 6) 4-Y-O+ **£1,714** (£527; £263) **Stalls** Low

Form RPR

22-0 **1** **Heathyards Pride**[47] 1069 10-9-11 80 MrStephenHarrison(3) 10 65
(R Hollinshead) *hld up: hdwy on outside over 3f out: edgd lft and led ins fnl f: pushed out* **5/2**[1]

-125 **2** *1¾* **William's Way**[49] 1053 8-10-9 73 MrCMartin(5) 12 76
(I A Wood) *hld up: rdn over 4f out: hdwy over 2f out: styd on to chse wnr towards fin* **9/1**

1123 **3** *¾* **My Mate Mal**[60] 923 6-9-13 70 MrJohnWilley(7) 5 67
(B Ellison) *t.k.h: led: rdn over 2f out: hdd ins fnl f: kpt on same pce* **7/1**

0032 **4** *½* **Mustajed**[14] 1758 9-10-3 66 MrPMillman(5) 2 68
(B R Millman) *prom: hdwy over 3f out: rdn and outpcd 2f out: kpt on ins fnl f* **11/2**[2]

3500 **5** *2¼* **Dream Of Fortune (IRE)**[11] 1840 6-10-2 70 (b) MrsEEvans 3 58
(P D Evans) *missed break: sn rcvrd and hld up in midfield: hdwy to chse ldr over 2f out to 1f out: sn no ex* **6/1**[3]

0000 **6** *2¾* **Resplendent Ace (IRE)**[7] 1980 6-10-1 64 MrJPFeatherstone(5) 6 58
(P Howling) *hld up: hdwy on outside over 2f out: edgd lft and no imp fr over 1f out* **14/1**

3443 **7** *1* **New Star (UAE)**[21] 1587 6-10-5 65 MrBenBrisbourne(3) 4 58
(W M Brisbourne) *prom: nt clr run over 2f out: rdn and effrt over 1f out: edgd lft and wknd ins fnl f* **12/1**

102- **8** *6* **Mista Rossa**[11] 7036 5-10-10 70 (v1) MissLHorner 9 51
(Jamie Snowden) *trckd ldrs: drvn and outpcd 3f out: sn btn* **16/1**

3000 **9** *2¾* **Aureate**[31] 1357 6-10-6 67 MrSWalker 7 42
(B Forsey) *pressed ldr: rdn over 3f out: wknd over 2f out* **8/1**

000- **10** *1½* **Mississippian (IRE)**[210] 6909 6-10-7 58 MissDLenge(7) 11 48
(Mrs D J Sanderson) *t.k.h early: hld up: pushed along over 3f out: sn btn* **40/1**

6/5 **11** *7* **Tuxsumdoin**[43] 1103 6-9-11 0 MrSDobson 8 20
(J R Weymes) *bhd: struggling 1/2-way: sn btn* **66/1**

12 *65* **Micksgirl**[152] 4-9-7 0 MrPTFinn(5) 1 —
(H E Haynes) *t.k.h in midfield: struggling after 6f: sn lost tch: t.o* **200/1**

2m 42.06s (0.96) **Going Correction** +0.025s/f (Slow) **12** Ran SP% **116.5**
Speed ratings (Par 101): **97,95,95,95,93 91,91,87,85,84 79,36**
toteswingers: 1&2 £5.00, 1&3 £2.60, 2&3 £11.10 CSF £25.30 TOTE £4.30: £2.30, £4.30, £1.10; EX 30.50.
Owner Miss Sarah Hollinshead **Bred** L A Morgan **Trained** Upper Longdon, Staffs

FOCUS
Five of the runners had a BHA rating between 70 and 80 in this fairly competitive claimer for amateur riders. The pace was not very strong but they finished quite well strung out and the heavily backed favourite ran out a decisive winner. The form is rated around the runner-up and it is probably not a race to be too positive about.

2183 FREE HORSE RACING TIPS AT BIGTIPS.CO.UK MAIDEN AUCTION STKS 5f 20y(P)
2:40 (2:41) (Class 6) 2-Y-O **£2,047** (£604; £302) **Stalls** Low

Form RPR
6 **1** **Sacrosanctus**[16] 1704 2-8-12 0 FrederikTylicki 3 70
(J A Glover) *cl up: drvn over 2f out: edgd lft and led ins fnl f: pushed out* **7/1**[3]
0 **2** *1* **Justbookie Dot Com (IRE)**[9] 1930 2-9-1 0 SebSanders 6 69
(Louise Best) *t.k.h: hld up in tch: drvn and hung lft over 1f out: styd on wl last 100yds to take 2nd cl home: nt rch wnr* **7/1**[3]
0 **3** *shd* **My Mate Al**[23] 1510 2-8-4 0 RichardKingscote 4 58
(Tom Dascombe) *led: rdn over 1f out: hdd and no ex wl ins fnl f: lost 2nd cl home* **14/1**
64 **4** *nk* **Nellie Ellis (IRE)**[7] 1981 2-8-7 0 PaulHanagan 2 60
(K A Ryan) *trckd ldrs: drvn over 2f out: kpt on same pce ins fnl f* **1/1**[1]
66 **5** *1 ½* **Ruby Alexander (IRE)**[22] 1541 2-8-7 0 JackMitchell 8 55
(R M Beckett) *prom on outside: drvn over 2f out: edgd lft over 1f out: sn no ex* **4/1**[2]
04 **6** *4* **Nalany**[13] 1794 2-8-4 0 FrankieMcDonald 7 37
(D Haydn Jones) *towards rr: drvn and outpcd 1/2-way: n.d after* **25/1**
05 **7** *5* **Whipperoo (IRE)**[10] 1864 2-8-4 0 AndrewHeffernan(3) 5 22
(Patrick Morris) *dwlt and wnt lft s: bhd and pushed along 1/2-way: nvr on terms* **33/1**
8 *5* **Zohan (IRE)** 2-8-9 0 SaleemGolam 1 6
(Peter Grayson) *s.i.s: bhd: struggling over 2f out: sn wknd* **25/1**

63.09 secs (0.79) **Going Correction** +0.025s/f (Slow) **8** Ran SP% **112.3**
Speed ratings (Par 91): **94,92,92,91,89 82,74,66**
toteswingers: 1&2 £4.90, 1&3 £6.90, 2&3 £7.40 CSF £51.75 TOTE £9.90: £2.00, £1.60, £2.60; EX 29.40.
Owner Paul J Dixon **Bred** Worksop Manor Stud **Trained** Babworth, Notts

FOCUS
The majority of runners had not shown much in this ordinary maiden auction in which the two market leaders were both a bit disappointing. The form should be treated with caution, although the winner showed a good atitude.

NOTEBOOK
Sacrosanctus dropped away into a remote sixth of seven in a modest 5f Thirsk maiden on debut. There was a suspicion that the gelded half-brother to modest 2m hurdle/chase winner Lerida might be one for later over longer distances but he attracted support this time and showed a very willing attitude to score under a prominent ride. (op 10-1 tchd 11-2)
Justbookie Dot Com(IRE) faded when 11l tenth at 28-1 in an ordinary 5.5f Warwick maiden on debut but he caught the eye with a fast finishing effort against the far rail here. He is an athletic-looking half-brother to fair/useful 2-y-o (and older winners) and should be capable of further progress. (op 10-1)
My Mate Al showed little on debut at Haydock last month but she put in an encouraging effort under front-running tactics on this second start. (op 10-1)
Nellie Ellis(IRE) had strong form claims on her promising runs at Ripon and at this track. The well-backed favourite tracked the pace for most of the way but faltered for a few strides when finding a clear run in the straight and could only plug on after that. (op 5-4 tchd 10-11)
Ruby Alexander(IRE) showed promise at single-figure odds in maidens at Kempton and Bath but she was a huge drifter in the market here and put in a fairly tame effort out wide. (op 5-2 tchd 9-2)

2184 FREE HORSE RACING TIPS AT BIGTIPS.CO.UK H'CAP 5f 216y(P)
3:10 (3:12) (Class 6) (0-55,55) 4-Y-O+ **£1,774** (£523; £262) **Stalls** Low

Form RPR
0500 **1** **Only A Game (IRE)**[9] 1928 5-8-12 **55** (vt[1]) GaryBartley(3) 10 64
(I W McInnes) *hld up: hdwy 2f out: rdn to ld ins fnl f: hld on wl* **16/1**
6506 **2** *nk* **Loyal Royal (IRE)**[23] 1534 7-8-12 **55** (bt) MichaelGeran(3) 6 63
(J M Bradley) *hld up in tch: hdwy 2f out: chsd wnr ins fnl f: r.o fin* **8/1**[3]
-046 **3** *½* **The History Man (IRE)**[10] 1884 7-9-0 **54** (p) KirstyMilczarek 3 60
(B D Leavy) *led: rdn over 2f out: edgd lft over 1f out: hdd ins fnl f: kpt on* **13/2**[1]
-255 **4** *½* **Namu**[9] 1929 7-8-12 **55** JackDean(3) 11 60+
(Miss T Spearing) *dwlt: bhd: hdwy on wd outside whn checked over 1f out: edgd lft and kpt on wl fnl f: nrst fin* **9/1**
050 **5** *shd* **Suhayl Star (IRE)**[68] 844 6-9-1 **55** SaleemGolam 4 60
(P Burgoyne) *pressed ldr: rdn 2f out: kpt on same pce ins fnl f* **14/1**
600 **6** *nk* **Albero Di Giuda (IRE)**[10] 1884 5-9-1 **55** (t) DarrylHolland 2 59
(F Sheridan) *t.k.h early: prom: effrt over 1f out: one pce ins fnl f* **12/1**
0054 **7** *hd* **Carnival Dream**[15] 1722 5-9-0 **54** PatrickMathers 8 57
(H A McWilliams) *hld up on outside: rdn 1/2-way: wandered over 1f out: kpt on ins fnl f* **33/1**
0234 **8** *½* **Dream Express (IRE)**[18] 1642 5-8-12 **55** MichaelStainton(3) 7 56
(P Howling) *plld hrd: hld up: drvn and carried hd high over 1f out: hdwy fnl f: swtchd lft and kpt on fin* **8/1**[3]
6105 **9** *¾* **Cheery Cat (USA)**[37] 1236 6-9-0 **54** (p) RobertWinston 13 55
(J Balding) *prom: drvn over 2f out: one pce fnl f: eased whn hld towards fin* **10/1**
5102 **10** *3 ½* **Metropolitan Chief**[37] 1236 6-9-0 **54** TomMcLaughlin 1 42
(P Burgoyne) *hld up ins: drvn over 2f out: no imp over 1f out* **9/1**
3306 **11** *2 ½* **Tamino (IRE)**[37] 1236 7-8-13 **53** J-PGuillambert 5 33
(P Howling) *in tch gng wl: lost pl 2f out: eased whn hld over 1f out* **7/1**[2]
00-0 **12** *1* **Prince Andjo (USA)**[9] 1928 4-9-1 **55** DavidNolan 9 32
(D Carroll) *trckd ldrs tl rdn and wknd fr 2f out* **14/1**
00 **13** *1* **Dickie Le Davoir**[34] 1270 6-8-10 **55** (v) BillyCray(5) 12 28
(R C Guest) *s.s: bhd and drvn over 2f out: nvr on terms* **11/1**

1m 14.91s (-0.09) **Going Correction** +0.025s/f (Slow) **13** Ran SP% **115.3**
Speed ratings (Par 101): **101,100,99,99,99 98,98,97,96,92 88,87,86**
toteswingers: 1&2 £44.30, 1&3 £23.50, 2&3 £17.00 CSF £133.96 CT £954.72 TOTE £26.60: £6.60, £3.60, £1.70; EX 183.60.
Owner Hall Farm Racing **Bred** Maggie And Eric Hemming **Trained** Catwick, E Yorks

FOCUS
A modest handicap in which most of the runners had been well held on their previous run. The pace was strong but they finished in a bunch. The winner is rated back to his best.
Albero Di Giuda(IRE) Official explanation: jockey said mare ran too freely

2185 OVER £1000 IN FREE BETS AT BIGTIPS.CO.UK H'CAP 5f 216y(P)
3:40 (3:41) (Class 6) (0-60,60) 3-Y-O **£1,774** (£523; £262) **Stalls** Low

Form RPR
-412 **1** **Jigajig**[17] 1667 3-8-13 **55** PaulHanagan 5 59
(K A Ryan) *mde all: rdn over 1f out: edgd lft ins fnl f: r.o* **11/8**[1]
0632 **2** *hd* **Miss Polly Plum**[20] 1605 3-8-4 **49** KellyHarrison(3) 9 52
(C A Dwyer) *t.k.h: hld up: hdwy 2f out: chsd wnr ins fnl f: r.o* **14/1**
-420 **3** *shd* **Dimaire**[14] 1760 3-9-2 **58** (b[1]) DarrylHolland 11 61
(D Haydn Jones) *hld up on outside: rdn 1/2-way: hdwy and hung lft over 1f out: kpt on wl fnl f* **8/1**[2]
346- **4** *¾* **Just The Tonic**[236] 6215 3-8-13 **55** PJMcDonald 6 55
(Mrs Marjorie Fife) *trckd ldrs: effrt over 1f out: chsd wnr briefly ins fnl f: hld towards fin* **9/1**[3]
160 **5** *½* **Cookie Galore**[20] 1605 3-9-2 **58** FrederikTylicki 2 57
(J A Glover) *dwlt: hld up on ins: hdwy and drvn over 1f out: kpt on ins fnl f* **10/1**
3336 **6** *2 ½* **Magenta Strait**[6] 2000 3-8-13 **60** PaulPickard(5) 10 51
(R Hollinshead) *bhd: effrt and hdwy on outside over 1f out: kpt on fnl f: nvr rchd ldrs* **20/1**
60-5 **7** *¾* **Winifred Jo**[37] 1222 3-9-1 **57** FrannyNorton 4 45
(J R Gask) *trckd ldrs: effrt and chsd wnr over 1f out to ins fnl f: sn wknd* **12/1**
0004 **8** *½* **Shawkantango**[26] 1477 3-8-8 **50** (v) GrahamGibbons 12 37
(D Shaw) *prom: drvn over 2f out: edgd lft u.p and wknd ent fnl f* **20/1**
063- **9** *1* **Anna's Boy**[229] 6381 3-8-11 **53** PhillipMakin 7 36
(A Berry) *bhd: drvn along 1/2-way: sme late hdwy: nvr on terms* **66/1**
4631 **10** *1 ¼* **Vilnius**[14] 1774 3-8-11 **58** IanBrennan(5) 8 37
(M R Channon) *in tch: drvn and outpcd 2f out: edgd lft and sn btn* **16/1**
0235 **11** *1* **Rathbawn Girl (IRE)**[20] 1605 3-9-1 **60** MichaelStainton(3) 1 36
(Miss J Feilden) *missed break: bhd: drvn over 2f out: nvr on terms* **10/1**
2356 **12** *2 ¾* **Taper Jean Girl (IRE)**[26] 1469 3-8-10 **52** (p) RobertWinston 13 19
(Mrs R A Carr) *pressed wnr: rdn over 2f out: wkng whn blkd over 1f out* **33/1**
650 **13** *8* **My Meteor**[15] 1731 3-9-3 **59** SebSanders 3 —
(A G Newcombe) *in tch on ins tl wknd over 2f out* **12/1**

1m 15.47s (0.47) **Going Correction** +0.025s/f (Slow) **13** Ran SP% **123.3**
Speed ratings (Par 97): **97,96,96,95,94 91,90,89,88,86 85,81,71**
toteswingers:1&2 £5.10, 2&3 £18.50, 1&3 £4.10 CSF £22.72 CT £131.08 TOTE £2.80: £1.70, £4.90, £1.20; EX 29.30.
Owner Mrs Maureen Eason **Bred** Miss D Fleming **Trained** Hambleton, N Yorks

FOCUS
Most of the runners were fairly exposed in this handicap for 3-y-os. There was a thrilling finish and the hot favourite just held off the closers. It is doubtful if he needed to improve.
Dimaire Official explanation: jockey said filly hung left-handed

2186 BIGTIPS.CO.UK FOR FREE BETS AND TIPS H'CAP 5f 20y(P)
4:10 (4:10) (Class 6) (0-60,60) 4-Y-O+ **£1,774** (£523; £262) **Stalls** Low

Form RPR
0500 **1** **Figaro Flyer (IRE)**[26] 1482 7-9-4 **60** J-PGuillambert 5 69
(P Howling) *hld up: hdwy over 1f out: led ins fnl f: kpt on wl* **7/1**
-412 **2** *¾* **Cavitie**[26] 1477 4-8-13 **55** DarryllHolland 4 61
(Andrew Reid) *in tch: drvn over 2f out: hdwy over 1f out: chsd wnr ins fnl f: r.o* **5/2**[1]
03-0 **3** *hd* **Sorrel Point**[26] 1477 7-8-5 **52** (vt) SimonPearce(5) 1 57
(H J Collingridge) *bhd: outpcd after 2f: gd hdwy on ins over 1f out: kpt on fnl f: nrst fin* **20/1**
0432 **4** *¾* **Kheley (IRE)**[9] 1929 4-8-11 **58** KierenFox(5) 6 61
(W M Brisbourne) *hld up: hdwy over 1f out: kpt on fnl f: nrst fin* **6/1**[3]
050- **5** *1 ¾* **Lady Vivien**[227] 6456 4-8-13 **55** PhillipMakin 9 51
(D H Brown) *dwlt: bhd: drvn 1/2-way: hdwy on outside over 1f out: kpt on fnl f: nvr able to chal* **10/1**
0035 **6** *nk* **Almaty Express**[37] 1234 8-8-10 **52** (b) FrederikTylicki 7 47
(J R Weymes) *sn drvn along in midfield: no imp tl styd on fnl f: nt gng pce to chal* **8/1**
5300 **7** *hd* **Tune Up The Band**[5] 2021 6-8-9 **51** RichardKingscote 8 45
(R J Hodges) *prom: rdn over 2f out: outpcd fnl f* **10/1**
600- **8** *½* **Pressed For Time (IRE)**[287] 4596 4-8-6 **48** ow1 (t) EddieCreighton 13 41
(E J Creighton) *led at decent gallop: rdn over 1f out: hdd ins fnl f: sn btn* **66/1**
3650 **9** *1 ½* **Bluebok**[5] 2021 9-8-10 **52** (bt) NickyMackay 11 39
(J M Bradley) *in tch: drvn and outpcd over 2f out: n.d after* **33/1**
-000 **10** *1* **Blessed Place**[13] 1799 10-8-5 **50** (tp) AshleyHamblett(3) 3 34
(D J S Ffrench Davis) *pressed ldr tl rdn and wknd fr 2f out* **16/1**
3434 **11** *nk* **Trick Or Two**[32] 1337 4-9-1 **57** (b) RobertWinston 10 40
(Mrs R A Carr) *t.k.h: trckd ldrs: drvn over 2f out: edgd lft and wknd fnl f* **11/2**[2]
406 **12** *½* **Norse Warrior (USA)**[73] 810 4-9-1 **57** SaleemGolam 2 38
(Peter Grayson) *bhd and sn drvn along: nvr on terms* **25/1**

61.97 secs (-0.33) **Going Correction** +0.025s/f (Slow) **12** Ran SP% **119.0**
Speed ratings (Par 101): **103,101,101,100,97 97,96,95,93,91 91,90**
toteswingers: 1&2 £6.70, 1&3 £31.10, 2&3 £13.20 CSF £23.95 CT £344.10 TOTE £11.90: £4.20, £1.20, £6.70; EX 34.10.
Owner S J Hammond **Bred** Mohammad Al Qatami **Trained** Newmarket, Suffolk

FOCUS
A modest handicap. The leaders went off fast and those who were held up dominated the finish. The winner did not need to match even his winter best.

2187 REGISTER FOR FREE TODAY AT BIGTIPS.CO.UK H'CAP (DIV I) 7f 32y(P)
4:40 (4:40) (Class 5) (0-70,70) 4-Y-O+ **£2,115** (£624; £312) **Stalls** High

Form RPR
504 **1** **Headache**[9] 1914 5-8-8 **65** (bt) SophieDoyle(5) 6 76
(B W Duke) *trckd ldrs: led over 1f out: r.o strly fnl f* **4/1**[2]
0-01 **2** *1 ¾* **Chief Red Cloud (USA)**[21] 1585 4-9-3 **69** FrederikTylicki 9 75
(J R Weymes) *hld up in midfield on outside: hdwy and ev ch 2f out: sn rdn: kpt on fnl f: nt rch wnr* **10/3**[1]
5430 **3** *¾* **Ravi River (IRE)**[9] 1914 6-8-13 **70** (v) RichardEvans(5) 11 74
(P D Evans) *dwlt: bhd and sn drvn along: hdwy on ins over 1f out: kpt on: nrst fin* **14/1**
3463 **4** *½* **Trade Centre**[10] 1877 5-9-1 **67** (p) DavidProbert 7 70
(R A Harris) *in tch: drvn and outpcd over 2f out: rallied over 1f out: kpt on ins fnl f* **9/1**
50-0 **5** *nk* **Buxton**[10] 1877 6-8-13 **65** (t) SebSanders 5 67
(R Ingram) *trckd ldrs: led over 2f out to 1f out: no ex ins fnl f* **7/1**[3]
2650 **6** *2* **Guildenstern (IRE)**[13] 1813 8-8-5 **57** SaleemGolam 12 53
(P Howling) *bhd: rdn over 2f out: kpt on fnl f: nvr able to chal* **25/1**
464- **7** *1 ¼* **Crystallize**[157] 7715 4-8-9 **61** StevieDonohoe 1 54
(A B Haynes) *midfield: drvn over 2f out: sn outpcd: plugged on fnl f: n.d* **20/1**
450- **8** *½* **Forzarzi (IRE)**[317] 3615 6-8-5 **57** oh1 ow1 PatrickMathers 3 49
(H A McWilliams) *hld up: rdn and hdwy over 1f out: no further imp fnl f* **40/1**

63-0 **9** *shd* **First Blade**[30] 1391 4-8-11 **63**.....................(p) AmirQuinn 4 54
(S R Bowring) *prom tl edgd lft and wknd over 1f out* **14/1**

3225 **10** *1 3/4* **Tevez**[6] 2009 5-8-10 **62**..................... AndreaAtzeni 2 49+
(D Donovan) *hld up: effrt whn no room fr over 2f out to ins fnl f: nt rcvr* **4/1**[2]

54-0 **11** *1* **Business Class (BRZ)**[42] 814 5-8-9 **61**..................... PJMcDonald 10 45
(Mrs Marjorie Fife) *cl up tl rdn and wknd wl over 1f out* **22/1**

5346 **12** *3 1/2* **Mocha Java**[15] 1737 7-8-6 **63**.....................(p) RossAtkinson(5) 8 38
(Matthew Salaman) *led tl rdn and hdd over 2f out: wknd wl over 1f out* **28/1**

1m 29.53s (-0.07) **Going Correction** +0.025s/f (Slow) 12 Ran SP% **117.8**
Speed ratings (Par 103): **101,99,98,97,97 94,93,92,92,90 89,85**
toteswingers: 1&2 £4.50, 1&3 £16.30, 2&3 £10.00 CSF £16.21 CT £173.53 TOTE £3.20: £1.10, £2.90, £4.70; EX 20.00.
Owner Brendan W Duke Racing **Bred** Bearstone Stud **Trained** Lambourn, Berks

FOCUS
They went a fair pace in this 7f handicap and two of the market leaders filled the first two positions. The form looks sound enough.
Ravi River(IRE) Official explanation: jockey said gelding hung right-handed
Mocha Java Official explanation: jockey said gelding hung right-handed

2188 REGISTER FOR FREE TODAY AT BIGTIPS.CO.UK H'CAP (DIV II) 7f 32y(P)
5:10 (5:11) (Class 5) (0-70,70) 4-Y-O+ **£2,115** (£624; £312) **Stalls** High

Form RPR

2243 **1** **Spinning Ridge (IRE)**[10] 1875 5-9-0 **66**.....................(b) DavidProbert 10 75
(R A Harris) *trckd ldr: led over 3f out: qcknd clr 2f out: kpt on wl fnl f* **4/1**[2]

006 **2** *1 3/4* **Running Flame (IRE)**[9] 1924 4-8-11 **63**..................... JamesDoyle 3 67
(A J McCabe) *in tch: rdn 1/2-way: hdwy over 1f out: wnt 2nd ins fnl f: r.o: nt rch wnr* **4/1**[2]

2403 **3** *3/4* **Cut And Thrust (IRE)**[37] 1238 4-8-13 **70**..................... KierenFox(5) 12 72
(M Wellings) *t.k.h: prom: effrt and chsd wnr 2f out: edgd lft: one pce and lost 2nd ins fnl f* **14/1**

40-0 **4** *hd* **Location**[21] 1585 4-8-5 **57**..................... PaulHanagan 8 58
(Ian Williams) *hld up: hdwy over 1f out: kpt on ins fnl f: nrst fin* **20/1**

5010 **5** *nk* **Straight Face (IRE)**[9] 1914 6-8-8 **67**.....................(b) MatthewCosham(7) 2 68
(P D Evans) *trckd ldrs: drvn over 2f out: no ex fnl f* **16/1**

6030 **6** *1 1/4* **The Graig**[33] 1293 6-8-4 **56** oh7.....................(t) NickyMackay 7 53
(J R Holt) *towards rr: hdwy u.p and edgd lft over 1f out: nrst fin* **25/1**

0004 **7** *1/2* **Bob Stock (IRE)**[40] 1170 4-8-6 **58**..................... JamieMackay 9 54
(W J Musson) *hld up: rdn over 2f out: hdd over 1f out: nvr able to chal* **8/1**[3]

3161 **8** *1* **Imperial Djay (IRE)**[13] 1812 5-8-10 **62**..................... RobertWinston 5 55+
(Mrs R A Carr) *hld up in midfield on ins: v little room fr 1/2-way: rdn over 1f out: sn no room: nt rcvr and eased ins fnl f* **7/2**[1]

12-0 **9** *1* **Blue Noodles**[25] 1492 4-8-13 **68**..................... AndrewHeffernan(3) 1 59
(P D Evans) *led to over 3f out: rdn and wknd fr 2f out* **10/1**

3510 **10** *1* **Woolston Ferry (IRE)**[21] 1585 4-8-4 **61**.....................(p) SimonPearce(5) 11 49
(David Pinder) *midfield on outside: hdwy over 3f out: rdn and wknd fr 2f out* **12/1**

60-0 **11** *1* **Silver Hotspur**[127] 114 6-8-10 **62**.....................(p) GrahamGibbons 4 47
(D Shaw) *missed break: t.k.h in rr: rdn over 2f out: nvr on terms* **20/1**

0000 **12** *3/4* **All About You (IRE)**[37] 1238 4-8-11 **63**..................... SaleemGolam 6 46
(P Howling) *bhd: drvn over 3f out: btn fnl 2f* **25/1**

1m 29.32s (-0.28) **Going Correction** +0.025s/f (Slow) 12 Ran SP% **119.9**
Speed ratings (Par 103): **102,100,99,98,98 97,96,95,94,93 92,91**
toteswingers: 1&2 £4.90, 1&3 £11.00, 2&3 £16.60 CSF £19.39 CT £205.78 TOTE £4.80: £2.20, £2.00, £5.20; EX 23.20.
Owner Robert & Nina Bailey **Bred** Eddie O'Leary **Trained** Earlswood, Monmouths

FOCUS
The second and quicker division of an ordinary handicap. The winner scored under an enterprising ride, recording a small personal best, and nothing got into it from behind.
The Graig Official explanation: jockey said gelding hung left-handed
Imperial Djay(IRE) Official explanation: jockey said gelding was denied a clear run

2189 BIGTIPS.CO.UK REGISTER FOR FREE TODAY H'CAP 1m 1f 103y(P)
5:40 (5:42) (Class 6) (0-60,60) 3-Y-O **£1,774** (£523; £262) **Stalls** Low

Form RPR

02-6 **1** **Al Shababiya (IRE)**[23] 1538 3-9-1 **60**..................... MartinLane(3) 11 65
(D M Simcock) *dwlt: t.k.h and sn in tch: hdwy on outside to ld over 2f out: edgd lft over 1f out: kpt on wl u.p fnl f* **14/1**

0-22 **2** *shd* **Celtic Ransom**[13] 1796 3-8-12 **59**..................... KierenFox(5) 8 64
(J W Hills) *led to over 2f out: rallied and ev ch over 1f out: edgd rt: kpt on wl fnl f: jst hld* **7/2**[2]

000- **3** *hd* **Celebrian**[179] 7451 3-8-12 **59**.....................(t) IanBrennan(5) 3 64+
(W R Swinburn) *t.k.h in midfield: stdy hdwy to trck ldrs over 3f out: effrt 2f out: nt clr run and swtchd rt ins fnl f: r.o* **13/2**[3]

5-30 **4** *1 1/4* **Red Amy**[13] 1796 3-9-0 **56**..................... DarryllHolland 9 58
(M L W Bell) *t.k.h: prom: drvn and outpcd over 3f out: rallied wl over 1f out: kpt on fin* **13/2**[3]

000- **5** *1* **Motrice**[209] 6921 3-9-4 **60**..................... SebSanders 7 60+
(Sir Mark Prescott) *dwlt: bhd: pushed along fr 4f out: drvn whn c wd st: hung lft over 1f out: styd on ins fnl f: nrst fin* **5/2**[1]

055 **6** *4 1/2* **Broughtons Swinger**[73] 812 3-9-1 **57**..................... JamieMackay 4 47
(W J Musson) *hld up: shkn up and hdwy wl over 1f out: nvr nr to chal* **40/1**

2543 **7** *hd* **Market Puzzle (IRE)**[25] 1495 3-9-1 **57**.....................(v[1]) TomMcLaughlin 5 47
(W M Brisbourne) *midfield: drvn and outpcd 4f out: styd on fr over 1f out: nvr rchd ldrs* **16/1**

0-00 **8** *3/4* **Vert Chapeau**[13] 1795 3-9-0 **56**.....................(b[1]) AndreaAtzeni 12 44
(E F Vaughan) *stdd s: hld up: pushed along over 3f out: shortlived effrt on ins over 1f out: n.d* **33/1**

400- **9** *1* **Suzi's A Smartlady (IRE)**[212] 6844 3-9-2 **58**..................... RobertWinston 6 44
(H J Collingridge) *trckd ldrs: drvn over 3f out: wknd fnl 2f* **20/1**

06-6 **10** *2 1/4* **Jamarjo (IRE)**[6] 1992 3-9-1 **57**..................... FrederikTylicki 10 39
(S Gollings) *prom tl rdn and wknd over 2f out* **16/1**

04-0 **11** *nse* **Pursestrings**[28] 1431 3-9-1 **57**..................... PaulHanagan 13 38
(R Charlton) *t.k.h: cl up tl rdn and wknd 2f out* **16/1**

30-6 **12** *1 3/4* **Charpoy Cobra**[23] 1537 3-9-2 **58**..................... KirstyMilczarek 2 36
(J A R Toller) *hld up: rdn over 3f out: sn struggling* **14/1**

2m 2.45s (0.75) **Going Correction** +0.025s/f (Slow) 12 Ran SP% **118.6**
Speed ratings (Par 97): **97,96,96,95,94 90,90,89,89,87 86,85**
toteswingers: 1&2 £8.40, 1&3 £17.00, 2&3 £7.20 CSF £61.47 CT £360.89 TOTE £20.70: £4.80, £2.00, £1.80; EX 50.30 Place 6: £69.06 Place 5: £37.83.
Owner Ahmad Al Shaikh **Bred** De Burgh Equine **Trained** Newmarket, Suffolk

FOCUS
A low-grade handicap, but there were several potential improvers involved and the first five finished a long way clear of the rest.
Charpoy Cobra Official explanation: jockey said filly never travelled; trainer said filly was found to be in season
T/Jkpt: Not won. T/Plt: £451.80. Pool £68,296.28 - 110.35 winning tickets. T/Qpdt: £15.90. Pool £5,954.09 - 276.11 winning tickets. RY

2190 - 2194a (Foreign Racing) - See Raceform Interactive

OVREVOLL (R-H)
Monday, May 17

OFFICIAL GOING: Turf: good

2195a WALTER NILSENS MINNELOP (LISTED RACE) (4YO+) (TURF) 1m 4f
5:25 (12:00) 4-Y-O+ **£64,171** (£21,390; £10,695; £6,417; £4,278)

RPR

1 **Alpacco (IRE)**[16] 8-9-2 0..................... ManuelMartinez 8 100
(Sandie Kjaer Nortoft, Denmark) **84/10**

2 *7* **Touch Of Hawk (FR)**[29] 1420 4-9-4 0..................... LennartHammer-Hansen 3 91
(Wido Neuroth, Norway) **6/4**[2]

3 *1 1/2* **Appel Au Maitre (FR)**[29] 1420 6-9-4 0..................... Jan-ErikNeuroth 9 88
(Wido Neuroth, Norway) **11/10**[1]

4 *hd* **Classical World (USA)**[16] 5-9-2 0..................... NikolajStott 4 86
(Torben Christensen, Denmark) **36/1**

5 *3* **Volo Cat (FR)**[16] 6-9-2 0..................... JacobJohansen 2 81
(Bent Olsen, Denmark) **47/1**

6 *1/2* **Alnitak (USA)**[246] 5933 9-9-2 0.....................(b) KimAndersen 5 80
(Bent Olsen, Denmark) **208/10**

7 *5 1/2* **Fricoteiro (ARG)**[218] 7-9-2 0..................... Per-AndersGraberg 7 72
(Niels Petersen, Norway) **169/10**

8 *2* **Percussionist (IRE)**[115] 2056 9-9-2 0..................... EspenSki 6 68
(J Howard Johnson) *racd in midfield: rdn appr 2f out: sn wknd* **15/2**[3]

9 *3* **Timely Production (IRE)** 4-9-2 0.....................(b) MadeleineSmith 1 64
(Madeleine Smith, Sweden) **40/1**

2m 35.7s (1.60) 9 Ran SP% **127.4**
PARI-MUTUEL (all including 1 krone stakes): WIN 9.39; PLACE 1.26, 1.23, 1.26; DF 33.62.
Owner Lone & Jens Westh **Bred** Manfred Hoffer **Trained** Denmark

NOTEBOOK
Percussionist(IRE) will now continue his carreer in Scandinavia.

1957 BRIGHTON (L-H)
Tuesday, May 18

OFFICIAL GOING: Good to firm (9.1)
Wind: virtualy nil Weather: overcast

2196 HARDINGS BAR AND CATERING H'CAP 5f 59y
2:20 (2:20) (Class 5) (0-70,69) 4-Y-O+ **£2,849** (£847; £423; £211) **Stalls** Low

Form RPR

2-10 **1** **Ajjaadd (USA)**[74] 806 4-9-2 **67**..................... GeorgeBaker 8 75
(T E Powell) *stdd s: racd wl off the pce in last trio: hdwy 1/2-way: rdn to chse ldng pair over 1f out: kpt on wl u.p to ld towards fin* **4/1**[2]

440- **2** *1/2* **Multahab**[193] 7280 11-8-4 **58**.....................(t) MarcHalford(3) 1 64
(M Wigham) *led and set gd gallop: grad crossed over to r on stands' rail in st: rdn clr wl over 1f out: hdd towards fin* **10/1**

2540 **3** *2 1/4* **Boho Chic**[23] 1547 4-8-6 **62**.....................(p) MatthewDavies(5) 2 60
(George Baker) *chsd clr ldng pair: rdn and effrt 1/2-way: chsd ldr over 1f out tl ins fnl f: wknd fnl 100yds* **10/3**[1]

0200 **4** *3/4* **Lucky Leigh**[4] 2087 4-9-3 **68**.....................(v) TedDurcan 6 63
(M R Channon) *s.i.s: bhd: rdn and no prog 2f out: plugged on u.p fnl f: nvr trbld ldrs* **5/1**[3]

4145 **5** *nk* **Sherjawy (IRE)**[8] 1963 6-9-4 **69**..................... SamHitchcott 7 63
(Miss Z C Davison) *sn pushed along and struggling to go pce in midfield: no prog u.p 2f out: plugged on ins fnl f* **4/1**[2]

040- **6** *3* **Mambo Spirit (IRE)**[160] 7682 6-9-1 **66**..................... MickyFenton 5 50
(Stef Higgins) *rrd as stalls opened and slowly away: bhd: effrt u.p ent fnl 2f: no prog: nvr trbld ldrs* **4/1**[2]

4050 **7** *3 3/4* **Slap And Tickle (IRE)**[6] 2021 4-8-4 **58** ow3..................... WilliamCarson(3) 4 28
(M D Squance) *taken down early: w ldr: rdn and struggling ent fnl 2f: wknd qckly over 1f: eased whn wl btn ins fnl f* **25/1**

620- **8** *15* **Gone'N'Dunnett (IRE)**[286] 4668 11-8-4 **55** oh10.....................(p) NickyMackay 3 —
(Mrs C A Dunnett) *taken down early: in midfield early but sn rdn along: dropped to rr over 3f out: lost tch 2f out: eased fnl f* **50/1**

61.88 secs (-0.42) **Going Correction** -0.05s/f (Good) 8 Ran SP% **114.6**
Speed ratings (Par 103): **101,100,96,95,94 90,84,60**
toteswingers:1&2:£10.00, 1&3:£4.90, 2&3:£10.20 CSF £43.00 CT £147.68 TOTE £4.10: £1.10, £3.20, £1.10; EX 40.80 Trifecta £181.70 Part won. Pool: £245.63 - 0.20 winning units..
Owner Katy & Lol Pratt **Bred** Darley **Trained** Reigate, Surrey

FOCUS
Despite the ground officially being good to firm the jockeys decided to adopt the strategy favoured on softer going and raced centre to stands' side. A weak race won by the only likely improver on paper. He ran his best race since he was a 2yo.
Mambo Spirit(IRE) Official explanation: jockey said gelding reared on leaving stalls

2197 WEATHERBYS BETTRENDS.CO.UK MAIDEN STKS 5f 213y
2:50 (2:51) (Class 5) 3-Y-O+ **£2,978** (£886; £442; £221) **Stalls** Low

Form RPR

30-0 **1** **Imperial Delight**[18] 1663 3-9-1 75..................... DaneO'Neill 6 80
(H Candy) *in tch in midfield: rdn and effrt ent fnl 2f: led 1f out: r.o strly and drew clr ins fnl f: eased towards fin* **10/3**[2]

2-32 **2** *3 1/4* **Frequency**[31] 1402 3-9-1 72..................... GeorgeBaker 3 70
(E A L Dunlop) *in tch: effrt and rdn 2f out: chsd wnr but edgd lft u.p ins fnl f: no prog and no ch w wnr fnl 100yds* **5/2**[1]

36-5 **3** *nk* **Gundaroo**[19] 1640 3-8-10 67..................... TedDurcan 5 64
(J L Dunlop) *stdd s: hld up in rr: hdwy and looking for run wl over 1f out: swtchd lft ent fnl f: kpt on u.p to press for 3rd towards fin: no ch w wnr* **13/2**[3]

4 *2* **Sammuramat (IRE)**[238] 6194 3-8-10 68..................... JerryO'Dwyer 1 58
(M G Quinlan) *in tch whn hmpd and lost pl after 1f: bhd after: hdwy and edging out rt over 1f out: kpt on to go 4th wl ins fnl f: nvr trbld ldrs* **12/1**

6 **5** *1 1/2* **Music Lover**[20] 1622 3-9-1 0..................... DavidProbert 11 58
(R A Harris) *sn prom: led after 1f: rdn ent fnl 2f: hdd 1f out: wknd qckly ins fnl f* **22/1**

2-04 **6** *6* **Itwasonlyakiss (IRE)**[19] 1639 3-8-10 66 .... JimmyQuinn 4 34
(J W Hills) *racd in last trio: pushed along and effrt ent fnl 2f: hld hd awkwardly and no prog over 1f out: wl btn fnl f* **11/1**

24-0 **7** *nk* **Sophie's Beau (USA)**[17] 1694 3-9-1 77 ....(b[1]) NickyMackay 9 40
(B J Meehan) *taken down early and ponied to s: awkward leaving stalls: sn chsng ldrs: wnt 2nd 1/2-way: rdn and ev ch ent fnl 2f: wknd qckly jst over 1f out: wl btn and eased ins fnl f* **10/3**[2]

0-60 **8** *2* **Thumberlina**[7] 2008 4-9-2 40 ....(p) WilliamCarson(3) 2 28
(Mrs C A Dunnett) *in tch in midfield on inner: rdn 2f out: wknd qckly over 1f out: wl btn fnl f* **200/1**

0 **9** *6* **Trader Way (GR)**[16] 1731 3-9-1 0 .... LiamKeniry 10 12
(P R Chamings) *racd keenly: led for 1f: chsd ldr tl 1/2-way: sn rdn and struggling: wl bhd and eased ins fnl f* **66/1**

0-0 **10** *8* **Spirit Of Normandy**[54] 980 3-8-10 0 .... KirstyMilczarek 8 —
(R Ingram) *taken down early: t.k.h: chsd ldrs for 2f: sn lost pl: wl bhd fnl 2f: eased ins fnl f: t.o* **80/1**

1m 10.04s (-0.16) **Going Correction** -0.05s/f (Good)
WFA 3 from 4yo 9lb **10** Ran SP% **111.7**
Speed ratings (Par 103): **99,94,94,91,89 81,81,78,70,59**
toteswingers:1&2:£3.60, 1&3:£4.60, 2&3:£2.90 CSF £11.33 TOTE £4.90: £1.90, £1.10, £2.20; EX 12.10 Trifecta £30.80 Pool: £382.59 - 9.19 winning units..
Owner A N Solomons **Bred** Coln Valley Stud **Trained** Kingston Warren, Oxon

FOCUS
Once again the field came centre-course. Bits and pieces of form for this class five maiden and it was won by the gelding with the highest official mark of 75. He may not have had to improve to win this modest race.
Sophie's Beau(USA) Official explanation: jockey said gelding had no more to give

2198 HARDINGS CATERING NO JOB TOO SMALL H'CAP 7f 214y
3:20 (3:20) (Class 6) (0-60,60) 4-Y-O+ **£2,072** (£616; £308; £153) **Stalls** Low

Form RPR

6266 **1** **Musical Script (USA)**[10] 1929 7-8-13 55 ....(b) DaneO'Neill 11 66
(Mouse Hamilton-Fairley) *stdd s: hld up in rr: stl last wl over 2f out: rdn and gd hdwy towards inner over 1f out: led fnl 100yds: sn in command: eased towards fin* **11/1**

3231 **2** *1 ¾* **Eager To Bow (IRE)**[28] 1441 4-9-2 58 .... GeorgeBaker 13 65+
(P R Chamings) *in tch in midfield: rdn and effrt 2f out: swtchd rt ins fnl f: kpt on wl fnl 100yds to go 2nd wl ins fnl f* **5/2**[1]

0601 **3** *nk* **Yourgolftravel Com**[19] 1633 5-9-2 58 .... StephenCraine 9 64
(M Wigham) *stdd s: hld up in rr: pushed along and hdwy ent fnl 2f: drvn and kpt on fnl f: wnt 3rd towards fin* **8/1**[3]

2350 **4** *1* **Yakama (IRE)**[19] 1633 5-8-9 51 ....(v) DavidProbert 14 55
(Mrs C A Dunnett) *chsd ldrs: rdn to ld over 2f out: hrd drvn over 1f out: kpt on wl tl hdd fnl 100yds: wknd towards fin* **14/1**

4440 **5** *½* **Inquisitress**[89] 591 6-8-4 46 .... NeilChalmers 16 49
(J J Bridger) *t.k.h: hld up in rr: rdn and hdwy towards stands' rail jst over 1f out: kpt on wl ins fnl f: nt rch ldrs* **50/1**

040- **6** *¾* **Fire King**[170] 7587 4-8-11 53 .... PatCosgrave 10 54
(J R Boyle) *chsd ldrs: effrt to chse ldr ent fnl 2f: drvn and ev ch wl over 1f out tl wknd ins fnl f* **5/1**[2]

60-0 **7** *2* **Some Time Good (IRE)**[10] 1922 4-8-13 55 ....(p) StevieDonohoe 5 52
(Miss J S Davis) *w ldrs: ev ch and rdn over 2f out: wknd u.p over 1f out* **50/1**

0460 **8** *1 ½* **Prince Valentine**[28] 1441 9-8-0 49 ....(p) HarryBentley(7) 8 42
(G L Moore) *in tch in midfield: rdn and effrt whn n.m.r 2f out: no prog and wl hld after* **33/1**

2400 **9** *¾* **Top Flight Splash**[28] 1441 4-8-3 48 ....(v) AndrewHeffernan(3) 3 39
(P D Evans) *chsd ldrs: nt qckning u.p whn sltly hmpd 2f out: wknd over 1f out* **16/1**

5-00 **10** *2 ¾* **Greystoke Prince**[127] 124 5-8-4 49 oh1 ow3 .... WilliamCarson(3) 7 34
(M D Squance) *a towards rr: rdn and no prog over 2f out: nvr a factor* **16/1**

-000 **11** *1* **Enlist**[38] 1226 6-9-1 57 .... MickyFenton 6 40
(B G Powell) *a towards rr: racing awkwardly and struggling wl over 3f out: bhd fnl 2f* **50/1**

34-0 **12** *2 ¼* **Dancer's Legacy**[19] 1636 5-8-10 52 ....(tp) TedDurcan 1 30
(J R Boyle) *chsd ldr: ev ch and rdn over 2f out: edgd lft 2f out: sn btn: eased ins fnl frlong* **20/1**

00-0 **13** *2 ½* **Lady Florence**[34] 1293 5-9-3 59 ....(b[1]) LiamKeniry 4 31
(A B Coogan) *led tl hdd and rdn over 2f out: sn wknd: wl btn and eased ins fnl f* **10/1**

-000 **14** *5* **Under Fire (IRE)**[15] 1771 7-8-7 49 .... KirstyMilczarek 12 9
(A W Carroll) *chsd ldrs tl wknd qckly ent fnl 2f: wl bhd and eased ins fnl f* **20/1**

0100 **15** *3 ¼* **Elusive Ronnie (IRE)**[34] 1300 4-8-12 54 ....(p) JimmyQuinn 15 7
(R A Teal) *a in rr: rdn and no rspnse over 3f out: eased ins fnl f* **33/1**

0-30 **16** *10* **Jazacosta (USA)**[34] 1304 4-9-4 60 .... IanMongan 2 —
(Miss Jo Crowley) *a towards rr: rdn and btn over 2f out: wl bhd and eased ins fnl f: t.o: burst blood vessel* **11/1**

1m 35.27s (-0.73) **Going Correction** -0.05s/f (Good) **16** Ran SP% **121.8**
Speed ratings (Par 101): **101,99,98,97,97 96,94,93,92,89 88,86,83,78,75 65**
toteswingers:1&2:£5.80, 1&3:£16.00, 2&3:£9.10 CSF £35.87 CT £241.13 TOTE £19.90: £4.20, £1.02, £2.30, £4.60; EX 49.80 Trifecta £188.00 Part won. Pool: £254.18 - 0.10 winning units..
Owner The Composers **Bred** Juddmonte Farms Inc **Trained** Bramshill, Hants

FOCUS
A competitive handicap. It was well run and the form looks sound.
Under Fire(IRE) Official explanation: jockey said gelding had a breathing problem
Jazacosta(USA) Official explanation: jockey said gelding bled from the nose

2199 WEATHERBYS BLOODSTOCK INSURANCE H'CAP 1m 3f 196y
3:50 (3:51) (Class 5) (0-70,70) 4-Y-O+ **£2,849** (£847; £423; £211) **Stalls** High

Form RPR

-642 **1** **Inspirina (IRE)**[8] 1961 6-9-0 66 .... TedDurcan 2 74
(R Ford) *mde all: rdn over 1f out: kpt on u.p ins fnl f* **11/8**[1]

06-1 **2** *¾* **Penang Cinta**[15] 1817 7-9-1 70 .... AndrewHeffernan(3) 4 77
(P D Evans) *chsd wnr thrght: rdn and effrt 2f out: drvn to press wnr ins fnl f: one pce and a hld* **2/1**[2]

1416 **3** *3 ½* **Carlton Scroop (FR)**[10] 1916 7-9-3 69 ....(b) JimmyQuinn 1 70
(J Jay) *chsd ldrs: drvn and one pce fr over 1f out* **4/1**[3]

010- **4** *10* **Zaif (IRE)**[178] 7490 7-8-8 60 ....(p) DavidProbert 3 45
(D J S Ffrench Davis) *v.s.a: a pushed along in last pair: lost tch 3f out* **8/1**

05-0 **5** *22* **Robbmaa (FR)**[15] 1759 5-8-4 56 oh11 .... KirstyMilczarek 5 —
(A W Carroll) *chsd ldrs: rdn and dropped to last 4f out: wl bhd fnl 2f: t.o* **40/1**

2m 30.84s (-1.86) **Going Correction** -0.05s/f (Good) **5** Ran SP% **109.0**
Speed ratings (Par 103): **104,103,101,94,79**
CSF £4.29 TOTE £2.60: £1.20, £1.10; EX 4.10.
Owner Miss Gill Quincey **Bred** Mohammad Al-Qatami **Trained** Butterton, Staffs

FOCUS
A weakish race, but it was quite well run and the form is sound.
Robbmaa(FR) Official explanation: jockey said gelding was unsuited by the good to firm ground

2200 LILY FOUNDATION H'CAP 6f 209y
4:20 (4:22) (Class 6) (0-60,60) 3-Y-O **£2,201** (£655; £327; £163) **Stalls** Centre

Form RPR

634- **1** **Rosedale**[203] 7097 3-9-1 57 .... LiamKeniry 4 63
(J A R Toller) *chsd ldrs: wnt 2nd over 2f out: rdn to ld over 1f out: drvn ins fnl f: jst hld on* **17/2**

10-0 **2** *nse* **Dutiful**[31] 1392 3-9-4 60 .... TedDurcan 7 66
(M R Channon) *bhd and struggling to go pce: hdwy u.p over 1f out: chsd wnr jst ins fnl f: r.o wl: jst failed* **15/2**

-556 **3** *3 ¼* **Prince Yarraman (IRE)**[26] 1495 3-8-10 57 .... SophieDoyle(5) 10 54
(J A Osborne) *midfield: rdn over 2f out: hdwy to chse ldrs and edgd lft 1f out: no ex and btn fnl 100yds* **13/2**[3]

0560 **4** *¾* **Singingintherain (IRE)**[7] 2005 3-9-2 58 .... StevieDonohoe 6 53
(R A Mills) *chsd ldr tl over 5f out: styd chsng ldrs: rdn 1/2-way: chsd wnr over 1f out tl ins fnl f: wknd fnl 100yds* **14/1**

0-12 **5** *2 ½* **Decency (IRE)**[19] 1643 3-9-4 60 .... GeorgeBaker 12 48
(E A L Dunlop) *taken down early: hld up in last trio: hdwy 1/2-way: chsd ldrs whn hung lft u.p ent fnl f: wknd fnl 150yds* **7/4**[1]

00-6 **6** *1 ¾* **Ridgeway Sapphire**[15] 1760 3-8-6 48 .... DavidProbert 11 32
(M D I Usher) *a in midfield: rdn over 2f out: plugged on same pce fnl 2f* **10/1**

4-00 **7** *3* **Arnie Guru**[11] 1873 3-9-4 60 .... JimmyQuinn 8 35
(M J Attwater) *sn bhd and pushed along: nvr on terms* **33/1**

-600 **8** *6* **Stay On Track (IRE)**[19] 1643 3-8-13 55 ....(b[1]) PatCosgrave 2 14
(E F Vaughan) *racd freely: sn led: clr 5f out tl hdd and rdn over 1f out: sn btn: wknd fnl f* **28/1**

0-06 **9** *34* **Sparkle Park**[23] 1542 3-8-4 46 ....(b) NickyMackay 5 —
(B J Meehan) *a bhd: lost tch over 2f out: virtually p.u fnl f: t.o* **25/1**

0500 **10** *2 ¾* **The Wonga Coup (IRE)**[22] 1578 3-9-3 59 .... IanMongan 1 —
(P M Phelan) *dwlt: sn rcvrd and chsd ldr over 5f out tl over 2f out: sn dropped out: wl bhd and virtually p.u fnl f* **5/1**[2]

1m 23.11s (0.01) **Going Correction** -0.05s/f (Good) **10** Ran SP% **114.6**
Speed ratings (Par 97): **97,96,93,92,89 87,84,77,38,35**
toteswingers:1&2:£5.00, 1&3:£7.20, 2&3:£6.40 CSF £67.85 CT £451.83 TOTE £6.50: £1.80, £1.90, £1.70; EX 38.20 TRIFECTA Not won..Show Willing was withdrawn. Price at time of withdrawal 16/1. Rule 4 does not apply
Owner Alan Gibson **Bred** Alan Gibson **Trained** Newmarket, Suffolk

FOCUS
Moderate form, with the favourite disappointing. The pace was sound though.
Sparkle Park Official explanation: jockey said filly hung left
The Wonga Coup(IRE) Official explanation: jockey said gelding was unsuited by the track

2201 RACING EXCELLENCE "HANDS AND HEELS" APPRENTICE SERIES H'CAP 1m 1f 209y
4:50 (4:53) (Class 6) (0-60,60) 4-Y-O+ **£2,201** (£655; £327; £163) **Stalls** High

Form RPR

-421 **1** **Four Kicks (IRE)**[10] 1922 4-8-12 56 .... RyanPowell(3) 1 62+
(J S Moore) *chsd ldr tl led over 4f out: mde rest: kpt on wl fr over 1f out* **5/4**[1]

4-40 **2** *1 ¼* **The Dial House**[114] 282 4-9-5 60 .... HollyHall 6 63
(J A Osborne) *t.k.h: chsd ldrs over 7f out: chsd wnr over 2f out: nudged along and kpt on same pce fnl f* **10/3**[2]

2405 **3** *shd* **Alfredtheordinary**[10] 1922 5-9-2 57 .... BarryAdams 5 59
(M R Channon) *hld up in tch: hdwy and rdn to dispute 2nd wl over 1f out: styd on same pce fnl f* **11/2**

-306 **4** *3 ¼* **Rosy Dawn**[19] 1636 5-8-5 46 oh1 .... MatthewCosham 4 42
(J J Bridger) *led tl over 4f out: rdn and outpcd over 2f out: one pce and n.d fr over 1f out* **12/1**

0003 **5** *1 ½* **Maximus Aurelius (IRE)**[7] 2012 5-9-1 56 ....(t) AdamBeschizza 3 49
(J Jay) *in tch: rdn and effrt over 2f out: wknd ent fnl f* **9/2**[3]

2m 4.11s (0.51) **Going Correction** -0.05s/f (Good) **5** Ran SP% **108.8**
Speed ratings (Par 101): **95,94,93,91,90**
CSF £5.47 TOTE £1.90: £1.10, £1.70; EX 6.80 Place 6 £16.67; Place 5 £8.07.
Owner James Clements **Bred** Fortview Stud **Trained** Upper Lambourn, Berks
■ Stewards' Enquiry : Barry Adams seven-day ban: failed to ride out for 2nd (Jun 1-7)

FOCUS
A moderate apprentice handicap. Muddling form, and doubtful whether the winner had to improve.
T/Plt: £48.50. Pool £70,904.42 - 1,065.04 winning tickets T/Qpdt: £20.80. Pool £3.798.48 - 134.96 winning tickets SP

CARLISLE (R-H)
Tuesday, May 18

OFFICIAL GOING: Good to firm
Wind: Breezy, half against Weather: Sunny, fine

2202 JOOLS HOLLAND IN CONCERT 3RD JULY MAIDEN AUCTION STKS 5f
6:30 (6:31) (Class 5) 2-Y-O **£2,729** (£806; £403) **Stalls** High

Form RPR

03 **1** **Choose Wisely (IRE)**[14] 1800 2-8-11 0 .... TonyHamilton 3 84+
(K A Ryan) *mde all: rdn and edgd rt fnl f: kpt on strly* **5/1**[3]

4 **2** *2* **Electric Waves (IRE)**[22] 1577 2-8-8 0 .... RichardMullen 6 74
(E S McMahon) *cl up: ev ch 1/2-way: edgd rt and kpt on same pce fnl f* **4/5**[1]

3 *4 ½* **Hayley Cropper** 2-8-6 0 .... AdrianNicholls 7 56+
(D Nicholls) *in tch: drvn thrght: hdwy to chse clr ldrs over 1f out: no imp* **16/1**

4 **4** *4 ½* **Peppercorn Rent (IRE)**[48] 1066 2-8-6 0 .... DavidAllan 4 40
(T D Easterby) *cl up: drvn and outpcd 2f out: n.d after* **10/1**

00 **5** *1 ¼* **Losing Draw (IRE)**[24] 1527 2-8-5 0 .... PJMcDonald 5 34
(P T Midgley) *t.k.h: trckd ldrs tl rdn and wknd wl over 1f out* **80/1**

6 *11* **Mercy Street** 2-8-12 0 .... AndrewElliott 2 —
(N Tinkler) *s.i.s: outpcd and bhd: no ch fr 1/2-way* **40/1**

7 *3* **Solo Whisper (IRE)** 2-9-3 0 .... FrederikTylicki 9 —
(J Howard Johnson) *dwlt: sn bhd and pushed along: nvr on terms* **9/2**[2]

8 *6* **Aprication (IRE)** 2-8-11 0 .... PhillipMakin 1 —
(J R Weymes) *dwlt: sn rdn in rr: nvr on terms* **40/1**

9 *9* **No Explanation** 2-8-10 0 .... LeeVickers 8 —
(D W Thompson) *dwlt: bhd and outpcd: hung rt and no ch fr 1/2-way*
100/1

61.01 secs (0.21) **Going Correction** -0.05s/f (Good) 9 Ran SP% **112.5**
Speed ratings (Par 93): **96,92,85,78,76 58,54,44,30**
toteswingers:1&2:£1.20, 1&3:£8.80, 2&3:£3.30 CSF £9.06 TOTE £5.80: £1.10, £1.02, £8.90; EX 11.50.
Owner D W Barker **Bred** Tom Kelly **Trained** Hambleton, N Yorks

FOCUS
On a bright and sunny evening the ground had dried out slightly and was reckoned 'very quick, not much in the way of good'. The stalls were placed on the far side but the whole field crossed to the quicker ground on the stands' side.

NOTEBOOK
Choose Wisely(IRE), who stepped up on his debut effort when a close third at Catterick, showed further improvement. Grabbing the stands' side rail he shrugged off the favourite's challenge and in the end won going away. He looks ideal nursery material but after spread eagling this field he can hardly expect a lenient mark. (op 9-2 tchd 11-2)
Electric Waves(IRE), fourth first time in a Windsor maiden that has worked out exceptionally well, was on her toes beforehand. She was soon upsides the winner but was the first to come under serious pressure and in the end was very much second best. The quick ground might not have been in her favour and she can surely go one better. (op 8-11 tchd 5-6)
Hayley Cropper, soon driven along, kept on to finish clear third best on her debut. This will have taught her something but she looks to be crying out for a step up to 6f already. (op 11-1)
Peppercorn Rent(IRE), on her toes beforehand, had shown ability on her debut on the all-weather. She showed plenty of early toe but looked another who will appreciate less quick ground. (op 14-1 tchd 16-1)
Losing Draw(IRE), well beaten on her first two starts, shaped a fraction better but may have to descend to claimers if she is to make her mark. (op 100-1)
Solo Whisper(IRE), a well backed newcomer, threw away his chance at the start but it was disappointing that he was unable to make up any of the leeway. (op 13-2 tchd 7-1)

2203 CARLISLE-RACES.CO.UK CLAIMING STKS 5f 193y
7:00 (7:02) (Class 6) 3-Y-O **£2,047** (£604; £302) **Stalls** High

Form RPR
3-00 **1** **Newbury Street**[22] [1584] 3-8-13 67 .... PaulHanagan 4 66
(R A Fahey) *hld up: pushed along 1/2-way: swtchd rt and hdwy 2f out: led ins fnl f: hld on wl* **4/1**[2]
0-0 **2** *nk* **Fleetwoodsands (IRE)**[43] [1114] 3-8-7 0 .... DavidAllan 6 59
(Miss Tracy Waggott) *dwlt: bhd: hdwy on outside 2f out: chsd wnr ins fnl f: r.o: jst hld* **200/1**
144- **3** *¾* **Pure Nostalgia (IRE)**[224] [6557] 3-8-12 61 .... FrederikTylicki 5 62
(J Howard Johnson) *led: rdn over 2f out: hdd ins fnl f: kpt on u.p towards fin* **7/2**[1]
6-03 **4** *1 ¾* **Angel Of Fashion (IRE)**[19] [1651] 3-9-2 72 .... AdrianNicholls 9 60
(D Nicholls) *trckd ldrs: effrt and ev ch over 1f out to ins fnl f: kpt on same pce* **9/2**[3]
1600 **5** *1 ¼* **Eight Hours**[8] [1968] 3-8-7 66 .... TonyHamilton 2 47
(R A Fahey) *prom: effrt over 2f out: edgd rt: kpt on same pce fnl f* **11/1**
05 **6** *nk* **Lucky Belle (IRE)**[14] [1809] 3-8-12 0 .... PhillipMakin 1 51
(M Dods) *hld up in tch: pushed along over 2f out: edgd rt over 1f out: no imp* **22/1**
2242 **7** *1 ¾* **Clear Ice (IRE)**[7] [1994] 3-8-4 62 ....(v) BillyCray(5) 7 42
(R C Guest) *prom tl edgd rt and outpcd fr 2f out* **9/2**[3]
-651 **8** *9* **Petrocelli**[7] [1987] 3-8-12 72 ....(b) JamesDoyle 3 17
(A J McCabe) *hld up in tch: shkn up 2f out: sn btn* **5/1**
5245 **9** *2 ¾* **Tealing**[25] [1505] 3-8-9 60 ....(e) PJMcDonald 8 5
(R C Guest) *cl up tl rdn and lost pl over 2f out: sn wknd* **22/1**

1m 13.89s (0.19) **Going Correction** -0.05s/f (Good) 9 Ran SP% **112.8**
Speed ratings (Par 97): **96,95,94,92,90 90,87,75,72**
toteswingers:1&2:£21.00, 1&3:£2.60, 2&3:£32.80 CSF £620.82 TOTE £3.70: £1.10, £46.10, £1.60; EX 446.30.Fleetwoodsands was claimed by Ollie Pears for £5,000
Owner J J Staunton **Bred** R A Fahey **Trained** Musley Bank, N Yorks

FOCUS
They all came towards the stands' side and the first two home were the last two in the early stages and both made their effort on the outside of the main body of the field. Modest claiming form.

2204 STARS OF X-FACTOR CONCERT 25TH JULY H'CAP 1m 1f 61y
7:30 (7:30) (Class 4) (0-80,85) 4-Y-O+ **£4,209** (£1,252; £625; £312) **Stalls** High

Form RPR
4-03 **1** **Templetuohy Max (IRE)**[10] [1926] 5-8-7 68 ....(v) GrahamGibbons 8 80
(J D Bethell) *cl up: wnt 2nd over 2f out: drvn to ld over 1f out: styd on strly fnl f* **6/1**[2]
0-51 **2** *3 ½* **Celtic Change (IRE)**[7] [1990] 6-9-10 85 6ex ....(bt) PhillipMakin 7 89
(M Dods) *led: rdn and hdd over 1f out: kpt on same pce fnl f* **11/4**[1]
-122 **3** *1 ¼* **Blue Spinnaker (IRE)**[34] [1296] 11-8-4 70 .... JamesSullivan(5) 4 72
(M W Easterby) *hld up: hdwy on outside 2f out: kpt on fnl f: nt rch first two* **7/1**[3]
0330 **4** *1 ¼* **Ella Woodcock (IRE)**[24] [1513] 6-8-6 67 .... DavidAllan 10 66
(E J Alston) *hld up in tch: effrt and hdwy over 2f out: edgd rt and no imp over 1f out* **8/1**
6300 **5** *6* **Wovoka (IRE)**[10] [1926] 7-8-7 68 ....(p) TonyHamilton 2 54
(K A Ryan) *hld up in tch: rdn over 2f out: wknd over 1f out* **8/1**
24-1 **6** *2 ¼* **High Office**[39] [1203] 4-9-0 75 .... PaulHanagan 6 56
(R A Fahey) *chsd ldr tl outpcd over 2f out: sn btn* **11/4**[1]
06-0 **7** *6* **Gallego**[15] [1779] 8-8-2 66 .... KellyHarrison(3) 3 33
(R J Price) *dwlt: hld up: rdn and edgd rt over 2f out: nvr on terms* **18/1**
0-60 **8** *1* **Rising Kheleyf (IRE)**[17] [1707] 4-8-8 69 .... PJMcDonald 1 34
(G A Swinbank) *prom tl rdn and wknd over 2f out* **16/1**

1m 55.91s (-1.69) **Going Correction** -0.05s/f (Good) 8 Ran SP% **113.5**
Speed ratings (Par 105): **105,101,100,99,94 92,87,86**
toteswingers:1&2:£3.00, 1&3:£4.60, 2&3:£6.60 CSF £22.53 CT £117.28 TOTE £8.80: £4.60, £1.10, £1.60; EX 19.30.
Owner Craig Monty **Bred** Jim Shanahan **Trained** Middleham Moor, N Yorks

FOCUS
A competitive 66-85 handicap run at a strong pace and they again all came stands' side. The front pair were always 1-2 and the winner is rated back to his best.

2205 BETFAIR H'CAP 6f 192y
8:00 (8:00) (Class 4) (0-85,85) 4-Y-O+ **£4,695** (£1,397; £698; £348) **Stalls** High

Form RPR
3010 **1** **Game Lad**[4] [2086] 8-8-10 77 ....(tp) DavidAllan 1 84
(T D Easterby) *hld up in tch: effrt and hdwy over 1f out: led ins fnl f: drvn out* **7/1**
-004 **2** *½* **Rio Cobolo (IRE)**[8] [1967] 4-7-13 71 oh2 ....(v) JamesSullivan(5) 8 77
(Paul Green) *hld up in tch: hdwy 2f out: ev ch ins fnl f: kpt on: hld nr fin* **9/1**
0503 **3** *½* **My Gacho (IRE)**[8] [1962] 8-9-3 84 ....(v) J-PGuillambert 5 89+
(M Johnston) *w ldr: clr of rest 1/2-way: rdn and led over 2f out: hdd ins fnl f: kpt on same pce* **7/1**
121- **4** *1 ½* **Ancient Cross**[213] [6846] 6-8-10 77 ....(bt) GrahamGibbons 4 78
(M W Easterby) *hld up: hdwy 2f out: rdn and kpt on same pce last 100yds* **7/2**[2]
0-00 **5** *2 ½* **Summer Dancer (IRE)**[15] [1752] 6-8-11 78 .... PhillipMakin 2 72
(P T Midgley) *t.k.h: hld up: rdn over 2f out: hdwy over 1f out: nvr rchd ldrs* **28/1**
4406 **6** *1 ¾* **Ra Junior (USA)**[17] [1707] 4-8-11 81 .... MichaelGeran(3) 6 70
(D Nicholls) *prom: drvn and outpcd over 2f out: n.d after* **11/2**[3]
352 **7** *2 ¾* **Nightjar (USA)**[17] [1707] 5-9-3 84 .... PaulHanagan 7 66
(K A Ryan) *chsd ldrs: drvn and hung rt over 2f out: sn btn* **3/1**[1]
-045 **8** *22* **Joseph Henry**[11] [1857] 8-9-4 85 .... AdrianNicholls 3 7
(D Nicholls) *set decent gallop: hdd over 2f out: sn wknd: eased whn no ch fnl f* **6/1**

1m 27.11s (0.01) **Going Correction** -0.05s/f (Good) 8 Ran SP% **115.3**
Speed ratings (Par 105): **97,96,95,94,91 89,86,61**
toteswingers:1&2:£20.20, 1&3:£8.10, 2&3:£18.60 CSF £67.69 CT £462.36 TOTE £15.80: £5.70, £5.30, £4.00; EX 86.80.
Owner T D Easterby **Bred** M H Easterby **Trained** Great Habton, N Yorks
■ Stewards' Enquiry : J-P Guillambert caution: used whip with excessive freauency

FOCUS
A competitive 71-85 handicap run at a breakneck pace and they again came stands' side. A return to form from the winner, with the third the best guide.
Game Lad Official explanation: trainer's rep said she had no explanation for the apparent improvement of form

2206 CHAMPION'S 60:60 HERE 24TH MAY H'CAP 5f 193y
8:30 (8:31) (Class 5) (0-75,72) 4-Y-O+ **£2,729** (£806; £403) **Stalls** High

Form RPR
1500 **1** **Wyatt Earp (IRE)**[10] [1924] 9-9-2 70 ....(p) AndrewMullen 7 81
(P Salmon) *mde all: rdn and edgd lft over 1f out: kpt on strly fnl f* **18/1**
1200 **2** *2 ¼* **Cornus**[3] [2113] 8-8-13 67 ....(be) JamesDoyle 10 71
(A J McCabe) *midfield: effrt and hdwy over 1f out: kpt on to go 2nd nr fin: nt rch wnr* **10/1**
00 **3** *nk* **Dickie Le Davoir**[1] [2184] 6-8-7 66 ....(v) BillyCray(5) 13 69
(R C Guest) *hld up: hdwy on outside 2f out: chsd wnr ins fnl f: kpt on same pce: lost 2nd towards fin* **16/1**
0202 **4** *hd* **Avontuur (FR)**[14] [1802] 8-8-11 70 ....(b) DeanHeslop(5) 2 72
(Mrs R A Carr) *sn drvn and cl up: ev ch over 2f out: kpt on u.p ins fnl f* **7/2**[1]
06-6 **5** *2* **Daring Dream (GER)**[18] [1673] 5-8-6 63 .... KellyHarrison(3) 5 59+
(J S Goldie) *bhd tl hdwy over 1f out: kpt on fnl f: nrst fin* **7/1**
-235 **6** *½* **Lucky Dan (IRE)**[7] [1988] 4-9-2 70 .... PaulMulrennan 3 64
(Paul Green) *chsd ldrs: drvn over 2f out: edgd rt and no ex over 1f out* **11/2**[2]
-006 **7** *hd* **Bid For Gold**[11] [1869] 6-8-12 66 .... TonyHamilton 8 60
(Jedd O'Keeffe) *racd wd in midfield: rdn over 2f out: no ex over 1f out* **6/1**[3]
0424 **8** *2 ½* **Guest Connections**[8] [1965] 7-8-9 63 ....(v) AdrianNicholls 1 49
(D Nicholls) *sn drvn and outpcd: shortlived effrt 2f out: sn no imp* **8/1**
00-4 **9** *2 ¼* **Hansomis (IRE)**[22] [1575] 6-8-6 60 .... PaulHanagan 11 38
(B Mactaggart) *cl up: rdn over 2f out: wknd over 1f out* **9/1**
10-4 **10** *6* **Botham (USA)**[16] [1717] 6-8-10 64 .... DanielTudhope 14 23
(J S Goldie) *hld up: pushed along over 2f out: nvr on terms* **12/1**
0-30 **11** *4 ½* **Grand Stitch (USA)**[14] [1804] 4-9-4 72 .... DavidNolan 4 17
(D Carroll) *in tch tl rdn and wknd over 2f out* **20/1**

1m 13.39s (-0.31) **Going Correction** -0.05s/f (Good) 11 Ran SP% **118.2**
Speed ratings (Par 103): **100,97,96,96,93 93,92,89,86,78 72**
toteswingers:1&2:£19.70, 1&3:£30.40, 2&3:£61.90 CSF £187.65 CT £2939.57 TOTE £32.00: £8.50, £2.30, £6.90; EX 207.90.
Owner Los Bandidos Racing **Bred** J W Parker And Keith Wills **Trained** Kirk Deighton, West Yorks
■ Stewards' Enquiry : Andrew Mullen one-day ban: careless riding (Jun 1)

FOCUS
Five withdrawals, all but one on account of the ground, in this modest 60-72 sprint handicap and once again they all made their way to the stands' side. The winner made all against the rail and the form is rated around the runner-up.
Wyatt Earp(IRE) Official explanation: trainer had no explanation for the apparent improvement in form

2207 BJORN AGAIN LIVE LADIES NIGHT 2ND AUGUST H'CAP 7f 200y
9:00 (9:00) (Class 6) (0-60,60) 4-Y-O+ **£2,047** (£604; £302) **Stalls** High

Form RPR
-010 **1** **Cheers For Thea (IRE)**[29] [1426] 5-9-4 60 ....(bt) DavidAllan 16 76+
(T D Easterby) *midfield: smooth hdwy to ld over 1f out: pushed clr fnl f* **3/1**[1]
50-3 **2** *3 ¾* **Desert Hunter (IRE)**[14] [1813] 7-8-11 53 .... FrederikTylicki 15 59
(Micky Hammond) *t.k.h: prom: effrt and ev ch 2f out: kpt on fnl f: nt pce of wnr* **13/2**[3]
3-05 **3** *nse* **Dean Iarracht (IRE)**[11] [1887] 4-8-7 52 ....(p) KellyHarrison(3) 9 58
(Miss Tracy Waggott) *w ldr: led fr over 2f tl over 1f out: kpt on u.p fnl f* **14/1**
5-52 **4** *2 ¼* **George Adamson (IRE)**[16] [1717] 4-9-0 56 .... PJMcDonald 2 57
(G A Swinbank) *in tch: rdn along 3f out: kpt on same pce appr fnl f* **13/2**[3]
-065 **5** *1 ½* **Call Of Duty (IRE)**[8] [1983] 5-8-9 51 .... DuranFentiman 17 48
(Mrs Dianne Sayer) *bhd: hdwy on outside over 2f out: no imp fnl f* **16/1**
0000 **6** *shd* **Redwater River**[10] [1928] 6-8-4 51 ....(b) DeanHeslop(5) 8 48
(Mrs R A Carr) *sn cl up: rdn over 3f out: one pce fr 2f out* **33/1**
-006 **7** *1 ¾* **Prime Circle**[20] [1631] 4-9-3 59 .... FrannyNorton 13 52
(A D Brown) *in tch: drvn along 3f out: no ex fr 2f out* **16/1**
5-33 **8** *hd* **Fathey (IRE)**[14] [1812] 4-8-13 58 .... BarryMcHugh(3) 1 51
(C Smith) *towards rr: drvn and outpcd over 3f out: rallied over 1f out: no imp* **13/2**[3]
00-4 **9** *5* **Raise All In (IRE)**[8] [1958] 4-8-2 49 ....(p) IanBrennan(5) 11 30
(I W McInnes) *dwlt: bhd: drvn over 3f out: nvr on terms* **40/1**
0-06 **10** *1* **Eyes Like A Hawk (IRE)**[14] [1813] 4-8-8 50 .... AndrewElliott 4 29
(Jedd O'Keeffe) *bhd: struggling over 3f out: sn btn* **33/1**
-004 **11** *nk* **Ask Dan (IRE)**[10] [1928] 4-8-11 53 ....(p) PhillipMakin 14 31
(M Dods) *led at decent gallop: hdd over 2f out: wknd over 1f out* **5/1**[2]
0-00 **12** *3 ¾* **Final Salute**[10] [1924] 4-9-4 60 .... PaulMulrennan 5 29
(B Smart) *bhd: drvn over 3f out: nvr on terms* **25/1**

513- **13** *8* **Social Rhythm**[199] 7173 6-8-12 **59**........................ MichaelO'Connell(5) 7 10
(A C Whillans) *missed break: bhd: sme hdwy wl over 2f out: sn rdn and wknd* **12/1**

1m 41.1s (1.10) **Going Correction** -0.05s/f (Good) 13 Ran SP% **120.0**
Speed ratings (Par 101): **92,88,88,85,84 84,82,82,77,76 76,72,64**
toteswingers:1&2:£7.50, 1&3:£40.00, 2&3:£19.30 CSF £21.33 CT £242.17 TOTE £4.30: £1.40, £1.90, £8.90; EX 25.80 Place 6 £645.54; Place 5 £487.71.
Owner Ron George **Bred** Crone Stud Farms Ltd **Trained** Great Habton, N Yorks

FOCUS
A modest 49-60 handicap run at a sound pace and, as in the previous five races, they came wide and raced towards the stands' side. Straightforward form.
Final Salute Official explanation: jockey said gelding hung right
T/Plt: £1,658.70. Pool £79,076.77 - 34.80 winning tickets T/Qpdt: £710.40. Pool £5,856.10 - 6.10 winning tickets RY

1667 MUSSELBURGH (R-H)
Tuesday, May 18

OFFICIAL GOING: Good to firm (7.2)
Wind: Light across Weather: Sunny and dry

2208 SCOTTISH RACING YOUR BETTER BET (S) STKS — 1m 1f
2:10 (2:10) (Class 6) 3-Y-O+ **£1,942** (£578; £288; £144) **Stalls** High

Form RPR

1111 **1** **Fremen (USA)**[12] 1839 10-9-9 80.................................. AdrianNicholls 5 74
(D Nicholls) *sn trcking ldr: hdwy 3f out: cl up 2f out: rdn to ld ent fnl f: sn drvn and kpt on towards fin* **8/13[1]**

06-0 **2** *¾* **Liberty Trail (IRE)**[18] 1672 4-9-4 71.................................. PhillipMakin 1 67
(N Wilson) *led: jinked lft after 1f: pushed along 3f out: rdn and jnd 2f out: drvn and hdd ent fnl f: rallied u.p and ev ch tl no ex last 50yds* **12/1**

100- **3** *5* **Joinedupwriting**[288] 4597 5-9-4 62.................................. TonyHamilton 3 57
(R M Whitaker) *trckd ldng pair: hdwy 3f out: rdn along 2f out: drvn and edgd rt over 1f out: sn one pce* **11/1[3]**

00-4 **4** *hd* **Rowan Lodge (IRE)**[34] 1293 8-9-1 62.....................(b) BarryMcHugh(3) 2 56
(Ollie Pears) *hld up in tch: effrt wl over 2f out and sn pushed along: rdn and n.m.r wl over 1f out: swtchd lft and drvn ent fnl f: kpt on same pce* **7/2[2]**

-060 **5** *1 ½* **Agricultural**[22] 1576 4-9-4 51.................................. PJMcDonald 7 53
(Mrs L B Normile) *hld up in rr: sme hdwy on outer wl over 2f out: sn rdn and no imp fr over 1f out* **100/1**

0-0 **6** *3 ¼* **Catcher Of Dreams (IRE)**[16] 1717 4-9-4 48.............(t) AndrewMullen 6 46
(A G Foster) *chsd ldrs on inner: rdn along wl over 2f out: drvn wl over 1f out and sn wknd* **100/1**

7 *7* **Takween (IRE)**[162] 1657 5-9-4 0.................................. FrederikTylicki 8 31
(J Howard Johnson) *hld up in rr: effrt 3f out: sn rdn along and nvr a factor* **12/1**

1m 53.68s (-0.22) **Going Correction** -0.375s/f (Firm) 7 Ran SP% **109.8**
Speed ratings (Par 101): **89,88,83,83,82 79,73**
toteswingers:1&2:£3.50, 1&3:£1.80, 2&3:£5.40 CSF £8.77 TOTE £1.50: £1.50, £4.20; EX 7.22.There was no bid for the winner
Owner Middleham Park Racing XXXV C King A Seed **Bred** Flaxman Holdings Ltd **Trained** Sessay, N Yorks

FOCUS
A very uncompetitive claimer in which only two counted according to the market. The pace was very moderate and the order hardly changed throughout the contest. It is doubtful if the first two were at their best.

2209 RACING UK THE UK'S BEST RACECOURSES LIVE H'CAP — 7f 30y
2:40 (2:41) (Class 6) (0-60,58) 3-Y-O **£1,942** (£578; £288; £144) **Stalls** High

Form RPR

043- **1** **Timeless Elegance (IRE)**[230] 6378 3-9-4 58............ FrederikTylicki 11 79
(J Howard Johnson) *mde all: rdn clr wl over 1f out: easily* **7/2[1]**

06-2 **2** *8* **Coolella (IRE)**[39] 1201 3-8-13 56.................................. MartinLane(3) 9 55
(J R Weymes) *trckd ldrs: hdwy to chse wnr wl over 2f out and sn rdn: drvn wl over 1f out and kpt on same pce* **6/1[3]**

00-6 **3** *1 ½* **High Resolution**[16] 1718 3-9-3 57.................................(p) PJMcDonald 5 52
(Miss L A Perratt) *hld up: hdwy over 2f out: sn rdn and kpt on ins fnl f* **12/1**

0-00 **4** *1 ½* **Dispol Kabira**[8] 1970 3-8-7 47.................................(p) PatrickMathers 10 38
(D W Thompson) *chsd ldrs on inner: rdn along 3f out: drvn 2f out and kpt on same pce* **40/1**

3523 **5** *4* **Lord's Seat**[27] 1465 3-8-9 49.................................. TonyHamilton 7 29
(A Berry) *chsd wnr: rdn along 3f out: grad wknd* **17/2**

556- **6** *3 ¼* **Dies Solis**[199] 7167 3-9-2 56.................................. PhillipMakin 6 27
(N Wilson) *hld up: towards rr fr 1/2-way* **4/1[2]**

0-55 **7** *1* **Ochilview Warrior (IRE)**[27] 1469 3-8-4 51........... MatthewLawson(7) 2 20
(R Bastiman) *towards rr: hdwy 3f out: rdn and hung rt 2f out: sn wknd* **16/1**

-304 **8** *6* **Sharp Shoes**[15] 1774 3-8-12 55.................................. BarryMcHugh(3) 4 7
(Mrs A Duffield) *chsd ldrs: rdn along wl over 2f out: sn wknd* **15/2**

5055 **9** *1* **Rescent**[27] 1465 3-8-5 45.................................. AndrewElliott 3 —
(Mrs R A Carr) *chsd ldrs on outer: rdn along 1/2-way: sn wknd* **12/1**

00-0 **10** *3* **Stanley Bridge**[18] 1667 3-8-5 45.................................. AndrewMullen 1 —
(A Berry) *stdd s: hld up: a in rr* **80/1**

0-00 **11** *½* **Mr Mohican (IRE)**[8] 1971 3-8-12 52.................................. PaulHanagan 8 —
(Mrs A Duffield) *awkward s and s.i.s: a in rr* **15/2**

1m 27.08s (-1.92) **Going Correction** -0.375s/f (Firm) 11 Ran SP% **115.5**
Speed ratings (Par 97): **103,93,92,90,85 82,81,74,73,69 69**
toteswingers:1&2:£4.10, 1&3:£10.30, 2&3:£10.30 CSF £24.02 CT £230.34 TOTE £5.20: £1.70, £2.10, £3.90; EX 18.30.
Owner Transcend Bloodstock LLP **Bred** Mrs M Togher **Trained** Billy Row, Co Durham

FOCUS
This was another race in which few got into it, though the pace was much more solid than in the opener. The winner made all in a quick time and was full value for the win.

2210 EUROPEAN BREEDERS' FUND MAIDEN STKS — 5f
3:10 (3:10) (Class 5) 2-Y-O **£3,238** (£963; £481; £240) **Stalls** Low

Form RPR

1 **Excel Bolt** 2-9-3 0.................................. PaulHanagan 1 87+
(B Smart) *mde all: rdn and qcknd clr appr fnl f: easily* **1/1[1]**

5 **2** *5* **Crimson Knot (IRE)**[18] 1668 2-8-7 0.................................. MarkCoumbe(5) 5 63
(A Berry) *trckd ldrs: hdwy to chse ldng pair wl over 1f out: sn rdn and kpt on ins fnl f: no ch w wnr* **20/1**

3 *1 ¾* **Dotty Darroch** 2-8-5 0.................................. MatthewLawson(7) 4 57
(R Bastiman) *dwlt and towards rr: hdwy wl over 1f out: sn rdn and kpt on ins fnl f: tk 3rd nr fin* **33/1**

06 **4** *¾* **Press Release**[12] 1835 2-9-3 0.................................(t) RichardKingscote 3 59
(Tom Dascombe) *cl up: rdn along over 2f out: hung bdly rt wl over 1f out: wknd ent fnl f* **9/4[2]**

4 **5** *2 ½* **Hollyhocks (IRE)**[11] 1864 2-8-9 0.................................. MartinLane(3) 2 45
(N Wilson) *chsd ldrs: rdn along 1/2-way: grad wknd* **22/1**

6 *5* **Calypso Magic (IRE)** 2-9-3 0.................................. FrederikTylicki 6 32
(J Howard Johnson) *in tch: rdn along 1/2-way: no hdwy* **11/2[3]**

7 *7* **Beachwood Bay** 2-9-3 0.................................. KevinGhunowa 7 7
(R Curtis) *s.i.s: a bhd* **33/1**

58.77 secs (-1.63) **Going Correction** -0.375s/f (Firm) 7 Ran SP% **111.1**
Speed ratings (Par 93): **98,90,87,86,82 74,62**
toteswingers:1&2:£3.10, 1&3:£13.10, 2&3:£23.90 CSF £24.52 TOTE £1.80: £1.10, £9.10; EX 19.30.
Owner Elders, Turton, Brown & Rhodes **Bred** P A Mason **Trained** Hambleton, N Yorks

FOCUS
An uncompetitive maiden, but a very impressive winner who can go on to better things.

NOTEBOOK
Excel Bolt ◆ was ready for this debut according to the market and could hardly have done it any easier, making every yard against the stands' rail and pulling right away from his rivals through the last furlong. Out of a winning juvenile sprinter, he looks a very nice sprinting prospect himself and may have another run before heading for the Norfolk Stakes. (op 6-5 tchd 5-6 and 5-4 in places)
Crimson Knot(IRE), green on her debut over C&D last month, stayed on again after getting outpaced mid-race and this was a good effort as her saddle reportedly slipped. She wasn't in the class of the winner, but should be able to find a small race in due course. (op 25-1)
Dotty Darroch, a £5,000 filly out of a sister to the useful Maze and Count Kristo, made some late progress from off the pace and is bred to appreciate further. (op 28-1)
Hollyhocks(IRE) looked in need of the run when fourth of five on her Hamilton debut earlier this month, but didn't really improve on that and was beaten entering the last 2f. (op 16-1 tchd 25-1)
Calypso Magic(IRE), a 70,000gns half-brother to two winning juveniles including the useful City Dancer, was soon struggling to lay up. (tchd 5-1)
Beachwood Bay, a £10,000 colt out of a dual winning juvenile sprinter, fluffed the start and then saw plenty of daylight on the wide outside. (op 20-1)

2211 SCOTTISH RACING H'CAP — 7f 30y
3:40 (3:41) (Class 5) (0-70,69) 4-Y-O+ **£3,238** (£963; £481; £240) **Stalls** High

Form RPR

2-01 **1** **Nufoudh (IRE)**[18] 1673 6-8-13 **64**.................................. FrederikTylicki 9 73
(Miss Tracy Waggott) *unruly stalls: sn chsng ldng pair: effrt whn n.m.r on inner over 2f out: sn rdn: led over 1f out: drvn and kpt on gamely ins fnl f* **11/4[1]**

0-03 **2** *¾* **Mister Jingles**[18] 1673 7-8-5 **56**.................................(p) PaulQuinn 5 63
(R M Whitaker) *trckd ldrs: hdwy 3f out: rdn along 2f out: styng on whn n.m.r and edgd rt ent fnl f: sn drvn and ev ch tl no ex towards fin* **14/1**

25-2 **3** *1 ½* **Jonny Lesters Hair (IRE)**[18] 1673 5-9-2 **67**............ GrahamGibbons 2 70
(T D Easterby) *trckd ldr: effrt and cl up over 2f out: sn rdn and ev ch: swtchd lft and drvn over 1f out: one pce ins fnl f* **4/1[2]**

5321 **4** *½* **Dhhamaan (IRE)**[14] 1813 5-7-13 **55** oh1.................(b) JamesSullivan(5) 8 57
(Mrs R A Carr) *led: rdn along over 2f out: drvn and hung lft over 1f out: sn hdd & wknd ins fnl f* **11/2[3]**

135- **5** *2 ½* **Cils Blancs (IRE)**[187] 7349 4-8-7 **58**.................................. PaulHanagan 4 53
(B Smart) *in tch: rdn to chse ldrs 3f out: kpt on same pce fnl 2f* **6/1**

4500 **6** *½* **Peter's Gift (IRE)**[8] 1967 4-8-6 **62**.................................(b[1]) AmyRyan(5) 7 55
(K A Ryan) *dwlt and towards rr: rdn along and hdwy 1/2-way: kpt on u.p fnl 2f: n.d* **20/1**

3-60 **7** *1 ¾* **Stellite**[18] 1672 10-8-13 **67**.................................. GaryBartley(3) 6 56
(J S Goldie) *a towards rr* **11/2[3]**

0-60 **8** *3 ½* **Inter Vision (USA)**[10] 1924 10-9-4 **69**.................................. DanielTudhope 3 48
(A Dickman) *dwlt and in rr: sme hdwy on outer 3f out: sn rdn and nvr a factor* **14/1**

20-0 **9** *2 ¼* **Shunkawakhan (IRE)**[18] 1673 7-8-4 **55**.................................(p) PJMcDonald 1 28
(Miss L A Perratt) *a towards rr* **40/1**

1m 27.7s (-1.30) **Going Correction** -0.375s/f (Firm) 9 Ran SP% **112.3**
Speed ratings (Par 103): **99,98,96,95,93 92,90,86,83**
toteswingers:1&2:£11.70, 1&3:£2.80, 2&3:£6.00 CSF £41.75 CT £151.60 TOTE £3.10: £1.10, £4.60, £1.30; EX 34.80.
Owner H Conlon **Bred** Swordlestown Stud **Trained** Spennymoor, Co Durham

FOCUS
Yet another contest where few got into it from off the pace. The pace was fair, but the winning time was still 0.62 seconds slower than the earlier 3-y-o handicap. The first three met over C/D last month and the front pair ran to similar marks. Straightforward if limited form.

2212 TURFTV MAIDEN STKS — 5f
4:10 (4:10) (Class 5) 3-Y-O+ **£2,590** (£770; £385; £192) **Stalls** Low

Form RPR

25 **1** **Fairy Shoes**[20] 1622 3-8-12 0.................................. PaulHanagan 1 70
(R A Fahey) *dwlt: sn trcking ldng pair: effrt and nt clr run 2f out: sn swtchd rt and rdn: styd on to chal ent fnl f: sn led and kpt on wl towards fin* **8/13[1]**

6-0 **2** *¾* **Mrs Mogg**[11] 1861 3-8-12 0.................................. RichardKingscote 4 67
(Tom Dascombe) *cl up: led after 1f: rdn 2f out: edgd lft and drvn ent fnl f: sn hdd and no ex towards fin* **5/1[3]**

0-4 **3** *4 ½* **Interest Free**[11] 1890 3-8-12 0.................................. GrahamGibbons 2 51
(T D Easterby) *qckly away and led 1f: cl up and ev ch tl rdn and wknd appr fnl f* **11/4[2]**

00- **4** *3* **Tai Hang (IRE)**[241] 6096 3-8-9 0.................................. GaryBartley(3) 3 40
(J S Goldie) *in tch: hdwy 2f out: sn rdn and one pce* **25/1**

0/65 **5** *12* **Lunar Lass**[32] 1345 5-9-3 41.................................. BarryMcHugh(3) 6 —
(D C Griffiths) *sn outpcd and a bhd* **100/1**

0/0- **6** *3 ½* **Compton Lad**[364] 2157 7-9-6 36.................................. JamesSullivan(5) 5 —
(D A Nolan) *cl up: rdn along 1/2-way: sn wknd* **200/1**

58.51 secs (-1.89) **Going Correction** -0.375s/f (Firm)
WFA 3 from 5yo+ 8lb 6 Ran SP% **110.6**
Speed ratings (Par 103): **100,98,91,86,67 62**
toteswingers:1&2:£1.30, 1&3:£1.30, 2&3:£1.50 CSF £4.12 TOTE £1.40: £1.10, £2.20; EX 3.50.
Owner R A Fahey **Bred** Mrs Sheila Oakes **Trained** Musley Bank, N Yorks

FOCUS
A very moderate maiden and only the four 3-y-o fillies really mattered. The front two pulled well clear of the others and the form is rated around the averages.

2213 RACING UK H'CAP 5f
4:40 (4:41) (Class 6) (0-65,65) 4-Y-0+ **£1,942** (£578; £288; £144) **Stalls** Low

Form RPR

0061 **1** **Chosen One (IRE)**[10] 1923 5-9-2 **63** JamesSullivan(5) 5 72
(Mrs R A Carr) *a cl up: rdn along wl over 1f out: drvn ins fnl f: styd on to ld nr fin* **9/2**[3]

2315 **2** *nk* **Verinco**[10] 1915 4-9-1 **64** (v) AdamCarter(7) 1 72
(B Smart) *led: rdn wl over 1f out: edgd rt ins fnl f: hdd and nt qckn nr fin* **4/1**[2]

3536 **3** *hd* **Mandarin Spirit (IRE)**[4] 2073 10-9-4 **65** (b) IanBrennan(5) 4 72+
(Miss L A Perratt) *dwlt and squeezed out shortly after s: hdwy 2f out: chsd ldrs and nt clr run over 1f out: swtchd rt and rdn ent fnl f: kpt on: nrst fin* **10/3**[1]

00-6 **4** *4* **Braille**[31] 1391 5-9-2 **58** GrahamGibbons 3 51
(T D Walford) *towards rr on inner: effrt 2f out and sn rdn: swtchd rt and drvn over 1f out: kpt on ins fnl f: nrst fin* **11/2**

0523 **5** *½* **Fasliyanne (IRE)**[22] 1569 4-8-7 **54** (b) AmyRyan(5) 8 45
(K A Ryan) *midfield: hdwy 1/2-way: chsd ldrs and n.m.r wl over 1f out: swtchd rt and rdn ent fnl f: kpt on same pce* **9/1**

0356 **6** *2 ¼* **Almaty Express**[1] 2186 8-8-1 **46** oh1 (b) MartinLane(3) 13 29
(J R Weymes) *in tch on wd outside: hdwy 1/2-way: sn rdn and wknd over 1f out* **12/1**

020- **7** *½* **Wicked Wilma (IRE)**[202] 7119 6-9-1 **62** MarkCoumbe(5) 11 43
(A Berry) *cl up: rdn 2f out and ev ch tl drvn and wknd ent fnl f* **22/1**

230- **8** *7* **Angelofthenorth**[277] 5008 8-8-6 **48** PatrickMathers 14 4
(C J Teague) *a towards rr* **33/1**

/4 **9** *½* **Socceroo**[22] 1569 5-8-9 **54** BarryMcHugh(3) 9 8
(D C Griffiths) *chsd ldrs: rdn along 2f out: wknd over 1f out: and sn eased* **14/1**

00-0 **10** *½* **Princess Charlmane (IRE)**[8] 1965 7-8-4 **51** (p) LanceBetts(5) 12 3
(C J Teague) *in tch towards outer: rdn along over 2f out and sn wknd* **25/1**

/00- **11** *½* **Barraland**[332] 3149 5-9-8 **64** DanielTudhope 6 15
(J S Goldie) *cl up: rdn along bef 1/2-way and sn wknd* **14/1**

00-0 **12** *shd* **Howards Prince**[16] 1723 7-7-12 **46** oh1 ow1 (p) MatthewLawson(7) 2 —
(D A Nolan) *cl up: rdn along 1/2-way and sn wknd* **100/1**

04-0 **13** *3 ½* **Clanachy**[22] 1569 4-8-4 **46** oh1 AndrewMullen 10 —
(A G Foster) *dwlt: a in rr* **40/1**

58.33 secs (-2.07) **Going Correction** -0.375s/f (Firm) **13** Ran SP% **122.2**
Speed ratings (Par 101): **101,100,100,93,93 89,88,77,76,75 75,74,69**
toteswingers:1&2:£5.60, 1&3:£5.70, 2&3:£5.30 CSF £22.31 CT £69.74 TOTE £4.30: £1.30, £1.20, £3.30; EX 26.80.
Owner David W Chapman **Bred** Carl Holt **Trained** Huby, N Yorks

FOCUS
A weak sprint handicap dominated by those drawn towards the stands' side with the first four home starting from the five lowest stalls. Those drawn high can be forgiven for apparently modest efforts. It was the pick of the three C/D time and the winner confirmed his recent improvement.
Socceroo Official explanation: trainer said mare lost its action but returned sound

2214 TURFTV.CO.UK APPRENTICE H'CAP 1m 6f
5:10 (5:11) (Class 6) (0-65,64) 4-Y-0+ **£2,266** (£674; £337; £168) **Stalls** High

Form RPR

363- **1** **Tillietudlem (FR)**[26] 5442 4-8-2 **45** IanBrennan(3) 11 54
(J S Goldie) *trckd ldng pair on inner: effrt over 2f out: rdn wl over 1f out: styd on to ld ins fnl f: drvn out* **7/4**[1]

0/00 **2** *½* **Planetarium**[16] 1720 5-9-7 **64** (p) MichaelO'Connell(3) 2 72
(P Monteith) *towards rr: pushed along 3f out: sn rdn and hdwy 2f out: drvn to ld briefly over 1f out: sn hung lft and hdd ins fnl f: kpt on same pce* **25/1**

20-3 **3** *5* **Petella**[18] 1671 4-8-8 **48** MartinLane 4 49
(C W Thornton) *hld up towards rr: hdwy 3f out: rdn to chse ldrs wl over 1f out: sn drvn and kpt on same pce ins fnl f* **4/1**[2]

40/- **4** *1 ½* **Perez (IRE)**[13] 1559 8-8-5 **48** (v) DeanHeslop(3) 6 47
(W Storey) *trckd ldrs: hdwy on outer 3f out: rdn and edgd lft 2f out: sn ev ch on wd outside tl drvn and one pce ent fnl f* **33/1**

00-0 **5** *½* **Paddy Partridge**[10] 1920 4-8-12 **55** (v[1]) RossAtkinson(3) 3 53
(Tom Dascombe) *trckd ldr: effrt 3f out: rdn over 2f out and sn ev ch tl drvn over 1f out: hung rt and wknd ins fnl f* **15/2**[3]

4 **6** *1* **Ocean Bright (USA)**[15] 1759 4-8-2 **45** (b) DeclanCannon(3) 10 42
(J G Given) *in tch: hdwy 3f out: rdn along 2f out: sn drvn and n.m.r over 1f out: swtchd lft and plugged on same pce* **4/1**[2]

0/55 **7** *1* **Without Equal**[24] 1526 4-8-0 **45** MatthewLawson(5) 1 41
(A Dickman) *dwlt: sn led: rdn along over 2f out: drvn over 1f out: hdd appr fnl f: wkng whn carried rt and n.m.r ins fnl f* **100/1**

44-0 **8** *2 ½* **Kyber**[18] 1671 9-8-5 **48** LanceBetts(3) 5 40
(J S Goldie) *trckd ldrs: hdwy 3f out: rdn along 2f out and ch: sn drvn and wknd over 1f out* **16/1**

405- **9** *3 ¾* **Ballade De La Mer**[202] 7118 4-8-4 **49** ow4 AdamCarter(5) 9 36
(A G Foster) *midfield: hdwy over 3f out: rdn to chse ldrs over 2f out: sn drvn and wknd* **16/1**

00-5 **10** *2 ¾* **Royal Flynn**[14] 1803 8-8-7 **50** (p) AmyRyan(3) 7 33
(Mrs K Walton) *a in rr* **10/1**

3m 4.13s (-1.17) **Going Correction** -0.375s/f (Firm) **10** Ran SP% **116.8**
Speed ratings (Par 101): **88,87,84,84,83 83,82,81,79,77**
toteswingers:1&2:£16.00, 1&3:£3.00, 2&3:£21.50 CSF £55.30 CT £161.32 TOTE £3.40: £1.50, £7.50, £2.00; EX 41.30 Place 6 £8.26; Place 5 £5.80.
Owner Mr & Mrs C J Smith **Bred** Bernard Ducasse **Trained** Uplawmoor, E Renfrews
■ Stewards' Enquiry : Ross Atkinson one-day ban: careless riding (Jun 1)

FOCUS
A modest apprentice staying handicap. A Flat personal best from the winner, who was on a good mark on his jumps form.
Perez(IRE) Official explanation: jockey said gelding hung left final 2f
T/Plt: £11.50. Pool £55,928.68 -3,540.86 winning tickets T/Qpdt: £5.30. Pool £2714.79 - 374.54 winning tickets JR

1915 NOTTINGHAM (L-H)
Tuesday, May 18
OFFICIAL GOING: Outer course - good to firm (7.5)
Wind: Almost nil Weather: Overcast

2215 NOTTINGHAMRACECOURSE.CO.UK H'CAP 6f 15y
2:00 (2:01) (Class 5) (0-70,70) 3-Y-O **£2,590** (£770; £385; £192) **Stalls** High

Form RPR

41-5 **1** **Belinsky (IRE)**[17] 1709 3-9-4 **70** J-PGuillambert 12 75
(N Tinkler) *mde virtually all: shkn up over 1f out: rdn out* **16/1**

-306 **2** *1 ¼* **Rainbow Six**[21] 1602 3-8-13 **65** AndreaAtzeni 10 66
(M Botti) *a.p: rdn to chse wnr ins fnl f: r.o* **10/1**

545- **3** *1 ¾* **Lutine Bell**[300] 4200 3-9-2 **68** SebSanders 7 63+
(Sir Mark Prescott) *s.s: sn pushed along in rr: r.o ins fnl f: wnt 3rd post: nrst fin* **8/1**[3]

-451 **4** *shd* **Tell Halaf**[11] 1873 3-9-3 **69** JamieSpencer 5 64+
(M L W Bell) *chsd ldrs: rdn over 2f out: styd on same pce ins fnl f: lost 3rd post* **5/2**[1]

-350 **5** *nse* **Tell Me A Story**[14] 1811 3-8-4 **63** ow1 JohnCavanagh(7) 13 58
(M Brittain) *s.i.s: hdwy 4f out: rdn over 1f out: r.o* **20/1**

56-4 **6** *nk* **Final Turn**[11] 1878 3-9-0 **66** FergusSweeney 3 60
(H Candy) *chsd ldrs: rdn over 2f out: no ex ins fnl f* **6/1**[2]

-020 **7** *nk* **A Pocketful Of Rye (IRE)**[15] 1753 3-8-1 **60** LeonnaMayor(7) 14 53+
(P Howling) *dwlt: hld up: nt clr run over 1f out: swtchd lft and r.o ins fnl f: nt clr run nr fin: nvr nrr* **11/1**

66-0 **8** *nse* **King's Approach (IRE)**[12] 1842 3-9-2 **68** (p) JoeFanning 6 60
(R A Harris) *chsd wnr: rdn over 1f out: no ex ins fnl f* **66/1**

00-3 **9** *½* **Speedyfix**[21] 1605 3-8-4 **56** oh9 (tp) FrannyNorton 4 47+
(Mrs C A Dunnett) *s.i.s: in rr and pushed along 1/2-way: r.o ins fnl f: nrst fin* **40/1**

2311 **10** *1* **Thaliwarru**[15] 1760 3-9-3 **69** SteveDrowne 1 57
(J R Gask) *mid-div: outpcd 1/2-way: rallied over 1f out: no ex wl ins fnl f* **17/2**

04-3 **11** *1 ¾* **South African Gold (USA)**[120] 218 3-9-1 **67** LukeMorris 11 49
(J M P Eustace) *chsd ldrs: lost pl over 3f out: n.d after* **28/1**

0636 **12** *½* **Itsthursdayalready**[48] 1058 3-9-0 **66** PaulMulrennan 8 46
(J G Given) *prom: rdn over 1f out: wknd fnl f* **11/1**

604- **13** *1 ¼* **Bubbelas**[239] 6169 3-8-13 **65** JimmyFortune 2 41
(J J Quinn) *hld up: rdn over 2f out: n.d* **25/1**

2040 **14** *1 ¼* **Marjolly (IRE)**[10] 1934 3-8-13 **65** (v[1]) TadhgO'Shea 9 37
(J Gallagher) *s.i.s: a in rr* **33/1**

1m 14.17s (-0.73) **Going Correction** -0.20s/f (Firm) **14** Ran SP% **115.1**
Speed ratings (Par 99): **96,94,92,91,91 91,91,90,90,88 86,85,84,82**
toteswingers:1&2:£49.80, 1&3:£21.60, 2&3:£25.70 CSF £148.13 CT £1380.62 TOTE £17.60: £6.20, £4.90, £4.20; EX 405.60.
Owner Wentdale Limited **Bred** Camogue Stud Ltd **Trained** Langton, N Yorks
■ Stewards' Enquiry : Leonna Mayor one-day ban: careless riding (Jun 1)

FOCUS
A moderate 3-y-o sprint handicap. The field came over to the stands' rail and those drawn high were no doubt at an advantage. The winner is rated up 5lb.
Speedyfix Official explanation: jockey said gelding hung left

2216 EUROPEAN BREEDERS' FUND MAIDEN STKS 6f 15y
2:30 (2:30) (Class 5) 2-Y-O **£3,561** (£1,059; £529; £264) **Stalls** High

Form RPR

0 **1** **Planet Waves (IRE)**[10] 1901 2-9-3 0 SebSanders 10 78
(C E Brittain) *chsd ldr: hung lft over 4f out: led over 2f out: rdn out* **10/3**[2]

4 **2** *1 ¼* **Trade Storm**[12] 1845 2-9-3 0 TadhgO'Shea 8 74
(J Gallagher) *s.i.s: hdwy over 4f out: rdn and hung rt over 1f out: chsd wnr ins fnl f: r.o* **11/1**

430 **3** *2* **Just For Leo (IRE)**[12] 1835 2-9-3 0 CathyGannon 12 68
(P D Evans) *led: hung lft 4f out: hung rt over 2f out: sn hdd: rdn over 1f out: no ex ins fnl f* **7/1**

4 *4 ½* **Excelebration (IRE)** 2-9-3 0 KierenFallon 9 62+
(M Botti) *s.i.s: hdwy over 4f out: wknd over 1f out* **11/4**[1]

5 *1 ½* **Roayh (USA)** 2-9-3 0 FrankieDettori 4 55+
(Saeed Bin Suroor) *chsd ldrs: rdn over 2f out: wknd over 1f out* **5/1**[3]

0 **6** *4 ½* **High Kickin**[29] 1421 2-8-12 0 JamesDoyle 2 37+
(A J McCabe) *prom: rdn 1/2-way: wknd 2f out* **66/1**

0 **7** *3 ¼* **Torteval (IRE)**[21] 1597 2-8-13 0 ow1 RichardEvans(5) 5 33+
(P D Evans) *s.i.s: sn pushed along in rr: nvr on terms* **66/1**

6 **8** *¾* **Whitby Jet (IRE)**[11] 1871 2-9-3 0 AndreaAtzeni 3 30+
(E F Vaughan) *s.i.s: sn in tch: rdn 1/2-way: wknd over 2f out* **125/1**

9 *3 ¾* **Fleet Captain** 2-9-3 0 JamieSpencer 13 18+
(K A Ryan) *s.s: hdwy over 2f out: sn rdn and wknd* **13/2**

10 *1* **Reachforthebucks** 2-9-3 0 SaleemGolam 11 15+
(G D Blake) *dwlt: a in rr* **100/1**

11 *2 ¾* **Liberty Cap (USA)** 2-9-3 0 RobertHavlin 7 2
(J H M Gosden) *prom: rdn over 4f out: sn lost pl* **12/1**

1m 14.62s (-0.28) **Going Correction** -0.20s/f (Firm) **11** Ran SP% **113.0**
Speed ratings (Par 93): **93,91,88,82,80 74,70,69,64,63 59**
toteswingers:1&2:£7.30, 1&3:£7.10, 2&3:£8.70 CSF £37.86 TOTE £3.40: £1.10, £3.20, £2.70; EX 40.80.
Owner Saeed Manana **Bred** Old Carhue Stud **Trained** Newmarket, Suffolk

FOCUS
Considering the preceding event, it was surprising the remainder elected to either stay or indeed go out to the middle. The third is the best guide and the first two are improving.

NOTEBOOK
Planet Waves(IRE) showed himself to be a progressive colt and, racing hard up against the stands' rail, came home a game winner. Stepping up a furlong made all the difference to this half-brother to last season's Group 1 Moyglare Stud winner Termagant, indeed he is bred to enjoy 1m plus next term. A step up in class now beckons and it wouldn't be that surprising if his trainer was eyeing something at Royal Ascot, but using the runner-up as a guide his Goodwood winner Sikeeb rates the classier of the two. (op 6-1)
Trade Storm was an eye-catcher when fourth to Brittain's Sikeeb at Goodwood on debut and this rates a step forward in defeat. He sensibly came to the near side with his challenge from 2f out and should not be that long in going one better. (op 12-1)
Just For Leo(IRE) was having his fourth outing and that made him the most experienced in this line up. He saw out the extra furlong sufficiently and ran his race despite again hanging, so rates the benchmark. (op 8-1 tchd 17-2)
Excelebration(IRE), a half-brother to this year's Lincoln third Mull Of Killough, was brought to the centre of the track and that cannot have helped his cause. The experience will not be lost on him, though, and better was evidently expected. (op 7-2)

Roayh(USA) is a well-bred $200,000 purchase and his trainer boasts a decent record with juveniles at the course. The yard is not firing on all cylinders yet, however, and it wasn't that surprising to see him drift in the betting, especially as he didn't have a great draw. He showed up well through the early parts, but also kept to the centre with his effort and ultimately looked in need of the run. (op 2-1)

2217 BOB CHAMPION'S 60:60 CHARITY CHALLENGE H'CAP 5f 13y
3:00 (3:01) (Class 6) (0-60,60) 3-Y-O **£2,047** (£604; £302) **Stalls** High

Form RPR

3305 **1** **Tamarind Hill (IRE)**[10] 1923 3-8-13 **55**........................(b) JamesDoyle 12 63
(A J McCabe) *racd stands' side: chsd ldrs: rdn to ld overall ins fnl f: r.o* **15/2**

-353 **2** ¾ **Pherousa**[15] 1784 3-9-4 **60**.......................... SteveDrowne 8 65
(M Blanshard) *racd stands' side: hld up in tch: rdn and ev ch ins fnl f: styd on: 2nd of 10 in gp* **13/2**[3]

5433 **3** 3 **Annia Galeria (IRE)**[15] 1774 3-8-8 **50**..........................(b) EddieAhern 14 44
(C A Dwyer) *racd stands' side: chsd ldrs: rdn over 1f out: styd on same pce ins fnl f: 3rd of 10 in gp* **8/1**

1-50 **4** *shd* **Midget**[14] 1811 3-9-4 **60**.......................... DavidNolan 11 54
(D Carroll) *racd stands' side: led overall: rdn over 1f out: hdd and no ex ins fnl f: 4th of 10 in gp* **6/1**[2]

2000 **5** *nse* **Lets Move It**[15] 1774 3-8-4 **46** oh1..........................(v) LukeMorris 16 40
(D Shaw) *racd stands' side: sn pushed along in rr: r.o wl ins fnl f: nrst fin: 5th of 10 in gp* **22/1**

0050 **6** *hd* **Pavement Games**[14] 1811 3-8-4 **46** oh1.......................... FrannyNorton 15 39
(R C Guest) *racd stands' side: chsd ldrs: rdn over 2f out: outpcd over 1f out: swtchd lft and r.o ins fnl f: 6th of 10 in gp* **12/1**

6-35 **7** 1¾ **Watch Chain (IRE)**[7] 2000 3-8-13 **55**.......................... DarryllHolland 10 42
(M H Tompkins) *racd stands' side: dwlt: hld up: hdwy on outer over 1f out: styd on same pce ins fnl f: 7th of 10 in gp* **11/2**[1]

3402 **8** *nk* **Duke Of Rainford**[24] 1535 3-8-12 **54**.......................... JamieSpencer 5 40+
(M Herrington) *racd far side: hld up: hdwy to ld that gp 1f out: r.o: no ch w stands' side: 1st of 6 in gp* **15/2**

0-60 **9** *nk* **Bird On The Wire**[7] 2000 3-8-7 **52**..........................(p) JackDean[(3)] 9 36
(W G M Turner) *racd stands' side: chsd ldrs: rdn over 1f out: wknd ins fnl f: 8th of 10 in gp* **33/1**

-030 **10** 1¾ **Gower Sophia**[27] 1468 3-8-4 **53** ow1.......................... JohnCavanagh[(7)] 13 31
(M Brittain) *s.i.s and hmpd s: sn chsng ldrs stands' side: rdn and wknd over 1f out: 9th of 10 in gp* **14/1**

00-4 **11** 1½ **Amoureuse**[27] 1468 3-8-4 **46** oh1.......................... JoeFanning 2 19
(D Carroll) *racd far side: chsd ldrs: rdn over 1f out: wknd ins fnl f: 2nd of 6 in gp* **16/1**

60-5 **12** 1¼ **Camacho Flyer (IRE)**[26] 1483 3-9-4 **60**..........................(v) TonyCulhane 3 28
(P T Midgley) *racd far side: prom: rdn and edgd rt over 1f out: sn wknd: 3rd of 6 in gp* **40/1**

6400 **13** 1¾ **Blue Neptune**[15] 1784 3-9-0 **56**..........................(v[1]) CathyGannon 4 18
(P D Evans) *led far side: rdn and hdd that gp 1f out: sn wknd: 4th of 6 in gp* **22/1**

4-65 **14** 1½ **Southwark Newshawk**[21] 1604 3-8-10 **52**..............(p) TomMcLaughlin 1 9
(Mrs C A Dunnett) *racd far side: prom: rdn 1/2-way: wknd over 1f out: 5th of 6 in gp* **66/1**

000- **15** 3½ **Lady Compton**[224] 6555 3-8-1 **46** oh1.......................... KellyHarrison[(3)] 6 —
(R Bastiman) *racd far side: sn outpcd: last of 6 in gp* **50/1**

1450 **16** 2½ **Ballyvonane (USA)**[41] 1162 3-8-11 **53**.......................... KierenFallon 7 —
(P Howling) *racd stands' side: s.i.s: a bhd: last of 10 in gp* **9/1**

60.35 secs (-0.65) **Going Correction** -0.20s/f (Firm) **16** Ran SP% **125.4**
Speed ratings (Par 97): **97,95,91,90,90 90,87,87,86,83 81,79,76,74,68 64**
toteswingers:1&2:£16.80, 1&3:£13.80, 2&3:£11.10 CSF £53.73 CT £415.11 TOTE £9.70: £2.40, £1.70, £1.70, £1.70; EX 75.10.
Owner A C Timms **Bred** Ballylinch Stud **Trained** Averham Park, Notts

FOCUS
Somewhat predictably the main group that raced on the near side dominated this poor 3-y-o sprint handicap. Not a race to be too positive about.
Gower Sophia Official explanation: trainer's rep said filly finished distressed

2218 PADDOCKS CONFERENCE CENTRE H'CAP 2m 9y
3:30 (3:30) (Class 5) (0-70,67) 4-Y-O+ **£2,590** (£770; £385; £192) **Stalls** Low

Form RPR

30-3 **1** **Rare Ruby (IRE)**[14] 1798 6-9-9 **67**.......................... JimmyFortune 3 75
(Jennie Candlish) *chsd ldrs: led over 3f out: rdn over 1f out: styd on gamely* **5/2**[1]

4046 **2** 1½ **Strikemaster (IRE)**[5] 2060 4-9-4 **64**..........................(b) JamieSpencer 2 71
(B Ellison) *hld up: hdwy 3f out: rdn over 1f out: hung lft and chsd wnr ins fnl f: styd on* **10/3**[2]

00-2 **3** 3 **Eijaaz (IRE)**[14] 1801 9-9-2 **60**..........................(p) SebSanders 1 63
(G A Harker) *hld up: hdwy over 3f out: chsd wnr 2f out tl rdn and no ex ins fnl f* **8/1**

1-63 **4** 9 **Unawatuna**[11] 1891 5-8-10 **57**.......................... KellyHarrison[(3)] 7 49
(Mrs K Walton) *chsd ldrs: rdn over 3f out: hung lft and wknd over 2f out* **7/2**[3]

26-0 **5** 6 **Ingenue**[136] 15 4-8-10 **56**..........................(v[1]) JoeFanning 5 41
(P Howling) *chsd ldr tl led 11f out: clr 9f out: rdn and hdd over 3f out: wknd over 1f out* **28/1**

410- **6** 9 **Court Princess**[139] 7873 7-9-2 **60**.......................... TonyCulhane 4 34
(George Baker) *hld up: rdn over 3f out: sn wknd* **22/1**

60-5 **7** 12 **Straight Laced**[20] 1623 4-8-9 **55**..........................(p) ShaneKelly 6 15
(W J Knight) *led 5f: chsd ldr tl rdn over 3f out: wknd over 2f out: t.o* **7/1**

4500 **8** 7 **Lava Steps (USA)**[14] 1807 4-8-9 **55**.......................... PaulMulrennan 8 6
(P T Midgley) *s.s: hld up: a in rr: rdn and wknd over 3f out: t.o* **18/1**

3m 31.54s (1.24) **Going Correction** +0.05s/f (Good)
WFA 4 from 5yo+ 2lb **8** Ran SP% **110.5**
Speed ratings (Par 103): **98,97,95,91,88 83,77,74**
toteswingers:1&2:£3.30, 1&3:£3.90, 2&3:£5.40 CSF £10.10 CT £51.84 TOTE £3.50: £1.80, £1.10, £2.30; EX 10.70.
Owner Mrs Judith Ratcliff **Bred** Robert And Michelle Dore **Trained** Basford Green, Staffs

FOCUS
This moderate staying handicap was run at a sound pace thanks to the headstrong Ingenue and the first three pulled clear in the home straight. A small personal best from the winner.

2219 RACING UK ON CHANNEL 432 FILLIES' H'CAP 1m 2f 50y
4:00 (4:00) (Class 4) (0-80,77) 3-Y-O **£5,828** (£1,734; £866; £432) **Stalls** Low

Form RPR

2-62 **1** **Ice Diva**[21] 1608 3-9-2 **72**.......................... TonyCulhane 6 83
(P W D'Arcy) *a.p: chsd ldr over 3f out: led over 2f out: rdn out* **5/1**[3]

-521 **2** 1 **Babycakes (IRE)**[8] 1982 3-9-6 **76** 6ex.......................... HayleyTurner 8 85+
(M L W Bell) *hld up: shkn up over 3f out: hdwy 2f out: sn rdn and edgd lft: chsd wnr fnl f: r.o* **6/1**

2133 **3** 1¾ **Sweet Child O'Mine**[22] 1571 3-9-7 **77**.......................... FrannyNorton 5 83
(R C Guest) *trckd ldrs: racd keenly: rdn over 2f out: styd on same pce ins fnl f* **9/1**

0-42 **4** 3¾ **Aegean Destiny**[21] 1601 3-8-1 **62**.......................... JohnFahy[(5)] 3 61
(J Mackie) *hld up: hdwy over 2f out: rdn and nt clr run over 1f out: swtchd rt: one pce* **11/1**

1- **5** 1¾ **Hudoo**[200] 7157 3-9-6 **76**.......................... FrankieDettori 7 72
(Saeed Bin Suroor) *s.i.s: rcvrd to ld after 1f but set stdy pce: qcknd over 3f out: rdn and hdd over 2f out: wknd ins fnl f* **5/2**[1]

04-2 **6** 1¼ **Wulfrida (IRE)**[26] 1485 3-9-7 **77**.......................... EddieAhern 4 70
(J R Fanshawe) *hld up: hdwy 1/2-way: rdn over 2f out: wknd over 1f out* **4/1**[2]

2303 **7** 1 **Sunrise Lyric (IRE)**[14] 1795 3-8-4 **60**.......................... JoeFanning 1 51
(P F I Cole) *hld up in tch: racd keenly: rdn over 2f out: wknd over 1f out* **20/1**

364 **8** 9 **Spicewood (USA)**[20] 1621 3-9-2 **72**.......................... RobertHavlin 2 46
(J H M Gosden) *hld up in tch: rdn over 3f out: wknd over 2f out* **16/1**

530- **9** 5 **Yankee Bright (USA)**[199] 7187 3-8-11 **67**.......................... PaulMulrennan 9 32
(J G Given) *led 1f: chsd ldr tl rdn over 3f out: wknd over 2f out* **25/1**

2m 12.54s (0.84) **Going Correction** +0.05s/f (Good) **9** Ran SP% **112.3**
Speed ratings (Par 98): **98,96,95,92,91 90,89,82,78**
toteswingers:1&2:£4.10, 1&3:£5.80, 2&3:£5.60 CSF £33.78 CT £258.91 TOTE £4.50: £1.10, £2.30, £2.30; EX 33.60.
Owner Mark & Sue Harniman **Bred** Elsdon Farms **Trained** Newmarket, Suffolk

FOCUS
A very competitive fillies' handicap for the class. It appeared to be run at an uneven pace and those racing handily were perfectly placed when the race became serious. Form to be fairly positive about.
Spicewood(USA) Official explanation: trainer said filly was unsuited by the good to firm ground

2220 IT'S LADIES' NIGHT 3RD JULY MAIDEN STKS 1m 75y
4:30 (4:30) (Class 5) 3-Y-O **£2,590** (£770; £385; £192) **Stalls** Centre

Form RPR

1 **Inqaath (IRE)** 3-9-3 0.......................... RichardHills 9 84+
(Sir Michael Stoute) *hld up: hdwy over 4f out: rdn and hung lft over 1f out: led ins fnl f: r.o wl* **13/2**[3]

5 **2** 2 **Tamarillo Grove (IRE)**[26] 1485 3-9-3 0.......................... GregFairley 4 78+
(B Smart) *chsd ldrs: rdn over 2f out: hung lft over 1f out: styd on* **13/2**[3]

3 *hd* **Bursary (CAN)** 3-9-3 0.......................... FrankieDettori 11 77+
(M Johnston) *led: hdd over 6f out: chsd ldr tl led again over 2f out: rdn over 1f out: hdd and no ex ins fnl f* **3/1**[2]

344- **4** 6 **Miss Antonia (IRE)**[210] 6920 3-8-12 71.......................... EddieAhern 7 59
(H R A Cecil) *chsd ldrs: rdn over 2f out: wknd over 1f out* **9/4**[1]

5 2½ **Quick Deal (USA)** 3-9-3 0.......................... RobertHavlin 14 58+
(J H M Gosden) *s.s and wnt rt: hld up: hdwy and hung lft fr over 2f out: nvr trbld ldrs* **14/1**

00- **6** 3 **Rock The Stars (IRE)**[153] 7773 3-9-0 0.......................... PatrickHills[(3)] 8 51
(J W Hills) *mid-div: rdn over 3f out: wknd over 2f out* **100/1**

0 **7** 1½ **Piddie's Power**[17] 1706 3-8-12 0.......................... SebSanders 3 43
(E S McMahon) *hld up: hmpd after 1f: hdwy over 3f out: wknd over 1f out* **40/1**

8 *nk* **Kayaan** 3-9-3 0.......................... TadhgO'Shea 1 47
(W J Haggas) *s.i.s: hld up: swtchd rt ins fnl f: nvr trbld ldrs* **22/1**

5 **9** 7 **Macie (IRE)**[11] 1872 3-8-12 0.......................... JimmyFortune 6 26
(J Noseda) *w ldr tl led over 6f out: rdn and hdd over 2f out: wknd wl over 1f out* **16/1**

00 **10** 2½ **Motirani**[15] 1766 3-9-3 0.......................... HayleyTurner 13 25
(M L W Bell) *hld up: a in rr* **28/1**

11 5 **Old Adage** 3-9-3 0.......................... JimCrowley 5 14
(Mrs A J Perrett) *s.s: hld up: pushed along 1/2-way: a in rr* **14/1**

0 **12** *hd* **Rileys Crane**[11] 1870 3-9-3 0.......................... TomMcLaughlin 10 13
(Mrs C A Dunnett) *chsd ldrs: rdn over 3f out: sn wknd* **150/1**

1m 46.3s (0.70) **Going Correction** +0.05s/f (Good) **12** Ran SP% **113.5**
Speed ratings (Par 99): **98,96,95,89,87 84,82,82,75,73 68,67**
toteswingers:1&2:£6.30, 1&3:£3.30, 2&3:£5.00 CSF £44.45 TOTE £7.40: £2.20, £1.40, £1.20; EX 54.30.
Owner Hamdan Al Maktoum **Bred** Gigginstown House Stud **Trained** Newmarket, Suffolk

FOCUS
The time wasn't great, but this will likely work out to be an above-average 3-y-o maiden and it was yet another race where the first three came clear of their rivals.

2221 COME RACING ON WEDNESDAY 2ND JUNE CLASSIFIED STKS 1m 75y
5:00 (5:01) (Class 6) 3-Y-O **£2,047** (£604; £302) **Stalls** Centre

Form RPR

0-60 **1** **Al Dafa (USA)**[32] 1362 3-9-0 65.......................... JamieSpencer 2 75
(M L W Bell) *pushed along and sn prom: hrd rdn fr over 3f out: swtchd lft over 1f out: led and hung lft ins fnl f: styd on u.p* **4/1**[1]

065- **2** *nk* **Strike A Deal (IRE)**[203] 7095 3-9-0 65.......................... JackMitchell 3 74
(C F Wall) *hld up in tch: rdn over 1f out: ev ch ins fnl f: styd on* **6/1**[2]

4123 **3** 4½ **Volatilis (IRE)**[8] 1977 3-8-9 65.......................... KierenFox[(5)] 11 64
(J W Hills) *led: rdn over 2f out: hdd and no ex ins fnl f* **4/1**[1]

30-5 **4** 3½ **Green For Luck (IRE)**[7] 1992 3-8-9 62.......................... JohnFahy[(5)] 14 56
(S Gollings) *hld up in tch: rdn over 2f out: wkng whn hung lft over 1f out* **33/1**

500- **5** *shd* **Comedy Act**[283] 4790 3-9-0 65.......................... SebSanders 4 56
(Sir Mark Prescott) *chsd ldr: rdn over 2f out: wknd over 1f out* **8/1**

2-04 **6** 2¼ **Bonnie Brae**[8] 1959 3-9-0 65.......................... TadhgO'Shea 6 51
(G G Margarson) *hld up: hdwy over 2f out: nvr on terms* **14/1**

565 **7** 4½ **Barnstorm**[22] 1586 3-9-0 65.......................... FrankieDettori 10 40
(M Johnston) *trckd ldrs: rdn over 2f out: wknd over 1f out* **9/1**

00 **8** 1 **Catawollow**[26] 1495 3-8-7 41..........................(e[1]) CharlesEddery[(7)] 9 38
(R C Guest) *hld up: shkn up over 3f out: nvr trbld ldrs* **125/1**

0-40 **9** 2½ **Springwell Giant (IRE)**[10] 1923 3-8-7 55.......................... NoraLooby[(7)] 12 32
(A J McCabe) *hld up: rdn over 3f out: n.d* **80/1**

0-60 **10** 1¾ **Silent Majority (IRE)**[21] 1608 3-9-0 65..........................(b[1]) KierenFallon 8 28
(E A L Dunlop) *s.i.s: a in rr* **6/1**[2]

000- **11** *shd* **Suzi's Challenger**[204] 7061 3-9-0 47.......................... DarryllHolland 1 28
(H J Collingridge) *hld up: rdn over 4f out: a in rr* **80/1**

00-0 **12** *nk* **Jemimaville (IRE)**[33] 1329 3-9-0 65.......................... TravisBlock 13 27
(G C Bravery) *hld up: pushed along 5f out: a in rr* **7/1**[3]

0P0- **13** 3¼ **Miss Isle Control**[212] 6874 3-8-7 35.......................... ConorQuish[(7)] 5 20
(A J McCabe) *hld up: wknd over 3f out* **200/1**

The Form Book, Raceform Ltd, Compton, RG20 6NL

6-30 **14** *13* **England (IRE)**[75] 788 3-9-0 63........................(b[1]) JimCrowley 7 —
(N P Littmoden) *hld up: wknd over 3f out* **25/1**

1m 46.15s (0.55) **Going Correction** +0.05s/f (Good) **14** Ran SP% **119.4**
Speed ratings (Par 97): **99,98,94,90,90 88,83,82,80,78 78,78,74,61**
toteswingers:1&2:£9.40, 1&3:£5.10, 2&3:£4.20 CSF £26.87 TOTE £5.50: £2.20, £3.70, £1.10; EX 41.30 Place 6 £149.76; Place 5 £40.78.
Owner Sheikh Marwan Al Maktoum **Bred** Darley **Trained** Newmarket, Suffolk

FOCUS
A poor 3-y-o classified event, but there were potential improvers lurking in the race. There was no hanging about early on and the chances of the majority were apparent 2f out. The winner ran his best race since his debut, with the third the best guide.
T/Jkpt: Not won. T/Plt: £792.90. Pool £87,439.37 - 80.50 winning tickets T/Qpdt: £14.70. Pool £5,006.64 - 250.98 winning tickets CR

1844 GOODWOOD (R-H)
Wednesday, May 19

OFFICIAL GOING: Good (good to firm in places on round course; 8.4)
Wind: Light, half against Weather: Sunny, warm

2223 E B F MEL WOOD "CELEBRATION OF LIFE" MAIDEN FILLIES' STKS — 6f
2:00 (2:00) (Class 5) 2-Y-O **£3,561** (£1,059; £529; £264) **Stalls** Low

Form RPR
1 **Memory (IRE)** 2-9-0 0........................ RichardHughes 4 89+
(R Hannon) *dwlt: t.k.h: hld up in last trio: gd prog and swtchd rt to outer 2f out: pushed into ld ins fnl f: qckly drew away* **9/4**[1]
2 *2 ¾* **Goodwood Treasure** 2-9-0 0........................ EddieAhern 10 76
(J L Dunlop) *prom on outer: pushed into ld over 1f out: hdd and outpcd ins fnl f* **11/1**
3 *1* **Elkmait** 2-9-0 0........................ SebSanders 6 73
(C E Brittain) *chsd ldrs and racd against rail: pushed along 2f out: effrt to take 3rd 1f out: outpcd after* **13/2**[3]
0 **4** *2 ¾* **Sheila's Star (IRE)**[51] 1043 2-9-0 0........................ LiamKeniry 2 65
(J S Moore) *mostly chsd ldr to 2f out: sn outpcd: plugged on* **7/1**
5 *shd* **Apazine (USA)** 2-9-0 0........................ RobertHavlin 3 64+
(J H M Gosden) *disp 2nd pl to 2f out: pushed along and steadily outpcd* **9/2**[2]
0 **6** *nk* **Atia**[23] 1577 2-9-0 0........................ DaneO'Neill 1 64
(J G Portman) *racd against nr side rail: led to over 1f out: fdd* **40/1**
7 *1 ¾* **Kalleidoscope** 2-9-0 0........................ AlanMunro 5 58
(M R Channon) *dwlt: mostly in last trio: pushed along and kpt on fr over 1f out: nvr a factor* **12/1**
8 *5* **Miss Dutee** 2-9-0 0........................ PatDobbs 8 43
(R Hannon) *chsd ldrs: pushed along 1/2-way: lost pl and btn 2f out* **12/1**
9 *6* **Broken Belle (IRE)** 2-9-0 0........................ MichaelHills 7 25+
(J W Hills) *dwlt: t.k.h and rn green: in tch: wandered and wknd rapidly 2f out* **33/1**
10 *2 ½* **Vow Of Silence** 2-8-11 0........................ AhmedAjtebi(3) 9 18
(Mahmood Al Zarooni) *hld up in last trio: brief effrt on outer 1/2-way: wknd rapidly 2f out* **9/1**

1m 14.52s (2.32) **Going Correction** +0.175s/f (Good) **10** Ran SP% **113.9**
Speed ratings (Par 90): **91,87,86,82,82 81,79,72,64,61**
toteswingers: 1&2 £5.00, 1&3 £3.00, 2&3 £12.60 CSF £27.96 TOTE £2.30: £1.10, £2.80, £2.80; EX 20.00.
Owner Highclere Thoroughbred Racing-Masquerade **Bred** Swordlestown Stud **Trained** East Everleigh, Wilts

FOCUS
Richard Hannon had won five of the last ten runnings of this maiden, including with subsequent French Guineas winner Elusive Wave in 2008, and the trainer introduced another smart-looking type in the shape of Memory. Time will tell with regard to what she beat.

NOTEBOOK
Memory(IRE) ◆, a 72,000gns purchase, who is out of a quite useful triple winner at around 1m, needed to pushed along through the early stages after missing the break, before then raced keenly in rear after a couple of furlongs. Just after halfway she made good headway, when all the while switching right and, in the open over 1f out, she fairly bounded clear late on without being overly pressured, ultimately taking a while to be pulled up after the line. This was an impressive performance and she'll surely now be pointed towards the Albany Stakes at Royal Ascot, although she might not want the ground too quick. (tchd 2-1 and 5-2)
Goodwood Treasure, a 10,000gns purchase, shaped nicely on debut. She showed good speed to chase the pace, and was one of the last off the bridle, although she was ultimately no match at all for the winner. (op 10-1 tchd 9-1)
Elkmait, a 20,000gns half-sister to Stubbs Art, has some size and scope. She kept on for pressure to pull clear of the remainder and should improve. (op 6-1 tchd 15-2)
Sheila's Star(IRE), an eyecatcher in a weaker race than this on debut 51 days earlier, came out on top in the bunch finish for fourth. She's entitled to progress again. (op 8-1 tchd 9-1)
Apazine(USA) showed plenty of speed to a point, but was one-paced when coming under mainly hands-and-heels pressure from about 2f out. This $190,000 purchase should come on for the run. (op 5-1 tchd 11-2)
Atia showed loads of natural speed and should be suited by a return to 5f. (op 28-1)

2224 BLUE SQUARE HEIGHT OF FASHION STKS (LISTED RACE) — 1m 1f 192y
2:35 (2:35) (Class 1) 3-Y-O **£23,704** (£8,964; £4,480; £2,240) **Stalls** High

Form RPR
430- **1** **Snow Fairy (IRE)**[207] 7033 3-9-0 102........................ EddieAhern 9 108
(E A L Dunlop) *stmbld bdly s: hld up last: stl there 3f out: gd prog and swtchd lft to outer over 2f out: led 1f out: styd on wl: readily* **9/4**[1]
3-10 **2** *3* **Pipette**[17] 1726 3-9-0 100........................ RichardHughes 2 102
(A M Balding) *trckd ldr over 2f: styd handy: pushed along to go 2nd again 3f out: cl enough and rdn over 1f out: wnr sn wnt by: kpt on* **10/3**[3]
1-64 **3** *nk* **Deirdre**[21] 1613 3-9-0 94........................ RobertHavlin 6 101
(J H M Gosden) *led: shkn up 2f out: hdd 1f out: readily outpcd* **20/1**
20-5 **4** *5* **Mudaaraah**[17] 1729 3-9-3 99........................ TedDurcan 1 94
(J L Dunlop) *hld up in last pair: rdn wl over 2f out: modest prog over 1f out: tk 4th ins fnl f* **12/1**
4-23 **5** *2 ¼* **Bella Swan**[21] 1613 3-9-0 99........................ AdamKirby 3 87
(W R Swinburn) *hld up in 5th: prog to dispute 2nd briefly 3f out: rdn over 2f out: wknd over 1f out* **10/1**
5-1 **6** *3* **Thaahira (USA)**[14] 1824 3-9-0 88........................ TadhgO'Shea 5 81
(M A Jarvis) *hld up in rr: rdn wl over 2f out: no prog and sn btn* **3/1**[2]
0-26 **7** *12* **Bint Doyen**[46] 1082 3-9-0 82........................ SebSanders 4 57
(C E Brittain) *t.k.h: trckd ldng pair 6f out: rdn on outer 3f out: sn wknd* **66/1**
4- **8** *15* **Wedding March (IRE)**[227] 6523 3-9-0 0........................ FrankieDettori 8 27
(Saeed Bin Suroor) *chsd ldr over 7f out tl wknd rapidly 3f out: t.o* **15/8**[1]

2m 6.92s (-1.08) **Going Correction** -0.075s/f (Good) **8** Ran SP% **113.6**
Speed ratings (Par 107): **101,98,98,94,92 90,80,68**
toteswingers: 1&2 £9.30, 1&3 £13.10, 2&3 £19.00 CSF £51.19 TOTE £15.90: £2.60, £1.50, £3.70; EX 63.00.
Owner Anamoine Limited **Bred** Windflower Overseas Holdings Inc **Trained** Newmarket, Suffolk
■ Stewards' Enquiry : Eddie Ahern one-day ban: careless riding (Jun 2)

FOCUS
The last winner of a version of this race to follow up in the Oaks was Love Divine in 2000, although Something Exciting and Rising Cross, successful in 2005 and 2006 respectively, were placed at Epsom. Plus, for the last two years the race has produced a Royal Ascot winner, with the 2008 victor Michita taking the Ribblesdale, and last season Moneycantbuyme adding the Sandringham. Not much of an Oaks trial at all this season, with only three of eight runners entered at Epsom, and the two most interesting contenders, Thaahira and Wedding March, disappointing to varying degrees. The pace seemed fair enough and the form is fair for the grade with a clear personal best from the winner.

NOTEBOOK
Snow Fairy(IRE) never raced beyond 7f as a juvenile, but she produced improved form over this longer trip on her return from 207 days off, again showing a liking for Goodwood (close third in last season's Prestige Stakes). She raced out the back after stumbling on leaving the stalls, but settled well and was travelling best of all towards the inside early in the straight. Once switched into the clear around 2f out, she found as much as promised, drawing nicely clear. She's not in the Oaks and probably wouldn't want much further than this trip, but whatever she's worth another try in Group company.
Pipette, disappointing in the Guineas, even allowing for an unfavourable draw, fared better on this step up in trip but was no match for the winner. This is probably about as good as she is just now. (op 5-1)
Deirdre, worth a try at this trip judged on her breeding (half-sister to 1m4f winner Duncan and 1m6f scorer Samuel), was allowed a soft lead and ran well. She's a likeable filly who could have more to offer as the season progresses. (op 14-1)
Mudaaraah was just in front of Snow Fairy in last season's Prestige Stakes, but she's yet to prove she has trained on fully. (op 11-1)
Bella Swan's pedigree offered encouragement that she might improve for the increase in distance, but that wasn't the case. (op 8-1)
Thaahira(USA) really impressed when winning her maiden at the Chester May Meeting, but this represented a rise in grade and she simply didn't look up to the task. (op 5-2)
Wedding March(IRE), fourth in the Marcel Boussac when with Andre Fabre last year, looked a shadow of her former self on her debut for Saeed Bin Suroor, a trainer who has now saddled 18 consecutive losers. Official explanation: jockey said filly was unsuited by the track (op 5-2)

2225 M-REAL STKS (H'CAP) — 1m 1f
3:10 (3:10) (Class 4) (0-85,84) 3-Y-O
£4,361 (£1,306; £653; £326; £163; £81) **Stalls** High

Form RPR
51-4 **1** **Soul Station (FR)**[26] 1502 3-9-2 82........................ RichardKingscote 9 96
(R Charlton) *mde all and set decent pce: kicked at least 2 l clr 2f out: edgd lft fnl f: hld on wl* **7/2**[3]
1-14 **2** *nk* **Hypnotized (USA)**[18] 1703 3-9-4 84........................ JamieSpencer 11 97+
(M L W Bell) *hld up in 5th: looking for room fr 3f out: prog to go 2nd over 1f out: drvn to cl on wnr fnl f: hld last 50yds* **5/2**[1]
1 **3** *5* **Beachfire**[22] 1590 3-9-0 80........................ RobertHavlin 6 82
(J H M Gosden) *hld up in 8th: pushed along 3f out: nt clr run briefly 2f out: rdn and styd on to take 3rd ins fnl f: n.d* **9/1**
-202 **4** *1* **Gallant Eagle (IRE)**[16] 1761 3-8-13 79........................ PatDobbs 10 80+
(S Kirk) *stdd s: hld up last: trbld passage whn looking for run against rail fr over 2f out: pushed along and styd on on fnl f to take 4th nr fin: no ch* **12/1**
00-6 **5** *nk* **Fame Is The Spur**[21] 1620 3-8-6 72........................ EddieAhern 8 71
(J W Hills) *hld up in 7th: nt clr run towards inner 2f out: prog over 1f out: disp 3rd ent fnl f: one pce* **25/1**
00-2 **6** *7* **Song To The Moon (IRE)**[21] 1620 3-8-8 74........................ DavidProbert 3 58
(A M Balding) *t.k.h: hld up in 6th: rdn wl over 3f out: wknd over 2f out* **16/1**
0-12 **7** *1* **Our Boy Barrington (IRE)**[23] 1582 3-8-11 77........................ RichardHughes 2 59
(R Hannon) *chsd wnr 2f: wnt 2nd again 3f out to over 1f out: wknd rapidly* **3/1**[2]
100- **8** *½* **Marsh Warbler**[292] 4488 3-9-3 83........................ FrankieDettori 1 63
(M Johnston) *chsd wnr after 2f to 3f out: sn wknd u.p* **9/1**
3236 **9** *3 ¼* **Green Earth (IRE)**[9] 1969 3-8-11 77........................ JimCrowley 7 50
(Mrs A J Perrett) *trckd ldng trio: rdn over 3f out: wknd over 2f out* **33/1**

1m 55.36s (-0.94) **Going Correction** -0.075s/f (Good) **9** Ran SP% **116.2**
Speed ratings (Par 101): **101,100,96,95,95 88,88,87,84**
toteswingers: 1&2 £2.80, 1&3 £10.00, 2&3 £6.10 CSF £12.77 CT £71.86 TOTE £4.30: £1.60, £1.10, £3.10; EX 14.30.
Owner Michael Pescod **Bred** Sugar Puss Corporation **Trained** Beckhampton, Wilts

FOCUS
This looked a good 3-y-o handicap, although Soul Station was allowed an uncontested lead and the time was almost four seconds over standard. He is rated up 8lb, and it is worth taking a solid view of this form.

2226 BLUESQUARE.COM COCKED HAT STKS (LISTED RACE) (C&G) — 1m 3f
3:45 (3:45) (Class 1) 3-Y-O
£22,708 (£8,608; £4,308; £2,148; £1,076; £540) **Stalls** Low

Form RPR
2 **1** **Rewilding**[38] 1254 3-9-0 110........................ FrankieDettori 6 113+
(Mahmood Al Zarooni) *trckd ldrs in 5th: prog over 2f out: pushed into ld over 1f out: sn clr: easily* **1/1**[1]
15-6 **2** *4* **Prizefighting (USA)**[35] 1313 3-9-0 105........................ RobertHavlin 3 103
(J H M Gosden) *hld up: 7th 4f out: pushed along and prog fr 2f out: r.o to take 2nd jst ins fnl f: no ch w wnr* **20/1**
2- **3** *½* **Very Good Day (FR)**[279] 4953 3-9-0 0........................ AlanMunro 4 102+
(M R Channon) *stdd s: hld up in last pair: last whn asked for effrt over 2f out: rn green but prog over 1f out: r.o to take 3rd ins fnl f and press runner-up* **25/1**
13-3 **4** *2 ¾* **Simenon (IRE)**[26] 1498 3-9-0 101........................ LiamKeniry 9 97
(A M Balding) *trckd ldng pair: pushed along 3f out: effrt against rail to dispute 2nd 1f out but no ch w wnr: wknd* **12/1**
12-6 **5** *3 ¼* **Waseet**[26] 1498 3-9-0 110........................ TedDurcan 1 91
(J L Dunlop) *hld up in last pair: effrt on outer 3f out: sn rdn: outpcd fr 2f out* **12/1**
1 **6** *hd* **Eavesdropper**[11] 1912 3-9-0 84........................ AhmedAjtebi 5 91
(Mahmood Al Zarooni) *hld up: 6th 4f out: shkn up 3f out: no real prog fnl 2f and readily outpcd* **22/1**

1-3 **7** 1 ½ **Rashaad (USA)**[18] 1702 3-9-0 99 ... TadhgO'Shea 2 88
(B W Hills) *trckd ldng pair: wnt 2nd 3f out and sn chalng: hanging and nt qckn over 2f out: wknd over 1f out* **8/1**[3]

5-32 **8** 1 **Averroes (IRE)**[14] 1823 3-9-0 90 ... AdamKirby 8 86
(C G Cox) *trckd ldr: led jst over 3f out: drvn and hdd over 1f out: wknd rapidly: b.b.v* **9/1**

312- **9** 35 **Kalypso King (USA)**[215] 6811 3-9-0 101 ... RichardHughes 7 23
(R Hannon) *led: rdn and hdd jst over 3f out: wknd rapidly: t.o and eased* **7/1**[2]

2m 24.93s (-1.57) **Going Correction** -0.075s/f (Good) **9** Ran SP% **112.0**
Speed ratings (Par 107): **102,99,98,96,94 94,93,92,66**
toteswingers: 1&2 £8.00, 1&3 £8.20, 2&3 £22.10 CSF £26.11 TOTE £2.10: £1.20, £4.80, £3.90; EX 29.50.
Owner Godolphin **Bred** Watership Down Stud **Trained** Newmarket, Suffolk

FOCUS
The only horse to win a version of this race and follow up in the Derby was Troy in 1979, but there have been plenty of other smart winners. This year's contest didn't look that strong a trial, and the early pace was just ordinary (time almost four seconds over standard), but there was at least a clear-cut winner, who is set to take his chance at Epsom. He was value for 6l and is rated on a par with the best British Derby challengers.

NOTEBOOK
Rewilding, switched to Mahmood Al Zarooni following his second in a Longchamp Group 2 first time up this season, readily outclassed this lot. He displayed a professional attitude, handled the undulations well, and will be suited by 1m4f, so it was no surprise that he is set to be supplemented for Epsom. It's clear that he has the attributes to run a decent race, it just remains to be seen whether he is quite good enough at this stage of his career, with Simon Crisford predicting the half-brother to Dar Re Mi will do better as gets older. Whatever the case, there is an interesting point to note regarding Rewilding's performance, with him defeating Simenon by exactly the same margin as the same owner's Chabal had in the Sandown Classic Trial. (op 6-5 after 6-4 and 11-8 in a place, tchd 5-4 in places)
Prizefighting(USA), trying his furthest trip to date, narrowly came out on top in the separate race for second. He has not gone as expected since his impressive debut success, but this was a little more encouraging and perhaps he'll do better again in time. (op 16-1)
Very Good Day(FR) ◆, 41/2l behind Waseet in a 1m Sandown maiden on his only previous start last August, has done well physically since he was last seen and ran a fine race for one so inexperienced, keeping on well from off the pace (missed the break) to battle out the minor honours. He didn't look totally comfortable on the track and/or was still green, and he can do better again. By the same sire as his owner/trainer's flagship horse, Youmzain, these connections may have another smart colt on their hands. (op 22-1)
Simenon(IRE) ran a respectable race but basically wasn't good enough. (op 9-1)
Waseet, set plenty to do after starting slowly, found little for pressure and couldn't reverse recent Sandown form with Simenon. (op 11-1 tchd 10-1)
Eavesdropper, a stable companion of the winner, was coltish in the paddock and found this much tougher than the Lingfield maiden he won on debut earlier in the month. (op 20-1)
Averroes(IRE), up in grade, seemed to be running well for a long way but it was disconcerting to see him drop out really tamely late on. Official explanation: trainer said colt bled (op 10-1 tchd 11-1)
Kalypso King(USA), taken quietly to post for his first start in 215 days, was allowed a soft lead but weakened quickly and virtually walked over the line. Official explanation: jockey said colt did not face the net (op 8-1 tchd 13-2)

2227 GOLDRING SECURITY SERVICES MAIDEN FILLIES' STKS 7f
4:20 (4:21) (Class 5) 3-Y-O
£3,115 (£933; £466; £233; £116; £58) **Stalls** High

Form RPR
0- **1** **Water Gipsy**[243] 6061 3-9-0 0 ... LiamKeniry 11 77
(G L Moore) *dwlt: settled in last trio: sme prog 2f out: 5th whn eased to outer over 1f out: r.o wl to ld last 100yds: one reminder and sn clr* **16/1**

-323 **2** 3 **Nimue (USA)**[12] 1861 3-9-0 82 ... JamieSpencer 2 69
(P F I Cole) *led at gd clip: gng much bttr than nrest pursuers 2f out: pushed along 1f out: hdd and no answer to wnr last 100yds: wknd nr fin* **6/4**[1]

0- **3** nk **Lathaat**[354] 2490 3-9-0 0 ... TadhgO'Shea 10 68
(J L Dunlop) *settled in 6th: pushed along fr 1/2-way: no prog tl styd on fnl f to take 3rd on post* **22/1**

04- **4** hd **Sign Of Life**[225] 6567 3-9-0 0 ... AdamKirby 5 68
(W R Swinburn) *chsd ldng trio: rdn and effrt 2f out: swtchd to inner over 1f out: wnt 2nd but hanging: one pce fnl f* **9/2**[3]

5 **5** hd **Chilli Green**[18] 1694 3-9-0 0 ... PatDobbs 7 67
(J Akehurst) *trckd ldng pair: rdn 2f out: nt qckn over 1f out: kpt on fnl f* **12/1**

0-06 **6** 3 ¾ **That's My Style**[12] 1882 3-9-0 70 ... FrankieDettori 9 57
(J H M Gosden) *chsd ldr: rdn over 2f out: lost 2nd over 1f out: wknd: sddle slipped* **4/1**[2]

7 nse **Fashion Tycoon (IRE)** 3-9-0 0 ... RichardHughes 1 57+
(R Hannon) *sn last and rn green: pushed along and kpt on fr over 1f out: nt disgracd* **12/1**

5 **8** ¾ **Confrontation**[26] 1504 3-9-0 0 ... ShaneKelly 8 63+
(D M Simcock) *trckd ldng trio: rdn 2f out: hld whn hmpd on inner over 1f out: wknd* **12/1**

06 **9** 3 ¼ **Ramble On Love**[22] 1590 3-9-0 0 ... FrankieMcDonald 6 46
(P Winkworth) *sltly awkward s: a in rr: struggling fr 3f out* **50/1**

10 7 **Marksbury** 3-9-0 0 ... StephenCraine 4 27
(J M P Eustace) *s.s: chsd along in rr bef 1/2-way: wknd and eased over 2f out* **50/1**

1m 28.23s (1.33) **Going Correction** -0.075s/f (Good) **10** Ran SP% **115.4**
Speed ratings (Par 96): **92,88,88,88,87 83,83,82,78,70**
toteswingers: 1&2 £9.20, 1&3 £32.80, 2&3 £8.50 CSF £39.60 TOTE £30.90: £7.80, £1.10, £3.70; EX 90.70.
Owner Mrs A E V Wadman **Bred** Mrs Susan Wadman **Trained** Lower Beeding, W Sussex

FOCUS
A reasonable fillies' maiden but tricky form to pin down and it has been rated around the averages. The second and sixth were clearly not at their best.
That's My Style Official explanation: jockey said saddle slipped
Fashion Tycoon(IRE) Official explanation: jockey said filly cocked its jaw

2228 RUK SUSSEX STAYERS STKS (H'CAP) 2m
4:55 (4:55) (Class 4) (0-80,80) 4-Y-O+
£4,533 (£1,348; £674; £336) **Stalls** Low

Form RPR
3-60 **1** **Brett Vale (IRE)**[11] 1902 4-9-11 80 ... DaneO'Neill 6 87
(P R Hedger) *stdd s: hld up: last tl gd prog on outer wl over 2f out: drvn and styd on wl to ld last 150yds* **22/1**

0-30 **2** ¾ **Epsom Salts**[23] 1579 5-9-2 76 ... RichardRowe(7) 3 84+
(P M Phelan) *stdd s: hld up in last pair: prog on inner over 2f out: trapped against rail tl fnd clr run jst over 1f out: styd on wl to take 2nd on post* **16/1**

342 **3** nse **Calculating (IRE)**[15] 1798 6-8-12 65 ... DavidProbert 5 71
(M D I Usher) *trckd ldrs in 5th: clsd threateningly 3f out: rdn over 2f out: drvn and upsides 1f out: one pce last 150yds* **12/1**

3-32 **4** 1 ¼ **Curacao**[18] 1690 4-9-9 78 ... EddieAhern 8 83
(Mrs A J Perrett) *led after 2f to 6f out: led again 3f out: drvn and pressed over 1f out: hdd and no ex last 150yds* **10/3**[3]

0-23 **5** 1 **Devil To Pay**[18] 1690 4-9-8 77 ... RichardHughes 7 80
(A King) *trckd ldng pair: pushed along 3f out: asked to chal over 1f out: nt qckn ent fnl f: fizzled out tamely* **3/1**[2]

00-0 **6** 15 **Missoula (IRE)**[11] 1902 7-9-10 77 ... SamHitchcott 4 62
(Miss Suzy Smith) *trckd ldng pair: pushed along 7f out: drvn and lost pl 3f out: sn wknd: t.o* **20/1**

03-3 **7** 1 ½ **Penang Princess**[17] 1736 4-9-11 80 ... JimCrowley 2 64
(R M Beckett) *led 2f: pressed ldr: led 6f out: kicked on 5f out: hdd 3f out: wknd rapidly over 1f out: t.o* **2/1**[1]

355- **8** 13 **Colonel Flay**[205] 7066 6-9-3 70 ... JackMitchell 9 38
(Mrs P N Dutfield) *hld up in 6th: wknd 3f out: t.o* **8/1**

3m 29.83s (0.83) **Going Correction** -0.075s/f (Good)
WFA 4 from 5yo+ 2lb **8** Ran SP% **115.2**
Speed ratings (Par 105): **94,93,93,92,92 84,84,77**
toteswingers: 1&2 £15.00, 1&3 £12.70, 2&3 £7.30 CSF £317.76 CT £4362.27 TOTE £34.50: £6.20, £3.60, £3.00; EX 139.80.
Owner P C F Racing Ltd **Bred** Mrs O Murtagh **Trained** Dogmersfield, Hampshire

FOCUS
A fair staying handicap. The lead was contested for some of the way, but even so the pace was not overly strong. The first two came from the rear and returned to something like their best, but the fancied horses were rather disappointing.
Brett Vale(IRE) Official explanation: trainer said, regarding apparent improvement in form, that the gelding ran too free on its previous run and benefited from being fitted with a tongue bit which helped it settle.

2229 TURFTV.CO.UK APPRENTICE STKS (H'CAP) 5f
5:30 (5:30) (Class 6) (0-65,62) 4-Y-O+
£2,590 (£770; £385; £192) **Stalls** Low

Form RPR
0-30 **1** **Avrilo**[7] 2021 4-8-10 53 ... AshleyMorgan 6 62
(M S Saunders) *hld up and racd on outer: prog 3f out: rdn to ld over 1f out: styd on wl* **4/1**[2]

24-2 **2** ¾ **Tiger Trail (GER)**[20] 1638 6-8-10 56 ... JohnFahy(3) 9 63
(Mrs N Smith) *stdd s: hld up last: smooth prog on outer fr 1/2-way: wnt 2nd 1f out: drvn to chal but nt qckn last 100yds* **9/2**[3]

6500 **3** 2 ¼ **Commandingpresence (USA)**[16] 1762 4-8-5 48 oh2 ... KierenFox 2 47
(J J Bridger) *settled in last pair: pushed along 1/2-way: rdn and prog over 1f out: styd on to take 3rd last 75yds* **16/1**

0-0 **4** 1 **The Lord**[11] 1915 10-8-12 60 ... MatthewCosham(5) 4 55
(W G M Turner) *lost pl against rail over 3f out: sn pushed along: nt clr run 2f out: prog to chse ldng pair jst ins fnl f: no imp: lost 3rd last 75yds* **10/1**

-526 **5** 2 ¼ **Desert Strike**[15] 1799 4-9-2 62 ... DuilioDaSilva(3) 5 49
(P F I Cole) *pressed ldrs tl fdd u.p over 1f out* **9/2**[3]

5503 **6** 2 ½ **Thoughtsofstardom**[4] 2123 7-8-4 54 ... LeonnaMayor(7) 8 32
(P S McEntee) *sn racd against rail: w ldrs 2f: struggling sn after 1/2-way* **3/1**[1]

06-0 **7** shd **Island Legend (IRE)**[11] 1915 4-9-3 60 ... DeclanCannon 11 38
(J M Bradley) *t.k.h on outer: pressed ldrs: led jst over 2f out to over 1f out: wknd* **13/2**

0-05 **8** shd **Louie's Lad**[17] 1737 4-8-6 49 ... (p) AmyBaker 10 26
(J J Bridger) *racd freely: led to jst over 2f out: sn wknd* **20/1**

59.05 secs (0.65) **Going Correction** +0.175s/f (Good) **8** Ran SP% **114.4**
Speed ratings (Par 101): **101,99,96,94,91 87,86,86**
toteswingers: 1&2 £5.30, 1&3 £6.90, 2&3 £9.80 TOTE £4.50: £1.80, £1.10, £5.20; EX 24.20 Place 6: £407.83 Place 5: £230.92.
Owner Paul Nicholas **Bred** D & S Horn **Trained** Green Ore, Somerset

FOCUS
A moderate apprentice handicap, and straightforward form.
T/Jkpt: Not won. T/Plt: £270.50. Pool: £95,877.34 - 258.67 winning tickets. T/Qpdt: £23.30 Pool: £5,951.94 - 188.27 winning tickets. JN

1908 LINGFIELD (L-H)
Wednesday, May 19

OFFICIAL GOING: Turf course - good to firm (7.7); all-weather - standard
Wind: modest, across Weather: warm and sunny

2230 LINGFIELD PARK OWNERS CLUB H'CAP (DIV I) 1m 3f 106y
1:50 (1:51) (Class 6) (0-60,60) 4-Y-O+
£1,706 (£503; £252) **Stalls** High

Form RPR
03-1 **1** **Mediterranean Sea (IRE)**[90] 599 4-8-10 52 ... RyanMoore 2 61
(J R Jenkins) *chsd ldng pair: wnt 2nd over 3f out: sn rdn: drvn ahd ent fnl f: kpt on wl u.p* **10/3**[2]

5016 **2** 1 **Ghufa (IRE)**[21] 1623 6-8-11 58 ... SimonPearce(5) 5 65+
(J Pearce) *stdd after s: hld up wl bhd: stl last ent st: hdwy on inner 3f out: modest 6th 2f out: r.o to chse wnr wl ins fnl f: nvr gng to get there* **11/4**[1]

540- **3** 2 ¾ **Mossmann Gorge**[263] 5246 8-8-4 46 oh1 ... (p) KevinGhunowa 4 49
(A Middleton) *chsd ldrs: rdn to chse ldng trio wl over 2f out: kpt on u.p to press ldrs 1f out: one pce after* **8/1**

210- **4** shd **Iguacu**[156] 7750 6-8-4 51 ... MatthewDavies(5) 8 53
(George Baker) *in tch in midfield: c wd bnd over 3f out: drvn and chsd ldng trio ent fnl 2f: one pce ins fnl f* **4/1**[3]

00-0 **5** 1 **Ledgerwood**[35] 1301 5-8-5 47 oh1 ow1 ... (p) NeilChalmers 6 48?
(A J Chamberlain) *led: clr 8f out: rdn wl over 2f out: hdd and drvn 1f out: wknd ins fnl f* **200/1**

-000 **6** 7 **Mixing**[21] 1623 8-8-4 46 oh1 ... AndreaAtzeni 3 35
(M J Attwater) *in tch in midfield: effrt u.p 3f out: no prog and wl hld fnl 2f* **40/1**

5300 **7** 6 **Ladies Dancing**[16] 1763 4-8-13 60 ... SophieDoyle(5) 1 39
(J A Osborne) *stdd after s: t.k.h: hld up in last trio: rdn and short-lived effrt 3f out: wl btn fnl 2f* **12/1**

2650 **8** 21 **Mid Wicket (USA)**[10] 539 4-8-8 50 ... SteveDrowne 10 —
(Mouse Hamilton-Fairley) *in tch in midfield: lost pl qckly downhill 4f out: bhd and rdn w no rspnse over 3f out: t.o and eased fr over 1f out* **10/1**

300 **9** 1 **Alternative Choice (USA)**[54] 989 4-9-0 56 ... J-PGuillambert 9 —
(N P Littmoden) *dwlt: a in rr: pushed along and struggling downhill 4f out: lost tch over 3f out: t.o* **20/1**

-605 **10** *1* **Fleur De'Lion (IRE)**[2] 2165 4-9-4 60 GeorgeBaker 11 —
(S Kirk) *chsd ldr tl over 3f out: sn lost pl u.p: wl bhd and eased fr over 1f out: t.o* **14/1**

2m 37.0s (5.50) **Going Correction** +0.525s/f (Yiel) **10** Ran SP% **112.0**
Speed ratings (Par 101): **101,100,98,98,97 92,88,72,72,71**
toteswingers: 1&2 £2.90, 1&3 £5.90, 2&3 £2.40 CSF £12.14 CT £64.54 TOTE £2.70: £1.10, £2.00, £2.90; EX 11.30 Trifecta £42.40 Pool: £254.41 - 4.43 winning units..
Owner Mrs Wendy Jenkins **Bred** D H W Dobson **Trained** Royston, Herts

FOCUS
The ground was officially good to firm, but the 6mm of water had been applied the previous day, the times were very much on the slow side and they were kicking the top off. The suspicion is that this was overwatered ground. This was a weak handicap although it was quicker than division one. The form is rated around the front pair.
Alternative Choice(USA) Official explanation: vet said gelding lost front left shoe

2231 LINGFIELD MARRIOTT HOTEL & COUNTRY CLUB MAIDEN STKS 1m 3f 106y
2:25 (2:27) (Class 5) 3-Y-O+ **£2,729** (£806; £403) **Stalls High**

Form RPR

1 **Ugalla** 3-7-13 0 HarryBentley(7) 1 74
(W J Knight) *hld up in tch towards rr: hdwy and pushed along 3f out: edgd lft and chse ldrs over 1f out: rdn to ld ins fnl f: r.o wl* **25/1**

00 **2** *1 ½* **Never Can Tell (IRE)**[6] 2050 3-8-1 0 SophieDoyle(5) 5 72
(J A Osborne) *led: rdn and hrd pressed 3f out: hdd wl over 1f out: sn lft in ld again: hdd and one pce ins fnl f* **40/1**

3 *1* **Treacle Tart**[40] 5-9-4 0 WilliamCarson(3) 4 70
(Eugene Stanford) *t.k.h: hdwy to chal over 2f out: pushed to ld wl over 1f out: sn hung bdly rt and hdd: stყd on same pce fnl f* **16/1**

32- **4** *4 ½* **Chincoteague (IRE)**[233] 6332 4-9-7 0 MartinDwyer 6 62
(B J Meehan) *chsd ldrs: rdn and unable qck wl over 2f out: drvn and btn ent fnl f* **4/1**[3]

3- **5** *9* **Wadnaan**[265] 5371 3-8-11 0 JoeFanning 7 52
(M Johnston) *chsd ldr: rdn and racd awkwardly 3f out: nt qckn and sn struggling: wl btn fnl 2f* **6/4**[1]

6-36 **6** *2 ½* **Pekan Three (IRE)**[14] 1824 3-8-11 75 TomQueally 12 48
(P F I Cole) *t.k.h: hld up wl in tch in midfield: rdn and btn 3f out: wl bhd fnl 2f* **3/1**[2]

0 **7** *1 ½* **Admiral Rodney**[21] 1627 3-8-11 0 MickyFenton 10 45
(Mrs P Sly) *stdd s: hld up in last pair: struggling downhill 4f out: lost tch over 3f out* **200/1**

6 **8** *7* **Drummers Drumming (USA)**[35] 1302 4-9-12 0 FergusSweeney 13 33
(J A Osborne) *hld up in last trio: rdn and lost tch over 3f out* **33/1**

00-0 **9** *2 ½* **Fiancee (IRE)**[21] 1620 4-9-7 62 PatCosgrave 2 24
(R Brotherton) *chsd ldrs: rdn and unable qck over 3f out: wknd u.p over 2f out: wl bhd fnl f* **150/1**

60 **10** *1* **Miss Formidable (IRE)**[35] 1302 3-8-6 0 AndreaAtzeni 11 22
(Luke Comer, Ire) *stdd after s: hld up in last trio: struggling downhill 4f out: sn lost tch* **100/1**

00-0 **11** *17* **Aintgottaname**[49] 1059 3-8-6 49 JimmyQuinn 14 —
(M J McGrath) *hld up towards rr: rdn and lost tch over 3f out: t.o* **200/1**

3 **12** *7* **Loyalty**[22] 1607 3-8-11 0 (v[1]) RyanMoore 9 —
(Sir Michael Stoute) *sn rdn along to chse ldrs 10f out: rdn along at times: dropped out rapidly over 3f out: sn wl bhd: t.o* **6/1**

2m 36.16s (4.66) **Going Correction** +0.525s/f (Yiel)
WFA 3 from 4yo+ 15lb **12** Ran SP% **117.0**
Speed ratings (Par 103): **104,102,102,98,92 90,89,84,82,81 69,64**
toteswingers: 1&2 £47.50, 2&3 £16.00, 1&3 not won. CSF £698.91 TOTE £35.70: £8.80, £10.50, £3.90; EX 408.50 TRIFECTA Not won..
Owner Mrs Alison Ruggles **Bred** Mrs A Ruggles **Trained** Patching, W Sussex

FOCUS
A modest maiden in which the market principals disappointed, and it was won by the one newcomer in the field. It was the quickest of the the three C/D races, although none were sound run.
Loyalty Official explanation: jockey said gelding did not handle the bends

2232 LINGFIELD PARK OWNERS CLUB H'CAP (DIV II) 1m 3f 106y
3:00 (3:02) (Class 6) (0-60,60) 4-Y-O+ **£1,706** (£503; £252) **Stalls High**

Form RPR

-134 **1** **Peintre D'Argent (IRE)**[20] 1635 4-8-4 53 HarryBentley(7) 10 67
(W J Knight) *chsd ldrs: c wd bnd over 3f out: rdn to ld over 2f out: gng clr whn rdr dropped whip wl over 1f out: wl clr fnl f: easily* **9/2**[2]

53-1 **2** *7* **Galiotto (IRE)**[20] 1635 4-9-3 59 GeorgeBaker 3 61
(C F Wall) *hld up in tch in midfield: clsd and trckd ldrs 4f out: rdn and fnd nil 3f out: no ch w wnr fnl 2f: plugged on fnl f to go 2nd towards fin* **11/10**[1]

00-2 **3** *¾* **Amroth**[16] 1756 4-8-10 52 RyanMoore 9 53
(P D Evans) *chsd ldr: rdn and ev ch 3f out: outpcd by wnr ent fnl 2f: wl btn after but kpt battling away for 2nd tl wl ins fnl f* **8/1**

00-0 **4** *½* **Rehabilitation**[39] 1226 5-8-12 54 (v) TomQueally 7 54
(W R Swinburn) *led: rdn and jnd 3f out: outpcd and no ch w wnr fnl 2f but kpt battling away for 2nd tl wl ins fnl f* **11/1**

0000 **5** *1 ¾* **Holyfield Warrior (IRE)**[39] 1225 6-8-9 51 HayleyTurner 8 48
(R J Smith) *hld up in tch: rdn and unable qck on inner wl over 2f out: no ch w wnr after* **33/1**

0-60 **6** *8* **Court Wing (IRE)**[29] 1437 4-7-13 46 oh1 SimonPearce(5) 1 30
(George Baker) *in tch: rdn and btn over 2f out: wl bhd fnl f* **50/1**

4-02 **7** *8* **Largem**[41] 1194 4-9-1 57 SimonWhitworth 6 27
(J R Jenkins) *racd in last trio: rdn and lost tch wl over 2f out* **14/1**

0252 **8** *10* **Pedasus (USA)**[8] 2012 4-9-4 60 (b) DarrylHolland 4 13
(T Keddy) *s.i.s: a in last pair: rdn and lost tch 3f out: t.o* **6/1**[3]

00-0 **9** *49* **Miskin Spirit**[16] 1762 4-8-4 46 oh1 LukeMorris 5 —
(B Palling) *v.s.a: a last: rdn 5f out: t.o fnl 3f* **50/1**

2m 38.99s (7.49) **Going Correction** +0.525s/f (Yiel) **9** Ran SP% **113.1**
Speed ratings (Par 101): **93,87,87,87,85 79,74,66,31**
toteswingers: 1&2 £1.80, 1&3 £4.70, 2&3 £1.70 CSF £9.49 CT £35.92 TOTE £3.20: £1.10, £1.30, £1.70; EX 9.60 Trifecta £81.30 Pool: £617.96 - 5.62 winning units..
Owner The Pro-Claimers **Bred** D Couper Snr **Trained** Patching, W Sussex

FOCUS
The slower of the two divisions by 1.99sec. Less than solid form, with the winner turning around Brighton form with the runner-up.

2233 COUNTRYSIDE DAY HERE ON JUNE 3RD H'CAP 1m 2f
3:35 (3:36) (Class 5) (0-70,70) 4-Y-O+ **£3,070** (£906; £453) **Stalls Low**

Form RPR

500- **1** **Dancing Jest (IRE)**[240] 6174 6-8-9 61 MartinDwyer 8 69
(Rae Guest) *mde all: edgd lft 3f out: rdn over 1f out: kpt on wl fnl f: edgd lft towards fin* **20/1**

6044 **2** *2* **Rocky's Pride (IRE)**[29] 1440 4-9-1 67 RyanMoore 4 73+
(A B Haynes) *chsd ldrs: rdn whn nt clr run 3f out: effrt on inner 2f out: chsd wnr and drvn 1f out: keeping on same pce and btn whn short of room towards fin* **5/1**[3]

05-0 **3** *¾* **Mons Calpe (IRE)**[12] 1883 4-9-4 70 (b) JoeFanning 11 73
(P F I Cole) *restless in stalls and s.i.s: sn bustled along and rcvrd to chse ldrs: rdn to press ldrs 3f out: nt qckn u.p 2f out: one pce and edging lft fnl f* **11/1**

03-0 **4** *½* **Barliffey (IRE)**[21] 1617 5-9-4 70 DarrylHolland 3 72+
(D J Coakley) *s.i.s: hld up in last trio: rdn over 2f out: hdwy ent fnl f: nt clr run and swtchd lft jst ins fnl f: kpt on: nvr rchd ldrs* **11/4**[1]

6-64 **5** *2 ¼* **Love In The Park**[21] 1623 5-9-1 67 PatCosgrave 5 64
(R Brotherton) *in tch in midfield: rdn and unable qck over 2f out: drvn and styd on same pce fr over 1f out* **7/2**[2]

6-00 **6** *1 ¾* **Catalan Bay (AUS)**[15] 1797 6-9-1 67 (t) SteveDrowne 9 61
(J R Gask) *t.k.h: chsd wnr: rdn ent fnl 3f: drvn and wknd ent fnl f* **14/1**

3104 **7** *½* **Hip Hip Hooray**[16] 1779 4-8-12 64 TomMcLaughlin 6 57
(L A Dace) *hld up in last trio: c wd bnd over 3f out: rdn 3f out: edging lft and plugged on same pce fr over 1f out: nvr trbld ldrs* **14/1**

0-65 **8** *10* **Lunar River (FR)**[16] 1763 7-8-7 59 (t) FergusSweeney 1 32
(David Pinder) *in tch in midfield: rdn and unable qck 3f out: wknd wl over 1f out: eased wl ins fnl f* **10/1**

5033 **9** *5* **Goose Green (IRE)**[9] 1961 6-9-1 67 ow1 GeorgeBaker 2 30
(R J Hodges) *hld up in last trio: rdn and short-lied effrt over 2f out: wl bhd and eased ins fnl f* **8/1**

2m 16.02s (5.52) **Going Correction** +0.525s/f (Yiel) **9** Ran SP% **112.2**
Speed ratings (Par 103): **98,96,95,95,93 92,91,83,79**
toteswingers: 1&2 £18.30, 1&3 £29.70, 2&3 £19.00 CSF £112.85 CT £1165.65 TOTE £29.00: £6.60, £1.90, £4.70; EX 187.30 TRIFECTA Not won..
Owner Mrs J E Lury and O T Lury **Bred** Knocklong House Stud **Trained** Newmarket, Suffolk

FOCUS
A modest handicap. The winner made all at an ordinary pace and this is muddling form.
Mons Calpe(IRE) Official explanation: jockey said gelding hung left
Barliffey(IRE) Official explanation: jockey said gelding did not handle the good to firm (loose on top) ground
Lunar River(FR) Official explanation: jockey said mare had no more to give
Goose Green(IRE) Official explanation: trainer said gelding was unsuited by the good to firm (loose on top) ground

2234 ARENALEISUREPLC.COM (S) STKS 6f (P)
4:10 (4:13) (Class 6) 3-Y-O+ **£2,047** (£604; £302) **Stalls Low**

Form RPR

5162 **1** **Chjimes (IRE)**[9] 1979 6-9-12 67 HayleyTurner 7 67
(C R Dore) *hld up in midfield: rdn and hdwy over 1f out: drvn to chal ins fnl f: styd on wl to ld towards fin* **5/1**[3]

0000 **2** *½* **Don Pele (IRE)**[9] 1979 8-9-12 58 (b) JoeFanning 1 65
(R A Harris) *chsd ldrs: wnt 2nd over 1f out: rdn to ld fnl 100yds: hdd and no ex towards fin* **25/1**

5550 **3** *¾* **Sweet Applause (IRE)**[11] 1929 4-9-7 60 TonyCulhane 2 58
(G Prodromou) *hld up in tch towards rr: hdwy to chse ldrs: gng wl jst over 1f out: rdn ins fnl f: fnd little and kpt on same pce fnl 100yds* **11/1**

1056 **4** *1* **Equinity**[8] 2010 4-9-7 57 (t) SaleemGolam 8 54
(J Pearce) *taken down early: hld up in last trio: rdn and effrt over 1f out: kpt on ins fnl f: nvr quite gng pce to rch ldrs* **20/1**

3200 **5** *nse* **Mutamared (USA)**[18] 1692 10-9-3 65 (t) RussKennemore(3) 3 53
(Andrew Reid) *led tl over 4f out: chsd ldr after tl led again 2f out: drvn ent fnl f: hdd fnl 100yds: wknd towards fin* **5/2**[1]

-140 **6** *1 ½* **Prince Namid**[28] 1482 8-9-12 67 LukeMorris 6 54
(J A T De Giles) *in tch: drvn and effrt over 1f out: kpt on same pce fnl f* **15/2**

1500 **7** *nk* **Muktasb (USA)**[12] 1885 9-9-12 57 (v) JimmyQuinn 5 53
(D Shaw) *awkward leaving stalls and s.i.s: bhd: stl 10th ent fnl f: styd on wl ins fnl f: nvr able to rch ldrs* **25/1**

2203 **8** *1 ½* **Romantic Queen**[9] 1979 4-8-10 62 (t) MatthewDavies(5) 10 38
(George Baker) *stdd and swtchd lft sn after s: bhd: rdn over 1f out: nvr gng pce to rch ldrs* **8/1**

-604 **9** *2* **Briannsta (IRE)**[8] 2008 8-9-3 49 (v) NataliaGemelova(3) 12 36
(J E Long) *crossing over sn after s: led over 4f out: rdn and hdd 2f out: wknd u.p ent fnl f* **33/1**

63 **10** *2* **Crazy Parachute**[20] 1639 3-8-11 0 RyanMoore 9 28
(G L Moore) *carried lft after s: racd keenly: chsd ldrs: rdn and struggling ent fnl 2f: lost pl bnd wl over 1f out: wl btn fnl f* **4/1**[2]

5206 **11** *11* **Arken Lad**[22] 1604 3-8-11 63 (b[1]) AndreaAtzeni 11 —
(D Donovan) *chsd ldrs: rdn and struggling 3f out: wl bhd fr over 1f out* **14/1**

1m 12.84s (0.94) **Going Correction** +0.125s/f (Slow)
WFA 3 from 4yo+ 9lb **11** Ran SP% **118.5**
Speed ratings (Par 101): **98,97,96,95,94 92,92,90,87,85 70**
toteswingers: 1&2 £17.70, 1&3 £10.70, 2&3 £49.10 CSF £128.94 TOTE £5.50: £2.30, £8.00, £3.80; EX 75.10 TRIFECTA Not won..There was no bid for the winner.
Owner Sean J Murphy **Bred** Morgan O'Flaherty **Trained** Cowbit, Lincs

FOCUS
Quite a competitive seller on paper, this has been rated around the runner-up to his winter form.

2235 STARBOROUGH CLAIMING STKS 7f (P)
4:45 (4:49) (Class 6) 3-Y-O+ **£2,047** (£604; £302) **Stalls Low**

Form RPR

420U **1** **Samarinda (USA)**[8] 1990 7-9-12 88 MickyFenton 8 83+
(Mrs P Sly) *broke v fast: mde all: rdn clr wl over 1f out: in n.d fnl f: comf* **11/4**[2]

1000 **2** *2* **Orchard Supreme**[16] 1767 7-9-11 87 RyanMoore 9 77+
(R Hannon) *hld up in tch in midfield: hdwy and rdn wl over 1f out: swtchd rt ent fnl f: sn chsng wnr: r.o but nvr able to chal* **15/8**[1]

0000 **3** *4* **Esteem Lord**[35] 1304 4-8-13 55 (b) MartinLane(3) 1 57
(Jamie Poulton) *chsd ldrs: rdn and nt pce of wnr wl over 1f out: kpt on but no ch w ldng pair ins fnl f* **40/1**

1-30 **4** *hd* **Hinton Admiral**[9] 1979 6-9-5 72 VinceSlattery 13 59
(M S Tuck) *stdd and dropped in bhd after s: n.m.r bnd ent fnl 2f: hdwy over 1f out: kpt on wl to press for 3rd at fin: nvr trbld ldrs* **25/1**

2310 **5** *1 ½* **Castleburg**[35] 1305 4-9-0 63 (be) FergusSweeney 11 50
(G L Moore) *t.k.h: hld up in rr: rdn and hdwy over 1f out: swtchd rt 1f out: kpt on but nvr any threat to ldrs* **11/1**

63/0 **6** *hd* **Ganache (IRE)**[28] 1477 8-9-2 48 GeorgeBaker 3 52
(P R Chamings) *plld hrd: chsd wnr over 5f out: rdn and nt pce of wnr wl over 1f out: lost 2nd 1f out: wknd fnl f* **40/1**

3433 **7** ¾ **Gone Hunting**[28] 1482 4-9-0 70 (t) SimonPearce(5) 10 53
(J Pearce) *bhd: rdn and wd bnd 2f out: kpt on but n.d* **15/2**

4523 **8** 1 ¼ **Ginger Grey (IRE)**[22] 1594 3-9-1 67 (p) HayleyTurner 7 52
(D R C Elsworth) *sn rdn along in rr: hdwy into midfield 4f out: rdn and outpcd wl over 1f out: wl btn fnl f* **5/1**[3]

6505 **9** nk **Goodbye Cash (IRE)**[16] 1815 6-8-11 60 StevieDonohoe 6 41
(R J Smith) *bhd: rdn and struggling jst over 2f out: n.d* **18/1**

6460 **10** 1 ¼ **Reach For The Sky (IRE)**[22] 1605 3-8-0 56 NickyMackay 12 33
(G Prodromou) *in tch in midfield: rdn and struggling whn wd bnd 2f out: wl bhd fr over 1f out* **66/1**

-000 **11** 5 **Stormburst (IRE)**[89] 615 6-8-12 45 NeilChalmers 5 25
(A J Chamberlain) *chsd ldrs tl wknd qckly u.p wl over 1f out: wl btn fnl f* **200/1**

0/00 **12** 10 **High Class Problem (IRE)**[48] 1078 7-8-9 48 (b) FrancisHayes(7) 4 2
(D C O'Brien) *dwlt: sn bustled along and hdwy into midfield 5f out: lost pl wl over 2f out: bhd fnl 2f* **100/1**

1m 25.46s (0.66) **Going Correction** +0.125s/f (Slow)
WFA 3 from 4yo+ 11lb **12** Ran SP% **115.2**
Speed ratings (Par 101): **101,98,94,93,92 91,91,89,89,87 82,70**
CSF £7.73 TOTE £3.80: £1.20, £1.70, £10.30; EX 9.30 Trifecta £231.80 Part won. Pool: £313.26 - 0.53 winning units..
Owner D Bayliss, T Davies, G Libson & P Sly **Bred** Gainsborough Farm Llc **Trained** Thorney, Cambs

FOCUS
Not a bad race for the class of contest but the first two did not need to be at their best with the third and sixth limiting the form.

2236 LINGFIELDPARK.CO.UK H'CAP 1m (P)
5:20 (5:21) (Class 5) (0-75,73) 4-Y-0+ **£3,070** (£906; £453) **Stalls** High

Form RPR

0-32 **1** **Mishrif (USA)**[8] 2009 4-9-3 72 (b) RyanMoore 10 84
(J R Jenkins) *mde all: rdn and clr over 1f out: kpt on wl fnl f: comf* **7/4**[1]

-526 **2** 2 ¾ **Land Hawk (IRE)**[26] 1508 4-8-6 66 SimonPearce(5) 3 72
(J Pearce) *chsd wnr thrght: rdn and nt pce of wnr over 1f out: kpt on same pce fnl f* **14/1**

4510 **3** 2 ¼ **Alqaahir (USA)**[11] 1914 8-8-11 73 KaseyLoftus(7) 5 74+
(P Butler) *dwlt: hld up in tch towards rr: hdwy into midfield over 2f out: rdn and kpt on to go 3rd wl ins fnl f: no threat to ldng pair* **16/1**

0-00 **4** ¾ **Mister Ross**[33] 1346 5-8-13 68 PatCosgrave 4 67
(J R Boyle) *dwlt: sn bustled up to chse ldrs: rdn and outpcd over 1f out: one pce and wl hld fnl f* **25/1**

5051 **5** 1 ¾ **Expensive Problem**[12] 1875 7-9-4 73 GeorgeBaker 2 68
(R J Smith) *hld up towards rr: hdwy on inner 2f out: rdn and disputing modest 3rd jst over 1f out: no imp and wl hld fnl f* **11/2**[2]

04-5 **6** nk **Kiss A Prince**[25] 1530 4-9-4 73 HayleyTurner 8 67
(D K Ivory) *dwlt: sn pushed up to chse ldrs: rdn and wknd over 1f out: wl hld fnl f* **8/1**[3]

05-0 **7** nk **Aurora Sky (IRE)**[25] 1530 4-8-13 68 J-PGuillambert 12 62
(J Akehurst) *stdd and swtchd lft after s: hld up in rr: sme hdwy fnl f: n.d* **33/1**

5254 **8** 1 ¾ **Pyrus Time (IRE)**[13] 1839 4-9-1 70 (p) LukeMorris 1 60
(R A Harris) *in tch in midfield: rdn and outpcd ent fnl 2f: no ch fnl f* **12/1**

1-14 **9** nk **Wunder Strike (USA)**[131] 84 4-8-13 68 (p) NickyMackay 7 57
(J R Boyle) *hld up in last trio: rdn and effrt wl over 1f out: n.d* **14/1**

3-05 **10** 2 ¾ **Emeebee**[26] 1509 4-9-4 73 StevieDonohoe 11 56
(W J Musson) *a bhd: rdn and struggling 3f out: wl bhd fnl 2f* **14/1**

3160 **11** shd **Fault**[7] 2024 4-8-13 68 (t) TomQueally 9 50
(Stef Higgins) *in tch in midfield: hdwy on outer 3f out: wknd qckly wl over 1f out* **8/1**[3]

/41- **12** 3 ¼ **First Service (IRE)**[180] 7464 4-8-10 70 JemmaMarshall(5) 6 45
(M J Attwater) *dwlt: a in rr: rdn and no rspnse over 2f out: wl bhd fnl f* **20/1**

1m 38.14s (-0.06) **Going Correction** +0.125s/f (Slow) **12** Ran SP% **119.1**
Speed ratings (Par 103): **105,102,100,99,97 97,96,95,94,92 92,88**
toteswingers: 1&2 £14.30, 1&3 £17.40, 2&3 £40.40 CSF £28.36 CT £314.40 TOTE £2.30: £1.10, £8.40, £6.30; EX 36.30 TRIFECTA Not won. Place 6: £1132.10 Place 5: £751.39 .
Owner Sheik Ahmad Yousuf Al Sabah **Bred** Mr & Mrs Theodore Kuster Et Al **Trained** Royston, Herts

FOCUS
A fair handicap. The winner was alloweed a pretty easy lead and the front pair were always 1-2.
Wunder Strike(USA) Official explanation: jockey said gelding had no more to give
T/Plt: £499.100. Pool:£55575.620 - 81.28 winning tickets. T/Qpdt: £159.60. Pool:£3580.23 - 16.60 winning tickets. SP

1904 HAYDOCK (L-H)
Thursday, May 20

OFFICIAL GOING: Good to firm (7.1)
Wind: Nil Weather: Cloudy turning fine

2238 SPORTECH PLC MAIDEN AUCTION STKS (DIV I) 6f
1:50 (1:53) (Class 5) 2-Y-O **£2,590** (£770; £385; £192) **Stalls** High

Form RPR

5 **1** **Minch Man**[36] 1294 2-8-9 0 AndrewElliott 12 80
(J R Weymes) *in tch: led 2f out: rdn over 1f out: hdd ins fnl f: rallied to regain ld post* **28/1**

2 shd **Imperialistic Diva (IRE)** 2-8-4 0 GrahamGibbons 11 75
(T D Easterby) *in tch: pushed along over 2f out: r.o to ld ins fnl f: hdd post* **12/1**

3 2 ½ **Bay Of Fires (IRE)** 2-8-4 0 AndreaAtzeni 6 67
(J Hetherton) *hld up: hdwy over 1f out: chsd front pair ins fnl f: nt qckn towards fin* **33/1**

6 **4** 4 ½ **Swendab (IRE)**[8] 2022 2-8-9 0 LukeMorris 8 59
(J G M O'Shea) *chsd ldrs: pushed along 2f out: rdn and hung lft over 1f out: no ex fnl 100yds* **12/1**

02 **5** 1 ½ **Colorado Gold**[16] 1793 2-8-13 0 PaulHanagan 1 58
(P F I Cole) *led: hdd after 2f: remained prom: rdn over 1f out: wknd ins fnl f* **5/2**[2]

6 2 **Witzend (IRE)** 2-8-13 0 PaulMulrennan 3 52
(Jedd O'Keeffe) *hld up: hdwy 2f out: sn chsd ldrs: wknd fnl 100yds* **80/1**

7 2 ¾ **Speed Gene (IRE)** 2-8-4 0 FrankieMcDonald 5 35
(R Hannon) *bmpd s: in rr: rdn over 1f out: no imp* **16/1**

5 **8** 1 **West Leake Bridge (IRE)**[12] 1901 2-9-2 0 MichaelHills 2 44
(B W Hills) *in tch: pushed along 2f out: rdn and ch over 1f out: wknd ent fnl f* **6/4**[1]

6 **9** 5 **Rational Act (IRE)**[33] 1389 2-8-11 0 DuranFentiman 7 24
(T D Easterby) *racd keenly in midfield: dropped away over 2f out* **33/1**

6 **10** 7 **Roman Dancer (IRE)**[19] 1686 2-8-13 0 TadhgO'Shea 9 —+
(J Gallagher) *rrd s: slowly away and rdr lost irons: rapid hdwy to ld after 2f: hdd 2f out: sn wknd* **9/1**[3]

0 **11** ½ **Commercial (IRE)**[14] 1845 2-8-11 0 FergusSweeney 4 —
(J A Osborne) *racd keenly in midfield: wknd over 1f out* **25/1**

1m 14.91s (1.41) **Going Correction** -0.125s/f (Firm) **11** Ran SP% **114.2**
Speed ratings (Par 93): **92,91,88,82,80 77,74,72,66,56 56**
toteswingers:1&2:£31.60, 1&3:£52.70, 2&3:£32.60 CSF £307.37 TOTE £45.10: £8.20, £4.60, £9.90; EX 285.50.
Owner J C S Wilson **Bred** J C S Wilson Bloodstock **Trained** Middleham Moor, N Yorks

FOCUS
This looked the weaker of the two divisions and the time was 0.26 seconds slower than the second leg, won by Premier Clarets. A big step up from the winner but no fluke.

NOTEBOOK
Minch Man improved significantly on the form he showed over 5f on debut at Beverley, proving game under pressure to deny a debutante filly. His attitude should ensure he's competitive during the nursery season. (op 50-1 tchd 25-1)
Imperialistic Diva(IRE) looked set to prevail narrowly for much of the final furlong, but even so it was a surprise to note afterwards that the filly touched 1.01 in running on Betfair. Out of a quite useful multiple 6f-1m winner, she was green in the paddock beforehand and is open to improvement. (op 16-1)
Bay Of Fires(IRE), a 3,500euros half-sister to 6.5f winner Derpat, and Cothrom Na Feinne, a 1m winner who was also successful over hurdles, didn't threaten the front two but pulled clear of the remainder in third. Quite a big filly, she's entitled to come on for this.
Swendab(IRE), who ran to only a moderate level on debut, lacked the speed of the front three and edged left under pressure. (op 11-1)
Colorado Gold showed plenty of speed but he found disappointingly little for pressure. (op 9-4 tchd 11-4)
West Leake Bridge(IRE) showed plenty of ability on debut over 5f at Ascot, but he was not in the same form this time, appearing to become a little unbalanced when under pressure. (op 11-8)
Roman Dancer(IRE) Official explanation: jockey said colt reared leaving the stalls and he lost his irons

2239 SPORTECH PLC MAIDEN AUCTION STKS (DIV II) 6f
2:20 (2:24) (Class 5) 2-Y-O **£2,590** (£770; £385; £192) **Stalls** High

Form RPR

2 **1** **Premier Clarets (IRE)**[16] 1806 2-8-13 0 PaulHanagan 6 86
(R A Fahey) *in tch: rdn to chse ldr over 1f out: r.o to ld fnl 110yds: wl on top at fin* **2/1**[2]

3362 **2** 2 **Master Macho (IRE)**[10] 1957 2-8-9 0 TadhgO'Shea 7 76
(M R Channon) *led: rdn over 1f out: hdd fnl 110yds: no ex cl home* **12/1**

2 **3** ¾ **Dr Green (IRE)**[14] 1845 2-8-13 0 RichardHughes 3 78
(R Hannon) *chsd ldrs: rdn over 1f out: styd on same pce ins fnl f* **1/1**[1]

4 **4** nk **Tarantella Lady**[19] 1686 2-8-8 0 PJMcDonald 4 73+
(G M Moore) *rn green in midfield: outpcd 2f out: styd on fnl f: nt pce to chal* **14/1**

2 **5** 7 **Tilliemint (IRE)**[19] 1704 2-8-4 0 GrahamGibbons 2 47
(T D Easterby) *in tch: rdn and outpcd over 2f out: no imp after* **7/1**[3]

6 **6** 2 **Wild Hysteria (IRE)**[16] 1800 2-8-9 0 MickyFenton 11 46
(T P Tate) *chsd ldr tl rdn over 1f out: wknd ins fnl f* **40/1**

7 1 **Moorland Boy** 2-8-11 0 FergusSweeney 10 45
(J A Osborne) *towards rr: rdn and sme hdwy 2f out: no imp on ldrs* **33/1**

8 3 ½ **Miss Cosette (IRE)** 2-8-4 0 AndrewMullen 9 27
(T D Barron) *dwlt: rn green and outpcd: nvr on terms* **25/1**

5 **9** 7 **Celtic Anu**[19] 1704 2-8-9 0 PaulMulrennan 5 11
(Patrick Morris) *s.i.s: stl looked green: bhd: wl outpcd fr 1/2-way* **80/1**

10 hd **Karafuse (IRE)** 2-8-4 0 DuranFentiman 8 6+
(T D Easterby) *walked out of stalls: a bhd* **50/1**

0 **11** 12 **Phair Winter**[36] 1292 2-8-5 0 ow1 AndrewElliott 1 —
(A D Brown) *prom: rdn 1/2-way: lost pl over 2f out: edgd rt and wknd wl over 1f out* **100/1**

1m 14.65s (1.15) **Going Correction** -0.125s/f (Firm) **11** Ran SP% **123.6**
Speed ratings (Par 93): **94,91,90,89,80 77,76,71,62,62 46**
toteswingers:1&2:£5.20, 1&3:£1.80, 2&3:£3.80 CSF £26.20 TOTE £3.70: £1.30, £3.50, £1.10; EX 26.10.
Owner The Matthewman Partnership **Bred** Killarkin Stud **Trained** Musley Bank, N Yorks
■ Stewards' Enquiry : Paul Hanagan two-day ban: used whip with excessive frequency (Jun 3, 6)

FOCUS
The time was 0.26 seconds quicker than the first division, which was won by Minch Man. The first four were clear and this is strong form for the grade.

NOTEBOOK
Premier Clarets(IRE) took a while to pick up but he was nicely on top at the line and confirmed the promise he showed when runner-up over 5f on debut at Newcastle, having been strongly supported beforehand. He looks useful. (op 5-2 tchd 3-1 in a place)
Master Macho(IRE), the most exposed in the line-up having been beaten five times already, put his experience to good use in a race where few got involved, but he was simply beaten by a better colt. (op 10-1)
Dr Green(IRE) failed to progress as one might have hoped from his promising debut effort. He showed speed to chase the pace, but never looked to be travelling all that strongly and was laboured under pressure. (tchd 6-5)
Tarantella Lady was under pressure throughout and didn't look totally comfortable on the quick ground, but she made some late headway, confirming the ability she showed on debut. Easier going ought to suit. (op 16-1)
Tilliemint(IRE) was beaten only a neck on debut over 5f at Thirsk, but she failed to improve on that form, coming under pressure by halfway and making only limited progress. (op 8-1 tchd 13-2)

2240 CLASSIC LODGES H'CAP 1m 2f 95y
2:50 (2:50) (Class 5) (0-75,73) 4-Y-0+ **£2,914** (£867; £433; £216) **Stalls** High

Form RPR

0-04 **1** **Visions Of Johanna (USA)**[14] 1840 5-8-10 65 RichardHughes 1 79
(Ian Williams) *in tch: shkn up to make prog bhd ldng pair 2f out: effrt to chal over 1f out: led narrowly ins fnl f: kpt up to work towards fin* **5/2**[2]

4053 **2** nk **Hawaana (IRE)**[13] 1883 5-9-3 72 PaulDoe 7 85+
(Miss Gay Kelleway) *chsd ldr: rdn to ld over 2f out: hdd narrowly ins fnl f: kpt on and continued to push wnr to the line* **7/2**[3]

-452 **3** 6 **Oriental Cavalier**[13] 1883 4-9-4 73 (v) GrahamGibbons 2 75
(R Hollinshead) *led: rdn and hdd over 2f out: continued to chse ldrs: no ex ins fnl f* **9/4**[1]

-611 **4** 3 ¾ **Bernix**[27] 1508 8-8-9 64 (p) TomEaves 8 58
(N Tinkler) *chsd ldrs: rdn over 3f out: sn outpcd: n.d after* **9/1**

5- **5** 1 ¾ **Holden Eagle**[211] 6941 5-9-3 72 (t) FergusSweeney 4 63
(A G Newcombe) *s.i.s: hld up: rdn 3f out: outpcd after* **7/1**

33-0 **6** 1 ¼ **Cavendish Road (IRE)**[96] 543 4-8-13 68 GregFairley 3 57
(N J Vaughan) *in tch: outpcd over 3f out: n.d after* **16/1**

-000 7 33 **Pitbull**[18] 1717 7-8-4 **59** oh10............(p) PatrickMathers 5 —
(A Berry) *missed break: in rr: rdn 4f out: sn lft wl bhd* **100/1**

2m 14.33s (-1.67) **Going Correction** +0.15s/f (Good) 7 Ran SP% **110.9**
Speed ratings (Par 103): **100,99,94,91,90 89,63**
toteswingers:1&2:£2.80, 1&3:£1.80, 2&3:£2.20 CSF £10.95 CT £20.02 TOTE £3.60: £2.30, £3.00; EX 13.30.
Owner Dr Marwan Koukash **Bred** David S Milch **Trained** Portway, Worcs
■ Stewards' Enquiry : Paul Doe two-day ban: used whip without giving gelding sufficient time to respond (Jun 7-8)

FOCUS
A strongly run race. They finished strung out behind the front two and this is ordinary handicap form. The race could be rated up to 3lb higher.

2241 WIN £3 MILLION AT FOOTBALLPOOLS.COM H'CAP 1m 30y
3:25 (3:26) (Class 3) (0-90,90) 4-Y-0+ **£9,066** (£2,697; £1,348; £673) **Stalls** Low

Form RPR

0416 1 **Ezdeyaad (USA)**[16] 1802 6-8-10 **82**............ PJMcDonald 1 91
(G A Swinbank) *in tch: swtchd rt over 2f out: led narrowly over 1f out: r.o u.p: hld on wl cl home* **9/2**[2]

1-52 2 *hd* **Jordaura**[22] 1617 4-8-12 **84**............ JerryO'Dwyer 6 92
(J R Holt) *hld up: hdwy 2f out: swtchd rt over 1f out: r.o ins fnl f: chalng fnl 100yds: jst hld* **7/1**

3-00 3 *1* **Fastnet Storm (IRE)**[14] 1837 4-9-4 **90**............ MickyFenton 10 96
(T P Tate) *led: rdn and hdd narrowly over 1f out: r.o u.p and continued to press wnr ins fnl f: hld fnl strides* **12/1**

35-0 4 *1 1/4* **Webbow (IRE)**[13] 1857 8-9-4 **90**............ TomEaves 2 93
(N Tinkler) *midfield: hdwy on inner 2f out: nt clr run briefly over 1f out: rdn to chse ldrs sn after: nt qckn ins fnl f* **3/1**[1]

6012 5 *1 3/4* **Just Bond (IRE)**[9] 1990 8-8-9 **84**............ BarryMcHugh(3) 3 83
(G R Oldroyd) *hld up in rr: rdn and hdwy over 1f out: kpt on to chse front quartet ins fnl f: nt pce to chal ldrs* **5/1**[3]

1101 6 *2 1/2* **Trans Sonic**[15] 1826 7-8-2 **79**............ JamesSullivan(5) 7 72
(J Hetherton) *handy: chsd ldr after 2f: rdn to chal over 2f out: lost 2nd wl over 1f out: wknd ins fnl f* **16/1**

01-5 7 *2 3/4* **Mujaadel (USA)**[19] 1707 5-8-5 **77**............(p) AndrewMullen 4 64
(D Nicholls) *chsd ldr for 2f: remained cl up: rdn and struggling to hold pl whn n.m.r over 1f out: sn wknd* **12/1**

120 8 *4 1/2* **Kidlat**[17] 1780 5-8-7 **82**............ MarcHalford(3) 8 62
(A Bailey) *in tch: shkn up 4f out: rdn and wknd 2f out: eased whn wl btn ins fnl f* **8/1**

223- 9 *3 3/4* **Gala Casino Star (IRE)**[174] 7560 5-9-2 **88**............ PaulHanagan 5 56
(R A Fahey) *hld up: pushed along 2f out: nvr on terms* **17/2**

3654 10 *2 1/2* **Carnivore**[36] 1306 8-8-4 **76**............ GrahamGibbons 9 38
(T D Barron) *midfield: pushed along over 2f out: wknd over 1f out* **16/1**

1m 43.43s (-1.27) **Going Correction** +0.15s/f (Good) 10 Ran SP% **121.1**
Speed ratings (Par 107): **107,106,105,104,102 100,97,93,89,86**
toteswingers:1&2:£6.50, 1&3:£14.30, 2&3:£17.20 CSF £37.68 CT £370.04 TOTE £6.30: £2.20, £1.90, £4.50; EX 43.00.
Owner B Boanson & M Wane **Bred** Caldara Farm **Trained** Melsonby, N Yorks
■ Stewards' Enquiry : Jerry O'Dwyer caution: used whip with excessive frequency

FOCUS
This was a good, competitive handicap, and the pace seemed fair.

NOTEBOOK
Ezdeyaad(USA) didn't get much of a run when beaten favourite at Catterick on his previous start, but he enjoyed a better trip this time and defied a 3lb higher mark than when successful at Musselburgh on his penultimate outing. He should remain competitive. (op 11-2)
Jordaura raced out the back after starting slowly and had to be switched from the inside with less than 2f to run. He stuck on all the way to the line once in the clear and this was a decent effort off a mark 3lb higher than when second at Ascot on his previous start. (op 5-1)
Fastnet Storm(IRE) had to go off quickly to get to the front from stall ten, and he was kept honest by Trans Sonic, so he did well to last for so long, proving game when joined over 1f out. (op 14-1)
Webbow(IRE), denied a clear run at Chester on his reappearance, again had his path blocked, although it's debatable whether or not he was that unlucky. When looking for room halfway up the straight, there seemed to be a narrow gap against the inside rail but he didn't take it, and when in the open late on, albeit too late, he was one-paced. Official explanation: jockey said gelding was denied a clear run (op 7-2 tchd 4-1 and 9-2 in a place)
Just Bond(IRE)'s rider sat quietly on him for much of the way following a slow start, but once under pressure he carried his head a touch high and didn't look to be striding out fully. (op 8-1)
Mujaadel(USA) was keeping on but appearing reluctant to take a narrow gap between runners when squeezed up inside the final 2f. (op 18-1)

2242 BETDAQ THE BETTING EXCHANGE H'CAP 7f 30y
4:00 (4:00) (Class 4) (0-80,80) 3-Y-O **£5,180** (£1,541; £770; £384) **Stalls** Low

Form RPR

15- 1 **Madam Macie (IRE)**[208] 7033 3-9-3 **79**............ GrahamGibbons 9 93
(J Hetherton) *mde all: qcknd clr 2f out: comf* **8/1**

41-2 2 *4 1/2* **Gene Autry (USA)**[17] 1776 3-9-4 **80**............ RichardHughes 7 90+
(R Hannon) *hld up: nt clr run 2f out and plenty to do: hdwy over 1f out: chsd wnr in vain wl ins fnl f: no ch* **11/10**[1]

-323 3 *1* **High Importance (USA)**[12] 1934 3-8-12 **74**............ PaulHanagan 5 73
(J Noseda) *chsd ldrs: wnt 2nd over 2f out: rdn and no imp on wnr over 1f out: lost 2nd wl ins fnl f: kpt on same pce* **9/2**[2]

514- 4 *1 3/4* **Emerald Girl (IRE)**[223] 6643 3-8-9 **71**............ FrederikTylicki 4 65
(R A Fahey) *racd keenly: chsd ldrs: rdn over 2f out: one pce over 1f out* **15/2**[3]

5-50 5 *4* **Khajaaly (IRE)**[20] 1659 3-8-8 **70**............ TadhgO'Shea 3 53
(E A L Dunlop) *hld up in midfield: rdn and hdwy to chse ldrs over 2f out: wknd 1f out* **15/2**[3]

10-6 6 *3 1/2* **Admire The View (IRE)**[29] 1480 3-9-2 **78**............ RichardMullen 8 52
(D R Lanigan) *hld up in midfield: rdn 2f out: no imp: wknd over 1f out* **14/1**

5-00 7 *1 1/4* **Hail Bold Chief (USA)**[16] 1804 3-8-8 **70**............ PJMcDonald 1 41
(G A Swinbank) *chsd wnr tl rdn over 2f out: wknd over 1f out* **40/1**

010 8 *1 1/4* **Skyfire**[29] 1476 3-8-13 **75**............ GregFairley 6 42
(M Johnston) *midfield: rdn 2f out: sn wknd* **16/1**

26-1 9 *1/2* **Master Of Dance (IRE)**[137] 22 3-9-2 **78**............ PaulMulrennan 2 44
(J G Given) *n.m.r and hmpd after 1f: a bhd: rdn over 1f out: nvr on terms* **25/1**

1m 30.98s (-1.72) **Going Correction** +0.15s/f (Good) 9 Ran SP% **119.3**
Speed ratings (Par 101): **101,95,94,92,88 84,82,81,80**
toteswingers:1&2:£4.90, 1&3:£7.20, 2&3:£2.20 CSF £17.79 CT £48.12 TOTE £10.90: £2.40, £1.10, £1.80; EX 23.60.
Owner R Fell & K Everitt **Bred** Michael McGlynn **Trained** Norton, N Yorks

FOCUS
A fair handicap, although the gallop was just ordinary with the winner allowed to dominate. The second met trouble but the form has been rated at something like face value.
Master Of Dance(IRE) Official explanation: jockey said colt suffered interference shortly after the start

2243 AMBROSE PLANT HIRE H'CAP 1m 3f 200y
4:35 (4:36) (Class 4) (0-85,83) 4-Y-0+ **£5,180** (£1,541; £770; £384) **Stalls** High

Form RPR

P12- 1 **Spirit Is Needed (IRE)**[235] 6313 4-9-4 **83**............ GregFairley 3 93+
(M Johnston) *mde all: rdn 2f out: abt 4 l clr 1f out: r.o wl* **5/1**[2]

110- 2 *2 1/2* **The Last Alzao (IRE)**[279] 5009 4-8-7 **72**............ PaulHanagan 5 78+
(R A Fahey) *in tch: clsd on outer 2f out: chsd wnr over 1f out: no imp* **13/2**[3]

15-4 3 *2* **Jawaab (IRE)**[12] 1907 6-8-11 **76**............ AdrianMcCarthy 7 79
(Mark Buckley) *hld up: rdn and hdwy over 1f out: kpt on to chse ldrs: nt quite pce to chal* **9/1**

431 4 *1/2* **Ahlawy (IRE)**[12] 1907 7-8-12 **77**............(t) MichaelHills 6 79
(F Sheridan) *hld up: hdwy 2f out: sn rdn to chse ldrs: kpt on: no ex fnl 75yds* **8/1**

36-0 5 *shd* **King's Head (IRE)**[26] 1512 7-8-7 **72**............ TomEaves 9 74
(Miss L A Perratt) *hld up: rdn 2f out: styd on ins fnl f: nt pce to rch ldrs* **16/1**

1-50 6 *1 3/4* **Bollin Greta**[12] 1925 5-8-5 **70**............ GrahamGibbons 8 69+
(T D Easterby) *hld up: hdwy 2f out: rdn whn nt clr run over 1f out: no imp on ldrs: one pce fnl f* **9/2**[1]

1-00 7 *3/4* **Caster Sugar (USA)**[17] 1780 4-9-0 **79**............ RichardMullen 2 77
(R Hannon) *midfield: effrt and hdwy to chse ldrs 4f out: wknd over 1f out* **9/2**[1]

60-0 8 *7* **El Diego (IRE)**[17] 1783 6-8-7 **72**............ TadhgO'Shea 4 59
(J R Gask) *chsd wnr: pushed along 5f out: rdn over 2f out: lost 2nd over 1f out: sn wknd* **15/2**

115- 9 *20* **Chookie Hamilton**[173] 7573 6-9-2 **81**............ PaulMulrennan 1 36
(N Wilson) *chsd ldrs: wkng whn n.m.r 3f out: bhd fnl 2f: eased whn wl btn fnl f* **20/1**

100- 10 *7* **Pictorial (USA)**[20] 1679 4-9-0 **79**............ AndreaAtzeni 10 23
(Daniel Mark Loughnane, Ire) *racd freely on outer: handy: rdn over 2f out: wknd over 1f out* **12/1**

2m 33.45s (-0.55) **Going Correction** +0.15s/f (Good) 10 Ran SP% **117.6**
Speed ratings (Par 105): **105,103,102,101,101 100,99,95,81,77**
toteswingers:1&2:£4.30, 1&3:£10.80, 2&3:£7.40 CSF £37.89 CT £287.35 TOTE £6.40: £2.50, £2.30, £3.90; EX 25.70.
Owner Mrs Joan Keaney **Bred** Mrs Joan Keaney **Trained** Middleham Moor, N Yorks

FOCUS
A fair handicap run at a decent pace. The winer impressed, the second ran a personal bedst and the form is rated around the third.
Bollin Greta Official explanation: jockey said mare was denied a clear run
Pictorial(USA) Official explanation: jockey said gelding had no more to give

2244 INJURED JOCKEYS FUND MAIDEN STKS 1m 3f 200y
5:05 (5:08) (Class 5) 3-Y-0+ **£2,914** (£867; £433; £216) **Stalls** High

Form RPR

0-2 1 **Acquainted**[15] 1820 3-8-7 0 ow1............ MichaelHills 6 81+
(B W Hills) *broke wl: chsd ldr: led over 3f out: r.o wl to draw clr over 1f out: eased fnl 100yds* **1/5**[1]

4 2 *6* **Cat O' Nine Tails**[16] 1809 3-8-6 0............ GregFairley 7 64
(M Johnston) *sn led: hdd over 3f out: rdn and outpcd by wnr over 1f out: no ch after* **10/1**[3]

3 *6* **Blazing Desert**[116] 6-10-0 0............ GrahamGibbons 2 60
(J J Quinn) *dwlt: hld up: pushed along to go pce over 2f out: styd on ins fnl f: nt pce to trble ldrs* **33/1**

4 *1 1/4* **Blackmore** 3-8-11 0............ RichardThomas 12 57
(R Charlton) *unruly bef r: missed break: in rr: hdwy over 1f out: kpt on but no imp on ldrs ins fnl f* **8/1**[2]

0- 5 *1 1/4* **Ocean Club**[211] 6943 3-8-11 0............ TadhgO'Shea 4 55
(B W Hills) *s.i.s: racd keenly: sn chsd ldrs: rdn 2f out: wknd over 1f out* **14/1**

0 6 *1 3/4* **Street Runner**[59] 963 4-10-0 0............ JerryO'Dwyer 11 54
(R Hollinshead) *hld up: pushed along 3f out: nvr on terms* **66/1**

0 7 *1 1/4* **Tinseltown**[24] 1572 4-10-0 0............ MickyFenton 8 52
(B S Rothwell) *prom: rdn over 3f out: hung lft and wknd over 1f out* **33/1**

4-55 8 *hd* **Brootommitty (IRE)**[26] 1528 3-8-6 **48**............ PaulHanagan 9 45
(N Wilson) *racd keenly: chsd ldrs after 2f: dropped to midfield 6f out: rdn and wknd 3f out* **66/1**

2m 35.58s (1.58) **Going Correction** +0.15s/f (Good)
WFA 3 from 4yo+ 17lb 8 Ran SP% **119.1**
Speed ratings (Par 103): **98,94,90,89,88 87,86,86**
toteswingers:1&2:£1.80, 1&3:£4.70, 2&3:£6.60 CSF £3.53 TOTE £1.10: £1.02, £1.90, £3.70; EX 3.60 Place 6 £350.89; Place 5 £25.41.
Owner Mr & Mrs G Middlebrook **Bred** Mr & Mrs G Middlebrook **Trained** Lambourn, Berks
■ Chickini was withdrawn (10/1, unruly at s). Deduct 5p in the £ under R4.

FOCUS
A weak maiden with no depth. The winner did not need to get close to her Cheshire Oaks form.
Tinseltown Official explanation: jockey said gelding hung left-handed
T/Jkpt: Not won. T/Plt: £938.10. Pool:£82,765.95 - 64.40 winning tickets T/Qpdt: £14.70. Pool:£6,397.85 - 321.28 winning tickets DO

2047 SALISBURY (R-H)
Thursday, May 20

OFFICIAL GOING: Good to firm (9.2)
Wind: Nil Weather: Bright

2245 E B F BATHWICK TYRES MAIDEN STKS 5f
6:00 (6:01) (Class 4) 2-Y-O **£4,695** (£1,397; £698; £348) **Stalls** High

Form RPR

3 1 **Approve (IRE)**[12] 1901 2-9-3 0............ EddieAhern 7 82
(W J Haggas) *trckd ldr tl led appr fnl 2f: rdn and edgd lft ins fnl f: styd on strly* **4/6**[1]

3 2 *1/2* **Remotelinx (IRE)**[19] 1695 2-9-3 0............ TedDurcan 4 80
(J W Hills) *bmpd s: chsd ldrs: wnt 2nd over 1f out: styng on to chal whn carried rt and lost stride patter: sn rcvrd but a jst hld by wnr* **5/1**[3]

0 3 *3 3/4* **May Be Some Time**[26] 1517 2-9-3 0............ ChrisCatlin 9 67
(W S Kittow) *led tl hdd appr fnl 2f: styd chsng wnr tl appr fnl f: sn one pce* **50/1**

4 *1/2* **Diamond Charlie (IRE)** 2-9-3 0............ DarryllHolland 1 65+
(S Dow) *slowly away: bhd: pushed along 1/2-way: hdwy fr 2f out: styd wl fnl f but nt rch ldrs* **12/1**

5 3 ¾ **Sarangoo** 2-8-12 0 DaneO'Neill 6 46+
(M S Saunders) *green and in rr: pushed along 2f out: styd on fnl f but nvr any threat* **40/1**
6 nse **Sleeping Wolf** 2-9-3 0 PatDobbs 3 51
(R Hannon) *bmpd s: sn chsng ldrs: styd on fr over 1f out but nvr a threat* **9/2**[2]
00 7 3 ¼ **Bathwick Nero**[8] 2022 2-8-12 0 CathyGannon 8 35
(P D Evans) *in tch: t.k.h and bmpd after 2f: styd prom tl wknd ins fnl 2f* **100/1**
05 8 nse **Bathwick Freeze**[9] 1999 2-8-9 0 AndrewHeffernan(3) 5 34
(P D Evans) *in tch: green and hung rt after 2f: wknd ins fnl 2f* **40/1**
9 1 ½ **Marmaduke** 2-9-3 0 NeilChalmers 2 34
(J J Bridger) *chsd ldrs to 1/2-way* **200/1**
6 10 2 ¼ **Miss Maudie (IRE)**[19] 1695 2-8-12 0 SteveDrowne 10 21
(J J Bridger) *s.i.s: a outpcd* **125/1**
11 2 **Captain Sharpe** 2-9-3 0 DavidProbert 11 19
(H J L Dunlop) *rdn sn after s: a in rr* **16/1**

61.46 secs (0.46) **Going Correction** -0.175s/f (Firm) **11** Ran SP% **117.5**
Speed ratings (Par 95): **89,88,82,81,75 75,70,70,67,64 60**
toteswingers:1&2:£1.30, 1&3:£8.60, 2&3:£16.10 CSF £4.29 TOTE £1.50: £1.02, £1.50, £10.40; EX 4.20.
Owner Highclere Thoroughbred Racing (Bahram) **Bred** Abbeville And Meadow Court Partners **Trained** Newmarket, Suffolk

FOCUS
A good gallop highlighted the superiority of the first two home, since both travelled noticeably well throughout, and they had the finish between them. The winner should go forward and rate higher.

NOTEBOOK
Approve(IRE) was all the rage, but he did not win as convincingly as the odds suggested. However, his tendency to wander left-handed suggested he was still green for this second run, and this scopey sort can be expected to improve as he gains experience. (op 4-5 tchd 10-11 in a place)
Remotelinx(IRE) was done no favours by the hanging winner but he had no chance of being awarded the race. However, he must be a good bet to complete a 3-2-1 in routine maiden company and looks capable of building on that later in the season. (op 11-2 tchd 6-1)
May Be Some Time showed much more early speed than he had on his debut, and looks effective setting the pace. He can put that to advantage in the coming months. (tchd 40-1)
Diamond Charlie(IRE), a Diamond Green debutant from a winning family, did well following an awkward start from an unhelpful draw. A potential improver, he has room for physical development and is worth a second look next time. (tchd 10-1)
Sarangoo was green and outpaced until running on late. A daughter of the speedy Piccolo, and from a stable noted for its sprinters, she can do better when she has learnt the game. (op 33-1)
Sleeping Wolf's lofty position in the betting probably owed something to the general form of the Richard Hannon-trained juveniles. He made a respectable debut but never threatened to live up to second-favouritism. (op 4-1 tchd 5-1)

2246 BATHWICK TYRES BOURNEMOUTH H'CAP 6f
6:30 (6:32) (Class 6) (0-65,65) 4-Y-0+ £2,914 (£867; £433; £216) Stalls High

Form RPR
4536 1 **Dvinsky (USA)**[37] 1276 9-9-1 62 (b) JimmyQuinn 17 69
(P Howling) *mde all: rdn fr over 2f out: hld on all out* **11/1**
5044 2 shd **Bollywood Style**[12] 1929 5-8-11 58 SteveDrowne 11 65
(J R Best) *mid-div: hdwy fr 2f out: str run fnl f: fin wl to take 2nd cl home: jst failed* **12/1**
0/0- 3 nk **Pragmatist**[358] 2381 6-8-11 61 JamesMillman(3) 16 67
(B R Millman) *chsd ldr: rdn and ev ch fr over 2f out: kpt on wl fnl f but a jst hld: lost 2nd last strides* **11/1**
-003 4 1 ¼ **The Wee Chief (IRE)**[98] 501 4-9-4 65 TedDurcan 13 67
(J C Fox) *chsd ldrs: rdn over 2f out: styd on same pce ins fnl f* **6/1**[1]
0-60 5 nk **Bateleur**[13] 1869 6-8-11 58 CathyGannon 14 59+
(M R Channon) *in rr: bdly hmpd over 2f out: hdwy approachin fnl f: kpt on wl cl home but nt rch ldrs* **14/1**
5-45 6 ½ **Plumage**[14] 1843 5-8-8 60 LeeNewnes(5) 4 59
(Miss Tor Sturgis) *s.i.s: plld hrd and sn chsng ldrs: rdn 2f out: styd on same pce ins fnl f* **16/1**
30-0 7 ¾ **Ghost Dancer**[25] 1547 6-9-4 65 (p) LukeMorris 2 62+
(J M Bradley) *stdd s and swtchd rt: plld hrd in rr: hdwy fr 2f out: styd on appr fnl f: nt qckn ins fnl f* **33/1**
60-0 8 ½ **Admiral Sandhoe (USA)**[21] 1637 4-8-13 60 EddieAhern 15 56
(Mrs A J Perrett) *in rr tl pushed along and hdwy on ins wl over 1f out: nvr gng pce to get into contention* **14/1**
300- 9 ¾ **Witchry**[195] 7275 8-8-6 58 MarkCoumbe(5) 18 51
(A G Newcombe) *in rr: pushed along and hdwy on ins over 1f out: styd on same pce ins fnl f* **16/1**
1323 10 ½ **Cwmni**[14] 1843 4-8-11 58 DavidProbert 12 49
(B Palling) *chsd ldrs: rdn and hung lft 2f out: wknd fnl f* **7/1**[2]
0-53 11 nse **Stamford Blue**[8] 2021 9-8-4 58 (b) JakePayne(7) 1 49
(R A Harris) *chsd ldrs: rdn over 2f out: hung rt and wknd fnl f* **17/2**[3]
6011 12 2 ½ **West Leake (IRE)**[16] 1799 4-8-13 60 DaneO'Neill 6 43
(P Burgoyne) *towards rr on outside: rdn and sme progs 2f out: nvr on terms and sn btn* **7/1**[2]
11-0 13 6 **Abhainn (IRE)**[17] 1762 4-8-10 57 PatCosgrave 5 21
(B Palling) *chsd ldrs over 3f* **16/1**
012- 14 ¾ **Connor's Choice**[180] 7480 5-9-3 64 ChrisCatlin 9 26
(Andrew Turnell) *chsd ldrs: rdn 2f out: sn btn* **16/1**
00-0 15 1 ½ **Rio Royale (IRE)**[38] 1258 4-9-2 63 PatDobbs 3 20
(Mrs A J Perrett) *bhd most of way* **10/1**
000- 16 4 ½ **Bold Argument (IRE)**[259] 5608 7-9-3 64 SamHitchcott 8 7
(Mrs P N Dutfield) *chsd ldrs tl rdn and stmbld 3f out: sn wknd* **20/1**

1m 13.69s (-1.11) **Going Correction** -0.175s/f (Firm) **16** Ran SP% **127.8**
Speed ratings (Par 101): **100,99,99,97,97 96,95,95,94,93 93,90,82,81,79 73**
toteswingers:1&2:£17.80, 1&3:£21.80, 2&3:£55.60 CSF £143.25 CT £1518.55 TOTE £14.70: £3.10, £4.30, £4.10, £2.50; EX 212.00.
Owner Richard Berenson **Bred** Eclipse Bloodstock & Tipperary Bloodstock **Trained** Newmarket, Suffolk

FOCUS
A competitive sprint handicap with a couple of less-exposed horses than usual finishing in the first five. High numbers were favoured and the form is rated around the second and third.

2247 BATHWICK TYRES H'CAP 6f
7:05 (7:05) (Class 4) (0-85,84) 4-Y-0+ £4,857 (£1,445; £722; £360) Stalls High

Form RPR
6444 1 **Secret Witness**[12] 1924 4-8-9 75 (b) ChrisCatlin 11 87
(R A Harris) *trckd ldr: led ins fnl 2f: drvn clr ins fnl f* **9/2**[2]
14-0 2 2 **Rapid Water**[18] 1727 4-8-13 79 DarryllHolland 1 85
(A M Balding) *broke fast fr outside draw and led: hdd ins fnl 2f: styd on u.p fr over 1f out and styd chsng wnr but no imp* **2/1**[1]
1/5- 3 ½ **Bold Tie**[352] 2562 4-8-9 75 PatDobbs 2 79
(R Hannon) *chsd ldrs: rdn over 2f out: styd on same pce fnl f* **16/1**
0-04 4 ¾ **Piscean (USA)**[13] 1874 5-9-2 82 JimmyQuinn 5 84
(T Keddy) *t.k.h: in tch: rdn and hdwy fr 2f out: kpt on fnl f but nvr a danger* **22/1**
00-0 5 ½ **Desert Icon (IRE)**[24] 1580 4-8-12 78 DavidProbert 4 78
(W J Knight) *t.k.h in rr: rdn 3f out: hdwy on outside over 1f out: styng on whn bmpd ins fnl f: sn rcvrd but nt rch ldrs* **6/1**[3]
-514 6 ½ **Sarah's Art (IRE)**[24] 1580 7-9-0 80 (t) PatCosgrave 6 79
(Stef Higgins) *in rr: rdn 2f out: swtchd lft over 1f out: styng on one pce u.p whn hung lft ins fnl f: sn no ex* **10/1**
00-0 7 ¾ **Smokey Ryder**[114] 299 4-8-5 78 JakePayne(7) 8 74
(R A Harris) *chsd ldrs: rdn over 2f out: wknd ins fnl f* **40/1**
300 8 ½ **Orpsie Boy (IRE)**[18] 1727 7-8-13 79 (b) SteveDrowne 9 74
(N P Littmoden) *outpcd most of way* **15/2**
0400 9 hd **Desert Dreamer (IRE)**[13] 1862 9-8-13 84 RichardEvans(5) 7 78
(P D Evans) *outpcd most of way: mod last prog* **40/1**
-340 10 5 **Viking Spirit**[19] 1692 8-9-3 83 (v) AdamKirby 3 61
(W R Swinburn) *in tch to 1/2-way* **12/1**
1-26 11 1 ½ **Perfect Act**[17] 1770 5-8-12 78 LukeMorris 10 51
(C G Cox) *chsd ldrs: rdn 1/2-way: wknd ins fnl 2f* **14/1**

1m 12.95s (-1.85) **Going Correction** -0.175s/f (Firm) **11** Ran SP% **116.1**
Speed ratings (Par 105): **105,102,101,100,100 99,98,97,97,90 88**
toteswingers:1&2:£2.10, 1&3:£24.90, 2&3:£18.60 CSF £13.40 CT £130.60 TOTE £7.60: £2.40, £1.10, £6.00; EX 16.60.
Owner Ridge House Stables Ltd **Bred** Cheveley Park Stud Ltd **Trained** Earlswood, Monmouths

FOCUS
The fast conditions continued to help those who raced prominently, with a high draw a help on the "straight" course. The form is rated at face value around the front three.

2248 BATHWICK TYRES SALISBURY H'CAP 1m 4f
7:40 (7:40) (Class 6) (0-65,65) 3-Y-0 £2,914 (£867; £433; £216) Stalls Low

Form RPR
6-34 1 **Firehawk**[17] 1815 3-8-8 55 CathyGannon 1 60
(P D Evans) *hld up in rr: drvn and hdwy on outside over 3f out: slt ld jst ins fnl 2f: styd on wl u.p whn strly chal thrght fnl f* **16/1**
4-41 2 shd **Leader Of The Land (IRE)**[9] 1989 3-9-4 65 6ex TedDurcan 14 70
(D R Lanigan) *t.k.h: trckd ldr tl led 4f out: narrowly hdd ins fnl 2f: sn drvn and rallied to press wnr fr over 1f out and stl upsides thrght fnl f: jst failed* **4/1**[3]
4035 3 3 ¼ **Spice Fair**[23] 1601 3-8-9 61 LeeNewnes(5) 10 64+
(M D I Usher) *t.k.h: hld up towards rr and stl keen over 5f out: hdwy on ins fr 2f out: continually looking for run fr over 1f out tl swtchd lft wl insd fnl f and fin wl to take 3rd but nvr any ch w ldng du* **16/1**
2121 4 nk **Captain Cool (IRE)**[13] 1880 3-9-4 65 PatDobbs 3 65
(R Hannon) *sn chsng ldrs: rdn along 3f out: styd on same pce fr over 1f out and lost 3rd nr fin* **7/2**[2]
00-6 5 1 ½ **Green Energy**[12] 1912 3-8-13 60 EddieAhern 12 57
(Mrs A J Perrett) *in rr tl hdwy 4f out: drvn to chse ldrs fr 2f out: wknd ins fnl f* **20/1**
00-2 6 1 ¼ **Red Barcelona (IRE)**[22] 1630 3-9-0 61 DarryllHolland 7 56
(M H Tompkins) *chsd ldrs: drvn along fr 4f out: wkng whn bmpd ins fnl f* **11/4**[1]
-055 7 1 **Highland Cadett**[73] 825 3-8-12 62 JamesMillman(3) 13 56
(B R Millman) *t.k.h: chsd ldrs: rdn over 2f out: wknd fnl f* **20/1**
00-4 8 nk **Almutaham (USA)**[26] 1521 3-8-9 56 JimmyQuinn 11 49
(J L Dunlop) *in rr: hdwy 4f out: rdn over 2f out and no imp on ldrs* **11/2**
00-4 9 20 **Flyinflyout**[19] 1696 3-8-9 59 (p) RobertLButler(3) 5 20
(Miss Sheena West) *racd on outside and t.k.h: wd bnd 7f out: chsd ldrs tl wknd fr 3f out* **33/1**
-350 10 9 **Mnarani (IRE)**[31] 1422 3-9-4 65 LukeMorris 2 12
(J S Moore) *chsd ldrs: rdn along 6f out: wknd fr 3f out* **33/1**
000- 11 ½ **Sefton Park**[218] 6772 3-8-8 55 (b[1]) PatCosgrave 4 1
(C R Egerton) *in rr: sme hdwy 4f out: sn rdn: bhd fnl 3f* **33/1**
0-05 12 20 **Swain's Quest (USA)**[14] 1847 3-9-3 64 DaneO'Neill 9 —
(Eve Johnson Houghton) *led tl hdd 4f out: sn rdn and wknd: eased whn no ch fnl 2f* **33/1**
5440 13 25 **Mister Pleau (USA)**[24] 1578 3-8-11 58 SteveDrowne 6 —
(J R Best) *chsd ldrs tl wknd 5f out: eased whn no ch fnl 2f* **66/1**

2m 35.16s (-2.84) **Going Correction** -0.175s/f (Firm) **13** Ran SP% **118.8**
Speed ratings (Par 97): **102,101,99,99,98 97,97,96,83,77 77,63,47**
toteswingers:1&2:£12.90, 1&3:£23.20, 2&3:£15.10 CSF £73.23 CT £1069.28 TOTE £23.60: £6.20, £1.50, £4.10; EX 108.20.
Owner W Clifford **Bred** J A Forsyth **Trained** Pandy, Monmouths

FOCUS
There was a good gallop, but it proved a fair pace for all, with the photo being shared between one runner who had been handy all the way and another who had been held up. The form is rated slightly on the solid side.
Spice Fair ◆ Official explanation: jockey said, regarding running and riding, that his instructions were to drop the gelding out, get him settled as he is keen and was trying this 1 1/2 mile trip for the first time. He added that the horse hung right and he had been hampered in his run by a weakening horse in the home straight, after which it had taken time to get the gelding re-balanced. The trainer confirmed these instructions, adding that the gelding has a tendency to pull very hard.

2249 BATHWICK TYRES ANDOVER MAIDEN FILLIES' STKS 6f
8:15 (8:16) (Class 5) 3-Y-0+ £3,885 (£1,156; £577; £288) Stalls High

Form RPR
455- 1 **Pose (IRE)**[231] 6418 3-8-12 78 PatDobbs 10 67
(R Hannon) *chsd ldrs: tl slt ld 2f out: kpt narrow advantage and rdn fr over 1f out: jst hld on* **5/4**[1]
2 shd **Valencha** 3-8-12 0 SteveDrowne 14 67+
(H Morrison) *s.i.s: in rr and continually green on ins but gd hdwy over 2f out: swtchd lft jst ins fnl f and again whn qckning smartly sn after: fin strly: jst failed: should improve* **10/1**
00-0 3 1 ¼ **Acquaviva**[13] 1872 3-8-9 42 (p) PatrickHills(3) 7 63
(Eve Johnson Houghton) *chsd ldr: rdn 3f out and stl upsides over 1f out and ins fnl f: styd on same pce fnl 100yds* **50/1**
- 4 2 **Bidruma** 3-8-12 0 DaneO'Neill 13 56
(Mike Murphy) *chsd ldrs: rdn over 2f out: outpcd fnl f* **22/1**
5 1 **Rare Tern (IRE)** 3-8-5 0 RosieJessop(7) 4 53+
(Sir Mark Prescott) *in rr: pushed along and styd on thrght fnl 2f but nvr gng pce to trble ldrs* **9/1**[3]
/ 6 ½ **Croeso Mawr** 4-9-7 0 AdamKirby 11 53
(J L Spearing) *in tch: pushed along and kpt on fr over 1f out but nvr gng pce to get into contention* **25/1**

4 **7** *1 ½* **Liel**[9] 2003 4-9-7 0 TedDurcan 15 49
(B J Meehan) *chsd ldrs: rdn over 2f out: wknd appr fnl f* **7/2**[2]
50- **8** *3 ½* **Thoughtful (IRE)**[237] 6241 3-8-12 0 EddieAhern 1 35+
(J W Hills) *in rr tl sme prog fr over 1f out* **9/1**[3]
0/0- **9** *shd* **Harley Fern**[195] 7278 4-9-0 31 MJMurphy(7) 2 37
(T T Clement) *outpcd most of way* **150/1**
540/ **10** *1 ½* **Turtle Dove**[707] 2982 5-9-7 58 NeilChalmers 5 32
(Mark Gillard) *led tl hdd 2f out: wknd qckly wl over 1f out* **66/1**
11 *2 ½* **Lilli Palmer (IRE)** 3-8-12 0 PaulFitzsimons 12 22
(Miss J R Tooth) *chsd ldrs 4f* **40/1**
60 **12** *2 ½* **Piccolo Blue**[38] 1257 3-8-7 0 (p) JohnFahy(5) 9 14
(C G Cox) *s.i.s: sn drvn along: mid-div 1/2-way: sn wknd* **25/1**
00- **13** *5* **Swirl Tango**[217] 6794 4-9-7 0 JimmyQuinn 8 —
(F Jordan) *pressed ldrs 4f* **150/1**

1m 14.78s (-0.02) **Going Correction** -0.175s/f (Firm)
WFA 3 from 4yo+ 9lb **13** Ran SP% **115.0**
Speed ratings (Par 100): **93,92,91,88,87 86,84,79,79,77 74,71,64**
toteswingers:1&2:£5.40, 1&3:£28.00, 2&3:£91.30 CSF £13.34 TOTE £1.80: £1.02, £3.80, £17.30; EX 12.50.
Owner Highclere Thoroughbred Racing(Childers)1 **Bred** Rathbarry Stud **Trained** East Everleigh, Wilts

FOCUS
The winner was the one with the previous figures, setting a fair standard for a maiden, but the fact that so many runners were still lightly raced this late in life suggests some weaknesses in the form. It is doubtful if the winner ran to her mark.

2250 BATHWICK TYRES SUPPORTS HEROS RE-HOMING RACEHORSES CLASSIFIED STKS 1m 1f 198y
8:45 (8:45) (Class 5) 3-Y-O **£3,238** (£963; £481; £240) **Stalls** High

Form RPR
01- **1** **Sea Of Heartbreak (IRE)**[195] 7276 3-9-0 70 SteveDrowne 4 83+
(R Charlton) *hld up in rr: stdy hdwy on outside fr 3f out: drvn to ld jst ins fnl f: r.o strly* **7/2**[2]
50-4 **2** *1* **Aattash (IRE)**[20] 1666 3-9-0 70 ChrisCatlin 10 81
(M R Channon) *led: rdn over 2f out: hdd jst ins fnl f: kpt on but nt pce of wnr* **15/2**
-360 **3** *4 ½* **Crunched**[24] 1582 3-9-0 70 PatCosgrave 5 72
(M L W Bell) *chsd ldr: rdn over 2f out: outpcd by ldng duo appr fnl f* **9/1**
03-5 **4** *4 ½* **Sandy Shaw**[23] 1602 3-9-0 68 DaneO'Neill 9 63
(J W Hills) *in rr and n.m.r 3f out: hdwy fr 2f out: kpt on but nvr gng pce to rch ldrs* **14/1**
604 **5** *½* **Southern Cape (IRE)**[43] 1165 3-9-0 68 EddieAhern 13 62
(D J Coakley) *chsd ldrs: rdn 3f out: wknd over 1f out* **10/1**
300- **6** *½* **Akula (IRE)**[244] 6066 3-9-0 70 DarryllHolland 6 61
(M H Tompkins) *stdd s: in rr: rdn: hdwy and swtchd lft wl over 1f out: styd on but nvr any threat* **16/1**
25-0 **7** *2* **Shabak Hom (IRE)**[17] 1761 3-9-0 70 StevieDonohoe 12 57
(D M Simcock) *in rr: rdn over 3f out: hung rt u.p whn mod hdwy ins fnl 2f* **6/1**[3]
5253 **8** *1 ¾* **Blues Forever (IRE)**[13] 1887 3-8-11 65 AndrewHeffernan(3) 1 54
(P D Evans) *chsd ldrs: rdn 3f out: wknd ins fnl 2f* **20/1**
60-6 **9** *3 ½* **Louisiana Gift (IRE)**[29] 1475 3-8-11 64 PatrickHills(3) 3 47
(J W Hills) *in tch: chsd ldrs 1/2-way: wknd 2f out* **50/1**
6-02 **10** *½* **Primary Colors**[23] 1602 3-9-0 70 (p) AdamKirby 8 46
(C G Cox) *in tch: rdn and sme prog over 3f out: nvr rchd ldrs and wknd 2f out* **3/1**[1]
1-05 **11** *nk* **Sounds Of Thunder**[17] 1778 3-9-0 68 JimmyQuinn 7 45
(H J L Dunlop) *rdn 4f out: bhd most of way* **16/1**
6560 **12** *32* **Gems**[30] 1461 3-9-0 52 (p) LukeMorris 2 —
(H J L Dunlop) *chsd ldrs: rdn 4f out: sn wknd* **66/1**

2m 7.96s (-1.94) **Going Correction** -0.175s/f (Firm) **12** Ran SP% **119.0**
Speed ratings (Par 99): **100,99,95,92,91 91,89,88,85,85 84,59**
toteswingers:1&2:£14.30, 1&3:£12.10, 2&3:£23.60 CSF £29.80 TOTE £4.50: £2.30, £4.00, £4.90; EX 27.60 Place 6 £78.73; Place 5 £58.60.
Owner D G Hardisty Bloodstock **Bred** D G Hardisty Bloodstock **Trained** Beckhampton, Wilts

FOCUS
A decent early gallop steadied somewhat after 3f, as the runners came off the loop, but there was no doubt about the horse with most potential. The winner could be rated 6-7lb higher but there are doubts over the strength of the form.
Akula(IRE) Official explanation: jockey said colt ran too free
Primary Colors Official explanation: jockey said colt ran too free
T/Plt: £123.70. Pool:£63,187.06 - 372.61 winning tickets T/Qpdt: £28.20. Pool:£4,785.30 - 125.22 winning tickets ST

1530 SANDOWN (R-H)
Thursday, May 20

OFFICIAL GOING: Good (good to firm in places; sprint 8.5, round 8.3)
Wind: Almost nil Weather: Sunny, warm

2251 PANMURE GORDON SMALL COMPANIES E B F MAIDEN FILLIES' STKS 5f 6y
5:50 (5:51) (Class 4) 2-Y-O **£4,533** (£1,348; £674; £336) **Stalls** High

Form RPR
1 **Maqaasid** 2-9-0 0 RichardHills 4 86+
(J H M Gosden) *lengthy: str: slowest away: hld up: last to 1/2-way: gd and sustained prog after: pushed along and r.o to ld last 100yds: promising* **7/2**[1]
2 *½* **Elshabakiya (IRE)** 2-9-0 0 NeilCallan 8 81+
(C E Brittain) *str: w'like: trckd ldng trio: shkn up 2f out: r.o to chal and upsides ins fnl f: no match for wnr nr fin* **6/1**[3]
3 *1 ¼* **Take Flight (IRE)** 2-9-0 0 FrankieDettori 3 77+
(J Noseda) *w'like: athletic: trckd ldrs on outer: rn green whn asked for effrt 2f out: r.o fnl f to take 3rd nr fin* **5/1**[2]
0 **4** *½* **Eucharist (IRE)**[24] 1577 2-9-0 0 RyanMoore 5 75
(R Hannon) *unf: scope: pressed ldr: rdn to ld jst over 1f out: hdd and one pce last 100yds* **6/1**[3]
4 **5** *2* **Good Morning Dubai (IRE)**[10] 1972 2-9-0 0 TomQueally 6 68
(B J Meehan) *w'like: led against rail to jst over 1f out: grad fdd* **7/2**[1]
6 *1 ¾* **Countess Ellen (IRE)** 2-9-0 0 RichardKingscote 7 61
(Tom Dascombe) *athletic: lw: s.i.s: wl in rr: struggling in last pair 2f out: styd on fnl f* **12/1**
03 **7** *nk* **Alexs Rainbow (USA)**[17] 1773 2-8-11 0 MartinLane(3) 9 60
(J Gallagher) *w'like: trckd ldng pair to 2f out: shkn up and steadily fdd* **100/1**
8 *1 ¾* **Mixed Emotions (IRE)** 2-8-11 0 PatrickHills(3) 10 54
(R Hannon) *leggy: s.i.s: sn chsd ldrs: outpcd and rdn 2f out: nvr on terms after* **33/1**
3 **9** *4 ½* **The Thrill Is Gone**[10] 1972 2-9-0 0 AlanMunro 2 38
(M R Channon) *leggy: s.i.s: a towards rr: wknd over 1f out* **10/1**
00 **10** *1 ¾* **Three Scoops**[12] 1930 2-9-0 0 JackMitchell 1 32
(D J S Ffrench Davis) *a in rr: rdn over 2f out: steadily wknd* **200/1**

62.29 secs (0.69) **Going Correction** -0.05s/f (Good) **10** Ran SP% **110.9**
Speed ratings (Par 92): **92,91,89,88,85 82,81,79,71,69**
toteswingers:1&2:£6.20, 1&3:£4.10, 2&3:£5.50 CSF £23.18 TOTE £5.70: £2.30, £1.30, £2.60; EX 10.90.
Owner Hamdan Al Maktoum **Bred** Shadwell Estate Company Limited **Trained** Newmarket, Suffolk

FOCUS
Course at outermost configuration, increasing distances of races on Round course by 8 yards. A quarter of an inch of rain had fallen on the previous Sunday and the ground, on the easy side at that stage, was deemed good. This was a fascinating juvenile fillies' maiden, featuring a clutch with fair form and several choicely bred newcomers. As has been the case in the past, it may well have relevance for Royal Ascot, with the winner looking a Queen Mary type. The fifth and seventh give the form some basic substance.

NOTEBOOK
Maqaasid, whose dam is closely related to 1,000 Guineas heroine Ghanaati, was well supported and scored with ease. Slowly away and last after a furlong, she began to close on the leaders 2f out and, weaving between rivals, got to the front inside the last. She was never touched with the whip and not overly pressed to score, so seems certain to win again in better company. The Queen Mary could be her next target. (op 3-1 tchd 4-1 in a place)
Elshabakiya(IRE), whose dam won over 6f as a two-year-old, was a lot quicker away than the winner, but even though she was travelling within herself 2f out, had no answer when her conqueror swept by. She ought to improve for this run and is sure to collect a some stage. (op 7-2)
Take Flight(IRE), a sister to Irish 1,000 Guineas winner Saoire, broke smartly and took a prominent position a few horse-widths off the far rail. She could not respond immediately when the winner quickened, but in keeping with her breeding, was going on nicely towards the finish and is another likely to score in the near future, possibly over a longer trip. (op 11-2 tchd 6-1)
Eucharist(IRE), from a stable with an outstanding record with its juveniles this term, had shown some ability when seventh on her debut and that experience had clearly not been lost on her, as she broke fast. She chased the pace throughout, going well, but was left behind inside the final furlong. (op 9-1 tchd 5-1)
Good Morning Dubai(IRE), representing a yard whose juveniles often improve significantly for a run, had finished just behind The Thrill Is Gone on her debut, but turned that form around. She broke fastest of all, establishing a handy lead after 2f, but looked one-paced when the principals engaged a higher gear. (op 4-1 tchd 10-3)
The Thrill Is Gone, a head in front of Good Morning Dubai first time out, does not seem to have improved from that debut effort. She was never really in the hunt here, even though she passed a couple of rivals in the closing stages. (op 9-1 tchd 8-1)

2252 PANMURE GORDON CORPORATE FINANCE H'CAP 1m 6f
6:20 (6:20) (Class 4) (0-85,85) 3-Y-O **£4,533** (£1,348; £674; £336) **Stalls** High

Form RPR
1133 **1** **Desert Recluse (IRE)**[13] 1880 3-8-11 **76** MartinLane(3) 6 82
(Pat Eddery) *hld up in 5th: moved clsr 4f out: rdn to ld 2f out: jnd ent fnl f: battled on wl* **8/1**
1132 **2** *1* **Rock A Doodle Doo (IRE)**[27] 1502 3-9-5 **81** FrankieDettori 9 86
(W Jarvis) *lw: hld up in last: taken to outer and gd prog over 2f out: wnt 2nd over 1f out: jnd wnr ent fnl f: nt qckn last 100yds* **5/1**[3]
3211 **3** *hd* **Atlantic Tiger (IRE)**[30] 1452 3-9-6 **82** RichardHills 7 87+
(M Johnston) *trckd ldr to 5f out: nt pce to hold pl and dropped to midfield over 2f out: n.m.r after: rdn and styd on wl fnl f: clsng at fin* **7/2**[1]
0-54 **4** *nse* **Stadium Of Light (IRE)**[50] 1060 3-8-4 **66** oh1 (t) NickyMackay 1 71
(H Morrison) *swtg: hld up and sn 6th: prog to trck ldrs over 3f out: short of room and rdn over 2f out: styd on wl fnl f: clsng at fin* **16/1**
533- **5** *4 ½* **Architrave**[217] 6805 3-8-10 **72** StevieDonohoe 2 70
(Sir Mark Prescott) *stdd s: hld up in 8th: rdn wl over 2f out: limited prog over 1f out: no imp after* **7/1**
3-23 **6** *¾* **Ebony Boom (IRE)**[18] 1735 3-8-12 **74** TomQueally 4 71
(H R A Cecil) *lw: trckd ldng pair: wnt 2nd 5f out: rdn to ld jst over 3f out: hdd 2f out: wknd fnl f* **8/1**
-221 **7** *5* **Deauville Post (FR)**[26] 1515 3-9-9 **85** RichardHughes 3 75
(R Hannon) *lw: hld up in last trio: pushed along 3f out: last whn nt clr run over 2f out: wknd over 1f out* **4/1**[2]
-151 **8** *1 ½* **Sir Pitt**[15] 1830 3-8-12 **74** (t) RyanMoore 8 62
(J H M Gosden) *trckd ldng trio: lost pl fr 5f out: brief effrt again on inner over 2f out: sn wknd* **17/2**
0-25 **9** *hd* **Iron Condor**[13] 1880 3-8-8 **70** HayleyTurner 5 58
(J M P Eustace) *led at gd pce: rdn and hdd jst over 3f out: wknd over 1f out* **20/1**

3m 4.40s (-0.10) **Going Correction** +0.125s/f (Good) **9** Ran SP% **114.8**
Speed ratings (Par 101): **105,104,104,104,101 101,98,97,97**
toteswingers:1&2:£13.00, 1&3:£8.90, 2&3:£4.50 CSF £47.38 CT £166.27 TOTE £17.60: £6.50, £1.10, £1.10; EX 60.80.
Owner Pat Eddery Racing (Storm Bird) **Bred** John Foley & Miss Ann Aungier **Trained** Nether Winchendon, Bucks

FOCUS
A decent three-year-old handicap, with most of the runners trying this trip for the first time. The round-course rail was unaltered since the April meeting, being at its outermost configuration in the back straight and on the bend, adding eight yards to all distances. The race was well run and there was trouble in the straight. The winner avoided it and continues to look progressive.

2253 PANMURE GORDON INSTITUTIONAL EQUITIES H'CAP 1m 14y
6:50 (6:54) (Class 4) (0-85,83) 3-Y-O **£4,533** (£1,348; £674; £336) **Stalls** High

Form RPR
14-0 **1** **Fontley**[27] 1502 3-8-12 **77** TomQueally 4 87+
(Eve Johnson Houghton) *hld up in last and detached: drvn and gd prog on wd outside over 2f out following runner-up: wnt 2nd over 1f out: styd on to ld ins fnl f* **50/1**
2-00 **2** *1 ½* **First Cat**[18] 1734 3-8-12 **77** RichardHughes 8 84
(R Hannon) *hld up in 12th and detached: rapid prog on wd outside over 3f out to ld over 2f out: drvn wl over 1f out: hdd and one pce ins fnl f* **10/1**
530- **3** *3* **Cultured Pride (IRE)**[237] 6241 3-8-10 **75** RichardKingscote 10 75
(R Hannon) *led: drvn and hdd over 2f out: lost 2nd over 1f out: no ch ldng pair after but hld on for 3rd* **66/1**
-033 **4** *½* **Yes Chef**[17] 1776 3-8-5 **73** MartinLane(3) 14 72+
(J Gallagher) *t.k.h: hld up in 11th: dropped to last over 2f out: taken to outer wl over 1f out: styd on after: pressed for 3rd nr fin* **16/1**

01- **5** *hd* **Treble Jig (USA)**[265] 5401 3-9-4 **83** .... RyanMoore 3 81+
(Sir Michael Stoute) *swtg: hld up towards rr: u.p and struggling over 2f out: kpt on fr over 1f out to press for 3rd ins fnl f: one pce last 100yds* **5/2**[1]

6-26 **6** *2* **Jutland**[27] 1502 3-9-1 **80** .... RichardHills 5 74
(M Johnston) *hld up towards rr on outer: rdn over 2f out: modest prog fr over 1f out: no hdwy fnl f* **9/2**[2]

25-1 **7** *nk* **Oriental Scot**[23] 1602 3-9-3 **82** .... FrankieDettori 1 75
(W Jarvis) *lw: trckd ldrs: rdn over 2f out: nt qckn and steadily lost pl over 1f out* **9/2**[2]

10- **8** *½* **Silver Rock (IRE)**[215] 6852 3-9-4 **83** .... GeorgeBaker 7 75
(M A Magnusson) *trckd ldr: upsides over 2f out: sn outpcd: grad fdd* **5/1**[3]

30-0 **9** *2 ¼* **Be Invincible (IRE)**[34] 1352 3-8-13 **78** .... NeilCallan 2 68
(B W Hills) *swtg: hld up in midfield: rdn over 2f out: plugging on at one pce and no ch whn squeezed out 1f out* **16/1**

415- **10** *½* **Come On Safari (IRE)**[183] 7434 3-8-12 **77** .... JimCrowley 11 63
(P Winkworth) *hld up in midfield: nt qckn over 2f out: steadily fdd over 1f out* **16/1**

4-14 **11** *4* **Fivefold (USA)**[12] 1913 3-8-13 **78** .... AlanMunro 13 55
(J Akehurst) *hld up in midfield: nt qckn over 2f out: struggling whn n.m.r sn after: wknd* **14/1**

31-6 **12** *2 ¼* **Scottish Boogie (IRE)**[30] 1453 3-8-12 **77** .... HayleyTurner 9 48
(S Kirk) *trckd ldrs: rdn and wknd fr over 2f out* **33/1**

1-14 **13** *3 ¼* **Prince Of Sorrento**[124] 203 3-8-11 **76** .... J-PGuillambert 12 40
(J Akehurst) *t.k.h: trckd ldng pair to 3f out: sn wknd* **33/1**

1m 44.04s (0.74) **Going Correction** +0.125s/f (Good) **13** Ran SP% **124.3**
Speed ratings (Par 101): **101,99,96,96,95 93,93,93,90,90 86,84,80**
toteswingers:1&2:£100.70, 1&3:£183.30, 2&3:£60.60 CSF £505.33 CT £28362.32 TOTE £66.90: £14.30, £2.70, £13.40; EX 834.60.
Owner Mrs Virginia Neale **Bred** Sarah J Leigh And Robin S Leigh **Trained** Blewbury, Oxon

FOCUS
An interesting handicap, run at a good gallop. The first two both came from the rear and the winner got back to her 2yo promise.

2254 HARRY PANMURE GORDON MEMORIAL H'CAP 1m 2f 7y
7:25 (7:25) (Class 4) (0-85,82) 3-Y-O **£4,533** (£1,348; £674; £336) **Stalls High**

Form RPR

61-1 **1** **Agent Archie (USA)**[23] 1608 3-8-10 **79** .... KierenFox(5) 13 87
(J R Best) *t.k.h: trckd ldng pair: rdn wl over 2f out: looked hld in 4th fr 2f out tl styd on wl to ld last 150yds: fended off rival after* **7/1**[3]

50-1 **2** *hd* **Quick Reaction**[29] 1475 3-9-0 **78** .... RichardHughes 10 86
(R Hannon) *hld up in last quartet: stdy prog fr over 2f out: rdn to chal and upsides ent fnl f: r.o but a jst hld* **14/1**

22-1 **3** *2* **Life And Soul (IRE)**[13] 1876 3-9-1 **79** .... PhilipRobinson 2 83
(Mrs A J Perrett) *trckd ldng pair: effrt to chal 2f out: narrow ld 1f out: sn hdd and no ex* **12/1**

5-1 **4** *½* **Hayzoom**[17] 1757 3-9-2 **80** .... JackMitchell 8 83+
(P W Chapple-Hyam) *s.i.s: hld up wl in rr: last over 2f out: prog on inner after: sltly checked 1f out: styd on: nrst fin* **12/1**

54-4 **5** *nse* **Missionaire (USA)**[17] 1761 3-9-1 **79** .... ShaneKelly 12 82
(W J Knight) *hld up in midfield disputing 7th: prog on inner over 2f out: cl up over 1f out but nt qckn: styd on ins fnl f* **13/2**[2]

001- **6** *¾* **Perfect Vision**[204] 7106 3-8-6 **70** .... AlanMunro 6 71
(C G Cox) *led: narrowly hdd 3f out: kpt on wl and stl nrly upsides 1f out: fdd* **20/1**

02-4 **7** *1 ¾* **Tiger Star**[33] 1393 3-8-11 **75** .... HayleyTurner 9 73
(J M P Eustace) *hld up in last quartet: pushed along fr 3f out: kpt on steadily fnl 2f but nvr threatened* **33/1**

41-6 **8** *½* **Spoken**[18] 1734 3-9-1 **79** .... RyanMoore 11 76
(R Charlton) *swtg: hld up in midfield disputing 7th: rdn on outer over 2f out: nt qckn: no imp on ldrs after* **11/4**[1]

0-21 **9** *shd* **Towbaat**[22] 1621 3-9-2 **80** .... FrankieDettori 4 77
(M A Jarvis) *lw: pressed ldr: led narrowly 3f out: drvn and pressed after: hdd 1f out: wknd rapidly last 150yds* **8/1**

-054 **10** *hd* **Sheila Toss (IRE)**[7] 2047 3-8-8 **72** .... RichardKingscote 3 68
(R Hannon) *hld up last: effrt on wd outside 3f out and sme prog: no hdwy over 1f out: wknd* **12/1**

0-10 **11** *9* **Signor Verdi**[14] 1834 3-9-4 **82** .... TomQueally 1 60
(B J Meehan) *racd wd thrght: trckd ldrs: rdn and nt qckn over 2f out: wknd wl over 1f out* **16/1**

0-14 **12** *6* **Midfielder (USA)**[54] 1018 3-9-0 **78** .... RobertHavlin 7 44
(J H M Gosden) *hld up in midfield disputing 7th: rdn and wknd over 2f out* **11/1**

-211 **13** *14* **Azlak (USA)**[42] 1189 3-9-0 **78** .... NeilCallan 5 16
(C E Brittain) *t.k.h: trckd ldrs: stl cl up 2f out: wknd rapidly over 1f out: eased: t.o* **16/1**

2m 11.39s (0.89) **Going Correction** +0.125s/f (Good) **13** Ran SP% **121.2**
Speed ratings (Par 101): **101,100,99,98,98 98,96,96,96,96 88,84,72**
toteswingers:1&2:£18.30, 1&3:£20.70, 2&3:£30.60 CSF £102.76 CT £1171.22 TOTE £7.50: £1.90, £6.90, £6.70; EX 86.50.
Owner D Gorton **Bred** Earle I Mack **Trained** Hucking, Kent
■ Stewards' Enquiry : Jack Mitchell caution: used whip without giving colt time to respond

FOCUS
Seven last-time-out winners lined up for this competitive handicap. The early pace was not great, but they quickened smartly turning for home and the time was significantly quicker than the following maiden. Sound form.

2255 PANMURE GORDON LIVERPOOL MAIDEN STKS 1m 2f 7y
8:00 (8:06) (Class 5) 3-4-Y-O **£3,238** (£963; £481; £240) **Stalls High**

Form RPR

1 **Sajjhaa** 3-8-7 0 .... FrankieDettori 3 83+
(M A Jarvis) *rangy: gd sort: lw: nt wl away but rcvrd steadily to trck ldrs after 4f: prog over 2f out: led over 1f out: pushed along firmly and drew rt away* **5/4**[1]

0-0 **2** *7* **Saggiatore**[34] 1356 3-8-7 0 .... HayleyTurner 13 69+
(E A L Dunlop) *swtg: trckd ldrs: pushed along and effrt on inner over 2f out: styd on to take 2nd ins fnl f* **25/1**

44 **3** *1 ¼* **White Finch (USA)**[26] 1538 3-8-7 0 .... LiamKeniry 7 66
(A M Balding) *swtg: pressed ldr: led over 2f out: hdd and easily outpcd over 1f out: lost 2nd ins fnl f* **33/1**

0-2 **4** *¾* **Mavalenta (IRE)**[22] 1621 3-8-7 0 .... RichardHills 15 65
(J W Hills) *trckd ldng pair: pushed along fr over 2f out: wl hld in 4th over 1f out: no imp after* **11/2**[3]

5 *¾* **Olympic Medal** 3-8-7 0 .... RichardKingscote 1 63+
(R Charlton) *unf: hld up in last: pushed along and prog on inner over 2f out: rchd 5th fnl f: kpt on* **25/1**

0 **6** *½* **Candotoo (IRE)**[22] 1621 3-8-7 0 .... AlanMunro 10 62
(J Noseda) *trckd ldrs: outpcd fr 2f out: n.d over 1f out* **66/1**

7 *hd* **Budding Daffodil** 3-8-7 0 .... ShaneKelly 5 62+
(W J Knight) *leggy: rn green in rr: pushed along and last over 2f out: shkn up and styd on quite takingly fnl f* **33/1**

00 **8** *nk* **Latent Light (USA)**[10] 1976 3-8-9 0 .... AshleyHamblett(3) 17 66
(E A L Dunlop) *lw: sn led: hdd over 2f out: wknd over 1f out* **100/1**

0-0 **9** *½* **Kathleen Frances**[36] 1314 3-8-2 0 .... AshleyMorgan(5) 9 60
(M H Tompkins) *hld up in 12th: pushed along and no prog 3f out: sme hdwy over 1f out: nvr on terms* **66/1**

3 **10** *3* **Weathervane**[17] 1757 3-8-12 0 .... RyanMoore 12 59
(J H M Gosden) *str: lw: trckd ldng pair: pushed along over 2f out: wknd wl over 1f out* **9/4**[2]

/6- **11** *½* **Gearbox (IRE)**[279] 5010 4-9-12 0 .... TomQueally 8 58
(H J L Dunlop) *w'like: hld up towards rr: shkn up and no prog over 2f out* **100/1**

5 **12** *nk* **Abu Wathab**[15] 1824 3-8-12 0 .... JackMitchell 11 57
(P W Chapple-Hyam) *s.i.s and bustled along early: rdn and effrt over 2f out: wknd over 1f out* **25/1**

03 **13** *1 ¼* **Indian Ghyll (IRE)**[14] 1847 4-9-12 0 .... RichardHughes 4 55
(R A Teal) *hld up in rr: sme prog into midfield over 3f out: no hdwy 2f out: wknd* **16/1**

2m 12.59s (2.09) **Going Correction** +0.125s/f (Good)
WFA 3 from 4yo 14lb **13** Ran SP% **118.9**
Speed ratings (Par 103): **96,90,89,88,88 87,87,87,87,84 84,83,82**
toteswingers:1&2:£8.00, 1&3:£13.70, 2&3:£40.50 CSF £44.05 TOTE £2.80: £1.80, £5.70, £10.20; EX 40.30.
Owner Sheikh Ahmed Al Maktoum **Bred** Darley **Trained** Newmarket, Suffolk

FOCUS
Only limited form to go on here, and the form horses disappointed, but plenty of potential and some smart pedigrees. The winner impressed but overall this is not form to be too positive about.

2256 PANMURE GORDON STOCKBROKING FILLIES' H'CAP 1m 1f
8:35 (8:36) (Class 4) (0-80,80) 3-Y-O+ **£4,533** (£1,348; £674; £336) **Stalls High**

Form RPR

3-31 **1** **Right Rave (IRE)**[10] 1977 3-8-10 **72** 6ex .... ShaneKelly 12 79
(P J McBride) *lw: trckd ldrs: prog 2f out: rdn to ld jst over 1f out: jnd ins fnl f: kpt on wl* **7/2**[2]

150- **2** *nk* **Cwm Rhondda (USA)**[246] 6003 5-9-10 **73** .... JackMitchell 5 81+
(P W Chapple-Hyam) *stdd s: hld up in last: gd prog on wd outside fr 2f out: jnd wnr 150yds out: edgd rt and nt qckn after: jst hld* **33/1**

5-1 **3** *1* **Circus Girl (IRE)**[31] 1431 3-9-0 **79** .... MartinLane(3) 2 83
(R M Beckett) *led: rdn and hdd jst over 1f out: kpt on wl but a hld ins fnl f* **14/1**

6-22 **4** *1* **Brushing**[31] 1426 4-9-6 **74** .... AshleyMorgan(5) 9 78+
(M H Tompkins) *hld up in rr: last and pushed along 2f out: stl last whn swtchd sharply lft to outer ent fnl f: r.o wl last 150yds: gaining at fin* **11/2**[3]

00-1 **5** *nse* **Sweet Clementine (IRE)**[22] 1620 3-9-4 **80** .... JimCrowley 13 81
(W J Knight) *trckd ldng pair: rdn and nt qckn wl over 1f out: one pce after* **15/2**

645- **6** *½* **Critical Path (IRE)**[188] 7366 4-9-10 **73** .... LiamKeniry 10 75+
(A M Balding) *hld up in midfield: rdn and nt qckn 2f out: no prog over 1f out: styd on ins fnl f* **12/1**

1-44 **7** *1* **Gifted Apakay (USA)**[13] 1876 3-8-11 **73** .... HayleyTurner 11 71
(E A L Dunlop) *hld up wl in rr: effrt on inner 2f out: no imp on ldrs 1f out* **25/1**

-1 **8** *nk* **Marie De Guise (IRE)**[13] 1881 3-9-4 **80** .... RyanMoore 4 78+
(Sir Michael Stoute) *lw: trckd ldng trio: rdn over 2f out: lost pl wl over 1f out: no ch after: plugged on ins fnl f* **5/2**[1]

20-1 **9** *1* **Lost Horizon (IRE)**[17] 1777 3-9-1 **77** .... RichardHughes 6 72
(R Hannon) *nt wl away but rcvrd fast to trck ldr after 2f: lost 2nd wl over 1f out: wknd fnl f* **10/1**

56-0 **10** *5* **Moonline Dancer (FR)**[7] 2047 3-9-1 **77** .... RichardKingscote 1 61
(R Hannon) *trckd ldrs: rdn over 2f out: wknd rapidly fnl f* **40/1**

/03- **11** *2* **Dream In Waiting**[203] 7141 4-9-13 **76** .... FrankieDettori 7 58
(B J Meehan) *a towards rr on outer: no prog 2f out: wkng whn bmpd jst ins fnl f* **16/1**

1m 58.75s (3.05) **Going Correction** +0.125s/f (Good)
WFA 3 from 4yo+ 13lb **11** Ran SP% **116.5**
Speed ratings (Par 102): **94,93,92,91,91 91,90,90,89,84 83**
Swingers:1&2:£20.20, 1&3:£17.40, 2&3:£123.10 CSF £117.27 CT £1471.96 TOTE £3.70: £1.10, £7.20, £4.60; EX 184.30 Place 6 £1,319.56; Place 5 £747.81.
Owner Jason Anderson **Bred** Garry Chong **Trained** Newmarket, Suffolk
■ Stewards' Enquiry : Ashley Morgan four-day ban: careless riding (Jun 3-6,7-8)

FOCUS
Most of the established four-year-olds looked exposed but several younger rivals hinted at untapped potential. Something of a muddling race, but the winner continues to improve.
T/Plt: £24,096.60. Pool:£77,571.29 - 2.35 winning tickets T/Qpdt: £952.40. Pool:£6,693.18 - 5.20 winning tickets JN

1993 SOUTHWELL (L-H)
Thursday, May 20

OFFICIAL GOING: Standard
Wind: Virtually nil Weather: Fine and dry

2257 BET HEINEKEN CUP FINAL - BETDAQ H'CAP (DIV I) 7f (F)
2:10 (2:10) (Class 6) (0-60,65) 4-Y-O+ **£1,748** (£520; £260; £129) **Stalls Low**

Form RPR

2121 **1** **Scruffy Skip (IRE)**[9] 1998 5-9-9 **65** 6ex .... (p) TomMcLaughlin 12 73
(Mrs C A Dunnett) *in tch: hdwy on outer 1/2-way: led 2f out: rdn over 1f out: edgd rt and styd on ins fnl f* **5/2**[1]

00-5 **2** *1 ½* **Sparky Vixen**[9] 1998 6-8-1 **46** oh1 .... KellyHarrison(3) 3 50
(C J Teague) *in tch on inner: effrt and n.m.r over 3f out: hdwy over 2f out: rdn to chse wnr over 1f out: drvn and edgd rt ins fnl f: one pce* **12/1**

-004 **3** *hd* **Fortezza**[13] 1884 4-8-4 **51** .... DeclanCannon(5) 6 54
(A J McCabe) *trckd ldrs: hdwy 3f out: rdn along 2f out: drvn ent fnl f and kpt on same pce* **9/2**[2]

3030 **4** *2 ¾* **Louisiade (IRE)**[16] 1813 9-7-13 **48** .... (p) CharlesEddery(7) 7 44
(R C Guest) *towards rr: pushed along 1/2-way: hdwy over 2f out: sn rdn and kpt on appr fnl f: nrst fin* **12/1**

-562 **5** *1* **Tenancy (IRE)**[9] 1998 6-8-4 **46** oh1 .... RoystonFfrench 4 39
(S A Harris) *led: rdn along 3f out: hdd 2f out and sn drvn: wknd over 1f out* **13/2**[3]

0-30 **6** 1 3/4 **Kingaroo (IRE)**27 1503 4-8-7 49 JamieMackay 11 38
(G Woodward) *chsd ldrs: rdn along over 3f out: drvn over 2f out and sn no imp* 12/1

0000 **7** 1 1/4 **Easy Wonder (GER)**9 2010 5-8-0 47 oh1 ow1 (v) BillyCray(5) 1 32
(I A Wood) *s.i.s: a in rr* 50/1

00-0 **8** 3/4 **Union Jack Jackson (IRE)**72 838 8-8-0 47 oh1 ow1(b) JohnFahy(5) 2 30
(John A Harris) *towards rr: hdwy on inner over 3f out: rdn to chse ldrs 2f out: sn drvn and wknd* 33/1

6-00 **9** 2 1/2 **Hilltop Legacy**45 1130 7-8-5 47 oh1 ow1 (b1) LiamJones 10 23
(J R Jenkins) *dwlt: sn rdn along on outer: bhd fr 1/2-way* 66/1

2503 **10** 1 3/4 **Spoof Master (IRE)**12 1929 6-9-0 56 (t) SebSanders 9 28
(C R Dore) *cl up: rdn along 3f out: drvn over 2f out and sn wknd* 15/2

0650 **11** 19 **Pipers Piping (IRE)**16 1812 4-9-4 60 J-PGuillambert 5 —
(P Howling) *cl up: rdn along 1/2-way: sn wknd: bhd and eased wl over 1f out* 8/1

1m 29.91s (-0.39) **Going Correction** -0.075s/f (Stan) 11 Ran SP% 112.4
Speed ratings (Par 101): **99,97,97,93,92 90,89,88,85,83 61**
toteswingers:1&2:£8.00, 1&3:£13.60, 2&3:£13.80 CSF £32.45 CT £128.89 TOTE £3.60: £2.10, £2.70, £2.20; EX 25.90 Trifecta £220.40 Part won. Pool: £297.83 - 0.43 winning units..
Owner C Dunnett, D Cooper, R Clarke & J Power **Bred** Darley **Trained** Hingham, Norfolk

FOCUS
A couple of modest performers in a very ordinary handicap in which five of the 12 were carrying more than their allotted handicap marks. The gallop was sound and the winner raced centre to stands' side in the straight. Straightforward form.

2258 FRONTCOVER MAKEUP MEDIAN AUCTION MAIDEN STKS 7f (F)
2:40 (2:40) (Class 5) 3-4-Y-O £3,238 (£963; £481; £240) Stalls Low

Form RPR

63 **1** **Wadi Wanderer (IRE)**28 1490 3-9-2 0 JamieSpencer 2 78
(E F Vaughan) *mde all: qcknd 2f out: rdn clr ent fnl f: kpt on wl* 10/1

2-02 **2** 2 3/4 **Primo De Vida (IRE)**28 1490 3-9-2 70 JimCrowley 12 71
(R M Beckett) *prom: cl up 1/2-way: rdn to chal 2f out and ev ch tl drvn ent fnl f and kpt on same pce* 15/8[1]

3 **3** 5 **Conceptual Art**23 1589 3-9-2 0 HayleyTurner 8 58
(M L W Bell) *trckd ldrs: hdwy over 2f out: rdn wl over 1f out: edgd rt and one pce ent fnl f* 7/2[3]

4 nk **Line Of Duty (IRE)** 3-9-2 0 RobertWinston 11 57
(G A Swinbank) *dwlt: hdwy on outer to join ldrs after 3f: rdn along: edgd lft and sltly outpcd 2f out: styd on ins fnl f* 20/1

5 2 1/2 **San Fermin (USA)** 3-8-13 0 AhmedAjtebi(3) 4 50
(Mahmood Al Zarooni) *dwlt: sn trcking ldrs on inner: hdwy over 2f out: rdn to chse ldng pair wl over 1f out: sn edgd rt and wknd* 2/1[2]

00 **6** 4 1/2 **Frontline Phantom (IRE)**12 1927 3-9-2 0 FrannyNorton 9 38
(J R Weymes) *a towards rr* 16/1

00-0 **7** 2 1/4 **Bold Hawk**9 2010 4-9-13 45 (v1) TomMcLaughlin 6 36
(Mrs C A Dunnett) *dwlt: a towards rr* 150/1

000- **8** 1 3/4 **Chardonnay Star (IRE)**184 7420 3-8-11 20 DavidNolan 10 22
(C J Teague) *prom: rdn along after 3f: sn lost pl and bhd* 200/1

1m 29.33s (-0.97) **Going Correction** -0.075s/f (Stan)
WFA 3 from 4yo 11lb 8 Ran SP% 111.2
Speed ratings (Par 103): **102,98,93,92,89 84,82,80**
toteswingers:1&2:£2.50, 1&3:£3.00, 2&3:£2.10 CSF £27.66 TOTE £9.80: £2.80, £1.10, £1.10; EX 20.00 Trifecta £59.10 Pool: £541.43 - 6.77 winning units..
Owner Mohamed Obaida **Bred** Rabbah Bloodstock Limited **Trained** Newmarket, Suffolk

FOCUS
No more than a fair maiden and one in which the gallop was an ordinary one. The winner raced up the centre in the straight and comprehensively turned around C/D form with the second.

2259 NSPCC CHILD'S VOICE APPEAL H'CAP 1m 3f (F)
3:15 (3:15) (Class 5) (0-70,69) 4-Y-O+ £2,590 (£770; £385; £192) Stalls Low

Form RPR

42-2 **1** **Speed Dating**9 1996 4-9-2 67 SebSanders 4 75+
(Sir Mark Prescott) *trckd ldrs on inner: swtchd rt and hdwy over 3f out: chal 2f out: rdn and led appr fnl f: sn drvn and edgd lft: kpt on* 10/11[1]

3-00 **2** nk **Northside Prince (IRE)**6 2084 4-9-3 68 RobertWinston 2 75
(G A Swinbank) *trckd ldng pair: cl up over 4f out: rdn to ld 2f out: drvn and hdd appr fnl f: rallied u.p ins fnl f: no ex last 50yds* 11/1

1344 **3** 1 1/4 **Magic Haze**12 1919 4-8-2 56 Louis-PhilippeBeuzelin(3) 10 61
(Miss S E Hall) *trckd ldrs: hdwy 1/2-way: led over 4f out: rdn along 3f out: hdd 2f out: swtchd rt and drvn appr fnl f: kpt on towards fin* 11/2[3]

545- **4** 1 **Gosforth Park**219 6766 4-8-4 55 oh3 FrannyNorton 1 58
(M Brittain) *led: pushed along 1/2-way: hdd over 4f out: rdn along 3f out: drvn wl over 1f out: kpt on same pce appr fnl f* 25/1

25-0 **5** 2 **Guga (IRE)**17 1756 4-8-10 61 JimCrowley 3 61
(Dr R D P Newland) *trckd ldr: rdn along 3f out: drvn over 2f out: kpt on same pce appr fnl f* 22/1

3-52 **6** 2 1/4 **Crystal Feather**43 1172 4-8-11 62 JamieSpencer 8 58
(E F Vaughan) *hld up in rr: hdwy 4f out: rdn to chse ldrs over 2f out: sn btn* 4/1[2]

4206 **7** 1 1/4 **Heathyards Junior**26 1526 4-8-13 69 DeclanCannon(5) 6 62
(A J McCabe) *in tch: rdn along over 4f out: sn wknd* 11/1

0/0- **8** 8 **Tilapia (IRE)**317 3721 6-9-2 67 StephenCraine 9 46
(Stef Higgins) *a in rr: bhd fnl 2f* 33/1

2m 26.8s (-1.20) **Going Correction** -0.075s/f (Stan) 8 Ran SP% 115.6
Speed ratings (Par 103): **101,100,99,99,97 96,95,89**
toteswingers:1&2:£4.00, 1&3:£2.40, 2&3:£5.10 CSF £12.35 CT £38.64 TOTE £1.90: £1.10, £3.00, £1.40; EX 12.90 Trifecta £50.40 Pool: £444.47 - 6.52 winning units..
Owner Cheveley Park Stud **Bred** Cheveley Park Stud Ltd **Trained** Newmarket, Suffolk

FOCUS
A modest handicap in which the gallop was just an ordinary one. The winner and second raced up the centre in the straight. Muddling form, and it is doubtful if the winner had to improve.

2260 BET CHAMPIONS LEAGUE FINAL - BETDAQ H'CAP 5f (F)
3:55 (3:56) (Class 2) (0-100,98) 3-Y-O £10,361 (£3,083; £1,540; £769) Stalls High

Form RPR

1-23 **1** **Confessional**13 1860 3-8-6 83 (p) DavidAllan 4 92+
(T D Easterby) *hmpd s and towards rr: gd hdwy 1/2-way and sn trcking ldrs: effrt to chal over 1f out: rdn and qcknd wl to ld jst ins fnl f: sn hung bdly lft: in command whn swvd bdly rt nr fin* 9/2[1]

11-4 **2** 1/2 **The Only Boss (IRE)**26 1523 3-8-13 90 JamieSpencer 6 95
(W J Haggas) *cl up: effrt 2f out: sn rdn and ev ch tl drvn ins fnl f: keeping on whn edgd lft last 100yds: whn hmpd nr fin* 5/1[2]

6-10 **3** 1/2 **Whozthecat (IRE)**19 1701 3-8-13 90 DavidNolan 5 93
(D Carroll) *led: rdn along 2f out: drvn and hdd jst ins fnl f: sn edgd lft: keeping on whn edgd lft last 100yds: n.m.r nr fin* 7/1

2-20 **4** 1 **Singeur (IRE)**19 1701 3-9-0 98 MatthewLawson(7) 1 97
(R Bastiman) *dwlt and towards rr: hdwy on wd outside 1/2-way: rdn wl over 1f out: styd on ins fnl f: nrst fin* 5/1[2]

1500 **5** 1 1/2 **Love Delta (USA)**19 1701 3-9-2 93 JoeFanning 8 87
(M Johnston) *chsd ldrs: rdn along 2f out: drvn and edgd lft wl over 1f out: sn one pce* 5/1[2]

0-54 **6** 3 3/4 **Dancing Freddy (IRE)**14 1836 3-8-2 79 oh1 FrannyNorton 3 60
(J G Given) *wnt rt s: chsd ldrs: rdn along 2f out: drvn over 1f out and grad wknd* 25/1

1-16 **7** nk **Falasteen (IRE)**13 1860 3-9-2 93 TonyHamilton 2 72
(R A Fahey) *cl up: rdn along over 2f out: drvn wl over 1f out and sn wknd* 6/1[3]

-056 **8** 1 1/4 **Comedy Hall (USA)**12 1917 3-8-11 88 RoystonFfrench 7 63
(M Johnston) *chsd ldrs: pushed along 1/2-way: sn rdn and wknd* 12/1

4511 **9** 1 1/4 **Kylladdie**17 1765 3-8-0 82 oh5 ow3 JohnFahy(5) 9 54
(S Gollings) *dwlt: racd on stands' rail: a in rr* 20/1

58.46 secs (-1.24) **Going Correction** -0.075s/f (Stan) 9 Ran SP% 111.3
Speed ratings (Par 105): **106,105,104,102,100 94,93,91,89**
toteswingers:1&2:£2.80, 1&3:£7.60, 2&3:£8.60 CSF £25.41 CT £148.66 TOTE £3.50: £1.10, £2.90, £3.10; EX 23.60 Trifecta £122.80 Pool: £516.38 - 3.11 winning units..
Owner T G & Mrs M E Holdcroft **Bred** Bearstone Stud **Trained** Great Habton, N Yorks

FOCUS
A valuable and a good-quality handicap for the track. The pace was sound and the winner raced up the centre for much of the way.An improved effort from the winner and the form should be of relevance back on turf.

NOTEBOOK
Confessional, tried in cheekpieces, is a reliable sort who turned in his best effort for his bang in-form yard on this Fibresand debut, despite hanging markedly both ways under pressure in the closing stages. He will reportedly be aimed at a Newmarket handicap at the end of the month and should continue to give a good account. (op 5-1 tchd 4-1)

The Only Boss(IRE) ◆ settled better than on his reappearance run at Ripon and returned to form on this first run on artificial surfaces, despite hanging left under a strong ride before being checked by the winner in the closing stages. This was only his fifth run and he's the type to win again. (op 6-1)

Whozthecat(IRE) had been again well beaten over 6f on his previous start but fared better on this all-weather debut returned to the minimum distance on this first run since being gelded. This was only his sixth race and, although he is high enough in the weights at present, he may be capable of further progress. (op 6-1 tchd 5-1 and 8-1)

Singeur(IRE) is a fairly reliable sort who ran creditably from his low draw returned to Fibresand. He should continue to give it his best shot but is likely to remain vulnerable from his current mark. Official explanation: jockey said colt missed the break (tchd 9-2)

Love Delta(USA) had won his three previous starts on this surface early in the year but he again had his limitations exposed from a mark in the 90s returned to an artificial surface, and he'll have to improve to win a competitive handicap from this sort of mark. (op 9-2 tchd 6-1)

Dancing Freddy(IRE)'s form has been patchy since his maiden win and he wasn't at his best on this Fibresand debut. He will have to show a fair bit more before he is a solid betting proposition either on sand or on turf. (op 20-1 tchd 18-1 and 28-1)

2261 CHAMPIONS 60:60 CHARITY CHALLENGE H'CAP 1m (F)
4:25 (4:27) (Class 3) (0-95,86) 3-Y-O £7,771 (£2,312; £1,155; £577) Stalls Low

Form RPR

1- **1** **Nazreef**177 7502 3-8-10 75 (t) TravisBlock 7 92+
(H Morrison) *prom on outer: hdwy 3f out: cl up 2f out: rdn to ld jst over 1f out: drvn and edgd lft ins fnl f: kpt on* 9/2[2]

1 **2** 1 1/4 **Capponi (IRE)**62 930 3-9-6 85 JoeFanning 3 98
(M Johnston) *dwlt: sn pushed along to chse ldrs on inner: effrt to chse ldng pair over 2f out: drvn over 1f out: kpt on u.p ins fnl f* 3/1[1]

2-12 **3** 1 3/4 **Dolphin Rock**18 1718 3-8-10 75 PhillipMakin 1 84
(T D Barron) *led: rdn along 2f out: drvn and hdd jst over 1f out: one pce ins fnl f* 9/2[2]

0100 **4** 4 1/2 **Premium Charge**13 1873 3-8-2 70 KellyHarrison(3) 4 69
(C A Dwyer) *chsd ldrs: rdn along 3f out: edgd rt over 2f out and sn one pce* 14/1

11-3 **5** 9 **Soul Heaven**36 1307 3-8-10 75 JamieSpencer 8 53
(M L W Bell) *stdd s and hld up in tch: effrt on outer 3f out: sn rdn and btn* 3/1[1]

-210 **6** 1 **Transmit (IRE)**5 2112 3-8-11 76 DavidAllan 6 52
(T D Easterby) *cl up: rdn along 3f out: wknd over 2f out* 8/1[3]

20-5 **7** 29 **Krymian**30 1442 3-9-2 84 Louis-PhilippeBeuzelin(3) 5 —
(Sir Michael Stoute) *sn rdn along in rr: bhd fr 1/2-way* 12/1

1m 41.21s (-2.49) **Going Correction** -0.075s/f (Stan) 7 Ran SP% 111.8
Speed ratings (Par 103): **109,107,106,101,92 91,62**
toteswingers:1&2:£1.70, 1&3:£5.00, 2&3:£2.80 CSF £17.54 CT £61.92 TOTE £6.30: £3.20, £2.90; EX 22.50 Trifecta £89.90 Pool: £372.31 - 3.06 winning units..
Owner Deborah Collett & M J Watson **Bred** M J Watson **Trained** East Ilsley, Berks
■ Stewards' Enquiry : Phillip Makin caution: used whip down the shoulder in the forehand position

FOCUS
A useful handicap for the track in which the first two had won their only previous starts and the third, who finished clear, looks a reliable yardstick. The gallop was a reasonable one and the winner raced up the centre in the straight.

NOTEBOOK
Nazreef ◆, sporting a first-time tongue-tie, had won his only previous start over this C&D and he showed improved form to follow up on this reappearance and handicap debut, despite edging left under pressure. He's the type to physically progress again and, although he has to show he's as good on turf as Fibresand (reportedly will not be risked on quick ground), he appeals strongly as the type to win more races.

Capponi(IRE) ◆, making his Fibresand debut after creating a good impression on his debut on Polytrack, bettered that form on this handicap debut, despite giving a few problems at the start. He's the type to make further progress for this yard and should be able to win again. (tchd 7-2)

Dolphin Rock has shown improved form on turf this year and ran right up to his best returned to Fibresand against two previous once-raced maiden winners. He pulled clear of the remainder and he looks sure to win a race away from the more progressive sorts on this surface. (op 5-1)

Premium Charge had previously won two 0-60 handicaps over 7f but, while not totally disgraced after hanging left, had his limitations firmly exposed in this stronger grade returned to a trip he's still to show that he truly stays. There will be easier opportunities than this one returned to that shorter trip. (op 22-1)

Soul Heaven looked to have sound prospects after showing he retains all his ability upped to this trip on his reappearance but he proved disappointing on this Fibresand debut. The return to Polytrack or to turf should suit, though, and he is worth another chance. Official explanation: trainer said gelding was unsuited by the fibresand (op 5-2)

Transmit(IRE) again failed to match the form of his maiden win returned to 1m on this AW debut and has a bit to prove at present. (op 10-1)

Krymian was beaten out of sight on this Fibresand debut and looks one to tread carefully with at present. (op 18-1 tchd 20-1)

2262 BET CHAMPIONSHIP PLAY OFF - BETDAQ FILLIES' H'CAP 7f (F)
4:55 (4:56) (Class 4) (0-85,83) 4-Y-0+ £4,533 (£1,348; £674; £336) Stalls Low

Form RPR

-004 1 **La Zamora**[15] 1827 4-8-8 **73** JamieSpencer 4 84
(T D Barron) *trckd ldrs: rapid hdwy on outer over 2f out: led wl over 1f out: sn rdn clr: comf* **8/1**

0004 2 3 ½ **Mozayada (USA)**[16] 1808 6-8-9 **74** FrannyNorton 5 76
(M Brittain) *led: rdn along over 2f out: hdd wl over 1f out: drvn and kpt on ins fnl f: no ch w wnr* **11/2**

11-0 3 shd **Salerosa (IRE)**[9] 1997 5-9-0 **79** SebSanders 6 81
(Mrs A Duffield) *hld up in rr: swtchd outside and hdwy 2f out: rdn to chse ldng pair over 1f out: sn drvn and one pce* **11/4**[1]

0-34 4 2 ½ **Sakhee's Pearl**[17] 1770 4-9-4 **83** StephenCraine 1 78
(Miss Gay Kelleway) *trckd ldrs: effrt over 2f out: sn rdn and one pce* **10/3**[3]

1-00 5 4 ½ **Kyleene**[12] 1933 4-8-4 **72** KellyHarrison(3) 3 55
(M D I Usher) *chsd ldr: rdn along over 2f out and sn wknd* **16/1**

11-3 6 ¾ **Ela Gorrie Mou**[17] 1775 4-8-5 **70** EddieCreighton 2 51
(P Charalambous) *a in rr: rdn along and outpcd fnl 2f* **3/1**[2]

1m 29.46s (-0.84) **Going Correction** -0.075s/f (Stan) **6** Ran SP% **107.1**
Speed ratings (Par 102): **101,97,96,94,88 88**
toteswingers:1&2:£4.90, 1&3:£4.50, 2&3:£4.00 CSF £45.12 TOTE £13.30: £7.90, £7.20; EX 30.20.
Owner J G Brown **Bred** Miss S J Smith **Trained** Maunby, N Yorks

FOCUS
A fair fillies' handicap but one in which the gallop was only an ordinary one. The winner was another to race up the centre in the straight. The form is ordinary with the winner getting back to her 3yo level.
Ela Gorrie Mou Official explanation: trainer said filly was unuited by the fibresand surface

2263 BET HEINEKEN CUP FINAL - BETDAQ H'CAP (DIV II) 7f (F)
5:25 (5:26) (Class 6) (0-60,60) 4-Y-0+ £1,748 (£520; £260; £129) Stalls Low

Form RPR

06-0 1 **Wotatomboy**[12] 1922 4-8-4 **46** oh1 PaulQuinn 9 56
(R M Whitaker) *cl up: led after 2f: rdn along and jnd 2f out: drvn ins fnl f and kpt on gamely towards fin* **6/1**

014 2 ½ **Gracie's Gift (IRE)**[24] 1585 8-9-4 **60** JamieSpencer 3 69
(R C Guest) *led 2f: cl up on inner: effrt to chal 2f out and sn rdn drvn ins fnl f and ev ch tl no ex nr fin* **3/1**[1]

0044 3 4 ½ **Vogarth**[9] 1998 6-8-2 **49** SophieDoyle(5) 6 46
(M C Chapman) *chsd ldrs: rdn along wl over 2f out: drvn and hung rt over 1f out: kpt on ins fnl f: nrst fin* **15/2**

-006 4 ¾ **Guertino (IRE)**[18] 1719 5-8-12 **54** DavidNolan 10 49
(C J Teague) *prom: rdn along over 2f out: drvn wl over 1f out: sn one pce* **13/2**

000/ 5 ¾ **Wainwright (IRE)**[962] 5866 10-8-4 **46** oh1 (tp) JoeFanning 8 39
(J Mackie) *in tch: hdwy to chse ldrs over 2f out: rdn wl over 1f out: drvn and edgd lft ins fnl f: one pce* **14/1**

000 6 ½ **Admirals Way**[18] 1723 5-7-11 **46** oh1 NathanAlison(7) 12 37
(C N Kellett) *prom: effrt and cl up 3f out: rdn over 2f out: drvn over 1f out: one pce whn n.m.r ins fnl f* **66/1**

3005 7 ½ **Fulford**[16] 1813 5-9-3 **59** FrannyNorton 2 51
(M Brittain) *hld up in rr: hdwy 2f out: rdn over 1f out: styng on whn nt clr run ins fnl f* **5/1**[2]

04-2 8 1 ½ **Cross Of Lorraine (IRE)**[16] 1813 7-8-10 **52** (b) TonyHamilton 4 38
(J Wade) *towards rr: hdwy on inner over 2f out: rdn wl over 1f out: sn wknd* **11/2**[3]

6623 9 ¾ **King's Sabre**[13] 1885 4-8-1 **50** (e) CharlesEddery(7) 11 34
(R C Guest) *dwlt and towards rr: hdwy 3f out: rdn to chse ldrs 2f out: sn drvn and wknd over 1f out* **14/1**

000- 10 ¾ **Hilltop Alchemy**[204] 7110 4-8-5 **47** oh1 ow1 (b[1]) RoystonFfrench 1 29
(J R Jenkins) *dwlt: a in rr* **66/1**

-000 11 18 **City For Conquest (IRE)**[13] 1885 7-8-1 **46** oh1 (b) KellyHarrison(3) 5 —
(John A Harris) *dwlt: a in rr* **33/1**

00-0 12 16 **Calypso Girl (IRE)**[55] 995 4-8-4 **46** oh1 LiamJones 7 —
(A M Hales) *a in rr* **33/1**

1m 29.59s (-0.71) **Going Correction** -0.075s/f (Stan) **12** Ran SP% **118.6**
Speed ratings (Par 101): **101,100,95,94,93 93,92,90,89,89 68,50**
toteswingers:1&2:£8.10, 1&3:£9.90, 2&3:£7.90 CSF £23.88 CT £140.36 TOTE £10.80: £3.50, £1.90, £4.40; EX 39.40 Trifecta £202.10 Part won. Pool: £273.14 - 0.58 winning units. Place 6 £62.19; Place 5 £42.22..
Owner Mrs Jill Willows **Bred** Hellwood Stud Farm **Trained** Scarcroft, W Yorks

FOCUS
Division two of a very ordinary handicap, in which half the field were out of the weights. The gallop was a fair one but those up with the pace held the edge, and the first two came down the centre in the straight. Weak form.
Hilltop Alchemy Official explanation: jockey said gelding was never travelling
T/Plt: £75.10. Pool:£59,863.87 - 581.73 winning tickets T/Qpdt: £40.80. Pool:£4,310.72 - 78.10 winning tickets JR

2264 - 2271a (Foreign Racing) - See Raceform Interactive

1800 CATTERICK (L-H)
Friday, May 21

OFFICIAL GOING: Good to firm (firm in places; 9.7)
Wind: Almost nil Weather: Sunny, hot

2272 EUROPEAN BREEDERS' FUND MAIDEN STKS 5f
2:20 (2:20) (Class 5) 2-Y-0 £3,275 (£967; £483) Stalls Low

Form RPR

1 **Snow Bear (IRE)** 2-8-12 0 GrahamGibbons 6 64
(J J Quinn) *chsd ldrs: effrt over 1f out: edgd lft and led ins fnl f: r.o wl* **3/1**[1]

4 2 ¾ **Miserere (IRE)**[11] 1964 2-8-12 0 PaulMulrennan 1 61
(J S Wainwright) *t.k.h: trckd ldrs on ins: effrt whn n.m.r briefly ins fnl f: kpt on wl to take 2nd cl home* **6/1**[3]

44 3 nk **Trading**[21] 1668 2-9-3 0 DavidAllan 3 65
(T D Easterby) *led: pushed along 2f out: hdd ins fnl f: kpt on same pce* **3/1**[1]

4 1 ½ **Miss Clairton** 2-8-12 0 SebSanders 5 55+
(Sir Mark Prescott) *rn green: sn pushed along bhd ldng gp: no imp tl hdwy over 1f out: edgd lft fnl f: kpt on wl: bttr for r* **13/2**

5 ¾ **Tancred Spirit** 2-8-12 0 TonyHamilton 8 52
(P T Midgley) *pressed ldr: pushed along 2f out: one pce fnl f* **20/1**

50 6 3 **Mandy's Princess (IRE)**[15] 1835 2-8-12 0 PaulHanagan 9 42
(R A Fahey) *dwlt: sn pushed along bhd main gp: outpcd 1/2-way: no imp over 1f out* **9/2**[2]

3 7 1 ¾ **Mr Khan**[14] 1864 2-9-3 0 FrederikTylicki 4 40
(James Moffatt) *chsd ldrs: drvn and outpcd 1/2-way: n.d after* **12/1**

8 16 **Buon Compleanno (IRE)** 2-8-7 0 MarkCoumbe(5) 2 —
(A Berry) *s.i.s: sn wl bhd: nvr on terms* **100/1**

9 1 ½ **Stevie Bee Party** 2-9-0 0 GaryBartley(3) 7 —
(I W McInnes) *s.i.s: a struggling in rr* **66/1**

60.19 secs (0.39) **Going Correction** -0.075s/f (Good) **9** Ran SP% **110.7**
Speed ratings (Par 93): **93,91,91,88,87 82,80,54,52**
Tote Swingers: 1&2 £4.60, 1&3 £3.60, 2&3 £5.30 CSF £19.96 TOTE £2.90: £1.10, £2.90, £1.30; EX 25.20.
Owner Bellwood Cottage Syndicate I **Bred** Ocal Bloodstock **Trained** Settrington, N Yorks

FOCUS
An ordinary juvenile maiden, run at a solid pace. A fair starting effort from the winner.

NOTEBOOK
Snow Bear(IRE) was a gambled-on favourite for her racecourse debut and she got the job done, running out a tenacious winner. An £8,800 breeze-up purchase, she is a precociously bred filly and there was a lot to like about her attitude when asked to win the race. (op 7-2 tchd 11-4)
Miserere(IRE) was ridden more patiently and just got up for second place having failed to get a clear run against the far rail from 2f out. She rates better than the bare form and ought to be found an opening at this level before long. (tchd 15-2)
Trading cut out most of the running and posted a game effort. His previous experience was a big advantage, though, and it's debatable just how much improvement he has in him. (op 11-4 tchd 10-3)
Miss Clairton ◆ was her yard's first juvenile runner of the campaign. She proved easy to back and was detached with 2f to run as she struggled to act on the undulating track. She eventually picked up strongly for pressure at the furlong pole, though, and finished with real purpose. The experience should not be lost on her, another furlong could suit better and it will be interesting to see what she does next time. (op 6-1 tchd 7-1)
Stevie Bee Party Official explanation: jockey said the gelding lost its action but returned sound

2273 YORKSHIRE4X4.COM (S) STKS 7f
2:50 (2:50) (Class 6) 3-4-Y-0 £2,047 (£604; £302) Stalls Low

Form RPR

2620 1 **Lord Fidelio (IRE)**[13] 1923 4-9-11 68 TomEaves 3 67+
(Ollie Pears) *trckd ldrs: hdwy to ld over 1f out: clr ins fnl f: drvn out* **4/1**[2]

-004 2 2 **Dispol Kabira**[3] 2209 3-8-9 47 PatrickMathers 2 52
(D W Thompson) *prom: effrt 2f out: chsd wnr ins fnl f: r.o* **50/1**

4-00 3 1 ¼ **Hettie Hubble**[17] 1804 4-9-0 48 FrederikTylicki 1 47
(D W Thompson) *t.k.h: cl up: effrt 2f out: kpt on same pce fnl f* **16/1**

6-02 4 2 ¾ **Liberty Trail (IRE)**[3] 2208 4-9-11 71 PhillipMakin 7 51
(N Wilson) *prom on outside: effrt over 2f out: no imp appr fnl f* **11/8**[1]

4660 5 ½ **Alphacino**[18] 1753 3-9-0 55 (p) PaulMulrennan 4 45
(B M R Haslam) *hld up: hdwy on ins over 1f out: kpt on same pce fnl f* **10/1**

0565 6 1 ½ **Captain Imperial (IRE)**[42] 1204 4-9-5 48 (b[1]) SebSanders 9 39
(R Bastiman) *t.k.h: led: rdn over 2f out: hung lft and hdd over 1f out: sn btn* **9/2**[3]

0205 7 4 ½ **Always Dixie (IRE)**[17] 1810 3-8-3 53 GregFairley 8 18
(M Johnston) *in tch on outside: outpcd 1/2-way: n.d after* **11/2**

05-0 8 11 **Miss Lauz**[11] 1966 3-8-3 0 (b[1]) AndrewMullen 5 —
(A Berry) *sn drvn along in rr: struggling fr 1/2-way: t.o* **150/1**

1m 25.54s (-1.46) **Going Correction** -0.275s/f (Firm)
WFA 3 from 4yo 11lb **8** Ran SP% **113.3**
Speed ratings (Par 101): **97,94,93,90,89 87,82,70**
Tote Swingers: 1&2 £10.90, 1&3 £7.90, 2&3 £20.50 CSF £150.72 TOTE £4.90: £1.80, £6.50, £3.10; EX 115.50.The winner was bought in for 3,200gns. Liberty Trail was claimed by Diamond Racing Ltd for £5000.
Owner Reuben Glynn **Bred** G S A Bloodstock Ptl Ltd **Trained** Norton, N Yorks

FOCUS
A weak seller, run at a strong pace.

2274 ELLERY HILL RATING RELATED MAIDEN STKS 7f
3:20 (3:22) (Class 6) 3-Y-0+ £2,047 (£604; £302) Stalls Low

Form RPR

00-0 1 **Ellies Image**[34] 1392 3-8-11 43 GrahamGibbons 10 58
(B P J Baugh) *cl up: rdn over 2f out: styd on fnl f: led towards fin* **150/1**

66/0 2 1 ¼ **Chambers (IRE)**[19] 1723 4-9-6 46 PaulPickard(5) 2 62
(E J Alston) *led: rdn over 2f out: kpt on fnl f: hdd towards fin* **40/1**

3-04 3 hd **Spavento (IRE)**[19] 1719 4-9-8 64 (b) DavidAllan 9 58
(E J Alston) *prom: effrt and drvn over 1f out: kpt on ins fnl f* **4/1**[2]

-004 4 1 **Tislaam (IRE)**[17] 1811 3-9-0 65 (p) PaulMulrennan 8 56
(J S Wainwright) *towards rr: hdwy on ins 2f out: kpt on ins fnl f: nrst fin* **12/1**

40-5 5 2 ¼ **Faithful Duchess (IRE)**[35] 1362 3-8-11 65 PaulHanagan 1 51+
(E A L Dunlop) *s.i.s: towards rr: hdwy whn nt clr run over 2f out: styd on fnl f: nrst fin* **11/4**[1]

5-00 6 1 ¼ **Star Addition**[38] 1276 4-9-11 50 DuranFentiman 11 49
(E J Alston) *dwlt: bhd and pushed along 1/2-way: hdwy on ins over 1f out: nvr able to chal* **33/1**

5-06 7 3 **Indian Violet (IRE)**[11] 1967 4-9-11 63 SebSanders 3 41
(D W Thompson) *towards rr on ins: drvn 3f out: no imp fnl 2f* **7/1**

3020 8 2 **Adam De Beaulieu (USA)**[27] 1514 3-9-0 65 (t) PhillipMakin 4 32
(B M R Haslam) *in tch: effrt and edgd rt 2f out: sn outpcd* **9/2**[3]

2/00 9 1 ½ **Northumberland**[18] 1754 4-9-6 61 MarkCoumbe(5) 7 32
(M C Chapman) *t.k.h: cl up tl wknd over 2f out* **40/1**

5-06 10 ½ **Alsufooh (USA)**[18] 1753 3-8-11 62 TadhgO'Shea 13 23
(M Johnston) *cl up on outside tl edgd lft and wknd 2f out* **15/2**

60-0 11 10 **Bravo Blue (IRE)**[45] 1143 3-8-11 25 GregFairley 5 —
(T H Caldwell) *towards rr on outside: sn drvn along: no ch fr 1/2-way* **250/1**

5-03 12 3 ¼ **Big Whitfield**[17] 1808 4-9-6 60 PatrickDonaghy(5) 6 —
(M Dods) *t.k.h: hld up in tch: rn wd bnd ent st: sn struggling* **8/1**

1m 25.28s (-1.72) **Going Correction** -0.275s/f (Firm)
WFA 3 from 4yo 11lb **12** Ran SP% **116.8**
Speed ratings (Par 101): **98,96,96,95,92 91,87,85,83,83 71,68**
Tote Swingers: 1&2 £104.90, 1&3 £58.20, 2&3 £38.20 CSF £2837.19 TOTE £68.70: £13.90, £14.70, £2.50; EX 1300.90.
Owner F Gillespie **Bred** Miss S M Potts **Trained** Audley, Staffs

FOCUS
A 0-65 maiden with a shock winner and the form is poor, with thed first two amongst the worst in. The front three were always prominent.
Faithful Duchess(IRE) Official explanation: jockey said reported the filly missed the break

Big Whitfield Official explanation: jockey said the gelding did not handle the bends

2275 JOHN SMITHS H'CAP 5f 212y
3:50 (3:50) (Class 4) (0-80,78) 3-Y-O+ £4,209 (£1,252; £625; £312) Stalls Low

Form RPR
51-4 1 **Gap Princess (IRE)**44 1152 6-9-4 71 SilvestreDeSousa 1 79
(G A Harker) hld up in tch: hdwy and swtchd rt over 1f out: led ins fnl f: kpt on wl 6/1
6230 2 nk **Green Park (IRE)**6 2134 7-9-9 76 (b) DavidNolan 5 83
(D Carroll) hld up in tch: hdwy on ins over 1f out: ev ch ins fnl f: kpt on: hld nr fin 11/1
60-3 3 1 **Mandalay King (IRE)**13 1924 5-9-3 70 PJMcDonald 2 74
(Mrs Marjorie Fife) dwlt: bhd and pushed along 1/2-way: hdwy wl over 1f out: edgd lft: kpt on u.p ins fnl f 9/4[1]
-220 4 1 3/4 **Mr Wolf**13 1924 9-8-10 68 (p) IanBrennan(5) 7 66
(J J Quinn) led: rdn over 1f out: hdd ins fnl f: kpt on same pce 11/4[2]
210- 5 1 **Makbullet**274 5198 3-9-2 78 FrederikTylicki 8 71
(J Howard Johnson) pressed ldr: drvn over 2f out: one pce whn n.m.r ins fnl f 7/1
0000 6 1 1/2 **Frognal (IRE)**20 1688 4-9-11 78 PaulMulrennan 4 73+
(Mrs R A Carr) trckd ldrs: effrt whn no room fr 2f out: nt rcvr 9/2[3]

1m 11.62s (-1.98) **Going Correction** -0.275s/f (Firm)
WFA 3 from 4yo+ 9lb 6 Ran SP% 110.7
Speed ratings (Par 105): **102,101,100,97,96 94**
Tote Swingers: 1&2 £5.50, 1&3 £2.60, 2&3 £4.10 CSF £61.37 CT £182.78 TOTE £5.80: £2.50, £3.90; EX 39.40.
Owner Brian Morton **Bred** D Veitch And Musagd Abo Salim **Trained** Thirkleby, N Yorks

FOCUS
A tight sprint handicap. The winner carried over her AW improvement to turf.
Frognal(IRE) Official explanation: jockey said the gelding was denied a clear ru

2276 SCORTON H'CAP 1m 3f 214y
4:20 (4:20) (Class 3) (0-95,88) 4-Y-O+ £6,799 (£2,023; £1,011; £505) Stalls Low

Form RPR
0-23 1 **Granston (IRE)**14 1889 9-9-6 85 DarryllHolland 2 93
(J D Bethell) t.k.h: prom: effrt and chsd ldr 2f out: styd on u.p fnl f: whip knocked out of rdrs hand cl home: led post 3/1[2]
265- 2 nse **Bergonzi (IRE)**217 6822 6-8-8 73 FrederikTylicki 3 81
(J Howard Johnson) prom: chsd ldr after 4f: led over 2f out: rdn and styd on wl: hdd post 6/1
0321 3 1 3/4 **Destinys Dream (IRE)**13 1925 5-8-8 76 KellyHarrison(3) 5 81
(Miss Tracy Waggott) stdd in last pl: smooth hdwy over 2f out: chsd ldrs over 1f out: kpt on same pce wl ins fnl f 11/8[1]
3-30 4 3 1/4 **Alcalde**19 1720 4-9-9 88 GregFairley 4 88
(M Johnston) chsd ldr tl rn wd and lost pl bnd after 4f: prom: drvn and outpcd 4f out: edgd lft and rallied 2f out: no imp 4/1[3]
0200 5 14 **River Ardeche**18 1751 5-8-5 75 PatrickDonaghy(5) 1 53
(B M R Haslam) led: rdn over 3f out: hdd over 2f out: sn btn 18/1

2m 33.25s (-5.65) **Going Correction** -0.275s/f (Firm) 5 Ran SP% 106.7
Speed ratings (Par 107): **107,106,105,103,94**
CSF £18.54 TOTE £3.00: £1.10, £2.60; EX 17.60.
Owner The Four Players Partnership **Bred** Yeomanstown Stud **Trained** Middleham Moor, N Yorks

FOCUS
Not the strongest of races for the class. It was run at a strong pace and the first pair, who came clear in a bobbing finish, are rated to form.

NOTEBOOK
Granston(IRE) just got the better of Bergonzi in a bobbing finish. He went in pursuit of the runner-up turning for home and had the kitchen sink thrown at him inside the final furlong. His jockey lost his whip, but it was too late in the day to make any difference. It was a much-deserved win for the 9-y-o, whose brother Our Kes won over 1m4f, and he is worth keeping to this sort of test. (op 11-4 tchd 10-3)
Bergonzi(IRE) won a 2m handicap at the course last term and unsurprisingly made his move rounding the home turn. He gave his all and only just lost out, but may have paid for running somewhat freely early on. This run should bring him on and he certainly deserves to go one better again, but will be going up in the weights for this. (op 13-2 tchd 11-2)
Destinys Dream(IRE) was very well backed off her 6lb higher mark for winning well at Thirsk 13 days earlier. She had the race run to suit and was produced with her chance, but was ultimately well held by the first two. (op 13-8 tchd 5-4 and 7-4 in places)
Alcalde, back down in trip, didn't handle the track at all well. He also failed to convince with his attitude and now has it to prove. (op 10-3 tchd 9-2 in a place)
River Ardeche went off too quickly and was a sitting duck off the final turn. (op 14-1)

2277 LESLIE PETCH H'CAP 1m 3f 214y
4:50 (4:51) (Class 5) (0-75,73) 3-Y-O+ £2,331 (£693; £346; £173) Stalls Low

Form RPR
503- 1 **Hel's Angel (IRE)**241 6182 4-10-0 73 SebSanders 2 80
(Mrs A Duffield) hld up: hdwy on outside over 1f out: led ins fnl f: kpt on gamely 9/1
513 2 shd **Parhelion**51 1060 3-8-9 71 (t) DarryllHolland 4 77
(Tim Vaughan) hld up in tch: pushed along after 4f: hdwy to chse ldrs 4f out: effrt and edgd lft 2f out: disp ld ins fnl f: kpt on: jst hld 11/2
-214 3 1 3/4 **Park's Prodigy**7 2085 6-9-3 62 SilvestreDeSousa 3 66
(G A Harker) t.k.h: sn cl up: rdn over 2f out: ev ch ins fnl f: hld towards fin 4/1[3]
00-1 4 3/4 **That'll Do Nicely (IRE)**30 1467 7-9-5 64 TomEaves 1 67+
(N G Richards) t.k.h: in tch: effrt whn nt clr run over 1f out: n.m.r briefly ins fnl f: r.o 9/4[1]
20-0 5 2 1/4 **Amazing King (IRE)**17 1807 6-9-4 63 LeeVickers 5 62
(P A Kirby) led: rdn over 2f out: hdd ins fnl f: sn outpcd 14/1
4-60 6 1/2 **Classic Contours (USA)**21 1671 4-9-4 68 IanBrennan(5) 6 66
(J J Quinn) trckd ldrs: effrt and rdn over 2f out: no ex fnl f 11/4[2]
006/ 7 1/2 **Maneki Neko (IRE)**539 5040 8-9-1 60 oh1 TonyHamilton 7 58
(E W Tuer) prom: rdn whn nt clr run over 1f out: sn outpcd 16/1

2m 36.53s (-2.37) **Going Correction** -0.275s/f (Firm)
WFA 3 from 4yo+ 17lb 7 Ran SP% 115.4
Speed ratings (Par 103): **96,95,94,94,92 92,92**
Tote Swingers: 1&2 £4.50, 1&3 £4.50, 2&3 £3.00 CSF £57.74 TOTE £10.60: £5.80, £5.20; EX 49.90.
Owner Mrs H Baines & Middleham Park Racing VII **Bred** S White **Trained** Constable Burton, N Yorks

FOCUS
Not a bad handicap for the class, run at a fair pace. Improvement from the first two, with the race rated around the third.

That'll Do Nicely(IRE) Official explanation: jockey said the gelding was denied a clear run

2278 RACING AGAIN ON SATURDAY 29TH MAY APPRENTICE H'CAP 5f
5:20 (5:20) (Class 6) (0-60,59) 4-Y-O+ £2,047 (£604; £302) Stalls Low

Form RPR
5-60 1 **Ask Jenny (IRE)**24 1595 8-9-4 58 DeclanCannon 2 67
(Patrick Morris) sn pushed along bhd main gp: hdwy over 1f out: swtchd rt and qcknd to ld wl ins fnl f: r.o 10/1
230- 2 3/4 **Arriva La Diva**259 5626 4-8-7 50 IanBrennan(3) 8 56
(J J Quinn) led: rdn 2f out: hdd wl ins fnl f: kpt on 11/2[3]
0-06 3 1/2 **Officer Mor (USA)**19 1723 4-8-0 45 RichardRowe(5) 3 50
(Mrs Dianne Sayer) prom: effrt over 2f out: kpt on wl ins fnl f 7/1
10-4 4 1/2 **Tongalooma**19 1723 4-8-13 53 PatrickDonaghy 5 56
(James Moffatt) cl up: rdn and hung rt over 1f out: keeping on same pce whn short of room cl home 5/1[2]
200- 5 nse **Windjammer**198 7241 6-8-5 50 (p) CharlesEddery(5) 11 53
(L A Mullaney) cl up: effrt and ev ch ins fnl f: kpt on same pce last 75yds 25/1
60-2 6 1 **Foreign Rhythm (IRE)**11 1965 5-8-6 46 DeanHeslop 6 45
(R E Barr) in tch: drvn along 2f out: kpt on same pce fnl f 7/2[1]
00-0 7 1/2 **Thunder Bay**19 1723 5-8-6 51 AdamCarter(5) 10 48
(R E Barr) chsd ldrs: drvn along 1/2-way: nt qckn fnl f 10/1
50-0 8 1 **Silvanus (IRE)**27 1534 5-9-1 55 PaulPickard 4 49
(P T Midgley) missed break: wl bhd tl edgd lft and hdwy over 1f out: nvr able to chal 11/2[3]
-050 9 nk **Cheveyo (IRE)**13 1923 4-9-0 59 BarryAdams(5) 7 51
(Patrick Morris) s.i.s: bhd and hung lft: sme hdwy over 1f out: nvr rchd ldrs 18/1
0006 10 4 **Red Cell (IRE)**11 1968 4-8-0 45 (p) MatthewLawson(5) 1 23
(I W McInnes) bhd and outpcd: no ch fr 1/2-way 25/1
0-00 11 4 **Royal Premium**19 1722 4-8-9 52 (b[1]) RosieJessop(3) 9 16
(James Moffatt) midfield on outside: struggling 1/2-way: sn wknd 20/1

59.19 secs (-0.61) **Going Correction** -0.075s/f (Good) 11 Ran SP% 118.1
Speed ratings (Par 101): **101,99,99,98,98 96,95,94,93,87 80**
Tote Swingers: 1&2 £8.40, 1&3 £15.10, 2&3 £10.10 CSF £62.76 CT £421.23 TOTE £14.70: £4.20, £2.90, £3.20; EX 71.70 Place 6: £4,792.89 Place 5: £3,159.05 .
Owner W J Crosbie **Bred** Mrs J Costelloe **Trained** Tarporley, Cheshire

FOCUS
A poor handicap, confined to apprentice riders. It was run at a solid pace and they finished in something of a heap. The form looks sound.
Silvanus(IRE) Official explanation: jockey said the gelding missed the break
T/Plt: £1,306.50.80. Pool: £49,487.27 - 27.65 winning units. T/Qpdt: £217.10. Pool: £3,474.43 - 11.84 winning units. RY

1755 CHEPSTOW (L-H)
Friday, May 21

OFFICIAL GOING: Good to firm (8.1)
Wind: Virtually nil Weather: Bright and warm

2279 WIN SATURDAY'S SCOOP6 JACKPOT WITH ISCOOPED6.CO.UK CLAIMING STKS 1m 14y
2:40 (2:43) (Class 5) 3-Y-O+ £2,590 (£770; £385; £192) Stalls High

Form RPR
4-00 1 **Cereal Killer (IRE)**7 2089 3-8-12 75 (b[1]) JimmyFortune 8 72
(R Hannon) trckd ldr: led over 2f out: rdn whn jnd 1f out: styd on wl u.p fnl 120yds 9/1
-001 2 1 **Shared Moment (IRE)**18 1771 4-9-1 58 (p) HayleyTurner 7 64
(J Gallagher) t.k.h: hld up in tch: hdwy fr 2f out: chal 1f out and sn rdn: styd upsides tl outpcd fnl 120yds 7/2[1]
00-3 3 2 1/4 **Jeremiah (IRE)**22 1637 4-9-6 66 (p) EddieAhern 1 64
(J G Portman) in tch: trckd ldrs 2f out: rdn over 1f out: styd on same pce fnl f 6/1[3]
60 4 1/2 **Pennfield Pirate**19 1735 3-8-8 0 (v[1]) TravisBlock 14 60
(H Morrison) led: rdn 3f out: hdd over 2f out: one pce fr over 1f out 50/1
1356 5 1/2 **Musashi (IRE)**18 1763 5-9-7 59 IanMongan 3 63
(Mrs L J Mongan) s.i.s: in rr: rdn along 3f out: sn styd on fr over 1f out and kpt on ins fnl f but nvr gng pce to get into contention 14/1
0600 6 1 1/4 **Noble Jack (IRE)**22 1634 4-9-6 73 FergusSweeney 13 59
(G L Moore) t.k.h towards rr: hdwy 3f out: rdn 2f out: no ex fnl f 7/2[1]
3200 7 nk **Ant Music (IRE)**8 2049 3-8-5 63 (b) LukeMorris 6 52
(J S Moore) in tch: rdn and sme prog 3f out: nvr on terms and wknd fnl f 8/1
0536 8 3 1/2 **Tuscan King**4 2168 3-8-7 66 (b) AndrewHeffernan(3) 2 49
(P D Evans) rdn 3f out: nvr gng pce to rch ldrs 4/1[2]
0-50 9 12 **Never Sold Out (IRE)**42 1208 5-9-3 50 TomMcLaughlin 9 19
(J G M O'Shea) a in rr 40/1
000 10 33 **Higenius**28 1505 3-8-5 36 ChrisCatlin 10 —
(D Burchell) rdn 1/2-way: sn bhd: t.o 200/1
00/ 11 35 **Berry Pomeroy**688 3604 5-9-8 0 KevinGhunowa 4 —
(L P Grassick) chsd ldrs to 1/2-way: t.o 200/1

1m 34.45s (-1.75) **Going Correction** -0.15s/f (Firm)
WFA 3 from 4yo+ 12lb 11 Ran SP% 111.9
Speed ratings (Par 103): **102,101,98,98,97 96,96,92,80,47 12**
Tote Swingers: 1&2 £4.00, 1&3 £8.60, 2&3 £4.80 CSF £38.48 TOTE £6.00: £2.70, £2.10, £1.30; EX 35.70 Trifecta £180.60 Pool: £587.42 - 2.40 winning units..
Owner The Major Shear **Bred** John Foley & Miss A Foley **Trained** East Everleigh, Wilts

FOCUS
The ground had been watered and was riding 'quick with no jar'. They raced down the centre of the track. Ordinary claiming form and straightforward form for the grade judged around the runner-up.

2280 PERSONAL SHOPPING SERVICE AT BRIDGEND DESIGNER OUTLET H'CAP 5f 16y
3:10 (3:11) (Class 3) (0-95,92) 4-Y-O+ £7,123 (£2,119; £1,059; £529) Stalls High

Form RPR
5-41 1 **Captain Carey**28 1506 4-8-11 85 TomMcLaughlin 7 94+
(M S Saunders) in tch: rdn fnl 2f out: qcknd to ld appr fnl f: readily 7/2[2]
3-00 2 1 1/4 **Abraham Lincoln (IRE)**19 1727 6-8-13 87 (p) LukeMorris 3 92
(R A Harris) wnt lft s: sn chsng ldrs: drvn to chal over 1f out: styd on fnl f but nt pce of wnr: hld on all out for 2nd 10/1
110- 3 shd **Olynard (IRE)**272 5263 4-9-4 92 JimCrowley 8 96+
(R M Beckett) in tch: rdn and hdwy fr 2f out: styd on wl fnl f: gng on cl home to press for 2nd but nt rch wnr 5/1[3]

0-53 **4** shd **Our Piccadilly (IRE)**7 2094 5-8-4 78 oh2 FrannyNorton 6 82
(W S Kittow) *rrd stalls: sn in tch: hdwy fr 2f out to chal over 1f out: styd on fnl f but nt pce of wnr* **8/1**
124- **5** ¾ **Hajoum (IRE)**199 7227 4-8-13 87 FrankieDettori 10 88+
(M Johnston) *bhd and sn pushed along stl struggling 2f out: hdwy fnl f: r.o wl cl home but nvr a threat* **10/3**1
230- **6** ½ **Triple Dream**223 6666 5-8-4 78 oh1 (p) ChrisCatlin 9 79
(J M Bradley) *t.k.h: in tch: hdwy over 1f out: sn edgd lft and kpt on but nvr gng pce to rch ldrs* **18/1**
10-0 **7** ¾ **Mythical Blue (IRE)**18 1779 4-8-4 78 oh4 RichardThomas 5 75
(J M Bradley) *led tl hdd appr fnl f: sn btn* **33/1**
40-0 **8** hd **Mattamia (IRE)**44 1174 4-9-0 91 JamesMillman(3) 2 87
(B R Millman) *hmpd s: sn recovred to chse ldrs and ev ch appr fnl f: wknd ins fnl f* **5/1**3
120- **9** 3½ **Tony The Tap**251 5860 9-9-2 90 HayleyTurner 4 73
(W R Muir) *sn rdn along: a outpcd* **16/1**
0-05 **10** 5 **Sharpened Edge**16 1827 4-8-4 78 oh6 NeilChalmers 1 43
(B Palling) *chsd ldrs tl hung lft over 2f out: wknd wl over 1f out* **25/1**

58.44 secs (-0.86) **Going Correction** -0.15s/f (Firm) **10** Ran SP% **116.8**
Speed ratings (Par 107): **100,98,97,97,96 95,94,94,88,80**
Tote Swingers: 1&2 £12.70, 1&3 £6.80, 2&3 £16.00 CSF £38.59 CT £179.32 TOTE £6.80: £1.90, £3.70, £1.80; EX 42.80 Trifecta £347.50 Pool: £549.52 - 1.17 winning units..
Owner M S Saunders **Bred** B Walters **Trained** Green Ore, Somerset

FOCUS
A fairly valuable and competitive sprint handicap in which they finished in a heap behind the progressive winner. The form is rated around the second and third.

NOTEBOOK
Captain Carey had a good season at three and is continuing in the same vein this year, following up his Wolverhampton win off this career-high mark. He travelled well before being sent to the front and had no problem with the faster ground. He should continue to give a good account and holds an entry in the Wokingham, although that would mean stepping up to 6f. (op 5-1)
Abraham Lincoln(IRE) had not shown much in two previous runs for this yard but had dropped 20lb since his Ballydoyle heyday and he ran a big race from an outside draw after going left out of the stalls. The cheekpieces sharpened him up. (op 9-1 tchd 17-2)
Olynard(IRE) had ground conditions to suit and ran with plenty of credit on this first start since August. He is entitled to come on from this but is currently 4lb above his highest winning mark. (op 9-2 tchd 4-1)
Our Piccadilly(IRE) did not get the best of breaks but that did not really affect her chance as she was soon racing in touch. She had been third at Newmarket a week earlier and this was another solid effort from 2lb out of the weights. (tchd 15-2 and 9-1)
Hajoum(IRE), trained by Saeed Bin Suroor last season, made a satisfactory debut for his new yard without looking entirely at home on the ground. All his previous runs were over 6f and the way he was keeping on late suggests he may not mind a return to that trip. (op 9-2)
Triple Dream was another to more than pay his way last year and he showed enough on this reappearance to suggest he will win races again this year, although he may have to come back down the weights again. (op 20-1)
Mythical Blue(IRE), 4lb wrong at the weights so effectively 6lb above his last winning mark, showed plenty of pace before fading late on. (op 25-1)
Mattamia(IRE) had no excuses with the ground this time but met trouble at the start and his draw was no help. Official explanation: jockey said that the gelding was hampered on leaving the stalls (tchd 9-2)
Tony The Tap, who reportedly incurred a small stress fracture after running in the Portland last autumn, was always outpaced after missing the break. (op 10-1)
Sharpened Edge showed pace but, not for the first time, she hung to her left under pressure. (op 40-1)

2281 PIMM'S MAIDEN STKS 1m 4f 23y
3:40 (3:41) (Class 5) 3-Y-O **£2,590** (£770; £385; £192) **Stalls Low**

Form RPR
004- **1** **Caucus**262 5542 3-9-3 77 SteveDrowne 2 82
(H Morrison) *w ldr tl led after 4f: hung rt and wd bnd 5f out: narrowly hdd appr fnl 3f: styd pressing ldr and slt ld again u.p jst ins fnl f: styd on strly* **4/1**2
4-62 **2** ¾ **Bombadero (IRE)**15 1847 3-9-3 82 EddieAhern 5 81
(J L Dunlop) *trckd ldrs tl led appr fnl 3f: rdn 2f out: narrowly hdd jst ins fnl f: styd upsides tl no ex fnl 50yds* **4/7**1
5 **3** ½ **Pilote Celebre**19 1735 3-9-3 0 JimmyFortune 7 80
(A M Balding) *hld up in tch: rdn 3f out: styd on fr 2f out and styd on strly to cl on ldng duo fnl f but a jst hld* **9/2**3
4- **4** 12 **Lileo (IRE)**206 7096 3-9-3 0 HayleyTurner 6 61
(Mrs N S Evans) *s.i.s: in rr: rdn over 3f out: modest prog and nvr any ch* **16/1**
5 ½ **Kalamill (IRE)**318 3723 3-9-3 0 ChrisCatlin 3 60
(S Lycett) *slt ld 4f: styd chsng wnr tl hung rt 5f out: wknd fr 4f out* **33/1**
0-0 **6** 1¾ **Sunshine Buddy**13 1932 3-8-9 0 RobertLButler(3) 4 52
(C J Down) *chsd ldrs tl wknd over 2f out* **80/1**

2m 38.93s (-0.07) **Going Correction** +0.075s/f (Good) **6** Ran SP% **111.9**
Speed ratings (Par 99): **103,102,102,94,93 92**
Tote Swingers: 1&2 £1.30, 1&3 £2.50, 2&3 £1.10 CSF £6.64 TOTE £4.60: £1.70, £1.40; EX 9.20.
Owner Normandie Stud Ltd **Bred** Normandie Stud Ltd **Trained** East Ilsley, Berks

FOCUS
The first two home set a decent standard in this maiden but there was no strength in depth. It was steadily run and the form may not be all that solid. It has been rated around the runner-up.
Pilote Celebre Official explanation: jockey said that the colt hung left under pressure.

2282 BRIDGEND DESIGNER OUTLET H'CAP 1m 2f 36y
4:10 (4:10) (Class 3) (0-95,93) 4-Y-O+ **£7,123** (£2,119; £1,059; £529) **Stalls Low**

Form RPR
1004 **1** **Cairnsmore**15 1831 4-9-4 93 FrankieDettori 4 101+
(M Johnston) *mde all: grad qcknd pce fr 3f out: kpt on wl fnl f and a doing enough* **2/1**2
03-2 **2** ½ **Mabuya (UAE)**15 1840 4-8-7 82 EddieAhern 2 89+
(P J Makin) *chsd wnr: rdn and hung bdly lft fr over 2f out: stl hanging but styd on thrght fnl f and a hld by wnr* **13/8**1
6-01 **3** 1½ **Tinshu (IRE)**18 1780 4-8-10 85 DaneO'Neill 6 89
(D Haydn Jones) *chsd ldrs: drvn along 3f out: styd on fr over 1f out but no imp on ldng duo* **9/2**3
0-46 **4** 2½ **Potentiale (IRE)**15 1840 6-8-5 80 (p) HayleyTurner 5 79
(J W Hills) *slowly away: in rr: clsd up 5f out: drvn 3f out: styd on same pce fnl 2f* **10/1**
6 **5** hd **Silver Point (FR)**16 1829 7-9-2 91 LukeMorris 1 90
(B Palling) *t.k.h: chsd ldrs: rdn over 3f out: nvr on terms and no ch fnl 2f* **22/1**
2413 **6** 4½ **Hollow Green (IRE)**15 1837 4-8-4 82 AndrewHeffernan(3) 3 72
(P D Evans) *rdn 4f out: a in rr* **10/1**

2m 9.55s (-1.05) **Going Correction** +0.075s/f (Good) **6** Ran SP% **112.1**
Speed ratings (Par 107): **107,106,105,103,103 99**
Tote Swingers: 1&2 £1.02, 1&3 £1.50, 2&3 £2.20 CSF £5.64 TOTE £2.20: £1.10, £2.30; EX 6.60.
Owner Sheikh Hamdan Bin Mohammed Al Maktoum **Bred** Darley **Trained** Middleham Moor, N Yorks

FOCUS
A fair handicap in which the winner set a steady pace. The third is a solid guide.

NOTEBOOK
Cairnsmore had things his own way in front under a good ride, winding it up in the straight and holding on well enough. He had run well returned to turf at Chester last time and was down in grade and racing off the same mark here. (tchd 15-8)
Mabuya(UAE) chased the winner throughout but did not help his rider in the latter stages and was just held when he hung in slightly behind the winner late on. Unlucky at Ffos Las last time and 2lb higher here, his turn will come but he is going to need a truer run race. (op 7-4 tchd 15-8)
Tinshu(IRE) ran her race off a 3lb higher mark on this different ground without quite reaching the first two. (op 6-1)
Potentiale(IRE) had the cheekpieces back on, but he stood still as the stalls opened and although he passed a couple of rivals late on he was never a threat. He finished further behind Mabuya than he had at Ffos Las. (op 11-1 tchd 12-1)
Silver Point(FR) could never get into the picture on this return to turf and drop in trip. (op 20-1 tchd 16-1 and 25-1)
Hollow Green(IRE) was disappointing on this quicker surface. (op 8-1)

2283 BRIDGEND DESIGNER OUTLET OPEN UNTIL 8PM WEEKNIGHTS H'CAP 6f 16y
4:40 (4:41) (Class 3) (0-90,87) 3-Y-O **£7,123** (£2,119; £1,059; £264; £264) **Stalls High**

Form RPR
-400 **1** **Ghostwing**15 1836 3-9-2 85 (v1) HayleyTurner 1 92+
(J Gallagher) *trckd ldrs and travelling wl 2f out: qcknd to ld jst ins fnl f: in command whn hung rt and carried hd high fnl 30yds* **25/1**
4-30 **2** 1 **Lowdown (IRE)**15 1836 3-9-4 87 FrankieDettori 4 91
(M Johnston) *trckd ldrs: chal fr 3f out and travelling comf whn led wl over 1f out: hdd jst ins fnl f: sn outpcd by wnr but kpt on for clr 2nd* **2/1**2
2-54 **3** 1¾ **Fly Silca Fly (IRE)**21 1663 3-8-10 79 AlanMunro 6 77
(M R Channon) *in rr but in tch: hdwy 2f out: styd on to take 3rd ins fnl f but no ch w ldng duo* **17/2**3
610- **4** 1 **Danny's Choice**238 6241 3-9-4 87 JimCrowley 3 82
(R M Beckett) *led: jnd fr 3f out: hdd wl over 1f out: styd on same pce* **12/1**
3121 **4** dht **Maoi Chinn Tire (IRE)**79 766 3-8-7 76 (p) LukeMorris 8 71
(J S Moore) *chsd ldrs: pushed along fr 4f out: styd in tch: kpt on same pce fr over 1f out* **16/1**
40-0 **6** 3 **Farmers Wish (IRE)**31 1453 3-8-7 76 FrannyNorton 7 65
(J L Spearing) *chsd ldrs: rdn along over 2f out: hanging lft and wknd fr 1f out: no ch whn n.m.r sn after* **18/1**
0-00 **7** ¾ **Hairspray**20 1701 3-9-2 85 ChrisCatlin 2 68
(M R Channon) *slowly away: in rr: sme hdwy over 2f out: nvr on terms and wknd ins fnl 2f* **25/1**
23-1 **8** 1 **Felsham**26 1546 3-8-11 80 DaneO'Neill 9 60
(H Candy) *s.i.s: in tch: pushed along over 2f out: no imp on ldrs and sn btn* **5/4**1

1m 10.53s (-1.47) **Going Correction** -0.15s/f (Firm) **8** Ran SP% **114.8**
Speed ratings (Par 103): **103,101,99,98,98 94,93,91**
Tote Swingers: 1&2 £8.80, 1&3 £28.50, 2&3 £4.30 CSF £75.76 CT £482.32 TOTE £47.40: £4.90, £1.60, £1.50; EX 120.30 Trifecta £205.70 Part won. Pool: £278.06 - 0.43 winning units..
Owner Mark Benton **Bred** D R Botterill **Trained** Chastleton, Oxon

FOCUS
They headed down the centre again in this fair handicap. It might not prove the most solid piece of form although the winner was arguably value for further.

NOTEBOOK
Ghostwing was awash with sweat in the preliminaries, albeit on a very warm day. He travelled well from his wide draw and burst clear a furlong out before putting his ears back and his head up with the race in the bag. Value for a greater margin of victory, his chances of following up depend on whether the headgear works so well again. The stewards considered his improvement in form compared with his last run at Chester, but decided not to hold an enquiry after hearing connections' explanation that the grey was suited by today's faster ground and the fitting of a visor. Official explanation: trainer said, regarding the apparent improvement of form, that the gelding appeared better suited by today's faster ground and the fitting of a first time visor today
Lowdown(IRE) briefly had his head in front, but could not hold off the winner. He is running well enough on a variety of surfaces and might not mind a return to 7f. (op 3-1)
Fly Silca Fly(IRE) is edging down the weights and she stayed on for third after losing her initial pitch. (op 13-2 tchd 9-1)
Danny's Choice made the running and should last longer with this seasonal debut under her belt. (tchd 14-1)
Maoi Chinn Tire(IRE) ran respectably back on turf, but his success on the Polytrack meant he was 16lb higher than when last seen in this sphere. (tchd 14-1)
Farmers Wish(IRE) faded after chasing the pace. (op 16-1)
Hairspray was never in it after a slow start and has become disappointing. (op 20-1)
Felsham, 6lb higher than when winning a weakish race at Bath over 5f, was keen in the paddock and did not go down to post well. Never within striking distance, he was reported to have run flat. The stewards decided not to hold an enquiry but ordered him to be routine tested. Official explanation: trainer said, regarding the running and riding, the gelding ran flat (op 11-8 tchd 6-4 and 13-8 in a place)

2284 BRIDGEND DESIGNER OUTLET FASHION H'CAP 1m 14y
5:10 (5:12) (Class 4) (0-85,83) 4-Y-O+ **£4,533** (£1,348; £674; £336) **Stalls High**

Form RPR
-056 **1** **Satwa Laird**13 1933 4-9-4 83 FrankieDettori 5 89
(E A L Dunlop) *trckd ldr: led wl over 2f out: kpt slt advantage whn chal over 1f out: edgd lft u.p ins fnl f: sn stened: hld on all out* **3/1**1
26-4 **2** shd **Effigy**15 1841 6-8-13 78 DaneO'Neill 8 84
(H Candy) *trckd ldrs: hdwy and rdn over 1f out: chsd wnr ins fnl f: and styd on strly cl home: jst failed* **9/2**2
50-1 **3** 1½ **Addwaitya**22 1645 5-9-2 81 IanMongan 2 84+
(Mrs L J Mongan) *s.i.s: in rr: pushed along 3f out: styd on u.p to dispute 2nd ins fnl f: outpcd fnl 100yds* **10/1**
-550 **4** ¾ **Jesse James (IRE)**15 1841 4-9-4 83 SteveDrowne 3 84
(J R Gask) *chsd ldrs: rdn to chal over 1f out: outpcd ins fnl f* **8/1**
26-0 **5** 1¼ **Ogre (USA)**21 1669 5-8-10 78 (t) AndrewHeffernan(3) 6 76
(P D Evans) *plld hrd: chsd ldrs: pushed along over 2f out: ev ch wl over 1f out: wknd ins fnl f* **9/2**2
400- **6** 3 **Roman Glory (IRE)**350 2674 4-9-0 79 EddieAhern 1 70
(B J Meehan) *prssed ldrs: ev ch 2f out: wknd qckly fnl f: eased* **16/1**

0-50 **7** 3/4 **Ocean Transit (IRE)**13 1933 5-8-9 **74** JimCrowley 7 63
(R J Price) *pressed ldrs tl over 2f out: wknd qckly over 1f out* **10/1**

3-34 **8** 2 3/4 **Southandwest (IRE)**11 1962 6-8-13 **78** (b1) JimmyFortune 9 61
(J S Moore) *slowly away: t.k.h: in rr: rdn over 2f out and no rspnse* **6/1**3

0-00 **9** 15 **Aroundthebay**27 1516 4-8-13 **78** (p) ChrisCatlin 4 27
(H J L Dunlop) *led tl hdd & wknd rapidly wl over 2f out* **33/1**

1m 34.28s (-1.92) **Going Correction** -0.15s/f (Firm) **9** Ran SP% **113.8**
Speed ratings (Par 105): **103,102,101,100,99 96,95,92,77**
Tote Swingers: 1&2 £4.10, 1&3 £2.40, 2&3 £5.20 CSF £16.03 CT £117.94 TOTE £2.00: £1.10, £3.10, £6.40; EX 11.00 Trifecta £215.90 Place 6: £25.64 Place 5: £10.76 .
Owner The Lamprell Partnership **Bred** The Policy Setters **Trained** Newmarket, Suffolk

FOCUS
An ordinary handicap and the time did not compare favourably with the claimer. The runer-up is a solid guide to the form.
Jesse James(IRE) Official explanation: jockey said the gelding lost a front shoe
Southandwest(IRE) Official explanation: jockey said that the gelding ran too free
T/Plt: £37.80. Pool: £64,802.35 - 1,250.46 winning units. T/Qpdt: £6.60. Pool: £4,218.95 - 469.10 winning units. ST

2238 HAYDOCK (L-H)
Friday, May 21

OFFICIAL GOING: Good to firm (7.3)
Wind: Light, half-against Weather: fine and sunny

2285 BETDAQ THE BETTING EXCHANGE APPRENTICE TRAINING SERIES H'CAP 1m 3f 200y
6:30 (6:31) (Class 5) (0-70,70) 4-Y-O+ **£3,238** (£963; £481; £240) **Stalls** High

Form RPR

0162 **1** **Ghufa (IRE)**2 2230 6-8-2 **58** SophieSilvester(5) 8 67
(J Pearce) *hld up in midfield: hdwy on outer to ld over 2f out: hld on wl towards fin* **4/1**2

31-4 **2** nk **Elite Land**28 173 7-8-11 **65** DaleSwift(3) 3 74
(B Ellison) *hld up in rr: hdwy on ins over 3f out: chal 1f out: no ex towards fin* **7/2**1

00-0 **3** 1 1/4 **Duty Free (IRE)**17 1807 6-8-11 **67** MatthewCosham(5) 10 74
(James Moffatt) *trckd ldrs: wnt 3rd over 5f out: led 3f out: sn hdd: styd on wl last 100yds* **12/1**

1323 **4** 4 1/2 **Magnitude**66 893 5-8-4 **60** DannyBrock(5) 2 59
(B P J Baugh) *chsd ldrs: one pce fnl 2f* **16/1**

5/6- **5** 8 **Stage Acclaim (IRE)**16 7212 5-8-7 **58** DavidKenny 7 45
(Dr R D P Newland) *mid-div: hdwy to chse ldrs 3f out: wknd appr fnl f* **13/2**3

31-0 **6** 1 1/4 **Parc Des Princes (USA)**25 1579 4-8-12 **70** FrancisHayes(7) 6 55
(A M Balding) *mid-div: drvn over 2f out: nvr nr ldrs* **15/2**

0006 **7** 1 1/4 **Mojeerr**6 2109 4-8-0 **56** oh11 (be) AdamBeschizza(5) 11 39
(A J McCabe) *in rr: drvn over 3f out: nvr on terms* **20/1**

2640 **8** 2 3/4 **Doubnov (FR)**35 1357 7-8-12 **68** (p) AlexEdwards(5) 4 46
(Ian Williams) *led 1f: wnt 2nd over 5f out: lost pl over 2f out* **9/1**

023 **9** 3 3/4 **Hunters Belt (IRE)**47 1103 6-8-10 **68** ShirleyTeasdale(7) 9 40
(N Wilson) *mid-div: effrt over 4f out: wknd over 2f out* **14/1**

0220 **10** 2 **Diamond Twister (USA)**14 1883 4-9-0 **65** (t) DuilioDaSilva 12 34
(J R Best) *trckd ldrs: led 6f out tl over 2f out: sn lost pl* **12/1**

0/0- **11** 3 1/2 **Charlie Green (IRE)**155 7790 5-7-12 **56** oh11 JordanDodd(7) 5 19
(Paul Green) *slowly away: a towards rr: bhd fnl 3f* **100/1**

5440 **12** 46 **Sacco D'Oro**42 1207 4-7-12 **56** oh4 JosephYoung(7) 1 —
(M Mullineaux) *tk fierce hold: sddle sn slipped: led after 1f: hdd 6f out: lost pl over 3f out: sn wl bhd: t.o* **33/1**

2m 34.83s (0.83) **Going Correction** +0.225s/f (Good) **12** Ran SP% **113.9**
Speed ratings (Par 103): **103,102,101,98,93 92,91,90,87,86 83,53**
Tote Swingers: 1&2 £2.70, 1&3 £13.80, 2&3 £12.10 CSF £17.23 CT £151.73 TOTE £4.00: £1.10, £2.60, £4.80; EX 18.40.
Owner Miss Emma Pearce **Bred** Shadwell Estate Company Limited **Trained** Newmarket, Suffolk

FOCUS
As is often the case in these types of races, the bare form might want treating with a little caution. These apprentices were of varying ability, and with the saddle soon slipping on Sacco D'Oro, who raced extremely freely in front for much of the way, the field were soon strung out. A personal best from the winner who was suited by the strong pace.
Duty Free(IRE) Official explanation: vet said gelding lost a left hind shoe
Sacco D'Oro Official explanation: jockey said that filly's saddle slipped

2286 E B F JIM CUNNINGHAM'S 70TH MAIDEN FILLIES' STKS 6f
7:00 (7:01) (Class 5) 2-Y-O **£3,432** (£1,021; £510; £254) **Stalls** High

Form RPR

1 **Fork Handles** 2-9-0 0 KierenFallon 1 73+
(M R Channon) *s.s: drvn to chse ldrs after 2f: led over 1f out: styd on wl last 100yds* **2/1**1

4 **2** 3 1/2 **Box Of Frogs (IRE)**14 1879 2-9-0 0 GrahamGibbons 4 57
(A J McCabe) *swvd rt s: sn w ldr: drvn 3f out: kpt on ins fnl f* **3/1**2

3 hd **Colourful Past (USA)** 2-8-11 0 AhmedAjtebi(3) 3 56
(Mahmood Al Zarooni) *swvd rt s: mde most: drvn over 2f out: hdd over 1f out: swtchd lft: kpt on same pce* **2/1**1

4 8 **Cerejeira (IRE)** 2-9-0 0 ShaneKelly 2 35
(E J Alston) *trckd ldrs: nt clr run 2f out: swtchd lft: wknd 1f out: eased ins fnl f* **5/1**3

1m 17.14s (3.64) **Going Correction** +0.025s/f (Good) **4** Ran SP% **108.3**
Speed ratings (Par 90): **83,78,78,67**
CSF £8.05 TOTE £3.20; EX 5.10.
Owner M Channon **Bred** Mike Channon Bloodstock Ltd **Trained** West Ilsley, Berks

FOCUS
A non-bonus fillies' maiden, and only four runners, three of whom were debutants, so hard to know exactly what to make of the form, but whatever the case, one of the newcomers Fork Handles was visually impressive. The winner is afforded 8lb improvement from her debut.

NOTEBOOK
Fork Handles ◆, a filly with size and scope, took the eye in the paddock, although she displayed plenty of signs of mental immaturity both beforehand and during the race. Edgy in the preliminaries, she was also slightly fractious in the stalls, meaning she was standing awkwardly as the gates opened and lost ground on her three rivals. She then had to be niggled along for the first half of the contest, but she gradually got the idea and was actually going quite well by the time she took over. Once in front, she displayed further signs of greenness, pricking her ears, but she was still able to clear away from the others and looked to be motoring crossing the line. This was a fine start considering she's a daughter of a King George winner, as well as a half-sister to 1m3f scorer, and provided she goes the right way, she could be decent. She's eligible for the Chesham Stakes at Royal Ascot and would be interesting if taking her chance. (op 9-4 tchd 15-8)
Box Of Frogs(IRE) put her experience to good use, showing speed against the rail, and as such may be a little flattered, but even so, this was a respectable effort and probably represented improve form. (op 11-4 tchd 4-1)
Colourful Past(USA), out of a high-class dual 1m winning juvenile, showed speed but didn't find a great deal for pressure. Her first-season trainer is now 0-9 with his juveniles, managing only one second placing in the process. (op 7-4 tchd 6-4)
Cerejeira(IRE), a £15,000 purchase, ran a little better than the beaten margin suggests, as she travelled well to a point and was then eased off late on once it was clear she wasn't picking up. (op 13-2 tchd 7-1 in places)

2287 CHESHIRE OAKS DESIGNER OUTLET CLASSIFIED STKS 6f
7:30 (7:31) (Class 4) 3-Y-O **£5,504** (£1,637; £818; £408) **Stalls** High

Form RPR

-022 **1** **Flaneur**7 2069 3-9-0 77 (b) GrahamGibbons 2 85
(T D Easterby) *trckd ldrs: swtchd rt over 3f out: led on stands' side over 1f out: drvn and edgd lft: kpt on wl towards fin* **9/2**3

10-0 **2** 3/4 **Excellent Guest**38 1279 3-9-0 78 SebSanders 5 83+
(G G Margarson) *dwlt: bdly hmpd after 1f: effrt on inner and hmpd 2f out: styd on wl fnl f: nt rch wnr* **12/1**

3-1 **3** 3/4 **Red Gulch**53 1050 3-9-0 79 KierenFallon 6 80+
(E A L Dunlop) *t.k.h: bdly hmpd after 1f: swtchd lft over 3f out: hdwy to chse ldrs 2f out: styd on appr fnl f: no ex ins fnl f* **6/4**1

-010 **4** nk **Vanilla Loan (IRE)**27 1535 3-9-0 72 AndreaAtzeni 3 79
(M Botti) *trckd ldrs on outer: effrt over 2f out: hrd rdn and hung lft over 1f out: kpt on same pce ins fnl f* **20/1**

4-44 **5** 1 **Mon Brav**18 1776 3-9-0 78 (b1) DavidNolan 9 76
(D Carroll) *led: wnt lft after 1f: hung lft: hdd over 1f out: wknd fnl 75yds* **4/1**2

321- **6** 2 **Goddess Of Light (IRE)**26 1557 3-9-0 75 ShaneKelly 8 70
(Daniel Mark Loughnane, Ire) *in rr: rdn over 2f out: styd on fnl f* **25/1**

-401 **7** 1/2 **Ventura Cove (IRE)**20 1709 3-9-0 78 PaulHanagan 1 72
(R A Fahey) *chsd ldrs on outside: hung lft and wkng whn hmpd jst ins fnl f* **10/1**

-224 **8** hd **Dusty Spirit**26 1546 3-8-9 76 (tp) MatthewDavies(5) 4 67
(W G M Turner) *stmbld s: sn chsng ldrs: rdn over 2f out: wknd over 1f out* **25/1**

435- **9** 4 **High Spice (USA)**205 7108 3-9-0 80 RichardMullen 7 61
(R M H Cowell) *s.i.s: hmpd after 1f: chsng ldrs 3f out: wknd and heavily eased last 100yds* **12/1**

1m 14.47s (0.97) **Going Correction** +0.025s/f (Good) **9** Ran SP% **115.1**
Speed ratings (Par 101): **101,100,99,98,97 94,93,93,88**
Tote Swingers: 1&2 £13.20, 1&3 £2.70, 2&3 £3.80 CSF £54.14 TOTE £4.70: £1.40, £3.30, £1.10; EX 52.00.
Owner Jeremy Gompertz **Bred** C R Mason **Trained** Great Habton, N Yorks

FOCUS
A competitive sprint, with only 8lb separating these 3-y-os at the weights. The runer-up was the chief sufferer of trouble with the race rated around the winner and fifth.
Vanilla Loan(IRE) Official explanation: vet said filly lost a shoe
Ventura Cove(IRE) Official explanation: jockey said the gelding hung left-handed

2288 NORTHERN RACING CLUB'S 30TH YEAR H'CAP 1m 30y
8:00 (8:01) (Class 4) (0-80,79) 3-Y-O **£6,476** (£1,927; £963; £481) **Stalls** Low

Form RPR

0622 **1** **Secretive**7 2089 3-8-13 **74** (b) JoeFanning 5 89
(M Johnston) *sn led: stdd pce: qcknd over 3f out: kpt on wl* **13/8**1

43-2 **2** 1 3/4 **King Of Reason**20 1694 3-9-4 **79** ShaneKelly 4 90
(D M Simcock) *hld up in rr: smooth hdwy on outside to chse wnr over 1f out: sn rdn and hung lft: swtchd rt ins fnl f: eased whn hld towards fin* **7/2**2

-212 **3** 5 **Layla's Lexi**8 2042 3-8-6 **67** TadhgO'Shea 3 67
(Ian Williams) *led early: chsd ldrs: drvn over 3f out: one pce* **7/2**2

0-03 **4** 8 **On The Cusp (IRE)**17 1810 3-8-6 **67** PaulHanagan 2 48
(M A Jarvis) *trckd ldrs: wnt 2nd over 2f out: wknd over 1f out* **5/1**3

0-05 **5** 2 **Royal Patriot (IRE)**14 1890 3-8-7 **68** SilvestreDeSousa 7 45
(Paul Green) *t.k.h: trckd ldr: effrt over 2f out: wknd over 1f out* **18/1**

6-00 **6** 1 3/4 **Ruler's Honour (IRE)**13 1927 3-8-6 **67** AndrewElliott 1 39
(T J Etherington) *t.k.h: dropped bk after 1f: drvn over 3f out: wknd 2f out* **16/1**

1m 45.36s (0.66) **Going Correction** +0.225s/f (Good) **6** Ran SP% **110.4**
Speed ratings (Par 101): **101,99,94,86,84 82**
Tote Swingers: 1&2 £1.90, 1&3 £2.00, 2&3 £3.00 CSF £7.25 TOTE £2.60: £1.50, £1.90; EX 7.00.
Owner Sheikh Hamdan Bin Mohammed Al Maktoum **Bred** T A Scothern **Trained** Middleham Moor, N Yorks

FOCUS
The distance from the 1m start to the winning post was 1m and 40 yards. A £10,000 handicap, but there wasn't much strength in depth. The pace, set by the winner Secretive, seemed fair, although that one appeared to get a breather in early in the straight. The first pair finished clear of the solid form.

2289 BETFRED H'CAP 1m 2f 95y
8:30 (8:30) (Class 5) (0-75,75) 3-Y-O **£3,885** (£1,156; £577; £288) **Stalls** High

Form RPR

31-0 **1** **Christopher Wren (USA)**30 1476 3-8-13 **75** KierenFox(5) 5 87+
(J R Best) *sn in rr: effrt over 3f out: styd on on outside over 2f out: led jst ins fnl f: styd on strly: v readily* **14/1**

006- **2** 1 1/4 **Tuscan Gold**213 6912 3-8-9 **66** SebSanders 1 75
(Sir Mark Prescott) *dwlt: sn chsng ldrs: chal over 3f out: edgd lft and led over 1f out: hdd jst ins fnl f: no ex* **7/2**2

0-32 **3** 1 **Gritstone**22 1652 3-9-2 **73** PaulHanagan 6 80
(R A Fahey) *led: edgd lft over 3f out: hdd over 1f out: styd on same pce* **11/8**1

63-3 **4** 4 **Another Magic Man (USA)**14 1876 3-9-2 **73** RobertWinston 9 73
(J R Best) *trckd ldrs: effrt over 3f out: hmpd and swtchd rt over 2f out: one pce* **14/1**

5 13 **Red Fighter (IRE)**237 6299 3-9-2 **73** AndreaAtzeni 3 48
(Daniel Mark Loughnane, Ire) *in rr: effrt on inner 4f out: wknd 2f out* **25/1**

-036 **6** 3 1/4 **Pullyourfingerout (IRE)**11 1975 3-9-1 **72** KierenFallon 4 41
(B G Powell) *sn chsng ldrs: drvn 3f out: lost pl over 1f out* **5/1**3

1334 **7** 5 **Miami Gator (IRE)**17 1810 3-8-7 **64** AndrewElliott 8 23
(J R Weymes) *chsd ldrs: lost pl over 2f out* **16/1**

0-45 **8** 2 1/2 **Damietta (USA)**31 1453 3-9-2 **73** JoeFanning 2 27
(M Johnston) *sn chsng ldrs: lost pl 3f out: eased whn bhd ins fnl f* **16/1**

600- **9** *11* **Diamondgeezer Luke (IRE)**[195] 7298 3-8-9 **66**............... ShaneKelly 7 —
(Patrick Morris) *in rr: lost pl over 2f out: bhd whn eased ins fnl f* **33/1**

2m 16.06s (0.06) **Going Correction** +0.225s/f (Good) 9 Ran SP% **112.9**
Speed ratings (Par 99): **96,95,94,91,80 78,74,72,63**
Tote Swingers: 1&2 £12.50, 1&3 £1.30, 2&3 £2.30 CSF £61.19 CT £112.21 TOTE £17.60: £4.10, £1.10, £1.30; EX 85.90.
Owner Kingsgate Racing **Bred** Rod D'Elia **Trained** Hucking, Kent

FOCUS
They finished spread out after going a good pace and, with the front two both scopey individuals, this looks pretty good for the grade. The first pair are rated up around 10lb and the first four finished clear.
Diamondgeezer Luke(IRE) Official explanation: jockey said that the gelding had no more to give

2290 GET RACING UK IN YOUR PUB 0870 351 8834 MAIDEN STKS 1m 2f 95y
9:00 (9:02) (Class 5) 3-Y-O+ **£3,561** (£1,059; £529; £264) **Stalls** High

Form RPR

6-42 **1** **Cultivar**[16] 1824 3-9-0 83........................ MichaelHills 2 83+
(B W Hills) *mde all: styd on strly fnl 2f: readily* **10/11**[1]

55 **2** *2 ½* **Hail Tiberius**[13] 1927 3-9-0 0........................ GrahamGibbons 1 78
(T D Walford) *s.i.s: t.k.h: effrt on inner over 3f out: styd on appr fnl f: tk 2nd last 75yds* **7/1**[3]

0-2 **3** *1* **Raqeeb (USA)**[23] 1627 3-9-0 0........................ TadhgO'Shea 8 76
(Sir Michael Stoute) *sn trcking ldrs on outside: chal over 3f out: kpt on same pce fnl 2f* **11/2**[2]

22- **4** *1 ½* **Faith Jicaro (IRE)**[311] 3944 3-8-9 0........................ ShaneKelly 7 68
(N J Vaughan) *hld up in rr: hdwy 4f out: styd on same pce fnl 2f* **16/1**

43 **5** *11* **Sheiling (IRE)**[17] 1809 3-8-9 0........................ PaulHanagan 12 47+
(R A Fahey) *in rr: outpcd 3f out: kpt on fnl f* **18/1**

6 *½* **Charming Man** 3-8-11 0........................ AhmedAjtebi(3) 10 51+
(Mahmood Al Zarooni) *s.s: rdn over 4f out: nvr on terms* **8/1**

/05- **7** *1 ½* **Sumbe (USA)**[377] 1872 4-10-0 82........................ RichardMullen 11 49
(M P Tregoning) *in tch on outside: effrt over 3f out: sn wl outpcd* **8/1**

8 *½* **Queen's Scholar (USA)** 3-8-9 0........................ JoeFanning 5 42+
(M Johnston) *hdwy to trck ldrs after 3f: wknd qckly over 1f out* **20/1**

50 **9** *5* **Ionaguru**[13] 1932 5-9-9 0........................ RobertWinston 4 34
(B D Leavy) *t.k.h: sn trcking ldrs: wd bnd over 5f out: lost pl over 2f out* **100/1**

0 **10** *19* **Annie Moyles**[10] 2003 4-9-9 0........................ DavidNolan 9 —
(C N Kellett) *s.i.s: in rr: bhd fnl 3f* **100/1**

446- **11** *¾* **Brasingaman Eric**[318] 3716 3-8-11 51...............(b[1]) RussKennemore(3) 3 —
(S Wynne) *trckd ldrs: lost pl over 3f out: sn bhd* **100/1**

0 **12** *¾* **Massachusetts**[25] 1581 3-9-0 0........................ KierenFallon 6 —
(B J Meehan) *t.k.h: trckd ldrs: rdn and lost pl over 6f out: sn wl bhd* **20/1**

2m 17.81s (1.81) **Going Correction** +0.225s/f (Good)
WFA 3 from 4yo+ 14lb 12 Ran SP% **126.1**
Speed ratings (Par 103): **89,87,86,85,76 75,74,74,70,55 54,53**
Tote Swingers: 1&2 £2.90, 1&3 £2.10, 2&3 £8.30 CSF £8.27 TOTE £1.80: £1.10, £1.70, £1.50; EX 11.80 Place 6 £8.59, Place 5 £4.90..
Owner K Abdulla **Bred** Juddmonte Farms Ltd **Trained** Lambourn, Berks

FOCUS
An interesting maiden with plenty of powerful connections represented, although the pace was modest (time 1.75 seconds slower than previous Class 5 handicap), with Cultivar allowed a soft lead. He set a decent standard and this is sound form.
T/Plt: £19.30. Pool: £57,675.16. 2,170.32 winning units. T/Qpdt: £2.70. Pool: £4,774.37. 1,281.67 winning units. WG

2208 MUSSELBURGH (R-H)
Friday, May 21

OFFICIAL GOING: Good to firm (7.3)
Wind: Nil Weather: Fine

2291 ROK THE NATIONS LOCAL BUILDER APPRENTICE H'CAP 5f
6:40 (6:41) (Class 6) (0-65,65) 3-Y-O **£2,590** (£770; £385; £192) **Stalls** Low

Form RPR

4121 **1** **Jigajig**[4] 2185 3-9-3 61 6ex........................ AmyRyan(3) 4 75
(K A Ryan) *led early: remained w ldr tl led again 2f out: rdn and r.o wl ins fnl f* **3/1**[1]

0-01 **2** *3* **Lees Anthem**[21] 1667 3-9-1 **59**........................ LanceBetts(3) 2 62
(C J Teague) *a.p: rdn to chse wnr fnl f: styd on same pce* **6/1**[3]

664- **3** *1 ½* **North Central (USA)**[272] 5253 3-9-7 **65**............... MichaelO'Connell(3) 1 63
(J Howard Johnson) *sn led: rdn and hdd 2f out: no ex ins fnl f* **4/1**[2]

6423 **4** *2* **Dower Glen**[21] 1667 3-9-3 **58**........................ MartinLane 8 49+
(N Wilson) *hld up in tch: rdn over 1f out: no ex fnl f* **13/2**

0-05 **5** *½* **Kristen Jane (USA)**[21] 1667 3-8-5 **46** oh1........................ JackDean 5 35
(Miss L A Perratt) *mid-div: prom: rdn 1/2-way: hung rt and no ex ins fnl f* **16/1**

00-0 **6** *3 ½* **Classlin**[21] 1667 3-8-10 **51**........................ AshleyHamblett 3 27
(J S Goldie) *hld up: rdn over 1f out: nvr on terms* **16/1**

55-0 **7** *1 ½* **Luv U Noo**[46] 1118 3-8-10 **54**........................ BillyCray(3) 10 25
(B Ellison) *s.i.s: outpcd: nvr nrr* **9/1**

4000 **8** *hd* **Blue Neptune**[3] 2217 3-8-8 **56**........................ KevinLundie(7) 9 26
(P D Evans) *hld up: rdn and swtchd rt over 1f out: nvr on terms* **25/1**

0-60 **9** *¾* **Royal Holiday (IRE)**[27] 1511 3-9-4 **64**........................ GarryWhillans(5) 6 31
(B Ellison) *sn outpcd* **25/1**

0-41 **10** *nk* **Monte Mayor One**[11] 1979 3-9-3 **61** 6ex...............(p) JamesSullivan(3) 7 27
(P Monteith) *prom: rdn 2f out: wknd over 1f out* **10/1**

59.01 secs (-1.39) **Going Correction** -0.30s/f (Firm) 10 Ran SP% **111.2**
Speed ratings (Par 97): **99,94,91,88,87 82,79,79,78,77**
Tote Swingers: 1&2 £2.40, 1&3 £4.50, 2&3 £4.30 CSF £19.74 CT £68.16 TOTE £3.60: £2.30, £2.80, £1.40; EX 16.00.
Owner Mrs Maureen Eason **Bred** Miss D Fleming **Trained** Hambleton, N Yorks

FOCUS
A modest handicap won in good fashion by an improving sprinter, who reversed recent C/D running with the second. The principals were all prominent throughout on the stand rail and nothing got into the race from further back.
Luv U Noo Official explanation: jockey said that filly missed the break

2292 EUROPEAN BREEDERS' FUND MAIDEN STKS 5f
7:10 (7:10) (Class 4) 2-Y-O **£5,828** (£1,734; £866; £432) **Stalls** Low

Form RPR

325 **1** **Molly Mylenis**[27] 1527 2-8-12 0........................ CathyGannon 5 65
(P D Evans) *mde all: rdn over 1f out: styd on wl* **2/1**[1]

0 **2** *nk* **Kheya (IRE)**[36] 1331 2-8-12 0........................ PJMcDonald 3 64
(G M Moore) *w wnr: rdn and ev ch fr over 1f out: styd on* **11/4**[2]

0462 **3** *2 ½* **Roodee Queen**[14] 1864 2-8-12 0........................ PaulMulrennan 2 55
(Patrick Morris) *trckd ldrs: racd keenly: nt clr run over 1f out: styd on same pce fnl f* **9/1**[3]

6 **4** *2* **Fast Shot**[17] 1806 2-9-3 0........................ DavidAllan 4 53
(T D Easterby) *chsd ldrs: rdn 2f out: edgd rt and wknd ins fnl f* **11/4**[2]

0 **5** *2 ½* **Liberty Ess (IRE)**[14] 1879 2-8-12 0........................ PhillipMakin 6 39
(K A Ryan) *chsd ldrs: rdn 1/2-way: wknd fnl f* **9/1**[3]

6 *22* **Immacolata (IRE)** 2-8-8 0 ow1........................ MarkCoumbe(5) 1 —
(A Berry) *s.s: outpcd* **33/1**

60.27 secs (-0.13) **Going Correction** -0.30s/f (Firm) 6 Ran SP% **109.6**
Speed ratings (Par 95): **89,88,84,81,77 42**
Tote Swingers: 1&2 £1.90, 1&3 £2.50, 2&3 £4.90 CSF £7.35 TOTE £2.10: £1.10, £3.20; EX 8.10.
Owner Terry Earle **Bred** Mrs G S Rees **Trained** Pandy, Monmouths

FOCUS
Weak maiden form and the winner is rated a fraction below her best. Once again the first two hugged the stand rail and held those positions throughout in a race run over two seconds slower than the opener.

NOTEBOOK
Molly Mylenis set the standard on her last two bits of form and without the visor she wore last time, always seemed just to have things under control. She's not good enough to win a novice event and will probably have to bide her time until nurseries come along. (tchd 9-4 and 5-2 in a place)
Kheya(IRE) had clearly benefited from her debut when in a race that has generally worked out quite well and showed improved form, pestering the winner all the way to the line. A half-sister to the Norfolk Stakes runner-up Art Advisor, this trip looks ideal for now. (op 7-2 tchd 9-2)
Roodee Queen has been steadily progressive at a low level and probably improved again while looking short of room on one or two occasions. She'd be up to winning a seller. (op 8-1 tchd 10-1)
Fast Shot, the only colt in the field, showed a bit of promise in better company on his debut but again left the impression he's more one for later in the season, perhaps over 6f in nurseries. (op 3-1 tchd 5-2)
Liberty Ess(IRE) only hinted at ability at Nottingham on her debut and didn't offer much more here, though she might have raced more towards the middle than ideal. (op 7-1 tchd 13-2)
Immacolata(IRE), a half-sister to the 5f winner Guto, hails from a yard rarely among 2yo winners these days and never showed after missing the break, flashing her tail. Official explanation: jockey said that the filly was slowly away (tchd 25-1)

2293 PDM H'CAP 7f 30y
7:40 (7:40) (Class 5) (0-70,70) 4-Y-O+ **£4,209** (£1,252; £625; £312) **Stalls** High

Form RPR

1312 **1** **Camerooney**[21] 1672 7-9-1 **70**........................ BarryMcHugh(3) 3 82
(B Ellison) *mde all: rdn clr fnl f: r.o wl* **7/4**[2]

-000 **2** *6* **Hosanna**[14] 1869 4-8-5 **57** oh11 ow1........................ PJMcDonald 2 53
(J Barclay) *s.i.s: rcvrd to chse wnr 6f out: rdn over 1f out: sn outpcd* **100/1**

60-0 **3** *shd* **Cold Quest (USA)**[42] 1204 6-7-13 **56** oh2........................ JamesSullivan(5) 1 52
(Miss L A Perratt) *unruly in stalls: hld up: rdn over 2f out: swtchd rt and styd on ins fnl f: nvr nrr* **28/1**

-011 **4** *1* **Nufoudh (IRE)**[3] 2211 6-9-4 **70** 6ex........................ FrederikTylicki 6 63+
(Miss Tracy Waggott) *trckd ldrs: plld hrd: rdn over 1f out: no ex fnl f* **11/10**[1]

1U-2 **5** *2 ¾* **Mr Lu**[13] 1928 5-8-4 **59**........................ KellyHarrison(3) 4 45+
(J S Goldie) *hld up: plld hrd: hdwy on outer wl over 1f out: wknd fnl f* **7/1**[3]

40-0 **6** *¾* **Minturno (USA)**[72] 853 4-9-0 **66**........................ PaulMulrennan 5 50
(Mrs A Duffield) *trckd ldrs: racd keenly: rdn over 1f out: wknd fnl f* **9/1**

1m 28.76s (-0.24) **Going Correction** -0.125s/f (Firm) 6 Ran SP% **110.9**
Speed ratings (Par 103): **103,96,96,94,91 90**
Tote Swingers: 1&2 £10.90, 1&3 £9.40, 2&3 £20.60 CSF £82.61 TOTE £2.30: £1.10, £15.50; EX 104.00.
Owner Mrs Jean Stapleton **Bred** Miss Dianne Hill **Trained** Norton, N Yorks

FOCUS
An uncompetitive handicap with half the field either out of form or out of the weights. The winner was able to dictate a steady pace and never looked in any danger, but this is not form to be getting carried away with for all that the winner is progressive.

2294 BERNARD HUNTER CRANE HIRE (S) STKS 5f
8:10 (8:10) (Class 6) 3-Y-O+ **£2,590** (£770; £385; £192) **Stalls** Low

Form RPR

5004 **1** **The Bear**[7] 2073 7-9-3 59........................ PaulMulrennan 4 69
(Miss L A Perratt) *chsd ldr: led 1f out: rdn out* **22/1**

0330 **2** *2 ½* **Stolt (IRE)**[6] 2136 6-9-0 82........................(v[1]) AshleyHamblett(3) 2 60
(N Wilson) *led: rdn and hdd 1f out: edgd rt ins fnl f: styd on same pce* **11/4**[1]

5363 **3** *shd* **Mandarin Spirit (IRE)**[3] 2213 10-9-3 65...............(b) FrederikTylicki 3 60
(Miss L A Perratt) *rrd in stalls prior to the s: sn pushed along towards rr: hdwy 1/2-way: rdn over 1f out: styd on* **11/4**[1]

00-3 **4** *5* **Raccoon (IRE)**[11] 1965 10-9-3 74........................ PJMcDonald 7 42
(Mrs R A Carr) *chsd ldrs: rdn over 1f out: wknd ins fnl f* **4/1**[2]

0221 **5** *4 ½* **Ingleby Star (IRE)**[7] 2073 5-9-6 70........................(p) MartinLane(3) 8 31
(N Wilson) *s.i.s: hdwy 1/2-way: sn rdn: wknd ins fnl f* **4/1**[2]

6-20 **6** *1* **Caribbean Coral**[4] 2166 11-9-3 62........................ PhillipMakin 1 22
(A B Haynes) *hld up: shkn up 2f out: wknd over 1f out* **9/1**[3]

000- **7** *3 ¼* **Fern House (IRE)**[206] 7086 8-8-12 43........................ MarkCoumbe(5) 5 10
(A Berry) *s.s: outpcd* **50/1**

58.76 secs (-1.64) **Going Correction** -0.30s/f (Firm) 7 Ran SP% **109.6**
Speed ratings (Par 101): **101,97,96,88,81 80,74**
Tote Swingers: 1&2 £11.10, 1&3 £5.50, 2&3 £2.10 CSF £75.35 TOTE £23.20: £10.10, £1.50; EX 108.40.There was no bid for the winner
Owner Cincinnati Club **Bred** P G Airey And R R Whitton **Trained** East Kilbride, South Lanarks

FOCUS
A routine seller here with a wide range of abilities on show. Once again the winner and runner-up dominated proceedings on the rail in a race run at a good clip. The winner is rated to last year's best with the rest 10lb+ off their recent form.
Caribbean Coral Official explanation: jockey said that the gelding hung left handed from half way
Fern House(IRE) Official explanation: jockey said that the gelding was slowly away

2295 RENNIES OF DUNFERMLINE H'CAP 1m 6f
8:40 (8:40) (Class 4) (0-80,73) 4-Y-O+ **£6,476** (£1,927; £963; £481) **Stalls** High

Form RPR

14-2 **1** **Jackday (IRE)**[14] 1891 5-9-2 **65**........................(p) DavidAllan 2 73
(T D Easterby) *hld up: hdwy over 3f out: rdn to ld over 1f out: edgd rt ins fnl f: styd on* **15/8**[1]

500- **2** *½* **Forrest Flyer (IRE)**[202] 7170 6-8-11 **60**........................ DanielTudhope 7 67
(J S Goldie) *a.p: led over 2f out: rdn and hdd over 1f out: styd on* **8/1**

1106 **3** *3 ½* **Wicked Daze (IRE)**[19] 1720 7-9-10 **73**........................ PhillipMakin 1 75
(Miss L A Perratt) *dwlt: hld up: hdwy 2f out: sn rdn: no ex ins fnl f* **11/2**[3]

644/ 4 1 **Danish Rebel (IRE)**28 3785 6-9-3 66 (t) PaulMulrennan 3 67
(G A Charlton) *chsd ldr: rdn and ev ch over 2f out: no ex fnl f* 11/1
-020 5 3/4 **Film Festival (USA)**14 1883 7-9-1 67 BarryMcHugh(3) 8 67
(B Ellison) *hld up: hdwy over 3f out: rdn over 1f out: no ex fnl f* 4/1[2]
2020 6 11 **Oddsmaker (IRE)**8 2060 9-9-4 67 (t) CathyGannon 4 51
(M A Barnes) *led: rdn and hdd over 2f out: wknd over 1f out* 9/1
252- 7 14 **Sonara (IRE)**70 3313 6-9-8 71 FrederikTylicki 6 36
(J Howard Johnson) *chsd ldrs: rdn over 4f out: hit rail sn after: wknd over 2f out* 8/1

3m 3.84s (-1.46) **Going Correction** -0.125s/f (Firm) 7 Ran SP% 110.7
Speed ratings (Par 105): **99,98,96,96,95 89,81**
Tote Swingers: 1&2 £6.50, 1&3 £2.00, 2&3 £4.00 CSF £16.38 CT £65.24 TOTE £3.10: £1.60, £4.60; EX 14.50.
Owner Mrs Jean P Connew **Bred** Mrs H D McCalmont **Trained** Great Habton, N Yorks

FOCUS
A weak race for the money with the top weight having an official mark of only 73. The pace was mostly a decent one, allowing those held up to dominate the finish, though the first three were arguably the best handicapped horses anyway. A personal best from the winner.
Oddsmaker(IRE) Official explanation: jocket said the gelding was unsuited by the going (good to firm).

2296 CANADA LIFE H'CAP 7f 30y
9:10 (9:10) (Class 5) (0-70,70) 3-Y-O **£4,209** (£939; £939; £312) **Stalls** High

Form RPR
240- 1 **Desert Forest (IRE)**217 6821 3-9-5 68 FrederikTylicki 5 71
(J Howard Johnson) *led: hdd over 4f out: rdn over 1f out: r.o to ld wl ins fnl f* 7/1
0522 2 1/2 **Killing Moon (USA)**6 2132 3-8-11 65 MichaelO'Connell(5) 9 67
(K A Ryan) *s.i.s: sn chsng ldrs: rdn over 1f out: r.o* 15/8[1]
1504 2 dht **Lockantanks**22 1651 3-9-7 70 PhillipMakin 8 72
(A B Haynes) *chsd wnr tl led over 4f out: rdn over 1f out: hdd ins fnl f: r.o* 9/1
6032 4 shd **Chinese Democracy (USA)**8 2049 3-8-6 55 CathyGannon 4 57
(P D Evans) *chsd ldrs: rdn to ld ins fnl f: sn hdd: r.o* 5/2[2]
30-3 5 hd **Could It Be Magic**15 1842 3-9-4 70 (p) JackDean(3) 1 71
(W G M Turner) *hld up: hdwy over 2f out: rdn and hung rt over 1f out: r.o* 6/1[3]
56-0 6 3 1/4 **Military Call**14 1869 3-9-7 70 PJMcDonald 6 62
(A C Whillans) *hld up: hdwy u.p over 1f out: no imp ins fnl f* 33/1
663- 7 1/2 **Chookie Avon**181 7493 3-8-11 63 MartinLane(3) 7 54
(N Wilson) *s.i.s: sn prom: rdn over 3f out: wknd fnl f* 20/1
45-0 8 4 1/2 **Brinscall**24 1593 3-9-2 68 BarryMcHugh(3) 3 47
(Julie Camacho) *hld up: rdn over 2f out: wknd over 1f out* 20/1
44-0 9 3 1/4 **Charity Fair**11 1971 3-7-11 51 oh2 JamesSullivan(5) 2 21
(A Berry) *s.i.s: hld up: rdn over 2f out: a in rr* 50/1

1m 30.77s (1.77) **Going Correction** -0.125s/f (Firm) 9 Ran SP% 114.6
Speed ratings (Par 99): **92,91,91,91,91 87,86,81,77**Place: Desert Forest £1.20 Killing Moon £1.10 Lockantanks £4.50 Ex: DF-KM £12.90 DF-L £31.80 CSF: DF,KM £9.79 DF,L £31.30 Tricast: DF,KM,L £60.55 DF,L,KM £82.84 Tote Swingers: DF&L £11.70, DF&KM £2.30, KM&L £7.30 TOTE £5.80 Place27 Owner.

FOCUS
A modest finale and another race run at a steady pace that heavily favoured those up with the pace. They finished in a heap but the first three were close to their marks.
T/Plt: £74.70. Pool: £52,561.91. 513.47 winning units. T/Qpdt: £29.50. Pool: £3,406.87. 85.30 winning units. CR

2007 YARMOUTH (L-H)
Friday, May 21

OFFICIAL GOING: Good to firm (watered; 7.8)
Wind: gentle breeze, across Weather: warm and sunny

2297 NORFOLK RACING CLUB BANHAM POULTRY MEDIAN AUCTION MAIDEN STKS 6f 3y
2:00 (2:01) (Class 6) 3-5-Y-O **£2,331** (£693; £346; £173) **Stalls** High

Form RPR
35-3 1 **Pirate's Song**10 2004 3-9-3 66 (t) RobertHavlin 7 58
(J A R Toller) *hld up wl in tch: hdwy wl over 2f out: ev ch ent fnl 2f: rdn and racd awkwardly over 1f out: drvn ahd fnl 75yds: kpt on* 7/4[1]
2 nk **Jemima Nicholas** 3-8-12 0 LiamJones 1 52+
(W J Haggas) *carried lft s and slowly away: sn pushed along and rn green in rr: hdwy and edging towards stands' rail ent fnl f: r.o wl to go 2nd nr fin: nt quite rch wnr* 5/1[3]
3 1/2 **Valenzani** 3-9-3 0 (b1) NickyMackay 8 55
(J H M Gosden) *in tch niggled along 4f out: hdwy wl over 2f out: led ent fnl 2f: drvn and hld hd awkwardly over 1f out: hdd and no ex fnl 75yds: lost 2nd nr fin* 15/8[2]
0-30 4 1 3/4 **Speedyfix**3 2215 3-9-3 47 (tp) AdrianMcCarthy 6 50
(Mrs C A Dunnett) *dwlt: in tch towards rr: hdwy over 2f out: rdn wl 1f out: chsd ldng trio jst ins fnl f: edgd lft and kpt on same pce fnl 100yds* 14/1
00 5 1 3/4 **Tigers Charm**10 2004 3-9-3 0 GeorgeBaker 2 44
(J M Bradley) *wnt bdly lft s: sn rcvrd and chsng ldrs: ev ch and hung rt whn rdn 2f out: outpcd and btn jst over 1f out* 50/1
0600 6 1 1/4 **Avonlini**13 1923 4-9-2 39 JemmaMarshall(5) 9 37
(B P J Baugh) *led tl hdd and rdn ent fnl 2f: wknd wl over 1f out* 125/1
0 7 1/2 **Avaricious**20 1685 3-8-12 0 JackMitchell 4 33
(C F Wall) *in tch in midfield: rdn and outpcd ent fnl 2f: plugged on same pce and wl hld after* 9/1
00 8 12 **Pappas Fc**10 2003 3-9-3 0 (p) DavidProbert 3 —
(J M Bradley) *chsd ldng pair tl over 2f out: sn rdn and struggling: wl bhd fnl f* 125/1
00/ 9 17 **Confident Warrior (IRE)**708 2981 5-9-7 0 (t) SimonPearce(5) 5 —
(J Pearce) *t.k.h: chsd ldrs tl 1/2-way: sn struggling: t.o and eased ins fnl f* 20/1

1m 14.38s (-0.02) **Going Correction** -0.10s/f (Good)
WFA 3 from 4yo+ 9lb 9 Ran SP% 112.8
Speed ratings (Par 101): **96,95,94,92,90 88,87,71,49**
Tote Swingers: 1&2 £2.30, 1&3 £1.20, 2&3 £1.90 CSF £10.52 TOTE £3.10: £1.10, £2.80, £1.10; EX 9.60.
Owner Saeed Manana **Bred** Genesis Green Stud Ltd And Thurso Ltd **Trained** Newmarket, Suffolk

FOCUS
The whole course was irrigated during the morning with 3mm of water being applied. The jockeys returned from the opener suggesting that the ground was quick enough but with no jar. This was a weak maiden with the time being well outside standard and the proximity of the 47-rated Speedyfix another negative. The bare form is anchored by the fourth and sixth.
Jemima Nicholas ◆ Official explanation: jockey said that the filly suffered interference leaving the stalls
Confident Warrior(IRE) Official explanation: jockey said that the gelding was unsuited by today's Good to Firm ground

2298 NORFOLK RACING CLUB TEAM-BARISTA H'CAP 7f 3y
2:30 (2:31) (Class 5) (0-70,70) 4-Y-O+ **£2,460** (£732; £365; £182) **Stalls** High

Form RPR
213- 1 **Wake Up Call**177 7519 4-9-4 70 GeorgeBaker 8 85+
(C F Wall) *broke wl: sn stdd and trckd ldrs: jnd ldr ent fnl 2f: rdn to ld ent fnl f: r.o wl to assert fnl 100yds: wl in command at fin* 4/5[1]
6651 2 1 1/2 **Sairaam (IRE)**13 1928 4-8-8 60 KirstyMilczarek 3 71
(C Smith) *sn led: rdn 2f out: clr w wnr over 1f out: hdd ent fnl f: no ex and btn fnl 100yds* 7/1[3]
1466 3 2 **Millfields Dreams**14 1875 11-8-11 68 (p) TobyAtkinson(5) 11 73
(P Leech) *hld up in rr: rdn ent fnl 3f: hdwy u.p over 1f out: chsd ldng pair jst over 1f out: one pce and no imp fnl f* 20/1
3222 4 4 **Dinner Date**57 981 8-8-0 59 ow1 LauraPike(7) 9 54
(T Keddy) *in tch in midfield: rdn and effrt ent fnl 2f: outpcd by ldng pair and drvn over 1f out: wl hld fnl f* 4/1[2]
460- 5 hd **Safari Guide**198 7246 4-8-11 63 JackMitchell 6 57
(P Winkworth) *t.k.h early: hld up in tch in midfield: effrt in centre over 2f out: rdn and no prog wl over 1f out: wl btn fnl f* 9/1
-130 6 1 1/2 **Athboy Auction**44 1170 5-7-11 56 oh10 NatashaEaton(7) 7 46
(H J Collingridge) *plld hrd: hld up wl in tch: rdn and unable qck 2f out: wknd over 1f out: wl btn fnl f* 66/1
0000 7 2 **Resplendent Alpha**21 1653 6-8-8 60 JimmyQuinn 2 45
(P Howling) *t.k.h: chsd ldrs tl lost pl qckly and dropped to rr over 2f out: wl btn wl over 1f out* 20/1
00-0 8 hd **Summers Target (USA)**32 1428 4-8-0 59 RyanClark(7) 1 43
(S C Williams) *t.k.h early: chsd ldr tl ent fnl 2f: sn rdn and lost pl: bhd fr over 1f out* 16/1
54-0 9 8 **Ettrick Mill**10 2004 4-8-11 63 DavidProbert 4 25
(J M Bradley) *a in rr: rdn and btn over 2f out: wl btn fr wl over 1f out* 40/1

1m 26.39s (-0.21) **Going Correction** -0.10s/f (Good) 9 Ran SP% 117.4
Speed ratings (Par 103): **97,95,93,88,88 86,84,83,74**
Tote Swingers: 1&2 £1.70, 1&3 £4.40, 2&3 £14.50 CSF £6.86 CT £67.27 TOTE £1.50: £1.10, £2.20, £4.30; EX 7.20.
Owner J G Lambton **Bred** Whatton Manor Stud **Trained** Newmarket, Suffolk

FOCUS
Just a modest event that very few got into. It was run at a steady pace in a time that was well over two seconds outside standard. The winner was the least exposed and is capable of better.

2299 NORFOLK RACING CLUB S&M SUPPLIES (AYLSHAM) H'CAP 1m 3y
3:00 (3:00) (Class 6) (0-60,60) 4-Y-O+ **£1,942** (£578; £288; £144) **Stalls** High

Form RPR
3504 1 **Yakama (IRE)**3 2198 5-8-9 51 (v) DavidProbert 2 59
(Mrs C A Dunnett) *stdd s: hld up in tch towards rr: prog 1/2-way: trckd ldrs gng wl ent fnl 2f: ev ch jst over 1f out: rdn ins fnl f: led fnl 75yds: kpt on* 10/3[1]
2004 2 hd **Libre**18 1772 10-7-13 46 oh1 AshleyMorgan(5) 8 53
(F Jordan) *hld up wl in tch in midfield: hdwy 3f out: jnd ldrs over 1f out: pushed ahd 1f out: hld hd awkwardly ins fnl f: hdd and no ex fnl 75yds* 12/1
5460 3 2 1/4 **Via Mia**88 666 4-8-13 55 PatCosgrave 9 57
(John A Harris) *chsd ldrs: wnt 2nd over 2f out: rdn to ld over 1f out: hdd 1f out: unable qck u.p after: btn whn n.m.r and eased towards fin* 20/1
165- 4 4 1/2 **Chantilly Dancer (IRE)**247 6001 4-8-6 51 Louis-PhilippeBeuzelin(3) 4 43
(M Quinn) *led: rdn ent fnl 2f: hdd and drvn over 1f out: nt pce of ldng trio ins fnl f: plugged on* 11/1
5666 5 1 1/4 **Djalalabad (FR)**10 2008 6-8-5 47 oh1 ow1 (t) SaleemGolam 1 36
(J Pearce) *stdd s: t.k.h: hld up wl in tch: chsd ldrs and rdn wl over 1f out: wl btn ent fnl f* 20/1
0300 6 nk **Grand Honour (IRE)**37 1304 4-8-11 53 JimmyQuinn 7 41
(P Howling) *hld up in tch towards rr: rdn and effrt 2f out: no real hdwy tl kpt on past btn horses fnl f: nvr trbld ldrs* 12/1
00-4 7 1 1/2 **Foxtrot Alpha (IRE)**17 1797 4-9-4 60 FrankieMcDonald 13 45
(P Winkworth) *hld up in tch in midfield: hdwy to chse ldrs over 3f out: rdn 2f out: sn edgd lft and wknd* 9/2[2]
4-40 8 1 1/2 **Feet Of Fury**10 2006 4-8-13 55 NeilCallan 3 36
(W M Brisbourne) *midfield: rdn and outpcd ent fnl 2f: no ch w ldrs fr over 1f out* 10/1
04-0 9 hd **Big Sur**24 1591 4-9-3 59 LiamKeniry 11 40+
(T Keddy) *stdd s: t.k.h: hld up in tch in rr: rdn and outpcd ent fnl 2f: n.d* 8/1
05-0 10 1 **Abu Dubai (IRE)**18 1771 4-8-13 55 PhilipRobinson 14 33
(J A Glover) *t.k.h: hld up wl in tch in midfield: rdn and btn 2f out: wl btn fr over 1f out* 15/2[3]
5-00 11 9 **Ardent Prince**58 976 7-7-13 46 oh1 AmyBaker(5) 5 4
(A B Haynes) *restless in stalls: stdd s and slowly away: hld up in tch in rr: rdn and lost tch over 2f out: wl bhd fnl f* 33/1
24-0 12 hd **If Only**27 1534 4-9-1 57 JamieMackay 10 14
(J Jay) *in tch in midfield: lost pl qckly and dropped to rr wl over 2f out: wl bhd fnl f* 14/1
0-00 13 1 1/4 **Amber Ridge**112 347 5-8-4 46 oh1 LiamJones 12 —
(B P J Baugh) *chsd ldr tl over 2f out: sn struggling u.p: wl bhd fnl f* 66/1

1m 39.39s (-1.21) **Going Correction** -0.10s/f (Good) 13 Ran SP% 117.6
Speed ratings (Par 101): **102,101,99,95,93 93,92,90,90,89 80,80,78**
Tote Swingers: 1&2 £7.40, 1&3 £15.60, 2&3 £43.10 CSF £41.70 CT £721.04 TOTE £3.00: £1.20, £4.30, £7.30; EX 30.20.
Owner Mark Riley **Bred** Azienda Agricola Robiati Angelo **Trained** Hingham, Norfolk

FOCUS
A weak handicap and not form to be positive about. The winner is rated close to his best. The time was almost two seconds outside standard.
Foxtrot Alpha(IRE) Official explanation: jockey said that the filly had no more to give.

2300 NORFOLK RACING CLUB EARLE ARMS AT HEYDON (S) STKS 5f 43y
3:30 (3:30) (Class 6) 2-Y-O **£1,683** (£501; £250; £125) **Stalls** High

Form RPR
405 1 **Mini Bon Bon**17 1800 2-8-0 0 NatashaEaton(7) 6 60
(A Bailey) *mde all: pushed clr over 1f out: in command fnl f: eased towards fin* 11/2[3]
202 2 1 3/4 **Calormen**30 1463 2-8-12 0 JimmyQuinn 4 58
(C A Dwyer) *chsd wnr thrght: shkn up and effrt wl over 1f out: drvn and nt qckn ent fnl f: one pce after* 7/4[2]

0320 **3** 1 ¾ **Ivan's A Star (IRE)**[17] 1793 2-8-12 0 LiamKeniry 5 52
(J S Moore) *chsd ldng pair: rdn and edging lft wl over 1f out: unable qck u.p over 1f out: one pce fnl f* **13/8**[1]

4 *shd* **Silence Is Bliss (IRE)** 2-8-5 0 RyanPowell(7) 3 51+
(J S Moore) *restless in stalls: v.s.a and lost many l s: wl detached in last: clsd over 1f out: r.o wl ins fnl f: gng on fin: nvr threatened ldrs* **13/2**

60 **5** ¾ **Coolree Pearl (IRE)**[9] 2022 2-8-2 0 AmyBaker(5) 1 44
(A B Haynes) *wnt lft s: chsd ldrs but sn niggled along: rdn 3f out: outpcd u.p over 2f out: plugged on same pce and wl hld fr over 1f out* **20/1**

64.39 secs (1.69) **Going Correction** -0.10s/f (Good) 5 Ran SP% **107.9**
Speed ratings (Par 91): **78,75,72,72,71**
CSF £14.98 TOTE £6.40: £2.60, £1.60; EX 16.20.There was no bid for the winner. Silence Is Bliss was the subject of a friendly claim. Calormen claimed by A G Juckes for £5,000.
Owner A Bailey **Bred** P Balding & W Clifford **Trained** Newmarket, Suffolk

FOCUS
This low-grade event was run in a time that was considerably beyond standard and the form is hard to get excited about. The winner was taking a big drop in class.

NOTEBOOK
Mini Bon Bon was a worthy winner, making every yard to convincingly prevail, having offered a little encouragement in each of her previous three runs. Dropped into selling company, she was entitled to be more competitive and so it proved. She clearly handles quick ground and will probably get a little further, which should open up options if connections choose to keep her at this sort of level. There were no bids for her in the ensuing auction. (op 4-1)

Calormen has now finished runner-up on three of four starts and looked a little short of finishing speed. He may be worth a try over 6f. (tchd 13-8 and 15-8)

Ivan's A Star(IRE) didn't live up to market expectations at Bath earlier in the month and this again was a little disappointing. Like the second, he simply couldn't find enough when push came to shove. (op 7-4)

Silence Is Bliss(IRE) ◆ completely missed the break but finished his race well. He made up most of the ground in the closing furlong and a half and 6f should be well within his compass. If he finds the usual improvement from a debut - and jumps out smartly - he should be very competitive in this sort of class next time. Official explanation: jockey said that the gelding was slowly away (op 10-1)

2301 NORFOLK RACING CLUB WARD-ROBES / K MANSFIELD & CO LTD H'CAP 5f 43y
4:00 (4:00) (Class 5) (0-75,75) 3-Y-O+ **£2,460** (£732; £365; £91; £91) **Stalls** High

Form RPR

12-3 **1** **Solemn**[10] 1988 5-9-9 **72** (b) GeorgeBaker 7 90
(J M Bradley) *chsd ldng pair on stands' rail: swtchd lft and hdwy to chse ldr over 1f out: rdn to ld 1f out: drew clr fnl f: eased towards fin* **9/2**[3]

3123 **2** 4 **Wreningham**[22] 1638 5-8-9 **61** oh1 WilliamCarson(3) 3 65
(S C Williams) *broke wl: led and grad crossed to stands' rail: rdn over 1f out: hdd 1f out: no ch w wnr ins fnl f but hld on for 2nd* **4/1**[2]

1242 **3** ¾ **Brynfa Boy**[7] 2094 4-9-8 **71** TonyCulhane 8 72
(P W D'Arcy) *stdd s: hld up in rr: stl last wl over 1f out: sn swtchd lft and hdwy: rdn and kpt on to go 3rd wl ins fnl f: nvr able to chal* **10/3**[1]

4133 **4** ½ **Love You Louis**[14] 1874 4-9-12 **75** PhilipRobinson 1 75
(J R Jenkins) *racd in centre pair: chsd ldrs: rdn over 1f out: wknd u.p 1f out* **8/1**

0-22 **4** *dht* **Danzoe (IRE)**[24] 1604 3-8-11 **68** (v1) JimmyQuinn 2 65
(Mrs C A Dunnett) *t.k.h: racd in centre pair: rdn wl over 1f out: wknd u.p ent fnl f* **10/1**

3033 **6** ¾ **Whiskey Junction**[11] 1963 6-9-12 **75** NeilCallan 5 72
(M Quinn) *chsd ldr tl over 1f out: sn outpcd u.p: one pce and wl hld fnl f* **11/2**

5101 **7** 4 **Rough Rock (IRE)**[10] 2010 5-8-9 **65** 6ex MJMurphy(7) 4 47
(C A Dwyer) *racd in last trio: pushed along and effrt ent fnl 2f: edgd lft and wl btn over 1f out* **8/1**

00-3 **8** 9 **Angelo Poliziano**[17] 1805 4-9-4 **67** PatCosgrave 6 17
(Mrs A Duffield) *dwlt: a in rr: rdn over 2f out: edge dlft and lost tch 2f out: wl bhd fnl f* **12/1**

61.21 secs (-1.49) **Going Correction** -0.10s/f (Good)
WFA 3 from 4yo+ 8lb 8 Ran SP% **115.7**
Speed ratings (Par 103): **103,96,95,94,94 93,87,72**
Tote Swingers: 1&2 £3.50, 1&3 £3.90, 2&3 £3.60 CSF £23.14 CT £67.71 TOTE £3.60: £1.20, £1.10, £1.60; EX 19.30.
Owner E A Hayward **Bred** Cheveley Park Stud Ltd **Trained** Sedbury, Gloucs

FOCUS
This looked a tight heat on paper with several holding decent claims. The time was only 0.21seconds outside standard and over three seconds quicker than the preceding juvenile seller. A personal best from the winner with tyhe form rated at face value.

2302 NORFOLK RACING CLUB HAMLYN FINANCIAL SERVICES H'CAP 1m 6f 17y
4:30 (4:30) (Class 6) (0-60,55) 4-Y-O+ **£1,942** (£578; £288; £144) **Stalls** High

Form RPR

2 **1** **If I Had Him (IRE)**[11] 1983 6-8-13 **50** TonyCulhane 6 59
(George Baker) *chsd ldr tl 10f out: rdn over 3f out: sltly outpcd 2f out: rallied u.p 1f out: led fnl 75yds: styd on wl: gng away at fin* **7/1**

56-4 **2** 1 ½ **Astroleo**[38] 1283 4-8-4 **46** AshleyMorgan(5) 8 53
(M H Tompkins) *led: rdn over 2f out: drvn and kpt on gamely tl hdd and no ex fnl 75yds* **4/1**[2]

0053 **3** *hd* **Dazzling Begum**[11] 1980 5-8-9 **46** SaleemGolam 1 54
(J Pearce) *in tch towards rr: rdn and effrt over 3f out: chsng ldrs u.p but nvr much room fr 2f out tl swtchd rt wl ins fnl f: kpt on* **11/1**

3403 **4** 1 ¾ **Dovedon Angel**[92] 599 4-8-10 **47** MickyFenton 3 51
(Miss Gay Kelleway) *stdd s: plld hrd early: hld up in last: gd hdwy on inner ent fnl 3f: chsd wnr and rdn 2f out: unable qck u.p 1f out: lost 2 pls ins fnl f* **33/1**

0-52 **5** ½ **City Stable (IRE)**[10] 2006 5-9-2 **53** StephenCraine 9 56
(M Wigham) *t.k.h: chsd ldng trio: effrt and rdn ent fnl 2f: edgd lft and no hdwy over 1f out* **15/8**[1]

-100 **6** 1 ¼ **Dulce Domum**[22] 1635 4-8-9 **46** JimmyQuinn 5 48
(A B Haynes) *chsd ldrs tl wnt 2nd 10f out tl 2f out: sn outpcd u.p: plugged on same pce and wl hld fnl f* **33/1**

0336 **7** ½ **Barbirolli**[11] 1984 8-8-2 **46** LauraPike(7) 11 47
(W B Stone) *t.k.h: hld up in last trio: rdn and styd on same pce fr over 2f out: nvr trbld ldrs* **16/1**

0-25 **8** 5 **Honorable Endeavor**[15] 1849 4-9-2 **53** (v) LiamKeniry 2 47
(E F Vaughan) *in tch in midfield: outpcd and dropped to rr 4f out: swtchd rt and rallied briefly ent fnl 2f: sn wknd* **5/1**[3]

4360 **9** 1 **Supernoverre (IRE)**[83] 621 4-9-4 **55** J-PGuillambert 4 48
(P Howling) *t.k.h: chsd ldrs tl stdd into midfield 12f out: dropped to rr and pushed along 3f out: wl btn fnl 2f* **8/1**

3m 12.57s (4.97) **Going Correction** -0.10s/f (Good) 9 Ran SP% **115.2**
Speed ratings (Par 101): **81,80,80,79,78 78,77,74,74**
Tote Swingers: 1&2 £6.30, 1&3 £6.90, 2&3 £6.80 CSF £35.03 CT £302.67 TOTE £8.30: £3.30, £1.20, £3.00; EX 29.30.
Owner Sir Alex Ferguson **Bred** Mrs J Morrissey **Trained** Moreton Morrell, Warwicks

FOCUS
The pace was only steady with the time over 12 seconds beyond standard and it largely favoured those who raced on the front end. The form is best judged around the second.

2303 NORFOLK RACING CLUB M.D. THOMPSON ELECTRICAL H'CAP 1m 2f 21y
5:00 (5:01) (Class 6) (0-55,58) 4-Y-O+ **£1,942** (£578; £288; £144) **Stalls** Low

Form RPR

0041 **1** **Iceman George**[10] 2006 6-9-0 **58** 6ex (v) WilliamCarson(3) 8 67
(G C Bravery) *dwlt: hld up in last trio: c wd bnd over 4f out and racd down centre in st: hdwy 4f out: rdn to ld wl over 1f out: kpt on wl u.p fnl f* **11/2**[2]

0-31 **2** ¾ **Sharp Sovereign (USA)**[10] 2012 4-8-7 **51** 6ex Louis-PhilippeBeuzelin(3) 3 59
(T D Barron) *led: rdn ent fnl 3f: hdd and drvn wl over 1f out: kpt on same pce fnl f* **7/4**[1]

0/0- **3** *nk* **Aestival**[214] 6910 4-8-12 **53** StevieDonohoe 12 61+
(Sir Mark Prescott) *hld up in tch towards rr: hdwy and edging lft wl over 2f out: flashed tail u.p but chsng ldrs over 1f out: keeping on whn rdr dropped reins fnl 100yds: edgd lft after and n.m.r nr fin* **9/1**

260- **4** 1 ½ **Mayfair's Future**[287] 4745 5-8-11 **52** NeilCallan 5 56
(J R Jenkins) *t.k.h: in tch: effrt to chse ldrs and rdn ent fnl 2f: no ex and btn ins fnl f* **14/1**

0-34 **5** 2 **Strike Force**[10] 2012 6-8-7 **53** TobyAtkinson(5) 2 53
(P Leech) *hld up in tch in midfield: hdwy and pushed along on inner 4f out: wknd u.p ent fnl f* **11/1**

1002 **6** 4 ½ **Jiggalong**[24] 1606 4-8-9 **50** PaulDoe 10 41
(Jim Best) *chsd ldrs: rdn to chse ldr over 2f out tl 2f out: wknd qckly over 1f out* **8/1**[3]

00-0 **7** 1 **Berriedale**[10] 2006 4-8-11 **52** PatCosgrave 4 41
(Mrs A Duffield) *hld up towards rr: pushed along bnd 6f out: hdwy over 2f out: rdn and btn over 1f out* **20/1**

40-0 **8** 2 ¼ **Tivers Song (USA)**[13] 1920 6-8-7 **48** (b) DavidProbert 6 32
(John A Harris) *stdd after s: hld up in tch in midfield: rdn and no hdwy over 2f out: wl btn over 1f out* **10/1**

00-0 **9** 8 **Mystic Touch**[27] 1539 4-8-12 **53** RobertHavlin 1 21
(A B Haynes) *stdd s: hld up in rr: hdwy and effrt whn hmpd over 2f out: sn btn and lost tch* **12/1**

-100 **10** 3 ¾ **Mekong Miss**[39] 1262 4-9-0 **55** JamieMackay 11 16
(J Jay) *chsd ldrs tl wknd u.p over 3f out: wl bhd fnl f* **28/1**

41-0 **11** 1 ¾ **Kristopher James (IRE)**[11] 1984 4-9-0 **55** LiamJones 9 12
(W M Brisbourne) *t.k.h: chsd ldr tl over 2f out: sn wknd: wl bhd fnl f* **25/1**

00-0 **12** 35 **Anasy (USA)**[11] 1983 4-8-7 **48** JimmyQuinn 7 —
(Miss Gay Kelleway) *chsd ldrs: wkng qckly whn sltly hmpd 4f out: t.o and eased ins fnl f* **50/1**

2m 8.82s (-1.68) **Going Correction** -0.10s/f (Good) 12 Ran SP% **118.7**
Speed ratings (Par 101): **102,101,101,99,98 94,93,92,85,82 81,53**
Tote Swingers: 1&2 £3.30, 1&3 £9.40, 2&3 £6.80 CSF £14.78 CT £87.71 TOTE £7.30: £2.30, £1.40, £3.20; EX 22.90 Place 6: £34.33 Place 5: £30.36 .
Owner John Mangan **Bred** T J And J Wells **Trained** Cowlinge, Suffolk

FOCUS
There was an honest pace in this low-grade race and the time was 3.32 seconds outside of standard. Solid form rated around the runner-up, with the winner to his best.
T/Jkpt: £7,339.80. Pool: £41,351.01 - 4 winning units. T/Plt: £23.00. Pool: £70,819.14 - 2,243.20 winning units. T/Qpdt: £11.90. Pool: £3,821.61 - 236.94 winning units. SP

2304 - 2308a (Foreign Racing) - See Raceform Interactive

1857 CHESTER (L-H)
Saturday, May 22

OFFICIAL GOING: Good to firm (8.2)
Rail dolled right out 7yards from 6f to finish with no 'drop in' and 5f races increased by 15yards, 6f by 18yards, 7f by 22y, 10f by 24y and 13f by 33yds.
Wind: Almost nil Weather: Hot and Sunny

2309 CRABBIES "SPIFFING" ALCOHOLIC GINGER BEER MAIDEN STKS 6f 18y
2:25 (2:25) (Class 4) 3-Y-O **£4,533** (£1,348; £674; £336) **Stalls** Centre

Form RPR

400- **1** **Little Scotland**[275] 5199 3-8-12 88 FrederikTylicki 2 70
(R A Fahey) *prom: chsd ldr over 3f out: rdn and nt qckn over 1f out: r.o ins fnl f: led towards fin* **5/6**[1]

4-43 **2** ¾ **Song Of Parkes**[21] 1685 3-8-12 70 RobertWinston 3 68
(E J Alston) *pushed along s: led after 1f: rdn on inner over 1f out whn jst over 2 l clr: hung lft after: worn down towards fin* **7/2**[3]

2-23 **3** 1 ¾ **Boy The Bell**[121] 253 3-8-10 66 JosephYoung(7) 4 67
(M Mullineaux) *in rr: effrt to go 3rd over 1f out: kpt on but nt pce to chal front pair fnl f* **14/1**

-022 **4** 4 ½ **Bilash**[7] 2114 3-9-3 70 JerryO'Dwyer 1 53
(R Hollinshead) *led for 1f: chsd ldr tl over 3f out: pushed along 2f out: rdn and dropped to last over 1f out: n.d after* **5/2**[2]

1m 15.33s (1.53) **Going Correction** +0.25s/f (Good) 4 Ran SP% **112.0**
Speed ratings (Par 101): **99,98,95,89**
CSF £4.32 TOTE £1.80; EX 2.80.
Owner David W Armstrong **Bred** Sir Eric Parker **Trained** Musley Bank, N Yorks

FOCUS
The ground had been watered throughout the week but was officially described as good to firm (GoingStick 8.2) on what was a warm and sunny day. The form is rated around the third and the winner didn't need to match her 2yo best.
Bilash Official explanation: jockey said colt did not handle the track

2310 LAMBS NAVY RUM H'CAP 5f 16y
2:55 (2:57) (Class 5) (0-75,75) 4-Y-O+ **£4,047** (£1,204; £601; £300) **Stalls** Low

Form RPR

2356 **1** **Lucky Dan (IRE)**[4] 2206 4-8-12 **69** FrannyNorton 9 79
(Paul Green) *bhd: nt clr run and hdwy over 1f out: swtchd lft sn after: str run to burst through gap between horses and ld fnl 110yds: r.o wl* **10/1**

4200 **2** *1 ½* **Not My Choice (IRE)**[7] 2113 5-8-7 **64** ow2................(t) RobertWinston 1 68
(D C Griffiths) *led but hrd at work: hdd over 3f out: chsd ldrs after: rdn and wnt 2nd over 1f out: chalng ins fnl f: no answer to wnr's kick towards fin* **4/1**[3]

5-54 **3** *¾* **Legal Eagle (IRE)**[15] 1888 5-9-3 **74**......................(v[1]) SilvestreDeSousa 3 75
(Paul Green) *w ldrs: lost pl over 3f out: in midfield 2f out: rallied ent fnl f: r.o towards fin* **11/4**[2]

0304 **4** *nk* **Methaaly (IRE)**[7] 2123 7-8-6 **70**............................(be) JosephYoung[(7)] 12 70
(M Mullineaux) *outpcd and bhd: prog ins fnl f: r.o wl: nrst fin* **20/1**

0-06 **5** *hd* **Ajara (IRE)**[26] 1588 4-8-3 **65**.. RossAtkinson[(5)] 7 65
(Tom Dascombe) *midfield: effrt over 1f out: kpt on ins fnl f: nt pce to chal* **40/1**

1612 **6** *hd* **Sir Geoffrey (IRE)**[11] 1988 4-9-4 **75**...........................(b) FrederikTylicki 4 74
(J A Glover) *w ldrs: led over 3f out: rdn over 1f out: hdd fnl 110yds: no ex* **2/1**[1]

4561 **7** *shd* **Step It Up (IRE)**[11] 2001 6-9-0 **71**................................ StephenCraine 10 69
(J R Boyle) *towards rr: rdn and hdwy on wd outside fnl f: styd on: nt pce to get to ldrs* **11/1**

4031 **8** *1* **Radiator Rooney (IRE)**[10] 2021 7-7-13 **61** oh5........... PaulPickard[(5)] 6 56+
(Patrick Morris) *towards rr: effrt whn nt clr run 1f out and again ins fnl f: unable to make further prog whn nowhere to go after* **12/1**

060- **9** *¾* **Baby Queen (IRE)**[286] 4829 4-8-7 **64** ow1.................. J-PGuillambert 8 56
(B P J Baugh) *racd keenly: chsd ldrs: rdn over 1f out: fdd ins fnl f: eased whn btn cl home* **25/1**

00-5 **10** *shd* **Harry Up**[12] 1979 9-8-4 **61** oh1.. AndrewElliott 5 53
(Andrew Reid) *gd spd w ldr tl rdn over 1f out: wknd fnl 110yds* **17/2**

-000 **11** *14* **Red Rosanna**[11] 1988 4-8-13 **70**.................................... JerryO'Dwyer 11 11
(R Hollinshead) *chsd ldrs: rdn over 2f out: wknd over 1f out: eased whn btn ins fnl f* **20/1**

61.82 secs (0.82) **Going Correction** +0.25s/f (Good) **11** Ran SP% **131.5**
Speed ratings (Par 103): **103,100,99,98,98 98,98,96,95,95 72**
toteswingers: 1&2 £19.40, 1&3 £7.40, 2&3 £2.90 CSF £53.62 CT £151.29 TOTE £12.80: £2.90, £1.80, £1.50; EX 70.20.
Owner Stephen Bell **Bred** Mountarmstrong Stud **Trained** Lydiate, Merseyside

FOCUS
There was a mad gallop to the first bend here, with the low-drawn horses keen to maintain their positions, but that resulted in a contested lead and the race was set up for a closer. The winner is rated back to his best.
Legal Eagle(IRE) Official explanation: jockey said gelding hung left-handed
Radiator Rooney(IRE) Official explanation: jockey said gelding was denied a clear run

2311 TSINGTAO CHINESE BEER H'CAP 7f 2y
3:25 (3:25) (Class 2) (0-100,99) 4-Y-0+ **£16,190** (£4,817; £2,407; £1,202) **Stalls** Low

Form RPR

02-4 **1** **Brae Hill (IRE)**[15] 1857 4-8-13 **94**........................... StevieDonohoe 5 103
(R A Fahey) *racd keenly: chsd ldr: rdn to ld over 1f out: kpt on wl and a doing enough towards fin* **11/4**[1]

03-1 **2** *½* **Dance And Dance (IRE)**[15] 1862 4-8-10 **91**................ RobertWinston 3 99
(E F Vaughan) *midfield: hdwy 2f out: chsd wnr wl ins fnl f: r.o towards fin but a looked hld* **6/1**

2051 **3** *1 ½* **Autumn Blades (IRE)**[15] 1857 5-9-4 **99**......................(v) FrannyNorton 1 103
(A Bailey) *racd keenly: hld up: rdn and hdwy over 1f out: r.o towards fin: nt pce to chal front pair* **9/2**[3]

0-40 **4** *shd* **Invincible Force (IRE)**[15] 1857 6-8-12 **93**..........(b) SilvestreDeSousa 10 96
(Paul Green) *gd pce to ld: rdn and hdd over 1f out: no ex towards fin* **12/1**

-020 **5** *¾* **Saucy Brown (IRE)**[20] 1727 4-8-10 **91**............................ PaulQuinn 9 92
(D Nicholls) *chsd ldrs: effrt 2f out: nt qckn over 1f out: styd on same pce ins fnl f* **14/1**

0200 **6** *½* **Flipando (IRE)**[14] 1900 9-9-1 **96**.................................... PhillipMakin 7 98+
(T D Barron) *hld up: hdwy over 1f out: nt clr run ins fnl f: nvr a danger* **6/1**

40-0 **7** *1 ¼* **Majuro (IRE)**[21] 1708 6-8-10 **91**................................... MickyFenton 4 88+
(C F Wall) *hld up: effrt whn denied a run ins fnl f: nvr a danger* **11/1**

3512 **8** *nse* **Dubai Dynamo**[6] 2141 5-8-13 **94**................................ AndrewElliott 8 90
(Mrs R A Carr) *midfield: hdwy over 3f out: pushed along over 2f out: wknd over 1f out* **4/1**[2]

00-0 **9** *¾* **Whistledownwind**[8] 2100 5-8-9 **90**............................. PJMcDonald 2 84
(D Nicholls) *chsd ldrs: rdn over 1f out: fdd ins fnl f* **28/1**

5206 **10** *½* **Carcinetto (IRE)**[15] 1857 8-8-11 **92**........................... StephenCraine 6 85
(P D Evans) *hld up: pushed along 4f out: rdn over 1f out: nvr able to land a blow* **22/1**

1m 26.23s (-0.27) **Going Correction** +0.075s/f (Good) **10** Ran SP% **123.9**
Speed ratings (Par 109): **104,103,101,101,100 100,98,98,97,97**
toteswingers: 1&2 £1.10, 1&3 £2.80, 2&3 £5.50 CSF £21.09 CT £75.84 TOTE £3.50: £1.90, £1.70, £1.80; EX 25.90 Trifecta £26.70 Pool: £353.36 - 9.76 winning units..
Owner Dr Marwan Koukash **Bred** James Doyle **Trained** Musley Bank, N Yorks

FOCUS
They didn't go mad early here and the pace held up pretty well. Straightforward form.

NOTEBOOK
Brae Hill(IRE), unlucky in running here at the May meeting on his reappearance, gained compensation with a trouble-free run. He held a prominent pitch throughout, saw his race out strongly, and looks firmly on the upgrade for his new connections. He is in the Wokingham, but the less valuable Buckingham Palace Stakes over this distance might be more his cup of tea. (op 3-1)
Dance And Dance(IRE) won a lower class event over this C&D at the May meeting and was 6lb higher this time. He had again been fortunate with the draw, though, and ran a sound race in defeat. (op 11-2 tchd 9-2)
Autumn Blades(IRE) had the unlucky Brae Hill back in fourth when successful here last time out, but he was 4lb worse off at the weights with that rival this time and it was no surprise to see the form reversed. (op 6-1)
Invincible Force(IRE) had the worst of the draw but he was sprightly from the gate and crossed over to make the running. He was allowed to go a sensible gallop in front and cannot have too many excuses.
Saucy Brown(IRE) was another who was never too far off the gallop, albeit a little wider than ideal. (op 12-1)
Flipando(IRE) could have done with a stronger all-round pace as he's a real come-from-behind performer. (op 11-2)
Majuro(IRE) Official explanation: jockey said gelding was denied a clear run
Dubai Dynamo had little chance after racing widest of all for most of the way. (op 11-2)

2312 CRABBIES "TICKETY BOO" ALCOHOLIC GINGER BEER E B F MAIDEN STKS 6f 18y
4:00 (4:00) (Class 4) 2-Y-0 **£4,857** (£1,445; £722; £360) **Stalls** Centre

Form RPR

1 **Amwell Pinot** 2-9-3 0.. FrannyNorton 1 77+
(A Bailey) *in tch: pushed along 2f out: r.o to ld 1f out: rdn out* **10/3**[3]

233 **2** *¾* **Alfraamsey**[7] 2127 2-9-3 0.. RobertWinston 7 75
(M R Channon) *s.i.s: sn in midfield: hdwy and effrt to chse ldrs over 2f out: styd on to take 2nd wl ins fnl f: unable to seriously chal wnr* **3/1**[2]

3 *1 ¾* **Lexington Bay (IRE)** 2-9-3 0.. FrederikTylicki 8 70+
(R A Fahey) *slowly away: bhd: hdwy over 1f out: r.o ins fnl f: nt trble front 2: shaped wl* **8/1**

4 **4** *1* **Tamareen (IRE)**[11] 2007 2-9-3 0.................................... WilliamBuick 3 67
(E A L Dunlop) *handy: moved upsides wl over 2f out: led over 1f out and sn leant on rival: hdd 1f out: no ex fnl 100yds* **15/8**[1]

0 **5** *½* **Addock And Egg**[28] 1517 2-8-12 0.............................. RossAtkinson[(5)] 5 65
(Tom Dascombe) *pushed along and sn towards rr: rdn over 2f out: kpt on ins fnl f: nvr able to chal* **20/1**

0 **6** *3 ½* **Merrjanah**[35] 1375 2-8-12 0.. J-PGuillambert 6 50
(C E Brittain) *midfield tl rdn and wknd over 2f out* **11/1**

003 **7** *nk* **The Best Mode (IRE)**[27] 1541 2-9-3 0.......................(v[1]) CathyGannon 4 56
(P D Evans) *racd keenly: gd to spd to ld after 1f: hdd over 1f out: sn n.m.r and hmpd: wknd fnl f* **11/1**

8 *2 ¾* **River Blade** 2-9-3 0.. MickyFenton 2 46
(W M Brisbourne) *led: hdd after 1f: chasd ldr after and pushed along: n.m.r and hmpd 3f out: rdn and wknd over 2f out* **25/1**

1m 16.41s (2.61) **Going Correction** +0.25s/f (Good) **8** Ran SP% **119.2**
Speed ratings (Par 95): **92,91,88,87,86 82,81,77**
toteswingers: 1&2 £2.30, 2&3 £6.80 CSF £14.51 TOTE £4.60: £1.60, £1.20, £2.40; EX 12.20.
Owner John Stocker **Bred** Darley **Trained** Newmarket, Suffolk

FOCUS
An ordinary maiden. The winner took advantage of his plum draw and the second set the level.

NOTEBOOK
Amwell Pinot is a half-brother to a 1m2f winner in France out of a dam from an outstanding middle-distance filly, so he's clearly bred to be decent, but it was a bit of a surprise that he had the pace to be effective over this trip, especially on his debut. However, he was drawn in stall one, got a nice trip throughout, and the leaders set a decent gallop out in front which helped set things up for him. He will come on for this, and a step up to 7f in due course should suit. (op 11-2 tchd 6-1 in places)
Alfraamsey looked to have plenty going for him despite a wide draw, but he wasn't best away, raced a little wide early and couldn't match the winner's finishing kick. He looks likely to remain vulnerable. (tchd 11-4)
Lexington Bay(IRE), whose price rose from 29,000gns as a foal to 85,000gns as a yearling, is a half-brother to dual Group 3 winner Confuchias. From the worst draw he was slowly away, but stuck to the inside virtually throughout and came home well for third without having a hard race. He'll come on for the experience and looks the type to progress.
Tamareen(IRE) showed bright speed but looked to be sent on plenty soon enough and didn't get home. He probably wouldn't mind dropping back to 5f. Official explanation: jockey said colt hung left-handed throughout (tchd 2-1)
Addock And Egg ran a better race up a furlong in distance, but he looks more of a handicap prospect in due course.
The Best Mode(IRE) had a visor on for the first time and went too fast in front to have a chance of getting home over this longer trip. (op 9-1)

2313 CRABBIES "WIZARD" ALCOHOLIC GINGER BEER H'CAP 1m 5f 89y
4:35 (4:56) (Class 3) (0-90,86) 4-Y-0+ **£9,066** (£2,697; £1,348; £673) **Stalls** Low

Form RPR

-525 **1** **Dazzling Light (UAE)**[8] 2096 5-8-13 **76**........................... WilliamBuick 6 85
(J S Goldie) *hld up in rr: hdwy on outer over 1f out: sn chsd wnr: r.o ins fnl f to ld fnl strides* **5/2**[2]

53/0 **2** *nk* **La Vecchia Scuola (IRE)**[17] 1821 6-9-5 **85**.................. GaryBartley[(3)] 7 93
(J S Goldie) *led: rdn abt 3 l clr over 1f out: worn down fnl strides* **20/1**

4101 **3** *3 ½* **Prince Picasso**[20] 1720 7-9-2 **79**...............................(b) FrederikTylicki 5 82
(R A Fahey) *midfield: effrt and hdwy 2f out: chsd ldrs over 1f out: kpt on but nt pce to chal front pair ins fnl f* **11/2**[3]

0041 **4** *1 ¼* **Hallstatt (IRE)**[14] 1916 4-8-12 **75**.............................. StephenCraine 1 76
(J Mackie) *chsd ldrs: wnt 2nd 3f out: rdn and lost 2nd over 1f out: styd on same pce ins fnl f* **10/1**

10-0 **5** *nse* **Saga De Tercey (FR)**[10] 2027 5-9-9 **86**........................ RobertWinston 3 87
(G A Swinbank) *chsd ldrs: rdn 2f out: nt qckn over 1f out: styd on same pce ins fnl f* **2/1**[1]

1544 **6** *½* **Paktolos (FR)**[15] 1863 7-9-3 **80**......................................(p) MickyFenton 2 80+
(John A Harris) *hld up: pushed along whn nt clr run jst over 1f out: kpt on wout troubling ldrs ins fnl f* **12/1**

2-01 **7** *1 ¼* **Heathyards Pride**[5] 2182 10-8-13 **76** 6ex........................ JerryO'Dwyer 4 74
(R Hollinshead) *hld up: rdn over 1f out: no imp fnl f* **25/1**

-335 **8** *8* **Hindu Kush (IRE)**[15] 1863 5-9-0 **77**............................. StevieDonohoe 8 63
(Ian Williams) *chsd ldr to 3f out: rdn and wknd 2f out* **15/2**

2m 56.0s (2.80) **Going Correction** +0.075s/f (Good) **8** Ran SP% **114.4**
Speed ratings (Par 107): **94,93,91,90,90 90,89,84**
toteswingers: 1&2 £13.00, 1&3 £8.20, 2&3 £30.20 CSF £49.56 CT £253.86 TOTE £3.40: £1.10, £4.50, £2.00; EX 52.30.
Owner M Mackay, S Bruce, J S Goldie **Bred** Darley **Trained** Uplawmoor, E Renfrews

FOCUS
Plenty of in-form horses here and the form looks solid for the level rated around the second and third. The race was delayed after a horse broke loose following the previous race.

NOTEBOOK
Dazzling Light(UAE) had run over shorter on her last two starts but stamina is her forte and she put up an impressive performance to pick up from last place and catch the front-running runner-up close home. Despite her ordinary strike-rate she looks to have more to offer as a stayer, and one shouldn't read too much into some of her defeats over further in the past as most came on ground that was too soft for her. She's very much a fast-ground mare. (op 11-4 tchd 3-1)
La Vecchia Scuola(IRE) finished down the field in the Chester Cup last time out but she wasn't without her supporters that day despite having been off the track since September 2008. This looked a far easier assignment and, having been handed an uncontested lead, she was always going to take quite a bit of passing. She might just have come up against an improving mare. (op 14-1)
Prince Picasso, who bounced back to winning form at Hamilton last time out, was 5lb higher here and ran an acceptable race in defeat. (op 9-2 tchd 6-1)
Hallstatt(IRE) was another 5lb higher for a recent success. He was well placed behind the leader but failed to pick up once switched to challenge, and perhaps the ground was on the fast side for him. (op 9-1)
Saga De Tercey(FR), back over a more suitable trip, also found disappointingly little once asked to challenge entering the straight. (op 4-1 tchd 15-8)
Paktolos(FR) Official explanation: jockey said gelding was denied a clear run

2314 LAMBRINI ORIGINAL H'CAP 1m 2f 75y
5:10 (5:31) (Class 4) (0-85,85) 4-Y-0+ **£5,504** (£1,637; £818; £408) **Stalls** High

Form RPR

-155 **1** **Paquerettza (FR)**[16] 1837 4-9-3 **84**................................... PhillipMakin 8 95+
(D H Brown) *chsd ldrs: wnt 2nd over 2f out: rdn to ld over 1f out: r.o wl and in command ins fnl f* **13/2**[3]

0-65 **2** *3* **Bullet Man (USA)**[15] 1889 5-8-13 **80**.............................. FrederikTylicki 6 85+
(R A Fahey) *led: kicked on over 2f out: rdn and hdd over 1f out: nt pce of wnr fnl 110yds* **4/1**[2]

54-2 **3** *1 ¼* **Norwegian Dancer (UAE)**[16] 1837 4-9-2 **83**.................. WilliamBuick 5 86
(E S McMahon) *midfield: hdwy over 2f out: styd on to chse ldrs over 1f out: styd on same pce fnl 100yds* **7/4**[1]

200 **4** *1 ¾* **Kidlat**[2] 2241 5-9-1 **82**.. FrannyNorton 3 81
(A Bailey) *chsd ldr to over 5f out: remained handy: pushed along over 2f out: one pce over 1f out* **8/1**

U0 **5** *1 ½* **Bagutta Sun**[28] 1519 4-8-13 **80**..............................(v[1]) RichardKingscote 7 76
(Tom Dascombe) *in tch: pushed along over 4f out: sn outpcd: n.d after* **25/1**

5-02 **6** *1* **Prince Of Johanne (IRE)**[14] 1907 4-9-4 **85**.................. MickyFenton 1 79
(T P Tate) *in rr: pushed along over 4f out: sme hdwy u.p over 1f out: sn swtchd rt: no imp after* **8/1**

51-0 **7** *1 ¼* **Dragon Slayer (IRE)**[15] 1883 8-8-4 **71** oh2.................... AndrewElliott 9 63
(John A Harris) *slowly away: hld up: n.m.r over 2f out: nvr able to get on terms* **33/1**

5432 **8** *8* **I'm In The Pink (FR)**[15] 1863 6-6-8 **73**...................... CathyGannon 10 64+
(P D Evans) *slowly away: hld up: u.p whn nt clr run and snatched up over 2f out: wl outpcd after: nvr on terms* **8/1**

0P-0 **9** *15* **Geneva Geyser (GER)**[10] 2031 4-8-13 **80**................(b) StephenCraine 2 26
(J M P Eustace) *ref to settle: midfield: hdwy 7f out: chsd ldr over 5f out: rdn 3f out: lost 2nd and wknd over 2f out* **14/1**

2m 10.68s (-1.52) **Going Correction** +0.075s/f (Good) **9** Ran SP% **116.5**
Speed ratings (Par 105): **109,106,105,104,103 102,101,94,82**
toteswingers: 1&2 £63.80, 1&3 £21.40, 2&3 £2.00 CSF £32.99 CT £65.18 TOTE £9.00: £2.30, £1.90, £1.50; EX 38.40.
Owner J B Smith & J M Smith **Bred** Newsells Park Stud **Trained** Maltby, S Yorks

FOCUS
The pace and time were good and the winner comprehensively reversed C/D form with the third.
Geneva Geyser(GER) Official explanation: trainer said he had no explanation for the poor form shown

2315 CRABBIES "STEADY ON" ALCOHOLIC GINGER BEER H'CAP 1m 3f 79y
5:45 (6:00) (Class 4) (0-80,80) 3-Y-O **£5,504** (£1,637; £818; £408) **Stalls** Low

Form RPR

213 **1** **Zuider Zee (GER)**[24] 1624 3-9-1 **77**.................................. WilliamBuick 1 89+
(J H M Gosden) *hld up: hdwy over 2f out: led 1f out: edgd lft ins fnl f: r.o: wl on top at fin* **2/1**[1]

021- **2** *1 ½* **Bowdler's Magic**[182] 7491 3-9-4 **80**.............................. J-PGuillambert 4 89+
(M Johnston) *racd keenly: a.p: rdn to chal and ev ch fr over 1f out: nt qckn fnl 75yds* **9/1**

01 **3** *nk* **Sunny Game**[26] 1581 3-9-4 **80**.. PhillipMakin 3 89+
(M L W Bell) *s.i.s: in rr: pushed along 2f out: c wd ent st wl over 1f out: prog ent fnl f: r.o: gng on at fin* **5/2**[2]

5-22 **4** *2* **I'm Super Too (IRE)**[12] 1969 3-8-12 **74**........................... PJMcDonald 6 79
(G A Swinbank) *led: rdn and hung rt whn hdd 1f out: no ex fnl 100yds* **13/2**

0323 **5** *13* **Layla's Boy**[22] 1666 3-8-7 **69**..(t) StevieDonohoe 5 51
(Ian Williams) *hld up: effrt 3f out: wknd over 2f out* **16/1**

22-1 **6** *1 ¼* **Saint Thomas (IRE)**[11] 1992 3-8-8 **70**.......................... RobertWinston 7 49
(J Mackie) *chsd ldr after 1f: effrt to chal 3f out: lost 2nd 2f out: wknd over 1f out* **14/1**

-622 **7** *15* **Monkton Vale (IRE)**[8] 2101 3-9-0 **76**........................... FrederikTylicki 8 28
(R A Fahey) *racd keenly: hld up: racd in midfield after 2f: rdn and wknd 3f out* **9/2**[3]

2m 28.1s (1.50) **Going Correction** +0.075s/f (Good) **7** Ran SP% **116.0**
Speed ratings (Par 101): **97,95,95,94,84 83,72**
toteswingers: 1&2 £6.10, 1&3 £1.40, 2&3 £23.80 CSF £21.41 CT £46.86 TOTE £3.10: £1.90, £5.60; EX 23.60 Place 6 £28.03, Place 5 £15.04.
Owner H R H Princess Haya Of Jordan **Bred** Graf U Grafin V Stauffenberg **Trained** Newmarket, Suffolk

FOCUS
Quite an interesting handicap for 3-y-os, and the three least experienced runners in the race came home clear. Good form for the grade and the race has been rated positively.
Saint Thomas(IRE) Official explanation: jockey said gelding slipped final bend and hung left into straight
Monkton Vale(IRE) Official explanation: jockey said gelding ran flat
T/Plt: £69.70 to a £1 stake Pool: £75,473.99. 790.38 winning tickets. T/Qpdt: £10.60 to a £1 stake. Pool: £3,313.71. 230.20 winning tickets. DO

2223 GOODWOOD (R-H)
Saturday, May 22

OFFICIAL GOING: Good (good to firm in places; 8.5)
Wind: Slight, across Weather: Glorious

2316 TOTESCOOP6 STKS (H'CAP) 6f
2:15 (2:16) (Class 2) (0-100,102) 3-Y-0+
£12,462 (£3,732; £1,866; £934; £466; £234) **Stalls** Low

Form RPR

-650 **1** **Parisian Pyramid (IRE)**[17] 1822 4-8-13 **88**...................... TomQueally 9 97
(K A Ryan) *chsd ldng pair: effrt to ld ent fnl 2f: hrd pressed and drvn ent fnl f: styd on gamely fnl f* **7/2**[1]

2-60 **2** *¾* **Jonny Mudball**[20] 1727 4-9-0 **89**......................................(t) HayleyTurner 2 95
(Tom Dascombe) *broke wl: stdd and t.k.h in midfield sn after s: switching out rt looking for run 2f out: drvn ent fnl f: styd on wl to snatch 2nd last stride* **8/1**

0001 **3** *nse* **Rileyskeepingfaith**[7] 2119 4-9-13 **102**............................(v) AlanMunro 8 108
(M R Channon) *hld up in tch in midfield: hdwy over 2f out: chsd wnr wl over 1f out: rdn and ev ch ent fnl f: unable qck ins fnl f and btn fnl 75yds: lost 2nd last stride* **5/1**[3]

11-0 **4** *shd* **Freeforaday (USA)**[21] 1701 3-8-2 **91**............................... KierenFox(5) 7 95
(J R Best) *hld up in rr: hdwy on outer ent fnl 2f: rdn to chse ldng pair over 1f out: kpt on same pce u.p fnl 150yds* **9/1**

24-4 **5** *1 ¼* **Son Of The Cat (USA)**[56] 1014 4-9-4 **93**...........................(t) PatDobbs 1 95
(B Gubby) *hld up in last trio: swtchd rt and hdwy over 1f out: styd on same pce u.p fnl f* **11/1**

63-6 **6** *¾* **Run For The Hills**[14] 1906 4-9-11 **100**.......................... RobertHavlin 3 99
(J H M Gosden) *hld up wl in tch in midfield: hdwy to chse wnr ent fnl 2f tl wl over 1f out: sn rdn and nt qckn: wknd ins fnl f* **12/1**

40-1 **7** *nse* **Spitfire**[51] 1076 5-9-1 **90**.. PhilipRobinson 4 89
(J R Jenkins) *stdd s: bhd: sn niggled along and racing awkwardly: edging rt and effrt u.p wl over 1f out: kpt on but nvr gng pce to rch ldrs* **12/1**

0004 **8** *9* **Mac Gille Eoin**[14] 1906 6-9-8 **97**....................................... SebSanders 5 67
(J Gallagher) *broke wl: led and crossed to stands' rail: hdd and rdn ent fnl 2f: fdd qckly over 1f out: wl btn and eased ins fnl f: b.b.v* **4/1**[2]

1042 **9** *nse* **Jarrow (IRE)**[8] 2090 3-8-6 **90**... GregFairley 6 58
(M Johnston) *chsd ldr tl over 2f out: sn dropped out: wl bhd fr over 1f out* **6/1**

1m 11.32s (-0.88) **Going Correction** +0.10s/f (Good)
WFA 3 from 4yo+ 9lb **9** Ran SP% **118.0**
Speed ratings (Par 109): **109,108,107,107,106 105,105,93,93**
toteswingers: 1&2 £7.60, 1&3 £4.50, 2&3 £5.80 CSF £32.70 CT £142.30 TOTE £4.30: £1.50, £2.80, £1.50; EX 36.20 Trifecta £288.20 Part won. Pool: £389.54 - 0.83 winning units..
Owner Dr Marwan Koukash **Bred** Illuminatus Investments **Trained** Hambleton, N Yorks

FOCUS
A typically competitive sprint handicap for the track. Straightforward form with the winner getting back to his best.

NOTEBOOK
Parisian Pyramid(IRE) stayed on strongly to register his first success since a C&D nursery off 20lb lower two years back. He had run well off a pound higher at Newmarket two starts back, and his latest Chester effort could be ignored (wide draw/5f), so it's possible he could start to progress again. (op 15-2)
Jonny Mudball, who had been disappointing in two previous outings this year, ran much more encouragingly. The return to a sound surface was a help and he would have given the winner a bit more to do had he been in the clear earlier. His yard is beginning to get going, so he could be a player in some of the top sprint handicaps this season. (op 11-2)
Rileyskeepingfaith, 5lb higher than when winning at Newbury a week earlier, improved travelling well and held every chance, but he may have seen daylight a bit too soon and couldn't quicken close home. (op 9-2)
Freeforaday(USA) challenged out wide but couldn't stay on as strongly as some. He was a progressive juvenile and should come on again. (op 11-1 tchd 8-1)
Son Of The Cat(USA) is 9lb higher than when winning his only handicap, but he ran well enough to suggest he can remain competitive.
Run For The Hills moved well, if a little keen, but his finishing effort was rather tame and this mark of 100 looks beyond him. (tchd 14-1)
Spitfire was never going the pace on ground that would have been quick enough for him.
Mac Gille Eoin was quickly across to lead on the stands' rail, and judged by the way he dropped right out, that clearly wasn't the place to be. Official explanation: trainer said horse bled (op 11-2)
Jarrow(IRE) has been running well, but he found this a bit too competitive and ultimately dropped right out. (op 5-1)

2317 TOTESWINGER STKS (H'CAP) 1m 4f
2:45 (2:47) (Class 2) (0-105,100) 4-Y-O+ **£22,666** (£6,744; £3,370; £1,683) **Stalls** Low

Form RPR

30-2 **1** **Final Victory**[31] 1472 4-8-8 **84**.. LiamKeniry 4 94
(A M Balding) *chsd ldrs: chsd ldr ent fnl 3f: pushed ahd over 1f out: rdn clr ins fnl f: r.o wl: comf* **9/1**

0-46 **2** *2 ¼* **Classic Vintage (USA)**[20] 1724 4-9-5 **95**.................... PhilipRobinson 8 101
(Mrs A J Perrett) *led for 1f: sn settled in tch in midfield: rdn to chse ldng trio 3f out: kpt on u.p to go 2nd ins fnl f: nvr gng pce to threaten wnr* **11/4**[1]

10/2 **3** *1 ¾* **Managua**[39] 1282 4-8-5 **81**.. AlanMunro 9 85
(M R Channon) *hld up in last trio: effrt and hanging rt wl over 2f out: swtchd lft 2f out: kpt wanting to hang rt but plugged on steadily fnl f to go 3rd nr fin: nvr gng pce to chal wnr* **11/1**

3553 **4** *nk* **Perpetually (IRE)**[12] 1960 4-8-12 **88**.............................. SebSanders 7 91
(M Johnston) *chsd ldrs after 2f: rdn to chse ldng pair 3f out: drvn and plugged on one pce fnl 2f out: lost 3rd nr fin* **9/2**[2]

2450 **5** *3 ¾* **Record Breaker (IRE)**[20] 1724 6-9-2 **92**..........................(b) GregFairley 5 89
(M Johnston) *chsd ldng pair after 2f: led over 3f out: drvn and hdd over 1f out: lost 2nd and fdd fnl 150yds* **11/2**[3]

262 **6** *1 ¾* **Sohcahtoa (IRE)**[9] 2044 4-8-11 **87**.................................. PatDobbs 10 81
(R Hannon) *hld up in last trio: effrt and no hdwy over 2f out: wl btn whn swtchd lft ins fnl f:* **7/1**

00-3 **7** *hd* **Via Galilei (IRE)**[14] 1911 5-9-10 **100**............................... JamieMoore 11 94
(G L Moore) *v.s.a: sn rcvrd and in tch in rr: rdn and edgd rt 2f out: no prog and nvr trbld ldrs* **20/1**

4-10 **8** *7* **Brunston**[21] 1697 4-9-1 **91**.. HayleyTurner 1 74
(R Charlton) *taken down early: led after 1f tl 6f out: chsd ldr after tl over 3f out: wknd qckly wl over 1f out: wl bhd and eased ins fnl f* **13/2**

6-00 **9** *15* **Liszt (IRE)**[17] 1821 4-9-2 **92**..(p) TomQueally 6 51
(Ian Williams) *rrd as stalls opened and v.s.a: early reminders: hdwy to press ldr after 2f: led 6f out tl pushed along and hdd over 3f out: sn dropped out: wl bhd and eased ins fnl f: t.o* **14/1**

2m 36.19s (-2.21) **Going Correction** 0.0s/f (Good) **9** Ran SP% **115.8**
Speed ratings (Par 109): **107,105,104,104,101 100,100,95,85**
toteswingers: 1&2 £3.40, 1&3 £6.10, 2&3 £5.30 CSF £34.13 CT £280.72 TOTE £10.10: £2.70, £1.70, £2.00; EX 28.70 Trifecta £217.00 Pool: £517.09 - 1.76 winning units..
Owner Sir Gordon Brunton **Bred** Sir Gordon Brunton **Trained** Kingsclere, Hants

FOCUS
A good handicap run at a sound gallop, and the form looks sound too.

NOTEBOOK
Final Victory, off the same mark as when a well-beaten second at Epsom on his reappearance, would have been suited by the way the race was run, given he stays 1m6f, and he could be called the winner from over a furlong out. He has improved again from three to four, and may well develop into a leading Ebor contender. (op 6-1)
Classic Vintage(USA), 5lb higher than when winning at last year's Glorious meeting here, ran a satisfactory race in a good handicap at Newmarket last time and looked the one to beat off a pound lower, but he was found wanting for pace and kept on all too late into second. He looks in need of a return to 1m6f. (op 7-2)
Managua, who was looked after when second at Yarmouth on his return from a lengthy absence, again shaped with plenty of promise. He stayed on late for third, despite hanging and not looking at home on the track, and remains interesting for good middle-distance handicaps. (op 10-1 tchd 8-1)
Perpetually(IRE) lacks a finishing kick and that was again evident. He is looking exposed. (op 9-1)
Record Breaker(IRE)looked the one to beat when racing into the lead over three furlongs out, but he was strongly pressed and then passed by the winner inside the final two furlongs. He has still to recapture his best form, but this was better and he will no doubt go well again in the Duke of Edinburgh at Royal Ascot (second last year). (tchd 5-1)
Brunston, winner of the Spring Cup over 1m on his reappearance, disappointed next time and the return to this sort of distance failed to help. (tchd 6-1)

Liszt(IRE) Official explanation: jockey said gelding reared as stalls opened

2318 TOTESPORT.COM STKS (REGISTERED AS THE ON THE HOUSE STAKES) (LISTED RACE) 1m
3:20 (3:21) (Class 1) 3-Y-O+

£22,708 (£8,608; £4,308; £2,148; £1,076; £540) **Stalls** High

Form RPR

-060 **1** **Beauchamp Xerxes**[92] 629 4-9-5 98 DaneO'Neill 6 104
(G A Butler) *taken down early: stdd s: t.k.h and hld up in last: hdwy over 2f out: rdn to ld ent fnl f: hld on cl home: all out* **20/1**

0623 **2** *hd* **Vitznau (IRE)**[12] 1974 6-9-5 99 PatDobbs 1 105+
(R Hannon) *hld up in last pair: n.m.r 2f out: plld out lft and hdwy ent fnl f: chsd wnr u.p ins fnl f: kpt on: nt quite rch wnr* **10/1**

-153 **3** *2 ¾* **Skysurfers**[56] 1022 4-9-5 113 TedDurcan 3 97
(Saeed Bin Suroor) *chsd ldrs: wnt 2nd over 2f out: led 2f out: sn rdn and hdd over 1f out: lost 2nd ins fnl f: eased whn btn towards fin* **4/1[3]**

15-1 **4** *2 ¾* **King Of Dixie (USA)**[24] 1614 6-9-8 109 GeorgeBaker 5 94+
(W J Knight) *hld up wl in tch: nt clr run on inner 2f out: swtchd arnd wkng rival wl over 1f out: no prog whn rdn ent fnl f* **6/4[1]**

1 **5** *4 ½* **Storm Ultralight (ARG)**[22] 1664 4-9-3 111 TomQueally 7 79
(Mahmood Al Zarooni) *chsd ldr tl led over 2f out: sn hanging rt and racing awkwardly: hdd 2f out: wknd qckly over 1f out: wl btn fnl f* **9/4[2]**

4500 **6** *5* **Yahrab (IRE)**[21] 1712 5-9-5 96 (b) SebSanders 2 69
(C E Brittain) *sn led: clr over 5f out: rdn and hdd over 2f out: hanging rt and dropped out qckly wl over 1f out: wl btn fnl f* **20/1**

1m 38.92s (-0.98) **Going Correction** 0.0s/f (Good) **6** Ran SP% **109.4**
Speed ratings (Par 111): **104,103,101,98,93 88**
toteswingers: 1&2 £5.90, 1&3 £14.90, 2&3 £3.40 CSF £176.56 TOTE £24.40: £6.90, £4.10; EX 102.30.
Owner Erik Penser **Bred** E Penser **Trained** Newmarket, Suffolk

FOCUS
Not a strong race for the grade, and muddling form, with both the Godolphin representatives failing to transfer their smart artificial surface form to turf, and the outcome fought out between two horses rated in the high 90s. The winner enjoyed a clearer run than some and the form is rated around him.

NOTEBOOK
Beauchamp Xerxes just managed to hold on in a head-bob. All he had to his name coming into the race was a maiden win, and he struggled to make an impact off a mark of 100 in Dubai this year, so it was hard to see this return to form coming. The form is worth little, however, with none of the first three in the betting coming up to expectations, and he will struggle to find another opportunity as good at this level. (op 22-1)
Vitznau(IRE) looked likely to go well in this type of event, despite having a bit to do at the weights, and he came with a strong challenge inside the final furlong, but just couldn't get up in time. (op 9-1 tchd 8-1)
Skysurfers, who twice ran well in Group races in Dubai this year, was weak in the market and, despite having moved up to lead two furlongs out, his finishing effort was rather tame. His stable is hardly in great form and he may improve. (op 7-2 tchd 9-2 and 3-1 in places)
King Of Dixie(USA), winner of a Listed race at Ascot on his reappearance, was conceding weight all round, but came in for good support to head the market. However, he was plenty keen enough early and didn't have much room against the rail, but he didn't find a great deal when switched out anyway. (op 2-1 tchd 9-4)
Storm Ultralight(ARG), a tidy winner on his debut for connections at Lingfield, didn't look happy on the track and became very awkward to ride. He deserves another chance, but is left with a bit to prove. Official explanation: jockey said colt was struck into (op 2-1, tchd 5-2 in places)
Yahrab(IRE) had a bit to find and dropped right out, having made the running. (op 16-1)

2319 E B F MAY 31ST AT GOODWOOD MAIDEN STKS 6f
3:50 (3:51) (Class 4) 2-Y-O **£6,476** (£1,927; £963; £481) **Stalls** Low

Form RPR

3 **1** **Avonmore Star**[19] 1764 2-9-3 0 GregFairley 11 86+
(R Hannon) *t.k.h: chsd ldrs: led gng wl over 1f out: sn pushed clr: r.o strly fnl f: comf* **7/1[2]**

0 **2** *3* **Numeral (IRE)**[20] 1728 2-9-3 0 PatDobbs 3 79+
(R Hannon) *hld up wl in tch on stands' rail: nt clr run fr over 2f out tl hdwy between horses to chse clr wnr ins fnl f: r.o wl for clr 2nd but nvr able to threaten wnr* **7/4[1]**

3 **3** *2* **Sylas Ings**[8] 2077 2-9-3 0 IanMongan 6 71
(P M Phelan) *led: rdn ent fnl 2f: hdd and nt pce of wnr over 1f out: kpt on one pce and wl hld fnl f* **8/1[3]**

4 *½* **Local Singer (IRE)** 2-9-3 0 TomQueally 7 70
(M R Channon) *t.k.h: trckd ldrs: effrt and ev ch 2f out: rdn and nt pce of wnr over 1f out: kpt on same pce and wl hld fnl f* **16/1**

5 *2 ¼* **Oliver's Gold** 2-9-3 0 PhilipRobinson 12 63
(Mrs A J Perrett) *racd keenly: chsd ldr tl ent fnl 2f: nt pce of wnr and btn over 1f out: wknd ins fnl f* **12/1**

6 *1* **Beacon Hill (IRE)** 2-9-3 0 RobertHavlin 10 60
(J H M Gosden) *t.k.h early: chsd ldrs: rdn and edging rt ent fnl 2f: wknd wl over 1f out* **10/1**

7 *¾* **Jamhoori** 2-9-3 0 JamieMackay 2 58+
(C E Brittain) *towards rr: rdn along and struggling over 2f out: styd on steadily ins fnl f: nvr trbld ldrs* **25/1**

8 *¾* **Rutterkin (USA)** 2-9-3 0 TedDurcan 5 55
(Mahmood Al Zarooni) *s.i.s: hld up in midfield: swtchd rt and hdwy on outer over 2f out: rdn ent fnl 2f: sn struggling and btn wl over 1f out* **10/1**

9 *1* **High On The Hog (IRE)** 2-9-3 0 DaneO'Neill 4 52
(J L Dunlop) *s.i.s: in tch towards rr: effrt and edging rt over 2f out: sn outpcd and btn ent fnl 2f* **14/1**

10 *¾* **Golden Taurus (IRE)** 2-9-3 0 GeorgeBaker 9 50
(J W Hills) *hld up in tch in midfield: rdn and struggling ent fnl 2f: wl bhd fr wl over 1f out* **20/1**

11 *3 ¾* **Toucan Tango (IRE)** 2-9-3 0 AlanMunro 8 39
(P W Chapple-Hyam) *s.i.s: a in rr: lost tch wl over 2f out: wl bhd fnl 2f* **12/1**

0 **12** *2 ¼* **Irie Ute**[8] 2077 2-9-3 0 LiamKeniry 1 32
(S Kirk) *in tch towards rr: rdn and lost tch over 2f out: sn wl bhd* **66/1**

13 *2 ¾* **Alltherightmoves (IRE)** 2-8-12 0 HayleyTurner 13 19
(Eve Johnson Houghton) *s.i.s: in tch in rr on outer tl lost tch qckly over 2f out: sn wl bhd* **16/1**

1m 13.12s (0.92) **Going Correction** +0.10s/f (Good) **13** Ran SP% **122.1**
Speed ratings (Par 95): **97,93,90,89,86 85,84,83,82,81 76,73,69**
toteswingers: 1&2 £3.70, 1&3 £8.00, 2&3 £5.30 CSF £19.53 TOTE £7.00: £1.90, £1.10, £2.10; EX 17.20.
Owner Ken Geering **Bred** Miss J R Tooth **Trained** East Everleigh, Wilts

FOCUS
This had the look of an interesting maiden, and those with experience came to the fore. Richard Hannon was responsible for the one-two, though not in the order the market suggested. The winner stepped forward on his ddebut run and the form is pitched towards the top end of the race averages.

NOTEBOOK
Avonmore Star, a promising third at Kempton on debut, improved a lot and relished the extra furlong, quickly going clear and getting first run on his stablemate. He may well have been the best on the day anyway, and it will be interesting to see where he goes next. (op 5-1)
Numeral(IRE), fancied for a good maiden at the Newmarket Guineas meeting (well held, having been slowly away and denied a clear run), was expected to have improved and the extra furlong looked in his favour, but he raced against the rail, which wasn't a wise move, and there was no room when his rider wanted to switch out. By the time the favourite was in the clear the winner had gone, but he should gain compensation at some stage. (op 15-8 tchd 9-4)
Sylas Ings showed plenty of promise when third at Newbury on his debut, and he again ran well without suggesting he had improved. (op 9-1 tchd 7-1)
Local Singer(IRE), from a yard whose juveniles tend to benefit from a run, showed plenty, coming to hold a chance inside the final two furlongs before getting outpaced. He did best of the newcomers. (op 20-1)
Oliver's Gold shaped well on this debut, if racing a little keenly, and should come on for the experience.
Beacon Hill(IRE), a £70,000 half-brother to a fair 6/7f winner, was backed beforehand and showed up well for a long way, but his lack of experience was evident and he faded, having raced a tad keenly early on. (op 18-1)
Jamhoori, very much bred for further, shaped most pleasingly in finishing a running-on seventh, coming home well in the final furlong. He will improve and should relish the chance to tackle 7f and more in time. (op 40-1)
Rutterkin(USA), whose trainer has yet to have a juvenile winner, showed enough to suggest he has a future. (tchd 11-1)
High On The Hog(IRE), related to winners over further, didn't show enough to make him of obvious interest for the immediate future. (tchd 16-1)

2320 TURFTV STKS (H'CAP) 5f
4:25 (4:25) (Class 5) (0-70,69) 3-Y-O **£3,238** (£963; £481; £240) **Stalls** Low

Form RPR

2231 **1** **Boogie Waltzer**[19] 1784 3-8-9 67 (t) RyanClark(7) 1 71
(S C Williams) *broke wl and rdr looking to go rt and r in centre: hmpd and stdd over 4f out: kpt gng rt tl in centre 3f out: effrt to chal and rdn 1f out: led fnl 50yds: hld on wl: all out* **10/3[1]**

450- **2** *shd* **Admirable Duchess**[233] 6418 3-9-1 66 GregFairley 6 70
(D J S Ffrench Davis) *short of room after s: t.k.h and sn rcvrd to press ldrs: led narrowly 3f out: rdn over 1f out: hdd fnl 50yds: kpt on wl: jst hld* **4/1[2]**

6310 **3** *nk* **Vilnius**[5] 2185 3-8-7 58 AlanMunro 4 60
(M R Channon) *w ldrs: rdn ent fnl 2f: sltly outpcd jst over 1f out: rallied u.p ins fnl f: kpt on wl* **5/1**

0-00 **4** *hd* **Avongate**[26] 1584 3-9-4 69 LukeMorris 3 71
(R A Harris) *w ldrs: rdn and ev ch ent fnl 2f: sltly outpcd over 1f out: hrd drvn and rallied ins fnl f: kpt on* **10/1**

-010 **5** *hd* **Lucky Flyer**[8] 2099 3-9-2 67 GeorgeBaker 8 68
(S Kirk) *broke wl: sn led and crossed to stands' rail: hdd 3f out but stl w ldrs: rdn 2f out: drvn and unable qck over 1f out: n.m.r and kpt on same pce ins fnl f* **9/2[3]**

40-0 **6** *¾* **Oasis Jade**[11] 2000 3-8-9 60 PatDobbs 7 58
(G L Moore) *hld up in last pair: carried sltly rt 3f out: effrt and rdn ent fnl 2f: edgd rt and no imp fnl f* **5/1**

2160 **7** *3* **Wanchai Whisper**[27] 1546 3-8-11 62 DaneO'Neill 5 50
(P R Hedger) *squeezed out sn after s: hld up in last pair: rdn and effrt 2f out: wknd ent fnl f* **10/1**

59.21 secs (0.81) **Going Correction** +0.10s/f (Good) **7** Ran SP% **112.8**
Speed ratings (Par 99): **97,96,96,96,95 94,89**
toteswingers: 1&2 £3.40, 1&3 £2.20, 2&3 £4.60 CSF £16.31 CT £63.89 TOTE £3.20: £1.90, £2.20; EX 18.30.
Owner Michael Edwards and John Parsons **Bred** Michael Edwards And John Parsons **Trained** Newmarket, Suffolk

FOCUS
Just a modest three-year-old sprint handicap, but it was competitive and the front five were separated by under half a length. Sound but ordinary form.

2321 FAMILY FUN ON MAY 31ST STKS (H'CAP) 1m 3f
5:00 (5:01) (Class 5) (0-70,70) 3-Y-O **£3,238** (£963; £481; £240) **Stalls** Low

Form RPR

000- **1** **Trovare (USA)**[204] 7146 3-9-1 67 PhilipRobinson 1 78+
(Mrs A J Perrett) *t.k.h: chsd ldrs: rdn over 2f out: ev ch over 1f out: flashed tail u.p: led fnl 100yds: styd on strly: in command whn edgd lft towards fin* **3/1[2]**

45-0 **2** *1 ½* **Boston Blue**[26] 1581 3-9-2 68 GeorgeBaker 4 76
(W J Knight) *dwlt and bustled along early: racd in last trio: effrt and hanging rt over 2f out: plld out lft 2f out: rdn and hdwy to ld over 1f out: hdd fnl 100yds: btn whn carried lft towards fin* **13/2**

5-23 **3** *3 ¼* **Gordon Flash**[12] 1975 3-9-4 70 PatDobbs 5 72
(R Hannon) *hld up in tch in midfield: hdwy and nt clr run 2f out: sn swtchd ins and rdn to press ldrs: wknd u.p ins fnl f* **7/4[1]**

05-0 **4** *2 ¼* **Apache Kid (IRE)**[32] 1450 3-8-8 60 LukeMorris 7 58
(D M Simcock) *hld up in last trio: effrt and rdn 4f out: drvn and no real prog 3f out: plugged on to go modest 4th ins fnl f: nvr trbld ldrs* **14/1**

01U5 **5** *½* **Until The Man (IRE)**[12] 1977 3-9-1 67 (p) IanMongan 2 64
(Mrs L J Mongan) *chsd ldr tl rdn to ld over 2f out: drvn and hdd over 1f out: wknd qckly 1f out* **8/1**

-505 **6** *9* **Halyard (IRE)**[12] 1975 3-9-0 66 DaneO'Neill 3 50
(W R Swinburn) *led tl hdd and rdn over 2f out: struggling whn hmpd 2f out: sn wl btn: eased ins fnl f* **5/1[3]**

0506 **7** *¾* **Orsett Lad (USA)**[26] 1578 3-8-1 58 KierenFox(5) 6 38
(J R Best) *stdd s: hld up in last: rdn and no prog over 3f out: wl bhd fr wl over 1f out* **20/1**

5341 **8** *46* **Beat Route**[52] 1060 3-8-11 68 JemmaMarshall(5) 8 —
(M J Attwater) *chsd ldrs tl rdn and lost pl qckly 3f out: t.o and virtually p.u fr over 1f out* **20/1**

2m 25.8s (-0.70) **Going Correction** 0.0s/f (Good) **8** Ran SP% **118.7**
Speed ratings (Par 99): **102,100,98,96,96 90,89,56**
toteswingers: 1&2 £6.50, 1&3 £2.10, 2&3 £4.10 CSF £23.86 CT £42.72 TOTE £4.00: £1.10, £2.90, £1.10; EX 24.30.
Owner John Connolly **Bred** James Heyward **Trained** Pulborough, W Sussex
■ Stewards' Enquiry : Pat Dobbs one-day ban: careless riding (Jun 6)

FOCUS
Run at a decent pace, this looks fair form for the grade and the race should produce winners. The unexposed winner was up 12lb on his 2yo form.

2322 RACING UK 6TH BIRTHDAY STKS (H'CAP) 1m
5:35 (5:36) (Class 3) (0-90,94) 4-Y-0+

£6,542 (£1,959; £979; £490; £244; £122) Stalls High

Form RPR

-034 **1** **Moynahan (USA)**[19] 1767 5-9-1 **87**.................................. GregFairley 12 96+
(P F I Cole) *hld up in tch towards rr: effrt whn bdly hmpd and lost pl wl over 1f out: swtchd lft over 1f out: rdn and gd hdwy on outer ent fnl f: r.o wl to ld fnl 75yds* **5/1**[3]

0-01 **2** ¾ **Mujood**[12] 1962 7-9-3 **94**...(v) JohnFahy(5) 8 101
(Eve Johnson Houghton) *in tch in midfield: lost pl and towards rr over 3f out: effrt u.p on outer over 2f out: drvn to chal 1f out: led ins fnl f: sn hdd and no ex* **8/1**

1-01 **3** 1 **South Cape**[24] 1618 7-9-0 **86** ow1.................................... GeorgeBaker 3 91
(G L Moore) *hld up in last trio: hdwy over 2f out: rdn to press ldrs ent fnl f: led fnl 150yds: hdd fnl 100yds: no ex* **3/1**[2]

00-0 **4** 2¾ **Aldermoor (USA)**[55] 1032 4-8-13 **85**.............................. SaleemGolam 9 84
(S C Williams) *chsd ldrs: led over 2f out: rdn wl over 1f out: hdd fnl 150yds: sn wknd* **25/1**

222- **5** 2¾ **Truism**[229] 6535 4-9-1 **87**.. PhilipRobinson 10 79
(Mrs A J Perrett) *t.k.h: hld up wl in tch: rdn and unable qck over 2f out: wknd ent fnl f* **9/4**[1]

0-02 **6** ¾ **Swift Chap**[16] 1841 4-8-13 **85**.. KirstyMilczarek 1 76
(B R Millman) *sn led: hdd over 4f out: rdn and outpcd whn jostled wl over 1f out: in rr and no threat to ldrs whn swtchd lft jst ins fnl f* **10/1**

2206 **7** nse **Pegasus Again (USA)**[32] 1455 5-8-10 **85**................ JamesMillman(3) 5 76
(R A Mills) *in tch in midfield: n.m.r on inner ent fnl 2f: rdn and unable qck wl over 1f out: wknd ent fnl f* **12/1**

0000 **8** ¾ **Kaolak (USA)**[21] 1697 4-9-3 **89**...(v) IanMongan 6 78
(J Ryan) *sn bustled along: hdwy to press ldr after 1f: led and pushed clr 4f out: hdd and rdn over 2f out: drvn over 1f out: wknd jst ins fnl f* **16/1**

5-00 **9** nk **The Which Doctor**[19] 1767 5-8-13 **85**.............................. PatDobbs 7 73
(J Noseda) *s.i.s: hld up in rr: looking for run on rail fr over 2f out: nvr clr run and nvr able to chal: swtchd lft ins fnl f* **7/1**

1m 38.39s (-1.51) **Going Correction** 0.0s/f (Good) **9** Ran SP% **122.6**
Speed ratings (Par 107): **107,106,105,102,99 99,98,98,97**
toteswingers: 1&2 £12.30, 1&3 £3.60, 2&3 £6.30 CSF £47.46 CT £144.78 TOTE £6.90: £3.00, £3.30, £1.50; EX 46.40 Place 6 £185.48, Place 5 £100.80.
Owner D S Lee **Bred** Stonestreet Mares Llc **Trained** Whatcombe, Oxon

FOCUS
A fair handicap made up of exposed handicappers. It was a bit of a messy race but the form appears sound enough.

NOTEBOOK
Moynahan(USA), who had twice run well off the same mark at Kempton this year, became short of room and was hampered, but his rider conjured a strong run out of him once he switched wide and the five-year-old got well on top close home. He fully deserved this first win since his two-year-old days.
Mujood has now finished runner-up in this race for three straight years. Though 5lb higher than when scoring at Brighton last time, he looked to be coming with a winning run inside the final furlong, but couldn't repel the winner's late effort. (op 6-1)
South Cape, 4lb higher than when winning at Ascot last time, briefly got to the front over half a furlong out, but the front pair stayed on too strongly for him. This was a good effort. (op 4-1, tchd 5-1 in places and 11-2 in a place)
Aldermoor(USA), racing beyond 7f for the first time, ran a fine race without suggesting he is going to prove better at this trip. (op 16-1)
Truism, runner-up on his final three starts last season, kept on at one pace and will need to improve to win off this mark. (op 7-2 tchd 2-1)
Swift Chap was a notable disappointment, slowly fading in the straight and failing to build on his latest effort. (op 11-1)
The Which Doctor got no run throughout the final two furlongs and crossed the line full of running. He will be of obvious interest next time. (op 8-1)
T/Plt: £245.40 to a £1 stake. Pool: £78,486.43. 233.42 winning tickets. T/Qpdt: £76.80 to a £1 stake. Pool: £3,157.64. 30.40 winning tickets. SP

2285 HAYDOCK (L-H)
Saturday, May 22

OFFICIAL GOING: Good to firm (7.6)
Wind: almost nil Weather: fine, sunny and very warm

2323 BETFRED "BOTH TEAMS SCORE...GOALS GALORE!" H'CAP 1m 3f 200y
2:00 (2:01) (Class 2) (0-100,91) 3-Y-0

£12,462 (£3,732; £1,866; £934; £466; £234) Stalls High

Form RPR

0-31 **1** **Awsaal**[20] 1735 3-9-4 **88**.. EddieAhern 4 103+
(J L Dunlop) *chsd ldrs: led over 2f out: sn rdn clr: styd on strly* **9/2**[2]

4-65 **2** 3½ **Private Story (USA)**[7] 2117 3-9-7 **91**................................ RyanMoore 8 100
(R Hannon) *hld up in rr: drvn over 3f out: styd on to chse wnr over 1f out* **6/1**[3]

0-11 **3** 4 **Gomrath (IRE)**[31] 1466 3-9-0 **84**.. ChrisCatlin 7 87
(M R Channon) *t.k.h in last: effrt over 3f out: styd on fnl f to take 3rd nr fin* **6/1**[3]

1-21 **4** ½ **Beat The Rush**[24] 1630 3-8-10 **80**.................................... PaulHanagan 2 82
(Julie Camacho) *trckd ldr: pushed along 4f out: outpcd over 2f out: styd on fnl f* **3/1**[1]

1003 **5** 1¾ **Munaawer (USA)**[8] 2101 3-8-8 **78**.......................................(p) NeilCallan 6 77
(J D Bethell) *hld up in midfield: effrt on ins over 3f out: one pce fnl 2f* **20/1**

4-1 **6** ¾ **Rawnaq (IRE)**[20] 1721 3-8-13 **83**.. TadhgO'Shea 5 81+
(M Johnston) *dwlt: sn chsng ldrs: lost pl over 3f out: hung lft and styd on ins fnl f* **6/1**[3]

12-5 **7** nk **Tominator**[16] 1833 3-9-7 **91**.. DarryllHolland 1 89
(R Hollinshead) *led: qcknd over 4f out: hdd over 2f out: wknd fnl f* **9/1**

212 **8** 9 **High On A Hill (IRE)**[12] 1975 3-8-9 **79**............................ WilliamBuick 3 69
(S Kirk) *chsd ldrs: drvn 4f out: lost pl over 1f out: eased and bhd wl ins fnl f* **15/2**

2m 33.33s (-0.67) **Going Correction** +0.15s/f (Good) **8** Ran SP% **112.6**
Speed ratings (Par 105): **105,102,100,99,98 98,97,91**
toteswingers:1&2:£5.00, 1&3:£7.20, 2&3:£8.20 CSF £30.43 CT £160.71 TOTE £5.50: £1.90, £1.50, £2.40; EX 27.60 Trifecta £181.60 Pool: £458.96 - 1.87 winning units..
Owner Hamdan Al Maktoum **Bred** Meon Valley Stud **Trained** Arundel, W Sussex

FOCUS
After a dry night, the going was good to firm. There was some fresh ground, however, as the rail was moved 2m on the bend. This looked a competitive handicap, but the winner was value for his winning distance and seems sure to be tried at a higher level. Strong form, rated fairly positively.

NOTEBOOK
Awsaal ◆ got off the mark at Salisbury last time over 1m4f and was unexposed. He holds an entry in the King Edward VII at Royal Ascot (he was also entered in Derby until recently) and looks a nice prospect judged by the way he kept on strongly under pressure. It's no surprise to see him making the progress that he is, because he has plenty of size about him, and can only improve again with this effort under his belt. He shapes like a stayer, with a bit of pace, in the making. (op 5-1)
Private Story(USA), who ran a week previously in a valuable handicap, was up in trip and seemed to stay it without a problem, but the winner was gone before he could respond. It was a sound performance, however. (tchd 11-2)
Gomrath(IRE) had made a bright start to this campaign, winning on his previous two starts, but ran here like he needed either a stronger pace to follow, or a step up to 1m6f. (op 11-2)
Beat The Rush has been in good heart this year and was 5lb higher than when winning on his last outing. Nicely supported in the betting, he was a little keen on the heels of the leader and then needed pushing along with 4f to go. He kept on but was no threat to the leading bunch. (op 4-1)
Munaawer(USA) never looked like winning but plugged on for pressure.
Rawnaq(IRE), unraced as a juvenile, progressed from his first outing to win an ordinary-looking Hamilton maiden by 5l. Slightly up in trip again, he ran moderately after starting slowly. He must be better than this and something may not have been right with him. (op 5-1)
Tominator, beaten just over 10l into 5th in the Chester Vase last time, had Listed form as a juvenile and enjoyed an easy lead, but he went backwards once the field caught him about 2f out.
High On A Hill(IRE) sat prominent early but could not go with his rivals once the pace quickened. He was reported to have been unsuited by the ground. Official explanation: trainer's rep said colt was unsuited by the good to firm ground (op 8-1)

2324 BETFRED SILVER BOWL (HERITAGE H'CAP) 1m 30y
2:30 (2:31) (Class 2) 3-Y-0

£46,732 (£13,995; £6,997; £3,502; £1,747; £877) Stalls Low

Form RPR

-312 **1** **Balducci**[21] 1703 3-8-3 **84**.. DavidProbert 3 96+
(A M Balding) *hld up in rr: hdwy on ins over 5f out: effrt over 3f out: wnt 2nd over 1f out: r.o u.p to ld ins fnl f* **4/1**[1]

2103 **2** ¾ **Al Farahidi (USA)**[19] 1781 3-8-4 **85**...........................(b[1]) AndrewMullen 6 95
(M Johnston) *led: clr over 6f out tl over 2f out: hdd and no ex last 100yds* **20/1**

-540 **3** 6 **Black Snowflake (USA)**[38] 1313 3-9-2 **97**..................... TadhgO'Shea 9 93+
(Mahmood Al Zarooni) *in rr: hdwy over 2f out: swtchd rt over 1f out: styd on to take 3rd fnl 100yds* **33/1**

15-2 **4** 1½ **Our Joe Mac (IRE)**[16] 1834 3-8-12 **93**.............................. PaulHanagan 8 86
(R A Fahey) *trckd ldrs: effrt 3f out: kpt on same pce* **4/1**[1]

114 **5** ½ **Hacienda (IRE)**[19] 1786 3-9-1 **96**...................................... RyanMoore 10 87
(M Johnston) *in rr: hdwy and swtchd rt over 2f out: kpt on wl fnl f* **15/2**[2]

50-2 **6** nk **Gunner Lindley (IRE)**[20] 1732 3-8-7 **88**............................ MichaelHills 7 79
(B W Hills) *chsd ldrs: one pce fnl 2f* **11/1**

5-11 **7** 1¼ **Ginger Jack**[92] 617 3-8-4 **85**.. RoystonFfrench 15 73
(M Johnston) *chsd ldrs: kpt on same pce fnl 2f* **16/1**

3-13 **8** nk **Huygens**[29] 1497 3-8-12 **93**.. DarryllHolland 1 80
(D J Coakley) *mid-div: hdwy on ins over 3f out: sn chsng ldrs: one pce fnl 2f* **8/1**[3]

5-06 **9** nk **Mark Twain (IRE)**[17] 1823 3-8-2 **86**................................ MartinLane(3) 2 72
(D M Simcock) *s.i.s: sn mid-div: one pce fnl 3f* **33/1**

20-2 **10** ½ **Unshakable Will (IRE)**[7] 2112 3-7-10 **82**................... DeclanCannon(5) 5 67
(B Smart) *trckd ldrs: t.k.h: fdd over 1f out* **11/1**

16-4 **11** 1¾ **Aerodynamic (IRE)**[19] 1781 3-8-7 **88**............................ AndreaAtzeni 12 69
(Pat Eddery) *chsd ldrs: wknd over 1f out* **16/1**

65-0 **12** 7 **Desert Auction (IRE)**[14] 1913 3-8-6 **87**........................ RichardMullen 16 52
(R Hannon) *in rr: hmpd bnd over 6f out: sme hdwy over 3f out: wkng whn hmpd over 1f out: eased ins fnl f* **40/1**

2231 **13** 15 **Mejd (IRE)**[10] 2025 3-7-12 **79** oh1.................................... CathyGannon 13 10
(M R Channon) *bhd: hmpd wd bnd over 6f out: t.o* **25/1**

0-42 **14** ¾ **High Twelve (IRE)**[9] 2045 3-9-2 **97**................................ WilliamBuick 17 26
(J H M Gosden) *bhd: wd bnd over 5f out: t.o* **12/1**

01-2 **15** 9 **Rakaan (IRE)**[14] 1913 3-8-9 **90**.. EddieAhern 14 —
(J A Osborne) *in rr: bhd whn eased over 1f out: t.o* **16/1**

1642 **16** 5 **Gumnd (IRE)**[16] 1846 3-8-6 **87**..(p) ChrisCatlin 11 —
(C E Brittain) *dwlt: in rr: hmpd bnd over 6f out: bhd and eased fnl f: t.o* **33/1**

1m 42.2s (-2.50) **Going Correction** +0.15s/f (Good) **16** Ran SP% **124.8**
Speed ratings (Par 105): **114,113,107,105,105 104,103,103,103,102 100,93,78,78,69 64**
toteswingers:1&2:£31.40, 1&3:£59.70, 2&3:£123.60 CSF £93.63 CT £2374.98 TOTE £4.80: £1.80, £8.10, £6.30, £2.10; EX 147.00 Trifecta £5888.20 Pool: £11,139.90 - 1.40 winning units..
Owner McMahon/Gorell/Pausewang/Russell **Bred** G Russell **Trained** Kingsclere, Hants

FOCUS
No Hubris, set to carry topweight of 9-7, was a non-runner. This usually goes to a very-useful sort that can go on to great things, both on the Flat and over Jumps. Jazz Messenger became a Grade 1-winning hurdler, Home Affairs finished third in the Jersey Stakes, and Anna Pavlova collected a couple of Group 2 victories. This year's winner looks right up to scratch, but it's fair to say that only two horses played a meaningful part in the outcome. The time was fast and this is good form.

NOTEBOOK
Balducci got shuffled back through the field early, but made his way into a prominent position about 2f from home before reeling in the second with every stride. He was in front a good 50 yards before the post and was maintaining his lead comfortably. One would imagine that the next logical target would be the Britanina Handicap at Royal Ascot. (tchd 9-2)
Al Farahidi(USA), blinkered for the first time, beat Balducci back in March and went a strong pace from the start, gaining a big advantage at one stage. It seemed as though the Mark Johnston-trained runner would be pegged back quite easily, considering how fast he seemed to go, but he stuck to his task well and only narrowly failed to collect. There is a good handicap in him during the summer. (tchd 25-1)
Black Snowflake(USA) was beaten a long way in the Fielden Stakes on his first run back in Britain, so this was better, although he never looked like winning after being held up. He had plenty of horses to negotiate up the straight.
Our Joe Mac(IRE), who narrowly failed to get up on his seasonal return at Chester from a terrible draw, pretty much had every chance in this but was unable to find another gear when needed. (op 9-2)
Hacienda(IRE) was unraced as a juvenile but quickly developed a good attitude, and won his first two starts. Not disgraced in an Irish Group 3 last time, he stayed on well after being ridden along, but was another who could not get there after being towards the rear. (op 13-2 tchd 6-1)
Gunner Lindley(IRE), an eyecatcher in the paddock, didn't run too badly on his first start of the season and once again here. The ground was probably as firm as he would want it. (op 14-1)

Ginger Jack, returned to turf chasing a hat-trick, looked a little green on occasions before running on again. He may have learnt plenty for this run and is not one to give up on yet. (op 14-1)

2325 BETFRED.COM TEMPLE STKS (GROUP 2) 5f
3:00 (3:02) (Class 1) 3-Y-0+

£56,770 (£21,520; £10,770; £5,370; £2,690; £1,350) **Stalls** Centre

Form				RPR
016-	**1**		**Kingsgate Native (IRE)**[274] 5233 5-9-4 118 ...... RyanMoore 4 (Sir Michael Stoute) *trckd ldrs: effrt 2f out: r.o to ld last 100yds: readily* **3/1**[1]	121
0-11	**2**	½	**Equiano (FR)**[21] 1700 5-9-4 114 ...... MichaelHills 6 (B W Hills) *led: edgd lft and hdd ins fnl f: no ex* **3/1**[1]	119
60-2	**3**	¾	**Borderlescott**[21] 1700 8-9-4 116 ...... NeilCallan 9 (R Bastiman) *chsd ldrs: styd on same pce fnl f* **7/2**[2]	116
61-0	**4**	¾	**Spin Cycle (IRE)**[21] 1700 4-9-4 107 ...... RichardMullen 5 (B Smart) *chsd ldrs towards far side: hung lft and kpt on same pce fnl f* **16/1**	114
16-6	**5**	3½	**Total Gallery (IRE)**[21] 1700 4-9-11 118 ...... JimmyFortune 10 (J S Moore) *hld up: swtchd lft after 1f: hdwy to chse ldrs over 2f out: fdd fnl 150yds* **8/1**	108
52-4	**6**	1	**Look Busy (IRE)**[17] 1822 5-9-1 104 ...... DanielTudhope 1 (A Berry) *in rr: styd on fnl 2f: nvr nr to chal* **16/1**	94
0-13	**7**	1	**Blue Jack**[21] 1700 5-9-4 110 ...... RichardKingscote 2 (Tom Dascombe) *chsd ldrs far side: wknd over 1f out* **6/1**[3]	94
4-62	**8**	½	**Benbaun (IRE)**[6] 2157 9-9-4 115 ......(v) PaulHanagan 3 (K A Ryan) *chsd ldrs: wknd appr fnl f* **15/2**	92
0-10	**9**	10	**Wi Dud**[35] 1406 6-9-4 103 ...... DarryllHolland 8 (K A Ryan) *dwlt: in rr: bhd and eased ins fnl f* **33/1**	56

58.92 secs (-2.08) **Going Correction** +0.075s/f (Good) **9 Ran SP% 124.1**

Speed ratings (Par 115): **115,114,113,111,106 104,103,102,86**

toteswingers:1&2:£2.40, 1&3:£3.90, 2&3:£3.40 CSF £13.18 TOTE £3.80: £1.50, £1.40, £1.40; EX 13.50 Trifecta £36.70 Pool: £1,532.21 - 30.86 winning units..

Owner Cheveley Park Stud **Bred** Peter McCutcheon **Trained** Newmarket, Suffolk

FOCUS
As one would expect, this was run at a terrific pace and a few of the runners didn't make much impact. The first three home confirmed this to be a good renewal of this Group 2 prize and Kingsgate Native is rated close to his best.

NOTEBOOK
Kingsgate Native(IRE), absent since finishing sixth in last year's Nunthorpe, in which he started favourite but finished behind Borderlescott and Benbaun, produced a classy-looking performance after tracking the pace. Said to look really well in the paddock before going to the start, and calmer in demeanour by his jockey, he is likely to take a lot of beating in the best sprints during the season. The King's Stand at Royal Ascot seems the likely target, although he is also in the Golden Jubilee. (op 9-2)

Equiano(FR) had returned to his best this season, collecting two victories from two starts, possibly due to a wind operation at the end of 2009. He set a good tempo out in front and rallied bravely under pressure. His target is the King's Stand, which makes sense considering how quickly he can go. (op 4-1)

Borderlescott is consistent and held a chance of winning this inside the final furlong before his effort flattened out a little. He will have a say in all the major sprints this year but may not head to Ascot if alternatives can be found. (op 4-1 tchd 5-1 in a place)

Spin Cycle(IRE) hasn't been up to this level in the past, so this was a fine effort, finishing on the heels of some classy opponents. (op 25-1 tchd 28-1)

Total Gallery(IRE), carrying a Group 1 penalty for winning the Prix De L'Abbaye last season, showed good pace just behind the leaders but is finding things difficult giving weight away. (op 17-2 tchd 9-1)

Look Busy(IRE) is an admirable mare who took this race last year when it was run in heavy ground. She ran on quite well after being outpaced, especially as both of her front shoes came off. Official explanation: vet said mare lost both front shoes (op 14-1)

Blue Jack has made a good start to his time with Tom Dascombe, but wasn't up to this grade. (op 5-1)

Benbaun(IRE) was a fine second in a Group 3 at Longchamp the previous weekend behind Marchand D'Or, finding plenty for pressure at the end of the race, but made little impression once horses started to appear around him. (op 7-1)

Wi Dud continues to disappoint but was reported to have been unsuited by the ground. Official explanation: jockey said colt was unsuited by the good to firm ground (op 40-1)

2326 BETFRED "FRED'S LUCKY NUMBERS" STKS (REGISTERED AS THE CECIL FRAIL STAKES) (LISTED RACE) (FILLIES) 6f
3:30 (3:31) (Class 1) 3-Y-0+

£22,708 (£8,608; £4,308; £2,148; £1,076; £540) **Stalls** Centre

Form				RPR
124-	**1**		**Beyond Desire**[245] 6090 3-8-7 105 ...... NeilCallan 3 (M A Jarvis) *t.k.h: trckd ldrs: edgd rt after 150yds: led over 1f out: styd on wl fnl f* **10/11**[1]	101+
35-0	**2**	2¼	**Astrophysical Jet**[14] 1918 3-8-7 93 ...... TadhgO'Shea 9 (E S McMahon) *swtchd lft after s: hld up: edgd rt over 4f out: nt clr run and swtchd lft 2f out: hung lft and styd on fnl f: tk 2nd nr fin* **12/1**	94+
002-	**3**	½	**Excellerator (IRE)**[207] 7090 4-9-2 94 ......(t) TonyCulhane 4 (George Baker) *trckd ldrs: hmpd after 150yds: rdn to chse wnr 1f out: no imp* **12/1**	94
4-50	**4**	¾	**Sea Of Leaves (USA)**[14] 1918 4-9-2 93 ...... DanielTudhope 2 (J S Goldie) *trckd ldrs on outer: effrt 2f out: kpt on same pce* **20/1**	92
2044	**5**	4	**Ishiadancer**[14] 1918 5-9-2 90 ...... RyanMoore 8 (E J Alston) *w ldr stands' side: edgd lft and wknd fnl f* **8/1**[3]	79
43-2	**6**	nk	**Poppy's Rose**[8] 2087 6-9-2 57 ...... DaleSwift 6 (T J Etherington) *led: hdd over 1f out: wknd ins fnl f* **100/1**	78?
6-30	**7**	nk	**Anglezarke (IRE)**[10] 2030 4-9-2 100 ...... PaulHanagan 5 (R A Fahey) *chsd ldrs: drvn over 2f out: sn outpcd* **11/4**[2]	77
50-6	**8**	4½	**Pretty Bonnie**[14] 1918 5-9-2 85 ...... EddieAhern 7 (A E Price) *chsd ldrs: drvn over 3f out: lost pl over 2f out* **20/1**	63
600-	**9**	¾	**King's Starlet**[218] 6814 4-9-2 92 ...... JimmyFortune 1 (H Morrison) *racd alone towards far side: w ldrs: wknd over 1f out: eased* **20/1**	60

1m 12.7s (-0.80) **Going Correction** +0.075s/f (Good)

WFA 3 from 4yo+ 9lb **9 Ran SP% 120.8**

Speed ratings (Par 108): **111,108,107,106,101 100,100,94,93**

toteswingers:1&2:£3.40, 1&3:£5.30, 2&3:£14.00 CSF £14.12 TOTE £1.80: £1.40, £2.40, £2.60; EX 14.70.

Owner Clipper Logistics **Bred** Pinnacle Bloodstock **Trained** Newmarket, Suffolk

FOCUS
A race dominated by the two three-year-olds in the field, who had both shown good form as juveniles. The sixth was too close for comfort and it is doubtful if the winner had to match her 2yo best.

NOTEBOOK
Beyond Desire was a little keen early but readily got away from her rivals when asked to quicken. Runner-up in the Lowther Stakes before disappointing in a Group 3 next time, she showed that she had trained on nicely, and can win a few good-quality contests this season. She is likely to head to Ireland next. (op 11-10 tchd 6-5 in places)

Astrophysical Jet, who had a sore throat when disappointing last time, travelled strongly behind a wall of horses down the stands'-side rail but then tended to hang left under pressure. She has a lot of size about her and is one to follow at a realistic level.

Excellerator(IRE), whose trainer reported before the race that she'd strengthened up over the winter, hasn't won since her racecourse debut and was having her first outing since October last year. Back up to 6f, she had every chance and shaped promisingly for the remainder of the year.

Sea Of Leaves(USA), who was behind the runner-up last time, went very close to gaining some black type and may be able to get some before too long. (op 14-1)

Ishiadancer, in front of Sea Of Leaves at Nottingham, never really got involved and arguably wants further.

Poppy's Rose, without a win since 2007, was trying Listed company for the first time and led early before weakening. It was a commendable effort for a horse rated almost 30lb below the second lowest-rated horse in the field. (op 150-1)

Anglezarke(IRE) ran fairly well in the Group 2 Duke Of York Stakes last time but never got competitive here. (op 7-2 tchd 4-1)

King's Starlet, making her seasonal debut, raced away from the main body of the field early and faltered in the latter stages.

2327 BETFRED "BEST BET FOR WORLD CUP" H'CAP 6f
4:05 (4:08) (Class 4) (0-85,85) 4-Y-0+ **£5,180** (£1,541; £770; £384) **Stalls** Centre

Form				RPR
204-	**1**		**Novellen Lad (IRE)**[238] 6282 5-9-3 **84** ...... RyanMoore 14 (E J Alston) *trckd ldrs: str run on stands' side to ld jst ins fnl f: r.o wl* **3/1**[1]	98+
200	**2**	3	**Indian Skipper (IRE)**[7] 2134 5-8-9 **76** ......(be) RoystonFfrench 2 (R C Guest) *s.s: hdwy over 2f out: styd on wl to take 2nd nr fin* **25/1**	80+
0544	**3**	1	**Fathsta (IRE)**[15] 1862 5-9-4 **85** ...... EddieAhern 3 (D M Simcock) *hld up: hdwy 2f out: styd on ins fnl f* **7/1**[3]	86
50-0	**4**	shd	**Mrs Penny (AUS)**[37] 1332 6-9-1 **82** ......(p) NeilCallan 4 (J R Gask) *chsd ldrs on outside: effrt 2f out: kpt on ins fnl f* **16/1**	82
6-34	**5**	hd	**Rowayton**[7] 2134 4-9-1 **82** ......(p) DarryllHolland 11 (J D Bethell) *chsd ldr: led over 1f out: hdd jst ins fnl f: hung rt and no ex* **11/2**[2]	82
145	**6**	2¼	**Absa Lutte (IRE)**[7] 2136 7-8-13 **80** ......(t) DanielTudhope 1 (Patrick Morris) *hld up: nt clr run over 2f out: kpt on fnl f* **20/1**	73
2404	**7**	1¼	**Kerrys Requiem (IRE)**[6] 2140 4-9-3 **84** ...... TonyCulhane 12 (M R Channon) *in rr: kpt on fnl 2f: nvr nr ldrs* **12/1**	73
344-	**8**	2	**First In Command (IRE)**[27] 1557 5-8-11 **78** ......(t) AndreaAtzeni 6 (Daniel Mark Loughnane, Ire) *chsd ldrs on outer: wknd appr fnl f* **11/1**	60
6033	**9**	2¼	**Lucky Numbers (IRE)**[15] 1862 4-9-1 **82** ...... PaulMulrennan 10 (Paul Green) *chsd ldrs: swtchd lft over 1f out: sn wknd* **9/1**	57
4-00	**10**	2¼	**Mandurah (IRE)**[21] 1711 6-8-9 **76** ...... DavidProbert 13 (B P J Baugh) *dwlt: nvr on terms* **16/1**	44
3232	**11**	2½	**Brierty (IRE)**[7] 2136 4-8-11 **78** ...... DavidNolan 7 (D Carroll) *chsd ldrs: lost pl over 1f out* **17/2**	38
5-00	**12**	2¾	**Time Medicean**[7] 2136 4-8-5 **72** ...... PaulHanagan 9 (P T Midgley) *dwlt: a outpcd and wl in rr* **40/1**	23
610-	**13**	1¾	**Crimea (IRE)**[202] 7202 4-8-13 **85** ...... MichaelO'Connell(5) 5 (D Nicholls) *led: hdd & wknd qckly over 1f out* **14/1**	30

1m 12.73s (-0.77) **Going Correction** +0.075s/f (Good) **13 Ran SP% 118.9**

Speed ratings (Par 105): **111,107,105,105,105 102,100,97,94,91 88,84,82**

toteswingers:1&2:£20.60, 1&3:£4.50, 2&3:£35.40 CSF £81.12 CT £392.11 TOTE £3.80: £1.50, £7.00, £2.00; EX 98.70.

Owner Con Harrington **Bred** Mrs Chris Harrington **Trained** Longton, Lancs

■ Rash Judgement was withdrawn (8/1, ref to ent stalls). Deduct 10p in the £ under R4.

FOCUS
Most of these had shown good form on their last start, so one would imagine the form is sound for the level. The winner impressed in a decent time.

Rowayton Official explanation: jockey said filly hung right

Absa Lutte(IRE) Official explanation: jockey said mare was denied a clear run

Mandurah(IRE) Official explanation: trainer's rep said gelding was unsuited by the good to firm ground

2328 BETFRED KINGSPIN H'CAP 1m 30y
4:40 (4:40) (Class 4) (0-80,80) 4-Y-0+ **£5,180** (£1,541; £770; £384) **Stalls** Low

Form				RPR
1224	**1**		**Sir George (IRE)**[14] 1926 5-8-11 **76** ...... BarryMcHugh(3) 3 (Ollie Pears) *t.k.h: trckd ldrs: led 2f out: styd on wl fnl f: drvn out* **9/4**[1]	83
303-	**2**	1	**Harriet's Girl**[204] 7149 4-8-11 **73** ...... NeilCallan 9 (J R Weymes) *hld up in rr: effrt over 3f out: hrd rdn and styd on to take 2nd nr fin* **10/1**	77
22-2	**3**	hd	**Peponi**[19] 1782 4-9-1 **77** ...... RyanMoore 6 (P J Makin) *trckd ldrs: t.k.h: effrt over 2f out: styd on same pce appr fnl f* **5/2**[2]	81
1-50	**4**	nse	**Mujaadel (USA)**[2] 2241 5-9-1 **77** ......(p) AndrewMullen 2 (D Nicholls) *sn led: hdd 2f out: hung lft and kpt on same pce* **9/1**	81
5-13	**5**	1	**King Of The Moors (USA)**[19] 1752 7-8-9 **71** ......(p) DavidProbert 8 (R C Guest) *led early: w ldr: kpt on same pce fnl f* **14/1**	72
050-	**6**	hd	**Bold Cross (IRE)**[252] 5887 7-9-2 **78** ...... PaulFitzsimons 4 (E G Bevan) *s.s: t.k.h: hdwy over 3f out: one pce appr fnl f* **12/1**	79
0-00	**7**	1½	**Block Party**[38] 1306 4-8-13 **75** ...... RichardMullen 5 (D M Simcock) *mid-div: effrt over 3f out: one pce fnl 2f* **7/1**[3]	72
0005	**8**	3¾	**Bolodenka (IRE)**[11] 1990 8-9-1 **77** ...... PaulHanagan 1 (R A Fahey) *chsd ldrs: effrt 3f out: wknd over 1f out* **10/1**	65
000-	**9**	8	**Stevie Gee (IRE)**[198] 7252 6-9-4 **80** ......(t) TadhgO'Shea 7 (Ian Williams) *in rr: rdn 3f out: no rspnse* **20/1**	49

1m 44.83s (0.13) **Going Correction** +0.15s/f (Good) **9 Ran SP% 119.1**

Speed ratings (Par 105): **100,99,98,98,97 97,96,92,84**

toteswingers:1&2:£4.90, 1&3:£2.40, 2&3:£4.70 CSF £26.77 CT £62.17 TOTE £3.20: £1.20, £3.10, £1.10; EX 30.90.

Owner Ian Bishop **Bred** Bernard Colclough **Trained** Norton, N Yorks

FOCUS
The leader did not go a strong pace, which helps to explain the bunch finish. This result may not be repeated if some of these met again later on in the season. It is doubtful if the winner needed to improve.

2329 BETFRED THE BONUS KING H'CAP 7f 30y
5:15 (5:15) (Class 5) (0-70,70) 3-Y-0 **£4,857** (£1,445; £722; £360) **Stalls** Low

Form				RPR
0-33	**1**		**Whitechapel**[15] 1890 3-9-4 **70** ...... PaulHanagan 1 (E J Alston) *hld up: hdwy over 3f out: squeezed through on ins to ld over 1f out: hld on gamely clsng stages* **10/3**[2]	76+

604- **2** *nk* **Redden**[196] 7289 3-9-1 **67** MichaelHills 5 72+
(W J Haggas) *trckd ldrs: effrt over 3f out: chal jst ins fnl f: rdn and no ex fnl 50yds* **5/4**[1]
2630 **3** *4* **Nadinska**[11] 2005 3-9-1 **67** ChrisCatlin 4 61
(M R Channon) *led: hdd over 1f out: edgd rt and fdd ins fnl f* **16/1**
30-4 **4** *1 1/4* **Frontline Boy (IRE)**[43] 1201 3-9-1 **67** NeilCallan 3 58
(J R Weymes) *trckd ldr: effrt over 3f out: one pce fnl 2f* **7/1**
2-10 **5** *hd* **Always Dazzling**[11] 2005 3-9-1 **67** RoystonFfrench 2 57
(M Johnston) *dwlt: in rr: hung lft and kpt on fnl 2f: nvr a threat* **7/1**
36-0 **6** *6* **Gold Crusher (USA)**[33] 1425 3-8-10 **65** BarryMcHugh(3) 7 39
(Julie Camacho) *mid-div: drvn 3f out: wknd over 1f out* **22/1**
7 *5* **Sapperton**[94] 3-8-12 **64** TonyCulhane 6 24
(George Baker) *chsd ldrs: drvn over 3f out: lost pl over 2f out: sn bhd* **6/1**[3]

1m 32.65s (-0.05) **Going Correction** +0.15s/f (Good) 7 Ran SP% **117.0**
Speed ratings (Par 99): **92,91,87,85,85 78,72**
toteswingers:1&2:£1.40, 1&3:£7.80, 2&3:£6.60 CSF £8.24 TOTE £3.80: £1.10, £1.40; EX 9.30 Place 6 £19.56; Place 5 £6.91.
Owner Mr & Mrs Middlebrook/Mr & Mrs Nicholson **Bred** Mr & Mrs G Middlebrook **Trained** Longton, Lancs

FOCUS
An ordinary-looking contest and it was not strongly run. The unexposed first pair pulled clear.
T/Jkpt: Not won. T/Plt: £20.50. Pool:£157,227.36 - 5,579.41 winning tickets T/Qpdt: £4.80. Pool:£5,074.26 - 769.34 winning tickets WG

2230 LINGFIELD (L-H)
Saturday, May 22

OFFICIAL GOING: Turf course - good to firm (firm in places); all-weather - standard
Wind: Nil Weather: Hot and sunny

2330 EUROPEAN BREEDERS' FUND MAIDEN FILLIES' STKS 6f
5:20 (5:27) (Class 5) 2-Y-O **£3,480** (£1,027; £514) **Stalls High**

Form RPR
4 **1** **Serena's Pride**[8] 2074 2-8-9 0 MatthewDavies(5) 4 78+
(A P Jarvis) *mde all: pushed clr fnl f: eased nr fin* **10/3**[1]
653 **2** *4 1/2* **Russian Ice**[12] 1978 2-9-0 0 EddieCreighton 6 64
(D K Ivory) *chsd wnr: rdn over 2f out: outpcd fnl f* **14/1**
3 *1 1/4* **Boastful (IRE)** 2-9-0 0 TedDurcan 1 60+
(Mahmood Al Zarooni) *dwlt: hld up: hdwy over 2f out: rdn over 1f out: styd on same pce fnl f* **5/1**[3]
4 *nk* **Grandmas Dream** 2-9-0 0 PaulDoe 11 59
(G C Bravery) *prom: rdn over 2f out: styd on same pce fnl f* **16/1**
5 *3 1/2* **Al Andalyya (USA)** 2-9-0 0 KevinGhunowa 7 48
(D R Lanigan) *hld up in tch: rdn over 1f out: sn wknd* **11/2**
6 *1* **Jolah** 2-8-11 0 NataliaGemelova(3) 10 45
(C E Brittain) *chsd ldrs: rdn over 2f out: wknd over 1f out* **6/1**
0 **7** *6* **Brandy Snap (IRE)**[12] 1972 2-8-11 0 PatrickHills(3) 3 27
(R Hannon) *prom: rdn over 2f out: wknd over 1f out* **11/1**
0 **8** *19* **Maxiyow (IRE)**[40] 1263 2-8-9 0 AshleyMorgan(5) 5 —
(B Palling) *sn outpcd and bhd* **33/1**
U **Manasha** 2-9-0 0 SebSanders 2 —
(J L Dunlop) *s.s: outpcd: eased fnl 4f: uns rdr over 1f out* **7/2**[2]

1m 11.3s (0.10) **Going Correction** -0.075s/f (Good) 9 Ran SP% **115.5**
Speed ratings (Par 90): **96,90,88,87,83 81,73,48,—**
toteswingers: 1&2 £3.20, 1&3 £3.90, 2&3 £6.80 CSF £49.92 TOTE £3.60: £1.40, £1.40, £3.50; EX 28.50.
Owner Baydoun & Harake Partnership **Bred** Mrs Ann Jarvis **Trained** Twyford, Bucks

FOCUS
After a very hot day, the ground was changed to good to firm, firm in places. This was an uncompetitive maiden run at just an ordinary gallop and those with previous experience filled the first two places. The form is rated around the time and the runner-up.

NOTEBOOK
Serena's Pride had shown promise against four previous winners on her debut and probably did not have to improve too much to beat a modest sort with plenty in hand in a race where the newcomers failed to land a blow. She should stay 7f and, although she enjoyed a fairly easy time of it in front, she is a highly regard sort who is capable of better and will reportedly be aimed at either the Queen Mary or the Albany. (tchd 3-1 and 7-2)
Russian Ice, the most experienced of these, had the run of the race and gave it her best shot back on turf and up to 6f for the first time. She is probably the best guide to this form and, although vulnerable to the better types in this grade, may be able to pick up a small race when the nursery season begins or in a lesser grade. (op 12-1 tchd 9-1)
Boastful(IRE), a 100,000gns half-sister to smart sprinter Lesson In Humility, showed a modest level of form after faring the best of those held up on this racecourse debut. She should be better for this experience and it will be a surprise if she cannot better this bare form at some stage. (op 9-2 tchd 11-2)
Grandmas Dream, who cost 26,000gns and has several winners from 5f-7f in her pedigree, was not disgraced after attracting a bit of support on this racecourse debut. Runners from this yard invariably improve for their debut outings and she may do better. (tchd 14-1)
Al Andalyya(USA), who cost $100,000 and is the first foal of a sister to 2003 St Leger winner Brian Boru and half-sister to smart Moon Search was the subject of much support through the day but had her limitations exposed after showing greenness on this debut run. However she had presumably been showing a fair bit at home and will be of more interest granted a stiffer test of stamina. (op 5-1 tchd 6-1)
Jolah, a 60,000euro yearling out of a fairly useful dual 6f winner, was backed before the start and showed speed before getting tired on this debut. She may do better. (op 16-1)
Manasha, a well-backed sister to a couple of juvenile winners, but who is missing her left eye, was soon tailed off after proving fractious in the stalls and after missing the break before eventually unshipping her rider. The market suggested she has plenty of ability but it will be prudent to tread carefully with her after this showing. Official explanation: jockey said filly was slowly away and never travelled (op 11-2 tchd 6-1 in a place)

2331 WHYTELEAFE TAVERN H'CAP 6f
5:55 (5:57) (Class 5) (0-75,74) 4-Y-O+ **£2,914** (£867; £433; £216) **Stalls High**

Form RPR
10- **1** **Aegean Shadow**[254] 5806 4-8-9 **65** TomQueally 6 75+
(H R A Cecil) *s.i.s: hdwy over 4f out: rdn to chse ldr over 1f out: styd on to ld nr fin* **2/1**[1]
4354 **2** *nk* **Another Try (IRE)**[23] 1641 5-8-3 **64** MatthewDavies(5) 8 73
(A P Jarvis) *w ldr tl led 1/2-way: rdn over 1f out: hung lft ins fnl f: hdd nr fin* **4/1**[3]
00-0 **3** *2 1/4* **Frank Street**[9] 2053 4-8-10 **66** LiamKeniry 12 68
(Eve Johnson Houghton) *chsd ldrs: rdn over 2f out: hung lft ins fnl f: styd on same pce* **16/1**
2513 **4** *1/2* **Lastkingofscotland (IRE)**[11] 2009 4-9-3 **73** (b) PaulDoe 4 73+
(Jim Best) *s.i.s: sn prom: rdn and swtchd lft over 1f out: no ex ins fnl f* **5/2**[2]
1455 **5** *1 1/4* **Sherjawy (IRE)**[4] 2196 6-8-6 **69** RichardRowe(7) 10 65
(Miss Z C Davison) *led to 1/2-way: rdn over 1f out: hung lft and wknd ins fnl f* **16/1**
5-44 **6** *1/2* **Cativo Cavallino**[11] 2009 7-8-4 **63** NataliaGemelova(3) 2 58+
(J E Long) *sn pushed along in rr: hung lft: styd on ins fnl f: nvr on terms* **20/1**
0-50 **7** *1/2* **Darcey**[11] 2009 4-8-12 **68** EddieCreighton 5 61
(Miss Amy Weaver) *sn pushed along in rr: rdn over 2f out: nvr trbld ldrs* **33/1**
-350 **8** *3/4* **Daddy's Gift (IRE)**[26] 1580 4-9-1 **74** PatrickHills(3) 9 65
(R Hannon) *chsd ldrs: rdn over 2f out: outpcd fr over 1f out* **12/1**
105- **9** *3/4* **Speak The Truth (IRE)**[160] 7739 4-8-6 **69** NathanAlison(7) 1 57
(J R Boyle) *s.i.s: sn pushed along in rr: nvr on terms* **50/1**
0-00 **10** *3/4* **Maxwell Hawke (IRE)**[22] 1653 4-8-11 **67** TedDurcan 3 53
(P W Chapple-Hyam) *chsd ldrs: rdn over 1f out: wknd fnl f* **12/1**

1m 10.27s (-0.93) **Going Correction** -0.075s/f (Good) 10 Ran SP% **118.7**
Speed ratings (Par 103): **103,102,99,98,97 96,95,94,93,92**
toteswingers: 1&2 £2.00, 1&3 £8.90, 2&3 £11.60 CSF £10.30 CT £100.98 TOTE £2.60: £1.10, £2.40, £4.30; EX 13.10.
Owner Theobalds Stud **Bred** Theobalds Stud **Trained** Newmarket, Suffolk

FOCUS
No more than a fair handicap run at an ordinary gallop and the first two pulled a few lengths clear in the closing stages. Straightforward form rated around the second, with the winner up 10lb.

2332 FILLIES FOLLOW THE LEADERS IN LETTINGS FILLIES' H'CAP 5f
6:25 (6:25) (Class 5) (0-70,70) 3-Y-O+ **£3,070** (£906; £453) **Stalls High**

Form RPR
-143 **1** **Liberty Lady (IRE)**[19] 1765 3-9-2 **68** PaulDoe 8 82
(D Donovan) *chsd ldrs: led over 1f out: rdn clr* **11/4**[2]
-301 **2** *3 3/4* **Avrilo**[3] 2229 4-8-7 **56** 6ex AshleyMorgan(5) 6 59+
(M S Saunders) *s.i.s: hdwy 1/2-way: rdn over 1f out: styd on same pce ins fnl f* **11/8**[1]
63-4 **3** *nk* **Matterofact (IRE)**[10] 2026 7-9-8 **66** SebSanders 3 68
(M S Saunders) *chsd ldr: led wl over 1f out: sn rdn and hdd: no ex ins fnl f* **5/1**[3]
4-05 **4** *1 1/4* **Littlemisssunshine (IRE)**[122] 241 5-9-8 **66** (t) LiamKeniry 5 64
(T B P Coles) *hld up in tch: plld hrd: rdn over 1f out: edgd lft and no imp fnl f* **16/1**
2-20 **5** *1/2* **South African (USA)**[14] 1929 4-9-2 **60** TomQueally 1 56
(M A Magnusson) *led: rdn and hdd wl over 1f out: wknd ins fnl f* **9/1**
0001 **6** *1 1/4* **White Shift (IRE)**[10] 2026 4-9-5 **70** JohnCavanagh(7) 7 61+
(P Howling) *stmbld s: sn pushed along in rr: wknd over 1f out* **11/1**

57.49 secs (-0.71) **Going Correction** -0.075s/f (Good)
WFA 3 from 4yo+ 8lb 6 Ran SP% **109.7**
Speed ratings (Par 100): **102,96,95,93,92 90**
toteswingers: 1&2 £1.50, 2&3 £2.20 CSF £6.59 CT £14.15 TOTE £3.70: £2.40, £1.10; EX 8.80.
Owner Mark Jones **Bred** Chris Giblett **Trained** Newmarket, Suffolk

FOCUS
A modest handicap run at a decent gallop. The winner is rated up 6lb with the second 6lb off her Goodwood win.
Avrilo Official explanation: jockey said filly missed the break
White Shift(IRE) Official explanation: jockey said filly stumbled leaving stalls

2333 "EXCELLENCE IN EQUINE" LINGFIELD EQUINE VETS (S) STKS 1m 4f (P)
6:55 (6:56) (Class 6) 3-Y-O **£2,047** (£604; £302) **Stalls Low**

Form RPR
0-30 **1** **Lauberhorn**[26] 1578 3-8-12 65 TomQueally 2 63
(Eve Johnson Houghton) *hld up: hdwy over 3f out: rdn to ld over 1f out: clr ins fnl f* **8/1**[3]
44-4 **2** *3 3/4* **Sassanian (IRE)**[40] 1264 3-8-5 58 LewisWalsh(7) 4 57
(Jane Chapple-Hyam) *s.i.s: hld up: hdwy over 1f out: r.o to go 2nd nr fin: nt trble wnr* **5/1**[2]
3630 **3** *hd* **Frameit (IRE)**[12] 1975 3-8-12 61 (b) LiamKeniry 3 57
(J S Moore) *a.p: chsd ldr over 5f out: rdn to ld over 2f out: hdd over 1f out: no ex ins fnl f: lost 2nd nr fin* **11/10**[1]
0064 **4** *2 1/2* **Tallawalla (IRE)**[31] 1466 3-8-7 54 TedDurcan 10 48
(M R Channon) *led: hdd over 10f out: chsd ldrs: rdn over 2f out: no ex fnl f* **5/1**[2]
4450 **5** *1/2* **Always De One**[12] 1982 3-8-7 52 LukeMorris 9 47
(Miss J Feilden) *prom: jnd ldr over 7f out: led over 5f out: rdn and hdd over 2f out: no ex fnl f* **12/1**
6-46 **6** *2 1/2* **Baggsy (IRE)**[94] 589 3-8-0 52 AdamBeschizza(7) 6 43
(Miss J Feilden) *trckd ldrs: racd keenly: rdn over 2f out: wknd over 1f out* **25/1**
46-6 **7** *18* **Spirit Land (IRE)**[40] 1264 3-8-7 51 AshleyMorgan(5) 5 19
(M H Tompkins) *hld up in tch: rdn and wknd over 2f out: eased fnl f* **16/1**
0 **8** *1/2* **Cromwellian**[11] 2011 3-8-12 0 CoryParish 8 18
(M R Channon) *led over 10f out: hdd over 7f out: rdn and wknd over 3f out* **50/1**
2400 **9** *126* **Brave Talk**[20] 1735 3-8-12 60 SebSanders 1 —
(S Kirk) *hld up: pushed along over 5f out: sn wknd and eased: virtually p.u fnl 3f: t.o* **12/1**

2m 36.33s (3.33) **Going Correction** +0.175s/f (Slow) 9 Ran SP% **119.1**
Speed ratings (Par 97): **95,92,92,90,90 88,76,76,—**
toteswingers: 1&2 £5.20, 2&3 £2.30 CSF £49.27 TOTE £20.70: £5.10, £1.60, £1.02; EX 38.90.The winner was bought in for 5,600gns.
Owner R F Johnson Houghton **Bred** Grasshopper 2000 Ltd **Trained** Blewbury, Oxon

FOCUS
A very ordinary seller and one run at a modest gallop. The winner, who raced towards the inside in the straight, was less exposed than most.
Brave Talk Official explanation: jockey said gelding hung badly

2334 T FROST (BAWTRY) RACING SADDLERS MAIDEN STKS (DIV I) 1m (P)
7:30 (7:33) (Class 5) 3-Y-O+ **£2,729** (£806; £403) **Stalls High**

Form RPR
02- **1** **Breakheart (IRE)**[213] 6930 3-9-1 0 LiamKeniry 3 71
(A M Balding) *chsd ldr: rdn over 1f out: styd on u.p to ld post* **10/3**[2]
0- **2** *hd* **Curlew (IRE)**[326] 3485 4-9-10 0 JamesMillman(3) 8 73
(C J Down) *led: rdn over 1f out: hdd post* **33/1**
2 **3** *1* **Significant Move**[35] 1381 3-9-1 0 SteveDrowne 5 68
(R Charlton) *chsd ldrs: rdn and hung lft over 1f out: styd on* **8/13**[1]

4 *1* **Sumerian** 3-8-10 0 .... SebSanders 12 61+
(Sir Mark Prescott) *broke wl: stdd and lost pl sn after s: hld up: racd on outside: shkn up over 1f out: r.o ins fnl f: nvr nr to chal* **20/1**

0 5 *3/4* **Dilys Maud**[15] 1872 3-8-10 0 .... RobertHavlin 1 59
(R Ingram) *prom: rdn over 2f out: styd on u.p* **50/1**

6 *nk* **Conciliatory** 3-8-10 0 .... SaleemGolam 10 58+
(Rae Guest) *s.i.s: hld up: hdwy over 2f out: rdn over 1f out: styd on* **66/1**

0- 7 *hd* **Suzhou**[196] 7288 3-8-10 0 .... PaulDoe 9 58
(D J Coakley) *hld up: hdwy over 2f out: rdn over 1f out: styd on* **50/1**

/ 8 *4* **Cheddar George** 4-9-13 0 .... TedDurcan 7 57+
(B J Meehan) *hld up: hmpd 5f out: styd on fnl f: n.d* **13/2**[3]

40 9 *3* **Craicajack (IRE)**[15] 1870 3-9-1 0 .... EddieCreighton 6 47
(E J Creighton) *prom: rdn over 2f out: wknd fnl f* **50/1**

10 *6* **Falcun** 3-9-1 0 .... KirstyMilczarek 4 33+
(L M Cumani) *dwlt: sn pushed along and a in rr: bhd fnl 3f* **25/1**

11 *1 1/4* **Saffron Hick (IRE)** 3-9-1 0 .... NickyMackay 2 30
(G A Butler) *hld up: rdn 1/2-way: lost tch fnl 3f* **40/1**

1m 40.13s (1.93) **Going Correction** +0.175s/f (Slow)
WFA 3 from 4yo 12lb 11 Ran SP% **119.7**
Speed ratings (Par 103): **97,96,95,94,94 93,93,89,86,80 79**
toteswingers: 1&2 £45.30, 1&3 £1.80, 2&3 £54.80 CSF £105.73 TOTE £4.10: £1.10, £10.10, £1.10; EX 245.00.
Owner J C Smith **Bred** Littleton Stud **Trained** Kingsclere, Hants

FOCUS
With the market leader disappointing, this took less winning than seemed likely and the proximity of the fifth and seventh suggest this bare form is no more than fair at best. The gallop was a modest one and the first three, who filled the first three placings throughout, came down the centre in the straight. It was the slower of the two divisions.
Cheddar George Official explanation: jockey said colt ran green

2335 T FROST (BAWTRY) RACING SADDLERS MAIDEN STKS (DIV II) 1m (P)
8:00 (8:02) (Class 5) 3-Y-O+ £2,729 (£806; £403) Stalls High

Form RPR

4- 1 **Capital Attraction (USA)**[221] 6759 3-9-1 0 .... TomQueally 1 88
(H R A Cecil) *a.p: lft in ld wl over 1f out: styd on wl* **9/2**[2]

-3 2 *2* **Azimuth (USA)**[19] 1769 3-9-1 0 .... GeorgeBaker 5 83
(J Noseda) *chsd ldrs: lft w ev ch wl over 1f out: sn rdn: styd on same pce ins fnl f* **4/6**[1]

4 3 *3 3/4* **Break Serve (USA)**[32] 1450 3-9-1 0 .... TedDurcan 10 74
(W R Swinburn) *hld up: hdwy over 2f out: no ex fnl f* **6/1**[3]

4 *5* **Tariq Too** 3-9-1 0 .... EddieCreighton 9 63+
(D M Simcock) *sn pushed along and rn green in rr: hdwy over 1f out: nvr nrr* **14/1**

4 5 *1 1/2* **Star Prospect (IRE)**[25] 1589 3-9-1 0 .... NickyMackay 7 59
(Luke Comer, Ire) *sn led: hdd over 6f out: rdn over 2f out: wknd over 1f out* **50/1**

6 *1 1/2* **Peaceful Means (IRE)**[6] 7-9-1 0 .... AdamBeschizza(7) 8 54
(J Jay) *s.i.s: sn pushed along and rn green in rr: nvr nrr* **40/1**

0 7 *9* **Farmer Palmer**[19] 1766 3-9-1 0 .... KirstyMilczarek 11 35
(Louise Best) *chsd ldrs: rdn over 2f out: sn wknd* **100/1**

8 *3/4* **Nelson's Bounty** 3-9-1 0 .... LiamKeniry 6 34
(P W D'Arcy) *hld up: rdn over 3f out: wknd over 2f out* **33/1**

9 *1 1/4* **Snow White Feet (IRE)** 3-8-10 0 .... LukeMorris 3 26
(H J L Dunlop) *s.i.s: pushed along in rr: wknd over 3f out* **66/1**

0- 10 *1/2* **Eye Of Eternity**[207] 7096 3-8-10 0 .... SaleemGolam 4 25
(Rae Guest) *mid-div: rdn over 3f out: wknd over 2f out* **66/1**

3- P **Ulzana (IRE)**[253] 5840 4-9-13 0 .... SebSanders 2 —
(Sir Mark Prescott) *chsd ldr: led over 6f out: stl hld the advantage whn broke down wl over 1f out: sn p.u* **14/1**

1m 38.66s (0.46) **Going Correction** +0.175s/f (Slow)
WFA 3 from 4yo+ 12lb 11 Ran SP% **117.1**
Speed ratings (Par 103): **104,102,98,93,91 90,81,80,79,78** —
toteswingers: 1&2 £1.50, 1&3 £3.50, 2&3 £1.90 CSF £7.66 TOTE £4.60: £1.10, £1.30, £1.10; EX 7.90.
Owner H E Sheikh Sultan Bin Khalifa Al Nahyan **Bred** WinStar Farm LLC **Trained** Newmarket, Suffolk

FOCUS
The second division of a fair maiden and this is the stronger race form-wise. The fotrm makes sense at face value. Although the gallop was an ordinary one, this was run about a second and a half quicker than the previous race and the winner and runner-up came down the centre in the straight.

2336 FROMTHESTABLES.COM H'CAP 1m 2f (P)
8:35 (8:37) (Class 6) (0-60,62) 3-Y-O £2,047 (£604; £302) Stalls Low

Form RPR

3262 1 **D'Urberville**[30] 1495 3-9-1 57 .... PaulDoe 14 66
(J R Jenkins) *chsd ldrs: led over 2f out: rdn over 1f out: styd on* **13/2**[3]

00-5 2 *1 1/2* **Baoli**[18] 1795 3-8-12 54 .... KirstyMilczarek 6 60
(L M Cumani) *chsd ldr: ev ch over 2f out: sn rdn: styd on u.p* **11/1**

-450 3 *nk* **Little Meadow (IRE)**[45] 1158 3-7-13 46 .... AmyBaker(5) 5 51
(Miss J Feilden) *chsd ldrs: rdn along fr over 4f out: styd on gamely* **40/1**

06-1 4 *1/2* **It's A Deal (IRE)**[18] 1795 3-8-12 54 .... LukeMorris 11 58
(P Winkworth) *prom: rdn over 2f out: styd on u.p* **15/2**

0-01 5 *1* **Mr Harmoosh (IRE)**[12] 1970 3-9-6 62 .... TomQueally 12 64+
(E F Vaughan) *hld up: nt clr run over 2f out: hdwy over 1f out: r.o: nt trble ldrs* **7/2**[1]

000- 6 *nse* **Sancho Panza**[285] 4839 3-8-8 50 .... SaleemGolam 3 52
(Miss J Feilden) *mid-div: rdn over 2f out: styd on ins fnl f: nt rch ldrs* **33/1**

-000 7 *3/4* **Denton Ryal**[23] 1643 3-8-3 52 .... AdamBeschizza(7) 13 53+
(M E Rimmer) *s.i.s: hld up: r.o ins fnl f: nrst fin* **25/1**

06-0 8 *2 1/2* **Finch Flyer (IRE)**[18] 1796 3-8-10 52 .... LiamKeniry 8 48
(G L Moore) *hld up: rdn over 2f out: r.o ins fnl f: nvr nrr* **20/1**

500- 9 *3* **Cheyenne Chant**[182] 7491 3-8-9 51 .... SebSanders 4 41
(Sir Mark Prescott) *led: rdn and hdd over 2f out: wknd over 1f out* **7/2**[1]

00-0 10 *1 1/4* **Donair**[19] 1766 3-9-1 57 .... (t) TedDurcan 2 44
(P F I Cole) *hld up: hdwy u.p over 1f out: sn wknd* **5/1**[2]

00-0 11 *1/2* **Dance With Chance (IRE)**[29] 1504 3-9-3 59 .... NickyMackay 7 45
(W R Swinburn) *hld up: rdn over 2f out: n.d* **14/1**

5-40 12 *2 3/4* **Rock Of Eire**[81] 762 3-8-9 51 .... (t) EddieCreighton 9 32
(E J Creighton) *hld up: racd keenly: rdn over 2f out: n.d* **40/1**

00-0 13 *3 1/4* **Silk Runner (IRE)**[25] 1589 3-9-4 60 .... GeorgeBaker 1 34
(J W Hills) *chsd ldrs tl rdn and wknd over 2f out* **25/1**

2m 7.78s (1.18) **Going Correction** +0.175s/f (Slow) 13 Ran SP% **121.5**
Speed ratings (Par 97): **102,100,100,100,99 99,98,96,94,93 92,90,88**
toteswingers: 1&2 £12.80, 1&3 £57.80, 2&3 £131.80 CSF £70.34 CT £2646.65 TOTE £6.00: £2.00, £7.70, £18.60; EX 85.70 Place 6 £3.37, Place 5 £1.79.
Owner Lehane Playford **Bred** Llety Stud **Trained** Royston, Herts

FOCUS
A moderate handicap run at just an ordinary gallop and another race on the sand that suited the prominent-racers. The winner raced against the inside rail in the straight. The form has been rated at face value.
T/Plt: £6.30 to a £1 stake. Pool: £48,625.39. 5,618.25 winning tickets. T/Qpdt: £2.20 to a £1 stake. Pool: £4,472.74. 1,461.90 winning tickets. CR

2115 NEWBURY (L-H)
Saturday, May 22

OFFICIAL GOING: Good to firm (8.3)
Wind: Virtually nil Weather: Starting sunny

2337 HILDON AMATEUR RIDERS' H'CAP 1m 2f 6y
6:05 (6:05) (Class 5) (0-70,67) 4-Y-O+ £2,498 (£774; £387; £193) Stalls Low

Form RPR

0324 1 **Mustajed**[5] 2182 9-10-2 60 .... MrPMillman(5) 8 70
(B R Millman) *in tch: swtchd to outside and styd on wl fr over 1f out: led fnl 120yds: r.o strly* **7/2**[1]

2124 2 *1 1/4* **Bajan Pride**[14] 1922 6-10-2 60 .... MrsVFahey(5) 2 68
(R A Fahey) *led 3f: styd trcking ldr tl led again ins fnl 2f: sn shkn up: hdd fnl 120yds and one pce* **4/1**[2]

/50- 3 *2 1/2* **Rock Relief (IRE)**[290] 4650 4-10-5 63 .... MrBMMorris(5) 7 66
(Sir Mark Prescott) *chsd ldrs: led ins fnl 4f: hdd ins fnl 2f: styd on same pce fnl f* **9/2**[3]

000- 4 *3/4* **Django Reinhardt**[254] 5809 4-9-11 53 .... MrDavidTurner(3) 5 54
(Miss S L Davison) *in tch: rdn over 2f out: styd on u.p fr over 1f out and styd on ins fnl f but no imp on ldng trio* **100/1**

340/ 5 *nk* **Shakedown**[551] 7362 5-10-7 60 .... MissSBrotherton 3 60
(Ian Williams) *chsd ldrs: rdn and one pce fr over 2f out* **8/1**

4350 6 *3* **Choral Festival**[19] 1756 4-10-2 62 ow4 .... (p) MrJackSalmon(7) 4 56
(J J Bridger) *chsd ldrs: rdn over 2f out: wknd fnl f* **14/1**

2004 7 *hd* **Barodine**[5] 2167 7-9-11 55 .... MrPPrince(5) 11 49
(R J Hodges) *chsd ldr: led after 3f: hdd ins fnl 4f: wknd appr fnl f* **15/2**

00-0 8 *2 3/4* **Northern Spy (USA)**[37] 1322 6-10-7 67 .... MrJCoffill-Brown(7) 1 56
(S Dow) *chsd ldrs: rdn 3f out: wknd fr 2f out* **16/1**

0-00 9 *3 3/4* **Magic Warrior**[12] 1983 10-9-9 53 oh8 .... MrsSarah-JaneFox(5) 6 34
(J C Fox) *slowly away: in rr: sme prog over 2f out: nvr nr ldrs* **66/1**

0-23 10 *10* **Amroth**[3] 2232 4-10-0 53 oh1 .... (p) MrsEEvans 10 14
(P D Evans) *racd on outside: bhd most of way* **11/2**

000- 11 *29* **Mytivil (IRE)**[345] 2858 4-10-7 65 .... MrNdeBoinville(5) 12 —
(Mrs H S Main) *slowly away: plld hrd and chsd ldrs on outside: wknd 4f out* **16/1**

000 12 *3/4* **Idol Deputy (FR)**[28] 1536 4-9-7 53 oh3 .... (p) MrMTStanley(7) 9 —
(M D I Usher) *bhd fr 1/2-way* **80/1**

2m 7.03s (-1.77) **Going Correction** -0.175s/f (Firm) 12 Ran SP% **120.8**
Speed ratings (Par 103): **100,99,97,96,96 93,93,91,88,80 57,56**
toteswingers: 1&2 £1.40, 1&3 £6.10, 2&3 £6.20 CSF £17.71 CT £65.68 TOTE £6.30: £2.90, £1.10, £3.10; EX 13.40.
Owner Mrs L S Millman **Bred** Shadwell Estate Company Limited **Trained** Kentisbeare, Devon

FOCUS
A moderate handicap, confined to amateur riders, which was run at a decent pace. The form looks sound enough amongst the principals.

2338 BATHWICK TYRES MAIDEN AUCTION FILLIES' STKS 6f 8y
6:35 (6:36) (Class 5) 2-Y-O £3,885 (£1,156; £577; £288) Stalls Centre

Form RPR

1 **Margot Did (IRE)** 2-8-6 0 .... HayleyTurner 6 82+
(M L W Bell) *in tch: hdwy over 2f out: led wl over 1f out: drvn clr ins fnl f: comf* **8/1**[3]

03 2 *2* **Two Feet Of Snow (IRE)**[14] 1930 2-8-4 0 .... FrankieMcDonald 15 72
(R Hannon) *in tch: hdwy fr 2f out: drvn and hung lft fr over 1f out: tk 2nd fnl 120yds but no ch w wnr* **12/1**

3 *3/4* **Elegant Muse** 2-8-6 0 .... EddieAhern 11 72+
(W R Swinburn) *mid-div: rdn over 2f out: hdwy over 1f out: styd on fnl f to take 3rd cl home but no ch w wnr* **16/1**

4 *nk* **Whoateallthepius (IRE)** 2-8-6 0 .... SimonWhitworth 9 71+
(R Hannon) *in tch: pushed along over 2f out: styd on fnl f: nt rch ldrs* **28/1**

2 5 *2 1/4* **Whisper Louise (IRE)**[38] 1294 2-8-6 0 .... JamieMackay 7 64
(Mrs P Sly) *chsd ldrs: rdn and edgd lft 2f out: wknd ins fnl f* **7/2**[1]

6 *1* **Delira (IRE)** 2-8-4 0 .... LiamJones 2 59
(J G Portman) *chsd ldrs: led over 3f out: hdd wl over 1f out: wknd ins fnl f* **20/1**

3 7 *1 1/2* **Looksmart**[8] 2088 2-8-8 0 .... AlanMunro 5 59
(R Hannon) *in tch: hdwy 1/2-way: drvn to chse ldrs 2f out: wknd fnl f* **7/2**[1]

8 *3/4* **Second Encore** 2-8-6 0 .... PaulEddery 12 54
(J S Moore) *s.i.s towards rr: rdn 3f out: sme hdwy 2f out: nvr rchd ldrs* **66/1**

34 9 *3* **Darwin Star**[14] 1930 2-8-1 0 .... SimonPearce(5) 3 45+
(D K Ivory) *led tl hdd over 3f out: hmpd 2f out: wknd fnl f* **16/1**

42 10 *1/2* **Fifth Commandment (IRE)**[12] 1972 2-8-8 0 .... FergusSweeney 13 46+
(J A Osborne) *pressed ldrs: rdn and ev ch 2f out: wkng whn crossed and swtchd rt over 1f out and wknd qckly* **9/2**[2]

0 11 *nk* **Rafella (IRE)**[12] 1972 2-8-8 0 .... JackMitchell 8 45
(R M Beckett) *s.i.s: outpcd tl sme late prog* **14/1**

0 12 *3/4* **Kissing Clara (IRE)**[26] 1577 2-8-1 0 ow4 .... LauraPike(7) 10 43
(J S Moore) *in tch 4f* **66/1**

13 *1 1/2* **One Fat Cat (IRE)** 2-8-4 0 .... NeilChalmers 4 34
(P M Phelan) *chsd ldrs over 3f* **40/1**

14 *7* **Pure Princess (IRE)** 2-8-3 0 .... JackDean(3) 1 15
(P M Phelan) *outpcd* **33/1**

15 *nk* **Fastada (IRE)** 2-8-5 0 .... AndrewHeffernan(3) 16 16
(J G Portman) *slowly away: a in rr* **25/1**

0 16 *4 1/2* **Seas Of Sorrow (IRE)**[8] 2077 2-8-1 0 .... SophieDoyle(5) 14 1
(B W Duke) *slowly away: a in rr* **40/1**

1m 12.14s (-0.86) **Going Correction** -0.175s/f (Firm) 16 Ran SP% **122.7**
Speed ratings (Par 90): **98,95,94,93,90 89,87,86,82,81 81,80,78,69,68 62**
toteswingers: 1&2 £23.60, 1&3 £67.10, 2&3 £65.50 CSF £93.01 TOTE £13.30: £3.60, £2.80, £7.60; EX 164.80.
Owner T Redman And P Philipps **Bred** N Hartery **Trained** Newmarket, Suffolk

FOCUS
An ordinary juvenile maiden, rated around the averages and the time. The winner scored with a bit in hand.

NOTEBOOK
Margot Did(IRE) ran out a clear-cut winner on her debut. She is bred to get a lot further down the line, but clearly has a deal of speed and it will be interesting to see where she is pitched in next as she is evidently a cut above this level. (op 6-1 tchd 12-1)
Two Feet Of Snow(IRE) posted a solid effort on this slight step up in distance and helps to set a sound standard. (op 11-1)
Elegant Muse, related to winners at around this trip, turned in a pleasing debut display and the experience will not be lost on her. (op 14-1)
Whoateallthepius(IRE) ◆, who has plenty of stamina on her dam's side of the pedigree, showed enough to suggest she would benefit for the run and it wouldn't be surprising to see her go very close next time.
Whisper Louise(IRE) probably ran close to her debut form over 5f and is another that helps to set the standard (op 9-2)
Delira(IRE), whose dam was a 7f-1m winner at three, showed enough on this racecourse debut to think she will go close next time. (op 16-1)
Looksmart failed to build on her initial run at Newmarket and can have no excuses. (op 9-2 tchd 3-1)
Darwin Star Official explanation: jockey said filly was unsuited by the good to firm ground
Seas Of Sorrow(IRE) Official explanation: jockey said filly missed the break

2339 RACING UK FOR YOUR PUB 0870 3518834 H'CAP 1m 7y(R)
7:05 (7:07) (Class 4) (0-80,80) 4-Y-O+ £4,533 (£1,348; £674; £336) Stalls Centre

Form RPR
52-1 1 **Play It Sam**24 1617 4-9-2 78 ... EddieAhern 12 92+
(W R Swinburn) *mde all: drvn along wl over 1f out: styd on strly fnl f: unchal* 7/2[1]
60-3 2 1 1/4 **Directorship**28 1530 4-9-1 77 ... DaneO'Neill 1 85
(P R Chamings) *in tch: rdn along fr 3f out: styd on to chse wnr ins fnl f but no imp* 14/1
4404 3 1 **Baylini**9 2044 6-8-13 75 ... HayleyTurner 2 81+
(Ms J S Doyle) *in rr: hdwy and n.m.r fr 2f out: hdwy over 1f out: squeezed through to chse ldrs ins fnl f: kpt on cl home* 12/1
21-1 4 1 1/4 **Compton Blue**10 2024 4-9-2 78 ...(b) RichardHughes 5 81
(R Hannon) *chsd ldrs: wnt 2nd wl over 1f out but no imp: wknd fnl 120yds* 7/2[1]
2416 5 shd **Halsion Chancer**7 2129 6-8-9 76 ... KierenFox(5) 9 79
(J R Best) *plld hrd: in rr on outside tl rdn and hdwy fr 2f out: hung bdly lft fr ins fnl f and no imp on ldrs* 8/1[3]
0241 6 1 3/4 **Kingswinford (IRE)**11 2009 4-9-0 79 ... AndrewHeffernan(3) 6 78
(P D Evans) *chsd ldrs: rdn along fr 3f out: wkng whn hmpd ins fnl f* 9/1
6-44 7 1 1/4 **Edgeworth (IRE)**24 1618 4-8-13 75 ... FergusSweeney 3 71
(B G Powell) *chsd ldrs: rdn 3f out: wknd ins fnl 2f* 12/1
605/ 8 1 3/4 **Acheekyone (IRE)**1078 2476 7-9-2 78 ... LiamJones 8 70
(B J Meehan) *stdd s: in rr: shkn up and no prog over 2f out* 20/1
-103 9 nk **Dingaan (IRE)**38 1306 7-9-4 80 ... JimmyFortune 7 71
(A M Balding) *chsd ldrs: rdn 2f out: sn edgd lft and wknd* 8/1[3]
241- 10 3/4 **Truly Asia (IRE)**213 6937 4-9-1 77 ... AlanMunro 4 66
(R Charlton) *pushed along over 2f out: swtchd lft and a in rr* 11/2[2]

1m 37.28s (97.28) 10 Ran SP% 118.9
toteswingers: 1&2 £17.60, 1&3 £19.10, 2&3 £37.70 CSF £56.84 CT £552.19 TOTE £4.70: £1.80, £4.00, £4.30; EX 53.90.
Owner P W Harris **Bred** Shortgrove Manor Stud **Trained** Aldbury, Herts
FOCUS
This race was run on the recently revived round mile. A modest handicap where it paid to race handy. The winner made all in a fair time and is still progressing.

2340 BATHWICK TYRES MAIDEN STKS 6f 8y
7:40 (7:43) (Class 5) 3-Y-O £3,238 (£963; £481; £240) Stalls Centre

Form RPR
52-2 1 **Strictly Dancing (IRE)**15 1861 3-8-12 85 ... JimmyFortune 2 80+
(A M Balding) *mde all: swtchd rt to stands' rail ins fnl 2f: jnd 1f out: responded wl to press and asserted fnl 100yds* 10/11[1]
4-3 2 1/2 **Poppy Seed**20 1731 3-8-12 0 ... RichardHughes 6 78+
(R Hannon) *chsd ldrs: wnt 2nd ins fnl 2f and sn grabbed stands' rail: drvn to chal 1f out: outpcd fnl 100yds* 6/5[2]
05-5 3 6 **Great Intrigue (IRE)**94 582 3-9-3 70 ... HayleyTurner 3 64
(J S Moore) *chsd ldrs: drvn along over 2f out: easily outpcd by ldng duo fr over 1f out* 22/1
0-0 4 shd **Aleqa**12 1966 3-8-12 0 ... AlanMunro 1 59+
(C F Wall) *stdd in rr tl hdwy to cl on ldrs over 2f out: readily outpcd by ldng duo fr over 1f out* 33/1
05 5 nk **Twice As Nice**11 2003 3-8-10 0 ... CharlesEddery(7) 4 63
(R Hannon) *chsd ldrs: rdn over 2f out: readily outpcd by ldng duo over 1f out* 10/1[3]
0- 6 3 3/4 **Brody's Boy**204 7145 3-9-3 0 ... FergusSweeney 7 51
(G L Moore) *stdd in rr: sme hdwy to get in tch over 2f out: sn rdn: wknd over 1f out* 66/1
0 7 hd **Serious Matters (IRE)**22 1659 3-9-3 0 ... EddieAhern 8 50
(W R Swinburn) *in tch 3f: sn pushed along and bhd* 25/1
8 25 **Picansort** 3-9-3 0 ... JimmyQuinn 5 —
(B R Johnson) *wnt bdly lft s and green: managed to get in tch 1/2-way but stl green and sn dropped away* 33/1

1m 12.08s (-0.92) **Going Correction** -0.175s/f (Firm) 8 Ran SP% 122.5
Speed ratings (Par 99): **99,98,90,90,89 84,84,51**
toteswingers: 1&2 £4.60, 1&3 £1.10, 2&3 £2.30 CSF £2.35 TOTE £1.80: £1.02, £1.10, £4.30; EX 2.20.
Owner J C Smith **Bred** Littleton Stud **Trained** Kingsclere, Hants
FOCUS
This looked a match between the two market leaders and they duly came well clear. The form is rated around the third.

2341 RELYON CLEANING NEWBURY H'CAP 1m 5f 61y
8:15 (8:16) (Class 5) (0-75,75) 4-Y-O+ £2,590 (£770; £385; £192) Stalls Low

Form RPR
0-00 1 **Phoenix Flight (IRE)**15 1863 5-9-8 74 ... RichardHughes 13 82
(H J Evans) *hld up in rr: n.m.r fr 3f out tl hdwy 2f out: swtchd and squeezed between horses 1f out: drvn to ld fnl 120yds: forged clr nr fin* 16/1
212/ 2 1 1/2 **Ski Sunday**399 434 5-9-0 66 ... EddieAhern 12 72
(N J Henderson) *plld hrd and sn stdd in bhd ldrs: chal over 3f out tl ld wl over 2f out: styd on u.p tl hdd and no ex fnl 120yds* 13/8[1]
-002 3 3/4 **Graylyn Ruby (FR)**10 2023 5-8-8 60 ... JimmyQuinn 8 65
(R Dickin) *chsd ldrs: rdn: swtchd lft to ins and styd on to chal over 1f out: kpt on to press for 2nd thrght fnl f but outpcd by wnr fnl 120yds* 11/1
4-62 4 hd **Seventh Hill**24 1623 5-8-8 60 ... FergusSweeney 7 65
(M Blanshard) *in rr: impr fr 4f out: rdn and styd on to press ldrs jst ins fnl f: one pce fnl 120yds* 25/1
4252 5 1/2 **Yemeni Princess (IRE)**19 1755 4-8-12 67 ... RussKennemore(3) 5 71
(B G Powell) *in rr tl hdwy on outside over 2f out: styng on whn pushed rt sn after: styd on fnl f but nvr rchd ldrs* 7/1[2]
1066 6 3/4 **Admirable Duque (IRE)**21 1690 4-9-6 72 ...(p) JamesDoyle 6 75
(D J S Ffrench Davis) *in rr: hdwy fr 3f out: rdn and swtchd rt over 2f out: styd on fnl f but nt rch ldrs* 11/1
536- 7 1 **Beauchamp Xenia**266 5430 4-8-10 62 ... DaneO'Neill 3 63
(H Candy) *stdd s: in rr: tried to improve fr 3f out and continually looking for a run: swtchd rt over 1f out: styd on fnl f but nt rch ldrs* 8/1[3]
20-6 8 nk **Outland (IRE)**19 1755 4-8-5 57 ... HayleyTurner 10 58
(M G Rimell) *led after 3f: kpt narrow advantage tl hdd wl over 2f out: wknd fnl f* 14/1
/422 9 shd **Laconicos (IRE)**12 1980 8-8-3 62 ...(t) LauraPike(7) 4 63
(W B Stone) *t.k.h: in tch: drvn to chse ldrs over 2f out: wknd ins fnl f* 25/1
25-1 10 1 1/4 **Capable Guest (IRE)**11 2013 8-9-0 66 ... AlanMunro 1 65
(M R Channon) *in rr: rdn and sme hdwy over 2f out: wknd 1f out* 25/1
45-4 11 15 **Lapina (IRE)**12 1980 6-8-2 59 ... SimonPearce(5) 9 35
(A Middleton) *led 3f: styd chsng ldrs tl wknd 3f out* 25/1
05/4 12 6 **Corredor Sun (USA)**14 1931 4-8-9 64 ...(p) RobertLButler(3) 2 31
(N A Twiston-Davies) *chsd ldrs 5f: rdn and bhd fnl 5f* 25/1

2m 49.95s (-2.05) **Going Correction** -0.175s/f (Firm) 12 Ran SP% 118.8
Speed ratings (Par 103): **99,98,97,97,97 96,96,95,95,95 85,82**
toteswingers: 1&2 £2.90, 1&3 £20.10, 2&3 £4.50 CSF £40.54 CT £307.87 TOTE £17.90: £3.70, £1.80, £3.40; EX 32.80.
Owner D Ross **Bred** Airlie Stud And Sir Thomas Pilkington **Trained** Broadwas, Worcs
FOCUS
A steadily run handicap that saw a host of chances. They finished well bunched and this looks ordinary form.

2342 DOWNLOAD THE FREE RACING UK IPHONE APP FILLIES' H'CAP 7f (S)
8:45 (8:48) (Class 5) (0-75,77) 3-Y-O+ £2,590 (£770; £385; £192) Stalls Centre

Form RPR
0-00 1 **Ken's Girl**19 1775 6-9-0 62 ... IanMongan 12 75
(W S Kittow) *mde virtually all: shkn up over 1f out: forged clr ins fnl f: unchal* 16/1
35-4 2 2 1/4 **Lady Pattern (IRE)**7 2120 3-8-12 71 ... TonyCulhane 11 74
(P W D'Arcy) *in tch: rdn and hdwy over 1f out: edgd lft but styd on to chse wnr ins fnl f but nvr any ch* 11/4[1]
4-20 3 1/2 **Goolagong (IRE)**22 1654 3-8-11 70 ... JackMitchell 4 72+
(R M Beckett) *hld up in rr: rdn 2f out: swtchd rt and hdwy over 1f out: styd on to take 3rd fnl 120yds to cl on 2nd but nvr any ch w wnr* 15/2[3]
00-3 4 nk **Russian Rave**36 1350 4-9-5 67 ... DaneO'Neill 6 72
(J G Portman) *chsd ldrs: rdn 2f out: one pce ins fnl f* 14/1
-302 5 1 1/4 **Light Dubai (IRE)**19 1775 4-9-2 64 ... AlanMunro 7 66
(M R Channon) *mid-div 1/2-way: drvn and hdwy over 1f out: kpt on same pce ins fnl f* 17/2
0-03 6 hd **Blue Again**22 1661 3-8-12 71 ... EddieAhern 3 68
(W R Swinburn) *chsd ldrs tl wknd ins fnl f* 14/1
-660 7 2 **Al Khimiya (IRE)**16 1850 3-8-11 70 ... HayleyTurner 8 62
(S Woodman) *hld up in rr tl styd on fnl f: nt rch ldrs* 20/1
40-5 8 2 3/4 **Cape Melody**19 1779 4-9-8 70 ... TravisBlock 14 58
(H Morrison) *stdd s: plld hrd towards rr: rdn 2f out: nvr gng pce to rch ldrs* 16/1
03-0 9 1/2 **La Pantera**19 1761 3-9-2 75 ... PatDobbs 5 58
(R Hannon) *t.k.h: stdd towards rr: rdn over 2f out and nvr gng pce to rch ldrs* 12/1
6006 10 3/4 **Ramamara (IRE)**16 1842 3-8-7 69 ... AndrewHeffernan(3) 13 50
(P D Evans) *dipped s: sn chsng ldrs: rdn 3f out: wknd wl over 1f out* 33/1
3-06 11 nk **Katehari (IRE)**26 1582 3-9-0 73 ...(v[1]) JimmyFortune 2 53
(A M Balding) *chsd ldrs: rdn over 2f out: wknd over 1f out* 12/1
10-2 12 1/2 **Tarita (IRE)**10 2025 3-9-4 77 ... RichardHughes 1 56
(R Hannon) *chsd ldrs tl wknd wl over 1f out* 3/1[2]
303- 13 3 1/4 **Blue Sparkle (IRE)**261 5604 3-8-9 68 ... JimmyQuinn 10 38
(Mrs A J Perrett) *outpcd* 20/1

1m 25.15s (-0.55) **Going Correction** -0.175s/f (Firm)
WFA 3 from 4yo+ 11lb 13 Ran SP% 126.9
Speed ratings (Par 100): **96,93,92,92,91 90,88,85,84,84 83,83,79**
toteswingers: 1&2 £43.60, 1&3 £53.50, 2&3 £2.80 CSF £62.04 CT £394.33 TOTE £26.70: £6.00, £1.10, £3.20; EX 132.60 Place 6 £73.78, Place 5 £48.88.
Owner Midd Shire Racing **Bred** D R Tucker **Trained** Blackborough, Devon
FOCUS
A wide-open fillies' handicap. The form is modest but seems sound enough.
Tarita(IRE) Official explanation: jockey said filly ran too free
T/Plt: £113.90 to a £1 stake. Pool: £75,956.45. 486.69 winning tickets. T/Qpdt: £29.10 to a £1 stake. Pool: £4,437.74. 112.70 winning tickets. ST

2095 YORK (L-H)
Saturday, May 22

OFFICIAL GOING: Good to firm (8.4)
Wind: Virtually nil Weather: Hot and sunny

2343 SPORTINGBET.COM CLAIMING STKS 1m 4f
2:05 (2:06) (Class 4) 4-Y-O+ £6,540 (£1,946; £972; £485) Stalls Centre

Form RPR
-146 1 **Trip The Light**8 2071 5-9-0 90 ...(v) LeeTopliss(7) 5 89
(R A Fahey) *hld up in tch: hdwy 4f out: led wl over 2f out: rdn clr over 1f out: kpt on strly ins fnl f* 5/4[1]
2-06 2 1 **Saloon (USA)**17 1828 6-8-11 69 ...(p) IvaMilickova 9 77
(Jane Chapple-Hyam) *hld up towards rr: hdwy 4f out: rdn to chse ldrs 2f out: drvn and styd on to chse wnr ins fnl f and ch tl no ex towards fin* 16/1
5105 3 2 1/2 **Kames Park (IRE)**10 2031 8-8-12 79 ... JimmyQuinn 4 74
(R C Guest) *hld up in rr: hdwy 3f out: effrt 2f out: rdn to chse ldrs over 1f out: sn drvn and one pce ins fnl f* 7/1
-000 4 3 3/4 **Mull Of Dubai**8 2096 7-8-13 89 ... MichaelGeran(3) 3 72
(D Nicholls) *hld up: hdwy on inner over 4f out: rdn to chse ldrs 2f out: drvn and one pce appr fnl f* 9/2[3]
-231 5 nk **Royal Straight**14 1919 5-8-11 70 ... TonyHamilton 8 67
(R A Fahey) *in tch: hdwy over 4f out: rdn to chse wnr over 2f out: drvn and wknd over 1f out* 10/3[2]

56-0 **6** *2 ¼* **Maybeme**[19] 1751 4-8-11 64 .... DuranFentiman 7 63
(N Bycroft) *hld up in rr: hdwy on outer wl over 3f out: rdn to chse ldrs 2f out: wknd over 1f out* **20/1**

06-0 **7** *30* **Daltaban (FR)**[18] 1803 6-8-5 45 .... BillyCray(5) 6 14
(P Salmon) *chsd ldrs: rdn along over 5f out: sn wknd* **150/1**

64 **8** *23* **Flockton Tobouggie**[7] 2131 4-8-9 0 .... TomEaves 10 —
(M W Easterby) *in tch: hdwy to chse clr ldng pair after 3f: rdn along 5f out and sn wknd* **33/1**

0-00 **9** *3 ½* **Sri Kuantan (IRE)**[21] 1689 6-8-10 60 .... (tp) SteveDrowne 1 —
(R C Guest) *t.k.h: chsd clr ldr tl led wl over 3f out: rdn and hdd wl over 2f out: wknd qckly* **50/1**

0565 **10** *2 ¾* **Border Fox**[29] 1507 7-8-9 45 .... (t) JoeFanning 2 —
(P Salmon) *plld hrd and sn clr: rdn along over 4f out: sn hdd & wknd qckly* **66/1**

2m 30.78s (-2.42) **Going Correction** -0.075s/f (Good) **10** Ran SP% **115.9**
Speed ratings (Par 105): **105,104,102,100,99 98,78,63,60,58**
toteswingers:1&2:£6.20, 1&3:£2.70, 2&3:£11.20 CSF £23.87 TOTE £2.20: £1.10, £4.30, £2.10; EX 22.20 Trifecta £81.10 Pool: £454.44 - 4.14 winning units..
Owner The Matthewman One Partnership **Bred** Darley **Trained** Musley Bank, N Yorks

FOCUS
A good claimer run at a strong pace. A repeat of his recent efforts probably sufficed for the winner.

2344 SPORTINGBET.COM CONDITIONS STKS 7f

2:35 (2:35) (Class 3) 3-Y-O+ **£8,095** (£2,408; £1,203; £601) **Stalls** Low

Form RPR

5-01 **1** **Harrison George (IRE)**[39] 1272 5-9-2 108 .... TonyHamilton 6 112
(R A Fahey) *chsd ldr: rdn along and sltly outpcd wl over 1f out: drvn and kpt on ins fnl f to ld nr fin* **5/2**[2]

403 **2** *nk* **Marching (AUS)**[14] 1904 6-9-2 107 .... RichardHills 4 111
(Mahmood Al Zarooni) *led: rdn and qcknd 2f out: jnd and drvn ent fnl f: sn edgd lft: hdd and no ex nr fin* **4/1**[3]

0110 **3** *nk* **Sirocco Breeze**[56] 1021 5-9-2 115 .... FrankieDettori 2 110
(Saeed Bin Suroor) *hld up in tch: hdwy over 2f out: swtchd lft and effrt to join ldr ent fnl f: sn rdn and ev ch tl nt qckn towards fin* **11/8**[1]

134- **4** *4 ½* **City Style (USA)**[203] 7186 4-9-2 109 .... JoeFanning 5 98
(Mahmood Al Zarooni) *chsd ldng pair: rdn along on inner wl over 2f out: sn edgd lft and wknd* **7/1**

5-00 **5** *2* **Able Master (IRE)**[13] 1955 4-9-2 100 .... SteveDrowne 3 93
(J R Gask) *dwlt: hdwy to chse ldrs 1/2-way: rdn along wl over 2f out: sn wknd* **12/1**

1m 24.0s (-1.30) **Going Correction** -0.075s/f (Good) **5** Ran SP% **110.9**
Speed ratings (Par 107): **104,103,103,98,95**
CSF £12.65 TOTE £2.90: £1.30, £2.30; EX 11.80.
Owner P D Smith Holdings Ltd **Bred** R P Ryan **Trained** Musley Bank, N Yorks

FOCUS
A quality conditions contest. The pace set by Marching didn't seem that strong, although the final time was only half a second above standard. The winner showed his Pontefract win didn't flatter him and the second is getting closer to his old Australian form.

NOTEBOOK
Harrison George(IRE) looked an improved performer when taking a 1m handicap by 7l off a mark of 95 last time and he confirmed that to be the case with a narrow success in this better company. He took a while to get on top, suggesting he won't mind going back up in trip, and he'll be worth his place in Listed company. (tchd 9-4)
Marching(AUS) was left alone in front for much of the way and can have no excuse. (op 9-2)
Sirocco Breeze, who enjoyed a successful spell on synthetics in Dubai earlier in the year, wasn't quite at his best after almost two months off. A naturally free-going type, the small field probably didn't suit and he was a bit keen early on. He briefly looked the winner when produced with his challenge in the straight, but his effort flattened out near the line. Although he could make no impression in the Al Quoz Sprint on his only previous try over 6f, on this evidence he will be well worth another shot over a sprint trip. (op 6-4)
City Style(USA), a non-runner when due to appear at Meydan in March, was having his first start for this trainer after an absence of 203 days. This galloping track promised to suit (he lost his action at Newmarket when last seen), but he still looked most ungainly, and as such, never appeared likely to get involved. He might come on for this, but looks best watched for the time being. (tchd 8-1)
Able Master(IRE) had plenty to find at the weights and he never threatened after starting slowly. Official explanation: jockey said gelding reared as stalls opened (tchd 11-1)

2345 STOWE FAMILY LAW LLP GRAND CUP (LISTED RACE) 1m 6f

3:10 (3:10) (Class 1) 4-Y-O+
£22,708 (£8,608; £4,308; £2,148; £1,076; £540) **Stalls** Low

Form RPR

54-2 **1** **Tactic**[28] 1529 4-9-0 103 .... JimmyQuinn 1 119+
(J L Dunlop) *trckd ldrs: hdwy on bit 4f out: led 2f out: shkn up and sn clr: easily* **10/1**

20-3 **2** *14* **Munsef**[15] 1859 8-9-0 110 .... TomEaves 6 99
(Ian Williams) *midfield: hdwy on inner 4f out: rdn to chse wnr wl over 1f out: sn drvn and kpt on: no ch w wnr* **13/2**[3]

00-0 **3** *5* **Macarthur**[20] 1724 6-9-0 101 .... ShaneKelly 9 92
(Jane Chapple-Hyam) *trckd ldr: led over 4f out: rdn along and hdd 2f out: sn drvn and hung lft: wknd wl over 1f out* **12/1**

13- **4** *nse* **Shahwardi (FR)**[47] 1135 4-9-3 103 .... SteveDrowne 5 95
(J R Gask) *plld hrd: hld up in rr: hdwy over 4f out: pushed along and sltly hmpd 3f out: chsd ldrs over 2f out: sn rdn and one pce* **20/1**

26-3 **5** *3* **Starfala**[14] 1898 5-8-9 105 .... JoeFanning 7 83
(P F I Cole) *hld up in rr: hdwy over 4f out: rdn 3f out: drvn and kpt on fnl 2f: n.d* **8/1**

/1-2 **6** *28* **Aajel (USA)**[24] 1615 6-9-0 106 .... RichardHills 4 49
(M P Tregoning) *set stdy pce: pushed along and hdd over 4f out: rdn over 3f out and sn hung lft: sn wknd and eased fnl 2f* **9/4**[1]

-300 **7** *18* **Mojave Moon**[24] 1615 4-9-0 105 .... (v) NickyMackay 8 23
(Mahmood Al Zarooni) *trckd ldrs: effrt over 4f out: sn rdn and btn: bhd and eased 3f out* **33/1**

11-1 **8** *1 ¼* **Highland Glen**[100] 512 4-9-0 106 .... TonyHamilton 3 22
(Saeed Bin Suroor) *t.k.h: hld up towards rr: pushed along 6f out: outpcd 4f out: sn bhd and eased* **8/1**

114- **9** *¾* **Caracciola (GER)**[296] 4457 13-9-0 105 .... DavidAllan 11 21
(N J Henderson) *chsd ldrs: rdn along and lost pl 1/2-way: bhd and eased fnl 3f* **10/1**

2-12 **10** *3 ½* **Age Of Reason (UAE)**[86] 712 5-9-0 109 .... FrankieDettori 10 16
(Saeed Bin Suroor) *hld up towards rr: sme hdwy over 4f out: sn rdn and btn: eased 3f out* **5/1**[2]

2m 54.96s (-5.24) **Going Correction** -0.075s/f (Good) **10** Ran SP% **116.6**
Speed ratings (Par 111): **111,103,100,100,98 82,72,71,70,68**
toteswingers:1&2:£9.00, 1&3:£99.80, 2&3:£20.70 CSF £73.52 TOTE £12.60: £3.90, £2.00, £3.90; EX 59.00 Trifecta £512.90 Part won. Pool: £693.11 - 0.20 winning units..
Owner Hamdan Al Maktoum **Bred** Shadwell Estate Company Limited **Trained** Arundel, W Sussex

FOCUS
In common with some other races on the card there was a surprise outcome to this decent-looking Listed contest, and in truth it's a difficult result to explain. The winner clearly improved but this is not form to take literally.

NOTEBOOK
Tactic pulled no less than 14l clear, but such a performance could not have been predicted, as his form was nothing out of the ordinary, and he was passed over by Richard Hills. The final time - a new course record - would seem to suggest this wasn't a fluke, although that might need treating with a little caution, as the rail had been moved out six metres from the 1m1f point to the entrance to the home straight, and in races over 1m or further, distances were 11 yards shorter than advertised. The winner was just 1-11 coming into this, but in fairness he had recorded a career-best RPR on his reappearance, and whatever way you look at this, it's clear he's very much improving. It's true a number of his rivals underperformed, but it was hard not to be taken by the ease with which he travelled before really finding for pressure, and for now at least this looks a performance to buy into. He apparently finished distressed, suggesting he had a hard race, but provided he's none the worse, he certainly deserves his place back in Group company.
Munsef, third in the Ormonde Stakes on his reappearance, seemed to run his race but he was no match whatsoever for the winner. (op 11-2)
Macarthur is nowhere near as good as he once was and, although managing third, he was still beaten a total of 19l. (op 16-1)
Shahwardi(FR), who was having his first start since leaving Alain de Royer-Dupre, played up a bit before the start and then was keen in the race itself. He was ultimately well held under his penalty.
Starfala is on a lengthy losing run and never featured. (op 7-1)
Aajel(USA), Hamdan Al Maktoum's apparent first string, was nowhere near the form he showed when runner-up in the Sagaro on his reappearance. Official explanation: trainer said gelding was unsuited by the good to firm ground (op 11-4)
Highland Glen Official explanation: jockey said gelding ran too free
Caracciola(GER), returning from an absence of 296 days, never looked like following up last year's success in this race and offered little. (op 11-1)
Age Of Reason(UAE) Official explanation: jockey said gelding lost its action

2346 SPORTINGBET.COM SPRINT (H'CAP) 5f

3:40 (3:40) (Class 2) (0-105,101) 3-Y-O+ **£25,904** (£7,708; £3,852; £1,924) **Stalls** High

Form RPR

0-32 **1** **Hamish McGonagall**[17] 1822 5-9-1 92 .... DavidAllan 11 107
(T D Easterby) *cl up: led 2f out: rdn and qcknd ent fnl f: kpt on wl* **7/2**[1]

1-01 **2** *1 ¼* **Ziggy Lee**[8] 2094 4-8-3 83 .... WilliamCarson(3) 15 94+
(S C Williams) *hmpd s and towards rr: hdwy over 1f out: n.m.r and swtchd rt ent fnl f: sn rdn and styd on to chse wnr: no imp towards fin: stmbld and fell after line* **10/1**

0-40 **3** *1* **Masta Plasta (IRE)**[17] 1822 7-9-7 101 .... MichaelGeran(3) 5 108
(D Nicholls) *prom: effrt and cl up wl over 1f out: sn rdn and ev ch tl drvn and one pce ins fnl f* **14/1**

-052 **4** *¾* **Feelin Foxy**[17] 1827 6-8-3 80 .... JoeFanning 14 84
(J G Given) *sltly hmpd s: midfield: hdwy to chse ldrs 2f out: sn rdn and edgd rt over 1f out: drvn and kpt on wl fnl f* **28/1**

-563 **5** *nk* **Indian Trail**[7] 2136 10-8-3 85 .... (b) BillyCray(5) 3 88
(D Nicholls) *midfield: hdwy 2f out: rdn to chse ldrs over 1f out: swtchd lft and drvn ent fnl f: kpt on* **14/1**

-134 **6** *shd* **Tabaret**[7] 2135 7-8-9 89 .... MichaelStainton(3) 2 92
(R M Whitaker) *prom: effrt 2f out and cl up: rdn and ev ch ent fnl f: sn drvn and one pce* **8/1**[3]

0-30 **6** *dht* **Rasaman (IRE)**[7] 2136 6-8-1 81 .... (v) KellyHarrison(3) 4 87+
(J S Goldie) *sn outpcd and bhd: hdwy over 1f out: styng on whn nt clr run ins fnl f: kpt on wl towards fin* **16/1**

0-6 **8** *½* **Secret Millionaire (IRE)**[9] 2058 3-8-1 89 .... Louis-PhilippeBeuzelin(3) 8 87
(Patrick Morris) *chsd ldrs: hdwy 2f out: sn rdn and kpt on same pce ent fnl f* **16/1**

0-54 **9** *shd* **River Falcon**[9] 2054 10-8-7 84 .... JimmyQuinn 6 85
(J S Goldie) *dwlt sn outpcd and bhd: hdwy over 1f out: nt clr run and swtchd lft jst ins fnl f: rdn and fin strly* **12/1**

130- **10** *½* **Invincible Lad (IRE)**[210] 7015 6-8-8 85 .... ShaneKelly 16 84
(E J Alston) *wnt lft s: chsd ldrs: hdwy 2f out: sn rdn and edgd lft: drvn and wknd appr fnl f* **20/1**

0-55 **11** *hd* **Sohraab**[17] 1822 6-9-5 96 .... (v1) TravisBlock 1 94
(H Morrison) *chsd ldrs on outer: rdn along 2f out: drvn and wknd over 1f out* **12/1**

4213 **12** *½* **Discanti (IRE)**[7] 2134 5-8-7 84 .... (t) DuranFentiman 7 80
(T D Easterby) *midfield: effrt and hdwy whn n.m.r over 1f out: sn rdn and no imp* **12/1**

03-1 **13** *½* **Johannes (IRE)**[9] 2054 7-9-3 101 .... LeeTopliss(7) 10 95
(R A Fahey) *towards rr: hdwy 1/2-way: rdn along 2f out: sme hdwy whn n.m.r ent fnl f: n.d* **6/1**[2]

604- **14** *2 ½* **Kingdom Of Light**[231] 6486 3-8-13 98 .... TonyHamilton 9 80
(J Howard Johnson) *chsd ldrs: rdn along over 2f out: grad wknd* **18/1**

-000 **15** *2 ¼* **Rievaulx World**[9] 2054 4-8-8 85 .... (p) TomEaves 13 62
(K A Ryan) *slt ld: rdn along and hdd 2f out: wknd over 1f out* **25/1**

20-0 **16** *8* **Cheveton**[36] 1353 6-9-5 96 .... FrankieDettori 12 45
(R J Price) *dwlt: a in rr* **12/1**

57.75 secs (-1.55) **Going Correction** -0.075s/f (Good)
WFA 3 from 4yo+ 8lb **16** Ran SP% **129.9**
Speed ratings (Par 109): **109,107,105,104,103 103,103,102,102,101 101,100,99,95,92 79**
toteswingers:1&2:£5.50, 1&3:£12.00, 2&3:£61.90 CSF £39.65 CT £483.57 TOTE £4.90: £1.60, £2.00, £4.40, £4.80; EX 33.40 Trifecta £601.90 Pool: £1,789.60 - 2.20 winning units..
Owner Reality Partnerships I **Bred** J P Coggan And Whitsbury Manor Stud **Trained** Great Habton, N Yorks

FOCUS
A good, competitive sprint handicap. Solid form with the winner back to his best.

NOTEBOOK
Hamish McGonagall, who was racing off the same mark as when runner-up at Chester on his reappearance, which was 6lb lower than when he ran fourth in this last year, won in decent style. He's now likely to be aimed at the Scottish Sprint Cup at Musselburgh in June, a race in which he finished fourth last season off a mark of 98. (op 4-1)
Ziggy Lee ran a good race off a mark 5lb higher than when successful at Newmarket last time. Having lost ground at the start, he took a while to get going, but he finished strongly once switched to the near-side rail in the latter stages. Shortly after the line he stumbled and fell, but fortunately he was soon back on his feet, appearing none the worse. (op 9-1 tchd 8-1)
Masta Plasta(IRE), 5lb higher than when winning this race in 2008, showed plenty of speed and didn't seem to have any excuses.
Feelin Foxy has yet to win off a mark this high but she ran respectably.
Indian Trail is usually seen at his absolute best when the leaders overdo it a bit, which wasn't the case this time.
Rasaman(IRE), with the visor re-fitted, got going too late but would still have finished slightly closer with a better run. Official explanation: jockey said gelding was denied a clear run
Invincible Lad(IRE) Official explanation: jockey said gelding jumped left on leaving stalls
Johannes(IRE) was disappointing off a 6lb higher mark than when winning over C&D on his previous start. Official explanation: jockey said gelding was denied a clear run (op 7-1)

Cheveton Official explanation: jockey said gelding was unsuited by the good to firm ground

2347 YORKSHIRE REGIMENT E B F MAIDEN FILLIES' STKS 6f
4:15 (4:15) (Class 3) 2-Y-O **£6,605** (£1,965; £982; £490) **Stalls** High

Form RPR
3 **1** **Singapore Lilly (IRE)**[12] 1957 2-9-0 0 SamHitchcott 2 75
(M R Channon) *trckd ldng pair on outer: hdwy 2f out and sn cl up: rdn and chal ent fnl f: kpt on to ld last 50yds* **3/1**[1]
03 **2** *hd* **Loves Theme (IRE)**[14] 1905 2-8-11 0 MarcHalford(3) 5 74
(A Bailey) *cl up: led 2f out: rdn over 1f out: drvn ins fnl f: hdd and no ex last 50yds* **9/2**[3]
3 *3 ¾* **Nicola's Dream** 2-9-0 0 TonyHamilton 4 63
(R A Fahey) *trckd ldrs: hdwy 2f out: rdn to chse ldng pair over 1f out: ch ent fnl f: kpt on same pce* **3/1**[1]
4 *1 ¾* **Paper Dreams (IRE)** 2-9-0 0 TomEaves 3 58+
(K A Ryan) *dwlt: sn in tch: effrt 1/2-way and chsd ldrs tl rdn and wknd wl over 1f out* **7/2**[2]
5 *2 ½* **Slatey Hen (IRE)** 2-9-0 0 JamesDoyle 1 50
(A J McCabe) *in tch: swtchd lft and hdwy to chse ldrs 2f out: sn rdn and wknd over 1f out* **10/1**
0 **6** *4* **Classic Gem (IRE)**[27] 1541 2-9-0 0 FrankieDettori 7 38
(Tom Dascombe) *led: rdn along and hdd 2f out: grad wknd* **7/1**

1m 12.84s (0.94) **Going Correction** -0.075s/f (Good) **6** Ran SP% **112.0**
Speed ratings (Par 94): **90,89,84,82,79 73**
toteswingers:1&2:£3.20, 1&3:£1.10, 2&3:£2.70 CSF £16.58 TOTE £3.40: £1.90, £2.30; EX 19.60.
Owner Mrs T Burns **Bred** Troy Cullen **Trained** West Ilsley, Berks

FOCUS
A non-bonus fillies' maiden and the form looks pretty average for the track. The first two stepped forward from their debuts.

NOTEBOOK
Singapore Lilly(IRE) confirmed the promise she showed when third on her debut at Brighton. She's not that big, but she has a good attitude and should be competitive in ordinary nurseries in due course. (op 11-4)
Loves Theme(IRE) improved on her debut effort when third at Haydock last time and this was another respectable performance. She was nicely clear of the remainder. (op 4-1)
Nicola's Dream, a £24,000 sister to 1m-1m2f winner Miss Sophisticat, fared best of the newcomers. She travelled okay, but was one paced under pressure and looks in need of further. (op 11-4)
Paper Dreams(IRE), a 15,000gns purchase, didn't offer a great deal but could improve for the experience. (op 5-1)
Slatey Hen(IRE), an £18,000 half-sister to very useful sprinter Masta Plasta, was easy to back and never featured. (op 9-1)

2348 SPORTINGBET.COM H'CAP 7f
4:50 (4:51) (Class 3) (0-90,88) 3-Y-O **£6,799** (£2,023; £1,011; £505) **Stalls** Low

Form RPR
2-21 **1** **Dherghaam (IRE)**[18] 1804 3-9-3 **84** RichardHills 3 98+
(E A L Dunlop) *mde most: pushed along and qckND clr appr fnl f: easily* **11/8**[1]
0-43 **2** *5* **William Morgan (IRE)**[20] 1718 3-8-11 **78** TonyHamilton 7 76
(R A Fahey) *chsd wnr: rdn along and sltly outpcd over 2f out: kpt on u.p ins fnl f: no ch w wnr* **4/1**[2]
000- **3** *1 ¾* **Step In Time (IRE)**[237] 6317 3-8-11 **78** JoeFanning 4 71
(M Johnston) *t.k.h: trckd ldng pair: hdwy 3f out: rdn along and ch 2f out: drvn over 1f out and sn one pce* **13/2**[3]
241- **4** *nk* **Tatiana Romanova (USA)**[206] 7114 3-8-10 **77** FranciscoDaSilva 2 69
(R A Fahey) *t.k.h: trckd ldrs on inner: effrt 3f out and sn rdn along: drvn wl over 1f out and sn btn* **11/1**
0-50 **5** *2 ½* **Exceedingly Bold**[10] 2028 3-9-7 **88** FrankieDettori 9 73
(Miss Gay Kelleway) *t.k.h: hld up in tch: hdwy 3f out: rdn along 2f out and sn no imp* **8/1**
4651 **6** *2* **Thrust Control (IRE)**[9] 2049 3-8-9 **76** TomEaves 6 56
(B Ellison) *plld hrd: hld up in rr: hdwy 3f out: rdn over 2f out and sn wknd* **7/1**
05-5 **7** *1 ½* **Ishtar Gate (USA)**[28] 1518 3-8-11 **78** ShaneKelly 8 54
(P F I Cole) *hld up: hdwy 1/2-way: rdn along over 2f out and sn wknd* **16/1**

1m 25.13s (-0.17) **Going Correction** +0.075s/f (Good) **7** Ran SP% **113.3**
Speed ratings (Par 103): **103,97,95,94,92 89,88**
toteswingers:1&2:£1.80, 1&3:£3.70, 2&3:£3.70 CSF £6.81 CT £25.27 TOTE £2.50: £1.80, £2.30; EX 6.00 Trifecta £50.30 Pool: £415.31 - 6.11 winning units..
Owner Hamdan Al Maktoum **Bred** Shadwell Estate Company Limited **Trained** Newmarket, Suffolk

FOCUS
An ordinary-looking handicap for the grade. The easy winner is rated up 11lb but this is one of several funny results on the card and it may not be form to take too literally.

NOTEBOOK
Dherghaam(IRE) readily followed up his recent Catterick maiden success and looks a pretty useful type. A hefty rise in the weights is inevitable, but he is clearly most progressive and is one to keep on side. (op 2-1 tchd 85-40 in a place)
William Morgan(IRE) coped with the drop back in trip from 1m, but the winner was much too good. (op 10-3)
Step In Time(IRE), returning from 237 days off, was a little keen early and found only the one pace for pressure. He's entitled to come on for this. (op 8-1 tchd 6-1)
Tatiana Romanova(USA) looked a fair type when winning her maiden at Musselburgh last October, but she appeared the stable second string for her return to action and she was duly well held. (op 13-2)

2349 BOLLINGER CHAMPAGNE CHALLENGE SERIES H'CAP (GENTLEMAN AMATEURS) (IN ASSOC WITH DAILY TELEGRAPH) 1m 4f
5:25 (5:25) (Class 4) (0-80,79) 4-Y-O+ **£6,308** (£1,956; £977; £488) **Stalls** Centre

Form RPR
2350 **1** **Sedgwick**[11] 1996 8-10-2 **65** MrCAHarris(5) 10 79
(S A Harris) *in tch: hdwy 4f out: effrt to chse ldr 2f out: rdn to chal wl over 1f out: led ent fnl f: kpt on wl towards fin* **20/1**
23-1 **2** *½* **Mr Freddy (IRE)**[24] 1631 4-11-7 **79** MrMSeston 11 92
(R A Fahey) *hld up towards rr: hdwy on inner 4f out: effrt to ld over 2f out: jnd and rdn wl over 1f out: drvn and hdd ent fnl f: rallied u.p towards fin* **13/8**[1]
6-02 **3** *8* **Red Kestrel (USA)**[14] 1925 5-11-3 **75** MrJoshuaMoore 12 75
(K A Ryan) *hld up in rr: hdwy on outer 4f out: rdn to chse ldrs 2f out: drvn over 1f out and kpt on same pce* **5/1**
00-6 **4** *hd* **Middlemarch (IRE)**[10] 1098 10-10-2 **65** (v) MrJMQuinlan(5) 4 65
(J S Goldie) *trckd ldng pair: hdwy over 3f out: rdn along wl over 2f out: drvn and kpt on same pce fr wl over 1f out* **16/1**
0603 **5** *1* **Bavarica**[8] 2081 8-10-9 **70** MrRBirkett(3) 9 68
(Miss J Feilden) *hld up in midfield: hdwy 4f out: rdn to chse ldrs over 2f out: sn drvn and kpt on same pce* **16/1**
6300 **6** *3 ¼* **Sea Land (FR)**[14] 1919 6-10-0 **65** oh13 MrJohnWilley(7) 3 58
(B Ellison) *hld up in rr: sme hdwy 3f out: rdn along over 2f out: n.d* **28/1**
0-20 **7** *¾* **Baltimore Jack (IRE)**[19] 1751 6-11-1 **73** MrSWalker 6 65
(T D Walford) *led: hdd over 7f out: rdn along 4f out: drvn over 2f out and grad wknd* **4/1**[2]
5115 **8** *15* **Jeer (IRE)**[9] 2060 6-11-7 **79** (b) MrOGreenall 5 47
(M W Easterby) *trckd ldr: led over 7f out: rdn along over 3f out: hdd wl over 2f out and sn wknd* **9/2**[3]
004 **9** *12* **Carnac (IRE)**[14] 1925 4-10-7 **70** MrCRNelson(5) 7 19
(J S Wainwright) *chsd ldrs: rdn along over 4f out and sn wknd* **14/1**

2m 33.15s (-0.05) **Going Correction** -0.075s/f (Good) **9** Ran SP% **119.6**
Speed ratings (Par 105): **97,96,91,91,90 88,87,77,69**
toteswingers:1&2:£5.50, 1&3:£5.80, 2&3:£2.70 CSF £54.91 CT £203.64 TOTE £37.80: £6.40, £1.30, £1.60; EX 160.60 TRIFECTA Not won. Place 6 £134.23, Place 5 £75.95.
Owner Wilf Hobson **Bred** G And Mrs Middlebrook **Trained** Carburton, Notts

FOCUS
A fair amateur riders' handicap. The first two finished clear and the form could be rated higher.
T/Plt: £73.70. Pool:£117,923.42 - 1,167.07 winning tickets T/Qpdt: £19.40. Pool:£4,667.55 - 177.90 winning tickets JR

2350 - 2351a (Foreign Racing) - See Raceform Interactive

1785 CURRAGH (R-H)
Saturday, May 22

OFFICIAL GOING: Good to firm

2352a T P WATERS EUROPEAN BREEDERS FUND MARBLE HILL STKS (LISTED RACE) 5f
2:40 (2:42) 2-Y-O **£25,884** (£7,566; £3,584; £1,194)

RPR
1 **Samuel Morse (IRE)**[41] 1243 2-9-1 JMurtagh 4 100+
(A P O'Brien, Ire) *trckd ldrs: 4th 1/2-way: nt clr run over 1f out: rdn to chal ins fnl f: kpt on wl to ld cl home* **9/4**[1]
2 *nk* **Purple Glow (IRE)**[6] 2146 2-8-12 KJManning 2 95
(J S Bolger, Ire) *hld up towards rr: swtchd 2f out: prog in 4th 1 1/2f out: rdn to ld over 1f out: kpt on: hdd cl home* **12/1**
3 *3* **So Stylish (USA)**[27] 1558 2-8-12 JAHeffernan 6 84
(A P O'Brien, Ire) *setttled bhd ldrs: 5th 1/2-way: rdn in 7th 2f out: 6th 1f out: kpt on fnl f* **7/1**
4 *shd* **High Award (IRE)**[22] 1674 2-9-1 WMLordan 8 87
(T Stack, Ire) *settled bhd ldrs: 6th 1/2-way: rdn 2f out: 5th 1f out: kpt on fnl f* **10/1**
5 *1 ¼* **Moment Of Weakness (IRE)**[14] 1935 2-9-1 FMBerry 1 82
(Mrs John Harrington, Ire) *led and disp: rdn and hdd over 1f out: no ex and kpt on one pce* **5/2**[2]
6 *3 ½* **Lightening Thief (IRE)**[22] 1674 2-9-1 RPCleary 5 70
(W McCreery, Ire) *prom: cl 3rd 1/2-way: rdn to chal over 1f out: no ex fnl f and wknd* **9/2**[3]
7 *3* **Jolly Snake (IRE)**[36] 1367 2-9-1 DPMcDonogh 7 59
(Gerard O'Leary, Ire) *prom on outer and disp: cl 2nd 1/2-way: rdn and wknd 1 1/2f out* **9/1**
8 *1 ¼* **Foolproof (IRE)**[19] 1785 2-9-1 PJSmullen 3 54
(John Joseph Murphy, Ire) *a towards rr* **33/1**

59.76 secs (-2.74) **Going Correction** -0.50s/f (Hard) **8** Ran SP% **119.7**
Speed ratings: **96,95,90,90,88 82,78,76**
CSF £31.84 TOTE £2.50: £1.40, £2.40, £2.60; DF 32.80.
Owner Michael Tabor **Bred** Strategy Bloodstock **Trained** Ballydoyle, Co Tipperary

FOCUS
They broke a minute for this contest, and despite it being run on a quick surface, it does suggest that there was plenty of quality on show. The early pacesetters went off at a tremendous rate and couldn't last it out. The winner impressed and there should be better to come.

NOTEBOOK
Samuel Morse(IRE) would have been an unlucky loser, and despite the fact that he didn't show blinding speed, he quickened to get into a challenging position over a furlong out. Briefly short of room, he quickened well through the gap between horses when it did appear and the way he closed the gap on the runner-up was impressive as it looked a tough task. He'll have no problem with an extra furlong and looks a very smart colt. The Coventry Stakes is his immediate target. (op 9/4 tchd 2/1)
Purple Glow(IRE) is undoubtedly a filly that's improving at a fair rate. She'll probably appreciate an extra furlong as well. Just ridden to go the pace at halfway, she picked up well to get to the front a furlong out and kept on really well under pressure. She was beaten by a smart colt, but deserves to take her chance in a race like the Albany Stakes if the evidence of this is to be believed. (op 10/1)
So Stylish(USA), another who is Albany Stakes bound, ran quite green and should continue to improve. She really got going only inside the last and came home well up the hill. One imagines this is the last time she'll run over the minimum trip. (op 6/1)
High Award(IRE) ran well but just appeared to roll around a bit on the fast ground inside the last and kept on at more or less the same pace. He ended up in the centre of the track and looks as though he'll be at his best on good ground at best.
Moment Of Weakness(IRE) did best of the pacemakers as he only gave way a furlong out. (op 5/2 tchd 11/4)
Lightening Thief(IRE) paid for racing up with the strong pace. (op 9/2 tchd 5/1)
Jolly Snake(IRE), on his turf debut, had run his race with a furlong and a half left.
Foolproof(IRE), predictably enough, was very much out of his depth.

2353a WEATHERBYS IRELAND GREENLANDS STKS (GROUP 3) 6f
3:10 (3:10) 3-Y-O+ **£38,827** (£11,349; £5,376; £1,792)

RPR
1 **Markab**[35] 1400 7-9-9 PatCosgrave 3 114
(H Candy) *mde all: chal 2f out: rdn and kpt on wl fnl f* **10/3**[1]
2 *2* **Snaefell (IRE)**[22] 1676 6-9-12 106 (p) PJSmullen 1 111
(M Halford, Ire) *chsd ldrs: 6th 1/2-way: hdwy to 2nd and chal 2f out: rdn and no ex 1f out: kpt on same pce fnl f* **14/1**
3 *3* **Alfred Nobel (IRE)**[41] 1244 3-9-5 112 JMurtagh 2 101
(A P O'Brien, Ire) *hld up in mid-div: 8th 1/2-way: 7th 2f out: rdn into 4th 1f out: no imp on ldrs: kpt on same pce fnl f* **9/2**[2]
4 *¾* **Six Of Hearts**[22] 1676 6-9-9 98 DJMoran 8 96
(Cecil Ross, Ire) *mid-div: 7th 1/2-way: rdn into 5th 1 1/2f out: 3rd 1f out: no imp on ldrs: kpt on same pce fnl f* **33/1**
5 *2* **Velvet Flicker (IRE)**[35] 1406 3-8-11 100 DPMcDonogh 5 84+
(Kevin Prendergast, Ire) *hld up towards rr: late hdwy in 9th over 1f out: kpt on same pce fnl f* **8/1**

6 1 **Luisant**35 1406 7-9-9 107 FMBerry 10 86+
(J A Nash, Ire) *hld up towards rr: hdwy on outer to 6th 1f out: rdn and no imp: kpt on same pce fnl f* **9/1**

7 1 **Invincible Ash (IRE)**22 1676 5-9-6 95 (b) GFCarroll 9 80
(M Halford, Ire) *mid-div: hdwy on outer to 7th 1f out: rdn and no imp: kpt on same pce fnl f* **33/1**

8 3 **Kitty Kiernan**310 4028 3-8-11 99 KJManning 11 68
(J S Bolger, Ire) *chsd ldrs on outer: 5th 1/2-way: rdn into 4th 1 1/2f out: no ex in 5th 1f out: kpt on one pce* **14/1**

9 2 1/2 **Jimmy Styles**224 6661 6-9-9 (p) RichardHughes 7 65
(C G Cox) *prom: 3rd 1/2-way: rdn 2f out: wknd over 1f out* **6/1**3

10 3/4 **Air Chief Marshal (IRE)**208 7072 3-9-0 110 JAHeffernan 4 61
(A P O'Brien, Ire) *prom: 2nd 1/2-way: rdn in 6th 2f out: no ex and sn wknd* **16/1**

11 7 **Rain Delayed (IRE)**22 1676 4-9-9 109 KLatham 6 40
(G M Lyons, Ire) *prom: 4th 1/2-way: rdn 2f out: no ex and sn wknd* **9/2**2

1m 10.86s (-4.14) **Going Correction** -0.50s/f (Hard)
WFA 3 from 4yo+ 9lb 11 Ran SP% **119.9**
Speed ratings: **113,110,106,105,102 101,100,96,92,91 82**
CSF £53.87 TOTE £4.80: £2.00, £3.80, £2.30; DF 71.60.
Owner Tight Lines Partnership **Bred** Shadwell Estate Company Limited **Trained** Kingston Warren, Oxon

FOCUS
The winner made all up the rail and little got into it from the rear. It is doubtful if the second ran to his best.

NOTEBOOK
Markab recorded his first Pattern success at the age of seven and only the second attempt. Fourth in last season's Wokingham and winner of the Great St Wilfrid at Ascot, he had run well in a Group 3 race at Ascot towards the end of last season and had begun the new campaign in bright style with a conditions-race win at Thirsk. Suited by quick ground and well drawn, he was in front from the start and asserted control through the last couple of furlongs. It remains to be seen whether he has improved sufficiently to win a race at this level on home territory, but there should be more opportunities for him in Ireland, and possibly on the continent as well. His connections are eyeing a crack at the King's Stand Stakes now. (op 4/1)
Snaefell(IRE) ran a fine race for a horse who has usually produced his best performances on soft ground (his two Group 3 wins have come on soft and heavy) and was very close to peak form here on the third run of the season. He seems at least as good ever now at the age of six, and can continue to pay his way at this level.
Alfred Nobel(IRE), last season's Railway and Phoenix Stakes winner, was soundly beaten in third, but this still marked a return to something like his juvenile best after a disappointing effort over a furlong further in the Loughbrown Stakes at the venue last month. Considering that he was carrying a Group 1 penalty, this was a stiff enough task against battle-hardened sprinters, but he may merit another try at 7f, since he doesn't seem to have the natural pace to live with the real speedsters. (op 7/2)
Six Of Hearts an honest-to-goodness handicapper, thoroughly justified trainer Cecil Ross's decision to aim high with a very game performance. He already had seven outings under his belt this year, having started off at Kempton in February, and this goes down as a career-best.
Velvet Flicker(IRE), who began to come good at the backend of a fairly busy juvenile season, has developed into a reliable sprinting filly. She could not confirm her Naas superiority over Snaefell but had Luisant behind again. (op 7/1)
Luisant ran quite creditably on ground that may have a bit quicker than ideal. (op 10/1)
Rain Delayed(IRE) was the main disappointment of the race, having won in promising fashion on his seasonal debut at Cork. Official explanation: jockey said gelding tired quickly and finished distressed (op 5/1)

2354a ABU DHABI IRISH 2,000 GUINEAS (GROUP 1) (ENTIRE COLTS & FILLIES) 1m
3:45 (3:48) 3-Y-O
£166,814 (£54,646; £25,884; £8,628; £5,752; £2,876)

RPR

1 **Canford Cliffs (IRE)**21 1699 3-9-0 RichardHughes 5 126+
(R Hannon) *settled mid-div: swtchd out in 6th 2f out: travelled wl into 2nd 1f out: rdn to ld last 200yds: comf* **9/4**1

2 3 **Free Judgement (USA)**19 1786 3-9-0 109 KJManning 3 117
(J S Bolger, Ire) *hld up towards rr: hdwy in 7th 1 1/2f out: rdn into 5th 1f out: kpt on wl fnl f to go 2nd: no ch w wnr* **25/1**

3 1 1/2 **Viscount Nelson (USA)**21 1699 3-9-0 108 (b1) PJSmullen 11 113
(A P O'Brien, Ire) *mid-div: 8th 1/2-way: hdwy in 5th 2f out: rdn in 4th 1 1/2f out: 3rd 1f out: no ex fnl f and kpt on same pce* **20/1**

4 1/2 **Steinbeck (IRE)**217 6849 3-9-0 JMurtagh 6 112+
(A P O'Brien, Ire) *sn hld up towards rr: rdn in 9th 1 1/2f out: 8th 1f out: kpt on fnl f* **9/2**2

5 hd **Xtension (IRE)**21 1699 3-9-0 AdamKirby 8 112
(C G Cox) *chsd ldrs: 5th 1/2-way: hdwy under 3f out: led 2 1/2f out: rdn and chal 1f out: hdd fnl 200yds: no ex and kpt on same pce* **5/1**3

6 2 **Keredari (IRE)**41 1244 3-9-0 106 FMBerry 7 107
(John M Oxx, Ire) *chsd ldrs: 4th 1/2-way: rdn 2f out: u.p in 3rd 1 1/2f out: no ex in 4th 1f out: kpt on same pce* **11/1**

7 1 3/4 **Sebastian Flyte**55 1038 3-9-0 107 WJSupple 10 103
(Francis Ennis, Ire) *mid-div: 7th 1/2-way: rdn 2f out: no ex 1 1/2f out: kpt on same pce* **66/1**

8 shd **Dynasty**19 1786 3-9-0 103 JAHeffernan 1 103
(A P O'Brien, Ire) *towards rr: rdn into 10th 1f out: no imp and kpt on one pce fnl f* **20/1**

9 nk **Noll Wallop (IRE)**55 1038 3-9-0 109 WMLordan 4 102
(T Stack, Ire) *in rr of mid-div thrght: nvr a factor* **8/1**

10 3 1/2 **Fencing Master**21 1699 3-9-0 116 CO'Donoghue 12 94
(A P O'Brien, Ire) *chsd ldrs: 6th 1/2-way: hdwy to 3rd 3f out: rdn in 5th and no ex 1 1/2f out: wknd fnl f* **9/2**2

11 3 1/2 **Oasis Dancer**21 1703 3-9-0 JimCrowley 13 86
(R M Beckett) *prom and disp: led 3f out: rdn and hdd 2 1/2f out: kpt on: wknd over 1f out* **16/1**

12 13 **Purple Heart (IRE)**20 1742 3-9-0 94 JPO'Brien 2 56
(A P O'Brien, Ire) *chsd ldrs: rdn in 3rd 1/2-way: wknd over 3f out* **150/1**

13 1 3/4 **Encompassing (IRE)**6 2151 3-9-0 100 SMLevey 9 52
(A P O'Brien, Ire) *led and disp in centre: drifted lft over 3f out: sn hdd: rdn and wknd over 2f out* **150/1**

1m 37.64s (-8.36) **Going Correction** -0.60s/f (Hard) 13 Ran SP% **125.3**
Speed ratings: **117,114,112,112,111 109,108,107,107,104 100,87,85**
CSF £76.32 TOTE £2.50: £1.40, £5.20, £8.90; DF 42.90.
Owner Heffer Syndicate, Mrs Roy & Mrs Instance **Bred** S And S Hubbard Rodwell **Trained** East Everleigh, Wilts

FOCUS
The pace was strong and there was a decent time for the grade. Canford Cliffs impressed, and is the season's leading 3yo at this stage on RPRs, but there are doubts over what he beat.

NOTEBOOK
Canford Cliffs(IRE) proved supreme, as last season's impressive Coventry Stakes winner proved his doubters seriously wrong with a display that stamps him as a top-class miler. Question marks had been raised by an unexpected defeat in the Greenham, and by his failure to reverse form with Dick Turpin at Newmarket, but there was considerable market confidence behind him here, and he delivered in terrific style under a well-executed ride by Richard Hughes, who settled him well before beginning his run from over a furlong and a half down, and getting to the front just inside the final furlong. He had looked an exceptional prospect at Royal Ascot, and Hannon and his team deserve a lot of credit for getting him back to a peak. Now, once again, there is much to look forward to with him. The St James's Palace Stakes, where he will meet Dick Turpin again, is his next target. (op 11/4)
Free Judgement(USA), winner of the 7f Tetrarch Stakes on an easier surface, saw out this extra furlong really well to prove how much progress he has made since contesting the Dewhurst as a 66-1 chance. He had been disappointing on his seasonal debut in a Guineas Trial at Leopardstown, but turned the tables here on the runner-up in that event, Viscount Nelson. His next race is likely to be the Jersey Stakes over 7f at Royal Ascot.
Viscount Nelson(USA) ran a perfectly respectable race in first-time blinkers, proving best of six runners for Aidan O'Brien, but could not confirm his Leopardstown superiority over Free Judgement. He may step up in trip for the Prix du Jockey Club.
Steinbeck(IRE), having only the third run of his career, never looked imposing his presence on the race, but kept on well enough through the last furlong to suggest that there could be a lot better to come. It would be no surprise to see him establish a presence as a genuine Group 1 horse in the coming months, and he could take on Canford Cliffs again at Ascot. (op 9/2 tchd 5/1)
Xtension(IRE) faded from early in the final furlong after a spell in the lead from around two and a half furlongs down, another failing to build on what he had shown at Newmarket when he finished only one place behind Canford Cliffs in fourth. (op 11/2)
Keredari(IRE), third to Free Judgement in last season's Killavullan Stakes, did not seem to stay on his first attempt at 1m, something that came as a surprise after a convincing Listed win over 7f on his reappearance. Perhaps the jump in standard simply found him out. (op 8/1)
Noll Wallop(IRE), winner of Leopardstown's 2,000 Guineas Trial on soft ground, could not handle the rise in grade. (op 7/1)
Fencing Master, who was well supported, dropped out tamely, failing to improve from Newmarket in the way that had been expected. He was reported to have tested clinically abnormal. Official explanation: vet said colt was found to be clinically abnormal post race (op 11/2)

2355a TRI EQUESTRIAN STKS (GROUP 3) (F&M) 1m
4:20 (4:20) 4-Y-O+ **£37,389** (£10,929; £5,176; £1,725)

RPR

1 **Shamwari Lodge (IRE)**21 1693 4-8-12 RichardHughes 9 102+
(R Hannon) *mde all: shkn up briefly ins fnl f: easily* **8/15**1

2 1 1/2 **Indiana Gal (IRE)**10 2037 5-8-13 99 ow1 (p) FMBerry 3 97+
(Patrick Martin, Ire) *hld up towards rr: rdn into 6th 1f out: styd on fnl f to 2nd on line* **20/1**

3 shd **Annabelle's Charm (IRE)**20 1725 5-8-12 KierenFallon 8 96
(L M Cumani) *chsd ldrs: 3rd 1/2-way: rdn in 4th 2f out: kpt on u.p in 3rd 1f out: 2nd and no imp on ldr fnl f: lost 2nd on line* **7/1**2

4 1 **Enchanted Evening (IRE)**363 2306 4-8-12 99 PJSmullen 5 93
(D K Weld, Ire) *chsd ldrs: 5th 1/2-way: rdn into 4th 1f out: no imp on ldrs: kpt on same pce fnl f* **12/1**

5 hd **Good Time Sue (IRE)**35 1408 6-8-12 86 (t) GFCarroll 2 93
(Ms M Dowdall Blake, Ire) *in rr of mid-div: hdwy in 6th 3f out: rdn in 5th and no imp 1f out: kpt on same pce fnl f* **33/1**

6 nk **Rose Hip (IRE)**13 1954 6-8-12 98 CDHayes 1 92
(Joseph G Murphy, Ire) *chsd ldrs: 4th 1/2-way: rdn in 3rd 2f out: 2nd 1 /2f out: no imp on ldr 1f out: no ex fnl f* **14/1**

7 1 **Choose Me (IRE)**238 6298 4-8-12 102 DPMcDonogh 6 90
(Kevin Prendergast, Ire) *a towards rr* **8/1**3

8 nk **Latin Love (IRE)**19 1787 4-8-12 101 JMurtagh 7 89
(David Wachman, Ire) *mid-div: 6th 1/2-way: 7th 2f out: nt clr run fr under 2f out: hmpd ins fnl f and eased* **12/1**

9 1 1/2 **Pollen (IRE)**19 1787 5-9-1 100 WJLee 4 89
(T Stack, Ire) *chsd ldr in 2nd: rdn 2f out: no ex in 4th 1 1/2f out: wknd* **14/1**

1m 41.35s (-4.65) **Going Correction** -0.60s/f (Hard) 9 Ran SP% **125.3**
Speed ratings: **99,97,97,96,96 95,94,94,93**
CSF £17.60 TOTE £1.50: £1.10, £4.90, £2.20; DF 15.40.
Owner Andrew Russell **Bred** Pier House Stud **Trained** East Everleigh, Wilts

FOCUS
This Group 3 was little more than a glorified handicap if you take the winner out of it. The pace was steady and the second and fourth are the best guides.

NOTEBOOK
Shamwari Lodge(IRE) won as she was entitled to. Making all, she was allowed a soft enough lead but once she was asked to quicken the pace her response was far too good for this bunch as she won the race with one spurt a furlong and a half out. She was the class filly in what was a poor Group 3 and she'll face some far stiffer tasks than this. The Windsor Forest Stakes at Ascot could be next for her. (op 8/13)
Indiana Gal(IRE)ran what would be a career best on paper but she didn't have to run vastly above her mark to achieve it. Held up off the pace for a late run, she kept on well up the hill inside the final furlong to get second spot close home. She's probably too high for handicaps and perhaps she might be able to pick up an ordinary Listed race somewhere, certainly not an impossible task on this evidence.
Annabelle's Charm(IRE) raced very handily on the inner, was asked just beyond halfway and despite being the first of the principals to come under pressure she did keep going gamely enough. It was a good run by a filly that probably needs further.
Enchanted Evening(IRE) ran a fair race on her return from an absence of a year. She raced handily, was caught for toe over a furlong out and just kept going at the same pace. She might be one of the few in this race that could be a genuine improver.
Good Time Sue(IRE) is rated 86 and being beaten less than three lengths does put this contest in perspective, even if she's a filly that always runs well at the Curragh. Not that far off the pace on the outside, she just kept on at one pace without threatening inside the last.
Rose Hip(IRE) ran out of steam inside the final furlong having been a shade too keen early on. (op 16/1)
Choose Me(IRE) was never a factor. (op 7/1)
Latin Love(IRE) was far too free early. Official explanation: jockey said filly ran short of room when attempting to challenge and was eased in the closing stages (op 10/1)
Pollen(IRE), racing on unsuitable ground, tracked the winner and travelled well most of the way but weakened once coming under pressure well over a furlong out.

2350 - 2357a (Foreign Racing) - See Raceform Interactive

2163 BATH (L-H)

Sunday, May 23

OFFICIAL GOING: Firm (10.0)

Wind: Nil Weather: Fine and sunny

2358 TOTEPLACEPOT MEDIAN AUCTION MAIDEN FILLIES' STKS — 5f 161y

2:05 (2:12) (Class 6) 2-Y-O — £2,072 (£616; £308; £153) Stalls Centre

Form				RPR
	1		**Tipsy Girl** 2-9-0 0 ... RobertWinston 13 (D J Coakley) *s.i.s: sn pushed along in rr: hdwy over 1f out: r.o to ld nr fin* **15/2**[3]	84+
	2	½	**Catalinas Diamond (IRE)** 2-8-9 0 ... SophieDoyle(5) 8 (B W Duke) *chsd ldrs: led and hung rt over 1f out: hdd nr fin* **50/1**	82+
5	3	6	**Kodiac Star (IRE)**[13] 1957 2-9-0 ... FergusSweeney 12 (J A Osborne) *prom: rdn 3f out: no ex fnl f* **28/1**	62
4	4	1 ¼	**Veil Of Night**[17] 1838 2-9-0 0 ... DaneO'Neill 15 (D Haydn Jones) *hld up: hdwy over 1f out: nt trble ldrs* **16/1**	57+
0	5	½	**Allegrissimo (IRE)**[16] 1879 2-9-0 0 ... AdamKirby 14 (C G Cox) *mid-div: sn pushed along: no imp fr over 1f out* **16/1**	56
3242	6	1 ¾	**Bajan Bullet**[12] 2007 2-9-0 0 ... CathyGannon 10 (P D Evans) *chsd ldrs: rdn 1/2-way: wknd over 1f out* **9/2**[2]	50
	7	¾	**Danzigs Grandchild (USA)** 2-9-0 0 ... LiamKeniry 11 (J S Moore) *s.i.s: outpcd: nvr nrr* **33/1**	47
	8	3 ¼	**Welsh Inlet (IRE)** 2-8-11 0 ... WilliamCarson(3) 7 (S C Williams) *s.s: in rr: rdn 1/2-way: n.d* **12/1**	36
2	9	*shd*	**Never Can Stop**[16] 1879 2-9-0 0 ... PatCosgrave 2 (J G Portman) *led: hdd over 3f out: rdn and wknd over 1f out* **2/1**[1]	35
	10	1	**Blaze On By** 2-9-0 0 ... PatDobbs 6 (R Hannon) *mid-div: rdn 1/2-way: wknd over 1f out* **9/1**	32
	11	1 ½	**Country Waltz** 2-9-0 0 ... AlanMunro 9 (M R Channon) *mid-div: rdn over 2f out: sn wknd* **11/1**	27
	12	3 ¾	**Elusive Vine (IRE)** 2-9-0 0 ... ChrisCatlin 5 (R A Harris) *s.i.s: outpcd* **28/1**	14
	13	5	**Lagan Lullaby** 2-9-0 0 ... ShaneKelly 4 (N P Mulholland) *chsd ldr: led over 3f out: hdd & wknd over 1f out* **80/1**	—

1m 10.56s (-0.64) **Going Correction** -0.225s/f (Firm) 13 Ran SP% **114.1**

Speed ratings (Par 88): **95,94,86,84,84 81,80,76,76,74 72,67,61**

toteswingers: 1&2 £69.00, 1&3 £45.90, 2&3 £54.00 CSF £345.85 TOTE £6.60: £2.00, £15.00, £13.40; EX 645.30 TRIFECTA Not won..

Owner Lawrence Alkin **Bred** Alpha Bloodstock Limited **Trained** West Ilsley, Berks

FOCUS

The start was delayed by over seven minutes, which was hardly ideal for these inexperienced juveniles, especially on such a hot day. The form is probably just fair overall but the first two finished clear and look decent.

NOTEBOOK

Tipsy Girl was representing a trainer who has shown a healthy level-stakes profit with his juveniles over the last five seasons, and who also shows a profit with his runner's at Bath. This 12,000gns purchase, first foal of a mare who was placed over 1m-1m2f, raced out the back for much of the way after starting slowly, but she picked up well late on to take advantage of the runner-up's waywardness. She should improve and her trainer thinks she will benefit from a step up in trip. (op 12-1)

Catalinas Diamond(IRE) showed good pace to hit the front in the straight and looked the winner for much of the closing stages, but she idled badly, pricking her ears and wandering around, handing the initiative to the winner. She's open to a deal of improvement and her natural speed should see her winning before long.

Kodiac Star(IRE) improved significantly on the form she showed on debut at Brighton, just as her trainer had predicted. Her best chance of success may come in nurseries in due course. (op 25-1)

Veil Of Night probably ran to a similar level as when fourth on debut at Ffos Las and is another who may be more of a nursery type. (tchd 14-1)

Allegrissimo(IRE) stepped up a little on her debut performance but was never really a threat. (op 18-1 tchd 20-1)

Bajan Bullet ran nowhere near her best form, fading after showing speed, and two of her last three performances have been poor. (op 7-2)

Never Can Stop, well backed when runner-up on her debut at Nottingham, proved most disappointing this time. She showed loads of speed, but stopped quickly and now has plenty to prove. (tchd 5-2 in a place)

2359 TOTESWINGER FLEXI BETTING H'CAP — 1m 5y

2:35 (2:40) (Class 6) (0-60,60) 3-Y-O — £1,942 (£578; £288; £144) Stalls Low

Form				RPR
-032	1		**Kingsdine (IRE)**[19] 1795 3-9-1 57 ... TomMcLaughlin 5 (M S Saunders) *chsd ldrs: hung rt and led over 1f out: rdn out* **9/2**[2]	62
-060	2	1 ½	**Sparkle Park**[5] 2200 3-8-1 46 ...(v[1]) Louis-PhilippeBeuzelin(3) 11 (B J Meehan) *chsd ldr tl led 1/2-way: rdn and hdd over 1f out: styd on same pce* **50/1**	47
4026	3	*nk*	**Sultan's Choice**[19] 1795 3-8-12 54 ...(v) CathyGannon 2 (P D Evans) *hld up: hdwy u.p over 1f out: r.o: nt rch ldrs* **9/1**	54+
2-50	4	*hd*	**Pie Poudre**[19] 1796 3-8-13 55 ... PatCosgrave 1 (R Brotherton) *s.i.s: hdwy over 3f out: rdn over 1f out: styd on same pce ins fnl f* **25/1**	55
06-1	5	¾	**Cool Kitten (IRE)**[24] 1643 3-8-7 56 ... HarryBentley(7) 7 (W J Knight) *mid-div: rdn over 3f out: hdwy over 1f out: nt rch ldrs* **7/2**[1]	54
5563	6	1 ¼	**Prince Yarraman (IRE)**[5] 2200 3-8-10 57 ... SophieDoyle(5) 16 (J A Osborne) *hld up: rdn over 3f out: r.o ins fnl f: nvr nrr* **7/1**[3]	52
006-	7	3 ¼	**Dancing Poppy**[223] 6722 3-9-4 60 ... DaneO'Neill 15 (R A Farrant) *chsd ldrs: rdn over 3f out: wknd fnl f* **25/1**	48
3240	8	½	**Clayton Flick (IRE)**[36] 1394 3-8-12 54 ... RobertHavlin 3 (A B Haynes) *prom: rdn over 3f out: wknd over 1f out* **25/1**	41
60-6	9	1 ½	**My Grand Duke (USA)**[19] 1796 3-8-6 48 ... ChrisCatlin 8 (J A Osborne) *led to 1/2-way: rdn over 2f out: wknd fnl f* **12/1**	31
00-0	10	¾	**Federal Reserve**[26] 1590 3-8-10 52 ... LiamKeniry 12 (M Madgwick) *chsd ldrs: rdn and lost pl over 3f out* **66/1**	34
-614	11	½	**Motty's Gift**[24] 1643 3-8-13 55 ... ShaneKelly 10 (W R Swinburn) *s.i.s: hld up: nvr on terms* **9/2**[2]	35
0-00	12	1 ¾	**Joan's Legacy**[84] 745 3-8-8 50 ... PatDobbs 13 (J C Fox) *hld up: a in rr* **40/1**	26
056-	13	1	**My Sister**[223] 6735 3-8-13 60 ... LeeNewnes(5) 14 (M D I Usher) *hld up: a in rr* **10/1**	34
000-	14	134	**Superhoops**[253] 5868 3-7-11 46 oh1 ... CharlesEddery(7) 9 (H S Howe) *hld up: in rr whn hung rt over 4f out: sn wl bhd: t.o* **100/1**	—

1m 40.3s (-0.50) **Going Correction** -0.225s/f (Firm) 14 Ran SP% **116.3**

Speed ratings (Par 97): **93,91,91,91,90 89,85,85,83,83 82,80,79,—**

toteswingers: 1&2 £26.00, 1&3 £10.00, 2&3 £64.30 CSF £221.81 CT £1988.83 TOTE £4.00: £1.10, £8.80, £2.80; EX 212.90 TRIFECTA Not won..

Owner M S Saunders **Bred** Deer Forest Stud Ltd **Trained** Green Ore, Somerset

FOCUS

A moderate 3-y-o handicap and few were ever seriously involved. The time was 0.39 seconds slower than the later Class 5 contest for older horses and the form makes some sense.

Motty's Gift Official explanation: jockey said gelding missed the break

My Sister Official explanation: jockey said filly never travelled

Superhoops Official explanation: jockey said saddle slipped

2360 TOTEQUADPOT H'CAP — 1m 2f 46y

3:05 (3:05) (Class 6) (0-65,65) 4-Y-O+ — £2,072 (£616; £308; £153) Stalls Low

Form				RPR
0-43	1		**Sunny Future (IRE)**[11] 2024 4-9-4 65 ... TomMcLaughlin 11 (M S Saunders) *hld up: hdwy over 2f out: rdn and hung lft over 1f out: led ins fnl f: r.o* **3/1**[2]	73
6600	2	2	**Hector Spectre (IRE)**[45] 1194 4-8-10 57 ...(p) RobertWinston 10 (Mrs N S Evans) *chsd ldr: rdn to ld over 1f out: hdd and unable qck ins fnl f* **20/1**	61
4-05	3	2 ¾	**Aspirational (IRE)**[11] 2023 4-8-4 51 ... LukeMorris 4 (B Palling) *led: rdn and hdd over 2f out: n.m.r over 1f out: styd on same pce* **9/1**	52
4211	4	*nk*	**Four Kicks (IRE)**[5] 2201 4-8-2 56 ... RyanPowell(7) 7 (J S Moore) *chsd ldrs: led over 2f out: rdn and hdd over 1f out: no ex fnl f* **15/8**[1]	54
6104	5	½	**Golden Prospect**[24] 1636 6-9-1 62 ... PaulFitzsimons 6 (Miss J R Tooth) *hld up: racd keenly: hdwy over 2f out: sn rdn: styd on* **25/1**	59
10-0	6	¾	**Lucy's Perfect**[20] 1755 4-8-7 54 ...(b) DavidProbert 2 (B R Millman) *s.i.s: hld up: hdwy 6f out: rdn over 2f out: sn wknd* **10/1**	49
5-10	7	1 ½	**Beaubrav**[25] 1623 4-9-4 65 ... LiamKeniry 3 (M Madgwick) *hld up in tch: lost pl over 4f out: n.d after* **5/1**[3]	57
	8	1 ¾	**Lindsay's Dream**[86] 4-9-3 64 ... RobertHavlin 1 (A B Haynes) *chsd ldr over 8f out: rdn over 3f out: wknd over 1f out* **40/1**	53
0-00	9	2 ½	**Catchmeifyoucan (FR)**[21] 1737 4-7-13 51 oh1 ...(b) SimonPearce(5) 8 (Andrew Turnell) *hld up: bhd 1/2-way: nvr on terms* **50/1**	35
0660	10	2 ¼	**Hatch A Plan (IRE)**[9] 2080 9-8-5 52 ... ChrisCatlin 9 (Mouse Hamilton-Fairley) *hld up: hdwy over 3f out: wknd over 1f out* **16/1**	31

2m 8.32s (-2.68) **Going Correction** -0.225s/f (Firm) 10 Ran SP% **114.4**

Speed ratings (Par 101): **101,99,97,96,96 95,94,93,91,89**

toteswingers: 1&2 £15.80, 1&3 £6.80, 2&3 £17.70 CSF £64.23 CT £484.86 TOTE £4.40: £1.70, £5.00, £2.70; EX 53.40 TRIFECTA Not won..

Owner M S Saunders **Bred** Mrs G Stanga **Trained** Green Ore, Somerset

FOCUS

A moderate contest run at a fair pace. The favourite disappointed but the winner is rated back towards his early form.

Golden Prospect Official explanation: jockey said gelding was denied a clear run

2361 TOTEEXACTA FLEXI BETTING H'CAP — 1m 3f 144y

3:35 (3:35) (Class 6) (0-60,60) 4-Y-O+ — £1,942 (£578; £288; £144) Stalls Low

Form				RPR
03-3	1		**Bedarra Boy**[13] 1983 4-8-5 47 ... DavidProbert 12 (D W P Arbuthnot) *chsd ldrs: led 2f out: rdn and hung lft ins fnl f: r.o* **7/2**[1]	55
00-3	2	1	**Touch Of Style (IRE)**[20] 1771 6-8-1 46 oh1 Louis-PhilippeBeuzelin(3) 11 (Matthew Salaman) *chsd ldrs: nt clr run over 2f out: sn rdn: r.o* **9/1**	52
302-	3	½	**Dhania (IRE)**[39] 6788 4-8-11 53 ... LiamKeniry 10 (C Gordon) *led: hdd over 7f out: chsd ldr tl led again over 2f out: sn hdd: styd on* **8/1**[3]	58
-402	4	*nk*	**The Dial House**[5] 2201 4-9-4 60 ...(t) ShaneKelly 2 (J A Osborne) *hld up: hdwy over 2f out: rdn over 1f out:* **4/1**[2]	65
-434	5	1 ½	**Ocean Of Peace (FR)**[65] 942 7-8-4 46 ... LukeMorris 7 (M R Bosley) *hld up: hdwy over 2f out: rdn over 1f out: nt trble ldrs* **17/2**	48
-606	6	½	**Jordan's Light (USA)**[19] 813 7-8-4 53 ...(b[1]) MatthewCosham(7) 6 (P D Evans) *hld up in tch: rdn over 2f out: no imp fnl f* **14/1**	54
0630	7	3 ¾	**Lean Burn (USA)**[17] 898 4-7-13 46 oh1 ...(bt[1]) SimonPearce(5) 3 (J F Panvert) *hld up: rdn over 2f out: nvr on terms* **33/1**	41
5360	8	3 ½	**Six Of Clubs**[24] 1635 4-8-3 48 oh1 ow2 ...(b) JackDean(3) 9 (W G M Turner) *hld up: racd keenly: hdwy over 3f out: rdn over 2f out: edgd rt over 1f out: wknd fnl f* **20/1**	37
64-6	9	1 ½	**Spinning Waters**[11] 2023 4-8-13 55 ...(p) RobertWinston 4 (Eve Johnson Houghton) *prom: rdn over 2f out: wknd over 1f out* **7/2**[1]	41
/05-	10	6	**Aston Boy**[412] 1156 5-8-4 46 oh1 ... FrannyNorton 1 (M Blanshard) *hld up: racd keenly: bhd fnl 4f* **16/1**	22
063/	11	2 ½	**Gainsborough's Art (IRE)**[24] 4298 5-8-8 50 ... ChrisCatlin 5 (C J Down) *chsd ldr tl led over 7f out: rdn and hdd over 2f out: sn wknd* **33/1**	22

2m 29.48s (-1.12) **Going Correction** -0.225s/f (Firm) 11 Ran SP% **119.3**

Speed ratings (Par 101): **94,93,93,92,91 91,88,86,85,81 79**

toteswingers: 1&2 £8.70, 1&3 £7.80, 2&3 £12.50 CSF £35.47 CT £236.68 TOTE £5.00: £1.90, £3.70, £3.30; EX 46.40 Trifecta £140.70 Part won. Pool: £190.13 - 0.73 winning units..

Owner P M Claydon **Bred** Mickley Stud & E Kent **Trained** Compton, Berks

FOCUS

Another moderate race. A personal best from the winner with the runner-up to form.

2362 TOTETRIFECTA FLEXI BETTING H'CAP — 1m 5y

4:10 (4:10) (Class 5) (0-70,72) 4-Y-O+ — £2,590 (£770; £385; £192) Stalls Low

Form				RPR
2060	1		**Jewelled**[19] 1797 4-9-2 66 ...(v[1]) SebSanders 2 (J W Hills) *chsd ldrs: rdn to ld ins fnl f: r.o* **9/1**	75
2431	2	2	**Spinning Ridge (IRE)**[6] 2188 5-9-8 72 6ex ...(b) DavidProbert 3 (R A Harris) *led: rdn over 1f out: hdd and unable qck ins fnl f* **11/4**[1]	76
5363	3	¾	**Perfect Class**[6] 2167 4-8-11 66 ... JohnFahy(5) 1 (C G Cox) *hld up: hdwy over 1f out: sn rdn: r.o* **7/2**[3]	69
-246	4	2 ½	**Capeability (IRE)**[48] 1133 4-9-4 68 ... ChrisCatlin 5 (M R Channon) *w ldr tl rn wd bnd over 4f out: rdn over 2f out: no ex fnl f* **13/2**	65
1300	5	1	**Wrighty Almighty (IRE)**[20] 1763 8-8-11 61 ... RichardKingscote 8 (P R Chamings) *s.i.s: hld up: hdwy over 1f out: sn rdn: no ex fnl f* **12/1**	56
-322	6	*hd*	**Full Victory (IRE)**[6] 2167 8-9-3 67 ... LiamKeniry 4 (R A Farrant) *prom: rdn over 2f out: no ex fnl f* **3/1**[2]	61
210-	7	2 ¼	**Bidable**[169] 7650 6-8-6 56 ... LukeMorris 6 (B Palling) *chsd ldrs: rdn over 2f out: wknd fnl f* **16/1**	45

1m 39.91s (-0.89) **Going Correction** -0.225s/f (Firm) 7 Ran SP% **110.8**

Speed ratings (Par 103): **95,93,92,89,88 88,86**

toteswingers: 1&2 £4.30, 1&3 £6.00, 2&3 £2.40 CSF £31.86 CT £99.41 TOTE £9.30: £3.90, £1.20; EX 39.40 Trifecta £257.60 Pool: £362.58 - 1.04 winning units..

Owner J W Hills **Bred** Wyck Hall Stud Ltd **Trained** Upper Lambourn, Berks

FOCUS
A modest handicap run in a time 0.39 seconds quicker than the earlier Class 6 event for 3-y-os. The form is rated through the third with the winner back to her best.
Full Victory(IRE) Official explanation: jockey said gelding was unsuited by the firm ground

2363 BET TOTESPORT AT TOTESPORT.COM H'CAP 2m 1f 34y
4:45 (4:45) (Class 6) (0-60,60) 4-Y-O+ **£1,942** (£578; £288; £144) **Stalls** Centre

Form RPR
61-5 **1** **Brave Bugsy (IRE)**[6] 2169 7-9-3 **55**..........................(v) JimmyFortune 2 61
(A M Balding) *pushed along early: sn prom: led over 8f out: rdn over 1f out: styd on wl* **9/4**[2]
02-5 **2** *2 ¾* **Brad's Luck (IRE)**[13] 1980 4-8-11 **51**.............................. FrannyNorton 1 54
(M Blanshard) *hld up in tch: rdn to chse wnr over 2f out: no imp fnl f* **10/1**
0401 **3** *2 ¾* **Spiritonthemount (USA)**[6] 2169 5-8-12 **53** 6ex....(b) WilliamCarson(3) 5 52
(P W Hiatt) *chsd ldrs: rdn over 5f out: outpcd over 2f out: styd on u.p fnl f* **9/2**[3]
3000 **4** *6* **Ladies Dancing**[4] 2230 4-9-1 **60**................................. SophieDoyle(5) 3 52
(J A Osborne) *hld up: hdwy over 3f out: rdn over 1f out: wkng whn stmbld ins fnl f* **20/1**
4-02 **5** *6* **Brandy Butter**[6] 2169 4-8-10 **50**....................................(bt) GregFairley 4 35
(D E Pipe) *chsd ldr: pushed along 6f out: rdn to chse wnr briefly 3f out: wknd over 1f out* **2/1**[1]
0303 **6** *6* **Party Palace**[6] 2165 6-8-10 **48**... DaneO'Neill 6 30
(H S Howe) *led: hdd over 8f out: rdn and wknd 2f out: eased fnl f* **11/2**

3m 46.38s (-5.52) **Going Correction** -0.225s/f (Firm)
WFA 4 from 5yo+ 2lb **6** Ran SP% **111.5**
Speed ratings (Par 101): **103,101,100,97,94 91**
toteswingers: 1&2 £4.00, 1&3 £2.70, 2&3 £3.70 CSF £23.27 TOTE £2.20: £1.10, £4.70; EX 18.00.
Owner West Mercia Fork Trucks Ltd **Bred** James F Hanly **Trained** Kingsclere, Hants

FOCUS
A moderate staying handicap that was run an ordinary pace until about halfway when Jimmy Fortune sent Brave Bugsy to the front. The winner reversed recent C/D form with the third and fifth.

2364 BET TOTEPOOL ON 0800 221 221 H'CAP 5f 161y
5:20 (5:21) (Class 4) (0-85,84) 3-Y-O+ **£4,533** (£1,348; £674; £336) **Stalls** Centre

Form RPR
204- **1** **Night Affair**[253] 5877 4-9-0 **73**.. AdamKirby 3 81
(D W P Arbuthnot) *chsd ldrs: rdn to ld over 1f out: r.o* **4/1**[3]
6161 **2** *1 ¼* **Beat The Bell**[24] 1641 5-9-6 **84**..................................... SophieDoyle(5) 4 88
(J A Osborne) *s.i.s: sn rcvrd to ld: hdd over 4f out: chsd ldr: rdn and ev ch over 1f out: styd on same pce ins fnl f* **13/8**[1]
4103 **3** *shd* **Kyllachy Storm**[6] 2166 6-8-11 **70**..........................(b) RichardKingscote 2 74
(R J Hodges) *hld up: rdn 1/2-way: r.o wl ins fnl f: nrst fin* **11/2**
00-1 **4** *1 ¾* **Orange Pip**[76] 828 5-9-7 **80**.. SebSanders 6 78
(P J Makin) *chsd ldr: led over 4f out: rdn and hdd over 1f out: styd on same pce ins fnl f* **10/3**[2]
1136 **5** *14* **Misaro (GER)**[16] 1874 9-9-1 **74**....................................(b) DavidProbert 5 26
(R A Harris) *chsd ldrs: rdn 1/2-way: wknd over 1f out* **5/1**

1m 10.04s (-1.16) **Going Correction** -0.225s/f (Firm)
WFA 3 from 4yo+ 9lb **5** Ran SP% **113.2**
Speed ratings (Par 105): **98,96,96,93,75**
CSF £11.33 TOTE £4.90: £1.60, £1.40; EX 11.40 Place 6 £935.49, Place 5 £144.46.
Owner Godfrey Wilson **Bred** Mrs C R D Wilson **Trained** Compton, Berks

FOCUS
Few runners, but this was still a fair sprint handicap. The form is rated around the front two.
Beat The Bell Official explanation: jockey said gelding slipped leaving stalls
Misaro(GER) Official explanation: jockey said gelding never travelled
T/Jkpt: Not won. T/Plt: £2,018.70 to a £1 stake. Pool: £83,321.77. 30.13 winning tickets. T/Qpdt: £72.30 to a £1 stake. Pool: £6,427.85. 65.70 winning tickets. CR

2365 - 2366a (Foreign Racing) - See Raceform Interactive

2350 CURRAGH (R-H)
Sunday, May 23

OFFICIAL GOING: Good to firm

2367a AIRLIE STUD GALLINULE STKS (GROUP 3) 1m 2f
2:40 (2:43) 3-Y-O **£31,637** (£9,247; £4,380; £1,460)

RPR
1 **Jan Vermeer (IRE)**[203] 7207 3-9-8 119.................................. JMurtagh 6 119+
(A P O'Brien, Ire) *chsd ldrs in 3rd: travelling best st: led over 1f out: sn qcknd to assert: v easily* **6/4**[1]
2 *1 ¾* **Bobbyscot (IRE)**[10] 2067 3-9-1 102...................................... WJSupple 8 104
(P D Deegan, Ire) *sn led: clr w 2nd appr st: rdn and reduced ld 2f out: hdd and kpt on same pce fr 1f out* **33/1**
3 *nk* **Shintoh (USA)**[7] 2151 3-9-1 103.. KJManning 5 103+
(J S Bolger, Ire) *chsd ldrs in 4th: rdn bef st: clsd 2f out: no imp and kpt on same pce fr 1f out* **5/2**[2]
4 *1* **Icon Dream (IRE)**[17] 1833 3-9-1 104............................... JamieSpencer 4 101+
(David Wachman, Ire) *sn racd in mod 5th: rdn to cl 2f out: swtchd to outer and no imp fr over 1f out: kpt on* **11/2**[3]
5 *½* **Fighting Brave (USA)**[56] 1038 3-9-1 103.......................... JAHeffernan 7 100
(A P O'Brien, Ire) *trckd ldr: clr of remainder appr st: rdn and reduced advantage 2f out: no ex and kpt on same pce fr 1f out* **8/1**
6 *7* **Troas (IRE)**[14] 1949 3-9-1.. FMBerry 3 86
(John M Oxx, Ire) *sn settled wl off pce towards rr: rdn bef st: sn no imp: no ex fr over 1f out* **12/1**
7 *3 ½* **Zayaan**[20] 1786 3-9-1 101.. DPMcDonogh 2 79
(Kevin Prendergast, Ire) *settled wl off pce in rr: rdn st: sn no imp: no ex fr over 1f out* **10/1**

2m 11.38s (-1.22) **Going Correction** -0.325s/f (Firm) **7** Ran SP% **114.8**
Speed ratings: **101,99,99,98,98 92,89**
CSF £51.49 TOTE £2.00: £1.60, £5.00; DF 31.10.
Owner Michael Tabor **Bred** Shadow Song Syndicate **Trained** Ballydoyle, Co Tipperary

FOCUS
The time was slowish and the second limits the form, but easy winner Jan Vermeer impressed and was value for at least 4l.

NOTEBOOK
Jan Vermeer(IRE) didn't disappoint on his reappearance. Held up by a bruised foot earlier in the campaign, he had worked well after racing here earlier this month and looked the real deal on his first outing since his runaway Criterium International success on heavy ground at Saint-Cloud last November. Always travelling, he loomed up ominously to take over at the furlong pole and his rider never had a moment's worry. Despite his 7lb penalty, he simply toyed with his six rivals and on this evidence looks a worthy Investec Derby contender. He hails from a stable which holds all the aces for the Epsom Classic with the first four in the betting, including current ante-post favourite St Nicholas Abbey, but no decision will be made for several days and he could go to Chantilly instead. His trainer, who was winning this race for the tenth time and for the fifth consecutive year, said he expected improvement from this.
Bobbyscot(IRE) had shaped well in a conditions event over 2f longer at Gowran Park and was expected to improve a bit from that seasonal comeback run. He brought them along at a steady pace until the winner took over and to his credit he galloped all the way to the line to hold second.
Shintoh(USA), who was well backed, came under pressure turning for home and, although he closed in the straight, he never looked likely to impose his presence stepping up to this longer journey. (op 5/2 tchd 11/4)
Icon Dream(IRE), one of two runners from the David Wachman yard, came into this after his narrow defeat in the Chester Vase on his most recent start. He struggled again on fast going and may well be more effective with some juice in the ground, as he showed on his previous start. (op 7/1)
Fighting Brave(USA), stable companion of the winner, was happy to track the leader and probably would have gone on had the pace not been run to suit the favourite. He had no more to offer a furlong and a half from home . (op 7/1)
Troas(IRE), a Leopardstown maiden winner, was held in this stronger company. (op 10/1)
Zayaan was held up last of the septet and was another who never got in a blow. (op 8/1)

2369a TATTERSALLS GOLD CUP (GROUP 1) 1m 2f 110y
3:40 (3:41) 4-Y-O+ **£123,451** (£37,831; £17,920; £5,973; £1,991)

RPR
1 **Fame And Glory**[20] 1789 4-9-0 128....................................... JMurtagh 5 124+
(A P O'Brien, Ire) *racd in mod 2nd: clsd fr bef st: led over 2f out: rdn clr fr over 1f out: styd on wl: impressive* **8/15**[1]
2 *7* **Recharge (IRE)**[20] 1789 4-9-0 107.................................... CDHayes 3 111
(Kevin Prendergast, Ire) *racd in mod 3rd: clsd bef st: 2nd over 2f out: sn no imp u.p and kpt on same pce* **25/1**
3 *nk* **Chinese White (IRE)**[21] 1741 5-8-11 113........................... PJSmullen 6 107
(D K Weld, Ire) *racd in mod 4th for most: clsd bef st: 3rd over 2f out: sn no imp and kpt on same pce u.p* **6/1**[3]
4 *½* **Halicarnassus (IRE)**[22] 1698 6-9-0 .... RyanMoore 1 109
(M R Channon) *racd wl off pce in rr: rdn st: styd on wout threatening fr 2f out* **33/1**
5 *13* **Cutlass Bay (UAE)**[21] 1747 4-9-0 ....(t) AhmedAjtebi 2 85
(Saeed Bin Suroor) *racd mainly in mod 5th: rdn over 4f out: no ex st* **3/1**[2]
6 *13* **Dixie Music (IRE)**[20] 1789 4-9-0 101.............................. JAHeffernan 4 60
(A P O'Brien, Ire) *sn led and clr: reduced ld bef st: hdd & wknd fr over 2f out* **66/1**

2m 13.57s (-6.43) **Going Correction** -0.325s/f (Firm) **6** Ran SP% **112.8**
Speed ratings: **117,111,111,111,101 92**
CSF £18.16 TOTE £1.90: £1.10, £4.40; DF 19.70.
Owner Derrick Smith **Bred** Ptarmigan Bloodstock And Miss K Rausing **Trained** Ballydoyle, Co Tipperary

FOCUS
The winner had nothing to beat, with the fifth running poorly on his first start for Saeed Bin Suroor and the fourth in bad form since returning from Dubai. It has been rated through the runner-up to his questionable best.

NOTEBOOK
Fame And Glory laid down a significant marker for the rest of the campaign. Last year's Irish Derby hero started the season with a disappointing and somewhat controversial defeat in a Listed race at the venue, but Aidan O'Brien's long-term strategy with the Montjeu colt has never been in doubt, and he supplemented his victory in the Group 3 Mooresbridge Stakes with an appropriately power-packed display on his return to Group 1 competition for the first time since a tame end to his 3-y-o career in Newmarket's Champion Stakes. Overshadowed by the exceptional Sea The Stars last year, he was always the horse most likely to fill the void in the middle-distance division this year, and the Coronation Cup now beckons, with a second attempt at the Arc already coming into focus. With stable companion Dixie Music supplying the pace, Murtagh settled Fame And Glory in second and he picked up effortlessly from 2f down, extending his margin of superiority over the Moorebridge runner-up Recharge, who could make no impression. Though the dismal performance of the Ballydoyle colt's main market rival could be used to question the validity of the form, the visual impression was of a horse who is really coming into his own as a 4-y-o. (op 8/11)
Recharge(IRE) patently failed to stay when a remote fifth to Fame And Glory in the Irish Derby, a race that brought his season to a premature close. He may continue to have stamina limitations as regards 1m4f, but it was a creditable effort.
Chinese White(IRE), a Listed winner at Gowran on her seasonal debut at Gowran, and in foal to Cape Cross, deservedly bettered her 2008 Irish Oaks finishing position by one place. (op 13/2)
Halicarnassus(IRE), winner of last season's Bosphorus Cup (Group 2) in Turkey, did not have the pace to put himself into serious contention, but stayed on well enough towards the finish. It was a reassuring display after flops on his final outing during a winter spell in Dubai and on his return to domestic action in the Jockey Club Stakes. He should benefit from a drop in class and a return to 1m4f.
Cutlass Bay(UAE) ran a stinker on his first run for Saeed Bin Suroor. He failed to find any sort of response after coming under pressure fully half a mile out and was a bitter disappointment. (op 9/4)

2370a ETIHAD AIRWAYS IRISH 1,000 GUINEAS (GROUP 1) (FILLIES) 1m
4:15 (4:21) 3-Y-O
£166,814 (£54,646; £25,884; £8,628; £5,752; £2,876)

RPR
1 **Bethrah (IRE)**[14] 1952 3-9-0 103.. PJSmullen 8 110+
(D K Weld, Ire) *sn mid-div: 11th 1/2-way: swtchd towards rail and hdwy fr over 1f out: r.o wl fnl f to ld on line* **16/1**
2 *hd* **Anna Salai (USA)**[28] 1566 3-9-0 .... AhmedAjtebi 12 110
(Mahmood Al Zarooni) *trckd ldrs: 3rd travelling wl under 3f out: led over 1 1/2f out: kpt on wl fnl f: hdd on line* **15/2**
3 *nk* **Music Show (IRE)**[21] 1726 3-9-0 .... RyanMoore 7 109
(M R Channon) *mid-div: 10th 1/2-way: hdwy to trck ldrs 1 1/2f out: 5th over 1f out: r.o u.p fnl f: nt quite get there* **3/1**[1]
4 *shd* **Remember When (IRE)**[21] 1741 3-9-0 .... CO'Donoghue 11 109
(A P O'Brien, Ire) *mid-div: 12th 1/2-way: hdwy to chse ldrs under 3f out: 4th u.p over 1f out: r.o fnl f wout rching ldrs* **20/1**
5 *hd* **Lillie Langtry (IRE)**[198] 7282 3-9-0 108.............................. JMurtagh 6 109+
(A P O'Brien, Ire) *in rr of mid-div: travelling wl and swtchd to outer fr over 1f out: r.o wl u.p fnl f: nt quite rch ldrs* **11/1**

6 1 ¾ **Lady Darshaan (IRE)**[21] 1726 3-9-0 .... RichardHughes 16 104
(J S Moore) *a.p: 4th under 3f out: 2nd 1 1/2f out: no ex and kpt on same pce fnl f* **16/1**

7 ½ **Crystal Gal (IRE)**[56] 1036 3-9-0 96 .... CDHayes 10 103?
(Kevin Prendergast, Ire) *towards rr: rdn into 7th fr 1f out: kpt on wout threatening* **66/1**

8 1 ¾ **Lolly For Dolly (IRE)**[20] 1787 3-9-0 .... WMLordan 14 99
(T Stack, Ire) *chsd ldrs: 6th under 3f out: no imp and kpt on same pce fr 1 1/2f out* **11/2[3]**

9 nk **Termagant (IRE)**[266] 5488 3-9-0 .... DPMcDonogh 2 98
(Kevin Prendergast, Ire) *towards rr: kpt on wout threatening u.p fr under 2f out* **8/1**

10 ¾ **Song Of My Heart (IRE)**[42] 1244 3-9-0 102 .... JamieSpencer 18 97
(David Wachman, Ire) *towards rr: no imp and kpt on same pce fr 2f out* **20/1**

11 nk **Blue Maiden**[21] 1726 3-9-0 .... KierenFallon 5 96
(P J McBride) *towards rr: no imp and kpt on same pce fr 2f out* **14/1**

12 1 ¾ **Atasari (IRE)**[14] 1952 3-9-0 105 .... (b[1]) DJMoran 3 92
(J S Bolger, Ire) *nvr bttr than mid-div* **33/1**

13 3 **Famous (IRE)**[20] 1787 3-9-0 103 .... JAHeffernan 17 85
(A P O'Brien, Ire) *sn chsd ldrs: 5th under 3f out: no ex fr 1 1/2f out* **33/1**

14 1 ¾ **Lady Springbank (IRE)**[56] 1036 3-9-0 104 .... JimCrowley 9 81
(P D Deegan, Ire) *mid-div: 9th 1/2-way: no ex fr 2f out* **20/1**

15 nk **Cnocandancer (IRE)**[20] 1791 3-9-0 .... WJLee 1 80
(T Stack, Ire) *towards rr for most: no imp fr under 3f out* **33/1**

16 nk **What About Me (IRE)**[42] 1244 3-9-0 94 .... DavidNolan 15 80
(Brian Nolan, Ire) *chsd ldrs: 7th 1/2-way: lost pl fr under 3f out: sn no ex* **100/1**

17 nk **Gile Na Greine (IRE)**[21] 1726 3-9-0 110 .... KJManning 19 79
(J S Bolger, Ire) *trckd ldrs: rdn under 3f out: struggling whn short of room and no ex fr 2f out* **5/1[2]**

18 3 ½ **Full Of Hope (IRE)**[14] 1952 3-9-0 92 .... SMLevey 4 71
(A P O'Brien, Ire) *sn led: hdd over 1 1/2f out: sn wknd* **100/1**

19 23 **Queen Of Troy (IRE)**[14] 1952 3-9-0 92 .... JPO'Brien 13 18
(A P O'Brien, Ire) *sn trckd ldr: rdn 1/2-way: wknd fr under 3f out* **100/1**

1m 37.49s (-8.51) **Going Correction** -0.65s/f (Hard) **19** Ran SP% **134.3**
Speed ratings: **116,115,115,115,115 113,112,111,110,110 109,108,105,103,103 102,102,98,75**
CSF £131.68 TOTE £16.10: £4.50, £2.70, £1.40, £4.60; DF 111.30.
Owner Hamdan Al Maktoum **Bred** Tullpark Limited **Trained** The Curragh, Co Kildare
■ Stewards' Enquiry : Ryan Moore caution: used whip with excessive frequency

FOCUS
A big field for this Classic produced a slightly unexpected but meritorious winner. It produced a blanket finish and some of these are likely to prove flattered by the result. The form is rated through the fifth, with improvement from the first two.

NOTEBOOK
Bethrah(IRE) raced only once at two and began the season with a low-key target in a Limerick maiden. She won that with authority, but a narrow win in Leopardstown's Derrinstown 1,000 Guineas Trial still left her with plenty of improvement to find at this level, which she duly did. Tucked in mid-division at half-way, she started to build momentum when switched to the inside over a furlong and came home best to prevail in a blanket-finish. She is clearly a very smart and resolute filly, and further improvement is on the cards. She is not in the Coronation Stakes but could be supplemented. (op 14/1)
Anna Salai(USA), a former French-trained Group 3 winner, making only the fourth appearance of her career, justified her supplementary entry with a solid effort. She struck for home a furlong and half down, but did not show the same turn of foot that she had produced when relegating the Prix Marcel Boussac winner Rosanara to third at Longchamp last month, and was just run out of it in a hectic finish. Like the winner, she is not in the Coronation Stakes. (op 7/1)
Music Show(IRE), who had suffered from track bias in the Newmarket equivalent, stuck to her task well to secure third place, and puts the form in a strong context having won the Nell Gwyn under a penalty that stemmed from last season's Rockfel Stakes win. She could run in the Coronation Stakes next. (op 3/1 tchd 7/2)
Remember When(IRE), a maiden having only her third start, proved best of Aidan O'Brien's runners, putting in a strong finish. She is a three-parts sister to Dylan Thomas, and having already shaped with promise when taking on her elders over a longer trip at Gowran she appeals as a filly who could win a good prize at around 1m2f. She holds an Oaks entry.
Lillie Langtry(IRE), who picked up an injury in last season's Breeder's Cup Juvenile Fillies Turf, lacked the benefit of a previous outing this term. She seemed to be travelling as well as anything under two furlongs but hit a bit of a flat spot before staying on again. There should be better to come from her, since the market indicated no strong confidence despite the riding arrangement. (op 10/1)
Lady Darshaan(IRE) raced in a handy position throughout before being swamped in the closing stages. (op 25/1)
Crystal Gal(IRE), a 96-rated outsider, made progress from the rear without getting close enough to challenge.
Lolly For Dolly(IRE) failed to deliver the performance that might have been expected having made it two from two with a smart-looking win in the Athasi Stakes. The quicker ground may not have suited her. (op 6/1)
Termagant(IRE) was found wanting on her first outing since winning the Moyglare Stud Stakes. (op 10/1 tchd 11/1)
Atasari(IRE), second to Bethrah at Leopardstown, was unable to make any significant impact.
Gile Na Greine(IRE), the Newmarket third, was already labouring when interference sealed her fate. She was never travelling according to her jockey, who thought she didn't handle the fast ground. Official explanation: jockey said filly became unbalanced and did not handle today's ground (op 11/2)

2368 - 2371a (Foreign Racing) - See Raceform Interactive

HOPPEGARTEN (R-H)
Sunday, May 23

OFFICIAL GOING: Turf: good

2372a DIANA-TRIAL (GROUP 2) (3YO FILLIES) (TURF) 1m 2f
3:55 (12:00) 3-Y-O **£35,398** (£13,274; £5,309; £3,539)

RPR

1 **Vanjura (GER)**[22] 1715 3-9-2 0 .... APietsch 2 102
(R Dzubasz, Germany) *settled in 3rd on rail: travelling smoothly: full of running ent st: tk ld 1 1/2f out: r.o ins fnl f: comf* **23/5[3]**

2 1 ¼ **Waldjagd** 3-9-2 0 .... EPedroza 4 100
(A Wohler, Germany) *racd in 2nd fr s: tk ld early in st: ct 1 1/2f out: r.o wl: no threat to wnr clsng stages* **3/1[2]**

3 10 **Elle Shadow (IRE)**[21] 3-9-2 0 .... AStarke 3 80
(P Schiergen, Germany) *led at fast pce: wnt several l clr: began to shorten stride ent st and sn hdd: tired qckly but hld on for 3rd* **2/5[1]**

4 8 **Nicea (GER)**[217] 6892 3-9-2 0 .... FilipMinarik 5 64
(P Schiergen, Germany) *a in rr: nvr threatened* **12/1**

5 24 **Val De Rama (GER)**[21] 3-9-2 0 .... AHelfenbein 1 16
(Uwe Ostmann, Germany) *racd in 4th: rdn bef st: nvr threatened* **11/1**

2m 6.40s (-0.30) **5** Ran SP% **130.3**
WIN (incl. 10 euro stake): 56. PLACES: 18, 12. SF: 193.
Owner German Racing Club **Bred** M Barth **Trained** Germany

[2271]LONGCHAMP (R-H)
Sunday, May 23

OFFICIAL GOING: Turf: good

2373a MONTJEU COOLMORE PRIX SAINT-ALARY (GROUP 1) (3YO FILLIES) (TURF) 1m 2f
1:35 (12:00) 3-Y-O **£126,415** (£50,575; £25,287; £12,632; £6,327)

RPR

1 **Sarafina (FR)**[20] 3-9-0 0 .... GeraldMosse 1 112
(A De Royer-Dupre, France) *racd in 5th fr s: qcknd wl early in st: hmpd by wkng rival 1 1/2f out and in turn hmpd anther rival on rail: qcknd wl and r.o strly to win comf* **13/8[1]**

2 ½ **Deluxe (USA)**[38] 3-9-0 0 .... MaximeGuyon 4 111
(A Fabre, France) *racd in 6th fr s: hrd rdn early in st and mde gd prog: r.o wl but outpcd by wnr ins fnl f* **7/2[2]**

3 1 ½ **Hibaayeb**[21] 1726 3-9-0 0 .... FrankieDettori 5 108
(Saeed Bin Suroor) *led after 1f and stl in front ent st: rdn and r.o wl: outpcd ins fnl f* **8/1**

4 ½ **Galaxidi**[28] 3-9-0 0 .... DavyBonilla 8 107
(F Head, France) *slowly in stride: racd towards rr: rdn early in st: short of room: fin wl whn in clr* **25/1**

5 2 **Plain Vanilla (FR)**[21] 1746 3-9-0 0 .... RonanThomas 9 103
(P Van De Poele, France) *towards rr fr s: rdn early in st but short of room: fin wl whn in clr* **25/1**

6 3 **Aruna (USA)**[28] 1566 3-9-0 0 .... Christophe-PatriceLemaire 6 97
(J E Pease, France) *racd towards rr: wd ent st: r.o clsng stages* **12/1**

7 nk **Dariole (FR)**[31] 1496 3-9-0 0 .... GregoryBenoist 3 96
(P Bary, France) *racd in 4th fr s: rdn early in st but fnd no ex: fdd* **7/1[3]**

8 ½ **T'As D'Beaux Yeux**[22] 3-9-0 0 .... OlivierPeslier 2 95
(D Smaga, France) *racd in 3rd: running on wl on rail whn hmpd by wnr 1 1/2f out: dropped bk qckly but r.o again clsng stages* **10/1**

9 2 **On Verra (IRE)**[21] 1746 3-9-0 0 .... ThierryThulliez 7 91
(F Doumen, France) *racd in 2nd and hld position tl hrd rdn early in st: wkng whn hampering subsequent wnr 1 1/2f out* **12/1**

2m 4.10s (0.10) **Going Correction** +0.30s/f (Good) **9** Ran SP% **116.1**
Speed ratings: **111,110,109,109,107 105,104,104,102**
WIN (incl. 1 euro stake): 2.20. PLACES: 1.20, 1.40, 2.00. DF: 2.50. SF: 2.90.
Owner H H Aga Khan **Bred** H H Aga Khan **Trained** Chantilly, France

FOCUS
It seems curious that a race framed as a trial for the Prix de Diane on June 13 has - and continues to retain - Group 1 status when other more informative trials such as the Derrinstown and Dante are supposedly lesser races. Having said that, a race that had spent some years in the doldrums received a much-needed boost 12 months ago when Stacelita won this en route to wins in the Diane and the Vermeille before being beaten just five lengths by Sea The Stars in the Arc.

NOTEBOOK
Sarafina(FR) was taking a massive step up in class on what was only her second start, less than three weeks after making her debut. After recent events in top fillies' races too, they must have also been pleased to see her keep the race after passing the post half a length clear of Deluxe, having been involved in scrimmaging as they raced into the final 2f of a race that had up to then been fairly uneventful. Underfoot conditions were much quicker than when she won on her debut and the extra 2f suited her well. Her connections have done well with fillies in recent seasons and there could well be plenty more to come from this one, who as well as having the Diane as an obvious target is also entered in the Irish Oaks the following month.
Deluxe(USA), as a half-sister to the likes of Banks Hill and Dansili, is bred to be special. Unbeaten in two starts, she came here instead of last week's Pouliches, which would have been the obvious target judged on her relations. However, it was clear to see why connections went for the option of the longer trip, as after looking short of a turn of foot when they straightened up she responded for pressure to finish well.
Hibaayeb, the sole Group 1 winner in the race, showed more like the level of form that won her the Fillies' Mile last September than when beating just one home in the Guineas last time. Her jockey made the decision to take up the running early on and she was only headed late on. Another try over this longer trip would be well worth it.
Galaxidi, second on her only previous start in a conditions race over 1m3f, did well to finish as close as she did having not got the smoothest passage as she had just two rivals behind when they straightened up.
Plain Vanilla(FR), one of the two behind her at the top of the straight, kept on through beaten horses on ground that was probably plenty quick enough.
Aruna(USA) raced widest down the straight and was unable to build on the promise of her fourth in a Group 3 at this track last time.
Dariole(FR) was the big disappointment of the race. Having won a Group 3 at Saint-Cloud over this trip last month she was expected to play a big part here. After racing in a fairly prominent position, she was shaken up three out and found little once ridden 2f from home. This ground was notably quicker than she has been winning on.
T'As D'Beaux Yeux was badly inconvenienced when she took a bump from the winner. She was the biggest sufferer from the trouble in the race and dropped away after that.
On Verra(IRE), second in the Prix Marcel Boussac on her final start last year, was eased when beaten. She looks best suited by a strong gallop.

2374a PRIX D'ISPAHAN (GROUP 1) (4YO+) (TURF) 1m 1f 55y
2:45 (12:00) 4-Y-O+ **£126,415** (£50,575; £25,287; £12,632; £6,327)

RPR

1 **Goldikova (IRE)**[197] 7308 5-8-13 0 .... OlivierPeslier 1 125+
(F Head, France) *racd in 3rd fr s: cruised to ld 2f out: wnt clr: r.o wl: rdn ins fnl f to hold clsng runner-up* **4/6[1]**

2 ½ **Byword**[22] 1716 4-9-2 0 .... MaximeGuyon 7 126
(A Fabre, France) *towards fr rr fr s: smooth prog early in st: outpcd by wnr fr 1 1/2f out but r.o strly fnl f* **7/2[2]**

3 10 **Wiener Walzer (GER)**[259] 5707 4-9-2 0 .... ADeVries 6 107
(J Hirschberger, Germany) *racd in 4th fr s: rdn 2f out: qcknd wl but had no answer to two ldrs* **14/1**

4 6 **Stacelita (FR)**[231] 6526 4-8-13 0 .... ChristopheSoumillon 4 93
(J-C Rouget, France) *w.w fr s: proged on outside early in st: threatened briefly but sn fdd* **9/2[3]**

5 *10* **Runaway**[45] 1197 8-9-2 0.....(p) ThierryJarnet 3 77
(R Pritchard-Gordon, France) *nvr figured* **66/1**

6 *1* **Next Vision (IRE)**[24] 4-9-2 0..... SHellyn 8 75
(J Hirschberger, Germany) *set fast pce w wnr's pcemaker: fell away qckly early in st* **100/1**

7 *20* **Celebrissime (IRE)**[343] 2953 5-9-2 0..... MickaelBarzalona 9 37
(F Head, France) *set fast pce: led into st: sn wknd and eased* **100/1**

8 *dist* **Board Meeting (IRE)**[231] 6525 4-8-13 0..... AnthonyCrastus 2 —
(E Lellouche, France) *prom early but fdd rapidly in st* **11/1**

1m 49.4s (-5.90) **Going Correction** -0.225s/f (Firm) **8** Ran SP% **118.9**
Speed ratings: **117,116,107,102,93 92,74,—**
WIN (incl. 1 euro stake): 2.10 (Goldikova coupled with Celebrissime), PLACES: 1.20, 1.20, 2.00. DF: 3.40. SF: 7.00.
Owner Wertheimer & Frere **Bred** Wertheimer Et Frere **Trained** France

FOCUS
Most of these were reappearaing and Goldikova is usually better for a run. The form is rated around the second.

NOTEBOOK
Goldikova(IRE) had been beaten first time out for the past two seasons, including in this contest 12 months ago when she finished unplaced for the only time in her 16-race career to date, but it is probably no coincidence that those two defeats came on softer ground. Back on her favoured quicker surface she showed emphatically that she retains all her brilliance at five and that she will again be just about the horse to beat over a mile this year, in France, Britain and the US. It is also fair to say, however, that this will probably turn out to be Goldikova's easiest assignment of the year, as if she goes to Royal Ascot next month she could face the likes of Paco Boy and Rip Van Winkle in the Queen Anne Stakes. She has never run at Ascot before, nor Churchill Downs, where a hat-trick in the Breeders' Cup Mile is the main goal, so there are imponderables ahead. This was more familiar territory, with the same pacemaker, stablemate Celebrissime, as last year in the line-up to help ensure a decent gallop. Also doing that was German-trained Next Vision, stablemate of third home Wiener Walzer. The front-running duo were mastered by Goldikova, who raced in third, just inside the 3f pole, after which she was always comfortably fending off Byword, who quickened well from the rear to get into a challenging position. This was Goldikova's eighth victory at the top level and she broke the track record to boot. The Prix Rothschild, Jacques Le Marois and Foret are again the plan before the Breeders' Cup. She had been rather difficult to load, as she can be at the start, but it made no difference in the race.
Byword put up a personal-best performance in chasing down Goldikova close home while giving her 3lb. Connections are considering the Prince of Wales's Stakes at Royal Ascot, for which Wiener Walzer and Board Meeting are also entered.
Wiener Walzer(GER) had the ground in his favour, but the distance was not so, having shown all his form over further. This was not a bad effort on his first foray outside Germany.
Stacelita(FR) was ridden far more patiently than normal. While one could perhaps understand connections not wanting her to get into a scrap with the two pacesetters, in hindsight she would have been better off racing handier. She did make up some ground in the final 3f, but it was all too late. Byword came from a not dissimilar position in rear, but Stacelita was not able to muster the same burst of acceleration to get into contention, and her jockey was not hard on her after her chance had gone. She can do much better when upped in trip, ridden closer to the pace and given softer ground.
Runaway has won only at Listed level.
Board Meeting(IRE) was beaten 4f out and was disappointing on this return.

2375a PRIX VICOMTESSE VIGIER (GROUP 2) (4YO+) (TURF) 1m 7f 110y
3:15 (12:00) 4-Y-0+ **£65,575** (£25,309; £12,079; £8,053; £4,026)

RPR

1 **Kite Wood (IRE)**[253] 5861 4-8-11 0..... FrankieDettori 3 112
(Saeed Bin Suroor) *sent st to ld: travelled smoothly: qcknd wl early in st and r.o wl to hold runner-up comf in clsng stages* **2/1**[2]

2 *3/4* **Kasbah Bliss (FR)**[21] 1748 8-8-11 0..... ThierryThulliez 2 109
(F Doumen, France) *w.w towards rr: qcknd wl early in st and r.o strly wout seriously threatening wnr ins fnl f* **6/5**[1]

3 *1 1/2* **Blek (FR)**[21] 1748 5-8-11 0..... AnthonyCrastus 6 107
(E Lellouche, France) *pursued ldr fr s: posed a threat ent st and r.o wl but no ex fnl f* **11/2**[3]

4 *1 1/2* **Green Tango (FR)**[21] 1748 7-8-11 0..... RonanThomas 7 106
(P Van De Poele, France) *racd bhd ldrs fr s: rdn early in st and r.o: no real threat to ldrs* **20/1**

5 *1* **Los Cristianos (FR)**[21] 4-8-11 0..... ThomasHuet 4 107
(A Couetil, France) *racd in rr fr s: proged early in st and r.o one pce* **16/1**

6 *5* **Buxted (IRE)**[36] 1382 4-8-11 0..... StevieDonohoe 5 101
(R A Mills) *4th fr s: nvr threatened in st and wknd qckly* **14/1**

7 *1* **Validor (FR)**[42] 1255 4-8-11 0.....(p) OlivierPeslier 1 100
(Y Fouin, France) *nvr prom: hrd rdn early in s: fdd* **25/1**

3m 20.0s (-1.50) **Going Correction** +0.30s/f (Good)
WFA 4 from 5yo+ 1lb **7** Ran SP% **115.3**
Speed ratings: **115,114,113,113,112 110,109**
WIN (incl. 1 euro stake): 3.80. PLACES; 1.90, 1.30. SF: 8.30.
Owner Godolphin **Bred** Elsdon Farms **Trained** Newmarket, Suffolk

NOTEBOOK
Kite Wood(IRE), having his first run since finishing second in last season's St Leger, was allowed a soft lead and took full advantage. He seems a more relaxed horse this year (was quite nervous last season, often sweating up) and is a high-class stayer.
Kasbah Bliss(FR) was set too much to do in a race run at a modest gallop and could not peg back the front-running winner. His main target is the Ascot Gold Cup, but it remains to be seen whether, at the age of eight, he is as good as he was.
Buxted(IRE) promised to be suited by the step up from 1m4f but he was below form. Perhaps this ground was too quick.

2202 CARLISLE (R-H)
Monday, May 24

OFFICIAL GOING: Good to firm (good in places; 6.9)
Outside rail from 4.5f to winning line moved in 4 to 5 yds.
Wind: Light, half against Weather: Fine and sunny

2376 UPPERBY PRIMARY SCHOOL MEDIAN AUCTION MAIDEN STKS 5f
2:15 (2:16) (Class 5) 2-Y-O **£3,238** (£963; £481; £240) **Stalls** High

Form RPR

1 **Marine Commando** 2-9-3 0..... PaulHanagan 2 87+
(R A Fahey) *swtchd rt after 1f: hld up in midfield: hdwy ins fnl 2f: edgd lft and led ins fnl f: pushed out: readily* **7/2**[2]

3 **2** *2 1/4* **Button Moon (IRE)**[11] 2048 2-8-12 0..... RichardThomas 13 74
(I A Wood) *led: rdn along 2f out: hdd ins fnl f: kpt on: nt pce of wnr* **7/2**[2]

3 *3* **Shoshoni Wind** 2-8-12 0..... PaulMulrennan 10 63+
(K A Ryan) *t.k.h: prom: effrt 2f out: hung rt appr fnl f: one pce* **15/2**[3]

6 **4** *1/2* **Dubai Celebration**[40] 1292 2-9-3 0..... TonyHamilton 14 66
(Jedd O'Keeffe) *cl up tl rdn and nt qckn appr fnl f* **16/1**

5 *1 3/4* **No Poppy (IRE)** 2-8-12 0..... DavidAllan 1 55+
(T D Easterby) *bhd and sn outpcd: hdwy 2f out: kpt on steadily fnl f: nvr nr ldrs* **40/1**

0 **6** *1* **Reachtothestars (USA)**[38] 1359 2-9-3 0..... PhillipMakin 9 56
(M Dods) *cl up: rdn and ev ch over 2f out: edgd rt and wknd appr fnl f* **9/4**[1]

04 **7** *2* **Mirror Lad**[39] 1319 2-9-3 0..... RichardSmith 3 49
(Tom Dascombe) *swtchd rt sn after s: bhd: effrt over 2f out: no imp over 1f out* **16/1**

8 *2 3/4* **Beyaz Villas** 2-9-0 0..... MichaelGeran(3) 7 39
(D Nicholls) *hld up: effrt on outside over 2f out: hung lft: sn outpcd* **25/1**

00 **9** *15* **Gunalt Penny Sweet**[13] 1986 2-8-7 0..... JamesSullivan(5) 8 —
(M W Easterby) *in tch tl edgd rt and wknd 2f out* **250/1**

5 **10** *2 3/4* **Chadford**[21] 1749 2-9-3 0..... DuranFentiman 5 —
(T D Walford) *in tch: drvn over 3f out: wknd over 2f out* **9/1**

11 *6* **Illawalla** 2-9-3 0..... PatrickMathers 11 —
(H A McWilliams) *s.i.s: sn outpcd and bhd: no ch fr 1/2-way* **150/1**

12 *2* **Bigalo's Vera B** 2-8-12 0..... FrederikTylicki 12 —
(L A Mullaney) *midfield: drvn and outpcd over 2f out: sn btn* **80/1**

62.17 secs (1.37) **Going Correction** +0.175s/f (Good) **12** Ran SP% **117.3**
Speed ratings (Par 93): **96,92,87,86,84 82,79,74,50,46 36,33**
Tote Swingers: 1&2 £3.10, 1&3 £6.30, 2&3 £4.70 CSF £15.75 TOTE £4.00: £2.50, £1.10, £4.30; EX 23.90.
Owner M Wynne **Bred** L J Vaessen **Trained** Musley Bank, N Yorks

FOCUS
This is often a decent maiden - it went to subsequent Norfolk winner South Central in 2008 - and this year's race looked a good contest and strong form for the track. The winner can rate higher still.

NOTEBOOK
Marine Commando made a winning debut in taking style. A half-brother to a dual 6f winner, his price-tag increased significantly the second time he went through the sales ring, and he is reportedly all speed at home, so much so that his trainer had concerns over him seeing out the stiff 5f. The fact he was a bit outpaced early can be put down to greenness, and that actually worked in his favour, as he had plenty in reserve for the finish, realising what it was all about in the final 2f and picking up really well once switched towards the inside. It was clear he was going to win once angled out to challenge the runner-up, and he ran on strongly to get well on top close home. Significant improvement can be expected with this experience behind him, and connections are right to consider a crack at Royal Ascot, with the Windsor Castle looking the likely target. (op 11-4 tchd 5-2 and 9-2 in places)
Button Moon(IRE) showed plenty when third to a smart-looking sort on her debut at Salisbury, and she set a clear standard of those with previous experience. Obviously a very speedy filly, she was soon out in front and briefly looked to have everything in trouble, but ultimately had no answer when the winner swept past. She has shown more than enough to win a maiden, and will be suited by running on a more speed-favouring track. (op 3-1 tchd 4-1)
Shoshoni Wind, half-sister to precocious 2-y-o Burnwynd Boy, was expected to benefit from the experience, so this has to go down as a very promising debut. She was unable to match the front pair, but there were plenty of positives to take from the performance and she should have no trouble winning a standard maiden. (op 7-1 tchd 9-1)
Dubai Celebration, who showed speed before fading on debut, was again up there early and saw his race out much better this time. (op 20-1)
No Poppy(IRE), whose pedigree is a blend of speed and stamina, was quickly outpaced, but she out in some good late work and clearly going to relish the step up top 6f.
Reachtothestars(USA), who showed a bit of ability when eighth in a fair maiden at Thirsk on debut, came in for strong support and was soon tracking the front-running runner-up, but he couldn't quicken from 2f out and slowly faded. He clearly has ability, but is unlikely to fulfil his potential until racing over at least 6f in handicaps. (op 7-2)
Mirror Lad is now qualified for a mark and should find an opportunity in nurseries. (op 14-1)
Beyaz Villas, bred to need further than this, can be expected to improve for the experience and do better in time. Official explanation: jockey said gelding hung left throughout
Chadford was disappointing, failing to build on his debut effort. Official explanation: trainer had no explanation for the poor form shown (op 14-1)

2377 RAUGHTON HEAD C OF E SCHOOL CLAIMING STKS 7f 200y
2:45 (2:45) (Class 6) 3-Y-O+ **£2,047** (£604; £302) **Stalls** High

Form RPR

3311 **1** **Royal Dignitary (USA)**[13] 1995 10-9-7 80..... MichaelGeran(3) 4 80
(D Nicholls) *mde all: qcknd 2f out: hld on wl fnl f* **9/4**[2]

-403 **2** *3/4* **Finsbury**[7] 2172 7-9-0 58..... GaryBartley(5) 6 71
(D Nicholls) *dwlt: hld up: nt clr run appr 2f out to over 1f out: kpt on wl fnl f* **20/1**

03-2 **3** *3/4* **Moody Tunes**[37] 1374 7-9-8 82..... AndrewElliott 5 74
(J R Weymes) *chsd wnr: effrt over 2f out: kpt on same pce fnl f* **7/4**[1]

0050 **4** *1 1/4* **Bolodenka (IRE)**[2] 2328 8-9-10 77..... PaulHanagan 8 73
(R A Fahey) *hld up in tch on ins: effrt and rdn over 2f out: no imp fnl f* **11/2**[3]

0-44 **5** *6* **Rowan Lodge (IRE)**[6] 2208 8-9-1 62.....(b) IanBrennan(5) 7 56
(Ollie Pears) *in tch: drvn over 2f out: wknd over 1f out* **10/1**

044- **6** *2 1/2* **Kings Point (IRE)**[243] 6217 9-9-8 77..... AndrewMullen 9 52
(D Nicholls) *trckd ldrs tl rdn and wknd over 1f out* **9/1**

4065 **7** *2 3/4* **Rub Of The Relic (IRE)**[28] 1575 5-8-12 57.....(v) PaulPickard(5) 2 41
(P T Midgley) *sn trcking ldrs: drvn and outpcd over 2f out: sn btn* **33/1**

0-30 **8** *52* **Welcome Bounty**[50] 1103 3-8-10 0..... PaulMulrennan 3 —
(Miss L A Perratt) *hld up on outside: rdn and hung lft ent st: sn btn: eased whn no ch fnl f* **100/1**

1m 42.38s (2.38) **Going Correction** +0.175s/f (Good)
WFA 3 from 5yo+ 12lb **8** Ran SP% **110.3**
Speed ratings (Par 101): **95,94,93,92,86 83,81,29**
Tote Swingers: 1&2 £9.60, 1&3 £2.00, 2&3 £5.90 CSF £42.72 TOTE £2.80: £2.30, £5.10, £1.02; EX 32.20.Finsbury was claimed by Mr Ken McGarrity for £5,000.
Owner Middleham Park Racing XXXVI **Bred** Bentley Smith, J Michael O'Farrell Jr , Joan Thor **Trained** Sessay, N Yorks

FOCUS
Not a bad little claimer and the time compared well with the later handicap. The form could be rated higher but that would suppose that the runner-up has improved.
Welcome Bounty Official explanation: jockey said colt hung left in straight

2378 RACING UK SKY 432 H'CAP (DIV I) 5f 193y
3:15 (3:15) (Class 6) (0-65,65) 4-Y-O+ **£1,706** (£503; £252) **Stalls** High

Form RPR

0-00 **1** **Ryedane (IRE)**[8] 2144 8-8-8 55.....(b) DavidAllan 6 65
(T D Easterby) *mde all: rdn 2f out: edgd lft and hld on wl fnl f* **6/1**

0-40 **2** *nk* **Hansomis (IRE)**[6] 2206 6-8-13 60..... FrederikTylicki 10 69
(B Mactaggart) *hld up: hdwy over 2f out: chsd wnr 1f out: kpt on u.p fin* **5/1**[2]

5- **3** 1 ¾ **Distant Vision (IRE)**^{219} 6856 7-8-4 **51** oh2 .... PatrickMathers 13 54
(H A McWilliams) *chsd ldrs: wnt 2nd over 2f out to 1f out: kpt on same pce* **50/1**

4340 **4** 3 ½ **Namir (IRE)**^{16} 1915 8-9-4 **65** .... DuranFentiman 12 57
(H J Evans) *towards rr and sn pushed along: hdwy over 1f out: kpt on: nrst fin* **12/1**

05-1 **5** ½ **Ace Of Spies (IRE)**^{22} 1723 5-9-0 **61** .... SilvestreDeSousa 11 51
(G A Harker) *prom: rdn and edgd lft 2f out: sn one pce* **11/4**^{1}

-543 **6** ¾ **Cool Art (IRE)**^{13} 2010 4-8-1 **53** ow1 .... IanBrennan$^{(5)}$ 9 41
(J S Wainwright) *hld up towards rr: effrt and drvn over 2f out: no imp fr over 1f out* **10/1**

2000 **7** ¾ **Misterisland (IRE)**^{48} 1148 5-7-13 **53** oh6 ow2 .... JosephYoung$^{(7)}$ 4 38
(M Mullineaux) *bhd on outside: hung lft ent st: sn rdn: hung rt ins fnl f: no imp* **50/1**

0303 **8** 1 ¼ **Soto**^{14} 1968 7-8-5 **57** .... (b) JamesSullivan$^{(5)}$ 2 38
(M W Easterby) *chsd wnr to over 2f out: wknd over 1f out* **11/1**

4000 **9** 1 ¼ **Ponting (IRE)**^{9} 2113 4-8-11 **63** .... PaulPickard$^{(5)}$ 3 40
(P T Midgley) *in tch on outside: rdn 1/2-way: wknd fr 2f out* **25/1**

3230 **10** *nk* **Megalo Maniac**^{13} 1998 7-8-4 **51** oh5 .... (v) PaulHanagan 8 27
(R A Fahey) *bhd and drvn along: nvr able to chal* **11/1**

345- **11** 4 **Tripbiyah (USA)**^{227} 6637 4-9-1 **62** .... PJMcDonald 5 26
(G A Swinbank) *hld up in tch: effrt and rdn over 2f out: wknd over 1f out* **11/2**^{3}

56-0 **12** 5 **Port Ronan (USA)**^{17} 1885 4-8-2 **52** oh6 ow1 .... (p) MartinLane$^{(3)}$ 1 —
(J S Wainwright) *chsd ldrs tl rdn and wknd over 2f out* **66/1**

660 **13** 9 **Boxer Shorts**^{75} 849 4-8-6 **53** .... AndrewElliott 7 —
(M Mullineaux) *midfield: struggling after 2f: sn btn* **40/1**

1m 14.55s (0.85) **Going Correction** +0.175s/f (Good) 13 Ran SP% **118.2**
Speed ratings (Par 101): **101,100,98,93,92 91,90,89,87,87 81,75,63**
Tote Swingers: 1&2 £8.90, 1&3 £80.20, 2&3 £37.10 CSF £34.48 CT £1424.94 TOTE £8.30: £2.80, £1.50, £19.50; EX 41.60.
Owner Ryedale Partners No 5 **Bred** Tally-Ho Stud **Trained** Great Habton, N Yorks

FOCUS
The first and slower division of what was a moderate sprint handicap. The form is rated through the winner.

2379 FANTAILS RESTAURANT SUPPORTS BOB CHAMPION'S CHARITY FILLIES' H'CAP — 1m 1f 61y
3:45 (3:46) (Class 5) (0-70,67) 3-Y-0 **£3,238** (£963; £481; £240) **Stalls** High

Form RPR

1636 **1** **Wedding Dream**^{81} 781 3-9-1 **64** .... SilvestreDeSousa 7 76
(K A Ryan) *mde all: rdn and flashed tail over 1f out: kpt on strly to go clr fnl f: edgd lft towards fin* **18/1**

-133 **2** 5 **Dazakhee**^{21} 1753 3-8-12 **61** .... TonyCulhane 6 62
(P T Midgley) *t.k.h: hld up: hdwy to chse wnr 2f out: sn rdn and edgd rt: one pce fnl f* **10/3**^{3}

45-0 **3** 4 ½ **Anaya**^{13} 2005 3-8-11 **65** .... RossAtkinson$^{(5)}$ 3 56
(Tom Dascombe) *trckd wnr: effrt over 2f out: wknd over 1f out* **12/1**

0-00 **4** 6 **Main Spring**^{26} 1620 3-9-4 **67** .... PhillipMakin 5 45
(M L W Bell) *in tch: drvn and reminders 4f out: shortlived effrt over 2f out: wknd over 1f out* **8/1**

-033 **5** 2 **Refuse To Wait (IRE)**^{9} 2132 3-9-0 **63** .... (b) DavidAllan 2 37
(T D Easterby) *prom: rdn and outpcd whn checked over 2f out: sn n.d* **15/8**^{1}

0-04 **6** *shd* **Cygnet Committee (IRE)**^{14} 1971 3-7-13 **53** oh5 .(b) JamesSullivan$^{(5)}$ 1 26
(J S Wainwright) *hld up: drvn along over 3f out: btn fnl 2f* **40/1**

30-6 **P** **Princess Emma**^{16} 1927 3-8-13 **62** .... PaulHanagan 8 —
(R A Fahey) *trckd ldrs: drvn over 3f out: broke down over 2f out: sn p.u: fatally injured* **11/4**^{2}

1m 58.67s (1.07) **Going Correction** +0.175s/f (Good) 7 Ran SP% **111.0**
Speed ratings (Par 96): **102,97,93,88,86 86,—**
Tote Swingers: 1&2 £9.00, 1&3 £9.10, 2&3 £9.70 CSF £72.54 CT £737.76 TOTE £21.60: £11.90, £2.00; EX 75.40.
Owner J H Henderson **Bred** Lofts Hall Stud **Trained** Hambleton, N Yorks

FOCUS
A low-grade fillies' handicap. The winner made all in a fair time and there seemed no fluke about it.
Refuse To Wait(IRE) Official explanation: jockey said filly suffered interference in running

2380 JOOLS HOLLAND/ALISON MOYET HERE 3RD JULY H'CAP — 6f 192y
4:15 (4:15) (Class 6) (0-60,60) 3-Y-0 **£2,047** (£604; £302) **Stalls** High

Form RPR

0042 **1** **Dispol Kabira**^{3} 2273 3-8-4 **46** oh1 .... PatrickMathers 10 50
(D W Thompson) *chsd ldrs: led over 2f out: hung lft over 1f out: drvn out fnl f* **11/2**^{3}

5-00 **2** ¾ **Luv U Noo**^{3} 2291 3-8-12 **54** .... TonyHamilton 9 56
(B Ellison) *hld up in tch: effrt on ins 2f out: chsd wnr appr fnl f: kpt on towards fin* **8/1**

00 **3** 1 ¼ **Lady Vyrnwy (IRE)**^{14} 1966 3-8-8 **50** .... PaulHanagan 1 49
(R A Fahey) *in tch: effrt and rdn 2f out: kpt on same pce ins fnl f* **12/1**

0-00 **4** 1 ½ **Scooby Dee**^{14} 1970 3-8-2 **49** ow3 .... AmyRyan$^{(5)}$ 2 44
(R M Whitaker) *bhd on outside: outpcd after 3f: rallied 2f out: edgd rt: kpt on ins fnl f: nrst fin* **8/1**

0550 **5** ¾ **Rescent**^{6} 2209 3-8-4 **46** oh1 .... AndrewElliott 4 39
(Mrs R A Carr) *chsd ldrs: drvn over 2f out: edgd rt and one pce over 1f out* **22/1**

6-22 **6** 2 ½ **Coolella (IRE)**^{6} 2209 3-8-11 **56** .... MartinLane$^{(3)}$ 11 42
(J R Weymes) *w ldr: led over 3f out to over 2f out: edgd lft and wknd appr fnl f* **9/4**^{1}

52-0 **7** *shd* **Dandarrell**^{23} 1685 3-9-4 **60** .... PaulMulrennan 5 46
(Julie Camacho) *hld up: pushed along 3f out: no imp fr 2f out* **9/1**

0-63 **8** 1 ½ **High Resolution**^{6} 2209 3-8-10 **57** .... JamesSullivan$^{(5)}$ 3 38
(Miss L A Perratt) *led to over 2f out: sn rdn: wknd over 1f out* **5/1**^{2}

04-0 **9** 12 **Hedgerow (IRE)**^{14} 1971 3-8-13 **55** ow1 .... DanielTudhope 7 4
(A Dickman) *hld up: hmpd after 1f: hdwy and hung rt over 2f out: sn btn* **12/1**

1m 29.63s (2.53) **Going Correction** +0.175s/f (Good) 9 Ran SP% **114.8**
Speed ratings (Par 97): **92,91,89,88,87 84,84,82,68**
Tote Swingers: 1&2 £18.30, 1&3 £5.90, 2&3 £13.50 CSF £48.42 CT £507.37 TOTE £6.30: £1.60, £3.80, £5.40; EX 49.60.
Owner J Greenbank **Bred** Silfield Bloodstock **Trained** Bolam, Co Durham

FOCUS
A very weak handicap. Straightforward form with the winner confirming her latest improvement and the second back to her 2yo form.
Hedgerow(IRE) Official explanation: jockey said filly suffered interference leaving stalls

2381 RACING UK SKY 432 H'CAP (DIV II) — 5f 193y
4:45 (4:46) (Class 6) (0-65,63) 4-Y-0+ **£1,706** (£503; £252) **Stalls** High

Form RPR

0-14 **1** **King Of Eden (IRE)**^{16} 1915 4-8-11 **56** .... DavidAllan 4 77+
(E J Alston) *cl up: led 1/2-way: rdn clr over 1f out: eased towards fin* **2/1**^{1}

33-0 **2** 6 **Elkhorn**^{17} 1885 8-8-2 **50** .... (b) MartinLane$^{(3)}$ 12 52
(Julie Camacho) *trckd ldrs: effrt over 2f out: chsd wnr over 1f out: kpt on: no imp* **11/1**

5-60 **3** ¾ **El Dececy (USA)**^{24} 1653 6-9-3 **62** .... AndrewElliott 11 61
(J Balding) *hld up: rdn and hdwy over 1f out: kpt on fnl f: nrst fin* **14/1**

1610 **4** 2 ¼ **Imperial Djay (IRE)**^{7} 2188 5-9-2 **61** .... PhillipMakin 3 53
(Mrs R A Carr) *hld up: hdwy on outside over 1f out: kpt on: nt pce to chal* **5/1**^{2}

405- **5** ½ **Optical Illusion (USA)**^{216} 6925 6-8-10 **55** .... PaulHanagan 8 46
(R A Fahey) *in tch: rdn over 2f out: no imp over 1f out* **10/1**

5-02 **6** *nk* **Two Turtle Doves (IRE)**^{17} 1885 4-8-7 **59** .... JosephYoung$^{(7)}$ 1 49
(M Mullineaux) *led to 1/2-way: rdn and edgd lft 2f out: sn one pce* **11/2**^{3}

0-40 **7** 2 **Avoncreek**^{88} 694 6-8-1 **49** oh4 .... KellyHarrison$^{(3)}$ 6 32
(B P J Baugh) *hld up: effrt on ins whn n.m.r over 1f out to ins fnl f: n.d* **50/1**

4240 **8** ¾ **Guest Connections**^{6} 2206 7-8-13 **63** .... (v) MichaelO'Connell$^{(5)}$ 7 44
(D Nicholls) *midfield on outside: rdn and hung rt wl over 1f out: sn outpcd* **16/1**

0-44 **9** 3 ¼ **Fyodorovich (USA)**^{13} 2010 5-7-13 **49** oh3 .... (v) JamesSullivan$^{(5)}$ 2 19
(J S Wainwright) *prom tl edgd rt and wknd over 1f out* **22/1**

2320 **10** 6 **Welcome Approach**^{12} 2021 7-8-8 **53** .... PaulMulrennan 10 4
(J R Weymes) *in tch tl rdn and wknd wl over 1f out* **9/1**

0002 **11** 8 **Bertbrand**^{14} 1968 5-8-4 **49** .... (v) SilvestreDeSousa 5 —
(I W McInnes) *hld up: rdn and hung rt 2f out: sn btn* **40/1**

1m 13.88s (0.18) **Going Correction** +0.175s/f (Good) 11 Ran SP% **114.1**
Speed ratings (Par 101): **105,97,96,93,92 91,89,88,83,75 65**
Tote Swingers: 1&2 £4.50, 1&3 £7.70, 2&3 £15.70 CSF £24.34 CT £245.74 TOTE £4.00: £1.80, £2.40, £3.30; EX 27.40.
Owner The Grumpy Old Geezers **Bred** Gainsborough Stud Management Ltd **Trained** Longton, Lancs

FOCUS
Nowhere near as competitive as the first division but the winner scored easily in a fast time. He can rate higher.
Avoncreek Official explanation: jockey said gelding was denied a clear run

2382 CUMBERLAND SHOW HERE 17TH JULY APPRENTICE H'CAP — 7f 200y
5:15 (5:16) (Class 6) (0-65,64) 4-Y-0+ **£2,047** (£604; £302) **Stalls** High

Form RPR

-000 **1** **Chicamia**^{61} 969 6-7-13 **51** oh5 ow1 .... JosephYoung$^{(7)}$ 13 57
(M Mullineaux) *bhd: n.m.r briefly over 2f out: hdwy wl over 1f out: styd on fnl f: led last stride* **125/1**

0-32 **2** *nse* **Desert Hunter (IRE)**^{6} 2207 7-8-8 **53** .... KellyHarrison 8 59
(Micky Hammond) *t.k.h: cl up: led over 2f out to over 1f out: led ins fnl f: kpt on: hdd last stride* **3/1**^{1}

0-66 **3** ¾ **Fortunate Bid (IRE)**^{28} 1575 4-9-2 **61** .... JamesSullivan 14 65
(Mrs L Stubbs) *hld up ins: stdy hdwy over 2f out: led over 1f out to ins fnl f: one pce towards fin* **9/2**^{2}

40/0 **4** ¾ **Custard Cream Kid (IRE)**^{14} 1967 4-8-7 **55** .... LeeTopliss$^{(3)}$ 7 57
(R A Fahey) *hld up: effrt and swtchd wd 2f out: edgd rt and kpt on fnl f: nrst fin* **14/1**

05- **5** 3 ¼ **Mister Maq**^{343} 2965 7-8-0 **50** oh4 .... (b) MatthewLawson$^{(5)}$ 9 45
(A Crook) *bhd tl hdwy over 1f out: kpt on fnl f: nvr able to chal* **33/1**

-003 **6** 1 **Hettie Hubble**^{3} 2273 4-8-2 **50** oh2 .... JohnCavanagh$^{(3)}$ 11 43
(D W Thompson) *midfield: pushed along over 2f out: no imp over 1f out* **16/1**

5-56 **7** ½ **Morocchius (USA)**^{28} 1574 5-9-3 **62** .... MartinLane 12 53
(Julie Camacho) *chsd ldrs: rdn 3f out: no ex over 1f out* **6/1**^{3}

445- **8** ½ **Eastern Hills**^{201} 7247 5-9-5 **64** .... (p) LanceBetts 10 54
(J S Wainwright) *cl up tl rdn and wknd over 1f out* **7/1**

-040 **9** 1 ¾ **Aussie Blue (IRE)**^{16} 1926 6-9-2 **61** .... AmyRyan 6 47
(R M Whitaker) *midfield: rdn 3f out: hdwy and hung rt fr 2f out: wknd ent fnl f* **8/1**

00-5 **10** 1 ¾ **Champain Sands (IRE)**^{22} 1717 11-8-12 **57** .... PaulPickard 2 39
(E J Alston) *hld up: effrt whn n.m.r 2f out: sn n.d* **13/2**

0-00 **11** 6 **Red China Blues (USA)**^{22} 1717 4-8-9 **54** .... DeanHeslop 5 22
(R E Barr) *in tch on outside: rdn over 2f out: sn wknd* **16/1**

-060 **12** 12 **Eyes Like A Hawk (IRE)**^{6} 2207 4-8-5 **50** .... RossAtkinson 3 —
(Jedd O'Keeffe) *cl up tl rdn and wknd fr 2f out* **50/1**

30/0 **13** 1 **Emirate Isle**^{26} 1574 6-9-3 **62** .... (b^{1}) MichaelO'Connell 4 —
(B Storey) *led to over 2f out: sn wknd* **33/1**

1m 43.43s (3.43) **Going Correction** +0.175s/f (Good) 13 Ran SP% **121.5**
Speed ratings (Par 101): **89,88,88,87,84 83,82,82,80,78 72,60,59**
Tote Swingers: 1&2 £97.20, 1&3 £4.50, 2&3 £48.60 CSF £484.30 CT £2222.59 TOTE £117.30: £20.30, £1.20, £1.60; EX 405.90 Place 6 £295.58, Place 5 £168.26.
Owner Abbey Racing **Bred** Limestone And Tara Studs **Trained** Alpraham, Cheshire

FOCUS
A massive shock for this concluding apprentices' handicap with the winner, 15lb wrong, showing his first real form. The time was slow and this is dubious form.
T/Jkpt: Not won. T/Plt: £377.50. Pool: £68,962.68 - 133.33 winning units. T/Qpdt: £78.40. Pool: £44.520 - 4,716.90 winning units. RY

2170 LEICESTER (R-H)
Monday, May 24

OFFICIAL GOING: Good to firm (firm in places; watered; 8.8)
Wind: Light behind Weather: Fine and sunny

2383 LADBROKES.COM H'CAP — 7f 9y
2:00 (2:01) (Class 5) (0-70,70) 3-Y-0+ **£2,590** (£770; £385; £192) **Stalls** Low

Form RPR

-560 **1** **Learo Dochais (USA)**^{27} 1595 4-9-5 **63** .... (p) PhilipRobinson 5 73
(M A Jarvis) *chsd ldr tl led 1/2-way: rdn over 1f out: r.o* **8/1**

66 **2** 1 ½ **Crocodile Bay (IRE)**^{13} 1998 7-8-12 **56** oh3 .... FrannyNorton 7 62
(R C Guest) *a.p: rdn to chse wnr over 1f out: r.o* **28/1**

2560 **3** 2 ½ **Eastern Gift**^{34} 1440 5-9-10 **68** .... JimmyFortune 2 67
(Miss Gay Kelleway) *hld up: hdwy u.p 2f out: r.o: nt rch ldrs* **20/1**

2635 **4** 2 ¼ **Billberry**^{25} 1634 5-8-9 **60** .... (t) RyanClark$^{(7)}$ 4 53+
(S C Williams) *hld up: hdwy 1/2-way: rdn over 1f out: no ex ins fnl f* **11/2**^{3}

43-3 **5** *1 ¾* **Plutocraft**[21] 1766 3-9-1 **70** WilliamBuick 6 58+
(J R Fanshawe) *hld up: hdwy 1/2-way: rdn over 1f out: wknd ins fnl f* **9/4**[1]

64-0 **6** *2 ¾* **Sweet Possession (USA)**[35] 1426 4-9-0 **58** NeilCallan 9 39+
(A P Jarvis) *led to 1/2-way: rdn over 1f out: wknd ins fnl f* **12/1**

-536 **7** *2 ¾* **Fly By Nelly**[117] 318 4-9-0 **58** SteveDrowne 3 32
(H Morrison) *hld up: hdwy u.p 2f out: wknd fnl f* **8/1**

0506 **8** *6* **Kheskianto (IRE)**[16] 1928 4-8-7 **56** oh4 MarkCoumbe(5) 10 13
(M C Chapman) *chsd ldrs: rdn 1/2-way: wknd over 2f out* **40/1**

5-65 **9** *23* **Cadeaux Fax**[21] 1762 5-9-1 **62** JamesMillman(3) 1 —
(B R Millman) *chsd ldrs: rdn over 2f out: sn wknd and eased: t.o* **10/3**[2]

-000 **10** *6* **Seneschal**[13] 2009 9-9-12 **70** KierenFallon 8 —
(A B Haynes) *prom: rdn 4f out: wknd over 2f out: t.o* **22/1**

1m 25.33s (-0.87) **Going Correction** -0.025s/f (Good)
WFA 3 from 4yo+ 11lb **10** Ran SP% **114.1**
Speed ratings (Par 103): **103,101,98,95,93 90,87,80,54,47**
Tote Swingers: 1&2 £22.50, 1&3 £20.90, 2&3 £30.90 CSF £208.78 CT £4355.08 TOTE £14.40: £3.20, £5.70, £5.80; EX 106.60 TRIFECTA Not won..
Owner Mrs Lynn Mernagh **Bred** D J Stable **Trained** Newmarket, Suffolk

FOCUS
A low-grade handicap and not too competitive. The field split into two groups and those on the near side seemed to be at an advantage, with the first three racing closest to the stands' rail, and those who raced on the far side appearing to go off too fast. The form doesn't look too solid.
Kheskianto(IRE) Official explanation: jockey said filly was struck into behind
Cadeaux Fax Official explanation: trainer had no explanation for the poor form shown
Seneschal Official explanation: jockey said gelding felt wrong behind

2384 LADBROKES.COM MAIDEN STKS (DIV I) 5f 218y
2:30 (2:30) (Class 4) 2-Y-O **£4,533** (£1,348; £674; £336) **Stalls** Low

Form RPR

1 **King Torus (IRE)** 2-9-3 0 RichardHughes 4 87+
(R Hannon) *hld up: shkn up over 2f out: hdwy to ld over 1f out: sn clr: edgd rt nr fin: readily* **6/4**[1]

5 **2** *5* **Tokum (IRE)**[13] 2007 2-9-3 0 WilliamBuick 6 68
(J Noseda) *hld up: rdn over 2f out: r.o u.p ins fnl f: no ch w wnr* **8/1**[3]

3 *1 ¼* **Postscript (IRE)** 2-9-3 0 TedDurcan 2 64
(Mahmood Al Zarooni) *prom: rdn over 2f out: edgd rt and no ex ins fnl f* **7/2**[2]

0 **4** *nk* **Pretium Sceleris**[22] 1728 2-9-3 0 NeilCallan 11 63
(M Botti) *w ldr tl led over 4f out: rdn and hdd over 1f out: no ex ins fnl f* **8/1**[3]

5 *nk* **Titus Two (IRE)** 2-9-3 0 JimmyFortune 8 62
(P W Chapple-Hyam) *prom: rdn over 2f out: and ev ch over 1f out: no ex ins fnl f* **20/1**

0 **6** *2* **Aramid (IRE)**[10] 2077 2-9-3 0 MichaelHills 10 56
(B W Hills) *led: hdd over 4f out: chsd ldr tl rdn over 2f out: wknd fnl f* **16/1**

7 *shd* **Silver Alliance** 2-9-3 0 ShaneKelly 3 56
(W R Swinburn) *chsd ldrs: rdn over 2f out: hung rt over 1f out: sn wknd* **22/1**

00 **8** *hd* **Bonjour Bongee**[11] 2059 2-9-3 0 JamesDoyle 7 55
(A J McCabe) *prom: rdn over 2f out: wknd over 1f out* **80/1**

0 **9** *nk* **Salvationist**[10] 2077 2-9-3 0 RichardMullen 9 54
(J L Dunlop) *s.i.s: in rr: rdn over 2f out: wknd over 1f out* **33/1**

0 **10** *6* **Market Maker (IRE)**[11] 2059 2-9-3 0 KierenFallon 5 37
(T D Easterby) *chsd ldrs: rdn and lost pl wl over 3f out: styng on although no ch whn eased fnl f* **12/1**

11 *22* **Eduardo** 2-9-3 0 TomEaves 1 —
(Jedd O'Keeffe) *s.s: outpcd: t.o* **100/1**

1m 13.35s (0.35) **Going Correction** -0.025s/f (Good) **11** Ran SP% **112.3**
Speed ratings (Par 95): **96,89,87,87,86 84,84,83,83,75 46**
Tote Swingers: 1&2 £3.70, 1&3 £4.20, 2&3 £6.00 CSF £12.52 TOTE £3.30: £1.10, £2.50, £1.30; EX 16.30 Trifecta £37.10 Pool: £369.50 - 7.37 winning units..
Owner Hitchcock & King **Bred** Whisperview Trading Ltd **Trained** East Everleigh, Wilts

FOCUS
A fair maiden and yet another impressive winner from the Hannon stable. He was value for further and looks Listed class at this stage.

NOTEBOOK
King Torus(IRE) is a half-brother to a sprint winner in Italy, out of a fast mare. Despite running green in the early stages, Hughes switched him towards the stands'-side rail (where he changed his lead leg) and he picked up impressively. This was his yard's 21st juvenile winner this year and he could head for the Chesham at Royal Ascot, with his connections expecting a longer trip to suit him in time. (op 5-4)
Tokum(IRE) ◆ was expected to run well on debut but was too green to do himself justice. He had clearly learnt plenty from that and ran creditably here doing good late work. He should shed his maiden tag soon. (op 10-1)
Postscript(IRE) is a half-brother to the very smart French sprinter Do The Honours, out of a smart mare at 6f-1m. He was wearing a noseband for his racecourse debut and ran green early on, before getting the hang of things and plugging on late. Horses from this yard seem to be better for the run so a bold showing next time can be expected. (op 6-1)
Pretium Sceleris was well beaten on debut but showed more promise on his second start. He looks capable of making his mark. Official explanation: jockey said colt hung left (op 11-2 tchd 5-1)
Titus Two(IRE) was a cheap purchase who ran well considering he looked in need of the experience. He will do better in time. (op 12-1)
Aramid(IRE) again shaped with promise but could be one who will fare better in handicaps. (tchd 18-1)
Market Maker(IRE) Official explanation: jockey said gelding was unsuited by the good to firm (firm in places) ground

2385 LADBROKES.COM HICKLING (S) STKS 5f 218y
3:00 (3:01) (Class 6) 3-5-Y-O **£1,942** (£578; £288; £144) **Stalls** Low

Form RPR

4-00 **1** **Sophie's Beau (USA)**[6] 2197 3-8-11 77 JimmyFortune 1 65
(B J Meehan) *trckd ldrs: rdn to ld and hung rt fr over 1f out: styd on u.p* **9/2**[2]

6-00 **2** *2 ¾* **Piazza San Pietro**[14] 1967 4-9-6 65 KierenFallon 9 58+
(A B Haynes) *hld up in tch: rdn and ev ch over 1f out: styd on same pce ins fnl f* **7/2**[1]

0242 **3** *1 ¼* **Bold Ring**[13] 2010 4-9-1 55 EddieCreighton 4 49
(E J Creighton) *hld up: rdn over 1f out: r.o ins fnl f: nt trble ldrs* **13/2**[3]

6230 **4** *nk* **King's Sabre**[4] 2263 4-9-6 50 (e) FrannyNorton 6 53
(R C Guest) *hld up: pushed along over 2f out: r.o ins fnl f: nvr nrr* **9/1**

0-05 **5** *1* **Come On Buckers (IRE)**[13] 2008 4-9-3 55 (v) AlanCreighton(3) 8 50
(E J Creighton) *led: rdn and hdd over 1f out: no ex fnl f* **22/1**

2-50 **6** *2* **Feeling Fragile (IRE)**[11] 2052 3-8-11 68 RyanMoore 2 41
(Pat Eddery) *trckd ldrs: rdn over 2f out: sn hung rt: wknd ins fnl f* **9/2**[2]

0610 **7** *5* **Titus Gent**[20] 1799 5-9-11 63 DavidProbert 3 32
(R A Harris) *chsd ldrs: rdn 1/2-way: wknd wl over 1f out* **7/2**[1]

0400 **8** *½* **Baby Judge (IRE)**[9] 2132 3-8-6 52 MarkCoumbe(5) 5 24
(M C Chapman) *chsd ldrs: rdn over 3f out: wknd over 2f out* **80/1**

0406 **9** *¾* **Mandhooma**[7] 2166 4-9-1 49 ChrisCatlin 7 18
(P W Hiatt) *prom: rdn over 2f out: wknd fnl f* **40/1**

1m 12.65s (-0.35) **Going Correction** -0.025s/f (Good)
WFA 3 from 4yo+ 9lb **9** Ran SP% **112.2**
Speed ratings (Par 101): **101,97,95,95,93 91,84,83,82**
Tote Swingers: 1&2 £5.50, 1&3 £3.40, 2&3 £8.50 CSF £19.68 TOTE £7.00: £2.30, £2.20, £1.40; EX 24.00 Trifecta £163.00 Pool: £257.73 - 1.17 winning units..The winner was sold to M Chapman for 5,700gns.
Owner Iraj Parvizi **Bred** Steve C Snowden & Doug Wilson **Trained** Manton, Wilts

FOCUS
An ordinary seller. The winner was a fair way off his 2yo form and again it was an advantage to race near the rail.
Titus Gent Official explanation: jockey said gelding never travelled

2386 LADBROKES.COM BELVOIR CASTLE H'CAP 1m 1f 218y
3:30 (3:30) (Class 4) (0-85,80) 3-Y-O **£4,209** (£1,252; £625; £312) **Stalls** High

Form RPR

610 **1** **Vulcanite (IRE)**[39] 1330 3-9-3 **76** JimCrowley 6 87+
(R M Beckett) *hld up: racd keenly: pushed along 3f out: hdwy over 1f out: r.o to ld wl ins fnl f: comf* **12/1**

4-51 **2** *½* **Buffett**[14] 1973 3-8-13 **72** KierenFallon 1 81+
(L M Cumani) *s.i.s: hld up: hdwy over 2f out: rdn to ld 1f out: sn edgd rt: hdd wl ins fnl f* **7/2**[3]

1-5 **3** *2 ¾* **Sierra Alpha**[22] 1734 3-9-6 **79** TedDurcan 4 83
(Mrs A J Perrett) *chsd ldrs: rdn and ev ch fr over 2f out tl no ex wl ins fnl f* **10/1**

01-0 **4** *½* **Mr Irons (USA)**[38] 1352 3-9-7 **80** RyanMoore 2 84+
(Sir Michael Stoute) *s.i.s: sn prom: pushed along over 3f out: rdn and ev ch over 1f out: n.m.r ins fnl f: styd on same pce* **9/4**[2]

25-1 **5** *1 ¼* **Flying Destination**[37] 1393 3-9-5 **78** ShaneKelly 3 78
(W J Knight) *t.k.h: w ldr tl led over 2f out: rdn and hdd 1f out: no ex* **16/1**

3-51 **6** *hd* **Udabaa (IRE)**[21] 1766 3-9-7 **80** RichardHills 7 83+
(M P Tregoning) *chsd ldrs: rdn and nt clr run over 2f out: swtchd rt over 1f out: styd on same pce* **15/8**[1]

6-54 **7** *4 ½* **Dynamic Drive (IRE)**[16] 1912 3-9-5 **78** AdamKirby 5 72
(W R Swinburn) *led: rdn and hdd over 2f out: hmpd over 1f out: wknd fnl f* **25/1**

2m 6.13s (-1.77) **Going Correction** -0.15s/f (Firm) **7** Ran SP% **114.3**
Speed ratings (Par 101): **101,100,98,98,97 96,93**
Tote Swingers: 1&2 £5.50, 2&3 £12.50 CSF £53.42 TOTE £7.60: £7.70, £1.30; EX 65.00.
Owner Mrs Barbara Facchino **Bred** Barouche Stud Ireland Ltd **Trained** Whitsbury, Hants

FOCUS
A fair handicap, but it was a bit of a messy race and it is hard to be too positive about the bare form. The race contained some likely improvers though and the winner is rated up 10lb.

2387 LADBROKES.COM CHARNWOOD FOREST FILLIES' CONDITIONS STKS 7f 9y
4:00 (4:00) (Class 2) 3-Y-O+ **£9,969** (£2,985; £1,492; £747) **Stalls** Low

Form RPR

13-0 **1** **Seta**[22] 1726 3-8-6 102 KierenFallon 4 109+
(L M Cumani) *trckd ldr tl led over 4f out: shkn up over 1f out: r.o: edgd rt nr fin* **6/4**[1]

4-52 **2** *1 ¾* **First City**[16] 1899 4-8-13 96 ShaneKelly 1 104
(D M Simcock) *trckd ldrs: wnt 2nd 4f out: rdn over 1f out: styd on same pce ins fnl f* **11/4**[3]

3030 **3** *7* **Souter's Sister (IRE)**[16] 1918 4-8-13 90 WilliamBuick 2 85
(M Botti) *hld up: rdn over 2f out: wknd over 1f out: wnt 3rd nr fin* **16/1**

254- **4** *nk* **Baileys Cacao (IRE)**[352] 2703 4-8-13 102 RichardHughes 3 84
(R Hannon) *led: hdd over 4f out: rdn and hung rt over 1f out: wknd fnl f: lost 3rd nr fin* **15/8**[2]

1m 25.36s (-0.84) **Going Correction** -0.025s/f (Good)
WFA 3 from 4yo 11lb **4** Ran SP% **107.3**
Speed ratings (Par 96): **103,101,93,92**
CSF £5.80 TOTE £2.70; EX 5.30.
Owner Miss Sarah J Leigh **Bred** Sarah J Leigh And Robin S Leigh **Trained** Newmarket, Suffolk

FOCUS
A very interesting fillies' event with the 3-y-o Seta beating her elders. She raced up the favoured rail and is rated up 6lb on her 2yo form and not far off the leading 3-y-o fillies. The race was slower than the earlier handicap.

NOTEBOOK
Seta had been beaten twice in pattern company since winning impressively on debut, although she was on the wrong side in the 1000 Guineas at Newmarket when last seen. Given an uncomplicated ride by Kieren Fallon, who never resorted to using his whip, she won in workmanlike style against the stands' rail. The quick ground would not have been that much to her liking, but she did what was asked of her. A tilt at the Coronation Stakes at Royal Ascot has been ruled out, ansd she is likely to run in a Listed race at Warwick next. (op 6-5 tchd 13-8)
First City had come up short when tried in Pattern races in her career to date but she gave the winner a race from 2f out. Despite carrying her head awkwardly, she ought to be up to winning races in future, but connections could seek valuable black type with her. Better ground would suit her. (op 4-1)
Souter's Sister(IRE) is becoming a disappointment and has lost her form. (op 14-1)
Baileys Cacao(IRE) set the slow early pace but ultimately dropped away as if the run was needed. She missed the second half of last season after putting up some creditable efforts in Group company. In time she should prove better than the bare result. Official explanation: jockey said filly moved poorly (op 2-1)

2388 LADBROKES.COM CLAIMING STKS 1m 1f 218y
4:30 (4:30) (Class 5) 4-Y-O+ **£2,590** (£770; £385; £192) **Stalls** High

Form RPR

0442 **1** **Rocky's Pride (IRE)**[5] 2233 4-8-9 67 NeilCallan 9 72+
(A B Haynes) *led after 1f: set stdy pce tl qcknd over 3f out: rdn over 1f out: eased ins fnl f* **5/2**[2]

010- **2** *5* **Saltagioo (ITY)**[19] 5725 6-9-3 80 RyanMoore 5 70
(A King) *hld up in tch: chsd wnr over 3f out: sn rdn and no imp* **6/5**[1]

00-0 **3** *2 ½* **Applaude**[16] 1919 5-8-9 57 (b) FrannyNorton 7 57
(R C Guest) *hld up: plld hrd: hdwy over 2f out: wnt 3rd over 1f out: nvr trbld ldrs* **22/1**

3526 **4** *1 ¼* **Quince (IRE)**[27] 1592 7-8-2 60 (v) SimonPearce(5) 3 53
(J Pearce) *hld up: rdn over 2f out: r.o ins fnl f: nvr nrr* **10/1**

3000 **5** *shd* **Sacrilege**[9] 2133 5-8-8 70 (b) MarkCoumbe(5) 4 59
(M C Chapman) *s.i.s: hld up: r.o ins fnl f: nrst fin* **25/1**

6 *½* **Macanta (USA)**[234] 6466 4-9-2 0 (t) NickyMackay 8 61
(G A Butler) *hld up: plld hrd: hdwy over 2f out: sn rdn: nt trble ldrs* **20/1**

0-00 **7** 3¾ **Firsaan (IRE)**[28] 1576 4-8-9 43 JoeFanning 6 46
(J R Norton) *chsd ldrs: rdn over 3f out: wknd wl over 1f out* **100/1**

5005 **8** ¾ **Dream Of Fortune (IRE)**[7] 2182 6-8-2 70 (b) MatthewCosham(7) 2 45
(P D Evans) *s.i.s: hld up: hdwy over 2f out: sn rdn and edgd rt: wknd over 1f out* **8/1**[3]

00/0 **9** 7 **Alright Chuck**[12] 2023 6-8-7 30 ChrisCatlin 11 29
(P W Hiatt) *prom: rdn over 3f out: wknd wl over 1f out* **200/1**

00-0 **10** 5 **Spume (IRE)**[14] 1980 6-8-10 44 RussKennemore(3) 1 25
(J Balding) *s.i.s: hld up: hdwy 1/2-way: rdn 4f out: wknd 3f out* **66/1**

/60- **11** 2¼ **Highway Magic (IRE)**[8] 4389 4-8-13 58 RichardMullen 10 20
(A P Jarvis) *led 1f: chsd wnr tl rdn over 3f out: sn wknd* **80/1**

2m 7.58s (-0.32) **Going Correction** -0.15s/f (Firm) 11 Ran SP% **111.4**
Speed ratings (Par 103): **95,91,89,88,87 87,84,83,78,74 72**
Tote Swingers: 1&2 £2.00, 1&3 £7.30, 2&3 £7.10 CSF £5.12 TOTE £2.70: £1.10, £2.50, £6.40; EX 7.10 Trifecta £86.00 Pool: £268.87 - 2.31 winning units..Rocky's Pride was claimed by Mr W. J. Musson for £6,000. Saltagioo was claimed by M. F. Harris for £10,000.
Owner Athos Racing **Bred** London Thoroughbred Services Ltd **Trained** Limpley Stoke, Bath

FOCUS
The winner got a very easy lead here and the form of this weak claimer is best rated through him.
Macanta(USA) Official explanation: jockey said filly was unsuited by the good to firm (firm in places) ground

2389 LADBROKES.COM MAIDEN STKS (DIV II) 5f 218y
5:00 (5:00) (Class 4) 2-Y-O **£4,533** (£1,348; £674; £336) **Stalls** Low

Form RPR

5 **1** **Sheer Courage (IRE)**[22] 1728 2-9-3 0 RyanMoore 7 96+
(R Hannon) *mde all: shkn up over 1f out: r.o strly to go clr fnl f: impressive* **13/8**[2]

2 10 **Residence And Spa (IRE)** 2-9-3 0 ChrisCatlin 9 66+
(T D Easterby) *s.i.s: hld up: hdwy over 1f out: r.o to go 2nd wl ins fnl f: no ch w wnr* **50/1**

2 **3** nk **Old Master Expert**[16] 1901 2-9-3 0 HayleyTurner 10 65
(M L W Bell) *hld up in tch: racd keenly: chsd wnr over 2f out: rdn over 1f out: wknd ins fnl f* **6/4**[1]

63 **4** 1¾ **Royal Opera**[18] 1845 2-9-0 0 JamesMillman(3) 5 60
(B R Millman) *chsd ldrs: rdn over 2f out: wknd fnl f* **16/1**

5 1½ **Stentorian (IRE)** 2-9-3 0 JoeFanning 3 55
(M Johnston) *rn green: sn pushed along and prom: wknd over 1f out* **16/1**

6 2½ **Georgina Bailey (IRE)** 2-8-12 0 JamesDoyle 4 43
(A J McCabe) *hld up: swtchd rt and sme hdwy wl over 1f out: sn wknd* **100/1**

7 5 **Emmeline Pankhurst (IRE)** 2-8-12 0 MichaelHills 6 28
(Miss J Feilden) *s.i.s: sn pushed along in rr: bhd fr 1/2-way* **13/2**[3]

0 **8** 8 **Diplomasi**[58] 1009 2-9-3 0 NeilCallan 2 9
(C E Brittain) *pushed along early: sn trcking wnr and racd keenly: rdn over 2f out: wknd wl over 1f out* **25/1**

0 **9** 8 **Triple Agent (IRE)**[42] 1263 2-9-3 0 PaulDoe 8 —
(A Bailey) *prom tl rdn and wknd over 2f out* **33/1**

1m 12.4s (-0.60) **Going Correction** -0.025s/f (Good) 9 Ran SP% **112.9**
Speed ratings (Par 95): **103,89,89,86,84 81,74,64,53**
Tote Swingers: 1&2 £12.00, 1&3 £1.60, 2&3 £9.70 CSF £87.13 TOTE £3.20: £1.10, £10.00, £1.10; EX 82.40 Trifecta £104.40 Pool: £342.98 - 2.43 winng units..
Owner The Socrates Partnership **Bred** A Stroud And J Hanly **Trained** East Everleigh, Wilts

FOCUS
A very impressive winner in this second division of the juvenile maiden as Sheer Courage thrashed what looked a fairly decent field.

NOTEBOOK
Sheer Courage(IRE) ◆ improved bundles for his debut at Newmarket and bounced off this quicker ground. He lengthened well close home under only a hand ride from Ryan Moore to score comfortably. This was a really taking performance and he could now head to Royal Ascot. He is also entered in some sales races at the end of the season so that is another option open to connections. (op 5-2 tchd 6-4)
Residence And Spa(IRE) was clueless in the early stages but did some good late work. He will get further in time and is sure to be winning races. (tchd 40-1)
Old Master Expert had the best form in the race but was blown away by an impressive winner. He is clearly up to winning races and looks a nice prospect. (op Evens)
Royal Opera was the most experienced runner in the race and he is the one to rate the race around. He should be winning races and now has the option of handicaps. (tchd 14-1)
Stentorian(IRE), a 110,000gns yearling by Street Cry, was too green to do himself justice on debut. He will have learnt plenty from this and a bold showing is expected next time. (op 14-1)
Emmeline Pankhurst(IRE) was fractious in the preliminaries and too green in the race to do herself justice. The money for her beforehand suggested she is well regarded and it would be no surprise to see her improve from this. Official explanation: trainer said filly was found to be in season (op 7-1 tchd 9-1)
Triple Agent(IRE) Official explanation: jockey said gelding moved poorly

2390 LADBROKES.COM COPLOW MAIDEN STKS 1m 3f 183y
5:30 (5:32) (Class 5) 3-Y-O **£2,590** (£770; £385; £192) **Stalls** High

Form RPR

423 **1** **Bay Willow (IRE)**[9] 2115 3-9-3 77 RichardHills 3 93+
(M Johnston) *led at stdy pce tl qcknd over 3f out: shkn up over 2f out: c clr fr over 1f out: eased ins fnl f* **10/11**[1]

3-3 **2** 6 **Sister Earth (IRE)**[34] 1451 3-8-12 0 WilliamBuick 2 73
(J H M Gosden) *chsd wnr: rdn over 2f out: hung rt over 1f out: styd on same pce* **11/2**[3]

632- **3** 4½ **Magnetic Force (IRE)**[228] 6607 3-9-3 75 RyanMoore 8 71
(Sir Michael Stoute) *chsd ldrs: rdn over 3f out: wknd fnl f* **9/4**[2]

4-6 **4** 2¼ **Mausin (IRE)**[38] 1356 3-8-12 0 TravisBlock 4 62+
(H Morrison) *hld up: hdwy 1/2-way: rdn and wknd over 1f out* **20/1**

5 6 **Rhyton (IRE)** 3-9-3 0 RichardMullen 1 58+
(Sir Michael Stoute) *sn pushed along and a in rr: wknd over 2f out* **33/1**

0-0 **6** 9 **Annelko**[37] 1393 3-9-3 0 RobertHavlin 6 46
(A B Haynes) *hld up: rdn and wknd over 2f out* **100/1**

0- **7** 2 **Amylyn**[201] 7244 3-8-12 0 JerryO'Dwyer 5 35
(J R Holt) *s.s: hld up: pushed along 1/2-way: sn bhd* **250/1**

0 **8** 3 **Jewellery (IRE)**[16] 1932 3-8-12 0 PatCosgrave 7 36
(J R Fanshawe) *chsd ldrs: rdn over 3f out: sn wknd* **33/1**

2m 30.77s (-3.13) **Going Correction** -0.15s/f (Firm) 8 Ran SP% **110.6**
Speed ratings (Par 99): **104,100,97,95,91 85,84,82**
Tote Swingers: 1&2 £2.70, 2&3 £2.30 CSF £5.86 TOTE £1.70: £1.10, £1.10, £1.50; EX 6.70 Trifecta £11.40 Pool: £408.55 - 26.49 winning units. Place 6 £367.78, Place 5 £27.92.
Owner Sheikh Hamdan Bin Mohammed Al Maktoum **Bred** Philip Brady **Trained** Middleham Moor, N Yorks

FOCUS
A modest maiden but a taking and progressive winner who was value for 9l.

T/Plt: £194.90. Pool: £71,842.44 - 269.01 winning units. T/Qpdt: £17.70. Pool: £6,321.06 - 262.80 winning units. CR

2130 THIRSK (L-H)
Monday, May 24

OFFICIAL GOING: Good to firm (firm in places; 10.8)
Wind: Light across Weather: Fine and dry

2391 CARPENTERS ARMS, FELIXKIRK (S) STKS 6f
6:25 (6:25) (Class 4) 2-Y-O **£4,274** (£1,271; £635; £317) **Stalls** High

Form RPR

35 **1** **Daas Rite (IRE)**[40] 1292 2-8-12 0 AlanMunro 8 66
(K A Ryan) *hld up: swtchd outside and hdwy 2f out: chal over 1f out: rdn to ld ent fnl f: kpt on* **9/4**[1]

63 **2** 2 **Madam Markievicz (IRE)**[23] 1704 2-8-7 0 (p) TonyHamilton 5 55
(M Dods) *t.k.h: chsd ldr: hdwy 2f out: rdn to ld briefly over 1f out: hdd ent fnl f: kpt on* **9/2**

12 **3** 6 **Tanked Up (IRE)**[25] 1647 2-8-12 0 BillyCray(5) 2 49
(D Nicholls) *sn led: rdn along 2f out: drvn and hdd appr fnl f and sn one pce* **7/2**[2]

4 1 **Artic Rose (IRE)** 2-8-4 0 WilliamCarson(3) 9 34
(S C Williams) *trckd ldrs: swtchd lft and hdwy over 1f out: rdn and rdr dropped reins jst ins fnl f: no imp* **12/1**

5 shd **Alhoni** 2-8-2 0 IanBrennan(5) 1 36+
(J J Quinn) *dwlt and wnt lft s: sn in rr: hdwy 2f out: kpt on ins fnl f: nrst fin* **14/1**

2 **6** 5 **Muse To Use**[8] 2139 2-8-7 0 PatrickMathers 7 19
(I W McInnes) *prom: rdn along 2f out: sn wknd* **4/1**[3]

03 **7** 2½ **Kodibelle (IRE)**[8] 2139 2-8-7 0 (b) DuranFentiman 6 11
(T D Easterby) *chsd ldrs: rdn along 1/2-way: sn wknd* **15/2**

1m 13.46s (0.76) **Going Correction** -0.125s/f (Firm) 7 Ran SP% **117.3**
Speed ratings (Par 95): **89,86,78,77,76 70,66**
Tote Swingers: 1&2 £2.30, 1&3 £1.70, 2&3 £7.60 CSF £13.32 TOTE £3.20: £1.50, £5.60; EX 11.10.There was no bid for the winner.
Owner Miss Deirdre McGuire & Mrs J Ryan **Bred** Mark & Pippa Hackett **Trained** Hambleton, N Yorks

FOCUS
A run-of-the-mill two-year-old seller. The time was fast for the grade but this is possibly not form to trust, although the winner looks a fair plater.

NOTEBOOK
Daas Rite(IRE), the paddock pick, came from well off the pace to win going away. He will be suited by a step up to seven and might be capable of adding a claimer before the nurseries start. (op 4-1)
Madam Markievicz(IRE), who hung badly on her second start, sported first-time cheekpieces. She was very keen but kept on to finish clear second best and should be able to find a similar event. (op 11-2)
Tanked Up(IRE) showed plenty of toe to take them along but he emptied badly. He is not exactly progressing and 5f looks his trip. (op 3-1 tchd 11-4)
Artic Rose(IRE), who has plenty of stamina on her dam's side, showed a measure of ability on her debut despite her rider getting his reins in a tangle. (op 10-1 tchd 14-1)
Alhoni, who started slowly and was soon being scrubbed along, made a little late ground and will have learnt from this. (op 12-1)
Muse To Use, claimed after finishing runner-up in a similar event first time at Ripon, showed plenty of dash but dropped right away in most disappointing fashion. (op 7-2)

2392 BLACK SHEEP BREWERY H'CAP 1m
6:55 (6:56) (Class 5) (0-75,72) 4-Y-O+ **£4,274** (£1,271; £635; £317) **Stalls** Low

Form RPR

1-21 **1** **Night Lily (IRE)**[17] 1877 4-9-1 69 TonyCulhane 3 83+
(P W D'Arcy) *trckd ldrs on inner: hdwy wl over 2f out: swtchd rt and effrt to chse ldr over 1f out: rdn to chal ent fnl f: styd on to ld fnl 100yds* **11/2**[3]

5-23 **2** ½ **Jonny Lesters Hair (IRE)**[6] 2211 5-8-13 67 DavidAllan 10 79
(T D Easterby) *led: rdn along 2f out: drvn and hung rt ins fnl f: hdd and no ex fnl 100yds* **9/2**[2]

6310 **3** 4½ **By Command**[16] 1926 5-9-0 68 (tp) AlanMunro 5 70+
(K A Ryan) *hld up towards rr: hdwy over 2f out: sn rdn and styd on ins fnl f: nrst fin* **18/1**

06-0 **4** ¾ **Ailsa Craig (IRE)**[16] 1926 4-8-10 64 PaulMulrennan 12 64
(E W Tuer) *prom: chsd ldr after 3f: rdn 2f out: kpt on same pce apperoaching fnl f* **33/1**

-316 **5** 2¾ **French Art**[16] 1926 5-9-4 72 (p) PhillipMakin 11 66
(N Tinkler) *hld up towards rr: hdwy on outer over 2f out: rdn and kpt on ins fnl f: nt rch ldrs* **7/1**

04-2 **6** 1 **Shadowtime**[16] 1926 5-8-11 65 AndrewMullen 7 57
(Miss Tracy Waggott) *chsd ldrs: hdwy 3f out: rdn along 2f out: sn drvn and btn* **85/40**[1]

-000 **7** 1½ **Violent Velocity (IRE)**[21] 1754 7-8-10 71 ShaneBKelly(7) 1 59
(J J Quinn) *hld up towards rr on inner: swtchd rt and hdwy 3f out: rdn and edgd rt wl over 1f out: sn no imp* **22/1**

643 **8** shd **I'm Frank**[22] 1721 4-9-0 68 PJMcDonald 2 56
(G A Swinbank) *dwlt and in rr tl sme late hdwy* **16/1**

-000 **9** 1 **Cherri Fosfate**[16] 1923 6-8-3 62 (t) IanBrennan(5) 6 48
(D Carroll) *dwlt: a towards rr* **40/1**

-260 **10** 2¼ **Sarwin (USA)**[35] 1426 7-8-11 65 RobertWinston 8 45
(G A Swinbank) *cl up: rdn along 3f out: sn wknd* **12/1**

051- **11** shd **Kildare Sun (IRE)**[221] 6806 8-8-11 65 (p) PaulHanagan 4 45
(J Mackie) *chsd ldrs: rdn wl over 2f out: sn drvn and wknd* **20/1**

3202 **12** 7 **Hits Only Jude (IRE)**[13] 1997 7-8-10 64 DavidNolan 9 28
(D Carroll) *chsd ldrs: rdn along 3f out: sn wknd* **12/1**

1m 37.48s (-2.62) **Going Correction** -0.25s/f (Firm) 12 Ran SP% **119.1**
Speed ratings (Par 103): **103,102,98,97,94 93,92,91,90,88 88,81**
Tote Swingers: 1&2 £7.50, 1&3 £28.20, 2&3 £19.40 CSF £29.22 CT £430.34 TOTE £6.00: £2.70, £1.30, £7.30; EX 34.00.
Owner K Snell **Bred** Keith Wills **Trained** Newmarket, Suffolk

FOCUS
A modest 62-72 handicap and the pace was not strong with the runner-up granted a fairly easy lead. He is rated back to his best though and the winner remains progressive.

The Form Book, Raceform Ltd, Compton, RG20 6NL

Shadowtime Official explanation: jockey said gelding was unsuited by the good to firm (firm in places) ground

2393 TURFTV MAIDEN STKS 7f
7:25 (7:29) (Class 5) 3-Y-O+ **£4,274** (£1,271; £635; £317) **Stalls** Low

Form RPR
5 **1** **Sailorman (IRE)**[34] 1450 3-9-2 0 GregFairley 3 76+
(M Johnston) *mde all: rdn 2f out: drvn over 1f out: styd on gamely towards fin* **85/40**[1]
65-2 **2** ¾ **Touch Tone**[13] 2003 3-8-11 75 RobertWinston 9 69
(B W Hills) *trckd ldrs on inner: hdwy 2f out: effrt and n.m.r over 1f out: swtchd rt and drvn ins fnl f: no ex towards fin* **85/40**[1]
2-02 **3** *shd* **Antarctic Desert (IRE)**[17] 1868 3-9-2 72 AlanMunro 8 74
(K A Ryan) *chsd wnr: rdn along 2f out: drvn over 1f out: kpt on u.p ins fnl f* **11/2**[2]
0-43 **4** 3 ¼ **Compton Park**[24] 1659 3-9-2 76 ShaneKelly 13 65
(W J Knight) *trckd ldrs: hdwy 3f out: rdn wl over 1f out: kpt on same pce ent fnl f* **15/2**[3]
5 **5** *nse* **Roose Blox (IRE)**[20] 1804 3-9-2 0 TonyHamilton 14 65
(R F Fisher) *stdd and swtchd lft s: hld up towards rr: hdwy towards outer over 2f out: rdn over 1f out: kpt on ins fnl f: nrst fin* **40/1**
6 ¾ **Hades (IRE)** 3-9-2 0 DavidAllan 5 63+
(T D Easterby) *s.i.s: in rr whn rn wd bnd after 2f: hdwy over 2f out: sn rdn and kpt on ins fnl f: nrst fin* **33/1**
0 **7** ¾ **Viking Warrior (IRE)**[23] 1706 3-9-2 0 PhillipMakin 12 61
(M Dods) *t.k.h: chsd ldrs: rdn along 2f out: no imp appr fnl f* **20/1**
0 **8** *nk* **Offspring**[49] 1116 3-8-11 0 DuranFentiman 16 55
(T D Easterby) *chsd ldrs on outer: effrt over 2f out: rdn wl over 1f out: kpt on same pce ins fnl f* **50/1**
64 **9** ½ **Smarty Sam (USA)**[10] 2072 3-9-2 0 PJMcDonald 4 59+
(G A Swinbank) *hld up towards rr: hdwy wl over 2f out: n.m.r and swtchd rt over 1f out: keeping on whn n.m.r ins fnl f* **18/1**
0/ **10** 1 ¼ **Olympian Order (IRE)**[635] 5387 4-9-13 0 AndrewElliott 2 60
(G A Swinbank) *hld up: effrt 3f out: sn rdn and no imp* **66/1**
11 *nk* **Leolene Starlight**[75] 5-9-8 0 FranciscoDaSilva 7 54
(J Hetherton) *chsd ldrs: rdn along 3f out: sn hung lft and wknd* **150/1**
6 **12** 1 ¼ **Ingleby King (USA)**[9] 2114 4-9-8 0 DeanHeslop(5) 6 54
(T D Barron) *dwlt and slty hmpd at s: a towards rr* **14/1**
00 **13** 3 **Marsh's Gift**[23] 1706 3-8-11 0 PaulPickard(5) 1 42
(R E Barr) *t.k.h: a in rr* **200/1**
00 **14** 2 ¾ **Accamelia**[20] 1804 4-9-8 0 PaulMulrennan 11 33
(C W Fairhurst) *in tch on inner: rdn along 3f out: grad wknd* **100/1**
/4 **15** 95 **Rosbertini**[17] 1868 4-9-8 0 AmyRyan(5) 10 —
(Miss L A Perratt) *rrd bdly and swvd violently lft s: a t.o* **80/1**

1m 25.38s (-1.82) **Going Correction** -0.25s/f (Firm)
WFA 3 from 4yo+ 11lb **15** Ran SP% **120.1**
Speed ratings (Par 103): **100,99,99,95,95 94,93,93,92,91 90,88,85,82,48**
Tote Swingers: 1&2 £2.80, 1&3 £5.30, 2&3 £2.90 CSF £5.55 TOTE £2.80: £1.10, £2.20, £1.10; EX 9.10.
Owner Sheikh Hamdan Bin Mohammed Al Maktoum **Bred** 6c Racing Ltd **Trained** Middleham Moor, N Yorks

FOCUS
Just an average maiden with plenty of deadwood. The form makes plenty of sense among the front three.

2394 WEATHERBYS BANK H'CAP 7f
7:55 (7:56) (Class 4) (0-85,85) 3-Y-O **£5,569** (£1,657; £828; £413) **Stalls** Low

Form RPR
406- **1** **Maison Brillet (IRE)**[248] 6048 3-8-4 71 oh3 PaulHanagan 3 76
(J Howard Johnson) *trckd ldrs: hdwy 2f out: rdn to chse ldr over 1f out: drvn ins fnl f: styd on to ld nr line* **13/2**
0-06 **2** *hd* **The Hermitage (IRE)**[24] 1656 3-8-6 73 GregFairley 4 77
(M Johnston) *led: rdn along 2f out: drvn ent fnl f: edgd rt: hdd and nt qckn nr line* **22/1**
1322 **3** 2 ¼ **Tiradito (USA)**[72] 884 3-9-2 83 (p) AndreaAtzeni 6 81
(M Botti) *hld up in rr: hdwy wl over 2f out: rdn over 1f out: kpt on wl fnl f: nrst fin* **5/1**
-000 **4** ½ **Ongoodform (IRE)**[23] 1701 3-9-4 85 TonyCulhane 7 82
(P W D'Arcy) *trckd ldrs: hdwy wl over 2f out: sn rdn and kpt on same pce fnl f* **10/3**[2]
313- **5** *hd* **Licence To Till (USA)**[149] 7846 3-9-2 83 JoeFanning 2 79
(M Johnston) *t.k.h: trckd ldng pair: effrt over 2f out: rdn wl over 1f out: drvn and one pce ent fnl f* **9/2**[3]
3341 **6** ¾ **Hot Spark**[9] 2112 3-8-8 75 (t) AlanMunro 5 71
(K A Ryan) *cl up: effrt over 2f out and ev ch tl sltly outpcd over 1f out: eased ins fnl f* **9/4**[1]
1-30 **7** 6 **Tres Amigos**[10] 2069 3-8-2 72 WilliamCarson(3) 1 50
(D Nicholls) *hld up in tch: effrt 3f out: rdn along over 2f out: sn wknd* **12/1**

1m 25.71s (-1.49) **Going Correction** -0.25s/f (Firm) **7** Ran SP% **114.1**
Speed ratings (Par 101): **98,97,95,94,94 93,86**
Tote Swingers: 1&2 £7.40, 1&3 £3.00, 2&3 £19.80 CSF £121.07 TOTE £12.90: £13.80, £21.00; EX 101.60.
Owner Mrs Mary Bird & J Howard Johnson **Bred** Liam Webb **Trained** Billy Row, Co Durham

FOCUS
A 71-85 three-year-olds' handicap. It was slower than the previous maiden and the form might not prove solid, with the first two seemingly back to their 2yo form.
Hot Spark Official explanation: trainer said colt was unsuited by the track

2395 WEATHERBYS BLOODSTOCK INSURANCE H'CAP 1m 4f
8:25 (8:25) (Class 4) (0-85,84) 4-Y-O+ **£5,569** (£1,657; £828; £413) **Stalls** Low

Form RPR
3213 **1** **Destinys Dream (IRE)**[3] 2276 5-8-7 76 KellyHarrison(3) 2 83+
(Miss Tracy Waggott) *hld up in rr: hdwy 3f out: n.m.r 2f out: sn swtchd ins and chal over 1f out: rdn and qcknd to ld ins fnl f* **13/8**[1]
6023 **2** 1 ¼ **Daaweitza**[13] 1996 7-8-7 80 ow1 (b) DaleSwift(7) 6 84
(B Ellison) *t.k.h: trckd ldng pair tl rapid hdwy to ld after 3f: rdn along over 2f out: drvn over 1f out: hdd ins fnl f* **3/1**[3]
-043 **3** 5 **Umverti**[16] 1925 5-8-4 70 oh7 PaulQuinn 5 66
(N Bycroft) *cl up 3f: trckd ldng pair: effrt on outer 3f out: rdn to chal whn edgd lft 2f out: ch tl drvn and one pce appr fnl f* **8/1**
216- **4** ½ **Act Of Kalanisi (IRE)**[253] 5909 4-9-4 84 GregFairley 3 79
(M Johnston) *led 3f: trckd ldr: hdwy and cl up 4f out: rdn along over 3f out: drvn whn n.m.r 2f out and sn wknd* **2/1**[2]

2m 34.21s (-1.99) **Going Correction** -0.25s/f (Firm) **4** Ran SP% **107.5**
Speed ratings (Par 105): **96,95,91,91**
CSF £6.60 TOTE £1.80; EX 7.90.
Owner H Conlon **Bred** Sean Burke **Trained** Spennymoor, Co Durham

FOCUS
A stop-start gallop to this four-runner 70-84 handicap. Weakish form and it's doubtful if the winner had to improve.

2396 WELCOME TO YORKSHIRE'S HERRIOT COUNTRY FILLIES' H'CAP 5f
8:55 (8:55) (Class 5) (0-70,70) 3-Y-O+ **£4,274** (£1,271; £635; £317) **Stalls** High

Form RPR
3-26 **1** **Poppy's Rose**[2] 2326 6-8-7 60 ow3 DaleSwift(7) 6 74
(T J Etherington) *trckd ldrs: hdwy 1/2-way: led wl over 1f out: rdn and hung lft ins fnl f: kpt on* **11/4**[1]
-601 **2** 2 **Ask Jenny (IRE)**[3] 2278 8-8-7 58 DeclanCannon(5) 2 65
(Patrick Morris) *slty hmpd s and towards rr: hdwy 2f out: rdn to chse wnr ent fnl f: sn drvn and edgd lft: kpt on* **8/1**
5235 **3** 1 ¼ **Fasliyanne (IRE)**[6] 2213 4-8-10 56 oh2 (b) AlanMunro 5 58
(K A Ryan) *trckd ldrs: hdwy over 2f out: rdn to chse ldrs over 1f out: drvn and kpt on same pce fnl f* **11/1**
-254 **4** ½ **Picnic Party**[13] 2004 3-9-0 68 PaulMulrennan 7 65
(D R C Elsworth) *sn led: rdn along 2f out: sn hdd: drvn and one pce fr over 1f out* **8/1**
00-5 **5** *nk* **Piste**[8] 2144 4-9-0 60 FrederikTylicki 10 59
(Miss T Jackson) *cl up on stands' rail: rdn along 2f out: sn one pce* **10/1**
0-66 **6** 1 ¾ **Revue Princess (IRE)**[10] 2087 5-9-0 60 (b) DavidAllan 9 53
(T D Easterby) *chsd ldrs: rdn along 2f out: sn one pce* **6/1**[3]
545- **7** 1 ½ **Oondiri (IRE)**[230] 6554 3-8-4 58 (p) DuranFentiman 11 42
(T D Easterby) *a towards rr* **16/1**
0000 **8** 3 **Red Rosanna**[2] 2310 4-9-3 70 LeeTopliss(7) 8 47
(R Hollinshead) *chsd ldrs: rdn along 2f out: sn wknd* **12/1**
155- **9** 15 **On The Piste (IRE)**[192] 7372 3-8-9 63 PaulHanagan 1 —
(L A Mullaney) *towards rr: rdn along and hung bdly lft 1/2-way: sn outpcd and bhd* **25/1**
-001 **U** **Mey Blossom**[10] 2087 5-8-12 61 MichaelStainton(3) 3 —
(R M Whitaker) *stmbld and uns rdr s* **4/1**[2]

58.89 secs (-0.71) **Going Correction** -0.125s/f (Firm)
WFA 3 from 4yo+ 8lb **10** Ran SP% **118.0**
Speed ratings (Par 100): **100,96,94,94,93 90,88,83,59,—**
Tote Swingers: 1&2 £5.50, 1&3 £9.30, 2&3 £24.60 CSF £25.73 CT £212.98 TOTE £3.90: £1.90, £3.60, £4.00; EX 35.60 Place 6 £552.74, Place 5 £266.19.
Owner Mrs Ann Morris **Bred** Mrs A Morris **Trained** Norton, N Yorks

FOCUS
A modest 58-70 sprint handicap. The winner showed her recent Listed effort didn't totally flatter her.
On The Piste(IRE) Official explanation: jockey said filly hung left-handed throughout
T/Plt: £966.00. Pool: £69,940.83 - 52.85 winning units. T/Qpdt: £204.60. Pool: £6,063.55 - 21.93 winning units. JR

2176 WINDSOR (R-H)
Monday, May 24

OFFICIAL GOING: Good to firm (8.2)
Stands' rail dolled out 10yds from 6f down to 3yds at the winning post. Top bend dolled out 8yds from innermost line adding 30yds to races of 1m or over.
Wind: Light, behind Weather: Sunny, hot

2397 E B F TIME 106.6 FM RADIO NOVICE STKS 5f 10y
6:10 (6:10) (Class 5) 2-Y-O **£3,367** (£1,002; £500; £250) **Stalls** High

Form RPR
2212 **1** **Scarlet Rocks (IRE)**[7] 2177 2-8-11 0 CathyGannon 3 81
(P D Evans) *racd freely: led: rdn and narrowly hdd over 1f out: hung lft fnl f: drvn to ld nr fin* **7/2**[3]
2 *hd* **Stone Of Folca** 2-8-9 0 KierenFox(5) 7 84+
(J R Best) *free to post: cl up: wnt 2nd bef 1/2-way gng wl: shkn up to ld narrowly over 1f out: hung lft fnl f: rdn and hdd nr fin* **16/1**
012 **3** ¾ **Joyously**[10] 2082 2-8-6 0 AndrewHeffernan(3) 8 76
(P D Evans) *settled towards rr: wnt 4th 2f out but hrd rdn: styd on u.p fnl f to take 3rd nr fin* **20/1**
613 **4** ½ **Fifth Ave**[10] 2095 2-8-11 0 FergusSweeney 6 76
(J A Osborne) *cl up: pressed ldng pair fr 1/2-way on outer: chal over 1f out: nt qckn fnl f* **5/2**[2]
5 2 ¼ **Eshoog (IRE)** 2-8-9 0 SebSanders 4 66
(C E Brittain) *s.s: last and wl off the pce to 1/2-way: effrt 2f out but hanging lft: no imp on ldrs over 1f out* **7/1**
4 **6** *nk* **Maggie's Treasure (IRE)**[17] 1871 2-9-0 0 TadhgO'Shea 5 72+
(J Gallagher) *s.i.s: hld up: gng wl enough but inclined to hang fr 2f out: nudged along and kpt on* **50/1**
143 **7** *hd* **Takeaway**[7] 2177 2-9-5 0 RichardHughes 2 74
(R Hannon) *settled off the pce in rr: effrt 1/2-way: no imp on ldrs over 1f out: btn after* **9/4**[1]
61 **8** 11 **Danube Dancer (IRE)**[13] 1999 2-9-0 0 LiamKeniry 1 30
(J S Moore) *pressed wnr 2f: wknd rapidly: t.o* **16/1**

60.73 secs (0.43) **Going Correction** -0.025s/f (Good) **8** Ran SP% **112.6**
Speed ratings (Par 93): **95,94,93,92,89 88,88,70**
Tote Swingers: 1&2 £15.90, 1&3 £7.90, 2&3 £10.10 CSF £54.17 TOTE £4.50: £1.20, £6.90, £6.90; EX 80.80 Trifecta £1185.80 Part won. Pool: £1602.47 - 0.93 winning units..
Owner Nick Shutts **Bred** Mountarmstrong Stud **Trained** Pandy, Monmouths

FOCUS
A hot little novice race featuring several speedy early-season sorts and two promising newcomers. The winner ran to her pre-race level.

NOTEBOOK
Scarlet Rocks(IRE), yet to finish out of the first two, has now won twice and her enthusiasm is undiminished despite a busy couple of months. A tough sort, she can be expected to keep up the good work for a while yet. (op 10-3)
Stone Of Folca, a Kodiac newcomer, ran a cracking race against some proven speedsters, showing excellent pace throughout. He is more useful than his odds would suggest and, while a maiden is there for the taking, connections should now be thinking of his longer term prospects.
Joyously's win was in a seller but she is better than a typical plater and looks the sort who will progress to make her mark in nurseries. This was another fine effort in novice company and there is more to come. (op 16-1)
Fifth Ave has solid early form and she provides a good line regarding the quality of the race, having run in listed company last time. Her pace will stand her in good stead if she switches to nurseries. (op 11-4 tchd 3-1 in places)
Eshoog(IRE) made an awkward start but was recovering encouragingly at the end. By Kyllachy out of a Primo Dominie mare, she is bred to be quick and can do much better with this debut behind her. (op 13-2)
Maggie's Treasure(IRE) Official explanation: jockey said colt hung left under pressure

Takeaway has done well at this trip but it is beginning to look as if he will be worth a try at 6f.
Official explanation: jockey said colt ran flat (op 3-1)

2398 SUNLEY H'CAP — 1m 67y

6:40 (6:40) (Class 5) (0-75,75) 3-Y-O — **£2,729** (£806; £403) **Stalls** High

Form — RPR

-043 **1** **Avon River**^{21} [1761] 3-9-4 **75**....................(b^{1}) RichardHughes 9 — 85
(R Hannon) *trckd ldr 3f: reminders over 3f out: wnt 2nd again over 2f out: pushed into ld over 1f out: sn 2 l clr: in n.d after* **5/1^{2}**

035 **2** 2 ¾ **Edition**^{21} [1766] 3-8-10 **67**.................... LukeMorris 10 — 71+
(J R Gask) *settled in 7th: rdn 3f out: swtchd sharply lft wl over 1f out: styd on u.str.p to take 2nd wl ins fnl f* **9/1**

0-12 **3** nk **The Shuffler**^{14} [1977] 3-8-11 **68**.................... JimmyFortune 4 — 71
(G L Moore) *racd quite keenly: hld up in 6th: pushed along over 2f out: effrt over 1f out: drvn and styd on to take 3rd ins fnl f* **5/2^{1}**

-120 **4** 1 **First Post (IRE)**^{24} [1657] 3-8-12 **69**.................... DaneO'Neill 1 — 70+
(D Haydn Jones) *hung bdly lft bnd 6f out and detached in last sn after: prog 3f out on outer: kpt on fnl 2f: nvr able to chal* **14/1**

50-0 **5** hd **Yabtree (IRE)**^{17} [1873] 3-8-11 **68**.................... SteveDrowne 5 — 68
(R Charlton) *hld up in 8th: effrt over 2f out: bmpd by rival wl over 1f out: kpt on same pce fnl f* **14/1**

66-3 **6** shd **Tamtara**^{88} [698] 3-8-10 **67**.................... TomQueally 12 — 67
(Mrs A J Perrett) *hld up in last trio: gng strly 3f out: effrt over 2f out: nt qckn over 1f out: styd on ins fnl f* **13/2^{3}**

6234 **7** 2 **Chateau Zara**^{14} [1977] 3-8-1 **63** ow1.................... JohnFahy$^{(5)}$ 6 — 58
(C G Cox) *led to over 1f out: wknd fnl f* **12/1**

01- **8** 1 ½ **Shoot The Pot (IRE)**^{155} [7825] 3-8-10 **67**.................... JimCrowley 11 — 59
(R M Beckett) *pushed up to trck ldng trio: rdn over 2f out: wknd over 1f out* **9/1**

0-35 **9** nk **Alice Cullen**^{13} [2004] 3-9-1 **72**.................... AdamKirby 8 — 63
(W R Swinburn) *chsd ldrs in 5th: rdn against nr side rail over 2f out: fdd over 1f out* **8/1**

00-6 **10** 8 **Emirates Hills**^{23} [1709] 3-9-1 **72**.................... LiamKeniry 3 — 45
(E F Vaughan) *chsd ldr after 3f to over 2f out: wknd rapidly* **33/1**

-060 **11** 12 **Annacaboe (IRE)**^{20} [1795] 3-8-4 **61** oh5.................... AdrianMcCarthy 2 — —
(D K Ivory) *a in last pair: struggling fr 1/2-way: t.o* **100/1**

1m 44.2s (-0.50) **Going Correction** -0.025s/f (Good) — **11** Ran SP% **114.6**
Speed ratings (Par 99): **101,98,97,96,96 96,94,93,92,84 72**
Tote Swingers: 1&2 £12.20, 1&3 £1.80, 2&3 £8.00 CSF £48.21 CT £139.93 TOTE £5.00: £2.90, £4.30, £1.10; EX 52.60 Trifecta £150.50 Pool: £2,278.28 - 11.20 winning units..
Owner Jim Horgan **Bred** Poulton Stud **Trained** East Everleigh, Wilts

FOCUS

Run at a decent pace, this featured some potential improvers and therefore ranks as an interesting contest. However, the winner was largely exposed. He is rated back to the best view of his 2yo form.

The Shuffler Official explanation: jockey said gelding ran too free
Tamtara Official explanation: jockey said filly hung right-handed

2399 SPORTINGBET.COM H'CAP — 6f

7:10 (7:10) (Class 4) (0-80,80) 4-Y-O+ — **£4,533** (£1,348; £674; £336) **Stalls** High

Form — RPR

4204 **1** **Anne Of Kiev (IRE)**^{9} [2113] 5-8-13 **75**....................(t) LukeMorris 13 — 87
(J R Gask) *hld up in 8th and off the pce: clsd fr 2f out: swtchd to inner and led ent fnl f: readily* **7/2^{1}**

24-0 **2** 2 ¼ **Greensward**^{26} [1618] 4-9-3 **79**.................... KierenFallon 11 — 84
(B J Meehan) *wl off the pce in 11th: pushed along 1/2-way: rdn and prog 2f out: styd on fnl f to take 2nd last stride* **7/2^{1}**

060- **3** shd **Victorian Bounty**^{344} [2946] 5-9-4 **80**.................... MickyFenton 5 — 84
(Stef Higgins) *pressed ldr and racd on outer: led over 1f out: hdd and one pce ent fnl f: lost 2nd last stride* **28/1**

-056 **4** ¾ **Phantom Whisper**^{18} [1848] 7-8-13 **75**.................... SebSanders 1 — 77
(B R Millman) *pressed ldrs and racd on outer: upsides over 1f out: one pce fnl f* **10/1**

15-3 **5** 1 ¾ **Berbice (IRE)**^{88} [696] 5-9-1 **77**....................(e) RichardHughes 10 — 73
(S Donohoe, Ire) *awkward s: hld up in abt 12th and wl off the pce: smooth prog over 2f out: trying to cl whn chopped off over 1f out: hanging and kpt on same pce after* **10/1**

-320 **6** nk **Make My Dream**^{10} [2094] 7-8-11 **73**.................... TadhgO'Shea 16 — 69
(J Gallagher) *chsd ldng trio: rdn over 2f out: no imp over 1f out: fdd* **17/2^{3}**

-000 **7** ¾ **Memphis Man**^{9} [2113] 7-8-5 **67**.................... CathyGannon 2 — 60
(P D Evans) *taken down early: hld up off the pce in abt 9th: sltly checked over 1f out and lost pl: styd on again ins fnl f* **18/1**

045 **8** hd **Hatta Stream (IRE)**^{24} [1659] 4-8-12 **74**.................... DaneO'Neill 15 — 66
(J Pearce) *chsd clr ldrs: rdn over 2f out: sn lost pl: plugged on again fnl f* **33/1**

5030 **9** 1 ½ **Vhujon (IRE)**^{68} [905] 5-8-7 **76**.................... KevinLundie$^{(7)}$ 6 — 64
(P D Evans) *taken down early: s.s: mostly in last trio: urged along fr over 2f out: kpt on: n.d* **28/1**

4-00 **10** hd **Lodi (IRE)**^{14} [1963] 5-8-12 **74** ow1....................(t) AdamKirby 8 — 61
(J Akehurst) *chsd clr ldrs: rdn bef 1/2-way: wandered over 1f out: wknd* **25/1**

525- **11** nse **Captainrisk (IRE)**^{285} [4914] 4-8-11 **73**....................(t) TomMcLaughlin 3 — 60
(Mrs C A Dunnett) *hld up in last trio: prog on wd outside over 2f out: no hdwy over 1f out: fdd and eased* **50/1**

140- **12** 1 ¾ **Gwilym (GER)**^{184} [7478] 7-8-9 **71**.................... TomQueally 14 — 52
(D Haydn Jones) *led to over 1f out: wknd rapidly fnl f* **28/1**

1005 **13** 2 **Spinning Bailiwick**^{91} [657] 4-9-3 **79**.................... JimmyFortune 7 — 54
(G L Moore) *stdd s: hld up in last pair and wl off the pce: nvr a factor* **40/1**

0-01 **14** hd **Sometsuke**^{7} [2166] 4-8-12 **74** 6ex.................... FergusSweeney 9 — 48+
(P J Makin) *chsd clr ldrs: rdn over 2f out: trying to cl but nt making much prog whn hmpd over 1f out: wknd* **9/2^{2}**

6550 **15** 7 **Earlsmedic**^{39} [1332] 5-9-4 **80**....................(v) SaleemGolam 12 — 32
(S C Williams) *nvr bttr than abt 10th: wknd 2f out: t.o* **20/1**

1m 12.05s (-0.95) **Going Correction** -0.025s/f (Good) — **15** Ran SP% **122.9**
Speed ratings (Par 105): **105,102,101,100,98 98,97,96,94,94 94,92,89,89,79**
Tote Swingers: 1&2 £2.20, 1&3 £58.90, 2&3 £44.70 CSF £13.63 CT £313.82 TOTE £3.60: £2.50, £1.20, £14.60; EX 17.70 Trifecta £341.10 Pool: £2904.43 - 6.30 winning units..
Owner P Bamford **Bred** Deerfield Farm **Trained** Sutton Veny, Wilts

FOCUS

Again the stands' rail appeared to be the place to be. Solid and straightforward form, with the winner back to her best.

Spinning Bailiwick Official explanation: jockey said filly lost its action

2400 SPORTINGBET.COM LEISURE STKS (LISTED RACE) — 6f

7:40 (7:40) (Class 1) 3-Y-O+
£22,708 (£8,608; £4,308; £2,148; £1,076; £540) **Stalls** High

Form — RPR

242- **1** **Triple Aspect (IRE)**^{226} [6661] 4-9-0 **109**.................... LiamJones 4 — 111+
(W J Haggas) *t.k.h: hld up bhd ldrs: plld out and effrt over 1f out: rdn to ld ins fnl f: r.o wl* **13/8^{1}**

3000 **2** ¾ **Sir Gerry (USA)**^{24} [1676] 5-9-0 **105**.................... SteveDrowne 7 — 108
(J R Best) *t.k.h: hld up in last pair: effrt over 1f out: rdn and r.o to take 2nd wl ins fnl f: a hld* **33/1**

36-0 **3** 1 **Edge Closer**^{12} [2030] 6-9-0 **102**.................... JimmyFortune 5 — 105
(R Hannon) *t.k.h: pressed ldr after 1f: upsides fr 2f out tl ins fnl f: styd on but outpcd* **7/1**

-330 **4** ½ **Fitz Flyer (IRE)**^{37} [1400] 4-9-0 **100**.................... KierenFallon 2 — 103
(D H Brown) *trckd ldrs: chal fr 2f out: nrly upsides ent fnl f: one pce last 100yds* **9/1**

40-0 **5** hd **Tax Free (IRE)**^{58} [1007] 8-9-0 **111**.................... FrannyNorton 6 — 103
(D Nicholls) *led after 1f: hrd pressed fr 2f out: hdd and fdd ins fnl f* **5/1^{3}**

31-6 **6** ¾ **Lucky General (IRE)**^{39} [1327] 3-8-7 **112** ow2.................... RichardHughes 9 — 100+
(R Hannon) *racd against nr side rail while ldrs racd towards centre: nt on terms fr 1/2-way: kpt on ins fnl f* **4/1^{2}**

30 **7** 1 **El Cambio (AUS)**^{80} [822] 6-9-0 **108**....................(v^{1}) TedDurcan 1 — 99
(Mahmood Al Zarooni) *hld up in last pair: prog on wd outside over 2f out: rdn and cl enough over 1f out: fdd* **20/1**

00-5 **8** 6 **Enderby Spirit (GR)**^{37} [1400] 4-9-0 **100**.................... TomEaves 8 — 78
(B Smart) *led 1f: sn lost pl: no ch fnl 2f* **12/1**

1m 11.56s (-1.44) **Going Correction** -0.025s/f (Good)
WFA 3 from 4yo+ 9lb — **8** Ran SP% **112.7**
Speed ratings (Par 111): **108,107,105,105,104 103,102,94**
Tote Swingers: 1&2 £15.00, 1&3 £6.00, 2&3 £9.90 CSF £60.19 TOTE £2.20: £1.02, £9.10, £2.90; EX 54.90 Trifecta £427.10 Pool: £750.34 - 1.10 winning units..
Owner Tony Bloom **Bred** Noel O'Callaghan **Trained** Newmarket, Suffolk

FOCUS

The pace was disappointing for a listed event, with the tempo only starting to quicken near the 2f pole, and the time was only 0.49sec quicker than the earlier handicap. Ordinary form for the grade and the winner did not need to match his previous best.

NOTEBOOK

Triple Aspect(IRE) had to switch after being stopped in his run, but he picked up well and was clearly the best horse in the race. Though lightly raced - which means he has few miles on the clock - he has had two good seasons so far and looks set for another in decent company. Trainer William Haggas, describing him as "very tough and genuine", has him entered for both the King's Stand and the Golden Jubilee at Royal Ascot and believes he is entitled to run in either, saying: "if he can find a little improvement he should run a good race." (op 2-1 tchd 9-4 in places)

Sir Gerry(USA), well up to this class two years ago, had some success in Dubai during the winter but his form had begun to tail off, so this was a welcome return to something like his best. He still has plenty to offer, but horses like him are never easy to place because of their lofty handicap mark. (op 28-1)

Edge Closer had a fruitless 2009 but his trainer has got him back to form and this was his best performance since August 2008. The challenge now will be to find a suitable race for him. (op 12-1)

Fitz Flyer(IRE) continues to maintain his AWT form on turf, if not quite good enough to beat these useful rivals. (op 11-1 tchd 17-2)

Tax Free(IRE) ran infinitely better than on his soft-ground seasonal debut, and is now within touching distance of his smart 2009 form. (op 4-1)

2401 BERKSHIRE LIFE MEDIAN AUCTION MAIDEN STKS — 1m 2f 7y

8:10 (8:12) (Class 5) 3-Y-O — **£2,729** (£806; £201; £201) **Stalls** Centre

Form — RPR

32-0 **1** **Nurture (IRE)**^{22} [1726] 3-8-12 **99**.................... JimCrowley 7 — 71
(R M Beckett) *mde virtually all: pushed along over 3f out: pressed and drvn fr 2f out: jnd fnl f: asserted nr fin* **8/15^{1}**

00- **2** ¾ **Centime**^{213} [6992] 3-8-12 0.................... TadhgO'Shea 14 — 69
(B J Meehan) *trckd ldng quartet: prog to go 2nd 2f out: sn chalng: upsides fnl f: no ex last 100yds* **40/1**

0 **3** ¾ **Norse Dame**^{21} [1766] 3-8-12 0.................... DaneO'Neill 8 — 68
(D R C Elsworth) *hld up in 10th: pushed along over 2f out: modest prog tl r.o wl fnl f: nrst fin* **50/1**

3 dht **My Manikato** 3-9-3 0.................... KierenFallon 5 — 73+
(L M Cumani) *rn green in 8th: shkn up over 3f out: no prog tl rdn and r.o fr over 1f out: nrst fin* **7/1^{2}**

4 **5** ¾ **Roanstar**^{14} [1976] 3-9-3 0.................... LiamKeniry 3 — 71
(A M Balding) *pressed wnr to 2f out: fdd ins fnl f* **8/1^{3}**

6 1 ¾ **Byrd In Hand (IRE)** 3-9-3 0.................... NeilChalmers 12 — 68
(J J Bridger) *hld up in 7th: prog and swtchd lft 2f out: tried to cl on ldrs over 1f out: one pce after* **100/1**

00 **7** ¾ **Gifted Lady (IRE)**^{28} [1581] 3-8-12 0.................... IanMongan 13 — 61
(P M Phelan) *restless preliminaries: dwlt: hld up in last trio: pushed along over 2f out: kpt on steadily: nrst fin* **66/1**

8 nk **Anacopa (USA)** 3-8-12 0.................... TedDurcan 6 — 60+
(Mahmood Al Zarooni) *trckd ldng pair to over 2f out: shkn up over 1f out: wknd and eased fnl f* **8/1^{3}**

35 **9** ½ **Business Bay (USA)**^{13} [2011] 3-9-3 0.................... JimmyFortune 4 — 64
(E F Vaughan) *settled in 6th: reminder on outer and effrt over 2f out: one pce over 1f out: fdd last 100yds* **25/1**

0-0 **10** ½ **Happy Mood**^{31} [1501] 3-8-12 0.................... FergusSweeney 10 — 58
(G L Moore) *t.k.h: trckd ldng trio to over 2f out: shkn up and wknd* **33/1**

6 **11** 6 **Technophobe (IRE)**^{14} [1976] 3-8-10 0.................... HarryBentley$^{(7)}$ 2 — 51
(W J Knight) *s.s: mostly in last: bhd fnl 2f* **25/1**

12 8 **Mr Muddle** 3-9-0 0.................... RobertLButler$^{(3)}$ 9 — 35
(Miss Sheena West) *a in last trio: reminder and no prog 3f out: sn bhd* **100/1**

60 **13** 1 **Oh Two**^{28} [1581] 3-8-12 0.................... SaleemGolam 1 — 28
(S C Williams) *nvr bttr than 9th: pushed along 4f out: sn struggling and bhd* **100/1**

2m 9.43s (0.73) **Going Correction** -0.025s/f (Good) — **13** Ran SP% **119.4**
Speed ratings (Par 99): **96,95,94,94,94 92,92,91,91,91 86,79,79**
Place: My Manikato £1.20 Norse Dame £5.60. CSF £43.96 TOTE £1.60: £1.10, £8.70; EX 38.10 TRIFECTA 13-9-5 £129.40 13-9-12 £164.20. Swingers: 1&2 £21.60, N&MM £0.90, C&MM £18.70, N&ND not won, C & ND not won, MM&ND not won. .
Owner R A Pegum & The Bloodstock Connection **Bred** John O'Connor **Trained** Whitsbury, Hants

FOCUS
Potentially a race of interest, with an ambitiously-campaigned winner and a number of newcomers from good stables. However, the form of some of those who chased home the favourite was poor, so the form has a hollow look until it becomes clear how it is working out. The pace was solid, with the field soon strung out by 20 lengths, though that partly reflects the huge difference in ability of the participants. The winner stood out on 2yo form but was some way below her best.
Anacopa(USA) Official explanation: jockey said filly had no more to give

2402 CENKOS SECURITIES H'CAP — 1m 3f 135y
8:40 (8:40) (Class 5) (0-75,75) 4-Y-O+ — **£2,729** (£806; £403) **Stalls** Centre

Form — RPR

03-0 **1** **Marju King (IRE)**[30] 1520 4-8-10 **67** .... FergusSweeney 2 — 73
(W S Kittow) *hld up in last: pushed along over 4f out: prog 3f out to go 2nd 2f out: sustained effrt to ld ins fnl f: styd on wl* **17/2**[3]

-001 **2** *2 3/4* **Maslak (IRE)**[10] 2081 6-8-12 **69** .... ChrisCatlin 3 — 70
(P W Hiatt) *led: rdn over 2f out: hdd and one pce ins fnl f* **2/1**[1]

5224 **3** *2 1/4* **Where's Susie**[7] 2165 5-8-8 **65** .... (p) RobertHavlin 5 — 62
(M Madgwick) *cl up: disp 2nd 3f out: rdn and nt qckn 2f out: one pce after* **9/2**[2]

0030 **4** *16* **Ramona Chase**[10] 2093 5-8-13 **75** .... (t) JemmaMarshall(5) 1 — 45
(M J Attwater) *mostly chsd ldr to 4f out: lost pl qckly and sn btn* **17/2**[3]

212- **5** *20* **Silent Act (USA)**[201] 7238 4-8-13 **70** .... JimCrowley 4 — 6
(Mrs A J Perrett) *cl up: chsd ldr 4f out: drvn 3f out: wknd rapidly 2f out: virtually p.u fnl f* **2/1**[1]

2m 28.86s (-0.64) **Going Correction** -0.025s/f (Good) — **5** Ran SP% **105.9**
Speed ratings (Par 103): **101,99,97,87,73**
CSF £23.88 TOTE £12.90: £5.80, £1.10; EX 27.90 Place 6 £35.31, Place 5 £7.02.
Owner Chris & David Stam **Bred** Hardys Of Kilkeel Ltd **Trained** Blackborough, Devon

FOCUS
An ordinary pace until the last three furlongs, with the winner overcoming the probable disadvantage of making his effort well wide of the stands' rail. Ordinary but sound form.
Silent Act(USA) Official explanation: jockey said filly stopped quickly
T/Plt: £39.10. Pool: £104,797.73 - 1,955.12 winning units. T/Qpdt: £10.50. Pool: £8,032.80 - 561.74 winning units. JN

2237 SAINT-CLOUD (L-H)
Monday, May 24

OFFICIAL GOING: Turf: good

2403a PRIX CORRIDA (GROUP 2) (4YO+ FILLIES & MARES) (TURF) — 1m 2f 110y
2:05 (12:00) 4-Y-O+ — **£65,575** (£25,309; £12,079; £8,053; £4,026)

RPR

1 **Plumania**[21] 1792 4-8-9 0 .... OlivierPeslier 5 — 109
(A Fabre, France) *settled in 4th on outer: qcknd wl early in st: cruised to ld over 1f out: r.o strly under hands and heels ride: comf* **14/1**[3]

2 *1 1/2* **Celimene (IRE)**[22] 1747 4-8-11 0 .... YannLerner 7 — 108
(C Lerner, France) *racd in 2nd fr s: rdn early in st:qcknd wl and r.o strly to hold 2nd on line* **11/4**[2]

3 *shd* **Daryakana (FR)**[162] 7744 4-9-2 0 .... GeraldMosse 3 — 113
(A De Royer-Dupre, France) *settled in rr: 5th ent st: rdn 2f out: r.o wl but hung in late and had to be stened: losing 2nd on line* **5/4**[1]

4 *shd* **Shemiyla (FR)**[21] 1792 4-8-11 0 .... Christophe-PatriceLemaire 6 — 108
(A De Royer-Dupre, France) *led fr s: rdn and qcknd wl early in st: hdd 1f out: r.o wl to line* **11/4**[2]

5 *1 1/2* **Biased**[21] 1792 4-8-9 0 .... MaximeGuyon 1 — 103
(M Delzangles, France) *racd in 4th on rail: rdn early in st: short of room whn attempting to chal ldr 1 1/2f out: r.o* **28/1**

6 *3/4* **La Boum (GER)**[21] 1792 7-8-9 0 .... ThierryJarnet 2 — 101
(Robert Collet, France) *settled towards rr fr s: r.o wl in st but n.d to ldrs* **25/1**

2m 13.6s (-6.00) — **6** Ran SP% **111.7**
WIN (incl. 1 euro stake): 12.20. PLACES: 3.50, 2.00. SF: 44.10.
Owner Wertheimer & Frere **Bred** Wertheimer Et Frere **Trained** Chantilly, France

NOTEBOOK
Plumania ran out a comfortable winner in a falsely-run contest. She will be aimed at the Prix Jean Romanet at Deauville and might take in the Grand Prix de Saint-Cloud beforehand.
Celimene(IRE) is a consistent sort and ran her race over her optimium trip.
Daryakana(FR), having her first outing of the season, lost her unbeaten record in a contest not run to suit. She will be better for the run and back over a longer trip.

1955 COLOGNE (R-H)
Monday, May 24

OFFICIAL GOING: Turf: good

2404a KARIN BARONIN VON ULLMANN - SCHWARZGOLD-RENNEN (GROUP 3) (3YO FILLIES) (TURF) — 1m
3:05 (3:18) 3-Y-0 — **£35,398** (£11,504; £4,424; £3,539; £1,769; £884)

RPR

1 **Prakasa (FR)**[23] 1715 3-9-2 0 .... EPedroza 2 — 97
(W Hickst, Germany) *racd in midfield fr s: travelled smoothly: qcknd up early in st on outside: ct ldr ins fnl f: battled hrd to win on line* **5/2**[1]

2 *1/2* **Reine Heureuse (GER)**[23] 1715 3-9-2 0 .... AHelfenbein 1 — 96
(Uwe Ostmann, Germany) *sent to ld fr s: set mod pce at first: qcknd down bkstretch: r.o wl u.p in st: fought hrd: lost r in fnl strides* **3/1**[2]

3 *2 1/2* **Mahamaya (GER)**[15] 3-9-2 0 .... AGoritz 8 — 90
(A Trybuhl, Germany) *settled in midfield: hit traffic problems ent st: swtchd to outside following wnr: r.o wl* **6/1**[3]

4 *3/4* **Madonje (GER)** 3-9-2 0 .... ADeVries 7 — 89
(J Hirschberger, Germany) *bkmarker fr s: hmpd by traffic problems in st: fnd room on outside and r.o wl* **20/1**

5 *3/4* **Aslana (IRE)**[23] 1715 3-9-2 0 .... AStarke 3 — 87
(P Schiergen, Germany) *broke smartly and racd in 3rd: stdd hrd whn ldr slowed: swtchd to outside: r.o wl* **6/1**[3]

6 *3* **Devilish Lips (GER)**[23] 1715 3-9-2 0 .... (b) THellier 6 — 80
(Andreas Lowe, Germany) *racd in 4th fr s: threatened briefly in st but fnd no ex and wknd* **7/1**

7 *2* **Ottofee (GER)**[49] 3-9-2 0 .... WCahill 5 — 75
(Andreas Lowe, Germany) *racd in midfield: nvr a threat* **33/1**

8 *1 3/4* **Don't Tell Mary (IRE)**[212] 7033 3-9-2 0 .... RichardKingscote 9 — 71
(Tom Dascombe) *trckd the ldr: plld hrd: briefly threatened in st but wknd* **8/1**

9 *10* **Perfect Eye (IRE)** 3-9-2 0 .... HenkGrewe 4 — 48
(Andreas Lowe, Germany) *settled in midfield: nvr figured* **12/1**

1m 36.64s (-1.75) — **9** Ran SP% **121.1**
WIN (incl. 10 euro stake): 47. PLACES: 18, 14, 18. SF: 89..
Owner Gestut Park Wiedingen **Bred** Gestut Park Wiedingen **Trained** Germany

NOTEBOOK
Prakasa(FR) finished really well to grab the long-time leader in the final strides. She will stay further judged on this effort.
Reine Heureuse(GER) did her best to make every yard but was picked off by the winner close to the line.

2405a MEHL MULHENS-RENNEN - GERMAN 2000 GUINEAS (GROUP 2) (3YO COLTS & FILLIES) (TURF) — 1m
4:15 (4:36) 3-Y-0 — **£88,495** (£26,548; £8,849; £8,849)

RPR

1 **Frozen Power (IRE)**[58] 1023 3-9-2 0 .... FrankieDettori 7 — 104
(Mahmood Al Zarooni) *settled towards rr travelling smoothly: swtchd wd on turn: qcknd wl and led early in st: r.o strly to win comf* **6/4**[1]

2 *nk* **Kite Hunter (IRE)**[29] 1564 3-9-2 0 .... ADeVries 2 — 103
(Mario Hofer, Germany) *sent to ld at mod pce: qcknd up on bkstretch: led into st: r.o wl: battled gamely to the line to hold on for 2nd* **16/1**

3 *nk* **Noble Alpha (IRE)**[202] 7231 3-9-2 0 .... (b) THellier 1 — 103
(Mario Hofer, Germany) *trckd ldr fr s: qcknd wl in st: wandered off st line and battled hrd to dead-heat for 3rd* **6/1**

3 *dht* **Russian Tango (GER)**[23] 3-9-2 0 .... EPedroza 6 — 103
(A Wohler, Germany) *racd in 5th fr s: qcknd wl in st but had to be checked whn making his move: c again to dead-heat for 3rd cl home* **3/1**[2]

5 *1 1/4* **Santino (GER)**[39] 3-9-2 0 .... Jean-BernardEyquem 5 — 100
(J-P Carvalho, Germany) *racd in 4th: mde gd prog arnd fnl turn: r.o wl in st: styd on* **33/1**

6 *shd* **Neatico (GER)**[197] 7314 3-9-2 0 .... AStarke 8 — 100
(P Schiergen, Germany) *racd in joint 2nd fr s: looked threatening early in st: checked whn short of room: perhaps unlucky* **7/2**[3]

7 *5* **Beagle Boy (IRE)**[50] 3-9-2 0 .... FranckBlondel 3 — 88
(A Wohler, Germany) *a towards the rr: nvr figured* **10/1**

8 *1/2* **Go Country (FR)**[29] 1564 3-9-2 0 .... AGoritz 4 — 87
(P Schiergen, Germany) *bkmarker fr s and nvr figured* **25/1**

1m 36.69s (-1.70) — **8** Ran SP% **123.3**
WIN (incl. 10 euro stake): 30. PLACES: 17, 26, NA 10, RT 6. SF: 379..
Owner Godolphin **Bred** Rathbarry Stud **Trained** Newmarket, Suffolk
■ Mahmood Al Zarooni's first Classic winner.

NOTEBOOK
Frozen Power(IRE), last seen finishing fifth in the UAE Derby, looked a non-stayer that day and the drop back to a mile promised to suit. Having travelled well off the pace he picked up in good style in the straight, staying on strongly and responding well to pressure to win by a narrow margin but a shade comfortably.
Kite Hunter(IRE), runner-up in a key trial in Germany for this race, did his best to make every yard but was caught in the latter stages. He is a fair marker to the form.
Russian Tango(GER) may have been slightly unlucky and was gaining again in the final stages.
Noble Alpha(IRE), having his first run of the year and wearing blinkers for the first time, came through to have every chance but lacked a change of gear at the crucial stage of the race.
Neatico(GER), a Group 3 winner in heavy ground at 2 making his seasonal debut, may stay a bit further later on in the season and certainly shaped with promise.

MUNICH (L-H)
Monday, May 24

OFFICIAL GOING: Turf: good

2406a ONEXTWO.COM - BAVARIAN CLASSIC (GROUP 3) (3YO) (TURF) — 1m 2f
2:45 (2:54) 3-Y-0 — **£28,318** (£8,849; £4,424; £2,654)

RPR

1 **Scalo**[22] 1745 3-9-2 0 .... GaetanMasure 3 — 105
(A Wohler, Germany) *slowly away: settled in rr: shkn up on fnl turn: grad picked up and qcknd wl 1 1/2f out: cruised to ld over 1f out: sn clr: comf* **3/5**[1]

2 *2* **Wheredreamsare** 3-9-2 0 .... APietsch 5 — 101
(W Hickst, Germany) *broke wl but settled towards rr: qckly chal ent st: r.o wl u.p: battled hrd ins fnl f but no ch w wnr* **3/1**[2]

3 *3* **Nightdance Paolo (GER)**[22] 1745 3-9-2 0 .... FilipMinarik 4 — 95
(P Schiergen, Germany) *broke wl: racd in 2nd trcking pcemaker: styd on wl in st but no threat to ldrs* **104/10**

4 *1 1/4* **Keep Cool**[22] 1745 3-9-2 0 .... DPorcu 2 — 93
(Andreas Lowe, Germany) *in rr fr s: plld hrd: briefly mde a move ent st but styd on one pce: no ex* **39/10**[3]

5 *3* **Lamool (GER)**[22] 1745 3-9-2 0 .... StefanieHofer 6 — 87
(Mario Hofer, Germany) *broke wl and racd keenly: mde move on ins rail in st and threatened briefly but wknd ins fnl f* **63/10**

6 *3/4* **Langley**[22] 1745 3-9-2 0 .... KKerekes 1 — 85
(A Wohler, Germany) *led fr s at str pce: qckly wknd in st and fdd to rr* **139/10**

2m 9.71s (0.74) — **6** Ran SP% **137.1**
WIN (incl. 10 euro stake): 16. PLACES: 10, 11. SF: 45..
Owner Gestut Ittlingen **Bred** Gestut Hof Ittlingen **Trained** Germany

FOCUS
The early pace was far from strong.

NOTEBOOK
Scalo, whose stablemate made the running at a modest tempo, took quite a while to get going, but once making his way to the front, he found a decent turn of gear and was a clear winner. He will be seen to better effect when there is more emphasis on stamina.
Wheredreamsare came away with the winner in the latter stages (he got first run on that rival) but had no answer to his acceleration. Scalo did lean on him inside the final furlong but he did not seem unlucky in any way.
Nightdance Paolo(GER) was beaten further by Scalo this time than when they clashed on their previous outing.
Keep Cool, held up, made his challenge around horses but had no chance of closing down the first two. He did not appear to have any obvious excuses.

2279 CHEPSTOW (L-H)

Tuesday, May 25

OFFICIAL GOING: Good to firm (8.4)

Wind: Modest, half behind Weather: Overcast

2407 LINDLEY CATERING MAIDEN AUCTION STKS — 5f 16y

2:20 (2:21) (Class 5) 2-Y-O — £2,719 (£809; £404; £202) Stalls High

Form — RPR

1 **Malice Or Mischief (IRE)** 2-8-11 0 ..... JimCrowley 6 — 76+
(R M Beckett) *trckd ldrs: wnt 2nd ent fnl 2f: ev ch fr wl over 1f out: rn green and rdn over 1f out: led wl ins fnl f: hld on cl home* — 9/1[3]

03 2 *hd* **Belle Bayardo (IRE)**[40] 1319 2-8-11 0 ow1 ..... TomMcLaughlin 3 — 75
(R A Harris) *led: rdn and pressed wl over 1f out: hdd wl ins fnl f: battled on gamely but hld nr fin* — 16/1

64 3 *2* **Rojo Boy**[12] 2059 2-8-13 0 ..... JimmyFortune 12 — 72+
(A M Balding) *in tch in midfield: pushed along after 2f: hdwy u.p to chse ldrs over 1f out: kpt on to go 3rd ins fnl f: nvr gng pce to rch ldrs* — 1/1[1]

2 4 *1* **Millyluvstobouggie**[8] 2176 2-8-0 0 ..... JohnFahy(5) 10 — 58
(C G Cox) *in tch in midfield: rdn and effrt 2f out: chsd ldng pair over 1f out: one pce and no imp ins fnl f* — 2/1[2]

54 5 *2 1/4* **King Of Cassis**[15] 1957 2-8-7 0 ..... JackDean(3) 11 — 55
(W G M Turner) *chsd ldr tl ent fnl 2f: wknd u.p over 1f out* — 16/1

00 6 *1* **Lady On Top (IRE)**[21] 1793 2-8-1 0 ..... AmyBaker(5) 8 — 48
(Mrs P N Dutfield) *in tch towards rr of main gp: bustled along and outpcd over 2f out: no threat to ldrs after: plugged on fnl f* — 100/1

0 7 *5* **Magical Star**[21] 1793 2-7-12 0 ..... CharlesEddery(7) 4 — 29
(R Hannon) *stdd after s: hld up in tch in main gp: rdn and struggling over 2f out: wl btn fnl f* — 28/1

8 *6* **Romany Gypsy** 2-8-4 0 ..... AndrewHeffernan(3) 1 — 9
(P D Evans) *s.i.s: sn pushed along and rn green in rr: lost tch 1/2-way* — 33/1

9 *4 1/2* **Lord Of The Storm** 2-8-5 0 ..... MatthewDavies(5) 2 — —
(W G M Turner) *in tch in rr of main gp tl 1/2-way: sn lost tch and wl bhd* — 66/1

10 *3 1/4* **Fair Dame (IRE)** 2-8-5 0 ..... ChrisCatlin 9 — —
(Mrs P N Dutfield) *v.s.a: rn green and sn wl outpcd in last: t.o fr 1/2-way* — 100/1

59.55 secs (0.25) **Going Correction** -0.05s/f (Good) — 10 Ran SP% **115.0**

Speed ratings (Par 93): **96,95,92,90,87 85,77,68,60,55**

toteswingers: 1&2 £4.70, 1&3 £3.30, 2&3 £6.10 CSF £127.35 TOTE £10.80: £2.00, £4.00, £1.50.

Owner Mrs Carolyn Thornton Roberts **Bred** Kilnamoragh Stud **Trained** Whitsbury, Hants

FOCUS

Several of these had fair form going into this. The winner made a nice start and the second improved again.

NOTEBOOK

Malice Or Mischief(IRE) overcame signs of greenness in the preliminaries. By Intikhab out of a Namaqualand mare, it would have been reasonable to assume that this fast 5f would have been a bit quick, and it was only close home that everything kicked into place. However, he wasn't knocked about and should be able to build on this, when a penalty could be negated by experience and an extra furlong. (op 8-1)

Belle Bayardo(IRE) has now improved with each of his three runs over the minimum trip and the tardy starts that blighted the first two efforts were a thing of the past here as he showed plenty of pace on the front end. He should win at this trip in this class. (op 14-1)

Rojo Boy was all the rage for this having shown the best public form on his latest of two outings when a readily held fourth to the well-regarded pair of Elzaam and Sir Reginald at York 12 days earlier. But that was over 6f and this quick 5f had him struggling to engage the gears mid-race. He did it willingly enough inside the last furlong but needs to go back to 6f when a race of this class will be well within his range. (op 11-8)

Millyluvstobouggie was beaten the minimum on debut at Windsor in a race that is impossible to evaluate at present but was just a bit flat here. It was only eight days earlier and the ground was quick enough so she's well worth another chance. (op 15-8 tchd 9-4)

King Of Cassis was having his third start of the month, the last coming 15 days earlier. He showed pace but was changing his legs when the leaders quickened and will appreciate some ease.

Lady On Top(IRE) was struggling for pace from halfway and might be better over a furlong further and held on to a bit longer.

Fair Dame(IRE) Official explanation: jockey said filly hung left

2408 LINDLEY CATERING CLASSIFIED STKS — 6f 16y

2:50 (2:50) (Class 6) 3-Y-O — £2,183 (£644; £322) Stalls High

Form — RPR

06-3 1 **Erebus (IRE)**[22] 1760 3-9-0 65 ..... JimmyFortune 6 — 69
(S Kirk) *t.k.h: pressed ldr: pushed into ld wl over 1f out: rdn and hung lft ent fnl f: styd on strly to assert fnl 100yds* — 2/1[1]

0-03 2 *2* **Acquaviva**[5] 2249 3-8-11 42 ..... (p) PatrickHills(3) 2 — 63
(Eve Johnson Houghton) *led: rdn ent fnl 2f: hdd wl over 1f out: unable qck u.p 1f out: btn fnl 100yds* — 9/1

-404 3 *3/4* **Leitzu (IRE)**[17] 1921 3-9-0 62 ..... KierenFallon 5 — 60
(M R Channon) *t.k.h: chsd ldng pair: rdn and effrt over 2f out: pressed ldrs u.p ent fnl f: one pce and btn fnl 100yds* — 3/1[2]

1-30 4 *3/4* **Two Kisses (IRE)**[17] 1934 3-9-0 65 ..... StevieDonohoe 1 — 58
(B G Powell) *in tch: rdn and outpcd wl over 2f out: plugged on fnl f: nvr gng pce to trble ldrs* — 15/2

0-62 5 *7* **Stef And Stelio**[35] 1449 3-9-0 63 ..... (p) RichardHughes 3 — 45
(G A Butler) *taken down early: stdd after s: t.k.h: hld up in tch: shkn up and effrt over 2f out: rdn and fnd nil 2f out: wl btn ins fnl f: eased fnl 50yds* — 7/2[3]

0-04 6 *14* **Hounds Ditch**[8] 2164 3-9-0 65 ..... (b) ChrisCatlin 4 — —
(Eve Johnson Houghton) *dwlt: a last: rdn and no rspnse over 3f out: wl bhd fr wl over 1f out* — 11/1

1m 11.58s (-0.42) **Going Correction** -0.05s/f (Good) — 6 Ran SP% **110.7**

Speed ratings (Par 97): **100,97,96,95,86 67**

toteswingers: 1&2 £2.80, 1&3 £2.10, 2&3 £4.00 CSF £19.65 TOTE £3.10: £1.30, £8.80.

Owner The Classics Partnership **Bred** R J Brennan And D Boocock **Trained** Upper Lambourn, Berks

FOCUS

An ordinary claissfied stakes. The winner has been rated up 5lb.

2409 LINDLEY CATERING (S) STKS — 7f 16y

3:20 (3:23) (Class 6) 3-4-Y-O — £2,047 (£604; £302) Stalls High

Form — RPR

0-05 1 **Set To Go**[8] 2172 3-8-8 55 ..... (b) RichardHughes 1 — 61
(H J L Dunlop) *led tl rdn and hdd 2f out: hrd drvn ent fnl f: ev ch and edgd rt u.p wl ins fnl f: led again towards fin: fin 1st: disqualified and plcd 2nd* — 16/1

5134 2 *nse* **Lastkingofscotland (IRE)**[3] 2331 4-9-11 73 ..... (b) PaulDoe 4 — 71
(Jim Best) *dwlt: in tch in last trio: hdwy 1/2-way: pushed into ld 2f out: rdn and wandered u.p ent fnl f: jnd and bmpd by rival wl ins fnl f: hdd and no ex towards fin: fin 2nd, nse: awrdd r* — 8/13[1]

2-00 3 *2 1/4* **Blue Noodles**[8] 2188 4-9-2 68 ..... AndrewHeffernan(3) 7 — 61+
(P D Evans) *chsd ldrs: wnt 2nd over 3f out tl over 2f out: drvn and unable qck wl over 1f out: styng on same pce and hld whn edgd lft and hmpd ins fnl f* — 5/1[2]

3105 4 *2 1/4* **Castleburg**[6] 2235 4-9-0 63 ..... (be) JimmyFortune 6 — 48
(G L Moore) *stdd s: t.k.h: hld up in tch towards rr: effrt and rdn 2f out: hld hd high and nt qckn over 1f out: wl btn ins fnl f* — 9/1

0430 5 *1/2* **Athaakeel (IRE)**[17] 1928 4-9-0 52 ..... LukeMorris 2 — 47
(R A Harris) *chsd ldrs: rdn ent fnl 2f: wknd u.p jst over 1f out* — 20/1

00-0 6 *6* **Banco Busto (IRE)**[12] 2050 3-8-4 41 ow1 ..... ChrisCatlin 5 — 27
(H S Howe) *s.i.s: a in rr: struggling and rdn 1/2-way: wl bhd fnl 2f* — 66/1

0-64 7 *3* **Dr Mathias**[61] 977 3-8-1 64 ..... MatthewCosham(7) 3 — 23
(P D Evans) *chsd ldr tl 1/2-way: sn lost pl and rdn: wl bhd fnl 2f* — 8/1[3]

1m 22.87s (-0.33) **Going Correction** -0.05s/f (Good)

WFA 3 from 4yo 11lb — 7 Ran SP% **111.8**

Speed ratings (Par 101): **99,98,96,93,93 86,82**

toteswingers: 1&2 £3.00, 1&3 £2.40, 2&3 £5.50 CSF £12.11 TOTE £1.70: £1.40, £4.80; EX 8.70.The winner was sold to Diamond Racing for 6,500gns.

Owner Hart Royal Partnership **Bred** D J And Mrs Brown **Trained** Lambourn, Berks

FOCUS

A weak seller in which the outcome was decided by the Stewards. The form is rated around the front pair.

2410 ABSOLUTE RECRUITMENT CELEBRATION H'CAP — 1m 14y

3:50 (3:57) (Class 5) (0-70,74) 4-Y-O+ — £3,561 (£1,059; £529; £264) Stalls High

Form — RPR

2-60 1 **Lord Of The Dance (IRE)**[11] 2080 4-8-10 61 ..... EddieAhern 6 — 67
(W M Brisbourne) *t.k.h: stdd after s: hld up wl in tch: effrt and rdn wl over 1f out: led ent fnl f: r.o wl ins fnl f* — 7/1[2]

05-6 2 *3/4* **Quiquillo (USA)**[19] 1843 4-8-13 67 ..... (b[1]) AndrewHeffernan(3) 8 — 71
(P D Evans) *stdd s: t.k.h: hld up wl in tch in last pair: hdwy to trck ldrs 3f out: rdn to press wnr ent fnl f: r.o wl but a hld fnl 150yds* — 18/1

2361 3 *3 1/4* **Rapid City**[8] 2172 7-9-9 74 6ex ..... PaulDoe 1 — 71
(Jim Best) *trckd ldrs: rdn ent fnl 2f: drvn and ev ch over 1f out: wknd ins fnl f* — 16/1[3]

020- 4 *1 3/4* **Oriental Girl**[225] 6733 5-8-12 63 ..... (p) RichardHughes 7 — 56
(J S Moore) *t.k.h: sn chsng ldr: rdn to ld ent fnl 2f: hdd ent fnl f: wknd and flashed tail ins fnl f* — 9/4[1]

13-0 5 *1/2* **It's A Mans World**[12] 2053 4-8-2 60 ..... MatthewCosham(7) 5 — 54
(P D Evans) *stdd s: tt.k.h: hld up wl in tch in last: rdn and nt pce of rivals wl over 1f out: plugged on same pce and no threat to ldrs fnl f* — 20/1

6-00 6 *hd* **Komreyev Star**[22] 1772 8-8-4 55 oh10 ..... (p) ChrisCatlin 3 — 46
(R E Peacock) *led at stdy gallop: rdn over 2f out: sn hdd and outpcd wl over 1f out: styd on one pce and wl hld fnl f* — 66/1

1m 35.86s (-0.34) **Going Correction** -0.05s/f (Good) — 6 Ran SP% **60.7**

Speed ratings (Par 103): **99,98,95,93,92 92**

toteswingers: 1&2 £4.00, 1&3 £2.60, 2&3 £2.10 CSF £27.01 CT £166.15 TOTE £4.20: £1.80, £4.50; EX 33.80.

Owner D C Rutter & H Clewlow **Bred** Bridgewater Equine Ltd **Trained** Great Ness, Shropshire

FOCUS

The well-backed 7/4 favourite Advertise got restless in the stalls and was led out, while Petomic (5/1) refused to enter them, taking the edge off this race. There was a 50p in the 3 deduction under R4. Weak form, with the last horse finishing close enough.

It's A Mans World Official explanation: jockey said gelding was denied a clear run

2411 BREWIN DOLPHIN H'CAP — 1m 2f 36y

4:20 (4:23) (Class 5) (0-75,74) 4-Y-O+ — £3,561 (£1,059; £529; £264) Stalls Low

Form — RPR

5121 1 **King's Masque**[19] 1840 4-8-12 68 ..... JimmyFortune 1 — 78
(B J Llewellyn) *a travelling strly: chsd ldr tl led gng wl 3f out: rdn and asserted ent fnl f: r.o strly: readily* — 11/4[1]

52-1 2 *2 3/4* **The Hague**[35] 1440 4-8-12 71 ..... AndrewHeffernan(3) 2 — 76
(P D Evans) *chsd ldrs: rdn and ev ch 3f out: drvn and nt pce of wnr ent fnl f: kpt on same pce after* — 11/2[3]

214- 3 *2* **Dishdasha (IRE)**[24] 848 8-9-3 73 ..... (t) EddieAhern 3 — 74
(Mrs A M Thorpe) *dwlt: t.k.h: hld up in midfield: swtchd out off of rail and effrt 2f out: sn chsng ldng pair and rdn: one pce and wl hld fnl f* — 9/1

0-05 4 *1 1/4* **Apex**[13] 2024 9-8-10 66 ..... TadhgO'Shea 7 — 64+
(M Hill) *racd wl off the pce in last pair: rdn and effrt whn nt clr run and swtchd lft 2f out: plugged on fnl f: nvr gng pce to threaten ldrs* — 12/1

2-34 5 *nse* **Bolanderi (USA)**[19] 485 5-8-13 74 ..... SimonPearce(5) 6 — 72
(Andrew Turnell) *wnt rt s: sn detached in last: hdwy on outer over 2f out: no imp whn rdn 2f out: plugged on same pce fnl f* — 12/1

10-0 6 *3/4* **Dove Cottage (IRE)**[29] 1579 8-9-0 70 ..... ChrisCatlin 8 — 66
(W S Kittow) *taken down early: led: rdn and hdd 3f out: wknd u.p over 1f out* — 9/2[2]

0-2 7 *7* **Silent Oasis**[8] 2173 4-9-2 72 ..... LukeMorris 5 — 60
(J S Moore) *in tch in midfield: rdn 3f out: wknd and edgd rt wl over 1f out: eased whn wl btn ins fnl f* — 11/4[1]

2m 9.30s (-1.30) **Going Correction** -0.05s/f (Good) — 7 Ran SP% **112.3**

Speed ratings (Par 103): **103,100,99,98,98 97,91**

toteswingers: 1&2 £4.60, 1&3 £3.60, 2&3 £4.90 TOTE £3.70: £2.70, £2.50; EX 19.50.

Owner B J Llewellyn **Bred** Deerfield Farm **Trained** Fochriw, Caerphilly

FOCUS

A tight handicap on paper. The winner showed himself to be as good on turf as he is on the AW.

Silent Oasis Official explanation: jockey said filly hung right

2412 LINDLEY CATERING H'CAP — 1m 4f 23y
4:50 (4:55) (Class 6) (0-60,66) 3-Y-O — **£2,072** (£616; £308; £153) **Stalls** Low

Form — RPR

00-0 **1** **Othello (IRE)**[15] 1977 3-9-0 **56**.....................(p) ChrisCatlin 8 58
(E F Vaughan) *dwlt: sn pushed along and hdwy to chse ldrs: pushed along 4f out: hdwy and rdn 2f out: swtchd rt jst ins fnl f: kpt on u.p to ld on post* **20/1**

00-5 **2** *nse* **Oak Leaves**[48] 1158 3-8-13 **55**..................... JimCrowley 16 57
(J G Portman) *chsd ldrs: wnt 2nd over 2f out: rdn to ld wl over 1f out: kpt on wl u.p tl hdd on post* **14/1**

00-0 **3** *1 1/4* **Helaku (IRE)**[38] 1381 3-9-2 **58**..................... RichardHughes 2 58+
(R Hannon) *taken down early: hld up towards rr: rdn and hdwy 2f out: nt clr run and swtchd rt 1f out: chsd ldrs u.p ins fnl f: one pce fnl 75yds* **5/1**[2]

0526 **4** *3/4* **Rosewood Lad**[18] 1880 3-8-5 **47**..................... TadhgO'Shea 7 46
(J S Moore) *taken down early: led tl 10f out: chsd ldr until rdn to ld again 3f out: drvn and hdd wl over 1f out: kpt on same pce and lost 2 pls ins fnl f* **12/1**

00-0 **5** *hd* **Spring Heather (IRE)**[29] 1581 3-8-13 **55**.....................(t) EddieAhern 1 53+
(J L Dunlop) *hld up wl in tch: n.m.r on inner fr over 2f out tl swtchd rt 1f out: kpt on steadily ins fnl f: styng on fin but unable to rch ldrs* **12/1**

0263 **6** *2 1/4* **Sultan's Choice**[2] 2359 3-8-9 **54**.....................(v) AndrewHeffernan[(3)] 17 49+
(P D Evans) *t.k.h early: stdd sn after s and dropped in towards rr after 1f: hdwy over 3f out: drvn to chse ldrs wl over 1f out: wknd jst ins fnl f* **7/1**[3]

0-06 **7** *nk* **Torran Sound**[14] 1989 3-8-6 **48**.....................(b[1]) LukeMorris 3 42
(J M P Eustace) *s.i.s: sn rdn along and hdwy to ld 10f out: rdn and hdd 3f out: wknd u.p jst over 1f out* **22/1**

3030 **8** *6* **Single Lady**[21] 1796 3-8-10 **55**.....................(p) RussKennemore[(3)] 4 40
(J S Moore) *sn towards rr: rdn 7f out: struggling u.p over 4f out: wl btn 2f out: plugged on past btn horses fnl f: n.d* **33/1**

0-00 **9** *1 1/4* **Antoella (IRE)**[14] 1989 3-8-8 **50**..................... StevieDonohoe 14 37
(Ian Williams) *t.k.h: hld up in rr: hdwy over 3f out: rdn and no prog 2f out: eased whn wl btn ins fnl f* **11/1**

00-0 **10** *2 1/4* **Philippa Jane**[21] 1796 3-8-2 **49**..................... MatthewDavies[(5)] 11 28
(P Winkworth) *plld hrd: hld up in midfield: rdn and btn over 2f out: no ch w ldrs fnl 2f* **25/1**

5430 **11** *3/4* **Market Puzzle (IRE)**[8] 2189 3-9-1 **57**..................... TomMcLaughlin 9 35
(W M Brisbourne) *hld up in rr: rdn and short-lived effrt on outer 3f out: wl btn fr wl over 1f out* **25/1**

-162 **12** *7* **Il Portico**[18] 1866 3-9-4 **60**..................... KierenFallon 5 27
(M R Channon) *chsd ldrs tl rdn and lost pl 3f out: wl bhd fr wl over 1f out* **3/1**[1]

500 **13** *3* **Bethlehem (IRE)**[36] 1432 3-9-4 **60**..................... TravisBlock 15 22
(H Morrison) *in tch: rdn and dropped out qckly 3f out: wl bhd fnl 2f* **9/1**

2m 40.47s (1.47) **Going Correction** -0.05s/f (Good) 13 Ran SP% **114.3**
Speed ratings (Par 97): **93,92,92,91,91 90,89,85,84,83 82,78,76**
toteswingers: 1&2 £62.00, 1&3 £22.40, 2&3 £24.20 CSF £208.95 CT £1043.96 TOTE £37.30: £9.90, £6.10, £1.80; EX 248.90 Place 6 £105.75, Place 5 £66.59.
Owner Hungerford Park Stud **Bred** Barronstown Stud **Trained** Newmarket, Suffolk
■ Stewards' Enquiry : Chris Catlin one-day ban: misuse of whip (Jun 8)

FOCUS
An extremely trappy handicap made slightly easier by the withdrawal of Mr Maximas (8/1) who got down in the stalls and damaged the saddle and Baltic Ben (14/1) who wouldn't load. There was a 15p in the £ R4 deduction. That left eight of the field moving up in distance of at least two furlongs. The fourth, fifth and seventh look the best guides.
Spring Heather(IRE) Official explanation: vet said filly had a breathing problem
T/Plt: £1,004.00 to a £1 stake. Pool: £55,647.79. 40.46 winning tickets. T/Qpdt: £148.90 to a £1 stake. Pool: £3,945.96. 19.60 winning tickets. SP

2330 LINGFIELD (L-H)
Tuesday, May 25

OFFICIAL GOING: Standard
Wind: Moderate, across Weather: Fine

2413 LINGFIELD MARRIOTT HOTEL & COUNTRY CLUB MEDIAN AUCTION MAIDEN STKS — 5f (P)
2:30 (2:30) (Class 6) 2-Y-O — **£2,047** (£604; £302) **Stalls** High

Form — RPR

6 **1** **Reckless Reward (IRE)**[12] 2048 2-9-3 0..................... PatDobbs 6 83+
(R Hannon) *chsd ldr: led over 1f out: rdn clr: comf* **5/4**[1]

323 **2** *4 1/2* **Stunning In Purple (IRE)**[15] 1981 2-8-12 0..................... NeilCallan 1 62
(A B Haynes) *led tl over 1f out: sn outpcd by wnr* **15/2**

3 *1/2* **Coeus** 2-9-3 0..................... SebSanders 5 65+
(Sir Mark Prescott) *chsd ldng pair: rdn over 2f out: styd on same pce* **5/2**[2]

0 **4** *2 1/4* **I Scream (IRE)**[15] 1972 2-8-7 0..................... DeclanCannon[(5)] 7 52
(D R C Elsworth) *sn pushed along in 5th: no hdwy fnl 2f* **25/1**

3 **5** *4* **Its You Again**[21] 1806 2-9-3 0..................... JerryO'Dwyer 9 43
(M G Quinlan) *towards rr: rdn 1/2-way: nt trble ldrs* **5/1**[3]

5 **6** *5* **Renesmee (IRE)**[15] 1981 2-8-12 0..................... DaneO'Neill 2 20
(Peter Grayson) *sn rdn into 4th: wknd 2f out* **100/1**

7 *3 1/4* **Minus Tolerance** 2-8-12 0..................... DavidProbert 4 8
(Miss S L Davison) *outpcd and rdn along: sn bhd* **33/1**

8 *1* **Mirabile Visu** 2-8-12 0..................... SamHitchcott 8 4
(Mrs H S Main) *outpcd and rdn along: sn bhd* **66/1**

9 *3/4* **Fairy Tales** 2-8-12 0..................... NeilChalmers 3 2
(J J Bridger) *settled in 6th: pushed along and n.d fnl 2f* **100/1**

60.48 secs (1.68) **Going Correction** +0.275s/f (Slow) 9 Ran SP% **111.7**
Speed ratings (Par 91): **97,89,89,85,79 71,65,64,63**
toteswingers: 1&2 £2.90, 1&3 £1.90, 2&3 £3.50 CSF £10.77 TOTE £2.20: £1.30, £1.30, £1.10; EX 9.70.
Owner W P Drew **Bred** Ken Carroll **Trained** East Everleigh, Wilts

FOCUS
Not the strongest of Lingfield maidens and few ever got into it. Yet another promising Hannon 2yo and the form has a solid feel to it.

NOTEBOOK
Reckless Reward(IRE) didn't enjoy a straightforward passage on his Salisbury debut 12 days earlier, but he still showed plenty of ability and was much more the finished article here. He was always travelling well on the shoulder of the leader and quickened up smartly once taking over in front over a furlong from home. He may not have beaten much, but is entitled to improve again and should find further opportunities. (op 11-8 tchd 6-4)
Stunning In Purple(IRE), in the frame in her first three starts including twice on Polytrack, tried to make her experience count from the stalls and made most of the running, but the winner was running all over her from the home bend. She is now starting to look exposed and may need to drop in grade in order to win a race, or wait until the nurseries start. (op 8-1 tchd 9-1)
Coeus, a £40,000 half-brother to a couple of winning sprinters, was well supported earlier in the day and he was close enough early, but he became outpaced by the front pair from the home bend and could only plug on from that point. Despite his speedy pedigree, he shaped as though in need of further. (tchd 11-4)
I Scream(IRE), last of 16 on her Windsor debut, ran much better even though she could never get to the leaders. She is likely to improve with racing. (op 33-1)
Its You Again, behind a subsequent winner when third on his Newcastle debut, didn't seem to handle the track here and looked particularly awkward on the home bend. He is worth another chance back on a straight track. (op 4-1 tchd 7-2)

2414 BET TEST MATCH CRICKET - BETDAQ (S) STKS — 1m (P)
3:00 (3:02) (Class 6) 3-5-Y-O — **£2,047** (£604; £302) **Stalls** High

Form — RPR

6006 **1** **Noble Jack (IRE)**[4] 2279 4-9-10 70..................... GeorgeBaker 9 73+
(G L Moore) *s.s: bhd tl hdwy into midfield after 3f: effrt on outer 2f out: led over 1f out: rdn clr* **5/1**[3]

0-46 **2** *2 1/4* **Douchkette (FR)**[28] 1591 4-9-0 57..................... NeilCallan 12 58
(John Berry) *in tch: effrt over 2f out: rdn to chal on rail over 1f out: one pce* **10/1**

-604 **3** *1* **Brave Decision**[14] 1995 3-8-7 61..................... AndreaAtzeni 5 58
(R M H Cowell) *prom: rdn 2f out: one pce appr fnl f* **8/1**

-400 **4** *hd* **Illuminative (USA)**[11] 2081 4-9-5 71..................... TomQueally 4 60
(Stef Higgins) *towards rr: rdn and styd on fnl 2f: nrst fin* **11/4**[1]

2442 **5** *1* **Kenswick**[8] 2172 3-8-0 55 ow1.....................(b) MartinLane[(3)] 7 51
(Pat Eddery) *chsd ldrs: rdn and one pce fnl 2f* **4/1**[2]

/05- **6** *5* **Fromthebeginning**[379] 1932 4-9-5 67..................... DaneO'Neill 1 46
(D R C Elsworth) *dwlt: sn chsng ldr: wknd and n.m.r ent st* **11/1**

2000 **7** *1 1/4* **Ant Music (IRE)**[4] 2279 3-8-12 65.....................(b) PatDobbs 6 46
(J S Moore) *led tl wknd over 1f out* **8/1**

000 **8** *4 1/2* **Greystoke Prince**[7] 2198 5-8-12 50.....................(t) CarolineKelly[(7)] 2 33
(M D Squance) *a towards rr: rdn and n.d fnl 3f* **50/1**

00-0 **9** *8* **Baycat (IRE)**[39] 1346 4-9-5 68.....................(b[1]) StephenCraine 10 15
(J G Portman) *chsd ldrs tl wknd over 2f out* **16/1**

10 *13* **Farmers Surprise** 3-8-3 0 ow1..................... FrankieMcDonald 8 —
(H J Evans) *in tch whn hmpd after 100yds: lost pl and rn green: sn bhd: no ch whn rn wd bnd 4f out* **66/1**

11 *dist* **Preset** 3-8-7 0..................... NickyMackay 3 —
(J M P Eustace) *s.i.s: rdr lost irons: sn t.o and virtually p.u* **33/1**

1m 40.34s (2.14) **Going Correction** +0.275s/f (Slow)
WFA 3 from 4yo+ 12lb 11 Ran SP% **115.3**
Speed ratings (Par 101): **100,97,96,96,95 90,89,84,76,63** —
toteswingers: 1&2 £6.50, 1&3 £8.10, 2&3 £12.10 CSF £52.46 TOTE £4.80: £1.60, £3.80, £4.20; EX 51.30.There was no bid for the winner. Illuminative was claimed by Miss Z. C. Davison for £6,000.
Owner M K George **Bred** Team Hogdala **Trained** Lower Beeding, W Sussex

FOCUS
A modest seller but the form looks sound.
Farmers Surprise Official explanation: jockey said filly hung right throughout
Preset Official explanation: jockey said he lost irons on leaving stalls

2415 FAIRWARP CLAIMING STKS — 7f (P)
3:30 (3:31) (Class 6) 3-Y-O+ — **£2,047** (£604; £302) **Stalls** Low

Form — RPR

4100 **1** **Lady Kent (IRE)**[34] 1482 4-9-7 70..................... PatCosgrave 6 78
(J R Boyle) *prom: drvn to press ldrs 1f out: grad wore down idling runner-up: got up fnl 30yds* **11/1**

1206 **2** *hd* **Fazbee (IRE)**[26] 1641 4-9-1 70.....................(b) TonyCulhane 11 71
(P W D'Arcy) *hld up in tch: effrt on bit ent st: shkn up and led 1f out: carried hd high and fnd little: hdd fnl 30yds* **8/1**

3020 **3** *1 1/4* **Dichoh**[8] 2167 7-9-10 73.....................(v) GeorgeBaker 9 77
(M Madgwick) *hld up towards rr: gd hdwy over 1f out: drvn to chal ins fnl f: no ex fnl 50yds* **8/1**

0312 **4** *1* **Craicattack (IRE)**[28] 1594 3-8-13 72.....................(p) TomQueally 5 70
(J S Moore) *chsd ldr: led 2f out tl 1f out: one pce* **7/1**[2]

1406 **5** *1/2* **Prince Namid**[6] 2234 8-8-9 67..................... KierenFox[(5)] 14 63
(J A T De Giles) *stdd into last pl s and taken to ins rail: rdn and styd on fnl 2f: nrst fin* **20/1**

0105 **6** *1* **Straight Face (IRE)**[8] 2188 6-9-2 67.....................(b) CathyGannon 13 62+
(P D Evans) *outpcd and sn bhd: styd on wl fnl f* **14/1**

1154 **7** *hd* **Kirsty's Boy (IRE)**[12] 2049 3-8-13 73..................... PatDobbs 12 66
(J S Moore) *mid-div on outer: rdn over 3f out: styd on fnl f* **15/2**[3]

0-16 **8** *1 1/4* **King's Caprice**[24] 1692 9-9-10 74..................... RichardThomas 7 66
(J C Fox) *chsd ldrs: outpcd whn n.m.r over 2f out: hld after* **8/1**

-240 **9** *1 1/2* **Welsh Artist**[27] 1619 3-8-13 70..................... NeilCallan 10 58
(Mrs A J Perrett) *chsd ldrs: pushed along over 2f out: wknd over 1f out* **10/1**

3210 **10** *2* **Army Of Stars (IRE)**[33] 1492 4-9-6 70.....................(p) FergusSweeney 3 53
(J A Osborne) *led tl 2f out: hrd rdn and wknd qckly 1f out* **9/1**

4303 **11** *3* **Ravi River (IRE)**[8] 2187 6-8-12 70 ow1.....................(v) RichardEvans[(5)] 2 42
(P D Evans) *mid-div: rdn and lost pl 3f out: sn bhd* **4/1**[1]

0 **12** *26* **Kamphora (IRE)**[17] 1932 5-9-9 0..................... WiaczeslawSzymczuk 8 —
(T T Clement) *outpcd in rr: wl bhd fnl 3f* **200/1**

1m 26.38s (1.58) **Going Correction** +0.275s/f (Slow)
WFA 3 from 4yo+ 11lb 12 Ran SP% **116.9**
Speed ratings (Par 101): **101,100,99,98,97 96,96,94,93,90 87,57**
toteswingers: 1&2 £17.40, 1&3 £14.60, 2&3 £13.80 CSF £94.95 TOTE £15.60: £4.20, £2.60, £2.70; EX 180.10.
Owner J-P Lim & Allen B Pope **Bred** Tally-Ho Stud **Trained** Epsom, Surrey

FOCUS
An ordinary claimer, but a race of changing fortunes. The quickest of the three C/D races and the winner looks back to her best.
Ravi River(IRE) Official explanation: jockey said gelding made a noise 1 1/2f out

2416 BETDAQ.CO.UK H'CAP — 7f (P)
4:00 (4:02) (Class 5) (0-75,75) 3-Y-O — **£3,412** (£1,007; £504) **Stalls** Low

Form — RPR

0-56 **1** **Tewin Wood**[42] 1279 3-9-1 **72**..................... FrannyNorton 12 79
(A Bailey) *plld hrd: prom: rdn to ld 1f out: styd on* **11/1**

1264 **2** *1 1/2* **Marosh (FR)**[42] 1279 3-9-2 **73**..................... GeorgeBaker 13 76+
(R M H Cowell) *stdd s and taken to ins rail in last pl: wd st: rapid hdwy over 1f out: weaved through and r.o to take 2nd nr fin* **11/2**[2]

323- **3** 1/2 **Baby Dottie**[206] 7177 3-8-12 **69** .... IanMongan 7 71
(P M Phelan) *disp ld: led ent st: hrd rdn and hdd 1f out: one pce* **12/1**

0-51 **4** 1 1/4 **Super Yellow**[14] 2000 3-8-12 **69** .... FergusSweeney 2 67
(J A Osborne) *in tch in 5th: sltly outpcd 3f out: kpt on again fnl f* **12/1**

05-0 **5** nse **Lutine Charlie (IRE)**[22] 1766 3-9-2 **73** .... DaneO'Neill 6 71
(P Winkworth) *hld up in midfield: effrt ent st: wnt 4th 1f out: no imp* **20/1**

5254 **6** 1/2 **Master Mylo (IRE)**[22] 1784 3-8-13 **70** .... TomQueally 9 67+
(D K Ivory) *towards rr: last whn v wd and rdn st: styd on wl fnl f* **22/1**

23-0 **7** 3/4 **Warning Song (USA)**[17] 1913 3-9-4 **75** .... PatDobbs 11 70+
(Mrs A J Perrett) *t.k.h in midfield: wd and rdn st: styd on fnl f* **20/1**

0300 **8** 1 1/4 **Transfixed (IRE)**[10] 2112 3-9-1 **72** .... CathyGannon 10 65
(P D Evans) *towards rr: sme hdwy whn hmpd 1f out: nvr rchd ldrs* **33/1**

0-45 **9** hd **Yarra River**[22] 1782 3-9-3 **74** .... DavidProbert 4 65
(A M Balding) *disp ld tl ent st: wknd fnl f* **7/1**[3]

100- **10** 2 **Fardyieh**[229] 6619 3-9-4 **75** .... NeilCallan 3 60
(C E Brittain) *chsd ldrs tl hrd rdn and wknd over 1f out* **16/1**

-240 **11** 1 1/4 **Giulietta Da Vinci**[18] 1873 3-8-6 **63** .... JimmyQuinn 5 45
(S Woodman) *a towards rr: rdn and n.d fnl 2f* **33/1**

04-2 **12** 1 **Redden**[3] 2329 3-8-10 **67** .... DarryllHolland 8 46
(W J Haggas) *in tch in 6th: rdn over 2f out: wknd wl over 1f out* **11/8**[1]

121- **13** 2 **Shark Man (IRE)**[197] 7319 3-9-1 **72** ....(b[1]) PaulFitzsimons 1 46
(Miss J R Tooth) *in tch on rail tl wknd 2f out* **40/1**

1m 26.74s (1.94) **Going Correction** +0.275s/f (Slow) **13** Ran SP% **121.8**
Speed ratings (Par 99): **99,97,96,95,95 94,93,92,92,89 88,87,85**
toteswingers: 1&2 £16.00, 1&3 £20.30, 2&3 £11.70 CSF £65.57 CT £787.62 TOTE £11.20: £2.60, £2.60, £3.50; EX 70.60.
Owner The Perle d'Or Partnership **Bred** Perle D'Or Partnership **Trained** Newmarket, Suffolk

FOCUS
An ordinary 3-y-o handicap in which the winning time was 0.36 seconds slower than the older-horse claimer. It paid to race prominently and the third helps set the standard.
Marosh(FR) Official explanation: jockey said gelding hung left
Transfixed(IRE) Official explanation: jockey said filly was denied a clear run
Redden Official explanation: trainer's rep said gelding was unsuited by the track

2417 HENRY STREETER H'CAP (DIV I) 1m (P)
4:30 (4:32) (Class 6) (0-60,60) 4-Y-0+ **£1,706** (£503; £252) **Stalls** High

Form RPR

0100 **1** **Batchworth Blaise**[12] 2053 7-8-6 **53** .... KierenFox[(5)] 12 65
(E A Wheeler) *s.s: outpcd and bhd tl gd hdwy on outer ent st: led 1f out: rdn out* **8/1**

0643 **2** 1 **Dr Wintringham (IRE)**[22] 1762 4-9-3 **59** .... DarryllHolland 1 69
(Karen George) *trckd ldrs: drvn to chal over 1f out: kpt on* **4/1**[2]

553 **3** 4 **Sir Mozart (IRE)**[31] 1534 7-9-2 **58** .... TomQueally 4 59
(B J Curley) *mid-div: rdn into 4th 2f out: pressed ldrs jst over 1f out: no ex fnl f* **7/4**[1]

005- **4** 1/2 **Cottonfields (USA)**[284] 4979 4-9-4 **60** ....(p) SamHitchcott 6 60
(Mrs H S Main) *led and set gd pce: hdd and rdn over 3f out: rallied on rail over 1f out: no ex fnl f* **33/1**

0443 **5** 1/2 **Kielty's Folly**[14] 1998 6-8-13 **55** .... TonyCulhane 3 54
(B P J Baugh) *mid-div: pushed along and struggling to hold pl 3f out: kpt on again fnl f* **12/1**

5330 **6** 1 1/2 **December**[14] 2010 4-9-0 **56** ....(vt) SebSanders 8 51
(Mrs C A Dunnett) *chsd ldr: led over 3f out tl wknd qckly 1f out* **11/2**[3]

6000 **7** 1 1/2 **Haasem (USA)**[26] 1633 7-8-10 **52** .... FergusSweeney 10 44
(J R Jenkins) *mid-div: brief effrt on rail ent st: hung lft and btn over 1f out* **20/1**

1000 **8** 2 1/4 **Elusive Ronnie (IRE)**[7] 2198 4-9-2 **58** ....(b) JackMitchell 2 44
(R A Teal) *mainly 5th tl rdn and wknd 3f out* **25/1**

/0-0 **9** 5 **Seven Royals (IRE)**[35] 1443 5-8-7 **49** .... FrankieMcDonald 5 24
(Miss A M Newton-Smith) *rrd s: s.i.s: a bhd: rdn and no ch fnl 3f* **50/1**

50-0 **10** 2 1/4 **Burnbrake**[40] 1323 5-8-13 **55** ....(v) PatDobbs 11 25
(L Montague Hall) *sn bhd: rdn 3f out: no ch after* **8/1**

000- **11** 3 3/4 **Novastasia (IRE)**[234] 6497 4-8-9 **51** .... NeilCallan 7 12
(D K Ivory) *chsd ldng pair tl 3f out: sn wknd* **25/1**

1m 40.51s (2.31) **Going Correction** +0.275s/f (Slow) **11** Ran SP% **119.0**
Speed ratings (Par 101): **99,98,94,93,93 91,90,87,82,80 76**
toteswingers: 1&2 £4.00, 1&3 £6.60, 2&3 £5.30 CSF £38.10 CT £83.83 TOTE £9.80: £2.80, £2.00, £1.80; EX 34.40.
Owner Astrod TA Austin Stroud & Co **Bred** Mrs D Price **Trained** Whitchurch-on-Thames, Oxon

FOCUS
Not a great race, but they went a good pace. The winner looks better than ever and the runner-up is rated to form.
Burnbrake Official explanation: trainer said gelding scoped dirty on return

2418 BET FRENCH OPEN TENNIS - BETDAQ H'CAP 7f (P)
5:00 (5:02) (Class 6) (0-55,55) 3-Y-0 **£2,047** (£604; £302) **Stalls** Low

Form RPR

000 **1** **Collect Art (IRE)**[35] 1450 3-8-5 **46** oh1 .... HayleyTurner 6 53+
(M L W Bell) *trckd ldng pair: wnt 2nd 2f out: led 1f out: rdn out* **11/4**[2]

00-0 **2** 1 **Naseby (USA)**[21] 1795 3-9-0 **55** .... RichardKingscote 12 59
(Miss S L Davison) *led: rdn over 2f out: hdd 1f out: kpt on wl* **20/1**

01 **3** 3 **Belle Park**[60] 993 3-8-7 **55** .... AdamBeschizza[(7)] 9 51
(Karen George) *in tch in 6th: drvn to chse ldrs over 1f out: one pce* **14/1**

-540 **4** 2 **Tregony Bridge**[26] 1643 3-8-9 **50** .... FergusSweeney 2 41+
(M Blanshard) *hld up towards rr: effrt on outer 2f out: styd on fnl f* **5/2**[1]

0-00 **5** 1/2 **Securitisation (IRE)**[33] 1495 3-8-9 **50** .... TomQueally 4 39
(B J Curley) *mid-div: effrt on outer 2f out: styd on same pce: unable to chal* **8/1**

-600 **6** 1 3/4 **Proper Littlemadam**[21] 1795 3-8-12 **53** .... AndreaAtzeni 7 37
(C N Kellett) *towards rr: rdn and struggling 3f out: styd on fnl f* **20/1**

00-0 **7** 1/2 **Dixi Heights**[28] 1593 3-9-0 **55** ....(b[1]) PatCosgrave 1 38+
(J R Boyle) *in rr gp whn bdly hmpd and dropped bk to last pl 5f out: rdn and styd on fr over 1f out: nvr nrr* **9/1**

00-0 **8** 3/4 **Tumbled Again**[50] 1127 3-8-9 **50** .... JamieMackay 13 31
(M E Rimmer) *sn rdn along: chsd ldrs tl no ex over 1f out* **14/1**

3300 **9** 3/4 **Roybuoy**[21] 1795 3-8-9 **50** ....(b) JimmyQuinn 3 29
(H J L Dunlop) *mid-div: n.m.r on rail 5f out: outpcd and btn over 2f out* **7/1**[3]

2400 **10** 3 **Clayton Flick (IRE)**[2] 2359 3-8-13 **54** .... NeilCallan 14 25
(A B Haynes) *stdd s and hld up in rr: hdwy and in tch ent st: hrd rdn and wknd over 1f out* **14/1**

2066 **11** nse **Miss Kitty Grey (IRE)**[22] 1784 3-8-8 **54** .... JemmaMarshall[(5)] 5 25
(J R Boyle) *chsd ldrs tl wknd over 2f out* **33/1**

0-60 **12** 6 **Aldorable**[21] 1796 3-9-0 **55** ....(b[1]) DarryllHolland 10 10
(R A Teal) *chsd ldr tl wknd 2f out: btn whn squeezed out ent st* **20/1**

1m 28.02s (3.22) **Going Correction** +0.275s/f (Slow) **12** Ran SP% **126.1**
Speed ratings (Par 97): **92,90,87,85,84 82,82,81,80,76 76,69**
toteswingers: 1&2 £16.90, 1&3 £11.50, 2&3 £72.40 CSF £65.75 CT £697.07 TOTE £3.10: £1.10, £11.60, £4.90; EX 108.80.
Owner R A Green **Bred** Pier House Stud **Trained** Newmarket, Suffolk

FOCUS
A very weak handicap and the winning time was much slower than the two earlier races over the same trip. It paid to race handily. The form is rated around the second and third and the winner is capable of better.
Tregony Bridge ◆ Official explanation: jockey said gelding reared on leaving stalls

2419 HENRY STREETER H'CAP (DIV II) 1m (P)
5:30 (5:34) (Class 6) (0-60,59) 4-Y-0+ **£1,706** (£503; £252) **Stalls** High

Form RPR

5-50 **1** **Amber Sunset**[95] 615 4-9-3 **58** .... NeilCallan 4 69
(J Jay) *t.k.h: trckd ldrs: led over 1f out: hung bdly rt ins fnl f: drvn out* **7/1**[2]

0566 **2** 1 1/2 **Signora Frasi (IRE)**[35] 1437 5-8-12 **53** .... DaneO'Neill 7 61
(A G Newcombe) *hld up in rr: hdwy on outer 2f out: rdn to chal 1f out: carried rt ins fnl f: kpt on* **4/1**[1]

3565 **3** 3 1/2 **Musashi (IRE)**[4] 2279 5-9-4 **59** ....(b) IanMongan 11 59+
(Mrs L J Mongan) *v.s.a: towards rr: effrt and wd st: r.o to take 3rd ins fnl f* **4/1**[1]

0420 **4** 2 1/4 **Count Ceprano (IRE)**[22] 1772 6-9-1 **56** .... SaleemGolam 9 50
(J Pearce) *mid-div: effrt and briefly nt clr run ent st: styd on same pce appr fnl f* **7/1**[2]

3105 **5** 2 1/4 **Royal Acclamation (IRE)**[17] 1922 5-8-3 **51** .... DavidKenny[(7)] 8 40
(H J Evans) *towards rr on outer: v wd home turn: styd on fnl f* **10/1**

405- **6** hd **Dilli Dancer**[223] 6777 5-8-9 **50** ....(e[1]) JimmyQuinn 5 39
(G D Blake) *prom: pressed ldr over 2f out: wknd 1f out* **25/1**

0003 **7** 1 1/2 **Esteem Lord**[6] 2235 4-8-11 **55** ....(b) MartinLane[(3)] 10 40
(Jamie Poulton) *mid-div: n.m.r and outpcd 2f out: kpt on again fnl f* **11/1**

4350 **8** hd **Clever Omneya (USA)**[50] 1129 4-8-8 **49** .... FergusSweeney 2 34
(J R Jenkins) *dwlt: sn in midfield: effrt and in tch ent st: no imp* **16/1**

006- **9** 1/2 **Action Girl**[164] 7732 5-8-12 **53** .... PatCosgrave 3 37
(R M H Cowell) *dwlt: led 1f: prom tl hrd rdn and wknd over 1f out* **25/1**

0/1- **10** 8 **Ain't Talkin'**[487] 267 4-8-5 **51** .... KierenFox[(5)] 6 16
(M J Attwater) *led after 1f tl wknd qckly over 1f out* **9/1**[3]

-022 **11** 1 3/4 **Great Bounder (CAN)**[120] 295 4-9-0 **55** .... RichardKingscote 1 16
(A B Haynes) *towards rr: rdn over 3f out: n.d after* **9/1**[3]

4500 **12** 1 1/4 **Oceans Edge**[95] 614 4-9-4 **59** ....(b[1]) StephenCraine 12 17
(J R Boyle) *sluggish s: sn chsng ldrs on outer: wknd 2f out* **12/1**

1m 40.4s (2.20) **Going Correction** +0.275s/f (Slow) **12** Ran SP% **123.7**
Speed ratings (Par 101): **100,98,95,92,90 90,88,88,88,80 78,77**
toteswingers: 1&2 £16.70, 1&3 £19.30, 2&3 £4.40 CSF £36.70 CT £132.24 TOTE £16.30: £5.20, £1.10, £3.20; EX 56.40 Place 6 £215.34, Place 5 £161.39.
Owner David J Orchard **Bred** Southill Stud **Trained**
■ Stewards' Enquiry : Neil Callan one-day ban: careless riding (Jun 10)

FOCUS
Another moderate handicap though the winning time was 0.11 seconds faster than the first division. The winner is rated in line with last year's best.
Musashi(IRE) Official explanation: jockey said gelding was slowly away
Great Bounder(CAN) Official explanation: jockey said gelding was unsuited by the kickback
T/Plt: £210.30 to a £1 stake. Pool: £53,386.07. 185.25 winning tickets. T/Qpdt: £98.90 to a £1 stake. Pool: £3,796.07. 28.40 winning tickets. LM

2138 RIPON (R-H)
Tuesday, May 25

OFFICIAL GOING: Good (good to firm in places) changing to good to soft after race 3 (3.10)
Wind: Light, half against Weather: Overcast

2420 E B F SAWLEY MAIDEN STKS 5f
2:10 (2:13) (Class 5) 2-Y-0 **£3,561** (£1,059; £529; £264) **Stalls** Low

Form RPR

1 **Sergeant Suzie** 2-8-7 0 .... JamesSullivan[(5)] 3 71+
(M Dods) *mde all stands' side: kpt on wl towards fin* **14/1**

2 1/2 **Sea Flower (IRE)** 2-8-12 0 .... GrahamGibbons 9 69+
(T D Easterby) *swtchd lft after s: w ldrs: chal over 1f out: no ex clsng stages* **7/2**[2]

3 3 3/4 **Insolenceofoffice (IRE)** 2-9-3 0 .... MickyFenton 1 61
(Mrs A Duffield) *drvn along: hmpd and lost pl after 150yds: outpcd: hdwy over 1f out: edgd rt and kpt on: will improve* **9/1**[3]

4 5 **Brave Dream** 2-9-3 0 .... JamieSpencer 5 43+
(K A Ryan) *sed slow: reminders sn after s: hdwy on outer over 2f out: hung rt: wknd over 1f out* **6/4**[1]

0 **5** 1 1/4 **Dark Times (IRE)**[31] 1510 2-8-12 0 .... AndrewElliott 6 33
(J R Weymes) *chsd ldrs: drvn over 2f out: wknd fnl 150yds* **33/1**

6 6 **Sister Sioux (IRE)** 2-8-5 0 .... MatthewLawson[(7)] 8 11
(R Bastiman) *dwlt: sn w ldrs on outer: sn drvn along: wknd over 1f out* **12/1**

7 1 1/2 **Bonded Spirit** 2-9-3 0 .... PaulMulrennan 4 11
(Mrs K Walton) *w ldrs: wknd over 2f out* **25/1**

62.22 secs (1.52) **Going Correction** +0.075s/f (Good) **7** Ran SP% **93.4**
Speed ratings (Par 93): **90,89,83,75,73 63,61**
toteswingers: 1&2 £4.80, 1&3 £4.60, 2&3 £3.00 CSF £38.85 TOTE £17.30: £6.30, £1.30; EX 27.30 Trifecta £130.90 Part won. Pool: £177.02 - 0.43 winning units..
Owner Mrs Suzanne Kirkup **Bred** R J Cornelius **Trained** Denton, Co Durham
■ Satin Love was withdrawn (3/1, unruly in stalls). R4 applies, deduct 25p in the £.

FOCUS
At the start of racing the ground was officially described as good, good to firm in places (GoingStick 8.7), but that proved to be totally misleading. For instance, both Graham Gibbons and Jamie Spencer reported after this opener that it was on the soft side of good, and many of the race times were well above standard. Only after the third race was the ground changed to good to soft, and considering there was nothing more than light drizzle in the morning, it seems the track had been overwatered. This opener seemed to lack depth and the form has been rated conservatively.

NOTEBOOK
Sergeant Suzie, a £3,500 half-brother to 1m winner Crosstar, and 6f winner Danny's Choice, out of a fairly useful 7f scorer, was well educated. She showed good speed against the near-side rail from the off and stuck on gamely for pressure, although it remains to be seen how much she will improve. (op 12-1)
Sea Flower(IRE) seemed to know her job, showing plenty of pace and keeping on well for pressure. This £6,000 purchase was clear of the remainder and should find a race. (op 11-2 tchd 6-1)

Insolenceofoffice(IRE), a £14,000 purchase, lacked the know how of the front two and, having been short of room early on, he was always struggling. There should be plenty of improvement forthcoming. (tchd 10-1)
Brave Dream, a £15,000 purchase, out of a triple 5f-1m winner, soon needed reminders after starting slowly and then hung right in the second half of the contest. A starting price of 6-4 strongly suggests much better was expected. (tchd 15-8)
Dark Times(IRE) was never going the required speed.

2421 ATTHERACES.COM IS FREE H'CAP — 1m 1f 170y
2:40 (2:40) (Class 5) (0-70,70) 4-Y-0+ — £2,914 (£867; £433; £216) Stalls High

Form — RPR
00-0 **1** **Northern Acres**[25] 1669 4-8-6 **63** .... BillyCray(5) 7 — 75
(D Nicholls) *trckd ldrs: effrt on ins 4f out: hrd rdn to ld last 100yds* **14/1**
5/0- **2** 2 ¼ **Smirfy's Silver**[269] 5438 6-8-10 **62** .... SilvestreDeSousa 8 — 69
(Mrs D J Sanderson) *sn led: hdd ins fnl f: no ex* **33/1**
3-52 **3** 2 ½ **Highkingofireland**[17] 1920 4-8-11 **63** ow2 .... AndrewElliott 6 — 65
(J R Weymes) *sn drvn along in midfield: hdwy over 3f out: wnt 3rd over 1f out: kpt on same pce* **7/1**[3]
34-0 **4** 4 ½ **Steel Trade**[17] 1926 4-8-13 **65** .... TomEaves 9 — 58
(M Brittain) *s.s: reminder and hdwy 6f out: kpt on to take n.d 4th last stride* **7/1**[3]
00-3 **5** shd **Joinedupwriting**[7] 2208 5-8-5 **62** .... AmyRyan(5) 13 — 55
(R M Whitaker) *prom: effrt 3f out: one pce* **9/2**[1]
50-0 **6** 1 ¼ **Highland Love**[17] 1920 5-8-4 **56** oh2 .... RoystonFfrench 5 — 46
(Jedd O'Keeffe) *hld up in rr: effrt 4f out: kpt on fnl 2f: nvr nr ldrs* **22/1**
0-06 **7** 1 ½ **Tres Froide (FR)**[17] 1919 5-8-5 **57** .... JoeFanning 11 — 44
(N Tinkler) *trckd ldrs: wknd over 1f out* **15/2**
0002 **8** ½ **Orpen Wide (IRE)**[9] 2142 8-8-10 **67** ....(b) MarkCoumbe(5) 2 — 53
(M C Chapman) *sn detached in last and drvn along: kpt on fnl 3f: nvr a factor* **16/1**
300- **9** 1 ¼ **Royal Composer (IRE)**[246] 6174 7-8-4 **56** oh4 .... PJMcDonald 4 — 40
(T D Easterby) *hld up in rr: effrt 3f out: nvr on terms* **25/1**
02-6 **10** 1 ¼ **Avitus**[17] 1920 4-8-4 **56** .... PaulHanagan 10 — 37
(Micky Hammond) *trckd ldrs: wkng whn hmpd 2f out* **6/1**[2]
145- **11** nk **Castlebury (IRE)**[289] 4821 5-8-10 **62** .... RobertWinston 1 — 43
(G A Swinbank) *hld up in rr: effrt on outside 4f out: nvr a factor* **14/1**
313- **12** nk **Tropical Duke (IRE)**[221] 6818 4-8-8 **60** .... PhillipMakin 3 — 40
(R E Barr) *in rr: drvn over 3f out: hmpd 2f out: nvr on terms* **10/1**
050- **13** nk **Fabled Dancer (IRE)**[260] 5731 4-8-4 **56** oh2 .... DuranFentiman 14 — 36
(E J Alston) *trckd ldrs: wknd 3f out* **25/1**
606/ **14** 2 ¾ **Paradise Walk**[513] 6235 6-8-10 **62** .... TonyHamilton 15 — 36
(E W Tuer) *led early: trckd ldr: wknd over 2f out* **25/1**

2m 5.13s (-0.27) **Going Correction** -0.05s/f (Good) — **14** Ran SP% **116.4**
Speed ratings (Par 103): **99,97,95,91,91 90,89,88,87,86 86,86,86,84**
toteswingers: 1&2 £82.60, 1&3 £39.00, 2&3 £91.70 CSF £418.82 CT £3470.96 TOTE £21.10: £6.80, £12.50, £2.30; EX 633.90 TRIFECTA Not won..
Owner Jim Dale **Bred** Darley **Trained** Sessay, N Yorks

FOCUS
A modest contest, but the time was quite good, being 1.97 seconds quicker than the following 61-80 handicap, albeit that was for 3-y-os. Pretty solid form, with a return to his best from the winner.

2422 WEATHERBYS BANK H'CAP — 1m 1f 170y
3:10 (3:10) (Class 4) (0-80,76) 3-Y-O — £4,533 (£1,348; £674; £336) Stalls High

Form — RPR
503 **1** **Yashrid (USA)**[15] 1959 3-9-0 **69** .... PhilipRobinson 4 — 76+
(M A Jarvis) *trckd ldrs: drvn 3f out: edgd lft over 1f out: sn led: jst hld on* **5/2**[1]
03-1 **2** nse **Music Of The Moor (IRE)**[41] 1297 3-9-6 **75** .... MickyFenton 1 — 81+
(T P Tate) *hld up in rr: stdy hdwy on outside over 3f out: chal 1f out: jst failed* **7/2**[2]
10-5 **3** 1 ½ **Tut (IRE)**[47] 1182 3-9-6 **75** .... AndrewElliott 8 — 78
(J R Weymes) *hld up: hdwy 3f out: chal over 1f out: styd on same pce ins fnl f* **25/1**
43-1 **4** 2 ¾ **Mighty Clarets (IRE)**[21] 1810 3-9-2 **71** .... PaulHanagan 7 — 68
(R A Fahey) *led early: trckd ldrs: effrt over 3f out: one pce whn nt clr run over 1f out* **4/1**[3]
-330 **5** 1 **Epic (IRE)**[28] 1608 3-9-3 **72** .... JoeFanning 2 — 67
(M Johnston) *sn led: hdd over 1f out: one pce* **9/1**
-504 **6** 3 ¼ **Vito Volterra (IRE)**[43] 1259 3-8-11 **66** .... PhillipMakin 5 — 54
(Michael Smith) *trckd ldrs: drvn 3f out: wknd fnl f* **7/1**
1-30 **7** nk **Jupiter Fidius**[25] 1658 3-9-4 **76** .... KellyHarrison(3) 6 — 66
(Mrs K Walton) *dwlt: hld up in rr: sme hdwy whn nt clr run over 1f out: wknd fnl 150yds* **10/1**
530- **8** 27 **Turf Trivia**[222] 6793 3-8-9 **64** .... PJMcDonald 3 — —
(G M Moore) *sn trcking ldrs: lost pl over 3f out: bhd and eased ins fnl f* **14/1**

2m 7.10s (1.70) **Going Correction** -0.05s/f (Good) — **8** Ran SP% **112.9**
Speed ratings (Par 101): **91,90,89,87,86 84,83,62**
toteswingers: 1&2 £1.10, 1&3 £18.20, 2&3 £20.10 CSF £10.95 CT £168.17 TOTE £3.30: £2.30, £1.20, £8.90; EX 10.20 Trifecta £250.00 Part won. Pool: £337.97 - 0.10 winning units..
Owner Sheikh Ahmed Al Maktoum **Bred** Darley **Trained** Newmarket, Suffolk

FOCUS
The ground was changed to good to soft after this contest. This was a fair handicap, but the time was 1.97 seconds slower than the earlier Class 5 handicap for older horses, suggesting they didn't go that quick. The form appears sound enough.
Jupiter Fidius Official explanation: jockey said gelding was unsuited by the good to soft ground

2423 NICK WILMOT-SMITH MEMORIAL H'CAP — 1m
3:40 (3:40) (Class 3) (0-95,92) 4-Y-0- £7,569 (£2,265; £1,132; £566; £282) Stalls High

Form — RPR
4401 **1** **Charlie Cool**[10] 2133 7-8-9 **83** ....(b) RobertWinston 10 — 94
(Mrs R A Carr) *trckd ldrs: effrt over 3f out: led over 1f out: hld on towards fin* **5/1**[3]
3-33 **2** hd **Off Chance**[17] 1899 4-8-12 **86** .... DuranFentiman 5 — 97
(T D Easterby) *dwlt: hdwy over 3f out: chsd wnr 1f out: kpt on wl towards fin* **5/2**[1]
30-5 **3** 2 ¾ **Bencoolen (IRE)**[40] 1333 5-8-13 **92** .... MichaelO'Connell(5) 4 — 97
(D Nicholls) *chsd ldrs: edgd rt and kpt on fnl f* **33/1**
-026 **4** nk **Billy Dane (IRE)**[18] 1889 6-9-0 **88** ....(p) PaulHanagan 6 — 92
(F P Murtagh) *led: hdd over 1f out: kpt on same pce* **13/2**
4-21 **5** 1 ½ **Osteopathic Remedy (IRE)**[24] 1708 6-9-1 **89** .... PhillipMakin 9 — 90
(M Dods) *trckd ldrs: drvn on outer over 3f out: hung lft and kpt on same pce appr fnl f* **9/2**[2]
00-0 **6** 1 **City Of The Kings (IRE)**[18] 1889 5-8-11 **85** .... SilvestreDeSousa 7 — 83
(G A Harker) *mid-div: rdn and hdwy over 2f out: one pce* **12/1**
21-0 **7** 2 ½ **Inheritor (IRE)**[130] 197 4-8-11 **85** .... TomEaves 3 — 77
(B Smart) *trckd ldr: chal over 2f out: hung lft and wknd fnl f* **25/1**
050- **8** 4 ½ **Jack Dawkins (USA)**[280] 5137 5-9-1 **92** .... MichaelGeran(3) 1 — 74
(D Nicholls) *dwlt: hld up in rr: effrt 3f out: lost pl over 1f out* **20/1**
0-06 **9** 1 ¾ **Reel Buddy Star**[11] 2086 5-8-4 **78** .... PJMcDonald 11 — 56
(G M Moore) *chsd ldrs: wknd over 2f out* **13/2**
0-00 **10** 8 **Peter Tchaikovsky**[13] 2027 4-8-11 **85** .... MickyFenton 8 — 45
(B S Rothwell) *s.i.s: detached in last: bhd fnl 3f* **40/1**
240- **11** nk **Ordoney (IRE)**[202] 7233 5-8-8 **82** .... PaulMulrennan 2 — 41
(J S Wainwright) *in rr: rdn and lost pl over 3f out* **28/1**

1m 39.56s (-1.84) **Going Correction** -0.05s/f (Good) — **11** Ran SP% **115.2**
Speed ratings (Par 107): **107,106,104,103,102 101,98,94,92,84 84**
toteswingers: 1&2 £4.90, 1&3 £25.20, 2&3 £15.00 CSF £16.32 CT £378.57 TOTE £6.70: £2.30, £1.40, £6.70; EX 20.00 Trifecta £295.90 Pool: £463.91 - 1.16 winning units..
Owner Middleham Park Racing Xxiv **Bred** Middle Park Stud Ltd **Trained** Huby, N Yorks

FOCUS
Probably an ordinary handicap for the grade, but at least they seemed to go a reasonable pace and the time was good, being 3.49 seconds quicker than the later 3-y-o maiden won by Law To Himself. Decent, solid form for the grade, the winner building on his Thirsk win.

NOTEBOOK
Charlie Cool coped with the overwatered ground to defy a 6lb rise for his recent success at Thirsk. He's thriving right now and could complete the hat-trick. (op 11-2 tchd 6-1)
Off Chance has an action that suggests she may ideally prefer quicker ground, but she still posted a very useful effort in defeat. She remains progressive and is one to keep on side. (op 11-4 tchd 3-1, 10-3 in places)
Bencoolen(IRE) plugged on for pressure but never looked like getting there and is probably a bit too high in the weights. (op 28-1)
Billy Dane(IRE) is another who seems to have little in hand off his current sort of rating. (tchd 6-1)
Osteopathic Remedy(IRE)'s trainer said beforehand that he hoped the course would be well watered but, despite conditions coming right for this gelding, he couldn't defy a 3lb rise for his recent Thirsk win, and also failed to confirm form with Billy Dane. Official explanation: jockey said gelding hung left (tchd 4-1 and 5-1)
Inheritor(IRE) Official explanation: jockey said gelding hung left

2424 WEATHERBYS BLOODSTOCK INSURANCE H'CAP — 1m 4f 10y
4:10 (4:10) (Class 5) (0-70,63) 4-Y-0+ — £2,914 (£867; £433; £216) Stalls High

Form — RPR
-223 **1** **Patavium (IRE)**[21] 1807 7-9-2 **61** .... PaulHanagan 5 — 69
(E W Tuer) *trckd ldr: chal 6f out: led over 2f out: edgd rt 1f out: hld on wl* **11/2**[3]
60-0 **2** ½ **Master Nimbus**[18] 1113 10-9-1 **60** .... GrahamGibbons 2 — 67
(J J Quinn) *hld up: hdwy to trck ldrs 7f out: rdn over 2f out: wnt 2nd jst ins fnl f: jst hld* **7/2**[2]
2143 **3** 2 ¾ **Park's Prodigy**[4] 2277 6-9-1 **60** .... SilvestreDeSousa 7 — 64
(G A Harker) *led: drvn 4f out: hdd over 2f out: one pce whn hmpd ins fnl f* **15/8**[1]
-000 **4** nse **Dispol Diva**[33] 1489 4-8-8 **53** ....(v) JoeFanning 8 — 56
(P T Midgley) *chsd ldr: drvn over 4f out: one pce appr fnl f* **12/1**
63-0 **5** 12 **Obara D'Avril (FR)**[11] 1803 8-7-12 **50** oh2 ow1 .... SoniaEaton(7) 3 — 34
(S G West) *sn trcking ldrs: effrt over 3f out: lost pl over 1f out* **20/1**
1643 **6** 15 **War Of The Roses (IRE)**[13] 2023 7-9-3 **62** .... J-PGuillambert 1 — 22
(R Brotherton) *hld up in rr: effrt over 3f out: rdn and hung lft over 2f out: wknd and eased over 1f out* **7/1**
23-0 **7** 1 ¾ **Regal Lyric (IRE)**[17] 1925 4-9-4 **63** .... MickyFenton 6 — 20
(T P Tate) *hld up in rr: hdwy 7f out: effrt over 3f out: rdn and lost pl over 2f out: eased over 1f out: sn bhd* **15/2**
00-4 **8** 19 **Kendalewood**[24] 1705 4-9-2 **61** .... DuranFentiman 4 — —
(T D Walford) *sn trcking ldrs: shkn up and lost pl after 3f: bhd fnl 3f: virtually p.u* **16/1**

2m 39.61s (2.91) **Going Correction** -0.05s/f (Good) — **8** Ran SP% **115.0**
Speed ratings (Par 103): **88,87,85,85,77 67,66,53**
toteswingers: 1&2 £4.80, 1&3 £2.10, 2&3 £4.70 CSF £25.24 CT £49.02 TOTE £5.80: £2.30, £2.10, £1.10; EX 26.90 Trifecta £47.80 Pool: £246.22 - 3.80 winning units..
Owner J A Nixon **Bred** M Channon **Trained** Great Smeaton, N Yorks
■ Stewards' Enquiry : Graham Gibbons one-day ban: misuse of whip (Jun 8)
Paul Hanagan one-day ban: careless riding (Jun 8)

FOCUS
A modest handicap and they didn't go much of a pace. The winner's best figure since he was a 2yo.
War Of The Roses(IRE) Official explanation: jockey said gelding was unsuited by the good to soft ground

2425 NICK HORSMAN 21ST BIRTHDAY MAIDEN STKS — 1m
4:40 (4:49) (Class 5) 3-Y-O — £2,914 (£867; £433; £216) Stalls High

Form — RPR
3 **1** **Law To Himself (IRE)**[33] 1485 3-9-3 0 .... PJMcDonald 13 — 73
(G A Swinbank) *uns rdr s and rn loose: chsd ldrs: drvn over 3f out: styd on strly appr fnl f: edgd lft ins fnl f: styd on to ld nr fin* **10/1**
3 **2** nk **Kathlatino**[21] 1804 3-8-12 0 .... FrederikTylicki 10 — 68
(Micky Hammond) *prom: styd on to chal over 1f out: led jst ins fnl f: edgd rt: hdd and no ex nr fin* **20/1**
32 **3** ¾ **Jay's Treaty (USA)**[15] 1959 3-9-3 0 .... JoeFanning 12 — 71+
(M Johnston) *trckd ldrs: led 2f out: hdd jst ins fnl f: hld whn squeezed out nr line* **11/4**[2]
62- **4** 2 ½ **Quite Sparky**[262] 5669 3-9-3 0 .... MickyFenton 9 — 65
(T P Tate) *led: hdd 2f out: wknd last 150yds* **4/1**[3]
00 **5** 2 **Nahab**[27] 1620 3-8-12 0 .... PaulHanagan 3 — 56+
(D R Lanigan) *dwlt: in rr: stdy hdwy over 2f out: gng on nicely at fin* **20/1**
6 ¾ **Silvery Moon (IRE)** 3-9-3 0 .... DuranFentiman 2 — 59+
(T D Easterby) *s.i.s: bhd: hdwy over 3f out: kpt on: nvr nr ldrs* **50/1**
7 2 ¼ **Honest Buck** 3-9-3 0 .... TomEaves 11 — 54
(Mrs K Walton) *s.s: bhd: styd on fnl 2f: nrst fin* **100/1**
42-4 **8** 1 **Music Maestro (IRE)**[18] 1872 3-9-3 80 .... MichaelHills 8 — 54
(B W Hills) *w ldr: chal over 3f out: wknd over 1f out: sn eased* **7/4**[1]
0- **9** 3 **Roman Sioux (IRE)**[227] 6679 3-8-10 0 .... MatthewLawson(7) 14 — 45
(R Bastiman) *chsd ldrs: wknd over 2f out* **100/1**
06 **10** 2 **Fantastic Favour**[27] 1627 3-9-3 0 .... TonyHamilton 7 — 40
(Jedd O'Keeffe) *in rr: sme hdwy over 2f out: nvr on terms* **100/1**
00 **11** 2 ½ **Blue Zealot (IRE)**[8] 2180 3-8-12 0 .... JamieSpencer 4 — 29
(M L W Bell) *mid-div: drvn 3f out: nvr a factor* **10/1**
00- **12** 4 **Patricks Lodge**[268] 5466 3-9-3 0 .... GrahamGibbons 1 — 25
(J D Bethell) *s.i.s: a in rr* **100/1**
00- **13** 1 ½ **Both Ends Burning (IRE)**[289] 4817 3-8-7 0 .... LanceBetts(5) 15 — 17
(J S Wainwright) *in tch: lost pl over 2f out* **100/1**
0-5 **14** 6 **Belgooree**[38] 1393 3-8-12 0 .... PaulMulrennan 6 — 3
(J G Given) *chsd ldrs: lost pl over 2f out: eased and sn bhd* **40/1**

00- **15** 2 ¾ **Swansea Jack**217 6922 3-9-0 0 (t) WilliamCarson(3) 5 1
(S C Williams) *s.i.s: in rr: bhd fnl 3f* **50/1**
1m 43.05s (1.65) **Going Correction** -0.05s/f (Good) **15** Ran SP% **122.0**
Speed ratings (Par 99): **89,88,87,85,83 82,80,79,76,74 71,67,66,60,57**
toteswingers: 1&2 £13.10, 1&3 £6.50, 2&3 £12.30 CSF £193.48 TOTE £13.00: £3.10, £4.80, £1.50; EX 142.10 Trifecta £261.30 Part won. Pool: £353.12 - 0.10 winning units..
Owner A Mallen **Bred** C Lilburn **Trained** Melsonby, N Yorks
■ Stewards' Enquiry : Joe Fanning three-day ban: misuse of whip (Jun 8-10)

FOCUS
Problem an ordinary maiden, and the time was 3.49 seconds slower than the earlier Class 3 handicap for older horses. The form seems sound enough rated around the third to fifth.
Belgooree Official explanation: jockey said filly had no more to give

2426 BET BRITISH WITH TOTEPOOL H'CAP 6f
5:10 (5:17) (Class 5) (0-75,75) 3-Y-O **£4,533** (£1,348; £674; £336) **Stalls** Low

Form				RPR
5-23	**1**		**Kellys Eye (IRE)**11 2069 3-9-3 **74** RobertWinston 10 (D H Brown) *in rr-div: hdwy on outer over 2f out: led appr fnl f: edgd lft and styd on strly: eased nr fin* **7/4**1	88+
1-00	**2**	3 ½	**Besty**11 2099 3-8-13 **70** TomEaves 9 (B Smart) *trckd ldr: led 2f out: hdd over 1f out: kpt on same pce* **20/1**	73
23-6	**3**	1 ¼	**We'll Deal Again**11 2099 3-8-4 **66** JamesSullivan(5) 4 (M W Easterby) *rrd s: t.k.h in midfield: effrt over 2f out: n.m.r over 1f out: kpt on ins fnl f* **10/1**	65+
-144	**4**	shd	**Trade Secret**11 2099 3-9-4 **75** PaulHanagan 8 (M Brittain) *chsd ldrs: kpt on same pce appr fnl f* **9/1**3	74
0-03	**5**	hd	**Bossy Kitty**25 1656 3-9-4 **75** SilvestreDeSousa 11 (N Tinkler) *in rr: hdwy on outside over 2f out: kpt on same pce* **12/1**	73
1356	**6**	1	**Slikback Jack (IRE)**39 1362 3-9-2 **73** FrederikTylicki 2 (J A Glover) *dwlt: in rr: nt clr run and swtchd outside over 1f out: kpt on: nvr nr ldrs* **9/1**3	68
31-3	**7**	2 ½	**Mark Anthony (IRE)**24 1709 3-9-1 **72** JamieSpencer 6 (K A Ryan) *led: hdd 2f out: wknd over 1f out* **5/2**2	59
0-00	**8**	3	**Arch Walker (IRE)**24 1706 3-8-8 **65** TonyHamilton 5 (Jedd O'Keeffe) *in rr: sme hdwy on outer over 2f out: edgd rt and lost pl over 1f out* **50/1**	42
5-04	**9**	3 ½	**Bitter Honey**60 991 3-8-4 **61** DuranFentiman 7 (E J Alston) *sn chsng ldrs: wknd over 1f out* **50/1**	27
166-	**10**	nk	**Fair Bunny**165 7707 3-8-7 **64** GrahamGibbons 1 (A D Brown) *sn outpcd: bhd fnl 2f* **40/1**	29
4-40	**11**	hd	**Mercers Row**21 1811 3-8-11 **68** PaulMulrennan 3 (A Dickman) *chsd ldrs: wkng whn n.m.r over 1f out* **33/1**	32

1m 13.56s (0.56) **Going Correction** +0.075s/f (Good) **11** Ran SP% **115.8**
Speed ratings (Par 99): **99,94,92,92,92 90,87,83,78,78 78**
toteswingers: 1&2 £11.60, 1&3 £6.60, 2&3 £19.20 CSF £44.17 CT £280.77 TOTE £3.20: £1.60, £5.40, £3.00; EX 49.80 Trifecta £338.50 Part won. Pool: £457.50 - 0.50 winning units. Place 6 £151.74, Place 5 £45.68.
Owner Ron Hull **Bred** Michael Downey And Roalso Ltd **Trained** Maltby, S Yorks

FOCUS
A modest sprint handicap. A clear personal best from the impressive winner with the form rated around the runner-up. The second favourite's poor run lends slight doubts to the form.
T/Jkpt: Not won. T/Plt: £254.80 to a £1 stake.Pool: £70,227.18. 201.20 winning tickets. T/Qpdt: £6.50 to a £1 stake. Pool: £5,856.78. 665.40 winning tickets. WG

AYR (L-H)
Wednesday, May 26

OFFICIAL GOING: Good to firm (9.6) changing to good to firm (firm in places) after race 1 (2.10)
Wind: Fresh, half against Weather: Sunny

2427 EBF BIRD SEMPLE SOLICITORS 10TH ANNIVERSARY MAIDEN STKS 6f
2:10 (2:10) (Class 4) 2-Y-O **£4,533** (£1,348; £674; £336) **Stalls** High

Form				RPR
	1		**Dubawi Gold** 2-9-3 0 PhillipMakin 6 (M Dods) *plld hrd early: mde virtually all: qcknd clr over 1f out: readily* **6/4**1	79+
	2	4 ½	**Sinadinou** 2-9-0 0 MichaelGeran(3) 8 (D Nicholls) *trckd ldrs: effrt over 1f out: chsd wnr ins fnl f: no imp* **20/1**	66+
4	**3**	1 ¼	**Night Singer**12 2068 2-9-3 0 FrederikTylicki 1 (J Howard Johnson) *cl up on outside: effrt and ev ch 2f out: one pce appr fnl f* **11/2**3	62
4	**4**	1 ½	**Crown Ridge (IRE)**11 2111 2-9-3 0 KierenFallon 2 (M R Channon) *prom: effrt 2f out: sn outpcd* **10/1**	58
	5	6	**Namwahjobo (IRE)** 2-9-0 0 GaryBartley(3) 3 (J S Goldie) *missed break: bhd and detached: styd on fnl f: nvr nrr* **12/1**	43+
	6	4	**Save The Bees** 2-9-3 0 PatrickMathers 7 (I W McInnes) *disp ld 2f: cl up: rdn whn n.m.r over 2f out: wknd wl over 1f out* **66/1**	28
	7	16	**Glitter Bug (IRE)** 2-9-3 0 GregFairley 5 (M Johnston) *rrd s: sn pushed along bhd ldng gp: effrt on outside 1/2-way: wknd 2f out* **7/2**2	—
	8	½	**Lexi's Boy (IRE)** 2-9-3 0 TomEaves 4 (K A Ryan) *s.i.s: sn wl bhd: no ch fr 1/2-way* **13/2**	—

1m 11.72s (-1.88) **Going Correction** -0.375s/f (Firm) **8** Ran SP% **114.0**
Speed ratings (Par 95): **97,91,89,87,79 74,52,52**
toteswingers: 1&2 £9.40, 1&3 £2.70, 2&3 £14.80 CSF £35.74 TOTE £2.10: £1.10, £5.90, £1.40; EX 36.90.
Owner Andrew Tinkler **Bred** A H Bennett **Trained** Denton, Co Durham

FOCUS
A race with a good history, two Gimcrack winners having taken it in the last four years, and it's quite possible we saw another smart sort in the shape of the well-backed Dubawi Gold. Time will tell what he beat.

NOTEBOOK
Dubawi Gold certainly knew his job and stayed on strongly to win with ease. Bought for 160,000gns just last month, he is related to numerous winners and impressed with how strongly he travelled on this racecourse debut, certainly showing enough speed to suggest he would have no trouble with a drop to 5f. A rise in grade is inevitable at some stage, with his trainer Michael Dods not ruling out a possible trip to Royal Ascot. (op 9-4 tchd 5-2 in places)
Sinadinou, an already gelded son of Dubai Destination who cost just 2,000gns, showed speed and stayed on again to take second, but the winner was in a different league. This was a promising start and any improvement should see him up to winning an ordinary maiden.
Night Singer, who beat just one home when fourth on his recent debut, has clearly improved from that initial outing and looks a likely type for nurseries. (op 5-1 tchd 6-1 in places)
Crown Ridge(IRE) showed ability when fourth at Doncaster on his recent debut and again did enough to suggest he will be winning races at some stage, probably once handicapping over 7f. (op 15-2)
Namwahjobo(IRE), who has plenty of speed in his pedigree, being related to Knot In Wood, but he wasn't the best away and showed signs of greenness. He did stay on late, though, and should learn from this. (op 14-1 tchd 11-1)
Save The Bees, a cheap purchase bred for further, showed up well to a point and should find more suitable opportunities. (tchd 80-1)
Glitter Bug(IRE), a half-brother to plenty of winners, was representing a trainer responsible for two of the five previous winners of this, but he left the stalls awkwardly and was quickly outpaced. He should improve, but evidently needs to. (op 3-1 tchd 4-1)
Lexi's Boy(IRE), a 30,000gns Verglas newcomer, wasn't the best away and quickly got left behind. He showed little, but is presumably thought capable of better. (op 7-1)

2428 WILLIAMHILL.COM - LIVE WORLD CUP MARKETS H'CAP 7f 50y
2:40 (2:41) (Class 4) (0-85,85) 4-Y-O+ **£4,727** (£1,406; £702; £351) **Stalls** High

Form				RPR
64-0	**1**		**Northern Fling**26 1672 6-8-8 **75** KierenFallon 3 (J S Goldie) *hld up: rdn 3f out: swtchd rt and hdwy 2f out: led 1f out: rdn out* **4/1**2	89
0-60	**2**	3 ½	**Celtic Sultan (IRE)**25 1688 6-9-4 **85** (b1) MickyFenton 5 (T P Tate) *t.k.h: led and clr: rdn and hdd 1f out: kpt on same pce* **3/1**1	90
5033	**3**	hd	**My Gacho (IRE)**8 2205 8-9-1 **82** (v) J-PGuillambert 1 (M Johnston) *cl up: chsd ldr 3f out: effrt 2f out: edgd lft and one pce fnl f* **9/2**3	86
6-00	**4**	3 ¼	**Euston Square**25 1707 4-9-0 **81** AndrewMullen 8 (D Nicholls) *bhd and sn pushed along: hdwy over 1f out: kpt on: nvr rchd ldrs* **20/1**	77
-104	**5**	4	**She's In The Money**12 2086 4-9-4 **85** FrederikTylicki 6 (R A Fahey) *prom tl edgd lft and outpcd wl over 1f out* **11/2**	70
10-0	**6**	3 ¼	**Stonehaugh (IRE)**19 1869 7-8-5 **72** RoystonFfrench 9 (J Howard Johnson) *hld up in tch: drvn over 2f out: edgd lft and sn wknd* **28/1**	48
11-0	**7**	1 ¼	**Espero (IRE)**32 1513 4-9-1 **82** TomEaves 2 (Miss L A Perratt) *in tch: effrt over 2f out: wknd appr fnl f* **9/2**3	55
06-0	**8**	2 ¾	**Star Links (USA)**13 2065 4-8-4 **71** oh4 RPCleary 7 (S Donohoe, Ire) *chsd clr ldr to 3f out: edgd lft and wknd appr 2f out* **12/1**	36

1m 29.4s (-4.00) **Going Correction** -0.375s/f (Firm) **8** Ran SP% **112.7**
Speed ratings (Par 105): **107,103,102,99,94 90,89,86**
toteswingers: 1&2 £3.60, 1&3 £4.20, 2&3 £3.90 CSF £15.91 CT £54.32 TOTE £5.10: £2.10, £1.60, £2.00; EX 17.20.
Owner Paul Moulton **Bred** Lady Juliet Tadgell **Trained** Uplawmoor, E Renfrews

FOCUS
A decent handicap that was run at a fast gallop thanks to Celtic Sultan. The form is rated around him and the third.

2429 WILLIAMHILL.COM GREYHOUND DERBY - WATCH ONLINE! FILLIES' H'CAP 1m
3:15 (3:15) (Class 5) (0-70,67) 4-Y-O+ **£2,849** (£847; £423; £211) **Stalls** Low

Form				RPR
3025	**1**		**Light Dubai (IRE)**4 2342 4-9-1 **64** KierenFallon 4 (M R Channon) *in tch: n.m.r fr 2f to 1f out: rdn to ld ins fnl f: hld on wl* **9/2**2	72
122-	**2**	nk	**Graceful Descent (FR)**215 6987 5-9-1 **67** GaryBartley(3) 5 (J S Goldie) *hld up last: rdn and hdwy wl over 1f out: styd on wl fnl f* **8/1**	74
503-	**3**	½	**Ykikamoocow**215 6984 4-9-3 **66** SilvestreDeSousa 7 (G A Harker) *cl up: led 2f out: sn rdn: hdd ins fnl f: kpt on same pce* **9/1**	72
5212	**4**	1	**Whipma Whopma Gate (IRE)**18 1922 5-9-4 **67** (v) DanielTudhope 3 (D Carroll) *prom: effrt over 2f out: one pce fnl f* **15/2**3	71
0101	**5**	nk	**Cheers For Thea (IRE)**8 2207 5-9-3 **66** 6ex (bt) DavidAllan 1 (T D Easterby) *hld up in tch: swtchd rt and hdwy over 2f out: rdn over 1f out: kpt on same pce fnl f* **13/8**1	69
01-3	**6**	2 ¾	**Clumber Place**18 1928 4-8-1 **55** BillyCray(5) 6 (R C Guest) *led to 2f out: sn rdn and flashed tail: wknd ins fnl f* **20/1**	52
2013	**7**	½	**Saving Grace**24 1717 4-8-1 **55** PaulPickard(5) 2 (E J Alston) *t.k.h: trckd ldrs: rdn over 2f out: wknd appr fnl f* **9/2**2	51

1m 41.37s (-2.43) **Going Correction** -0.375s/f (Firm) **7** Ran SP% **112.1**
Speed ratings (Par 100): **97,96,96,95,94 92,91**
toteswingers: 1&2 £5.00, 1&3 £6.70, 2&3 £10.00 CSF £37.54 TOTE £5.80: £2.70, £3.30; EX 41.40.
Owner Mrs M Findlay **Bred** Peter O'Brien **Trained** West Ilsley, Berks

FOCUS
An ordinary but competitive little fillies' handicap. The winner is rated in line with last year's handicap form.

2430 SCOTTISH SUN MISS SCOTLAND 2010 H'CAP 1m 7f
3:50 (3:50) (Class 6) (0-60,57) 4-Y-O+ **£2,266** (£674; £337; £168) **Stalls** Low

Form				RPR
63-1	**1**		**Tillietudlem (FR)**8 2214 4-8-7 **46** ow1 KierenFallon 2 (J S Goldie) *chsd ldrs: pushed along over 2f out: led over 1f out: styd on strly to go clr fnl f* **8/15**1	58+
05-4	**2**	3 ½	**Los Nadis (GER)**13 1671 6-8-13 **56** MichaelO'Connell(5) 4 (P Monteith) *cl up: effrt and ev ch over 1f out: kpt on same pce fnl f* **5/1**2	63
60-5	**3**	¾	**Knock Three Times (IRE)**19 1891 4-8-1 **45** JamesSullivan(5) 7 (W Storey) *hld up in tch: hdwy over 2f out: rdn and hung lft over 1f out: one pce fnl f* **20/1**	51
0-61	**4**	2 ¾	**Alloro**12 2085 6-8-5 **48** PaulPickard(5) 3 (A Kirtley) *led tl rdn and hdd over 1f out: sn no ex* **15/2**3	50
020/	**5**	5	**Mutadarrej (IRE)**7 1939 6-8-12 **57** LFRoche(7) 8 (Mrs Y Dunleavy, Ire) *hld up: rdn over 3f out: no imp fnl 2f* **40/1**	53
00-6	**6**	7	**Davids City (IRE)**31 506 6-8-7 **45** SilvestreDeSousa 5 (G A Harker) *bhd: hdwy and prom 1/2-way: rdn and wknd over 2f out* **14/1**	32
205-	**7**	2	**Marillos Proterras**310 4142 4-8-8 **47** TomEaves 1 (Mrs A Duffield) *hld up: drvn over 3f out: sn wknd* **20/1**	31
00-0	**8**	2	**Bogula (IRE)**51 1113 4-8-8 **47** (v1) RoystonFfrench 6 (Mrs A Duffield) *cl up: rdn over 3f out: wknd over 2f out* **33/1**	29

3m 19.11s (-1.29) **Going Correction** -0.375s/f (Firm)
WFA 4 from 6yo 1lb **8** Ran SP% **115.2**
Speed ratings (Par 101): **88,86,85,84,81 77,76,75**
toteswingers: 1&2 £2.10, 1&3 £4.50, 2&3 £8.00 CSF £3.26 CT £24.26 TOTE £1.50: £1.10, £1.60, £4.00; EX 3.90.
Owner Mr & Mrs C J Smith **Bred** Bernard Ducasse **Trained** Uplawmoor, E Renfrews

FOCUS
A weak staying handicap, but it was sound run and the form looks solid enough for the grade. The winner did not need to improve on his Musselburgh form.

2431 WILLIAMHILL.COM - HOME OF BETTING H'CAP 5f
4:25 (4:26) (Class 3) (0-90,89) 4-Y-O+ £7,771 (£2,312; £1,155; £577) Stalls High

Form				RPR
4045	1		**Five Star Junior (USA)**[11] 2119 4-9-7 **89** .... KierenFallon 7 (Mrs L Stubbs) *in tch: effrt over 2f out: led ins fnl f: hld on wl u.p* **15/2**[3]	99
-050	2	hd	**The Nifty Fox**[13] 2054 6-9-2 **84** .... DavidAllan 6 (T D Easterby) *hld up: hdwy over 1f out: edgd lft and kpt on wl fnl f: jst hld* **10/1**	93
300-	3	1 1/2	**Hypnosis**[221] 6843 7-8-9 **77** .... RoystonFfrench 12 (N Wilson) *trckd ldr: rdn and ev ch over 1f out: edgd lft ins fnl f: hld towards fin* **33/1**	81
-431	4	3/4	**Sirenuse (IRE)**[11] 2136 4-9-1 **83** .... TomEaves 11 (B Smart) *t.k.h: led: rdn over 1f out: hdd ins fnl f: nt qckn* **9/4**[1]	84+
06-4	5	1/2	**City Dancer (IRE)**[26] 1670 4-9-3 **88** .... MichaelGeran(3) 9 (D Nicholls) *dwlt: bhd tl hdwy over 1f out: kpt on fnl f: nrst fin* **15/2**[3]	88
-004	6	1 1/2	**Rothesay Dancer**[18] 1923 7-8-4 **75** .... KellyHarrison(3) 10 (J S Goldie) *hld up: hdwy appr fnl f: nrst fin* **16/1**	69
1-16	7	2 3/4	**Igoyougo**[11] 2136 4-8-11 **79** .... SilvestreDeSousa 8 (G A Harker) *chsd ldrs: drvn and outpcd over 2f out: n.d after* **5/1**[2]	63
0-02	8	shd	**Doctor Parkes**[11] 2134 4-9-4 **86** .... MickyFenton 1 (E J Alston) *racd wd fr low draw in midfield: pushed along and no imp fr 1/2-way* **5/1**[2]	70+
2215	9	4 1/2	**Ingleby Star (IRE)**[5] 2294 5-8-0 **75** ....(p) ShirleyTeasdale(7) 2 (N Wilson) *racd wd in tch fr low draw: drvn and outpcd 1/2-way: sn btn* **40/1**	43+
1-60	10	4 1/2	**Royal Intruder**[21] 1822 5-9-7 **89** .... RPCleary 5 (S Donohoe, Ire) *towards rr: drvn after 2f: sn struggling* **16/1**	40
24-4	11	1/2	**Grissom (IRE)**[47] 1200 4-8-10 **78** .... PhillipMakin 3 (A Berry) *bhd: rdn and outpcd after 2f: sn btn* **18/1**	28

57.33 secs (-2.77) **Going Correction** -0.375s/f (Firm) 11 Ran SP% **119.1**
Speed ratings (Par 107): **107,106,104,103,102 99,95,95,88,80 80**
toteswingers: 1&2 £9.20, 1&3 £26.40, 2&3 £40.10 CSF £81.34 CT £2379.65 TOTE £9.50: £3.60, £4.00, £8.30; EX 80.70.
Owner Moyns Park Stud **Bred** Robert W Sanford **Trained** Norton, N Yorks

FOCUS
They went a very fast gallop thanks to Sirenuse. The first two are rated back to their best.

NOTEBOOK
Five Star Junior(USA), who would have needed a strong pace to win at this distance, has been shaping as though a return to form wasn't far away, albeit over 6f, and having got to the front inside the final furlong, he held on well for his first win in 15 months. (op 7-1)
The Nifty Fox, who ideally needs a slower surface, came with a strong run between runners inside the final furlong, but couldn't quite get up in time. He has never won off a mark as high as this, but is clearly capable. (op 9-1)
Hypnosis, the only runner without a previous run this season, has run well off this sort of mark in the past and she kept on the best she could back in third without quite being able to match the front pair. (tchd 40-1 in places)
Sirenuse(IRE), 4lb higher than when making all at Thirsk latest, was soon in a clear lead, but she was always going to be vulnerable at the business end, and ultimately lost out on the places. She's quick and can continue to put her speed to good use over an easier 5f. (op 11-4)
City Dancer(IRE) finished on the heels of the leaders and could be up to winning once dropped a further few pounds. (op 7-1)
Rothesay Dancer, 2lb higher this time round, could never get into it, but did run on. (tchd 20-1 in places)
Igoyougo didn't seem to have the pace and was disappointing. (op 7-1)
Doctor Parkes was always wide and failed to build on his Thirsk second. (tchd 9-2 and 11-2)

2432 RAEBURN H'CAP 6f
4:55 (4:57) (Class 6) (0-60,64) 3-Y-O £2,266 (£674; £337; £168) Stalls High

Form				RPR
43-1	1		**Timeless Elegance (IRE)**[8] 2209 3-9-8 **64** 6ex........ FrederikTylicki 4 (J Howard Johnson) *mde all: rdn and qcknd clr over 1f out: readily* **1/2**[1]	80+
0-40	2	4 1/2	**Amoureuse**[8] 2217 3-7-13 **46** oh1........ BillyCray(5) 10 (D Carroll) *chsd wnr: rdn 2f out: kpt on fnl f: no imp* **25/1**	42
2-00	3	hd	**Ya Boy Sir (IRE)**[26] 1667 3-8-5 **52** .... JamesSullivan(5) 9 (N Wilson) *prom: rdn over 2f out: hdwy over 1f out: one pce fnl f* **50/1**	48
005-	4	1	**Weetentherty**[313] 4035 3-9-0 **56** ....(v) PhillipMakin 11 (J S Goldie) *sn pushed along in tch: effrt and edgd lft fr over 1f out: nt clr run ins fnl f: no imp* **33/1**	52+
003-	5	1/2	**Thinking**[203] 7242 3-9-4 **60** ....(p) DavidAllan 8 (T D Easterby) *chsd ldrs: drvn over 2f out: outpcd fnl f* **12/1**[3]	51
05-6	6	2	**Mr Prize Fighter**[27] 1648 3-8-5 **47** .... RoystonFfrench 13 (I W McInnes) *bhd and outpcd: hdwy over 1f out: nvr rchd ldrs* **50/1**	32
00-0	7	1/2	**Monsieur Pontaven**[39] 1401 3-7-11 **46** oh1........ MatthewLawson(7) 12 (R Bastiman) *dwlt: bhd: rdn 1/2-way: hdwy over 1f out: nvr able to chal* **33/1**	29
63-0	8	3	**Anna's Boy**[9] 2185 3-8-11 **53** .... TomEaves 5 (A Berry) *bhd and outpcd: sme late hdwy: nvr on terms* **66/1**	26
-055	9	1	**Kristen Jane (USA)**[5] 2291 3-8-1 **46** oh1........ KellyHarrison(3) 1 (Miss L A Perratt) *towards rr: effrt and swtchd lft 2f out: sn no imp* **28/1**	16
06-0	10	3	**Lady Lube Rye (IRE)**[32] 1511 3-8-10 **57** .... PaulPickard(5) 3 (N Wilson) *in tch on outside: hung lft and outpcd over 2f out: sn btn* **22/1**	18+
3103	11	shd	**Vilnius**[4] 2320 3-9-2 **58** .... KierenFallon 2 (M R Channon) *midfield on outside: shkn up 2f out: sn btn* **3/1**[2]	18+
0-00	12	2 1/2	**Velle Est Valere**[27] 1648 3-8-4 **46** oh1........ SilvestreDeSousa 7 (C J Teague) *towards rr: drvn and outpcd over 2f out: sn btn* **40/1**	—
02	13	4	**The Bay Bandit**[61] 998 3-8-13 **55** .... RPCleary 6 (S Donohoe, Ire) *midfield: drvn over 2f out: sn wknd* **14/1**	—

1m 11.17s (-2.43) **Going Correction** -0.375s/f (Firm) 13 Ran SP% **131.4**
Speed ratings (Par 97): **101,95,94,93,92 90,89,85,84,80 79,76,71**
toteswingers: 1&2 £10.10, 1&3 £15.20, 2&3 £70.70 CSF £28.15 CT £468.02 TOTE £1.70: £1.10, £7.00, £11.40; EX 26.40.
Owner Transcend Bloodstock LLP **Bred** Mrs M Togher **Trained** Billy Row, Co Durham

FOCUS
A weak and uncompetitive handicap. It was all about the well-in winner, who was value for 6l.

2433 DUMFRIES & GALLOWAY STANDARD APPRENTICE H'CAP 1m 1f 20y
5:25 (5:26) (Class 6) (0-60,60) 4-Y-O+ £2,266 (£674; £337; £168) Stalls Low

Form				RPR
	1		**Sports Casual**[1024] 4239 7-8-0 **46** oh1........ LFRoche(5) 8 (Mrs Y Dunleavy, Ire) *hld up: hdwy on outside over 2f out: edgd lft and styd on fnl f: led nr fin* **10/1**	53
202-	2	nk	**Bed Fellow (IRE)**[201] 7113 6-8-7 **51** .... AdamCarter(3) 1 (P Monteith) *chsd ldr: rdn and led 2f out: kpt on fnl f: hdd nr fin* **10/1**	57
306-	3	1	**Al Wasef (USA)**[319] 3857 5-9-0 **60** .... PaulNorton(5) 4 (J S Goldie) *hld up in tch: rdn over 2f out: hdwy over 1f out: kpt on fnl f* **9/1**	64
05-6	4	1/2	**Papa's Princess**[22] 1812 6-8-3 **47** .... MatthewLawson(3) 5 (James Moffatt) *prom: effrt and rdn over 2f out: one pce fnl f* **18/1**	50
4053	5	1 1/2	**Alfredtheordinary**[8] 2201 5-9-2 **57** .... CharlesEddery 9 (M R Channon) *rdr slow to remove blindfold: missed break: hld up: rdn and outpcd over 2f out: styd on fnl f: nrst fin* **13/2**[3]	56
0-03	6	1	**Cold Quest (USA)**[5] 2293 6-8-13 **54** .... GarryWhillans 7 (Miss L A Perratt) *prom: effrt over 2f out: edgd lft over 1f out: no ex fnl f* **9/1**	51
0-64	7	2	**Nesno (USA)**[18] 1920 7-9-1 **56** ....(b) LeeTopliss 6 (M Dods) *led to 2f out: sn rdn and outpcd* **7/4**[1]	49
0000	8	nk	**Stateside (CAN)**[37] 1427 5-8-9 **55** .... MarzenaJeziorek(5) 3 (R A Fahey) *t.k.h: hld up in tch: shkn up over 2f out: wknd over 1f out* **4/1**[2]	47
00-0	9	36	**Just Call Me Dave (USA)**[12] 2072 4-8-5 **46** oh1........(b[1]) DavidKenny 2 (Mrs L Williamson) *towards rr: drvn 1/2-way: hung rt bnd appr st: sn lost tch* **50/1**	—

1m 56.4s (-2.00) **Going Correction** -0.375s/f (Firm) 9 Ran SP% **115.1**
Speed ratings (Par 101): **93,92,91,91,90 89,87,87,55**
toteswingers: 1&2 £12.60, 1&3 £13.50, 2&3 £9.50 CSF £104.22 CT £934.58 TOTE £21.80: £8.80, £4.10, £2.90; EX 113.60 Place 6 £119.12, Place 5 £70.85.
Owner Mrs Y Dunleavy **Bred** Deerfield Farm **Trained** Turloughmore, Co Galway
■ The first winner for Irish-based trainer Yvonne Dunleavy.

FOCUS
A dire apprentice handicap which was steadily run. Not a race to be positive about.
T/Jkpt: £3,164.30 to a £1 stake. Pool: £35,654.40. 8.00 winning tickets. T/Plt: £146.80 to a £1 stake. Pool: £75,201.79. 373.84 winning tickets. T/Qpdt: £23.10 to a £1 stake. Pool: £4,211.22. 134.75 winning tickets. RY

1986 BEVERLEY (R-H)
Wednesday, May 26

OFFICIAL GOING: Good to firm (9.0)
Wind: Light against Weather: Overcast and dry

2434 BEVERLEY-RACECOURSE.CO.UK MAIDEN FILLIES' STKS 7f 100y
6:30 (6:31) (Class 5) 3-Y-O+ £2,590 (£770; £385; £192) Stalls High

Form				RPR
0-22	1		**Copper Penny**[19] 1881 3-8-10 78........ TedDurcan 5 (D R Lanigan) *trckd ldrs: hdwy on outer over 2f out: rdn to ld over 1f out: hung rt ins fnl f: styd on strly* **4/5**[1]	75+
34-	2	3 3/4	**Shaluca**[209] 7140 3-8-10 0........ GrahamGibbons 2 (E S McMahon) *t.k.h: chsd ldr: hdwy 3f out: chal over 2f out: rdn and ev ch over 1f out: kpt on same pce ins fnl f* **6/1**[3]	66
	3	1/2	**Wasara** 3-8-10 0........ NeilCallan 6 (C E Brittain) *trckd ldrs: hdwy wl over 2f out: chsd ldng pair 2f out: sn rdn: edgd lft ent fnl f and kpt on same pce ent fnl f* **22/1**	64
6	4	1/2	**Medici Palace**[28] 1621 3-8-10 0........ EddieAhern 1 (J R Fanshawe) *t.k.h: hld up: tk clsr order on outer whn rn green and hung lft over 3f out: effrt and chsd ldrs whn green and hung rt appr fnl f: one pce* **4/1**[2]	63+
5	5	1/2	**Red Skies (IRE)**[26] 1654 3-8-10 0........ DuranFentiman 9 (Mrs L Stubbs) *dwlt: sn in midfield: effrt wl over 2f out: sn rdn and no imp* **10/1**	62
	6	2 3/4	**Patroller (USA)**[1251] 7-9-7 0........ JamieSpencer 7 (K A Ryan) *led: rdn along over 2f out: drvn and hdd over 1f out: sn wknd* **25/1**	59
0	7	5	**Zamid (FR)**[25] 1685 3-8-10 0........ PaulHanagan 10 (R A Fahey) *s.i.s: a in rr* **28/1**	43
-44	8	3/4	**Greeley Bright (USA)**[16] 1966 3-8-10 0........ LeeVickers 3 (J G Given) *rrd s and slowly away: a towards rr* **22/1**	41
000-	9	6	**Mujada**[25] 4995 5-9-7 39........ PaulMulrennan 8 (M W Easterby) *chsd ldng pair: rdn along 3f out: drvn 2f out and sn wknd* **200/1**	30
03-0	10	29	**Falcon's Tribute (IRE)**[49] 1153 8-9-7 57........ FrankieDettori 4 (P Salmon) *dwlt: a in rr: bhd and eased fnl 2f: b.b.v* **50/1**	—

1m 32.43s (-1.37) **Going Correction** -0.275s/f (Firm)
WFA 3 from 5yo+ 11lb 10 Ran SP% **117.4**
Speed ratings (Par 100): **96,91,91,90,90 86,81,80,73,40**
toteswingers: 1&2 £2.40, 1&3 £4.90, 2&3 £15.60 CSF £5.49 TOTE £2.20: £1.10, £1.10, £6.50; EX 6.30.
Owner Saif Ali & Saeed H Altayer **Bred** Barry Taylor **Trained** Newmarket, Suffolk

FOCUS
The going was described as good to firm, although 5mm of water had been applied since the previous day, and that was on top of 10mm put on the track on Sunday and Monday. The GoingStick reading was 9.5. They went a fair pace and this looks sound if ordinary fillies' form.

2435 KEVIN DONKIN MEMORIAL H'CAP 1m 1f 207y
7:00 (7:02) (Class 4) (0-85,85) 4-Y-O+ £4,533 (£1,348; £674; £336) Stalls High

Form				RPR
16	1		**Submariner (USA)**[20] 1831 4-9-1 **82** .... FrankieDettori 4 (M Johnston) *mde most: swtchd lft to centre of crse over 2f out and sn pushed clr: rdn appr fnl f and styd on strly* **11/4**[2]	95
50-6	2	4 1/2	**Changing The Guard**[14] 2027 4-9-4 **85** .... PaulHanagan 3 (R A Fahey) *t.k.h: trckd ldrs: hdwy to chse wnr 2f out: sn rdn: drvn and no imp fnl f* **85/40**[1]	89
-213	3	hd	**King Fingal (IRE)**[12] 2084 5-8-9 **81** .... IanBrennan(5) 6 (J J Quinn) *trckd ldrs on inner: hdwy over 3f out: effrt over 2f out and sn rdn: drvn appr fnl f and kpt on same pce* **4/1**[3]	85
1531	4	nk	**Taaresh (IRE)**[19] 1867 5-8-3 **75** .... JohnFahy(5) 2 (K A Morgan) *hld up in rr: hdwy on inner over 2f out: rdn to chse ldrs over 1f out: drvn and one pce ins fnl f* **9/2**	78
30-0	5	7	**Snowed Under**[9] 2173 9-8-12 **79** .... DarryllHolland 1 (J D Bethell) *sn chsng wnr: rdn along wl over 2f out: drvn wl over 1f out and sn wknd* **16/1**	68
2202	6	11	**Thunderstruck**[25] 1684 5-9-1 **82** ....(p) EddieAhern 5 (J A Glover) *dwlt: sn chsng ldrs on outer: rdn along 3f out: wknd over 2f out* **8/1**	49

2m 3.89s (-3.11) **Going Correction** -0.275s/f (Firm) 6 Ran SP% **113.8**
Speed ratings (Par 105): **101,97,97,97,91 82**
toteswingers: 1&2: £1.10, 1&3: £2.30, 2&3: £1.80 CSF £9.26 TOTE £3.70: £2.10, £1.10; EX 12.00.

Owner Sheikh Hamdan Bin Mohammed Al Maktoum **Bred** Darley **Trained** Middleham Moor, N Yorks

FOCUS

Something of a tactical affair, as Frankie Dettori dictated a stop-start gallop in front. The winner had the run of the race but still built on his Folkestone win and the form seems sound at face value.

2436 HILARY NEEDLER TROPHY (LISTED RACE) (FILLIES) 5f

7:30 (7:32) (Class 1) 2-Y-O

£17,031 (£6,456; £3,231; £1,611; £807; £405) **Stalls** High

Form				RPR
14	**1**		**Geesala (IRE)**[12] 2095 2-8-12 0 .... JamieSpencer 10 (K A Ryan) *mde all: rdn over 1f out: drvn and edgd rt ins fnl f: kpt on* **8/1**	85
62	**2**	*1 ¼*	**Lady Royale**[15] 1986 2-8-12 0 .... PJMcDonald 3 (G R Oldroyd) *chsd ldrs: pushed along and sltly outpcd 1/2-way: rdn wl over 1f out: styd on strly ins fnl f* **40/1**	81
23	**3**	*hd*	**Malpas Missile (IRE)**[20] 1835 2-8-12 0 .... RichardKingscote 15 (Tom Dascombe) *in tch: gd hdwy on outer 2f out: rdn to chal and hung lft ent fnl f: sn drvn and ev ch tl no ex last 100yds* **7/2**[1]	80
213	**4**	*¾*	**Meandmyshadow**[12] 2082 2-8-12 0 .... FrannyNorton 14 (A D Brown) *chsd ldrs: hdwy and cl up 1/2-way: rdn whn hmpd ent fnl f: sn swtchd lft and kpt on same pce* **22/1**	77
	5	*¾*	**Mawjoodah** 2-8-9 0 .... NeilCallan 11 (C E Brittain) *dwlt: sn in tch: chsd ldrs 1/2-way: rdn and green wl over 1f out: kpt on same pce ins fnl f* **20/1**	71+
012	**6**	*nse*	**Inagh River**[12] 2074 2-8-12 0 .... PatDobbs 6 (R Hannon) *sn pushed along and in rr: rdn 1/2-way: swtchd rt and hdwy over 1f out: kpt on ins fnl f: nrst fin* **7/1**[3]	74
31	**7**	*hd*	**First Class Favour (IRE)**[22] 1800 2-8-12 0 .... GrahamGibbons 7 (T D Easterby) *chsd ldrs: rdn along 2f out: sn wknd* **10/1**	73
2	**8**	*1*	**Orchid Street (USA)**[11] 2130 2-8-12 0 .... TadhgO'Shea 8 (Mrs A Duffield) *t.k.h: hld up: hdwy 2f out: rdn wl over 1f out: swtchd rt ent fnl f and no imp* **13/2**[2]	70
31	**9**	*¾*	**Lenjawi Pride**[16] 1981 2-8-12 0 .... RichardSmith 4 (Tom Dascombe) *sn pushed along: a in rr* **12/1**	67
42	**10**	*4 ½*	**Miserere (IRE)**[5] 2272 2-8-12 0 .... PaulMulrennan 12 (J S Wainwright) *dwlt: hdwy and cl up after 1f: rdn along over 2f out and wknd qckly* **16/1**	51
015	**U**		**Misty Morn**[14] 2032 2-8-12 0 .... DarryllHolland 13 (A D Brown) *rrd stalls: fly-leapt and uns rdr s* **40/1**	—

62.82 secs (-0.68) **Going Correction** -0.175s/f (Firm) 11 Ran SP% **95.8**

Speed ratings (Par 98): **98,96,95,94,93 93,92,91,90,82** —

toteswingers: 1&2 £57.80, 1&3 £3.40, 2&3 £31.40 CSF £199.28 TOTE £8.30: £2.60, £10.80, £1.30; EX 204.00.

Owner John J Brennan **Bred** Paul & T J Monaghan **Trained** Hambleton, N Yorks

■ Dress Up (7/2JF) was withdrawn at the start on vet's advice; Rule 4 applies, deduction 20p in the £.

FOCUS

Four non-runners plus the late withdrawal of joint-favourite Dress Up and the early unseating of Misty Morn meant that this race lost a lot of its competitiveness, and only five of the ten remaining were previous winners. As a result, the form looks decidedly below par for the grade. The compressed finish adds weight to the theory that this was a weak renewal.

NOTEBOOK

Geesala(IRE) was well held behind Primo Lady in another Listed race at York last time, but this well-watered ground suited her better and so did the stiffer track. She showed good speed from the off, came up the centre of the track and stayed on strongly to see off her challengers. Another furlong is going to suit her and connections are now eyeing a Group 3 race at Naas. (op 10-1)

Lady Royale ran a fairly promising race in a maiden here last time but this was another step up. Drawn low, she was always towards the stands' side and finished really strongly to take second. Like the winner, she shapes like she wants 6f sooner rather than later.

Malpas Missile(IRE) was wisely brought over to race as near to the centre of the track as possible. She gave Geesala a race for half a furlong inside the last, but eventually the winner's greater stamina saw her through. A confidence-boosting maiden win might do her good before a return to better company.

Meandmyshadow showed up well for a long way before getting tightened up approaching the furlong pole. She stayed on again afterwards and posted a solid effort. (op 20-1)

Mawjoodah, who cost 60,000gns, is out of a half-sister to smart sprinter Sir Gerry. The only newcomer in the field, she received 3lb from the rest and wasn't disgraced considering her lack of experience. (op 22-1 tchd 25-1)

Inagh River looked to hold solid claims on her Newbury effort, but she was desperately weak in the betting and really struggled to go the early pace. She did stay on late, but wasn't helped by racing more towards the far side in the closing stages. (op 6-1)

First Class Favour(IRE), who has a fast-ground pedigree and won her maiden on firm ground, may not have been suited by the well-watered surface here. (op 12-1)

2437 WEATHERBYS BLOODSTOCK INSURANCE CONDITIONS STKS 5f

8:00 (8:01) (Class 3) 3-Y-O

£7,025 (£2,223; £1,197) **Stalls** High

Form				RPR
0-2	**1**		**Burning Thread (IRE)**[25] 1685 3-8-7 0 ow2 .... DaleSwift(7) 2 (T J Etherington) *cl up: rdn to ld wl over 1f out: drvn ins fnl f and kpt on strly* **25/1**	93
112-	**2**	*2*	**Coolminx (IRE)**[228] 6677 3-8-13 96 .... PaulHanagan 3 (R A Fahey) *chsd ldng pair: rdn along and outpcd 1/2-way: styd on u.p ins fnl f: tk 2nd on line* **7/4**[2]	85
14-5	**3**	*shd*	**Living It Large (FR)**[13] 2058 3-9-1 90 .... TonyHamilton 1 (R F Fisher) *led: rdn along and hdd wl over 1f out: drvn and one pce ins fnl f* **11/2**[3]	87
-123	**F**		**Mister Hughie (IRE)**[12] 2075 3-8-12 99 .... JamieSpencer 4 (M R Channon) *s.i.s and in rr: gd hdwy 2f out: swtchd rt to trck wnr whn clipped heels and fell appr fnl f* **10/11**[1]	—

62.17 secs (-1.33) **Going Correction** -0.175s/f (Firm) 4 Ran SP% **108.0**

Speed ratings (Par 103): **103,99,99,**—

CSF £66.58 TOTE £17.60; EX 30.10.

Owner Tim Etherington **Bred** James Lombard **Trained** Norton, N Yorks

FOCUS

An eventful race despite the small field. The winner beat the other pair well enough and clearly improved, but it is hard to know how literally to take this.

NOTEBOOK

Burning Thread(IRE) showed good pace from the start here and had all but the favourite, who clipped his heels and fell, beaten a furlong out. He ran on strongly while racing more towards the unfavoured inside rail, and there didn't look to be too much fluke about this. He's clearly a useful sprinter and the Portland was mentioned as a long-term aim. (op 20-1)

Coolminx(IRE) had not been seen since finishing second in a Listed race on her final start at two, but she looked a big player in this company if ready to go first time up. She ran as though she needed it and is entitled to be sharper next time. (op 13-8)

Living It Large(FR), who is probably at his best on a sharper track, could have done without Burning Thread taking him on for the lead as he likes to dominate. (op 6-1 tchd 8-1)

Mister Hughie(IRE) looked to hold strong claims on paper, but he sweated up beforehand and missed the break, giving away three lengths at the start. It took him a while to get back into the race, but the pace up front was good and, as they approached the final furlong, it looked as though Spencer was just delaying his challenge as late as possible. He was angling the colt towards the inside rail when he clipped the heels of the winner and went down (op 11-10 tchd 5-6)

2438 RACING AGAIN ON SATURDAY 29 MAY H'CAP 1m 100y

8:30 (8:31) (Class 5) (0-70,70) 3-Y-O

£2,914 (£867; £433; £216) **Stalls** High

Form				RPR
625-	**1**		**Robens Rock (IRE)**[217] 6932 3-9-2 68 .... FrankieDettori 1 (M Johnston) *sn led: swtchd lft to centre of trck wl over 2f out: sn pushed clr: eased nr fin* **5/2**[2]	83+
-253	**2**	*2 ½*	**Banks And Braes**[16] 1973 3-9-1 70 .... PatrickHills(3) 4 (R Hannon) *hld up in rr: hdwy on inner over 2f out: rdn to chse ldng pair over 1f out: drvn and kpt on ins fnl f: tk 2nd on line* **6/1**	74
-131	**3**	*nse*	**Tribal Myth (IRE)**[23] 1753 3-8-12 64 .... JamieSpencer 5 (K A Ryan) *trckd ldr: effrt to chal wl over 2f out: sn rdn: kpt on same pce: lost 2nd nr line* **2/1**[1]	68
210-	**4**	*5*	**Raleigh Quay (IRE)**[219] 6895 3-9-4 70 .... PaulMulrennan 7 (Micky Hammond) *trckd ldrs on inner: hdwy 1/2-way: rdn along wl over 2f out and sn one pce* **18/1**	62
05-2	**5**	*5*	**Emerald Glade (IRE)**[22] 1810 3-8-6 58 .... GrahamGibbons 2 (T D Easterby) *chsd ldrs: lost pl and towards rr 1/2-way: n.d after* **9/2**[3]	39
0452	**6**	*2 ¼*	**Battle Study (IRE)**[15] 1992 3-8-13 65 .... JamesDoyle 6 (A J McCabe) *hld up: effrt and sme hdwy 3f out: rdn over 2f out and sn wknd* **9/1**	41
40-0	**7**	*8*	**Bubber (IRE)**[11] 2132 3-8-4 56 oh4 .... PaulHanagan 3 (R A Fahey) *t.k.h: chsd ldrs: rdn along wl over 2f out: sn wknd* **22/1**	13

1m 45.65s (-1.95) **Going Correction** -0.275s/f (Firm) 7 Ran SP% **114.0**

Speed ratings (Par 99): **98,95,95,90,85 83,75**

toteswingers: 1&2: £4.80, 1&3: £1.10, 2&3: £4.30 CSF £17.70 TOTE £3.70: £2.10, £3.40; EX 18.30.

Owner R S Brookhouse **Bred** Longueville B'Stk & H Lascelles B'Stk **Trained** Middleham Moor, N Yorks

FOCUS

Just a modest handicap, but it was taken apart by Robens Rock, who was running in a handicap for the first time on his debut for the Mark Johnston yard. He was value double the actual margin and the form has been rated at face value.

2439 LUCKY IN LOVE RACENIGHT 17 JUNE H'CAP 1m 4f 16y

9:00 (9:00) (Class 5) (0-70,70) 3-Y-O

£2,914 (£867; £433; £216) **Stalls** High

Form				RPR
-412	**1**		**Leader Of The Land (IRE)**[6] 2248 3-9-0 66 .... TedDurcan 2 (D R Lanigan) *hld up in rr: tk clsr order 5f out: smooth hdwy 3f out: led on bit wl over 1f out: pushed clr ent fnl f: eased nr fin* **5/6**[1]	82+
00-1	**2**	*5*	**Corr Point (IRE)**[9] 2175 3-8-7 59 6ex .... (t) GrahamGibbons 5 (J A Osborne) *led: jnd after 2f and disp ld tl rdn and tk advantage again over 2f out: drvn and hdd wl over 1f: kpt on: no ch w wnr* **9/4**[2]	64
041	**3**	*2 ¾*	**Meetings Man (IRE)**[19] 1866 3-8-12 64 .... PaulHanagan 1 (Micky Hammond) *t.k.h: cl up: disp ld after 2f: rdn along 3f out: drvn and one pce fnl 2f* **7/1**[3]	65
3-52	**4**	*3 ¾*	**Palawi (IRE)**[24] 1721 3-8-13 70 .... IanBrennan(5) 4 (J J Quinn) *chsd ldng pair: rdn along 3f out: drvn over 2f out and sn one pce* **10/1**	65

2m 37.65s (-2.15) **Going Correction** -0.275s/f (Firm) 4 Ran SP% **106.9**

Speed ratings (Par 99): **99,95,93,91**

CSF £2.87 TOTE £1.70; EX 3.10 Place 6 £491.19, Place 5 £352.23.

Owner Saeed H Altayer **Bred** Rabbah Bloodstock Limited **Trained** Newmarket, Suffolk

FOCUS

With only four taking part and no confirmed front-runner, this promised to be a tactical affair, but in actual fact Meetings Man and Corr Point took each other on, set a strong pace in front, and rather set things up for the favourite. The winner was value for further and the form is taken at something like face value.

T/Plt: £703.70 to a £1 stake. Pool: £74,954.97. 77.75 winning tickets. T/Qpdt: £299.00 to a £1 stake. Pool: £4,889.22. 12.10 winning tickets. JR

1838 FFOS LAS (L-H)

Wednesday, May 26

OFFICIAL GOING: Good to firm (8.9)

Wind: Modest, across Weather: Overcast, muggy

2440 E.B.F./FREE RACING WITH ODDSCHECKER.COM WEDNESDAY MAIDEN STKS 5f

2:30 (2:31) (Class 5) 2-Y-O

£3,753 (£1,108; £554) **Stalls** High

Form				RPR
2	**1**		**Marlinka**[15] 1999 2-8-12 0 .... SteveDrowne 6 (R Charlton) *mde all: rdn clr ent fnl f: r.o strly: easily* **6/5**[1]	82+
4303	**2**	*6*	**Just For Leo (IRE)**[8] 2216 2-9-3 0 .... (p) CathyGannon 2 (P D Evans) *w wnr tl outpcd and rdn wl over 1f out: 3rd and wl hld ins fnl f: kpt on again fnl 100yds to go 2nd again nr fin: no ch w wnr* **9/2**[3]	66
0	**3**	*½*	**Uncle Dermot (IRE)**[14] 2022 2-9-3 0 .... FergusSweeney 5 (B G Powell) *wnt lft s: chsd clr ldng pair: clsd 1/2-way: wnt 2nd wl over 1f out: rdn and nt pce of wnr ent fnl f: lost 2nd nr fin* **16/1**	64
	4	*1 ¼*	**Imogen Louise (IRE)** 2-8-12 0 .... RichardMullen 1 (D Haydn Jones) *s.i.s: rn v green and hung bdly lft sn after s: wl detached in last: pushed along and hdwy over 1f out: kpt on fnl f: nvr trbld ldrs* **33/1**	55+
	5	*2 ¾*	**Pabusar** 2-9-3 0 .... JimCrowley 4 (R M Beckett) *restless in stalls: awkward leaving stalls and v.s.a: sn pushed along and outpcd: hdwy and edging lft 2f out: no prog and btn 1f out: eased ins fnl f* **15/8**[2]	54+

57.20 secs (-0.20) **Going Correction** -0.125s/f (Firm) 5 Ran SP% **107.2**

Speed ratings (Par 93): **96,86,85,83,79**

CSF £6.60 TOTE £1.70: £1.10, £2.50; EX 3.00.

Owner Elite Racing Club **Bred** Elite Racing Club **Trained** Beckhampton, Wilts

FOCUS

This was an uncompetitive maiden and, excluding the winner, the form probably adds up to little. The exposed runner-up produced a slightly lesser effort.

NOTEBOOK

Marlinka was only just caught over an extra half-furlong on her Warwick debut and showed the benefit of that experience. With the stands' rail to help her, she shared the early advantage and, once asked to stretch, had little difficulty in pulling clear of her rivals over the last furlong or so. She can improve further and may run in a fillies' conditions stakes next, or she might turn out at Royal Ascot. (op 5-4 tchd 11-8 and 11-10)

Just For Leo(IRE), the most experienced in the field, had cheekpieces fitted for the first time on this return to the minimum trip. He showed good speed in the early stages alongside the favourite and stayed on to regain second after getting outpaced after halfway. He appears to need the extra furlong now, but looks exposed. (tchd 4-1)

Uncle Dermot(IRE), who showed pace before fading when well backed for his Bath debut, put in an effort coming to the last furlong but couldn't go through with it. He will need to improve again if he is to win races. (op 14-1 tchd 20-1)

Imogen Louise(IRE), a half-sister to two Flat winners at up to 1m2f and a winning hurdler, proved clueless in the early stages and tailed herself off, but she wasn't beaten that far at the line. She needs plenty more time and a stiffer test. (op 25-1)

Pabusar, a half-brother to the dual winning sprinter Thaliwarru, completely missed the break and proved far too green to do himself justice. (tchd 13-8 and 2-1)

2441 SITESERV RECYCLING MAIDEN STKS 6f

3:05 (3:05) (Class 5) 3-Y-O+ **£2,523** (£755; £377; £188; £94) **Stalls** High

Form RPR

-352 **1** **Sheer Force (IRE)**[19] 1872 3-9-1 74 ShaneKelly 3 79
(W J Knight) *t.k.h: trckd ldrs: hdwy between horses to ld wl over 1f out: sn rdn: r.o strly and drew clr ins fnl f: easily* **3/1**[2]

3 **2** 4 ½ **Beauty Pageant (IRE)**[16] 1966 3-8-10 0 RichardMullen 4 60
(E S McMahon) *chsd ldng pair: rdn and ev ch wl over 1f out: edgd lft u.p and nt pce of wnr ins fnl f* **4/1**[3]

2- **3** 1 ¾ **Praesepe**[151] 7843 3-8-10 0 LiamJones 1 54
(W J Haggas) *wnt lft s: hld up in tch in midfield: effrt and rdn 2f out: sn swtchd lft and chsd ldng pair: wknd u.p ins fnl f* **2/1**[1]

0004 **4** 3 ½ **Bahkov (IRE)**[23] 1771 4-9-5 44 (t) SimonPearce(5) 6 50
(Andrew Turnell) *awkward leaving stalls and slowly away: sn wl bhd and nudged along: swtchd lft and sme hdwy wl over 1f out: nvr trbld ldrs* **66/1**

00 **5** ¾ **Euroquip Boy (IRE)**[15] 2003 3-9-1 0 JimCrowley 7 45
(M J Scudamore) *led tl rdn and hdd wl over 1f out: wknd qckly and wl btn fnl f* **66/1**

5 **6** 1 ½ **Masteeat (USA)**[55] 1075 3-8-10 0 SteveDrowne 8 36
(J R Best) *in tch in last trio: rdn and outpcd over 2f out: no ch fr wl over 1f out* **33/1**

60 **7** ½ **Amends (USA)**[23] 1766 3-9-1 0 RobertWinston 2 39
(J R Best) *sn outpcd and nudged along in rr: carried lft wl over 1f out: nvr trbld ldrs* **16/1**

0- **8** 8 **Fighting Talk (IRE)**[245] 6214 3-9-1 0 JoeFanning 5 13
(M Johnston) *w ldr tl over 2f out: sn rdn and wknd qckly wl over 1f out: wl bhd and eased ins fnl f* **3/1**[2]

68.59 secs (-1.11) **Going Correction** -0.125s/f (Firm)
WFA 3 from 4yo 9lb **8** Ran SP% **115.1**
Speed ratings (Par 103): **102,96,93,89,88 86,85,74**
toteswingers: 1&2 £2.70, 1&3 £2.30, 2&3 £1.60 CSF £15.46 TOTE £4.40: £1.30, £1.30, £1.02; EX 14.60 Trifecta £39.80 Pool: £552.75 - 10.26 winning units..
Owner Bluehills Racing Limited **Bred** Victor Stud Bloodstock Ltd **Trained** Patching, W Sussex

FOCUS
A weak and uncompetitive older-horse maiden in which only half the field could be given a realistic chance. It could rate improved form from the winner, but that look unlikely on balance.

2442 PETER REES RETIREMENT H'CAP 5f

3:40 (3:43) (Class 4) (0-80,80) 3-Y-O **£4,209** (£1,252; £625; £312) **Stalls** High

Form RPR

31-0 **1** **Kingsgate Choice (IRE)**[13] 2052 3-9-1 74 RobertWinston 1 83+
(J R Best) *stdd s: t.k.h: hld up in tch: rdn and effrt wl over 1f out: led ins fnl f: r.o strly: readily* **6/1**[3]

34-0 **2** 2 ¼ **Six Diamonds**[23] 1765 3-9-0 73 JimCrowley 5 74
(H Morrison) *sn chsng ldr: rdn to ld over 1f out: hdd and no ex ins fnl f: nt pce of wnr fnl 100yds* **11/2**[2]

35-5 **3** ½ **Fear Nothing**[12] 2099 3-9-2 75 (v¹) RichardMullen 6 74
(E S McMahon) *bustled along leaving stalls: sn led and racd keenly: hdd and rdn over 1f out: hung lft u.p 1f out: styd on one pce fnl f* **11/10**[1]

3-05 **4** hd **Autocracy**[23] 1784 3-8-6 65 (b) LiamJones 4 63
(W J Haggas) *stdd s: hld up in tch: rdn and effrt over 1f out: one pce and no ch w wnr whn swtchd rt ins fnl f* **11/2**[2]

22-0 **5** 4 ½ **Valmina**[13] 2052 3-8-8 72 (t) SimonPearce(5) 3 54
(Andrew Turnell) *racd towards centre: in tch: rdn and unable qck ent fnl 2f: wknd and wl btn ent fnl f* **25/1**

-360 **6** 1 ¼ **Yurituni**[18] 1917 3-9-7 80 TonyCulhane 7 58
(Eve Johnson Houghton) *stdd s: trckd ldrs: pushed along and unable qck 2f out: rdn and btn over 1f out* **9/1**

56.55 secs (-0.85) **Going Correction** -0.125s/f (Firm) **6** Ran SP% **106.5**
Speed ratings (Par 101): **101,97,96,96,89 87**
toteswingers: 1&2 £3.20, 1&3 £2.60, 2&3 £2.20 CSF £33.25 TOTE £6.80: £2.30, £1.60; EX 19.90.
Owner John Mayne **Bred** Michael Staunton **Trained** Hucking, Kent
■ Electioneer was withdrawn (11/1, ref to ent stalls). Deduct 5p in the £ under R4.

FOCUS
A fair 3-y-o sprint handicap run at a decent clip. The winner is unexposed and the form is rated around the second.

2443 O'BRIEN CHARTERED ACCOUNTANTS H'CAP 1m (R)

4:15 (4:15) (Class 4) (0-85,84) 4-Y-O+ **£4,209** (£1,252; £625; £312) **Stalls** Low

Form RPR

5-55 **1** **Opus Maximus (IRE)**[20] 1841 5-9-3 83 JoeFanning 5 92
(M Johnston) *led and set stdy gallop: qcknd ent fnl 2f: rdn and hrd pressed ent fnl f: hdd ins fnl f: kpt on wl u.p to ld again nr fin* **7/4**[1]

0602 **2** nk **Hazzard County (USA)**[18] 1914 6-8-4 73 MartinLane(3) 1 81
(D M Simcock) *t.k.h: hld up in last pair: hdwy 2f out: rdn to chal ent fnl f: led narrowly ins fnl f: outbattled and hdd nr fin* **9/4**[2]

5-05 **3** 2 ¼ **Masai Moon**[21] 1826 6-9-1 84 JamesMillman(3) 2 87
(B R Millman) *t.k.h: chsd wnr tl rdn and unable qck ent fnl 2f: kpt on same pce fnl f* **10/3**[3]

-540 **4** 1 ¼ **Prohibition (IRE)**[125] 245 4-8-13 79 TonyCulhane 4 79
(W J Haggas) *stdd s: hld up in tch in last: effrt on rail and nt clr run 2f out tl over 1f out: sn rdn and unable qck: btn 1f out* **8/1**

333- **5** 14 **First Bay (IRE)**[14] 6137 4-8-10 76 (tp) LiamJones 3 44
(W K Goldsworthy) *dwlt: sn bustled up to disput 2nd: rdn over 3f out: wknd u.p and dropped to last over 2f out: sn lost tch* **12/1**

1m 39.4s (-1.10) **Going Correction** -0.125s/f (Firm) **5** Ran SP% **109.0**
Speed ratings (Par 105): **100,99,97,96,82**
CSF £5.83 TOTE £3.40: £4.70, £1.10; EX 6.30.
Owner Jim McGrath **Bred** Mrs Anne Marie Burns **Trained** Middleham Moor, N Yorks

FOCUS
Not the strongest handicap for the grade and they only went a steady early pace. The winner is getting back to last season's form.

2444 HM PLANT HITACHI H'CAP 1m 2f (R)

4:45 (4:45) (Class 2) (0-100,100) 4-Y£0t092 (£3,020; £1,510; £755; £376) **Stalls** Low

Form RPR

0-03 **1** **Sandor**[13] 2044 4-8-8 90 SteveDrowne 4 96+
(P J Makin) *hld up in tch in last pair: rdn 3f out: nt clr run and switching rt over 1f out: str run on outer ins fnl f to ld fnl 50yds* **11/2**[2]

3151 **2** ½ **Follow The Flag (IRE)**[13] 2044 6-7-13 86 (p) DeclanCannon(5) 3 90
(A J McCabe) *t.k.h: trckd ldng pair: rdn and effrt ent fnl 2f: ev ch whn edgd lft u.p ins fnl f: led fnl 75yds: sn hdd and no ex towards fin* **12/1**

50-1 **3** nk **Shavansky**[29] 1600 6-8-9 94 ow2 JamesMillman(3) 1 98+
(B R Millman) *v.s.a: sn rcvrd and in tch in last: reminder over 2f out: nt clr run and switching out rt fr wl over 1f out: eventually in the clr and r.o wl fnl 100yds: nt rch ldrs* **8/1**

11-6 **4** nk **Shamali**[25] 1697 5-9-4 100 TonyCulhane 6 102
(W J Haggas) *led at stdy gallop: rdn ent fnl 2f: drvn 1f out: hdd fnl 75yds: no ex and lost 3 pls after* **5/6**[1]

1-00 **5** 1 ½ **Proponent (IRE)**[96] 632 6-9-1 97 RichardMullen 5 97
(R Charlton) *t.k.h: chsd ldr: rdn and unable qck 2f out: styng on same pce and btn whn short of room ins fnl f* **8/1**

2135 **6** hd **December Draw (IRE)**[26] 1665 4-9-3 99 ShaneKelly 2 98
(W J Knight) *hld up in tch: effrt and nt clr run on inner 2f out: swtchd rt and rdn over 1f out: unable qck and styd on same pce fnl f* **7/1**[3]

2m 6.51s (-1.89) **Going Correction** -0.125s/f (Firm) **6** Ran SP% **112.4**
Speed ratings (Par 109): **102,101,101,101,99 99**
toteswingers: 1&2 £3.80, 1&3 £6.30, 2&3 £3.90 CSF £61.96 TOTE £9.70: £5.90, £6.90; EX 22.00.
Owner Keith And Brian Brackpool **Bred** Southcourt Stud **Trained** Ogbourne Maisey, Wilts

FOCUS
The best race on the card, but not the most satisfactory outcome with an ordinary pace leading to traffic problems for a couple. The favourite disappointed but the winner and third were close to their Newmarket form.

NOTEBOOK
Sandor, 3lb better off with Follow The Flag for a length beating at Newmarket earlier this month, needs to be produced as late as possible so the fact that he had to change course in order to get a clear run was probably a help to him. He produced a telling turn of foot when switched wide to hit the front around 50yds from the line and this quick ground was no problem to him at all. (op 5-1 tchd 9-2 and 6-1)
Follow The Flag(IRE), already twice a winner under similar conditions so far this month, saw plenty of daylight on the wide outside but had every chance and kept on well despite edging away to his left late on. He ran very close to the Newmarket form with the winner. (tchd 14-1)
Shavansky ◆, 6lb higher than when scraping home on his Nottingham reappearance including the 2lb overweight, can be considered unlucky. He gave away ground at the start and then got stuck behind a wall of horse when trying for a run over a furlong out, but took off once switched to the wide outside and finished strongly. He would have gone very close otherwise and can gain compensation whilst the ground remains fast. (tchd 9-1)
Shamali, who ran well for a long way on his first start since July at Newmarket at the start of this month, tried to make all and attempted to quicken from the front, but he was worn down well inside the last half-furlong. This race may have come soon enough and he is 8lb above his last winning mark, but he looked a progressive sort last year and he shouldn't be given up on just yet. (op Evens tchd 11-10)
Proponent(IRE), unplaced in two starts at Meydan at the start of the year, was 5lb higher than when signing off last season with victory in a Newmarket handicap. He raced keenly in second place for much of the way and those exertions seemed to tell on him inside the last furlong. (tchd 17-2)
December Draw(IRE) was 17lb higher than when last on turf due to a successful spell on Polytrack in the meantime, including making the frame in Listed company. He didn't have a lot of room to play with on the inside passing the 2f pole, but saw daylight in plenty of time had he been good enough, and he may have found this ground quicker than ideal. (tchd 15-2)

2445 DAVIES H'CAP 1m 6f (R)

5:15 (5:15) (Class 5) (0-75,75) 4-Y-O+ **£2,914** (£867; £433; £216) **Stalls** Low

Form RPR

414 **1** **Lady Eclair (IRE)**[15] 2014 4-8-11 65 JoeFanning 7 73+
(M Johnston) *chsd ldr tl led over 2f out: rdn clr 2f out: styd on wl: eased towards fin* **5/1**

2-30 **2** 1 ¼ **Moonbeam Dancer (USA)**[11] 2126 4-8-13 70 MartinLane(3) 2 74
(D M Simcock) *dwlt: in tch in rr: rdn over 4f out: effrt u.p on outer over 3f out: no ch w wnr fr over 1f out: plugged on to go 2nd nr fin* **85/40**[2]

-055 **3** nk **Divinatore**[32] 1520 4-8-2 56 (b¹) FrankieMcDonald 5 59
(D Haydn Jones) *chsd ldng pair: rdn and swtchd rt over 2f out: chsd wnr fnl 2f: kpt on but no imp: lost 2nd nr fin* **10/1**

0213 **4** 6 **Little Sark (IRE)**[23] 1816 5-8-8 62 CathyGannon 1 57
(P D Evans) *chsd ldrs: rdn 3f out: struggling u.p ent fnl 2f: no ch fr over 1f out* **4/1**[3]

10-3 **5** 18 **Benozzo Gozzoli**[36] 1446 4-8-2 56 NickyMackay 4 39
(H Morrison) *led tl rdn and hdd over 2f out: sn struggling u.p: wl btn over 1f out: eased ins fnl f* **2/1**[1]

3m 3.77s (-0.03) **Going Correction** -0.125s/f (Firm) **5** Ran SP% **111.1**
Speed ratings (Par 103): **95,94,94,90,80**
CSF £16.13 TOTE £5.10: £8.20, £1.10; EX 14.40 Place 6 £117.31, Place 5 £69.84.
Owner Netherfield House Stud **Bred** Lynch Bages Ltd & Samac Ltd **Trained** Middleham Moor, N Yorks

FOCUS
A few of these had question marks against them on the fast ground and the form is ordinary. The winner is rated back to something like her Kempton level. The early pace was good before steadying at halfway.
T/Plt: £83.80 to a £1 stake. Pool: £54,740.95. 476.83 winning tickets. T/Qpdt: £41.00 to a £1 stake. Pool: £3,058.50. 55.10 winning tickets. SP

1985 CHANTILLY (R-H)

Wednesday, May 26

OFFICIAL GOING: Turf: good to soft

2446a PRIX ALY KHAN (CONDITIONS) (4YO+) (GENTLEMEN RIDERS) (TURF) 6f

2:25 (12:00) 4-Y-O+ **£14,601** (£5,840; £4,380; £2,920; £1,460)

RPR

1 **Mister Chop (FR)**[48] 5-10-6 0 (b) MrChristopheGuimard 1 87
(T Lemer, France) **20/1**

2 6 **Lisselan Gardens (USA)**9 7-10-6 0 MrDBellocq 12 68
(Mme J Bidgood, Spain) 14/1
3 hd **Psy Chic (FR)**6 6-10-6 0 MrChristopheGard 7 67
(Robert Collet, France) 83/10
4 snk **Livandar (FR)**29 1611 4-10-12 0 MrFlorentGuy 9 73
(Mlle M Henry, France) 5/2[1]
5 2 **Randonneur (USA)**48 4-10-9 0 (p) MrYannickMergirie 6 63
(E Lellouche, France) 7/2[2]
6 snk **Zizany (IRE)**9 7-10-6 0 MrJeremieLaurent-Joye 8 60
(Robert Collet, France) 32/1
7 3/4 **Calbuco (FR)**9 6-10-6 0 MrGuyD'Arexy 58
(B Dutruel, France) 11/2
8 2 **Arc De Triomphe (GER)**4 8-10-6 0 (p) MrThibaudMace 51
(J Morin, France) 73/1
9 2 **Principe Uromonte (IRE)**36 4-10-6 0 MathieuDelage 10 45
(Ecurie Prince Rose, Belgium) 94/1
10 nse **Sacho (GER)**178 12-10-6 0 MrEtienneMerle 45
(W Kujath, Germany) 25/1
0 **Venado (SWI)**48 9-10-6 0 MrPascalBenoist 5 —
(P Benoist, France) 104/1
0 **Peter Island (FR)**16 1963 7-10-6 0 (b) MrJean-PhilippeBoisgontier —
(J Gallagher) *broke smartly: rdn to ld after 1 1/2f along rail: hdd at 1/2-way: rdn 2f out: fdd qckly: eased* 48/10[3]

1m 10.8s (-0.60) 12 Ran SP% **115.8**
WIN (incl. 1 euro stake): 20.70. PLACES: 5.30, 4.10, 3.50. DF: 95.80. SF: 177.20.
Owner Mme Geraldine Bouquil **Bred** Alain Chopard **Trained** France

NOTEBOOK
Peter Island(FR)showed his usual blistering early pace but dropped away after being headed and was allowed to come home in his own time.

2447 - (Foreign Racing) - See Raceform Interactive

2427 AYR (L-H)

Thursday, May 27

OFFICIAL GOING: Good to firm (firm in places; 9.9)
Wind: Breezy, half against Weather: Cloudy

2448 EUROPEAN BREEDERS' FUND MAIDEN STKS 5f
2:20 (2:23) (Class 4) 2-Y-O **£4,533** (£1,348; £674; £336) **Stalls** High

Form RPR
2 1 **Where's Romeo (IRE)**19 1930 2-9-3 0 GrahamGibbons 9 82
(D H Brown) *mde all: hrd pressed fr over 1f out: hld on wl fnl f* 15/8[1]
5 2 3/4 **Extra Power (IRE)**13 2077 2-9-3 0 KierenFallon 5 80+
(M R Channon) *trckd ldrs: nt clr run briefly over 1f out: squeezed through and ev ch ins fnl f: kpt on: hld nr fin* 11/2[3]
2 3 1 1/2 **Lexi's Hero (IRE)**13 2068 2-9-3 0 PaulHanagan 8 74
(K A Ryan) *pressed wnr: ev ch and rdn over 1f out: one pce ins fnl f* 4/1[2]
2 4 shd **Imperialistic Diva (IRE)**7 2238 2-8-12 0 DavidAllan 6 71+
(T D Easterby) *t.k.h: hld up in tch on ins: nt clr run fr 1/2-way: swtchd lft over 1f out: stl bhd horses but kpt on towards fin: improve* 7/1
6 5 5 **Evening Dress**30 1597 2-8-12 0 RoystonFfrench 7 51
(M Johnston) *chsd ldrs: drvn and outpcd over 2f out: n.d after* 33/1
6 1 **Key Lago (IRE)** 2-9-3 0 PhillipMakin 3 56+
(M Dods) *t.k.h: prom: effrt and swtchd lft over 1f out: wknd ins fnl f* 6/1
4 7 9 **Mr Optimistic**29 1626 2-8-10 0 LeeTopliss(7) 1 20
(R A Fahey) *prom on outside: struggling over 2f out: sn btn* 12/1
8 19 **Majestic Max (IRE)** 2-9-3 0 AdrianNicholls 4 —
(D Nicholls) *s.i.s: bhd: outpcd after 2f: sn lost tch* 25/1

59.79 secs (-0.31) **Going Correction** -0.20s/f (Firm) 8 Ran SP% **111.4**
Speed ratings (Par 95): **94,92,90,90,82 80,66,35**
Tote Swingers: 1&2 £3.40, 1&3 £2.20, 2&3 £4.00 CSF £11.76 TOTE £2.60: £1.10, £1.80, £1.50; EX 13.60.
Owner J C Fretwell **Bred** Patrick Hayes **Trained** Maltby, S Yorks

FOCUS
A heavy shower fell before the first race and there was 0.6mm of overnight rain. In addition the racecourse put 5mm of water on overnight on the home bend, home straight and the pull-up area. This was probably a pretty decent contest, as a few of these had shown promise in their previous starts. The fourth home looked particularly unlucky. The winning time was quicker than the 51-70 rated 3-y-o handicap that followed.

NOTEBOOK
Where's Romeo(IRE), an athletic sort, caught the eye on his first start after showing good speed (his trainer felt he should have won by about five or 6l with luck) and made no mistake this time after grabbing the stands'-side rail. Evidently quite well regarded by David Brown, he should have a leading chance if tried in conditions company next time, but connections did seem to indicate that he will be at his best when there is a bit of ease in the ground. (op 5-2)
Extra Power(IRE), a respectable fifth at Newbury on his debut over 6f, got a little outpaced at one stage and a bit short of room, but came through to look a likely winner before his effort flattened out. He wasn't beaten far and should win a maiden at least. (op 9-2 tchd 4-1)
Lexi's Hero(IRE), a nice looker, was green on his first outing but looked more professional here. A sixth furlong is sure to be within his scope. (op 11-2)
Imperialistic Diva(IRE), who was slowly away, looked very unlucky, as she had little room on at least two occasions. She flew home once in the clear and may have won if the gap had opened about 1f out. Official explanation: jockey said filly was denied a clear run (op 6-1)
Evening Dress didn't achieve a great deal in this but will surely do better later on in the year. A win of any description for her would be valuable for this nicely bred filly.
Key Lago(IRE), a half-brother to winners, was keen under restraint and didn't get home. He is no doubt capable of better but it was a little alarming to see his ears go flat back under pressure. If that was just greenness, he should improve. (op 5-1)
Mr Optimistic, whose debut race had produced three winners already, raced prominently before weakening. (op 10-1 tchd 14-1)
Majestic Max(IRE), a 26,000euro foal, is a half-brother to the smart Yarra but was far too green in this to do himself justice. (op 20-1)

2449 PAUL MACLAGAN, BELHAVEN'S BEST MANAGER 2009 H'CAP 5f
2:50 (2:51) (Class 5) (0-70,66) 3-Y-O **£2,914** (£650; £650; £216) **Stalls** High

Form RPR
0-66 1 **Patch Patch**24 1750 3-9-7 66 PhillipMakin 4 70
(M Dods) *carried rt sn after s: t.k.h: chsd ldrs: effrt over 1f out: kpt on to ld towards fin* 11/2[2]
-160 2 3/4 **Taborcillo**13 2099 3-9-6 65 (b[1]) GrahamGibbons 2 66+
(T D Barron) *dwlt: sn cl up: rdn over 2f out: effrt over 1f out: styd on fnl f* 7/1[3]
0-06 2 dht **Classlin**6 2291 3-8-6 51 PaulHanagan 9 52
(J S Goldie) *hmpd sn after s: t.k.h: in tch: effrt whn nt clr run over 1f out: styd on wl fnl f: nrst fin* 25/1
1211 4 nk **Jigajig**6 2291 3-8-11 61 6ex AmyRyan(5) 1 61+
(K A Ryan) *swtchd rt sn after s: led: rdn 2f out: kpt on fnl f tl hdd and no ex towards fin* 4/5[1]
2- 5 3/4 **Grace And Virtue (IRE)**14 2063 3-8-11 56 FrederikTylicki 3 53
(S Donohoe, Ire) *carried rt sn after s: w ldr to ins fnl f: kpt on same pce* 14/1
4234 6 2 1/2 **Dower Glen**6 2291 3-8-13 58 (p) KierenFallon 7 46+
(N Wilson) *in tch: effrt on outside over 1f out: wknd ins fnl f* 7/1[3]
-410 7 nk **Monte Mayor One**6 2291 3-9-1 60 FrannyNorton 8 47
(P Monteith) *hld up: rdn over 2f out: no imp fnl f* 20/1
5-00 8 hd **Lieu Day Louie (IRE)**13 2069 3-8-10 55 TomEaves 6 41
(N Wilson) *t.k.h: hld up: rdn and edgd lft over 1f out: sn wknd* 9/1
40- 9 1/2 **Psychopathicsandra (IRE)**212 7079 3-8-0 50 oh2 ow3 BillyCray(5) 5 35
(A Berry) *chsd ldrs tl rdn and wknd over 1f out* 100/1

60.31 secs (0.21) **Going Correction** -0.20s/f (Firm) 9 Ran SP% **122.2**
Speed ratings (Par 99): **90,88,88,88,87 83,82,82,81**
Place: Taborcillo £2.50 Classlin £5.00 Ex: Patch Patch-T £23.80 PP-C £62.70 CSF: PP-T £22.63 PP-C £67.08 Tricast: PP-T-C £465.58 PP-C-T £498.29 Tote Swingers: PP&C £6.40, PP&T £10.80, C&T £25.70 TOTE £3.70: £1.30.
Owner J M & Mrs E E Ranson **Bred** Mrs A M Young **Trained** Denton, Co Durham

FOCUS
A modest handicap and the winning time was slower than the 2-y-o maiden on the same card. There was a bunch finish. The form is rated around the runner-up, but looks a bit muddling.

2450 JOHNSTON OILS - J GAS LTD H'CAP 6f
3:20 (3:21) (Class 4) (0-85,85) 3-Y-O **£5,180** (£1,541; £770; £384) **Stalls** High

Form RPR
21-6 1 **Glen Shiel (USA)**13 2069 3-8-8 75 RoystonFfrench 7 86
(M Johnston) *prom: hdwy to ld over 1f out: drvn out fnl f* 9/2[2]
3330 2 2 1/4 **Breathless Kiss (USA)**40 1399 3-8-13 80 PaulHanagan 3 83
(K A Ryan) *chsd ldrs: effrt and wnt 2nd over 1f out: kpt on u.p fnl f* 13/2[3]
004- 3 3 3/4 **Eternal Instinct**211 7115 3-8-11 78 KierenFallon 6 69
(J S Goldie) *hld up in tch: effrt and hdwy over 1f out: flashed tail ins fnl f: no imp* 9/2[2]
311- 4 1 **Melody In The Mist (FR)**277 5292 3-8-6 73 GrahamGibbons 5 61
(T D Barron) *dwlt: hld up: shkn up and stdy hdwy over 1f out: fdd ins fnl f* 9/1
10-0 5 8 **Coin From Heaven (IRE)**19 1917 3-8-9 83 LeeTopliss(7) 2 45
(R A Fahey) *chsd clr ldr: drvn over 2f out: wknd over 1f out* 9/2[2]
32-1 6 12 **Mutafajer**20 1870 3-9-4 85 (v) TadhgO'Shea 4 9
(Saeed Bin Suroor) *led and sn clr: hdd over 1f out: sn wknd* 7/4[1]

1m 12.25s (-1.35) **Going Correction** -0.20s/f (Firm) 6 Ran SP% **114.2**
Speed ratings (Par 101): **101,98,93,91,81 65**
Tote Swingers: 1&2 £4.20, 1&3 £5.40, 2&3 £4.40 CSF £33.11 TOTE £5.20: £3.60, £4.10; EX 33.80.
Owner Sheikh Hamdan Bin Mohammed Al Maktoum **Bred** Marablue Farm Llc **Trained** Middleham Moor, N Yorks

FOCUS
The pace set by Mutafajer was much too strong, and it was noticeable that none of the other riders tried to go with him. It is doubtful how much winning this took and the form has not been rated too positively.
Mutafajer Official explanation: jockey said colt ran too free

2451 BURNS FESTIVAL H'CAP 1m
3:50 (3:51) (Class 5) (0-75,75) 4-Y-O+ **£3,238** (£963; £481; £240) **Stalls** Low

Form RPR
100- 1 **Justonefortheroad**227 6731 4-9-4 75 PaulHanagan 2 88
(R A Fahey) *mde all: rdn over 2f out: styd on strly: unchal* 11/4[2]
6-65 2 2 **Daring Dream (GER)**9 2206 5-8-3 63 KellyHarrison(3) 1 71
(J S Goldie) *prom: effrt and chsd wnr 3f out: kpt on u.p fnl f: nt rch wnr* 7/2[3]
0-05 3 7 **Aldaado (IRE)**20 1867 4-8-11 68 PhillipMakin 5 60
(M Dods) *prom: effrt over 2f out: edgd lft and outpcd wl over 1f out* 5/2[1]
-656 4 2 1/2 **Green Agenda**23 1808 4-8-5 62 RoystonFfrench 7 48
(M Johnston) *towards rr: effrt over 2f out: sn no imp* 6/1
0-00 5 10 **Barataria**27 1653 8-8-0 64 MatthewLawson(7) 4 27
(R Bastiman) *rrd s: bhd: effrt on outside over 3f out: nvr on terms* 25/1
060- 6 7 **Secret Hero**44 1288 4-7-13 61 oh1 (p) JamesSullivan(5) 6 8
(Lee Smyth, Ire) *chsd wnr: rdn over 3f out: wknd over 2f out* 25/1
30-0 7 2 **Cara's Request (AUS)**41 1361 5-9-1 72 AdrianNicholls 8 14
(D Nicholls) *plld hrd: cl up tl rdn and wknd over 2f out* 7/1

1m 40.3s (-3.50) **Going Correction** -0.35s/f (Firm) 7 Ran SP% **111.9**
Speed ratings (Par 103): **103,101,94,91,81 74,72**
Tote Swingers: 1&2 £2.60, 1&3 £2.30, 2&3 £3.70 CSF £12.24 CT £25.30 TOTE £2.60: £1.10, £1.90; EX 12.80.
Owner The Pontoon Partnership **Bred** Wellsummers Farm & Hammarsfield B'Stock **Trained** Musley Bank, N Yorks

FOCUS
Quite a few of these had been not running well on recent starts, so this is likely to be weak form. The form has been rated at face value.
Barataria Official explanation: jockey said gelding missed the break

2452 ACCESS PLUS H'CAP 1m 2f
4:20 (4:20) (Class 4) (0-80,77) 4-Y-O+ **£5,180** (£1,541; £770; £384) **Stalls** Low

Form RPR
-031 1 **Templetuohy Max (IRE)**9 2204 5-9-1 74 6ex (v) GrahamGibbons 5 83
(J D Bethell) *mde all: rdn over 1f out: kpt on wl fnl f* 13/8[1]
00-0 2 1/2 **Jewelled Dagger (IRE)**27 1669 6-8-12 74 GaryBartley(3) 1 82
(J S Goldie) *chsd wnr to over 4f out: rdn over 2f out: chsd wnr again ent fnl f: r.o* 7/1[2]
2-60 3 3 3/4 **Starla Dancer (GER)**20 1863 4-9-4 77 PaulHanagan 4 78
(R A Fahey) *trckd ldrs: wnt 2nd over 4f out: rdn over 2f out: no ex fnl f* 13/8[1]
010- 4 4 **Shy Glance (USA)**230 6648 8-9-1 74 FrannyNorton 2 67
(P Monteith) *t.k.h: prom tl outpcd fnl 2f* 15/2[3]
B63- 5 1 1/2 **Talk Of Saafend (IRE)**288 4896 5-8-9 68 RoystonFfrench 6 58
(P Monteith) *hld up in tch: outpcd 3f out: n.d after* 14/1

2m 8.57s (-3.43) **Going Correction** -0.35s/f (Firm) 5 Ran SP% **107.1**
Speed ratings (Par 105): **99,98,95,92,91**
CSF £12.66 TOTE £2.70: £1.10, £3.40; EX 12.20.
Owner Craig Monty **Bred** Jim Shanahan **Trained** Middleham Moor, N Yorks

FOCUS
An ordinary handicap. Much like the previous race, the winning rider takes plenty of credit for getting his mount home first. The winner is rated better than ever.

2453 VICTOR CHANDLER CLAIMING STKS 6f
4:50 (4:51) (Class 6) 3-Y-O+ **£2,388** (£705; £352) **Stalls** Low

Form RPR
0201 1 **Abbondanza (IRE)**[17] 1968 7-9-8 80 AdrianNicholls 3 79
(D Nicholls) *pressed ldr: rdn over 2f out: led over 1f out: edgd lft ins fnl f: kpt on wl* **4/6**[1]
-600 2 ½ **Stellite**[9] 2211 10-8-13 67 GaryBartley(3) 6 71
(J S Goldie) *hld up: hdwy over 1f out: swtchd lft ins fnl f: styd on to chse wnr towards fin* **16/1**
60-6 3 ¾ **Artsu**[41] 1365 5-9-3 70 PhillipMakin 4 70
(M Dods) *stdd bhd ldrs: effrt and rdn over 1f out: chsd wnr ins fnl f: no ex towards fin* **4/1**[2]
/00- 4 2¼ **Saxford**[377] 2035 4-9-12 99 DuranFentiman 1 71
(Mrs L Stubbs) *led tl drvn and hdd over 1f out: no ex ins fnl f* **11/2**[3]
5 10 **Non Tiscordardime**[14] 2063 3-8-6 61 (p) PaulHanagan 2 28
(Niall Moran, Ire) *chsd ldrs tl rdn and wknd over 2f out* **20/1**
00-0 6 11 **Geojimali**[20] 1869 8-9-4 68 FrederikTylicki 5 —
(J S Goldie) *hld up: rdn and struggling over 2f out: sn lost tch* **20/1**

1m 12.05s (-1.55) **Going Correction** -0.20s/f (Firm)
WFA 3 from 4yo+ 9lb **6 Ran SP% 110.8**
Speed ratings (Par 101): **102,101,100,97,84 69**
Tote Swingers: 1&2 £3.20, 1&3 £1.40, 2&3 £3.30 CSF £12.92 TOTE £1.80: £1.30, £3.20; EX 11.80.
Owner Middleham Park Racing XXXI **Bred** M Nolan **Trained** Sessay, N Yorks

FOCUS
A fair claimer. The winner probably ran to a similar level to Redcar.

2454 UP TO £125 FREE BET AT VICTORCHANDLER.COM H'CAP 7f 50y
5:20 (5:22) (Class 6) (0-60,60) 4-Y-O+ **£2,266** (£674; £337; £168) **Stalls** High

Form RPR
U-25 1 **Mr Lu**[6] 2293 5-9-3 59 FrederikTylicki 1 70+
(J S Goldie) *t.k.h: in tch: hdwy over 1f out: led ins fnl f: pushed out* **5/2**[1]
-000 2 1¾ **Fiefdom (IRE)**[29] 1628 8-8-12 54 (v[1]) PatrickMathers 10 60
(I W McInnes) *prom: effrt 2f out: chsd wnr ins fnl f: kpt on: no imp* **9/1**
6064 3 nk **King's Jester (IRE)**[69] 939 8-8-11 53 (b) AdrianNicholls 4 58
(Lee Smyth, Ire) *midfield: effrt whn nt clr run over 2f out: hdwy over 1f out: kpt on ins fnl f* **14/1**
05-5 4 nk **Optical Illusion (USA)**[3] 2381 6-8-6 55 LeeTopliss(7) 11 59+
(R A Fahey) *hld up: stdy hdwy on outside over 2f out: effrt over 1f out: kpt on same pce fnl f* **4/1**[2]
4600 5 ¾ **Whatyouwoodwishfor (USA)**[23] 1808 4-9-1 60 (b) BarryMcHugh(3) 2 62
(R A Fahey) *t.k.h: led: rdn 2f out: hdd ins fnl f: one pce* **9/1**
-061 6 3 **Obe Brave**[13] 2105 7-8-7 54 (b) JamesSullivan(5) 14 48
(Lee Smyth, Ire) *prom: effrt over 1f out: no ex ins fnl f* **16/1**
050- 7 nk **Glenluji**[208] 7174 5-8-1 46 KellyHarrison(3) 9 39
(J S Goldie) *stdd s: hld up: stdy hdwy over 1f out: kpt on fnl f: nvr nr ldrs* **9/1**
0002 8 1½ **Hosanna**[6] 2293 4-8-4 46 oh1 PaulHanagan 8 35
(J Barclay) *t.k.h: cl up: rdn over 1f out: wknd ins fnl f* **11/2**[3]
/00- 9 6 **Anthemion (IRE)**[325] 3683 13-7-11 46 oh1 MatthewLawson(7) 13 19
(Mrs J C McGregor) *s.i.s: hld up: hdwy on outside and prom 3f out: wknd over 1f out* **80/1**
0-00 10 nse **Maison Dieu**[19] 1923 7-9-0 56 FrannyNorton 12 29
(A Berry) *cl up tl rdn and wknd over 1f out* **33/1**
0-40 11 ½ **Raise All In (IRE)**[9] 2207 4-8-6 48 (b) RoystonFfrench 6 20
(I W McInnes) *bhd: drvn and outpcd 1/2-way: sn btn* **33/1**
000/ 12 20 **Brace Of Doves**[611] 5968 8-8-0 47 oh1 ow1 BillyCray(5) 7 —
(D W Whillans) *bhd: struggling 1/2-way: nvr on terms* **66/1**

1m 32.24s (-1.16) **Going Correction** -0.35s/f (Firm) **12 Ran SP% 115.1**
Speed ratings (Par 101): **92,90,89,89,88 85,84,82,76,76 75,52**
Tote Swingers: 1&2 £8.00, 1&3 £7.80, 2&3 £11.30 CSF £22.67 CT £205.20 TOTE £2.90: £1.10, £3.80, £4.70; EX 37.10 Place 6: £96.37 Place 5: £75.03.
Owner The Greens Committee **Bred** Whitwell Bloodstock **Trained** Uplawmoor, E Renfrews
■ Jord (9/1, upset in stalls) was withdrawn. R4 applies, deduct 10p in the £.

FOCUS
This was another race on the day where the early pace was not strong, but it did see a gamble landed. Modest form with the winner rated back to his best.
Anthemion(IRE) Official explanation: jockey said gelding missed the break
T/Plt: £447.70 to a £1 stake. Pool: £66,775.12 - 108.87 winning units. T/Qpdt: £24.50 to a £1 stake. Pool: £3,964.85 - 119.30 winning units. RY

2196 BRIGHTON (L-H)
Thursday, May 27

OFFICIAL GOING: Good to firm (watered; 9.1)
Rail realignment increased distances by about 25yds.
Wind: virtually nil Weather: cloudy, chilly changing to sunny and pleasant after Race 3

2455 BRIGHTON FESTIVAL 4TH, 5TH, 6TH AUGUST H'CAP 1m 3f 196y
2:10 (2:10) (Class 5) (0-70,70) 4-Y-O+ **£2,978** (£886; £442; £221) **Stalls** High

Form RPR
6-12 1 **Penang Cinta**[9] 2199 7-8-13 70 RichardEvans(5) 4 74+
(P D Evans) *chsd ldr: rdn and unable qck 3f out: kpt on ins fnl f to ld fnl 75yds: in command and eased nr fin* **15/8**[1]
6125 2 ½ **What's Up Doc (IRE)**[17] 1961 9-8-13 65 DaneO'Neill 2 68
(Mrs Lawney Hill) *led: gng best ent fnl 2f: rdn and hanging lft fr over 1f out: hdd and no ex fnl 75yds* **9/4**[2]
-435 3 1¾ **Calzaghe (IRE)**[44] 1283 6-8-9 61 PaulDoe 5 61
(Jim Best) *chsd ldrs: rdn over 3f out: plugged on same pce u.p fnl 2f: nvr quite gng pce to chal ldrs* **11/4**[3]
660- 4 ½ **Sand Repeal (IRE)**[217] 6969 8-8-2 61 oh3 ow5 AdamBeschizza(7) 3 61
(Miss J Feilden) *hld up wl in tch: rdn and effrt over 2f out: unable qck and kpt on one pce fnl 2f* **12/1**
10-4 5 ¾ **Zaif (IRE)**[9] 2199 7-8-5 60 AshleyHamblett(3) 1 58
(D J S Ffrench Davis) *hld up wl in tch: effrt and rdn over 2f out: unable qck and styd on one pce fnl 2f* **14/1**

2m 34.63s (1.93) **Going Correction** +0.10s/f (Good) **5 Ran SP% 106.6**
Speed ratings (Par 103): **97,96,95,95,94**
Tote Swingers: 1&2 £5.80, 1&3 £1.40, 2&3 £3.90 CSF £5.93 TOTE £2.50: £1.80, £1.10; EX 6.40.
Owner Trevor Gallienne **Bred** Mrs A K H Ooi **Trained** Pandy, Monmouths

FOCUS
Rail realignment increased distances by about 25yds. After 4mm of rain over the previous 24 hours the ground had slightly eased from Good to Firm, Firm in places to Good to Firm with a decent covering of grass. A small field for this 56-70 handicap with, on paper, only three of the five that could be seriously considered on recent form. It was run at just an ordinary pace with the time being more than five seconds outside RP Standard. Muddling form, with the fourth a doubt.

2456 NORFOLK ARMS ARUNDEL H'CAP 7f 214y
2:40 (2:40) (Class 6) (0-60,61) 4-Y-O+ **£2,072** (£616; £308; £153) **Stalls** Low

Form RPR
1002 1 **Lady Lam**[17] 1958 4-8-12 53 RichardHughes 2 60
(S Kirk) *t.k.h: trckd ldrs: rdn to chse ldr over 1f out: drvn ins fnl f: r.o wl to ld nr fin* **11/4**[2]
0-00 2 nk **Lady Florence**[9] 2198 5-9-4 59 StevieDonohoe 3 65
(A B Coogan) *led tl over 5f out: chsd ldr after tl led again ent fnl 2f: edgd lft u.p ent fnl f: kpt on wl tl hdd and no ex nr fin* **13/2**
2661 3 2 **Musical Script (USA)**[9] 2198 7-9-6 61 6ex (b) DaneO'Neill 4 63
(Mouse Hamilton-Fairley) *stdd s: hld up in rr: hdwy on inner ent fnl 2f: disputing 2nd whn nt clr run 1f out: sn swtchd rt and rdn: no imp and btn fnl 100yds* **15/8**[1]
4600 4 nk **Prince Valentine**[9] 2198 9-8-8 49 (p) FergusSweeney 7 50
(G L Moore) *hld up in last pair: shkn up and effrt towards centre ent fnl 2f: kpt on u.p ins fnl f: nvr gng pce to rch ldrs* **14/1**
0306 5 nse **The Graig**[10] 2188 6-8-8 49 (t) JerryO'Dwyer 5 50
(J R Holt) *hld up wl in tch: rdn and effrt towards centre over 2f out: unable qck u.p over 1f out: kpt on ins fnl f* **11/1**
0-06 6 1¾ **Annes Rocket (IRE)**[14] 2053 5-9-3 58 PatDobbs 6 55
(J C Fox) *plld hrd early: hld up wl in tch: effrt and rdn over 1f out: unable qck and n.m.r jst ins fnl f: wknd fnl 100yds* **5/1**[3]
0000 7 5 **Affirmatively**[24] 1775 5-7-13 45 AmyBaker(5) 1 30
(A W Carroll) *plld hrd: chsd ldr tl led over 5f out: hdd ent fnl 2f: wknd ent fnl f* **50/1**

1m 37.71s (1.71) **Going Correction** +0.10s/f (Good) **7 Ran SP% 108.4**
Speed ratings (Par 101): **95,94,92,92,92 90,85**
Tote Swingers: 1&2 £1.02, 1&3 £28.50, 2&3 £5.50 CSF £18.47 TOTE £2.90: £1.10, £6.30; EX 15.40.
Owner J B J Richards **Bred** J B J Richards **Trained** Upper Lambourn, Berks

FOCUS
A low-grade affair run at just a fair pace. The winner ran to her AW mark.
Affirmatively Official explanation: jockey said mare ran too free

2457 ALICE IN RACELAND 6TH JUNE MAIDEN AUCTION STKS 5f 213y
3:10 (3:10) (Class 5) 2-Y-O **£2,849** (£847; £423; £211) **Stalls** Low

Form RPR
032 1 **Two Feet Of Snow (IRE)**[5] 2338 2-8-8 0 RichardHughes 4 72
(R Hannon) *chsd ldng pair: rdn to chse ldr wl over 1f out: drvn to chal jst ins fnl f: led fnl 75yds: styd on wl* **4/7**[1]
3622 2 1½ **Master Macho (IRE)**[7] 2239 2-8-13 0 SamHitchcott 1 73
(M R Channon) *led: rdn 2f out: drvn ent fnl f: hdd and no ex fnl 75yds* **9/4**[2]
00 3 1 **Kissing Clara (IRE)**[5] 2338 2-8-10 0 ow2 StevieDonohoe 5 67+
(J S Moore) *racd in last pair: rdn and no prog ent fnl 2f: kpt on wl ins fnl f: wnt 3rd towards fin* **50/1**
53 4 1¼ **Kodiac Star (IRE)**[4] 2358 2-8-10 0 FergusSweeney 3 63
(J A Osborne) *chsd ldr tl over 1f out: outpcd u.p ent fnl f: styd on same pce after* **14/1**[3]
04 5 5 **Silly Billy (IRE)**[15] 2022 2-9-3 0 PatDobbs 2 55
(S Kirk) *in tch in midfield: rdn and unable qck ent fnl 2f: no threat to ldrs after* **16/1**
6 22 **Sister June (IRE)** 2-8-6 0 EddieCreighton 6 —
(E J Creighton) *s.i.s: sn swishing tail and pushed along in last: lost tch ent fnl 2f: t.o* **50/1**

1m 11.81s (1.61) **Going Correction** +0.10s/f (Good) **6 Ran SP% 110.9**
Speed ratings (Par 93): **93,91,89,88,81 52**
Tote Swingers: 1&2 £1.02, 1&3 £28.50, 2&3 £5.50 CSF £1.98 TOTE £1.70: £1.30, £1.10; EX 1.80.
Owner Alpine Racing **Bred** Paulyn Limited **Trained** East Everleigh, Wilts

FOCUS
A weak maiden with the odds-on favourite having to dig deep to come out on top in a race run at an ordinary pace. Straightforward form, and the winner didn't have to improve.

NOTEBOOK
Two Feet Of Snow(IRE) had been progressing with each run and it would have been disappointing had she not collected after her effort when runner-up at Newbury last time. She tracked the leader for much of the way with her rider having to get fairly serious coming up the hill but she won going away after hitting the front in the final 75 yards. One of the yard's lesser lights in the two-year-old division, she will stick to being campaigned at 6f. (op 8-11)
Master Macho(IRE) has been knocking on the door and once again came out second best after trying to make all. It will be a surprise, with his connections, if he does not go one better before long in a similar contest.
Kissing Clara(IRE) had shown precious little in her two previous runs so her proximity to the principals casts a big cloud over the form, although this was a step in the right direction if taken at face value. She was doing all her best work towards the latter part of the race without ever threatening. (tchd 66-1)
Kodiac Star(IRE) was very green on debut but stepped up on that when third last time. She can be given another chance after chasing the pace for much of the way, but seemed not to handle the undulations that well before fading inside the distance. (op 12-1)
Silly Billy(IRE) was a little disappointing as she could never get on terms after a promising effort last time. He was nonetheless conceding weight all round here. (op 12-1)

2458 TOTEPOOL FLEXI BETTING H'CAP 5f 213y
3:40 (3:40) (Class 5) (0-75,79) 4-Y-O+ **£2,978** (£886; £442; £221) **Stalls** Low

Form RPR
-501 1 **Poppanan (USA)**[24] 1779 4-8-10 72 AdamBeschizza(7) 3 82+
(S Dow) *t.k.h: trckd ldng pair: swtchd rt and hdwy between horses ent fnl f: led fnl 100yds: r.o wl: readily* **5/4**[1]
-040 2 1¼ **Highland Harvest**[105] 501 6-8-10 65 StevieDonohoe 2 71
(Jamie Poulton) *led: rdn wl over 1f out: hdd and nt pce of wnr fnl 100yds* **5/1**[3]
4250 3 ½ **Magical Speedfit (IRE)**[12] 2123 5-9-1 70 DaneO'Neill 5 74
(G G Margarson) *chsd ldr: rdn wl over 1f out: drvn and nt qiucken ent fnl f: styd on same pce after* **2/1**[2]
000 4 4 **Divine Force**[31] 1580 4-9-3 72 (p) SimonWhitworth 1 64
(M Wigham) *awkward leaving stalls and s.i.s: t.k.h: hld up in last: clipped heels and stmbld after 1f: rdn and no prog wl over 1f out: wl hld fnl f* **6/1**

1m 11.29s (1.09) **Going Correction** +0.10s/f (Good) **4 Ran SP% 108.7**
Speed ratings (Par 103): **96,94,93,88**
CSF £7.53 TOTE £2.30; EX 6.80.

Owner Joe Cole **Bred** Liberation Farm And Brandywine Farm Llc **Trained** Epsom, Surrey
FOCUS
A small but quite competitive field for this 61-75 sprint handicap. The winner is rated up a length on his Windsor success.

2459 BRIGHTON RACECOURSE AND CONFERENCE CENTRE H'CAP 6f 209y
4:10 (4:10) (Class 6) (0-65,65) 3-Y-O £2,201 (£655; £327; £163) Stalls Centre

Form RPR
5-65 1 **Interakt**[35] 1486 3-9-3 **64** SamHitchcott 6 66
(M R Channon) *dwlt: sn rcvrd and chsd ldr tl led over 2f out: rdn and edging rt fr wl over 1f out: hld on nr fin* **13/8**[1]
5-44 2 ½ **Young Simon**[30] 1604 3-9-2 **63** (v[1]) DaneO'Neill 3 64
(G G Margarson) *t.k.h: hld up wl in tch in last pair: rdn over 2f out: hdwy u.p towards centre ent fnl f: pressed wnr fnl 75yds: hld nr fin* **7/2**[3]
2350 3 2½ **Rathbawn Girl (IRE)**[10] 2185 3-8-3 **57** AdamBeschizza(7) 2 51
(Miss J Feilden) *stdd s: t.k.h: hld up in tch: hdwy to chse ldrs over 4f out: chsd wnr wl over 1f out: rdn and unable qck ent fnl f: wknd fnl 150yds* **8/1**
65 4 1¾ **Starwatch**[103] 538 3-8-11 **58** NeilChalmers 4 47
(J J Bridger) *led tl over 2f out: wknd u.p ent fnl f* **10/1**
0334 5 3¾ **Hill Of Miller (IRE)**[24] 1760 3-8-11 **61** (t) WilliamCarson(3) 1 40
(Rae Guest) *plld hrd: chsd ldrs tl rdn and wknd wl over 1f out: wl btn fnl f* **9/4**[2]

1m 24.19s (1.09) **Going Correction** +0.10s/f (Good) **5** Ran SP% **111.3**
Speed ratings (Par 97): **97,96,93,91,87**
CSF £7.75 TOTE £2.80: £1.10, £1.60; EX 5.50.
Owner Heart Of The South Racing **Bred** P C Hunt **Trained** West Ilsley, Berks
FOCUS
A small but tight little 51-65 handicap run at a fair pace. Weakish form, rated around the winner.
Hill Of Miller(IRE) Official explanation: trainer said gelding was unsuited by the track

2460 MATTHEW CLARK DRINKS H'CAP 1m 1f 209y
4:40 (4:41) (Class 6) (0-65,63) 3-Y-O £2,201 (£655; £327; £163) Stalls High

Form RPR
000- 1 **Bona Fortuna**[202] 7266 3-9-0 **59** StevieDonohoe 4 76+
(Sir Mark Prescott) *mde all: rdn clr 2f out: wl clr ent fnl f: eased fnl 75yds* **8/1**
-015 2 6 **Mr Harmoosh (IRE)**[5] 2336 3-9-3 **62** AndreaAtzeni 1 63
(E F Vaughan) *hld up in tch in midfield: rdn and effrt ent fnl 2f: sn wl outpcd by wnr but plugged on to go 2nd ins fnl f: no ch w wnr* **13/8**[1]
00-0 3 1¼ **Tom Wade (IRE)**[17] 1977 3-9-3 **62** JackMitchell 7 61
(M A Jarvis) *chsd wnr for 1f: rdn over 2f out: chsd wnr and hung rt 2f out: sn outpcd by wnr and wl btn 1f out: lost 2nd ins fnl f* **5/1**[3]
2306 4 3¾ **Dane Cottage**[10] 2175 3-9-4 **63** PaulDoe 6 54
(Miss Gay Kelleway) *t.k.h early: hld up in tch towards rr: hdwy to chse ldrs 5f out: rdn ent fnl 3f: wknd u.p enterung fnl 2f* **9/2**[2]
0-60 5 2¼ **Cuckoo Rock (IRE)**[17] 1977 3-9-0 **59** StephenCraine 9 46
(J G Portman) *chsd ldrs: rdn over 2f out: unable qck and struggling whn hmpd 2f out: wl hld after* **9/1**
000- 6 2 **Vadition (IRE)**[194] 7390 3-7-13 **49** oh4 AmyBaker(5) 2 32
(J J Bridger) *hld up in last trio: rdn and struggling over 2f out: wl btn fnl 2f* **50/1**
2166 7 6 **Take My Hand**[12] 2132 3-9-3 **62** SamHitchcott 3 33
(M R Channon) *t.k.h: hld up in last pair: rdn and no reponse 3f out: wl btn fnl 2f* **10/1**
456- 8 2 **Mrs Puff (IRE)**[197] 7334 3-8-7 **52** SimonWhitworth 5 19
(P D Evans) *stdd s: hld up in last pair: rdn and lost tch 3f out* **22/1**
0-60 9 ½ **My Grand Duke (USA)**[4] 2359 3-7-13 **49** oh1 SimonPearce(5) 8 15
(J A Osborne) *stdd s: plld hrd: chsd wnr after 1f tl over 2f out: sn wknd* **12/1**

2m 4.72s (1.12) **Going Correction** +0.10s/f (Good) **9** Ran SP% **117.1**
Speed ratings (Par 97): **99,94,93,90,88 86,82,80,80**
Tote Swingers: 1&2 £4.50, 1&3 £7.10, 2&3 £3.70 CSF £21.73 CT £74.40 TOTE £12.80: £2.90, £3.30, £1.90; EX 16.20 Trifecta £105.60 Pool: £249.79 - 1.75 winning units. Place 6: £12.52 Place 5: £9.06 .
Owner S Munir **Bred** W And R Barnett Ltd **Trained** Newmarket, Suffolk
FOCUS
A moderate 51-65 middle distance handicap run at a sound pace. The winner is clearly a long way ahead of this mark and the form is rated around the runner-up.
T/Plt: £17.50 to a £1 stake. Pool: £51,498.59 - 2,145.35 winning units. T/Qpdt: £24.50 to a £1 stake. Pool: £3,177.25 - 602.67 winning units. SP

2082 NEWCASTLE (L-H)
Thursday, May 27

OFFICIAL GOING: Good (good to firm in places; 7.5)
Bend after winning post and at 1m2f area moved in to provide fresh ground down back straight.
Wind: moderate half against Weather: Overcast and light showers

2461 LA TAXIS MAIDEN FILLIES' STKS 6f
6:25 (6:27) (Class 4) 2-Y-O £4,415 (£1,321; £660; £330; £164) Stalls Centre

Form RPR
4 1 **Idiom (IRE)**[13] 2088 2-9-0 0 TadhgO'Shea 8 82+
(Mahmood Al Zarooni) *hld up towards rr: smooth hdwy over 2f out: swtchd lft and effrt to chal over 1f out: led ent fnl f and sn clr* **7/2**[2]
442 2 5 **Silca Conegliano (IRE)**[10] 2163 2-9-0 0 KierenFallon 5 67
(M R Channon) *wnt rt s: sn led: rdn along and jnd wl over 1f out: drvn and hdd ent fnl f: sn one pce* **6/4**[1]
405 3 2 **Lady Platinum Club**[13] 2095 2-9-0 0 PJMcDonald 9 61+
(G R Oldroyd) *trckd ldrs on inner: effrt over 2f out: rdn wl over 1f out: kpt on same pce appr fnl f* **6/1**[3]
4 hd **So Belle** 2-9-0 0 NeilCallan 6 60+
(K A Ryan) *trckd ldrs: swtchd lft and hdwy over 2f out: rdn along wl over 1f out: kpt on same pce* **14/1**
5 5 **Louis Girl** 2-9-0 0 TonyHamilton 7 45
(R A Fahey) *hld up: hdwy 2f out: rdn and kpt on same pce appr fnl f* **9/1**
6 shd **Damascus Symphony** 2-9-0 0 AndrewElliott 2 45
(J D Bethell) *s.i.s and in rr: pushed along 1/2-way: styd on appr fnl f* **33/1**
7 1 **Unwrapit (USA)** 2-9-0 0 TomEaves 4 42
(B Smart) *cl up: rdn along over 2f out: sn wknd* **12/1**
8 2 **Regal Kiss** 2-9-0 0 JoeFanning 3 36
(M Johnston) *cl up on outer: rdn along wl over 2f out: grad wknd* **16/1**
9 13 **Elsie's Star** 2-9-0 0 DavidAllan 1 —
(T D Easterby) *dwlt: a towards rr: rdn along over 2f out: sn outpcd and bhd* **16/1**

1m 17.5s (2.90) **Going Correction** 0.0s/f (Good) **9** Ran SP% **115.6**
Speed ratings (Par 92): **84,77,74,74,67 67,66,63,46**
Tote Swingers: 1&2 £1.30, 1&3 £6.10, 2&3 £3.40 CSF £9.11 TOTE £5.20: £1.90, £1.10, £1.50; EX 8.30.
Owner Godolphin **Bred** Mountarmstrong Stud **Trained** Newmarket, Suffolk
■ Stewards' Enquiry : Tadhg O'Shea one-day ban: careless riding (Jun 10)
FOCUS
There had been some sharp showers since the irrigation of the track was completed on Monday and the going was officially described as good, good to firm in places. Just three of the runners had previous experience in this fillies' maiden and they filled the first three places in a race where the field finished well strung out. The first two raced against the rail and the impressive winner is rated up 19lb, with the next two below form.
NOTEBOOK
Idiom(IRE) showed promise when 13-2 fourth in an ordinary 6f Newmarket fillies' maiden on debut. There was no sign of her hanging this time and she manoeuvred her way through some potential traffic problems to win in impressive style under a confident ride. There may not have been much strength in depth in this race but the scopey half-sister to useful winners Capable Guest (7f-1m4f) and Petardias Magic (5f/6f) looks a nice type and should go on to better things. (tchd 3-1)
Silca Conegliano(IRE) set the standard on her narrow defeat in a Bath maiden ten days earlier. She was heavily backed to get off the mark on the fourth attempt and things looked to be going well under positive tactics for a long way, but she could not respond to the surging run of the winner and was eventually well held. (op 7-4 tchd 2-1)
Lady Platinum Club seemed to show improvement when 6l fifth of seven at 25-1 in a 5f York Listed event last time. She had an interesting chance if confirming that form but could only plug on when things got serious at the two furlong pole. (op 8-1 tchd 11-2)
So Belle moved quite well for a long way before hanging and showing signs of inexperience in the closing stages. This was a fair debut effort from a filly whose sales price took a dramatic rise to 30,000gns last month. (op 9-1)
Louis Girl ran very green but did a bit of late work to finish a remote fifth. She should be a lot more streetwise next time and several of her siblings were successful during their two-year-old campaigns. (op 8-1 tchd 10-1)

2462 IPC SECURITY H'CAP 7f
7:00 (7:00) (Class 4) (0-80,83) 4-Y-O+ £4,415 (£1,321; £660; £330; £164) Stalls Centre

Form RPR
3-21 1 **Tagseed (IRE)**[16] 2004 4-9-4 **80** TadhgO'Shea 9 92+
(W J Haggas) *set stdy pce: qcknd 3f out: rdn wl over 1f out: kpt on wl fnl f* **15/8**[1]
15-3 2 1 **Major Phil (IRE)**[16] 1997 4-9-0 **76** KierenFallon 10 82
(L M Cumani) *trckd ldrs on inner: pushed along 3f out: swtchd lft and rdn to chse wnr 2f out: drvn over 1f out: kpt on same pce ins fnl f* **3/1**[2]
0101 3 ¾ **Game Lad**[9] 2205 8-9-7 **83** 6ex (tp) DavidAllan 6 87
(T D Easterby) *hld up in rr: hdwy on outer over 2f out: rdn to chse ldrs over 1f out: kpt on ins fnl f* **10/1**
1-00 4 1¾ **Piquante**[26] 1684 4-8-6 **68** JoeFanning 5 67
(N Tinkler) *in tch: hdwy 3f out: chsd ldng pair wl over 1f out: sn rdn and one pce ent fnl f* **20/1**
-504 5 3½ **Legal Legacy**[26] 1707 4-9-1 **77** TomEaves 4 67
(M Dods) *hld up and bhd: hdwy 2f out: sn rdn and kpt on ins fnl f: nvr nr ldrs* **11/2**[3]
50-0 6 5 **Who's Shirl**[28] 1650 4-8-0 **67** PaulPickard(5) 2 43
(C W Fairhurst) *t.k.h: cl up: rdn along wl over 2f out and grad wknd* **18/1**
44-6 7 1¾ **The Galloping Shoe**[20] 1867 5-8-12 **74** PJMcDonald 3 46
(A C Whillans) *hld up towards rr: rdn along over 3f out: nvr a factor* **20/1**
630- 8 ½ **Olympic Dream**[272] 5409 4-8-10 **72** TonyHamilton 7 42
(R A Fahey) *trckd ldng pair: rdn along wl over 2f out: sn wknd* **12/1**
00 9 3¼ **Signore Momento (IRE)**[42] 1332 4-8-13 **75** AndrewElliott 8 36
(Miss Amy Weaver) *chsd ldrs: rdn along 3f out and sn wknd* **40/1**
40-1 10 20 **Averoo**[19] 1924 5-8-5 **67** (p) PaulQuinn 1 —
(M D Squance) *wnt lft s: a in rr: bhd and eased fnl f* **14/1**

1m 27.8s (-0.90) **Going Correction** 0.0s/f (Good) **10** Ran SP% **115.8**
Speed ratings (Par 105): **105,103,103,101,97 91,89,88,85,62**
Tote Swingers: 1&2 £4.60, 1&3 £4.00, 2&3 £1.30 CSF £7.01 CT £42.83 TOTE £2.60: £1.10, £1.60, £1.60; EX 9.20.
Owner Hamdan Al Maktoum **Bred** Miss A R Byrne **Trained** Newmarket, Suffolk
FOCUS
There were three last-time-out winners involved in this competitive handicap. The first four raced on the rail and the two market leaders finished first and second. The form looks solid.
Averoo Official explanation: jockey said gelding never travelled

2463 GOSFORTH DECORATING & BUILDING SERVICES MAIDEN FILLIES' STKS 1m 2f 32y
7:35 (7:39) (Class 5) 3-Y-O+ £3,238 (£963; £481; £240) Stalls Centre

Form RPR
4 1 **Akinoshirabe (JPN)**[20] 1881 3-8-10 0 KierenFallon 1 72+
(L M Cumani) *trckd ldrs on inner: pushed along over 2f out: rdn to chse ldr ins fnl f: styd on to ld fnl 50yds* **11/2**[2]
42-2 2 ¾ **Scorn (USA)**[14] 2050 3-8-10 79 RobertHavlin 2 70
(J H M Gosden) *set stdy pce: qcknd over 3f out: rdn over 1f out: edgd rt and drvn ins fnl f: hdd and no ex fnl 50yds* **9/4**[1]
0-4 3 1¾ **Best Intent**[20] 1882 3-8-10 0 NeilCallan 9 67
(M A Jarvis) *trckd ldrs: hdwy 3f out: rdn to chse ldng pair over 1f out: drvn and one pce ins fnl f* **9/4**[1]
3-0 4 ¾ **Infanta (IRE)**[20] 1881 3-8-10 0 (v[1]) JoeFanning 6 65
(Mahmood Al Zarooni) *cl up: effrt to chal over 2f out: rdn wl over 1f out and ev ch tl drvn ent fnl f and sn wknd* **20/1**
0 5 1¼ **Najlaa**[27] 1654 3-8-10 0 TadhgO'Shea 10 63+
(W J Haggas) *t.k.h: trckd ldrs: effrt on outer over 2f out: sn rdn and one pce fr over 1f out* **11/1**[3]
6 hd **Maid Of Meft** 3-8-10 0 TonyHamilton 7 63
(Miss L A Perratt) *s.i.s and bhd: hdwy over 3f out: swtchd rt and rdn 2f out: styd on appr fnl f: nrst fin* **100/1**
06- 7 2¼ **By Request**[262] 5718 4-9-10 0 TomEaves 3 59+
(Sir Mark Prescott) *midfield: effrt and sme hdwy over 3f out: rdn over 2f out and n.d* **25/1**
05 8 1¾ **Fantastic Sam (IRE)**[11] 2143 3-8-10 0 PJMcDonald 12 55
(Mrs K Walton) *midfield: rdn along 3f out: sn no imp* **80/1**
00/3 9 8 **Dolly Royal (IRE)**[25] 1722 5-9-5 53 PaulPickard(5) 5 39
(R Johnson) *t.k.h early: a towards rr* **66/1**
0/5 10 10 **Born To Frill**[24] 1777 5-9-3 0 DaleSwift(7) 11 19
(Miss L C Siddall) *a in rr* **200/1**

11 *1* **Crianza** 4-9-10 0 AndrewElliott 8 17
(N Tinkler) *a in rr* **150/1**

2m 14.65s (2.75) **Going Correction** -0.025s/f (Good)
WFA 3 from 4yo+ 14lb 11 Ran SP% **98.7**
Speed ratings (Par 100): **88,87,86,85,84 84,82,81,74,66 65**
Tote Swingers: 1&2 £2.80, 1&3 £1.70, 2&3 £1.50 CSF £12.12 TOTE £5.90: £1.40, £1.10, £1.20; EX 14.20.
Owner N L Tinkler **Bred** Darley Japan K K **Trained** Newmarket, Suffolk

FOCUS
A fair fillies' maiden run at a reasonable pace. Island Dreams was heavily backed but refused to enter the stalls. There are one or two doubts about the race and it may pay not to be too positive about the form.
By Request Official explanation: jockey said filly hung right-handed in straight
Dolly Royal(IRE) Official explanation: jockey said mare hung right-handed in straight

2464 LA TAXIS H'CAP 2m 19y
8:10 (8:10) (Class 6) (0-65,63) 4-Y-0+ £1,942 (£578; £288; £144) Stalls Low

Form RPR
6-53 **1** **Silent Lucidity (IRE)**13 2085 6-8-7 45 (p) TonyHamilton 2 54
(P D Niven) *a.p: hdwy to ld 3f out: rdn clr 2f out: styd on strly* **8/1**
10-6 **2** *4 1/2* **Spiders Star**20 1891 7-9-6 63 PaulPickard(5) 5 67
(S G West) *hld up and bhd: hdwy on wd outside 3f out: rdn wl over 1f out: styd on appr fnl f: tk 2nd towards fin* **11/1**
0201 **3** *3/4* **They All Laughed**23 1803 7-9-3 55 (p) PhillipMakin 11 58
(Mrs Marjorie Fife) *hld up in rr: hdwy over 3f out: rdn to chse ldrs wl over 1f out: drvn and kpt on ins fnl f* **15/2**3
1-14 **4** *nk* **Sendali (FR)**23 1803 6-9-1 53 GrahamGibbons 8 55
(J D Bethell) *hld up: hdwy on inner into midfield 1/2-way: effrt whn n.m.r wl over 2f out: sn swtchd rt and rdn: chsd wnr over 1f out: drvn fnl f: lost 2nd towards fin* **7/2**1
2242 **5** *2 1/2* **Spring Breeze**13 2085 9-8-7 50 (v) IanBrennan(5) 9 49
(J J Quinn) *in tch: rdn along and outpcd over 4f out: swtchd outside 2f out: kpt on u.p fnl f* **5/1**2
0-02 **6** *3/4* **Drop The Hammer**23 1803 4-8-10 50 TadhgO'Shea 1 48
(J Hetherton) *led 2f: chsd ldr tl rdn along over 2f out and grad wknd* **8/1**
0-00 **7** *1* **Mt Desert**36 1467 8-8-12 50 DavidAllan 7 47
(E W Tuer) *midfield: pushed along and lost pl over 6f out: sn in rr* **16/1**
060- **8** *2* **Cripsey Brook**9 6768 12-8-10 48 TomEaves 3 45
(K G Reveley) *chsd ldrs: rdn along and lost pl over 5f out: wkng whn n.m.r on inner over 2f out* **28/1**
0/-4 **9** *5* **Perez (IRE)**9 2214 8-8-5 48 (v) DeanHeslop(5) 10 37
(W Storey) *trckd ldrs: rdn along over 4f out: wknd 3f out* **33/1**
2110 **10** *12* **Aaman (IRE)**112 409 4-9-7 61 JoeFanning 4 35
(E F Vaughan) *cl up: led after 2f: rdn along and hdd 3f out: wknd qckly and bhd whn eased fnl f* **7/2**1

3m 38.35s (-1.05) **Going Correction** -0.025s/f (Good)
WFA 4 from 6yo+ 2lb 10 Ran SP% **115.7**
Speed ratings (Par 101): **101,98,98,98,96 96,96,95,92,86**
Tote Swingers: 1&2 £17.10, 1&3 £12.00, 2&3 £11.20 CSF £91.51 CT £688.38 TOTE £8.40: £2.40, £5.90, £4.60; EX 97.20.
Owner P D Niven **Bred** Mrs Jacqueline Donnelly **Trained** Barton-le-Street, N Yorks

FOCUS
A modest staying handicap run at a decent pace. Orinary form for the grade, the winner reversing recent form with the fifth.
Spring Breeze Official explanation: trainer had no explanation for the poor form shown
Cripsey Brook Official explanation: jockey said gelding was denied a clear run
Perez(IRE) Official explanation: trainer said gelding had a breathing problem
Aaman(IRE) Official explanation: jockey said colt hung right-handed throughout

2465 JONNY CRAIB 40TH BIRTHDAY H'CAP 6f
8:40 (8:41) (Class 3) (0-90,90) 4-Y-0 £6,938 (£2,076; £1,038; £519; £258) Stalls Centre

Form RPR
-061 **1** **Damika (IRE)**12 2134 7-9-1 90 MichaelStainton(3) 11 101
(R M Whitaker) *cl up nr stands' rail: rdn to ld over 1f out: drvn and kpt on wl fnl f: rdr dropped whip towards fin* **5/1**1
4-01 **2** *3/4* **Noodles Blue Boy**16 1988 4-8-8 80 TonyHamilton 3 88
(Ollie Pears) *a.p: hdwy 2f out: rdn and ev ch over 1f out tl drvn: edgd rt and nt qckn wl ins fnl f* **12/1**
-500 **3** *1* **Hotham**26 1688 7-9-1 87 TadhgO'Shea 2 92
(N Wilson) *hld up towards rr: hdwy 2f out: rdn over 1f out: styd on ins fnl f: nrst fin* **20/1**
3-06 **4** *1 1/4* **Master Rooney (IRE)**31 1573 4-8-13 85 TomEaves 12 86
(B Smart) *racd nr stands' rail: led: rdn along 2f out: drvn and hdd over 1f out: kpt on same pce ins fnl f* **11/2**2
0-12 **5** *1 3/4* **Leonid Glow**12 2113 5-8-1 78 PatrickDonaghy(5) 6 73
(M Dods) *hld up in rr: hdwy 2f out: swtchd lft and rdn over 1f out: styng on whn n.m.r ins fnl f* **6/1**3
6-51 **6** *2* **Mullglen**26 1711 4-8-5 77 (tp) DuranFentiman 13 66
(T D Easterby) *chsd ldrs towards stands' rail: rdn along wl over 1f out: drvn whn n.m.r and wknd ins fnl f* **16/1**
-000 **7** *3/4* **Ishetoo**14 2054 6-8-11 88 (b1) IanBrennan(5) 5 75
(Ollie Pears) *trckd ldrs: hdwy and cl up 2f out: rdn and edgd rt over 1f out: n.m.r and wknd ins fnl f* **12/1**
350- **8** *2 1/4* **Ursula (IRE)**187 7478 4-8-6 78 RichardKingscote 1 57
(J R Weymes) *in tch on outer: rdn along wl over 1f out: wknd appr fnl f* **33/1**
-055 **9** *shd* **Red Cape (FR)**12 2134 7-8-12 84 AndrewElliott 4 63
(Mrs R A Carr) *prom: rdn along 2f out: grad wknd* **8/1**
0-00 **10** *1 3/4* **Hamoody (USA)**14 2054 6-8-12 87 ow1 MichaelGeran(3) 8 60
(D Nicholls) *chsd ldrs: rdn along 2f out: sn wknd* **9/1**
0-16 **11** *8* **Sunrise Safari (IRE)**13 2100 7-9-0 86 (v) PaulHanagan 9 34+
(R A Fahey) *in tch: rdn along 2f out: wkng whn n.m.r appr fnl f: sn eased* **6/1**3
00-1 **12** *3* **Bond City (IRE)**42 1332 8-9-1 87 PJMcDonald 7 25+
(G R Oldroyd) *prom: rdn along over 2f out: sn edgd rt and wknd over 1f out* **18/1**
2040 **D** *14* **Onceaponatime (IRE)**22 1826 5-8-4 76 oh4 PaulQuinn 10 —
(M D Squance) *a in rr: bhd fnl 2f: fin 14th, disq: (prohibited substance)* **14/1**

1m 14.69s (0.09) **Going Correction** 0.0s/f (Good) 13 Ran SP% **122.6**
Speed ratings (Par 107): **103,102,100,99,96 94,93,90,89,87 76,72,54**
Tote Swingers: 1&2 £18.60, 1&3 £23.00, 2&3 £26.50 CSF £67.01 CT £1163.71 TOTE £6.30: £2.20, £4.70, £9.90; EX 86.00.
Owner G B Bedford **Bred** Patrick J Monahan **Trained** Scarcroft, W Yorks

FOCUS
There was a lively market for this decent sprint handicap. The field gradually drifted towards the stands' rail and the winner is getting closer to his old form.

NOTEBOOK
Damika(IRE) landed a gamble when cashing in on a lenient mark in a 6f Thirsk handicap 12 days earlier. The money arrived for him again and he defied a 4lb higher mark with a bit in hand. He will be hit with another rise for this success but the versatile 7-y-o was rated 106 at his peak in 2008, and should continue to be a force in 6f/7f handicaps. (op 7-1 tchd 15-2)
Noodles Blue Boy ran a big race back at 6f in a bid to follow up his fast finishing win off 6lb lower in a 5f Beverley handicap last time. He has a record of 212122 at this track since last June. (op 10-1)
Hotham moved smoothly for a long way down the centre of the track but couldn't find the decisive kick needed to challenge the front pair. He remains a bit high in the weights after three wins and a few near-misses in the second half of last season but there was quite a bit to like about this revived effort. (op 16-1)
Master Rooney(IRE) had not fired in two runs this season but he gave it a fair shot to land a gamble under a forcing ride against the stands' rail in this contest. (op 7-1)
Leonid Glow, a drifter on course, ran a solid enough race and would have finished a bit closer if not checked approaching the two furlong pole. (op 7-2)
Mullglen posted a personal best with cheekpieces applied when winning over 5f at Thirsk last time but the combination of a 4lb rise and step up to a stiff 6f blunted his powers. (tchd 14-1)
Sunrise Safari(IRE) was stopped in his tracks at a crucial stage and wasn't given a hard time after that. He was reported to have lost a shoe. (op 8-1)
Bond City(IRE) Official explanation: jockey said gelding hung right-handed

2466 PARKLANDS GOLF COURSE H'CAP 1m 3y(S)
9:15 (9:15) (Class 4) (0-85,83) 3-Y-O £4,415 (£1,321; £660; £330; £164) Stalls Centre

Form RPR
31-0 **1** **Tres Coronas (IRE)**15 2033 3-9-1 80 (b) GrahamGibbons 6 85
(T D Barron) *mde all: sn clr: 8 l ahd at 1/2-way: rdn and qcknd over 2f out: drvn ins fnl f: hld on gamely towards* **5/2**1
0 **2** *hd* **Ejteyaaz**14 2058 3-9-3 82 PaulHanagan 4 86
(R A Fahey) *hld up in rr: hdwy 2f out: rdn over 1f out: str run ins fnl f: jst hld* **14/1**
03-1 **3** *1/2* **Miss Mittagong (USA)**20 1882 3-9-4 83 RichardKingscote 3 86
(R M Beckett) *trckd ldng pair: hdwy to chse wnr over 2f out: rdn wl over 1f out: drvn ins fnl f: ch tl nt qckn towards fin* **11/4**2
3-61 **4** *3/4* **Brannagh (USA)**17 1959 3-8-12 77 (t) TomEaves 5 78
(J Noseda) *chsd ldrs: rdn along 3f out: drvn wl over 1f out: kpt on wl ins fnl f* **9/2**
22-2 **5** *38* **Huntingfortreasure**19 1927 3-9-0 79 PhillipMakin 2 —
(M Dods) *hld up towards rr: effrt 3f out: sn rdn along and btn: eased over 1f out* **4/1**3
26-1 **6** *19* **Battlemaiden (IRE)**31 1571 3-9-1 80 JoeFanning 1 —
(M Johnston) *chsd wnr: rdn along 3f out: sn wknd and bhd whn eased over 1f out* **9/2**

1m 42.34s (-1.06) **Going Correction** 0.0s/f (Good) 6 Ran SP% **118.3**
Speed ratings (Par 101): **104,103,103,102,64 45**
Tote Swingers: 1&2 £8.20, 1&3 £2.80, 2&3 £21.60 CSF £36.92 TOTE £3.80: £1.80, £5.50; EX 40.20 Place 6: £56.37 Place 5: £47.31.
Owner J Cringan & D Pryde **Bred** Denis McDonnell **Trained** Maunby, N Yorks

FOCUS
A fascinating handicap featuring four last-time-out winners. The pace was strong and there was an exciting finish in which the most exposed runner in the field just prevailed. The form is pretty sound.
Huntingfortreasure Official explanation: jockey said gelding never travelled
Battlemaiden(IRE) Official explanation: trainer had no explanation for the poor form shown
T/Plt: £110.90 to a £1 stake. Pool: £72,744.51- 478.76 winning tickets. T/Qpdt: £115.60 to a £1 stake. Pool:£4,862.12 - 31.10 winning tickets. JR

2251 SANDOWN (R-H)
Thursday, May 27

OFFICIAL GOING: Good to firm (good in places; sprint 8.6, round 8.9)
Wind: Light, half against Weather: Fine but cloudy

2467 BLUESQ.COM ON YOUR IPHONE H'CAP 1m 2f 7y
6:05 (6:07) (Class 4) (0-85,82) 4-Y-0+ £4,533 (£1,348; £674; £336) Stalls High

Form RPR
55-5 **1** **Jo'Burg (USA)**14 2044 6-8-11 75 RyanMoore 11 88
(Lady Herries) *s.s and lft abt 6 l: latched on to bk of field after 2f: brought to wd outside and gd prog fr 2f out: sustained effrt to ld last 150yds: urged along and styd on wl* **4/1**1
6-05 **2** *1/2* **Resurge (IRE)**19 1907 5-8-13 77 FergusSweeney 8 89
(W S Kittow) *t.k.h: trckd ldng pair: effrt gng wl 2f out: led jst over 1f out: hdd last 150yds: styd on but hld* **11/2**2
0-06 **3** *3 1/2* **Uncle Fred**21 1846 5-9-2 80 JimCrowley 7 85
(P R Chamings) *trckd ldng trio: effrt over 2f out: led briefly over 1f out: outpcd fnl f* **22/1**
50-6 **4** *1/2* **Dubai Crest**24 1780 4-9-3 81 JimmyFortune 12 87+
(Mrs A J Perrett) *trckd ldng quartet on inner: looking for room fr 3f out: cl up but nowhere to go 2f out: tried for run over 1f out and hmpd: styd on fnl f* **8/1**
-024 **5** *3/4* **Laudatory**21 1837 4-9-4 82 AdamKirby 10 85
(W R Swinburn) *hld up in midfield disputing 6th: rdn over 2f out: sme prog over 1f out but nt threatening ldrs: kpt on* **8/1**
-336 **6** *1 3/4* **Mannlichen**15 2031 4-8-13 77 (b1) FrankieDettori 5 76
(M Johnston) *led after 1f: narrowly hdd over 3f out: led again 2f out to over 1f out: wknd fnl f* **13/2**3
560- **7** *2* **Admiral Dundas (IRE)**215 7014 5-8-12 76 RichardHughes 9 71
(K C Bailey) *hld up in last pair: detached over 2f out: rdn and kpt on fr over 1f out: no ch* **16/1**
3010 **8** *hd* **Waahej**29 1631 4-8-2 73 LauraPike(7) 1 68
(P W Hiatt) *hld up in 10th: rdn and effrt on outer 3f out: limited prog 2f out: no hdwy over 1f out* **25/1**
0-13 **9** *2* **Addwaitya**6 2284 5-9-3 81 IanMongan 2 72
(Mrs L J Mongan) *pushed along in rr early: prog to dispute 6th on outer after 4f: drvn 3f out: no real prog 2f out: wknd fnl f* **16/1**
1150 **10** *6* **Franco Is My Name**24 1780 4-9-4 82 DaneO'Neill 4 61
(P R Hedger) *hld up in 9th: rdn and effrt on outer wl over 2f out: no prog wl over 1f out: wknd rapidly* **16/1**
4631 **11** *1* **Make Amends (IRE)**13 2080 5-8-8 72 JimmyQuinn 3 49
(R J Hodges) *hld up in midfield disputing 6th: rdn over 2f out: wknd rapidly over 1f out* **12/1**

22-0 **12** *1 ½* **Rumble Of Thunder (IRE)**[14] 2044 4-9-3 **81** .... JamieSpencer 6 55
(D W P Arbuthnot) *t.k.h: led 1f: led again narrowly over 3f out to 2f out: wknd rapidly* **17/2**

2m 8.14s (-2.36) **Going Correction** -0.10s/f (Good) **12** Ran SP% **115.0**
Speed ratings (Par 105): **105,104,101,101,100 99,97,97,96,91 90,89**
toteswingers: 1&2 £7.10, 1&3 £13.60, 2&3 £33.00 CSF £23.99 CT £426.81 TOTE £3.80: £1.10, £3.00, £8.20; EX 31.90.
Owner Seymour Bloodstock (uk) Ltd **Bred** Tim Cooper **Trained** Patching, W Sussex

FOCUS
A competitive-looking handicap. It didn't look strong run, but compared favourably with the later Group 3 and the form is taken at face value. Jo'Burg showed his best form since he was a 2yo.
Dubai Crest ◆ Official explanation: jockey said gelding was denied a clear run
Rumble Of Thunder(IRE) Official explanation: jockey said gelding ran too free and hung both ways

2468 £66 OF FREE BETS AT BLUESQ.COM NATIONAL STKS (LISTED RACE) 5f 6y
6:35 (6:37) (Class 1) 2-Y-O

£15,327 (£5,810; £2,907; £1,449; £726; £364) **Stalls** High

Form RPR
1 **1** **Dinkum Diamond (IRE)**[14] 2048 2-9-0 0 .... DaneO'Neill 1 99+
(H Candy) *trckd ldng pair: pushed along and prog to ld 1f out: rdn out and styd on wl* **9/4**[2]

21 **2** *1 ¼* **Chilworth Lad**[19] 1901 2-9-0 0 .... RyanMoore 3 95
(M R Channon) *s.i.s: in tch in 5th: pushed along 1/2-way: prog on outer over 1f out to dispute 2nd last 150yds: styd on but no real imp on wnr* **6/1**[3]

11 **3** *hd* **Cape To Rio (IRE)**[10] 2177 2-9-0 0 .... RichardHughes 4 94
(R Hannon) *settled in 4th: pushed along 2f out: styd on to dispute 2nd last 150yds: no real imp on wnr* **11/8**[1]

2121 **4** *3 ¼* **Scarlet Rocks (IRE)**[3] 2397 2-8-9 0 .... JimmyQuinn 2 77
(P D Evans) *racd keenly: led to 1f out: wknd* **14/1**

32 **5** *1* **Foghorn Leghorn**[14] 2048 2-9-0 0 .... JimmyFortune 5 78
(P W Chapple-Hyam) *trckd ldr: chal and upsides over 1f out gng wl: wknd fnl f* **16/1**

1 **6** *2* **Nasharra (IRE)**[10] 2171 2-9-0 0 .... JamieSpencer 7 71
(K A Ryan) *hld up in last: shkn up over 1f out: hanging and no rspnse* **8/1**

61.88 secs (0.28) **Going Correction** +0.10s/f (Good) **6** Ran SP% **110.8**
Speed ratings (Par 101): **101,99,98,93,91 88**
toteswingers: 1&2 £3.20, 1&3 £1.10, 2&3 £2.50 CSF £15.39 TOTE £2.60: £1.40, £2.50; EX 16.60.
Owner Eight Star Syndicate **Bred** Ms H W Topping **Trained** Kingston Warren, Oxon

FOCUS
This is often a decent race, though you have to go back to Russian Valour in 2003 to find the last winner who went on to follow up at Royal Ascot. This looked one of the weaker recent renewals but the winner was quite impressive.

NOTEBOOK
Dinkum Diamond(IRE) proved too good. Tidy winner of what is looking to be a decent Salisbury maiden on debut, showing a nice change of gear, he was always going nicely in behind the leaders and, having been asked for his effort inside the final 2f, he stayed on strongly to get on top inside the final furlong. It wasn't a performance that screamed Royal Ascot winner, but he will take his chance, as he is entitled to, with the Norfolk Stakes the aim. (op 10-3 tchd 7-2 in places)
Chilworth Lad did really well to get second considering he was slowly away, keeping on in a manner to suggest he will relish an extra furlong. He responded really well to pressure inside the final 2f and will presumably be Ascot-bound as well. (op 8-1)
Cape To Rio(IRE), bidding to emulate last year's winning stablemate Monsieur Chevalier, who had also won at Folkestone and Windsor, didn't win as his 1-4 odds entitled him to last time, and it was no surprise to see him lose his unbeaten record here. Racing on the inside of the winner early, he couldn't quicken when initially asked for his effort and, for all that he did stay on inside the final furlong, the winner was edging away from him again as they crossed the line. It's thought 6f will suit better, but he may bypass Ascot in favour of Glorious Goodwood. (op Evens)
Scarlet Rocks(IRE), already having her eighth start of the season, was 1l behind Cape To Rio at Windsor, and won at that same venue earlier in the week. There are reasons for believing she didn't run up to her best, though, as she was keen in front and had nothing left for the finish. (op 12-1 tchd 11-1)
Foghorn Leghorn, runner-up to the winner at Salisbury, doesn't have much in the way of scope and he emptied inside the final furlong. (op 14-1 tchd 20-1)
Nasharra(IRE), winner of a four-runner race at Leicester on debut, would have wanted to be up with the pace, but wasn't the best away and then didn't look comfy under pressure when trying to close. (op 9-1 tchd 11-1)

2469 BLUE SQUARE HENRY II STKS (GROUP 2) 2m 78y
7:10 (7:13) (Class 1) 4-Y-O+

£56,770 (£21,520; £10,770; £5,370; £2,690; £1,350) **Stalls** Centre

Form RPR
1-00 **1** **Akmal**[29] 1615 4-9-0 106 .... RichardHills 6 111
(J L Dunlop) *mde all: pushed along 3f out: hrd pressed and drvn ent fnl f: plld out more last 100yds* **4/1**[2]

45-1 **2** *1 ½* **Saptapadi (IRE)**[40] 1380 4-9-0 100 .... RyanMoore 4 109+
(Sir Michael Stoute) *uns rdr and cantered off on way to post: hld up in 6th: prog over 2f out: wnt 2nd over 1f out: chal and upsides ent fnl f: nt qckn and hld last 100yds* **6/1**[3]

121- **3** *1 ¾* **Darley Sun (IRE)**[222] 6851 4-9-0 109 .... FrankieDettori 8 107
(Saeed Bin Suroor) *trckd wnr: shkn up wl over 2f out: no imp and lost 2nd over 1f out: one pce* **2/1**[1]

0431 **4** *½* **Illustrious Blue**[29] 1615 7-9-2 108 .... JimCrowley 10 106
(W J Knight) *stdd s: t.k.h: hld up: last to over 6f out: rdn on outer over 2f out: no prog tl styd on jst over 1f out: clsng on 3rd nr fin* **7/1**

0024 **5** *¾* **Montaff**[29] 1615 4-9-0 102 .... RichardHughes 3 106
(M R Channon) *hld up in 7th: rdn over 2f out: kpt1 on fr over 1f out: n.d* **14/1**

/000 **6** *1* **Balkan Knight**[12] 2116 10-9-2 100 .... JimmyFortune 5 104?
(D R C Elsworth) *dwlt: hld up in 8th: dropped to last over 6f out: effrt and pushed along over 2f out: modest prog over 1f out: one pce after* **28/1**

243/ **7** *1 ¼* **Eradicate (IRE)**[19] 5114 6-9-2 104 .... JamieSpencer 9 103
(N J Henderson) *mostly trckd ldng pair to 2f out: grad fdd fnl f* **10/1**

10-5 **8** *½* **Furmigadelagiusta**[60] 1031 6-9-2 107 .... JimmyQuinn 1 102
(R A Fahey) *trckd ldrs in 5th: rdn over 2f out: steadily wknd fr over 1f out* **33/1**

-412 **9** *10* **Sabotage (UAE)**[12] 2116 4-9-0 110 .... TedDurcan 7 90
(Saeed Bin Suroor) *trckd ldng trio to 2f out: wknd tamely and eased* **13/2**

3m 37.92s (-0.78) **Going Correction** -0.10s/f (Good)
WFA 4 from 6yo+ 2lb **9** Ran SP% **115.6**
Speed ratings (Par 115): **97,96,95,95,94 94,93,93,88**
toteswingers: 1&2 £6.60, 1&3 £2.00, 2&3 £3.20 CSF £28.29 TOTE £6.80: £1.70, £2.40, £1.40; EX 40.80 Trifecta £296.80 Pool: £4,752.99 - 11.85 winning units..
Owner Hamdan Al Maktoum **Bred** Shadwell Estate Company Limited **Trained** Arundel, W Sussex

FOCUS
A really good renewal of this Group 2 contest, despite the late defection of likely favourite Opinion Poll, who would have found this ground too fast. Mr Dinos (2003) and Papineau (2004) went on to Gold Cup glory having taken this, and there was more than one contender to emerge here for Ascot's staying showpiece. The pace was a stop-start one, the excellent Richard Hills having his wicked way with them on the front-running Akmal. There is a bit of doubt over the bare form but the first two are rated to personal bests and the third was close to his best.

NOTEBOOK
Akmal, who was a prolific-winning 3-y-o, was given an excellent front-running ride by Richard Hills and found plenty when strongly challenged inside the final furlong to get off the mark for the season. It was obvious beforehand that he may be allowed an easy time of it on the front, which certainly wasn't the case when he pulled hard having been restrained at Ascot last time, and having stacked the field up before the home turn, he kicked again 3f out and gave the impression he was only doing enough, as he readily pulled out more when needed in the final 75 yards. It's unlikely things will fall so kindly at Ascot, and he will be faced with an extra 4f, but certainly gives the impression he will stay, and it would be no surprise were this likeable sort to make the frame. (op 5-1 tchd 11-2)
Saptapadi(IRE), who got rid of Ryan Moore and went for a little canter on the way to post, came into this as a complete unknown, but showed himself more than up to the level. Easy winner of a Doncaster maiden at 2-7 on his reappearance, he had twice shown fair form in defeat in Derby trials at three, and the fact his trainer was willing to put this brother to the stables smart stayer Patkai in this looked significant. He showed a good change of pace to come and challenge, and looked the winner with the momentum behind him, but had no answer when Akmal pulled out extra close home. This effort suggests he can make into a high-class stayer, though this year's Gold Cup may come a bit too soon. (op 9-2)
Darley Sun(IRE) made a highly satisfactory debut for Godolphin. Runner-up in the Doncaster Cup on his only previous try at Group level, he was very much expected to improve for this outing and simply lacked the finishing speed of the front pair. Considering how well he progressed with racing at three (started off by winning off just 69), it's reasonable to expect him to get better as the season progresses, and the extra 4f of the Gold Cup will be right up his street, so Dettori could have a tough decision in choosing between this one and Kite Wood, who made a wining reappearance in France at the weekend. (op 5-2)
Illustrious Blue, who won the Sagaro Stakes at Ascot contested by Akmal, deserves plenty of credit considering he was held up right at the back in a race that wouldn't have been run to suit. Throw in the fact he was conceding 2lb to those in front of him and he is perfectly entitled to go to Ascot. (op 11-2 tchd 8-1)
Montaff, another from the Ascot race, again ran well without suggesting he is quite up to winning a Group 2. He hasn't actually won since his maiden as a 2-y-o, and connections may well want to put him in a conditions race at some point. (op 20-1)
Balkan Knight, runner-up in this in both 2007 and 2008, ran about as well as could have been expected and will stand more of a chance back down in grade. (op 40-1 tchd 50-1 in places)
Eradicate(IRE), winner of the Swinton over hurdles at Haydock earlier in the month, had never previously run beyond 1m4f and his stamina wasn't up to it. (op 11-1 tchd 12-1)
Furmigadelagiusta had it to prove in this grade, especially on ground that would have been plenty quick enough, and he slowly faded. (op 28-1)
Sabotage(UAE), who had run so well when second at Newbury and was expected to be suited by the longer trip, was the one to disappoint. Looking at the way he dropped out, it was probable something was amiss. Official explanation: trainer had no explanation for the poor form shown (tchd 11-2)

2470 BLUE SQUARE BRIGADIER GERARD STKS (GROUP 3) 1m 2f 7y
7:45 (7:47) (Class 1) 4-Y-O+

£36,900 (£13,988; £7,000; £3,490; £1,748; £877) **Stalls** High

Form RPR
6-40 **1** **Stotsfold**[21] 1832 7-9-0 111 .... AdamKirby 8 118
(W R Swinburn) *hld up in last trio: prog fr 2f out to ld jst over 1f out: drvn and styd on wl* **7/1**[3]

56-2 **2** *nk* **Tazeez (USA)**[27] 1664 6-9-0 113 .... RichardHills 6 117
(J H M Gosden) *led: wound it up fr over 2f out: rdn and hdd jst over 1f out: styd on to press wnr but a jst hld* **9/1**

42-1 **3** *1 ¾* **Glass Harmonium (IRE)**[33] 1532 4-9-3 114 .... RyanMoore 2 116+
(Sir Michael Stoute) *hld up last: rdn over 2f out: prog on outer over 1f out: styd on to take 3rd last 100yds: nt gng pce to threaten* **13/8**[1]

112- **4** *1 ¼* **Prince Siegfried (FR)**[208] 7188 4-9-0 114 .... TedDurcan 9 113+
(Saeed Bin Suroor) *trckd ldng pair: rdn 2f out: cl up whn nt clr run briefly 1f out: one pce after* **8/1**

1-46 **5** *4 ½* **Steele Tango (USA)**[33] 1532 5-9-3 112 .... DaneO'Neill 3 105
(R A Teal) *hld up in last trio: effrt on outer over 2f out: no prog and btn over 1f out: fdd* **25/1**

11-5 **6** *¾* **Lady Jane Digby**[13] 2071 5-8-11 106 .... GregFairley 7 97
(M Johnston) *trckd ldng trio: rdn 3f out: sn struggling: grad fdd* **16/1**

31-2 **7** *½* **Peligroso (FR)**[19] 1911 4-9-0 109 .... FrankieDettori 5 99
(Saeed Bin Suroor) *chsd ldr: rdn over 2f out: lost 2nd and wknd quite qckly fr over 1f out* **17/2**

50-1 **8** *21* **Sri Putra**[42] 1328 4-9-3 111 .... PhilipRobinson 1 60
(M A Jarvis) *trckd ldng trio on outer: rdn over 2f out: wknd rapidly sn after: t.o* **7/2**[2]

2m 5.73s (-4.77) **Going Correction** -0.10s/f (Good) **8** Ran SP% **114.2**
Speed ratings (Par 113): **115,114,113,112,108 108,107,90**
toteswingers: 1&2 £12.40, 1&3 £3.90, 2&3 £8.60 CSF £66.87 TOTE £8.20: £2.50, £2.90, £1.80; EX 89.00 Trifecta £237.70 Pool: £616.95 - 1.92 winning units..
Owner P W Harris **Bred** Pendley Farm **Trained** Aldbury, Herts

FOCUS
This wouldn't have been the strongest running of what is traditionally an informative Group 3 contest, and the pace wasn't the best. The solid Stotsfold was close to his best with Tazeez rated to last year's Ascot form and Glass Harmonium a shade off his reappearance win.

NOTEBOOK
Stotsfold, last year's third who ran no sort of race after the ground had gone against him at Chester latest, held major claims if able to repeat the sort of form shown when third in last season's Arlington Million, and having been brought with a well-timed challenge, he gradually wore down the front-running Tazeez. A stiff 1m2f suits him best and he will again be campaigned internationally. (op 8-1)
Tazeez(USA), who wasn't at all suited by Lingfield when runner-up on the Polytrack on his reappearance, showed on several occasions last season that he is well up to this level, and Richard Hills gave him an excellent ride, but the pair weren't able to repel Stotsfold in the final strides. He's likely to have another crack at the Prince Of Wales's Stakes. (tchd 17-2)
Glass Harmonium(IRE) had much expected of him, having made a winning reappearance over C&D, but he wasn't the best away, having appeared to anticipate the start, and then found himself with too much ground to make up having been held up last and caught behind runners for the best part of as furlong as his rivals were engaging top gear. That said, once seeing daylight his response was gradual rather than immediate, and as has been the impression given by the son of Verglas on more than one occasion, he looks ready for 1m4f, with slightly slower ground also likely to help. He was penalised, but has work to do if he is to develop into a genuine Group 1 performer. (op 11-8 tchd 7-4)

Prince Siegfried(FR), the joint-highest on official ratings, progressed well towards the end of last season and this effort suggests he has gone on again from three to four. Though not getting the clearest of runs, it didn't affect his finishing position, and he may well be placed to win at this level, possibly abroad. Official explanation: jockey said gelding was denied a clear run (op 10-1 tchd 11-1)
Steele Tango(USA) ran about as well as could have been expected, again finishing well behind Glass Harmonium. (op 33-1 tchd 22-1)
Lady Jane Digby finds this trip too short and can expect to find much more suitable tasks as the season progresses. (tchd 14-1)
Peligroso(FR) ran well against a most progressive sort in a conditions race at Lingfield latest, but this ground was plenty quick enough for him and he failed to run his race. (op 11-1)
Sri Putra's reappearance win hadn't been working out, but he was still entitled to run well, so the fact he dropped out so tamely strongly suggests that something was amiss. It later emerged he had got very worked up in the stables before the race, so it's probably safe to give him another chance. Official explanation: trainer's rep said colt got upset in stables before race (op 4-1)

2471 BRITAIN'S GOT TALENT BINGO AT MECCABINGO.COM HERON STKS (LISTED RACE) 1m 14y

8:20 (8:22) (Class 1) 3-Y-O

£22,708 (£8,608; £4,308; £2,148; £1,076; £540) **Stalls** High

Form RPR

1-1 **1** **Fallen Idol**[34] 1497 3-8-12 98 ... WilliamBuick 2 107+
(J H M Gosden) *dwlt: in last trio tl shkn up and effrt on outer 2f out: cl u.p to take 3rd 1f out: drvn and styd on to ld post* **6/4**[1]

42-1 **2** *hd* **The Rectifier (USA)**[37] 1442 3-8-12 82 ... MickyFenton 5 106
(Stef Higgins) *sn led at mod pce: kicked on over 2f out: hrd pressed fnl f: hdd last stride* **28/1**

10 **3** *hd* **Aldovrandi (IRE)**[11] 2159 3-8-12 102 ... MartinDwyer 4 106
(M Botti) *hld up in 6th: prog to go 2nd over 1f out: str chal fnl f: jst hld nr fin and lost 2nd* **8/1**[3]

5-10 **4** *1 ¾* **Lord Zenith**[26] 1699 3-9-3 102 ... JimmyFortune 6 107+
(A M Balding) *trckd ldng pair: rdn and nt qckn wl over 1f out: kpt on same pce fnl f* **11/2**[2]

1120 **5** *nk* **Greyfriarschorista**[26] 1699 3-8-12 99 ... GregFairley 8 101+
(M Johnston) *trckd ldng trio: rdn whn pce lifted 2f out: hanging and nt qckn over 1f out: one pce after* **11/1**

041- **6** *1 ¼* **Big Audio (IRE)**[279] 5214 3-9-3 105 ... (v[1]) FrankieDettori 1 103
(Saeed Bin Suroor) *sn trckd ldr: rdn whn pce lifted 2f out: lost 2nd and nt qckn over 1f out: fdd* **11/1**

41-2 **7** *3 ¾* **Zaahy (USA)**[47] 1221 3-8-12 100 ... RyanMoore 7 90
(P W Chapple-Hyam) *hld up in last trio: shkn up 2f out: no prog and btn over 1f out* **17/2**

33-1 **8** *1 ½* **Cumulus Nimbus**[21] 1846 3-8-12 91 ... RichardHughes 9 86
(R Hannon) *taken down early and walked to post: stdd s: hld up in last: pushed along 2f out: no prog over 1f out: eased* **18/1**

16-1 **9** *12* **No Hubris (USA)**[34] 1500 3-8-12 102 ... JamieSpencer 3 59
(P F I Cole) *trckd ldng quartet: rdn 2f out: wknd rapidly over 1f out* **8/1**[3]

1m 42.6s (-0.70) **Going Correction** -0.10s/f (Good) **9** Ran SP% **113.5**
Speed ratings (Par 107): **99,98,98,96,96 95,91,90,78**
toteswingers: 1&2 £8.90, 1&3 £5.70, 2&3 £26.40 CSF £50.21 TOTE £2.30: £1.20, £5.40, £2.60; EX 57.20.
Owner Normandie Stud Ltd **Bred** Normandie Stud Ltd **Trained** Newmarket, Suffolk

FOCUS
A muddling Listed contest run in a modest time. There is a doubt over the apparent improvement from the runner-up and at face value the winner did not need to improve. The third and fourth are rated to their marks.

NOTEBOOK
Fallen Idol, who until recently held a Group 1 St James's Palace Stakes entry, made the step up from handicaps, and although only winning narrowly, he did well to win at all. Not the best away (apparently got his head caught briefly as the stalls opened), he was then held up in rear off a steady gallop, and considering it was only his third start, it said a lot about his ability that he was able to get up. Although only beating an 82-rated rival, that one may have been underrated and had the run of the race, so it shouldn't be held against him. Gosden expects him to improve further, with 1m2f likely to be within range at some point. He will head to a 1m Group 3 at Chantilly next month. (tchd 13-8 and 7-4 in places)
The Rectifier(USA), who is held in the highest regard by his trainer, had only won a Folkestone maiden, but he showed himself to be useful with this effort, just failing to hold on under a well-judged ride by Micky Fenton. His handicap rating is going to suffer badly as a result, however, and it will be interesting whether connections opt to stick to this level or run him in the Britannia at Royal Ascot. (op 25-1)
Aldovrandi(IRE), who only beat one home in the French Guineas, had earlier won at Kempton and he travelled like a decent horse, but couldn't quicken well enough close home. This is about his level for the time being. (op 9-1)
Lord Zenith, who was far from disgraced in the 2,000 Guineas, would have preferred a stronger pace and wasn't helped by the 5lb penalty. (op 6-1 tchd 5-1)
Greyfriarschorista, well beaten in the 2,000 Guineas, didn't get the best of trips, but was hanging under pressure and couldn't go on inside the final furlong. (op 14-1 tchd 10-1)
Big Audio(IRE), last year's Chesham winner, wearing a first-time visor on this debut for Godolphin, looked in need of the run, fading inside the final furlong under his penalty. (op 12-1 tchd 9-1)
Zaahy(USA), beaten by Lord Zenith at Lingfield last month, was beaten much further by that rival despite a 5lb swing at the weights. (op 8-1 tchd 9-1)
Cumulus Nimbus, walked to post early, was very slow leaving the stalls and found this a lot tougher than the race he won at Goodwood on his reappearance. (op 12-1 tchd 20-1)
No Hubris(USA), who has always been thought a bit of, had won narrowly on his reappearance and was expected to have come on for the run, but he stopped very quickly and something was presumably amiss. (op 9-1)

2472 BLUE SQUARE SUPPORTING MARIE CURIE WHITSUN CUP H'CAP 1m 14y

8:50 (8:55) (Class 3) (0-95,95) 4-Y-O+

£9,346 (£2,799; £1,399; £700; £349; £175) **Stalls** High

Form RPR

20-4 **1** **Flora Trevelyan**[19] 1899 4-8-10 87 ... TedDurcan 4 104+
(W R Swinburn) *t.k.h: trckd ldng pair: pushed along and prog to ld over 1f out: sn clr: in n.d fnl f: eased last 75yds* **10/3**[1]

11-0 **2** *5* **Ithinkbest**[26] 1697 4-8-9 86 ... RyanMoore 7 91
(Sir Michael Stoute) *settled in 7th: rdn over 2f out: prog u.p wl over 1f out: won battle for 2nd nr fin* **13/2**

-230 **3** *nk* **Dunn'o (IRE)**[20] 1857 5-9-2 93 ... PhilipRobinson 5 97
(C G Cox) *racd freely: led at str pce: hdd and outpcd over 1f out: lost 2nd nr fin* **11/2**[3]

10-4 **4** *2 ¼* **Invisible Man**[12] 2124 4-9-4 95 ... FrankieDettori 10 94
(Saeed Bin Suroor) *trckd ldng pair: rdn and nt qckn 2f out and lost pl: kpt on again fnl f* **9/1**

0-05 **5** *shd* **Kavachi (IRE)**[21] 1846 7-8-6 83 ... FergusSweeney 3 82
(G L Moore) *hld up disputing 8th: drvn wl over 2f out: styd on u.p over 1f out: nrst fin* **12/1**

20-0 **6** *½* **Woodcote Place**[24] 1767 7-8-10 87 ... JimCrowley 1 85+
(P R Chamings) *s.i.s: hld up disputing 8th: gng wl whn effrt on outer 3f out: drvn 2f out to chse ldng pair briefly: wknd fnl f* **25/1**

0-05 **7** *2 ¾* **Docofthebay (IRE)**[14] 2057 6-9-1 92 ... JimmyFortune 12 83
(J A Glover) *trckd ldrs in 6th: rdn and no prog over 2f out: limited hdwy over 1f out: no threat* **9/2**[2]

2-26 **8** *¾* **Chapter And Verse (IRE)**[33] 1533 4-8-7 84 ... AndreaAtzeni 6 74
(Mike Murphy) *hld up in last pair: drvn wl over 2f out: limited prog over 1f out: nvr a factor* **25/1**

2000 **9** *3 ¼* **Benandonner (USA)**[40] 1383 7-8-10 87 ... MartinDwyer 2 69
(Mike Murphy) *pressed ldr to 2f out: wknd rapidly* **33/1**

4100 **10** *6* **Arachnophobia (IRE)**[24] 1767 4-8-8 85 ... WilliamBuick 11 53
(Pat Eddery) *dropped to last pair after 3f: struggling after: no ch fnl 3f* **33/1**

450- **11** *1 ½* **Ballinteni**[189] 6812 8-8-10 87 ... DaneO'Neill 9 52
(N P Littmoden) *chsd ldng quartet: u.p 3f out: sn lost pl* **66/1**

1m 40.84s (-2.46) **Going Correction** -0.10s/f (Good) **11** Ran SP% **102.7**
Speed ratings (Par 107): **108,103,102,100,100 99,97,96,93,87 85**
toteswingers: 1&2 £4.20, 1&3 £2.80, 2&3 £7.40 CSF £17.39 CT £71.68 TOTE £3.70: £1.50, £2.40, £2.20; EX 15.30 Place 6: £18.32 Place 5: £8.48.
Owner P W Harris **Bred** Pendley Farm **Trained** Aldbury, Herts

FOCUS
A decent handicap, run at a fast pace. Solid form, with the winner a big improver and the second rated to form.

NOTEBOOK
Flora Trevelyan won in the style of a filly destined for better things. Unlucky not to finish closer on her reappearance at Ascot, she had no trouble getting a clear run this time, and gradually increased her lead having gone to the front over 1f out. Top handicaps, or more likely pattern races, will now have to come under consideration, and she can be expected to gain black type at some point if this win is anything to go by. (op 3-1 tchd 11-4)
Ithinkbest, who made no show on his reappearance at Newmarket, was able to race off 2lb lower this time and he came with a steady challenge, just winning the battle for second. On this evidence a stiffer test is required, and it's possible we have still to see the best of him. (op 7-1)
Dunn'o(IRE), 1lb higher than when winning this last year, set a good gallop, but raced freely. It says a lot that he only just managed to lose second. (op 6-1)
Invisible Man, a bit disappointing on his debut for the yard at Newmarket, again ran as though this mark may be a little beyond him. (op 7-1 tchd 10-1)
Kavachi(IRE), third a year ago, needs a decent gallop, which he got, but he still got going all too late. He is nearing a return to top form, and will be of interest for a decent handicap at York next month, a race he won a year ago. (op 16-1)
Woodcote Place's stamina didn't look up to it in a strongly-run race, but he could be of interest back at 7f.
Docofthebay(IRE) was disappointing considering the race was run to suit. (op 8-1)
T/Jkpt: Not won. T/Plt: £33.40 to a £1 stake. Pool: £135,984.80 - 2,969.11 winning tickets.
T/Qpdt: £3.10 to a £1 stake. Pool: £8,556.46 - 1,992.16 winning tickets. JN

2182 WOLVERHAMPTON (A.W) (L-H)

Thursday, May 27

OFFICIAL GOING: Standard
Wind: Fresh across Weather: Cloudy with sunny spells

2473 SPONSOR A RACE BY CALLING 01902 390000 MAIDEN FILLIES' STKS (DIV I) 1m 141y(P)

2:00 (2:04) (Class 5) 3-Y-O+ **£2,115** (£624; £312) **Stalls** Low

Form RPR

6- **1** **Naddwah**[227] 6730 3-8-12 0 ... NeilCallan 6 71
(M A Jarvis) *led: hdd over 7f out: chsd ldrs: led and hung rt fr over 1f out: rdn out* **9/4**[1]

2 *¾* **Librettista (AUS)** 4-9-8 0 ... KirstyMilczarek 11 69
(L M Cumani) *got loose prior to the s: led after 1f: rdn and hdd over 1f out: edgd rt: styd on* **33/1**

6 **3** *½* **Fancy Vivid (IRE)**[24] 1769 3-8-12 0 ... RichardMullen 7 69
(Sir Michael Stoute) *chsd ldrs: rdn over 1f out: r.o* **7/2**[2]

6 **4** *hd* **Sooraah**[41] 1355 3-8-12 0 ... LiamJones 2 68+
(W J Haggas) *hld up in tch: hmpd over 5f out: rdn over 1f out: r.o* **15/2**

2-2 **5** *½* **Wishformore (IRE)**[34] 1504 3-8-12 0 ... LukeMorris 12 67
(J S Moore) *chsd ldrs: pushed along 1/2-way: styd on u.p* **8/1**

2 **6** *nk* **Tartaria**[23] 1809 4-9-11 0 ... WilliamBuick 9 68
(D M Simcock) *hld up in tch: rdn over 2f out: styd on* **15/2**

7 *½* **Fork Lightning (USA)** 3-8-12 0 ... SebSanders 5 65
(Sir Mark Prescott) *s.i.s: hld up: hdwy over 2f out: swtchd lft fnl f: r.o: nt rch ldrs* **6/1**[3]

-30 **8** *1 ¾* **Heaven Forbid**[20] 1882 3-8-12 0 ... TedDurcan 10 61
(J R Fanshawe) *stdd s: hld up: hdwy over 1f out: r.o: nt trble ldrs* **11/1**

03 **9** *2 ¾* **Sula Two**[16] 2003 3-8-12 0 ... SteveDrowne 13 55
(R J Hodges) *ind ldr over 7f out tl rdn over 2f out: wknd fnl f* **40/1**

0 **10** *1* **Jasmin Rai**[33] 1538 3-8-12 0 ... ShaneKelly 1 53
(D Donovan) *hld up: rdn over 2f out: n.d* **100/1**

0- **11** *1* **Miss Chaumiere**[301] 4460 3-8-12 0 ... HayleyTurner 3 50
(M L W Bell) *mid-div: wknd over 1f out* **66/1**

12 *20* **Hannah Hawk** 3-8-12 0 ... TomMcLaughlin 8 4
(Lucinda Featherstone) *sn outpcd* **100/1**

1m 50.49s (-0.01) **Going Correction** -0.05s/f (Stan)
WFA 3 from 4yo 13lb **12** Ran SP% **119.1**
Speed ratings (Par 100): **98,97,96,96,96 96,95,94,91,90 89,72**
Tote Swingers: 1&2 £14.60, 1&3 £2.90, 2&3 £22.70 CSF £90.10 TOTE £3.10: £1.40, £4.50, £1.50; EX 81.30.
Owner Sheikh Ahmed Al Maktoum **Bred** Darley **Trained** Newmarket, Suffolk

FOCUS
They didn't go a great tempo in the first division of this fillies' maiden and it was an advantage to race close to the pace. The form seems to make a fair bit of sense through.

2474 WATCH LIVE SPORT AT LADBROKES.COM MAIDEN STKS 5f 20y(P)

2:30 (2:30) (Class 4) 2-Y-O **£4,857** (£1,445; £722; £360) **Stalls** Low

Form RPR

243 **1** **Yarooh (USA)**[12] 2130 2-8-12 0 ... NeilCallan 5 77+
(C E Brittain) *chsd ldr tl led ins fnl f: shkn up and r.o wl* **5/2**[2]

00 **2** *2 ½* **Henrys Air**[19] 1930 2-9-3 0 ... TomMcLaughlin 3 70
(D G Bridgwater) *led: rdn over 1f out: hdd and unable qck ins fnl f* **100/1**

3 1 3/4 **Black Moth (IRE)** 2-9-3 0 MartinDwyer 8 64
(B J Meehan) *chsd ldrs: pushed along 1/2-way: styd on same pce fnl f* 15/8[1]
4 3 1/2 **Finn's Rainbow** 2-9-3 0 SilvestreDeSousa 1 51+
(K A Ryan) *s.i.s: hld up: hdwy over 1f out: nvr nrr* 8/1
5 1 **Krypton Factor** 2-9-3 0 SebSanders 4 48
(Sir Mark Prescott) *pushed along and prom: rdn 1/2-way: wknd over 1f out* 11/2[3]
0 6 1 3/4 **Rum Sun N Sand (USA)**[17] 1972 2-8-12 0 HayleyTurner 2 36
(J W Hills) *mid-div: rdn over 1f out: nvr on terms* 16/1
7 shd **Golden Compass** 2-8-12 0 SaleemGolam 10 36+
(G C Bravery) *s.i.s: sn pushed along in rr: n.d* 13/2
8 2 1/2 **Lord Cornwall (IRE)** 2-9-3 0 SteveDrowne 7 32
(J R Gask) *mid-div: effrt 1/2-way: edgd lft and wknd over 1f out* 22/1
9 2 **Cinq Heavens (IRE)** 2-9-3 0 RichardKingscote 6 25
(Tom Dascombe) *mid-div: rdn over 3f out: sn wknd* 25/1

62.31 secs (0.01) **Going Correction** -0.05s/f (Stan) 9 Ran SP% **118.2**
Speed ratings (Par 95): **97,93,90,84,83 80,80,76,72**
Tote Swingers: 1&2 £9.80, 1&3 £2.00, 2&3 £26.60 CSF £242.27 TOTE £3.70: £2.50, £23.00, £1.02; EX 87.30.
Owner Mohammed Al Shafar **Bred** Sequel Thoroughbreds LLC **Trained** Newmarket, Suffolk

FOCUS
There were whispers for a couple of the newcomers in this maiden, but in the end experience won the day and the form behind the winner looks decidedly modest. The winner got back towards her debut form.

NOTEBOOK
Yarooh(USA) was a disappointing odds-on favourite at Thirsk last time, but still boasted the best form having previously run well in a couple of Newmarket maidens. She was always going well behind the leader and had little trouble in picking him off a furlong out, but this was a modest race and she looks one for nurseries later on. (op 9-4)
Henrys Air, well held in his first two starts, ran a blinder from the front at massive odds and only the winner was able to get past him. He may have been flattered, however, as he enjoyed the run of the race and it may not be wise to get too carried away.
Black Moth(IRE), a 55,000gns half-brother to four winners including the high-class Majestic Missile, was always in about the same place and plugged on under pressure over the last 2f. He did fare best of the newcomers, but is nothing special on this evidence. (op 9-4 tchd 3-1 and 7-4)
Finn's Rainbow, a 22,000gns colt out of a half-sister to Binary File and Hawksbill, stayed on from well off the pace up the inside rail but probably achieved little. Official explanation: jockey said colt was slowly away (op 12-1)
Krypton Factor, a 20,000gns half-brother to a couple of winning sprinters, was off the bridle from an early stage and needs more time. (op 6-1)
Golden Compass, out of a half-sister to a winning hurdler, was the subject of major market support earlier in the day, but she missed the break from the outside stall and was never seen with a chance. (op 6-1 tchd 5-1)

2475 BEST ODDS GUARANTEED AT LADBROKES.COM FILLIES' H'CAP 7f 32y(P)
3:00 (3:00) (Class 4) (0-85,85) 3-Y-O+ £5,180 (£1,541; £770; £384) Stalls High

Form RPR
0-20 1 **All The Nines (IRE)**[12] 2113 4-9-3 79 DeclanCannon(5) 4 87
(Mrs D J Sanderson) *sn pushed along to ld: rdn over 1f out: jst hld on* 20/1
-412 2 hd **Faithful One (IRE)**[10] 2170 3-8-12 80 TedDurcan 11 83+
(D R Lanigan) *hld up in tch: rdn over 2f out: r.o wl ins fnl f* 7/2[1]
110- 3 nk **Wasmi (IRE)**[230] 6643 3-8-9 77 NeilCallan 1 79
(C E Brittain) *chsd wnr: rdn and ev ch ins fnl f: r.o: b.b.v* 13/2
-423 4 1 **Night Trade (IRE)**[12] 2112 3-8-10 78 SilvestreDeSousa 8 77
(Mrs D J Sanderson) *chsd ldrs: rdn over 1f out: styd on* 9/2[2]
120- 5 3/4 **Midnight Fantasy**[226] 6765 4-9-4 75 SaleemGolam 2 76
(Rae Guest) *chsd ldrs: outpcd over 2f out: r.o ins fnl f* 12/1
2-1 6 shd **Mainstay**[27] 1654 4-9-12 83 WilliamBuick 12 84+
(J H M Gosden) *s.i.s: hld up: rdn and hung lft over 1f out: swtchd rt and r.o ins fnl f: nrst fin* 5/1[3]
00-4 7 1/2 **Suzie Quw**[31] 1588 4-8-13 73 MartinLane(3) 3 73
(J R Weymes) *prom: rdn over 2f out: styd on same pce ins fnl f* 16/1
1-13 8 1/2 **Diapason (IRE)**[128] 225 4-9-6 77 RichardKingscote 6 75
(Tom Dascombe) *hld up: rdn over 1f out: nt trble ldrs* 12/1
4-00 9 1 3/4 **Seradim**[19] 1899 4-10-0 85 (v[1]) HayleyTurner 10 79
(P F I Cole) *mid-div: lost pl 1/2-way: n.d after* 15/2
1110 10 nk **Catherines Call (IRE)**[12] 2120 3-8-9 77 ShaneKelly 7 66
(D Donovan) *hld up: rdn over 1f out: n.d* 14/1

1m 28.71s (-0.89) **Going Correction** -0.05s/f (Stan)
WFA 3 from 4yo+ 11lb 10 Ran SP% **114.9**
Speed ratings (Par 102): **103,102,102,101,100 100,99,99,97,96**
Tote Swingers: 1&2 £13.20, 1&3 £20.60, 2&3 £5.30 CSF £87.80 CT £529.18 TOTE £26.20: £6.50, £1.10, £2.40; EX 112.10.
Owner R J Budge **Bred** Deerpark Stud **Trained** Wiseton, Notts

FOCUS
This race continued the trend of the previous two races in that those that raced handily were at an advantage and nothing could get into it from off the pace. The winner is rated back to her best.
Wasmi(IRE) Official explanation: trainer's rep said filly bled from the nose

2476 BET AFTER THE OFF AT LADBROKES.COM H'CAP 2m 119y(P)
3:30 (3:30) (Class 5) (0-70,64) 4-Y-O+ £2,456 (£725; £362) Stalls Low

Form RPR
21 1 **If I Had Him (IRE)**[6] 2302 6-9-1 56 6ex TonyCulhane 4 71+
(George Baker) *chsd ldrs: pushed along over 6f out: rdn over 3f out: led and hung lft over 1f out: styd on dourly* 3/1[1]
02/3 2 3/4 **Ultimate Quest (IRE)**[16] 2014 5-9-2 57 SebSanders 13 71
(Sir Mark Prescott) *chsd ldr after 1f: led 4f out: rdn and hdd over 2f out: styd on gamely* 5/1[2]
053- 3 4 1/2 **Dee Cee Elle**[263] 4862 6-8-1 47 (p) KierenFox(5) 9 56
(D Burchell) *hld up: hdwy over 3f out: rdn over 1f out: no imp fnl f* 33/1
3314 4 3 **Broughtons Point**[21] 1849 4-8-13 56 JamieMackay 5 61
(W J Musson) *hld up: hdwy over 1f out: hung lft fnl f: nvr nr to chal* 8/1[3]
6121 5 2 3/4 **Bold Adventure**[37] 1459 6-9-6 61 TomQueally 3 63+
(W J Musson) *hld up: nt clr run 3f out: sn pushed along: styd on ins fnl f: nvr nr to chal* 5/1[2]
00/2 6 8 **Moon Star (GER)**[19] 1931 9-9-9 64 NeilCallan 12 56
(R Curtis) *hld up: hdwy 7f out: rdn and wknd over 1f out* 9/1
/523 7 4 1/2 **Pearl (IRE)**[24] 1768 6-8-8 49 (tp) HayleyTurner 8 36
(Mrs A M Thorpe) *prom: rdn over 4f out: wknd over 3f out* 9/1
10-1 8 3 1/2 **Picot De Say**[24] 1758 8-9-3 58 RichardThomas 10 41
(B J Llewellyn) *hld up: a in rr* 11/1
0-05 9 11 **Paddy Partridge**[9] 2214 4-8-12 55 (b[1]) RichardKingscote 2 24
(Tom Dascombe) *led: hdd 4f out: rdn and weakened 2 out: t.o* 25/1
0-63 10 1 3/4 **Lastroseofsummer (IRE)**[85] 777 4-9-3 60 DavidProbert 11 27
(Rae Guest) *s.i.s: hld up and a in rr: t.o* 8/1[3]
20/0 P **Snow's Ride**[22] 1828 10-9-5 60 RobertWinston 7 —
(M Herrington) *chsd ldrs: rdn and lost pl 7f out: sn bhd: t.o whn p.u over 4f out* 66/1

3m 37.44s (-4.36) **Going Correction** -0.05s/f (Stan)
WFA 4 from 5yo+ 2lb 11 Ran SP% **117.2**
Speed ratings (Par 103): **108,107,105,104,102 99,96,95,90,89** —
Tote Swingers: 1&2 £5.60, 1&3 £26.10, 2&3 £28.50 CSF £17.16 CT £413.01 TOTE £4.70: £2.20, £2.40, £7.10; EX 19.90.
Owner Sir Alex Ferguson **Bred** Mrs J Morrissey **Trained** Moreton Morrell, Warwicks

FOCUS
A modest staying handicap, run at a decent pace, and another race where those that raced prominently were favoured, with the first two home always up there. They finished clear and the form is rated fairly positively.
Bold Adventure Official explanation: jockey said gelding was denied a clear run

2477 WOLVERHAMPTON-RACECOURSE.CO.UK CLAIMING STKS 1m 141y(P)
4:00 (4:01) (Class 6) 3-Y-O+ £2,047 (£604; £302) Stalls Low

Form RPR
1-00 1 **Calahonda**[20] 1883 4-9-4 75 NeilCallan 8 75
(P W D'Arcy) *chsd ldrs: led over 1f out: rdn out* 15/2
3515 2 1/2 **Atacama Sunrise**[16] 2013 4-9-1 60 DavidProbert 10 71
(G Prodromou) *hld up: hdwy over 1f out: sn rdn: r.o* 16/1
2120 3 hd **Plush**[21] 1837 7-9-8 81 RossAtkinson(5) 5 83+
(Tom Dascombe) *s.i.s: hld up: hdwy over 1f out: rdr dropped whip 1f out: r.o* 3/1[2]
3-23 4 shd **Moody Tunes**[3] 2377 7-9-6 75 MartinLane(3) 3 78
(J R Weymes) *chsd ldrs: rdn and ev ch over 1f out: edgd rt ins fnl f: r.o* 5/1[3]
6004 5 1 **Flowing Cape (IRE)**[10] 2172 5-9-8 88 GeorgeBaker 4 75
(R Hollinshead) *hld up: nt clr run over 2f out: hdwy and hung lft over 1f out: sn rdn: r.o* 6/4[1]
2121 6 6 **Tous Les Deux**[24] 1815 7-9-8 68 EamonDehdashti(5) 2 66
(Dr J R J Naylor) *hld up: rdn over 2f out: hdwy over 1f out: styd on same pce fnl f* 16/1
0034 7 3/4 **Fifty Cents**[48] 1208 6-9-5 62 SteveDrowne 13 56
(M F Harris) *led over 6f out: rdn and hdd over 1f out: wknd fnl f* 25/1
060- 8 3 **Duke Of Normandy (IRE)**[195] 7369 4-9-7 48 JamieMackay 9 52
(B P J Baugh) *led: hdd over 6f out: chsd ldr: rdn over 2f out: wknd fnl f* 100/1
0000 9 nse **Machinate (USA)**[24] 1772 8-9-4 48 LiamJones 11 48
(W M Brisbourne) *chsd ldrs: rdn over 2f out: wknd fnl f* 80/1
3650 10 3/4 **Yorksters Prince (IRE)**[30] 1608 3-8-5 63 KierenFox(5) 7 52
(G Prodromou) *s.i.s: hld up: sme hdwy over 1f out: sn wknd* 33/1
4/0- 11 12 **Rebellious Spirit**[505] 79 7-9-9 77 JamesDoyle 6 24
(S Curran) *chsd ldrs: rdn over 2f out: wknd wl over 1f out* 16/1
/-00 12 3/4 **Longoria (IRE)**[47] 1241 5-9-4 69 TomMcLaughlin 12 17
(Lucinda Featherstone) *sn pushed along and a in rr: wknd over 2f out: fin lame* 50/1

1m 49.39s (-1.11) **Going Correction** -0.05s/f (Stan)
WFA 3 from 4yo+ 13lb 12 Ran SP% **122.1**
Speed ratings (Par 101): **102,101,101,101,100 95,94,91,91,91 80,79**
Tote Swingers: 1&2 £12.40, 1&3 £5.40, 2&3 £8.40 CSF £118.41 TOTE £7.90: £2.40, £5.40, £1.10; EX 102.00.
Owner Gongolphin & Racing **Bred** Eurostrait Ltd **Trained** Newmarket, Suffolk

FOCUS
A typical claimer with a wide range of abilities amongst the runners but a decent race of its type with five of the field officially rated 75 or above. The winner did not need to be at her best with the runner-up looking the best guide.
Flowing Cape(IRE) Official explanation: jockey said gelding was denied a clear run
Rebellious Spirit Official explanation: jockey said gelding stopped quickly
Longoria(IRE) Official explanation: vet said mare finished lame left-fore

2478 SPONSOR A RACE BY CALLING 01902 390000 MAIDEN FILLIES' STKS (DIV II) 1m 141y(P)
4:30 (4:31) (Class 5) 3-Y-O+ £2,115 (£624; £312) Stalls Low

Form RPR
0 1 **Titbit**[38] 1431 3-8-12 0 TomQueally 2 76+
(H R A Cecil) *hld up: hdwy over 1f out: r.o to ld nr fin: comf* 11/1
-6 2 1/2 **Frances Stuart (IRE)**[26] 1694 3-8-12 0 DavidProbert 11 71
(A M Balding) *a.p: chsd ldr over 5f out: rdn 2f out: lft in ld over 1f out: hdd nr fin* 9/1
3 1 1/4 **Almiranta** 3-8-12 0 SebSanders 7 68
(Sir Mark Prescott) *sn pushed along and prom: rdn over 2f out: styd on: fin lame* 18/1
0- 4 1 1/2 **Gwenllian (IRE)**[201] 7288 3-8-12 0 SaleemGolam 6 65+
(Ian Williams) *prom: nt clr run over 2f out: rdn over 1f out: r.o* 66/1
4 5 nk **Valeur**[24] 1766 3-8-12 0 RichardMullen 13 64
(Sir Michael Stoute) *prom: rdn over 1f out: no ex ins fnl f* 11/4[2]
00- 6 nse **Highland Jewel (IRE)**[227] 6730 3-8-12 0 LukeMorris 3 64
(C G Cox) *hld up: rdn over 2f out: r.o ins fnl f: nrst fin* 22/1
60- 7 1/2 **Quality Mover (USA)**[281] 5165 3-8-12 0 NickyMackay 9 63
(D M Simcock) *mid-div: rdn over 2f out: styd on ins fnl f: nt trble ldrs* 25/1
4- 8 3/4 **Chicane**[194] 7396 3-8-12 0 LiamJones 4 61
(W J Haggas) *mid-div: hdwy over 2f out: styd on same pce fnl f* 14/1
00 9 2 **Asterales**[29] 1620 3-8-12 0 JamieMackay 5 57
(W J Musson) *s.i.s: hld up: nvr on terms* 100/1
10 1 1/2 **Miss Flash Dancer** 4-9-11 0 FrankieMcDonald 10 55
(C C Bealby) *dwlt: hld up: sme hdwy over 2f out: wknd over 1f out* 100/1
56 11 1/2 **Eden Nights (USA)**[10] 2180 3-8-12 0 WilliamBuick 1 52+
(J H M Gosden) *hld up: shkn up over 2f out: hung rt 1f out: nvr nr to chal* 7/2[3]
12 8 **Daisy Dolittle** 3-8-12 0 TomMcLaughlin 8 34
(J R Holt) *chsd ldr 3f: remained handy: rdn over 2f out: wknd over 1f out* 100/1
63- R **Queen's Envoy**[210] 7135 3-8-12 0 KirstyMilczarek 12 —
(L M Cumani) *led tl swvd lft and crashed through rails jst over 1f out* 5/2[1]

1m 51.21s (0.71) **Going Correction** -0.05s/f (Stan)
WFA 3 from 4yo 13lb 13 Ran SP% **120.4**
Speed ratings (Par 100): **94,93,92,91,90 90,90,89,87,86 86,79,**—
Tote Swingers: 1&2 £17.80, 1&3 £17.80, 2&3 £15.00 CSF £102.97 TOTE £22.00: £5.80, £4.70, £2.10; EX 127.70.
Owner Bloomsbury Stud & Mrs Bruce Bossom **Bred** Penelope Bossom & Bloomsbury Stud **Trained** Newmarket, Suffolk

The Form Book, Raceform Ltd, Compton, RG20 6NL

FOCUS
The winning time was 0.72 seconds slower than the first division. Muddling form to this dramatic race but the winner was quite impressive.
Almiranta Official explanation: vet said filly finished lame left-fore

2479 PLAY POKER AT LADBROKES.COM H'CAP — 1m 1f 103y(P)
5:00 (5:01) (Class 3) (0-90,88) 3-Y-O **£7,569** (£2,265; £1,132; £566; £282) **Stalls** Low

Form | | | | RPR
20-5 **1** **Sea Lord (IRE)**[21] 1834 3-9-2 **86**........ RobertWinston 3 97
(M Johnston) *plld hrd: led after 1f: rdn and edgd rt wl over 1f out: styd on* **6/1**
-123 **2** 1 ¾ **Power Series (USA)**[25] 1730 3-9-4 **88**........ WilliamBuick 8 95+
(J H M Gosden) *hld up in tch: racd keenly: rdn and hung lft fnl f: styd on* **4/1**[2]
11-4 **3** 1 ½ **Nafura**[21] 1850 3-9-1 **85**........(v[1]) TedDurcan 4 89
(Saeed Bin Suroor) *a.p: chsd wnr 2f out: rdn and hung rt 1f out: styd on same pce ins fnl f* **5/1**[3]
201- **4** 3 ½ **Kings Bayonet**[244] 6254 3-8-13 **83**........ TomQueally 6 80+
(H R A Cecil) *trckd ldrs: plld hrd: rdn over 1f out: n.m.r and wknd ins fnl f* **4/1**[2]
41 **5** *hd* **Bakongo (IRE)**[33] 1538 3-8-9 **79**........ HayleyTurner 7 75
(M L W Bell) *hld up: hdwy over 2f out: rdn over 1f out: wknd ins fnl f* **10/3**[1]
2160 **6** 1 **Exceedthewildman**[12] 2117 3-8-11 **86**........(p) KierenFox[(5)] 2 80
(J S Moore) *hld up: rdn over 2f out: n.d* **12/1**
223- **7** 1 ¼ **Pytheas (USA)**[211] 7121 3-8-7 **77**........ DavidProbert 5 69
(M J Attwater) *led 1f: chsd ldr tl rdn 2f out: wknd fnl f* **14/1**

1m 59.65s (-2.05) **Going Correction** -0.05s/f (Stan) 7 Ran SP% **108.4**
Speed ratings (Par 103): **107,105,104,101,100 99,98**
Tote Swingers: 1&2 £3.70, 1&3 £3.00, 2&3 £4.10 CSF £26.86 CT £112.94 TOTE £9.10: £4.80, £5.10; EX 18.90.
Owner Sheikh Hamdan Bin Mohammed Al Maktoum **Bred** Darley **Trained** Middleham Moor, N Yorks

FOCUS
The best race on the card, but they only went a modest pace which caused a few to pull hard and the winner had a fairly easy lead. The form has been rated around the second and third but may not be totally reliable.

NOTEBOOK
Sea Lord(IRE), making his AW debut, was one of those who took a keen grip early, but being out in front was very much in his favour as things turned out. He hung away to his right off the final bend which meant that he came down the centre of the track in the home straight, but that is no bad thing here either and he kept on finding plenty. However, he doesn't seem to run two races alike and this form must have a question mark against it, so he may be one to take on next time. (op 8-1)
Power Series(USA), up another 1lb having shown good form so far this year and proven at this track, raced keenly early and was then off the bridle near the back of the field over 2f from home, but he finished well and this was another good effort from him under the circumstances. (op 9-2 tchd 5-1)
Nafura, a dual winner over a furlong shorter here last autumn, had a first-time visor replacing the cheekpieces and she travelled nicely behind the leaders against the inside rail, but once off the bridle she started to hang and was never doing enough. She looks held off a mark 11lb higher than her last win. (op 7-2)
Kings Bayonet, making his handicap debut and not seen since winning a 7f maiden here last September, pulled furiously in midfield and when an effort was asked for there was nothing there. This should at least have taken the freshness out of him. Official explanation: jockey said gelding ran too free (op 11-4)
Bakongo(IRE), making her handicap debut after winning a C&D fillies' maiden last month, tried to make an effort on the inside of the track after turning for home, but it came to little. She is better than this effort suggests and is still open to improvement. (op 7-2 tchd 3-1)
Exceedthewildman, a four-time winner on Polytrack during a busy winter, never landed a blow from off the pace and looks exposed now.
Pytheas(USA), placed in five of his six outings for Mark Johnston at two, was making his debut for his new yard after seven months off having been gelded in the meantime. He was another to race keenly up with the early pace and blew up passing the 2f pole. (op 20-1)

2480 BOOK EARLY FOR CHRISTMAS H'CAP — 1m 141y(P)
5:30 (5:33) (Class 6) (0-60,60) 3-Y-O **£2,047** (£604; £302) **Stalls** Low

Form | | | | RPR
600 **1** **True Pleasure (IRE)**[26] 1706 3-8-11 **53**........ TomQueally 13 57
(J D Bethell) *stdd and swtchd lft sn after s: bhd: stl last and plenty to do over 2f out: swtchd rt and hdwy over 1f out: r.o wl u.p to ld nr fin* **40/1**
06-0 **2** ½ **Dauntsey Park (IRE)**[17] 1977 3-8-10 **57**........ RossAtkinson[(5)] 12 60
(Miss Tor Sturgis) *hld up: hdwy over 1f out: rdn and r.o wl ins fnl f* **16/1**
4-05 **3** *nk* **Mini Max**[33] 1537 3-8-13 **55**........ HayleyTurner 4 57
(B W Duke) *led over 7f out: rdn clr over 1f out: hdd nr fin* **8/1**
50-0 **4** *nk* **Fire Raiser**[25] 1731 3-9-4 **60**........ DavidProbert 2 61
(A M Balding) *hld up in tch: rdn over 2f out: r.o* **9/2**[1]
5230 **5** 2 **Golden Ratio (IRE)**[16] 2005 3-9-4 **60**........(b) LukeMorris 9 57
(J R Gask) *hld up: hdwy over 2f out: rdn over 1f out: hung lft: r.o* **14/1**
-125 **6** 2 ¼ **Decency (IRE)**[9] 2200 3-9-4 **60**........ GeorgeBaker 11 52+
(E A L Dunlop) *led 1f: chsd ldrs: wnt 2nd over 2f out: rdn and edgd rt over 1f out: no ex ins fnl f* **11/2**[2]
0-45 **7** 3 **Lucky Diva**[17] 1959 3-9-3 **59**........ JamesDoyle 10 44
(S Kirk) *sn pushed along in rr: styd on fnl f: nvr nrr* **14/1**
006 **8** 3 **Togoaviking**[20] 1872 3-9-3 **59**........ LiamJones 3 37
(W J Haggas) *chsd ldrs: rdn over 2f out: wknd over 1f out* **8/1**
4-06 **9** 6 **Revoltinthedesert**[47] 1237 3-8-11 **53**........ NickyMackay 8 17
(M Botti) *hld up: sme hdwy wl over 2f out: wknd sn after* **20/1**
55-0 **10** 6 **Cosmic Orbit**[42] 1335 3-9-3 **59**........ TonyCulhane 1 9
(R Curtis) *bhd: pushed along over 3f out: nvr on terms* **14/1**
0 **11** ½ **Marjustar (IRE)**[36] 1477 3-8-8 **50**........ PatCosgrave 7 —
(J R Boyle) *mid-div: rdn over 2f out: wknd over 1f out* **6/1**[3]
005- **12** 1 ¾ **Mosqueta**[206] 7213 3-9-1 **60**........ MartinLane[(3)] 6 —
(P D Evans) *prom: hmpd over 3f out: wknd over 2f out* **8/1**
000 **13** 11 **Baxter (IRE)**[20] 1870 3-8-12 **54**........ SebSanders 5 —
(J W Hills) *sn chsng ldr: rdn 4f out: wknd over 2f out* **28/1**

1m 51.06s (0.56) **Going Correction** -0.05s/f (Stan) 13 Ran SP% **117.7**
Speed ratings (Par 97): **95,94,94,94,92 90,87,84,79,74 73,72,62**
Tote Swingers: 1&2 £52.40, 1&3 £43.90, 2&3 £41.20 CSF £568.52 CT £5736.49 TOTE £51.50: £14.40, £7.50, £1.90; EX 453.30 Place 6: £211.08 Place 5: £127.04 .
Owner T R Lock **Bred** Michael O'Mahony **Trained** Middleham Moor, N Yorks

FOCUS
A moderate handicap, but several of these were potential improvers after the three obligatory runs in maidens. However, the leaders may have done too much too soon as they fell in a heap late on and the front pair came from miles off the pace. The winning time was 0.57 seconds slower than the first division of the fillies' maiden. The form is sound if limited at face value but the way the race was run lends serious doubts.

T/Plt: £475.30 to a £1 stake. Pool: £61,862.71 - 95 winning units. T/Qpdt: £605.10 to a £1 stake. Pool: £4,007.25 - 4.90 winning units. CR

[2455] BRIGHTON (L-H)
Friday, May 28

OFFICIAL GOING: Good to firm (watered; 9.3)
Rail realignment increased distances by about 25yds.
Wind: modest, across Weather: sunny

2485 TOTESWINGER FLEXI BETTING H'CAP — 5f 59y
2:00 (2:00) (Class 5) (0-70,70) 3-Y-O+ **£2,978** (£886; £442; £221) **Stalls** Low

Form | | | | RPR
3012 **1** **Avrilo**[6] 2332 4-8-12 **56** oh3........ TomMcLaughlin 3 67
(M S Saunders) *t.k.h: w ldrs: rdn to ld wl over 1f out: r.o wl ins fnl f* **3/1**[1]
2004 **2** 1 **Lucky Leigh**[10] 2196 4-9-7 **65**........ SamHitchcott 7 72
(M R Channon) *in tch in midfield: rdn over 2f out: hdwy u.p over 1f out: wnt 2nd jst ins fnl f: sn pressing wnr: no ex and btn fnl 50yds* **12/1**
6012 **3** *nk* **Ask Jenny (IRE)**[4] 2396 8-8-9 **58**........ DeclanCannon[(5)] 8 64
(Patrick Morris) *stdd and dropped in after s: hld up in last pair: n.m.r briefly 2f out: hdwy u.p and edging lft over 1f out: kpt on ins fnl f* **11/2**
2503 **4** 1 ½ **Magical Speedfit (IRE)**[1] 2458 5-9-12 **70**........ SebSanders 4 71
(G G Margarson) *in tch in last trio: effrt and rdn to chse ldrs ent fnl f: nt qckn and no prog fnl 150yds* **7/2**[2]
5403 **5** 1 ½ **Boho Chic**[10] 2196 4-9-4 **62**........(p) JimmyQuinn 6 57
(George Baker) *chsd ldng trio: hdwy to chse wnr over 1f out tl jst ins fnl f: wknd fnl 100yds* **9/2**[3]
0006 **6** 3 **Simple Rhythm**[25] 1779 4-9-9 **70**........ MarcHalford[(3)] 5 54
(J Ryan) *w ldrs tl led 3f out: rdn and hdd wl over 1f out: wknd u.p jst over 1f out* **10/1**
0310 **7** 2 **Radiator Rooney (IRE)**[6] 2310 7-8-12 **56**........ StephenCraine 1 33
(Patrick Morris) *s.i.s: hld up in tch in rr: rdn and effrt on inner ent fnl 2f: no prog and btn ent fnl f* **8/1**
0000 **8** 7 **Blue Neptune**[7] 2291 3-8-4 **56**........ LukeMorris 2 8
(P D Evans) *led for 2f: rdn and wknd 2f out: wl bhd and eased ins fnl f* **50/1**

62.76 secs (0.46) **Going Correction** +0.175s/f (Good)
WFA 3 from 4yo+ 8lb 8 Ran SP% **110.6**
Speed ratings (Par 103): **103,101,100,98,96 91,88,76**
toteswingers:1&2:£6.60, 1&3:£2.80, 2&3:£6.90 CSF £36.71 CT £179.16 TOTE £4.60: £1.50, £3.90, £1.30; EX 28.30 Trifecta £104.00 Pool: £407.64 - 2.90 winning units..
Owner Paul Nicholas **Bred** D & S Horn **Trained** Green Ore, Somerset

FOCUS
A modest sprint handicap. The winner is getting his act together and is rated up 5lb.
Simple Rhythm Official explanation: trainer said filly was unsuited by the good to firm ground

2486 E B F TOTEPLACEPOT MAIDEN STKS — 5f 213y
2:30 (2:30) (Class 5) 2-Y-O **£3,154** (£944; £472; £236; £117) **Stalls** Low

Form | | | | RPR
1 **Cafe Elektric** 2-9-3 0........ SebSanders 3 85+
(Sir Mark Prescott) *chsd ldng pair: hdwy to join ldrs over 2f out: led ent fnl 2f: rdn over 1f out: styd on wl to assert ins fnl f* **6/5**[1]
2 1 **Afkar (IRE)** 2-9-3 0........ JimmyQuinn 6 82+
(C E Brittain) *in tch in last pair: hdwy to chse wnr 2f out: ev ch and rdn over 1f out: no ex and btn fnl 100yds* **9/4**[2]
54 **3** 14 **Sarandjam**[12] 2138 2-9-3 0........ SamHitchcott 5 40
(M R Channon) *w ldr tl 2f out: sn hung lft and outpcd by ldng pair: no ch fr over 1f out* **7/1**
0 **4** 1 ¾ **Joe Junior**[30] 1612 2-9-3 0........ DavidProbert 2 35
(Miss Gay Kelleway) *sn led: hdd and rdn ent fnl 2f: outpcd by ldng pair wl over 1f out: wl btn whn n.m.r on rail over 1f out* **13/2**[3]
0 **5** *nse* **Moorland Boy**[8] 2239 2-9-3 0........ FergusSweeney 4 35
(J A Osborne) *dwlt: t.k.h early: a in rr: rdn and outpcd by ldng pair wl over 1f out: no ch after* **14/1**

1m 11.15s (0.95) **Going Correction** +0.175s/f (Good) 5 Ran SP% **108.7**
Speed ratings (Par 93): **100,98,80,77,77**
CSF £3.99 TOTE £1.90: £1.30, £1.30; EX 4.30.
Owner Cheveley Park Stud **Bred** Cheveley Park Stud Ltd **Trained** Newmarket, Suffolk

FOCUS
No depth to this maiden but the front two, both newcomers from top yards, came miles clear and obviously have futures. Both are capable of improving on the bare form.

NOTEBOOK
Cafe Elektric ◆ is bred to make a 2-y-o being the first foal of dual winning 2-y-o Shanghai Lily and he justified strong market support to make a winning debut. He broke well but was soon being urged along and didn't look totally at ease on the track, although that may have been due to the very quick ground. Still, he was going best entering the final two furlongs and kept on well enough to readily hold off Afkar in the closing stages. (op 6-4 tchd 13-8 in a place)
Afkar(IRE) ◆, who looked a picture in the paddock, didn't break well and was always playing catch-up but he stuck to his task well and drew right away from the others. This experience won't have been lost on him and he'll soon be going one better for a yard with a decent crop of juveniles. (op 2-1)
Sarandjam set the form standard of those to have raced but he was 14 lengths behind the runner-up so was outclassed. Nurseries, probably over further, beckon for him now. (op 13-2 tchd 6-1 and 15-2)

2487 TOTEQUADPOT (S) STKS — 1m 1f 209y
3:05 (3:05) (Class 6) 3-5-Y-O **£1,942** (£578; £288; £144) **Stalls** High

Form | | | | RPR
30-1 **1** **Timocracy**[31] 1592 5-10-0 **76**........ SteveDrowne 4 73
(A B Haynes) *mde all: rdn over 2f out: hrd pressed and drvn ent fnl 2f: forged ahd ins fnl f: clr fnl 100yds: kpt on* **4/9**[1]
-405 **2** 1 ¾ **Bussell Along (IRE)**[18] 1976 4-9-3 **55**........(tp) SebSanders 5 58
(Stef Higgins) *stdd s: hld up in tch in last pair: hdwy 4f out: rdn and ev ch ent fnl 2f: edgd lft and no ex jst ins fnl f: hld on for 2nd nr fin* **8/1**[3]
6 **3** ½ **Seriy Tzarina**[71] 920 4-9-3 0........ FergusSweeney 3 57
(A G Newcombe) *in tch: pushed along and rn green wl over 2f out: outpcd and edgd lft wl over 1f out: swtchd rt jst ins fnl f: styd on wl fnl 100yds to go 3rd nr fin* **50/1**
-462 **4** ½ **Douchkette (FR)**[3] 2414 4-9-3 **57**........ LukeMorris 2 56
(John Berry) *t.k.h: chsd ldr for 2f: in tch after: rdn over 2f out: drvn and plugged on same pce fr over 1f out* **11/4**[2]
00-0 **5** *hd* **Lytton**[51] 1149 5-9-8 **58**........ StephenCraine 1 61
(R Ford) *stdd s: hld up in last pair: effrt on inner and rdn ent fnl 2f: chsd ldng pair wl over 1f out: drvn and btn jst ins fnl f: lost 2 pls wl ins fnl f* **33/1**

300 **6** *19* **Better Be Blue (IRE)**[24] [1795] 3-8-3 45 JimmyQuinn 6 31
(A W Carroll) *t.k.h: chsd ldr after 2f tl over 2f out: wknd qckly wl over 1f out: wl bhd and eased ins fnl f* **66/1**

2m 6.34s (2.74) **Going Correction** +0.175s/f (Good)
WFA 3 from 4yo+ 14lb **6** Ran SP% **113.4**
Speed ratings (Par 101): **96,94,94,93,93 78**
toteswingers:1&2:£1.40, 1&3:£4.70, 2&3:£6.10 CSF £5.13 TOTE £1.70: £1.30, £1.50; EX 4.40.There was no bid for the winner. Seriy Tzarina was claimed by Gay Kelleway for £5,000
Owner Ms J Loylert **Bred** Gainsborough Stud Management Ltd **Trained** Limpley Stoke, Bath

FOCUS
Desperately weak, even for this grade, and not form to be dwelling on. The winner made hard work of seeing off some dubious opposition.

2488 TOTEEXACTA FLEXI BETTING H'CAP 1m 1f 209y
3:40 (3:40) (Class 6) (0-60,60) 4-Y-O+ **£2,072** (£616; £308; £153) **Stalls** High

Form RPR

/0-3 **1** **Aestival**[7] [2303] 4-8-11 **53** SebSanders 9 72+
(Sir Mark Prescott) *mde all: rdn over 2f out: rn green wl over 1f out: styd on strly and clr 1f out: easily* **4/6**[1]

2114 **2** *6* **Four Kicks (IRE)**[5] [2360] 4-8-9 **56** KierenFox(5) 3 63
(J S Moore) *chsd ldng pair: rdn and effrt ent fnl 2f: outpcd by wnr over 1f out: 2nd and wl hld fnl f* **9/4**[2]

0000 **3** *2* **Bere Davis (FR)**[13] [2109] 5-9-0 **56** (p) PatCosgrave 2 59
(P D Evans) *chsd wnr: rdn and tried to chal jst over 2f out: outpcd by wnr over 1f out: 3rd and wl btn ins fnl f* **8/1**[3]

4405 **4** *¾* **Inquisitress**[10] [2198] 6-8-4 **46** NeilChalmers 5 48
(J J Bridger) *t.k.h early: hld up in tch: plld out and rdn wl over 1f out: no prog and wl hld fnl f* **25/1**

50-5 **5** *6* **Kashmina**[29] [1636] 5-9-1 **60** RussKennemore(3) 8 50
(Miss Sheena West) *hld up in tch: rdn and shortlived effrt over 2f out: wl btn fr wl over 1f out* **20/1**

-000 **6** *¾* **Shouldntbethere (IRE)**[31] [1592] 6-7-13 **46** oh1 AmyBaker(5) 7 34
(Mrs P N Dutfield) *heavily restrained s and slowly away: hld up in rr: clsd and in tch 1/2-way: rdn and btn over 2f out* **50/1**

R-00 **7** *99* **Willie Ever**[28] [663] 6-9-2 **58** (be) TomMcLaughlin 6 —
(D G Bridgwater) *s.i.s: veered rt and virtually ref to r sn after s: continued wl t.o* **100/1**

2m 5.67s (2.07) **Going Correction** +0.175s/f (Good) **7** Ran SP% **113.4**
Speed ratings (Par 101): **98,93,91,91,86 85,6**
toteswingers:1&2:£1.50, 1&3:£1.20, 2&3:£2.50 CSF £2.26 CT £4.59 TOTE £2.10: £1.20, £1.50; EX 3.10 Trifecta £12.70 Pool: £352.39 - 20.53 winning units..
Owner Lady Katharine Watts **Bred** Miss K Rausing **Trained** Newmarket, Suffolk

FOCUS
A weak handicap run only marginally quicker than the seller. The unexposed winner can do better still and the form is rated around the runner-up.

2489 TOTETRIFECTA FLEXI BETTING H'CAP 1m 3f 196y
4:15 (4:15) (Class 6) (0-55,62) 4-Y-O+ **£2,072** (£616; £308; £153) **Stalls** High

Form RPR

0360 **1** **Free Falling**[73] [898] 4-8-7 **45** (v) DavidProbert 8 53
(Miss Gay Kelleway) *mde all: clr fr 8f out: rdn ent fnl 2f: kpt plugging on and a holding runner-up fr over 1f out* **12/1**

02-3 **2** *1 ¾* **Dhania (IRE)**[5] [2361] 4-9-1 **53** SebSanders 7 58
(C Gordon) *chsd ldng pair tl wnt 2nd 4f out: rdn and unable qck ent fnl 2f: edgd lft u.p and one pce fr over 1f out* **11/4**[2]

3064 **3** *3 ¾* **Rosy Dawn**[10] [2201] 5-8-7 **45** NeilChalmers 5 44
(J J Bridger) *chsd wnr tl 4f out: rdn and one pce ent fnl 2f: sltly hmpd and swtchd rt over 1f out: no imp fnl f* **16/1**

5552 **4** *3* **Stanley Rigby**[29] [1635] 4-8-10 **48** JackMitchell 6 42
(C F Wall) *bustled along leaving stalls: hld up in tch towards rr: prog into midfield 4f out: rdn ent fnl 2f: sn hung lft and no prog: wnt modest 4th ins fnl f* **6/4**[1]

2020 **5** *2 ¾* **Turner's Touch**[29] [1635] 8-8-10 **48** (b) AmirQuinn 4 38
(G L Moore) *dwlt: sn in tch in midfield: rdn and no hdwy over 2f out: wl btn over 1f out* **16/1**

6066 **6** *10* **Jordan's Light (USA)**[3] [2361] 7-9-1 **53** (v) PatCosgrave 10 27
(P D Evans) *dropped in towards rr after s: hld up towards rr: rdn and shortlived effrt wl over 2f out: no hdwy and wl btn fnl 2f* **9/1**

000 **7** *15* **Behest**[20] [1932] 5-8-12 **50** TomMcLaughlin 9 —
(D G Bridgwater) *s.i.s: a in last pair: rdn and toiling bdly over 3f out: sn lost tch: t.o fr wl over 1f out* **33/1**

0026 **8** *40* **Jiggalong**[7] [2303] 4-8-12 **50** PaulDoe 2 —
(Jim Best) *stdd s: hld up in tch: rdn and dropped to rr over 4f out: lost tch rapidly over 3f out: virtually p.u fnl 2f: t.o* **5/1**[3]

2m 34.42s (1.72) **Going Correction** +0.175s/f (Good) **8** Ran SP% **115.7**
Speed ratings (Par 101): **101,99,97,95,93 86,76,50**
toteswingers:1&2:£7.30, 1&3:£14.30, 2&3:£6.10 CSF £45.77 CT £542.86 TOTE £16.00: £4.20, £2.50, £5.40; EX 68.90 Trifecta £373.50 Part won. Pool: £504.72 - 0.52 winning units..
Owner A C Entertainment Technologies Ltd **Bred** Fittocks Stud Ltd **Trained** Exning, Suffolk

FOCUS
The front two were both long-standing maidens coming into this and, like the previous race, the winner was allowed to dominate from the outset, so very weak handicap form. The winner is rated somewhere near her old level.
Jiggalong Official explanation: jockey said filly ran flat

2490 BET TOTEPOOL AT TOTESPORT.COM H'CAP 6f 209y
4:50 (4:50) (Class 6) (0-65,71) 4-Y-O+ **£2,201** (£655; £327; £163) **Stalls** Low

Form RPR

0-05 **1** **Buxton**[11] [2187] 6-9-4 **65** (t) SebSanders 2 76+
(R Ingram) *stdd s: hld up in tch in rr: clsd to trck rivals gng wl ent fnl f: swtchd rt and rdn jst ins fnl f: qcknd and led ins fnl f: sn clr: readily* **5/1**[3]

6013 **2** *2 ½* **Yourgolftravel Com**[10] [2198] 5-8-11 **58** StephenCraine 8 63
(M Wigham) *stdd s: hld up in tch towards rr: swtchd to outer and effrt ent fnl 2f: rdn to ld wl over 1f out: hld hd high u.p and edging lft over 1f out: hdd and nt pce of wnr ins fnl f* **9/4**[1]

5041 **3** *1* **Yakama (IRE)**[7] [2299] 5-8-10 **57** 6ex (v) DavidProbert 3 59
(Mrs C A Dunnett) *stdd s: hld up in tch: hdwy and waiting for clr run over 1f out: squeezed through and ev ch 1f out: nt pce of wnr ins fnl f: kpt on* **7/1**

5066 **4** *3 ½* **Carmenero (GER)**[20] [1914] 7-9-4 **65** FergusSweeney 1 58
(C R Dore) *t.k.h early: stdd after s: hld up in tch towards rr: rdn and effrt on inner wl over 1f out: drvn and ev ch 1f out: wknd fnl 150yds* **12/1**

1206 **5** *¾* **Unlimited**[25] [1762] 8-9-0 **61** JimmyQuinn 5 52
(A W Carroll) *plld hrd: stdd s but sn chsng ldrs: ev ch and rdn 2f out: stl ev ch ent fnl f: wknd qckly jst ins fnl f* **10/1**

0442 **6** *¾* **Bollywood Style**[8] [2246] 5-8-11 **58** SteveDrowne 6 47
(J R Best) *chsd ldr: rdn over 2f out: stl ev ch ent fnl f: wknd qckly jst ins fnl f* **9/2**[2]

1211 **7** *2 ¾* **Scruffy Skip (IRE)**[8] [2257] 5-9-10 **71** 6ex (p) TomMcLaughlin 7 52
(Mrs C A Dunnett) *led: rdn ent fnl 2f: hdd wl over 1f out: stl ev ch ent fnl f: wknd qckly 1f out* **6/1**

20 **8** *nk* **Mackintosh (IRE)**[52] [1142] 4-8-0 **52** DeclanCannon(5) 4 32
(Patrick Morris) *chsd ldrs: rdn and effrt towards inner jst over 2f out: wkng whn n.m.r jst over 1f out: wl btn ins fnl f* **20/1**

1m 24.17s (1.07) **Going Correction** +0.175s/f (Good) **8** Ran SP% **113.9**
Speed ratings (Par 101): **100,97,96,92,91 90,87,86**
toteswingers:1&2:£5.40, 1&3:£8.20, 2&3:£5.10 CSF £16.55 CT £78.11 TOTE £8.50: £2.60, £1.90, £2.90; EX 21.40 Trifecta £113.20 Pool: £492.89 - 3.22 winning units..
Owner Peter J Burton **Bred** Sharon Ingram **Trained** Epsom, Surrey

FOCUS
Quite a competitive little handicap for the grade but it was won in fine style by the gambled-on Buxton, who returned to form with a bang.
Unlimited Official explanation: jockey said gelding ran too free

2491 BET TOTEPOOL ON 0800 221 221 H'CAP 5f 213y
5:25 (5:25) (Class 5) (0-75,73) 3-Y-O **£2,719** (£809; £404; £202) **Stalls** Low

Form RPR

6-00 **1** **Universal Circus**[13] [2120] 3-9-4 **73** SamHitchcott 3 76
(M R Channon) *taken down early: hld up in last pair: rdn 2f out: nt clr run and swtchd rt over 1f out: hrd drvn and r.o wl ins fnl f to ld towards fin* **8/1**

0060 **2** *nk* **Ramamara (IRE)**[6] [2342] 3-9-0 **69** JamesDoyle 2 71
(P D Evans) *dwlt: sn rcvrd and chsng ldrs: swtchd ins and effrt over 2f out: drvn ahd ent fnl f: kpt on u.p tl hdd and no ex towards fin* **10/1**

-514 **3** *2* **Super Yellow**[3] [2416] 3-9-0 **69** FergusSweeney 4 65
(J A Osborne) *led: rdn ent fnl 2f: hrd drvn and hdd ent fnl f: no ex and btn fnl 75yds* **6/4**[1]

3454 **4** *1 ¼* **Barlaman (USA)**[70] [933] 3-8-12 **67** (t) SebSanders 6 59
(C E Brittain) *hld up in tch in last pair: effrt on outer wl over 1f out: edging lft and btn fnl 150yds* **9/2**[2]

0-05 **5** *1 ¼* **Ice Cool Lady (IRE)**[20] [1934] 3-8-13 **73** (v) JohnFahy(5) 7 61
(W R Swinburn) *chsd ldrs: rdn and effrt 2f out: wknd u.p ent fnl f* **9/2**[2]

5221 **6** *1 ½* **Tom Folan**[15] [2046] 3-8-8 **66** (p) RussKennemore(3) 5 49
(Andrew Reid) *racd keenly: pressed ldr: rdn ent fnl 2f: stl ev ch tl wknd jst ins fnl f* **11/2**[3]

1m 11.18s (0.98) **Going Correction** +0.175s/f (Good) **6** Ran SP% **112.0**
Speed ratings (Par 99): **100,99,96,95,93 91**
toteswingers:1&2:£8.70, 1&3:£3.30, 2&3:£3.90 CSF £76.74 TOTE £12.30: £6.70, £6.30; EX 101.90 Place 6 £11.31; Place 5 £4.83.
Owner Anne & Steve Fisher **Bred** Wansdyke Farms Limited **Trained** West Ilsley, Berks

FOCUS
A decent gallop to this weakish handicap. The favourite disappointed and it's doubtful if the first two recaptured their old form.
Tom Folan Official explanation: jockey said filly ran too free
T/Plt: £14.30 to a £1 stake. Pool:£57,654.89 - 2,940.44 winning tickets T/Qpdt: £7.00 to a £1 stake. Pool:£3,797.34 - 399.74 winning tickets SP

2323 HAYDOCK (L-H)
Friday, May 28

OFFICIAL GOING: Good to firm (good in places; watered; 7.4)
Rail realignment increased distances on round course by 16yards.
Wind: light 1/2 against Weather: fine

2492 TURFTV.CO.UK H'CAP (FOR LADY AMATEUR RIDERS) 1m 2f 95y
6:40 (6:42) (Class 5) (0-75,72) 4-Y-O+ **£2,966** (£912; £456) **Stalls** High

Form RPR

10-2 **1** **The Last Alzao (IRE)**[8] [2243] 4-10-2 **72** MrsVFahey(5) 5 82
(R A Fahey) *trckd ldrs: led over 2f out: edgd lft over 1f out: hld on towards fin* **15/8**[2]

0650 **2** *nk* **Rub Of The Relic (IRE)**[4] [2377] 5-9-0 **58** oh1 (be) MissHDukes(7) 9 67
(P T Midgley) *led: hdd over 2f out: swtchd rt over 1f out: rallied: no ex towards fin* **25/1**

0532 **3** *½* **Hawaana (IRE)**[8] [2240] 5-10-7 **72** MissEJJones 3 80
(Miss Gay Kelleway) *hld up in rr: hdwy over 3f out: upsides over 1f out: styd on wl ins fnl f* **13/8**[1]

34-6 **4** *7* **Simonside**[39] [1427] 7-9-10 **68** MissFrancesHarper(7) 8 63
(B Ellison) *stmbld sn after s: hld up towards rr: drvn and edgd lft over 3f out: swtchd rt and kpt on fnl f* **16/1**

-402 **5** *shd* **Weetfromthechaff**[13] [2131] 5-9-2 **58** oh1 (t) MissAngelaBarnes(5) 4 53
(M A Barnes) *t.k.h in rr: hdwy over 3f out: edgd lft and one pce fnl 2f* **16/1**

201- **6** *5* **Edas**[212] [7113] 8-9-13 **69** MissHCuthbert(5) 2 55
(T A K Cuthbert) *t.k.h: sn trcking ldrs: edgd rt and wknd over 1f out* **10/1**[3]

610- **7** *½* **Masterofceremonies**[272] [5438] 7-9-6 **64** MissALMurphy(7) 1 49
(W M Brisbourne) *swvd lft s: effrt over 3f out: wknd over 2f out* **18/1**

200- **8** *½* **Peaceful Rule (USA)**[270] [5520] 4-9-10 **68** MissJWalker(7) 7 52
(D Nicholls) *racd wd: chsd ldrs: lost pl after 3f: nvr a factor after* **25/1**

00-0 **9** *3* **Mississippian (IRE)**[11] [2182] 6-9-0 **58** (e[1]) MissDLenge(7) 6 36
(Mrs D J Sanderson) *t.k.h: trckd ldrs: wnt 2nd after 2f: chal over 5f out: wknd over 2f out* **22/1**

2m 18.23s (2.23) **Going Correction** +0.225s/f (Good) **9** Ran SP% **111.0**
Speed ratings (Par 103): **88,87,87,81,81 77,77,76,74**
toteswingers:1&2:£10.20, 1&3:£1.30, 2&3:£7.30 CSF £49.65 CT £85.61 TOTE £2.20: £1.70, £7.50, £1.10; EX 46.30.
Owner G Devlin **Bred** G Devlin **Trained** Musley Bank, N Yorks

FOCUS
Rail alignment out of the back straight meant that the distance from the 1m start to the winning post was actually 1m 51yards. There was 4mm of rain overnight added to the watered turf and the winning rider in the first described the ground as 'beautiful'. Times suggested the ground was riding close to good. They went a reasonable pace in this ordinary handicap for lady amateurs. Three pulled clear to contest a tight finish, including a pair who were ahead of the handicapper, and although the runner-up appeared to run above himself the form has a fairly sound look to it. The race has been rated at face value.

2493 E B F MHA LIGHTING MAIDEN STKS 6f
7:10 (7:14) (Class 5) 2-Y-O **£3,432** (£1,021; £510; £254) **Stalls** High

Form RPR

3 **1** **Rerouted (USA)**[15] [2059] 2-9-3 **0** MichaelHills 9 82+
(B W Hills) *trckd ldrs: led over 2f out: hung lft over 1f out: rdn and r.o: kpt on wl towards fin* **2/5**[1]

2 ¾ **Dortmund** 2-9-3 0 TedDurcan 7 80+
(Mahmood Al Zarooni) *dwlt: hld up in midfield: effrt on wd outside over 2f out: chsd wnr over 1f out: hung lft: no ex wl ins fnl f* **10/1**[3]

3 2 ¼ **Polar Kite (IRE)** 2-9-3 0 TonyHamilton 10 73+
(R A Fahey) *gave problems in stalls: s.i.s: sn trcking ldrs: styd on wl to take 3rd last 100yds: will improve* **25/1**

4 2 ¾ **Capaill Liath (IRE)** 2-9-3 0 PaulEddery 5 65+
(B W Hills) *chsd ldrs: kpt on same pce fnl 2f* **50/1**

5 nk **Arabian Star (IRE)** 2-9-3 0 TadhgO'Shea 11 64
(M R Channon) *dwlt: sn chsng ldrs: kpt on same pce fnl 2f* **20/1**

6 6 **Newzflash** 2-9-3 0 GrahamGibbons 6 46
(T D Barron) *led: hung lft and hdd over 2f out: wknd over 1f out* **40/1**

0 7 1 ¼ **Velvet Underground (IRE)**[20] 1901 2-9-3 0 MartinDwyer 4 42
(B J Meehan) *chsd ldrs: wknd over 1f out* **7/1**[2]

6 8 3 **Captain Loui (IRE)**[12] 2138 2-9-3 0 StevieDonohoe 8 33
(K A Ryan) *chsd ldrs: lost pl over 1f out* **50/1**

9 4 ½ **Mediplomat** 2-9-3 0 WilliamBuick 1 20
(M Botti) *swvd lft s: in rr: sme hdwy over 2f out: sn wknd* **20/1**

10 1 **Bold Bidder** 2-8-12 0 RoystonFfrench 3 12+
(K A Ryan) *s.s: reminders after s: a in rr: bhd whn swvd rt over 2f out* **33/1**

50 11 23 **Angle Knight (USA)**[22] 1845 2-9-3 0 KierenFallon 2 —
(B J Meehan) *rrd s: sn drvn along and outpcd: bhd whn hmpd over 2f out: virtually p.u* **40/1**

1m 15.02s (1.52) **Going Correction** +0.15s/f (Good) 11 Ran SP% **118.1**
Speed ratings (Par 93): **95,94,91,87,86 78,77,73,67,65 35**
toteswingers:1&2:£2.90, 1&3:£6.00, 2&3:£9.30 CSF £4.14 TOTE £1.50: £1.10, £1.70, £6.50; EX 5.40.
Owner K Abdulla **Bred** Juddmonte Farms Inc **Trained** Lambourn, Berks

FOCUS
In all likelihood this was a decent maiden. The winner brought good form into the race and won well enough. The stalls were placed on the stands' side but the action took place down the centre of the track.

NOTEBOOK
Rerouted(USA) was sent off a well-supported favourite after his third to Elzaam in what looked a warm race at York on his debut, and he looked the part in the preliminaries. He did not have things all his own way in the race and needed to work to see off the runner-up but was nicely on top at the line despite holding his head at a slightly awkward angle. Likely to have learnt more from this second run, he looks a useful colt but may not turn out as good as Spinning Queen, who won this race for the Hills yard five years ago before progressing to Group 1 glory. (op 8-15 tchd 8-13 in places)
Dortmund was noticeably green, but he showed definite promise and an ordinary maiden is his for the taking. Following a slightly slow start he improved nicely once angled to the outside of the field before drifting back across in the latter stages, always just held by the winner. Out of an unraced half-sister to Godolphin's Arc winner Marienbard, he will have no problem with another furlong. (tchd 9-1 and 12-1)
Polar Kite(IRE) ◆ is a brother to the useful Icemancometh and a half-brother to a couple of other winners. After becoming a littled stirred up in the stalls he made a very pleasing debut, displaying a nice attitude as he ran on for third inside the last. Provided he is not aimed too high he is another who should not be long in winning. (tchd 20-1 and 28-1)
Capaill Liath(IRE), the winner's stablemate, was green on the way to the start but travelled quite nicely in the race until he was outpaced by the principals when things began to get serious. Out of a half-sister to Middle Park winner Fard, he is a half-brother to three winners including this year's speedy handicapper Masamah. There should be better to come from him. (tchd 40-1)
Arabian Star(IRE) looks to have ability too, and although he is by Green Desert the dam won over 1m4f and he is likely to appreciate a bit further than this. (op 16-1)
Newzflash, a half-brother to winning miler Dolphin Rock, faded after showing pace. (op 33-1)
Velvet Underground(IRE), who had the benefit of a previous race, weakened after chasing the pace. (op 9-1)
Bold Bidder, the only filly on show, was green both before the race and during it and was always outpaced at the back. She is bred to do better, being a half-brother to the useful Right Answer out of a half-sister to sprinting ace Mind Games, but may need more time. (op 50-1)

2494 TURFTV H'CAP 5f
7:40 (7:40) (Class 4) (0-85,81) 3-Y-O **£5,180** (£1,541; £770; £384) **Stalls** High

Form RPR

-011 1 **Hoof It**[14] 2099 3-9-4 **81** GrahamGibbons 3 99+
(M W Easterby) *mde all: shkn up 1f out: wnt clr: v easily* **1/2**[1]

314- 2 4 ½ **Durham Express (IRE)**[223] 6841 3-8-11 **74** TonyHamilton 4 71
(M Dods) *trckd ldrs: drvn over 2f out: wnt 2nd 1f out: no ch w wnr* **17/2**

1245 3 1 ½ **Texas Queen**[25] 1750 3-8-10 **73** TedDurcan 1 65
(M R Channon) *hld up in rr: swtchd rt after s: hdwy and swtchd outside over 1f out: kpt on same pce* **6/1**[3]

3323 4 1 ¼ **Maldon Prom (IRE)**[15] 2046 3-8-11 **74** (b[1]) ShaneKelly 2 61
(C A Dwyer) *chsd wnr: rdn 2f out and carried hd high: wknd 1f out* **5/1**[2]

61.58 secs (0.58) **Going Correction** +0.15s/f (Good) 4 Ran SP% **108.1**
Speed ratings (Par 101): **101,93,91,89**
CSF £5.22 TOTE £1.50; EX 5.10.
Owner A Chandler & L Westwood **Bred** Bond Thoroughbred Corporation **Trained** Sheriff Hutton, N Yorks

FOCUS
This had an uncompetitive look about it beforehand and that impression was borne out in the race as the progressive Hoof It won easily. The form is rated around the second.

2495 HALLIWELL JONES BMW "JOY" H'CAP 1m 6f
8:10 (8:10) (Class 5) (0-75,74) 4-Y-O+ **£2,914** (£867; £433; £216) **Stalls** Low

Form RPR

1-22 1 **Kazbow (IRE)**[17] 2014 4-9-6 **73** KierenFallon 1 82
(L M Cumani) *trckd ldr: chal over 4f out: led over 3f out: edgd lft over 1f out: jst hld on* **6/4**[1]

14-1 2 hd **My Mate Max**[20] 1931 5-9-6 **73** (p) GrahamGibbons 6 82
(R Hollinshead) *drvn to ld: hdd over 3f out: rallied and almost upsides whn squeezed and hmpd 100yds out: kpt on gamely: jst hld* **11/4**[2]

0-14 3 5 **Locum**[17] 2013 5-9-0 **67** TedDurcan 5 69
(M H Tompkins) *hld up: hdwy on ins over 3f out: drvn 2f out: kpt on to take n.d 3rd ins fnl f* **5/1**[3]

2304 4 ¾ **Chocolate Caramel (USA)**[27] 1689 8-9-4 **71** TonyHamilton 2 72
(R A Fahey) *chsd ldrs: drvn over 3f out: one pce* **12/1**

60/0 5 23 **Dalhaan (USA)**[36] 1484 5-9-7 **74** (t) StevieDonohoe 3 43
(Ian Williams) *hld up: hdwy to trck ldrs 9f out: rdn 4f out: hung lft: nvr a threat: eased whn wl btn 1f out: lame* **5/1**[3]

-126 6 9 **Leyte Gulf (USA)**[105] 529 7-9-0 **67** FrankieMcDonald 4 23
(C C Bealby) *dwlt: hld up in rr: hdwy over 3f out: sn rdn: nvr a threat: eased whn wl btn 1f out* **25/1**

3m 6.33s (5.13) **Going Correction** +0.225s/f (Good) 6 Ran SP% **111.5**
Speed ratings (Par 103): **103,102,100,99,86 81**
toteswingers:1&2:£1.10, 1&3:£1.70, 2&3:£3.10 CSF £5.74 TOTE £2.20: £1.10, £2.30; EX 6.20.
Owner Bruce Corman **Bred** Airlie Stud **Trained** Newmarket, Suffolk

FOCUS
Just an ordinary handicap, but the first two served up a cracking and controversial finish after being locked together for the length of the home straight. The pace slackened briefly down the far side but soon picked up again and this was a decent test at the trip. Only the first two ever mattered, and they both recorded personal bests.
Dalhaan(USA) Official explanation: jockey said gelding hung left-handed; vet said gelding returned lame right-fore
Leyte Gulf(USA) Official explanation: jockey said gelding had no more to give

2496 TURFTV MAIDEN STKS 1m 30y
8:40 (8:40) (Class 5) 3-Y-O+ **£2,914** (£867; £433; £216) **Stalls** Low

Form RPR

432 1 **Blues Music (IRE)**[70] 930 3-9-2 **73** MichaelHills 2 78+
(B W Hills) *trckd ldrs: swtchd rt to chse wnr 2f out: styd on to ld last 75yds* **9/4**[2]

3 2 ¾ **Rule Breaker (IRE)**[17] 1991 3-9-2 0 RoystonFfrench 5 76+
(M Johnston) *led: drvn over 3f out: hdd and no ex ins fnl f* **11/8**[1]

3 4 ½ **Pedantic** 3-9-2 0 KierenFallon 7 65
(L M Cumani) *chsd ldrs: drvn over 5f out: edgd lft and styd on same pce fnl 2f: tk 3rd last 50yds* **6/1**

05 4 ¾ **Glacial**[25] 1769 3-9-2 0 TedDurcan 6 64
(E F Vaughan) *trckd wnr: kpt on one pce fnl 2f* **7/2**[3]

400- 5 3 ¾ **Piccolo Express**[292] 4819 4-10-0 **50** GrahamGibbons 1 58
(B P J Baugh) *t.k.h: hdwy over 3f out: sn chsng ldrs: wknd fnl f* **66/1**

6 26 **Tender Appeal** 3-8-11 0 PaulEddery 8 —
(C W Moore) *in rr: drvn 4f out: sn lost pl* **125/1**

7 nk **Colamandis** 3-8-11 0 PatrickMathers 4 —
(H A McWilliams) *dwlt: in rr: lost pl 3f out: sn bhd* **100/1**

1m 45.98s (1.28) **Going Correction** +0.225s/f (Good)
WFA 3 from 4yo 12lb 7 Ran SP% **112.7**
Speed ratings (Par 103): **98,97,92,92,88 62,61**
toteswingers:1&2:£1.10, 1&3:£4.80, 2&3:£2.30 CSF £5.56 TOTE £2.80: £1.40, £1.10; EX 6.10.
Owner B W Hills **Bred** Dermot Cantillon & The Irish National **Trained** Lambourn, Berks

FOCUS
Not much depth to this maiden, which was run just at a fair pace. The winner did not need to improve on his AW form at face value but the form could be rated at least 5lb higher if the fifth was ignored.

2497 CHESHIRE OAKS DESIGNER OUTLET MAIDEN STKS 1m 3f 200y
9:10 (9:11) (Class 5) 3-Y-O+ **£2,914** (£867; £433; £216) **Stalls** High

Form RPR

0-2 1 **Mataaleb**[34] 1521 3-8-11 0 TadhgO'Shea 1 88+
(M A Jarvis) *mde all: qcknd 6f out: drvn over 3f out: clr over 1f out: v readily* **7/2**[3]

5 2 5 **Reality Show (IRE)**[15] 2043 3-8-11 0 TedDurcan 6 82+
(Mahmood Al Zarooni) *s.i.s: sn chsng ldrs: shkn up 6f out: drvn over 3f out: tk modest 2nd over 1f out: no ch w wnr* **6/5**[1]

3-5 3 2 ¼ **Wadnaan**[9] 2231 3-8-11 0 RoystonFfrench 3 76
(M Johnston) *chsd ldrs: reminders over 5f out: outpcd and lost pl over 3f out: edgd rt and kpt on fnl f: tk modest 3rd towards fin* **10/1**

2 4 1 ¼ **Rule Maker**[14] 2083 3-8-11 0 WilliamBuick 2 74
(J Noseda) *t.k.h: trckd wnr: effrt over 3f out: wknd over 1f out* **5/2**[2]

0-6 5 7 **Silkenveil (IRE)**[14] 2072 3-8-7 0 ow1 TonyHamilton 4 59
(R A Fahey) *t.k.h in last: effrt over 3f out: rdn and lost pl over 2f out* **40/1**

2m 38.64s (4.64) **Going Correction** +0.225s/f (Good)
WFA 3 from 4yo 17lb 5 Ran SP% **107.8**
Speed ratings (Par 103): **90,86,85,84,79**
CSF £7.82 TOTE £3.70: £3.50, £1.60; EX 8.90 Place 6 £3.03; Place 5 £2.47.
Owner Hamdan Al Maktoum **Bred** Shadwell Estate Company Limited **Trained** Newmarket, Suffolk

FOCUS
Some good stables were represented in this maiden, in which the winner dictated a very steady pace. It turned into a sprint up the straight, but Mataaleb impressed and is rated up a stone.
T/Plt: £4.50 to a £1 stake. Pool:£61,925.06 - 9,828.98 winning tickets T/Qpdt: £3.20 to a £1 stake. Pool:£3,037.68 - 688.34 winning tickets WG

2461 NEWCASTLE (L-H)
Friday, May 28

OFFICIAL GOING: Good (7.3)
Bend after winning post and at 1m20f area moved in to provide fresh ground down back straight.
Wind: Breezy, half against Weather: Cloudy

2498 WARD HADAWAY MEDIAN AUCTION MAIDEN STKS 6f
2:10 (2:12) (Class 6) 2-Y-O **£2,590** (£770; £385; £192) **Stalls** Centre

Form RPR

0 1 **Move In Time**[15] 2059 2-9-3 0 RichardMullen 14 79+
(B Smart) *prom stands' side: led that gp over 1f out: edgd rt: overall ldr ins fnl f: kpt on strly: 1st of 7 in gp* **10/1**[3]

2 2 ¼ **Sophie's Hero** 2-9-3 0 PJMcDonald 6 72+
(K A Ryan) *dwlt: sn prom far side: effrt 2f out: led that gp wl ins fnl f: nt pce of stands' side wnr: 1st of 8 in gp* **28/1**

2 3 nk **Ahtoug**[20] 1905 2-9-3 0 TedDurcan 4 71
(Mahmood Al Zarooni) *trckd far side ldr: led that gp and overall ldr over 1f out: hdd wl ins fnl f: kpt on: 2nd of 8 in gp* **4/9**[1]

4 1 ½ **Eland Ally** 2-9-3 0 MickyFenton 2 67+
(T P Tate) *prom far side: drvn and outpcd 1/2-way: rallied over 1f out: kpt on nrst fin: 3rd of 8 in gp* **28/1**

4 5 ½ **Mysterious Bounty (IRE)**[24] 1806 2-9-3 0 PhillipMakin 15 65
(M Dods) *led stands' side to over 1f out: kpt on same pce fnl f: 2nd of 7 in gp* **11/2**[2]

03 6 2 ½ **Anddante (IRE)**[12] 2138 2-9-3 0 PaulHanagan 5 61+
(T D Easterby) *led and overall ldr far side: hdd over 1f out: no ex: 4th of 8 in gp* **11/1**

7 4 ½ **Wanchai Minx** 2-8-7 0 MatthewDavies(5) 3 42+
(A P Jarvis) *hld up bhd ldng gp far side: effrt over 2f out: nt pce to chal: 5th of 8 in gp* **66/1**

8 ½ **Mr Shifter** 2-9-3 0 DuranFentiman 12 43
(Mrs L Stubbs) *hld up in tch stands' side: pushed along over 2f out: no imp fnl f: 3rd of 7 in gp* **100/1**

9 nk **Roman Ruler (IRE)** 2-9-0 0 KellyHarrison(3) 11 42
(C W Fairhurst) *dwlt: bhd stands' side: pushed along over 2f out: nvr rchd ldrs: 4th of 7 in gp* **100/1**

0 **10** *2 3/4* **Aprication (IRE)**[10] 2202 2-9-3 0 SilvestreDeSousa 8 34
(J R Weymes) *cl up stands' side tl rdn and wknd wl over 1f out: 5th of 7 in gp* **100/1**

11 *2 1/4* **Kodicil (IRE)** 2-9-3 0 GrahamGibbons 7 27
(T D Walford) *in tch far side: rdn over 2f out: sn btn: 6th of 8 in gp* **100/1**

12 *1 3/4* **Livinadream** 2-8-12 0 AndrewElliott 1 20+
(N Tinkler) *missed break: bhd far side: pushed along over 2f out: nvr on terms: 7th of 8 in gp* **100/1**

13 *2 1/4* **Green Pastures (IRE)** 2-9-3 0 FrederikTylicki 10 15
(J Howard Johnson) *chsd stands' side ldrs tl rdn and wknd over 2f out: 6th of 7 in gp* **50/1**

4 **14** *13* **Dark Dune (IRE)**[21] 1886 2-9-3 0 RobertWinston 13 —
(T D Easterby) *w stands' side ldrs tl rdn and wknd over 2f out: last of 7 in gp* **33/1**

15 *2* **Downtown Boy (IRE)** 2-9-3 0 JoeFanning 9 —
(T P Tate) *s.i.s: sn prom far side: rdn and wknd over 2f out: last of 8 in gp* **66/1**

1m 17.01s (2.41) **Going Correction** +0.15s/f (Good) **15** Ran SP% **121.8**
Speed ratings (Par 91): **93,90,89,87,86 83,77,76,76,72 69,67,64,47,44**
toteswingers:1&2:£42.00, 1&3:£6.10, 2&3:£11.80 CSF £253.34 TOTE £10.20: £2.10, £5.20, £1.10; EX 204.40.
Owner A Turton, J Blackburn & R Bond **Bred** Bond Thoroughbred Corporation **Trained** Hambleton, N Yorks

FOCUS
A split was always likely for this juvenile maiden, what with there being so many runners, and the winner raced stands' side, but there wasn't much between the two groups. A messy race and a number of these are better than the bare form.

NOTEBOOK
Move In Time travelled before picking up strongly for pressure and probably would have won regardless of which side he raced. 33-1 and well held in what looked a decent York maiden on debut, he had clearly learnt a lot from that and was a different proposition this time, getting well on top close home. He is thought of very highly, but won't be rushed, as he is a big horse. (op 9-1)
Sophie's Hero, who is related to plenty of winners, came out best of the far-side group. From a yard that has started well with its 2-y-os, he wasn't the best away, but came to challenge over 2f out and stayed on get the better of the favourite, though found he wasn't quite on terms with the winner.
Ahtoug looked very promising when just denied on his debut at Haydock and he was a very skinny price to go one better, but didn't go away having got to the front on his side, and looked one paced in the closing stages. (op 8-13)
Eland Ally, whose trainer has his juveniles in good form, shaped encouragingly in fourth, staying on well inside the final furlong, and natural progress should see him capable of winning a maiden. (op 25-1)
Mysterious Bounty(IRE), fourth over 5f at the course on debut, took them along against the stands' rail, but was readily brushed aside by the winner and didn't give the impression he particularly improved for the extra furlong. He may need a slower surface. (op 5-1)
Anddante(IRE) is now qualified for a mark and should be capable of winning in nurseries. (op 12-1)
Wanchai Minx, whose dam was a half-sister to a couple of juvenile winners, shaped well enough to suggest she has a future. (op 80-1)
Mr Shifter, who is already gelded, finished third on the stands' side and will find easier opportunities.

2499 MITIE MEDIAN AUCTION MAIDEN STKS 1m 4f 93y
2:45 (2:47) (Class 6) 3-4-Y-O £2,590 (£770; £385; £192) Stalls Low

Form RPR

6-52 **1** **Widezain (IRE)**[38] 1447 3-8-10 70 TedDurcan 6 81+
(M R Channon) *pressed ldr: led 3f out: sn qcknd clr: eased ins fnl f* **15/8**[1]

546- **2** *9* **Urban Clubber**[310] 4190 3-8-10 68 FrederikTylicki 4 63
(J Howard Johnson) *prom: rdn 3f out: chsd clr ldr 2f out: no imp* **11/4**[2]

32-0 **3** *1 3/4* **Brink**[32] 1571 3-8-5 65 PJMcDonald 3 55
(T J Pitt) *hld up last: nt clr run over 2f out: swtchd rt and hdwy over 1f out: no imp* **11/2**

0 **4** *4 1/2* **Sposalizio (IRE)**[17] 2011 3-8-10 0 RichardMullen 2 53
(Sir Michael Stoute) *chsd ldrs: outpcd and carried hd high over 2f out: btn over 1f out* **9/2**[3]

00-0 **5** *3 1/4* **Short Supply (USA)**[20] 1920 4-9-8 49 GrahamGibbons 1 44
(T D Walford) *led to 3f out: sn rdn: wknd fr 2f out* **50/1**

2m 45.28s (-0.32) **Going Correction** -0.05s/f (Good)
WFA 3 from 4yo 17lb **5** Ran SP% **97.0**
Speed ratings (Par 101): **99,93,91,88,86**
CSF £5.49 TOTE £1.80: £1.02, £2.60; EX 6.70.
Owner Jaber Abdullah **Bred** Silk Fan Syndicate **Trained** West Ilsley, Berks

FOCUS
A weak maiden, even more so with the late withdrawal of Nezhenka, who refused to enter the stalls (11/2, deduct 15p in the £ under R4). The pace was steady. An improved effort from the winner but doubts over what he beat.

2500 TSG ENTERPRISE SOLUTIONS H'CAP 1m 4f 93y
3:20 (3:20) (Class 6) (0-60,59) 4-Y-O+ £2,201 (£655; £327; £163) Stalls Low

Form RPR

-524 **1** **George Adamson (IRE)**[10] 2207 4-9-1 56 PJMcDonald 3 68+
(G A Swinbank) *in tch: effrt whn nt clr run over 2f to 1f out: styd on wl fnl f to ld last 25yds* **11/2**[1]

2 *3/4* **Tenhoo**[198] 7343 4-8-3 49 PaulPickard(5) 6 56
(E J Alston) *hld up: hdwy over 2f out: chsd wnr last 25yds: r.o* **16/1**

54-0 **3** *1* **San Deng**[21] 1891 8-8-6 47 PaulHanagan 1 53
(Micky Hammond) *cl up: drvn over 2f out: led ent fnl f: hdd and no ex last 25yds* **15/2**

5-16 **4** *shd* **Shekan Star**[24] 1807 8-8-7 55 MatthewLawson(7) 12 61
(K G Reveley) *hld up: rdn along 3f out: hdwy on outside over 1f out: kpt on towards fin* **10/1**

4252 **5** *1* **Lisbon Lion (IRE)**[18] 1984 5-8-12 53 FrederikTylicki 11 57
(James Moffatt) *hld up: hdwy 2f out: kpt on ins fnl f: nrst fin* **13/2**[2]

0/05 **6** *nk* **Gulf Coast**[32] 1576 5-9-0 55 GrahamGibbons 15 59
(T D Walford) *cl up: led over 2f out to ent fnl f: kpt on same pce* **11/2**[1]

1-00 **7** *1 1/2* **Bollin Freddie**[32] 1576 6-8-5 53 ShaneBKelly(7) 8 54
(A J Lockwood) *in tch: stdy hdwy over 3f out: rdn 2f out: kpt on same pce fnl f* **25/1**

-204 **8** *4* **Orkney (IRE)**[13] 2109 5-9-1 59 (b) BarryMcHugh(3) 13 54
(Julie Camacho) *hld up in midfield on outside: drvn 3f out: no imp over 1f out* **7/1**[3]

3520 **9** *1 1/2* **Fitzwarren**[44] 1296 9-8-5 46 (tp) SilvestreDeSousa 2 38
(A D Brown) *led to over 2f out: rdn and wknd appr fnl f* **12/1**

0/0- **10** *1 1/2* **Chip N Pin**[22] 3499 6-8-4 45 (b) DuranFentiman 5 35
(T D Easterby) *chsd ldrs tl rdn and wknd over 2f out* **9/1**

04-0 **11** *1* **Dechiper (IRE)**[14] 2085 8-8-13 59 PatrickDonaghy(5) 14 47
(R Johnson) *hld up: shortlived effrt over 2f out: sn rdn and wknd* **16/1**

0-06 **12** *9* **Catcher Of Dreams (IRE)**[10] 2208 4-8-7 48 (t) AndrewMullen 7 22
(A G Foster) *midfield: rdn over 2f out: sn wknd* **66/1**

000- **13** *11* **Media Stars**[213] 7080 5-8-4 45 PaulQuinn 10 1
(R Johnson) *t.k.h: hld up: rdn 3f out: sn wknd* **50/1**

400- **14** *10* **Fenners (USA)**[167] 6558 7-8-0 46 JamesSullivan(5) 4 —
(M W Easterby) *midfield on ins: rdn over 3f out: sn lost pl* **16/1**

2m 44.57s (-1.03) **Going Correction** -0.05s/f (Good) **14** Ran SP% **120.1**
Speed ratings (Par 101): **101,100,99,99,99 98,97,95,94,93 92,86,79,78**
toteswingers:1&2:£27.10, 1&3:£9.00, 2&3:£27.30 CSF £93.60 CT £671.94 TOTE £4.10: £1.20, £9.40, £4.00; EX 139.50.
Owner Mrs S Sanbrook **Bred** Miss O O'Connor & Stephanie Von Schilcher **Trained** Melsonby, N Yorks

FOCUS
A low-grade handicap that saw any number in with a chance a furlong out. Sound form, and the winner is a bit better than the bare result.
Shekan Star Official explanation: jockey said mare missed the break
Fenners(USA) Official explanation: jockey said gelding had a breathing problem

2501 DELOITTE CLASSIFIED STKS 1m 2f 32y
3:55 (3:56) (Class 6) 3-Y-O £2,201 (£655; £327; £163) Stalls Centre

Form RPR

00-5 **1** **Comedy Act**[10] 2221 3-9-0 65 PaulHanagan 4 77+
(Sir Mark Prescott) *mde all: qcknd 2f out: kpt on strly fnl f: unchal* **3/1**[2]

5-31 **2** *5* **So Bazaar (IRE)**[21] 1887 3-9-0 61 PJMcDonald 6 67
(G A Swinbank) *chsd wnr: effrt over 2f out: edgd lft: kpt on fnl f: no imp* **5/1**

425- **3** *nse* **Mason Hindmarsh**[212] 7116 3-8-11 65 BarryMcHugh(3) 5 67
(Karen McLintock) *chsd ldrs: rdn over 2f out: kpt same pce fnl f* **7/2**[3]

40-2 **4** *1* **Big Wave Bay (IRE)**[51] 1158 3-9-0 65 RichardMullen 1 65+
(A P Jarvis) *prom: rdn and outpcd over 2f out: rallied over 1f out: kpt on fnl f: no imp* **2/1**[1]

000- **5** *7* **Forethought**[224] 6821 3-9-0 62 JoeFanning 3 51
(P Howling) *in tch: drvn and outpcd over 2f out: n.d after* **20/1**

0-55 **6** *nk* **Brananx (USA)**[43] 1335 3-9-0 65 RobertWinston 8 50
(K A Ryan) *t.k.h: hld up: rdn 3f out: nvr on terms* **6/1**

00-0 **7** *3 1/2* **Acol**[14] 2072 3-9-0 40 FrederikTylicki 2 43
(A G Foster) *t.k.h: hld up in tch: drvn over 2f out: sn outpcd* **100/1**

060- **8** *34* **Light Nights (IRE)**[192] 7419 3-8-9 42 LanceBetts(5) 7 —
(T D Easterby) *hld up in tch: struggling 4f out: sn btn: t.o* **66/1**

2m 13.64s (1.74) **Going Correction** -0.05s/f (Good) **8** Ran SP% **118.8**
Speed ratings (Par 97): **91,87,86,86,80 80,77,50**
toteswingers:1&2:£9.70, 1&3:£10.90, 2&3:£6.40 CSF £18.98 TOTE £3.30: £1.10, £2.40, £2.50; EX 24.30.
Owner Neil Greig - Osborne House **Bred** Floors Farming & The Duke Of Devonshire **Trained** Newmarket, Suffolk

FOCUS
Not at all a strong heat and the first three were in the same order throughout. The winner is on the upgrade.

2502 EMIRATES NEWCASTLE TO DUBAI FILLIES' H'CAP 1m 3y(S)
4:30 (4:30) (Class 5) (0-75,75) 3-Y-O £3,238 (£963; £481; £240) Stalls Centre

Form RPR

60-5 **1** **Path Of Peace**[21] 1861 3-8-10 67 JoeFanning 6 77+
(J D Bethell) *trckd ldrs: nt clr run over 2f out: hdwy to ld appr fnl f: rdn clr* **13/2**

1-60 **2** *3 3/4* **Excellent Day (IRE)**[13] 2120 3-9-4 75 RobertWinston 3 74
(M R Channon) *dwlt and swtchd rt s: hld up: hdwy and swtchd lft 2f out: effrt and chsd wnr ins fnl f: r.o* **5/1**

0-52 **3** *1 1/4* **Red Scintilla**[29] 1648 3-8-5 62 SilvestreDeSousa 4 58
(N Tinkler) *t.k.h: cl up: led over 2f out to appr fnl f: one pce* **4/1**[3]

6-04 **4** *3/4* **Dance For Julie (IRE)**[32] 1571 3-8-10 72 PatrickDonaghy(5) 1 66
(B M R Haslam) *hld up: hdwy and prom 2f out: rdn and no ex fnl f* **9/1**

4-23 **5** *3* **Chushka**[36] 1488 3-8-10 67 RichardMullen 5 55
(B Smart) *t.k.h: trckd ldrs: effrt 2f out: wknd ins fnl f* **5/2**[1]

600- **6** *12* **Wood Fair**[247] 6215 3-8-2 62 KellyHarrison(3) 2 22
(J R Weymes) *w ldr: led after 3f to over 2f out: sn wknd* **33/1**

31- **7** *10* **Chardonnay**[231] 6638 3-9-4 75 PJMcDonald 7 12
(G A Swinbank) *led 3f: cl up tl rdn and lost pl over 2f out: sn btn* **7/2**[2]

1m 43.93s (0.53) **Going Correction** +0.15s/f (Good) **7** Ran SP% **113.7**
Speed ratings (Par 96): **102,98,97,96,93 81,71**
toteswingers:1&2:£5.50, 1&3:£4.40, 2&3:£3.40 CSF £38.02 TOTE £9.00: £4.80, £2.30; EX 40.00.
Owner Mrs R D Peacock **Bred** Mrs R D Peacock **Trained** Middleham Moor, N Yorks

FOCUS
A modest fillies' handicap. The winner progressed again and the runner-up ran to form.
Chushka Official explanation: jockey said filly was unsuited by the good ground
Chardonnay Official explanation: jockey said filly hung right-handed throughout

2503 BIZA TAX & DUTY FREE H'CAP 1m 3y(S)
5:05 (5:08) (Class 6) (0-60,60) 3-Y-O £2,072 (£616; £308; £153) Stalls Centre

Form RPR

00 **1** **Catawollow**[10] 2221 3-7-13 46 oh1 (e) BillyCray(5) 11 51
(R C Guest) *prom stands' side: drvn over 2f out: rallied over 1f out: led ins fnl f: kpt on wl: 1st of 9 in gp* **16/1**

202- **2** *1* **Jozafeen**[225] 6797 3-8-11 60 MatthewLawson(7) 8 63+
(R Bastiman) *chsd stands' side ldrs: led and rdn over 2f out: hdd ins fnl f: kpt on same pce: 2nd of 9 in gp* **20/1**

-002 **3** *1 1/2* **Broctune Papa Gio**[18] 1971 3-8-0 47 PaulPickard(5) 5 47+
(K G Reveley) *led far side: rdn clr of that gp 2f out: kpt on wl: nt pce of first two stands' side: 1st of 6 in gp* **12/1**

0-02 **4** *1 1/2* **Dutiful**[10] 2200 3-9-4 60 RobertWinston 14 56
(M R Channon) *prom stands' side: drvn over 2f out: rallied over 1f out: kpt on fin: 3rd of 9 in gp* **11/4**[1]

000- **5** *3 1/4* **Lighterman**[299] 4557 3-8-1 46 oh1 KellyHarrison(3) 4 35+
(E J Alston) *dwlt: hld up far side: hdwy to chse far side ldr 2f out: edgd lft and kpt on: no imp: 2nd of 6 in gp* **28/1**

6-05 **6** *1 3/4* **French Seventyfive**[18] 1971 3-8-12 54 DuranFentiman 15 39
(T D Walford) *hld up stands' side: rdn over 2f out: hdwy over 1f out: nvr rchd ldrs: 4th of 9 in gp* **12/1**

-000 **7** *hd* **Barastar**[13] 2132 3-8-9 51 SilvestreDeSousa 16 35
(N Tinkler) *hld up stands' side: rdn and hdwy 2f out: no imp fnl f: 5th of 9 in gp* **33/1**

000- **8** *3 3/4* **Chichina (USA)**[223] 6858 3-8-8 **50** JoeFanning 7 26
(M Johnston) *bhd stands' side: outpcd 1/2-way: sme late hdwy: nvr on terms: 6th of 9 in gp* **9/1**

4503 **9** *1 1/2* **Cross The Boss (IRE)**[18] 1971 3-9-0 **56** (t) JerryO'Dwyer 10 28
(B M R Haslam) *led stands' side to over 2f out: rdn and wknd over 1f out: 7th of 9 in gp* **7/1**[3]

0-00 **10** *hd* **Russian Brigadier**[43] 1336 3-8-6 **48** RichardMullen 2 20
(M Brittain) *prom far side: drvn and outpcd 3f out: no imp fnl 2f: 3rd of 6 in gp* **25/1**

-000 **11** *11* **Electric City (IRE)**[24] 1810 3-8-13 **60** PatrickDonaghy(5) 3 6
(M G Quinlan) *hld up in tch far side: rdn over 2f out: sn wknd: 4th of 6 in gp* **50/1**

0550 **12** *3 1/4* **Spirited Lady (IRE)**[41] 1392 3-8-13 **58** BarryMcHugh(3) 9 —
(R A Fahey) *cl up on outside of stands' side gp: rdn and wknd 3f out: 8th of 9 in gp* **16/1**

0-00 **13** *2 1/4* **Bring Sweets (IRE)**[18] 1970 3-8-4 **46** oh1 PJMcDonald 13 —
(B Ellison) *w stands' side ldrs tl wknd over 2f out: last of 9 in gp* **9/2**[2]

0-40 **14** *4 1/2* **No Quarter (IRE)**[13] 2132 3-9-0 **56** (p) FrederikTylicki 1 —
(A Dickman) *trckd far side ldrs tl wknd over 2f out: 5th of 6 in gp* **14/1**

000- **15** *6* **Silvermine Bay (IRE)**[238] 6441 3-8-4 **51** MatthewDavies(5) 6 —
(A P Jarvis) *trckd far side ldrs untl rdn and wknd fr over 2f out* **28/1**

1m 45.97s (2.57) **Going Correction** +0.15s/f (Good) **15** Ran SP% **121.6**
Speed ratings (Par 97): **92,91,89,88,84 83,82,79,77,77 66,63,60,56,50**
toteswingers:1&2:£33.50, 1&3:£42.70, 2&3:£21.40 CSF £313.27 CT £4026.61 TOTE £18.40: £5.00, £2.70, £3.40; EX 400.80.
Owner Bamboozelem **Bred** Worksop Manor Stud **Trained** Stainforth, S Yorks

FOCUS
A moderate handicap, and the winner again came from those racing stands' side. A clear personal best from the winner.
Bring Sweets(IRE) Official explanation: jockey said gelding hung left-handed throughout

2504 NEWCASTLE INTERNATIONAL AIRPORT 75TH ANNIVERSARY H'CAP 6f
5:40 (5:40) (Class 5) (0-70,70) 3-Y-0+ **£3,238** (£963; £481; £240) **Stalls** Centre

Form RPR

10-3 **1** **Just Sam (IRE)**[25] 1754 5-9-2 **68** DaleSwift(7) 6 79
(R E Barr) *mde all: rdn 2f out: kpt on strly fnl f* **11/2**[3]

0/60 **2** *2* **Tawzeea (IRE)**[13] 2113 5-9-11 **70** JoeFanning 10 75
(J D Bethell) *dwlt: t.k.h and sn prom: chsd wnr over 2f out to appr fnl f: styd on to regain 2nd nr fin* **9/1**

03 **3** *1/2* **Dickie Le Davoir**[10] 2206 6-9-2 **66** (v) BillyCray(5) 7 69+
(R C Guest) *dwlt: hld up: hdwy on outside 2f out: edgd rt and chsd wnr appr fnl f: no ex and lost 2nd cl home* **11/1**

0-64 **4** *3 3/4* **Braille**[10] 2213 5-8-13 **58** DuranFentiman 12 49
(T D Walford) *t.k.h: prom: rdn 2f out: edgd lft: kpt on same pce* **10/1**

5034 **5** *2* **Apache Ridge (IRE)**[21] 1869 4-9-6 **70** AmyRyan(5) 4 55
(K A Ryan) *cl up tl rdn and wknd appr fnl f* **9/2**[2]

3542 **6** *2* **Another Try (IRE)**[6] 2331 5-9-0 **64** MatthewDavies(5) 5 42
(A P Jarvis) *in tch: drvn over 2f out: sn no imp* **7/2**[1]

0-60 **7** *3/4* **Caranbola**[42] 1365 4-8-10 **62** JohnCavanagh(7) 11 38
(M Brittain) *bhd: rdn over 2f out: nvr rchd ldrs* **8/1**

4114 **8** *2 3/4* **Whispered Times (USA)**[14] 2069 3-8-8 **65** KellyHarrison(3) 2 32
(Miss Tracy Waggott) *cl up on outside tl rdn and wknd fr 2f out* **13/2**

210- **9** *1/2* **Arjemis**[251] 6103 4-8-13 **58** SilvestreDeSousa 9 23
(C R Wilson) *hld up: effrt and swtchd lft over 2f out: wknd over 1f out* **20/1**

600 **10** *11* **Inter Vision (USA)**[10] 2211 10-9-10 **69** FrederikTylicki 3 —
(A Dickman) *chsd ldrs tl rdn and wknd over 2f out* **14/1**

1m 15.57s (0.97) **Going Correction** +0.15s/f (Good)
WFA 3 from 4yo+ 9lb **10** Ran SP% **119.1**
Speed ratings (Par 103): **103,99,100,94,92 89,88,84,84,69**
toteswingers:1&2:£2.20, 1&3:£5.30, 2&3:£3.30 CSF £55.43 CT £533.23 TOTE £6.30: £2.20, £3.30, £2.90; EX 72.90 Place 6 £436.51; Place 5 £343.10.
Owner P Cartmell **Bred** John J Carroll **Trained** Seamer, N Yorks

FOCUS
The stands' rail again proved crucial in this modest handicap. A personal best from the winner, who made all.
T/Plt: £414.70 to a £1 stake. Pool:£73,051.18 - 128.58 winning tickets T/Qpdt: £305.80 to a £1 stake. Pool:£4,009.59 - 9.70 winning tickets RY

2123 NEWMARKET (Rowley Mile) (R-H)
Friday, May 28

OFFICIAL GOING: Good to firm (watered; 8.5)
Far side track used.
Wind: Light half-behind Weather: Cloudy with sunny spells

2505 CHEMTEST E B F MAIDEN FILLIES' STKS 6f
2:20 (2:22) (Class 4) 2-Y-0 **£5,180** (£1,541; £770; £384) **Stalls** High

Form RPR

0 **1** **Al Sharood**[20] 1901 2-9-0 0 FrankieDettori 7 86+
(Mahmood Al Zarooni) *w ldr tl led over 4f out: hdd over 1f out: rallied to ld wl ins fnl f* **10/3**[2]

2 *nk* **Googlette (IRE)** 2-9-0 0 JamieSpencer 6 85+
(E F Vaughan) *chsd ldrs: led over 1f out: sn rdn and edgd rt: hdd wl ins fnl f* **33/1**

3 *3* **Cape Dollar (IRE)** 2-9-0 0 RyanMoore 3 76+
(Sir Michael Stoute) *a.p: outpcd 2f out: rallied ins fnl f: r.o* **8/1**

06 **4** *4 1/2* **On Wings Of Love (IRE)**[26] 1728 2-9-0 0 FrannyNorton 9 63
(A Bailey) *mid-div: rdn over 2f out: wnt 4th over 1f out: no imp fnl f* **9/1**

5 *3 1/2* **Bakoura** 2-9-0 0 RichardHills 1 52+
(J L Dunlop) *s.i.s: hdwy over 4f out: rdn and wknd over 1f out* **10/1**

6 *1* **Royal Liaison** 2-9-0 0 HayleyTurner 12 49
(M L W Bell) *hld up: rdn over 2f out: nvr trbld ldrs* **22/1**

7 *3/4* **Eljowzah (IRE)** 2-9-0 0 NeilCallan 2 47+
(C E Brittain) *mid-div: rdn 1/2-way: wknd 2f out* **20/1**

8 *hd* **Spanish Pride (IRE)** 2-9-0 0 IanMongan 4 46+
(J L Dunlop) *sn outpcd: last 1/2-way: r.o wl ins fnl f: nrst fin* **50/1**

5 **9** *3/4* **Apazine (USA)**[9] 2223 2-9-0 0 WilliamBuick 8 44
(J H M Gosden) *chsd ldrs tl rdn and wknd over 1f out* **6/1**[3]

5 **10** *1 1/4* **Koha (USA)**[11] 2176 2-9-0 0 JimCrowley 13 40
(D K Ivory) *led: hdd over 4f out: remained handy tl hung rt and wknd over 1f out* **20/1**

11 *1 1/4* **Wafeira** 2-9-0 0 TomQueally 11 37+
(H R A Cecil) *s.s: hdwy over 3f out: wknd over 2f out* **11/4**[1]

12 *3 3/4* **Volcanic Dust (IRE)** 2-9-0 0 AdrianMcCarthy 5 25
(E A L Dunlop) *hld up: racd keenly: hdwy over 3f out: wknd over 1f out* **66/1**

13 *8* **Pearl Haven** 2-9-0 0 LiamJones 10 —
(P W D'Arcy) *s.s: a in rr: bhd fr 1/2-way* **66/1**

1m 11.76s (-0.44) **Going Correction** +0.025s/f (Good) **13** Ran SP% **116.0**
Speed ratings (Par 92): **103,102,98,92,87 86,85,85,84,82 81,76,65**
totewingers:1&2:£20.20, 2&3:£19.70, 1&3:£5.10 CSF £115.16 TOTE £3.60: £1.20, £8.10, £2.40; EX 167.90.
Owner Godolphin **Bred** Darley **Trained** Newmarket, Suffolk

FOCUS
The course was watered earlier in the week but sunshine and a breeze resulted in the ground riding Good to firm. This fillies' maiden has not produced any stars in recent years, the best recent winners being Kissing the Camera, who scored at Listed level, and Bicoastal, who was Group placed. This looked a cracking race and could rate higher with the first three appearing decent recruits.

NOTEBOOK
Al Sharood, related to mainly milers, had made a decent start in an Ascot maiden looking as if she would be better for the experience. That proved to be the case, as she jumped smartly and made the running. She looked in trouble when the runner-up took the advantage in the Dip, but put her experience of good use up the hill to regain the lead near the line. She looks capable of going on again from this and may go for the Albany Stakes at Royal Ascot. (op 9-2 tchd 3-1)
Googlette(IRE) ◆, a speedily bred filly related to couple of 5f winners, knew her job on this debut and travelled like the best horse in the race for much of the way. She went to the front in the Dip but wandered up the hill and lost out to her more experienced rival near the finish. She was clear of the remainder and looks sure to be winning soon, although she could take on the winner again at Royal Ascot.
Cape Dollar(IRE), out of an unraced half-sister to a couple of middle-distance winners from the family of Imagine, was another to show promise for the future on this debut. She was no match for the first pair but was making inroads into their advantage up the climb to the line. She should also win races, possibly over a little further.
On Wings Of Love(IRE), the most experienced runner in the line-up, had shown promise on both runs over 5f here. She stayed on in her own time and, now qualified for a handicap mark, may make her mark in that sphere later in the season. (op 8-1)
Bakoura, the first foal of a 1m winner from the family of Shadayid, looked as if she would benefit from this debut and ran pretty well considering she was rather isolated on the outside of the field. Official explanation: jockey said filly ran green (op 9-1)
Royal Liaison, a £33,000 half-sister to a dual 6f winner whose dam was Listed placed at 6f, showed ability on this debut despite displaying signs of inexperience. (op 25-1)
Eljowzah(IRE), an 85,000gns half-sister to Pure Poetry, missed the break before staying on late. (op 16-1)
Spanish Pride(IRE) ◆, a sister to Spanish Hidalgo and related to other middle-distance winners, was outpaced early before catching the eye doing her best work in the closing stages. She is likely to need further in time and is another who should improve for the experience.
Apazine(USA) did not build on her Goodwood debut, fading in the cloing stages. (op 5-1)
Wafeira, out of a mare who won a 7f Listed race on her debut, impressed beforehand but totally blew the start and the effort required to get back into contention ultimately told. She can be given another chance. Official explanation: jockey said filly was slowly away (op 3-1 tchd 5-2)

2506 LLOYDS TSB COMMERCIAL H'CAP 1m 2f
2:55 (2:55) (Class 4) (0-85,81) 4-Y-0+ **£5,180** (£1,541; £770; £384) **Stalls** Centre

Form RPR

6-66 **1** **Ellemujie**[30] 1617 5-9-2 **79** FrankieDettori 1 91
(D K Ivory) *chsd ldrs: led ins fnl f: rdn out* **4/1**[2]

5-51 **2** *1/2* **Feathered Crown (FR)**[11] 2173 4-9-3 **80** 6ex TomQueally 3 91
(H R A Cecil) *chsd ldr tl led over 3f out: rdn and hdd ins fnl f: r.o* **1/1**[1]

4-00 **3** *1* **Ouster (GER)**[26] 1724 4-9-4 **81** (t) KierenFallon 7 90
(D R C Elsworth) *chsd ldrs: rdn and ev ch over 1f out: styd on* **8/1**[3]

0/1- **4** *3 1/2* **Silent Applause**[343] 3114 7-8-3 **69** Louis-PhilippeBeuzelin(3) 8 71
(Dr J D Scargill) *led over 6f: rdn over 2f out: styd on same pce appr fnl f* **10/1**

0-23 **5** *1 1/2* **Goodwood Starlight (IRE)**[11] 2181 5-8-11 **77** RobertLButler(3) 2 76
(Miss Sheena West) *hld up: racd keenly: rdn over 2f out: hung rt and no imp fr over 1f out* **12/1**

-003 **6** *1/2* **Archie Rice (USA)**[14] 2093 4-8-10 **73** SaleemGolam 5 71
(T Keddy) *s.v.s: rdn over 2f out: nvr on terms* **17/2**

4150 **7** *1 3/4* **Raptor (GER)**[26] 1724 7-8-11 **81** MJMurphy(7) 4 76
(M E Rimmer) *chsd ldrs: rdn and ev ch over 2f out: wknd over 1f* **20/1**

2m 4.83s (-0.97) **Going Correction** +0.025s/f (Good) **7** Ran SP% **113.2**
Speed ratings (Par 105): **104,103,102,100,98 98,97**
toteswingers:1&2:£2.10, 1&3:£3.80, 2&3:£3.60 CSF £8.21 CT £28.27 TOTE £4.00: £2.00, £1.20; EX 11.30.
Owner Mrs J A Cornwell **Bred** Mrs J A Cornwell **Trained** Radlett, Herts

FOCUS
An ordinary handicap but the runners were closely matched on the ratings. The pace was steady until picking up in the last 3f and the first three came clear of the rest. The form is a bit muddling with the form best rated around the placed horses.

2507 PETERS ELWORTHY & MOORE MAIDEN STKS 1m 2f
3:30 (3:33) (Class 4) 3-Y-0 **£5,180** (£1,541; £770; £384) **Stalls** Centre

Form RPR

1 **Film Score (USA)** 3-9-3 0 FrankieDettori 5 94+
(Mahmood Al Zarooni) *s.i.s: hld up: hdwy over 3f out: chsd ldr over 1f out: rdn to ld wl ins fnl f* **10/1**[3]

3-30 **2** *3/4* **Mata Keranjang (USA)**[12] 2159 3-9-3 106 (t) JamieSpencer 9 92
(P F I Cole) *chsd ldrs: led wl over 2f out: rdn and edgd lft over 1f out: hdd wl ins fnl f* **11/8**[1]

3 *6* **Heart Of Hearts** 3-8-12 0 IanMongan 8 75+
(H R A Cecil) *mid-div: outpcd over 4f out: hdwy over 2f out: styd on to go 3rd nr fin: nt trble ldrs* **16/1**

24 **4** *1/2* **All Action (USA)**[15] 2043 3-9-3 0 TomQueally 7 79
(H R A Cecil) *prom: shkn up and hung rt fr over 2f out: wknd fnl f: lost 3rd nr fin* **7/4**[2]

0- **5** *2* **Baibars (USA)**[219] 6943 3-9-3 0 (b[1]) NickyMackay 3 75?
(G A Butler) *led: rdn and hdd wl over 2f out: wknd fnl f* **100/1**

0 **6** *4 1/2* **Court Circle**[32] 1581 3-9-3 0 RyanMoore 13 66
(Sir Michael Stoute) *prom: shkn up over 3f out: wknd 2f out* **10/1**[3]

7 *1 1/4* **Rio Tinto** 3-9-3 0 DaraghO'Donohoe 11 64
(Mahmood Al Zarooni) *dwlt: hld up: hdwy 1/2-way: wknd 3f out* **33/1**

8 *4 1/2* **Cotton Mill** 3-9-3 0 KierenFallon 12 55
(W Jarvis) *chsd ldrs: pushed along 4f out: wknd wl over 2f out* **40/1**

9 *1/2* **Aneel** 3-9-3 0 HayleyTurner 4 54
(J Noseda) *swvd lft s: a towards rr: wknd over 3f out* **66/1**

10 *27* **Strophic** 3-9-3 0 GeorgeBaker 6 —
(J Noseda) *s.i.s: hld up: wknd over 3f out: t.o* **40/1**

11 1 3/4 **Telescopic** 3-8-12 0 ... WilliamBuick 10 —
(W Jarvis) *hld up: a in rr: rdn over 4f out: sn lost tch: t.o* **66/1**

2m 5.08s (-0.72) **Going Correction** +0.025s/f (Good) 11 Ran SP% **114.3**
Speed ratings (Par 101): **103,102,97,97,95 92,91,87,87,65 64**
toteswingers:1&2:£5.10, 1&3:£12.70, 2&3:£6.90 CSF £23.12 TOTE £11.60: £2.50, £1.20, £3.80; EX 30.20.
Owner Godolphin **Bred** Gallagher's Stud **Trained** Newmarket, Suffolk

FOCUS
A maiden that has been dominated by the big Newmarket yards with the best previous winner being the subsequent multiple Listed and Group winner Tranquil Tiger. This year's renewal looked an interesting affair with a number of newcomers having quality pedigrees, but the time was 0.25secs slower than the preceding handicap. The runner-up is rated below his best but the winner still looks a smart prospect.

2508 EDMONDSON HALL SOLICITORS & SPORTS LAWYERS H'CAP 7f
4:05 (4:05) (Class 3) (0-95,94) 4-Y-O+ **£9,066** (£2,697; £1,348; £673) **Stalls** High

Form RPR
5120 **1** **Dubai Dynamo**[6] 2311 5-9-4 **94** ... HayleyTurner 12 106
(Mrs R A Carr) *s.i.s: hld up: hdwy over 2f out: rdn over 1f out: str run to ld post* **10/1**

15-3 **2** *hd* **St Moritz (IRE)**[13] 2124 4-9-3 **93** ... FrankieDettori 15 104
(M Johnston) *led 1f: chsd ldr to 1/2-way: led again wl over 1f out: sn hdd: rallied to ld wl ins fnl f: hdd post* **7/2**[1]

-210 **3** *3/4* **Crown Choice**[20] 1900 5-8-11 **87** ... AdamKirby 14 96
(W R Swinburn) *chsd ldrs: rdn to ld over 1f out: sn hung rt: hdd and unable qck wl ins fnl f* **4/1**[2]

26-5 **4** *2 1/2* **Bounty Box**[20] 1918 4-9-4 **94** ... GeorgeBaker 16 97
(C F Wall) *chsd ldrs: rdn and ev ch over 1f out: styd on same pce ins fnl f* **11/1**

0-30 **5** *shd* **Kay Gee Be (IRE)**[20] 1900 6-8-12 **88** ... KierenFallon 7 90
(W Jarvis) *hmpd s: hld up: hdwy u.p over 1f out: r.o: nt rch ldrs* **6/1**[3]

- **6** *nse* **Decent Fella (IRE)**[323] 3833 4-8-11 **87** ...(t) LiamKeniry 4 89+
(A M Balding) *hld up: nt clr run over 2f out: hung rt and hdwy over 1f out: r.o wl: nrst fin* **6/1**[3]

1100 **7** *3/4* **Mahadee (IRE)**[41] 1383 5-9-2 **92** ...(b) TomQueally 3 92
(C E Brittain) *hld up: rdn over 2f out: sn hung lft: r.o ins fnl f: nvr trbld ldrs* **22/1**

250- **8** *1 1/4* **Quanah Parker (IRE)**[328] 3622 4-8-10 **89** ... MichaelStainton(3) 1 86
(R M Whitaker) *chsd ldrs: rdn over 2f out: no ex fnl f* **20/1**

1-23 **9** *2 1/2* **Brother Cha (IRE)**[20] 1933 4-8-6 **82** ... WilliamBuick 8 72
(M G Quinlan) *plld hrd: led 6f out: rdn and hung rt fr over 2f out: hdd wl over 1f out: wknd ins fnl f* **14/1**

2060 **10** *1 1/2* **Carcinetto (IRE)**[6] 2311 8-9-2 **92** ... JimCrowley 5 78
(P D Evans) *mid-div: rdn and wknd over 2f out* **50/1**

4-30 **11** *2 3/4* **One Way Or Another (AUS)**[20] 1900 7-8-9 **90** ... SimonPearce(5) 11 69+
(J R Gask) *chsd ldrs: rdn over 2f out: hung rt and wknd over 1f out* **6/1**[3]

36-0 **12** *1* **Baunagain (IRE)**[13] 2119 5-8-7 **83** ... RobertHavlin 10 59
(P W Chapple-Hyam) *plld hrd and prom: trckd ldr 1/2-way tl hmpd and wknd 2f out* **100/1**

030- **13** *3* **Maswerte (IRE)**[226] 6773 4-8-1 **82** ... TobyAtkinson(5) 2 50
(M Wigham) *hld up: wknd over 2f out* **66/1**

1m 24.25s (-1.15) **Going Correction** +0.025s/f (Good) 13 Ran SP% **122.7**
Speed ratings (Par 107): **107,106,105,103,102 102,102,100,97,96 92,91,88**
toteswingers:1&2:£9.70, 1&3:£10.90, 2&3:£6.40 CSF £44.52 CT £156.36 TOTE £15.20: £4.20, £2.20, £2.00; EX 75.80.
Owner The Bottom Liners **Bred** T K & Mrs P A Knox **Trained** Huby, N Yorks

FOCUS
A good, competitive handicap that was won by ill-fated former course specialist Plum Pudding in 2008, and by the very useful Roaring Forte last season. An open race on paper, it produced a good finish with those racing towards the far side appearing to have an advantage. The winner looked better than ever and the placed horses both recorded personal bests on turf.

NOTEBOOK
Dubai Dynamo has had a busy time of it this season but swooped late to gain his third success of the year. A consistent performer, he is already due to go up 5lb from tomorrow, so will not find it easy to follow up unless the Handicapper revises his opinion in view of this narrow success.
St Moritz(IRE) ◆ was dropping back to the trip over which he gained his two wins on Polytrack. He made a bold bid to give his rider a four-timer, battling his way to the front inside the last, but the winner swooped fast and late, giving him no chance to respond. He is clearly progressive and could be the sort for a race such as the Buckingham Palace Handicap at Royal Ascot. (op 4-1 tchd 5-1 in places and 9-2 in places)
Crown Choice, another progressive performer from a yard that has recently struck form, looked the most likely winner when hitting the front in the Dip but could not sustain his effort up the hill. He has yet to win on turf but looks more than capable of doing so, and a flat track might suit him best. (op 5-1 tchd 11-2 in a place)
Bounty Box had gained all her previous wins at 6f and did not run badly considering she saw plenty of daylight. (op 9-1)
Kay Gee Be(IRE) has not won since October 2007 but is pretty consistent and has only just dropped back to that last winning mark. He ran his race without ever looking likely to win, and a return to further will probably be in his favour. (op 7-1 tchd 15-2 in a place)
Decent Fella(IRE) ◆, a lightly raced ex-Irish colt having his first run for the yard, was held up towards the centre of the track early but then got stopped in his run when trying to make headway over 2f out. He finished well once switched and can be rated better than the bare form. (op 15-2 tchd 8-1)
Mahadee(IRE) did well early in the year but has struggled in better races since. He raced nearest the stands' side throughout which may not have been the place to be. (op 25-1)
Quanah Parker(IRE) ran with credit on this seasonal debut and should be better for the run. (tchd 22-1 in a place)
Brother Cha(IRE), having his first start since returning to Mick Quinlan, again pulled too hard and needs to learn to settle if he is ever to fulfil his potential. (op 11-1)
Carcinetto(IRE) Official explanation: jockey said mare was slowly away
One Way Or Another(AUS) was beginning to struggle when appearing to lose his action in the Dip and was allowed to come home in his own time. (tchd 11-2)

2509 ELECHECK H'CAP 1m 4f
4:40 (4:40) (Class 3) (0-90,89) 4-Y-O+ **£9,066** (£2,697; £1,348; £673) **Stalls** High

Form RPR
0-60 **1** **Martyr**[26] 1724 5-9-2 **87** ... RyanMoore 4 96
(R Hannon) *trckd ldrs: nt clr run and swtchd rt over 1f out: r.o to ld wl ins fnl f* **9/4**[1]

12-1 **2** *1/2* **Spirit Is Needed (IRE)**[8] 2243 4-9-4 **89** 6ex ... GregFairley 8 97
(M Johnston) *led: rdn and edgd lft over 1f out: hdd wl ins fnl f* **7/2**[2]

4-11 **3** *1 1/2* **Sherman McCoy**[33] 1544 4-9-1 **89** ... JamesMillman(3) 3 95
(B R Millman) *chsd ldr: rdn over 2f out: led briefly over 1f out: no ex wl ins fnl f* **5/1**[3]

5-20 **4** *1 1/2* **Cool Strike (UAE)**[14] 2096 4-9-4 **89** ...(v) LiamKeniry 1 93
(A M Balding) *prom: racd keenly: rdn over 2f out: styd on same pce ins fnl f* **13/2**

42-0 **5** *1/2* **Featherweight (IRE)**[25] 1783 4-8-9 **80** ... KierenFallon 2 83
(B W Hills) *hld up: shkn up over 2f out: rdn over 1f out: edgd rt and no imp ins fnl f* **6/1**

20-0 **6** *1* **Hevelius**[37] 1472 5-9-4 **89** ... AdamKirby 7 90
(W R Swinburn) *wnt lft s: hld up: effrt over 2f out: no ex fnl f* **9/1**

0-00 **7** *4* **Far From Old (IRE)**[13] 2126 7-9-3 **88** ... JamieSpencer 6 83
(M L W Bell) *hmpd s: hld up: rdn over 1f out: hung rt and wknd ins fnl f* **20/1**

2m 32.81s (-0.69) **Going Correction** +0.025s/f (Good) 7 Ran SP% **112.0**
Speed ratings (Par 107): **103,102,101,100,100 99,97**
toteswingers:1&2:£3.00, 1&3:£3.50, 2&3:£2.80 CSF £9.77 CT £33.54 TOTE £3.30: £1.90, £1.40; EX 10.20.
Owner Highclere Thoroughbred Racing (Delilah) **Bred** D Maroun **Trained** East Everleigh, Wilts

FOCUS
A decent handicap and fair form, with the winner rated up a length on his previous year's success. The third and fourth set the level.

NOTEBOOK
Martyr was bidding to follow up last year's success off a 2lb higher mark. Well backed in the morning so that he was sent off favourite, he was never far away and, although briefly denied a run over a furlong out, his rider switched quickly and his mount responded to pressure to take advantage of a gap nearest the rail inside the last furlong. (op 2-1 tchd 15-8 and 5-2 in places)
Spirit Is Needed(IRE) has progressed well since an unfortunate start to his career last June. He made the running and his rider got a breather into him about halfway before quickening up 3f out. He responded to pressure but the older, more experienced winner ran him down near the finish. He looks one to keep on-side despite having jumped up the handicap. (op 5-2)
Sherman McCoy, another progressive type this season, was 6lb higher than for his previous success but ran his race and only gave best up the hill. He confirmed previous form with Cool Strike on worse terms so still appears to be improving. (op 7-1)
Cool Strike(UAE) was meeting today's third for the third time and, as on the previous two occasions, came off second-best. He seems best when ridden from the front. (op 7-1 tchd 8-1)
Featherweight(IRE) was back on her favoured fast ground but is probably best suited by a turning track and more positive tactics. (op 10-1)
Hevelius lost his action and finished distressed last time but this was much better, although he could not sustain his effort in the closing stages. (tchd 10-1)
Far From Old(IRE) is struggling for form since coming to this country from France and never got out of last place. Nevertheless, his handicap mark is dropping quickly, so once he acclimatises he could prove well handicapped.

2510 HOME OF RACING CLASSIFIED STKS 1m
5:15 (5:15) (Class 5) 3-Y-O **£3,885** (£1,156; £577; £288) **Stalls** High

Form RPR
2-23 **1** **Finest Reserve (IRE)**[28] 1658 3-9-0 75 ...(v[1]) KierenFallon 3 81
(M R Channon) *hmpd s: sn chsng ldr: rdn over 2f out: outpcd over 1f out: rallied and hung rt ins fnl f: r.o to ld towards fin* **9/2**[2]

14-6 **2** *3/4* **Venutius**[16] 2033 3-9-0 75 ... FrankieDettori 5 79
(E S McMahon) *set stdy pce tl qcknd over 2f out: clr 1f out: hung rt ins fnl f: rdn and hdd towards fin* **7/4**[1]

2-56 **3** *3* **Mountrath**[22] 1844 3-9-0 74 ... LiamKeniry 6 72
(B R Johnson) *plld hrd and prom: rdn over 1f out: styd on same pce* **13/2**

55-5 **4** *3 1/4* **Invincible Prince (IRE)**[17] 2002 3-9-0 75 ...(b) JimCrowley 1 65
(R M Beckett) *hmpd s: hld up: hdwy over 3f out: rdn over 2f out: hung rt and no ex fnl f* **15/2**

30-3 **5** *5* **Cultured Pride (IRE)**[8] 2253 3-9-0 75 ... RichardKingscote 4 53
(R Hannon) *edgd lft s: hld up: rdn over 2f out: wknd over 1f out* **6/1**[3]

6-00 **6** *4* **Moonline Dancer (FR)**[8] 2256 3-9-0 75 ... RyanMoore 7 44
(R Hannon) *prom: rdn over 2f out: wknd over 1f out* **9/1**

4223 **7** *5* **Christmas Coming**[36] 1486 3-9-0 69 ... HayleyTurner 8 33
(D R C Elsworth) *hld up: pushed along 1/2-way: wknd over 2f out* **20/1**

0-50 **8** *13* **The Starboard Bow**[26] 1734 3-9-0 75 ... WilliamBuick 9 3
(S Kirk) *hld up: rdn over 3f out: wknd over 2f out: t.o* **16/1**

1m 37.17s (-1.43) **Going Correction** +0.025s/f (Good) 8 Ran SP% **114.6**
Speed ratings (Par 99): **108,107,104,101,96 92,87,74**
toteswingers:1&2:£3.20, 1&3:£4.40, 2&3:£5.10 CSF £12.83 TOTE £5.30: £1.70, £1.20, £2.40; EX 13.30.
Owner Mrs E F Clarke **Bred** Wardstown Stud Ltd **Trained** West Ilsley, Berks

FOCUS
A really tight classified stakes with little between the majority of the field on official ratings. The pace was sound but the first three held those positions throughout, but the form looks ordinary with the third the best guide to the level.
The Starboard Bow Official explanation: jockey said colt was unsuited by the good to firm ground

2511 BOLLINGER CHAMPAGNE CHALLENGE SERIES H'CAP (FOR GENTLEMAN AMATEUR RIDERS) 1m 2f
5:50 (5:51) (Class 5) (0-70,70) 4-Y-O+ **£3,123** (£968; £484; £242) **Stalls** Centre

Form RPR
260- **1** *shd* **Lucayan Dancer**[253] 6012 10-10-9 **65** ow5 ... MrSebSpencer(7) 3 73
(N Bycroft) *sn chsng ldr: led over 4f out: hdd over 2f out: stl ev ch fr there: r.o: fin 2nd, shd: awrdd r* **17/2**

5-42 **2** *shd* **Rosco Flyer (IRE)**[14] 2080 4-10-10 **64** ... MrTJCannon(5) 9 72
(R A Teal) *chsd ldrs: pushed along 1/2-way: led over 2f out to over 1f out: hmpd ins fnl f: r.o: fin 3rd, shd, shd: plcd 2nd* **3/1**[1]

10-3 **3** **Prince Golan (IRE)**[112] 426 6-10-6 **58** ... MrMPrice(3) 7 66
(R J Price) *hld up: hdwy over 4f out: led over 1f out: rdn and hung lft ins fnl f: all out: fin 1st: disq: plcd 3rd* **12/1**

6035 **4** *3 3/4* **Bavarica**[6] 2349 8-11-4 **70** ... MrRBirkett(3) 8 70
(Miss J Feilden) *hld up in tch: rdn over 1f out: no ex ins fnl f* **6/1**[3]

5-03 **5** *1* **Mons Calpe (IRE)**[9] 2233 4-11-7 **70** ...(b) MrJoshuaMoore 6 68
(P F I Cole) *led: hdd over 4f out: sn rdn: n.m.r over 2f out: no ex fnl f* **10/3**[2]

0060 **6** *1 1/2* **Mojeerr**[7] 2285 4-10-7 **56** oh6 ...(be) MrSWalker 2 51
(A J McCabe) *hld up: rdn over 2f out: no ex fnl f* **8/1**

2250 **7** *3 1/4* **Tevez**[11] 2187 5-10-6 **62** ... MrARawlinson(7) 4 51
(D Donovan) *hld up: hdwy 1/2-way: rdn over 1f out: wknd fnl f* **8/1**

005- **8** *9* **Jenny Soba**[165] 7751 7-10-2 **56** oh11 ... MrJPFeatherstone(5) 5 27
(Lucinda Featherstone) *prom: lost pl 6f out: bhd whn rdn over 3f out: hung rt over 2f out* **25/1**

0-30 **9** *1/2* **Maybe I Wont**[20] 1920 5-10-2 **58** ...(p) MrWFeatherstone(7) 1 28
(Lucinda Featherstone) *racd wd: chsd ldrs: rdn over 3f out: wknd over 2f out* **8/1**

2m 6.73s (0.93) **Going Correction** +0.025s/f (Good) 9 Ran SP% **117.8**
Speed ratings (Par 103): **96,96,97,93,93 91,89,82,81**
toteswingers:1&2:£6.80, 1&3:£12.00, 2&3:£6.10 CSF £34.96 CT £389.73 TOTE £8.60: £2.10, £2.20, £4.00; EX 51.60 Place 6 £14.99; Place 5 £4.13.
Owner N Bycroft **Bred** The National Stud Owner Breeders Club Ltd **Trained** Brandsby, N Yorks

FOCUS
A modest amateurs' handicap in which the last two successful riders were again taking part. It produced a desperate finish in which the three principals were involved in a bumping match in the closing stages, initiating a stewards' inquiry and the disqualification of the first past the post. The form is perhaps not the most solid.
Mons Calpe(IRE) Official explanation: jockey said gelding hung left
T/Jkpt: Not won. T/Plt: £32.70 to a £1 stake. Pool:£102,361.26 - 2,279.12 winning tickets T/Qpdt: £5.50 to a £1 stake. Pool:£5,551.03 - 746.26 winning tickets CR

1626 PONTEFRACT (L-H)
Friday, May 28

OFFICIAL GOING: Good to firm (watered; 9.1)
Temporary rail in place from 6f bend.
Wind: Light half behind Weather: Fine and dry

2512 ST. JOHN AMBULANCE H'CAP — 1m 4y
6:30 (6:30) (Class 5) (0-75,75) 4-Y-0+ — £2,914 (£867; £433; £216) Stalls Low

Form — RPR
03-2 **1** **Harriet's Girl**[6] 2328 4-9-2 **73** AndrewElliott 6 — 80
(J R Weymes) *hld up: hdwy to trck ldrs 1/2-way: effrt to chal 2f out: rdn to ld jst ins fnl f: drvn and edgd lft towards fin* **9/2**[2]
-012 **2** ½ **Chief Red Cloud (USA)**[11] 2187 4-8-12 **69** NeilCallan 5 — 75
(J R Weymes) *plld hrd: chsd ldrs on inner: rdn 2f out: styd on to chal ins fnl f: ev ch tl no ex nr fin* **5/1**[3]
3-04 **3** nk **North Cape (USA)**[21] 1883 4-9-2 **73** TonyCulhane 2 — 78
(H Candy) *trckd ldr: hdwy and cl up over 2f out: rdn to ld wl over 1f out: drvn and hdd jst ins fnl f: kpt on wl u.p towards fin* **6/4**[1]
0101 **4** 7 **Very Well Red**[24] 1797 7-9-1 **75** WilliamCarson(3) 1 — 64
(P W Hiatt) *led: rdn over 2f out: drvn and hdd wl over 1f out: grad wknd* **13/2**
000- **5** ½ **Betteras Bertie**[219] 6946 7-8-10 **67** PhillipMakin 3 — 55
(M Brittain) *dwlt and in rr: sme hdwy over 2f out: sn rdn and n.d* **16/1**
6000 **6** 2¼ **Negotiation (IRE)**[13] 2129 4-9-4 **75** FrannyNorton 4 — 58
(M Quinn) *chsd ldrs: rdn along over 3f out: sn wknd* **8/1**
00- **7** 10 **Bold Diktator**[223] 6861 8-8-0 **62** IanBrennan(5) 8 — 22
(R M Whitaker) *a towards rr: rdn along 3f out: sn outpcd and bhd* **25/1**

1m 43.39s (-2.51) **Going Correction** -0.225s/f (Firm) 7 Ran SP% **109.0**
Speed ratings (Par 103): **103,102,102,95,94 92,82**
toteswingers:1&2:£4.00, 1&3:£3.30, 2&3:£2.20 CSF £24.38 CT £43.13 TOTE £4.20: £1.50, £2.90; EX 21.50.
Owner Ray Bailey **Bred** J Sankey **Trained** Middleham Moor, N Yorks

FOCUS
A minor handicap run at a decent pace. The three market leaders pulled a long way clear of the rest and the time was 0.11 seconds under standard. The form looks pretty solid.
Betteras Bertie Official explanation: jockey said gelding missed the break

2513 CONSTANT SECURITY SERVING YORKSHIRE RACECOURSES H'CAP — 1m 4f 8y
7:00 (7:00) (Class 4) (0-85,85) 4-Y-0+ — £4,533 (£1,348; £674; £336) Stalls Low

Form — RPR
56-0 **1** **Rajeh (IRE)**[37] 1472 7-9-2 **83** LiamJones 4 — 93
(J L Spearing) *trckd ldng pair: hdwy to chse ldr after 3f: rdn to chal over 2f out: led wl over 1f out: drvn and edgd lft ins fnl f: kpt on gamely* **12/1**
12-6 **2** 3 **Eton Fable (IRE)**[18] 1960 5-8-12 **79** (p) TravisBlock 8 — 84
(W J H Ratcliffe) *set stdy pce: qcknd over 4f out: rdn and qcknd over 2f out: drvn and hdd wl over 1f out: kpt on same pce u.p ins fnl f* **16/1**
36-3 **3** 1½ **Lady Luachmhar (IRE)**[20] 1907 4-9-1 **82** PaulHanagan 7 — 85
(R A Fahey) *t.k.h early: hld up in tch: hdwy over 4f out: rdn along 3f out: drvn to chse ldng pair over 1f out: sn no imp* **5/4**[1]
1-60 **4** 3¾ **Blue Nymph**[16] 2031 4-8-7 **79** IanBrennan(5) 2 — 76
(J J Quinn) *hld up: hdwy over 4f out: rdn along over 2f out and sn one pce* **8/1**
-223 **5** 8 **Embsay Crag**[21] 1863 4-8-7 **81** LeeTopliss(7) 6 — 65
(Mrs K Walton) *t.k.h: prom: pushed along and lost pl whn rn wd bnd bef 1/2-way: sn rdn and bhd* **3/1**[2]
-504 **6** ¾ **Sirgarfieldsobers (IRE)**[16] 2031 4-9-4 **85** MickyFenton 1 — 68
(B S Rothwell) *chsd ldr 3f: prom tl rdn along 3f out: wknd 2f out* **5/1**[3]

2m 37.66s (-3.14) **Going Correction** -0.225s/f (Firm) 6 Ran SP% **110.8**
Speed ratings (Par 105): **101,99,98,95,90 89**
toteswingers:1&2:£10.70, 1&3:£5.10, 2&3:£3.70 CSF £154.23 CT £392.68 TOTE £13.50: £3.30, £3.80; EX 95.30.
Owner Miss C Ive **Bred** Mrs C S Acham **Trained** Kinnersley, Worcs

FOCUS
Not a strong handicap for the grade. The majority of runners had been well held on their latest run. The early pace was steady and nothing got into it from behind. The winner is rated to last summer's form.
Embsay Crag Official explanation: jockey said gelding hung right-handed throughout
Sirgarfieldsobers(IRE) Official explanation: jockey said gelding hung both ways

2514 DRURY PSM YOUNGSTERS CONDITIONS STKS — 6f
7:30 (7:31) (Class 2) 2-Y-0
£9,346 (£2,799; £1,399; £700; £349; £175) Stalls Low

Form — RPR
041 **1** **Galtymore Lad**[17] 1986 2-9-0 0 TonyCulhane 5 — 95
(M R Channon) *wnt lft s: cl up: rdn to ld 1 1/2f out: sn hung lft and drvn clr ent fnl f: kpt on* **11/1**
1 **2** 4 **Clarke Lane (USA)**[20] 1905 2-9-0 0 NeilCallan 4 — 83
(M A Jarvis) *trckd ldrs whn sltly hmpd after 2f and sn rdn along: outpcd wl over 2f out: hdwy on outer to chse wnr over 1f out: hung lft and drvn ins fnl f: no imp* **2/1**[1]
12 **3** 5 **My Son Max**[13] 2127 2-9-0 0 PatDobbs 6 — 68
(R Hannon) *hld up: swtchd to inner and hdwy 1/2-way: swtchd rt and effrt 2f out: rdn to chse wnr wl over 1f out: sn drvn and one pce* **2/1**[1]
1 **4** 1 **Twist Of Silver (USA)**[15] 2041 2-8-6 0 PaulHanagan 2 — 57
(J Noseda) *led: rdn along over 2f out: drvn and hdd 1 1/2f out: sn wknd* **5/1**[2]
1 **5** 2 **Dads Amigo**[25] 1749 2-8-11 0 PhillipMakin 3 — 56
(D H Brown) *sltly hmpd and squeezed out s: hdwy to trck ldrs 1/2-way: rdn along over 2f out and sn btn* **8/1**[3]
01 **6** hd **Mayhab**[17] 2007 2-9-0 0 PhilipRobinson 1 — 58
(C E Brittain) *cl up on inner: rdn along over 2f out and ev ch tl wknd wl over 1f out* **12/1**

1m 16.41s (-0.49) **Going Correction** -0.225s/f (Firm) 6 Ran SP% **110.5**
Speed ratings (Par 99): **94,88,82,80,78 77**
toteswingers:1&2:£8.70, 1&3:£5.70, 2&3:£1.20 CSF £32.39 TOTE £16.50: £5.10, £1.40; EX 47.80.
Owner Mrs M Findlay **Bred** Bearstone Stud **Trained** West Ilsley, Berks

FOCUS
A hot conditions race involving five last-time-out winners. The 11-1 winner did the job in impressive style and looks a useful prospect. The form could have been rated a few pounds higher or lower.

NOTEBOOK
Galtymore Lad showed significant improvement when justifying a landslide of support in an ordinary 5f Beverley maiden on his third start. He faced some much stiffer opposition this time but attracted support at big prices and powered clear for an emphatic success. The £28,000 yearling is out of a useful 5f winner at two, and the highly progressive type will be targeted for one of the races at Royal Ascot. (op 10-1 tchd 12-1)
Clarke Lane(USA) showed fighting spirit when beating a well-backed Godolphin rival in a 6f Haydock maiden on her debut this month. He was no match for the runaway winner this time but showed a good attitude to keep battling away out wide and finished a long way clear of the third. (op 5-2 tchd 11-4 in a place)
My Son Max overcame inexperience when making a successful debut at Nottingham and set the standard on his close second behind useful Klammer at Newmarket this month. He was ridden patiently and looked a potential threat early in the straight but his effort petered out. (op 9-4 tchd 5-2)
Twist Of Silver(USA) coasted home when a 13l odds-on winner in a three-runner maiden at Newmarket on debut. It was hard to know what she achieved on that occasion and she was comfortably outgunned this time. (op 4-1)
Dads Amigo gradually got the hang of things when pouncing late at Beverley on debut but he was caught flat-footed when the pace increased in this much stronger race and finished well held. (op 9-1)
Mayhab faded after making a brief effort against the far rail around the final turn. (op 10-1 tchd 15-2)

2515 CONSTANT SECURITY SERVICES H'CAP — 1m 4y
8:00 (8:01) (Class 4) (0-85,85) 3-Y-0 — £4,533 (£1,348; £674; £336) Stalls Low

Form — RPR
2110 **1** **Azlak (USA)**[8] 2254 3-8-11 **78** (b[1]) NeilCallan 6 — 85
(C E Brittain) *led 1f: trckd ldr: effrt and hung rt home turn: rdn to ld and hung sharply lft wl over 1f out: drvn ins fnl f: jst hld on* **10/1**
1333 **2** hd **Sweet Child O'Mine**[10] 2219 3-8-10 **77** FrannyNorton 7 — 84
(R C Guest) *trckd ldrs: hdwy over 2f out: rdn whn n.m.r and swtchd rt wl over 1f out: sn chsng wnr: drvn and kpt on ins fnl f: jst hld* **7/2**[2]
-002 **3** ¾ **First Cat**[8] 2253 3-8-10 **77** PatDobbs 3 — 82
(R Hannon) *hld up and bhd: stdy hdwy 3f out: effrt on outer wl over 1f out: rdn to chse ldng pair whn hung lft and awkward 1f out: sn drvn and kpt on towards fin* **9/4**[1]
24-3 **4** 2½ **Elmfield Giant (USA)**[14] 2072 3-8-7 **74** PaulHanagan 5 — 74
(R A Fahey) *prom: led after 1f: rdn along over 2f out: drvn and hdd wl over 1f out: grad wknd* **7/1**
22-3 **5** 1 **Taste The Victory (USA)**[20] 1927 3-8-8 **75** PJMcDonald 2 — 72
(G A Swinbank) *hld up in tch: hdwy 3f out: rdn along wl over 1f out: sn no imp* **9/2**[3]
6-10 **6** 3¼ **Much Acclaimed (IRE)**[26] 1730 3-9-4 **85** MickyFenton 1 — 75
(T P Tate) *trckd ldrs: hdwy over 3f out: rdn along over 2f out: sn wknd* **9/2**[3]

1m 43.8s (-2.10) **Going Correction** -0.225s/f (Firm) 6 Ran SP% **110.9**
Speed ratings (Par 101): **101,100,100,97,96 93**
toteswingers:1&2:£5.70, 1&3:£3.60, 2&3:£2.00 CSF £43.25 TOTE £12.30: £6.60, £2.00; EX 42.70.
Owner Saeed Manana **Bred** Rabbah Bloodstock Llc **Trained** Newmarket, Suffolk

FOCUS
A decent handicap run at a fair pace. The form looks sound enough.

2516 MSK FILLIES' H'CAP — 1m 2f 6y
8:30 (8:30) (Class 5) (0-70,70) 3-Y-0+ — £3,238 (£963; £481; £240) Stalls Low

Form — RPR
43-0 **1** **City Vaults Girl (IRE)**[16] 2033 3-9-5 **70** PaulHanagan 5 — 76
(R A Fahey) *set stdy pce: rdn and qcknd wl over 2f out: drvn over 1f out: styd on gamely u.p ins fnl f* **5/1**
25-0 **2** ¾ **Aquarius Star (IRE)**[46] 1260 3-9-5 **70** DaneO'Neill 6 — 74+
(Pat Eddery) *hld up in rr: hdwy 3f out: rdn to chse ldng pair wl over 1f out: drvn ins fnl f: kpt on* **7/2**[2]
20-5 **3** 1½ **Chantilly Pearl (USA)**[21] 1883 4-9-12 **63** FrederikTylicki 3 — 65+
(J G Given) *hld up in tch: pushed along and sltly outpcd wl over 2f out: swtchd rt and rdn to chse ldrs over 1f out: drvn and kpt on ins fnl f: nrst fin* **11/4**[1]
0-40 **4** 1½ **Chichen Daawe**[20] 1920 4-9-0 51 oh4 PJMcDonald 2 — 50
(B Ellison) *sn trcking wnr: rdn along over 2f out: drvn over 1f out: grad wknd ent fnl f* **10/1**
400- **5** 5 **Al Joza**[237] 6477 3-9-0 **65** NeilCallan 1 — 53
(C E Brittain) *trckd ldrs on inner: effrt over 2f out: sn rdn and wknd wl over 1f out* **4/1**[3]
6115 **6** 1½ **Sudden Impulse**[14] 2084 9-9-13 **64** SilvestreDeSousa 7 — 50
(A D Brown) *trckd ldrs: effrt 3f out: sn rdn: wknd wl over 1f out* **7/1**
4400 **7** 6 **Sacco D'Oro**[7] 2285 4-8-8 **52** JosephYoung(7) 4 — 26
(M Mullineaux) *t.k.h: chsd ldrs on inner: rdn along 3f out and sn wknd* **16/1**

2m 15.27s (1.57) **Going Correction** -0.225s/f (Firm)
WFA 3 from 4yo+ 14lb 7 Ran SP% **113.0**
Speed ratings (Par 100): **84,83,82,81,77 75,71**
toteswingers:1&2:£2.50, 1&3:£1.50, 2&3:£2.50 CSF £22.23 CT £56.61 TOTE £5.10: £2.60, £2.40; EX 26.90.
Owner City Vaults Racing **Bred** Davin Investments Ltd **Trained** Musley Bank, N Yorks

FOCUS
A modest fillies' handicap run at a steady pace. The winner was given a shrewd front-running ride and the form has been taken at face value.

2517 BIG FELLAS NIGHTCLUB PONTEFRACT MAIDEN STKS — 6f
9:00 (9:00) (Class 5) 3-Y-0 — £2,914 (£867; £433; £216) Stalls Low

Form — RPR
62-6 **1** **Robinson Cruso**[28] 1659 3-9-3 84 (p) PhilipRobinson 6 — 89
(M A Jarvis) *mde all: rdn clr wl over 1f out: styd on strly* **11/4**[1]

425- **2** 2½ **King Of Windsor (IRE)**[225] 6802 3-9-3 83 .... PaulHanagan 5 81
(R M Beckett) *trckd ldrs: hdwy over 2f out: rdn to chse wnr ent fnl f: kpt on* **7/2**[3]

3 **3** 2 **Feel The Heat**[13] 2114 3-9-3 0 .... FrannyNorton 9 75+
(B Smart) *hld up: hdwy over 2f out: rdn wl over 1f out: styd on ins fnl f: nrst fin* **10/1**

0- **4** ½ **Times Ahead (USA)**[294] 4756 3-9-3 0 .... NeilCallan 1 73
(P W Chapple-Hyam) *chsd wnr: rdn along over 2f out: drvn wl over 1f out: grad wknd* **6/1**

2 **5** nse **Kielder (IRE)**[21] 1890 3-9-3 0 .... PhillipMakin 7 73+
(T D Barron) *chsd ldrs on outer: rdn along wl over 1f out: sn one pce* **3/1**[2]

6 **6** 5 **Haafhd Sharp**[18] 1966 3-8-12 0 .... JerryO'Dwyer 3 52
(M G Quinlan) *in tch: hdwy on inner over 2f out: rdn to chse ldrs wl over 1f out: drvn and wknd appr fnl f* **40/1**

0 **7** 3 **Marteau**[61] 1029 3-9-3 0 .... PatDobbs 4 47
(K A Ryan) *dwlt: a in rr* **16/1**

32-6 **8** 3½ **Olney Lass**[46] 1269 3-8-9 71 .... KellyHarrison(3) 2 31
(W J H Ratcliffe) *chsd ldng pair: rdn along over 2f out: wknd wl over 1f out* **14/1**

9 50 **Gypsy Style** 3-8-12 0 .... PJMcDonald 10 —
(Mrs K Walton) *s.i.s: a bhd* **20/1**

1m 16.15s (-0.75) **Going Correction** -0.225s/f (Firm) 9 Ran SP% **117.0**
Speed ratings (Par 99): **96,92,90,89,89 82,78,73,7**
toteswingers:1&2:£2.30, 1&3:£5.70, 2&3:£5.30 CSF £12.83 TOTE £3.30: £1.10, £1.10, £3.20; EX 11.00 Place 6 £2510.19; Place 5 £942.49.
Owner P D Smith **Bred** D G Hardisty Bloodstock & Marston Stud **Trained** Newmarket, Suffolk

FOCUS
A decent maiden. The first two home had BHA ratings in the low 80s and the form looks solid enough rated through the first two.
Olney Lass Official explanation: trainer's rep said filly was unsuited by the good to firm ground
T/Plt: £1,440.80 to a £1 stake. Pool:£63,101.36 - 31.97 winning tickets T/Qpdt: £61.30 to a £1 stake. Pool:£4,308.89 - 52.00 winning tickets JR

2518 - 2521a (Foreign Racing) - See Raceform Interactive

2434 BEVERLEY (R-H)

Saturday, May 29

OFFICIAL GOING: Good to firm (9.3)
Wind: Light across Weather: Overcast and light rain

2522 PAUL-PICKARD.CO.UK MEDIAN AUCTION MAIDEN STKS 5f
2:10 (2:11) (Class 4) 2-Y-O £3,885 (£1,156; £577; £288) **Stalls** High

Form RPR

1 **Ladies Are Forever** 2-8-9 0 .... BarryMcHugh(3) 5 85+
(G R Oldroyd) *cl up: led over 2f out: shkn up and qcknd clr ent fnl f: easily* **17/2**

4 **2** 6 **Ice Trooper**[18] 1986 2-8-12 0 .... JamesSullivan(5) 10 68
(Mrs L Stubbs) *sn led: rdn along and hdd over 2f out: drvn and kpt on fnl f: no ch w wnr* **7/2**[2]

3 4 **Philharmonic Hall** 2-9-3 0 .... TonyHamilton 8 54
(R A Fahey) *trckd ldrs: hdwy 2f out: sn rdn and kpt on same pce* **4/1**[3]

2 **4** 1½ **Last Destination (IRE)**[26] 1749 2-9-3 0 .... SilvestreDeSousa 1 49
(N Tinkler) *hld up: hdwy 2f out: sn rdn: chsd ldrs and edgd rt over 1f out: no imp fnl f* **9/4**[1]

60 **5** 3¾ **Rational Act (IRE)**[9] 2238 2-9-3 0 .... FrederikTylicki 2 35
(T D Easterby) *chsd ldrs on outer: rdn along over 2f out: edgd rt and wknd wl over 1f out* **20/1**

50 **6** 1¼ **Blind Stag (IRE)**[26] 1749 2-8-12 0 .... PaulPickard(5) 9 31
(P T Midgley) *chsd ldrs on inner: rdn along 2f out: grad wknd* **8/1**

7 1 **Marina Belle** 2-8-12 0 .... RoystonFfrench 3 22
(M Johnston) *prom: pushed along and green after 1f: sn rdn along: lost pl and bhd bef 1/2-way* **8/1**

0 **8** 3 **Stevie Bee Party**[8] 2272 2-8-12 0 .... IanBrennan(5) 4 16
(I W McInnes) *dwlt: a in rr* **100/1**

9 20 **Pinotage** 2-9-3 0 .... PaulQuinn 7 —
(R M Whitaker) *s.i.s: a bhd* **25/1**

62.19 secs (-1.31) **Going Correction** -0.225s/f (Firm) 9 Ran SP% **115.3**
Speed ratings (Par 95): **101,91,85,82,76 74,73,68,36**
toteswingers:1&2:£8.60, 1&3:£11.80, 2&3:£3.50 CSF £37.67 TOTE £12.60: £2.40, £1.30, £2.60; EX 56.40.
Owner R C Bond **Bred** Bond Thoroughbred Corporation **Trained** Brawby, N Yorks

FOCUS
A dry night, but a bit of drizzle started to fall shortly before racing. Jockeys in the opener reported the ground to be "pretty good". An ordinary maiden overall which was dominated by the first two. The winner raced some way off the inside rail and was really impressive. She could have been rated in the high 80s.

NOTEBOOK
Ladies Are Forever ◆ was the subject of good pre-race reports and made a highly impressive debut. Well away, she matched strides with the runner-up before easing ahead around two furlongs out and careering right away in the last 100 yards. A sister to this season's progressive sprinter Hoof It, out of a half-sister to Wokingham winner Ratio, she is regarded by her trainer as his best two-year-old. She will have no problem with a sixth furlong and her trainer is already thinking ahead to the Group 2 Lowther Stakes at York in August, but she is still a bit unfurnished and won't be overraced this year. (op 8-1)
Ice Trooper, who had been fourth over the course and distance on his debut earlier this month, was the subject of support. He was better away from the stalls this time and showed bright pace from his berth nearest the fence, but could do nothing when the winner engaged overdrive inside the final furlong. He still finished a clear of the rest and should soon be winning. (op 5-1 tchd 11-2)
Philharmonic Hall, a half-brother to the useful Philharmonic, is a nice type and he shaped with plenty of promise back in third, albeit beaten 10l by the useful winner. An ordinary race should soon be found for him. (tchd 7-2 and 9-2)
Last Destination(IRE) set the standard on his narrow debut defeat here, but he was disappointing and could never get into the race from his low draw. He was running on when it was all over and may require a stiffer test now. (op 2-1)
Rational Act(IRE) ran respectably without suggesting that the drop in trip was what he wanted. (op 28-1)
Blind Stag(IRE), whose jockey had the race named after him, finished closer to Last Destination than he had here last time but he had a decent draw on this occasion and does not seem to be progressing. (op 15-2 tchd 9-1)
Marina Belle is a half-sister to Marinas Charm who won for Mark Johnston as a juvenile, out of a smart sprinter for the stable. She broke well but looked markedly green and very quickly found herself dropping back through the field until she had only one behind her. She made a little late progress and can leave this running behind in time. (op 7-1 tchd 6-1)
Pinotage Official explanation: jockey said colt ran green

2523 BERYL AND JOE TURNER MEMORIAL H'CAP 1m 1f 207y
2:40 (2:40) (Class 5) (0-75,75) 4-Y-O+ £3,070 (£906; £453) **Stalls** High

Form RPR

0325 **1** **General Tufto**[15] 2093 5-8-10 72 .... (b) BillyCray(5) 2 81
(C Smith) *hld up in rr: gd hdwy on inner over 2f out: swtchd lft and effrt over 1f out: rdn and styd on to ld jst ins fnl f: styd on strly* **5/1**

5-40 **2** 2½ **Veroon (IRE)**[21] 1925 4-9-4 75 .... (p) FrederikTylicki 3 79
(J G Given) *trckd ldr: clsd up 3f out: rdn to ld 1 1/2f out: drvn ent fnl f: sn hdd and one pce* **15/8**[1]

065- **3** 1 **Trumpstoo (USA)**[196] 6384 4-8-4 61 .... FranciscoDaSilva 1 63
(R A Fahey) *trckd ldng pair on inner: hdwy 3f out: swtchd lft and effrt over 2f out: rdn to chal over 1f out and ev ch tl drvn and one pce ins fnl f* **4/1**[3]

-135 **4** 4 **King Of The Moors (USA)**[7] 2328 7-8-13 70 .... (p) RoystonFfrench 5 64
(R C Guest) *set stdy pce: qcknd over 3f out: rdn along over 2f out: hdd and drvn 1 1/2f out: sn wknd* **7/2**[2]

3-00 **5** 2 **Solis**[70] 451 4-8-0 62 .... IanBrennan(5) 4 52
(J J Quinn) *stmbld bdly and lost 5 l s: tk clsr order 1/2-way: chsd ldrs over 3f out: sn rdn and wknd wl over 1f out* **11/2**

2m 6.95s (-0.05) **Going Correction** -0.225s/f (Firm) 5 Ran SP% **109.1**
Speed ratings (Par 103): **91,89,88,85,83**
CSF £14.52 TOTE £4.50: £2.00, £1.40; EX 14.10.
Owner Phil Martin & Trev Sleath **Bred** Hascombe And Valiant Studs **Trained** Temple Bruer, Lincs

FOCUS
A modest handicap run at no more than an ordinary pace. Straightforward form, the winner matching his AW best.
Trumpstoo(USA) Official explanation: jockey said gelding slipped on leaving stalls
Solis Official explanation: jockey said gelding stumbled at start

2524 GILBERT JOHNSON 80 NOT OUT STKS (H'CAP) 7f 100y
3:10 (3:10) (Class 4) (0-80,77) 4-Y-O+ £4,533 (£1,348; £674; £336) **Stalls** High

Form RPR

-005 **1** **Summer Dancer (IRE)**[11] 2205 6-9-3 76 .... MickyFenton 7 84
(P T Midgley) *hld up in rr: hdwy on inner over 2f out: swtchd lft over 1f out and sn rdn: styd on u.p ins fnl f to ld nr fin* **14/1**

2350 **2** nk **Ansells Pride (IRE)**[31] 1628 7-8-7 66 .... SilvestreDeSousa 4 73
(B Smart) *chsd ldr: hdwy to ld wl over 1f out: drvn ins fnl f: hdd and no ex nr fin* **7/1**

30-5 **3** 1½ **Observatory Star (IRE)**[26] 1752 7-9-4 77 .... (tp) FrederikTylicki 9 80
(T D Easterby) *trckd ldrs: hdwy over 2f out: rdn to chse ldr over 1f out: sn drvn and kpt on same pce ins fnl f* **5/1**[3]

2002 **4** ¾ **Indian Skipper (IRE)**[7] 2327 5-8-13 77 .... (be) BillyCray(5) 5 80+
(R C Guest) *dwlt: hld up and bhd: hdwy on inner 2f out: nt clr run and swtchd lft over 1f out: rdn and n.m.r ins fnl f: kpt on towards fin* **6/1**

6402 **5** 3¼ **Kipchak (IRE)**[18] 1995 5-8-2 66 .... (p) JamesSullivan(5) 1 59
(C R Dore) *sn led: rdn along over 2f out: drvn and hdd wl over 1f out: wknd appr fnl f* **16/1**

60-2 **6** nse **Celtic Lynn (IRE)**[25] 1808 5-9-0 73 .... TonyHamilton 6 66
(M Dods) *in tch: hdwy on outer over 2f out: rdn wl over 1f out and sn no imp* **6/1**

-065 **7** ½ **Glenmuir (IRE)**[25] 1802 7-8-4 68 .... IanBrennan(5) 3 60
(J J Quinn) *towards rr: pushed along after 3f: rdn and sme hdwy on wd outside over 2f out: n.d* **7/2**[1]

0-00 **8** 4 **Desert Falls**[15] 2086 4-8-13 72 .... DaraghO'Donohoe 8 54
(R M Whitaker) *chsd ldng pair: rdn along over 2f out: sn wknd* **18/1**

2031 **9** 4 **Elusive Fame (USA)**[18] 1997 4-8-11 70 .... (b) RoystonFfrench 2 42
(M Johnston) *chsd ldrs: rdn along over 2f out: sn wknd* **9/2**[2]

1m 31.21s (-2.59) **Going Correction** -0.225s/f (Firm) 9 Ran SP% **116.0**
Speed ratings (Par 105): **105,104,102,102,98 98,97,93,88**
toteswingers:1&2:£16.00, 1&3:£4.70, 2&3:£6.90 CSF £108.38 CT £568.60 TOTE £14.50: £3.40, £2.50, £1.30; EX 147.10.
Owner The Howarting's Partnership **Bred** Eddie O'Leary **Trained** Westow, N Yorks

FOCUS
Just an ordinary handicap, but the pace was brisk and the form ought to prove solid. The winner is rated close to last year's best.
Desert Falls Official explanation: jockey said gelding had no more to give

2525 BRIAN YEARDLEY CONTINENTAL TWO YEAR OLD TROPHY CONDITIONS STKS 5f
3:40 (3:40) (Class 2) 2-Y-O £9,346 (£2,799; £1,399; £700; £349) **Stalls** High

Form RPR

51 **1** **Boundless Spirit**[15] 2068 2-9-2 0 .... RoystonFfrench 4 88
(B Smart) *mde all: clr 1/2-way: rdn wl over 1f out: drvn ins fnl f: hld on wl* **4/1**[3]

1 **2** 1 **Chiswick Bey (IRE)**[63] 1009 2-9-2 0 .... TonyHamilton 3 84
(R A Fahey) *chsd wnr: rdn along and sltly outpcd 2f out: drvn and styd on wl fnl f* **2/1**[2]

1 **3** hd **On The High Tops (IRE)**[25] 1806 2-9-0 0 .... MickyFenton 5 81
(T P Tate) *hld up in tch: hdwy 1/2-way: chsd wnr wl over 1f out: rdn and ch ins fnl f: sn drvn and one pce last 100yds* **7/4**[1]

112 **4** 6 **Bathwick Bear (IRE)**[24] 1819 2-9-6 0 .... CathyGannon 2 66
(P D Evans) *chsd ldrs: rdn along over 2f out: sn drvn and outpcd appr fnl f* **11/2**

14 **5** 1 **Orientalist**[14] 2127 2-9-2 0 .... SilvestreDeSousa 1 58
(Eve Johnson Houghton) *chsd ldrs: rdn along 1/2-way: sn outpcd and in rr* **14/1**

62.22 secs (-1.28) **Going Correction** -0.225s/f (Firm) 5 Ran SP% **111.7**
Speed ratings (Par 99): **101,99,99,89,87**
CSF £12.62 TOTE £5.00: £1.80, £1.60; EX 18.70.
Owner Pinnacle Invincible Spirit Partnership **Bred** Silfield Bloodstock **Trained** Hambleton, N Yorks

FOCUS
All five were previous winners in this warm conditions race, which last year saw subsequent Group 1 scorer Hearts Of Fire beaten into second by Archers Road. The pace was sound although the time was slightly slower than the maiden which opened the card. Boundless Spirit improved again and probably has a bit more to offer.

NOTEBOOK
Boundless Spirit was a good way behind Bathwick Bear on his debut but he won well at Hamilton next time and improved again here. Making all at a fast pace, he was getting a bit tired as the line loomed and his lead was being reduced, but held on well to give his trainer his second win in this race in three years, following Able Master in 2008. He will go to Ascot, either for the Windsor Castle or the Norfolk Stakes. (op 5-1)
Chiswick Bey(IRE) had deliberately been given a break to allow him to strengthen since his win in an ordinary renewal of the Brocklesby in late March. He chased the winner for much of the trip and rallied close home, sugggesting that there are more races to be won with him, perhaps over 6f. These different underfoot conditions were not a problem. (op 3-1)

On The High Tops(IRE), who was in receipt of weight from his rivals, travelled quite well nearest the rail. He improved to challenge for second but could not get to the winner and was held close home. (op 2-1)
Bathwick Bear(IRE) who lost his unbeaten record in the Lily Agnes at Chester, was attempting to concede 4lb or more to his rivals. Struggling from halfway, he is not really progressing. Official explanation: vet said colt returned lame right-fore (op 3-1)
Orientalist was taken off his feet on this drop back down to the minimum trip, even on this stiff track. (op 10-1)

2526 BRANTINGHAM CONDITIONS STKS 5f
4:15 (4:15) (Class 2) 3-Y-0+ **£10,592** (£3,172; £1,586; £793; £396) **Stalls** High

Form				RPR
2-46	**1**		**Look Busy (IRE)**[7] 2325 5-8-7 104 .... PatrickMathers 1 (A Berry) *slipped and dwlt s: hld up: hdwy 2f out: swtchd rt and hdwy on inner appr fnl f: rdn and qcknd to ld last 100yds* **7/4**[1]	106
-403	**2**	½	**Masta Plasta (IRE)**[7] 2346 7-8-12 101 .... MichaelGeran 5 (D Nicholls) *led: rdn along 2f out: drvn ent fnl f: hdd last 100yds: kpt on* **9/2**	109
11-1	**3**	*hd*	**Kaldoun Kingdom (IRE)**[62] 1032 5-8-12 102 .... TonyHamilton 6 (R A Fahey) *trckd ldrs: hdwy and cl up 1/2-way: rdn and ev ch over 1f out tl drvn ins fnl f and nt qckn last 50yds* **11/4**[2]	108
3304	**4**	1 ¾	**Fitz Flyer (IRE)**[5] 2400 4-8-12 100 .... RoystonFfrench 3 (D H Brown) *cl up: rdn along over 2f out: drvn over 1f out: kpt on same pce u.p ins fnl f* **7/2**[3]	102
60-0	**5**	6	**Tombi (USA)**[21] 1904 6-8-12 101 .... (p) FrederikTylicki 2 (J Howard Johnson) *cl up on outer: rdn along over 2f out: wknd over 1f out* **14/1**	81

61.66 secs (-1.84) **Going Correction** -0.225s/f (Firm) **5** Ran SP% **110.1**
Speed ratings (Par 109): **105,104,103,101,91**
CSF £9.89 TOTE £2.20: £1.10, £3.40; EX 6.00.
Owner A Underwood **Bred** Tom And Hazel Russell **Trained** Cockerham, Lancs

FOCUS
A decent conditions race run in a time 0.66secs outside the RP standard. The winner did not need to her match her best and the next two ran to form.

NOTEBOOK
Look Busy(IRE) was without a win since taking Haydock's Temple Stakes just over a year ago, but ran well in the same race last week considering she lost both front shoes. Dropped in from her outside stall after a slow start, she had to wait for a run, but a gap opened up for her against the rail inside the last and she quickened up to lead. Also successful in this event two years ago, and now unbeaten in three starts over course and distance, she had 7lb plus in hand of her rivals on adjusted official figures and was below her best in victory. She is likely to head for the Group 2 Sapphire Stakes at the Curragh on Irish Derby day next. (op 9-4)
Masta Plasta(IRE), back in conditions company, made the running and battled on well, but could not repel the winner's challenge inside the last. He retains a lot of ability, but is one of those 'twilight' sprinters who is difficult to place successfully and he's without a win since October 2008. (op 5-1 tchd 11-2)
Kaldoun Kingdom(IRE) ran a fine race stepping out of handicap company and might even have poked his nose in front for a few strides before going down fighting. Considering that 6f and easy ground are his optimum conditions this was a fine run, and he deserves a crack at a Listed race now. (op 5-2 tchd 9-4)
Fitz Flyer(IRE), making a quick reappearance, ran his race with no apparent excuses. He is likely to prove hard to win with in the short term. (op 3-1 tchd 4-1)
Tombi(USA), fitted with cheekpieces for the first time, was in trouble by halfway and has now beaten just one rival in his last three starts. This was only his third ever run over 5f and it was too sharp for him. (op 12-1 tchd 16-1)

2527 NICK WATTS 50TH BIRTHDAY H'CAP 1m 100y
4:50 (4:50) (Class 5) (0-70,70) 4-Y-0+ **£2,914** (£867; £433; £216) **Stalls** High

Form				RPR
4-26	**1**		**Shadowtime**[5] 2392 5-9-0 66 .... AndrewMullen 8 (Miss Tracy Waggott) *hld up: hdwy 3f out: rdn to ld wl over 1f out: sn jnd: drvn and hdd ent fnl f: rallied wl u.p to ld nr line* **2/1**[1]	77
0605	**2**	*nk*	**Ninth House (USA)**[21] 1926 8-8-3 60 .... (t) JamesSullivan(5) 1 (Mrs R A Carr) *hld up: hdwy 3f out: effrt to chal wl over 1f out: rdn to ld ent fnl f: sn drvn: hdd and no ex nr fin* **12/1**	70
-006	**3**	5	**Northern Flyer (GER)**[26] 1754 4-8-1 58 .... (p) IanBrennan(5) 11 (J J Quinn) *chsd ldng pair: effrt whn nt clr run over 1f out: swtchd lft and rdn ent fnl f: one pce* **8/1**	57+
60-3	**4**	½	**Flying Silks (IRE)**[36] 1508 4-8-13 65 .... (b[1]) LukeMorris 12 (J R Gask) *chsd ldrs: hdwy over 2f out and sn rdn: drvn and kpt on same pce ent fnl f* **5/1**[2]	63
00-4	**5**	1 ½	**Polish World (USA)**[33] 1574 6-7-13 56 oh6 .... PaulPickard(5) 2 (P T Midgley) *cl up: rdn along over 2f out and ev ch tl drvn: edgd rt and wknd appr fnl f* **18/1**	50+
435-	**6**	4	**Postman**[295] 4741 4-9-4 70 .... FrederikTylicki 3 (B Smart) *in tch: hung bdly lft bnd at 1/2-way: rdn to chse ldrs over 2f out: sn drvn and n.d* **16/1**	55
3103	**7**	3	**By Command**[5] 2392 5-8-11 68 .... (tp) AmyRyan(5) 10 (K A Ryan) *hld up in midfield: hdwy over 2f out: sn rdn and nvr nr ldrs* **6/1**[3]	46
-040	**8**	3 ¼	**Coole Dodger (IRE)**[22] 1891 5-8-4 56 oh3 .... FranciscoDaSilva 4 (B Ellison) *hld up in rr: sme hdwy over 2f out: sn rdn and nvr a factor* **20/1**	27
0016	**9**	1 ½	**Provost**[50] 1204 6-8-7 59 .... (b) TonyHamilton 9 (M W Easterby) *a towards rr* **20/1**	26
50-3	**10**	*nk*	**One Scoop Or Two**[21] 1922 4-8-4 56 oh5 .... DaraghO'Donohoe 5 (R Hollinshead) *a towards rr* **20/1**	22
0-45	**11**	2 ¾	**Nuit Sombre (IRE)**[29] 1673 10-8-8 60 .... (v) SilvestreDeSousa 13 (G A Harker) *set str pce: rdn along over 2f out: hdd and drvn wl over 1f out: sn wknd* **12/1**	20
6-00	**12**	1	**Tanforan**[21] 1926 8-8-3 60 .... BillyCray(5) 6 (B P J Baugh) *dwlt: a in rr* **33/1**	18
0-06	**13**	5	**Green Passion (USA)**[35] 1520 4-8-6 58 .... (b[1]) RoystonFfrench 7 (M Johnston) *chsd ldrs: edgd lft bnd at 1/2-way: rdn along over 2f out and sn wknd* **20/1**	4

1m 44.03s (-3.57) **Going Correction** -0.225s/f (Firm) **13** Ran SP% **123.9**
Speed ratings (Par 103): **108,107,102,102,100 96,93,90,88,88 85,84,79**
toteswingers:1&2:£6.50, 1&3:£7.80, 2&3:not won CSF £26.62 CT £177.43 TOTE £2.90: £1.10, £3.30, £3.30; EX 34.90.
Owner H Conlon **Bred** Darley **Trained** Spennymoor, Co Durham

FOCUS
The pace in this modest handicap was strong courtesy of Nuit Sombre and the field was quickly strung out. The first two came clear to fight out the finish and the winner rates a 4lb personal best.
Flying Silks(IRE) Official explanation: jockey said gelding hung right
Polish World(USA) Official explanation: jockey said gelding hung right
Coole Dodger(IRE) Official explanation: jockey said saddle slipped
Tanforan Official explanation: jockey said gelding slipped at start

2528 HAPPY 50TH BIRTHDAY GRAHAM HALLETT H'CAP 5f
5:25 (5:25) (Class 5) (0-75,75) 4-Y-0+ **£2,914** (£867; £433; £216) **Stalls** High

Form				RPR
0611	**1**		**Chosen One (IRE)**[11] 2213 5-8-4 66 .... JamesSullivan(5) 15 (Mrs R A Carr) *chsd ldrs: hdwy 2f out: led over 1f out: sn jnd and rdn: drvn ins fnl f and kpt on wl towards fin* **11/4**[1]	76
-406	**2**	½	**Select Committee**[18] 1988 5-8-6 68 .... IanBrennan(5) 13 (J J Quinn) *towards rr: hdwy 1/2-way: swtchd rt and rdn to chal over 1f out: drvn and ev ch ins fnl f tl nt qckn towards fin* **7/2**[2]	76
43-0	**3**	½	**Tyfos**[14] 2113 5-8-13 75 .... BillyCray(5) 2 (B P J Baugh) *prom: rdn and cl up 2f out: drvn over 1f out and ev ch tl nt qckn wl ins fnl f* **16/1**	81
12-5	**4**	*nk*	**Cheyenne Red (IRE)**[22] 1869 4-8-8 70 .... PatrickDonaghy(5) 6 (M Dods) *towards rr: hdwy over 2f out: rdn over 1f out: styd on ins fnl f: nrst fin* **5/1**[3]	75+
-031	**5**	¾	**Perlachy**[113] 431 6-8-13 70 .... (v) LukeMorris 5 (D Shaw) *chsd ldrs: rdn along 2f out: drvn over 1f out and one pce fnl f* **28/1**	72
-502	**6**	1 ¼	**Milton Of Campsie**[15] 2073 5-9-3 74 .... MickyFenton 8 (J Balding) *midfield: hdwy 1/2-way: rdn to chse ldrs over 1f out: drvn and one pce ins fnl f* **9/1**	72
0-00	**7**	¾	**Bravely (IRE)**[14] 2136 6-8-13 70 .... PatrickMathers 1 (T D Easterby) *wnt lft s and bhd: hdwy wl over 1f out: sn rdn and styd on wl fnl f: nrst fin* **20/1**	65
0060	**8**	¾	**King Of Swords (IRE)**[18] 1988 6-8-8 65 .... (p) SilvestreDeSousa 4 (N Tinkler) *towards rr: hdwy wl over 1f out: sn rdn and no imp* **8/1**	58
3144	**9**	*nse*	**Colorus (IRE)**[28] 1710 7-8-10 72 .... (p) PaulPickard(5) 7 (W J H Ratcliffe) *led: rdn along 2f out: drvn wl over 1f out: sn hdd & wknd* **22/1**	64
14-0	**10**	¾	**Rainy Night**[42] 1391 4-8-7 64 .... DaraghO'Donohoe 12 (R Hollinshead) *chsd ldrs: rdn along 2f out: grad wknd* **12/1**	54
-160	**11**	¾	**Dispol Grand (IRE)**[35] 1524 4-8-11 68 .... TonyHamilton 9 (P T Midgley) *cl up: rdn along 2f out: wknd over 1f out* **28/1**	55
0-06	**12**	2 ½	**Divine Spirit**[21] 1923 9-8-4 61 oh4 .... RoystonFfrench 14 (M Dods) *a in rr* **18/1**	39
1100	**13**	18	**Lord Of The Reins (IRE)**[18] 1988 6-9-1 72 .... FrederikTylicki 11 (J G Given) *sn rdn along in rr: outpcd and bhd fr 1/2-way* **14/1**	—

62.00 secs (-1.50) **Going Correction** -0.225s/f (Firm) **13** Ran SP% **128.2**
Speed ratings (Par 103): **103,102,101,100,99 97,96,95,95,94 92,88,60**
toteswingers:1&2:£3.10, 1&3:£20.80, 2&3:£40.00 CSF £12.31 CT £140.68 TOTE £4.40: £1.50, £2.40, £6.30; EX 18.60 Place 6: £82.57 Place 5: £42.68.
Owner David W Chapman **Bred** Carl Holt **Trained** Huby, N Yorks

FOCUS
An ordinary sprint handicap and the fourth race on the card over the minimum trip. The time was only 0.34sec slower than the earlier Class 2 conditions stakes. The first two were both drawn high, traditionally a plus here, but ended up contesting the finish some distance away from the inside rail. Solid form.
T/Plt: £117.90 to a £1 stake. Pool of £56,272.68 - 348.21 winning tickets. T/Qpdt: £47.60 to a £1 stake. Pool of £2,976.50 - 46.20 winning tickets. JR

2272 CATTERICK (L-H)
Saturday, May 29

OFFICIAL GOING: Good to firm changing to good (good to firm in places) after race 4 (3.25)
Wind: Breezy, half behind Weather: Overcast

2529 TOTEPLACEPOT (S) STKS 1m 3f 214y
1:55 (1:55) (Class 6) 4-Y-0+ **£2,047** (£604; £302) **Stalls** Low

Form				RPR
3006	**1**		**Sea Land (FR)**[7] 2349 6-8-11 52 .... PJMcDonald 8 (B Ellison) *plld hrd: hld up in tch: hdwy over 2f out: led ins fnl f: kpt on wl* **11/4**[2]	58
4365	**2**	½	**New England**[18] 2006 8-8-11 53 .... LukeMorris 1 (N J Vaughan) *trckd ldrs: hdwy to ld over 1f out: hdd ins fnl f: kpt on: hld nr fin* **6/4**[1]	57
/550	**3**	¾	**Without Equal**[11] 2214 4-7-13 38 .... MatthewLawson(7) 6 (A Dickman) *t.k.h: sn cl up: led over 2f to 1f out: kpt on same pce ins fnl f* **16/1**	51
3360	**4**	4	**Barbirolli**[8] 2302 8-8-11 43 .... JerryO'Dwyer 2 (W B Stone) *prom: effrt over 2f out: outpcd over 1f out* **4/1**[3]	50
50-0	**5**	12	**Kochanski (IRE)**[10] 130 4-8-6 51 .... (b[1]) GrahamGibbons 4 (J R Weymes) *t.k.h: led 5f: cl up: led again briefly over 2f out: wknd over 1f out* **8/1**	25
0000	**6**	15	**Pitbull**[9] 2240 7-8-7 47 ow1 .... (v[1]) MarkCoumbe(5) 3 (A Berry) *plld hrd: hld up: hdwy on ins to ld after 5f: hdd over 2f out: sn wknd* **28/1**	7

2m 40.36s (1.46) **Going Correction** -0.025s/f (Good) **6** Ran SP% **107.1**
Speed ratings (Par 101): **94,93,93,90,82 72**
toteswingers:1&2:£1.10, 1&3:£8.80, 2&3:£5.50 CSF £6.56 TOTE £3.80: £1.80, £1.30; EX 7.00.There was no bid for the winner.
Owner Brian Ellison **Bred** Tarworth Bloodstock Ltd **Trained** Norton, N Yorks

FOCUS
A weak seller run at a steady pace and rated around the runner-up.

2530 TOTEEXACTA FLEXI BETTING MEDIAN AUCTION MAIDEN STKS 5f
2:25 (2:26) (Class 6) 3-Y-0 **£2,388** (£705; £352) **Stalls** Low

Form				RPR
24	**1**		**Philosophers Stone (FR)**[42] 1401 3-9-3 0 .... GrahamGibbons 6 (T D Barron) *cl up: drvn 2f out: led ins fnl f: kpt on wl* **8/15**[1]	60+
0-00	**2**	1	**Loss Leader (IRE)**[19] 1971 3-8-12 45 .... LanceBetts(5) 7 (T D Easterby) *led: rdn over 1f out: hdd ins fnl f: r.o* **16/1**	56
0	**3**	½	**Mottley Crewe**[14] 2114 3-9-3 0 .... PJMcDonald 3 (M Dods) *t.k.h early: prom: effrt over 1f out: kpt on ins fnl f* **8/1**[3]	54
3040	**4**	1 ½	**Sharp Shoes**[11] 2209 3-9-3 54 .... JimmyQuinn 2 (Mrs A Duffield) *t.k.h: trckd ldrs: rdn whn n.m.r briefly over 1f out: one pce fnl f* **7/1**[2]	49
0-0	**5**	5	**Rio's Girl**[19] 1966 3-8-9 0 .... MichaelStainton(3) 1 (R M Whitaker) *rdr lost iron sn after s: in tch tl rdn and outpcd fnl 2f* **22/1**	26+
-	**6**	1	**Red Roar (IRE)** 3-8-7 0 .... MarkCoumbe(5) 8 (A Berry) *s.i.s: bhd and outpcd: short lived effrt over 1f out: nvr on terms* **25/1**	22

-024 **7** *5* **Nabrina (IRE)**[52] 1155 3-8-5 52 .... JohnCavanagh(7) 4 4
(M Brittain) *in tch: drvn after 2f: struggling fnl 2f* **14/1**
8 *1 ¾* **Lord Lansing (IRE)** 3-9-3 0 .... AndrewElliott 5 3
(J R Weymes) *s.i.s: a outpcd and bhd* **18/1**
59.59 secs (-0.21) **Going Correction** -0.025s/f (Good) **8** Ran SP% **114.8**
Speed ratings (Par 97): **100,98,97,95,87 85,77,74**
toteswingers: 1&2 £3.30, 1&3 £3.70, 2&3 £16.10 CSF £11.46 TOTE £1.80: £1.10, £2.60, £1.90; EX 17.00.
Owner Peter Jones **Bred** Headquarters Stud Uk **Trained** Maunby, N Yorks
FOCUS
A very weak maiden, but the time was'nt bad. The fourth looks the best guide to the form.
Rio's Girl Official explanation: jockey said he lost an iron leaving stalls
Nabrina(IRE) Official explanation: jockey said filly was unbalanced throughout

2531 TOTEQUADPOT H'CAP 7f
2:55 (2:56) (Class 5) (0-75,73) 4-Y-0+ **£3,412** (£1,007; £504) **Stalls** Low

Form RPR
6104 **1** **Imperial Djay (IRE)**[5] 2381 5-8-6 **61** .... PJMcDonald 4 70+
(Mrs R A Carr) *hld up: hdwy over 2f out: str run fnl f: led last stride* **6/1**[3]
-500 **2** *shd* **Glenridding**[21] 1926 6-8-12 **67** .... (p) LeeVickers 9 76
(J G Given) *led: qcknd clr ent st: kpt on fnl f: hdd last stride* **14/1**
1443 **3** *1* **Smalljohn**[25] 1802 4-8-7 **69** .... (v) AdamCarter(7) 1 75
(B Smart) *trckd wnr: rdn and outpcd over 2f out: no imp tl styd on fnl f: hld cl home* **9/2**[1]
0114 **4** *5* **Nufoudh (IRE)**[8] 2293 6-8-10 **68** .... KellyHarrison(3) 2 61
(Miss Tracy Waggott) *in tch: effrt over 2f out: no imp wl over 1f out* **8/1**
-000 **5** *nk* **Bold Marc (IRE)**[28] 1707 8-9-4 **73** .... AndrewElliott 3 65
(J R Weymes) *prom: drvn over 2f out: sn one pce* **5/1**[2]
6-51 **6** *1* **Hobson**[26] 1762 5-8-11 **73** .... AmyScott(7) 5 62
(Eve Johnson Houghton) *hld up: drvn over 2f out: no imp tl sme late hdwy: nvr rchd ldrs* **9/2**[1]
1-03 **7** *shd* **Salerosa (IRE)**[9] 2262 5-9-4 **73** .... JimmyQuinn 7 62
(Mrs A Duffield) *hld up in tch: rdn over 2f out: btn over 1f out* **10/1**
0042 **8** *3 ¾* **Rio Cobolo (IRE)**[11] 2205 4-9-3 **72** .... (v) RobertHavlin 6 51
(Paul Green) *t.k.h: hld up in tch: effrt over 2f out: btn fnl f* **9/2**[1]
106- **9** *17* **Dark Moment**[224] 6847 4-9-4 **73** .... (p) DanielTudhope 8 6
(A Dickman) *hld up on outside: drvn and outpcd 3f out: sn wknd: t.o* **16/1**
1m 25.9s (-1.10) **Going Correction** -0.025s/f (Good) **9** Ran SP% **118.2**
Speed ratings (Par 103): **105,104,103,98,97 96,96,92,72**
toteswingers:1&2 £18.10, 2&3 £12.40, 1&3 £6.90 CSF £87.11 CT £420.04 TOTE £9.30: £2.70, £5.10, £2.00; EX 123.10.
Owner Hollinbridge Partnership **Bred** D Veitch And Musagd Abo Salim **Trained** Huby, N Yorks
FOCUS
An open handicap on paper but, in truth, little got into it. A clear personal best from the winner with the third the best guide.

2532 TOTETRIFECTA FLEXI BETTING H'CAP 7f
3:25 (3:25) (Class 3) (0-90,89) 4-Y-0+ **£7,771** (£2,312; £1,155; £577) **Stalls** Low

Form RPR
24-5 **1** **Hajoum (IRE)**[8] 2280 4-9-2 **87** .... AndrewElliott 4 97
(M Johnston) *chsd ldr: rdn 1/2-way: rallied over 1f out: led ins fnl f: kpt on wl* **6/1**
21-4 **2** *½* **Ancient Cross**[11] 2205 6-8-6 **77** .... (t) JimmyQuinn 8 86
(M W Easterby) *s.i.s: hld up in tch: effrt over 2f out: chsd wnr ins fnl f: r.o fin* **9/2**[3]
00-0 **3** *2 ½* **Beaver Patrol (IRE)**[14] 2119 8-9-0 **85** .... RobertHavlin 5 87
(Eve Johnson Houghton) *trckd ldrs: drvn and outpcd over 2f out: rallied appr fnl f: r.o* **20/1**
00-1 **4** *nk* **Turn Me On (IRE)**[25] 1802 7-8-4 **82** .... LukeStrong(7) 3 83
(T D Walford) *in tch: effrt over 2f out: edgd lft over 1f out: kpt on same pce fnl f* **10/1**
2-62 **5** *½* **Cheviot (USA)**[19] 1962 4-9-2 **87** .... (b) JackMitchell 1 87
(M A Jarvis) *t.k.h: led: qcknd clr over 2f out: hung lft over 1f out: hdd and no ex ins fnl f* **11/2**
2220 **6** *½* **Internationaldebut (IRE)**[21] 1900 5-9-4 **89** .... TonyCulhane 9 87
(P T Midgley) *t.k.h: hld up: effrt over 2f out: kpt on: nvr able to chal* **7/2**[1]
033 **7** *2* **Beckermet (IRE)**[15] 2086 8-9-1 **86** .... PJMcDonald 7 79
(Mrs R A Carr) *prom: rdn and outpcd 2f out: no imp over 1f out* **4/1**[2]
23-0 **8** *2 ¼* **Gala Casino Star (IRE)**[9] 2241 5-8-8 **86** .... MarzenaJeziorek(7) 6 73
(R A Fahey) *t.k.h: in tch tl outpcd fr 2f out* **14/1**
0-10 **9** *nk* **Malcheek (IRE)**[29] 1672 8-8-11 **82** .... DuranFentiman 2 68
(T D Easterby) *missed break: bhd: effrt over 2f out: btn over 1f out* **14/1**
1m 25.5s (-1.50) **Going Correction** -0.025s/f (Good) **9** Ran SP% **117.3**
Speed ratings (Par 107): **107,106,103,103,102 102,99,97,96**
toteswingers:1&2 £4.50, 2&3 £19.60, 1&3 £25.50 CSF £33.71 CT £514.36 TOTE £9.40: £1.60, £1.70, £6.10; EX 33.30 TRIFECTA Not won..
Owner Sheikh Hamdan Bin Mohammed Al Maktoum **Bred** Darley **Trained** Middleham Moor, N Yorks
FOCUS
A strong gallop to this handicap thanks to Cheviot, who ran similarly to Glenridding in the previous race, kicking clear turning for home but being run down. Fair form for the grade.
NOTEBOOK
Hajoum(IRE) was always tracking the speed and although he wasn't travelling as well as Ancient Cross, he found loads for pressure and saw out the final furlong in ultra-game style. This was his first try at 7f, but he clearly has no trouble with the trip and may well have improved for it. (tchd 15-2)
Ancient Cross, who was well supported, travelled smoothly off the pace and looked a huge threat when moving up on the outside of Hajoum but, while he kept on well, could never master that rival. On this evidence, he can win off this sort of mark. (op 11-2)
Beaver Patrol(IRE) finished well from off the pace, improving on his return, and there is no doubt he's dangerously well handicapped nowadays, having dropped the best part of a stone in the last year. (op 25-1)
Turn Me On(IRE) couldn't quite run to the same level as when winning as last time, but he loves to bounce off fast ground so the rain might have not have helped his chance. (op 11-1 tchd 9-1)
Cheviot(USA) probably went too hard early and dropped away. (op 4-1)
Internationaldebut(IRE) kept on from the back but was quite keen through the early stages, despite the decent gallop. (op 4-1)
Beckermet(IRE) was front rank early but was on the retreat entering the final furlong, and his lengthy losing run continues. (op 6-1)

2533 TOTESWINGER FLEXI BETTING H'CAP 1m 7f 177y
4:00 (4:01) (Class 5) (0-70,63) 4-Y-0+ **£2,590** (£770; £385; £192) **Stalls** Low

Form RPR
030/ **1** **Dan's Heir**[447] 146 8-8-8 **50** .... (p) DeanHeslop(5) 6 57
(W Storey) *hld up: effrt 3f out: hdwy on outside over 1f out: led ins fnl f: styd on wl* **40/1**
-303 **2** *1 ½* **Amir Pasha (UAE)**[25] 1803 5-9-0 **54** .... (p) KellyHarrison(3) 4 59
(Micky Hammond) *t.k.h: prom: rdn over 2f out: hdwy over 1f out: ev ch ins fnl f: edgd lft and one pce towards fin* **15/2**
00-2 **3** *¾* **Smugglers Bay (IRE)**[16] 2060 6-9-12 **63** .... (b) PJMcDonald 5 67
(T D Easterby) *stdd s: hld up in tch: effrt over 2f out: kpt on ins fnl f: tk 3rd cl home* **5/1**[3]
0-62 **4** *nk* **Spiders Star**[2] 2464 7-9-9 **63** .... GaryBartley(3) 7 67
(S G West) *t.k.h: hld up: stdy hdwy on outside 1/2-way: effrt over 2f out: one pce whn n.m.r: eased down and ct for 3rd cl home* **85/40**[2]
2425 **5** *2 ¼* **Spring Breeze**[2] 2464 9-8-8 **50** .... (v) LanceBetts(5) 3 51
(J J Quinn) *trckd ldrs: rdn over 4f out: outpcd 2f out: no imp fnl f* **15/8**[1]
/655 **6** *¾* **Decibel**[14] 2131 6-9-3 **54** .... StephenCraine 8 54
(K A Ryan) *dictated ordinary gallop: rdn clr ent st: hdd ins fnl f: sn wknd* **10/1**
6466 **7** *5* **Haka Dancer (USA)**[3] 1983 7-8-12 **49** .... (p) LeeVickers 2 43
(P A Kirby) *t.k.h: chsd ldr: rdn over 4f out: wknd over 2f out* **20/1**
3m 37.93s (5.93) **Going Correction** +0.075s/f (Good)
WFA 4 from 5yo+ 2lb **7** Ran SP% **111.5**
Speed ratings (Par 103): **88,87,86,86,85 85,82**
toteswingers:1&2 £12.10, 2&3 £3.40, 1&3 £10.80 CSF £289.46 CT £1748.74 TOTE £34.30: £7.50, £2.10; EX 145.80.
Owner Peter W Tomlinson **Bred** R P Williams **Trained** Muggleswick, Co Durham
FOCUS
A steady pace to this 2m handicap and muddling form. The form is rated around the second and fourth and is far from solid.

2534 BET TOTEPOOL AT TOTESPORT.COM H'CAP 5f 212y
4:35 (4:36) (Class 4) (0-85,84) 4-Y-0+ **£4,533** (£1,348; £674; £336) **Stalls** Low

Form RPR
-455 **1** **Favourite Girl (IRE)**[13] 2140 4-8-8 **74** .... (v[1]) DuranFentiman 4 83
(T D Easterby) *mde all: crossed over to stands' rail ent st: sn rdn: hld on wl fnl f* **6/1**[3]
-002 **2** *½* **Solar Spirit (IRE)**[21] 1923 5-8-6 **72** .... SaleemGolam 8 79
(J J Quinn) *cl up: effrt over 2f out: kpt on fnl f: hld cl home: slipped and fell sn after fin* **7/1**
0006 **3** *¾* **Frognal (IRE)**[8] 2275 4-8-10 **76** .... PJMcDonald 7 81
(Mrs R A Carr) *hld up: hdwy stands' rail over 1f out: kpt on fnl f: nrst fin* **4/1**[1]
3561 **4** *½* **Lucky Dan (IRE)**[7] 2310 4-8-8 **74** .... RobertHavlin 2 79+
(Paul Green) *hld up in tch: effrt whn nt clr run over 1f out: swtchd rt ins fnl f: r.o* **5/1**[2]
-006 **5** *¾* **Haajes**[22] 1888 6-9-0 **80** .... (t) TonyCulhane 3 81
(P T Midgley) *hld up in tch: drvn along 1/2-way: rallied over 1f out: one pce ins fnl f* **8/1**
-535 **6** *1 ½* **Floor Show**[15] 2086 4-8-11 **80** .... AshleyHamblett(3) 9 76
(N Wilson) *hld up: effrt on outside of gp over 1f out: no imp fnl f* **6/1**[3]
2302 **7** *nk* **Green Park (IRE)**[8] 2275 7-8-11 **77** .... (b) JimmyQuinn 10 72
(D Carroll) *hld up: hdwy on outside over 1f out: kpt on same pce fnl f* **9/1**
00-0 **8** *1 ¼* **Galpin Junior (USA)**[28] 1688 4-9-4 **84** .... PaulQuinn 5 79
(D Nicholls) *cl up: rdn over 2f out: one pce whn hmpd ins fnl f* **20/1**
050- **9** *5* **Sharp Bullet (IRE)**[240] 6434 4-8-10 **76** .... IvaMilickova 1 51
(A Berry) *cl up tl rdn and lost pl over 1f out: btn whn hung rt ins fnl f* **33/1**
-045 **10** *11* **Bosun Breese**[28] 1711 5-8-4 **75** .... DeanHeslop(5) 6 15
(T D Barron) *stmbld bdly s: hld up in tch: wknd over 2f out: eased whn no ch over 1f out* **8/1**
1m 13.21s (-0.39) **Going Correction** +0.075s/f (Good) **10** Ran SP% **117.7**
Speed ratings (Par 105): **105,104,103,102,101 99,99,97,90,76**
toteswingers: 1&2 £10.60, 1&3 £6.50, 2&3 £9.90 CSF £48.09 CT £189.87 TOTE £8.00: £2.70, £1.90, £3.00; EX 56.50.
Owner Peter C Bourke **Bred** Limestone And Tara Studs **Trained** Great Habton, N Yorks
FOCUS
The notable point about this contest was that the field came stands' side in the straight, suggesting the jockeys felt the rain was getting into the ground. The winner is rated in line with her latter 3yo form.
Bosun Breese Official explanation: jockey said gelding hung right-handed throughout

2535 BET TOTEPOOL ON 0800 221 221 MEDIAN AUCTION MAIDEN FILLIES' STKS 5f 212y
5:10 (5:11) (Class 6) 3-4-Y-0 **£2,388** (£705; £352) **Stalls** Low

Form RPR
06- **1** **Royal Cheer**[256] 5957 3-8-10 0 .... JackMitchell 2 46
(Mrs A Duffield) *in tch: drvn over 2f out: styd on wl fnl f: ct eased down wnr cl home* **22/1**
2-42 **2** *hd* **Vaultage (USA)**[19] 1982 3-8-10 69 .... TomMcLaughlin 7 49+
(E A L Dunlop) *dwlt: sn prom: wnt 2nd over 3f out: rdn to ld over 1f out: hung lft: 2 l clr ins fnl f: eased and ct cl home* **8/15**[1]
6006 **3** *hd* **Avonlini**[8] 2297 4-9-0 39 .... JimmyQuinn(5) 3 47
(B P J Baugh) *prom: rdn over 2f out: kpt on wl fnl f: nrst fin* **33/1**
56 **4** *¾* **Masteeat (USA)**[3] 2441 3-8-10 0 .... RobertHavlin 6 43
(J R Best) *hld up in tch: effrt and shkn up over 1f out: kpt on fnl f: nvr nr to chal* **11/1**[3]
0-0 **5** *½* **Zelos Spirit**[18] 2004 3-8-10 0 .... SaleemGolam 1 41
(Rae Guest) *t.k.h: prom: rdn over 2f out: one pce fnl f* **11/1**[3]
300- **6** *1 ¾* **Royal Record**[225] 6820 3-8-3 59 .... JohnCavanagh(7) 5 35
(M Brittain) *dwlt: bhd and sn rdn along: sme hdwy over 1f out: nvr rchd ldrs* **4/1**[2]
7 *½* **Dashing Beauty (IRE)**[199] 7340 4-9-5 0 .... PJMcDonald 4 34
(M G Quinlan) *rrd s: bhd and pushed along: sme late hdwy: nvr on terms* **16/1**
8 *5* **Best Known Secret (IRE)** 4-9-5 0 .... KevinGhunowa 9 20
(C C Bealby) *led tl hung lft and hdd over 1f out: sn wknd* **16/1**
460- **9** *14* **Ed's A Red**[256] 5958 3-8-6 33 ow1 .... MarkCoumbe(5) 8 —
(A Berry) *s.i.s: bhd and outpcd: nvr on terms* **40/1**
1m 16.13s (2.53) **Going Correction** +0.075s/f (Good)
WFA 3 from 4yo 9lb **9** Ran SP% **123.4**
Speed ratings (Par 98): **86,85,85,84,83 81,80,74,55**
toteswingers: 1&2 £7.10, 2&3 £8.00, 1&3 £37.80 CSF £36.33 TOTE £22.70: £7.70, £1.02, £9.60; EX 112.00 Place 6: £277.93 Place 5: £227.01.
Owner Mrs D G Garrity **Bred** Tattersalls Scoundrels & Trickledown Stud **Trained** Constable Burton, N Yorks
FOCUS
A very weak fillies' auction maiden but a controversial finish as Tom McLaughlin eased up on Vaultage thinking he had the race in the bag only to get collared on the line by the fast-finishing Royal Cheer. Vaultage has been rated a length winner and the proximity of the third limits the form.
T/Plt: £305.50 to a £1 stake. Pool of £52,318.53 - 124.99 winning tickets. T/Qpdt: £141.50 to a £1 stake. Pool of £3,042.45 - 15.90 winning tickets. RY

2492 HAYDOCK (L-H)

Saturday, May 29

OFFICIAL GOING: Good (good to soft in places) changing to good to soft after race 1 (2.00)

Rail realignment increased distances on Round course by 25yards

Wind: Light half-behind Weather: Raining

2536 SPORTS360.CO.UK ACHILLES STKS (LISTED RACE) 5f

2:00 (2:01) (Class 1) 3-Y-0+

£22,708 (£8,608; £4,308; £2,148; £1,076; £540) Stalls Centre

Form				RPR
134-	1		**High Standing (USA)**[244] 6304 5-9-3 112 ..... RyanMoore 2 (W J Haggas) *unruly in stalls: hld up: hdwy over 1f out: rdn to ld and edgd rt wl ins fnl f: r.o* **9/4**[1]	114+
4-01	2	½	**Rose Blossom**[16] 2058 3-8-4 97 ..... PaulHanagan 5 (R A Fahey) *w ldr tl led 3f out: rdn and hdd wl ins fnl f* **5/1**	104
0160	3	2½	**Judd Street**[17] 2030 8-9-3 105 ..... (v) KierenFallon 1 (Eve Johnson Houghton) *sn pushed along in rr: r.o fnl f: nt trble ldrs* **12/1**	103
2-00	4	¾	**Impressible**[21] 1918 4-8-12 85 ..... DavidProbert 4 (S C Williams) *led 1f: chsd ldrs: rdn 1/2-way: styd on same pce fnl f* **20/1**	95
-416	5	¾	**Inxile (IRE)**[17] 2030 5-9-7 108 ..... AdrianNicholls 9 (D Nicholls) *unruly in stalls: led 4f out: hdd 3f out: rdn over 1f out: no ex* **3/1**[2]	101
2253	6	1	**Elnawin**[21] 1906 4-9-3 104 ..... TadhgO'Shea 7 (R Hannon) *hld up: shkn up over 1f out: nvr on terms* **9/2**[3]	94
30-0	7	2¼	**Invincible Lad (IRE)**[7] 2346 6-9-3 83 ..... StevieDonohoe 6 (E J Alston) *mid-div: rdn 1/2-way: wknd fnl f* **14/1**	86
-2	8	6	**Nollaig Shona (IRE)**[12] 2164 3-8-4 0 ..... GregFairley 8 (J W Mullins) *mid-div: sn pushed along: wknd over 1f out* **100/1**	56

61.32 secs (0.32) **Going Correction** +0.35s/f (Good)

WFA 3 from 4yo+ 8lb **8** Ran SP% **110.7**

Speed ratings (Par 111): **111,110,106,105,103 102,98,89**

toteswingers: 1&2 £2.10, 1&3 £7.20, 2&3 £11.40 CSF £12.94 TOTE £3.30: £1.10, £1.90, £2.70; EX 11.40 Trifecta £48.90 Pool: of £710.23 - 10.73 winning units..

Owner Tony Bloom **Bred** Dr Melinda Blue **Trained** Newmarket, Suffolk

FOCUS

The rain had got into the ground, which was officially given as good, good to soft in places at the start of racing, and that description was changed to good to soft all over following this opener. They went a strong pace throughout and this looks like good form for the grade, but the fourth is a slight doubt.

NOTEBOOK

High Standing(USA) has won when fresh in the past, so an eight-month absence wasn't too much of a concern, and he coped with the drop in trip to record his first victory over 5f. He lacked the natural early speed of some of these, but in any case he's a hold-up performer and crucially got a decent gallop to chase. Plus the easing of the ground was in his favour in that it helped bring his stamina into play. He had upwards of 7lb in hand on official figures, and 10lb to spare over the runner-up (that one has improved in fairness), so this isn't a performance to get carried away with, but even so, there was plenty to like. Ryan Moore didn't have to be too hard on him, and there should be more to come when he returns to his optimum distance of 6f. It's likely that he'll now be aimed at the Golden Jubilee, although that will demand much more. (op 5-2 tchd 11-4)

Rose Blossom ◆ has always been highly regarded and she's now realising her potential. She proved suited by a forward ride when winning a conditions race at York last time and, again allowed to stride on (Richard Fahey has, for now at least, given up trying to teach her to settle), she produced a career-best performance. This effort is all the more creditable considering, not only was she was hassled up front by Inxile, who faded, but the softish going probably blunted her finishing speed. This out-and-out speedster can make further progress. (op 4-1)

Judd Street ran a respectable race but he simply wasn't quite good enough. (op 10-1 tchd 9-1)

Impressible had plenty to find at the weights but she improved for the return to easy ground and it would probably be unwise to use her to hold the form down. She was a most impressive winner when last racing on ground with soft in the description (Hamilton last August) and it's clear she's decent when conditions are in her favour. (op 18-1)

Inxile(IRE) faded after showing early speed. (op 4-1)

Elnawin was never competitive and probably wants better ground. (tchd 7-2)

Invincible Lad(IRE) was out of his depth. (op 18-1)

Nollaig Shona(IRE) didn't run at all badly and evidently has ability.

2537 J.W. LEES SANDY LANE STKS (LISTED RACE) 6f

2:30 (2:31) (Class 1) 3-Y-0

£22,708 (£8,608; £4,308; £2,148; £1,076; £540) Stalls Centre

Form				RPR
0-	1		**Bewitched (IRE)**[17] 2036 3-8-9 98 ..... KierenFallon 9 (Charles O'Brien, Ire) *hld up in tch: rdn to ld and hung lft wl ins fnl f: r.o* **5/1**[1]	108
1	2	¾	**Rainfall (IRE)**[28] 1706 3-8-9 94 ..... GregFairley 1 (M Johnston) *w ldr: rdn to ld ins fnl f: sn hdd and edgd lft: unable qck* **8/1**	106
1-10	3	2¾	**Mister Manannan (IRE)**[13] 2157 3-9-3 106 ..... AdrianNicholls 4 (D Nicholls) *led: rdn over 1f out: hdd and no ex ins fnl f* **13/2**[3]	106
20-1	4	3¼	**Angel's Pursuit (IRE)**[15] 2075 3-9-3 111 ..... RobertWinston 2 (R Hannon) *hld up in tch: rdn: hung lft and wknd over 1f out* **6/1**[2]	96
6-26	5	½	**Corporal Maddox**[15] 2075 3-9-3 105 ..... (t) TomQueally 7 (H R A Cecil) *hld up: rdn over 1f out: n.d* **5/1**[1]	94
11-4	6	5	**Layla's Hero (IRE)**[72] 927 3-9-3 104 ..... StevieDonohoe 6 (D M Simcock) *rrd s: a bhd* **5/1**[1]	79
113-	7	1¾	**Quarrel (USA)**[252] 6105 3-9-0 108 ..... RyanMoore 5 (W J Haggas) *chsd ldrs: rdn 1/2-way: wknd over 2f out* **5/1**[1]	71
16-	8	1	**Khattaab (USA)**[240] 6426 3-9-0 98 ..... TadhgO'Shea 3 (B W Hills) *sn pushed along in rr: wknd over 2f out* **16/1**	68

1m 13.73s (0.23) **Going Correction** +0.35s/f (Good) **8** Ran SP% **111.3**

Speed ratings (Par 107): **112,111,107,103,102 95,93,92**

toteswingers: 1&2 £11.30, 1&3 £7.30, 2&3 £16.40 CSF £42.28 TOTE £5.30: £1.60, £2.80, £2.10; EX 44.50 Trifecta £353.70 Pool: £678.73 - 1.42 winning units..

Owner Mrs John Magnier **Bred** Monsieur J C Coude **Trained** Straffan, Co Kildare

FOCUS

This looked a decent Listed contest beforehand, but it was run in gloomy conditions and few were ever involved. The main action was up the middle of the track. Tricky form to pin down, with the first two progressive.

NOTEBOOK

Bewitched(IRE) ◆, a handicap winner at Naas off a mark of 85 on her reappearance, showed improved form on this rise in class. Able to keep tabs on the two leaders, who finished second and third respectively, she picked up well for pressure and was nicely on top at the line, despite edging left late on. Both her trainer and jockey believe she ideally wants quicker ground, so there may be more to come.

Rainfall(IRE) ◆, a wide-margin winner over 7f on debut, proved herself a smart filly on this step up in class. Having shown plenty of speed to just about match strides with Mister Manannan, she stuck on willingly once passed by the winner and this was a fine effort in defeat. She won't mind going back up in trip (dam won over 1m4f) and looks the type to keep improving. (tchd 7-1)

Mister Manannan(IRE) simply didn't see out this trip on the easy ground. A very fast horse, he's at his best when the emphasis is solely on speed. (op 9-2)

Angel's Pursuit(IRE), successful in a Listed event at Newbury on his reappearance, failed to show his best form this time and it seems the easy ground was no use to him. (op 11-2 tchd 5-1)

Corporal Maddox didn't improve for the fitting of a tongue-tie. (op 7-1 tchd 8-1)

Layla's Hero(IRE) was disappointing on his debut for David Simcock after a 72-day break. He lost ground when rearing slightly as the stalls opened and was never travelling, which is puzzling considering he has plenty of form on this sort of going. (op 6-1)

Quarrel(USA), having his first start since finishing third in last year's Mill Reef, was using this as a stepping stone towards the Jersey Stakes according to William Haggas, but he seemed totally unsuited by the conditions and underperformed. Official explanation: trainer's rep said colt was unsuited by the good to soft ground (op 11-2)

2538 EBF JOAN WESTBROOK PINNACLE STKS (LISTED RACE) (F&M) 1m 3f 200y

3:00 (3:01) (Class 1) 4-Y-0+

£22,708 (£8,608; £4,308; £2,148; £1,076; £540) Stalls High

Form				RPR
41-2	1		**Les Fazzani (IRE)**[23] 1832 6-9-1 108 ..... PaulHanagan 3 (K A Ryan) *mde all: clr over 4f out: rdn over 1f out: all out* **9/2**[2]	112+
12-4	2	hd	**Polly's Mark (IRE)**[42] 1382 4-8-12 102 ..... RichardHughes 5 (C G Cox) *hld up: hdwy u.p fr over 2f out: chsd wnr ins fnl f: hung lft: r.o: jst failed* **7/2**[1]	109
212-	3	5	**Rosika**[212] 7131 4-8-12 96 ..... RyanMoore 10 (Sir Michael Stoute) *hld up: pushed along 4f out: hdwy u.p fr over 1f out: wnt 3rd wl ins fnl f: nrst fin* **13/2**[3]	101
40-1	4	¾	**Barshiba (IRE)**[21] 1898 6-9-1 111 ..... HayleyTurner 8 (D R C Elsworth) *sn trcking wnr: racd keenly: rdn and hung lft fr over 2f out: lost 2nd and no ex ins fnl f* **9/2**[2]	103
505-	5	9	**Flame Of Gibraltar (IRE)**[212] 7131 4-8-12 97 ..... TomQueally 7 (H R A Cecil) *s.i.s: hld up: hdwy over 3f out: wknd over 1f out* **16/1**	85
20-6	6	8	**Victoria Montoya**[22] 1859 5-8-12 95 ..... (v[1]) DavidProbert 4 (A M Balding) *trckd ldrs: racd keenly: rdn and wknd over 3f out* **25/1**	73
120-	7	34	**Cassique Lady (IRE)**[261] 5796 5-8-12 99 ..... RobertWinston 2 (Mrs L Wadham) *prom: racd keenly: rdn and wknd over 3f out: t.o* **33/1**	—
36-	8	1	**Becqu Adoree (FR)**[258] 5929 4-8-12 108 ..... KierenFallon 6 (L M Cumani) *unruly prior to loading: hld up: hdwy over 4f out: wknd over 3f out: t.o* **7/2**[1]	—
12-4	9	39	**Three Moons (IRE)**[27] 1725 4-8-12 104 ..... TedDurcan 1 (H J L Dunlop) *prom: rdn over 3f out: sn wknd: t.o* **10/1**	—

2m 36.99s (2.99) **Going Correction** +0.60s/f (Yiel) **9** Ran SP% **115.9**

Speed ratings (Par 111): **111,110,107,107,101 95,73,72,46**

toteswingers:1&2 £4.80, 2&3 £7.50, 1&3 £4.70 CSF £20.74 TOTE £5.50: £2.00, £1.40, £2.10; EX 21.60 Trifecta £178.10 Pool: £897.80 - 3.73 winning units..

Owner Dr Marwan Koukash **Bred** J Erhardt And Mrs J Schonwalder **Trained** Hambleton, N Yorks

FOCUS

A decent enough fillies' Listed contest, although few of these were suited by the ground. The pace was strong and they raced up the middle of the track in the straight. The winner looks better than ever and the form seems solid.

NOTEBOOK

Les Fazzani(IRE) had opened up a clear lead by the time she reached the straight, and she had just enough left to hold on, improving on her second-placing in this race last year. The winner, who reappeared with a good second in Group 3 company, relishes this sort of ground and has a fine attitude. This was a smart effort under her penalty and she should continue to go well when there is give underfoot. (op 5-1)

Polly's Mark(IRE), fourth in a hot renewal of the John Porter on her reappearance, found this easier and just failed to reel in the front-running winner, having taken a while to get going. (op 5-1)

Rosika plugged on into third without ever looking likely to win. She probably wants better ground, and she also shaped as though she will stay 2m. (op 6-1)

Barshiba(IRE), who, like the winner, was carrying a penalty, was much too keen early on and couldn't follow up her recent Listed success. (op 4-1)

Flame Of Gibraltar(IRE) lost ground with a slow start and was never competitive. (tchd 14-1)

Victoria Montoya needs further and probably wants a quicker surface. (op 18-1 tchd 16-1)

Becqu Adoree(FR), an ex-French trained filly who was making her debut for Luca Cumani after an absence of 258 days, should have been suited by the ground but she showed nothing. Official explanation: trainer's rep said filly finished distressed (op 4-1 tchd 9-2 in places)

Three Moons(IRE) Official explanation: jockey said filly had no more to give

2539 TIMEFORM JURY STKS (REGISTERED AS THE JOHN OF GAUNT STAKES) (GROUP 3) 7f 30y

3:30 (3:32) (Class 1) 4-Y-0+

£36,900 (£13,988; £7,000; £3,490; £1,748; £877) Stalls Low

Form				RPR
04-3	1		**Main Aim**[17] 2030 5-9-0 117 ..... RyanMoore 9 (Sir Michael Stoute) *sn chsng ldr: led 2f out: rdn and edgd rt over 1f out: r.o* **2/1**[1]	116
0-34	2	¾	**Doncaster Rover (USA)**[17] 2030 4-9-0 109 ..... RobertWinston 8 (D H Brown) *chsd ldrs: rdn to chal over 2f out: styd on u.p* **10/1**[3]	114
120-	3	¾	**Dream Eater (IRE)**[244] 6304 5-9-0 114 ..... (t) DavidProbert 5 (A M Balding) *chsd ldrs: rdn over 2f out: styd on: wnt 3rd nr fin* **12/1**	112
50-3	4	½	**Lord Shanakill (USA)**[14] 2118 4-9-0 118 ..... TomQueally 2 (H R A Cecil) *sn led: hdd 2f out: rdn over 1f out: no ex ins fnl f: lost 3rd nr fin* **2/1**[1]	111
24-4	5	2	**Georgebernardshaw (IRE)**[21] 1904 5-9-0 105 ..... StevieDonohoe 1 (D M Simcock) *chsd ldrs: rdn over 2f out: no ex fnl f* **20/1**	105
0311	6	2¼	**Lovelace**[21] 1904 6-9-0 106 ..... AdrianNicholls 6 (D Nicholls) *hld up: rdn over 2f out: edgd lft: nt trble ldrs* **10/1**[3]	99
54-2	7	1¾	**Dream Lodge (IRE)**[33] 1570 6-9-0 108 ..... PaulHanagan 3 (R A Fahey) *hld up: rdn over 3f out: nvr on terms* **25/1**	94
0513	8	7	**Autumn Blades (IRE)**[7] 2311 5-9-0 99 ..... (v) FrannyNorton 4 (A Bailey) *hld up: hdwy over 3f out: wknd over 2f out* **50/1**	76
2622	9	19	**Mia's Boy**[21] 1904 6-9-0 105 ..... RichardHughes 7 (C A Dwyer) *s.i.s: hld up: shkn up over 2f out: sn wknd and eased: t.o* **8/1**[2]	24

1m 33.69s (0.99) **Going Correction** +0.60s/f (Yiel) **9** Ran SP% **114.2**

Speed ratings (Par 113): **104,103,102,101,99 96,94,86,65**

toteswingers: 1&2 £7.90, 1&3 £4.80, 2&3 £11.50 CSF £23.63 TOTE £2.50: £1.10, £3.00, £3.10; EX 26.80 Trifecta £206.80 Pool: £1635.38 - 5.85 winning units..

Owner K Abdulla **Bred** Juddmonte Farms Ltd **Trained** Newmarket, Suffolk

FOCUS
A quality contest, although it proved hard to make up significant amounts of ground, and with the time only 0.15 seconds quicker than the later Class 3 handicap for 3-y-os, it seems the pace was not that quick. They came stands' side in the straight. The winner did not need to be at his best with the level set around the second and third.

NOTEBOOK
Main Aim had to work hard to gain his first success since taking this race last year. Always close up, he responded well enough to pressure but could never get away from his rivals. It's possible he could do better back on quicker ground (although not too quick) but he'll still appeal as one to take on when upped in grade, with his record in Group 1 and Group 2 contests 0-6. It's possible he'll go to Royal Ascot, presumably for the Golden Jubilee, but his main target is said to be the Prix Maurice de Gheest. (op 7-4 tchd 9-4 in places)
Doncaster Rover(USA) was unproven over a trip this far and he looked set to drop away when coming under strong pressure early in the straight, but he stuck on really gamely. He was slightly short of room against the near-side rail late on, as the winner edged slightly into his path, but he was not unlucky. On this evidence he may even get 1m. (op 14-1)
Dream Eater(IRE) made a pleasing return from a 244-day break on ground that was probably softer than ideal. (op 10-1 tchd 14-1)
Lord Shanakill(USA) ran below the form he showed in the Lockinge on his reappearance, and perhaps he didn't appreciate the easy ground. (op 11-4)
Georgebernardshaw(IRE) had conditions to suit on just his second start for this yard but he was always being held. He's looked something of an underachiever for a while now. (op 16-1 tchd 22-1)
Lovelace had won both his starts since joining this yard, but he couldn't confirm recent C&D placings with Georgebernardshaw and probably didn't appreciate the ground. (tchd 8-1)
Mia's Boy should have been suited by the conditions but he didn't really travel that well after missing the break and dropped away in the straight, giving the impression something was amiss. (op 10-1 tchd 11-1)

2540 EBF R DRAPER LTD MAIDEN STKS — 5f
4:10 (4:10) (Class 5) 2-Y-O — **£3,432** (£1,021; £510; £254) **Stalls** Centre

Form	Pos	Dist	Horse	Jockey	RPR
	1		**Ballista (IRE)** 2-9-3 0 (Tom Dascombe) *trckd ldrs: plld hrd: hmpd over 1f out: r.o to ld nr fin* **7/1**[2]	RichardKingscote 4	89+
2	**2**	*nk*	**Royal Exchange**[43] 1351 2-9-3 0 (R Hannon) *led: shkn up over 1f out: hung lft ins fnl f: hdd nr fin* **30/100**[1]	RichardHughes 3	88+
	3	*5*	**Barkston Ash** 2-9-3 0 (E J Alston) *s.i.s: and wnt lft s: hdwy 1/2-way: rdn and hung rt over 1f out: wknd ins fnl f* **22/1**	SebSanders 2	70
0	**4**	*2 3/4*	**Bussa**[16] 2048 2-9-3 0 (P D Evans) *chsd ldrs: rdn 1/2-way: wknd over 1f out* **10/1**[3]	KierenFallon 5	60
	5	*2 3/4*	**Countrywide Flame** 2-9-3 0 (K A Ryan) *s.i.s: sn chsng ldrs: rdn and wknd over 1f out* **12/1**	PaulHanagan 6	50
06	**6**	*2 1/4*	**Love Club**[24] 1819 2-9-3 0 (B P J Baugh) *prom: jnd ldr over 3f out: hmpd over 1f out: sn hung lft and wknd* **33/1**	DavidProbert 1	42

62.78 secs (1.78) **Going Correction** +0.35s/f (Good) **6** Ran SP% **113.5**
Speed ratings (Par 93): **99,98,90,86,81 78**
toteswingers: 1&2 £2.00, 1&3 £6.30, 2&3 £3.80 CSF £9.81 TOTE £8.30: £2.30, £1.10; EX 14.50.
Owner Well Done Top Man Partnership **Bred** Sj Partnership **Trained** Malpas, Cheshire

FOCUS
The time of this maiden was most impressive, being only 1.46 seconds slower than the 5-y-o High Standing managed in an earlier Listed contest. They raced stands' side and the first two, who came clear, are very useful types.

NOTEBOOK
Ballista(IRE) ◆, an 11,000euros half-brother to five winners, would appear to be well-above average, for not only did he record a quick time, but he defeated a colt who had already shown useful form, and there was 5l back to the third. Fitted with a cross noseband, he was keen through the first furlong, before travelling powerfully just in behind the pace, and he then found plenty for pressure without having to be given too hard a race. He may well be Royal Ascot material. (tchd 8-1)
Royal Exchange didn't seem to improve on the form he showed when second in a hot Newbury maiden on debut, although in fairness he probably ran into quite a useful colt. This ground probably wasn't ideal and he ought to be winning soon enough. (op 2-5 tchd 4-9 in places)
Barkston Ash, an £8,000 first foal, shaped nicely on debut. He showed his inexperience when going left as the stalls opened, and he couldn't go with the front two late on, but this was still a fair effort. (op 20-1)
Bussa was outpaced from about halfway and looks to need further. (op 9-1 tchd 17-2 and 11-1 in places)
Countrywide Flame seemed to need this experience.

2541 SPORTS 360 SPORTS ADVERTISING SPECIALISTS STKS (H'CAP) — 2m 45y
4:45 (4:46) (Class 2) (0-100,100) 4-Y-O+
£12,462 (£3,732; £1,866; £934; £466; £234) **Stalls** Low

Form	Pos	Dist	Horse	Jockey	RPR
42-5	**1**		**Dayia (IRE)**[27] 1736 6-8-10 **85** (J Pearce) *hld up in tch: lost pl over 10f out: hdwy 3f out: led over 1f out: styd on* **14/1**	SimonPearce(5) 6	97+
0-12	**2**	*hd*	**My Arch**[35] 1525 8-8-8 **81** (Ollie Pears) *hld up: hdwy over 4f out: pushed along over 3f out: hrd rdn fr over 2f out: r.o wl and edgd lft towards fin: nt quite get up* **10/1**	BarryMcHugh(3) 3	92
2-02	**3**	*3 1/4*	**Crackentorp**[15] 2096 5-9-7 **91** (T D Easterby) *hld up: hdwy 1/2-way: rdn and ev ch over 1f out: wknd wl ins fnl f* **5/1**[2]	RyanMoore 10	98+
6-14	**4**	*1/2*	**Stanstill (IRE)**[15] 2071 4-9-7 **93** (G A Swinbank) *led: rdn over 2f out: hdd over 1f out: wknd ins fnl f* **10/1**	PhilipRobinson 9	99
0-65	**5**	*1 1/2*	**Topolski (IRE)**[27] 1724 4-8-12 **84** (A M Balding) *chsd ldr: rdn over 4f out: hung lft and wknd over 1f out* **11/1**	DavidProbert 11	88
01-3	**6**	*1 1/2*	**Aaim To Prosper (IRE)**[21] 1902 6-9-4 **88** (B J Meehan) *chsd ldrs: rdn over 1f out: wknd ins fnl f* **9/2**[1]	RichardHughes 2	90
132-	**7**	*1 1/2*	**Mith Hill**[41] 6676 9-8-10 **80** (Ian Williams) *prom: outpcd 4f out: styd on ins fnl f* **20/1**	StevieDonohoe 12	81
24-6	**8**	*4*	**Bollin Felix**[52] 1151 6-9-1 **85** (T D Easterby) *hld up: nt clr run over 3f out: sn rdn: nvr on terms* **11/2**[3]	(p) SebSanders 16	81
45-5	**9**	*13*	**Hawk Mountain (UAE)**[27] 1720 5-9-0 **84** (J J Quinn) *chsd ldrs: rdn over 3f out: wknd over 2f out* **14/1**	GrahamGibbons 17	64
443-	**10**	*17*	**Cosmic Sun**[260] 5823 4-9-8 **94** (R A Fahey) *hld up: a in rr* **9/1**	PaulHanagan 4	54
610-	**11**	*33*	**Urban Poet (USA)**[224] 6854 4-10-0 **100** (Saeed Bin Suroor) *prom: rdn over 4f out: wknd over 3f out: t.o* **16/1**	TedDurcan 13	20
0/50	**12**	*2 1/2*	**Raincoat**[24] 1821 6-9-7 **91** (F J Brennan) *s.i.s: hld up: hdwy over 5f out: wknd over 3f out: t.o* **12/1**	KierenFallon 1	8

3m 44.14s (8.14) **Going Correction** +0.60s/f (Yiel)
WFA 4 from 5yo+ 2lb **12** Ran SP% **118.4**
Speed ratings (Par 109): **103,102,101,101,100 99,98,96,90,81 65,64**
toteswingers:1&2 £34.40, 2&3 £8.80, 1&3 £29.70 CSF £146.86 CT £807.13 TOTE £18.90: £4.00, £3.50, £2.20; EX 195.90.
Owner Lady Green **Bred** Shadwell Estate Company Limited **Trained** Newmarket, Suffolk

FOCUS
A good staying handicap run at a fair pace in the conditions, and they raced middle to stands' side in the straight. The form looks pretty solid with the winner generally progressive.

NOTEBOOK
Dayia(IRE) improved on the form she showed over 1m6f at Salisbury on her reappearance. Although having raced enthusiastically under a hold-up ride, she had enough left to produce a sustained challenge up the centre of the track in the straight and, having worked her way to the front, she was all out to hold on after edging left. She had plenty in her favour - the ease in the ground helped - and things might be tougher off a higher mark next time. (tchd 16-1)
My Arch responded well to pressure but he was unable to go with Dayia when she went by and then only just failed to reel that rival in. He's holding his form well and is one to keep on-side. (op 7-1)
Crackentorp, trying 2m for the first time, seemed to stay the trip okay, although didn't get it as well as the front two. (op 6-1 tchd 9-2)
Stanstill(IRE), another trying 2m for the first time, wasn't ridden as though stamina was an issue and he grabbed the stands' rail early in the straight. Looking at where the winner raced, that was not an advantage. Alan Swinbank's gelding faded into fourth but this was still a respectable showing. (tchd 9-1 and 11-1 in places)
Topolski(IRE) didn't convince that he got the trip on this first run beyond 1m4f. (tchd 10-1)
Aaim To Prosper(IRE) seemed to have conditions to suit but he proved a little disappointing, failing to build on the form he showed on his reappearance. He has won in headgear in the past and it would be no surprise to see blinkers or a visor back on next time. (op 5-1 tchd 11-2)
Bollin Felix, 1lb lower than when runner-up in this race last year, failed to pick up after being slightly short of room 3f out. (tchd 13-2)

2542 SPORTS 360 AND RACHEL 10TH ANNIVERSARY H'CAP — 7f 30y
5:20 (5:20) (Class 3) (0-95,95) 3-Y-O **£8,095** (£2,408; £1,203; £601) **Stalls** Low

Form	Pos	Dist	Horse	Jockey	RPR
2303	**1**		**Navajo Chief**[17] 2028 3-9-3 **94** (A P Jarvis) *w ldr: led over 5f out: rdn and hung lft over 1f out: styd on wl* **17/2**[3]	KierenFallon 12	103
61	**2**	*2 1/4*	**Eton Forever (IRE)**[26] 1769 3-9-1 **92** (M A Jarvis) *chsd ldrs: rdn to chse wnr fnl f: no ex towards fin* **5/4**[1]	PhilipRobinson 10	95
015-	**3**	*2*	**Colepeper**[232] 6643 3-9-4 **95** (M Johnston) *led: hdd over 5f out: styd chsng wnr: rdn over 1f out: no ex fnl f* **12/1**	GregFairley 1	93
1-0	**4**	*4*	**Rock 'N' Royal**[17] 2028 3-8-5 **82** (R A Fahey) *hld up: hdwy over 2f out: sn rdn: hung lft and no imp fr over 1f out* **20/1**	PaulHanagan 5	69
10-	**5**	*3 3/4*	**Quiet**[260] 5825 3-8-10 **87** (R Charlton) *hld up: shkn up over 2f out: nvr on terms* **7/2**[2]	RyanMoore 11	64
25-0	**6**	*4 1/2*	**Bond Fastrac**[17] 2028 3-8-10 **90** (G R Oldroyd) *chsd ldrs: rdn over 2f out: sn hung lft and wknd* **20/1**	BarryMcHugh(3) 6	55
1-0	**7**	*2 3/4*	**Elspeth's Boy (USA)**[28] 1699 3-8-10 **87** (J R Best) *s.i.s: hld up: nvr on terms* **9/1**	TedDurcan 4	45
00-0	**8**	*4*	**She's A Character**[17] 2028 3-8-11 **88** (R A Fahey) *hld up: hdwy 1/2-way: wknd over 2f out* **16/1**	RichardHughes 9	35
1010	**9**	*1 3/4*	**Niran (IRE)**[23] 1834 3-8-10 **87** (C E Brittain) *chsd ldrs: rdn over 3f out: hung lft and wknd over 1f out* **14/1**	SebSanders 2	29

1m 33.84s (1.14) **Going Correction** +0.60s/f (Yiel) **9** Ran SP% **117.0**
Speed ratings (Par 103): **103,100,98,93,89 84,81,76,74**
toteswingers:1&2 £3.20, 2&3 £5.40, 1&3 £10.60 CSF £19.79 CT £129.01 TOTE £8.20: £2.10, £1.20, £3.10; EX 17.30 Place 6: £59.78 Place 5: £29.86 .
Owner Geoffrey Bishop **Bred** Eurostrait Ltd **Trained** Twyford, Bucks

FOCUS
A decent 3yo handicap run at a fair pace, and the time was very good, being only 0.15 seconds slower than Main Aim recorded in an earlier Group 3. The main action was middle to far side in the straight. The winner had started to look exposed but is rated up 9lb.

NOTEBOOK
Navajo Chief didn't get the best of runs in a similar race at York on his previous start, but he was given a no-nonsense ride by Fallon this time and responded gamely. He's clearly very useful, but whether he's up to defying a rise remains to be seen. (op 7-1)
Eton Forever(IRE), the winner of a decent maiden over 1m on Polytrack last time, coped with the drop in trip but was always being held by the enterprisingly ridden winner. He should yet be capable of better. (op 6-4)
Colepeper was the only runner to stick tight against the far rail in the straight, which may or may not have been a wise decision. Returning from 232 days off, he kept on well for much of the closing stages, before tiring late on, and he should stay further. (op 10-1 tchd 14-1)
Rock 'N' Royal fared better than on his reappearance and could build on this. (op 16-1)
Quiet, a winner on debut before finishing last in the May Hill, offered little after 260 days off. (op 7-1)
Bond Fastrac Official explanation: jockey said colt had no more to give
T/Plt: £64.70 to a £1 stake. Pool of £138,722.44 - 1,564.02 winning tickets. T/Qpdt: £12.90 to a £1 stake. Pool of £7,049.63 - 403.60 winning tickets. CR

2505 NEWMARKET (Rowley Mile) (R-H)
Saturday, May 29

OFFICIAL GOING: Good to firm changing to good after race 2 (2:45)
Stands' side track used.
Wind: medium, against Weather: raining

2543 NOVAE BLOODSTOCK INSURANCE FAIRWAY STKS (LISTED RACE) — 1m 2f
2:15 (2:15) (Class 1) 3-Y-O
£22,708 (£8,608; £4,308; £2,148; £1,076; £540) **Stalls** Low

Form	Pos	Dist	Horse	Jockey	RPR
4-11	**1**		**Green Moon (IRE)**[14] 2117 3-9-0 **96** (H J L Dunlop) *chsd ldng pair: wnt 2nd 4f out: rdn along over 2f out: led wl over 1f out: clr ent fnl f: styd on wl* **2/1**[1]	JamieSpencer 5	108
10-4	**2**	*2 1/4*	**Red Badge (IRE)**[36] 1497 3-9-0 **92** (R Hannon) *hld up in tch in last pair: rdn and effrt over 2f out: chsd clr wnr ent fnl f: edgd lft u.p jst ins fnl f: kpt on but nvr gng pce to chal wnr* **12/1**[3]	PatDobbs 2	103

2135 **3** 3 ½ **Miss Starlight**[24] 1820 3-8-9 99 ShaneKelly 1 91
(P J McBride) *hld up in tch in last pair: rdn along 3f out: chsd ldng pair ent fnl f: one pce and wl hld after* **12/1**[3]

2-21 **4** 3 ¾ **Alrasm (IRE)**[24] 1823 3-9-0 102 RichardHills 3 89
(M A Jarvis) *led: hdd wl over 1f out: rdn and edgd lft over 1f out: 4th and fading whn hmpd ins fnl f* **2/1**[1]

3-20 **5** 21 **Ameer (IRE)**[21] 1945 3-9-3 105 FrankieDettori 4 50
(Saeed Bin Suroor) *in tch: pushed along 1/2-way: hdwy to chse ldng pair over 3f out: rdn and edgd rt 2f out: wknd qckly over 1f out: eased fnl f* **10/3**[2]

1425 **6** 7 **Kinky Afro (IRE)**[28] 1715 3-8-9 99 LiamKeniry 6 28
(J S Moore) *chsd ldr tl 4f out: rdn and dropped to rr 3f out: lost tch ent fnl 2f: t.o and eased ins fnl f* **25/1**

2m 6.77s (0.97) **Going Correction** +0.275s/f (Good) **6** Ran SP% **109.0**
Speed ratings (Par 107): **107,105,102,99,82 77**
toteswingers:1&2:£5.20, 1&3:£3.90, 2&3:£8.20 CSF £24.74 TOTE £3.10: £2.30, £4.80; EX 21.60.

Owner Mrs Ben Goldsmith **Bred** Goldsmith Bloodstock Partnership **Trained** Lambourn, Berks

FOCUS
Stands' side track used. Despite 2mm of rain in the morning the going description remained unchanged as Good to firm before the first race. However, the rain closed in just before the first and a crosswind blowing into the stands may have contributed to a modest time despite what appeared a sound gallop. The runners raced up the centre of the track. This Listed race has thrown up some subsequently very good winners in recent years, most notably St Leger victor Lucarno, Champion Stakes winner David Junior and Breeders' Cup Turf hero Red Rocks. This year's renewal looked a tight affair judged on official ratings but was won in emphatic fashion. The form looks sound enough rated through the third.

NOTEBOOK
Green Moon(IRE) ◆ has progressed from winning his maiden to take a competitive handicap at Newbury and stepped up again here. He took over running into the Dip and drew away without being asked for maximum effort. His connections believe he will be suited by 1m4f and he is in the King Edward VII Stakes at Royal Ascot, but the Hampton Court at this trip looks a viable alternative. (op 5-2)

Red Badge(IRE), stepping up in trip, tracked the winner throughout but could not respond when that rival went on before staying on steadily up the hill. There could be a decent handicap in him at around this trip, although finishing so close to an improving sort may cause the Handicapper to react. (op 9-1)

Miss Starlight was probably suited by the arrival of the rain and ran her race. She went after the winner running down into the Dip but could find no more on the climb to the line. There is a similar race to be won with her against her own sex. (op 10-1)

Alrasm(IRE) was sent off favourite and, having already won over 1m4f, was given a positive ride. He appeared to be going well enough over 2f out but stopped pretty quickly once headed by the winner and his rider reported the colt was too keen. He had been narrowly beaten by today's third earlier this season and was 7lb better off today, which suggests he ran below-par here. Official explanation: jockey said gelding ran too keen (op 7-4 tchd 5-2 in a place)

Ameer(IRE) looks to have gone backwards after a promising start to the season. He also seems to have temperament problems as he was being pushed along at an early stage, then came on the bridle travelling strongly before fading tamely once the race began in earnest. He looks one to avoid for betting purposes until he offers something more positive. (op 4-1)

Kinky Afro(IRE) ran fifth in the German 1000 Guineas last time but lost her place around halfway here, ran no sort of race and the rider reported she hung left. However, she did not perform that well on her only previous try at the track and may not like it. Official explanation: jockey said filly hung left (op 20-1)

2544 HOME OF RACING H'CAP 1m
2:45 (2:49) (Class 3) (0-90,89) 3-Y-O £7,771 (£2,312; £1,155; £577) Stalls Low

Form RPR

12-4 **1** **Business As Usual**[17] 2028 3-9-3 88 NeilCallan 10 101+
(M A Jarvis) *t.k.h early: chsd ldrs: swtchd rt and bmpd rival over 6f out: led gng wl over 2f out: hrd pressed over 1f out: rdn and kpt on wl fnl f: asserted towards fin* **9/1**

01-1 **2** ½ **Ransom Note**[29] 1658 3-9-1 86 MichaelHills 6 98+
(B W Hills) *in tch: hdwy over 3f out: rdn and ev ch 2f out: hrd drvn and kpt on ins fnl f: no ex and btn towards fin* **15/8**[1]

3-22 **3** 3 ¾ **Spa's Dancer (IRE)**[23] 1844 3-8-9 80 FrankieDettori 7 83
(J W Hills) *prom: led 3f out: sn hdd: nt pce of ldng pair ent fnl f: wl hld ins fnl f but plugged on for clr 3rd* **8/1**[3]

3-00 **4** 5 **Syrian**[23] 1834 3-9-4 89 JamieSpencer 2 81
(M L W Bell) *stdd s: hld up in rr: hdwy ent fnl 3f: edgd rt and rdn 2f out: chsd ldng trio but continued to edge rt over 1f out: wl btn ent fnl f* **16/1**

0-01 **5** ¾ **One Good Emperor (IRE)**[15] 2089 3-8-5 81 KierenFox(5) 13 71
(J R Best) *t.k.h early: hld up in tch on outer: effrt and rdn wl over 2f out: no prog and wl btn over 1f out* **17/2**

31-5 **6** nk **Dubai Set**[27] 1732 3-9-2 87 PatDobbs 5 76
(R Hannon) *chsd ldrs: rdn and unable qck ent 3f out: wl hld but plugged on u.p fr over 1f out* **11/1**

314- **7** ¾ **Dashing Doc (IRE)**[256] 5970 3-8-1 77 DeclanCannon(5) 12 64
(D R C Elsworth) *chsd ldrs: bmpd over 6f out: rdn wl over 2f out: edgd lft and struggling 2f out: wl btn over 1f out* **25/1**

343- **8** 6 **Munsarim (IRE)**[225] 6810 3-8-8 79 RichardHills 3 53
(J L Dunlop) *hld up in rr on stands' rail: nt clr run 4f out tl over 2f out: no ch after* **4/1**[2]

60-0 **9** 13 **The Human League**[28] 1703 3-8-13 84 SamHitchcott 8 28
(M R Channon) *in tch in midfield: rdn and struggling ent fnl 3f: wl bhd fnl 2f: t.o* **33/1**

13-0 **10** 10 **San Cassiano (IRE)**[21] 1913 3-9-4 89 JimCrowley 4 10
(R M Beckett) *a in rr: struggling and rdn over 3f out: lost tch wl over 2f out: t.o and eased ins fnl f* **25/1**

6420 **11** 5 **Gumnd (IRE)**[7] 2324 3-8-11 85 AhmedAjtebi(3) 9 —
(C E Brittain) *led tl 3f out: sn struggling: wkng whn hmpd and stmbld 2f out: wl bhd and eased ins fnl f: t.o* **25/1**

1m 40.07s (1.47) **Going Correction** +0.275s/f (Good) **11** Ran SP% **115.1**
Speed ratings (Par 103): **103,102,98,93,93 92,91,85,72,62 57**
toteswingers:1&2:£3.50, 1&3:£5.50, 2&3:£3.50 CSF £24.53 CT £144.30 TOTE £8.20: £2.40, £1.30, £1.80; EX 23.20 Trifecta £112.20 Pool: £708.44 - 5.67 winning units..

Owner P Makin **Bred** Paulyn Limited **Trained** Newmarket, Suffolk

FOCUS
A decent 3-y-o handicap that often falls to an improving sort and it was dominated by a pair who fit that description. Unlike the first race, the field raced more towards the stands' rail. The firs two pulled clear and look ahead of their marks.

NOTEBOOK
Business As Usual ◆ was a decent juvenile and had put up a fine effort on his return to action at York. However, he was a significant market drifter beforehand but proved the doubters wrong with a game effort. Held up just off the pace, unlike in his previous starts when he made the running, he was a little keen before coming through to hit the front around the quarter-mile pole. He then held off the favourite who had the advantage of the stands' rail and looks the sort who can make his mark in something like the Britannia Handicap at Royal Ascot, providing he is high enough handicapped to get a run. (op 5-1 tchd 9-2)

Ransom Note has been improving well and was a strongly supported favourite despite a 9lb rise for his previous success. He tracked the winner from the start and came through to deliver his challenge running into the Dip. He had every chance and kept trying, but the winner proved too strong. (op 7-2 tchd 4-1 in places)

Spa's Dancer(IRE) is still a maiden and has been placed in his last five starts. He was in the front rank throughout near the stands' rail and stuck on, although proving no match for the first two. He should find a race before long. (op 17-2)

Syrian appeared to miss the break but was held up, so that might have been intentional. He made ground from the back without ever looking a threat, but he does not give the impression he is putting everything in and his rider reported the gelding hung both ways, so headgear might be applied before too long. Official explanation: jockey said gelding hung both ways

One Good Emperor(IRE), a C&D winner here earlier in the month, was 8lb higher and appeared to run his race more towards the centre of the track, although the trainer reported he was unsuited by the rain-softened ground. Official explanation: trainer said colt was unsuited by the good to firm ground (op 15-2 tchd 9-1 and 10-1 in a place)

Dubai Set, stepping up in distance, only ran on past beaten rivals in the closing stages. (op 10-1 tchd 12-1)

Munsarim(IRE) was well supported on this handicap debut but was already beginning to struggle when hampered near the rail over 2f out. (op 7-2 tchd 9-2 in places)

2545 CORAL.CO.UK SPRINT (H'CAP) 6f
3:20 (3:21) (Class 2) (0-105,102) 3-Y-O
£24,924 (£7,464; £3,732; £1,868; £932; £468) Stalls Low

Form RPR

0-56 **1** **Swilly Ferry (USA)**[28] 1701 3-9-1 96 MichaelHills 4 108+
(B W Hills) *racd on stands' side: hld up towards rr: hdwy 2f out: rdn and chsd ldr ins fnl f: r.o wl to ld fnl 50yds: gng away at fin* **12/1**[3]

0-02 **2** 1 **Excellent Guest**[8] 2287 3-7-5 79 RyanPowell(7) 8 88
(G G Margarson) *racd in centre: chsd ldrs: wnt overall 2nd and rdn over 1f out: led jst ins fnl f: rdn and hdd fnl 50yds: no ex: 1st of 6 in gp* **16/1**

-231 **3** 2 ¼ **Confessional**[9] 2260 3-8-6 87 (p) DavidAllan 12 89
(T D Easterby) *racd in centre: led that gp and prom: rdn to ld overall 2f out: edgd lft u.p 1f out: sn hdd: nt pce of ldng pair fnl 100yds: jst hld 3rd: 2nd of 6 in gp* **14/1**

-001 **4** shd **Russian Rock (IRE)**[12] 2179 3-8-2 88 JohnFahy(5) 15 89
(R A Teal) *racd on far side: in tch: effrt u.p wl over 1f out: chsd ldrs and hrd drvn ent fnl f: styd on same pce fnl 150yds: 1st of 4 in gp* **20/1**

1-22 **5** nk **Gene Autry (USA)**[9] 2242 3-8-1 82 FrankieMcDonald 18 83
(R Hannon) *racd on far side: hld up in tch: effrt and rdn wl over 1f out: edgd lft u.p jst ins fnl f: styd on same pce fnl 150yds: 2nd of 4 in gp* **7/1**[1]

12-4 **6** nk **Side Glance**[27] 1732 3-8-9 90 LiamKeniry 13 90
(A M Balding) *stdd s and sn swtchd to r in centre gp: hld up towards rr: pushed along and effrt 2f out: rdn and kpt on fr over 1f out: unable to rch ldrs: 3rd of 6 in gp* **12/1**[3]

22-2 **7** 1 ½ **Bagamoyo**[28] 1701 3-9-1 96 PatCosgrave 10 91
(J R Fanshawe) *swtchd to r in stands' side gp after s: hdwy ent fnl 2f: drvn and unable qck over 1f out: edgd rt and btn ins fnl f: 2nd of 7 in gp* **8/1**[2]

-343 **8** ½ **Below Zero (IRE)**[22] 1865 3-9-0 95 JoeFanning 3 88
(M Johnston) *racd stands' side: broke wl: prom overall tl wknd u.p jst ins fnl f: 3rd of 7 in gp* **33/1**

-302 **9** 1 ¾ **Lowdown (IRE)**[8] 2283 3-8-9 90 FrankieDettori 14 78
(M Johnston) *racd in centre: in tch: rdn and unable qck wl over 1f out: wknd over 1f out: 4th of 6 in gp* **12/1**[3]

23-4 **10** nk **Take Ten**[36] 1499 3-8-11 92 RichardHills 17 79
(M Johnston) *racd on far side: led that gp and prom overall: rdn wl over 1f out: wknd qckly fnl 150yds: 3rd of 4 in gp* **12/1**[3]

00-2 **11** 2 **Pastoral Player**[45] 1315 3-9-0 95 WilliamBuick 7 75
(H Morrison) *swtchd to r in centre after 1f: hld up in tch towards rr: hdwy ent fnl 2f: rdn and fnd little over 1f out: wl btn 1f out: 5th of 6 in gp* **7/1**[1]

3-01 **12** 1 ¾ **Folly Bridge**[21] 1917 3-8-6 87 RichardMullen 5 62
(R Charlton) *racd on stands' side: in tch tl struggling u.p ent fnl 2f: wl btn over 1f out: 4th of 7 in gp* **12/1**[3]

66-0 **13** ½ **Footstepsofspring (FR)**[28] 1701 3-8-6 87 JamieMackay 19 60
(W J Musson) *racd on far side: a in rr: rdn and struggling ent fnl 2f: n.d: 4th of 4 in gp* **66/1**

5211 **14** 1 ¾ **Jack My Boy (IRE)**[28] 1701 3-8-12 93 (b) NeilCallan 1 60
(P D Evans) *racd stands' side: broke wl: overall ldr tl hdd over 2f out: sn struggling u.p: wl btn ins fnl f: 5th of 7 in gp* **8/1**[2]

5-06 **15** 1 **Di Stefano**[15] 2090 3-8-7 88 (v) SamHitchcott 9 52
(M R Channon) *racd on stands' side: towards rr: drvn and struggling ent fnl 2f: wl btn over 1f out: 6th of 7 in gp* **40/1**

116- **16** 7 **Walk On Water**[268] 5606 3-8-12 93 EddieAhern 11 35
(H R A Cecil) *racd in centre: wl in tch tl wknd qckly whn rdn wl over 1f out: wl bhd fnl f: 6th of 6 in gp* **12/1**[3]

336- **17** 9 **Above Limits (IRE)**[231] 6660 3-9-7 102 JamieSpencer 6 15
(D M Simcock) *racd on stands' side: a in rr: lost tch and hung bdly rt wl over 1f out: eased ins fnl f: 7th of 7 in gp* **20/1**

1m 13.29s (1.09) **Going Correction** +0.325s/f (Good) **17** Ran SP% **122.3**
Speed ratings (Par 105): **105,103,100,100,100 99,97,97,94,94 91,89,88,86,85 75,63**
toteswingers:1&2:£58.90, 1&3:£43.90, 2&3:£62.40 CSF £180.04 CT £2810.06 TOTE £13.70: £3.20, £4.00, £3.70, £6.30; EX 329.70 Trifecta £8762.70 Pool: £16578.16 - 1.40 winning units..

Owner John C Grant **Bred** Kilboy Estate Inc **Trained** Lambourn, Berks

FOCUS
The ground was changed to good following the previous race. A very competitive sprint handicap that has been won by some top sorts in recent years. The field split initially into three groups but most ended up nearer the stands' rail. The form makes sense with the third rated to previous 5f form.

NOTEBOOK
Swilly Ferry(USA) came right up the stands' side and picked up well to get to the front on the climb to the line. The winner of a valuable sales race last season, these good handicaps are his level and he looks capable of getting another furlong in time. Meanwhile, there is a valuable handicap at York the weekend before Royal Ascot which could prove an ideal target. (tchd 16-1 in a place)

Excellent Guest, who looked a little unlucky on his previous start, had a clear run this time and, when he got the better of the long-time leader, he looked set for compensation. However, he could not respond to the late challenge of the winner up the rail. (tchd 25-1 in a place)

Confessional has developed into a pretty consistent sprinter and the headgear has seemed to help. He ran well under a positive ride, only getting run out of it on the climb to the line. He is another who could go to York, where the track should suit him. (op 12-1)

Russian Rock(IRE) benefited from the drop back from 7f to 5f last time and ran pretty well on his first try at this trip. He was keeping on at the end and looks worth another try at it.
Gene Autry(USA) was the subject of good market support on this drop back from 7f. He raced in the group nearest the centre of the course, along with the fourth, but did not appear to last home up the hill and was reported as hanging left. He is another who might prefer a flatter track. Official explanation: jockey said colt hung left (op 9-1 tchd 10-1 in places)
Side Glance was held up at the back towards the centre but switched more towards the stands' side in the closing stages and stayed on well. A return to 7f should be in his favour. (op 11-1)
Bagamoyo had been pretty consistent up to now but could never land a blow having been held up early. He did stay on in manner that suggests he might be worth trying at 7f.
Below Zero(IRE) showed up for a long way up the stands' side and did best of the Johnston trio.
Pastoral Player, whose problems with the stalls looked to have been cured by a gelding operation last time, was held up off the pace and switched towards the centre. However, from that point he was unable to get competitive and only ran on late. He is probably better than the bare form indicates. (tchd 15-2)
Jack My Boy(IRE), who had beaten Bagamoyo over C&D last time, showed up nearest the rail but was already in trouble when the winner swept past going into the Dip. (tchd 15-2 and 17-2 in a place)
Above Limits(IRE)'s rider reported that the filly ran too free. Official explanation: jockey said filly ran too free (tchd 25-1)

2546 KING CHARLES II STKS (LISTED RACE) 7f
3:55 (3:55) (Class 1) 3-Y-O **£22,708** (£8,608; £4,308; £2,148; £1,076) **Stalls** Low

Form RPR

0-5 **1** **Field Of Dream**[16] 2045 3-9-4 95 .... J-PGuillambert 3 109
(L M Cumani) *t.k.h: chsd ldrs: rdn along 3f out: hrd drvn over 1f out: styd on wl ins fnl f to ld fnl 75yds* **33/1**

3-10 **2** ½ **Red Jazz (USA)**[28] 1699 3-9-4 113 .... MichaelHills 1 108
(B W Hills) *chsd ldr: rdn to chal over 1f out: stl ev ch and drvn 1f out: after tl no ex fnl 50yds* **5/4**[1]

4-41 **3** nk **Rodrigo De Torres**[28] 1687 3-9-0 103 .... EddieAhern 4 103
(H R A Cecil) *wnt rt s: sn rcvrd to ld and crossed to r on stands' rail: rdn and kpt on wl ent fnl f: hdd and no ex fnl 75yds* **4/1**[3]

21-1 **4** 2 ¾ **Dafeef**[27] 1732 3-9-0 102 .... FrankieDettori 2 96
(Saeed Bin Suroor) *stdd and dropped in bhd after s: t.k.h: hld up in tch: swtchd rt and hdwy over 2f out: drvn and unable qck over 1f out: wknd jst ins fnl f* **5/2**[2]

321- **5** 1 ¼ **Electric Feel**[217] 7033 3-8-13 99 .... MartinDwyer 5 91
(M Botti) *pushed rt s: sn swtchd lft and dropped in bhd: a last: rdn and styd on same pce fr wl over 1f out* **7/1**

1m 27.4s (2.00) **Going Correction** +0.325s/f (Good) 5 Ran SP% **108.5**
Speed ratings (Par 107): **101,100,100,96,95**
CSF £73.63 TOTE £24.70: £3.80, £1.10; EX 53.00.
Owner Exors Of The Late L Cashman **Bred** Grundy Bloodstock S R L **Trained** Newmarket, Suffolk

FOCUS
This Listed race has produced a number of subsequent Group winners in recent years and has been a decent guide to the Jersey Stakes at Royal Ascot, with both Jeremy and Tariq following up their successes here, while Fokine finished runner-up. The small field stuck close to the stands' rail but the runner that raced widest of the quintet caused a major surprise. The form is a bit muddling and although there are grounds for rating it higher, it looks less than straightforward.

NOTEBOOK
Field Of Dream, a soft-ground Listed winner in Italy, had beaten only one home in two previous starts for his current trainer. However, those runs were both on fast going and perhaps the rain-softened ground and settling better made the difference. He was held up early and was the first under pressure, but he kept responding and stayed on best up the hill to pass the duo on his inside. Connections had no immediate plans for him. (tchd 40-1 in a place)
Red Jazz(USA), who made all to win the Free Handicap here earlier in the season, got a lead from the third this time before delivering his challenge running into the Dip. He could not get past the leader, though, and it was only when the winner went past that he picked up again. (op 11-8 tchd 6-5, 6-4 in places and 13-8 in a place)
Rodrigo De Torres had looked an improved performer this season and set out to make all the running. He battled well to initially hold off the runner-up but that left him vulnerable to a late challenge and he was run out of it up the hill. Both his previous wins have been on flat tracks, and he looks capable of scoring at this level on a suitable course. (op 3-1 tchd 9-2 in a place)
Dafeef had done little wrong in three previous starts apart from hanging on the second occasion. The rain-softened ground was probably in his favour but after having every chance 2f out, the response under pressure was minimal. He may just not be up to this class. (op 11-4 tchd 3-1 in places and 10-3 in a place)
Electric Feel, the only filly in the line-up, is already a Listed winner and Group placed so her paddock value is assured. However, she was always at the rear on this seasonal debut and might be better for the outing. (op 8-1)

2547 EBF JOE AGGIO 30TH BIRTHDAY MAIDEN STKS 6f
4:30 (4:32) (Class 4) 2-Y-O **£5,180** (£1,541; £770; £384) **Stalls** Low

Form RPR

1 **Libranno** 2-9-3 0 .... PatCosgrave 12 85
(R Hannon) *mde all: grad crossed over to r on stands' rail rdn wl over 1f out: hld on wl ins fnl f* **25/1**

2 nk **Ecliptic (USA)** 2-9-0 0 .... AhmedAjtebi(3) 13 84
(Mahmood Al Zarooni) *chsd ldrs: wnt 2nd 2f out: sn rdn along and rn green over 1f out: ev ch 1f out: edgd rt u.p ins fnl f: kpt on but hld fnl 75yds* **13/2**[3]

2 **3** 1 ¾ **King Of Jazz (IRE)**[15] 2077 2-9-3 0 .... PatDobbs 11 79
(R Hannon) *chsd wnr tl 2f out: 3rd and rdn wl over 1f out: styd on same pce and no imp fnl f* **3/1**[1]

4 4 ½ **Whaileyy (IRE)** 2-9-3 0 .... RichardMullen 6 67+
(Sir Michael Stoute) *in tch in midfield: rdn and hdwy ent fnl 2f: chsd ldng trio ent fnl f: sn outpcd* **14/1**

5 3 ½ **Dffar (IRE)** 2-9-3 0 .... NeilCallan 9 55
(C E Brittain) *in tch: hmpd after 1f: rdn and unable qck ent fnl 2f: wknd over 1f out: no ch w ldrs ins fnl f* **7/1**

6 **6** ¾ **Blue Dazzler (IRE)**[15] 2077 2-9-3 0 .... AdamKirby 16 53
(Mrs A J Perrett) *in tch on outer: hdwy to chse ldrs ent fnl 3f: wknd u.p over 1f out: wl btn fnl f* **6/1**[2]

7 2 ¼ **Canada Fleet (CAN)** 2-9-3 0 .... JamieSpencer 10 46
(E A L Dunlop) *v.s.a: bhd: hdwy on outer 3f out: rdn and wknd wl over 1f out: wl btn fnl f* **20/1**

6 **8** shd **Early Applause**[45] 1309 2-9-3 0 .... MichaelHills 8 46
(B W Hills) *dwlt: sn wl in tch in midfield: hdwy to chse ldrs ent fnl 2f: rdn and btn wl over 1f out* **10/1**

0 **9** hd **Talk Talk (IRE)**[15] 2077 2-9-3 0 .... MartinDwyer 4 45
(B J Meehan) *t.k.h: hld up in tch hmpd after 1f and again after 4f out: rdn and btn 2f out* **9/1**

0 **10** 1 ¼ **Freedom Trail**[12] 2176 2-8-12 0 .... DaneO'Neill 14 36
(D R C Elsworth) *chsd ldrs tl rdn and wknd ent fnl 2f: wl bhd fnl f* **20/1**

11 2 **Surrey Star (IRE)** 2-9-3 0 .... LiamKeniry 7 35+
(R A Teal) *s.i.s: hld up in tch towards rr: hdwy and rdn whn stmbld 2f out: edging rt and n.d after* **50/1**

12 ¾ **Magic Cross** 2-8-7 0 .... TobyAtkinson(5) 3 28
(P J McBride) *s.i.s: rn green: in tch towards rr tl rdn and wknd over 2f out: wl bhd fnl f* **66/1**

13 2 ¼ **Tagansky** 2-9-3 0 .... JimCrowley 2 26+
(S Dow) *s.i.s: sn in tch hmpd and lost pl 4f out: bhd whn hung rt 2f out: ease whn btn* **33/1**

14 ½ **One Cool Bex** 2-9-3 0 .... ShaneKelly 5 25
(P J McBride) *in tch towards rr: rdn and btn over 2f out: wl bhd fr wl over 1f out* **50/1**

15 9 **Key West (IRE)** 2-9-3 0 ....(b[1]) WilliamBuick 15 —
(J H M Gosden) *coltish in paddock: dwlt: sn rcvrd and in tch in midfield: rdn and wknd qckly ent fnl 2f: wl bhd and eased ins fnl f* **12/1**

1m 15.08s (2.88) **Going Correction** +0.375s/f (Good) 15 Ran SP% **120.3**
Speed ratings (Par 95): **95,94,92,86,81 80,77,77,77,75 72,71,68,68,56**
toteswingers:1&2:£48.30, 1&3:£21.90, 2&3:£7.10 CSF £170.59 TOTE £32.00: £7.20, £2.50, £1.90; EX 174.70 Trifecta £327.60 Part won. Pool of £442.78 - 0.50 winning units..
Owner Mcdowell Racing **Bred** O McDowell **Trained** East Everleigh, Wilts

FOCUS
This maiden had thrown up a few horses that went on to be Group placed but the best recent winner was the high-class Tariq, who returned to win the preceding Listed race the season after taking this on his debut. This looked a fair maiden with the field strung out behind the first three.

NOTEBOOK
Libranno ◆ looked the stable second string on jockey bookings but proved that wrong by making just about all the running. He ran on straight and true up the hill, which in the end proved decisive. A 26,000gns first foal of a 7f juvenile winner from a prolific winning family, he has clearly inherited ability and has a fair bit of size about him, so can be expected to improve with this behind him. (op 40-1)
Ecliptic(USA), the first foal of a 1m1f Grade 1 winner in the USA, was well backed and put up a decent effort. He looked the most likely winner when drawing upsides the leader a furlong out but tended to wander under pressure and could not get past his rival, who kept straight. He should also be better for the experience. (op 11-1)
King Of Jazz(IRE), a £48,000 son of Acclamation, ran with plenty of promise on his debut at Newbury. He was sent off favourite but was easy to back. He tracked his stable companion from the start but failed to make any impression in the closing stages, despite finishing clear of the rest. (op 9-4 tchd 7-2)
Whaileyy(IRE) ◆, a 120,000gns half-brother to 1m1f Listed winner from the family of Lomond, made an encouraging debut, especially considering he was rather hampered by Dffar early on. He looks sure to come on a fair amount for the run.
Dffar(IRE), a 50,000gns first foal of a filly who was third in the Marcel Boussac, was rather green on this debut, wandering about early and hampering one or two of his rivals. However, he showed plenty of ability and will know more next time. (op 8-1 tchd 6-1)
Blue Dazzler(IRE) has something of a middle-distance pedigree but had made a promising debut over 6f at Newbury on fast ground. He ran well from his draw on the outside of the field and can be expected to win races over longer trips in time. (op 7-1 tchd 15-2 and 8-1 in places)
Canada Fleet(CAN), a $150,000 first foal of a multiple winner in the USA, also showed some promise after missing the break.
Early Applause had previous experience but failed to take a hand and might be the sort for nurseries later in the season. (tchd 9-1 and 11-1)
Talk Talk(IRE), another who had previous experience, also failed to take a hand and might be the sort for nurseries later in the season. (op 10-1)

2548 ROWLEY MILE MAIDEN STKS 1m
5:05 (5:09) (Class 4) 3-Y-O **£5,180** (£1,541; £770; £384) **Stalls** Low

Form RPR

1 **Qanoon (USA)** 3-9-3 0 .... RichardHills 4 89+
(W J Haggas) *trckd ldrs: hdwy to chse ldr ent fnl 2f: disp 1f out: r.o wl to go clr fnl 100yds: readily* **4/1**[2]

22 **2** 1 ¾ **Soviet Secret**[19] 1976 3-9-3 0 .... ShaneKelly 7 83
(P J McBride) *w ldr tl led 3f out: rdn clr w wnr wl over 1f out: disp 1f out: nt pce of wnr fnl 150yds* **11/4**[1]

35- **3** 7 **Penangdouble O One**[196] 7390 3-9-3 0 .... JimCrowley 1 66
(R M Beckett) *pushed along early: chsd ldrs: rdn wl over 2f out: 3rd and outpcd by ldng pair wl over 1f out: wl btn but kpt on to hold 3rd fnl f* **13/2**[3]

60 **4** 1 **Majestatic**[39] 1442 3-9-3 0 .... SamHitchcott 6 64
(S W James) *led tl 3f out: sn rdn: drvn and outpcd by ldng pair wl over 1f out: wl hld and plugged on same pce fnl f* **66/1**

5 nk **Wise Up** 3-9-3 0 .... MichaelHills 2 63
(B W Hills) *broke wl: t.k.h and grad stdd bk into midfield: pushed along and effrt over 2f out: pressing for 3rd but no ch w ldrs over 1f out: kpt on same pce fnl f* **8/1**

0- **6** ½ **Profligate (IRE)**[210] 7182 3-8-12 0 .... AlanMunro 5 57+
(W Jarvis) *stdd s: t.k.h: hld up in tch in last pair: rdn and effrt over 2f out: no ch w ldrs fr wl over 1f out: plugged on fnl f* **33/1**

7 ¾ **Majestic Bright** 3-8-12 0 .... J-PGuillambert 8 55
(L M Cumani) *in tch on outer: pushed along and effrt over 2f out: ev ch of 3rd but no ch w ldng pair over 1f out: no ex ins fnl f* **9/1**

5 **8** 3 ¼ **Dhaafer**[14] 2128 3-9-3 0 .... LiamJones 9 52
(W J Haggas) *s.i.s: a in rr: rdn and struggling over 2f out: wl bhd fr wl over 1f out* **16/1**

9 1 **Attrition** 3-9-3 0 .... MartinDwyer 3 50
(Andrew Reid) *stdd s: plld hrd: hld up in last pair: rdn and effrt over 2f out: outpcd and no ch w ldrs fr wl over 1f out: n.m.r and eased ins fnl f* **50/1**

1m 40.29s (1.69) **Going Correction** +0.375s/f (Good) 9 Ran SP% **93.4**
Speed ratings (Par 101): **106,104,97,96,95 95,94,91,90**
toteswingers:1&2 £2.90, 2&3 £3.20, 1&3 £4.60 CSF £9.72 TOTE £4.00: £1.70, £1.20, £1.10; EX 10.10 Trifecta £47.20 Pool: £304.48 - 4.77 winning units..
Owner Hamdan Al Maktoum **Bred** Highfield Stock Farm Et Al **Trained** Newmarket, Suffolk
■ Mureb (11/4) withdrawn (bolted to s); deducton 25p in £ from all bets.

FOCUS
This maiden has been dominated by the major Newmarket yards, but the market was thrown into confusion when the market leader Mureb bolted going to the start and was subsequently withdrawn. The time was 0.22secs slower than the earlier handicap over the trip and the runner-up sets the level to C&D form.

2549 COURSE OF CHAMPIONS H'CAP 1m 6f
5:40 (5:41) (Class 4) (0-85,85) 4-Y-O+ **£5,180** (£1,541; £770; £384) **Stalls** Centre

Form RPR

60-5 **1** **Perfect Shot (IRE)**[21] 1902 4-9-6 82 .... MartinDwyer 8 94+
(J L Dunlop) *t.k.h: hld up in tch in midfield: styd far side 10f out: effrt to ld wl over 1f out: jinked lft but gng clr 1f out: r.o wl: easily* **4/1**[2]

1-33 **2** 6 **Mildoura (FR)**[38] 1472 5-9-9 **85** IanMongan 3 89
(Mrs L J Mongan) *t.k.h: chsd ldrs: styd far side 10f out: ev ch and drvn over 2f out: pushed rt 2f out: chsd clr wnr 1f out: no imp* **8/1**

1-46 **3** 3 1/4 **Abayaan**[29] 1655 4-9-2 **78** (p) ShaneKelly 7 77
(Jane Chapple-Hyam) *led: styd far side 10f out: hdd: drvn and edgd rt wl over 1f out: no ch w wnr fnl f: hld on for 3rd* **13/2**

2-30 **4** 1/2 **Hawridge King**[21] 1902 8-8-12 **74** AlanMunro 5 72
(W S Kittow) *chsd ldr: c centre 10f out: rdn and unable qck over 3f out: plugged on same pce fnl 2f* **8/1**

5 1/2 **According**[112] 4-9-9 **85** EddieAhern 2 83+
(N J Henderson) *chsd ldrs: c centre 10f out: led that gp over 3f out: edgd rt whn rdn wl over 2f out: pressing ldrs ent fnl 2f: wknd ent fnl f* **7/2**[1]

5446 **6** 3 **Paktolos (FR)**[7] 2313 7-9-3 **79** (p) FergusSweeney 6 72
(John A Harris) *hld up in last trio: c centre 10f out: rdn and btn over 3f out: no ch but plugged on fnl f* **16/1**

212- **7** 8 **Bollin Judith**[210] 7170 4-8-8 **70** DavidAllan 1 52
(T D Easterby) *in tch in midfield: c centre 10f out: pushed along 4f out: wl btn 3f out* **7/1**

41-0 **8** 1 3/4 **Lombok**[21] 1902 4-8-8 **70** JamieSpencer 10 50
(M L W Bell) *t.k.h: hld up in last trio: styd far side 10f out: rdn and effrt to press ldrs 3f out: wknd qckly over 2f out* **5/1**[3]

10-0 **9** 3 1/4 **Never Ending Tale**[38] 1474 5-9-6 **82** LiamKeniry 9 57
(E F Vaughan) *stdd s: t.k.h: hld up in rr: styd far side 10f out: rdn and lost tch wl over 3f out* **28/1**

3m 3.21s (4.71) **Going Correction** +0.425s/f (Yiel) **9** Ran SP% **116.3**
Speed ratings (Par 105): **103,99,97,97,97 95,90,89,88**
toteswingers:1&2:£7.20, 1&3:£6.30, 2&3:£8.80 CSF £36.20 CT £204.53 TOTE £4.70: £1.30, £2.90, £2.60; EX 40.40 Trifecta £409.40 Part won. Pool of £553.36 - 0.62 winning units. Place 6: £50.65 Place 5: £21.94 .
Owner Sir Philip Wroughton **Bred** David Jamison Bloodstock **Trained** Arundel, W Sussex

FOCUS
A fair stayers' handicap in which subsequent Group 2 winner Finalmente was the best recent winner. The early pace was modest and the field split into two almost equal groups turning into the long straight before converging more towards the far side running into the Dip. The form is not straightforward.
T/Jkpt: Not won. T/Plt: £145.20 to a £1 stake. Pool:£133,457.17 - 670.89 winning tickets T/Qpdt: £31.00 to a £1 stake. Pool:£7,105.75 - 169.15 winning tickets SP

2550 - 2558a (Foreign Racing) - See Raceform Interactive

1715 DUSSELDORF (R-H)
Saturday, May 29

OFFICIAL GOING: Turf: good

2559a PREIS DER FREUNDE UND FORDERER DES DUSSELDORF REITER UND RENNVEREINS (GROUP 3) (3YO+) (TURF) 1m
5:00 (5:06) 3-Y-O+
£28,318 (£9,734; £4,867; £2,654; £1,769; £1,327)

RPR

1 **Abbashiva (GER)**[48] 1251 5-9-0 0 EFrank 1 98
(T Mundry, Germany) *a.p: trckd pce: r.o wl in st: hit front 2f out: a fnd more ins fnl f* **41/5**

2 3/4 **Alianthus (GER)**[20] 5-9-0 0 ADeVries 4 96
(J Hirschberger, Germany) *broke wl: led after 1f: r.o wl u.p in st: hdd 2f out: battled wl to line* **16/5**[1]

3 1 **Sanjii Danon (GER)**[48] 1251 4-9-2 0 APietsch 7 96
(W Hickst, Germany) *in rr fr s: travelling wl: swung wd into st: r.o wl in st* **4/1**[3]

4 3/4 **Sehrezad (IRE)**[28] 1716 5-9-4 0 JiriPalik 10 96
(Andreas Lowe, Germany) *a.p fr s: mde early move in st: r.o wl but no threat to ldrs* **33/10**[2]

5 1 **Magic Eye (IRE)**[170] 7704 5-8-11 0 THellier 13 87
(Andreas Lowe, Germany) *settled towards rr: gd move towards end of bk-stretch: hit traffic problems ent st: r.o wl whn fnd room: fin fast* **169/10**

6 1 3/4 **Polarix**[23] 1855 4-9-0 0 FabriceVeron 2 86
(H-A Pantall, France) *broke fast: led briefly: remained prom: r.o wl in st wout threatening* **156/10**

7 2 1/2 **Usbeke (GER)**[20] 4-9-2 0 HenkGrewe 11 82
(J-P Carvalho, Germany) *racd in midfield: threatened briefly early in st: but no imp* **25/1**

8 1/2 **Le Big (GER)**[203] 7303 6-9-4 0 EPedroza 3 83
(U Stoltefuss, Germany) *cl up fr s: early move in st: hmpd briefly by tiring horses: r.o wl whn clr ins fnl f* **13/2**

9 1 **Earl Of Fire (GER)**[20] 1955 5-9-4 0 DominiqueBoeuf 12 80
(W Baltromei, Germany) *settled in midfield: swung wd in fnl turn: looked to be travelling wl but mde no imp in clsng stages* **69/10**

10 nk **Atlantic Sport (USA)**[20] 5-9-0 0 AStarke 9 76
(P Schiergen, Germany) *prom early: sn btn in st* **189/10**

11 nk **Beltanus (GER)**[20] 6-9-0 0 AHelfenbein 8 75
(T Potters, Germany) *a towards rr: nvr a threat* **161/10**

12 3/4 **Sabantuy**[37] 4-9-0 0 MSuerland 6 73
(C Von Der Recke, Germany) *a towards the rr* **61/1**

13 6 **Mharadono (GER)**[20] 7-9-0 0 SHellyn 5 60
(P Hirschberger, Germany) *prom early: qckly fdd in st* **68/1**

1m 35.57s (-5.59) **13** Ran SP% **133.3**
WIN (incl. 10 euro stake): 92. PLACES: 25, 17, 21. SF: 370..
Owner Gestut Brummerhof **Bred** Frau N Schuoler **Trained** Germany

2543 NEWMARKET (Rowley Mile) (R-H)
Sunday, May 30

OFFICIAL GOING: Good (8.1)
Stands' side track used. There was a strong tailwind up the straight.
Wind: strong, half behind Weather: bright and breezy

2560 JOSE HAIR DESIGN & MALE GROOMING LADIES' H'CAP (AMATEURS) (IN MEMORY OF LUCINDA STOPFORD-SACKVILLE) 1m 4f
2:20 (2:20) (Class 5) (0-70,70) 4-Y-O+
£3,123 (£968; £484; £242) **Stalls** Centre

Form RPR

0-05 **1** **Haljaferia (UAE)**[15] 2109 4-9-11 **65** MissLAllan(5) 1 72
(D R C Elsworth) *t.k.h early: hld up in tch in midfield: effrt to chal wl over 1f out: rdn to ld over 1f out: kpt on fnl f: rdn out* **13/2**[3]

1233 **2** 1 1/2 **My Mate Mal**[13] 2182 6-10-0 **70** MissCScott(7) 5 75
(W B Stone) *led: jnd 3f out: pushed along 2f out: hdd over 1f out: styd on same pce fnl f* **14/1**

600- **3** 1/2 **Sheila's Castle**[164] 7785 6-9-4 **60** MissCBoxall(7) 7 64
(S Regan) *stdd s: t.k.h: hld up towards rr: swtchd lft and hdwy 2f out: kpt on steadily fnl f: nt rch ldrs* **12/1**

463- **4** 2 **Drawn Gold**[181] 7594 6-9-4 **58** MissRKneller(5) 8 59
(R Hollinshead) *s.i.s: sn rcvrd and chsd ldr 10f out: pushed along and outpcd ent fnl 2f: swtchd lft wl over 1f out: plugged on fnl f* **13/2**[3]

0002 **5** 2 3/4 **Broughtons Paradis (IRE)**[19] 2013 4-9-11 **60** MissLHorner 9 57
(W J Musson) *t.k.h early: trckd ldrs: hdwy to join ldr 3f out: rdn ent 2f out: wknd ent fnl f* **5/1**[2]

205- **6** 2 1/2 **Ovthenight (IRE)**[14] 5028 5-10-0 **63** (b[1]) MissGAndrews 2 56
(Mrs P Sly) *chsd ldr for 2f: styd chsng ldrs tl rdn and no rspnse 4f out: btn over 2f out: edgd rt u.p fr over 1f out* **10/3**[1]

20-5 **7** 1 1/2 **What A Day**[22] 1919 4-9-2 **56** oh2 MissPhillipaTutty(5) 4 46
(J J Quinn) *t.k.h: hld up in tch towards rr: rdn and no hdwy over 2f out: nvr trbld ldrs* **11/1**

0033 **8** 3 **Moscow Oznick**[19] 2013 5-9-12 **61** MissSBrotherton 10 46
(D Donovan) *in tch: rdn and no rspnse over 2f out: wl btn fnl 2f* **13/2**[3]

0-30 **9** 9 **Dimashq**[23] 1891 8-9-2 **56** oh4 MissWGibson(5) 3 27
(P T Midgley) *hld up in last pair: rdn and no hdwy wl over 3f out: n.d* **28/1**

4663 **10** 60 **Millfields Dreams**[9] 2298 11-9-13 **67** (p) MissJodieHughes(5) 6 —
(P Leech) *a in rr: rdn and lost tch 4f out: t.o and eased fr over 1f out* **16/1**

2m 32.05s (-1.45) **Going Correction** -0.175s/f (Firm) **10** Ran SP% **111.8**
Speed ratings (Par 103): **97,96,95,94,92 90,89,87,81,41**
toteswingers:1&2:£7.10, 1&3:£23.50, 2&3:£21.80 CSF £88.96 CT £1046.31 TOTE £8.10: £2.60, £3.70, £5.30; EX 77.60 TRIFECTA Not won..
Owner The Howarting's Partnership **Bred** Darley **Trained** Newmarket, Suffolk

FOCUS
This is weak form, the winner in line with his Doncaster latest.
Millfields Dreams Official explanation: jockey said gelding pulled up lame

2561 STABLECARE MAIDEN STKS 5f
2:55 (2:56) (Class 4) 2-Y-O
£5,180 (£1,541; £770; £384) **Stalls** Low

Form RPR

5 **1** **Swiss Dream**[20] 1972 2-8-12 0 JimmyFortune 5 82+
(D R C Elsworth) *trckd ldrs gng wl: hdwy 2f out: rdn to ld ent fnl f: r.o strly: readily* **7/4**[1]

42 **2** 2 1/4 **Bunce (IRE)**[29] 1686 2-9-3 0 RyanMoore 4 79
(R Hannon) *w ldr: pushed into ld wl over 1f out: rdn and hdd ent fnl f: no ch w wnr but kpt on for clr 2nd* **15/8**[2]

2 **3** 3 **Mujrayaat (IRE)**[13] 2171 2-9-3 0 RichardHills 2 68+
(M A Jarvis) *in tch in midfield: effrt to chse ldng pair wl over 1f out: edgd lft whn rdn over 1f out: outpcd by ldng pair ent fnl f: wl hld after* **5/2**[3]

0 **4** 5 **Blade Pirate**[33] 1603 2-9-3 0 MichaelHills 3 50
(J Ryan) *led tl hdd and rdn wl over 1f out: sn wknd* **33/1**

5 3 1/4 **Sirens** 2-8-12 0 (t) DavidProbert 8 34
(P S McEntee) *pressed ldrs on outer tl 1/2-way: sn rdn and struggling: wl btn over 1f out* **25/1**

6 4 1/2 **Jamaica Grande** 2-9-3 0 JerryO'Dwyer 9 22
(P S McEntee) *s.i.s: sn pushed along and outpcd in rr: nvr on terms* **66/1**

7 3 1/4 **Bridget The Fidget** 2-8-12 0 EddieCreighton 1 6
(E J Creighton) *awkward leaving stalls and v.s.a: rn green and sn pushed along in rr: nvr on terms* **40/1**

8 14 **Knudstrup Noble (IRE)** 2-8-10 0 LeonnaMayor(7) 7 —
(P S McEntee) *v.s.a and wnt lft and rt after s: rn v green and a wl bhd: t.o fr 1/2-way* **100/1**

59.02 secs (-0.08) **Going Correction** -0.175s/f (Firm) **8** Ran SP% **111.4**
Speed ratings (Par 95): **93,89,84,76,71 64,59,36**
toteswingers:1&2:£1.60, 1&3:£1.80, 2&3:£1.30 CSF £4.99 TOTE £2.70: £1.10, £1.10, £1.10; EX 5.20 Trifecta £11.50 Pool: £950.12 - 61.10 winning units..
Owner Lordship Stud **Bred** Lordship Stud **Trained** Newmarket, Suffolk

FOCUS
A decent enough juvenile maiden. The winner impressed in seeing off a couple of nice colts.

NOTEBOOK
Swiss Dream picked up nicely after travelling well, improving significantly on her debut effort. She's quite well regarded by David Elsworth and will be pointed towards Royal Ascot for either the Queen Mary or the Albany. (op 9-4)
Bunce(IRE) showed good speed throughout and there was plenty to like about the way he kept on once passed. He simply found one too good, but ought to be able to win a maiden at some point. (op 7-4 tchd 2-1 in places)
Mujrayaat(IRE) wasn't that well away and ended up having to be switched out wider than ideal with his challenge. He still looked green when placed under pressure, and as such he probably didn't improve on the form of his debut, but there should be better to come. (op 2-1 tchd 15-8 and 11-4 in a place)
Blade Pirate showed early speed against the stands' rail and this was a big improvement on his first effort.
Sirens, fitted with a tongue-tie for her debut, fared best of McEntee trio but was still well held. (op 50-1)

2562 JOHNS PRACTICE H'CAP 1m 2f
3:30 (3:30) (Class 2) (0-100,94) 3-Y-O
£11,656 (£3,468; £1,733; £865) **Stalls** Low

Form RPR

1112 **1** **Monterosso**[15] 2117 3-9-4 **94** FrankieDettori 4 111
(M Johnston) *chsd ldng pair tl wnt 2nd over 2f out: rdn to ld over 1f out: edgd lft but styd on strly to draw clr ins fnl f: comf* **5/2**[1]

3-11 **2** 3 3/4 **Caldercruix (USA)**[20] 1969 3-8-11 **87** JamieSpencer 2 96
(T P Tate) *led: rdn over 2f out: hdd over 1f out: one pce and btn jst ins fnl f: kpt on for clr 2nd* **8/1**

5-31 **3** 2 **Moose Moran (USA)**[15] 2115 3-8-9 **85** TomQueally 5 90
(H R A Cecil) *hld up in tch in midfield: rdn and effrt ent fnl 2f: chsd ldng pair but hanging lft over 1f out: no imp and wl hld after* **7/2**[2]

6-31 **4** 1 3/4 **Florentine Ruler (USA)**[14] 2143 3-8-8 **84** EddieAhern 8 86
(H R A Cecil) *chsd ldrs: rdn and unable qck over 2f out: wknd u.p over 1f out: wl hld fnl f* **6/1**

6-1 **5** 1 1/4 **Oriental Cat**[16] 2072 3-8-9 **85** RobertHavlin 7 84
(J H M Gosden) *hld up in tch in midfield: effrt and switching out rt 2f out: edgd lft u.p and btn over 1f out* **10/1**

0-40 **6** 8 **Stags Leap (IRE)**[46] 1313 3-8-12 **88** RyanMoore 1 71
(R Hannon) *chsd ldr: rdn ent fnl 3f: lost 2nd over 2f out and sn struggling: wl bhd fr over 1f out* **25/1**

5-26 **7** 11 **Right Step**[15] 2117 3-8-11 **87** AlanMunro 9 48
(A P Jarvis) *hld up in last pair: rdn and struggling wl over 2f out: lost tch 2f out* **9/2**[3]

1-4 **8** *21* **Commissionaire**[37] 1500 3-9-0 **90**.................................. WilliamBuick 6 9
(J H M Gosden) *stdd and dropped in bhd after s: t.k.h: hld up in last: rdn and lost tch wl over 2f out: t.o and eased fnl f* **16/1**

2m 0.72s (-5.08) **Going Correction** -0.175s/f (Firm) course record **8** Ran SP% **113.2**
Speed ratings (Par 105): **113,110,108,107,106 99,90,74**
toteswingers:1&2:£3.10, 1&3:£2.60, 2&3:£5.80 CSF £22.75 CT £68.81 TOTE £3.30: £1.10, £2.00, £1.80; EX 21.70 Trifecta £31.00 Pool: £730.16 - 17.38 winning units..
Owner Sheikh Hamdan Bin Mohammed Al Maktoum **Bred** Darley **Trained** Middleham Moor, N Yorks

FOCUS
A hot-looking 3-y-o handicap and the pace seemed fair, but few were ever involved. The progressive winner posted a smart effort.

NOTEBOOK
Monterosso found the rapidly improving Green Moon 4l too good in a red-hot handicap at Newbury last time, but there was nothing of that one's calibre in opposition on this occasion and he readily gained his fourth win from his last five starts. Never that far away, he travelled strongly before finding plenty for pressure. He looks the type to go on improving. (op 11-4 tchd 3-1 in places)
Caldercruix(USA), twice a winner at Redcar this year, ran well off an 8lb higher mark. It was the furthest trip he had tried to date, but although ultimately no match for the winner, he saw his race out well and his effort was all the more creditable considering he was hassled up front by Stags Leap, who ended up dropping away. (op 5-1)
Moose Moran(USA), a Newbury maiden winner on his previous start, looked rather ungainly under pressure this time, carrying his head a touch high, and it may be that he is still immature, or perhaps he just didn't appreciate the undulations. (tchd 4-1)
Florentine Ruler(USA) won his maiden by a wide margin at Ripon last time, but this was tougher and he was well held. (op 17-2)
Oriental Cat, a Hamilton maiden winner on his reappearance, was disappointing on this switch to handicap company. (tchd 12-1)

2563 LONG MELFORD LADY JANE CLOTHING & SADDLERY H'CAP 6f
4:05 (4:05) (Class 2) (0-100,100) 4-Y-O+ **£11,656** (£3,468; £1,733; £865) **Stalls** Low

Form RPR
0-43 **1** **Noverre To Go (IRE)**[22] 1903 4-8-11 **93**................(t) RichardKingscote 2 106
(Tom Dascombe) *trckd ldrs gng wl: hdwy to ld over 1f out: drvn and edgd lft 1f out: hld on wl ins fnl f* **9/2**[2]
34-0 **2** *nk* **Himalya (IRE)**[16] 2100 4-9-4 **100**.. RyanMoore 4 112
(J Noseda) *taken down early: ponied to s: stdd s: hld up in rr: hdwy: nt clr run and swtchd rt jst over 1f out: chsd wnr jst ins fnl f: n.m.r briefly ins fnl f: kpt on but hld towards fin* **9/2**[2]
3-66 **3** *2* **Run For The Hills**[8] 2316 4-9-2 **98**.................................. WilliamBuick 8 104
(J H M Gosden) *hld up towards rr: hdwy and n.m.r 2f out: sn swtchd rt and rdn: chsd ldng pair 1f out: kpt on same pce fnl f* **6/1**[3]
5052 **4** *4* **Shifting Star (IRE)**[15] 2119 5-8-10 **92**.............................. ShaneKelly 11 85
(W R Swinburn) *in tch: rdn to press ldrs 2f out: edgd lft u.p over 1f out: nt pce of ldng trio fnl f* **4/1**[1]
002- **5** *¾* **Copper Dock (IRE)**[14] 2145 6-8-9 **96**................................. BACurtis(5) 6 86
(T G McCourt, Ire) *towards rr: effrt and nt clr run over 1f out: kpt on u.p fnl f: nvr gng pce to chal ldrs* **16/1**
01-0 **6** *¾* **Nota Bene**[16] 2100 8-9-4 **100**.. DaneO'Neill 12 88
(D R C Elsworth) *taken down early: in tch on outer: rdn and effrt 2f out: wknd u.p jst ins fnl f* **25/1**
0060 **7** *1 ¼* **Matsunosuke**[46] 1295 8-8-10 **92**.................................... TonyCulhane 10 76
(A B Coogan) *stdd to rr after s: sn detached in last: styd on past btn horses fnl f: n.d* **33/1**
63-1 **8** *2* **Imperial Guest**[40] 1438 4-8-8 **90**...................................... SebSanders 9 78+
(G G Margarson) *hld up in rr: effrt and rdn whn nt clr run and hmpd over 1f out: nvr trbld ldrs* **9/1**
-463 **9** *½* **Angus Newz**[28] 1727 7-8-4 **86** oh2...............................(v) FrannyNorton 7 62
(M Quinn) *w ldr: rdn to ld wl over 1f out: sn hdd but stl 2nd 1f out: wknd qckly fnl f* **10/1**
100- **10** *1 ¼* **Ancien Regime (IRE)**[232] 6661 5-9-4 **100**....................(t) FrankieDettori 3 72
(Saeed Bin Suroor) *taken down early: chsd ldrs: rdn ent fnl 2f: wkng whn hmpd over 1f out: wl btn fnl f* **8/1**
1410 **11** *2 ¾* **Billy Red**[93] 722 6-8-4 **86**...(b) JimmyQuinn 5 49
(J R Jenkins) *led tl hdd and rdn wl over 1f out: wkng whn stmbld over 1f out: sn fdd and wl bhd fnl f* **33/1**

69.99 secs (-2.21) **Going Correction** -0.175s/f (Firm) course record **11** Ran SP% **116.5**
Speed ratings (Par 109): **107,106,103,98,97 96,94,92,91,89 86**
toteswingers:1&2:£5.90, 1&3:£6.60, 2&3:£5.60 CSF £24.32 CT £122.86 TOTE £4.70: £1.30, £2.00, £1.80; EX 25.10 Trifecta £139.70 Pool: £850.10 - 4.50 winning units..
Owner Duddy Duddy Heeney McBride **Bred** Gestut Gorlsdorf **Trained** Malpas, Cheshire

FOCUS
A good, competitive sprint handicap. They went a strong pace and that, combined with a tailwind, resulted in a time only 0.43 seconds off the track record. The winner improved to the tune of 6lb.

NOTEBOOK
Noverre To Go(IRE) was always well placed, tracking the leaders, and having travelled strongly, he found enough when produced with his challenge. This represents a career-best performance and he'll surely now be aimed at the Wokingham. (op 5-1 tchd 11-2 in places)
Himalya(IRE) was tucked away towards the inside for much of the way and had to wait for a gap. He ran on well when in the clear and was closing on the winner all the way to the line, but he's a notoriously difficult ride and, as such, couldn't be described as unlucky. (op 7-1)
Run For The Hills had to wait for a clear run before challenging wider than ideal and, despite running on, he was always being held. (op 15-2)
Shifting Star(IRE) raced without cover for most of the way and faded in the closing stages. He can do better. (op 9-2 tchd 5-1)
Copper Dock(IRE) is better than he showed as he didn't get the best of runs through and also failed to convince that the track suited. (op 20-1 tchd 14-1)
Matsunosuke is reliant on the leaders going too fast, but even so Tony Culhane seemed to overdo the waiting tactics, holding the gelding up in a detached last until 2f out. Still, a run like this could help the horse's confidence, as he had broken a blood vessel only two starts back. (op 22-1)
Imperial Guest, 5lb higher than when winning at Brighton on his reappearance, was short of room over 1f out but it's debatable whether he was really picking up before that incident. (tchd 10-1)

2564 HOME OF RACING MAIDEN STKS 7f
4:40 (4:44) (Class 4) 3-Y-O £5,180 (£1,541; £770; £384) **Stalls** Low

Form RPR
3- **1** **Man Of Action (USA)**[212] 7146 3-9-3 0......................... WilliamBuick 15 95+
(J H M Gosden) *mde all: grad crossed over to stands' rail rdn ent fnl f: pushed along hands and heels and a doing enough fnl f* **5/4**[1]
0- **2** *¾* **Highland Knight (IRE)**[229] 6759 3-9-3 0.................(t) JimmyFortune 10 93
(A M Balding) *wnt lft s: in tch: hdwy to chse ldrs 4f out: rdn to chse wnr and edgd lft jst over 2f out: pressed wnr over 1f out: a hld fnl f* **14/1**
0 **3** *1 ¼* **Ertikaan**[15] 2121 3-9-3 0... RichardHills 8 89+
(M A Jarvis) *n.m.r sn after s: midfield tl hdwy to chse ldrs 4f out: chse ldng pair wl over 1f out: styd on same pce fnl f* **9/1**[3]
4 *7* **Pearl Huntsman (USA)** 3-9-3 0.................................. RyanMoore 4 70+
(J Noseda) *restless stalls: s.i.s and rn green: towards rr: hdwy into midfield 1/2-way: stl modest 9th over 1f out: styd on after: swtchd rt ins fnl f: wnt 4th towards fin: nvr trbld ldrs* **20/1**
0-3 **5** *½* **Tap Dance Way (IRE)**[23] 1872 3-8-12 0......................... LiamKeniry 11 64
(P R Chamings) *chsd ldrs: rdn and edgd lft u.p ent fnl 2f: wknd and wl btn 1f out: lost modest 4th towards fin* **9/1**[3]
6 *4 ½* **Bernie's Moon (USA)** 3-8-12 0................................. MartinDwyer 3 52+
(B J Meehan) *racd wl off the pce in midfield: pushed along 1/2-way: styd on steadily fr over 1f out: nvr trbld ldrs* **40/1**
03 **7** *1 ¼* **Excellent Aim**[23] 1878 3-9-3 0...................................... ShaneKelly 13 53
(Jane Chapple-Hyam) *chsd wnr tl over 2f out: wknd qckly wl over 1f out* **20/1**
4-0 **8** *nk* **Freedom Pass (USA)**[23] 1870 3-8-12 0.................. KirstyMilczarek 5 48
(J A R Toller) *racd wl off the pce in midfield: rdn 4f out: nvr trbld ldrs* **100/1**
3 **9** *2 ¼* **Bursary (CAN)**[12] 2220 3-9-3 0................................... FrankieDettori 6 47
(M Johnston) *chsd ldng piar: rdn and struggling whn sltly hmpd ent fnl 2f: sn wknd: wl btn and eased wl ins fnl f* **2/1**[2]
06- **10** *2 ½* **Lyric Poet (USA)**[261] 5831 3-9-0 0....................... WilliamCarson(3) 12 40
(G C Bravery) *s.i.s: sn pushed along in rr: n.d* **100/1**
\- **11** *hd* **Trecase** 3-9-3 0.. SebSanders 1 39
(A W Carroll) *s.i.s: hld up wl bhd: nvr on terms* **100/1**
00- **12** *2 ¼* **Footsie (IRE)**[219] 6992 3-8-12 0..................................... TomQueally 7 28
(J G Given) *s.i.s: a bhd* **40/1**
13 *2* **Upset** 3-9-3 0.. JerryO'Dwyer 14 28
(P J O'Gorman) *sn pushed along and wl bhd: nvr on terms* **100/1**
14 *8* **Faustina** 3-8-12 0... DaneO'Neill 2 —
(Miss Amy Weaver) *v.s.a: a wl bhd: t.o fnl 3f* **100/1**
15 *6* **Dirakh Shan** 3-9-3 0.. J-PGuillambert 16 —
(L M Cumani) *restless stalls: v.s.a: a wl bhd: t.o fr 1/2-way* **33/1**
00 **16** *6* **Just My Girl**[19] 2011 3-8-12 0.. SaleemGolam 9 —
(P Leech) *chsd ldrs for 3f: sn wknd: t.o fnl 2f* **100/1**

1m 22.95s (-2.45) **Going Correction** -0.175s/f (Firm) **16** Ran SP% **127.7**
Speed ratings (Par 101): **107,106,104,96,96 91,89,89,86,83 83,81,78,69,62 55**
toteswingers:1&2:£6.10, 2&3:£12.90, 1&3:£4.00 CSF £21.87 TOTE £2.20: £1.20, £4.10, £1.90; EX 22.30 Trifecta £145.70 Pool: £728.62 - 3.70 winning units..
Owner H R H Princess Haya Of Jordan **Bred** Gainesway Thoroughbreds Ltd **Trained** Newmarket, Suffolk

FOCUS
Not many got into this but the first three came clear and look above average. The winning time was 1.36 seconds quicker than the later Class 5 handicap for the 3-y-os and the winner looks a smart prospect.
Highland Knight(IRE) Official explanation: jockey said colt hyung left throughout

2565 ROTARY CLUB OF NEWMARKET EBF FILLIES' H'CAP 6f
5:15 (5:18) (Class 4) (0-85,84) 3-Y-O £5,828 (£1,734; £866; £432) **Stalls** Low

Form RPR
-543 **1** **Fly Silca Fly (IRE)**[9] 2283 3-8-12 **78**.................................... AlanMunro 6 83
(M R Channon) *chsd ldr for over 1f: sn pushed along: drvn and chsd ldr ent fnl f: kpt on to ld wl ins fnl f* **7/1**[2]
6-05 **2** *½* **Bahati (IRE)**[15] 2120 3-9-3 **83**....................................... PatCosgrave 12 86
(J G Portman) *chsd ldrs: rdn to ld over 1f out: drvn ent fnl f: hdd and no ex wl ins fnl f* **7/1**[2]
2-31 **3** *¾* **Bonheurs Art (IRE)**[23] 1890 3-8-6 **72**.............................. EddieAhern 1 73
(B W Hills) *in tch towards rr: effrt and hanging rt wl over 1f out: squeezed through on rail ins fnl f: styng wl fin: unable to rch ldng pair* **11/2**[1]
320- **4** *¾* **Chaussini**[212] 7147 3-8-13 **79**... RobertHavlin 3 78
(J A R Toller) *hld up in tch in midfield: rdn and hdwy over 1f out: styd on same pce ins fnl f* **14/1**
1-10 **5** *hd* **Key Light (IRE)**[15] 2120 3-8-10 **76**................................... MichaelHills 5 74
(J W Hills) *led: rdn and hdd over 1f out: kpt on same pce u.p fnl f* **7/1**[2]
2216 **6** *2* **Tom Folan**[2] 2491 3-7-11 **70** oh4...............................(p) HarryBentley(7) 10 62
(Andrew Reid) *in tch on outer: rdn and hdwy to chse ldrs over 1f out: no ex and btn fnl 100yds* **25/1**
16-0 **7** *¾* **Secret Queen**[28] 1732 3-9-1 **84**.................(b[1]) Louis-PhilippeBeuzelin(3) 8 73
(B J Meehan) *dwlt: hdwy to chse ldr over 4f out: drvn and lost 2nd over 1f out: hrd rdn and btn jst ins fnl f* **14/1**
112- **8** *¾* **Sabatini (IRE)**[164] 7786 3-8-9 **80**............................. SimonPearce(5) 11 67
(J Pearce) *s.i.s: in tch on outer: rdn and unable qck wl over 1f out: wknd ent fnl f* **14/1**
0104 **9** *½* **Vanilla Loan (IRE)**[9] 2287 3-8-9 **75**............................... WilliamBuick 7 60
(M Botti) *in tch in midfield: rdn and effrt over 1f out: no prog and btn 1f out* **11/2**[1]
2-15 **10** *¾* **Mount Juliet (IRE)**[33] 1593 3-8-4 **70**.............................. MartinDwyer 2 53
(M Botti) *a in rr: rdn along 1/2-way: no prog and n.d* **15/2**[3]

1m 11.51s (-0.69) **Going Correction** -0.175s/f (Firm) **10** Ran SP% **103.9**
Speed ratings (Par 98): **97,96,95,94,94 91,90,89,88,87**
toteswingers:1&2:£9.10, 1&3:£5.40, 2&3:£6.00 CSF £44.60 CT £217.18 TOTE £5.70: £2.30, £2.70, £1.30; EX 48.50 TRIFECTA Not won. e..
Owner Aldridge Racing Partnership **Bred** Glenlogan Park Stud **Trained** West Ilsley, Berks

FOCUS
Just a fair fillies' handicap and again it paid to race prominently. Ordinary form.

2566 NEWMARKETEXPERIENCE.CO.UK H'CAP 7f
5:50 (5:52) (Class 5) (0-70,70) 3-Y-O £3,238 (£963; £481; £240) **Stalls** Low

Form RPR
356- **1** **Rockabilly Rebel**[272] 5526 3-8-13 **65**.............................. MichaelHills 11 75
(B W Hills) *chsd ldrs tl led 3f out: rdn ent fnl 2f: edgd lft u.p ins fnl f: kpt on wl* **9/1**[3]
4514 **2** *1 ½* **Tell Halaf**[12] 2215 3-9-3 **69**... JamieSpencer 1 75+
(M L W Bell) *stdd s: hld up wl bhd: hdwy 3f out: hdwy wl over 1f out: hrd drvn and disputing 2nd ins fnl f: chsd wnr but no imp fnl 50yds* **5/2**[1]
45-3 **3** *nk* **Lutine Bell**[12] 2215 3-9-2 **68**....................................... SebSanders 15 73
(Sir Mark Prescott) *stdd and swtchd rt across towards stands' side after s: bhd: hdwy ent fnl 2f: rdn and chsd ldrs over 1f out: chsd wnr ins fnl f: no imp and lost 2nd fnl 50yds* **3/1**[2]
34-1 **4** *¾* **Rosedale**[12] 2200 3-8-10 **62**... LiamKeniry 2 65
(J A R Toller) *hld up towards rr: hdwy 3f out: chsd wnr rdn jst over 1f out: keeping on same pce whn swtchd rt ins fnl f: no ex fnl 100yds* **10/1**
30-0 **5** *3* **Spinning Spirit (IRE)**[19] 2000 3-8-10 **62**......................... TomQueally 10 57
(J G Given) *led for 1f: chsd ldrs after: rdn 3f out: wknd fnl f* **25/1**
3345 **6** *1 ¾* **Hill Of Miller (IRE)**[3] 2459 3-8-9 **61**......................(t) MartinDwyer 14 52
(Rae Guest) *hld up towards rr: hdwy 1/2-way: rdn to chse wnr wl over 1f out tl jst over 1f out: wknd fnl f* **16/1**

2546 **7** 1 1/4 **Master Mylo (IRE)**[5] 2416 3-9-4 **70** AlanMunro 7 58
(D K Ivory) *in tch in midfield: pushed along after 2f: rdn and wknd wl over 1f out* **16/1**

2250 **8** 3 1/2 **Takajan (IRE)**[99] 638 3-9-0 **69** Louis-PhilippeBeuzelin(3) 5 48
(S Kirk) *in tch in midfield: rdn and unable qck 3f out: drvn and wl btn over 1f out* **33/1**

5230 **9** hd **Ginger Grey (IRE)**[11] 2235 3-9-1 **67** (b) FrankieDettori 9 45
(D R C Elsworth) *s.i.s: bhd: hdwy on outer over 2f out: rdn and no prog over 1f out: wknd fnl f* **9/1**[3]

4-30 **10** 1/2 **South African Gold (USA)**[12] 2215 3-8-13 **65** (t) LukeMorris 8 42
(J M P Eustace) *sn rdn along in midfield: nvr trbld ldrs* **50/1**

1-5 **11** 4 **Black Baccara**[17] 2046 3-8-11 **70** LeonnaMayor(7) 12 36
(P S McEntee) *awkward leaving stalls: racd freely and led after 1f: hdd 3f out: rdn and wknd wl over 1f out* **50/1**

1005 **12** 1 1/2 **Highland Bridge**[32] 1619 3-9-1 **67** (b[1]) DaneO'Neill 6 29
(D R C Elsworth) *chsd ldrs tl rdn and struggling 1/2-way: wl btn fnl 2f* **20/1**

0-00 **13** 4 1/2 **Baileys Vision**[17] 2042 3-8-1 **56** KellyHarrison(3) 3 —
(C A Dwyer) *chsd ldrs tl rdn and struggling whn hung rt 3f out: wl btn fnl 2f* **40/1**

6322 **14** 2 **Miss Polly Plum**[13] 2185 3-8-4 **56** oh5 JimmyQuinn 13 —
(C A Dwyer) *stdd after s: t.k.h: hld up in towards rr: rdn and lost tch over 2f out* **20/1**

4-04 **15** 14 **Kings 'n Dreams**[32] 1619 3-9-3 **69** JimmyFortune 4 —
(D K Ivory) *sltly hmpd s: nvr gng and sn in rr: t.o whn veered rt ins fnl f* **12/1**

1m 24.31s (-1.09) **Going Correction** -0.175s/f (Firm) **15** Ran SP% **124.8**
Speed ratings (Par 99): **99,97,96,96,92 90,89,85,85,84 79,78,73,70,54**
toteswingers:1&2:£6.20, 1&3:£11.40, 2&3:£2.30 CSF £30.31 CT £89.75 TOTE £12.00: £3.40, £1.30, £1.80; EX 46.50 Trifecta £120.60 Pool: £456.57 - 2.80 winning units. Place 6 £42.57; Place 5 £5.69.
Owner P Cunningham & Phil Cunningham **Bred** Clive Dennett **Trained** Lambourn, Berks

FOCUS
A fair 3-y-o handicap for the grade and they went a decent pace. The form looks sound.
Baileys Vision Official explanation: jockey said filly hung right
Kings 'n Dreams Official explanation: jockey said gelding was reluctant to race
T/Jkpt: Part won. £24,370.90 to a £1 stake. Pool:£34,325.34 - 0.50 winning tickets. T/Plt: £65.20 to a £1 stake. Pool:£115,683.00 - 1,294.48 winning tickets T/Qpdt: £11.50 to a £1 stake. Pool:£7,493.00 - 480.57 winning tickets SP

2567 - 2569a (Foreign Racing) - See Raceform Interactive

1948 LEOPARDSTOWN (L-H)
Sunday, May 30

OFFICIAL GOING: Good to firm

2570a VODAFONE IRELAND FOUNDATION SUPPORTS GAISCE BALLYCORUS STKS (GROUP 3) 7f
3:45 (3:45) 3-Y-O+ **£34,513** (£10,088; £4,778; £1,592)

RPR

1 **Six Of Hearts**[8] 2353 6-9-9 98 DJMoran 6 104
(Cecil Ross, Ire) *settled bhd ldrs: 4th 1/2-way: rdn into 2nd 1f out: styd on to ld fnl 150yds: kpt on wl* **10/1**[3]

2 1/2 **Duff (IRE)**[21] 1954 7-10-0 115 FMBerry 2 108
(Edward Lynam, Ire) *j.rt out of stalls and led: rdn over 1f out: hdd fnl 150yds: no ex and kpt on same pce* **8/13**[1]

3 1 3/4 **Croisultan (IRE)**[49] 1246 4-9-9 105 CO'Donoghue 3 98
(Liam McAteer, Ire) *settled bhd ldrs: 3rd 1/2-way: nt clr run fr 1f out: no imp in 3rd fnl 100yds* **12/1**

4 1 1/4 **King Jock (USA)**[21] 1954 9-9-9 107 PShanahan 5 95
(Tracey Collins, Ire) *chsd ldr in cl 2nd: rdn 1 1/2f out: no ex in 4th 1f out: kpt on same pce* **9/4**[2]

5 dist **Purple Land (USA)**[18] 2038 3-8-12 KJManning 4 —
(J S Bolger, Ire) *hmpd s: sn trailing and virtually p.u: completely t.o* **18/1**

1m 28.29s (-0.41) **Going Correction** +0.025s/f (Good)
WFA 3 from 4yo+ 11lb **5** Ran SP% **114.7**
Speed ratings: **103,102,100,99,—**
CSF £17.86 TOTE £13.70: £1.50, £1.10; DF 30.00.
Owner Round Tower Syndicate **Bred** Skymarc & Castlemartin Stud **Trained** Mullingar, Co Westmeath

FOCUS
A typically tactical affair and a personal best from the winner.

NOTEBOOK
Six Of Hearts provided Cecil Ross with a career highlight on the Flat. He picked up best to take over inside the final furlong after the tempo increased. The winning trainer admitted after it was hard to see him winning, which was fully nderstandable considering he was rated 17lb inferior to Eddie Lynam's hot pot. "Leaving off the cheekpieces has rejuvenated him," added Ross of his 6yo, who knuckled down in tenacious fashion when the race unfolded in the straight to record his biggest win. (op 9/1)
Duff(IRE) was expected to step up on his seasonal bow when fourth behind Famous Name here. He had ground conditions and trip in his favour but his trainer had raised concern beforehand about him having to shoulder 10st and it didn't help. Edging right out of stall 2, he caused plenty of early interference. He soon settled into his customary front-running role and led into the straightHe was unable to raise his game enough when the winner took over, but overall it was a disappointing display. (op 5/6 tchd 4/7)
Croisultan(IRE) ran another consistent race without looking a potential threat. He didn't enjoy the clearest of passages when the race took shape in the straight and this ground was probably too lively for him when he was asked to go about his business. His rider reported afterwards that his mount hung left. Official explanation: jockey said gelding hung left throughout (op 8/1)
King Jock(USA) was fancied to put it up to the favourite but had to settle for the minor honours after he tracked the favourite from the outset and couldn't raise his game in the straight. (op 2/1 tchd 5/2)
Purple Land(USA) was ponied to the straight and was the main sufferer in what was a rough start. He was soon detached and tailed off at the end of the back straight and came home a street adrift. Official explanation: jockey said colt lost its action and felt lame for a number of strides soon after start (op 16/1 tchd 20/1)

2571a SEAMUS & ROSEMARY MCGRATH MEMORIAL SAVAL BEG STKS (LISTED RACE) 1m 6f
4:15 (4:15) 4-Y-O+ **£28,761** (£8,407; £3,982; £1,327)

RPR

1 **Profound Beauty (IRE)**[260] 5891 6-9-3 113 PJSmullen 2 107+
(D K Weld, Ire) *settled bhd ldrs: 5th 1/2-way: hdwy in 2nd 3 1/2f out: travelled wl to chal 1 1/2f out: led 1f out: rdn and kpt on wl ins fnl f* **4/1**[2]

2 1/2 **Age Of Aquarius (IRE)**[23] 1859 4-9-6 117 JMurtagh 3 109+
(A P O'Brien, Ire) *trckd ldr in 2nd: led 4f out: rdn and chal fr 1 1/2f out: hdd 1f out: no ex ins fnl f and kpt on same pce* **2/5**[1]

3 13 **Caesar's Song (IRE)**[14] 5-9-1 CDHayes 7 86
(Patrick O Brady, Ire) *hld up towards rr: rdn into 5th 3f out: no imp in 4th 2f out: mod 3rd 1f out: kpt on same pce* **50/1**

4 2 1/2 **Loch Long (IRE)**[36] 7263 4-9-1 96 PShanahan 5 83
(Tracey Collins, Ire) *chsd ldrs: 3rd 1/2-way: rdn in 4th 3f out: no imp in 3rd 2f out: kpt on one pce* **33/1**

5 6 **Keep It Cool (IRE)**[10] 2268 6-9-1 75 (tp) WMLordan 4 74
(P F O'Donnell, Ire) *rrd leaving stalls and towards rr: rdn in 6th 3f out: kpt on one pce* **66/1**

6 10 **Donegal (USA)**[45] 1343 5-9-1 95 (b) JAHeffernan 6 60
(Robert Alan Hennessy, Ire) *led: hdd 4f out: rdn in 3rd 3f out: wknd ent st* **50/1**

P **Haralan (IRE)**[42] 1417 4-9-1 103 (t) FMBerry 1 —
(John M Oxx, Ire) *chsd ldrs: 4th 1/2-way: p.u 6f out* **6/1**[3]

2m 58.64s (-2.36) **Going Correction** +0.025s/f (Good) **7** Ran SP% **114.1**
Speed ratings: **107,106,99,97,94 88,—**
CSF £6.05 TOTE £5.40: £1.20, £1.10; DF 10.40.
Owner Moyglare Stud Farm **Bred** Moyglare Stud Farm Ltd **Trained** The Curragh, Co Kildare

FOCUS
This was steadily run and although the first two came clear, the third and fifth finished close enough.

NOTEBOOK
Profound Beauty(IRE) put up what must be considered a career-best performance in winning this, with plenty of reason to believe that there's a good bit more to come from this mare. Held up as usual and travelling well to the turn in, she moved up to challenge the favourite over a furlong out and did enough to win and probably showed a lack of race fitness in the very late stages. However, this performance does give plenty of cause for thinking she could well be better than ever this season. The Melbourne Cup is her long-term aim. (op 7/2)
Age Of Aquarius(IRE) came here on the back of quite a narrow defeat by Harbinger at Chester and there's little reason for thinking he didn't run up to that here. Tracking the early leader, he travelled strongly into the lead off the home bend but to his credit he found plenty when headed and made the winner work hard. It was a good performance and the way the first two pulled clear does put both of them in a very positive light. It will take a very good horse to beat either of them over this trip as the season progresses. The Gold Cup at Ascot remains his target. (op 2/5 tchd 4/9)
Caesar's Song(IRE) came here on the back of a success in a Limerick bumper, but kept going well and can expect a rating of close to 100. Where that puts him time will tell but he's obviously a pretty good horse.
Loch Long(IRE) is a solid enough mid-90s rated horse but he's realistically only racing for small shares of prize money in races like this. He ran on at one pace in the straight past a couple of beaten horses. He's capable of winning a conditions race or a nice handicap.
Keep It Cool(IRE) reared badly coming out of the stalls and was never a factor.
Donegal(USA) was pushed up to lead early on but weakened quickly once headed before the turn in
Haralan(IRE) broke down badly and was pulled up beyond halfway. Official explanation: broke down badly and was pulled up beyond halfway.

2572 - 2573a (Foreign Racing) - See Raceform Interactive

2155 KREFELD (R-H)
Sunday, May 30

OFFICIAL GOING: Turf: good

2574a GROSSER EHRMANN STEHER CUP (GROUP 3) (4YO+) (TURF) 2m
3:40 (3:51) 4-Y-O+ **£28,318** (£8,849; £4,424; £2,654)

RPR

1 **Tres Rock Danon (FR)**[28] 1748 4-8-11 0 JiriPalik 3 113
(W Hickst, Germany) *hld up in 3rd on rail: a.p: travelling smoothly: chal early in st: r.o wl to gain ld and drew clr ins fnl f* **11/2**[3]

2 4 **Brisant (GER)**[334] 3493 8-8-11 0 MSuerland 8 107
(R Suerland, Germany) *a gng wl fr s bhd ldrs: mde move early in st: r.o wl to chse eventual wnr home* **25/1**

3 2 **Eye Of The Tiger (GER)**[21] 1956 5-9-4 0 ADeVries 6 112
(J Hirschberger, Germany) *hld up in midfield travelling wl: passed horses arnd fnl turn: effrt on outside in st but no ex* **7/4**[1]

4 3 **Caudillo (GER)**[29] 7-9-0 0 HenkGrewe 4 105
(Dr A Bolte, Germany) *racd in midfield: no imp in st* **13/2**

5 1 3/4 **Frantic Storm (GER)**[29] 4-8-11 0 APietsch 2 102
(W Hickst, Germany) *bkmarker fr s: rn through tired horses in st* **9/1**

6 1 3/4 **Yes Mr President (IRE)**[16] 2071 5-9-0 0 JoeFanning 1 101
(M Johnston) *reluctant ldr fr s: set mod pce at first: asked to qckn: led field into st: r.o briefly but sn hdd and btn* **9/2**[2]

7 1/2 **Tarkheena Prince (USA)**[211] 5-9-0 0 AHelfenbein 7 100
(C Von Der Recke, Germany) *prom in 2nd fr s: trcking pce: pressed ldr tl st: no ex: wknd* **14/1**

8 5 **Speedy Catcher (IRE)**[26] 4-9-0 0 DominiqueBoeuf 5 97
(H-A Pantall, France) *broke wl: tk v t.k.h: settled in midfield: nvr a threat in st* **11/1**

3m 25.51s (205.51)
WFA 4 from 5yo+ 2lb **8** Ran SP% **112.1**
WIN (incl. 10 euro stake): 62. PLACES: 15, 21, 10. SF: 1,495..
Owner Stall D'Angelo **Bred** Haras De Chevotel & Morton Bloodstock **Trained** Germany

NOTEBOOK
Yes Mr President(IRE), trying this level again, made the running at a steady gallop but faded pretty tamely once headed in the straight.

1540 SAN SIRO (R-H)
Sunday, May 30

OFFICIAL GOING: Turf: good

2575a OAKS D'ITALIA (GROUP 2) (3YO FILLIES) (TURF) 1m 3f
3:15 (12:00) 3-Y-O **£176,991** (£77,876; £42,477; £21,238)

RPR

1 **Contredanse (IRE)**[17] 2047 3-8-11 0 KierenFallon 1 104
(L M Cumani) *broke wl: settled in 2nd: led ent fnl 2 1/2f: hrd rdn fnl f: hld on fnl strides fr fast-fining runner-up* **9/4**[2]

2 shd **Middle Club**[38] 1496 3-8-11 0 RichardHughes 9 104
(R Hannon) *broke wl: trckd ldrs in 3rd: moved 2nd ent fnl 2f: hrd rdn and no imp on eventual wnr tl fnl 100yds: r.o strly* **33/20**[1]

3 1 1/2 **Isantha (GER)** 3-8-11 0 ... EPedroza 6 101
(T Mundry, Germany) *broke wl to trck ldrs in 4th: in tch ent fnl 3f: hrd rdn and ev ch fnl 2f: no imp on ldng pair: styd on gamely* **247/10**

4 7 **Cronsa (GER)**[29] 1713 3-8-11 0 ... MircoDemuro 7 89
(S Botti, Italy) *slowly away: settled in rr: hdwy on outer ent st to go 5th: hrd rdn fnl 2f: styd on* **106/10**

5 1 **Siyaadah**[64] 1023 3-8-11 0 ... AhmedAjtebi 11 87
(Mahmood Al Zarooni) *settled nr rr on outer: asked for effrt ent fnl 3f: no imp and hrd rdn fnl 2f: styd on* **558/100**[3]

6 hd **Saldennahe (GER)**[21] 3-8-11 0 ... AStarke 8 87
(P Schiergen, Germany) *settled midfield: rdn to stay in tch fnl 4f: hrd rdn fnl 2f: no ex* **127/20**

7 2 1/2 **Monblue**[21] 3-8-11 0 ... DVargiu 10 82
(B Grizzetti, Italy) *slowly away: settled midfield on outer: rdn ent fnl 3f to keep position: hrd rdn fnl 2f: wknd* **187/10**

8 1 1/2 **Blessed Luck (IRE)**[224] 6892 3-8-11 0 ... NPinna 2 79
(S Botti, Italy) *broke wl: lost position and settled midfield: hrd rdn whn pce increased fnl 3f: no imp* **143/10**

9 2 1/2 **In My Secret Life (IRE)** 3-8-11 0 ... PierantonioConvertino 12 75
(C M De Petra, Italy) *slowly away and hld up in rr: hrd rdn and no imp fnl 3f* **66/1**

10 nk **Sadowa Destination**[29] 1713 3-8-11 0 ... CColombi 5 74
(B Grizzetti, Italy) *broke wl to ld: set decent pce: rdn ent fnl 3f: hdd fnl 2 1/2f: sn wknd: eased fnl f* **187/10**

11 2 **Super Motiva**[56] 3-8-11 0 ... MEsposito 3 71
(S Cannavo', Italy) *in rr: hrd rdn ent fnl 3f: no imp* **17/2**

12 5 **Mabura (IRE)**[29] 1713 3-8-11 0 ... FabioBranca 4 62
(S Botti, Italy) *broke wl: lost position and settled midfield: effrt and hrd rdn fnl 3f: eased fnl 2f* **106/10**

2m 14.7s (-3.90) 12 Ran SP% **147.1**
WIN (incl. 1 euro stake): 3.25. PLACES: 1.52, 1.37, 3.42. DF: 8.55.
Owner S Stuckey **Bred** Ahdaab Syndicate **Trained** Newmarket, Suffolk

NOTEBOOK
Contredanse(IRE), the winner of handicaps at Windsor and Salisbury, the latter off a mark of 84, handled the step up in trip and grade to take this classic narrowly. She is clearly progressive and this will have secured her paddock value.
Middle Club, a consistent performer on a sound surface, was also stepping up in trip and only lost out after responding to pressure and finishing well.

2576a PREMIO CARLO VITTADINI (EX TURATI) (GROUP 2) (3YO+) (TURF) 1m
4:30 (12:00) 3-Y-0+ £61,946 (£27,256; £14,867; £7,433)

RPR

1 **Pressing (IRE)**[14] 2152 7-9-12 0 ... NeilCallan 1 118
(M A Jarvis) *broke wl: settled in 3rd for 4f: prog whn swtchd to rail fnl 2f: rdn and sn two l clr: a holding chalrs* **11/10**[1]

2 1 **Summit Surge (IRE)**[64] 1022 6-9-7 0 ... KierenFallon 5 111
(L M Cumani) *settled midfield on rail: asked for effrt ent fnl 3f: swtchd to outer 2f out: styd on under hrd ride to snatch 2nd on line* **13/2**

3 snk **Win For Sure (GER)**[21] 5-9-7 0 ... EPedroza 9 111
(A Wohler, Germany) *slowly away: hld up in midfield on out for 5f: rdn and hdwy to take 2nd fnl 2f: hrd rdn fnl f: ct on line for 2nd* **43/20**[2]

4 2 1/4 **Fanunalter**[43] 1377 4-9-7 0 ... RichardHughes 10 105
(M Botti) *slowly away: hld up in rr: hdwy on inner ent st: no room fnl 2f: swtchd to outer: r.o fnl f* **123/20**[3]

5 2 1/4 **Marshade (ITY)**[42] 1418 3-8-9 0broke wl: stdd to trck ldrs for 4f: in tch and ev ch at 3f: travelling wl whn outpcd fnl 2f: hrd rdn and no ex fnl f FabioBranca 3 100
(S Botti, Italy) **78/10**

6 3/4 **Diocleziano (USA)**[14] 5-9-7 0 ... (b) LManiezzi 7 99
(R Menichetti, Italy) *steaded in midfield for 4f: lost position whn outpcd 3f out: styd on fnl f* **72/1**

7 2 1/4 **Integral (GER)**[21] 6-9-7 0 ... PierantonioConvertino 8 93
(R Rohne, Germany) *slowly away: rdn to be prom after 1f: trckd ldr for 5f: rdn and ev ch fnl 2f: wknd whn hrd rdn fnl f* **57/1**

8 3 **King Of Sydney (USA)**[28] 1747 4-9-7 0 ... THellier 2 87
(Mario Hofer, Germany) *slowly away: hld up in rr: effrt and no imp fnl 3f* **174/10**

9 nk **Relco Italy (IRE)**[14] 4-9-7 0 ... DVargiu 6 86
(B Grizzetti, Italy) *broke wl to ld: set stdy pce for 4f: rdn ent fnl 3f: hrd rdn: hdd and no ex fnl 2f: wknd fnl f* **47/1**

10 5 **Abaton**[21] 4-9-7 0 ... MircoDemuro 4 74
(Vittorio Caruso, Italy) *v.s.a: hld up in rr: effrt on outer to stay in tch ent st: no imp* **113/10**

1m 36.5s (-5.60)
WFA 3 from 4yo+ 12lb 10 Ran SP% **136.8**
WIN (incl. 1 euro stake): 2.09. PLACES: 1.17, 1.50, 1.28. DF: 6.65.
Owner Gary A Tanaka **Bred** Agricola Del Parco **Trained** Newmarket, Suffolk

2376 CARLISLE (R-H)
Monday, May 31

OFFICIAL GOING: Good to firm (6.9)
Old stable bend moved out 3yds increasing distance of races of 6f and over by 4metres.
Wind: Slight, half-against. Weather: Cloudy

2577 EUROPEAN BREEDERS' FUND MAIDEN STKS 5f
2:20 (2:21) (Class 5) 2-Y-O £3,885 (£1,156; £577; £288) Stalls High

Form RPR

1 **Honeymead (IRE)** 2-8-12 0 ... PaulHanagan 7 76+
(R A Fahey) *chsd ldrs: effrt over 1f out: styd on wl fnl f: led last stride* **2/1**[2]

2 2 nse **Defence Council (IRE)**[15] 2138 2-9-3 0 ... FrederikTylicki 6 81+
(J Howard Johnson) *led: rdn over 1f out: kpt on wl fnl f: hdd last stride* **10/11**[1]

3 11 **Shy Bird** 2-8-12 0 ... DavidAllan 5 36
(J A Glover) *w ldr tl rdn and wknd over 1f out* **14/1**

4 1 1/4 **Golden Blaze** 2-9-3 0 ... DarrenMoffatt 4 37
(James Moffatt) *s.i.s: rn green in rr: hdwy and hung rt 2f out: sn no imp* **33/1**

5 nse **Ad Value (IRE)** 2-9-3 0 ... AndrewElliott 1 37
(G A Swinbank) *prom: rdn and rn green 2f out: sn wknd* **8/1**[3]

30 6 2 **Mr Khan**[10] 2272 2-8-12 0 ... IanBrennan(5) 3 30
(James Moffatt) *chsd ldrs tl rdn and wknd fr 2f out* **40/1**

7 6 **Indian Giver** 2-8-12 0 ... PatrickMathers 2 —
(H A McWilliams) *s.i.s: bhd and outpcd: no ch fnl 2f* **100/1**

63.24 secs (2.44) **Going Correction** +0.275s/f (Good) 7 Ran SP% **109.9**
Speed ratings (Par 93): **91,90,73,71,71 68,58**
toteswingers: 1&2 £2.70, 1&3 £2.40, 2&3 £1.30 CSF £3.77 TOTE £3.70: £2.40, £1.10; EX 4.10.
Owner Mrs H Steel **Bred** London Thoroughbred Services Ltd **Trained** Musley Bank, N Yorks

FOCUS
On a bright breezy afternoon the ground was described good to firm all around. Five of the seven were newcomers and the race developed on the far side of the track. The first two finished clear and the form looks solid at this level.

NOTEBOOK
Honeymead(IRE), coming from an in-form yard, was able to make a winning debut. Never far off the pace, she showed a willing attitude and will get further in due course as well. (op 7-4)
Defence Council(IRE), runner-up on his debut, lost little in defeat; he appears to be all speed and can go one better in similar company shortly, especially on a sharp track. (op Evens)
Shy Bird, who showed some early dash before weakening inside the final furlong, led home the remainder. (op 12-1)
Ad Value(IRE) attracted some support beforehand but was well held. (op 12-1)

2578 X-FACTOR CONCERT HERE 25TH JULY H'CAP 5f 193y
2:55 (2:55) (Class 5) (0-70,74) 4-Y-O+ £2,590 (£770; £385; £192) Stalls High

Form RPR

0345 1 **Apache Ridge (IRE)**[3] 2504 4-9-4 70 ... (b) PaulHanagan 5 77
(K A Ryan) *trckd ldrs: effrt over 1f out: led ins fnl f: drvn out* **15/2**

0050 2 1/2 **Klynch**[16] 2113 4-8-10 67 ... (b) JamesSullivan(5) 2 73
(Mrs R A Carr) *trckd ldrs: effrt and rdn over 1f out: swtchd and styd on fnl f: nrst fin* **18/1**

-005 3 1/2 **Hazelrigg (IRE)**[16] 2113 5-9-0 66 ... (v[1]) DavidAllan 6 70
(T D Easterby) *w ldr: led and carried hd awkwardly over 1f out: hung rt and hdd ins fnl f: one pce* **3/1**[1]

0-33 4 1 1/2 **Mandalay King (IRE)**[10] 2275 5-9-1 70 ... KellyHarrison(3) 4 69
(Mrs Marjorie Fife) *t.k.h: hld up in tch: effrt over 1f out: kpt on same pce ins fnl f* **5/1**[2]

0-31 5 3/4 **Just Sam (IRE)**[3] 2504 5-9-1 74 6ex ... DaleSwift(7) 11 71
(R E Barr) *led tl rdn and hdd over 1f out: kpt on same pce* **3/1**[1]

05-3 6 nk **Elijah Pepper (USA)**[137] 171 5-8-3 60 ... DeanHeslop(5) 8 61+
(T D Barron) *hld up in tch: drvn and outpcd over 2f out: rallied appr fnl f: kpt on: no imp* **13/2**[3]

3044 7 2 1/4 **Methaaly (IRE)**[9] 2310 7-8-11 70 ... (be) JosephYoung(7) 10 59
(M Mullineaux) *s.i.s: bhd and rdn along: no imp fnl 2f* **10/1**

00-0 8 4 1/2 **Captain Scooby**[37] 1524 4-9-1 70 ... MichaelStainton(3) 1 44
(R M Whitaker) *in tch: drvn and outpcd over 2f out: sn n.d* **20/1**

1000 9 2 1/4 **Nacho Libre**[61] 1063 5-9-4 70 ... (b) PatrickMathers 7 37
(M W Easterby) *s.s: a outpcd and bhd* **33/1**

1m 14.79s (1.09) **Going Correction** +0.275s/f (Good) 9 Ran SP% **113.8**
Speed ratings (Par 103): **103,102,101,99,98 98,95,89,86**
toteswingers: 1&2 £17.70, 1&3 £4.70, 2&3 £15.00 CSF £127.90 CT £491.71 TOTE £7.60: £2.00, £5.20, £1.60; EX 144.70.
Owner Aidan Heeney **Bred** Allevamento Ficomontanino Srl **Trained** Hambleton, N Yorks

FOCUS
A good gallop for this handicap and it favoured those racing up with the pace. Ordinary form, with the winner reversing Newcastle form with the fifth.
Elijah Pepper(USA) Official explanation: jockey said gelding was denied a clear run

2579 EDINBURGH WOOLLEN MILL CUMBERLAND PLATE TRIAL H'CAP 1m 1f 61y
3:30 (3:30) (Class 4) (0-80,79) 4-Y-O+ £5,180 (£1,541; £770; £384) Stalls High

Form RPR

-224 1 **Brushing**[11] 2256 4-8-8 74 ... AshleyMorgan(5) 11 84+
(M H Tompkins) *in tch: hdwy over 2f out: led ins fnl f: rdn out* **11/4**[1]

-516 2 1 **Danehillsundance (IRE)**[20] 1990 6-9-4 79 ... (t) RobertWinston 4 87
(D H Brown) *hld up and bhd: hdwy on wd outside 2f out: edgd rt and kpt on fnl f: wnt 2nd nr fin* **12/1**

3215 3 1/2 **Hydrant**[28] 1751 4-8-8 69 ... GregFairley 5 76
(P Salmon) *pressed ldr: rdn to ld over 2f out: hdd ins fnl f: kpt on same pce* **18/1**

205- 4 hd **Tepmokea (IRE)**[275] 5419 4-9-4 79 ... PaulHanagan 10 85
(R A Fahey) *t.k.h: cl up: effrt 2f out: one pce fnl f* **7/2**[2]

1123 5 3 3/4 **Zaplamation (IRE)**[24] 1867 5-8-2 68 ... IanBrennan(5) 3 66
(J J Quinn) *hld up on ins: effrt 2f out: no imp fnl f* **15/2**

-000 6 3 1/4 **Wind Shuffle (GER)**[8] 1867 7-8-7 68 ... FrederikTylicki 7 59
(J S Goldie) *led to over 2f out: rdn and wknd over 1f out* **10/1**

-504 7 hd **Mujaadel (USA)**[9] 2328 5-9-2 77 ... (p) AndrewMullen 1 68
(D Nicholls) *hld up: hdwy on outside 2f out: no ex fnl f* **18/1**

0-66 8 1/2 **Hurlingham**[24] 1883 6-8-1 67 ... (v[1]) JamesSullivan(5) 8 57
(M W Easterby) *hld up in midfield: effrt whn nt clr run over 2f out: nvr able to chal* **16/1**

3600 9 2 1/2 **Royal Power (IRE)**[48] 1272 7-8-13 77 ... MichaelGeran(3) 9 61
(D Nicholls) *midfield: drvn and effrt 2f out: edgd rt and sn outpcd* **14/1**

-431 10 6 **Bollin Dolly**[15] 2142 7-9-1 76 ... DavidAllan 2 47
(T D Easterby) *trckd ldrs: drvn 3f out: wknd wl over 1f out* **5/1**[3]

0206 11 3/4 **Oddsmaker (IRE)**[10] 2295 9-8-4 65 oh1 ... (t) PaulQuinn 12 34
(M A Barnes) *t.k.h: in tch tl rdn and wknd over 2f out* **50/1**

1m 57.6s **Going Correction** +0.125s/f (Good) 11 Ran SP% **119.1**
Speed ratings (Par 105): **105,104,103,103,100 97,97,96,94,89 88**
CSF £38.08 CT £510.56 TOTE £3.40: £1.30, £3.80, £6.30; EX 44.90.
Owner Dullingham Park **Bred** Dullingham Park **Trained** Newmarket, Suffolk

FOCUS
They went a very strong gallop for this 66-80 handicap and the first two home had nothing to do with the early pace. The winner should do better from here.
Hurlingham Official explanation: jockey said gelding was denied a clear run
Bollin Dolly Official explanation: trainer had no explanation for the poor form shown

2580 LLOYD MOTORS CARLISLE BELL TRIAL H'CAP 7f 200y
4:05 (4:06) (Class 4) (0-80,80) 4-Y-O+ £5,180 (£1,541; £770; £384) Stalls High

Form RPR

-232 1 **Jonny Lesters Hair (IRE)**[7] 2392 5-8-5 67 ... DavidAllan 7 78
(T D Easterby) *led to over 1f out: styd on wl u.p fnl f: regained ld cl home* **9/4**[1]

6-6 2 hd **Silver Rime (FR)**[52] 1202 5-9-1 77 ... RobertWinston 9 88
(Miss L A Perratt) *dwlt: sn in tch: effrt and drvn over 1f out: led ins fnl f: kpt on: hdd cl home* **9/1**

5100 3 2 **Border Owl (IRE)**[38] 1508 5-8-4 66 oh3 ... GregFairley 2 72
(P Salmon) *w ldr: led over 1f out to ins fnl f: kpt on same pce* **20/1**

6-50 4 3/4 **Astrodonna**[19] 2024 5-8-1 68.................................(p) AshleyMorgan(5) 3 72
(M H Tompkins) *bhd: drvn and hdwy on outside 2f out: kpt on ins fnl f* 14/1
6640 5 1/2 **Thunderball**[44] 1374 4-9-1 77.......................... FrederikTylicki 4 80
(J A Glover) *dwlt: hld up: effrt over 1f out: edgd rt: kpt on sam pce fnl f* 9/1
-613 6 nk **Come And Go (UAE)**[16] 2133 4-9-4 80.......................... AndrewElliott 5 82
(G A Swinbank) *trckd ldrs tl rdn and nt qckn appr fnl f* 7/2[2]
60-3 7 3 **Arabian Spirit**[15] 2142 5-9-1 77.......................... PaulHanagan 1 73
(R A Fahey) *hld up: rdn over 2f out: no imp over 1f out* 4/1[3]
-030 8 5 **Salerosa (IRE)**[2] 2531 5-8-11 73.......................... StephenCraine 6 57
(Mrs A Duffield) *in tch tl rdn and wknd over 1f out* 11/1
260- 9 1 **Lucy Brown**[201] 7327 4-8-7 74.......................... JamesSullivan(5) 8 56
(M W Easterby) *hld up: rdn over 2f out: sn wknd* 33/1

1m 41.52s (1.52) **Going Correction** +0.125s/f (Good) 9 Ran SP% 115.7
Speed ratings (Par 105): **97,96,94,94,93 93,90,85,84**
CSF £23.79 CT £326.05 TOTE £2.10: £1.10, £4.30, £6.50; EX 24.50.
Owner Reality Partnerships II **Bred** Gary O'Reilly **Trained** Great Habton, N Yorks

FOCUS
Another strong pace for this 1m handicap and the winner confirmed his recent return to his best.
Salerosa(IRE) Official explanation: jockey said reins snapped leaving stalls

2581 LISA WILSON YOUNG RACEGOERS FIRST-TIME H'CAP (DIV I) 5f
4:40 (4:41) (Class 6) (0-60,59) 3-Y-O+ **£1,706** (£503; £252) **Stalls** High

Form RPR
0-00 1 **Silvanus (IRE)**[10] 2278 5-9-6 55.......................... PaulHanagan 9 66
(P T Midgley) *plld hrd: prom on ins: shkn up to ld ins fnl f: comf* 7/1
0-44 2 1 1/2 **Tongalooma**[10] 2278 4-9-4 53.......................... DarrenMoffatt 10 59
(James Moffatt) *led tl edgd lft and hdd over 1f out: rallied and ev ch ins fnl f: kpt on: nt rch wnr* 9/1
4-30 3 nk **Comptonspirit**[44] 1391 6-9-8 57.......................... RobertWinston 7 62
(B P J Baugh) *prom: effrt whn nt clr run over 1f out: kpt on u.p ins fnl f* 6/1[3]
055- 4 hd **Red River Boy**[319] 3999 5-8-10 48.......................... KellyHarrison(3) 5 52
(C W Fairhurst) *cl up: led over 1f out to ins fnl f: kpt on same pce* 7/1
50-5 5 1/2 **Lady Vivien**[14] 2186 4-9-0 54.......................... IanBrennan(5) 1 56
(D H Brown) *trckd ldrs on outside: effrt over 1f out: kpt on same pce fnl f* 15/2
-402 6 1/2 **Hansomis (IRE)**[7] 2378 6-9-9 58.......................... FrederikTylicki 8 58
(B Mactaggart) *cl up tl rdn and kpt on same pce appr fnl f* 3/1[1]
6254 7 1 1/4 **Miss Daawe**[17] 2087 6-9-3 59..........................(p) DaleSwift(7) 4 55
(B Ellison) *in tch: effrt 2f out: no imp fnl f* 4/1[2]
0003 8 shd **Commander Wish**[17] 2073 7-8-8 50..........................(p) DavidKenny(7) 3 46
(Lucinda Featherstone) *stdd s: hld up: rdn over 2f out: nvr able to chal* 11/1
00-0 9 1/2 **Fern House (IRE)**[10] 2294 8-8-6 46 ow1.......................... MarkCoumbe(5) 2 40
(A Berry) *hld up: rdn over 2f out: sn no imp* 50/1

62.59 secs (1.79) **Going Correction** +0.275s/f (Good)
WFA 3 from 4yo+ 8lb 9 Ran SP% 116.3
Speed ratings (Par 101): **96,93,93,92,92 91,89,89,88**
toteswingers: 1&2 £13.20, 1&3 £7.90, 2&3 £11.40 CSF £68.41 CT £402.52 TOTE £11.60: £3.40, £4.50, £2.20; EX 103.50.
Owner Colin Alton **Bred** Barronstown Stud And Mrs T Stack **Trained** Westow, N Yorks

FOCUS
Division one of a wide open, run-of-the-mill, 46-60 sprint. Again it paid not to be far off the pace. It was the slower division and this is modest form.

2582 LISA WILSON YOUNG RACEGOERS FIRST-TIME H'CAP (DIV II) 5f
5:15 (5:15) (Class 6) (0-60,58) 3-Y-O+ **£1,706** (£503; £252) **Stalls** High

Form RPR
-050 1 **Lake Chini (IRE)**[51] 1236 8-9-7 55..........................(b) DavidAllan 6 67
(M W Easterby) *trckd ldrs: effrt and rdn 2f out: styd on wl fnl f: led towards fin* 8/1
2353 2 nk **Fasliyanne (IRE)**[7] 2396 4-9-5 53..........................(b) StephenCraine 10 64
(K A Ryan) *t.k.h: led: rdn over 1f out: kpt on fnl f: hdd towards fin* 10/3[1]
4020 3 5 **Duke Of Rainford**[13] 2217 3-8-12 54.......................... PaulHanagan 2 44
(M Herrington) *hld up: hdwy over 1f out: chsd ldrs ins fnl f: no imp* 5/1[2]
00-0 4 1/2 **Rio Sands**[20] 1988 5-9-7 58.......................... MichaelStainton(3) 3 49
(R M Whitaker) *pressed ldr tl rdn and wknd over 1f out* 11/2[3]
302- 5 3/4 **Embra (IRE)**[188] 7503 5-9-3 58.......................... DaleSwift(7) 5 47
(T J Etherington) *s.i.s: bhd and outpcd: hdwy on outside over 1f out: nvr able to chal* 7/1
0-00 6 3/4 **Darcy's Pride (IRE)**[35] 1569 6-8-13 52..........................(t) IanBrennan(5) 1 38
(P T Midgley) *prom on outside tl rdn and wknd over 1f out* 12/1
-063 7 1/2 **Officer Mor (USA)**[10] 2278 4-8-11 45.......................... FrederikTylicki 9 29
(Mrs Dianne Sayer) *hld up in tch: outpcd over 3f out: n.d after* 5/1[2]
5-3 8 3 3/4 **Distant Vision (IRE)**[7] 2378 7-9-1 49.......................... PatrickMathers 4 20
(H A McWilliams) *in tch: rdn over 2f out: wknd over 1f out* 15/2

61.78 secs (0.98) **Going Correction** +0.275s/f (Good)
WFA 3 from 4yo+ 8lb 8 Ran SP% 114.9
Speed ratings (Par 101): **103,102,94,93,92 91,90,84**
CSF £35.03 CT £149.32 TOTE £14.30: £4.70, £1.10, £2.30; EX 45.30.
Owner Mrs Jean Turpin **Bred** Paul McEnery **Trained** Sheriff Hutton, N Yorks

FOCUS
Again it proved best to race up with the pace for division two of this 46-60 sprint handicap. It was run nearly a second quicker than the first division and with the first two clear, the form is rated slightly positively.

2583 JOOLS HOLLAND LIVE HERE 3RD JULY H'CAP 1m 1f 61y
5:45 (5:46) (Class 6) (0-65,64) 4-Y-O+ **£1,942** (£578; £288; £144) **Stalls** High

Form RPR
4032 1 **Finsbury**[7] 2377 7-8-13 59.......................... FrederikTylicki 9 69+
(Miss L A Perratt) *hld up: effrt whn nt clr run 2f out: hdwy over 1f out: led wl ins fnl f: styd on wl* 5/1[2]
0655 2 1 **Call Of Duty (IRE)**[13] 2207 5-8-5 51 oh2 ow1.......................... GregFairley 1 58
(Mrs Dianne Sayer) *led: rdn clr over 1f out: hdd wl ins fnl f: r.o* 16/1
0-62 3 3 1/2 **Mohawk Ridge**[35] 1575 4-9-4 64.......................... DavidAllan 2 64+
(M Dods) *hld up in tch: effrt over 2f out: n.m.r over 1f out: kpt on fnl f: nt rch first two* 5/2[1]
053 4 shd **Dean Iarracht (IRE)**[13] 2207 4-8-3 52..........................(p) KellyHarrison(3) 4 52
(Miss Tracy Waggott) *hld up in midfield: effrt over 2f out: edgd rt over 1f out: one pce fnl f* 15/2
0000 5 2 1/2 **Stateside (CAN)**[5] 2433 5-8-9 55.......................... PaulHanagan 7 49
(R A Fahey) *chsd ldr: rdn 3f out: no ex appr fnl f* 7/1[3]
240- 6 2 1/2 **Regent's Secret (USA)**[19] 5947 10-8-1 52..........................(v) IanBrennan(5) 3 41
(J S Goldie) *hld up: drvn 3f out: no imp fr 2f out* 15/2
50-0 7 9 **Forzarzi (IRE)**[14] 2187 6-8-9 55.......................... PatrickMathers 10 24
(H A McWilliams) *hld up in tch: rdn over 2f out: wknd over 1f out* 40/1
46-1 8 12 **Arashi**[37] 1520 4-8-11 64..........................(p) DavidKenny(7) 5 6
(Lucinda Featherstone) *t.k.h: prom on outside tl wknd fr 2f out* 8/1
4025 9 6 **Weetfromthechaff**[3] 2492 5-8-11 57..........................(t) StephenCraine 6 —
(M A Barnes) *prom tl rdn and wknd 2f out* 14/1
400- 10 10 **Elliwan**[132] 7499 5-8-3 54..........................(vt[1]) JamesSullivan(5) 8 —
(M W Easterby) *bhd: struggling 4f out: sn btn* 20/1

1m 58.45s (0.85) **Going Correction** +0.125s/f (Good) 10 Ran SP% 112.1
Speed ratings (Par 101): **101,100,97,96,94 92,84,73,68,59**
toteswingers: 1&2 £9.40, 1&3 £3.40, 2&3 £7.40 CSF £77.95 CT £242.63 TOTE £5.10: £1.30, £4.20, £1.40; EX 100.70 Place 6 £61.73, Place 5 £56.42..
Owner Ken McGarrity **Bred** O Pointing **Trained** East Kilbride, South Lanarks

FOCUS
An ordinary 51-65 handicap. It was run at a sound pace and the winner was held up early. The winner confirmed his latest improvement and the runner-up's beffort effort was no fluke.
T/Plt: £135.50 to a £1 stake. Pool: £39,132.27 - 210.75 winning tickets. T/Qpdt: £30.60 to a £1 stake. Pool: £2,621.10 - 63.20 winning tickets. RY

2407 CHEPSTOW (L-H)
Monday, May 31

OFFICIAL GOING: Good
Wind: Virtually nil Weather: Overcast

2584 PAT BIFFEN 70TH BIRTHDAY H'CAP 5f 16y
2:30 (2:32) (Class 6) (0-60,60) 3-Y-O **£1,942** (£578; £288; £144) **Stalls** High

Form RPR
0020 1 **Boga (IRE)**[20] 2000 3-8-3 48.......................... WilliamCarson(3) 4 53
(R J Hodges) *chsd ldrs: led appr fnl f: drvn out* 12/1
6300 2 1 3/4 **Exceed Power**[28] 1774 3-9-1 57.......................... WilliamBuick 2 56
(D M Simcock) *s.i.s: drvn along and outpcd tl styd on appr fnl f and tk 2nd fnl 75yds but no ch w wnr* 11/2[3]
0063 3 nk **Gemma's Delight (IRE)**[20] 2000 3-8-10 52..........................(v[1]) ShaneKelly 1 50
(J W Unett) *chsd ldrs: drvn to take 2nd ins fnl f: nvr any ch w wnr and lost 2nd fnl 75yds* 6/1
306 4 1 1/2 **Force To Spend**[14] 2174 3-9-1 57.......................... JimCrowley 5 50
(N P Littmoden) *outpcd: rdn along 1/2-way: stl struggling under sme hdwy appr fnl f: kpt on cl home but nvr a threat* 9/2[2]
-530 5 nk **Ishipink**[28] 1774 3-7-13 48 oh1 ow2.......................... MatthewCosham(7) 3 40
(R J Hodges) *sn led: hdd appr fnl f: wknd fnl 120yds* 13/2
400- 6 1 3/4 **Satin Princess (IRE)**[193] 7453 3-8-4 46 oh1.......................... KirstyMilczarek 8 31
(A M Hales) *chsd ldrs: ev ch wl over 1f out: wknd fnl f and eased whn no ch* 25/1
50-0 7 1/2 **Brave Ghurka**[24] 1873 3-9-4 60.......................... LiamKeniry 6 43
(S Kirk) *chsd ldrs: rdn 1/2-way: wknd ins fnl 2f* 13/2
-032 8 1 1/2 **Acquaviva**[6] 2408 3-9-1 60..........................(p) PatrickHills(3) 7 38
(Eve Johnson Houghton) *squeezed s: nvr travelling after and a bdly outpcd* 11/4[1]

59.96 secs (0.66) **Going Correction** -0.175s/f (Firm) 8 Ran SP% 112.7
Speed ratings (Par 97): **87,84,83,81,80 78,77,74**
toteswingers: 1&2 £32.60, 1&3 £10.00, 2&3 £4.10 CSF £73.90 CT £437.58 TOTE £18.30: £5.00, £1.90, £1.90; EX 112.20 Trifecta £214.70 Part won. Pool £290.19 - 0.42 winning units..
Owner Miss R Dobson **Bred** Cathal Ennis **Trained** Charlton Mackrell, Somerset

FOCUS
Weak handicap form. The runner-up is rated below her recent best with the fifth rated to her latest mark.
Satin Princess(IRE) Official explanation: jockey said filly hung left-handed
Acquaviva Official explanation: trainer's rep said regarding runing that the filly was always outpaced

2585 LINDLEY CATERING MAIDEN STKS 1m 4f 23y
3:05 (3:05) (Class 5) 3-Y-O **£2,590** (£770; £385; £192) **Stalls** Low

Form RPR
4- 1 **Countess Comet (IRE)**[228] 6792 3-8-12 0.......................... JimCrowley 10 79+
(R M Beckett) *trckd ldrs: wnt 3rd 5f out: wnt 2nd ins fnl 3f: led appr fnl 2f: pushed clr over 1f out: comf* 7/2[3]
2-4 2 2 3/4 **Prince Of Dreams**[25] 1851 3-9-3 0.......................... ShaneKelly 3 77
(W J Knight) *narrow advantage tl def ld over 4f out: rdn and hdd appr fnl 2f: no ch w wnr appr fnl f: styd on wl for 2nd* 5/2[2]
20- 3 3/4 **Donna Elvira**[215] 7106 3-8-9 0.......................... PatrickHills(3) 2 71
(R Hannon) *mid-div: hdwy over 3f out: styd on fr 2f out: one pce ins fnl f* 14/1
0-0 4 1 **Juwireya**[18] 2051 3-8-12 0.......................... KirstyMilczarek 4 69+
(M P Tregoning) *in tch: drvn and hdwy 3f out: styd on fnl 2f but nvr gng pce to get into contention* 25/1
0-0 5 3 1/4 **High Ransom**[45] 1356 3-8-12 0.......................... PhilipRobinson 6 64+
(M A Jarvis) *bhd: stl plenty to do over 3f out: styd on fr 2f out but stl inexperienced: gng on fnl f but nvr any thrr* 11/1
0 6 6 **Ancient Greece**[56] 1127 3-9-3 0.......................... DaraghO'Donohoe 1 60
(George Baker) *bhd tl hdwy over 3f out: rdn 2f out and nvr rchd ldrs: wknd fnl f* 50/1
3-2 7 4 1/2 **Radio Wave**[17] 2092 3-8-12 0.......................... WilliamBuick 7 47
(J H M Gosden) *pressed ldr to 4f out: styd cl 2nd: rdn over 3f out: sn struggling and wknd wl over 2f out: eased whn no ch fnl f* 5/4[1]
00- 8 20 **Jinksy Minx**[178] 7624 3-8-12 0.......................... SamHitchcott 8 15
(Miss Suzy Smith) *chsd ldrs in 3rd tl rdn 5f out: wknd over 3f out* 50/1
00-0 9 46 **Superhoops**[8] 2359 3-9-3 35.......................... LiamKeniry 5 —
(H S Howe) *a bhd: t.o fr 1/2-way* 150/1
05 10 26 **Rumballina**[34] 1607 3-8-12 0.......................... TravisBlock 9 —
(Miss Amy Weaver) *in tch tl rdn 6f out: sn wknd and t.o* 100/1

2m 36.35s (-2.65) **Going Correction** -0.175s/f (Firm) 10 Ran SP% 119.7
Speed ratings (Par 99): **101,99,98,98,95 91,88,75,53,35**
toteswingers: 1&2 £7.10, 1&3 £2.90, 2&3 £2.80 CSF £12.90 TOTE £4.60: £1.20, £1.30, £3.80; EX 15.70 Trifecta £125.80 Pool £229.52 - 1.35 winning units..
Owner Lady Cobham & Giles Irwin **Bred** Lady Cobham **Trained** Whitsbury, Hants

FOCUS
Potentially quite a warm maiden for the track with the winner an improver, although the form looks just fair rated around the placed horses.

Radio Wave Official explanation: trainer had no explanation for the poor form shown

2586 EUROPEAN BREEDERS' FUND FILLIES' H'CAP 1m 4f 23y
3:40 (3:40) (Class 5) (0-75,74) 4-Y-0+ £3,885 (£1,156; £577; £288) Stalls Low

Form RPR

550/ **1** **Dolcetto (IRE)**[697] 3629 5-8-6 **62** .... MarcHalford(3) 7 71+
(A King) *hld up in rr tl stdy hdwy 3f out to ld jst ins fnl 2f: shkn up and clr fnl f: comf* 9/1

350 **2** 2 ½ **Setter's Princess**[28] 1757 4-8-4 **57** ow1 .... SimonWhitworth 5 59
(R J Hodges) *trckd ldrs: drvn to chal appr fnl 2f: chsd wnr sn after and edgd lft over 1f out: nvr any ch but kpt on wl for clr 2nd* 8/1

00-0 **3** 2 **Shy**[17] 2080 5-8-11 **64** .... JimCrowley 2 63
(B R Millman) *chsd ldrs: rdn 4f out: outpcd over 3f out: styd on u.p fnl 2f and tk readily hld 3rd cl home* 11/4[1]

55-2 **4** shd **Ragdollianna**[14] 2165 6-9-5 **72** .... LiamKeniry 8 71+
(M J McGrath) *s.i.s: in rr: rdn over 3f out: styd on fnl 2f but nvr gng pce to get into contention* 6/1[3]

65-6 **5** ½ **Princess Flame (GER)**[83] 114 8-8-5 **58** .... KirstyMilczarek 4 56
(B G Powell) *sn chsng ldr: drvn to take slt advantage over 2f out: hdd jst ins fnl 2f: wkng whn tightened up over 1f out* 8/1

50-3 **6** 1 ¾ **Lyra's Daemon**[25] 1840 4-9-7 **74** .... GeorgeBaker 3 69
(W R Muir) *led tl hdd over 2f out: wknd wl over 1f out* 3/1[2]

-645 **7** ½ **Love In The Park**[12] 2233 5-8-9 **65** .... WilliamCarson(3) 1 59
(R Brotherton) *chsd ldrs: rdn and lost pl 3f out: nvr in contention after* 6/1[3]

-230 **8** 1 ½ **Amroth**[9] 2337 4-7-13 **59** oh4 ow4 .... MatthewCosham(7) 6 51
(P D Evans) *a towards rr* 12/1

2m 39.29s (0.29) **Going Correction** -0.175s/f (Firm) **8** Ran SP% **120.2**
Speed ratings (Par 100): **92,90,89,88,88 87,87,86**
toteswingers: 1&2 £13.00, 1&3 £15.00, 2&3 £7.90 CSF £81.58 CT £254.81 TOTE £14.00: £3.00, £3.70, £1.20; EX 105.10 TRIFECTA Not won..
Owner Mrs Lesley Field **Bred** Exors R E Sangster & Mrs S Magnier **Trained** Barbury Castle, Wilts

FOCUS
A steady pace to this contest and a whole host of chances 2f out. The form looks muddling and limited, despite the winner impressing.
Lyra's Daemon Official explanation: trainer said filly ran flat

2587 ROBERT MOTTRAM MEMORIAL H'CAP 1m 14y
4:15 (4:20) (Class 5) (0-70,70) 3-Y-O £2,914 (£867; £433; £216) Stalls High

Form RPR

66-4 **1** **Trewarthenick**[34] 1594 3-8-13 **65** .... SamHitchcott 9 70+
(A M Balding) *chsd ldrs: hrd rdn over 3f out: styd on wl to ld appr fnl f: drvn out* 12/1

5-31 **2** ¾ **Candleshoe (IRE)**[28] 1775 3-9-4 **70** .... JimCrowley 10 73
(R Hannon) *broke wl: stdd in tch: hdwy over 2f out: chsd wnr fnl f: kpt on but a hld* 7/2[1]

00-0 **3** ½ **Mount Athos (IRE)**[54] 1164 3-8-9 **64** .... PatrickHills(3) 15 66+
(J W Hills) *in rr: swtchd lft to outside and hdwy over 2f out: styd on wl fnl f to hold 3rd: nt gng pce to trble ldng duo* 9/1[3]

00-0 **4** nk **Bramshill Lady (IRE)**[20] 2000 3-8-10 **62** .... RichardThomas 6 65+
(Pat Eddery) *chsd ldrs tl n.m.r on stands' rail and lost position 2f out: styd on again ins fnl f: gng on cl home* 33/1

-006 **5** ½ **First In The Queue (IRE)**[21] 1973 3-9-4 **70** .... LiamKeniry 3 70
(S Kirk) *got loose coming out of paddock: in rr: rdn 3f out: hdwy fr 2f out: kpt on ins fnl f: nt rch ldrs* 14/1

-405 **6** nk **White Dart**[16] 2110 3-9-4 **70** .... WilliamBuick 4 69
(M R Channon) *trckd ldr 5f out: led over 2f out: hdd appr fnl f: wknd fnl 120yds* 5/1[2]

00-0 **7** 1 ¼ **Diamondgeezer Luke (IRE)**[10] 2289 3-8-12 **64** ...... TomMcLaughlin 11 62+
(Patrick Morris) *in rr: hdwy and nt clr run 2f out: swtchd lft and hdwy over 1f out and n.m.r: kpt on ins fnl f: nvr a threat* 33/1

030- **8** 2 ½ **Ashkalara**[255] 6055 3-8-11 **63** .... DaraghO'Donohoe 12 54
(H S Howe) *broke wl: stdd in rr: hdwy and hmpd over 2f out: styd on again fnl f: nt rch ldrs* 50/1

0-35 **9** ½ **Could It Be Magic**[10] 2296 3-9-1 **70** ....(v[1]) JackDean(3) 5 59
(W G M Turner) *chsd ldrs: rdn 2f out: wknd appr fnl f* 10/1

000- **10** 3 **Madj's Baby**[283] 5212 3-8-5 **57** .... KirstyMilczarek 14 39
(H S Howe) *chsd ldrs: rdn 2f out: wknd wl over 1f out* 40/1

0-54 **11** nk **Onyx Of Arabia (IRE)**[17] 2089 3-9-3 **69** ....(b) RichardKingscote 7 51
(B J Meehan) *in rr towards outside: pushed along over 2f out: a struggling* 7/2[1]

5-04 **12** shd **So Surreal (IRE)**[20] 2005 3-9-3 **69** ....(b) GeorgeBaker 2 51
(G L Moore) *in rr: hdwy on outside over 2f out: nvr rchd ldrs and sn wknd* 16/1

40-0 **13** 5 **Rigid**[30] 1696 3-8-4 **59** .... WilliamCarson(3) 8 29
(A W Carroll) *in rr: sme hdwy towards outside over 2f out: sn wknd* 25/1

-505 **14** 31 **Khajaaly (IRE)**[11] 2242 3-9-2 **68** ....(b[1]) ShaneKelly 1 —
(E A L Dunlop) *sn led: hdd over 2f out: sn wknd* 11/1

1m 34.83s (-1.37) **Going Correction** -0.175s/f (Firm) **14** Ran SP% **122.9**
Speed ratings (Par 99): **99,98,97,97,96 96,95,92,92,89 89,89,84,51**
toteswingers: 1&2 £21.80, 1&3 £42.90, 2&3 £13.50 CSF £52.70 CT £414.20 TOTE £19.60: £4.70, £2.10, £3.80; EX 104.50 TRIFECTA Not won..
Owner Marcus Evans **Bred** Miss G Abbey **Trained** Kingsclere, Hants

FOCUS
A good pace to this handicap, thanks to the front-running Khajaaly. The form looks reasonable enough for the grade and is rated slighly positively.
So Surreal(IRE) Official explanation: jockey said filly never travelled
Khajaaly(IRE) Official explanation: jockey said colt ran too free in first time blinkers

2588 LINDLEY CATERING FILLIES' H'CAP 6f 16y
4:50 (4:51) (Class 5) (0-70,70) 3-Y-O £2,914 (£867; £433; £216) Stalls High

Form RPR

00-4 **1** **Sweet Pilgrim**[24] 1870 3-8-12 **64** .... JimCrowley 11 70
(M D I Usher) *chsd ldrs: led 2f out: drvn and hld on wl fnl f* 14/1

6-02 **2** ½ **Mrs Mogg**[13] 2212 3-8-10 **62** .... RichardKingscote 1 66+
(Tom Dascombe) *stdd s: swtchd rt and off pce tl hdwy 2f out: nt clr run over 1f out: swtchd sharply lft jst ins fnl f and qcknd between horses: r.o to take 2nd cl home: nt rch wnr* 6/1[2]

0-61 **3** nk **Scarcity (IRE)**[34] 1605 3-9-0 **66** .... WilliamBuick 6 69
(E A L Dunlop) *hld up in tch: hdwy 3f out: chsd wnr over 1f out: kpt on fnl f but a jst hld: lsot 2nd cl home* 15/8[1]

6-53 **4** 3 **Gundaroo**[13] 2197 3-8-13 **65** .... ShaneKelly 9 63+
(J L Dunlop) *in tch: hdwy 3f out: drvn and styd on fr over 1f out: nvr gng pce to chal* 8/1[3]

0324 **5** ¾ **Chinese Democracy (USA)**[10] 2296 3-8-4 **56** oh1 SimonWhitworth 10 47
(P D Evans) *chsd ldrs: rdn and slt ld 3f out: hdd 2f out: fading whn hmpd jst ins fnl f* 6/1[2]

0-06 **6** 2 ½ **Oasis Jade**[9] 2320 3-8-7 **59** .... LiamKeniry 8 42
(G L Moore) *chsd ldrs: rdn over 2f out: wknd over 1f out* 28/1

-000 **7** nse **Joan's Legacy**[8] 2359 3-8-4 **56** oh6 ....(b[1]) KirstyMilczarek 3 39
(J C Fox) *pressed ldrs: rdn 3f out: wknd over 1f out* 50/1

0602 **8** 2 ¼ **Ramamara (IRE)**[3] 2491 3-9-0 **66** .... TomMcLaughlin 4 42
(P D Evans) *in tch: rdn 1/2-way: wknd ins fnl 2f* 8/1[3]

0 **9** 2 **Boragh Jamal (IRE)**[21] 1977 3-8-13 **68** .... PatrickHills(3) 5 37
(B J Meehan) *s.i.s: in rr and t.k.h: sme prog over 2f out: nvr on terms and wknd over 1f out* 10/1

035- **10** 16 **Miskin Nights**[314] 4163 3-9-4 **70** .... GeorgeBaker 7 —
(B Palling) *slt ld tl hdd 3f out: wknd 2f out* 33/1

343- **11** 6 **Kenyan Cat**[217] 7061 3-9-2 **68** .... DaraghO'Donohoe 2 —
(George Baker) *slowly away: sn wl bhd: hung lft fnl 3f* 10/1

1m 11.32s (-0.68) **Going Correction** -0.175s/f (Firm) **11** Ran SP% **118.8**
Speed ratings (Par 96): **97,96,95,91,90 87,87,84,81,60 52**
CSF £95.42 CT £239.28 TOTE £20.70: £3.90, £1.50, £1.10; EX 119.30 Trifecta £240.70 Part won. Pool £325.29 - 0.10 winning units..
Owner Mr & Mrs Richard Hames And Friends **Bred** R And Mrs Hames **Trained** Upper Lambourn, Berks

FOCUS
No great depth to this fillies' handicap but the first three came nicely clear. The form is rated around those in the frame behind the winner.
Gundaroo Official explanation: jockey said filly was denied a clear run
Kenyan Cat Official explanation: jockey said filly hung left

2589 LINDLEY CATERING H'CAP (DIV I) 6f 16y
5:25 (5:27) (Class 6) (0-60,60) 4-Y-O+ £1,619 (£481; £240; £120) Stalls High

Form RPR

-456 **1** **Plumage**[11] 2246 5-9-4 **60** .... LiamKeniry 10 67
(Miss Tor Sturgis) *trckd ldrs: rdn 2f out: styd on wl fnl f to ld fnl 120yds: hld on wl* 13/2[2]

-000 **2** nk **What Katie Did (IRE)**[27] 1799 5-8-13 **55** ....(p) RichardKingscote 6 61+
(J M Bradley) *trckd ldrs: hdwy whn nt clr run over 1f out: str run ins fnl f: fin strly: nt quite get up* 20/1

0002 **3** ½ **Don Pele (IRE)**[12] 2234 8-8-13 **55** ....(b) TomMcLaughlin 1 60
(R A Harris) *in tch: drvn to chse ldrs 2f out: str chal jst ins fnl f: no ex cl home and lost 2nd* 9/1[3]

50-0 **4** nk **Bermondsey Bob (IRE)**[24] 1884 4-8-5 **50** ow2 .... JackDean(3) 3 54
(J L Spearing) *chsd ldrs: wnt 2nd 3f out: led ins fnl 2f: edgd rt appr fnl f: hdd and one pce fnl 120yds* 14/1

-126 **5** ½ **Charles Parnell (IRE)**[102] 602 7-9-4 **60** .... DaraghO'Donohoe 2 62
(S P Griffiths) *in rr tl styd on fr 2f out: kpt on ins fnl f: nvr quite gng pce to rch ldrs* 16/1

-030 **6** ½ **Desert Pride**[27] 1799 5-8-9 **51** ....(v) WilliamBuick 13 55+
(W S Kittow) *trckd ldrs: n.m.r and swtchd rt 1f out: rdn and kpt on: nvr gng pce to get into contention* 11/4[1]

6035 **7** nk **Dualagi**[19] 2026 6-8-10 **52** .... JimCrowley 4 51
(M R Bosley) *in rr: hdwy 1/2-way: hrd drvn 2f out: styng on same pce whn n.m.r ins fnl f* 11/1

1-00 **8** ¾ **Abhainn (IRE)**[11] 2246 4-9-0 **56** .... ShaneKelly 8 53
(B Palling) *s.i.s: towards rr: hdwy fr 2f out: kpt on ins fnl f: nvr rchd ldrs* 12/1

060- **9** 1 **Wooden King (IRE)**[288] 5065 5-8-8 **50** .... LiamJones 7 44
(M S Saunders) *slt ld tl hdd ins fnl 2f: btn whn pushed rt appr fnl f* 12/1

4000 **10** nk **Dynamo Dave (USA)**[32] 1633 5-8-4 **46** oh1 ....(v) RichardThomas 14 39
(M D I Usher) *broke wl: outpcd: sme hdwy 2f out: nvr gng pce to get into contention* 22/1

0400 **11** 1 ¼ **Mazzola**[14] 2166 4-9-3 **59** .... GeorgeBaker 9 48
(J M Bradley) *chsd ldrs tl wknd fnl f* 10/1

2340 **12** 1 **Dream Express (IRE)**[14] 2184 5-8-12 **54** .... AmirQuinn 5 40
(P Howling) *outpcd most of way* 12/1

0-00 **13** 1 ¼ **Blushing Maid**[40] 1477 4-8-7 **49** .... KirstyMilczarek 11 31
(H S Howe) *chsd ldrs: wkng whn sltly hmpd 1f out* 33/1

0000 **14** 8 **Stormburst (IRE)**[12] 2235 6-8-4 **46** oh1 .... SimonWhitworth 12 2
(A J Chamberlain) *slowly away: a bhd* 40/1

3500 **15** 44 **Trading Nation (USA)**[41] 1441 4-8-12 **57** .... WilliamCarson(3) 15 —
(P W Hiatt) *bolted to s: early spd: sn wl bhd: t.o* 12/1

1m 11.26s (-0.74) **Going Correction** -0.175s/f (Firm) **15** Ran SP% **125.2**
Speed ratings (Par 101): **97,96,95,95,94 94,93,92,91,91 89,88,86,75,15**
toteswingers: 1&2 £26.40, 1&3 £14.50, 2&3 £38.00 CSF £139.58 CT £1221.39 TOTE £9.90: £3.60, £4.60, £4.00; EX 166.20 TRIFECTA Not won..
Owner Mrs N L Young **Bred** The Duke Of Devonshire & Floors Farming **Trained** Lambourn, Berks

FOCUS
A modest handicap in which not much separated several on the line, so not form to be getting excited about. The form looks straightforward but modest.
Dualagi Official explanation: trainer said mare banged its head on stalls
Abhainn(IRE) Official explanation: jockey said gelding suffered interference at start
Stormburst(IRE) Official explanation: jockey said mare was slowly away
Trading Nation(USA) Official explanation: jockey said gelding bolted to the start

2590 LINDLEY CATERING H'CAP (DIV II) 6f 16y
5:55 (5:57) (Class 6) (0-60,60) 4-Y-O+ £1,619 (£481; £240; £120) Stalls High

Form RPR

0463 **1** **The History Man (IRE)**[14] 2184 7-9-1 **57** ....(p) KirstyMilczarek 6 66
(B D Leavy) *chsd ldrs: slt ld jst ins fnl f: hld on all out* 7/1[3]

25- **2** hd **Nativity**[161] 7835 4-8-7 **52** .... JackDean(3) 14 61
(J L Spearing) *in tch: hdwy 2f out: str run to chal ins fnl f: no ex last strides* 12/1

000- **3** 1 **Emiratesdotcom**[251] 6188 4-8-3 **48** ow1 .... WilliamCarson(3) 15 54
(J M Bradley) *chsd ldr: led appr fnl 2f: sn rdn: edgd rt u.p appr fnl f and hdd jst ins fnl f: no ex* 18/1

-033 **4** ½ **Sermons Mount (USA)**[32] 1633 4-8-13 **55** ....(b[1]) TravisBlock 8 59
(Mouse Hamilton-Fairley) *sn led: hdd appr fnl 2f: styd pressing ldrs: kpt on same pce fnl 75yds* 6/1[2]

4544 **5** ¾ **Hart Of Gold**[19] 2021 6-8-10 **52** ....(b) RichardThomas 12 54
(R A Harris) *chsd ldrs: rdn over 2f out: wknd fnl 50yds* 10/1

5301 **6** ½ **Sirjosh**[20] 2008 4-8-6 **53** .... BillyCray(5) 10 53+
(D Donovan) *in rr: rdn 1/2-way: hdwy and hmpd 1f out: swtchd rt and r.o: gng on cl home* 8/1

5062 **7** nse **Loyal Royal (IRE)**[14] 2184 7-8-7 **50** ....(bt) RichardKingscote 11 50
(J M Bradley) *s.i.s: in rr tl hdwy over 2f out: chsd ldrs over 1f out: fdd fnl 50yds* 7/1[3]

The Form Book, Raceform Ltd, Compton, RG20 6NL

0000 **8** 3/4 **Resplendent Alpha**[10] 2298 6-8-13 **55**............................ JimCrowley 9 52
(P Howling) *in rr: styd on fr over 1f out: kpt on cl home but nvr a threat* **16/1**

006- **9** 1 1/4 **Lily Wood**[168] 7753 4-8-8 **50**.............................(v[1]) ShaneKelly 2 43
(J W Unett) *chsd ldrs: rdn over 2f out: wknd appr fnl f* **33/1**

4000 **10** 1 **Top Flight Splash**[13] 2198 4-8-4 **46** oh1.................(v) SimonWhitworth 5 36
(P D Evans) *in rr 1/2-way: sme late prog* **20/1**

-530 **11** shd **Stamford Blue**[11] 2246 9-8-11 **60**.................................(b) JakePayne(7) 3 50
(R A Harris) *chsd ldrs tl wknd over 1f out* **14/1**

-605 **12** hd **Bateleur**[11] 2246 6-9-2 **58**.. WilliamBuick 13 47
(M R Channon) *mid-div: drvn along fr 1/2-way: sme prog over 1f out and effrt ins fnl f: nvr gng pce to get into contention and swtchd lft 1f out: sn fdd* **10/3**[1]

-005 **13** nk **Talamahana**[19] 2021 5-8-4 **46** oh1.........................(v) DaraghO'Donohoe 1 34
(A B Haynes) *chsd ldrs over 4f* **33/1**

000- **14** 5 **Charlietoo**[270] 5610 4-9-4 **60**... PaulFitzsimons 7 32
(E G Bevan) *chsd ldrs 4f* **50/1**

0/0- **15** 8 **Ensign's Trick**[223] 6924 6-8-6 **48**.. LiamJones 4 —
(W M Brisbourne) *slowly away: a in rr* **50/1**

1m 11.07s (-0.93) **Going Correction** -0.175s/f (Firm) **15** Ran SP% **122.6**
Speed ratings (Par 101): **99,98,97,96,95 95,95,94,92,91 90,90,90,83,72**
toteswingers:1&2 £17.40, 2&3 £0.00, 1&3 £67.20 CSF £85.16 CT £1496.00 TOTE £8.90: £2.70, £5.60, £7.00; EX 110.30 TRIFECTA Not won. Place 6 £218.91, Place 5 £59.36..
Owner D E Simpson & R Farrington-Kirkham **Bred** J Beckett **Trained** Forsbrook, Staffs

FOCUS
Another modest line-up and once again a bunched finish. The race was slightly quicker than the first division and the form is sound but modest.
T/Plt: £727.30 to a £1 stake. Pool:£63,695.84 - 63.93 winning tickets. T/Qpdt: £40.10 to a £1 stake. Pool: £4,509.50 - 83.20 winning tickets. ST

2316 GOODWOOD (R-H)

Monday, May 31

OFFICIAL GOING: Good (good to firm in places; 8.6)
First 2f of 1mile course moved out 5yards but all distances as advertised.
Wind: Moderate, across (towards stands) Weather: Cloudy

2591 GOODWOOD FAMILY FUN DAY (S) STKS 5f
2:00 (2:00) (Class 4) 2-Y-O **£4,857** (£1,445; £722; £360) **Stalls** Low

Form RPR

2226 **1** **Belle Royale (IRE)**[16] 2130 2-8-7 0.................................. KierenFallon 1 64
(W M Brisbourne) *hanging rt thrght: mde virtually all: hung rt fr 1/2-way and ended nr far side rail: in command over 1f out: styd on wl* **5/4**[1]

6532 **2** 2 3/4 **Russian Ice**[9] 2330 2-8-7 0.................................. EddieCreighton 5 54
(D K Ivory) *sn pushed along: rdn to chse ldng pair 1/2-way: edgd rt after: tk 2nd ins fnl f: no threat to wnr* **5/2**[2]

6626 **3** 1/2 **Crazy In Love**[15] 2139 2-8-2 0.................................(b) RossAtkinson(5) 4 52
(W G M Turner) *hanging rt thrght: w wnr to 2f out: hung rt and ended against far side rail: lost 2nd ins fnl f* **28/1**

0 **4** 2 1/2 **Speed Gene (IRE)**[11] 2238 2-8-7 0.......................... FrankieMcDonald 3 43
(R Hannon) *hld up bhd ldrs: shkn up 1/2-way: edgd rt and no prog over 1f out* **8/1**

0 **5** 1 1/4 **One Fat Cat (IRE)**[9] 2338 2-8-2 0....................................... KierenFox(5) 6 39
(P M Phelan) *chsd ldng pair to 1/2-way: edgd rt and fdd fnl 2f* **4/1**[3]

6 4 **Livia Quarta (IRE)** 2-8-7 0... JamesDoyle 2 24
(E J Creighton) *squeezed out s: a last: struggling fnl 2f* **25/1**

59.58 secs (1.18) **Going Correction** +0.025s/f (Good) **6** Ran SP% **111.4**
Speed ratings (Par 95): **91,86,85,81,79 73**The winner was bought in for 7,500gns..The winner was bought in for 7,500gns.
Owner Peter Mort **Bred** Dxb Ltd **Trained** Great Ness, Shropshire

FOCUS
A fairly weak seller rated through the third but could rate higher.

NOTEBOOK
Belle Royale(IRE) managed to make all despite hanging right over to the far side. The form shown on her second and third starts was more than good enough to win this and she can probably pay her way in low-grade nurseries later in the season. (op 11-8 tchd 6-4)
Russian Ice looked the danger to the favourite on form and duly chased her home, but never got close enough to seriously challenge having been a bit outpaced on this drop to 5f. She should find a race at this level. (op 9-4)
Crazy In Love bounced back from a moderate effort at Ripon, seeming to appreciate the return to 5f, but she too ended up against the far rail having hung right. Official explanation: jockey said filly hung right (op 25-1)
Speed Gene(IRE), never involved over 6f at Haydock on her debut, didn't seem helped by the drop in trip, but confirmed this is her level. (tchd 15-2)
One Fat Cat(IRE), well beaten in a Newbury maiden on debut, was backed on this drop in grade, but disappointed. (op 13-2)

2592 WATCH RACING UK VETERANS' H'CAP 6f
2:35 (2:35) (Class 4) (0-80,79) 6-Y-O+ **£4,209** (£1,252; £625; £312) **Stalls** Low

Form RPR

0136 **1** **Alfresco**[28] 1767 6-8-7 **68** ow1..(b) KierenFallon 8 77
(J R Best) *trckd clr ldr over 3f out: clsd to ld wl over 1f out: pressed ins fnl f: drvn and styd on* **4/1**[2]

1033 **2** nk **Kyllachy Storm**[8] 2364 6-8-8 **69**..(b) AlanMunro 1 77
(R J Hodges) *hld up: rdn and effrt over 1f out: r.o against nr side rail fnl f: wnt 2nd nr fin and clsd on wnr* **14/1**

2/11 **3** hd **Tubby Isaacs**[16] 2113 6-9-1 **76**.. NeilCallan 5 83
(D K Ivory) *s.s: hld up in last pair: prog on outer over 2f out: wnt 2nd over 1f out w hd high: chal ent fnl f: nt qckn and lost 2nd nr fin* **13/8**[1]

2002 **4** 1 1/2 **Cornus**[13] 2206 8-8-6 **67**..(be) JamesDoyle 7 69
(A J McCabe) *prom in chsng gp: lost pl and rdn 1/2-way: effrt over 1f out: one pce* **20/1**

6-06 **5** 1/2 **Barons Spy (IRE)**[17] 2091 9-9-4 **79**............................... JamieSpencer 6 80
(R J Price) *chsd clr ldr over 2f: lost pl over 2f out and rdn: one pce and nvr on terms after* **10/1**

1002 **6** hd **Even Bolder**[30] 1691 7-8-10 **76**.. KierenFox(5) 2 76
(E A Wheeler) *plld hrd: hld up: effrt 2f out: rdn and disp 2nd briefly over 1f out: fnd nil* **10/1**

-621 **7** 2 3/4 **Rocker**[24] 1874 6-9-3 **78**.. RyanMoore 3 69
(G L Moore) *hld up in last pair: pushed along over 2f out: nvr nr ldrs* **17/2**

0564 **8** 3 3/4 **Phantom Whisper**[7] 2399 7-8-11 **75**...........................(b) JamesMillman(3) 9 54
(B R Millman) *led and sn wl clr: wknd and hdd wl over 1f out* **11/2**[3]

1m 11.54s (-0.66) **Going Correction** +0.025s/f (Good) **8** Ran SP% **113.6**
Speed ratings: **105,104,104,102,101 101,97,92**
CSF £56.01 CT £125.54 TOTE £4.40: £1.30, £2.70, £1.20; EX 52.80.
Owner Mrs A M Riney **Bred** Usk Valley Stud **Trained** Hucking, Kent

FOCUS
A decent little sprint handicap, limited to horses aged six of older, and Phantom Whisper set a fast gallop. The runner-up is rated close to his best and sets the level.
Phantom Whisper Official explanation: jockey said gelding ran too free

2593 FESTIVAL STKS (LISTED RACE) 1m 1f 192y
3:10 (3:10) (Class 1) 4-Y-O+
£22,708 (£8,608; £4,308; £2,148; £1,076; £540) **Stalls** High

Form RPR

0-00 **1** **Class Is Class (IRE)**[17] 2096 4-8-12 94..........................(v) RyanMoore 9 116
(Sir Michael Stoute) *trckd ldrs: cl up on inner 2f out: eased out and effrt over 1f out: drvn to ld last 150yds: styd on wl* **14/1**

11-3 **2** 1 3/4 **Laaheb**[37] 1532 4-9-1 112.. RichardHills 6 115
(M A Jarvis) *prog to trck ldng pair after 4f: wnt 2nd wl over 2f out and sn chalng: narrow ld wl over 1f out tl hdd and one pce last 150yds* **9/4**[1]

-115 **3** shd **Drunken Sailor (IRE)**[87] 820 5-8-12 107....................(b) KierenFallon 7 112
(L M Cumani) *hld up and mostly in last pair: wound up on outer over 2f out: prog over 1f out to chal ent fnl f: nt qckn: kpt on nr fin* **15/2**

0-52 **4** 1 3/4 **Indian Days**[19] 2027 5-8-12 104.. PaulMulrennan 5 109
(J G Given) *mde most: narrowly hdd wl over 1f out: upsides ent fnl f: fdd last 100yds* **6/1**[3]

0-04 **5** nse **Traffic Guard (USA)**[23] 1898 6-8-12 110...................... JamieSpencer 2 108+
(P F I Cole) *trckd ldng pair 4f: lost pl: effrt but nt clr run 2f out: snatched up over 1f out: drvn and r.o ins fnl f: no ch to rcvr* **6/1**[3]

63-3 **6** 1/2 **Palavicini (USA)**[46] 1328 4-8-12 112.................................. EddieAhern 8 107+
(J L Dunlop) *hld up and mostly in last pair: looking for run over 2f out: swtchd out wd over 1f out but ldrs already gone: styd on fnl 150yds* **3/1**[2]

0-22 **7** 4 1/2 **Safari Sunup (IRE)**[31] 1665 5-8-12 100.............................. IanMongan 4 98
(P Winkworth) *hld up in tch: rdn to chse ldrs over 2f out: losing pl whn hmpd and snatched up over 1f out* **25/1**

310- **8** 7 **Chock A Block (IRE)**[219] 7031 4-9-1 107..................... FrankieDettori 1 87
(Saeed Bin Suroor) *mostly pressed ldr to wl over 2f out: wknd rapidly* **16/1**

2m 5.00s (-3.00) **Going Correction** +0.025s/f (Good) **8** Ran SP% **112.5**
Speed ratings (Par 111): **113,111,111,110,110 109,106,100**
CSF £44.37 TOTE £16.70: £3.70, £1.10, £1.90; EX 51.60.
Owner R Ahamad & P Scott **Bred** P And C Scott & Exors Of The Late N Ahamad **Trained** Newmarket, Suffolk

FOCUS
This was certainly an open Listed contest, and the early pace was just a steady one. It was perhaps slightly disappointing that it went to the lowest-rated runner but the form appears sound rated around the runner-up and fourth.

NOTEBOOK
Class Is Class(IRE), carrying an official mark of just 94, but he has always been well thought of, and the visor, which he raced to freely in over 1m4f at York first time, was clearly a large factor in his dramatic improvement. The drop to 1m2f was clearly an advantage too, as having been moved out to challenge, he picked up really well and was nicely on top at the line. He may be capable of fulfilling that early potential now, and a reproduction of this effort could see him go close in the Wolferton Handicap at Royal Ascot. (tchd 16-1)
Laaheb, rated 112 following a highly progressive first season at three, shaped nicely enough when third in a Group 3 at Sandown on his reappearance, and he looked the one to beat back at this level, despite the penalty. He was weak in the market, though, and having come through to take it up over 1f out, he was readily done for toe by the winner late on. He has yet suggest he's made as much progress as expected from three to four, though it's still relatively early days for him. (op 15-8)
Drunken Sailor(IRE), twice a winner in handicaps in Dubai earlier in the year, the latest of which came off 104, came with a strong challenge out wide and held every chance, but as with the runner-up, he had no answer when the winner hot top gear in the final 100 yards. He too looks a likely type for the Wolferton. (tchd 7-1)
Indian Days ran really well under a positive ride in a handicap at York last time, and he put up another solid effort in defeat back up in grade, but it's approaching two years since he last won a race. (op 13-2 tchd 11-2)
Traffic Guard(USA) was certainly unlucky not to finish closer, twice being denied a clear run when trying to close and finding himself out of time once getting going again inside the final furlong. Official explanation: jockey said horse suffered interference in running (op 8-1)
Palavicini(USA) is another who can count himself unlucky as he found himself with nowhere to go when looking for a run towards the final 2f, and then finding the principals away and gone by the time he switched out and got going, flashing home in sixth. He can be rated a good bit better than the bare form. (op 7-2 tchd 4-1 in places)
Safari Sunup(IRE) has run two good races this season, but this was another step up and he was already in trouble when cut up 1f out. Official explanation: jockey said gelding suffered interference in running (op 33-1 tchd 20-1)
Chock A Block(IRE), a progressive sort last year but saddled with a penalty for this reappearance, comes from a yard struggling for winners and he dropped out tamely having been right up there early. (tchd 12-1)

2594 GOLF AT GOODWOOD MAIDEN AUCTION STKS 6f
3:45 (3:47) (Class 5) 2-Y-O **£3,238** (£963; £481; £240) **Stalls** Low

Form RPR

1 **Crown Prosecutor (IRE)** 2-8-13 0................................. KierenFallon 9 80+
(B J Meehan) *dwlt: sn trckd ldrs: effrt and shkn up over 1f out: drvn and r.o fnl f to ld last 50yds* **3/1**[2]

2 nk **Sonning Rose (IRE)** 2-8-6 0.. AlanMunro 2 72+
(M R Channon) *awkward s: wl in rr: stl nrr last than first over 1f out: gd prog after: styd on wl to take 2nd fnl stride* **20/1**

23 **3** nse **Dr Green (IRE)**[11] 2239 2-9-1 0.. RyanMoore 13 81
(R Hannon) *mde most in centre: hrd pressed thrght: drvn fnl f: hdd last 50yds* **13/8**[1]

5 **4** hd **Major Conquest (IRE)**[17] 2078 2-8-12 0.......................... RichardHills 6 77
(J W Hills) *dwlt: t.k.h: hld up bhd ldrs: prog to go 2nd over 1f out and looked threatening: nt qckn ins fnl f* **9/1**

40 **5** shd **Reposer (IRE)**[23] 1930 2-8-10 0.. SteveDrowne 12 75
(J R Best) *trckd ldrs on outer: prog over 2f out: cl up over 1f out: chal ins fnl f: no ex last 100yds* **16/1**

6 2 3/4 **Sonoran Sands (IRE)** 2-9-0 0... JamesDoyle 1 71+
(J S Moore) *pressed ldng pair: stl cl up over 1f out: fdd ins fnl f* **50/1**

7 hd **Folly Drove** 2-8-1 0.. JohnFahy(5) 14 62+
(J G Portman) *free to post: difficult to load: dwlt: sn in tch bhd ldrs: pushed along over 2f out: kpt on without threatening: nt disgracd* **66/1**

40 **8** 2 1/2 **Reginald Claude**[34] 1603 2-8-11 0.................................. HayleyTurner 7 60
(M D I Usher) *towards rr: pushed along 1/2-way: no prog after tl kpt on ins fnl f* **40/1**

60 **9** 3 1/4 **Roman Dancer (IRE)**[11] 2238 2-8-13 0............................. NeilCallan 10 52+
(J Gallagher) *pressed ldr to over 1f out: wknd rapidly fnl f* **16/1**

10 3/4 **Believe It Or Not (IRE)** 2-9-0 0....................................... FergusSweeney 5 51
(J S Moore) *wl on terms w ldrs tl wknd jst over 1f out* **28/1**

0 **11** 1 ¾ **Sky Booster**16 2111 2-8-12 0 EddieAhern 8 43+
(W J Haggas) *in tch in midfield: shkn up and no prog 2f out: wknd over 1f out* **16/1**

12 nk **Standout** 2-8-10 0 JamieSpencer 11 41+
(R Hannon) *s.s and wnt lft: a wl in rr: nvr a factor* **8/1**3

13 2 **Star Commander** 2-8-11 0 SimonPearce(5) 3 41
(M H Tompkins) *dwlt: nvr on terms w ldrs: struggling sn after 1/2-way* **66/1**

14 2 ¾ **Sensational Love (IRE)** 2-8-9 0 StevieDonohoe 15 25
(R A Mills) *dwlt: a wl in rr: nvr a factor* **20/1**

0 **15** 29 **Impulse Dancer**18 2048 2-8-4 0 NeilChalmers 4 —
(J J Bridger) *spd 2f: wknd rapidly: t.o: lame* **200/1**

1m 12.43s (0.23) **Going Correction** +0.025s/f (Good) **15** Ran SP% **122.7**
Speed ratings (Par 93): **99,98,98,98,98 94,94,90,86,85 83,82,80,76,37**
toteswingers: 1&2 £22.00, 1&3 £2.20, 2&3 £11.60 CSF £70.00 TOTE £4.70: £2.00, £5.70, £1.10; EX 109.10.
Owner Mrs M Findlay & Sangster Family **Bred** Edmond And Richard Kent **Trained** Manton, Wilts

FOCUS
An ordinary maiden in truth, though the winner is highly regarded, and it should still produce a few winners. The form looks up to scratch for the track, rated through the third.

NOTEBOOK
Crown Prosecutor(IRE), who had reportedly been going well at home, including in a few bits of work for Kieren Fallon, and the partnership prevailed narrowly after perhaps being eased a stride or two prematurely. Though a half-brother to a hurdler, there is plenty of speed in his pedigree, and the talk afterwards was that the Coventry Stakes will be next, but he will need to leave this form a long way behind if he is going to be up to winning a race like that. (op 9-2 tchd 5-1 in a place)
Sonning Rose(IRE), an 11,000gns half-sister to several winners, got well behind, not being helped by an awkward start, but she rattled home once getting an idea of what was required and very nearly got up. She should be capable of winning an ordinary maiden with this experience behind her. (op 28-1)
Dr Green(IRE) set a solid, if somewhat unspectacular, standard and he seemed to run his race without quite being good enough. He has done enough to win a small race, but hardly seems to be progressing. (op 15-8)
Major Conquest(IRE) travelled really nicely and briefly looked the winner, but couldn't quicken sufficiently late on. He is clearly learning and appeals as a likely sort for nurseries. (op 13-2)
Reposer(IRE) bounced back from a very poor effort at Warwick, challenging wide, and is another likely type for nurseries.
Sonoran Sands(IRE), a 21,000gns son of Footstepsinthesand, showed plenty of pace to lead towards the stands' side and should be able to cope with 5f, though it's likely he will see his race out better with this experience behind him. (op 100-1)
Folly Drove was a bit of a handful before the race, but shaped nicely enough and should improve for a yard that does quite well with juvenile fillies. (tchd 80-1)
Reginald Claude was noted staying on late and will be one to look out for in handicaps.
Roman Dancer(IRE), who has plenty of speed, is another who can make his mark in handicaps in due course.
Believe It Or Not(IRE), entered in a couple of sales races, showed pace before fading. (op 40-1)
Sky Booster has shown little in two starts and may need more time. (op 14-1)
Standout, another newcomer, was always outpaced. (op 11-2 tchd 5-1)
Impulse Dancer Official explanation: vet said filly returned lame right-hind

2595 RACING UK ON SKY 432 H'CAP 7f

4:20 (4:22) (Class 2) (0-100,100) 4-Y-0+ **£10,361** (£3,083; £1,540; £769) **Stalls** High

Form RPR

10-6 **1** **Tropical Paradise (IRE)**30 1693 4-9-2 **98** IanMongan 4 106
(P Winkworth) *cl up bhd ldrs in 6th: effrt on outer 2f out: drvn to ld narrowly over 1f out: jst hld on* **25/1**

06-0 **2** shd **Signor Peltro**23 1900 7-9-0 **96** FergusSweeney 13 103+
(H Candy) *stdd s: hld up in last trio: stl there 2f out: swtchd out wd over 1f out: gd prog fnl f: clsd on wnr fin: jst failed* **9/1**3

0410 **3** ½ **Thebes**23 1900 5-8-11 **93** FrankieDettori 14 99
(M Johnston) *racd keenly bhd ldng pair: got through against rail to chal over 1f out: nrly upsides ins fnl f: no ex* **5/2**1

00-6 **4** 1 **Spanish Bounty**16 2119 5-8-6 **88** EddieAhern 6 91
(J G Portman) *led: edgd lft off rail fr 2f out: narrowly hdd over 1f out: one pce last 150yds* **16/1**

30-3 **5** ¾ **Nasri**33 1614 4-9-2 **98** KierenFallon 9 99
(D M Simcock) *hld up towards rr in abt 11th: pushed along 3f out: sme prog but n.m.r over 1f out: kpt on: no real danger* **12/1**

-543 **6** ½ **Light From Mars**37 1519 5-9-1 **100** JamesMillman(3) 1 102+
(B R Millman) *pressed ldng pair: rdn and nt quite gng pce to hold pl whn bmpd and squeezed out over 1f out: one pce fnl f* **9/1**3

U0-6 **7** ½ **Cyflymder (IRE)**121 358 4-8-12 **94** RyanMoore 7 93
(R Hannon) *hld up in last pair: stl there 2f out: taken to outer jst over 1f out: styd on last 150yds: no ch* **14/1**

-015 **8** shd **Getcarter**23 1903 4-7-12 **87** CharlesEddery(7) 8 85+
(R Hannon) *dwlt: hld up in 10th: pushed along over 2f out: nt great deal of room after: kpt on fnl f: no ch* **12/1**

00-0 **9** 1 ¼ **Pravda Street**26 1826 5-8-4 **86** oh1 HayleyTurner 3 81
(P F I Cole) *pressed ldr to over 1f out: fdd fnl f* **50/1**

-006 **10** nk **Huzzah (IRE)**23 1900 5-8-4 **86** JimmyQuinn 2 80+
(B W Hills) *rrd bdly s and lft abt 8 l: latched on to bk of field after 2f: pushed along on inner over 2f out: no ch whn nt clr run 1f out* **8/1**2

10- **11** ½ **Jeninsky (USA)**225 6886 5-8-10 **92** AlanMunro 5 85
(Rae Guest) *trckd ldrs in 7th on outer: nt qckn 2f out: fdd fnl f* **25/1**

-012 **12** hd **Mujood**9 2322 7-8-9 **96** (v) JohnFahy(5) 11 88
(Eve Johnson Houghton) *nvr bttr than midfield: rdn over 2f out: no prog: fdd fnl f* **10/1**

40-0 **13** shd **Seamus Shindig**23 1903 8-8-5 **87** FrankieMcDonald 12 79
(H Candy) *racd freely in midfield on inner: snatched up 1/2-way: no prog 2f out: wknd fnl f* **25/1**

2140 **14** ¾ **Bravo Echo**23 1900 4-8-10 **92** NeilCallan 10 82
(M J Attwater) *trckd ldng quartet: rdn and sing to lose pl whn bmpd over 1f out: wknd* **9/1**3

1m 25.97s (-0.93) **Going Correction** +0.025s/f (Good) **14** Ran SP% **120.2**
Speed ratings (Par 109): **109,108,108,107,106 105,105,105,103,103 102,102,102,101**
toteswingers: 1&2 £55.00, 1&3 £18.60, 2&3 £7.40 CSF £228.94 CT £795.71 TOTE £39.00: £9.70, £2.90, £1.10; EX 374.70.
Owner S Lovelace & R Muddle **Bred** George E McMahon **Trained** Chiddingfold, Surrey

FOCUS
A really competitive handicap and it produced a cracking finish. The winner is generally progressive and the second is rated a length off last year's best.

NOTEBOOK
Tropical Paradise(IRE) had been far from disgraced in a 1m Listed race at the track on her reappearance, and was only 1lb higher than when last winning, so it was therefore rather surprising to see her returned at 25-1. Always well placed, she really did dig in having got to the front inside the final furlong, and not for the first time gave the impression she would stay 1m. She looks capable of gaining black type at some stage. (op 28-1 tchd 33-1 in places)
Signor Peltro, whose low draw was of no real advantage being a hold-up horse, picked up takingly once switched and asked for his effort over 1f out, looking for all the world as though his momentum would carry him past the winner, but he couldn't quite get up. He will presumably head for the Buckingham Palace Stakes. (op 13-2)
Thebes had every opportunity after a gap appeared against the rail, but couldn't stay on as strongly as the front pair. (op 4-1 tchd 9-4)
Spanish Bounty, who has yet to win beyond 6f, led them until over 1f out and didn't curl up once headed, keeping on for fourth.
Nasri shaped a bit more encouragingly, keeping on having been a bit tightened up, but it was not enough to claim he was unlucky.
Light From Mars was drawn lowest of all, but got across to race prominently and it was no surprise he found a few too quick at the finish. (op 10-1)
Cyflymder(IRE) made a lot of ground in the final 1.5f, staying on strongly down the outside having been switched to the outer. He is one to watch out for in something similar. (tchd 12-1)
Pravda Street showed up well for a long way from a low draw, although ultimately faded. (tchd 40-1)
Huzzah(IRE) lost all chance when rearing at the start and then found things not going his way when trying to keep on late. This run is safely ignored. Official explanation: jockey said gelding reared leaving stalls (op 17-2 tchd 9-1 in places)

2596 JUNE FRIDAY EVENINGS AT GOODWOOD H'CAP 1m

4:55 (4:56) (Class 6) (0-65,67) 4-Y-0+ **£3,238** (£963; £481; £240) **Stalls** High

Form RPR

06-0 **1** **Kilburn**44 1374 6-9-4 **65** SteveDrowne 9 75
(A J Lidderdale) *mde all at decent pce: kicked 2 l clr 2f out: styd on u.p fnl f* **16/1**

0-60 **2** 1 ¾ **Bomber Command (USA)**17 2080 7-9-4 **65** (v) RichardHills 4 71
(J W Hills) *hld up in midfield in 9th: prog on outer over 2f out: wnt 2nd over 1f out: styd on but no real imp* **12/1**

0-42 **3** ½ **Moon Lightning (IRE)**28 1771 4-9-0 **61** RyanMoore 12 66
(M H Tompkins) *t.k.h: trckd ldng quartet: effrt 2f out: swtchd to rail over 1f out: styd on to take 3rd nr fin* **3/1**2

044 **4** ¾ **Cruise Control**29 1737 4-8-4 **51** oh1 HayleyTurner 11 54
(R J Price) *trckd ldng pair on inner: eased out and rdn to dispute 2nd over 1f out: kpt on same pce after* **25/1**

0003 **5** shd **Bere Davis (FR)**3 2488 5-8-9 **56** KierenFallon 16 59
(P D Evans) *pressed wnr: rdn over 2f out: hld and lost 2nd over 1f out: n.m.r sn after: one pce* **11/4**1

4600 **6** shd **Trafalgar Square**24 1875 8-8-11 **58** (v1) NeilCallan 2 61
(M J Attwater) *settled in 10th: rdn 3f out: no prog tl styd on wl fnl f: nrst fin* **12/1**

405- **7** ¾ **Transfer**238 6547 5-9-3 **64** IanMongan 10 65
(C P Morlock) *t.k.h: hld up in 8th: effrt 2f out: swtchd lft over 1f out: kpt on but n.d* **18/1**

50-5 **8** hd **Second To Nun (IRE)**36 4-8-4 **51** JimmyQuinn 6 53+
(M Blanshard) *trckd ldrs in 6th: effrt over 2f out: tried to dispute 2nd over 1f out but sn squeezed out: one pce after* **33/1**

4204 **9** 2 **Count Ceprano (IRE)**6 2419 6-8-4 **56** SimonPearce(5) 13 52
(J Pearce) *trckd ldrs on inner in 7th: rdn and nt qckn 2f out: no imp after* **9/1**3

0/00 **10** nk **Blue Aura (IRE)**23 1929 7-8-13 **60** (v1) FergusSweeney 15 55
(B G Powell) *hld up in last quartet: pushed along over 2f out: rmodest late prog: no ch* **16/1**

2050 **11** nse **Harare**28 1762 9-9-0 **61** (v) JamesDoyle 3 56
(R J Price) *hld up towards rr in 11th: pushed along and no prog over 2f out: plugged on fnl f* **33/1**

1001 **12** ¾ **Batchworth Blaise**6 2417 7-8-7 **59** 6ex KierenFox(5) 5 52
(E A Wheeler) *hld up in last quartet: effrt on wd outside 3f out: no prog 2f out: sn btn* **12/1**

1040 **13** 1 ¾ **Hip Hip Hooray**12 2233 4-9-1 **62** FrankieMcDonald 8 51
(L A Dace) *stdd s and swtchd rt: hld up in last trio: stl there whn swtchd to inner 2f out: nvr nr ldrs* **25/1**

-601 **14** 7 **Lord Of The Dance (IRE)**6 2410 4-9-6 **67** 6ex EddieAhern 1 40
(W M Brisbourne) *hld up in abt 12th: rdn and no prog over 2f out* **11/1**

0030 **15** 17 **Esteem Lord**6 2419 4-8-10 **57** (b) StevieDonohoe 7 —
(Jamie Poulton) *chsd ldng pair to over 2f out: wknd rapidly* **40/1**

4650 **F** **See Elsie Play**28 1763 4-8-7 **54** (p) EddieCreighton 14 —
(Miss Z C Davison) *s.s: wl in rr tl broke down and fell 2f out* **28/1**

1m 38.69s (-1.21) **Going Correction** +0.025s/f (Good) **16** Ran SP% **129.6**
Speed ratings (Par 101): **107,105,104,104,103 103,103,102,100,100 100,99,98,91,74** —
toteswingers: 1&2 £29.80, 1&3 £15.90, 2&3 £11.40 CSF £194.14 CT £778.08 TOTE £17.10: £4.60, £3.50, £1.10, £4.20; EX 220.10.
Owner Royal Windsor Racing Club **Bred** B Walters **Trained** Eastbury, Berks

FOCUS
A modest handicap, but it was certainly competitive and the form looks solid with the third, fourth and fifth close to their latest marks.
Cruise Control Official explanation: jockey said gelding hung left
Bere Davis(FR) Official explanation: jockey said gelding hung left
Second To Nun(IRE) Official explanation: jockey said filly suffered interference 2f out
Blue Aura(IRE) Official explanation: jockey said gelding stumbled leaving stalls

2597 TOTEEXACTA H'CAP 1m 4f

5:30 (5:31) (Class 5) (0-70,68) 4-Y-0+ **£3,238** (£963; £481; £240) **Stalls** Low

Form RPR

42-0 **1** **Seventh Cavalry (IRE)**17 2080 5-9-2 **66** RyanMoore 5 75
(A King) *hld up in 8th: prog over 2f out to go 2nd over 1f out: chal ent fnl f: drvn ahd last 100yds* **7/2**2

606- **2** ¾ **Megalala (IRE)**209 7225 9-8-8 **58** NeilChalmers 2 66
(J J Bridger) *led at decent pce: urged along over 3f out: kpt on but hdd last 100yds* **33/1**

1621 **3** ½ **Ghufa (IRE)**10 2285 6-8-7 **62** SimonPearce(5) 8 69
(J Pearce) *settled in last: detached whn reminder over 3f out: gd prog fr 2f out: r.o to take 3rd fnl f: fin strly* **4/1**3

2-20 **4** 4 **Carter**21 1980 4-8-10 **60** PaulMulrennan 9 61
(W M Brisbourne) *mostly chsd ldr to over 1f out: wknd fnl f* **17/2**

4-60 **5** nk **Spinning Waters**8 2361 4-8-0 **55** (b1) JohnFahy(5) 6 55
(Eve Johnson Houghton) *in tch: effrt over 2f out: one pce and no imp fr over 1f out* **14/1**

5043 **6** 1 ¾ **Valdan (IRE)**29 1720 6-9-4 **68** KierenFallon 1 69
(P D Evans) *in tch: effrt on outer 3f out: disp 2nd 2f out but hanging rt: wknd over 1f out: eased fnl f* **4/1**3

615 **7** 1 **Two Oclock John**23 1931 4-9-0 **64** JimmyQuinn 4 60
(H J Collingridge) *in tch towards rr: taken to outer and shkn up over 2f out: sn no imp* **20/1**

-000 8 2 ¾ **Dubai Gem**[25] 1849 4-8-9 **59** .... StevieDonohoe 7 50
(Jamie Poulton) *trckd ldrs: rdn to dispute 2nd 2f out: wknd over 1f out* **14/1**

32-4 9 14 **Chincoteague (IRE)**[12] 2231 4-9-2 **66** .... EddieAhern 3 35
(B J Meehan) *chsd ldng pair to 1/2-way: rdn and wknd over 3f out: eased whn no ch over 1f out: t.o* **3/1**[1]

2m 37.23s (-1.17) **Going Correction** +0.025s/f (Good) **9** Ran SP% **118.8**
Speed ratings (Par 103): **104,103,103,100,100 99,98,96,87**
toteswingers: 1&2 £22.70, 1&3 £4.30, 2&3 £14.10 CSF £108.35 CT £489.26 TOTE £4.80: £2.50, £7.70, £1.30; EX 137.10 Place 6 £22.89, Place 5 £19.16..
Owner W H Ponsonby **Bred** N Reid **Trained** Barbury Castle, Wilts

FOCUS
A low-grade handicap that was soundly run and the first five were pretty close to their marks.
Valdan(IRE) Official explanation: jockey said gelding hung badly right
Chincoteague(IRE) Official explanation: trainer said filly was unsuited by the track
T/Jkpt: Not won. T/Plt: £18.30 to a £1 stake. Pool:£99,876.72 - 3,966.28 winning tickets. T/Qpdt: £10.70 to a £1 stake. Pool:£4,240.13 - 291.07 winning tickets JN

2383 LEICESTER (R-H)

Monday, May 31

OFFICIAL GOING: Good to firm (good in places; 8.3)
Wind: Light, behind. Weather: Overcast

2598 ENDERBY MEDIAN AUCTION MAIDEN STKS 5f 2y
2:05 (2:06) (Class 5) 2-Y-O **£3,238** (£963; £481; £240) **Stalls Low**

Form RPR

1 **Little Lion Man** 2-9-3 0 .... MartinDwyer 1 79+
(P W Chapple-Hyam) *s.i.s: sn trcking ldrs: led over 1f out: shkn up and r.o wl* **1/1**[1]

6 2 2 ¼ **Zarazar**[53] 1180 2-9-3 0 .... JimmyFortune 2 69
(P D Evans) *led: edgd rt 2f out: sn rdn and hdd: styd on same pce ins fnl f* **7/2**[3]

3 nk **Loki's Revenge** 2-9-3 0 .... DaneO'Neill 4 68
(W Jarvis) *chsd ldr: rdn and ev ch over 1f out: styd on same pce ins fnl f* **5/2**[2]

4 1 ½ **Cornish Quest** 2-9-3 0 .... PatCosgrave 3 64+
(M H Tompkins) *dwlt: sn prom: pushed along 1/2-way: kpt on wl enough but nvr trbld ldrs* **16/1**

62.74 secs (2.74) **Going Correction** +0.025s/f (Good) **4** Ran SP% **106.7**
Speed ratings (Par 93): **79,75,74,72**
CSF £4.65 TOTE £2.00; EX 5.10.
Owner The Triple Crown Partnership **Bred** Cheveley Park Stud Ltd **Trained** Newmarket, Suffolk

FOCUS
With selective watering the going was described as good to firm, good in places. Little to go on with three of the four runners making their debuts for this maiden sprint run in a time just over three seconds slower than RP standard.

NOTEBOOK
Little Lion Man, a son of Kyllachy whose prodigy have plenty of speed about them, made a very satisfactory start to his career. After being a little slow coming out of the stalls, he travelled comfortably behind the front pair before taking the lead over a furlong out, only having to be pushed out to score readily. He looked well in the paddock beforehand and connections were very hopeful after some pleasing work at home. It's hard to assess what he achieved and he can only build on this. (op 5-4 tchd 10-11and 11-8 in places)
Zarazar had the benefit of a run which stood him in good stead here as he was soon at the front. He did his best to use his little experience to good effect but lacked the pace of the winner when headed. (op 10-3 tchd 5-1)
Loki's Revenge, by the same sire as the winner, also possessed plenty of speed on his dam's side. He broke well to sit prominently but lacked the pace of the winner nearing the final furlong. This was an encouraging debut as he was probably the greenest of the four so he should come on for this. (op 9-4)
Cornish Quest shaped with some promise, and although never having the pace to get on terms, he was staying on towards the finish. His breeding suggests he will do better over further in time (op 12-1)

2599 LEICESTERSHIRE LIFE H'CAP 5f 218y
2:40 (2:40) (Class 4) (0-80,77) 3-Y-O **£4,533** (£1,348; £674; £336) **Stalls Low**

Form RPR

21-0 1 **London Gold**[23] 1917 3-9-4 **77** .... DaneO'Neill 4 86
(H Candy) *chsd ldrs: rdn over 1f out: styd on to ld wl ins fnl f* **9/4**[1]

034- 2 ¾ **Pin Cushion**[231] 6737 3-9-4 **77** .... MartinDwyer 1 83
(B J Meehan) *chsd ldr: led over 2f out: edgd rt and hdd wl ins fnl f* **17/2**

6-13 3 2 ¼ **Kakapuka**[28] 1750 3-8-12 **74** .... RussKennemore(3) 7 73
(Mrs A L M King) *hld up: hdwy over 2f out: rdn and hung rt over 1f out: styd on same pce fnl f* **4/1**[3]

-210 4 1 ½ **Kummel Excess (IRE)**[55] 1147 3-8-10 **74** .... MatthewDavies(5) 8 68
(George Baker) *hld up: hdwy over 2f out: rdn over 1f out: no ex ins fnl f* **28/1**

3-03 5 2 ¼ **Imjin River (IRE)**[17] 2099 3-8-13 **72** .... PatCosgrave 3 59
(M H Tompkins) *chsd ldrs: rdn over 2f out: wknd ins fnl f* **7/2**[2]

-1P0 6 20 **Call To Arms (IRE)**[14] 2170 3-9-4 **77** .... AdrianNicholls 2 —
(M Johnston) *led: rdn and hdd over 2f out: wknd and eased over 1f out: t.o* **7/1**

-546 7 25 **Dancing Freddy (IRE)**[11] 2260 3-9-2 **75** .... JimmyFortune 5 —
(J G Given) *prom: pushed along 1/2-way: rdn and wknd wl over 1f out: eased: t.o* **15/2**

1m 12.91s (-0.09) **Going Correction** +0.025s/f (Good) **7** Ran SP% **111.2**
Speed ratings (Par 101): **101,100,97,95,92 65,32**
Tote Swingers: 1&2 £7.00, 1&3 £2.40, 2&3 £5.70 CSF £20.83 CT £68.76 TOTE £3.10: £2.60, £5.50; EX 20.20.
Owner John Simms **Bred** John Simms **Trained** Kingston Warren, Oxon

FOCUS
An open 6f 66-80 handicap ran at a strong pace. The front pair are unexposed and the form is rated on the positive side.
Call To Arms(IRE) Official explanation: jockey said gelding stopped quickly
Dancing Freddy(IRE) Official explanation: jockey said colt lost right-fore shoe and its action

2600 GILMORTON (S) STKS 1m 1f 218y
3:15 (3:15) (Class 6) 3-5-Y-O **£1,942** (£578; £288; £144) **Stalls High**

Form RPR

0-11 1 **Timocracy**[3] 2487 5-9-12 76 .... TonyCulhane 12 72
(A B Haynes) *chsd ldr: led wl over 2f out: sn rdn and hdd: rallied to ld ins fnl f: all out* **4/6**[1]

5-05 2 hd **Guga (IRE)**[11] 2259 4-9-7 55 .... (p) JimmyFortune 3 67
(Dr R D P Newland) *s.i.s: hld up: hdwy over 3f out: hrd rdn fr over 1f out: r.o* **7/1**[3]

0-03 3 2 ¼ **Applaude**[7] 2388 5-9-7 57 .... (b) MartinDwyer 8 62
(R C Guest) *a.p: led over 2f out: rdn over 1f out: hdd and no ex ins fnl f* **11/2**[2]

1-00 4 ½ **Ravens Rose**[37] 1537 3-7-13 59 .... Louis-PhilippeBeuzelin(3) 6 55
(J G Portman) *chsd ldrs: rdn and ev ch over 2f out: no ex ins fnl f* **10/1**

0466 5 12 **Major Pop (USA)**[24] 1866 3-8-6 62 ow2 .... (p) BarryMcHugh(3) 11 38
(R A Fahey) *s.i.s: hdwy 6f out: stmbld over 5f out: sn given reminders: wknd over 2f out* **10/1**

00 6 4 **Annie Moyles**[10] 2290 4-9-2 0 .... JerryO'Dwyer 5 24
(C N Kellett) *led: rdn and hdd wl over 2f out: wknd over 1f out* **66/1**

0 7 5 **Red Smokey (IRE)**[48] 1278 3-8-2 0 .... JamieMackay 4 13
(M H Tompkins) *hld up: a in rr: bhd fnl 3f* **33/1**

P0-0 8 6 **Miss Isle Control**[13] 2221 3-8-2 34 .... NickyMackay 10 —
(A J McCabe) *prom tl rdn and wknd wl over 2f out: t.o* **66/1**

0- 9 5 **Apurna**[236] 6595 5-8-13 57 .... RobertLButler(3) 9 —
(John A Harris) *hld up: a in rr: bhd fnl 4f: t.o* **28/1**

2m 8.69s (0.79) **Going Correction** +0.025s/f (Good)
WFA 3 from 4yo+ 14lb **9** Ran SP% **115.4**
Speed ratings (Par 101): **97,96,95,94,85 81,77,73,69**
Tote Swingers: 1&2 £2.80, 1&3 £7.10, 2&3 £2.90 CSF £5.75 TOTE £1.50: £1.02, £2.30, £1.30; EX 7.40.The winner was bought in for 6,500gns
Owner Ms J Loylert **Bred** Gainsborough Stud Management Ltd **Trained** Limpley Stoke, Bath

FOCUS
A weak seller in which the winner did not have to match his best.
Apurna Official explanation: jockey said mare slipped going into bend out of back straight

2601 LEICESTER MERCURY FAMILY FUN DAY FILLIES' H'CAP 7f 9y
3:50 (3:50) (Class 4) (0-80,78) 4-Y-O+
£6,231 (£1,866; £933; £467; £233; £117) **Stalls Low**

Form RPR

-445 1 **Arabian Pearl (IRE)**[16] 2129 4-8-9 **69** .... (b) JackMitchell 8 83
(P W Chapple-Hyam) *chsd ldr: rdn to ld and hung rt fr over 1f out: styd on* **4/1**[2]

415- 2 3 ¾ **Penzena**[175] 7664 4-8-12 **72** .... JimmyFortune 4 76
(A M Balding) *sn led: rdn and hdd over 1f out: styd on same pce fnl f* **7/2**[1]

3602 3 1 ½ **My Best Bet**[27] 1797 4-9-2 **76** .... MickyFenton 3 76
(Stef Higgins) *trckd ldrs racd keenly: rdn over 1f out: styd on same pce* **7/2**[1]

6-05 4 1 ¼ **Ogre (USA)**[10] 2284 5-9-2 **76** .... (t) DaneO'Neill 5 73
(P D Evans) *hld up in tch: rdn over 2f out: no ex fr over 1f out* **11/2**[3]

-066 5 ½ **Perfect Friend**[42] 1428 4-8-3 **70** .... RichardRowe(7) 7 65
(S Kirk) *hld up: hdwy over 4f out: rdn over 1f out: hung lft and wknd fnl f* **25/1**

50-4 6 3 ½ **Poppet's Lovein**[27] 1802 4-9-4 **78** .... RobertHavlin 2 64
(A B Haynes) *hld up: hdwy over 2f out: rdn and wknd wl over 1f out* **7/1**

55-5 7 4 ½ **Cut The Cackle (IRE)**[28] 1770 4-9-1 **75** .... AdamKirby 1 49
(P Winkworth) *unruly in stalls: broke wl: plld hrd: sn stdd and lost pl: rdn and wknd over 2f out* **12/1**

120- 8 2 **Romanticize**[345] 3163 4-8-12 **75** .... Louis-PhilippeBeuzelin(3) 6 43
(Dr J D Scargill) *hld up: hdwy 4f out: sn rdn: wknd over 2f out* **10/1**

1m 26.11s (-0.09) **Going Correction** +0.025s/f (Good) **8** Ran SP% **113.0**
Speed ratings (Par 102): **101,96,95,93,93 89,83,81**
Tote Swingers:1&2:£3.60, 2&3:£1.40, 1&3:£4.70 CSF £17.93 CT £52.67 TOTE £8.00: £3.20, £1.40, £1.10; EX 18.00.
Owner Arabian Shield 2004 **Bred** Derek Veitch And Eamon McEvoy **Trained** Newmarket, Suffolk

FOCUS
A tight fillies' handicap with very little between the front five in the betting. The winner is rated back to her best, backed up by the second.

2602 FOREST H'CAP 1m 1f 218y
4:25 (4:26) (Class 5) (0-70,70) 4-Y-O+ **£3,238** (£963; £481; £240) **Stalls High**

Form RPR

5020 1 **Scamperdale**[17] 2080 8-8-10 **62** .... JackMitchell 8 68
(B P J Baugh) *hld up: hdwy over 2f out: rdn to ld over 1f out: sn hung rt: r.o* **9/1**

6-00 2 1 ½ **Folio (IRE)**[17] 2080 10-8-8 **60** .... TonyCulhane 2 63+
(W J Musson) *hld up: rdn over 2f out: hdwy over 1f out: r.o* **6/1**[3]

-040 3 nk **Kyle Of Bute**[23] 1919 4-8-4 **56** oh1 .... JamieMackay 3 58+
(B P J Baugh) *hld up in tch: plld hrd: nt clr run and swtchd rt over 1f out: r.o* **14/1**

555 4 ¾ **Daniel Thomas (IRE)**[14] 2167 8-8-13 **68** .... (p) RussKennemore(3) 5 69
(Mrs A L M King) *s.s: hld up: rdn over 1f out: nt clr run: swtchd lft and r.o ins fnl f: nt rch ldrs* **20/1**

120- 5 1 ½ **Dream Of Olwyn (IRE)**[208] 7248 5-9-4 **70** .... LeeVickers 6 68
(J G Given) *chsd ldr: rdn over 2f out: sn hung rt: no ex ins fnl f* **11/1**

6-00 6 nk **Gallego**[13] 2204 8-8-8 **63** .... BarryMcHugh(3) 10 60+
(R J Price) *hld up: rdn over 2f out: nt clr run over 1f out: r.o: nvr trbld ldrs* **40/1**

/0-2 7 nk **Smirfy's Silver**[6] 2421 6-8-10 **62** .... PatCosgrave 7 59
(Mrs D J Sanderson) *set stdy pce tl qcknd over 3f out: rdn over 2f out: hdd over 1f out: no ex ins fnl f* **4/1**[2]

20-4 8 1 ¼ **Beauchamp Xiara**[17] 2081 4-9-1 **67** .... DaneO'Neill 9 61+
(H Candy) *chsd ldrs: rdn over 2f out: nt clr run fr over 1f out: eased ins fnl f* **9/4**[1]

2125 9 3 ½ **King's Icon (IRE)**[15] 1241 5-9-2 **68** .... (p) NickyMackay 4 55
(M Wigham) *hld up: rdn over 2f out: nvr on terms* **11/1**

2m 10.64s (2.74) **Going Correction** +0.025s/f (Good) **9** Ran SP% **105.6**
Speed ratings (Par 103): **90,88,88,87,86 86,86,85,82**
Tote Swingers:1&2:£25.70, 2&3:£9.30, 1&3:£25.70 CSF £51.15 CT £549.51 TOTE £8.50: £3.10, £2.00, £6.00; EX 63.80.
Owner Saddle Up Racing **Bred** Mrs J A Prescott **Trained** Audley, Staffs

FOCUS
The fancied Dancing Jest was withdrawn after playing up in the stalls and injuring her rider before this modest 56-70 middle-distance handicap, run at a steady pace. Several found trouble in a messy race. The winner showed his first turf form for nearly three years and the runner-up is rated to last year's level.

Beauchamp Xiara Official explanation: jockey said filly was denied a clear run

2603 ADRENALIN TATTOOS LUTON 10TH ANNIVERSARY MEDIAN AUCTION MAIDEN STKS — 1m 60y
5:00 (5:01) (Class 5) 3-Y-O — **£2,590** (£770; £385; £192) **Stalls** High

Form / RPR

00-4 **1** — **Veni Vedi Veci (IRE)**[26] 1824 3-8-12 72 — JimmyFortune 5 — 81+
(A M Balding) *mde all: rdn clr over 1f out: r.o* — **7/2**[2]

6- **2** 1 ½ — **Mazamorra (USA)**[211] 7199 3-8-12 0 — JerryO'Dwyer 8 — 76
(M Botti) *a.p: rdn to chse wnr and hung lft over 1f out: r.o* — **16/1**

53-4 **3** 1 ½ — **Christmas Carnival**[44] 1381 3-9-3 80 — MartinDwyer 2 — 78
(B J Meehan) *trckd ldrs: racd keenly: wnt 2nd over 2f out tl rdn over 1f out: no ex ins fnl f* — **8/11**[1]

4 3 ¼ — **Eastern Magic** 3-9-3 0 — JackMitchell 9 — 70
(R Hollinshead) *s.i.s: hld up: r.o ins fnl f: nrest at fin* — **66/1**

05- **5** 1 ¼ — **Before The War (USA)**[184] 7580 3-9-3 0 — DaneO'Neill 6 — 67
(L M Cumani) *hld up in tch: rdn over 2f out: styd on same pce appr fnl f* — **16/1**

0-3 **6** shd — **Lathaat**[12] 2227 3-8-12 0 — TadhgO'Shea 7 — 62
(J L Dunlop) *plld hrd: trckd wnr tl rdn over 2f out: wknd over 1f out* — **13/2**[3]

7 3 ½ — **Dazzled** 3-8-12 0 — PatCosgrave 1 — 54
(J R Fanshawe) *hld up: rdn over 2f out: wknd over 2f out* — **16/1**

06- **8** 2 ¾ — **Weliketobouggie**[313] 4201 3-9-3 0 — RobertHavlin 3 — 53
(A M Hales) *chsd ldrs tl rdn and wknd over 2f out* — **80/1**

0 **9** nk — **Shut Up Shapiro (IRE)**[24] 1870 3-9-3 0 — TonyCulhane 4 — 52
(George Baker) *hld up: rdn over 3f out: a in rr* — **66/1**

1m 46.29s (1.19) **Going Correction** +0.025s/f (Good) — **9 Ran SP% 115.3**
Speed ratings (Par 99): **95,93,92,88,87 87,83,81,80**
Tote Swingers: 1&2 £41.20, 1&3 £1.10, 2&3 £4.20 CSF £55.89 TOTE £5.90: £1.50, £6.70, £1.02; EX 58.20.
Owner Favourites Racing VIII **Bred** Meadowlands Stud **Trained** Kingsclere, Hants

FOCUS
Not the strongest of maidens. The favourite set the standard with a mark of 80, but disappointed. The winner made all at just an ordinary pace and the form is a little fluid with the winner and third setting the level.

2604 TIGERS APPRENTICE H'CAP — 1m 3f 183y
5:35 (5:35) (Class 6) (0-60,60) 4-Y-O+ — **£2,590** (£770; £385; £192) **Stalls** High

Form / RPR

000- **1** — **Channel Crossing**[221] 6969 8-8-6 47 — JohnCavanagh 8 — 54
(R Ford) *mde all: rdn over 3f out: styd on* — **17/2**

60/0 **2** 1 ¼ — **Contradiktive (IRE)**[38] 1503 4-8-0 46 oh1 — (b[1]) HarryBentley(5) 1 — 51
(J R Boyle) *chsd wnr over 7f: sn rdn: rallied and hung rt fnl f wnt 2nd again fnl 50yds* — **9/2**[2]

450- **3** 1 — **Carbon Print (USA)**[166] 5484 5-8-10 54 — RichardRowe(3) 2 — 57
(P R Webber) *s.i.s: hld up: hdwy over 3f out: rdn over 1f out: kpt on* — **7/1**

10-4 **4** nk — **Iguacu**[12] 2230 6-8-7 51 — NathanAlison(3) 7 — 54
(George Baker) *s.i.s: sn hld up in tch: chsd wnr over 4f out: rdn over 1f out: no ex ins fnl f* — **11/4**[1]

5264 **5** 7 — **Quince (IRE)**[7] 2388 7-9-0 60 — (v) SophieSilvester(5) 9 — 52
(J Pearce) *hld up: nvr on terms* — **9/2**[2]

3434 **6** shd — **Trysting Grove (IRE)**[53] 1188 9-8-8 49 — RyanClark 5 — 41
(E G Bevan) *hld up: hdwy over 3f out: rdn over 2f out: wknd over 1f out* — **5/1**[3]

050/ **7** 28 — **Adjami (IRE)**[37] 4493 9-8-2 50 — (p) IanBurns(7) 6 — —
(John A Harris) *prom to 1/2-way: t.o* — **20/1**

66/0 **8** 16 — **Ernmoor**[20] 2012 8-8-0 46 oh1 — AdamBeschizza(5) 3 — —
(A E Price) *plld hrd and prom: sddle slipped over 8f out: wknd over 3f out: t.o* — **16/1**

2m 33.46s (-0.44) **Going Correction** +0.025s/f (Good) — **8 Ran SP% 113.4**
Speed ratings (Par 101): **102,101,100,100,95 95,76,66**
Tote Swingers:1&2:£10.40, 2&3:£10.10, 1&3:£16.50 CSF £45.60 CT £282.88 TOTE £11.50: £3.70, £1.70, £3.40; EX 37.30 Place 6 £19.97, Place 5 £10.10..
Owner Miss Gillian Milner **Bred** M H Dixon **Trained** Butterton, Staffs

FOCUS
An open but weak apprentice 46-60 handicap run at a good pace. The winner showed his first form since the summer of 2008 but this is not a race to be too positive about.
Ernmoor Official explanation: jockey said saddle slipped
T/Plt: £168.10 to a £1 stake. Pool:£45,958.21 - 199.55 winning tickets T/Qpdt: £104.30 to a £1 stake. Pool:£3,274.07 - 23.22 winning tickets CR

1964 REDCAR (L-H)
Monday, May 31

OFFICIAL GOING: Good to firm (9.2)
Wind: Virtually nil Weather: Dry with sunny periods

2605 BUY YOUR TICKETS ON-LINE @ REDCARRACING.CO.UK MAIDEN AUCTION STKS — 5f
2:25 (2:26) (Class 5) 2-Y-O — **£2,524** (£745; £372) **Stalls** Centre

Form / RPR

4 **1** — **Silence Is Bliss (IRE)**[10] 2300 2-8-2 0 — RyanPowell(7) 8 — 67+
(J S Moore) *prom on outer: hdwy over 2f out: led 1 1/2f out: rdn and edgd rt ent fnl f: kpt on* — **10/3**[2]

4623 **2** 1 ½ — **Roodee Queen**[10] 2292 2-8-5 0 — SaleemGolam 3 — 58+
(Patrick Morris) *trckd ldrs: effrt and swtchd rt wl over 1f out: rdn to chse wnr and edgd lft ins fnl f: kpt on* — **4/1**[3]

3 2 ¼ — **Chestival (IRE)** 2-8-4 0 — PJMcDonald 1 — 49
(Patrick Morris) *cl up: led over 2f out: rdn and hdd 1 1/2f out: drvn and kpt on same pce fnl f* — **9/1**

0 **4** shd — **Moving Picture**[61] 1065 2-8-10 0 — TomEaves 2 — 55
(B M R Haslam) *led: pushed along 1/2-way: hdd and rdn 2f out: kpt on same pce appr fnl f* — **14/1**

005 **5** 3 — **Dispol Snapper (IRE)**[16] 2111 2-8-11 0 — JoeFanning 6 — 45
(P T Midgley) *in tch: rdn along and outpcd over 2f out: hung lft wl over 1f out: n.d* — **12/1**

6 1 ¾ — **Hereselle (IRE)** 2-8-5 0 — GrahamGibbons 7 — 32
(T D Barron) *in tch: rdn along 1/2-way: sn outpcd and bhd* — **5/2**[1]

7 nse — **Plumsum** 2-8-4 0 — FranciscoDaSilva 4 — 31
(N Bycroft) *a towards rr: rdn along over 2f out and sn outpcd* — **20/1**

60.56 secs (1.96) **Going Correction** 0.0s/f (Good) — **7 Ran SP% 100.8**
Speed ratings (Par 93): **84,81,78,77,73 70,70**
toteswinger: 1&2 £2.10, 1&3 £4.00, 2&3 £3.60 CSF £13.00 TOTE £2.90: £1.70, £1.80; EX 13.10.
Owner J S Moore **Bred** Mrs E Thompson **Trained** Upper Lambourn, Berks

FOCUS
This was a really weak juvenile maiden, a seller in all but name.

NOTEBOOK
Silence Is Bliss(IRE) caught the eye keeping on well after a slow start in selling company on his debut and he clearly learnt from that experience. He showed plenty of early speed this time and kept on well to win readily, but this is moderate form. (op 7-2)
Roodee Queen ran her race but simply found one too good and she's now 0-6. She probably needs dropping in grade. (op 7-2)
Chestival(IRE) made little appeal on pedigree but she showed ability, displaying plenty of natural speed. (op 12-1)
Moving Picture showed nothing on his debut on Fibresand back in March but this was better.
Hereselle(IRE) is related to a few winners and was prominent in the betting, but she showed little. (tchd 11-4 and 3-1 in a place)

2606 MARKET CROSS JEWELLERS MAIDEN H'CAP — 1m 6f 19y
3:00 (3:01) (Class 6) (0-65,65) 3-Y-O — **£1,842** (£544; £272) **Stalls** Low

Form / RPR

-543 **1** — **Dubara Reef (IRE)**[20] 1989 3-8-2 46 — SilvestreDeSousa 2 — 50
(Paul Green) *trckd ldrs on inner: hdwy over 3f out: rdn to ld over 1f out: drvn ins fnl f and kpt on wl towards fin* — **10/3**[2]

006- **2** nk — **Escape Artist**[292] 4888 3-8-5 49 — GrahamGibbons 10 — 52+
(T D Easterby) *hld up towards rr: gd hdwy on outer wl over 2f out: rdn to chse ldrs over 1f out: drvn to chal and hung lft ins fnl f: ev ch tl no ex towards fin* — **3/1**[1]

00-6 **3** 1 ¾ — **Dubawi King**[16] 2131 3-8-4 48 — JoeFanning 9 — 49+
(N Tinkler) *hld up and bhd: hdwy 3f out: swtchd rt and chsd ldrs 2f out: rdn over 1f out and sn edgd lft: drvn and styd on ins fnl f* — **20/1**

466- **4** 1 — **Leopard Hills (IRE)**[313] 4187 3-9-0 65 — LeeTopliss(7) 5 — 64
(J Howard Johnson) *hld up in tch: hdwy over 3f out: chsd ldrs 2f out: sn rdn: n.m.r and drvn 1f out: kpt on same pce ins fnl f* — **16/1**

6303 **5** nk — **Frameit (IRE)**[9] 2333 3-8-10 61 — (b) RyanPowell(7) 6 — 61+
(J S Moore) *led: rdn clr 4f out: drvn 2f out: hdd wl over 1f out: edgd lft and wkng whn hmpd ins fnl f* — **7/1**[3]

4-64 **6** ¾ — **Tia Juana (IRE)**[21] 1982 3-9-4 62 — PJMcDonald 8 — 60
(B M R Haslam) *hld up in rr: hdwy 3f out: rdn to chse ldrs wl over 1f out: drvn and ch on inner ins fnl f: wknd last 100yds* — **16/1**

0-50 **7** ¾ — **Henry Havelock**[20] 1992 3-9-1 59 — TonyHamilton 7 — 58+
(C Grant) *chsd ldr: rdn along 3f out: drvn 2f out: one pce and hld whn hmpd ins fnl f* — **33/1**

000 **8** 5 — **I Got Music**[35] 1572 3-7-11 46 oh1 — PaulPickard(5) 13 — 36
(K G Reveley) *midfield: hdwy on wd outside and in tch 1/2-way: rdn along 3f out: drvn over 2f out and kpt on same pce* — **20/1**

5264 **9** 1 ¾ — **Rosewood Lad**[6] 2412 3-8-5 49 ow2 — SaleemGolam 14 — 36
(J S Moore) *chsd ldrs: rdn along wl over 2f out: drvn and wkng whn n.m.r over 1f out* — **8/1**

60-4 **10** 1 ¾ — **Lady Pacha**[24] 1866 3-8-2 46 oh1 — (v[1]) FrannyNorton 1 — 31
(T J Pitt) *hld up in rr: hdwy on inner 4f out: rdn 3f out: wknd over 2f out* — **12/1**

-050 **11** nse — **Swain's Quest (USA)**[11] 2248 3-9-3 61 — TomQueally 4 — 46
(Eve Johnson Houghton) *chsd ldrs on inner: rdn along over 3f out: wknd over 2f out* — **16/1**

000- **12** 2 ¼ — **Priestley (IRE)**[199] 7376 3-7-11 46 oh1 — DeclanCannon(5) 11 — 28
(J G Given) *chsd ldrs: hdwy over 3f out: rdn along over 2f out: sn wknd* — **16/1**

0-00 **13** 21 — **Lucky Traveller**[21] 1970 3-8-2 46 oh1 — DuranFentiman 12 — —
(T D Easterby) *a in rr: rdn along over 4f out: sn lost tch and bhd* — **25/1**

3m 7.49s (2.79) **Going Correction** 0.0s/f (Good) — **13 Ran SP% 119.2**
Speed ratings (Par 97): **92,91,90,90,90 89,89,86,85,84 84,83,71**
toteswinger: 1&2 £2.60, 1&3 £9.20, 2&3 £29.00 CSF £12.86 CT £175.07 TOTE £3.60: £1.10, £1.40, £6.40; EX 14.90.
Owner The Four Aces **Bred** M Duffy **Trained** Lydiate, Merseyside

FOCUS
A moderate contest for maidens with very little solid form on show, and not form to dwell on.
Frameit(IRE) Official explanation: jockey said gelding hung right-handed
Rosewood Lad Official explanation: jockey said gelding hung left-handed

2607 TOTEEXACTA FLEXI BETTING H'CAP — 1m 2f
3:35 (3:35) (Class 4) (0-85,85) 3-Y-O — **£5,180** (£1,541; £770; £384) **Stalls** Low

Form / RPR

2-13 **1** — **Gold Rules**[20] 2002 3-9-7 85 — J-PGuillambert 5 — 93+
(L M Cumani) *t.k.h: hld up in rr: swtchd rt and hdwy wl over 1f out: rdn to chal ent fnl f: kpt on u.p to ld nr fin* — **7/2**[2]

0-21 **2** ½ — **Shimmering Moment (USA)**[18] 2051 3-9-3 81 — TomQueally 1 — 88
(H R A Cecil) *trckd ldng pair on inner: hdwy 3f out: rdn to ld 1 1/2f out: drvn ent fnl f: hdd and no ex nr fin* — **2/1**[1]

2-40 **3** nk — **Aquarian Spirit**[16] 2117 3-9-2 80 — TonyHamilton 6 — 86
(R A Fahey) *cl up: led 3f out: rdn 2f out: hdd 1 1/2f out and sn drvn: ev ch tl no ex towards fin* — **9/1**

2143 **4** 5 — **Beneath**[16] 2125 3-9-2 80 — AndreaAtzeni 4 — 76
(Pat Eddery) *hld up: hdwy over 3f out: rdn along 2f out: drvn and no imp over 1f out* — **11/2**

01-1 **5** 3 — **Judiciary (IRE)**[17] 2101 3-9-4 82 — TedDurcan 2 — 72
(Mahmood Al Zarooni) *trckd ldng pair: hdwy over 3f out: chal over 2f out: sn rdn and wknd wl over 1f out* — **9/2**[3]

-442 **6** 11 — **Omaruru (IRE)**[17] 2072 3-8-7 71 — JoeFanning 3 — 39
(M Johnston) *set stdy pce: rdn along 4f out: hdd 3f out and sn wknd: eased wl over 1f out* — **6/1**

2m 7.77s (0.67) **Going Correction** 0.0s/f (Good) — **6 Ran SP% 113.4**
Speed ratings (Par 101): **97,96,96,92,89 81**
toteswinger: 1&2 £1.60, 1&3 £1.70, 2&3 £10.90 CSF £11.16 TOTE £5.10: £2.10, £1.60; EX 12.60.
Owner Leonidas Marinopoulos **Bred** Langham Hall Stud **Trained** Newmarket, Suffolk

FOCUS
A decent 3-y-o handicap run at a fair pace with the first three all rated as improvers.

2608 TOTETRIFECTA FLEXI BETTING ZETLAND GOLD CUP (H'CAP) — 1m 2f
4:10 (4:10) (Class 2) (0-105,99) 3-Y-O+ **£22,666** (£6,744; £3,370; £1,683) **Stalls** Low

Form / RPR

0-14 **1** — **Forte Dei Marmi**[19] 2027 4-9-3 92 — J-PGuillambert 8 — 104+
(L M Cumani) *hld up in tch: smooth hdwy over 2f out: trckd ldr over 1f out: swtchd lft and effrt to chal ent fnl f: rdn and qcknd to ld last 100yds* — **4/1**[2]

03-1 **2** 1 — **Sweet Lightning**[25] 1831 5-9-4 93 — TomEaves 5 — 103+
(M Dods) *trckd ldrs: smooth hdwy to ld over 2f out: jnd and rdn ent fnl f: hdd and nt qckn last 100yds* — **11/4**[1]

3010 **3** 1 1/2 **Albaqaa**[30] 1697 5-9-3 **99**........ LeeTopliss(7) 10 106
(R A Fahey) *s.i.s: hld up and bhd: hdwy 3f out: rdn to chse ldrs 2f out: drvn and kpt on ins fnl f: nrst fin* **7/1**[3]

1214 **4** 2 1/2 **Fujin Dancer (FR)**[20] 1990 5-8-0 **80** ow1........(p) AmyRyan(5) 4 86+
(K A Ryan) *hld up in midfield: hdwy on inner and nt clr run wl over 1f out: swtchd rt and rdn ent fnl f: kpt on* **16/1**

1512 **5** 1/2 **Follow The Flag (IRE)**[5] 2444 6-8-6 **86**........(p) DeclanCannon(5) 7 87
(A J McCabe) *trckd ldrs: hdwy over 3f out: rdn to chse ldrs 2f out: sn drvn: edgd lft and one pce appr fnl f* **14/1**

0-62 **6** 2 **Changing The Guard**[5] 2435 4-8-10 **85**........ TonyHamilton 1 82
(R A Fahey) *trckd ldng pair: effrt wl over 2f out and sn rdn: drvn and wknd over 1f out* **8/1**

0504 **7** 2 **Reve De Nuit (USA)**[26] 1829 4-8-8 **88**........ TobyAtkinson(5) 12 81
(A J McCabe) *hld up in midfield: effrt on outer over 3f out: rdn along over 2f out: sn no imp* **33/1**

21-1 **8** 1 1/2 **Oneofapear (IRE)**[24] 1889 4-8-12 **87**........ PJMcDonald 2 77
(G A Swinbank) *led: rdn along 3f out: hdd over 2f out and sn drvn: grad wknd* **8/1**

0232 **9** hd **Daaweitza**[7] 2395 7-8-4 **79**........(b) RoystonFfrench 3 69
(B Ellison) *dwlt: a towards rr* **16/1**

4422 **10** 1 **Rosbay (IRE)**[17] 2084 6-8-5 **80**........ DuranFentiman 9 68
(T D Easterby) *hld up: a towards rr* **16/1**

0041 **11** nse **Cairnsmore**[10] 2282 4-9-8 **97**........ JoeFanning 11 85
(M Johnston) *cl up: effrt over 3f out: rdn along over 2f out: sn wknd: fin lame* **8/1**

2m 4.75s (-2.35) **Going Correction** 0.0s/f (Good) 11 Ran SP% **119.8**
Speed ratings (Par 109): **109,108,107,105,104 103,101,100,100,99 99**
toteswinger: 1&2 £2.90, 1&3 £5.50, 2&3 £5.20 CSF £15.71 CT £76.24 TOTE £4.80: £1.90, £1.80, £2.30; EX 16.90 Trifecta £106.60 Pool £597.98 - 4.15 winning units..
Owner Fittocks Stud **Bred** Fittocks Stud **Trained** Newmarket, Suffolk

FOCUS
A quality handicap run at a decent pace. The first two look progressive, the third is a solid guide and the fourth was close to form.

NOTEBOOK
Forte Dei Marmi ◆ didn't find as much as had looked likely when apparently unsuited by really quick ground at York last time, and there was some doubt over his participation here, with conditions again fast, but he coped just fine. A strong-travelling type, he was given a patient ride and responded well when coming under pressure to win convincingly. He looks a Group horse in the making but can stick to handicaps for the time being. He's in the Royal Hunt Cup, for which he has picked a 5lb penalty, but it remains to be seen whether he would be suited by the drop back to 1m, and perhaps the Wolferton Handicap will be his race should connections send him to Ascot. In the slightly longer term, the John Smith's Cup looks the logical target.
Sweet Lightning ◆, 3lb higher than when winning at Chester on his reappearance/debut for this yard, probably got to the front a bit too soon after making effortless headway, but it's unlikely he would have beaten the winner whatever the case. He looks the type to make further improvement. (op 7-2)
Albaqaa plugged on in the straight after being dropped in from his wide draw, but he was never a threat to the front pair. (op 13-2 tchd 15-2)
Fujin Dancer(FR) lost his place after being short of room against the rail around 2f out, and as such he can be rated a bit better than the bare form. Official explanation: jockey said gelding was denied a clear run (op 20-1)
Follow The Flag(IRE) is in tremendous form right now and this was another decent effort.
Changing The Guard was not at his best.
Oneofapear(IRE) couldn't defy a mark 5lb higher than when winning at Ripon on his reappearance. Official explanation: jockey said gelding was unsuited by the good to firm ground (op 15-2)
Daaweitza Official explanation: jockey said gelding missed the break
Cairnsmore, 4lb higher than when making all at Chepstow last time, couldn't dominate and was well beaten. Official explanation: vet said gelding returned lame (op 7-1)

2609 RACING UK ON SKY 432 MEDIAN AUCTION MAIDEN STKS 6f
4:45 (4:47) (Class 5) 3-Y-O £2,396 (£712; £356; £177) Stalls Centre

Form RPR

33 **1** **Feel The Heat**[3] 2517 3-9-3 0........ TomEaves 5 79
(B Smart) *cl up: led wl over 2f out: rdn wl over 1f out: drvn ins fnl f and kpt on wl* **3/1**[2]

42 **2** 3/4 **Ezra Church (IRE)**[20] 1991 3-9-3 0........ GrahamGibbons 4 77
(T D Barron) *led: rdn along and hdd wl over 2f out: drvn over 1f out: kpt on u.p fnl f* **4/5**[1]

4-23 **3** 2 1/2 **Powerful Pierre**[24] 1868 3-8-12 71........(p) PatrickDonaghy(5) 1 69
(Jedd O'Keeffe) *chsd ldrs: rdn along and outpcd 1/2-way: styd on u.p appr fnl f* **8/1**[3]

4 shd **Panama Jack** 3-9-3 0........ TonyHamilton 6 69+
(R A Fahey) *towards rr: hdwy over 2f out: rdn wl over 1f out: kpt on ins fnl f: nrst fin* **9/1**

0-4 **5** 1/2 **Mighty Aphrodite**[30] 1685 3-8-12 0........ SaleemGolam 3 62
(Rae Guest) *chsd ldrs: rdn along over 2f out: drvn wl over 1f out: wknd ent fnl f* **9/1**

400 **6** 2 1/2 **Pelmanism**[16] 2114 3-9-3 67........ PJMcDonald 2 59
(K A Ryan) *cl up: rdn along over 2f out: sn drvn and wknd over 1f out* **25/1**

00-0 **7** 8 **Woldgate**[21] 1967 3-8-10 57........ GarethEdwards(7) 7 33
(G R Oldroyd) *hung lft thrght: in rr tl outpcd and bhd fr wl over 2f out* **50/1**

1m 11.82s (0.02) **Going Correction** 0.0s/f (Good) 7 Ran SP% **117.5**
Speed ratings (Par 99): **99,98,94,94,93 90,79**
toteswinger: 1&2 £1.50, 1&3 £2.50, 2&3 £2.80 CSF £6.01 TOTE £4.20: £2.00, £1.10; EX 6.90.
Owner T G & Mrs M E Holdcroft **Bred** Bearstone Stud **Trained** Hambleton, N Yorks

FOCUS
An ordinary maiden with the winner improving and the placed horses rated to form.

2610 TOTESWINGER FLEXI BETTING H'CAP 1m 6f 19y
5:20 (5:20) (Class 6) (0-65,63) 4-Y-O+ £1,748 (£520; £260; £129) Stalls Low

Form RPR

414- **1** **Simple Jim (FR)**[24] 7080 6-8-13 **55**........ SilvestreDeSousa 9 64+
(J Hetherton) *hld up towards rr: gd hdwy on outer wl over 2f out: rdn to chse ldrs over 1f out: hung lft and styd on ins fnl f: led nr line* **4/1**[2]

46 **2** shd **Ocean Bright (USA)**[13] 2214 4-8-3 **45**........(b) FrannyNorton 11 53
(J G Given) *trckd ldng pair: hdwy 3f out: rdn to chal wl over 1f out: drvn to ld wl ins fnl f: edgd rt and bmpd: hdd nr line* **14/1**

405- **3** 1 **Zefooha (FR)**[243] 6385 6-9-4 **60**........ DuranFentiman 8 67
(T D Walford) *led to 1/2-way: prom tl led again over 3f out: rdn 2f out: drvn over 1f out: hdd and no ex wl ins fnl f* **9/1**

1006 **4** 2 1/4 **Dulce Domum**[10] 2302 4-7-12 **45**........ DeclanCannon(5) 4 49
(A B Haynes) *trckd ldrs on inner: effrt 4f out: rdn along 3f out: drvn wl over 1f out: kpt on same pce ins fnl f* **22/1**

0-02 **5** 4 **Master Nimbus**[6] 2424 10-9-4 **60**........(t) GrahamGibbons 3 58
(J J Quinn) *trckd ldrs: hdwy 4f out: cl up wl over 2f out and sn rdn: drvn and ev ch over 1f out: wknd ent fnl f* **13/8**[1]

06/0 **6** 3/4 **Maneki Neko (IRE)**[10] 2277 8-9-2 **58**........ TonyHamilton 2 55
(E W Tuer) *trckd ldr: led 1/2-way: rdn along 4f out: hdd over 3f out: cl up tl drvn and wknd appr fnl f* **20/1**

5221 **7** 1 **Blackstone Vegas**[21] 1984 4-8-12 **54**........(v) PJMcDonald 12 50
(D Shaw) *in tch: effrt over 4f out: rdn along 3f out: drvn and no imp fnl 2f* **10/1**

3-05 **8** 1 **Obara D'Avril (FR)**[6] 2424 8-8-0 **47**........(p) PaulPickard(5) 10 41
(S G West) *a towards rr* **33/1**

60-0 **9** shd **Cripsey Brook**[4] 2464 12-7-13 **48**........ MatthewLawson(7) 1 42
(K G Reveley) *a towards rr* **16/1**

5-60 **10** 1/2 **Hi Dancer**[18] 2060 7-9-2 **63**........ AmyRyan(5) 7 57
(B M R Haslam) *midfield: hdwy over 3f out: rdn along wl over 2f out: sn wknd* **11/2**[3]

0/0- **11** 7 **Crosby Jemma**[26] 221 6-8-4 **46** ow1........ RoystonFfrench 5 30
(M E Sowersby) *a towards rr* **16/1**

3m 7.16s (2.46) **Going Correction** 0.0s/f (Good) 11 Ran SP% **123.1**
Speed ratings (Par 101): **92,91,91,90,87 87,86,86,86,85 81**
toteswinger: 1&2 £10.50, 1&3 £8.40, 2&3 £18.70 CSF £60.06 CT £490.94 TOTE £5.50: £2.30, £4.40, £2.80; EX 49.60 Place 6 £23.98, Place 5 £8.02..
Owner R G Fell **Bred** Snc Haras Des Peltrais, Laurent Thibault **Trained** Norton, N Yorks

FOCUS
A moderate race run at a steady pace and the form is somewhat muddling, with the third and fourth the best guides.
Master Nimbus Official explanation: trainer had no explanation for the poor form shown
T/Plt: £35.40 to a £1 stake. Pool:£50,518.51. 1,038.84 winning tickets T/Qpdt: £12.80 to a £1 stake. Pool:£2,528.10. 146.10 winning tickets JR

2615 - (Foreign Racing) - See Raceform Interactive

2598 LEICESTER (R-H)
Tuesday, June 1

OFFICIAL GOING: Good to firm (good in places) changing to good after race 1 (2:15)
Wind: Light half-behind Weather: Raining

2616 E B F FOREST MAIDEN FILLIES' STKS 5f 2y
2:15 (2:17) (Class 4) 2-Y-O £5,180 (£1,541; £770; £384) Stalls Low

Form RPR

1 **Crying Lightening (IRE)** 2-9-0 0........ MartinDwyer 6 84+
(P W Chapple-Hyam) *s.i.s: hdwy 1/2-way: r.o to ld and edgd rt towards fin* **7/2**[2]

2 **2** 1/2 **Elshabakiya (IRE)**[12] 2251 2-9-0 0........ NeilCallan 7 82+
(C E Brittain) *plld hrd and prom: led over 1f out: sn rdn: hung lft ins fnl f: hdd towards fin* **11/8**[1]

2 **3** 1 1/4 **Catalinas Diamond (IRE)**[9] 2358 2-8-9 0........ SophieDoyle(5) 9 78
(B W Duke) *hld up: hdwy 2f out: rdn and edgd lft ins fnl f: no ex towards fin* **15/2**

6 **4** 3 1/4 **Countess Ellen (IRE)**[12] 2251 2-9-0 0........ RichardKingscote 5 66
(Tom Dascombe) *led 4f out: rdn and hdd over 1f out: edgd lft and no ex fnl f* **6/1**[3]

5 1 **Star Today** 2-9-0 0........ KierenFallon 3 62
(B J Meehan) *w ldrs: pushed along 1/2-way: styd on same pce appr fnl f* **15/2**

6 shd **My Elliemay** 2-9-0 0........ CathyGannon 8 62
(P D Evans) *prom: rdn 1/2-way: styd on same pce fr over 1f out* **66/1**

7 nk **Princess Izzy** 2-9-0 0........ PatCosgrave 1 61
(M H Tompkins) *hld up in tch: rdn 1/2-way: styd on same pce appr fnl f* **66/1**

8 hd **Water Ice** 2-9-0 0........ RichardSmith 4 60
(Tom Dascombe) *led 1f: chsd ldrs: rdn over 1f out: no ex* **50/1**

9 5 **Dubai Affair** 2-9-0 0........ SteveDrowne 2 42
(H Morrison) *dwlt: sn pushed along in rr: lost tch over 1f out* **20/1**

61.77 secs (1.77) **Going Correction** 0.0s/f (Good) 9 Ran SP% **111.9**
Speed ratings (Par 92): **85,84,82,77,75 75,74,74,66**
toteswingers:1&2:£2.10, 1&3:£4.10, 2&3:£2.90 CSF £8.19 TOTE £3.90: £1.30, £1.30, £1.80; EX 13.60 Trifecta £72.50 Pool: £422.67 - 4.31 winning units..
Owner J Barton & C Pizarro **Bred** Paulyn Limited **Trained** Newmarket, Suffolk

FOCUS
The ground was changed to good following this opener. A non-bonus maiden, but it appeared to be a red-hot contest nonetheless. They looked a quality bunch of fillies in the paddock, the form is rated around the placed horses and the race should produce some nice winners.

NOTEBOOK
Crying Lightening(IRE) ◆, a £26,000 first foal of a 1m winner, created a fine impression on debut and could be quite smart. Having recovered from a sluggish start to track the leaders, she travelled well before showing a fine attitude under pressure, really lengthening and responding well to a couple of taps with the whip. It was no surprise to hear afterwards that she may go to Royal Ascot, and the Queen Mary was mentioned as the likely target, although it may well be that another furlong will suit her better in due course, so perhaps the Albany will be considered. (tchd 3-1)
Elshabakiya(IRE), a promising second on debut at Sandown, raced keenly through the early stages this time and was picked off late on by a potentially above-average type. The owner's racing manager Bruce Raymond said before that this daughter of Diktat is Clive Brittain's best filly, and she certainly has the size and scope to do better. The general feeling is that she'll appreciate a step up in trip, although she will need to settle better in future. (op Evens tchd 6-4)
Catalinas Diamond(IRE) confirmed the ability she showed when second on debut at Bath (probably would have won had she not run green) but simply ran into a couple of useful types. Clear of the remainder, she's pretty decent in her own right and is one to keep on-side. (op 10-1 tchd 7-1)
Countess Ellen(IRE), well backed, improved on the form she showed when 51/2l behind today's runner-up on debut and is going the right way. (op 14-1 tchd 16-1)
Star Today ◆, an 80,000euros half-sister to, among others, smart 7f-1m performer Mia's Boy out of a quite useful 1m2f winner, showed good early speed but was clueless when first coming off the bridle before keeping on reasonably well near the line. There should be improvement forthcoming. (op 13-2 tchd 8-1)
My Elliemay showed plenty of ability on debut.
Princess Izzy ran better than her position suggests.
Water Ice looks to have her share of ability. (op 80-1)

2617 STATHERN CLAIMING STKS 7f 9y
2:45 (2:46) (Class 6) 3-Y-O £1,942 (£578; £288; £144) Stalls Low

Form RPR

1214 **1** **Maoi Chinn Tire (IRE)**[11] 2283 3-9-0 74........(p) RichardHughes 3 73
(J S Moore) *led to 1/2-way: rdn to ld over 1f out: r.o: eased nr fin* **6/4**[1]

3100 **2** *nk* **Juicy Pear (IRE)**[18] 2089 3-8-7 72..............................(v[1]) IanBurns(7) 5 72
(M L W Bell) *hld up in tch: racd keenly: rdn over 1f out: r.o* **13/2**
1540 **3** *2* **Kirsty's Boy (IRE)**[7] 2415 3-8-10 70.............................. LiamKeniry 7 63
(J S Moore) *chsd ldr tl led 1/2-way: rdn and hdd over 1f out: no ex ins fnl f* **5/1**[2]
6510 **4** *shd* **Petrocelli**[14] 2203 3-7-13 70..............................(b) DeclanCannon(5) 8 57
(A J McCabe) *chsd ldrs: rdn over 1f out: hung lft and styd on same pce ins fnl f* **20/1**
4000 **5** *4* **Baby Judge (IRE)**[8] 2385 3-7-13 52.............................. SophieDoyle(5) 1 46
(M C Chapman) *prom: rdn over 2f out: wknd ins fnl f* **66/1**
-001 **6** *8* **Sophie's Beau (USA)**[8] 2385 3-8-13 74.............................. MarkCoumbe(5) 2 38
(M C Chapman) *plld hrd and sn prom: rdn over 2f out: wknd over 1f out* **10/1**
21-0 **7** *2 1/4* **Tucker's Law**[25] 1873 3-8-6 65.............................. FergusSweeney 4 20
(B R Millman) *hld up: plld hrd: hdwy over 2f out: rdn and wknd over 1f out* **10/1**
1330 **8** *6* **Moors Gorse**[21] 2005 3-7-13 62.............................. DavidProbert 6 —
(R Hollinshead) *free to post: half rrd s: plld hrd and hdwy over 4f out: rdn 1/2-way: wknd over 1f out: eased* **11/2**[3]

1m 27.18s (0.98) **Going Correction** 0.0s/f (Good) **8** Ran SP% **109.8**
Speed ratings (Par 97): **94,93,91,91,86 77,74,68**
toteswingers:1&2:£3.40, 1&3:£2.60, 2&3:£4.40 CSF £10.61 TOTE £2.80: £1.40, £2.10, £1.50; EX 10.40 Trifecta £44.40 Pool: £411.21 - 6.85 winning units..
Owner W Adams & J S Moore **Bred** Mrs E Thompson **Trained** Upper Lambourn, Berks

FOCUS
The first four finishers, who came clear, were all officially rated in the 70s and this was a fair claimer. The form is not that solid though with the winner the best guide, and not a race to view positively.

2618 ABBEY PARK H'CAP 7f 9y
3:15 (3:15) (Class 4) (0-80,80) 3-Y-O **£4,209** (£1,252; £625; £312) **Stalls** Low

Form RPR
5-16 **1** **Maid In Heaven (IRE)**[29] 1776 3-9-3 **76**.............................. ShaneKelly 6 91+
(W R Swinburn) *a.p: swtchd rt over 1f out: r.o to ld nr fin: readily* **8/1**
4-21 **2** *nk* **Suited And Booted (IRE)**[29] 1782 3-9-6 **79**.............................. RichardHughes 10 91
(R Hannon) *s.i.s: hld up: hdwy over 2f out: rdn to ld ins fnl f: hdd nr fin* **9/2**[2]
-062 **3** *2 1/4* **The Hermitage (IRE)**[8] 2394 3-9-0 **73**.............................. RoystonFfrench 11 79
(M Johnston) *chsd ldr tl led 4f out: rdn and edgd lft over 1f out: hdd and unable qck ins fnl f* **12/1**
6516 **4** *2 1/4* **Thrust Control (IRE)**[10] 2348 3-9-1 **74**.............................. FranciscoDaSilva 4 74
(B Ellison) *s.i.s: hld up: rdn over 2f out: styd on fnl f: nt trble ldrs* **33/1**
3-13 **5** *5* **Red Gulch**[11] 2287 3-9-6 **79**.............................. FrankieDettori 9 66
(E A L Dunlop) *hld up in tch: rdn over 1f out: wknd fnl f* **3/1**[1]
3000 **6** *3/4* **Transfixed (IRE)**[7] 2416 3-8-13 **72**.............................. CathyGannon 3 57
(P D Evans) *chsd ldrs: rdn 1/2-way: wknd over 1f out* **40/1**
30-4 **7** *1* **Merchant Of Medici**[24] 1934 3-8-11 **70**.............................. MartinDwyer 14 52
(W R Muir) *s.i.s: hdwy over 4f out: rdn and wknd over 1f out* **12/1**
2-20 **8** *6* **Rolling Hills (IRE)**[19] 2052 3-9-1 **74**.............................. DaneO'Neill 12 40
(H Candy) *hld up: rdn 1/2-way: sn wknd* **15/2**[3]
0-20 **9** *7* **Kilmanseck**[34] 1619 3-8-11 **70**.............................. NeilCallan 7 17
(Eve Johnson Houghton) *mid-div: rdn 1/2-way: wknd 2f out* **25/1**
1-60 **10** *1/2* **Scottish Boogie (IRE)**[12] 2253 3-9-1 **74**.............................. WilliamBuick 8 19
(S Kirk) *hld up: rdn and wknd over 2f out* **9/1**
61-0 **11** *1 1/2* **Number One Guy**[18] 2089 3-8-13 **72**.............................. PatCosgrave 15 13
(M H Tompkins) *hld up: rdn 1/2-way: wknd over 2f out* **12/1**
420- **12** *13* **Quaker Parrot**[157] 7846 3-9-7 **80**.............................. RichardKingscote 2 —
(Tom Dascombe) *led 3f: chsd ldrs: rdn over 2f out: sn wknd: t.o* **40/1**
40-6 **13** *4 1/2* **Fairy Promises (USA)**[32] 1658 3-9-5 **78**.............................. AndreaAtzeni 5 —
(Pat Eddery) *chsd ldrs tl wknd wl over 2f out: t.o* **14/1**

1m 25.92s (-0.28) **Going Correction** 0.0s/f (Good) **13** Ran SP% **117.5**
Speed ratings (Par 101): **101,100,98,95,89 88,87,80,72,72 70,55,50**
toteswingers:1&2:£7.60, 1&3:£10.50, 2&3:£5.90 CSF £41.72 CT £432.57 TOTE £9.90: £2.70, £2.10, £3.80; EX 72.60 Trifecta £233.40 Part won. Pool: £315.45 - 0.42 winning units..
Owner Delightful Dozen **Bred** Mrs C Hartery **Trained** Aldbury, Herts

FOCUS
A fair handicap run in a time 1.26 seconds quicker than the earlier claimer won by the 74-rated Maoi Chinn Tire. The form looks decent for the grade with unexposed sorts fighting out the finish.

2619 SWANNINGTON H'CAP (DIV I) 1m 1f 218y
3:45 (3:48) (Class 6) (0-65,68) 3-Y-O **£2,266** (£674; £337; £168) **Stalls** High

Form RPR
0-51 **1** **Comedy Act**[4] 2501 3-9-10 **68** 5ex.............................. SebSanders 11 81+
(Sir Mark Prescott) *mde all: rdn over 1f out: hmpd ins fnl f: styd on gamely* **5/6**[1]
654 **2** *nk* **Shades Of Grey**[19] 2051 3-9-7 **65**.............................. AdamKirby 10 74
(C G Cox) *unruly bhd the stalls: a.p: rdn over 3f out: chsd wnr and hung rt fr over 1f out: ev ch ins fnl f: styd on* **33/1**
4162 **3** *3* **Buona Sarah (IRE)**[31] 1696 3-9-5 **63**.............................. PatCosgrave 13 66
(J R Boyle) *a.p: rdn over 3f out: styd on same pce fnl f* **7/1**[2]
-222 **4** *1* **Celtic Ransom**[15] 2189 3-9-3 **61**.............................. MartinDwyer 2 62
(J W Hills) *chsd wnr tl rdn over 1f out: no ex ins fnl f* **8/1**[3]
2636 **5** *3* **Sultan's Choice**[7] 2412 3-8-10 **54**..............................(v) CathyGannon 3 49
(P D Evans) *hld up in tch: rdn over 3f out: styd on same pce fnl 2f* **33/1**
2-06 **6** *7* **Akamon**[24] 1934 3-9-7 **65**.............................. FrankieDettori 8 46
(E A L Dunlop) *broke wl: stdd and lost pl over 7f out: hdwy over 3f out: wknd over 2f out* **9/1**
00-3 **7** *1/2* **Celebrian**[15] 2189 3-9-3 **61**..............................(t) ShaneKelly 6 41
(W R Swinburn) *hld up: rdn over 3f out: nvr on terms* **10/1**
-605 **8** *nk* **Bandear (IRE)**[53] 1205 3-9-0 **58**.............................. NeilCallan 9 37
(C E Brittain) *hld up: hdwy over 4f out: rdn and wknd over 3f out* **16/1**
0-06 **9** *13* **Sunshine Buddy**[11] 2281 3-8-11 **55**.............................. StevieDonohoe 7 —
(C J Down) *s.i.s: hld up: a in rr: rdn and wknd over 3f out* **100/1**
033- **10** *9* **Admiral Breese**[166] 7781 3-8-13 **57**.............................. JimCrowley 4 —
(R Hollinshead) *hld up: hdwy 1/2-way: rdn and wknd 3f out: t.o* **40/1**
-564 **11** *16* **A P Ling**[106] 564 3-8-8 **52**.............................. DavidProbert 1 —
(C N Kellett) *chsd ldrs tl rdn and wknd over 3f out: t.o* **100/1**
250- **12** *15* **Rainsborough**[163] 7824 3-9-3 **61**.............................. RobertWinston 5 —
(S Curran) *mid-div: plld hrd: hdwy 7f out: rdn and wknd over 3f out: t.o* **66/1**

2m 9.87s (1.97) **Going Correction** 0.0s/f (Good) **12** Ran SP% **114.9**
Speed ratings (Par 97): **92,91,89,88,86 80,80,79,69,62 49,37**
toteswingers:1&2:£7.20, 1&3:£3.50, 2&3:£14.00 CSF £45.15 CT £128.74 TOTE £1.80: £1.10, £6.10, £2.00; EX 19.00 Trifecta £68.90 Pool: £394.87 - 4.24 winning units..
Owner Neil Greig - Osborne House **Bred** Floors Farming & The Duke Of Devonshire **Trained** Newmarket, Suffolk

FOCUS
The faster of the two divisions and probably a decent enough race for the grade. The form looks sound overall rated around those in the frame behind the winner.

2620 SWANNINGTON H'CAP (DIV II) 1m 1f 218y
4:15 (4:15) (Class 6) (0-65,65) 3-Y-O **£2,266** (£674; £337; £168) **Stalls** High

Form RPR
0556 **1** **Broughtons Swinger**[15] 2189 3-8-11 **55**.............................. StevieDonohoe 8 68
(W J Musson) *mde all: shkn up 3f out: pushed clr over 1f out: unchal* **22/1**
0440 **2** *6* **Sharakti (IRE)**[15] 2175 3-8-9 **58**.............................. DeclanCannon(5) 10 59
(A J McCabe) *chsd ldrs: pushed along 1/2-way: rdn to chse wnr over 2f out: hung rt fr over 1f out: styd on same pce fnl f* **14/1**
035- **3** *1/2* **Fine Lace (IRE)**[165] 7804 3-9-3 **61**.............................. LiamKeniry 3 61+
(D J S Ffrench Davis) *s.i.s: hld up: rdn over 3f out: hdwy over 2f out: styd on: nt trble ldrs* **40/1**
6-25 **4** *2* **One Cool Poppy (IRE)**[36] 1578 3-8-12 **56**.............................. DavidProbert 12 52
(H J L Dunlop) *chsd ldrs: rdn over 2f out: styd on same pce appr fnl f* **11/2**[3]
0-54 **5** *nk* **Catchanova (IRE)**[15] 2168 3-9-3 **61**.............................. WilliamBuick 2 56
(Eve Johnson Houghton) *trckd ldrs: plld hrd: rdn over 2f out: wknd ins fnl f* **5/1**[2]
0550 **6** *2 1/2* **Highland Cadett**[12] 2248 3-8-13 **60**.............................. JamesMillman(3) 9 50
(B R Millman) *hld up: hdwy over 3f out: rdn and wknd over 1f out* **6/1**
-033 **7** *2 1/4* **Ice Viking (IRE)**[27] 1830 3-9-5 **63**.............................. PaulMulrennan 5 49
(J G Given) *hld up: hdwy 4f out: rdn: hung rt and wknd over 1f out* **15/2**
004- **8** *5* **Storm Hawk (IRE)**[225] 6901 3-9-7 **65**.............................. AndreaAtzeni 1 41
(Pat Eddery) *hld up: rdn over 3f out: hung rt and wknd over 2f out* **8/1**
50-6 **9** *hd* **Amno Dancer (IRE)**[35] 1608 3-9-4 **62**.............................. TedDurcan 7 38+
(M H Tompkins) *hld up: effrt and nt clr run over 3f out: nvr on terms: eased fnl f* **9/2**[1]
5500 **10** *27* **Heliocentric**[29] 1757 3-9-7 **65**..............................(p) RichardHughes 11 —
(R Hannon) *chsd ldrs: rdn over 4f out: wknd 3f out: t.o* **11/1**
2050 **11** *7* **Always Dixie (IRE)**[11] 2273 3-8-8 **52**.............................. RoystonFfrench 6 —
(M Johnston) *hld up in tch: rdn and wknd over 3f out: t.o* **25/1**

2m 10.17s (2.27) **Going Correction** 0.0s/f (Good) **11** Ran SP% **113.0**
Speed ratings (Par 97): **90,85,84,83,82 80,79,75,75,53 47**
toteswingers:1&2:£58.80, 1&3:£46.50, 2&3:£34.00 CSF £283.76 CT £11568.47 TOTE £27.70: £8.80, £6.20, £6.80; EX 226.80 TRIFECTA Not won..
Owner Broughton Thermal Insulation **Bred** Michael E Broughton **Trained** Newmarket, Suffolk

FOCUS
A moderate contest run slower than the first leg and in which it paid to race prominently. The winner made surprise improvement but the runner-up is rated in line with previous handicap form.

2621 OADBY OPEN MAIDEN STKS 5f 218y
4:45 (4:46) (Class 4) 2-Y-O **£4,857** (£1,445; £722; £360) **Stalls** Low

Form RPR
5 **1** **Roayh (USA)**[14] 2216 2-9-3 0.............................. FrankieDettori 12 84+
(Saeed Bin Suroor) *mde all: pushed clr fr over 1f out: comf* **9/4**[1]
5 **2** *2 1/4* **Greek Islands (IRE)**[16] 2138 2-9-0 0.............................. AhmedAjtebi(3) 7 75+
(Mahmood Al Zarooni) *prom: rdn over 2f out: hung rt fr over 1f out: styd on to go 2nd towards fin: nt trble wnr* **9/1**
3 **3** *1 1/4* **Battle Of Britain**[21] 2007 2-9-3 0.............................. TedDurcan 6 72
(Mahmood Al Zarooni) *hld up: hdwy over 2f out: rdn to chse wnr and hung rt fr over 1f out: styd on same pce ins fnl f: lost 2nd towards fin* **6/1**[2]
4 *5* **Ice Magic** 2-9-3 0.............................. PatCosgrave 13 57
(M H Tompkins) *s.i.s: outpcd: hdwy over 1f out: nt rch ldrs* **40/1**
6 **5** *nk* **Beacon Hill (IRE)**[10] 2319 2-9-3 0.............................. WilliamBuick 9 56
(J H M Gosden) *prom: chsd wnr over 2f out tl rdn over 1f out: wknd ins fnl f* **9/4**[1]
6 *1* **Bobbyow** 2-9-3 0.............................. DavidProbert 8 53
(B Palling) *chsd ldrs: rdn over 2f out: wknd over 1f out* **33/1**
7 *1 3/4* **Fantasy Fry** 2-9-3 0.............................. SteveDrowne 5 47
(H Morrison) *hld up: sme hdwy over 2f out: nt trble ldrs* **25/1**
8 *3/4* **Right Said Fred (IRE)** 2-9-3 0.............................. JimCrowley 10 45
(R M Beckett) *s.i.s: hdwy over 4f out: wknd over 1f out* **8/1**[3]
9 *3 1/2* **Place And Chips** 2-9-3 0.............................. RichardKingscote 1 35
(Tom Dascombe) *dwlt: outpcd: nvr on terms* **16/1**
0 **10** *2 3/4* **Romany Gypsy**[7] 2407 2-8-12 0.............................. CathyGannon 3 21
(P D Evans) *mid-div: rdn 1/2-way: wknd 2f out* **80/1**

1m 13.57s (0.57) **Going Correction** 0.0s/f (Good) **10** Ran SP% **113.3**
Speed ratings (Par 95): **96,93,91,84,84 82,80,79,74,71**
toteswingers:1&2:£5.00, 1&3:£3.20, 2&3:£4.70 CSF £23.20 TOTE £4.40: £1.50, £3.30, £1.10; EX 21.30 Trifecta £22.00 Pool: £344.73 - 11.56 winning units..
Owner Godolphin **Bred** Overrbook Farm **Trained** Newmarket, Suffolk

FOCUS
Some powerful connections were represented, but few of these took the eye beforehand and this looked just a fair juvenile maiden. The third is the best initial guide while the winner was a big improver.

NOTEBOOK
Roayh(USA) stepped up hugely on the form he showed on his debut at Nottingham, travelling strongly before finding plenty for pressure. Although this may not have been that strong a race, the winner seems to be quite useful and a rise in grade surely awaits. (op 11-4)
Greek Islands(IRE), although no match for the winner, finished a clear second and this was an improvement on the form he showed first time up at Ripon. (op 17-2 tchd 8-1)
Battle Of Britain still looked pretty green, hanging right under pressure, and he probably didn't improve much, if at all, on his debut third at Yarmouth. (op 7-2)
Ice Magic, a 12,500gns half-brother to, among others, 7f-1m4f winner Exceedthewildman, ran green from the off, missing the break and needing to be niggled along throughout, and he can do better in due course. (tchd 33-1)
Beacon Hill(IRE) failed to see his race out and has not really gone on from his first outing. (op 5-1)

2622 SIS H'CAP 5f 2y
5:15 (5:16) (Class 5) (0-75,75) 4-Y-O+ **£3,238** (£963; £481; £240) **Stalls** Low

Form RPR
200- **1** **Foxy Music**[319] 4043 6-9-7 **75**.............................. ShaneKelly 10 86
(E J Alston) *w ldr: led over 3f out: rdn out* **25/1**
40-3 **2** *1 1/4* **Spring Green**[27] 1827 4-9-6 **74**.............................. SteveDrowne 2 81+
(H Morrison) *chsd ldrs: rdn over 1f out: r.o to go 2nd post* **7/2**[1]
3034 **3** *nk* **Cape Royal**[21] 2001 10-9-1 **69**..............................(bt) RichardKingscote 1 74
(J M Bradley) *led: hdd over 3f out: rdn and hung rt fr over 1f out: sn ev ch: unable qck ins fnl f: lost 2nd post* **16/1**
0050 **4** *hd* **The Tatling (IRE)**[21] 1988 13-9-2 **70**.............................. FrankieDettori 14 75+
(J M Bradley) *hld up: r.o ins fnl f: nrst fin* **11/1**

10-4 **5** ¾ **Brandywell Boy (IRE)**[15] 2166 7-8-10 **64**.................. RichardThomas 9 66
(D J S Ffrench Davis) *mid-div: hdwy 1/2-way: rdn over 1f out: styd on same pce ins fnl f* **20/1**
0060 **6** 2 ¾ **Guto**[24] 1915 7-8-8 **62**.. TravisBlock 16 54
(W J H Ratcliffe) *mid-div: 1/2-way u.p 1/2-way: no ex ins fnl f* **33/1**
40-0 **7** 1 ½ **Supermassive Muse (IRE)**[50] 1266 5-8-13 **67**............(p) TedDurcan 13 54
(E S McMahon) *hld up: rdn 1/2-way: styd on ins fnl f: nvr nrr* **12/1**
6126 **8** ¾ **Sir Geoffrey (IRE)**[10] 2310 4-9-7 **75**..............................(b) JimCrowley 7 59
(J A Glover) *chsd ldrs: rdn 2f out: hung rt over 1f out: wknd ins fnl f* **8/1**
4564 **9** ¾ **The Jobber (IRE)**[18] 2094 9-9-4 **72**.............................. NeilCallan 17 53
(M Blanshard) *hld up: plld hrd: hdwy 1/2-way: rdn over 1f out: wknd ins fnl f* **11/2**[3]
/5-3 **10** 1 ¾ **Bold Tie**[12] 2247 4-9-7 **75**.. RichardHughes 6 50
(R Hannon) *prom: rdn 1/2-way: wknd fnl f* **4/1**[2]
6204 **11** ¾ **Sands Crooner (IRE)**[16] 2144 7-9-0 **68**.....................(v) PaulMulrennan 3 40
(J G Given) *hld up: rdn 1/2-way: n.d* **12/1**
1202 **12** 2 ½ **Grudge**[21] 2001 5-9-4 **72**.......................................(be) RobertWinston 8 35
(C R Dore) *chsd ldrs: rdn 1/2-way: wknd over 1f out* **8/1**

60.70 secs (0.70) **Going Correction** 0.0s/f (Good) **12** Ran SP% **121.0**
Speed ratings (Par 103): **94,92,91,91,90 85,83,82,80,78 76,72**
toteswingers:1&2:£24.60, 1&3:£49.60, 2&3:£18.40 CSF £111.06 CT £1518.31 TOTE £34.00: £10.00, £1.30, £6.50; EX 143.80 TRIFECTA Not won. Place 6 £240.24; Place 5 £181.39.
Owner G M & Mrs C Baillie **Bred** G M & C Baillie & Springs Equestrian **Trained** Longton, Lancs

FOCUS
A modest sprint handicap with the winner back to his best and the placed horses close to form.
Bold Tie Official explanation: jockey said that the gelding lost its action
Sands Crooner(IRE) Official explanation: jockey said that the gelding had a breathing problem.
T/Jkpt: £18,848.30 to a £1 stake. Pool:£53,093.94 - 2.00 winning tickets T/Plt: £134.10 to a £1 stake. Pool:£93,967.78 - 511.40 winning tickets T/Qpdt: £101.20 to a £1 stake. Pool:£4,501.44 - 32.90 winning tickets CR

2605 REDCAR (L-H)
Tuesday, June 1

OFFICIAL GOING: Good to firm changing to good (good to firm in places in chute) after race 1 (2:30)
Wind: Nil Weather: Overcast and raining

2623 EUROPEAN BREEDERS' FUND MEDIAN AUCTION MAIDEN FILLIES' STKS 6f
2:30 (2:30) (Class 5) 2-Y-O **£3,302** (£982; £491; £245) **Stalls** Centre

Form RPR
2 **1** **Lady Del Sol**[22] 1964 2-9-0 0.. PJMcDonald 6 78+
(G R Oldroyd) *cl up: rdn along and sltly outpcd wl over 1f out: styd on ins fnl f to ld nr fin* **12/1**
2 **2** nk **Madany (IRE)**[18] 2088 2-9-0 0.. RichardHills 3 77
(B W Hills) *cl up: led 1/2-way: pushed clr wl over 1f out: rdn ins fnl f: hung lft last 75yds: hdd nr fin* **1/2**[1]
3 2 **Bahamian Sunset** 2-9-0 0... PaulHanagan 7 71+
(R A Fahey) *t.k.h: trckd ldrs: hdwy 2f out: rdn over 1f out: kpt on ins fnl f* **8/1**[2]
4 5 **Susiesstaying** 2-9-0 0.. TonyHamilton 4 56
(P T Midgley) *in tch: effrt over 2f out: sn rdn and kpt on fnl f* **50/1**
3 **5** nk **Hayley Cropper**[14] 2202 2-9-0 0.. AdrianNicholls 8 55
(D Nicholls) *led: pushed along and hdd 1/2-way: rdn along 2f out: grad wknd* **11/1**[3]
6 3 **Playful Girl (IRE)** 2-9-0 0.. DavidAllan 2 46
(T D Easterby) *in rr tl sme late hdwy* **25/1**
0 **7** hd **Miss Cosette (IRE)**[12] 2239 2-9-0 0................................. PhillipMakin 9 46
(T D Barron) *towards rr: pushed along 1/2-way: swtchd rt and hdwy 2f out: sn rdn and n.d* **20/1**
42 **8** 5 **Box Of Frogs (IRE)**[11] 2286 2-9-0 0................................ JamesDoyle 10 31
(A J McCabe) *dwlt: sn chsng ldrs on outer: rdn along wl over 2f out: sn wknd* **16/1**
9 6 **Antipas (IRE)** 2-9-0 0.. AndrewElliott 5 13
(J R Weymes) *a in rr: outpcd and bhd fr 1/2-way* **100/1**
10 10 **Somebody Loves You** 2-9-0 0... StephenCraine 1 —
(Mrs A Duffield) *s.i.s: a in rr: bhd fr 1/2-way* **66/1**

1m 11.83s (0.03) **Going Correction** 0.0s/f (Good) **10** Ran SP% **112.7**
Speed ratings (Par 90): **99,98,95,89,88 84,84,77,69,56**
toteswingers:1&2:£3.00, 1&3:£4.00, 2&3:£2.20 CSF £17.41 TOTE £10.70: £2.60, £1.10, £1.10; EX 22.40.
Owner R C Bond **Bred** Bond Thoroughbred Corporation **Trained** Brawby, N Yorks

FOCUS
Straightforward maiden form with the winenr improved and the runner-up coming from a sound-looking previous start.

NOTEBOOK
Lady Del Sol ran well when second over 5f on debut here 22 days previously and this extra furlong made the difference. She looked like playing second fiddle when coming under pressure near the furlong marker, but that was clearly still down to greenness as she found an extra gear nearing the finish. The best is still to come from her and, while she has a touch to prove with her attitude, connections do look to have a useful prospect on their hands. (op 10-1)
Madany(IRE) was all the rage to go one better than her initial second at Newmarket last month and things looked good for her backers when she eased to the front after halfway. She was travelling all over the winner at the furlong marker, but could only find the same pace when asked to settle the issue and was picked off late on. This could be deemed disappointing, but she has probably run up to her debut form and was a clear second-best. (tchd 4-9)
Bahamian Sunset is related to winners over this trip and was representing a stable that remains in decent form. She lost out by refusing to settle early on, but still showed a deal of ability and was nicely clear in third. It's fair to expect her to go very close next time out. (op 10-1)
Susiesstaying caught the eye staying on by far the best of those that raced from off the pace and this was a pleasing debut effort. She will enjoy another furlong in due course.
Hayley Cropper showed the benefit of her debut run a fortnight earlier, but failed to see out the extra furlong as might have been expected and a drop back to the minimum looks in order. (op 12-1)

2624 RACING UK SKY 432 (S) STKS 7f
3:00 (3:00) (Class 6) 3-5-Y-O **£1,842** (£544; £272) **Stalls** Centre

Form RPR
-034 **1** **Angel Of Fashion (IRE)**[14] 2203 3-8-6 68.................. AdrianNicholls 6 61
(D Nicholls) *t.k.h: trckd ldrs: hdwy 2f out: rdn to chal and edgd lft over 1f out: led ins fnl f: rdn out* **9/2**[2]
-024 **2** 1 ¾ **Liberty Trail (IRE)**[11] 2273 4-9-7 70.................................. JamesDoyle 7 65
(P D Evans) *led: rdn along 2f out: drvn and edgd lft over 1f out: hdd ins fnl f: kpt on* **8/1**
1341 **3** 1 ¼ **Lastkingofscotland (IRE)**[7] 2409 4-9-13 73...............(b) PaulHanagan 2 68
(P D Evans) *dwlt: sn in tch: hdwy 3f out: swtchd rt and effrt 2f out: sn rdn and ev ch: drvn ent fnl f and kpt on same pce* **6/4**[1]
2304 **4** shd **King's Sabre**[8] 2385 4-9-7 49..(e) FrannyNorton 1 62
(R C Guest) *stdd s and hld up in rr: hdwy over 2f out: rdn over 1f out: sn swtchd lft and kpt on same pce* **20/1**
-003 **5** ¾ **Blue Noodles**[7] 2409 4-9-2 67...................................... RichardEvans[(5)] 4 60
(P D Evans) *cl up: rdn along over 2f out: drvn over 1f out and grad wknd* **8/1**
5305 **6** 12 **Deely Plaza**[16] 2162 3-8-11 67......................................(p) FrederikTylicki 9 23
(J A Glover) *cl up: rdn along over 3f out: sn wknd* **8/1**
060- **7** 1 ¾ **Home Before Dark**[251] 6219 4-9-7 37............................ TonyHamilton 8 23
(R M Whitaker) *chsd ldrs: rdn along 3f out: sn wknd* **100/1**
2-00 **R** **Jimwil (IRE)**[22] 1967 4-9-4 65......................................(b) KellyHarrison[(3)] 5 —
(M Dods) *ref to r; tk no part* **13/2**[3]

1m 24.51s (0.01) **Going Correction** 0.0s/f (Good)
WFA 3 from 4yo 10lb **8** Ran SP% **110.6**
Speed ratings (Par 101): **99,97,95,95,94 80,78,—**
toteswingers:1&2:£5.20, 1&3:£3.20, 2&3:£2.90 CSF £37.13 TOTE £6.20: £2.10, £1.20, £1.10; EX 44.20.The winner was bought in for 4,200gns. Lastkingofscotland was claimed by John A. Harris for £6,000.
Owner K Farragher S Creaton B Atkinson **Bred** Grangemore Stud **Trained** Sessay, N Yorks

FOCUS
A modest seller with the winner not having to improve much on previous efforts this season. The form is limited by the proximity of the 49-rated fourth..

2625 WEATHERBYS BLOODSTOCK INSURANCE H'CAP 1m 1f
3:30 (3:31) (Class 5) (0-70,70) 4-Y-0+ **£2,396** (£712; £356; £177) **Stalls** Low

Form RPR
06-5 **1** **King's Counsel (IRE)**[41] 1296 4-8-4 **53**................(v) SilvestreDeSousa 6 65
(J Hetherton) *mde most: clr 1/2-way: rdn and qcknd wl over 2f out: kpt on strly fnl f* **4/1**[1]
2-60 **2** 3 **Avitus**[7] 2421 4-8-7 **56**.. FrederikTylicki 7 61
(Micky Hammond) *hld up in midfield: hdwy on outer 4f out: rdn to chse wnr wl over 1f out: drvn: edgd lft and no imp fnl f* **12/1**
-041 **3** nk **Visions Of Johanna (USA)**[12] 2240 5-9-7 **70**.............. PJMcDonald 10 75
(Ian Williams) *trckd ldrs: hdwy 2f out: rdn wl over 1f out: kpt on same pce ins fnl f* **5/1**[2]
-526 **4** 1 ¾ **Crystal Feather**[12] 2259 4-8-13 **62**.................................... TomQueally 3 65+
(E F Vaughan) *hld up in midfield: hdwy 3f out: effrt and n.m.r wl over 1f out: sn rdn and no imp* **5/1**[2]
4-04 **5** ¾ **Steel Trade**[7] 2421 4-9-2 **65**.. DavidAllan 1 64
(M Brittain) *dwlt and towards rr: hdwy 3f out: swtchd ins and rdn wl over 1f out: sn no imp* **13/2**[3]
4001 **6** 2 ½ **Dream Win**[22] 1967 4-8-10 **59**... TomEaves 8 53
(B Ellison) *hld up in rr: hdwy over 2f out: swtchd rt and rdn over 1f out: nvr rchd ldrs* **4/1**[1]
4603 **7** 6 **Via Mia**[11] 2299 4-8-5 **54**..(p) PaulHanagan 4 35
(John A Harris) *chsd wnr: rdn along over 3f out: drvn over 2f out: grad wknd* **9/1**
13-0 **8** 2 ¼ **Tropical Duke (IRE)**[7] 2421 4-8-11 **60**............................ PhillipMakin 9 36
(R E Barr) *prom: rdn along wl over 2f out: sn drvn and wknd* **10/1**
-000 **9** ½ **Amber Ridge**[11] 2299 5-8-0 **54** oh6 ow3..........................(p) BillyCray[(5)] 5 28
(B P J Baugh) *a in rr: rdn along over 3f out: nvr a factor* **100/1**
0-35 **10** 6 **Joinedupwriting**[7] 2421 5-8-13 **62**................................ TonyHamilton 2 23
(R M Whitaker) *chsd ldrs: rdn along over 3f out: sn wknd* **16/1**

1m 53.19s (0.19) **Going Correction** 0.0s/f (Good) **10** Ran SP% **120.3**
Speed ratings (Par 103): **99,96,96,94,93 91,86,84,83,78**
toteswingers:1&2:£11.90, 1&3:£4.20, 2&3:£13.90 CSF £55.51 CT £250.10 TOTE £5.50: £1.60, £4.70, £1.50; EX 65.70.
Owner R G Fell **Bred** Peter And Jackie Grimes **Trained** Norton, N Yorks

FOCUS
A moderate handicap where the winner dictated. The runner-up is rated to form.
Crystal Feather Official explanation: jockey said the filly was denied a clear run

2626 WEATHERBYS BANK H'CAP 5f
4:00 (4:01) (Class 4) (0-85,78) 4-Y-0+ **£4,209** (£1,252; £625; £312) **Stalls** Centre

Form RPR
5614 **1** **Lucky Dan (IRE)**[3] 2534 4-9-3 **74**.................................... FrannyNorton 3 83
(Paul Green) *hld up in rr: hdwy wl over 1f out and sn rdn: drvn ent fnl f: kpt on to ld nr fin* **4/1**[2]
4062 **2** nk **Select Committee**[3] 2528 5-8-11 **68**.......................(v) GrahamGibbons 6 76
(J J Quinn) *trckd ldrs: hdwy 2f out: swtchd rt and effrt over 1f out: rdn to ld ent fnl f: drvn and edgd lft last 100yds: hdd nr fin* **3/1**[1]
-203 **3** 1 ¾ **Dispol Kylie (IRE)**[18] 2087 4-8-8 **65**................................. JoeFanning 8 67
(P T Midgley) *wnt rt s: sn cl up: rdn and ev ch over 1f out: drvn and kpt on same pce ins fnl f* **8/1**
4306 **4** nk **Incomparable**[18] 2094 5-9-7 **78**..............................(tp) FrederikTylicki 5 81
(J A Glover) *chsd ldr: rdn along 2f out: drvn and one pce ent fnl f: hld whn n.m.r nr fin* **7/1**
3240 **5** 1 ½ **Lucky Art (USA)**[17] 2136 4-8-9 **71**............................ JamesSullivan[(5)] 7 67
(Mrs R A Carr) *led: rdn 2f out: drvn and hdd ent fnl f: sn wknd* **8/1**
-516 **6** ½ **Mullglen**[5] 2465 4-9-6 **77**...(tp) DavidAllan 4 71
(T D Easterby) *racd wd: prom: rdn 2f out: sn drvn: hung lft and wknd appr fnl f* **5/1**
4-34 **7** 1 ¾ **Evelyn May (IRE)**[18] 2094 4-9-1 **72**.................................. MichaelHills 2 59
(B W Hills) *racd wd: in tch: rdn along over 2f out: sn wknd* **9/2**[3]

57.94 secs (-0.66) **Going Correction** 0.0s/f (Good) **7** Ran SP% **114.6**
Speed ratings (Par 105): **105,104,101,101,98 98,95**
toteswingers:1&2:£3.30, 1&3:£5.10, 2&3:£4.80 CSF £16.49 CT £90.20 TOTE £3.50: £1.80, £3.40; EX 19.20.
Owner Stephen Bell **Bred** Mountarmstrong Stud **Trained** Lydiate, Merseyside

FOCUS
A fair sprint and the form looks straightforward and sound.

2627 BUY YOUR TICKETS ON-LINE @ REDCARRACING.CO.UK MAIDEN STKS 1m 2f
4:30 (4:31) (Class 5) 3-Y-0+ **£2,396** (£712; £356; £177) **Stalls** Low

Form RPR
64-2 **1** **Grey Bunting**[36] 1581 3-8-13 75.. MichaelHills 7 75
(B W Hills) *trckd ldrs: hdwy 3f out: led 2f out: rdn and edgd lft over 1f out: kpt on wl* **2/1**[1]
2 2 ¼ **Music City (IRE)** 3-8-13 0.. JoeFanning 4 71
(M Johnston) *trckd ldr: cl up 4f out: chal 3f out: rdn and ev ch 2f out: sn drvn and kpt on same pce appr fnl f* **9/4**[2]

4-40 **3** *1* **Weekend Millionair (IRE)**[22] 1973 3-8-13 74................ JamesDoyle 3 69
(P D Evans) *sn led: jnd and rdn along 3f out: hdd 2f out and sn drvn: one pce appr fnl f* **13/2**

4 *¾* **Opening Nite (IRE)** 3-8-13 0.. PaulHanagan 10 67
(R A Fahey) *dwlt: sn trcking ldrs: hdwy over 3f out: rdn 2f out: kpt on same pce appr fnl f* **10/1**

0 **5** *4 ½* **Sinatramania**[18] 2072 3-8-10 0.. KellyHarrison(3) 9 58
(Miss Tracy Waggott) *midfield: hdwy over 3f out: rdn to chse ldrs 2f out: wknd over 1f out* **50/1**

65 **6** *2 ½* **Robbie Burnett**[21] 1991 3-8-13 0.. PJMcDonald 2 53
(G A Swinbank) *trckd ldrs on inner: rdn along over 3f out: wknd over 2f out* **16/1**

00 **7** *2 ¼* **Siberian Sunset (IRE)**[17] 2131 4-9-12 0........................ AndrewElliott 8 50
(G A Swinbank) *hld up towards rr: sme hdwy over 2f out: nvr a factor* **40/1**

66U **8** *6* **On The Right Path**[17] 2131 3-8-8 0........................... JamesSullivan(5) 5 37
(Paul Murphy) *chsd ldrs: pushed along 1/2-way: sn rdn and wknd over 3f out* **100/1**

9 *18* **Suleimah** 3-8-8 0... PatrickMathers 1 —
(C J Teague) *v.s.a and a bhd* **100/1**

10 *½* **Clearly Cryptonite (USA)** 3-8-13 0................................ TomQueally 6 36
(H R A Cecil) *dwlt and reminders after s: sn rdn along and a bhd* **11/2**[3]

2m 9.19s (2.09) **Going Correction** 0.0s/f (Good)
WFA 3 from 4yo 13lb 10 Ran SP% **114.2**
Speed ratings (Par 103): **91,89,88,87,84 82,80,75,61,60**
toteswingers:1&2:£2.40, 1&3:£2.60, 2&3:£4.40 CSF £6.43 TOTE £2.70: £1.10, £1.50, £1.30; EX 8.50.
Owner The Hon Mrs J M Corbett & C Wright **Bred** C A Cyzer **Trained** Lambourn, Berks

FOCUS
A fair maiden rated around the winner and third.
Suleimah Official explanation: jockey said the filly missed the break
Clearly Cryptonite(USA) Official explanation: jockey said the gelding had no more to give

2628 WIN A VIP DAY OUT @ REDCARRACING.CO.UK H'CAP 6f
5:00 (5:01) (Class 5) (0-70,70) 3-Y-O **£2,396** (£712; £356; £177) **Stalls** Centre

Form RPR

355- **1** **Pepper Lane**[228] 6819 3-8-2 56................................ JamesSullivan(5) 13 71
(J Hetherton) *hld up: gd hdwy 2f out: rdn to chse ldr over 1f out: kpt on to ld ins fnl f* **7/1**

0-20 **2** *¾* **Sharp Eclipse**[21] 2000 3-9-2 65.............................. SilvestreDeSousa 12 77
(K A Ryan) *trckd ldrs on outer: hdwy to ld 2f out: rdn and edgd lft over 1f out: drvn and hdd ins fnl f: kpt on* **9/2**[1]

631 **3** *4* **Carrie's Magic**[22] 1966 3-9-7 70.. PhillipMakin 6 70+
(T D Barron) *hld up: hdwy over 2f out: swtchd lft and rdn to chse ldrs over 1f out: drvn and kpt on same pce ins fnl f* **5/1**[2]

46-4 **4** *1 ¼* **Just The Tonic**[15] 2185 3-8-6 55.. PJMcDonald 10 51+
(Mrs Marjorie Fife) *dwlt and in rr: hdwy wl over 2f out: sn rdn and styd on appr fnl f: nrst fin* **7/1**

-233 **5** *nk* **Boy The Bell**[10] 2309 3-8-12 68.. JosephYoung(7) 9 63
(M Mullineaux) *prom: rdn over 2f out and ev ch tl drvn and wknd appr fnl f* **20/1**

0-43 **6** *2 ½* **Interest Free**[14] 2212 3-8-11 60.. PaulHanagan 11 47
(T D Easterby) *cl up: effrt over 2f out and ev ch tl rdn wl over 1f out and grad wknd* **8/1**

1140 **7** *nk* **Whispered Times (USA)**[4] 2504 3-8-13 65.............. KellyHarrison(3) 8 51+
(Miss Tracy Waggott) *chsd ldrs: rdn along and outpcd 1/2-way: styd on fnl f* **6/1**[3]

-445 **8** *hd* **Seven Of Diamonds (IRE)**[22] 1966 3-8-10 59..............(tp) DavidAllan 2 44
(T D Easterby) *cl up: rdn along over 2f out: sn drvn and wknd* **9/1**

55-0 **9** *3* **On The Piste (IRE)**[8] 2396 3-8-11 63........................... GaryBartley(3) 3 38
(L A Mullaney) *chsd ldrs: swtchd lft and rdn over 2f out: hung bdly lft wl over 1f out: wknd* **40/1**

-105 **10** *½* **Always Dazzling**[10] 2329 3-9-2 65.. JoeFanning 5 39
(M Johnston) *chsd ldrs: cl up 1/2-way: rdn 2f out and sn wknd* **10/1**

0-02 **11** *½* **Hanbelation (USA)**[22] 1966 3-9-4 67................................ TomQueally 7 39
(E F Vaughan) *led: rdn along 1/2-way: hdd 2f out and sn wknd* **11/1**

00-6 **12** *9* **Royal Record**[3] 2535 3-8-10 59.. TomEaves 1 —
(M Brittain) *midfield: hdwy to chse ldrs after 2f: rdn along 1/2-way and sn wknd* **33/1**

1m 11.37s (-0.43) **Going Correction** 0.0s/f (Good) 12 Ran SP% **122.8**
Speed ratings (Par 99): **102,101,95,94,93 90,89,89,85,84 84,72**
toteswingers:1&2:£11.70, 1&3:£8.80, 2&3:£4.80 CSF £39.26 CT £180.19 TOTE £9.80: £3.70, £1.60, £1.10; EX 47.20.
Owner Mrs Lynne Lumley & K Nicholson **Bred** Conor J C Parsons & Brian M Parsons **Trained** Norton, N Yorks

FOCUS
A moderate 3-y-o sprint handicap. The form looks good with the first pair coming clear late on and could be rated a little higher.

2629 WEDDING RECEPTIONS @ REDCAR RACECOURSE AMATEUR RIDERS' MAIDEN H'CAP 6f
5:30 (5:30) (Class 6) (0-60,60) 4-Y-O+ **£1,780** (£547; £273) **Stalls** Centre

Form RPR

030- **1** **Green Poppy**[227] 6856 4-9-13 52.. MrJNewman(7) 8 62
(B Smart) *qckly away: mde all: clr 1/2-way: styd on wl* **9/2**[2]

0043 **2** *3 ½* **Fortezza**[12] 2257 4-10-2 51..(p) MrPCollington(3) 2 50
(A J McCabe) *in tch: hdwy to chse ldrs over 2f out: rdn wl over 1f out: styd on ins fnl f: nt trble wnr* **5/2**[1]

0000 **3** *nk* **Misterisland (IRE)**[8] 2378 5-9-9 46 oh1.............. MissMMullineaux(5) 3 44
(M Mullineaux) *sltly hmpd s: sn in tch: hdwy to chse ldrs over 2f out: sn rdn: kpt on ins fnl f* **12/1**

000- **4** *nk* **Karate Queen**[334] 3541 5-9-9 46 oh1........................... MissRKneller(5) 4 43
(R E Barr) *dwlt: sltly hmpd s: towards rr: hdwy over 2f out: rdn wl over 1f: kpt on ins fnl f: nrst fin* **25/1**

-000 **5** *nk* **Red China Blues (USA)**[8] 2382 4-10-3 54........................ MissVBarr(5) 7 50
(R E Barr) *wnt lft s: sn prom: chsd wnr after 2f: rdn over 2f out: grad wknd* **9/1**

/0-5 **6** *1 ¼* **Quadrifolio**[39] 1503 4-10-2 48 oh1 ow2............................ MrSWalker 10 40
(Paul Green) *chsd ldrs: rdn along 2f out: drvn over 1f out: sn one pce* **10/1**

0500 **7** *1* **Cheveyo (IRE)**[11] 2278 4-10-6 55....................(t) MrStephenHarrison(3) 5 44
(Patrick Morris) *dwlt and towards rr tl styd on fnl 2f: nrst fin* **10/1**

4/52 **8** *¾* **Ivestar (IRE)**[112] 476 5-10-7 60..................(tp) MissCharlotteHolmes(7) 6 46
(B M R Haslam) *s.i.s and bhd tl styd on fnl 2f: nvr rchd ldrs* **20/1**

/00- **9** *3 ¼* **Boy Racer (IRE)**[216] 7118 5-10-4 50.. MrSDobson 11 26
(C J Teague) *dwlt: hdwy to chse ldrs after 2f: rdn over 2f out and sn wknd* **33/1**

60-0 **10** *2 ¼* **Balzarine**[22] 1966 4-10-0 46 oh1.. MissSBrotherton 1 15
(C J Teague) *in tch: rdn along 1/2-way: sn hung lft and wknd* **14/1**

000- **11** *1 ¼* **Towthorpe**[260] 5954 4-10-9 60.. MrJMoorman(5) 9 25
(M Brittain) *chsd ldrs: rdn along bef 1/2-way: sn wknd* **6/1**[3]

060- **12** *5* **Bold Bomber**[180] 7615 4-9-9 48.. MissACraven(7) 15 —
(Paul Green) *chsd ldrs on wd outside: rdn along bef 1/2-way: sn wknd* **20/1**

/655 **13** *9* **Lunar Lass**[14] 2212 5-9-7 46 oh1.................... MrJosephPalmowski(7) 13 —
(D C Griffiths) *prom: rdn along bef 1/2-way: sn wknd and bhd fnl 2f* **80/1**

1m 12.67s (0.87) **Going Correction** 0.0s/f (Good) 13 Ran SP% **121.1**
Speed ratings (Par 101): **94,89,88,88,88 86,85,84,79,76 75,68,56**
toteswingers:1&2:£3.80, 1&3:£17.20, 2&3:£9.80 CSF £15.25 CT £134.82 TOTE £7.90: £2.30, £1.60, £6.80; EX 19.50 Place 6 £6.74; Place 5 £5.88.
Owner Jeffrey Hobby **Bred** Gainsborough Stud Management Ltd **Trained** Hambleton, N Yorks

FOCUS
An amateur riders' maiden handicap and five were out of the weights, so obviously this was poor stuff. The winner is rated to the best of her old form but there is little solid overall.
T/Plt: £13.40 to a £1 stake. Pool:£65,261.76 3,553.02 winning tickets T/Qpdt: £13.40 to a £1 stake. Pool:£4,118.50 226.10 winning tickets JR

2297 YARMOUTH (L-H)
Tuesday, June 1

OFFICIAL GOING: Good to firm (good in places; 7.4)
Back straight and bends dolled out 3metres.
Wind: modest, across Weather: dull, just starting to rain

2630 EUROPEAN BREEDERS' FUND / HOTPOINT HOME APPLIANCE NOVICE STKS 6f 3y
5:45 (5:46) (Class 5) 2-Y-O **£3,532** (£1,057; £528; £264; £131) **Stalls** High

Form RPR

1 **1** **Margot Did (IRE)**[10] 2338 2-8-11 0.. HayleyTurner 4 88+
(M L W Bell) *trckd ldrs and a gng wl: led on bit 2f out: cruised clr ins fnl f: nt extended* **4/9**[1]

0123 **2** *¾* **Joyously**[8] 2397 2-8-9 0.. ChrisCatlin 1 78
(P D Evans) *led: rdn and hdd 2f out: hrd drvn and stl w wnr after tl brushed aside ins fnl f: edgd lft towards fin* **9/2**[2]

3 *2 ¼* **Al Burkaan (IRE)** 2-9-0 0.. RyanMoore 3 76+
(E A L Dunlop) *dwlt: sn in tch: swtchd lft over 2f out: rdn along to chse ldng pair wl over 1f out: styd on same pce fr over 1f out* **15/2**[3]

101 **4** *8* **Novabridge**[33] 1647 2-9-5 0.. RobertHavlin 5 57
(A B Haynes) *w ldr: rdn over 1f out: struggling u.p wl over 1f out: wl btn whn edgd lft ent fnl f* **14/1**

6 **5** *21* **Sister June (IRE)**[5] 2457 2-8-9 0.. TadhgO'Shea 2 —
(E J Creighton) *sn swishing tail and racing v awkwardly in last: lost tch 1/2-way: t.o* **200/1**

1m 15.12s (0.72) **Going Correction** -0.05s/f (Good) 5 Ran SP% **106.4**
Speed ratings (Par 93): **93,92,89,78,50**
CSF £2.50 TOTE £1.30: £1.10, £2.30; EX 2.30.
Owner T Redman And P Philipps **Bred** N Hartery **Trained** Newmarket, Suffolk

FOCUS
A dry night and day saw the ground changed to good to firm, good in places. The winning rider reported the ground as "good to firm with no jar". There were three previous winners in the race but, although not a competitive race, the winner looks a useful prospect. The gallop was a reasonable one and the runner-up sets the level.

NOTEBOOK
Margot Did(IRE) ◆ again created a favourable impression to beat a reliable yardstick with a good deal more in hand than the winning margin suggests. The Albany at Royal Ascot, her next intended target, will be a much stiffer test but she is well worth a try in stronger company and she appeals as the type to win more races. (tchd 2-5 and 1-2)
Joyously has improved steadily with every run and, while flattered by her proximity to the easy winner, seemed to give it her best shot and she looks the best guide to the worth of this form. Her stable does very well with this type and she should continue to give a good account. (op 4-1)
Al Burkaan(IRE), out of a half-sister to a fairly useful French juvenile, was nibbled at in the market and showed ability at an ordinary level, despite his greenness on this racecourse debut. He was not knocked about and should come on for this experience. (op 17-2 tchd 7-1)
Novabridge, the winner of two of his three races, faced a stiff task conceding weight all round and was quickly left behind when the tempo increased. He should be seen to better effect in ordinary nursery company in due course. (op 12-1)
Sister June(IRE) faced a very tough task at the weights and as on her debut, did not show anywhere near enough to suggest she would be of much short-term interest.

2631 BETTER FURNITURE AT SOUTHTOWN ROAD (S) STKS 6f 3y
6:15 (6:19) (Class 6) 2-Y-O **£1,683** (£501; £250; £125) **Stalls** High

Form RPR

0 **1** **Tupelo (IRE)**[64] 1043 2-8-6 0.. LiamJones 5 60
(P W D'Arcy) *t.k.h: chsd ldrs: rdn and hung rt ent fnl 2f: chsd ldr wl over 1f out: ev ch and drvn over 1f out: led wl ins fnl f: drvn out* **9/4**[2]

4 **2** *½* **Artic Rose (IRE)**[8] 2391 2-8-3 0.. WilliamCarson(3) 8 59
(S C Williams) *racd alone on stands' rail: overall ldr: rdn wl over 1f out: hung lft and hld hd high ent fnl f: hdd wl ins fnl f: no ex towards fin* **11/2**[3]

545 **3** *hd* **King Of Cassis**[7] 2407 2-8-8 0.. JackDean(3) 3 63
(W G M Turner) *in tch: rdn to chse ldng pair wl over 1f out: hung rt u.p ins fnl f: swtchd lft fnl 75yds: styd on towards fin: nt able to rch ldrs* **7/4**[1]

565 **4** *8* **Dancing With Fire**[16] 2139 2-8-6 0.. ChrisCatlin 2 34
(D Donovan) *in tch towards rr: rdn and outpcd 1/2-way: rallied and hdwy ent fnl 2f: wknd u.p over 1f out* **20/1**

0 **5** *1* **Battenberg**[35] 1603 2-8-8 0 ow2.. JerryO'Dwyer 7 33
(Miss Amy Weaver) *in tch towards rr: u.p and struggling over 3f out: no threat to ldrs after* **16/1**

26 **6** *3* **Muse To Use**[8] 2391 2-8-6 0..(p) HayleyTurner 4 22
(I W McInnes) *chsd ldr tl wl over 1f out: sn hrd drvn and wknd over 1f out: no ch fnl f* **8/1**

0 **7** *2 ¼* **No Peace (IRE)**[50] 1263 2-7-13 0..(b[1]) RyanPowell(7) 1 15
(G G Margarson) *dwlt: sn in tch: hdwy to chse ldrs 1/2-way: rdn and wknd over 1f out: wl btn fnl f* **11/1**

0 **8** *12* **Little Nuthatch (IRE)**[41] 1463 2-8-6 0.. SaleemGolam 6 —
(P D Evans) *a bhd: lost tch over 2f out: t.o* **40/1**

1m 15.7s (1.30) **Going Correction** -0.05s/f (Good) 8 Ran SP% **115.0**
Speed ratings (Par 91): **89,88,88,77,76 72,69,53**
toteswingers:1&2:£5.10, 1&3:£1.90, 2&3:£3.90 CSF £15.30 TOTE £4.00: £1.40, £1.40, £1.10; EX 23.90.There was no bid for the winner.
Owner Stapleford Racing Ltd **Bred** Ms Marie Walsh **Trained** Newmarket, Suffolk

FOCUS

A modest seller in which the gallop was sound. The three market leaders pulled clear in the closing stages, with the third the best guide to the level.

NOTEBOOK

Tupelo(IRE), down in grade, attracted plenty of support and bettered her debut form over this longer trip, despite racing keenly and edging off a true line under pressure. She is not very big and, given this was not much of a race, would not be an obvious one to follow up. (op 5-1)

Artic Rose(IRE) bettered her debut run after racing away from the main centre group for much of the way. She showed a tendency to hang left in the closing stages and, although capable of picking up a similarly modest event, may not be one to take too short a price about. (tchd 8-1)

King Of Cassis looked to have solid prospects dropped in grade and upped in distance but, although not beaten far, was again below his best. He would not be one to take too short a price about. Official explanation: jockey said that the colt hung right (op 6-4 tchd 6-5)

Dancing With Fire again had his limitations exposed in this grade and will have to show a fair bit more before he is worth a bet. (op 16-1)

Battenberg, whose rider posted 2lb of overweight, gave trouble before the start and was quickly left behind when the tempo increased. (op 18-1 tchd 20-1)

No Peace(IRE) Official explanation: jockey said that the filly hung right

2632 INDESIT HOME APPLIANCE MAIDEN STKS — 1m 3y

6:45 (6:48) (Class 5) 3-Y-O+ — £2,590 (£578; £578; £192) Stalls High

Form — RPR

0 **1** **Shesells Seashells**[25] 1881 3-8-9 0 ChrisCatlin 11 — 68+
(C F Wall) *stdd s: hld up in tch in midfield: hdwy ent fnl 2f: swtchd rt over 1f out: chal jst ins fnl f: rdn and styd on wl to ld fnl 50yds* — **25/1**

0 **2** *nk* **Free As A Lark**[25] 1882 3-8-9 0 JackMitchell 12 — 67+
(C F Wall) *hld up wl in toiuch: rdn to chal over 1f out: led ent fnl f: drvn ins fnl f: hdd and no ex fnl 50yds* — **4/1**[2]

2 *dht* **Captivator** 3-8-9 0 HayleyTurner 4 — 70+
(J R Fanshawe) *stdd s: hld up in tch towards rr: hdwy 1/2-way: chsd ldrs and nt clr run 1f out: swtchd lft ins fnl f: styd on wl fnl 100yds: nt quite rch wnr* — **9/1**

0-0 **4** *2 1/4* **Fidler Bay**[29] 1757 4-9-11 0 FrankieMcDonald 10 — 70
(H Candy) *chsd ldrs: rdn along over 2f out: ev ch u.p over 1f out: no ex and one pce ins fnl f* — **66/1**

4-0 **5** *1 1/4* **Top Tigress**[49] 1278 3-8-9 0 RyanMoore 3 — 59
(Sir Michael Stoute) *chsd ldr tl led ent fnl 3f: drvn and hrd pressed 2f out: hdd ent fnl f: wknd fnl 100yds* — **9/2**[3]

6 *1 3/4* **Hear The Roar (IRE)** 3-9-0 0 NickyMackay 15 — 59
(J R Boyle) *s.i.s: bhd: pushed along wl over 2f out: rdn and hdwy over 1f out: kpt on steadily fnl f: nvr threatened ldrs* — **28/1**

0 **7** *1 1/2* **Kayaan**[14] 2220 3-9-0 0 TadhgO'Shea 5 — 56+
(W J Haggas) *awkward leaving stalls and s.i.s: sn rcvrd and chsd ldrs after 1f: chsd ldr 3f out: ev ch u.p 2f out: wknd 1f out* — **9/2**[3]

06- **8** *4* **One Cool Slash (IRE)**[164] 7806 3-8-9 0 JimmyQuinn 8 — 41
(M J McGrath) *chsd ldrs: rdn wl over 2f out: wknd u.p 2f out: wl btn fnl f* — **100/1**

0-0 **9** *1 3/4* **Rowan Light**[32] 1661 4-9-3 0 RobertLButler(3) 13 — 40+
(J R Boyle) *a towards rr: pushed along and rn green wl over 2f out: sme modest late hdwy: nvr trbld ldrs* — **66/1**

10 *3/4* **Melinoise** 3-8-6 0 WilliamCarson(3) 14 — 35
(Rae Guest) *s.i.s: a in rr: rdn and struggling over 4f out: n.d* — **33/1**

11 *1* **Mandate** 3-9-0 0 RobertHavlin 6 — 38
(J A R Toller) *dwlt: sn rcvrd and in tch: rdn and wknd over 2f out: wl btn over 1f out* — **20/1**

0-0 **12** *2* **Eye Of Eternity**[10] 2335 3-8-9 0 SaleemGolam 16 — 28
(Rae Guest) *s.i.s: a in rr: n.d* — **50/1**

13 *3 1/2* **Mont Ras (IRE)** 3-9-0 0 KierenFallon 9 — 25+
(E A L Dunlop) *v.s.a: sn pushed along in tch after 2f out: rdn 1/2-way: hdwy to chse ldrs ent fnl 2f: wknd wl over 1f out: wl btn 1f out: eased wl ins fnl f* — **10/3**[1]

14 *3/4* **Marcus Antonius** 3-9-0 0 MickyFenton 2 — 23
(J R Boyle) *s.i.s: sn in midfield but rn v green: rdn and lost pl 1/2-way: wl bhd fnl 2f* — **14/1**

00 **15** *2* **Rileys Crane**[14] 2220 3-9-0 0 TomMcLaughlin 7 — 18
(Mrs C A Dunnett) *t.k.h: led tl ent fnl 3f: wknd qckly over 2f out: wl bhd fr over 1f out* — **100/1**

1m 41.75s (1.15) **Going Correction** -0.05s/f (Good)
WFA 3 from 4yo 11lb — 15 Ran SP% **118.0**
Speed ratings (Par 103): **92,91,91,89,88 86,84,80,79,78 77,75,71,71,69**
PL: Captivator £1.40, Free As A Lark £1.90 EX: SS/CP £189.30 SS/FL £106.50 CSF: SS/CP £109.48 SS/FL £57.34 toteswingers:SS&CP:£21.40, CP&FL:£5.20, SS&FL:£21.00 TOTE £40.30: £10.60.
Owner Get To The Bar Racing **Bred** G A E And J Smith Bloodstock Ltd **Trained** Newmarket, Suffolk

FOCUS

No more than a fair maiden and one run at just an ordinary gallop. The field raced in the centre and the form is rated around one of the runners-up and fifth, while the third looked unlucky and is rated as the winner.

Fidler Bay Official explanation: jockey that the gelding ran green
Hear The Roar(IRE) Official explanation: jockey said that the gelding ran green
Mont Ras(IRE) Official explanation: jockey said that the colt was slowly away
Marcus Antonius Official explanation: jockey said that the gelding ran green

2633 CANNON COOKING H'CAP — 1m 3y

7:20 (7:23) (Class 6) (0-60,60) 3-Y-O — £1,942 (£578; £288; £144) Stalls High

Form — RPR

00-6 **1** **Rock The Stars (IRE)**[14] 2220 3-9-2 **58** SebSanders 5 — 65
(J W Hills) *stdd s: hld up towards rr: hdwy on far side 2f out: rdn over 1f out: str run ins fnl f to ld nr fin* — **7/1**[3]

0-54 **2** *hd* **Green For Luck (IRE)**[14] 2221 3-9-2 **58** JackMitchell 2 — 64
(S Gollings) *taken down early: rrd as stalls opened: sn rcvrd and chsng ldrs: rdn to ld 2f out: hrd rdn ent fnl f: kpt on wl tl hdd nr fin* — **11/1**

6140 **3** *1 1/4* **Motty's Gift**[9] 2359 3-8-13 **55** (v) ChrisCatlin 8 — 58
(W R Swinburn) *in tch in midfield: rdn over 3f out: hdwy and edgd lft 2f out: u.p to chse ldrs over 1f out: hrd drvn and pressed ldr 1f out: no ex and btn fnl 75yds* — **10/1**

0000 **4** *3/4* **Denton Ryal**[10] 2336 3-8-2 **51** AdamBeschizza(7) 7 — 52
(M E Rimmer) *hld up towards rr: hdwy over 2f out: squeezed through and bmpd rival wl over 1f out: chsd ldrs ldrs ent fnl f: styd on same pce fnl 150yds* — **25/1**

3030 **5** *hd* **Sunrise Lyric (IRE)**[14] 2219 3-9-2 **58** RyanMoore 16 — 59
(P F I Cole) *stdd and dropped in bhd after s: hld up in rr: hdwy wl over 1f out: rdn to chse ldr 1f out: no ex u.p fnl 150yds* — **9/2**[2]

56-2 **6** *1 1/2* **Man In The Mirror (IRE)**[42] 1461 3-8-9 **54** (p) AshleyHamblett(3) 12 — 51
(P L Gilligan) *t.k.h: chsd ldr tl over 2f out: unable qck u.p wl over 1f out: kpt on same pce fr over 1f out* — **16/1**

60-0 **7** *2 1/4* **Wavertree Bounty**[42] 1461 3-8-8 **50** HayleyTurner 3 — 42
(J Ryan) *stdd s: hld up towards rr: hdwy 1/2-way: chsd ldrs and rdn 2f out: wknd u.p over 1f out* — **33/1**

6053 **8** *3/4* **Chandrayaan**[19] 2049 3-9-3 **59** (v) SamHitchcott 4 — 49
(J E Long) *in tch in midfield: hdwy 3f out: chsng ldrs rdn 2f out: edgd rt u.p and bmpd wl over 1f out: wknd u.p over 1f out* — **14/1**

0-00 **9** *7* **Fasette**[49] 1278 3-8-8 **55** AshleyMorgan(5) 15 — 28
(M H Tompkins) *in tch: rdn and unable qck ent fnl 2f: wl btn over 1f out* — **16/1**

00 **10** *3/4* **Marjustar (IRE)**[5] 2480 3-8-8 **50** NickyMackay 6 — 22
(J R Boyle) *led tl rdn and hdd 2f out: wknd u.p over 1f out: wl btn ins fnl f* — **20/1**

6620 **11** *1 1/2* **Mack's Sister**[28] 1796 3-9-4 **60** JimmyQuinn 14 — 28
(D K Ivory) *t.k.h: hld up in tch: rdn and nt qckn ent fnl 2f: wl btn over 1f out* — **14/1**

30-0 **12** *6* **Labretella (IRE)**[40] 1495 3-8-10 **52** ow2 MickyFenton 10 — 6
(S A Harris) *taken down early but dismntd and eventually led to s: hld up in rr: effrt towards stands' side over 2f out: no prog whn nt clr run 2f out: sn hung lft and wl btn* — **40/1**

-052 **13** *6* **All Moving Parts (USA)**[22] 1970 3-9-2 **58** KierenFallon 9 — —
(J S Wainwright) *a towards rr: rdn 4f out: wl btn fnl 2f* — **3/1**[1]

0-00 **14** *4* **Tumbled Again**[7] 2418 3-8-5 **50** (b[1]) MarcHalford(3) 1 — —
(M E Rimmer) *in tch: rdn over 3f out: lost pl wl over 2f out: sn wl bhd: t.o* — **66/1**

050 **15** *19* **Trelicia**[50] 1257 3-9-1 **60** WilliamCarson(3) 13 — —
(S C Williams) *in tch towards rr: rdn and hung rt ent fnl 2f: sn wl bhd: eased ins fnl f: t.o* — **9/1**

1m 41.57s (0.97) **Going Correction** -0.05s/f (Good) — 15 Ran SP% **123.7**
Speed ratings (Par 97): **93,92,91,90,90 89,86,86,79,78 76,70,64,60,41**
toteswingers:1&2:£18.20, 1&3:£7.90, 2&3:£27.50 CSF £79.26 CT £803.08 TOTE £9.50: £4.30, £3.00, £4.00; EX 83.70.
Owner David Cohen **Bred** Bernard Cooke **Trained** Upper Lambourn, Berks

FOCUS

A moderate handicap run at a fair gallop in which the field fanned across the course in the last quarter mile. The third, fourth and fifth are rated close to recent handicap form.

All Moving Parts(USA) Official explanation: jockey that the gelding lost action

2634 BENNETTSONLINE.CO.UK H'CAP — 7f 3y

7:50 (7:52) (Class 6) (0-60,60) 3-Y-O — £1,942 (£578; £288; £144) Stalls High

Form — RPR

0001 **1** **Collect Art (IRE)**[7] 2418 3-8-9 **51** 6ex (v[1]) HayleyTurner 9 — 65+
(M L W Bell) *t.k.h: in tch: rdn and effrt 2f out: drvn to chal over 1f out: led jst ins fnl f: styd on* — **10/3**[2]

0660 **2** *1* **Miss Kitty Grey (IRE)**[7] 2418 3-8-12 **54** RobertHavlin 7 — 65
(J R Boyle) *in tch in midfield: pushed along over 3f out: rdn and hdwy over 1f out: chsd wnr fnl 100yds: kpt on but no imp after* — **66/1**

00-6 **3** *2 1/2* **Micky P**[42] 1442 3-8-13 **58** WilliamCarson(3) 3 — 62
(S C Williams) *t.k.h: w ldrs: rdn ent fnl 2f: wknd u.p ins fnl f* — **9/2**[3]

-046 **4** *1 1/4* **Bonnie Brae**[14] 2221 3-9-4 **60** (b[1]) SebSanders 6 — 61
(G G Margarson) *t.k.h: chsd ldr tl led 4f out: rdn 2f out: hrd drvn over 1f out: hdd jst ins fnl f: wknd fnl 100yds* — **9/1**

0003 **5** *1* **Eywa**[21] 2005 3-9-3 **59** KierenFallon 2 — 57+
(W Jarvis) *in tch: rdn and unable qck ent fnl 2f: outpcd wl over 1f out: edgd rt but plugged on again fnl f: nt pce to rch ldrs* — **9/4**[1]

0044 **6** *2 1/4* **Tislaam (IRE)**[11] 2274 3-9-4 **60** (p) MickyFenton 10 — 52
(J S Wainwright) *stdd after s: t.k.h: hld up in last trio: rdn and effrt 2f out: no hdwy and wl hld ent fnl f* — **10/1**

5006 **7** *1/2* **Bell's Ocean (USA)**[35] 1605 3-8-11 **53** JerryO'Dwyer 8 — 44
(J Ryan) *led tl 4f out: rdn over 2f out: wknd u.p over 1f out* — **33/1**

0-00 **8** *nse* **Dixi Heights**[7] 2418 3-8-13 **55** (b) PatCosgrave 11 — 46
(J R Boyle) *hld up in tch towards rr: effrt u.p and no prog 2f out: nvr trbld ldrs* — **16/1**

0006 **9** *6* **Chocolate Cookie (IRE)**[22] 1982 3-9-2 **58** TomMcLaughlin 5 — 32
(Miss M E Rowland) *stdd after s: hld up in tch: rdn wl over 2f out: wknd ent fnl 2f: wl bhd over 1f out* — **14/1**

0200 **10** *1 1/4* **A Pocketful Of Rye (IRE)**[14] 2215 3-9-1 **60** MichaelStainton(3) 13 — 31
(P Howling) *a in rr: rdn over 2f out: lost tch wl over 1f out* — **14/1**

00-0 **11** *11* **Tudor Princess**[32] 1661 3-9-3 **59** ChrisCatlin 1 — —
(W R Muir) *chsd ldrs: rdn and hung lft over 2f out: sn wknd: t.o fnl f* **16/1**

1m 26.73s (0.13) **Going Correction** -0.05s/f (Good) — 11 Ran SP% **120.7**
Speed ratings (Par 97): **97,95,93,91,90 87,87,87,80,78 66**
toteswingers:1&2:£20.90, 1&3:£3.10, 2&3:£27.30 CSF £194.07 CT £1037.10 TOTE £4.30: £1.50, £14.10, £1.80; EX 154.80.
Owner R A Green **Bred** Pier House Stud **Trained** Newmarket, Suffolk

FOCUS

Another moderate handicap and one run at an ordinary gallop. the placed horses set the level and with the time reasonable the race has been rated slightly positively.

2635 MEDIUM UK / BENNETTS H'CAP — 6f 3y

8:25 (8:26) (Class 5) (0-75,81) 4-Y-O+ — £2,460 (£732; £365; £182) Stalls High

Form — RPR

-002 **1** **Piazza San Pietro**[8] 2385 4-8-11 **65** RobertHavlin 10 — 72
(A B Haynes) *hld up wl in tch towards rr: rdn and hdwy over 1f out: drvn and ev ch 1f out: kpt on wl to ld last stride* — **12/1**

0-66 **2** *shd* **Requisite**[17] 2123 5-8-7 **61** (v) HayleyTurner 5 — 68
(I A Wood) *stdd after s: hld up in tch in rr: hdwy wl over 1f out: rdn to chal ent fnl f: led ins fnl f: hdd last stride* — **15/2**[3]

0336 **3** *nse* **Whiskey Junction**[11] 2301 6-9-6 **74** SebSanders 2 — 80
(M Quinn) *led: rdn over 1f out: hdd ins fnl f: kpt on wl tl no ex nr fin* **13/2**[2]

5361 **4** *nk* **Dvinsky (USA)**[12] 2246 9-8-11 **65** (b) JimmyQuinn 7 — 70
(P Howling) *w ldr thrght: rdn wl over 1f out: unable qck u.p wl ins fnl f* — **10/1**

1010 **5** *3/4* **Rough Rock (IRE)**[11] 2301 5-8-10 **64** AndreaAtzeni 4 — 67
(C A Dwyer) *in tch: pushed along and effrt over 1f out: edging rt ins fnl f: kpt on same pce fnl 100yds* — **9/1**

2041 **6** *1/2* **Anne Of Kiev (IRE)**[8] 2399 5-9-13 **81** 6ex (t) SteveDrowne 1 — 82
(J R Gask) *in tch: rdn and unable qck wl over 1f out: styd on one pce ins fnl f* — **11/8**[1]

0066 **7** *3 1/4* **Simple Rhythm**[4] 2485 4-8-9 **70** JoshCrane(7) 8 — 61
(J Ryan) *chsd ldrs: hdwy to join ldrs ent fnl 2f: rdn and wknd jst over 1f out* — **28/1**

25-0 **8** *3 1/4* **Captainrisk (IRE)**[8] 2399 4-9-5 **73** (t) TomMcLaughlin 6 — 54
(Mrs C A Dunnett) *hld up in tch towards rr: rdn and unable qck ent fnl 2f: wl btn over 1f out* — **20/1**

0-25 **9** *3 1/2* **Amosite**[17] 2123 4-9-1 **69** KierenFallon 9 — 38
(J R Jenkins) *w ldrs tl 2f out: sn struggling: wl btn fnl f* — **16/1**

00-2 **10** *nk* **Maryolini**[21] 2008 5-8-4 **58** oh1 ow2 ChrisCatlin 3 26
(T Keddy) *a towards rr: rdn and no hdwy ent fnl 2f: n.d after* **14/1**
1m 13.26s (-1.14) **Going Correction** -0.05s/f (Good) **10** Ran SP% **114.7**
Speed ratings (Par 103): **105,104,104,104,103 102,98,94,89,89**
toteswingers:1&2:£4.60, 1&3:£12.40, 2&3:£6.10 CSF £97.29 CT £654.30 TOTE £12.00: £3.60, £1.80, £2.40; EX 101.30.
Owner K Corke **Bred** T E Pocock **Trained** Limpley Stoke, Bath

FOCUS
Exposed performers in a fair handicap and the form looks straightforward. The gallop was only an ordinary one for a sprint and the first five finished in a heap. The field raced centre to stands' side from halfway and the first two were closest to the rail.
Anne Of Kiev(IRE) Official explanation: jockey said the mare lost her action

2636 HYUNDAI AT CONSTITUTION MOTORS H'CAP 1m 2f 21y
8:55 (8:55) (Class 6) (0-55,61) 4-Y-O+ **£1,942** (£578; £288; £144) **Stalls** Low

Form RPR
0-31 **1** **Aestival**[4] 2488 4-9-6 **61** 6ex SebSanders 4 83+
(Sir Mark Prescott) *chsd ldr tl led gng wl 4f out: clr fr wl over 2f out: eased ins fnl f: v easily* **4/9**[1]
0042 **2** *4 ½* **Libre**[11] 2299 10-8-2 **48** AshleyMorgan(5) 5 56
(F Jordan) *hld up in tch in midfield: hdwy to chse ldng pair 4f out: chsd clr wnr over 2f out: no imp* **16/1**
050 **3** *3 ¾* **Comrade Cotton**[41] 1478 6-8-7 **51** MarcHalford(3) 6 52
(J Ryan) *hld up towards rr: hdwy on inner 3f out: swtchd rt over 1f out: wnt modest 3rd ins fnl f: no ch w wnr* **33/1**
0005 **4** *½* **Holyfield Warrior (IRE)**[13] 2232 6-8-7 **48** HayleyTurner 10 48
(R J Smith) *hld up wl bhd in last pair: hdwy to chal for placings 1f out: kpt on: no ch w wnr* **25/1**
3602 **5** *1 ¼* **Mister Frosty (IRE)**[35] 1592 4-8-12 **53** SaleemGolam 2 50
(G Prodromou) *led tl hdd and rdn 4f out: no ch w wnr fr 3f out: lost 2 pls ins fnl f* **10/1**[2]
4345 **6** *2 ¼* **Ocean Of Peace (FR)**[9] 2361 7-8-5 **46** JimmyQuinn 9 39
(M R Bosley) *hld up towards rr: pushed along and effrt over 2f out: no hdwy fnl 2f: n.d* **22/1**
6-62 **7** *4* **Al Rayanah**[39] 1507 7-8-7 **55** RichardOld(7) 3 40
(G Prodromou) *hld up wl bhd in last: swtchd wd 3f out: nvr on terms* **16/1**
3000 **8** *12* **Alternative Choice (USA)**[13] 2230 4-8-12 **53** J-PGuillambert 8 14
(N P Littmoden) *in tch in midfield: rdn and struggling 4f out: wl bhd fnl 2f* **50/1**
0000 **9** *1 ¼* **Haasem (USA)**[7] 2417 7-8-11 **52** KierenFallon 1 10
(J R Jenkins) *chsd ldrs tl wknd u.p 4f out: towards rr whn hmpd 3f out: sn lost tch* **12/1**[3]
4000 **10** *9* **Achromatic**[33] 1635 4-8-8 **49** (b[1]) ChrisCatlin 11 —
(W R Swinburn) *chsd ldrs tl wknd u.p wl over 3f out: wl bhd fnl 2f* **22/1**
2m 9.61s (-0.89) **Going Correction** -0.05s/f (Good) **10** Ran SP% **115.2**
Speed ratings (Par 101): **101,97,94,94,93 91,88,78,77,70**
toteswingers:1&2:£2.80, 1&3:£12.40, 2&3:£68.70 CSF £7.67 CT £115.98 TOTE £1.40: £1.02, £2.80, £8.30; EX 8.50 Place 6 £90.00; Place 5 £82.12.
Owner Lady Katharine Watts **Bred** Miss K Rausing **Trained** Newmarket, Suffolk

FOCUS
A moderate handicap run at a fair gallop and won in ready fashion by the one progressive horse in the field. He looks way ahead of his current mark and the runner-up is rated to his winter all-weather form.
Alternative Choice(USA) Official explanation: jocket said that the gelding lost a shoe
T/Plt: £106.60 to a £1 stake. Pool:£68,912.81 - 471.67 winning tickets T/Qpdt: £127.00 to a £1 stake. Pool:£5,014.40 - 29.20 winning tickets SP

TABY (R-H)
Tuesday, June 1
OFFICIAL GOING: Turf: good

2637a STOCKHOLMS STORA PRIS (GROUP 3) (4YO+) (TURF) 1m 1f 165y
8:04 (12:00) 4-Y-O+ **£60,606** (£21,645; £10,389; £6,926; £4,329)

RPR
1 **Tertullus (FR)**[31] 7-9-2 0 EspenSki 8 105
(Rune Haugen, Norway) *racd in midfield: hdwy 3f out: led 2f out: sn clr: r.o wl u.p* **36/1**
2 *2* **Touch Of Hawk (FR)**[15] 2195 4-9-2 0 LennartHammer-Hansen 6 101
(Wido Neuroth, Norway) *plld hrd in rr first 3f: eighth 3f out: r.o to dispute 2nd 2f out: styd on wout getting to wnr* **77/10**
3 *2* **Theatrical Award (NOR)**[21] 2020 5-8-11 0 CarlosLopez 4 92
(Michael Taylor, Norway) *short of room on rail first f: settled in midfield: r.o ins fnl 2f to take 3rd fnl f: kpt on same pce* **18/1**
4 *½* **Smart Enough**[282] 5302 7-9-2 0 ManuelMartinez 11 96
(Fredrik Reuterskiold, Sweden) *hld up towards rr: styd on u.p fnl 2f: nvr threatened* **74/10**
5 *nk* **Kings Gambit (SAF)**[26] 1832 6-9-2 0 JamieSpencer 5 95
(T P Tate) *chsd ldrs: cl up whn rdn and nt qckn 2f out: styd on ins fnl f* **23/10**[1]
6 *¾* **Volo Cat (FR)**[15] 2195 6-9-2 0 ManuelSantos 7 94
(Bent Olsen, Denmark) *last: hdwy on outside 2 1/2f out: r.o wl fnl f: nvr nrr* **50/1**
7 *1* **Palermo (GER)**[31] 4-9-2 0 AlanMunro 12 91
(Cathrine Erichsen, Norway) *chsd ldrs: 3rd and ev ch 2f out: sn rdn and no ex* **10/1**
8 *¾* **Perks (IRE)**[31] 5-9-2 0 KimAndersen 1 90
(Jessica Long, Sweden) *plld early: settled towards rr: last 2f out: mde sme late hdwy: n.d* **34/1**
9 *1 ¼* **Sehoy (USA)**[232] 6724 4-9-2 0 JacobJohansen 3 87
(Lennart Reuterskiold Jr, Sweden) *disp ld early: 2nd after 1 1/2f: led 3f out tl hdd 2f out and fdd* **104/10**
10 *2* **Peas And Carrots (DEN)**[233] 7-9-2 0 Per-AndersGraberg 9 83
(Lennart Reuterskiold Jr, Sweden) *chsd ldrs: rdn and btn 2f out* **54/10**[3]
11 *2 ½* **Alpacco (IRE)**[15] 2195 8-9-2 0 EddieAhern 2 78
(Sandie Kjaer Nortoft, Denmark) *disp ld early: led after 1 1/2f: hdd 3f out: sn rdn and wknd* **102/10**
12 *hd* **Luca Brasi (FR)**[21] 2020 6-9-2 0 RafaelSchistl 10 77
(Francisco Castro, Sweden) *w ldrs: slipped and lost pl first bnd: midfield and clsng 3f out: sn rdn and dropped away* **49/10**[2]
1m 57.8s (-1.50) **12** Ran SP% **125.9**
PARI-MUTUEL (all including 1sek stake): WIN 36.79; PLACE 6.10, 3.63, 9.34; DF 304.65.
Owner Stall Nor & Lagulise Racing **Bred** H Volz **Trained** Norway

NOTEBOOK
Kings Gambit(SAF), a winner at this trip in April, was up in grade and could not go with the leader when the pace quickened before keeping on to the finish.

1763 KEMPTON (A.W) (R-H)
Wednesday, June 2
OFFICIAL GOING: Standard
Wind: Almost Nil Weather: Sunny, warm

2638 SUMMER SERIES IS HERE MEDIAN AUCTION MAIDEN STKS 5f (P)
5:50 (5:51) (Class 6) 2-Y-O **£2,047** (£604; £302) **Stalls** High

Form RPR
0 **1** **Excello**[16] 2176 2-8-12 0 IanMongan 10 87+
(M S Saunders) *sn trckd ldr: clsd to ld over 1f out: and briefly rn green: sprinted clr* **7/1**
30 **2** *4* **The Thrill Is Gone**[13] 2251 2-8-12 0 AlanMunro 12 73
(M R Channon) *prom bhd ldr: rdn and effrt over 1f out: styd on fnl f to take 2nd last 75yds* **6/1**[3]
32 **3** *1 ½* **Button Moon (IRE)**[9] 2376 2-8-12 0 RichardThomas 2 67
(I A Wood) *fast away fr wd draw: led and sn crossed to rails: hdd and no answer to wnr over 1f out: lost 2nd last 75yds* **6/4**[1]
4 *3 ¼* **Palindromic (IRE)** 2-9-3 0 NeilCallan 11 61
(J R Gask) *s.s: sn in tch on inner: trckd ldrs gng wl enough 1/2-way: outpcd over 1f out: no ch after* **12/1**
045 **5** *nk* **Silly Billy (IRE)**[6] 2457 2-9-3 0 LiamKeniry 6 59
(S Kirk) *prom bhd ldr: rdn 2f out: outpcd fr over 1f out* **20/1**
05 **6** *6* **Allegrissimo (IRE)**[10] 2358 2-8-12 0 (b[1]) AdamKirby 5 33
(C G Cox) *struggling in midfield after 2f and reminder: rn wd bnd 2f out: drvn and kpt on to take remote 6th nr fin* **16/1**
0 **7** *1* **Lord Of The Storm**[8] 2407 2-9-0 0 JackDean(3) 1 34
(W G M Turner) *outpcd and wl bhd in last pair: modest late prog on inner: nvr a factor* **100/1**
8 *2 ¼* **Furiosa (IRE)** 2-8-12 0 EddieCreighton 7 21
(E J Creighton) *dwlt: drvn into midfield 1/2-way: wl outpcd fnl 2f* **66/1**
9 *¾* **Cold Secret** 2-9-3 0 DaneO'Neill 9 23
(D R C Elsworth) *s.s: wl bhd in last: sme v modest late prog* **7/2**[2]
0 **10** *7* **Zohan (IRE)**[16] 2183 2-9-3 0 AdrianMcCarthy 8 —
(Peter Grayson) *drvn in midfield after 2f: outpcd and c wd bnd 2f out: sn wl bhd* **100/1**
03 **11** *3 ¾* **My Mate Al**[16] 2183 2-8-12 0 RichardSmith 3 —
(Tom Dascombe) *nvr on terms: wl btn whn rn wd bnd 2f out* **25/1**
60 **12** *4 ½* **Miss Maudie (IRE)**[13] 2245 2-8-12 0 DavidProbert 4 —
(J J Bridger) *hanging lft thrght: already struggling whn v wd 3f out to 2f out: t.o: sddle slipped* **200/1**
60.59 secs (0.09) **Going Correction** -0.05s/f (Stan) **12** Ran SP% **115.2**
Speed ratings (Par 91): **97,90,88,83,82 72,71,67,66,55 49,42**
toteswingers: 1&2 £6.00, 1&3 £2.50, 2&3 £2.80. CSF £45.31 TOTE £10.90: £3.80, £1.10, £1.90; EX 56.40.
Owner Chris Scott **Bred** Whatton Manor Stud **Trained** Green Ore, Somerset

FOCUS
There did not seem to be a great deal of strength in depth in this juvenile maiden auction but they finished well strung out and the two main form contenders finished placed, so the form could work out. The winner improved markedly on her debut while the runner-up is rated back to her debut form.

NOTEBOOK
Excello looked inexperienced but showed a bit of ability when ninth in a Windsor maiden on debut. The £24,000 filly looked a different proposition this time, travelling well just behind the pace and unleashing a good turn of foot to power clear just inside the final furlong. She is open to further progress and her style and pedigree suggest she should stay an extra furlong or two this season. (op 8-1)
The Thrill Is Gone was a bit disappointing at Sandown last time in a bid to build on her promising 50-1 third on debut, but the speedily bred half-sister to a couple of useful 5f winners bounced back with a fair effort switched to Polytrack. (op 9-2 tchd 13-2)
Button Moon(IRE) set the standard on her third behind a subsequent listed winner on debut and clear second to a well-backed Richard Fahey-trained newcomer at Carlisle last week. She made a swift move to grab the early lead from an outside draw and things looked to be going well for a long way, but she could not respond when the winner attacked and then lost the battle for second. She was reported to have lost a shoe. Official explanation: jockey said filly lost a left-fore shoe (op 7-4 tchd 15-8)
Palindromic(IRE) was never dangerous but showed some promise on debut. He is an 11,000gns half-brother to fair 5f 2-y-o winner Night Trade. (op 10-1 tchd 14-1)
Silly Billy(IRE) had been beaten 5l+ in three previous starts and it was a similar story on AW debut. He is not really progressing.
Cold Secret, out of a Lowther Stakes winner who has been a good source of juvenile winners, was well backed on this debut but never got anywhere near the leaders after missing the break. (op 4-1 tchd 3-1)
Miss Maudie(IRE) Official explanation: jockey said filly hung left and saddle slipped

2639 DIGIBET.COM H'CAP 5f (P)
6:20 (6:21) (Class 5) (0-70,68) 3-Y-O+ **£2,590** (£770; £385; £192) **Stalls** High

Form RPR
1 **Captain Coke (IRE)**[19] 2104 3-9-4 **68** AndreaAtzeni 7 74
(Denis P Quinn, Ire) *chsd ldrs on outer: shkn up 2f out: clsd 1f out: pushed into ld last 50yds: readily* **15/2**
6-00 **2** *1* **Island Legend (IRE)**[14] 2229 4-9-7 **64** (b[1]) ChrisCatlin 11 70
(J M Bradley) *led: drvn and over a l clr ent fnl f: hung lft and hdd last 50yds: wknd* **7/1**
0110 **3** *hd* **West Leake (IRE)**[13] 2246 4-9-3 **60** LiamKeniry 10 65+
(P Burgoyne) *settled in midfield: effrt over 1f out: plenty to do and nt clrest of runs ent fnl f: drvn and r.o last 150yds* **13/2**[3]
300- **4** *½* **Steelcut**[169] 7758 6-9-7 **67** RussKennemore(3) 8 70
(Andrew Reid) *chsd ldng trio: u.p and nt qckn over 1f out: lost pl: styd on again fnl 100yds* **12/1**
-205 **5** *nk* **South African (USA)**[11] 2332 4-9-6 **63** GeorgeBaker 6 65
(M A Magnusson) *chsd ldr: rdn and no imp over 1f out: losing pl whn n.m.r last 100yds* **12/1**
1334 **6** *hd* **Love You Louis**[12] 2301 4-9-10 **67** RichardHughes 4 68
(J R Jenkins) *pushed along to stay in tch over 3f out: effrt on outer over 1f out: rdn ent fnl f: styd on but no ch: eased last strides* **4/1**[1]
0-60 **7** *1* **Edith's Boy (IRE)**[89] 806 4-9-9 **66** SebSanders 12 64
(S Dow) *chsd ldng pair: rdn and nt qckn on inner over 1f out: lost pl ins fnl f* **6/1**[2]

5001 **8** *1* **Figaro Flyer (IRE)**[16] 2186 7-9-7 **64** .... J-PGuillambert 9 58
(P Howling) *awkward s: settled in last trio: pushed along fr 2f out: styd on steadily fnl f: nvr nr ldrs* **8/1**

6500 **9** *1* **Pipers Piping (IRE)**[13] 2257 4-9-2 **59** .... SaleemGolam 1 50
(P Howling) *stdd fr wd draw but racd wd: a in last trio: reminder over 1f out: nvr nr ldrs* **33/1**

3-43 **10** *½* **Matterofact (IRE)**[11] 2332 7-9-3 **60** .... TomMcLaughlin 5 49
(M S Saunders) *s.i.s: settled in last trio: pushed along quite vigorously 2f out: reminder over 1f out: nvr nr ldrs* **8/1**

222/ **11** *7* **Herotozero (IRE)**[25] 1938 6-9-7 **64** ....(b) NeilCallan 3 28
(Gerard O'Leary, Ire) *racd wd: sn rdn in midfield: lost grnd bnd 2f out: sn bhd* **10/1**

60.58 secs (0.08) **Going Correction** -0.05s/f (Stan)
WFA 3 from 4yo+ 7lb 11 Ran SP% **121.5**
Speed ratings (Par 103): **97,95,95,94,93 93,91,90,88,87 76**
toteswingers: 1&2 £14.90, 1&3 £13.30, 2&3 £6.30. CSF £61.30 CT £368.08 TOTE £10.00: £3.30, £3.70, £1.50; EX 89.10.
Owner Peter A Quinn **Bred** Fintan Walsh **Trained** Sixmilebridge, Co. Clare

FOCUS
A minor sprint handicap. It was run at a good pace but they finished in a bunch. The placed horses set the level.
Figaro Flyer(IRE) Official explanation: jockey said gelding missed the break

2640 DIGIBET REDFERN H'CAP 1m 2f (P)
6:50 (6:51) (Class 3) (0-95,94) 4-Y-0+
£6,542 (£1,959; £979; £490; £244; £122) **Stalls** High

Form RPR

161 **1** **Submariner (USA)**[7] 2435 4-9-1 **88** 6ex .... FrankieDettori 6 97+
(M Johnston) *prog on outer to ld after 2f: hdd after 4f: styd prom: rdn to ld 1f out: styd on wl* **2/1**[1]

4-50 **2** *½* **Classic Punch (IRE)**[19] 2096 7-9-4 **91** .... WilliamBuick 10 99
(D R C Elsworth) *led 2f: settled bhd ldrs: rdn 3f out: prog to chal over 1f out: pressed wnr after: nt qckn last 100yds* **40/1**

11-6 **3** *2* **Luc Jordan**[27] 1837 4-9-0 **87** .... J-PGuillambert 13 91
(L M Cumani) *hld up in 9th: prog over 2f out: rdn wl over 1f out: styd on to take 3rd nr fin: nvr rchd ldrs* **5/2**[2]

65 **4** *nse* **Silver Point (FR)**[12] 2282 7-9-2 **89** .... DavidProbert 9 93
(B Palling) *chsd ldrs: rdn 3f out: styd on u.p fnl f: nvr able to chal* **28/1**

1331 **5** *½* **Mr Hichens**[27] 1841 5-9-0 **87** .... TadhgO'Shea 8 90
(Karen George) *prog arnd outer to ld 8f out: drvn 2f out: hdd 1f out: wknd nr fin* **20/1**

4262 **6** *2¼* **The Kyllachy Kid**[30] 1767 4-8-12 **85** ....(p) IanMongan 3 84
(S Gollings) *prom: mostly chsd ldr after 2f to over 1f out: wknd* **20/1**

20-0 **7** *shd* **Greylami (IRE)**[42] 1474 5-9-5 **92** .... JimmyFortune 14 94+
(R A Mills) *hld up in 7th: effrt 3f out: pushed along and styng on whn squeezed out jst over 1f out: nt rcvr* **8/1**[3]

560- **8** *2* **Stevie Thunder**[235] 6665 5-9-0 **87** .... StevieDonohoe 2 81
(Ian Williams) *dwlt: hld up in last pair: detached 3f out: pushed along and kpt on steadily fnl 2f* **25/1**

5006 **9** *nk* **Yahrab (IRE)**[11] 2318 5-9-7 **94** .... NeilCallan 1 88
(C E Brittain) *hld up in abt 8th: effrt 3f out: rdn and no hdwy over 2f out: n.d after* **16/1**

1500 **10** *1* **Franco Is My Name**[6] 2467 4-8-12 **85** .... DaneO'Neill 7 77
(P R Hedger) *hld up in 11th: prog on outer 3f out: rdn 2f out: no hdwy over 1f out: fdd* **14/1**

-302 **11** *½* **Wise Dennis**[35] 1618 8-8-11 **84** .... TomQueally 11 75
(A P Jarvis) *dwlt: hld up in 10th: n.m.r on inner 6f out: rdn and no prog over 2f out* **16/1**

-135 **12** *7* **Highly Regal (IRE)**[18] 2124 5-8-12 **85** ....(b) LiamKeniry 12 62
(R A Teal) *t.k.h: hld up in 12th: rdn and no prog 3f out* **16/1**

2626 **13** *2* **Sohcahtoa (IRE)**[11] 2317 4-9-7 **94** ....(b) RichardHughes 4 67
(R Hannon) *prog on outer to go prom 8f out: wknd rapidly 3f out: sn bhd* **16/1**

2026 **14** *18* **Thunderstruck**[7] 2435 5-9-0 **87** ....(p) ChrisCatlin 5 24
(J A Glover) *dwlt: a last and nvr gng wl: t.o* **40/1**

2m 6.21s (-1.79) **Going Correction** -0.05s/f (Stan) 14 Ran SP% **124.9**
Speed ratings (Par 107): **105,104,103,102,102 100,100,99,98,98 97,92,90,76**
toteswingers: 1&2 £54.30, 1&3 £1.50, 2&3 £13.00. CSF £109.73 CT £221.66 TOTE £3.00: £1.80, £18.00, £1.20; EX 117.20.
Owner Sheikh Hamdan Bin Mohammed Al Maktoum **Bred** Darley **Trained** Middleham Moor, N Yorks

FOCUS
A decent handicap. The pace was steady but the favourite and least exposed runner in the field got the job done in professional style and the clear second favourite finished third. The form looks solid despite the prominent racers appearing to be favoured.

NOTEBOOK
Submariner(USA) made it two wins from three runs when making all in a Beverley handicap last week. He had a penalty to defy and couldn't maintain an uncontested lead on AW debut but kept his composure and showed a good attitude to forge his way back to the front inside the final furlong. The long-striding individual looks a very likeable and progressive type who should have scope for further improvement. (op 5-2 tchd 11-4)
Classic Punch(IRE) had shown regressive form since a second over this trip at Newmarket last August but he burst back to life off a career-low mark on belated AW debut and went close to springing a 40-1 surprise.
Luc Jordan ran a solid enough race but could not quite get into a threatening position off the uneven pace. He ended his 3-y-o campaign with a hat-trick and could continue his progress in more strongly run handicaps this season. (op 7-2 tchd 4-1)
Silver Point(FR) stayed on well under a strong ride on his third run for a new yard. His record of 3-5 on AW tracks in France, included a Listed win, and he could make a big impact off a potentially lenient mark off a faster pace next time. (op 25-1)
Mr Hichens was a triple winner on Polytrack during the winter and powered clear over 1m at Ffos Las last month. The revitalised performer couldn't deal with an 8lb higher mark in a stronger race back at 1m2f but ran respectably under a positive ride and pulled clear of the sixth.
Highly Regal(IRE) Official explanation: jockey said gelding ran too free

2641 EUROPEAN BREEDERS' FUND MAIDEN FILLIES' STKS (DIV I) 6f (P)
7:20 (7:21) (Class 5) 2-Y-O £3,626 (£1,079; £539; £269) **Stalls** High

Form RPR

1 **Hooray** 2-9-0 0 .... SebSanders 11 87+
(Sir Mark Prescott) *tk v t.k.h: trckd ldng pair: wnt 2nd over 2f out: led over 1f out: r.o wl* **7/2**[2]

2 *2½* **Jetfire** 2-9-0 0 .... JimmyFortune 7 77+
(P F I Cole) *led: rdn and hdd over 1f out: styd on wl enough and clr of rest but no ch w wnr* **20/1**

3 *5* **Zabeel Park (USA)** 2-9-0 0 .... FrankieDettori 3 62+
(Saeed Bin Suroor) *chsd ldr to over 2f out: shkn up and sn outpcd: hld on for 3rd* **6/1**[3]

03 **4** *¾* **Hoppy's Flyer (FR)**[39] 1510 2-9-0 0 .... RichardSmith 6 60
(Tom Dascombe) *chsd ldng quartet: outpcd over 2f out: effrt and kpt on fr over 1f out: n.d* **25/1**

3 **5** *2¾* **Take Flight (IRE)**[13] 2251 2-9-0 0 .... WilliamBuick 5 52
(J Noseda) *settled at rr of main gp: effrt over 2f out: nt pce to trble ldrs over 1f out: no prog after* **10/11**[1]

6 *1¾* **Sukhothai (USA)** 2-9-0 0 .... TomQueally 4 47
(H R A Cecil) *racd wd: hld up at bk of main gp: pushed along over 2f out: no real prog* **14/1**

0 **7** *½* **Disco Doll**[33] 1660 2-9-0 0 .... SaleemGolam 1 45
(G D Blake) *dropped in fr wd draw: hld up in rr of main gp: nt clr run on inner over 2f out: sn wl outpcd* **100/1**

3 **8** *2¼* **Elkmait**[14] 2223 2-9-0 0 .... NeilCallan 10 38
(C E Brittain) *rring bdly in stalls bef s: rrd s: rcvrd to chse ldng trio to over 1f out: wknd* **7/1**

9 *9* **I Dreamed A Dream** 2-9-0 0 .... ChrisCatlin 12 11+
(D K Ivory) *s.v.s: a t.o* **80/1**

10 *7* **Zafrina** 2-9-0 0 .... AdrianMcCarthy 9 —
(Peter Grayson) *dwlt: rcvrd to chse ldrs: wknd rapidly over 2f out: t.o* **100/1**

1m 13.17s (0.07) **Going Correction** -0.05s/f (Stan) 10 Ran SP% **119.9**
Speed ratings (Par 90): **97,93,87,86,82 80,79,76,64,55**
toteswingers: 1&2 £11.90, 1&3 £4.10, 2&3 £9.10. CSF £72.84 TOTE £3.60: £1.10, £10.90, £1.40; EX 123.60.
Owner Cheveley Park Stud **Bred** Cheveley Park Stud Ltd **Trained** Newmarket, Suffolk

FOCUS
An interesting fillies' maiden, involving a number of well-bred types from powerful yards. The pace was fairly steady and hot favourite was disappointing but there was plenty to like about the performance of the winner. Not an easy race to race with the first three newcomers, but it could be a decent event.

NOTEBOOK
Hooray raced enthusiastically just behind the pace and kicked clear after seizing the initiative against the far rail inside the final 2f. She is a half-sister to Hypnotic, a useful triple 7f-1m winner at two for the same yard, including in Listed company in France. The daughter of Invincible Spirit looks a potentially useful prospect for the Sir Mark Prescott winning machine that has started to whirl into gear recently. (op 5-1 tchd 10-3)
Jetfire ran a promising race under a forcing ride on debut. She is out of a multiple 5f-6f winner and looks a speedy type. (op 25-1)
Zabeel Park(USA), a 500,000gns half-sister to Finsceal Beo who completed the English/Irish 1000 Guineas double, showed signs of ability under a prominent ride on debut and should improve for the experience. (op 5-1 tchd 9-2)
Hoppy's Flyer(FR) did some good late work from some way off the pace on this step up to 6f. She seems to be quietly progressing and could have a profitable time in nurseries over a bit further.
Take Flight(IRE) stayed on nicely when third at 5-1 in a 5f Sandown maiden on debut. The sister to Irish 1000 Guineas winner Saoire was a heavily backed favourite on AW debut but could only find a short-lived effort under a confident ride. (op 11-10 tchd 6-4 in places)
Sukhothai(USA), a first foal of smart 7f-1m winner Succession, looked inexperienced but showed a glimmer of promise out wide on debut. (op 12-1)
Disco Doll Official explanation: trainer said filly was found to be lame right-hind on return home
Elkmait, a promising third behind useful Memory in a Goodwood fillies' maiden on debut, was a bit keen after rearing badly in the stalls and put in a tame effort on her second run. (op 6-1 tchd 5-1)

2642 EUROPEAN BREEDERS' FUND MAIDEN FILLIES' STKS (DIV II) 6f (P)
7:50 (7:54) (Class 5) 2-Y-O £3,626 (£1,079; £539; £269) **Stalls** High

Form RPR

1 **Lily Again** 2-9-0 0 .... JamieSpencer 1 80+
(P F I Cole) *trckd ldng pair: prog to ld over 2f out: tended to edge rt after: drvn over 1f out: in command fnl f* **13/2**[3]

2 *2* **Zanazzi (USA)** 2-9-0 0 .... WilliamBuick 8 74+
(J H M Gosden) *trckd ldng quartet: tapped for pce and lost pl over 2f out: effrt over 1f out: styd on wl to take 2nd last 50yds* **9/4**[1]

22 **3** *½* **Jambo Bibi (IRE)**[30] 1764 2-9-0 0 .... RichardHughes 7 72
(R Hannon) *mde most to over 2f out: chsd wnr after: no imp ent fnl f: lost 2nd last 50yds* **9/4**[1]

340 **4** *2½* **Darwin Star**[11] 2338 2-9-0 0 .... DaneO'Neill 5 65
(D K Ivory) *chsd ldrs in 6th: effrt 1/2-way: rdn to go 3rd briefly 1f out: one pce after* **14/1**

6 **5** *½* **Paris Is Burning**[19] 2074 2-9-0 0 .... LiamKeniry 2 63
(J S Moore) *in tch on outer: effrt over 2f out: no imp on ldrs over 1f out: one pce* **4/1**[2]

0 **6** *2¾* **Chilworth Lass (IRE)**[23] 1972 2-9-0 0 .... ChrisCatlin 3 55
(M R Channon) *w ldr: sltly brushed by wnr over 2f out: hanging and wknd over 1f out* **33/1**

7 *7* **Evaso Nice** 2-9-0 0 .... DavidProbert 6 34
(D Donovan) *t.k.h: trckd ldng pair to 1/2-way: wknd rapidly over 1f out* **25/1**

8 *5* **Te Amo Jen** 2-8-11 0 .... RussKennemore(3) 11 19
(B G Powell) *in tch in rr to 1/2-way: sn bhd* **50/1**

9 *5* **Ellie In The Pink (IRE)** 2-9-0 0 .... TomQueally 4 4
(A P Jarvis) *awkward to load: v.s.i.s: rn green and a wl detached* **20/1**

040 **10** *6* **Terrys Flutter**[23] 1972 2-9-0 0 .... J-PGuillambert 10 —
(M A Allen) *in tch in rr to 1/2-way: sn bhd: t.o* **50/1**

1m 13.93s (0.83) **Going Correction** -0.05s/f (Stan) 10 Ran SP% **117.0**
Speed ratings (Par 90): **92,89,88,85,84 81,71,65,58,50**
toteswingers: 1&2 £1.80, 1&3 £3.70, 2&3 £3.00 CSF £20.60 TOTE £7.10: £1.90, £1.80, £1.10; EX 16.80.
Owner R A Instone **Bred** R A Instone **Trained** Whatcombe, Oxon

FOCUS
The second division of a fillies' maiden. The pace was only fair but a newcomer beat the two market leaders in taking style. The third and fourth set the level.

NOTEBOOK
Lily Again moved well just behind the pace and was never in any serious danger after seizing the advantage inside the final two furlongs. She is a big powerful half-sister to quite useful dual 7f winner Pravda Street and represents a yard that is 4-10 with juveniles so far this season. (op 7-1 tchd 6-1)
Zanazzi(USA) couldn't find an immediate response when the winner went for home but stayed on nicely to post an encouraging effort on debut. The $360,000 half-sister to Breeders' Cup Sprint winner Speightstown, will have learned a lot from this initial experience and should be able to win a similar race. (op 2-1 tchd 5-2)
Jambo Bibi(IRE) had strong claims on her quick-fire runner-up efforts here and at Lingfield around a month ago. She was very weak in the market but put in a fair effort under a positive ride and shaped like a return to 5f could suit. (op 13-8 tchd 5-2)
Darwin Star ran respectably on AW debut but she has an uneven four-race profile and has not really managed to build on her 5l fourth at Warwick on her second start. (op 12-1)

Paris Is Burning showed promise at 40-1 faced with a stiff assignment in a fillies' conditions race at Newbury on debut. She was the subject of sustained support this time but could not make any inroads on the leaders out wide. (op 10-1)

2643 DIGIBET CASINO H'CAP 7f (P)
8:20 (8:23) (Class 6) (0-65,65) 4-Y-0+ **£2,047** (£604; £302) **Stalls** High

Form RPR

40-6 **1** **Mambo Spirit (IRE)**[15] 2196 6-9-3 **63**.................... TomQueally 9 76
(Stef Higgins) *mde all: stretched away over 2f out: drvn over 1f out: styd on wl: unchal* **12/1**

6530 **2** 2 ¾ **Harting Hill**[22] 2009 5-9-2 **62**.................... PatDobbs 14 68
(M P Tregoning) *a in ldng trio: rdn over 2f out: wnt 2nd wl over 1f out: styd on but no imp on wnr* **6/1**[1]

-220 **3** ¾ **Landucci**[16] 2172 9-9-5 **65**....................(p) JamesDoyle 12 69
(S Curran) *chsd wnr: rdn 2f out: one pce and sn lost 2nd but clr of rest after* **12/1**

510/ **4** 2 ¾ **Al Aqabah (IRE)**[755] 1930 5-9-5 **65**.................... JimmyFortune 11 61
(B Gubby) *dwlt: sn in midfield in abt 7th: rdn over 2f out: plugged on to take 4th ins fnl f: no ch* **12/1**

-501 **5** 1 ¼ **Amber Sunset**[8] 2419 4-9-4 **64** 6ex.................... NeilCallan 3 57
(J Jay) *chsd ldng trio: outpcd fr over 2f out: no imp after: lost 4th ins fnl f* **6/1**[1]

6613 **6** *nk* **Musical Script (USA)**[6] 2456 7-9-4 **64**....................(b) DaneO'Neill 4 56
(Mouse Hamilton-Fairley) *nt that wl away: settled in last trio: rdn over 2f out: sme prog over 1f out but no ch* **15/2**[2]

30-0 **7** ½ **Yankee Storm**[25] 1929 5-9-2 **62**.................... JimmyQuinn 10 53
(H J Collingridge) *in tch in midfield in 8th: rdn over 2f out: no prog* **6/1**[1]

00/0 **8** *hd* **Beat Up**[26] 1877 4-9-2 **62**.................... SaleemGolam 6 52
(G D Blake) *racd wd: in tch: effrt and prom in chsng gp 2f out: no imp: fdd fnl f* **33/1**

0503 **9** ¾ **Blue Charm**[35] 1628 6-9-5 **65**.................... JamieSpencer 5 53
(I W McInnes) *t.k.h and stdd in last: effrt on wd outside over 2f out: v modest late prog* **12/1**

5-00 **10** ½ **Aurora Sky (IRE)**[14] 2236 4-9-5 **65**.................... LiamKeniry 7 52
(J Akehurst) *awkward s: rcvrd to rch 10th after 2f: effrt on inner over 2f out: sn no prog* **11/1**

033- **11** 3 **Hilltop Artistry**[330] 3708 4-9-5 **65**.................... RichardHughes 13 44
(J R Jenkins) *chsd ldrs in abt 6th: rdn over 2f out: no prog: wknd over 1f out* **8/1**[3]

0-00 **12** ½ **Head Down**[26] 1877 4-9-5 **65**.................... GeorgeBaker 8 42
(M R Bosley) *in tch in 9th: rdn over 2f out: lost pl and wl btn wl over 1f out* **16/1**

2-60 **13** 1 **Beauchamp Wizard**[34] 1637 5-9-3 **63**.................... SebSanders 2 38
(G A Butler) *dropped in fr wd draw and hld up in 12th: effrt on outer over 2f out: sn no prog* **25/1**

1m 25.59s (-0.41) **Going Correction** -0.05s/f (Stan) **13** Ran SP% **117.5**
Speed ratings (Par 101): **100,96,96,92,91 91,90,90,89,88 85,84,83**
toteswingers: 1&2 £23.30, 1&3 £30.40, 2&3 £5.80 CSF £80.97 CT £895.24 TOTE £10.80: £7.00, £1.30, £4.70; EX 121.10.
Owner That's The Spirit **Bred** R Warren **Trained** Lambourn, Berks
■ Stewards' Enquiry : Neil Callan one-day ban: failed to ride to draw (Jun 20)

FOCUS
A modest handicap that is rated at face value around the first two. Nothing got into it from behind and the first three filled those positions throughout.
Aurora Sky(IRE) Official explanation: jockey said filly was slowly away

2644 WHO CAN RUN A MILE FASTEST H'CAP (LONDON MILE QUALIFIER) 1m (P)
8:50 (8:54) (Class 4) (0-80,81) 3-Y-0 **£4,209** (£1,252; £625; £312) **Stalls** High

Form RPR

0431 **1** **Avon River**[9] 2398 3-9-8 **81** 6ex....................(b) RichardHughes 12 88
(R Hannon) *mde all: rdn clr fr 2f out: hld on nr fin* **9/2**[2]

2-40 **2** ½ **White Devil**[30] 1761 3-9-4 **77**.................... JimmyFortune 13 83+
(A M Balding) *trckd ldrs: nt clr run briefly over 2f out: prog to go 2nd over 1f out: clsd on wnr fnl f: post c too sn* **6/1**

22-0 **3** 2 ¼ **Be A Devil**[25] 1913 3-9-3 **76**.................... DaneO'Neill 2 77+
(W R Muir) *dropped in fr wd draw and hld up last: stl there 2f out: gd prog jst over 1f out: r.o to take 3rd nr fin: hopeless task* **12/1**

-561 **4** *nk* **Tewin Wood**[8] 2416 3-9-5 **78** 6ex.................... FrannyNorton 10 78
(A Bailey) *t.k.h: hld up in midfield: rdn over 2f out: prog on outer over 1f out: styd on fnl f* **8/1**

-062 **5** ¾ **Swiss Cross**[18] 2110 3-9-7 **80**....................(v[1]) TomQueally 6 78
(G A Butler) *t.k.h: hld up in 6th: prog to chse wnr briefly wl over 1f out: outpcd after: lost 2 pls nr fin* **11/2**[3]

3126 **6** 3 **Purple Gallery (IRE)**[21] 2025 3-8-11 **73**....................(p) RussKennemore[(3)] 7 64
(J S Moore) *hld up in rr on outer: rdn and struggling 3f out: last pair 2f out: kpt on fnl f* **25/1**

631 **7** ¾ **Wadi Wanderer (IRE)**[13] 2258 3-9-2 **75**.................... JamieSpencer 9 65
(E F Vaughan) *nt wl away: hld up in rr: prog on inner over 2f out: jnd chsers wl over 1f out: wknd fnl f* **4/1**[1]

3200 **8** *shd* **Tenacestream (CAN)**[21] 2033 3-9-3 **76**.................... SteveDrowne 3 65
(J R Best) *t.k.h in midfield: nt qckn over 2f out: tried to make prog over 1f out: no imp* **25/1**

05-1 **9** 1 **He's Invincible**[35] 1619 3-9-1 **74**....................(b) MartinDwyer 11 61
(B J Meehan) *chsd wnr 3f: prom tl wknd 2f out* **8/1**

-306 **10** 1 ½ **Ferris Wheel (IRE)**[16] 2170 3-8-13 **72**.................... WilliamBuick 8 56
(P F I Cole) *chsd wnr after 3f to wl over 1f out: wknd* **25/1**

5-50 **11** 4 ½ **Ishtar Gate (USA)**[11] 2348 3-8-13 **72**.................... NeilCallan 14 45
(P F I Cole) *prom on inner: drvn over 2f out: disp 2nd wl over 1f out: sn wknd* **25/1**

22-0 **12** 2 ¼ **Rare Malt (IRE)**[40] 1501 3-9-3 **76**.................... GeorgeBaker 5 44
(Miss Amy Weaver) *hld up in rr: no prog over 2f out: wknd rapidly over 1f out* **33/1**

1m 38.97s (-0.83) **Going Correction** -0.05s/f (Stan) **12** Ran SP% **116.1**
Speed ratings (Par 101): **102,101,99,98,98 95,94,94,93,91 87,85**
toteswingers: 1&2 £6.50, 1&3 £9.50, 2&3 £5.20 CSF £28.56 CT £307.93 TOTE £5.20: £2.70, £1.60, £4.70; EX 40.10.
Owner Jim Horgan **Bred** Poulton Stud **Trained** East Everleigh, Wilts

FOCUS
A fair handicap run at a decent pace and worth rating at face value.

2645 KEMPTON.CO.UK APPRENTICE H'CAP 1m 4f (P)
9:20 (9:22) (Class 6) (0-65,65) 4-Y-0+ **£2,047** (£604; £302) **Stalls** Centre

Form RPR

/0-0 **1** **Tilapia (IRE)**[13] 2259 6-9-1 **63**.................... FrancisHayes[(7)] 9 69
(Stef Higgins) *hld up in midfield: prog over 2f out to go 2nd over 1f out: rdn to ld ins fnl f: styd on* **50/1**

3506 **2** ½ **Choral Festival**[11] 2337 4-9-0 **58**....................(v[1]) RyanClark[(3)] 11 63
(J J Bridger) *trckd ldrs: prog to ld over 2f out: drvn and worn down ins fnl f* **14/1**

01-6 **3** 2 **Annambo**[22] 2013 10-9-4 **62**.................... DavidKenny[(3)] 6 64
(Andrew Reid) *hld up wl in rr: rdn and prog over 2f out: styd on wl to take 3rd last strides* **16/1**

4/00 **4** *hd* **Sumner (IRE)**[18] 2109 6-9-10 **65**....................(bt[1]) KierenFox 13 66
(F Sheridan) *trckd ldrs: rdn and cl up over 2f out: kpt on to chse ldng pair ins fnl f: no imp: lost 3rd last strides* **12/1**

4/0- **5** 1 ½ **Jocheski (IRE)**[27] 147 6-9-4 **59**.................... MatthewDavies 10 58
(A G Newcombe) *racd freely early: mde most to over 4f out: led again briefly wl over 2f out: nt qckn over 1f out: fdd fnl f* **12/1**

4030 **6** 1 ¾ **Altimatum (USA)**[22] 2012 4-9-2 **60**....................(t) DuilioDaSilva[(3)] 8 56
(P F I Cole) *trckd ldrs in 6th: rdn over 2f out: no prog over 1f out: fdd* **33/1**

50-6 **7** *nk* **Lilly Royal (IRE)**[56] 1179 4-9-5 **60**.................... DeclanCannon 5 56
(B Palling) *hld up in last trio: u.p 3f out: styd on fr over 1f out: n.d* **20/1**

1361 **8** *nk* **Lytham (IRE)**[35] 1623 9-9-6 **64**.................... TobyAtkinson[(3)] 2 59
(A W Carroll) *t.k.h: hld up towards rr: effrt on outer over 2f out: rdn and no prog over 1f out* **10/3**[2]

0-40 **9** ½ **Uncle Keef (IRE)**[43] 1459 4-8-12 **58**....................(p) KatiaScallan[(5)] 7 53
(M P Tregoning) *hld up in last trio: rdn over 2f out: modest late prog: nvr on terms* **7/1**[3]

50-3 **10** *nk* **Rock Relief (IRE)**[11] 2337 4-9-4 **62**.................... RosieJessop[(3)] 1 56
(Sir Mark Prescott) *dwlt: t.k.h and racd wd: prog and prom 1/2-way: lost pl whn wd bnd 3f out: no prog 2f out: wknd* **9/4**[1]

02-0 **11** 1 ¼ **Guiseppe Verdi (USA)**[131] 261 6-9-4 **59**.................... RossAtkinson 14 51
(Miss Tor Sturgis) *chsd ldr 4f: styd cl up: rdn over 3f out: wknd wl over 1f out* **14/1**

120/ **12** 1 ¾ **Rickety Bridge (IRE)**[854] 358 7-9-5 **65**.................... HarryBentley[(5)] 4 54
(P R Chamings) *dwlt: hld up: a in last trio: rdn and no prog over 2f out* **11/1**

240- **13** 6 **D'Artagnans Dream**[219] 7049 4-9-2 **57**....................(v[1]) SimonPearce 12 37
(G D Blake) *t.k.h: wnt 2nd after 4f: led over 4f out: wd bnd 3f out: sn hdd & wknd rapidly* **25/1**

2m 35.51s (1.01) **Going Correction** -0.05s/f (Stan) **13** Ran SP% **122.8**
Speed ratings (Par 101): **94,93,92,92,91 90,89,89,89,89 88,87,83**
toteswingers: 1&2 £133.00, 1&3 £52.70, 2&3 £53.40 CSF £639.15 CT £11178.11 TOTE £62.40: £12.60, £2.90, £4.30; EX 812.60 Place 6: £60.85, Place 5: £47.20 ..
Owner Something Fishy **Bred** G D Waters **Trained** Lambourn, Berks

FOCUS
An ordinary apprentice handicap. It was run at a steady pace and a shock winner was chased home by six other runners who were sent off at biggish prices.
Lytham(IRE) Official explanation: jockey said gelding ran too free
T/Plt: £160.10 to a £1 stake. Pool: £62,346.95. 284.21 winning tickets. T/Qpdt: £28.10 to a £1 stake. Pool: £5,128.37. 134.80 winning tickets. JN

2215 NOTTINGHAM (L-H)
Wednesday, June 2

OFFICIAL GOING: Good to firm (good in places) changing to good to firm after race 5 (4.15)
All races on outer track. Rail moved out 2m from turn out of dog leg, round top bend and as far as 4.5f out, increasing distances by 7yds.
Wind: Light against Weather: Sun breaking through

2646 TOTEPLACEPOT H'CAP (DIV I) 6f 15y
2:10 (2:11) (Class 5) (0-70,70) 4-Y-0+ **£2,266** (£674; £337; £168) **Stalls** High

Form RPR

5066 **1** **Bahamian Lad**[18] 2113 5-9-3 **66**....................(p) JerryO'Dwyer 3 76
(R Hollinshead) *w ldr tl led 1/2-way: rdn over 1f out: edgd lft ins fnl f: styd on* **7/2**[1]

0142 **2** 1 ½ **Gracie's Gift (IRE)**[13] 2263 8-8-13 **62**.................... JamieSpencer 9 67
(R C Guest) *chsd ldrs: rdn over 2f out: styd on same pce wl ins fnl f* **4/1**[2]

0-00 **3** 2 ¾ **George Thisby**[18] 2129 4-9-4 **70**.................... JamesMillman[(3)] 7 66
(B R Millman) *chsd ldrs: rdn: outpcd and hung lft over 2f out: rallied over 1f out: hung rt ins fnl f: styd on same pce* **7/2**[1]

0060 **4** 1 ¼ **Steel City Boy (IRE)**[25] 1915 7-8-6 **55**.................... PaulHanagan 8 47
(D Shaw) *s.s: hld up: hdwy over 2f out: rdn over 1f out: no ex ins fnl f* **11/1**

0-03 **5** *nk* **Frank Street**[11] 2331 4-9-2 **65**....................(b[1]) JimmyFortune 11 56
(Eve Johnson Houghton) *prom: rdn over 1f out: no ex fnl f* **7/2**[1]

100- **6** 2 ½ **Villaruz (IRE)**[165] 7815 4-8-10 **59**.................... ShaneKelly 5 42
(J W Unett) *hld up: hdwy u.p 2f out: wknd fnl f* **28/1**

4245 **7** 9 **Nabeeda**[77] 912 5-8-2 **51**.................... FrannyNorton 10 5
(M Brittain) *led: hung lft 4f out: hdd 1/2-way: wknd over 1f out* **6/1**[3]

1m 13.55s (-1.35) **Going Correction** -0.275s/f (Firm) **7** Ran SP% **112.7**
Speed ratings (Par 103): **98,96,92,90,90 86,74**
toteswingers: 1&2 £4.60, 1&3 £3.80, 2&3 £4.40. CSF £17.19 CT £50.84 TOTE £3.90: £2.30, £2.30; EX 18.70 Trifecta £113.60 Pool: £348.77 - 2.27 winning units..
Owner Graham Brothers Racing Partnership **Bred** J D Graham **Trained** Upper Longdon, Staffs

FOCUS
After just 1mm of rain the previous day, the ground was described as Good to firm, good in places. A modest sprint handicap hit by four non-runners. The field raced towards the nearside rail, though the first three home all raced furthest from it. The form looks straightforward for the grade rated around the first two.

2647 TOTEPLACEPOT H'CAP (DIV II) 6f 15y
2:40 (2:46) (Class 5) (0-70,67) 4-Y-0+ **£2,266** (£674; £337; £168) **Stalls** High

Form RPR

-500 **1** **Exceedingly Good (IRE)**[46] 1391 4-8-3 **49**.................... CathyGannon 6 58
(S R Bowring) *plld hrd and prom: led over 3f out: rdn over 1f out: r.o* **33/1**

0024 **2** 1 **Cornus**[2] 2592 8-9-7 **67**....................(be) JamesDoyle 11 73
(A J McCabe) *chsd ldrs: rdn and swtchd lft over 1f out: chsd wnr ins fnl f: r.o* **7/2**[2]

4513 **3** ¾ **Fuzzy Cat**[22] 2008 4-9-1 **61** .... GrahamGibbons 8 64
(T D Barron) *sn w ldrs: rdn over 2f out: styd on same pce ins fnl f* **5/2**[1]

-235 **4** 1½ **Sea Crest**[42] 1470 4-8-12 **58** .... AlanMunro 10 57+
(M Brittain) *hld up: rdn and swtchd lft over 2f out: r.o ins fnl f: nt trble ldrs* **10/1**

-400 **5** 1¼ **Avoncreek**[9] 2381 6-7-13 **48** oh3 .... KellyHarrison(3) 1 43
(B P J Baugh) *prom: rdn over 2f out: edgd rt 1f out: styd on same pce* **33/1**

12-0 **6** *hd* **Connor's Choice**[13] 2246 5-9-3 **63** .... ChrisCatlin 9 57
(Andrew Turnell) *dwlt: in rr tl styd on fnl f: nvr nrr* **16/1**

0-00 **7** 1¾ **Silver Hotspur**[16] 2188 6-8-6 **52** .... (v1) PaulHanagan 2 40
(D Shaw) *s.i.s: nvr on terms* **14/1**

4631 **8** 1¼ **The History Man (IRE)**[2] 2590 7-9-3 **63** 6ex .... (p) KirstyMilczarek 5 51
(B D Leavy) *chsd ldrs: rdn over 2f out: wkng whn n.m.r 1f out* **8/1**

0-00 **9** ¾ **Ghost Dancer**[13] 2246 6-9-5 **65** .... (p) GeorgeBaker 3 47
(J M Bradley) *s.i.s: hld up: hdwy over 2f out: wknd ins fnl f* **17/2**

/000 **10** 3½ **Northumberland**[12] 2274 4-8-7 **58** ow3 .... MarkCoumbe(5) 7 29
(M C Chapman) *unruly on the way to post: chsd ldrs: rdn over 3f out: wknd 2f out* **66/1**

606- **11** *15* **Lieutenant Pigeon**[315] 4203 5-8-9 **55** .... FrannyNorton 4 —
(R C Guest) *sn led: hdd over 3f out: wknd over 2f out* **6/1**[3]

1m 13.64s (-1.26) **Going Correction** -0.275s/f (Firm) **11** Ran SP% **115.7**
Speed ratings (Par 103): **97,95,94,92,91 90,88,86,85,81 61**
toteswingers: 1&2 £31.20, 1&3 £22.00, 2&3 £3.00. CSF £142.71 CT £413.56 TOTE £35.60: £8.50, £1.40, £1.60; EX 328.40 Trifecta £317.40 Part won. Pool: £428.92 - 0.50 winning units..
Owner S R Bowring **Bred** Martin Francis Ltd **Trained** Edwinstowe, Notts
■ Stewards' Enquiry : Cathy Gannon one-day ban: used whip in incorrect place (Jun 20)

FOCUS
A more competitive contest than the first division, though the winning time was 0.09 seconds slower. Again the field raced towards the nearside rail and the form is moderate, with the runner-up pretty exposed and the fifth limiting things from out of the handicap.
Exceedingly Good(IRE) Official explanation: trainer said, regarding apparent improvement in form, that the filly had benefited from a change in tactics, being held up and also back to 6f
Connor's Choice Official explanation: jockey said gelding stumbled leaving stalls
The History Man(IRE) Official explanation: jockey said gelding missed the break

2648 TOTEQUADPOT H'CAP 5f 13y
3:10 (3:20) (Class 5) (0-70,70) 3-Y-O **£2,729** (£806; £403) **Stalls** High

Form RPR

550- **1** **Perfect Blossom**[293] 4928 3-8-7 **56** .... PaulHanagan 14 64+
(K A Ryan) *hld up in tch: rdn to chse ldr over 1f out: r.o to ld wl ins fnl f* **7/2**[1]

-224 **2** ½ **Danzoe (IRE)**[12] 2301 3-9-4 **67** .... (v) TomMcLaughlin 6 73
(Mrs C A Dunnett) *s.i.s: hld up: hdwy over 1f out: sn rdn: r.o* **13/2**[3]

400- **3** *nk* **Star Twilight**[181] 7619 3-8-10 **59** .... RobertWinston 5 64
(D Shaw) *sn led: rdn over 1f out: hdd and unable qck wl ins fnl f* **40/1**

50-2 **4** 3½ **Admirable Duchess**[11] 2320 3-9-4 **67** .... GregFairley 8 59
(D J S Ffrench Davis) *chsd ldr tl rdn over 1f out: no ex ins fnl f* **13/2**[3]

4-02 **5** 2¼ **Macroy**[22] 2000 3-8-11 **63** .... JamesMillman(3) 1 47
(B R Millman) *prom: rdn 1/2-way: hung rt over 1f out: wknd fnl f* **11/1**

3051 **6** ¾ **Tamarind Hill (IRE)**[15] 2217 3-8-12 **61** .... (b) JamesDoyle 12 43
(A J McCabe) *chsd ldrs: rdn 1/2-way: wknd fnl f* **5/1**[2]

2510 **7** *nk* **Flaxen Lake**[30] 1784 3-9-3 **66** .... (p) GeorgeBaker 9 47
(J M Bradley) *mid-div: rdn 1/2-way: wknd over 1f out* **9/1**

0040 **8** ½ **Shawkantango**[16] 2185 3-8-2 **51** oh3 .... (v) PatrickMathers 11 30
(D Shaw) *s.i.s: hld up: sme hdwy u.p and hung lft over 1f out: wknd fnl f* **50/1**

6-00 **9** ½ **King's Approach (IRE)**[15] 2215 3-9-2 **65** .... (p) ChrisCatlin 4 42
(R A Harris) *chsd ldrs tl rdn and wknd over 1f out* **16/1**

-004 **10** ½ **Avongate**[11] 2320 3-9-6 **69** .... LukeMorris 15 44
(R A Harris) *sn outpcd* **12/1**

0506 **11** 4½ **Pavement Games**[15] 2217 3-8-2 **51** oh6 .... FrannyNorton 10 10
(R C Guest) *s.i.s: a in rr* **16/1**

-504 **12** *shd* **Midget**[15] 2217 3-8-11 **60** .... DavidNolan 13 19
(D Carroll) *s.i.s: sn chsng ldrs: rdn 1/2-way: wknd wl over 1f out* **12/1**

15-0 **13** 1¾ **Tartufo Dolce (IRE)**[30] 1750 3-9-7 **70** .... PaulMulrennan 7 22
(J G Given) *chsd ldrs: rdn 1/2-way: wknd wl over 1f out* **25/1**

59.57 secs (-1.43) **Going Correction** -0.275s/f (Firm) **13** Ran SP% **119.3**
Speed ratings (Par 99): **100,99,98,93,89 88,87,87,86,85 78,78,75**
toteswingers: 1&2 £7.90, 1&3 £36.00, 2&3 £45.50. CSF £25.14 CT £813.26 TOTE £6.10: £2.20, £2.10, £13.10; EX 33.40 TRIFECTA Not won..
Owner Mrs Ann Morris **Bred** Mrs A Morris **Trained** Hambleton, N Yorks

FOCUS
A big field for this modest sprint handicap in which they raced centre to stands' side, but few ever really got into it. The runner-up is the best guide to the level.
Tartufo Dolce(IRE) Official explanation: trainer's rep said filly was unsuited by the good to firm (good in places) ground

2649 TOTESWINGER E B F MAIDEN STKS 5f 13y
3:45 (3:46) (Class 5) 2-Y-O **£3,561** (£1,059; £529; £264) **Stalls** High

Form RPR

1 **Forjatt (IRE)** 2-9-3 0 .... FrankieDettori 2 79+
(M A Jarvis) *green to post: racd in 3rd pl tl rdn to chse ldr over 1f out: hung lft and r.o to ld wl ins fnl f* **6/4**[1]

2 *hd* **Gold Pearl (USA)** 2-9-0 0 .... WilliamCarson(3) 3 78+
(S C Williams) *trckd ldr: racd keenly: led over 1f out: rdn: hung lft and hdd wl ins fnl f* **15/8**[2]

5 **3** 4½ **Slatey Hen (IRE)**[11] 2347 2-8-12 0 .... FrederikTylicki 1 57
(A J McCabe) *sn led: rdn and hdd over 1f out: wknd ins fnl f* **12/1**

4 **4** 2¼ **Brave Dream**[8] 2420 2-9-3 0 .... JamieSpencer 4 54
(K A Ryan) *dwlt: hld up: swtchd lft 1/2-way: sn rdn: hung rt and wknd over 1f out* **3/1**[3]

60.07 secs (-0.93) **Going Correction** -0.275s/f (Firm) **4** Ran SP% **107.5**
Speed ratings (Par 93): **96,95,88,84**
CSF £4.56 TOTE £1.90; EX 5.20.
Owner Sheikh Ahmed Al Maktoum **Bred** Michael Downey & Roalso Ltd **Trained** Newmarket, Suffolk

FOCUS
Just the four runners, but an interesting maiden in which the two newcomers proved far too good for the pair with experience. The level is rather fluid with the third and fourth making minor progress on previous marks.

NOTEBOOK
Forjatt(IRE), a 60,000gns half-brother to a winning juvenile sprinter, tracked the leaders early but then appeared to run green when coming under pressure 2f from home. It took him a while to respond, but he did eventually and nailed the runner-up in the very closing stages. He should have learnt plenty from this and can go on to better things. (op Evens)

Gold Pearl(USA), who was sold for 85,000gns as a 2-y-o, and is half-brother to two winners including the 1000 Guineas runner-up Arch Swing, was well backed for this debut. He was keen enough against the nearside rail in the early stages, but still looked the likely winner when taking over in front over a furlong from home, only to have the race snatched from him late on. He should go one better before too long. (op 11-4)

Slatey Hen(IRE), a well-held fifth of six on her York debut last month, took them along until collared over a furlong from home. She may need her sights lowering if she is to win a race. (op 17-2 tchd 14-1)

Brave Dream, a disappointing favourite on his Ripon debut eight days earlier when looking green, missed the break and though he tried to make an effort on the outside entering the last 2f, it came to little and he again seemed to be hanging. He has a few questions to answer now. Official explanation: jockey said colt missed the break (op 4-1 tchd 5-1)

2650 TOTESUPER7 H'CAP 1m 6f 15y
4:15 (4:16) (Class 5) (0-70,70) 3-Y-O **£2,590** (£770; £385; £192) **Stalls** Low

Form RPR

3-22 **1** **Dream Spinner**[26] 1880 3-9-7 **70** .... JimmyFortune 5 76+
(J L Dunlop) *sn led: hrd rdn fnl f: styd on gamely* **9/4**[1]

-313 **2** ½ **Blinka Me**[16] 2175 3-8-11 **60** .... PatCosgrave 2 65
(M H Tompkins) *led early: chsd wnr: rdn over 3f out: edgd lft over 1f out: styd on gamely* **12/1**

5-45 **3** 1½ **Pena Dorada (IRE)**[16] 2175 3-9-4 **67** .... (p) AndrewElliott 1 70
(J R Weymes) *chsd ldrs: rdn over 3f out: styd on* **20/1**

-544 **4** 2¼ **Stadium Of Light (IRE)**[13] 2252 3-9-6 **69** .... (t) SteveDrowne 6 69
(H Morrison) *prom: rdn over 3f out: outpcd over 2f out: rallied over 1f out: no ex ins fnl f* **7/2**[3]

-444 **5** ½ **Dr Finley (IRE)**[26] 1880 3-9-0 **70** .... IanBurns(7) 7 69
(M L W Bell) *prom: rdn 3f out: styd on same pce fnl f* **10/1**

1214 **6** 4½ **Captain Cool (IRE)**[13] 2248 3-9-2 **65** .... PatDobbs 8 58
(R Hannon) *hld up: rdn over 3f out: wknd 2f out* **15/2**

-640 **7** *9* **Dr Mathias**[8] 2409 3-9-1 **64** .... CathyGannon 4 44
(P D Evans) *hld up: rdn over 4f out: wknd 3f out* **40/1**

62-3 **8** *14* **Molon Labe (IRE)**[35] 1630 3-9-7 **70** .... JamieSpencer 3 31
(T P Tate) *hld up: rdn over 4f out: wknd over 3f out: t.o* **3/1**[2]

3m 3.00s (-4.30) **Going Correction** -0.275s/f (Firm) **8** Ran SP% **113.7**
Speed ratings (Par 99): **101,100,99,98,98 95,90,82**
toteswingers: 1&2 £5.00, 1&3 £6.70, 2&3 £10.60. CSF £30.32 CT £427.72 TOTE £3.40: £1.50, £3.20, £5.20; EX 30.60 Trifecta £231.40 Part won. Pool: £312.75 - 0.83 winning units..
Owner Bluehills Racing Limited **Bred** Hesmonds Stud Ltd **Trained** Arundel, W Sussex

FOCUS
The pace was nothing special in this staying handicap and it favoured those that raced handily, with the order never changing that much. The runner-up ran close to previous form with the third, while the fourth is rated close to Sandown form.

2651 TOTEPOOL FLEXI BETTING CONDITIONS STKS 1m 75y
4:50 (4:50) (Class 2) 3-Y-O+
£9,969 (£2,985; £1,492; £747; £372; £187) **Stalls** Centre

Form RPR

25-0 **1** **Rio De La Plata (USA)**[89] 823 5-9-1 114 .... FrankieDettori 8 112+
(Saeed Bin Suroor) *a.p: chsd ldr 5f out: shkn up to ld wl ins fnl f: r.o* **6/4**[1]

3633 **2** 1¼ **Balcarce Nov (ARG)**[20] 2057 5-9-1 103 .... JamieSpencer 6 109
(T P Tate) *chsd ldrs: led wl over 5f out: rdn over 1f out: hdd and unable qck wl ins fnl f* **7/4**[2]

34-4 **3** *6* **City Style (USA)**[11] 2344 4-9-1 106 .... AhmedAjtebi 7 95
(Mahmood Al Zarooni) *hld up: outpcd over 3f out: styd on u.p fr over 1f out: nvr on terms* **9/1**

063- **4** *nk* **Captain Brilliance (USA)**[221] 7019 5-9-1 102 .... ShaneKelly 2 95
(J Noseda) *hld up in tch: rdn over 2f out: sn outpcd* **6/1**[3]

0600 **5** 3¼ **Carcinetto (IRE)**[5] 2508 8-8-10 90 .... CathyGannon 1 82
(P D Evans) *led: hdd wl over 5f out: chsd ldrs: rdn over 3f out: wknd wl over 1f out* **33/1**

0-04 **6** *9* **Aspectus (IRE)**[104] 610 7-9-1 105 .... FergusSweeney 3 66
(J A Osborne) *prom tl rdn and wknd over 2f out* **16/1**

000- **7** *25* **Gessabelle**[238] 6591 3-7-13 45 .... (t) LeonnaMayor 4 —
(P S McEntee) *chsd ldr over 2f: wknd over 4f out: t.o* **250/1**

1m 42.25s (-3.35) **Going Correction** -0.275s/f (Firm)
WFA 3 from 4yo+ 11lb **7** Ran SP% **109.9**
Speed ratings (Par 109): **105,103,97,97,94 85,60**
toteswingers: 1&2 £1.30, 1&3 £2.90, 2&3 £2.50. CSF £3.96 TOTE £2.50: £1.10, £1.70; EX 4.50 Trifecta £15.90 Pool: £305.97 - 14.16 winning units..
Owner Godolphin **Bred** Jose De Camargo, Robert N Clay Et Al **Trained** Newmarket, Suffolk

FOCUS
The going was changed to Good to firm all round before this race. Possible favourite Cityscape was withdrawn during the morning, but that still left this a tough-looking puzzle to sort out. The early pace did not look really strong, which may explain why two runners stretched away from the rest. The winner is rated 6lb off best with the runner-up to form.

NOTEBOOK
Rio De La Plata(USA), absent since one disappointing effort at Meydan, was nicely clear of his rivals on BHA ratings but had not won a race of any description since 2007. Representing a trainer who had won this race in the last ten years with Librettist and Dubai Destination, he moved well just behind the leader and, after taking a little while to get going, was a comfortable enough winner. Connections have given him some good entries, but it would be a little surprising if he was up to winning those, so the Group 3 Prix Messidor, a race they won with Librettist after taking this contest in 2006, would seem a sensible target before bigger plans are made. (tchd 11-8 and 13-8 tchd 5-4 in a place)

Balcarce Nov(ARG) has developed into a consistent and tough handicapper, and his latest third came in a strong contest at York. He was allowed to dominate his rivals quite a way from home and pulled out plenty for pressure, but found the winner too strong for him in the final half a furlong. He is a solid marker. (op 11-4)

City Style(USA) made only a fair comeback in late May for this trainer (formerly with Saeed Bin Suroor) but did not impress with his head carriage under pressure here. He may not be straightforward. (op 5-1)

Captain Brilliance(USA) had a respectable first-time-out record, so he was interesting for that fact alone. Off since a good effort in a conditions race at York when a visor, absent here, was fitted for the first time, he looked very one paced when the tempo increased and made no impression. (tchd 9-2)

Carcinetto(IRE) probably ran up to somewhere near her best and is running quite well at present. (tchd 40-1)

Aspectus(IRE), who ran one fair race in Dubai from two starts in the spring, did most of his winning in Germany at about 1m (he did win a Group 2 over 1m3f at a 3-y-o) but put up a thoroughly lacklustre performance in this. (op 12-1)

2652 BET TOTEPOOL AT TOTESPORT.COM E B F FILLIES' H'CAP 1m 75y

5:25 (5:26) (Class 4) (0-85,85) 3-Y-O £6,476 (£1,927; £963; £481) Stalls Centre

Form				RPR
41-2	1		**Forest Crown**[27] 1850 3-9-5 **83** JimCrowley 3 (R M Beckett) *mde all: racd keenly: shkn up over 1f out: edgd rt: comf* 10/3[2]	97+
1-	2	2 3/4	**Field Day (IRE)**[214] 7183 3-9-7 **85** MartinDwyer 11 (B J Meehan) *a.p: chsd wnr over 2f out tl rdn and edgd rt over 1f out: wnt 2nd again towards fin* 3/1[1]	93+
5-42	3	3/4	**Lady Pattern (IRE)**[11] 2342 3-8-8 **72** TonyCulhane 4 (P W D'Arcy) *chsd ldrs: rdn over 2f out: wnt 2nd over 1f out tl no ex wl ins fnl f* 15/2	78
-031	4	1 1/4	**Gobama**[20] 2042 3-9-0 **78** PhilipRobinson 5 (J W Hills) *hld up: plld hrd: styd on fr over 1f out: nvr trbld ldrs* 6/1	81
0-00	5	2 1/4	**Sunarise (IRE)**[20] 2047 3-9-2 **80** PatDobbs 10 (R Hannon) *chsd wnr tl rdn over 2f out: wknd fnl f* 20/1	78
61-	6	2 1/2	**Avon Lady**[230] 6786 3-8-8 **72** PatCosgrave 6 (J R Fanshawe) *hld up: hdwy over 2f out: rdn and wknd over 1f out* 20/1	64
61	7	1/2	**My Nan Nell (IRE)**[83] 864 3-8-11 **75** TedDurcan 7 (M Botti) *hld up: rdn and hung rt fr over 1f out: nvr on terms* 10/1	66
1144	8	1	**Dream On Buddy (IRE)**[37] 1582 3-8-10 **74** RobertWinston 1 (B W Hills) *hld up: hdwy over 2f out: rdn: hung lft and wknd over 1f out* 9/2[3]	63
41-4	9	2	**Tatiana Romanova (USA)**[11] 2348 3-8-12 **76** TonyHamilton 9 (R A Fahey) *hld up: rdn 1/2-way: a in rr* 28/1	60

1m 43.96s (-1.64) **Going Correction** -0.275s/f (Firm) 9 Ran SP% 114.4
Speed ratings (Par 98): **97,94,93,92,90 87,87,86,84**
toteswingers: 1&2 £2.40, 1&3 £5.40, 2&3 £4.80. CSF £13.19 CT £68.47 TOTE £3.50: £1.60, £1.10, £3.60; EX 12.50 Trifecta £52.50 Pool: £159.70 - 2.25 winning units..
Owner The Eclipse Partnership **Bred** Car Colston Hall Stud **Trained** Whitsbury, Hants

FOCUS
A decent fillies' handicap and a few were well backed, but this was another race where those that raced up with the pace were favoured and, as such, the form may not be rock-solid.

2653 BET TOTEPOOL ON 0800 221 221 "HANDS AND HEELS" APPRENTICE SERIES H'CAP 1m 2f 50y

5:55 (5:57) (Class 6) (0-60,57) 4-Y-O+ £2,047 (£604; £302) Stalls Low

Form				RPR
0034	1		**King Zeal (IRE)**[22] 2006 6-9-0 **53** JamesRogers 11 (B D Leavy) *chsd ldrs: wnt 2nd 4 out: shkn up to ld over 2f out: pushed clr fnl f* 7/1[3]	68
-022	2	4 1/2	**Major Promise**[25] 1919 5-9-0 **56** LewisWalsh(3) 1 (Jane Chapple-Hyam) *s.i.s: sn pushed along into mid-div: hdwy 1/2-way: pushed along over 3f out: styd on to go 2nd wl ins fnl f: no ch w wnr* 7/2[2]	61
-312	3	1	**Sharp Sovereign (USA)**[12] 2303 4-8-11 **53** AnthonyBetts(3) 3 (T D Barron) *led: pushed along and hdd over 2f out: no ex fnl f* 5/4[1]	56+
0-00	4	4	**Tivers Song (USA)**[12] 2303 6-8-7 **46** (b) SoniaEaton 10 (John A Harris) *hld up: hdwy over 2f out: wknd over 1f out* 16/1	42
0606	5	4	**Mojeerr**[5] 2511 4-8-6 **48** (be) NoraLooby(3) 12 (A J McCabe) *s.s: bhd: mod late prog: nvr nrr* 16/1	36
-000	6	3 3/4	**Kingsmaite**[26] 1884 9-8-6 **45** (b) JakePayne 9 (S R Bowring) *chsd ldrs: outpcd 7f out: hdwy 4f out: wknd over 2f out* 22/1	26
2224	7	1 1/4	**Dinner Date**[12] 2298 8-9-4 **57** NatashaEaton 8 (T Keddy) *hld up: pushed along over 3f out: nvr on terms* 17/2	35
4000	8	7	**Sacco D'Oro**[5] 2516 4-8-8 **50** JosephYoung(3) 5 (M Mullineaux) *w ldr over 4f: wknd over 2f out* 33/1	15
	9	1 1/4	**Hawk Junior (IRE)**[705] 3463 4-8-6 **45** MatthewCosham 6 (Patrick Morris) *in rr: wknd 4f out* 25/1	8
-000	10	53	**Catchmeifyoucan (FR)**[10] 2360 4-8-11 **50** (t) RichardRowe 4 (Andrew Turnell) *prom tl wknd over 3f out: t.o* 40/1	—

2m 11.04s (-0.66) **Going Correction** -0.275s/f (Firm) 10 Ran SP% 115.0
Speed ratings (Par 101): **91,87,86,83,80 77,76,70,69,27**
toteswingers: 1&2 £4.70, 1&3 £4.60, 2&3 £1.70. CSF £30.03 CT £50.40 TOTE £7.00: £1.70, £1.10, £1.80; EX 37.70 Trifecta £80.60 Part won. Pool: £108.97 - 0.52 winning units.Place 6: £31.36, Place 5: £12.95..
Owner Deborah Hart & Alan Jackson **Bred** Janus Bloodstock **Trained** Forsbrook, Staffs

FOCUS
A moderate "hands and heels" apprentice handicap with seven of the ten runners maidens coming into it. The winner is rated back to his best with the runner-up to latest course form.
Hawk Junior(IRE) Official explanation: jockey said gelding ran green
Catchmeifyoucan(FR) Official explanation: jockey said gelding lost its action
T/Plt: £32.30 to a £1 stake. Pool: £57,653.87. 1,302.09 winning tickets. T/Qpdt: £10.20 to a £1 stake. Pool: £3,409.24. 246.20 winning tickets. CR

2420 RIPON (R-H)

Wednesday, June 2

OFFICIAL GOING: Good (8.7)
Wind: virtually nil Weather: Fine and dry

2654 E B F EURA AUDIT UK MAIDEN STKS 6f

6:40 (6:41) (Class 5) 2-Y-O £3,561 (£1,059; £529; £264) Stalls Low

Form				RPR
	1		**Waltz Darling (IRE)** 2-9-3 0 PaulHanagan 8 (R A Fahey) *in tch: hdwy to trck ldrs 1/2-way: rdn to chse ldr over 1f out: styd on to ld ins fnl f: kpt on strly* 6/1[3]	81+
2	2	1 1/2	**Sea Flower (IRE)**[8] 2420 2-8-12 0 DavidAllan 2 (T D Easterby) *led: rdn along wl over 1f out: drvn ins fnl f: sn hdd and no ex towards fin* 15/8[1]	71+
4	3	3 3/4	**Paper Dreams (IRE)**[11] 2347 2-8-12 0 GrahamGibbons 12 (K A Ryan) *prom: effrt to chse ldr 1/2-way: rdn along 2f out: drvn and one pce fr over 1f out* 5/1[2]	60
	4	2 1/4	**Hortensis** 2-8-7 0 LanceBetts(5) 5 (T D Easterby) *in tch: hdwy on inner to trck ldrs 1/2-way: rdn along 2f out: sn one pce* 28/1	53+
03	5	1 3/4	**Hi Ho Ron**[19] 2068 2-9-3 0 PhillipMakin 11 (D H Brown) *midfield: effrt over 2f out: sn rdn along and no imp fr wl over 1f out* 13/2	53
	6	1 1/4	**Lady Amakhala** 2-8-12 0 PJMcDonald 4 (G M Moore) *s.i.s and bhd: rdn along 1/2-way: swtchd outside wl over 1f out: styd on ins fnl f: nrst fin* 50/1	44+
4	7	3/4	**Silver Shine (IRE)**[16] 2171 2-9-3 0 MichaelHills 7 (W J Haggas) *in tch: rdn along 1/2-way: n.d* 8/1	47
0	8	nk	**Jealousy Defined (IRE)**[22] 1986 2-8-12 0 SilvestreDeSousa 1 (N Tinkler) *dwlt: a towards rr* 50/1	41
	9	1 1/4	**Willow's Wish** 2-8-12 0 TomEaves 6 (G M Moore) *s.i.s: bhd tl sme late hdwy* 33/1	37
05	10	1/2	**Sky Diamond (IRE)**[55] 1180 2-9-3 0 PaulMulrennan 3 (J G Given) *chsd ldrs to 1/2-way: sn wknd* 14/1	41
6	11	5	**Mercy Street**[15] 2202 2-9-3 0 AndrewElliott 10 (N Tinkler) *dwlt: a in rr* 100/1	26
	12	1 1/4	**Baby Driver** 2-9-3 0 FrederikTylicki 9 (J Howard Johnson) *prom: rdn along and lost pl bef 1/2-way: sn in rr* 14/1	22

1m 13.83s (0.83) **Going Correction** -0.075s/f (Good) 12 Ran SP% 114.8
Speed ratings (Par 93): **91,89,84,81,78 77,76,75,73,73 66,64**
toteswingers: 1&2 £2.50, 1&3 £6.20, 2&3 £3.00. CSF £16.48 TOTE £5.80: £2.00, £1.10, £1.80; EX 17.20.
Owner Mike Browne **Bred** Ms Natalie Cleary **Trained** Musley Bank, N Yorks

FOCUS
An average juvenile maiden where a low draw was an advantage. The placed horses appeared to step up on their respective debuts.

NOTEBOOK
Waltz Darling(IRE) is half-brother to a dual sprint winner at two and showed a professional attitude to come out on top of his battle with the more experienced runner-up. He has plenty of scope and speed, but on the dam's side of his pedigree he should have little trouble staying further down the line. This rates yet another promising juvenile this season from his yard. (op 11-2 tchd 5-1)
Sea Flower(IRE) showed the benefit of her debut outing here eight days earlier and was soon racing in the lead against the stands' rail. She ultimately failed to see out the extra furlong, but was nicely clear of the remainder and obviously has it in her to win races this summer. (op 9-4)
Paper Dreams(IRE), representing a stable with a good record in this race, lacked the pace to go with the first pair yet kept on respectably in third. She wasn't helped by the draw and it was a step up on her debut effort 11 days previously. (op 9-2 tchd 13-2)
Hortensis is out of a dam that won over this trip at two and she turned in a pleasing debut run. She ought to get closer next time out. (op 33-1)
Hi Ho Ron, who comes from an in-form yard, was one paced and failed to run up to the level of his improved third at Hamilton. (op 8-1 tchd 6-1)
Lady Amakhala showed her inexperience and, bred to get further, should relish being faced with a stiffer test in due course.
Silver Shine(IRE) Official explanation: jockey said colt was unsuited by the track

2655 BET TOTEPOOL TO SUPPORT YOUR SPORT (S) H'CAP 1m 4f 10y

7:10 (7:10) (Class 6) (0-60,60) 4-5-Y-O £2,590 (£770; £385; £192) Stalls High

Form				RPR
3522	1		**Tropical Bachelor (IRE)**[18] 2109 4-8-13 **60** JohnFahy(5) 6 (T J Pitt) *hld up in rr: stdy hdwy over 4f out: trckd ldrs 3f out: led over 1f out: sn rdn clr* 7/2[1]	73
0004	2	7	**Dispol Diva**[8] 2424 4-8-11 **53** (v) JoeFanning 2 (P T Midgley) *a.p: led 4f out: rdn along over 2f out: drvn and hdd over 1f out: kpt on same pce* 4/1[2]	55
0-50	3	2	**What A Day**[3] 2560 4-8-12 **54** GrahamGibbons 8 (J J Quinn) *trckd ldrs: effrt 4f out: rdn along wl over 2f out: plugged on same pce to take 3rd nr fin* 5/1[3]	53
0400	4	nk	**Coole Dodger (IRE)**[4] 2527 5-8-11 **53** (p) RoystonFfrench 7 (B Ellison) *stdd s and hld up: rapid hdwy on outer to ld after 3f: rdn along and hdd 4f out: sn drvn and grad wknd* 6/1	51
/056	5	6	**Gulf Coast**[5] 2500 5-8-13 **55** DuranFentiman 11 (T D Walford) *led 3f: chsd ldrs: rdn along over 4f out and grad wknd* 7/2[1]	44
0-05	6	3 1/4	**Ledgerwood**[14] 2230 5-8-4 **46** oh1 (p) NeilChalmers 1 (A J Chamberlain) *s.i.s and bhd: sme late hdwy: nvr a factor* 28/1	30
343-	7	17	**Melkatant**[232] 6766 4-8-5 **47** PaulHanagan 5 (N Bycroft) *t.k.h early: chsd ldrs: pushed along over 5f out: sn lost pl and bhd fnl 3f* 11/1	3
2-06	8	9	**Musigny (USA)**[26] 1887 4-9-1 **57** PhillipMakin 10 (Miss S E Hall) *chsd ldrs 3f: midfield tl rdn along and wknd 5f out: sn bhd* 25/1	—
00/6	9	5	**James Junior**[17] 700 4-7-13 **46** oh1 JamesSullivan(5) 3 (P D Niven) *a towards rr: rdn along over 4f out: sn bhd* 66/1	—
-04U	10	23	**Bertie Smalls**[21] 2023 4-8-4 **46** oh1 (b) LiamJones 9 (M H Tompkins) *trckd ldrs: chsd ldr after 3f: rdn along over 4f out: sn wknd* 16/1	—

2m 36.86s (0.16) **Going Correction** +0.10s/f (Good) 10 Ran SP% 118.4
Speed ratings: **103,98,97,96,92 90,79,73,69,54**
toteswingers: 1&2 £2.50, 1&3 £2.70, 2&3 £8.00. CSF £17.62 CT £70.54 TOTE £3.90: £1.20, £2.80, £1.70; EX 10.10.The winner was bought in for £6,500.
Owner M & A McBride,M Brennan & J Kilbride **Bred** George Ward **Trained** Norton, N Yorks

FOCUS
A moderate handicap, run at a good gallop. The winner is rated back to his best with the placed horses a few pounds of their recent best.
Coole Dodger(IRE) Official explanation: jockey said gelding ran too free

2656 RIPON FARM SERVICES H'CAP 6f

7:40 (7:41) (Class 4) (0-85,85) 3-Y-O £4,533 (£1,348; £674; £336) Stalls Low

Form				RPR
-231	1		**Kellys Eye (IRE)**[8] 2426 3-9-2 **80** 6ex RobertWinston 3 (D H Brown) *midfield: hdwy 1/2-way: effrt and n.m.r 2f out: sn swtchd rt and rdn to chal over 1f out: led ent fnl f: sn drvn and edgd lft: kpt on strly* 13/8[1]	91+
4006	2	2 1/4	**Nubar Boy**[20] 2052 3-8-5 **72** MartinLane(3) 6 (P D Evans) *trckd ldrs: effrt and n.m.r 2f out: gd hdwy over 1f out: swtchd lft and rdn to chse ldng pair ent fnl f: drvn and one pce last 100yds* 33/1	76
-152	3	hd	**Esuvia (IRE)**[17] 2140 3-9-3 **81** TomEaves 11 (B Smart) *trckd ldrs: hdwy on outer and cl up 1/2-way: rdn to ld briefly over 1f out: drvn and hdd ent fnl f: kpt on same pce towards fin* 9/1	84
51	4	2	**Timeless Stride (IRE)**[26] 1878 3-8-9 **76** Louis-PhilippeBeuzelin(3) 4 (Sir Michael Stoute) *trckd ldrs: n.m.r and swtchd rt 2f out: rdn to chse ldrs over 1f out: sn drvn and one pce appr fnl f* 9/2[2]	73
1523	5	2 3/4	**Solstice**[17] 2140 3-9-1 **82** BarryMcHugh(3) 7 (Julie Camacho) *in tch: hdwy to chse ldrs 1/2-way: rdn along wl over 1f out: sn one pce* 12/1	70
516-	6	nk	**Walvis Bay (IRE)**[207] 7290 3-9-5 **83** MickyFenton 8 (T P Tate) *cl up: rdn to ld over 2f out: drvn and hdd wl over 1f out: grad wknd* 10/1	70

52-1 **7** *1* **Masked Dance (IRE)**^{30} [1776] 3-9-5 **83**......................(p) PaulHanagan 10 67
(K A Ryan) *cl up: effrt over 2f out: sn rdn and ev ch tl drvn and wknd over 1f out* **5/1**^{3}

2-10 **7** *dht* **Johannesgray (IRE)**^{27} [1836] 3-9-0 **78**......................... AdrianNicholls 2 62
(D Nicholls) *hld up towards rr: hdwy 1/2-way: effrt and n.m.r over 1f out: sn rdn and btn* **22/1**

15-3 **9** *7* **Cape Kimberley**^{37} [1584] 3-8-10 **74**......................... PaulMulrennan 1 35
(J G Given) *led: rdn along 1/2-way: sn hdd & wknd* **33/1**

13-5 **10** *1 1/2* **Licence To Till (USA)**^{9} [2394] 3-9-5 **83**......................... JoeFanning 12 39
(M Johnston) *a towards rr* **12/1**

60-0 **11** *nse* **Celestial Tryst**^{48} [1334] 3-8-11 **75**......................... PJMcDonald 9 31
(G M Moore) *s.i.s: a in rr* **100/1**

1m 12.24s (-0.76) **Going Correction** -0.075s/f (Good) **11** Ran SP% **118.6**
Speed ratings (Par 101): **102,99,98,96,92 92,90,90,81,79 79**
toteswingers: 1&2 £24.30, 1&3 £4.70, 2&3 £65.40. CSF £76.31 CT £401.43 TOTE £2.00: £1.02, £13.40, £4.20; EX 96.80.
Owner Ron Hull **Bred** Michael Downey And Roalso Ltd **Trained** Maltby, S Yorks

FOCUS
A competitive sprint and again it was a help to be drawn low. The winner improved again and the placed horses ran to form.
Cape Kimberley Official explanation: jockey said gelding was unsuited by the track

2657 DIRECTORS CUP (HANDICAP STKS) 6f
8:10 (8:12) (Class 3) (0-95,94) 4-Y-O+ **£7,569** (£2,265; £1,132; £566; £282) **Stalls** Low

Form RPR

00-2 **1** **Tajneed (IRE)**^{49} [1295] 7-9-3 **90**......................... AdrianNicholls 6 101
(D Nicholls) *a cl up: rdn to ld over 1f out: drvn ins fnl f: kpt on wl towards fin* **11/2**^{2}

-002 **2** *3/4* **Abraham Lincoln (IRE)**^{12} [2280] 6-9-0 **87**......................(p) LukeMorris 3 95
(R A Harris) *dwlt: sn in midfield: hdwy to trck ldrs 1/2-way: swtchd rt and rdn over 1f out: chal ent fnl f and ev ch tl drvn and no ex last 75yds* **14/1**

0450 **3** *3 3/4* **Joseph Henry**^{15} [2205] 8-8-7 **85**......................... BillyCray$^{(5)}$ 8 81
(D Nicholls) *cl up: rdn and ev ch 2f out tl drvn and one pce ent fnl f* **20/1**

231- **4** *hd* **Eton Rifles (IRE)**^{255} [6135] 5-9-5 **92**......................... FrederikTylicki 4 88+
(J Howard Johnson) *in tch: hdwy to trck ldrs 1/2-way: swtchd rt and rdn over 1f out: drvn and kpt on same pce ins fnl f* **10/3**^{1}

00-0 **5** *2 1/4* **Northern Dare (IRE)**^{81} [887] 6-8-12 **85**......................... PaulHanagan 2 74
(R A Fahey) *in tch: hdwy to chse ldrs 1/2-way: effrt and n.m.r wl over 1f out: sn rdn and kpt on same pce* **7/1**^{3}

1346 **6** *1 3/4* **Tabaret**^{11} [2346] 7-8-12 **88**......................... MichaelStainton$^{(3)}$ 5 71
(R M Whitaker) *cl up: led wl over 2f out: sn rdn: hdd and drvn over 1f out: sn wknd* **12/1**

0065 **7** *1/2* **Haajes**^{4} [2534] 6-8-7 **80**......................(t) PaulMulrennan 12 61
(P T Midgley) *bhd tl sme late hdwy* **20/1**

2-06 **8** *shd* **Marine Boy (IRE)**^{33} [1664] 4-9-7 **94**......................... RichardKingscote 10 75
(Tom Dascombe) *towards rr fr 1/2-way* **22/1**

-030 **9** *1* **Courageous (IRE)**^{31} [1727] 4-9-3 **90**......................... TomEaves 1 68
(B Smart) *led: rdn along and hdd over 2f out: wknd wl over 1f out* **7/1**^{3}

-042 **10** *2 1/2* **Esprit De Midas**^{48} [1332] 4-9-3 **90**......................... MichaelHills 9 60
(K A Ryan) *midfield: rdn along 1/2-way: sn wknd* **15/2**

40-0 **11** *4* **Shotley Mac**^{26} [1888] 6-8-10 **83** ow1......................(b) PhillipMakin 14 40
(N Bycroft) *a in rr: bhd fr 1/2-way* **28/1**

26-0 **12** *4* **Excusez Moi (USA)**^{49} [1295] 8-9-5 **92**......................(v^{1}) PJMcDonald 13 36
(Mrs R A Carr) *v s.i.s and bhd: hdwy and midfield 1/2-way: effrt and n.m.r over 2f out: sn rdn and wknd* **14/1**

0-56 **13** *10* **Cerito**^{32} [1691] 4-8-4 **77**......................... NickyMackay 11 —
(J R Boyle) *rdn along and towards rr on outer: lost tch and bhd fr 1/2-way* **40/1**

1m 11.37s (-1.63) **Going Correction** -0.075s/f (Good) **13** Ran SP% **116.0**
Speed ratings (Par 107): **107,106,101,100,97 95,94,94,93,89 84,79,65**
toteswingers: 1&2 £15.40, 1&3 £39.40, 2&3 £120.20. CSF £70.62 CT £1429.23 TOTE £7.40: £2.50, £7.00, £9.50; EX 109.50.
Owner Alex Nicholls & Finola Devaney **Bred** R Hodgins **Trained** Sessay, N Yorks

FOCUS
A decent handicap and sound form rated around the principals.

NOTEBOOK
Tajneed(IRE) extended his C&D record to 3-3 under a positive ride. He took it up full of running soon after 2f out and picked up again once the runner-up came at him nearing the business end. He is best at this distance and he was 2lb lower than when landing the big one here last August. (op 9-2 tchd 7-2)
Abraham Lincoln(IRE) ◆ was the only real threat to the winner inside the final furlong and looked as though he may get on top, but that rival proved strongest when it mattered. He is back in top form and his turn isn't looking far off once more. (op 16-1)
Joseph Henry was never far away on this drop back in trip and ran one of his better races, but remains hard to win with
Eton Rifles(IRE) was making his seasonal comeback and proved popular. He didn't get the best of passages, but was not unlucky and ideally needs an easier surface. This was still an encouraging return. (op 4-1 tchd 9-2 and 3-1)
Northern Dare(IRE) was never seriously involved, but this was better back from a break and he is currently 2lb lower than when last winning. (op 6-1)
Tabaret caught the eye running on late from out the back, but was passing tired horses and needs dropping back to the minimum trip. (op 14-1 tchd 16-1)
Marine Boy(IRE) Official explanation: jockey said gelding hung left throughout

2658 SIS PICTURE SERVICES MAIDEN STKS 1m 1f 170y
8:40 (8:42) (Class 5) 3-Y-O+ **£2,914** (£867; £433; £216) **Stalls** High

Form RPR

5-20 **1** **Red Fantasy (IRE)**^{21} [2029] 3-8-7 100 ow1......................... MichaelHills 6 72
(B W Hills) *trckd ldng pair: hdwy 3f out: led 3f out: rdn ent fnl f: drvn and kpt on towards fin* **2/5**^{1}

2 *1/2* **Mainland (USA)** 4-9-10 0......................... PaulMulrennan 9 75+
(K A Ryan) *dwlt and in rr: hdwy on inner 3f out: rdn over 1f out: styd on strly ins fnl f* **40/1**

0 **3** *2 3/4* **Queen's Scholar (USA)**^{12} [2290] 3-8-6 0......................... JoeFanning 7 64
(M Johnston) *trckd ldrs: hdwy 4f out: rdn to chse wnr 2f out: drvn over 1f out: kpt on same pce* **14/1**

4 *1/2* **Invitee** 3-8-6 0......................... HayleyTurner 8 63+
(E A L Dunlop) *hld up in tch: hdwy 3f out: rdn over 2f out: drvn and kpt on appr fnl f* **6/1**^{2}

05- **5** *nk* **Sadler's Mark**^{210} [7244] 3-8-11 0......................... MickyFenton 3 67
(T P Tate) *hld up: hdwy on outer over 3f out: rdn to chse ldrs 2f out: drvn and wknd over 1f out* **8/1**^{3}

4 **6** *1 1/4* **Line Of Duty (IRE)**^{13} [2258] 3-8-11 0......................... PJMcDonald 2 64
(G A Swinbank) *led 2f: prom tl rdn along and sltly outpcd over 2f out: kpt on u.p ins fnl f* **14/1**

00-0 **7** *4* **Peaceful Rule (USA)**^{5} [2492] 4-9-10 68......................... AdrianNicholls 5 57
(D Nicholls) *cl up: led after 2f: rdn along 4f out: hdd 3f out: drvn 2f out and grad wknd appr fnl f* **25/1**

3-0 **8** *4 1/2* **Retrato (USA)**^{30} [1757] 3-8-6 0......................... PaulHanagan 4 42
(Rae Guest) *trckd ldrs: hdwy over 3f out: rdn over 2f out: wknd wl over 1f out* **25/1**

9 *17* **Arkas**^{107} 4-9-5 0......................... PaddyAspell 1 —
(C R Wilson) *s.i.s: a in rr: outpcd and bhd fnl 3f* **125/1**

2m 6.47s (1.07) **Going Correction** +0.10s/f (Good)
WFA 3 from 4yo 13lb **9** Ran SP% **121.1**
Speed ratings (Par 103): **99,98,96,96,95 94,91,87,74**
toteswingers: 1&2 £7.30, 1&3 £28.60, 2&3 £2.40. CSF £35.73 TOTE £1.20: £1.02, £8.20, £2.40; EX 34.70.
Owner R J Arculli **Bred** Eugene O'Donnell & Westbury Bloodstock **Trained** Lambourn, Berks

FOCUS
A fair maiden, but the form is muddling with the winner running well below her mark.
Peaceful Rule(USA) Official explanation: jockey said gelding ran too free

2659 ATTHERACES.COM IS FREE H'CAP 2m
9:10 (9:10) (Class 5) (0-75,75) 4-Y-O+ **£2,914** (£867; £433; £216) **Stalls** Low

Form RPR

45-5 **1** **Miss Keck**^{56} [1150] 6-9-1 **66**......................... PJMcDonald 5 78
(G A Swinbank) *hld up: stdy hdwy over 5f out: chsd ldrs 3f out: rdn to chse ldr over 1f out: led ent fnl f: kpt on strly* **7/1**

-433 **2** *3* **Royal Trooper (IRE)**^{20} [2060] 4-9-6 **72**......................... PaulMulrennan 6 80
(J G Given) *prom: led after 2f: rdn clr 2f out: drvn and hdd ent fnl f: kpt on same pce* **10/1**

5-34 **3** *2* **King In Waiting (IRE)**^{20} [2060] 7-8-9 **60**......................... GrahamGibbons 10 66
(J Hetherton) *t.k.h early: trckd ldr: effrt 3f out: rdn along over 2f out: drvn wl over 1f out and kpt on same pce* **10/3**^{2}

2-22 **4** *1 3/4* **Gaselee (USA)**^{27} [1849] 4-9-4 **70**......................... JoeFanning 2 74
(Rae Guest) *trckd ldrs: hdwy and cl up 4f out: rdn along over 2f out: sn drvn and kpt on same pce* **9/4**^{1}

0-23 **5** *4* **Smugglers Bay (IRE)**^{4} [2533] 6-8-7 **63**......................(b) LanceBetts$^{(5)}$ 3 62
(T D Easterby) *t.k.h: hld up: hdwy over 4f out: rdn along 3f out: nvr rchd ldrs* **10/1**

220- **6** *3/4* **Ursis (FR)**^{54} [3510] 9-9-0 **70**......................... JohnFahy$^{(5)}$ 4 68
(S Gollings) *hld up: hdwy to trck ldrs 1/2-way: effrt 3f out: rdn along over 2f out: sn drvn and btn* **25/1**

21-5 **7** *4* **Saborido (USA)**^{19} [2081] 4-9-3 **69**......................... JimCrowley 11 62
(Mrs A J Perrett) *led 2f: prom tl rdn along over 3f out and sn wknd* **5/1**^{3}

/26- **8** *6* **Basalt (IRE)**^{186} [7573] 6-9-10 **75**......................... GregFairley 1 61
(T J Pitt) *towards rr: rdn along 6f out: nvr a factor* **16/1**

10-6 **9** *6* **Court Princess**^{15} [2218] 7-8-5 **56** oh1......................... PaulHanagan 7 35
(George Baker) *chsd ldrs on inner: rdn along 4f out: sn wknd* **20/1**

0-16 **10** *32* **Spruzzo**^{19} [2085] 4-8-4 **56** oh3......................... DuranFentiman 9 —
(C W Thornton) *s.i.s: a in rr: bhd fnl 3f* **33/1**

35/- **11** *5* **Jetta Joy (IRE)**^{567} [7285] 5-8-5 **56** oh4......................... RoystonFfrench 8 —
(Mrs A Duffield) *a in rr: bhd fnl 3f* **40/1**

3m 31.81s (0.01) **Going Correction** +0.10s/f (Good)
WFA 4 from 5yo+ 1lb **11** Ran SP% **121.1**
Speed ratings (Par 103): **103,101,100,99,97 97,95,92,89,74 71**
toteswingers: 1&2 £23.90, 1&3 £6.70, 2&3 £6.20. CSF £73.52 CT £280.67 TOTE £10.70: £3.00, £4.50, £1.40; EX 80.10 Place 6: £55.13, Place 5: £42.69..
Owner Alan Wright **Bred** The Woodhaven Stud **Trained** Melsonby, N Yorks

FOCUS
A modest staying handicap, run at a sound gallop and the form looks solid enough rated around the placed horses.
Jetta Joy(IRE) Official explanation: jockey said mare never travelled
T/Plt: £22.80 to a £1 stake. Pool: £77,658.10. 2479.04 winning tickets. T/Qpdt: £11.10 to a £1 stake. Pool: £5,744.77. 381.80 winning tickets. JR

2068 HAMILTON (R-H)
Thursday, June 3

OFFICIAL GOING: Good to firm (good in places; 9.9)
Rail realignment around the loop reduced advertised increased distances on Round course by about 8yds.
Wind: Slight, across Weather: Cloudy, fine

2667 LANARK SILVER BELL RACENIGHT NEXT WEEK MAIDEN AUCTION STKS 6f 5y
2:10 (2:11) (Class 6) 2-Y-O **£2,590** (£770; £385; £192) **Stalls** Low

Form RPR

5 **1** **Krypton Factor**^{7} [2474] 2-9-1 0......................... PaulMulrennan 1 74
(Sir Mark Prescott) *mde all: hung rt thrght: rdn and hld on wl fnl f* **1/1**^{1}

2 *hd* **Dr Noverre (IRE)** 2-9-1 0......................... StephenCraine 5 73+
(K A Ryan) *dwlt: chsd ldng gp: effrt and hdwy over 1f out: kpt on wl fnl f: jst hld* **7/2**^{2}

3 *1 3/4* **Lexi's Princess (IRE)** 2-8-6 0......................... GrahamGibbons 4 59
(K A Ryan) *w ldrs: rdn 2f out: kpt on same pce ins fnl f* **5/1**^{3}

4 **4** *4* **Golden Blaze**^{3} [2577] 2-8-11 0......................... DarrenMoffatt 2 52
(James Moffatt) *prom: drvn and outpcd 1/2-way: rallied fnl f: no imp* **18/1**

66 **5** *2* **Wild Hysteria (IRE)**^{14} [2239] 2-8-11 0......................... MickyFenton 3 46
(T P Tate) *t.k.h: cl up: hung rt thrght: rdn 2f out: wknd fnl f* **13/2**

50 **6** *7* **Celtic Anu**^{14} [2239] 2-8-6 0......................... JamesSullivan$^{(5)}$ 6 25
(Patrick Morris) *s.i.s: sn outpcd and struggling: no ch fr 1/2-way* **40/1**

1m 11.7s (-0.50) **Going Correction** -0.20s/f (Firm) **6** Ran SP% **109.9**
Speed ratings (Par 91): **95,94,92,87,84 75**
Tote Swingers: 1&2 £1.80, 1&3 £2.30, 2&3 £2.50 CSF £4.48 TOTE £1.70: £1.10, £1.20; EX 5.30.

Owner Lady Fairhaven & The Hon C & H Broughton **Bred** Lady Fairhaven **Trained** Newmarket, Suffolk

FOCUS
This was probably an average little juvenile maiden. The front three can all do better than this whatever the true worth of this form proves to be.

NOTEBOOK
Krypton Factor was all the rage to step up on his 5f Polytrack debut a week earlier and duly obliged, but certainly made his rider earn his fee in doing so. He was always front rank and had the benefit of the stands' rail but took an age to shake off the two that duelled on the lead with him, though, and hung right away from the rail under maximum pressure from the furlong marker. Ultimately he was all out to score, but was clearly racing lazily and rates better than the bare margin. He has scope and it is likely this experience will see him go forward again. (op 11-8 tchd 7-4 in a place)

Dr Noverre(IRE) ◆ is a half-brother to Mark Anthony, who scored over this trip at two for his stable last year. He only found his full stride entering the final furlong and was motoring home as the winner drifted across the track. The line came a stride too soon for him, but he can be expected to step up on this next time and should take some beating. (op 3-1 tchd 4-1)
Lexi's Princess(IRE) had been withdrawn in the stalls on her intended debut in the Brocklesby in March. She knew her job and kept on well for pressure, but left the impression this test was too sharp. (op 4-1)
Golden Blaze struggled to go the pace and will be better off over a stiffer test. (op 20-1 tchd 16-1)

2668 CHEQUE CENTRE CLAIMING STKS 6f 5y
2:40 (2:40) (Class 6) 3-5-Y-O **£2,047** (£604; £302) **Stalls** Low

Form RPR
230 **1** **Caprio (IRE)**[36] 1625 5-9-10 84 NickyMackay 1 81+
(J R Boyle) *dwlt: sn prom on outside: rdn to ld appr fnl f: kpt on wl* **11/8**[1]
-614 **2** ½ **Cawdor (IRE)**[24] 1968 4-9-2 75 TomEaves 5 71
(Mrs L Stubbs) *led tl rdn and hdd appr fnl f: kpt on towards fin* **3/1**[3]
2420 **3** *nk* **Clear Ice (IRE)**[16] 2203 3-8-3 60 (v) FrannyNorton 3 63
(R C Guest) *cl up: rdn and outpcd over 1f out: r.o ins fnl f* **9/1**
-001 **4** 2½ **Newbury Street**[16] 2203 3-8-8 67 TonyHamilton 2 60
(R A Fahey) *prom: effrt over 1f out: kpt on same pce fnl f* **9/4**[2]
-006 **5** 3¾ **Star Addition**[13] 2274 4-9-2 50 DavidAllan 4 50
(E J Alston) *cl up tl rdn and outpcd over 2f out: edgd rt and btn fnl f* **20/1**

1m 11.05s (-1.15) **Going Correction** -0.20s/f (Firm)
WFA 3 from 4yo+ 8lb **5 Ran SP% 112.6**
Speed ratings (Par 101): **99,98,97,94,89**
CSF £6.05 TOTE £2.20: £1.70, £1.40; EX 5.60.
Owner M Khan X2 **Bred** P Rabbitte **Trained** Epsom, Surrey

FOCUS
A fairly tight claimer, and a bit of a muddling race. The comfortable winner did not need to be at his best.

2669 LANARKSHIRE CHAMBER OF COMMERCE H'CAP 5f 4y
3:10 (3:11) (Class 6) (0-65,65) 3-Y-O+ **£2,388** (£705; £352) **Stalls** Low

Form RPR
-001 **1** **Musical Bridge**[18] 2144 4-10-0 65 (b) TomEaves 1 76
(Mrs L Williamson) *racd w one other stands' side: prom: effrt 2f out: led last 100yds: pushed out* **11/4**[1]
05-0 **2** 2½ **Sandwith**[20] 2073 7-9-9 60 LNewman 10 62
(A G Foster) *prom: rdn 1/2-way: edgd lft and led briefly ins fnl f: kpt on same pce* **11/1**
4100 **3** *2* **Monte Mayor One**[7] 2449 3-9-1 59 TonyHamilton 11 51
(P Monteith) *bhd tl hdwy over 1f out: kpt on fnl f: nrst fin* **28/1**
3200 **4** ½ **Welcome Approach**[10] 2381 7-9-2 53 AndrewElliott 3 46
(J R Weymes) *in tch: rdn 1/2-way: effrt over 1f out: kpt on ins fnl f* **9/2**[2]
246- **5** ¾ **Cayman Fox**[181] 7634 5-9-10 61 (e) PJMcDonald 8 51
(James Moffatt) *t.k.h: led at str gallop: hdd ins fnl f: sn wknd* **13/2**
5-30 **6** *nse* **Distant Vision (IRE)**[3] 2582 7-8-12 49 PatrickMathers 2 39
(H A McWilliams) *racd w wnr stands' side: hld up in tch: effrt over 1f out: edgd rt: sn no imp* **14/1**
00-0 **7** *4* **Barraland**[16] 2213 5-9-11 62 (v) FrederikTylicki 6 38
(J S Goldie) *chsd ldrs: rdn and outpcd 2f out: n.d after* **12/1**
-066 **8** *5* **Mr Rooney (IRE)**[24] 1965 7-8-9 46 oh1 FrannyNorton 5 4
(A Berry) *bhd and sn rdn along: no ch fr 1/2-way* **100/1**
-250 **9** 1¾ **Kyzer Chief**[18] 2144 5-9-9 60 PhillipMakin 7 11
(R E Barr) *in tch tl rdn and wknd over 1f out* **5/1**[3]
/0-6 **10** ½ **Compton Lad**[16] 2212 7-8-4 46 oh1 PaulPickard(5) 4 —
(D A Nolan) *cl up: rdn 1/2-way: wknd over 1f out* **100/1**
0-00 **11** 1½ **Howards Prince**[16] 2213 7-8-4 46 oh1 (p) JamesSullivan(5) 9 —
(D A Nolan) *midfield: outpcd 1/2-way: sn btn* **100/1**
0041 **12** *31* **The Bear**[13] 2294 7-9-13 64 PaulMulrennan 12 —
(Miss L A Perratt) *bolted to post: bhd and outpcd after 2f: sn lost tch: t.o* **7/1**

58.99 secs (-1.01) **Going Correction** -0.20s/f (Firm)
WFA 3 from 4yo+ 7lb **12 Ran SP% 116.5**
Speed ratings (Par 101): **100,96,92,92,90 90,84,76,73,72 70,20**
Tote Swingers: 1&2 £9.30, 1&3 £17.10, 2&3 £40.00 CSF £34.14 CT £702.71 TOTE £3.80: £1.80, £3.80, £8.40; EX 39.50.
Owner John Conway **Bred** John Starbuck **Trained** Saighton, Cheshire

FOCUS
A weak sprint handicap. The winner is rated back this old best.
The Bear Official explanation: jockey said gelding ran too free to post

2670 PRESTIGE SCOTLAND H'CAP (QUALIFIER FOR THE SCOTTISH TROPHY HANDICAP SERIES FINAL) 1m 65y
3:40 (3:42) (Class 5) (0-70,66) 4-Y-O+ **£3,238** (£963; £481; £240) **Stalls** High

Form RPR
62 **1** **Crocodile Bay (IRE)**[10] 2383 7-8-8 53 FrannyNorton 6 62
(R C Guest) *chsd clr ldr: smooth hdwy over 2f out: rdn to ld ins fnl f: r.o* **9/2**[2]
00-0 **2** 1¼ **Anthemion (IRE)**[7] 2454 13-8-2 47 oh2 AndrewMullen 2 53
(Mrs J C McGregor) *led: clr 1/2-way: hdd ins fnl f: kpt on same pce* **66/1**
-652 **3** ¾ **Daring Dream (GER)**[7] 2451 5-9-0 62 GaryBartley(3) 10 66+
(J S Goldie) *dwlt: hld up: rdn over 2f out: styd on fnl f: nrst fin* **11/8**[1]
-036 **4** ¾ **Cold Quest (USA)**[8] 2433 6-8-9 54 FrederikTylicki 9 57
(Miss L A Perratt) *hld up in tch: effrt and rdn over 2f out: kpt on same pce fnl f* **8/1**
5-64 **5** *1* **Papa's Princess**[8] 2433 6-8-2 47 DarrenMoffatt 7 47
(James Moffatt) *in tch: effrt over 2f out: kpt on same pce fnl f* **12/1**
-000 **6** ¾ **Silly Gilly (IRE)**[26] 1928 6-8-1 51 JamesSullivan(5) 3 50
(R E Barr) *hld up in tch: rdn over 2f out: effrt over 1f out: nt qckn fnl f* **9/1**
6105 **7** ¾ **Wrongwayround (IRE)**[18] 2142 4-9-7 66 PJMcDonald 5 63
(G A Swinbank) *hld up: rdn and outpcd over 2f out: edgd rt and styd on fnl f: no imp* **5/1**[3]
0-00 **8** *6* **Primo Way**[32] 1717 9-8-5 50 DuranFentiman 8 33
(D A Nolan) *bhd: rdn over 3f out: sme hdwy on ins over 2f out: sn wknd* **33/1**
0/00 **9** *6* **Emirate Isle**[10] 2382 6-9-3 62 (p) TomEaves 1 31
(B Storey) *prom: rdn 4f out: wknd fnl 2f* **40/1**
0/3- **10** *2* **Ten To The Dozen**[501] 210 7-8-12 57 PatrickMathers 4 22
(D W Thompson) *dwlt: hld up: drvn over 3f out: btn fr 2f out* **28/1**

1m 45.18s (-3.22) **Going Correction** -0.375s/f (Firm) **10 Ran SP% 116.1**
Speed ratings (Par 103): **101,99,99,98,97 96,95,89,83,81**
Tote Swingers: 1&2 £31.90, 1&3 £2.40, 2&3 £22.70 CSF £272.68 CT £628.31 TOTE £5.80: £2.10, £17.70, £1.10; EX 264.70.
Owner Stan Wright **Bred** James And Joe Brannigan **Trained** Stainforth, S Yorks

FOCUS
This ordinary handicap was run at a sound pace, but it still proved a race where it paid to race handily. The winner is ratest to his recent form, with the second showing his best form for a couple of years.

2671 SODEXO STOP HUNGER CHARITY H'CAP 6f 5y
4:10 (4:11) (Class 5) (0-70,70) 4-Y-O+ **£2,914** (£867; £433; £216) **Stalls** Low

Form RPR
-141 **1** **King Of Eden (IRE)**[10] 2381 4-8-13 62 6ex DavidAllan 4 71
(E J Alston) *trckd ldrs: rdn 2f out: edgd rt: led 1f out: pushed out* **8/11**[1]
2-54 **2** 1¼ **Cheyenne Red (IRE)**[5] 2528 4-9-7 70 PhillipMakin 10 75
(M Dods) *prom: hdwy and ev ch 1f out: kpt on fnl f* **3/1**[2]
03-1 **3** *shd* **Tadalavil**[27] 1869 5-9-6 69 TomEaves 1 74
(Miss L A Perratt) *led to 1f out: kpt on u.p* **16/1**
033 **4** *hd* **Dickie Le Davoir**[6] 2504 6-9-2 65 (v) FrannyNorton 9 69
(R C Guest) *bhd and sn outpcd: hdwy over 1f out: swtchd rt and styd on ins fnl f: nrst fin* **10/1**[3]
0036 **5** 1¾ **Hettie Hubble**[10] 2382 4-8-2 51 oh3 NickyMackay 8 50
(D W Thompson) *cl up on outside: pushed along 2f out: edgd rt: one pce fnl f* **50/1**
0540 **6** *hd* **Carnival Dream**[17] 2184 5-8-5 54 PatrickMathers 6 52
(H A McWilliams) *cl up: effrt and ev ch appr fnl f: kpt on same pce* **50/1**
0-40 **7** *nk* **Botham (USA)**[16] 2206 6-8-10 62 GaryBartley(3) 2 59
(J S Goldie) *bhd: pushed along 1/2-way: plugged on fnl f: no imp* **20/1**
6-00 **8** 2¼ **Sea Salt**[32] 1719 7-9-5 68 TonyHamilton 5 58
(R E Barr) *towards rr: drvn and outpcd 1/2-way: n.d after* **33/1**
2400 **9** *2* **Guest Connections**[10] 2381 7-8-12 61 (v) AdrianNicholls 3 45
(D Nicholls) *midfield: drvn after 2f: outpcd fnl 2f* **14/1**
0200 **10** *4* **Sendreni (FR)**[34] 1672 6-9-1 69 IanBrennan(5) 7 40
(Mrs J C McGregor) *hld up: rdn and edgd rt 1/2-way: sn wknd* **66/1**

1m 10.54s (-1.66) **Going Correction** -0.20s/f (Firm) **10 Ran SP% 117.7**
Speed ratings (Par 103): **103,101,101,100,98 98,97,94,92,86**
Tote Swingers: 1&2 £1.60, 1&3 £3.80, 2&3 £6.00 CSF £2.81 CT £17.96 TOTE £1.70: £1.10, £1.10, £2.10; EX 3.50.
Owner The Grumpy Old Geezers **Bred** Gainsborough Stud Management Ltd **Trained** Longton, Lancs

FOCUS
A moderate sprint handicap and once again the near side was the place to be. The winner was 6lb off his impressive Carlisle win with the runner-up to form.
Guest Connections Official explanation: jockey said gelding hung right throughout

2672 TURFTV H'CAP 1m 5f 9y
4:40 (4:49) (Class 5) (0-70,71) 4-Y-O+ **£2,914** (£867; £433; £216) **Stalls** Low

Form RPR
4141 **1** **Lady Eclair (IRE)**[8] 2445 4-9-10 71 6ex JoeFanning 7 81+
(M Johnston) *pressed ldr: rdn and led over 2f out: edgd rt 1f out: styd on strly* **1/1**[1]
-433 **2** *3* **Birkside**[40] 1539 7-8-13 60 PaulMulrennan 5 64
(Miss L A Perratt) *prom: effrt over 2f out: styd on u.p fnl f: wnt 2nd last stride* **7/1**[3]
3-00 **3** *hd* **Safebreaker**[47] 1398 5-9-2 68 (p) AmyRyan(5) 4 72+
(K A Ryan) *led: rdn and hdd over 2f out: rallied: n.m.r 1f out: kpt on same pce fnl f: lost 2nd last stride* **15/2**
/002 **4** 1½ **Planetarium**[16] 2214 5-9-1 67 (p) MichaelO'Connell(5) 1 68
(P Monteith) *hld up in tch: outpcd over 3f out: rallied and hung rt over 2f out: no imp fnl f* **10/1**
26-4 **5** *6* **Madamlily (IRE)**[30] 1807 4-9-4 65 GrahamGibbons 6 57
(J J Quinn) *trckd ldrs tl wknd over 2f out* **5/2**[2]
340- **6** *21* **Safin (GER)**[15] 1568 10-8-11 58 (t) TomEaves 2 19
(Mrs S C Bradburne) *cl up tl wknd fr 4f out: t.o* **20/1**

2m 47.74s (-6.16) **Going Correction** -0.375s/f (Firm) **6 Ran SP% 116.7**
Speed ratings (Par 103): **103,101,101,100,96 83**
Tote Swingers: 1&2 £1.90, 1&3 £2.40, 2&3 £3.90 CSF £9.51 TOTE £2.00: £1.10, £3.60; EX 7.60.
Owner Netherfield House Stud **Bred** Lynch Bages Ltd & Samac Ltd **Trained** Middleham Moor, N Yorks
■ Northside Prince was withdrawn (7/2, broke out of stalls). Deduct 20p in the £ under R4. New market formed.
■ Stewards' Enquiry : Joe Fanning three-day ban: careless riding (Jun 20-22)

FOCUS
This was run at an average pace and it was weakened by the withdrawal of Northside Prince (7/2, broke out of stalls, . The second sets the level.

2673 BETFAIR RACING EXCELLENCE APPRENTICE TRAINING SERIES H'CAP 1m 3f 16y
5:10 (5:13) (Class 6) (0-65,65) 3-Y-O **£2,388** (£705; £352) **Stalls** Low

Form RPR
00-1 **1** **Bona Fortuna**[7] 2460 3-9-10 65 6ex RosieJessop 1 78+
(Sir Mark Prescott) *hld up and bhd: plenty to do over 4f out: hdwy over 3f out: led 1f out: pushed out* **1/3**[1]
413 **2** *2* **Meetings Man (IRE)**[8] 2439 3-9-6 64 DaleSwift(3) 4 68
(Micky Hammond) *hld up: hdwy over 2f out: chsd wnr ins fnl f: no ex* **4/1**[2]
0-45 **3** 2¼ **Storm Command (IRE)**[35] 1652 3-9-0 58 (v[1]) AdamCarter(3) 5 58
(B Smart) *led 2f: chsd ldr: rdn over 3f out: hung lft: one pce over 1f out* **16/1**
435 **4** 1½ **Sheiling (IRE)**[13] 2290 3-9-5 65 MarzenaJeziorek(5) 3 62
(R A Fahey) *hld up: rdn over 4f out: kpt on fnl f: nvr rchd ldrs* **12/1**[3]
040- **5** 1¼ **Goodison Park**[233] 6762 3-9-3 58 JohnCavanagh 7 53
(A G Foster) *prom: drvn and outpcd over 3f out: n.d after* **20/1**
3144 **6** *1* **Vittachi**[66] 1054 3-9-1 56 GarryWhillans 8 49
(A C Whillans) *in tch tl rdn and outpcd over 3f out: n.d after* **14/1**
000- **7** 2½ **Star Of Kalani (IRE)**[218] 7120 3-8-2 46 oh1 (b[1]) MatthewLawson(3) 6 35
(R D Wylie) *led after 2f: rdn clr fr 4f out: wknd and hdd 1f out: sn lost pl* **50/1**
0-00 **8** *17* **Hotgrove Boy**[24] 1971 3-8-6 47 oh1 ow1 DavidKenny 2 —
(A G Foster) *hld up: drvn over 4f out: hung lft and wknd over 3f out* **66/1**

2m 23.16s (-2.44) **Going Correction** -0.375s/f (Firm) **8 Ran SP% 123.5**
Speed ratings (Par 97): **93,91,89,88,87 87,85,73**
Tote Swingers: 1&2 £1.80, 1&3 £3.60, 2&3 £3.20 CSF £2.41 CT £10.25 TOTE £1.50: £1.10, £1.20, £3.20; EX 2.80 Place 6: £7.03 Place 5: £5.55..
Owner S Munir **Bred** W And R Barnett Ltd **Trained** Newmarket, Suffolk
■ Stewards' Enquiry : Marzena Jeziorek two-day ban: careless riding (Jun 20-21)

FOCUS
A modest race run at a sound pace. The winner was value for extra and had more to offer. The form is sound but weak apart from the winner.
T/Plt: £7.40 to a £1 stake. Pool: £39,592.78 - 3,892.41. T/Qpdt: £4.90 to a £1 stake. Pool: £3,082.06 - 461.60. RY

[2413]LINGFIELD (L-H)

Thursday, June 3

OFFICIAL GOING: Turf course - good to firm (firm in places; 9.4) all-weather - standard

Wind: gentle breeze, half against Weather: warm and sunny

2674 HONDA - BEST NAME ON GRASS MAIDEN FILLIES' STKS 1m 2f
2:20 (2:21) (Class 5) 3-Y-O+ **£2,729** (£806; £403) **Stalls** Low

Form RPR

3 **1** **Sharedah (IRE)**[21] 2043 3-8-9 0 RichardHills 9 74
(Sir Michael Stoute) *led after 1f: mde rest: rdn ent fnl 2f: kpt on gamely fnl f* **8/15**[1]

2 *nk* **Dolphina (USA)** 3-8-9 0 TomQueally 12 73
(H R A Cecil) *led for 1f: chsd wnr after: rdn over 2f out: pressed wnr and drvn over 1f out: kpt on but a jst hld fnl f* **7/1**[2]

3 *1 3/4* **Eastern Paramour (IRE)**[46] 5-9-5 0 JamesMillman(3) 10 70
(B R Millman) *in tch: effrt and edging lft over 2f out: chsd ldng pair over 1f out: kpt on same pce ins fnl f* **100/1**

4 *1 1/2* **Sensationally** 3-8-9 0 JimCrowley 8 67+
(R M Beckett) *s.i.s: hld up in rr: hdwy ent fnl 3f: n.m.r wl over 1f out: styd on wl ins fnl f: nt rch ldrs* **10/1**[3]

32- **5** *1 3/4* **Inner Angel**[196] 7451 3-8-9 0 LukeMorris 3 63
(R A Teal) *s.i.s: hld up in tch in midfield: rdn and unable qck 3f out: edging lft u.p 2f out: kpt on same pce after* **12/1**

5-5 **6** *nse* **Al Jaadl**[27] 1881 3-8-9 0 AlanMunro 14 63
(W Jarvis) *t.k.h: chsd ldrs: rdn to chse ldng pair over 2f out: wknd u.p over 1f out* **11/1**

0 **7** *7* **Budding Daffodil**[14] 2255 3-8-9 0 ShaneKelly 13 49
(W J Knight) *hld up in tch in midfield: slipped bnd over 3f out: sn struggling u.p: no ch w ldrs fnl 2f* **14/1**

00 **8** *3 1/4* **Tymora (USA)**[26] 1932 3-8-9 0 EddieAhern 5 43+
(H R A Cecil) *chsd ldng pair tl rdn and struggling over 2f out: wkng and wl btn whn n.m.r and hmpd wl over 1f out* **25/1**

0 **9** *6* **Greeley's Qik Chic (USA)**[17] 2180 3-8-9 0 TonyCulhane 11 31
(George Baker) *t.k.h: hld up in tch in midfield: lost pl on downhill run over 4f out: bhd whn rn wd bnd over 3f out: no ch after* **100/1**

50-6 **10** *2 1/2* **Red Willow**[24] 1959 4-9-8 45 SamHitchcott 7 26
(J E Long) *in tch in midfield: lost pl and dropped to rr on downhill run 4f out: rdn over 3f out: wl btn after* **100/1**

11 *10* **Belvidera**[65] 4-9-8 0 TomMcLaughlin 6 6
(Mrs C A Dunnett) *a in rr: pushed along and struggling bdly over 5f out: t.o fnl 3f* **200/1**

12 *18* **Ericaceous** 3-8-9 0 DavidProbert 2 —
(Mrs C A Dunnett) *in tch in midfield tl wknd rapidly over 3f out: t.o fnl 2f* **100/1**

2m 10.01s (-0.49) **Going Correction** -0.30s/f (Firm)
WFA 3 from 4yo+ 13lb 12 Ran SP% **117.8**
Speed ratings (Par 100): **89,88,87,86,84 84,79,76,71,69 61,47**
Tote Swingers: 1&2 £3.00, 1&3 £17.80, 2&3 £30.60 CSF £4.60 TOTE £1.60: £1.02, £2.10, £15.20; EX 7.00 Trifecta £246.90 Part won. Pool: £333.70 - 0.84 winning units..
Owner Hamdan Al Maktoum **Bred** Shadwell Estate Company Limited **Trained** Newmarket, Suffolk

FOCUS

This was a modest maiden and it paid to be up there, with the front three on the pace throughout. The winner did not need to match her debut form.

Budding Daffodil Official explanation: jockey said filly slipped on bend

Tymora(USA) Official explanation: jockey said filly lost its action

2675 POLARIS RANGER - HARDEST WORKING SMOOTHEST RIDING H'CAP 1m 3f 106y
2:50 (2:51) (Class 6) (0-60,60) 3-Y-O **£2,047** (£604; £302) **Stalls** High

Form RPR

6-46 **1** **Goldtrek (USA)**[24] 1977 3-9-4 60 SteveDrowne 16 78+
(R Charlton) *broke wl to ld and crossed to rail: rdn and hrd pressed over 3f out: kpt on gamely fnl f* **12/1**

00-5 **2** *nk* **Motrice**[17] 2189 3-9-3 59 SebSanders 15 76+
(Sir Mark Prescott) *sn bustled along to chse ldrs: chsd wnr 6f out: rdn to chal 3f out: hrd drvn 2f out: nt qckn u.p and a jst hld fnl f* **9/2**[2]

00-0 **3** *3 3/4* **Super Duplex**[24] 1977 3-8-13 55 IanMongan 3 66
(P M Phelan) *stdd after s: hld up towards rr: hdwy 1/2-way: clr in ldng quintet 4f out: rdn to chse ldng pair 2f out: edgd lft u.p ent fnl f: no ex and beat fnl 100yds* **12/1**

-304 **4** *4 1/2* **Red Amy**[17] 2189 3-9-0 56 JamieSpencer 2 59+
(M L W Bell) *s.i.s: hld up in rr: lost tch 4f out and rn wd bnd over 3f out: prog to go modest 6th over 1f out: r.o wl ins fnl f: wnt 4th towards fin: nvr trbld ldrs* **5/1**[3]

0-50 **5** *3/4* **Seattle Speight (USA)**[23] 1989 3-9-1 57 ShaneKelly 7 59
(W J Knight) *chsd ldrs: wnt 3rd 5f out: rdn and nt qckn 3f out: wknd and flashing tail u.p over 1f out* **25/1**

0440 **6** *nk* **Nurai**[27] 1880 3-8-10 52 TonyCulhane 9 53
(P W D'Arcy) *chsd wnr for 1f: styd chsng ldrs: rdn and unable qck ent fnl 3f: wknd 2f out* **8/1**

0-52 **7** *13* **Oak Leaves**[9] 2412 3-8-13 55 JimCrowley 8 34
(J G Portman) *t.k.h: hld up in tch in midfield: outpcd by ldrs in 6th 4f out: no prog after and wl btn 2f out* **13/2**

0-03 **8** *1/2* **Helaku (IRE)**[9] 2412 3-9-2 58 (p) RyanMoore 11 36
(R Hannon) *hmpd and lost pl sn after s: hld up wl in rr: lost tch w ldrs over 4f out: no ch after* **4/1**[1]

-040 **9** *1 1/4* **Specialising**[23] 1989 3-8-10 52 SamHitchcott 1 28
(M R Channon) *taken down early: stdd s: t.k.h and hld up in rr: lost tch over 4f out: nvr on terms* **16/1**

00-0 **10** *1/2* **Red Eddie**[30] 1795 3-8-13 55 HayleyTurner 6 30
(S Dow) *chsd ldrs: rdn and struggling 5f out: wl btn fnl 3f* **40/1**

00-0 **11** *3/4* **Calm And Serene (USA)**[31] 1782 3-8-10 52 NeilCallan 4 26
(Rae Guest) *in tch in midfield tl outpcd 4f out: rdn and wl btn over 3f out* **66/1**

00-0 **12** *5* **Suzi's Challenger**[16] 2221 3-8-5 47 JimmyQuinn 14 13
(H J Collingridge) *t.k.h: hld up in midfield tl lost pl over 4f out: wl bhd fnl 3f* **40/1**

0-35 **13** *3 1/4* **Captain Clint (IRE)**[23] 1989 3-7-13 46 SimonPearce(5) 10 —
(M H Tompkins) *t.k.h: chsd ldrs tl wknd over 4f out: wl bhd fr wl over 2f out* **16/1**

-600 **14** *11* **Aldorable**[9] 2418 3-8-13 55 LukeMorris 13 —
(R A Teal) *stdd s: a in rr: lost tch over 4f out: t.o* **66/1**

000- **15** *6* **Downtoobusiness**[283] 5312 3-8-10 52 ChrisCatlin 12 —
(Karen George) *t.k.h: chsd wnr after 1f tl 6f out: lost pl qckly 5f out: t.o fnl 2f* **50/1**

2m 28.9s (-2.60) **Going Correction** -0.30s/f (Firm) 15 Ran SP% **120.1**
Speed ratings (Par 97): **97,96,94,90,90 90,80,80,79,78 78,74,72,64,60**
Tote Swingers: 1&2 £39.70, 1&3 £25.80, 2&3 £18.80 CSF £62.27 CT £677.66 TOTE £14.70: £4.20, £2.70, £3.70; EX 84.60 TRIFECTA Not won..
Owner AXOM (XVII) **Bred** Kenneth Lejeune & Charles Simon **Trained** Beckhampton, Wilts

FOCUS

A moderate handicap contested by 15 maidens and several were taking a significant step up in trip. This was another race where it was crucial to be handy with the first two home in those positions throughout, and several of these hung badly off the final bend. The form has been rated slightly on the positive side.

Helaku(IRE) Official explanation: jockey said colt was hampered at start and had no chance after

2676 YAMAHA - WHEN YOU NEED REAL HORSEPOWER H'CAP 1m 3f 106y
3:20 (3:33) (Class 6) (0-55,55) 4-Y-O+ **£2,047** (£604; £302) **Stalls** High

Form RPR

536- **1** **Le Corvee (IRE)**[177] 5246 8-8-1 47 KierenFox(5) 1 54
(A W Carroll) *chsd ldr for 2f: styd chsng ldrs: rdn to chal 3f out: clr w rival over 2f out: led wl over 1f out: kpt on wl fnl f* **5/1**[1]

0063 **2** *nk* **Prickles**[24] 1984 5-8-7 48 TadhgO'Shea 7 54
(Karen George) *racd keenly: sn led: rdn and clr w wnr over 2f out: hdd wl over 1f out: kpt on gamely u.p ins fnl f* **6/1**[2]

4034 **3** *3/4* **Dovedon Angel**[13] 2302 4-8-6 47 DavidProbert 12 52+
(Miss Gay Kelleway) *stdd after s: hld up in last trio: c wd amd slipped bnd over 3f out: rdn and hdwy to chse ldng pair 2f out: pressed ldrs and drvn ent fnl f: one pce and no imp on ldrs ins fnl f* **5/1**[1]

4000 **4** *7* **Catholic Hill (USA)**[54] 1225 5-8-10 51 NeilChalmers 15 44
(Mark Gillard) *t.k.h: hld up: rdn and outpcd by ldng pair 3f out: one pce and wl hld fnl 2f* **16/1**

0000 **5** *1 1/4* **Behest**[6] 2489 5-8-9 50 CathyGannon 9 41
(D G Bridgwater) *s.i.s: hld up in last pair: effrt u.p towards inner over 2f out: nvr trbld ldrs* **40/1**

00-5 **6** *2 1/2* **Christophers Quest**[26] 1920 5-8-11 52 (t) PaulFitzsimons 8 38
(Miss N A Lloyd-Beavis) *chsd ldr after 2f tl over 3f out: sn outpcd u.p: wl btn and edgd lft ins fnl f* **10/1**

6050 **7** *nk* **Fleur De'Lion (IRE)**[15] 2230 4-8-7 55 RichardRowe(7) 2 41
(S Kirk) *hld up in last trio: rdn and no real prog over 2f out: wl btn whn n.m.r ins fnl f* **25/1**

006- **8** *1/2* **Top Seed (IRE)**[231] 6806 9-8-9 50 StevieDonohoe 4 35
(R Brotherton) *t.k.h: hld up towards rr: slipped bnd over 3f out: sn rdn and no hdwy 3f out: nvr trbld ldrs* **7/1**[3]

503 **9** *1/2* **Comrade Cotton**[2] 2636 6-8-7 51 (p) MarcHalford(3) 10 35
(J Ryan) *stdd after s: hld up in rr: rdn and no hdwy wl over 2f out: n.d* **6/1**[2]

40-3 **10** *1/2* **Mossmann Gorge**[15] 2230 8-8-5 46 oh1 (p) KevinGhunowa 11 29
(A Middleton) *t.k.h: chsd ldrs: hdwy to dispute 2nd over 3f out: outpcd u.p 3f out: wl btn fnl 2f* **5/1**[1]

05-0 **11** *4 1/2* **Aston Boy**[11] 2361 5-8-5 46 oh1 JimmyQuinn 3 22
(M Blanshard) *dwlt: sn bustled along and in tch: lost pl on downhill run and dropped to in rr over 3f out: trying to make hdwy whn nt clr run on over 1f out: no ch and eased ins fnl f* **20/1**

2m 30.23s (-1.27) **Going Correction** -0.30s/f (Firm) 11 Ran SP% **117.1**
Speed ratings (Par 101): **92,91,91,86,85 83,83,82,82,82 78**
Tote Swingers: 1&2 £9.60, 1&3 £7.10, 2&3 £5.70 CSF £33.67 CT £158.91 TOTE £7.10: £2.50, £2.60, £1.60; EX 48.50 Trifecta £258.50 Part won. Pool: £349.45 - 0.10 winning units..
Owner A W Carroll **Bred** Forenaghts Stud And David O'Reilly **Trained** Cropthorne, Worcs

FOCUS

Another moderate handicap and with the early pace modest a few were inclined to pull. As in the earlier turf races, several of these had a real problem with the home bend and again those that raced handily were at a major advantage. The first three pulled well clear and the winner is rated to last year's form.

Dovedon Angel Official explanation: jockey said filly slipped on bend

Catholic Hill(USA) Official explanation: jockey said gelding ran too free

Behest Official explanation: jockey said mare hung left

Top Seed(IRE) Official explanation: jockey said gelding ran too free and slipped on bend

2677 JOHN DEERE - NOTHING RUNS LIKE A DEERE MEDIAN AUCTION MAIDEN STKS 6f (P)
3:50 (3:58) (Class 6) 2-Y-O **£2,388** (£705; £352) **Stalls** Low

Form RPR

3 **1** **Coeus**[9] 2413 2-9-3 0 SebSanders 6 87+
(Sir Mark Prescott) *mde all: drew wl clr ent fnl 2f: styd on strly: easily* **11/10**[1]

26 **2** *5* **Indian Narjes**[17] 2176 2-8-12 0 ChrisCatlin 11 67
(M R Channon) *chsd wnr thrght: rdn over 2f out: nt pce of wnr ent fnl 2f: no ch w wnr after but kpt on for clr 2nd* **7/1**

0 **3** *6* **Captain Dimitrios**[17] 2163 2-8-12 0 RichardEvans(5) 3 54
(P D Evans) *chsd ldng pair but nvr on terms: rdn and no prog wl over 2f out: no ch threat to ldng pair after: plugged on* **16/1**

4 *2 1/4* **Degly Bo (IRE)** 2-9-3 0 JimmyFortune 9 47
(P W Chapple-Hyam) *outpcd in midfield: swtchd to outer 3f out: kpt on same pce and no threat to ldrs after* **4/1**[2]

5 *3/4* **Zakon (IRE)** 2-9-3 0 RobertWinston 2 45+
(D J Coakley) *s.i.s: wl off the pce towards rr: sme hdwy on inner 2f out: nvr on terms* **6/1**[3]

6 *2 1/2* **Spirit Of Oakdale (IRE)** 2-9-3 0 AdamKirby 4 38
(W R Swinburn) *s.i.s: sn rdn along and wl outpcd towards rr: plugged on fr 2f out: n.d* **14/1**

00 **7** *3/4* **Bendigedig**[26] 1930 2-8-12 0 JamesDoyle 5 30
(S Kirk) *chsd ldng trio but nvr on terms: wknd u.p over 2f out* **100/1**

8 *1 1/4* **Amistress** 2-8-12 0 TomQueally 10 27
(Eve Johnson Houghton) *sn outpcd and rdn along towards rr: nvr on terms* **20/1**

9 *12* **Arctic Reach** 2-9-3 0 (b[1]) SaleemGolam 8 —
(G D Blake) *s.i.s: sn rdn along and a wl bhd: t.o* **66/1**

10 *3/4* **Nice Chimes (IRE)** 2-8-7 0 SophieDoyle(5) 1 —
(B W Duke) *wl off the pce in midfield: rdn and wl btn ent fnl 2f: t.o* **40/1**

0 **11** *12* **Hannah Cann**[43] 1463 2-8-12 0 AdrianMcCarthy 7 —
(Peter Grayson) *racd off the pce in midfield: rdn along and struggling over 3f out: t.o fnl f* **200/1**

1m 13.1s (1.20) **Going Correction** +0.15s/f (Slow) 11 Ran SP% **117.1**
Speed ratings (Par 91): **98,91,83,80,79 76,75,73,57,56 40**
Tote Swingers: 1&2 £3.00, 1&3 £9.00, 2&3 £11.00 CSF £9.18 TOTE £2.00: £1.10, £2.00, £5.40; EX 11.50 Trifecta £50.80 Pool: £385.25 - 5.61 winning units..

Owner William Charnley & Richard Pegum **Bred** Lilac Bloodstock & Redmyre Bloodstock **Trained** Newmarket, Suffolk

FOCUS

An uncompetitive maiden and although this race was on the Polytrack, it followed the trend of the turf races by favouring those that raced handily. The first three held those positions throughout. The winner is a very useful recruit and an Ascot possible.

NOTEBOOK

Coeus, who shaped as though this extra furlong would suit when third on his debut here nine days earlier, hit the gates running and ran his rivals into the ground. He was ridden right out to the line which would have taught him something and, whilst this wasn't a strong contest, he seem sure to progress with racing. (op 11-8 tchd 13-8 in a place)

Indian Narjes, a disappointing favourite at Windsor last time after a promising debut at Ffos Las, was soon ridden into a handy position from the outside stall and had every chance, but the winner was toying with her from the home bend. She may need to drop in class in order to win a race, or wait until the nurseries start. (op 6-1)

Captain Dimitrios, who showed some ability on his Bath debut, is bred to handle this surface and he ran well having been up there from the start, but he was done for foot over the last couple of furlongs and was reported to have hung right. There should be a small race in him. Official explanation: jockey said colt hung right

Degly Bo(IRE), a 70,000gns foal and a half-brother to four winners including the very useful Nashmiah, ran on again after getting outpaced at halfway but he will need to improve a good deal on this if he is to win a race. (op 7-2 tchd 3-1)

Zakon(IRE), a 39,000gns colt out of a half-sister to the Listed winner Savarain and the recent Zetland Gold Cup winner Forte Dei Marmi, looked very green and disorganised for most of the contest, but he did show a little ability and looks one for later on. (op 7-1 tchd 15-2)

Arctic Reach Official explanation: trainer said that on return home colt was found to be jarred up

2678 GODFREYS - LAWN & LEISURE SPECIALIST (S) STKS — 7f (P)

4:20 (4:25) (Class 6) 3-Y-0+ — **£2,047** (£604; £302) **Stalls** Low

Form				RPR
304	**1**		**Hinton Admiral**[15] 2235 6-9-7 60 ... StevieDonohoe 9 (M S Tuck) *in tch in midfield: pushed along to chse ldng pair 3f out: rdn and effrt wl over 1f out: led fnl 150yds: r.o wl* **7/1**	71
2062	**2**	½	**Fazbee (IRE)**[9] 2415 4-9-8 70 ... (v) TonyCulhane 8 (P W D'Arcy) *stdd after s: hld up towards rr: hdwy to chse ldrs ent fnl 2f: swtchd rt and pushed along over 1f out: chsd wnr wl ins fnl f: kpt on but nvr gng to rch wnr* **7/4**[1]	71
-120	**3**	1¼	**Fol Liam**[47] 1374 4-9-8 70 ... (p) DeclanCannon(5) 12 (A J McCabe) *in tch in midfield: hdwy 3f out: chsd ldrs and rdn wl over 1f out: styd u.p to chse wnr fnl 100yds: no ex and lost 2nd wl ins fnl f* **4/1**[2]	72
1056	**4**	2½	**Straight Face (IRE)**[9] 2415 6-9-8 66 ... (b) RichardEvans(5) 6 (P D Evans) *towards rr: effrt into midfield over 2f out: swtchd wd wl over 1f out: kpt on fnl f to go 4th towards fin: nvr gng pce to rch ldrs* **16/1**	66
/00-	**5**	½	**Nomoretaxes (BRZ)**[25] 3736 8-9-4 72 ... (tp) WilliamCarson(3) 7 (Miss D Mountain) *chsd ldr: rdn and unable qck ent fnl 2f: lost 2nd over 1f out: styd on same pce fnl f* **50/1**	58
2110	**6**	hd	**Waterloo Dock**[37] 1596 5-9-13 64 ... (v) SebSanders 4 (M Quinn) *sn pushed up to ld: rdn clr wl over 1f out: drvn ent fnl f: hdd fnl 150yds: wknd qckly fnl 100yds* **10/1**	64
4330	**7**	2	**Gone Hunting**[15] 2235 4-9-2 70 ... (t) SimonPearce(5) 5 (J Pearce) *racd off the pce in midfield: effrt and rdn towards inner ent fnl 2f: nvr gng pce to rch ldrs* **13/2**[3]	52
4/	**8**	13	**Broughtons Dream**[574] 7207 4-9-2 0 ... JamieMackay 14 (W J Musson) *hld up towards rr on outer: outpcd wl over 2f out: wl btn over 1f out* **10/1**	12
0050	**9**	1¾	**Kathleen Kennet**[44] 1437 10-8-11 49 ... KierenFox(5) 1 (M R Bosley) *s.i.s: sn rdn along: a towards rr: wl bhd fr wl over 1f out* **40/1**	—
4-00	**10**	2¾	**If Only**[13] 2299 4-9-7 57 ... (b) NeilCallan 11 (J Jay) *wnt lft s and v.s.a: sn u.p: nvr on terms* **16/1**	—
5600	**11**	12	**Gems**[14] 2250 3-8-6 49 ... (p) DavidProbert 3 (H J L Dunlop) *dwlt: sn rdn along and hdwy to chse ldrs: wknd 3f out: wl bhd fr wl over 1f out* **66/1**	—
0	**12**	1¼	**Preset**[9] 2414 3-8-11 0 ... LukeMorris 10 (J M P Eustace) *chsd ldrs tl over 3f out: sn lost pl u.p: wl bhd fnl f* **100/1**	—

1m 26.13s (1.33) **Going Correction** +0.15s/f (Slow)

WFA 3 from 4yo+ 10lb — **12** Ran SP% **119.0**

Speed ratings (Par 101): **98,97,96,93,92 92,90,75,73,70 56,54**

Tote Swingers: 1&2 £4.20, 1&3 £5.40, 2&3 £2.90 CSF £19.49 TOTE £5.80: £2.40, £1.10, £2.30; EX 26.40 Trifecta £92.20 Pool: £241.80 - 1.94 winning units..Winner was bought in for 5,200gns.

Owner M Bell **Bred** Gainsborough Stud Management Ltd **Trained** Oldbury on the Hill, Gloucs

FOCUS

A moderate seller and plenty of headgear on show. The form is rated around the runner-up.

2679 GODFREYS - A GREAT DEAL MORE THAN MOWERS FILLIES' H'CAP — 6f (P)

4:50 (4:52) (Class 5) (0-75,72) 3-Y-0 — **£3,070** (£906; £453) **Stalls** Low

Form				RPR
5-1	**1**		**Dever Dream**[17] 2174 3-9-7 **72** ... RyanMoore 7 (W J Haggas) *hld up in tch in last pl: hdwy and switching rt wl over 1f out: led ent fnl f: stormed wl clr: easily* **4/9**[1]	92+
4436	**2**	10	**Mrs Boss**[21] 2049 3-8-13 **67** ... JamesMillman(3) 4 (B R Millman) *chsd ldrs: rdn 3f out: outpcd and wl btn over 1f out: plugged on ins fnl f to go modest 2nd nr fin* **12/1**[3]	55
0-10	**3**	nk	**Faited To Pretend (IRE)**[44] 1453 3-9-7 **72** ... AndreaAtzeni 8 (M Botti) *chsd ldr: rdn and ev ch wl over 1f out: nt pce of wnr and wl btn ins fnl f: tired and lost 2nd nr fin* **8/1**[2]	59
3102	**4**	1¾	**Caramelita**[35] 1640 3-9-5 **70** ... TomQueally 3 (J R Jenkins) *in tch in last pair: effrt u.p on inner 2f out: no hdwy and btn 1f out* **12/1**[3]	51
-341	**5**	5	**Katy's Secret**[23] 1994 3-8-7 **65** ... Mary-AnnParkin(7) 6 (W Jarvis) *t.k.h: chsd ldrs on outer: wknd qckly wl over 1f out: wl btn fnl f* **8/1**[2]	30
00	**6**	4½	**Boragh Jamal (IRE)**[3] 2588 3-9-3 **68** ... (b[1]) EddieAhern 1 (B J Meehan) *led: rdn wl over 1f out: hdd ent fnl f: sn wl btn: eased ins fnl f* **20/1**	19

1m 12.84s (0.94) **Going Correction** +0.15s/f (Slow) — **6** Ran SP% **111.6**

Speed ratings (Par 96): **99,85,85,82,76 70**

Tote Swingers: 1&2 £2.60, 1&3 £2.00, 2&3 £7.20 CSF £6.94 CT £19.72 TOTE £1.40: £1.10, £3.80; EX 7.30 Trifecta £29.50 Pool: £176.45 - 4.42 winning units. Place 6: £14.33 Place 5: £11.33..

Owner Options O Syndicate **Bred** F C T Wilson **Trained** Newmarket, Suffolk

FOCUS

As uncompetitive a handicap as you are likely to see and not many sprints are won by such a margin.

Boragh Jamal(IRE) Official explanation: jockey said filly lost its action

T/Plt: £19.70 to a £1 stake. Pool: £61,985.59 - 2,296.64 winning units. T/Qpdt: £4.20 to a £1 stake. Pool: £3,383.59 - 590.10 winning units. SP

2467 SANDOWN (R-H)

Thursday, June 3

OFFICIAL GOING: Good to firm (round course: 8.8 sprint course: far side - 8.5; stands' side - 8.3)

Course at innermost configuration.

Wind: Light, half behind Weather: Sunny, warm

2680 DRIVERS JONAS DELOITTE MAIDEN AUCTION STKS — 5f 6y

6:10 (6:11) (Class 5) 2-Y-O — **£3,238** (£963; £481; £240) **Stalls** High

Form				RPR
04	**1**		**Eucharist (IRE)**[14] 2251 2-8-8 0 ... RichardHughes 1 (R Hannon) *hld up at rr of main gp: prog fr 2f out: wnt 3rd and shkn up ent fnl f: r.o to ld last stride: shade clever* **8/1**	75
6222	**2**	shd	**Master Macho (IRE)**[7] 2457 2-8-9 0 ... ChrisCatlin 6 (M R Channon) *mde most: drvn over 1f out: styd on but hdd last stride* **8/1**	76
4	**3**	1	**Diamond Charlie (IRE)**[14] 2245 2-8-11 0 ... HayleyTurner 13 (S Dow) *racd against rail: pressed ldr thrght: drvn 2f out: hld ins fnl f and lost 2nd last 100yds* **6/1**	74
2	**4**	1½	**Cocohatchee**[52] 1256 2-8-9 0 ... JimmyQuinn 4 (P M Phelan) *chsd ldrs on outer: rdn and effrt over 1f out: hung rt ent fnl f: styd on: nvr able to chal* **11/2**[3]	67
032	**5**	½	**Belle Bayardo (IRE)**[9] 2407 2-8-9 0 ... LukeMorris 11 (R A Harris) *racd against rail: cl up bhd ldng pair: drvn 2f out: one pce fr over 1f out* **9/2**[2]	65
025	**6**	1¼	**Colorado Gold**[14] 2238 2-8-13 0 ... (b[1]) JimmyFortune 8 (P F I Cole) *chsd ldrs: rdn 2f out: no imp whn sltly checked 1f out and bmpd sn after: kpt on* **16/1**	66
32	**7**	2	**Remotelinx (IRE)**[14] 2245 2-9-2 0 ... MichaelHills 9 (J W Hills) *t.k.h: hld up at rr of main gp: looking for room fr 2f out: keeping on but plenty to do whn bmpd jst ins fnl f: nt rcvr* **10/3**[1]	67
03	**8**	3	**May Be Some Time**[14] 2245 2-8-11 0 ... FergusSweeney 10 (W S Kittow) *chsd ldrs and racd against rail: hmpd 2f out: steadily fdd* **22/1**	47
5	**9**	2¾	**Kyncraighe (IRE)**[22] 2022 2-8-13 0 ... TedDurcan 3 (Eve Johnson Houghton) *mostly in 10th and nvr on terms w ldrs: no prog fnl 2f* **16/1**	36
	10	1½	**Midnight Feast** 2-8-9 0 ... JimCrowley 7 (P Winkworth) *s.v.s: rn green and immediately wl bhd: passed 2 stragglers by 1/2-way: nvr in it* **22/1**	27
0	**11**	1¾	**Marmaduke**[14] 2245 2-8-9 0 ... NeilChalmers 2 (J J Bridger) *chsd ldng pair to 1/2-way: losing pl whn squeezed out over 1f out* **150/1**	21
	12	2	**Foxy's Mint** 2-8-4 0 ... FrankieMcDonald 12 (R Hannon) *s.s: reminders after 1f: outpcd thrght* **40/1**	9
0	**13**	¾	**Shutterbug**[24] 1972 2-8-3 0 ... WilliamCarson(3) 5 (S C Williams) *outpcd and a detached* **100/1**	8

60.67 secs (-0.93) **Going Correction** -0.175s/f (Firm) — **13** Ran SP% **117.7**

Speed ratings (Par 93): **100,99,98,95,95 93,89,85,80,78 75,72,71**

Tote Swingers: 1&2 £4.60, 1&3 £7.60, 2&3 £11.40 CSF £66.74 TOTE £8.30: £2.80, £3.30, £2.30; EX 51.40.

Owner Mrs J Wood **Bred** M Kelly **Trained** East Everleigh, Wilts

■ Stewards' Enquiry : Chris Catlin two-day ban: used whip without giving colt time to respond (Jun 22-23)

FOCUS

A pretty decent maiden auction, with the runner-up providing several solid lines of form, but the lack of unexposed potential improvers and debutants from big stables suggests it has limitations.

NOTEBOOK

Eucharist(IRE), who did well to overcome stall 1, was given a fine ride by Hughes, who managed to get her covered up and produced her late. She has been steadily improving in 5f maidens and gives the impression that 6f will be no problem.

Master Macho(IRE), finishing second for the fourth race running, is running his heart out but again found one to deny him his just reward, in this case agonisingly close to the winning line. He has tremendous early speed and can surely break the sequence. (tchd 9-1)

Diamond Charlie(IRE) confirmed the promise of his debut, this time showing much more early pace. He is good enough to win a routine maiden. (op 8-1)

Cocohatchee, who ran into a smart youngster first time out, was keen to post. He looks capable of landing a run-of-the-mill maiden and should be suited by 6f. (op 6-1 tchd 9-2)

Belle Bayardo(IRE), on his toes in the paddock, had previously been inching closer in maidens but this was a better race and he was beaten fair and square despite being well drawn. He might still win a lesser race of this type but nurseries are becoming a more attractive option. (tchd 5-1)

Colorado Gold, fitted with blinkers after disappointing last time, ran respectably but is falling short in this company. He is looking more and more like a nursery type. (tchd 14-1)

Remotelinx(IRE) did not live up to the promise of his first two races but he did not get the run of the race and in any case may now appreciate an extra furlong. Official explanation: jockey said bit slipped through mouth and colt hung right (op 3-1 tchd 7-2)

2681 DAN FROST MEMORIAL H'CAP — 5f 6y

6:45 (6:46) (Class 4) (0-85,85) 3-Y-0+ — **£4,533** (£1,348; £674; £336) **Stalls** High

Form				RPR
005-	**1**		**Palisades Park**[286] 5218 3-9-5 **83** ... JimmyFortune 7 (R Hannon) *hld up in rr: prog against rail fr over 1f out: dream run through fnl f: led last 50yds* **33/1**	90
00-1	**2**	½	**Osiris Way**[33] 1691 8-10-0 **85** ... JimCrowley 15 (P R Chamings) *racd against rail: trckd ldng pair: wnt 2nd wl over 1f out: rdn to ld jst ins fnl f: styd on: collared last 50yds* **11/1**	93
-012	**3**	hd	**Noodles Blue Boy**[7] 2465 4-9-9 **80** ... RyanMoore 3 (Ollie Pears) *chsd ldrs on outer: u.p bef 1/2-way: looked to be struggling over 1f out: r.o after: tk 3rd nr fin* **9/2**[2]	87+
0-00	**4**	shd	**Invincible Lad (IRE)**[5] 2536 6-9-12 **83** ... RichardHughes 11 (E J Alston) *hld up in rr: nt clr run over 1f out: swtchd lft ent fnl f: drvn and r.o: nrst fin* **9/2**[2]	90+
-044	**5**	½	**Piscean (USA)**[14] 2247 5-9-10 **81** ... JimmyQuinn 14 (T Keddy) *s.s: detached in last: gd prog against rail over 1f out: clsng whn nt clr run ins fnl f: r.o nr fin* **14/1**	87+
5-00	**6**	hd	**Macdillon**[19] 2119 4-9-11 **82** ... FergusSweeney 17 (W S Kittow) *racd against rail: hld up in midfield: prog and cl up bhd ldrs 1f out gng wl enough: rdn and styd on same pce last 100yds* **8/1**	86
2113	**7**	¾	**Master Lightfoot**[41] 1506 4-9-7 **78** ... ShaneKelly 2 (W R Swinburn) *fast away fr wd draw: led and crossed to rail: edgd lft and hdd jst ins fnl f: swamped for pls nr fin* **18/1**	80

221- **8** *1* **Present Alchemy**[278] 5422 4-9-9 **80**.....(t) EddieAhern 16 78+
(H Morrison) *hld up in midfield: looking for room and trapped bhd rivals fr 1/2-way tl last 100yds: r.o but all ch gone* **4/1**[1]

3-40 **9** *1 ½* **Equuleus Pictor**[50] 1295 6-9-9 **83**..... JackDean(3) 8 76
(J L Spearing) *t.k.h early: hld up bhd ldrs: rdn and nt qckn over 1f out: fdd ins fnl f* **33/1**

2-31 **10** *¾* **Solemn**[13] 2301 5-9-13 **84**.....(b) GeorgeBaker 10 74
(J M Bradley) *chsd ldrs and cl up: rdn wl over 1f out: fdd fnl f* **15/2**[3]

05-0 **11** *nse* **Tagula Night (IRE)**[26] 1903 4-9-11 **82**.....(vt) AdamKirby 6 72
(W R Swinburn) *a in rr: u.p and no prog 2f out* **16/1**

00-1 **12** *nk* **Efistorm**[52] 1266 9-9-10 **81**..... LiamKeniry 5 70
(C R Dore) *hld up in rr: rdn and no prog 2f out: no ch whn sltly checked 1f out* **20/1**

5610 **13** *1 ¾* **Step It Up (IRE)**[12] 2310 6-9-0 **71**..... RobertHavlin 1 53
(J R Boyle) *fast away fr wd draw: chsd ldr to wl over 1f out: wknd* **33/1**

60.09 secs (-1.51) **Going Correction** -0.175s/f (Firm)
WFA 3 from 4yo+ 7lb **13** Ran SP% **119.0**
Speed ratings (Par 105): **105,104,103,103,102 102,101,99,97,96 96,95,92**
Tote Swingers: 1&2 £42.30, 1&3 £9.40, 2&3 £7.20 CSF £350.15 CT £2008.27 TOTE £31.50: £8.00, £3.90, £1.90; EX 641.60.
Owner D Powell, R Dollar, Derek & Jean Clee **Bred** Dunchurch Lodge Stud Co **Trained** East Everleigh, Wilts

■ Stewards' Enquiry : Richard Hughes three-day ban: careless riding (Jun 20-22)

FOCUS
The combination of a strong sprint gallop and stiff track set this up for the finishers. The first two and the fifth all raced on the rail. Decent form.
Piscean(USA) Official explanation: jockey said gelding was slowly away and denied a clear run
Present Alchemy ◆ Official explanation: jockey said colt was denied a clear run

2682 OCM CAPITAL MARKETS H'CAP — 7f 16y
7:15 (7:19) (Class 4) (0-85,84) 3-Y-O **£4,533** (£1,348; £674; £336) **Stalls** High

Form RPR

0-01 **1** **Imperial Delight**[16] 2197 3-9-3 **78**..... DaneO'Neill 12 86
(H Candy) *t.k.h: hld up in 5th: swtchd lft and effrt over 1f out: wnt 2nd ins fnl f: drvn and r.o to ld last strides* **9/2**[3]

160- **2** *hd* **Dylanesque**[222] 7013 3-9-2 **77**..... PhilipRobinson 9 84
(M A Jarvis) *trckd ldng pair: squeezed through to take 2nd 2f out: rdn to ld ent fnl f: hdd last strides* **9/1**

-140 **3** *½* **Fivefold (USA)**[14] 2253 3-9-0 **75**..... AlanMunro 8 81
(J Akehurst) *racd freely: led: drvn and hdd ent fnl f: kpt on wl but lost 2nd last 100yds* **14/1**

210- **4** *2* **Oil Strike**[208] 7290 3-9-9 **84**..... JimCrowley 1 85+
(P Winkworth) *hld up last: plenty to do whn prog on outer 2f out: drvn over 1f out: kpt on into 4th fnl f: nt pce to threaten* **10/1**

44-3 **5** *¾* **Lay Claim (USA)**[19] 2110 3-9-3 **78**..... RyanMoore 2 77
(Sir Michael Stoute) *hld up in 10th: effrt on outer over 2f out: sme prog over 1f out: nvr gng pce to threaten ldrs* **3/1**[1]

45-0 **6** *¾* **Kurtanella**[32] 1732 3-9-6 **81**..... RichardHughes 10 78
(R Hannon) *stdd s: hld up in 9th: effrt on inner over 2f out: hrd rdn and sme prog over 1f out: one pce and no imp fnl f* **16/1**

-422 **7** *2 ¼* **Streets Of War (USA)**[23] 2004 3-9-3 **78**..... RobertHavlin 6 68
(P W Chapple-Hyam) *trckd ldng trio: effrt over 2f out: hanging and nt qckn wl over 1f out: wknd* **4/1**[2]

6-45 **8** *4* **Kerchak (USA)**[22] 2025 3-8-12 **73**..... J-PGuillambert 11 53
(W Jarvis) *settled in 6th: rdn 3f out: no rspnse: wl btn over 1f out* **16/1**

50-0 **9** *shd* **Goodwood Maestro**[26] 1913 3-9-2 **77**..... EddieAhern 7 56
(J L Dunlop) *hld up in 8th: pushed along over 2f out: no prog and btn after* **14/1**

24-4 **10** *½* **Lean Machine**[19] 2122 3-9-2 **77**..... JimmyFortune 5 55
(R Hannon) *hld up in 7th: rdn over 2f out: no prog: wknd over 1f out: eased* **9/1**

026 **11** *6* **Avonside (IRE)**[27] 1870 3-8-4 **65** oh3..... NeilChalmers 3 27
(J J Bridger) *trckd ldr: rdn whn squeezed out jst over 2f out: wknd* **66/1**

1m 28.11s (-1.39) **Going Correction** -0.05s/f (Good) **11** Ran SP% **118.9**
Speed ratings (Par 101): **105,104,104,101,101 100,97,93,92,92 85**
Tote Swingers: 1&2 £19.90, 1&3 £16.80, 2&3 £31.40 CSF £45.38 CT £531.93 TOTE £6.80: £1.90, £3.70, £5.80; EX 57.80.
Owner A N Solomons **Bred** Coln Valley Stud **Trained** Kingston Warren, Oxon

FOCUS
There was a solid gallop, but the first three home were all in the leading five throughout and the finishers were always arriving too late. Fairly ordinary form, with the third the best guide.
Avonside(IRE) Official explanation: jockey said gelding suffered interference in running

2683 DRIVERS JONAS DELOITTE H'CAP — 1m 14y
7:50 (7:52) (Class 3) (0-90,89) 4-Y-O+ **£6,799** (£2,023; £1,011; £505) **Stalls** High

Form RPR

0-5 **1** **Dukes Art**[36] 1625 4-9-0 **80**..... RobertHavlin 3 90
(J A R Toller) *hld up in midfield: prog 2f out to chse ldrs over 1f out: styd on wl fnl f to ld last strides* **14/1**

0-32 **2** *hd* **Directorship**[12] 2339 4-8-13 **79**..... RichardKingscote 9 88
(P R Chamings) *trckd ldrs: led 2f out and kicked on: styd on fnl f: hdd last strides* **5/1**[2]

1-02 **3** *1 ½* **Ithinkbest**[7] 2472 4-9-6 **86**..... RyanMoore 15 92
(Sir Michael Stoute) *trckd ldrs: wnt 3rd over 2f out: sn drvn: tried to cl on ldng pair 1f out: outpcd last 75yds* **9/4**[1]

4165 **4** *nk* **Halsion Chancer**[12] 2339 6-8-10 **76**..... RobertWinston 8 81
(J R Best) *s.s: sn in 10th: rdn 3f out: prog u.p 2f out: r.o fr over 1f out: nrst fin* **14/1**

54-0 **5** *hd* **Rafiqa (IRE)**[26] 1899 4-9-8 **88**..... JackMitchell 2 93+
(C F Wall) *stdd s fr wd draw: hld up last: ambitious aim up inner over 2f out and nowhere to go tl wl over 1f out: r.o after: nrst fin* **14/1**

3-13 **6** *1 ¾* **Tudor Key (IRE)**[28] 1846 4-9-4 **84**..... NeilCallan 12 85
(Mrs A J Perrett) *led: rdn and hdd 2f out: grad fdd fnl f* **11/1**

20-0 **7** *½* **Nezami (IRE)**[145] 108 5-9-9 **89**..... DaneO'Neill 16 88
(J Akehurst) *mostly in same pl: rdn over 2f out: no imp on ldrs over 1f out but kpt on* **40/1**

41-0 **8** *5* **Truly Asia (IRE)**[12] 2339 4-8-11 **77**..... SteveDrowne 1 65
(R Charlton) *hld up in last trio: pushed along 3f out: sme prog into 8th whn checked 1f out: eased* **16/1**

00-4 **9** *1 ¾* **Habshan (USA)**[36] 1617 10-9-2 **82**..... AlanMunro 7 66
(C F Wall) *t.k.h: trckd ldrs: nt qckn over 2f out: steadily wknd over 1f out* **16/1**

6-00 **10** *3 ¼* **Titan Triumph**[26] 1900 6-9-5 **85**.....(t) JimCrowley 14 61
(W J Knight) *hld up in last trio: nt clr run over 2f out to wl over 1f out: no prog after* **16/1**

500- **11** *1 ½* **Isphahan**[187] 7575 7-9-2 **82**..... JimmyFortune 11 55
(A M Balding) *hld up in 11th: shkn up and no prog over 2f out: sn no ch* **16/1**

0-20 **12** *6* **Hail Promenader (IRE)**[36] 1617 4-9-4 **84**..... MichaelHills 4 43
(B W Hills) *racd wd: trckd ldrs: lost pl over 2f out: steadily wknd and eased* **9/1**[3]

15- **13** *nk* **In Footlights (USA)**[322] 4020 4-9-7 **87**..... TedDurcan 17 45
(Saeed Bin Suroor) *trckd ldrs: rdn over 2f out: sn wknd* **10/1**

20-6 **14** *64* **Mut'Ab (USA)**[43] 1481 5-8-11 **77**.....(b) SebSanders 6 —
(C E Brittain) *trckd ldr to 3f out: wknd rapidly: t.o and eased* **40/1**

1m 41.46s (-1.84) **Going Correction** -0.05s/f (Good) **14** Ran SP% **123.3**
Speed ratings (Par 107): **107,106,105,105,104 103,102,97,95,92 91,85,84,20**
Tote Swingers: 1&2 £18.20, 1&3 £3.70, 2&3 £19.70 CSF £84.47 CT £228.38 TOTE £16.10: £3.50, £1.80, £1.90; EX 119.20.
Owner Buckingham Thoroughbreds I **Bred** Fern Hill Stud & M Green **Trained** Newmarket, Suffolk

FOCUS
A fair pace gave all the runners a chance, and there was a mix of prominent runners and hold-up types involved in the finish. Pretty sound form, with the winner generally progressive.

NOTEBOOK
Dukes Art had looked better at 7f than 1m last year, but the way he finished here suggests that the longer trip is ideal these days. He has been gradually progressive since last summer, and though he will probably go up 1-2lb for this, he is lightly raced and largely unexposed at this trip, so he is likely to remain competitive off the higher mark. (op 16-1)
Directorship had been running up to his best in two earlier races this season, and this was another sound effort in defeat. He is on a sporting mark and has done well at Sandown in the past, so he can always be given extra consideration if returning to this course. (op 15-2)
Ithinkbest, who seems suited by the track, has hit the groove now and 1m is probably his best trip on turf, though he has won at 1m1f on the Wolverhampton Polytrack. He should find a race on grass off this sort of mark. (tchd 5-2)
Halsion Chancer has been finding it tougher off a higher mark since winning here in April. However, in general his recent turf form compares with his more regular Polytrack performances and on this evidence he should stay a bit further. (op 16-1)
Rafiqa(IRE) ◆ improved significantly on her seasonal debut, having weaved her way through from the rear in the home straight. She is coming back to form and is one to consider from now on. (op 16-1)
Tudor Key(IRE) remains in generally good shape, but he is dropping just short of the form shown when winning at Windsor in April. (tchd 10-1)
Nezami(IRE) still looked a little high in the weights on this return to turf, but he was not beaten far.
Mut'Ab(USA) Official explanation: jockey said gelding moved poorly

2684 SPAR MAIDEN STKS — 1m 2f 7y
8:25 (8:34) (Class 5) 3-Y-O **£3,238** (£963; £481; £240) **Stalls** High

Form RPR

6-36 **1** **Kensei (IRE)**[20] 2089 3-9-3 77..... JimCrowley 10 81+
(R M Beckett) *trckd ldrs: led over 2f out gng easily: shkn up and drew clr over 1f out: eased nr fin* **7/1**[2]

0-0 **2** *2 ¾* **Out Of Eden**[50] 1314 3-9-3 0..... TomQueally 17 75
(H R A Cecil) *hld up bhd ldrs: effrt over 2f out: rdn to chse wnr over 1f out: no imp* **7/1**[2]

65 **3** *1* **Whitby Jack**[26] 1912 3-9-3 0..... GeorgeBaker 16 73
(G L Moore) *prom: trckd ldr 1/2-way: led briefly wl over 2f out: chsd wnr to over 1f out: one pce* **16/1**

2 **4** *nk* **Direct Answer (USA)**[26] 1912 3-9-3 0..... RyanMoore 3 72
(Sir Michael Stoute) *settled off the pce towards rr: effrt 3f out: struggling to make prog tl styd on fr over 1f out: gng on at fin* **11/10**[1]

06 **5** *1 ½* **Formulation (IRE)**[31] 1766 3-9-3 0..... SteveDrowne 5 69+
(H Morrison) *dwlt: hld up wl in rr: pushed along 3f out: inclined to hang but decent prog fr 2f out: nrst fin* **25/1**

40 **6** *¾* **Montparnasse (IRE)**[19] 2115 3-9-3 0..... EddieAhern 13 68+
(B J Meehan) *dwlt: hld up wl in rr: nudged along and stdy prog fr over 2f out: nvr nr ldrs* **20/1**

7 *7* **Judicious** 3-9-3 0..... RichardMullen 4 54
(Sir Michael Stoute) *sed slowest of all: hld up in last: modest prog fr 3f out: rn into trble 1f out: styng on takingly nr fin* **12/1**

50 **8** *4* **Abu Wathab**[14] 2255 3-9-3 0..... JimmyFortune 7 46
(P W Chapple-Hyam) *chsd ldr to 1/2-way: shkn up and wknd over 2f out* **50/1**

9 *½* **Voysey (IRE)** 3-9-3 0..... NeilCallan 6 45
(Mrs A J Perrett) *wl plcd bhd ldrs tl shkn up and wknd over 2f out* **40/1**

5 **10** *1 ½* **Quick Deal (USA)**[16] 2220 3-9-3 0..... WilliamBuick 1 42
(J H M Gosden) *led to wl over 2f out: sn wknd* **8/1**[3]

11 *hd* **Dynamic Air (USA)** 3-9-3 0..... RobertHavlin 15 42+
(J H M Gosden) *nvr bttr than midfield: wknd on inner fr 2f out* **25/1**

0-6 **12** *17* **That's Showbiz**[23] 2011 3-9-3 0..... ShaneKelly 8 8
(W J Knight) *prom: shkn up over 2f out: wandered and wknd rapidly* **100/1**

0 **13** *1 ½* **Southwark Newsman**[47] 1393 3-9-3 0..... TomMcLaughlin 12 5
(Mrs C A Dunnett) *dwlt: a wl in rr: rdn and no prog 3f out* **125/1**

14 *14* **Gilderoy** 3-9-3 0..... SebSanders 14 —
(D J S Ffrench Davis) *dwlt: a in last trio: shkn up and no prog 3f out: t.o* **100/1**

0-3 **15** *nk* **Ticket To Paradise**[18] 2143 3-9-3 0..... TedDurcan 2 —
(D R Lanigan) *chsd ldrs on outer: rdn over 4f out: wknd 3f out: t.o* **20/1**

2m 9.00s (-1.50) **Going Correction** -0.05s/f (Good) **15** Ran SP% **121.7**
Speed ratings (Par 99): **104,101,101,100,99 98,93,90,89,88 88,74,73,62,62**
Tote Swingers: 1&2 £8.30, 1&3 £9.30, 2&3 £23.20 CSF £50.67 TOTE £6.10: £1.60, £2.00, £3.80; EX 46.10.
Owner J C Smith **Bred** Paget Bloodstock Ltd **Trained** Whitsbury, Hants

FOCUS
With the race going to the most exposed runner, and the form of the runner-up nothing special, this had the look of an ordinary maiden for the track, but there should be winners in the line-up. They went just a medium gallop.
Judicious Official explanation: jockey said colt missed the break

2685 HCC INTERNATIONAL INSURANCE H'CAP — 1m 2f 7y
8:55 (9:01) (Class 4) (0-80,80) 4-Y-O+ **£4,533** (£1,348; £674; £336) **Stalls** High

Form RPR

06-1 **1** **Agapanthus (GER)**[24] 1961 5-9-0 **71**..... TomQueally 13 79+
(B J Curley) *trckd ldrs in abt 6th: rdn over 2f out: no prog over 1f out: tk off ent fnl f: str run to ld post* **6/1**[2]

-162 **2** *shd* **Penchesco (IRE)**[20] 2093 5-9-4 **75**..... RyanMoore 3 83
(Mrs A J Perrett) *trckd ldr after 2f: rdn to ld wl over 1f out: drvn 2 l clr ins fnl f: nailed on the post* **13/2**[3]

0036 **3** *1 ¾* **Archie Rice (USA)**[6] 2506 4-9-2 **73**..... JimmyFortune 11 77
(T Keddy) *led: rdn and hdd wl over 1f out: kpt on same pce after* **16/1**

500- **4** *1* **Union Island (IRE)**[253] 6209 4-9-9 **80** NeilCallan 16 82
(A King) *chsd ldr 2f: styd prom: rdn to chse ldng pair over 2f out: one pce after* **11/1**

1- **5** *3/4* **Fastback (IRE)**[205] 4-9-2 **73** JimCrowley 1 74
(R M Beckett) *trckd ldng pair: rdn over 2f out: no imp over 1f out: one pce* **13/2**[3]

030- **6** *3/4* **Tanto Faz (IRE)**[87] 6724 5-9-3 **74** DavidProbert 15 73
(J J Quinn) *trckd ldrs on inner: rdn whn n.m.r wl over 1f out: kpt on same pce after* **5/1**[1]

6-62 **7** *1 3/4* **Black N Brew (USA)**[40] 1530 4-9-1 **72** RobertWinston 7 68
(J R Best) *hld up in midfield: rdn and limited prog over 2f out: no hdwy over 1f out: fdd* **14/1**

2513 **8** *1/2* **Buddy Holly**[17] 2173 5-9-6 **80** MartinLane(3) 12 75
(Pat Eddery) *hld up in midfield: a abt same pl: rdn and no prog over 2f out* **9/1**

00 **9** *shd* **Monte Cavallo (SAF)**[21] 2044 5-9-7 **78** StephenCraine 9 72+
(M Wigham) *s.s: hld up in last: stuck bhd rivals fr over 2f out tl plld out 1f out: pushed along and kpt on: nvr nr ldrs* **33/1**

054- **10** *1/2* **Sagredo (USA)**[199] 7413 6-9-2 **73** GeorgeBaker 4 66
(Jonjo O'Neill) *hld up towards rr on outer: rdn over 2f out: no prog* **33/1**

-030 **11** *3/4* **Bowsers Brave (USA)**[28] 1844 4-9-1 **72** PatDobbs 6 64
(M P Tregoning) *a in rr: rdn 3f out: struggling fnl 2f* **10/1**

50-2 **12** *3 1/2* **Cwm Rhondda (USA)**[14] 2256 5-9-5 **76** JackMitchell 17 61
(P W Chapple-Hyam) *rrng as stalls opened and v.s.a: effrt fr last pair over 2f out: sn btn* **7/1**

/0-0 **13** *4 1/2* **Nizhoni Dancer**[31] 1780 4-9-6 **77** TedDurcan 5 53
(C F Wall) *s.i.s: pushed along early to rch midfield: rdn 3f out: sn wknd* **22/1**

2m 10.31s (-0.19) **Going Correction** -0.05s/f (Good) **13** Ran SP% **120.3**
Speed ratings (Par 105): **98,97,96,95,95 94,93,92,92,92 91,88,85**
Tote Swingers: 1&2 £6.80, 1&3 £18.10, 2&3 £24.80 CSF £44.23 CT £597.93 TOTE £7.40: £2.50, £2.50, £5.70; EX 48.90 Place 6: £529.95 Place 5: £158.42 .
Owner Curley Leisure **Bred** Gestut Schlenderhan **Trained** Newmarket, Suffolk

FOCUS
An ordinary gallop made it hard to come from too far back. The winner produced his best British run so far.
Tanto Faz(IRE) Official explanation: jockey said gelding finished lame
Monte Cavallo(SAF) Official explanation: jockey said gelding missed the break
Sagredo(USA) Official explanation: jockey said gelding hung left
T/Jkpt: Not won. T/Plt: £2,281.20 to a £1 stake. Pool £82,23.62 - 30.12 winning units. T/Qpdt: £132.90 to a £1 stake. Pool £6,612.42 - 36.80 winning tickets. JN

2358 BATH (L-H)
Friday, June 4

OFFICIAL GOING: Good to firm (firm in places; 9.6)
Wind: mild breeze across Weather: sunny

2687 EBF BATH ALES HOP POLE MAIDEN STKS 5f 161y
6:25 (6:27) (Class 5) 2-Y-O £3,626 (£1,079; £539; £269) Stalls Centre

Form RPR

3 **1** **Black Moth (IRE)**[8] 2474 2-9-3 0 MartinDwyer 8 80+
(B J Meehan) *mde all: drifted lft fnl f: kpt on strly: rdn out* **5/2**[2]

3 **2** *1 1/2* **Postscript (IRE)**[11] 2384 2-9-3 0 DaraghO'Donohoe 5 75
(Mahmood Al Zarooni) *chsd ldrs: pushed along over 3f out: rn green but kpt on to go 2nd ins fnl f: nt pce of wnr* **9/4**[1]

3 *1 1/2* **Falkland Flyer (IRE)** 2-9-3 0 ChrisCatlin 10 70+
(M R Channon) *sltly slowly away: sn mid-div on outer: hdwy 3f out to chse ldrs: sn rdn: kpt on but nt pce to chal* **14/1**

4 **4** *1/2* **Diamond Vine (IRE)**[18] 2163 2-9-3 0 GeorgeBaker 11 68
(R A Harris) *trckd ldrs: rdn over 2f out: edgd lft over 1f out: kpt on same pce* **14/1**

U2 **5** *1* **Kojak (IRE)**[23] 2022 2-9-3 0 PatDobbs 7 65
(R Hannon) *towards rr: hdwy over 2f out: chsng ldrs u.p over 1f out whn bmpd: hung lft: no ex* **11/4**[3]

0 **6** *1/2* **Aurivorous**[25] 1972 2-8-12 0 RichardKingscote 3 58
(Jonjo O'Neill) *in tch tl wknd 2f out* **80/1**

7 *3/4* **Buddy Miracle** 2-8-12 0 NeilChalmers 2 56+
(A M Balding) *s.i.s: nvr bttr than mid-div: wknd fnl f* **22/1**

5 **8** *1 1/2* **Sarangoo**[15] 2245 2-8-12 0 TomMcLaughlin 12 51
(M S Saunders) *chsd ldr: rdn over 2f out: wknd over 1f out* **12/1**

03 **9** *1* **He's The Star (IRE)**[23] 2022 2-8-12 0 RichardEvans(5) 1 52
(P D Evans) *s.i.s: sn mid-div: wknd over 2f out* **25/1**

50 **10** *13* **Capa Cruz (IRE)**[25] 1978 2-9-3 0 RichardThomas 4 9
(R A Harris) *chsd ldrs tl wknd 2f out* **100/1**

11 *8* **Adzing (IRE)** 2-9-3 0 LiamKeniry 9 —
(R A Harris) *edgd rt leaving stalls: a towards rr* **100/1**

0 **12** *2* **Titian Queen**[18] 2163 2-8-7 0 SophieDoyle(5) 6 —
(Mrs P N Dutfield) *sn outpcd and a detached* **100/1**

1m 11.13s (-0.07) **Going Correction** -0.15s/f (Firm) **12** Ran SP% **119.4**
Speed ratings (Par 93): **94,92,90,89,88 87,86,84,83,65 55,52**
toteswingers:1&2 £1.20, 1&3 £9.40, 2&3 £6.20 CSF £8.31 TOTE £5.10: £1.80, £1.10, £6.50; EX 8.60.
Owner Sangster Family & Mrs M Findlay **Bred** Victor Stud Bloodstock & Brendan Cummins **Trained** Manton, Wilts

FOCUS
A fair maiden won in good style, although those behind look modest. The placed horses are up to winning races.

NOTEBOOK
Black Moth(IRE) stepped up on his debut Wolverhampton fourth. Soon to the fore, he kept rolling out in front, maintaining his advantage throughout the final furlong despite still looking green. Only time will tell what this form is worth but he's entitled to go on from here and he is a half-brother to the high-class Majestic Missile, so he could prove useful in the long term. (op 9-4 tchd 100-30)
Postscript(IRE) looked like he was struggling approaching the final furlong but he rallied and came home quite strongly. Slightly easier ground would probably not go amiss and he'll soon be getting off the mark. (op 7-2 tchd 15-8)
Falkland Flyer(IRE) provided plenty of encouragement on this debut, travelling well despite being trapped wide, and he will rank highly next time if building on this. (op 16-1)
Diamond Vine(IRE) confirmed the promise of his debut and should be found a winning opportunity Official explanation: jockey said colt hung left-handed (op 12-1)
Kojak(IRE) never landed a blow and clearly isn't going forward. (op 9-4 tchd 7-2)

2688 BATH ALES SPA FILLIES' H'CAP 5f 11y
6:55 (6:57) (Class 5) (0-70,69) 3-Y-O £2,719 (£809; £404; £202) Stalls Centre

Form RPR

0105 **1** **Lucky Flyer**[13] 2320 3-9-5 **67** LiamKeniry 6 72
(S Kirk) *prom: rdn to ld over 1f out: hld on wl* **15/2**

2544 **2** *nk* **Picnic Party**[11] 2396 3-9-6 **68** GeorgeBaker 3 72
(D R C Elsworth) *stdd s: hdwy but hung rt 2f out: sn rdn to chse ldrs: r.o fnl 100yds: clsng at fin* **7/2**[2]

3532 **3** *nse* **Pherousa**[17] 2217 3-9-1 **63** FrannyNorton 1 69+
(M Blanshard) *chsd ldrs: nt clrest of runs but pushed along over 1f out: rdn and kpt on fnl f: clsng at fin* **9/4**[1]

2166 **4** *1 1/4* **Tom Folan**[5] 2565 3-9-4 **66** (p) MartinDwyer 2 65
(Andrew Reid) *chsd ldrs: snatched up 3f out: effrt over 1f out: kpt on but no ex fnl 75yds* **4/1**[3]

-560 **5** *3 1/4* **Avonvalley**[22] 2052 3-9-7 **69** TomMcLaughlin 5 57
(M S Saunders) *sn pushed along in cl 4th/5th: rdn over 3f out: fdd fnl f* **9/2**

5526 **6** *1/2* **True Red (IRE)**[23] 2026 3-8-4 **52** ow1 (b) ChrisCatlin 4 38
(Mrs N S Evans) *led tl rdn over 1f out: wknd sn after* **16/1**

61.28 secs (-1.22) **Going Correction** -0.15s/f (Firm) **6** Ran SP% **108.8**
Speed ratings (Par 96): **103,102,102,100,95 94**
toteswingers:1&2 £7.20, 1&3 £1.30, 2&3 £2.50 CSF £31.40 TOTE £7.90: £4.70, £2.20; EX 37.00.
Owner Gracelands Stud Partnership **Bred** R V Young **Trained** Upper Lambourn, Berks
■ Stewards' Enquiry : George Baker caution: used whip with excessive frequency
Liam Keniry two-day ban: used whip with excessive force (Jun 20-21)

FOCUS
An ordinary fillies' handicap.
Picnic Party Official explanation: jockey said filly hung right-handed from 2f out
Tom Folan Official explanation: vet said filly lost an off-fore shoe

2689 BATH ALES GEM H'CAP 5f 161y
7:30 (7:31) (Class 4) (0-85,84) 3-Y-O+ £4,533 (£1,348; £674; £336) Stalls Centre

Form RPR

444- **1** **Drawnfromthepast (IRE)**[202] 7395 5-9-7 **82** SophieDoyle(5) 4 91
(J A Osborne) *chsd ldrs: rdn to ld ent fnl f: kpt on wl* **20/1**

05-6 **2** *3/4* **Filligree (IRE)**[20] 2134 5-9-11 **84** WilliamCarson(3) 10 91
(Rae Guest) *mid-div: rdn over 2f out: little imp tl r.o fnl f: wnt 2nd nr fin* **7/1**[3]

4441 **3** *nk* **Secret Witness**[15] 2247 4-9-12 **82** (b) ChrisCatlin 6 88
(R A Harris) *led: hdd briefly 2f out: rdn and hdd ent fnl f: no ex* **8/1**

0-04 **4** *2* **Mrs Penny (AUS)**[13] 2327 6-9-11 **81** (p) LiamKeniry 8 80+
(J R Gask) *towards rr: pushed along over 3f out: clsng steadily whn nt best of runs over 1f out: kpt on fnl f* **9/1**

40-0 **5** *3/4* **Gwilym (GER)**[11] 2399 7-9-1 **71** JimCrowley 9 67
(D Haydn Jones) *w ldr: rdn to ld briefly 2f out: one pce fnl f* **20/1**

0332 **6** *1 1/2* **Kyllachy Storm**[4] 2592 6-8-13 **69** RichardKingscote 3 61
(R J Hodges) *chsd ldrs: rdn over 2f out: sn one pce* **9/2**[2]

561 **7** *nk* **Desperate Dan**[25] 1965 9-8-9 **72** (v) MarkPower(7) 5 63
(A B Haynes) *chsd ldrs: rdn and ev ch 2f out: fdd fnl f* **16/1**

30-6 **8** *1 3/4* **Triple Dream**[14] 2280 5-9-7 **77** (p) GeorgeBaker 12 62
(J M Bradley) *sn struggling in rr on outer: nvr a threat* **4/1**[1]

33-6 **9** *1/2* **Silver Guest**[49] 1361 5-9-1 **71** CathyGannon 7 54
(M R Channon) *towards rr: hdwy u.p 2f out: fdd fnl f* **11/1**

54-2 **10** *shd* **Johnstown Lad (IRE)**[12] 2366 6-9-7 **77** (t) MartinDwyer 1 60
(Daniel Mark Loughnane, Ire) *chsd ldrs: rdn over 2f out: wknd ent fnl f* **8/1**

-245 **11** *1 1/2* **Nepotism**[18] 2179 3-8-8 **72** LukeMorris 11 48
(M S Saunders) *sn u.p: a towards rr* **12/1**

0016 **12** *3 1/2* **White Shift (IRE)**[13] 2332 4-9-0 **70** FrannyNorton 2 36
(P Howling) *mid-div: rdn and no imp over 2f out: fdd fnl f* **28/1**

69.52 secs (-1.68) **Going Correction** -0.15s/f (Firm)
WFA 3 from 4yo+ 8lb **12** Ran SP% **117.8**
Speed ratings (Par 105): **105,104,103,100,99 97,97,95,94,94 92,87**
toteswingers:1&2 £66.90, 1&3 £40.70, 2&3 £12.20 CSF £149.73 CT £1247.45 TOTE £29.70: £6.90, £3.10, £2.90; EX 280.90.
Owner H R H Prince of Saxe-Weimar **Bred** D And Mrs D Veitch **Trained** Upper Lambourn, Berks
■ Stewards' Enquiry : William Carson three-day ban: used whip with excessive frequency without giving mare time to respond (Jun 20-22)

FOCUS
Run-of-the-mill handicap form.
Mrs Penny(AUS) Official explanation: jockey said mare suffered interference in running
White Shift(IRE) Official explanation: jockey said filly lost its action

2690 BATH ALES SALAMANDER H'CAP 1m 2f 46y
8:00 (8:02) (Class 5) (0-70,71) 4-Y-O+ £2,719 (£809; £404; £202) Stalls Centre

Form RPR

-311 **1** **Aestival**[3] 2636 4-9-4 **67** 12ex ChrisCatlin 9 83+
(Sir Mark Prescott) *led for 2f: trckd ldr: did nt handle bnd too wl over 4f out: led over 3f out: sn in command: pushed out* **2/5**[1]

-050 **2** *3* **Bramalea**[93] 777 5-8-12 **61** JimCrowley 6 68
(B W Duke) *mid-div: hdwy u.p fr over 2f out: styd on fnl f: wnt 2nd nr fin: no ch w wnr* **25/1**

0-06 **3** *1/2* **Sgt Schultz (IRE)**[21] 2081 7-9-2 **65** LiamKeniry 3 71
(J S Moore) *trckd ldrs: rdn over 3f out: kpt on gamely to chse wnr over 1f out: no ex whn lost 2nd nr fin* **12/1**[3]

-431 **4** *2 1/4* **Sunny Future (IRE)**[12] 2360 4-9-8 **71** 6ex TomMcLaughlin 7 73
(M S Saunders) *trckd ldrs: rdn to chse wnr 3f out tl over 1f out: no ex fnl f* **9/2**[2]

-000 **5** *6* **Una Pelota (IRE)**[28] 1863 4-9-7 **70** (t) RichardKingscote 4 60
(Tom Dascombe) *mid-div: rdn over 2f out: wknd fnl f* **25/1**

0330 **6** *13* **Goose Green (IRE)**[16] 2233 6-9-1 **64** GeorgeBaker 8 42
(R J Hodges) *hld up towards rr: nvr able to get on terms: eased whn btn fnl f* **16/1**

0 **7** *39* **One Cool Pussy (IRE)**[29] 1852 4-8-11 **60** MartinDwyer 1 —
(Daniel Mark Loughnane, Ire) *rrd leaving stalls: steadily rcvrd to ld after 2f: rdn and hdd over 3f out: sn btn: eased fr over 1f out* **28/1**

2m 7.45s (-3.55) **Going Correction** -0.325s/f (Firm) **7** Ran SP% **114.3**
Speed ratings (Par 103): **101,98,98,96,91 81,50**
toteswingers:1&2 £5.30, 1&3 £3.70, 2&3 £7.50 CSF £16.94 CT £60.64 TOTE £1.50: £1.10, £7.10; EX 11.80.
Owner Lady Katharine Watts **Bred** Miss K Rausing **Trained** Newmarket, Suffolk

FOCUS
A modest handicap but the winner is on a roll.

One Cool Pussy(IRE) Official explanation: jockey said filly was slowly away

2691 BATH ALES SWAN H'CAP — 1m 5f 22y
8:35 (8:35) (Class 6) (0-60,60) 4-Y-O+ £2,072 (£616; £308; £153) Stalls High

Form RPR

-624 1 **Seventh Hill**[13] 2341 5-9-4 **60** FergusSweeney 4 67
(M Blanshard) *mid-div: hdwy 3f out: sn pushed along: rdn ent fnl f: led fnl 100yds: styd on strly* **5/2**[1]

06 2 1 1/4 **Street Runner**[15] 2244 4-9-2 **58** GeorgeBaker 3 63
(R Hollinshead) *chsd clr ldng pair: clsd on ldrs 4f out: rdn 3f out: ch ent fnl f: styd on* **16/1**

2-32 3 3/4 **Dhania (IRE)**[7] 2489 4-8-11 **53** LiamKeniry 7 57
(C Gordon) *trckd ldr clr of rest: rdn to ld over 2f out: kpt on tl hdd fnl 100yds: no ex* **11/2**[3]

05-0 4 2 **Googoobarabajagal (IRE)**[31] 1758 4-8-4 **46** oh1 (v[1]) ChrisCatlin 8 47
(W S Kittow) *hld up: hdwy 3f out: sn rdn: styd on same pce fnl 2f* **11/2**[3]

4052 5 3/4 **Bussell Along (IRE)**[7] 2487 4-8-13 **55** (tp) FrannyNorton 6 55
(Stef Higgins) *hld up: hdwy u.p over 2f out: 4th ent fnl f: no further imp* **8/1**

0040 6 nse **Barodine**[13] 2337 7-8-12 **54** RichardKingscote 5 54
(R J Hodges) *hld up: rdn over 3f out: little prog: nvr a danger* **8/1**

0-25 7 9 **Act Three**[32] 1759 6-8-11 **53** (t) JimCrowley 2 39
(Mouse Hamilton-Fairley) *squeezed out but stdd s: rdn 3f out: nvr a factor* **4/1**[2]

-000 8 2 3/4 **Warrior Nation (FR)**[23] 2023 4-8-4 **46** oh1 (b) NeilChalmers 9 27
(A J Chamberlain) *sn led at gd pce: clr w one other: rdn and hdd over 2f out: wknd ent fnl f* **50/1**

0666 9 22 **Jordan's Light (USA)**[7] 2489 7-8-11 **53** (b) CathyGannon 1 —
(P D Evans) *mid-div: rdn 4f out: sn wknd: eased over 1f out* **16/1**

2m 50.58s (-1.42) **Going Correction** -0.325s/f (Firm) 9 Ran SP% **115.3**
Speed ratings (Par 101): **91,90,89,88,88 88,82,80,67**
toteswingers:1&2 £9.40, 1&3 £2.20, 2&3 £26.20 CSF £45.58 CT £203.83 TOTE £2.80: £1.10, £7.10, £1.10; EX 34.60.
Owner Stanley Hinton **Bred** Mascalls Stud **Trained** Upper Lambourn, Berks

FOCUS
A weak handicap and not form to dwell on for too long.
Act Three Official explanation: jockey said mare was unsuited by the good to firm (firm in places) ground
Jordan's Light(USA) Official explanation: jockey said gelding lost its action; vet said gelding finished lame

2692 BATH ALES WELLINGTON MEDIAN AUCTION MAIDEN STKS — 1m 5y
9:05 (9:06) (Class 6) 3-Y-O £2,072 (£616; £308; £153) Stalls Low

Form RPR

0-42 1 **Aattash (IRE)**[15] 2250 3-9-3 75 ChrisCatlin 2 80
(M R Channon) *mde all: rdn whn hrd pressed over 1f out: kpt on strly to assert ins fnl f: rdn out* **10/3**[3]

2-30 2 2 1/4 **Youm Jamil (USA)**[30] 1824 3-9-3 80 MartinDwyer 4 75
(B J Meehan) *trckd ldr: rdn to chal but edgd rt over 1f out: hld on to 2nd but no ex fnl f* **5/4**[1]

3 3 hd **Linnens Star (IRE)**[20] 2128 3-9-3 0 JimCrowley 3 75
(R M Beckett) *t.k.h early trckd ldrs: rdn to chal over 1f out: kpt on but no ex fnl f* **7/4**[2]

5- 4 25 **Peckforton Castle**[196] 7463 3-9-3 0 LiamKeniry 5 —
(Patrick Morris) *rrd stalls: in last pair but in tch tl pce qcknd over 3f out: wl btn* **28/1**

000 5 29 **Pappas Fc**[14] 2297 3-9-3 30 (p) RichardKingscote 1 —
(J M Bradley) *sltly slowly away: in last pair but in tch tl pce qckned over 3f out: t.o* **50/1**

1m 39.12s (-1.68) **Going Correction** -0.325s/f (Firm) 5 Ran SP% **109.3**
Speed ratings (Par 97): **95,92,92,67,38**
CSF £7.85 TOTE £3.90: £2.40, £1.10; EX 7.80 Place 6 £65.36; Place 5 £47.10.
Owner Sheikh Ahmed Al Maktoum **Bred** Oghill House Stud **Trained** West Ilsley, Berks

FOCUS
This concerned only three in truth and they finished miles clear.
T/Plt: £44.00 to a £1 stake. Pool:£49,584.62 - 822.00 winning tickets T/Qpdt: £8.00 to a £1 stake. Pool:£4,570.46 - 421.32 winning tickets TM

2529 CATTERICK (L-H)
Friday, June 4

OFFICIAL GOING: Good to firm (9.4)
Wind: light 1/2 behind Weather: fine and sunny

2693 EUROPEAN BREEDERS' FUND MAIDEN STKS — 5f
1:50 (1:51) (Class 5) 2-Y-O £3,302 (£982; £491; £245) Stalls Low

Form RPR

1 **Clipthorne** 2-8-9 0 BarryMcHugh(3) 7 73+
(Ollie Pears) *swvd rt s: mid-div: outpcd over 2f out: hdwy and swtchd rt 1f out: fin strly to ld fnl strides* **25/1**

20 2 hd **Orchid Street (USA)**[9] 2436 2-8-12 0 JackMitchell 6 72
(Mrs A Duffield) *chsd ldrs: styd on to chal wl ins fnl f: no ex* **10/11**[1]

5 3 1/2 **Lady Kildare (IRE)**[20] 2130 2-8-12 0 TonyHamilton 2 70
(Jedd O'Keeffe) *w ldr: led over 1f out: hdd nr fin* **10/1**

4 4 1 1/2 **Miss Clairton**[14] 2272 2-8-12 0 SebSanders 13 65
(Sir Mark Prescott) *chsd ldrs: kpt on same pce over 1f out* **11/4**[2]

02 5 hd **Kheya (IRE)**[14] 2292 2-8-12 0 TomEaves 1 64
(G M Moore) *led tl over 1f out: one pce* **15/2**[3]

6 1 1/2 **Fol Pickle** 2-8-12 0 MichaelO'Connell(5) 5 64+
(D Nicholls) *chsd ldrs: one pce fnl 2f* **16/1**

0 7 1 **Bellemere**[32] 1749 2-8-7 0 JamesSullivan(5) 14 55
(M W Easterby) *in tch: kpt on same pce fnl 2f* **40/1**

8 6 **Buzz Law (IRE)** 2-9-0 0 KellyHarrison(3) 8 38
(J R Weymes) *s.i.s: outpcd and a bhd* **100/1**

0 9 2 **Buon Compleanno (IRE)**[14] 2272 2-8-7 0 MarkCoumbe(5) 12 26
(A Berry) *towards rr: hung bdly lft over 3f out* **200/1**

10 3 1/4 **Mossgorda (IRE)** 2-9-3 0 DavidAllan 15 20
(J R Weymes) *s.s: bhd whn hmpd sn after s* **80/1**

000 11 7 **Gunalt Penny Sweet**[11] 2376 2-8-12 0 (b[1]) GrahamGibbons 9 —
(M W Easterby) *sn outpcd in rr: bhd fnl 2f* **125/1**

4 U **Novalist**[31] 1800 2-8-10 0 MatthewLawson(7) 11 —
(R Bastiman) *v free to post: sddle sn slipped: bucked and uns rdr sn after s* **33/1**

59.36 secs (-0.44) **Going Correction** -0.275s/f (Firm) 12 Ran SP% **118.5**
Speed ratings (Par 93): **92,91,90,88,88 85,84,74,71,66 54,—**
toteswingers:1&2:£10.40, 1&3:£40.20, 2&3:£2.90 CSF £48.18 TOTE £58.30: £8.40, £1.02, £4.10; EX 85.30.
Owner Mrs J E Morton **Bred** Wilderbrook Stud **Trained** Norton, N Yorks

FOCUS
On a dry and sunny day the ground was described as good to firm all around. The jockeys reported the ground to be "very quick" after the first. Not much strength in depth in this maiden and the first five home were all fillies. The pace was sound and the form looks ordinary but solid enough.

NOTEBOOK
Clipthorne got home in front despite running green. There should be more to come from her and she should improve plenty for this experience. (op 22-1 tchd 20-1)
Orchid Street(USA), having her third quick start, again showed ability and should be able to go one better shortly. She will stay further in due course. (op 6-4)
Lady Kildare(IRE), prominently ridden, appeared to better her first run and can make her mark at some stage as well. (op 11-1 tchd 12-1)
Miss Clairton, also having her second start, ran okay to a point without really looking like winning. She holds an entry in a claimer and that might the form in some context. (op 9-4 tchd 3-1)
Kheya(IRE), the early leader, weakened towards the finish and looks more of a nursery type later in the season. (op 13-2 tchd 11-2)
Fol Pickle, coming from a good yard, made a satisfactory start to his career and looks the type to improve in time. (op 14-1)
Novalist Official explanation: jockey said saddle slipped

2694 YORKSHIRE4X4.COM ADVENTURE ACTIVITIES (S) STKS — 1m 5f 175y
2:25 (2:25) (Class 6) 4-Y-O+ £2,047 (£604; £302) Stalls Low

Form RPR

3044 1 **Chocolate Caramel (USA)**[7] 2495 8-8-12 71 TonyHamilton 5 64
(R A Fahey) *chsd ldrs: effrt and stmbld bnd over 3f out: wnt 2nd over 1f out: kpt on to ld last 75yds* **5/6**[1]

45-0 2 1 **Castlebury (IRE)**[10] 2421 5-8-12 62 (b) RobertWinston 4 63
(G A Swinbank) *t.k.h: trckd ldrs: led over 2f out: hdd and no ex wl ins fnl f* **13/2**[3]

5-10 3 2 3/4 **Capable Guest (IRE)**[13] 2341 8-9-4 66 SamHitchcott 8 65
(M R Channon) *hld up in rr: effrt 3f out: swtchd rt over 1f out: kpt on to take 3rd ins fnl f* **11/4**[2]

5-50 4 4 1/2 **Mister Fizzbomb (IRE)**[16] 1296 7-8-12 59 (v) DavidNolan 2 52
(J S Wainwright) *led tl over 2f out: wknd jst ins fnl f* **28/1**

60 5 1 **Drummers Drumming (USA)**[16] 2231 4-8-12 0 TomEaves 1 51
(J A Osborne) *hld up wl in tch: outpcd and lost pl over 2f out: kpt on fnl f* **10/1**

6-00 6 2 1/4 **Daltaban (FR)**[13] 2343 6-8-12 36 GregFairley 3 48?
(P Salmon) *chsd ldr: drvn over 4f out: edgd rt 2f out: sn wknd* **125/1**

050- 7 12 **Mceldowney**[205] 7332 8-8-7 45 MarkCoumbe(5) 6 31
(M C Chapman) *hld up in rr: reminders over 5f out: bhd fnl 3f* **100/1**

0-00 8 8 **Spume (IRE)**[11] 2388 6-8-12 44 (t) SebSanders 7 20
(J Balding) *trckd ldrs: drvn 4f out: hung lft and lost pl over 2f out: sn eased and bhd* **28/1**

3m 2.23s (-1.37) **Going Correction** -0.20s/f (Firm) 8 Ran SP% **112.3**
Speed ratings (Par 101): **95,94,92,90,89 88,81,77**
toteswingers:1&2:£2.40, 1&3:£1.10, 2&3:£4.00 CSF £6.66 TOTE £2.00: £1.10, £1.60, £1.10; EX 6.80.There was no bid for the winner. Capable Guest was claimed by G. M. Moore for £6,000
Owner Jonathan Gill **Bred** Sierra Thoroughbreds **Trained** Musley Bank, N Yorks

FOCUS
A run-of-the-mill seller run at a sound pace.
Spume(IRE) Official explanation: jockey said gelding was unsuited by the good to firm ground

2695 LIONWELD KENNEDY CENTENARY SPRINT H'CAP — 5f
3:00 (3:00) (Class 5) (0-70,70) 3-Y-O+ £2,331 (£693; £346; £173) Stalls Low

Form RPR

-000 1 **Nomoreblondes**[19] 2144 6-9-7 **63** (p) PaulMulrennan 4 75
(P T Midgley) *mde all: styd on strly to forge clr ins fnl f* **11/1**

20-0 2 2 1/4 **Wicked Wilma (IRE)**[17] 2213 6-9-0 **61** MarkCoumbe(5) 1 65
(A Berry) *chsd wnr: kpt on same pce fnl f* **12/1**

6-25 3 3/4 **Ravenfield (IRE)**[20] 2114 3-8-12 **68** DaleSwift(7) 10 66+
(D H Brown) *sn outpcd and in rr: hdwy and edgd lft over 1f out: styd on wl to take 3rd nr line* **9/2**[2]

3152 4 nk **Verinco**[17] 2213 4-9-3 **66** (v) AdamCarter(7) 3 66
(B Smart) *mid-div: rdn and outpcd over 2f out: hdwy on inner over 1f out: kpt on same pce* **9/4**[1]

4600 5 1 1/4 **Spirit Of Coniston**[19] 2144 7-9-2 **58** FrederikTylicki 2 54
(P T Midgley) *chsd ldrs on ins: nt clr run over 1f out: hung lft and kpt on same pce* **10/1**

0-30 6 3/4 **Angelo Poliziano**[14] 2301 4-9-9 **65** (b) SebSanders 7 58
(Mrs A Duffield) *wnt lft s: outpcd and in rr: hung lft and sme hdwy over 1f out: nvr a factor* **13/2**[3]

0-34 7 hd **Raccoon (IRE)**[14] 2294 10-9-12 **68** TomEaves 8 60
(Mrs R A Carr) *chsd ldrs: fdd fnl f* **11/1**

142- 8 1/2 **Bertie Southstreet**[181] 7645 7-9-4 **65** (v) JamesO'Reilly(5) 5 55
(J O'Reilly) *chsd ldrs: wknd over 1f out* **11/1**

1-00 9 2 **Secret Venue**[34] 1711 4-10-0 **70** TonyHamilton 9 53
(Jedd O'Keeffe) *in rr-div on outside: wknd over 1f out* **12/1**

000- 10 1 1/4 **Molly Two**[229] 6877 5-8-10 **52** DuranFentiman 6 31
(L A Mullaney) *bmpd s: mid-div: lost pl over 1f out* **40/1**

57.98 secs (-1.82) **Going Correction** -0.275s/f (Firm)
WFA 3 from 4yo+ 7lb 10 Ran SP% **114.2**
Speed ratings (Par 103): **103,99,98,97,95 94,94,93,90,88**
toteswingers:1&2:£13.40, 1&3:£14.10, 2&3:£25.30 CSF £132.14 CT £694.93 TOTE £14.50: £6.50, £4.50, £1.80; EX 201.40.
Owner Anthony D Copley **Bred** P John And Redmyre Bloodstock **Trained** Westow, N Yorks

FOCUS
A run-of-the-mill 51-70 sprint handicap.
Nomoreblondes Official explanation: trainer said, regarding apparent improvement in form, that the yards runners are in better form having previously been under a cloud.
Spirit Of Coniston Official explanation: jockey said gelding hung left throughout

2696 LYDIA'S 18TH BIRTHDAY CELEBRATION H'CAP — 5f 212y
3:35 (3:35) (Class 4) (0-85,82) 4-Y-O+ £4,209 (£1,252; £625; £312) Stalls Low

Form RPR

-543 1 **Legal Eagle (IRE)**[13] 2310 5-8-8 **74** JamesSullivan(5) 5 82
(Paul Green) *led 1f: jnd ldr over 2f out: edgd lft and led over 1f out: hld on wl towards fin* **10/3**[1]

0-14 **2** ½ **Turn Me On (IRE)**[6] 2532 7-9-0 **82** .... LukeStrong(7) 7 88
(T D Walford) *in tch: pushed along and hdwy over 2f out: hung lft and wnt 2nd jst ins fnl f: kpt on towards fin* **5/1**[3]

-101 **3** nk **Sir Nod**[49] 1365 8-9-2 **77** .... TomEaves 3 82+
(Julie Camacho) *trckd ldrs: nt clr run over 1f out: styd on same pce fnl 100yds* **13/2**

3020 **4** nk **Green Park (IRE)**[6] 2534 7-9-2 **77** ....(b) DavidNolan 2 81+
(D Carroll) *hld up: hdwy on ins over 2f out: n.m.r over 1f out: kpt on same pce ins fnl f* **7/1**

0-10 **5** 2¾ **Dametime (IRE)**[12] 2366 4-9-5 **80** .... SebSanders 6 75
(Daniel Mark Loughnane, Ire) *chsd ldrs: upsides over 2f out: wknd fnl f* **9/1**

04-0 **6** 3¼ **Devil You Know (IRE)**[20] 2113 4-9-1 **76** .... PaulMulrennan 1 63+
(M W Easterby) *s.i.s: drvn to ld after 1f: hdd over 1f out: sn wknd: eased fnl 50yds* **6/1**

0043 **7** 3½ **Istiqdaam**[58] 1152 5-8-12 **73** ....(b) GrahamGibbons 4 47
(M W Easterby) *sn outpcd and detached in last: nvr on terms* **7/2**[2]

1m 11.55s (-2.05) **Going Correction** -0.20s/f (Firm) 7 Ran SP% **112.1**
Speed ratings (Par 105): **105,104,103,103,99 95,90**
toteswingers:1&2:£16.60, 1&3:£6.60, 2&3:£3.80 CSF £19.34 TOTE £2.40: £1.10, £3.50; EX 22.70.
Owner Paul Boyers **Bred** John Cooke **Trained** Lydiate, Merseyside

FOCUS
Despite only seven runners, this was a wide-open 66-85 handicap. The early pace was generous to say the least.
Istiqdaam Official explanation: jockey said gelding never travelled

2697 CHAMPIONS 60:60 MAIDEN STKS — 1m 3f 214y
4:15 (4:18) (Class 5) 3-Y-O+ — £2,331 (£693; £346; £173) Stalls Low

Form — RPR

04- **1** **Monterey (IRE)**[233] 6772 3-8-11 0 .... RobertHavlin 2 86+
(R A Mills) *trckd ldrs: led and hung bdly rt over 2f out: drvn clr on stands' side over 1f out: eased ins fnl f* **9/2**[2]

30-0 **2** 7 **Yankee Bright (USA)**[17] 2219 3-8-8 65 ow2 .... PaulMulrennan 4 70
(J G Given) *chsd ldrs: swtchd rt 2f out: kpt on to take modest 2nd ins fnl f* **40/1**

33-5 **3** 1 **Architrave**[15] 2252 3-8-11 72 .... SebSanders 3 71
(Sir Mark Prescott) *chsd ldrs: drvn to ld over 3f out: hdd over 2f out: kpt on same pce* **5/4**[1]

42 **4** 2¼ **Cat O' Nine Tails**[15] 2244 3-8-6 0 .... GregFairley 10 63
(M Johnston) *led: hdd over 3f out: one pce fnl 2f* **9/1**

5 1 **Donny Briggs**[44] 5-9-12 0 .... DavidAllan 6 66+
(T D Easterby) *s.i.s: drvn and sme hdwy 7f out: swtchd outside over 2f out: kpt on: styng on at fin* **66/1**

3 **6** 1 **Blazing Desert**[15] 2244 6-9-12 0 .... GrahamGibbons 8 65
(J J Quinn) *t.k.h in rr: hdwy over 2f out: kpt on: nvr nr ldrs* **25/1**

462 **7** 7 **Ocean Bright (USA)**[4] 2610 4-9-7 42 .... LeeVickers 12 48
(J G Given) *sn in tch: wknd 2f out* **16/1**

66- **8** 3 **New World Symphony (IRE)**[283] 5324 3-8-11 0 .... FrederikTylicki 13 49
(J Howard Johnson) *hld up in mid-div: effrt over 3f out: wknd over 2f out* **100/1**

0 **9** 12 **Neptune's Girl (IRE)**[18] 2180 3-8-3 0 .... Louis-PhilippeBeuzelin(3) 7 24
(Sir Michael Stoute) *in rr: reminders over 5f out: drvn 4f out: sn bhd* **12/1**

5 **10** ½ **Nabari (JPN)**[22] 2050 3-8-6 0 .... KirstyMilczarek 9 24
(L M Cumani) *prom: lost pl over 2f out* **5/1**[3]

4-0 **11** 3½ **Destiny Blue (IRE)**[27] 1912 3-8-11 0 .... TomEaves 11 23
(J A Osborne) *hld up in rr: pushed along over 6f out: nvr on terms* **28/1**

12 11 **Finellas Fortune**[16] 5-9-2 0 .... MichaelO'Connell(5) 14 —
(G M Moore) *s.i.s: sn chsng ldrs: lost pl over 4f out: t.o 3f out* **100/1**

0 **13** 49 **Quitao (GER)**[34] 1705 3-8-11 0 .... AdrianNicholls 5 —
(M Johnston) *in rr: sn drvn along: lost tch over 3f out: sn t.o: virtually p.u* **40/1**

2m 34.29s (-4.61) **Going Correction** -0.20s/f (Firm)
WFA 3 from 4yo+ 15lb 13 Ran SP% **118.5**
Speed ratings (Par 103): **107,102,101,100,99 98,94,92,84,83 81,74,41**
toteswingers:1&2:£9.00, 1&3:£11.00, 2&3:£5.10 CSF £179.11 TOTE £5.30: £1.50, £10.30, £1.10; EX 166.10.
Owner T G Mills, J Humphreys, Mrs S Ecclestone **Bred** Swettenham Stud **Trained** Headley, Surrey

FOCUS
Plenty of dead wood in the maiden which was run at a good pace with the leaders kicking for home a long way out.
Nabari(JPN) Official explanation: trainer said, regarding running, that the filly was unsuited by the track

2698 PEN HILL H'CAP (DIV I) — 5f 212y
4:45 (4:45) (Class 6) (0-65,71) 3-Y-O+ — £1,706 (£503; £252) Stalls Low

Form — RPR

10-0 **1** **Arjemis**[7] 2504 4-9-6 **58** .... SilvestreDeSousa 7 65
(C R Wilson) *rrd s: in rr: hdwy on outside over 2f out: hung lft and styd on to ld last 150yds* **16/1**

64-3 **2** 1 **North Central (USA)**[14] 2291 3-9-5 **65** .... FrederikTylicki 3 67
(J Howard Johnson) *trckd ldr on ins: led over 1f out: hdd and no ex ins fnl f* **2/1**[1]

2330 **3** 1¼ **Bentley**[39] 1585 6-8-11 **49** ....(v) PaulMulrennan 6 49
(J G Given) *chsd ldrs: styd on same pce fnl f* **11/1**

-065 **4** 1¼ **Dancing Wave**[27] 1928 4-8-9 **52** .... MarkCoumbe(5) 4 49
(M C Chapman) *led: hdd over 1f out: one pce* **12/1**

605 **5** hd **Cookie Galore**[18] 2185 3-8-8 **54** .... DavidAllan 1 48
(J A Glover) *hld up: hdwy on outer 2f out: sltly hmpd 1f out: kpt on same pce* **8/1**

1050 **6** 2 **Cheery Cat (USA)**[18] 2184 6-9-1 **53** ....(p) GregFairley 2 43
(J Balding) *chsd ldrs: hung lft over 1f out: one pce* **5/1**[3]

-640 **7** hd **He's A Humbug (IRE)**[35] 1653 6-9-7 **64** .... JamesO'Reilly(5) 10 53
(J O'Reilly) *chsd ldrs: rdn over 2f out: wknd appr fnl f* **14/1**

3-00 **8** 35 **First Blade**[18] 2187 4-9-7 **62** ....(p) RussKennemore(3) 5 —
(S R Bowring) *rrd s and hit hd on stalls: in rr: sn drvn along: bhd and eased over 1f out: virtually p.u: t.o* **7/2**[2]

1m 12.18s (-1.42) **Going Correction** -0.20s/f (Firm)
WFA 3 from 4yo+ 8lb 8 Ran SP% **111.9**
Speed ratings (Par 101): **101,99,98,96,96 93,93,46**
toteswingers:1&2:£9.00, 1&3:£11.00, 2&3:£5.10 CSF £46.39 CT £378.42 TOTE £18.70: £4.50, £1.30, £2.00; EX 53.20.
Owner David Bartlett **Bred** Mrs Andrea Bartlett **Trained** Manfield, N Yorks

FOCUS
Division one of the 46-65 handicap, run at a furious pace.
First Blade Official explanation: jockey said gelding hit its head on stalls as they opened

2699 PEN HILL H'CAP (DIV II) — 5f 212y
5:15 (5:15) (Class 6) (0-65,65) 3-Y-O+ — £1,706 (£503; £252) Stalls Low

Form — RPR

3030 **1** **Soto**[11] 2378 7-9-5 **57** ....(b) PaulMulrennan 8 68
(M W Easterby) *mde all: qcknd after 2f: drvn rt out: unchal* **16/1**

6042 **2** 2¼ **Divertimenti (IRE)**[28] 1884 6-8-12 **53** ....(b) RussKennemore(3) 7 57
(S R Bowring) *chsd wnr thrght: styd on same pce fnl f: nvr to able chal* **9/2**[2]

0-06 **3** shd **Minturno (USA)**[14] 2293 4-9-11 **63** .... TomEaves 2 67
(Mrs A Duffield) *chsd ldrs: outpcd after 2f: hdwy and swtchd inner over 2f out: styd on same pce fnl f* **9/2**[2]

5046 **4** hd **Aqua Vitae (IRE)**[25] 1971 3-8-11 **57** .... GregFairley 5 58
(M Johnston) *chsd ldng pair: one pce fnl 2f* **13/2**[3]

2-55 **5** 3½ **Real Diamond**[21] 2087 4-9-10 **65** ....(p) BarryMcHugh(3) 10 58
(Ollie Pears) *chsd ldrs: outpcd over 3f out: hdwy over 2f out: kpt on: nvr nr to chal* **15/2**

0006 **6** ½ **Redwater River**[17] 2207 6-8-7 **50** ....(b) DeanHeslop(5) 9 41
(Mrs R A Carr) *rrd s: hdwy on outside 2f out: nvr nr ldrs* **7/2**[1]

000- **7** ½ **Ursus**[175] 7709 5-9-2 **54** .... SilvestreDeSousa 3 44
(C R Wilson) *mid-div: outpcd after 2f: kpt on fnl 2f: nvr a factor* **8/1**

046- **8** ½ **Rainbow Bay**[247] 6379 7-8-8 **46** ....(p) AndrewMullen 1 34
(Miss Tracy Waggott) *in rr: kpt on fnl 2f: nvr a factor* **12/1**

0-00 **9** 8 **Fern House (IRE)**[4] 2581 8-8-6 **49** oh1 ow3 .... MarkCoumbe(5) 4 13
(A Berry) *s.i.s: a in rr: bhd fnl 2f* **40/1**

60-0 **10** 6 **Pacific Pride**[24] 1988 7-9-0 **57** ....(v) IanBrennan(5) 6 3
(J J Quinn) *mid-div: lost pl 2f out: sn bhd* **16/1**

1m 12.13s (-1.47) **Going Correction** -0.20s/f (Firm)
WFA 3 from 4yo+ 8lb 10 Ran SP% **116.7**
Speed ratings (Par 101): **101,98,97,97,92 92,91,90,80,72**
toteswingers:1&2:£8.60, 1&3:£16.00, 2&3:£6.70 CSF £86.74 CT £395.23 TOTE £24.20: £4.10, £1.10, £2.60; EX 78.90.
Owner W H & Mrs J A Tinning **Bred** David Sugars And Bob Parker **Trained** Sheriff Hutton, N Yorks

FOCUS
Similar to the first division, this 46-65 was run at a furious pace.
Redwater River Official explanation: jockey said gelding reared as stalls opened

2700 BOOK A PUNTERS PACKAGE H'CAP — 7f
5:45 (5:45) (Class 5) (0-70,70) 3-Y-O+ — £2,456 (£725; £362) Stalls Low

Form — RPR

-040 **1** **Maze (IRE)**[27] 1924 5-9-9 **70** .... MichaelO'Connell(5) 14 78
(D Nicholls) *hld up in mid-div on outside: effrt over 2f out: styd on to ld last 75yds* **5/1**[2]

-032 **2** 1¼ **Mister Jingles**[17] 2211 7-8-11 **58** ....(v) AmyRyan(5) 11 63
(R M Whitaker) *mid-div on outer: hdwy over 2f out: chsd ldrs ins fnl f: kpt on to take 2nd nr fin* **13/2**[3]

44-3 **3** hd **Pure Nostalgia (IRE)**[17] 2203 3-8-6 **63** .... IanBrennan(5) 7 63
(J Howard Johnson) *led: hdd wl ins fnl f: no ex* **9/1**

6505 **4** ½ **Classic Descent**[31] 1808 5-8-11 **58** ....(t) JamesSullivan(5) 10 61
(Mrs R A Carr) *v.s.a: t.k.h towards rr: hdwy on outer over 2f out: nt clr run over 1f out: styd on wl ins fnl f* **14/1**

0000 **5** nk **Nacho Libre**[4] 2578 5-10-0 **70** ....(b) LeeVickers 13 72
(M W Easterby) *s.i.s: hdwy on ins over 2f out: kpt on same pce fnl f* **33/1**

10-4 **6** ¾ **Raleigh Quay (IRE)**[9] 2438 3-9-4 **70** .... FrederikTylicki 8 66
(Micky Hammond) *s.i.s: hdwy on outer over 2f out: kpt on fnl f* **12/1**

6155 **7** ½ **Sixties Rock**[25] 1967 3-7-12 **55** .... PaulPickard(5) 4 50
(J A Glover) *mid-div: effrt and chsd ldrs over 2f out: hung rt and one pce* **13/2**[3]

330 **8** 1¼ **Bajan Flash**[34] 1706 3-9-4 **70** .... TomEaves 3 61
(B Smart) *in rr: hdwy on ins over 2f out: edgd rt: one pce whn heavily eased towards fin* **13/2**[3]

0421 **9** ½ **Dispol Kabira**[11] 2380 3-8-5 **57** 7ex .... PatrickMathers 5 47
(D W Thompson) *mid-div: drvn over 2f out: one pce* **20/1**

66-0 **10** 1¼ **Fair Bunny**[10] 2426 3-8-12 **64** .... SilvestreDeSousa 2 51
(A D Brown) *sn chsng ldrs: wknd jst ins fnl f* **28/1**

0-32 **11** 2¼ **Rio Caribe (IRE)**[25] 1967 3-9-4 **70** ....(p) DuranFentiman 1 50
(T D Walford) *chsd ldrs: wknd appr fnl f* **9/2**[1]

5650 **12** 1¼ **Barnstorm**[17] 2221 3-8-10 **62** .... GregFairley 6 39
(M Johnston) *chsd ldrs on outer: hung bdly rt and lost pl jst ins fnl f* **15/2**

00-0 **13** 2¼ **William Arnold**[32] 1753 3-7-13 **51** oh6 .... PaulQuinn 9 22
(C W Fairhurst) *mid-div: lost pl over 3f out* **100/1**

1m 25.6s (-1.40) **Going Correction** -0.20s/f (Firm)
WFA 3 from 4yo+ 10lb 13 Ran SP% **121.3**
Speed ratings (Par 103): **100,98,98,97,97 96,96,94,94,92 90,88,86**
toteswingers:1&2:£8.90, 1&3:£17.80, 2&3:£14.10 CSF £36.89 CT £301.00 TOTE £9.20: £3.50, £4.20, £2.00; EX 56.30 Place 6 £25.41; Place 5 £14.97.
Owner Centaur Global Partnership I **Bred** Millsec Limited **Trained** Sessay, N Yorks

FOCUS
Another wide open handicap run at a solid tempo.
Maze(IRE) Official explanation: trainer's rep said, regarding apparent improvement in form, that the gelding was better suited by the change in tactics, being held up.
Sixties Rock Official explanation: jockey said gelding hung right-handed
T/Plt: £96.60 to a £1 stake. Pool:£33,449.13 - 252.70 winning tickets T/Qpdt: £40.30 to a £1 stake. Pool:£2,893.50 - 53.00 winning tickets WG

2109 DONCASTER (L-H)
Friday, June 4

OFFICIAL GOING: Good to firm (good in places; watered; 8.7)
Wind: Light across Weather: Fine and dry

2701 CROWNHOTEL-BAWTRY.COM MAIDEN AUCTION STKS — 6f
6:05 (6:05) (Class 5) 2-Y-O — £3,238 (£963; £481; £240) Stalls High

Form — RPR

4 **1** **Excelebration (IRE)**[17] 2216 2-8-12 0 .... NeilCallan 3 80+
(M Botti) *hmpd s: sn cl up: led 2f out: rdn and qcknd clr over 1f out: edgd rt and kpt on strly fnl f* **4/6**[1]

2 2½ **Belgian Bill** 2-9-1 0 .... TonyCulhane 5 75+
(George Baker) *wnt bdly lft s: plld hrd early and in tch: effrt 2f out: sn swtchd rt: swtchd lft and rdn ent fnl f: styd on strly: nt rch wnr* **15/2**[3]

0 **3** 1¼ **Silken Thoughts**[21] 2078 2-8-10 0 .... MickyFenton 7 66
(John Berry) *led: rdn along 1/2-way: hdd 2f out: kpt on same pce fnl f* **16/1**

4 nk **Midnight Rider (IRE)** 2-9-1 0 .... JackMitchell 8 70
(C F Wall) *t.k.h: chsd ldrs: rdn along wl over 1f out: kpt on same pce ent fnl f* **8/1**

5 6 **Finnker (IRE)** 2-8-11 0 ow2 .... RobertWinston 1 48+
(J J Quinn) *wnt bdly lft and lost several l s: bhd and keen: sme hdwy over 1f out: n.d* **7/1**[2]

6 1 1/2 **Il Battista** 2-8-9 0 .... RichardMullen 6 41
(A J McCabe) *dwlt: sn pushed along in rr: rdn 1/2-way: n.d* **25/1**

3 7 3 3/4 **Annalika**[22] [2041] 2-8-1 0 .... KellyHarrison(3) 2 25
(W J H Ratcliffe) *chsd ldrs on outer: rdn along 1/2-way: wknd over 2f out* **28/1**

8 6 **Henry Chettle (IRE)** 2-8-4 0 .... DeclanCannon(5) 4 12
(D C Griffiths) *hmpd s: a in rr* **50/1**

1m 12.8s (-0.80) **Going Correction** -0.35s/f (Firm) **8** Ran SP% **110.5**
Speed ratings (Par 93): **91,87,86,85,77 75,70,62**
toteswingers:1&2:£2.90, 1&3:£4.90, 2&3:£8.70 CSF £5.54 TOTE £1.60: £1.02, £1.20, £5.60; EX 6.10.
Owner Giuliano Manfredini **Bred** Owenstown Stud **Trained** Newmarket, Suffolk

FOCUS
10mm of water was applied to the entire course on Wednesday and Thursday, but despite a dry night and hot day, the ground remained "good to firm, good in places". The riders reported the ground to be as the official. \n\x\x An uncompetitive maiden and one run at a moderate gallop. The winner is impressed but this is tricky form to pin down.

NOTEBOOK
Excelebration(IRE) had shown promise on his debut in a race that was franked by Roayh at Leicester earlier in the week and he probably did not have to improve too much to win with plenty of hand. Although this was not a strong race, he should be able to progress further and should have no problems with 7f. (op 5-6)
Belgian Bill, out of a half-sister to high-class US miler Hawksley Hill, attracted a bit of support in the day and shaped with a degree of promise on this debut, despite his apparent greenness. He should come on for this experience, should stay a bit further and is capable of picking up a minor event. (op 7-1)
Silken Thoughts had offered little at Newbury on her debut but she had the run of the race and showed a fair bit more this time. She has a bit of physical scope and will be of more interest once the nursery season begins. (tchd 20-1 in a place)
Midnight Rider(IRE), out of a dual 6f-7f winner, was fairly easy to back beforehand but was far from disgraced on this debut. Her trainer's newcomers are invariably better for a run and she is entitled to improve for this experience. (op 13-2)
Finnker(IRE) took the eye in the paddock as a strong sort with scope, but this half-brother to a 5f juvenile winner in Italy was far too green to do himself justice on his debut. He should come on a good deal for this outing. Official explanation: jockey said colt ran green (tchd 13-2)

2702 SOCIETY LIFESTYLE & LEISURE MAGAZINE H'CAP 1m (R)
6:35 (6:37) (Class 5) (0-75,75) 3-Y-O **£3,238** (£963; £481; £240) **Stalls** Low

Form RPR
2-22 1 **Cabal**[32] [1777] 3-9-6 **74** .... RichardMullen 9 80+
(Sir Michael Stoute) *midfield: swtchd rt and hdwy 3f out: effrt to chse ldrs 2f out: rdn and styng on to chal whn sltly hmpd ent fnl f: drvn and kpt on wl to ld nr fin* **14/1**

25-1 2 shd **Robens Rock (IRE)**[9] [2438] 3-9-6 **74** 6ex .... NeilCallan 15 80
(M Johnston) *dwlt: hung rt and racd wd: sn cl up: effrt to ld 2f out: rdn and hung rt ent fnl f: sn drvn: hdd and no ex nr fin* **11/8**[1]

-601 3 1 1/2 **Al Dafa (USA)**[17] [2221] 3-9-3 **71** .... (v[1]) HayleyTurner 8 74
(M L W Bell) *hld up: hdwy wl over 2f out: rdn over 1f out: styd on ins fnl f: nrst fin* **15/2**[3]

1332 4 nk **Dazakhee**[11] [2379] 3-8-7 **61** .... TonyCulhane 10 63+
(P T Midgley) *dwlt and hld up in rr: stdy hdwy on inner wl over 2f out: n.m.r and swtchd rt over 1f out: styd on ins fnl f: nrst fin* **16/1**

3-34 5 1 1/4 **Another Magic Man (USA)**[14] [2289] 3-9-3 **71** .... RobertWinston 12 70
(J R Best) *chsd ldrs: hdwy 3f out: rdn wl over 1f out: swtchd lft and drvn ent fnl f: kpt on same pce* **11/1**

5-05 6 1 1/4 **Inpursuitoffreedom**[25] [1973] 3-8-7 **66** .... TobyAtkinson(5) 3 62
(P J McBride) *squeezed out s and in rr: hdwy 3f out: swtchd outside and rdn to chse ldrs wl over 1f out: edgd lft and no imp ins fnl f* **18/1**

-446 7 1/2 **Jack O'Lantern**[19] [2143] 3-9-7 **75** .... TonyHamilton 7 70
(R A Fahey) *trckd ldrs on inner: effrt over 2f out: rdn wl over 1f out: kpt on same pce* **33/1**

006 8 2 **Frontline Phantom (IRE)**[15] [2258] 3-8-5 **62** .... KellyHarrison(3) 13 52
(J R Weymes) *nvr bttr than midfield* **66/1**

033- 9 nk **Grams And Ounces**[166] [7825] 3-8-11 **65** .... KirstyMilczarek 5 55
(Miss Amy Weaver) *hld up in rr: hdwy 3f out and rdn over 2f out: nvr rchd ldrs* **50/1**

66-1 10 3 3/4 **Durham Town (IRE)**[99] [692] 3-9-2 **70** .... SebSanders 2 51
(D K Ivory) *t.k.h: chsd ldrs: rdn along wl over 2f out: drvn wl over 1f out and grad wknd* **20/1**

6361 11 1/2 **Wedding Dream**[11] [2379] 3-9-2 **70** 6ex .... StephenCraine 1 50
(K A Ryan) *led: rdn along 3f out: hdd 2f out and sn wknd* **9/1**

06-0 12 3 3/4 **Gibraltar Lass (USA)**[153] [9] 3-7-13 **56** oh4
Louis-PhilippeBeuzelin(3) 14 27
(H J Collingridge) *a in rr* **100/1**

04-0 13 6 **Bubbelas**[17] [2215] 3-8-8 **62** .... GrahamGibbons 11 19
(J J Quinn) *towards rr: effrt and sme hdwy 4f out: rdn along 3f out and sn wknd* **33/1**

2-2 14 38 **George Benjamin**[24] [1993] 3-9-6 **74** .... AdrianNicholls 4 —
(D Nicholls) *chsd ldrs: rdn along 3f out: drvn and wknd wl over 1f out: bhd and eased fnl f* **7/1**[2]

1m 37.43s (-2.27) **Going Correction** -0.35s/f (Firm) **14** Ran SP% **117.6**
Speed ratings (Par 99): **97,96,95,95,93 92,92,90,89,86 85,81,75,37**
toteswingers:1&2:£5.50, 1&3:£13.20, 2&3:£3.10 CSF £31.30 CT £171.19 TOTE £16.80: £3.40, £1.20, £1.30; EX 24.70.
Owner Cheveley Park Stud **Bred** Cheveley Park Stud Ltd **Trained** Newmarket, Suffolk

FOCUS
A couple of previous winners in a fair handicap. The gallop was a reasonable one and this form looks reliable.
Dazakhee Official explanation: jockey said filly was denied a clear run
Gibraltar Lass(USA) Official explanation: jockey said filly slipped on bend
George Benjamin Official explanation: trainer said gelding returned lame

2703 MOSS PROPERTIES FILLIES' H'CAP 1m 2f 60y
7:10 (7:10) (Class 3) (0-95,93) 4-Y-O+ **£7,771** (£2,312; £1,155; £577) **Stalls** Low

Form RPR
-353 1 **Desert Kiss**[32] [1767] 5-8-13 **85** .... ShaneKelly 7 92
(W R Swinburn) *mde all: qcknd over 2f out: rdn over 1f out: kpt on gamely u.p ins fnl f* **9/2**[3]

26-2 2 1 **Lady Artemisia (IRE)**[48] [1379] 4-9-0 **86** .... AndreaAtzeni 1 91+
(M Botti) *trckd ldrs: hdwy over 3f out: effrt and n.m.r on inner over 2f out: rdn to chse wnr over 1f out: drvn ins fnl f: no imp* **2/1**[1]

-013 3 nk **Tinshu (IRE)**[14] [2282] 4-8-13 **85** .... RichardMullen 3 90
(D Haydn Jones) *trckd ldng pair: hdwy to chse wnr over 2f out: rdn wl over 1f out: drvn ins fnl f: kpt on* **7/1**

22-2 4 4 1/2 **Graceful Descent (FR)**[9] [2429] 5-7-13 **74** oh7 .... KellyHarrison(3) 5 70
(J S Goldie) *hld up in tch: hdwy 3f out: rdn along over 2f out: sn one pce* **10/1**

133- 5 1 **Fanditha (IRE)**[217] [7148] 4-8-13 **85** .... KirstyMilczarek 6 79
(L M Cumani) *hld up in tch: hdwy over 3f out: rdn over 2f out: n.d* **4/1**[2]

U05 6 1 **Bagutta Sun**[13] [2314] 4-8-5 **77** .... (b[1]) HayleyTurner 8 69
(Tom Dascombe) *chsd wnr: rdn along over 3f out: drvn over 2f out and sn wknd* **25/1**

15-6 7 1 3/4 **Anice Stellato (IRE)**[22] [2044] 4-9-1 **87** .... NeilCallan 2 76
(R M Beckett) *trckd ldrs: effrt 4f out: rdn along 3f out: wknd 2f out* **9/2**[3]

2m 6.53s (-2.87) **Going Correction** -0.35s/f (Firm) **7** Ran SP% **115.1**
Speed ratings (Par 104): **104,103,102,99,98 97,96**
toteswingers:1&2:£2.40, 1&3:£4.70, 2&3:£4.80 CSF £14.16 CT £61.41 TOTE £3.60: £1.20, £2.40; EX 10.70.
Owner The Capers **Bred** C R Mason **Trained** Aldbury, Herts

FOCUS
Mainly exposed sorts in a decent quality fillies' handicap but a steady pace until the last quarter-mile means this bare form is not reliable.

NOTEBOOK
Desert Kiss, back against her own sex, has been racing around 1m but benefited from an astute tactical ride to make her first run over this trip a winning one. It remains to be seen whether she will be as effective in a truly-run race over this trip but nevertheless she is a reliable sort who should continue to give it her best shot. (op 5-1 tchd 11-2 in a place)
Lady Artemisia(IRE), who ran well in a race that threw up winners over course and distance on her first run for this yard, ran to a similar level. She left the strong impression a stronger overall gallop would have suited and she is more than capable of picking up a similar event. (op 9-4 tchd 5-2)
Tinshu(IRE) is a reliable sort who again gave it her best shot, despite hanging left, over this trip on fast ground. Easier ground and a better gallop would be more to her liking but she has very little margin for error from her current mark. (op 13-2)
Graceful Descent(FR) ◆ looks a fair bit better than the bare facts suggest after being held up in a slowly run race. She will be able to race from a 5lb lower mark in future and will be of much more interest granted a much stronger overall test of stamina. She is one to keep an eye on. (op 18-1)
Fanditha(IRE), having her first run for Luca Cumani, was fairly easy to back just before the off and could never land a blow after being dropped out in a slowly run race. She should be better for this run and will also be of more interest when a stiffer stamina test looks likely. (op 10-3 tchd 9-2)
Bagutta Sun, tried in blinkers this time, again had her limitations exposed and has plenty to prove. (op 22-1)
Anice Stellato(IRE) could have been expected to fare better than this, even allowing for the slow gallop. She will have to show a fair bit more before she is worth a bet. (op 5-1 tchd 4-1)

2704 FUNKYFASCINATORS.CO.UK H'CAP 1m 4f
7:40 (7:40) (Class 5) (0-70,70) 3-Y-O **£3,238** (£963; £481; £240) **Stalls** Low

Form RPR
0-11 1 **Bona Fortuna**[1] [2673] 3-9-2 **65** 6ex .... SebSanders 2 80+
(Sir Mark Prescott) *reminders s and sn led: rdn along over 3f out: drvn over 2f out: hdd over 1f out: hrd drvn and rallied gamely to ld last 75yds* **4/5**[1]

-124 2 hd **Shelfah (IRE)**[25] [1975] 3-9-7 **70** .... NeilCallan 5 84+
(M A Jarvis) *trckd wnr: hdwy 3f out: rdn to chal over 2f out: drvn to ld over 1f out: hdd and no ex last 75yds* **3/1**[2]

54-2 3 9 **Astral Flower**[24] [2011] 3-9-6 **69** .... RichardMullen 1 69
(Sir Michael Stoute) *trckd ldng pair: pushed along 4f out: rdn 3f out: sn drvn and outpcd fnl 2f* **5/1**[3]

-424 4 1 1/2 **Aegean Destiny**[17] [2219] 3-8-12 **61** .... StephenCraine 6 59
(J Mackie) *hld up in rr: hdwy over 4f out: rdn to chse ldrs 3f out: drvn and outpcd fnl 2f* **16/1**

4526 5 6 **Battle Study (IRE)**[9] [2438] 3-8-11 **65** .... DeclanCannon(5) 4 53
(A J McCabe) *chsd ldrs: rdn along over 4f out: wknd fnl 3f* **25/1**

634 6 11 **Trojan Gift (USA)**[21] [2083] 3-8-12 **61** .... TomEaves 3 31
(Julie Camacho) *chsd ldrs: rdn along 1/2-way: wknd over 4f out* **33/1**

2m 30.32s (-4.58) **Going Correction** -0.35s/f (Firm) **6** Ran SP% **109.9**
Speed ratings (Par 99): **101,100,94,93,89 82**
toteswingers:1&2:£1.60, 1&3:£1.50, 2&3:£1.10 CSF £3.22 TOTE £2.00: £1.40, £1.70; EX 3.40.
Owner S Munir **Bred** W And R Barnett Ltd **Trained** Newmarket, Suffolk
■ Stewards' Enquiry : Seb Sanders one-day ban: used whip with excessive frequency (Jun 21)

FOCUS
Not a competitive race and a race run at just a moderate gallop until the tempo lifted turning for home.

2705 FLY TO DUBLIN WITH AERLINGUS.COM H'CAP 1m (S)
8:15 (8:15) (Class 4) (0-80,78) 4-Y-O+ **£5,180** (£1,541; £770; £384) **Stalls** High

Form RPR
6052 1 **Ninth House (USA)**[6] [2527] 8-7-12 **60** .... (t) JamesSullivan(5) 11 70
(Mrs R A Carr) *hld up in midfield: hdwy to trck ldrs 3f out: effrt to chse ldr wl over 1f out and sn rdn: drvn ins fnl f: styd on wl to ld nr fin* **3/1**[1]

6405 2 1/2 **Thunderball**[4] [2580] 4-9-6 **77** .... (b) FrederikTylicki 4 86
(J A Glover) *chsd ldr: led after 2f: clr 1/2-way: rdn wl over 1f out: drvn ins fnl f: hdd and no ex nr fin* **9/1**

0045 3 2 1/4 **Flowing Cape (IRE)**[8] [2477] 5-9-5 **76** .... RobertWinston 7 80
(R Hollinshead) *hld up in midfield: hdwy 3f out: nt clr run and swtchd rt over 1f out: swtchd lft and rdn jst ins fnl f: styd on* **8/1**

50-6 4 3 1/2 **Bold Cross (IRE)**[13] [2328] 7-9-6 **77** .... PaulFitzsimons 8 73
(E G Bevan) *dwlt and in rr: hdwy on outer 1/2-way: rdn along over 2f out: drvn and kpt on ins fnl f* **5/1**[2]

4-02 5 3 1/2 **Arizona John (IRE)**[20] [2133] 5-9-7 **78** .... StephenCraine 6 66
(J Mackie) *chsd ldrs: rdn along over 2f out: drvn over 1f out: hld whn n.m.r ent fnl f: wknd* **11/2**[3]

-043 6 3/4 **Spavento (IRE)**[14] [2274] 4-8-0 **60** .... (b) KellyHarrison(3) 3 46
(E J Alston) *trckd ldrs: hdwy 1/2-way: rdn along over 2f out: drvn and edgd rt over 1f out: sn wknd* **16/1**

51-0 7 1 **Kildare Sun (IRE)**[11] [2392] 8-8-8 **65** .... (p) GrahamGibbons 10 49
(J Mackie) *led 2f: chsd ldr: rdn along over 2f out: drvn and n.m.r over 1f out: sn wknd* **20/1**

4003 8 6 **Stanley Goodspeed**[22] [2053] 7-8-11 **68** .... (t) SebSanders 1 38
(J W Hills) *racd wd: hld up in rr: hdwy and in tch 1/2-way: rdn over 2f out and sn wknd* **9/1**

0205 9 2 1/2 **Film Festival (USA)**[14] [2295] 7-8-8 **65** .... TomEaves 2 29
(B Ellison) *chsd ldng pair: rdn along 3f out: wknd over 2f out* **8/1**

-050 **10** *4* **Lakeman (IRE)**[24] [1990] 4-8-11 **68** .... TonyHamilton 9 23
(B Ellison) *a in rr* **50/1**

03-0 **11** *7* **Dream In Waiting**[15] [2256] 4-9-4 **75** .... NeilCallan 5 14
(B J Meehan) *trckd ldrs on inner: effrt and n.m.r over 2f out: sn rdn and wknd* **18/1**

1m 35.95s (-3.35) **Going Correction** -0.35s/f (Firm) course record **11** Ran SP% **117.1**
Speed ratings (Par 105): **102,101,99,95,92 91,90,84,82,78 71**
toteswingers:1&2:£6.60, 1&3:£7.50, 2&3:£5.20 CSF £30.62 CT £201.86 TOTE £2.80: £1.80, £3.20, £3.20; EX 52.00.
Owner Michael Hill **Bred** Juddmonte Farms Inc **Trained** Huby, N Yorks

FOCUS
Exposed performers in a fair handicap and one run at an ordinary gallop.

2706 JCT600 MERCEDES-BENZ SOUTH YORKSHIRE MAIDEN STKS 7f
8:45 (8:51) (Class 5) 3-Y-O **£3,238** (£963; £481; £240) **Stalls** High

Form RPR

4-22 **1** **Tesslam**[31] [1804] 3-9-3 78 .... NeilCallan 10 81
(M A Jarvis) *mde all: pushed clr over 2f out: kpt on* **1/3**[1]

2 *3 ¼* **City Ground (USA)** 3-9-3 0 .... JackMitchell 9 72+
(M A Jarvis) *dwlt: t.k.h and hld up towards rr: hdwy 3f out: chsd ldrs 2f out: swtchd lft and rdn to chse wnr ent fnl f: no imp* **6/1**[2]

0 **3** *5* **Music Festival (USA)**[59] [1137] 3-9-3 0 .... FrederikTylicki 8 59
(J S Goldie) *chsd ldrs: rdn over 2f out: sn drvn: kpt on same pce: tk 3rd nr line* **25/1**

-006 **4** *nk* **Ruler's Honour (IRE)**[14] [2288] 3-8-10 63 .... DaleSwift(7) 2 58
(T J Etherington) *chsd ldrs: rdn over 2f out: drvn wl over 1f out: sn one pce: lost 3rd nr fin* **25/1**

5 *4* **Lady Anthracite** 3-8-12 0 .... TomEaves 7 42
(B Smart) *chsd ldrs: rdn along over 2f out: sn wknd* **20/1**

40 **6** *2 ½* **Elle Est**[36] [1648] 3-8-12 0 .... RobertWinston 4 35
(E J Alston) *t.k.h: chsd ldrs: rdn along over 2f out and sn wknd* **12/1**[3]

0 **7** *3* **Rockie Bright**[42] [1504] 3-8-12 0 .... LeeVickers 1 27
(J G Given) *s.i.s: a in rr* **33/1**

8 *2 ½* **Happy The Man (IRE)** 3-9-3 0 .... TonyHamilton 6 26
(T D Easterby) *s.i.s: a in rr* **16/1**

9 *12* **Shesasnip** 3-8-12 0 .... GrahamGibbons 5 —
(R Hollinshead) *cl up: rdn along over 3f out: sn wknd and bhd fnl 2f* **40/1**

1m 24.85s (-1.45) **Going Correction** -0.35s/f (Firm) **9** Ran SP% **120.7**
Speed ratings (Par 99): **94,90,84,84,79 76,73,70,56**
toteswingers:1&2:£1.30, 1&3:£3.60, 2&3:£12.00 CSF £2.66 TOTE £1.20: £1.02, £1.30, £6.50; EX 2.60 Place 6 £4.55; Place 5 £3.60.
Owner Sheikh Ahmed Al Maktoum **Bred** Darley **Trained** Newmarket, Suffolk

FOCUS
A most uncompetitive maiden in which the gallop was an ordinary one.
Elle Est Official explanation: trainer said filly was unsuited by the good to firm (good in places) ground
T/Plt: £4.40 to a £1 stake. Pool:£48,548.35 - 7,939.43 winning tickets T/Qpdt: £3.00 to a £1 stake. Pool:£3,576.00 - 866.70 winning tickets JR

1471 EPSOM (L-H)
Friday, June 4

OFFICIAL GOING: Good (good to firm in places; 8.4; home straight - far side 8.6; stands' side 8.8)
The course was dolled out up to 5yds from the 6f point to the winning line, adding approximately 10yds to race distances.
Wind: light, behind Weather: sunny and warm

2707 INVESTEC DIOMED STKS (GROUP 3) 1m 114y
1:40 (1:41) (Class 1) 3-Y-O+
£36,900 (£13,988; £7,000; £3,490; £1,748; £877) **Stalls** Low

Form RPR

03-1 **1** **Bushman**[25] [1974] 6-9-4 109 .... WilliamBuick 8 115
(D M Simcock) *t.k.h: chsd ldrs: wnt 2nd 4f out: rdn to chal 2f out: led ent fnl f: hld on gamely fnl 100yds* **11/1**

-120 **2** *nk* **Alexandros**[69] [1025] 5-9-7 115 .... FrankieDettori 2 117+
(Saeed Bin Suroor) *lw: hld up in tch in midfield: 5th st: plld out and effrt over 2f out: awkward hd carriage and edgd lft u.p wl over 1f out: str chal ins fnl f: nt qckn and hld towards fin* **9/2**[3]

1-12 **3** *½* **Mabait**[27] [1900] 4-9-4 108 .... KierenFallon 9 113+
(L M Cumani) *lw: t.k.h: hld up in tch towards rr: 7th st: rdn and hdwy on outer ent fnl 2f: pressed ldrs ins fnl f: no ex and one pce fnl 100yds* **10/3**[2]

1-35 **4** *2 ¼* **The Cheka (IRE)**[20] [2118] 4-9-4 110 .... TomQueally 5 109+
(Eve Johnson Houghton) *in tch in midfield: 4th st: effrt to chse ldng pair and rdn 3f out: one pce and struggling whn nt clr run and hmpd 1f out: plugged on same pce after* **5/1**

0601 **5** *¾* **Beauchamp Xerxes**[13] [2318] 4-9-4 101 .... DaneO'Neill 4 106
(G A Butler) *stdd s: hld up in last pair: 8th st: hdwy on inner ent fnl 2f: styng on whn nt clr run and swtchd rt ins fnl f: nvr gng pce to rch ldrs* **25/1**

0-62 **6** *nk* **Ordnance Row**[25] [1974] 7-9-4 108 .... RichardHughes 6 105
(R Hannon) *led: rdn ent fnl 2f: hdd u.p ent fnl f: wknd fnl 150yds* **16/1**

12-1 **7** *2* **Penitent**[69] [1008] 4-9-4 109 .... JMurtagh 3 101
(W J Haggas) *t.k.h: hld up in tch towards rr: 6th st: rdn and unable qck ent fnl 3f: styd on same pce after and nvr able to chal* **11/4**[1]

-011 **8** *1* **Harrison George (IRE)**[13] [2344] 5-9-4 109 .... PaulHanagan 1 98
(R A Fahey) *racd keenly: chsd ldr tl 4f out: 3rd st: struggling u.p 3f out: bhd fnl 2f* **9/1**

-140 **9** *1* **Classic Colori (IRE)**[19] [2159] 3-8-6 100 .... RichardKingscote 7 94
(Tom Dascombe) *stdd s: hld up in last: rdn and no prog over 2f out: n.d* **40/1**

1m 43.03s (-3.07) **Going Correction** -0.125s/f (Firm)
WFA 3 from 4yo+ 12lb **9** Ran SP% **115.1**
Speed ratings (Par 113): **108,107,107,105,104 104,102,101,100**
toteswingers:1&2:£7.50, 1&3:£8.70, 2&3:£3.00 CSF £59.71 TOTE £18.70: £4.10, £1.20, £1.20; EX 53.30 Trifecta £240.40 Pool: £10,335.90 - 31.81 winning units..
Owner Khalifa Dasmal **Bred** Darley **Trained** Newmarket, Suffolk
■ The first Group winner for David Simcock.
■ Stewards' Enquiry : William Buick caution: careless riding.

FOCUS
A combination of horses proven at around this sort of level and some progressive types trying to make the step up made for a quality Group 3 contest. The pace was not overly strong (time 0.25 secs slower than the 100-rated Tartan Gigha managed in the following handicap), with Ordnance Row allowed his own way. The winner rates a length personal best but this form may not prove too solid.

NOTEBOOK
Bushman looked an improved performer when a clear-cut winner of a Windsor Listed race on his reappearance (career-best RPR) and he confirmed that to be the case with a game effort on this return to Group company. Always well placed, he came under pressure fully 3f out and looked vulnerable when strongly pressed on his outside by a couple of rivals (who both traded at odds on in running) inside the final furlong, but he proved most determined. There's nothing for him at Royal Ascot according to David Simcock, and this is his sort of level. (op 10-1 tchd 9-1)
Alexandros, runner-up in this race as a 3-y-o, again had to settle for second, although he emerges as the best horse at the weights seeing as he was carrying a 3lb penalty. Produced with every chance, he briefly looked the winner inside the final furlong - touched 1.16 on Betfair - but was just held. He was inclined to edge slightly left late on and that might have cost him. Official explanation: jockey said horse hung left (op 4-1 tchd 5-1)
Mabait ◆ was not helped by stall nine and could be considered slightly unlucky. Having got warm beforehand, he was a bit keen for a furlong or so when caught wide, and then had to be settled further back than ideal to get some cover. He looked a big threat when produced with his chance out wide in the straight - touched 1.25 on Betfair - but his run flattened out near the line, which was no surprise all things considered. He's up to this level. (op 3-1 tchd 11-4)
The Cheka(IRE) didn't find as much as had looked likely and was weakening when carried slightly left inside the final furlong. Perhaps he'll be worth another try over 7f. (op 6-1)
Beauchamp Xerxes, who was mounted on course, raced out the back after starting slowly and, although keeping on after being switched off the rail, he was never a threat. This was tougher than the Goodwood Listed race he won last time.
Ordnance Row could not take advantage of being allowed a soft lead and continues below his best form.
Penitent, winner of the Lincoln off a mark of 98 on his only previous start this year, struggled on this rise in grade, but in fairness the ground was probably quicker than ideal, and also time may show him to be best suited by shorter distances. Official explanation: trainer's rep said gelding was unsuited by the good (good to firm in places) ground (op 7-2)
Harrison George(IRE) raced keenly early on and may have been unsuited by the track. (op 10-1)
Classic Colori(IRE), who played up in the parade ring, never featured after starting slowly. (op 33-1)

2708 INVESTEC MILE (H'CAP) 1m 114y
2:10 (2:11) (Class 2) (0-105,100) 4-Y-O+
£18,693 (£5,598; £2,799; £1,401; £699; £351) **Stalls** Low

Form RPR

0621 **1** **Tartan Gigha (IRE)**[34] [1697] 5-9-10 **100** .... KierenFallon 10 108
(M Johnston) *in tch in midfield: rdn and effrt wl over 2f out: chsd ldr jst over 1f out: styd on wl u.p fnl f to ld last stride* **6/1**[2]

200- **2** *shd* **Set The Trend**[272] [5663] 4-9-3 **93** .... JimmyFortune 8 101
(A M Balding) *lw: chsd ldrs: effrt to chse ldr over 2f out: rdn to ld wl over 1f out: sn hung lft into rail: hrd drvn fnl f: kpt on wl tl hdd last stride* **7/2**[1]

4041 **3** *½* **Vainglory (USA)**[20] [2124] 6-8-13 **92** .... MartinLane(3) 12 99
(D M Simcock) *lw: in tch: rdn 4f out: outpcd u.p over 3f out: rallied on outer ent fnl f: styd on wl fnl f: nt quite rch ldng pair* **14/1**

6215 **4** *nk* **Gaily Noble (IRE)**[45] [1455] 4-9-0 **90** .... JimCrowley 4 96
(A B Haynes) *chsd ldrs: rdn to cl 3f out: kpt on wl u.p fnl f: nt quite pce to chal ldrs* **25/1**

1-30 **5** *1 ½* **Mull Of Killough (IRE)**[48] [1383] 4-9-6 **96** .... JAHeffernan 3 101+
(J L Spearing) *stdd after s: hld up in rr: rdn and effrt over 3f out: gd hdwy u.p 2f out: looking to switch out but hld in over 1f out: chsng ldrs and styng on whn nt clr run wl ins fnl f: eased towards fin* **9/1**

6232 **6** *1 ¼* **Vitznau (IRE)**[13] [2318] 6-9-10 **100** .... RichardHughes 2 100
(R Hannon) *hld up wl bhd: gd hdwy 2f out: rdn and chsng ldrs 1f out: no imp fnl 100yds* **8/1**[3]

4560 **7** *1* **Extraterrestrial**[28] [1857] 6-9-8 **98** .... FrankieDettori 7 95+
(R A Fahey) *hld up in rr: effrt but switching rt to outer 2f out: styd on wl fnl f but nvr gng pce to rch ldrs* **11/1**

4-25 **8** *1 ¼* **Sunnyside Tom (IRE)**[19] [2141] 6-8-8 **84** .... RoystonFfrench 11 78
(R A Fahey) *sn led: rdn and hdd wl over 1f out: wknd fnl f* **33/1**

-522 **9** *3 ¼* **Jordaura**[15] [2241] 4-8-10 **86** .... JamieSpencer 1 73
(J R Holt) *hld up off the pce in midfield: rdn and effrt 3f out: no prog and btn over 1f out* **8/1**[3]

-215 **10** *2 ¼* **Osteopathic Remedy (IRE)**[10] [2423] 6-8-13 **89** .... PhillipMakin 14 71
(M Dods) *dwlt: sn pushed up to chse ldrs: wnt 2nd over 5f out: wknd and edgd lft u.p 2f out: wl btn and eased ins fnl f* **16/1**

0006 **11** *½* **Ocean's Minstrel**[41] [1519] 4-9-5 **95** .... JerryO'Dwyer 5 76
(J Ryan) *hld up in rr: rdn and no prog over 2f out: n.d* **20/1**

3052 **12** *nk* **Audemar (IRE)**[20] [2124] 4-8-9 **85** .... MartinDwyer 9 65
(E F Vaughan) *chsd ldr tl over 5f out: rdn and effrt over 3f out: wkng whn hmpd on rail wl over 1f out: wl btn after* **11/1**

0120 **13** *4 ½* **Mujood**[4] [2595] 7-9-6 **96** ....(v) TomQueally 13 66
(Eve Johnson Houghton) *s.i.s: bhd early: hdwy into midfield 5f out: rdn and struggling 4f out: lost pl and wl bhd fnl 2f* **25/1**

50-3 **14** *6* **Deadly Secret (USA)**[24] [1990] 4-8-8 **84** .... PaulHanagan 6 40
(R A Fahey) *restless in stalls: stdd s: t.k.h and hld up in rr: rdn and lost tch 3f out* **14/1**

1m 42.78s (-3.32) **Going Correction** -0.125s/f (Firm) **14** Ran SP% **120.0**
Speed ratings (Par 109): **109,108,108,108,106 105,104,103,100,98 98,98,94,88**
toteswingers:1&2:£3.00, 1&3:£10.20, 2&3:£20.60 CSF £25.71 CT £289.30 TOTE £4.60: £2.20, £2.10, £4.80; EX 24.70 Trifecta £400.90 Pool: £1,354.61 - 2.50 winning units..
Owner Exors of the Late Mrs I Bird **Bred** Gainsborough Stud Management Ltd **Trained** Middleham Moor, N Yorks

FOCUS
A hot handicap and they went a strong pace. The winning time was 0.25 seconds faster than the Diomed.

NOTEBOOK
Tartan Gigha(IRE) had been put up 5lb for his Newmarket success last month and was therefore 12lb higher than when taking this last year, but this performance once again showed that proven ability to handle this demanding track means so much. Not that he ever looked that happy during the contest, though he was never too far off the pace and responded gamely when Fallon asked him to get closer inside the last 3f. He still looked held by the runner-up until a last-gasp effort took him to the front in the final stride. He is now a top-priced 20-1 for the Royal Hunt Cup, for which he picks up a 5lb penalty. (op 11-2 tchd 9-2)
Set The Trend was having his first start since September and his first on quick ground, but he made a successful racecourse debut last year, so he can go well fresh and market support suggested he was thought fit enough. Always in a handy position, he was sent to the front passing the 2f pole and looked likely to win until cut down in the very last stride. He remains unexposed and on this evidence has a big handicap in him. (op 6-1)
Vainglory(USA), raised 5lb for his Newmarket win last month, was 3lb higher than when beaten less than a length into third in this race two years ago. Having raced in mid-division on the outside of the field, he came off the bridle rounding Tattenham Corner, but to his great credit he kept battling away and was right alongside the front pair passing the line. He remains competitive off this mark. (op 16-1)

Gaily Noble(IRE), having his first start on turf since September, was another off the bridle a fair way out but he too stayed on well over the last 2f. A four-time winner on Polytrack, he is yet to score on turf, but should put that right before long, perhaps back over a bit further. (op 22-1 tchd 40-1 in a place)
Mull Of Killough(IRE), whose effort in the Newbury Spring Cup can basically be ignored, didn't look happy on the track here, but he made up good ground over the last 2f and seemed to have run his race when running out of room close home. He didn't see the racecourse until April of last year, so still has a bit of scope. (op 15-2)
Vitznau(IRE) usually runs well at this track and was fourth in this race off 2lb higher two years ago. Given plenty to do, he made up plenty of ground over the last couple of furlongs but was never getting there in time. (op 7-1)
Extraterrestrial, one of three representing the Fahey yard and still 3lb above his highest winning mark, was also given a lot to do and though he made up some late ground, he was never a threat. He would probably have preferred an easier surface. (op 14-1)
Sunnyside Tom(IRE) was responsible for the strong pace, but he had nothing left when headed 2f from home and is still 10lb higher than for his most recent win last August. (op 40-1 tchd 50-1 in a place)
Jordaura, edging up the weights after two recent narrow defeats and now 10lb higher than for his Doncaster success at the end of last season, could never get involved but he did look ill-at-ease on the track, so is well worth another chance. (op 7-1)
Ocean's Minstrel Official explanation: trainer said colt sustained a cut to near-fore

2709 INVESTEC CORONATION CUP (GROUP 1) 1m 4f 10y
2:45 (2:49) (Class 1) 4-Y-O+

£127,732 (£48,420; £24,232; £12,082; £6,052; £3,037) **Stalls** Centre

Form				RPR
-311	**1**		**Fame And Glory**[12] 2369 4-9-0 128 JMurtagh 8 *(A P O'Brien, Ire) sn chsng ldrs: clr in ldng trio over 8f out: wnt 2nd 7f out: pushed into ld over 3f out: jnd and rdn 2f out: forged ahd jst ins fnl f: styd on wl and in command fnl 100yds* **5/6**[1]	127+
23-1	**2**	1 ½	**Sariska**[22] 2055 4-8-11 118 JamieSpencer 5 (M L W Bell) *hld up in midfield: allowed ldng trio to go clr 7f out: clsd on ldrs 5f out: 3rd st: pushed up to chal wnr 2f out: drvn over 1f out: no ex and btn jst ins fnl f* **5/2**[2]	121
541-	**3**	1 ¼	**High Heeled (IRE)**[223] 7031 4-8-11 115 WilliamBuick 1 (J H M Gosden) *stdd s: hld up in rr: hdwy 5f out: 7th: st: rdn and effrt on outer wl over 2f out: chsd ldng pair and edging lft jst ins fnl f: kpt on same pce after* **25/1**	119
20-0	**4**	¾	**Youmzain (IRE)**[69] 1026 7-9-0 125 (v) KierenFallon 9 (M R Channon) *hld up in rr: hdwy 5f out: 6th st: rdn to chse ldrs 2f out: keeping on one pce whn hung bdly lft jst ins fnl f: one pce after* **8/1**[3]	121
3-05	**5**	1 ¾	**Cavalryman**[69] 1026 4-9-0 120 FrankieDettori 2 (Saeed Bin Suroor) *taken down early: hld up in midfield: hdwy 5f out: 5th st: rdn and nt clr run wl over 1f out: sn swtchd lft to rail: keeping on and pressing for 3rd whn nt clr run and bdly hmpd ins fnl f: no ch after* **9/1**	121+
6-13	**6**	4 ½	**South Easter (IRE)**[29] 1832 4-9-0 105 (t) RyanMoore 4 (W J Haggas) *led briefly: chsd ldr tl 10f out: allowed ldng trio to go clr over 8f out: lost pl 5f out: 7th and struggling st: no threat to ldrs after* **33/1**	111
2-01	**7**	5	**Jukebox Jury (IRE)**[34] 1698 4-9-0 118 (v) RoystonFfrench 3 (M Johnston) *t.k.h early: chsd ldrs: wnt 2nd and sn clr in ldng trio over 8f out: 4th and rdn st: wknd 3f out: wl bhd fnl 2f* **16/1**	103
/00-	**8**	10	**Bashkirov**[12] 2368 5-9-0 92 RPWalsh 6 (Luke Comer, Ire) *a towards rr: pushed along and struggling in last 5f out: 8th st: sn lost tch:* **125/1**	87
-446	**9**	14	**Dixie Music (IRE)**[12] 2369 4-9-0 101 JAHeffernan 10 (A P O'Brien, Ire) *s.i.s: sn bustled up to ld: wnt clr w 2 rivals over 8f out: rdn and hdd over 3f out: dropped out qckly over 2f out: t.o and virtually p.u ins fnl f* **125/1**	65

2m 33.42s (-5.48) **Going Correction** -0.125s/f (Firm) **9** Ran SP% **118.5**
Speed ratings (Par 117): **113,112,111,110,109 106,103,96,87**
toteswingers:1&2:£1.20, 1&3:£6.70, 2&3:£8.70 CSF £3.07 TOTE £2.00: £1.10, £1.60, £5.60; EX 4.00 Trifecta £31.20 Pool: £5,672.15 - 134.11 winning units..
Owner D Smith, Mrs J Magnier, M Tabor **Bred** Ptarmigan Bloodstock And Miss K Rausing **Trained** Ballydoyle, Co Tipperary

FOCUS
Not always the strongest of Group 1 contests, but this year's race looked a high-class edition featuring, among others, last year's Derby runner-up and the Oaks winner, and it was that pair who dominated. The gallop set by the winner's stablemate Dixie Music, who recovered from a slow start, seemed even - not favouring any one running style - and that view is backed up by a time 2.35 seconds quicker than the Oaks later on the card. Fame And Glory produced a top-class effort, 3lb off his 3yo best at face value, with Sariska running her best race bar the Irish Oaks.

NOTEBOOK
Fame And Glory found himself in front early in the straight, which might have been soon enough for most horses, but Aidan O'Brien's colt is very much a stayer rather than a quickener, and it was the best place for him to be considering how the race unfolded. He looked vulnerable when Sariska loomed up apparently travelling the better of the pair, but Johnny Murtagh's mount kept responding to pressure and was ultimately a convincing winner. Despite having a hard season last year, Fame And Glory has returned better than ever and is now 3-4 for the campaign. It's possible he'll now be aimed at the Prince Of Wales's Stakes, but although he managed to win the Tattersalls Gold Cup over 1m21/2f last time, that was a weak renewal run at a very strong pace, and he seems better suited by this trip. (tchd Evens)
Sariska, last year's dual Oaks winner who returned with victory in the Group 2 Middleton Stakes, raced further back than Fame And Glory, but the pace was good and she made up her ground readily. She traded short on Betfair when still travelling well and putting pressure on the winner approaching 2f out, but once off the bridle she was always being held. Although she clearly handles this type of ground, she's always looked best suited by some give underfoot, and she can do better again when getting her optimum conditions. She's a possible for the King George, and apparently has the Arc as her long-term aim. (op 7-2)
High Heeled(IRE), third to Sariska in last year's Oaks before winning a Listed race and a Group 3, had been sold out of the Barry Hills yard for 600,000gns since she was last seen. Pitched into Group 1 company - against colts - for her first run in 223 days, she ran a terrific race and will surely have delighted her new connections. Having raced a bit further back than might have been ideal, both the winner and runner-up got a start on her by the time she reached the straight, and she was always being held. She's entitled to come on for this and could do even better when there is some cut in the ground, which has always seemed to suit her best. John Gosden said beforehand the filly was likely to be aimed at the Lancashire Oaks. (op 33-1)
Youmzain(IRE), runner-up in this race for the last two years, had a visor re-fitted following a disappointing effort in Dubai on his reappearance, but he got warm beforehand and was again below his very best. He was only 1l behind Sariska and in front of High Heeled turning into the straight, and was produced with every chance, but he did not look all that keen, seeming inclined to edge to his left. (tchd 9-1 in places)
Cavalryman, fifth in the Sheema Classic when last seen, appeared to travel well enough into the race but he was denied a clear run when trying to switch out around 2f out, and was again short of room against the rail late on. He couldn't be considered unlucky - just a bit better than he showed - and has yet to rediscover the form he showed for Andre Fabre last year, but he can be given another chance on a more conventional track, with easier ground also likely to help. He may re-oppose the winner in the Prince of Wales's Stakes at Royal Ascot. (tchd 8-1)
South Easter(IRE) recovered from a stumble on leaving the stalls to race prominently early on, but he gradually lost his position, looking set to finish well out the back, and it was a surprise he was as close as sixth at the line. (tchd 50-1 in a place)
Jukebox Jury(IRE), winner of the Jockey Club Stakes in a first-time visor on his return to Britain, was given a positive ride but found little for pressure. Perhaps the track didn't suit. (op 14-1 tchd 12-1)

2710 INVESTEC CHALLENGE (H'CAP) 1m 2f 18y
3:25 (3:26) (Class 2) 4-Y-O+

£24,924 (£7,464; £3,732; £1,868; £932; £468) **Stalls** Low

Form				RPR
-000	**1**		**Fiery Lad (IRE)**[76] 946 5-9-8 **105** KierenFallon 10 (L M Cumani) *sn pushed along and wl bhd: clsd and in tch 1/2-way: rdn and effrt whn nt clr run wl over 1f out: swtchd rt and drvn over 1f out: str run to ld fnl 100yds: r.o wl* **12/1**	114
0304	**2**	¾	**Ramona Chase**[11] 2402 5-7-12 **81** oh6 (t) NickyMackay 5 (M J Attwater) *hld up towards rr: hmpd 8f out: rdn and gd hdwy ent fnl 2f: drvn to ld ent fnl f: hdd and one pce fnl 100yds* **40/1**	88
01-1	**3**	1	**Thin Red Line (IRE)**[29] 1837 4-8-12 **95** PhillipMakin 3 (M Dods) *in tch in midfield: effrt u.p to chse ldrs 2f out: kpt on same pce u.p fnl f* **11/2**[3]	100+
3-10	**4**	shd	**Red Jade**[48] 1378 5-8-4 **87** PaulHanagan 6 (R A Fahey) *in tch in midfield: effrt u.p 3f out: chsd ldrs and drvn 2f out: styd on one pce fnl f* **14/1**	92
0-31	**5**	1 ¼	**Antinori (IRE)**[99] 706 4-9-2 **102** (v) AhmedAjtebi(3) 2 (Mahmood Al Zarooni) *stdd s: hld up wl off the pce towards rr: effrt on outer over 2f out: chsng ldrs but hanging lft fr over 1f out: no imp ins fnl f* **11/2**[3]	104
3353	**6**	¾	**Tartan Gunna**[23] 2027 4-8-5 **88** JoeFanning 9 (M Johnston) *hld up in midfield: effrt on inner and nt clr run ent fnl 2f: swtchd arnd wkng rival and drvn to chse ldrs over 1f out: wknd jst ins fnl f* **10/3**[1]	89
20-1	**7**	nk	**Kings Destiny**[35] 1665 4-9-10 **107** PhilipRobinson 1 (M A Jarvis) *racd keenly: chsd ldrs: rdn to ld ent fnl 2f: drvn and hdd ent fnl f: wknd ins fnl f* **4/1**[2]	107+
-026	**8**	2 ¾	**Swift Chap**[13] 2322 4-8-1 **84** DavidProbert 7 (B R Millman) *sn pushed up to ld and set gd gallop tl hdd 5f out: rdn to ld again 3f out tl hdd 2f out: wknd over 1f out* **22/1**	79
0606	**9**	hd	**Victoria Sponge (IRE)**[27] 1899 4-8-5 **87** ow1 RoystonFfrench 8 (S C Williams) *rrd as stalls opened and s.i.s: bhd: c stands' side st: rdn and effrt over 2f out: nvr trbld ldrs* **20/1**	82
042-	**10**	1 ¾	**Australia Day (IRE)**[229] 6302 7-8-12 **95** MartinDwyer 11 (P R Webber) *racd keenly: pressed ldr tl led 5f out tl rdn and hdd 3f out: wknd u.p over 2f out* **10/1**	86
0510	**11**	11	**Sand Tiger (IRE)**[23] 2027 4-7-8 **84** MarzenaJeziorek(7) 4 (R A Fahey) *in tch tl lost pl qckly over 2f out: wl bhd fnl f* **33/1**	53
12-0	**12**	22	**Leceile (USA)**[29] 1831 4-8-6 **89** WilliamBuick 12 (W J Haggas) *racd keenly: pressed ldrs tl wknd qckly over 3f out: t.o and eased fnl f* **12/1**	14

2m 5.86s (-3.84) **Going Correction** -0.125s/f (Firm) **12** Ran SP% **119.5**
Speed ratings (Par 109): **110,109,108,108,107 106,106,104,104,102 94,76**
toteswingers:1&2:£64.90, 1&3:£16.70, 2&3:£39.90 CSF £431.29 CT £2925.81 TOTE £13.90: £3.40, £11.40, £2.30; EX 629.70 TRIFECTA Not won..
Owner Samanda Racing **Bred** Ken Carroll **Trained** Newmarket, Suffolk

FOCUS
Another decent handicap that has been won by some smart performers in recent years, including the likes of Vintage Premium and Eccentric. With several who like to force the pace in opposition, they were always likely to go a decent tempo, and it was Swift Chap and Australia Day who disputed the lead for most of the way, but they both eventually blew out and merely set it up for the closers.

NOTEBOOK
Fiery Lad(IRE) had been disappointing so far this year for his new yard, and was without a win since November 2008, but he didn't go off unbacked. Dropped right out here, he almost has to be ridden like a non-trier and the strong pace proved to be right up his street. After making progress passing the 3f pole, he had to be switched out wide in order to get a run, but took off once there and hit the front in the last 50 yards. Having won this so well off a mark of 105, he will probably have to go back up into Pattern company after, but he would still be entitled to plenty of respect at that level now that he has returned to form, provided the race is run to suit. (op 16-1)
Ramona Chase, without a win since his fourth start at two, looks a shadow of the horse who chased home Conduit over C&D at this meeting two years ago, but this was a cracking effort from 6lb 'wrong'. Another held up well off the pace early, he scythed through the field to lead over a furlong out and looked like winning until swamped by the winner in the last 50 yards. He was already due to drop another 3lb before this, but looks sure to be raised again for this effort. (op 50-1 tchd 100-1 in a place)
Thin Red Line(IRE), raised 8lb after making a successful debut for the yard on his return to action at Chester last month, had every chance passing the 2f pole and stayed on well to fare best of those to race closer to the pace. There are more decent handicaps to be won with him. (op 5-1)
Red Jade came off the bridle fully half a mile from, but he kept staying on and was still bang there with every chance a furlong from home. This was a decent effort considering he is 6lb higher than when scoring on his Doncaster reappearance in March, whilst he has shown his very best form on much softer ground. (op 12-1)
Antinori(IRE) looked like playing a part when moving up on the outside 3f from home, but he then started to hang and was making little impression thereafter. He may just have needed this first start since winning off 6lb lower at Meydan in February. (op 7-1)
Tartan Gunna, now back on his last winning mark, had his chance just behind the leaders coming to the last 2f, but was then made to look one paced. (op 7-2 tchd 4-1 in places)
Kings Destiny, raised 7lb for his all-the way success on his reappearance on the Lingfield Polytrack in April, was forced to take a lead this time and travelled enthusiastically until taking over in front 2f from home, but he was swamped before reaching the furlong pole. He was reported to have not handled the ground, but still looks to be on a stiff mark now. Official explanation: jockey said gelding was unsuited by the good (good to firm in places) ground (op 9-2 tchd 5-1)
Victoria Sponge(IRE), unplaced all four starts for her new yard this year, had an eventful race as she almost decapitated her rider when jumping in the air as the stalls opened, giving away ground, and was then brought over to race alone against the stands' rail after turning in, which did her no favours at all.
Australia Day(IRE) Official explanation: jockey said gelding hung right

Leceile(USA), who made all for both of her victories last season, was up there on the outside of the leaders early, but was far too keen and stopped very quickly entering the last 3f. (tchd 11-1)

2711 INVESTEC OAKS (GROUP 1) (FILLIES) 1m 4f 10y
4:05 (4:07) (Class 1) 3-Y-O

£208,118 (£78,892; £39,482; £19,686; £9,861; £4,949) **Stalls** Centre

Form				RPR
30-1	1		**Snow Fairy (IRE)**[16] 2224 3-9-0 107 RyanMoore 15 (E A L Dunlop) *stdd after s: hld up in rr: 14th st: rdn and hdwy but bhd wall of horses 2f out: sn switching lft towards rail: str burst to chal 1f out: led ins fnl f: r.o wl* **9/1**	116
33-1	2D	nk	**Meeznah (USA)**[21] 2092 3-9-0 85 TedDurcan 11 (D R Lanigan) *lw: hld up towards rr: hmpd over 4f out: 11th st: swtchd rt and bmpd rival over 2f out: gd hdwy to chal wl over 1f out: sltly outpcd by wnr ins fnl f: rallied gamely: fin 2nd, nk: subs disq (ACP in sample)* **25/1**	115
4	2	2	**Remember When (IRE)**[12] 2370 3-9-0 110 JMurtagh 4 (A P O'Brien, Ire) *w'like: scope: stdd s: hld up in rr: 12th st: hdwy towards inner over 2f out: swtchd rt and gd hdwy ent fnl 2f: rdn to ld over 1f out: hdd ins fnl f: btn fnl 100yds: fin 3rd, nk & 2l: subs plced 2nd* **8/1**	112
1-10	3	4	**Rumoush (USA)**[33] 1726 3-9-0 107 RichardHills 2 (M P Tregoning) *lw: pushed along after s: in tch in midfield: 7th st: rdn and effrt to chse ldrs whn hmpd over 1f out: sn outpcd by ldrs: kpt on ins fnl f to go 4th towards fin: fin 4th, nk, 2l & 4l, subs plcd 3rd* **13/2**[3]	108+
2-11	4	3/4	**Gertrude Bell**[30] 1820 3-9-0 105 WilliamBuick 14 (J H M Gosden) *chsd ldrs: 3rd st: sn rdn and ev ch: led ent fnl 2f: hdd over 1f out: nt pce of ldrs and beginning to struggle whn hmpd 1f out: lost 4th towards fin: fin 5th, subs plcd 4th* **16/1**	104+
3-41	5	3 3/4	**Akdarena**[23] 2037 3-9-0 113 (vt[1]) KJManning 13 (J S Bolger, Ire) *led: swishing tail early: rdn and hrd pressed over 3f out: hdd ent fnl 2f: wknd u.p over 1f out: fin 6th, plcd 5th* **6/1**[2]	98
1-11	6	2 1/2	**Aviate**[23] 2029 3-9-0 107 TomQueally 1 (H R A Cecil) *hld up wl in tch: 5th st: rdn and edging rt over 2f out: unable qck whn sltly hmpd 2f out: wknd wl over 1f out: fin 7th, plcd 6th* **7/2**[1]	94+
5245	7	nk	**Bikini Babe (IRE)**[23] 2029 3-9-0 97 KierenFallon 12 (M Johnston) *chsd ldrs: rdn and 6th st: struggling whn bmpd by rival over 2f out: drvn and wknd 2f out: fin 8th, plcd 7th* **33/1**	94
1-42	8	1/2	**Timepiece**[27] 1909 3-9-0 105 EddieAhern 10 (H R A Cecil) *lw: hld up towards rr: 9th st: rdn and no prog wl over 2f out: nvr trbld ldrs: fin 9th, plcd 8th* **7/1**	93
10-3	9	2 1/4	**Champagnelifestyle**[30] 1820 3-9-0 102 MichaelHills 8 (B W Hills) *t.k.h: chsd ldrs: hdwy and 4th st: drvn and unable qck over 2f out: wknd wl over 1f out: fin 10th, plcd 9th* **25/1**	89
	10	1	**Awe Inspiring (IRE)**[35] 1680 3-9-0 0 JAHeffernan 5 (A P O'Brien, Ire) *lw: hld up in rr: 13th st: short-lived effrt on inner 3f out: nvr trbld ldrs: fin 11th, plcd 10th* **40/1**	88
-431	11	1 1/4	**Marie De Medici (USA)**[33] 1729 3-9-0 102 JoeFanning 6 (M Johnston) *swtg: chsd ldr: 2nd st: drvn and ev ch wl over 2f out: wknd qckly u.p wl over 1f out: fin 12th, plcd 11th* **40/1**	86
10-0	12	nk	**Cabaret (IRE)**[23] 2029 3-9-0 107 CO'Donoghue 7 (A P O'Brien, Ire) *hld up towards rr: 10th and effrt on outer st: struggling u.p over 2f out: wl btn over 1f out: fin 13th, plcd 12th* **40/1**	85
1-3	13	3 1/4	**Ceilidh House**[27] 1909 3-9-0 98 JimCrowley 3 (R M Beckett) *lw: a bhd: pushed along and nt travelling downhill 5f out: 15th st: lost tch 3f out: fin 14th, plcd 13th* **16/1**	80
1	14	nse	**Sajjhaa**[15] 2255 3-9-0 0 FrankieDettori 9 (M A Jarvis) *hld up in tch in midfield: hdwy and 8th st: sn rdn and no hdwy: wl btn and eased fr over 1f out: fin 15th, plcd 14th* **8/1**	80

2m 35.77s (-3.13) **Going Correction** -0.125s/f (Firm) **15** Ran SP% **124.3**
Speed ratings (Par 110): **105,104,103,100,100 97,96,95,95,94 93,92,92,90,90**
toteswingers:1&2:£42.60, 1&3:£16.30, 2&3:£44.50 CSF £230.28 CT £1878.58 TOTE £12.30: £4.20, £8.50, £3.10; EX 312.10 Trifecta £7758.20 Part won. Pool: £10,484.05 - 0.53 winning units..
Owner Anamoine Limited **Bred** Windflower Overseas Holdings Inc **Trained** Newmarket, Suffolk
■ A second Oaks for Ed Dunlop following on from Ouija Board in 2004, and a first British Classic for Ryan Moore.

FOCUS
This year's Oaks looked a fascinating contest beforehand, with a case to be made for several of the runners, resulting in a wide-open betting heat. Plus there were enough classy-looking fillies in the line up to believe at least one of them could stamp themselves as a really top-notch performer, although it rates a slightly below scratch Oaks overall. While every bit as competitive as anticipated, several of the likely candidates disappointed to varying degrees, and it was quite a rough race, with several horses bumping each other at various stages, and it was muddling, too, with the pace, that had looked genuine early on, appearing to steady at about halfway. The time - 2.35 seconds slower than the earlier Coronation Cup - backs up that view, and three of the first four could be classed as some of the speedier types in the line up. All things considered, the result needs treating with caution, but a few of the beaten runners are likely to do better in due course.

NOTEBOOK
Snow Fairy(IRE) hardly looked a potential Oaks winner earlier in her career (cost just 1,800euros as a yearling, was beaten in a nursery at two, and was an extremely doubtful stayer), and even after winning the race formerly known as the Lupe in quite taking style, she was still hard to fancy seeing as she didn't even hold an entry at the time. However, she was supplemented at a cost of £20,000 and being a tough, experienced filly, who is not short of pace, she was clearly well equipped to deal with how the race unfolded. Held up well out the back for most of the way, she was faced with a wall of horses when trying to pick up early in the straight, and really had to force her way through, displaying a fine attitude in the process. She ended up tight against the far rail in the final furlong, and looked set to win by around 1l or so at one stage, but she became unbalanced near the line, jinking into the rail, and that very nearly let the runner-up back in. She could go some way to showing this wasn't a fluke if allowed her chance in the Nassau Stakes later in the season, for she certainly won't mind dropping back in trip and handles Goodwood extremely well. In the mean time it's likely that she'll supplemented for the Irish Oaks. It has been reported that she is set to stay in training at four. (op 14-1 tchd 16-1 in places)
Meeznah(USA) ◆, a Newmarket maiden winner on her reappearance, who was officially rated just 85, ran a mighty race in defeat for one so inexperienced and looks worth taking from race. According to Ted Durcan she wasn't totally at home around this track, and she didn't get the best of runs around 2f out, but she still produced a sustained effort when in the clear, in the end just missing out. This performance is all the more creditable considering she looks a thorough stayer, yet split two fillies with plenty of natural speed, and she's entitled to come on a lot for the experience. A more galloping course ought to suit better, making her a major player for the Irish Oaks, which is said to be her target. Subs. disqualified having tested positive for ACP. (op 33-1)
Remember When(IRE) ◆, fourth in the Irish Guineas on just her third start, didn't quite see out this longer trip, although she still looked green when narrowly in front over 1f out and it's possible that her lack of experience found her out as much as her lack of stamina. She's actually still a maiden, but there should be plenty more to come and this close relation of Dylan Thomas is a most promising filly. (op 9-1 tchd 15-2)
Rumoush(USA) ◆ didn't seem to cope with the downhill run into the straight and, according to Richard Hills, she then didn't handle the camber in the straight, changing her legs, although the jockey was satisfied that she got the trip. She was also bumped about a bit around 2f out and is undoubtedly better than she showed. (op 6-1 tchd 7-1)
Gertrude Bell, the Cheshire Oaks winner, was always well placed, but she's essentially a stayer and just lacked the pace of some of these. A stronger end-to-end gallop would have suited better. (tchd 20-1)
Akdarena impressed when beating older rivals from the front in a 1m2f Group 3 last time, but this was tougher. With a visor replacing blinkers, she again led but could never get away from her rivals. (op 13-2 tchd 11-2)
Aviate, the Musidora winner, didn't come down the hill very well according to connections and Tom Queally also felt she didn't stay. (op 5-1 tchd 6-1 in places)
Bikini Babe(IRE) was never too far away but basically wasn't good enough. (op 40-1)
Timepiece, just like stablemate Aviate, was said to have failed to come down the hill sufficiently well. We've probably yet to see the best of her. (op 9-1 tchd 10-1in places)
Champagnelifestyle was said to have done well since taking third in the Cheshire Oaks, but she failed to justify her connections' positive comments.
Awe Inspiring(IRE) failed to prove herself up to his grade. (op 50-1)
Marie De Medici(USA) ran well for a long way but ultimately looked a non-stayer.
Ceilidh House was a major disappointment but in fairness it seems she didn't handle the track, and easier ground should suit her better as well. Official explanation: trainer said filly was found to have a temperature (op 14-1)
Sajjhaa, an impressive Sandown maiden winner on her sole previous start, simply failed to handle the track and can certainly be given another chance. Those close to the filly hold her in the highest regard, as is evidenced by Michael Jarvis, who thinks she'll prove well suited by a 1m2f on a galloping track, suggesting she could go straight back into Group 1 company for the Pretty Polly in Ireland. Official explanation: jockey said filly was unsuited by the track (op 6-1)

2712 INVESTEC SURREY STKS (LISTED RACE) 7f
4:50 (4:50) (Class 1) 3-Y-O

£22,708 (£8,608; £4,308; £2,148; £1,076; £540) **Stalls** Low

Form				RPR
116-	1		**Shakespearean (IRE)**[223] 7017 3-9-5 107 (t) FrankieDettori 1 (Saeed Bin Suroor) *lw: mde all: pushed along and styd on strly fr over 1f out: unchal* **11/4**[1]	114
42-1	2	1 3/4	**Yaa Wayl (IRE)**[29] 1834 3-8-13 94 PhilipRobinson 3 (M A Jarvis) *swtg: chsd ldrs: rdn and styd on fr 2f out: disp 2nd 1f out: chsd wnr ins fnl f but no imp* **15/2**[3]	103
1-30	3	3/4	**Mon Cadeaux**[19] 2159 3-8-13 100 JimmyFortune 6 (A M Balding) *t.k.h: in tch: rdn and styd on u.p fr 2f out: disp 2nd over 1f out tl ins fnl f: nvr any imp on wnr: styd on same pce* **10/3**[2]	101
2-01	4	1 1/4	**Kaptain Kirkup (IRE)**[23] 2028 3-8-13 102 PhillipMakin 2 (M Dods) *chsd wnr: rdn and no imp fr 2f out: wknd fnl f* **11/4**[1]	98
1-66	5	1 1/2	**Lucky General (IRE)**[11] 2400 3-8-13 112 RichardHughes 4 (R Hannon) *hld up towards rr but in tch: pushed along over 2f out: styd on same pce fr over 1f out and nvr in contention* **8/1**	94
1-46	6	1/2	**Layla's Hero (IRE)**[6] 2537 3-9-3 104 JamieSpencer 5 (D M Simcock) *pushed along fr s and nvr really travelling: mod prog fnl f* **12/1**	96+
-145	7	1 1/2	**Clairvoyance (IRE)**[27] 1899 3-8-8 89 NickyMackay 8 (J H M Gosden) *lw: t.k.h in tch: swtchd rt rdn 2f out: no imp and sn wknd* **16/1**	83+
54-1	8	3 1/4	**Curtains**[45] 1436 3-8-8 93 TomQueally 7 (S Dow) *swtg: hld up towards rr but in tch: hdwy towards outside over 2f out: nvr rchd ldrs: sn btn* **33/1**	74

1m 21.65s (-1.65) **Going Correction** -0.125s/f (Firm) **8** Ran SP% **115.8**
Speed ratings (Par 107): **104,102,101,99,98 97,95,92**
toteswingers:1&2:£3.90, 1&3:£2.50, 2&3:£5.80 CSF £24.49 TOTE £3.20: £1.50, £2.00, £1.40; EX 20.60 Trifecta £75.10 Pool: £1,041.24 - 10.25 winning units..
Owner Godolphin **Bred** Mrs H Owen **Trained** Newmarket, Suffolk

FOCUS
An interesting Listed event run in a time 0-75sec slower than the following handicap. Few got into it. The winner enjoyed the run of the race but produced a smart effort.

NOTEBOOK
Shakespearean(IRE) was a smart juvenile for Mark Johnston in 2009 and was last seen finishing sixth behind St Nicholas Abbey in the Racing Post Trophy. Making his debut for Godolphin, there was the danger that this big colt wouldn't be suited by the undulations of Epsom, but Dettori fired him straight into the lead from the inside draw and his supporters never had many moments of concern. He looks ready for a step back up into Group company now and connections will consider aiming him at either the St James's Palace or the Jersey Stakes. (op 10-3 tchd 5-2 and 7-2 in places)
Yaa Wayl(IRE), narrow winner of a Chester handicap off 88 on his return last month, ran a blinder as he had plenty to find at these weights and pulled like a train in the early stages, yet still battled on to snatch second. There are more decent prizes to be won with him. (op 7-1)
Mon Cadeaux, down to a more realistic level after finishing well beaten in the French 2,000 Guineas, also deserves credit for hanging in there for as long as he did as he was all over the place coming down the hill. He can win at this sort of level. (op 9-2)
Kaptain Kirkup(IRE), up in class after winning a York handicap off 94 last month from which the third and fourth have won since, was always in a good position behind the winner, but he could never get to him and was run out of the places inside the last furlong. (tchd 3-1 in places)
Lucky General(IRE), best in at the weights on the strength of his success in the Goffs Million Sprint at The Curragh last September, met a bit of trouble at the top of the hill, but only made limited progress from off the pace and his stamina for this trip remains unproven. (op 13-2)
Layla's Hero(IRE), a dual Listed winner at two, was disappointing at Haydock on his debut for the yard six days earlier. Trying this trip for the first time, he was knocked back to last after getting squeezed out exiting the gates and is worth another chance. (tchd 11-1)
Clairvoyance(IRE), unplaced on her turf debut at Ascot last month and dropped to 7f for the first time, had plenty to do at the weights and found it all happening too quickly.
Curtains, who made hard work of landing odds of 1-5 in a Brighton maiden on her return from a lengthy absence in April, was trying beyond 6f for the first time and didn't get home after seeing plenty of daylight on the outside of the field. (op 28-1)

2713 INVESTEC OPPORTUNITY STKS (H'CAP) 7f
5:25 (5:26) (Class 2) (0-100,99) 3-Y-O

£12,462 (£3,732; £1,866; £934; £466; £234) **Stalls** Low

Form				RPR
24-1	1		**Cansili Star**[28] 1872 3-8-9 **85** PhilipRobinson 9 (M A Jarvis) *lw: in tch: gd hdwy fr 2f out: str chal ins fnl f: led fnl 30yds: all out* **7/1**[3]	95
5-32	2	nk	**Treadwell (IRE)**[23] 2028 3-9-4 **94** FergusSweeney 5 (J A Osborne) *chsd ldrs: led ins fnl 2f: sn hrd drvn: hdd and outpcd fnl 30yds* **7/1**[3]	103
-311	3	2	**Kajima**[27] 1934 3-8-6 **82** ow1 RichardHughes 7 (R Hannon) *lw: trckd ldrs: rdn over 1f out: outpcd by ldng duo ins fnl f and readily hld whn hung rt nr fin* **10/3**[2]	86

13-3 **4** *nk* **Citrus Star (USA)**[34] 1687 3-9-9 **99** .... AlanMunro 4 103+
(C F Wall) *lw: slowly away and wl bhd over 3f out: hdwy ins fnl 2f: n.m.r over 1f out: styd on wl thrght fnl f: gng on cl home* **12/1**

-505 **5** *shd* **Nosedive**[27] 1917 3-9-2 **92** .... JMurtagh 8 95
(W J Haggas) *in rr: rdn and hdwy over 2f out: styd on wl fnl f but nvr gng pce to rch ldrs* **14/1**

1-30 **6** *½* **Gramercy (IRE)**[33] 1732 3-8-9 **85** .... JamieSpencer 2 87+
(M L W Bell) *in rr: rdn and hdwy 2f out but sn hanging lft: kpt on fnl f but nvr a threat* **7/1**[3]

3154 **7** *3¼* **Duellist**[24] 2002 3-8-8 **84** .... JoeFanning 1 78+
(M Johnston) *chsd ldrs: rdn over 2f out: sn unbalanced on camber and hung lft: wknd wl over 1f out* **10/1**

2-11 **8** *2¼* **Kingston Acacia**[24] 2005 3-8-4 **80** oh4 ....(v) DavidProbert 10 68
(A M Balding) *t.k.h: chsd ldr tl ld wl over 2f out: hdd ins fnl 2f: wknd sn after* **16/1**

31-0 **9** *3½* **Whistleinthewind (IRE)**[20] 2117 3-8-7 **83** .... PaulHanagan 3 63
(G L Moore) *a in rr* **20/1**

1032 **10** *6* **Al Farahidi (USA)**[13] 2324 3-9-4 **94** ....(b) FrankieDettori 6 59
(M Johnston) *led tl hdd wl over 2f out: sn btn* **3/1**[1]

1m 20.9s (-2.40) **Going Correction** -0.125s/f (Firm) **10** Ran SP% **119.7**
Speed ratings (Par 105): **108,107,105,105,104 104,100,98,94,87**
toteswingers:1&2:£9.10, 1&3:£5.20, 2&3:£6.60 CSF £56.84 CT £196.34 TOTE £7.00: £2.80, £2.40, £1.80; EX 83.90 Trifecta £354.80 Pool: £1,414.74 - 2.95 winning units. Place 6 £206.32; Place 5 £102.36.
Owner A D Spence **Bred** Hascombe And Valiant Studs **Trained** Newmarket, Suffolk

FOCUS
A decent 3-y-o handicap and, with several that had been successful from the front before in opposition, a solid pace was always likely. They were soon well spread out and the winning time was 0.75 seconds faster than the Listed event. Good, solid handicap form.

NOTEBOOK
Cansili Star, who made the most of a track bias when making all to beat a subsequent winner in a Lingfield maiden on his reappearance last month, again showed his liking for a downhill track. He crept into the race gradually and then stayed on to hit the front well inside the last furlong. Now that he has got the winning habit, he may well be capable of more and, given his liking for a switchback track, he could be worth keeping in mind for something at Glorious Goodwood. (op 6-1 tchd 8-1 in places)
Treadwell(IRE), just ahead of two subsequent winners when runner-up to Kaptain Kirkup (fourth in the preceding Listed race) at York last month, was 3lb well in compared to his new mark. He travelled powerfully behind the leaders before taking over 1f from home, but couldn't resist the winner's late challenge despite keeping on gamely. He is now likely to be aimed at the Buckingham Palace. (op 17-2 tchd 9-1)
Kajima, bidding for a hat-trick off a 7lb higher mark, including the overweight, was never too far away and didn't have much room to play with on a couple of occasions in the home straight, including inside the last furlong, but he still looked third-best on merit. (op 4-1)
Citrus Star(USA), who didn't seem to get home over this trip when third of five in a Doncaster conditions event on his reappearance last month, ran a remarkable race as he missed the break and had an enormous amount of ground to make up turning in, but he finished in great style to snatch fourth and is worth keeping in mind. (op 11-1)
Nosedive, still without a win since his racecourse debut, albeit often in the face of some stiff tasks, stayed on from the middle of the field over the last 2f despite hanging down the camber in the home straight. He will be suited by a return to a more conventional track. (op 12-1 tchd 16-1 in places)
Gramercy(IRE), who pulled his chance away at Salisbury last time, following an encouraging return in a hot Newbury handicap, gave himself plenty to do and though he made up some ground when switched out wide, he could never get to the leaders. (op 8-1 tchd 17-2)
Duellist, back down to probably his optimum trip, but encountering quick ground for the first time, didn't handle the track at all well and found little once off the bridle. (op 12-1)
Kingston Acacia, 4lb 'wrong' and therefore 11lb higher in her bid for a hat-trick, was soon serving it up to the leader from the widest stall and took over in front passing the 2f pole, but whilst her earlier efforts may have contributed to the favourite's demise, it also meant that she had run her race once headed over 1f from home.
Whistleinthewind(IRE), well beaten over 1m2f on his Newbury return, was trying a trip this short for the first time, but he barely went a yard.
Al Farahidi(USA), who finished clear of the rest when runner-up to Balducci in the Betfred Silver Bowl last month when sporting first-time blinkers, was put up 9lb for that and he was soon setting a decent pace and racing enthusiastically. However, he put up little resistance when headed over 2f out and was eventually eased right off. He is much better than this. (tchd 11-4 and 10-3)
T/Jkpt: Not won. T/Plt: £502.90 to a £1 stake. Pool:£238,313.08 - 345.87 winning tickets T/Qpdt: £69.90 to a £1 stake. Pool:£11,412.63 - 120.65 winning tickets ST

2591 GOODWOOD (R-H)

Friday, June 4

OFFICIAL GOING: Straight course - good; round course - good to firm (watered; straight 8.5, round 9.0)
First 2f of mile course dolled out 5yds. Rail from 5f dolled out 6yds increasing distances by about 12yds.
Wind: light, across Weather: warm and sunny

2714 GOODWOOD FARM SHOP STKS (H'CAP) (FOR AMATEUR RIDERS) 1m 1f
6:15 (6:16) (Class 5) (0-70,70) 4-Y-O+ **£2,498** (£774; £387; £193) **Stalls** High

Form RPR

06-2 **1** **Megalala (IRE)**[4] 2597 9-9-12 **61** ow3 .... MrJackSalmon(7) 9 70
(J J Bridger) *led for 2f: chsd ldr after tl rdn to ld again 2f out: styd on gamely fnl f* **5/1**[2]

0340 **2** *1¼* **Fifty Cents**[8] 2477 6-10-1 **62** .... MrCMartin(5) 14 68
(M F Harris) *dwlt: sn rcvrd and chsng ldrs: rdn and n.m.r on inner 2f out: swtchd arnd wkng rival over 1f out: r.o wl to go 2nd nr fin* **7/1**[3]

0-00 **3** *hd* **King Columbo (IRE)**[24] 2009 5-10-11 **67** .... MissGAndrews 10 73
(Miss J Feilden) *chsd ldrs: rdn to chal 2f out: ev ch after tl no ex and btn fnl 100yds* **9/1**

0300 **4** *¾* **Ivory Lace**[36] 1634 9-11-0 **70** .... MrSWalker 11 74+
(S Woodman) *hld up wl off pce towards rr: effrt and rdn wl over 2f out: r.o wl ins fnl f: nt rch ldrs* **12/1**

00-4 **5** *hd* **Django Reinhardt**[13] 2337 4-9-6 **51** .... MrDavidTurner(3) 4 54
(Miss S L Davison) *hld up off the pce towards rr: gd hdwy towards inner ent fnl 2f: kpt on same pce unde press ins fnl f* **14/1**

-006 **6** *1* **Gallego**[4] 2602 8-10-4 **63** .... MrMPrice(3) 7 64+
(R J Price) *stdd s: hld up wl bhd: c wd over 3f out: styd on strly fnl f: nt rch ldrs* **17/2**

0-00 **7** *hd* **Northern Spy (USA)**[13] 2337 6-10-2 **65** .... MrJCoffill-Brown(7) 3 66
(S Dow) *racd off the pce in midfield: rdn and hung lft fr over 3f out: styd on fnl f: nt rch ldrs* **20/1**

4145 **8** *1½* **Charlie Smirke (USA)**[21] 2080 4-10-13 **69** .... MrJoshuaMoore 8 67
(G L Moore) *hld up in midfield: effrt to chse ldrs whn sltly hmpd ent fnl 2f: wknd ent fnl f* **9/2**[1]

10-0 **9** *shd* **Masterofceremonies**[7] 2492 7-10-1 **64** ....(p) MissALMurphy(7) 12 61
(W M Brisbourne) *racd off the pce in midfield: rdn and hdwy 3f out: no imp ent fnl frlong* **16/1**

0400 **10** *10* **Whodunit (UAE)**[28] 1883 6-10-1 **62** ....(b) MrJMQuinlan(5) 13 37
(P W Hiatt) *chsd ldr tl led 6f out tl 2f out: sn wknd* **25/1**

-600 **11** *1* **Chadwell Spring (IRE)**[28] 1875 4-10-6 **65** .... MrRBirkett(3) 15 38
(Miss J Feilden) *chsd ldrs tl wknd u.p wl over 1f out* **11/1**

40/5 **12** *1½* **Shakedown**[13] 2337 5-10-2 **58** .... MissSBrotherton 2 28
(Ian Williams) *stdd after s: hld up towards rr: effrt and edgd rt over 2f out: wknd wl over 1f out* **9/1**

0-00 **13** *10* **Mississippian (IRE)**[7] 2492 6-9-6 **55** ....(t) MissDLenge(7) 6 3
(Mrs D J Sanderson) *s.i.s: a bhd* **40/1**

0/6- **14** *7* **Persian Buddy**[485] 397 4-10-4 **67** .... MrDanielBurchell(7) 5 —
(Jamie Poulton) *wnt lft s and v.s.a: a in rr* **40/1**

1m 58.25s (1.95) **Going Correction** -0.025s/f (Good) **14** Ran SP% **119.9**
Speed ratings (Par 103): **90,88,88,88,87 86,86,85,85,76 75,74,65,59**
toteswingers:1&2:£10.50, 1&3:£20.00, 2&3:£14.60 CSF £38.14 CT £309.29 TOTE £5.70: £2.20, £2.60, £3.70; EX 53.10.
Owner Tommy Ware **Bred** Joseph Gallagher **Trained** Liphook, Hants
■ Stewards' Enquiry : Miss D Lenge three-day ban: used whip when out of contention.
Mr R Birkett caution: used whip when out of contention.
Mr Daniel Burchell two-day ban: used whip when out of contention (tbn)

FOCUS
A typically moderate handicap for amateur riders. There was a sound pace on and the form looks fair enough.
King Columbo(IRE) Official explanation: vet said gelding had been struck into and lost a shoe

2715 NEW FORESTS EUROPEAN BREEDERS' FUND MAIDEN STKS 6f
6:45 (6:45) (Class 5) 2-Y-O **£3,885** (£1,156; £577; £288) **Stalls** Low

Form RPR

2 **1** **Neebras (IRE)**[21] 2078 2-9-3 0 .... FrankieDettori 5 93+
(Mahmood Al Zarooni) *stdd s and swtchd rt to r towards centre: hld up towards rr: hdwy 1/2-way: rdn to ld 1f out: r.o strly and sn clr: easily* **1/2**[1]

5 **2** *4* **Arabian Star (IRE)**[7] 2493 2-9-3 0 .... AlanMunro 8 79
(M R Channon) *hld up in tch in midfield: hdwy over 2f out: rdn to ld over 1f out: hdd 1f out: sn outpcd by wnr but kpt on for clr 2nd* **9/1**[3]

3 *2½* **Spokesperson (USA)** 2-9-0 0 .... AhmedAjtebi(3) 4 72
(Mahmood Al Zarooni) *hld up towards rr: rdn along and effrt over 2f out: swtchd lft over 1f out: kpt on to go 3rd ins fnl f: no ch w wnr* **25/1**

4 *1¾* **Frankish Dynasty (GER)** 2-9-3 0 .... KierenFallon 3 66
(P F I Cole) *chsd ldrs: ev ch and rdn 2f out: wknd jst over 1f out* **16/1**

5 *nk* **Cadeaux Pearl** 2-9-3 0 .... RichardHughes 6 65+
(R Hannon) *s.i.s: hld up in rr: hdwy 1/2-way: rdn and no prog over 1f out* **3/1**[2]

0 **6** *9* **Reachforthebucks**[17] 2216 2-9-3 0 ....(b[1]) DaneO'Neill 1 42
(G D Blake) *led tl rdn and hdd over 1f out: wknd qckly: wl btn and eased ins fnl f* **50/1**

00 **7** *1* **Salvationist**[11] 2384 2-9-3 0 .... JimmyFortune 7 35
(J L Dunlop) *a bhd and sn pushed along: lost tch 1/2-way: wl bhd fnl 2f* **50/1**

5 **8** *1¼* **Oliver's Gold**[13] 2319 2-9-3 0 .... PhilipRobinson 2 32
(Mrs A J Perrett) *t.k.h: chsd ldrs tl struggling u.p 1/2-way: wl bhd fnl 2f* **12/1**

1m 12.04s (-0.16) **Going Correction** -0.025s/f (Good) **8** Ran SP% **123.0**
Speed ratings (Par 93): **100,94,91,89,88 76,75,73**
toteswingers:1&2:£2.50, 1&3:£3.90, 2&3:£8.90 CSF £7.28 TOTE £1.40: £1.02, £2.80, £4.90; EX 7.70.
Owner Godolphin **Bred** Michael E Wates **Trained** Newmarket, Suffolk

FOCUS
This often works out to be a good juvenile maiden and the easy winner could be an Ascot 2-y-o.

NOTEBOOK
Neebras(IRE) opened his account at the second time of asking with a comfortable success and handed a compliment to Coventry hopeful Strong Suit in the process. He had pulled clear of the rest when second to that rival on debut at Newbury and had been snapped up by Godolphin since then. He wasn't helped by having to race widest of all throughout and rates value for even further. A rise in class now awaits him and a stiffer test ought to suit before the season's end. (op 4-5)
Arabian Star(IRE) stepped up on the level of his debut form and should be capable of finding an ordinary maiden. He should also relish racing over another furlong in due course. (op 8-1)
Spokesperson(USA), the winner's stable companion, turned in a pleasing enough debut effort and is sure to know more next time. This $125,000 purchase is another that will come into his own over further.
Frankish Dynasty(GER) knew his job and showed enough to think he will be sharper for the initial experience. (op 22-1)
Cadeaux Pearl, whose trainer was chasing a hat-trick in this race, attracted good support for his racecourse debut. He ran distinctly green, however, after missing the kick and was never a serious player. It won't be surprising to see him get plenty closer next time out. (op 5-2 tchd 9-4)
Oliver's Gold Official explanation: jockey said colt jumped awkwardly and hung right

2716 WHEB GROUP STKS (REGISTERED AS THE TAPSTER STAKES) (LISTED RACE) 1m 4f
7:20 (7:20) (Class 1) 4-Y-O+ **£23,704** (£8,964; £4,480; £2,240) **Stalls** Low

Form RPR

131- **1** **Holberg (UAE)**[350] 3090 4-9-0 113 .... FrankieDettori 1 117+
(Saeed Bin Suroor) *mde all: pushed clr over 1f out: styd on strly: easily* **3/1**[1]

213- **2** *6* **Manighar (FR)**[222] 7047 4-9-9 114 .... KierenFallon 6 115+
(L M Cumani) *stdd s: t.k.h and hld up in midfield: rdn and effrt ent fnl 2f: no ch w wnr fnl f: kpt on u.p to go 2nd fnl 75yds* **7/1**

01-1 **3** *1* **Opinion Poll (IRE)**[58] 1176 4-9-3 109 .... PhilipRobinson 2 107
(M A Jarvis) *chsd ldrs: rdn over 2f out: chsd clr wnr and edging rt u.p over 1f out: no imp and wl btn ins fnl f: lost 2nd fnl 75yds* **10/3**[2]

15-1 **4** *1½* **King Of Wands**[41] 1529 4-9-0 105 .... WilliamBuick 3 102
(J H M Gosden) *hld up in tch towards rr: hdwy to chse ldrs after 3f: wnt 2nd over 5f out: rdn and unable qck wl over 2f out: no ch w wnr fnl f: wknd and n.m.r wl ins fnl f* **7/2**[3]

/44- **5** *3¼* **Blue Monday**[293] 5059 9-9-0 115 .... SteveDrowne 8 96
(R Charlton) *stdd after s: hld up in last pair: effrt and rdn wl over 2f out: outpcd and btn wl over 1f out* **8/1**

10-0 **6** *3¼* **Red Merlin (IRE)**[20] 2116 5-9-0 103 ....(v) AdamKirby 4 91
(C G Cox) *stdd s: t.k.h: hld up in last pair: rdn and no prog wl over 2f out: wl btn fnl 2f* **14/1**

00-5 **7** ¾ **Snoqualmie Girl (IRE)**[28] 1859 4-8-12 102 DaneO'Neill 9 88
(D R C Elsworth) *t.k.h: hld up in tch towards rr: rdn and no rspnse 3f out: wl btn fnl 2f* **20/1**

P054 **8** 7 **Halicarnassus (IRE)**[12] 2369 6-9-9 110 AlanMunro 10 88
(M R Channon) *chsd wnr tl over 5f out: wknd u.p wl over 3f out: wl bhd fr over 2f out* **12/1**

2m 34.62s (-3.78) **Going Correction** -0.025s/f (Good) 8 Ran SP% **113.0**
Speed ratings (Par 111): **111,107,106,105,103 101,100,95**
toteswingers:1&2:£2.20, 1&3:£2.00, 2&3:£4.70 CSF £23.81 TOTE £4.50: £2.10, £2.00, £1.10; EX 12.00.
Owner Godolphin **Bred** Darley **Trained** Newmarket, Suffolk

FOCUS
It's a shame Duncan was withdrawn, but this was still a strong Listed contest. It was another front-running master-class from Dettori.

NOTEBOOK
Holberg(UAE) ◆ was having his first outing since landing the Queen's Vase at Royal Ascot nearly a year earlier, and his new connections were expecting him to improve a good deal for the run. If that is to be the case they have a very exciting prospect on their hands, as he has always looked a horse that would excel as he matured and he is clearly not just a stayer. (op 4-1)
Manighar(FR) ◆ was having his first outing in Britain for new connections and, easy to back, was not that surprisingly doing his best work towards the finish. Considering he had a penalty here he looks a decent acquisition and is sure to improve a deal for the run. (op 5-1)
Opinion Poll(IRE) created quite an impression on his return at Nottingham in April and proved popular despite dropping in trip. He moved well through the race, but lacked the speed to get really serious and clearly wants a stiffer test. This ground was also probably quick enough for him. (op 3-1)
King Of Wands ran close to his previous Ripon form despite not looking in love with the track. He too also wants a stiffer test ideally. (op 4-1 tchd 3-1)
Blue Monday was never in the hunt from out the back, but should be all the better for this seasonal return. Official explanation: vet said gelding finished lame left-hind (op 9-1 tchd 10-1)

2717 SOIL ASSOCIATION CLASSIFIED STKS 1m 3f
7:50 (7:52) (Class 5) 3-Y-O £3,238 (£963; £481; £240) Stalls Low

Form RPR

46-2 **1** **Roxy Flyer (IRE)**[22] 2051 3-9-0 74 JimmyQuinn 7 80
(Mrs A J Perrett) *t.k.h: hld up wl in tch: nt clr run over 2f out: hdwy between horses and drvn 1f out: edgd lft u.p but r.o strly to ld fnl 75yds: kpt edging lft but hld on wl nr fin* **9/2**[2]

0-00 **2** ½ **Meglio Ancora**[21] 2079 3-9-0 74 KierenFallon 4 79
(J G Portman) *stdd after s: hld up in rr: nt clr run on inner and switching rt to outer fr 2f out: drvn and str run to chal fnl 75ds: hld nr fin* **9/1**

03-1 **3** 1¾ **Eltheeb**[34] 1696 3-9-0 73 RichardHills 1 76
(J L Dunlop) *t.k.h: in tch: chsd ldr 7f out: led over 2f out: drvn over 1f out: hdd fnl 75yds: no ex* **9/4**[1]

-140 **4** 2¾ **Midfielder (USA)**[15] 2254 3-9-0 75 (p) WilliamBuick 2 71
(J H M Gosden) *s.i.s and pushed along early: in tch in last trio: hdwy to chse ldrs over 4f out: rdn to chse ldr ent fnl 2f: one pce and looked btn whn carried lft jst ins fnl f: wknd fnl 100yds* **12/1**

-302 **5** shd **First Fandango**[18] 2168 3-9-0 75 MichaelHills 8 71
(J W Hills) *t.k.h: chsd ldr for 1f: styd in tch: rdn and effrt ent fnl 2f: keeping on same pce whn n.m.r jst ins fnl f* **13/2**[3]

53-3 **6** 1¼ **Hill Tribe**[37] 1620 3-9-0 74 JimmyFortune 5 68
(J R Gask) *led tl 9f out: styd chsng ldrs: effrt u.p and switching to inner wl over 1f out: wknd ent fnl f* **15/2**

03-0 **7** 3½ **Knockdolian (IRE)**[48] 1387 3-9-0 72 SteveDrowne 6 62
(R Charlton) *stdd after s: hld up in last pair: rdn and no hdwy wl over 2f out: nvr threatened ldrs* **13/2**[3]

20-4 **8** 16 **Banana Republic (IRE)**[20] 2115 3-9-0 72 RichardHughes 3 33
(P F I Cole) *chsd ldr after 1f: led 9f out tl over 2f out: wknd u.p wl over 1f out: wl bhd and eased ins fnl f* **8/1**

2m 26.03s (-0.47) **Going Correction** -0.025s/f (Good) 8 Ran SP% **116.2**
Speed ratings (Par 99): **100,99,98,96,96 95,92,81**
toteswingers:1&2:£5.10, 1&3:£1.40, 2&3:£3.70 CSF £44.70 TOTE £4.80: £1.20, £3.60, £1.40; EX 55.80.
Owner Mr & Mrs F Cotton Mrs S Conway **Bred** Narvick International **Trained** Pulborough, W Sussex
■ Stewards' Enquiry : Jimmy Quinn one-day ban: careless riding (Jun 20)

FOCUS
A fair 3-y-o classified stakes, run at an average sort of pace.
Meglio Ancora Official explanation: jockey said gelding hung right
Hill Tribe Official explanation: jockey said filly hung left throughout

2718 ORGANIC RESEARCH CENTRE MAIDEN FILLIES' STKS 1m
8:25 (8:28) (Class 5) 3-Y-O+ £3,238 (£963; £481; £240) Stalls High

Form RPR

1 **Bougainvilia (IRE)** 3-8-12 0 SteveDrowne 12 80+
(R Hannon) *v.s.a: bhd: hdwy 5f out: swtchd lft and gd hdwy to chse ldrs over 1f out: clipped heels and hmpd jst over 1f out: swtchd lft and str run jst ins fnl f: led last stride* **25/1**

5- **2** shd **Mirror Lake**[218] 7135 3-8-12 0 TomQueally 9 77
(Mrs A J Perrett) *in tch: rdn and effrt over 2f out: drvn and ev ch over 1f out: led jst ins fnl f: r.o wl: hdd last stride* **9/2**[2]

0 **3** 1½ **Ishraaqat**[37] 1621 3-8-12 0 TadhgO'Shea 16 73
(M P Tregoning) *chsd ldrs: rdn over 2f out: pressing ldrs ent fnl f: kpt on same pce fnl 150yds* **8/1**[3]

5-03 **4** ½ **Madhaaq (IRE)**[29] 1844 3-8-12 0 RichardHills 6 72
(J L Dunlop) *stdd s: hld in last trio: plld out and hdwy over 2f out: drvn to chse ldrs over 1f out: no ex and one pce fnl 150yds* **10/3**[1]

0- **5** ½ **Romancea (USA)**[322] 4055 3-8-12 0 DaneO'Neill 4 71
(E F Vaughan) *stdd s: hld up wl in rr: hdwy towards inner jst over 2f out: switching lft to outer over 1f out: gd hdwy to chse ldrs 1f out: no ex fnl 150yds* **50/1**

0-43 **6** nse **Easy Terms**[46] 1431 3-8-10 72 ow1 JamesMillman(3) 10 74+
(B R Millman) *in tch in midfield: nt clr run on inner and switching lft over 1f out: nt clr run again and switching bk rt jst ins fnl f: kpt on wl fnl 75yds: nt rch ldrs* **16/1**

64 **7** 1¾ **Sooraah**[8] 2473 3-8-12 0 KierenFallon 2 67
(W J Haggas) *chsd ldrs: rdn and ev ch ent fnl 2f: led over 1f out tl hdd jst ins fnl f: wknd fnl 150yds* **8/1**[3]

0 **8** 6 **Anacopa (USA)**[11] 2401 3-8-9 0 AhmedAjtebi(3) 8 53
(Mahmood Al Zarooni) *led: hrd pressed and rdn over 2f out: hdd over 1f out: wknd qckly fnl f* **10/1**

0- **9** 1¾ **Shianda**[216] 7183 3-8-12 0 DavidProbert 5 49
(G L Moore) *in tch in midfield: rdn and effrt on outer 3f out: wknd ent fnl 2f* **66/1**

10 2¼ **Annie Bonita** 3-8-12 0 EddieCreighton 7 44
(Mrs A J Perrett) *s.i.s: sn in tch in midfield: rdn and unable qck over 2f out: btn whn sltly hmpd over 1f out* **66/1**

43- **11** 1 **Serious Drinking (USA)**[235] 6741 4-9-9 0 AdamKirby 3 45
(W R Swinburn) *stdd s t.k.h: hld up in rr: effrt whn hmpd over 2f out: n.d* **10/1**

0-24 **12** 2½ **Mavalenta (IRE)**[15] 2255 3-8-12 74 MichaelHills 14 36
(J W Hills) *chsd ldr: rdn to chal wl over 2f out: wknd wl over 1f out: wl btn and eased ins fnl f* **10/1**

00 **13** nk **Ayam Zainah**[18] 2180 3-8-12 0 AlanMunro 11 35
(M R Channon) *chsd ldrs tl wknd u.p 3f out: wl btn over 1f out* **33/1**

05- **14** 5 **Sweet Secret**[223] 7029 3-8-12 0 RichardHughes 1 24
(R Hannon) *a bhd: lost tch 3f out* **10/1**

1m 39.34s (-0.56) **Going Correction** -0.025s/f (Good)
WFA 3 from 4yo 11lb 14 Ran SP% **117.5**
Speed ratings (Par 100): **101,100,99,98,98 98,96,90,88,86 85,83,82,77**
toteswingers:1&2:£16.40, 1&3:£35.30, 2&3:£12.60 CSF £122.48 TOTE £20.90: £5.10, £1.80, £3.60; EX 106.50.
Owner William Durkan **Bred** Cathal Ryan **Trained** East Everleigh, Wilts

FOCUS
An average fillies' maiden, run at a fair pace.
Serious Drinking(USA) Official explanation: jockey said filly ran too free early stages

2719 FRANKIE FILLIES AND FROCKS ON 11 JUNE H'CAP 6f
8:55 (8:58) (Class 5) (0-70,67) 4-Y-O+ £3,238 (£963; £481; £240) Stalls Low

Form RPR

0-10 **1** **Averoo**[8] 2462 5-9-7 67 (p) AdamKirby 3 78
(M D Squance) *hld up in rr of main gp: stl plenty to do and switching rt to outer wl over 1f out: hdwy and drvn over 1f out: edgd lft u.p 1f out: led ins fnl f: r.o wl* **12/1**

5002 **2** 1½ **Peopleton Brook**[20] 2123 8-8-12 58 (t) KierenFallon 14 64
(B G Powell) *towards rr: hdwy on outer 2f out: drvn to press wnr ins fnl f: no ex and btn fnl 75yds* **4/1**[1]

0-00 **3** 1¾ **Rio Royale (IRE)**[15] 2246 4-9-0 60 (p) EddieCreighton 6 60
(Mrs A J Perrett) *chsd ldr: rdn and ev ch over 2f out: drvn and outpcd over 1f out: rallied u.p ins fnl f: kpt on* **25/1**

3426 **4** ½ **Captain Kallis (IRE)**[23] 2021 4-8-13 59 AlanMunro 10 58
(D J S Ffrench Davis) *chsd ldrs: led ent fnl 2f: sn rdn: hdd ins fnl f: one pce fnl 150yds* **8/1**

6-00 **5** hd **Spiritual Art**[133] 259 4-9-0 67 HarryBentley(7) 9 65
(L A Dace) *in tch: nt clr and switching rt whn hmpd over 1f out: swtchd rt again 1f out: kpt on ins fnl f: unable to rch ldrs* **16/1**

/0-3 **6** 1¼ **Pragmatist**[15] 2246 6-8-13 62 JamesMillman(3) 1 56
(B R Millman) *led: rdn over 2f out: hdd 2f out: keeping on same pce u.p whn edgd lft and bdly bmpd 1f out: no threat to ldrs after* **9/2**[2]

0402 **7** nk **Highland Harvest**[8] 2458 6-9-5 65 IanMongan 8 58
(Jamie Poulton) *in tch in midfield: swtchd rt and effrt ent fnl 2f: no imp and btn 1f out* **9/1**

0034 **8** nk **The Wee Chief (IRE)**[15] 2246 4-9-5 65 DaneO'Neill 4 57+
(J C Fox) *s.i.s: hld up in tch: effrt but nvr much room against stands' rail over 1f out: rdn and barging match w rival 1f out: nvr threatened ldrs* **11/2**[3]

5003 **9** ½ **Commandingpresence (USA)**[16] 2229 4-8-2 48 oh2 DavidProbert 7 39
(J J Bridger) *chsd ldrs: rdn over 2f out: unable qck and nt clr run wl over 1f out: one pce and wl hld fnl f* **16/1**

345- **10** nse **Forest Dane**[155] 7890 10-8-8 59 JohnFahy(5) 12 49
(Mrs N Smith) *hld up wl in tch: pushed along and effrt 2f out: rdn and nt qckning whn carried lft ent fnl f: wknd fnl f* **12/1**

0050 **11** 21 **Shadow Bay (IRE)**[18] 2178 4-8-4 50 (p) TadhgO'Shea 15 —
(Miss Z C Davison) *sn outpcd in rr: t.o fnl 2f* **12/1**

6-56 **12** 22 **Hellbender (IRE)**[107] 580 4-9-5 65 RichardHughes 13 —
(S Kirk) *sn outpcd in rr: t.o fr 1/2-way: virtually p.u ins fnl f* **8/1**

1m 12.44s (0.24) **Going Correction** -0.025s/f (Good) 12 Ran SP% **124.5**
Speed ratings (Par 103): **97,95,92,92,91 90,89,89,88,88 60,31**
toteswingers:1&2:£30.60, 1&3:£151.30, 2&3:£9.80 CSF £62.55 CT £1239.87 TOTE £16.60: £5.20, £2.30, £8.20; EX 76.90 Place 6 £75.75; Place 5 £25.01.
Owner Miss K Squance **Bred** Mrs H Johnson Houghton & Mrs R F Johnson Hought **Trained** Newmarket, Suffolk
■ Stewards' Enquiry : James Millman three-day ban: careless riding (Jun 20-22)

FOCUS
A competitive sprint for the grade.
Highland Harvest Official explanation: jockey said gelding was denied a clear run 2 1/2f out
The Wee Chief(IRE) Official explanation: jockey said gelding suffered interference in running
Hellbender(IRE) Official explanation: trainer said gelding was unsuited by the good ground
T/Plt: £75.70 to a £1 stake. Pool:£53,606.69 - 516.83 winning tickets T/Qpdt: £35.70n to a £1 stake. Pool:£3,953.30 - 81.80 winning tickets SP

2473 WOLVERHAMPTON (A.W) (L-H)
Friday, June 4

OFFICIAL GOING: Standard
Wind: Light behind Weather: Sunny

2720 BET EPSOM DERBY - BETDAQ H'CAP (DIV I) 5f 20y(P)
1:30 (1:30) (Class 6) (0-55,61) 3-Y-O+ £1,433 (£423; £211) Stalls Low

Form RPR

00-0 **1** **Pressed For Time (IRE)**[18] 2186 4-8-12 47 (vt[1]) EddieCreighton 7 59
(E J Creighton) *chsd ldr tl led 2f out: rdn out* **14/1**

-001 **2** 2 **Silvanus (IRE)**[4] 2581 5-9-12 61 6ex MickyFenton 6 66
(P T Midgley) *a.p: rdn to chse wnr over 1f out: hung lft ins fnl f: styd on* **11/4**[1]

6006 **3** ½ **Albero Di Giuda (IRE)**[18] 2184 5-9-1 55 (bt[1]) DeclanCannon(5) 11 58
(F Sheridan) *s.i.s: sn pushed along: edgd lft wl over 3f out: hmpd sn after: hdwy and hung rt over 1f out: r.o* **12/1**

3566 **4** 1½ **Almaty Express**[17] 2213 8-8-13 51 (b) AshleyHamblett(3) 1 49+
(J R Weymes) *prom: hmpd and lost pl wl over 3f out: r.o ins fnl f: nt rch ldrs* **11/2**[2]

3-03 **5** 1 **Sorrel Point**[18] 2186 7-8-13 53 (vt) SimonPearce(5) 8 47+
(H J Collingridge) *sn bhd: racd wd: r.o ins fnl f: nvr nrr* **7/1**

0630 **6** ½ **Meikle Barfil**[38] 1598 8-8-11 49 (bt) WilliamCarson(3) 5 41
(J M Bradley) *chsd ldrs: rdn over 1f out: no ex fnl f* **14/1**

0000 **7** hd **Blessed Place**[18] 2186 10-8-8 48 BillyCray(5) 3 39
(D J S Ffrench Davis) *led: hdd 2f out: wknd ins fnl f* **16/1**

3000 **8** shd **Tune Up The Band**[18] 2186 6-9-2 51 ow1 GeorgeBaker 10 42
(R J Hodges) *hld up in tch: rdn over 1f out: edgd lft and no ex fnl f* **6/1**[3]

The Form Book, Raceform Ltd, Compton, RG20 6NL

505 9 2 3/4 **Suhayl Star (IRE)**18 2184 6-9-6 55 LukeMorris 13 36
(P Burgoyne) *chsd ldrs tl rdn and wknd over 1f out* 9/1
5034 10 1/2 **Nawaaff**65 1072 5-8-12 47 FrannyNorton 4 26
(M Quinn) *mid-div: sn pushed along: hmpd wl over 3f out: rdn 1/2-way: wknd wl over 1f out* 12/1
0-00 11 23 **Woodcote (IRE)**114 477 8-8-11 46 oh1 (v) AdrianMcCarthy 12 —
(Peter Grayson) *s.i.s: hdwy over 3f out: wknd 1/2-way: t.o* 100/1
63.15 secs (0.85) **Going Correction** +0.20s/f (Slow) 11 Ran SP% 114.4
Speed ratings (Par 101): **101,97,97,94,93 92,91,91,87,86 49**
toteswingers:1&2:£22.20, 1&3:£33.10, 2&3:£4.50 CSF £50.99 CT £487.17 TOTE £19.60: £5.70, £2.00, £2.10; EX 74.50 TRIFECTA Not won..
Owner P Cafferty **Bred** Richard O' Hara **Trained** Wormshill, Kent
FOCUS
This low-grade sprint featured a number of front runners and very few got involved.

2721 BET EPSOM DERBY - BETDAQ H'CAP (DIV II) 5f 20y(P)
2:00 (2:01) (Class 6) (0-55,55) 3-Y-O+ **£1,433** (£423; £211) **Stalls** Low

Form RPR
023- 1 **Mansii**237 6674 5-9-1 50 (t) ShaneKelly 8 59
(P J McBride) *hld up in tch: shkn up and edgd lft ins fnl f: r.o to ld nr fin: readily* 3/1[1]
60-0 2 1/2 **Double Carpet (IRE)**55 1234 7-9-1 55 RossAtkinson(5) 11 62
(G Woodward) *chsd ldrs: rdn 1/2-way: led over 1f out: hdd nr fin* 33/1
-005 3 3/4 **You'relikemefrank**38 1598 4-8-11 46 (p) AndrewElliott 3 50
(J Balding) *hld up: plld hrd: hmpd over 3f out: hung lft and r.o wl ins fnl f: nt rch ldrs* 15/2
4340 4 1 1/4 **Trick Or Two**18 2186 4-9-6 55 (b) PJMcDonald 7 55
(Mrs R A Carr) *hld up: hdwy: nt clr run and swtchd lft over 1f out: styd on same pce ins fnl f* 11/2[3]
6500 5 3/4 **Bluebok**18 2186 9-8-12 50 (bt) JackDean(3) 6 47
(J M Bradley) *chsd ldrs: rdn whn hmpd over 1f out: styd on same pce* 11/1
2402 6 nk **Best One**23 2021 6-9-4 53 (b) ChrisCatlin 12 49
(R A Harris) *mid-div: hdwy 2f out: rdn over 1f out: styd on same pce ins fnl f* 14/1
4060 7 1 1/4 **Norse Warrior (USA)**18 2186 4-9-3 52 (v) AdrianMcCarthy 1 44
(Peter Grayson) *s.i.s: sn outpcd: last and rdn 1/2-way: r.o ins fnl f: nrst fin* 18/1
5202 8 shd **Ten Down**39 1583 5-9-5 54 FrannyNorton 5 45
(M Quinn) *w ldr: rdn and ev ch over 1f out: no ex fnl f* 10/3[2]
-055 9 shd **Come On Buckers (IRE)**11 2385 4-9-3 55 (b) AlanCreighton(3) 10 46
(E J Creighton) *hld up: rdn 1/2-way: nvr on terms* 14/1
0-50 10 1 1/2 **Winifred Jo**18 2185 3-8-13 55 LukeMorris 9 40
(J R Gask) *s.i.s: a in rr* 11/1
040 11 nk **Triskaidekaphobia**55 1234 7-8-12 47 (t) PaulFitzsimons 4 31
(Miss J R Tooth) *led: rdn and hdd over 1f out: wknd ins fnl f* 20/1
63.65 secs (1.35) **Going Correction** +0.20s/f (Slow)
WFA 3 from 4yo+ 7lb 11 Ran SP% 118.2
Speed ratings (Par 101): **97,96,95,93,91 91,89,89,89,86 86**
toteswingers:1&2:£55.60, 1&3:£8.60, 2&3:£55.60 CSF £104.17 CT £708.68 TOTE £4.20: £1.60, £14.80, £2.80; EX 160.50 TRIFECTA Not won..
Owner P J McBride **Bred** Coln Valley Stud **Trained** Newmarket, Suffolk
FOCUS
The second leg of this sprint handicap, and again plenty of front-runners in evidence, but the time was half a second slower than the first division.
Trick Or Two Official explanation: jockey said saddle slipped

2722 GREAT OFFERS AT WOLVERHAMPTON-RACECOURSE.CO.UK (S) STKS 5f 216y(P)
2:35 (2:36) (Class 6) 3-Y-O **£1,774** (£523; £262) **Stalls** Low

Form RPR
5134 1 **Anjomarba (IRE)**24 1994 3-8-9 64 (p) JackDean(3) 7 63
(W G M Turner) *chsd ldrs: rdn and hung lft fr over 1f out: r.o to ld wl ins fnl f* 12/1
-233 2 3/4 **Powerful Pierre**4 2609 3-8-7 71 PatrickDonaghy(5) 6 60
(Jedd O'Keeffe) *sn pushed along to ld: rdn over 2f out: hdd wl ins fnl f* 5/2[1]
0 3 3/4 **Eviction (IRE)**68 1029 3-8-12 0 (b1) FrannyNorton 4 60+
(E S McMahon) *hld up: hdwy over 1f out: r.o: nt rch ldrs* 17/2[2]
3110 4 nk **Thaliwarru**17 2215 3-9-3 69 ShaneKelly 2 62
(J R Gask) *hld up in tch: nt clr run over 1f out: rdn: nt clr run and swtchd rt ins fnl f: r.o* 5/2[1]
13 5 1/2 **Belle Park**10 2418 3-8-5 55 AdamBeschizza(7) 8 55
(Karen George) *s.i.s: hdwy u.p fr over 1f out: nt rch ldrs* 25/1
3366 6 shd **Magenta Strait**18 2185 3-8-12 59 ChrisCatlin 9 55
(R Hollinshead) *chsd ldr: chal 2f out: sn rdn: edgd lft and no ex ins fnl f* 17/2[2]
0-44 7 1 **Frontline Boy (IRE)**13 2329 3-8-12 65 AndrewElliott 3 52
(J R Weymes) *chsd ldrs: rdn over 1f out: hung lft and no ex ins fnl f* 9/1[3]
03-3 8 2 3/4 **Lexi's Layla (IRE)**49 1345 3-8-7 65 StevieDonohoe 5 38
(D M Simcock) *hld up in tch: rdn over 2f out: hung lft and wknd fnl f* 10/1
0- 9 6 **Sostenuto**221 7061 3-8-7 0 FrankieMcDonald 1 19
(T H Caldwell) *s.i.s: a in rr* 80/1
1m 16.6s (1.60) **Going Correction** +0.20s/f (Slow) 9 Ran SP% 110.1
Speed ratings (Par 97): **97,96,95,94,93 93,92,88,80**
toteswingers:1&2:£4.70, 1&3:£36.20, 2&3:£4.10 CSF £39.15 TOTE £21.70: £1.10, £1.10, £5.30; EX 50.30 TRIFECTA Not won..There was no bid for the winner.
Owner Marbary Partnership **Bred** Tally-Ho Stud **Trained** Sigwells, Somerset
■ Stewards' Enquiry : Patrick Donaghy one-day ban: careless riding (Jun 20)
FOCUS
Not a bad seller and reasonably competitive on paper, with a number of these dropping into the grade for the first time.
Thaliwarru Official explanation: jockey said gelding hung left
Sostenuto Official explanation: vet said filly lost a right-fore shoe

2723 BET TEST MATCH CRICKET - BETDAQ H'CAP 1m 4f 50y(P)
3:10 (3:11) (Class 5) (0-75,74) 4-Y-O+ **£2,456** (£725; £362) **Stalls** Low

Form RPR
5-40 1 **Proud Times (USA)**22 2060 4-9-7 74 PJMcDonald 3 83
(G A Swinbank) *chsd ldr: led 10f out: hdd over 8f out: led again 5f out: rdn and hdd over 1f out: rallied to ld post* 4/1[2]
2-21 2 nse **Speed Dating**15 2259 4-9-4 71 StevieDonohoe 12 80+
(Sir Mark Prescott) *s.i.s: hld up: hdwy 7f out: led over 1f out: sn rdn: hdd post* 10/3[1]
2131 3 3/4 **Cozy Tiger (USA)**25 1980 5-8-12 65 TonyCulhane 8 73
(W J Musson) *hld up: hdwy over 7f out: rdn over 1f out: r.o* 4/1[2]
24- 4 2 1/2 **Starkat**232 6794 4-9-5 72 ShaneKelly 2 76+
(Jane Chapple-Hyam) *chsd ldrs: lost pl 8f out: hdwy over 2f out: rdn over 1f out: styd on: eased nr fin* 9/1
-035 5 6 **Mons Calpe (IRE)**7 2511 4-9-3 70 (b) ChrisCatlin 5 64
(P F I Cole) *prom: chsd wnr over 3f out to over 2f out: rdn and wknd over 1f out* 12/1
4163 6 1 1/2 **Carlton Scroop (FR)**5 2199 7-8-8 68 (b) AdamBeschizza(7) 11 60
(J Jay) *s.i.s: hld up: rdn over 2f out: nvr on terms* 20/1
1252 7 4 1/2 **William's Way**18 2182 8-9-3 70 GeorgeBaker 7 55
(I A Wood) *hld up: rdn over 2f out: a in rr* 9/2[3]
0-01 8 13 **Khun John (IRE)**60 1134 7-8-11 64 SaleemGolam 4 28
(W J Musson) *hld up: hdwy over 2f out: sn rdn: hung lft and wknd* 16/1
226/ 9 14 **Pertemps Networks**428 7617 6-8-9 69 DavidSimmonson(7) 6 10
(M W Easterby) *chsd ldr tl led over 10f out: sn hdd: led again over 8f out: hdd 5f out: rdn and wknd over 2f out: t.o* 20/1
1003 10 7 **Zerzura**37 1623 4-9-1 68 FrannyNorton 1 —
(P Howling) *racd keenly: led: hdd over 10f out: remained handy tl rdn and wknd over 2f out: t.o* 25/1
2m 42.87s (1.77) **Going Correction** +0.20s/f (Slow) 10 Ran SP% 118.2
Speed ratings (Par 103): **102,101,101,99,95 94,91,83,73,69**
toteswingers:1&2:£6.00, 1&3:£5.90, 2&3:£4.30 CSF £17.48 CT £57.19 TOTE £7.60: £1.10, £1.50, £2.40; EX 27.40 Trifecta £199.60 Part won. Pool: £269.84 - 0.10 winning units..
Owner J Townson **Bred** Timothy Thornton & Meg & Mike Buckley **Trained** Melsonby, N Yorks
FOCUS
A tight middle-distance handicap with a number of interesting contenders. Although the early pace did not look that strong the field came home strung out, and only three mattered in the straight.
Zerzura Official explanation: jockey said gelding lost its action

2724 ENJOY EXECUTIVE HOSPITALITY AT WOLVERHAMPTON CLAIMING STKS 1m 1f 103y(P)
3:45 (3:45) (Class 6) 3-Y-O **£1,774** (£523; £262) **Stalls** Low

Form RPR
6001 1 **True Pleasure (IRE)**8 2480 3-8-4 53 FrannyNorton 8 58
(J D Bethell) *hld up: hdwy 2f out: n.m.r ins fnl f: r.o to ld towards fin* 15/8[1]
3500 2 1/2 **Mnarani (IRE)**15 2248 3-8-9 64 (b1) LukeMorris 1 62
(J S Moore) *chsd ldr tl led over 1f out: sn rdn: hung lft ins fnl f: hdd towards fin* 6/1[3]
-400 3 2 3/4 **Danceintothelight**31 1810 3-8-13 65 StevieDonohoe 5 60
(K A Ryan) *led: rdn and hdd over 1f out: styd on same pce fnl f* 7/1
-466 4 3 1/4 **Baggsy (IRE)**13 2333 3-8-4 50 CathyGannon 3 44
(Miss J Feilden) *chsd ldrs: rdn over 3f out: wknd fnl f* 16/1
2203 5 3 **Mary Helen**25 1982 3-8-8 59 ShaneKelly 6 42
(W M Brisbourne) *hld up: hdwy over 2f out: sn rdn: hung lft and wknd fnl f* 9/4[2]
0300 6 1 1/4 **Single Lady**10 2412 3-7-9 55 RyanPowell(7) 2 33
(J S Moore) *chsd ldrs: lost pl over 5f out: hdwy 2f out: wknd over 1f out* 9/1
00 7 5 **Marju's Reward (IRE)**30 1825 3-8-12 0 PJMcDonald 4 33
(G A Swinbank) *hld up: a in rr: pushed along 6f out: rdn over 4f out: wknd 2f out* 25/1
0-00 8 5 **Bravo Blue (IRE)**14 2274 3-8-8 25 FrankieMcDonald 7 18
(T H Caldwell) *prom: rdn and wknd 2f out* 200/1
2m 3.51s (1.81) **Going Correction** +0.20s/f (Slow) 8 Ran SP% 112.6
Speed ratings (Par 97): **99,98,96,93,90 89,85,80**
toteswingers:1&2:£3.20, 1&3:£2.80, 2&3:£5.00 CSF £13.32 TOTE £2.70: £1.20, £2.90, £4.10; EX 18.10 Trifecta £130.60 Part won. Pool: £176.62 - 0.30 winning units..
Owner T R Lock **Bred** Michael O'Mahony **Trained** Middleham Moor, N Yorks
■ Stewards' Enquiry : Luke Morris three-day ban: careless riding (Jun 20-22)
FOCUS
A moderate but tightly knit claimer.

2725 BET FRENCH OPEN TENNIS - BETDAQ H'CAP 1m 141y(P)
4:25 (4:25) (Class 5) (0-70,70) 3-Y-O **£2,456** (£725; £181; £181) **Stalls** Low

Form RPR
6-36 1 **Tamtara**11 2398 3-9-4 67 PatCosgrave 9 74+
(Mrs A J Perrett) *chsd ldrs: rdn over 1f out: led and edgd lft ins fnl f: r.o* 11/4[1]
3340 2 2 **Miami Gator (IRE)**14 2289 3-9-3 66 (v1) AndrewElliott 6 68
(J R Weymes) *led early: chsd ldr tl led over 5f out: rdn over 1f out: hdd and unable qck ins fnl f* 9/1
144- 3 1 1/2 **Ever So Bold**189 7551 3-9-5 68 CathyGannon 7 66
(W R Muir) *hld up: hdwy over 2f out: rdn over 1f out: styd on: nt trble ldrs* 8/1
6-55 3 dht **Granite Girl**22 2042 3-9-6 69 ShaneKelly 1 67
(P J McBride) *hld up in tch: nt clr run and dropped in rr 7f out: hdwy over 1f out: sn rdn and hung lft: no ex ins fnl f* 4/1[2]
0-24 5 3 1/4 **Indian Valley (USA)**22 2042 3-9-4 70 WilliamCarson(3) 5 61
(Rae Guest) *sn led: hdd over 5f out: chsd ldr: rdn over 2f out: wknd ins fnl f* 9/2[3]
50-5 6 2 **Shayla**44 1464 3-9-3 66 PJMcDonald 10 52
(G A Swinbank) *hld up: hdwy over 5f out: rdn over 2f out: wknd over 1f out* 13/2
-304 7 3/4 **Two Kisses (IRE)**10 2408 3-9-2 65 StevieDonohoe 3 50
(B G Powell) *hld up: hdwy over 2f out: hung lft and wknd over 1f out* 20/1
440 8 4 1/2 **Marrimeclaire (IRE)**27 1932 3-9-2 65 SaleemGolam 8 39
(B J McMath) *pushed along in rr early: hdwy over 6f out: rdn and wknd over 2f out* 12/1
535- 9 9 **Gracelightening**266 5839 3-9-4 67 JamesDoyle 4 21
(Paul Green) *chsd ldrs: hmpd 7f out: rdn over 5f out: wknd 3f out* 20/1
1m 51.79s (1.29) **Going Correction** +0.20s/f (Slow) 9 Ran SP% 116.5
Speed ratings (Par 99): **102,100,98,98,96 94,93,89,81**
PL: ESB £0.70, GG £1.20 TRI: TM/MG/ESB £86.43 TM/MG/GG £48.31.
toteswingers:TM&MG:£7.40, MG&GG:£3.70, TM&GG:£2.20, MG&ESB:£3.70, TM&ESB:£4.00 CSF £28.83 TOTE £4.30: £1.60, £3.20; EX 38.90 Trifecta £42.20 Part won. Pool: £114.18 - 0.42 winning units..
Owner Mr & Mrs R Scott **Bred** Mr & Mrs R & P Scott **Trained** Pulborough, W Sussex
■ Stewards' Enquiry : Shane Kelly two-day ban: careless riding (Jun 20-21)
FOCUS
A modest contest, but several handicap debutants added interest.
Granite Girl Official explanation: jockey said filly hung left

2726 STAY AT THE WOLVERHAMPTON HOLIDAY INN H'CAP (DIV I) 7f 32y(P)
5:00 (5:00) (Class 6) (0-60,64) 4-Y-O+ **£1,433** (£423; £211) **Stalls** High

Form RPR
-125 1 **The City Kid (IRE)**92 791 7-8-12 54 SaleemGolam 3 65
(G D Blake) *hld up: hdwy 3f out: rdn to ld and hung lft wl ins fnl f: r.o* 12/1

0606 2 2 **El Libertador (USA)**[18] 2167 4-9-3 59 LiamJones 9 65
(E A Wheeler) *chsd ldrs: led over 2f out: rdn and hdd over 1f out: led again ins fnl f: sn hdd and unable qck* 7/1
0-50 3 2½ **Mr Skipiton (IRE)**[27] 1929 5-9-0 59 JackDean(3) 5 58+
(B J McMath) *a.p: rdn to ld over 1f out: hdd and no ex ins fnl f* 5/1[3]
0432 4 ½ **Fortezza**[3] 2629 4-8-9 51 (p) JamesDoyle 6 49
(A J McCabe) *mid-div: hdwy over 2f out: rdn over 1f out: styd on same pce fr over 1f out* 9/2[2]
6506 4 dht **Guildenstern (IRE)**[18] 2187 8-9-0 56 PatCosgrave 8 54
(P Howling) *hld up: hdwy over 1f out: r.o: nt rch ldrs* 18/1
00-5 6 ½ **Piccolo Express**[7] 2496 4-8-8 50 J-PGuillambert 10 46
(B P J Baugh) *hld up: hdwy over 2f out: rdn over 1f out: styd on same pce* 7/1
4324 7 4 **Kheley (IRE)**[18] 2186 4-8-10 57 KierenFox(5) 4 42
(W M Brisbourne) *led: hdd 6f out: chsd ldrs: rdn over 2f out: wknd over 1f out* 9/1
600- 8 3 **Queen Of Thebes (IRE)**[245] 6439 4-9-3 59 CathyGannon 2 36
(S Kirk) *s.i.s: hld up: rdn and hung lft over 1f out: n.d* 16/1
3214 9 9 **Dhhamaan (IRE)**[17] 2211 5-8-12 54 (b) PJMcDonald 7 7
(Mrs R A Carr) *led 6f out: rdn and hdd over 2f out: wknd over 1f out* 3/1[1]
035/ 10 ¾ **Gee Ceffyl Bach**[584] 7053 6-8-2 49 RossAtkinson(5) 1 —
(G Woodward) *prom to 1/2-way* 50/1

1m 30.74s (1.14) **Going Correction** +0.20s/f (Slow) 10 Ran SP% **115.6**
Speed ratings (Par 101): **101,98,95,95,95 94,90,86,76,75**
toteswingers:1&2:£18.20, 1&3:£11.50, 2&3:£8.60 CSF £92.61 CT £492.71 TOTE £6.80: £1.60, £3.40, £1.70; EX 107.00 TRIFECTA Not won..
Owner Luke McGarrigle **Bred** T B And Mrs T B Russell **Trained** Wendover, Bucks

FOCUS
A moderate handicap and a number with questions to answer.
Fortezza Official explanation: jockey said filly hung right-handed througout
Dhhamaan(IRE) Official explanation: trainer said, regarding running, that the gelding performs well when dominating but missed the break

2727 STAY AT THE WOLVERHAMPTON HOLIDAY INN H'CAP (DIV II) 7f 32y(P)
5:35 (5:35) (Class 6) (0-60,60) 4-Y-O+ £1,433 (£423; £211) Stalls High

Form RPR
-400 1 **Feet Of Fury**[14] 2299 4-8-10 52 (p) LiamJones 2 59
(W M Brisbourne) *chsd ldrs: rdn over 2f out: r.o to ld nr fin* 16/1
0000 2 ¾ **Towy Boy (IRE)**[24] 2008 5-8-3 50 (bt) BillyCray(5) 3 55
(I A Wood) *led: rdn over 1f out: hdd nr fin* 14/1
-0 3 nk **Whispering Spirit (IRE)**[58] 1149 4-9-2 58 (v) SaleemGolam 11 62
(Mrs A Duffield) *a.p: rdn to chse ldr over 1f out: styd on* 22/1
-160 4 1½ **Short Cut**[31] 1799 4-8-9 51 (t) StevieDonohoe 4 51+
(Ian Williams) *hld up: hdwy over 2f out: sn rdn: styd on* 5/1[3]
64-0 5 1¼ **Crystallize**[18] 2187 4-8-13 60 AmyBaker(5) 7 57+
(A B Haynes) *dwlt: hld up: rdn over 2f out: r.o ins fnl f: nrst fin* 5/1[3]
6432 6 ½ **Dr Wintringham (IRE)**[10] 2417 4-8-10 59 AdamBeschizza(7) 6 54+
(Karen George) *hld up: rdn over 2f out: styd on ins fnl f: nvr trbld ldrs* 10/3[1]
4435 7 nk **Kielty's Folly**[10] 2417 6-8-10 55 JackDean(3) 1 49
(B P J Baugh) *prom: lost pl 5f out: rdn over 2f out: styd on same pce fnl f* 4/1[2]
-010 8 1¾ **Portrush Storm**[27] 1922 5-8-5 50 ow1 AshleyHamblett(3) 12 40
(R E Peacock) *hld up in tch: rdn over 2f out: wknd over 1f out* 16/1
0-00 9 1 **Admiral Sandhoe (USA)**[15] 2246 4-9-3 59 PatCosgrave 10 46
(Mrs A J Perrett) *chsd ldr 6f out: rdn over 2f out: wknd ins fnl f* 15/2
-000 10 5 **Silver Hotspur**[2] 2647 6-9-4 60 (v) PJMcDonald 9 33
(D Shaw) *dwlt: hld up: a in rr* 25/1

1m 31.04s (1.44) **Going Correction** +0.20s/f (Slow) 10 Ran SP% **114.8**
Speed ratings (Par 101): **99,98,97,96,94 94,93,91,90,84**
toteswingers:1&2:£22.80, 1&3:£24.00, 2&3:£27.00 CSF £216.21 CT £4977.54 TOTE £23.50: £8.00, £7.50, £7.40; EX 85.40 TRIFECTA Not won. Place 6 £20.37; Place 5 £8.07.
Owner Stratford Bards Racing No 2 **Bred** The National Stud **Trained** Great Ness, Shropshire

FOCUS
The second leg of this moderate handicap was run 0.30secs slower than the first.
Crystallize Official explanation: jockey said gelding hit its head on stalls and missed the break
T/Plt: £88.50 to a £1 stake. Pool:£35,006.63 - 288.60 winning tickets T/Qpdt: £10.80 to a £1 stake. Pool:£3,503.64 - 238.24 winning tickets CR

2728 - 2735a (Foreign Racing) - See Raceform Interactive

2701 DONCASTER (L-H)
Saturday, June 5

OFFICIAL GOING: Good to firm (8.7)
Wind: Virtually nil Weather: Warm and dry

2736 SPORTINGBET H'CAP 7f
2:20 (2:22) (Class 3) (0-90,92) 4-Y-O+ £11,333 (£3,372; £1,685; £841) Stalls High

Form RPR
31-1 1 **Day Of The Eagle (IRE)**[21] 2129 4-9-1 84 J-PGuillambert 2 97
(L M Cumani) *hld up: gd hdwy over 2f out: r.o strly fr over 1f out to ld ins fnl 100yds: edgd lft but hld on nr fin* 6/1[2]
-053 2 hd **Masai Moon**[10] 2443 6-8-10 82 (b[1]) JamesMillman(3) 9 94
(B R Millman) *trckd ldrs: smooth hdwy to ld wl over 1f out: hdd ins fnl 1f: rallied: jst failed* 14/1
00-0 3 4½ **Magaling (IRE)**[22] 2100 4-8-10 86 DavidSimmonson(7) 7 86
(M W Easterby) *slowly away and hld up: swtchd lft and niggled along 1/2-way: kpt on wl for hands and heels fr over 1f out: nrst fin* 66/1
1-41 4 hd **Watch Amigo (IRE)**[36] 1653 4-8-11 80 ShaneKelly 14 79
(W R Swinburn) *dwlt: sn rcvrd to trck ldrs racing keenly: swtchd lft to chal over 2f out: kpt on same pce* 5/2[1]
0205 5 1½ **Saucy Brown (IRE)**[14] 2311 4-9-7 90 AndrewMullen 4 85
(D Nicholls) *trckd ldrs: rdn along over 2f out: kpt on same pce* 12/1
40-0 6 ¾ **Mister Hardy**[70] 1008 5-9-0 90 MarzenaJeziorek(7) 12 83
(R A Fahey) *chsd ldrs: outpcd over 2f out: kpt on wl fnl f* 16/1
-036 7 ¾ **Mountain Cat (IRE)**[20] 2141 6-9-0 83 PJMcDonald 8 74
(G A Swinbank) *hld up in midfield: rdn along over 2f out: kpt on wout ever troubling ldrs* 28/1
-020 8 1 **Pearly Wey**[21] 2134 7-8-10 79 AndrewElliott 3 71+
(I W McInnes) *hld up in midfield: niggled along over 2f out: briefly short of room over 1f out: kpt on wout troubling ldrs* 40/1
-602 9 nk **Celtic Sultan (IRE)**[10] 2428 6-9-2 85 MickyFenton 6 73
(T P Tate) *led: trckd over towards rail 3f out: hdd and hmpd appr fnl 2f: sn rdn along and no imp* 14/1
-253 10 1½ **Shaded Edge**[28] 1914 6-8-0 74 ow2 JohnFahy(5) 10 58
(D W P Arbuthnot) *hld up: rdn along 3f out: sn no hdwy* 33/1
4-51 11 ½ **Hajoum (IRE)**[7] 2532 4-9-9 92 RoystonFfrench 16 74
(M Johnston) *cl up: rdn along over 2f out: wknd over 1f out* 8/1[3]
0006 12 ¾ **Rainbow Mirage (IRE)**[33] 1752 6-8-11 80 TadhgO'Shea 17 60
(E S McMahon) *chsd ldrs: rdn along over 2f out: wknd fnl f* 25/1
-443 13 ½ **Dancing Maite**[21] 2113 5-8-4 73 MarcHalford 5 52
(S R Bowring) *cl up: edgd rt and led briefly 2f out: sn rdn and wknd over 1f out* 18/1
0330 14 ¾ **Beckermet (IRE)**[7] 2532 8-9-2 85 HayleyTurner 13 62
(Mrs R A Carr) *hld up in midfield: nvr a factor* 20/1
2206 15 2¼ **Internationaldebut (IRE)**[7] 2532 5-9-5 88 NeilCallan 1 59+
(P T Midgley) *midfield: rdn along and no real imp whn sltly short of room over 1f out: allowed to coast fnl f* 9/1
40-0 16 8 **Mr Macattack**[29] 1862 5-9-0 83 (t) RichardKingscote 11 32
(Tom Dascombe) *hld up: rdn and sn no hdwy over 2f out: eased fnl f* 8/1[3]

1m 23.94s (-2.36) **Going Correction** -0.15s/f (Firm) 16 Ran SP% **126.2**
Speed ratings (Par 107): **107,106,101,101,99 98,97,96,96,94 94,93,92,91,89 80**
toteswingers: 1&2 £16.70, 1&3 £104.40, 2&3 £45.80 CSF £83.93 CT £5235.98 TOTE £4.90: £1.60, £2.90, £12.70, £1.30; EX 90.70 TRIFECTA Not won..
Owner Chris Wright & Andy MacDonald **Bred** Swersky & Associates **Trained** Newmarket, Suffolk
■ Stewards' Enquiry : Marc Halford three-day ban: careless riding (Jun 20-22)
Shane Kelly one-day ban: careless riding (Jun 22)

FOCUS
This was a good, competitive handicap and they went a strong pace.

NOTEBOOK
Day Of The Eagle(IRE) ◆ defied an 8lb rise for his win at Newmarket on his reappearance, but not for the first time he proved wayward under pressure. He didn't travel through the first couple of furlongs, but with the pace strong the leaders ended up coming back to him and he had passed all bar the runner-up approaching the final furlong. When asked to go past that rival he hung right, before then hanging left once Guillambert had switched his whip, and he very nearly threw this away. There's no doubt he is significantly better than the margin suggests, indeed he could eventually be quite smart, but while he doesn't look ungenuine, he will need to mature and learn to run straight if he's to fulfil his potential. (op 5-1)
Masai Moon tanked along for much of the way, clearly responding to first-time blinkers, and having just failed to take advantage of the winner's waywardness, he was clear of the remainder. Whether the headgear works as well in future remains to be seen. (tchd 12-1)
Magaling(IRE), a former stablemate of the winner, improved on what he showed on his debut for this yard/reappearance under an apprentice having only his fourth ride in public. He should build on this. (op 80-1)
Watch Amigo(IRE), 11lb higher than when bolting in a weaker race over C&D, took an age to pick up and this was a rather lacklustre performance. (op 4-1)
Saucy Brown(IRE) was never that far away but his head was a bit high under pressure and he was comfortably held. (tchd 14-1)
Mr Macattack Official explanation: jockey said gelding never travelled

2737 SPORTINGBET.COM H'CAP 1m (S)
2:50 (2:50) (Class 2) (0-100,91) 3-Y-O £16,190 (£4,817; £2,407; £1,202) Stalls High

Form RPR
0-51 1 **Sea Lord (IRE)**[9] 2479 3-9-7 91 GregFairley 8 97
(M Johnston) *set modest pce: qcknd over 2f out: styd on wl whn chal fr over 1f out* 9/2[2]
5-11 2 ¾ **Haatheq (USA)**[19] 2170 3-9-1 85 RichardHills 5 89
(J L Dunlop) *trckd wnr: qcknd to have ev ch over 1f out: kpt on tl no ex fnl 100yds* 6/5[1]
-110 3 hd **Ginger Jack**[14] 2324 3-9-1 85 RoystonFfrench 4 89
(M Johnston) *cl up: outpcd whn ldr qcknd over 2f out: kpt on wl fnl f* 11/2[3]
4-20 4 ¾ **Strong Vigilance (IRE)**[33] 1769 3-8-7 77 HayleyTurner 3 79
(M L W Bell) *in tch: racd keenly: hdwy to chse ldrs over 1f out: kpt on same pce fnl f* 6/1
15-0 5 4 **Flip Flop (IRE)**[35] 1703 3-8-13 83 PaulEddery 7 76
(B W Hills) *rrd and lost 5 l s: in tch by 1/2-way: drvn and brief hdwy over 1f out: wknd fnl f* 10/1
40-0 6 2¼ **Bahamian Music (IRE)**[21] 2110 3-8-10 80 FranciscoDaSilva 6 68
(R A Fahey) *hld up: drvn 1/2-way: sn no imp* 25/1
2310 7 1¾ **Mejd (IRE)**[14] 2324 3-8-8 78 (v[1]) TadhgO'Shea 1 62
(M R Channon) *hld up: hdwy to trck ldrs 1/2-way: drvn and sn wknd fnl 2f* 12/1

1m 38.23s (-1.07) **Going Correction** -0.15s/f (Firm) 7 Ran SP% **113.9**
Speed ratings (Par 105): **99,98,98,97,93 91,89**
toteswingers: 1&2 £1.50, 1&3 £2.40, 2&3 £2.90 CSF £10.25 CT £29.18 TOTE £6.30: £3.30, £1.50; EX 12.00 Trifecta £67.80 Pool: £357.47 - 3.90 winning units..
Owner Sheikh Hamdan Bin Mohammed Al Maktoum **Bred** Darley **Trained** Middleham Moor, N Yorks

FOCUS
They went a steady pace and it paid to race prominently.

NOTEBOOK
Sea Lord(IRE) got away with setting a modest gallop and stayed on well to defy a 5lb higher mark than when winning on Polytrack last time. He's clearly progressing, but will be up in the weights again next time and won't always have things his own way. (op 13-2 tchd 7-1)
Haatheq(USA), twice a winner over 7f at Leicester this year, was 9lb higher but he showed himself up to his new mark. The impression was that he might have won had he really knuckled down and taken the gap between the winner and the near rail in the closing stages, but while by no means ungenuine, he seemed a bit intimidated, being inclined to edge left. There should be more to come. (op Evens tchd 5-4)
Ginger Jack was always well placed and had his chance. (op 5-1 tchd 9-2)
Strong Vigilance(IRE) is better than he showed. With the steady pace no use to him, he pulled hard and then couldn't make an impression, with the leaders simply not stopping. (op 8-1)
Flip Flop(IRE) lost ground with an awkward start and was never particularly competitive. (tchd 9-1)

2738 SPORTINGBET.COM CONDITIONS STKS 1m 2f 60y
3:25 (3:26) (Class 2) 3-Y-O £19,428 (£5,781; £2,889; £1,443) Stalls Low

Form RPR
21 1 **Afsare**[21] 2128 3-8-12 90 J-PGuillambert 1 108+
(L M Cumani) *cl up on inner: swtchd rt over 2f out: shkn up to ld over 1f out: sn clr: eased fnl 75yds: impressive* 11/4[2]
5-12 2 4½ **Wigmore Hall (IRE)**[35] 1702 3-8-12 101 HayleyTurner 3 96
(M L W Bell) *slowly away: hld up: impr to r in tch 5f out: hdwy over 2f out: kpt on but no match for wnr* 5/4[1]
-000 3 1¾ **Dubai Miracle (USA)**[77] 945 3-8-12 95 NeilCallan 4 93+
(D M Simcock) *hld up: short of room over 2f out: kpt on wout ever threatening* 16/1
3-34 4 3¾ **Simenon (IRE)**[17] 2226 3-8-12 101 LiamKeniry 2 86
(A M Balding) *led: hdd over 2f out: already wkng whn short of room over 1f out* 7/2[3]

The Form Book, Raceform Ltd, Compton, RG20 6NL

16 **5** 2½ **Eavesdropper**[17] 2226 3-8-12 96 ....(t) TadhgO'Shea 5 81
(Mahmood Al Zarooni) *cl up: led over 2f out: hung lft and hdd over 1f out: sn wknd* **13/2**

2m 7.16s (-2.24) **Going Correction** -0.15s/f (Firm) **5** Ran SP% **112.5**
Speed ratings (Par 105): **110,106,105,102,100**
CSF £6.82 TOTE £4.00: £2.00, £1.10; EX 7.90.
Owner Sheikh Mohammed Obaid Al Maktoum **Bred** Darley **Trained** Newmarket, Suffolk
■ Stewards' Enquiry : Hayley Turner 4-day ban: careless riding (Jun 20-23)

FOCUS
The pace was not that strong (time under standard, but so were two other races on this six-race card) and some of these probably failed to give their true running, making it difficult to establish the worth of the form. Whatever the case, though, Afsare won in the manner of a potential Group 1 horse.

NOTEBOOK
Afsare ◆, having shaped with immense promise on debut, this good-looking, scopey son of Dubawi wasn't particularly impressive when off the mark at Newmarket last time, not helping himself by hanging left, but he showed himself to be very smart on this step up in trip. It was clear from an early stage that he's well regarded seeing as he was once entered in the St James's Palace Stakes, and his participation in this contest was also quite telling, with Luca Cumani, such as expert placer of handicappers, passing up the opportunity to try and exploit an official mark of just 90. Always well placed, tracking the leaders, the winner was still going easily when switched into the clear approaching the final 2f, and despite displaying a knee action and not appearing totally comfortable on the fast ground, he quickened up most impressively. Eased near the line, he looked value for at least 7l. It's possible that Royal Ascot will come too soon for him, and in any case the ground there may be plenty quick enough, but whatever, he's obviously due a rise in grade. (op 3-1)
Wigmore Hall(IRE) was unsuited by the lack of pace in the race, although it's unlikely he would have troubled the winner whatever the case. Having been held up in last position early on, Hayley Turner took him to the outside at about halfway, obviously not wanting to get caught out, but the gelding, at this point racing with no cover, ended up being keen. Once under pressure in the straight, he further compromised his chance by being inclined to edge left. He can probably do better off a stronger gallop. (tchd 11-8)
Dubai Miracle(USA), without the blinkers on this step up in trip, was short of room when carried left towards the rail by the runner-up around 3f out and was one paced from that point onwards.
Simenon(IRE) may have found the ground a bit too quick and was in trouble when squeezed for room around 2f out. (op 4-1)
Eavesdropper, tried in a tongue-tie for the first time, was hanging badly left in the straight and that cost him his chance. Official explanation: jockey said colt hung left (op 6-1)

2739 WIN AT SPORTINGBET.COM H'CAP — 1m 4f
3:55 (3:55) (Class 4) (0-85,83) 4-Y-0+ **£5,180** (£1,541; £770; £384) **Stalls** Low

Form RPR
5-43 **1** **Jawaab (IRE)**[16] 2243 6-9-1 **77** .... ShaneKelly 5 83
(Mark Buckley) *trckd ldr: stl on bridle 2f out: qcknd to ld narrowly appr fnl 1f: kpt on wl* **5/1**[2]
3501 **2** ½ **Sedgwick**[14] 2349 8-8-13 **75** .... LiamKeniry 9 80
(S A Harris) *racd keenly in midfield: hdwy over 2f out: drvn to chse ldrs over 1f out: kpt on wl fnl f* **6/1**[3]
30-0 **3** hd **Aleatricis**[24] 2031 5-9-1 **77** .... PatCosgrave 7 82+
(J J Quinn) *trckd ldr: briefly tapped for spd whn pce increased over 2f out: styd on wl fnl f* **5/1**[2]
13-4 **4** ½ **Akbabend**[73] 974 4-9-7 **83** .... RoystonFfrench 8 87
(M Johnston) *set stdy pce: qcknd over 2f out: drvn and hdd appr fnl 1f: kpt on* **7/2**[1]
1053 **5** hd **Kames Park (IRE)**[14] 2343 8-9-1 **77** .... PaulEddery 10 81+
(R C Guest) *hld up: short of room 3f out: swtchd rt over 2f out: hdwy over 1f out: styd on wl fnl f: nrst fin* **8/1**
130- **6** 2 **High Ambition**[180] 6878 7-9-3 **79** .... FranciscoDaSilva 2 79
(R A Fahey) *v.s.a: sn rcvrd to be hld up in tch: niggled 4f out: drvn and sn one pce fnl 2f* **8/1**
5-04 **7** 2¼ **French Applause (IRE)**[20] 2142 4-8-11 **73** .... MickyFenton 3 70
(T P Tate) *racd keenly in midfield: rdn whn pce increased over 2f out: sn no imp* **10/1**
0115 **8** 2¼ **Chalice Welcome**[13] 1960 7-9-4 **80** .... HayleyTurner 4 73
(N B King) *hld up: brief hdwy wd over 3f out: drvn 2f out: sn btn* **14/1**
6-06 **9** 2¾ **Maybeme**[14] 2343 4-8-4 **66** ow2 .... AndrewElliott 6 55
(N Bycroft) *racd in midfield on outer: sn btn whn pce qcknd over 2f out* **11/1**

2m 35.56s (0.66) **Going Correction** -0.15s/f (Firm) **9** Ran SP% **116.2**
Speed ratings (Par 105): **92,91,91,91,91 89,88,86,84**
toteswingers: 1&2 £3.50, 1&3 £7.50, 2&3 £5.00 CSF £35.25 CT £158.24 TOTE £7.10: £2.20, £2.10, £2.30; EX 37.10 Trifecta £123.80 Part won. Pool: £167.34 - 0.41 winning units..
Owner C C Buckley **Bred** Hascombe And Valiant Studs **Trained** Castle Bytham, Stanford

FOCUS
The pace was modest, resulting in a time over four seconds above standard (on a card where many of the races dipped under standard), and the first five finishers were covered by only around 1 1/2l at the line, so this is suspect form.

2740 E B F SPORTINGBET.COM MAIDEN FILLIES' STKS — 6f 110y
4:30 (4:33) (Class 4) 2-Y-0 **£4,533** (£1,348; £674; £336) **Stalls** High

Form RPR
1 **Miss Boops (IRE)** 2-9-0 0 .... AdamKirby 8 71+
(M G Quinlan) *dwlt: hld up in midfield: hdwy over 2f out: rdn over 1f out: r.o strly fnl f to ld nr fin* **20/1**
2 ½ **Mama Lulu (USA)** 2-9-0 0 .... HayleyTurner 10 70+
(M L W Bell) *trckd ldrs: gd hdwy to ld 1f out: rdn and edgd lft fnl f: hdd nr fin* **6/4**[1]
0 **3** nk **Sixty Roses (IRE)**[22] 2088 2-9-0 0 .... ShaneKelly 4 69+
(J L Dunlop) *dwlt: hld up and rn green initially: swtchd rt over 2f out: rdn over 1f out: r.o strly fnl f: nrst fin* **25/1**
4 1½ **Makheelah** 2-9-0 0 .... NeilCallan 2 65
(C E Brittain) *trckd ldrs: impr to chal 2f out: drvn to ld narrowly over 1f out: hdd 1f out: no ex fnl 100yds* **7/1**[3]
5 1¾ **Mabsam** 2-9-0 0 .... RichardHills 7 60+
(E A L Dunlop) *dwlt: hld up: hdwy over 2f out: kpt on for hand riding* **4/1**[2]
6 3½ **Smart Red** 2-9-0 0 .... PaulEddery 3 50
(M R Channon) *hld up: gd hdwy to chse ldrs over 1f out: wknd ins fnl f* **9/1**
3 **7** 1½ **Colourful Past (USA)**[15] 2286 2-9-0 0 .... TadhgO'Shea 6 46+
(Mahmood Al Zarooni) *trckd ldrs: rdn over 2f out: wknd over 1f out* **4/1**[2]
6 **8** 1 **Georgina Bailey (IRE)**[12] 2389 2-9-0 0 .... JamesDoyle 5 43
(A J McCabe) *midfield: rdn over 2f out: wknd over 1f out* **25/1**
9 ½ **Bright Dictator (IRE)** 2-9-0 0 .... LeeVickers 1 42
(J G Given) *racd in narrow ld: rdn and hdd over 1f out: sn wknd* **25/1**
06 **10** 2¾ **High Kickin**[18] 2216 2-9-0 0 .... PatCosgrave 9 34
(A J McCabe) *w ldr: rdn over 2f out: sn wknd* **33/1**

1m 20.58s (0.68) **Going Correction** -0.15s/f (Firm) **10** Ran SP% **121.7**
Speed ratings (Par 92): **90,89,89,87,85 81,79,78,77,74**
toteswingers: 1&2 £11.00, 1&3 £29.10, 2&3 £11.10 CSF £50.17 TOTE £29.30: £7.10, £1.10, £7.60; EX 86.40 TRIFECTA Not won..
Owner Cillian S Ryan **Bred** Swordlestown Stud **Trained** Newmarket, Suffolk

FOCUS
This looked just a fair fillies' maiden.

NOTEBOOK
Miss Boops(IRE), a daughter of Johannesburg, travelled in the middle of the pack before responding well to strong pressure to get up near the line. She may improve from this experience. (op 16-1)
Mama Lulu(USA) proved reluctant to go into the stalls, swishing her tail on occasions, but she was fine in the race itself. Having travelled well for much of the way, she briefly looked set to win without having to be given too hard a time, but she was picked off near the line. This first foal of a Group 3 winner evidently has plenty of ability. (op 2-1 tchd 9-4 and 11-8)
Sixty Roses(IRE), reported by Shane Kelly to have been unsuited by good to firm ground, and to have run green, when beaten a long way on debut at Newmarket, still seemed badly in need of this experience. Racing well out the back after a sluggish start, she had too much to do, but there was plenty to like about the manner in which she ran on.
Makheelah, a 50,000gns half-sister to 7f winner Duke Of Homberg, seemed well educated and had her chance. (op 15-2)
Mabsam, a £50,000 first foal, started slowly and shaped a though in need of this experience. (op 5-1)
Colourful Past(USA) may not have achieved much when third in a four-runner race on debut. (op 7-2)

2741 SPORTINGBET.COM MAIDEN STKS — 5f
5:05 (5:07) (Class 5) 3-Y-0+ **£3,885** (£1,156; £577; £288) **Stalls** High

Form RPR
5 **1** **Tabiet**[29] 1868 3-8-12 0 .... LeeVickers 5 61
(James Moffatt) *midfield: chsd along 1/2-way: hdwy over 1f out: drvn and r.o strly to ld fnl 100yds: hld on wl* **50/1**
44 **2** shd **Gold Gleam (USA)**[19] 2174 3-9-3 0 .... ShaneKelly 2 65
(J Noseda) *cl up: rdn to chal ent fnl f: styd on strly: jst failed* **5/1**
5-53 **3** ¾ **Fear Nothing**[10] 2442 3-8-10 74 ....(v) DavidKenny(7) 4 63
(E S McMahon) *led: drvn over 1f out: hdd and no ex fnl 100yds* **15/8**[1]
44- **4** 2¼ **Burnt Cream**[256] 6179 3-8-12 0 .... J-PGuillambert 11 49
(B Smart) *w ldr: drvn over 1f out and remained w ev ch tl wknd fnl 100yds* **9/2**[3]
40 **5** ¾ **Liel**[16] 2249 4-9-5 0 .... TadhgO'Shea 6 50+
(B J Meehan) *restrained into rr early: outpcd bef 1/2-way: kpt on wl fr over 1f out: nrst fin* **11/1**
/40 **6** ¾ **Socceroo**[18] 2213 5-9-5 54 .... LiamKeniry 10 47?
(D C Griffiths) *trckd ldrs: swtchd rt over 1f out: sn drvn and no imp* **25/1**
00 **7** shd **Serious Matters (IRE)**[14] 2340 3-9-3 0 .... AdamKirby 8 49
(W R Swinburn) *midfield: rdn 2f out and sn one pce: wknd fnl f* **20/1**
6 **8** ¾ **Patroller (USA)**[10] 2434 7-9-5 0 .... NeilCallan 7 44
(K A Ryan) *s.i.s: hld up: outpcd 1/2-way: nvr a factor* **4/1**[2]
9 3 **Spirit Of Dixie** 3-8-12 0 .... GregFairley 1 30
(J A Glover) *chsd ldrs tl wknd after 1/2-way* **25/1**
00 **10** nk **Zamid (FR)**[10] 2434 3-8-5 0 .... MarzenaJeziorek(7) 9 29
(R A Fahey) *slowly away: sn outpcd and a in rr* **33/1**

60.06 secs (-0.44) **Going Correction** -0.15s/f (Firm)
WFA 3 from 4yo+ 7lb **10** Ran SP% **115.3**
Speed ratings (Par 103): **97,96,95,92,90 89,89,88,83,83**
toteswingers: 1&2 £23.20, 1&3 £17.60, 2&3 £3.00 CSF £269.48 TOTE £69.90: £10.00, £2.10, £1.50; EX 409.80 Trifecta £440.50 Part won. Pool: £595.38 - 0.41 winning units. Place 6: £19.94, Place 5: £8.78..
Owner R R Whitton **Bred** R R Whitton **Trained** Cartmel, Cumbria

FOCUS
A modest sprint maiden.
T/Plt: £32.20 to a £1 stake. Pool: £1,601.23. 1,601.23 winning tickets. T/Qpdt: £22.50 to a £1 stake. Pool: £3,018.73. 99.20 winning tickets. AS

2707 EPSOM (L-H)
Saturday, June 5

OFFICIAL GOING: Good to firm (derby course 8.6; sprint course 8.9)
Course at normal configuration.
Wind: Virtually nil Weather: Warm and sunny

2742 INVESTEC VINCENT O'BRIEN H'CAP — 1m 2f 18y
1:40 (1:41) (Class 2) (0-105,93) 3-Y-0
£31,155 (£9,330; £4,665; £2,335; £1,165; £585) **Stalls** Low

Form RPR
2-11 **1** **Dandino**[36] 1657 3-8-10 **82** .... PaulMulrennan 11 96+
(J G Given) *hld up in tch in midfield: effrt and nt clr run 2f out: swtchd lft over 1f out: rdn and qcknd to ld 1f out: r.o strly* **17/2**
2-13 **2** 2 **Life And Soul (IRE)**[16] 2254 3-8-7 **79** .... EddieAhern 9 86
(Mrs A J Perrett) *chsd ldrs tl wnt 2nd 7f out: rdn and ev ch wl over 1f out: stl ev ch tl outpcd by wnr fnl f: kpt on gamely to hold 2nd* **16/1**
1-10 **3** 1 **Verdant**[21] 2117 3-9-3 **89** .... RyanMoore 1 94+
(Sir Michael Stoute) *broke wl: chsd ldrs: stdd bk but stl wl in tch after 2f: rdn and effrt on inner 2f out: nt clr run and swtchd rt over 1f out: kpt on wl ins fnl f: unable to rch wnr* **11/4**[1]
1232 **4** ½ **Power Series (USA)**[9] 2479 3-9-4 **90** .... WilliamBuick 10 94+
(J H M Gosden) *swtg: t.k.h: hld up in last trio: hdwy and nt clr run over 2f out: swtchd rt wl over 1f out: styd on wl u.p on outer fnl f: unable to rch ldrs* **25/1**
21-0 **5** ½ **Fine Sight**[30] 1834 3-8-9 **81** .... SteveDrowne 5 84
(R Hannon) *led: rdn wl over 2f out: hdd 1f out: no ex and styd on same pce after* **40/1**
0-12 **6** ½ **Quick Reaction**[16] 2254 3-8-10 **82** .... RichardHughes 12 84
(R Hannon) *stdd and dropped in bhd after s: hdwy on outer 4f out: rdn and no real prog over 2f out: kpt on u.p fr over 1f out: nt pce to rch ldrs* **11/1**
4132 **7** ¾ **Paintball (IRE)**[34] 1734 3-8-7 **79** .... MartinDwyer 13 80
(W R Muir) *lw: stdd and swtchd lft after s: hld up in rr: effrt on inner over 2f out: nt clr run and swtchd rt over 1f out: kpt on ins fnl f: nvr able to rch ldrs* **28/1**

5-24 **8** *1* **Our Joe Mac (IRE)**[14] 2324 3-9-7 **93**.............................. PaulHanagan 8 92
(R A Fahey) *chsd ldrs: rdn and unable qck ent fnl 2f: wknd u.p ent fnl f* **12/1**

1661 **9** *nk* **Arlequin**[24] 2033 3-9-3 **89**.............................. PhilipRobinson 4 87+
(J D Bethell) *t.k.h: hld up in tch in midfield: effrt on inner ent fnl 2f: keeping on but stl plenty to do whn nt clr run and hmpd over 1f out: no threat to ldrs after* **5/1**[2]

2024 **10** *hd* **Gallant Eagle (IRE)**[17] 2225 3-8-7 **79**.............................. JamieSpencer 7 77+
(S Kirk) *swtg: plld hrd: hld up towards rr: effrt and nt clr run ent fnl 2f: swtchd lft jst over 1f out: nvr trbld ldrs* **20/1**

12-1 **11** *3 ½* **Constant Contact**[33] 1781 3-9-4 **90**.............................. JimmyFortune 3 81+
(A M Balding) *lw: chsd ldr tl 7f out: styd chsng ldrs: rdn and unable qck ent fnl 2f: btn whn faltered and lost action briefly 1f out* **7/1**[3]

-103 **12** *¾* **Doctor Zhivago**[21] 2117 3-9-2 **88**.............................. FrankieDettori 2 77
(M Johnston) *dwlt: sn bustled along in last trio: swtchd to outer and rdn ent fnl 3f: no prog and n.d* **7/1**[3]

2m 7.73s (-1.97) **Going Correction** -0.125s/f (Firm) **12** Ran SP% **115.3**
Speed ratings (Par 105): **102,100,99,99,98 98,97,97,96,96 93,93**
toteswingers:1&2 £22.70, 1&3 £7.70, 2&3 £10.60 CSF £125.25 CT £471.17 TOTE £9.70: £2.40, £5.10, £1.40; EX 190.30 Trifecta £1114.90 Pool: £2,561.46 - 1.70 winning units..
Owner Elite Racing Club **Bred** Elite Racing Club **Trained** Willoughton, Lincs
■ Stewards' Enquiry : William Buick two-day ban: careless riding (Jun 20-21)
Ryan Moore two-day ban: careless riding (Jun 22-23)

FOCUS
Parts of the track were watered on Friday evening, but with the ongoing hot weather the going was officially amended to good to firm before racing. Jockeys in the first confirmed that it was riding quick. The pace was fairly steady and the time was 1.73secs outside standard. Run last year in memory of Sir Clement Freud and named this year after Derby great Vincent O'Brien, this is always a warm handicap. Subsequent triple Group/Grade 1 winner Conduit won it two years ago and Lailani, Enforcer, Stage Gift and Zaham are other winners in the past decade to make their mark in Pattern races. This looked an up-to-scratch renewal, although the top-weight raced off 12lb below the race ceiling. The form should work out and winners will emerge from the race. It was a bit of a messy race but the progressive Dandino was the best horse on the day. The fifth rather limits the form.

NOTEBOOK
Dandino ◆ was unbeaten this term in a Redcar maiden and a Doncaster handicap and he made it three from three with an impressive success. Settling well in midfield, he briefly had to wait for a run just as the leaders were kicking for home before quickening up very smartly to lead inside the last, showing a powerful action as he came clear. It would be no surprise to see him make up into a Listed performer at least, later in the season, but he will remain in handicap company for now with the King George V at Royal Ascot his intended target. He would be suited by the 1m4f of that race, judged on the way he was running on at the end here. (op 15-2)
Life And Soul(IRE) tracked the pace and tried to get past the long-time leader in the straight, but took time to master him, and by the time he had the winner had bounded past. He handled the fast ground well and this was a solid effort from a colt who is still on the upgrade. He reversed Sandown form with the sixth. (op 22-1)
Verdant, winner of a hot handicap at Sandown first time out before encountering trouble in the London Gold Cup at Newbury, was a sixth consecutive favourite in this race for Sir Michael Stoute, and the fourth to be beaten, although the yard has won it three times in recent years including with Conduit two years ago. Never far from the leaders on the inside, he was sent for a run on the rail but the gap quickly closed on him and he had to be switched out, costing him momentum. He kept on when in the clear and would certainly have finished nearer than he did, without beating the winner. There is still a big handicap in him. (tchd 3-1)
Power Series(USA), in the same ownership as the third, was held up two-thirds of the way down the field. One of several who had to be switched for a run, he stayed on well down the outside in the straight. He might be worth a try over 1m4f but gives the impression he is a bit of a tricky ride. (op 20-1)
Fine Sight, in the second colours of the Queen, made the running at his own pace, gradually increasing the tempo in the home straight. He relinquished his lead only at the furlong pole and faded out of the places in the last 100 yards or so as his stamina for this longer trip was put to the test, finishing a place ahead of his connections' first string.
Quick Reaction, a course winner at two, was up a further 4lb for his narrow defeat at Sandown. Again held up in rear, he made late progress without reaching the principals. (tchd 12-1)
Paintball(IRE), whose yard won this with Enforcer five years ago, was dropped in from his wide draw and still at the back entering the straight, before making decent progress against the fence. This was his first taste of fast ground and while he was not discredited he might prefer easier conditions. (tchd 33-1)
Our Joe Mac(IRE) was well enough placed turning in and appeared to have no real excuses other than the longer trip, over which he was unproven. (op 11-1)
Arlequin went up no less than 11lb for his wide-margin York victory He gave the impression that the ground was faster than he would have liked and could never get into the action, although he was another who met with a troubled passage. He was reported by his rider to have been unsuited by the track. Official explanation: jockey said colt was unsuited by the track (op 17-2 tchd 10-1 in a place)
Gallant Eagle(IRE) may have finished a bit closer with a clear run but again hinted that he may not be straightforward. (op 16-1)
Constant Contact, 3lb higher than at Windsor, was well placed turning into the straight but could not quicken up and may not have seen out the longer trip. He was reported by Jimmy Fortune to have lost his action. Official explanation: jockey said colt lost its action (op 6-1)
Doctor Zhivago, always at the back, was seemingly unsuited by the ground. (op 8-1)

2743 INVESTEC WOODCOTE STKS (LISTED RACE) 6f
2:10 (2:10) (Class 1) 2-Y-O

£17,031 (£6,456; £3,231; £1,611; £807; £405) **Stalls** High

Form RPR

14 **1** **High Award (IRE)**[14] 2352 2-9-0 0.............................. JMurtagh 5 98
(T Stack, Ire) *led for 1f: styd pressing ldr tl pushed ahd over 2f out: rdn clr over 1f out: styd on wl fnl f* **7/1**

1 **2** *1 ½* **Dubawi Gold**[10] 2427 2-9-0 0.............................. PhillipMakin 8 94+
(M Dods) *str: plld hrd: hld up wl in tch: rdn and effrt wl over 1f out: drvn ent fnl f: sn chsng wnr: kpt on but no real imp* **5/2**[1]

21 **3** *hd* **Premier Clarets (IRE)**[16] 2239 2-9-0 0.............................. PaulHanagan 6 93
(R A Fahey) *unf: scope: tall: lw: t.k.h early: chsd ldrs: rdn and effrt over 2f out: drvn to press wnr wl over 1f out: nt pce of wnr over 1f out: kpt on same pce fnl f* **11/2**[3]

31 **4** *¾* **Approve (IRE)**[16] 2245 2-9-0 0.............................. EddieAhern 9 91+
(W J Haggas) *str: t.k.h: hld up in tch towards rr: effrt on inner ent fnl 2f: nt clr run and switching rt over 1f out: hanging lft but kpt on fnl f: nt pce to threaten wnr* **15/2**

1 **5** *1 ¼* **Casual Glimpse**[35] 1695 2-9-0 0.............................. RichardHughes 7 87
(R Hannon) *str: scope: lw: wnt lft s: in tch towards rr: plld out and effrt on outer over 2f out: hanging lft but no prog over 1f out: wknd fnl f* **5/1**[2]

325 **6** *½* **Foghorn Leghorn**[9] 2468 2-9-0 0.............................. JimmyFortune 1 85
(P W Chapple-Hyam) *stdd after s: hld up in tch: rdn and hdwy ent fnl 2f: btn u.p jst over 1f out: wknd qckly ins fnl f* **14/1**

31 **7** *2 ¼* **Singapore Lilly (IRE)**[14] 2347 2-8-9 0.............................. AlanMunro 4 74
(M R Channon) *leggy: sn bustled along towards rr: rdn and no hdwy over 2f out: wl btn over 1f out* **16/1**

3213 **8** *¾* **Saucy Buck (IRE)**[24] 2032 2-9-0 0.............................. TonyCulhane 3 76
(M R Channon) *stdd after s: bhd and sn detached in last: n.d* **25/1**

21 **9** *nk* **Where's Romeo (IRE)**[9] 2448 2-9-0 0.............................. RichardMullen 2 82
(D H Brown) *w'like: dwlt: sn pushed along and hdwy to ld after 1f: hdd and rdn over 2f out: wknd over 1f out: wl btn and eased fnl 150yds* **7/1**

69.23 secs (-0.17) **Going Correction** -0.125s/f (Firm) **9** Ran SP% **113.8**
Speed ratings (Par 101): **96,94,93,92,91 90,87,86,86**
toteswingers: 1&2 £4.60, 1&3 £7.40, 2&3 £3.80. CSF £24.46 TOTE £7.30: £2.20, £1.90, £2.30; EX 27.50 Trifecta £163.30 Pool: £2,007.16 - 9.09 winning units..
Owner M Tabor, D Smith & Mrs John Magnier **Bred** Mrs T Stack And Mrs Jane Rowli **Trained** Golden, Co Tipperary

FOCUS
This juvenile Listed race is seldom a strong race for the grade and rarely produces future stars, but usually falls to a precocious juvenile. Nine of the last ten winners had already won a race and the other had finished runner-up on his only previous start. The track configuration suggests that a low draw is important, but it had been won by horses drawn as high as 11 twice in the previous three years. With the field smaller this season the pace was steadier than normal, and that caused a couple to pull too hard in the early stages.

NOTEBOOK
High Award(IRE), a soft-ground winner at the Curragh on his debut, had wandered when fourth in a Listed race on fast ground on his previous start. Stepping up in trip, this diminutive son of Holy Roman Emperor settled well up with the pace and, when asked for an effort, quickly took the lead and came home for a comfortable victory. He looks sure to be kept on the go and Royal Ascot, where he has several options, might be on the agenda, while he has entries in some big sales races later on. (op 6-1)
Dubawi Gold, a 160,000gns breeze-up purchase and related to numerous winners, had taken a 6f maiden on his debut. With the ground no problem he was sent off a well-backed favourite, but compromised his chance by pulling too hard in the early stages. In the circumstances, this was a decent effort, and he will be happier back on a more conventional track with a better gallop. Official explanation: jockey said colt ran too free (op 4-1)
Premier Clarets(IRE), a £25,000 half-brother to a number of winners at 5f-1m2f, had been narrowly beaten on his debut before scoring next time over 6f on fast ground. However, like the runner-up, he pulled too hard in the early stages and can be given another chance back on a flatter track when the pace is stronger. Official explanation: jockey said colt ran too free (tchd 6-1)
Approve(IRE) ◆ ran well in a decent Ascot maiden before taking a 5f maiden at Salisbury, the form of which is not working out. Stepping up in trip, he was dropped in from his outside draw before making good progress nearest the rail from 2f out. He had to be switched towards the outside to get a clear run and finished well, suggesting that he is progressing with racing. Official explanation: jockey said colt hung left closing stages (tchd 8-1)
Casual Glimpse, a 40,000gns half-brother to five winners, had the beating of Approve on a line through others, but he missed the break from his wide draw and was always struggling, looking unsuited by the camber. He ran on late, and can prove he is better than this back on a more conventional track. (op 9-2 tchd 4-1)
Foghorn Leghorn, the only maiden in the race, had nevertheless posted promising efforts on his first two starts before a fifth in the National Stakes suggested he was not progressing. Stepping up in trip, he was never far away before his effort flattened out in the closing stages.
Singapore Lilly(IRE), the only filly in the line-up, had scored over this trip at York but never got competitive against the colts. (tchd 14-1)
Saucy Buck(IRE) was always struggling in rear on this step up in trip and grade. (op 33-1)
Where's Romeo(IRE), a £14,000 half-brother to juvenile winner Hold On Tiger, had made all to win an Ayr maiden on his second start and adopted the same tactics on this step up in trip once it was clear there was no early pace. However, he was quickly brushed aside by the winner in the straight and faded tamely, being allowed to come home in his own time once his chance had gone. Official explanation: jockey said colt was unsuited by the good to firm ground (op 6-1 tchd 8-1 in a place)

2744 PRINCESS ELIZABETH STKS SPONSORED BY INVESTEC (GROUP 3) (F&M) 1m 114y
2:40 (2:40) (Class 1) 3-Y-O+

£36,900 (£13,988; £7,000; £3,490; £1,748; £877) **Stalls** Low

Form RPR

1- **1** **Antara (GER)**[245] 6500 4-9-9 116.............................. FrankieDettori 5 111+
(Saeed Bin Suroor) *w'like: scope: lw: dwlt: sn chsng ldrs: 4th st: smooth hdwy to ld ent fnl 2f: clr wl over 1f out: pushed along ins fnl f: a holding on* **15/8**[1]

66-3 **2** *nk* **Reggane**[28] 1908 4-9-6 113..............................(t) GeraldMosse 7 108+
(A De Royer-Dupre, France) *hld up off the pce towards rr: 7th st: plld out and effrt ent fnl 2f: str run on outer but edging lft over 1f out: chsd clr wnr 1f out: r.o wl and clsng fin but nvr quite getting to wnr* **2/1**[2]

-530 **3** *2* **Pachattack (USA)**[23] 2057 4-9-6 100..............................(p) RyanMoore 3 104+
(G A Butler) *hld up in last trio: 6th st: effrt and rdn jst over 2f out: styng on whn hmpd over 1f out: no ch w wnr but styd on wl ins fnl f* **14/1**

0-50 **4** *¾* **Please Sing**[35] 1693 4-9-6 92.............................. AlanMunro 1 101
(M R Channon) *t.k.h: hld up wl in tch: hdwy and 3rd st: rdn and effrt over 2f out: nt clr run and swtchd rt over 1f out: kpt on u.p fnl f but no threat to ldrs* **16/1**

-224 **5** *nse* **Aspectoflove (IRE)**[35] 1693 4-9-6 104.............................. TedDurcan 8 101+
(Saeed Bin Suroor) *lw: hld up in last pair: 9th st: c wd and rdn over 2f out: no prog tl styd on wl ins fnl f: nvr threatened ldrs* **9/1**[3]

-465 **6** *1 ¾* **Jira**[35] 1713 3-8-8 94.............................. ChrisCatlin 2 95
(C E Brittain) *b.hind: chsd ldr: 2nd st: rdn and ev ch over 2f out: nt pce of wnr wl over 1f out: wknd fnl f* **33/1**

05-0 **7** *hd* **Sarah Park (IRE)**[28] 1899 5-9-6 90.............................. MartinDwyer 4 97?
(B J Meehan) *swtg: hld up in tch in midfield: 5th st: rdn and effrt over 2f out: keeping on same pce u.p whn sltly hmpd over 1f out: plugged on same pce after* **28/1**

-522 **8** *nk* **First City**[12] 2387 4-9-6 98.............................. AhmedAjtebi 9 96
(D M Simcock) *stdd after s: t.k.h: hld up in last pair: 8th st: rdn and effrt on inner wl over 1f out: kpt on but nvr gng pce to threaten ldrs* **14/1**

00-5 **9** *2 ¼* **Penny's Gift**[28] 1908 4-9-6 104..............................(b[1]) RichardHughes 6 91
(R Hannon) *lw: sn led: rdn and hdd ent fnl 2f: outpcd by wnr wl over 1f out: lost 2nd 1f out: sn wknd: eased towards fin* **9/1**[3]

1m 42.78s (-3.32) **Going Correction** -0.125s/f (Firm)
WFA 3 from 4yo+ 12lb **9** Ran SP% **113.7**
Speed ratings (Par 113): **109,108,106,106,106 104,104,104,102**
toteswingers: 1&2 £1.90, 1&3 £6.30, 2&3 £6.50. CSF £5.70 TOTE £2.60: £1.40, £1.20, £3.80; EX 5.90 Trifecta £53.10 Pool: £6,869.04 - 95.71 winning units..
Owner Godolphin **Bred** Th Gehrig **Trained** Newmarket, Suffolk

FOCUS
A reasonable renewal of this fillies' Group 3. The pace looked only steady but the time was respectable, just 0.48secs outside the standard. The two who fought out the finish were joint top-rated on adjusted official figures and the form looks sound enough with the winner not needing to match her best German form.

NOTEBOOK

Antara(GER) was conceding a 3lb penalty, having won at this level on her final start for German trainer Roland Dzubasz at Hoppegarten in October. Making her debut for Goldolphin, she travelled well just off the pace before coming with a smooth run that took her a couple of lengths clear. The runner-up was cutting into her lead late on, but she was always holding her and gave the impression she could have pulled out a little more if required. The winner is already proven at 1m2f and this uncomplicated filly looks well capable of handling a step up to Group 2 level. Her jockey feels she will be seen to even greater effect on a more conventional track, and she will head to Ascot for the Windsor Forest Stakes next. (op 2-1)

Reggane, whose trainer also saddled the runner-up in this last year, Alnadana, was slightly disappointing at Lingfield last month but this trip was more in her favour. Held up, she was left with a fair bit of ground to make up the way the race unfolded and although she finished well, despite edging to her left, she could never quite get to the winner. Last year's Coronation Stakes second is a very smart filly but perhaps not the easiest of rides. (op 9-4 tchd 5-2 in places)

Pachattack(USA) had cheekpieces back on instead of blinkers. After being slightly impeded by the runner-up, she ran on well for third, confirming that she will be suited by a return to 1m2f. Her Goodwood maiden victory as a 2yo remains her only win. (op 12-1)

Please Sing, representing last season's winning stable, has not won since taking the Cherry Hinton as a 2yo and had been out of sorts so far this term, but this was a better effort as she stuck on for fourth. She may remain hard to place successfully though. (op 18-1 tchd 20-1)

Aspectoflove(IRE), the winner's stablemate, was another with an awful lot of ground to make up in the straight. She ran on late and would have got up for fourth in another couple of strides. (op 8-1 tchd 10-1)

Jira, the only 3yo in the field, faced a tough task in this company and faded in the final furlong after racing close behind the pace.

Sarah Park(IRE) had a great deal to find on these terms and did not prove up to the task.

First City, runner-up to Seta in a conditions event last time, raced keenly in rear and made just a little progress in the straight. She did not really handle the track. (op 12-1)

Penny's Gift set the pace and was still in second with a furlong to run before dropping quickly back through the field. (op 10-1 tchd 17-2)

2745 INVESTEC ENTREPRENEURIAL DASH" (HERITAGE H'CAP) 5f

3:15 (3:15) (Class 2) 3-Y-O+

£46,732 (£13,995; £6,997; £3,502; £1,747; £877) **Stalls** High

Form	Pos	Dist	Horse / details	Jockey	RPR
0300	**1**		**Bertoliver**[21] 2136 6-8-6 **83** (S C Williams) *b. off hind: chsd ldr tl pushed into ld ent fnl 2f: clr 1f out: kpt on u.p: jst lasted* **33/1**	JackMitchell 15	92
4-11	**2**	*nk*	**Hawkeyethenoo (IRE)**[34] 1727 4-8-11 **88** (J S Goldie) *restless in stalls: s.i.s: bhd: stl plenty to do over 1f out: str run against stands' rail fnl f: swtchd lft fnl 50yds: nt quite rch wnr* **5/1**[1]	TedDurcan 14	96+
1252	**3**	*1*	**Rocket Rob (IRE)**[45] 1471 4-8-8 **85** (M Botti) *towards rr: rdn and n.m.r over 1f out: swtchd rt jst ins fnl f: r.o wl to go 3rd last strides: nt rch ldrs* **9/1**	MartinDwyer 16	89+
0-35	**4**	*hd*	**Judge 'n Jury**[23] 2054 6-9-8 **99** (R A Harris) *chsd ldrs: rdn 2f out: chsd clr ldr jst ins fnl f: kpt on but lost 2 pls nr fin* **20/1**	PhilipRobinson 9	103
4032	**5**	*hd*	**Masta Plasta (IRE)**[7] 2526 7-9-7 **101** (D Nicholls) *chsd ldrs: rdn ent fnl 2f: kpt on u.p fnl f: nvr quite gng pce to rch ldrs* **20/1**	MichaelGeran(3) 2	104+
6-45	**6**	*½*	**City Dancer (IRE)**[10] 2431 4-8-11 **88** (D Nicholls) *v.s.a: wl bhd: last and looking for clr run over 1f out: swtchd to stands' rail and str run fnl 150yds: unable to rch ldrs* **16/1**	FrannyNorton 17	89+
30-1	**7**	*nk*	**Fathom Five (IRE)**[45] 1471 6-9-3 **94** (C F Wall) *lw: in tch: rdn and effrt over 1f out: kpt on steadily u.p fnl f: btn whn n.m.r towards fin* **8/1**[3]	AlanMunro 18	94
5635	**8**	*1 ¼*	**Indian Trail**[14] 2346 10-8-3 **85** (D Nicholls) *racd off the pce in midfield: effrt u.p and edgd rt ins fnl f: styd on same pce ins fnl f* **9/1**	(v) BillyCray(5) 12	81
-021	**9**	*nk*	**Moorhouse Lad**[36] 1670 7-9-6 **97** (B Smart) *swtg: chsd ldng pair: rdn wl over 1f out: chsd clr wnr jst over 1f out tl ins fnl f: wknd towards fin* **16/1**	JimCrowley 4	92
0-04	**10**	*½*	**Oldjoesaid**[22] 2100 6-9-2 **93** (K A Ryan) *lw: s.i.s: wl bhd: swtchd lft to centre and hdwy jst over 1f out: kpt on fnl f: nvr threatened ldrs* **9/1**	JamieSpencer 7	86+
4212	**11**	*1*	**Glamorous Spirit (IRE)**[77] 948 4-8-13 **90** (R A Harris) *led and grad crossed towards stands' side: hdd and rdn ent fnl 2f: wknd ins fnl f* **33/1**	ChrisCatlin 1	79
0-22	**12**	*½*	**Captain Dunne (IRE)**[21] 2135 5-9-8 **99** (T D Easterby) *lw: s.i.s: a towards rr: nt clr run ent fnl f: kpt on fnl f: n.d* **7/1**[2]	JimmyFortune 10	86+
4-00	**13**	*nk*	**Strike Up The Band**[31] 1822 7-9-6 **97** (D Nicholls) *in tch: rdn and effrt wl over 1f out: one pce and no imp ins fnl f* **25/1**	RichardHughes 6	83
10-0	**14**	*hd*	**Crimea (IRE)**[14] 2327 4-8-8 **85** (D Nicholls) *swtg: racd off the pce towards rr: swtchd lft and hmpd ent fnl f: n.d* **40/1**	PaulQuinn 8	71
00-0	**15**	*nse*	**Safari Mischief**[28] 1903 7-8-11 **88** (P Winkworth) *a towards rr: drvn and effrt over 1f out: nvr trbld ldrs* **28/1**	(b[1]) LukeMorris 13	73
6300	**16**	*2*	**Hoh Hoh Hoh**[45] 1471 8-8-13 **90** (R J Price) *in tch: rdn and effrt 2f out: no prog and btn jst ins fnl f* **33/1**	EddieAhern 11	68
1325	**17**	*nse*	**Jaconet (USA)**[21] 2135 5-9-1 **92** (T D Barron) *swtg: a wl outpcd towards rr: n.d* **14/1**	(b) PhillipMakin 5	70
-120	**18**	*½*	**Bajan Tryst (USA)**[84] 887 4-8-11 **88** (K A Ryan) *s.i.s: a bhd: n.d* **20/1**	PaulHanagan 19	64
-130	**19**	*2 ¾*	**Le Toreador**[23] 2054 5-9-4 **95** (K A Ryan) *a towards rr in centre: wl btn 1f out: eased towards fin* **50/1**	(tp) WilliamBuick 3	61

54.22 secs (-1.48) **Going Correction** -0.05s/f (Good) **19** Ran SP% **123.5**

Speed ratings (Par 109): **109,108,106,106,106 105,105,103,102,101 100,99,98,98,98 95,95,94,89**

toteswingers: 1&2 £35.30, 1&3 £36.70, 2&3 £6.30. CSF £172.22 CT £1126.71 TOTE £41.70: £6.10, £1.80, £2.20, £5.30; EX 219.90 Trifecta £3214.30 Pool: £35,717.23 - 8.22 winning units..

Owner Mrs A Shone **Bred** Pillar To Post Racing **Trained** Newmarket, Suffolk

FOCUS

A typically red-hot edition of the 'Dash', it was run at a blistering pace and in a time inside the standard. High numbers proved favoured, with the principals racing close to the stands' rail. The winner reversed April form with the thirdf and seventh and the runner-up is rated to form at face value.

NOTEBOOK

Bertoliver was a surprise winner off bottom weight. Never too far from the action, he surged into a clear lead shortly after the two pole and held off the late flourish of the runner-up, despite his rider's saddle slipping inside the final furlong. From the stable that won this with Hogmaneigh three years ago, he had run well over course and distance at the spring meeting but had been been well held in two subsequent starts in well-contested handicaps. Official explanation: trainer said, regarding apparent improvement in form, that the gelding had been out of form. (tchd 40-1 in a place)

Hawkeyethenoo(IRE) was ridden by Ted Durcan as Kieren Fallon was delayed in traffic. After a slow break he was nearer last than first for much of the way, but picked up really strongly in the last furlong or so and flew home against the stands' rail for second. This highly progressive sprinter is well at home over 6f too and will go for the Wokingham next provided he gets in.

Rocket Rob(IRE), another to finish well from the back on the stands' side, had not run since finishing second to Fathom Five, a place ahead of Bertoliver, here in April. He made up his ground alongside the runner-up and grabbed third on the line. (op 10-1)

Judge 'n Jury was up with the pace all the way and still in second close home, only to be relegated two places in the last few strides. He remains a smart sprinter.

Masta Plasta(IRE) represented a trainer with a fine record in this event, having sent out four winners in the previous eight runnings. He did best of the yard's five runners this time, running a thoroughly creditable race under top weight from stall 2. (op 22-1 tchd 28-1 in a place)

City Dancer(IRE) ◆ ran a most eyecatching race on her third run for the yard. A little slowly away, she was caught behind a wall of horses at the back of the field but finished very fast for sixth when a passage presented itself on the fence. There is surely a decent sprint handicap to be won with her before long.

Fathom Five(IRE), 3lb higher than when winning here in April, ran another decent race at a track he likes, albeit from a favourable draw. He probably found the ground a little faster than he'd have liked. (op 9-1)

Indian Trail, another of the Nicholls phalanx, ran his usual race and is still 3lb higher than when taking this event a year ago, his most recent win. (op 8-1)

Moorhouse Lad, contesting his first handicap since July 2007, showed fine speed but could not sustain it. (op 20-1)

Oldjoesaid ◆ made late progress from the back after being switched to the outside and remains very much one to be interested in, perhaps when he's returned to 6f. (tchd 10-1 in a place)

Glamorous Spirit(IRE), representing the connections of the fourth home, was having her first run on turf this year. Drawn one, she showed blistering pace to lead down the centre of the track and edged over towards the stands' side before gradually fading once headed by the winner. There are not many quicker sprinters than her.

Captain Dunne(IRE), last year's runner-up, was 4lb higher this time round and officially a pound well in. He missed the break and was never a threat but hinted that he remains in decent form. He was reported to have anticipated the start and banged his head on the stalls. Official explanation: jockey said gelding anticipated the start and banged its head on stalls (tchd 15-2 in a place)

2746 INVESTEC DERBY (GROUP 1) (ENTIRE COLTS & FILLIES) 1m 4f 10y

4:00 (4:00) (Class 1) 3-Y-O

£771,504 (£292,456; £146,364; £72,978; £36,557; £18,346) **Stalls** Centre

Form	Pos	Dist	Horse / details	Jockey	RPR
1-2	**1**		**Workforce**[23] 2056 3-9-0 108 (Sir Michael Stoute) *lw: towards rr: hdwy and 6th st: rdn and gd hdwy to chse clr ldr over 3f out: clsng 2f out: led over 1f out: sn clr and in command: styd on wl* **6/1**[3]	RyanMoore 8	129+
23	**2**	*7*	**At First Sight (IRE)**[27] 1951 3-9-0 104 (A P O'Brien, Ire) *led after 1f: wnt clr over 5f out: 8 l clr and drvn 3f out: hdd over 1f out: no ch w wnr after: hld on for 2nd* **100/1**	JAHeffernan 6	117
21	**3**	*½*	**Rewilding**[17] 2226 3-9-0 115 (Mahmood Al Zarooni) *dwlt: towards rr: 8th st: sn rdn and no real prog: styd on and edging lft fr over 1f out: wnt 3rd jst ins fnl f: kpt on to press for 2nd nr fin: no ch w wnr* **9/2**[2]	FrankieDettori 11	116+
1-1	**4**	*4*	**Jan Vermeer (IRE)**[13] 2367 3-9-0 119 (A P O'Brien, Ire) *w'like: scope: lw: t.k.h early: hld up in tch: 7th st: sn rdn and nt pce of wnr: disputing modest 3rd and drvn ent fnl 3f: no imp on ldng pair and n.d after: lost 3rd ins fnl f* **9/4**[1]	JMurtagh 12	110
4-1	**5**	*hd*	**Midas Touch**[27] 1951 3-9-0 115 (A P O'Brien, Ire) *str: chsd ldrs: 3rd st: sn drvn and no prog: no ch w ldrs fnl 2f: plugged on* **6/1**[3]	CO'Donoghue 4	109
13-0	**6**	*½*	**Al Zir (USA)**[35] 1699 3-9-0 110 (Saeed Bin Suroor) *lw: s.i.s: t.k.h and sn wl in tch: 5th st: sn drvn and no prog: disputing modest 3rd fr 3f out tl no ex fnl f* **14/1**	KierenFallon 2	108
0-13	**7**	*hd*	**Coordinated Cut (IRE)**[23] 2056 3-9-0 107 (M L W Bell) *lw: t.k.h: hld up in rr: 11th st: sn wl outpcd and no ch: sme hdwy past btn horses over 1f out: nvr any ch* **20/1**	JamieSpencer 9	108+
5-04	**8**	*3 ¾*	**Buzzword**[20] 2159 3-9-0 112 (Mahmood Al Zarooni) *lw: stdd s: hld up in rr: last st: sn rdn and wl outpcd: no ch fnl 3f* **40/1**	AhmedAjtebi 10	102
6-33	**9**	*1 ¾*	**Hot Prospect**[28] 1910 3-9-0 101 (M A Jarvis) *swtg: stdd after s: hld up towards rr: 10th st: sn rdn and struggling: wl btn fr over 2f out* **50/1**	PhilipRobinson 3	102
0-21	**10**	*16*	**Azmeel**[29] 1858 3-9-0 109 (J H M Gosden) *t.k.h: led for 1f: chsd ldrs after: 4th and rdn st: sn struggling and btn: no ch fnl 2f: wl bhd and eased ins fnl f: t.o* **14/1**	WilliamBuick 5	74
13-1	**11**	*1 ¾*	**Ted Spread**[30] 1833 3-9-0 105 (M H Tompkins) *in tch on outer: pushed along and nt travelling downhill 5f out: 9th and wkng st: wl bhd fnl 2f: eased ins fnl f: t.o* **28/1**	MichaelHills 7	71
1-21	**12**	*2*	**Bullet Train**[28] 1910 3-9-0 109 (H R A Cecil) *lw: chsd ldrs: wnt 2nd 9f out: 2nd st: sn rdn and struggling: wknd ent fnl 3f and wl bhd fnl 2f: eased ins fnl f: t.o* **13/2**	TomQueally 1	68

2m 31.33s (-7.57) **Going Correction** -0.125s/f (Firm) course record **12** Ran SP% **117.8**

Speed ratings (Par 113): **120,115,115,112,112 111,111,109,108,97 96,94**

toteswingers: 1&2 £54.70, 1&3 £5.30, 2&3 £58.00. CSF £525.99 CT £2936.94 TOTE £6.50: £2.20, £14.20, £1.50; EX 541.90 Trifecta £4255.10 Pool: £4,255.10 - 4.10 winning units..

Owner K Abdulla **Bred** Juddmonte Farms Ltd **Trained** Newmarket, Suffolk

■ Ryan Moore's first Derby win, following the previous day's Oaks, and Sir Michael Stoute's fifth.

FOCUS

Britain's premier Classic and the joint smallest field in recent times, although the same number of runners as in 2009. The most successful sires in recent years have been Montjeu, who was represented by Coordinated Cut and Jan Vermeer, and Sadler's Wells, whose sole runner was Bullet Train. Their Derby-winning sons Motivator (Hot Prospect) and Galileo (At First Sight and Midas Touch), also had runners. This year's race resulted in a straight duel between Newmarket and Coolmore, with no trainers from elsewhere represented, and resulted in a victory for Headquarters. The hot weather meant the race took place on good to firm ground, despite selective overnight watering, and and the removal of a rail to provide fresh racing ground ensured the time was more than 2.09secs faster than the Coronation Cup the previous day. The astounding aspect though, was that the winning time was a track record, beating Lammtarra's track record 1995 time by the best part of a second. The time assuages doubts over the strength of the race given the Ballydoyle defections, as well as the runner-up's rather surprising effort, and Workforce is entitled to rate among the best Derby-wiinning performances of the last decade, just a pound behind Authorized and High Chaparral. If At First Sight can confirm his improvement this could be rated the best winning performance since Generous 20 years ago.

NOTEBOOK

Workforce ◆, whose dam is a sister to St Leger winner Brian Boru, had won on his sole juvenile start over 7f at Goodwood (next seven home to have run since have all won), and was second favourite for this when reappearing in the Dante. However, he was beaten by Cape Blanco (who represented Coolmore in the French Derby) there, and displayed a very awkward head carriage, despite staying on well to the line. It transpired that the bit had slipped through his mouth, which explains him hanging. There was some doubt about the ground, as connections had made no secret of the fact that they didn't want it too quick, but in the event he handled it with no problem. Held up early, he moved up rounding the turn into the straight and got a good split towards the inside of the track. When asked to go after the leader 3f out, he picked up really well and, in closing that rival down, drew right away from the others. He found more once in front and came home in a manner that evoked memories of his trainer's first Derby winner, Shergar, nearly 30 years previously. At the same time he overcame the statistic that no horse beaten in the Dante had ever previously gone on to win the Derby. This was only his third start, so there looks sure to be more to come, with the Irish Derby the obvious target and then possibly the King George. However, connections might consider the Arc, as he is almost certain to get suitable ground at Longchamp in the autumn, and bookmakers were quoting him as 4-1 favourite for that race. (op 13-2 tchd 7-1 and 8-1 in a place)

At First Sight(IRE), the pacemaker, was first home of the Coolmore contingent. A maiden winner last July, he was not seen again until making the running and being touched off in the Ballysax Stakes in April on similar ground to today's. He was then used as a pacemaker when third behind Midas Touch in the Derrinstown. Stepping up in trip, he was given a fine ride, with Seamie Heffernan setting a reasonable gallop but gradually winding it up and stealing an advantage rounding Tattenham Corner. He kept galloping and, although unable to respond when the winner went past, stayed on to finish a comfortable second. Connections may take him off pacemaking duties next time.

Rewilding ◆, a half-brother to Dar Re Mi formerly trained in France, had finished runner-up in Prix Noailles on soft ground before being transferred to Godolphin. He had been supplemented into this after running out the easy winner of a Goodwood Listed contest on his first start in Britain and looked sure to appreciate this trip. Held up early, he stayed on past beaten rivals in the straight, and his rider reported that he could make up into a St Leger horse later in the season. (tchd 5-1 in places)

Jan Vermeer(IRE), the well-backed favourite, suffered a bruised foot early in the season but returned to win the Group 3 Gallinule Stakes 13 days previously. He had originally been on course for the Prix du Jockey Club, but was switched to this when his connections' long-time ante-post favourite St Nicholas Abbey suffered a setback. He was settled in mid-division before making headway to chase his stable companion early in the straight but had no answer when the winner went past and could plug on at only the one pace. Johnny Murtagh reported that he was never happy on the colt, but the trainer said the colt lost both front shoes, so better can be expected. (op 11-4 tchd 3-1 in places)

Midas Touch had finished behind Jan Vermeer in two of his three juvenile starts, winning a 7f maiden on soft in between. He had returned to win the Derrinstown in a very good time, with today's runner-up back in third. Like the favourite, he had his chance when coming to join the chasing group but could not pick up again. His rider reported that the colt was unsuited by the track. (op 13-2 tchd 11-2, 8-1 in a place)

Al Zir(USA) looked a decent prospect when winning his first two starts and had finished third behind St Nicholas Abbey and Elusive Pimpernel in the Racing Post Trophy but ran to a similar level when behind those two colts in finishing ninth in the 2000 Guineas. He was taking a big step up in trip and ran his race, but was not sure to stay on pedigree and that looked to be the case, although his rider reported that the colt is still immature and is likely to appreciate a drop back to 1m2f.

Coordinated Cut(IRE) cost 325,000gns and did much to justify that outlay when winning a valuable 1m2f sales race at Newmarket on his reappearance. He finished third in the Dante next time, three-quarters of a length behind today's winner, so had a bit to find. Held up and keen early, he stayed on quite well in the straight and appeals as the sort to do better at this trip on a more conventional track. (op 16-1)

Buzzword, supplemented for this after a good effort in the Poulains backed up by subsequent work, was taking a big step up in trip, which his pedigree suggested was not sure to suit. He was held up at the back and only kept on in his own time in the straight. (tchd 50-1)

Hot Prospect had a lot to find with both Bullet Train and Coordinated Cut on this season's form but had shown in the past he handles fast ground. He did not get the best of runs, being hampered on the downhill run and again in the straight, but never got into contention and probably needs a drop in grade now.

Azmeel, a narrow winner of the Dee Stakes, had a bit to find on this step up in trip and was not sure to stay on pedigree. He raced prominently in the early stages but dropped away in the straight, and it appeared the stamina concerns were justified. (op 12-1)

Ted Spread made a good start to his 3-y-o season by winning the Chester Vase, but the runner-up there finished behind Jan Vermeer subsequently, which suggested he had something to find on form. He raced just off the pace early but was being niggled at around the halfway mark and dropped away once in line for home. (op 33-1)

Bullet Train, in the first colours of the winning owner, had made all to win the Lingfield Derby Trial. He was unsurprisingly ridden positively but dropped away in the straight in a manner that suggested something was amiss, but he reportedly did not come down the hill. He can be given the chance to prove this running all wrong. (op 7-1)

2747 INVESTEC SUREFOOTED H'CAP — 1m 4f 10y

4:45 (4:48) (Class 2) (0-100,100) 4-Y-0+

£12,462 (£3,732; £1,866; £934; £466; £234) **Stalls** Centre

Form	Pos	Btn	Horse / details	RPR
14-0	**1**		**Fortuni (IRE)**^{22} 2096 4-8-8 **85** .... SebSanders 6 (Sir Mark Prescott) *sltly hmpd s: sn led and mde rest: pushed clr 4f out: rdn and kpt on wl fnl 3f: eased towards fin* **9/1**	101+
60-4	**2**	4½	**Cill Rialaig**^{45} 1474 5-8-13 **90** .... SteveDrowne 1 (H Morrison) *in tch: rdn and barging match w rival wl over 2f out: chsd clr wnr ent fnl 2f: no imp u.p after but kpt on for 2nd* **8/1**^{3}	97
0004	**3**	¾	**Mull Of Dubai**^{14} 2343 7-8-8 **85** .... FrannyNorton 13 (D Nicholls) *t.k.h: hld up in rr: hdwy ent fnl 2f: switching lft to inner over 1f out: kpt on wl ins fnl f: no ch w wnr* **33/1**	91+
00-1	**4**	1	**Coin Of The Realm (IRE)**^{45} 1472 5-9-9 **100** .... RyanMoore 3 (G L Moore) *t.k.h: hld up in midfield: swtchd rt and rdn ent fnl 2f: kpt on u.p fnl f: no ch w wnr* **11/4**^{1}	104
5040	**5**	2½	**Reve De Nuit (USA)**^{5} 2608 4-8-6 **88** .... DeclanCannon(5) 7 (A J McCabe) *hmpd s: t.k.h: hld up towards rr: rdn and effrt ent fnl 2f: edging lft and hdwy over 1f out: kpt on: nvr trbld ldrs* **33/1**	88
0-64	**6**	nk	**Dubai Crest**^{9} 2467 4-8-4 **81** .... PaulHanagan 10 (Mrs A J Perrett) *t.k.h: chsd ldrs tl grad stdd and towards rr 7f out: rdn and hdwy u.p ent fnl 2f: kpt on: no ch w wnr* **8/1**^{3}	81
245-	**7**	1	**Seeking The Buck (USA)**^{290} 5170 6-8-13 **90** .... JimCrowley 17 (R M Beckett) *lw: chsd ldrs: drvn and edging lft over 2f out: wknd ins fnl f* **13/2**^{2}	88
-464	**8**	2	**Potentiale (IRE)**^{15} 2282 6-7-13 **81** oh2........(p) KierenFox(5) 11 (J W Hills) *lw: t.k.h: hld up towards rr: rdn and hdwy ent fnl 2f: edging lft wl over 1f out: no hdwy and wl hld fnl f* **33/1**	76
60-6	**9**	¾	**Plaisterer**^{34} 1725 5-9-4 **95** .... JackMitchell 5 (C F Wall) *bdly hmpd s and s.i.s: hld up in rr: rdn and effrt in centre over 2f out: no prog and nvr trbld ldrs* **20/1**	89
1-12	**10**	4½	**Aurorian (IRE)**^{33} 1783 4-8-10 **87** .... RichardHughes 14 (R Hannon) *hld up in tch in midfield: rdn and effrt over 2f out: no prog and wl hld whn n.m.r over 1f out: nvr threatened ldrs* **8/1**^{3}	74
0-00	**11**	3¼	**Pevensey (IRE)**^{34} 1724 8-8-11 **88** ....(p) ChrisCatlin 16 (J J Quinn) *dweit: bustled along early: hdwy to chse wnr 9f out tl over 3f out: wknd qckly ent fnl 2f: wl btn fnl f* **33/1**	69
1201	**12**	½	**King Olav (UAE)**^{26} 1960 5-9-0 **91** .... JamieSpencer 8 (A W Carroll) *lw: chsd wnr tl 9f out: rdn to chse clr wnr again over 3f out tl over 2f out: wknd qckly wl over 1f out: wl btn fnl f* **12/1**	72
32-4	**13**	14	**Resplendent Light**^{26} 1960 5-8-9 **86** .... MartinDwyer 4 (W R Muir) *t.k.h: chsd ldrs: rdn and struggling over 3f out: wkng and btn whn n.m.r on inner over 1f out: wl btn after* **25/1**	44
15-5	**14**	2¾	**Recession Proof (FR)**^{24} 2027 4-8-7 **89** .... IanBrennan(5) 15 (J J Quinn) *stmbld s and s.i.s: t.k.h: hld up in rr: rdn and lost tch qckly 3f out: t.o fnl f* **9/1**	43

2m 34.68s (-4.22) **Going Correction** -0.125s/f (Firm) **14** Ran SP% **121.4**

Speed ratings (Par 109): **109,106,105,104,103 102,102,100,100,97 95,94,85,83**

toteswingers: 1&2 £16.30, 1&3 £70.80, 2&3 £58.50. CSF £73.44 CT £2242.83 TOTE £11.90: £3.30, £2.70, £10.20; EX 109.60 TRIFECTA Not won.

Owner Pacific International Management **Bred** Moyglare Stud Farm Ltd **Trained** Newmarket, Suffolk

FOCUS

Quite a competitive handicap on paper, but in the event it proved a one-horse race. The time was more than three seconds slower than the Derby, but still inside the standard.

NOTEBOOK

Fortuni(IRE) was soon in front and dictating his own pace, and when Sanders asked him to quicken off the home turn he produced a fine response, stretching clear to win eased down. Representing a yard in great form, he came here unexposed on turf, with just two previous tries on it, and left his York running in May well behind, settling much better allowed to bowl along in front. While he had the run of things here, he is obviously on the upgrade and looks well capable of winning again, although the handicapper will be stepping in. Official explanation: trainer said, regarding apparent improvement in form, that the gelding appeared better suited by the change of tactics, making the running. (tchd 8-1)

Cill Rialaig was proven at this track and her yard won this with another mare, Salim Toto, in 2002. She was never too far from the pace and stuck on well to hold second in the last couple of furlongs, but never had a prayer with the winner. (op 15-2 tchd 9-1)

Mull Of Dubai did best of those who came from off the pace, making up a lot of ground against the rail up the straight. This was his best effort of the year and he is now 4lb lower than when scoring for another yard last July.

Coin Of The Realm(IRE) won this race 12 months ago and went up 12lb for winning the Great Met over course and distance in April, which put him on the limit for this 81-100 affair. After racing keenly he stayed on in the straight for a creditable fourth without reaching the principals. (tchd 5-2, 3-1 in places)

Reve De Nuit(USA), who has largely been disappointing this year, had only two behind him at the quarter-mile pole but was staying on well at the end. This is not the first time he shaped as if he will get further than this.

Dubai Crest, whose stable won this event in both 2006 and 2007, lost a prominent early pitch but was running on at the end. He remains capable of winning a nice handicap and may be worth trying over this trip again. (op 10-1)

Seeking The Buck(USA), a winner over 1m2f at this fixture a year ago but off the track since August, was close enough entering the straight but then came off worse in a barging match with the runner-up and faded out of contention for the places. (op 8-1)

Aurorian(IRE) came here in good heart but could never advance beyond mid-division. (tchd 9-1)

Recession Proof(FR), another of the more fancied contenders, was always in rear after a tardy start. (tchd 7-1)

2748 INVESTEC DISTINCTIVE H'CAP — 6f

5:20 (5:21) (Class 2) (0-100,100) 4-Y-0+

£12,462 (£3,732; £1,866; £934; £466; £234) **Stalls** High

Form	Pos	Btn	Horse / details	RPR
2006	**1**		**Flipando (IRE)**^{14} 2311 9-9-4 **94** .... PhillipMakin 13 (T D Barron) *taken down early: stdd and short of room sn after s: wl bhd in last trio: effrt on outer over 1f out: str run fnl 100yds to ld last strides* **9/1**^{3}	102
4301	**2**	nk	**Fol Hollow (IRE)**^{21} 2135 5-9-3 **96** .... MichaelGeran(3) 4 (D Nicholls) *awkward leaving stalls: sn w ldr: ev ch fr over 3f out: rdn ent fnl 2f: drvn over 1f out: led wl ins fnl f: hdd last strides* **16/1**	103
56-0	**3**	½	**Something (IRE)**^{79} 916 8-9-2 **92** .... PaulQuinn 14 (D Nicholls) *swtg: bhd: swtchd rt to outer and effrt over 1f out: r.o wl to press ldrs wl ins fnl f: no ex towards fin* **14/1**	97
2-20	**4**	hd	**We Have A Dream**^{28} 1903 5-8-11 **87** .... MartinDwyer 3 (W R Muir) *led: rdn and kpt on gamely fr over 2f out tl hdd and no ex wl ins fnl f: lost 2 pls cl home* **20/1**	92
6501	**5**	½	**Parisian Pyramid (IRE)**^{14} 2316 4-9-1 **91** .... JamieSpencer 2 (K A Ryan) *chsd ldrs: rdn over 2f out: swtchd lft and drvn ent fnl f: kpt on wl nt quite pce to rch ldrs* **11/2**^{1}	94
-663	**6**	nk	**Run For The Hills**^{6} 2563 4-9-8 **98** .... WilliamBuick 9 (J H M Gosden) *hld up wl bhd in last trio: bhd a wall of horses and swtchd rt to outer fr 2f out: nt clr run 1f out tl ins fnl f: r.o wl fnl 100yds: unable to rch ldrs* **8/1**^{2}	100+
4562	**7**	shd	**Baldemar**^{22} 2100 5-9-3 **93** .... PaulHanagan 6 (R A Fahey) *chsd ldrs: effrt u.p over 2f out: swtchd lft and drvn 1f out: styd on fnl f: nt quite pce to chal ldrs* **11/2**^{1}	95
0550	**8**	nk	**Red Cape (FR)**^{9} 2465 7-8-11 **82** .... IanBrennan(5) 16 (Mrs R A Carr) *hld up in midfield: swtchd rt and hdwy 2f out: kpt on same pce and no imp ins fnl f* **25/1**	83
65-5	**9**	½	**King's Wonder**^{47} 1423 5-8-5 **86** .... BillyCray(5) 12 (D Nicholls) *taken down early: t.k.h: hld up towards rr: racd awkwardly downhill over 4f out: effrt and hanging lft fr 3f out: hdwy on inner over 1f out: kpt on: nt threaten ldrs* **16/1**	85
10-3	**10**	¾	**Olynard (IRE)**^{15} 2280 4-9-2 **92** .... JimCrowley 7 (R M Beckett) *chsd ldrs: rdn and unable qck 3f out: styd on same pce u.p fnl f* **12/1**	89
0022	**11**	¾	**Abraham Lincoln (IRE)**^{3} 2657 6-8-11 **87** ....(p) LukeMorris 15 (R A Harris) *lw: t.k.h: hld up in midfield: effrt 2f out: nt clr run and swtchd ins ent fnl f: nvr able to chal* **12/1**	82+
0150	**12**	¾	**Getcarter**^{5} 2595 4-8-11 **87** .... RichardHughes 11 (R Hannon) *taken down early: in tch in midfield: pushed along on downhill run over 4f out: effrt to chse ldrs and drvn over 1f out: btn jst ins fnl f: eased towards fin* **11/1**	79
5060	**13**	nk	**Pusey Street Lady**^{21} 2119 6-8-7 **86** .... MartinLane(3) 10 (J Gallagher) *restless in stalls: in tch in midfield: rdn and no prog ent fnl 2f: drvn and one pce fr over 1f out* **28/1**	77
0040	**14**	2	**Mac Gille Eoin**^{14} 2316 6-9-6 **96** .... ChrisCatlin 8 (J Gallagher) *chsd ldrs: rdn over 2f out: wknd u.p ent fnl f* **12/1**	81

-410 **15** 1 1/4 **Everymanforhimself (IRE)**77 944 6-9-10 **100**............ RyanMoore 5 81
(K A Ryan) *lw: s.i.s: a bhd: n.d* **16/1**
4413 **16** 3 3/4 **Secret Witness**1 2689 4-8-7 **83** ow1.............(b) KierenFallon 1 52
(R A Harris) *b.hind: a towards rr: effrt and rdn on inner ent fnl 2f: no prog and btn 1f out: eased ins fnl f* **8/1**2
67.60 secs (-1.80) **Going Correction** -0.125s/f (Firm) **16** Ran SP% **130.8**
Speed ratings (Par 109): **107,106,105,105,105 104,104,104,103,102 101,100,100,97,95 90**
toteswingers: 1&2 £52.10, 1&3 £8.60, 2&3 £40.80. CSF £152.32 CT £2120.55 TOTE £13.10: £2.40, £5.30, £3.60, £3.80; EX 274.50 Trifecta £1713.20 Pool: £2,315.22 - 0.20 winning units. Place 6: £198.01, Place 5: £80.75..
Owner Mrs J Hazell **Bred** Denis McDonnell **Trained** Maunby, N Yorks

FOCUS
This good, competitive handicap was dominated by David Nicholls in the first half of the decade, when he trained four successive winners. He was represented by three runners this time and they all ran with credit. With a big field, the pace was good, the time was 1.63secs faster than the earlier juvenile Listed race, and it produced a blanket finish, with the first eight covered by about two lengths.

NOTEBOOK
Flipando(IRE) has been best known in the past as a 7f/miler but caused a surprise when winning over 6f at Wolverhampton earlier in the year, and did the same here. Settled out the back in the early stages, his rider did not hurry him but asked for everything only when his mount started to run in the last 2f. The gelding responded well and swept right down the outside to hit the front near the finish. A really good servant for connections, this was his tenth success, during which time he has amassed nearly £1/4m in prize-money. (op 12-1)
Fol Hollow(IRE) ◆ did best of the Nicholls trio. Always close to the pace from his low draw, he delivered his final challenge to hit the front inside the last furlong, only to be collared on the line. Better known as a 5f performer, he is in good form and could well find compensation before long, although it would be no surprise to see him aimed for one of the big handicaps at Goodwood later on. (op 14-1)
Something(IRE), third in this race last season, like the winner, was held up out the back. He got first run on that rival but could not pick up quite as well. He looks to be finding some form and is equally adept over 7f. (op 11-1)
We Have A Dream is pretty effective on undulating tracks and bounced back from a disappointing effort at Ascot last time. He showed plenty of pace and can pick up another race before too long.
Parisian Pyramid(IRE) looks to have found his form again for his new trainer. He was another who was never far away, stayed on, and could be interesting if sent to Goodwood, as both his wins have been gained there. (op 6-1 tchd 8-1 in places)
Run For The Hills ◆ looked one of the unlucky ones. Held up at the back with the winner, he did not really handle the hill, or the camber in the straight, but was staying on well at the finish to end up on the heels of the placed horses. He seems to be coming back to his juvenile form and is one to note if returning to Newmarket, a track he has gone well on in the past. (op 10-1)
Baldemar was sent off joint-favourite, having won this race last season off an 11lb lower mark and run well at York on his last outing. He chased the leaders from the start but could not find a change of gear in the closing stages. (op 13-2)
Red Cape(FR) has been rather struggling of late but showed plenty of dash from his wide draw. He hit form around this time last season and has now slipped back to a pound above his last winning mark.
King's Wonder, the third of the Nicholls trio, was having just his second start for his current trainer and did not fare badly, running on as if he will appreciate a return to 7f in future. (tchd 20-1)
Olynard(IRE) was progressive last season and ran pretty well but was found out in this grade against some battle-hardened rivals. He might appreciate a return to a flatter track. (op 10-1)
Abraham Lincoln(IRE) did not get the best of runs and can be forgiven this effort. (tchd 14-1 in places)
Getcarter chased the leaders from the start but weakened late on and is another who might be best on a flatter track. (op 14-1)
Mac Gille Eoin has a good record in this race, having won it in 2008 and finished a close second last year. He appeared to have his chance but faded in the last 2f. He can be given another chance, especially if returning to this track. (tchd 14-1)
T/Jkpt: Not won. T/Plt: £165.70 to a £1 stake. Pool: £337,274.47. 1,485.26 winning tickets.
T/Qpdt: £63.00 to a £1 stake. Pool: £13,272.72. 155.90 winning tickets. SP

2674 LINGFIELD (L-H)
Saturday, June 5

OFFICIAL GOING: Turf course - good to firm (9.5); all-weather - standard
Stands rail moved in 2m.
Wind: Mild, behind Weather: Sunny

2749 E B F PREMIER PENSIONS MANAGEMENT CONSULTANCY LTD MAIDEN FILLIES' STKS 6f
5:15 (5:16) (Class 5) 2-Y-O **£3,302** (£982; £491; £245) **Stalls** High

Form RPR
1 **Fanny May** 2-9-0 0.................. EddieAhern 7 73+
(D J Coakley) *mid-div: hdwy over 2f out: pushed along to chal over 1f out: kpt on fnl f: led fnl stride: pushed out* **9/2**2
420 **2** nse **Fifth Commandment (IRE)**14 2338 2-8-9 0.......... SophieDoyle(5) 9 73
(J A Osborne) *chsd ldrs: led wl over 2f out: sn hrd pressed: kpt on: hdd fnl stride* **13/2**
4422 **3** 1 **Silca Conegliano (IRE)**9 2461 2-9-0 0.............. AlanMunro 8 70
(M R Channon) *prom: rdn and ev ch fr 2f out: no ex fnl 75yds* **6/4**1
5 **4** 1 **Al Andalyya (USA)**14 2330 2-9-0 0.............. TomMcLaughlin 10 67
(D R Lanigan) *mid-div: rdn and hdwy 2f out: kpt on same pce fnl f* **5/1**3
5 nk **Sceal Nua (IRE)** 2-9-0 0.............. FrankieMcDonald 3 66
(R Hannon) *chsd ldrs: rdn over 2f out: kpt on same pce fnl f* **20/1**
0 **6** 4 **Miss Dutee**17 2223 2-9-0 0.............. DaneO'Neill 12 54
(R Hannon) *led tl wl over 2f out: sn rdn: wknd fnl f* **16/1**
7 6 **Kaifi (IRE)** 2-9-0 0.............. RichardMullen 13 36
(C E Brittain) *s.i.s: a towards rr* **16/1**
8 5 **Sottovoce** 2-9-0 0.............. TonyCulhane 11 21
(S Dow) *s.i.s: sn in mid-div: outpcd fr 3f out* **12/1**
9 3 1/4 **Mystica (IRE)** 2-9-0 0.............. RichardThomas 2 11
(D J S Ffrench Davis) *s.i.s: a towards rr* **33/1**
10 8 **Veuveveuvevoom** 2-8-11 0.............. RussKennemore(3) 6 —
(G P Enright) *dwlt: racd green: hung bdly lft: nvr a danger: fin on far side rails* **80/1**
0 **11** 4 1/2 **Pure Princess (IRE)**14 2338 2-9-0 0.............. IanMongan 1 —
(P M Phelan) *s.i.s: a towards rr* **66/1**
12 1 3/4 **Hazy Ridge** 2-9-0 0.............. RobertHavlin 4 —
(M Madgwick) *hung lft: a towards rr* **33/1**
1m 10.52s (-0.68) **Going Correction** -0.325s/f (Firm) **12** Ran SP% **121.0**
Speed ratings (Par 90): **91,90,89,88,87 82,74,67,63,52 46,44**
toteswingers: 1&2 £6.10, 1&3 £3.20, 2&3 £4.50 CSF £33.17 TOTE £5.40: £1.60, £2.10, £1.30; EX 40.10.
Owner Chris Van Hoorn **Bred** C T Van Hoorn **Trained** West Ilsley, Berks

FOCUS
Just a run-of-the-mill juvenile fillies' maiden and they finished compressed. The winner is the type to do a little better than the bare form.

NOTEBOOK
Fanny May, a first-time-out half-sister to prolific winner Sweet Pickle, knew her job and broke well. Always in the leading group, a few horse widths off the stands' rail, she launched a strong challenge in the final furlong and got her head in front just before the post. A daughter of Nayef, she is entitled to appreciate longer trips in time, but her immediate future almost certainly depends on how the handicapper treats her. (op 11-2 tchd 6-1)
Fifth Commandment(IRE) had started her career with two commendable runs, but her latest had been disappointing, so this was return to form. She was quickly away and soon in front, bang up against the stands' rail. She did not see out the trip quite as well as the winner, though, and was caught close home. Her record suggests she will find her niche in nurseries. (op 9-2 tchd 7-1)
Silca Conegliano(IRE) lined up with the best form, although her latest run did not suggest she was progressing and this was probably a step backwards. She was never far away, but lacked finishing zip and was losing ground on the first two in the dying strides. (op 15-8 tchd 5-4)
Al Andalyya(USA), fifth on debut in an ordinary maiden here two weeks previously, improved a little on that display. She will need to make further progress to win an average maiden, but, given another run, should be no forlorn hope when nurseries start. (op 13-2)
Sceal Nua(IRE), whose dam never won, did well enough to suggest she can rectify that family omission at some stage. She showed good speed throughout and stayed on encouragingly in the closing stages. (op 25-1)
Mystica(IRE) Official explanation: jockey said filly ran green
Veuveveuvevoom Official explanation: jockey said filly hung violently left

2750 PREMIER PENSIONS MANAGEMENT LTD H'CAP 7f
5:50 (5:51) (Class 5) (0-70,70) 4-Y-O+ **£2,914** (£867; £433; £216) **Stalls** High

Form RPR
5-02 **1** **Space Station**33 1762 4-9-7 **70**..............(b1) SebSanders 12 84
(S Dow) *mid-div on stands' side rails: edgd lft over 2f out: rdn and hdwy whn gap appeared over 1f out: led ins fnl f: r.o: rdn out* **2/1**1
-236 **2** 1 3/4 **For Life (IRE)**26 1963 8-9-2 **70**.............. SophieDoyle(5) 9 79
(J E Long) *racd keenly: led: rdn wl over 1f out: sn edgd sltly lft: hdd ins fnl f: kpt on but no ex* **20/1**
-000 **3** 3 **Hustle (IRE)**21 2123 5-9-5 **68**.............. EddieAhern 3 69
(Miss Gay Kelleway) *mid-div: rdn and hdwy fr 2f out: kpt on same pce fnl f* **7/1**2
6354 **4** 3/4 **Billberry**12 2383 5-8-3 **59**..............(t) RyanClark(7) 5 58+
(S C Williams) *hld up: swtchd lft and hdwy 2f out: sn rdn: kpt on same pce fnl f* **8/1**3
5-30 **5** shd **Steel Free (IRE)**32 1797 4-9-7 **70**..............(v1) RobertHavlin 10 69
(M Madgwick) *trckd ldr: rdn 2f out: kpt on same pce fnl f* **25/1**
4125 **6** 3 3/4 **Copperwood**29 1877 5-9-6 **69**.............. DaneO'Neill 1 57
(M Blanshard) *hld up bhd: swtchd lft and hdwy 2f out: sn rdn: fdd ins fnl f* **18/1**
2110 **7** 2 1/4 **Scruffy Skip (IRE)**8 2490 5-9-6 **69**..............(p) TomMcLaughlin 11 51
(Mrs C A Dunnett) *chsd ldrs tl wknd 2f out* **14/1**
/1-5 **8** 3/4 **Cape Quarter (USA)**21 2133 4-9-6 **69**.............. TonyCulhane 7 49
(W J Haggas) *s.i.s: a towards rr* **2/1**1
3030 **9** 1 3/4 **Ravi River (IRE)**11 2415 6-9-1 **69**..............(v) RichardEvans(5) 2 45
(P D Evans) *mid-div on outer tl wknd 2f out* **33/1**
-030 **10** 4 **Purus (IRE)**21 2129 8-8-13 **62**.............. JackMitchell 8 27
(R A Teal) *in tch tl rdn 2f out: fdd* **16/1**
1m 20.37s (-2.93) **Going Correction** -0.325s/f (Firm) **10** Ran SP% **119.6**
Speed ratings (Par 103): **103,101,97,96,96 92,89,88,86,82**
toteswingers: 1&2 £9.90, 1&3 £4.90, 2&3 £17.30 CSF £52.97 CT £254.25 TOTE £2.80: £1.30, £5.70, £1.70; EX 41.40.
Owner Mr & Mrs Chua, Moore & Jurd **Bred** Juddmonte Farms Ltd **Trained** Epsom, Surrey
■ Stewards' Enquiry : Ryan Clark two-day ban: careless riding (Jun 20-21)

FOCUS
A modest contest, with the top weight rated just 70.

2751 PREMIER PENSIONS MANAGEMENT ACTUARIAL LTD FILLIES' H'CAP 5f
6:20 (6:21) (Class 5) (0-70,68) 3-Y-O+ **£3,070** (£906; £453) **Stalls** High

Form RPR
0121 **1** **Avrilo**8 2485 4-9-7 **61**.............. TomMcLaughlin 6 72+
(M S Saunders) *disp ld: qcknd clr ent fnl f: readily* **3/1**1
-353 **2** 1 1/4 **Green Velvet**24 2026 5-9-6 **60**.............. SebSanders 1 62+
(P J Makin) *towards rr of midfield: swtchd to stands' side after 1f: nt clr run whn making prog u.p over 1f out: r.o ins fnl f: fin 3rd, 11/2l &1 1/4l: plcd 2nd* **5/1**3
0123 **3** 1/2 **Ask Jenny (IRE)**8 2485 8-9-0 **61**.............. AdamBeschizza(7) 5 60
(Patrick Morris) *mid-div: sn pushed along: rdn over 2f out: kpt on ins fnl f: fin 4th, plcd 3rd* **17/2**
5220 **4** nk **Fine Silk (USA)**22 2094 4-9-11 **65**..............(p) JerryO'Dwyer 7 64
(M G Quinlan) *chsd ldrs: rdn 2f out: sn one pce: edgd lft ins fnl f: fin 5th, plcd 4th* **10/1**
-065 **5** 1 **Ajara (IRE)**14 2310 4-9-11 **65**.............. RichardSmith 3 60
(Tom Dascombe) *mid-div: effrt wl over 1f out: fdd ins fnl f: fin 6th, plcd 5th* **20/1**
0000 **6** nk **Town House**39 1598 8-8-9 **49** oh4.............. TonyCulhane 10 43
(B P J Baugh) *disp ld tl wknd ent fnl f: fin 7th, plcd 6th* **33/1**
55-0 **7** 1 **Corton Charlemagne (IRE)**22 2094 4-10-0 **68**.......... JimmyFortune 8 59+
(Rae Guest) *dwlt bdly: in rr: nt best of runs fr over 1f out: nvr a danger: fin 8th, plcd 7th* **10/3**2
-054 **8** 2 **Littlemisssunshine (IRE)**14 2332 5-9-4 **65**..........(t) RosieJessop(7) 9 49+
(T B P Coles) *v awkward leaving stalls: towards rr: sme prog over 2f out: wknd 1f out: fin 9th, plcd 8th* **6/1**
9 7 **Spring Horizon (IRE)**210 7296 4-8-11 **51**..........(p) KirstyMilczarek 2 9
(Miss Z C Davison) *s.i.s: towards rr: wknd 2f out: fin 10th, plcd 9th* **28/1**
60-0 **D** 1 1/2 **Baby Queen (IRE)**14 2310 4-9-8 **62**.............. JackMitchell 4 67
(B P J Baugh) *chsd ldrs: rdn whn outpcd by wnr ent fnl f: kpt on but readily hld: fin 2nd, 11/2l: rdr weighed in light: disqualified* **16/1**
56.84 secs (-1.36) **Going Correction** -0.325s/f (Firm) **10** Ran SP% **115.7**
Speed ratings (Par 100): **97,92,91,91,89 89,87,84,73,94**
toteswingers: 1&2 £4.10, 1&3 £5.50, 2&3 £8.30 CSF £17.59 CT £117.39 TOTE £3.40: £1.80, £2.70, £2.70; EX 17.00.
Owner Paul Nicholas **Bred** D & S Horn **Trained** Green Ore, Somerset

FOCUS
A modest affair, but several had solid form at this level.
Corton Charlemagne(IRE) Official explanation: jockey said filly was slowly away and denied a clear run

Spring Horizon(IRE) Official explanation: jockey said filly was slowly away

2752 PREMIER PENSIONS MANAGEMENT ADMINISTRATIONS LTD (S) STKS 1m 4f (P)

6:50 (6:50) (Class 6) 3-Y-O+ **£2,047** (£604; £302) **Stalls** Low

Form RPR

-111 **1** **Timocracy**[5] 2600 5-10-0 75 (v[1]) TonyCulhane 5 71
(A B Haynes) *mde all: hrd rdn and looked to be fighting losing battle fr over 2f out: battled on gamely: jst hld on* **10/3**[3]

3613 **2** *nse* **Rapid City**[11] 2410 7-10-0 68 RichardHughes 4 71
(Jim Best) *stdd s: hdwy bk st to join wnr 5f out: travelling all over wnr fr 2f out: rdn ent fnl f: kpt on but could nt gain advantage: jst failed* **7/4**[1]

0056 **3** *5* **Sunset Boulevard (IRE)**[25] 2006 7-10-0 53 ChrisCatlin 3 62
(Miss Tor Sturgis) *hld up in last pair: hdwy over 4f out: rdn over 2f out: kpt on same pce* **14/1**

6400 **4** *2 ½* **Doubnov (FR)**[15] 2285 7-10-0 66 (p) JamieSpencer 7 58
(Ian Williams) *hld up: rdn over 2f out: sn one pce: wnt 4th fnl f* **11/4**[2]

1444 **5** *3 ¼* **Zero Cool (USA)**[39] 1592 6-10-0 63 (p) JamieMoore 2 53
(G L Moore) *racd in 4th: rdn 3f out: wknd ent fnl f* **15/2**

060/ **6** *4* **Gold Ring**[809] 5533 10-10-0 70 (t) NeilChalmers 6 46
(Mark Gillard) *chsd ldrs: rdn over 2f out: wknd over 1f out* **16/1**

0/05 **P** **Turnham Green**[87] 841 4-9-3 31 AnthonyFreeman(7) 8 —
(S Curran) *trckd wnr tl 5f out: sn rdn: wknd 3f out: p.u over 1f out* **66/1**

2m 36.1s (3.10) **Going Correction** +0.15s/f (Slow) **7 Ran SP% 111.9**
Speed ratings (Par 101): **95,94,91,89,87 85,—**
toteswingers: 1&2 £1.60, 1&3 £10.50, 2&3 £5.40 CSF £9.15 TOTE £4.10: £2.50, £2.10; EX 5.80.The winner was bought in for 6,800gns.
Owner Ms C Berry **Bred** Gainsborough Stud Management Ltd **Trained** Limpley Stoke, Bath
■ Stewards' Enquiry : Anthony Freeman one-day ban: failed to ride to draw (Jun 20)

FOCUS
An ordinary contest, even by selling standards, and lacking depth. The first two are rated to form but this would not be the most solid. .
Turnham Green Official explanation: vet said gelding returned lame left-fore

2753 PREMIER WEALTH PLANNING H'CAP 1m 2f (P)

7:20 (7:22) (Class 6) (0-60,60) 3-Y-O **£2,047** (£604; £302) **Stalls** Low

Form RPR

0-52 **1** **Baoli**[14] 2336 3-8-13 **55** KirstyMilczarek 4 65
(L M Cumani) *trckd ldr: led over 3f out: drifted rt fr over 1f out: hld on wl fnl f: drvn out* **11/2**[3]

006 **2** *½* **Resolute Road**[21] 2121 3-9-2 **58** WilliamBuick 1 67+
(B W Hills) *broke wl: sn taken bk to trck ldrs: rdn 2f out: wnt 2nd ins fnl f: carried rt towards fin: styd on* **7/2**[2]

3106 **3** *½* **Sheila's Bond**[59] 1158 3-8-5 **54** RyanPowell(7) 11 62
(J S Moore) *hld up towards rr: hdwy on outer over 2f out: sn rdn: styng on wl whn checked towards fin: hld after* **16/1**

060- **4** *1* **Luck Of The Draw (IRE)**[239] 6627 3-9-4 **60** SebSanders 12 66+
(Sir Mark Prescott) *trckd ldrs: rdn to chal 2f out: styd on but no ex ins fnl f* **6/4**[1]

0-40 **5** *5* **Flyinflyout**[16] 2248 3-8-11 **56** (p) RobertLButler(3) 14 52
(Miss Sheena West) *mid-div: effrt over 2f out: fdd fnl f* **33/1**

0-00 **6** *hd* **Federal Reserve**[13] 2359 3-8-8 **50** ow1 RobertHavlin 5 46
(M Madgwick) *mid-div: rdn over 2f out: styd on fnl f* **80/1**

3500 **7** *shd* **Pascalina**[26] 1975 3-8-13 **55** TomQueally 6 52
(J Akehurst) *t.k.h in tch: rdn over 2f out: sn outpcd* **16/1**

4-35 **8** *shd* **Jennerous Blue**[135] 254 3-8-8 **50** EddieCreighton 10 45
(D K Ivory) *s.i.s: towards rr: rdn wl over 2f out: styd on fr over 1f out: nvr a danger* **33/1**

5-44 **9** *3 ¾* **Land Of Plenty (IRE)**[135] 254 3-7-11 **46** RosieJessop(7) 7 34
(Jamie Poulton) *mid-div: rdn 3f out: wknd ent fnl f* **20/1**

6-02 **10** *shd* **Dauntsey Park (IRE)**[9] 2480 3-8-11 **58** RossAtkinson(5) 13 46
(Miss Tor Sturgis) *s.i.s: towards rr: sme prog u.p whn c wd over 2f out: sn hung lft: wknd* **14/1**

-000 **11** *3 ½* **Arnie Guru**[18] 2200 3-8-13 **55** LukeMorris 8 36
(M J Attwater) *a towards rr* **50/1**

55-0 **12** *4 ½* **Qaraqum (USA)**[36] 1659 3-9-1 **57** EddieAhern 3 29
(D J Coakley) *led tl over 3f out: sn wknd* **15/2**

2m 8.79s (2.19) **Going Correction** +0.15s/f (Slow) **12 Ran SP% 121.6**
Speed ratings (Par 97): **97,96,96,95,91 91,91,91,88,88 85,81**
toteswingers: 1&2 £4.10, 1&3 £17.30, 2&3 £13.70 CSF £24.72 CT £299.72 TOTE £6.60: £2.20, £1.20, £5.60; EX 25.50.
Owner Andrew Patey **Bred** W M Johnstone **Trained** Newmarket, Suffolk
■ Stewards' Enquiry : Kirsty Milczarek two-day ban: careless riding (Jun 20-21)
William Buick one-day ban: careless riding (Jun 22)

FOCUS
A poor contest, with the top weight rated 60.

2754 PREMIER BENEFITS SOLUTIONS LTD MAIDEN STKS (DIV I) 1m (P)

7:50 (7:53) (Class 5) 3-Y-O **£2,729** (£806; £403) **Stalls** High

Form RPR

3- **1** **Sarrsar**[221] 7095 3-9-3 0 PhilipRobinson 2 87+
(M A Jarvis) *trckd ldr: led over 2f out: sn rn a little green: r.o strly to draw clr: eased wl ins fnl f* **8/15**[1]

00- **2** *6* **Claimant (IRE)**[316] 4286 3-9-3 0 PaulFitzsimons 1 68
(Miss J R Tooth) *s.i.s: sn in mid-div: hdwy 3f out: sn rdn: kpt on to go 2nd ins fnl f: no ch w wnr* **50/1**

3 *½* **Bitter Fortune (USA)** 3-9-3 0 JamieSpencer 8 67+
(J Noseda) *s.i.s: racd green towards rr: pushed along over 4f out: r.o strly fr over 1f out: 3rd towards fin: promising* **8/1**[3]

2U0- **4** *1 ¾* **Spanish Acclaim**[285] 5318 3-9-3 0 NeilChalmers 7 63
(A M Balding) *led: sn clr: rdn and hdd over 2f out: sn btn* **25/1**

00-4 **5** *½* **Fancy Star**[100] 692 3-9-3 67 WilliamBuick 12 62
(B W Hills) *trckd ldrs: rdn to press wnr briefly 2f out: sn hld: no ex whn lost 2 pls ins fnl f* **11/2**[2]

0-30 **6** *3 ½* **Double Fortune**[50] 1358 3-8-12 69 TomQueally 5 49
(Jamie Poulton) *trckd ldrs: rdn 4f out: wknd wl over 1f out* **16/1**

0 **7** *1 ½* **Nelson's Bounty**[14] 2335 3-9-3 0 TonyCulhane 11 50
(P W D'Arcy) *a towards rr* **40/1**

8 *2* **Jovial (IRE)** 3-9-3 0 EddieAhern 4 46
(D J Coakley) *s.i.s: a towards rr* **16/1**

00 **9** *15* **Farmer Palmer**[14] 2335 3-9-3 0 KirstyMilczarek 9 11
(Louise Best) *mid-div: rdn 4f out: wknd wl over 1f out* **66/1**

44- **10** *3 ¼* **Silken Aunt**[183] 7630 3-8-12 0 RobertHavlin 3 —
(J A R Toller) *mid-div: rdn 3f out: wknd wl over 1f out* **16/1**

06 **11** *8* **Silver Astralis**[39] 1607 3-8-12 0 (p) TomMcLaughlin 10 —
(Mrs C A Dunnett) *rdn over 4f out: a towards rr* **100/1**

1m 39.51s (1.31) **Going Correction** +0.15s/f (Slow) **11 Ran SP% 120.1**
Speed ratings (Par 99): **99,93,92,90,90 86,85,83,68,65 57**
toteswingers: 1&2 £9.00, 1&3 £2.80, 2&3 £28.60 CSF £57.45 TOTE £1.40: £1.10, £13.50, £2.30; EX 58.80.
Owner Sheikh Ahmed Al Maktoum **Bred** Darley **Trained** Newmarket, Suffolk

FOCUS
An ordinary maiden lacking depth.
Nelson's Bounty Official explanation: jockey said gelding hung right

2755 PREMIER BENEFITS SOLUTIONS LTD MAIDEN STKS (DIV II) 1m (P)

8:20 (8:20) (Class 5) 3-Y-O **£2,729** (£806; £403) **Stalls** High

Form RPR

0-2 **1** **Highland Knight (IRE)**[6] 2564 3-9-3 0 (t) JimmyFortune 11 86
(A M Balding) *mde all: qcknd clr wl over 1f out: readily* **6/5**[1]

4 **2** *4 ½* **Zakiy**[36] 1659 3-9-3 0 (t) JamieSpencer 7 76
(W J Haggas) *trckd ldrs: rdn over 2f out: chsd wnr wl over 1f out: kpt on but nvr any ch* **11/4**[2]

-400 **3** *2* **Texan Star (IRE)**[33] 1761 3-9-3 70 (b[1]) WilliamBuick 12 71
(J H M Gosden) *racd wd early: prom: rdn to chse wnr 2f out: sn hung lft: kpt on same pce* **22/1**

33 **4** *4 ½* **Conceptual Art**[16] 2258 3-9-3 0 TomQueally 8 61
(M L W Bell) *trckd ldrs: rdn over 2f out: styd on same pce* **20/1**

3 **5** *3 ¾* **Wasara**[10] 2434 3-8-12 0 ChrisCatlin 5 47
(C E Brittain) *swtchd rt over 1f out: nvr threatened: a mid-div* **8/1**

0 **6** *½* **Fork Lightning (USA)**[9] 2473 3-8-12 0 SebSanders 3 46
(Sir Mark Prescott) *little slow away: racd keenly in midfield after 1f: rdn over 3f out: one pce fnl 2f* **9/2**[3]

7 *½* **Aldo** 3-9-3 0 DaneO'Neill 1 50
(A J Lidderdale) *s.i.s: towards rr: sme late prog: nvr a factor* **100/1**

00 **8** *¾* **Rocky Mood (IRE)**[30] 1844 3-9-3 0 EddieAhern 10 48
(W R Swinburn) *nvr bttr than mid-div* **40/1**

9 *2 ½* **Red Storm Rising** 3-9-3 0 RichardMullen 2 42
(K A Morgan) *s.i.s: a towards rr* **66/1**

10 *6* **Final Try** 3-9-0 0 RobertLButler(3) 6 29
(P Butler) *s.i.s: a towards rr* **150/1**

05 **11** *¾* **Hope She Does (USA)**[29] 1870 3-8-12 0 FrankieMcDonald 9 22
(Mrs L C Jewell) *a towards rr* **100/1**

1m 38.83s (0.63) **Going Correction** +0.15s/f (Slow) **11 Ran SP% 117.1**
Speed ratings (Par 99): **102,97,95,92,88 87,87,86,84,78 77**
toteswingers: 1&2 £2.40, 1&3 £6.30, 2&3 £18.30 CSF £4.28 TOTE £2.00: £1.02, £1.10, £8.80; EX 5.00 Place 6 £15.19, Place 5 £11.08.
Owner J C Smith **Bred** Littleton Stud **Trained** Kingsclere, Hants

FOCUS
This looked stronger than the first division.
T/Plt: £8.20 to £1 stake. Pool: £33,888.88. 2,989.36 winning tickets. T/Qpdt: £3.00 to a £1 stake. Pool: £6,500.04. 1,577.32 winning tickets. TM

2291 MUSSELBURGH (R-H)

Saturday, June 5

OFFICIAL GOING: Good to firm (7.3)
Rail moved 3m along whole of track. Course at innermost configuration and all distances as advertised.
Wind: Light across Weather: Fine and dry

2756 TOTESPORT 0800 221221 TARTAN SPRINT TROPHY H'CAP (CONSOLATION RACE FOR THE SCOTTISH SPRINT CUP) 5f

2:05 (2:06) (Class 3) 3-Y-O+
£7,788 (£2,332; £1,166; £583; £291; £146) **Stalls** Low

Form RPR

-413 **1** **Lost In Paris (IRE)**[25] 2001 4-9-4 **75** (v[1]) DavidAllan 3 84
(T D Easterby) *cl up: effrt wl over 1f out: rdn to ld ent fnl f: sn drvn and edgd rt: kpt on wl* **5/2**[1]

2150 **2** *½* **Ingleby Star (IRE)**[10] 2431 5-9-2 **73** (p) RobertWinston 2 80
(N Wilson) *trckd ldrs: effrt and nt clr run over 1f out: swtchd rt ent fnl f: sn rdn and kpt on wl towards fin* **20/1**

0123 **3** *1* **Ridley Didley (IRE)**[20] 2144 5-8-7 **67** WilliamCarson(3) 9 70
(N Wilson) *cl up: rdn to ld over 1f out: drvn and hdd ent fnl f: no ex last 100yds* **11/2**[3]

3633 **4** *1 ½* **Mandarin Spirit (IRE)**[15] 2294 10-8-10 **67** (b) TomEaves 1 65
(Miss L A Perratt) *midfield: hdwy 2f out: sn rdn and kpt on ins fnl f: nrst fin* **12/1**

00-3 **5** *¾* **Hypnosis**[10] 2431 7-9-6 **77** TonyHamilton 6 72
(N Wilson) *led: rdn 2f out: sn hdd & wknd ent fnl f* **9/1**

3302 **6** *4 ½* **Stolt (IRE)**[15] 2294 6-9-4 **75** DanielTudhope 11 54
(N Wilson) *cl up on outer: rdn along 2f out: sn wknd* **16/1**

03-0 **7** *hd* **Distant Sun (USA)**[57] 1200 6-8-9 **69** BarryMcHugh(3) 7 47
(Miss L A Perratt) *dwlt and bhd tl sme late hdwy* **18/1**

0-00 **8** *1 ¼* **Barraland**[2] 2669 5-8-5 **62** (v) SilvestreDeSousa 5 36
(J S Goldie) *midfield: rdn along and towards rr fr 1/2-way* **18/1**

-306 **9** *1 ¼* **Rasaman (IRE)**[14] 2346 6-9-10 **81** (v) FrederikTylicki 8 50
(J S Goldie) *a outpcd in rr* **7/2**[2]

-620 **10** *3 ¾* **Taurus Twins**[22] 2094 4-9-6 **77** (b) JimmyQuinn 10 33
(R J Price) *a in rr* **9/1**

58.40 secs (-2.00) **Going Correction** -0.275s/f (Firm) **10 Ran SP% 115.0**
Speed ratings (Par 107): **105,104,102,100,99 91,91,89,87,81**
toteswingers:1&2 £7.90, 1&3 £2.50, 2&3 £116.50 CSF £55.37 CT £260.01 TOTE £2.50: £1.10, £6.50, £1.80; EX 49.60 Trifecta £139.40 Pool: £341.15 - 1.81 winning units..
Owner W H Ponsonby **Bred** Yeomanstown Stud **Trained** Great Habton, N Yorks

FOCUS
Quick ground for this valuable card and a competitive opener, but it was dominated by horses who raced on or close to the pace. The official winning time of 58.4 seconds was a tenth of a second inside Racing Post standard, so pretty rapid, but not as quick as the juveniles 30 minutes later. The winner is rated back to his Catterick form.

NOTEBOOK
Lost In Paris(IRE) was well backed beforehand despite getting turned over at odds-on last time, but the confidence proved justified on this occasion as he stayed on best having raced hard up the rail throughout. Whether the first-time visor made the difference it is hard to say, but the change of headgear certainly did no harm and, having broke smartly to race prominently up the favoured rail, he saw this out in grand style to defy a 4lb rise in pretty emphatic fashion. (op 3-1 tchd 9-4)

Ingleby Star(IRE) had appeared to have gone off the boil recently but he bounced right back to form here, giving the winner most to do by keeping on really stoutly for pressure and there is a race in him off this sort of mark, despite having done all his winning off slightly lower ratings. (op 28-1)

Ridley Didley(IRE), who travelled smoothly out wide, continued his good run of form, although he looked like going on entering the final furlong but was soon mastered by the winner. He does not appear to have much, if anything, in hand of the assessor now. (op 5-1)

Mandarin Spirit(IRE) kept on well up the inside but, having lacked a bit of tactical speed mid-race, he never really got close. (op 14-1)

Hypnosis weakened in the final furlong and her winless run now stretches back the best part of two years. (op 6-1)

Barraland Official explanation: jockey said gelding ran flat

Rasaman(IRE), who looked extremely well in the paddock, got outpaced after a couple of furlongs and could never get anywhere near. This was clearly not his true running. Official explanation: jockey said gelding never travelled (op 4-1)

2757 TOTEPOOL EDINBURGH CASTLE CONDITIONS STKS 5f

2:35 (2:35) (Class 2) 2-Y-O

£15,577 (£4,665; £2,332; £1,167; £582; £292) **Stalls** Low

Form				RPR
1	**1**		**Excel Bolt**[18] 2210 2-9-0 0 ... TomEaves 4 *(B Smart) led: rdn along 2f out: hdd wl over 1f out: drvn and rallied ins fnl f to ld on line* **4/6**[1]	97+
12	**2**	*shd*	**Cocktail Charlie**[24] 2032 2-9-0 0 ... DavidAllan 6 *(T D Easterby) cl up: led wl over 1f out: rdn ins fnl f: drvn last 100yds: hdd on line* **7/2**[2]	97+
6134	**3**	*3 ¼*	**Fifth Ave**[12] 2397 2-8-6 0 ... FergusSweeney 1 *(J A Osborne) hld up in rr: hdwy 2f out: rdn over 1f out: kpt on ins fnl f: nrst fin* **11/1**	77
3315	**4**	*¾*	**Style And Panache (IRE)**[19] 2177 2-8-9 0 ... CathyGannon 2 *(P D Evans) chsd ldrs: rdn along 2f out: drvn and one pce appr fnl f* **33/1**	77
1	**5**	*2*	**Oneladyowner**[21] 2111 2-8-11 0 ... GrahamGibbons 5 *(D H Brown) dwlt and in rr: rdn along and hdwy wl over 1f out: no imp fnl f* **14/1**	72
1	**6**	*3*	**Jamesway (IRE)**[66] 1065 2-9-0 0 ... TonyHamilton 3 *(R A Fahey) chsd ldrs: rdn along 2f out: sn wknd* **7/1**[3]	64
015U	**7**	*5*	**Misty Morn**[10] 2436 2-8-6 0 ... SilvestreDeSousa 7 *(A D Brown) chsd ldng pair: rdn along over 2f out: sn wknd* **66/1**	38

58.31 secs (-2.09) **Going Correction** -0.275s/f (Firm) 7 Ran SP% **114.1**

Speed ratings (Par 99): **105,104,99,98,95 90,82**

toteswingers: 1&2 £1.10, 1&3 £3.30, 2&3 £2.10. CSF £3.24 TOTE £1.70: £1.20, £1.20; EX 3.10 Trifecta £22.50 Pool: £473.89 - 15.58 winning units..

Owner Elders, Turton, Brown & Rhodes **Bred** P A Mason **Trained** Hambleton, N Yorks

FOCUS

This looked a warm juvenile conditions race on paper and a few of these have been talked of as Royal Ascot possibles. They clocked a faster time than the older horses in the first race, which bodes well for the strength of the form. Listed form in all but name, worthy of the decent prize.

NOTEBOOK

Excel Bolt ◆ was expected to prove different class after such an impressive debut but although ultimately victorious, he was forced to pull out all the stops by Cocktail Charlie, with the pair clear. He shot from the gates and was soon taking the field along, but he suddenly looked in major trouble over a furlong out when coming under pressure and was passed by Cocktail Charlie. The raced looked all but over, but to his credit he rallied gamely up the rail, a position that may well have been to the winner's benefit, and got back up right on the line. Next stop will be either the Norfolk Stakes or the Windsor Castle, with the trainer leaning towards the former at this stage. (op 10-11 tchd 8-13)

Cocktail Charlie ◆ looks all about speed and ran a blinder. Although collared, he has done enough to deserve a crack at a big prize and is highly regarded by Tim Easterby. (op 3-1 tchd 4-1)

Fifth Ave stayed on from a long way back, and on this evidence the filly looks sure to be suited by the step up to 6f. (op 17-2 tchd 12-1)

Style And Panache(IRE) has not achieved anywhere near as much as some of these in her previous races and, unsurprisingly, she lacked the speed of the front two but was not disgraced and doubtless she will hold her own in nurseries later in the season. Official explanation: jockey said filly hung right-handed (op 25-1)

Oneladyowner, who got a little worked up beforehand and fluffed the break, was far from disgraced in the circumstances, keeping on well, and is capable of better. (op 11-1 tchd 10-1)

Jamesway(IRE) was close to the speed early but he dropped away disappointingly. (tchd 17-2)

2758 TOTESPORT.COM EDINBURGH CUP HERITAGE H'CAP 1m 4f 100y

3:10 (3:10) (Class 2) (0-105,104) 3-Y-O

£49,848 (£14,928; £7,464; £3,736; £1,864; £936) **Stalls** High

Form				RPR
5-12	**1**		**Harris Tweed**[21] 2125 3-8-3 **86** ... LiamJones 11 *(W J Haggas) prom: led after 2f: rdn clr wl over 1f out: drvn out* **4/1**[1]	99+
20-2	**2**	*5*	**Sing Sweetly**[23] 2043 3-7-12 **81** oh4 ... JamieMackay 14 *(G A Butler) chsd ldrs: effrt and hdwy 3f out: rdn 2f out: drvn and kpt on ins fnl f: no ch w wnr* **8/1**	86
-111	**3**	*nse*	**Corsica (IRE)**[22] 2070 3-9-7 **104** ... JoeFanning 7 *(M Johnston) a.p: chsd wnr fr 1/2-way: rdn along wl over 2f out: drvn over 1f out: kpt on same pce* **6/1**[3]	109
42-2	**4**	*2*	**Opera Gal (IRE)**[29] 1876 3-7-12 **81** oh5 ... DavidProbert 12 *(A M Balding) t.k.h: a.p: rdn along 3f out: drvn 2f out: kpt on same pce* **16/1**	83
21-2	**5**	*hd*	**Bowdler's Magic**[14] 2315 3-7-13 **82** ... SilvestreDeSousa 2 *(M Johnston) hld up and bhd: hdwy wl over 2f out: rdn wl over 1f out: drvn and kpt on ins fnl f: nrst fin* **15/2**	84+
1322	**6**	*½*	**Rock A Doodle Doo (IRE)**[16] 2252 3-7-10 **84** ... SimonPearce(5) 10 *(W Jarvis) hld up and bhd: hdwy wl over 2f out: sn swtchd lft: rdn and hung bdly rt 1f out: kpt on ins fnl f: nrst fin* **10/1**	85+
2131	**7**	*1 ¾*	**Zuider Zee (GER)**[14] 2315 3-7-13 **82** ... NickyMackay 1 *(J H M Gosden) hld up in rr: hdwy on wd outside wl over 2f out: rdn wl over 1f out: sn drvn and no imp* **5/1**[2]	80
1-01	**8**	*nse*	**Spanish Duke (IRE)**[34] 1734 3-8-5 **88** ... JimmyQuinn 4 *(J L Dunlop) hld up in midfield: hdwy on outer 3f out: rdn to chse ldrs 2f out: sn drvn and no imp* **8/1**	86
1-30	**9**	*¾*	**Mister Angry (IRE)**[31] 1823 3-8-0 **83** ... AndreaAtzeni 5 *(M Johnston) chsd ldrs: rdn along over 2f out: drvn wl over 1f out: grad wknd* **40/1**	80
2-34	**10**	*¾*	**Bonfire Knight**[21] 2117 3-7-11 **83** ow1 ... AndrewHeffernan(3) 9 *(J J Quinn) hld up in tch: effrt 3f out: rdn along over 2f out: sn drvn and no imp* **12/1**	79
-113	**11**	*2 ½*	**Gomrath (IRE)**[14] 2323 3-8-0 **83** ... CathyGannon 8 *(M R Channon) hld up in midfield: effrt and hdwy 4f out: rdn along wl over 2f out: sn drvn and wknd wl over 1f out* **16/1**	75
4-30	**12**	*nk*	**Ingleby Spirit**[21] 2117 3-7-11 **83** ... NataliaGemelova(3) 15 *(R A Fahey) a in rr* **25/1**	74
-403	**13**	*2 ¼*	**Aquarian Spirit**[5] 2607 3-7-12 **81** oh1 ... DuranFentiman 3 *(R A Fahey) midfield whn rn wd bnd after 2f and towards rr: hdwy on outer and in tch 1/2-way: rdn along over 3f out: sn wknd* **20/1**	69
-114	**14**	*3 ¼*	**Bebopalula (IRE)**[28] 1909 3-8-1 **84** ow2 ... AdrianNicholls 13 *(B W Hills) t.k.h: led 2f: prom: rdn along over 3f out: sn wknd* **16/1**	67
0-33	**15**	*1*	**Wild Rose**[23] 2047 3-7-12 **84** oh1 ow3 ... Louis-PhilippeBeuzelin(3) 6 *(M L W Bell) a towards rr* **25/1**	65

2m 36.8s (-5.20) **Going Correction** -0.275s/f (Firm) 15 Ran SP% **134.3**

Speed ratings (Par 105): **106,102,102,101,101 100,99,99,99,98 96,96,95,93,92**

toteswingers: 1&2 £13.40, 1&3 £6.70, 2&3 £25.90. CSF £38.47 CT £205.77 TOTE £5.90: £1.90, £2.00, £3.90; EX 50.40 Trifecta £307.20 Part won. Pool: £415.26 - 0.50 winning units..

Owner B Haggas **Bred** J B Haggas **Trained** Newmarket, Suffolk

FOCUS

Musselburgh's richest race and a hotly contested handicap featuring a host of improving/unexposed 3yos. The presence of 104-rated Corsica at the top of the weights meant that everything else carried 8st 5lb or less. The pace was red hot from the outset and the track record time of 2min 40.93sec was smashed to pieces by Harris Tweed. He looks sure to rate higher still.

NOTEBOOK

Harris Tweed ◆ shaved over four seconds off the course record time. He led early, kicked for home in the straight and galloped right away from his rivals in the final two furlongs in relentless style, marking himself down as a Pattern-class performer in the making. To see his race out so strongly having been on the sharp end of such a strong pace is wildly impressive and he could be some tool over middle distances. (op 5-1)

Sing Sweetly ◆, who was 4lb out of the handicap, travelled well up the inside and kept on stoutly, shaping as though she probably wants a stiffer test of stamina if anything. (op 12-1)

Corsica(IRE) ◆ ran a blinder in third under such a big weight, conceding a stone and 4lb to the winner, which, with the benefit of hindsight, was an impossible task. Like the winner, the step up to Listed company, at least, beckons and he remains a progressive colt. (op 7-1)

Opera Gal(IRE) ran well, seeing the longer trip out despite racing from 5lb out of the weights, and there is more to come from her with experience. (op 20-1)

Bowdler's Magic was taken off his feet in the first half of the race, but he picked up in really good style in the straight and looks the type to do better over a longer trip. (op 8-1)

Rock A Doodle Doo(IRE) also finished well and continues to progress.

Zuider Zee(GER) couldn't repeat his Chester form off his new higher mark. Official explanation: trainer had no explanation for the poor form shown (tchd 11-2)

Spanish Duke(IRE) Official explanation: jockey said gelding didn't handle the bend

2759 TOTESCOOP6 SCOTTISH SPRINT CUP H'CAP STKS 5f

3:40 (3:42) (Class 2) (0-105,99) 3-Y-O+

£31,155 (£9,330; £4,665; £2,335; £1,165; £585) **Stalls** Low

Form				RPR
-321	**1**		**Hamish McGonagall**[14] 2346 5-9-10 **99** ... DavidAllan 12 *(T D Easterby) cl up: rdn to ld 1 1/2f out: drvn and edgd rt ins fnl f: hld on wl* **5/1**[2]	109
0-24	**2**	*nk*	**Striking Spirit**[21] 2119 5-9-5 **94** ... AdrianNicholls 6 *(D Nicholls) trckd ldrs: hdwy over 2f out: rdn to chal over 1f out: ev ch tl drvn ins fnl f and no ex towards fin* **9/1**	103
02-1	**3**	*1 ¼*	**Ingleby Lady**[22] 2100 4-9-8 **97** ... GrahamGibbons 5 *(T D Barron) dwlt: sn chsng ldrs on inner: swtchd rt 1/2-way: hdwy 2f out: rdn to chse ldrs over 1f out: kpt on strly towards fin* **6/1**[3]	102+
02-1	**4**	*nk*	**Masamah (IRE)**[31] 1822 4-9-8 **97** ... StevieDonohoe 10 *(K A Ryan) led: rdn along 2f out: sn hdd and drvn: kpt on fnl f* **8/1**	101
-012	**5**	*½*	**Ziggy Lee**[14] 2346 4-8-8 **86** ... WilliamCarson(3) 3 *(S C Williams) chsd ldrs: effrt 2f out: sn rdn and ev ch tl drvn and one pce ins fnl f* **7/2**[1]	88
0502	**6**	*1 ¼*	**The Nifty Fox**[10] 2431 6-8-8 **86** ... BarryMcHugh(3) 8 *(T D Easterby) midfield: hdwy 2f out: swtchd rt and rdn to chse ldrs ent fnl f: sn drvn and one pce* **14/1**	84
36-1	**7**	*1 ¼*	**Lenny Bee**[52] 1295 4-9-3 **92** ... RobertWinston 14 *(D H Brown) chsd ldrs: rdn and ev ch 2f out: drvn over 1f out and gradally wknd* **8/1**	85
-200	**8**	*½*	**Green Manalishi**[31] 1822 9-9-5 **94** ... (p) TomEaves 4 *(K A Ryan) in tch: effrt 2f out: sn rdn and kpt on same pce ent fnl f* **22/1**	85
00-5	**9**	*¾*	**Valery Borzov (IRE)**[28] 1906 6-9-8 **97** ... TonyHamilton 1 *(R A Fahey) dwlt and towards rr tl sme late hdwy* **14/1**	86
20-0	**10**	*1 ¾*	**Tony The Tap**[15] 2280 9-8-12 **87** ... DavidProbert 16 *(W R Muir) chsd ldrs on outer: rdn along over 2f out: grad wknd* **33/1**	69
-540	**11**	*hd*	**River Falcon**[14] 2346 10-8-7 **82** ... AndreaAtzeni 9 *(J S Goldie) in rr tl sme late hdwy* **14/1**	63
000-	**12**	*2 ¼*	**Hogmaneigh (IRE)**[238] 6678 7-9-8 **97** ... SaleemGolam 7 *(J S Goldie) sn rdn along: a in rr* **25/1**	70
5003	**13**	*¾*	**Hotham**[9] 2465 7-8-12 **87** ... DanielTudhope 15 *(N Wilson) s.i.s: a in rr* **25/1**	58
00-0	**14**	*¾*	**Roker Park (IRE)**[40] 1573 5-9-4 **93** ... StephenCraine 17 *(K A Ryan) swtchd lft s and towards rr whn hmpd after 1 1/2f and bhd after* **33/1**	61
-504	**U**		**Sea Of Leaves (USA)**[14] 2326 4-9-3 **92** ... FrederikTylicki 11 *(J S Goldie) in tch whn n.m.r: bmpd: then stmbld and uns rdr after 1 1/2f* **18/1**	—

57.85 secs (-2.55) **Going Correction** -0.275s/f (Firm) 15 Ran SP% **128.6**

Speed ratings (Par 109): **109,108,106,106,105 103,101,100,99,96 96,92,91,90,—**

toteswingers: 1&2 £4.90, 1&3 £6.50, 2&3 £9.70. CSF £49.61 CT £291.85 TOTE £5.50: £1.70, £2.90, £2.80; EX 45.50 Trifecta £194.20 Pool: £842.51 - 3.21 winning units..

Owner Reality Partnerships I **Bred** J P Coggan And Whitsbury Manor Stud **Trained** Great Habton, N Yorks

■ Stewards' Enquiry : David Allan one-day ban: failed to ride to draw (Jun 20)

Stevie Donohoe one-day ban: failed to ride to draw (Jun 20)

FOCUS

A hot 5f handicap but, like the opener, they posted a slower time than the two-year-old race, adding further credence to the strength of that particular piece of form. Hamish McGonagall was better than ever and confirmed York form with the favourite.

NOTEBOOK

Hamish McGonagall defied top weight and a 7lb rise for his York win in grand style, breaking well and getting across to race prominently before sticking on really strongly to hold on well. He is really in the groove right now and this has to be something close to a career-best.

Striking Spirit ran another cracking race in defeat, coming home strongly, and is handicapped to win again, but the suspicion is it will come over another furlong.

Ingleby Lady was forced to switch wide having raced along the rail early and she stayed on well and is another who will fare even better back up to 6f.

Masamah(IRE) could not keep his rivals at bay having made the running and his new mark looks high enough for now. (tchd 15-2)

Ziggy Lee was well backed to turn recent York form around with Hamish McGonagall and he had every chance having raced in touch with the leaders, but he could not quite muster the speed to get in a telling challenge. (op 5-1)

Hotham Official explanation: jockey said gelding was hampered by fallen rider

2760 CREATING EVENTS WITH SOUND AND VISION (S) STKS 1m 1f
4:15 (4:20) (Class 4) 3-Y-0+ **£5,180** (£1,541; £770; £384) **Stalls** High

Form RPR

1111 **1** **Fremen (USA)**[18] 2208 10-9-8 80 AdrianNicholls 1 86
(D Nicholls) *cl up: led after 1 1/2f and set stdy pce: qcknd wl over 2f out: rdn over 1f out: kpt on gamely ins fnl f* **2/1**[1]

040 **2** *1* **Mount Hadley (USA)**[31] 1826 6-9-3 83 (v) StevieDonohoe 2 79
(G A Butler) *trckd ldrs: swtchd lft and effrt 2f out: rdn to chse wnr and hung rt ins fnl f: drvn and kpt on wl towards fin* **3/1**[2]

44-6 **3** *2 3/4* **Kings Point (IRE)**[12] 2377 9-8-12 72 MichaelO'Connell(5) 5 73
(D Nicholls) *led 1 1/2f: cl up on inner: rdn along wl over 2f out: drvn over 1f out: sn one pce* **14/1**

0504 **4** *hd* **Bolodenka (IRE)**[12] 2377 8-9-3 74 TonyHamilton 3 72
(R A Fahey) *trckd ldrs: hdwy to chse wnr 1/2-way: rdn over 2f out: drvn wl over 1f out: sn one pce* **11/1**

-000 **5** *shd* **Lang Shining (IRE)**[31] 1829 6-9-3 89 FergusSweeney 6 72
(J A Osborne) *hld up in rr: swtchd lft and hdwy over 2f out: rdn over 1f out: sn drvn and no imp* **3/1**[2]

4066 **6** *2* **Ra Junior (USA)**[18] 2205 4-8-12 78 AmyRyan(5) 4 68
(D Nicholls) *hld up in tch: effrt over 3f out: rdn along over 2f out: n.d* **5/1**[3]

1m 52.56s (-1.34) **Going Correction** -0.275s/f (Firm) **6** Ran SP% **115.0**
Speed ratings (Par 105): **98,97,94,94,94 92**
toteswingers: 1&2 £3.00, 1&3 £7.90, 2&3 £5.50. CSF £8.59 TOTE £2.90: £1.10, £1.50; EX 8.00.There was no bid for the winner.
Owner Middleham Park Racing XXXV C King A Seed **Bred** Flaxman Holdings Ltd **Trained** Sessay, N Yorks

FOCUS
Quite a competitive heat for the grade but most of these find winning extremely difficult nowadays. It was steadily run and the form is a bit muddling. The winner is rated to last year's best.

2761 STEPHEN HAY AND ASSOCIATES LTD H'CAP (FOR THE TRADESMAN'S DERBY) 1m 4f 100y
4:50 (4:52) (Class 4) (0-80,80) 4-Y-0+
£7,788 (£2,332; £1,166; £583; £291; £146) **Stalls** High

Form RPR

0040 **1** **Just Lille (IRE)**[24] 2031 7-9-7 80 (v[1]) BarryMcHugh(3) 3 93
(Mrs A Duffield) *mde all: rdn along 3f out: drvn over 1f out: styd on gamely* **11/2**[3]

-014 **2** *3* **Antigua Sunrise (IRE)**[22] 2096 4-9-8 78 TonyHamilton 7 86
(R A Fahey) *trckd ldng pair on inner: hdwy to chse wnr 3f out: rdn wl over 1f out: drvn ins fnl f: one pce towards fin* **7/4**[1]

000- **3** *4 1/2* **Annibale Caro**[13] 5334 8-8-6 62 SaleemGolam 5 63
(J S Goldie) *dwlt: hld up in rr: hdwy on inner over 2f out: rdn to chse ldng pair over 1f out: sn drvn and no imp* **16/1**

4-53 **4** *5* **Veiled Applause**[56] 1013 7-9-8 78 GrahamGibbons 2 71
(J J Quinn) *hld up in tch: hdwy 3f out: rdn along to chse ldrs 12f out: sn drvn and btn* **10/1**

6-05 **5** *2 1/2* **King's Head (IRE)**[16] 2243 7-9-1 71 (p) TomEaves 1 60
(Miss L A Perratt) *chsd wnr: pushed along over 3f out: rdn wl over 2f out and sn wknd* **9/1**

0-64 **6** *2 1/2* **Middlemarch (IRE)**[14] 2349 10-8-5 61 (v) AndreaAtzeni 4 47
(J S Goldie) *hld up: a towards rr* **12/1**

0061 **7** *3 1/2* **Sea Land (FR)**[7] 2529 6-7-12 54 oh2 CathyGannon 8 34
(B Ellison) *hld up: a towards rr* **16/1**

21 **8** *1* **Royal Swain (IRE)**[21] 2131 4-9-3 73 RobertWinston 6 52
(G A Swinbank) *trckd ldrs: pushed along over 4f out: rdn 3f out: sn btn and eased fnl f* **15/8**[2]

2m 37.4s (-4.60) **Going Correction** -0.275s/f (Firm) **8** Ran SP% **125.1**
Speed ratings (Par 105): **104,102,99,95,94 92,90,89**
toteswingers: 1&2 £5.10, 1&3 £34.20, 2&3 £11.40. CSF £17.20 CT £156.16 TOTE £8.30: £2.10, £1.30, £5.60; EX 27.30.
Owner Miss Helen Wynne **Bred** Sweetmans Bloodstock **Trained** Constable Burton, N Yorks

FOCUS
A fair handicap and another front-running winner. She was entitled to win this on her best form.
Royal Swain(IRE) Official explanation: jockey said, gelding hung right-handed in straight, lost its action having been unsuited by the good to firm ground.

2762 TURFTV IN BETTING SHOPS H'CAP 7f 30y
5:25 (5:25) (Class 4) (0-80,78) 3-Y-0 **£5,180** (£1,541; £770; £384) **Stalls** High

Form RPR

11-6 **1** **Jeannie Galloway (IRE)**[21] 2112 3-9-7 78 TonyHamilton 6 88
(R A Fahey) *trckd ldrs: hdwy on inner over 4f out: swtchd lft and effrt to chal 2f out: sn rdn: drvn ins fnl f: edgd rt and led last 50yds* **9/2**[3]

5-62 **2** *nk* **Engulf (IRE)**[21] 2121 3-9-4 75 LiamJones 4 84
(W J Haggas) *hld up: hdwy and in tch 1/2-way: smooth prog 2f out: chal over 1f out: rdn ins fnl f and ev ch tl drvn and nt qckn nr fin* **5/4**[1]

-655 **3** *1* **Amenable (IRE)**[21] 2112 3-9-2 73 AdrianNicholls 9 79
(D Nicholls) *led: rdn along over 2f out: drvn over 1f out: hdd: n.m.r and wknd last 50yds* **7/2**[2]

000- **4** *6* **Thescottishsoldier**[220] 7116 3-7-13 59 oh14 AndrewHeffernan(3) 5 49
(A G Foster) *hld up: hdwy over 2f out: n.m.r and swtchd lft over 1f out: sn rdn and kpt on ins fnl f* **40/1**

54-0 **5** *1 1/2* **Key Breeze**[42] 1511 3-8-8 65 StevieDonohoe 8 51
(K A Ryan) *dwlt: hdwy on inner over 2f out: sn rdn and one pce* **22/1**

6-06 **6** *2* **Military Call**[15] 2296 3-8-7 67 BarryMcHugh(3) 7 47
(A C Whillans) *a towards rr* **20/1**

0006 **7** *4 1/2* **Transfixed (IRE)**[4] 2618 3-8-13 70 (v[1]) CathyGannon 3 38
(P D Evans) *t.k.h: chsd ldng pair: rdn along wl over 2f out: sn wknd* **18/1**

2220 **8** *1 1/4* **Magic Omen (USA)**[33] 1761 3-9-4 75 JoeFanning 2 40
(M Johnston) *cl up: rdn along over 2f out: sn drvn and wknd* **6/1**

2-12 **9** *2 1/4* **Master Leon**[134] 268 3-9-5 76 (v) TomEaves 1 35
(B Smart) *racd wd: cl up: rdn along 3f out: drvn over 2f out and sn wknd* **8/1**

1m 26.39s (-2.61) **Going Correction** -0.275s/f (Firm) **9** Ran SP% **127.1**
Speed ratings (Par 101): **111,110,109,102,100 98,93,92,89**
toteswingers: 1&2 £3.20, 1&3 £5.30, 2&3 £1.80. CSF £11.48 CT £24.39 TOTE £6.30: £1.30, £1.10, £1.80; EX 17.10 Place 6: £20.00, Place 5: £10.47..
Owner David Renwick **Bred** G And J Bloodstock **Trained** Musley Bank, N Yorks

FOCUS
A brisk gallop to this 7f handicap. Ordinary form. The winner and third came from the same Doncaster race last month with the winner posting a clear personal best.
T/Plt: £30.50 to a £1 stake. Pool: £76,420.08. 1,824.94 winning tickets. T/Qpdt: £11.80 to a £1 stake. Pool: £3,198.83. 199.90 winning tickets. JR

2498 NEWCASTLE (L-H)
Saturday, June 5

OFFICIAL GOING: Good to firm (good in places; 7.7)
Wind: Light, half behind Weather: Fine

2763 NESTLE CONFECTIONERY CHARITY MAIDEN AUCTION STKS 6f
6:35 (6:35) (Class 5) 2-Y-O **£3,238** (£963; £481; £240) **Stalls** Low

Form RPR

3 **1** **Shoshoni Wind**[12] 2376 2-8-12 0 PJMcDonald 4 88+
(K A Ryan) *t.k.h: trckd ldr: led after 1f: drvn clr over 1f out: pushed rt out* **5/2**[2]

25 **2** *5* **Tilliemint (IRE)**[16] 2239 2-8-4 0 (b[1]) DuranFentiman 7 65
(T D Easterby) *trckd ldrs: wnt 2nd over 2f out: sn rdn and no imp* **7/2**[3]

0 **3** *1 1/2* **Second Encore**[14] 2338 2-8-6 0 JimmyQuinn 1 63
(J S Moore) *t.k.h: trckd ldrs: effrt over 2f out: wnt 3rd over 1f out: one pce* **9/4**[1]

44 **4** *5* **Crown Ridge (IRE)**[10] 2427 2-8-13 0 SamHitchcott 2 55
(M R Channon) *led 1f: chsd wnr: drvn over 2f out: wknd 1f out* **8/1**

5 *1 3/4* **Sky Falcon (USA)** 2-8-11 0 RoystonFfrench 5 47
(M Johnston) *rrd s: sn drvn along in rr: hdwy over 3f out: wknd 2f out* **9/2**

6 *24* **Disco Des** 2-8-13 0 SilvestreDeSousa 6 —
(C Grant) *s.s: sn outpcd and bhd: t.o 2f out* **22/1**

1m 13.34s (-1.26) **Going Correction** -0.35s/f (Firm) **6** Ran SP% **115.2**
Speed ratings (Par 93): **98,91,89,82,80 48**
toteswingers: 1&2 £2.80, 1&3 £2.10, 2&3 £1.30 CSF £12.11 TOTE £2.90: £1.10, £2.40; EX 10.00.
Owner Hambleton Racing Ltd XVI **Bred** Mrs A F Tullie **Trained** Hambleton, N Yorks

FOCUS
After the current dry spell, the track was watered throughout the week to maintain the good to firm, good in places ground. The race developed on the far side of the track and afterwards the jockeys reported it to be good fast ground. Probably just an ordinary maiden auction stakes but the form looks solid enough. The winner produced a big step up from her debut.

NOTEBOOK
Shoshoni Wind, who had shown a clear sign of ability on her debut at Carlisle over 5f, put up a nice performance. Making all the running, she relished the extra furlong and looks to have a very straightforward attitude. She can go on from this. (op 9-4 tchd 2-1 and 11-4)
Tilliemint(IRE), coming from the yard who took this race last year, ran okay in her first-time blinkers and looks the ideal type for a nursery. (op 10-3 tchd 11-4)
Second Encore, who made her debut in a maiden at Newbury that is working out well, never looked happy and is surely better than this. (op 5-1)
Crown Ridge(IRE), having his third start, might have to drop down in grade to lose the maiden tag. (op 9-1 tchd 10-1)
Sky Falcon(USA), running for a respected stable, ran green and showed little. (op 3-1)

2764 FEVERSHAMARMSHOTEL.COM H'CAP 7f
7:05 (7:05) (Class 5) (0-70,69) 4-Y-0+ **£3,238** (£963; £481; £240) **Stalls** Low

Form RPR

6512 **1** **Sairaam (IRE)**[15] 2298 4-9-0 62 MickyFenton 11 72
(C Smith) *racd alone stands' side: w ldrs: overall ldr 4f out: edgd lft ins fnl f: styd on* **6/1**[2]

1041 **2** *1 1/4* **Imperial Djay (IRE)**[7] 2531 5-9-2 64 JimmyQuinn 8 71
(Mrs R A Carr) *hld up in rr: effrt and n.m.r 2f out: upsides 1f out: kpt on to take 2nd nr fin* **11/4**[1]

2500 **3** *hd* **Tevez**[8] 2511 5-8-11 59 SamHitchcott 1 65
(D Donovan) *dwlt: sn chsng ldrs: drvn 3f out: styd on to ld far side 150yds out: kpt on same pce* **11/1**

2/-0 **4** *1 1/4* **Frontline Girl (IRE)**[28] 1926 4-8-11 59 AndrewElliott 7 62
(J R Weymes) *chsd ldrs: upsides 1f out: kpt on same pce* **18/1**

340- **5** *1* **Rosko**[290] 5160 6-9-0 69 DaleSwift(7) 5 69
(B Ellison) *trckd ldrs: upsides 1f out: fdd towards fin* **6/1**[2]

3260 **6** *5* **Seldom (IRE)**[49] 1395 4-8-7 62 JohnCavanagh(7) 12 49
(M Brittain) *racd alone centre: chsd ldrs: wknd over 1f out* **12/1**

0024 **7** *nse* **Toby Tyler**[36] 1653 4-9-3 65 (p) PaulMulrennan 9 51
(P T Midgley) *chsd ldrs: led far side over 2f out: hung lft and hdd that side 150yds out: sn wknd* **7/1**[3]

-030 **8** *1 3/4* **Big Whitfield**[15] 2274 4-8-4 57 PatrickDonaghy(5) 10 39
(M Dods) *led far side gp: hdd over 2f out: wknd 1f out* **33/1**

-004 **9** *nk* **Piquante**[9] 2462 4-9-5 67 SilvestreDeSousa 4 48
(N Tinkler) *in rr: effrt over 2f out: kpt on: nvr nr ldrs* **6/1**[2]

/005 **10** *3/4* **Loyal Knight (IRE)**[32] 1812 5-7-11 50 oh5 (t) PaulPickard(5) 3 29
(P T Midgley) *dwlt: a in rr* **33/1**

0-06 **11** *1 3/4* **Who's Shirl**[9] 2462 4-9-0 65 KellyHarrison(3) 6 39
(C W Fairhurst) *t.k.h: trckd ldrs: drvn 3f out: sn lost pl* **20/1**

-600 **12** *2* **Rising Kheleyf (IRE)**[18] 2204 4-9-4 66 PJMcDonald 2 35
(G A Swinbank) *chsd ldrs: lost pl over 1f out* **16/1**

1m 25.69s (-3.01) **Going Correction** -0.35s/f (Firm) **12** Ran SP% **119.8**
Speed ratings (Par 103): **103,101,101,99,98 93,93,91,90,89 87,85**
toteswingers: 1&2 £3.20, 1&3 £9.70, 2&3 £8.50 CSF £22.55 CT £182.28 TOTE £5.40: £1.50, £1.50, £4.00; EX 17.20.
Owner Phil Martin & Trev Sleath **Bred** Shadwell Estate Company Limited **Trained** Temple Bruer, Lincs

FOCUS
A wide-open 51-70 handicap run at a sound pace and there were still six horses with a chance with just over a furlong to run.
Toby Tyler Official explanation: jockey said gelding hung left-handed
Who's Shirl Official explanation: jockey said filly ran too free

2765 ROWNTREE'S FRUIT PASTILLES H'CAP 2m 19y
7:35 (7:35) (Class 6) (0-65,65) 4-Y-0+ **£1,942** (£578; £288; £144) **Stalls** Low

Form RPR

660/ **1** **Jeu De Roseau (IRE)**[6] 436 6-8-7 47 ShaneKelly 5 60
(C Grant) *hld up in tch: wnt 2nd over 2f out: rdn to ld over 1f out: styd on strly* **4/1**[2]

0-33 **2** *3* **Petella**[18] 2214 4-8-2 46 KellyHarrison(3) 7 55
(C W Thornton) *hld up in rr: drvn 5f out: hdwy over 2f out: styd on to take 2nd 1f out: no imp* **5/1**[3]

0462 **3** *4 1/2* **Strikemaster (IRE)**[18] 2218 4-9-3 65 (b) DaleSwift(7) 6 69
(B Ellison) *hld up in rr: hdwy 6f out: styd on to take 3rd 1f out: kpt on same pce* **13/8**[1]

230- **4** *9* **Border Tale**[10] 5734 10-8-8 48 (v) PaulMulrennan 12 41
(James Moffatt) *hld up towards rr: drvn over 3f out: hdwy on ins over 2f out: nvr nr ldrs* **12/1**

-614 5 1/2 **Alloro**10 2430 6-8-2 47 PaulPickard(5) 4 39
(A Kirtley) *led: hdd over 1f out: sn wknd* 14/1
4-00 6 7 **Dechiper (IRE)**8 2500 8-9-1 55 GrahamGibbons 3 39
(R Johnson) *dwlt: hld up in rr: drvn over 4f out: hrd rdn over 2f out: sn wknd* 7/1
0530 7 1/2 **Ferney Boy**45 1467 4-9-6 61 PJMcDonald 8 44
(G A Swinbank) *hld up in rr: hdwy 4f out: sn drvn: nvr on terms* 12/1
00-0 8 3 3/4 **Media Stars**8 2500 5-8-1 46 ow1 DeanHeslop(5) 1 25
(R Johnson) *chsd ldr: drvn 5f out: wknd appr fnl f: eased towards fin* 50/1
6P0- 9 4 **Humourous (IRE)**16 4873 8-8-8 48 (t) PatrickMathers 11 22
(B Storey) *sn chsng ldrs: sn pushed along: lost pl over 4f out: sn bhd* 40/1
0- 10 22 **Kathleen Cox (IRE)**204 7369 5-8-5 45 RoystonFfrench 9 —
(Niall Moran, Ire) *gave problems in stalls: sn chsng ldrs: drvn along 7f out: lost pl over 3f out: sn bhd and eased: t.o* 40/1

3m 31.18s (-8.22) **Going Correction** -0.475s/f (Firm)
WFA 4 from 5yo+ 1lb **10** Ran SP% **116.2**
Speed ratings (Par 101): **101,99,97,92,92 89,88,86,84,73**
toteswingers: 1&2 £2.50 CSF £24.01 CT £44.61 TOTE £5.30: £1.90, £2.20, £1.10; EX 26.80.
Owner W Raw **Bred** P Connolly **Trained** Newton Bewley, Co Durham

FOCUS
No great surprises in this race, with the first three in the betting filling the places. It was run at a very sound gallop thanks to Alloro, who weakened inside the final furlong.

2766 BLUE RIBAND H'CAP 1m 2f 32y
8:05 (8:05) (Class 5) (0-75,73) 4-Y-0+ **£3,238** (£963; £481; £240) **Stalls** Centre

Form RPR
5241 1 **George Adamson (IRE)**8 2500 4-8-9 61 PJMcDonald 5 70+
(G A Swinbank) *trckd ldrs: nt clr run over 2f out: sn swtchd rt: led 1f out: drvn out* 7/4[1]
-045 2 1 1/2 **Steel Trade**4 2625 4-8-10 62 DavidAllan 8 68
(M Brittain) *dwlt: hld up in last: drvn 4f out: edgd rt and hdwy 2f out: edgd lft and styd on to take 2nd last 150yds* 13/2
0-14 3 1 1/2 **That'll Do Nicely (IRE)**15 2277 7-8-12 64 PaulMulrennan 4 70+
(N G Richards) *hld up: nt clr run on inner over 2f out tl jst ins fnl f: r.o to take 3rd last 100yds* 7/2[2]
4-16 4 1 1/2 **High Office**18 2204 4-9-7 73 TonyHamilton 7 73
(R A Fahey) *trckd ldrs: effrt over 2f out: led briefly over 1f out: fdd ins fnl f* 11/2[3]
-006 5 1 1/4 **Casino Night**22 2084 5-8-8 65 DeanHeslop(5) 2 63
(R Johnson) *t.k.h: led after 1f: hdd over 1f out: fdd jst ins fnl f* 33/1
-053 6 1 1/2 **Aldaado (IRE)**9 2451 4-8-13 65 (p) TomEaves 6 60
(M Dods) *prom: sn drvn along: reminders 4f out: one pce fnl 3f* 8/1
0-65 7 1 3/4 **Tilos Gem (IRE)**53 1277 4-9-3 69 RoystonFfrench 3 60
(M Johnston) *led 1f: chsd ldr: effrt over 3f out: upsides over 1f out: wknd 1f out* 8/1

2m 10.73s (-1.17) **Going Correction** -0.475s/f (Firm) **7** Ran SP% **112.5**
Speed ratings (Par 103): **85,83,82,81,80 79,77**
toteswingers: 1&2 £4.30, 1&3 £1.10, 2&3 £13.80 CSF £13.26 CT £35.05 TOTE £3.10: £2.00, £2.00; EX 11.10.
Owner Mrs S Sanbrook **Bred** Miss O O'Connor & Stephanie Von Schilcher **Trained** Melsonby, N Yorks

FOCUS
A good pace for this very tight handicap, in which all seven runners had some sort of chance inside the final furlong.
That'll Do Nicely(IRE) Official explanation: jockey said gelding was denied a clear run

2767 MARIE CURIE MAIDEN STKS 1m 2f 32y
8:35 (8:35) (Class 5) 3-Y-0+ **£3,238** (£963; £481; £240) **Stalls** Centre

Form RPR
5-55 1 **Boss's Destination**24 2033 3-8-12 74 PJMcDonald 3 77
(G A Swinbank) *led: drvn over 3f out: hdd over 1f out: hung rt and led last 150yds: kpt on wl* 9/4[2]
505 2 1 1/2 **Osgood**21 2115 3-8-12 72 SamHitchcott 5 74
(M R Channon) *stdd s: hld up in last: effrt over 3f out: edgd lft and led over 1f out: hdd ins fnl f: no ex* 7/2[3]
3 1/2 **Ceoil An Aith (IRE)** 4-9-6 0 RoystonFfrench 4 70+
(M Johnston) *chsd ldr: effrt over 3f out: hung bdly lft over 2f out: n.m.r and outpcd over 1f out: styd on wl fnl 150yds: will improve* 10/1
6- 4 1 3/4 **Choice**228 6921 3-8-7 0 ShaneKelly 2 69+
(Sir Michael Stoute) *trckd ldrs: effrt over 2f out: upsides but keeping on same pce whn squeezed out over 1f out: fdd ins fnl f* 11/10[1]

2m 14.09s (2.19) **Going Correction** -0.475s/f (Firm)
WFA 3 from 4yo 13lb **4** Ran SP% **109.7**
Speed ratings (Par 103): **72,70,70,69**
CSF £9.97 TOTE £2.90; EX 10.80.
Owner G H Bell **Bred** Overbury Stallions Ltd **Trained** Melsonby, N Yorks

FOCUS
Despite there being only four runners in this maiden, it ended up becoming quite messy with the runners getting on top of each other with just over a furlong to run.

2768 QUALITY STREET MATCHMAKERS H'CAP 5f
9:05 (9:05) (Class 5) (0-75,75) 3-Y-O **£3,238** (£963; £481; £240) **Stalls** Low

Form RPR
41-0 1 **Commanche Raider (IRE)**22 2069 3-9-7 75 PhillipMakin 7 80+
(M Dods) *mid-div: drvn over 2f out: hdwy appr fnl f: r.o to ld last strides* 3/1[2]
-012 2 hd **Lees Anthem**15 2291 3-8-5 59 PatrickMathers 4 63
(C J Teague) *chsd ldrs: narrow ld 75yds out: hdd post* 12/1
341- 3 3/4 **Jack Luey**205 7352 3-8-8 65 AndrewHeffernan(3) 8 66
(L A Mullaney) *led: hdd ins fnl f: no ex* 25/1
3-63 4 1/2 **We'll Deal Again**11 2426 3-8-12 66 GrahamGibbons 9 66
(M W Easterby) *w ldrs: kpt on same pce ins fnl f* 7/1
1431 5 nk **Liberty Lady (IRE)**14 2332 3-9-7 75 ShaneKelly 2 73+
(D Donovan) *rrd and swvd rt s: chsd ldrs: kpt on ins fnl f: n.m.r nr fin* 11/4[1]
0-50 6 2 1/2 **Camacho Flyer (IRE)**18 2217 3-7-11 56 (v) PaulPickard(5) 11 45
(P T Midgley) *racd w ldrs on wd outside: wknd last 75yds* 20/1
-035 7 3/4 **Bossy Kitty**11 2426 3-9-6 74 SilvestreDeSousa 5 61
(N Tinkler) *sltly hmpd s: hdwy 3f out: kpt on same pce fnl f* 17/2
11-4 8 nk **Melody In The Mist (FR)**9 2450 3-8-13 72 DeanHeslop(5) 3 58
(T D Barron) *hmpd s: in rr: kpt on fnl 2f: nvr nr ldrs* 16/1
03-5 9 2 3/4 **Thinking**10 2432 3-8-6 60 ow1 (p) DavidAllan 6 36
(T D Easterby) *mid-div: sme hdwy over 2f out: nvr nr ldrs* 8/1

410- 10 7 **Cian Rooney (IRE)**301 4803 3-9-4 72 MickyFenton 1 23
(Mrs A Duffield) *t.k.h in rr: swtchd rt after 1f: nvr on terms: eased ins fnl f* 33/1
1444 11 16 **Trade Secret**11 2426 3-9-6 74 TomEaves 10 —
(M Brittain) *s.i.s: in rr: wl bhd fnl 2f: virtually p.u* 13/2[3]

60.18 secs (-0.92) **Going Correction** -0.35s/f (Firm) **11** Ran SP% **124.3**
Speed ratings (Par 99): **90,89,88,87,87 83,82,81,77,65 40**
toteswingers: 1&2 £12.60, 1&3 £5.60, 2&3 £90.70 CSF £40.64 CT £793.09 TOTE £4.00: £2.00, £6.10, £11.30; EX 61.90 Place 6 £88.31, Place 5 £46.64.
Owner Doug Graham **Bred** Epona Bloodstock Ltd **Trained** Denton, Co Durham
■ Stewards' Enquiry : Patrick Mathers three-day ban: weighed in 2lb heavier (Jun 20-22)

FOCUS
A wide-open 56-75 handicap run at a sound tempo and it proved hard to make ground from off the pace.
Liberty Lady(IRE) Official explanation: jockey said filly reared on leaving stalls
Cian Rooney(IRE) Official explanation: jockey said gelding lost its action
Trade Secret Official explanation: jockey said colt moved poorly throughout
T/Plt: £259.10 to a £1 stake. Pool: £66,145.31. 186.34 winning tickets. T/Qpdt: £96.90 to a £1 stake Pool: £4,910.70. 37.50 winning tickets. WG

2769 - 2775a (Foreign Racing) - See Raceform Interactive

BELMONT PARK (L-H)
Saturday, June 5

OFFICIAL GOING: Dirt: fast; turf: firm

2776a BELMONT STKS (GRADE 1) (3YO) (DIRT) 1m 4f (D)
11:32 (11:35) 3-Y-O **£370,370** (£123,456; £67,901; £37,037; £18,518)

RPR
1 **Drosselmeyer (USA)**28 3-9-0 0 MESmith 7 116
(William Mott, U.S.A) 13/1
2 3/4 **Fly Down (USA)**28 3-9-0 0 JRVelazquez 5 115
(Nicholas Zito, U.S.A) 26/5[2]
3 nk **First Dude (USA)**21 2137 3-9-0 0 RADominguez 11 114
(Dale Romans, U.S.A) 59/10[3]
4 1 1/2 **Game On Dude (USA)**28 3-9-0 0 (b) MGarcia 8 112
(Bob Baffert, U.S.A) 17/1
5 3 3/4 **Stay Put (USA)**35 3-9-0 0 (b) HJTheriotII 10 106
(Steve Margolis, U.S.A) 26/1
6 1 1/4 **Interactif (USA)**56 3-9-0 0 JJCastellano 12 105
(Todd Pletcher, U.S.A) 198/10
7 2 1/2 **Stately Victor (USA)**35 1714 3-9-0 0 AGarcia 9 101
(Michael J Maker, U.S.A) 143/10
8 3/4 **Ice Box (USA)**35 1714 3-9-0 0 JLezcano 6 100
(Nicholas Zito, U.S.A) 37/20[1]
9 4 1/2 **Make Music For Me (USA)**35 1714 3-9-0 0 (b) JRosario 4 93
(Alexis Barba, U.S.A) 123/10
10 11 1/4 **Dave In Dixie (USA)**63 3-9-0 0 CHBorel 1 76
(John W Sadler, U.S.A) 147/10
11 19 1/2 **Spangled Star (USA)**42 3-9-0 0 (b) GKGomez 2 47
(Richard Dutrow Jr, U.S.A) 233/10
12 1/2 **Uptowncharlybrown (USA)**49 3-9-0 0 RMaragh 3 103
(Kiaran McLaughlin, U.S.A) 109/10

2m 31.57s (2.61) **12** Ran SP% **119.9**
PARI-MUTUEL (all including $2 stake): WIN 28.00; PLACE (1-2) 11.60, 6.80; SHOW (1-2-3) 7.70, 5.10, 4.90; SF 144.50.
Owner WinStar Farm LLC **Bred** Aaron U Jones & Marie D Jones **Trained** USA

FOCUS
A weak-looking Belmont Stakes and they went a steady pace. Basically an unsatisfactory renewal.

NOTEBOOK
Drosselmeyer(USA) got first run on Fly Down and that enabled him to reverse recent Dwyer Stakes form with that rival.
Fly Down(USA) had today's winner 6l behind him when landing the Dwyer Stakes over 1m1f at this course last time and it's not difficult to argue that he would have confirmed placings with that rival had Velazquez got after him sooner. He finished strongly, but all too late and his rider should have been proactive considering the lack of pace in the race.
First Dude(USA), a game second in the Preakness last time, was allowed to set modest fractions but he still didn't see out this longer trip. As well as a lack of stamina, it's also possible this came plenty soon enough following his recent exertions.
Ice Box(USA) benefited from being held up off an overly strong pace when winning the Florida Derby and again when second in the Kentucky Derby, but the steady gallop was no use to him this time.

2777 - (Foreign Racing) - See Raceform Interactive

2615 LONGCHAMP (R-H)
Saturday, June 5

OFFICIAL GOING: Turf: good

2778a PRIX DU PALAIS-ROYAL (GROUP 3) (3YO+) (TURF) 7f
2:50 (12:00) 3-Y-O+ **£35,398** (£14,159; £10,619; £7,079; £3,539)

RPR
1 **Dalghar (FR)**30 1855 4-9-3 0 Christophe-PatriceLemaire 7 117
(A De Royer-Dupre, France) *led briefly s: hdd after 1f: cruised to ld at 1/2-way: rdn 1f out: sn wnt clr: won comf* 11/10[1]
2 2 1/2 **Colonial (IRE)**14 2357 3-8-7 0 MaximeGuyon 2 106
(A Fabre, France) *grabbed ld after a f: hdd at 1/2-way: rdn 1 1/2f out: no ch w wnr: r.o wl* 2/1[2]
3 1 1/2 **Salut L'Africain (FR)**39 1611 5-9-3 0 (p) IoritzMendizabal 5 106
(Robert Collet, France) *racd in 6th fr s: effrt 2f out: r.o wl ins fnl f* 11/1
4 3/4 **Slickly Royal (FR)**49 6-9-3 0 (b) AnthonyCrastus 1 104
(P Demercastel, France) *racd in 3rd on rail fr s pulling hrd: rdn 1 1/2f out: threatened briefly: no ex fnl f: styd on* 19/1
5 3/4 **Too Nice Name (FR)**16 2271 3-8-7 0 GregoryBenoist 6 98
(Robert Collet, France) *in rr fr s: hrd rdn 1 1/2f out: r.o wl but no threat to ldrs* 19/1
6 2 **Blue And Gold (FR)**44 4-9-0 0 YannLerner 9 94
(C Lerner, France) *settled towards rr: rdn 2f out: styd on: no ex* 53/1
7 2 **Only Green (IRE)**211 7285 4-9-0 0 MickaelBarzalona 3 88
(F Head, France) *racd in 5th bhd ldrs: rdn 2f out: briefly threatened but wknd fr 1f out* 12/1

8 ½ **Lutece Eria (FR)**[61] 4-9-0 0 AlexandreRoussel 4 87
(C Diard, France) *racd cl bhd ldrs fr s: rdn 2f out on outside: grad fdd to rr* **9/1**[3]

1m 17.4s (-3.30)
WFA 3 from 4yo+ 10lb 8 Ran SP% **118.8**
WIN (incl. 1 euro stake): 2.10. PLACES: 1.10, 1.20, 1.70. DF: 2.00. SF: 4.10.
Owner H H Aga Khan **Bred** H H The Aga Khan's Studs S C **Trained** Chantilly, France

NOTEBOOK
Dalghar(FR) is a progressive sort and gained his first Group win with something in hand. He could well reappear in the Queen Anne over another furlong, although that is another step up from this. He can win more races at around this trip and the Prix de la Foret looks a suitable long-term target.
Colonial(IRE), a dual Listed winner, is also progressing but, after making much of the running, the winner proved too speedy.
Salut L'Africain(FR) ran a reasonable race but all his best form has been at shorter trips.

2485 BRIGHTON (L-H)
Sunday, June 6

OFFICIAL GOING: Good to firm (firm in places; watered; 9.1)
All rails on Inner and distances as advertised.
Wind: medium, against Weather: sunny and warm

2779 AUGUST FESTIVAL HERE 4TH, 5TH, 6TH H'CAP 5f 213y
2:30 (2:31) (Class 6) (0-55,55) 4-Y-0+ **£2,072** (£616; £308; £153) **Stalls** Low

Form RPR

0-16 1 **Boldinor**[101] 694 7-9-0 **54** DavidProbert 8 63
(M R Bosley) *rrd s and s.i.s: bhd: hdwy and rdn 3f out: drvn and chsd ldrs ent fnl f: led fnl 150yds: kpt on wl towards fin* **25/1**

3016 2 ½ **Sirjosh**[6] 2590 4-8-8 **53** DeclanCannon(5) 7 60
(D Donovan) *s.i.s: bhd: stl plenty to do and rdn 2f out: gd hdwy on outer ent fnl f: pressed wnr wl ins fnl f: no ex towards fin* **5/1**[1]

2554 3 1 ¼ **Namu**[20] 2184 7-8-10 **53** (p) JackDean(3) 4 58+
(Miss T Spearing) *hld up in tch: effrt on inner wl over 1f out: rdn whn hmpd ent fnl f: switchd rt jst ins fnl f: styd on wl fnl 100yds* **11/2**[2]

0002 4 ¾ **What Katie Did (IRE)**[6] 2589 5-9-1 **55** (p) LiamKeniry 13 56
(J M Bradley) *t.k.h: hld up in tch: effrt and rdn 2f out: edgd lft u.p ent fnl f: kpt on same pce ins fnl f* **7/1**[3]

5656 5 shd **Captain Imperial (IRE)**[16] 2273 4-7-13 **46** (t) MatthewLawson(7) 5 46
(R Bastiman) *taken down early: s.i.s: bhd: rdn and hdwy over 1f out: drvn and styd on wl fnl f: nt rch ldrs* **11/1**

0350 6 ¾ **Dualagi**[6] 2589 6-8-12 **52** JimCrowley 10 50+
(M R Bosley) *hmpd s and s.i.s: hld up in last trio: hdwy and nt clr run 2f out tl jst over 1f out: fnlly in the clr and styd on fnl f: nvr trbld ldrs* **11/1**

4026 7 nse **Best One**[2] 2721 6-8-13 **53** (b) KevinGhunowa 1 51
(R A Harris) *led: rdn over 2f out: hrd drvn and hung lft 1f out: sn collided w rival and hdd: nt rcvr and btn after* **15/2**

0000 8 2 **Top Flight Splash**[6] 2590 4-8-3 **46** oh1 MartinLane(3) 12 50+
(P D Evans) *hld up towards rr: swtchd ins and hdwy 2f out: rdn and pressing wnr whn gap clsd and bdly hmpd jst ins fnl f: nt rcvr and btn after* **14/1**

5445 9 hd **Hart Of Gold**[6] 2590 6-8-12 **52** (b) LukeMorris 9 43
(R A Harris) *taken down early: racd keenly: chsd ldrs: rdn ent fnl 2f: edgd lft u.p over 1f out: wknd ins fnl f* **8/1**

05-6 10 1 ¾ **Dilli Dancer**[12] 2419 5-8-7 **47** (e) SaleemGolam 15 32
(G D Blake) *in tch in midfield: rdn and unable qck 2f out: wkng whn n.m.r jst over 1f out: wl btn fnl f* **14/1**

0000 11 1 **Conjecture**[89] 839 8-8-10 **50** TomQueally 6 32
(R Bastiman) *taken down early: w ldr tl wl over 1f out: wkng u.p whn n.m.r and hmpd ent fnl f: wl btn fnl f* **14/1**

1055 12 1 **Royal Acclamation (IRE)**[12] 2419 5-8-4 **51** DavidKenny(7) 11 30+
(H J Evans) *stmbld and wnt lft s: s.i.s: hld up towards rr: effrt and nt clr run fr 2f out tl 1f out: no ch* **12/1**

4060 13 ¾ **Mandhooma**[13] 2385 4-8-3 **46** oh1 WilliamCarson(3) 14 22
(P W Hiatt) *dwlt: sn revovered and chsng ldrs: wknd u.p over 1f out: eased whn wl btn ins fnl f* **33/1**

40/0 14 2 ½ **Turtle Dove**[17] 2249 5-9-1 **55** NeilChalmers 3 23
(Mark Gillard) *chsd ldrs tl rdn and wknd qckly ent fnl 2f: wl btn and eased ins fnl f* **66/1**

1m 11.11s (0.91) **Going Correction** +0.125s/f (Good) 14 Ran SP% **120.1**
Speed ratings (Par 101): **98,97,95,94,94 93,93,90,90,88 86,85,84,81**
Tote Swingers: 1&2 £31.10, 1&3 £14.30, 2&3 £7.70 CSF £144.21 CT £811.05 TOTE £31.00: £6.80, £2.40, £1.50; EX 157.60 TRIFECTA Not won..
Owner Ron Collins **Bred** Ron Collins **Trained** Chalfont St Giles, Bucks
■ Stewards' Enquiry : Kevin Ghunowa five-day ban: careless riding (Jun 20-24)
Martin Lane one-day ban: careless riding (Jun 20)

FOCUS
They went an overly strong pace in this moderate handicap, suiting those held up, but it still proved very competitive, and a rough contest, too, with plenty of these bumping each other. As such, some of the beaten runners are better than they showed.
Dualagi ◆ Official explanation: jockey said mare was denied a clear run
Royal Acclamation(IRE) ◆ Official explanation: jockey said gelding suffered interference in running

2780 BRIGHTON JOHN SMITH'S DAY 4TH AUGUST H'CAP 7f 214y
3:00 (3:00) (Class 6) (0-60,60) 3-Y-O **£2,072** (£616; £308; £153) **Stalls** Low

Form RPR

-001 1 **Princess Lexi (IRE)**[27] 1971 3-8-9 **51** StevieDonohoe 2 56
(Ian Williams) *mde most: rdn ent fnl 2f: hdd over 1f out: drvn and kpt on gamely to ld again fnl 75yds: styd on wl* **7/2**[2]

0-60 2 1 **Louisiana Gift (IRE)**[17] 2250 3-9-1 **60** (p) PatrickHills(3) 6 63
(J W Hills) *chsd ldng pair: rdn and unable qck ent fnl 2f: drvn to chse ldng pair ent fnl f: hung bdly rt after but kpt on to go 2nd nr fin* **7/1**

-053 3 hd **Mini Max**[10] 2480 3-9-0 **56** (b[1]) DaneO'Neill 4 58
(B W Duke) *dwlt and pushed along early: hdwy into midfield 5f out: rdn to chse ldr 2f out: drvn to ld over 1f out: hdd and no ex fnl 75yds* **3/1**[1]

06-0 4 1 **Atakora (IRE)**[55] 1261 3-9-2 **58** (e[1]) JimCrowley 7 58
(Mrs A J Perrett) *hld up in last: rdn and effrt ent fnl 2f: no real prog tl styd on u.p fnl 150yds: nt pce to rch ldrs* **9/2**[3]

0-02 5 2 **Naseby (USA)**[12] 2418 3-9-2 **58** DavidProbert 5 53
(Miss S L Davison) *w ldr tl rdn and unable qck ent fnl 2f: btn whn edgd lft ins fnl f* **7/2**[2]

0-00 6 1 ½ **Gazamali (IRE)**[60] 1164 3-8-8 **50** FrankieMcDonald 1 42
(H J Evans) *t.k.h: hld up in tch in last trio: switching rt looking for run 2f out: no prog and btn ent fnl f* **25/1**

0550 7 shd **Gulf Punch**[47] 1461 3-8-1 **46** oh1 (p) Louis-PhilippeBeuzelin(3) 3 38
(M F Harris) *hld up in tch towards rr: rdn and effrt jst over 2f out: swtchd lft and wnt between horses 1f out: no prog fnl f: wl hld whn n.m.r fnl 150yds* **16/1**

0-00 8 21 **Aintgottaname**[18] 2231 3-8-5 **47** CathyGannon 8 —
(M J McGrath) *chsd ldrs: rdn ent fnl 3f: wknd u.p over 1f out: btn whn short of room and hmpd 1f out: eased ins fnl f* **33/1**

1m 37.5s (1.50) **Going Correction** +0.125s/f (Good) 8 Ran SP% **112.8**
Speed ratings (Par 97): **97,96,95,94,92 91,91,70**
Tote Swingers: 1&2 £4.90, 1&3 £2.60, 2&3 £5.00 CSF £27.25 CT £80.95 TOTE £3.60: £2.10, £2.60, £1.02; EX 26.10 Trifecta £190.20 Pool: £386.77 - 1.50 winning units..
Owner Dr Marwan Koukash **Bred** Epona Bloodstock Ltd And P A Byrne **Trained** Portway, Worcs
■ Stewards' Enquiry : Louis-Philippe Beuzelin two-day ban: careless riding (Jun 20-21)

FOCUS
A weak contest.
Louisiana Gift(IRE) Official explanation: jockey said gelding hung both ways

2781 BRIGHTON LADIES DAY 5TH AUGUST H'CAP 1m 1f 209y
3:30 (3:30) (Class 6) (0-65,60) 4-Y-0+ **£2,072** (£616; £308; £153) **Stalls** High

Form RPR

4054 1 **Inquisitress**[9] 2488 6-8-6 **45** NeilChalmers 6 51
(J J Bridger) *chsd ldng pair tl hdwy to ld 7f out: mde rest: rdn 2f out: edging rt u.p over 1f out: jst hld on: all out* **7/1**

0132 2 nse **Yourgolftravel Com**[9] 2490 5-9-6 **59** StephenCraine 2 68+
(M Wigham) *stdd s: hld up in last pair: effrt on inner whn bdly hmpd and snatched up 2f out: swtchd rt and rdn wl over 1f out: chsd wnr 1f out: kpt on u.p fnl f: jst failed* **5/6**[1]

0300 3 5 **Foxtrot Bravo (IRE)**[113] 540 4-8-6 **45** (b[1]) DavidProbert 3 41
(Miss S L Davison) *led tl 7f out: chsd wnr after: rdn and edgd sltly lft 2f out: btn and lost 2nd 1f out: wknd fnl f* **13/2**[3]

222- 4 14 **Ubiquitous**[291] 5152 5-8-11 **50** SaleemGolam 4 18
(S Dow) *chsd ldr tl 7f out: chsd ldrs after tl wknd u.p wl over 1f out: eased wl ins fnl f* **9/2**[2]

4530 5 7 **Shake On It**[12] 1241 6-9-6 **59** JimCrowley 5 13
(M R Hoad) *stdd s: hld up in last: rdn and effrt 2f out: wl btn over 1f out: eased ins fnl f* **9/1**

2m 6.11s (2.51) **Going Correction** +0.125s/f (Good) 5 Ran SP% **108.6**
Speed ratings (Par 101): **94,93,89,78,73**
CSF £13.18 TOTE £6.90: £3.60, £1.20; EX 15.00.
Owner C Marshall T Wallace J J Bridger **Bred** A Saccomando **Trained** Liphook, Hants

FOCUS
A misleading one-two in this moderate handicap, with Inquisitress appearing to nick this under a fine tactical ride from Neil Chalmers, while Yourgolftravel Com was denied a clear run at a crucial stage. There wasn't that much pace on through the early stages and the time was over six seconds above standard.
Yourgolftravel Com Official explanation: jockey said gelding was denied a clear run

2782 HANNAH RICHARDSON BIRTHDAY MAIDEN STKS 1m 3f 196y
4:00 (4:01) (Class 5) 3-Y-O+ **£2,719** (£809; £404; £202) **Stalls** High

Form RPR

-236 1 **Ebony Boom (IRE)**[17] 2252 3-8-12 72 TomQueally 1 77
(H R A Cecil) *mde all: gng best and pushed along wl over 1f out: in command ent fnl f: easily* **4/6**[1]

5-53 2 3 ¼ **Baltimore Clipper (USA)**[27] 1976 3-8-12 74 JimCrowley 5 72
(P F I Cole) *chsd wnr for 2f: in tch after: rdn to chse wnr over 2f out: hld hd high and racd awkwardly fr wl over 1f out: hung lft and no hdwy over 1f out: btn ent fnl f* **6/4**[2]

3 9 **Joan D'Arc (IRE)** 3-8-4 0 WilliamCarson(3) 4 54
(M G Quinlan) *hld up in tch: c centre and rdn ent fnl 3f: btn over 1f out: heavily eased wl ins fnl f* **12/1**[3]

00-6 4 14 **Vadition (IRE)**[10] 2460 3-8-2 42 AmyBaker(5) 6 30
(J J Bridger) *chsd wnr after 2f: rdn ent fnl 3f: lost 2nd over 2f out and sn wl bhd* **66/1**

2m 36.71s (4.01) **Going Correction** +0.125s/f (Good)
WFA 3 from 4yo 15lb 4 Ran SP% **109.2**
Speed ratings (Par 103): **91,88,82,73**
CSF £1.95 TOTE £1.50; EX 1.80.
Owner Pkd Partnership **Bred** Ammerland Verwaltung Gmbh **Trained** Newmarket, Suffolk

FOCUS
A seriously uncompetitive maiden and not form to dwell on.

2783 HARDINGS BAR AND CATERING SERVICES H'CAP 6f 209y
4:30 (4:31) (Class 5) (0-75,73) 4-Y-0+ **£2,719** (£809; £404; £202) **Stalls** Centre

Form RPR

10-1 1 **Aegean Shadow**[15] 2331 4-9-4 **70** TomQueally 2 84+
(H R A Cecil) *trckd ldrs: gng wl but nt clr run wl over 1f out: carried lft and barging match w rivals ent fnl f: rdn and qckdn to ld fnl 50yds: wl in command fin* **10/3**[1]

5433 2 1 **Rondeau (GR)**[31] 1848 5-9-5 **71** JimCrowley 10 78
(P R Chamings) *stdd s: t.k.h: hld up in tch in rr: rdn and effrt on outer wl over 1f out: chal and edgd lft u.p ent fnl f: led fnl 150yds: hdd and nt pce of wnr fnl 50yds* **5/1**[3]

56-1 3 hd **Ocean Countess (IRE)**[38] 1634 4-9-5 **71** CathyGannon 8 78+
(Miss J Feilden) *in tch in last trio: pushed along over 4f out: rdn over 2f out: unable qck and sltly hmpd over 1f out: swtchd rt and styd on wl fnl f: wnt 3rd last strides* **9/2**[2]

00-5 4 hd **Choreography**[38] 1637 7-9-3 **69** (p) DaneO'Neill 9 75
(Jim Best) *t.k.h: hld up in tch towards rr: rdn and hdwy 2f out: led and edgd lft u.p over 1f out: hdd fnl 150yds: no ex and lost 2 pls towards fin* **17/2**

-051 5 2 **Buxton**[9] 2490 6-9-6 **72** (t) PatCosgrave 7 73+
(R Ingram) *stdd s: hld up in tch in last trio: nt clr run fr over 2f out tl wl ins fnl f: kpt on but nvr able to chal* **6/1**

0-00 6 1 **Hi Shinko**[25] 2024 4-9-4 **73** JamesMillman(3) 3 71
(B R Millman) *t.k.h: w ldrs: led over 2f out: rdn ent fnl 2f: hdd over 1f out: stl pressing ldrs and keeping on same pce whn carried lft and squeezed out 1f out: one pce and hld after* **15/2**

0564 7 nse **Straight Face (IRE)**[3] 2678 6-8-13 **65** (b) JamesDoyle 4 63
(P D Evans) *w ldrs: ev ch and rdn over 2f out: nt qckning u.p whn short of room over 1f out: styd on same pce after* **25/1**

0-20 8 1 ¾ **Mr Fantozzi (IRE)**[76] 568 5-8-2 **54** oh2 DavidProbert 1 53+
(D Donovan) *sn pushed up to ld: hdd and rdn wl over 2f out: stl ev ch but hrd drvn tl pushed lft: collided w rail and bdly hmpd ent fnl f: nt rcvr* **10/1**

4312 **9** *nse* **Spinning Ridge (IRE)**[14] 2362 5-9-6 **72**..........................(b) LukeMorris 6 65
(R A Harris) *chsd ldrs: rdn and effrt 2f out: sn edgd rt u.p: drvn and edging lft whn short of room and lost pl jst over 1f out: no threat to ldrs fnl f* **11/1**

4501 **10** *12* **Timeteam (IRE)**[20] 2178 4-9-1 **70**...................................... MartinLane(3) 5 31
(P D Evans) *stood stl as stalls opened and lost many l s: nvr on terms* **20/1**

1m 23.74s (0.64) **Going Correction** +0.125s/f (Good) **10** Ran SP% **120.5**
Speed ratings (Par 103): **101,99,99,99,97 95,95,93,93,80**
Tote Swingers: 1&2 £3.70, 1&3 £4.20, 2&3 £7.20 CSF £20.63 CT £78.85 TOTE £2.70: £1.10, £3.40, £1.60; EX 19.80 Trifecta £89.80 Pool: £404.28 - 3.33 winning units..
Owner Theobalds Stud **Bred** Theobalds Stud **Trained** Newmarket, Suffolk
■ Stewards' Enquiry : Dane O'Neill four-day ban: careless riding (Jun 20-23)

FOCUS
A fair handicap, but it was quite a rough race in the closing stages.
Buxton Official explanation: jockey said gelding was denied a clear run
Spinning Ridge(IRE) Official explanation: jockey said gelding stumbled and lost its action briefly 1 1/2f out
Timeteam(IRE) Official explanation: jockey said gelding was slowly away and all but refused to race

2784 HARDINGS CATERING H'CAP 5f 59y
5:00 (5:01) (Class 5) (0-70,70) 3-Y-O **£2,719** (£809; £404; £202) **Stalls** Low

Form RPR
3503 **1** **Rathbawn Girl (IRE)**[10] 2459 3-7-13 **55**................. AdamBeschizza(7) 7 56
(Miss J Feilden) *dwlt: sn niggled along: hdwy to trck ldrs on inner 3f out: nt clr run and barging match w rival over 1f out: drvn through gap to ld ins fnl f: jst lasted: all out* **9/2**[2]

654 **2** *shd* **Starwatch**[10] 2459 3-8-6 **55**... NeilChalmers 3 56+
(J J Bridger) *chsd ldrs: gng wl but nt enough room fr 2f out tl ins fnl f: str run fnl 100yds: jst failed* **7/1**[3]

5100 **3** *2 ½* **Flaxen Lake**[4] 2648 3-9-3 **66**...(p) LiamKeniry 6 58
(J M Bradley) *chsd ldr: rdn ent fnl 2f: edgd rt u.p over 1f out: no ex and btn ins fnl f* **7/1**[3]

3-50 **4** *½* **Kings Of Leo**[20] 2179 3-9-7 **70**....................................(be[1]) PatCosgrave 5 61
(J R Boyle) *led: rdn 2f out: edgd lft over drvn and edgd rt u.p ent fnl f: no ex and btn ins fnl f* **10/1**

0-23 **5** *½* **Suzy Alexander**[20] 2174 3-9-3 **66**.. TomQueally 1 55
(G G Margarson) *hld up in tch: hdwy to press ldrs on outer ent fnl 2f: rdn and unable qck 1f out: btn fnl 150yds* **8/11**[1]

63.41 secs (1.11) **Going Correction** +0.125s/f (Good) **5** Ran SP% **110.2**
Speed ratings (Par 99): **96,95,91,91,90**
CSF £32.20 TOTE £5.10: £1.90, £3.10; EX 44.00 Place 6: £29.09 Place 5: £12.68 .
Owner J W Reynolds **Bred** Mrs Kathleen Reynolds **Trained** Exning, Suffolk

FOCUS
A modest sprint handicap and the one-two might have been different had the runner-up enjoyed a better trip.
Starwatch Official explanation: jockey said gelding was denied a clear run
T/Plt: £48.80 to a £1 stake. Pool: £73,120.70. 1,093.77 winning tickets. T/Qpdt: £22.60 to a £1 stake. Pool: £3,957.26. 129.31 winning tickets. SP

2257 SOUTHWELL (L-H)
Sunday, June 6

OFFICIAL GOING: Standard
Wind: light 1/2 behind Weather: fine, light rain race 8

2785 EUROPEAN BREEDERS' FUND MAIDEN STKS 5f (F)
2:20 (2:25) (Class 5) 2-Y-O **£3,480** (£1,027; £514) **Stalls** High

Form RPR
0 **1** **Waking Warrior**[33] 1806 2-9-3 0...................................... TonyHamilton 2 79+
(K A Ryan) *trckd ldr: led over 2f out: shkn up and wnt clr appr fnl f: easily* **9/2**[2]

60 **2** *4* **Captain Loui (IRE)**[9] 2493 2-9-3 0..............................(b[1]) PJMcDonald 5 65
(K A Ryan) *dwlt: reminders after s: sn chsng ldrs: hung lft over 2f out: wnt 2nd over 1f out: edgd rt: no ch w wnr* **16/1**

002 **3** *2 ¼* **Henrys Air**[10] 2474 2-9-3 0.. TomMcLaughlin 7 57
(D G Bridgwater) *chsd ldrs: rdn over 2f out: kpt on same pce* **9/2**[2]

4 *1* **Hernando Torres** 2-8-12 0.................................. JamesSullivan(5) 10 53+
(M W Easterby) *dwlt: outpcd after 1f: stdy hdwy 2f out: styd on steadily fnl f: will improve* **25/1**

00 **5** *1 ¾* **Jossy Johnston (IRE)**[29] 1905 2-9-3 0........................... ShaneKelly 12 47
(E J Alston) *v free to post: chsd ldrs: rdn and edgd lft over 2f out: one pce* **9/1**

00 **6** *½* **Phair Winter**[17] 2239 2-8-12 0................................ SilvestreDeSousa 9 40
(A D Brown) *chsd ldrs: fdd fnl f* **100/1**

7 *6* **Silent Blessing** 2-9-3 0.. GrahamGibbons 11 23
(R M H Cowell) *chsd ldrs: hung lft: rdn and lost pl after 1f: nvr a factor after* **7/2**[1]

8 *½* **Twisted Wings (IRE)** 2-8-12 0... DavidAllan 8 16
(T D Easterby) *dwlt: sn outpcd and wl bhd: sme late hdwy* **7/1**[3]

0400 **9** *hd* **Terrys Flutter**[4] 2642 2-8-12 0...(tp) ChrisCatlin 6 16
(M A Allen) *led tl over 2f out: wknd over 1f out* **40/1**

0 **10** *6* **No Explanation**[19] 2202 2-9-3 0................................... PatrickMathers 4 —
(D W Thompson) *mid-div: lost pl over 2f out* **125/1**

11 *2* **Silver Writer** 2-9-3 0... PaulMulrennan 1 —
(M W Easterby) *dwlt: sn outpcd and bhd* **14/1**

58.55 secs (-1.15) **Going Correction** -0.40s/f (Stan) **11** Ran SP% **101.7**
Speed ratings (Par 93): **93,86,83,81,78 77,68,67,67,57 54**
Tote Swingers: 1&2 £15.00, 1&3 £3.50, 2&3 £6.60 CSF £55.19 TOTE £5.10: £1.40, £4.60, £1.10; EX 60.50.
Owner Hambleton Racing Ltd XVII **Bred** Rosyground Stud **Trained** Hambleton, N Yorks

FOCUS
Very few got into what looked a moderate maiden. Waking Warrior is potentially a decent 2yo, but he didn't beat much.

NOTEBOOK
Waking Warrior ◆ could be called the winner before halfway. He had failed to fire on his debut at Newcastle, never recovering from a sluggish start, but his trainer has his 2-y-os in cracking form at present, and he had clearly learnt a lot from that dinitial effort. Soon taking along up on the pace, he readily drew clear, and this Super Sprint entrant looks a useful prospect. (op 4-1 tchd 7-2)
Captain Loui(IRE), well beaten on both previous starts, wasn't the best away, and didn't look straightforward in the first-time blinkers, but did at least post an improved effort. He's a likely sort for nurseries. (tchd 14-1)
Henrys Air showed much-improved form when second at 100/1 in a fair maiden at Wolverhampton latest, but he didn't seem quite as effective on this Fibresand surface. He will be one for nurseries. (op 4-1)
Hernando Torres kept on having been outpaced and looked a bit green early. (op 20-1)
Jossy Johnston(IRE) is now qualified for a mark and should fare better in low-grade nurseries. (op 8-1 tchd 7-1)
Silent Blessing, whose brother won his only race over C&D, was soon in trouble and never threatened to make headway. He was clearly expected to fare much better, and should learn from the experience. (op 11-1)
Twisted Wings(IRE) was soon in trouble, but should improve for the experience. (tchd 17-2)
Terrys Flutter Official explanation: trainer said filly finished distressed

2786 SHANE W DARBY MEMORIAL CLAIMING STKS 1m 4f (F)
2:50 (2:50) (Class 5) 3-Y-O+ **£2,729** (£806; £403) **Stalls** Low

Form RPR
-010 **1** **Heathyards Pride**[15] 2313 10-9-6 78........................... GrahamGibbons 2 62
(R Hollinshead) *hld up: hdwy to trck ldrs 8f out: wnt 2nd 4f out: drvn 3f out: led over 1f out: styd on wl: eased towards fin* **2/5**[1]

/ **2** *1 ¼* **Trojan Reef**[58] 4-9-9 0.......................................(t) TobyAtkinson(5) 6 67
(G A Butler) *led after 1f: drvn over 3f out: hdd over 1f out: kpt on same pce* **10/3**[2]

5503 **3** *3 ½* **Without Equal**[8] 2529 4-9-0 42.. DanielTudhope 4 47
(A Dickman) *chsd ldrs: pushed along over 5f out: hung lft over 1f out: one pce* **25/1**

/0-0 **4** *1 ¾* **Rebellious Spirit**[10] 2477 7-9-6 72............................... BarryMcHugh(3) 3 53
(S Curran) *led 1f: hdwy 4f out: one pce fnl 3f* **14/1**[3]

2040 **5** *7* **Cragganmore Creek**[67] 1071 7-9-3 42....................(v) KellyHarrison(3) 8 39
(D Morris) *t.k.h: sn trcking ldr: lost pl over 4fwknd 3f out* **33/1**

/00- **6** *13* **Hippodrome (IRE)**[63] 918 8-8-13 50......................(p) MarkCoumbe(5) 1 16
(John A Harris) *in rr: reminders 6f out: lost pl over 3f out: sn bhd* **40/1**

2m 38.63s (-2.37) **Going Correction** -0.225s/f (Stan) **6** Ran SP% **110.4**
Speed ratings (Par 103): **98,97,94,93,89 80**
Tote Swingers: 1&2 £1.10, 1&3 £2.60, 2&3 £6.00 CSF £1.85 TOTE £1.20: £1.10, £1.50; EX 2.10.
Owner Miss Sarah Hollinshead **Bred** L A Morgan **Trained** Upper Longdon, Staffs

FOCUS
A claimer that concerned only two.

2787 AMBITIONS PERSONNEL (S) STKS 7f (F)
3:20 (3:28) (Class 6) 3-Y-O **£2,047** (£604; £302) **Stalls** Low

Form RPR
2010 **1** **Buzz Bird**[27] 1970 3-8-13 56.. GrahamGibbons 11 72+
(T D Barron) *w ldrs on wd outside: drvn over 3f out: led over 2f out: drew clr jst ins fnl f: heavily eased fnl 75yds* **13/8**[1]

3363 **2** *6* **Blue Zephyr**[26] 1994 3-8-12 60..(b) ShaneKelly 3 55
(W R Muir) *s.i.s: sn chsng ldrs: wnt 2nd and edgd lft 2f out: kpt on same pce fnl f* **9/1**[3]

0-44 **3** *5* **Shercon (IRE)**[30] 1887 3-8-12 49............................ DaraghO'Donohoe 1 41
(N Tinkler) *chsd ldrs: sn pushed along: styd on appr fnl f: tk modest 3rd clsng stages* **16/1**

6005 **4** *1 ¼* **Eight Hours**[19] 2203 3-9-4 60....................................(v[1]) TonyHamilton 10 44
(R A Fahey) *chsd ldrs on outer: one pce fnl 2f* **11/2**[2]

6-00 **5** *2* **Infinity World**[46] 1465 3-8-6 56 ow2............................. BarryMcHugh(3) 6 29
(G R Oldroyd) *led tl over 2f out: wknd 1f out* **22/1**

3560 **6** *3 ¼* **Taper Jean Girl (IRE)**[20] 2185 3-8-13 50.....................(p) PJMcDonald 2 24
(Mrs R A Carr) *chsd ldrs: wknd over 1f out* **12/1**

0 **7** *3 ¼* **Du Plessis**[30] 1878 3-8-7 0 ow2.. DaleSwift(7) 5 17
(B Ellison) *chsd ldrs: sn drvn along: outpcd over 4f out: no threat after* **11/1**

-064 **8** *14* **Star Cruiser (USA)**[26] 1987 3-8-12 50..............................(b) DavidAllan 7 —
(T D Easterby) *w ldrs: lost pl over 2f out: eased fnl f* **25/1**

000 **9** *3* **Just My Girl**[7] 2564 3-8-2 0.......................................(bt[1]) TobyAtkinson(5) 9 —
(P Leech) *swtchd lft after s: in rr: bhd fnl 5f* **50/1**

0 **10** *4* **Rodrigo Fontana**[32] 1825 3-8-12 0.............................. SilvestreDeSousa 8 —
(Sir Mark Prescott) *chsd ldrs: outpcd over 3f out: sn lost pl* **12/1**

1m 28.03s (-2.27) **Going Correction** -0.225s/f (Stan) **10** Ran SP% **103.2**
Speed ratings (Par 97): **103,96,90,89,86 83,79,63,59,55**
Tote Swingers: 1&2 £3.10, 1&3 £3.60, 2&3 £5.60 CSF £12.20 TOTE £2.40: £1.10, £2.20, £5.10; EX 8.70.The winner was bought in for £4,250.
Owner Twinacre Nurseries Ltd **Bred** Twinacre Nurseries Ltd **Trained** Maunby, N Yorks

FOCUS
A weak seller.

2788 SAM BOLDY MEMORIAL H'CAP (DIV I) 1m (F)
3:50 (3:53) (Class 6) (0-60,60) 4-Y-O+ **£1,706** (£503; £252) **Stalls** Low

Form RPR
32-0 **1** **Celtic Step**[29] 1926 6-9-2 **58**... DavidAllan 5 65
(P D Niven) *sn drvn along: sn chsng ldrs: led 1f out: edgd lft: carried hd high and swished tail: narrowly hdd 75yds out: kpt on to regain ld nr line* **9/4**[1]

006 **2** *hd* **Admirals Way**[17] 2263 5-8-4 **45** oh1.............................. FrannyNorton 10 53
(C N Kellett) *hld up towards rr: stdy hdwy over 3f out: effrt over 2f out: chal jst ins fnl f: led narrowly 75yds out: hdd and no ex nr fin* **50/1**

4344 **3** *3 ½* **Kladester (USA)**[45] 1492 4-9-0 **56**...............................(p) TonyHamilton 3 57+
(M Herrington) *w ldrs: led over 2f out: hdd 1f out: keeping on same pce whn sn hmpd* **7/1**[3]

-306 **4** *2 ½* **Kingaroo (IRE)**[17] 2257 4-8-6 **48**.. ChrisCatlin 6 41
(G Woodward) *led tl over 2f out: wknd appr fnl f* **12/1**

453- **5** *hd* **Noche De Reyes**[188] 7599 5-8-11 **53**.................................. ShaneKelly 7 45
(E J Alston) *w ldrs: wknd over 1f out* **9/1**

25-0 **6** *¾* **Croeso Cusan**[60] 1177 5-8-13 **55**... SebSanders 9 46
(J L Spearing) *hld up in rr: hdwy over 2f out: chsng ldrs over 1f out: sn wknd* **9/2**[2]

4-00 **7** *9* **Business Class (BRZ)**[20] 2187 5-8-13 **60**.................(p) DeanHeslop(5) 2 30
(Mrs Marjorie Fife) *chsd ldrs: drvn over 3f out: lost pl over 2f out* **12/1**

600- **8** *4* **Navajo Joe (IRE)**[249] 6383 5-9-3 **59**..............................(vt[1]) TomEaves 4 20
(R Johnson) *t.k.h: trckd ldrs: wknd over 2f out* **7/1**[3]

0060 **9** *4* **Escardo (GER)**[26] 2006 7-8-8 **50**.................................(v[1]) JimmyQuinn 11 1
(D G Bridgwater) *sn drvn along on outer in rr: bhd fnl 2f* **28/1**

0160 **10** *5* **Provost**[8] 2527 6-9-2 **58**...(b) GrahamGibbons 8 —
(M W Easterby) *s.i.s: reminders on outside after 1f: hdwy over 4f out: lost pl over 2f out: sn bhd* **15/2**

1m 42.0s (-1.70) **Going Correction** -0.225s/f (Stan) **10** Ran SP% **116.5**
Speed ratings (Par 101): **99,98,95,92,92 91,82,78,74,69**
Tote Swingers: 1&2 £25.50, 1&3 £6.20, 2&3 £38.80 CSF £131.19 CT £714.39 TOTE £2.90: £1.10, £12.40, £4.10; EX 92.30.
Owner Mrs Muriel Ward **Bred** Woodcote Stud Ltd **Trained** Barton-le-Street, N Yorks
■ Stewards' Enquiry : David Allan three-day ban: careless riding (Jun 21-23)

FOCUS
The first division of a moderate handicap.

2789 SAM BOLDY MEMORIAL H'CAP (DIV II) 1m (F)
4:20 (4:21) (Class 6) (0-60,60) 4-Y-O+ £1,706 (£503; £252) Stalls Low

Form					RPR
50-4	1		**Liteup My World (USA)**45 1494 4-8-10 59 ... DaleSwift(7) 3 (B Ellison) *sn chsng ldrs: led over 1f out: edgd rt: drew clr* **3/1**1		72
2320	2	4	**Tomintoul Star**45 1489 4-8-12 54 ... PJMcDonald 7 (Mrs R A Carr) *dwlt: hld up towards rr: hdwy over 3f out: wnt 2nd 1f out: no imp* **3/1**1		58
260	3	2 1/4	**Fitzolini**41 1575 4-8-13 55 ...(p) JimmyQuinn 6 (A D Brown) *w ldr: rdn over 2f out: one pce appr fnl f* **6/1**3		54
0-52	4	5	**Sparky Vixen**17 2257 6-8-2 47 ... KellyHarrison(3) 1 (C J Teague) *chsd ldrs: wknd over 1f out* **8/1**		34
6-01	5	1/2	**Wotatomboy**17 2263 4-8-8 50 ... PaulQuinn 4 (R M Whitaker) *led tl over 1f out: sn wknd* **7/2**2		36
50-0	6	8	**Woodsley House (IRE)**37 1673 8-9-1 57 ...(p) RobertHavlin 2 (A G Foster) *in rr: sn pushed along: outpcd over 4f out: sme hdwy 3f out: nvr a factor: eased ins fnl f* **20/1**		25
0000	7	3/4	**All About You (IRE)**20 2188 4-9-4 60 ... JerryO'Dwyer 8 (P Howling) *towards rr on outer: effrt over 4f out: sn lost pl and bhd* **16/1**		26
006-	8	3 3/4	**Royal Applord**351 3174 5-9-2 58 ... J-PGuillambert 9 (N Tinkler) *chsd ldrs: drvn over 4f out: wknd over 2f out* **20/1**		15
-006	9	1 3/4	**Komreyev Star**12 2410 8-8-4 46 oh1 ... ChrisCatlin 5 (R E Peacock) *chsd ldrs on outer: outpcd over 4f out: sn lost pl and bhd* **18/1**		—

1m 41.25s (-2.45) **Going Correction** -0.225s/f (Stan) 9 Ran SP% **118.3**
Speed ratings (Par 101): **103,99,96,91,91 83,82,78,77**
Tote Swingers: 1&2 £3.60, 1&3 £5.80, 2&3 £4.70 CSF £12.40 CT £49.15 TOTE £4.50: £1.50, £1.10, £1.60; EX 18.60.
Owner Carr, Marucci, Amin, Duggan, Gilligan **Bred** Ocala Horses, Llc **Trained** Norton, N Yorks

FOCUS
This looked the stronger of the two divisions.

2790 ATRIUM H'CAP (DIV I) 6f (F)
4:50 (4:53) (Class 6) (0-65,65) 4-Y-O+ £1,706 (£503; £252) Stalls Low

Form				RPR
40-4	1		**Efisio Princess**82 892 7-9-7 65 ... RichardThomas 3 (J E Long) *chsd ldrs: narrow ld over 1f out: kpt on towards fin* **6/1**3	73
5625	2	nk	**Tenancy (IRE)**17 2257 6-8-4 48 ... ChrisCatlin 4 (S A Harris) *led: narrowly hdd over 1f out: hrd rdn and kpt on: no ex towards fin* **3/1**1	55
-304	3	1	**Cardinal**89 836 5-8-8 52 ...(t) GrahamGibbons 5 (R M H Cowell) *drvn to chse ldrs: outpcd 3f out: hdwy on inner 2f out: chsng ldrs jst ins fnl f: kpt on same pce* **7/2**2	56
2-56	4	2 1/2	**Fantasy Fighter (IRE)**122 404 5-9-2 60 ... JimmyQuinn 10 (J J Quinn) *chsd ldrs: drvn 3f out: one pce appr fnl f* **15/2**	56
5000	5	1 1/4	**Mister Incredible**30 1885 7-8-2 46 oh1 ...(v) FrannyNorton 8 (J M Bradley) *trckd ldrs: effrt over 3f out: one pce fnl 2f* **18/1**	38
0-00	6	6	**Future Gem**43 1524 4-9-5 63 ...(p) DanielTudhope 6 (A Dickman) *chsd ldrs: drvn 3f out: wknd over 1f out* **25/1**	36
-600	7	5	**Beauchamp Wizard**4 2643 5-9-5 63 ... SebSanders 2 (G A Butler) *dwlt: hld up in rr: rdn over 2f out: hung rt and sn wknd* **15/2**	20
000/	8	nk	**Prigsnov Dancer (IRE)**620 6218 5-8-10 54 ... PaulMulrennan 1 (O Brennan) *chsd ldrs: lost pl over 1f out* **10/1**	10
3060	F		**Kyle (IRE)**40 1596 6-9-0 58 ... ShaneKelly 9 (C R Dore) *chsd ldrs on outer: clipped heels and fell after 1f: fatally injured* **8/1**	—

1m 15.2s (-1.30) **Going Correction** -0.225s/f (Stan) 9 Ran SP% **114.3**
Speed ratings (Par 101): **99,98,97,93,92 84,77,77,—**
Tote Swingers: 1&2 £4.20, 1&3 £4.90, 2&3 £1.80 CSF £24.09 CT £72.36 TOTE £9.10: £2.60, £1.30, £1.70; EX 35.10.
Owner Miss M B Fernandes **Bred** Mrs A Yearley **Trained** Caterham, Surrey

FOCUS
A very modest handicap.

2791 ATRIUM H'CAP (DIV II) 6f (F)
5:20 (5:22) (Class 6) (0-65,64) 4-Y-O+ £1,706 (£503; £252) Stalls Low

Form				RPR
1422	1		**Gracie's Gift (IRE)**4 2646 8-9-5 62 ... GrahamGibbons 2 (R C Guest) *chsd ldrs: drvn 3f out: wnt 2nd 2f out: led 150yds out: jst hld on* **6/5**1	70
0063	2	nse	**Albero Di Giuda (IRE)**2 2720 5-8-7 55 ...(bt) BillyCray(5) 10 (F Sheridan) *led: 5 l clr 3f out: edgd lft over 1f out: hdd ins fnl f: rallied: jst failed* **10/1**	63
001U	3	1 1/2	**Mey Blossom**13 2396 5-9-1 61 ... MichaelStainton(3) 7 (R M Whitaker) *chsd ldrs: wnt 3rd 2f out: kpt on wl fnl f* **10/1**	64
5006	4	2 1/2	**Peter's Gift (IRE)**19 2211 4-9-2 64 ...(b) AmyRyan(5) 6 (K A Ryan) *dwlt: bhd: hdwy on outside 2f out: styd on ins fnl f* **13/2**2	59+
6254	5	1 1/4	**Calmdownmate (IRE)**45 1491 5-9-2 59 ... PJMcDonald 5 (Mrs R A Carr) *chsd ldrs: outpcd over 4f out: hdwy over 2f out: kpt on fnl f* **7/1**3	50
0064	6	1 1/4	**Guertino (IRE)**17 2263 5-8-9 52 ...(v1) PatrickMathers 9 (C J Teague) *racd wd: reminders after s: outpcd and in rr: sme late hdwy* **9/1**	39
00/5	7	1/2	**Wainwright (IRE)**17 2263 10-8-2 45 ...(tp) SilvestreDeSousa 4 (J Mackie) *chsd ldrs: hung rt and one pce fnl 2f* **9/1**	30
0/30	8	1/2	**Dolly Royal (IRE)**10 2463 5-8-4 52 ... PaulPickard(5) 8 (R Johnson) *sn outpcd and in rr: sme late hdwy: nvr on terms* **33/1**	36
000	9	2 3/4	**Brazilian Brush (IRE)**30 1884 5-8-2 45 ...(bt) FrannyNorton 1 (J M Bradley) *prom: outpcd over 2f out: lost pl over 1f out* **12/1**	20
060-	10	1	**Andrasta**200 7427 5-8-5 48 ... ChrisCatlin 3 (S A Harris) *chsd ldrs: lost pl over 1f out* **40/1**	20

1m 15.31s (-1.19) **Going Correction** -0.225s/f (Stan) 10 Ran SP% **122.5**
Speed ratings (Par 101): **98,97,95,92,90 89,88,87,84,82**
Tote Swingers: 1&2 £12.30, 1&3 £37.30, 2&3 £38.90 CSF £15.70 CT £94.91 TOTE £2.20: £1.30, £4.40, £3.00; EX 20.50.
Owner S Hussey **Bred** Richard O'Hara **Trained** Stainforth, S Yorks

FOCUS
They went a good clip in this second division.

2792 CORAL.CO.UK H'CAP 1m 4f (F)
5:50 (5:53) (Class 6) (0-65,63) 3-Y-O £2,047 (£604; £302) Stalls Low

Form				RPR
30-0	1		**Killusty Fancy (IRE)**27 1977 3-9-0 61 ... BillyCray(5) 10 (D J S Ffrench Davis) *trckd ldrs: t.k.h: drvn over 3f out: wnt cl 2nd jst ins fnl f: styd on to ld last strides* **28/1**	68
600-	2	hd	**Consult**207 7326 3-8-3 45 ... SilvestreDeSousa 1 (Sir Mark Prescott) *dwlt: led after 1f: drvn 5f out: hdd and edgd rt over 2f out: led over 1f out: hdd nr fin* **15/8**1	52+
000	3	3 1/4	**Best Of Broadway (IRE)**31 1851 3-8-13 55 ...(b1) TedDurcan 7 (D R Lanigan) *trckd ldrs: smooth hdwy to chal 4f out: led over 2f out tl over 1f out: wknd fnl 100yds* **9/2**3	56
00-0	4	3/4	**Moonlight Blaze**100 717 3-8-5 50 ... KellyHarrison(3) 9 (C W Fairhurst) *in rr: hdwy over 5f out: outpcd over 3f out: rallied over 1f out: kpt on* **66/1**	50
030-	5	3 1/2	**Budva**183 7638 3-9-3 59 ... TravisBlock 3 (H Morrison) *led 1f: chsd ldrs: rdn and edgd rt over 2f out: wknd over 1f out* **7/2**2	54
5-03	6	7	**Anaya**13 2379 3-9-1 62 ...(v1) RossAtkinson(5) 2 (Tom Dascombe) *chsd ldrs: rdn and outpcd over 3f out: wknd over 1f out: eased ins fnl f* **14/1**	45
0-03	7	17	**Tom Wade (IRE)**10 2460 3-9-4 60 ... PhilipRobinson 4 (M A Jarvis) *sn drvn along: chsd ldrs: reminders over 5f out: lost pl over 2f out: sn bhd: virtually p.u* **7/2**2	16
0-11	8	10	**Usquaebach**69 1048 3-9-7 63 ... JerryO'Dwyer 5 (M G Quinlan) *v awkward to load: in rr: drvn over 5f out: sn bhd: virtually p.u* **9/1**	3
00-0	9	2 3/4	**Chardonnay Star (IRE)**17 2258 3-8-4 46 ow1 ... PatrickMathers 6 (C J Teague) *in rr: sn bhd: t.o 3f out: virtually p.u* **66/1**	—

2m 39.73s (-1.27) **Going Correction** -0.225s/f (Stan) 9 Ran SP% **120.5**
Speed ratings (Par 97): **95,94,92,92,89 85,73,67,65**
Tote Swingers: 1&2 £10.20, 1&3 £23.00, 2&3 £4.90 CSF £83.92 CT £301.96 TOTE £36.30: £5.60, £1.90, £1.60; EX 178.80 Place 6: £9.00 Place 5: £3.28.
Owner Mrs F Houlihan **Bred** Mrs F Houlihan **Trained** Lambourn, Berks

FOCUS
An interesting handicap that saw a late plunge on Consult, but having asserted and looked the winner, he was grabbed in the final strides by Killusty Fancy.
Tom Wade(IRE) Official explanation: trainer said gelding never travelled
T/Jkpt: £1,527 to a £1 stake. Pool: £76,350.86. 35.50 winning tickets. T/Plt: £12.90 to a £1 stake. Pool: £66,692.66. 3,771.14 winning tickets. T/Qpdt: £4.20 to a £1 stake. Pool: £4,485.01. 785.32 winning tickets. WG

2446 CHANTILLY (R-H)
Sunday, June 6

OFFICIAL GOING: Turf: soft

2800a PRIX DE ROYAUMONT (GROUP 3) (3YO FILLIES) (TURF) 1m 4f
1:35 (12:00) 3-Y-O £35,398 (£14,159; £10,619; £7,079; £3,539)

			RPR
1		**Lady's Purse**37 1681 3-9-0 0 ... MaximeGuyon 9 (H-A Pantall, France) *towards rr on outer fr s: swung wd into st: qcknd wl 1 1/2f out: r.o strly to ld wl ins fnl f* **6/1**3	101
2	3/4	**Pearl Away (FR)**29 1946 3-9-0 0 ... ChristopheSoumillon 2 (Y De Nicolay, France) *midfield fr s: burst through between horses to grab ld at dist: r.o wl but hdd wl ins fnl f* **11/4**1	100
3	2 1/2	**Never Forget (FR)**21 2156 3-9-0 0 ... AnthonyCrastus 1 (E Lellouche, France) *a.p bhd ldrs: hrd rdn 1 1/2f out: r.o wl: ev ch: nt qckn ins fnl f* **7/2**2	96
4	hd	**Foundation Filly**33 1818 3-9-0 0 ... ThierryThulliez 7 (F Doumen, France) *settled towards rr: qcknd wl early in st: short of room whn trying to chal 1 1/2f out: fin strly whn clr* **16/1**	96
5	snk	**Gallic Star (IRE)**35 1729 3-9-0 0 ... RyanMoore 5 (M R Channon) *in rr fr s: qcknd wl 1 1/2f out: fin strly but too late* **14/1**	95
6	snk	**Sinndarina (FR)**45 1496 3-9-0 0 ...(b1) OlivierPeslier 4 (P Demercastel, France) *one of early ldrs and stl prom in st: outpcd 1 1/2f out but c again to fin wl* **11/1**	95
7	3/4	**Oekaki (FR)**60 3-9-0 0 ... DavyBonilla 6 (Y Barberot, France) *one of early ldrs and stl prom ent st: began to fade at dist and wknd* **10/1**	94
8	nk	**Seeking Solace**21 2156 3-9-0 0 ... MickaelBarzalona 8 (A Fabre, France) *racd towards rr: mde move early in st but no ex fnl f: fdd* **7/2**2	94
9	2 1/2	**Cracking Lass (IRE)**25 2029 3-9-0 0 ... MartinDwyer 3 (R A Fahey) *a in rr: nvr threatened* **14/1**	90

2m 31.7s (0.70) **Going Correction** +0.30s/f (Good) 9 Ran SP% **122.0**
Speed ratings: **109,108,106,106,106 106,106,105,104**
PARI-MUTUEL (all including 1 euro stakes): WIN 4.20 (Lady's Purse coupled with Seeking Solace). PLACES: 2.40, 1.30, 1.40. DF: 12.00. SF: 33.20.
Owner Sheikh Mohammed **Bred** Bumble Bloodstock **Trained** France

NOTEBOOK
Lady's Purse, a Listed winner over 1m2f last time, stayed on well to claim the runner-up late on.
Pearl Away(FR), a Listed winner and runner-up at this level last time, appreciated the longer trip but could not hold off the strong-finishing winner.
Never Forget(FR), a Listed winner last time, ran her race but may have found the ground softer than ideal on this step up in grade.
Gallic Star(IRE), upped in trip, was doing her best work at the finish.
Cracking Lass(IRE), who had her stamina to prove, was always near the back.

2801a PRIX DE SANDRINGHAM (GROUP 2) (3YO FILLIES) (TURF) 1m
2:15 (12:00) 3-Y-O £65,575 (£25,309; £12,079; £8,053; £4,026)

			RPR
1		**Joanna (IRE)**21 2158 3-8-11 0 ... ChristopheSoumillon 6 (J-C Rouget, France) *w.w: qcknd wl to cl on ldrs early in st: rdr biding his time tl ins fnl f: unleashed fine burst to go clr: comfortable* **11/4**2	103
2	2	**Kali (GER)**36 1715 3-9-2 0 ... MaximeGuyon 2 (W Hickst, Germany) *smartly away: following clr ldr: grabbed the ld early in st but no answer to wnr ins fnl f: r.o wl* **10/1**	103

3 shd **Evaporation (FR)**[18] 2237 3-8-11 0 OlivierPeslier 5 98
(C Laffon-Parias, France) *last into the st: mde gd prog on outside at dist: fin wl* **20/1**

4 nse **Kartica**[18] 2237 3-8-11 0 FrankieDettori 4 98
(P Demercastel, France) *w.w in midfield: mde gd prog in centre of st 1 1/2f out: fin wl* **16/1**

5 1 **Liliside (FR)**[21] 2158 3-8-11 0 Jean-BernardEyquem 3 96
(F Rohaut, France) *racd bhd eventual wnr fr s: swtchd towards rail in st: short of room at dist: c again to fin wl* **2/1**[1]

6 hd **Carioca (IRE)**[23] 2098 3-8-11 0 MircoDemuro 11 95
(M Botti) *3rd into st: rdn early in st: r.o wl clsng stages* **14/1**

7 shd **Ercolini (IRE)**[42] 3-8-11 0 JMurtagh 1 95
(F Rodriguez Puertas, Spain) *towards the rr early in st: r.o in st: no ex clsng stages* **16/1**

8 nk **Lixirova (FR)**[59] 1196 3-8-11 0 Christophe-PatriceLemaire 9 94
(D Smaga, France) *qckly to the ld: stl in front early in st: hrd rdn 1 1/2f out: no ex: wknd* **20/1**

9 1 1/2 **Ayun Tara (FR)**[21] 2158 3-8-11 0 GregoryBenoist 8 91
(X Nakkachdji, France) *at rr fr s: racd wd in st: no ex: fdd* **28/1**

10 3/4 **Gotlandia (FR)**[42] 1566 3-8-11 0 RyanMoore 7 89
(Y De Nicolay, France) *racd bhd the gp following the clr ldr: proged on outside in st but qckly fdd* **7/1**[3]

11 **Barouda (FR)**[21] 2158 3-8-11 0 GeraldMosse 10 89
(J-M Beguigne, France) *towards rr fr s: no imp in st* **9/1**

1m 38.7s (0.70) **Going Correction** +0.30s/f (Good) 11 Ran SP% **123.0**
Speed ratings: **108,106,105,105,104 104,104,104,102,102 102**
PARI-MUTUEL (all including 1 euro stakes): WIN 3.80. PLACES: 1.80, 3.40, 2.80. DF: 17.70. SF: 28.10.
Owner Hamdan Al Maktoum **Bred** Giovanni Faldutto **Trained** Pau, France

NOTEBOOK
Joanna(IRE) had shown herself to be a smart performer when defeating subsequent dual Classic winner Special Duty in the Prix Imprudence in April, before being promoted to third behind that filly in the Poule d'Essai des Pouliches on her latest start. She won this in the style of a top-class performer and could be aimed at the Falmouth stakes at Newmarket. She handles good ground but is well suited by soft.
Kali(GER), the winner of the German 1000 Guineas, got the better of a blanket finish for second and proved herself a high-class performer. The soft ground proved no problem.
Evaporation(FR), runner-up in a Listed race last time, finished well from well back and only just failed to grab the runner-up spot.

2802a PRIX DU JOCKEY CLUB (GROUP 1) (3YO COLTS & FILLIES) (TURF) 1m 2f 110y

3:04 (12:00) 3-Y-O **£758,495** (£303,451; £151,725; £75,796; £37,964)

RPR

1 **Lope De Vega (IRE)**[21] 2159 3-9-2 0 MaximeGuyon 20 124+
(A Fabre, France) *broke wl: trckd ldr tl wnt on gng wl 3f out: sn clr: comf* **12/1**

2 3 **Planteur (IRE)**[56] 1254 3-9-2 0 AnthonyCrastus 10 116
(E Lellouche, France) *disp 3rd: wnt 2nd 3f out: sn rdn and unable to go w ldr: styd on but no imp fnl 300yds* **9/2**[2]

3 3/4 **Pain Perdu (FR)**[42] 1567 3-9-2 0 FrankieDettori 18 115
(N Clement, France) *disp 3rd: rdn 2f out: styd on same pce* **25/1**

4 1/2 **Behkabad (FR)**[27] 1985 3-9-2 0 Christophe-PatriceLemaire 13 114+
(J-C Rouget, France) *hld up in midfield: bmpd 3f out: plld wd st and r.o fnl 300yds* **8/1**

5 hd **Viscount Nelson (USA)**[15] 2354 3-9-2 0 (b) CO'Donoghue 6 114
(A P O'Brien, Ire) *racd in 7th: rdn 2f out: kpt on wout qckning* **25/1**

6 1/2 **Lumineux**[17] 3-9-2 0 OlivierPeslier 2 113
(A Fabre, France) *settled in midfield: hdwy on rail 2f out: styd on at one pce* **20/1**

7 shd **Ice Blue**[29] 1947 3-9-2 0 RyanMoore 3 112
(P Bary, France) *plld hrd on rail and racd in 4th: disp 3rd st: rdn 2f out: no ex fnl f* **5/1**[3]

8 2 **Handsome Devil**[29] 1947 3-9-2 0 JohanVictoire 11 109
(E Lellouche, France) *hld up towards rr: hdwy 2 1/2f out: styd on one pce fnl 300yds* **33/1**

9 3/4 **Dancing David (IRE)**[30] 1858 3-9-2 0 MartinDwyer 21 107
(B J Meehan) *racd in 6th: rdn 2 1/2f out: no ex* **66/1**

10 1 **Cape Blanco (IRE)**[24] 2056 3-9-2 0 JMurtagh 7 105
(A P O'Brien, Ire) *racd in 8th: plld wd ent st and bmpd rival: sn rdn and unable qck* **2/1**[1]

11 shd **Ivory Land (FR)**[21] 2160 3-9-2 0 GeraldMosse 19 105
(A De Royer-Dupre, France) *hld up: hdwy 2 1/2f out: plugged on same pce* **66/1**

12 1 1/2 **Green Rock (FR)**[29] 1947 3-9-2 0 GregoryBenoist 23 102
(Mme M Bollack-Badel, France) *midfield: c wd st: effrt 2 1/2f out: wknd fnl f* **100/1**

13 1/2 **Shamalgan (FR)**[21] 2159 3-9-2 0 ThierryJarnet 22 101
(A Savujev, Czech Republic) *hld up: mde sme prog st: sn one pce* **40/1**

14 1 1/2 **Royal Bench (IRE)**[62] 3-9-2 0 IoritzMendizabal 12 98
(Robert Collet, France) *nvr in contention* **33/1**

15 3 **Russian Dream (FR)**[27] 1985 3-9-2 0 (p) FredericSpanu 8 92
(T Castanheira, France) *nvr in a position to chal* **100/1**

16 1/2 **No Risk At All (FR)**[27] 1985 3-9-2 0 ChristopheSoumillon 5 91
(J-P Gallorini, France) *racd in midfield: rdn and nt qckn 2f out: eased fnl f* **16/1**

17 2 1/2 **Celtic Celeb (IRE)**[21] 2160 3-9-2 0 ThierryThulliez 17 86
(F Doumen, France) *n.d* **66/1**

18 1/2 **Tip Toe (FR)**[27] 1985 3-9-2 0 FranckBlondel 9 85
(F Doumen, France) *racd in midfield: bmpd st: sn rdn and wknd fnl 2f* **50/1**

19 snk **Classic Hero (GER)**[27] 3-9-2 0 WilliamMongil 5 85
(H-W Hiller, Germany) *a bhd* **200/1**

20 1/2 **Big Creek (IRE)**[7] 3-9-2 0 MircoDemuro 16 84
(B Grizzetti, Italy) *nvr threatened ldrs* **150/1**

21 2 1/2 **Prince Pretender (FR)**[27] 3-9-2 0 FlavienPrat 4 79
(J-P Gallorini, France) *a bhd* **200/1**

22 dist **Vivre Libre**[38] 3-9-2 0 (b[1]) SamuelFargeat 14 —
(E Lellouche, France) *led tl hdd & wknd 3f out* **250/1**

2m 7.10s (-1.70) **Going Correction** +0.30s/f (Good) **22** Ran SP% **124.1**
Speed ratings: **118,115,115,114,114 114,114,112,112,111 111,110,110,108,106 106,104,104,104,103 101,—**
PARI-MUTUEL (all including 1 euro stakes): WIN 11.20; PLACE 3.70, 2.40, 4.50; DF 21.00; SF 60.60.
Owner Gestut Ammerland **Bred** Gestut Ammerland **Trained** Chantilly, France

FOCUS
The decision to lop two a furlong and a half off the Prix Du Jockey Club trip in 2005 seemed to achieve little other than attract more runners and this year's field was bigger still - the biggest since 1858 - after France Galop decided to increase the safety limit just a few days prior to the race. With that in mind, the draw once again looked like being a key factor with no winner in the last ten years being drawn higher than 11 and, perhaps more significantly, only five winners since starting stalls were introduced in 1960 racing from stall 14 or higher. They appeared to go steady and the first three were always prominent.

NOTEBOOK
Lope De Vega(IRE)'s supposedly disadvantageous draw in stall 20 proved to be no barrier and he followed up his impressive win in the Poule d'Essai Des Poulains with another taking Classic win. Whereas on the previous occasion he was held up, he raced prominently from the off this time, tracking the pacemaker until his confident jockey made his move as they straightened up before pulling clear over two furlongs out to win comfortably. The extra step up in trip proved to be no problem, indeed, he hardly saw a rival throughout the whole of the race and Guyon's biggest battle probably came in the preliminaries where the colt, who is said to be a handful at home, looked a tad reluctant to enter the stalls after sweating up a bit. Connections said afterwards that they feel this is as far as he will get and he could now drop back to a mile with the Prix Jacques Le Marois at Deauville a possible. Due to his excitable nature he is unlikely to be sent on his travels too often, although his trainer said afterwards overseas trips could be on the cards if he stays in racing next year.
Planteur(IRE) came here off the back of a win in a Group 2 in April over this trip at Longchamp where he had Epsom Derby third Rewilding a length and a half behind in second. Although he got closest to the winner here, he never looked like giving him a contest.
Pain Perdu(FR), another to race prominently, was unable to go with the winner late on. This represented another step up in company for him and he has come a long way since winning an apprentice handicap in March. The decision by connections to supplement him looks fully justified and understandably they were thrilled by this effort.
Behkabad(FR) repeated the efforts of his half-brother Beheshtam last year in coming fourth. He finished best of all and is worth another try over this trip having dictated when winning for a third time, over 1m1f, on his previous start.
Viscount Nelson(USA) was already having his fourth start of the season. Breeding suggested that the Irish Guineas third would be suited by this extra distance and that proved to be the case.
Lumineuxdid not have the finishing kick of Behkabad and Viscount Nelson.
Ice Blue had won over half a furlong further last time. He raced not far behind the leaders but was unable to get competitive, having been ridden from the top of the straight. He was another to get warm before the race started and, having run free early on, used up too much energy.
Handsome Devil finished one place behind Ice Blue for the third race on the bounce. He was another who stayed on at one pace late on.
Dancing David(IRE) failed to get a blow like so many of them and was ridden along from over two furlongs out.
Cape Blanco(IRE)'s Dante form was given a massive boost after the impressive win of Workforce - who finished behind him in the York race - at Epsom the day before. However, he lost his unbeaten record in disappointing fashion. He ran wide off the final bend and was never able to get a blow in after. His jockey was not overly hard on him when it became evident late on that he was not going to be involved in the shake-up.

2803a GRAND PRIX DE CHANTILLY (GROUP 2) (4YO+) (TURF) 1m 4f

3:50 (12:00) 4-Y-O+ **£65,575** (£25,309; £12,079; £8,053; £4,026)

RPR

1 **Allied Powers (IRE)**[31] 1856 5-8-11 0 IoritzMendizabal 5 115
(M L W Bell) *w.w in rr: rdn 1 1/2f out: r.o strly ins fnl f: grabbed ld 50yds out: comf* **7/2**[3]

2 1 **Timos (GER)**[31] 1856 5-8-11 0 ChristopheSoumillon 2 113
(T Doumen, France) *led: relinquished ld after 3f: racd in 2nd ent st: grabbed ld at dist: wandered rt and lft causing problems to rivals bhd: hdd 50yds out: styd on wl and edgd 2nd on line* **12/1**

3 nse **Pouvoir Absolu**[62] 1135 5-8-11 0 (b) AnthonyCrastus 3 113
(E Lellouche, France) *racd in 2nd initially: settled in 3rd: hrd rdn in st: hmpd by 2nd ins fnl f: styd on wl* **15/8**[1]

4 3/4 **Chinchon (IRE)**[35] 1747 5-9-0 0 OlivierPeslier 1 115
(C Laffon-Parias, France) *racd in 4th fr s: rdn at dist: prog blocked on two occasions: unlucky* **5/2**[2]

5 2 **Roatan**[35] 5-8-11 0 Christophe-PatriceLemaire 4 109
(P Bary, France) *racd in 3rd initially but sent to ld after 3f: led in st: hdd at dist: hrd rdn but fnd no ex: fdd* **9/2**

2m 33.9s (2.90) **Going Correction** +0.30s/f (Good) 5 Ran SP% **111.5**
Speed ratings: **102,101,101,100,99**
PARI-MUTUEL (all including 1 euro stakes): WIN 6.80. PLACES: 3.20, 4.60. SF: 33.90.
Owner David Fish And Edward Ware **Bred** Saad Bin Mishrif **Trained** Newmarket, Suffolk

NOTEBOOK
Allied Powers(IRE), given a good hold-up ride, ground down the leading pair deep inside the last for a fairly comfortable victory. He may go for the Grand Prix de Saint-Cloud or the Hardwicke Stakes next. This was the 1,000th training success of Michael Bell's career.
Timos(GER), behind Allied Powers at Longchamp last time, was worn down by his old rival late on.
Pouvoir Absolu gets further and was staying on at the end.
Chinchon(IRE) was the worst affected by the runner-up's antics.

2804a PRIX DU GROS-CHENE (GROUP 2) (3YO+) (TURF) 5f

4:25 (12:00) 3-Y-O+ **£65,575** (£25,309; £12,079; £8,053; £4,026)

RPR

1 **Planet Five (USA)**[40] 1611 4-9-2 0 Christophe-PatriceLemaire 2 112
(P Bary, France) *racd in 6th: hdwy 1 1/2f out: led fnl 50yds* **10/1**

2 snk **Piccadilly Filly (IRE)**[239] 6660 3-8-6 0 EddieCreighton 3 106
(E J Creighton) *broke wl and sn led: rdn and r.o wl fnl f: hdd fnl 50yds* **16/1**

3 1/2 **Marchand D'Or (FR)**[21] 2157 7-9-2 0 DavyBonilla 10 110
(M Delzangles, France) *hld up: rdn and r.o fnl 300yds* **1/1**[1]

4 nk **Delvita (FR)**[266] 5928 6-8-13 0 GregoryBenoist 6 106
(J-V Toux, France) *a.p: no ex fnl f* **20/1**

5 snk **Mood Music**[21] 2157 6-9-2 0 (b) MaximeGuyon 8 108
(Mario Hofer, Germany) *racd in 4th: wnt 2nd and ev ch 1f out: wknd fnl 100yds* **12/1**

6 1 **Tertio Bloom (SWE)**[26] 2019 5-9-2 0 GeraldMosse 1 105
(Fredrik Reutersköld, Sweden) *hld up: last whn hdwy 2f out: r.o fnl f: no ex last 100yds* **16/1**

7 1/2 **Kolokol (IRE)**[21] 2157 3-8-9 0 ChristopheSoumillon 9 100
(D Prod'Homme, France) *racd in midfield: no imp fnl f* **13/2**[3]

8 2 **Dolled Up (IRE)**[21] 2158 3-8-6 0 IoritzMendizabal 4 90
(Robert Collet, France) *hld up: nvr able to chal* **6/1**[2]

9 2 **Black Mambazo (IRE)**[21] 2157 5-9-2 0 MircoDemuro 5 89
(L Riccardi, Italy) *bmpd s: sn trcking ldrs: 2nd and ev ch 2f out: sn rdn and unable qck: eased fnl f* **6/1**[2]

10 *10* **Manzila (FR)**[21] 2157 7-8-13 0....(b) RonanThomas 7 50
(Mme C Barande-Barbe, France) *chsd ldrs: rdn and wknd qckly fnl 2f* **40/1**

58.60 secs (0.50) **Going Correction** +0.475s/f (Yiel)
WFA 3 from 4yo+ 7lb **10** Ran SP% **127.7**
Speed ratings: **115,114,113,113,113 111,110,107,104,88**
PARI-MUTUEL (all including 1 euro stakes): WIN 7.80; PLACE 2.10, 5.20, 1.30; DF 104.50; SF 208.20.
Owner Niarchos Family **Bred** Flaxman Holdings Ltd **Trained** Chantilly, France

NOTEBOOK
Planet Five(USA), a son of the high-class filly Six Perfections, was dropping down in trip but has a decent record at this track and caused a bit of an upset coming up the stands'-side rail. He will probably return to further and be aimed at the Prix Maurice de Gheest in August.
Piccadilly Filly(IRE), having her first start of the season, once again showed a lot of pace and was only caught late on. She looks to have trained on and will go next for the Sapphire Stakes at the Curragh on Irish Derby day.
Marchand D'Or(FR) was tucked in behind ready for a late thrust, but momentarily edged left when making his run and could not get on terms. It was reported that he had lost a front shoe. He has rediscovered his form for his new trainer this season, will appreciate a return to further and another crack at the July Cup looks likely.

2372 HOPPEGARTEN (R-H)
Sunday, June 6

OFFICIAL GOING: Turf: good

2805a BENAZET-RENNEN - PREIS DER DEUTSCHEN BESITZER (GROUP 3) (3YO+) (TURF) 6f
3:20 (3:25) 3-Y-0+

£28,318 (£9,734; £4,867; £2,654; £1,769; £1,327)

RPR

1 **Amico Fritz (GER)**[28] 1955 4-9-6 0.... FabriceVeron 1 106
(H-A Pantall, France) *cl up bhd ldr fr s: trcking pce: mde move jst under 2f out: r.o wl: led ins fnl f: drew clr* **29/10**[2]

2 *3/4* **Indomito (GER)**[236] 4-9-6 0.... AStarke 4 104
(P Vovcenko, Germany) *in rr: shkn up at 1/2-way: responded wl: fin strly ins fnl f* **13/2**

3 *1/2* **Contat (GER)**[28] 1955 7-9-6 0.... RJuracek 7 102
(P Vovcenko, Germany) *a.p: racd bhd ldr: chal 2f out: r.o but no ex clsng stages* **6/4**[1]

4 *1 1/2* **Walero (GER)**[28] 1955 4-9-6 0.... AHelfenbein 5 97
(Uwe Ostmann, Germany) *led fr s: r.o whn chal in st: hdd and no ex ins fnl f* **43/10**[3]

5 *3/4* **Nareion (GER)**[28] 1955 4-9-6 0.... YannLerner 3 95
(W Baltromei, Germany) *racd in 3rd: briefly threatened in st: no ex* **43/10**[3]

6 *4* **Shinko's Best (IRE)**[28] 1955 9-9-6 0.... APietsch 2 82
(A Kleinkorres, Germany) *racd in midfield: tired qckly in st* **151/10**

7 *5* **Paradise Rain**[13] 3-8-9 0.... JBojko 6 63
(Manfred Hofer, Germany) *racd towards bk of field: nvr threatened* **148/10**

69.50 secs (69.50)
WFA 3 from 4yo+ 8lb **7** Ran SP% **129.3**
WIN (Incl. 10 euro stake): 39. PLACES: 12, 14, 10. SF: 282.
Owner Alexandre Pereira **Bred** A Pereira **Trained** France

2806a GROSSER PREIS DER HAUPTSTADTREGION (GROUP 2) (4YO+) (TURF) 1m 3f
4:30 (4:35) 4-Y-0+

£35,398 (£13,716; £5,752; £3,539; £2,212; £1,327)

RPR

1 **Night Magic (GER)**[21] 2152 4-9-3 0.... KKerekes 1 109+
(W Figge, Germany) *racd in 6th: galloping freely: cruised to be prom arnd fnl turn: r.o strly and led cl home: easily* **33/10**[3]

2 *1 1/4* **Sordino (GER)**[336] 3670 4-9-0 0.... APietsch 4 104
(W Hickst, Germany) *racd in 4th: swtchd to outer ent st: r.o wl to go 2nd* **29/10**[2]

3 *3/4* **Miss Europa (IRE)**[21] 2155 4-9-0 0.... AStarke 3 103
(P Schiergen, Germany) *racd in 2nd bhd ldr: led early in st: r.o wl but unable to wstand first two in clsng stages* **14/5**[1]

4 *hd* **Liang Kay (GER)**[63] 1111 5-9-0 0.... YannLerner 6 102
(Uwe Ostmann, Germany) *racd in rr: r.o wl in st and briefly looked a threat but no ex clsng stages* **19/5**

5 *nse* **Steuben (GER)**[31] 1856 4-9-0 0.... ADeVries 7 102
(J Hirschberger, Germany) *racd in 5th: threatened briefly in st but no ex* **58/10**

6 *1/2* **White Lightning (GER)**[28] 8-9-0 0.... RJuracek 9 101
(U Stech, Germany) *racd in 3rd: r.o wl in st but no threat* **176/10**

7 *8* **Assahab (GER)**[28] 7-9-0 0.... WPanov 8 88
(U Stech, Germany) *bkmarker fr s and mde no prog in st* **30/1**

8 *15* **Ordenstreuer (IRE)**[28] 4-9-0 0....(b) THellier 2 62
(R Dzubasz, Germany) *set fast pce fr outset and sn several l clr: c bk to field ent st and sn btn* **10/1**

2m 15.9s (135.90) **8** Ran SP% **128.4**
WIN (incl. 10 euro stake): 43. PLACES: 19, 18, 16. SF: 243.
Owner Stall Salzburg **Bred** Gestut Etzean **Trained** Germany

1639 FOLKESTONE (R-H)
Monday, June 7

OFFICIAL GOING: Straight course - good to firm (good in places); round course - good (good to firm in places)
Wind: fresh, slightly behind Weather: partly cloudy, breezy

2807 ASHFORD DESIGNER OUTLET OPEN TILL 8PM WEEKNIGHTS H'CAP 6f
2:15 (2:15) (Class 4) (0-85,85) 3-Y-0 **£4,857** (£1,445; £722; £360) **Stalls** Low

Form RPR

50-2 **1** **Duster**[31] 1873 3-8-10 **74**.... SteveDrowne 3 82
(H Morrison) *mde all: rdn 2f out: styd on wl to draw clr fnl 100yds: comf* **5/2**[2]

0-50 **2** *2 1/2* **Planet Red (IRE)**[52] 1352 3-9-6 **84**.... RichardHughes 2 85
(R Hannon) *reminders sn after s: chsd wnr thrght: swtchd rt off of stands' rail over 3f out: rdn over 2f out: drvn to press wnr over 1f out: edgd rt and btn ins fnl f* **4/1**[3]

0-10 **3** *5* **Sard**[23] 2120 3-9-1 **79**.... PhilipRobinson 5 64
(M A Jarvis) *hld up in last trio: hdwy 1/2-way: rdn to chse ldng pair wl over 1f out: btn 1f out and no ch fnl f* **9/4**[1]

6221 **4** *1 1/2* **Diamond Johnny G (USA)**[39] 1639 3-8-9 **73**....(t) EddieCreighton 6 53
(E J Creighton) *t.k.h: hld up in last trio: rdn and effrt over 2f out: no prog and wl btn over 1f out* **14/1**

3606 **5** *1/2* **Yurituni**[12] 2442 3-8-11 **75**.... TonyCulhane 1 54
(Eve Johnson Houghton) *hld up in rr: pushed along and effrt over 2f out: no hdwy and wl btn over 1f out* **16/1**

103- **6** *3 1/4* **Trailblazing**[247] 6471 3-9-7 **85**.... FrankieDettori 4 53
(M Johnston) *dwlt: sn chsd ldng pair: effrt and clsd 1/2-way: rdn and wknd wl over 1f out: wl bhd fnl f* **4/1**[3]

1m 11.06s (-1.64) **Going Correction** -0.20s/f (Firm) **6** Ran SP% **111.9**
Speed ratings (Par 101): **102,98,92,90,89 85**
toteswingers:1&2:£2.10, 1&3:£1.60, 2&3:£2.30 CSF £12.75 TOTE £3.40: £1.40, £2.70; EX 12.70.
Owner M T Bevan **Bred** Paddock Space **Trained** East Ilsley, Berks

FOCUS
There was 8mm of rain overnight but good to firm was still part of the official ground description on the straight and round course. This looked a competitive handicap but the winner blew his rivals away under a forcing ride, and they finished well strung out. The winner had the rail, but the form is rated at face value.
Yurituni Official explanation: jockey said filly lost its action

2808 FREE 2 HOUR PERSONAL SHOPPING EXPERIENCE CLAIMING STKS 6f
2:45 (2:45) (Class 6) 3-Y-0+ **£2,047** (£604; £302) **Stalls** Low

Form RPR

021 **1** **Piazza San Pietro**[6] 2635 4-9-4 62.... RobertHavlin 4 74
(A B Haynes) *hld up in tch: swtchd rt and hdwy ent fnl 2f: rdn to ld over 1f out: kpt on wl fnl f* **6/1**

6002 **2** *3/4* **Silver Wind**[21] 2178 5-9-10 78....(v) KierenFallon 7 78
(P D Evans) *chsd ldrs: effrt and ev ch 2f out: drvn and rdr dropped whip over 1f out: chsd wnr fnl f: styd on but a hld* **9/4**[2]

0600 **3** *1 1/4* **Matsunosuke**[8] 2563 8-10-0 92.... TonyCulhane 5 78
(A B Coogan) *stdd after s: hld up in last: swtchd rt and effrt 2f out: rdn to chse ldrs over 1f out: one pce and no imp fnl f* **2/1**[1]

3406 **4** *3/4* **Lindoro**[21] 2172 5-9-2 80....(p) JerryO'Dwyer 2 63
(M G Quinlan) *led: jnd and rdn 2f out: hdd over 1f out: one pce and btn fnl f* **10/1**

-000 **5** *7* **Aroundthebay**[17] 2284 4-9-9 74....(p) RichardHughes 1 48
(H J L Dunlop) *chsd ldrs: rdn and unable qck over 2f out: drvn and wl btn over 1f out: eased wl ins fnl f* **11/2**[3]

030- **6** *8* **Jimmy Ryan (IRE)**[222] 7122 9-9-2 65.... SebSanders 3 15
(T D McCarthy) *taken down early and led to s: racd freely: sn chsng ldr: rdn and wknd qckly ent fnl 2f: wl bhd and eased ins fnl f* **16/1**

0303 **7** *10* **Bahama Baileys**[28] 1958 5-9-0 48.... PatCosgrave 8 —
(C A Dwyer) *sn pushed along in last pair: rdn and struggling 1/2-way: lost tch ent fnl 2f: eased ins fnl f* **33/1**

1m 11.7s (-1.00) **Going Correction** -0.20s/f (Firm)
WFA 3 from 4yo+ 8lb **7** Ran SP% **111.7**
Speed ratings (Par 101): **98,97,95,94,85 74,61**
.Matsunosuke was clamied by R. A. Harris for £12,000. Piazza San Pietro was subject to a friendly claim for £7,000.\n\x\x
Owner K Corke **Bred** T E Pocock **Trained** Limpley Stoke, Bath

FOCUS
A decent claimer. It was run at a good pace but the leading form contender, who was a weak favourite, was a bit disappointing. The winner looks the best guide.
Silver Wind Official explanation: jockey said whip was knocked out of his hand 1f out

2809 ASHFORD DESIGNER OUTLET, JUNCTION 10 M20 H'CAP 5f
3:15 (3:15) (Class 6) (0-60,60) 4-Y-0+ **£2,047** (£604; £302) **Stalls** Low

Form RPR

5036 **1** **Thoughtsofstardom**[19] 2229 7-9-1 **57**....(be) FrankieDettori 5 64
(P S McEntee) *chsd ldr: swtchd rt off of rail and rdn to ld jst over 1f out: edgd lft jst ins fnl f: kpt on wl* **3/1**[1]

20-0 **2** *3/4* **The Name Is Frank**[25] 2053 5-9-2 **58**....(t) NeilChalmers 2 65+
(Mark Gillard) *taken down early: broke wl but sn outpcd and lost pl: towards rr and nt clr run over 1f out: swtchd rt and hdwy on outer ent fnl f: r.o strly to go 2nd towards fin: nt rch wnr* **11/2**

4264 **3** *3/4* **Captain Kallis (IRE)**[3] 2719 4-9-3 **59**.... KierenFallon 8 61
(D J S Ffrench Davis) *chsd ldng pair: rdn over 2f out: chsd wnr ent fnl f: kpt on same pce: lost 2nd towards fin* **7/2**[2]

0162 **4** *nk* **Bookiesindex Boy**[53] 1320 6-8-11 **53**....(b) StephenCraine 1 54
(J R Jenkins) *hld up wl off the pce in midfield: hdwy 2f out: drvn and chsd ldrs ent fnl f: kpt on but nt pce to rch wnr* **5/1**[3]

0-01 **5** *3 1/2* **Pressed For Time (IRE)**[3] 2720 4-8-11 **53** 6ex....(vt) EddieCreighton 7 41
(E J Creighton) *sn led and crossed to r on stands' rail: rdn and hdd jst over 1f out: wknd qckly 1f out: wl btn whn edgd rt ins fnl f* **7/1**

-206 **6** *1/2* **Caribbean Coral**[17] 2294 11-9-4 **60**....(v) RobertHavlin 3 46
(A B Haynes) *chsd ldrs but a struggling to go pce: rdn ent fnl 2f: styd on one pce and nvr able to chal* **16/1**

0500 **7** *nk* **Shadow Bay (IRE)**[3] 2719 4-8-8 **50**....(b[1]) SamHitchcott 6 35
(Miss Z C Davison) *wl outpcd towards rr: rdn 1/2-way: sme hdwy u.p wl over 1f out: no hdwy and wl hld fnl f* **16/1**

0-60 **8** *1 1/2* **Riggs (IRE)**[123] 402 4-8-4 **46** oh1.... AdrianMcCarthy 9 26
(Peter Grayson) *a outpcd in last trio: rdn and no hdwy fr over 2f out* **100/1**

4426 **9** *3/4* **Bollywood Style**[10] 2490 5-9-4 **60**.... SteveDrowne 10 37
(J R Best) *a wl bhd in last trio: n.d* **10/1**

500/ **10** *1 1/4* **Jucebabe**[641] 5626 7-7-13 **46**.... SimonPearce(5) 4 18
(John R Upson) *t.k.h early but a bhd: lost tch 2f out* **25/1**

59.50 secs (-0.50) **Going Correction** -0.20s/f (Firm) **10** Ran SP% **117.5**
Speed ratings (Par 101): **96,94,93,93,87 86,86,83,82,80**
toteswingers:1&2:£5.50, 1&3:£2.60, 2&3:£5.30 CSF £19.98 CT £61.92 TOTE £4.30: £1.70, £1.20, £2.10; EX 26.50 Trifecta £129.90 Pool: £356.39 - 2.03 winning units..
Owner Eventmaker Racehorses **Bred** B Bargh **Trained** Newmarket, Suffolk

FOCUS
A modest sprint handicap. The winner showed his best turf form for two years.

The Name Is Frank Official explanation: jockey said gelding was denied a clear run

2810 ASHFORDDESIGNEROUTLET.COM H'CAP 2m 93y
3:45 (3:46) (Class 5) (0-70,70) 4-Y-0+ **£3,070** (£906; £453) **Stalls** Low

Form RPR

211 **1** **On Terms (USA)**[32] [1849] 4-9-4 **65** TomQueally 11 81+
(S Dow) *mde all: pushed clr wl over 2f out: in n.d fnl 2f: v easily* **9/4**[1]

/21- **2** *7* **Ambrose Princess (IRE)**[23] [4301] 5-8-11 **57** (p) PatCosgrave 1 62
(M J Scudamore) *t.k.h early: chsd ldrs: rdn and nt pce of wnr wl over 2f out: chsd clr wnr over 1f out: no imp but kpt on for clr 2nd* **13/2**[3]

404- **3** *3 ¼* **Sir Freddie**[313] [4442] 4-9-8 **69** PatDobbs 3 70+
(Lady Herries) *t.k.h: hld up in last trio: clsd 5f out: effrt on outer ent fnl 3f: sn outpcd and no ch w wnr: styd on fnl f to go 3rd nr fin* **14/1**

2-52 **4** *nk* **Brad's Luck (IRE)**[15] [2363] 4-8-4 **51** TadhgO'Shea 8 52
(M Blanshard) *chsd wnr for 2f: chsd ldng pair: drvn to chse clr wnr over 2f out: no imp after: lost 2 pls fr over 1f out* **20/1**

0-33 **5** *1 ½* **Bell Island**[30] [1931] 6-9-5 **65** (v) SebSanders 4 64
(Lady Herries) *hld up in last trio: hdwy into midfield and wl in tch 5f out: rdn and nt pce of wnr 3f out: wl btn fnl 2f* **7/1**

-040 **6** *6* **Sweetheart**[30] [1902] 6-9-10 **70** StevieDonohoe 9 62
(Jamie Poulton) *racd in midfield: clsd and wl in tch 5f out: rdn and unable qck 3f out: sn struggling and no ch fnl 2f* **7/2**[2]

1-51 **7** *1 ¼* **Brave Bugsy (IRE)**[15] [2363] 7-9-0 **60** (v) LiamKeniry 10 50
(A M Balding) *pushed along early: hdwy to chse ldr after 3f: rdn and lost pl wl over 2f out: wl btn fnl 2f* **8/1**

4013 **8** *4 ½* **Spiritonthemount (USA)**[15] [2363] 5-8-3 **52** oh1 ow1(b) WilliamCarson(3) 7 37
(P W Hiatt) *dwlt: sn pushed along and nvr gng wl in rr: clsd 5f out: rdn and effrt on outer 4f out: btn and swtchd rt 3f out: sn lost tch* **20/1**

0-25 **9** *14* **Group Leader (IRE)**[46] [1493] 4-9-2 **63** FrankieDettori 12 31
(J R Jenkins) *hld up in midfield: clsd and in tch 5f out: rdn and outpcd 3f out: wl btn 2f out: eased ins fnl f: t.o* **14/1**

3m 39.92s (2.72) **Going Correction** -0.025s/f (Good)
WFA 4 from 5yo+ 1lb **9** Ran SP% **112.8**
Speed ratings (Par 103): **92,88,86,86,85 82,82,80,73**
toteswingers:1&2:£4.10, 1&3:£5.90, 2&3:£7.10 CSF £16.73 CT £160.68 TOTE £2.40: £1.10, £2.70, £5.20; EX 16.40 Trifecta £186.80 Pool: £419.06 - 1.66 winning units..
Owner S Dow **Bred** Juddmonte Farms Inc **Trained** Epsom, Surrey

FOCUS
A fairly competitive staying handicap, involving three last-time-out winners and four others who finished placed on their latest run. It was run at a stop-start gallop and the favourite hammered her rivals. She was value for a bit extra and the form seems sound.
Sir Freddie Official explanation: jockey said gelding hung left

2811 JOY IS DISCOVERING YOUR FAVOURITE BRANDS H'CAP 1m 4f
4:15 (4:16) (Class 6) (0-60,58) 4-Y-0+ **£2,047** (£604; £302) **Stalls** Low

Form RPR

0533 **1** **Dazzling Begum**[17] [2302] 5-8-3 **48** SimonPearce(5) 7 59+
(J Pearce) *racd wl off the pce in rr: clsd 5f out: stl plenty to do ent st: hdwy and swtchd lft over 1f out: led jst ins fnl f: drew clr fnl 100yds* **15/2**

3-31 **2** *2* **Bedarra Boy**[15] [2361] 4-8-11 **51** SebSanders 9 57
(D W P Arbuthnot) *chsd ldrs and clr in ldng quartet: rdn wl over 2f out: drvn and pressed ldr ent fnl f: nt pce of wnr ins fnl f: wnt 2nd fnl 100yds* **7/2**[2]

650- **3** *nk* **Dark Energy**[22] [7695] 6-8-13 **53** (t) PatCosgrave 8 59
(M J Scudamore) *chsd clr ldng quartet: clsd 5f out: drvn and hdwy over 1f out: led ent fnl f: sn hdd and nt pce of wnr ins fnl f: lost 2nd fnl 100yds* **10/1**

0-55 **4** *1 ¼* **Kashmina**[10] [2488] 5-9-1 **58** RobertLButler(3) 6 62
(Miss Sheena West) *hld up wl off the pce in last trio: clsd 5f out: rdn and c wd ent st: styd on u.p fnl f: nvr trbld ldrs* **25/1**

2250 **5** *4 ½* **Silken Promise (USA)**[35] [1763] 4-9-3 **57** (b[1]) FrankieDettori 2 54
(T B P Coles) *chsd ldrs and clr in ldng quartet: wnt 2nd ent fnl 3f: rdn to ld over 1f out: hdd and wandered u.p 1f out: sn wknd* **15/2**

-666 **6** *¾* **Drum Major (IRE)**[74] [983] 5-9-2 **56** (b) TomQueally 5 52
(Jim Best) *disp ld at fast gallop: led and clr 4f out: drvn wl over 2f out: hdd over 1f out: wknd qckly 1f out* **5/1**[3]

00-1 **7** *shd* **Channel Crossing**[7] [2604] 8-8-2 **49** ow2 JohnCavanagh(7) 11 44
(R Ford) *disp ld at fast gallop tl 4f out: rdn ent fnl 3f: wknd wl over 1f out* **3/1**[1]

3604 **8** *1* **Barbirolli**[9] [2529] 8-7-13 **46** ow1 LauraPike(7) 10 40
(W B Stone) *racd off the pce in midfield: clsd 5f out: rdn and no prog over 2f out: wl btn fnl f* **11/1**

600/ **9** *19* **Dora Explora**[729] [5189] 6-9-4 **58** StevieDonohoe 3 21
(Mrs L C Jewell) *stdd and dropped in bhd after s: a in rr: pushed along 7f out: lost tch wl over 2f out: t.o and eased ins fnl f* **80/1**

-020 **10** *2* **Largem**[19] [2232] 4-8-12 **52** SimonWhitworth 1 12
(J R Jenkins) *stdd and dropped in bhd after s: a wl bhd in last trio: lost tch wl over 2f out: t.o and eased ins fnl f* **20/1**

00-6 **11** *½* **Very Distinguished**[150] [82] 4-8-5 **48** WilliamCarson(3) 4 —
(M G Quinlan) *racd off the pce in midfield: clsd and in tch 5f out: rdn and btn over 2f out: wl btn over 1f out: eased ins fnl f: t.o* **33/1**

2m 39.99s (-0.91) **Going Correction** -0.025s/f (Good) **11** Ran SP% **117.6**
Speed ratings (Par 101): **102,100,100,99,96 96,96,95,82,81 81**
toteswingers:1&2:£4.10, 1&3:£12.50, 2&3:£8.10 CSF £32.75 CT £268.99 TOTE £5.80: £1.40, £2.00, £3.30; EX 28.80 Trifecta £197.70 Not won. Pool: £267.22 - 0.10 winning units..
Owner Macniler Racing Partnership **Bred** Ian Bryant **Trained** Newmarket, Suffolk

FOCUS
A minor handicap run at a surprisingly good pace. The winner is rated to her best.

2812 PLUMBASE.COM MEDIAN AUCTION MAIDEN STKS 1m 1f 149y
4:45 (4:48) (Class 5) 3-4-Y-0 **£2,729** (£806; £403) **Stalls** Centre

Form RPR

03- **1** **Mecox Bay (IRE)**[298] [4953] 3-8-13 0 LiamKeniry 1 77
(A M Balding) *chsd ldr: rdn to chal over 2f out: led 2f out: edgd lft u.p and hdd over 1f out: hrd drvn and kpt on wl fnl f to ld again last stride* **5/1**

2 *shd* **Cockney (IRE)** 3-8-13 0 FrankieDettori 4 76+
(M Johnston) *dwlt: sn pushed up into midfield: hdwy to chse ldrs 4f out: c wd st: sn rdn and ev ch: led over 1f out: kpt on u.p fnl f: hdd last stride* **7/4**[1]

6- **3** *4 ½* **Blitzed**[220] [7146] 3-8-13 0 FergusSweeney 6 67+
(G L Moore) *chsd ldrs: rdn and unable qck whn nt clr run and swtchd rt over 1f out: edgd rt and outpcd by ldng pair 1f out: one pce fnl f* **2/1**[2]

6-0 **4** *1 ½* **Affirmable**[21] [2180] 3-8-9 0 ow1 SebSanders 7 62+
(J W Hills) *racd in midfield: rdn and effrt wl over 3f out: hdwy and chsng whn nt clr run and hmpd over 1f out: sn swtchd lft: one pce fnl f* **4/1**[3]

/6-0 **5** *1* **Gearbox (IRE)**[18] [2255] 4-9-12 0 TomQueally 8 63+
(H J L Dunlop) *trckd ldrs: shkn up and hmpd over 1f out: one pce and no threat to ldrs fnl f* **25/1**

50 **6** *7* **Sirdave**[28] [1976] 4-9-9 0 WilliamCarson(3) 5 53+
(P W Hiatt) *led: rdn over 2f out: hdd over 1f out: wknd qckly fnl f* **25/1**

7 *¾* **Plan A (IRE)** 3-8-13 0 JerryO'Dwyer 9 45
(M G Quinlan) *a in rr: sme hdwy 5f out: rdn and btn wl over 2f out* **33/1**

564 **8** *13* **Masteeat (USA)**[9] [2535] 3-8-3 44 KierenFox(5) 2 13
(J R Best) *restless in stalls: v.s.a: a bhd: lost tch 3f out* **25/1**

9 *19* **Ancestral Dream** 3-8-13 0 StevieDonohoe 10 —
(Andrew Reid) *s.i.s: sn pushed along and a bhd: t.o fnl 2f* **50/1**

5 **10** *28* **Mujdy (IRE)**[79] [949] 3-8-13 0 FrankieMcDonald 3 —
(Miss Z C Davison) *s.i.s: a bhd: lost tch wl over 3f out: wl t.o fnl 2f* **100/1**

2m 6.17s (1.27) **Going Correction** -0.025s/f (Good)
WFA 3 from 4yo 13lb **10** Ran SP% **123.8**
Speed ratings (Par 103): **93,92,89,88,87 81,81,70,55,33**
toteswingers:1&2:£3.70, 1&3:£3.20, 2&3:£2.10 CSF £14.43 TOTE £4.40: £1.30, £1.60, £1.10; EX 22.50 Trifecta £31.30 Pool: £580.09 - 13.69 winning units. Place 6 £42.54; Place 5 £19.05.
Owner E N Kronfeld **Bred** Glending Bloodstock **Trained** Kingsclere, Hants

FOCUS
A fair maiden which was quite truly run. The first two pulled clear of the rest and the four market leaders filled the first four positions. The form is rated around the third and fourth.
Masteeat(USA) Official explanation: jockey said filly reared on leaving stalls
T/Plt: £37.10. to a £1 stake. Pool:£76,256.75 - 1,499.70 winning tickets T/Qpdt: £6.60. to a £1 stake. Pool:£5,063.10 - 563.30 winning tickets SP

2512 PONTEFRACT (L-H)
Monday, June 7

OFFICIAL GOING: Good to firm (good in places; 8.8)
Temporary rail in place from 6f bend.
Wind: Light against Weather: Overcast and showers

2813 JK AND JOEL BREAKFAST SHOW - RADIO AIRE MAIDEN AUCTION FILLIES' STKS 6f
6:45 (6:46) (Class 5) 2-Y-0 **£3,238** (£963; £481; £240) **Stalls** Low

Form RPR

2 **1** **Sonning Rose (IRE)**[7] [2594] 2-8-6 0 AlanMunro 1 84+
(M R Channon) *trckd ldrs: effrt and nt clr run 1 1/2f out: swtchd rt and rdn to chal ins fnl f: kpt on to ld last 100yds: comf* **1/1**[1]

25 **2** *1 ¼* **Whisper Louise (IRE)**[16] [2338] 2-8-4 0 JamieMackay 9 76
(Mrs P Sly) *hld up in tch: hdwy on outer 2f out: rdn to ld 1f out and sn edgd lft: hdd and nt qckn last 100yds* **3/1**[2]

2 **3** *4 ½* **Abidhabidubai**[49] [1421] 2-8-4 0 GrahamGibbons 7 63
(J J Quinn) *cl up: led wl over 2f out: rdn and hdd 1f out: kpt on same pce* **5/1**[3]

0 **4** *1 ¼* **Sapphire Girl**[49] [1421] 2-8-4 0 PaulHanagan 3 59
(R A Fahey) *trckd ldrs: hdwy wl over 2f out: rdn over 1f out and sn one pce* **11/1**

00 **5** *2 ½* **Freedom Trail**[9] [2547] 2-8-13 0 JimmyFortune 6 60
(D R C Elsworth) *t.k.h: led: hdd wl over 2f out: sn rdn and wknd wl over 1f out* **14/1**

6 **6** *4* **Damascus Symphony**[11] [2461] 2-8-10 0 JoeFanning 2 45
(J D Bethell) *s.i.s: a in rr* **25/1**

0 **7** *5* **Whats For Pudding (IRE)**[23] [2130] 2-8-4 0 AndrewElliott 8 24
(D Carroll) *cl up: rdn along over 2f out: sn edgd lft and wknd* **80/1**

1m 19.5s (2.60) **Going Correction** +0.15s/f (Good) **7** Ran SP% **111.7**
Speed ratings (Par 90): **88,86,80,78,75 70,63**
toteswingers:1&2:£1.20, 1&3:£2.00, 2&3:£2.70 CSF £3.90 TOTE £1.70: £1.10, £2.20; EX 5.00.
Owner Alf Heaney & Alec Tuckerman **Bred** Mark Commins **Trained** West Ilsley, Berks

FOCUS
Little strength in depth, but decent maiden form for fillies only. It was run at a steady pace, all the runners still closely bunched turning for home. The winning margin understates the winner's superiority and she has better to come.

NOTEBOOK
Sonning Rose(IRE) ◆ had shaped with plenty of promise on her debut at Goodwood behind a likely useful sort and she confirmed that she's probably of similar potential herself with a cosy success gained despite seemingly being caught by surprise when the runner-up went for home early in the straight. She left the impression that had this race been more strongly run race she'd have won by quite some way, and she looks a viable candidate for the Albany Stakes at Royal Ascot. (op 6-5 tchd 5-4)
Whisper Louise(IRE), favourite for a stronger race than this at Newbury last time (first two have both won since) held a good chance on debut form and made a brave attempt to give her yard their first 2yo winner since Speciosa in 2005 but ultimately had no answer to the winner late on. She's going to prove vulnerable kept to maidens. (op 7-2 tchd 4-1 in places)
Abidhabidubai had finished second to the subsequent Hilary Needler winner Geesala on her debut but didn't really benefit from this longer trip as had seemed likely then despite being best placed turning for home. If the handicapper takes that first run at face value, she's unlikely to be treated leniently when moving into nurseries. (op 10-3)
Sapphire Girl had finished over five lengths behind Abidhabidubai on her debut when sent off joint favourite but an entry for her in a claimer later in the week suggests she's one of the stable lesser lights. She stayed on late when the race was all but over and would be interesting in that grade at 7f. (op 12-1)
Freedom Trail, out of her depth at Newmarket last time after a mildly encouraging debut, had a fair bit to find on form. She was readily left behind after getting the run of the race and is another that needs a drop in grade. (op 20-1)
Damascus Symphony had started to get the hang of things late on her debut and looked a potential improver but was slowly away and never landed a blow after taking a keen hold. (op 28-1 tchd 33-1)

2814 TONY BETHELL MEMORIAL H'CAP 2m 1f 22y
7:15 (7:16) (Class 4) (0-80,80) 4-Y-0+ **£4,533** (£1,348; £674; £336) **Stalls** Low

Form RPR

5-51 **1** **Miss Keck**[5] [2659] 6-9-2 **72** 6ex PJMcDonald 6 82
(G A Swinbank) *in tch: hdwy 6f out: effrt to chse ldr 3f out: rdn to ld jst over 1f out: drvn ins fnl f hld on wl towards fin* **9/2**[1]

0120 **2** *½* **Dan Buoy (FR)**[25] [2060] 7-8-5 **66** (b) BillyCray(5) 3 75
(R C Guest) *led and sn wl clr: eased and given breather 5f out: rdn over 2f out: hdd and drvn jst over 1f out: rallied gamely u.p and ev ch ins fnl f tl no ex towards fin* **7/1**

-624 **3** *8* **Spiders Star**[9] [2533] 7-8-2 **63** PaulPickard(5) 8 63
(S G West) *hld up in rr: hdwy over 4f out: n.m.r on inner and swtchd wd 2f out: rdn and hung lft over 1f out: drvn and hung lft ins fnl f: kpt on to take 3rd nr line* **7/1**

15-0 **4** *shd* **Bijou Dan**[22] 1150 9-8-6 **67**............................. PatrickDonaghy(5) 4 67
(G M Moore) *hld up in rr: hdwy 5f out: effrt 3f out: rdn 2f out: styd on u.p appr fnl f: nrst fin* **28/1**

243/ **5** *1* **Mutual Friend (USA)**[9] 3165 6-9-10 **80**..................(b) JimmyFortune 11 79
(D E Pipe) *hld up towards rr: hdwy over 4f out: chsd ldng pair 2f out and sn rdn: drvn over 1f out and one pce: lost 3rd towards fin* **11/2**[3]

004- **6** *30* **Inchnadamph**[222] 7117 10-9-7 **77**..........................(t) PaulHanagan 2 43
(T J Fitzgerald) *hld up: hdwy 5f out: rdn to chse ldrs 3f out: sn drvn and wknd* **15/2**

0-00 **7** *4 ½* **Judgethemoment (USA)**[23] 2126 5-9-10 **80**........(p) SilvestreDeSousa 9 41
(Jane Chapple-Hyam) *chsd clr ldr: cl up 7f out: rdn along 4f out: wknd 3f out* **7/1**

423 **8** *18* **Calculating (IRE)**[19] 2228 6-8-9 **65**............................ MickyFenton 10 6
(M D I Usher) *chsd ldrs: rdn along over 4f out: wknd over 3f out and eased fnl 2f* **5/1**[2]

/04- **9** *14* **Shore Thing (IRE)**[42] 5530 7-8-9 **68**..................(p) AndrewHeffernan(3) 1 —
(B J Llewellyn) *midfield: hdwy 1/2-way: chsd ldrs over 4f out: rdn along over 3f out: sn wknd and eased* **10/1**

3m 44.65s (0.05) **Going Correction** +0.15s/f (Good)
WFA 4 from 5yo+ 1lb 9 Ran SP% **112.0**
Speed ratings (Par 105): **105,104,101,100,100 86,84,75,69**
toteswingers:1&2:£4.90, 1&3:£5.10, 2&3:£11.50 CSF £34.45 CT £213.97 TOTE £5.10: £2.50, £2.40, £2.00; EX 24.10.
Owner Alan Wright **Bred** The Woodhaven Stud **Trained** Melsonby, N Yorks

FOCUS
A fair staying handicap run at a decent pace so testing stamina thoroughly. The first pair finished clear and this is sound form.
Calculating(IRE) Official explanation: jockey said gelding hung left throughout

2815 MR WOLF SPRINT H'CAP — 6f
7:45 (7:46) (Class 3) (0-90,90) 3-Y-O **£9,714** (£2,890; £1,444; £721) **Stalls** Low

Form RPR

1 **1** **Bated Breath**[49] 1425 3-9-7 **90**.............................. JimmyFortune 10 102+
(R Charlton) *wnt rt s: hld up in tch: smooth hdwy 2f out: chsd ldr over 1f out: rdn and qcknd wl fnl f to ld last 75yds* **4/6**[1]

-002 **2** *¾* **Besty**[13] 2426 3-8-2 **71** oh1.................................... SilvestreDeSousa 3 81
(B Smart) *led: rdn and qcknd 2f out: drvn ent fnl f: hdd and no ex last 75yds* **15/2**[2]

14-4 **3** *4* **Emerald Girl (IRE)**[18] 2242 3-8-2 **71** oh1...................... AndrewElliott 8 68
(R A Fahey) *in tch: hdwy on outer to chse ldrs 2f out: sn rdn and kpt on same pce appr fnl f* **16/1**

-060 **4** *½* **Di Stefano**[9] 2545 3-9-1 **84**.. AlanMunro 1 80
(M R Channon) *hld up and bhd: hdwy and swtchd rt wl over 1f out: sn rdn and styd on ins fnl f: nrst fin* **22/1**

0-35 **5** *1* **Ballodair (IRE)**[24] 2069 3-8-6 **75**....................................... PaulHanagan 6 67
(R A Fahey) *towards rr: rdn along over 2f out: hdwy on inner over 1f out: sn no imp* **12/1**

0560 **6** *nk* **Comedy Hall (USA)**[18] 2260 3-9-4 **87**............................... JoeFanning 4 78
(M Johnston) *cl up: rdn along over 2f out: drvn wl over 1f out and sn wknd* **10/1**

1-51 **7** *1 ¾* **Belinsky (IRE)**[20] 2215 3-8-3 **75**.................. Louis-PhilippeBeuzelin(3) 9 61
(N Tinkler) *cl up on outer: rdn aliong over 2f out: drvn wl over 1f out and sn wknd* **25/1**

201- **8** *shd* **Golden Shaheen (IRE)**[229] 6943 3-9-3 **86**.............(v) RoystonFfrench 2 72
(M Johnston) *s.i.s and in rr: rdn along whn bmpd wl over 1f out: n.d* **8/1**[3]

-100 **9** *2 ¾* **Amary (IRE)**[38] 1663 3-9-4 **87**... MickyFenton 5 64
(C E Brittain) *swtchd lft s: sn chsng ldrs on inner: rdn along 2f out: sn wknd* **66/1**

1m 16.93s (0.03) **Going Correction** +0.15s/f (Good) 9 Ran SP% **115.2**
Speed ratings (Par 103): **105,104,98,98,96 96,93,93,90**
toteswingers:1&2:£2.60, 1&3:£6.10, 2&3:£9.70 CSF £5.99 CT £43.73 TOTE £1.70: £1.10, £2.00, £2.30; EX 6.60.
Owner K Abdulla **Bred** Juddmonte Farms Ltd **Trained** Beckhampton, Wilts
■ Stewards' Enquiry : Paul Hanagan caution: careless riding

FOCUS
None too competitive a race despite the money on offer but a useful performance from the winner, who looks sure to go on to better things. The second produced a personal best too. The pace soon picked up after a steady first couple of furlongs.

NOTEBOOK
Bated Breath ◆'s impressive C&D win on debut had been franked since by wins for the second and third and lines of form thorough them suggested he was potentially very well treated despite an opening mark of 90. He didn't win by far, but considering he had to race wide from the outside stall and then, from what wasn't a great position at halfway, ran down one who had got first run as the first two pulled clear, this has to be marked up as a good step forward. He's probably Listed class at least, and will be even better given a chance at 7f. (op 8-13 tchd 8-15)
Besty ran an excellent race albeit under a very smart front-running ride. His trainer said beforehand easy ground suits him ideally, but he moves like a horse who shouldn't have a problem handling fast ground. (op 17-2 tchd 9-1)
Emerald Girl(IRE) looked on a fair mark on the pick of her 2-y-o form but didn't get going until too late and probably wants 7f as her reappearance at that trip had suggested. (op 14-1)
Di Stefano had beaten just two rivals in three races this year but ran a better race down 4lb with the visor he wore last time left off, staying on well from a poor position turning in without being given a hard time. He's very well handicapped now if he can build on this. (op 20-1 tchd 25-1)
Ballodair(IRE) had a bit to do on balance and didn't really convince with his stamina for this stiff 6f as the race was run. (op 14-1)
Comedy Hall(USA) has proved disappointing this year and is in need of much more respite from the handicapper than he has been getting. (op 14-1)
Belinsky(IRE) had things fall right when winning at Nottingham and dropped out tamely facing a stiff task up 5lb as well as sharply in grade. She might not prove the easiest to place. (op 22-1)
Golden Shaheen(IRE) ◆, a ready all-the-way winner of an AW maiden when last seen for Godolphin last year, is arguably very well handicapped on the form he showed on his penultimate start and left the impression here that he is worth another chance when stepped back up in trip, looking rusty early and soon badly placed but staying on when the race was all but over. Official explanation: jockey said gelding missed the break (op 10-1)

2816 BAR LIQUID - PONTEFRACT NUMBER ONE BAR H'CAP — 1m 2f 6y
8:15 (8:17) (Class 4) (0-85,85) 3-Y-O **£4,533** (£1,348; £674; £336) **Stalls** Low

Form RPR

1101 **1** **Azlak (USA)**[10] 2515 3-9-3 **81**...............................(b) JimmyFortune 7 88+
(C E Brittain) *mde all: rdn 1 1/2f out: drvn ins fnl f: kpt on wl* **7/1**

0-53 **2** *¾* **Tut (IRE)**[13] 2422 3-8-12 **76**... AndrewElliott 5 81+
(J R Weymes) *trckd ldrs: hdwy 2f out: rdn to chse wnr ins fnl f: sn drvn and edgd lft: styd on wl towards fin* **14/1**

25-3 **3** *2* **Mason Hindmarsh**[10] 2501 3-8-2 **66** oh1........................ PaulHanagan 4 67
(Karen McLintock) *prom: effrt to chal 2f out: sn rdn and ev ch tl drvn and one pce fnl f* **13/2**[3]

523 **4** *1 ¼* **Forsyth**[24] 2083 3-8-9 **73**.. PJMcDonald 2 72
(G A Swinbank) *trckd ldrs: hdwy 3f out: rdn over 1f out: swtchd lft ins fnl f: drvn and one pce whn n.m.r nr fin* **10/1**

-240 **5** *3 ¼* **Brooklands Bay (IRE)**[26] 2033 3-8-11 **75**............... SilvestreDeSousa 1 67+
(J R Weymes) *hld up towards rr: sme hdwy over 2f out: sn rdn and no imp over 1f out* **14/1**

01-4 **6** *1 ¼* **Forgotten Army (IRE)**[26] 2033 3-8-6 **70**.......................... TedDurcan 6 60
(M H Tompkins) *hld up in rr: effrt and sme hdwy 2f out: sn rdn and nvr a factor* **11/4**[1]

3305 **7** *nse* **Epic (IRE)**[13] 2422 3-8-5 **69**.. JoeFanning 3 58
(M Johnston) *hld up towards rr: hdwy 3f out: rdn to chse ldrs 2f out: sn wknd* **16/1**

1 **8** *1 ¾* **Pass Muster**[24] 2083 3-9-4 **85**.................................. AhmedAjtebi(3) 8 71
(Mahmood Al Zarooni) *dwlt: sn cl up: rdn along 3f out: drvn 2f out and sn wknd* **7/2**[2]

552 **9** *3* **Hail Tiberius**[17] 2290 3-9-0 **78**................................ GrahamGibbons 9 58
(T D Walford) *t.k.h early: chsd ldrs: rdn along 3f out: sn wknd* **13/2**[3]

2m 14.12s (0.42) **Going Correction** +0.15s/f (Good) 9 Ran SP% **116.4**
Speed ratings (Par 101): **104,103,101,100,98 97,97,95,93**
toteswingers:1&2:£12.30, 1&3:£12.50, 2&3:£18.50 CSF £99.22 CT £669.12 TOTE £7.40: £3.10, £4.50, £2.20; EX 73.90.
Owner Saeed Manana **Bred** Rabbah Bloodstock Llc **Trained** Newmarket, Suffolk

FOCUS
A fair handicap but one that was run at something of an uneven gallop with the eventual winner dictating things. He is not necessarily flattered though given his progressive profile.
Forgotten Army(IRE) Official explanation: trainer said colt was unsuited by the good to firm (good in places) ground
Pass Muster Official explanation: jockey said colt never travelled

2817 £35 FATHERS DAY ON JUNE 20TH PACKAGE H'CAP — 6f
8:45 (8:46) (Class 5) (0-70,70) 3-Y-O+ **£2,914** (£867; £433; £216) **Stalls** Low

Form RPR

5-36 **1** **Elijah Pepper (USA)**[7] 2578 5-9-7 **60**......................... GrahamGibbons 7 69
(T D Barron) *chsd ldrs: rdn along 2f out: swtchd rt and drvn ent fnl furlng: edgd rt and kpt on wl to ld nr line* **7/2**[1]

0334 **2** *hd* **Dickie Le Davoir**[4] 2671 6-9-9 **65**......................(v) AndrewHeffernan(3) 5 73
(R C Guest) *bhd and rdn along bef 1/2-way: hdwy on wd outside 2f out: str run over 1f out: led ins fnl f: sn drvn: hdd and no ex nr line* **5/1**[3]

2002 **3** *1 ¼* **Not My Choice (IRE)**[16] 2310 5-9-11 **64**.....................(t) JimmyFortune 1 68
(D C Griffiths) *led: rdn along 2f out: drvn over 1f out: hdd ins fnl f: one pce towards fin* **5/1**[3]

6400 **4** *¾* **He's A Humbug (IRE)**[3] 2698 6-9-6 **64**................... JamesO'Reilly(5) 6 66
(J O'Reilly) *in rr: hdwy on inner wl over 1f out: rdn and styd on ins fnl f: nrst fin* **28/1**

4-00 **5** *1 ½* **Rainy Night**[9] 2528 4-9-4 **62**...................................... BillyCray(5) 12 59
(R Hollinshead) *chsd ldrs: effrt 2f out: sn rdn and kpt on same pce ent fnl f* **10/1**

0060 **6** *1 ½* **Bid For Gold**[20] 2206 6-9-11 **64**................................... TonyHamilton 4 56
(Jedd O'Keeffe) *trckd ldng pair: effrt over 2f out: rdn wl over 1f out: hld whn hmpd ent fnl f* **4/1**[2]

020- **7** *1 ¼* **Sea Rover (IRE)**[189] 7595 6-9-12 **65**................................ AlanMunro 10 53
(M Brittain) *cl up: rdn and ev ch over 1f out: sn drvn and wknd ins fnl f* **11/1**

0502 **8** *1 ½* **Klynch**[7] 2578 4-9-9 **67**.......................................(b) JamesSullivan(5) 8 51
(Mrs R A Carr) *chsd ldrs: rdn wl over 1f out: sn wknd* **7/1**

6001 **9** *1 ½* **Pretty Orchid**[63] 1114 5-8-8 **52**.............................(p) PaulPickard(5) 2 31
(P T Midgley) *a in rr* **22/1**

1m 18.27s (1.37) **Going Correction** +0.15s/f (Good)
WFA 3 from 4yo+ 8lb 9 Ran SP% **113.3**
Speed ratings (Par 103): **96,95,94,93,91 89,87,85,83**
toteswingers:1&2:£2.80, 1&3:£2.90, 2&3:£5.50 CSF £20.65 CT £86.06 TOTE £2.80: £1.10, £2.90, £2.10; EX 16.00.
Owner Wensleydale Bacon Limited **Bred** Liberation Farm & Oratis Thoroughbreds **Trained** Maunby, N Yorks
■ Stewards' Enquiry : Andrew Heffernan one-day ban: used whip with excessive frequency (Jun 21)
Graham Gibbons four-day ban: careless riding (Jun 22-25)

FOCUS
A modest handicap run at a strong pace with the complexion of the race changing more than once in the home straight. Sound form.

2818 HEAVEN LAP DANCING BAR H'CAP — 5f
9:15 (9:16) (Class 5) (0-75,72) 4-Y-O+ **£2,914** (£867; £433; £216) **Stalls** Low

Form RPR

2462 **1** **Riflessione**[21] 2166 4-9-5 **70**...................................(b) JoeFanning 2 79
(R A Harris) *trckd ldng pair: swtchd rt and hdwy wl over 1f out: sn chal: rdn to ld ins fnl f: kpt on wl* **7/1**

-006 **2** *1 ¼* **Darcy's Pride (IRE)**[7] 2582 6-7-11 **53** oh1.................... PaulPickard(5) 1 58
(P T Midgley) *towards rr: hdwy on inner wl over 1f out: sn rdn and styd on ins fnl f: nrst fin* **25/1**

2204 **3** *nse* **Mr Wolf**[17] 2275 9-9-2 **67**.......................................(p) TonyHamilton 10 71
(J J Quinn) *led: rdn wl over 1f out: drvn and hdd ins fnl f: kpt on* **5/1**[2]

-261 **4** *½* **Poppy's Rose**[14] 2396 6-8-11 **69**...................................... DaleSwift(7) 6 72
(T J Etherington) *trckd ldrs on inner: effrt 2f out: sn rdn and kpt on same pce fnl f* **10/3**[1]

6111 **5** *2* **Chosen One (IRE)**[9] 2528 5-8-13 **69**......................... JamesSullivan(5) 7 64
(Mrs R A Carr) *cl up: rdn along wl over 1f out: sn drvn and wknd fnl f* **11/2**[3]

3404 **6** *¾* **Namir (IRE)**[14] 2378 8-8-12 **63**................................... GrahamGibbons 5 58+
(H J Evans) *in tch: rdn and effrt 2f out: styng on whn n.m.r ins fnl f: one pce* **12/1**

0-04 **7** *½* **Rio Sands**[7] 2582 5-8-7 **58**... DaraghO'Donohoe 8 49
(R M Whitaker) *in tch on outer: effrt 2f out: sn rdn and no imp appr fnl f* **33/1**

-054 **8** *hd* **Baybshambles (IRE)**[27] 1988 6-9-1 **66**............................ PaulHanagan 3 56
(R E Barr) *hld up: a towards rr* **13/2**

0600 **9** *2* **King Of Swords (IRE)**[9] 2528 6-8-12 **63**....................... AndrewElliott 11 46
(N Tinkler) *chsd ldrs: rdn along 2f out: grad wknd* **11/1**

5026 **10** *9* **Milton Of Campsie**[9] 2528 5-9-7 **72**............................... JimmyFortune 4 23+
(J Balding) *hld up in rr: hdwy and wd st: rdn over 1f out: sn wknd and eased fnl f* **13/2**

63.83 secs (0.53) **Going Correction** +0.15s/f (Good) 10 Ran SP% **117.1**
Speed ratings (Par 103): **101,99,98,98,94 93,92,92,89,75**
toteswingers:1&2:£25.90, 1&3:£5.90, 2&3:£33.80 CSF £163.93 CT £979.08 TOTE £9.50: £3.40, £10.50, £1.70; EX 256.30 Place 6 £63.69; Place 5 £54.64.
Owner Paul Moulton **Bred** Tom & Evelyn Yates **Trained** Earlswood, Monmouths
■ Stewards' Enquiry : Tony Hamilton two-day ban: used whip in incorrect place (Jun 21-22)

FOCUS
A fair handicap run at a good pace and the result seemed the right one. The winner is rated to his best.
Namir(IRE) Official explanation: jockey said gelding was denied a clear run
Baybshambles(IRE) Official explanation: jockey said gelding lost its near-fore shoe
Milton Of Campsie Official explanation: jockey said mare lost its action in straight
T/Jkpt: £3,550.00 to a £1 stake. Pool:£10,000.00 - 2.00 winning tickets T/Plt: £38.00 to a £1 stake. Pool:£85,665.49 - 1,641.59 winning tickets T/Qpdt: £17.00 to a £1 stake. Pool:£6,177.14 - 268.31 winning tickets JR

2397 WINDSOR (R-H)
Monday, June 7

OFFICIAL GOING: Good to firm (good in places) changing to good after race 5 (8:30)
Stands' rail dolled out 18yds at 6f down to 7yds at winning post. Top bend dolled out 2yds from innermost line adding 9yds to races of one mile plus.
Wind: Light, behind Weather: Overcast, rain from race 2

2819 SPORTINGBET.COM E B F MEDIAN AUCTION MAIDEN STKS — 6f
6:30 (6:31) (Class 5) 2-Y-O — £3,480 (£1,027; £514) Stalls High

Form — RPR

1 **Major Dude** 2-9-3 0 ... RichardHughes 15 — 84+
(R Hannon) trckd ldrs: led wl over 2f out: pushed along and clr fnl f: readily — 8/11[1]

2 2 ¾ **Perfect Pastime** 2-9-3 0 ... AdamKirby 8 — 73
(W R Swinburn) cl up: rdn to chse wnr jst over 1f out: styd on but no imp — 16/1

3 1 ¼ **Miss Moneypenni** 2-8-12 0 ... JimCrowley 3 — 64
(N P Littmoden) pressed ldr to 1/2-way: outpcd over 1f out: pushed along and kpt on — 33/1

4 nk **Cathcart Castle** 2-9-3 0 ... SamHitchcott 16 — 68
(M R Channon) trckd ldrs: green and pushed along briefly 4f out: effrt 2f out: styd on fnl f — 14/1[3]

5 nk **St Oswald** 2-9-3 0 ... SteveDrowne 5 — 67+
(R Charlton) wl in rr: pushed along over 2f out: styd on wl fnl f: nrst fin — 14/1[3]

6 2 ¾ **Arctic Mirage** 2-9-3 0 ... DaneO'Neill 7 — 59
(M Blanshard) s.i.s: t.k.h and hld up in last quartet: sme prog on outer over 2f out: shkn up over 1f out: v green and wandering after — 25/1

7 ½ **Robber Stone** 2-9-3 0 ... PaulEddery 14 — 57
(M R Channon) plld hrd: hld up in tch: outpcd fr 2f out — 33/1

8 2 ¾ **Quadra Hop (IRE)** 2-9-3 0 ... TonyCulhane 4 — 49
(B Palling) led to wl over 2f out: chsd wnr to jst over 1f out: hanging and wknd — 33/1

0 9 shd **Gower Rules (IRE)**[21] 2163 2-8-13 0 ow1 ... LeeNewnes(5) 10 — 50
(M D I Usher) wl in rr: struggling in last pair over 2f out: styd on last 100yds — 100/1

10 ½ **Nutley Copse** 2-8-12 0 ... DavidProbert 6 — 42
(A M Balding) s.i.s: v green early and wl in rr: no real prog — 25/1

0 11 nk **Regal Bullet (IRE)**[56] 1263 2-9-3 0 ... JimmyQuinn 9 — 47
(D K Ivory) dwlt: rcvrd into midfield over 3f out: rn green and outpcd over 2f out: fdd — 40/1

12 1 **Sammy Alexander** 2-9-3 0 ... MarcHalford 13 — 44
(G G Margarson) showed inexperience in preliminaries: a wl in rr — 66/1

32 13 1 **Littleportnbrandy (IRE)**[49] 1429 2-8-12 0 ... KierenFallon 1 — 36
(P D Evans) sn chsd ldrs: shkn up and outpcd over 2f out: wknd and eased over 1f out — 4/1[2]

14 2 **Snow Trooper** 2-9-3 0 ... EddieCreighton 11 — 35
(D K Ivory) nvr bttr than midfield: rdn bef 1/2-way: wknd 2f out — 100/1

1m 14.5s (1.50) **Going Correction** +0.05s/f (Good) — 14 Ran SP% 119.5
Speed ratings (Par 93): **92,88,86,86,85 82,81,77,77,77 76,75,74,71**
toteswingers:1&2:£7.30, 1&3:£11.70, 2&3:£58.30 CSF £13.24 TOTE £2.00: £1.20, £4.30, £5.80; EX 19.80 Trifecta £269.40 Part won. Pool: £364.09 - 0.91 winning units..
Owner Michael Pescod & Justin Dowley **Bred** M Humby And I Wilson **Trained** East Everleigh, Wilts

FOCUS
Little experience on show, and a disappointing early tempo, but the odds-on favourite had no trouble demonstrating his superiority and is another useful juvenile for his yard. The lack of pace meant it was hard to come from behind, and prominent runners dominated.

NOTEBOOK
Major Dude, a well made, scopey sort, was noisy at first and then colty in the paddock, and even though he was able to claim the advantage of the stands' rail, he still wanted to hang through inexperience. By Sakhee out of a (sadly untalented) Dilum mare, he looks a decent prospect, though he needs to improve to be ranked among the best in a stable full of juvenile talent. (tchd 4-5 and 5-6 in places)
Perfect Pastime, by Pastoral Pursuits out of a Desert King mare, was favoured by racing handily but deserves credit for chasing home the clear market leader. He should improve and take a similar race.
Miss Moneypenni, from a stable not noted for its debutant winners, made a sound debut. She has scope and, though she needs time to strengthen to her full potential, she is already good enough to win a routine maiden.
Cathcart Castle had a useful draw and shaped quite well in staying on better than most. He should soon step up on this promising first effort. (op 16-1)
St Oswald ◆, a Royal Applause newcomer out of a St Jovite mare, was the biggest eyecatcher. He ran on encouragingly when it was too late, and should leave this behind second time out. (op 16-1)
Arctic Mirage, who is bred to be quick, wandered all over the place in the last 2f. Already gelded for this debut, there has to be some concern about that but he showed enough to suggest that there could be some improvement in him when mentally tuned up. Official explanation: jockey said gelding ran green (op 66-1)
Robber Stone, making a satisfactory debut, needs to calm down a bit, but he would not have been helped in that respect by the weak early tempo. (op 50-1)
Quadra Hop(IRE) Official explanation: jockey said colt hung left
Littleportnbrandy(IRE) Official explanation: jockey said filly moved poorly throughout

2820 SOUTH AFRICA IS OPEN FOR BUSINESS CLAIMING STKS — 1m 3f 135y
7:00 (7:00) (Class 5) 3-Y-O — £2,593 (£765; £383) Stalls Low

Form — RPR

-406 1 **Stags Leap (IRE)**[8] 2562 3-9-6 88 ... (v[1]) RichardHughes 4 — 69+
(R Hannon) cl up: led over 3f out: racd against rail after: stl on bit 1f out: shkn up and fnd enough to win cosily — 10/11[1]

4-42 2 ¾ **Sassanian (IRE)**[16] 2333 3-9-0 61 ... ShaneKelly 2 — 62
(Jane Chapple-Hyam) led: rdn and hdd on either side over 3f out: hd high after: kpt on again fnl f to take 2nd last 100yds — 17/2

1623 3 1 **Buona Sarah (IRE)**[6] 2619 3-9-0 63 ... PatCosgrave 5 — 60
(J R Boyle) cl up: chal over 3f out: hrd rdn 2f out: wl hld fnl f: lost 2nd last 100yds — 2/1[2]

4 1 ½ **Tweedledrum** 3-8-13 0 ... DavidProbert 3 — 57+
(A M Balding) lft abour 12 l: v green early: ct up w rest after 5f: rdn 3f out: nvr posed a threat but kpt on — 4/1[3]

00-0 5 18 **Daryainur (IRE)**[23] 2115 3-8-4 44 ... JamesRogers(7) 1 — 24
(W De Best-Turner) cl up tl wknd over 3f out: t.o — 100/1

2m 31.95s (2.45) **Going Correction** +0.05s/f (Good) — 5 Ran SP% 117.2
Speed ratings (Par 99): **93,92,91,90,78**
CSF £10.46 TOTE £1.60: £1.10, £4.10; EX 5.40.Stags Leap was claimed by P. Monteith for £16,000
Owner Mrs J Wood **Bred** P McCartan & Paddy Twomey **Trained** East Everleigh, Wilts

FOCUS
An uncompetitive claimer in which the pace was just a modest one. The winner was unimpressive in beating inferior rivals.

2821 K & L GATES H'CAP — 1m 2f 7y
7:30 (7:32) (Class 4) (0-80,80) 4-Y-O+ — £4,533 (£1,348; £674; £336) Stalls Low

Form — RPR

-006 1 **Brouhaha**[21] 2173 6-8-10 76 ... SoniaEaton(7) 11 — 86
(Tom Dascombe) stdd s: hld up in last trio: gd prog fr over 2f out: led ent fnl f: drifted lft but styd on wl — 20/1

0666 2 1 ¾ **Admirable Duque (IRE)**[16] 2341 4-8-12 71 ... (p) RobertWinston 7 — 77
(D J S Ffrench Davis) settled towards rr: rdn wl over 3f out: prog fr 2f out: wnt 2nd ins fnl f: outpcd by wnr — 8/1[3]

/53- 3 1 **Wild Desert (FR)**[465] 549 5-9-6 79 ... JamieSpencer 1 — 83
(A King) led 2f: chsd ldr to 7f out: rdn in 3rd 3f out: kpt on to dispute 2nd ent fnl f: no ex — 14/1

0005 4 nse **Sacrilege**[9] 2388 5-8-1 65 ... (p) SophieDoyle(5) 3 — 69
(M C Chapman) taken down early and walked to post: s.s: wl in rr: detached in last 4f out: prog fr 2f out: fnlly r.o ins fnl f: nrly snatched 3rd — 40/1

-04 5 1 ½ **Opera Prince**[63] 1133 5-8-13 72 ... SebSanders 4 — 73+
(Lady Herries) wnt 2nd 7f out: jnd ldr 5f out: protracted battle after: narrow ld over 1f out but nthing lft to fend off later chalrs: hdd & wknd ent fnl f — 9/2[2]

0245 6 ¾ **Laudatory**[11] 2467 4-9-7 80 ... (p) AdamKirby 13 — 79+
(W R Swinburn) led after 2f: jnd 5f out: drvn 3f out: narrowly hdd over 1f out: sn wknd — 4/1[1]

135- 7 shd **Gunslinger (FR)**[76] 7841 5-9-4 77 ... PatCosgrave 5 — 76
(M J Scudamore) hld up in midfield: rdn over 3f out: no real hdwy 2f out: kpt on u.p — 14/1

4-56 8 3 **Kiss A Prince**[19] 2236 4-8-8 67 ... HayleyTurner 10 — 60
(D K Ivory) nvr bttr than midfield: dropped to rr u.p over 2f out: n.d after — 10/1

6-10 9 ½ **Arashi**[7] 2583 4-8-5 64 ... (p) JimmyQuinn 9 — 56
(Lucinda Featherstone) hld up towards rr: effrt on outer over 3f out: no prog 2f out: wknd over 1f out — 25/1

/000 10 1 ¾ **Track Record**[26] 2031 5-9-5 78 ... JimCrowley 14 — 67
(Jonjo O'Neill) stdd s: hld up in last trio: limited prog on outer over 3f out: no hdwy and btn 2f out — 16/1

6/0- 11 1 ½ **Blue Spartan (IRE)**[13] 1603 5-9-5 78 ... SteveDrowne 2 — 64
(C J Mann) chsd ldrs: rdn in 4th 4f out: wknd 2f out — 40/1

30-5 12 5 **Sequillo**[21] 2181 4-9-7 80 ... RichardHughes 12 — 56
(R Hannon) chsd ldrs: rdn over 2f out: clsd enough wl over 1f out: wknd rapidly — 4/1[1]

-140 13 14 **Wunder Strike (USA)**[19] 2236 4-8-8 67 ... (p) NickyMackay 6 — 15
(J R Boyle) hld up in rr: sme prog on outer over 3f out: shkn up and dropped to rr again over 2f out: t.o — 20/1

2m 7.74s (-0.96) **Going Correction** +0.05s/f (Good) — 13 Ran SP% 115.8
Speed ratings (Par 105): **105,103,102,102,101 100,100,98,98,96 95,91,80**
toteswingers:1&2:£44.30, 1&3:£64.10, 2&3:£29.40 CSF £158.84 CT £2311.30 TOTE £26.30: £7.40, £2.80, £4.00; EX 279.20 TRIFECTA Not won..
Owner Grant Thornton Racing Club **Bred** Mrs Rosamund Furlong **Trained** Malpas, Cheshire

FOCUS
A modest early tempo changed dramatically after the home turn, with Laudatory and Opera Prince injecting significant pace and racing several lengths clear, but ultimately it did neither of them any good. A turf personal best from the winner.
Wunder Strike(USA) Official explanation: jockey said gelding had no more to give

2822 SPORTINGBET.COM H'CAP — 5f 10y
8:00 (8:00) (Class 4) (0-85,85) 3-Y-O — £4,857 (£1,445; £722; £360) Stalls High

Form — RPR

1-01 1 **Kingsgate Choice (IRE)**[12] 2442 3-9-3 81 ... RobertWinston 5 — 97+
(J R Best) hld up bhd ldrs: prog to ld jst over 1f out: shkn up and sn clr — 7/4[1]

3-61 2 2 **Humidor (IRE)**[23] 2114 3-8-11 75 ... SteveDrowne 4 — 81
(R Charlton) t.k.h: hld up in last: stl there 2f out: prog over 1f out: pushed along and r.o to take 2nd nr fin: no ch to chal — 6/1[3]

-042 3 ½ **Ignatieff (IRE)**[21] 2179 3-9-1 79 ... DuranFentiman 3 — 83
(Mrs L Stubbs) led: drvn and hdd jst over 1f out: no ch w wnr after: lost 2nd nr fin — 8/1

2403 4 1 ¼ **Leleyf (IRE)**[21] 2179 3-8-7 71 ... SamHitchcott 9 — 70
(M R Channon) pressed ldr to over 1f out: steadily fdd — 8/1

10-4 5 ¾ **Danny's Choice**[17] 2283 3-9-7 85 ... JimCrowley 8 — 81+
(R M Beckett) settled towards rr: pushed along 2f out: keeping on one pce whn light reminder ins fnl f: nvr nr ldrs — 11/4[2]

0016 6 ¾ **Sophie's Beau (USA)**[6] 2617 3-8-1 70 ... SophieDoyle(5) 7 — 63
(M C Chapman) chsd ldrs: rdn wl over 1f out: sn outpcd — 25/1

322- 7 ½ **La Fortunata**[228] 6971 3-8-8 72 ... JimmyQuinn 1 — 63
(Mike Murphy) prom: rdn over 1f out: wknd fnl f — 12/1

-424 8 3 ½ **Lucky Mellor**[95] 783 3-9-2 80 ... RichardHughes 2 — 57
(D K Ivory) in tch towards rr: effrt on wd outside 1/2-way: lft bhd over 1f out — 12/1

60.00 secs (-0.30) **Going Correction** +0.05s/f (Good) — 8 Ran SP% 118.8
Speed ratings (Par 101): **104,100,100,98,96 95,94,89**
toteswingers:1&2:£3.10, 1&3:£5.30, 2&3:£9.60 CSF £13.57 CT £68.93 TOTE £3.10: £1.90, £2.40, £1.90; EX 12.80 Trifecta £139.10 Pool: £233.24 - 1.24 winning units..
Owner John Mayne **Bred** Michael Staunton **Trained** Hucking, Kent

FOCUS
A decent sprint handicap for the money, but it is likely the winner will prove to be way above this class as he matures. He was value for a bit extra on the day.

Danny's Choice Official explanation: jockey said filly was denied a clear run

2823 WIN A HOLIDAY WITH SUN INTERNATIONAL H'CAP 1m 67y
8:30 (8:31) (Class 5) (0-75,75) 4-Y-O+ £2,729 (£806; £403) Stalls High

Form RPR

1-20 **1** **Crazy Chris**[114] 546 5-9-4 **72** DavidProbert 10 83
(B Palling) *mde all: 2 l clr wl over 1f out: drvn and hrd pressed ins fnl f: hld on wl* **20/1**

-211 **2** *hd* **Night Lily (IRE)**[14] 2392 4-9-7 **75** TonyCulhane 13 86
(P W D'Arcy) *t.k.h early: trckd ldng pair: drvn to go 2nd wl over 1f out: clsd u.p fnl f: jst hld* **9/2**[1]

04-2 **3** *hd* **Saturn Way (GR)**[31] 1877 4-9-2 **70** LiamKeniry 2 80
(P R Chamings) *hld up towards rr: stdy prog on outer over 2f out: drvn to cl on ldrs fnl f: chal last 100yds: jst hld* **10/1**

4043 **4** *3/4* **Baylini**[16] 2339 6-9-2 **75** SophieDoyle(5) 5 83
(Ms J S Doyle) *taken down early: hld up in midfield: stdy prog on outer over 2f out: rdn over 1f out: pressed ldrs fnl f: nt qckn last 100yds* **11/2**[2]

24-6 **5** *4 1/2* **Wilfred Pickles (IRE)**[26] 2024 4-9-7 **75** JamieSpencer 11 73
(Miss Jo Crowley) *hld up in midfield: swtchd off rail and effrt over 2f out: drvn and no imp on ldrs over 1f out* **11/2**[2]

-440 **6** *1* **Edgeworth (IRE)**[16] 2339 4-9-6 **74** FergusSweeney 7 70
(B G Powell) *taken down early: prom bhd ldrs: rdn over 3f out: lost pl u.p over 1f out: n.d after* **16/1**

-314 **7** *1/2* **Magroom**[26] 2024 6-9-4 **72** HayleyTurner 6 67
(R J Hodges) *hld up in last trio: wl off the pce 1/2-way: prog on outer over 2f out: no hdwy over 1f out* **16/1**

3165 **8** *1 1/2* **French Art**[14] 2392 5-9-3 **71** (p) KierenFallon 14 62
(N Tinkler) *hld up towards rr: drvn and effrt on inner 2f out: no prog over 1f out* **9/2**[1]

-000 **9** *1 3/4* **Cheam Forever (USA)**[26] 2024 4-9-5 **73** RichardKingscote 3 60
(R Charlton) *chsd wnr to wl over 1f out: wknd* **8/1**[3]

030- **10** *1 3/4* **Becuille (IRE)**[207] 7360 5-9-2 **70** (b) EddieAhern 4 56
(B J Meehan) *trckd ldng pair: rdn over 2f out: sn lost pl: eased wl over 1f out* **33/1**

0002 **11** *nk* **Orchard Supreme**[19] 2235 7-9-3 **74** PatrickHills(3) 8 56
(R Hannon) *settled in midfield: rdn wl over 2f out and no prog: wknd over 1f out* **20/1**

-050 **12** *5* **Emeebee**[19] 2236 4-9-7 **75** RobertWinston 1 46
(W J Musson) *hld up last: wl detached and rdn 1/2-way: no prog* **33/1**

3500 **13** *3 1/4* **Daddy's Gift (IRE)**[16] 2331 4-9-2 **70** RichardHughes 9 33
(R Hannon) *hld up in last trio: off the pce 1/2-way: rdn and no prog 3f out: sn no ch* **16/1**

1m 43.11s (-1.59) **Going Correction** +0.05s/f (Good) **13** Ran SP% **120.4**
Speed ratings (Par 103): **109,108,108,107,103 102,101,100,98,96 96,91,88**
toteswingers:1&2:£8.50, 1&3:£66.40, 2&3:£6.60 CSF £104.79 CT £1004.36 TOTE £20.30: £5.60, £1.50, £2.80; EX 79.90 Trifecta £415.10 Part won. Pool: £561.04 - 0.30 winning units..

Owner E R Griffiths **Bred** E R Griffiths **Trained** Tredodridge, Vale Of Glamorgan

FOCUS
There was a decent tempo, with the pace-setter hanging on to win. Sound form, with the first four clear.

Emeebee Official explanation: jockey said gelding was unsuited by the track

2824 CHAMPION'S 60:60 CHARITY CHALLENGE CLASSIFIED STKS 6f
9:00 (9:00) (Class 5) 3-Y-O £2,593 (£765; £383) Stalls High

Form RPR

4-32 **1** **Vanilla Rum**[21] 2174 3-9-0 75 DaneO'Neill 1 80
(H Candy) *dwlt: hld up in rr: prog on wd outside fr 2f out: rdn to ld last strides: jst hld on* **4/1**[2]

-445 **2** *nse* **Mon Brav**[17] 2287 3-9-0 75 (b) JamieSpencer 9 80
(D Carroll) *racd freely: mde most towards nr side rail: drvn 2f out: hdd last strides: styd on* **10/3**[1]

2425 **3** *1 3/4* **Starlight Muse (IRE)**[37] 1685 3-9-0 75 SebSanders 5 74
(E S McMahon) *chsd ldrs: effrt 2f out: wnt 3rd fnl f: nt pce to chal* **20/1**

3566 **4** *shd* **Slikback Jack (IRE)**[13] 2426 3-9-0 72 RobertWinston 11 74+
(J A Glover) *cl up against nr side rail: chal 2f out to over 1f out: no ex fnl f* **6/1**[3]

2235 **5** *1/2* **R Woody**[110] 577 3-9-0 75 SteveDrowne 10 72+
(D K Ivory) *stdd s: hld up in last pair: shuffled along fr 2f out: styd on steadily: nrst fin* **20/1**

5460 **6** *1/2* **Dancing Freddy (IRE)**[7] 2599 3-9-0 75 PaulMulrennan 3 71
(J G Given) *sn w ldrs: rdn over 2f out: nt qckn over 1f out: fdd* **33/1**

221- **7** *1/2* **Adventure Story**[212] 7288 3-9-0 75 RichardHughes 2 69
(R Hannon) *hld up in tch: effrt on outer over 2f out: nt qckn u.p over 1f out: fdd ins fnl f* **6/1**[3]

0-20 **8** *1/2* **Fawley Green**[25] 2052 3-9-0 75 HayleyTurner 8 68+
(W R Muir) *stdd s: hld up last: shuffled along and kpt on steadily fnl 2f: nvr nr ldrs* **10/1**

0062 **9** *hd* **Nubar Boy**[5] 2656 3-8-11 72 (t) MartinLane(3) 4 67+
(P D Evans) *hld up: gng strly over 2f out: shuffled along and nt qckn over 1f out: no threat after* **7/1**

2240 **10** *1* **Dusty Spirit**[17] 2287 3-8-11 74 (t) JackDean(3) 7 64
(W G M Turner) *racd freely: w ldr to 1/2-way: wknd 2f out* **16/1**

2-50 **11** *5* **Grand Zafeen**[23] 2112 3-9-0 75 KierenFallon 6 48
(M R Channon) *w ldrs to 1/2-way: wknd u.p 2f out* **12/1**

1m 13.89s (0.89) **Going Correction** +0.05s/f (Good) **11** Ran SP% **119.3**
Speed ratings (Par 99): **96,95,93,93,92 92,91,90,90,89 82**
toteswingers:1&2:£5.60, 1&3:£6.70, 2&3:£18.20 CSF £17.52 TOTE £4.00: £1.20, £1.30, £6.60; EX 24.20 Place 6 £115.83; Place 5 £74.34. Not won..

Owner Trevor Stone & Friends **Bred** Charley Knoll Partnership **Trained** Kingston Warren, Oxon

■ Stewards' Enquiry : Jamie Spencer one-day ban: careless riding (Jun 21)

FOCUS
As the rain got further into the ground, the runners spread wide across the track and it became increasingly helpful to race towards the far side. The early pace was weak, leaving many with a chance in the last 2f, and they were bunched at the line. The winner was among the least exposed.

Fawley Green Official explanation: jockey said gelding lost a near-fore shoe

T/Plt: £108.50 to a £1 stake. Pool:£97,505.98 - 656.01 winning tickets T/Qpdt: £57.90 to a £1 stake. Pool:£7,623.56 - 97.42 winning tickets JN

2825 - 2827a (Foreign Racing) - See Raceform Interactive

2034 NAAS (L-H)
Monday, June 7

OFFICIAL GOING: Good to firm

2828a COOLMORE STUD FILLIES' STKS (GROUP 3) 6f
4:10 (4:11) 2-Y-O £57,522 (£16,814; £7,964; £2,654)

RPR

1 **Radharcnafarraige (IRE)**[26] 2034 2-8-12 KJManning 7 99
(J S Bolger, Ire) *cl up in 3rd: led travelling wl over 2f out: sn qcknd clr: kpt on wl ins fnl f: easily* **2/1**[1]

2 *3* **Emerald Ring (IRE)**[22] 2146 2-8-12 WMLordan 3 90
(David Wachman, Ire) *hld up in tch: 6th 1/2-way: 3rd and hdwy under 2f out: mod 2nd 1f out: styd on wl* **10/1**

3 *2 1/2* **Juliet Capulet (IRE)**[25] 2059 2-8-12 JAHeffernan 8 83
(A P O'Brien, Ire) *s.i.s and hld up in rr: r.o wl fr 1 1/2f out* **25/1**

4 *hd* **Cat Fire (IRE)**[5] 2660 2-8-12 DPMcDonogh 2 82
(Kevin Prendergast, Ire) *hld up towards rr: rdn 2f out: kpt on same pce u.p fr over 1f out* **11/1**

5 *3/4* **Anadolu (IRE)**[10] 2518 2-8-12 PShanahan 6 80
(Tracey Collins, Ire) *upset in stalls: cl up in 2nd: rdn and outpcd under 2f out: no ex fr over 1f out* **8/1**

6 *2 1/2* **Catherineofaragon (IRE)**[24] 2102 2-8-12 JMurtagh 1 72
(A P O'Brien, Ire) *hld up: 5th and effrt over 1 1/2f out: no imp: one pce* **3/1**[2]

7 *4 1/2* **Foot Perfect (IRE)**[9] 2550 2-8-12 FMBerry 4 59
(David Marnane, Ire) *chsd ldrs in 4th: rdn after 1/2-way: no ex fr 2f out* **8/1**

8 *7* **Geesala (IRE)**[12] 2436 2-8-12 PJSmullen 5 47
(K A Ryan) *led: rdn and hdd over 2f out: sn wknd: eased fnl f* **4/1**[3]

1m 10.43s (-2.77) **8** Ran SP% **121.8**
CSF £25.43 TOTE £2.90: £1.20, £2.80, £6.60; DF 38.50.

Owner Ms Grainne Seoige **Bred** J S Bolger **Trained** Coolcullen, Co Carlow

FOCUS
The time was good and the race has been rated in line with recent renewals.

NOTEBOOK
Radharcnafarraige(IRE) ◆ had made a favourable impression over this course and trip last month and she ran out the impressive winner of this Group 3 event. She settled in third from her nearside draw and once she took over 2f out she soon had her chasing rivals in trouble. She once again relished the decent surface and, although she edged left inside the final furlong when idling, the half-sister to Blas Ceoil did the job well. The Albany Stakes over this trip is next according to her trainer, who won both races two years ago with Cuis Ghaire. (op 5/2)
Emerald Ring(IRE), third on her debut behind Purple Glow, kept on well inside the final furlong without threatening. On this evidence, the half-sister to the useful 1m juvenile scorer Kingdom Of Naples, looks a future winner when upped in trip.
Juliet Capulet(IRE) looked up against it based on her two runs at Naas and York. She was another to shape well after a slow start and she can hopefully build on this pleasing display.
Cat Fire(IRE) was the subject of bullish reports before her debut win over this trip at Fairyhouse last Wednesday. She was making a quick reappearance in search of some black type and just failed after staying on under pressure inside the final furlong. (op 10/1)
Anadolu(IRE) was tackling this trip for the second time in her career. She had previously bolted home in a Dundalk sprint but she wasn't helped when she became upset loading up. She raced close to the pace early but couldn't go with the winner.
Catherineofaragon(IRE) was his principal fancy to score for the race sponsors. This furlong longer trip looked sure to suit the daughter of Holy Roman Emperor, having her third career start, but the Phoenix Stakes entry, who is closely related to group 1 juvenile winner Rumplestiltskin, never got in a telling blow. Official explanation: jockey said filly ran green throughout this race (op 3/1 tchd 7/2)
Geesala(IRE), successful twice from three starts all over 5f, looked a worthy challenger going up in trip, but she dropped away after taking them along until after halfway and her rider accepted the situation. Official explanation: jockey said filly needs more ease in the ground

2829 - 2831a (Foreign Racing) - See Raceform Interactive

2623 REDCAR (L-H)
Tuesday, June 8

OFFICIAL GOING: Good (good to firm in places; .8.7)
Wind: moderate 1/2 behind Weather: light showers

2832 CHAMPION'S 60:60 CHARITY CHALLENGE MEDIAN AUCTION MAIDEN STKS 6f
2:00 (2:01) (Class 5) 2-Y-O £2,396 (£712; £356; £177) Stalls Centre

Form RPR

3 **1** **Bay Of Fires (IRE)**[19] 2238 2-8-12 0 SilvestreDeSousa 8 71
(J Hetherton) *w ldrs: hung lft over 2f out: led over 1f out: dived rt: hung rt ins fnl f: jst hld on* **5/1**

6 **2** *shd* **Tinkertown (IRE)**[26] 2059 2-9-3 0 JamieSpencer 4 76
(P F I Cole) *w ldrs on outer: edgd rt and chal ins fnl f: jst failed* **4/1**[2]

4 **3** *hd* **Local Singer (IRE)**[17] 2319 2-9-3 0 AlanMunro 1 75
(M R Channon) *mid-div: hdwy on outside over 2f out: sn chsng ldrs: styd on to chal ins fnl f: no ex nr fin* **9/2**[3]

622 **4** *1 1/4* **Lady Royale**[13] 2436 2-8-12 0 PJMcDonald 16 67
(G R Oldroyd) *w ldrs: hung lft over 2f out: keeping on same pce whn sltly hmpd 1f out* **5/2**[1]

42 **5** *1/2* **Ice Trooper**[10] 2522 2-9-3 0 TomEaves 7 70
(Mrs L Stubbs) *led: hdd over 1f out: hmpd 1f out: sn wknd* **10/1**

5 **6** *1* **No Poppy (IRE)**[15] 2376 2-8-12 0 DavidAllan 5 62+
(T D Easterby) *mid-div: kpt on wl fnl f* **11/1**

6 **7** *2 3/4* **Witzend (IRE)**[19] 2238 2-9-3 0 TonyHamilton 14 59
(Jedd O'Keeffe) *hld up in rr: kpt on fnl 2f: nvr trbld ldrs* **100/1**

8 *2 3/4* **Cool In The Shade** 2-8-7 0 PaulPickard(5) 6 46
(P T Midgley) *chsd ldrs: wknd over 1f out* **100/1**

6 **9** *1* **Another Wise Kid (IRE)**[53] 1359 2-9-3 0 TonyCulhane 3 50
(P T Midgley) *hld up in rr: sme hdwy whn hmpd over 2f out: wknd over 1f out* **16/1**

10 *3* **Louis Vee (IRE)** 2-9-3 0 PaulMulrennan 11 39
(J G Given) *chsd ldrs: wknd over 1f out* **66/1**

0 **11** *1 1/4* **Roman Ruler (IRE)**[11] 2498 2-9-0 0 KellyHarrison(3) 13 35
(C W Fairhurst) *trckd ldrs: drvn over 2f out: sn wknd* **100/1**

50 **12** *1 1/4* **Chadford**[15] 2376 2-9-3 0 PhillipMakin 12 31
(T D Walford) *caused problems in stalls: t.k.h in rr: nvr a factor* **66/1**

00 **13** *nk* **Market Maker (IRE)**[15] 2384 2-8-12 0 LanceBetts(5) 2 30
(T D Easterby) *trckd ldrs: drvn over 3f out: lost pl 2f out* **100/1**

The Form Book, Raceform Ltd, Compton, RG20 6NL

14 2 **Bernisdale** 2-8-12 0 SebSanders 15 19
(G M Moore) *in rr div: drvn over 2f out: nvr a factor* **40/1**

0 15 4 **Illawalla**[15] 2376 2-9-3 0 PatrickMathers 9 12
(H A McWilliams) *s.i.s: bhd fnl 2f* **200/1**

0 16 11 **Key Impeller**[36] 1749 2-9-0 0 BarryMcHugh(3) 10 —
(Ollie Pears) *chsd ldrs lost pl 3f out: eased whn bhd ins fnl f* **50/1**

1m 12.86s (1.06) **Going Correction** +0.05s/f (Good) **16** Ran SP% **118.6**
Speed ratings (Par 93): **94,93,93,91,91 89,86,82,81,77 75,73,73,70,65 50**
toteswingers: 1&2 £7.00, 1&3 £6.10, 2&3 £4.60 CSF £24.26 TOTE £7.30: £2.50, £2.20, £2.40; EX 31.20 Trifecta £59.40 Pool: £184.76 - 2.30 winning units..
Owner P Bamford J M Binns R G Fell & K Everitt **Bred** Duncan A McGregor **Trained** Norton, N Yorks

FOCUS
Following 8mm of rain on Sunday and 3mm overnight, the ground eased to good, good to firm in places. The riders reported that it was "nice, decent ground". A fair juvenile maiden and one run at a reasonable gallop. The field converged in the centre. The form is rated around the time and the principals.

NOTEBOOK
Bay Of Fires(IRE), from a yard in really good form, stepped up a fair bit on her debut form to get off the mark, despite drifting markedly right in the closing stages. On this evidence she should prove equally effective over 7f (backed up by pedigree) and it will be interesting to see if she can improve on this next time. (op 13-2)
Tinkertown(IRE) had shown ability as well as marked greenness on his debut in a much stronger York maiden and he bettered that effort, despite unseating his rider before the start and tending to edge off a true line under pressure. He should be even better suited by 7f and is more than capable of picking up a similar event. (op 7-2)
Local Singer(IRE) showed promise on his debut and, after attracting support, he ran at least as well in what looks a reasonable maiden for the track. He should have no problems with a bit further and is also capable of picking up a minor event. (op 6-1)
Lady Royale, the form pick who had shown improvement with each of her first three starts, including in Listed company on her previous start but, after hanging left, she failed to improve in the anticipated manner for the step up to 6f. She is starting to look exposed, but it will be a bit of a surprise if she is not able to pick up a small race. (op 2-1 tchd 11-4)
Ice Trooper is a steadily progressive sort who finished much closer to Lady Royale than he had done at Beverley on his debut. While vulnerable to the better sorts in this grade, he will be interesting once the nursery season kicks in. (op 11-1 tchd 12-1 in a place)
No Poppy(IRE) ◆, who showed clear signs of ability on her debut, again showed promise over this longer trip. She looks more about stamina than speed, and she too will be of more interest in ordinary nursery company in due course. (op 14-1 tchd 10-1)

2833 WIN A VIP DAY OUT @ REDCARRACING.CO.UK APPRENTICE (S) STKS 1m 6f 19y
2:30 (2:31) (Class 6) 4-6-Y-O **£1,842** (£544; £272) **Stalls** Low

Form RPR

6-00 1 **Andorn (GER)**[24] 2109 6-8-9 54 AnthonyBetts(5) 5 51
(P A Kirby) *trckd ldrs: t.k.h: wnt 2nd 6f out: effrt over 3f out: led appr fnl f: styd on wl* **5/6**[1]

0-00 2 2 3/4 **Media Stars**[3] 2765 5-9-0 37 SoniaEaton 6 47
(R Johnson) *trckd ldrs: led 7f out: qckng over 5f out: hdd appr fnl f: kpt on same pce* **10/1**

05-0 3 4 1/2 **Ballade De La Mer**[21] 2214 4-8-6 40 JamesRogers(3) 3 36
(A G Foster) *trckd ldrs: carried wd bnd over 4f out: swtchd lft: one pce fnl 2f: tk 3rd jst ins fnl f* **10/1**

/0-0 4 4 1/2 **Starbougg**[5] 1807 6-8-4 41 LukeStrong(5) 2 30
(K G Reveley) *led 1f: chsd ldrs: swung wd bnd over 4f out: racd wd: wknd over 1f out* **5/1**[3]

43-0 5 2 1/2 **Melkatant**[6] 2655 4-8-9 47 MatthewLawson 4 26
(N Bycroft) *led after 1f: hdd 7f out: rallied and upside over 3f out: wknd qckly fnl f* **4/1**[2]

3m 10.06s (5.36) **Going Correction** +0.325s/f (Good) **5** Ran SP% **109.4**
Speed ratings: **97,95,92,90,88**
CSF £9.73 TOTE £1.50: £1.02, £5.90.There was no bid for the winner.
Owner Preesall Garage **Bred** Gestut Schlenderhan **Trained** Castleton, N Yorks

FOCUS
A very weak race, even for this grade, and one in which the pace was very steady to the straight. A strong candidate for worst race of the year.

2834 ANDERSON BARROWCLIFF H'CAP 7f
3:00 (3:03) (Class 5) (0-70,69) 3-Y-O **£2,396** (£712; £356; £177) **Stalls** Centre

Form RPR

6-44 1 **Just The Tonic**[7] 2628 3-8-7 55 PJMcDonald 9 63
(Mrs Marjorie Fife) *trckd ldrs: edgd rt and led jst ins fnl f: hld on towards fin* **11/1**

5300 2 1/2 **Dazeen**[36] 1750 3-9-0 62 (p) TonyCulhane 15 69
(P T Midgley) *in rr: hdwy and swtchd lft over 2f out: chsng ldrs 1f out: hrd rdn and kpt on towards fin* **10/1**

0-04 3 1 1/4 **Aleqa**[17] 2340 3-9-3 65 AlanMunro 6 69
(C F Wall) *chsd ldrs: kpt on same pce fnl f* **12/1**

0-01 4 1 **Ellies Image**[18] 2274 3-8-12 60 PatrickMathers 7 61
(B P J Baugh) *chsd ldrs: sn pushed along: kpt on same pce appr fnl f* **20/1**

5046 5 1/2 **Vito Volterra (IRE)**[14] 2422 3-9-3 65 PhillipMakin 10 65
(Michael Smith) *w ldr: led over 2f out: hdd jst ins fnl f: no ex* **15/2**[3]

0-26 6 3/4 **Jimmy The Poacher (IRE)**[31] 1921 3-9-6 68 DavidAllan 13 66+
(T D Easterby) *in rr: sn pushed along: styd on wl appr fnl f* **5/1**[2]

0-00 7 1 1/2 **Scarboro Warning (IRE)**[38] 1709 3-8-12 65 JamesO'Reilly(5) 2 59
(J O'Reilly) *hld up in rr: hdwy on outside over 2f out: hung lft and one pce* **66/1**

5-33 8 shd **Lutine Bell**[9] 2566 3-9-6 68 SebSanders 4 61
(Sir Mark Prescott) *mid-div: drvn over 3f out: one pce* **11/8**[1]

-002 9 1 3/4 **Luv U Noo**[15] 2380 3-8-8 56 TonyHamilton 5 45
(B Ellison) *chsd ldrs: wknd over 1f out* **18/1**

34-0 10 3/4 **Kalahari Desert (IRE)**[36] 1750 3-8-9 60 MichaelStainton(3) 1 46
(R M Whitaker) *hld up towards rr: effrt over 2f out: nvr nr ldrs* **22/1**

-420 11 nk **Choc'A'Moca (IRE)**[36] 1753 3-8-0 53 ow2 (b) BillyCray(5) 3 39
(D Carroll) *led tl over 2f out: wknd over 1f out* **20/1**

003 12 1 3/4 **Lady Vyrnwy (IRE)**[15] 2380 3-8-2 50 SilvestreDeSousa 16 31
(R A Fahey) *chsd ldrs: wknd over 1f out* **16/1**

540- 13 1 **Venture Girl (IRE)**[260] 6169 3-8-9 57 DuranFentiman 14 35
(T D Easterby) *in rr and sn drvn along: nvr on terms* **33/1**

00-4 14 shd **Tai Hang (IRE)**[21] 2212 3-7-13 50 oh5 KellyHarrison(3) 8 28
(J S Goldie) *mid-div: lost pl over 2f out* **50/1**

5-00 15 nk **Brinscall**[18] 2296 3-9-0 65 (b[1]) BarryMcHugh(3) 12 42
(Julie Camacho) *chsd ldrs: lost pl over 1f out* **40/1**

10 16 1 **Steed**[25] 2069 3-9-7 69 TomEaves 11 43
(K A Ryan) *in rr: rdn over 3f out: nvr on terms* **20/1**

1m 25.54s (1.04) **Going Correction** +0.05s/f (Good) **16** Ran SP% **134.3**
Speed ratings (Par 99): **96,95,94,92,92 91,89,89,87,86 86,84,83,83,82 81**
toteswingers: 1&2 £21.00, 1&3 £21.40, 2&3 £16.90 CSF £116.97 CT £1438.19 TOTE £13.70: £2.90, £2.60, £3.20, £3.80; EX 161.00 Trifecta £278.20 Part won. Pool of £376.01 - 0.10 winning units..
Owner R W Fife **Bred** West Dereham Abbey Stud **Trained** Stillington, N Yorks

FOCUS
A modest handicap in which the market leader proved disappointing. The first two are rated back towards their 2yo form. The gallop was a reasonable one.

2835 JOHN SMITH'S REDCAR STRAIGHT-MILE CHAMPIONSHIP H'CAP (QUALIFIER) 1m
3:35 (3:35) (Class 3) (0-95,94) 3-Y-O+
£6,542 (£1,959; £979; £490; £244; £122) **Stalls** Centre

Form RPR

-540 1 **Kiwi Bay**[25] 2086 5-9-5 85 TomEaves 4 99
(M Dods) *hld up in rr: hdwy on outer over 2f out: chsng ldrs 1f out: r.o to ld cl home* **9/1**

4011 2 nk **Charlie Cool**[14] 2423 7-9-3 88 (b) JamesSullivan(5) 2 101
(Mrs R A Carr) *mid-div: effrt over 2f out: led over 1f out: hdd and no ex nr fin* **7/2**[1]

-512 3 6 **Celtic Change (IRE)**[21] 2204 6-9-5 85 (bt) PhillipMakin 9 85
(M Dods) *sn w ldrs: led 4f out: hdd over 1f out: one pce* **13/2**[3]

-060 4 1 1/4 **Reel Buddy Star**[14] 2423 5-8-9 75 PJMcDonald 7 72
(G M Moore) *chsd ldrs: kpt on same pce appr fnl f* **10/1**

0-53 5 1 1/4 **Observatory Star (IRE)**[10] 2524 7-8-11 77 (tp) SebSanders 5 71
(T D Easterby) *hld up in rr: effrt and nt clr run over 2f out: kpt on fnl f* **8/1**

-006 6 2 **Collateral Damage (IRE)**[26] 2057 7-10-0 94 (t) DavidAllan 6 83
(T D Easterby) *mid-div: effrt over 2f out: nvr trbld ldrs* **8/1**

-020 7 3/4 **Handsome Falcon**[24] 2133 6-9-1 81 TonyHamilton 1 68
(R A Fahey) *mid-div: effrt over 2f out: wknd appr fnl f* **33/1**

-304 8 shd **Lucky Dance (BRZ)**[43] 1570 8-9-8 88 LNewman 12 75
(A G Foster) *swvd rt s: sn w ldrs: wknd over 1f out* **25/1**

-020 9 2 1/2 **Karaka Jack**[38] 1703 3-8-13 90 GregFairley 8 71
(M Johnston) *led tl 4f out: wknd over 1f out* **4/1**[2]

1404 10 1 1/2 **Exit Smiling**[23] 2141 8-9-4 84 TonyCulhane 3 62
(P T Midgley) *chsd ldrs: lost pl over 1f out* **12/1**

0125 11 5 **Just Bond (IRE)**[19] 2241 8-9-1 84 BarryMcHugh(3) 10 51
(G R Oldroyd) *prom: lost pl 2f out* **16/1**

50-0 12 8 **Jack Dawkins (USA)**[14] 2423 5-9-10 90 AdrianNicholls 11 38
(D Nicholls) *in rr: bhd fnl 3f* **25/1**

1m 36.6s (-1.40) **Going Correction** +0.05s/f (Good)
WFA 3 from 5yo+ 11lb **12** Ran SP% **121.1**
Speed ratings (Par 107): **109,108,102,101,100 98,97,97,94,93 88,80**
toteswingers: 1&2 £10.00, 1&3 £10.90, 2&3 £3.60 CSF £40.58 CT £230.47 TOTE £8.20: £2.00, £2.20, £2.10; EX 71.20 Trifecta £262.70 Pool: £394.18 - 1.11 winning units..
Owner Kiwi Racing **Bred** Templeton Stud **Trained** Denton, Co Durham

FOCUS
A good, competitive handicap in which the first two pulled clear. The gallop was a reasonable one and the form is taken at something like face value.

NOTEBOOK
Kiwi Bay hadn't been at his best over 7f in a race where it paid to race prominently on his previous start, but he appreciated the decent gallop back up in trip and ran as well as he ever has done to thwart the hat-trick bid of the runner-up. He's effective over 7f when the gallop is a generous one and the type to win more races when things pan out his way. (op 15-2)
Charlie Cool has had his enthusiasm rekindled by his in-form trainer and bettered the form of his previous Ripon victory from this 5lb higher mark. He pulled clear of the remainder and, although he will be up in the weights again, he has won off marks in the high 90's and low 100's in Dubai and should continue to give it his best shot. (op 4-1 tchd 9-2 in places)
Celtic Change(IRE) wasn't disgraced back in trip and fared the best of those up with the reasonable gallop. He doesn't have much room for manoeuvre from this mark but will be always worth a second look when it seems as though he may get an uncontested lead. (tchd 6-1)
Reel Buddy Star ◆ attracted support at double figure odds and finished closer to the runner-up than he had done at Ripon on his previous start. He has slipped back to a reasonable mark and there will be easier handicaps to tackle than this one in the near future. (op 16-1 tchd 20-1)
Observatory Star(IRE) is essentially a reliable sort but that consistency has earned him little respite from the handicapper. Although not disgraced, he has not won for nearly two years and is going to need things to slot perfectly into place.
Collateral Damage(IRE), in such good form in the second half of last season, was backed but again had his limitations exposed from a mark in the mid 90's and will have to show a fair bit more before he is a betting proposition. (op 15-2 tchd 6-1)
Karaka Jack, the only 3-y-o in the race, was the disappointment. He folded tamely in the last quarter mile and was again a long way below his useful Sandown form in April. He is best watched at present. (op 11-2 tchd 6-1 in a place)

2836 RACING UK CHANNEL 432 MAIDEN CLAIMING STKS 6f
4:10 (4:11) (Class 6) 2-Y-O **£1,842** (£544; £272) **Stalls** Centre

Form RPR

35 1 **Hayley Cropper**[7] 2623 2-8-6 0 AdrianNicholls 2 61+
(D Nicholls) *w ldr: led over 2f out: shkn up and styd on strly fnl f: v readily* **7/4**[1]

253 2 3 **Mica Mika (IRE)**[29] 1964 2-8-11 0 TonyHamilton 3 55
(R A Fahey) *chsd ldrs: rdn to chse wnr 1f out: kpt on same pce* **5/2**[2]

3 1 3/4 **Brian Sprout** 2-8-13 0 PaulMulrennan 1 52
(J R Weymes) *dwlt: in rr: drvn over 3f out: styd on fnl 2f: tk 3rd nr fin* **20/1**

0 4 3/4 **River Blade**[17] 2312 2-8-9 0 MickyFenton 4 46
(W M Brisbourne) *led: hdd over 2f out: fdd fnl f* **8/1**

00 5 8 **Stevie Bee Party**[10] 2522 2-8-5 0 PatrickMathers 8 18
(I W McInnes) *chsd ldrs: drvn 3f out: lost pl over 1f out* **100/1**

04 6 3 3/4 **Moving Picture**[8] 2605 2-8-13 0 TomEaves 9 14
(B M R Haslam) *t.k.h: sn trcking ldrs: wkng whn bmpd over 1f out* **12/1**

506 7 4 **Blind Stag (IRE)**[10] 2522 2-8-8 0 ow1 TonyCulhane 5 1+
(P T Midgley) *stdd s: tk fierce hold: sn trcking ldrs: hung bdly rt over 2f out: stmbld over 1f out: sn eased* **7/2**[3]

0 8 nse **Plumsum**[8] 2605 2-8-8 0 FranciscoDaSilva 6 —
(N Bycroft) *dwlt: in rr: drvn over 3f out: lost pl over 1f out* **50/1**

1m 13.45s (1.65) **Going Correction** +0.05s/f (Good) **8** Ran SP% **113.7**
Speed ratings (Par 91): **91,87,84,83,73 68,62,62**
toteswingers: 1&2 £1.80, 1&3 £5.10, 2&3 £5.40 CSF £6.16 TOTE £1.70: £1.02, £2.60, £5.00; EX 6.20 Trifecta £53.80 Pool: £403.36 - 5.54 winning units..
Owner Mrs Jackie Love & David Nicholls **Bred** R J & S A Carter **Trained** Sessay, N Yorks

FOCUS
A modest claimer run at a reasonable gallop. The first four finished clear and the form is limited behind the easy winner.

NOTEBOOK
Hayley Cropper hadn't got home over this trip at this track on her previous start but proved herself fully effective at the trip to win with something to spare. This wasn't much of a race but she may be capable of a little better. (op 2-1 tchd 13-8)
Mica Mika(IRE) has his obvious limitations, but he was far from disgraced upped to this trip for the first time against one that had shown promise in maidens. He should be able to pick up a similar event. (op 2-1)
Brian Sprout, the only newcomer in the field and the first foal of a half-sister to multiple 5f-7f scorer Welcome Approach, showed a modicum of ability after running green on this racecourse debut. He should stay 7f and is entitled to improve for this experience. (op 16-1)
River Blade had been soundly beaten in a Chester maiden on her debut but fared better in this lesser event. Low-grade nurseries will be the way forward with her in due course. (op 10-1)
Blind Stag(IRE), who was eased down after clipping heels with River Blade and stumbling passing the quarter mile pole, looks better than the bare form. However he has failed to confirm debut promise and, given the way he pulled and hung before meeting trouble, remains one to have reservations about. Official explanation: jockey said that the colt hung badly right handed in the final two furlongs (op 5-1)

2837 LADIES' DAY ON SATURDAY 19TH JUNE MEDIAN AUCTION MAIDEN STKS 1m

4:45 (4:46) (Class 6) 3-5-Y-O **£1,842** (£544; £272) **Stalls** Centre

Form RPR
65-2 **1** **Strike A Deal (IRE)**[21] 2221 3-8-8 70 AlanMunro 11 66
(C F Wall) *chsd ldrs: drvn over 2f out: led over 1f out: hld on towards fin* **15/8**[1]
2 ½ **Silvan Stream** 3-8-8 0 PJMcDonald 3 65
(J D Bethell) *s.s: hdwy over 2f out: chsd wnr 1f out: no ex towards fin* **25/1**
04 **3** 4 **Director General (USA)**[40] 1648 3-8-10 0 BarryMcHugh(3) 7 61
(Julie Camacho) *w ldrs: led over 2f out: hdd over 1f out: kpt on same pce* **28/1**
32 **4** hd **Kathlatino**[14] 2425 3-8-8 0 TomEaves 12 55
(Micky Hammond) *chsd ldrs: kpt on same pce appr fnl f* **7/2**[3]
5 hd **Sheikhtothemusic** 3-8-8 0 PaulMulrennan 10 55
(J G Given) *sn chsng ldrs: drvn over 2f out: kpt on fnl f* **40/1**
0 **6** 1 ½ **Leolene Starlight**[15] 2393 5-9-5 0 FranciscoDaSilva 8 54
(J Hetherton) *chsd ldrs: drvn and hung lft 3f out: one pce* **50/1**
0 **7** 3 ¼ **Colamandis**[11] 2496 3-8-8 0 PatrickMathers 1 43
(H A McWilliams) *racd wd: led: hdd over 2f out: wknd qckly jst ins fnl f* **200/1**
62-4 **8** ¾ **Quite Sparky**[14] 2425 3-8-13 77 MickyFenton 5 46
(T P Tate) *mid-div: drvn over 2f out: wknd and hung rt over 1f out* **2/1**[2]
55 **9** 8 **Red Skies (IRE)**[13] 2434 3-8-8 0 DuranFentiman 13 22
(Mrs L Stubbs) *w ldrs: wknd 2f out* **12/1**
00-5 **10** 5 **Lighterman**[11] 2503 3-8-13 40 SebSanders 2 15
(E J Alston) *racd wd: chsd ldrs: lost pl 2f out* **40/1**
11 12 **Octaviana** 3-8-8 0 DavidAllan 9 —
(E J Alston) *dwlt: in rr: bhd fnl 2f: eased* **50/1**

1m 39.71s (1.71) **Going Correction** +0.05s/f (Good)
WFA 3 from 5yo 11lb 11 Ran SP% **114.6**
Speed ratings (Par 101): **93,92,88,88,88 86,83,82,74,69 57**
toteswingers:1&2 £13.10, 2&3 £24.70, 1&3 £6.90 CSF £52.91 TOTE £2.60: £1.50, £7.80, £4.50; EX 61.90 Trifecta £375.40 Part won. Pool of 507.42 - 0.82 winning units..
Owner Racingeight Partners **Bred** Tally-Ho Stud **Trained** Newmarket, Suffolk

FOCUS
An ordinary maiden lacking anything in the way of strength in depth. The gallop was not strong and the first two pulled clear in the closing stages. This is inlikely to prove sound form.

2838 YORKSHIRE RACING SUMMER FESTIVAL H'CAP 1m 2f

5:15 (5:16) (Class 6) (0-55,55) 3-Y-O **£1,842** (£544; £272) **Stalls** Low

Form RPR
500- **1** **Valantino Oyster (IRE)**[359] 2940 3-8-0 46 oh1 IanBrennan(5) 1 56+
(J Howard Johnson) *chsd ldrs: effrt and swtchd rt over 3f out: wandered: led over 1f out: hld on wl nr fin* **7/2**[1]
5054 **2** nk **Destiny's Dancer**[24] 2132 3-8-4 50 PatrickDonaghy(5) 14 57
(B M R Haslam) *hld up in rr: swtchd rt 2f out: styd on strly to chse wnr last 75yds: hld at line* **8/1**
-004 **3** 3 ¾ **Miss Whippy**[28] 1989 3-8-13 54 SebSanders 6 53
(P Howling) *led tl over 7f out: chsd ldr: styd on same pce fnl f* **8/1**
-046 **4** nk **Cygnet Committee (IRE)**[15] 2379 3-8-5 46 (b) PJMcDonald 2 44
(J S Wainwright) *in tch: swtchd rt over 2f out: sn chsng ldrs: one pce* **33/1**
4300 **5** 1 **Market Puzzle (IRE)**[14] 2412 3-8-12 53 PaulMulrennan 13 49
(W M Brisbourne) *chsd ldrs: led over 7f out: hdd appr fnl f: one pce* **20/1**
-004 **6** nk **Scooby Dee**[15] 2380 3-8-1 47 ow1 AmyRyan(5) 9 43
(R M Whitaker) *chsd ldrs: one pce fnl 2f* **8/1**
-000 **7** hd **Bring Sweets (IRE)**[11] 2503 3-8-5 46 oh1 (b[1]) FranciscoDaSilva 4 41
(B Ellison) *hld up towards rr: hdwy on ins over 3f out: sn upsides ldr: hung lft over 1f out: one pce* **14/1**
000 **8** nk **Marsh's Gift**[15] 2393 3-8-11 55 BarryMcHugh(3) 5 50
(R E Barr) *s.i.s: t.k.h: hdwy over 2f out: kpt on: nvr nr ldrs* **25/1**
0000 **9** ½ **Barastar**[11] 2503 3-8-6 47 AndrewElliott 10 41
(N Tinkler) *in rr: kpt on fnl 2f: nvr nr ldrs* **20/1**
5-53 **10** 1 ¼ **Emeralds Spirit (IRE)**[32] 1866 3-8-5 46 oh1 SilvestreDeSousa 8 37
(J R Weymes) *s.s: hdwy on ins over 3f out: nvr nr ldrs* **13/2**[3]
-060 **11** 3 ¾ **Light The City (IRE)**[71] 1054 3-8-0 46 oh1 JamesSullivan(5) 12 30
(Mrs R A Carr) *mid-div: hung lft over 2f out: sn wknd* **33/1**
-056 **12** 3 **French Seventyfive**[11] 2503 3-8-10 51 DuranFentiman 7 29
(T D Walford) *in rr: sn pushed along: nvr on terms* **12/1**
000 **13** 7 **One More Tico**[23] 2143 3-8-7 48 RoystonFfrench 11 12
(M Johnston) *chsd ldrs: drvn 8f out: lost pl 3f out: eased whn bhd ins fnl f* **33/1**
0400 **14** 4 ½ **Specialising**[5] 2675 3-8-11 52 AlanMunro 3 —
(M R Channon) *t.k.h: trckd ldrs: sltly hmpd over 3f out: lost pl over 2f out: eased ins fnl f* **9/2**[2]

2m 10.16s (3.06) **Going Correction** +0.325s/f (Good) 14 Ran SP% **123.6**
Speed ratings (Par 97): **100,99,96,96,95 95,95,95,94,93 90,88,82,79**
toteswingers: 1&2 £10.00, 1&3 £7.90, 2&3 £6.50 CSF £29.41 CT £211.82 TOTE £4.30: £1.60, £3.10, £1.90; EX 34.50 TRIFECTA Not won. Place 6: £72.75 Place 5: £30.61.
Owner J Howard Johnson **Bred** Des Vere Hunt Farm Co And Jack Ronan **Trained** Billy Row, Co Durham

FOCUS
A moderate handicap but one in which the first two, who finished clear, both look a bit better than the bare form, which is sound but limited. The gallop was an ordinary one.
Emeralds Spirit(IRE) Official explanation: jockey said that the filly missed the break
T/Plt: £95.50 to a £1 stake. Pool of £68,323.38 - 522.14 winning tickets T/Qpdt: £28.40 to a £1 stake. Pool:£4,836.60 - 125.90 winning tickets WG

2245 SALISBURY (R-H)

Tuesday, June 8

OFFICIAL GOING: Good
Wind: Moderate across Weather: Overcast, showers

2839 "COME SHOPPING AT CASTLEPOINT" BOURNEMOUTH MAIDEN AUCTION STKS 6f

2:15 (2:17) (Class 5) 2-Y-O **£3,238** (£963; £481; £240) **Stalls** High

Form RPR
03 **1** **Honourable Knight (IRE)**[35] 1793 2-8-9 0 KierenFallon 12 70
(M D I Usher) *pressed ldrs: drvn to chal fr ins fnl 2f: led fnl 50yds: rdn out* **8/1**[3]
3 **2** hd **With Hindsight (IRE)**[22] 2163 2-9-2 0 PhilipRobinson 4 76
(C G Cox) *slt advantage: rdn along to maintain it fr ins fnl 2f tl hdd and no ex fnl 50yds* **7/2**[1]
3 hd **Hard Bargain (IRE)** 2-8-12 0 EddieAhern 16 71
(D J Coakley) *pressed ldrs: upsides fr 2f out and stl ev ch fnl 50yds: no ex cl home* **12/1**
0 **4** 2 ½ **Standout**[8] 2594 2-8-9 0 RyanMoore 13 61
(R Hannon) *chsd ldrs: tl drvn and outpcd 1/2-way: styd on again fr 2f out and ins fnl f but nvr gng pce of ldng trio* **11/2**[2]
5 1 ½ **Slim Shadey** 2-8-9 0 LiamKeniry 2 56+
(J S Moore) *chsd ldrs tl outpcd 2f out: drvn and styd on again ins fnl f: gng on cl home* **16/1**
6 1 ¾ **Cheers** 2-8-8 0 ow1 RichardHughes 8 50+
(R Hannon) *in rr: plenty to do over 2f out: pushed along and hdwy over 1f out: fin wl: gng on cl home* **8/1**[3]
5 **7** ¾ **Titus Two (IRE)**[15] 2384 2-8-12 0 JimmyFortune 18 52
(P W Chapple-Hyam) *chsd ldrs: rdn over 2f out: wknd fnl f* **11/2**[2]
8 ½ **Slumbering Sioux** 2-8-11 0 TedDurcan 14 49
(H J L Dunlop) *in tch: sn outpcd: sme prog fr over 1f out: nvr any threat* **28/1**
9 nk **Valeo Si Vales (IRE)** 2-9-2 0 FergusSweeney 17 54
(J A Osborne) *s.i.s: sn in tch: pushed along and styd on same pce fnl 2f* **40/1**
10 ¾ **Whodathought (IRE)** 2-8-9 0 PatDobbs 5 44+
(R Hannon) *s.i.s: green and wl bhd 1/2-way stl plenty to do 2f out gd prog over 1f out: fin wl* **16/1**
11 shd **Nothing To Hide (IRE)** 2-8-9 0 JamesDoyle 3 44
(D J S Ffrench Davis) *in rr and drvn along 1/2-way: kpt on fr over 1f out: nvr a threat* **100/1**
12 nse **Bathwick Siesta** 2-8-9 0 PatCosgrave 9 44
(J G Portman) *s.i.s: hdwy over 2f out: nvr a threat and one pce fr over 1f out* **80/1**
0 **13** shd **King Bling (IRE)**[25] 2077 2-9-2 0 DaneO'Neill 11 51
(S Kirk) *in rr and hmpd 3f out: sme late prog* **50/1**
04 **14** 3 ½ **I Scream (IRE)**[14] 2413 2-7-13 0 DeclanCannon(5) 15 28
(D R C Elsworth) *chsd ldrs: rdn over 2f out: sn wknd* **20/1**
15 ¾ **Foxtrot Golf (IRE)** 2-9-2 0 JimCrowley 10 38
(P Winkworth) *outpcd most of way* **16/1**
16 4 ½ **Bajan Bear** 2-8-9 0 SteveDrowne 1 17
(M Blanshard) *s.i.s: sn chsng ldrs: wknd over 2f out* **40/1**
17 ½ **Manchester Stanley** 2-8-12 0 ShaneKelly 6 19
(J A Osborne) *outpcd most of way* **40/1**
18 ½ **Bert And Ernie** 2-8-9 0 CoryParish 7 14
(M R Channon) *spd over 3f* **80/1**

1m 15.91s (1.11) **Going Correction** -0.10s/f (Good) 18 Ran SP% **121.5**
Speed ratings (Par 93): **88,87,87,84,82 79,78,78,77,76 76,76,76,71,70 64,64,63**
toteswingers: 1&2 £5.00, 1&3 £28.60, 2&3 £14.30 CSF £32.96 TOTE £10.60: £3.20, £1.20, £5.30; EX 42.10.
Owner Bryan Fry **Bred** Mohammed Al Sulaim **Trained** Upper Lambourn, Berks

FOCUS
The main action took place towards the far side. Plenty of runners for this maiden, but the first three finishers raced in the front three positions for much of the way, with few getting involved. The bare form is probably just fair, and a bit below the usual Salisbury standard.

NOTEBOOK
Honourable Knight(IRE) proved suited by the step up in trip and improved on the form he showed when third at Bath last time. He was being urged along in typical Fallon style by halfway, but kept responding and showed a good attitude, especially as the runner-up gave him less room than ideal near the line. He should make a fair nursery type/handicapper. (op 11-1)
With Hindsight(IRE) got a bit warm beforehand and probably didn't improve a great deal, if at all, on the form he showed when third on debut at Bath. He kept on for pressure, but could never get away from his rivals and edged right when tiring near the line. His yard is not in much form at present. (op 11-4 tchd 9-2)
Hard Bargain(IRE), a £9,000 purchase who is closely related to, among others, 1m winners Dance Pass (stayed 1m4f) and Sense Of Purpose, was well educated. He travelled well on the pace for much of the way but was just worried out of it near the line. While maybe not open to as much improvement as some of these, he should be winning before too long. (op 10-1 tchd 14-1)
Standout, down the field in a decent enough maiden at Goodwood on debut, appeared well fancied this time and duly showed improved form, but he could make no impression on the front three. (op 13-2 tchd 3-1)
Slim Shadey showed some early speed but was outpaced from halfway. That was hardly surprising considering he's a half-brother to, among others, 1m4f winner Nora Chrissie, and this was a pleasing debut. (op 14-1)
Cheers ◆, an 11,000gns purchase who carried 1lb overweight, was the eyecatcher of the race. She broke well enough, but was soon behind and it was most pleasing to see her finish so well in a race where few made up significant amounts of ground. (op 7-1)
Titus Two(IRE) didn't break that sharply and, although soon tracking the pace, the response was limited when he came under serious pressure. He had shown ability on debut, but this was disappointing. (op 6-1 tchd 13-2)
Whodathought(IRE) seemed badly in need of the experience but made some late headway and has ability. (op 33-1)

2840 "COME SHOPPING AT CASTLEPOINT" EMPRISE SERVICES CLAIMING STKS 6f 212y

2:45 (2:48) (Class 5) 3-Y-O+ **£3,238** (£963; £481; £240) **Stalls** High

Form RPR
2416 **1** **Kingswinford (IRE)**[17] 2339 4-9-6 79 AndrewHeffernan(3) 4 79
(P D Evans) *chsd ldrs: drvn to ld jst ins fnl 2f: hrd rdn fnl f: hld on all out* **11/4**[1]
0020 **2** nk **Orchard Supreme**[1] 2823 7-9-12 74 RyanMoore 7 81
(R Hannon) *hld up towards rr: hdwy over 2f out: chsd wnr fnl f: drvn to chal fnl 100yds but a hld* **11/2**[2]

1001 **3** 1 1/2 **Lady Kent (IRE)**[14] 2415 4-9-3 72 ..... PatCosgrave 13 68
(J R Boyle) *trckd ldrs: n.m.r on ins fr 2f out: swtchd lft fr over 1f out: hrd drvn and styd on to chse ldng duo fnl f but no imp* **8/1**

0030 **4** 1/2 **Stanley Goodspeed**[4] 2705 7-9-5 68 .....(t) RichardHills 10 69
(J W Hills) *in rr tl hdwy on ins over 2f out: rdn and hung rt over 1f out: sme prog fnl f: nvr a threat* **10/1**

-160 **5** 1/2 **King's Caprice**[14] 2415 9-9-5 73 ..... RichardThomas 9 70+
(J C Fox) *s.i.s: pushed along 4f out: hdwy over 2f out: styng on whn bdly hmpd over 1f out: one pce after* **16/1**

5042 **6** 3 3/4 **Lockantanks**[18] 2296 3-8-9 70 ..... KierenFallon 12 53
(A B Haynes) *chsd ldrs: led briefly 2f out and sn hdd: wknd appr fnl f* **10/1**

5300- **7** 5 **Stamford Blue**[8] 2590 9-9-4 60 .....(b) LukeMorris 2 43
(R A Harris) *in tch: chsd ldrs and rdn over 2f out: wknd appr fnl f* **28/1**

5-35 **8** 1 **Berbice (IRE)**[15] 2399 5-9-11 77 .....(e) RichardHughes 11 47
(S Kirk) *s.i.s: hld up in rr: swtchd lft over 2f out: sn rdn and no prog* **6/1**[3]

4450 **9** 8 **Hart Of Gold**[2] 2779 6-8-9 52 .....(b) JakePayne(7) 1 16
(R A Harris) *t.k.h: chsd ldrs 4f* **40/1**

04 **10** 6 **Affordable (IRE)**[23] 2143 3-8-11 0 ..... SamHitchcott 3 —
(M R Channon) *s.i.s: rdn and hung lft 3f out: a towards rr* **22/1**

4-06 **11** 1 1/4 **Sweet Possession (USA)**[15] 2383 4-9-2 56 .....(v[1]) JimmyFortune 5 —
(A P Jarvis) *chsd ldrs to 1/2-way* **20/1**

1-66 **12** 13 **Admin (IRE)**[22] 2179 3-8-11 77 .....(v[1]) JimCrowley 8 —
(R M Beckett) *led: t.k.h and sn clr: hdd & wknd rapidly 2f out* **17/2**

1m 27.75s (-1.25) **Going Correction** -0.10s/f (Good)
WFA 3 from 4yo+ 10lb **12** Ran SP% **117.0**
Speed ratings (Par 103): **103,102,100,100,99 95,89,88,79,72 71,56**
toteswingers: 1&2 £6.40, 1&3 £4.20, 2&3 £8.20 CSF £15.84 TOTE £2.50: £1.10, £2.70, £4.00; EX 22.90.
Owner Nick Shutts **Bred** J Costello **Trained** Pandy, Monmouths
■ Stewards' Enquiry : Pat Cosgrave three-day ban: careless riding (June 22, 23, 24)

FOCUS
A fair claimer, although the pace was overly strong with Admin racing freely in a clear lead. The winner did not need to match his recent best.
King's Caprice Official explanation: jockey said gelding was denied a clear run
Berbice(IRE) Official explanation: jockey said gelding had no more to give
Admin(IRE) Official explanation: jockey said that the gelding ran too free

2841 "COME SHOPPING AT CASTLEPOINT" DOUGLAND SUPPORT SERVICES MAIDEN STKS (DIV I) 6f 212y

3:20 (3:21) (Class 5) 3-Y-O **£3,561** (£1,059; £529; £264) **Stalls** High

Form RPR

02- **1** **Poltergeist (IRE)**[298] 4986 3-9-3 0 ..... RichardHughes 11 73+
(R Hannon) *trckd ldrs: shkn up to ld ins fnl f: strly pressed cl home but won cosily* **4/9**[1]

2 1/2 **Warm Memories** 3-9-3 0 ..... RyanMoore 4 71+
(Sir Michael Stoute) *stdd s: in rr tl hdwy fr 3f out: styd on wl fnl f to chse wnr fnl 50yds but a readily hld* **4/1**[2]

0 **3** 3/4 **Poppy Golightly**[37] 1731 3-8-12 0 ..... RichardKingscote 12 64
(R J Hodges) *led: rdn ins fnl 2f: hdd ins fnl f: outpcd fnl 50yds* **66/1**

4 1 1/4 **Laser Ruby** 3-8-12 0 ..... JimmyFortune 7 61
(A M Balding) *chsd ldrs: drvn to chal jst ins fnl f: sn no ex and wknd fnl 75yds* **14/1**

00 **5** 3/4 **Our Drama Queen (IRE)**[22] 2180 3-8-12 0 ..... PatDobbs 2 59
(R Hannon) *stdd s: in rr tl styd on fr over 1f out: fin wl but nvr a threat* **20/1**

50- **6** 2 1/2 **Accountable**[279] 5571 3-9-3 0 ..... FergusSweeney 9 57
(B G Powell) *in rr: pushed along 1/2-way: nvr gng pce to get into contention* **100/1**

00- **7** 1 **Krysanthe**[209] 7326 3-8-12 0 ..... SteveDrowne 10 50
(M Blanshard) *t.k.h: chsd ldrs: pushed along over 2f out: n.d after* **100/1**

65 **8** 3/4 **Music Lover**[21] 2197 3-9-3 0 ..... LukeMorris 5 53
(R A Harris) *chsd ldrs: j. path whn in 2nd 3f out: styd pressing ldrs tl 1f out: wknd sn after* **20/1**

00- **9** 3/4 **Compton Way**[213] 7289 3-9-3 0 ..... WilliamBuick 6 51
(B W Hills) *chsd ldrs: rdn 2f out: sn wknd* **33/1**

0- **10** 3 1/2 **Wet Feet**[300] 4900 3-9-3 0 ..... JimCrowley 1 41
(P R Chamings) *stdd s: chsd ldrs 1/2-way tl wknd wl over 1f out* **12/1**[3]

11 11 **Monte Mayor Two (IRE)** 3-9-3 0 ..... DaneO'Neill 8 11
(D Haydn Jones) *s.i.s: rdn and green over 3f out: a bhd* **66/1**

1m 29.71s (0.71) **Going Correction** -0.10s/f (Good) **11** Ran SP% **121.0**
Speed ratings (Par 99): **91,90,89,88,87 84,83,82,81,77 65**
toteswingers: 1&2 £7.00, 1&3 £6.10, 2&3 £4.60 CSF £2.36 TOTE £1.50: £1.10, £1.10, £12.50; EX 2.80.
Owner Highclere Thoroughbred Racing (Diomed) **Bred** Breeding Capital Plc **Trained** East Everleigh, Wilts

FOCUS
The 'right' two horses finished first and second, but the pace had been steady and the proximity of some modest-looking rivals limits the bare form. The time was 0.90 seconds slower than the second division won by 83-rated Chica Whopa. is doubtful if the winner had to get close to his 2yo form.

2842 "COME SHOPPING AT CASTLEPOINT" DOUGLAND SUPPORT SERVICES MAIDEN STKS (DIV II) 6f 212y

3:55 (3:59) (Class 5) 3-Y-O **£3,561** (£1,059; £529; £264) **Stalls** High

Form RPR

1 **Chica Whopa (IRE)**[225] 7071 3-8-12 83 ..... RichardHughes 3 78+
(R Hannon) *t.k.h: chsd ldrs: led ins fnl 2f: hrd drvn and r.o wl fnl f* **6/1**[3]

4 **2** nk **Give Your Verdict (USA)**[33] 1844 3-9-3 0 ..... RyanMoore 6 82+
(Sir Michael Stoute) *trckd ldrs: drvn to chse wnr fnl f: kpt on u.p but a hld* **4/5**[1]

0- **3** 3 1/4 **Night Sky**[239] 6730 3-8-12 0 ..... FergusSweeney 9 68
(P J Makin) *in rr: puhed along and hdwy fr 2f out: styd on for narrow 3rd wl ins fnl f but no ch w ldng duo* **40/1**

62- **4** nse **Hooligan Sean**[274] 5722 3-8-10 0 ..... AmyScott(7) 2 73
(H Candy) *sn led: narrowly hdd ins fnl 2f: hung bdly lft wl over 1f out: styd disputing one pce 2nd thrght fnl f* **11/1**

5-0 **5** 3 **Ajool (USA)**[39] 1654 3-8-12 0 ..... RichardHills 4 60
(B W Hills) *t.k.h: trckd ldrs: styng on same pce whn sltly hmpd and swtchd rt wl over 1f out: sn no ex* **16/1**

3-0 **6** nk **Tenessee**[52] 1381 3-9-3 0 ..... PhilipRobinson 1 67
(C G Cox) *sn pressing ldr and stl upsides over 1f out: wkng whn bdly hmpd wl over 1f out* **4/1**[2]

4 **7** nse **Whisper Wind**[38] 1694 3-9-3 0 ..... LiamKeniry 7 64
(G L Moore) *chsd ldrs: rdn 2f out: wknd wl over 1f out* **33/1**

8 2 1/2 **Chasse Coeur** 3-8-12 0 ..... DavidProbert 11 52
(A M Balding) *wnt lft s and bmpd: towards rr most of way* **25/1**

9 6 **Miss Tenacious** 3-8-12 0 ..... RichardKingscote 8 36
(R J Hodges) *stdd s: a towards rr* **100/1**

0 **10** 5 **Correlandie (USA)**[22] 2174 3-8-12 0 ..... SteveDrowne 10 23
(J R Gask) *bmpd s: sn in tch: rdn over 3f out: sn bhd* **80/1**

1m 28.81s (-0.19) **Going Correction** -0.10s/f (Good) **10** Ran SP% **115.5**
Speed ratings (Par 99): **97,96,92,92,89 89,89,86,79,73**
toteswingers: 1&2 £2.50, 1&3 £39.60, 2&3 £16.30 CSF £10.83 TOTE £5.40: £1.60, £1.10, £12.30; EX 11.80.
Owner William Durkan **Bred** Ballyhane Stud **Trained** East Everleigh, Wilts

FOCUS
The time was 0.90 seconds quicker than the steadily run first division and this looked to have more strength in depth. The form is rated around the front two.

2843 E B F MARGADALE FILLIES' H'CAP 1m 1f 198y

4:30 (4:33) (Class 4) (0-85,80) 3-Y-O+ **£6,476** (£1,927; £963; £481) **Stalls** High

Form RPR

01-1 **1** **Sea Of Heartbreak (IRE)**[19] 2250 3-9-12 78 ..... SteveDrowne 1 91+
(R Charlton) *trckd ldrs: drvn and qcknd to ld ins fnl 2f: styd on strly fnl f* **5/2**[1]

2-22 **2** 2 1/4 **Scorn (USA)**[12] 2463 3-9-12 78 ..... WilliamBuick 9 84
(J H M Gosden) *s.i.s: in rr: hdwy 3f out: swtchd lft to outside and hdwy fr 2f out: chsd wnr ins fnl f and kpt on but a readily hld* **9/1**

5212 **3** 1 **Babycakes (IRE)**[21] 2219 3-9-13 79 ..... HayleyTurner 4 83
(M L W Bell) *trckd ldrs: led travelling smoothly over 2f out: hdd ins fnl 2f: sn rdn and one pce: lost 2nd ins fnl f* **4/1**[2]

-10 **4** 1/2 **Marie De Guise (IRE)**[19] 2256 3-9-13 79 ..... RyanMoore 6 82+
(Sir Michael Stoute) *in rr: in tch: drvn along over 3f out: styd on fr over 1f out: kpt on cl home: nvr a threat* **9/2**[3]

4-12 **5** shd **On Khee**[34] 1830 3-9-1 67 ..... TravisBlock 8 69+
(H Morrison) *in tch: hdwy and drvn 3f out: chsng ldrs on ins fr 2f out: nvr seeing much daylight tl over 1f out: kpt on same pce* **17/2**

0-1 **6** 3 **Lucky Breeze (IRE)**[28] 2011 3-10-0 80 ..... ShaneKelly 5 76
(W J Knight) *in rr: t.k.h: pushed along over 2f out and nvr in contention* **14/1**

5-13 **7** 1/2 **Circus Girl (IRE)**[19] 2256 3-10-0 80 ..... JimCrowley 2 75
(R M Beckett) *led tl hdd over 2f out: wknd wl over 1f out* **9/1**

0-1 **8** 15 **On Her Way**[42] 1607 3-9-9 75 ..... PatCosgrave 3 40
(H R A Cecil) *reluctant to post: chsd ldr and t.k.h: stl t.k.h over 3f out: shkn up over 2f out: n.m.r sn after and qckly dropped away* **9/1**

-006 **9** 45 **Moonline Dancer (FR)**[11] 2510 3-9-3 69 .....(b[1]) RichardHughes 7 —
(R Hannon) *towards rr most of way* **22/1**

2m 8.95s (-0.95) **Going Correction** -0.10s/f (Good) **9** Ran SP% **118.3**
Speed ratings (Par 102): **99,97,96,96,95 93,93,81,45**
toteswingers: 1&2 £6.20, 2&3 £3.20, 1&3 not won. CSF £26.92 CT £89.43 TOTE £2.40: £1.10, £1.90, £2.50.
Owner D G Hardisty Bloodstock **Bred** D G Hardisty Bloodstock **Trained** Beckhampton, Wilts

FOCUS
This was a fair fillies' handicap featuring some unexposed types. The pace was sound enough and the form looks pretty solid, with anpother step up from the winner.
Moonline Dancer(FR) Official explanation: jockey said that the filly had a breathing problem

2844 "COME SHOPPING AT CASTLEPOINT" INDUSTRIAL CLEANING EQUIPMENT H'CAP 6f 212y

5:00 (5:03) (Class 6) (0-65,65) 3-Y-O **£2,914** (£867; £433; £216) **Stalls** High

Form RPR

0321 **1** **Kingsdine (IRE)**[16] 2359 3-9-4 62 ..... TomMcLaughlin 15 71
(M S Saunders) *hld up in tch: hdwy 3f out: led 2f out: hrd drvn fr over 1f out: styd on wl and in command nr fin* **10/1**

4043 **2** 1 1/2 **Leitzu (IRE)**[14] 2408 3-9-4 62 ..... KierenFallon 1 67
(M R Channon) *sn in tch: chsd ldrs and rdn 3f out: styd on to chse wnr fnl f but a hld* **10/1**

-405 **3** 1/2 **Lady Willa (IRE)**[29] 1982 3-9-2 60 ..... NeilChalmers 9 64
(Mark Gillard) *in rr: pushed along and hdwy fr 2f out: styd on wl to take 3rd ins fnl f: gng on cl home* **40/1**

-530 **4** 3/4 **Mellifera**[26] 2042 3-9-7 65 ..... AdamKirby 18 67
(W R Swinburn) *mid-div: pushed along 3f out: hdwy over 1f out: styd on strly ins fnl f: gng on cl home* **7/1**[1]

56-0 **5** 1/2 **One Hit Wonder**[36] 1769 3-9-2 60 ..... TravisBlock 14 60
(Mouse Hamilton-Fairley) *chsd ldrs: ev ch fr 3f out tl ins fnl 2f: outpcd ins fnl f* **33/1**

3-04 **6** 1/2 **Imperial Warrior**[32] 1873 3-9-2 60 ..... SteveDrowne 4 59
(H Morrison) *chsd ldr: chal over 3f out tl 2f out: wkng whn eged lft ins fnl f* **9/1**[3]

3456 **7** 1 **Hill Of Miller (IRE)**[9] 2566 3-9-3 61 .....(t) DavidProbert 5 57
(Rae Guest) *in tch: drvn to chse ldrs on outside 2f out: hld whn pushed lft and unbalanced ins fnl f: wknd* **16/1**

006 **8** nk **Michael's Nook**[24] 2122 3-9-1 59 ..... IanMongan 17 54
(W S Kittow) *in rr: hdwy over 2f out: styd on ins fnl f: nvr a threat* **12/1**

2340 **9** 3/4 **Chateau Zara**[15] 2398 3-8-11 60 ..... JohnFahy(5) 2 53
(C G Cox) *chsd ldrs: rdn and styd on same pce fnl 2f* **12/1**

2430 **10** 1/2 **Larkrise Star**[29] 1982 3-9-6 64 ..... FergusSweeney 6 56
(D K Ivory) *slt ld tl hdd 2f out: wknd fnl f* **33/1**

240- **11** 1 1/4 **Lady Slippers (IRE)**[225] 7058 3-9-6 64 ..... TedDurcan 8 53
(H J L Dunlop) *s.i.s: styd on fnl 2f: nvr in contention* **12/1**

505 **12** 1 3/4 **Madlool (IRE)**[62] 1164 3-9-7 65 ..... RichardHills 16 54
(W J Haggas) *in rr: styd on fr 2f out: nvr rchd ldrs* **9/1**[3]

03-0 **13** 8 **Panpiper**[24] 2122 3-9-7 65 ..... RyanMoore 7 27
(G L Moore) *rdn along over 2f out: towards rr most of way* **20/1**

5-15 **14** nk **Sonny G (IRE)**[32] 1873 3-8-12 61 ..... KierenFox(5) 11 23
(J R Best) *chsd ldrs: rdn 3f out: wknd fr 2f out* **9/1**[3]

03-0 **15** 6 **Blue Sparkle (IRE)**[17] 2342 3-9-7 65 .....(b[1]) JimCrowley 10 10
(Mrs A J Perrett) *in rr: sme hdwy on outside 3f out: nvr rchd ldrs and hung lft 2f out* **20/1**

-004 **16** 3/4 **First Term**[28] 2000 3-9-3 61 ..... RichardHughes 13 4
(R Hannon) *mid-div: sme hdwy 3f out: wknd sn after* **8/1**[2]

-052 **17** 8 **Set To Go**[14] 2409 3-9-2 60 .....(b) EddieAhern 3 —
(H J L Dunlop) *chsd ldrs: rdn over 2f out and wknd qckly* **14/1**

1m 28.46s (-0.54) **Going Correction** -0.10s/f (Good) **17** Ran SP% **125.3**
Speed ratings (Par 97): **99,97,96,95,95 94,93,93,92,91 90,88,79,78,72 71,62**
toteswingers: 1&2 £12.70, 1&3 £70.90, 2&3 £94.90 CSF £101.82 CT £3970.75 TOTE £15.90: £3.50, £2.30, £8.70, £2.30; EX 94.00.
Owner M S Saunders **Bred** Deer Forest Stud Ltd **Trained** Green Ore, Somerset

FOCUS
A modest handicap run at a fair pace. A clear personal best from the winner.
Madlool(IRE) Official explanation: jockey said that the colt was never travelling

First Term Official explanation: jockey said that the filly lost its action.

2845 "COME SHOPPING AT CASTLEPOINT" BOURNEMOUTH H'CAP 1m 4f

5:30 (5:31) (Class 5) (0-75,75) 4-Y-O+ **£3,238** (£963; £481; £240) **Stalls** High

Form RPR

3-35 **1** **Strathcal**[24] 2126 4-9-7 **75**................................. SteveDrowne 5 84
(H Morrison) *in rr tl gd hdwy on outside over 2f out: led and hung rt over 1f out: re-chal ins fnl f: all out* **13/8**[1]

6/0- **2** *nk* **All The Winds (GER)**[202] 5-9-6 **74**........................ LiamKeniry 3 83
(S Lycett) *trckd ldrs: led travelling wl appr fnl 2f: hdd over 1f out: rallied to press wnr ins fnl f: no xtra cl home* **16/1**

0-45 **3** *4* **Zaif (IRE)**[12] 2455 7-8-3 **57**............................... RichardThomas 6 59
(D J S Ffrench Davis) *in rr: hdwy fr 2f out: styd on to take 3rd last strides: no ch w ldng duo* **20/1**

-051 **4** *shd* **Haljaferia (UAE)**[9] 2560 4-9-3 **71** 6ex...................... KierenFallon 4 73
(D R C Elsworth) *chsd ldrs: rdn over 2f out: disp 3rd ins fnl f: nvr any ch w ldng duo and styd on same pce: lost 3rd last strides* **7/2**[2]

640- **5** *shd* **Gloucester**[31] 6244 7-9-7 **75**............................... PatCosgrave 8 77
(M J Scudamore) *in tch: rdn along 3f out: outpcd 2f out: styd on fnl f: nvr a threat* **8/1**

2-12 **6** *3* **The Hague**[14] 2411 4-9-0 **71**.......................... AndrewHeffernan(3) 2 68
(P D Evans) *in tch: chsd ldrs fr 4f out: effrt u.p 3f out: chsd ldrs 2f out: hung rt and wknd over 1f out* **6/1**[3]

34-6 **7** *6* **Coiled Spring**[33] 1847 4-9-4 **72**............................ JimCrowley 1 59
(Mrs A J Perrett) *led 1f: styd chsng ldr: chal over 3f out tl over 2f out: wknd sn after* **7/1**

030 **8** *5* **Indian Ghyll (IRE)**[19] 2255 4-9-5 **73**..................... RichardHughes 7 52
(R A Teal) *led after 1f: rdn to hold narrow advantage over 3f out: hdd & wknd over 2f out* **20/1**

2m 35.74s (-2.26) **Going Correction** -0.10s/f (Good) **8 Ran SP% 113.6**
Speed ratings (Par 103): **103,102,100,100,100 98,94,90**
toteswingers: 1&2 £4.70, 1&3 £9.70, 2&3 £13.80 CSF £30.26 CT £375.12 TOTE £2.20: £1.02, £2.20, £4.60; EX 46.50.
Owner The Caledonian Racing Society **Bred** Mrs R F Johnson Houghton **Trained** East Ilsley, Berks

FOCUS
An ordinary handicap for the grade and the pace seemed modest. The form is rated around the fourth.

2846 AXMINSTER CARPETS APPRENTICE H'CAP (RACING EXCELLENCE INITIATIVE) (WHIPS CARRIED BUT NOT USED) 6f

6:00 (6:00) (Class 5) (0-75,75) 4-Y-O+ **£3,238** (£963; £481; £240) **Stalls** High

Form RPR

00-0 **1** **Hazytoo**[95] 802 6-9-2 **67**.................................... DebraEngland 7 76
(P J Makin) *trckd ldrs: wnt 2nd appr fnl f: chal sn after and qcknd to ld cl home* **16/1**

-020 **2** *nk* **My Learned Friend (IRE)**[31] 1914 6-9-3 **75**.......... ThomasBrown(7) 10 83
(A M Balding) *sn led: kpt narrow advantage and pushed along wl over 1f out: hdd cl home* **3/1**[1]

5-30 **3** *1 ¼* **Bold Tie**[7] 2622 4-9-10 **75**.................................. CharlesEddery 3 79+
(R Hannon) *in rr: hdwy and swtchd lft to outside wl over 1f out: r.o to take 3rd wl ins fnl f: no imp on ldng duo* **8/1**

05-0 **4** *1 ¼* **Speak The Truth (IRE)**[17] 2331 4-8-13 **67**..............(p) NathanAlison(3) 5 67
(J R Boyle) *slowly away: in rr but in tch 1/2-way: hdwy and hung rt fr 2f out: styd on fnl f but nvr a threat* **16/1**

00-4 **5** *1* **Super Frank (IRE)**[26] 2053 7-8-9 **60**........................(p) RyanClark 4 57
(J Akehurst) *chsd ldrs: pushed along over 2f out: pressed ldrs over 1f out: wknd ins fnl f* **9/2**[3]

0022 **6** *½* **Peopleton Brook**[4] 2719 8-8-7 **58**..........................(t) RyanPowell 2 53
(B G Powell) *in rr: hdwy on outside over 1f out: nvr gng pce to get into contention* **7/1**

0660 **7** *1 ¼* **Simple Rhythm**[7] 2635 4-8-9 **67**............................ JoshCrane(7) 8 58
(J Ryan) *chsd ldr: chal over 3f out tl ins fnl 2f: wknd fnl f* **11/2**

1365 **8** *1 ¾* **Misaro (GER)**[16] 2364 9-9-3 **73**..........................(b) JakePayne(5) 6 59
(R A Harris) *chsd ldrs over 4f* **12/1**

2251 **9** *6* **War And Peace (IRE)**[26] 2053 6-8-12 **68**........... MatthewCosham(5) 1 34
(P D Evans) *outpcd* **4/1**[2]

1m 14.63s (-0.17) **Going Correction** -0.10s/f (Good) **9 Ran SP% 121.6**
Speed ratings (Par 103): **97,96,94,93,91 91,89,87,79**
toteswingers:1&2 £13.80, 2&3 £6.40, 1&3 £12.70 CSF £67.26 CT £435.55 TOTE £15.30: £3.00, £1.70, £1.70; EX 104.50 Place 6: £19.08 Place 5: £7.59.
Owner Wedgewood Estates **Bred** Mrs Liza Judd **Trained** Ogbourne Maisey, Wilts

FOCUS
A modest handicap in which these apprentices were not allowed to use their whips, and few were ever involved. Straightforward, sound form.
T/Jkpt: Not won. T/Plt: £10.10 to a £1 stake. Pool of £82,221.06 - 5,885.22 winning tickets T/Qpdt: £3.90 to a £1 stake. Pool of £5,034.24 - 936.08 winning tickets ST

2522 BEVERLEY (R-H)

Wednesday, June 9

OFFICIAL GOING: Good (good to soft in places; 8.4)
Wind: Light, across Weather: Overcast and damp

2848 CELEBRATE YOUR BIRTHDAY HERE CLAIMING STKS 5f

2:00 (2:01) (Class 6) 2-Y-O **£2,428** (£722; £361; £180) **Stalls** High

Form RPR

644 **1** **Nellie Ellis (IRE)**[23] 2183 2-8-6 0............................ SilvestreDeSousa 10 65
(K A Ryan) *led 2f: cl up tl rdn to ld and edgd lft over 1f out: kpt on strly fnl f* **15/8**[1]

632 **2** *1* **Madam Markievicz (IRE)**[16] 2391 2-8-10 0..................(p) PhillipMakin 2 65
(M Dods) *chsd ldrs: effrt 2f out: sn rdn: styd on ins fnl f* **2/1**[2]

5 **3** *1 ¾* **Alhoni**[16] 2391 2-8-6 0.. GrahamGibbons 5 55+
(J J Quinn) *in tch: rdn along 1/2-way: hdwy over 1f out: kpt on ins fnl f: nrst fin* **14/1**

266 **4** *hd* **Muse To Use**[8] 2631 2-8-0 0.................................. DuranFentiman 8 48
(I W McInnes) *trckd ldrs: rdn along to chse ldng pair ent fnl f: sn drvn and one pce* **33/1**

123 **5** *2 ¼* **Tanked Up (IRE)**[16] 2391 2-8-7 0.............................. AdrianNicholls 6 47
(D Nicholls) *cl up: led after 2f: rdn along 2f out: hdd over 1f out: wknd qckly ins fnl f* **10/3**[3]

506 **6** *3* **Mandy's Princess (IRE)**[19] 2272 2-8-6 0........................ PJMcDonald 9 35
(R A Fahey) *dwlt: sn in tch on inner: rdn along 2f out and sn btn* **11/1**

40 **7** *1 ½* **Mrs Nisbett (IRE)**[30] 1978 2-8-0 0.............................. PaulQuinn 4 24
(A J McCabe) *in tch: rdn along over 2f out: wknd wl over 1f out* **33/1**

0 **8** *20* **Golda Go**[36] 1800 2-7-11 0................................. PaulPickard(5) 3 —
(P T Midgley) *dwlt: a in rr: outpcd and wl bhd fr 1/2-way* **100/1**

63.54 secs (0.04) **Going Correction** -0.025s/f (Good) **8 Ran SP% 113.1**
Speed ratings (Par 91): **98,96,93,93,89 84,82,50**
toteswingers: 1&2 £1.80, 1&3 £6.70, 2&3 £7.60 CSF £5.73 TOTE £2.80: £1.10, £1.10, £4.90; EX 7.10.
Owner Mrs Margaret Forsyth **Bred** Mrs E Thompson **Trained** Hambleton, N Yorks

FOCUS
It was dry overnight, but there had been 5mm of rain the previous day and the ground was officially described as good, good to soft in places, with an overall GoingStick reading of 8.4. A typical claimer, but improved efforts from the front two on the face of things.

NOTEBOOK
Nellie Ellis(IRE) benefited from the drop into claiming company and gained her first success at the fourth attempt, despite wandering around under pressure and idling, rather than really knuckling down. She'll need to learn to focus better if she's to progress outside of this sort of company. (op 9-4)
Madam Markievicz(IRE), who had three of these rivals behind when runner-up in a Thirsk seller over 6f last time, confirmed the form but simply found the winner too good. (op 11-4)
Alhoni proved unsuited by the drop in trip and couldn't reverse debut form with Madam Markievicz. She finished reasonably well, though, and ought to find a little race back over further. (op 18-1)
Muse To Use finished second in a seller on debut when with Michael Dods but she's struggled since. (op 40-1)
Tanked Up(IRE) should have been suited by this drop in trip, but he faded after showing speed and perhaps the ground was easier than ideal, especially on a stiff track. (op 15-8 tchd 7-4 in a place)

2849 LUCKY IN LOVE NIGHT NEXT THURSDAY H'CAP 5f

2:30 (2:31) (Class 6) (0-65,65) 3-Y-O+ **£2,590** (£770; £385; £192) **Stalls** High

Form RPR

-001 **1** **Ryedane (IRE)**[16] 2378 8-9-7 **58**..............................(b) DavidAllan 13 73
(T D Easterby) *in tch towards inner: hdwy 2f out: rdn to chal over 1f out: hung lft ent fnl f: sn led and kpt on strly* **4/1**[1]

/00- **2** *3 ¼* **Azygous**[297] 5073 7-8-8 **52**............................... DavidSimmonson(7) 17 55
(G P Kelly) *led: rdn clr over 1f out: edgd lft and hdd ins fnl f: kpt on same pce* **25/1**

0516 **3** *hd* **Tamarind Hill (IRE)**[7] 2648 3-8-12 **61**..................(b) DeclanCannon(5) 15 61
(A J McCabe) *chsd ldng pair: rdn along wl over 1f out: drvn ins fnl f and kpt on same pce* **12/1**

65-5 **4** *hd* **Timber Treasure (USA)**[30] 1968 6-9-11 **62**..........(b) SilvestreDeSousa 5 64+
(Paul Green) *hmpd s and towards rr: hdwy 2f out: rdn over 1f out: styd on strly ins fnl f: nrst fin* **16/1**

02-5 **5** *½* **Embra (IRE)**[9] 2582 5-9-7 **58**................................... GregFairley 2 58
(T J Etherington) *chsd ldrs on outer: rdn along 2f out: drvn over 1f out: one pce ins fnl f* **12/1**

-6R6 **6** *½* **Greek Secret**[43] 1598 7-8-13 **55**.........................(b) JamesO'Reilly(5) 10 53
(J O'Reilly) *in tch: rdn along 1/2-way: hdwy wl over 1f out: chsd ldrs ent fnl f: kpt on same pce* **22/1**

6000 **7** *¾* **Tournedos (IRE)**[43] 1598 8-9-1 **57**.........................(b) JamesSullivan(5) 6 53+
(Mrs R A Carr) *rrd and almost uns rdr s: hdwy towards outer and in tch 1/2-way: rdn to chse ldrs wl over 1f out: sn drvn and one pce* **14/1**

100- **8** *shd* **Danum Dancer**[162] 7870 6-9-11 **62**...............................(b) PaulQuinn 3 57
(N Bycroft) *hmpd s and bhd: hdwy on outer 1/2-way: rdn to chse ldrs over 1f out: drvn and no imp fnl f* **28/1**

2033 **9** *½* **Dispol Kylie (IRE)**[8] 2626 4-10-0 **65**........................ PatCosgrave 1 59
(P T Midgley) *towards rr: hdwy 2f out: sn rdn: kpt on ins fnl f: n.d* **10/1**

-060 **10** *nk* **Divine Spirit**[11] 2528 9-9-6 **57**..............................(b) PhillipMakin 14 49
(M Dods) *midfield on inner: effrt 2f out: sn rdn and no imp appr fnl f* **8/1**[3]

560- **11** *1 ½* **Yungaburra (IRE)**[318] 4355 6-9-11 **62**......................... LeeVickers 8 49
(T J Pitt) *towards rr: hdwy wl over 1f out: sn rdn and no imp* **33/1**

45-0 **12** *½* **Joyeaux**[29] 1988 8-8-7 **58**..................................... DuranFentiman 9 43
(Ollie Pears) *sltly hmpd s: a towards rr* **11/1**

2345 **13** *1* **Fashion Icon (USA)**[44] 1569 4-8-13 **50**....................... PJMcDonald 7 32
(J Hetherton) *midfield: effrt 2f out: sn rdn and no hdwy* **8/1**[3]

644 **14** *5* **Braille**[12] 2504 5-9-6 **57**..................................(b[1]) GrahamGibbons 11 21
(T D Walford) *chsd ldr: rdn along 2f out: wkng whn bmpd and wnt lft over 1f out* **7/1**[2]

00-0 **15** *1 ¾* **Caledonia Princess**[55] 1337 4-10-0 **65**...................(b) TonyCulhane 12 22
(F J Brennan) *hld up in midfield effrt and n.m.r 2f out: rdn and hld whn hmpd over 1f out: bled fr nose* **28/1**

30-1 **16** *1* **Green Poppy**[8] 2629 4-9-7 **58** 6ex.................................. TomEaves 4 12
(B Smart) *hmpd s: sn chsd ldrs: rdn along wl over 1f out: sn wknd* **8/1**[3]

63.03 secs (-0.47) **Going Correction** -0.025s/f (Good)
WFA 3 from 4yo+ 7lb **16 Ran SP% 129.2**
Speed ratings (Par 101): **102,96,96,96,95 94,93,93,92,91 89,88,87,79,76 74**
toteswingers: 1&2 £71.00, 1&3 £14.80, 2&3 £73.10 CSF £122.19 CT £822.00 TOTE £4.80: £1.80, £7.70, £2.90, £4.10.
Owner Ryedale Partners No 5 **Bred** Tally-Ho Stud **Trained** Great Habton, N Yorks

FOCUS
The GoingStick suggested that the middle of the track represented the slowest ground (7.5 compared to 8.8 far side, and 8.9 stands' side), but disconcertingly that seemed to be totally misleading as far as this race was concerned, with the main action taking place centre field late on. This was just a modest sprint handicap, but it was competitive enough and unsurprisingly they went a decent pace and there are one or two doubts about the form.
Tournedos(IRE) Official explanation: jockey said gelding reared at start
Caledonia Princess Official explanation: jockey said filly bled from the nose
Green Poppy Official explanation: trainer had no explanation for the poor form shown

2850 WATCH FOOTBALL HERE 2/3 JULY H'CAP 7f 100y

3:00 (3:00) (Class 5) (0-70,70) 4-Y-O+ **£4,209** (£1,252; £625; £312) **Stalls** High

Form RPR

0-45 **1** **Polish World (USA)**[11] 2527 6-7-11 **51** oh1................ PaulPickard(5) 3 66
(P T Midgley) *mde all: rdn clr over 2f out: kpt on strly fnl f* **10/1**

1-40 **2** *2 ½* **Amethyst Dawn (IRE)**[37] 1751 4-9-4 **67**........................ DavidAllan 1 76+
(T D Easterby) *in tch: hdwy on outer over 2f out: rdn wl over 1f out: drvn to chse wnr ins fnl f: no imp towards fin* **7/2**[1]

0063 **3** *1* **Northern Flyer (GER)**[11] 2527 4-8-3 **57**..................(p) IanBrennan(5) 7 63
(J J Quinn) *trckd ldng pair on inner: effrt over 2f out: rdn to chse wnr over 1f out: drvn and one pce ins fnl f* **9/2**[2]

0002 **4** *3 ½* **Fiefdom (IRE)**[13] 2454 8-8-6 **55**........................(v) GrahamGibbons 14 50
(I W McInnes) *towards rr: hdwy on inner 2f out: sn rdn and no imp appr fnl f: fin 5th, plcd 4th* **10/1**

5030 **5** *¾* **Blue Charm**[7] 2643 6-9-1 **64**..................................... PJMcDonald 15 57
(I W McInnes) *dwlt: towards rr: effrt over 2f out and sn rdn along: kpt on appr fnl f: fin 6th, plcd 5th* **16/1**

3502 **6** *¾* **Ansells Pride (IRE)**[11] 2524 7-9-6 **69**............................ TomEaves 5 60
(B Smart) *chsd wnr: rdn along 2f out: drvn over 1f out: sn wknd: fin 7th, plcd 6th* **11/2**

-663 **7** 1 3/4 **Fortunate Bid (IRE)**[16] 2382 4-8-8 **60**........................ BarryMcHugh(3) 12 47
(Mrs L Stubbs) *in tch: hdwy over 2f out: rdn wl over 1f out: grad wknd: fin 8th, plcd 7th* **5/1**[3]

0-06 **8** 2 1/4 **Burns Night**[40] 1669 4-9-2 **70**........................ MichaelO'Connell(5) 8 51
(G A Harker) *dwlt: a in rr: fin 9th, plcd 8th* **16/1**

320- **9** 1 3/4 **This Ones For Eddy**[221] 7192 5-8-13 **62**........................ PhillipMakin 10 38
(J Balding) *in tch on inner: rdn along over 2f out: sn wknd: fin 10th, plcd 9th* **16/1**

2606 **10** 1/2 **Seldom (IRE)**[4] 2764 4-8-6 **62**........................ JohnCavanagh(7) 11 37
(M Brittain) *midfield: rdn along 1/2-way: sn wknd: fin 11th, plcd 12th* **33/1**

4-20 **11** 7 **Cross Of Lorraine (IRE)**[20] 2263 7-8-3 **52**..........(b) FranciscoDaSilva 6 —
(J Wade) *dwlt: sn chsng ldrs: rdn along wl over 2f out: sn wknd: fin 12th plcd 11th* **50/1**

5054 **D** 3/4 **Classic Descent**[5] 2700 5-8-4 **58**..........................(t) JamesSullivan(5) 13 62
(Mrs R A Carr) *towards rr: hdwy on outer wl over 2f out: rdn over 1f out: styd on strly ins fnl f: nrst fin: fin 4th: disqualified and plcd last: rdr failed to weigh in* **6/1**

1m 32.95s (-0.85) **Going Correction** -0.025s/f (Good) 12 Ran SP% **127.5**
Speed ratings (Par 103): **103,100,99,94,93 92,90,87,85,85 77,98**
toteswingers: 1&2 £18.10, 1&3 £24.00, 2&3 £11.40 CSF £48.39 CT £190.58 TOTE £14.10: £4.70, £1.20, £2.50; EX 130.20.
Owner C R Green **Bred** Racehorse Management, Llc **Trained** Westow, N Yorks
■ Stewards' Enquiry : James Sullivan three-day ban: failed to weigh in (Jun 23-25)

FOCUS
A modest handicap that was soundly run and the form makes sense rated around the third and fourth to their recent best.

2851 NEW FIXTURE NEXT THURSDAY EVENING H'CAP 1m 1f 207y
3:30 (3:30) (Class 5) (0-70,67) 4-Y-0+ **£4,209** (£1,252; £625; £312) **Stalls** High

Form RPR

0-06 **1** **Highland Love**[15] 2421 5-8-8 **52**........................ TonyCulhane 4 62
(Jedd O'Keeffe) *trckd ldr: hdwy to ld 3f out: rdn clr wl over 1f out: kpt on wl u.p fnl f* **7/1**[3]

2411 **2** 1 1/2 **George Adamson (IRE)**[4] 2766 4-9-9 **67** 6ex............... PJMcDonald 10 74+
(G A Swinbank) *dwlt: sn in tch on inner: hdwy wl over 2f out: rdn to chse wnr over 1f out: drvn and kpt on ins fnl f: nt rch wnr* **15/8**[1]

-623 **3** 1 1/2 **Mohawk Ridge**[9] 2583 4-9-6 **64**........................ PhillipMakin 6 68+
(M Dods) *trckd ldrs: hdwy over 2f out: rdn wl over 1f out: kpt on u.p fnl f* **3/1**[2]

6502 **4** 1/2 **Rub Of The Relic (IRE)**[12] 2492 5-8-13 **62**.............(be) PaulPickard(5) 5 65
(P T Midgley) *led: rdn along and hdd 3f out: drvn wl over 1f out: kpt on same pce* **18/1**

4004 **5** 1 1/4 **Coole Dodger (IRE)**[7] 2655 5-8-9 **53**..........................(p) TomEaves 11 54
(B Ellison) *s.i.s: t.k.h towards rr: gd hdwy on inner over 2f out: rdn to chse ldrs wl over 1f out: sn drvn and no imp fnl f* **9/1**

00-0 **6** 1 1/4 **Royal Composer (IRE)**[15] 2421 7-8-6 **50**........................ DavidAllan 1 48
(T D Easterby) *prom: effrt 3f out: rdn along over 2f out: drvn and kpt on same pce fr over 1f out* **25/1**

06/0 **7** 3/4 **Paradise Walk**[15] 2421 6-8-10 **59**........................ JamesSullivan(5) 9 56
(E W Tuer) *trckd ldrs: hdwy 3f out: chsd wnr 2f out: sn rdn and hung lft: wknd wl over 1f out* **25/1**

00-4 **8** 2 1/4 **Petsas Pleasure**[26] 2093 4-9-1 **62**........................ BarryMcHugh(3) 3 54
(Ollie Pears) *s.i.s and bhd: hdwy wl over 2f out: rdn to chse ldrs wl over 1f out: sn wknd* **9/1**

-564 **9** 3 1/4 **Holiday Cocktail**[51] 1427 8-9-3 **61**..........................(p) GrahamGibbons 2 47
(J J Quinn) *midfield: rdn along 3f out: sn wknd* **8/1**

400- **10** 7 **Efidium**[226] 7062 12-8-13 **57**........................ PaulQuinn 8 29
(N Bycroft) *a in rr* **66/1**

2m 8.16s (1.16) **Going Correction** -0.025s/f (Good) 10 Ran SP% **117.8**
Speed ratings (Par 103): **94,92,91,91,90 89,88,86,84,78**
toteswingers: 1&2 £3.00, 1&3 £4.20, 2&3 £2.10 CSF £20.42 CT £49.24 TOTE £8.00: £2.40, £1.20, £1.60.
Owner John & Susan Robertson **Bred** Farmers Hill Stud **Trained** Middleham Moor, N Yorks

FOCUS
Just a modest handicap and again it paid to race handy. The form is rated at face value.
Highland Love Official explanation: trainer said, regarding apparent improvement in form, that the gelding was better suited by the course and being given a more positive ride.

2852 RACING UK MAIDEN STKS 7f 100y
4:00 (4:01) (Class 5) 3-Y-0+ **£2,914** (£867; £433; £216) **Stalls** High

Form RPR

32 **1** **Rule Breaker (IRE)**[12] 2496 3-8-13 0........................ SilvestreDeSousa 9 86+
(M Johnston) *mde all: pushed clr over 2f out: rdn over 1f out: styd on strly* **11/10**[1]

3-02 **2** 6 **Advertisement (USA)**[37] 1766 3-8-13 78........................ TomEaves 10 71
(J Noseda) *a chsng wnr: rdn over 2f out: drvn over 1f out: kpt on: no ch w wnr* **7/2**[3]

6 **3** 5 **Silvery Moon (IRE)**[15] 2425 3-8-13 0........................ DavidAllan 1 59+
(T D Easterby) *s.i.s and bhd: hdwy over 2f out: rdn over 1f out: styd on strly ins fnl f: nrst fin* **18/1**

300- **4** 1 1/4 **State Fair**[219] 7209 3-8-13 76........................ StephenCraine 11 55
(Julie Camacho) *chsd ldrs: rdn along wl over 2f out: sn one pce* **16/1**

0/0 **5** 1 1/4 **Olympian Order (IRE)**[16] 2393 4-9-9 0........................ PJMcDonald 12 56
(G A Swinbank) *in tch: rdn along 3f out: sn one pce* **40/1**

60 **6** 1 3/4 **Ingleby King (USA)**[16] 2393 4-9-9 0........................ GrahamGibbons 2 52
(T D Barron) *a towards rr* **33/1**

0-32 **7** 1/2 **Fifty Moore**[39] 1706 3-8-13 85........................ PatCosgrave 6 47
(Jedd O'Keeffe) *prom: rdn and hung bdly lft over 2f out: sn drvn and wknd* **5/2**[2]

0 **8** 3/4 **Verluga (IRE)**[25] 2114 3-8-13 0........................ LeeVickers 4 45
(T D Easterby) *a towards rr* **50/1**

9 7 **Roydmore** 3-8-13 0........................ FranciscoDaSilva 7 27
(R A Fahey) *s.i.s: a bhd* **66/1**

000- **10** 10 **Frill A Minute**[218] 7220 6-8-13 25........................ JamesSullivan(5) 3 —
(Miss L C Siddall) *chsd ldrs: rdn along 1/2-way: sn wknd* **100/1**

1m 33.35s (-0.45) **Going Correction** -0.025s/f (Good)
WFA 3 from 4yo+ 10lb 10 Ran SP% **119.4**
Speed ratings (Par 103): **101,94,88,87,85 83,83,82,74,62**
toteswingers: 1&2 £2.20, 1&3 £4.90, 2&3 £8.00 CSF £5.35 TOTE £2.40: £1.30, £2.10, £3.00; EX 5.70.
Owner Sheikh Hamdan Bin Mohammed Al Maktoum **Bred** Declan Hyland And Lillian Montgomery **Trained** Middleham Moor, N Yorks

FOCUS
An uncompetitive maiden - the runner-up, fourth and seventh were below their official marks of 78, 76 and 85 respectively - and a prominent ride once again proved beneficial. The fifth is probably the best guide.
Silvery Moon(IRE) ◆ Official explanation: jockey said gelding ran too free to post

2853 TURFTV BETTING SHOP SERVICE H'CAP 1m 4f 16y
4:30 (4:30) (Class 6) (0-55,55) 3-Y-O **£2,590** (£770; £385; £192) **Stalls** High

Form RPR

000 **1** **Captain John Nixon**[25] 2121 3-8-0 **46** oh1................ JamesSullivan(5) 6 54
(Pat Eddery) *trckd ldrs: hdwy 3f out: rdn to ld jst over 1f out: drvn and edgd lft ins fnl f: kpt on wl* **9/2**[2]

0-63 **2** 1 1/2 **Dubawi King**[9] 2606 3-8-8 **49** ow1........................ TonyCulhane 10 55
(N Tinkler) *hld up towards rr: hdwy over 3f out: rdn wl over 1f out: drvn to chal and ev ch ent fnl f: sltly hmpd and one pce last 100yds* **8/1**

00-0 **3** 1/2 **Pleasant Way (IRE)**[53] 1393 3-9-0 **55**........................ PJMcDonald 9 60
(D R Lanigan) *a.p: effrt 3f out: rdn to chse ldr 2f out: drvn and ev ch over 1f out: one pce ins fnl f* **12/1**

5431 **4** nk **Dubara Reef (IRE)**[9] 2606 3-8-13 **54** 6ex.................. SilvestreDeSousa 3 58
(Paul Green) *hld up: hdwy 3f out: rdn 2f out: styd on appr fnl f: n.m.r whn swtchd rt and kpt on towards fin* **7/1**[3]

000- **5** 2 1/2 **Straversjoy**[186] 7638 3-8-6 **47**........................ GrahamGibbons 12 49+
(R Hollinshead) *hld up in rr: hdwy over 3f out: effrt to chse ldrs and nt clr run on inner 2f out: sn rdn and kpt on same pce appr fnl f* **14/1**

06-2 **6** 1/2 **Escape Artist**[9] 2606 3-8-8 **49**........................ DavidAllan 8 49
(T D Easterby) *trckd ldrs on inner: hdwy 3f out: rdn 2f out: sn drvn and one pce* **11/10**[1]

03-0 **7** 6 **Miss Wendy**[29] 2011 3-9-0 **55**........................ PatCosgrave 2 45
(M H Tompkins) *hld up: a in rr* **33/1**

00-0 **8** 3/4 **Star Of Kalani (IRE)**[6] 2673 3-8-5 **46** oh1..........................(b) PaulQuinn 1 35
(R D Wylie) *hld up: stdy hdwy 1/2-way: led 3f out: rdn clr 2f out: sn drvn: hdd over 1f out and wknd qckly* **16/1**

0-40 **9** 2 3/4 **Lady Pacha**[9] 2606 3-8-0 **46** oh1..........................(b[1]) IanBrennan(5) 11 30
(T J Pitt) *reminders s to ld on inner: rdn along 4f out: hdd 3f out: sn drvn and grad wknd* **25/1**

00-0 **10** 13 **Patricks Lodge**[15] 2425 3-8-5 **46** oh1........................ FranciscoDaSilva 5 10
(J D Bethell) *a in rr: bhd fnl 3f* **66/1**

-000 **11** 24 **Russian Brigadier**[12] 2503 3-8-8 **49** ow3........................ TomEaves 4 —
(M Brittain) *disp ld: rdn along over 3f out: sn wknd and bhd fnl 2f* **50/1**

2m 41.64s (1.84) **Going Correction** -0.025s/f (Good) 11 Ran SP% **119.9**
Speed ratings (Par 97): **96,95,94,94,92 92,88,87,86,77 61**
toteswingers: 1&2 £6.90, 1&3 £7.40, 2&3 £10.10 CSF £40.08 CT £411.83 TOTE £5.90: £2.20, £1.70, £3.70; EX 48.40 Place 6 £31.85, Place 5 £22.75.
Owner Paul Dean **Bred** Patrick Eddery Ltd **Trained** Nether Winchendon, Bucks
■ Stewards' Enquiry : James Sullivan caution: careless riding

FOCUS
Some unexposed types lined up and this wasn't too bad a race for the grade. They went a fair pace and the form looks reasonable for the grade.
Captain John Nixon Official explanation: trainer's rep said, regarding apparent improvement in form, that the gelding had been slow to learn but benefited from the step up in trip.
Straversjoy ◆ Official explanation: jockey said filly was denied a clear run
T/Plt: £75.50 to a £1 stake. Pool: £64,195.41. 620.39 winning tickets. T/Qpdt: £12.00 to a £1 stake. Pool: £4,421.61. 271.84 winning tickets. JR

2667 HAMILTON (R-H)
Wednesday, June 9

OFFICIAL GOING: Good to firm (good in places; 9.8)
Rail realignment around the loop reduced distances on round course by about 8yds.
Wind: Breezy, across Weather: Cloudy, dry

2854 WORLD CUP DAY NEXT WEDNESDAY AMATEUR RIDERS' H'CAP 6f 5y
6:35 (6:35) (Class 6) (0-60,60) 4-Y-0+ **£2,307** (£709; £354) **Stalls** Centre

Form RPR

/520 **1** **Ivestar (IRE)**[8] 2629 5-10-7 **60**....................(vt) MissCharlotteHolmes(7) 13 66
(B M R Haslam) *missed break: bhd: plenty to do 1/2-way: hdwy over 1f out: str run fnl f: led cl home* **40/1**

-603 **2** nk **El Dececy (USA)**[16] 2381 6-11-0 **60**..........................(p) MrSWalker 1 65
(J Balding) *t.k.h: trckd ldrs: led over 2f out: edgd rt over 1f out: kpt on u.p fnl f: hdd cl home* **1/1**[1]

-000 **3** nse **Final Salute**[22] 2207 4-10-3 **54**..........................(v) MrJNewman(5) 4 59
(B Smart) *t.k.h: prom: disp ld fr 1/2-way: rdn and kpt on fnl f: jst hld* **8/1**[3]

4005 **4** 1 1/4 **Avoncreek**[7] 2647 6-9-7 **46** oh1........................ MissStefaniaGandola(7) 8 47
(B P J Baugh) *prom: outpcd 2f out: kpt on fnl f: nrst fin* **14/1**

/300 **5** 2 1/4 **Dolly Royal (IRE)**[3] 2791 5-10-1 **52**..........................(p) MrAdamNicol(5) 2 46
(R Johnson) *bhd tl hdwy over 1f out: kpt on fnl f: nrst fin* **40/1**

4000 **6** 1/2 **Guest Connections**[6] 2671 7-10-7 **60**....................(v) MissJWalker(7) 10 52
(D Nicholls) *towards rr: pushed along and effrt over 1f out: nvr able to chal* **14/1**

/00- **7** 1 1/2 **Calley Ho**[333] 3862 4-10-1 **54**........................ MissTSyddall(7) 9 41
(Mrs L Stubbs) *disp ld to 1/2-way: no ex over 1f out* **100/1**

50-0 **8** nk **Glenluji**[13] 2454 5-9-9 **46**........................ MrJMQuinlan(5) 7 32
(J S Goldie) *fly-jmpd s: hld up: sme hdwy over 1f out: nvr able to chal* **16/1**

-026 **9** 1 1/2 **Two Turtle Doves (IRE)**[16] 2381 4-10-7 **58**....... MissMMullineaux(5) 15 40
(M Mullineaux) *prom tl rdn and no ex over 1f out* **5/1**[2]

0630 **10** nk **Officer Mor (USA)**[9] 2582 4-9-9 **46** oh1........................ MissECSayer(5) 6 27
(Mrs Dianne Sayer) *slt ld to over 2f out: hung rt and no ex over 1f out* **25/1**

0020 **11** 1/2 **Hosanna**[13] 2454 4-10-1 **52**........................ CallumWhillans(5) 11 31
(J Barclay) *prom tl rdn and no ex wl over 1f out* **33/1**

00-4 **12** hd **Karate Queen**[8] 2629 5-9-9 **46** oh1........................ MissVBarr(5) 3 24
(R E Barr) *s.i.s: sn midfield: sme hdwy wl over 1f out: nvr rchd ldrs* **12/1**

000/ **13** 12 **Merlins Dreams**[1092] 2563 7-9-10 **47** oh1 ow1............ MrCAHarris(5) 16 —
(S A Harris) *dwlt: t.k.h in rr: shkn up and edgd rt over 2f out: nvr on terms* **50/1**

000- **14** 7 **Quicks The Word**[284] 5443 10-9-9 **46** oh1............ MissHCuthbert(5) 14 —
(T A K Cuthbert) *towards rr on outside: struggling 1/2-way: sn btn* **40/1**

1m 13.3s (1.10) **Going Correction** +0.025s/f (Good) 14 Ran SP% **121.7**
Speed ratings (Par 101): **93,92,92,90,87 87,85,84,82,82 81,81,65,56**
toteswingers: 1&2 £27.80, 1&3 £54.20, 2&3 £4.30 CSF £79.75 CT £420.51 TOTE £64.10: £14.40, £1.02, £3.10; EX 80.40.
Owner Blue Lion Racing VIII **Bred** Grenane House Stud & Hatta International Bloodstoc **Trained** Middleham Moor, N Yorks
■ Charlotte Holmes's first winner.
■ Stewards' Enquiry : Miss V Barr one-day ban: careless riding (tbn)

FOCUS
A dearth of recent form in a very modest amateur riders' handicap rendered this a very uncompetitive affair despite the numbers. The main action unfolded on the half of the track nearest the stands' rail but the form is not solid with the winner showing his first form for two years.
Ivestar(IRE) Official explanation: trainer said, regarding apparent improvement in form, that the gelding was suited by the fast pace.

2855 EUROPEAN BREEDERS' FUND MAIDEN STKS 6f 5y
7:05 (7:05) (Class 4) 2-Y-O £4,533 (£1,348; £674; £336) Stalls Low

Form				RPR
	1		**Soraaya (IRE)** 2-8-12 0 ChrisCatlin 2 (M R Channon) *cl up: led gng wl over 2f out: drvn out fnl f* **15/8**1	82+
	2	2 3/4	**Nawaashi** 2-8-12 0 TadhgO'Shea 3 (M Johnston) *trckd ldrs: hdwy to chse wnr over 2f out: effrt over 1f out: kpt on same pce fnl f* **5/2**2	74+
	3	4 1/2	**Dunmore Boy (IRE)** 2-9-3 0 PaulHanagan 1 (R A Fahey) *dwlt: t.k.h: sn prom: effrt 2f out: outpcd appr fnl f* **15/8**1	65+
	4	4 1/2	**Not So Bright (USA)** 2-9-3 0 PaulMulrennan 4 (J G Given) *wnt rt s: sn led: hdd over 2f out: wknd over 1f out* **10/1**3	52

1m 12.87s (0.67) **Going Correction** +0.025s/f (Good) 4 Ran SP% **107.2**
Speed ratings (Par 95): **96,92,86,80**
CSF £6.68 TOTE £3.50; EX 7.00.
Owner Sheikh Ahmed Al Maktoum **Bred** Keogh Family **Trained** West Ilsley, Berks

FOCUS
Only four runners, all newcomers, and not easy to know what to make of the form, but the time at least was 0.43 seconds faster than the first race. The trainers of the first two are getting going with their juveniles now and the form is rated around the averages.

NOTEBOOK
Soraaya(IRE), a 55,000 guineas yearling and a half-sister to two winning 2yos, one of them smart, made an encouraging debut. She looked to be travelling the best from halfway and was never in much danger once hitting the front. From a yard where most of its youngsters have needed a run this year, she'll improve and will stay 7f. (tchd 2-1)
Nawaashi is a Green Desert filly related to some winners at around this trip but she did not look like giving her stable their third win in this race with a newcomer despite a satisfactory debut. She also left the impression she'll get 7f this year. (op 10-3 tchd 7-2)
Dunmore Boy(IRE) cost 28,000 euros as a yearling and is from a smart family but he didn't offer much, always in the last pair. He's in good hands, though, and is entitled to come on for the experience. (op 7-4 tchd 13-8)
Not So Bright(USA), a half-brother to three winners in the USA, is from a yard that do not get many debut 2yo winners. He shaped as if needing the run and was not given a hard time after taking the runners along. He should progress so long as the flash of his tail he gave when headed was a sign of inexperience and nothing else. (op 8-1 tchd 11-1)

2856 HAMILTON-PARK.CO.UK H'CAP 6f 5y
7:35 (7:35) (Class 4) (0-80,80) 4-Y-O+ £6,476 (£1,927; £963; £481) Stalls Centre

Form				RPR
-110	1		**Tangerine Trees**25 2113 5-9-6 **77** PaulHanagan 6 (B Smart) *mde all: rdn 2f out: hld on wl fnl f* **7/4**1	85
0024	2	nk	**Indian Skipper (IRE)**11 2524 5-9-6 **77** (be) FrannyNorton 7 (R C Guest) *missed break: hld up: hdwy over 2f out: kpt on wl fnl f: wnt 2nd nr fin but a hld* **5/1**3	84
-125	3	1	**Leonid Glow**13 2465 5-9-7 **78** PhillipMakin 5 (M Dods) *prom: stdy hdwy to chse wnr over 1f out: sn rdn: kpt on same pce ins fnl f* **11/4**2	82
0-00	4	1 1/4	**Protector (SAF)**39 1688 9-9-9 **80** (t) LNewman 3 (A G Foster) *prom: effrt over 2f out: kpt on same pce fnl f* **12/1**	80
3-13	5	3 3/4	**Tadalavil**6 2671 5-8-12 **69** PaulMulrennan 4 (Miss L A Perratt) *t.k.h: trckd wnr: rdn over 2f out: wknd over 1f out* **11/2**	57
-400	6	3	**Botham (USA)**6 2671 6-8-5 **62** ChrisCatlin 9 (J S Goldie) *towards rr: outpcd after 2f: no imp fnl 2f* **16/1**	40
2000	7	6	**Sendreni (FR)**6 2671 6-8-9 **69** (p) BarryMcHugh(3) 1 (Mrs J C McGregor) *in tch: rdn over 2f out: sn wknd* **80/1**	28

1m 11.58s (-0.62) **Going Correction** +0.025s/f (Good) 7 Ran SP% **109.9**
Speed ratings (Par 105): **105,104,103,101,96 92,84**
toteswingers: 1&2 £2.60, 1&3 £2.00, 2&3 £2.80 CSF £10.03 CT £20.23 TOTE £2.30: £1.10, £4.10; EX 9.00.
Owner Tangerine Trees Partnership **Bred** Mrs B A Matthews **Trained** Hambleton, N Yorks

FOCUS
A fair handicap run at a decent pace and no obvious excuses for the beaten runners. The form looks straightforward but ordinary.

2857 LANARK SILVER BELL H'CAP 1m 4f 17y
8:05 (8:06) (Class 3) (0-90,91) 4-Y-O+ £22,666 (£6,744; £3,370; £1,683) Stalls High

Form				RPR
0401	1		**Just Lille (IRE)**4 2761 7-9-3 **86** 6ex (v) BarryMcHugh(3) 13 (Mrs A Duffield) *enterprisingly rdn: mde all: qcknd clr over 4f out: kpt on strly fnl 2f: unchal* **12/1**	98
1411	2	5	**Lady Eclair (IRE)**6 2672 4-8-10 **76** 6ex PaulMulrennan 15 (M Johnston) *chsd wnr thrght: clr of rest over 3f out: kpt on fr 2f out: nt rch wnr* **12/1**	80
260-	3	3 1/4	**Citizenship**216 7263 4-8-12 **78** (t) StevieDonohoe 8 (Ian Williams) *hld up in midfield on ins: hdwy to chse clr ldng pair 3f out: no imp fnl 2f* **28/1**	77
0-41	4	1 1/4	**Jedi**33 1863 4-9-9 **89** RyanMoore 6 (Sir Michael Stoute) *hld up in midfield: pushed along over 3f out: plugged on fr 2f out: nvr able to chal* **7/4**1	86
10-0	5	nk	**Lochiel**26 2096 6-9-5 **90** MichaelO'Connell(5) 5 (Mrs L B Normile) *hld up: swtchd lft and hdwy 3f out: kpt on fr 2f out: nvr rchd ldrs* **66/1**	86
5251	6	1/2	**Dazzling Light (UAE)**18 2313 5-9-0 **83** GaryBartley(3) 4 (J S Goldie) *hld up: hdwy over 2f out: nvr rchd ldrs* **12/1**	79+
4505	7	nk	**Record Breaker (IRE)**18 2317 6-9-9 **89** (b) RoystonFfrench 7 (M Johnston) *hld up: rdn 4f out: plugged on fnl 2f: no imp* **9/2**2	84
0-63	8	3/4	**Persian Peril**28 2031 6-9-1 **81** TadhgO'Shea 12 (G A Swinbank) *hld up: effrt and rdn over 2f out: kpt on same pce* **25/1**	75
0/23	9	1 1/4	**Managua**18 2317 4-9-0 **80** ChrisCatlin 1 (M R Channon) *uns rdr and loose briefly bef s: midfield: rdn over 3f out: edgd rt: no ex fnl 2f* **16/1**	72
0535	10	nk	**Kames Park (IRE)**4 2739 8-8-11 **77** FrannyNorton 9 (R C Guest) *hld up: pushed along over 2f out: nvr rchd ldrs* **40/1**	68
16-4	11	10	**Act Of Kalanisi (IRE)**16 2395 4-9-3 **83** GregFairley 2 (M Johnston) *chsd ldrs tl rdn and wknd over 3f out* **25/1**	58
121	12	2	**Veloso (FR)**35 1829 8-9-6 **86** PhillipMakin 14 (J A Glover) *in tch tl rdn and wknd fr 3f out* **10/1**	58
3-12	13	25	**Mr Freddy (IRE)**18 2349 4-9-5 **85** PaulHanagan 3 (R A Fahey) *t.k.h: in tch tl wknd over 3f out* **5/1**3	17

2m 32.9s (-5.70) **Going Correction** -0.30s/f (Firm) 13 Ran SP% **124.3**
Speed ratings (Par 107): **107,103,101,100,100 100,99,99,98,98 91,90,73**
toteswingers: 1&2 £25.80, 1&3 £106.60, 2&3 £113.50 CSF £146.09 CT £3945.03 TOTE £18.30: £4.20, £3.70, £10.00; EX 50.20.
Owner Miss Helen Wynne **Bred** Sweetmans Bloodstock **Trained** Constable Burton, N Yorks

FOCUS
The official distances for all races over 1m or more were reduced by approximately 8 yards due to realignment of the rail on the loop. What looked a competitive race turned into something of a procession. Few were able to make much impression from off the pace under the fast conditions and probably not form to take at face value despite the first two running close to their best/recent marks.

NOTEBOOK
Just Lille(IRE) was second in this race last year off a mark of 87 and, 1lb lower here despite bouncing back to form in great style at Musselburgh at the weekend, made the most of a good piece of placing to win in thumping fashion. For all she might have been allowed a bit of rope in front, she had little trouble maintaining a clear advantage and was able to be eased late. Sweetened up by a recent schooling session over hurdles, this was her fourth course win and the third time she has won successive races within five days. (tchd 14-1)
Lady Eclair(IRE) ◆ has been progressive at a lower level and ran very well. She did not seem inconvenienced by another slight step back in trip. She's not had much racing and should win more races. (tchd 11-1)
Citizenship did well last season and made an encouraging reappearance. He's 11lb higher than his last winning mark, but this performance suggests he might well improve a bit more this year. (tchd 33-1)
Jedi was probably found out by the combination of the track and the fast conditions. He left the impression that he will be suited by a longer trip. (op 15-8 tchd 2-1 in places)
Lochiel had been third in this last year when with Alan Swinbank and put a modest recent comeback behind him with a good effort considering he came from further back than most. He can go well next time if things pan out more in his favour.
Dazzling Light(UAE) ◆'s run is best ignored. She had done well at Chester last time to catch up one that had gone clear and had a trouble passage trying to come from too far back. She remains in good heart. (op 11-1 tchd 14-1)
Record Breaker(IRE), who won this race last year, was dropped in grade but made only laboured progress. (op 13-2)
Managua, who unseated his rider before the start and got loose, is very lightly raced but might do better at a slightly shorter trip. (tchd 14-1)
Veloso(FR) did not to give his running, but may have found this too much of a speed test from a stiff turf mark. (op 20-1)
Mr Freddy(IRE) left the impression that all wasn't well. Official explanation: trainer had no explanation for the poor form shown (op 9-2)

2858 RACING UK (S) STKS 1m 65y
8:35 (8:35) (Class 6) 4-Y-O+ £2,590 (£770; £385; £192) Stalls High

Form				RPR
2315	1		**Royal Straight**18 2343 5-9-3 70 PaulHanagan 1 (R A Fahey) *in tch: effrt and rdn over 2f out: led ins fnl f: jst hld on* **15/8**2	69
6002	2	shd	**Stellite**13 2453 10-9-0 65 GaryBartley(3) 2 (J S Goldie) *hld up: hdwy over 2f out: kpt on wl fnl f: jst hld* **16/1**	68
3111	3	hd	**Royal Dignitary (USA)**16 2377 10-9-3 80 AdrianNicholls 6 (D Nicholls) *t.k.h: led 2f: chsd ldr: effrt over 2f out: kpt on fnl f: one pce whn blkd towards fin: dead-heated for 3rd: awrdd 3rd outrt* **10/11**1	68
24-0	4	dht	**San Silvestro (IRE)**14 2172 5-9-0 60 (b1) BarryMcHugh(3) 7 (Mrs A Duffield) *t.k.h: led after 2f: rdn and edgd lft 2f out: hdd ins fnl f: rallied: jst hld: dead-heated for 3rd, shd & hd: plcd 4th* **22/1**	68
0321	5	8	**Finsbury**9 2583 7-9-3 70 PaulMulrennan 3 (Miss L A Perratt) *hld up: effrt over 2f out: btn over 1f out* **15/2**3	49
02-2	6	7	**Bed Fellow (IRE)**14 2433 6-9-3 53 PhillipMakin 4 (P Monteith) *t.k.h: trckd ldrs tl rdn and wknd over 2f out* **50/1**	32

1m 47.01s (-1.39) **Going Correction** -0.30s/f (Firm) 6 Ran SP% **111.1**
Speed ratings (Par 101): **94,93,93,93,85 78**
toteswingers: 1&2 £4.30, 1&3 £1.02, 2&3 £4.20 CSF £28.23 TOTE £2.40: £1.10, £4.90; EX 34.90.The winner was sold to Ken McGarrity for 8,000gns.
Owner McAndrew Utilities Limited **Bred** Brook Stud Bloodstock & Leydens Farm Stud **Trained** Musley Bank, N Yorks

FOCUS
A fair seller that produced an exciting finish. The demoted fourth looks the best guide to the level.

2859 BOOK NOW FOR CASH FOR KIDS NIGHT H'CAP (QUALIFIER FOR THE SCOTTISH TROPHY HANDICAP SERIES FINAL) 1m 1f 36y
9:05 (9:07) (Class 5) (0-70,68) 4-Y-O+ £3,238 (£963; £481; £240) Stalls High

Form				RPR
033	1		**Applaude**9 2600 5-8-10 **55** (b) FrannyNorton 5 (R C Guest) *hld up: stdy hdwy over 2f out: effrt and swtchd lft over 1f out: qcknd to ld ins fnl f: comf* **8/1**2	67
0130	2	3	**Saving Grace**14 2429 4-8-10 **55** DuranFentiman 10 (E J Alston) *t.k.h: chsd ldr: led over 1f out: hdd ins fnl f: kpt on: nt pce of wnr* **9/1**3	61
2600	3	1 3/4	**Sarwin (USA)**16 2392 7-9-4 **63** AndrewElliott 7 (G A Swinbank) *prom: rdn over 2f out: hdwy over 1f out: kpt on same pce ins fnl f* **12/1**	65
0-02	4	1 1/2	**Anthemion (IRE)**6 2670 13-8-4 **49** oh4 AdrianNicholls 9 (Mrs J C McGregor) *led: rdn over 2f out: hdd over 1f out: kpt on same fnl f* **12/1**	48
1235	5	1	**Zaplamation (IRE)**9 2579 5-9-6 **68** BarryMcHugh(3) 3 (J J Quinn) *prom: effrt over 2f out: kpt on same pce fnl f* **9/4**1	65
06-3	6	2 1/2	**Al Wasef (USA)**14 2433 5-9-1 **60** PhillipMakin 6 (J S Goldie) *hld up in tch: rdn over 2f out: no imp over 1f out* **8/1**2	52
0/04	7	1 1/4	**Custard Cream Kid (IRE)**16 2382 4-8-9 **54** PaulHanagan 8 (R A Fahey) *hld up: effrt over 2f out: no ex over 1f out* **9/4**1	43
020/	8	1	**Tiger King (GER)**465 7177 9-8-2 **52** PatrickDonaghy(5) 2 (P Monteith) *hld up: rdn and outpcd over 2f out: n.d after* **50/1**	39
6564	9	3/4	**Green Agenda**13 2451 4-8-13 **58** (v1) RoystonFfrench 1 (M Johnston) *missed break: bhd: rdn 1/2-way: nvr on terms* **16/1**	44

1m 56.5s (-3.20) **Going Correction** -0.30s/f (Firm) 9 Ran SP% **117.0**
Speed ratings (Par 103): **102,99,97,96,95 93,92,91,90**
toteswingers: 1&2 £8.90, 1&3 £14.60, 2&3 £35.80 CSF £78.24 CT £864.49 TOTE £8.10: £1.60, £3.90, £4.50; EX 75.70 Place 6 £636.40, Place 5 £428.30.
Owner Stan Wright **Bred** G Reed **Trained** Stainforth, S Yorks

FOCUS
A modest finale run at a decent pace, and the form is rated through the runner-up backed up by the fourth to his recent course mark.
Green Agenda Official explanation: jockey said gelding missed the break
T/Plt: £1,688.60 to a £1 stake. Pool: £66,159.36. 28.60 winning tickets. T/Qpdt: £285.10 to a £1 stake. Pool: £6,115.00. 15.87 winning tickets. RY

2536 HAYDOCK (L-H)

Wednesday, June 9

OFFICIAL GOING: Good (good to firm in places) changing to good to soft (good in places) after race 1 (2.20)

Rail realignment increased advertised distances on round course by 25yds.

Wind: Moderate, half behind Weather: Overcast, light rain 1st 2 races

2860 PHS WASHROOM SERVICES MAIDEN STKS — 1m 3f 200y

2:20 (2:22) (Class 5) 3-Y-O+ — **£2,914** (£867; £433; £216) Stalls High

Form — RPR

2-3 **1** **Very Good Day (FR)**[21] 2226 3-8-13 0 — AlanMunro 2 — 80
(M R Channon) *in rr-div: hdwy over 3f out: sn drvn: styd on to ld appr fnl f: rdn out* — **4/9**[1]

24-6 **2** 1 1/4 **Cotillion**[37] 1757 4-10-0 73 — StevieDonohoe 13 — 78
(Ian Williams) *s.i.s: hdwy and swtchd rt over 3f out: styd on to take 2nd towards fin* — **25/1**

6 **3** 1/2 **Joseph Lister**[38] 1735 3-8-13 0 — MartinDwyer 12 — 77
(J H M Gosden) *w ldrs: led after 2f: hdd and no ex appr fnl f* — **25/1**

4 1 1/2 **Emerging Artist (FR)** 4-10-0 0 — FrankieDettori 6 — 75
(M Johnston) *sn w ldrs: kpt on same pce fnl f* — **11/1**[3]

06 **5** 1 1/2 **Candotoo (IRE)**[20] 2255 3-8-8 0 — TomQueally 7 — 67
(J Noseda) *in tch: hdwy to chse ldrs 3f out: shkn up over 1f out: kpt on* — **25/1**

0 **6** 7 **Tigranes The Great (IRE)**[27] 2043 3-8-13 0 — JerryO'Dwyer 15 — 61
(M Botti) *in rr: hdwy over 3f out: kpt on steadily fnl f* — **100/1**

330- **7** nse **Kansai Spirit (IRE)**[278] 5649 4-10-0 80 — RobertHavlin 8 — 61
(J H M Gosden) *hld up: hmpd after 3f: hdwy to chse ldrs 7f out: c wd over 4f out and racd alone stands' side: edgd lft over 2f out: wknd over 1f out* — **16/1**

0-2 **8** 3 **Ellbeedee (IRE)**[32] 1932 3-8-8 0 — PhilipRobinson 14 — 51
(M A Jarvis) *trckd ldrs: stmbld after 3f: hdwy to chal over 3f out: wknd over 1f out* — **9/2**[2]

9 8 **Kuantan Two (IRE)** 3-8-13 0 — PaulHanagan 4 — 44
(P F I Cole) *sn in rr and pushed along: bhd fnl 3f* — **50/1**

0-5 **10** 7 **Ocean Club**[20] 2244 3-8-13 0 — MichaelHills 5 — 32
(B W Hills) *trckd ldrs: t.k.h: wknd over 2f out* — **28/1**

11 19 **Tobermory Boy** 3-8-13 0 — PaulMulrennan 10 — —
(J G Given) *s.s: a bhd: t.o 4f out* — **100/1**

/06- **12** 3 1/4 **Pergamon (IRE)**[132] 1780 4-9-11 78 — (t) RobertLButler(3) 11 — —
(Miss C Dyson) *chsd ldrs: lost pl over 3f out* — **100/1**

60 **13** 1 1/4 **Roxy Spirit (IRE)**[47] 1504 3-8-1 0 — JosephYoung(7) 17 — —
(M Mullineaux) *chsd ldrs: sn pushed along: lost pl 4f out: sn bhd* — **150/1**

0 **14** 14 **Hannah Hawk**[13] 2473 3-8-8 0 — AndrewElliott 9 — —
(Lucinda Featherstone) *led 2f: lost pl 4f out: sn bhd* — **100/1**

2m 38.3s (4.30) **Going Correction** +0.375s/f (Good)
WFA 3 from 4yo 15lb — **14** Ran SP% **123.2**
Speed ratings (Par 103): **98,97,96,95,94 90,90,88,82,78 65,63,62,53**
toteswingers: 1&2 £5.90, 1&3 £7.10, 2&3 £24.40 CSF £23.01 TOTE £1.40: £1.10, £5.00, £6.90; EX 18.30.
Owner Jaber Abdullah **Bred** Darley Stud Management Co Ltd **Trained** West Ilsley, Berks

■ Stewards' Enquiry : Stevie Donohoe five-day ban: rode without first passing the doctor and misleading clerk of scales (Aug 12-16)

FOCUS
Rain began to fall before the first and the official going description was amended to good to soft, good in places after this race. Rider Alan Munro reported after the opener that the ground was 'slow on top but not very deep'. This was not the most competitive of maidens, being run at a steady pace and developing into something of a muddling affair. The runners came down the centre of the course in the home straight. The runner-up is rated close to his 3-y-o form but not a race to be too positive about.

2861 E B F PHS WORKPLACE SLIP TESTING MAIDEN FILLIES' STKS — 6f

2:50 (2:51) (Class 5) 2-Y-O — **£3,432** (£1,021; £510; £254) Stalls High

Form — RPR

0 **1** **Sweetie Time**[26] 2088 2-9-0 0 — SteveDrowne 3 — 85+
(M L W Bell) *chsd ldrs on outer: effrt over 2f out: led over 1f out: drew clr* — **11/1**

2 3 3/4 **Khor Sheed** 2-9-0 0 — KirstyMilczarek 5 — 74+
(L M Cumani) *led: t.k.h: hdd over 1f out: kpt on same pce* — **9/2**[3]

3 1/2 **Galloping Queen (IRE)** 2-9-0 0 — AlanMunro 7 — 74+
(M R Channon) *s.i.s: outpcd: hung lft and reminders after 1f: hdwy over 1f out: styd on to take 3rd nr line* — **8/1**

0 **4** nk **Wafeira**[12] 2505 2-9-0 0 — TomQueally 6 — 71
(H R A Cecil) *dwlt: sn w ldr: kpt on same pce fnl f* — **2/1**[1]

60 **5** 3/4 **West Stand**[25] 2130 2-9-0 0 — PaulMulrennan 2 — 69
(Mrs K Walton) *dwlt: sn chsd ldrs: one pce fnl 2f* — **20/1**

0 **6** 3 1/2 **Bold Bidder**[12] 2493 2-9-0 0 — PaulHanagan 8 — 59
(K A Ryan) *w ldrs: wknd over 1f out* — **11/1**

7 7 **Half Truth (IRE)** 2-8-11 0 — AhmedAjtebi(3) 4 — 38+
(Mahmood Al Zarooni) *chsd ldrs: drvn 7f out: lost pl over 2f out: eased whn bhd ins fnl f* — **9/4**[2]

0 **8** 9 **Indian Giver**[9] 2577 2-9-0 0 — PatrickMathers 9 — —
(H A McWilliams) *s.i.s: in rr: hung lft and wknd 2f out: wl bhd whn eased ins fnl f* — **100/1**

1m 15.17s (1.67) **Going Correction** -0.10s/f (Good) — **8** Ran SP% **115.8**
Speed ratings (Par 90): **84,79,78,77,76 72,62,50**
toteswingers: 1&2 £9.00, 1&3 £6.10, 2&3 £4.70 CSF £60.52 TOTE £13.30: £2.70, £2.20, £1.80; EX 80.60.
Owner Lordship Stud **Bred** Lordship Stud **Trained** Newmarket, Suffolk

FOCUS
Fair maiden fillies' form, although tricky to pin down and it could be rated up to 10lb higher. The pace was pretty strong and the first three look nice fillies, while the fifth is probably trhe best guide.

NOTEBOOK
Sweetie Time came from a little way off the generous gallop to strike the front on the outer of the field before coming away for an emphatic win. This was a considerable improvement on what she displayed on her debut and she is likely to step up in grade for the Listed Empress Stakes at Newmarket next month. She should stay 7f on this evidence. (op 17-2 tchd 12-1)

Khor Sheed was Luca Cumani's first 2yo runner of the year. She helped push the pace all the way, but after mastering the fourth home and taking a narrow lead, she was quickly eclipsed by the winner. This was a decent effort the way the race panned out, and the half-sister to Prix d'Ispahan winner Prince Kirk should soon be going one better. (tchd 6-1)

Galloping Queen(IRE) ◆ was slow to stride then veered to her left. She was green in rear for much of the way, indeed she was still only sixth with half a furlong to run, but then ran on very nicely without her rider being too hard on her. With normal improvement a maiden should come her way. (tchd 10-1)

Wafeira disappointed on her debut at Newmarket after missing the break but this flatter track was expected to suit. Again a bit slow to leave the stalls, she soon recovered to dispute the lead but could muster only the one pace at the business end. She probably deserves one more chance. (op 6-4 tchd 11-8)

West Stand broke better than on her first two starts and stepped up on her previous efforts on this first try at 6f. She finished a little too close to some runners from top yards for comfort as far as her opening handicap mark is concerned. (tchd 25-1)

Bold Bidder knew a lot more than she had on her debut, but after racing up with the pace nearest the stands' rail, she faded approaching the final furlong. (op 16-1 tchd 9-1)

Half Truth(IRE) is a half-sister to the July Cup winner Fleeting Spirit, and could have been expected to do better than she did on this debut. She may not have handled the rain-eased ground. (op 4-1)

Indian Giver Official explanation: jockey said filly moved poorly throughout

2862 PHS WASHROOM CONSUMABLES H'CAP — 6f

3:20 (3:21) (Class 3) (0-95,93) 3-Y-O — **£9,066** (£2,697; £1,348; £673) Stalls High

Form — RPR

0-33 **1** **Sunraider (IRE)**[32] 1917 3-9-3 **89** — MichaelHills 7 — 101+
(B W Hills) *trckd one other stands' side: effrt 2f out: hung lft: led jst ins fnl f: r.o strly: v readily* — **11/4**[1]

1-41 **2** 2 1/4 **Little Garcon (USA)**[40] 1663 3-9-1 **87** — MartinDwyer 5 — 92
(M Botti) *t.k.h: effrt over 2f out: kpt on to take 2nd ins fnl f* — **8/1**

16-6 **3** 1 1/4 **Walvis Bay (IRE)**[7] 2656 3-8-11 **83** — MickyFenton 4 — 84
(T P Tate) *led one other stands' side: trckd ldrs: led over 1f out: hdd jst ins fnl f: no ex* — **7/1**

3430 **4** 2 1/4 **Below Zero (IRE)**[11] 2545 3-9-7 **93** — FrankieDettori 2 — 87
(M Johnston) *led: hdd over 1f out: edgd rt and sn wknd* — **17/2**

-31 **5** 6 **Ginger Ted (IRE)**[26] 2069 3-8-9 **81** — (p) PhilipRobinson 6 — 55
(R C Guest) *t.k.h: chsd ldr: lost pl over 1f out* — **3/1**[2]

2122 **6** 1 1/2 **Diman Waters (IRE)**[26] 2099 3-8-9 **81** — RyanMoore 3 — 51
(E J Alston) *chsd ldrs: rdn over 2f out: lost pl over 1f out* — **7/2**[3]

4001 **7** 4 **Ghostwing**[19] 2283 3-9-5 **91** — (v) RobertWinston 1 — 48
(J Gallagher) *sn chsng ldrs: effrt over 2f out: wknd over 1f out* — **10/1**

1m 12.44s (-1.06) **Going Correction** -0.10s/f (Good) — **7** Ran SP% **117.1**
Speed ratings (Par 103): **103,100,98,95,87 85,80**
toteswingers: 1&2 £5.90, 1&3 £4.40, 2&3 £13.90 CSF £26.00 TOTE £3.00: £1.40, £4.00; EX 31.00.
Owner Ron Young & SW Group Logistics Ltd **Bred** Lodge Park Stud **Trained** Lambourn, Berks

FOCUS
A decent handicap, but a few of these disappointed and the form may not prove too solid. A group of five raced down the centre of the track with the other two, the winner included, nearer the stands' side, but still a long way off the rail. The groups merged from the two pole. The winner came clear up the stands' side and the placed horses were clear of the rest of their group.

NOTEBOOK
Sunraider(IRE) got a tow from Walvis Bay before coming through strongly for a decisive win. Connections had been wary of running him on the advertised fast ground, but the rain was ideal and he did this well. A seventh furlong would not trouble him, but he obviously has plenty of pace for this trip. (op 9-4 tchd 3-1)

Little Garcon(USA), a narrow winner at Lingfield latest, had not run on turf since his racecourse debut last year. Held up, he refused to settle for a long way but picked up nicely for second late on. Still unexposed on fast ground, he should find a race in the coming weeks. (op 6-1)

Walvis Bay(IRE) was another favoured by the easing conditions and, after coming over to lead the winner some way apart from the others, he was only run out of second late on. He was due to be dropped 2lb before this. (op 10-1)

Below Zero(IRE), eased 2lb following his handicap debut at Newmarket, led the main body of the field until fading inside the last. He began the season over 1m but has plenty of pace. (tchd 8-1 and 11-1)

Ginger Ted(IRE)'s Hamilton win has received several boosts, but the 4lb rise in the weights for that success took him up to a career-high mark. He has never been the most consistent and could not get in a blow after racing keenly behind the leaders. This ground should have suited him. His jockey reported that he ran too free. Official explanation: jockey said gelding ran too free (op 4-1 tchd 9-2)

Diman Waters(IRE) had been in fine form this year, with three seconds to well handicapped sprinters to accompany a win here. All his races this term had been over 5f though, and the extra furlong on rain-softened ground proved too much for him. His trainer confirmed that he was unsuited by the ground. Official explanation: trainer said gelding was unsuited by the good to soft (good in places) ground (op 4-1 tchd 3-1)

Ghostwing won emphatically in a first-time visor at Chepstow, but that was on fast ground and these conditions were no good to him. He is one to treat with caution in any case. (op 14-1 tchd 16-1)

2863 PHS WORKPLACE MATTING H'CAP — 1m 30y

3:50 (3:50) (Class 4) (0-80,79) 3-Y-O — **£5,180** (£1,541; £770; £384) Stalls Low

Form — RPR

-123 **1** **Dolphin Rock**[20] 2261 3-9-3 **75** — TomQueally 3 — 83
(T D Barron) *led 1f: w ldr: led over 3f out: chal over 1f out: r.o gamely* — **9/2**[1]

0-00 **2** 1/2 **Pintura**[32] 1934 3-8-9 **67** — StevieDonohoe 12 — 74
(D M Simcock) *in rr: hdwy and swtchd stands' side over 2f out: styd on wl ins fnl f: jst hld* — **20/1**

3-1 **3** hd **Pentominium**[106] 671 3-9-1 **73** — FrankieDettori 7 — 79+
(M Johnston) *hmpd s: in rr: hdwy over 2f out: chal jst ins fnl f: no ex* — **8/1**

1-60 **4** 3/4 **Spoken**[20] 2254 3-9-5 **77** — SteveDrowne 10 — 82
(R Charlton) *t.k.h: trckd ldrs: hdwy on outside to chal 1f out: hung lft and styd on same pce* — **11/2**[2]

-432 **5** 1 **William Morgan (IRE)**[18] 2348 3-9-6 **78** — PaulHanagan 15 — 80
(R A Fahey) *chsd ldrs: swtchd lft after 1f: drvn over 3f out: chal over 1f out: kpt on one pce* — **8/1**

-414 **6** 1/2 **Bin Shamardal (IRE)**[30] 1969 3-9-6 **78** — MichaelHills 4 — 79
(B W Hills) *trckd ldrs: hung lft and chal over 1f out: wknd towards fin* — **11/1**

0352 **7** 4 1/2 **Edition**[16] 2398 3-8-9 **67** — RobertHavlin 11 — 58
(J R Gask) *mid-div: effrt to chse ldrs over 3f out: wknd fnl f* — **9/2**[1]

10-0 **8** 7 **Cono Zur (FR)**[30] 1969 3-9-6 **78** — RoystonFfrench 1 — 53
(M Johnston) *led after 1f: hdd over 3f out: lost pl over 1f out* — **25/1**

-210 **9** 3 1/2 **Towbaat**[20] 2254 3-9-6 **78** — PhilipRobinson 2 — 45
(M A Jarvis) *trckd ldrs: effrt over 3f out: lost pl over 1f out* — **6/1**[3]

-300 **10** 1/2 **Jupiter Fidius**[15] 2422 3-9-2 **74** — PaulMulrennan 6 — 40
(Mrs K Walton) *mid-div: drvn over 4f out: wknd over 1f out* — **25/1**

2-33 **11** 6 **Golden Tiger**[97] 782 3-8-10 **68** — MickyFenton 9 — 20
(T P Tate) *chsd ldrs: lost pl after 3f: rdn over 3f out: sn bhd* — **16/1**

00-6 12 *22* **Irish Eyes**[39] 1706 3-8-12 **75**.................................. PatrickDonaghy(5) 13 —
(Jedd O'Keeffe) *in rr: rdn over 3f out: sn lost tch: t.o* **50/1**

1m 46.41s (1.71) **Going Correction** +0.375s/f (Good) **12** Ran SP% **116.9**
Speed ratings (Par 101): **101,100,100,99,98 98,93,86,83,82 76,54**
toteswingers: 1&2 £28.00, 1&3 £5.00, 2&3 £44.20 CSF £98.79 CT £712.81 TOTE £5.90: £2.70, £7.20, £2.40.
Owner Mia Racing **Bred** Mia Racing **Trained** Maunby, N Yorks

FOCUS
A wide-open handicap, and solid enough form. The runners again headed for the centre of the track in the home straight.
Spoken Official explanation: jockey said colt hung left
Towbaat Official explanation: trainer's rep said filly was unsuited by the good to soft (good in places) ground

2864 PHS WATER SAVING H'CAP — 1m 30y
4:20 (4:20) (Class 5) (0-70,70) 4-Y-0+ **£2,914** (£867; £433; £216) **Stalls** Low

Form RPR

-000 **1** **Tanforan**[11] 2527 8-8-8 **57**.................................. SteveDrowne 7 69
(B P J Baugh) *in rr: hdwy over 3f out: chal 1f out: led post* **25/1**

0-34 **2** *nse* **Flying Silks (IRE)**[11] 2527 4-9-1 **64**..................(b) RobertHavlin 1 76
(J R Gask) *trckd ldrs: narrow ld over 1f out: hdd nr fin: no ex* **11/4**[1]

-005 **3** *3 ¾* **Just Timmy Marcus**[121] 467 4-8-9 **58**.................. RobertWinston 5 61
(B P J Baugh) *prom: chsng ldrs 3f out: n.m.r 2f out: edgd lft and one pce fnl f* **8/1**[3]

0005 **4** *2 ¾* **Bold Marc (IRE)**[11] 2531 8-9-7 **70**.................. AndrewElliott 10 67
(J R Weymes) *w ldr: led over 4f out: hdd over 2f out: fdd fnl f* **12/1**

-560 **5** *2 ¼* **Morocchius (USA)**[16] 2382 5-8-11 **60**..................(p) RoystonFfrench 9 52
(Julie Camacho) *s.s: t.k.h in rr: hmpd bnd over 5f out: hdwy 3f out: one pce appr fnl f* **8/1**[3]

0-50 **6** *3* **Champain Sands (IRE)**[16] 2382 11-8-6 **55** ow1.............. AlanMunro 6 40
(E J Alston) *trckd ldrs: led over 2f out: hdd over 1f out: sn wknd* **22/1**

201 **7** *1 ¼* **Lord Fidelio (IRE)**[19] 2273 4-9-5 **68**.................. JamesDoyle 12 50
(P D Evans) *prom: hung lft and chsng ldrs over 2f out: wknd over 1f out* **8/1**[3]

2626 **8** *½* **Boo**[11] 752 8-8-7 **56**..................(v) MartinDwyer 8 37
(J W Unett) *in rr: hdwy 3f out: wknd over 1f out* **14/1**

666- **9** *hd* **Lady Bluesky**[318] 4347 7-8-1 **55**.................. PatrickDonaghy(5) 2 35
(A C Whillans) *s.s: in rr whn hmpd twice bnd over 5f out: sme hdwy 2f out: nvr on terms* **16/1**

45-0 **10** *1 ¾* **Eastern Hills**[16] 2382 5-8-7 **61**.................. LanceBetts(5) 13 37
(J S Wainwright) *mid-div: effrt and chsng ldrs 3f out: wknd over 1f out* **10/1**

160- **11** *1 ¾* **Funky Munky**[254] 6349 5-8-12 **61**.................. MickyFenton 4 33
(A C Whillans) *mid-div: effrt over 3f out: wknd 2f out* **14/1**

0-00 **12** *5* **Forzarzi (IRE)**[9] 2583 6-8-6 **55**..................(p) PatrickMathers 11 16
(H A McWilliams) *in rr: hmpd bnd over 5f out: hdwy on wd outside to chse ldrs over 2f out: sn wknd* **66/1**

100- **13** *7* **Lujano**[212] 7322 5-9-6 **69**.................. RyanMoore 3 14
(Ollie Pears) *led tl over 4f out: lost pl over 1f out: eased towards fin* **7/1**[2]

1m 47.48s (2.78) **Going Correction** +0.375s/f (Good) **13** Ran SP% **118.2**
Speed ratings (Par 103): **96,95,92,89,87 84,82,82,82,80 78,73,66**
toteswingers: 1&2 £21.30, 1&3 £42.40, 2&3 £5.80 CSF £90.71 CT £646.10 TOTE £34.20: £7.60, £1.80, £2.60; EX 153.20.
Owner Miss S M Potts **Bred** Bearstone Stud **Trained** Audley, Staffs

FOCUS
A pretty modest handicap, run in a time just over a second slower than the earlier race for 3-y-os. The first two pulled clear to fight out a good finish but the form is ordinary rated around the first two and fourth.
Tanforan Official explanation: Trainer's rep said, regarding apparent improvement in form, that the gelding takes a few runs before hitting form.

2865 PHS PAPER PRODUCTS H'CAP — 1m 2f 95y
4:55 (4:55) (Class 4) (0-85,85) 4-Y-0+ **£5,180** (£1,541; £770; £384) **Stalls** High

Form RPR

52- **1** **Itlaaq**[244] 6613 4-9-5 **83**.................................. RichardHills 6 97
(J L Dunlop) *hld up towards rr: hdwy over 3f out: led 2f out: hld on towards fin* **11/4**[1]

6-13 **2** *hd* **Satwa Moon (USA)**[91] 852 4-8-13 **77**.................. FrankieDettori 14 90
(E A L Dunlop) *chsd ldrs: chal over 1f out: styd on towards fin* **11/1**

4-60 **3** *¾* **The Galloping Shoe**[13] 2462 5-8-8 **72** ow1.............. SteveDrowne 4 84
(A C Whillans) *in rr: drvn over 5f out: hdwy over 3f out: chal over 1f out: styd on same pce last 100yds* **40/1**

32-2 **4** *2 ½* **Plymouth Rock (IRE)**[63] 1156 4-9-5 **83**.................. RyanMoore 1 90
(J Noseda) *trckd ldrs: chal over 2f out: one pce* **7/2**[2]

0-31 **5** *1 ¾* **Magic Echo**[26] 2084 6-9-5 **83**.................. JamesDoyle 12 87
(M Dods) *hld up towards rr: hdwy on outer over 2f out: kpt on same pce: nvr trbld ldrs* **14/1**

420- **6** *1 ½* **Sanctuary**[262] 6138 4-9-3 **81**.................. TomQueally 8 82
(B Smart) *dwlt: sn trcking ldrs: one pce fnl 2f* **17/2**

3-61 **7** *7* **Putra One (IRE)**[37] 1780 4-9-3 **81**.................. PhilipRobinson 11 69
(M A Jarvis) *led 3f: w ldrs: led over 3f out: hdd 2f out: sn wknd* **6/1**[3]

-026 **8** *4 ½* **Prince Of Johanne (IRE)**[18] 2314 4-9-7 **85**.................. MickyFenton 5 64
(T P Tate) *s.i.s: sn pushed along: hdwy on ins over 3f out: lost pl over 1f out* **16/1**

-500 **9** *hd* **Moheebb (IRE)**[34] 1837 6-9-7 **85**..................(b) RobertWinston 10 64
(Mrs R A Carr) *sn chsng ldrs: wknd over 1f out* **25/1**

-652 **10** *1* **Bullet Man (USA)**[18] 2314 5-9-3 **81**.................. MartinDwyer 13 58
(R A Fahey) *led after 2f: hdd 4f out: hung lft and wknd 2f out* **7/1**

14-0 **11** *8* **Royal Defence (IRE)**[30] 1962 4-9-6 **84**..................(p) RobertHavlin 9 46
(Matthew Salaman) *t.k.h: sn trcking ldrs: hung lft and lost pl over 2f out* **50/1**

40-0 **12** *9* **Ordoney (IRE)**[15] 2423 5-8-11 **80**.................. LanceBetts(5) 15 25
(J S Wainwright) *w ldrs: t.k.h: led 4f out: sn hdd: lost pl over 2f out: sn bhd: sddle slipped* **50/1**

2m 17.38s (1.38) **Going Correction** +0.375s/f (Good) **12** Ran SP% **117.3**
Speed ratings (Par 105): **97,96,96,94,92 91,86,82,82,81 75,67**
toteswingers: 1&2 £6.30, 1&3 £24.90, 2&3 £17.60 CSF £33.00 CT £984.16 TOTE £3.20: £1.10, £3.90, £10.80; EX 28.80 Place 6 £131.94, Place 5 £91.53.
Owner Hamdan Al Maktoum **Bred** Shadwell Estate Company Limited **Trained** Arundel, W Sussex

FOCUS
A competitive handicap run at just an average pace but the form looks sound. The race should produce winners.
Ordoney(IRE) Official explanation: jockey said saddle slipped
T/Jkpt: Not won. T/Plt: £137.90 to a £1 stake. Pool: £68,629.82. 363.22 winning tickets. T/Qpdt: £19.90 to a £1 stake. Pool: £4,760.87. 176.76 winning tickets. WG

2638 KEMPTON (A.W) (R-H)
Wednesday, June 9

OFFICIAL GOING: Standard
Wind: Fresh, across towards stands Weather: Fine but cloudy

2866 KEMPTON.CO.UK APPRENTICE H'CAP — 1m (P)
6:20 (6:20) (Class 5) (0-70,70) 4-Y-0+ **£2,590** (£770; £385; £192) **Stalls** High

Form RPR

6411 **1** **Quiet Mountain (IRE)**[44] 1574 5-9-4 **64**.................. MatthewDavies 5 75+
(Ollie Pears) *hld up in 8th: hanging sltly whn asked for effrt on wd outside over 2f out: sn gd prog: rdn to ld ins fnl f* **4/1**[1]

5302 **2** *1 ¼* **Harting Hill**[7] 2643 5-8-11 **62**.................. KatiaScallan(5) 6 70+
(M P Tregoning) *racd wd: prom: chsd ldr wl over 1f out: clsd ent fnl f but wnr sn wnt past* **13/2**[3]

5100 **3** *1 ¼* **Teen Ager (FR)**[33] 1875 6-8-12 **61**.................. RyanClark(3) 11 66
(P Burgoyne) *trckd ldr: led 2f out and kicked on: hdd & wknd ins fnl f* **14/1**

5653 **4** *1 ¼* **Musashi (IRE)**[15] 2419 5-8-5 **58**..................(b) CharlotteJenner(7) 7 60+
(Mrs L J Mongan) *s.v.s: wl bhd in last: stl there 3f out: pushed along and styd on wl fnl 2f: tk 4th ins fnl f* **12/1**

5262 **5** *3* **Land Hawk (IRE)**[21] 2236 4-9-7 **67**.................. SimonPearce 2 62
(J Pearce) *chsd ldrs: rdn over 2f out: no imp on ldrs: wnt 4th briefly ins fnl f* **4/1**[1]

-005 **6** *2* **Kyleene**[20] 2262 4-9-7 **70**.................. AmyScott(3) 10 61
(M D I Usher) *chsd ldrs: rdn over 2f out and sn struggling: n.d fr over 1f out* **18/1**

/000 **7** *nse* **Blue Aura (IRE)**[9] 2596 7-9-0 **60**.................. DeanHeslop 12 51
(B G Powell) *led at str pce to 2f out: wknd* **16/1**

436 **8** *¾* **Ejeed (USA)**[29] 2009 5-9-0 **60**..................(p) RossAtkinson 8 49
(Miss Z C Davison) *towards rr: pushed along in 9th sn after 1/2-way: effrt u.p over 2f out: sn no prog* **11/1**

1216 **9** *1* **Tous Les Deux**[13] 2477 7-9-8 **68**.................. AmyBaker 4 54
(Dr J R J Naylor) *wl in rr: rdn in 10th 1/2-way: bmpd along and effrt 2f out: sn no prog* **14/1**

032- **10** *9* **Co Dependent (USA)**[467] 716 4-9-10 **70**.................. SophieDoyle 14 36
(J A Osborne) *nt wl away but sn chsd ldrs and keen early: shoved along bef 1/2-way: wknd over 2f out* **11/2**[2]

1000 **11** *3 ¾* **Sapphire Prince (USA)**[46] 1530 4-9-1 **61**..................(bt[1]) KierenFox 9 18
(J R Best) *prom tl wknd over 2f out: sn bhd* **20/1**

0000 **12** *10* **State General (IRE)**[33] 1877 4-8-8 **61**.................. GeorgeDowning(7) 13 —
(A W Carroll) *a wl in rr: detached in last pair 1/2-way: t.o* **25/1**

1m 39.69s (-0.11) **Going Correction** +0.025s/f (Slow) **12** Ran SP% **117.8**
Speed ratings (Par 103): **101,99,98,97,94 92,92,91,90,81 77,67**
toteswingers: 1&2 £4.20, 1&3 £18.50, 2&3 £28.30 CSF £29.19 CT £338.30 TOTE £2.90: £1.10, £4.10, £8.50; EX 26.50.
Owner O'Brien, Moll, Spencer, Vaux, Davies **Bred** Mrs P Grubb **Trained** Norton, N Yorks

FOCUS
A moderate handicap, confined to apprentice riders. There was a fair pace on and the form looks sound enough for the class.
Musashi(IRE) Official explanation: jockey said gelding missed the break

2867 KEMPTON FOR OUTDOOR EVENTS MAIDEN AUCTION STKS — 6f (P)
6:50 (6:51) (Class 5) 2-Y-0 **£2,590** (£770; £385; £192) **Stalls** High

Form RPR

1 **Striking Priorite** 2-8-9 0.................................. WilliamBuick 3 69+
(R Charlton) *trckd ldng pair: wnt 2nd 1/2-way: pushed into ld wl over 1f out: shkn up ent fnl f: sn drew clr* **10/3**[1]

06 **2** *2 ½* **Lady Morganna (IRE)**[29] 2007 2-8-0 0.................. KierenFox(5) 4 58
(Miss Gay Kelleway) *led to over 4f out: styd prom: tried to chal over 1f out: kpt on to take 2nd nr fin* **14/1**

40 **3** *½* **Comrade Bond**[27] 2059 2-8-10 0.................. TedDurcan 1 61
(M H Tompkins) *s.i.s: rcvrd to ld over 4f out: hdd wl over 1f out: kpt on but lost 2nd nr fin* **9/2**[2]

4 *2* **Laugh Or Cry** 2-8-9 0.................. JimCrowley 11 54
(P J Makin) *chsd ldrs in 6th: shkn up and outpcd 2f out: kpt on one pce fnl f* **9/2**[2]

5 *½* **Camache Queen (IRE)** 2-8-8 0.................. EddieAhern 8 52+
(D J Coakley) *chsd ldng pair: rdn and outpcd fr 2f out: one pce after* **10/3**[1]

6 *1* **Avalon Bay** 2-8-10 0.................. MartinLane(3) 5 54
(Pat Eddery) *awkward and green s: rcvrd to chse ldng quartet: shkn up and outpcd 2f out: no prog after* **11/1**[3]

0 **7** *1 ½* **Stacey**[44] 1577 2-8-4 0.................. NeilChalmers 9 40
(M Blanshard) *walked to post and mounted at s: wl in rr and nvr on terms: sme prog 2f out* **50/1**

8 *1 ¾* **Thank You Joy** 2-7-13 0.................. DannyBrock(7) 10 37
(J R Jenkins) *outpcd and bhd: effrt over 2f out: sn no prog* **25/1**

9 *4* **Local Diktator** 2-8-11 0.................. LukeMorris 12 30
(R A Harris) *wl in rr early: latched on to ldng gp 1/2-way: sn outpcd and rdn: fdd* **16/1**

0 **10** *1 ¾* **Snapshott (IRE)**[64] 1136 2-8-12 0.................. LiamKeniry 7 26
(R A Harris) *sn off the pce: rdn after 2f: wd and green bnd 1/2-way: sn bhd* **40/1**

11 *50* **Arakan Ridge (IRE)** 2-8-11 0.................. RichardThomas 2 —
(R A Harris) *s.v.s: v green and a t.o* **33/1**

1m 14.28s (1.18) **Going Correction** +0.025s/f (Slow) **11** Ran SP% **114.6**
Speed ratings (Par 93): **93,89,89,86,85 84,82,80,74,72 5**
toteswingers: 1&2 £7.80, 1&3 £4.10, 2&3 £6.50 CSF £49.41 TOTE £4.80: £1.50, £4.70, £2.30; EX 42.10.
Owner Peter Webb, R Meaney & J Palfreymann **Bred** Longdon Stud Ltd **Trained** Beckhampton, Wilts

FOCUS
An ordinary juvenile maiden and the form is fluid, with the runner-up rated to her debut mark.

NOTEBOOK
Striking Priorite hails from a decent stable, but cost very little and was drawn poorly for this racecourse debut. The money came for him, though, and he went in with a ready success. He knew his job, negating his low draw, and was going easily 2f out. Once the penny dropped after he was asked to take the race there was only going to be one winner and this already gelded 2-y-o clearly has an engine. (op 7-2 tchd 4-1)
Lady Morganna(IRE) was having her third outing and showed her experience by getting to the front early from her moderate stall. She kept on gamely for pressure and returned to something near her debut form, so rates the best guide for the form.

Comrade Bond had the benefit of two previous spins and was dropping in class, but he too had a poor draw on the outside. His previous experience saw him front rank early, despite him missing the break, and he held every chance. A horse that will benefit switching to nurseries, he should get another furlong in due course. (op 5-1 tchd 13-2)

Laugh Or Cry, speedily bred, was well drawn and attracted support. He ultimately shaped as though this initial outing would do him a deal of good. (tchd 4-1)

Camache Queen(IRE) was another speedily bred newcomer with a good draw. She hit a flat spot before running on when the race was effectively over and will know more next time. (op 7-2 tchd 11-4)

Avalon Bay, yet another with plenty of pace in his pedigree, showed ability and ought to be all the better for this debut outing. Dropping back to the minimum might also suit in the short term. (op 8-1)

Arakan Ridge(IRE) Official explanation: jockey said colt ran green

2868 DIGIBET H'CAP — 6f (P)

7:20 (7:20) (Class 5) (0-75,78) 3-Y-O — **£2,590** (£770; £385; £192) **Stalls** High

Form				RPR
5-11	**1**		**Dever Dream**[6] 2679 3-9-10 **78** 6ex ... RichardHughes 9 (W J Haggas) *trckd ldng pair: cruised up to ld over 1f out: pushed along firmly whn pressed ent fnl f: sn asserted* **4/9**[1]	97+
06-5	**2**	1 ¼	**Gojeri (IRE)**[72] 1050 3-9-1 **69** ... JackMitchell 2 (M A Jarvis) *chsd ldng pair: pushed along bef 1/2-way: prog u.p to go 2nd over 1f out: tried to chal ent fnl f: kpt on but readily hld* **16/1**	80
5-51	**3**	2 ¾	**Dungannon**[23] 2164 3-9-7 **75** ... JimmyFortune 6 (A M Balding) *settled in 6th: rdn wl over 2f out: prog on outer fr wl over 1f out: styd on u.p to take 3rd nr fin* **6/1**[2]	77
6151	**4**	¾	**Knightfire (IRE)**[44] 1584 3-9-7 **75** ... (t) ShaneKelly 11 (W R Swinburn) *chsd clr ldrs in 5th: rdn wl over 2f out: tried to cl over 1f out: one pce* **8/1**[3]	75
423	**5**	nk	**Sulis Minerva (IRE)**[43] 1599 3-9-4 **72** ... (t) LukeMorris 3 (J R Gask) *stdd s: hld up in last quartet and wl off the pce: stdy prog whn bmpd 2f out and hmpd sn after: rallied fnl f: styng on fin* **33/1**	74+
-010	**6**	nk	**Do More Business (IRE)**[33] 1873 3-8-4 **63** ... KierenFox(5) 1 (P M Phelan) *wl off the pce in last quartet: wd bnd 4f out: rdn and kpt on fr over 2f out: n.d* **28/1**	61
-000	**7**	1	**King's Approach (IRE)**[7] 2648 3-8-11 **65** ... (b[1]) LiamKeniry 10 (R A Harris) *chsd clr ldr to 2f out: wknd* **50/1**	59
2220	**8**	1	**Torres Del Paine**[27] 2052 3-9-3 **71** ... PatDobbs 4 (J C Fox) *sn in 7th and nt on terms: swtchd sharply lft 2f out: no prog after* **33/1**	62
1166	**9**	7	**Silver Linnet (IRE)**[37] 1765 3-8-11 **65** ... (b) EddieAhern 5 (M G Quinlan) *led: sn wl clr: hdd & wknd rapidly over 1f out* **33/1**	34
4531	**10**	3	**St Ignatius**[97] 784 3-9-4 **72** ... (b) DaneO'Neill 8 (K O Cunningham-Brown) *a wl in rr and off the pce: struggling fr 1/2-way* **33/1**	31
1600	**11**	3	**Wanchai Whisper**[18] 2320 3-8-9 **63** ... FergusSweeney 12 (P R Hedger) *s.i.s: hld up and sn wl bhd: nvr a factor* **20/1**	13
6-00	**12**	36	**Strike Shot**[34] 1842 3-8-11 **65** ... WilliamBuick 7 (W R Muir) *a bhd: lost tch 1/2-way: wl t.o* **50/1**	—

1m 12.01s (-1.09) **Going Correction** +0.025s/f (Slow) **12 Ran SP% 124.4**

Speed ratings (Par 99): **108,106,102,101,101 100,99,98,88,84 80,32**

toteswingers: 1&2 £4.90, 1&3 £2.80, 2&3 £4.40 CSF £9.28 CT £29.26 TOTE £1.30: £1.02, £5.70, £2.40; EX 13.20.

Owner Options O Syndicate **Bred** F C T Wilson **Trained** Newmarket, Suffolk

■ Stewards' Enquiry : Pat Dobbs three-day ban: careless riding (Jun 23-25)

FOCUS

A fair handicap for the class run at a sound pace and rated around the third and fourth.

2869 DIGIBET.COM H'CAP — 1m 4f (P)

7:50 (7:51) (Class 4) (0-85,81) 3-Y-O — **£4,209** (£1,252; £625; £312) **Stalls** Centre

Form				RPR
4-13	**1**		**Arctic Cosmos (USA)**[26] 2079 3-9-4 **78** ... WilliamBuick 3 (J H M Gosden) *hld up in 9th: plld out wd and gd prog over 2f out to ld over 1f out: wl in command after: pushed out* **3/1**[2]	93
1-53	**2**	4 ½	**Sierra Alpha**[16] 2386 3-9-5 **79** ... TedDurcan 4 (Mrs A J Perrett) *trckd ldr: hung lft and lost 2nd bnd 3f out: sn drvn: styd on fr 2f out to chse wnr fnl f: no ch* **16/1**	86
2-12	**3**	½	**Activate**[26] 2079 3-9-5 **79** ... HayleyTurner 11 (M L W Bell) *trckd ldrs in 5th: effrt over 2f out: rdn and no rspnse sn after: kpt on fr over 1f out to press for 2nd ins fnl f* **2/1**[1]	86
-120	**4**	1	**Dromore (IRE)**[25] 2117 3-9-7 **81** ... JimmyFortune 9 (A M Balding) *t.k.h: hld up in last trio: prog on inner over 2f out: tried to cl over 1f out: outpcd after* **8/1**[3]	86
32-3	**5**	1	**Magnetic Force (IRE)**[16] 2390 3-8-12 **72** ... RichardMullen 12 (Sir Michael Stoute) *trckd ldng pair: wnt 2nd 3f out: rdn and hanging over 2f out: cl enough over 1f out: fdd* **12/1**	75
1116	**6**	2 ¾	**Keenes Royale**[64] 1138 3-9-5 **79** ... (t) JimCrowley 7 (R M Beckett) *trckd ldrs in 6th: gng strly over 3f out: rdn and nt qckn over 2f out: no imp after: fdd ins fnl f* **11/1**	78
3410	**7**	2 ¼	**Beat Route**[18] 2321 3-8-3 **68** ... JemmaMarshall(5) 6 (M J Attwater) *led: hrd pressed over 2f out: hdd & wknd over 1f out* **66/1**	63
4-45	**8**	1	**Missionaire (USA)**[20] 2254 3-9-4 **78** ... ShaneKelly 5 (W J Knight) *dwlt: hld up last: effrt wl over 2f out: limited prog and n.d fr over 1f out* **14/1**	72
1	**9**	3 ¾	**Ugalla**[21] 2231 3-8-10 **77** ... HarryBentley(7) 1 (W J Knight) *racd wd: hld up in 8th: rdn 4f out: sn struggling and wd bnd 3f out* **10/1**	65
1250	**10**	1	**Calypso Star (IRE)**[30] 1975 3-9-3 **77** ... PatDobbs 2 (R Hannon) *hld up in last trio: rdn and no prog wl over 2f out* **25/1**	63
215	**11**	6	**Goodlukin Lucy**[50] 1452 3-9-0 **77** ... MartinLane(3) 8 (Pat Eddery) *hld up in 7th: rdn and no prog over 2f out: sn wknd* **50/1**	54
1-00	**12**	6	**Higgy's Ragazzo (FR)**[26] 2079 3-9-2 **76** ... RichardHughes 10 (R Hannon) *chsd ldng trio: c v wd bnd 3f out and sn ended up against nr side rail: wknd rapidly* **9/1**	43

2m 33.15s (-1.35) **Going Correction** +0.025s/f (Slow) **12 Ran SP% 124.4**

Speed ratings (Par 101): **105,102,101,101,100 98,97,96,93,93 89,85**

toteswingers: 1&2 £15.60, 1&3 £2.00, 2&3 £6.90 CSF £53.03 CT £122.50 TOTE £2.90: £1.10, £7.80, £1.40; EX 75.80.

Owner Ms Rachel D S Hood **Bred** Sheridan & Iadora Farm **Trained** Newmarket, Suffolk

■ Stewards' Enquiry : William Buick one-day ban: careless riding (Jun 23)

FOCUS

A good handicap and an impressive winner. The form looks pretty sound with the first six fairly close to form.

Beat Route Official explanation: vet said colt lost right front shoe

Higgy's Ragazzo(FR) Official explanation: jockey said bit slipped through colt's mouth

2870 DIGIBET CASINO H'CAP — 1m 3f (P)

8:20 (8:21) (Class 6) (0-55,55) 4-Y-O+ — **£2,047** (£604; £302) **Stalls** High

Form				RPR
1000	**1**		**Litenup (IRE)**[29] 2006 4-9-2 **52** ... (t) TedDurcan 5 (A J Lidderdale) *pushed up fr wd draw to ld after 1f: mde rest: drvn 2f out: hrd pressed fr over 1f out: battled on wl* **16/1**	59
-046	**2**	¾	**Champagne Fizz (IRE)**[49] 1478 4-9-4 **54** ... DaneO'Neill 9 (Miss Jo Crowley) *hld up in 7th: rdn over 2f out: prog over 1f out: styd on to win battle for 2nd* **5/1**[2]	60
0-44	**3**	nse	**Iguacu**[9] 2604 6-8-10 **51** ... MatthewDavies(5) 8 (George Baker) *dwlt: hld up in last quartet: smooth prog fr 3f out: rdn 2f out: grad clsd fnl f: hld whn rdr dropped whip nr fin* **11/4**[1]	57
0-50	**4**	nk	**Straight Laced**[22] 2218 4-9-3 **53** ... (v[1]) JimCrowley 10 (W J Knight) *led 1f: chsd wnr after: hrd rdn 3f out: lost 2nd 2f out: kpt on u.p after* **9/1**	58
3652	**5**	nse	**New England**[11] 2529 8-9-1 **51** ... LukeMorris 13 (N J Vaughan) *t.k.h: trckd ldng trio: wnt 2nd 2f out and sn chalng: hld ins fnl f: lost out in battle for 2nd fin* **10/1**	56
3306	**6**	2 ¼	**December**[15] 2417 4-9-4 **54** ... (vt) RichardMullen 2 (Mrs C A Dunnett) *dwlt: hld up in last pair: prog over 2f out: rchd 6th fnl f: no imp after* **14/1**	55
4220	**7**	shd	**Laconicos (IRE)**[18] 2341 8-8-12 **55** ... (t) LauraPike(7) 12 (W B Stone) *t.k.h: hld up in 9th: little room on inner 3f out and lost pl: nt clr run over 2f out: kpt on fr over 1f out: no ch* **11/2**[3]	59+
0-00	**8**	2 ¼	**Some Time Good (IRE)**[22] 2198 4-8-13 **52** ... (p) RussKennemore(3) 7 (Miss J S Davis) *trckd ldng trio: hrd rdn and nt qckn wl over 2f out: wknd fnl f* **20/1**	49
00-3	**9**	nse	**Filun**[60] 1226 5-9-5 **55** ... (t) IanMongan 6 (A Middleton) *dwlt: hld up in last pair: wd bnd 3f out: drvn and effrt over 2f out: no imp over 1f out: wknd* **12/1**	52
60-4	**10**	3 ¼	**Mayfair's Future**[19] 2303 5-9-2 **52** ... RichardHughes 1 (J R Jenkins) *hld up in 8th: rdn over 2f out: no prog over 1f out: wknd fnl f* **8/1**	43
1000	**11**	10	**Mekong Miss**[19] 2303 4-9-5 **55** ... ShaneKelly 11 (J Jay) *chsd ldrs in 6th: rdn over 2f out: sn wknd: eased* **25/1**	28
0500	**12**	3 ¼	**Fleur De'Lion (IRE)**[6] 2676 4-9-5 **55** ... JimmyFortune 4 (S Kirk) *hld up in last quartet: rdn and wd bnd 3f out: sn wknd: t.o* **33/1**	22
330/	**13**	21	**Arniecoco**[256] 3483 5-8-13 **54** ... (p) SladeO'Hara(5) 14 (Ms E L McWilliam) *disp 2nd pl to over 4f out: sn lost pl: wknd rapidly over 2f out: wl t.o* **50/1**	—

2m 22.5s (0.60) **Going Correction** +0.025s/f (Slow) **13 Ran SP% 122.7**

Speed ratings (Par 101): **98,97,97,97,97 95,95,93,93,91 84,81,66**

toteswingers: 1&2 £24.30, 1&3 £11.40, 2&3 £4.60 CSF £93.37 CT £296.90 TOTE £25.50: £6.40, £1.80, £2.30; EX 185.20.

Owner A C Entertainment Technologies Ltd **Bred** Rathasker Stud **Trained** Eastbury, Berks

FOCUS

A weak handicap. With only 4lb covering the field, it wasn't that surprising to see such a close finish. The form is muddling rated around the first three

Laconicos(IRE) Official explanation: jockey said gelding was denied a clear run

Some Time Good(IRE) Official explanation: jockey said gelding hung right in straight

Filun Official explanation: jockey said gelding was slowly away

2871 BOOK KEMPTON TICKETS ON 0844 579 3008 FILLIES' H'CAP — 7f (P)

8:50 (8:52) (Class 5) (0-70,70) 3-Y-O — **£2,590** (£770; £385; £192) **Stalls** High

Form				RPR
6600	**1**		**Al Khimiya (IRE)**[18] 2342 3-9-5 **68** ... JimCrowley 3 (S Woodman) *mde all and crossed fr wd draw: drvn over 1f out: kpt on wl fnl f* **10/1**	73
-066	**2**	¾	**That's My Style**[21] 2227 3-9-7 **70** ... WilliamBuick 10 (J H M Gosden) *trckd ldng pair: drvn to go 2nd on inner wl over 1f out: chal after but hld ins fnl f* **10/1**	73
-513	**3**	¾	**Flouncing (IRE)**[23] 2178 3-9-7 **70** ... RichardHughes 12 (W J Haggas) *hld up in midfield: clsd on ldrs fr 2f out: pressed ldng pair 1f out: n.m.r but also nt pce to deliver telling blow* **3/1**[1]	71
23-3	**4**	nk	**Baby Dottie**[15] 2416 3-9-6 **69** ... IanMongan 8 (P M Phelan) *trckd ldng trio: rdn and nt qckn wl over 1f out: styd on ins fnl f: nrst fin* **9/2**[3]	69
-036	**5**	nse	**Blue Again**[18] 2342 3-9-7 **70** ... AdamKirby 9 (W R Swinburn) *hld up towards rr: prog over 2f out: drvn over 1f out: nt pce to threaten but kpt on: nrst fin* **4/1**[2]	70+
10-0	**6**	½	**Cat Hunter**[27] 2042 3-9-4 **67** ... EddieAhern 5 (Mrs A J Perrett) *chsd ldrs in 5th: rdn and nt qckn 2f out: kpt on fnl f: nvr able to chal* **16/1**	66
-060	**7**	1 ½	**Katehari (IRE)**[18] 2342 3-9-7 **70** ... (v) JimmyFortune 1 (A M Balding) *sn chsd wnr: drvn and lost 2nd wl over 1f out: stl chsng ldrs ent fnl f: fdd* **25/1**	64
3316	**8**	¾	**Posy Fossil (USA)**[41] 1640 3-8-12 **64** ... (t) WilliamCarson(3) 13 (S C Williams) *chsd ldrs: pushed along on inner and nt qckn over 2f out: no hdwy after* **12/1**	56
-040	**9**	1 ¼	**So Surreal (IRE)**[9] 2587 3-9-6 **69** ... (b) GeorgeBaker 6 (G L Moore) *nvr bttr than midfield: u.p and no prog 2f out* **25/1**	58
222-	**10**	½	**Zubova**[162] 7864 3-9-6 **69** ... (t) TedDurcan 7 (Rae Guest) *awkward s: hld up in last pair: brief effrt over 2f out: sn no prog* **16/1**	57
5-25	**11**	2	**Madame Roulin (IRE)**[29] 2005 3-9-1 **64** ... HayleyTurner 4 (M L W Bell) *dwlt: hld up last: shkn up and no rspnse 3f out: pushed along after and n.d* **22/1**	46
00-6	**12**	2 ¼	**Highland Jewel (IRE)**[13] 2478 3-9-1 **64** ... LukeMorris 11 (C G Cox) *awkward s: a in rr: u.p and no prog over 2f out* **8/1**	40
-020	**13**	nse	**Hanbelation (USA)**[8] 2628 3-9-1 **67** ... MartinLane(3) 14 (E F Vaughan) *nvr bttr than midfield: wknd 2f out* **40/1**	43

1m 26.67s (0.67) **Going Correction** +0.025s/f (Slow) **13 Ran SP% 126.4**

Speed ratings (Par 96): **97,96,95,94,94 94,92,91,90,89 87,84,84**

toteswingers: 1&2 £9.40, 1&3 £12.70, 2&3 £9.50 CSF £107.84 CT £397.25 TOTE £15.30: £4.60, £3.00, £1.30; EX 100.60.

Owner Al Khimiya Partnership **Bred** Plantation Stud **Trained** East Lavant, W Sussex

FOCUS

A moderate 3-y-o handicap and not form to be too confident about, with the form rated around the first two and fourth.

Blue Again Official explanation: jockey said filly ran too free

2872 BOOK NOW FOR BEST OF BRITISH NIGHT H'CAP 7f (P)
9:20 (9:20) (Class 4) (0-80,80) 4-Y-O+ £4,209 (£1,252; £625; £312) Stalls High

Form RPR

3-43 **1** **Cape Rock**[26] 2091 5-9-7 80 ... JimCrowley 4 92
(W J Knight) *racd keenly: led after 1f: drvn over 1f out: styd on wl fnl f: hld on* 7/1

2-20 **2** ½ **Clockmaker (IRE)**[50] 1450 4-9-4 77 ... WilliamBuick 3 88
(J H M Gosden) *racd wd early: prog to chse wnr after 2f: drvn and nt qckn 2f out: dropped to 3rd over 1f out: rallied fnl f: clsng nr fin* 11/2[3]

-631 **3** 2 ¼ **Regeneration (IRE)**[32] 1933 4-9-6 79 ... HayleyTurner 5 84
(M L W Bell) *t.k.h: led 1f: trckd ldng pair after 2f: rdn to chse wnr over 1f out and tried to chal: lost 2nd and fdd ins fnl f* 5/2[2]

-101 **4** ½ **Quasi Congaree (GER)**[34] 1848 4-9-2 75 ... (t) RichardHughes 13 79+
(I A Wood) *hld up towards rr: plenty to do whn asked for effrt over 1f out: styd on: no ch to chal* 16/1

-260 **5** ¾ **Defector (IRE)**[32] 1933 4-9-2 75 ... GeorgeBaker 11 77
(W R Muir) *chsd ldrs on outer: rdn and nt qckn over 2f out: kpt on fnl f* 20/1

5606 **6** ½ **Totally Focussed (IRE)**[30] 1962 5-9-7 80 ... (v[1]) EddieAhern 8 80+
(S Dow) *hld up in rr: effrt 2f out: shkn up and nt qckn over 1f out: kpt on* 25/1

-321 **7** hd **Mishrif (USA)**[21] 2236 4-9-6 79 ... (b) JimmyFortune 10 79
(J R Jenkins) *sn in 4th: shkn up 2f out: nt qckn and wl hld over 1f out: fdd* 2/1[1]

-560 **8** 1 ½ **Hellbender (IRE)**[5] 2719 4-9-1 74 ... JamesDoyle 12 70
(S Kirk) *t.k.h: hld up in midfield on inner: no imp on ldrs over 1f out* 50/1

-200 **9** 1 **Sunshine Always (IRE)**[101] 747 4-9-4 77 ... KirstyMilczarek 9 70
(T D McCarthy) *hld up in rr: shkn up 2f out: kpt on but nvr a threat* 33/1

-000 **10** 3 **Block Party**[18] 2328 4-9-0 73 ... TedDurcan 6 58
(D M Simcock) *a towards rr on outer: struggling 2f out* 16/1

04-0 **11** nk **Leverage (IRE)**[33] 1862 4-9-1 79 ... TobyAtkinson(5) 14 63
(M Wigham) *v awkward s and for 1st 100yds: wl bhd: nvr involved* 25/1

-560 **12** 2 ½ **Cerito**[7] 2657 4-8-13 77 ... MatthewDavies(5) 7 54
(J R Boyle) *a towards rr: rdn and no prog over 2f out: wknd over 1f out* 66/1

1m 25.2s (-0.80) **Going Correction** +0.025s/f (Slow) **12** Ran SP% **120.4**
Speed ratings (Par 105): **105,104,101,101,100 99,99,97,96,93 93,90**
toteswingers: 1&2 £4.20, 1&3 £3.60, 2&3 £3.20 CSF £42.65 CT £121.11 TOTE £10.30: £2.70, £3.30, £1.10; EX 45.20 Place 6 £18.88, Place 5 £7.31.
Owner Mrs B Sumner **Bred** Bricklow Ltd **Trained** Patching, W Sussex

FOCUS
A fair handicap and yet another race where it proved an advantage to be handy. The form looks reasonable rated around the third, fourth and fifth.
Mishrif(USA) Official explanation: jockey said gelding ran too free
Sunshine Always(IRE) Official explanation: jockey said gelding was slowly away
Leverage(IRE) Official explanation: jockey said gelding was slowly away
T/Plt: £15.60 to a £1 stake. Pool: £69,712.08. 3,256.07 winning tickets. T/Qpdt: £5.70 to a £1 stake. Pool: £5,622.31. 721.61 winning tickets. JN

2630 YARMOUTH (L-H)
Wednesday, June 9

OFFICIAL GOING: Good (7.1)
Wind: Virtually nil Weather: Cloudy, dry

2873 FREE RACING WITH ODDSCHECKER.COM WEDNESDAYS MAIDEN AUCTION STKS 5f 43y
2:10 (2:11) (Class 5) 2-Y-O £2,590 (£770; £385; £192) Stalls High

Form RPR

22 **1** **Leiba Leiba**[33] 1871 2-8-10 0 ... SebSanders 5 72+
(M Botti) *t.k.h: hld up wl in tch: hdwy to trck ldr 2f out: rdn to ld over 1f out: r.o wl* 4/11[1]

04 **2** 4 **Joe Junior**[12] 2486 2-9-0 0 ... DavidProbert 9 62
(Miss Gay Kelleway) *led: rdn ent fnl 2f: hdd over 1f out: no ch w wnr ins fnl f but kpt on for clr 2nd* 33/1

3 2 ¼ **Hawk Moth (IRE)** 2-8-8 0 ... JackDean(3) 2 51
(J L Spearing) *in tch towards rr: pushed along and nt pce of ldrs wl over 1f out: rdn and kpt on to go 3rd ent fnl f: no ch w ldng pair* 18/1

0 **4** 2 ¼ **Volcanic Dust (IRE)**[12] 2505 2-8-7 0 ... HayleyTurner 3 38+
(E A L Dunlop) *t.k.h: hld up in tch towards rr: rdn and rn green ent fnl 2f: plugged on to go modest 4th ins fnl f: nvr trbld ldrs* 12/1[3]

3 **5** 1 **Dotty Darroch**[22] 2210 2-7-12 0 ... MatthewLawson(7) 6 33
(R Bastiman) *s.i.s: sn bustled along in last pair: hdwy on outer 1/2-way: wknd over 1f out: no ch fnl f* 6/1[2]

0030 **6** ½ **The Best Mode (IRE)**[18] 2312 2-8-11 0 ... AndrewHeffernan(3) 4 40
(P D Evans) *chsd ldng pair: rdn and edgd rt wl over 1f out: wknd u.p over 1f out: wl btn fnl f* 16/1

7 ½ **Sabratha (IRE)** 2-8-4 0 ... DaraghO'Donohoe 7 28+
(B J Curley) *v.s.a: rn green and sn pushed along in rr: hdwy ent fnl 2f: nt clr run and swtchd rt wl over 1f out: nvr trbld ldrs* 50/1

0 **8** 2 ¼ **Key To The Motion (IRE)**[43] 1597 2-8-4 0 ... JimmyQuinn 1 20
(P T Midgley) *dwlt: sn rcvrd and in tch in midfield: rdn ent fnl 2f: wknd qckly u.p over 1f out: wl btn fnl f* 66/1

04 **9** 5 **Blade Pirate**[10] 2561 2-8-10 0 ... MarcHalford 8 8
(J Ryan) *chsd ldr tl 2f out: wkng u.p whn sltly hmpd wl over 1f out: wl bhd and eased ins fnl f* 25/1

63.43 secs (0.73) **Going Correction** -0.05s/f (Good) **9** Ran SP% **116.7**
Speed ratings (Par 93): **88,81,78,74,72 72,71,67,59**
toteswingers: 1&2 £6.90, 1&3 £6.60, 2&3 £10.90 CSF £24.86 TOTE £1.30: £1.02, £7.70, £4.30; EX 15.70 Trifecta £81.50 Pool: £361.44 - 3.28 winning units..
Owner Dachel Stud **Bred** Dachel Stud **Trained** Newmarket, Suffolk

FOCUS
A weak-looking maiden in which the winner ran to form.

NOTEBOOK
Leiba Leiba, a half-brother to the Listed placed Tia Mia, looked to have been handed another great chance to collect his first victory, and this time he didn't disappoint. He got to the front about 1f out and kept on strongly to claim the win. (op 1-2, tchd 4-7 in a place)
Joe Junior showed good pace up the stands' side rail but was unable to match the winner for gears in the latter stages. (op 22-1)
Hawk Moth(IRE) attracted market support on his debut and shaped well after looking green. Considering his size, he ought to improve. (op 28-1 tchd 14-1)
Volcanic Dust(IRE), a half-sister to winners, went off an unfancied 66/1 shot on her first start at Newmarket but showed a bit more in this after racing keenly. She still looked inexperienced under pressure, so is another who can make progress.
Dotty Darroch shaped nicely on her debut when starting at 33/1 (the winner of that race has gone on to win again) but was never in this, racing wide of the pack. Official explanation: jockey said filly missed the break (op 7-1 tchd 8-1)
Sabratha(IRE) wasn't the quickest away, but caught the eye towards the end of the contest, as she was making progress when finding little room. She is bred to need about 1m in time. (op 33-1)

2874 PLEASUREWOOD HILLS MAIDEN H'CAP 1m 3y
2:40 (2:40) (Class 6) (0-65,60) 4-Y-O+ £1,942 (£578; £288; £144) Stalls High

Form RPR

3044 **1** **King's Sabre**[8] 2624 4-8-11 50 ... (e) PaulEddery 3 61+
(R C Guest) *taken down early: stdd and awkward leaving stalls: hld up in rr: hdwy on outer 3f out: rdn to ld ent fnl f: hung bdly rt but asserting 1f out: clr fnl 100yds: eased towards fin* 11/2[2]

6 **2** 2 ½ **Macanta (USA)**[16] 2388 4-9-5 58 ... NickyMackay 14 63
(G A Butler) *t.k.h: hld up in tch: hdwy over 3f out: led ent fnl 2f: drvn wl over 1f out: hdd ent fnl f: styd on same pce after* 5/1[1]

20-0 **3** shd **Rascal In The Mix (USA)**[32] 1919 4-8-6 50 ... AmyRyan(5) 4 55
(R M Whitaker) *hld up wl in tch: hdwy to join ldrs over 2f out: ev ch and rdn 2f out: nt pce of wnr 1f out: plugged on same pce fnl f* 18/1

000- **4** 3 **Exopuntia**[259] 6217 4-8-6 52 ... AdamBeschizza(7) 7 50+
(Miss J Feilden) *stdd s: t.k.h: hld up wl in rr: rdn along and hdwy over 1f out: edgd rt but styd on fnl f: wnt 4th on line: nvr trbld ldrs* 33/1

0-00 **5** nse **Summers Target (USA)**[19] 2298 4-8-12 54 ... (t) WilliamCarson(3) 15 52
(S C Williams) *stdd s: t.k.h: hld up in rr: swtchd rt and effrt u.p 2f out: hung lft and no prog ent fnl f* 14/1

444 **6** nk **Cruise Control**[9] 2596 4-8-11 50 ... (p) HayleyTurner 10 47
(R J Price) *hld up in tch in midfield: hdwy over 2f out: chsd ldrs and rdn over 1f out: hung lft u.p and btn 1f out* 6/1[3]

06-0 **7** 2 **Action Girl**[15] 2419 5-8-12 51 ... (p) RichardMullen 9 44
(R M H Cowell) *chsd ldrs: rdn ent fnl 2f: wknd u.p over 1f out: wl hld fnl f* 16/1

60-0 **8** nk **Duke Of Normandy (IRE)**[13] 2477 4-8-8 47 ... JamieMackay 12 39
(B P J Baugh) *led: hdd and rdn ent fnl 2f: wknd u.p over 1f out* 22/1

6/00 **9** 1 ½ **Ernmoor**[9] 2604 8-8-6 45 ... CathyGannon 5 34
(A E Price) *chsd ldrs: rdn over 2f out: wkng whn n.m.r over 1f out: n.d fnl f* 20/1

5400 **10** 2 **Montego Breeze**[48] 1490 4-8-6 45 ... (p) DaraghO'Donohoe 1 29
(John A Harris) *in tch on outer: rdn 3f out: kpt on u.p tl wknd over 1f out: wl btn fnl f* 50/1

466- **11** 10 **Croeso Ynol**[266] 6005 4-8-9 48 ... SebSanders 13 9
(H J Evans) *stdd s: t.k.h: hld up in rr: effrt and hung lft over 2f out: lost tch wl over 1f out: eased ins fnl f* 12/1

0-00 **12** ½ **Forced Opinion (USA)**[82] 942 5-8-7 46 ... JimmyQuinn 8 6
(K A Morgan) *stdd s: hld up towards rr: hdwy over 3f out: rdn over 2f out: wknd qckly wl over 1f out: wl btn and eased ins fnl f* 14/1

030- **13** ½ **Galley Slave (IRE)**[9] 4519 5-8-3 45 ... (b) AndrewHeffernan(3) 6 4
(M C Chapman) *in tch tl struggling and rdn 1/2-way: wl bhd fnl 2f: eased ins fnl f* 16/1

656- **14** 5 **Rebel Woman**[196] 7517 4-8-13 52 ... FergusSweeney 11 —
(J A Osborne) *stdd s: t.k.h and hld up towards rr: hdwy 3f out: rdn and no prog over 2f out: wl btn and eased ent fnl f* 13/2

2U0- **15** 7 **Princess Aliuska**[296] 5093 5-9-7 60 ... DavidProbert 2 —
(C Smith) *chsd ldr tl over 2f out: sn wknd u.p: wl btn and eased fnl f: t.o* 12/1

1m 41.0s (0.40) **Going Correction** -0.05s/f (Good) **15** Ran SP% **119.4**
Speed ratings (Par 101): **96,93,93,90,90 90,88,87,86,84 74,73,73,68,61**
toteswingers: 1&2 £5.50, 1&3 £40.50, 2&3 £40.50 CSF £31.05 CT £480.91 TOTE £8.40: £3.10, £2.90, £4.60; EX 23.40 Trifecta £87.30 Pool: £118.04 - 1.00 winning units..
Owner Future Racing (Notts) Limited **Bred** Cheveley Park Stud Ltd **Trained** Stainforth, S Yorks

FOCUS
When the top weight for a handicap hasn't finished within 16l of a winner in any of its races, one is fairly safe in presuming that the contest took little winning. The placed horses set the level.
Ernmoor Official explanation: jockey said gelding hung left
Rebel Woman Official explanation: jockey said filly lost its action

2875 GREAT YARMOUTH LADIES NIGHT H'CAP (DIV I) 7f 3y
3:10 (3:10) (Class 6) (0-60,60) 3-Y-O+ £1,619 (£481; £240; £120) Stalls High

Form RPR

6602 **1** **Miss Kitty Grey (IRE)**[8] 2634 3-8-8 45 ... NickyMackay 2 56+
(J R Boyle) *chsd ldrs: rdn to ld 2f out: kpt on wl fnl f* 9/4[1]

0-0 **2** 2 **Bold Diktator**[12] 2512 8-9-7 58 ... (v[1]) AmyRyan(5) 1 63
(R M Whitaker) *in tch rdn and effrt on outer ent fnl 2f: chsd wnr over 1f out: one pce and no imp ins fnl f* 25/1

2-50 **3** 3 **Many Welcomes**[44] 1585 5-9-4 55 ... JemmaMarshall(5) 8 52
(B P J Baugh) *in tch in midfield: rdn and effrt ent fnl 2f: chsd ldng pair u.p ent fnl f: plugged on but no imp* 11/1

0000 **4** 1 ½ **Easy Wonder (GER)**[20] 2257 5-8-13 45 ... CathyGannon 5 38
(I A Wood) *hld up in tch towards rr: rdn and effrt ent fnl 2f: plugged on steadily u.p fnl f: no ch w ldrs* 40/1

0-55 **5** 2 ¾ **Faithful Duchess (IRE)**[19] 2274 3-9-4 60 ... JamieSpencer 10 41
(E A L Dunlop) *stdd s: hld up in last pair: hdwy 3f out: pressed ldrs and rdn 2f out: hung lft u.p and btn over 1f out: wknd fnl f* 3/1[2]

1-36 **6** 2 ½ **Clumber Place**[14] 2429 4-9-8 54 ... PaulEddery 6 33
(R C Guest) *t.k.h: chsd ldr tl led and rdn over 2f out: sn hdd: wknd qckly over 1f out: wl btn fnl f* 9/1

003- **7** 1 ¼ **Baby Rock**[285] 5406 5-9-5 58 ... RoryHanley(7) 7 33
(C F Wall) *pressed ldrs: pushed along ent fnl 2f: wknd over 1f out: wl btn fnl f* 10/1

000 **8** 2 **Major Eradicator (USA)**[23] 2174 3-8-13 55 ... RichardMullen 9 21
(R M H Cowell) *dwlt: sn pushed along: hdwy into midfield: edging lft and btn wl over 1f out: wl bhd fnl f* 13/2[3]

000 **9** ¾ **Greystoke Prince**[15] 2414 5-8-6 45 ... CarolineKelly(7) 4 18
(M D Squance) *led tl over 2f out: wknd qckly wl over 1f out: wl btn and eased fnl f* 33/1

6140 **10** 22 **Resplendent Nova**[54] 1350 8-9-6 52 ... JimmyQuinn 3 —
(P Howling) *in tch tl dropped to rr and rdn w no rspnse wl over 3f out: lost tch 2f out: t.o and virtually p.u fnl f* 8/1

1m 27.56s (0.96) **Going Correction** -0.05s/f (Good)
WFA 3 from 4yo+ 10lb **10** Ran SP% **116.9**
Speed ratings (Par 101): **92,89,86,84,81 78,77,74,74,48**
toteswingers: 1&2 £9.60, 1&3 £8.30, 2&3 £50.70 CSF £65.30 CT £534.58 TOTE £4.10: £1.60, £5.50, £3.50; EX 92.60 Trifecta £166.60 Part won. Pool: £225.22 - 0.41 winning units..
Owner Inside Track Racing Club **Bred** C Amerian **Trained** Epsom, Surrey

FOCUS
The first division of a moderate handicap and the level is fluid with little solid form amongst those behind the winner.
Greystoke Prince Official explanation: jockey said saddle slipped

The Form Book, Raceform Ltd, Compton, RG20 6NL

Resplendent Nova Official explanation: jockey said gelding lost its action

2876 GREAT YARMOUTH LADIES NIGHT H'CAP (DIV II) 7f 3y
3:40 (3:40) (Class 6) (0-60,58) 3-Y-0+ **£1,619** (£481; £240; £120) **Stalls** High

Form RPR

0011 **1** **Collect Art (IRE)**[8] 2634 3-9-2 **58** 6ex..........................(v) HayleyTurner 10 71
(M L W Bell) *w ldr tl led ent fnl 3f: rdn and drew clr w runner-up over 1f out: hdd 1f out: hrd drvn ins fnl f: kpt on to ld again nr fin* **7/4**[1]

440- **2** *hd* **Via Aurelia (IRE)**[226] 7061 3-8-9 **51**.......................... JamieSpencer 6 63
(J R Fanshawe) *stdd after s: hld up in last pair: swtchd rt and hdwy gng wl 2f out: upsides wnr and clr of field over 1f out: rdn to ld 1f out: hrd drvn and edgd lft u.p ins fnl f: hdd nr fin* **3/1**[2]

-200 **3** *9* **Eye For The Girls**[27] 2053 4-9-8 **54**.......................... CathyGannon 8 50+
(M R Channon) *in tch: rdn and struggling whn hmpd and lost pl over 2f out: sn swtchd rt and drvn: no ch w ldrs but kpt on to go modest 3rd fnl 100yds* **16/1**

-000 **4** *3* **Clerical (USA)**[112] 576 4-8-13 **45**..........................(p) J-PGuillambert 9 32+
(R M H Cowell) *in tch: rdn and edgd lft 2f out: wl outpcd by ldrs over 1f out: wnt modest 3rd 1f out tl fnl 100yds* **40/1**

0050 **5** *3* **Loyal Knight (IRE)**[4] 2764 5-8-13 **45**..........................(t) JimmyQuinn 4 21
(P T Midgley) *racd alone in centre tl 3f out: in tch in midfield: rdn and btn ent fnl 2f: no ch fr wl over 1f out* **14/1**

0005 **6** *1 ½* **Baby Judge (IRE)**[8] 2617 3-8-5 **52** ow3..........................(b) MarkCoumbe(5) 5 20
(M C Chapman) *led tl hdd and rdn ent fnl 3f: wknd u.p wl over 1f out: wl btn fnl f* **50/1**

0413 **7** *1 ¾* **Yakama (IRE)**[12] 2490 5-9-10 **56**..........................(v) DavidProbert 1 23
(Mrs C A Dunnett) *dwlt and pushed along early: in tch in rr: rdn and hdwy 3f out: drvn and btn 2f: wl bhd fnl f* **6/1**[3]

0505 **8** *1 ¼* **Whotsit (IRE)**[50] 1443 4-9-8 **54**..........................(b) DaraghO'Donohoe 7 33
(Miss Amy Weaver) *chsd ldrs: rdn and edgd rt jst over 2f out: 3rd and outpcd by ldng pair over 1f out: lost 3rd 1f out: heavily eased ins fnl f* **22/1**

0500 **9** *2* **Slap And Tickle (IRE)**[22] 2196 4-9-3 **52**.......................... WilliamCarson(3) 3 10
(M D Squance) *taken down early: stdd s and dropped in bhd: swtchd lft and effrt over 2f out: nt clr run and squeezed out ent fnl 2f: wl bhd after* **40/1**

3-05 **10** *7* **It's A Mans World**[15] 2410 4-9-9 **58**..........................(v) AndrewHeffernan(3) 2 —
(P D Evans) *in tch: rdn and lost pl over 2f out: lost tch u.p 2f out: t.o and eased ins fnl f* **7/1**

1m 26.93s (0.33) **Going Correction** -0.05s/f (Good)
WFA 3 from 4yo+ 10lb **10** Ran SP% **111.9**
Speed ratings (Par 101): **96,95,85,82,78 76,74,73,71,63**
toteswingers: 1&2 £2.20, 1&3 £3.60, 2&3 £44.70 CSF £6.22 CT £56.81 TOTE £2.30: £1.10, £2.00, £3.10; EX 6.90 Trifecta £42.40 Pool: £415.85 - 7.25 winning units..
Owner R A Green **Bred** Pier House Stud **Trained** Newmarket, Suffolk
■ Stewards' Enquiry : Daragh O'Donohoe two-day ban: careless riding (Jun 23-24)

FOCUS
Two horses pulled well clear of the remainder in this, which suggested that they can both can be followed next time. the form is tricky to pin down but the winner is improving.
Yakama(IRE) Official explanation: jockey said gelding never travelled
Whotsit(IRE) Official explanation: trainer said gelding lost its action

2877 WELL BALANCED LEDGER AT JHSIMPSON.CO.UK H'CAP 6f 3y
4:10 (4:13) (Class 4) (0-85,85) 3-Y-0+ **£4,163** (£1,246; £623; £311; £155) **Stalls** High

Form RPR

1-32 **1** **Deacon Blues**[32] 1917 3-9-1 **81**.......................... JamieSpencer 3 96+
(J R Fanshawe) *stdd after s: hld up in last pair: hdwy over 2f out: rdn and qcknd to ld 1f out: r.o strly: comf* **5/6**[1]

4630 **2** *3 ½* **Angus Newz**[10] 2563 7-9-12 **84**.......................... SebSanders 2 88
(M Quinn) *chsd ldrs: rdn and ev ch 2f out: led over 1f out tl 1f out: nt pce of wnr ins fnl f but hld on for 2nd* **12/1**[3]

0-10 **3** *½* **Street Power (USA)**[32] 1900 5-9-13 **85**.......................... AdamKirby 1 87
(J R Gask) *stdd s and dropped in bhd: hld up in rr: pushed along and hdwy over 2f out: rdn wl over 1f out: hdwy between horses ent fnl f: pressing for 2nd fnl f but no ch w wnr* **11/4**[2]

211- **4** *hd* **Fantasy Gladiator**[258] 6230 4-9-3 **75**.......................... DaraghO'Donohoe 5 76
(R M H Cowell) *s.i.s: niggled along and bhd early: hdwy into midfield 4f out: rdn and pressed ldr wl over 1f out: hung lft and nt pce of wnr 1f out: styd on same pce fnl f* **16/1**

4300 **5** *1 ¼* **Bel Cantor**[35] 1826 7-9-3 **82**.......................... AdamBeschizza(7) 6 79
(W J H Ratcliffe) *led: rdn over 2f out: hdd & wknd over 1f out* **14/1**

0450 **6** *2* **Hatta Stream (IRE)**[16] 2399 4-9-0 **72**.......................... SaleemGolam 8 63
(J Pearce) *in tch: rdn and unable qck ent fnl 2f: wknd u.p jst over 1f out* **33/1**

0300 **7** *2 ¼* **Vhujon (IRE)**[16] 2399 5-8-13 **74**.......................... AndrewHeffernan(3) 7 58
(P D Evans) *chsd ldrs: rdn and effrt over 2f out: wknd u.p over 1f out: wl btn fnl f* **20/1**

-000 **8** *8* **Desert Falls**[11] 2524 4-8-6 **69**.......................... AmyRyan(5) 4 27
(R M Whitaker) *w ldr: rdn over 2f out: wknd qckly and bhd fr over 1f out* **25/1**

1m 13.54s (-0.86) **Going Correction** -0.05s/f (Good)
WFA 3 from 4yo+ 8lb **8** Ran SP% **113.0**
Speed ratings (Par 105): **103,98,97,97,95 93,90,79**
toteswingers: 1&2 £3.00, 1&3 £1.20, 2&3 £2.90 CSF £12.07 CT £20.77 TOTE £2.00: £1.10, £1.10, £1.30; EX 8.00 Trifecta £14.10 Pool: £726.75 - 37.88 winning units..
Owner Jan & Peter Hopper & Michelle Morris **Bred** Mr & Mrs K W Grundy, Mr & Mrs P Hopper **Trained** Newmarket, Suffolk

FOCUS
An interesting handicap, but one in which only a couple of the runners looked possible improvers for the future. The winner is improving and the runner-up is rated to her Newmarket form.

2878 BENNETTS THE ELECTRICAL EXPERTS APPRENTICE (S) STKS 1m 1f
4:40 (4:40) (Class 6) 3-Y-0 **£1,683** (£501; £250; £125) **Stalls** Low

Form RPR

-000 **1** **Fasette**[8] 2633 3-8-4 55.......................... AshleyMorgan(3) 1 59
(M H Tompkins) *hld up in last trio: hdwy to chse ldrs 4f out: rdn to ld over 1f out: hung rt ent fnl f: styd on wl to go clr fnl 150yds* **7/1**

6043 **2** *5* **Brave Decision**[15] 2414 3-8-12 59.......................... WilliamCarson 10 53
(R M H Cowell) *sn led: hung bdly rt bnd over 4f out: racd on stands' rail fnl 3f: rdn wl over 2f out: hdd over 1f out: one pce and no ch w wnr fnl 150yds* **9/4**[1]

6365 **3** *1* **Sultan's Choice**[8] 2619 3-8-13 54..........................(v) AndrewHeffernan 4 52
(P D Evans) *in tch: chsd ldrs 4f out: rdn and nt qckn ent fnl 2f: hrd drvn and styd on one pce fr over 1f out: wnt 3rd nr fin* **9/2**[2]

5636 **4** *½* **Prince Yarraman (IRE)**[17] 2359 3-8-12 55....... Louis-PhilippeBeuzelin 3 50
(J A Osborne) *chsd ldrs: rdn and pressing ldr wl over 2f out: styng on one pce whn carried rt 1f out: no ch w wnr fnl 150yds* **9/2**[2]

4505 **5** *nk* **Always De One**[18] 2333 3-8-0 51.......................... AdamBeschizza(7) 9 44
(Miss J Feilden) *hld up in last trio: hdwy to chse ldrs 4f out: rdn 2f out: styng on same pce whn carried rt 1f out: wl hld whn rdr dropped whip nr fin* **10/1**

5002 **6** *13* **Mnarani (IRE)**[5] 2724 3-8-7 58..........................(b) RyanPowell(5) 2 20
(J S Moore) *chsd ldr: carried rt bnd over 4f out: swtchd lft and rdn 3f out: hung lft and rt over 1f out: wl btn ent fnl f* **6/1**[3]

0 **7** *9* **Faustina**[10] 2564 3-8-7 0.......................... MarcHalford 7 —
(Miss Amy Weaver) *s.i.s and hmpd s: a last trio: short of room bnd 6f out: lost tch 3f out* **40/1**

00-0 **8** *16* **Gessabelle**[7] 2651 3-8-0 45..........................(t) LeonnaMayor(7) 5 —
(P S McEntee) *chsd ldrs: struggling and rdn over 3f out: wl bhd fnl 2f: t.o* **33/1**

00-0 **9** *9* **Naughty Norris**[24] 2143 3-8-7 35.......................... MatthewLawson(5) 6 —
(R Bastiman) *in tch in midfield tl lost pl qckly over 4f out: t.o fnl 2f* **66/1**

1m 57.43s (1.63) **Going Correction** -0.05s/f (Good) **9** Ran SP% **109.9**
Speed ratings (Par 97): **90,85,84,84,83 72,64,50,42**
toteswingers: 1&2 £4.00, 1&3 £5.80, 2&3 £2.40 CSF £21.28 TOTE £9.00: £3.10, £2.10, £1.10; EX 26.40 Trifecta £91.80 Pool: £423.40 - 3.41 winning units..There was no bid for the winner.
Owner Raceworld **Bred** D D And Mrs Jean P Clee **Trained** Newmarket, Suffolk
■ Stewards' Enquiry : Ashley Morgan two-day ban: careless riding (23-24 June)
William Carson three-day ban: careless riding (23-25 June)

FOCUS
With the highest-rated horse having an official rating of 59, this was only a moderate contest of its type. The third and fourth are rated close to recent handicap form.

2879 GREAT YARMOUTH MERCURY H'CAP 6f 3y
5:10 (5:12) (Class 6) (0-65,65) 3-Y-0 **£1,942** (£578; £288; £144) **Stalls** High

Form RPR

0464 **1** **Bonnie Brae**[8] 2634 3-9-2 **60**..........................(b) SebSanders 9 76
(G G Margarson) *hld up towards rr: hdwy over 2f out: rdn to ld over 1f out: edgd lft u.p but r.o strly fnl f: comf* **5/1**[2]

-202 **2** *4 ½* **Sharp Eclipse**[8] 2628 3-9-7 **65**.......................... JamieSpencer 16 67
(K A Ryan) *led: rdn and hdd over 1f out: drvn and btn ent fnl f: hld on for 2nd ins fnl f* **11/8**[1]

1256 **3** *½* **Decency (IRE)**[13] 2480 3-9-1 **59**.......................... NickyMackay 10 59
(E A L Dunlop) *taken down early: chsd ldrs: rdn and unable qck wl over 1f out: drvn and btn ent fnl f: kpt on same pce fnl f* **7/1**[3]

3220 **4** *nk* **Miss Polly Plum**[10] 2566 3-8-7 **51**.......................... JimmyQuinn 13 50
(C A Dwyer) *t.k.h: chsd ldr tl wl over 1f out: styd on same pce u.p fr over 1f out* **20/1**

-304 **5** *hd* **Speedyfix**[19] 2297 3-8-6 **50**..........................(tp) DavidProbert 7 48
(Mrs C A Dunnett) *chsd ldrs: rdn and unable qck wl over 1f out: drvn and one pce ent fnl f* **10/1**

00-0 **6** *1 ¾* **Ellen Vannin (IRE)**[57] 1280 3-8-8 **55**.......................... PatrickHills(3) 6 48
(Eve Johnson Houghton) *chsd ldrs: rdn and unable qck wl over 1f out: wl btn but plugged on again ins fnl f* **40/1**

0-30 **7** *1 ¾* **Batgirl**[27] 2042 3-8-13 **57**.......................... TomMcLaughlin 8 44
(John Berry) *sn pushed along in rr: rdn and no hdwy 1/2-way: styd on steadily past btn horses fr over 1f out: nvr trbld ldrs* **33/1**

4203 **8** *4 ½* **Clear Ice (IRE)**[6] 2668 3-9-2 **60**..........................(v) PaulEddery 3 33
(R C Guest) *in tch in midfield: rdn and sn btn ent fnl 2f: wl bhd fr over 1f out* **14/1**

0060 **9** *nk* **Bell's Ocean (USA)**[8] 2634 3-8-9 **53**..........................(v[1]) MarcHalford 1 25
(J Ryan) *in tch in midfield: rdn and unable qck 1/2-way: wknd u.p wl over 1f out* **22/1**

5060 **10** *4* **Pavement Games**[7] 2648 3-8-2 **46** oh1.......................... JamieMackay 14 5
(R C Guest) *stdd s: t.k.h: hld up in rr: rdn and btn over 2f out: nvr on terms* **66/1**

5-66 **11** *2 ½* **Mr Prize Fighter**[14] 2432 3-7-12 **49** ow3.......................... MatthewLawson(7) 5 —
(I W McInnes) *a towards rr and nvr gng wl: lost tch wl over 1f out* **33/1**

000 **12** *1 ¼* **Aim'Ees Star**[23] 2174 3-8-3 **47** oh1 ow1.......................... DaraghO'Donohoe 15 —
(John A Harris) *s.i.s: sn pushed along: a bhd: lost tch 2f out* **100/1**

-650 **13** *2 ½* **Southwark Newshawk**[22] 2217 3-8-4 **48**.......................... CathyGannon 11 —
(Mrs C A Dunnett) *a towards rr and struggling 1/2-way: wl bhd fr wl over 1f out* **100/1**

0005 **14** *¾* **Lets Move It**[22] 2217 3-8-3 **47** oh1 ow1..........................(v) LiamJones 4 —
(D Shaw) *in tch in midfield: rdn and struggling 1/2-way: wl bhd fr wl over 1f out* **50/1**

-350 **15** *9* **Watch Chain (IRE)**[22] 2217 3-8-4 **53**..........................(b[1]) AshleyMorgan(5) 2 —
(M H Tompkins) *in tch in midfield: rdn and struggling 1/2-way: wl bhd fr over 1f out: t.o* **9/1**

1m 12.8s (-1.60) **Going Correction** -0.05s/f (Good) **15** Ran SP% **119.9**
Speed ratings (Par 97): **108,102,101,100,100 98,96,90,89,84 80,79,75,74,62**
toteswingers: 1&2 £3.10, 1&3 £5.60, 2&3 £4.10 CSF £11.06 CT £50.63 TOTE £5.80: £1.70, £1.10, £2.20; EX 14.30 Trifecta £36.80 Pool: £504.95 - 10.51 winning units..
Owner Mrs T A Foreman **Bred** Rosyground Stud **Trained** Newmarket, Suffolk

FOCUS
An ordinary handicap and. although the winner looked much improved here, the form is taken at face value.
Miss Polly Plum Official explanation: jockey said filly ran too free
Bell's Ocean(USA) Official explanation: vet said filly hit its head on stalls and bled from the mouth
Pavement Games Official explanation: trainer's rep said filly was unsuited by the good ground

2880 FOOTBALL IN THE COMMUNITY H'CAP 1m 2f 21y
5:40 (5:42) (Class 6) (0-60,60) 4-Y-0+ **£1,942** (£578; £288; £144) **Stalls** Low

Form RPR

-052 **1** **Guga (IRE)**[9] 2600 4-8-13 **55**..........................(b[1]) SebSanders 5 67
(Dr R D P Newland) *t.k.h: mde all: rdn over 2f out: drvn clr over 1f out: in command fnl f: rdn out* **5/2**[1]

2210 **2** *1 ½* **Blackstone Vegas**[9] 2610 4-8-12 **54**..........................(v) JimmyQuinn 1 63
(D Shaw) *chsd ldrs: wnt 2nd 4f out: rdn and no prog ent fnl 2f: btn but kpt on u.p fnl f* **5/1**[2]

0422 **3** *4* **Libre**[8] 2636 10-8-2 **49**.......................... AshleyMorgan(5) 8 50
(F Jordan) *stdd after s: hld up in tch in midfield: rdn and effrt over 2f out: hld hd high and no imp on ldrs fr over 1f out* **6/1**

00-0 **4** *1* **Hits Only Cash**[26] 2093 8-9-4 **60**.......................... DaraghO'Donohoe 4 59
(J Pearce) *t.k.h: hld up towards rr: rdn and outpcd wl over 2f out: plugged on fnl f: no ch w wnr* **16/1**

5-06 **5** *1 ¼* **Croeso Cusan**[3] 2788 5-8-13 **55**.......................... TomMcLaughlin 7 52
(J L Spearing) *taken down early: stdd s: hld up in last: hdwy on outer over 3f out: chsd ldrs and rdn ent fnl 2f: fnd little u.p and wknd over 1f out* **8/1**

5434 **6** *8* **Naheell**[46] 1539 4-8-11 **53**..(v[1]) SaleemGolam 6 34
(G Prodromou) *s.i.s: a in last trio: rdn and no rspnse ent fnl 4f: wl btn fnl 2f* **7/1**

-330 **7** *2* **Fathey (IRE)**[22] 2207 4-9-1 **57**.............................. DavidProbert 10 34
(C Smith) *chsd wnr tl 4f out: sn rdn: wknd u.p over 2f out: wl bhd fr over 1f out* **11/2**[3]

6600 **8** *3 ¾* **Naledi**[30] 1984 6-8-4 **46**.. LiamJones 11 15
(R J Price) *stdd s: hld up in last trio: rdn and no prog 4f out: wl bhd fnl 2f* **25/1**

2m 9.60s (-0.90) **Going Correction** -0.05s/f (Good) **8** Ran SP% **108.2**
Speed ratings (Par 101): **101,99,96,95,94 88,86,83**
toteswingers: 1&2 £2.70, 1&3 £2.50, 2&3 £3.10 CSF £13.26 CT £55.96 TOTE £3.10: £1.10, £1.90, £1.30; EX 15.40 Trifecta £17.50 Pool: £179.96 - 7.59 winning units. Place 6 £8.28, Place 5 £6.25.
Owner C E Stedman, R J Corsan & J A Provan **Bred** Azienda Agricola Loreto Luciani **Trained** Claines, Worcs

FOCUS
A moderate contest, and it was further weakened when Pedasus refused to go into the stalls. The form is rated around the principals.
Fathey(IRE) Official explanation: trainer said gelding was unsuited by the good ground
T/Plt: £11.80 to a £1 stake. Pool: £59,412.62. 3,657.21winning tickets. T/Qpdt: £3.90 to a £1 stake. Pool: £4,354.41. 815.23 winning tickets. SP

2860 HAYDOCK (L-H)
Thursday, June 10

OFFICIAL GOING: Good to soft (good in places) changing to good after race 2 (7.20)
Rail realignment increased distances on round course by 25yds.
Wind: Moderate, half-behind Weather: Part cloudy

2881 BETDAQ BETTING EXCHANGE APPRENTICE TRAINING SERIES H'CAP 1m 3f 200y
6:50 (6:50) (Class 5) (0-70,70) 4-Y-0+ **£2,914** (£867; £433; £216) **Stalls** High

Form RPR

6213 **1** **Ghufa (IRE)**[10] 2597 6-8-11 **62**.................................. SophieSilvester(5) 2 73+
(J Pearce) *hld up: nt clr run 2f out: sn swtchd rt: prog ins fnl f: r.o to ld fnl 100yds: pushed out* **2/1**[1]

3032 **2** *1* **Amir Pasha (UAE)**[12] 2533 5-8-6 **55**..............................(v) AdamCarter(3) 5 64
(Micky Hammond) *in tch: rdn 2f out: led 1f out: hdd fnl 100yds: hld after* **13/2**[3]

0012 **3** *6* **Maslak (IRE)**[17] 2402 6-9-8 **68**... RyanClark 3 67
(P W Hiatt) *led: hdd narrowly after 4f: remained w ldr: rdn to regain ld 2f out: hdd 1f out: wknd fnl 100yds* **11/4**[2]

10/6 **4** *½* **Ubi Ace**[38] 1751 4-9-5 **70**.. LukeStrong(5) 4 69
(T D Walford) *racd keenly: w ldr: led after 4f: hdd 2f out: stl ch 1f out: wknd ins fnl f* **7/1**

3234 **5** *¾* **Magnitude**[20] 2285 5-8-6 **57**...(p) DannyBrock(5) 8 54
(B P J Baugh) *handy: rdn 2f out: wknd ins fnl f* **13/2**[3]

/004 **6** *3 ¾* **Sumner (IRE)**[8] 2645 6-9-0 **65**...................................(bt) FrancisHayes(5) 7 56
(F Sheridan) *s.s: racd on outer and hdwy to trck ldrs after 3f: lost pl over 4f out: toiling fnl 3f* **16/1**

50-0 **7** *17* **Fabled Dancer (IRE)**[16] 2421 4-8-6 **52**.......................... JohnCavanagh 6 16
(E J Alston) *hld up: pushed along and outpcd over 4f out: lost tch over 1f out* **25/1**

2m 35.78s (1.78) **Going Correction** +0.275s/f (Good) **7** Ran SP% **108.9**
Speed ratings (Par 103): **102,101,97,97,96 94,82**
toteswingers:1&2 £3.50, 2&3 £2.50, 1&3 £1.30 CSF £13.91 CT £30.75 TOTE £1.60: £1.10, £2.90; EX 12.40.
Owner Miss Emma Pearce **Bred** Shadwell Estate Company Limited **Trained** Newmarket, Suffolk

FOCUS
A dry night and warm day. Exposed performers in a modest handicap. The gallop was a moderate one but the first two pulled clear in the closing stages and the second recorded a small personal best.

2882 BEST HORSERACING SKY CHANNEL 432 MAIDEN STKS (C&G) 6f
7:20 (7:19) (Class 5) 2-Y-0 **£2,914** (£867; £433; £216) **Stalls** High

Form RPR

3 **1** **Al Aasifh (IRE)**[39] 1728 2-9-0 0.. FrankieDettori 8 93+
(Saeed Bin Suroor) *racd keenly: trckd ldrs: led wl over 1f out: stretched clr ins fnl f: eased down towards fin* **2/5**[1]

3 **2** *7* **Falkland Flyer (IRE)**[6] 2687 2-9-0 0.............................. AlanMunro 6 70
(M R Channon) *a.p: rdn over 1f out: no ch and nt pce of wnr fnl f* **9/1**[3]

002 **3** *2* **Fred Willetts (IRE)**[26] 2111 2-8-11 0..................... AndrewHeffernan(3) 4 64
(P D Evans) *led: hdd 4f out: remained prom: rdn over 1f out: one pce fnl f* **33/1**

4 **4** *1 ¼* **Indian Ballad (IRE)**[33] 1905 2-9-0 0.......................... GrahamGibbons 10 60
(E S McMahon) *cl up: led 4f out: hdd wl over 1f out: rdn and fdd ins fnl f* **16/1**

5 **5** *2* **Red Marling (IRE)**[55] 1351 2-9-0 0..................................... PaulEddery 9 57
(B W Hills) *racd keenly: hld up: pushed along and hdwy over 1f out: kpt on wout troubling ldrs* **12/1**

6 *2 ¼* **Cotton Spirit** 2-9-0 0.. PaulHanagan 3 48
(R A Fahey) *s.i.s: towards rr: pushed along 1/2-way: sn outpcd: nvr rchd chalng position* **16/1**

7 *hd* **Elusivity (IRE)** 2-9-0 0.. PatDobbs 5 47
(R Hannon) *missed break: sn in midfield: rdn over 1f out: outpcd fnl f* **6/1**[2]

8 *4 ½* **Marster Parkes** 2-9-0 0... ShaneKelly 7 33
(E J Alston) *rn green: a bhd* **50/1**

6 **9** *5* **Save The Bees**[15] 2427 2-9-0 0.. PJMcDonald 1 18
(I W McInnes) *in tch: racd wd of field: rdn over 2f out: sn wknd* **100/1**

1m 13.44s (-0.06) **Going Correction** -0.025s/f (Good) **9** Ran SP% **121.1**
Speed ratings (Par 93): **99,89,87,85,82 79,79,73,66**
toteswingers:1&2 £1.40, 2&3 £9.40, 1&3 £8.00 CSF £5.57 TOTE £1.50: £1.10, £1.10, £6.20; EX 5.10.
Owner Godolphin **Bred** Rockfield Farm **Trained** Newmarket, Suffolk

FOCUS
This race has thrown up a couple of smart performers in Alzerra and Spinning Queen in recent years and, although this race had very little in the way of strength in depth, the winner looks potentially very useful at least, especially as the runner-up is rated to his debut mark. The gallop was a reasonable one and, after this race, the ground was changed to 'good'.

NOTEBOOK
Al Aasifh(IRE) ◆, who ran well in a race that produced winners at Newmarket on his debut, was very well backed and fully confirmed that promise to win an uncompetitive maiden by a wide margin, despite being eased in the closing stages. He's already a useful sort and one that fully deserves a step up in class. He should prove equally effective over 7f and may be aimed at a race at the July meeting at Newmarket next month. (op 1-2 tchd 1-3)
Falkland Flyer(IRE) had shown ability at a modest level in an ordinary Bath maiden on his debut and ran at least as well over this slightly longer distance. He runs and is bred to be suited by further in due course and, while likely to remain vulnerable against the better types in this grade, he should be able to pick up a minor event in due course. (op 8-1)
Fred Willetts(IRE) showed much improved form on his previous start at Doncaster and again ran to a similar level over this longer trip. Runners from this yard are invariably kept busy, and he will be of more interest either dropped in grade or when the nursery season begins.
Indian Ballad(IRE) failed to build on the form shown over course and distance on his debut but was again far from disgraced and is another that will be seen to better effect in nurseries.
Red Marling(IRE) wasn't knocked about after travelling strongly to halfway on this first run for two months. He has plenty of winners in his pedigree and should do better in ordinary nurseries in due course. (op 10-1)
Cotton Spirit is from a yard that has had juvenile debut winners this term but he was easy to back and only hinted at ability after running green on this racecourse debut. He should improve given time. (op 14-1)
Elusivity(IRE), from a stable that has been banging in winners all season, attracted a bit of support but ran green and was eventually well beaten. He too should leave this bare form behind. (op 15-2 tchd 8-1)

2883 MICK FRANKLAND RETIREMENT H'CAP 5f
7:50 (7:51) (Class 4) (0-80,80) 3-Y-0+ **£5,828** (£1,734; £866; £432) **Stalls** High

Form RPR

0330 **1** **Lucky Numbers (IRE)**[19] 2327 4-9-9 **80**................... JamesSullivan(5) 1 93
(Paul Green) *j.lft s: racd in midfield: hdwy over 2f out: led over 1f out: r.o ins fnl f: wl on top at fin* **4/1**[1]

11-6 **2** *1 ¾* **Lesley's Choice**[160] 2 4-9-8 **74**..............................(b) PaulHanagan 11 80
(F J Brennan) *led: rdn and hdd over 1f out: stuck on u.p: nt gng pce of wnr ins fnl f* **9/1**

-005 **3** *nse* **Coleorton Choice**[34] 1888 4-9-9 **80**...........................(p) PaulPickard(5) 9 86
(R Hollinshead) *towards rr: rdn and hdwy over 1f out: styd on ins fnl f: chalng for pls at fin* **17/2**

-000 **4** *nk* **Mandurah (IRE)**[19] 2327 6-9-8 **74**........................... SilvestreDeSousa 13 79
(B P J Baugh) *midfield: rdn and hdwy over 1f out: chsd ldrs ins fnl f: styd on: nt qckn fnl strides* **13/2**

0622 **5** *hd* **Select Committee**[9] 2626 5-8-12 **69**............................(p) IanBrennan(5) 6 73
(J J Quinn) *midfield: hdwy over 1f out: chal ins fnl f: styd on same pce fnl 100yds* **11/2**[3]

-606 **6** *shd* **Garstang**[132] 345 7-8-9 **61** oh1...(b) AlanMunro 5 65
(J Balding) *racd keenly: towards rr: hdwy 2f out: rdn to chal jst over 1f out: hung rt u.p fnl 100yds: nt qckn cl home* **25/1**

0-00 **7** *4 ½* **Supermassive Muse (IRE)**[9] 2622 5-8-8 **67**............(p) DavidKenny(7) 4 55
(E S McMahon) *prom: rdn 2f out: hung lft and wknd ins fnl f* **12/1**

-000 **8** *shd* **Bravely (IRE)**[12] 2528 6-9-3 **69**.. PJMcDonald 10 56+
(T D Easterby) *rrd s: bhd: u.p over 1f out: kpt on ins fnl f: unable to chal ldrs* **8/1**

-432 **9** *1 ¾* **Song Of Parkes**[19] 2309 3-8-11 **70**...................................... ShaneKelly 3 51
(E J Alston) *pressed ldr: rdn over 1f out: sn edgd rt and wknd* **5/1**[2]

-000 **10** *¾* **Time Medicean**[19] 2327 4-9-2 **68**..................................... TonyCulhane 15 46
(P T Midgley) *hld up: pushed along over 1f out: nvr on terms* **20/1**

60-0 **11** *1 ½* **Errigal Lad**[26] 2113 5-9-9 **75**......................................(p) PhillipMakin 7 48
(J Balding) *midfield: swtchd rt 2f out: sn rdn: outpcd over 1f out* **25/1**

50-0 **12** *3 ½* **Sharp Bullet (IRE)**[12] 2534 4-9-6 **72**................................ AdamKirby 12 32
(A Berry) *s.i.s: sn prom: rdn over 2f out: wknd over 1f out* **33/1**

60.16 secs (-0.84) **Going Correction** -0.025s/f (Good)
WFA 3 from 4yo+ 7lb **12** Ran SP% **120.1**
Speed ratings (Par 105): **105,102,102,101,101 101,93,93,91,89 87,81**
toteswingers:1&2 £9.40, 2&3 £10.30, 1&3 £7.40 CSF £38.92 CT £300.69 TOTE £6.00: £1.90, £4.10, £4.10; EX 65.60.
Owner Men Behaving Badly Two **Bred** Rory O'Brien **Trained** Lydiate, Merseyside

FOCUS
Exposed performers in a fair handicap. The gallop was sound and the form looks straightforward, with the third the best guide.
Lucky Numbers(IRE) Official explanation: trainer said, regarding apparent improvement in form, that the gelding was better suited by the good ground.
Bravely(IRE) Official explanation: jockey said gelding reared leaving stalls
Song Of Parkes Official explanation: trainer had no explanation for the poor form shown

2884 RACING UK HOME OF FLAT RACING H'CAP 7f 30y
8:20 (8:21) (Class 4) (0-85,85) 3-Y-0 **£5,828** (£1,734; £866; £432) **Stalls** Low

Form RPR

3-1 **1** **Victory Ide Say (IRE)**[40] 1685 3-9-7 **85**........................... AlanMunro 13 96+
(P W Chapple-Hyam) *hld up: swtchd rt and hdwy 2f out: rdn over 1f out: r.o to ld wl ins fnl f: pushed out towards fin* **15/8**[1]

3416 **2** *1 ½* **Hot Spark**[17] 2394 3-8-11 **75**.......................................(t) GrahamGibbons 1 82
(K A Ryan) *led: rdn over 1f out: hdd wl ins fnl f: kpt on same pce cl home* **11/2**[3]

023- **3** *2 ¾* **Fleeting Echo**[225] 7108 3-9-4 **82**....................................... PatDobbs 11 82
(R Hannon) *hld up: hdwy 2f out: rdn to chse ldrs over 1f out: styd on same pce fnl 110yds* **16/1**

01-4 **4** *1 ¾* **Saharia (IRE)**[26] 2112 3-9-4 **82**... ShaneKelly 8 77
(J Noseda) *trckd ldrs: wnt 2nd 2f out: rdn over 1f out: lost 2nd ins fnl f: no ex fnl 100yds* **3/1**[2]

-331 **5** *2* **Whitechapel**[19] 2329 3-8-12 **76**.. EddieAhern 3 65
(E J Alston) *midfield: rdn over 1f out: kpt on ins fnl f: nt gng pce to chal* **8/1**

0620 **6** *2* **Nubar Boy**[3] 2824 3-8-5 **72**...............................(t) AndrewHeffernan(3) 4 56
(P D Evans) *midfield: hdwy 3f out: effrt to chse ldrs and carried hd awkwardly 2f out: wknd fnl f* **10/1**

3-56 **7** *10* **Tukitinyasok (IRE)**[71] 1070 3-9-3 **81**............................ PaulHanagan 14 38
(R F Fisher) *hld up: hdwy over 5f out: sn chsd ldrs: rdn over 2f out: sn wknd* **50/1**

0623 **8** *1* **The Hermitage (IRE)**[9] 2618 3-8-12 **76**...................... RoystonFfrench 9 30
(M Johnston) *prom: w ldr over 5f out: rdn over 2f out: sn lost 2nd: wknd over 1f out* **14/1**

-000 **9** *1 ¼* **Toga Tiger (IRE)**[26] 2112 3-8-8 **72**................................... TonyCulhane 6 23
(P T Midgley) *in rr: niggled along over 4f out: nvr on terms* **33/1**

350- **10** *1 ¾* **Lava Lamp (GER)**[215] 7290 3-8-8 **72**.............................. FrannyNorton 7 18
(G A Harker) *s.i.s: a bhd* **33/1**

31-0 11 29 **Chardonnay**[13] 2502 3-8-9 73 PJMcDonald 12 —
(G A Swinbank) *in tch: rdn over 3f out: sn wknd* 25/1
1m 31.38s (-1.32) **Going Correction** +0.275s/f (Good) 11 Ran SP% 119.6
Speed ratings (Par 101): **104,102,99,97,94 92,81,80,78,76 43**
toteswingers:1&2 £4.30, 2&3 £13.20, 1&3 £6.70 CSF £12.32 CT £133.02 TOTE £3.70: £1.10, £1.50, £5.70; EX 15.60.
Owner P W Chapple-Hyam **Bred** Rathasker Stud **Trained** Newmarket, Suffolk

FOCUS
A useful-looking handicap in which the early gallop was only an ordinary one and the winner, who is rated a big improver, looks the type to make further progress. The first six pulled clear.
Toga Tiger(IRE) Official explanation: jockey said gelding slipped on bend
Chardonnay Official explanation: jockey said filly hung badly right-handed

2885 TURFTV.CO.UK H'CAP 1m 30y
8:50 (8:50) (Class 4) (0-85,85) 4-Y-O+ £5,828 (£1,734; £866; £432) Stalls Low

Form RPR
4161 1 **Ezdeyaad (USA)**[21] 2241 6-9-7 85 PJMcDonald 3 94
(G A Swinbank) *mde all: rdn over 1f out: r.o ins fnl f: plld out more towards fin* 7/1
-200 2 1 1/2 **Happy Anniversary (IRE)**[33] 1933 4-9-3 81 SilvestreDeSousa 5 87
(Mrs D J Sanderson) *trckd ldrs: rdn over 3f out: hung lft u.p fr 2f out: chsd wnr over 1f out: sn ev ch: no ex fnl 50yds* 15/2
01-1 3 1 **Keys Of Cyprus**[40] 1707 8-9-5 83 AdrianNicholls 4 86
(D Nicholls) *hld up in midfield: rdn 2f out: prog ins fnl f: gng on at fin* 14/1
2-11 4 1 1/4 **Play It Sam**[19] 2339 4-9-5 83 AdamKirby 1 83
(W R Swinburn) *s.i.s: sn rcvrd to trck ldrs: effrt over 2f out: rdn over 1f out: one pce fnl 100yds* 2/1[1]
4000 5 1 1/4 **Desert Dreamer (IRE)**[21] 2247 9-8-12 81 RichardEvans(5) 6 79
(P D Evans) *in rr: rdn over 2f out: styd on fr over 1f out: unable to rch ldrs: eased fnl 50yds* 66/1
0420 6 shd **Rio Cobolo (IRE)**[12] 2531 4-8-3 72 (v) JamesSullivan(5) 9 69
(Paul Green) *hld up: rdn over 2f out: kpt on ins fnl f: nt gng pce to trble ldrs* 25/1
3226 7 1/2 **Full Victory (IRE)**[18] 2362 8-8-0 67 (b) AndrewHeffernan(3) 7 63
(R A Farrant) *midfield: rdn and nt qckn over 2f out: one pce over 1f out* 25/1
6-02 8 3 1/4 **Captain Dancer (IRE)**[55] 1361 4-9-0 78 RobertWinston 2 67
(B W Hills) *chsd wnr to 2f out: wknd qckly over 1f out* 6/1[3]
6111 9 9 **Dajen**[66] 1128 4-8-8 79 LauraPike(7) 10 47
(D M Simcock) *midfield: rdn over 2f out: sn wknd* 11/2[2]
14-6 10 14 **Arrivederla (IRE)**[43] 1625 4-9-5 83 JamesDoyle 8 19
(H J L Dunlop) *hld up in rr: rdn and no imp over 2f out: eased whn n.d over 1f out* 8/1
/26- 11 11 **Riqaab (IRE)**[408] 1581 5-8-9 73 GrahamGibbons 11 —
(M W Easterby) *a bhd: pushed along and outpcd over 3f out* 25/1
1m 44.98s (0.28) **Going Correction** +0.275s/f (Good) 11 Ran SP% 118.1
Speed ratings (Par 105): **105,103,102,101,100 99,99,96,87,73 62**
toteswingers:1&2 £7.80, 2&3 £33.80, 1&3 £16.80 CSF £56.45 CT £722.32 TOTE £12.60: £4.00, £4.00, £6.70; EX 73.60.
Owner B Boanson & M Wane **Bred** Caldara Farm **Trained** Melsonby, N Yorks
■ Stewards' Enquiry : Adam Kirby one-day ban: careless riding (Jun 24)

FOCUS
Several previous winners in another useful handicap. The gallop was reasonable throughout and the winner likes this track and beat two rivals who are rated close to form.
Happy Anniversary(IRE) Official explanation: jockey said filly hung left-handed
Play It Sam Official explanation: jockey said gelding missed the break
Arrivederla(IRE) Official explanation: jockey said filly lost its action
Riqaab(IRE) Official explanation: jockey said gelding slipped on the bend

2886 SIMPLY RED HERE ON 17TH JULY H'CAP 1m 2f 95y
9:20 (9:21) (Class 5) (0-70,70) 3-Y-O £2,914 (£867; £433; £216) Stalls High

Form RPR
603- 1 **Aktia (IRE)**[204] 7430 3-9-4 67 KirstyMilczarek 10 78+
(L M Cumani) *hld up: racd in midfield after 3f: hdwy 3f out: led over 2f out: rdn over 1f out: kpt on wl* 3/1[1]
650- 2 1/2 **The Caped Crusader (IRE)**[317] 4396 3-8-12 64 BarryMcHugh(3) 4 72
(Ollie Pears) *hld up: hdwy 2f out: rdn over 1f out: wnt 2nd ins fnl f: styd on but looked hld towards fin* 33/1
5-00 3 1 1/4 **Shabak Hom (IRE)**[21] 2250 3-9-4 67 EddieAhern 1 73
(D M Simcock) *missed break: hld up: hdwy over 2f out: styd on to chse ldrs ins fnl f: hld fnl strides* 8/1
0-0 4 2 1/4 **Rezwaan**[45] 1582 3-9-7 70 ShaneKelly 7 72
(Jane Chapple-Hyam) *trckd ldrs: led over 3f out: hdd over 2f out: rdn over 1f out whn stl chalng: no ex fnl 75yds* 8/1
0540 5 4 **Sheila Toss (IRE)**[21] 2254 3-9-7 70 PatDobbs 9 64
(R Hannon) *trckd ldrs: chal 3f out: rdn over 1f out: wknd fnl 100yds* 5/1[2]
0-13 6 2 1/2 **Lord Raglan (IRE)**[33] 1921 3-9-5 68 PhillipMakin 3 57
(J R Weymes) *hld up: wnt into midfield 5f out: rdn to chse ldrs over 2f out: one pce fnl f* 11/2[3]
50-4 7 4 **Baraconti (IRE)**[37] 1804 3-9-7 70 PaulHanagan 8 52
(R A Fahey) *towards rr: niggled along over 4f out: nvr able to chal* 6/1
-312 8 1 1/2 **So Bazaar (IRE)**[13] 2501 3-9-2 65 PJMcDonald 12 44
(G A Swinbank) *sn chsd ldr: chal 3f out: rdn over 2f out: wknd over 1f out* 15/2
2305 9 19 **Golden Ratio (IRE)**[14] 2480 3-8-9 58 (b) FrannyNorton 2 —
(J R Gask) *trckd ldrs: effrt 3f out: wknd 2f out* 20/1
-300 10 20 **Tres Amigos**[17] 2394 3-9-5 68 AdrianNicholls 6 —
(D Nicholls) *led: hdd over 3f out: wknd qckly over 2f out* 25/1
2520 11 11 **Inside Track (IRE)**[71] 1070 3-9-2 70 RichardEvans(5) 5 —
(P D Evans) *racd keenly in midfield: pushed along and lost pl 4f out: lft bhd fnl 3f* 33/1
2m 15.96s (-0.04) **Going Correction** +0.275s/f (Good) 11 Ran SP% 119.8
Speed ratings (Par 99): **99,98,97,95,92 90,87,86,71,55 46**
toteswingers:1&2 £32.10, 2&3 £41.40, 1&3 £17.10 CSF £122.60 CT £730.07 TOTE £4.60: £2.20, £13.10, £1.70; EX 152.60 Place 6 £85.89, Place 5 £44.06..
Owner Mrs M Marinopoulos **Bred** Swordlestown Stud **Trained** Newmarket, Suffolk

FOCUS
A modest handicap run at a reasonable gallop and probably fair form, with the third back to his best on this easier ground.
Tres Amigos Official explanation: jockey said gelding had no more to give
Inside Track(IRE) Official explanation: jockey said gelding lost its action on bend
T/Plt: £92.80 to a £1 stake. Pool: £70,878.3 - 557.46 winning tickets. T/Qpdt: £35.20 to a £1 stake. Pool: £4,894.00 - 102.70 winning tickets. DO

2337 NEWBURY (L-H)
Thursday, June 10

OFFICIAL GOING: Good to firm (good in places; 7.4)
Rails moved out increasing distances on round course by about 16m.
Wind: Brisk across Weather: Overcast

2887 7 BEDFORD ROW BARRISTERS CHAMBERS MAIDEN STKS (C&G) 6f 110y
2:00 (2:00) (Class 4) 2-Y-O £4,533 (£1,348; £674; £336) Stalls Centre

Form RPR
42 1 **Trade Storm**[23] 2216 2-9-0 0 TomQueally 12 84
(J Gallagher) *chsd ldr: led ins fnl 2f: pushed clr fnl f: comf* 12/1[3]
2 2 1 1/4 **Dortmund**[13] 2493 2-8-11 0 AhmedAjtebi(3) 1 81
(Mahmood Al Zarooni) *led: pushed along and hdd ins fnl 2f: sn outpcd by wnr but kpt on fnl f* 11/10[1]
3 nk **Hamlool (IRE)** 2-9-0 0 JimmyFortune 11 80+
(C E Brittain) *s.i.s: sn in tch and chsd ldrs 1/2-way: styd on wl to press for 2nd wl ins fnl f but no ch w wnr* 33/1
4 1/2 **Cult Classic (IRE)** 2-9-0 0 RyanMoore 16 78+
(R Hannon) *chsd sole opponent on stands' side tl c lft fr ins fnl 3f and hung lft to join main gp 2f out: stl green but r.o wl fnl f: gng on cl home* 14/1
5 1 **Fight The Chance (IRE)** 2-9-0 0 KierenFallon 14 76
(M R Channon) *in tch: hdwy fr 2f out: kpt on same pce ins fnl f* 16/1
6 1 3/4 **Waiter's Dream** 2-9-0 0 MartinDwyer 3 71
(B J Meehan) *chsd ldrs: pushed along over 2f out: kpt on same pce ins fnl f* 20/1
03 7 1 1/2 **Uncle Dermot (IRE)**[15] 2440 2-9-0 0 FergusSweeney 5 67
(B G Powell) *in rr tl hdwy over 2f out: nvr rchd ldrs and fdd ins fnl f* 66/1
8 2 3/4 **Four Nations (USA)** 2-9-0 0 AdamKirby 4 59
(Mrs A J Perrett) *s.i.s: in rr: pushed along 1/2-way: sme prog fr over 1f out* 100/1
9 3 1/2 **Red Presence (IRE)** 2-9-0 0 RichardKingscote 13 49
(Tom Dascombe) *outpcd and pushed along 1/2-way: nvr nrr* 16/1
10 1 3/4 **Knox Overstreet** 2-9-0 0 TonyCulhane 7 45
(Tom Dascombe) *chsd ldrs tl wknd 2f out* 80/1
11 4 **Glenavon** 2-9-0 0 JimCrowley 6 34
(Mrs A J Perrett) *in tch: rdn along: hung lft and green over 2f out: n.d after* 33/1
12 3/4 **Dubarshi** 2-9-0 0 IanMongan 10 32
(Miss Jo Crowley) *outpcd* 100/1
13 7 **Blue Cossack (IRE)** 2-9-0 0 LiamKeniry 9 12
(M D I Usher) *a outpcd* 100/1
4 14 9 **Welsh Dancer**[33] 1901 2-9-0 0 RichardHughes 15 —
(R Hannon) *led sole opponent on stands' side tl ins fnl 3f: nvr on terms after and sn no ch: eased* 15/8[2]
1m 19.45s (0.15) **Going Correction** -0.225s/f (Firm) 14 Ran SP% 124.9
Speed ratings (Par 95): **90,88,88,87,86 84,82,79,75,73 69,68,60,49**
toteswingers: 1&2 £4.30, 1&3 £23.80, 2&3 £11.30 CSF £25.83 TOTE £12.10: £2.70, £1.50, £5.50; EX 36.70.
Owner Universal Racing **Bred** G T Lucas **Trained** Chastleton, Oxon

FOCUS
This is always an informative juvenile maiden and last year it was a very hot affair, with subsequent Group 1 winners Arcano and Showcasing fighting out the finish. This year, with a horse having his third run coming out on top, it is most unlikely to work out so well, but there were still a host of encouraging performances. The field were inclined to converge more towards the far side of the track in the main and few landed a serious blow from off the pace.

NOTEBOOK
Trade Storm was always front rank and eventually came home a clear-cut winner. This confirmed the promise of his much-improved second at Nottingham 23 days earlier (race working out well) and he is clearly a progressive colt. His previous experience was clearly a notable advantage here, but he ought to improve further for a stiffer test as he matures, and it will be interesting to see where connections pitch him in next as he looks better than a nursery horse. (op 9-1)
Dortmund was very popular to go one better than his debut second 13 days earlier and, never far away, he held every chance. He didn't see it out like the winner and perhaps found the race coming a little too soon, but ought to be found an opening soon. (op 11-8 tchd 6-4 in places)
Hamlool(IRE), whose stable had won the two maidens previously contested by Trade Storm, made a pleasing debut considering he found it plenty sharp enough. He is bred to get further and looks one to be with next time. (op 28-1)
Cult Classic(IRE) was the second string from his powerful stable on jockey bookings and the market suggested the run would be needed. He turned in an eyecatching effort, keeping towards the near side early on and doing some decent late work when joining the main group. He appears another that will relish another furlong and shouldn't remain a maiden for long. (op 11-1)
Fight The Chance(IRE), whose dam was a 6f winner at two, came under pressure around halfway and lacked the pace to seriously get involved. He was keeping on nicely inside the final furlong, however, and should be plenty sharper with the experience under his belt.
Waiter's Dream ran as though his racecourse debut was needed. He was staying on with promise late on and, with plenty of stamina on his dam's side, is another to take out of the race. (tchd 18-1)
Four Nations(USA) is another that is out of a dam with plenty of stamina in her pedigree and he left the impression he will get closer next time out.
Knox Overstreet Official explanation: jockey said colt hung left-handed
Welsh Dancer was very well backed to improve on his promising debut effort over 5f at Ascot last month. He found himself in the wrong place to be keeping to the stands' side, but ultimately ran too badly to be true and something must have gone amiss. Official explanation: jockey said colt lost its action (op 11-4 tchd 3-1 in places)

2888 PERTEMPS H'CAP 1m (S)
2:30 (2:32) (Class 5) (0-75,75) 3-Y-O £3,238 (£963; £481; £240) Stalls Centre

Form RPR
6-00 1 **Lost In The Moment (IRE)**[35] 1844 3-9-5 73 RyanMoore 5 85+
(J Noseda) *trckd ldrs: pushed along and n.m.r 3f out: swtchd rt over 2f out: drvn to ld wl over 1f out: edgd rt to stands' rail fnl f: drvn out* 2/1[1]
0-00 2 1 1/4 **Be Invincible (IRE)**[21] 2253 3-9-6 74 RobertWinston 6 82
(B W Hills) *slt ld tl over 4f out: styd upsides and rdn to take narrow advantage 2f out: hdd wl over 1f out: styd on same pce u.p fnl f* 18/1
645- 3 1 1/4 **Beaumont's Party (IRE)**[223] 7145 3-8-13 70 PatrickHills(3) 8 75
(R Hannon) *in tch: hdwy over 2f out: styd on wl fr over 1f out: r.o ins fnl f and sn edgd rt: no imp on ldng duo* 16/1
-140 4 3 1/4 **Prince Of Sorrento**[21] 2253 3-9-4 72 DaneO'Neill 7 69
(J Akehurst) *s.i.s: in rr and t.k.h: hdwy fr 3f out: drvn to chse ldrs fr over 1f out: outpcd ins fnl f* 20/1
3-00 5 3 3/4 **Warning Song (USA)**[16] 2416 3-9-5 73 AdamKirby 14 61
(Mrs A J Perrett) *in rr tl hdwy fr 2f out: r.o fnl f and kpt on cl home: nvr a threat* 22/1

-345 **6** *1* **Another Magic Man (USA)**[6] 2702 3-9-3 **71** SteveDrowne 2 56
(J R Best) *pressed ldrs: rdn over 2f out: wknd appr fnl f* **16/1**

-225 **7** *2 1/4* **Red Yarn**[105] 698 3-9-1 **69** FergusSweeney 3 49
(G L Moore) *chsd ldrs after 2f: rdn over 2f out: wknd wl over 1f out* **50/1**

24-0 **8** *3 3/4* **Wild Rockette**[28] 2042 3-9-5 **73** MartinDwyer 11 44
(B J Meehan) *w ldr: slt advantage over 4f out tl narrowly hdd 2f out: wknd qckly over 1f out* **25/1**

6-41 **9** *1 1/4* **Trewarthenick**[10] 2587 3-9-3 **71** 6ex JimmyFortune 12 39
(A M Balding) *pressed ldrs: rdn over 2f out: wknd wl over 2f out* **10/1**

-001 **10** *7* **Cereal Killer (IRE)**[20] 2279 3-9-3 **71** (b) JimCrowley 15 22
(R Hannon) *chsd ldrs: rdn over 2f out: sn btn* **20/1**

0065 **11** *nse* **First In The Queue (IRE)**[10] 2587 3-9-2 **70** LiamKeniry 16 21
(S Kirk) *towards rr most of way* **10/1**

00-3 **12** *1/2* **Decree Absolute (USA)**[44] 1602 3-9-0 **68** PaulFitzsimons 9 18
(Miss J R Tooth) *s.i.s: sn chsng ldrs: rdn 3f out and sn btn* **100/1**

0334 **13** *shd* **Yes Chef**[21] 2253 3-9-5 **73** KierenFallon 10 23+
(J Gallagher) *chsd ldrs: wkng whn hmpd over 2f out* **5/1**[2]

-312 **14** *2 3/4* **Candleshoe (IRE)**[10] 2587 3-9-2 **70** RichardHughes 13 13
(R Hannon) *in tch: rdn over 3f out: sn btn* **15/2**[3]

15-0 **15** *19* **Many A Slip**[38] 1776 3-9-3 **71** TomQueally 4 —
(J L Dunlop) *bhd most of way* **33/1**

1m 37.97s (-1.73) **Going Correction** -0.225s/f (Firm) **15** Ran SP% **120.6**
Speed ratings (Par 99): **99,97,96,93,89 88,86,82,81,74 74,73,73,70,51**
toteswingers: 1&2 £15.70, 1&3 £19.00, 2&3 £62.50 CSF £38.99 CT £475.85 TOTE £3.30: £1.60, £8.90, £6.80; EX 61.80.
Owner M Tabor & Mrs Susan Roy **Bred** Rockhart Trading Ltd **Trained** Newmarket, Suffolk

FOCUS
A competitive enough 3-y-o handicap for the class. They went an average pace and, while the majority raced down the centre, the winner came home against the stands' rail so there appeared no bias. The form looks sound with the third the best guide.
Lost In The Moment(IRE) Official explanation: trainer said, regarding apparent improvement in form, that the colt is in good form and had a realistic chance on its last run in a maiden.
Yes Chef Official explanation: jockey said colt had been struck into behind

2889 LORD WEINSTOCK MEMORIAL STKS (REGISTERED AS THE BALLYMACOLL STUD STAKES) (LISTED RACE) (FILLIES) 1m 2f 6y

3:05 (3:08) (Class 1) 3-Y-O

£22,708 (£8,608; £4,308; £2,148; £1,076; £540) **Stalls** Low

Form RPR

1-23 **1** **Eleanora Duse (IRE)**[29] 2029 3-8-12 103 RyanMoore 2 109+
(Sir Michael Stoute) *trckd ldrs: rdn to ld 2f out: styd on wl fnl f* **11/4**[2]

4-14 **2** *2 1/4* **Pink Symphony**[29] 2029 3-8-12 100 JimmyFortune 5 104
(P F I Cole) *in rr but in tch: hdwy fr 3f out: n.m.r over 2f out: drvn and styd on fr over 1f out: kpt on u.p ins fnl f to take 2nd last stride* **10/1**

42-1 **3** *nse* **Shimmering Surf (IRE)**[28] 2050 3-8-12 84 IanMongan 3 104
(P Winkworth) *sn chsng ldrs: rdn and one pce 2f out: styd on again to press for 2nd fnl f: a hld by wnr* **10/1**

2-06 **4** *2* **Lady Darshaan (IRE)**[18] 2370 3-8-12 108 RichardHughes 8 100
(J S Moore) *sn chsng ldr: rdn to chal over 2f out: wknd ins fnl f* **9/4**[1]

1- **5** *2 1/4* **Kithonia (FR)**[280] 5604 3-8-12 77 TomQueally 6 95+
(H R A Cecil) *chsd ldrs: rdn and edgd lft over 2f out: wknd fnl f* **15/2**

21-0 **6** *1 1/4* **Diam Queen (GER)**[56] 1330 3-8-12 87 KierenFallon 4 93
(L M Cumani) *pushed along after s: pushed along and sme hdwy over 2f out: nvr rchd ldrs: wknd fnl f* **20/1**

2-01 **7** *3/4* **Nurture (IRE)**[17] 2401 3-8-12 97 (p) JimCrowley 7 91
(R M Beckett) *in rr: pushed along and sme prog over 3f out: nvr nr ldrs: wknd wl over 1f out* **20/1**

-643 **8** *3 1/4* **Deirdre**[22] 2224 3-8-12 99 WilliamBuick 1 85
(J H M Gosden) *led: rdn: hdd and edgd lft 2f out: sn btn* **11/2**[3]

2m 7.04s (-1.76) **Going Correction** -0.05s/f (Good) **8** Ran SP% **112.3**
Speed ratings (Par 104): **105,103,103,101,99 98,98,95**
toteswingers:1&2 £3.20, 2&3 £8.00, 1&3 £5.90 CSF £28.93 TOTE £3.80: £1.70, £2.10, £3.30; EX 27.00.
Owner Ballymacoll Stud **Bred** Ballymacoll Stud Farm Ltd **Trained** Newmarket, Suffolk

FOCUS
A strong Listed event for 3-y-o fillies. It was run at a sound pace and it saw the Musidora third and fourth fill the first two places. The pair are rated to that form but it is fairly ordinary for the grade.

NOTEBOOK
Eleanora Duse(IRE) deservedly resumed winning ways on this drop into Listed company and confirmed the promise of her previous third in the Musidora. She was produced with a well-timed challenge to lead and was always doing enough despite drifting right under pressure. That was likely still down to inexperience and the best of her has probably still to be seen. She looks the sort to enjoy racing over 1m4f and is in very good hands. (op 3-1 tchd 9-4 and 10-3 in places)
Pink Symphony, who won her maiden over C&D, travelled nicely through the race, but never looked like getting to the winner when that one asserted. She ran very close to her last-time-out form with the winner so helps to set a good standard, and she too now looks well worth a try over an extra 2f. (tchd 12-1)
Shimmering Surf(IRE) came into this with an official mark of 84, but she is highly regarded and does not hold down this form. She remains open to improvement and ought to be up to winning one of these over the distance. (tchd 9-1 and 14-1)
Lady Darshaan(IRE) had contested both the domestic and Irish 1000 Guineas on her two previous outings this term. She ran a big race at the Curragh 18 days earlier and was unsurprisingly popular. Ponied to the start, she took up a handy position and was well placed when things got serious. She failed to see out the longer trip like the principals, though, and dropping back to 1m in this grade should see her deservedly back to winning ways. (tchd 2-1 and 3-1)
Kithonia(FR) won her sole outing last term and was making her belated 3-y-o debut. She ran well considering she had reportedly been slow to come to hand this year and should improve a bundle for the outing. On this evidence 1m4f should also pose her few problems. (op 7-1 tchd 13-2)
Diam Queen(GER) was representing a yard with a decent record in the race, but had plenty to find on official figures and had run disappointingly on her debut at this trip when resuming in April. She tended to run in snatches and was outclassed, but this was still a step in the right direction. (op 16-1)
Nurture(IRE) was equipped with first-time cheekpieces and was another that found this all too hot. She is not simple to place. (op 25-1)
Deirdre finished third behind subsequent Oaks heroine Snow Fairy over this trip at Goodwood on her previous outing and so had to be of interest. She was a sitting duck from the front, however, and ultimately shaped as though something went amiss. (op 6-1 tchd 9-2)

2890 SPORTINGBET.COM MAIDEN FILLIES' STKS (DIV I) 1m 2f 6y

3:40 (3:42) (Class 5) 3-Y-O **£3,885** (£1,156; £577; £288) **Stalls** Low

Form RPR

4-3 **1** **Nouriya**[55] 1358 3-9-0 0 RyanMoore 2 96+
(Sir Michael Stoute) *trckd ldrs: led over 2f out: pushed along and in command thrght fnl f: edgd rt fnl 120yds* **8/11**[1]

4 **2** *3* **Marywell**[33] 1932 3-9-0 0 WilliamBuick 7 90
(J H M Gosden) *hld up towards rr: stdy hdwy fr 2f out to trck wnr 2f out: sn drvn and kpt on: readily hld thrght fnl f: stl qcknd to go wl clr of 3rd* **10/3**[2]

0-26 **3** *8* **Issabella Gem (IRE)**[27] 2076 3-9-0 89 RichardHughes 1 74
(C G Cox) *chsd ldrs: rdn over 2f out and sn no ch w ldng duo: kpt on to take wl-hld 3rd fnl f* **7/1**[3]

0 **4** *3/4* **Gale Green**[28] 2051 3-9-0 0 DaneO'Neill 9 73
(H Candy) *led tl hdd over 2f out: sn rdn and no ch w ldng duo: outpcd for wl hld 3rd fnl f* **50/1**

32-0 **5** *nse* **Old Money**[59] 1260 3-9-0 75 TomQueally 8 72
(H J L Dunlop) *in tch: rdn and hdwy to chse ldrs over 2f out: sn no ch w ldng duo and one pce fnl f* **25/1**

5 **6** *3 3/4* **Blast Furnace (IRE)**[55] 1356 3-9-0 0 JimmyFortune 10 65
(P W Chapple-Hyam) *chsd ldr: rdn 3f out: wknd 2f out* **11/1**

0 **7** *1* **Starshine**[28] 2043 3-9-0 0 SteveDrowne 4 63
(R Charlton) *s.i.s: in rr: sme hdwy and drvn 4f out: wknd ins fnl 3f* **33/1**

00 **8** *4 1/2* **Dolphin's Dream**[43] 1621 3-9-0 0 KierenFallon 3 54
(B J Meehan) *chsd ldrs: rdn ins fnl 3f: wknd over 2f out* **66/1**

9 *1/2* **Precious Spring (IRE)** 3-9-0 0 JimCrowley 6 53
(E A L Dunlop) *s.i.s: sme prog on outside 3f out: nvr rchd ldrs and sn wknd* **66/1**

10 *4 1/2* **Callisto Light** 3-9-0 0 AdamKirby 5 44
(W R Swinburn) *s.i.s: bhd most of way* **80/1**

2m 8.00s (-0.80) **Going Correction** -0.05s/f (Good) **10** Ran SP% **114.8**
Speed ratings (Par 96): **101,98,92,91,91 88,87,84,83,80**
toteswingers: 1&2 £1.90, 1&3 £2.10, 2&3 £3.90 CSF £2.99 TOTE £1.70: £1.10, £1.10, £2.20; EX 4.10.
Owner Saleh Al Homaizi & Imad Al Sagar **Bred** Saleh Al Homaizi **Trained** Newmarket, Suffolk

FOCUS
Some decent pedigrees on show in this fillies' maiden, and the form looks solid with the two market leaders pulling clear. The winning time was just under a second slower than the preceding Listed contest. The third and sixth give the form a solid look.

2891 SPORTINGBET.COM MAIDEN FILLIES' STKS (DIV II) 1m 2f 6y

4:15 (4:15) (Class 5) 3-Y-O **£3,885** (£1,156; £577; £288) **Stalls** Low

Form RPR

5-25 **1** **Mujdeya**[28] 2051 3-9-0 80 RyanMoore 10 86
(J H M Gosden) *trckd ldr: led wl over 2f out: pushed clr over 1f out: comf* **9/4**[1]

03 **2** *7* **Norse Dame**[17] 2401 3-9-0 0 DaneO'Neill 6 72
(D R C Elsworth) *in tch: pushed along and hdwy over 2f out: styd on fnl f: tk 2nd fnl 50yds* **10/1**

5-20 **3** *3/4* **Miss Miracle**[36] 1820 3-9-0 90 WilliamBuick 5 71
(C G Cox) *led tl hdd wl over 2f out: sn no ch w wnr but kpt on tl lost mod 2nd fnl 50yds* **6/1**

0-6 **4** *3 1/4* **Craighall**[33] 1932 3-9-0 0 JimCrowley 8 64
(D M Simcock) *chsd ldrs: pushed along: hung lft and no ch fnl 2f* **14/1**

5 *1 3/4* **Kitty Wells** 3-9-0 0 KierenFallon 3 61+
(L M Cumani) *in rr: pushed along 4f out: styd on fr over 1f out: nvr a threat to plcd horses* **7/2**[2]

0- **6** *shd* **Riccoche (IRE)**[201] 7491 3-9-0 0 LiamKeniry 1 60
(E F Vaughan) *in rr: pushed along 4f out: styd on fr over 1f out: nvr a threat to plcd horses* **100/1**

6 **7** *1/2* **Tulle (IRE)**[28] 2051 3-9-0 0 MartinDwyer 4 59
(B J Meehan) *in tch: rdn 3f out: wknd fr 2f out* **8/1**

8 *5* **Maroon** 3-9-0 0 RobertWinston 2 49
(B W Hills) *chsd ldrs: pushed along 3f out: wknd fr 2f out* **9/2**[3]

9 *12* **Sunshineofyourlove** 3-9-0 0 TomQueally 9 25
(J W Hills) *s.i.s: a in rr* **66/1**

2m 8.94s (0.14) **Going Correction** -0.05s/f (Good) **9** Ran SP% **114.8**
Speed ratings (Par 96): **97,91,90,88,86 86,86,82,72**
toteswingers: 1&2 £5.20, 1&3 £2.90, 2&3 £7.30 CSF £26.26 TOTE £2.20: £1.10, £3.10, £2.50; EX 29.30.
Owner Hamdan Al Maktoum **Bred** Shadwell Estate Company Limited **Trained** Newmarket, Suffolk

FOCUS
This second division of the fillies' maiden looked very much the weaker of the pair. The time was the best part of a second slower than the first division and the form is rated around the third and fourth.

2892 BATHWICK TYRES NEWBURY H'CAP 7f (S)

4:50 (4:50) (Class 5) (0-75,75) 3-Y-O **£3,238** (£963; £481; £240) **Stalls** Centre

Form RPR

4-62 **1** **Love Match**[30] 2005 3-9-2 **70** SteveDrowne 4 81
(R Charlton) *hld up in rr: stdy hdwy over 1f out: qckdn to ld fnl 150yds: drvn clr* **7/1**

0-43 **2** *2 1/2* **Alkhataaf (USA)**[26] 2122 3-9-7 **75** JimmyFortune 2 79
(J L Dunlop) *t.k.h: chsd ldrs: drvn and qckdn to ld jst ins fnl f: hdd fnl 150yds: sn outpcd* **7/2**[2]

4203 **3** *1 3/4* **Dimaire**[24] 2185 3-8-6 **60** (b) CathyGannon 8 60
(D Haydn Jones) *chsd ldrs: rdn and hung rt 2f out: drvn to chal and hung lft over 1f out: outpcd ins fnl f* **22/1**

-322 **4** *1* **Frequency**[23] 2197 3-9-2 **70** RyanMoore 9 67
(E A L Dunlop) *in rr: pushed along but nt much day light over 2f out: drvn and kpt on ins fnl f: nvr gng pce to rch ldrs* **9/2**[3]

2440 **5** *hd* **Robust Wish (USA)**[30] 2002 3-9-7 **75** MartinDwyer 11 71
(B J Meehan) *in rr: rdn and last over 2f out: sltly hmpd appr fnl f: r.o ins fnl f: nvr a threat* **28/1**

2234 **6** *1* **Lago Indiano (IRE)**[29] 2025 3-9-7 **75** (p) TomQueally 3 69
(Mrs A J Perrett) *pressed ldrs tl slt ld over 2f out: hdd jst ins fnl f: sn wknd* **11/1**

0-00 **7** *1* **Dream Number (IRE)**[44] 1593 3-9-2 **70** KierenFallon 1 61
(W R Muir) *sn pressing ldrs: chal over 2f out tl hdd & wknd jst ins fnl f* **16/1**

31-5 **8** *shd* **Elusive Trader (USA)**[28] 2052 3-9-6 **74** JimCrowley 6 65
(R M Beckett) *chsd ldrs: rdn over 2f out: wknd appr fnl f* **3/1**[1]

5-53 **9** *2 1/2* **Great Intrigue (IRE)**[19] 2340 3-9-2 **70** IanMongan 7 54
(J S Moore) *chsd ldrs: rdn 2f out: wknd fnl f* **25/1**

2-40 **10** *1 1/4* **Music Maestro (IRE)**[16] 2425 3-9-7 **75** RobertWinston 5 55
(B W Hills) *slt ld tl narrowly hdd over 2f out: wknd sn after* **12/1**

2500 **11** *1/2* **Takajan (IRE)**[11] 2566 3-9-1 **69** LiamKeniry 12 48
(S Kirk) *t.k.h in rr: sme hdwy and in tch whn hmpd 2f out: sn btn* **50/1**

0-66 **12** 3/4 **Admire The View (IRE)**[21] 2242 3-9-7 75 DaneO'Neill 10 52
(D R Lanigan) *nvr beyond mid-div* 14/1

1m 26.23s (0.53) **Going Correction** -0.225s/f (Firm) **12** Ran SP% **120.1**
Speed ratings (Par 99): **87,84,82,81,80 79,78,78,75,74 73,72**
toteswingers:1&2 £4.10, 2&3 £11.80, 1&3 £13.20 CSF £30.87 CT £533.32 TOTE £7.70: £2.60, £1.80, £7.20; EX 37.00.
Owner Lady Rothschild **Bred** The Rt Hon Lord Rothschild **Trained** Beckhampton, Wilts

FOCUS
A modest 3-y-o handicap, run at a sound pace. the form looks solid rated around those in the frame behind the winner.
Alkhataaf(USA) Official explanation: jockey said colt ran too free
Dream Number(IRE) Official explanation: jockey said filly hung right-handed
Takajan(IRE) Official explanation: vet said gelding bled from the nose

2893 BATHWICK TYRES SWINDON H'CAP 1m 4f 5y
5:20 (5:20) (Class 5) (0-75,74) 3-Y-O **£3,238** (£963; £481; £240) **Stalls** Low

Form RPR

06-4 **1** **Domination**[57] 1299 3-9-0 67 SteveDrowne 12 88+
(H Morrison) *trckd ldrs: led over 2f out: rdn and styd on strly fr over 1f out: readily* 7/1[3]

5031 **2** 3 1/4 **Yashrid (USA)**[16] 2422 3-9-7 74 WilliamBuick 1 88
(M A Jarvis) *chsd ldrs: rdn over 2f out: styd on u.p to chse wnr over 1f out: kpt on but nvr any ch* 10/1

4-04 **3** 1 3/4 **Fantastic Cuix (FR)**[30] 2011 3-9-4 71 KierenFallon 9 83+
(L M Cumani) *in tch: drvn along fr over 3f out: styd on thrght fnl f to take 3rd cl home but no ch w ldng duo* 11/2[2]

00-1 **4** nk **Trovare (USA)**[19] 2321 3-9-5 72 RyanMoore 7 83
(Mrs A J Perrett) *chsd ldrs: rdn along fr 4f out: one pce fr 2f out but styd on for 3rd over 1f out tl lost 3rd cl home* 2/1[1]

5-02 **5** 1/2 **Aquarius Star (IRE)**[13] 2516 3-9-5 72 DaneO'Neill 13 82+
(Pat Eddery) *in rr: pushed along hdwy: nt clr run and swtchd rt over 2f out: hdwy and edgd lft fnl f: kpt on cl home: nvr a threat* 14/1

0353 **6** 3 3/4 **Spice Fair**[21] 2248 3-8-8 64 PatrickHills(3) 11 68+
(M D I Usher) *stdd s: t.k.h in rr tl surged through to dispute ld over 5f out: led 3f out: hdd over 2f out: wknd wl over 1f out* 12/1

-341 **7** 2 **Firehawk**[21] 2248 3-8-7 60 CathyGannon 5 61
(P D Evans) *in rr: rdn and hdwy whn hmpd over 2f out: n.d after* 16/1

51-2 **8** 2 1/4 **Fairy Flight (USA)**[41] 1666 3-9-6 73 JimCrowley 4 71
(W J Knight) *chsd ldrs: rdn 4f out: wknd 2f out* 12/1

5132 **9** 3/4 **Parhelion**[20] 2277 3-9-7 74 (t) FergusSweeney 10 70
(Tim Vaughan) *in rr: hdwy to chse ldrs 6f out: rdn on outside 3f out and sn btn* 20/1

6-03 **10** 7 **Milnagavie**[40] 1696 3-9-1 68 RichardHughes 2 53
(R Hannon) *led tl hdd 3f out: wknd 2f out* 16/1

00-5 **11** 4 1/2 **Miniyamba (IRE)**[40] 1696 3-8-13 66 MartinDwyer 8 44
(J L Dunlop) *mid-div: rdn 5f out and sn bhd* 25/1

5-55 **12** 3 **Golden Waters**[33] 1909 3-9-5 72 TomQueally 3 45
(Eve Johnson Houghton) *chsd ldrs: drvn along 3f out: wknd over 2f out* 33/1

3-20 **13** 12 **Royal Etiquette (IRE)**[35] 1851 3-9-7 74 JimmyFortune 6 28
(H J L Dunlop) *in rr: sme hdwy 4f out: wknd 3f out* 33/1

2m 35.14s (-0.36) **Going Correction** -0.05s/f (Good) **13** Ran SP% **118.6**
Speed ratings (Par 99): **99,96,95,95,95 92,91,89,89,84 81,79,71**
toteswingers:1&2 £9.80, 2&3 £13.20, 1&3 £9.10 CSF £71.18 CT £414.28 TOTE £8.20: £2.50, £4.40, £2.30; EX 63.50.
Owner Michael Kerr-Dineen & Bob Tullett **Bred** M Kerr-Dineen **Trained** East Ilsley, Berks

FOCUS
An open 3-y-o middle-distance handicap full of potential improvers. The fifth and sixth set the level and are rated close to their marks.
Spice Fair Official explanation: jockey said gelding hung right-handed
Royal Etiquette(IRE) Official explanation: jockey said gelding ran too free

2894 BOLLINGER CHAMPAGNE CHALLENGE SERIES H'CAP (FOR GENTLEMAN AMATEUR RIDERS) 1m 2f 6y
5:50 (5:50) (Class 5) (0-70,70) 4-Y-O+ **£3,123** (£968; £484; £242) **Stalls** Low

Form RPR

0354 **1** **Bavarica**[13] 2511 8-11-2 68 MrRBirkett(3) 3 79
(Miss J Feilden) *trckd ldrs: wnt 2nd over 1f out: pushed along to ld fnl 120yds: hld on wl* 10/1

6-21 **2** nk **Megalala (IRE)**[6] 2714 9-10-10 64 6ex MrJackSalmon(5) 9 75
(J J Bridger) *led: pushed along and styd on wl fr over 2f out: hdd fnl 120yds: kpt on: a jst hld* 13/2[2]

0535 **3** 4 1/2 **Alfredtheordinary**[15] 2433 5-10-1 57 MrCBishop(7) 4 59
(M R Channon) *chsd ldrs: rdn to go 2nd 2f out: no imp and outpcd into 3rd over 1f out* 16/1

0-45 **4** nk **Django Reinhardt**[6] 2714 4-9-13 51 MrDavidTurner(3) 15 52
(Miss S L Davison) *chsd ldrs: drvn along 3f out: styd on same pce fr over 1f out* 11/1

0-31 **5** nse **Prince Golan (IRE)**[13] 2511 6-10-10 62 MrMPrice(3) 10 63
(R J Price) *in rr: rdn over 3f out: styd on towards outside fr 2f out: fin wl: nvr a threat* 16/1

1-06 **6** 1 3/4 **Parc Des Princes (USA)**[20] 2285 4-10-11 67 (v[1]) MrARawlinson(7) 12 64
(A M Balding) *in rr: hdwy towards outside 3f out: no imp and one pce fnl 2f* 8/1[3]

5554 **7** 1/2 **Daniel Thomas (IRE)**[10] 2602 8-11-0 68 (p) MrOJMurphy(5) 2 64
(Mrs A L M King) *in rr: swtchd rt fr rails to outside 3f out: styd on fnl 2f: nvr nr ldrs* 14/1

112- **8** hd **Sircozy (IRE)**[171] 7831 4-11-6 69 MrJoshuaMoore 8 65
(G L Moore) *chsd ldrs: rdn 3f out: wknd appr fnl f* 7/2[1]

1-00 **9** nk **Lunar Limelight**[61] 1225 5-10-10 59 MrSWalker 7 54
(P J Makin) *in tch: hdwy 3f out: drvn and styd on fnl 2f: nvr gng pce to get into contention* 12/1

620/ **10** 3/4 **Black Coffee**[27] 4024 5-11-4 70 (p) MrBenBrisbourne(3) 6 64
(W M Brisbourne) *in rr: sme hdwy towards outside fr 2f out: nvr nr ldrs* 10/1

0-06 **11** 2 3/4 **Lucy's Perfect**[18] 2360 4-9-11 51 (b) MrPMillman(5) 16 39
(B R Millman) *chsd ldrs: rdn 4f out: wknd ins fnl 2f* 14/1

6600 **12** 3 **Hatch A Plan (IRE)**[18] 2360 9-9-9 51 oh2 MrTGarner(7) 11 33
(Mouse Hamilton-Fairley) *chsd ldrs tl wknd ins fnl 3f* 40/1

0306 **13** nk **Altimatum (USA)**[8] 2645 4-10-11 60 (t) MrMSeston 14 42
(P F I Cole) *nvr bttr than mid-div: bhd fnl 3f* 33/1

60-2 **14** 2 1/4 **Lucayan Dancer**[13] 2511 10-11-1 69 MrSebSpencer(5) 13 46
(N Bycroft) *a in rr* 12/1

3330 **15** 26 **Gordon Road (IRE)**[7] 2093 4-11-0 68 (p) MrJMQuinlan(5) 1 —
(M G Quinlan) *nvr bttr than mid-div: bhd fnl 4f* 33/1

2m 10.49s (1.69) **Going Correction** -0.05s/f (Good) **15** Ran SP% **122.0**
Speed ratings (Par 103): **91,90,87,86,86 85,85,84,84,84 81,79,79,77,56**
toteswingers: 1&2 £9.80, 1&3 £9.10, 2&3 £13.20 CSF £73.05 CT £1054.15 TOTE £10.60: £3.90, £1.40, £5.00; EX 60.60 Place 6: £57.27 Place 5: £31.27 .
Owner Miss J Feilden **Bred** Juddmonte Farms **Trained** Exning, Suffolk

FOCUS
A typically moderate handicap for gentleman amateur riders. The pace was sound and the third is rated close to recent marks.
T/Jkpt: Not won. T/Plt: £94.60 to a £1 stake. Pool of £78,966.70 - 609.27 winning tickets. T/Qpdt: £7.10 to a £1 stake. Pool of £4,825.45 - 499.18 winning tickets. ST

2646 NOTTINGHAM (L-H)
Thursday, June 10

OFFICIAL GOING: good to soft (soft in places; 6.2)
All races on outer track. Rail moved out 2m from turn out of dog leg, round top bend and as far as 4.5f out, increasing distances by circa 7yds.
Wind: moderate behind Weather: Overcast and showers

2895 EUROPEAN BREEDERS' FUND MAIDEN STKS 6f 15y
2:20 (2:20) (Class 5) 2-Y-O **£3,561** (£1,059; £529; £264) **Stalls** High

Form RPR

04 **1** **Bussa**[12] 2540 2-9-3 0 SilvestreDeSousa 1 77
(P D Evans) *wnt lft s: sn prom: tk slt ld 1/2-way: rdn over 2f out: drvn and hdd over 1f out: rallied u.p to ld last 100yds: gamely* 12/1[3]

4 **2** hd **Capaill Liath (IRE)**[13] 2493 2-9-3 0 MichaelHills 5 76
(B W Hills) *prom: cl up 1/2-way: rdn to ld over 1f out: sn drvn and hung persistently lft: hdd and no ex last 100yds* 4/11[1]

40 **3** 10 **Silver Shine (IRE)**[8] 2654 2-9-3 0 EddieAhern 6 48+
(W J Haggas) *rrd s and s.i.s: bhd: hdwy 1/2-way: rdn over 2f out: kpt on same pce* 14/1

4 1 1/2 **Roman Strait** 2-9-3 0 PaulHanagan 4 42
(M Blanshard) *in rr: pushed along and hdwy 1/2-way: rdn over 2f out: sn one pce* 16/1

5 1 3/4 **Spartic** 2-9-3 0 JamesDoyle 3 37
(A J McCabe) *chsd ldrs: pushed along 1/2-way: rdn over 2f out and sn wknd* 25/1

6 11 **Brave Tiger (IRE)** 2-9-3 0 (t) GrahamGibbons 2 4
(S C Williams) *led: pushed along and hdd 1/2-way: sn rdn and wknd 2f out* 15/2[2]

1m 16.81s (1.91) **Going Correction** +0.30s/f (Good) **6** Ran SP% **109.2**
Speed ratings (Par 93): **99,98,85,83,81 66**
toteswingers: 1&2 £2.20, 1&3 £8.10, 2&3 £1.70 CSF £16.23 TOTE £7.90: £2.70, £1.10; EX 20.00.
Owner Nick Shutts **Bred** Natton House Thoroughbreds & Mark Woodall **Trained** Pandy, Monmouths

FOCUS
After 20mm of rain between Saturday and Tuesday and another 5mm overnight the ground on a dry but breezy afternoon was soft. A modest maiden with three of the six runners making their debuts but the first three home were the ones with previous experience. The winner improved on this third start while the runner-up was too free.

NOTEBOOK
Bussa, having his third start, proved very determined and in the end just edged out the favourite. A first winner for first-season sire Iceman, nurseries beckon and, quite stoutly bred on his dam's side, he will be suited by a step up to 7f. (op 17-2 tchd 14-1)
Capaill Liath(IRE), backed to the exclusion of the others, had finished fourth first time behind a better fancied stablemate in a decent maiden at Haydock. Much too keen after taking charge, he edged left and seemed to get worried out of it in the end. (op 4-7)
Silver Shine(IRE), unsuited by the undulations at Ripon on his second start, started slowly and had to settle for a modest third place in the end. This at least opens up the nursery route for him but he is obviously no great shakes. (op 10-1)
Roman Strait showed no obvious promise on his debut. (op 14-1 tchd 20-1 in a place)
Brave Tiger(IRE), who showed plenty of early dash, wore a tongue-tie on his first start and in the end dropped right away. (tchd 7-1 and 8-1)

2896 LADIES NIGHT ON SATURDAY 3RD JULY H'CAP 6f 15y
2:50 (2:51) (Class 6) (0-65,65) 3-Y-O+ **£2,047** (£604; £302) **Stalls** High

Form RPR

0000 **1** **Memphis Man**[17] 2399 7-9-9 65 RichardEvans(5) 11 78
(P D Evans) *hld up towards rr: hdwy 1/2-way: chsd ldrs 2f out: sn swtchd rt and effrt to chse ldr ent fnl f: sn chal: drvn and kpt on to ld on line* 4/1[2]

0-04 **2** nse **Bermondsey Bob (IRE)**[10] 2589 4-8-11 48 SamHitchcott 6 61
(J L Spearing) *a.p: led wl over 2f out: rdn over 1f out: edgd rt ins fnl f: sn drvn: hdd on line* 11/1

0-55 **3** 4 1/2 **Piste**[17] 2396 4-9-7 58 PaulHanagan 1 57
(Miss T Jackson) *hld up: swtchd rt after 2f and sn in tch: hdwy 2f out: rdn over 1f out: styng on whn bmpd ent fnl f: kpt on: nrst fin* 14/1

0664 **4** 1 1/4 **Carmenero (GER)**[13] 2490 7-9-12 63 EddieAhern 4 58
(C R Dore) *chsd ldrs on wd outside: rdn along 2f out: drvn over 1f out: kpt on same pce* 33/1

50-1 **5** 2 1/2 **Secret City (IRE)**[34] 1884 4-9-3 61 (b) MatthewLawson(7) 9 48
(R Bastiman) *cl up: led briefly over 2f out: sn rdn: edgd lft and hdd wl over 1f out: drvn: wandered and wknd appr fnl f* 10/1

0604 **6** nk **Steel City Boy (IRE)**[8] 2646 7-9-4 55 GrahamGibbons 15 41
(D Shaw) *hld up towards rr: hdwy 1/2-way: in tch and rdn along 2f out: kpt on same pce appr fnl f* 28/1

-201 **7** nk **Charles Darwin (IRE)**[44] 1595 7-10-0 65 FrannyNorton 8 50
(M Blanshard) *trckd ldrs: hdwy 1/2-way: rdn along 2f out: drvn and no imp appr fnl f* 18/1

5133 **8** 1/2 **Fuzzy Cat**[8] 2647 4-9-4 60 DeanHeslop(5) 12 43
(T D Barron) *reminders after s: sn chsng ldrs and led after 1 1/2f: rdn along 1/2-way: hdd over 2f out: sn drvn and wkng whn sltly hmpd ent fnl f* 9/4[1]

4324 **9** 3 **Fortezza**[6] 2726 4-8-9 51 (p) DeclanCannon(5) 14 24
(A J McCabe) *s.i.s: a in rr* 8/1

4025 **10** 1 **Kipchak (IRE)**[12] 2524 5-9-12 63 (p) HayleyTurner 17 33
(C R Dore) *led 1 1/2f: sn pushed along and lost pl 1/2-way: sn towards rr* 7/1[3]

3303 **11** shd **Bentley**[6] 2698 6-8-12 49 (v) PaulMulrennan 7 19
(J G Given) *in tch: rdn along wl over 2f out: sn wknd* 33/1

0-04 12 30 **French Wind**[106] 683 3-9-0 **59** .... TedDurcan 10 —
(Pat Eddery) *chsd ldrs: rdn along bef 1/2-way: wknd qckly: bhd and eased fnl 2f* **33/1**

1m 16.28s (1.38) **Going Correction** +0.30s/f (Good)
WFA 3 from 4yo+ 8lb 12 Ran SP% **116.0**
Speed ratings (Par 101): **102,101,95,94,90 90,90,89,85,84 84,44**
toteswingers: 1&2 £15.90, 1&3 £22.20, 2&3 £23.90 CSF £44.55 CT £558.61 TOTE £9.30: £3.10, £3.70, £9.50; EX 53.00.
Owner Mrs I M Folkes **Bred** R T And Mrs Watson **Trained** Pandy, Monmouths

FOCUS
A modest 48-65 sprint handicap and they raced in one group centre to stands' side. The runner-up is rated in line with his best form.
Secret City(IRE) Official explanation: jockey said gelding hung right
Fortezza Official explanation: jockey said filly hung right

2897 FIND US ON FACEBOOK H'CAP 1m 6f 15y
3:25 (3:25) (Class 5) (0-75,75) 4-Y-0+ **£2,590** (£770; £385; £192) **Stalls** Low

Form RPR

0-60 1 **Outland (IRE)**[19] 2341 4-8-2 **56** oh1 .... SilvestreDeSousa 9 67
(M G Rimell) *hld up in tch: hdwy to trck ldr over 4f out: effrt to ld over 2f out and sn rdn clr: drvn and styd on strly fnl f* **7/2**[2]

0-31 2 3 **Rare Ruby (IRE)**[23] 2218 6-9-2 **70** .... PaulHanagan 4 77
(Jennie Candlish) *hld up in tch: hdwy over 4f out: rdn along and sltly outpcd over 2f out: sn drvn and styd on to chse wnr ent fnl f: sn no imp* **9/4**[1]

-630 3 1 **Lastroseofsummer (IRE)**[14] 2476 4-8-5 **59** .... DavidProbert 5 65
(Rae Guest) *chsd ldr 3f: prom: rdn along to chse wnr over 2f out: sn drvn and one pce ent fnl f* **12/1**

3311 4 6 **Dunaskin (IRE)**[12] 834 10-9-0 **68** ....(b) PaulEddery 6 65
(R C Guest) *sn chsng ldr: led over 5f out: clr 4f out: rdn along and hdd over 2f out: sn drvn and grad wknd* **8/1**

15-0 5 10 **Sally Forth**[55] 1357 4-9-7 **75** ....(b[1]) RichardMullen 2 58
(R Charlton) *reminders s: in rr: pushed along after 6f: effrt and rdn 4f out: nvr a factor* **17/2**

2134 6 2 ½ **Little Sark (IRE)**[15] 2445 5-8-3 **60** .... AndrewHeffernan(3) 1 40
(P D Evans) *hld up: a in rr* **25/1**

-310 7 5 **Slip**[15] 2173 5-9-1 **69** .... HayleyTurner 10 42
(C R Dore) *trckd ldrs: hdwy to chse ldr over 4f out: rdn along over 3f out: sn wknd* **20/1**

2-0 8 30 **Pass The Port**[38] 1783 9-9-7 **75** .... MichaelHills 7 6
(D Haydn Jones) *hld up towards rr: hdwy over 4f out: rdn along over 3f out: wknd qckly: sn bhd and eased fnl 2f* **14/1**

2-41 9 30 **Cote D'Argent**[29] 2023 7-9-4 **72** ....(t) PhilipRobinson 3 —
(C J Down) *led: rdn along and hdd over 5f out: wknd qckly and bhd 3f out: sn eased* **7/1**[3]

3m 10.42s (3.12) **Going Correction** +0.30s/f (Good) 9 Ran SP% **110.1**
Speed ratings (Par 103): **103,101,100,97,91 90,87,70,53**
toteswingers: 1&2 £3.20, 1&3 £11.30, 2&3 £7.50 CSF £10.84 CT £74.75 TOTE £5.10: £1.70, £1.50, £5.10; EX 10.60.
Owner Rob Douglas **Bred** St Simon Foundation **Trained** Leafield, Oxon

FOCUS
The outer course was in use and the ground was soft. A modest 56-75 stayers' handicap and the pace was not strong. The form looks straightforward rated around the first three.
Cote D'Argent Official explanation: trainer said gelding had a breathing problem

2898 BETFAIR H'CAP 1m 75y
4:00 (4:03) (Class 3) (0-95,94) 3-Y-0 **£7,771** (£2,312; £1,155; £577) **Stalls** Centre

Form RPR

1- 1 **Decorative (IRE)**[284] 5478 3-9-0 **87** .... PhilipRobinson 5 99+
(M A Jarvis) *hld up in rr: hdwy on outer 3f out: rdn to chse ldr wl over 1f out: chal appr fnl f: drvn to ld last 100yds: styd on wl towards fin* **7/4**[1]

2-1 2 1 ¾ **Bintalwaadi**[44] 1589 3-8-11 **84** .... RichardHills 6 93+
(E A L Dunlop) *led: rdn along over 2f out: jnd and drvn appr fnl f: hdd and no ex last 100yds* **3/1**[2]

0-31 3 6 **Subtefuge**[30] 2002 3-8-6 **86** .... CharlesEddery(7) 4 80
(H R A Cecil) *t.k.h: trckd ldrs on outer: chsd ldr fr 1/2-way: rdn along 3f out: drvn over 2f out: kpt on same pce* **8/1**

0-26 4 1 ½ **Gunner Lindley (IRE)**[19] 2324 3-9-1 **88** .... MichaelHills 2 79
(B W Hills) *chsd ldrs: rdn along 3f out: drvn 2f out and kpt on same pce* **7/2**[3]

15-3 5 hd **Colepeper**[12] 2542 3-9-7 **94** .... RoystonFfrench 1 84
(M Johnston) *t.k.h: chsd ldr on inner: rdn along and lost pl over 4f out: drvn wl over 2f out: sn btn* **8/1**

2-01 6 6 **Count Bertoni (IRE)**[33] 1921 3-8-3 **76** ....(p) PaulHanagan 3 52
(S Gollings) *squeezed out shortly after s: t.k.h in rr: rdn along over 3f out and sn outpcd* **18/1**

1m 49.3s (3.70) **Going Correction** +0.60s/f (Yiel) 6 Ran SP% **111.1**
Speed ratings (Par 103): **105,103,97,95,95 89**
toteswingers: 1&2 £1.40, 1&3 £4.30, 2&3 £4.90 CSF £7.03 TOTE £2.30: £1.40, £1.80; EX 6.90.
Owner Highclere Thoroughbred Racing Royal Pal **Bred** Barouche Stud (ire) Ltd **Trained** Newmarket, Suffolk

FOCUS
A very interesting 76-94 handicap for 3-y-os and the first two pulled clearl of three solid markers.

NOTEBOOK
Decorative(IRE), impressive winner on her only previous starts at Yarmouth in August, injured a knee and could not run again. Formerly a 1000 Guineas entry, she made her handicap bow here from a possibly lenient mark of 87. After a tardy start she showed a bright turn of foot to move into a challenging position. On the soft ground she took time to gain the upper hand but was firmly in command at the line. She looks Listed class at least and should have a bright future. (op 15-8 tchd 2-1)
Bintalwaadi, off the mark at the second attempt on the AW at Lingfield in April, wore a blanket for stalls entry but still gave problems. She slowed the pace down from the front before going for home straightening up. She was firmly put in her place in the end by another unexposed filly but finished clear of the rest, and is much better than her rating here of just 84. She has a pronounced knee action and might not appreciate quick ground. (tchd 4-1)
Subtefuge, fifth behind Decorative at Yarmouth, was 8lb higher than for her Warwick success. Quite keen, she carries her head high and in the end, like the rest, was outclassed by the first two. (op 5-1 tchd 9-1)
Gunner Lindley(IRE), a first-time-out soft-ground maiden winner at two, has struggled from this sort of mark in handicap company since and it was the same story here. (op 5-1)
Colepeper, runner-up over 7f at Haydock on his return just 12 days earlier, was flat out and making no impression early in the home straight. (op 15-2 tchd 6-1)
Count Bertoni(IRE), winner here from a 2lb lower mark in a Class 5 event, found this Class 3 much too competitive and never figured after being left short of room at the start. (op 22-1 tchd 16-1)

2899 NOTTINGHAMRACECOURSE.CO.UK MAIDEN STKS (DIV I) 1m 75y
4:35 (4:36) (Class 5) 3-Y-O+ **£2,266** (£674; £337; £168) **Stalls** Centre

Form RPR

1 **Rock N Roll Ransom** 3-9-0 0 .... J-PGuillambert 2 83+
(L M Cumani) *trckd ldrs: hdwy to chse ldr over 4f out: shkn up over 2f out: led 1 1/2f out: comf* **2/1**[2]

50 2 2 **Dhaafer**[12] 2548 3-9-0 0 .... RichardHills 1 74
(W J Haggas) *chsd ldr: rdn along and sltly outpcd wl over 2f out: swtchd rt ent fnl f: styd on to chse wnr: sn no imp* **12/1**

00-2 3 3 **Rasselas (IRE)**[25] 2143 3-9-0 76 .... MichaelHills 12 67
(B W Hills) *t.k.h: led: rdn along and jnd over 2f out: hdd 1 1/2f out and sn wknd* **13/8**[1]

4 8 **Belle Boleyn** 3-8-9 0 .... TedDurcan 11 42+
(C F Wall) *bhd: hdwy over 3f out: rdn wl over 1f out: styd on ins fnl f: tk 4th nr fin* **18/1**

050- 5 hd **Ilkley**[261] 6181 3-8-4 48 .... JamesSullivan(5) 5 42
(M W Easterby) *in tch: hdwy over 3f out: rdn to chse ldng pair over 2f out: sn wknd* **100/1**

6 6 **Mashatu** 3-9-0 0 .... EddieAhern 6 33
(J R Fanshawe) *in tch: rdn along 4f out: sn outpcd* **7/2**[3]

0 7 14 **Crianza**[14] 2463 4-9-6 0 .... DaraghO'Donohoe 10 —
(N Tinkler) *hmpd s and a bhd* **200/1**

0 8 ¾ **Defence Of Realm (GER)**[49] 1485 3-8-9 0 .... MatthewDavies(5) 4 —
(George Baker) *chsd ldrs: rdn along 4f out: drvn over 3f out and sn wknd* **25/1**

00 9 nk **Massachusetts**[20] 2290 3-9-0 0 .... HayleyTurner 8 —
(B J Meehan) *a in rr: bhd fnl 3f* **33/1**

10 24 **Crimson Queen** 3-8-10 0 ow1 .... MickyFenton 7 —
(R Brotherton) *s.i.s: a towards rr: outpcd and wl bhd fnl 3f* **150/1**

11 3 ½ **Santo Subito (IRE)**[207] 9-9-6 0 .... MarkCoumbe(5) 9 —
(M C Chapman) *a in rr: bhd fr 1/2-way* **250/1**

1m 50.43s (4.83) **Going Correction** +0.60s/f (Yiel)
WFA 3 from 4yo+ 11lb 11 Ran SP% **115.9**
Speed ratings (Par 103): **99,97,94,86,85 79,65,65,64,40 37**
toteswingers:1&2 £6.40, 2&3 £3.30, 1&3 £2.00 CSF £24.79 TOTE £3.70: £1.50, £4.50, £1.02; EX 32.90.
Owner Castle Down Racing **Bred** Meon Valley Stud **Trained** Newmarket, Suffolk

FOCUS
A maiden lacking any real strength in depth but in the end a winner of real potential. There was little to go on formwise but it looks an average rce at best.
Belle Boleyn Official explanation: jockey said, regarding running and riding, that his orders were, as it was the filly's first run, to establish a position amongst the pack, avoid racing wide and do his best, adding that having suffered interference at start and being carried wide, he was obliged to settle in the rear, when asked to make progress in home straight it became unbalanced and showed signs of greenness.
Crianza Official explanation: jockey said filly suffered interference at start

2900 NOTTINGHAMRACECOURSE.CO.UK MAIDEN STKS (DIV II) 1m 75y
5:10 (5:10) (Class 5) 3-Y-0+ **£2,266** (£674; £337; £168) **Stalls** Centre

Form RPR

0- 1 **Uphold**[223] 7146 3-9-0 0 .... MichaelHills 1 83+
(B W Hills) *mde all: rdn clr 2f out: styd on strly* **10/3**[2]

0/ 2 7 **Supa Seeker (USA)**[616] 6425 4-9-11 0 .... JamesDoyle 9 64
(A W Carroll) *in tch: hdwy on outer 3f out: rdn to chse wnr over 1f out: sn edgd lft and kpt on: no ch w wnr* **200/1**

/0 3 nk **Cheddar George**[19] 2334 4-9-11 0 .... EddieAhern 5 63
(B J Meehan) *trckd ldrs: hdwy on inner 3f out: rdn 2f out: drvn and one pce appr fnl f* **15/2**[3]

0- 4 1 **Jubail (IRE)**[301] 4945 3-9-0 0 .... RichardMullen 3 58
(A King) *hld up towards rr: hdwy over 3f out: rdn to chse ldrs wl over 1f out: kpt on: nrst fin* **22/1**

45- 5 3 ¾ **Mushreq (USA)**[251] 6451 3-9-0 0 .... RichardHills 6 49
(Sir Michael Stoute) *midfield: hdwy to chse ldrs 3f out: rdn along over 2f out: sn hung lft and no hdwy fr over 1f out* **11/10**[1]

6 1 ¼ **Gracie May** 3-8-9 0 .... DavidProbert 2 41
(R Hollinshead) *chsd ldrs: rdn along 3f out: drvn 2f out and sn one pce* **66/1**

6 7 1 ½ **Peaceful Means (IRE)**[15] 2335 7-9-6 0 .... MickyFenton 10 40
(J Jay) *prom: rdn along over 3f out: drvn over 2f out: sn wknd* **14/1**

0 8 13 **Mont Ras (IRE)**[9] 2632 3-9-0 0 .... TedDurcan 7 —
(E A L Dunlop) *s.i.s: a in rr* **20/1**

0-0 9 1 **Miss Chaumiere**[14] 2473 3-8-9 0 .... HayleyTurner 8 —
(M L W Bell) *chsd wnr: rdn along over 3f out: sn wknd* **40/1**

00- 10 1 ¾ **Singing Scott (IRE)**[215] 7288 3-8-7 0 .... MatthewLawson(7) 11 —
(R Bastiman) *s.i.s: a bhd* **150/1**

11 4 ½ **Tattler** 3-9-0 0 .... RoystonFfrench 4 —
(M Johnston) *s.i.s: a bhd* **11/1**

1m 51.05s (5.45) **Going Correction** +0.60s/f (Yiel)
WFA 3 from 4yo+ 11lb 11 Ran SP% **111.7**
Speed ratings (Par 103): **96,89,88,87,83 82,81,68,67,65 60**
toteswingers:1&2 £49.90, 2&3 £75.80, 1&3 £2.80 CSF £570.13 TOTE £3.60: £1.10, £36.50, £6.30; EX 208.80.
Owner K Abdulla **Bred** Juddmonte Farms Ltd **Trained** Lambourn, Berks

FOCUS
Very little to go on here with none of the runners yet having earned an official rating. The time was almost half a second slower than division one. The form is tricky to pin down but the third and fourth are probably the best guides.
Singing Scott(IRE) Official explanation: jockey said gelding missed the break

2901 NOTTINGHAM RACECOURSE HEN AND STAG PARTIES FILLIES' H'CAP 1m 2f 50y
5:40 (5:41) (Class 5) (0-75,74) 3-Y-0 **£2,590** (£770; £385; £192) **Stalls** Low

Form RPR

00-2 1 **Centime**[17] 2401 3-8-12 **65** .... EddieAhern 8 70+
(B J Meehan) *hld up in rr: gd hdwy on wd outside 3f out: chsd ldrs wl over 1f out: sn rdn: edgd lft ent fnl f: sn led: drvn out* **7/1**

0-02 2 1 **Saggiatore**[21] 2255 3-9-3 **70** .... HayleyTurner 1 73
(E A L Dunlop) *in tch on inner: hdwy 3f out: effrt 2f out: n.m.r over 1f out: swtchd rt and rdn ent fnl f: ev ch tl drvn and no ex last 75yds* **11/2**[3]

005 3 ½ **Nahab**[16] 2425 3-9-1 **68** .... TedDurcan 13 70+
(D R Lanigan) *hld up in midfield: hdwy 3f out: rdn along and n.m.r 2f out: sn drvn and kpt on ins fnl f: tk 3rd nr line* **9/4**[1]

56-0 **4** *hd* **My Sister**18 2359 3-8-4 **57**............ DavidProbert 10 59
(M D I Usher) *cl up: rdn to chal wl over 1f out: drvn and ev ch ent fnl f: wknd last 100yds: lost 3rd nr line* **25/1**

3-54 **5** *3 1/4* **Sandy Shaw**21 2250 3-8-13 **66**............ MichaelHills 5 62
(J W Hills) *sn led: rdn along 3f out: drvn over 1f out: hdd jst ins fnl f: sn wknd* **16/1**

22-4 **6** *nse* **Faith Jicaro (IRE)**20 2290 3-9-6 **73**............ JamesDoyle 6 68
(N J Vaughan) *chsd ldrs: effrt 3f out and sn rdn: drvn 2f out and sn one pce* **16/1**

0-00 **7** *1 1/2* **Happy Mood**17 2401 3-8-9 **62**............ PaulMulrennan 11 54
(G L Moore) *chsd ldrs: hdwy over 3f out: rdn and wkng whn edgd rt and n.m.r 2f out* **33/1**

3640 **8** *1* **Spicewood (USA)**23 2219 3-9-3 **70**............ NickyMackay 4 60
(J H M Gosden) *prom: effrt 3f out and sn rdn: drvn 2f out and grad wknd appr fnl f* **20/1**

04-0 **9** *12* **Jasmeno**52 1431 3-8-11 **64**............ TravisBlock 12 30
(H Morrison) *chsd ldrs: rdn along over 3f out: sn wknd* **14/1**

00-6 **10** *3/4* **Lily Rio (IRE)**34 1881 3-8-9 **62**............ FrannyNorton 9 27
(W R Muir) *a in rr* **40/1**

2-44 **11** *3/4* **Skyrider (IRE)**24 2180 3-9-7 **74**............ RichardMullen 7 37
(R Charlton) *dwlt: a in rr* **10/3**2

560 **U** **Eden Nights (USA)**14 2478 3-8-12 **68**.......... Louis-PhilippeBeuzelin(3) 2 —
(J H M Gosden) *rrd and uns rdr in stalls at s* **20/1**

2m 19.74s (8.04) **Going Correction** +0.60s/f (Yiel) **12** Ran SP% **118.9**
Speed ratings (Par 96): **91,90,89,89,87 87,85,85,75,74 74,—**
toteswingers:1&2 £4.10, 2&3 £4.40, 1&3 £6.70 CSF £42.18 CT £115.73 TOTE £11.80: £3.40, £2.20, £1.10; EX 37.50.
Owner Car Colston Hall Stud **Bred** Car Colston Hall Stud **Trained** Manton, Wilts

FOCUS
A modest 57-74 three-year-olds' fillies' handicap, although the winner and third could prove better than the bare form.
Skyrider(IRE) Official explanation: jockey said filly was unsuited by the good to soft (soft in places) ground

2902 BOOK TODAY FOR FAMILY DAY 10TH JULY H'CAP 1m 2f 50y
6:10 (6:11) (Class 6) (0-60,60) 4-Y-O+ **£2,047** (£604; £302) **Stalls** Low

Form RPR

0341 **1** **King Zeal (IRE)**8 2653 6-8-4 **53**............ JamesRogers(7) 2 69+
(B D Leavy) *mde all: rdn clr over 2f out: drvn over 1f out: kpt on wl fnl f* **9/4**1

5124 **2** *5* **Marjury Daw (IRE)**64 1172 4-9-4 **60**............ PaulMulrennan 12 66
(J G Given) *in tch: hdwy to trck ldng pair 1/2-way: effrt to chse wnr over 2f out and sn rdn: drvn wl over 1f out: no imp fnl f* **5/1**2

0-56 **3** *1 3/4* **Quadrifolio**9 2629 4-8-4 **46** oh1............ NickyMackay 15 49
(Paul Green) *chsd ldrs: hdwy 3f out: sn rdn: drvn and kpt on same pce fnl 2f* **14/1**

05-0 **4** *1/2* **Jenny Soba**13 2511 7-8-4 **46** oh1............ NeilChalmers 14 48
(Lucinda Featherstone) *sn rdn along and bhd: hdwy on wd outside over 3f out: styd on u.p fnl 2f: tk 4th nr fin* **12/1**

05-5 **5** *1 1/4* **Sanctum**66 1134 4-8-9 **54**............ Louis-PhilippeBeuzelin(3) 7 53
(Dr J D Scargill) *chsd ldrs: rdn along 4f out: drvn 3f out: plugged on same pce* **7/1**3

460- **6** *14* **Freda's Rose (IRE)**224 7142 6-8-6 **48**............ PaulQuinn 16 19
(O Brennan) *bhd tl sme hdwy fnl 3f: nvr nr ldrs* **33/1**

-640 **7** *2 1/4* **Nesno (USA)**15 2433 7-8-8 **55**............(p) PatrickDonaghy(5) 8 22
(M Dods) *chsd wnr: effrt and cl up over 4f out: rdn along 3f out: sn drvn and wknd* **5/1**2

-060 **8** *20* **Tres Froide (FR)**16 2421 5-8-13 **55**............ DaraghO'Donohoe 13 —
(N Tinkler) *a towards rr: bhd fnl 3f* **10/1**

-300 **9** *6* **Starburst**75 1012 5-9-4 **60**............ DavidProbert 5 —
(Miss Gay Kelleway) *s.i.s: sn in midfield: rdn along 4f out and sn wknd* **9/1**

000- **10** *1 3/4* **Punta Galera (IRE)**295 5150 7-8-4 **46** oh1............(v) AndrewMullen 10 —
(Paul Green) *a in rr: bhd fnl 3f* **33/1**

-000 **11** *1* **Firsaan (IRE)**17 2388 4-8-6 **48** oh1 ow2............ SamHitchcott 1 —
(J R Norton) *chsd ldrs on inner: rdn along 4f out: sn wknd and bhd fnl 3f* **40/1**

2m 17.26s (5.56) **Going Correction** +0.60s/f (Yiel) **11** Ran SP% **118.4**
Speed ratings (Par 101): **101,97,95,95,94 83,81,65,60,59 58**
toteswingers: 1&2 £4.30, 1&3 £7.90, 2&3 £16.40 CSF £12.94 CT £129.67 TOTE £2.70: £1.10, £1.40, £6.40; EX 18.40 Place 6: £23.43 Place 5:£18.86.
Owner Deborah Hart & Alan Jackson **Bred** Janus Bloodstock **Trained** Forsbrook, Staffs

FOCUS
A very modest 46-60 handicap, a seller in all but name. The winner is rated close to his course form of the previous week with the runner-up running up to her best.
Starburst Official explanation: jockey said mare missed the break
Punta Galera(IRE) Official explanation: jockey said gelding lost its action on bend
Firsaan(IRE) Official explanation: trainer said gelding was unsuited by the good to soft (soft in places) ground
T/Plt: £44.20 to a £1 stake. Pool: £36,920.48 - 608.43 winning ticket. T/Qpdt: £11.20 to a £1 stake. Pool: £3,088.02 203.80 winning tickets. JR

2873 YARMOUTH (L-H)
Thursday, June 10

OFFICIAL GOING: Good (7.5)
Wind: fresh, behind Weather: dull, misty and cold

2903 FLEGG INVESTMENT CLUB MAIDEN STKS 6f 3y
2:10 (2:17) (Class 5) 3-Y-O+ **£2,719** (£809; £404; £202) **Stalls** High

Form RPR

0 **1** **Dashing Beauty (IRE)**12 2535 4-9-0 0............ WilliamCarson(3) 12 71
(M G Quinlan) *racd alone on stands' rail: chsd ldrs: rdn and ev ch 2f out: led ent fnl f: edgd lft u.p but styd on wl fnl 150yds* **50/1**

2 *1 1/4* **Oh So Spicy** 3-8-9 0............ JackMitchell 8 65
(C F Wall) *chsd ldrs: rdn and pressed ldrs fr wl over 1f out: kpt on same pce fnl 100yds* **14/1**

0 **3** *nk* **Divine Call**41 1661 3-9-0 0............ LiamJones 6 69
(W J Haggas) *dwlt: sn bustled along and in tch: rdn and effrt ent fnl 2f: led over 1f out: edgd rt u.p and hdd ent fnl f: one pce fnl 150yds* **4/6**1

-422 **4** *8* **Vaultage (USA)**12 2535 3-8-9 69............(p) TomMcLaughlin 7 38
(E A L Dunlop) *dwlt: bustled along after s: sn wl in tch: rdn ent fnl 2f: wknd: wl btn 1f out* **5/2**2

0 **5** *1 3/4* **Attrition**12 2548 3-9-0 0............ PatCosgrave 1 38
(Andrew Reid) *led tl rdn and hdd over 1f out: wknd qckly and wl btn fnl f* **12/1**3

-046 **6** *1/2* **Hounds Ditch**16 2408 3-9-0 60............(b) RobertHavlin 10 36
(Eve Johnson Houghton) *dwlt: sn rdn and struggling to go pce: wl bhd 1/2-way: styd on past btn horses fnl f: n.d* **33/1**

7 *nk* **Shamarlane** 3-8-4 0............ TobyAtkinson(5) 3 30
(M Wigham) *s.i.s: sn rdn along and wl bhd: nvr on terms* **33/1**

66 **8** *1 3/4* **Haafhd Sharp**13 2517 3-8-9 0............ JerryO'Dwyer 4 25
(M G Quinlan) *chsd ldr tl ent fnl 2f: sn wknd: wl bhd fnl f* **33/1**

9 *4* **Cinderella** 3-8-9 0............ AndrewElliott 5 12
(Lucinda Featherstone) *s.i.s: sn rdn and a wl bhd* **100/1**

00 **10** *3 1/2* **Whispering Ridge**24 2174 3-9-0 0............ ChrisCatlin 9 —
(M Wellings) *chsd ldrs tl 1/2-way: sn dropped out: wl bhd fnl 2f* **250/1**

1m 12.92s (-1.48) **Going Correction** -0.25s/f (Firm)
WFA 3 from 4yo 8lb **10** Ran SP% **115.1**
Speed ratings (Par 103): **99,97,96,86,83 83,82,80,75,70**
toteswingers: 1&2 £16.60, 1&3 £10.80, 2&3 £3.80 CSF £574.85 TOTE £41.10: £6.20, £1.90, £1.10; EX 282.30 TRIFECTA Not won..
Owner Mrs J Quinlan **Bred** Duncan A McGregor **Trained** Newmarket, Suffolk

FOCUS
Following a dry night the going remained good with a GoingStick reading of 7.5. A modest-looking maiden with the race being delayed after the unruly Masteeat broke out underneath the stalls before being withdrawn. Not a race to rate too positively and the bare form is probably modest.
Shamarlane Official explanation: jockey said filly was slowly away

2904 MR KING FILLIES' H'CAP 6f 3y
2:40 (2:42) (Class 5) (0-75,74) 3-Y-O+ **£2,460** (£732; £365; £182) **Stalls** High

Form RPR

-662 **1** **Requisite**9 2635 5-9-1 **61**............(v) GeorgeBaker 6 75
(I A Wood) *hld up wl in tch: swtchd rt and squeezed through on stands' rail to ld 1f out: r.o strly and clr fnl 100yds: comf* **9/4**1

0-06 **2** *2 3/4* **Farmers Wish (IRE)**20 2283 3-9-2 **73**............ JackDean(3) 1 76
(J L Spearing) *pressed ldrs: rdn and ev ch wl over 1f out: drvn and nt gng pce of wnr ins fnl f* **7/1**2

0622 **3** *3/4* **Fazbee (IRE)**7 2678 4-9-8 **68**............(v) SebSanders 4 70
(P W D'Arcy) *in tch in last: rdn and effrt over 1f out: no real prog and no ch w wnr ins fnl f: plugged on to go 3rd nr fin* **9/4**1

-103 **4** *3/4* **Faited To Pretend (IRE)**7 2679 3-9-4 **72**............ AndreaAtzeni 7 70
(M Botti) *led: rdn over 1f out: hdd 1f out: wknd jst ins fnl f* **12/1**3

20-5 **5** *2 1/4* **Midnight Fantasy**14 2475 4-10-0 **74**............ SaleemGolam 2 67
(Rae Guest) *hld up wl in tch: rdn and effrt over 1f out: no real prog and btn 1f out* **7/1**2

0-40 **6** *5* **Suzie Quw**14 2475 4-9-11 **71**............(p) AndrewElliott 5 48
(J R Weymes) *dwlt: in tch: rdn wl over 2f out: wknd u.p wl over 1f out: wl bhd fnl f* **20/1**

0042 **7** *6* **Lucky Leigh**13 2485 4-9-7 **67**............ ChrisCatlin 3 25
(M R Channon) *w ldr: rdn 2f out: wknd qckly over 1f out: wl bhd fnl f* **7/1**2

1m 11.9s (-2.50) **Going Correction** -0.25s/f (Firm)
WFA 3 from 4yo+ 8lb **7** Ran SP% **111.5**
Speed ratings (Par 100): **106,102,101,100,97 90,82**
toteswingers: 1&2 £2.90, 1&3 £1.60, 2&3 £2.80 CSF £17.96 CT £36.93 TOTE £2.00: £1.20, £3.40; EX 16.10 Trifecta £59.70 Pool: £326.77 - 4.05 winning units..
Owner Paddy Barrett **Bred** Darley **Trained** Upper Lambourn, Berks

FOCUS
A competitive 56-75 fillies' handicap run at a good pace. The level is fluid with those in the frame behind the winner not looking solid.

2905 GREAT YARMOUTH SEALIFE CENTRE (S) STKS 7f 3y
3:15 (3:15) (Class 6) 2-Y-O **£1,683** (£501; £250; £125) **Stalls** High

Form RPR

01 **1** **Tupelo (IRE)**9 2631 2-8-7 0............ KierenFox(5) 6 67
(P W D'Arcy) *chsd ldr unti led over 4f out: hung rt and sddle slipped over 2f out: rdn and hung rt again wl over 1f out: drew clr 1f out: rdn out: comf* **2/1**2

42 **2** *4 1/2* **Artic Rose (IRE)**9 2631 2-8-3 0............ WilliamCarson(3) 4 50
(S C Williams) *led and crossed to r on stands' rail: hdd over 4f out: hmpd and swtchd lft wl over 1f out: sn drvn and one pce after* **7/2**3

06 **3** *2 1/2* **Chilworth Lass (IRE)**8 2642 2-8-6 0............ ChrisCatlin 9 44
(M R Channon) *hld up wl in tch: rdn and hung lft ent fnl 2f: no imp: hung rt and hmpd rival ins fnl f: hld on for 3rd* **13/8**1

605 **4** *nk* **Coolree Pearl (IRE)**20 2300 2-8-6 0............ JimmyQuinn 7 45
(A B Haynes) *bhd: outpcd and pushed along wl over 3f out: plugged on fr over 1f out: clsng on 3rd whn nt clr run and swtchd lft ins fnl f: kpt on to press for 3rd nr fin: nvr trbld ldrs* **16/1**

00 **5** *4 1/2* **No Peace (IRE)**9 2631 2-8-6 0............(v1) MarcHalford 3 32
(G G Margarson) *reminders sn after s: chsd ldrs: drvn and nt qckn ent fnl 2f: wknd and edgd lft u.p over 1f out* **28/1**

00 **6** *2 1/2* **Prison Cat (IRE)**30 1999 2-8-3 0............ MartinLane(3) 2 25
(E F Vaughan) *s.i.s: in tch in midfield: rdn 4f out: struggling and losing pl 1/2-way: no ch fnl 2f* **20/1**

00 **7** *13* **Crystal Set (IRE)**29 2022 2-8-6 0............ AmyBaker(5) 1 —
(A B Haynes) *s.i.s: a bhd: struggling u.p 4f out: t.o fnl 2f* **66/1**

0 **8** *12* **Te Amo Jen**8 2642 2-8-6 0............ FrankieMcDonald 8 —
(B G Powell) *in tch in midfield: rdn 5f out: struggling and lost pl 1/2-way: wl bhd fnl 2f: t.o* **40/1**

0 **9** *6* **Knudstrup Noble (IRE)**11 2561 2-8-11 0............ TomMcLaughlin 5 —
(P S McEntee) *in tch in midfield: rdn and struggling 4f out: wl bhd fnl 2f: t.o and eased ins fnl f* **33/1**

1m 26.57s (-0.03) **Going Correction** -0.25s/f (Firm) **9** Ran SP% **114.6**
Speed ratings (Par 91): **90,84,82,81,76 73,58,45,38**
toteswingers: 1&2 £2.10, 1&3 £1.30, 2&3 £2.50 CSF £8.79 TOTE £2.50: £1.10, £2.50, £1.02; EX 9.70 Trifecta £12.10 Pool: £456.43 - 27.69 winning units..There was no bid for the winner.
Owner Stapleford Racing Ltd **Bred** Ms Marie Walsh **Trained** Newmarket, Suffolk
■ Stewards' Enquiry : Chris Catlin two-day ban: careless riding (Jun 24-25)

FOCUS
An uncompetitive seller won in a convincing manner but the form is limited.

NOTEBOOK
Tupelo(IRE) put up an improved effort when justifying support and landing a C&D seller here last time, and once again confirmed her superiority over the runner-up quite comfortably. Soon at the head of affairs, there was a scare for her supporters when the saddle slipped over 2f out but she never looked in any danger after her rider managed to regain the momentum when rocking the saddle back into place. She saw out the 7f well and is clearly progressing. She looks capable of holding her own when stepping up slightly in grade, and will be staying with present connections after the subsequent auction failed to attract a bid. (tchd 7-4)

Artic Rose(IRE) had a 6lb pull at the weights with the winner and was well fancied to turn around the half-length deficit but could never do so after the winner went on at halfway, although she did keep on well enough for second. (op 11-4)
Chilworth Lass(IRE) was well supported down to favouritism on this drop down to selling company, but she was under pressure a long way out and never got competitive. (op 9-4)
Coolree Pearl(IRE) was held up well off the pace to see out this step up in trip. She stayed on strongly in the latter stages and might be worth another look in a similar heat but was never a threat here. (tchd 14-1)
No Peace(IRE) raced prominently before tiring over a furlong out, and continues to make little appeal. (tchd 33-1)

2906 EASTERN DAILY PRESS CLASSIFIED STKS — 1m 3y
3:50 (3:51) (Class 6) 3-Y-O — £1,942 (£578; £288; £144) Stalls High

Form — RPR

1233 **1** **Volatilis (IRE)**[23] 2221 3-9-0 64 ...... SebSanders 11 — 72+
(J W Hills) *trckd ldrs: led gng wl 2f out: rdn clr over 1f out: in n.d fnl f: eased towards fin* **13/8**[1]

0152 **2** *5* **Mr Harmoosh (IRE)**[14] 2460 3-8-11 62 ...... MartinLane(3) 12 — 60
(E F Vaughan) *stdd s: hld up in last pair: rdn and hdwy wl over 1f out: no ch w wnr fnl f: kpt on to go 2nd fnl 100yds* **7/2**[2]

0-60 **3** *hd* **Charpoy Cobra**[24] 2189 3-9-0 55 ...... RobertHavlin 3 — 60
(J A R Toller) *in tch: rdn and effrt ent fnl 2f: pressing for 2nd but no ch w wnr fnl f: kpt on* **33/1**

-200 **4** *1 ½* **Abhar (USA)**[59] 1261 3-8-9 63 ...... KierenFox(5) 7 — 56
(J R Best) *led tl 2f out: sn rdn and nt pce of wnr over 1f out: wl btn 1f out: lost 2 pls fnl 100yds* **16/1**

0610 **5** *2* **Sternian**[28] 2042 3-9-0 61 ...... JamieMackay 9 — 51
(M E Rimmer) *stdd s: hld up in last pair: rdn and sme hdwy over 1f out: kpt on: nvr gng pce to rch ldrs* **20/1**

0-00 **6** *3 ¾* **Jemimaville (IRE)**[23] 2221 3-8-11 64 ...... WilliamCarson(3) 10 — 43
(G C Bravery) *in tch in midfield: rdn 1/2-way: struggling u.p over 2f out: wl btn over 1f out* **20/1**

060- **7** *½* **Regal Rave (USA)**[227] 7056 3-9-0 59 ...... AndreaAtzeni 6 — 42
(J R Best) *chsd ldr: rdn over 2f out: wknd u.p wl over 1f out* **50/1**

3306 **8** *1 ½* **Tilsworth Glenboy**[47] 1522 3-9-0 63 ...... StevieDonohoe 1 — 38
(J R Jenkins) *in tch in midfield: rdn and no prog ent fnl 2f: btn whn n.m.r wl over 1f out* **7/1**[3]

442 **9** *4* **Young Simon**[14] 2459 3-9-0 64 ......(v) MarcHalford 5 — 29
(G G Margarson) *t.k.h early: hld up in tch in midfield: rdn and lost pl 1/2-way: bhd whn n.m.r wl over 1f out* **9/1**

5-40 **10** *3* **Brave Enough (USA)**[44] 1601 3-9-0 62 ...... GeorgeBaker 2 — 22
(M A Magnusson) *chsd ldrs: wknd u.p ent fnl 2f: wl bhd fnl f* **20/1**

1400 **11** *17* **Ana Moutabahi**[45] 1582 3-9-0 65 ......(p) PaulDoe 4 — —
(Jim Best) *dwlt: sn rdn along: in tch in midfield: drvn and struggling wl over 2f out: wl bhd and eased fnl f: t.o* **14/1**

1m 38.26s (-2.34) **Going Correction** -0.25s/f (Firm) — 11 Ran SP% 114.6
Speed ratings (Par 97): **101,96,95,94,92 88,88,86,82,79 62**
toteswingers: 1&2 £1.70, 1&3 £17.00, 2&3 £25.80 CSF £6.01 TOTE £2.80: £1.30, £1.10, £8.50; EX 6.40 Trifecta £131.80 Pool: £425.69 - 2.39 winning units..
Owner P Abberley **Bred** G J King **Trained** Upper Lambourn, Berks

FOCUS
A run-of-the-mill 0-65 handicap, with the two at the head of the market filling stalls 11 and 12 against the nearside rail and proceeding to fill the principal places. The form is limited but the winner looks improved.
Ana Moutabahi Official explanation: jockey said colt stumbled early

2907 CHC HELICOPTERS AT CHC.CA H'CAP — 2m
4:25 (4:26) (Class 6) (0-60,58) 4-Y-O+ — £1,942 (£578; £288; £144) Stalls High

Form — RPR

-400 **1** **Uncle Keef (IRE)**[8] 2645 4-9-4 58 ......(b[1]) GeorgeBaker 2 — 67
(M P Tregoning) *hld up in last pair: hdwy on inner 4f out: nt clr run and swtchd rt over 2f out: upsides ldr gng best 2f out: rdn 1f out: fnd little u.p and stl upsides tl pushed ahd nr fin* **6/1**[3]

-33 **2** *nk* **Hassadin**[38] 1758 4-8-5 45 ...... AndrewElliott 1 — 54
(A B Haynes) *mde most: rdn wl over 3f out: jnd 2f out: kpt battling on u.p tl hdd: no ex nr fin* **12/1**

3144 **3** *1 ½* **Broughtons Point**[14] 2476 4-9-1 55 ...... JamieMackay 11 — 62
(W J Musson) *stdd after s: hld up in last pair: smooth hdwy 3f out: chsd ldng pair and rdn over 1f out: kpt hanging lft and one pce fnl f* **9/2**[2]

14-0 **4** *13* **Snowberry Hill (USA)**[31] 1983 7-8-11 50 ...... JimmyQuinn 3 — 42
(Lucinda Featherstone) *in tch in midfield: hdwy 5f out: chsd ldr and rdn wl over 2f out tl 2f out: wknd over 1f out* **33/1**

4-56 **5** *¾* **Rock Tech**[63] 1188 5-8-9 48 ...... AdrianMcCarthy 8 — 39
(J R Jenkins) *t.k.h: hld up in tch towards rr: rdn and sme hdwy ent fnl 4f: struggling and wl btn over 2f out: no ch but plugged on fnl f* **100/1**

6025 **6** *¾* **Mister Frosty (IRE)**[9] 2636 4-8-13 53 ...... SaleemGolam 9 — 43
(G Prodromou) *chsd ldrs: wnt 2nd over 4f out tl over 2f out: wknd u.p wl over 1f out: wl btn fnl f* **33/1**

6-42 **7** *1 ¾* **Astroleo**[20] 2302 4-8-2 47 ...... AshleyMorgan(5) 4 — 35
(M H Tompkins) *prom early: sn in midfield: rdn and effrt on outer over 3f out: wknd 2f out: wl btn over 1f out* **13/2**

-250 **8** *3 ¼* **Honorable Endeavor**[20] 2302 4-8-7 50 ......(b[1]) MartinLane(3) 7 — 34
(E F Vaughan) *hld up in tch towards rr: rdn and hdwy ent fnl 4f: swtchd rt and drvn over 2f out: wknd ent fnl 2f: sn wl bhd* **20/1**

0-21 **9** *3 ¼* **Any Given Moment (IRE)**[38] 1759 4-9-3 57 ...... ChrisCatlin 13 — 37
(D M Simcock) *chsd ldrs: wknd u.p over 3f out: wl btn fnl 2f* **2/1**[1]

3-11 **10** *56* **Mediterranean Sea (IRE)**[22] 2230 4-9-3 57 ...... PaulDoe 14 — —
(J R Jenkins) *dwlt: sn bustled along: in tch in midfield: rdn and dropped out qckly over 4f out: t.o and virtually p.u fnl 2f* **12/1**

231/ **11** *4* **That Look**[12] 6060 7-9-5 58 ...... TomMcLaughlin 16 — —
(D E Cantillon) *w ldr tl rdn and struggling over 4f out: sn bhd: t.o and virtually p.u fnl 2f* **12/1**

6-14 **12** *22* **Three Boars**[36] 1828 8-9-1 54 ......(b) PatCosgrave 15 — —
(S Gollings) *stdd s: in tch in midfield: dropped to last and rdn 6f out: lost tch over 4f out: t.o and virtually p.u fnl 2f* **33/1**

3m 30.07s (-4.53) **Going Correction** -0.25s/f (Firm)
WFA 4 from 5yo+ 1lb — 12 Ran SP% 116.8
Speed ratings (Par 101): **101,100,100,93,93 92,91,90,88,60 58,47**
toteswingers:1&2 £20.60, 2&3 £11.60, 1&3 £9.80 CSF £70.03 CT £356.12 TOTE £10.20: £4.70, £5.40, £1.20; EX 105.40 Trifecta £357.10 Part won. Pool: £482.62 - 0.76 winning units..
Owner R A H Evans **Bred** Premier Bloodstock **Trained** Lambourn, Berks

FOCUS
A low-grade staying handicap that was run at just an ordinary pace and the front three came well clear of the remainder. The form is rated around the placed horses for now.
Any Given Moment(IRE) Official explanation: trainer had no explanation for the poor form shown
Mediterranean Sea(IRE) Official explanation: jockey said filly never travelled

2908 MOULTON NURSERIES H'CAP — 1m 6f 17y
5:00 (5:00) (Class 5) (0-70,70) 3-Y-O — £2,460 (£732; £365; £182) Stalls High

Form — RPR

0-52 **1** **Motrice**[7] 2675 3-8-10 59 ...... SebSanders 7 — 73+
(Sir Mark Prescott) *stdd s: t.k.h: hld up in last pair: hdwy 4f out: rdn to chse ldr whn lft in ld ent fnl 2f: r.o strly and clr fnl f: eased towards fin* **4/6**[1]

-664 **2** *4 ½* **Head Hunted**[38] 1778 3-8-9 61 ...... MartinLane(3) 6 — 67
(D M Simcock) *in tch: hdwy to chse ldr ent fnl 4f: rdn wl over 2f out: lft w ev ch ent fnl 2f: drvn and outpcd by wnr over 1f out and wl hld fnl f* **11/1**

0-26 **3** *5* **Red Barcelona (IRE)**[21] 2248 3-8-6 60 ...... AshleyMorgan(5) 1 — 59
(M H Tompkins) *hld up towards rr: rdn and effrt over 3f out: no prog and wl btn 2f out: plugged on fnl f to go modest 3rd fnl 75yds* **7/1**[3]

0-01 **4** *½* **Othello (IRE)**[16] 2412 3-8-11 60 ...... ChrisCatlin 4 — 58
(E F Vaughan) *stdd after s: hld up in last pair: rdn and hung lft 3f out: 3rd and no threat to ldrs wl over 1f out: lost modest 3rd fnl 75yds* **20/1**

0-00 **5** *12* **Free Grain**[28] 2051 3-8-10 59 ...... JimmyQuinn 8 — 41
(J L Dunlop) *chsd ldr tl ent fnl 4f: wknd u.p 3f out: wl btn fnl 2f* **28/1**

600 **6** *18* **Oh Two**[17] 2401 3-8-3 52 ...... AndreaAtzeni 5 — 8
(S C Williams) *chsd ldrs tl over 4f out: sn struggling u.p: t.o fnl 2f* **66/1**

3334 **7** *19* **Corres (IRE)**[27] 2079 3-9-7 70 ...... GeorgeBaker 2 — —
(D R C Elsworth) *stmbld s: sn led: pushed clr and c towards centre wl over 4f out: rdn and stmbld bdly over 2f out: sn eased and hdd: virtually p.u fnl 2f* **7/2**[2]

3m 6.96s (-0.64) **Going Correction** -0.05s/f (Good) — 7 Ran SP% 112.7
Speed ratings (Par 99): **99,96,93,93,86 76,65**
toteswingers:1&2 £3.70, 2&3 £8.90, 1&3 £1.70 CSF £8.68 CT £24.67 TOTE £1.50: £1.10, £6.70; EX 9.50 Trifecta £42.50 Pool: £274.41 - 4.77 winning units..
Owner Miss K Rausing **Bred** Miss K Rausing **Trained** Newmarket, Suffolk

FOCUS
A small filed but a competitive handicap, with the long-time leader Corres kicking clear over 3f out and forcing the rest of the field to come under pressure. He stumbled badly when holding a diminishing advantage before being eased down. The third and fourth are rated a few pounds off recent marks.
Corres(IRE) Official explanation: jockey said colt stumbled approximately 1 1/2f out.

2909 GREAT YARMOUTH TOURIST AND INFORMATION CENTRE H'CAP — 1m 3f 101y
5:30 (5:30) (Class 6) (0-65,65) 3-Y-O — £1,942 (£578; £288; £144) Stalls Low

Form — RPR

0-00 **1** **Kathleen Frances**[21] 2255 3-9-0 63 ...... AshleyMorgan(5) 1 — 72
(M H Tompkins) *t.k.h: wl in tch: rdn to chal 2f out: led 1f out: edgd rt but asserted ins fnl f: kpt on wl: eased nr fin* **13/2**

5-04 **2** *½* **Apache Kid (IRE)**[19] 2321 3-9-0 58 ...... JimmyQuinn 4 — 66
(D M Simcock) *hld up in tch: pushed along over 4f out: rdn and chsd ldrs over 1f out: kpt on u.p fnl f: wnt 2nd wl ins fnl f* **5/1**[3]

6-54 **3** *1* **Bondage (IRE)**[24] 2175 3-9-7 65 ...... PatCosgrave 9 — 71
(J R Fanshawe) *chsd ldrs: rdn and effrt wl over 2f out: led 2f out: drvn and hdd 1f out: one pce ins fnl f* **4/1**[2]

0004 **4** *1 ½* **Denton Ryal**[9] 2633 3-8-0 51 ...... AdamBeschizza(7) 6 — 54
(M E Rimmer) *hld up in tch towards rr: rdn and effrt wl over 2f out: drvn to chse ldrs over 1f out: styd on same pce fnl f* **25/1**

0-35 **5** *nse* **Astronomer's Dream**[134] 308 3-8-13 60 ...... MartinLane(3) 12 — 63
(E F Vaughan) *t.k.h: stdd after s: hld up in midfield: hdwy over 3f out: edging lft wl over 1f out: effrt on rail ent fnl f: no imp fnl 150yds* **50/1**

000- **6** *4* **Allannah Abu**[224] 7135 3-9-3 61 ...... SebSanders 10 — 58
(Sir Mark Prescott) *chsd ldrs: wnt 2nd over 5f out tl jst over 2f out: unable qck 2f out: wknd jst ins fnl f* **11/2**

5561 **7** *3 ¼* **Broughtons Swinger**[9] 2620 3-9-3 61 6ex ...... StevieDonohoe 5 — 52
(W J Musson) *led: rdn ent fnl 3f: drvn and hdd 2f out: wknd ent fnl f* **11/4**[1]

0-00 **8** *4* **Dance With Chance (IRE)**[19] 2336 3-8-12 56 ...... AndreaAtzeni 14 — 40
(W R Swinburn) *hld up in last trio: drvn and no rspnse 4f out: wl bhd fnl 2f* **25/1**

6-26 **9** *6* **Man In The Mirror (IRE)**[9] 2633 3-8-7 54 ......(p) AshleyHamblett(3) 7 — 28
(P L Gilligan) *t.k.h: chsd ldr tl over 5f out: styd chsng ldrs: struggling u.p over 3f out: wl bhd fnl 2f* **20/1**

1620 **10** *shd* **Il Portico**[16] 2412 3-9-1 59 ......(v[1]) ChrisCatlin 3 — 33
(M R Channon) *dwlt: a in last trio: rdn and toiling bdly over 3f out: wl bhd fnl 2f* **14/1**

00-6 **11** *1* **Sancho Panza**[19] 2336 3-8-5 49 ...... SaleemGolam 8 — 21
(Miss J Feilden) *in tch: lost pl and pushed along 6f out: rallied u.p on outer over 4f out: wknd qckly wl over 2f out:* **20/1**

000- **12** *55* **Ava Doll**[208] 7388 3-8-2 46 oh1 ...... AdrianMcCarthy 13 — —
(J R Jenkins) *stdd and dropped in bhd after s: a in rr: lost tch rapidly over 4f out: t.o and virtually p.u fnl 2f* **100/1**

2m 28.79s (0.09) **Going Correction** -0.05s/f (Good) — 12 Ran SP% 118.9
Speed ratings (Par 97): **97,96,95,94,94 91,89,86,82,82 81,41**
toteswingers:1&2 £6.50, 2&3 £4.40, 1&3 £6.70 CSF £35.87 CT £149.28 TOTE £11.20: £5.00, £3.30, £1.90; EX 40.50 Trifecta £126.10 Pool of £185.86 - 1.09 winning units. Place 6: £11.32 Place 5: £7.28 .
Owner Russell Trew Ltd **Bred** Russell Trew Ltd **Trained** Newmarket, Suffolk

FOCUS
A weak, low-grade handicap run at a sound pace with the first two improvers and the third and fourth close to their marks, suggesting the form is sound.
Kathleen Frances Official explanation: trainer said, regarding apparent improvement in form, that the filly had been very backward, ran very green last time and was better suited by the longer trip.
T/Plt: £22.40 to a £1 stake. Pool £58,166.10 - 1,887.63 winning tickets. T/Qpdt: £4.20 to a £1 stake. Pool £4,614.09 - 808.63 winning tickets. SP

2910 - 2911a (Foreign Racing) - See Raceform Interactive

2567 LEOPARDSTOWN (L-H)
Thursday, June 10

OFFICIAL GOING: Good (good to firm in places)

2912a BALLYOGAN STKS (GROUP 3) (F&M) — 6f
7:05 (7:07) 3-Y-O+ — £34,513 (£10,088; £4,778; £1,592)

RPR

1 **Gilt Edge Girl**[46] 1545 4-9-6 ...... LukeMorris 1 — 109
(C G Cox) *trckd ldrs on inner in 3rd: wnt 2nd and pushed along to chal under 2f out: led jst over 1f out: hrd rdn and kpt on wl* **9/1**

2 *1 ¼* **Beyond Desire**[19] 2326 3-8-12 ...... PJSmullen 4 — 103
(M A Jarvis) *racd keenly and trckd ldrs in 4th: wnt 3rd early st: 2nd fnl f and kpt on one pce wout matching wnr* **7/4**[1]

3 ½ **Distinctive**[39] 1726 3-9-1 .... TomEaves 2 104+
(B Smart) *settled on inner in 5th: 4th early st: swtchd rt over 1f out: kpt on one pce into 3rd fnl f* **6/1**[3]

4 1 ¾ **Miss Gorica (IRE)**[3] 2827 6-9-6 106 .... WMLordan 8 98
(Ms Joanna Morgan, Ire) *led and showed gd spd: rdn ent st and pressed fr under 2f out: hdd jst over 1f out: no ex fnl f* **10/3**[2]

5 3 **Full Of Hope (IRE)**[18] 2370 3-8-12 92 .... SMLevey 5 86
(A P O'Brien, Ire) *chsd ldrs in 8th: nvr a threat: rdn along ent st: wnt mod 5th fnl f* **25/1**

6 nk **Glorified**[33] 1937 3-8-12 .... JMurtagh 3 85
(David Wachman, Ire) *slowly away: chsd ldrs mainly 7th: no threat fr 2f out* **6/1**[3]

7 1 ¼ **Invincible Ash (IRE)**[19] 2353 5-9-6 94 ....(b) GFCarroll 7 83
(M Halford, Ire) *outpcd in rr: kpt on one pce u.p fr 2f out wout threatening* **25/1**

8 2 **Atasari (IRE)**[18] 2370 3-8-12 103 .... KJManning 10 75
(J S Bolger, Ire) *trckd ldr in 2nd: pushed along ent st: sn no ex: eased whn btn fnl f* **7/1**

9 3 ½ **Velvet Flicker (IRE)**[19] 2353 3-8-12 99 .... DPMcDonogh 9 64
(Kevin Prendergast, Ire) *trckd ldrs on outer in 6th: rdn and no ex fr 2f out* **12/1**

10 5 **Queen Of Troy (IRE)**[18] 2370 3-8-12 92 .... CO'Donoghue 6 48
(A P O'Brien, Ire) *a towards rr* **25/1**

1m 13.13s (-0.97) **Going Correction** 0.0s/f (Good)
WFA 3 from 4yo+ 8lb **10** Ran SP% **129.7**
Speed ratings: **106,104,103,101,97 96,95,92,87,81**
CSF £27.61 TOTE £9.00: £1.90, £1.10, £2.60; DF 21.00.
Owner Wood Street Syndicate V & C J Harper **Bred** Whitsbury Manor Stud **Trained** Lambourn, Berks

FOCUS
The form looks sound rated around the placed horses.

NOTEBOOK
Gilt Edge Girl became the seventh British-trained winner of the race in the past nine years. A Listed winner over 5f at Bath in April on her previous start, the winner was always close up on the inside and hit the front over 1f out, keeping on gamely to the line and confirming that she is on the upgrade. (op 8/1)
Beyond Desire had won a Listed event over this trip at Haydock last month when she raced keenly. She was again a bit free here before going third into the straight and launching her challenge under pressure over 1f out. She soon had every chance but was well held towards the finish. (op 7/4 tchd 15/8)
Distinctive, dropping back in trip after running fifth in the 1,000 Guineas at Newmarket, had won a Group 3 event over this trip at Ayr last season. Fourth on the inside turning for home, she was soon ridden and kept on steadily when switched right inside the final furlong.
Miss Gorica(IRE), making a quick reappearance following her Listed win over 5f at Naas on Monday, broke out of the stalls before the start. She made the running until giving best under pressure over 1f out from where she could raise no extra. (op 5/1)
Full Of Hope(IRE), dropping in trip after finishing in rear in the Irish 1,000 Guineas in which she led until a furlong and a half out, kept on in the straight without ever posing a threat.
Glorified, winner of a 7f maiden at Dundalk on her only previous start, missed the break and could make little impression from a furlong and a half out, having been fifth into the straight. (op 8/1)

2913 - 2916a (Foreign Racing) - See Raceform Interactive

2357 MAISONS-LAFFITTE (R-H)
Thursday, June 10

OFFICIAL GOING: Turf: good to soft

2917a PRIX LA FLECHE (LISTED RACE) (2YO) (TURF) 5f
12:15 (12:00) 2-Y-O **£24,336** (£9,734; £7,300; £4,867; £2,433)

RPR

1 **Miss Liberty (FR)**[8] 2-8-10 0 .... MaximeGuyon 4 101
(Mme Pia Brandt, France) **58/10**[3]

2 1 **Magic Potion (FR)**[20] 2-8-10 0 .... Christophe-PatriceLemaire 6 98
(P Bary, France) **31/1**

3 ¾ **Lone Cat (FR)**[20] 2-8-10 0 .... ChristopheSoumillon 3 95
(Y De Nicolay, France) **78/10**

4 snk **Captain Chop (FR)**[38] 2-9-0 0 .... FlavienPrat 5 98
(D Guillemin, France) **7/2**[2]

5 1 ½ **Choose Wisely (IRE)**[23] 2202 2-9-0 0 .... StephenCraine 8 93
(K A Ryan) *smartly away: led in centre of trck: rdn 2f out: outpcd: no ex fnl f: styd on* **9/1**

6 ¾ **Belle Aumone (FR)**[15] 2-8-10 0 .... GregoryBenoist 10 86
(S Jesus, France) **13/1**

7 1 ½ **Kfar Sama (FR)**[37] 2-8-10 0 .... ThierryJarnet 9 81
(D Guillemin, France) **29/1**

8 1 **Lady Jak (FR)**[20] 2-8-10 0 .... RonanThomas 7 77
(J-V Toux, France) **35/1**

9 2 **Irish Chope (FR)**[8] 2-8-10 0 .... TonyPiccone 11 70
(C Boutin, France) **66/1**

10 nk **Crespo Crispado (SPA)**[8] 2-9-0 0 .... IoritzMendizabal 1 73
(C Boutin, France) **14/1**

11 **Melody Dawn (USA)**[14] 2-8-10 0 .... OlivierPeslier 2 —
(C Laffon-Parias, France) **2/1**[1]

60.60 secs (60.60) **11** Ran SP% **116.2**
WIN (incl. 1 euro stake): 6.80. PLACES: 2.30, 7.10, 2.60. DF: 72.60. SF: 186.80.
Owner Ecurie D Primes **Bred** Ecurie D **Trained** France

2584 CHEPSTOW (L-H)
Friday, June 11

OFFICIAL GOING: Good to firm (9.1)
Wind: Virtually nil Weather: Bright early

2918 EUROPEAN BREEDERS' FUND NOVICE STKS 6f 16y
6:25 (6:26) (Class 4) 2-Y-O **£4,857** (£1,445; £722; £360) **Stalls** High

Form RPR

1232 1 **Joyously**[10] 2630 2-8-6 0 .... AndrewHeffernan(3) 7 78
(P D Evans) *mde all: rdn over 2f out: edgd lft u.p appr fnl f: hld on gamely* **11/1**

51 2 ½ **Bilko Pak (IRE)**[53] 1429 2-9-5 0 .... PatDobbs 5 86
(R Hannon) *chsd wnr: rdn over 2f out: styd on u.p thrght fnl f but nt quite rch wnr* **6/1**[3]

1 3 hd **Cafe Elektric**[14] 2486 2-9-5 0 .... SebSanders 4 85
(Sir Mark Prescott) *s.i.s: sn pushed along and trcking ldrs: drvn again wl over 2f out: styd on wl u.p fnl f and gng on to press for 2nd fnl 75yds but nt quite rch wnr* **5/6**[1]

41 4 2 **Memen (IRE)**[28] 2077 2-9-5 0 .... JamieSpencer 2 79
(P F I Cole) *chsd ldrs: rdn over 2f out: styd on same pce fr over 1f out* **5/2**[2]

0 5 15 **Symphony Of Love**[31] 1999 2-8-4 0 .... KierenFox(5) 6 24
(D Burchell) *green and sn wl bhd* **150/1**

1m 11.6s (-0.40) **Going Correction** -0.35s/f (Firm) **5** Ran SP% **106.4**
Speed ratings (Par 95): **88,87,87,84,64**
CSF £63.73 TOTE £18.50: £8.90, £3.20; EX 21.70.
Owner Nick Shutts **Bred** N Shutts **Trained** Pandy, Monmouths
■ Stewards' Enquiry : Andrew Heffernan caution: used whip down shoulder in the forehand.

FOCUS
A warm little novice race in which four of the five runners had winning form. The winner is rated to form with the placed horses close to their marks.

NOTEBOOK
Joyously made all and proved too tough to pass. Despite looking vulnerable to her less-exposed rivals, the ultra-consistent daughter of Needwood Blade galloped on relentlessly through the final 2f, though edging left, doing more than enough to keep the colts at bay. (op 9-1 tchd 12-1)
Bilko Pak(IRE) ran a solid race on his first try at 6f, keeping on well but never really looking like getting to the winner. (op 11-2 tchd 7-1)
Cafe Elektric could go down as a shade unfortunate given he was forced to sit and wait for the gap to come up the rail. The winner had already gone by the time he got clear but he was closing at the finish. He is quite highly thought-of and it would be no surprise if he proved much better than he showed here. (op 8-11)
Memen(IRE) looked a nice prospect when winning at Newbury. He dropped off the tail of the front in the final furlong and now has a bit to prove. (op 10-3)

2919 LINDLEY CATERING MAIDEN H'CAP 6f 16y
6:55 (6:55) (Class 5) (0-70,70) 3-Y-0+ **£2,719** (£809; £404; £202) **Stalls** High

Form RPR

-043 1 **Joe Packet**[29] 2052 3-9-7 70 .... StephenCraine 13 82
(J G Portman) *trckd ldrs: wnt 2nd 2f out: drvn and styd on strly fnl f to ld last strides* **5/1**[2]

0334 2 nk **Sermons Mount (USA)**[11] 2590 4-9-0 55 ....(b) JamieSpencer 9 68
(Mouse Hamilton-Fairley) *led: pushed along over 2f out: hrd rdn and kpt on fr over 1f out: ct last strides* **4/1**[1]

60-0 3 3 **Bathwick Xaara**[84] 933 3-8-9 58 .... RichardKingscote 2 59
(J G Portman) *chsd ldrs: pushed along over 2f out: kpt on fnl f but no ch w ldng duo* **50/1**

0306 4 nk **Desert Pride**[11] 2589 5-8-10 51 .... FrannyNorton 12 53
(W S Kittow) *chsd ldrs: rdn over 2f out: styd on fnl f to cl on 3rd but no ch w ldng duo* **11/2**[3]

/00- 5 2 ½ **Bouggie Daize**[321] 4326 4-10-0 69 .... SebSanders 8 63
(C G Cox) *in tch: hdwy 3f out: sn pushed along: nvr quite gng pce to rch ldrs and wknd fnl f* **17/2**

5-05 6 1 ¼ **Lutine Charlie (IRE)**[17] 2416 3-9-4 67 .... JimCrowley 4 55
(P Winkworth) *chsd ldrs: rdn over 2f out: wknd ins fnl f* **8/1**

00-3 7 1 ¾ **Emiratesdotcom**[11] 2590 4-8-6 50 oh3 .... WilliamCarson(3) 3 35
(J M Bradley) *s.i.s: bhd and sn struggling: hdwy over 1f out: styd on cl home but nvr any threat* **7/1**

03-2 8 1 ½ **Law Of Attraction (IRE)**[44] 1622 3-9-7 70 .... LukeMorris 7 48
(J R Gask) *s.i.s: in rr: pushed along 1/2-way: mod prog fnl 2f* **10/1**

005 9 1 ¼ **Tigers Charm**[21] 2297 3-8-1 50 oh1 .... DavidProbert 10 24
(J M Bradley) *chsd ldrs: rdn over 3f out: wknd ins fnl 2f* **33/1**

24/- 10 1 ¼ **On The Feather**[624] 6223 4-9-7 65 .... JamesMillman(3) 5 37
(B R Millman) *in rr and bhd: modest prog fnl f* **28/1**

3056 11 ½ **Deely Plaza**[10] 2624 3-9-4 67 .... PatDobbs 11 35
(J A Glover) *chsd ldrs: rdn 3f out: sn btn* **28/1**

4552 12 1 ½ **Libertino (IRE)**[52] 1457 3-8-13 65 .... AndrewHeffernan(3) 14 29
(J Gallagher) *rdn fr stalls: bhd fr 1/2-way* **10/1**

6/0- 13 20 **Rose De Rita**[354] 3204 5-8-9 50 oh5 .... FrankieMcDonald 6 —
(L P Grassick) *in tch to 1/2-way: sn lost tch* **100/1**

1m 10.04s (-1.96) **Going Correction** -0.35s/f (Firm)
WFA 3 from 4yo+ 8lb **13** Ran SP% **117.2**
Speed ratings (Par 103): **99,98,94,94,90 89,86,84,83,81 80,78,52**
toteswingers:1&2:£2.70, 1&3:£67.80, 2&3:£67.80 CSF £23.74 CT £930.78 TOTE £10.10: £3.10, £1.40, £21.30; EX 29.10.
Owner Stuart McPhee **Bred** Stuart McPhee Bloodstock Ltd **Trained** Compton, Berks

FOCUS
A modest bunch, as is implied by the type of race, and nothing got into it from off the pace. The form is limited, with the runner-up the best guide.

2920 LINDLEY CATERING H'CAP 7f 16y
7:30 (7:31) (Class 5) (0-70,70) 4-Y-0+ **£2,914** (£867; £433; £216) **Stalls** High

Form RPR

4326 1 **Dr Wintringham (IRE)**[7] 2727 4-8-13 62 .... JerryO'Dwyer 6 83+
(Karen George) *trckd ldrs: led ins fnl 2f: pushed clr over 1f out: eased fnl 75yds* **6/1**[2]

0-61 2 2 ½ **Mambo Spirit (IRE)**[9] 2643 6-9-6 69 6ex .... TomQueally 10 79
(Stef Higgins) *disp ld tl led wl over 2f out: hdd ins fnl 2f: sn one pce but clsd on eased down wnr cl home* **11/4**[1]

5-00 3 1 ½ **Abu Dubai (IRE)**[21] 2299 4-8-2 51 .... JamieMackay 5 57
(J A Glover) *chsd ldrs: rdn over 2f out and sn one pce: kpt on again ins fnl f as wnr eased down fnl 75yds* **25/1**

10-0 4 shd **Bidable**[19] 2362 6-8-6 55 .... DavidProbert 11 61
(B Palling) *prom early: sn pushed along: outpcd fr 3f out: styd on again as wnr eased down fnl 75yds* **10/1**

2065 5 1 ¼ **Unlimited**[14] 2490 8-8-10 59 .... SebSanders 8 61
(A W Carroll) *s.i.s: in rr: pushed along and sme hdwy over 2f out: kpt on as wnr eased down fnl 75yds: nvr a threat* **6/1**[2]

010- 6 nk **You've Been Mowed**[240] 6778 4-8-10 62 .... WilliamCarson(3) 14 63
(R J Price) *disp ld tl wl over 2f out: wknd fnl f* **12/1**

-006 7 1 ½ **Prince Rossi (IRE)**[47] 1543 6-8-8 57 ....(v) JimCrowley 13 54
(A E Price) *chsd ldrs: rdn over 2f out and sn btn* **7/1**[3]

1600 8 ½ **Fault**[23] 2236 4-9-4 67 ....(t) MickyFenton 9 63
(Stef Higgins) *rdn along 1/2-way: a struggling to go pce* **7/1**[3]

0100 9 1 ½ **Portrush Storm**[7] 2727 5-8-2 51 oh2 ....(p) CathyGannon 12 43
(R E Peacock) *outpcd most of way* **25/1**

6565 10 2 ¼ **Mountain Pass (USA)**[36] 1839 8-8-5 54 ....(tp) RichardThomas 4 40
(B J Llewellyn) *outpcd most of way* **22/1**

0-34 11 ½ **Russian Rave**[20] 2342 4-9-4 67 StephenCraine 3 52
(J G Portman) *chsd ldrs to 1/2-way* **8/1**
1m 21.77s (-1.43) **Going Correction** -0.35s/f (Firm) 11 Ran SP% **120.2**
Speed ratings (Par 103): **94,91,89,89,87 87,85,85,83,80 80**
toteswingers:1&2:£4.90, 1&3:£51.70, 2&3:£52.80 CSF £22.78 CT £387.38 TOTE £5.20: £1.30, £3.80, £22.20; EX 31.10.
Owner Mrs Isabel Fraser **Bred** Peter Molony **Trained** Higher Eastington, Devon
FOCUS
Run-of the-mill low-grade handicap form but fairly sound with the placed horses to form.

2921 LINDLEY CATERING MAIDEN FILLIES' STKS 1m 4f 23y
8:05 (8:09) (Class 5) 3-Y-0+ **£2,590** (£770; £385; £192) **Stalls** Low

Form RPR
2-4 1 **Desert Sage**[28] 2076 3-8-12 0 JimCrowley 6 83+
(R M Beckett) *reluctant to enter stalls: trckd ldrs in 3rd tl wnt 2nd 5f out: led ins fnl 4f: pushed along 2f out: asserted wl over 1f out and a in command fnl f* **11/10**[1]
20-3 2 1 ½ **Donna Elvira**[11] 2585 3-8-9 0 PatrickHills(3) 10 80
(R Hannon) *in tch: hdwy to trck ldrs 3f out: rdn over 2f out: styd on to chse wnr fnl 120yds but a comf hld* **10/1**[3]
3 3 1 ½ **Heart Of Hearts**[14] 2507 3-8-12 0 TomQueally 3 78
(H R A Cecil) *trckd ldrs: wnt 2nd over 3f out: sn rdn and effrt: nvr quite upsides: outpcd wl over 1f out: no ex and lost 2nd fnl 120yds* **11/4**[2]
26 4 11 **Tartaria**[15] 2473 4-9-13 0 JamieSpencer 12 60
(D M Simcock) *t.k.h early: in rr tl hdwy 5f out: disp cl 3rd over 3f out: sn pushed along: hung lft and btn over 2f out* **14/1**
6 5 1 ¼ **Businessmoney Judi**[36] 1851 4-9-10 0 JamesMillman(3) 11 58
(B R Millman) *s.i.s: towards rr: hdwy over 3f out: nvr anywhere nr ldrs and styd on same pce fr over 2f out* **50/1**
6 8 **Deejan (IRE)**[90] 5-9-13 0 DavidProbert 4 46
(B Palling) *slowly away: led after 1f: hdd ins fnl 4f: wknd rapidly* **33/1**
7 nk **Intimate Whisper** 4-9-13 0 FergusSweeney 1 45
(H Candy) *chsd ldrs: rdn 4f out: wknd qckly over 3f out* **66/1**
0 8 24 **Snow White Feet (IRE)**[20] 2335 3-8-12 0 MickyFenton 2 7
(H J L Dunlop) *led 1f: chsd ldr to 5f out: sn wknd* **100/1**
0 9 19 **Farmers Surprise**[17] 2414 3-8-5 0 DavidKenny(7) 8 —
(H J Evans) *sn bhd* **100/1**
10 1 ¼ **Fraam Lea**[121] 4-9-10 0 RobertLButler(3) 9 —
(A E Price) *s.i.s: sn bhd* **125/1**
2m 35.26s (-3.74) **Going Correction** -0.35s/f (Firm)
WFA 3 from 4yo+ 15lb 10 Ran SP% **99.2**
Speed ratings (Par 100): **98,97,96,88,87 82,82,66,53,52**
toteswingers:1&2:£2.10, 1&3:£1.10, 2&3:£1.80 CSF £8.71 TOTE £1.80: £1.02, £1.40, £1.10; EX 9.90.
Owner J H Richmond-Watson **Bred** J H Richmond-Watson **Trained** Whitsbury, Hants
■ Stewards' Enquiry : Richard Mullen one-day ban: used whip when trying to get filly into stalls (Jun 25)
FOCUS
Little depth to this maiden but the winner is decent and the first three finished well clear.

2922 OFFICE IMAGE H'CAP 1m 2f 36y
8:40 (8:40) (Class 5) (0-75,74) 4-Y-0+ **£2,914** (£867; £433; £216) **Stalls** Low

Form RPR
45-6 1 **Critical Path (IRE)**[22] 2256 4-9-5 72 DavidProbert 1 83
(A M Balding) *trckd ldrs: wnt 2nd and rdn 2f out: narrow ld appr fnl f: hld on all out* **5/2**[2]
1211 2 shd **King's Masque**[17] 2411 4-9-7 74 JamieSpencer 8 85
(B J Llewellyn) *sn trcking ldr: led over 2f out: sn rdn: narrowly hdd appr fnl f: rallied u.str.p to press wnr cl home: jst failed* **2/1**[1]
00 3 4 ½ **Ocean Transit (IRE)**[21] 2284 5-9-5 72 TomQueally 2 74
(R J Price) *set mod pce and tried to qckn over 3f out: hdd over 2f out: sn outpcd by ldng duo but styd on fr over 1f out for wl hld 3rd* **16/1**
100- 4 1 ¾ **Integria**[232] 6977 4-9-1 68 SebSanders 10 67
(Miss Venetia Williams) *in rr but in tch off mod pce: hdwy 3f out: drvn to chse ldrs over 2f out: sn readily outpcd* **20/1**
6002 5 ½ **Hector Spectre (IRE)**[19] 2360 4-8-6 59 (p) FrankieMcDonald 5 57
(Mrs N S Evans) *t.k.h in rr: off mod pce: hdwy and pushed along 3f out: in tch over 2f out: styd on same pce* **25/1**
6310 6 nk **Make Amends (IRE)**[15] 2467 5-9-5 72 RichardKingscote 7 69
(R J Hodges) *s.i.s: hld up in rr off mod pce: shkn up 2f out: styd on fnl f but nvr any threat* **7/1**[3]
4320 7 hd **I'm In The Pink (FR)**[14] 2314 6-9-2 72 AndrewHeffernan(3) 3 69
(P D Evans) *chsd ldrs off mod pce: rdn 3f out: styd on same pce and no ch fnl 2f* **10/1**
0630 8 nse **Mr Udagawa**[30] 2024 4-9-2 69 RichardThomas 6 65
(B J Llewellyn) *towards rr off mod pce: hdwy to cl on ldrs 3f out: sn rdn: styd on same pce and no ch fnl 2f* **33/1**
3120 9 nk **Spinning Ridge (IRE)**[5] 2783 5-9-5 72 (b) LukeMorris 9 68
(R A Harris) *s.i.s: in rr of mod pce: rdn 3f out and mod prog: styd on same pce and nvr nr ldrs* **11/1**
0224 10 1 **Ermine Grey**[39] 1763 9-8-4 62 KierenFox(5) 4 56
(A W Carroll) *t.k.h: chsd ldrs off mod pce: rdn 3f out and sn bhd* **12/1**
2m 11.62s (1.02) **Going Correction** -0.35s/f (Firm) 10 Ran SP% **117.0**
Speed ratings (Par 103): **81,80,77,75,75 75,75,75,74,74**
toteswingers:1&2:£3.20, 1&3:£16.90, 2&3:£11.60 CSF £7.70 CT £63.48 TOTE £3.30: £1.30, £1.02, £10.60; EX 9.00.
Owner Trebles Holford Thoroughbreds **Bred** Trebles Holford Farm Thoroughbreds **Trained** Kingsclere, Hants
FOCUS
A steady pace to this handicap but a cracking finish. There was little depth in the race and not one to be too positive about.

2923 SUNSHINE RADIO H'CAP 2m 49y
9:10 (9:11) (Class 6) (0-65,62) 4-Y-0+ **£1,942** (£578; £288; £144) **Stalls** Low

Form RPR
43 1 **Salontyre (GER)**[39] 1759 4-9-6 58 (p) JamieSpencer 12 69
(B J Llewellyn) *in tch: rdn and hdwy over 3f out to ld over 2f out: forged clr u.p fnl f* **5/2**[1]
00-0 2 3 ¼ **Vertueux (FR)**[29] 409 5-9-1 52 SebSanders 3 59
(A W Carroll) *in tch: rdn and hdwy over 3f out: chsd wnr 2f out: nrly on terms 1f out: sn one pce* **4/1**[2]
0023 3 3 ¼ **Graylyn Ruby (FR)**[20] 2341 5-9-10 61 LukeMorris 6 64+
(R Dickin) *trckd ldr: led 9f out: sn clr and sddle slipped: racd wd: kpt ld tl hdd over 2f out: styd on same pce* **13/2**
0525 4 3 ¼ **Bussell Along (IRE)**[7] 2691 4-9-3 55 (tp) TomQueally 8 54
(Stef Higgins) *hld up in rr tl rdn and sme hdwy over 3f out: nvr on terms and no ch fnl 2f* **16/1**
0-10 5 2 ½ **Picot De Say**[15] 2476 8-9-5 56 RichardThomas 9 52
(B J Llewellyn) *hld up in rr and t.k.h: rdn and mod prog over 3f out: nvr nr ldrs and sn dropped away* **5/1**[3]
0/0- 6 2 **Synonymy**[33] 2760 7-8-8 45 (b) FrannyNorton 2 39
(M Blanshard) *in tch: rdn and effrt over 3f out: nvr on terms and sn btn* **33/1**
36-0 7 3 ½ **Beauchamp Xenia**[20] 2341 4-9-10 62 (b[1]) FergusSweeney 11 52
(H Candy) *hld up in rr: mod prog 4f out: sn rdn and dropped away* **5/1**[3]
310- 8 45 **Bute Street**[224] 7154 5-8-12 49 RichardKingscote 7 —
(R J Hodges) *led tl hdd 9f out: wknd 4f out: t.o* **14/1**
3m 45.13s (6.23) **Going Correction** -0.35s/f (Firm)
WFA 4 from 5yo+ 1lb 8 Ran SP% **110.7**
Speed ratings (Par 101): **70,68,66,65,63 62,61,38**
toteswingers:1&2:£1.30, 1&3:£5.10, 2&3:£9.30 CSF £11.61 CT £52.82 TOTE £2.50: £1.02, £3.00, £4.00; EX 14.40 Place 6: £54.79 Place 5: £4.60.
Owner Alex James **Bred** Gestut Wittekindshof **Trained** Fochriw, Caerphilly
FOCUS
Not much of a staying handicap and somewhat muddling with the third close to his recent best.
Graylyn Ruby(FR) Official explanation: jockey said saddle slipped
T/Plt: £27.70 to a £1 stake. Pool:£56,221.24 - 1,476.37 winning tickets T/Qpdt: £2.30 to a £1 stake. Pool:£5,474.84 - 1,690.94 winning tickets ST

2714 GOODWOOD (R-H)
Friday, June 11

OFFICIAL GOING: Good (8.0)
First 2f of mile course dolled out 5yds. Rail from 5f on the lower bend dolled out 6 yds increasing distances by about 10yds.
Wind: light breeze Weather: dry

2924 SOUTHERN DAILY ECHO MAIDEN H'CAP 1m 6f
6:15 (6:16) (Class 5) (0-75,75) 3-Y-0 **£3,238** (£963; £481; £240) **Stalls** High

Form RPR
5-02 1 **Boston Blue**[20] 2321 3-9-5 71 GeorgeBaker 8 87+
(W J Knight) *trckd ldrs: jnd ldrs 3f out: rdn to ld over 1f out: styd on wl: comf* **4/1**[2]
5-04 2 1 ¼ **Regal Park (IRE)**[36] 1847 3-9-9 75 RyanMoore 4 87
(J Noseda) *s.i.s: towards rr: hdwy over 3f out: wnt 4th and rdn 2f out: styd on wl fnl f: wnt 2nd towards fin: nt rch wnr* **7/4**[1]
002 3 1 ¼ **Never Can Tell (IRE)**[23] 2231 3-9-1 72 SophieDoyle(5) 9 82
(J A Osborne) *w ldr: led after 2f and stdd pce: quicked pce 3f out whn pressed: sn rdn: hdd over 1f out: kpt on same pce* **16/1**
6-60 4 7 **Aalya (IRE)**[29] 2050 3-8-12 64 TadhgO'Shea 3 64
(J L Dunlop) *s.i.s: towards rr: rn wd on bnd over 4f out: rdn over 3f out: no imp tl styd on fnl f but nvr a threat* **18/1**
4445 5 nk **Dr Finley (IRE)**[9] 2650 3-9-4 70 HayleyTurner 6 70
(M L W Bell) *hld up in rr of mid-div: hdwy over 3f out: sn rdn: one pce fnl 2f* **5/1**
-233 6 1 **Gordon Flash**[20] 2321 3-9-2 68 RichardHughes 7 66
(R Hannon) *led for 2f: w ldr: rdn wl over 2f out: ev ch over 1f out: wknd fnl f* **9/2**[3]
0-65 7 5 **Green Energy**[22] 2248 3-8-6 58 GregFairley 1 49
(Mrs A J Perrett) *trckd ldrs: rdn over 3f out: grad fdd fr over 2f out* **20/1**
53-5 8 2 ¾ **Dubai Phantom (USA)**[37] 1830 3-9-1 67 J-PGuillambert 5 55
(D M Simcock) *t.k.h: mid-div: rdn over 3f out: sn btn* **40/1**
0-05 9 dist **Spring Heather (IRE)**[17] 2412 3-8-4 56 (t) DaraghO'Donohoe 2 —
(J L Dunlop) *t.k.h: mid-div: in rr whn rn wd on bnd over 4f out: wknd over 2f out: heavily eased fnl f* **14/1**
3m 10.01s (6.41) **Going Correction** +0.275s/f (Good) 9 Ran SP% **116.2**
Speed ratings (Par 99): **92,91,90,86,86 85,82,81,—**
toteswingers:1&2:£1.70, 1&3:£12.30, 2&3:£7.30 CSF £11.46 CT £99.65 TOTE £6.10: £1.80, £1.10, £4.80; EX 15.90.
Owner Mr & Mrs I H Bendelow **Bred** Ballykilbride Stud **Trained** Patching, W Sussex
FOCUS
The first 2f of the 1m course was dolled out five yards and the running rail from the 5f mark on the lower bend to the winning post was dolled out six yards, so increasing distances by approx ten yards.A fair staying maiden handicap in which most of the runners were having their first try at the trip but, for all that, few of them looked open to significant improvement or got into things anyway on account of just a fair gallop. The front pair looks progressive and the form appears reasonable.

2925 FRANKIE'S 23RD ANNIVERSARY MAIDEN STKS 1m
6:45 (6:45) (Class 5) 3-Y-0 **£3,238** (£963; £481; £240) **Stalls** High

Form RPR
6 1 **Hear The Roar (IRE)**[10] 2632 3-9-3 0 NickyMackay 8 82+
(J R Boyle) *trckd ldr: led 2f out on strly: rdn out* **9/1**[3]
3- 2 3 **Mureb (USA)**[221] 7209 3-9-3 0 (t) FrankieDettori 1 76
(Saeed Bin Suroor) *sn swtchd to ins rail: led: rdn and hdd 2f out: no ex fnl f: fdd fnl 65yds* **8/11**[1]
4 3 1 **Tariq Too**[20] 2335 3-9-3 0 HayleyTurner 11 73+
(D M Simcock) *mid-div: rdn wl over 2f out: sn swtchd lft: styd on fr over 1f out: clsng on 2nd nring fin* **9/1**[3]
6 4 1 ¼ **Byrd In Hand (IRE)**[18] 2401 3-9-3 0 NeilChalmers 10 70
(J J Bridger) *trckd ldrs: rdn 3f out: kpt on same pce fnl 2f* **20/1**
0-0 5 4 **Shianda**[7] 2718 3-8-12 0 AmirQuinn 4 56
(G L Moore) *s.i.s: sn pushed along and bhd: swtchd lft and styd on fr 2f out: nvr trbld ldrs* **100/1**
6 3 **Silver Colors (USA)** 3-8-12 0 RyanMoore 2 49+
(J Noseda) *little slowly away: sn mid-div: rn green and pushed along wl over 3f out: styd on same pce fr 2f out* **11/2**[2]
54- 7 6 **Gypsy Boy (USA)**[279] 5664 3-9-3 0 KevinGhunowa 7 40
(F J Brennan) *snatched up on rails 4f out: a towards rr* **33/1**
0-6 8 ¾ **Brody's Boy**[20] 2340 3-9-3 0 GeorgeBaker 3 38
(G L Moore) *stdd s: a towards rr* **66/1**
3 9 5 **Startle**[27] 2121 3-9-3 0 RichardHughes 5 27
(R Hannon) *s.i.s: sn trcking ldrs: rdn 3f out: wknd 2f out* **9/1**[3]
50 10 9 **Confrontation**[23] 2227 3-8-12 0 ShaneKelly 9 1
(D M Simcock) *in tch: rdn 3f out: wknd 2f out* **25/1**

The Form Book, Raceform Ltd, Compton, RG20 6NL

05-0 11 *dist* **Rosie's Magic**[27] 2122 3-8-5 37 .... JamesRogers(7) 6 —
(W De Best-Turner) *mid-div tl 3f out: t.o* **100/1**

1m 40.82s (0.92) **Going Correction** +0.275s/f (Good) 11 Ran SP% **118.3**
Speed ratings (Par 99): **106,103,102,100,96 93,87,87,82,73** —
toteswingers:1&2:£4.40, 1&3:£17.60, 2&3:£2.70 CSF £15.54 TOTE £16.10: £2.50, £1.30, £1.50; EX 25.40.
Owner Mcatavey Developments Ltd **Bred** Chris McHale And Oghill House Stud **Trained** Epsom, Surrey

FOCUS
No more than a fair maiden in all probability, and one that was dominated by the first two from the start with little else getting competitive. The runner-up is the best guide to the level.

2926 FREDDIE DUFF STKS (H'CAP) 7f
7:20 (7:20) (Class 4) (0-85,85) 4-Y-0+ **£4,533** (£1,348; £674; £336) **Stalls** High

Form RPR
-624 1 **My Kingdom (IRE)**[32] 1963 4-9-2 **80** ....(t) GeorgeBaker 10 90+
(H Morrison) *mid-div: travelling wl but nt clr run on rail tl jst over 2f out: swtchd lft over 1f out: sltly impeded ins fnl f: led fnl 110yds: r.o wl: drifted lft towards fin* **11/2**[3]
11-4 2 *1* **Santefisio**[28] 2091 4-9-5 **83** .... JimmyFortune 6 90+
(P J Makin) *hld up last quartet: smooth hdwy over 2f out: nt best of runs but rdn over 1f out: r.o wl fnl f: hld in 2nd whn carried lft nr finsh* **11/4**[1]
22-5 3 *3/4* **Truism**[20] 2322 4-9-7 **85** .... RyanMoore 4 90
(Mrs A J Perrett) *mid-div: hdwy fr 3f out: rdn and ev ch ent fnl f: kpt on but no ex* **10/3**[2]
0 4 *3/4* **L'Hirondelle (IRE)**[44] 1625 6-8-12 **76** .... KierenFallon 1 79
(M J Attwater) *prom: led over 2f out: sn rdn: hdd fnl 110yds: kpt on but no ex* **25/1**
0061 5 *nk* **Noble Jack (IRE)**[17] 2414 4-8-8 **72** .... TravisBlock 12 74
(G L Moore) *prom tl snatched up on rails after 3f: trckd ldrs: swtchd off rails for effrt over 2f out: kpt on same pce fnl f* **16/1**
0-06 6 *shd* **Woodcote Place**[15] 2472 7-9-7 **85** .... LiamKeniry 5 87+
(P R Chamings) *dwlt: bhd: swtchd lft and hdwy over 2f out: sn rdn: kpt on fnl f: nrst fin* **7/1**
0-03 7 *2 1/4* **Beaver Patrol (IRE)**[13] 2532 8-9-6 **84** .... RobertHavlin 3 80
(Eve Johnson Houghton) *trckd ldrs: effrt over 2f out: fdd fnl f* **9/1**
030- 8 *2 3/4* **Zebrano**[209] 7395 4-9-0 **78** .... RichardHughes 2 66
(A B Haynes) *a towards rr* **28/1**
120- 9 *nk* **Leadenhall Lass (IRE)**[242] 6731 4-8-3 **72** .... JemmaMarshall(5) 8 60
(P M Phelan) *s.i.s: a towards rr* **66/1**
5504 10 *4* **Jesse James (IRE)**[21] 2284 4-9-3 **81** .... SteveDrowne 7 58
(J R Gask) *led after 1f: rdn and hdd over 2f out: wknd over 1f out* **12/1**
0-05 11 *4* **Desert Icon (IRE)**[22] 2247 4-8-12 **76** .... ShaneKelly 9 42
(W J Knight) *led for 1f: trckd ldrs: rdn 3f out: wknd over 1f out* **12/1**

1m 28.38s (1.48) **Going Correction** +0.275s/f (Good) 11 Ran SP% **117.7**
Speed ratings (Par 105): **105,103,103,102,101 101,99,95,95,91 86**
toteswingers:1&2:£4.50, 1&3:£5.00, 2&3:£2.30 CSF £20.65 CT £60.22 TOTE £8.80: £3.70, £1.10, £1.20; EX 24.70.
Owner Wood Street Syndicate V **Bred** Irish National Stud **Trained** East Ilsley, Berks
■ Stewards' Enquiry : George Baker two-day ban: careless riding (Jun 25-26)

FOCUS
A fairly useful handicap run at just a fair pace initially and those dropped right out were left with a bit to do once the pace picked up into the straight. Even so, the first two are better than the distances back to the rest suggest, although the form is slightly muddling.

2927 CRIMBOURNE STUD STKS (H'CAP) 1m 1f 192y
7:55 (7:55) (Class 3) (0-90,90) 3-Y-0 **£6,799** (£2,023; £1,011; £505) **Stalls** High

Form RPR
01-5 1 **Treble Jig (USA)**[22] 2253 3-9-0 **83** .... RyanMoore 5 93+
(Sir Michael Stoute) *led after 1f: styd on strly to assert fnl 110yds: drvn out* **15/8**[1]
1-46 2 *1 1/2* **Hidden Glory**[31] 2002 3-8-8 **77** .... AndreaAtzeni 10 84
(Pat Eddery) *trckd ldrs: ch whn wandered u.p over jst over 1f out: kpt on but hld fnl f* **9/2**[3]
4321 3 *1/2* **Blues Music (IRE)**[14] 2496 3-8-9 **78** .... MichaelHills 4 84
(B W Hills) *in tch: rdn over 2f out: hdwy over 1f out: kpt on fnl f* **4/1**[2]
5-15 4 *1 3/4* **Flying Destination**[18] 2386 3-8-8 **77** .... ShaneKelly 3 79
(W J Knight) *trckd ldrs: rdn in cl 3rd fr 2f out: kpt on same pce fnl f* **18/1**
0-00 5 *2 1/4* **Blakey's Boy**[27] 2117 3-9-1 **84** .... FrankieDettori 7 82
(J L Dunlop) *hld up wl off pce: clsd on ldng gp 4f out: travelling ok and cl enough 2f out: sn rdn: nt pce to chal: fdd fnl 100yds* **13/2**
1320 6 *2 1/4* **Paintball (IRE)**[6] 2742 3-8-10 **79** .... MartinDwyer 2 72
(W R Muir) *in tch: effrt whn short of room briefly 2f out: wknd fnl f* **7/1**
4143 7 *9* **Understory (USA)**[32] 1969 3-8-5 **74** .... GregFairley 8 49
(M Johnston) *led for 1f: w wnr: rdn over 3f out: wknd 2f out* **12/1**

2m 9.81s (1.81) **Going Correction** +0.275s/f (Good) 7 Ran SP% **111.8**
Speed ratings (Par 103): **103,101,101,100,98 96,89**
toteswingers:1&2:£3.50, 1&3:£1.60, 2&3:£11.10 CSF £9.96 CT £28.46 TOTE £2.40: £1.50, £3.20; EX 16.20.
Owner K Abdulla **Bred** Juddmonte Farms Inc **Trained** Newmarket, Suffolk

FOCUS
The feature event of the night but weakened by three withdrawals and not much more than an ordinary handicap as things turned out. The gallop was just a fair one and the winner was able to dictate. He is unexposed and looks sure to do better, while the fourth is the best guide to the form.

NOTEBOOK
Treble Jig(USA) had made big strides from his first run to his second last year and, up 2f in trip, did so again for all he was well served by being able to lead. It could be argued he was well in on a line through the horse he had beaten in his maiden, and he won well enough to think that when his stamina is tested more he can improve further. He has a willing attitude, which is more than can be said for some of those behind him here. (op 6-5 after 11-10 in places tchd 2-1)
Hidden Glory looked very interesting back up in trip with his reappearance form working out very well and though he failed to land substantial market support he acquitted himself well behind a progressive rival. He might have fared better had he kept a straighter course, but would still have been only second best on the day. (op 8-1 tchd 10-3)
Blues Music(IRE)'s Haydock win had been boosted since by a win for the runner-up and he's probably better than being held up off the steady gallop here showed him to be. Out of a mare who was a 1m4f winner in Ireland, he's worth another chance when his stamina is tested more. (op 5-1)
Flying Destination was readily held in a handicap last time having won a weakish maiden the time before and had no excuses. (op 25-1)
Blakey's Boy was highly tried as a juvenile, and it's easy to see why as he almost certainly has more ability than he cares to show, travelling well into contention here then finding nothing off the bridle with his head at an awkward angle. He might do better back at 1m, but looks one to treat with caution. (op 8-1)
Paintball(IRE) was back down in grade after getting a bit far back at Epsom last time under quicker conditions but seemed unsuited again by this race developing into too much of a speed test. (op 8-1 tchd 6-1)
Understory(USA) dropped out very quickly and presumably wasn't right for all he looked to have work to do from a handicapping perspective. (op 9-1)

2928 HILDON STKS (H'CAP) 6f
8:30 (8:30) (Class 4) (0-85,83) 3-Y-0 **£4,533** (£1,348; £674; £336) **Stalls** Low

Form RPR
2121 1 **Rio Mist**[29] 2052 3-9-6 **81** .... RichardHughes 2 93
(R Hannon) *led for 1f: trckd ldr: swtchd rt over 1f out: qcknd up wl to ld ins fnl f: sn clr: impressive* **7/1**
1-22 2 *3 1/2* **Rule Of Nature**[36] 1836 3-9-7 **82** .... RyanMoore 7 83
(Sir Michael Stoute) *wnt rt s: led after 1f: rdn and hung rt jst over 1f out: hdd ins fnl f: nt pce of wnr* **6/5**[1]
-133 3 *1 3/4* **Kakapuka**[11] 2599 3-9-0 **75** .... KierenFallon 5 70
(Mrs A L M King) *trckd ldrs: rdn over 2f out: kpt on same pce* **8/1**
34-2 4 *3* **Pin Cushion**[11] 2599 3-9-2 **77** .... MartinDwyer 3 63
(B J Meehan) *awkward leaving stalls: last but in tch: swtchd rt 2f out: sn rdn: nvr gng pce to get on terms* **6/1**[3]
1-01 5 *7* **London Gold**[11] 2599 3-9-8 **83** 6ex .... DaneO'Neill 4 46
(H Candy) *prom: rdn over 2f out: wknd over 1f out* **3/1**[2]
1310 6 *11* **Private Olley**[86] 901 3-8-6 **67** .... GregFairley 1 —
(J Akehurst) *broke wl: trckd ldrs early: struggling fr half way* **33/1**

1m 12.86s (0.66) **Going Correction** +0.275s/f (Good) 6 Ran SP% **111.3**
Speed ratings (Par 101): **106,101,99,95,85 71**
toteswingers:1&2:£1.20, 1&3:£2.90, 2&3:£3.10 CSF £15.71 CT £66.11 TOTE £6.30: £3.40, £1.10; EX 7.70.
Owner The Early Bath Partnership **Bred** Mount Coote Stud **Trained** East Everleigh, Wilts

FOCUS
Four of the field had good recent credentials, so despite the numbers it was a competitive affair and a credit to the winner that she could win so emphatically. The runner-up sets the standard.
London Gold Official explanation: vet said colt was lame right-fore

2929 EBF L K BENNETT FILLIES' STKS (H'CAP) 6f
9:00 (9:01) (Class 3) (0-95,94) 3-Y-0+ **£10,037** (£2,986; £1,492; £745) **Stalls** Low

Form RPR
4040 1 **Kerrys Requiem (IRE)**[20] 2327 4-9-2 **82** ....(v[1]) SamHitchcott 11 93
(M R Channon) *sn nudged along towards rr: hdwy over 2f out: led over 1f out: r.o: rdn out* **12/1**
60-0 2 *2* **Perfect Flight**[41] 1692 5-9-2 **82** .... DaneO'Neill 6 87
(M Blanshard) *hld up towards rr: hdwy 3f out: rdn 2f out: chsd wnr ent fnl f: kpt on but a hld* **33/1**
01-3 3 *1* **Plume**[27] 2120 3-8-8 **82** .... RichardHughes 5 82
(R Hannon) *trckd ldrs: ev ch 2f out: sn rdn: kpt on same pce fnl f* **1/1**[1]
0-60 4 *1* **Pretty Bonnie**[20] 2326 5-9-1 **84** .... NataliaGemelova(3) 9 83
(A E Price) *trckd ldrs: rdn over 2f out: kpt on same pce* **25/1**
0050 5 *1* **Spinning Bailiwick**[18] 2399 4-8-11 **77** .... LiamKeniry 8 72
(G L Moore) *mid-div: rdn 3f out: nvr gng pce to threaten* **66/1**
02-3 6 *nse* **Excellerator (IRE)**[20] 2326 4-9-8 **93** ....(t) MatthewDavies(5) 2 88
(George Baker) *trckd ldrs: rdn over 2f out: sn one pce* **13/2**[2]
0600 7 *1 1/2* **Pusey Street Lady**[6] 2748 6-9-3 **86** .... MartinLane(3) 1 76
(J Gallagher) *in tch: swtchd off rails 3f out: sn rdn: wknd ent fnl f* **14/1**
/65- 8 *nk* **What's Up Pussycat (IRE)**[320] 4358 4-10-0 **94** .... StevieDonohoe 3 83
(D M Simcock) *s.i.s: swtchd off rails after 2f: a towards rr* **20/1**
40-0 9 *shd* **Seeking Dubai**[34] 1918 3-9-1 **89** .... KierenFallon 4 76
(E F Vaughan) *sn outpcd: a towards rr* **20/1**
04-1 10 *10* **Night Affair**[19] 2364 4-8-10 **76** .... MartinDwyer 10 33
(D W P Arbuthnot) *wnt rt s: sn w ldr: led over 2f out: hdd over 1f out: wknd* **7/1**[3]
12-3 11 *3 3/4* **Belle Des Airs (IRE)**[51] 1481 4-9-7 **87** .... GeorgeBaker 7 32
(R M Beckett) *led tl over 2f out: sn hung rt: wknd over 1f out* **7/1**[3]

1m 13.18s (0.98) **Going Correction** +0.275s/f (Good)
WFA 3 from 4yo+ 8lb 11 Ran SP% **120.5**
Speed ratings (Par 104): **104,101,100,98,97 97,95,94,94,81 76**
toteswingers:1&2:£102.00, 1&3:£7.10, 2&3:£7.40 CSF £359.91 CT £771.16 TOTE £21.00: £4.80, £8.30, £1.10; EX 258.60 Place 6: £5.82 Place 5: £3.80.
Owner M Channon **Bred** Mrs T V Ryan **Trained** West Ilsley, Berks
■ Stewards' Enquiry : Dane O'Neill caution: careless riding.

FOCUS
Competitive enough fare, though not the result that the market suggested at the end of a well-run race in which the early leaders finished well held. The winner returned to form in the headgear with the runner-up to last year's form.

NOTEBOOK
Kerrys Requiem(IRE)'s temperament has often let her down but this hard ride has always had a decent race in her, and benefited greatly from a good pace as well as what was a long overdue try in headgear to win with some authority. Whether she will repeat this next time, however, is anybody's guess. (op 16-1)
Perfect Flight had a patchy 2009 and didn't show much on her reappearance but she's always been in her element on an easy surface and clearly retains a fair amount of ability. Her immediate prospects probably depend largely on the weather.
Plume looked an interesting runner back in trip and was backed accordingly, but she didn't find what looked likely after travelling strongly. The trip wasn't the issue, and it may be that she's the type that shows more at home than she does on the track. (tchd 5-4, 11-8 in places and 4-5 in places)
Pretty Bonnie, back in handicaps for first time this year, ran respectably without ever really threatening. (op 33-1)
Spinning Bailiwick had been really progressive on AW over the winter but looks a bit too high in the weights on turf. (tchd 50-1)
Excellerator(IRE), who was down in grade after her encouraging Listed race third on her comeback, didn't look entirely straightforward and remains winless since her juvenile debut. (op 6-1 tchd 11-2)
What's Up Pussycat(IRE), an ex Irish filly, looked on a stiff enough mark and probably found this sharp 6f an insufficient test of stamina on her first run for her new yard. (tchd 33-1 in places)
Night Affair probably did too much too soon in front. (op 9-1)
Belle Des Airs(IRE), second in this race last year off a 7lb lower mark, failed to get home. (op 15-2 tchd 6-1)

T/Plt: £8.70 to a £1 stake. Pool:£71,139.97 - 5,927.65 winning tickets T/Qpdt: £3.90 to £1 stake. Pool:£3,800.37 - 720.14 winning tickets TM

2680 SANDOWN (R-H)

Friday, June 11

OFFICIAL GOING: Good (round 8.4; sprint 8.1; home straight - far side 8.3, stands' side 8.1)

Sprint track at full width. Rail on home bend at mid configuration and dolled out 5yds up the straight increasing distances on round course by 5yds.

Wind: virtually nil Weather: overcast

2930 TOTEPLACEPOT E B F MAIDEN STKS 5f 6y

2:10 (2:12) (Class 4) 2-Y-O **£4,857** (£1,445; £722; £360) **Stalls** High

Form				RPR
52	1		**Extra Power (IRE)**[15] 2448 2-9-3 0 KierenFallon 3 (M R Channon) *mde all: set stdy gallop tl rdn and qcknd 2f out: kpt on wl and a holding rivals fnl f* **10/11**[1]	82+
	2	1 1/4	**Sweet Cecily (IRE)** 2-8-12 0 RyanMoore 5 (R Hannon) *chsd wnr tl over 3f out: rdn: outpcd and lost pl over 2f out: rallied strly ins fnl f: r.o wl snatched 2nd on post* **16/1**	73+
422	3	nse	**Bunce (IRE)**[12] 2561 2-9-3 0 RichardHughes 2 (R Hannon) *t.k.h: trckd ldrs tl wnt 2nd over 3f out: rdn wl over 1f out: drvn and tried to chal ent fnl f: kpt on same pce: lost 2nd on post* **7/4**[2]	77
0	4	1 1/4	**Golden Taurus (IRE)**[20] 2319 2-9-3 0 MichaelHills 6 (J W Hills) *t.k.h: broke wl: sn stdd and hld up in tch: effrt to dispute 2nd and rdn wl over 1f out: no ex fnl f and btn fnl 100yds* **33/1**	73
	5	3 1/2	**Quality Art (USA)** 2-9-3 0 GeorgeBaker 1 (G L Moore) *s.i.s: sn swtchd rt and hld up wl in tch in last: rdn and effrt 2f out: no imp and btn ins fnl f: nt pushed after* **20/1**	60+
	6	2 3/4	**Qenaa** 2-8-12 0 RichardHills 4 (M Johnston) *s.i.s: rn green and sn bustled along in last pair: rdn and wknd ent fnl 2f* **14/1**[3]	45+

63.48 secs (1.88) **Going Correction** +0.075s/f (Good) **6** Ran SP% **109.0**

Speed ratings (Par 95): **87,85,84,82,77 72**

toteswingers:1&2:£3.50, 1&3:£1.02, 2&3:£2.80 CSF £15.94 TOTE £1.70: £1.10, £3.90; EX 16.10.

Owner Jaber Abdullah **Bred** Mrs Rita Kent **Trained** West Ilsley, Berks

FOCUS

A fair maiden but the early pace wasn't that strong. The winner is rated to form with the third a length or so off.

NOTEBOOK

Extra Power(IRE), who was a well-backed favourite, dominated from start to finish having been soon sent to the front. Racing near the far-side rail may have been a help, but it was basically a good ride from Fallon which got the job done, and he looks to be progressing with racing. He might go for a conditions race somewhere next. (op 6-4 tchd 4-5)

Sweet Cecily(IRE), whose dam won over this trip at three, beat the stable's first string to the runner-up spot and shaped with plenty of promise on her debut, albeit having enjoyed the possible benefit of racing next to the far rail. (op 10-1)

Bunce(IRE) could have done with the leader setting a stronger pace as he always wanted to go quicker. He remains capable of winning a similar event, but nurseries will also be an option for him soon. (op 6-4 tchd 5-4, 2-1 in places)

Golden Taurus(IRE) showed a lot more than on his debut at Goodwood, appearing to appreciate the drop back to the minimum trip. (op 50-1)

Quality Art(USA), who cost a lot at the breeze-ups, was very slowly away and was too green to do himself justice on his debut. (op 16-1)

Qenaa, a half-sister to four-time 6f-7f winner at El Bosque, was also green and can be expected to do better for this experience. Official explanation: jockey said filly ran green (op 8-1 tchd 16-1)

2931 TOTESWINGER FLEXI BETTING H'CAP 5f 6y

2:40 (2:41) (Class 5) (0-75,72) 3-Y-O **£3,885** (£1,156; £577; £288) **Stalls** High

Form				RPR
22-4	1		**Drift And Dream**[29] 2046 3-9-8 **71** TedDurcan 4 (C F Wall) *chsd ldrs: wnt 2nd 3f out: rdn to ld ent fnl f: kpt on wl fnl f* **4/1**[3]	78
5323	2	3/4	**Pherousa**[7] 2688 3-9-0 **63** SteveDrowne 3 (M Blanshard) *t.k.h: hld up in tch in last trio: swtchd lft and effrt on outer 2f out: rdn wl over 1f out: kpt on wl fnl f to go 2nd last strides: nt quite pce to rch wnr* **12/1**	67
2242	3	shd	**Danzoe (IRE)**[9] 2648 3-9-4 **67** (v) TomQueally 2 (Mrs C A Dunnett) *in tch towards rr: rdn and effrt on outer ent fnl 2f: kpt on u.p ins fnl f: wnt 3rd nr fin: nvr quite pce to rch wnr* **7/1**	71
531	4	nk	**Special Quality (USA)**[37] 1825 3-9-9 **72** FrankieDettori 5 (R M H Cowell) *led and grad crossed to r on far rail: rdn wl over 1f out: drvn and hdd ent fnl f: kpt on same pce after: lost 2 pls towards fin* **9/4**[2]	75
-046	5	4 1/2	**Itwasonlyakiss (IRE)**[24] 2197 3-8-11 **60** (t) MichaelHills 1 (J W Hills) *in tch in rr: rdn and effrt 2f out: no prog and btn whn edgd rt jst over 1f out* **33/1**	47
045-	6	3	**Galatian**[228] 7058 3-9-6 **72** JamesMillman(3) 6 (B R Millman) *stdd s: hld up in tch: rdn and struggling 2f out: wl btn over 1f out* **12/1**	48
6-46	7	3 3/4	**Final Turn**[24] 2215 3-9-2 **65** DaneO'Neill 8 (H Candy) *chsd ldr: sltly hmpd: swtchd lft and lost 2nd over 3f out: wknd u.p over 1f out: wl btn fnl f* **2/1**[1]	27
3064	8	8	**Force To Spend**[11] 2584 3-8-8 **57** J-PGuillambert 7 (N P Littmoden) *chsd ldrs: rdn 1/2-way: wknd wl over 1f out: wl bhd fnl f* **25/1**	—

62.10 secs (0.50) **Going Correction** +0.075s/f (Good) **8** Ran SP% **118.8**

Speed ratings (Par 99): **99,97,97,97,89 85,79,66**

toteswingers:1&2:£6.00, 1&3:£7.00, 2&3:£8.40 CSF £52.03 CT £331.18 TOTE £5.50: £1.60, £2.70, £2.20; EX 70.40.

Owner Lady Juliet Tadgell **Bred** Lady Juliet Tadgell **Trained** Newmarket, Suffolk

FOCUS

Just a modest handicap, but the pace set by Special Quality was decent. The winner stepped up on last year's course form with the placed horses to recent marks.

Galatian Official explanation: jockey said gelding denied a clear run

Final Turn Official explanation: jockey said colt never travelled

2932 TOTEQUADPOT E B F MAIDEN STKS 7f 16y

3:15 (3:18) (Class 4) 2-Y-O **£4,857** (£1,445; £722; £360) **Stalls** High

Form				RPR
2	1		**Ecliptic (USA)**[13] 2547 2-9-0 0 AhmedAjtebi(3) 3 (Mahmood Al Zarooni) *chsd ldr tl led after 1f: rdn and hdd over 1f out: stl pressing ldr but one pce whn lft wl clr fnl 100yds* **5/4**[1]	89
0	2	8	**Surrey Star (IRE)**[13] 2547 2-9-3 0 LiamKeniry 4 (R A Teal) *led for 1f: chsd wnr after tl ent fnl 2f: rdn and wknd over 1f out: wl btn whn lft 2nd fnl 100yds* **100/1**	69
0	3	3 3/4	**Jamhoori**[20] 2319 2-9-3 0 NeilCallan 13 (C E Brittain) *chsd ldrs: rdn and no prog over 3f out: no ch w ldng trio fnl 2f: lft modest 3rd fnl 100yds* **8/1**[3]	60
0	4	1/2	**Tarjeyh (IRE)**[28] 2078 2-9-3 0 PatDobbs 16 (M P Tregoning) *t.k.h early: hld uip in tch: outpcd by ldrs and rdn over 3f out: no ch after: lft modest 4th fnl 100yds* **25/1**	58+
6	5	1 1/4	**Presto Volante (IRE)**[28] 2078 2-9-3 0 RyanMoore 2 (Mrs A J Perrett) *s.i.s and bustled along early: wl bhd: rdn over 4f out: edging rt over 2f out: kpt on fnl f: nvr trbld ldrs* **14/1**	55+
	6	1 1/2	**Aspantau (IRE)** 2-9-3 0 KierenFallon 9 (M P Tregoning) *racd off the pce towards rr: pushed along and reminder over 4f out: sme prog into midfield over 3f out: nvr trbld ldrs* **20/1**	52+
	7	2 3/4	**Purification (IRE)** 2-9-3 0 WilliamBuick 6 (J H M Gosden) *wl off pce towards rr: rdn and sme hdwy into midfield over 3f out: nvr trbld ldrs* **9/1**	45+
	8	hd	**Dr Darcey** 2-9-3 0 RichardHughes 11 (R Hannon) *chsd ldrs: rdn and struggling 4f out: wl btn fnl 3f* **16/1**	44
	9	5	**Jacobs Son** 2-9-3 0 StevieDonohoe 15 (R A Mills) *dwlt: t.k.h: hld up in midfield tl hmpd and lost pl over 5f out: bhd after: rdn and no prog over 3f out* **20/1**	32+
	10	3	**Time To Work (IRE)** 2-9-3 0 JimmyFortune 8 (A M Balding) *midfield and jst in tch: rdn and struggling 4f out: wl btn fnl 3f* **16/1**	24+
	11	1 3/4	**Ahlaain (USA)** 2-9-3 0 FergusSweeney 1 (D M Simcock) *s.i.s: rn green early: a bhd: nvr on terms* **100/1**	20
	12	5	**Cantonese Cat (IRE)** 2-9-3 0 MartinDwyer 12 (B J Meehan) *restless in stalls: fly j. as stalls opened and s.i.s: a bhd: nvr on terms: t.o* **50/1**	7
	13	7	**Denices Moonlight** 2-9-3 0 RichardHills 10 (M Johnston) *in tch: rdn and struggling 4f out: wl btn fnl 3f: t.o fr over 1f out* **25/1**	—
	14	4 1/2	**Isitfridayyet (IRE)** 2-9-3 0 TomQueally 5 (J G Given) *a in rr: lost tch wl over 3f out: t.o* **66/1**	—
	U		**Toolain (IRE)** 2-9-3 0 FrankieDettori 7 (M A Jarvis) *chsd ldng pair: pushed along to chal 2f out: led over 1f out: edgd rt ins fnl f: cocked jaw: hung bdly lft and uns rdr fnl 100yds* **4/1**[2]	91+

1m 30.46s (0.96) **Going Correction** +0.25s/f (Good) **15** Ran SP% **126.6**

Speed ratings (Par 95): **104,94,90,90,88 86,83,83,77,74 72,66,58,53,—**

toteswingers:1&2:£95.50, 1&3:£6.70, 2&3:£95.50 CSF £250.40 TOTE £2.10: £1.10, £13.60, £4.10; EX 247.00.

Owner Godolphin **Bred** Darley **Trained** Newmarket, Suffolk

FOCUS

The first 7f juvenile maiden of the year in this country and a dramatic finish. The winner was lucky but is rated a slight improver .

NOTEBOOK

Ecliptic(USA) ran well in defeat on his debut at Newmarket and looked to hold obvious claims here, with the extra furlong sure to suit on breeding. His measure had been taken by Toolain 1½f out, but then Dettori was unseated from that rival and he took full advantage of his good fortune to run out a clear winner. He remains a useful prospect but he won't want to be meeting Toolain again in the near future, as he was lucky to beat him here. (op 7-4 tchd 15-8, 2-1 in a place)

Surrey Star(IRE), given a positive ride, got a lot closer to Ecliptic than he did on his debut at Newmarket. The step up in distance suited and another run will bring nurseries into the equation.

Jamhoori looked likely to appreciate this extra furlong, both judged on his debut run and on pedigree. Nicely drawn, he shaped pretty well, but is another likely to be seen to better effect once handicapped. (op 12-1 tchd 14-1)

Tarjeyh(IRE) ◆, whose jockey wore the owner's second colours, shaped with distinct promise, but ran green once his rider asked for more in the closing stages. His sales price went up from 16,000gns as a foal to 220,000gns as a yearling, and he looks a very interesting type for when the nurseries come round. (op 20-1)

Presto Volante(IRE), sixth in Strong Suit's maiden on his debut, was staying on at the finish, looking to appreciate the extra furlong. (tchd 12-1)

Aspantau(IRE) cost 110,000gns and is bred to come into his own over middle distances next season. He showed some ability. (op 16-1)

Purification(IRE) was pretty green but he's closely related to May Hill winner Pollenator and better can be expected on the back of this debut experience. (op 7-1 tchd 11-1)

Toolain(IRE) ◆ looked to be in the process of winning comfortably when he veered left after being hit with the whip and deposited his rider, who'd lost his balance, on the ground. He would have run out a taking winner from a solid yardstick had his rider stayed aboard, and looks perfectly capable of making amends soon, as it was just greenness which saw him edge left. (tchd 7-2 and 9-2)

2933 THE MOUSETRAP CHALLENGE CUP (H'CAP) 1m 14y

3:50 (3:52) (Class 4) (0-85,85) 3-Y-O **£5,180** (£1,541; £770; £384) **Stalls** Centre

Form				RPR
4-01	1		**Fontley**[22] 2253 3-9-8 **84** TomQueally 7 (Eve Johnson Houghton) *dwlt: hld up in last trio: rdn and effrt over 2f out: edgd rt but chal 2f out: rdn to ld over 1f out: kpt on wl ins fnl f* **8/1**	92+
1-04	2	1	**Mr Irons (USA)**[18] 2386 3-9-4 **80** RyanMoore 1 (Sir Michael Stoute) *led: jnd ent 3f out: rdn 2f out: hdd over 1f out: drvn and kpt on same pce fnl f* **3/1**[2]	84
0023	3	1/2	**First Cat**[14] 2515 3-9-4 **80** RichardHughes 8 (R Hannon) *stdd s: t.k.h: hld up in tch in rr: rdn and effrt wl over 1f out: chsd ldrs ins fnl f: kpt on but nt pce to chal wnr* **8/1**	83
21	4	shd	**Innocuous**[31] 1993 3-9-4 **80** WilliamBuick 5 (D M Simcock) *bmpd s: t.k.h and sn chsng ldng pair: n.m.r on rail 2f out tl over 1f out: rdn and one pce ent fnl f: swtchd lft and kpt on fnl 75yds* **7/2**[3]	83+
6-10	5	2	**Master Of Dance (IRE)**[22] 2242 3-9-0 **76** JimmyFortune 3 (J G Given) *stdd s: hld up in tch in last pair: rdn 3f out: effrt on outer over 2f out: styd on same pce u.p fnl f* **25/1**	74
1103	6	3/4	**Ginger Jack**[6] 2737 3-9-9 **85** FrankieDettori 4 (M Johnston) *chsd ldr: upsides ent fnl 3f: rdn and unable qck 2f out: drvn and outpcd jst over 1f out: one pce and btn jst ins fnl f* **15/8**[1]	81
0-00	7	7	**The Human League**[13] 2544 3-9-3 **79** PaulEddery 6 (M R Channon) *t.k.h: hld up in tch in midfield: rdn and unable qck over 2f out: wknd wl over 1f out* **50/1**	59
10-3	8	1 1/2	**Wasmi (IRE)**[15] 2475 3-9-2 **78** NeilCallan 2 (C E Brittain) *chsd ldrs: rdn over 2f out: wknd and wl btn whn edgd rt jst over 1f out* **28/1**	55

1m 43.94s (0.64) **Going Correction** +0.25s/f (Good) **8** Ran SP% **113.5**

Speed ratings (Par 101): **106,105,104,104,102 101,94,93**

toteswingers:1&2:£4.20, 1&3:£3.90, 2&3:£4.20 CSF £31.50 CT £201.86 TOTE £7.20: £1.70, £1.50, £2.90; EX 27.40.

Owner Mrs Virginia Neale **Bred** Sarah J Leigh And Robin S Leigh **Trained** Blewbury, Oxon

FOCUS
A decent handicap and the form looks reasonable with the third the best guide, backed up by the fourth.

2934 TOTEEXACTA FLEXI BETTING H'CAP 1m 2f 7y
4:25 (4:25) (Class 3) (0-90,89) 4-Y-0+
£6,542 (£1,959; £979; £490; £244; £122) Stalls High

Form				RPR
5-51	1		**Jo'Burg (USA)**[15] 2467 6-8-12 81 .... MartinLane(3) 9 *(Lady Herries) s.i.s: hld up in last trio: hdwy and c to r alone on stands' rail wl over 3f out: rdn 3f out: led wl over 1f out: kpt on wl fnl f* 5/1[2]	91
0-10	2	1 1/2	**Bugaku**[36] 1837 5-9-4 84 .... RyanMoore 13 *(Sir Michael Stoute) hld up in tch towards rr: rdn along 3f out: hdwy u.p on inner over 1f out: squeezed through on rail ins fnl f to go 2nd nr fin: nt pce to chal wnr* 4/1[1]	91+
0000	3	nk	**Kaolak (USA)**[20] 2322 4-9-5 85 .... PhilipRobinson 4 *(J Ryan) led: rdn and hdd 2f out: drvn to ld main gp and chsng wnr 1f out: kpt on same pce: lost 2nd nr fin* 33/1	91
-402	4	1 3/4	**Veroon (IRE)**[13] 2523 4-8-9 75 ....(p) TomQueally 11 *(J G Given) hld up wl in tch: rdn and effrt to chse ldrs 2f out: drvn and kpt on same pce ins fnl f* 20/1	78
-403	5	hd	**Rowan Tiger**[28] 2080 4-8-5 71 .... NickyMackay 8 *(J R Boyle) t.k.h: hld up wl in tch: rdn and chsd ldrs 2f out: drvn and kpt on same pce fnl f* 12/1	74
1622	6	2 1/4	**Penchesco (IRE)**[8] 2685 5-8-9 75 .... TedDurcan 12 *(Mrs A J Perrett) t.k.h: mostly chsd ldr: rdn to ld 2f out: sn hdd by wnr: drvn jst over 1f out: wknd ins fnl f* 11/2[3]	73
41-4	7	1 1/4	**At Wits End**[39] 1780 4-8-9 75 .... KirstyMilczarek 6 *(J A R Toller) t.k.h: chsd ldrs: rdn and unable qckn over 2f out: wknd u.p jst over 1f out* 12/1	71
513-	8	1/2	**Wing Play (IRE)**[195] 7574 5-9-7 87 ....(p) ShaneKelly 3 *(H Morrison) stdd after s: hld up in tch in last trio: swtchd lft 2f out: rdn and no real prog over 1f out: plugged on same pce fnl f* 12/1	82
-661	9	1 1/2	**Ellemujie**[14] 2506 5-9-4 84 .... FrankieDettori 2 *(D K Ivory) t.k.h: hld up wl in tch: rdn and unable qck over 2f out: wknd wl over 1f out: wl hld fnl f* 7/1	76
-052	10	1 1/2	**Resurge (IRE)**[15] 2467 5-9-1 81 .... FergusSweeney 1 *(W S Kittow) t.k.h: chsd ldrs: rdn and unable qck over 2f out: drvn and wknd wl over 1f out: no ch fnl f* 10/1	70
50-0	11	9	**Ballinteni**[15] 2472 8-9-4 84 ....(v[1]) DaneO'Neill 10 *(N P Littmoden) t.k.h: hld up in tch towards rr: rdn and effrt over 2f out: no prog and wl btn over 1f out* 66/1	55
500	12	1 3/4	**Cluain Alainn (IRE)**[30] 2031 4-8-10 76 .... StevieDonohoe 5 *(Ian Williams) a bhd: rdn and no rspnse over 5f out: no ch fnl 4f* 22/1	43
1000	13	19	**Mahadee (IRE)**[14] 2508 5-9-5 89 ....(b) NeilCallan 7 *(C E Brittain) in tch in midfield: rdn wl over 2f out: wknd u.p wl over 1f out: wl btn and heavily eased fnl 100yds: t.o* 12/1	18

2m 11.24s (0.74) **Going Correction** +0.25s/f (Good) 13 Ran SP% **118.0**
Speed ratings (Par 107): **107,105,105,104,104 102,101,100,99,98 91,89,74**
toteswingers:1&2:£5.10, 1&3:£30.40, 2&3:£37.70 CSF £23.84 CT £602.18 TOTE £5.10: £1.70, £1.80, £8.90; EX 30.30.
Owner Seymour Bloodstock (uk) Ltd **Bred** Tim Cooper **Trained** Patching, W Sussex

FOCUS
A decent handicap and preparation paid off for connections of the winner here. The form is a bit muddling, although the runner-up is to her turf best.

NOTEBOOK
Jo'Burg(USA) was shrewdly angled over towards the stands' side entering the straight to race on what turned out to be quicker ground. Like the winner of the previous race, he now qualifies for the £100,000 bonus available to horses who have won two handicaps at this track and go on to win the heritage handicap on Variety Club day, but he has the added advantage of being proven over this C&D. Quicker ground won't be a problem for him when he returns here in August. (op 9-2)
Bugaku, a disappointing favourite at Chester last time, won the race on the far side, staying on strongly next to the rail to get past the long-time leader. His profile suggests he's best fresh, so he might not be one to be backing if making a quick reappearance. (op 11-2 tchd 6-1)
Kaolak(USA) has slipped to a good mark and bounced back to form under a positive ride. He took a lot of passing and might be one to keep in mind when he returns to Goodwood, where he has a good record.
Veroon(IRE) has done all his winning in Class 5 races and found this grade of race a touch too strong for him.
Rowan Tiger, who raced keenly early, is perhaps a little more effective over 1m4f. (op 14-1)
Penchesco(IRE), 3lb well in following his narrow defeat over this C&D eight days earlier, hit the front 2f out but weakened from a furlong out. He was another who had raced keenly in the early stages and probably paid for that later on. (op 7-1)

2935 TOTETRIFECTA FLEXI BETTING H'CAP 1m 2f 7y
4:55 (4:56) (Class 5) (0-75,75) 3-Y-O £3,885 (£1,156; £577; £288) Stalls High

Form				RPR
0-33	1		**Diamond Duchess (IRE)**[29] 2042 3-9-7 73 ....(b) TedDurcan 9 *(D R Lanigan) bhd: stl in last pair and rdn 3f out: hdwy over 2f out: edgd lft u.p and chsd ldr over 1f out: rdn to ld 1f out: styd on wl* 11/2[3]	83
0330	2	2 1/4	**Ice Viking (IRE)**[10] 2620 3-8-11 63 ....(b[1]) SteveDrowne 3 *(J G Given) bhd and sn niggled along: stl last and rdn over 3f out: gd hdwy and swtchd rt 2f out: styd on to chse wnr ins fnl f: no imp fnl 100yds* 20/1	68
3-45	3	2 1/2	**Whiepa Snappa (IRE)**[25] 2168 3-8-12 64 .... IanMongan 5 *(P M Phelan) chsd ldrs: rdn to ld ent fnl 2f: drvn and hdd 1f out: wknd ins fnl f* 11/1	64
433-	4	4	**Elvira Madigan**[177] 7763 3-9-4 70 .... JimmyFortune 7 *(A M Balding) towards rr and racing awkwardly: rdn: wandering and hld hd high over 2f out: hdwy and edging rt over 1f out: chsd ldr trio but no imp fnl f* 8/1	62
01-6	5	4 1/2	**Perfect Vision**[22] 2254 3-9-4 70 .... PhilipRobinson 13 *(C G Cox) dwlt: sn rcvrd and wl in tch: rdn 3f out: wknd u.p wl over 1f out: wl btn fnl f* 5/1[2]	53
-224	6	1 3/4	**I'm Super Too (IRE)**[20] 2315 3-9-8 74 .... KierenFallon 4 *(G A Swinbank) t.k.h: hld up towards rr: hdwy over 3f out: rdn and chsd ldrs over 2f out: wknd over 1f out: wl btn fnl f* 5/2[1]	54
644	7	4 1/2	**New Code**[31] 1993 3-9-0 66 .... DaneO'Neill 1 *(W R Muir) in tch in midfield: effrt and rdn ent fnl 3f: wknd and wl btn fnl 2f: eased wl ins fnl f* 40/1	37
0-43	8	2	**Rose Alba (IRE)**[39] 1778 3-8-12 64 .... MartinDwyer 2 *(J L Dunlop) chsd ldr tl led over 3f out: drvn and hdd ent fnl 2f: wknd over 1f out: wl btn and eased ins fnl f* 12/1	31
-240	9	3 3/4	**Katchmore (IRE)**[46] 1582 3-8-11 63 .... NeilCallan 10 *(M Blanshard) t.k.h: hld up towards rr: rdn and effrt 3f out: no real prog and wl btn fnl 2f: eased ins fnl f* 22/1	22
04-0	10	2 1/4	**Chat De Soie (IRE)**[53] 1433 3-8-8 60 .... LiamKeniry 14 *(J S Moore) hld up in tch in midfield: rdn and lost pl over 3f out: wl bhd fr over 2f out* 100/1	15
30-3	11	2 1/4	**Swift Return**[106] 692 3-9-6 72 .... SaleemGolam 8 *(S C Williams) hld up towards rr: sme hdwy into midfield over 3f out: rdn and no prog 3f out: wl btn fr over 2f out* 33/1	22
43-5	12	3 1/2	**Cloudy City (USA)**[99] 781 3-9-8 74 .... FrankieDettori 12 *(M Johnston) chsd ldrs: rdn and struggling wl over 3f out: wknd 3f out: wl bhd fnl 2f: t.o* 8/1	17
23-0	13	2 1/2	**Pytheas (USA)**[15] 2479 3-9-9 75 .... WilliamBuick 11 *(M J Attwater) led tl over 3f out: wknd u.p over 2f out: wl bhd and eased ins fnl f: t.o* 20/1	13

2m 11.17s (0.67) **Going Correction** +0.25s/f (Good) 13 Ran SP% **119.1**
Speed ratings (Par 99): **99,98,97,95,92 95,91,89,86,85 83,80,78**
toteswingers:1&2:£23.40, 1&3:£11.10, 2&3:£32.30 CSF £117.47 CT £1178.84 TOTE £7.30: £2.50, £9.30, £4.70; EX 172.90 Trifecta £348.60 Part won. Pool: £471.19 - 0.10 winning units. Place 6 £178.89; Place 5 £102.94.
Owner Saif Ali **Bred** R N Auld **Trained** Newmarket, Suffolk

FOCUS
A modest handicap run at a good gallop, which set things up for the hold-up horses. As a result of what happened in the previous race the whole field crossed over to the stands' side in the straight. Neither of the first two look completely straightforward.
I'm Super Too(IRE) Official explanation: jockey said gelding ran too free and lost its action
Pytheas(USA) Official explanation: jockey said gelding ran flat
T/Plt: £180.80 to a £1 stake. Pool:£58,536.31 - 236.26 winning tickets T/Qpdt: £55.30 to a £1 stake. Pool:£4,837.03 - 64.72 winning tickets SP

2343 YORK (L-H)
Friday, June 11

OFFICIAL GOING: Good (good to soft in places) changing to good after race 3 (3:25)
Wind: Light across Weather: Cloudy- sunny periods

2936 WIN A MILLION POUNDS WITH SPORTINGBET.COM E B F MAIDEN STKS 5f
2:20 (2:20) (Class 3) 2-Y-O £6,929 (£2,061; £1,030; £514) Stalls High

Form				RPR
24	1		**Imperialistic Diva (IRE)**[15] 2448 2-8-12 0 .... DavidAllan 7 *(T D Easterby) trckd ldrs: hdwy 2f out and sn cl up: rdn to chal over 1f out: drvn ins fnl f: led last 100yds* 11/8[1]	80
	2	nk	**Mayson** 2-9-3 0 .... PaulHanagan 9 *(R A Fahey) trckd ldrs: hdwy and cl up over 2f out: effrt and ev ch over 1f out: sn rdn and no ex towards fin* 13/2[3]	84
	3	3/4	**Miss Mediator (USA)** 2-8-12 0 .... PhillipMakin 4 *(M Dods) chsd ldr: hdwy 2f out: rdn to ld briefly ent fnl f: sn edgd lft: hdd and no ex last 100yds* 8/1	77
252	4	1 1/4	**Tilliemint (IRE)**[6] 2763 2-8-12 0 ....(b) RobertWinston 1 *(T D Easterby) led: rdn along wl over 1f out: drvn and hdd ent fnl f: one pce* 12/1	72
	5	1 1/2	**Close To The Edge (IRE)** 2-8-9 0 .... BarryMcHugh(3) 3 *(J S Wainwright) dwlt: sn chsng ldrs: rdn along and swtchd lft wl over 1f out: kpt on same pce fnl f* 66/1	67
2222	6	7	**Master Macho (IRE)**[8] 2680 2-9-3 0 .... ChrisCatlin 8 *(M R Channon) cl up on stands' rail: rdn along 1/2-way: wknd 2f out* 10/3[2]	46
4	7	3/4	**Cerejeira (IRE)**[21] 2286 2-8-12 0 .... EddieAhern 2 *(E J Alston) in tch on outer: rdn along over 2f out: grad wknd* 20/1	39
	8	3 1/4	**Goodmanyourself** 2-9-3 0 .... TonyCulhane 10 *(P T Midgley) dwlt: a outpcd in rr* 50/1	32
	9	3/4	**Da'Quonde (IRE)** 2-8-12 0 .... TomEaves 5 *(B Smart) s.i.s: a bhd* 14/1	24
	10	nk	**Assertion** 2-9-3 0 .... AlanMunro 6 *(M Brittain) wnt rt s: in tch: rn green and hung lft 1/2-way: sn outpcd and bhd* 66/1	28

60.14 secs (0.84) **Going Correction** +0.15s/f (Good) 10 Ran SP% **113.7**
Speed ratings (Par 97): **99,98,97,95,92 81,80,75,74,73**
toteswingers:1&2:£4.10, 1&3:£5.10, 2&3:£8.30 CSF £10.19 TOTE £2.30: £1.10, £2.50, £3.00; EX 10.10 Trifecta £169.60 Pool: £330.12 - 1.44 winning units..
Owner Miss N McFarlane **Bred** Bigwigs Bloodstock **Trained** Great Habton, N Yorks

FOCUS
No overnight rain and a dry, warm day. The going was described as "good, good to soft in places" and the riders described the ground as "on the easy side and patchy in places". Last year's race went to a very useful sort in Falasteen but, although this bare form is no more than fair, a couple of the newcomers shaped with plenty of promise and this race should throw up winners. The gallop was a reasonable one.

NOTEBOOK
Imperialistic Diva(IRE), an unlucky loser at Ayr, had no traffic problems this time and turned in her best effort to win in workmanlike fashion. She shapes as though the step up to 6f will be in her favour and, although she would not be guaranteed to confirm placings with either the second or third should they meet next time, she should be able to win again. (op 15-8 tchd 5-4 and 2-1 in places)
Mayson ◆, a late foal, has plenty of winners in his pedigree (mainly over sprint distances) and he shaped promisingly on this racecourse debut when chasing home a more experienced type. He has plenty of scope, should come on a fair bit for this experience, should stay 6f and appeals strongly as the type to win a similar event. (op 7-1 tchd 11-2)
Miss Mediator(USA), from a yard on the mark with juvenile newcomers in recent weeks, had reportedly missed a bit of work and was easy to back but shaped pleasingly on this racecourse debut, despite racing with the choke out and running green when asked for an effort. She is more than capable of winning a race of this nature. (tchd 12-1)
Tilliemint(IRE), with the blinkers again fitted, was allowed to dominate and probably turned in her best effort yet. She looks the best guide to the worth of this form and, although vulnerable to the better types in this grade, should pick up a minor event in due course. (op 10-1 tchd 9-1)
Close To The Edge(IRE), a £30,000 half-sister to several winners from 5f-1m, showed ability at an ordinary level, despite running green, on this racecourse debut. She should be better for the experience, though is likely to remain vulnerable in this grade.
Master Macho(IRE), who raced more towards the stands' rail than any of his rivals, was a fair way below his best. He has been a tough sort but is fully exposed. Official explanation: jockey said colt was unsuited by the good (good to soft places) ground (op 3-1 tchd 11-4)

2937 SPORTINGBET.COM WORLD CUP BETTING STKS (H'CAP) 1m 208y
2:50 (2:51) (Class 4) (0-80,80) 4-Y-O+ £6,799 (£2,023; £1,011; £505) Stalls Low

Form				RPR
22-0	1		**Kindest**[34] 1933 4-9-5 76 .... JackMitchell 3 *(C F Wall) trckd ldrs: smooth hdwy 4f out: led wl over 2f out: rdn and edgd rt wl over 1f out: drvn ent fnl f: kpt on gamely* 9/1[3]	85+

0060 2 *nk* **Chosen Forever**28 2093 5-8-11 71 BarryMcHugh(3) 1 79
(G R Oldroyd) *in tch: hdwy wl over 2f out: rdn over 1f out: ev ch ins fnl f: drvn and nt qckn towards fin* 16/1

1223 3 1 1/4 **Blue Spinnaker (IRE)**24 2204 11-8-8 70 JamesSullivan(5) 9 75
(M W Easterby) *hld up: hdwy wl over 2f out: rdn over 1f out: styd on strly ins fnl f* 7/1²

5040 4 *shd* **Mujaadel (USA)**11 2579 5-9-3 77 (p) MichaelGeran(3) 17 82
(D Nicholls) *hld up towards rr: hdwy 3f out: rdn wl over 1f out: styd on strly ins fnl f: nrst fin* 22/1

4220 5 *shd* **Rosbay (IRE)**11 2608 6-9-4 80 LanceBetts(5) 2 85
(T D Easterby) *midfield on inner: hdwy 3f out: rdn along over 2f out: styd on appr fnl f: nrst fin* 9/1³

-304 6 *hd* **Desert Vision**28 2084 6-9-8 79 (vt) PaulMulrennan 8 84
(M W Easterby) *trckd ldrs: hdwy and cl up 4f out: effrt over 2f out: rdn and ev ch over 1f out: drvn and one pce fnl f* 25/1

0-30 7 3/4 **Arabian Spirit**11 2580 5-9-6 77 PaulHanagan 18 80
(R A Fahey) *hld up towards rr: hdwy 3f out: rdn along 2f out: styd on fnl f: nrst fin* 14/1

4-00 8 *nk* **Kinsya**84 394 7-8-8 70 AshleyMorgan(5) 7 72
(M H Tompkins) *hld up towards rr: hdwy over 2f out: sn rdn: styd on ins fnl f: nrst fin* 13/2¹

261 9 1 1/4 **Shadowtime**13 2527 5-9-1 72 AndrewMullen 16 72
(Miss Tracy Waggott) *chsd ldrs: rdn along wl over 2f out: drvn over 1f out and grad wknd* 10/1

1150 10 3/4 **Jeer (IRE)**20 2349 6-9-7 78 (b) DavidAllan 11 76
(M W Easterby) *hld up towards rr: stdy hdwy on wd outside 3f out: rdn 2f out: no imp fr over 1f out* 20/1

0300 11 1 1/4 **Iron Out (USA)**25 2173 4-9-3 79 PaulPickard(5) 13 75
(R Hollinshead) *prom: effrt 4f out: cl up and rdn along whn hmpd wl over 1f out: sn drvn and grad wknd* 50/1

3251 12 1 1/4 **General Tufto**13 2523 5-9-0 76 (b) BillyCray(5) 15 69
(C Smith) *hld up and bhd: swtchd outside and hdwy wl over 2f out: sn rdn and nvr rchd ldrs* 20/1

25-0 13 *shd* **Best Prospect (IRE)**76 1011 8-9-6 77 (vt¹) PhillipMakin 5 70
(M Dods) *midfield: hdwy over 3f out: rdn along over 2f out: sn btn* 18/1

4523 14 3 **Oriental Cavalier**22 2240 4-9-2 73 (v) RobertWinston 4 59
(R Hollinshead) *in tch: hdwy 3f out: rdn along 2f out and sn btn* 9/1³

26-0 15 7 **Muftarres (IRE)**48 1513 5-9-7 78 (t) TonyCulhane 6 50
(P T Midgley) *a in rr* 28/1

0666 16 2 1/2 **Ra Junior (USA)**6 2760 4-9-7 78 (b) AdrianNicholls 12 44
(D Nicholls) *led 2f: cl up tl rdn to ld again 4f out: drvn 3f out: sn hdd & wknd* 33/1

411/ 17 2 1/4 **Duke Of Touraine (IRE)**545 1575 5-9-4 75 TomEaves 14 37
(B M R Haslam) *a bhd* 16/1

0363 18 2 3/4 **Archie Rice (USA)**8 2685 4-9-2 73 JimmyQuinn 20 29
(T Keddy) *chsd ldrs: hdwy to ld after 2f: rdn along and hdd 4f out: cl up tl drvn and wknd 2f out* 20/1

-011 19 17 **Dabbers Ridge (IRE)**39 1754 8-8-13 73 GaryBartley(3) 10 —
(I W McInnes) *a bhd: fin lame* 16/1

1m 52.43s (0.43) **Going Correction** +0.15s/f (Good) 19 Ran SP% 125.3
Speed ratings (Par 105): **104,103,102,102,102 102,101,101,100,99 98,97,97,94,88 86,84,81,66**
toteswingers:1&2:£48.60, 1&3:£10.20, 2&3:£35.10 CSF £128.93 CT £1111.57 TOTE £11.80: £2.80, £6.00, £1.90, £6.80; EX 230.40 TRIFECTA Not won..
Owner Peter Botham **Bred** Gainsborough Stud Management Ltd **Trained** Newmarket, Suffolk

FOCUS
Not too many progressive sorts but a fair handicap and one run at a fair gallop. The field fanned across the course in the last quarter mile and this form, which looks solid with the third to sixth all close to their marks, should prove reliable.
Desert Vision Official explanation: jockey said gelding hung right
Shadowtime Official explanation: jockey said gelding ran too free
Dabbers Ridge(IRE) Official explanation: vet said horse finished lame

2938 SPORTINGBET.COM BET ON YOUR IPHONE STAYERS STKS (H'CAP) 2m 88y
3:25 (3:25) (Class 3) (0-90,87) 4-Y-0+ **£11,009** (£3,275; £1,637; £817) Stalls Low

Form RPR

3-51 1 **Deauville Flyer**30 2031 4-9-6 84 RobertWinston 10 100+
(T D Easterby) *hld up: smooth hdwy over 4f out: chal on bit 2f out: sn led: rdn and edgd lft over 1f out: sn clr* 6/1²

0-21 2 3 1/2 **The Last Alzao (IRE)**14 2492 4-8-13 77 PaulHanagan 5 86
(R A Fahey) *hld up: hdwy and in tch 5f out: effrt 3f out: rdn to chal 2f out: drvn and kpt on same pce fnl f* 8/1³

210- 3 1/2 **Dulcie**224 7151 4-8-7 76 AshleyMorgan(5) 7 84
(M H Tompkins) *midfield: stdy hdwy 5f out: effrt 3f out: sn rdn and ev ch tl drvn and kpt on same pce fnl f* 6/1²

4-60 4 10 **Bollin Felix**13 2541 6-9-6 83 (b) DavidAllan 9 79
(T D Easterby) *in tch: hdwy over 6f out: led over 3f out: sn rdn and hdd 2f out: sn drvn and btn* 6/1²

0-05 5 2 1/2 **Saga De Tercey (FR)**20 2313 5-9-8 85 EddieAhern 12 78
(G A Swinbank) *in tch: rdn along 4f out: drvn over 2f out: plugged on same pce* 11/2¹

5046 6 1/2 **Sirgarfieldsobers (IRE)**14 2513 4-9-1 84 PaulPickard(5) 6 77
(B S Rothwell) *hld up and bhd: sme hdwy 4f out: rdn along 3f out: nvr nr ldrs* 20/1

100/ 7 3 **Backbord (GER)**405 2609 8-9-5 82 (t) AlanMunro 11 71
(Mrs L Wadham) *bhd: rdn along 1/2-way: sme hdwy u.p 3f out: plugged on: nvr nr ldrs* 20/1

4-36 8 3 3/4 **Bogside Theatre (IRE)**48 1525 6-8-11 79 ow2 MichaelO'Connell(5) 4 64
(G M Moore) *cl up: effrt to dispute ld 4f out: sn rdn: drvn 3f out and sn wknd* 12/1

536- 9 1/2 **Rugell (ARG)**152 5-9-5 87 JohnFahy(5) 3 71
(C G Cox) *in tch: rdn along over 3f out: sn wknd* 33/1

4332 10 1 1/2 **Royal Trooper (IRE)**9 2659 4-8-8 72 PaulMulrennan 8 54
(J G Given) *midfield: hdwy 6f out: effrt to chse ldr 3f out: rdn over 2f out and sn wknd* 10/1

-224 11 3 1/4 **Gaselee (USA)**9 2659 4-8-6 70 ChrisCatlin 1 48
(Rae Guest) *chsd ldrs: hdwy 7f out: cl up 5f out: rdn along over 3f out and sn wknd* 11/1

5-50 12 5 **Hawk Mountain (UAE)**13 2541 5-9-5 82 TomEaves 13 54
(J J Quinn) *a in rr: niggled along bef 1/2-way: nvr a factor* 14/1

0-05 13 30 **Kimberley Downs (USA)**41 1689 4-9-1 82(v) Louis-PhilippeBeuzelin(3) 2 18
(N Wilson) *set str pce: rdn along 5f out: hdd over 3f out and wknd qckly* 50/1

3m 32.4s (-2.10) **Going Correction** +0.15s/f (Good)
WFA 4 from 5yo+ 1lb 13 Ran SP% 115.6
Speed ratings (Par 107): **111,109,109,104,102 102,101,99,98,98 96,94,79**
toteswingers:1&2:£4.00, 1&3:£6.10, 2&3:£6.80 CSF £49.05 CT £301.20 TOTE £6.60: £2.40, £2.20, £2.20; EX 34.50 Trifecta £314.10 Pool: £544.79 - 1.28 winning units..
Owner Mr And Mrs J D Cotton **Bred** Harts Farm And Stud **Trained** Great Habton, N Yorks

FOCUS
A useful handicap. A decent gallop saw the field soon strung out and this was a good test of stamina. The first three pulled clear of the remainder and this form looks solid, with the winner progressive and the fourth to this year's form.

NOTEBOOK
Deauville Flyer ◆ is a progressive sort and strong-travelling type who turned in his best effort from this 4lb higher mark. This strong test of stamina suited him down to the ground, he goes on most ground (though ideally suited by decent ground) and appeals strongly as the sort to pick up a decent handicap at some point this year. He will be interesting if making the cut for the Northumberland Plate. (op 11-2 tchd 13-2 in places)
The Last Alzao(IRE) ◆, 5lb higher than when successful over 1m2f on her previous start, ran right up to her best jumping up markedly in distance. She's a very versatile sort - and a progressive one too - and she is more than capable of adding to her tally this summer on good or on quicker ground. (op 15-2 tchd 7-1)
Dulcie ◆ was a steadily progressive type last year and beat Deauville Flyer over C&D last autumn, but failed to confirm those placings behind a race-fit rival on this first run since October. However, the way he travelled through the race and the fact he pulled clear of the rest suggests this was an improved performance and it will be a surprise if he does not win races this year. (op 8-1)
Bollin Felix, a stable-companion of the winner, hasn't been at his very best this season but he has slipped to the same mark as his last victory and was far from disgraced with the blinkers back on, especially as he was ridden closer to the pace than the three progressive sorts that finished ahead of him. There will be easier opportunities than this one and he is worth another chance. (tchd 11-2 and 13-2)
Saga De Tercey(FR) looked a progressive sort last year but he's been essentially disappointing since his last win over this trip in August and, although he's in good hands and not one to write off yet, he'll have to show a fair bit more before he's a solid betting proposition from his current mark. (op 6-1 tchd 13-2)
Sirgarfieldsobers(IRE)'s form has been patchy since winning his maiden but he failed to get home over this much longer trip. The return to distances around 1m4f will be to his liking but he may have to drop further in the weights before he is able to win in handicap company. (op 18-1)
Backbord(GER), absent since running over fences last May, should be better for this run. A thorough test of stamina suits. (op 22-1 tchd 25-1)
Royal Trooper(IRE) Official explanation: jockey said gelding ran flat

2939 SKF ROUS (S) STKS 6f
4:00 (4:01) (Class 4) 2-Y-O **£6,799** (£2,023; £1,011; £505) Stalls High

Form RPR

1 **Sweet Cheeks (IRE)** 2-8-6 0 PaulHanagan 9 69+
(R A Fahey) *midfield: pushed along and hdwy to chse ldrs over 2f out: swtchd rt and rdn to ld over 1f out: clr ins fnl f* 12/1

2 4 **Thakeham (IRE)**22 2266 2-8-11 0 PatCosgrave 11 62
(P D Evans) *cl up: led 1/2-way: rdn and hdd over 1f out: sn drvn and kpt on* 11/2²

0 3 *nk* **Mossgorda (IRE)**7 2693 2-8-11 0 AndrewElliott 16 61
(J R Weymes) *dwlt and in rr: hdwy 2f out: swtchd lft and rdn over 1f out: styd on wl fnl f: nrst fin* 125/1

00 4 3/4 **Triple Agent (IRE)**18 2389 2-8-11 0 (v) JoeFanning 10 59
(A Bailey) *cl up: rdn along 2f out and ev ch tl drvn and wknd ins fnl f* 25/1

5322 5 1 1/4 **Russian Ice**11 2591 2-8-6 0 EddieCreighton 8 50
(D K Ivory) *in tch: hdwy to chse ldrs wl over 2f out: rdn over 1f out: kpt on same pce* 6/1³

0 6 1 1/4 **Silver Writer**5 2785 2-8-6 0 JamesSullivan(5) 18 51+
(M W Easterby) *bhd: pushed along 1/2-way: rdn over 2f out: styng on whn n.m.r and swtchd lft over 1f out: kpt on ins fnl f: nrst fin* 66/1

0 7 *nk* **Buzz Law (IRE)**7 2693 2-8-8 0 KellyHarrison(3) 17 50
(J R Weymes) *chsd ldrs: hdwy over 2f out: sn rdn and kpt on same pce fnl f* 66/1

5453 8 *shd* **King Of Cassis**10 2631 2-8-8 0 (b¹) JackDean(3) 2 50
(W G M Turner) *cl up: rdn along 2f out: drvn and wknd over 1f out* 7/1

351 9 1 1/2 **Daas Rite (IRE)**18 2391 2-8-11 0 AlanMunro 3 46
(K A Ryan) *towards rr and sn rdn along: drvn over 2f out: sme late hdwy: nvr a factor* 6/4¹

10 *nse* **Thirteen Shivers** 2-8-4 0 DavidSimmonson(7) 12 52+
(M W Easterby) *v.s.a and lost many l s: hdwy over 2f out: swtchd rt to stands' rails and in tch whn n.m.r over 1f out: sn wknd* 100/1

00 11 *shd* **Jealousy Defined (IRE)**9 2654 2-8-3 0 Louis-PhilippeBeuzelin(3) 15 40
(N Tinkler) *in tch: rdn along wl over 2f out: grad wknd* 100/1

40 12 1 3/4 **Vienna Woods (IRE)**32 1981 2-8-6 0 JimmyQuinn 14 35
(B M R Haslam) *chsd ldrs: rdn along 1/2-way: grad wknd* 20/1

030 13 1/2 **He's The Star (IRE)**7 2687 2-8-11 0 PhillipMakin 1 38
(P D Evans) *cl up: rdn along 2f out: hung lft and wknd over 1f out* 16/1

0 14 3 1/4 **Karafuse (IRE)**22 2239 2-8-6 0 DavidAllan 6 24
(T D Easterby) *s.i.s: a in rr* 20/1

15 5 **Ice Girl** 2-8-6 0 PaulMulrennan 4 9
(M W Easterby) *dwlt and bmpd s: a towards rr* 33/1

60 16 *nse* **Mercy Street**9 2654 2-8-11 0 (p) TomEaves 7 14
(N Tinkler) *dwlt: a in rr* 100/1

0455 17 *shd* **Silly Billy (IRE)**9 2638 2-8-11 0 EddieAhern 19 13
(S Kirk) *swtchd lft s: chsd ldrs: rdn along over 2f out and sn wknd* 16/1

543 18 2 1/2 **Sarandjam**14 2486 2-8-11 0 ChrisCatlin 5 6
(M R Channon) *led to 1/2-way: cl up tl rdn along 2f out and sn wknd* 16/1

00 19 7 **Whats For Pudding (IRE)**4 2813 2-7-13 0 NeilFarley(7) 13 —
(D Carroll) *chsd ldrs: rdn along 1/2-way: sn wknd* 100/1

1m 14.33s (2.43) **Going Correction** +0.15s/f (Good) 19 Ran SP% 131.6
Speed ratings (Par 95): **89,83,83,82,80 78,78,78,76,76 76,73,73,68,62 62,62,58,49**
toteswingers:1&2:£15.30, 1&3:£202.10, 2&3:£134.70 CSF £76.71 TOTE £10.80: £2.60, £2.50, £40.60; EX 136.10 TRIFECTA Not won..The winner was bought in for 14,000gns
Owner G Devlin **Bred** Terry McQuaid **Trained** Musley Bank, N Yorks
■ Stewards' Enquiry : David Simmonson caution: failed to ride out to line.

FOCUS
A valuable seller but those with previous form looked modest at best. The gallop was sound and the winner, who raced towards the stands' rail, looks the type to win more races with those close up setting the level.

NOTEBOOK

Sweet Cheeks(IRE) ◆, the first foal of a half-sister to a classy triple 6f juvenile winner, was easy to back but turned in a convincing display on this debut to beat several more experienced rivals with something in hand. She should be better for this experience, was bought in for 14,000gns and will be interesting when the nursery season begins. (op 9-1 tchd 8-1)

Thakeham(IRE) has improved steadily with every outing and it's not unreasonable to think he ran right up to his best on his first start for his in-form trainer. There will be easier opportunities in this grade and he is sure to be placed to best advantage. (op 9-1)

Mossgorda(IRE), soundly beaten after a slow start over 5f on his debut, did not forfeit as much ground this time but caught the eye with the way he made headway late on. Judging by his run-style and his pedigree, a further step up in trip will suit and he may be able to win a minor event. (op 100-1)

Triple Agent(IRE) had shown precious little but shaped much better dropped in grade and with the visor refitted. There is stamina on the dam's side of his pedigree, and the way he stuck on here suggested the step up to 7f could suit. (op 20-1 tchd 33-1 in a place)

Russian Ice has been a reliable yardstick over sprint distances and she was not disgraced returned to her optimum distance. She has had a few chances but should be able to pick up a weak race in this grade. (op 5-1 tchd 15-2)

Silver Writer had been well beaten after a slow start on his debut on Fibresand but fared better over this longer trip on this first run on turf. There is stamina in his pedigree and he may be capable of a little better over further. (tchd 100-1 in a place)

King Of Cassis Official explanation: jockey said colt hung right

Daas Rite(IRE), the only previous winner in the field, was never travelling with much fluency and was the disappointment of the race. However, he is only lightly raced and is worth another chance. Official explanation: trainer had no explanation for the poor form shown (op 5-2 tchd 11-8)

Thirteen Shivers hinted at ability after a very slow start and after meeting trouble when starting to make ground. He is entitled to improve for this outing.

Vienna Woods(IRE) Official explanation: jockey said filly hung right

He's The Star(IRE) Official explanation: jockey said colt hung right

Silly Billy(IRE) Official explanation: jockey said colt hung left

2940 SPORTINGBET.COM WORLD CUP DAILY OFFERS STKS (H'CAP) 5f

4:35 (4:35) (Class 3) (0-90,90) 3-Y-0+ **£8,095** (£2,408; £1,203; £601) **Stalls** High

Form RPR

0030 **1** **Hotham**[6] 2759 7-9-11 **87** PaulHanagan 2 97
(N Wilson) *chsd ldrs: swtchd rt and rdn to chse ldr over 1f out: led ins fnl f: kpt on wl* **18/1**

4551 **2** 1 ¼ **Favourite Girl (IRE)**[13] 2534 4-9-1 **77** (v) DavidAllan 3 83
(T D Easterby) *in tch: effrt 2f out: sn rdn and edgd rt wl over 1f out: drvn and styd on ins fnl f* **8/1**[3]

0524 **3** nk **Feelin Foxy**[20] 2346 6-9-4 **80** PaulMulrennan 12 84
(J G Given) *chsd ldng pair: rdn wl over 1f out: drvn and kpt on ins fnl f* **14/1**

10-0 **4** 1 ¾ **Go Go Green (IRE)**[53] 1423 4-9-10 **86** PhillipMakin 9 84
(D H Brown) *towards rr: hdwy 2f out: sn rdn and kpt on ins fnl f: nrst fin* **14/1**

-004 **5** nse **Invincible Lad (IRE)**[8] 2681 6-9-7 **83** PatCosgrave 1 81
(E J Alston) *chsd ldrs: rdn along and hung rt wl over 1f out: drvn and one pce ins fnl f* **9/1**

-411 **6** ¾ **Captain Carey**[21] 2280 4-9-13 **89** TomMcLaughlin 14 84+
(M S Saunders) *sn pushed along and towards rr on outer: hdwy 2f out: rdn and kpt on ins fnl f: nrst fin* **7/2**[1]

0-50 **7** nk **Desert Phantom (USA)**[27] 2119 4-10-0 **90** JoeFanning 11 87+
(D M Simcock) *chsd ldrs: rdn along whn n.m.r and hmpd wl over 1f out: kpt on ins fnl f* **12/1**

-400 **8** nk **Equuleus Pictor**[8] 2681 6-9-4 **83** JackDean(3) 4 76
(J L Spearing) *dwlt and towards rr: hdwy on outer 2f out: sn rdn and kpt on ins fnl f: nt rch ldrs* **17/2**

-345 **9** ½ **Rowayton**[20] 2327 4-9-5 **81** (p) AlanMunro 8 72
(J D Bethell) *in rr tl sme late hdwy* **7/1**[2]

3-21 **10** 1 ¼ **Atlantic Story (USA)**[146] 204 8-9-7 **88** (b) JamesSullivan(5) 5 75
(M W Easterby) *led: rdn over 1f out: hdd & wknd qckly ins fnl f* **10/1**

0-35 **11** ¾ **Hypnosis**[6] 2756 7-9-1 **77** TonyHamilton 10 61
(N Wilson) *chsd ldr: rdn along 2f out: sn hung lft and wknd* **25/1**

000- **12** hd **Tyrannosaurus Rex (IRE)**[293] 5247 6-8-12 **77** GaryBartley(3) 6 60
(D Shaw) *hld up: hdwy 2f out: rdn whn n.m.r and swtchd lft over 1f out: sn wknd* **33/1**

0445 **13** hd **Piscean (USA)**[8] 2681 5-9-5 **81** JimmyQuinn 7 64
(T Keddy) *s.i.s: a bhd* **16/1**

301 **14** 4 **Luscivious**[68] 1099 6-9-5 **81** (b) ChrisCatlin 13 49
(J A Glover) *chsd ldrs to 1/2-way: sn wknd* **14/1**

59.39 secs (0.09) **Going Correction** +0.15s/f (Good) **14** Ran SP% **121.1**

Speed ratings (Par 107): **105,103,102,99,99 98,97,97,96,94 93,93,92,86**

toteswingers:1&2:£20.00, 1&3:£33.00, 2&3:£10.70 CSF £156.48 CT £2149.85 TOTE £19.20: £4.80, £2.80, £3.10; EX 140.70 TRIFECTA Not won..

Owner Far 2 Many Sues **Bred** Capt J H Wilson **Trained** Sandhutton, N Yorks

FOCUS

Mainly exposed sorts but another useful handicap in which the gallop was a strong one. Those held up were at a disadvantage and the bulk of the runners came down the centre but the form looks straightforward.

NOTEBOOK

Hotham hadn't been at his best after a tardy start from a wide draw and after meeting early trouble in a competitive handicap at Musselburgh on his previous start, but he bounced back to form with a career-best effort. He is effective over 6f and, although this was his 69th career start, it will be interesting to see if this can be improved upon. (op 20-1)

Favourite Girl(IRE), who broke a losing run in a first-time visor over 6f last time, ran at least as well in this stronger event from this higher mark. The return to 6f will be in her favour and she should continue to give a good account.

Feelin Foxy is 10lb higher than her last win on turf but she appreciated the decent gallop and extended her run of creditable efforts. Equally effective on artificial surfaces, she should continue to give it her best shot. (op 12-1 tchd 11-1)

Go Go Green(IRE) ◆ bettered his reappearance form and, given all his wins have been at tracks with stiff uphill finishes, he probably deserves plenty of credit over this fast 5f. He should be spot-on now, and is one to keep an eye on, especially back at Pontefract, the scene of three of his wins. (op 16-1)

Invincible Lad(IRE) had run right up to his best when a close fourth at Sandown but failed to build on that this time, and life will be tougher from now on as he is due to go up 2lb in future handicaps. (op 13-2 tchd 10-1 in a place)

Captain Carey is probably a bit better than the bare facts in a race where the leaders never came back to the field and is worth another chance. (op 9-2)

Desert Phantom(USA) lost all chance when badly hampered at a crucial stage and is better than the bare form. Official explanation: jockey said colt was denied a clear run (op 16-1)

Hypnosis Official explanation: jockey said mare hung left

Piscean(USA) Official explanation: jockey said gelding was slow away

2941 FUTURE CLEANING SERVICES APPRENTICE STKS (H'CAP) 1m 4f

5:05 (5:06) (Class 4) (0-80,80) 4-Y-0+ **£5,180** (£1,541; £770; £384) **Stalls** Centre

Form RPR

5221 **1** **Tropical Bachelor (IRE)**[9] 2655 4-8-5 **66** 6ex JohnFahy(5) 4 77
(T J Pitt) *hld up in rr: hdwy on inner over 3f out: rdn to chse ldrs 2f out: styd on u.p to ld ins fnl f* **11/2**[2]

230 **2** 2 ¼ **Hunters Belt (IRE)**[21] 2285 6-8-10 **66** Louis-PhilippeBeuzelin 3 73
(N Wilson) *dwlt: hld up in rr: gd hdwy over 4f out: swtchd lft 3f out: chsd ldr over 2f out: sn rdn and kpt on u.p fnl f* **20/1**

1341 **3** nk **Peintre D'Argent (IRE)**[23] 2232 4-8-0 **63** HarryBentley(7) 2 70
(W J Knight) *prom: hdwy 4f out: led over 3f out: rdn along 2f out: drvn and hdd ins fnl f: one pce* **7/1**

-433 **4** 2 **Ahmedy (IRE)**[55] 1398 7-8-11 **70** IanBrennan(3) 6 73
(J J Quinn) *in tch on inner: smooth hdwy 4f out: sltly hmpd 3f out: rdn to chse ldng pair over 2f out: sn drvn and no imp appr fnl f* **11/1**

4-64 **5** 1 **Simonside**[14] 2492 7-8-7 **66** PatrickDonaghy(3) 12 68
(B Ellison) *chsd ldrs: rdn along 3f out: drvn over 2f out: kpt on same pce* **14/1**

2231 **6** 1 ½ **Patavium (IRE)**[17] 2424 7-8-9 **68** JamesSullivan(3) 16 67
(E W Tuer) *chsd ldrs on outer: effrt and hdwy over 3f out: rdn over 2f out: sn drvn and no imp* **12/1**

5-45 **7** 1 **Country Road (IRE)**[63] 1208 4-8-5 **68** DavidSimmonson(7) 10 66
(M W Easterby) *dwlt and in rr: hdwy on inner 3f out: sn rdn and nvr nr ldrs* **22/1**

0-01 **8** 1 ½ **Northern Acres**[17] 2421 4-8-10 **69** BillyCray(3) 5 64+
(D Nicholls) *hld up towards rr: hdwy over 3f out: n.m.r over 2f out: rdn wl over 1f out: n.d* **5/1**[1]

2-60 **9** 2 ¾ **Omokoroa (IRE)**[30] 2031 4-9-7 **80** AshleyMorgan(3) 15 71
(M H Tompkins) *hld up: hdwy on wd outside 4f out: rdn to chse ldrs over 2f out: sn drvn and wknd* **6/1**[3]

00- **10** 6 **Red Fama**[321] 4332 6-8-13 **72** DeclanCannon(3) 1 53
(N Bycroft) *midfield: effrt and sme hdwy over 4f out: rdn along over 3f out and sn wknd* **33/1**

100- **11** 2 ¼ **Joe Jo Star**[62] 5067 8-9-1 **76** LeeTopliss(5) 11 54
(R A Fahey) *trckd ldng pair: hdwy to ld briefly 4f out: sn hdd and rdn: wknd over 2f out* **8/1**

1350 **12** 2 ½ **Brockfield**[34] 1925 4-8-4 **65** JohnCavanagh(5) 9 39
(M Brittain) *chsd ldrs: rdn along over 4f out: sn wknd* **28/1**

0433 **13** 5 **Umverti**[18] 2395 5-8-4 **63** SimonPearce(3) 7 29
(N Bycroft) *led 1f: prom: rdn along over 3f out: drvn and wknd wl over 2f out* **14/1**

21-4 **14** 6 **Shifting Gold (IRE)**[87] 330 4-8-11 **70** ow2 (b) MichaelO'Connell(3) 13 26
(K A Ryan) *led after 1f: rdn along and hdd 4f out: drvn and wkng whn hung rt over 2f out: sn bhd* **20/1**

0040 **15** ½ **Carnac (IRE)**[20] 2349 4-8-9 **68** LanceBetts(3) 14 23
(J S Wainwright) *midfield: rdn along 4f out: sn wknd* **40/1**

2m 33.44s (0.24) **Going Correction** +0.15s/f (Good) **15** Ran SP% **122.0**

Speed ratings (Par 105): **105,103,103,101,101 100,99,98,96,92 91,89,86,82,81**

toteswingers:1&2:£58.80, 1&3:£9.70, 2&3:£41.00 CSF £119.90 CT £793.90 TOTE £8.80: £3.00, £8.00, £2.00; EX 299.30 TRIFECTA Not won. Place 6 £730.73; Place 5 £495.30.

Owner The Bachelor Party **Bred** George Ward **Trained** Norton, N Yorks

■ Stewards' Enquiry : Louis-Philippe Beuzelin one-day ban: careless riding (Jun 25)

FOCUS

A fair handicap run at just an ordinary early gallop. The runner-up is rated to the best view of his maiden form with the tird to the best view of her Lingfield effort.

Northern Acres Official explanation: jockey said gelding was denied a clear run

T/Jkpt: Not won. T/Plt: £1,019.10 to a £1 stake. Pool:£105,652.43 - 75.68 winning tickets T/Qpdt: £563.10 to a £1 stake. Pool:£5,479.34 - 7.20 winning tickets JR

2942 - 2949a (Foreign Racing) - See Raceform Interactive

2687 BATH (L-H)

Saturday, June 12

OFFICIAL GOING: Good to firm (9.3)

Wind: Moderate across Weather: Bright periods

2950 E B F FSB 24/7 LEGAL ADVICE LINE NOVICE STKS 5f 11y

2:15 (2:16) (Class 4) 2-Y-0 **£4,533** (£1,348; £674; £336) **Stalls** Centre

Form RPR

1 **1** **Jollywood (IRE)**[26] 2163 2-9-0 0 SebSanders 3 79
(R Hannon) *chsd ldrs: rdn and styd on wl fnl f: led last strides* **3/1**[2]

41 **2** hd **Silence Is Bliss (IRE)**[12] 2605 2-8-9 0 RyanPowell(7) 2 81
(J S Moore) *chsd ldrs: led ins fnl 2f: rdn and kpt on fnl f: ct last strides* **16/1**

1343 **3** 1 ¼ **Fifth Ave**[7] 2757 2-8-6 0 SophieDoyle(5) 5 72
(J A Osborne) *hmpd s: in rr: in tch: nt much daylight fr ins fnl 2f: hdwy between horses ins fnl f to take 3rd nr fin: nt rch ldrs* **11/4**[1]

1214 **4** ¾ **Scarlet Rocks (IRE)**[16] 2468 2-9-2 0 CathyGannon 4 73
(P D Evans) *veered rt s: sn disputing ld tl led after 2f: hdd ins fnl 2f: one pce fnl f* **10/3**[3]

5152 **5** ½ **Pick A Little**[33] 1978 2-9-2 0 DaneO'Neill 1 72
(B W Duke) *disp ld 2f: styd chsng ldrs tl wknd fnl f* **33/1**

1 **6** 1 ½ **Malice Or Mischief (IRE)**[18] 2407 2-9-2 0 JimCrowley 6 67
(R M Beckett) *bmpd s: sn chsng ldrs: rdn 2f out: little rspnse and wknd appr fnl f* **11/4**[1]

62.45 secs (-0.05) **Going Correction** -0.025s/f (Good) **6** Ran SP% **110.2**

Speed ratings (Par 95): **99,98,96,95,94 92**

toteswingers: 1&2 £23.20, 1&3 £1.50, 2&3 £8.20 CSF £42.17 TOTE £3.90: £2.60, £6.70; EX 59.80.

Owner Mrs J Wood **Bred** Tony O'Dwyer **Trained** East Everleigh, Wilts

FOCUS

This was a decent little novice stakes and is best rated around the third and fourth.

NOTEBOOK

Jollywood(IRE) got up to win in the final stride. Soon settled just in behind the speed, she couldn't match the runner-up when that one went on inside the final 2f. But she really came home strongly and looks to be crying out for 6f. She holds no notable entries and it will be interesting to see what mark the Handicapper gives her. (op 5-2 tchd 10-3 and 7-2 in a place)

Silence Is Bliss(IRE) ◆ is progressing fast. Unlucky not to win a seller on debut, he got off the mark at Redcar latest and looked all over the winner when quickening up to lead, but couldn't repel the winner's late charge. He is in the Super Sprint, and is the type who could easily go well there. (op 25-1)

Fifth Ave, who won her maiden over C&D, has been kept busy and she would almost certainly have been right in the mix with the front pair with a bit more luck, getting squeezed out at the start and then finding daylight all too late. She can be rated better than the bare form. Official explanation: jockey said filly suffered interference at start (op 3-1 tchd 5-2)

Scarlet Rocks(IRE), having her ninth start of the season, has been taking her racing well and showed plenty of speed despite veering right out of the gates, but couldn't race on inside the final 2f. This was below her previous best. Official explanation: jockey said filly jumped right leaving stalls (tchd 3-1 and 7-2)

Pick A Little had plenty to find with the best of these and ran about as well as could have been expected. He will find life easier in nurseries. Official explanation: jockey said colt was denied a clear run (op 25-1)

Malice Or Mischief(IRE) got a bump at the start and then found disappointingly little under pressure. She won on debut at Chepstow, and probably deserves another chance. (op 7-2)

2951 FSB LOBBYING FOR SMALL BUSINESS MAIDEN AUCTION STKS 5f 11y
2:45 (2:47) (Class 6) 2-Y-O £1,683 (£501; £250; £125) **Stalls** Centre

Form RPR

4202 **1** **Fifth Commandment (IRE)**[7] 2749 2-8-6 0.............. SophieDoyle(5) 12 80+
(J A Osborne) *mde all: c clr fr 2f out: easily* **3/1**[2]

6 **2** *3 ¼* **Delira (IRE)**[21] 2338 2-8-4 0.. FrankieMcDonald 9 61
(J G Portman) *awkward leaving stalls: sn chsng ldrs: pushed along and outpcd 2f out: rallied and r.o fnl f: tk 2nd last strides: no ch w wnr* **5/2**[1]

06 **3** *hd* **Atia**[24] 2223 2-8-11 0.. StephenCraine 10 67
(J G Portman) *chsd ldrs: wnt 2nd 2f out: sn rdn and no imp on wnr: lost 2nd last strides* **33/1**

05 **4** *1 ¾* **Moorland Boy**[15] 2486 2-8-11 0.. DaneO'Neill 13 61
(J A Osborne) *s.i.s: bhd: pushed along 2f out: styd on wl fnl f to cl on ldrs: nvr any ch w wnr* **33/1**

20 **5** *nse* **Lovat Lane**[35] 1930 2-8-4 0.. CathyGannon 1 54
(Eve Johnson Houghton) *chsd ldrs: rdn over 2f out: wknd fnl f* **11/1**

0 **6** *1* **Robber Stone**[5] 2819 2-8-9 0.. SamHitchcott 7 55
(M R Channon) *s.i.s: sn chsng ldrs: rdn over 2f out: wknd fnl f* **6/1**[3]

6232 **7** *1 ¼* **Roodee Queen**[12] 2605 2-7-13 0.............................. AdamBeschizza(7) 3 50
(Patrick Morris) *hmpd s: in rr: mid-div 1/2-way: sn pushed along: styd on fnl f: nvr a threat* **16/1**

00 **8** *3* **Rafella (IRE)**[21] 2338 2-8-11 0.. JimCrowley 11 42
(R M Beckett) *s.i.s: in rr: pushed along over 2f out: mod prog fnl f* **12/1**

000 **9** *½* **Three Scoops**[23] 2251 2-7-13 0.. BillyCray(5) 4 33
(D J S Ffrench Davis) *wnt lft s: outpcd* **100/1**

3 **10** *3 ½* **Chestival (IRE)**[12] 2605 2-8-1 0............................ AndrewHeffernan(3) 6 21
(Patrick Morris) *chsd ldr to 2f out: wknd qckly* **20/1**

0 **11** *9* **Nice Chimes (IRE)**[9] 2677 2-8-4 0.. LukeMorris 5 —
(B W Duke) *wnt lft s: chsd ldrs over 2f: wknd rapidly* **100/1**

45 **U** **So Is She (IRE)**[28] 2127 2-7-13 0.............................. NatashaEaton(7) 2 —
(A Bailey) *bmpd and uns rdr sn after s* **13/2**

62.28 secs (-0.22) **Going Correction** -0.025s/f (Good) 12 Ran SP% **115.7**
Speed ratings (Par 91): **100,94,94,91,91 90,88,83,82,76 62,—**
toteswingers: 1&2 £1.10, 1&3 £19.10, 2&3 £25.90 CSF £10.13 TOTE £3.30: £1.80, £1.10, £9.70; EX 10.70 Trifecta £148.10 Part won. Pool: £200.18 - 0.10 winning units..
Owner Danny Durkan **Bred** Keatly Overseas Ltd **Trained** Upper Lambourn, Berks

FOCUS
Few got into this maiden auction but the form looks solid rated around the placed horses.

NOTEBOOK
Fifth Commandment(IRE) ◆ showed plenty of speed to lead from her wide draw and raced clear inside the final 2f. Narrowly denied over 6f at Lingfield a week ago, the daughter of Holy Roman Emperor was not bothered by the shorter trip and is fully entitled to take her chance in the Super Sprint. (op 11-4 tchd 9-4)

Delira(IRE) made a promising debut over 6f at Newbury and she was readily outpaced by the winner on this drop in trip. She did stay on well for second, though, and can find a race returning to 6f. (op 7-2 tchd 9-4)

Atia improved on her two previous efforts and will be of obvious interest for nurseries. (tchd 28-1)

Moorland Boy ◆ made good late headway over a trip short of what will prove his best. He is certainly one to keep an eye out for in nurseries. (tchd 28-1)

Lovat Lane showed speed but doesn't look to have gone on from a promising debut effort. (op 8-1 tchd 12-1)

Robber Stone is another likely sort for nurseries. (op 10-1)

Roodee Queen was unable to recover after being hampered at the start. (tchd 14-1)

Rafella(IRE) is another likely sort for nurseries, especially over further. (op 9-1)

So Is She(IRE) would have been a player had she not received a bump and parted company with her rider at the start. (op 11-2)

2952 FSB MOBILE CARD PAYMENT H'CAP 1m 3f 144y
3:20 (3:21) (Class 6) (0-60,57) 4-Y-O+ £1,683 (£501; £250; £125) **Stalls** Low

Form RPR

0-32 **1** **Touch Of Style (IRE)**[20] 2361 6-8-1 47.................. AdamBeschizza(7) 5 59
(Matthew Salaman) *chsd ldrs: wnt 2nd over 4f out: led wl over 2f out: sn hrd drvn: c clr appr fnl f* **9/2**[2]

00-6 **2** *3 ¾* **Looks The Business (IRE)**[16] 1539 9-9-4 57.................. DaneO'Neill 6 62
(A B Haynes) *chsd ldrs: led 9f out: rdn and hdd wl over 2f out: no ch w wnr appr fnl f: eased nr fin* **10/1**

-063 **3** *5* **Minder**[32] 2006 4-9-4 57..(p) TonyCulhane 8 54
(J G Portman) *slowly away and wl bhd tl rdn and gradual prog over 3f out: styd on to take 3rd fnl 120yds: no ch w ldng duo* **10/3**[1]

36-1 **4** *½* **Le Corvee (IRE)**[9] 2676 8-8-13 52.................................... SebSanders 9 48
(A W Carroll) *chsd ldrs: rdn 3f out: wknd fr 2f out and lost mod 3rd fnl 120yds* **6/1**[3]

3601 **5** *15* **Free Falling**[15] 2489 4-8-10 49..(v) JimCrowley 10 20
(Miss Gay Kelleway) *led tl hdd 9f out: rdn and btn 3f out* **9/2**[2]

600- **6** *3* **Be Kind**[238] 6859 4-8-7 46.. FrankieMcDonald 11 11
(Karen George) *in tch: rdn and wknd 4f out* **50/1**

0-6 **7** *nk* **Piper's Song (IRE)**[154] 100 7-8-11 50........................ StephenCraine 1 15
(Patrick Morris) *in rr tl hdwy to trck ldrs 5f out: wknd 3f out* **20/1**

5-65 **8** *8* **Princess Flame (GER)**[12] 2586 8-9-0 56.............. RussKennemore(3) 4 7
(B G Powell) *in tch tl wknd 6f out* **7/1**

3502 **9** *¾* **Setter's Princess**[12] 2586 4-9-1 57........................ WilliamCarson(3) 7 7
(R J Hodges) *chsd ldrs tl wknd 6f out* **6/1**[3]

0005 **10** *43* **Behest**[9] 2676 5-8-4 46..(p) AndrewHeffernan(3) 3 —
(D G Bridgwater) *prom early: wknd qckly 7f out: t.o* **33/1**

2m 29.15s (-1.45) **Going Correction** -0.125s/f (Firm) 10 Ran SP% **119.3**
Speed ratings (Par 101): **99,96,93,92,82 80,80,75,74,46**
toteswingers: 1&2 £10.50, 1&3 £4.70, 2&3 £5.10 CSF £48.91 CT £171.29 TOTE £6.50: £2.20, £3.20, £1.10; EX 52.00 TRIFECTA Not won..
Owner Michael Barden **Bred** Yeomanstown Stud **Trained** Upper Lambourn, Berks

FOCUS
A low-grade handicap and although the time was reasonable, not form to be too positive about.

2953 FSB INDEPENDENT FINANCIAL SERVICES H'CAP 1m 3f 144y
3:55 (3:55) (Class 5) (0-70,70) 3-Y-O £2,590 (£770; £385; £192) **Stalls** Low

Form RPR

2532 **1** **Banks And Braes**[17] 2438 3-9-7 70.................................... JimCrowley 5 75
(R Hannon) *trckd ldrs tl lost position bnd 5f out: swtchd to outside and hdwy over 2f out: drvn to go 2nd wl over 1f out: hrd rdn fnl 120yds to ld last strides* **6/5**[1]

301 **2** *hd* **Lauberhorn**[21] 2333 3-9-2 65.. SebSanders 1 70
(Eve Johnson Houghton) *in rr but in tch: hdwy on ins fr 4f out: chsd ldrs 3f out: rdn to ld wl over 1f out: hdd and no ex last strides* **7/1**

44-0 **3** *2 ¼* **Lovely Eyes (IRE)**[37] 1847 3-8-13 65........................ MartinLane(3) 6 66
(D M Simcock) *chsd ldrs tl dropped in rr over 6f out: swtchd rt to outside 2f out: styd on to take 3rd wl ins fnl f: nt rch ldng duo* **8/1**

0366 **4** *3* **Pullyourfingerout (IRE)**[22] 2289 3-9-4 70.............. RussKennemore(3) 4 66
(B G Powell) *led: rdn over 2f out: hdd over 1f out: wknd ins fnl f* **6/1**[3]

-405 **5** *2 ¼* **Leaving Alone (USA)**[30] 2049 3-9-0 66.................... PatrickHills(3) 7 58
(R Hannon) *in rr but in tch: hdwy on ins 3f out: sn u.p and nvr quite on terms: wknd ins fnl f* **12/1**

6-14 **6** *3* **It's A Deal (IRE)**[21] 2336 3-8-5 54.. LukeMorris 2 41
(P Winkworth) *chsd ldr: chal 7f out: wknd 2f out* **4/1**[2]

2m 31.11s (0.51) **Going Correction** -0.125s/f (Firm) 6 Ran SP% **111.0**
Speed ratings (Par 99): **93,92,91,89,87 85**
toteswingers: 1&2 £1.30, 1&3 £2.70, 2&3 £1.80 CSF £9.97 TOTE £2.00: £1.40, £3.50; EX 8.00.
Owner The Queen **Bred** The Queen **Trained** East Everleigh, Wilts

FOCUS
A modest 3-y-o handicap run at an ordinary gallop and best rated through the runner-up.

Pullyourfingerout(IRE) Official explanation: jockey said colt hung right-handed throughout

2954 FSB TELECOM H'CAP 5f 161y
4:30 (4:30) (Class 4) (0-80,80) 3-Y-O+ £4,403 (£1,310; £654; £327) **Stalls** Centre

Form RPR

0-45 **1** **Brandywell Boy (IRE)**[11] 2622 7-8-5 62.............................. BillyCray(5) 6 71
(D J S Ffrench Davis) *in tch: hdwy over 2f out: drvn to ld wl over 1f out: rdn out* **6/1**

1456 **2** *nk* **Absa Lutte (IRE)**[21] 2327 7-9-13 79..............................(t) StephenCraine 7 87
(Patrick Morris) *stdd s: hld up in rr tl stdy hdwy to trck ldrs 2f out: chsd wnr u.p 1f out: styd on: a jst hld* **8/1**

5011 **3** *nk* **Poppanan (USA)**[16] 2458 4-9-3 76.......................... AdamBeschizza(7) 3 87+
(S Dow) *in rr but in tch: hdwy over 1f out: styng on whn nt clr run ins fnl f and swtchd rt fnl 100yds: fin wl* **9/4**[1]

1211 **4** *3* **Avrilo**[7] 2751 4-9-4 70.. DaneO'Neill 1 67
(M S Saunders) *in tch: hdwy to press ldrs ins fnl 2f: sn hrd drvn: wknd ins fnl f* **5/1**[3]

440 **5** *2 ¾* **Colorus (IRE)**[14] 2528 7-9-1 70....................................(p) MartinLane(3) 2 58
(W J H Ratcliffe) *pressed ldr: chal u.p over 2f out: wknd appr fnl f* **18/1**

-456 **6** *2 ¼* **Lithaam (IRE)**[103] 750 6-8-8 67....................................(p) RyanClark(7) 9 48
(J M Bradley) *mde most: jnd over 2f out: hdd & wknd wl over 1f out* **25/1**

3363 **7** *4* **Whiskey Junction**[11] 2635 6-9-9 75.................................... SebSanders 8 42
(M Quinn) *chsd ldrs to 1/2-way: sn btn* **5/2**[2]

0-16 **8** *¾* **Little Edward**[33] 1979 12-9-11 80.......................... WilliamCarson(3) 11 45
(R J Hodges) *chsd ldrs to 1/2-way: sn wknd* **16/1**

1m 10.29s (-0.91) **Going Correction** -0.025s/f (Good)
WFA 3 from 4yo+ 8lb 8 Ran SP% **116.4**
Speed ratings (Par 105): **105,104,104,100,96 93,88,87**
toteswingers: 1&2 £5.10, 1&3 £3.80, 2&3 £4.90 CSF £53.50 CT £140.37 TOTE £6.40: £1.70, £2.90, £1.30; EX 48.30 Trifecta £177.50 Pool: £177.50 - 1.19 winning units..
Owner P B Gallagher **Bred** Mountarmstrong Stud **Trained** Lambourn, Berks

FOCUS
Not a bad sprint for the grade and straightforward form rated around the first two.

Whiskey Junction Official explanation: jockey said gelding never travelled

2955 FSB FUEL CARD H'CAP 1m 2f 46y
5:05 (5:05) (Class 6) (0-55,55) 4-Y-O+ £2,047 (£604; £302) **Stalls** Low

Form RPR

0/0- **1** **Cyril The Squirrel**[404] 1728 6-7-13 47.................... AdamBeschizza(7) 2 56
(Karen George) *chsd ldrs: rdn to chal 2f out: led ins fnl f: drvn out* **14/1**

0000 **2** *1 ½* **Under Fire (IRE)**[25] 2198 7-8-4 48.................... AndrewHeffernan(3) 13 54
(A W Carroll) *sn led: hdd 2f out: styd chalng and led again over 1f out: hdd ins fnl f: no ex ins fnl 100yds* **33/1**

-605 **3** *½* **Spinning Waters**[12] 2597 4-8-9 50..................................(b) LukeMorris 4 55
(Eve Johnson Houghton) *chsd ldrs: rdn over 2f out: styd on same pce fnl f* **7/1**[3]

0220 **4** *1 ¼* **Great Bounder (CAN)**[18] 2419 4-9-0 55............................ SebSanders 3 58
(Michael Blake) *sn chsng ldrs: rdn over 2f out: styd on same pce fr over 1f out* **8/1**

04-5 **5** *½* **Flying Squad (UAE)**[52] 1478 6-8-9 50..........................(t) SamHitchcott 15 52
(M F Harris) *chsd ldrs: rdn over 3f out: slt ld appr fnl 2f: hdd over 1f out: sn wknd* **4/1**[2]

40-6 **6** *¾* **Fire King**[25] 2198 4-8-11 52.. DaneO'Neill 11 52
(A B Haynes) *sn chsng ldrs: rdn 3f out: one pce fnl 2f* **5/2**[1]

0006 **7** *1 ¼* **James Pollard (IRE)**[37] 1839 5-7-12 46 oh1..........(t) RichardRowe(7) 16 44
(B J Llewellyn) *s.i.s: in rr: pushed along 3f out: styd on fr 2f out: nvr a threat* **20/1**

541 **8** *¾* **Noah Jameel**[35] 1920 8-8-4 50.. BillyCray(5) 14 46
(A G Newcombe) *towards rr: sme hdwy on outside fr 3f out: kpt on fnl 2f: nvr a threat* **15/2**

0054 **9** *hd* **Holyfield Warrior (IRE)**[11] 2636 6-7-12 46............. CharlesEddery(7) 6 42
(R J Smith) *s.i.s: in rr: hdwy 6f out: rdn 3f out: wknd 2f out* **12/1**

0406 **10** *1 ½* **Barodine**[8] 2691 7-8-8 52.. WilliamCarson(3) 1 45
(R J Hodges) *mid-div: rdn and sme prog over 2f out: nvr rchd ldrs and sn wknd* **11/1**

50-0 **11** *8* **Lilly Blue (IRE)**[26] 2167 4-8-9 53..............................(t) RussKennemore(3) 5 30
(R Brotherton) *towards rr most of way* **25/1**

5-00 **12** *¾* **Aston Boy**[9] 2676 5-8-2 46 oh1.. MartinLane(3) 8 21
(M Blanshard) *a in rr* **40/1**

-606 **13** *2 ½* **Court Wing (IRE)**[24] 2232 4-8-0 46 oh1........................ SimonPearce(5) 7 16
(George Baker) *chsd ldrs to 3f out: sn wknd* **66/1**

646- **14** *12* **Rose Of Coma (IRE)**[228] 7094 4-8-0 48............................ RyanPowell(7) 9 —
(A G Juckes) *in tch: sme hdwy on outside over 3f out: sn wknd* **33/1**

30- **15** *33* **Grove View Star**[178] 7766 5-9-0 **55**............................ StephenCraine 10 —
(Patrick Morris) *v awkward leaving stalls: lost many l: a bhd* **16/1**

2m 9.36s (-1.64) **Going Correction** -0.125s/f (Firm) 15 Ran SP% **130.9**
Speed ratings (Par 101): **101,99,99,98,98 97,96,95,95,94 88,87,85,75,49**
toteswingers: 1&2 £2.20, 1&3 £4.00, 2&3 £4.40 CSF £441.29 CT £3519.43 TOTE £18.70: £4.20, £9.60, £2.80; EX 563.90 TRIFECTA Not won..
Owner R E Baskerville **Bred** R E Baskerville **Trained** Higher Eastington, Devon

FOCUS
Bit of a surprise result in this moderate handicap and modest form rated around the third and fourth.
Grove View Star Official explanation: jockey said gelding missed the break

2956 FSB CARE FOR ITS MEMBERS FILLIES' H'CAP 1m 5y
5:35 (5:35) (Class 5) (0-70,70) 3-Y-O+ **£2,331** (£693; £346; £173) **Stalls** Low

Form RPR

115- **1** **Seasonal Cross**[240] 6790 5-9-3 **66**............................ NathanAlison[(7)] 7 74
(S Dow) *s.i.s: hld up in rr: stdy hdwy on outer fr over 2f out: drvn and qcknd to ld fnl 75yds: pushed out* **9/1**

1463 **2** *3/4* **Pastello**[26] 2168 3-8-9 **65**............................ PatrickHills[(3)] 2 68
(R Hannon) *s.i.s: in rr: hdwy fr 3f out: drvn and qcknd to ld ins fnl f: hdd and outpcd fnl 75yds* **8/1**

0-50 **3** *nk* **Second To Nun (IRE)**[12] 2596 4-8-6 **51**.................. WilliamCarson[(3)] 5 57
(M Blanshard) *led: rdn fr 2f out: hdd ins fnl f: no ex fnl 75ds* **12/1**

-203 **4** *1 1/4* **Goolagong (IRE)**[21] 2342 3-9-3 **70**............................ JimCrowley 3 70
(R M Beckett) *chsd ldrs: rdn and kpt on fr 2f out: nvr quite gng pce to chal: edgd lft cl home* **2/1**[1]

0-40 **5** *shd* **Beauchamp Xiara**[12] 2602 4-9-11 **67**............................ DaneO'Neill 8 69
(H Candy) *mid-div: rdn along over 2f out: hdwy appr fnl f: kpt on cl home: could nt rch ldrs* **8/1**

3633 **6** *1* **Perfect Class**[20] 2362 4-9-10 **66**............................(v) LukeMorris 4 66
(C G Cox) *chsd ldrs: rdn over 2f out: outpcd fnl f* **7/1**

0251 **7** *1/2* **Light Dubai (IRE)**[17] 2429 4-9-11 **67**............................ TonyCulhane 11 66
(M R Channon) *stdd s: in rr: sme hdwy and nt clr run over 2f out: nvr gng pce to get into contention after* **6/1**[2]

5662 **8** *nse* **Signora Frasi (IRE)**[18] 2419 5-8-8 **53**.................. RussKennemore[(3)] 1 52
(A G Newcombe) *in tch: hdwy on ins 3f out: n.m.r over 2f out and nvr seeing much daylight after so nvr in contention* **12/1**

0601 **9** *nk* **Jewelled**[20] 2362 4-10-0 **70**............................(v) SebSanders 12 68
(J W Hills) *stdd s: in rr: sme hdwy on ins: styng on same pce whn hmpd cl home* **13/2**[3]

06-0 **10** *1/2* **Dancing Poppy**[20] 2359 3-8-1 **57**.................. AndrewHeffernan[(3)] 9 51
(R A Farrant) *chsd ldrs: rdn 3f out: wknd 2f out* **28/1**

00-0 **11** *3 1/4* **Madj's Baby**[12] 2587 3-7-8 **54** ow2.................. RyanPowell[(7)] 10 41
(H S Howe) *chsd ldrs: rdn 3f out: wknd 2f out* **50/1**

1m 42.24s (1.44) **Going Correction** -0.125s/f (Firm)
WFA 3 from 4yo+ 11lb 11 Ran SP% **126.5**
Speed ratings (Par 100): **87,86,85,84,84 83,83,83,82,82 79**
toteswingers: 1&2 £26.00, 1&3 £20.60, 2&3 £21.20 CSF £85.25 CT £893.71 TOTE £12.50: £2.50, £2.70, £4.90; EX 133.20 TRIFECTA Not won. Place 6 £192.18; Place 5 £33.76.
Owner Mrs Alicia Aldis **Bred** Adrienne And Michael Barnett **Trained** Epsom, Surrey

FOCUS
This was just a modest fillies' handicap, though it looks sure to produce winners at a similar level, with the winner progressive and the runner-up to the balance of his form.
Signora Frasi(IRE) Official explanation: jockey said mare was denied a clear run
T/Plt: £479.40 to a £1 stake. Pool: £54,047.74 - 82.30 winning tickets T/Qpdt: £53.00 to a £1 stake. Pool: £3,630.91 - 50.62 winning tickets ST

[2616]LEICESTER (R-H)
Saturday, June 12
OFFICIAL GOING: Good to firm (good in places; 8.4)
Wind: Almost nil Weather: Sunny

2957 3M INNOVATION H'CAP 5f 218y
5:00 (5:00) (Class 5) (0-70,70) 3-Y-O+ **£2,914** (£867; £433; £216) **Stalls** Centre

Form RPR

0-50 **1** **Cape Melody**[21] 2342 4-10-0 **68**............................(b[1]) TravisBlock 13 78
(H Morrison) *hld up: rdn and hdwy 2f out: led ins fnl f: r.o wl to draw away: eased cl home* **11/4**[1]

4560 **2** *3 3/4* **Shannon Golden**[36] 1885 4-8-6 **49** oh4.................. AshleyHamblett[(3)] 6 47
(S R Bowring) *racd keenly: a.p: rdn 2f out: nt qckn: hung rt over 1f out: styd on to take 2nd fnl strides: no imp on wnr* **16/1**

0422 **3** *nk* **Divertimenti (IRE)**[8] 2699 6-8-13 **53**............................(b) MarcHalford 3 50
(S R Bowring) *led: hung rt u.p fr 2f out: hdd ins fnl f: outpcd by wnr after: lost 2nd fnl strides* **6/1**[3]

0166 **4** *3/4* **Sophie's Beau (USA)**[5] 2822 3-9-3 **65**............................ PhillipMakin 10 58
(M C Chapman) *s.i.s: hld up: rdn and hdwy over 1f out: styd on ins fnl f: one pce fnl strides* **9/2**[2]

4046 **5** *shd* **Namir (IRE)**[5] 2818 8-9-9 **63**............................ DuranFentiman 8 57
(H J Evans) *midfield: rdn 2f out: prog and styd on ins fnl f: nt pce to chal* **17/2**

0242 **6** *nk* **Cornus**[10] 2647 8-9-9 **68**............................(be) TobyAtkinson[(5)] 4 61+
(A J McCabe) *hld up: rdn 2f out: hdwy over 1f out: kpt on ins fnl f: nt pce to get to ldrs* **6/1**[3]

0105 **7** *3/4* **Rough Rock (IRE)**[11] 2635 5-9-3 **64**............................ MJMurphy[(7)] 11 55
(C A Dwyer) *chsd ldrs: rdn over 1f out: fdd fnl 110yds* **7/1**

3240 **8** *1 3/4* **Kheley (IRE)**[8] 2726 4-9-13 **67**............................ EddieAhern 5 52
(W M Brisbourne) *in tch: rdn over 2f out: wknd fnl f* **12/1**

2005 **9** *4* **Mutamared (USA)**[24] 2234 10-9-7 **68**............................(t) DavidKenny[(7)] 12 41
(Andrew Reid) *chsd ldrs: rdn over 2f out: wknd over 1f out* **14/1**

1m 12.38s (-0.62) **Going Correction** -0.20s/f (Firm)
WFA 3 from 4yo+ 8lb 9 Ran SP% **116.7**
Speed ratings (Par 103): **96,91,90,89,89 89,88,85,80**
toteswingers:1&2:£15.20, 1&3:£7.00, 2&3:£12.40 CSF £50.35 CT £249.30 TOTE £5.80: £1.60, £4.20, £2.10; EX 109.90.
Owner Morrison, Eavis, Usher **Bred** Mrs A Savage **Trained** East Ilsley, Berks

FOCUS
A modest handicap, the top weight being rated 68, and depleted by a raft of withdrawals, so not the most solid form.

2958 SEAN NOLAN 60TH BIRTHDAY MAIDEN FILLIES' STKS 5f 218y
5:30 (5:32) (Class 4) 2-Y-O **£4,533** (£1,348; £674; £336) **Stalls** Centre

Form RPR

4 **1** **So Belle**[16] 2461 2-9-0 0............................ MickyFenton 14 72
(K A Ryan) *handy: rdn and edgd lft whn led over 1f out: r.o willingly whn pressed ins fnl f: plld out a little more fnl strides* **13/2**[3]

6 **2** *1/2* **Royal Liaison**[15] 2505 2-9-0 0............................ HayleyTurner 9 71
(M L W Bell) *hld up: hdwy over 2f out: intimidated over 1f out: chalng upsides wnr ins fnl f: hld fnl strides* **15/2**

50 **3** *hd* **Apazine (USA)**[15] 2505 2-9-0 0............................ NickyMackay 12 70
(J H M Gosden) *hld up: hdwy over 2f out: rdn to chse ldrs over 1f out: r.o u.p ins fnl f: a looked hld* **10/1**

064 **4** *2 1/4* **On Wings Of Love (IRE)**[15] 2505 2-9-0 0............................ MarcHalford 8 63
(A Bailey) *midfield: rdn and hdwy over 1f out: styd on ins fnl f: nt pce to rch ldrs* **10/1**

5 *1/2* **Feather Falls (USA)** 2-8-11 0............................ AhmedAjtebi[(3)] 13 62
(Mahmood Al Zarooni) *dwlt: racd in midfield: hdwy 1/2-way: led over 2f out: hdd and jinked lft whn intimidated over 1f out: no ex ins fnl f* **6/1**[2]

6 *1/2* **Miss Exhibitionist** 2-9-0 0............................ JackMitchell 3 60
(P W Chapple-Hyam) *racd keenly in midfield: hdwy over 2f out: rdn to chse ldrs over 1f out: styd on same pce fnl 110yds* **8/1**

0 **7** *2 3/4* **Water Ice**[11] 2616 2-9-0 0............................ RichardKingscote 15 52
(Tom Dascombe) *racd keenly: prom: lost pl 4f out: outpcd: rdn 2f out: kpt on ins fnl f: no imp on ldrs* **16/1**

5 **8** *5* **Mawjoodah**[17] 2436 2-9-0 0............................ JamieMackay 11 37
(C E Brittain) *racd keenly: prom tl rdn and wknd over 1f out* **13/8**[1]

0 **9** *3* **Alltherightmoves (IRE)**[21] 2319 2-9-0 0............................ EddieAhern 1 28
(Eve Johnson Houghton) *led: rdn and hdd over 2f out: wknd qckly over 1f out* **50/1**

0 **10** *1/2* **Liberty Green (IRE)**[56] 1375 2-8-9 0............................ TobyAtkinson[(5)] 5 27
(A J McCabe) *racd keenly: prom: rdn over 2f out: sn wknd* **66/1**

11 *25* **Shot Silk** 2-9-0 0............................ J-PGuillambert 2 —
(N P Littmoden) *dwlt: in tch: rdn and wknd over 1f out* **66/1**

1m 13.48s (0.48) **Going Correction** -0.20s/f (Firm) 11 Ran SP% **117.6**
Speed ratings (Par 92): **88,87,87,84,83 82,79,72,68,67 34**
toteswingers:1&2:£7.00, 1&3:£12.10, 2&3:£10.00 CSF £54.34 TOTE £7.50: £1.50, £1.20, £6.70; EX 76.00.
Owner Leavy Grant Devaney Hillen **Bred** Brook Stud Bloodstock Ltd **Trained** Hambleton, N Yorks

FOCUS
A run-of-the-mill juvenile fillies' maiden. The form is rated to the bottom of the averages for the grade.

NOTEBOOK
So Belle, a mildly encouraging fourth on her Newcastle debut, showed improved form to get off the mark. Always up with the pace, although racing on her own wide of the others in the middle of the course, she took control inside the final furlong. She is bred to stay farther than this and may well continue her progression when stepped up in trip. (op 7-1 tchd 5-1)

Royal Liaison, two places behind On Wings Of Love at Newmarket 15 days previously, comfortably reversed that form. On breeding, this seems as far as she wants to go at this stage, but she stayed on nicely and may handle farther. (op 8-1 tchd 7-1)

Apazine(USA) had shown only moderate ability in two previous outings, so this appears to be a step forward. She holds big race entries, which suggest she is held in some regard but, on this evidence, nurseries will be more her metier. (op 9-1)

On Wings Of Love(IRE) had already run three times and her record did not suggest she was especially progressive, so her presence in fourth puts the form into perspective. She might well have finished closer, too, but for a slowish start, and she was making ground inside the final furlong. (op 8-1 tchd 7-1)

Feather Falls(USA), who cost $100,000, will need to improve considerable on this if she is recoup a significant part of that outlay. Her all-American pedigree suggests she may be better on dirt or Polytrack. (op 13-2)

Mawjoodah was prominent until the 1f pole but faded. Official explanation: jockey said filly stopped very quickly (op 5-2)

2959 3M HEALTHCARE H'CAP 7f 9y
6:00 (6:00) (Class 4) (0-80,80) 3-Y-O+ **£4,533** (£1,348; £674; £336) **Stalls** Centre

Form RPR

0453 **1** **Flowing Cape (IRE)**[8] 2705 5-9-4 **75**............................ PaulPickard[(5)] 1 84
(R Hollinshead) *dwlt: in rr: hdwy over 3f out: led over 1f out: pushed out fnl 100yds: a looked in command* **8/1**[2]

3362 **2** *3/4* **Seasider**[28] 2129 5-9-6 **79**............................ LauraPike[(7)] 2 86
(D M Simcock) *dwlt: hld up: hdwy 3f out: rdn to chse ldrs over 1f out: wnt 2nd ins fnl f: chal fnl 100yds but a looked hld* **9/1**[3]

-000 **3** *1 3/4* **Lodi (IRE)**[19] 2399 5-9-4 **70**............................(tp) J-PGuillambert 7 72
(J Akehurst) *racd keenly in midfield: rdn and hdwy over 1f out to chse ldrs: styd on u.p fnl 100yds: nt pce to chal front pair* **10/1**

4451 **4** *nk* **Arabian Pearl (IRE)**[12] 2601 4-9-10 **76**............................(b) JackMitchell 3 77
(P W Chapple-Hyam) *in tch: led gng wl over 2f out: sn rdn: hdd over 1f out: no ex fnl 75yds* **9/4**[1]

0006 **5** *4* **Negotiation (IRE)**[15] 2512 4-9-6 **72**............................ EddieAhern 9 63
(M Quinn) *midfield: effrt 2f out: rdn over 1f out: kpt on but no imp on ldrs ins fnl f: allowed to coast home fnl 100yds* **18/1**

5601 **6** *3* **Learo Dochais (USA)**[19] 2383 4-9-1 **67**..................(p) PhilipRobinson 11 50
(M A Jarvis) *led: hdd over 2f out: sn rdn: wknd over 1f out* **9/4**[1]

60-0 **7** *1/2* **Lucy Brown**[12] 2580 4-9-1 **72**............................ JamesSullivan[(5)] 12 53
(M W Easterby) *racd keenly: prom: rdn and wknd over 2f out* **40/1**

60-5 **8** *1 3/4* **Oh So Saucy**[35] 1914 6-8-13 **72**............................ RoryHanley[(7)] 4 48
(C F Wall) *midfield: hdwy over 2f out: hung rt u.p whn outpcd over 1f out* **14/1**

4/2- **9** *3 3/4* **San Antonio**[359] 3076 10-9-10 **76**............................ MickyFenton 8 42
(Mrs P Sly) *prom: lost pl over 5f out: outpcd over 3f out: n.d after* **33/1**

4033 **10** *2 1/4* **Cut And Thrust (IRE)**[26] 2188 4-9-4 **70**............................ LiamJones 6 30
(M Wellings) *chsd ldrs: rdn over 2f out: wknd over 1f out* **25/1**

1m 26.01s (-0.19) **Going Correction** -0.20s/f (Firm) 10 Ran SP% **112.9**
Speed ratings (Par 105): **93,92,90,89,85 81,81,79,74,72**
toteswingers:1&2:£7.70, 1&3:£5.90, 2&3:£4.80 CSF £73.50 CT £738.15 TOTE £8.60: £2.80, £1.30, £3.40; EX 91.00.
Owner John L Marriott **Bred** David Maher **Trained** Upper Longdon, Staffs

FOCUS
A competitive handicap in which few could be discounted. The placed horses are rated in line with their recent best.

2960 LEICESTER MERCURY WORLD CUP SPRINT H'CAP 5f 2y
6:30 (6:30) (Class 3) (0-95,91) 3-Y-O
£7,788 (£2,332; £1,166; £583; £291; £146) **Stalls** Low

Form RPR
0-15 **1** **Monsieur Joe (IRE)**[42] 1701 3-9-7 **91** EddieAhern 1 104
(W R Swinburn) *hld up: hdwy over 2f out: sn rdn: wnt 2nd over 1f out: led fnl 110yds: r.o: wl on top at fin* **7/2**[2]
3-44 **2** 1 ½ **Racy**[42] 1701 3-9-0 **87** Louis-PhilippeBeuzelin(3) 6 95
(Sir Michael Stoute) *led: edgd lft fr jst over 1f out: hdd fnl 110yds: nt gng pce of wnr towards fin* **7/4**[1]
-60 **3** 2 **Secret Millionaire (IRE)**[21] 2346 3-8-12 **87** JamesSullivan(5) 3 88
(Patrick Morris) *chsd ldrs: wnt 2nd 3f out: rdn over 2f out: lost 2nd over 1f out: swtchd rt jst ins fnl f: one pce fnl 75yds* **10/1**
3-13 **4** 1 ¼ **Kanaf (IRE)**[29] 2090 3-8-11 **81** TadhgO'Shea 7 77
(E A L Dunlop) *dwlt: in rr: pushed along over 3f out: hdwy wl over 1f out: kpt on ins fnl f: nt gng pce to chal* **9/2**[3]
15- **5** 2 ¾ **Amitola (IRE)**[225] 7147 3-9-4 **88** PhillipMakin 5 74
(T D Barron) *chsd ldrs: rdn and nt qckn over 2f out: wknd ins fnl f* **9/2**[3]
4-53 **6** 3 **Living It Large (FR)**[17] 2437 3-9-6 **90** TonyHamilton 2 66
(R F Fisher) *in tch: pushed along over 2f out: wknd over 1f out* **12/1**
2-30 **7** 4 **Tillys Tale**[29] 2099 3-8-3 **78** PaulPickard(5) 4 39
(P T Midgley) *prom: lost pl 3f out: sn pushed along: outpcd fnl 2f* **33/1**

59.04 secs (-0.96) **Going Correction** -0.20s/f (Firm) 7 Ran SP% **114.7**
Speed ratings (Par 103): **99,96,93,91,87 82,75**
toteswingers:1&2:£1.70, 1&3:£6.20, 2&3:£10.80 CSF £10.13 TOTE £5.00: £3.20, £1.10; EX 10.90.
Owner Mrs Helen Checkley **Bred** Nicola And Eleanor Kent **Trained** Aldbury, Herts

FOCUS
A decent handicap, the top weight being rated 91, and it looked open. The first two reversed placings compared with their previous meeting, while the third sets the level.

NOTEBOOK
Monsieur Joe(IRE), half a length behind today's runner-up last time out, renewed rivalry on the same terms and turned the form around. Second in the early stages, he came under pressure at halfway and the response was not immediate. He had built momentum by the 1f pole, however and, racing under the stands' rail, hit the front with 50 yards left. He is consistent and this stiff 5f appears to suit. (tchd 4-1)
Racy, fourth in two warm 6f handicaps at Newmarket earlier this term, had beaten today's winner last time but was dropping in distance and tried to run the legs off his rivals. Quickly away, he was in a clear lead with 2f left, but could not maintain the gallop and had no response when the winner came past him. (op 15-8 tchd 2-1)
Secret Millionaire(IRE) is 6lb higher than when winning over this trip on Polytrack last term and may need a little help with his rating. He was always chasing the pace. (op 8-1 tchd 11-1)
Kanaf(IRE), who pulled hard over 6f last time out, was back over the distance of his previous maiden victory, but did himself no favours with a poor start. He tried hard to make up the lost ground, but never looked likely to get into contention. (op 4-1 tchd 7-2)
Amitola(IRE), fifth in Listed company on the second of her two starts last season, was making her handicap debut. She was slightly awkward jumping out of the stalls, however, and never closer than fourth. (op 8-1)

2961 ENGLAND V USA H'CAP 1m 1f 218y
7:00 (7:00) (Class 5) (0-75,75) 4-Y-O+ **£3,238** (£963; £481; £240) **Stalls** High

Form RPR
0201 **1** **Scamperdale**[12] 2602 8-8-12 **66** JackMitchell 1 79+
(B P J Baugh) *hld up: hdwy gng wl 3f out: led over 1f out: qcknd abt 3 l clr jst ins fnl f: in command whn idled towards fin: a doing enough* **8/1**
0413 **2** nk **Visions Of Johanna (USA)**[11] 2625 5-9-2 **70** TonyHamilton 9 80
(Ian Williams) *midfield: rdn and hdwy 2f out: wnt 2nd ins fnl f: clsd on idling wnr towards fin: hld* **9/2**[2]
0-0 **3** 6 **Welsh Anthem**[39] 1797 4-8-12 **66** (p) HayleyTurner 4 64
(W R Muir) *chsd ldrs: rdn and ev ch over 1f out: no ex fnl 110yds* **20/1**
6-65 **4** 1 ¾ **Sceilin (IRE)**[26] 2173 6-8-6 **65** (t) JamesSullivan(5) 7 59
(J Mackie) *hld up: rdn and hdwy on outer over 2f out: styd on ins fnl f: nt rch ldrs* **7/1**[3]
0-05 **5** ½ **Snowed Under**[17] 2435 9-9-7 **75** PhilipRobinson 11 68
(J D Bethell) *chsd clr ldr: led 2f out: rdn and hdd over 1f out: btn ins fnl f* **12/1**
6403 **6** 1 ½ **Singbella**[35] 1920 4-8-6 **60** (p) TadhgO'Shea 10 50
(C G Cox) *racd keenly: in tch: rdn over 3f out: one pce over 1f out* **17/2**
0100 **7** ¾ **Waahej**[16] 2467 4-8-8 **69** LauraPike(7) 13 58
(P W Hiatt) *in tch: rdn and no imp over 1f out: n.d fnl f* **17/2**
1640 **8** 4 ½ **Paint The Town Red**[33] 1980 5-7-13 **56** oh3 Louis-PhilippeBeuzelin(3) 2 36
(H J Collingridge) *hld up: rdn over 3f out: hdwy into midfield over 1f out: eased whn no imp ins fnl f* **50/1**
0020 **9** 1 ¾ **Orpen Wide (IRE)**[18] 2421 8-8-8 **65** (b) KellyHarrison(3) 3 41
(M C Chapman) *a towards rr: sn niggled along: nvr on terms* **40/1**
5314 **10** ¾ **Taaresh (IRE)**[17] 2435 5-9-7 **75** PhillipMakin 5 50
(K A Morgan) *midfield: effrt over 2f out: no imp on ldrs: wknd fnl f* **4/1**[1]
0-20 **11** 2 ¾ **Silent Oasis**[18] 2411 4-9-1 **74** RossAtkinson(5) 8 43
(J S Moore) *midfield: rdn over 3f out: sn wknd* **25/1**
0110 **12** 1 ¼ **West End Lad**[35] 1926 7-8-13 **74** (b) LeeTopliss(7) 6 41
(S R Bowring) *led: sn clr: hdd 2f out: wknd qckly over 1f out* **18/1**
664/ **13** 9 **Celtic Dragon**[626] 6202 5-9-1 **69** EddieAhern 12 18
(Mrs A J Perrett) *in tch: wknd qckly 3f out: eased* **17/2**

2m 4.92s (-2.98) **Going Correction** -0.20s/f (Firm) 13 Ran SP% **119.3**
Speed ratings (Par 103): **103,102,97,96,96 94,94,90,89,88 86,85,78**
toteswingers:1&2:£9.40, 1&3:£11.90, 2&3:£15.30 CSF £42.19 CT £709.16 TOTE £11.60: £3.60, £1.80, £6.60; EX 47.60.
Owner Saddle Up Racing **Bred** Mrs J A Prescott **Trained** Audley, Staffs

FOCUS
A modest handicap with the winner value for further and the second to last year's best.

2962 KICK-OFF H'CAP 5f 218y
7:25 (7:25) (Class 6) (0-60,61) 3-Y-O **£2,590** (£770; £385; £192) **Stalls** Centre

Form RPR
0-63 **1** **Micky P**[11] 2634 3-9-1 **57** JackMitchell 2 68+
(S C Williams) *racd alone on stands' rail: in tch: led 2f out: edgd rt ins fnl f: r.o wl: in command fnl 100yds* **5/2**[1]
3025 **2** 2 ¼ **Drumpellier (IRE)**[52] 1468 3-8-10 **57** PaulPickard(5) 8 61
(P T Midgley) *racd towards nr side: led: rdn and hdd 2f out: kpt on ins fnl f but nt pce of wnr* **14/1**
0-50 **3** 3 ½ **Dragonessa (IRE)**[32] 2000 3-8-13 **55** DavidProbert 11 48
(B Palling) *racd towards far side: a.p: rdn over 1f out: sn edgd lft: styd on same pce ins fnl f: nt pce of front pair* **10/1**[3]
5-00 **4** nk **Rosiliant (IRE)**[32] 2000 3-8-10 **50** ow2 (b) PhilipRobinson 9 44
(C G Cox) *racd towards nr side: a.p: rdn over 1f out: kpt on same pce ins fnl f* **12/1**
3666 **5** 3 **Magenta Strait**[8] 2722 3-8-5 **52** TobyAtkinson(5) 5 34
(R Hollinshead) *sn outpcd bhd nr side gp: hdwy u.p over 1f out: kpt on ins fnl f: nt pce of ldrs* **16/1**
50-1 **6** hd **Perfect Blossom**[10] 2648 3-9-0 **61** MichaelO'Connell(5) 13 43
(K A Ryan) *racd towards far side: a.p: rdn over 1f out: no ex ins fnl f* **10/3**[2]
1606 **7** 1 ½ **Sweet Mirasol (IRE)**[32] 1994 3-8-5 **50** (t) AshleyHamblett(3) 12 27
(Miss M E Rowland) *racd towards far side: chsd ldrs: rdn and nt qckn 2f out: one pce fnl f: uns rdr jst after line* **50/1**
6055 **8** 2 ½ **Cookie Galore**[8] 2698 3-8-11 **52** ow1 PhillipMakin 7 22
(J A Glover) *s.i.s: racd toward nr side: bhd: rdn and hdwy over 2f out: one-pced over 1f out* **12/1**
5-60 **9** 1 **Crushing (IRE)**[33] 1970 3-8-2 **49** PatrickDonaghy(5) 6 15
(Julie Camacho) *racd towards nr side: midfield: rdn 2f out: outpcd over 1f out* **22/1**
0-00 **10** 1 ¼ **Brave Ghurka**[12] 2584 3-8-13 **55** RichardKingscote 4 17
(S Kirk) *racd towards nr side: midfield: rdn and wknd over 1f out* **40/1**
06-1 **11** 3 ¼ **Royal Cheer**[14] 2535 3-8-9 **51** MickyFenton 16 2
(Mrs A Duffield) *racd towards far side: chsd ldrs: rdn 2f out: wknd over 1f out* **12/1**
-000 **12** ¾ **Baileys Vision**[13] 2566 3-8-8 **53** (v) KellyHarrison(3) 14 2
(C A Dwyer) *racd towards far side: midfield: outpcd fnl 2f* **33/1**
50-0 **13** 11 **Thoughtful (IRE)**[23] 2249 3-9-1 **57** EddieAhern 10 —
(J W Hills) *racd towards far side: chsd ldrs: rdn and wknd 2f out: eased whn btn over 1f out* **12/1**
660- **14** 4 ½ **Daisy Brown**[248] 6589 3-8-11 **53** J-PGuillambert 17 —
(N Tinkler) *racd towards far side: in tch: pushed along 1/2-way: wknd 2f out: eased whn btn fnl f* **25/1**
5360 **15** 2 **Seek The Cash (USA)**[78] 988 3-9-2 **58** NickyMackay 18 —
(M Quinn) *racd towards far side and in rr: outpcd 3f out: nvr on terms* **33/1**
0306 **16** 1 ¼ **City Gossip (IRE)**[49] 1536 3-8-11 **53** (b[1]) HayleyTurner 15 —
(Miss M E Rowland) *missed break: racd towards far side: a bhd* **25/1**

1m 11.91s (-1.09) **Going Correction** -0.20s/f (Firm) 16 Ran SP% **126.4**
Speed ratings (Par 97): **99,96,91,90,86 86,84,81,80,78 74,73,58,52,49 48**
toteswingers:1&2:£8.50, 1&3:£9.70, 2&3:£11.30 CSF £37.96 CT £333.69 TOTE £3.70: £1.40, £1.90, £3.30, £2.80; EX 52.70 Place 6 £232.63; Place 5 £120.23.
Owner O Pointing **Bred** O Pointing **Trained** Newmarket, Suffolk

FOCUS
Not much better than a seller, with the top weight rated 61, and the field split into at least three groups, making the form hard to evaluate. The form is a bit mesy but the runner-up is the best guide rated back to her juvenile form.
Royal Cheer Official explanation: trainer said filly was unsuited by the good to firm (good in places) ground
Seek The Cash(USA) Official explanation: jockey said colt never travelled
T/Plt: £568.20 to a £1 stake. Pool:£32,109.76 - 41.25 winning tickets T/Qpdt: £22.40 to a £1 stake. Pool:£3,685.57 - 121.68 winning tickets DO

2749 LINGFIELD (L-H)
Saturday, June 12

OFFICIAL GOING: Turf course - good to soft; all-weather - standard
Stands' rail moved in 2m.
Wind: Almost nil Weather: Fine

2963 BET ON ENGLAND V USA AT LADBROKES.COM MEDIAN AUCTION MAIDEN FILLIES' STKS 5f
5:50 (5:52) (Class 5) 2-Y-O **£2,729** (£806; £403) **Stalls** High

Form RPR
302 **1** **The Thrill Is Gone**[10] 2638 2-9-0 0 ChrisCatlin 3 70
(M R Channon) *pressed ldr: led over 1f out: rdn to assert fnl f: hld on to dwindling ld fin* **7/4**[1]
20 **2** ½ **Never Can Stop**[20] 2358 2-9-0 0 SaleemGolam 5 68
(J G Portman) *dwlt and n.m.r s: sn pushed along in last trio: rchd midfield 2f out: rdn and gd prog against rail 1f out: wnt 2nd and clsd on wnr fin* **7/1**
3 **3** 1 **Kokojo (IRE)**[26] 2176 2-9-0 0 FergusSweeney 11 65
(B G Powell) *trckd ldrs: effrt over 1f out: rdn to chse wnr jst ins fnl f: nt qckn: lost 2nd nr fin* **3/1**[2]
5 **4** ¾ **Sirens**[13] 2561 2-8-7 0 (t) LeonnaMayor(7) 14 62
(P S McEntee) *led: rdn and hdd over 1f out: nt qckn* **20/1**
04 **5** ¾ **Volcanic Dust (IRE)**[3] 2873 2-9-0 0 DaraghO'Donohoe 15 59+
(E A L Dunlop) *dwlt: t.k.h: hld up in last trio: shuffled along and taking prog fnl f: do bttr* **10/1**
6 nk **Amber Mist** 2-8-9 0 KierenFox(5) 7 58+
(David Pinder) *rn green and wl outpcd in last: taken to wd outside and kpt on fr 1/2-way: nrst fin* **25/1**
534 **7** 1 ½ **Kodiac Star (IRE)**[16] 2457 2-8-9 0 SophieDoyle(5) 12 53
(J A Osborne) *trckd ldrs: outpcd 2f out: shkn up and nt qckn over 1f out: fdd* **4/1**[3]
0 **8** 2 ¾ **Laugia**[26] 2176 2-9-0 0 SimonWhitworth 8 43
(J R Jenkins) *a towards rr: pushed along 1/2-way: sn btn* **66/1**
0 **9** 1 ¼ **Evaso Nice**[10] 2642 2-8-9 0 DeclanCannon(5) 9 38
(D Donovan) *chsd ldrs to 1/2-way: sn rdn and wknd* **40/1**
0 **10** 1 ¼ **Fairy Tales**[18] 2413 2-9-0 0 NeilChalmers 4 34
(J J Bridger) *pressed ldng pair on outer to 2f out: wknd rapidly* **150/1**
600 **11** 2 ¼ **Miss Maudie (IRE)**[10] 2638 2-9-0 0 JerryO'Dwyer 10 26
(J J Bridger) *a towards rr: struggling sn after 1/2-way* **200/1**

60.20 secs (2.00) **Going Correction** +0.175s/f (Good) 11 Ran SP% **116.7**
Speed ratings (Par 90): **91,90,88,87,86 85,83,78,76,74 71**
toteswingers:1&2:£4.50, 1&3:£2.90, 2&3:£4.60 CSF £14.11 TOTE £2.50: £1.10, £1.10, £1.20; EX 21.20.
Owner Mr & Mrs Christopher Wright **Bred** Stratford Place Stud **Trained** West Ilsley, Berks
■ Stewards' Enquiry : Fergus Sweeney one-day ban: careless riding (Jun 26)

FOCUS
A modest juvenile maiden but the form looks reasonable rated through the third.

NOTEBOOK
The Thrill Is Gone had been placed twice previously and probably didn't have to step up much on that form to get off the mark. Her willing attitude should hold her in good stead in nurseries but she isn't an obvious one to improve much further. (op 7-2)

Never Can Stop possibly failed to cope with the firm ground at Bath last time as she's been runner-up on her two other starts, finishing here as though a step up to 6f or more is sure to suit, a view which is backed up by her pedigree. (op 6-1)
Kokojo(IRE) confirmed she has a fair level of ability and a race should come her way at some stage, though she's always likely to be vulnerable to progressive sorts near to hand. (op 5-2 tchd 9-4 and 10-3)
Sirens has shown speed on both starts and is likely to continue to improve with racing. (op 12-1)
Volcanic Dust(IRE) ◆ was held up in a race in which it paid to race handily and kept on well in the closing stages without being knocked about. She'll be suited by a step back up to 6f and, now eligible for a mark, is very much one to look out for in nurseries. Official explanation: jockey said filly suffered interference shortly after start and was denied a clear run 2f out (op 11-1 tchd 12-1)
Amber Mist, a newcomer by Haafhd, was palpably green early on but showed clear ability as she gradually got the hang of things after halfway and can only improve. (op 16-1)
Kodiac Star(IRE) had made the frame on her last two starts and was a shade disappointing, the fact she was in trouble by halfway suggesting the drop back in trip perhaps wasn't in her favour. (tchd 7-2)

2964 GOT THE FEELING, GET TO LADBROKES H'CAP — 6f
6:20 (6:22) (Class 6) (0-60,63) 3-Y-0+ — £2,047 (£604; £302) Stalls High

Form — RPR
06 **1** **Doctor Hilary**[26] 2178 8-9-10 **60**.....................(v) ChrisCatlin 14 — 69
(M R Hoad) *racd against rail: mde all: drvn and styd on wl fr over 1f out* **28/1**

2300 **2** 1 1/2 **Bobs Dreamflight**[35] 1929 4-9-5 **60**.................... MarkCoumbe(5) 16 — 70+
(D K Ivory) *racd against rail: hld up bhd ldrs: effrt over 1f out: wnt 2nd ins fnl f: tried to chal on inner and no room: hld after* **10/1**

4360 **3** 3/4 **Ejeed (USA)**[3] 2866 5-9-3 **58**...................(b) GemmaGracey-Davison(5) 9 — 60
(Miss Z C Davison) *pressed ldrs: wnt 2nd 1/2-way: chal over 1f out: hld ins fnl f and sn outpcd* **13/2**[3]

60-5 **4** 1 1/4 **Safari Guide**[22] 2298 4-9-10 **60**...................... FrankieMcDonald 10 — 58
(P Winkworth) *cl up bhd ldrs: nt qckn and outpcd over 1f out: styd on again fnl f* **12/1**

0162 **5** 3/4 **Sirjosh**[6] 2779 4-8-12 **53**.......................... DeclanCannon(5) 13 — 49+
(D Donovan) *s.i.s: hld up in last trio: pushed along and swtchd fr rail to outer 2f out: styd on u.p: nrst fin* **9/2**[2]

4-22 **6** hd **Tiger Trail (GER)**[24] 2229 6-9-7 **57**..................... GeorgeBaker 12 — 52
(Mrs N Smith) *s.i.s: hld up in last trio and racd against rail: effrt 2f out: styd on fnl f: nvr gng pce to threaten* **10/3**[1]

000 **7** 4 1/2 **Gifted Lady (IRE)**[19] 2401 3-8-11 **60**..................... KierenFox(5) 15 — 39
(P M Phelan) *stdd s: mostly last and appeared nt gng wl: pushed along and passed several rivals fnl f* **12/1**

0023 **8** nk **Don Pele (IRE)**[12] 2589 8-9-6 **56**...................(b) RichardThomas 11 — 36
(R A Harris) *towards rr and sn pushed along: nvr on terms: no ch over 1f out* **8/1**

050 **9** 2 **Suhayl Star (IRE)**[8] 2720 6-9-4 **54**........................ NeilCallan 3 — 27
(P Burgoyne) *cl up to 2f out: steadily wknd* **25/1**

3060 **10** 1 **Tamino (IRE)**[26] 2184 7-9-2 **52**........................ JimmyQuinn 5 — 22
(P Howling) *racd towards outer: wl in tch in midfield: nudged along and steadily fdd fnl 2f* **20/1**

0600 **11** shd **Norse Warrior (USA)**[8] 2721 4-9-0 **50**................(v) AdrianMcCarthy 8 — 20
(Peter Grayson) *s.s and early reminder: racd wd: a in rr and struggling* **66/1**

005- **12** nk **Rosa Gurney (IRE)**[249] 6563 3-8-5 **56**..................... IanBurns(7) 6 — 23
(J R Best) *awkward s: a in rr: taken to outer and no prog over 2f out* **33/1**

4561 **13** 2 3/4 **Plumage**[12] 2589 5-9-13 **63**........................ LiamKeniry 2 — 23
(Miss Tor Sturgis) *chsd wnr to 1/2-way: sn wknd* **12/1**

5503 **14** hd **Sweet Applause (IRE)**[24] 2234 4-9-8 **58**................. SaleemGolam 1 — 17
(G Prodromou) *racd along on far side: nt on terms fr 1/2-way* **28/1**

0 **15** 10 **Spring Horizon (IRE)**[7] 2751 4-8-13 **49**..................(p) FergusSweeney 4 — —
(Miss Z C Davison) *s.i.s: t.k.h: w ldrs to 1/2-way: sn wknd: t.o* **80/1**

1m 12.1s (0.90) **Going Correction** +0.175s/f (Good) **15** Ran SP% **119.0**
WFA 3 from 4yo+ 8lb
Speed ratings (Par 101): **101,99,98,96,95 95,89,88,86,84 84,84,80,80,66**
toteswingers:1&2:£45.20, 1&3:£33.10, 2&3:£14.80 CSF £269.44 CT £2100.63 TOTE £54.20: £13.70, £7.10, £5.80; EX 421.60.
Owner double-r-racing.com **Bred** The Lavington Stud **Trained** Lewes, E Sussex
■ Stewards' Enquiry : Declan Cannon one-day ban: careless riding (Jun 26)

FOCUS
A poor handicap in which the rail draw proved a decisive factor.
Ejeed(USA) Official explanation: vet said gelding lost a right-fore shoe
Tiger Trail(GER) Official explanation: jockey said gelding suffered interference shortly after start
Don Pele(IRE) Official explanation: jockey said gelding never travelled
Spring Horizon(IRE) Official explanation: trainer said filly suffered a breathing problem

2965 BET IN-PLAY AT LADBROKES.COM H'CAP — 7f
6:50 (6:53) (Class 6) (0-55,55) 3-Y-0+ — £2,047 (£604; £302) Stalls High

Form — RPR
0060 **1** **Prime Circle**[25] 2207 4-9-8 **54**.....................(p) SteveDrowne 16 — 62
(A D Brown) *racd against rail: hld up: prog fr over 2f out: dream run through fnl f to ld last 100yds* **10/1**

3043 **2** 1 1/4 **Cardinal**[6] 2790 5-9-6 **52**.........................(t) ShaneKelly 12 — 57
(R M H Cowell) *dwlt: cl up on outer of ldrs: rdn to go 2nd 2f out: drvn ahd ent fnl f: hdd and outpcd last 100yds* **3/1**[1]

3/06 **3** 1 1/2 **Ganache (IRE)**[24] 2235 8-9-4 **50**...................... GeorgeBaker 1 — 51
(P R Chamings) *wl away fr wd draw: crossed to press ldr to 2f out: kpt on wl u.p after* **20/1**

6252 **4** 3/4 **Tenancy (IRE)**[6] 2790 6-9-2 **48**..................... ChrisCatlin 13 — 47
(S A Harris) *led but racd jst off rail: drifted lft fr 3f out and lft gap: hdd and nt qckn ent fnl f* **13/2**[2]

0-00 **5** 1 3/4 **Yankee Storm**[10] 2643 5-9-7 **53**....................(v[1]) JimmyQuinn 5 — 47+
(H J Collingridge) *hld up wl in rr: prog fr 3f out towards outer: drvn to cl on ldrs 1f out: kpt on but nvr able to chal* **20/1**

-440 **6** 1/2 **Kinigi (IRE)**[137] 296 4-8-8 **47**...................... JakePayne(7) 14 — 39
(R A Harris) *trckd ldrs against rail: rdn over 2f out: edgd off rail after: nt qckn fr over 1f out: plugged on* **7/1**[3]

2003 **7** shd **Eye For The Girls**[3] 2876 4-9-8 **54**..................... CathyGannon 9 — 46+
(M R Channon) *dwlt: hld up wl in rr: sme prog over 2f out: no imp over 1f out: kpt on fnl f* **9/1**

6040 **8** 3 1/4 **Briannsta (IRE)**[24] 2234 8-9-2 **48**...................(b) RichardThomas 10 — 31
(J E Long) *chsd ldrs: rdn 3f out: steadily wknd fnl 2f* **33/1**

/0-0 **9** 3 1/4 **Ensign's Trick**[12] 2590 6-8-11 **48**..................... KierenFox(5) 6 — 23
(W M Brisbourne) *racd on outer of ldrs: prom tl wknd 2f out* **66/1**

0-50 **10** 4 1/2 **Dawson Creek (IRE)**[59] 1301 6-8-11 **48**.................. AshleyMorgan(5) 4 — 11
(B Gubby) *racd in centre: nvr on terms: eased whn no ch fnl f* **16/1**

0052 **11** shd **Grey Boy (GER)**[40] 1772 9-8-13 **52**................... GeorgeDowning(7) 2 — 14
(A W Carroll) *racd wd: nvr on terms w ldrs: wknd 2f out: eased fnl f* **14/1**

-000 **12** 6 **Ymir**[40] 1772 4-9-6 **52**..............................(p) LiamKeniry 7 — —
(M J Attwater) *a towards rr: no prog 2f out: eased whn no ch fnl f* **12/1**

05-1 **13** 1/2 **My Flame**[33] 1958 5-9-9 **55**........................... NeilCallan 11 — —
(J R Jenkins) *cl up against rail: u.p 3f out: sn wknd: eased fnl f* **9/1**

-200 **14** 8 **Mr Fantozzi (IRE)**[6] 2783 5-9-1 **52**................... DeclanCannon(5) 8 — —
(D Donovan) *a towards rr: wknd over 2f out: eased over 1f out* **8/1**

000 **15** 14 **Faraday's Fancy (IRE)**[43] 1659 4-9-3 **49**................ FrankieMcDonald 3 — —
(Miss A M Newton-Smith) *mostly last and a struggling: eased over 1f out: t.o* **80/1**

1m 24.9s (1.60) **Going Correction** +0.175s/f (Good) **15** Ran SP% **126.5**
Speed ratings (Par 101): **97,95,93,93,91 90,90,86,82,77 77,70,70,61,45**
toteswingers:1&2:£21.00, 1&3:£44.80, 2&3:£14.30 CSF £39.84 CT £636.30 TOTE £4.10: £1.10, £1.60, £8.40; EX 57.00.
Owner S Pedersen **Bred** Gainsborough Stud Management Ltd **Trained** Yedingham, N Yorks

FOCUS
A weak handicap rated around the placed horses.
Ganache(IRE) Official explanation: jockey said gelding jumped right
Tenancy(IRE) Official explanation: jockey said gelding hung left

2966 BET AFTER THE OFF AT LADBROKES.COM H'CAP — 1m 2f (P)
7:20 (7:21) (Class 5) (0-70,69) 4-Y-0+ — £3,070 (£906; £453) Stalls Low

Form — RPR
-100 **1** **Beaubrav**[20] 2360 4-9-6 **68**..........................(t) ChrisCatlin 11 — 76
(M Madgwick) *hld up in rr: prog on wd outside fr 3f out: wnt 2nd ent fnl f: drvn and clsd to ld last 100yds* **7/1**[3]

40 **2** 1 **Pyrus Time (IRE)**[24] 2236 4-9-6 **68**.................... RichardThomas 5 — 74
(R A Harris) *trckd ldrs: n.m.r over 2f out: plld out and prog jst over 1f out: clsd threateningly fnl f: wnt 2nd but fnd little* **11/1**

4445 **3** 1/2 **Zero Cool (USA)**[7] 2752 6-8-13 **61**...................(p) JimmyFortune 4 — 66
(G L Moore) *trckd ldr gng wl: led over 1f out: drvn fnl f: hdd and no ex last 100yds* **8/1**

-000 **4** 2 1/2 **Aurora Sky (IRE)**[10] 2643 4-9-1 **63**.................... LiamKeniry 10 — 63
(J Akehurst) *disp 2nd to over 2f out: steadily fdd u.p fnl f but hld on for 4th* **14/1**

-620 **5** nk **Al Rayanah**[11] 2636 7-8-7 **55**.......................... SaleemGolam 13 — 54
(G Prodromou) *s.s: hld up in last pair: pushed along 3f out: stl wl in rr over 1f out: swtchd out wd and styd on fnl f* **25/1**

0330 **6** 1/2 **Moscow Oznick**[13] 2560 5-8-10 **63**...............(p) DeclanCannon(5) 7 — 61
(D Donovan) *trckd ldrs: cl up and rdn 2f out: stl chsng but nt qckn jst over 1f out: plugged on* **14/1**

0050 **7** 1 1/4 **Dream Of Fortune (IRE)**[19] 2388 6-8-12 **65**..........(vt) RichardEvans(5) 9 — 61
(P D Evans) *dwlt: hld up in last trio: gng easily 3f out: sme prog over 1f out: nt clr run against rail briefly fnl f: shkn up and one pce* **13/2**[2]

-650 **8** 3/4 **Lunar River (FR)**[24] 2233 7-9-0 **62**..................(t) FergusSweeney 8 — 56
(David Pinder) *hld up in midfield: rdn over 2f out: no prog over 1f out: fdd* **12/1**

0643 **9** 1/2 **Rosy Dawn**[15] 2489 5-8-2 **50** oh5...................... NeilChalmers 1 — 43
(J J Bridger) *led to over 1f out: sn wknd* **16/1**

260/ **10** 1 1/4 **Reload (IRE)**[166] 7447 7-9-7 **69**...................... JerryO'Dwyer 6 — 60
(Mrs S J Humphrey) *dwlt: hld up in last pair: pushed along 3f out: n.d after: sme prog on wd outside fnl f* **16/1**

1226 **11** 2 1/4 **Blue Tango (IRE)**[33] 1961 4-9-6 **68**...................(b) JimmyQuinn 2 — 54
(Mrs A J Perrett) *trckd ldrs: stl cl up and rdn 2f out: wknd rapidly over 1f out* **4/1**[1]

3100 **12** 1 1/4 **Vinces**[115] 588 6-9-3 **65**............................. GeorgeBaker 14 — 49
(T D McCarthy) *hld up in midfield: rdn over 2f out: no prog: wknd over 1f out* **8/1**

10-0 **13** 18 **Foxtrot Charlie**[29] 2080 4-9-5 **67**...................(v[1]) IanMongan 12 — 15
(P Winkworth) *racd wd: trckd ldrs: u.p over 4f out: wknd 3f out: t.o* **20/1**

2m 5.66s (-0.94) **Going Correction** +0.125s/f (Slow) **13** Ran SP% **117.8**
Speed ratings (Par 103): **108,107,106,104,104 104,103,102,102,101 99,98,83**
toteswingers:1&2:£7.10, 1&3:£25.60, 2&3:£25.20 CSF £80.67 CT £633.98 TOTE £8.80: £2.90, £2.50, £1.50; EX 122.40.
Owner The B B Partnership **Bred** Star Pointe Ltd,Brosnan And Williamson **Trained** Denmead, Hants

FOCUS
A moderate handicap and sound form in a modest handicap. The third and fourth are rated to their marks.
Reload(IRE) Official explanation: jockey said gelding never travelled
Foxtrot Charlie Official explanation: jockey said gelding never travelled

2967 LADBROKESPOKER.COM H'CAP — 1m (P)
7:50 (7:51) (Class 6) (0-60,60) 4-Y-0+ — £2,047 (£604; £302) Stalls High

Form — RPR
334- **1** **Leelu**[195] 7591 4-9-1 **57**.............................. NeilCallan 10 — 65
(D W P Arbuthnot) *racd wd early: trckd ldr 5f out: rdn to ld 2f out: kpt on wl and a holding on* **8/1**

5003 **2** 3/4 **Tevez**[7] 2764 5-8-13 **60**.......................... DeclanCannon(5) 7 — 66+
(D Donovan) *dwlt: sn in midfield: effrt and nt clr run 2f out: plenty to do after: drvn and r.o fnl f to take 2nd last stride* **13/2**

0010 **3** shd **Batchworth Blaise**[12] 2596 7-8-11 **58**.................. KierenFox(5) 9 — 64
(E A Wheeler) *s.s: bhd early: prog on wd outside 3f out: drvn to chse wnr over 1f out: kpt on but hld ins fnl f: lost 2nd last stride* **11/2**[2]

-355 **4** 1/2 **Pha Mai Blue**[82] 966 5-9-3 **59**........................ GeorgeBaker 8 — 64
(J R Boyle) *prom: rdn to chse ldng pair over 2f out: disp 2nd jst over 1f out: nt qckn* **8/1**

5360 **5** 3/4 **Fly By Nelly**[19] 2383 4-9-0 **56**....................... SteveDrowne 12 — 59
(H Morrison) *hld up in rr: prog on outer 3f out: nt qckn 2f out: styd on ins fnl f: nrst fin* **8/1**

62 **6** 1/2 **Macanta (USA)**[3] 2874 4-9-2 **58**...................... WilliamBuick 2 — 60
(G A Butler) *s.s: hld up in rr but in tch: effrt on inner 2f out: sme prog over 1f out: one pce fnl f* **6/1**[3]

3006 **7** 3/4 **Grand Honour (IRE)**[22] 2299 4-9-1 **57**.................. JimmyQuinn 11 — 57
(P Howling) *hld up in tch: effrt 2f out: cl enough over 1f out: nt qckn: wknd last 100yds* **33/1**

0-40 **8** 4 **Foxtrot Alpha (IRE)**[22] 2299 4-9-2 **58**................(t) ChrisCatlin 5 — 48
(P Winkworth) *t.k.h: trckd ldr 3f: styd cl up: nt qckn wl over 1f out: wknd fnl f* **20/1**

6534 **9** 1 **Musashi (IRE)**[3] 2866 5-9-2 **58**......................(b) IanMongan 1 — 46
(Mrs L J Mongan) *s.v.s: rapid rcvry and rchd 3rd by 1/2-way: stl chsng ldrs 2f out: wknd over 1f out* **4/1**[1]

00-0 **10** 11 **Queen Of Thebes (IRE)**[8] 2726 4-9-1 **57**................ JimmyFortune 3 — 18
(S Kirk) *dwlt: pushed up to ld: hdd 2f out: wknd rapidly* **33/1**

-000 **11** shd **Pab Special (IRE)**[36] 1877 7-9-4 **60**................... FrankieMcDonald 6 — 21
(B R Johnson) *t.k.h: trckd ldrs: effrt on outer 3f out: squeezed out over 2f out: sn wknd rapidly* **16/1**

100 **12** *48* **Woolston Ferry (IRE)**[26] 2188 4-9-4 **60**..................... FergusSweeney 4 —
(David Pinder) *s.v.s: no rcvry and allowed to amble arnd* **22/1**

1m 39.72s (1.52) **Going Correction** +0.125s/f (Slow) **12** Ran SP% **117.2**
Speed ratings (Par 101): **97,96,96,95,94 94,93,89,88,77 77,29**
toteswingers:1&2:£10.70, 1&3:£12.30, 2&3:£5.60 CSF £55.74 CT £311.00 TOTE £10.50: £1.40, £3.40, £4.20; EX 61.40.
Owner Philip Banfield **Bred** P Banfield **Trained** Compton, Berks

FOCUS
An ordinary handicap featuring some real characters. The form is muddling and not straightforward, with those in the frame behind the winner setting an ordinary standard.
Pha Mai Blue Official explanation: jockey said gelding hung left throughout
Musashi(IRE) Official explanation: jockey said gelding was slowly away
Woolston Ferry(IRE) Official explanation: jockey said gelding got its head stuck over starting gate and lost confidence

2968 BEST ODDS GUARANTEED AT LADBROKES.COM MEDIAN AUCTION MAIDEN STKS — 7f (P)
8:20 (8:22) (Class 6) 3-4-Y-O — **£2,047** (£604; £302) **Stalls** Low

Form / RPR

0-2 **1** **Kakatosi**[28] 2122 3-8-13 0.. JimmyFortune 3 77+
(A M Balding) *mde all: kicked on 2f out: drvn and styd on wl fnl f* **2/5**[1]

2 **2** *1 ¾* **City Ground (USA)**[8] 2706 3-8-13 0.................................. NeilCallan 14 72
(M A Jarvis) *prog on wd outside to chse wnr over 3f out: rdn and tried to chal over 1f out: styd on but readily hld* **8/1**[3]

3 *2* **Space War** 3-8-13 0.. WilliamBuick 5 67+
(J H M Gosden) *green in preliminaries: dwlt: sn in midfield: 7th 2f out: pushed along and styd on wl to take 3rd fnl f* **9/2**[2]

00 **4** *2* **Nelson's Bounty**[7] 2754 3-8-13 0.. IanMongan 6 61+
(P W D'Arcy) *hld up wl in rr: no ch whn rn into trble over 1f out: pushed along and styd on wl to take 4th nr fin* **100/1**

0-0 **5** *1* **Suzhou**[21] 2334 3-8-8 0... CathyGannon 2 54
(D J Coakley) *cl up: chsd ldng pair 2f out to 1f out: fdd* **25/1**

46- **6** *1 ¼* **Mufti (IRE)**[285] 5527 3-8-13 0... ShaneKelly 11 55+
(J Noseda) *mostly in midfield: wl outpcd and no ch whn nt clr run over 1f out: styd on fnl f* **12/1**

0 **7** *hd* **Picansort**[21] 2340 3-8-13 0... JimmyQuinn 8 55
(B R Johnson) *dwlt: hld up in last pair: nudged along and kpt on steadily fr over 1f out* **100/1**

8 *1 ¼* **Queenie's Star (IRE)** 3-8-3 0.............................. JemmaMarshall(5) 10 46
(M J Attwater) *dwlt: wl in rr: nvr a factor: pushed along and sme prog on inner over 1f out* **100/1**

0 **9** *shd* **Lilli Palmer (IRE)**[23] 2249 3-8-8 0............................. PaulFitzsimons 1 46
(Miss J R Tooth) *chsd wnr after 3f to over 3f out: stl cl up over 2f out: wknd* **100/1**

5- **10** *¾* **Scottish Glen**[352] 3319 4-9-9 0... LiamKeniry 9 53
(P R Chamings) *cl up: stl wl in tch over 2f out: wknd* **100/1**

55 **11** *¾* **Chilli Green**[24] 2227 3-8-8 0... ChrisCatlin 7 42
(J Akehurst) *racd wd: trckd ldrs: wd bnd 2f out and wknd* **25/1**

4 **12** *4 ½* **Well Overdue (IRE)**[44] 1644 4-9-4 0............................ SophieDoyle(5) 12 39
(J A Osborne) *settled in rr: pushed along and no prog over 2f out: no ch after* **66/1**

0 **13** *2 ¼* **Fashion Tycoon (IRE)**[24] 2227 3-8-9 0 ow1................ SteveDrowne 13 25
(R Hannon) *dwlt: rn green and a towards rr: hung rt bnd 2f out: bhd after: b.b.v* **33/1**

-0 **14** *dist* **Battleship Grey**[36] 1878 3-8-13 0................................ FergusSweeney 4 —
(D K Ivory) *plld hrd: chsd wnr 3f: sn dropped out rapidly: t.o whn virtually p.u fnl 2f* **100/1**

1m 25.39s (0.59) **Going Correction** +0.125s/f (Slow)
WFA 3 from 4yo 10lb **14** Ran SP% **126.5**
Speed ratings (Par 101): **101,99,96,94,93 91,91,90,90,89 88,83,80,—**
toteswingers:1&2:£3.10, 1&3:£2.90, 2&3:£4.70 CSF £4.79 TOTE £1.70: £1.10, £1.50, £1.30; EX 5.80 Place 6 £121.33; Place 5 £88.20.
Owner Robert E Tillett **Bred** T E Pocock **Trained** Kingsclere, Hants

FOCUS
An average maiden that should produce its share of winners, although there are several down the field whose proximity raises doubts.
Nelson's Bounty Official explanation: jockey said gelding was denied a clear run
Fashion Tycoon(IRE) Official explanation: trainer's rep said filly bled from the nose
Battleship Grey Official explanation: jockey said gelding was unrideable
T/Plt: £465.90 to a £1 stake. Pool:£57,039.09 - 89.37 winning tickets T/Qpdt: £26.50 to a £1 stake. Pool:£4,779.73 - 133.38 winning tickets JN

2930 SANDOWN (R-H)
Saturday, June 12

OFFICIAL GOING: Good (good to firm in places; round 8.5; sprint 8.3; home straight - far side 8.3, stands' side 8.4)
Sprint track at full width. Rail on home bend at mid configuration and dolled out 5yds up the straight increasing distances on round course by 5yds.
Wind: light, half behind Weather: cloudy, brighter spells

2969 TOTEPLACEPOT H'CAP — 1m 1f
1:45 (1:45) (Class 3) (0-90,88) 3-Y-O — **£7,123** (£2,119; £1,059; £529) **Stalls** High

Form / RPR

13 **1** **Beachfire**[24] 2225 3-9-1 **80**.. WilliamBuick 7 93
(J H M Gosden) *dwlt: sn rdn along in last: reminders after 1f: stl last and rdn ent fnl 2f: gd hdwy to ld 1f out: rn wl and clr fnl 100yds* **9/2**[3]

-020 **2** *2 ½* **New Christmas (USA)**[31] 2033 3-9-4 **83**........................(b[1]) MartinDwyer 2 90
(B J Meehan) *pressed ldrs: led over 3f out: rdn wl over 2f out: hdd 1f out and nt pce of wnr ins fnl f: hld on for 2nd* **15/2**

-266 **3** *shd* **Jutland**[23] 2253 3-8-13 **78**.. GregFairley 9 85
(M Johnston) *chsd ldr: rdn wl over 2f out: drvn and outpcd by wnr ins fnl f* **8/1**

1-1 **4** *½* **Nazreef**[23] 2261 3-9-3 **82**...(t) TravisBlock 8 88
(H Morrison) *t.k.h: trckd ldrs: rdn and pressed ldrs 2f out: drvn and styd on same pce fr over 1f out* **5/2**[1]

31- **5** *2 ½* **Revered**[224] 7182 3-9-6 **85**.. RyanMoore 1 85
(Sir Michael Stoute) *dwlt and flashing tail after s: hld up in last trio: rdn and effrt ent fnl 2f: swtchd rt and bmpd rival over 1f out: rdn and btn ent fnl f* **11/4**[2]

1-00 **6** *1 ½* **Whistleinthewind (IRE)**[8] 2713 3-9-2 **81**......................(p) GeorgeBaker 4 78
(G L Moore) *hld up ion last trio: pushed along and no prog 2f out: swtchd lft and styd on same pce fnl f: nvr trbld ldrs* **33/1**

1-40 **7** *2 ½* **Commissionaire**[13] 2562 3-9-7 **86**......................................(b[1]) NeilCallan 5 77
(J H M Gosden) *hld up wl in tch: rdn and effrt ent fnl 2f: drvn and nt qckning whn bdly bmpd over 1f out: wl btn after* **50/1**

145- **8** *2 ½* **Extreme Warrior (IRE)**[329] 4086 3-9-9 **88**......................(b) TedDurcan 3 74
(D R Lanigan) *led tl hdd over 3f out: rdn 3f out: styd pressing ldrs tl wknd u.p jst over 1f out: eased wl ins fnl f* **25/1**

1-56 **9** *1* **Dubai Set**[14] 2544 3-9-6 **85**...(b[1]) RichardHughes 6 69
(R Hannon) *t.k.h: hld up wl in tch: rdn and effrt 3f out: drvn and plugging on same pce whn pushed rt over 1f out: wl btn after: eased wl ins fnl f* **11/1**

1m 54.98s (-0.72) **Going Correction** +0.05s/f (Good) **9** Ran SP% **113.4**
Speed ratings (Par 103): **105,102,102,102,100 98,96,94,93**
toteswingers:1&2:£8.30, 1&3:£6.70, 2&3:£11.60 CSF £36.43 CT £260.42 TOTE £6.20: £2.20, £2.60, £2.40; EX 46.60.
Owner H R H Princess Haya Of Jordan **Bred** Bridgewater Equine Ltd **Trained** Newmarket, Suffolk
■ Stewards' Enquiry : Ryan Moore two-day ban: careless riding (Jun 26-27)

FOCUS
The sprint course was set to its full width, while the round course was mid-configuration on home bend, dolled out 5yds up the home straight, which added 5yds to round course distances. The runners headed towards the stands' side on turning into the home straight, which was the only time on the card that they did. The form looks sound rated around those in the framen behind the winner.

NOTEBOOK
Beachfire didn't show a great deal of enthusiasm throughout the first furlong, indeed the jockey was giving him reminders to keep him interested. However, he was back on the bridle by the time the field turned in and, after being ridden to make his move, he stayed on strongly to land an unlikely looking victory by a comfortable margin. Buick reported that his mount just has his own way of doing things and isn't necessarily ungenuine. (op 7-2)
New Christmas(USA) had blinkers fitted for the first time after a poor effort at York, and ran much better here, although he did have the run of the race. (op 10-1 tchd 11-1)
Jutland, dropped 2lb since his last outing, was always prominent and stayed on for pressure. (op 9-1 tchd 10-1)
Nazreef ◆ was chasing a hat-trick on his first outing on turf - his previous victories came at Southwell. A really imposing sort, he got caught flat-footed and edged left a little once under pressure, but kept finding a bit extra and can certainly be given another chance. (op 7-2)
Revered, having her first start since landing a maiden at Newmarket the previous October, wore a blanket for stalls entry and flashed her tail a few times after breaking from them. She had every chance as the race developed, but got outpaced at a crucial stage. (op 5-2)
Whistleinthewind(IRE), in cheekpieces for the first time, kept on but failed to look dangerous. (op 28-1 tchd 25-1)
Commissionaire had blinkers on for the first time after running miserably at Newmarket on his handicap debut. He was the stable's second string on jockey bookings and looked tricky under pressure. The interference he suffered made no obvious difference to his finishing position.
Extreme Warrior(IRE), up in trip on his seasonal debut, kept good company at two but was most disappointing here. The jockey reported his mount had no more to give after making the running. Official explanation: jockey said gelding had no more to give (op 20-1)
Dubai Set, with blinkers on for the first time, and stepping up in trip again, pulled too hard in the early stages to have much left for the finish. (op 10-1 tchd 17-2)

2970 TOTESCOOP6 H'CAP — 7f 16y
2:20 (2:20) (Class 3) (0-90,90) 3-Y-O — **£7,123** (£2,119; £1,059; £529) **Stalls** High

Form / RPR

1-20 **1** **Rakaan (IRE)**[21] 2324 3-9-9 **90**... GeorgeBaker 8 99
(J A Osborne) *racd off the pce towards rr: effrt to chse ldng trio over 2f out: clsng but edging rt over 1f out: drvn to ld and lft in command fnl 100yds: rdn out* **15/2**[3]

212 **2** *3* **Bohemian Melody**[52] 1480 3-9-0 **81**................................ JerryO'Dwyer 6 84
(M Botti) *chsd ldng pair: sltly outpcd over 3f out: plld out and rdn over 2f out: led ent fnl f: edgd lft and rt u.p: hdd and eased fnl 100yds: pushed along again towards fin* **4/1**[1]

0004 **3** *1 ¼* **Ongoodform (IRE)**[19] 2394 3-9-2 **83**.............................. JimmyFortune 7 81
(P W D'Arcy) *chsd ldr: pushed ahd over 2f out: drvn and hdd ent fnl f: no ex and btn fnl 150yds* **9/2**[2]

3-13 **4** *2 ¾* **Shamir**[70] 1086 3-8-12 **79**.. FergusSweeney 5 69
(Miss Jo Crowley) *racd in midfield: rdn and outpcd by ldrs over 3f out: styd on same pce fnl 2f* **8/1**

5-06 **5** *1* **Kurtanella**[9] 2682 3-8-13 **80**.. RichardHughes 2 67
(R Hannon) *dropped in bhd after s: hld up wl off the pce in last trio: rdn and effrt over 2f out: plugged on u.p fnl f: nvr trbld ldrs* **12/1**

-004 **6** *¾* **Syrian**[14] 2544 3-9-6 **87**.. TedDurcan 1 72
(M L W Bell) *taken down early: stdd and s.i.s: t.k.h: hld up wl off the pce in last: rdn and effrt on outer over 2f out: hld hd awkwardly and no prog fr over 1f out* **15/2**[3]

1-5 **7** *hd* **Muwakaba (USA)**[29] 2098 3-9-6 **87**.................................... RyanMoore 4 72
(Sir Michael Stoute) *taken down early: stdd s: t.k.h: hld up wl off the pce in last pair: rdn and hanging rt 2f out: no prog and swtchd lft over 1f out: nvr a factor* **9/2**[2]

3-50 **8** *7* **Licence To Till (USA)**[10] 2656 3-9-0 **81**............................ GregFairley 9 47
(M Johnston) *t.k.h: hld up in midfield: rdn and no prog over 3f out: no ch fnl 2f* **12/1**

4200 **9** *¾* **Gumnd (IRE)**[14] 2544 3-9-2 **83**.......................................(b[1]) NeilCallan 3 47
(C E Brittain) *racd keenly: led: rdn and hdd over 2f out: wknd qckly wl over 1f out: wl btn fnl f* **16/1**

1m 29.25s (-0.25) **Going Correction** +0.05s/f (Good) **9** Ran SP% **112.3**
Speed ratings (Par 103): **103,99,98,95,93 93,92,84,83**
toteswingers:1&2:£5.80, 1&3:£9.00, 2&3:£4.80 CSF £36.24 CT £149.98 TOTE £10.00: £2.80, £1.80, £1.90; EX 50.10 Trifecta £303.60 Part won. Pool: £410.32 - 0.70 winning units..
Owner J A Osborne **Bred** L Mulryan & M Fahy **Trained** Upper Lambourn, Berks

FOCUS
It seemed quite likely that the field may head over to the stands' side once again as they make their way into the home straight but, refreshingly, the jockey on the leader stayed towards the inside rail and the remainder followed him. The placed horses set the level.

NOTEBOOK
Rakaan(IRE), never sighted in the Betfred Silver Bowl on his previous start, looks the sort of horse who needs everything to fall right for him, so the way this race unfolded suited him. Under another fine hold-up ride by Baker, he picked off the two horses in front of him in the final stages and was a good winner. Whether he will do the same next time is open to debate. Official explanation: trainer had no explanation for the apparent improvement in form. (op 9-1)
Bohemian Melody, having his first outing on turf, is nicely bred and a lovely looking sort. He sat just off the early leader and moved into a challenging position at what seemed the right time. Once in front he started to edge both left and right, which may suggest he was feeling the ground - his jockey was also quick to ease him once Rakaan went past. It initially looked as though Jerry O'Dwyer may have mistaken the half-a-furlong marker for the winning post, but the jockey later reported the reason he stopped riding was due to shooting pain in his legs. Thankfully, it made no difference to the outcome. Undoubtedly there is more to come from Bohemian Melody and he is one to follow. (op 11-4)

Ongoodform(IRE), dropped 2lb since his last start, had his chance but didn't get home up the stiff uphill finish. (op 7-1 tchd 15-2)
Shamir showed some good form on the AW during the autumn/winter, and ran as though he needed this after a 70-day absence. He will be better judged on turf next time. (op 7-1 tchd 13-2)
Kurtanella looked fairly treated on her winning effort in a nursery last season, but didn't get going early enough here after being held up towards the rear. (op 11-1)
Syrian, who was taken down early, gave the impression he was not completely straightforward last time and did little to dispel that theory here. (op 9-1 tchd 13-2)
Muwakaba(USA), taken down early, disappointed on her return to action this season is a small-field Listed race, her first effort on turf. A handler accompanied her at the start and she was keen in the rear, which suggests she is possibly a bit highly strung. (tchd 5-1 and 4-1 in places)
Licence To Till(USA) didn't run with much distinction on his previous outing at Thirsk over 6f and seems to be regressing. (op 16-1)
Gumnd(IRE) had been disappointing on his previous two outings, so connections reached for the blinkers for the first time. Quickly away, he got over to the rail and had it his own way in front until tiring once joined. (op 22-1)

2971 TOTESPORT 0800 221 221 H'CAP 7f 16y
2:55 (2:58) (Class 2) (0-100,99) 3-Y-O+

£9,969 (£2,985; £1,492; £747; £372; £187) **Stalls** High

Form RPR

2103 **1** **Crown Choice**[15] 2508 5-9-3 **88** TedDurcan 8 98
(W R Swinburn) *hld up towards rr: hdwy on outer 2f out: hung rt but rdn to ld 1f out: jst hld on* **11/2**[3]

-540 **2** *shd* **Rulesn'regulations**[35] 1903 4-9-4 **89** GeorgeBaker 14 99
(Matthew Salaman) *t.k.h early: hld up in tch in midfield: switching out lft and rdn 2f out: chsng ldrs whn slt hmpd ent fnl f: chsd wnr fnl 100yds: kpt on wl: jst failed* **40/1**

-600 **3** *1* **Kyllachy Star**[70] 1085 4-9-1 **86** StevieDonohoe 4 93
(R A Fahey) *hld up towards rr: switching to outer and effrt ent fnl 2f: kpt on u.p to go 3rd fnl 75yds: nt able to rch ldng pair* **33/1**

0060 **4** *1* **Huzzah (IRE)**[12] 2595 5-9-1 **86** JimmyQuinn 12 91
(B W Hills) *t.k.h early: hld up in tch: hdwy 4f out: rdn to chse ldr 2f out: n.m.r 1f out: styd on same pce ins fnl f* **9/2**[2]

10/1 **5** *¾* **Coasting**[29] 2091 5-9-11 **96** RyanMoore 9 99
(Mrs A J Perrett) *hld up in rr: stl last over 2f out and switching to outer: swtchd bk rt and squeezed between horses over 1f out: drvn to chse ldrs 1f out: no imp fnl 100yds* **7/2**[1]

156 **6** *¾* **Bullwhip (IRE)**[37] 1834 3-9-1 **96** WilliamBuick 11 93+
(J H M Gosden) *hld up towards rr: switching lft over 2f out: sn rdn and hdwy: drvn and edging rt for run ent fnl f: no imp fnl 150yds* **10/1**

0532 **7** *¾* **Masai Moon**[7] 2736 6-9-0 **88** (b) JamesMillman(3) 10 87
(B R Millman) *t.k.h: hld up in midfield early: hdwy to chse ldr over 4f out: led over 3f out: rdn and edgd lft over 1f out: hdd 1f out: wknd ins fnl f* **15/2**

3501 **8** *2* **Den's Gift (IRE)**[40] 1767 6-8-13 **89** (b) JohnFahy(5) 6 82
(C G Cox) *dashed up to ld after 1f: hdd over 3f out: rdn over 2f out: keeping on same pce whn sltly hmpd and swtchd lft over 1f out: wknd jst ins fnl f* **18/1**

10-0 **9** *½* **Jeninsky (USA)**[12] 2595 5-9-7 **92** AndreaAtzeni 13 84
(Rae Guest) *t.k.h: hld up in midfield: rdn and hdwy 2f out: chsng ldrs and drvn whn sltly hmpd ent fnl f: wknd ins fnl f* **20/1**

5130 **10** *3 ¾* **Autumn Blades (IRE)**[14] 2539 5-9-9 **99** (v) DeclanCannon(5) 3 81
(A Bailey) *stdd after s: hld up in rr: plld out and effrt ent fnl 2f: sn edging rt and no prog: wl hld fnl f* **33/1**

0-10 **11** *1* **Guilded Warrior**[36] 1857 7-9-2 **87** FergusSweeney 16 66
(W S Kittow) *w ldr early: lost pl and in midfield 4f out: dropped towards rr and n.m.r over 2f out: no threat to ldrs fnl 2f* **16/1**

0-60 **12** *½* **Cyflymder (IRE)**[12] 2595 4-9-8 **93** RichardHughes 2 71
(R Hannon) *hld up in tch in midfield: rdn and effrt on outer 2f out: no prog and btn whn hung rt ins fnl f* **12/1**

50-0 **13** *1 ½* **Quanah Parker (IRE)**[15] 2508 4-8-13 **87** MichaelStainton(3) 7 61
(R M Whitaker) *t.k.h: chsd ldrs: rdn 3f out: wkng whn short of room ent fnl 2f: wl bhd fnl f* **20/1**

1-00 **14** *27* **Captain Macarry (IRE)**[35] 1900 5-8-10 **86** (v) IanBrennan(5) 15 —
(J J Quinn) *racd freely: led for 1f: chsd ldrs after tl wknd qckly wl over 2f out: wl bhd and eased ins fnl f: t.o* **28/1**

1-00 **15** *3* **Big Bay (USA)**[42] 1697 4-9-3 **88** ShaneKelly 1 —
(Jane Chapple-Hyam) *chsd ldrs tl wknd qckly over 2f out: wl bhd and eased ins fnl f: t.o* **66/1**

1m 29.24s (-0.26) **Going Correction** +0.05s/f (Good)
WFA 3 from 4yo+ 10lb **15** Ran SP% **118.3**
Speed ratings (Par 109): **103,102,101,100,99 98,98,95,95,90 89,89,87,56,53**
toteswingers:1&2:£40.60, 1&3:£33.30, 2&3:£139.80 CSF £217.40 CT £6646.27 TOTE £6.10: £2.50, £12.40, £8.00; EX 269.60 TRIFECTA Not won..
Owner P W Harris **Bred** Howard Barton Stud **Trained** Aldbury, Herts
■ Stewards' Enquiry : Michael Stainton three-day ban: careless riding (Jun 26-28)

FOCUS
The pace seemed sound as one would expect for a big-field handicap, and there didn't seem too many hard luck stories. The third is rated to last year's course form and sets the level.

NOTEBOOK
Crown Choice ◆ has been running well all season and gained his first win on turf by a narrow margin. He came with a sweeping run a furlong out that got him to the front, but he appeared to idle a little once there and edged right. He should remain competitive next time if kept to a similar level. (op 6-1 tchd 7-1)
Rulesn'regulations ◆ was disappointing at Ascot last time, but the form he showed before that wasn't too bad at all, although he was behind Crown Choice at Lingfield in April on the AW. He didn't get the gaps exactly when his jockey probably wanted them, and he was slightly unlucky. (op 33-1)
Kyllachy Star, back on turf after three races on Polytrack, ran on again after getting outpaced. A C&D winner, the further he went the better he looked.
Huzzah(IRE), who didn't rear this time leaving the stalls and had ear plugs in, has been coming down the weights after a spell without success and put up a solid performance. He had finished in front of Crown Choice in the Victoria Cup. (op 11-2 tchd 6-1 in a place)
Coasting had been off for over 1,000 days before making an excellent comeback at Newmarket. The worry, of course, was whether he could repeat that effort. Held up in rear, he had a bit to do but came to have a chance before finding one pace. The jockey reported that his mount had met some interference early. Official explanation: jockey said gelding suffered interference early on (op 4-1)
Bullwhip(IRE), who was warm in the paddock, still looked open to more improvement on only his fourth start but found a few traffic problems from his starting position up the home straight. He didn't look really unlucky but might be capable of better. (tchd 9-1)
Masai Moon hasn't won for a while and got a hefty hike in the weights for finishing second in first-time blinkers last time. The headgear was kept on and he raced a bit keenly in them (the jockey reported afterwards that his mount was too free) until weakening over a furlong out. Official explanation: jockey said gelding ran too free (tchd 13-2)

2972 TOTESPORT.COM SCURRY STKS (LISTED RACE) 5f 6y
3:30 (3:33) (Class 1) 3-Y-O

£22,708 (£8,608; £4,308; £2,148; £1,076; £540) **Stalls** High

Form RPR

0-21 **1** **Burning Thread (IRE)**[17] 2437 3-8-13 95 WilliamBuick 9 87
(T J Etherington) *mde all: rdn and forged ahd over 1f out: kpt on gamely u.p fnl f* **17/2**

6-4 **2** *½* **Reignier**[45] 1616 3-8-13 98 RyanMoore 1 85
(J R Weymes) *hld up in tch towards rr: rdn and effrt wl over 1f out: kpt on wl u.p fnl f: wnt 2nd last strides* **5/2**[1]

36-0 **3** *hd* **Above Limits (IRE)**[14] 2545 3-8-8 98 TedDurcan 2 79
(D M Simcock) *sn pressing wnr: rdn over 1f out: kpt pressing wnr but a jst hld fnl f: lost 2nd last strides* **8/1**

-143 **4** *½* **Duchess Dora (IRE)**[30] 2058 3-8-8 95 IanBrennan 3 77
(J J Quinn) *t.k.h: hld up wl in tch: rdn and effrt over 1f out: drvn and kpt on fnl f: nvr quite enough pce to chal* **11/4**[2]

55-0 **5** *½* **Tawaabb**[30] 2058 3-8-13 97 JimmyFortune 8 81
(M R Channon) *trckd ldrs on far rail: n.m.r over 1f out tl ent fnl f: styd on same pce fnl f* **7/1**

2214 **6** *1* **Diamond Johnny G (USA)**[5] 2807 3-8-13 73 (t) EddieCreighton 4 77
(E J Creighton) *in tch in last trio: pushed along 1/2-way: rdn and outpcd wl over 1f out: kpt on ins fnl f: nvr gng pce to threaten ldrs* **80/1**

-030 **7** *2* **Duplicity**[59] 1315 3-9-2 97 RichardHughes 7 73
(R Hannon) *stdd after s: hld up in last: plld out lft and effrt wl over 1f out: no real prog and styd on one pce ins fnl f* **11/2**[3]

350- **8** *2 ¾* **Red Avalanche (IRE)**[245] 6660 3-8-13 100 (t) NeilCallan 6 60
(P F I Cole) *chsd ldrs: rdn and unable qck 2f out: wknd over 1f out: wl btn fnl f* **16/1**

60.48 secs (-1.12) **Going Correction** -0.125s/f (Firm) **8** Ran SP% **111.9**
Speed ratings (Par 107): **103,102,101,101,100 98,95,91**
toteswingers:1&2:£4.40, 1&3:£11.70, 2&3:£4.70 CSF £28.79 TOTE £8.70: £2.50, £1.30, £2.80; EX 28.60 Trifecta £296.20 Pool: £1,092.92 - 2.73 winning units..
Owner Tim Etherington **Bred** James Lombard **Trained** Norton, N Yorks
■ Stewards' Enquiry : William Buick two-day ban: used whip with excessive frequency without giving gelding time to respond (Jun 26-27)

FOCUS
A few of these had clashed before, some in the Cornwallis Stakes last season and a couple this year at York. There wasn't a lot of distance between most of them at the end, so this is probably only ordinary form for the level. The form is muddling with the proximity of the sixth raising doubts over the form.

NOTEBOOK
Burning Thread(IRE) was the least exposed of these and came into this off the back of a seemingly surprise success in a small-field conditions event (favourite for that race fell). Exuberant from the off, he got to the rail and showed a great attitude under pressure to hang on. He will need to raise his game again now, but he has the scope to do so. The horse is due to have a little break now. (op 5-1 tchd 9-2)
Reignier, dropping in trip after a promising return at Ascot in April, attracted a lot of market support but could never quite get on terms after emerging from stall 1. He is an admirably consistent sort. (op 4-1 tchd 9-4 and 9-2 in a place)
Above Limits(IRE) was well beaten on her first start for this stable at Newmarket (jockey reported the filly ran to free that day) but this was a much more positive effort, and did at least prove she had trained on. (op 7-1)
Duchess Dora(IRE) had not been beaten over C&D in two previous starts, but didn't get home as strongly as those in front of her after being a bit free early. (tchd 5-2 and 3-1)
Tawaabb was keen tucked in behind the winner but had his chance when the gap opened. (op 15-2 tchd 8-1)
Diamond Johnny G(USA), making a fairly quick reappearance, was the first off the bridle but his jockey never stopped pushing him along, and the pair ran on inside the final furlong. (op 66-1 tchd 100-1)
Duplicity ◆ beat a subsequent Group 1 winner when taking the Listed Rose Bowl Stakes last year, and had not been completely disgraced in his last two starts this season. The feeling is that he needs more ease in the ground, but he ran better than his final position suggests here, and may not be far off another success. A return to 6f should help, considering how well he stayed on. (op 13-2 tchd 7-1)
Red Avalanche(IRE), the highest rated of these on official figures, had the tongue-tie back on for his seasonal debut, but he got knocked about in the middle of the pack quite a lot. He can be given another chance. (op 14-1 tchd 12-1)

2973 MORE WORLD CUP BETTING AT TOTESPORT.COM H'CAP 5f 6y
4:05 (4:08) (Class 4) (0-80,80) 4-Y-O+ **£5,180** (£1,541; £770; £384) **Stalls** High

Form RPR

00-4 **1** **Steelcut**[10] 2639 6-8-13 **70** MartinDwyer 11 83
(Andrew Reid) *mde all: rdn clr over 1f out: in command but edging lft fnl f: comf* **16/1**

-101 **2** *2 ¼* **Ajjaadd (USA)**[25] 2196 4-9-0 **71** JimmyFortune 6 76
(T E Powell) *chsd wnr thrght: rdn and nt pce of wnr over 1f out: styd on same pce u.p and no imp fnl f* **7/1**

0-05 **3** *nk* **Gwilym (GER)**[8] 2689 7-8-12 **69** NeilCallan 5 73
(D Haydn Jones) *t.k.h: chsd ldng pair thrght: rdn and unable qck over 1f out: kpt on same pce u.p fnl f* **16/1**

330- **4** *1* **Luminous Gold**[245] 6666 5-8-13 **70** TedDurcan 3 70
(C F Wall) *fly-jmpd leaving stalls: in tch: rdn and styd on same pce fr over 1f out* **8/1**

2423 **5** *hd* **Brynfa Boy**[22] 2301 4-9-2 **73** RichardHughes 2 72+
(P W D'Arcy) *stdd s: hld up in last pair: switching rt to far rail and hdwy jst over 1f out: kpt on fnl f: nvr trbld ldrs* **7/2**[1]

0-32 **6** *½* **Spring Green**[11] 2622 4-9-4 **75** GeorgeBaker 9 72
(H Morrison) *hld up wl in tch: rdn and unable qck wl over 1f out: one pce whn n.m.r 1f out: nvr gng pce to chal ldrs* **9/2**[2]

0-60 **7** *nse* **Triple Dream**[8] 2689 5-9-2 **76** (p) JackDean(3) 1 73+
(J M Bradley) *hld up in tch towards rr: rdn and effrt on outer 2f out: plugged on same pce and no imp fnl f* **25/1**

6100 **8** *½* **Step It Up (IRE)**[9] 2681 6-8-8 **70** JohnFahy(5) 13 66
(J R Boyle) *chsd ldrs on far rail: rdn 2f out: struggling and edgd lft 1f out: wknd qckly ins fnl f* **6/1**[3]

6210 **9** *2 ¼* **Rocker**[12] 2592 6-9-6 **77** RyanMoore 4 67+
(G L Moore) *hld up towards rr: effrt on far rail over 1f out: stl plenty to do whn hmpd and squeezed out 1f out: no ch after* **15/2**

3064 **10** *½* **Incomparable**[11] 2626 5-9-7 **78** (bt) WilliamBuick 7 64
(J A Glover) *t.k.h: hld up in tch towards rr: rdn and effrt wl over 1f out: no prog and nvr trbld ldrs* **14/1**

0-00 **11** *3* **Zowington**[29] 2094 8-9-4 **75**..........(p) SaleemGolam 8 50
(S C Williams) *stdd s: sn detached in last and switching towards centre: a bhd* **33/1**

60.33 secs (-1.27) **Going Correction** -0.125s/f (Firm) 11 Ran SP% **115.3**
Speed ratings (Par 105): **105,101,100,99,99 98,98,97,93,92 88**
toteswingers:1&2:£20.10, 1&3:£28.30, 2&3:£21.30 CSF £121.44 CT £1858.43 TOTE £18.60: £4.40, £1.50, £5.40; EX 133.00.
Owner A S Reid **Bred** Mrs B Skinner **Trained** Mill Hill, London NW7
■ Stewards' Enquiry : Martin Dwyer three-day ban: used whip in incorrect place (Jun 26-28)
Richard Hughes one-day ban: careless riding (Jun 26)

FOCUS
As is usually the case over the 5f course here, especially in big fields, a high draw looked essential, especially after the winner of the previous race (a Listed contest over the same trip) made every yard up the rail. However, even though he was drawn 11, it seems more likely that Steelcut, rated 3lb higher on turf than he is on the AW, came home a decisive winner because he was left alone in front. The placed horses are rated close to their form and set the standard.

2974 BET ON ENGLAND V USA AT TOTESPORT.COM MAIDEN STKS 1m 2f 7y
4:40 (4:45) (Class 5) 3-Y-O **£3,238** (£963; £481; £240) **Stalls** High

Form RPR

1 **Channel Squadron (IRE)** 3-9-3 0.......... IanMongan 3 86+
(H R A Cecil) *awkward leaving stalls and v.s.a: bhd and rn green: rdn and sme hdwy over 2f out: 7th and stl plenty do over 1f out: str run ent fnl f: led fnl 100yds: styd on strly* **8/1**[3]

24 **2** *2* **Direct Answer (USA)**[9] 2684 3-9-3 0.......... RyanMoore 10 82
(Sir Michael Stoute) *dwlt and bustled along leaving stalls: towards rr and niggled along at times: rdn and hdwy over 2f out: drvn to chal 2f out: led over 1f out: hdd and nt pce of wnr fnl 100yds* **4/5**[1]

0- **3** *1 ¾* **Flotation (USA)**[224] 7183 3-8-12 0.......... WilliamBuick 6 73
(B W Hills) *sn chsng ldr: rdn to chal over 2f out: drvn to ld wl over 1f out: sn hdd: no ex and btn ins fnl f* **12/1**

0 **4** *2* **Rio Tinto**[15] 2507 3-9-3 0.......... TedDurcan 2 74
(Mahmood Al Zarooni) *t.k.h: hld up in tch on outer: hdwy to chse ldrs 3f out: rdn and hung bdly rt wl over 1f out: no prog ent fnl f* **10/1**

06 **5** *7* **Balatoma (IRE)**[30] 2050 3-8-12 0.......... RichardHughes 9 60+
(M P Tregoning) *sn pushed up to ld: rdn ent fnl 2f: hdd wl over 1f out: btn jst over 1f out: eased ins fnl f* **12/1**

0 **6** *½* **Lamps**[47] 1581 3-9-3 0.......... MartinDwyer 8 59
(B J Meehan) *a in rr: rdn and struggling over 3f out: nvr trbld ldrs* **11/2**[2]

60 **7** *1* **Technophobe (IRE)**[19] 2401 3-9-3 0.......... ShaneKelly 1 57
(W J Knight) *in tch in midfield: rdn and outpcd by ldrs 3f out: n.d after* **66/1**

0-6 **8** *½* **Profligate (IRE)**[14] 2548 3-8-12 0.......... SteveDrowne 5 58+
(W Jarvis) *in tch in midfield: hdwy to chse ldrs 1/2-way: effrt but hanging rt over 2f out: btn wl over 1f out: eased fnl f: sddle slip* **28/1**

0 **9** *½* **Telescopic**[15] 2507 3-8-12 0.......... StevieDonohoe 4 50
(W Jarvis) *a in rr: rdn and struggling over 3f out: wl btn fnl 2f* **100/1**

-0 **10** *½* **Trecase**[13] 2564 3-9-3 0.......... AndreaAtzeni 7 54
(A W Carroll) *chsd ldrs tl wknd qckly ent fnl 2f: eased fnl f* **100/1**

11 *½* **Hawkeshead** 3-9-3 0.......... JimmyFortune 11 53
(W J Haggas) *dwlt: in tch towards rr: pushed along 7f out: rdn and struggling over 3f out: wl btn fnl 2f* **20/1**

2m 11.29s (0.79) **Going Correction** +0.05s/f (Good) 11 Ran SP% **118.2**
Speed ratings (Par 99): **98,96,95,93,87 87,86,86,85,85 85**
toteswingers:1&2:£3.00, 1&3:£8.10, 2&3:£4.60 CSF £14.50 TOTE £8.60: £1.90, £1.10, £3.30; EX 17.30.
Owner G Schoeningh **Bred** Barronstown Stud **Trained** Newmarket, Suffolk

FOCUS
Probably only a fair maiden, but a few of these may go on to be at least useful with time. The form level is fluid, although the winner looks potentially smart.
Profligate(IRE) ◆ Official explanation: jockey said saddle slipped

2975 40 LIVE FOOTBALL MARKETS AT TOTESPORT.COM H'CAP 1m 6f
5:15 (5:16) (Class 4) (0-85,91) 4-Y-O+ **£5,180** (£1,541; £770; £384) **Stalls** High

Form RPR

22-0 **1** **Outrageous Request**[69] 1101 4-9-0 **76**.......... AndreaAtzeni 6 84
(Pat Eddery) *led for 2f: chsd ldr tl over 5f out: rdn over 2f out: drvn to ld again ins fnl f: styd on wl* **12/1**

31-5 **2** *1 ¼* **Crocus Rose**[48] 1544 4-9-1 **77**.......... JimmyQuinn 7 83
(H J L Dunlop) *t.k.h: hld up wl in tch: hdwy to join ldrs gng wl over 2f out: wanting to hang rt after but nudged ahd 2f out: rdn and hdd ins fnl f: hrd rdn and nt qckn fnl 75yds* **20/1**

-463 **3** *nk* **Abayaan**[14] 2549 4-9-0 **76**.......... ShaneKelly 4 82
(Jane Chapple-Hyam) *chsd ldrs: wnt 2nd over 5f out: ev ch and rdn over 2f out: stl ev ch tl no ex u.p ins fnl f* **10/1**

-302 **4** *nk* **Epsom Salts**[24] 2228 5-9-2 **78**.......... IanMongan 5 83+
(P M Phelan) *stdd s and s.i.s: hld up in rr: hdwy 5f out: rdn and hdwy on outer 3f out: chsng ldrs but hanging rt wl over 1f out: plld out lft over 1f out: styd on one pce u.p fnl f* **15/2**

1-30 **5** *1 ¼* **Incendo**[31] 2031 4-8-13 **75**.......... WilliamBuick 10 80+
(J R Fanshawe) *stdd after s: hld up in rr: bhd a wall of horses and swtchd sharply rt 2f out: hdwy on rail to chse ldrs ent fnl f: swtchd lft and rt ins fnl f: no imp fnl 100yds* **7/1**[3]

51-4 **6** *4 ½* **Grey Granite (IRE)**[40] 1783 4-9-1 **77**.......... JimmyFortune 12 74
(W Jarvis) *t.k.h: chsd ldr tl led after 2f: rdn and hdd 2f out: btn ent fnl f: eased wl ins fnl f* **13/2**[2]

0-42 **7** *1 ½* **Highland Legacy**[41] 1736 6-9-8 **84**.......... RichardHughes 13 79
(M L W Bell) *hmpd sn after s: hld up in rr: plld out and rdn over 2f out: no real prog: plugged on fnl f: nvr trbld ldrs* **9/4**[1]

421/ **8** *¾* **Pathos (GER)**[1043] 4166 6-9-4 **80**.......... RyanMoore 9 74
(G L Moore) *hld up in tch: rdn and effrt 2f out: styng on one pce whn hmpd over 1f out: n.d after* **13/2**[2]

00-5 **9** *1 ½* **Brooklyn Spirit**[47] 1579 4-8-4 **71**..........(p) JohnFahy[(5)] 14 63
(C G Cox) *t.k.h: chsd ldrs: rdn and unable qck over 2f out: wkng whn sltly hmpd over 1f out* **16/1**

-604 **10** *nk* **Blue Nymph**[15] 2513 4-8-9 **76**..........(t) IanBrennan[(5)] 3 67
(J J Quinn) *pushed along leaving stalls: in tch in midfield: rdn and struggling 3f out: n.d fnl 2f* **20/1**

0414 **11** *2 ½* **Hallstatt (IRE)**[21] 2313 4-8-12 **74**.......... SteveDrowne 15 62
(J Mackie) *hmpd sn after s: hld up towards rr: rdn whn bdly hmpd 2f out: no ch after* **16/1**

3m 5.47s (0.97) **Going Correction** +0.05s/f (Good) 11 Ran SP% **119.8**
Speed ratings (Par 105): **99,98,98,97,97 94,93,93,92,92 90**
toteswingers:1&2:£18.20, 1&3:£11.70, 2&3:£19.10 CSF £231.49 CT £2469.87 TOTE £15.60: £3.90, £4.00, £3.30; EX 145.90 Place 6 £447.40; Place 5 £159.39.
Owner P J J Eddery **Bred** Patrick Eddery Ltd **Trained** Nether Winchendon, Bucks
■ Stewards' Enquiry : William Buick two-day ban: careless riding (Jun 28-29)

FOCUS
This was probably a fair handicap for the class, as plenty of them could be given a chance, but there was a distinct lack of pace in the early stages. The form is a bit muddling with the fourth the best guide.
Incendo ◆ Official explanation: jockey said gelding was denied a clear run
Grey Granite(IRE) Official explanation: jockey said colt ran too free
T/Plt: £366.60 to a £1 stake. Pool:£89,119.88 - 177.42 winning tickets T/Qpdt: £38.00 to a £1 stake. Pool:£7,179.21 - 139.72 winning tickets SP

2936 YORK (L-H)
Saturday, June 12

OFFICIAL GOING: Good (good to firm on home bend; 7.3)
Wind: moderate 1/2 against Weather: fine and sunny

2976 QUEEN MOTHER'S CUP LADY AMATEUR RIDERS H'CAP 1m 4f
2:05 (2:05) (Class 3) (0-95,95) 3-Y-O+ **£12,492** (£3,874; £1,936; £968) **Stalls** Centre

Form RPR

1331 **1** **Desert Recluse (IRE)**[23] 2252 3-8-3 **81**.......... MissRachelKing[(3)] 16 97
(Pat Eddery) *hld up in midfield: stdy hdwy 1/2-way: chsd ldrs 3f out: effrt over 2f out: rdn to ld wl over 1f out: sn clr and styd on wl* **11/1**

-304 **2** *6* **Alcalde**[22] 2276 4-9-12 **86**.......... MissLHorner 7 92
(M Johnston) *chsd ldrs: hdwy 4f out: rdn along over 2f out: edgd lft wl over 1f out: kpt on: no ch w wnr* **28/1**

-023 **3** *1 ¼* **Crackentorp**[14] 2541 5-10-4 **92**.......... MissJCoward 18 96
(T D Easterby) *prom: hdwy over 3f out: sn rdn: kpt on same pce fr wl over 1f out* **13/2**[1]

60- **4** *2* **Siberian Tiger (IRE)**[49] 7293 5-10-7 **95**..........(p) MissEJJones 6 96
(M Wigham) *hld up in rr: hdwy over 3f out: rdn over 2f out: drvn to chse ldrs and hung lft wl over 1f out: kpt on same pce fnl f* **16/1**

0142 **5** *3* **Antigua Sunrise (IRE)**[7] 2761 4-9-1 **78**.......... MissLAllan[(3)] 10 74
(R A Fahey) *trckd ldrs: hdwy to chse ldr 1/2-way: led wl over 3f out: rdn and hdd wl over 1f out: sn wknd* **15/2**[3]

6221 **6** *3 ¾* **Southern Regent (IND)**[32] 1996 9-9-5 **79**.......... MissIsabelTompsett 5 69
(J J Quinn) *midfield: hdwy 1/2-way: rdn to chse ldrs over 3f out: drvn over 2f out and sn one pce* **33/1**

1461 **6** *dht* **Trip The Light**[21] 2343 5-9-13 **90**..........(v) MrsVFahey[(3)] 1 80
(R A Fahey) *chsd ldrs: lost pl and towards rr after 2f: hdwy on inner 3f out: rdn and kpt on appr fnl f* **9/1**

2320 **8** *1 ¼* **Daaweitza**[12] 2608 7-9-1 **78**..........(b) MissNVorster[(3)] 3 66
(B Ellison) *sn led: rdn along 5f out: hdd wl over 3f out and grad wknd* **33/1**

1330 **9** *nk* **Shadows Lengthen**[29] 2096 4-10-1 **92**..........(b) MissJoannaMason[(3)] 4 80
(M W Easterby) *midfield: hdwy over 4f out: rdn to chse ldrs over 3f out: sn drvn and grad wknd* **20/1**

0043 **10** *½* **Mull Of Dubai**[7] 2747 7-9-8 **85**.......... MissKECooper[(3)] 12 72
(D Nicholls) *hld up towards rr: hdwy on wd outside 4f out: rdn over 2f out: sn no imp* **8/1**

1-02 **11** *½* **Bow To No One (IRE)**[35] 1902 4-9-11 **88**.......... MissLEBurke[(3)] 15 74
(A P Jarvis) *hld up on inner in rr: hdwy over 3f out: swtchd rt over 2f out: n.d* **12/1**

4-0 **12** *½* **Bothy**[38] 1829 4-10-0 **88**.......... MissSBrotherton 13 73
(B Ellison) *a in rr* **16/1**

2133 **13** *1 ½* **King Fingal (IRE)**[17] 2435 5-9-7 **81**.......... MissZoeLilly 9 64
(J J Quinn) *chsd ldrs: rdn along over 3f out: drvn and wknd over 2f out* **25/1**

01-6 **14** *2 ¼* **Edas**[15] 2492 8-9-2 **79** oh7 ow3.......... MissHCuthbert[(3)] 2 58
(T A K Cuthbert) *s.i.s and bhd: sme hdwy towards outer 4f out: rdn 3f out and no further prog* **100/1**

2-12 **15** *3* **Spirit Is Needed (IRE)**[15] 2509 4-10-4 **92**.......... MissNCarberry 17 66
(M Johnston) *midfield: pushed along 4f out: rdn over 3f out and sn wknd* **7/1**[2]

400- **16** *17* **Conquisto**[35] 7573 5-9-11 **85**.......... MsKWalsh 14 32
(S Gollings) *chsd ldrs: rdn along over 4f out: sn wknd* **15/2**[3]

251- **17** *1 ½* **Just Like Silk (USA)**[301] 5028 4-9-9 **86**.......... MissPhillipaTutty[(3)] 11 31
(G A Butler) *a in rr: bhd fnl 3f* **16/1**

340- **18** *10* **Twisted**[363] 2943 4-8-10 **76**.......... MissSMStaveley[(6)] 19 5
(M W Easterby) *chsd ldr: rdn along over 4f out: wknd over 3f out* **80/1**

2m 31.93s (-1.27) **Going Correction** +0.10s/f (Good)
WFA 3 from 4yo+ 15lb 18 Ran SP% **124.3**
Speed ratings (Par 107): **108,104,103,101,99 97,97,96,96,95 95,95,94,92,90 79,78,71**
toteswingers:1&2:£116.20, 1&3:£18.30, 2&3:£154.70 CSF £301.52 CT £2180.41 TOTE £18.00: £3.40, £11.10, £1.80, £5.60; EX 647.70 Trifecta £1170.60 Part won. Pool: £1581.90 - 0.10 winning units..
Owner The Hill Top Partnership **Bred** John Foley & Miss Ann Aungier **Trained** Nether Winchendon, Bucks
■ Stewards' Enquiry : Miss Zoe Lilly two-day ban: used whip when out of contention (tbn)

FOCUS
The ground had dried out since the previous day's meeting and the official going description was changed to good, good to firm in places on the home bend. A race for amateur riders in which the leaders went off much too fast and set it up for the closers. The placed horses are the best guides to the form.

NOTEBOOK
Desert Recluse(IRE), the only 3-y-o in the field, sneaked in at the bottom of the weights. A progressive performer since upped in trip this year, he gets further than this and the good gallop suited him. He had an awkward draw to overcome but being dropped in off the decent pace was the way to go and he stayed on strongly to win going away. He'll take a hit from the Handicapper now but could yet be capable of better again back over further. (op 14-1)
Alcalde beat Crackentorp over 1m3f at Warwick last autumn and again got the better of his old rival. He is on a mark he can be expected to remain competitive off, but also vulnerable to an improver. (op 25-1)
Crackentorp ◆, who like the winner was poorly drawn, travelled well through the race, albeit closer to the pace than the first two, and put up a solid effort. (op 7-1)
Siberian Tiger(IRE), a quirky type last seen running over hurdles in April, was another to benefit from being ridden patiently in a strongly run race. (op 12-1)
Antigua Sunrise(IRE) raced out wide and had too much use made of her. In the circumstances she was far from disgraced to hang on for fifth place. (op 8-1)
Trip The Light, on his toes beforehand, confirmed recent C&D claiming form with Mull Of Dubai. (op 11-1)
Shadows Lengthen Official explanation: trainer said gelding was unsuited by the good (good to firm places) ground
Mull Of Dubai won this race last year and got to race off a 4lb lower mark this time around, but failed to run to his best.

Spirit Is Needed(IRE) Official explanation: jockey said gelding never travelled

2977 LADBROKES.COM STKS (H'CAP) 1m 208y
2:40 (2:43) (Class 2) (0-105,105) 3-Y-0+**£17,485** (£5,202; £2,600; £1,298) **Stalls Low**

Form RPR

11-2 **1** **Distant Memories (IRE)**[60] 1274 4-9-13 **104** .... JamieSpencer 4 113
(T P Tate) *trckd ldrs: chal over 2f out: r.o gamely to ld towards fin* **11/4**[1]

0-30 **2** ½ **Oratory (IRE)**[35] 1900 4-9-0 **91** .... RobertWinston 5 99
(R Hannon) *trckd ldrs: led over 2f out: hdd and no ex towards fin* **10/1**

4-20 **3** 2¼ **Dream Lodge (IRE)**[14] 2539 6-10-0 **105** .... TonyHamilton 2 108
(R A Fahey) *in rr: hdwy on ins over 2f out: styd on fnl f* **14/1**

4-30 **4** ¾ **Demolition**[77] 1015 6-9-2 **93** .... PaulHanagan 11 94
(R A Fahey) *chsd ldrs: chal over 3f out: kpt on same pce over 1f out* **16/1**

100- **5** *nk* **Royal Destination (IRE)**[252] 6480 5-9-7 **98** .... FrankieDettori 10 99+
(J Noseda) *mid-div: effrt 3f out: nt clr run over 2f out: kpt on fnl f* **7/1**[3]

0-00 **6** *1* **Medici Pearl**[42] 1708 6-8-10 **87** oh2 .... DavidAllan 1 86
(T D Easterby) *mid-div: hdwy over 3f out: one pce fnl 2f* **33/1**

3536 **7** ½ **Tartan Gunna**[8] 2710 4-8-10 **87** oh1 .... RichardHills 7 85
(M Johnston) *s.i.s: in rr: hdwy on wd outside over 2f out: nvr nr ldrs* **6/1**[2]

-055 **8** 1¼ **Kavachi (IRE)**[16] 2472 7-8-10 **87** oh5 .... RichardMullen 13 82
(G L Moore) *swtchd lft after s: in rr div: drvn over 3f out: one pce fnl 2f* **20/1**

-551 **9** 1¾ **Opus Maximus (IRE)**[17] 2443 5-8-10 **87** oh2 .... JoeFanning 12 78
(M Johnston) *chsd ldrs: hung lft and wknd over 1f out* **20/1**

-234 **10** *hd* **Moody Tunes**[16] 2477 7-8-5 **87** oh5 .... JamesSullivan(5) 8 78
(J R Weymes) *chsd ldrs: drvn over 3f out: sn outpcd: wknd whn hmpd 2f out* **50/1**

3-5 **11** *8* **General Eliott (IRE)**[49] 1533 5-9-6 **97** .... TomQueally 14 71
(P F I Cole) *swtchd lft after s: in rr: bhd fnl 2f* **33/1**

0-53 **12** 1½ **Bencoolen (IRE)**[18] 2423 5-9-1 **92** .... AdrianNicholls 9 63
(D Nicholls) *w ldrs: edgd lft and lost pl 2f out* **22/1**

0224 **13** 1½ **Elliptical (USA)**[37] 1846 4-8-12 **89** .... KierenFallon 6 57
(G A Butler) *led: t.k.h: hdd over 2f out: sn hmpd and wknd* **6/1**[2]

1m 50.82s (-1.18) **Going Correction** +0.10s/f (Good) **13** Ran SP% **111.1**
Speed ratings (Par 109): **109,108,106,105,105 104,104,103,101,101 94,93,91**
toteswingers:1&2:£10.10, 1&3:£12.30, 2&3:£63.20 CSF £23.12 CT £212.79 TOTE £3.50: £1.40, £3.80, £5.10; EX 32.90 Trifecta £420.80 Pool: £1,723.19 - 3.03 winning units..
Owner Mrs Fitri Hay **Bred** Kildaragh Stud **Trained** Tadcaster, N Yorks

FOCUS
Six of the 14 runners were running from out of the weights in this 87-105 handicap. They went a solid gallop and the form looks sound rated through the third.

NOTEBOOK
Distant Memories(IRE) showed a really good attitude and put his head down to get the better of a duel with Oratory in the closing stages, especially considering that the ground had dried out more than ideal. He deserves another crack at a Listed race now. (op 5-1)
Oratory(IRE) had his stamina to prove over this longer trip, but he actually improved for it, pushing the winner all the way. He'll go up again now despite not winning, though, which might keep him in check for the time being. (tchd 9-1 and 11-1)
Dream Lodge(IRE), who stuck to the inside for most of the race, came from the back of the pack to take third without threatening the first two. He's likely to remain opposable in handicaps off his current mark. (op 12-1 tchd 11-1)
Demolition was stuck three wide around the bend and ran quite well in the circumstances to take fourth. He is better over further but his current career-high mark doesn't make things easy. (tchd 12-1)
Royal Destination(IRE), last seen finishing out the back in the Cambridgeshire, won first time out last season, but ran as though needing this outing. (op 8-1)
Medici Pearl, 2lb out of the handicap, travelled well enough into the race but she didn't see it out. She has never won beyond 1m. (op 20-1)
Tartan Gunna, despite being 1lb wrong at the weights, was racing off a 1lb lower mark than when last successful. He's probably more effective when ridden prominently, but he missed the break and was always struggling to get into it. (op 13-2)
Bencoolen(IRE) Official explanation: jockey said gelding had no more to give
Elliptical(USA) was far too keen in front and it wasn't a great surprise to see him hit the wall with over 2f to run. Official explanation: jockey said gelding ran too free early stages (op 5-1)

2978 REG GRIFFIN MEMORIAL TROPHY (HERITAGE H'CAP) 6f
3:15 (3:16) (Class 2) (0-105,104) 3-Y-0**£64,760** (£19,270; £9,630; £4,810) **Stalls High**

Form RPR

26-1 **1** **Victoire De Lyphar (IRE)**[56] 1376 3-8-7 **90** .... AdrianNicholls 5 97
(D Nicholls) *chsd ldrs: rdn along 1/2-way: drvn over 2f out: led over 1f out: kpt on gamely fnl f* **9/1**

4-65 **2** 1¼ **Iver Bridge Lad**[45] 1616 3-9-4 **101** ....(b[1]) AlanMunro 3 104
(J Ryan) *bhd: hdwy over 2f out: rdn wl over 1f out: styd on wl towards fin* **33/1**

-204 **3** *hd* **Singeur (IRE)**[23] 2260 3-9-0 **97** .... FrankieDettori 19 99
(R Bastiman) *hld up towards rr: smooth hdwy 2f out: rdn ent fnl f and ev ch tl drvn and no ex last 75yds* **20/1**

0-20 **4** *1* **Pastoral Player**[14] 2545 3-8-12 **95** .... HayleyTurner 11 94
(H Morrison) *dwlt and bhd: swtchd rt and hdwy over 2f out: rdn over 1f out: edgd lft ins fnl f: kpt on: nrst fin* **12/1**

2-46 **5** ½ **Side Glance**[14] 2545 3-8-7 **90** .... DavidProbert 8 88
(A M Balding) *a chsng ldrs: rdn along 2f out: drvn over 1f out: kpt on same pce ent fnl f* **8/1**[3]

5-02 **6** 3½ **Astrophysical Jet**[21] 2326 3-8-11 **94** .... TadhgO'Shea 1 80
(E S McMahon) *chsd ldrs on outer: hdwy to ld 1/2-way: rdn over 2f out: hdd over 1f out: drvn and wknd ins fnl f* **18/1**

5055 **7** ½ **Nosedive**[8] 2713 3-8-9 **92** .... LiamJones 4 77
(W J Haggas) *towards rr: rdn along 1/2-way: styd on fr wl over 1f out: nrst fin* **20/1**

15-1 **8** *hd* **Madam Macie (IRE)**[23] 2242 3-8-6 **89** .... KierenFallon 13 73
(D O'Meara) *in tch: pushed along and outpcd 1/2-way: rdn and hdwy 2f out: kpt on ins fnl f: nrst fin* **7/1**[2]

5-04 **9** ¾ **Colonel Mak**[35] 1917 3-8-7 **90** .... TomEaves 12 72
(T D Barron) *chsd ldrs: rdn along over 2f out: drvn and no imp over 1f out* **25/1**

0-61 **10** *2* **Magical Macey (USA)**[43] 1656 3-8-6 **89** ....(b) RichardMullen 20 64
(T D Barron) *chsd ldrs on wd outside: rdn along over 2f out: sn edgd lft and wknd* **33/1**

-160 **11** *shd* **Falasteen (IRE)**[23] 2260 3-8-10 **93** .... PaulHanagan 15 68
(R A Fahey) *nvr bttr than midfield* **25/1**

3-44 **12** *1* **Tomintoul Singer (IRE)**[30] 2058 3-8-11 **94** .... TomQueally 6 66
(H R A Cecil) *prom: effrt and cl up 2f out: sn rdn and wknd over 1f out* **18/1**

0111 **13** *nse* **Hoof It**[15] 2494 3-8-11 **94** .... GrahamGibbons 10 66
(M W Easterby) *cl up: rdn along over 2f out: wknd over 1f out* **17/2**

3020 **14** *6* **Lowdown (IRE)**[14] 2545 3-8-7 **90** .... RichardHills 7 42
(M Johnston) *a towards rr* **20/1**

12-2 **15** *nse* **Coolminx (IRE)**[17] 2437 3-8-10 **93** .... TonyHamilton 18 45
(R A Fahey) *chsd ldrs: rdn along 1/2-way: sn wknd* **25/1**

04-0 **16** ½ **Kingdom Of Light**[21] 2346 3-8-12 **95** .... PaulMulrennan 14 46
(J Howard Johnson) *cl up: rdn along 1/2-way: wknd over 2f out* **40/1**

2-22 **17** 3¼ **Midnight Martini**[30] 2058 3-8-12 **95** .... DavidAllan 17 35
(T D Easterby) *prom: rdn along over 2f out: sn drvn and wknd* **6/1**[1]

3-40 **18** 2¾ **Take Ten**[14] 2545 3-8-7 **90** .... JoeFanning 9 21
(M Johnston) *chsd ldrs: rdn along wl over 2f out: sn wknd* **20/1**

-561 **19** ½ **Swilly Ferry (USA)**[14] 2545 3-9-7 **104** .... MichaelHills 2 34
(B W Hills) *midfield: rdn along and bhd fr 1/2-way* **12/1**

1-42 **20** *6* **The Only Boss (IRE)**[23] 2260 3-8-9 **92** .... JamieSpencer 16 3
(W J Haggas) *slt ld to 1/2-way: sn rdn and wknd* **12/1**

1m 11.63s (-0.27) **Going Correction** +0.10s/f (Good) **20** Ran SP% **130.9**
Speed ratings (Par 105): **105,103,103,101,101 96,95,95,94,91 91,90,90,82,82 81,77,73,72,64**
toteswingers:1&2:£128.90, 1&3:£96.80, 2&3:£122.20 CSF £289.82 CT £5861.08 TOTE £11.40: £3.00, £8.90, £4.30, £3.60; EX 385.00 Trifecta £12419.00 Pool: £43,634.58 - 2.60 winning units..
Owner Middleham Park Racing Xviii **Bred** Mrs Monica Hackett **Trained** Sessay, N Yorks
■ Stewards' Enquiry : Adrian Nicholls caution: used whip with excessive frequency.

FOCUS
A competitive renewal as usual; the early pace was strong and the front-runners paid for their early efforts. The form looks sound with the third and fifth running close to previous Newmarket form.

NOTEBOOK
Victoire De Lyphar(IRE) won on his debut for David Nicholls in April, and had then been clearly targeted at this valuable handicap as he'd been off the track for 56 days afterwards. He didn't travel as well as at Doncaster as he was under pressure from an early stage, but he responded and kept on really strongly as the leaders hit the wall. This speed-favouring course was probably not ideal for him and better again can be expected on a stiffer track, or perhaps even back over 7f, a distance he ran well over at two. (tchd 10-1)
Iver Bridge Lad, wearing blinkers for the first time, was held up off the pace before coming through to take second inside the last. The return to more patient tactics certainly suited him, and the good pace allowed him to settle better.
Singeur(IRE) may have found 5f too short at Southwell last time and appreciated the return to six. He too was held up off the pace and was undoubtedly helped by the way the race was run, but he was poorly drawn and looked to post a personal best in third. (tchd 16-1)
Pastoral Player disappointed at Newmarket last time but this was more like it. Another given a waiting ride before finishing well, the quicker the ground the better it is for him. (op 14-1)
Side Glance ◆ probably needs 7f really, but this race was run at such a good gallop that it brought his stamina in to play. He remains capable of better when returned to a longer trip. (op 12-1)
Astrophysical Jet, runner-up in a Listed event last time out, performed best of those who were in the front rank throughout. She deserves credit for that and will be a different proposition when not forced to go so fast early. (tchd 20-1)
Nosedive was another to stay on past beaten horses from the back of the field, but he has a pretty exposed look about him now. (op 25-1)
Madam Macie(IRE) was always going to struggle to dominate in this competitive field, especially over a furlong shorter trip. Not only did she fail to lead but she struggled to go the pace in the early stages, and a return to 7f surely beckons. (op 8-1)
Midnight Martini had too much use made of her in contesting a disputed lead. She simply helped set the race up for the closers. Official explanation: trainer had no explanation for the poor form shown (op 15-2 tchd 8-1 in a place)

2979 DANIEL PRENN ROYAL YORKSHIRE STKS (H'CAP) 1m 2f 88y
3:50 (3:50) (Class 2) (0-100,92) 3-Y-0 **£14,247** (£4,239; £2,118; £1,058) **Stalls Low**

Form RPR

10 **1** **Rebel Soldier (IRE)**[57] 1352 3-9-5 **88** .... FrankieDettori 8 109+
(J Noseda) *mde all: qcknd over 3f out: edgd lft and wnt clr over 1f out: easily* **3/1**[1]

-340 **2** *8* **Bonfire Knight**[7] 2758 3-8-13 **82** .... GrahamGibbons 1 85
(J J Quinn) *chsd ldrs: drvn over 3f out: chsd wnr over 1f out: no ch w wnr* **9/1**

5-16 **3** 1½ **Thaahira (USA)**[24] 2224 3-9-5 **88** .... RichardHills 6 88
(M A Jarvis) *hld up: hdwy over 2f out: kpt on fnl f* **4/1**[2]

02 **4** *nse* **Ejteyaaz**[16] 2466 3-9-0 **83** .... PaulHanagan 3 83
(R A Fahey) *t.k.h towards rr: effrt over 3f out: sn outpcd: styd on fnl f* **5/1**[3]

46-0 **5** *3* **Mingun Bell (USA)**[28] 2117 3-9-2 **85** .... TomQueally 9 80
(H R A Cecil) *hld up in tch: hdwy to chse ldrs over 3f out: wknd over 1f out* **16/1**

1-50 **6** *shd* **Antoniola (IRE)**[28] 2110 3-8-10 **79** .... DavidAllan 4 73
(T D Easterby) *hld up in rr: hdwy on ins over 2f out: wknd over 1f out* **12/1**

-421 **7** 1¼ **Cultivar**[22] 2290 3-9-1 **84** .... MichaelHills 2 76
(B W Hills) *trckd ldrs: effrt 3f out: wknd over 1f out* **11/2**

41- **8** 4½ **Solicitor**[207] 7420 3-8-12 **81** .... JoeFanning 5 64
(M Johnston) *sn chsng ldrs: lost pl 2f out* **7/1**

06-1 **9** 1¼ **Maison Brillet (IRE)**[19] 2394 3-8-6 **75** .... PJMcDonald 7 56
(J Howard Johnson) *sn chsng ldrs: drvn over 3f out: wknd 2f out* **25/1**

2m 10.14s (-2.36) **Going Correction** +0.10s/f (Good) **9** Ran SP% **117.0**
Speed ratings (Par 105): **113,106,105,105,102 102,101,98,97**
toteswingers:1&2:£6.50, 1&3:£3.70, 2&3:£14.10 CSF £31.38 CT £110.16 TOTE £3.40: £1.50, £2.20, £1.90; EX 29.80 Trifecta £66.40 Pool: £1,400.46 - 15.59 winning units..
Owner The Honorable Earle I Mack **Bred** En Garde Syndicate **Trained** Newmarket, Suffolk

FOCUS
A decent handicap but the top-weight weighed in 8lb below the ceiling for the race. The winner was a cut above these and the runner-up sets the level for the form.

NOTEBOOK
Rebel Soldier(IRE) impressed when winning on his debut on the Polytrack but was never travelling when disappointing at Newbury subsequently. Upped a good deal in distance, he soon got to the front and Dettori dominated the race throughout. The way he stretched clear in the straight suggested he could be a Pattern-class performer, but the John Smith's Cup looks an ideal target for him in the short term, providing he gets into the race. (op 4-1)
Bonfire Knight appreciated the drop back in trip having found 1m4f too far last time. The winner was in a different parish but he held off the rest well for second. (op 10-1 tchd 8-1)
Thaahira(USA) won a maiden at Chester that in hindsight may have been overrated as she again failed to live up to the promise she showed there. Having sweated up beforehand, she was given a patient ride, but found just the one pace under pressure. (tchd 9-2)
Ejteyaaz, stepping up 2f in distance, didn't look to improve for it. (op 4-1)
Mingun Bell(USA), who had beaten only one rival home in his previous three starts, shaped a bit better this time without suggesting a return to the winner's enclosure is imminent. (tchd 18-1)
Antoniola(IRE) didn't improve for the longer trip. (op 14-1 tchd 16-1)

Cultivar is possibly a better horse when allowed to lead. Official explanation: jockey said colt ran flat (op 5-1 tchd 6-1)

2980 LEONARD SAINER E B F MAIDEN STKS 6f
4:20 (4:20) (Class 3) 2-Y-O **£6,929** (£2,061; £1,030; £514) **Stalls** High

Form RPR

2 **1** **Sir Reginald**[30] 2059 2-9-3 0 PaulHanagan 5 78
(R A Fahey) *cl up: rdn along 2f out: kpt on to ld ent fnl f: sn edgd rt: drvn and kpt on wl towards fin* **4/9**[1]

643 **2** ½ **Rojo Boy**[18] 2407 2-9-3 0 DavidProbert 6 77
(A M Balding) *chsd ldrs: sltly hmpd after 1f and towards rr: hdwy over 2f out and sn rdn: drvn and edgd lft ent fnl f: kpt on towards fin* **13/2**[2]

3 1 **Cathedral Spires** 2-9-3 0 TomEaves 9 74
(J Howard Johnson) *cl up: effrt 2f out: sn rdn and ev ch whn hmpd jst ins fnl f: one pce after* **66/1**

3 **4** hd **Nicola's Dream**[21] 2347 2-8-12 0 PJMcDonald 8 68
(R A Fahey) *trckd ldrs: hdwy 2f out: sn rdn and kpt on ins fnl f: nrst fin* **16/1**

00 **5** ½ **Bellemere**[8] 2693 2-8-12 0 GrahamGibbons 10 66
(M W Easterby) *led: rdn along 2f out: drvn and hdd ent fnl f: wknd* **66/1**

0 **6** 3¾ **Fleet Captain**[25] 2216 2-9-3 0 JamieSpencer 7 62
(K A Ryan) *dwlt and towards rr: hdwy 1/2-way: swtchd rt and effrt to chal over 1f out: rdn and hld whn sltly hmpd ins fnl f: sn eased* **25/1**

7 1¾ **My Mate Jake (IRE)** 2-9-3 0 PaulMulrennan 2 55
(J G Given) *in tch: rdn along 1/2-way: sn wknd* **28/1**

8 2 **Peters Spirit (IRE)** 2-8-12 0 FranciscoDaSilva 1 44
(R A Fahey) *sn outpcd and a in rr* **33/1**

9 9 **Memorabilia** 2-9-3 0 JoeFanning 3 22
(M Johnston) *sn rdn along: a towards rr* **14/1**

4 **10** 7 **Frankish Dynasty (GER)**[8] 2715 2-9-3 0 KierenFallon 4 1
(P F I Cole) *prom: rdn along over 2f out: sn wknd* **15/2**[3]

1m 13.86s (1.96) **Going Correction** +0.10s/f (Good) **10** Ran SP% **120.1**
Speed ratings (Par 97): **90,89,88,87,87 82,79,77,65,55**
toteswingers:1&2:£1.70, 1&3:£18.80, 2&3:£38.60 CSF £3.78 TOTE £1.40: £1.10, £1.50, £13.20; EX 3.40.
Owner Jim McGrath **Bred** Jeremy Green And Sons **Trained** Musley Bank, N Yorks

FOCUS
A fair maiden but the form is not as good as looked possible.

NOTEBOOK
Sir Reginald set a decent standard on his second to Coventry Stakes bound Elzaam on his debut here at the Dante meeting, so it was understandable that he was sent off a short price. He got the job done, albeit in workmanlike style, and judging by his multiple sales-race entries, it'll be a surprise if the big plan this year isn't to try to bag a big pot somewhere. (op 1-2 tchd 2-5)
Rojo Boy, who was back in fourth in the race in which Sir Reginald finished second on his debut, proved unsuited by the drop back to 5f at Chepstow last time and the return to six clearly helped. He was closing the winner down at the finish and really does deserve to get off the mark at a lesser track. (op 7-1)
Cathedral Spires, who is already gelded, was an unconsidered outsider but did best of the newcomers. Considering it was his debut he had quite a hard race. (tchd 50-1)
Nicola's Dream, stablemate of the winner, had finished third in a fillies' maiden over the C&D on her debut but found this tougher. (op 14-1)
Bellemere showed good early speed but didn't quite see it out. She'll be one for nurseries in due course.
Fleet Captain ran a lot better than he did on his debut. He was keeping on when hampered inside the last.

2981 MICHAEL SOBELL MAIDEN STKS 1m
4:55 (4:55) (Class 4) 3-Y-O **£6,540** (£1,946; £972; £485) **Stalls** Low

Form RPR

42 **1** **Zakiy**[7] 2755 3-9-3 0 (t) JamieSpencer 1 84
(W J Haggas) *led: rdn along 3f out: hdd over 2f out: cl up: drvn over 1f out: rallied ent fnl f: led last 100yds: kpt on grimly* **9/2**[3]

222 **2** ½ **Soviet Secret**[14] 2548 3-9-3 81 KierenFallon 4 82
(P J McBride) *trckd ldrs: hdwy 4f out: led over 2f out: rdn wl over 1f out: drvn ent fnl f: hdd and no ex last 100yds* **2/1**[2]

3-5 **3** 2½ **Chelsea Morning (USA)**[45] 1620 3-8-12 0 MichaelHills 6 72
(B W Hills) *trckd wnr: cl up 3f out: rdn along 2f out: drvn and one pce fr over 1f out* **11/1**

422 **4** 1½ **Ezra Church (IRE)**[12] 2609 3-9-3 77 GrahamGibbons 5 73
(T D Barron) *trckd ldrs: hdwy over 3f out: rdn along wl over 2f out: sn drvn and one pce* **8/1**

0 **5** shd **Safwaan**[59] 1308 3-9-3 0 RichardHills 2 73
(W J Haggas) *dwlt: in tch: effrt 3f out and sn rdn: drvn wl over 1f out and one pce* **13/8**[1]

6 24 **Maitre 'D** 3-9-3 0 AlanMunro 3 18
(C N Kellett) *a towards rr: rdden along over 3f out: sn outpcd and bhd* **50/1**

1m 41.01s (2.21) **Going Correction** +0.10s/f (Good) **6** Ran SP% **111.0**
Speed ratings (Par 101): **92,91,89,87,87 63**
toteswingers:1&2:£2.20, 1&3:£3.60, 2&3:£3.40 CSF £13.63 TOTE £5.70: £2.90, £1.60; EX 14.30.
Owner Saleh Al Homaizi & Imad Al Sagar **Bred** Saleh Al Homaizi **Trained** Newmarket, Suffolk

FOCUS
No more than a fair maiden but the form looks sound rated around the placed horses.

2982 CHARLES HENRY MEMORIAL STKS (H'CAP) 6f
5:25 (5:27) (Class 4) (0-80,80) 3-Y-O+ **£7,123** (£2,119; £1,059; £529) **Stalls** High

Form RPR

-101 **1** **Averoo**[8] 2719 5-9-6 72 (p) KierenFallon 20 82
(M D Squance) *sn detached in rr: rapid hdwy stands' side 1f out: fin strly to ld nr fin* **9/1**

-461 **2** ½ **Misplaced Fortune**[27] 2140 5-10-0 80 (v) JoeFanning 2 89
(N Tinkler) *hld up towards rr: gd hdwy over 1f out: led last 50yds: hdd fnl strides* **10/1**

3-03 **3** 1¼ **Tyfos**[14] 2528 5-9-9 75 RobertWinston 14 80
(B P J Baugh) *chsd ldrs: styd on to chal last 100yds: no ex* **11/1**

0430 **4** hd **Istiqdaam**[8] 2696 5-9-6 72 (b) GrahamGibbons 19 76
(M W Easterby) *in rr: hdwy 2f out: styd on ins fnl f* **12/1**

-004 **5** ½ **Protector (SAF)**[3] 2856 9-10-0 80 (t) LNewman 5 82
(A G Foster) *chsd ldrs: rdn and outpcd over 2f out: hdwy to chse ldrs jst ins fnl f: no ex last 50yds* **33/1**

-302 **6** 1¼ **Atlantic Beach**[27] 2144 5-9-1 67 AdrianNicholls 8 65
(J Hetherton) *chsd ldrs: kpt on same pce fnl 150yds* **11/2**[1]

5356 **7** ¾ **Floor Show**[14] 2534 4-9-10 79 MichaelGeran(3) 3 75
(N Wilson) *racd towards far side: chsd ldr: edgd lft and kpt on same pce fnl f* **12/1**

0661 **8** nk **Bahamian Lad**[10] 2646 5-9-4 70 (p) TomQueally 15 65
(R Hollinshead) *in tch: effrt over 1f out: kpt on same pce* **12/1**

6141 **9** ½ **Lucky Dan (IRE)**[11] 2626 4-9-11 77 PaulMulrennan 16 70
(Paul Green) *mid-div: kpt on fnl f: nvr nr ldrs* **8/1**[3]

50-0 **10** shd **Ursula (IRE)**[16] 2465 4-9-11 77 AndrewElliott 9 70
(J R Weymes) *mid-div: swtchd lft and styd on fnl f: nvr nr ldrs* **18/1**

5001 **11** hd **Wyatt Earp (IRE)**[25] 2206 9-9-10 76 (p) JamieSpencer 4 68
(P Salmon) *racd towards far side: led: edgd rt over 1f out: hdd & wknd fnl 50yds* **15/2**[2]

-361 **12** hd **Elijah Pepper (USA)**[5] 2817 5-8-13 65 6ex RichardMullen 11 57
(T D Barron) *in rr div: swtchd lft and sme hdwy over 1f out: nvr on terms* **16/1**

4010 **13** 1¾ **Ventura Cove (IRE)**[22] 2287 3-9-6 80 PaulHanagan 17 66
(R A Fahey) *a towards rr* **20/1**

0204 **14** 1½ **Green Park (IRE)**[8] 2696 7-9-11 77 (b) DavidNolan 18 58
(D Carroll) *in rr: swtchd lft over 1f out: kpt on: nvr a factor* **20/1**

01- **15** ½ **Vested Interest**[345] 3547 3-9-0 79 LanceBetts(5) 10 59
(J S Wainwright) *chsd ldrs: wknd appr fnl f* **50/1**

0063 **16** 1 **Frognal (IRE)**[14] 2534 4-9-10 76 PJMcDonald 7 53
(Mrs R A Carr) *dwlt: sn in tch: wknd appr fnl f* **11/1**

0450 **17** 2 **Bosun Breese**[14] 2534 5-9-9 75 DavidAllan 13 45
(T D Barron) *in rr: sme hdwy over 2f out: sn wknd* **40/1**

-0U3 **18** 2½ **Northern Bolt**[36] 1869 5-9-8 77 (v) GaryBartley(3) 1 39
(I W McInnes) *s.s: lft to r alone far side: a in rr* **25/1**

-000 **19** 1¾ **Peter Tchaikovsky**[18] 2423 4-9-9 75 TomEaves 12 32
(B S Rothwell) *s.i.s: a bhd* **40/1**

1m 11.9s **Going Correction** +0.10s/f (Good)
WFA 3 from 4yo+ 8lb **19** Ran SP% **131.4**
Speed ratings (Par 105): **104,103,101,101,100 99,98,97,97,96 96,96,94,92,91 90,87,84,81**
toteswingers:1&2:£11.80, 1&3:£30.00, 2&3:£27.40 CSF £94.38 CT £1058.63 TOTE £8.30: £2.20, £2.30, £3.10, £4.70; EX 76.90 Place 6 £146.44; Place 5 £45.54.
Owner Miss K Squance **Bred** Mrs H Johnson Houghton & Mrs R F Johnson Hought **Trained** Newmarket, Suffolk

FOCUS
A competitive handicap and an incredible finish. The form looks solid rated around the third and fourth.
Northern Bolt Official explanation: jockey said gelding missed the break
T/Jkpt: £19,024.8. Pool:£26,795.58 - 1.00 winning ticket. T/Plt: £189.20 to a £1 stake. Pool:£189,307.41 - 730.11 winning tickets T/Qpdt: £21.90 to a £1 stake. Pool:£7,954.68 - 267.90 winning tickets JR

2983 - 2989a (Foreign Racing) - See Raceform Interactive

2736 DONCASTER (L-H)
Sunday, June 13

OFFICIAL GOING: Good (good to soft in places on round course; 7.4)
Wind: Moderate, half against Weather: Fine, light rain race 3 onwards, becoming heavier

2990 CROWNHOTEL-BAWTRY.COM E B F MEDIAN AUCTION MAIDEN STKS 6f
2:20 (2:22) (Class 4) 2-Y-O **£4,533** (£1,348; £674; £336) **Stalls** High

Form RPR

3 **1** **Formosina (IRE)**[30] 2078 2-9-3 0 RyanMoore 12 94+
(J Noseda) *hld up towards rr: gd hdwy to ld over 2f out: sprinted clr over 1f out: v easily* **4/11**[1]

2 7 **Restless Bay (IRE)** 2-9-3 0 GeorgeBaker 4 73+
(R Hollinshead) *dwlt: towards rr on outer: edgd rt and hdwy over 2f out: swtchd stands' side 1f out: r.o to take 2nd nr line* **50/1**

3 ½ **King Of The Celts (IRE)** 2-9-3 0 DavidAllan 10 71
(T D Easterby) *sn chsng ldrs: wnt 2nd over 1f out: styd on same pce* **16/1**

2332 **4** 1 **Alfraamsey**[22] 2312 2-9-3 0 ChrisCatlin 7 68
(M R Channon) *chsd ldrs: one pce fnl 2f* **11/2**[2]

5 2¼ **Toparichi** 2-8-12 0 AshleyMorgan(5) 2 61+
(M H Tompkins) *sn wl outpcd and drvn along: hmpd over 2f out: kpt on: nvr on terms* **66/1**

6 1 **Lady Gar Gar** 2-8-12 0 PaulMulrennan 8 53+
(G R Oldroyd) *s.s: in rr: swtchd lft over 2f out: kpt on* **33/1**

6 **7** shd **George Woolf**[46] 1626 2-9-3 0 JamesDoyle 1 58
(A J McCabe) *swvd lft s: sn chsng ldrs: wknd over 1f out* **66/1**

6 **8** ¾ **Jamaica Grande**[14] 2561 2-9-3 0 JerryO'Dwyer 5 56
(P S McEntee) *chsd ldrs: hung lft and wknd over 1f out* **100/1**

9 3 **Arctic Cat (IRE)** 2-9-3 0 PJMcDonald 9 47
(G A Swinbank) *chsd ldrs: lost pl over 2f out* **33/1**

6 **10** hd **Newzflash**[16] 2493 2-9-3 0 PhillipMakin 11 46
(T D Barron) *chsd ldrs: lost pl 2f out* **25/1**

4 **11** ½ **Finn's Rainbow**[17] 2474 2-9-3 0 JamieSpencer 3 45
(K A Ryan) *led tl over 2f out: lost pl over 1f out* **8/1**[3]

12 1 **Dance For Livvy (IRE)** 2-8-12 0 TomEaves 6 37
(B M R Haslam) *dwlt: sn in midfield: lost pl over 2f out* **66/1**

1m 12.94s (-0.66) **Going Correction** -0.15s/f (Firm) **12** Ran SP% **122.8**
Speed ratings (Par 95): **98,88,88,86,83 82,82,81,77,76 76,74**
toteswingers: 1&2 £8.60, 1&3 £3.20, 2&3 £36.80 CSF £47.11 TOTE £1.40: £1.10, £11.80, £3.60; EX 35.80 Trifecta £477.10 Pool: £760.89 - 1.18 winning units..
Owner Daniel Pittack **Bred** Oak Lodge Bloodstock **Trained** Newmarket, Suffolk

FOCUS
An uncompetitive maiden and a promising winner. The fourth helps set the level.

NOTEBOOK
Formosina(IRE) was a well-held third on debut last month, but that came in a hot maiden at Newbury and the pair that finished in front of him there are both highly rated juveniles. He confirmed the promise of that run with a bloodless success in this lesser race and is clearly a very useful prospect. He got very warm before the start and still showed a little inexperience through the race, so one would think there should be plenty more to come after this confidence booster. The easier ground was also no bother to him. This paid another compliment to his conqueror at Newbury, Strong Suit who is due to contest the Coventry at Royal Ascot. (op 8-15)
Restless Bay(IRE), who cost 22,000gns and is bred to enjoy a little further. He was doing his best work inside the final furlong and looks well up to winning races. (tchd 40-1)
King Of The Celts(IRE) was starting off his career over a trip likely to prove plenty sharp enough according to his pedigree. He should relish being faced with a stiffer test and, in keeping with many juveniles from his yard, ought to come on a good deal for the outing. (op 12-1)
Alfraamsey wasn't helped by having to make his challenge more towards the centre of the course, but came into this having been placed on his four previous outings and does set a sensible guide to the form. He is starting to look exposed, but it was the easiest ground he had encountered to date and does deserve an opening. (op 9-2 tchd 6-1)
Toparichi ◆ caught the eye doing some decent late work having been outpaced early on. He should improve a deal for the initial experience, is another bred to enjoy a stiffer test and is one to keep an eye on as his yard's juveniles usually need their debut outing.

Lady Gar Gar was another that got outpaced and ran green, before staying on with a degree of promise late on. (op 28-1 tchd 25-1)

2991 POLYPIPE H'CAP 1m (R)
2:55 (2:57) (Class 4) (0-85,83) 4-Y-0+ £4,533 (£1,348; £674; £336) Stalls Low

Form RPR
5-32 1 **Major Phil (IRE)**[17] 2462 4-9-2 78 KierenFallon 7 89+
(L M Cumani) *mid-div: effrt over 2f out: styd on wl to take 2nd 100yds out: str burst to ld towards fin* 11/4[1]
4-03 2 ¾ **Mac's Power (IRE)**[29] 2129 4-9-3 79 (t) AdamKirby 2 88+
(J R Fanshawe) *trckd ldrs: swtchd outside 3f out: qcknd to ld 2f out: sn 3 l clr: no ex and hdd nr fin* 5/1[2]
1500 3 1 ¼ **Raptor (GER)**[16] 2506 7-9-4 80 (b) NickyMackay 5 86
(M E Rimmer) *chsd ldrs: effrt over 2f out: styd on to take 3rd last 75yds* 40/1
2002 4 1 ½ **Happy Anniversary (IRE)**[3] 2885 4-9-5 81 (p) JoeFanning 3 84
(Mrs D J Sanderson) *chsd ldr: chal 2f out: kpt on one pce* 6/1[3]
6-42 5 ¾ **Effigy**[23] 2284 6-9-4 80 FergusSweeney 1 81
(H Candy) *chsd ldrs: one pce fnl 2f* 12/1
2610 6 1 ½ **Shadowtime**[2] 2937 5-8-10 72 AndrewMullen 9 70
(Miss Tracy Waggott) *chsd ldrs: effrt over 2f out: one pce* 9/1
-000 7 1 **Smarty Socks (IRE)**[57] 1374 6-9-3 79 FranciscoDaSilva 11 74
(D O'Meara) *in rr: styd on fnl 2f: nvr nr ldrs* 40/1
0-20 8 hd **Marvo**[43] 1697 6-9-1 82 AshleyMorgan(5) 13 77
(M H Tompkins) *hld up towards rr: effrt over 2f out: nvr nr ldrs* 7/1
4052 9 2 ½ **Thunderball**[9] 2705 4-9-4 80 (b) ChrisCatlin 6 69
(J A Glover) *set str pce: t.k.h: hdd 2f out: sn wknd* 12/1
1354 10 1 ½ **King Of The Moors (USA)**[15] 2523 7-8-7 69 (p) FrannyNorton 4 55
(R C Guest) *chsd ldrs: wknd 2f out* 28/1
-136 11 1 ¼ **Tudor Key (IRE)**[10] 2683 4-9-7 83 RyanMoore 10 66
(Mrs A J Perrett) *slipped leaving stalls: swtchd lft after s: in rr: effrt over 2f out: hung bdly lft over 1f out: eased ins fnl f* 6/1[3]
5404 12 11 **Prohibition (IRE)**[18] 2443 4-8-13 75 TonyCulhane 12 32
(W J Haggas) *swtchd lft sn after s: in rr: bhd fnl 2f* 25/1
0200 13 1 **Pearly Wey**[8] 2736 7-9-2 78 (p) TomEaves 8 33
(I W McInnes) *t.k.h in rr: wknd 2f out: sn bhd* 40/1

1m 36.88s (-2.82) **Going Correction** -0.15s/f (Firm) 13 Ran SP% 124.4
Speed ratings (Par 105): **108,107,106,104,103 102,101,101,98,97 95,84,83**
toteswingers: 1&2 £4.70, 1&3 £20.40, 2&3 £45.40 CSF £15.83 CT £456.08 TOTE £2.40: £1.10, £3.00, £11.70; EX 20.50 TRIFECTA Not won..
Owner Leonidas Marinopoulos **Bred** Roger Macnair **Trained** Newmarket, Suffolk

FOCUS
A fair handicap and a good winning time.
Tudor Key(IRE) Official explanation: jockey said gelding slipped badly coming out of stalls and hung right thereafter

2992 BIG JOHN AT BREAKFAST H'CAP 6f
3:30 (3:33) (Class 3) (0-95,96) 3-Y-0+ £6,799 (£2,023; £1,011; £505) Stalls High

Form RPR
30-0 1 **Baby Strange**[58] 1349 6-9-4 85 FrannyNorton 6 96
(D Shaw) *hld up: hdwy over 2f out: str run to ld last 150yds: styd on wl* 33/1
-602 2 1 ¼ **Jonny Mudball**[22] 2316 4-9-8 89 (t) RichardKingscote 11 96
(Tom Dascombe) *w ldr: led over 1f out: hdd and no ex last 100yds* 13/2[2]
-020 3 hd **Doctor Parkes**[18] 2431 4-9-4 85 EddieAhern 12 91
(E J Alston) *led tl over 1f out: no ex ins fnl f* 16/1
4503 4 1 **Joseph Henry**[11] 2657 8-8-12 84 BillyCray(5) 10 87
(D Nicholls) *w ldrs: styd on same pce ins fnl f* 33/1
1-1 5 hd **Poet's Place (USA)**[131] 380 5-9-6 87 PhillipMakin 8 93+
(T D Barron) *dwlt: hld up: hdwy and n.m.r over 2f out: styng on whn nt clr run and eased fnl 50yds* 6/1[1]
3466 6 ¾ **Tabaret**[11] 2657 7-9-3 87 MichaelStainton(3) 4 87
(R M Whitaker) *w ldrs: no ex ins fnl f* 22/1
0-21 7 nse **Tajneed (IRE)**[11] 2657 7-10-1 96 AdrianNicholls 16 96
(D Nicholls) *w ldrs stands' side: kpt on same pce fnl f* 6/1[1]
60-1 8 1 **Definightly**[43] 1692 4-9-8 89 FergusSweeney 18 86
(R Charlton) *hld up stands' side: hdwy 2f out: kpt on ins fnl f: nt rch ldrs* 17/2
0-10 9 nk **Bond City (IRE)**[17] 2465 8-9-6 87 PaulMulrennan 7 83
(G R Oldroyd) *chsd ldrs: kpt on same pce fnl f* 66/1
00 10 nse **Cheveton**[22] 2346 6-9-8 92 WilliamCarson(3) 17 88
(R J Price) *chsd ldrs stands' side: sn drvn along: one pce fnl 2f* 20/1
0-05 11 shd **Northern Dare (IRE)**[11] 2657 6-9-2 83 PaulHanagan 9 78
(R A Fahey) *chsd ldrs: one pce fnl 2f* 11/1
06-6 12 shd **Captain Ramius (IRE)**[58] 1349 4-9-13 94 JamieSpencer 13 95+
(K A Ryan) *trckd ldrs: keeping on same pce whn nt clr run and eased fnl 50yds* 20/1
-300 13 shd **One Way Or Another (AUS)**[16] 2508 7-9-8 89 GeorgeBaker 14 84+
(J R Gask) *hld up stands' side: effrt and nt clr run wl over 1f out: nt clr run jst ins fnl f: nt rcvr* 8/1
4120 14 ½ **New Leyf (IRE)**[36] 1903 4-9-1 82 AdamKirby 15 75
(J R Gask) *chsd ldrs stands' side: one pce fnl 2f* 7/1[3]
0-00 15 nk **Seamus Shindig**[13] 2595 8-8-11 85 AmyScott(7) 1 77
(H Candy) *hld up in midfield towards far side: drvn over 2f out: nvr a factor* 28/1
0-00 16 2 ¼ **Fullandby (IRE)**[58] 1353 8-10-0 95 GregFairley 20 80
(T J Etherington) *s.i.s: reminders after s: hdwy stands' side over 2f out: wknd over 1f out* 20/1
6-00 17 ½ **Excusez Moi (USA)**[11] 2657 8-9-9 90 PJMcDonald 3 73
(Mrs R A Carr) *s.v.s: sme hdwy over 2f out: nvr on terms* 33/1
-404 18 59 **Invincible Force (IRE)**[22] 2311 6-9-12 93 (b) KierenFallon 5 —
(Paul Green) *s.s: mid-div on far side: lost pl over 2f out: sn eased and bhd: virtually p.u* 16/1

1m 11.57s (-2.03) **Going Correction** -0.15s/f (Firm) 18 Ran SP% 128.5
Speed ratings (Par 107): **107,105,105,103,103 102,102,101,100,100 100,100,100,99,99 96,95,16**
toteswingers: 1&2 £58.30, 1&3 £96.90, 2&3 £30.30 CSF £222.17 CT £3628.11 TOTE £54.20: £7.80, £2.00, £4.10, £6.40; EX 519.70 TRIFECTA Not won..
Owner Market Avenue Racing Club Ltd **Bred** Michael John Williamson **Trained** Sproxton, Leics

FOCUS
A typically competitive sprint handicap for the class and track. The runners ended up merging down the centre of the track and, despite the winner coming from out the back, it didn't prove easy to land a blow from off the pace.

NOTEBOOK
Baby Strange was asked for everything shortly after passing the 2f marker and eventually mowed down rivals to score readily. He is reliant on things falling jut right in his races, but is a very capable sprinter on his day and was 5lb lower than his last winning mark. His profile doesn't suggest a follow-up is on the cards, but it was just his second outing over the year and his first on turf since last July, so there could well be more improvement him next time out.
Jonny Mudball was always in the firing line and kept on gamely for maximum pressure, but again managed to find one too good off this mark. Slightly quicker ground is probably better for him, though, and this lightly raced sprinter should still be capable of going one better again sooner rather than later. (op 7-1 tchd 11-2)
Doctor Parkes made a bold bid and showed his true colours again. This looks his best trip nowadays and his turn is not looking far off again.
Joseph Henry took them along down the centre of the course and ran his race, rating a sound benchmark. (tchd 28-1)
Poet's Place(USA) came into this unbeaten in two previous runs on Fibresand and is reportedly difficult to train, hence he was returning from a 131-day break. Racing off a 12lb higher mark, he travelled nicely and did not get a lot of room 2f out, but did not quicken instantly when in the clear. He may need more of a test on turf and remains progressive. (op 7-1)
Tabaret posted another creditable effort and he too sets the level. (op 25-1)
Tajneed(IRE) had his chance but was anchored by a 6lb higher mark for winning again at Ripon 11 days earlier. (op 11-2 tchd 13-2)
Definightly was 4lb higher than when scoring at Goodwood in a lesser contest 43 days previously and didn't appear to have any real excuses. Perhaps stepping back up a furlong would now suit him. (op 8-1 tchd 15-2)
One Way Or Another(AUS) ◆ was having his first run at the track since a luckless run over C&D on his comeback. He was still on the bridle off the pace at the furlong marker and his rider only got serious with him when the race was effectively over, but in fairness he didn't look to get the best of passages. He may not be the easiest ride, but is better than he showed and there should be one of these in him during the summer. Official explanation: jockey said gelding was denied a clear run (tchd 17-2)
Invincible Force(IRE) Official explanation: jockey said gelding was slow away

2993 DONCASTER FREE PRESS LIFE IS LOCAL CLASSIFIED STKS 1m 2f 60y
4:05 (4:07) (Class 5) 3-Y-O £3,238 (£963; £481; £240) Stalls Low

Form RPR
3603 1 **Crunched**[24] 2250 3-9-0 69 JamieSpencer 1 74
(M L W Bell) *led 3f: regained ld 3f out: hrd rdn and kpt on fnl f: all out* 4/1[2]
-300 2 ¾ **Heaven Forbid**[17] 2473 3-9-0 68 EddieAhern 2 73
(J R Fanshawe) *trckd ldrs: chal 3f out: no ex wl ins fnl f* 17/2
0-15 3 1 ¼ **Flag Of Glory**[30] 2089 3-9-0 70 GeorgeBaker 11 70
(C F Wall) *reluctant to go to s: trckd ldrs: chal 2f out: styd on same pce ins fnl f* 7/2[1]
-044 4 ¾ **Dance For Julie (IRE)**[16] 2502 3-8-9 70 PatrickDonaghy(5) 4 69
(B M R Haslam) *s.s: hdwy on outer 4f out: chsng ldrs and drvn over 2f out: kpt on same pce fnl f* 14/1
3-14 5 hd **Mighty Clarets (IRE)**[19] 2422 3-9-0 70 PaulHanagan 6 68
(R A Fahey) *chsd ldrs: rdn over 2f out: one pce* 9/2[3]
-500 6 1 ½ **The Starboard Bow**[16] 2510 3-9-0 70 NeilCallan 5 66
(S Kirk) *hld up towards rr: effrt and hung rt 3f out: kpt on fnl f* 50/1
320 7 ½ **Laverre (IRE)**[36] 1927 3-9-0 70 DavidAllan 8 65
(T D Easterby) *hmpd s: in rr: hdwy on ins over 3f out: one pce fnl 2f* 11/1
-23 8 2 ¼ **Search For The Key (USA)**[33] 1993 3-9-0 68 RyanMoore 10 60
(P F I Cole) *wnt lft s: hld up in midfield: effrt over 2f out: wknd 2f out* 9/1
4402 9 hd **Sharakti (IRE)**[12] 2620 3-8-9 57 DeclanCannon(5) 7 60
(A J McCabe) *hmpd s: hdwy over 4f out: outpcd fnl 2f* 40/1
04-0 10 8 **Storm Hawk (IRE)**[12] 2620 3-9-0 62 AndreaAtzeni 3 53
(Pat Eddery) *drvn along to chse ldrs: led after 3f: hdd 3f out: lost pl over 1f out: eased ins fnl f* 28/1
50-6 11 6 **Snoqualmie Star**[31] 2042 3-9-0 68 KierenFallon 12 41
(D R C Elsworth) *t.k.h: hdwy to trck ldrs over 4f out: rdn and wknd over 2f out: eased ins fnl f* 7/1
-400 12 23 **Marafong**[37] 1878 3-8-7 70 AdamBeschizza(7) 9 —
(Miss J Feilden) *hmpd s: in rr: lost pl 3f out: sn bhd: heavily eased* 50/1

2m 9.38s (-0.02) **Going Correction** -0.15s/f (Firm) 12 Ran SP% 118.2
Speed ratings (Par 99): **101,100,99,98,98 97,97,95,95,88 83,65**
toteswingers: 1&2 £6.40, 1&3 £4.70, 2&3 £12.90 CSF £36.95 TOTE £4.80: £1.40, £4.30, £2.20; EX 44.30 Trifecta £148.80 Pool: £913.26 - 4.54 winning units..
Owner R P B Michaelson **Bred** D J And Mrs Deer **Trained** Newmarket, Suffolk

FOCUS
There was a fair pace on in this 3-y-o classified event and the form looks sound enough for the type of contest.
Laverre(IRE) Official explanation: jockey said filly suffered interference shortly after start
Snoqualmie Star Official explanation: jockey said filly lost its action

2994 DONCASTER FREE PRESS PROPERTY GUIDE MAIDEN STKS 1m 4f
4:35 (4:38) (Class 5) 3-Y-0+ £2,590 (£770; £385; £192) Stalls Low

Form RPR
1 **Shubaat** 3-8-12 0 NeilCallan 12 85+
(M A Jarvis) *trckd ldrs: wnt 2nd 3f out: shkn up to ld over 1f out: drvn 6 l clr: eased nr fin* 9/4[1]
0 2 4 **La Concorde (FR)**[31] 2043 3-8-7 0 RyanMoore 11 71
(Sir Michael Stoute) *chsd ldrs: pushed along 7f out: wnt 3rd over 2f out: tk n.d 2nd last 75yds* 8/1[3]
-0 3 1 **Old Hundred (IRE)**[31] 2043 3-8-12 0 AdamKirby 13 74
(J R Fanshawe) *in tch: hdwy over 3f out: wnt 4th over 2f out: styd on to take 3rd towards fin* 16/1
52 4 ¾ **Reality Show (IRE)**[16] 2497 3-8-5 0 AntiocoMurgia(7) 9 73
(Mahmood Al Zarooni) *led: hdd over 1f out: wknd fnl 150yds* 9/4[1]
5 2 ¼ **Royal Dalakhani (IRE)** 3-8-7 0 LiamJones 3 64+
(P W D'Arcy) *in tch: sn pushed along: outpcd over 2f out: kpt on fnl f* 20/1
00 6 7 **Anis Etoile**[38] 1847 5-9-8 0 IvaMilickova 8 53
(John Berry) *in rr: hdwy over 3f out: edgd rt: nvr a factor* 150/1
50 7 ¾ **Sleep Over**[36] 1932 5-9-8 0 PaulHanagan 2 52+
(D Morris) *trckd ldrs: effrt over 2f out: wknd 2f out* 33/1
8 15 **Fuzzypeg (IRE)** 3-8-7 0 EddieAhern 10 28
(J R Fanshawe) *in rr: last 4f out: kpt on fnl 2f: nvr on terms* 12/1
0 9 ¾ **Four Quartets (GER)**[54] 1450 4-9-13 0 FrannyNorton 15 32
(D Shaw) *in rr: hung rt thrght: nvr on terms* 100/1
0 10 ½ **Benamy Boy**[69] 1119 4-9-13 0 ChrisCatlin 5 31
(N Bycroft) *stdd s: hld up in rr: nvr on terms* 125/1
0-5 11 5 **Baibars (USA)**[16] 2507 3-8-12 0 (b) KierenFallon 4 23
(G A Butler) *chsd ldrs: rdn over 2f out: wknd 2f out* 6/1[2]
3533 12 nk **Ancient Times (USA)**[76] 1046 3-8-12 72 PaulMulrennan 14 23
(Joss Saville) *w ldrs: wknd qckly over 2f out* 16/1

05 **13** *7* **Sinatramania**[12] 2627 3-8-9 0 KellyHarrison(3) 6 11
(Miss Tracy Waggott) *mid-div: hdwy 7f out: lost pl over 2f out* **66/1**

000- **14** *26* **Little Buddy**[256] 6386 3-8-9 0 WilliamCarson(3) 1 —
(R J Price) *t.k.h in rr: sme hdwy over 4f out: wknd 3f out: sn bhd: t.o* **100/1**

15 *2 3/4* **Ebur Mac**[227] 6-9-13 0 PaulQuinn 7 —
(N Bycroft) *mid-div: wknd 5f out: sn bhd: t.o* **33/1**

2m 32.02s (-2.88) **Going Correction** -0.15s/f (Firm)
WFA 3 from 4yo+ 15lb **15** Ran SP% **122.0**
Speed ratings (Par 103): **104,101,100,100,98 94,93,83,83,82 79,79,74,57,55**
toteswingers: 1&2 £5.90, 1&3 £13.60, 2&3 £20.70 CSF £21.44 TOTE £3.50: £1.90, £2.00, £5.30; EX 23.80 Trifecta £313.60 Pool: £457.78 - 1.08 winning units..
Owner Sheikh Ahmed Al Maktoum **Bred** Darley **Trained** Newmarket, Suffolk

FOCUS
An average maiden.
Four Quartets(GER) Official explanation: jockey said gelding hung right throughout
Baibars(USA) Official explanation: jockey said colt had no more to give

2995 DONCASTERJOBSTODAY.CO.UK APPRENTICE H'CAP 1m 6f 132y
5:10 (5:10) (Class 5) (0-70,78) 4-Y-0+ **£2,590** (£770; £385; £192) **Stalls** Low

Form RPR

3-11 **1** **Tillietudlem (FR)**[18] 2430 4-8-4 **53** IanBrennan(3) 13 62+
(J S Goldie) *sn chsng ldrs: drvn 4f out: chal over 1f out: styd on to ld towards fin* **9/4**[1]

-531 **2** *1* **Silent Lucidity (IRE)**[17] 2464 6-8-5 **51** (p) WilliamCarson 9 59
(P D Niven) *trckd ldrs: led over 2f out: edgd lft: kpt on: hdd and no ex clsng stages* **6/1**

14-1 **3** *1 1/4* **Simple Jim (FR)**[13] 2610 6-8-11 **57** AndreaAtzeni 7 63+
(D O'Meara) *hld up in rr: gd hdwy and swtchd to outer 2f out: styd on strly to snatch clsng 3rd nr line* **11/2**[3]

2150 **4** *1* **Sir Sandicliffe (IRE)**[105] 748 6-8-2 **51** KierenFox(3) 4 56
(W M Brisbourne) *chsd ldrs: wnt 3rd over 1f out: kpt on same pce* **12/1**

0601 **5** *1 3/4* **Royal Premier (IRE)**[33] 2014 7-8-7 **56** SimonPearce(3) 12 59
(H J Collingridge) *in tch: drvn 7f out: sn outpcd: hdwy over 2f out: one pce* **20/1**

400- **6** *shd* **Favours Brave**[18] 6951 4-8-11 **60** LanceBetts(3) 2 63
(T D Easterby) *led 3f: chsd ldr: led over 3f out: hdd over 2f out: one pce* **20/1**

2211 **7** *2 1/2* **Tropical Bachelor (IRE)**[2] 2941 4-9-13 **78** 6ex JohnFahy(5) 6 77
(T J Pitt) *hld up in rr: hdwy over 3f out: chsng ldrs 2f out: fdd fnl 75yds* **5/1**[2]

243 **8** *3 1/2* **Amical Risks (FR)**[54] 1462 6-8-3 **54** (p) DavidKenny(5) 3 49
(Joss Saville) *s.s: in rr: hdwy 4f out: sn chsng ldrs: wknd jst ins fnl f* **11/1**

00 **9** *8* **Tinseltown**[24] 2244 4-8-6 **55** (b) PaulPickard(3) 5 39
(B S Rothwell) *in tch: rdn whn hmpd and swtchd rt 3f out: sn wknd* **33/1**

-000 **10** *10* **Spume (IRE)**[9] 2694 6-7-12 **51** oh6 (t) AndrewSmith(7) 11 22
(J Balding) *drvn to chse ldrs: led after 3f: hdd over 3f out: lost pl over 2f out* **100/1**

2012 **11** *2* **Red Wine**[36] 1916 11-9-2 **62** Louis-PhilippeBeuzelin 14 31
(J A Glover) *hld up in rr: hdwy on outer over 3f out: wknd over 1f out: sn eased* **8/1**

6065 **12** *10* **Mojeerr**[11] 2653 4-7-12 **51** oh3 (tp) NoraLooby(7) 8 —
(A J McCabe) *hld up in rr: hdwy on outer 7f out: wknd over 2f out: sn bhd and eased* **33/1**

000 **13** *47* **Sri Kuantan (IRE)**[22] 2343 6-8-9 **60** CharlesEddery(5) 1 —
(R C Guest) *chsd ldrs: swtchd rt 3f out: sn wknd: eased ins fnl f: virtually p.u: t.o* **50/1**

3m 8.07s (0.67) **Going Correction** -0.15s/f (Firm) **13** Ran SP% **122.6**
Speed ratings (Par 103): **90,89,88,88,87 87,85,84,79,74 73,68,43**
toteswingers: 1&2 £4.40, 1&3 £3.80, 2&3 £6.00 CSF £14.88 CT £70.04 TOTE £3.40: £1.40, £2.60, £2.10; EX 21.10 Trifecta £26.00 Pool: £364.52 - 10.34 winning units. Place 6 £56.26, Place 5 £41.67.
Owner Mr & Mrs C J Smith **Bred** Bernard Ducasse **Trained** Uplawmoor, E Renfrews

FOCUS
A very competitive handicap of its type with five last-time-out winners in attendance.
T/Jkpt: Not won. T/Plt: £96.70 to a £1 stake Pool: £90,224.95. 681.06 winning tickets. T/Qpdt: £53.80 to a £1 stake. Pool: £4,806.13. 66.07 winning tickets. WG

2839 SALISBURY (R-H)
Sunday, June 13

OFFICIAL GOING: Good to firm (9.1)
Far rail moved out 6yds over the final 6f.
Wind: Virtually nil Weather: Sunny and very warm

2996 ALBERT SAMUEL "CITY BOWL" H'CAP 1m 4f
2:00 (2:03) (Class 4) (0-85,84) 4-Y-0+ **£4,857** (£1,445; £722; £360) **Stalls** High

Form RPR

-003 **1** **Ouster (GER)**[16] 2506 4-9-4 **81** JimmyFortune 6 89
(D R C Elsworth) *hld up towards rr: hdwy over 2f out: rdn into narrow advantage wl over 1f out: styd on: hld on wl* **9/2**[3]

-512 **2** *1/2* **Feathered Crown (FR)**[16] 2506 4-9-5 **82** TomQueally 1 90
(H R A Cecil) *mid-div: hdwy to ld 2f out: sn rdn and narrowly hdd: styd pressing wnr: hld fnl 50yds* **5/2**[1]

3-04 **3** *2 1/4* **Wiggy Smith**[27] 2173 11-9-1 **78** DaneO'Neill 9 82
(H Candy) *hld up bhd: rdn whn swtchd to centre 3f out: hdwy sn after: styd on fnl f: wnt 3rd towards fin* **17/2**

0-50 **4** *hd* **Sequillo**[6] 2821 4-9-3 **80** RichardHughes 11 83
(R Hannon) *hld up bhd: swtchd lft and hdwy over 2f out: chsng ldrs whn swtchd rt over 1f out: drifted rt ent fnl f: kpt on same pce* **11/1**

65-0 **5** *nk* **Dakiyah (IRE)**[161] 25 6-9-5 **82** (p) IanMongan 3 85
(Mrs L J Mongan) *mid-div: hdwy to hold ev ch u.p 2f out: kpt on same pce* **33/1**

-121 **6** *1 1/2* **Penang Cinta**[17] 2455 7-8-7 **73** AndrewHeffernan(3) 2 73
(P D Evans) *led for 1f: trckd ldrs: rdn over 2f out: one pce after* **16/1**

0-06 **7** *nk* **Dove Cottage (IRE)**[19] 2411 8-8-5 **68** FrankieMcDonald 10 68
(W S Kittow) *led after 1f: rdn and hdd 2f out: sn one pce* **40/1**

3-22 **8** *2 1/2* **Mabuya (UAE)**[23] 2282 4-9-7 **84** (b[1]) SebSanders 8 80
(P J Makin) *racd keenly: trckd ldrs: ch whn rdn over 2f out: fading whn short of room on rails ent fnl f* **7/2**[2]

3-44 **9** *1* **Akbabend**[8] 2739 4-9-5 **82** RobertWinston 7 76
(M Johnston) *trckd ldr: rdn and ev ch 2f out: wknd over 1f out* **13/2**

/00- **10** *3 1/4* **Novikov**[100] 6633 6-9-1 **83** (t) RichardEvans(5) 4 72
(P D Evans) *mid-div: rdn and no imp whn nt clr run on rails over 1f out: fdd* **33/1**

2m 35.19s (-2.81) **Going Correction** -0.10s/f (Good) **10** Ran SP% **115.4**
Speed ratings (Par 105): **105,104,103,103,102 101,101,99,99,97**
toteswingers: 1&2 £3.70, 1&3 £8.50, 2&3 £5.90 CSF £15.72 CT £91.60 TOTE £6.90: £2.30, £1.10, £3.20; EX 17.10.
Owner Raymond Tooth **Bred** Newsells Park Stud Ltd **Trained** Newmarket, Suffolk

FOCUS
The far rail was out 18ft over the final 6f because the area was cut up by the 95 runners at Tuesday's meeting. No rain since that meeting meant that the course was watered with 4mm on Saturday, but the going was still described as good to firm, and drying out. The early pace wasn't that strong here and a few pulled for their heads early.
Ouster(GER) Official explanation: trainer said colt ran without tongue strap that had come adrift and could not be re-fitted

2997 PICADOR CHEVROLET H'CAP 5f
2:30 (2:31) (Class 4) (0-85,88) 3-Y-0+ **£4,857** (£1,445; £722; £360) **Stalls** Centre

Form RPR

21-0 **1** **Present Alchemy**[10] 2681 4-9-9 **80** (t) SteveDrowne 3 95+
(H Morrison) *in tch: hdwy 2f out: sn rdn: led ent fnl f: r.o wl* **3/1**[1]

-310 **2** *2* **Solemn**[10] 2681 5-9-9 **80** (b) LiamKeniry 5 88
(J M Bradley) *trckd ldrs: rdn over 2f out: kpt on fnl f: wnt 2nd nr fin: no ch w wnr* **11/2**[2]

0-30 **3** *nk* **Russian Spirit**[31] 2054 4-9-12 **83** PhilipRobinson 8 90
(M A Jarvis) *prom: rdn to ld wl over 1f out: hdd ent fnl f: no ex: lost 2nd nr fin* **6/1**[3]

6530 **4** *1* **Ocean Blaze**[30] 2094 6-9-9 **80** TomQueally 9 83
(B R Millman) *prom: rdn and ev ch over 1f out: no ex ins fnl f* **12/1**

-006 **5** *nse* **Macdillon**[10] 2681 4-9-11 **82** (b[1]) IanMongan 4 85
(W S Kittow) *s.i.s: sn pushed along in rr: rdn 3f out: kpt on fnl f: nrst fin* **12/1**

4-02 **6** *1/2* **Rapid Water**[24] 2247 4-9-9 **80** JimmyFortune 6 81
(A M Balding) *trckd ldrs: rdn over 2f out: kpt on same pce fnl f* **3/1**[1]

0-00 **7** *2 3/4* **Mythical Blue (IRE)**[23] 2280 4-9-3 **74** JimCrowley 11 65
(J M Bradley) *led: rdn and hdd wl over 1f out: fdd ent fnl f* **20/1**

05-1 **8** *6* **Palisades Park**[10] 2681 3-9-10 **88** RichardHughes 10 55+
(R Hannon) *hld up: nt best of runs fr over 1f out: eased whn no ch ins fnl f* **11/2**[2]

59.92 secs (-1.08) **Going Correction** -0.10s/f (Good)
WFA 3 from 4yo+ 7lb **8** Ran SP% **115.2**
Speed ratings (Par 105): **104,100,100,98,98 97,93,83**
toteswingers: 1&2 £4.90, 1&3 £6.10, 2&3 £6.60 CSF £19.99 CT £93.40 TOTE £4.00: £1.10, £2.00, £3.20; EX 26.60.
Owner Normandie Stud Ltd **Bred** Normandie Stud Ltd **Trained** East Ilsley, Berks

FOCUS
Four of these took each other on at Sandown ten days earlier but the form was turned around here.
Palisades Park Official explanation: jockey said colt lost its action

2998 BETFAIR MAIDEN FILLIES' STKS 1m
3:05 (3:05) (Class 5) 3-Y-O **£3,885** (£1,156; £577; £288) **Stalls** High

Form RPR

-62 **1** **Frances Stuart (IRE)**[17] 2478 3-9-0 0 JimmyFortune 8 78+
(A M Balding) *mde all: styd on strly to assert fnl f: rdn out* **8/1**[3]

-436 **2** *3 1/4* **Easy Terms**[9] 2718 3-8-11 72 JamesMillman(3) 10 71
(B R Millman) *trckd ldrs disputing 2nd: rdn over 2f out: a being hld but kpt on for clr 2nd ins fnl f* **13/2**[2]

0-5 **3** *1* **Treasure Way**[27] 2180 3-9-0 0 LiamKeniry 1 69
(P R Chamings) *trckd wnr disputing 2nd: rdn over 2f out: kpt on but no ex fnl f* **12/1**

4 *1* **Egmarey (IRE)** 3-9-0 0 TedDurcan 6 70+
(D R Lanigan) *hld up towards rr: hdwy whn nt clr run on rails wl over 1f out: swtchd lft whn nt clr run again jst ins fnl f: r.o: nrst fin: promising* **28/1**

5 *1/2* **Akhmatova** 3-9-0 0 TomQueally 14 65+
(G A Butler) *s.i.s: towards rr: hdwy 2f out: keeping on whn nt clr run briefly ins fnl f: promising* **14/1**

3 **6** *1 1/2* **Madonna Dell'Orto**[27] 2180 3-9-0 0 ShaneKelly 4 62
(W R Swinburn) *in tch: rdn over 2f out: kpt on same pce* **2/1**[1]

03 **7** *nse* **Queen's Scholar (USA)**[11] 2658 3-9-0 0 RobertWinston 12 62
(M Johnston) *trckd wnr disputing 2nd: rdn over 2f out: fdd fnl f* **8/1**[3]

8 *1 1/2* **Lady Berta** 3-9-0 0 RichardHughes 9 58+
(R Hannon) *swtchd lft over 1f out: nvr bttr than mid-div* **8/1**[3]

0-5 **9** *1/2* **Romancea (USA)**[9] 2718 3-9-0 0 DaneO'Neill 13 57
(E F Vaughan) *in tch: rdn over 2f out: wknd fnl f* **13/2**[2]

10 *2 3/4* **Converre** 3-9-0 0 JackMitchell 5 51
(G A Butler) *rdn 3f out: a towards rr* **66/1**

11 *1/2* **Fleeting Glance (IRE)** 3-9-0 0 TadhgO'Shea 7 50+
(B J Meehan) *racd keenly: hld up: hdwy over 3f out: rdn to chse ldrs in centre over 2f out: lost action and eased over 1f out* **20/1**

0-56 **12** *29* **Patachou**[103] 760 3-9-0 48 (v) SebSanders 11 —
(R J Smith) *a towards rr: t.o fr over 1f out* **100/1**

000- **13** *nk* **Khazara**[235] 6930 3-9-0 39 RobertHavlin 3 —
(A King) *nvr bttr than mid-div: wknd over 2f out: t.o* **80/1**

1m 41.84s (-1.66) **Going Correction** -0.10s/f (Good) **13** Ran SP% **119.6**
Speed ratings (Par 96): **104,100,99,98,98 96,96,95,94,91 91,62,62**
toteswingers: 1&2 £5.80, 1&3 £19.10, 2&3 £14.30 CSF £57.40 TOTE £5.50: £1.60, £2.10, £6.20; EX 60.80.
Owner Lowther Racing **Bred** D G Hardisty Bloodstock **Trained** Kingsclere, Hants

FOCUS
Not many got into this.
Fleeting Glance(IRE) Official explanation: jockey said filly hung left

2999 BATHWICK TYRES CATHEDRAL STKS (LISTED RACE) 6f
3:40 (3:40) (Class 1) 3-Y-0+
£22,708 (£8,608; £4,308; £2,148; £1,076; £540) **Stalls** High

Form RPR

0002 **1** **Sir Gerry (USA)**[20] 2400 5-9-4 105 RobertWinston 5 110+
(J R Best) *in tch but towards rr of gp: rdn whn c wd w str run ent fnl f: drifted sltly rt nring fin: led cl home* **17/2**

2536 **2** *nk* **Elnawin**[15] 2536 4-9-4 103 DaneO'Neill 4 109
(R Hannon) *trckd ldrs: rdn into narrow advantage jst over 2f out: sn hrd pressed: kpt on gamely: hdd fnl strides* **9/1**

0-14 **3** *nse* **Angel's Pursuit (IRE)**[15] 2537 3-9-0 109 RichardHughes 6 111
(R Hannon) *a.p: rdn to press ldr and ev ch fr over 2f out: drifted lft but upsides thrght fnl f: kpt on* **5/1**[3]

15-0 **4** *shd* **Jimmy Styles**[22] 2353 6-9-4 105.................................(p) PhilipRobinson 7 109
(C G Cox) *in tch: rdn to chse ldrs over 2f out: kpt on wl w wnr ins fnl f* **6/1**

100- **5** *3/4* **Palace Moon**[246] 6661 5-9-4 105....................................(t) SteveDrowne 9 109+
(H Morrison) *rrd leaving stalls: in tch but towards rr of gp: nt clr run over 2f out: hdwy wl over 1f out: mounting chal whn squeezed out and snatched up ent fnl f: kpt on but no ch after* **9/4**[1]

1103 **6** *3/4* **Sirocco Breeze**[22] 2344 5-9-4 110.. TedDurcan 2 106+
(Saeed Bin Suroor) *taken down early: hld up: hdwy 3f out: rdn to chse ldrs 2f out: keeping on same pce but hld in 6th whn squeezed out nr fin* **4/1**[2]

000- **7** *3 3/4* **Knot In Wood (IRE)**[222] 7232 8-9-4 108......................... TonyHamilton 8 92
(R A Fahey) *trckd ldrs: rdn over 2f out: wknd ins fnl f* **16/1**

1603 **8** *3/4* **Judd Street**[15] 2536 8-9-4 104..(v) TomQueally 1 89
(Eve Johnson Houghton) *in tch: tk clsr order 3f out: rdn to chal 2f out: wknd fnl f* **14/1**

12-0 **9** *1 3/4* **Kalypso King (USA)**[25] 2226 3-8-10 101................ FrankieMcDonald 10 82
(R Hannon) *led tl rdn over 2f out: wknd fnl f* **33/1**

1m 12.55s (-2.25) **Going Correction** -0.10s/f (Good)
WFA 3 from 4yo+ 8lb **9** Ran SP% **117.7**
Speed ratings (Par 111): **111,110,110,110,109 108,103,102,100**
toteswingers: 1&2 £14.20, 1&3 £10.00, 2&3 £6.80 CSF £83.49 TOTE £9.00: £2.30, £4.10, £3.20; EX 87.70.
Owner Mrs Gerry Galligan **Bred** Dr Catherine Wills **Trained** Hucking, Kent

FOCUS
A competitive Listed sprint on paper and in reality too, as four crossed the line close together.

NOTEBOOK
Sir Gerry(USA) likes to challenge from way back so this stiff finish was always going to suit him better than Windsor, where he ran surprisingly well off a fairly modest gallop last time. He is clearly returning to form now and, while the Golden Jubilee, his intended target at Royal Ascot this week, will be a big step up in class for him, he does at least have previous, in that he finished third in the race in 2008, and form figures of 1333 at Ascot confirm his liking for the venue. (op 11-1 tchd 12-1)
Elnawin ran a sound race here but has looked a difficult horse to place over the past two seasons, and that's unlikely to change soon. (op 10-1)
Angel's Pursuit(IRE) was saddled with a 4lb penalty for his win on his reappearance, but the ground suited him better than at Haydock last time, where it had turned too soft. He did well to be in the mix at the finish considering he was plenty keen enough early, and a more patient ride, like he received at Newbury, will suit him in future. Official explanation: two-day ban: careless riding (Jun 27-28) (tchd 6-1 in places)
Jimmy Styles, who could have settled better through the early stages, shaped with a good deal more promise than on his reappearance at the Curragh. He won the Ayr Gold Cup last year having run just eight days earlier so it wouldn't be a surprise to see him turn out for the Wokingham at Royal Ascot. (op 8-1 tchd 10-1)
Palace Moon, who had a tongue tie on for the first time, fly-jumped as the stalls opened and was tightened up for room when being brought with a challenge between Angel's Pursuit and Elnawin a furlong out. In the circumstances it was a perfectly acceptable reappearance run and he should be able to build on it. Official explanation: jockey said gelding was denied a clear run (op 11-4 tchd 3-1 in a place)
Sirocco Breeze, given a patient ride out the back, briefly threatened down the outside before his effort flattened out. His four previous wins have come over 7f and he might need to return to that distance to be seen at his best. (tchd 9-2 in places)
Knot In Wood(IRE) probably just needed this to blow the cobwebs away. He is another who has proved he can win following a short break though, so he too might well turn up in the Wokingham on Saturday. (op 12-1)
Judd Street won this race last year but, having raced keenly towards the outer, he had little energy left for the final 2f. (op 10-1 tchd 9-1)

3000 BRIDGET SWIRE MEMORIAL MAIDEN STKS 6f
4:15 (4:15) (Class 2) 2-Y-O **£7,771** (£2,312; £1,155; £577) **Stalls** High

Form RPR

54 **1** **Major Conquest (IRE)**[13] 2594 2-9-3 0.......................... SebSanders 10 80
(J W Hills) *trckd ldr: rdn over 2f out: led jst ins fnl f: kpt on: rdn out* **3/1**[2]

2 *3/4* **Jaahiz (IRE)** 2-9-3 0.. JimmyFortune 9 78+
(R Hannon) *wnt rt s: mid-div: rdn 2f out: clsd on ldrs enterig fnl f: r.o wl: wnt 2nd nr fin* **12/1**

3 *1* **Florestans Match** 2-8-12 0.. JimCrowley 2 70+
(R M Beckett) *trckd ldrs: led jst over 1f out: rdn whn drifted lft sn after and hdd: no ex* **10/1**

52 **4** *2 3/4* **Arabian Star (IRE)**[9] 2715 2-9-3 0....................................... AlanMunro 5 67
(M R Channon) *trckd ldrs: rdn over 2f out: kpt on but nt pce to mount chal* **2/1**[1]

0 **5** *1/2* **Dubai Affair**[12] 2616 2-8-12 0.. SteveDrowne 1 60
(H Morrison) *led: sn swtchd to far side rails: rdn 2f out: hdd jst over 1f out: swtchd lft whn hld sn after: no ex* **20/1**

6 *3 3/4* **El Mansour (USA)** 2-9-3 0.. PhilipRobinson 8 54
(C G Cox) *chsd ldrs tl outpcd 3f out: nvr bk on terms* **7/1**

7 *2 1/4* **Aldwick Bay (IRE)** 2-9-3 0.. RichardHughes 12 47
(R Hannon) *little slowly away: mainly towards rr: nvr on terms* **13/2**[3]

00 **8** *3/4* **Torteval (IRE)**[26] 2216 2-9-3 0.. ShaneKelly 6 45
(P D Evans) *mid-div tl wknd 2f out* **66/1**

9 *1 1/4* **Futurism** 2-9-3 0.. FrankieMcDonald 4 43+
(R Hannon) *a towards rr* **40/1**

0 **10** *nse* **Cold Secret**[11] 2638 2-9-3 0.. DaneO'Neill 7 41+
(D R C Elsworth) *mid-div tl outpcd 3f out* **12/1**

11 *1/2* **Madame Kintyre** 2-8-12 0.. JamesMillman 3 34
(B R Millman) *chsd ldrs tl wandered and wknd fr 2f out* **33/1**

12 *4 1/2* **Alshazah** 2-9-3 0.. TomQueally 11 26
(B R Millman) *s.i.s: a struggling in rr* **25/1**

1m 14.56s (-0.24) **Going Correction** -0.10s/f (Good) **12** Ran SP% **124.1**
Speed ratings (Par 99): **97,96,94,91,90 85,82,81,79,79 78,72**
toteswingers: 1&2 £14.50, 1&3 £9.50, 2&3 £18.00 CSF £38.62 TOTE £5.20: £1.70, £3.50, £3.40; EX 54.90.
Owner T J W Ellis **Bred** Deer Forest Stud **Trained** Upper Lambourn, Berks

FOCUS
A modest maiden in which the winner is rated a fractional improver while the placed horses can do better.

NOTEBOOK
Major Conquest(IRE), following on from Formosina's runaway win at Doncaster earlier in the day, provided another timely boost to the form of Coventry Stakes favourite Strong Suit. Fifth, but beaten over 15l by Richard Hannon's colt at Newbury, he improved on that to finish a close fourth at Goodwood second time out. Apparently he's been a bit of a handful at home but this proved his easiest task to date and he got the job done in professional style. He could be a nice nursery type. (op 4-1)
Jaahiz(IRE), a half-brother to six winners including Cherry Hinton winner Applaud, got outpaced mid-race before finishing really strongly once switched to the outside. This was a promising debut and he wouldn't need to find too much improvement to win something similar. (tchd 11-1)
Florestans Match is a half-sister to three maidens but she showed enough on her debut to suggest she can buck the family trend. She looked the most likely winner heading to the 2f pole, but was just outstayed in the end. (op 14-1 tchd 16-1)
Arabian Star(IRE) raced prominently for most of the way. He has stamina on his dam's side and might be suited by further once switched to nurseries. (tchd 9-4)
Dubai Affair showed a good deal more than on her debut over 5f at Leciester. A half-sister to the stable's 3-y-o filly Queen's Grace, this stiff 6f seemed to stretch her stamina. (op 25-1)
El Mansour(USA) showed signs of greenness and is entitled to improve for the experience. (op 13-2)
Aldwick Bay(IRE), seemingly the stable's first string based on jockey bookings, failed to land a blow but wasn't given a hard race. He's bred to appreciate further than this. (op 6-1 tchd 7-1)
Futurism was very green through the early stages, struggling to keep in touch with the pack, but he was just beginning to stay on when hampered by the hanging El Mansour, and his rider took things pretty easy afterwards. Official explanation: jockey said colt suffered interference in running (op 50-1)
Madame Kintyre Official explanation: jockey said filly had no more to give

3001 WATERAID MILDREN CONSTRUCTION FILLIES' H'CAP 6f 212y
4:45 (4:47) (Class 5) (0-75,78) 3-Y-O+ **£3,238** (£963; £481; £240) **Stalls** Centre

Form RPR

1 **1** **Moretta Blanche**[29] 2121 3-10-0 78...................................... JimCrowley 5 85+
(R M Beckett) *confidently rdn: hld up: smooth prog whn swtchd lft 2f out: shkn up to ld ent fnl f: r.o: readily* **13/8**[1]

-305 **2** *3/4* **Steel Free (IRE)**[8] 2750 4-9-13 67..................................... RobertHavlin 9 74
(M Madgwick) *trckd ldr: rdn and ev ch 2f out tl ent fnl f: kpt on but nt pce of wnr* **10/1**

0-06 **3** *1/2* **Cat Hunter**[4] 2871 3-9-3 67... TedDurcan 1 68
(Mrs A J Perrett) *hld up: rdn and hdwy 2f out: styd on ins fnl f: wnt 3rd fnl strides* **16/1**

-001 **4** *shd* **Ken's Girl**[22] 2342 6-10-0 68... IanMongan 3 73
(W S Kittow) *led: rdn 2f out: hdd ent fnl f: no ex* **11/1**

0665 **5** *2 1/4* **Perfect Friend**[13] 2601 4-10-0 68................................... JimmyFortune 7 67
(S Kirk) *in tch: rdn over 2f out: kpt on same pce fnl f* **7/1**[3]

0-0 **6** *1 1/4* **Les Yeux Bleus (IRE)**[29] 2110 3-9-11 75.................. KirstyMilczarek 12 67
(L M Cumani) *trckd ldrs: rdn and ch whn hung lft 2f out: one pce after* **20/1**

30-0 **7** *nk* **Ashkalara**[13] 2587 3-8-10 60.. TomQueally 6 51
(H S Howe) *in tch: rdn over 2f out: one pce after: fdd fnl 100yds* **10/1**

-602 **8** *nk* **Excellent Day (IRE)**[16] 2502 3-9-11 75............................... AlanMunro 4 65
(M R Channon) *trckd ldrs: rdn and ev ch 2f out: fdd fnl f* **8/1**

1- **9** *79* **Marrayah**[300] 5109 3-9-8 72... TadhgO'Shea 2 —
(M A Jarvis) *hld up in tch tl lost action 2f out: virtually p.u* **7/2**[2]

1m 27.57s (-1.43) **Going Correction** -0.10s/f (Good)
WFA 3 from 4yo+ 10lb **9** Ran SP% **121.1**
Speed ratings (Par 100): **104,103,102,102,99 98,98,97,7**
toteswingers: 1&2 £8.00, 1&3 £11.20, 2&3 £18.50 CSF £20.80 CT £206.78 TOTE £2.60: £1.10, £5.40, £5.40; EX 34.70.
Owner P K Gardner **Bred** Springcombe Park Stud **Trained** Whitsbury, Hants

FOCUS
This didn't look a strong race and it looked open to one of the unexposed fillies in the line-up to take advantage on their handicap debuts.
Marrayah Official explanation: jockey said filly lost its action

3002 BATHWICK TYRES RACING EXCELLENCE "HANDS AND HEELS" APPRENTICE SERIES H'CAP 1m
5:20 (5:21) (Class 6) (0-65,65) 3-Y-O **£2,914** (£867; £433; £216) **Stalls** High

Form RPR

0-61 **1** **Rock The Stars (IRE)**[12] 2633 3-9-3 62............................. HollyHall(3) 8 72
(J W Hills) *confidently rdn in last: stdy prog in centre fr over 2f out: led ins fnl f: won gng away: comf* **3/1**[1]

5060 **2** *2 1/4* **Orsett Lad (USA)**[22] 2321 3-8-8 55...................................... IanBurns(5) 5 60
(J R Best) *hld up in last pair: hdwy over 3f out: rdn and ev ch ins fnl f: kpt on to go clr 2nd but no ch w wnr* **14/1**

5604 **3** *1 1/4* **Singingintherain (IRE)**[26] 2200 3-9-0 56.............. MatthewCosham 1 58
(R A Mills) *led: rdn over 2f out: hdd ins fnl f: no ex* **20/1**

0-04 **4** *2 1/4* **Fire Raiser**[17] 2480 3-8-10 60.................................... ThomasBrown(8) 3 57
(A M Balding) *sn trcking ldrs: rdn wl over 2f out: kpt on same pce fnl f* **15/2**

005- **5** *nk* **State Visit**[232] 7024 3-9-4 63..................................(b) JamesRogers(3) 14 59
(W R Muir) *trckd ldrs: rdn wl over 2f out: kpt on same pce* **16/1**

5506 **6** *3/4* **Highland Cadett**[12] 2620 3-9-1 57..................................... SoniaEaton 11 51
(B R Millman) *hld up towards rr: sme late hdwy: nvr a factor* **8/1**

3245 **7** *1 1/2* **Chinese Democracy (USA)**[13] 2588 3-8-5 55........... KevinLundie(8) 10 46
(P D Evans) *awkward leaving stalls: towards rr: hdwy 3f out: sn rdn: no further imp* **6/1**[3]

5103 **8** *1/2* **Kathindi (IRE)**[62] 1264 3-9-6 65.................................... RyanPowell(3) 6 55
(J S Moore) *in tch: rdn over 2f out: fdd fnl f* **16/1**

06-5 **9** *1 3/4* **Fever Tree**[47] 1589 3-9-3 59... MJMurphy 7 45
(P J Makin) *nvr bttr than mid-div: wknd fnl f* **16/1**

-450 **10** *hd* **Lucky Diva**[17] 2480 3-9-0 56.. RichardRowe 13 41
(S Kirk) *trckd ldrs: rdn wl over 2f out: wknd ent fnl f* **28/1**

6-15 **11** *1* **Cool Kitten (IRE)**[21] 2359 3-9-0 56..................................... HarryBentley 12 39
(W J Knight) *a towards rr* **9/2**[2]

604 **12** *19* **Pennfield Pirate**[23] 2279 3-9-2 58...................................(v) BarryAdams 2 —
(H Morrison) *s.i.s: sn in mid-div: rdn 4f out: sn btn* **12/1**

00-0 **13** *2 3/4* **Jinksy Minx**[13] 2585 3-8-4 46 oh1... JakePayne 4 —
(Miss Suzy Smith) *chsd ldrs for over 4f: sn bhd* **50/1**

1m 42.46s (-1.04) **Going Correction** -0.10s/f (Good) **13** Ran SP% **122.5**
Speed ratings (Par 97): **101,98,97,95,94 94,92,92,90,90 89,70,67**
toteswingers: 1&2 £15.20, 1&3 £16.90, 2&3 £39.30 CSF £48.26 CT £766.21 TOTE £3.90: £2.00, £4.60, £4.80; EX 46.70 Place 6 £193.03, Place 5 £116.08.
Owner David Cohen **Bred** Bernard Cooke **Trained** Upper Lambourn, Berks
■ Stewards' Enquiry : Ryan Powell three-day ban: careless riding (tbn)

FOCUS
A modest race for apprentices run at a solid gallop.
Pennfield Pirate Official explanation: jockey said gelding was slowly away and never travelled
T/Plt: £366.20 to a £1 stake. Pool: £53,534.63. 106.70 winning tickets. T/Qpdt: £94.10 to a £1 stake Pool: £3,159.40. 24.84 winning tickets. TM

3003 - 3006a (Foreign Racing) - See Raceform Interactive

1674 CORK (R-H)

Sunday, June 13

OFFICIAL GOING: Good to firm

3007a KERRY GROUP NOBLESSE STKS (GROUP 3) (F&M) 1m 4f

4:50 (4:50) 3-Y-0+ **£48,893** (£14,292; £6,769; £2,256)

RPR

1 **Grace O'Malley (IRE)**[32] 2037 4-9-12 100 PJSmullen 2 101
(D K Weld, Ire) mde virtually all: jnd and strly pressed fr over 2f out: kpt on wl fnl f: all out to ld again on line **7/2**[3]

2 *shd* **Karasiyra (IRE)**[42] 1741 3-8-10 91 ow1 FMBerry 4 99+
(John M Oxx, Ire) chsd ldr in 2nd: rdn to dispute ld over 2f out: kpt on wl fnl f: hdd on line **3/1**[2]

3 *nk* **Unity (IRE)**[11] 2666 3-8-10 99 ow1 (p) JMurtagh 6 99+
(David Wachman, Ire) chsd ldrs in 4th: rdn in cl 3rd 2f out: disp ld briefly 1f out: kpt on wl fnl f: no ex cl home **2/1**[1]

4 *4* **She's Our Mark**[32] 2037 6-9-12 106 DMGrant 3 94+
(Patrick J Flynn, Ire) hld up in 5th: rdn in mod 5th 2 1/2f out: kpt on one pce over 1f out **5/1**

5 *nk* **Lady Lupus (IRE)**[32] 2037 3-8-9 94 (p) JPO'Brien 5 91
(A P O'Brien, Ire) chsd ldrs in 3rd: rdn in 4th 2 1/2f out: swtchd and drifted lft under 2f out: no ex fnl f **12/1**

6 *1 3/4* **Indiana Gal (IRE)**[22] 2355 5-9-9 99 (p) CDHayes 1 87+
(Patrick Martin, Ire) hld up in last: rdn and no imp st **7/1**

2m 35.7s (-12.20)
WFA 3 from 4yo+ 15lb **6** Ran SP% **117.4**
CSF £15.23 TOTE £4.20: £2.10, £2.10; DF 20.70.
Owner Mrs C L Weld **Bred** Hawthorn Villa Stud **Trained** The Curragh, Co Kildare

FOCUS
The first two were prominent throughout and the race has been rated through the winner and third to their best.

NOTEBOOK
Grace O'Malley(IRE) repeated last year's victory in this race in tremendously game fashion. Setting out to make all at an even pace, she had the inside rail and used it to her full advantage in the straight when challenged fiercely by her two main rivals. Whether she was headed or not is hard to say, but if she was it was only very briefly and her reserves of courage were fully tested. The trip and good ground would seem to be the key and she may go now to the Lancashire Oaks. She's in foal to Shamardal and it looks as though her racing career is approaching its end.
Karasiyra(IRE), carrying 1lb overweight, tracked the winner and was ridden up to dispute early in the straight, and in fairness to her she certainly didn't shirk the issue inside the last furlong and a half. She saw out the trip admirably and it wouldn't be a surprise to see her take her chance in the Irish Oaks. (op 4/1)
Unity(IRE), carrying 1lb overweight, had her resolution questioned before she won a maiden at Fairyhouse just over a week ago and it will probably be questioned again after this. Racing just behind the lead, she moved up on the outside of the two leaders to challenge and look the likely winner at that point, but as soon as she got there she couldn't or wouldn't go past. It may not be fair to judge her resolution on that as the winner is undoubtedly tough, but questions do remain. (op 5/2)
She's Our Mark was ridden to get the trip but didn't pick up when asked to race early in the straight, and in the end just kept on at one pace. (op 7/2)
Lady Lupus(IRE) drifted left in the straight having travelled well to the turn-in. She wasn't good enough anyway. (op 10/1)
Indiana Gal(IRE) briefly looked like getting into the race early in the straight before weakening. Official explanation: trainer said mare was found to be in season post-race

3008 - 3013a (Foreign Racing) - See Raceform Interactive

2800 CHANTILLY (R-H)

Sunday, June 13

OFFICIAL GOING: Turf: soft

3014a PRIX DU LYS (GROUP 3) (3YO COLTS & GELDINGS) (TURF) 1m 4f

1:35 (12:00) 3-Y-0 **£35,398** (£14,159; £10,619; £7,079; £3,539)

RPR

1 **Goldwaki (GER)**[40] 1818 3-8-11 0 OlivierPeslier 3 109
(A Fabre, France) bkmarker fr s: swtchd wd in st: rdn 1 1/2f out: qckd wl: grabbed ld 100yds out: r.o wl **6/4**[1]

2 *1* **Mashoor (FR)**[33] 3-8-11 0 MaximeGuyon 6 107
(A Fabre, France) racd in 4th fr s: hld that position into st: rdn 2f out: qcknd wl: grabbed ld 1f out: hdd 100yds out: r.o wl **3/1**[2]

3 *2 1/2* **Le Larron (IRE)**[13] 3-8-11 0 GeraldMosse 1 103
(A De Royer-Dupre, France) racd in 2nd fr s: 3rd into st: grabbed ld briefly 1 1/2f out: outpcd: styd on wl fnl f **9/2**

4 *1* **Prizefighting (USA)**[25] 2226 3-8-11 0 WilliamBuick 5 102
(J H M Gosden) racd in 5th: rdn early in st on rail: fnd no room to chal: swtchd to wd outside: qcknd wl but too late: fin wl **4/1**[3]

5 *1* **Lamool (GER)**[20] 2406 3-8-11 0 DominiqueBoeuf 4 100
(Mario Hofer, Germany) led fr s and stl in front 1 1/2f out: rdn and hdd 1f out: fdd **20/1**

6 *3* **Into Wain (USA)**[29] 2125 3-8-11 0 MartinDwyer 2 95
(D M Simcock) cl up bhd ldrs fr s: wnt 2nd early in st: rdn 2f out: no ex: fdd **20/1**

2m 31.4s (0.40) **Going Correction** +0.20s/f (Good) **6** Ran SP% **112.7**
Speed ratings: **106,105,103,103,102 100**
WIN (incl. 1 euro stake): 1.80. PLACES: 1.30, 1.40. SF: 4.00.
Owner Wertheimer & Frere **Bred** Wertheimer & Frere **Trained** Chantilly, France

NOTEBOOK
Goldwaki(GER) ran out a cosy winner and extended his unbeaten record. Effective on all sorts of ground, he will be supplemented into the Group 1 Grand Prix de Paris on July 14 next.
Prizefighting(USA), beaten in Listed company on his last two starts, could only stay on one-paced and wasn't up to it in this company. He's likely to remain difficult to place.
Into Wain(USA) is rated 83 and was predictably outclassed in this grade.

3015a PRIX DE DIANE (GROUP 1) (3YO FILLIES) (TURF) 1m 2f 110y

3:04 (12:00) 3-Y-0 **£404,530** (£161,840; £80,920; £40,424; £20,247)

RPR

1 **Sarafina (FR)**[21] 2373 3-9-0 0 Christophe-PatriceLemaire 7 118+
(A De Royer-Dupre, France) settled in 6th: tk clsr order st: chal on outside to ld appr fnl f: r.o wl **5/4**[1]

2 *1 1/2* **Rosanara (FR)**[28] 2158 3-9-0 0 GeraldMosse 3 114
(A De Royer-Dupre, France) racd in 7th: moved clsr ins fnl 2f: swtchd outside horses 350yds out: styd on u.p to take 2nd fnl 110yds **4/1**[2]

3 *1 1/2* **Sandbar**[36] 1946 3-9-0 0 OlivierPeslier 5 111
(F Rohaut, France) racd in 8th: rdn to make hdwy 2f out: wnt 3rd 1 1/2f out: kpt on u.p **6/1**

4 *1 1/2* **Deluxe (USA)**[21] 2373 3-9-0 0 (p) MaximeGuyon 2 108+
(A Fabre, France) racd in 5th: on heels of ldng trio st: u.p whn bmpd 1 1/2f out: kpt on at one pce **5/1**[3]

5 *1* **Zagora (FR)**[42] 1746 3-9-0 0 ChristopheSoumillon 1 106
(J-C Rouget, France) racd in 4th: rdn to ld ins fnl 2f: hdd appr fnl f: wknd and lost 4th ins fnl 100yds **13/2**

6 *6* **A Media Luz (FR)**[36] 1946 3-9-0 0 ThierryThulliez 4 95
(Y Fouin, France) plld early: swapped 2nd and 3rd pls tl 2nd and ev ch st: sn rdn and wknd: btn whn bmpd 1 1/2f out **40/1**

7 *2 1/2* **Valasyra (FR)**[13] 3-9-0 0 ThierryJarnet 6 90
(A De Royer-Dupre, France) led tl hdd & wknd ins fnl 2f **100/1**

8 *10* **Heaven's Vault (IRE)**[36] 1946 3-9-0 0 IoritzMendizabal 9 71
(Robert Collet, France) nvr in contention **33/1**

9 *20* **Bridge Of Peace**[24] 3-9-0 0 Jean-BernardEyquem 8 33
(J-Y Artu, France) swapped 2nd and 3rd pls tl grad fdd fr 3f out **100/1**

2m 7.80s (-1.00) **Going Correction** +0.20s/f (Good) **9** Ran SP% **116.1**
Speed ratings: **111,109,108,107,107 102,100,93,79**
PARI-MUTUEL (all including 1 euro stakes): WIN 1.70 (combined with Rosanara and Valasyra); PLACE 1.10, 1.70, 1.50; DF 7.80; SF 8.10.
Owner H H Aga Khan **Bred** H H Aga Khan **Trained** Chantilly, France

FOCUS
With recent winners including the likes of Egyptband, Aquarelliste, Nebaraska Tornado, Divine Proportions and the great Zarkava two years ago, there is no doubt that the fortunes of the Prix de Diane have been reversed over the last ten years. While only two of the dozen who went to post came into this race with Group 1 wins under their belt, the profile of the winning filly is often of one who will go on to better things.

NOTEBOOK
Sarafina(FR), representing the same connections as Zarkava, pulled hard in the early stages, despite the presence of a pacemaker. Settled towards the rear before making headway from three out, she showed she was without doubt the best in the race as she won by a length and a half. There were, however, signs of greenness in her effort down the home straight, as she switched her lead leg at least once. It is important to remember that this was only her third start (Zarkava was having her fifth in this two years ago) but she is already a dual Group 1 winner. With that in mind it is probably fairly safe to suggest we have not seen the best of her yet. She has an entry in the Irish Oaks but is unlikely to take that up due to fears that 1m4f may be too far for her. The Prix Jean Romanet at Deauville and then the Prix de l'Opera look likely targets for later in the year. If her progression continues she will take all the beating in those.
Rosanara(FR) was following a similar path to Zarkava but has now been beaten in all four starts since winning the Boussac last season. She did not get the clearest of runs over three out and was then switched before keeping on at one pace, but never looked like being a serious threat to her stablemate. She looks like being aimed at the Prix Vermeille next.
Sandbar had only one rival behind as they raced past the chateau, before finishing best of all. She looks to have stamina and could be of interest over further. Connections reported the ground was too soft for her.
Deluxe(USA), who is a half-sister to Banks Hill and Dansili, looked short of a turn of pace just as she had in the Saint-Alary three weeks earlier. She again lugged to her right when coming under pressure before keeping on at one pace.
Zagora(FR) should have been suited by the step up in trip and cut in ground. She was among the most experienced on show here and, after racing prominently, took it up over a furlong from home. However, she wandered around in the lead and, although she may have hit the front too soon, it is doubtful she would have been good enough to trouble the winner if ridden more patiently.
A Media Luz(FR) lost all chance when clouted by Deluxe.
Valasyra(FR) carried out pace-making duties as required.
Heaven's Vault(IRE) looked out of her depth.
Bridge Of Peace dropped away as would be expected in this company after racing up with the pace.

3016a PRIX PAUL DE MOUSSAC (GROUP 3) (3YO COLTS & GELDINGS) (TURF) 1m

3:50 (12:00) 3-Y-0 **£35,398** (£14,159; £10,619; £7,079; £3,539)

RPR

1 **Sormiou (FR)**[24] 2271 3-8-10 0 AlexandreRoussel 3 100
(C Diard, France) racd towards rr fr s: rdn 2f out: swtchd towards rail: qcknd wl 1 1/2f: out: c through to ld 100yds out: r.o wl **20/1**

2 *1* **Blue Panis (FR)**[44] 1682 3-8-10 0 ThierryThulliez 4 98
(F Chappet, France) led fr s and stl in front ent fnl f: r.o wl but ct and hdd fnl 100yds **18/1**

3 *snk* **Emerald Commander (IRE)**[224] 7207 3-8-10 0 MickaelBarzalona 1 98
(Saeed Bin Suroor) racd in 3rd: rdn 1 1/2f out: wandered lft: r.o wl whn stened: outpcd ins fnl 100yds **9/4**[1]

4 *nk* **Ramble On (FR)**[22] 2357 3-8-10 0 OlivierPeslier 2 97
(G Botti, Italy) racd in 3rd and stl prom 2f out: rdn 1/1/2f out: r.o wl but outpcd fnl 100yds **20/1**

5 *snk* **Fallen Idol**[17] 2471 3-8-10 0 WilliamBuick 6 97
(J H M Gosden) bkmarker fr s: rdn 2f out: swtchd wdst of all: outpcd but r.o wl ins fnl f **9/2**[3]

6 *1* **Chasing Halos (USA)**[25] 3-8-10 0 MaximeGuyon 8 94
(A Fabre, France) racd towards rr: rdn 2f out: r.o but no ex fnl f **11/4**[2]

7 *2* **Noble Alpha (IRE)**[20] 2405 3-8-10 0 (b) GeraldMosse 5 90
(Mario Hofer, Germany) racd in 5th fr s: rdn 2f out: outpcd: styd on but eased cl home **12/1**

8 *10* **Foreteller**[34] 1985 3-8-10 0 (b1) ChristopheSoumillon 7 67
(D Smaga, France) racd in 3rd: rdn early in st: fnd no ex: outpcd: wknd **11/2**

1m 37.1s (-0.90) **Going Correction** +0.20s/f (Good) **8** Ran SP% **113.5**
Speed ratings: **112,111,110,110,110 109,107,97**
WIN (incl. 1 euro stake): 18.30. PLACES: 4.00, 4.70, 3.00. DF: 58.90. SF: 147.80.
Owner Maurice Aubry **Bred** *unknown **Trained** France

NOTEBOOK
Sormiou(FR) showed a good turn of foot to make up ground from the rear and hit the front inside the last. He will go for the Group 1 Prix Jean Prat next.
Emerald Commander(IRE) had ground conditions to suit and ran a sound race on his seasonal reappearance. He can be expected to come on for this.

Fallen Idol was never a threat, failing to pick up from the back until it was too late. A stronger pace would probably have suited him.

3017a PRIX DU CHEMIN DE FER DU NORD (GROUP 3) (4YO+) (TURF) 1m
4:25 (12:00) 4-Y-0+ **£35,398** (£14,159; £10,619; £7,079; £3,539)

RPR

1 **Fuisse (FR)**[38] 1855 4-8-11 0 Christophe-PatriceLemaire 10 114
(Mme C Head-Maarek, France) *chsd ldrs: 3rd st: rdn ins fnl 2f but did nt qckn immediately: r.o u.p ins fnl f to ld 100yds out* **5/2**[1]

2 ¾ **Vertigineux (FR)**[43] 1716 6-8-11 0 PhilippeSogorb 5 112
(Mme C Dufreche, France) *racd in midfield: 5th st: rdn and ev ch whn short of room 1f out: r.o strly fnl 100yds* **9/1**

3 ½ **Slickly Royal (FR)**[8] 2778 6-8-11 0 (b) AnthonyCrastus 2 111
(P Demercastel, France) *a.p: swept through on rail to ld 3f out: 3 l clr st: rdn and wandered 1 1/2f out: hdd and no ex fnl 100yds* **25/1**

4 shd **Elusive Wave (IRE)**[43] 1716 4-8-8 0 ChristopheSoumillon 4 108
(J-C Rouget, France) *plld hrd early: chsd ldr: settled in 4th tl followed Slickly Royal through and 2nd st: rdn 1 1/2f out: kpt on same pce* **5/2**[1]

5 snk **Sweet Hearth (USA)**[18] 4-8-8 0 GeraldMosse 6 107
(A De Royer-Dupre, France) *hld up: 7th st: hdwy to go 5th 1 1/2f out: one pce* **6/1**[3]

6 1½ **Freminius (GER)**[13] 2615 6-8-11 0 DominiqueBoeuf 1 107
(W Baltromei, Germany) *last: hdwy 2f out: kpt on at same pce fnl f* **11/1**

7 4 **Numerologie (FR)**[24] 4-8-8 0 AlexisBadel 7 95
(Mme M Bollack-Badel, France) *hld up towards rr: r.o fnl f: n.d* **33/1**

8 nk **Border Patrol**[50] 1531 4-9-0 0 WilliamBuick 9 100
(R Charlton) *a bhd* **5/1**[2]

9 15 **Konig Bernard (FR)**[18] 4-8-11 0 MaximeGuyon 8 62
(W Baltromei, Germany) *propped coming out of stalls: racd in midfield tl rdn and nt qckn 1 1/2f out: eased fnl f* **14/1**

10 8 **Rectangulaire (FR)**[38] 1855 4-8-11 0 TonyPiccone 3 44
(Mme C Head-Maarek, France) *sn led: hdd and dropped out fnl 3f* **100/1**

1m 36.9s (-1.10) **Going Correction** +0.20s/f (Good) **10** Ran SP% **120.9**
Speed ratings: **113,112,111,111,111 110,106,105,90,82**
PARI-MUTUEL (all including 1 euro stakes): WIN 1.90 (coupled with Rectangulaire); PLACE 1.30, 2.40, 3.80; DF 9.00; SF 6.90.
Owner Haras Du Quesnay **Bred** Alec & Ghislaine Head **Trained** Chantilly, France

NOTEBOOK
Fuisse(FR), last year's Prix du Jockey Club runner-up in what proved to be an injury curtailed season, ran out a 3l winner of a Listed race at Longchamp last time out and took this return to Group company in his stride. He won a shade comfortably and will now be aimed at the Prix Messidor, before a possible tilt at the Champion Stakes in the autumn.
Border Patrol had the ground in his favour but proved disappointing, never threatening to get involved.

2404 COLOGNE (R-H)
Sunday, June 13

OFFICIAL GOING: Turf: good

3018a OPPENHEIM-UNION-RENNEN (GROUP 2) (3YO) (TURF) 1m 3f
4:00 (12:00) 3-Y-0
£53,097 (£18,584; £8,849; £4,424; £2,212; £1,327)

RPR

1 **Zazou (GER)**[28] 2159 3-9-2 0 THellier 2 103
(Mario Hofer, Germany) *settled in midfield travelling smoothly: swtchd wd ent st: qcknd wl to grab ld ent fnl f: r.o strly to win comf* **21/10**[2]

2 2 **Lindentree**[20] 3-9-2 0 YannLerner 7 100
(W Hickst, Germany) *bkmarker fr s: mde move early in st: r.o wl to ld 1 1/2f out: ct ent fnl f: r.o wl but no match for wnr* **174/10**

3 2 **Baschar**[31] 3-9-2 0 AHelfenbein 5 96
(M G Mintchev, Germany) *racd towards rr: r.o wl in st: styd on wl but no threat to first two* **206/10**

4 1 **Next Hight (IRE)**[21] 3-9-2 0 AGoritz 4 94
(P Schiergen, Germany) *joint ldr fr s: hdd 1 1/2f out: styd on one pce fnl f* **218/10**

5 ¾ **Scalo**[20] 2406 3-9-2 0 EPedroza 3 93
(A Wohler, Germany) *racd promly bhd ldrs travelling wl: fnd no room down st and unable to chal: unlucky* **4/5**[1]

6 5 **Nordfalke (IRE)**[31] 3-9-2 0 FilipMinarik 6 84
(P Schiergen, Germany) *racd in midfield: mde move at end of bkstretch: briefly threatened on st: no ex fnl 2f* **57/10**

7 4 **Wheredreamsare**[20] 2406 3-9-2 0 APietsch 1 77
(W Hickst, Germany) *joint ldr early: stl prom ent st: qckly btn and wknd* **56/10**[3]

2m 18.1s (-2.70) **7** Ran SP% **132.3**
WIN (incl. 10 euro stake): 31. PLACES: 16, 28, 30. SF: 408.
Owner WH Sport International **Bred** Gestut Fahrhof **Trained** Germany

NOTEBOOK
Zazou(GER) was settled in behind before coming with a sweeping run down the centre of the course. His main rival endured a torrid time getting a run, but he won this nicely and is a classy individual, as his effort in the French 2,000 Guineas showed.
Lindentree led into the latter stages after getting to the front but did not look in the same league as the winner when that horse quickened past him.
Baschar never looked like winning but did stay on quite nicely.
Next Hight(IRE) was swallowed up readily as the pack closed in.
Scalo was tucked into the chasing pack, and got no run whatsoever when wanting to make his effort up the inside rail. His final position can be safely ignored and he remains an exciting prospect. It is, however, impossible to know whether he would have won without suffering any interference.
Nordfalke(IRE) looks on the small side and did not get home after holding every chance.

2575 SAN SIRO (R-H)
Sunday, June 13

OFFICIAL GOING: Turf: good

3019a GRAN PREMIO DI MILANO (GROUP 1) (3YO+) (TURF) 1m 4f
5:00 (12:00) 3-Y-0+ **£119,469** (£52,566; £28,672; £14,336)

RPR

1 **Jakkalberry (IRE)**[28] 2152 4-9-7 0 FabioBranca 5 122
(E Botti, Italy) *settled in rr: hdwy ent st to trck ldrs: no room 2 1/2f out and swtchd rt to chal between horses: r.o wl ent fnl 1 1/2f to chal ldr: led fnl f and sn wnt 1 l up: a holding 2nd* **174/10**

2 ¾ **Getaway (GER)**[35] 1956 7-9-7 0 ADeVries 7 121
(J Hirschberger, Germany) *broke wl: steaded to trck ldrs in 4th: prog ent fnl 3 1/2f to chal for ld: rdn and a l clr ent fnl 2f: chal and no ex whn passed by wnr ent fnl f: styd on* **27/20**[1]

3 3¼ **Campanologist (USA)**[28] 2152 5-9-7 0 FrankieDettori 8 116
(Saeed Bin Suroor) *broke wl and trckd ldrs tl ent st: prog to chal for ld 3f out: hrd rdn fnl 2 1/2f: no imp on two ldrs: styd on fnl f* **13/5**[2]

4 2½ **Quijano (GER)**[78] 1026 8-9-7 0 AStarke 9 112
(P Schiergen, Germany) *broke wl: trckd gp on outer: racd in midfield for 6f: prog on outer ent fnl 3f: no ex whn asked and hrd rdn 2f out: styd on* **7/1**

5 2½ **Estejo (GER)**[50] 1540 6-9-7 0 DPorcu 10 108
(R Rohne, Germany) *broke wl: racd w ldr and tk over in front after 2f and set stdy pce tl 4f out: rdn to stay in tch w ldrs ent fnl 3f: sn hrd rdn and no ex: wknd* **27/1**

6 hd **Sant'Antonio (ITY)**[36] 1943 5-9-7 0 UmbertoRispoli 2 108
(S Botti, Italy) *settled in midfield on inner: hdwy ent fnl 3f to chal ldrs: hrd rdn fnl 2 1/2f: rallied briefly u.str.p tl 1 1/2f: sn no ex* **758/100**

7 2¼ **Heedas**[63] 4-9-7 0 CDemuro 3 104
(L Riccardi, Italy) *racd in midfield and t.k.h for 4f: moved rt ent fnl 3f to chal: ev ch 2 1/12f out: hrd rdn and no imp fnl f* **162/10**

8 ¾ **Permesso**[36] 1943 5-9-7 0 GMarcelli 1 103
(G Pucciatti, Italy) *slowly away and a towards rr* **162/10**

9 snk **Voila Ici (IRE)**[28] 2152 5-9-7 0 MircoDemuro 6 108+
(Vittorio Caruso, Italy) *broke wl and settled in midfield for 4f: stdy prog to go 3rd after 6f: chal for ld ent fnl 3f: no imp u.str ride fnl 2f: wknd* **18/5**[3]

10 dist **Seul Blue (ITY)**[50] 1540 4-9-7 0 LManiezzi 4 —
(R Menichetti, Italy) *sweated up bdly: broke wl: settled in 2nd for a m: effrt to stay in tch fnl 3 1/2f: no imp: eased fnl f* **45/1**

2m 29.6s (-1.90) **10** Ran SP% **139.0**
WIN (incl. 1 euro stake): 18.41. PLACES: 2.11, 1.29, 1.47. DF: 108.14.
Owner Effevi **Bred** Azienda Agricola Allevamento Deni **Trained** Italy

NOTEBOOK
Campanologist(USA) had his chance when brought to challenge from 3f down but the first two saw their races out better. Rattling quick ground suits him best.

2577 CARLISLE (R-H)
Monday, June 14

OFFICIAL GOING: Good (good to soft in places; 6.9)
The old stable bend was moved out 2m from the inside, adding 4m for all races over 6f or above. Conditions seemed softer than 'good'.
Wind: Slight, half behind Weather: Overcast, dry

3020 BLUCHER SOCIAL CLUB CAFFREY'S MAIDEN AUCTION STKS 5f 193y
2:15 (2:16) (Class 5) 2-Y-0 **£2,729** (£806; £403) **Stalls** High

Form RPR

1 **Tro Nesa (IRE)** 2-8-6 0 RoystonFfrench 8 67
(Mrs A Duffield) *trckd ldrs: pushed along 1/2-way: led 1f out: hld on wl* **40/1**

56 2 1¼ **No Poppy (IRE)**[6] 2832 2-8-6 0 ow2 DavidAllan 10 63+
(T D Easterby) *in tch: pushed along 1/2-way: hdwy whn nt clr run appr fnl f: swtchd lft: styd on ins fnl f: tk 2nd towards fin: could nt rch wnr* **11/4**[2]

3 ¾ **Ajaafa** 2-8-9 0 PaulMulrennan 9 64
(J G Given) *chsd ldrs: effrt and chal over 1f out: kpt on same pce ins fnl f* **22/1**

2 4 ¾ **Sophie's Hero**[17] 2498 2-9-2 0 JamieSpencer 4 69
(K A Ryan) *led: rdn over 2f out: hdd 1f out: kpt on same pce* **6/5**[1]

5 1 **Dr Red Eye** 2-8-11 0 ow2 PhillipMakin 3 61
(J A Glover) *dwlt: hld up: hdwy and edgd rt fr 2f out: kpt on ins fnl f: nrst fin* **28/1**

5 6 3¾ **Louis Girl**[18] 2461 2-8-8 0 TonyHamilton 5 46
(R A Fahey) *rn green in rr: pushed along 1/2-way: no imp* **20/1**

3 7 ¾ **Philharmonic Hall**[16] 2522 2-8-9 0 PaulHanagan 2 45
(R A Fahey) *cl up: rdn and ev ch 1/2-way tl wknd appr fnl f* **7/2**[3]

6 8 3¼ **Sister Sioux (IRE)**[20] 2420 2-7-13 0 MatthewLawson(7) 6 32
(R Bastiman) *dwlt: t.k.h in rr: pushed along 1/2-way: sn btn* **100/1**

1m 18.1s (4.40) **Going Correction** +0.45s/f (Yiel) **8** Ran SP% **110.3**
Speed ratings (Par 93): **88,86,85,84,83 78,77,72**
toteswingers: 1&2 £7.20, 1&3 £16.30, 2&3 £7.00 CSF £137.42 TOTE £37.90: £7.20, £1.80, £5.90; EX 116.90 TRIFECTA Not won..
Owner Rasio Cymru Racing **Bred** Lynnlodge Stud & Arthur Finnan **Trained** Constable Burton, N Yorks

FOCUS
This looked just a modest juvenile maiden.

NOTEBOOK
Tro Nesa(IRE), a £9,000 purchase who is out of a fair 7f winner, seemed quite well educated and stayed on strongly to make a successful introduction. She should be open to some improvement and ought to do okay in nurseries in due course. (op 50-1)
No Poppy(IRE), despite having a speedy pedigree, lacks pace. Carrying 2lb overweight, she found this stiff 6f on easy ground an insufficient test, looking in need of further. (tchd 5-2 and 3-1)
Ajaafa, a 3,500gns purchase, was never far away and kept on to the line, posting a respectable effort on debut. (op 16-1)
Sophie's Hero did not progress from his promising debut, fading late on after showing early speed. Perhaps he wants quicker ground. (op 11-10 tchd 5-4 and 11-8 in places)
Dr Red Eye, another carrying 2lb overweight, ran as though in need of the experience. (op 40-1 tchd 25-1)

Philharmonic Hall finished a tired horse after keeping the early leader Sophie's Hero honest and was disappointing. (tchd 3-1 and 4-1)

3021 HOLMESIDE HALL LABOUR CLUB GROLSCH CLAIMING STKS 1m 1f 61y
2:45 (2:45) (Class 6) 3-Y-O+ £2,047 (£604; £302) Stalls High

Form RPR
3603 1 **Cobo Bay**[29] 2141 5-9-13 87.....(v) JamieSpencer 4 85+
(K A Ryan) *mde all: pushed clr fr over 2f out: easily* 11/10[2]
014- 2 9 **Night Knight (IRE)**[11] 6439 4-9-6 63.....(p) TonyHamilton 6 59
(C Grant) *chsd ldrs: rdn and chsd wnr over 1f out: no imp fnl f* 16/1[3]
1111 3 11 **Fremen (USA)**[9] 2760 10-9-10 85..... AdrianNicholls 5 40
(D Nicholls) *dwlt: sn chsng wnr: rdn 3f out: lost 2nd over 1f out: wknd* 10/11[1]
0-00 4 19 **Its Beyond Me**[41] 1801 6-8-12 40.....(p) MichaelO'Connell(5) 1 —
(F P Murtagh) *hld up in tch: drvn and outpcd after 3f: rallied and prom over 3f out: hung rt and wknd fnl 2f* 80/1
630- 5 13 **Roman History (IRE)**[279] 4944 7-9-3 48.....(p) DavidAllan 3 —
(Miss Tracy Waggott) *in tch: struggling over 3f out: sn btn* 66/1
000/ 6 29 **Inchmarlow (IRE)**[917] 7103 7-9-8 32..... DuranFentiman 2 —
(T H Caldwell) *t.k.h: hld up in tch: struggling over 3f out: sn btn* 125/1

2m 1.55s (3.95) **Going Correction** +0.55s/f (Yiel) 6 Ran SP% **109.4**
Speed ratings (Par 101): **104,96,86,69,57 32**
toteswingers: 1&2 £1.02, 2&3 £2.60, 1&3 not won. CSF £15.84 TOTE £1.60: £1.10, £5.00; EX 12.10.Cobo Bay was claimed by C. R. Dore for £15,000.
Owner The C H F Partnership **Bred** The C H F Partnership **Trained** Hambleton, N Yorks

FOCUS
This claimer was a straight match on paper, with Cobo Bay and Fremen well clear of the remainder at the weights, but with the latter well below his best, the former won unchallenged.
Fremen(USA) Official explanation: trainer had no explanation for the poor form shown

3022 BEDLINGTON STATION WORTHINGTON'S H'CAP 7f 200y
3:15 (3:15) (Class 5) (0-70,69) 4-Y-O+ £2,590 (£770; £385; £192) Stalls High

Form RPR
6-04 1 **Ailsa Craig (IRE)**[21] 2392 4-9-1 63..... TonyHamilton 5 79
(E W Tuer) *chsd ldr: rdn to ld over 1f out: edgd rt ins fnl f: drvn out* 8/1
0544 2 2¾ **Classic Descent**[5] 2850 5-8-5 58.....(t) JamesSullivan(5) 9 67+
(Mrs R A Carr) *hld up: hdwy on outside over 2f out: chsd wnr ins fnl f: r.o* 13/2
6552 3 5 **Call Of Duty (IRE)**[14] 2583 5-8-6 54..... PaulHanagan 2 52
(Mrs Dianne Sayer) *led: rdn and hdd over 1f out: outpcd and lost 2nd ins fnl f* 5/2[1]
00-5 4 ¾ **Major Magpie (IRE)**[56] 1426 8-9-2 64.....(p) PhillipMakin 4 60
(M Dods) *hld up: rdn over 3f out: no imp fnl 2f* 7/1
0646 5 2¾ **Guertino (IRE)**[8] 2791 5-8-10 58..... PatrickMathers 7 48
(C J Teague) *dwlt: bhd: drvn 1/2-way: no imp fr over 2f out* 33/1
4026 6 1¼ **Hansomis (IRE)**[14] 2581 6-8-9 62..... IanBrennan(5) 11 49
(B Mactaggart) *hld up: rdn on outside over 2f out: nvr able to chal* 14/1
0-06 7 shd **Stonehaugh (IRE)**[19] 2428 7-9-7 69..... RoystonFfrench 12 56
(J Howard Johnson) *hld up in tch on ins: rdn 3f out: outpcd fnl 2f* 25/1
-322 8 nse **Desert Hunter (IRE)**[21] 2382 7-8-3 54..... KellyHarrison(3) 6 40
(Micky Hammond) *t.k.h: trckd ldr: rdn 3f out: edgd rt and wknd wl over 1f out* 4/1[2]
3-06 9 1 **Cavendish Road (IRE)**[25] 2240 4-9-4 66..... KirstyMilczarek 8 50
(N J Vaughan) *prom: drvn over 3f out: wknd wl over 1f out* 16/1
1030 10 6 **By Command**[16] 2527 5-9-5 67.....(tp) JamieSpencer 10 37
(K A Ryan) *t.k.h: hld up towards rr: rdn over 3f out: sn btn: eased whn no ch fnl f* 6/1[3]

1m 44.27s (4.27) **Going Correction** +0.55s/f (Yiel) 10 Ran SP% **119.1**
Speed ratings (Par 103): **100,97,92,91,88 87,87,87,86,80**
toteswingers: 1&2 £10.80, 1&3 £6.00, 2&3 £5.60 CSF £60.53 CT £173.04 TOTE £7.80: £2.20, £3.10, £1.70; EX 75.00 TRIFECTA Not won..
Owner E Tuer **Bred** P J B O'Callaghan **Trained** Great Smeaton, N Yorks

FOCUS
A modest handicap which was well run and in which few were ever involved. The form is rated around the winner.
Desert Hunter(IRE) Official explanation: jockey said gelding was unsuited by the good (good to soft places) ground

3023 BARROW CENTRAL WMC MAGNER'S FILLIES' H'CAP 6f 192y
3:45 (3:46) (Class 4) (0-80,80) 3-Y-O £4,857 (£1,445; £722; £360) Stalls High

Form RPR
4-43 1 **Emerald Girl (IRE)**[7] 2815 3-8-11 70..... PaulHanagan 5 77
(R A Fahey) *hld up in tch: effrt 2f out: squeezed through to ld ins fnl f: rdn out* 3/1[2]
3302 2 1¼ **Breathless Kiss (USA)**[18] 2450 3-9-7 80..... JamieSpencer 1 84
(K A Ryan) *hld up: swtchd lft and hdwy over 1f out: drifted lft to stands' side: kpt on fnl f: could nt rch ldr* 9/2
34-2 3 1¾ **Shaluca**[19] 2434 3-8-9 68..... GrahamGibbons 3 67
(E S McMahon) *dwlt: sn in tch: rdn over 2f out: n.m.r briefly over 1f out: kpt on u.p ins fnl f* 7/2[3]
5-00 4 1¾ **Tartufo Dolce (IRE)**[12] 2648 3-8-5 64..... RoystonFfrench 7 58
(J G Given) *t.k.h: pressed ldr: rdn and ev ch over 1f out: kpt on same pce ins fnl f* 40/1
3-11 5 1¾ **Timeless Elegance (IRE)**[19] 2432 3-9-0 78..... IanBrennan(5) 2 68
(J Howard Johnson) *plld hrd early: led to ins fnl f: sn btn* 9/4[1]
0-20 6 9 **Tarita (IRE)**[23] 2342 3-9-3 76..... SebSanders 6 41
(R Hannon) *stdd s: hld up: rdn 3f out: btn over 1f out* 9/1
00-6 7 3 **Wood Fair**[17] 2502 3-8-2 61 oh4.....(p) AndrewElliott 4 18
(J R Weymes) *cl up: chal after 2f to 3f out: wknd wl over 1f out* 40/1

1m 31.38s (4.28) **Going Correction** +0.55s/f (Yiel) 7 Ran SP% **111.1**
Speed ratings (Par 98): **97,95,93,91,89 79,75**
toteswingers: 1&2 £2.50, 1&3 £2.60, 2&3 £3.10 CSF £15.82 CT £45.70 TOTE £3.50: £1.50, £2.30; EX 13.90 Trifecta £55.90 Pool: £419.48 - 5.55 winning units..
Owner M Wynne **Bred** Tally-Ho Stud **Trained** Musley Bank, N Yorks

FOCUS
A fair fillies' handicap, although the pace looked overly strong in the conditions. Slight improvement from the first two.
Tarita(IRE) Official explanation: jockey said filly missed the break and never travelled

3024 KING'S ARMS AT STAINTON CARLING H'CAP 5f
4:15 (4:16) (Class 5) (0-70,70) 3-Y-O+ £2,590 (£770; £385; £192) Stalls High

Form RPR
-303 1 **Comptonspirit**[14] 2581 6-9-1 57..... GrahamGibbons 1 68
(B P J Baugh) *mde all: rdn 2f out: hrd pressed fnl f: edgd rt: hld on gamely u.p* 12/1
0053 2 nse **Hazelrigg (IRE)**[14] 2578 5-9-10 66.....(vt) DavidAllan 6 77
(T D Easterby) *in tch: hdwy over 1f out: chal fnl f: kpt on u.p: jst hld* 11/4[2]
3532 3 6 **Fasliyanne (IRE)**[14] 2582 4-9-1 57.....(v) JamieSpencer 7 46
(K A Ryan) *prom on outside: rdn and edgd rt over 1f out: sn outpcd* 5/1[3]
6225 4 1¼ **Select Committee**[4] 2883 5-9-9 70.....(v) IanBrennan(5) 9 55
(J J Quinn) *hld up in tch: effrt over 1f out: no imp fnl f* 17/2
0000 5 1½ **Tournedos (IRE)**[5] 2849 8-8-10 57.....(b) JamesSullivan(5) 8 37
(Mrs R A Carr) *cl up: ev ch and rdn over 1f out: sn wknd* 16/1
0000 6 1¼ **Silver Hotspur**[10] 2727 6-8-9 51 oh2.....(v) FrannyNorton 2 26
(D Shaw) *dwlt: bhd: pushed along over 2f out: nvr rchd ldrs* 50/1
0023 7 ¾ **Not My Choice (IRE)**[7] 2817 5-9-8 64.....(t) SebSanders 11 36
(D C Griffiths) *racd far side w one other: in tch to 1/2-way: sn outpcd* 12/1
0022 8 1¾ **Besty**[7] 2815 3-9-7 70..... TomEaves 3 33
(B Smart) *disp ld to 1/2-way: wknd over 1f out* 9/4[1]
6046 9 2¼ **Steel City Boy (IRE)**[4] 2896 7-8-11 53..... PaulHanagan 10 11
(D Shaw) *racd far side w one other: rdn 1/2-way: sn n.d* 12/1

62.26 secs (1.46) **Going Correction** +0.45s/f (Yiel)
WFA 3 from 4yo+ 7lb 9 Ran SP% **115.5**
Speed ratings (Par 103): **106,105,96,94,91 89,88,85,82**
toteswingers: 1&2 £5.10, 1&3 £6.40, 2&3 £3.20 CSF £45.19 CT £193.12 TOTE £14.50: £2.90, £1.60, £1.10; EX 55.10 Trifecta £202.00 Pool: £354.98 - 1.30 winning units..
Owner G B Hignett **Bred** Mrs F Wilson **Trained** Audley, Staffs

FOCUS
The main action took place towards the near side of the track. Two of these - Not My Choice and Steel City Boy - stayed far side throughout but they had no chance. The firfst two could have been rated higher but seemed advantaged by racing against the rail.
Select Committee Official explanation: jockey said gelding was denied a clear run
Besty Official explanation: trainer said gelding ran flat

3025 CRICKETERS AT BLACKHILL COORS LIGHT H'CAP 1m 1f 61y
4:45 (4:45) (Class 5) (0-70,66) 4-Y-O+ £2,590 (£770; £385; £192) Stalls High

Form RPR
1242 1 **Bajan Pride**[23] 2337 6-9-3 62..... PaulHanagan 10 71+
(R A Fahey) *trckd ldrs gng wl: led over 2f out: rdn over 1f out: kpt on wl ins fnl f* 7/2[2]
53-5 2 2 **Noche De Reyes**[8] 2788 5-8-8 53.....(p) DavidAllan 1 57+
(E J Alston) *prom: n.m.r and outpcd 2f out: rallied to chse wnr ins fnl f: r.o* 15/2
534 3 1 **Dean Iarracht (IRE)**[14] 2583 4-8-4 52.....(p) KellyHarrison(3) 3 54
(Miss Tracy Waggott) *hld up: hdwy and prom over 1f out: kpt on same pce ins fnl f* 6/1[3]
050 4 ½ **Switched Off**[19] 1927 5-9-0 64.....(b) JamesSullivan(5) 4 65+
(M W Easterby) *hld up: hdwy whn nt clr run over 3f out tl swtchd rt and hdwy over 1f out: drifted rt: no imp ins fnl f* 28/1
0065 5 ¾ **Star Addition**[11] 2668 4-8-5 50..... DuranFentiman 2 49+
(E J Alston) *midfield: drvn whn nt clr run 3f out: effrt u.p over 1f out: edgd rt and sn no imp* 40/1
0-30 6 ¾ **Rock Relief (IRE)**[12] 2645 4-9-2 61..... SebSanders 6 59
(Sir Mark Prescott) *in tch: reminders after 2f: drvn fr 4f out: rallied: one pce ins fnl f* 11/4[1]
0006 7 6 **Pitbull**[16] 2529 7-8-5 50 oh2 ow3.....(b[1]) PatrickMathers 8 34
(A Berry) *bhd: shortlived effrt over 2f out: sn wknd* 100/1
0006 8 ½ **Wind Shuffle (GER)**[14] 2579 7-9-3 65..... GaryBartley(3) 12 48
(J S Goldie) *led to over 2f out: sn rdn and wknd over 1f out* 7/2[2]
-550 9 10 **Supercast (IRE)**[87] 941 7-9-7 66.....(t) KirstyMilczarek 5 27
(N J Vaughan) *prom tl edgd rt and wknd fr 2f out* 20/1
6430 10 10 **I'm Frank**[21] 2392 4-9-7 66..... PJMcDonald 11 5
(G A Swinbank) *midfield: struggling 4f out: sn btn* 12/1
00- 11 7 **Napoletano (ITY)**[292] 5342 4-7-13 49..... PaulPickard(5) 7 —
(R Johnson) *towards rr: rdn along over 3f out: sn wknd* 66/1

2m 1.82s (4.22) **Going Correction** +0.55s/f (Yiel) 11 Ran SP% **118.0**
Speed ratings (Par 103): **103,101,100,99,99 98,93,92,83,75 68**
toteswingers: 1&2 £4.80, 1&3 £4.90, 2&3 £6.10 CSF £28.60 CT £154.64 TOTE £4.40: £2.00, £1.90, £3.30; EX 31.40 Trifecta £137.50 Pool: £256.55 - 1.38 winning units..
Owner R A Fahey **Bred** Plantation Stud **Trained** Musley Bank, N Yorks

FOCUS
A weak handicap for the grade, but at least the pace was decent. They raced stands' side in the straight. The form makes sense, with the third helping to set the standard.

3026 WORKINGTON ROYAL BRITISH LEGION STONE'S H'CAP (DIV I) 5f 193y
5:15 (5:16) (Class 6) (0-60,64) 3-Y-O+ £1,706 (£503; £252) Stalls High

Form RPR
0011 1 **Ryedane (IRE)**[5] 2849 8-10-0 64 6ex.....(b) DavidAllan 3 77
(T D Easterby) *mde all: drvn over 1f out: styd on strly fnl f* 11/8[1]
55-4 2 2 **Red River Boy**[14] 2581 5-8-9 48..... KellyHarrison(3) 9 55
(C W Fairhurst) *prom: nt clr run and swtchd rt over 1f out: chsd wnr ins fnl f: r.o* 11/2[3]
0-00 3 1 **Monsieur Pontaven**[19] 2432 3-7-13 50 oh1 ow4... MatthewLawson(7) 5 51
(R Bastiman) *hld up and bhd: hdwy over 1f out: kpt on ins fnl f: nrst fin* 40/1
0501 4 shd **Lake Chini (IRE)**[14] 2582 8-9-10 60.....(b) GrahamGibbons 11 63
(M W Easterby) *sn drvn along towards rr: hdwy u.p 2f out: one pce ins fnl f* 7/2[2]
-015 5 1 **Wotatomboy**[8] 2789 4-8-11 50..... MichaelStainton(3) 12 50
(R M Whitaker) *cl up: effrt and ev ch over 1f out: no ex ins fnl f* 11/2[3]
3546 6 2½ **Turf Time**[54] 1477 3-8-4 53..... PaulPickard(5) 10 43
(J A Glover) *cl up tl rdn and wknd over 1f out* 12/1
0063 7 hd **Avonlini**[16] 2535 4-9-0 50..... SebSanders 6 41
(B P J Baugh) *chsd ldrs tl drvn and wknd over 1f out* 20/1
000 8 9 **Maison Dieu**[18] 2454 7-9-3 53..... PatrickMathers 8 15
(A Berry) *in tch to 1/2-way: sn wknd* 40/1

1m 16.19s (2.49) **Going Correction** +0.45s/f (Yiel)
WFA 3 from 4yo+ 8lb 8 Ran SP% **112.4**
Speed ratings (Par 101): **101,98,97,96,95 92,91,79**
toteswingers: 1&2 £3.30, 1&3 £14.00, 2&3 £23.10 CSF £8.94 CT £193.19 TOTE £2.30: £1.50, £1.10, £11.70; EX 11.30 Trifecta £172.40 Part won. Pool £233.04 - 0.42 winning units..
Owner Ryedale Partners No 5 **Bred** Tally-Ho Stud **Trained** Great Habton, N Yorks
■ Stewards' Enquiry : Kelly Harrison one-day ban: careless riding (Jun 28)

The Form Book, Raceform Ltd, Compton, RG20 6NL

FOCUS
A moderate sprint handicap. They raced stands' side in the straight and again the near rail looked the place to be, with Ryedane the latest to take advantage. This was his best form since late 2007.

3027 WORKINGTON ROYAL BRITISH LEGION STONE'S H'CAP (DIV II) 5f 193y
5:45 (5:45) (Class 6) (0-60,60) 3-Y-0+ £1,706 (£503; £252) Stalls High

Form RPR
0005 1 **Red China Blues (USA)**[13] 2629 4-9-1 **51** PatrickMathers 4 59
(R E Barr) *prom: drvn over 2f out: rallied to ld over 1f out: hld on wl fnl f* **14/1**
-553 2 ½ **Piste**[4] 2896 4-9-8 **58** PaulHanagan 8 65
(Miss T Jackson) *plld hrd: hld up: hdwy on outside over 2f out: ev ch ins fnl f: kpt on: hld nr fin* **9/4**[1]
0-02 3 1 ¾ **Fleetwoodsands (IRE)**[27] 2203 3-8-11 **60** IanBrennan(5) 7 59
(Ollie Pears) *hld up in tch: hdwy: squeezed through and bmpd over 1f out: r.o ins fnl f: nrst fin* **8/1**
3030 4 ½ **Bentley**[4] 2896 6-8-12 **48** (v) RoystonFfrench 2 47
(J G Given) *chsd ldrs: drvn over 2f out: one pce whn bmpd over 1f out* **13/2**[3]
3-02 5 2 ½ **Elkhorn**[21] 2381 8-9-0 **50** (b) TomEaves 1 41
(Julie Camacho) *trckd ldrs tl shkn up: edgd rt and outpcd over 1f out* **5/2**[2]
-436 6 nse **Interest Free**[13] 2628 3-9-0 **58** DavidAllan 9 47
(T D Easterby) *led to over 1f out: sn outpcd* **7/1**
30-0 7 10 **Hot Rod Mamma (IRE)**[70] 1118 3-8-6 **50** PJMcDonald 6 —
(Mrs Dianne Sayer) *pressed ldr: rdn and ev ch over 2f out: wkng whn bmpd over 1f out* **12/1**
-000 8 18 **Fern House (IRE)**[10] 2699 8-8-10 **46** oh1 TonyHamilton 5 —
(A Berry) *dwlt: hld up: struggling over 2f out: sn btn* **50/1**
40-0 9 7 **Psychopathicsandra (IRE)**[18] 2449 3-7-13 **48** oh1 ow2 BillyCray(5) 12 —
(A Berry) *bhd: struggling 1/2-way: sn wknd* **66/1**

1m 16.15s (2.45) **Going Correction** +0.45s/f (Yiel)
WFA 3 from 4yo+ 8lb 9 Ran SP% **114.1**
Speed ratings (Par 101): **101,100,98,97,94 93,80,56,47**
toteswingers: 1&2 £9.30, 1&3 £11.60, 2&3 £4.50 CSF £45.23 CT £278.32 TOTE £26.00: £6.90, £2.60, £5.30; EX 76.90 Trifecta £144.40 Part won. Pool £195.27 - 0.10 winning units. Place 6: £141.31 Place 5: £46.08.
Owner Brian Morton **Bred** Spooky Hollow Racing **Trained** Seamer, N Yorks
■ Stewards' Enquiry : David Allan two-day ban: careless riding (Jun 28-29)
Ian Brennan two-day ban: careless riding (Jun 28-29)

FOCUS
The time was almost identical to the first division, and the main action was again near side in the straight. A modest race which has not been rated too positively.
Fern House(IRE) Official explanation: trainer's rep said gelding finished distressed
T/Plt: £205.70 to a £1 skake. Pool: £56,231.17 - 199.46 winning tickets T/Qpdt: £29.10 to a £ stake Pool: £4,437.89 - 112.60 winning tickets RY

1999 WARWICK (L-H)
Monday, June 14

OFFICIAL GOING: Good (6.4)
Wind: Light half-against Weather: Cloudy with sunny spells

3028 RACING UK AMATEUR RIDERS' H'CAP 1m 4f 134y
6:25 (6:28) (Class 6) (0-60,60) 4-Y-0+ £1,977 (£608; £304) Stalls Low

Form RPR
525 1 **City Stable (IRE)**[24] 2302 5-10-5 **56** MrJMQuinlan(5) 6 67+
(M Wigham) *hld up: racd keenly: hdwy 2f out: led on bit 1f out: r.o wl* **10/3**[2]
60-4 2 3 ½ **Sand Repeal (IRE)**[18] 2455 8-10-4 **53** MrRBirkett(3) 5 58
(Miss J Feilden) *chsd ldrs: rdn and ev ch 1f out: styd on same pce* **9/1**
63-4 3 1 **Drawn Gold**[15] 2560 6-10-8 **57** MrStephenHarrison(3) 4 60
(R Hollinshead) *unruly in stalls: dwlt: hld up: swtchd rt and c stands' side 2f out: hdwy u.p over 1f out: hung lft and r.o ins fnl f: nrst fin* **3/1**[1]
-503 4 1 ½ **What A Day**[12] 2655 4-10-6 **52** MrSWalker 1 53
(J J Quinn) *a.p: rdn over 2f out: styd on same pce fnl f* **6/1**[3]
200- 5 3 ¼ **Hurricane Thomas (IRE)**[229] 7127 6-10-7 **58** MissPhillipaTutty(5) 8 54
(R A Fahey) *led over 8f: led again over 2f out: rdn: hdd & wknd 1f out* **20/1**
022- 6 ¾ **It's Josr**[237] 6918 5-10-1 **52** (b) MrCMartin(5) 2 47
(I A Wood) *hld up: racd keenly: hdwy over 4f out: wknd over 1f out* **8/1**
2200 7 ¾ **Laconicos (IRE)**[5] 2870 8-10-7 **60** (t) MissCScott(7) 12 53
(W B Stone) *dwlt: racd keenly and hdwy 10f out: chsd ldr 6f out to 4f out: wknd over 1f out* **22/1**
0-30 8 1 **Mossmann Gorge**[11] 2676 8-9-9 **46** oh1 (p) MissJodieHughes(5) 9 38
(A Middleton) *chsd ldrs: led 4f out: hdd over 2f out: wknd fnl f* **50/1**
5125 9 10 **Jackie Kiely**[42] 1755 9-10-6 **55** (tp) MrPCollington(3) 11 31
(R Brotherton) *hld up: rdn over 3f out: nvr on terms* **16/1**
6556 10 9 **Decibel**[16] 2533 6-10-6 **52** MrJoshuaMoore 3 13
(K A Ryan) *chsd ldrs: rdn over 3f out: wknd 2f out: t.o* **8/1**
0/0- 11 20 **Bungie**[375] 133 6-10-0 **46** oh1 MissEJJones 10 —
(Jennie Candlish) *prom: racd keenly: wknd 4f out: t.o* **80/1**
400- 12 54 **Wusuul**[414] 1535 5-10-1 **54** ow2 MissKatySquires(7) 13 —
(J W Mullins) *chsd ldrs: lost pl 1/2-way: bhd fnl 4f: t.o* **50/1**

2m 49.26s (4.66) **Going Correction** +0.125s/f (Good) 12 Ran SP% **114.7**
Speed ratings (Par 101): **90,87,87,86,84 83,83,82,76,71 58,25**
toteswingers: 1&2 £10.50, 1&3 £4.70, 2&3 £4.90 CSF £30.36 CT £98.52 TOTE £6.70: £3.50, £5.10, £1.10; EX 36.00.
Owner G Swan **Bred** Ballymacoll Stud Farm Ltd **Trained** Newmarket, Suffolk
■ Jack Quinlan's first Flat winner.

FOCUS
The time of this opening amateur riders' handicap suggested the rain had got into the ground. City Stable finally took advantage of a decent mark and the second was close to his latest Brighton form.

3029 EUROPEAN BREEDERS' FUND MAIDEN FILLIES' STKS 5f
6:55 (6:57) (Class 5) 2-Y-0 £3,626 (£1,079; £539; £269) Stalls Low

Form RPR
42 1 **Electric Waves (IRE)**[27] 2202 2-9-0 0 RichardMullen 8 76+
(E S McMahon) *chsd ldrs: led 4f out: shkn up over 1f out: r.o wl* **6/4**[2]
45 2 1 ¾ **Good Morning Dubai (IRE)**[25] 2251 2-9-0 0 KierenFallon 5 69+
(B J Meehan) *mid-div: pushed along and hdwy over 1f out: rdn to chse wnr ins fnl f: r.o* **5/4**[1]
06 3 3 **Aurivorous**[10] 2687 2-9-0 0 HayleyTurner 3 58
(Jonjo O'Neill) *led 1f: chsd wnr tl no ex ins fnl f* **20/1**
4 2 ½ **Princess Dayna** 2-9-0 0 RichardSmith 4 49
(Tom Dascombe) *dwlt: hld up: pushed along 1/2-way: hdwy over 1f out: sn rdn: hung rt and wknd ins fnl f* **20/1**
06 5 1 ¼ **Miss Dutee**[9] 2749 2-9-0 0 PatDobbs 6 44
(R Hannon) *chsd ldrs: rdn over 1f out: wknd fnl f* **16/1**
6 ½ **Instructress** 2-9-0 0 EddieAhern 10 43
(R M H Cowell) *s.s: swtchd lft and r.o ins fnl f: nvr nrr* **14/1**[3]
0 7 1 ½ **Country Waltz**[22] 2358 2-9-0 0 SamHitchcott 7 37
(M R Channon) *prom: rdn 1/2-way: hung rt and wknd over 1f out* **66/1**
8 2 **Dallas Legend (IRE)** 2-9-0 0 AlanMunro 2 30
(J Ryan) *s.i.s: sn drvn along: a in rr* **25/1**
9 2 ½ **Compton Lass** 2-8-11 0 RussKennemore(3) 1 21
(B G Powell) *s.s: a in rr* **50/1**
0 10 1 ½ **Shesanindian (IRE)**[49] 1577 2-9-0 0 (v[1]) NeilCallan 9 16
(A W Carroll) *s.i.s: hdwy over 3f out: rdn and wknd over 1f out* **100/1**

62.49 secs (2.89) **Going Correction** +0.325s/f (Good) 10 Ran SP% **114.8**
Speed ratings (Par 90): **89,86,81,77,75 74,72,69,65,62**
toteswingers: 1&2 £1.10, 2&3 £10.50, 1&3 not won. CSF £3.29 TOTE £3.50: £1.20, £1.02, £2.30; EX 4.10.
Owner J C Fretwell **Bred** Ms Michelle Lyons **Trained** Lichfield, Staffs

FOCUS
A fillies' maiden that concerned only two.

NOTEBOOK
Electric Waves(IRE), the deposed favourite, came out on top. The form of both her previous runs had worked out well and she simply proved too speedy for the runner-up, leading after 1f and keeping on well having been brought across to the stands' rail in the straight. The stiff finish wasn't to her advantage at Carlisle last time, and though she didn't look entirely straightforward in the preliminaries, she should make her mark in nurseries. (op 11-8 tchd 15-8)
Good Morning Dubai(IRE), the well-backed favourite, showed plenty of pace in a good maiden at Sandown last time, but she was ridden with more restraint on this occasion and, though staying on inside the final furlong, she never looked like getting to the winner. An extra furlong will suit on this evidence and she can win an ordinary maiden at some point. (op 6-4 tchd 10-11)
Aurivorous showed good speed and will be of interest once handicapping. (op 16-1)
Princess Dayna, a daughter of Green Desert, looked green on this debut and should improve. (op 25-1)
Miss Dutee will be of more interest once contesting nurseries and should benefit from an extra furlong.
Instructress, a half-sister to 5f 2-y-o winner Smooch, got a bit worked up in the stalls and ran as though she would improve for the experience. (op 20-1 tchd 25-1)

3030 TURFTV H'CAP 6f
7:25 (7:25) (Class 6) (0-65,65) 3-Y-0 £2,729 (£806; £403) Stalls Low

Form RPR
-523 1 **Red Scintilla**[17] 2502 3-9-3 **61** EddieAhern 2 69
(N Tinkler) *hld up in tch: rdn over 2f out: rdr dropped whip sn after: led ins fnl f: edgd rt: r.o* **11/2**[2]
-006 2 1 **Gazamali (IRE)**[8] 2780 3-8-1 **50** JohnFahy(5) 5 55
(H J Evans) *s.i.s: hld up: hdwy over 1f out: rdn and r.o* **33/1**
600- 3 1 **Rebecca Romero**[284] 5589 3-8-2 **46** oh1 CathyGannon 1 48
(D J Coakley) *chsd ldrs: led over 2f out: rdn and hung lft over 1f out: hdd ins fnl f: styd on same pce* **11/1**
0633 4 2 ¼ **Gemma's Delight (IRE)**[14] 2584 3-8-8 **52** (p) HayleyTurner 10 47+
(J W Unett) *prom: outpcd 2f out: styd on u.p ins fnl f* **9/1**
0464 5 nse **Aqua Vitae (IRE)**[10] 2699 3-8-13 **57** GregFairley 11 52
(M Johnston) *sn pushed along in rr: hdwy over 2f out: rdn over 1f out: edgd rt and no ex fnl f* **9/1**
6360 6 1 ½ **Itsthursdayalready**[27] 2215 3-9-5 **63** (b[1]) PaulMulrennan 9 53
(J G Given) *hld up in tch: rdn over 1f out: no ex* **12/1**
-025 7 nse **Macroy**[12] 2648 3-9-2 **63** JamesMillman(3) 6 53
(B R Millman) *chsd ldrs: led 1/2-way: hdd over 2f out: wknd ins fnl f* **8/1**[3]
250- 8 3 ½ **James Barrymore**[179] 7788 3-9-7 **65** PaulFitzsimons 14 43
(Miss J R Tooth) *hld up: styd on ins fnl f: nvr nrr* **40/1**
5163 9 nk **Tamarind Hill (IRE)**[5] 2849 3-8-11 **60** (b) DeclanCannon(5) 8 38
(A J McCabe) *led to 1/2-way: wknd over 1f out* **8/1**[3]
2000 10 1 **A Pocketful Of Rye (IRE)**[13] 2634 3-8-12 **59** AndrewHeffernan(3) 12 33
(P Howling) *s.s: nvr on terms* **25/1**
-402 11 ½ **Amoureuse**[19] 2432 3-7-9 **46** NeilFarley(7) 4 19
(D Carroll) *chsd ldrs: rdn over 2f out: wknd over 1f out* **11/1**
-054 12 1 **Autocracy**[19] 2442 3-9-5 **63** (b) KierenFallon 3 33
(W J Haggas) *unruly in stalls: dwlt: hld up: nt clr run over 2f out: rdn and edgd lft over 1f out: wknd ins fnl f* **4/1**[1]
1003 13 2 ¼ **Flaxen Lake**[8] 2784 3-9-6 **64** (p) GeorgeBaker 13 26
(J M Bradley) *w ldr to 1/2-way: wknd over 1f out* **20/1**
-000 14 3 ½ **Strike Shot**[5] 2868 3-9-7 **65** (b[1]) MartinDwyer 17 16
(W R Muir) *s.i.s: sn prom: rdn over 2f out: wknd over 1f out* **33/1**
000 15 2 ½ **Paphos**[28] 2174 3-8-3 **50** ow2 WilliamCarson(3) 16 —
(S C Williams) *s.i.s: sn pushed along in rr: wknd over 2f out* **25/1**
35-0 16 46 **Miskin Nights**[14] 2588 3-9-7 **65** DavidProbert 15 —
(B Palling) *chsd ldrs over 3f: eased: t.o* **33/1**

1m 14.12s (2.32) **Going Correction** +0.325s/f (Good) 16 Ran SP% **125.7**
Speed ratings (Par 97): **97,95,94,91,91 89,89,84,84,82 82,80,77,73,69 8**
toteswingers: 1&2 £45.70, 1&3 £20.70, 2&3 £32.80 CSF £188.92 CT £1299.15 TOTE £8.50: £1.80, £7.70, £2.70, £3.80; EX 322.80.
Owner Philip A Jarvis **Bred** Philip A Jarvis **Trained** Langton, N Yorks

FOCUS
Just a low-grade 3-y-o handicap, but the time was not bad and it might be worth giving the form a chance.
Itsthursdayalready Official explanation: jockey said gelding ran too free

3031 VOUTE SALES WARWICKSHIRE OAKS STKS (LISTED RACE) (F&M) 1m 2f 188y
7:55 (7:56) (Class 1) 4-Y-0+
£22,708 (£8,608; £4,308; £2,148; £1,076; £540) Stalls Low

Form RPR
1-56 1 **Lady Jane Digby**[18] 2470 5-8-12 104 GregFairley 10 99
(M Johnston) *a.p: chsd ldr over 4f out: rdn to ld over 1f out: styd on wl* **4/1**[1]
20-0 2 ¾ **Cassique Lady (IRE)**[16] 2538 5-8-12 94 EddieAhern 8 98
(Mrs L Wadham) *hld up: racd keenly: hdwy over 3f out: rdn to chse wnr fnl f: r.o* **18/1**
6-22 3 3 ¼ **Lady Artemisia (IRE)**[10] 2703 4-8-12 87 AlanMunro 2 92+
(M Botti) *hld up: hdwy u.p over 1f out: r.o: nt rch ldrs* **13/2**[3]
334- 4 shd **Saphira's Fire (IRE)**[177] 7809 5-8-12 106 MartinDwyer 3 92
(W R Muir) *hld up in tch: rdn over 2f out: styd on* **5/1**[2]
50-0 5 ½ **Uvinza**[31] 2071 4-8-12 94 (v[1]) DavidProbert 5 91
(W J Knight) *chsd ldrs: rdn over 1f out: styd on same pce* **9/1**

-424 **6** *1* **Honimiere (IRE)**[32] 2055 4-8-12 107 NeilCallan 6 89
(G A Swinbank) *trckd ldr tl led 1/2-way: rdn and hdd over 1f out: no ex ins fnl f* **8/1**

61-5 **7** *1* **Danehill's Pearl (IRE)**[85] 957 4-8-12 100 HayleyTurner 11 87
(Tom Dascombe) *s.s: hld up: rdn over 2f out: n.d* **20/1**

-000 **8** *hd* **Caster Sugar (USA)**[25] 2243 4-8-12 78 PatDobbs 7 87?
(R Hannon) *hld up: rdn over 2f out: nvr on terms* **66/1**

36-0 **9** *1/2* **Becqu Adoree (FR)**[16] 2538 4-8-12 108 KierenFallon 9 86
(L M Cumani) *hld up in tch: tk clsr order over 3f out: rdn over 1f out: wknd fnl f* **5/1**[2]

043- **10** *5* **Club Tahiti**[320] 4422 4-8-12 87 LiamJones 1 77
(A W Carroll) *s.i.s: hld up: rdn over 2f out: wknd over 1f out* **20/1**

1551 **P** **Paquerettza (FR)**[23] 2314 4-8-12 90 PaulMulrennan 4 —
(D H Brown) *led to 1/2-way: sn wknd: bhd whn p.u and dismntd over 3f out* **15/2**

2m 18.67s (-2.43) **Going Correction** +0.125s/f (Good) **11** Ran SP% **115.8**
Speed ratings (Par 111): **113,112,110,110,109 108,108,108,107,104** —
toteswingers:1&2 £14.50, 2&3 £27.90, 1&3 £5.70 CSF £75.14 TOTE £4.90: £2.10, £6.40, £4.10; EX 49.20.
Owner Miss K Rausing **Bred** Miss K Rausing **Trained** Middleham Moor, N Yorks
■ Stewards' Enquiry : Alan Munro two-day ban: used whip with excessive frequency without giving filly time to respond (Jun 28-29)

FOCUS
This is often a well-contested Listed event and the fact they went 4-1 the field suggested it was an open contest. It was a little muddling and the time was only ordinary. The winner did not need to be at her best.

NOTEBOOK
Lady Jane Digby found this a lot easier than the Group 3 Brigadier Gerard Stakes she ran in at Sandown last time, and Greg Fairley ensured she was in a position to strike for home early in the straight, getting to the front over 1f out and running on well to hold last year's winner Cassique Lady. Already twice a winner at Pattern level (won a Group 3 at Bremen last year), she is a tough and genuine filly who looks sure to gain more black type at some point this season. (op 10-3 tchd 9-2)
Cassique Lady(IRE), rated 10lb inferior to the winner, had shown next to nothing on her last two starts, including on her reappearance, but she closed to chase up the principals turning for home and stayed on well to challenge the winner, but never looked like getting past. This form is very much close to her best. (op 22-1)
Lady Artemisia(IRE), though only rated 87, is a very consistent filly and it was no surprise to see her run well, keeping on late to just snatch third. (op 17-2 tchd 9-1)
Saphira's Fire(IRE), who often ran well without winning last season, made a satisfactory comeback, and like many from the yard, should come on for this initial outing. (op 6-1)
Uvinza, over 7l behind the winner at Hamilton, travelled well in the first-time visor and got closer this time, but couldn't quicken from over 1f out. (op 12-1)
Honimiere(IRE) hasn't built on her Newmarket second to Strawberrydaiquiri, though this was better than her latest York effort. (tchd 15-2)
Becqu Adoree(FR), who had a pony to help her down to the start, moved closer before the home turn, but found little and has yet to offer much encouragement in two starts since joining current connections. (op 4-1 tchd 11-2)
Paquerettza(FR), a good winner off 84 at Chester, led early, but went wrong down the far side and was dismounted having been pulled up. Something was clearly amiss. Official explanation: trainer said filly finished distressed (op 10-1 tchd 7-1)

3032 WARWICK FOR CONFERENCES H'CAP — 1m 2f 188y
8:25 (8:26) (Class 6) (0-65,64) 4-Y-O+ — £2,047 (£604; £302) Stalls Low

Form RPR

0500 **1** **Harare**[14] 2596 9-9-0 60 (v) WilliamCarson(3) 1 66
(R J Price) *hld up in tch: racd keenly: rdn over 1f out: edgd rt and r.o to ld nr fin* **8/1**

6404 **2** *nk* **Farncombe (IRE)**[15] 970 4-8-9 52 HayleyTurner 7 57
(M J Scudamore) *led: rdn over 1f out: hdd nr fin* **18/1**

-204 **3** *nk* **Carter**[14] 2597 4-9-1 58 PaulMulrennan 13 63
(W M Brisbourne) *sn chsng ldr: rdn and hung lft over 1f out: ev ch ins fnl f: styd on* **7/2**[1]

00-0 **4** *1* **Fantino**[30] 2109 4-9-3 60 DavidProbert 6 63
(J Mackie) *chsd ldrs: rdn over 3f out: styd on same pce ins fnl f* **5/1**[2]

5-04 **5** *1* **Jenny Soba**[4] 2902 7-7-13 45 AndrewHeffernan(3) 8 46
(Lucinda Featherstone) *pushed along early in mid-div: hrd drvn fr over 4f out: styd on u.p: nt gng pce to chal* **6/1**[3]

005/ **6** *3/4* **Shipboard Romance (IRE)**[16] 7701 5-8-2 45 (t) CathyGannon 4 45
(M G Rimell) *hld up: rdn over 2f out: r.o: nt trble ldrs* **10/1**

05-0 **7** *1/2* **Transfer**[14] 2596 5-9-6 63 EddieAhern 11 62
(C P Morlock) *prom: rdn over 3f out: no ex ins fnl f* **6/1**[3]

3200 **8** *2 1/2* **Desert Fairy**[37] 1919 4-8-5 48 ow1 (v[1]) GregFairley 2 43
(J W Unett) *s.i.s: hld up: rdn 1/2-way: nvr on terms* **25/1**

0-53 **9** *13* **Horsley Warrior**[68] 1172 4-9-0 64 DavidKenny(7) 5 35
(E S McMahon) *hld up: a in rr: rdn and lost tch over 2f out* **13/2**

-000 **10** *3 3/4* **Polish Power (GER)**[42] 1755 10-8-13 56 (p) RobertHavlin 3 20
(P G Murphy) *s.i.s: a in rr* **18/1**

006/ **11** *20* **Royal Indulgence**[632] 6136 10-8-10 53 LiamJones 9 —
(W M Brisbourne) *s.i.s: plld hrd: hdwy 8f out: wknd over 3f out: t.o* **33/1**

2m 22.03s (0.93) **Going Correction** +0.125s/f (Good) **11** Ran SP% **118.3**
Speed ratings (Par 101): **101,100,100,99,99 98,98,96,86,84 69**
toteswingers:1&2 £89.30, 2&3 £15.80, 1&3 £8.60 CSF £142.77 CT £599.30 TOTE £15.90: £4.40, £5.60, £2.90; EX 79.30.
Owner Mrs P A Wallis **Bred** Limestone Stud **Trained** Ullingswick, H'fords
■ Stewards' Enquiry : William Carson one-day ban: used whip with excessive frequency (Jun 28)
Hayley Turner caution: used whip with excessive frequency.

FOCUS
A tight handicap, and there was little to separate the front three at the line. Muddling and rather weak form.
Royal Indulgence Official explanation: jockey said gelding ran too free

3033 PRICEWATERHOUSECOOPERS H'CAP — 7f 26y
8:55 (8:56) (Class 4) (0-85,84) 4-Y-O+ — £5,828 (£1,734; £866; £432) Stalls Low

Form RPR

12-0 **1** **Mr Rainbow**[70] 1117 4-9-7 84 NeilCallan 2 93+
(G A Swinbank) *trckd ldrs: racd keenly: shkn up to ld over 1f out: hung rt ins fnl f: drvn out* **15/8**[1]

0322 **2** *1* **Ocean Legend (IRE)**[31] 2091 5-9-1 83 JohnFahy(5) 8 89
(A W Carroll) *chsd ldrs: swtchd lft over 1f out: rdn to chse wnr and hung rt ins fnl f: r.o* **4/1**[2]

5041 **3** *1 1/4* **Headache**[28] 2187 5-8-2 70 (bt) SophieDoyle(5) 6 73
(B W Duke) *chsd ldr: rdn and ev ch over 1f out: styd on same pce ins fnl f* **13/2**

3-20 **4** *hd* **Lochan Mor**[40] 1826 4-9-3 80 HayleyTurner 7 82
(M L W Bell) *led: rdn and hdd over 1f out: styd on same pce ins fnl f* **5/1**[3]

1030 **5** *nk* **Dingaan (IRE)**[23] 2339 7-9-1 78 DavidProbert 5 80
(A M Balding) *hld up: rdn over 1f out: r.o: nt rch ldrs* **9/1**

0515 **6** *1 3/4* **Buxton**[8] 2783 6-8-9 72 (t) RobertHavlin 3 72+
(R Ingram) *hld up: hdwy whn hmpdf 1f out: could nt rcvr* **10/1**

1203 **7** *1 1/4* **Fol Liam**[11] 2678 4-7-13 67 ow2 (p) DeclanCannon(5) 4 61
(A J McCabe) *hld up in tch: rdn over 1f out: wknd ins fnl f* **11/1**

1m 26.08s (1.48) **Going Correction** +0.125s/f (Good) **7** Ran SP% **112.2**
Speed ratings (Par 105): **96,94,93,93,92 90,89**
toteswingers:1&2 £1.90, 2&3 £2.70, 1&3 £3.40 CSF £9.03 CT £38.07 TOTE £3.70: £2.60, £2.60; EX 9.30 Place 6: £38.86 Place 5: £24.18.
Owner Guy Reed **Bred** G Reed **Trained** Melsonby, N Yorks

FOCUS
A fair handicap. The form makes a bit of sense and the winner posted a personal best.
T/Jkpt: Not won. T/Plt: £29.30 to a £1 stake. Pool: £54,904.15 - 1,363.90 winning tickets. T/Qpdt: £16.30 to a £1 stake. Pool: £3,725.91- 168.62 winning tickets CR

2819 WINDSOR (R-H)
Monday, June 14

OFFICIAL GOING: Good (7.5)
Stands rail dolled out 18yds at 6f down to 7yds at winning post. Top bend dolled out 2yds from innermost line, adding 9yds to races of one mile and over.
Wind: fresh, against Weather: overcast

3034 E B F BRITISH LEISURE SHOW MAIDEN STKS — 5f 10y
6:10 (6:12) (Class 4) 2-Y-O — £4,533 (£1,348; £674; £336) Stalls High

Form RPR

0 **1** **Believe It Or Not (IRE)**[14] 2594 2-9-3 0 LiamKeniry 11 76
(J S Moore) *chsd ldrs: swtchd lft over 2f out: hrd drvn to press ldrs jst ins fnl f: kpt on wl to ld wl ins fnl f* **11/2**[2]

2 *hd* **Enthusing (IRE)** 2-9-3 0 DaneO'Neill 8 75+
(D R C Elsworth) *dwlt: towards rr: switching lft to centre wl over 1f out: rdn and hdwy to chse ldrs ent fnl f: kpt on wl to press wnr cl home: gng on fin* **8/1**

2226 **3** *1/2* **Master Macho (IRE)**[3] 2936 2-9-3 0 ChrisCatlin 10 73
(M R Channon) *awkward leaving stalls: sn rcvrd to ld: rdn and edging lft u.p wl over 1f out: hdd and no ex wl ins fnl f* **11/4**[1]

50 **4** *1* **Sarangoo**[10] 2687 2-8-12 0 FergusSweeney 6 65
(M S Saunders) *chsd ldrs: rdn wl over 1f out: chsd ldr ent fnl f: no ex and btn fnl 75yds* **12/1**

50 **5** *6* **Koha (USA)**[17] 2505 2-8-12 0 SteveDrowne 1 43+
(D K Ivory) *chsd ldr: rdn and ev ch over 1f out: btn 1f out and wknd qckly fnl f* **12/1**

00 **6** *1 1/4* **Marmaduke**[11] 2680 2-9-3 0 NeilChalmers 12 44+
(J J Bridger) *s.i.s: sn niggled along in rr: struggling 1/2-way: styd on past btn horses fr over 1f out: nvr threatened ldrs* **100/1**

60 **7** *hd* **Ree's Rascal (IRE)**[31] 2078 2-9-0 0 RobertLButler(3) 5 47+
(J R Boyle) *wnt lft sn after s: bhd: struggling 1/2-way: kpt on past btn horses fnl f: nvr trbld ldrs* **50/1**

0 **8** *nse* **Mixed Emotions (IRE)**[25] 2251 2-8-12 0 RichardHughes 2 46+
(R Hannon) *t.k.h: hld up in midfield: rdn and btn wl over 1f out: heavily eased ins fnl f* **6/1**[3]

9 *3* **Poetically** 2-9-3 0 StephenCraine 9 32
(J G Portman) *s.i.s: sn rcvrd and chsng ldrs: rdn and wknd qckly wl over 1f out: wl bhd fnl f* **14/1**

00 **10** *3/4* **Regal Bullet (IRE)**[7] 2819 2-9-3 0 JimmyQuinn 4 29
(D K Ivory) *s.i.s: a bhd: lost tch over 2f out* **100/1**

62.57 secs (2.27) **Going Correction** +0.275s/f (Good) **10** Ran SP% **93.4**
Speed ratings (Par 95): **92,91,90,89,79 77,77,77,72,71**
toteswingers: 1&2 £6.60, 1&3 £4.20, 2&3 £2.70 CSF £29.55 TOTE £6.70: £2.00, £2.90, £1.20; EX 31.00 Trifecta £110.20 Pool £1102.17 - 7.40 winning units..
Owner Jimmy & Susie Wenman **Bred** Ballyhane Stud **Trained** Upper Lambourn, Berks

FOCUS
A routine juvenile contest in which the early favourite Pabusar went down in the stalls during the loading process, and was withdrawn (3/1, deduct 25p in the £ under R4).

NOTEBOOK
Believe It Or Not(IRE), finding a gap through the pack just when he needed it, improved significantly on his debut run at Goodwood but the market moved suggests it was not unexpected. (op 12-1)
Enthusing(IRE), by Noverre out of a Zafonic mare and likely to stay at least 1m in due course, was on the leggy side for this debut but looked pretty straight. He had to switch wide to make his run, and in the circumstances did well to reach second place, but normal improvement should see him win one of these. (op 6-1)
Master Macho(IRE) continues to show plenty of pace but is finding it hard to hold off less-exposed rivals. He ought to be capable of winning a race but has had plenty of chances now. (op 7-2 tchd 4-1)
Sarangoo ran her best race to date and might yet win a maiden. However, she is now qualified for nurseries and that looks the obvious option. (op 20-1 tchd 22-1)
Koha(USA) has not yet repeated the promise of her first run, and is unlikely to win a maiden if this is any guide, but at least her debut performance would give her a chance in nurseries now she is qualified. (tchd 10-1)
Marmaduke put in his best performance yet. Though it was nothing to get excited about, he will be more at home in nurseries and ought to be suited by 6f and even further. (op 150-1)
Ree's Rascal(IRE) was reported to have been denied a clear run three times, and then crowded and intimidated in the closing stages, so some improvement should be forthcoming. Official explanation: jockey said, regarding running and riding, that his orders were to drop the colt in and try to finish well, adding that it was denied a clear run on three occasions and was crowded and intimidated in the closing stages; trainer confirmed, adding that it has a tendancy to be free and buzzed up at home.
Mixed Emotions(IRE) Official explanation: jockey said bit slipped through filly's mouth

3035 PSP ASSOCIATION TRIBUTE (S) STKS — 6f
6:40 (6:44) (Class 5) 2-Y-O — £2,456 (£725; £362) Stalls High

Form RPR

4 **1** **Whoatealthepius (IRE)**[23] 2338 2-8-8 0 ow2 RichardHughes 16 71+
(R Hannon) *a gng wl: trcking ldrs: cruised ahd ent fnl f: c readily clr fnl f: nt extended* **4/11**[1]

444 **2** *4* **Crown Ridge (IRE)**[9] 2763 2-8-11 0 ChrisCatlin 2 58
(M R Channon) *chsd ldrs and jst abt in tch: rdn and hdwy in centre 2f out: chsd wnr fnl f: no imp and no ch* **11/1**[2]

3 *1/2* **A Little Bit Dusty** 2-8-8 0 JackDean(3) 5 57
(W G M Turner) *s.i.s: rn green and sn rdn along off the pce in midfield: swtchd to centre ent fnl 2f: kpt on to go 3rd fnl 100yds: no ch w wnr* **20/1**

The Form Book, Raceform Ltd, Compton, RG20 6NL

	4	2 1/2	**Painters Easel (IRE)** 2-8-4 0 RyanPowell(7) 8 (J S Moore) *s.i.s: sn wl off the pce towards rr: rdn and hdwy 2f out: swtchd lft and styd on wl in centre to go 4th wl ins fnl f: nvr trbld ldrs* **66/1**	49
00	5	shd	**Indian Dip**[34] 1999 2-8-6 0 SimonWhitworth 1 (F J Brennan) *broke wl: sn crossed towards stands' rail and chsd ldrs: wknd u.p over 1f out* **66/1**	44
6334	6	2	**Johnny Hancocks (IRE)**[35] 1978 2-8-11 0 JamesDoyle 6 (P D Evans) *disp ld: bmpd 3f out: sn led: drvn ent fnl 2f: hdd ent fnl f: sn wknd* **12/1**[3]	43
6	7	3/4	**Livia Quarta (IRE)**[14] 2591 2-8-6 0 LukeMorris 12 (E J Creighton) *awkward leaving stalls: sn rcvrd and chsng ldrs: edgd lft towards centre and rdn jst over 2f out: swtchd lft and hrd drvn over 1f out: sn wknd* **100/1**	35
	8	6	**Castle Kirk (IRE)** 2-8-6 0 KierenFox(5) 13 (P M Phelan) *s.i.s: sn rdn and along and a outpcd in midfield: n.d* **25/1**	22
00	9	1 3/4	**Sky Booster**[14] 2594 2-8-11 0 TadhgO'Shea 15 (W J Haggas) *chsd ldrs tl rdn and wknd qckly ent fnl 2f: wl bhd fnl f* **11/1**[2]	17
0	10	3/4	**Bert And Ernie**[6] 2839 2-8-11 0 CoryParish 11 (M R Channon) *s.i.s: sn rdn along: nvr on terms* **33/1**	15
	11	2	**Columba's Boy** 2-8-11 0 EddieCreighton 10 (D K Ivory) *racd off the pce in midfield: rdn and struggling 1/2-way: wl btn fnl 2f* **66/1**	9
	12	2 1/2	**Pahente** 2-8-11 0 LiamKeniry 3 (J S Moore) *s.i.s: sn wl outpcd in rr: n.d* **66/1**	—
05	13	2 1/4	**Battenberg**[13] 2631 2-8-6 0 (b1) NickyMackay 9 (Miss Amy Weaver) *disp ld: edgd lft and bmpd rival 3f out: sn hdd: wknd rapidly over 2f out: wl bhd fr over 1f out* **66/1**	—
0	14	7	**I Dreamed A Dream**[12] 2641 2-8-1 0 SimonPearce(5) 14 (D K Ivory) *s.i.s: a wl outpcd in rr: t.o* **40/1**	—
	15	8	**Petronilla** 2-8-6 0 SaleemGolam 7 (W J Musson) *v.s.a: sn wl detached in last: t.o fr 1/2-way* **33/1**	—

1m 15.93s (2.93) **Going Correction** +0.275s/f (Good) **15** Ran SP% **123.1**
Speed ratings (Par 93): **91,85,85,81,81 78,77,69,67,66 63,60,57,48,37**
toteswingers: 1&2 £2.50, 1&3 £3.90, 2&3 £9.80 CSF £4.46 TOTE £1.40: £1.10, £2.60, £4.90; EX 6.00 Trifecta £38.90 Pool: £1757.09 - 33.40 winning units..The winner was bought by D Ivory for £25,200.

Owner R Morecombe & F Jones **Bred** Moygaddy Stud **Trained** East Everleigh, Wilts

FOCUS

A run-of-the-mill seller with the exception of the winner.

NOTEBOOK

Whoateallthepius(IRE) looked much better class than this on the basis of a promising debut fourth in a Newbury maiden, and so it proved. She had the perfect draw, and the 2lb overweight wasn't even the slightest inconvenience. However, it was somewhat disconcerting that no attempt was made by connections to buy her back as the auction racked up a near-record price for the course. (tchd 1-3)

Crown Ridge(IRE) had shown minor promise when finishing fourth in three maidens. The drop to selling company would have produced dividends had the winner not been in the line-up, so he must have a chance of winning a similar race. (op 12-1)

A Little Bit Dusty, by Needwood Blade, is bred to be speedy, but he took too long to get going on this first appearance from a poor draw. The fact that he had already been gelded and started off in a seller is not encouraging, but he should be sharper next time and ran as if likely to stay 7f. (op 50-1)

Painters Easel(IRE), by Modigliani out of a Giant's Causeway mare, was another gelding debuting at this lowly level. However, he ran reasonably well in the end and was finishing as if likely to do even better over a longer trip.

Indian Dip did not do too badly in trying to overcome a low stall, but sellers are her scene. (op 80-1)

Johnny Hancocks(IRE) has plenty of early pace, so 5f sellers should suit him best. (op 10-1)

Castle Kirk(IRE) Official explanation: jockey said colt ran green

Battenberg Official explanation: jockey said filly became unbalanced under pressure

3036 METROPOLITAN HOTEL, LONDON SUPPORTS PSP ASSOCIATION H'CAP 1m 67y

7:10 (7:10) (Class 5) (0-75,75) 4-Y-0+ **£2,729** (£806; £403) **Stalls** High

Form				RPR
1-36	1		**Ela Gorrie Mou**[25] 2262 4-9-2 **70** RobertWinston 11 (P Charalambous) *chsd ldng trio: rdn and effrt 2f out: edgd rt u.p and chal wl over 1f out: sn led: kpt edging rt: styd on wl ins fnl f* **11/2**[2]	83
-001	2	2	**Calahonda**[18] 2477 4-8-11 **70** KierenFox(5) 12 (P W D'Arcy) *hld up in midfield: rdn and hdwy 2f out: chsd ldng pair over 1f out: kpt on u.p to go 2nd nr fin: nt gng pce to rch wnr* **6/1**[3]	78
6-01	3	nk	**Kilburn**[14] 2596 6-9-3 **71** SteveDrowne 7 (A J Lidderdale) *led: rdn and hdd over 1f out: nt clr run and swtchd lft jst ins fnl f: kpt on same pce after: lost 2nd nr fin* **6/1**[3]	78
6022	4	5	**Hazzard County (USA)**[19] 2443 6-9-6 **74** WilliamBuick 10 (D M Simcock) *hld up towards rr: rdn and effrt wl over 1f out: no imp fnl f* **11/4**[1]	70
30-0	5	2 3/4	**Becuille (IRE)**[7] 2823 5-9-2 **70** (b) TadhgO'Shea 13 (B J Meehan) *t.k.h: chsd ldng pair: wnt 2nd 4f out: rdn and chal over 2f out: struggling whn sltly hmpd wl over 1f out: sn wknd* **14/1**	59
-602	6	1/2	**Bomber Command (USA)**[14] 2596 7-8-10 **67** (v) PatrickHills(3) 4 (J W Hills) *in tch: rdn and unable qck ent fnl 2f: wknd over 1f out* **9/1**	55
-345	7	1 3/4	**Bolanderi (USA)**[20] 2411 5-9-4 **72** RichardHughes 6 (Andrew Turnell) *hld up in last trio: rdn and no hdwy wl over 1f out: n.d* **12/1**	56
53-4	8	5	**Piccolo Mondo**[38] 1875 4-9-1 **69** (p) JimCrowley 5 (P Winkworth) *chsd ldr tl 4f out: rdn and wkng whn hmpd wl over 1f out: sn wl btn* **6/1**[3]	42
4-00	9	1 1/4	**Red Suede Shoes**[131] 394 4-9-2 **75** (p) SimonPearce(5) 8 (J Pearce) *stdd after s: a in rr: rdn and no hdwy 2f out: n.d* **20/1**	45
300-	10	nk	**Doric Echo**[39] 6824 4-8-13 **67** DaneO'Neill 9 (C P Morlock) *hld up in last trio: rdn and no prog ent fnl 2f: wl btn over 1f out* **66/1**	36

1m 44.02s (-0.68) **Going Correction** 0.0s/f (Good) **10** Ran SP% **115.5**
Speed ratings (Par 103): **103,101,100,95,92 92,90,85,84,84**
toteswingers: 1&2 £9.20, 1&3 £4.80, 2&3 £5.70 CSF £38.11 CT £208.54 TOTE £7.00: £2.60, £3.30, £2.00; EX 45.30 Trifecta £226.60 Pool: £1163.85 - 3.80 winning units..

Owner P Charalambous **Bred** Peter Charles **Trained** Newmarket, Suffolk

■ The first training success for Peter Charalambous.

■ Stewards' Enquiry : Robert Winston one-day ban: careless riding (Jun 28)

FOCUS

There was a decent pace, but the first three were all in the first five throughout and nothing got close from behind. High numbers were favoured but the form has been rated at face value.

3037 SPORTINGBET.COM H'CAP 6f

7:40 (7:41) (Class 4) (0-80,80) 4-Y-0+ **£4,533** (£1,348; £674; £336) **Stalls** High

Form				RPR
-053	1		**Gwilym (GER)**[2] 2973 7-8-10 **69** JimCrowley 16 (D Haydn Jones) *hld up in tch: rdn and effrt over 1f out: led ins fnl f: r.o wl* **6/1**[2]	78
0060	2	1/2	**Lujeanie**[49] 1580 4-9-4 **77** FergusSweeney 15 (D K Ivory) *hld up in tch in rr: plenty to do ent fnl f: switching lft and str run ins fnl f: chsd wnr towards fin: could nt quite rch wnr* **40/1**	84
6621	3	1/2	**Requisite**[4] 2904 5-8-9 **68** 6ex (v) RichardHughes 14 (I A Wood) *hld up in tch towards rr: bhd a wall of horses and swtchd rt over 1f out: stl plenty to do 1f out: r.o wl ins fnl f: wnt 3rd last strides: could nt rch ldrs* **5/1**[1]	74+
60-3	4	nk	**Victorian Bounty**[21] 2399 5-9-7 **80** MickyFenton 5 (Stef Higgins) *broke fast and sn led: rdn and hdd over 1f out: kpt on u.p: no ex fnl 75yds* **7/1**[3]	85
5426	5	hd	**Another Try (IRE)**[17] 2504 5-8-3 **67** ow1 MatthewDavies(5) 7 (A P Jarvis) *chsd ldrs: rdn and effrt wl over 1f out: pressed ldrs 1f out: kpt on u.p fnl f* **28/1**	71
3400	6	1	**Viking Spirit**[25] 2247 8-9-7 **80** ShaneKelly 10 (W R Swinburn) *t.k.h: stdd s: hld up in tch towards rr: nt clr run over 1f out: swtchd lft ent fnl f: r.o: nt able to rch ldrs* **16/1**	81+
6-00	7	1/2	**Baunagain (IRE)**[17] 2508 5-9-7 **80** JackMitchell 12 (P W Chapple-Hyam) *taken down early: dwlt: t.k.h: hld up in tch in midfield: hdwy to chse ldrs wl over 1f out: drvn ent fnl f: no ex fnl 150yds* **18/1**	79
5-50	8	1/2	**Cut The Cackle (IRE)**[14] 2601 4-9-0 **73** LukeMorris 6 (P Winkworth) *rrd s: v slowly and wl bhd: rdn and switching lft wl over 1f out: r.o u.p fnl f: nvr rchd ldrs* **16/1**	71+
3206	9	hd	**Make My Dream**[21] 2399 7-8-13 **72** TadhgO'Shea 1 (J Gallagher) *t.k.h: hld up in midfield on outer: rdn and effrt wl over 1f out: no prog fnl f* **25/1**	69+
0001	10	1/2	**Memphis Man**[4] 2896 7-8-5 **71** 6ex KevinLundie(7) 9 (P D Evans) *taken down early: towards rr: rdn and effrt on outer wl over 1f out: nvr trbld ldrs* **12/1**	67
5-00	11	1/2	**Tagula Night (IRE)**[11] 2681 4-9-5 **78** (vt) AdamKirby 11 (W R Swinburn) *w ldr: rdn to ld over 1f out: hdd ins fnl f: wknd qckly fnl 100yds* **7/1**[3]	72
50-5	12	1	**Francis Walsingham (IRE)**[28] 2166 4-8-9 **68** (t) SteveDrowne 13 (H Morrison) *hld up in tch towards rr: n.m.r wl over 1f out tl ent fnl f: kpt on ins fnl f: nvr able to chal* **16/1**	59+
0001	13	1/2	**Imprimis Tagula (IRE)**[30] 2123 6-9-1 **74** (v) RobertWinston 8 (A Bailey) *chsd ldrs: rdn and struggling whn hmpd over 1f out: n.d fnl f* **6/1**[2]	63
210-	14	1/2	**Fleeting Star (USA)**[268] 6112 4-9-5 **78** (v) TomQueally 4 (J Noseda) *hld up in tch in midfield: rdn and edgd lft over 1f out: wknd u.p jst ins fnl f* **16/1**	66
05-6	15	10	**C'Mon You Irons (IRE)**[49] 1580 5-9-0 **73** IanMongan 3 (M R Hoad) *chsd ldrs on outer: rdn and hanging lft fr over 2f out: btn over 1f out: eased ins fnl f* **14/1**	29

1m 13.89s (0.89) **Going Correction** +0.275s/f (Good) **15** Ran SP% **123.1**
Speed ratings (Par 105): **105,104,103,103,103 101,101,100,100,99 98,97,96,96,82**
toteswingers: 1&2 £68.00, 1&3 £3.10, 2&3 £41.30 CSF £238.52 CT £959.75 TOTE £10.10: £3.80, £14.60, £1.60; EX 257.10 TRIFECTA Not won..

Owner S Kon, D Llewelyn and J Runeckles **Bred** B Krutmann **Trained** Efail Isaf, Rhondda C Taff

FOCUS

A competitive sprint handicap with plenty in contention a furlong out. The first three home came from the three highest stalls but that appeared to be a coincidence because they were wide apart at the finish, spread across the track with other runners between them. The form has been taken at face value.

Requisite Official explanation: jockey said mare was denied a clear run

Cut The Cackle(IRE) Official explanation: jockey said filly reared leaving stalls

Imprimis Tagula(IRE) Official explanation: jockey said gelding hung right

3038 SPORTINGBET.COM MAIDEN STKS 1m 2f 7y

8:10 (8:15) (Class 5) 3-Y-0+ **£2,729** (£806; £403) **Stalls** Centre

Form				RPR
06	1		**Court Circle**[17] 2507 3-9-0 0 WilliamBuick 4 (Sir Michael Stoute) *hld up in tch in midfield: rdn and hdwy to chal over 1f out: led fnl 100yds: r.o wl* **12/1**[3]	80
	2	1/2	**Marching Song (USA)**[33] 4-9-13 0 RichardHughes 10 (Andrew Turnell) *chsd ldr: pushed ahd over 3f out: rdn and kpt on wl 2f out: hdd and no ex fnl 100yds* **22/1**	79
	3	1/2	**Mountain Hiker (IRE)** 3-9-0 0 ShaneKelly 11 (J Noseda) *in tch in midfield: pushed along: outpcd and rn green over 2f out: switching lft over 1f out: styd on wl ins fnl f: gng on fin* **14/1**	78+
-32	4	3/4	**Azimuth (USA)**[23] 2335 3-9-0 0 TomQueally 5 (J Noseda) *chsd ldrs: wnt 2nd over 3f out: rdn to chal over 2f out: nt qckn u.p wl over 1f out: one pce and btn fnl 150yds* **10/11**[1]	76
45	5	3	**Roanstar**[21] 2401 3-9-0 0 LiamKeniry 8 (A M Balding) *t.k.h: chsd ldrs: rdn and edging lft wl over 1f out: unable qck and btn ent fnl f* **7/1**[2]	70
	6	9	**Jakeys Girl** 3-8-4 0 KierenFox(5) 7 (P M Phelan) *s.i.s: a towards rr: in tch tl wknd u.p wl over 2f out: wl btn fnl 2f* **100/1**	47
0/6	7	2 1/2	**Daniel Defoe (USA)**[58] 1380 4-9-10 0 Louis-PhilippeBeuzelin(3) 1 (Sir Michael Stoute) *sn pushed up to ld: rdn and hdd over 4f out: wknd 2f out: wl btn over 1f out* **33/1**	47
	8	3/4	**Isobar (GER)** 4-9-13 0 J-PGuillambert 12 (L M Cumani) *stdd s: hld up in last trio: lost tch wl over 2f out: n.d* **12/1**[3]	46
0	9	5	**Marcus Antonius**[13] 2632 3-9-0 0 StephenCraine 2 (J R Boyle) *s.i.s: rdn along thrght: towards rr: sme hdwy into midfield 5f out: struggling u.p 4f out: wl bhd fnl 2f* **100/1**	36
	10	1	**Jinn And Tinick** 4-9-8 0 JamesDoyle 3 (A W Carroll) *s.i.s: sn pushed along in rr: rdn and lost tch wl over 2f out* **100/1**	29
6-44	11	6	**Suhailah**[54] 1479 4-9-3 45 JemmaMarshall(5) 6 (M J Attwater) *chsd ldrs tl wknd 3f out: wl bhd fnl 2f* **100/1**	17

2m 10.29s (1.59) **Going Correction** 0.0s/f (Good)
WFA 3 from 4yo 13lb **11** Ran SP% **98.2**
Speed ratings (Par 103): **93,92,92,91,89 82,80,79,75,74 69**
toteswingers: 1&2 £75.80, 1&3 £4.20, 2&3 £16.30 CSF £157.23 TOTE £9.50: £1.90, £4.50, £3.10; EX 117.80 TRIFECTA Not won..

Owner Cheveley Park Stud **Bred** Cheveley Park Stud Ltd **Trained** Newmarket, Suffolk
■ Mortbet was withdrawn (4/1, refused to enter stalls). Deduct 20p in the £ under R4.

FOCUS
A modest-looking maiden in which a solid gallop left a group of just five in contention in the last 2f. The winner is progressing.
Jakeys Girl Official explanation: jockey said filly ran in snatches

3039 VERBATIM DIGITAL STORAGE H'CAP — 1m 2f 7y
8:40 (8:40) (Class 5) (0-75,75) 3-Y-O — **£2,729** (£806; £403) **Stalls** Centre

Form — RPR

-540 **1** **Onyx Of Arabia (IRE)**[14] [2587] 3-8-13 **67**......................(b) TadhgO'Shea 4 76
(B J Meehan) *s.i.s: hld up in last trio: hdwy over 2f out: rdn to ld ent fnl f: r.o strly and clr fnl 100yds* **25/1**

0-25 **2** *3* **Plus Ultra (IRE)**[39] [1851] 3-9-2 **70**.................................. TomQueally 13 75+
(H R A Cecil) *dwlt and bustled along early: sn in tch in midfield: nt clr run over 2f out tl swtchd lft over 1f out: sn nt clr run again and swtchd lft ent fnl f: kpt on wl to go 2nd nr fin: no ch w wnr* **5/1**[2]

0-24 **3** *nk* **Big Wave Bay (IRE)**[17] [2501] 3-8-11 **65**...................... RobertWinston 7 67
(A P Jarvis) *in tch: rdn and effrt over 2f out: drvn and ev ch 2f out: led over 1f out: sn hdd and nt gng pce of wnr ins fnl f: lost 2nd nr fin* **16/1**

6013 **4** *1* **Al Dafa (USA)**[10] [2702] 3-9-4 **72**...................................... JamieSpencer 2 72+
(M L W Bell) *stdd after s and hld up in last trio: effrt and swtchd lft over 2f out: sn drvn and hdwy to chse ldrs over 1f out: one pce ins fnl f* **13/8**[1]

3204 **5** *4* **Thundering Home**[35] [1973] 3-9-1 **69**.......................... WilliamBuick 11 61
(M J Attwater) *s.i.s: bhd: clsd and in tch 1/2-way: swtchd lft and effrt u.p 2f out: no imp and wl btn ent fnl f* **14/1**

01-0 **6** *nk* **Shoot The Pot (IRE)**[21] [2398] 3-8-11 **65**......................... JimCrowley 10 57
(R M Beckett) *led tl 7f out: chsd ldr after tl led again over 3f out: rdn and hdd over 1f out: wknd ins fnl f* **7/1**[3]

2500 **7** *4* **Calypso Star (IRE)**[5] [2869] 3-9-1 **72**...........................(b[1]) PatrickHills(3) 9 56
(R Hannon) *chsd ldrs: rdn and nt qckning whn n.m.r ent fnl 2f: wknd over 1f out: wl btn fnl f* **12/1**

0-43 **8** *1 1/4* **Thereafter (USA)**[51] [1537] 3-8-13 **67**............................ SteveDrowne 14 48
(R Charlton) *in tch in midfield: rdn over 3f out: wknd u.p ent fnl 2f: wl btn fnl f* **15/2**

14-0 **9** *6* **Dashing Doc (IRE)**[16] [2544] 3-9-7 **75**................................ DaneO'Neill 1 44
(D R C Elsworth) *a towards rr: racd awkwardly on bnd 6f out: effrt on outer whn squeezed out and hmpd over 2f out: no ch after* **12/1**

540- **10** *2 3/4* **Rodrigo De Freitas (IRE)**[242] [6793] 3-8-8 **62**................ NickyMackay 8 26
(J R Boyle) *chsd ldr tl led 7f out tl over 3f out: wkng u.p whn n.m.r jst over 2f out: wknd qckly wl over 1f out* **66/1**

3-04 **11** *hd* **Infanta (IRE)**[18] [2463] 3-8-11 **72**..................................(v) AntiocoMurgia(7) 5 35
(Mahmood Al Zarooni) *hld up towards rr: rdn and effrt on outer wl over 2f out: pushed lft over 2f out: sn wl btn* **20/1**

0060 **12** *8* **Togoaviking**[18] [2480] 3-8-3 **57**.. JimmyQuinn 6 —
(H J L Dunlop) *taken down early: chsd ldrs: wkng u.p whn pushed lft over 2f out: sn wl bhd* **66/1**

2m 9.27s (0.57) **Going Correction** 0.0s/f (Good) **12** Ran SP% **118.6**
Speed ratings (Par 99): **97,94,94,93,90 90,86,85,81,78 78,72**
toteswingers: 1&2 £29.10, 1&3 £40.80, 2&3 £15.10 CSF £142.86 CT £2095.33 TOTE £46.10: £8.60, £1.60, £5.90; EX 143.90 TRIFECTA Not won..
Owner Miss A Al-Hejailan **Bred** Ballyhane Stud & Allez B Stock 2 P Ship **Trained** Manton, Wilts
■ Stewards' Enquiry : Jamie Spencer two-day ban: careless riding (Jun 28-29)

FOCUS
This followed the pattern of previous races at 1m plus, with a small group dominating in the last 2f. The pace looked ordinary, only quickening 3f out, but the hold-up horses did best. The form seems sound.
Plus Ultra(IRE) Official explanation: jockey said gelding was denied a clear run

3040 A C BECK H'CAP — 1m 3f 135y
9:05 (9:05) (Class 5) (0-70,69) 4-Y-O+ — **£2,729** (£806; £403) **Stalls** Centre

Form — RPR

6031 **1** **Granny McPhee**[46] [1636] 4-9-7 **69**.............................. RobertWinston 11 77
(A Bailey) *s.i.s: hld up in rr: hdwy over 3f out: rdn to chal and edgd rt u.p wl over 1f out: led ins fnl f: kpt on u.p* **10/3**[1]

0025 **2** *nk* **Broughtons Paradis (IRE)**[15] [2560] 4-8-10 **58**............... TonyCulhane 7 68+
(W J Musson) *stdd s: hld up in tch in midfield: effrt on inner whn nt clr run and bdly hmpd jst over 1f out: swtchd lft jst ins fnl f: rn wl on to go 2nd last strides: nt quite able to rch wnr* **10/3**[1]

5062 **3** *hd* **Choral Festival**[12] [2645] 4-8-2 **57**...............................(v) RyanClark(7) 5 64
(J J Bridger) *chsd ldrs: rdn to ld jst over 2f out: edgd sltly rt u.p jst over 1f out: hdd ins fnl f: unable qck and lost 2nd last strides* **10/1**

0-03 **4** *3 3/4* **Shy**[14] [2586] 5-9-0 **62**.. JimCrowley 1 62
(B R Millman) *led for 2f: ev ch and rdn wl over 2f out: unable qck and n.m.r jst over 1f out: wknd ins fnl f* **7/2**[2]

0054 **5** *1 1/2* **Sacrilege**[7] [2821] 5-8-12 **65**..(p) MarkCoumbe(5) 4 63
(M C Chapman) *s.i.s and rel to r early: racd in last: rdn and hdwy on outer 2f out: kpt on same pce and no prog over 1f out* **11/1**

-554 **6** *1/2* **Kashmina**[7] [2811] 5-8-8 **59** ow1.. RobertLButler(3) 2 56
(Miss Sheena West) *s.i.s: hld up towards rr: rdn over 3f out: hdwy on outer ent fnl 2f out: no prog over 1f out: wl hld ins fnl f* **12/1**

56-5 **7** *1* **Lucky Score (IRE)**[41] [101] 4-9-0 **62**.................................... LiamKeniry 6 57
(Mouse Hamilton-Fairley) *hld up in last trio: switching ins and rdn ent fnl 2f: edging lft and plugged on fr over 1f out: nvr gng pce to threaten ldrs* **20/1**

1-00 **8** *5* **Aine's Delight (IRE)**[31] [2080] 4-8-13 **61**.................... RichardHughes 8 48
(Andrew Turnell) *t.k.h: hld up wl in tch: rdn and wknd over 2f out: wl btn over 1f out* **8/1**[3]

0400 **9** *4 1/2* **Hip Hip Hooray**[14] [2596] 4-8-12 **60**.................................. ChrisCatlin 10 39
(L A Dace) *chsd ldr tl led after 2f: rdn and hdd jst over 2f out: sn wknd: wl bhd fnl f* **16/1**

0006 **10** *7* **Mixing**[26] [2230] 8-8-2 **50** oh5.. JimmyQuinn 3 17
(M J Attwater) *chsd ldrs: rdn and nt qckning whn short of room jst over 2f out: sn wknd and wl bhd* **40/1**

2m 31.21s (1.71) **Going Correction** 0.0s/f (Good) **10** Ran SP% **117.7**
Speed ratings (Par 103): **94,93,93,91,90 89,89,85,82,78**
toteswingers: 1&2 £4.90, 1&3 £5.20, 2&3 £6.10 CSF £14.74 CT £100.90 TOTE £4.60: £1.30, £1.10, £3.70; EX 19.10 Trifecta £147.20 Pool: £328.23 - 1.65 winning units. Place 6: £225.00 Place 5: £160.75.
Owner Middleham Park Racing XXVI & Alan Bailey **Bred** Sugar Puss Corporation **Trained** Newmarket, Suffolk
■ Stewards' Enquiry : Ryan Clark four-day ban: careless riding (Jun 28-Jul 1)

FOCUS
Just an ordinary pace in a race dominated by fillies, but the winner overcame a slow start and everyone had a fair chance. The race followed the pattern of the evening and took shape against the stands' rail. The winner showed her best form since she was a 2yo.

T/Plt: £656.20 to a £1 stake. Pool: £79,476.56 - 88.41 winning tickets T/Qpdt: £718.60 to a £1 stake. Pool:£5,146.79 - 5.30 winning tickets SP

3041 - 3043a (Foreign Racing) - See Raceform Interactive

HOLLYWOOD PARK (L-H)
Monday, June 14

OFFICIAL GOING: Cushion track: fast

3044a VANITY H'CAP (GRADE 1) (3YO+ FILLIES & MARES) (CUSHION TRACK) — 1m 1f (D)
12:37 (12:45) 3-Y-O+ — **£74,074** (£24,691; £14,814; £7,407; £2,469)

RPR

1 **Zenyatta (USA)**[65] [1242] 6-9-3 **0**... MESmith 5 122+
(John Shirreffs, U.S.A) *hld up last on rail: c five-wd fnl turn: styd on strly u.p to ld cl home* **1/2**[1]

2 *1/2* **St Trinians**[100] 5-8-8 **0**... MGarcia 2 110
(Mike Mitchell, U.S.A) *racd in 5th: moved clsr 3f out: 4th st: led 1f out: ct cl home* **2/1**[2]

3 *6* **Zardana (BRZ)**[45] 6-8-6 **0**.. VEspinoza 3 95
(John Shirreffs, U.S.A) *plld early and chsd ldrs: chal for ld 1f out: no ex* **68/10**[3]

4 *6 1/4* **Will O Way (USA)**[148] 4-8-2 **0**.. TBaze 4 78
(Vladimir Cerin, U.S.A) *broke wl: settled in 4th: wl plcd st: wknd* **64/1**

5 *1 1/2* **Miss Silver Brook (USA)**[28] 4-8-0 **0**................................... JTalamo 1 73
(Julio C Canani, U.S.A) *sn led: hdd 1f out: wknd* **46/1**

6 *1/2* **Cherryblossommiss (USA)**[78] 5-8-0 **0**..........................(b) RBejarano 6 72
(John W Sadler, U.S.A) *chsd ldr tl wknd st* **202/10**

1m 49.01s (0.77) **6** Ran SP% **121.2**
PARI-MUTUEL (all including $2 stake): WIN 3.00; PLACE (1-2) 2.10, 2.20; DF 3.20; SF 5.60.
Owner Mr & Mrs Jerome S Moss **Bred** Maverick Production Limited **Trained** USA
■ Zenyatta passed Citation, Cigar, and Mister Frisky for consecutive wins in modern times in races not restricted to state breds.

NOTEBOOK
Zenyatta(USA) gained an unprecedented third straight win in this race to take her career record to 17-17, but it was hard work. Held up a long way off an ordinary pace, she looked in trouble after swinging widest of all into the straight, with the runner-up, who got first run, proving tough to pass. However, the great mare found enough to get on top in the final strides. While probably a little way short of her best form, this was certainly one of Zenyatta's most gutsy performances.

2777 LONGCHAMP (R-H)
Monday, June 14

OFFICIAL GOING: Turf: good to soft

3045a LA COUPE (GROUP 3) (4YO+) (TURF) — 1m 2f
2:05 (12:00) 4-Y-O+ — **£35,398** (£14,159; £10,619; £7,079; £3,539)

RPR

1 **Stacelita (FR)**[22] [2374] 4-9-3 0................................ ChristopheSoumillon 2 121
(J-C Rouget, France) *broke smartly: sn in front travelling smoothly: rdn 1 1/2f out: sn clr: comf* **8/13**[1]

2 *1 1/2* **Court Canibal**[43] [1747] 5-8-11 0.. OlivierPeslier 1 112
(M Delzangles, France) *racd towards rr fr s: fnlly rdn 1 1/2f: qcknd wl ins fnl f and grabbed 2nd in fnl strides* **10/1**[3]

3 *shd* **Russian Cross (IRE)**[19] 5-8-11 0.................................... MaximeGuyon 6 112
(A Fabre, France) *racd cl to ld fr s: rdn early in st and r.o wl: lost 2nd cl home* **10/3**[2]

4 *1 1/2* **Soberania (GER)**[19] [2447] 4-8-8 0................................(p) JohanVictoire 4 106
(J De Roualle, France) *racd in 3rd fr s: rdn early in st: styd on wl* **16/1**

5 *3/4* **World Heritage**[45] [1683] 4-8-11 0................. Christophe-PatriceLemaire 3 107
(P Bary, France) *racd in 4th fr s: hrd rdn 2f out: mde no imp* **11/1**

6 *3/4* **Starlish (IRE)**[43] [1747] 5-9-2 0.. AnthonyCrastus 5 111
(E Lellouche, France) *bkmarker fr s: c wd into st: hrd rdn but fnd no ex* **12/1**

2m 8.90s (4.90) **6** Ran SP% **116.0**
WIN (incl. 1 euro stake): 1.70. PLACES: 1.40, 2.90. SF: 9.30.
Owner Martin S Schwartz **Bred** J P J Dubois **Trained** Pau, France

NOTEBOOK
Stacelita(FR), returned to more positive tactics on easier ground, got back to winning ways with an all-the-way success. She was always dominating this field and connections will now look to return her to Group 1 company, with the likes of the Nassau Stakes or Prix Jean Romanet likely targets, before a tilt at the Breeders' Cup Filly & Mare Turf at the backend.

1898 ASCOT (R-H)
Tuesday, June 15

OFFICIAL GOING: Good (standside: 9.2, centre 9.0, farside 9.4, round course 8.6)
Round course rail positioned 3m out from the inside line from about 9f to home straight increasing Old Mile by 6yds, 10f by 9yd and 12f and over by 12yds.

3046 QUEEN ANNE STKS (GROUP 1) — 1m (S)
2:30 (2:30) (Class 1) 4-Y-O+
£141,925 (£53,800; £26,925; £13,425; £6,725; £3,375) **Stalls** Centre

Form — RPR

31-1 **1** **Goldikova (IRE)**[23] [2374] 5-8-11 130.............................. OlivierPeslier 1 125+
(F Head, France) *t.k.h: travelled wl and trckd ldng pair: rdn and qcknd to ld over 1f out: 3 l clr 1f out: kpt on fnl f and a holding runner-up* **11/8**[1]

2-11 **2** *nk* **Paco Boy (IRE)**[31] [2118] 5-9-0 124................................ RichardHughes 6 127+
(R Hannon) *t.k.h: hld up in rr: switching rt wl over 1f out: nt clr run briefly over 1f out: rdn and qcknd between horses ent fnl f: sn chsng clr wnr: r.o strly: nvr quite getting to wnr* **11/4**[2]

20-3 **3** *3 1/4* **Dream Eater (IRE)**[17] [2539] 5-9-0 114.......................(t) JimmyFortune 10 119
(A M Balding) *stdd s: hld up in last trio: swtchd rt and effrt wl over 1f out: drvn and kpt on fnl f: wnt 3rd fnl 75yds: no ch w ldng pair* **50/1**

20-0 **4** ¾ **Zacinto**[31] 2118 4-9-0 122 RyanMoore 3 118
(Sir Michael Stoute) *in tch in midfield: rdn and effrt wl over 1f out: nt gng pce of wnr over 1f out: chsd clr wnr over 1f out tl jst ins fnl f: kpt on same pce u.p after: lost 3rd fnl 75yds* **20/1**

/1-1 **5** 2 **Dalghar (FR)**[10] 2778 4-9-0 111 Christophe-PatriceLemaire 8 114
(A De Royer-Dupre, France) *stdd s: t.k.h: hld up in midfield: effrt and rdn ent fnl 2f: drvn and edgd rt jst over 1f out: wknd ent fnl f* **14/1**

110- **6** 1½ **Rip Van Winkle (IRE)**[220] 7311 4-9-0 129 JMurtagh 5 110
(A P O'Brien, Ire) *racd keenly: pressed ldr tl rdn to ld over 2f out: hdd and nt pce of wnr over 1f out: wknd qckly ent fnl f* **4/1**[3]

42-2 **7** 4 **Ouqba**[31] 2118 4-9-0 119 RichardHills 7 100
(B W Hills) *dwlt: sn in tch in midfield: rdn 2f out: sn struggling: wl btn over 1f out* **16/1**

5104 **8** 15 **Cat Junior (USA)**[52] 1531 5-9-0 114 (bt) FrankieDettori 9 66
(B J Meehan) *racd alone towards centre for 3f: chsd ldrs tl rdn and wknd qckly wl over 1f out: wl bhd and eased ins fnl f* **50/1**

4131 **9** 18 **Calming Influence (IRE)**[80] 1022 5-9-0 116 AhmedAjtebi 4 24
(Mahmood Al Zarooni) *t.k.h: led tl over 2f out: sn dropped out: wl t.o and virtually p.u ins fnl f* **40/1**

14-4 **P** **Pipedreamer**[31] 2118 6-9-0 118 JamieSpencer 2 —
(K A Ryan) *stdd s: hld up in last: rdn and no hdwy wl over 1f out: eased and rdr looking down jst over 1f out: p.u and dismntd nr finsh* **33/1**

1m 37.74s (-2.86) **Going Correction** +0.125s/f (Good) course record **10** Ran SP% **115.4**
Speed ratings (Par 117): **119,118,115,114,112 111,107,92,74,—**
Tote Swingers: 1&2 £1.50, 1&3 £25.60, 2&3 £23.40 CSF £4.79 CT £115.87 TOTE £2.50: £1.20, £1.50, £9.60; EX 5.30 Trifecta £190.20 Pool: £8,987.63 - 34.96 winning units..

Owner Wertheimer & Frere **Bred** Wertheimer Et Frere **Trained** France

FOCUS
A genuinely vintage Queen Anne with Europe's three top milers clashing. There was a slight worry as to whether it would become tactical with no obvious pace in the race, but there was a sound gallop set on the near side and the form looks solid with the classy first pair coming clear. This is Goldikova's best ever figure apart from last year's Prix Jacques Le Marois.

NOTEBOOK
Goldikova(IRE) had won with something in hand on her reappearance at Longchamp in the Prix D'Ispahan last month, when breaking the track record, and her trainer's assessment in the lead up to this race that he had never had her better proved to be spot-on. She stood out in the preliminaries and, despite having become notorious for her antics entering the stalls, she walked in at the first attempt here without any bother. Her master jockey Olivier Peslier had her settled in the ideal position through the first half of the race, and she moved up going ominously well at the three-furlong marker. Peslier went to the front plenty soon enough, as he had done when taking over from her pacemaker on her previous outing, and her acceleration in going clear ultimately won her the day as Paco Boy motored home to look a real threat late on. She doesn't do a great deal towards the end of her races under such tactics but always looked to be holding off her big rival where it mattered. It was her ninth success at the top level, her ninth consecutive win over the distance and she now goes down as one of the all-time greats. She also became the first filly or mare to win the Queen Anne since it was upgraded to Pattern status back in 1971.The ground was perfect for her and her connections are to be highly commended for keeping her in training as a 5-y-o. She has now won on both her British raids to date, having taken the Falmouth Stakes last July. She will reportedly now be left off till August when she will try to repeat last year's success in the Prix Jacques le Marois and then the Prix de la Foret, back over 7f. No doubt her campaign revolves around her hat-trick bid in the Breeders' Cup Mile, though, and, while it will be a serious training feat to keep her in such form until November, betting against her going in again there would be unwise. Freddie Head did sound a warning about possible soft ground at Churchill Downs, however, and will call it a day with her when she tells him she has had enough. (op 13-8)

Paco Boy(IRE) came into this defence of his win here last year in the form of his life, having beaten Ouqba in the Lockinge a month earlier. Admittedly it was an uninspiring running of that Group 1, but his proven record over C&D was a notable advantage. He had been beaten into third by Goldikova the only previous time the pair had met, in the Prix du Moulin in 2008, but that came on easier ground than he prefers and he has not really looked back since then. In contrast to the winner he was ridden with restraint here and could have settled better through the early parts. As usual he travelled powerfully when asked to improve and it was apparent he was the only real threat to her around 2f out. He didn't get the best of passages when looking to make his move nearing the furlong marker, and when first looking at his narrow margin of defeat it is fair to assume he was unlucky. That was not the case, though, as he needs to be ridden that way and it was only the winner's turn of foot that made him look momentarily out of his ground. He finished a clear second and probably ran a personal-best in defeat, so connections can still be proud of his run. His trainer later said he will now most likely head to France next for the Marois where he could re-oppose Goldikova, and then the Prix de la Foret, which he won in 2008. (op 7-2)

Dream Eater(IRE) ran a big race and improved a deal on his fifth in what was a weaker renewal of the race last year. It was probably a career-best in defeat for him too and certainly deserves to get his head back in front. His connections could aim him at the Summer Mile back here next month and are likely to travel him later on this year, with Turkey and Hong Kong under consideration.

Zacinto had looked a real improver when chasing home Rip Van Winkle at the course in the Queen Elizabeth II Stakes last season. He had bombed out on his two previous starts since, including when coming home a distant last in the Lockinge last month, but was on much better terms with himself in the preliminaries this time. He lacked the pace to get seriously involved, but is clearly getting back on track and it will be interesting to see where he is pitched in next. (op 16-1)

Dalghar(FR) sprang into prominence for this when winning well in a Group 3 at Longchamp just ten days earlier. The step back up in trip was fine for him, but he was coltish in the paddock on this first away trip and also took a hold through the early parts of the race. That didn't help his chances of seeing out the extra furlong in this much classier company, but he did have plenty to find with the market leaders here and probably ran close enough to his previous level. (op 11-1)

Rip Van Winkle(IRE) was the big disappointment of the race. He was expected to play a big part here after slamming Paco Boy in the Sussex Stakes last term and following up in the Queen Elizabeth II Stakes here. He was bidding to become the first horse to win this on his seasonal debut, however, and proved easy to back after his trainer Aidan O'Brien had sounded warnings about his fitness. He looked as though the run would do him good beforehand and unsurprisingly set out to make it a test, but ultimately looked to pay for doing too much through the first half. It is fair to expect a good deal of improvement from him, but it does leave him with something to prove all the same. (tchd 9-2 in places)

Ouqba, second to Paco Boy on his return, had won the Jersey Stakes over 7f at this meeting last year on his only previous run at the course. It was hard to see him reversing form with the runner-up, but he ran way below his Lockinge form and never looked totally happy.

Cat Junior(USA) was the likely front-runner in the race. However, after he broke and found himself racing alone down the centre of the track, he tracked in behind early pacesetters and his fate was apparent not long after.

Calming Influence(IRE), a dual winner in Dubai earlier this year, paid for doing plenty on the front end and was predictably outclassed.

Pipedreamer, who had finished fourth to Paco Boy on his return, was never really going after a sluggish start and he finished lame on his left fore. Official explanation: vet's said horse was lame (left fore) (op 50-1)

3047 KING'S STAND STKS (BRITISH LEG OF THE GLOBAL SPRINT CHALLENGE) (GROUP 1) 5f

3:05 (3:06) (Class 1) 3-Y-O+

£170,310 (£64,560; £32,310; £16,110; £8,070; £4,050) **Stalls** Centre

Form RPR

-112 **1** **Equiano (FR)**[24] 2325 5-9-4 114 MichaelHills 2 123
(B W Hills) *dipped leaving stalls: sn led: edgd rt fr over 1f out: sn rdn: r.o gamely ins fnl f: kpt finding more* **9/2**[3]

5-11 **2** 1½ **Markab**[24] 2353 7-9-4 110 PatCosgrave 9 117
(H Candy) *broke wl: chsd ldrs: rdn over 1f out: wnt cl 2nd ins fnl f: nt qckn towards fin* **14/1**

0-23 **3** nk **Borderlescott**[24] 2325 8-9-4 114 NeilCallan 10 116
(R Bastiman) *midfield: effrt 2f out: hdwy to chse ldrs over 1f out: r.o u.p ins fnl f: nt quite pce of front 2 but gng on at fin* **16/1**

4 ¾ **Nicconi (AUS)**[101] 5-9-4 117 (v[1]) FrankieDettori 8 116+
(David Hayes, Australia) *s.i.s: racd off the pce: nt clr run 2f out: sn swtchd lft: prog over 1f out: r.o ins fnl f: gng on at fin but nt pce to rch ldrs* **10/3**[2]

024- **5** hd **Bould Mover**[248] 6660 3-8-12 107 GrahamGibbons 5 111
(F J Brennan) *chsd ldrs: wnt 2nd 3f out: rdn over 1f out: lost 2nd ins fnl f: styd on same pce fnl 100yds* **66/1**

16-1 **6** 1¼ **Kingsgate Native (IRE)**[24] 2325 5-9-4 118 RyanMoore 7 108+
(Sir Michael Stoute) *midfield: pushed along 2f out: n.m.r over 1f out: sn swtchd rt: failed to pick-up: nvr able to chal ldrs* **5/2**[1]

1-04 **7** nk **Spin Cycle (IRE)**[24] 2325 4-9-4 110 RichardMullen 3 107
(B Smart) *towards rr: swtchd rt and hdwy jst over 2f out: rdn to chse ldrs and edgd rt over 1f out: no ex fnl 100yds* **25/1**

05-0 **8** 2 **Amour Propre**[45] 1700 4-9-4 110 DaneO'Neill 6 100
(H Candy) *hld up in midfield: effrt 2f out: rdn and hung rt over 1f out: no imp on ldrs: one pce fnl f* **25/1**

-130 **9** 1¾ **Blue Jack**[24] 2325 5-9-4 110 RichardKingscote 1 93
(Tom Dascombe) *s.i.s: bhd: rdn over 1f out: kpt on ins fnl f: nt gng pce to threaten ldrs* **33/1**

10 5 **Gold Trail (AUS)**[30] 2153 6-9-4 112 (b) MichaelRodd 4 75
(Gary Portelli, Australia) *w ldr to 3f out: pushed along and outpcd over 2f out: dropped away over 1f out* **10/1**

6-65 **11** 5 **Total Gallery (IRE)**[24] 2325 4-9-4 116 RichardHughes 11 57
(J S Moore) *hld up: pushed along 3f out: dropped away over 1f out: eased whn btn ins fnl f* **9/1**

-103 **12** 8 **Mister Manannan (IRE)**[17] 2537 3-8-12 106 AdrianNicholls 12 27
(D Nicholls) *off the pce: hdwy to go in tch after 1f: rdn over 2f out: sn lost pl and wknd: eased whn btn over 1f out* **25/1**

59.00 secs (-1.50) **Going Correction** +0.125s/f (Good) course record
WFA 3 from 4yo+ 7lb **12** Ran SP% **117.4**
Speed ratings (Par 117): **117,114,114,112,112 110,110,106,104,96 88,75**
Tote Swingers: 1&2 £13.50, 1&3 £12.30, 2&3 £26.30 CSF £60.41 CT £946.35 TOTE £6.10: £1.40, £4.70, £3.20; EX 94.40 Trifecta £1021.80 Pool: £15,176.03 - 10.99 winning units..
Owner J Acheson **Bred** Ecurie Skymarc Farm **Trained** Lambourn, Berks

FOCUS
An up-to-scratch rather than strong edition of the King's Stand Stakes, with a couple of the more fancied contenders below par. The winner produced a personal bedst and the form looks solid. The time was quick, exactly a second inside the RP standard. Fleeting Spirit was a notable absentee, kept back for the Golden Jubilee on Saturday, but otherwise the leading domestic 5f sprinters were present, including the first five home in last month's Temple Stakes at Haydock. The race had become something of a foreign benefit in recent years and there had been no British-trained winner since The Tatling in 2004, but the sole overseas challengers this year were a pair from Australia, the country responsible for four of the previous seven winners. The field soon split into two groups, the pace looking to be with those racing near the stands' side rather than the five stationed a little way apart from the others closer to the centre of the track. The two groups merged in the final furlong and a half.

NOTEBOOK
Equiano(FR), who won this two years ago when trained in Spain by Mauricio Delcher-Sanchez, became the first horse to regain the King's Stand since Elbio in 1993, in the days when it was a Group 2. He struggled for a time to to find his form after joining Barry Hills, but a wind operation has paid off handsomely and he followed wins on the Rowley Mile in the Abernant and Palace House this spring with a second to Kingsgate Native in the Temple Stakes. Drawn two, he almost blew things at the start when stumbling badly, but he recovered very quickly and showed fine speed to make just about all the running nearest the stands' fence, running on strongly and never being seriously challenged. The Nunthorpe is the obvious target - he has finished fourth and eighth in the last two renewals - but he could run first in the Group 2 Sapphire Stakes at the Curragh on Irish Derby day next. (op 8-1)

Markab was fourth in the Wokingham at last year's Royal meeting and only gained his first Group win last month. He had never run at the top level, nor had he raced over the minimum trip, but ran a cracker. Leading the group of five who raced away from the rail, he moved into second place overall with a furlong left and battled on willingly, although never able to reach the winner. Sure to be suited by a step back up in trip, the July Cup has been ruled out and he will head to Deauville and the Prix Maurice de Gheest over an extended 6f.

Borderlescott, another who has been fourth in the Wokingham in his time, came here with solid efforts in the Palace House and Temple under his belt. He stayed on well inside the final furlong to claim third, going two places better than last year, and everything points at this stage to him running a big race in his bid for a third Nunthorpe in August. (tchd 20-1 in places)

Nicconi(AUS) matched the profile of the four Australian winners of this, Choisir, Takeover Target, Miss Andretti and Scenic Blast, in that he had won the Lightning Stakes at Flemington in January, and like them he had run in the Newmarket Handicap there too. A first runner in this country for his trainer, he had been going well on the Newmarket gallops but was usurped as favourite on the day. Expected to go well in the first-time headgear, and with a good record fresh, he was dropping back to his optimum trip. After rather missing the kick he raced in rear, with Dettori opting to switch him to the stands' side. He made decent late headway, getting up for fourth close home, and may run in the July Cup before being retired to stud. (op 3-1 tchd 11-4)

Bould Mover reached the frame in the Flying Childers and Cornwallis last year when trained by Roger Curtis, but he looked to have a stiff task on this belated seasonal debut. He showed bright pace and was still disputing second at the furlong pole before fading under pressure. A game colt, he is clearly a smart sprinter and should continue to acquit himself well, but may find it difficult to get his head in front against his elders.

Kingsgate Native(IRE), only tenth in this race for John Best two years ago before winning the Golden Jubilee four days later, had Equiano and three more of today's opponents behind when winning the Temple, his first start since a gelding operation. Always in midfield, he was not given a hard time after being buffeted by Amour Propre over a furlong out but ran on nicely enough. There will be another day for him. (op 3-1)

Spin Cycle(IRE), the Temple fourth, was outpaced through the early part of the race but recovered to reach fifth place with a furlong or so left before weakening. This was another decent effort but he is likely to remain vulnerable against the best sprinters. (op 33-1)

Amour Propre, a stablemate of the runner-up, has had excuses in his last three outings, finishing distressed bidding for a repeat win in the Palace House last time when only ninth to Equiano. He raced in midfield here, rather lacking cover, and was already held when becoming involved in a bumping match with Kingsgate Native. (op 20-1)

Blue Jack was a little slow to break from the number one stall and was last for much of the way before running past beaten rivals late on. He is not quite up to this level. (tchd 40-1 in a place)

Gold Trail(AUS), the second of the Australian raiders, won the Grade 1 Railway Stakes in New Zealand on New Year's Day and was fourth in the International Sprint in Singapore last time. He matched strides with Equiano for a quarter of a mile before gradually fading. (op 9-1)

Total Gallery(IRE) had been saddled with a Grade 1 penalty for last year's Abbaye win in both of his starts this spring, finishing fifth in the Temple latest. Better was expected of him racing on level terms again, and his trainer made confident noises, but he didn't travel like he usually does and was always towards the rear before his rider eased him off. This was not his running. (op 8-1)

Mister Manannan(IRE) had recovered from a tardy start to chase the pace down the centre, but was already in trouble when being eased right down. Reported to have hung left, he has bags of pace but is not up to this grade at this stage. Official explanation: jockey said colt hung left (op 28-1)

3048 ST JAMES'S PALACE STKS (GROUP 1) (ENTIRE COLTS) 1m (R)

3:50 (3:51) (Class 1) 3-Y-O

£141,925 (£53,800; £26,925; £13,425; £6,725; £3,375) **Stalls** High

Form RPR

-231 **1** **Canford Cliffs (IRE)**[24] 2354 3-9-0 122 .... RichardHughes 6 123+
(R Hannon) stdd s: hld up towards rr: rdn and gd hdwy switching rt over 1f out: chsd ldrs and edgd out lft 1f out: r.o strly u.p to ld fnl 75yds **11/4**[1]

-122 **2** *1* **Dick Turpin (IRE)**[30] 2159 3-9-0 119 .... RyanMoore 1 120
(R Hannon) chsd ldrs: wnt 2nd over 5f out: rdn to ld over 1f out: edgd rt u.p ins fnl f: hdd fnl 75yds: no ex **5/1**[2]

11-0 **3** *¾* **Hearts Of Fire**[45] 1699 3-9-0 114 .... (t) JimmyFortune 2 119+
(Pat Eddery) stdd s: t.k.h: hld up in last: rdn and hdwy towards inner wl over 1f out: n.m.r and switching lft 1f out: running on whn nt clr run again on rail and swtchd lft fnl 75yds: kpt on **33/1**

1-20 **4** *½* **Siyouni (FR)**[30] 2159 3-9-0 118 .... Christophe-PatriceLemaire 3 117
(A De Royer-Dupre, France) hld up in last pair: stl gng wl 2f out: swtchd out lft and rdn over 1f out: kpt on u.p fnl f: unable to rch ldrs **5/1**[2]

3-5 **5** *¾* **Noble's Promise (USA)**[45] 1714 3-9-0 116 .... KierenFallon 9 115
(Kenneth McPeek, U.S.A) in tch in midfield: rdn wl over 2f out: effrt u.p to press ldrs 2f out: edgd lft and one pce ent fnl f **12/1**

616- **6** *1* **Beethoven (IRE)**[220] 7307 3-9-0 117 .... (v) JPO'Brien 4 113
(A P O'Brien, Ire) chsd ldrs: rdn 2f out: unable qck and edgd lft 1f out: wknd ins fnl f **50/1**

11 **7** *½* **Makfi**[45] 1699 3-9-0 122 .... OlivierPeslier 5 115
(M Delzangles, France) hld up in tch towards rr: plld out lft and rdn over 1f out: no prog ent fnl f: btn whn nt clr run and eased wl ins fnl f **11/4**[1]

14-4 **8** *1 ½* **Steinbeck (IRE)**[24] 2354 3-9-0 115 .... JMurtagh 7 114+
(A P O'Brien, Ire) sn led: rdn and hdd over 1f out: keeping on same pce u.p whn hmpd and snatched up fnl 100yds: no ch and nt pushed after **15/2**[3]

50 **9** *25* **Encompassing (IRE)**[24] 2354 3-9-0 100 .... SMLevey 8 51
(A P O'Brien, Ire) dwlt: sn pushed up and chsd ldr after 1f tl over 5f out: wknd qckly ent fnl 2f: wl bhd fnl f **200/1**

1m 39.55s (-1.15) **Going Correction** +0.20s/f (Good) **9** Ran SP% **111.5**

Speed ratings (Par 113): **113,112,111,110,110 109,108,107,82**

Tote Swingers: 1&2 £1.50, 1&3 £14.40, 2&3 £13.80 CSF £15.91 CT £354.01 TOTE £4.00: £1.30, £2.40, £6.70; EX 11.80 Trifecta £351.30 Pool: £19,290.46 - 40.62 winning units..

Owner Heffer Syndicate, Mrs Roy & Mrs Instance **Bred** S And S Hubbard Rodwell **Trained** East Everleigh, Wilts

■ Stewards' Enquiry : Jimmy Fortune three-day ban: careless riding (Jun 29-Jul 1)
Kieren Fallon one-day ban: careless riding (Jun 29)

FOCUS

A decent running of this defining event for the 3-y-o milers, with six of the nine-strong field having already won at the top level and two of them Classic winners. Canford Cliffs was yet another winner to follow up success from the Irish 2000 Guineas but probably didn't need to improve on his Curragh form. His stable-companion Dick Turpin gives the form a solid look in second.

NOTEBOOK

Canford Cliffs(IRE) upheld the tradition of Irish Guineas winners and followed up his win at the Curragh last month under a very confident ride from Richard Hughes. He found the strong early pace right up his street as it enabled him to settle under restraint, which had also been the case when he destroyed his rivals on his previous outing. He was travelling strongly turning for home and, despite having around five lengths to make up on the leaders, Hughes delayed his effort until nearing the furlong marker. Once out in the clear he responded strongly to run down his stablemate Dick Turpin and was well on top at the finish. His success is made more meritorious as he lost a shoe off the home bend. A turning mile such as this is evidently tailor-made for him and he is obviously still improving. With that in mind the Sussex Stakes at Glorious Goodwood next month looks an ideal race for him next and, although he would be taking on his elders for the first time there, if his connections' belief that he could be better than Paco Boy is accurate, he ought to take all the beating. (op 5-2 tchd 9-4)

Dick Turpin(IRE) had twice beaten Canford Cliffs on their previous match ups, when winning the Greenham on his return and then finishing second to Makfi in the 2,000 Guineas at Newmarket in May. He followed up that effort with another sterling display when runner-up to subsequent Prix Du Jockey Club hero Lope De Vega in the Franch Guineas earlier this month. His stable companion had not shown his true colours on either of those previous encounters, though, and, despite running another massive race here, it confirms him second-best. This very likeable colt continues on an upward curve himself. (op 7-1)

Hearts Of Fire ◆ had run 13th on his comeback in the 2,000 Guineas and was the hard-luck story of this race. Equipped with a first-time tongue tie, he would have no doubt given the winner more of a race had he not been denied room when staying on with purpose when upsides him nearing the furlong marker. He was then hampered again when he went to the inside by Dick Turpin and couldn't recover sufficiently when pulled out into the clear. This will have no doubt delighted his connections and it is remarkable progression when remembering he won the Brocklesby on debut at two. There should be more to come from him and he is now likely to head over to France for the Prix Jean Prat, a Group 1 over 1m1f. (tchd 50-1 in a place)

Siyouni(FR) had found trouble on his two previous runs since resuming, including behind Dick Turpin in the French Guineas, but had beaten that rival in the Prix Jean Luc Lagardere on his final outing at two. He was a little keen to post, but settled well enough out the back in the race and came from a similar position as the winner turning for home. He lacked anything like that rival's speed when asked for an effort, and surprisingly came wide with his challenge when staying on late in the day. It looked as though that was not the best place to be and, although he could be rated a little better than the bare form, it may be that 1m2f is now what he wants. (op 11-2 tchd 6-1)

Noble's Promise(USA) is a Grade 1 winner in his homeland and had finished a respectable fifth in the Kentucky Derby on his last start. Settled in midfield on this drop back in trip and return to turf, he ran a solid enough race, but was another not really helped by making his challenge more towards the centre of the track. Kieren Fallon reported that the colt hung left. Official explanation: jockey said colt hung left (op 14-1 tchd 16-1)

Beethoven(IRE), last year's Dewhurst winner, was having his first outing since running sixth at the Breeders' Cup and posted a creditable display. He should come on a bundle for the run, but while St Nicholas Abbey may yet prove an exception, the 3-y-os from Ballydoyle this year do look some way below the powerful operation's normal standard. (tchd 100-1 in a place)

Makfi was the disappointment. Granted Canford Cliffs had failed to settle when he beat him at Newmarket last month, but this was only his third outing and he was still open to any amount of improvement. He was upsides his old rival 2f out, but was just starting to be niggled at that stage. He was left behind when the winner asserted and was another that was brought more towards the middle from the furlong marker, being held before getting slightly hampered. This leaves him with it to now prove, but he was later reported to have coughed after the race and the vet found his throat to be inflamed. It's too soon to be writing him off and he could also enjoy stepping up in distance. Official explanation: trainer said colt was suffering from a throat infection (op 5-2)

Steinbeck(IRE) had finished fourth on his comeback behind Canford Cliffs at the Curragh and was the pick of Johnny Murtagh. It was surprising to see him so handy this time, but much more so that he quickly went to the front. After doing so much early he was in trouble before the final furlong and held after meeting some trouble, after which he was eased off. It was reported that he had lost a front shoe. Official explanation: jockey said colt lost a front shoe (op 7-1)

Encompassing(IRE) was again down for pace-making duties, but never actually got to the front.

3049 COVENTRY STKS (GROUP 2) 6f

4:25 (4:27) (Class 1) 2-Y-O

£56,770 (£21,520; £10,770; £5,370; £2,690; £1,350) **Stalls** Centre

Form RPR

1 **1** **Strong Suit (USA)**[32] 2078 2-9-1 0 .... RichardHughes 8 115+
(R Hannon) hld up off the pce: nt clr run wl over 2f out: hdwy whn nt clr run and checked over 1f out: sn swtchd rt to make grnd: abt 3 l to find on ldr 1f out: wnt 2nd 150yds out: str run to ld on nod at post **15/8**[1]

1 **2** *nse* **Elzaam (AUS)**[33] 2059 2-9-1 0 .... RichardHills 5 112+
(M A Jarvis) prom: led over 2f out: rdn over 1f out: running on abt 2 l up 150yds out: hdd on nod at post **3/1**[2]

51 **3** *2 ½* **Roayh (USA)**[14] 2621 2-9-1 0 .... FrankieDettori 3 104
(Saeed Bin Suroor) led: hdd over 2f out: rdn over 1f out: no ex fnl 75yds **22/1**

1 **4** *2 ¼* **Samuel Morse (IRE)**[24] 2352 2-9-1 0 .... RyanMoore 2 98
(A P O'Brien, Ire) hld up: hdwy 1/2-way: rdn to chse ldrs over 1f out: lugged rt ins fnl f: no imp on front trio fnl 100yds **7/1**

11 **5** *1* **Klammer**[31] 2127 2-9-1 0 .... ShaneKelly 7 95
(Jane Chapple-Hyam) hld up: pushed along over 2f out: hdwy over 1f out: hung rt ins fnl f: styd on but nt pce to chal **20/1**

1 **6** *2 ½* **Zoffany (IRE)**[34] 2035 2-9-1 0 .... JMurtagh 6 88
(A P O'Brien, Ire) racd keenly: prom: pushed along and nt qckn 2f out: n.m.r whn outpcd over 1f out: no imp after **9/2**[3]

0411 **7** *¾* **Galtymore Lad**[18] 2514 2-9-1 0 .... TonyCulhane 13 85
(M R Channon) in tch: pushed along over 2f out: nt qckn over 1f out: kpt on one pce ins fnl f **20/1**

5 **8** *½* **Mullins Way (USA)**[29] 2163 2-9-1 0 .... (b[1]) GrahamGibbons 4 83
(F J Brennan) s.i.s: bustled along early: in rr: gd hdwy to press ldrs over 3f out: rdn over 1f out: wknd ins fnl f **100/1**

1 **9** *1 ¼* **Amwell Pinot**[24] 2312 2-9-1 0 .... KierenFallon 10 80
(A Bailey) chsd ldrs: lost pl over 3f out: outpcd after **50/1**

12 **10** *nk* **Chiswick Bey (IRE)**[17] 2525 2-9-1 0 .... PaulHanagan 12 79
(R A Fahey) broke wl: chsd ldrs: dropped to midfield after 2f: pushed along 3f out: no imp after **50/1**

01 **11** *1 ¼* **Move In Time**[18] 2498 2-9-1 0 .... TomEaves 14 75
(B Smart) in tch: effrt to chse ldrs over 2f out: wknd ent fnl f **66/1**

01 **12** *3 ¾* **Planet Waves (IRE)**[28] 2216 2-9-1 0 .... SebSanders 15 64
(C E Brittain) prom: rdn over 2f out: sn lost pl: struggling over 1f out: bhd fnl f **40/1**

51 **13** *8* **Sheer Courage (IRE)**[22] 2389 2-9-1 0 .... JimmyFortune 11 40
(H J Brown, South Africa) hld up in rr: rdn 2f out: nvr on terms **14/1**

1m 14.29s (-0.11) **Going Correction** +0.125s/f (Good) **13** Ran SP% **119.8**

Speed ratings (Par 105): **105,104,101,98,97 93,92,92,90,90 88,83,72**

Tote Swingers: 1&2 £2.60, 1&3 £8.00, 2&3 £14.10 CSF £6.64 CT £94.06 TOTE £3.00: £1.50, £1.80, £3.50; EX 9.40 Trifecta £109.60 Pool: £13,302.07 - 89.78 winning units..

Owner Mrs J Wood **Bred** Mcdowell Farm, Gainsborough Farm Et Al **Trained** East Everleigh, Wilts

FOCUS

Four of the previous five Coventry winners went on to win in Group 1 company, with the last three, Henrythenavigator, Art Connoisseur and now Canford Cliffs all scoring at the top level at the Royal meeting 12 months on. This year's edition has plenty to live up to but the first two home, who came clear to contest a terrific finish, look very smart colts. The runners raced in a bunch down the centre of the track and the pace was solid. The time was 0.79secs outside the standard but the winner was value for a length and the form looks sound and reliable.

NOTEBOOK

Strong Suit(USA) ◆'s trainer has dominated the 2-y-o scene this season, sending out nearly 30 individual winners, and this one was widely acknowledged to be his best juvenile. Comfortable winner of the same Newbury maiden won by his stablemate Canford Cliffs last year, the form has been franked by victories for the next two home. Held up towards the back, the colt endured more than his share of trouble and was quite badly hampered by Mullins Bay over a furlong out as he attempted to pick up the leaders. Still only third with a furlong to run, he powered past Roayh before going out after Elzaam, finishing fast to claim him on the nod. He was value for further given his interrupted passage and would have been a decidedly unlucky loser had he not got up. Described by his trainer as not as naturally brilliant as Canford Cliffs, and a slower learner, he will prove hard to beat for the time being at least and is as short as 7/1 favourite for next spring's 2,000 Guineas. His next assignment will be either the July Stakes at Newmarket or the Richmond at Goodwood; the yard won the latter race last year with Dick Turpin. He ought to get 7f this season if required. (op 2-1 tchd 5-2 in a place and 9-4 in places)

Elzaam(AUS), winner of a strong maiden at the York May meeting, tackled the long-time leader from halfway. Getting on top before the last, he looked sure to win when going a couple of lengths clear, but he was collared right on the line as the winner came home fast. He was in front a little sooner than would have been ideal and might have become a little lonely, and loses nothing in defeat. Clear of the third, he will have learned from the experience and a race at this level should be found for him this summer. (op 9-2)

Roayh(USA), successful at Leicester latest, showed fine natural pace to lead and, although no match in the end for the big two, he stuck on well for a very creditable third. He is very useful and it would be interesting to know where he stands among the Godolphin juveniles. (op 25-1 tchd 33-1 in a place)

Samuel Morse(IRE), attempting to give Aidan O'Brien a sixth Coventry winner, was unbeaten in two races at the Curragh, a heavy-ground maiden and the Listed Marble Hill Stakes. Stepping up in trip, he was outpaced by the principals in the latter stages but stuck on well enough for a respectable fourth despite looking to hang to his right. He could prove the better prospect of the O'Brien pair. (op 11-2)

Klammer, hitherto unbeaten in two starts, stayed on well from a little off the pace despite appearing to be hanging a little. He will not mind a step up to 7f.

Zoffany(IRE), two from two before this, was Johnny Murtagh's choice over Samuel Morse. Taking a rather keen hold, the colt already seemed beaten when slightly hampered over a furlong out but to his credit did run on again through the final furlong. (op 5-1)

Galtymore Lad came here with a progressive profile but was found wanting on this rise in grade, albeit far from disgraced from his outside draw. (tchd 22-1 and 25-1 in places)
Mullins Way(USA), the sole maiden in the line-up following his debut fifth (for Roger Curtis) at Bath, shaped with plenty of promise. Equipped with blinkers this time, he recovered from a slow start to race up with the leaders before his exertions began to tell. An ordinary race should soon come his way.
Amwell Pinot showed early pace before fading. He is bred to need a fair bit further in time. (op 40-1)
Chiswick Bey(IRE) was expected to improve for the longer trip but was one of the first in trouble. (op 40-1)
Move In Time, well behind Elzaam on his debut before winning at Newcastle, came from the yard which won this with Hellvelyn four years ago. He could never get into the action, with a high draw not helping his cause.
Planet Waves(IRE), who had Roayh back in fifth when winning at Nottingham, could not sustain his pace for long here from the widest draw. (op 33-1)
Sheer Courage(IRE), a former stablemate of the winner, was always at the back of the field. He is expected to race in Dubai now. (op 12-1)

3050 ASCOT STKS (H'CAP) 2m 4f

5:00 (5:02) (Class 2) (0-95,95) 4-Y-O+

£31,155 (£9,330; £4,665; £1,750; £1,750; £585) **Stalls** High

Form RPR

131/ **1** **Junior**[68] 3216 7-9-0 **85**....................(b) SebSanders 16 96
(D E Pipe) *mde all: clr fr 12f out: rdn and styd on wl fnl 3f: unchal* **17/2**[3]

5/3- **2** *5* **Elyaadi**[16] 2572 6-9-9 **94**.................... FMBerry 12 100+
(John Queally, Ire) *stdd and dropped in bhd after s: hld up in last pair: rdn and hdwy over 2f out: styd on wl fnl f to snatch 2nd cl home: impossible task* **14/1**

1-36 **3** *½* **Aaim To Prosper (IRE)**[17] 2541 6-9-3 **88**.................... FrankieDettori 3 94
(B J Meehan) *racd in midfield: hdwy and rdn 5f out: disp 2nd and chsng clr ldr over 3f out: edgd lft u.p and no imp over 1f out* **16/1**

504- **4** *shd* **Ghimaar**[9] 6008 5-9-5 **90**.................... KierenFallon 14 95
(N J Henderson) *hld up in midfield: hdwy on outer 7f out: rdn to dispute 2nd and chsng clr wnr over 3f out: no imp on ldrs whn sltly hmpd and pushed lft over 1f out: kpt on same pce after* **7/2**[1]

2-51 **4** *dht* **Dayia (IRE)**[17] 2541 6-9-0 **90**.................... SimonPearce(5) 8 95
(J Pearce) *in tch in main gp: rdn and no imp on wnr 4f out: keeping on and edging out lft fr 2f out: pressing for placings nr fin: no ch w wnr* **16/1**

0-40 **6** *1 ¾* **Rangefinder**[23] 2368 6-9-0 **85**....................(p) JamieSpencer 15 89
(Jane Chapple-Hyam) *hld up towards rr: hdwy and weaving through 3f out: switching rt over 2f out: chsng plcd horse ent fnl f: styng on same pce and n.m.r ins fnl f: no ch w wnr* **16/1**

203- **7** *nk* **Sleepy Hollow**[66] 6734 5-9-0 **85**.................... SteveDrowne 7 88
(H Morrison) *racd in midfield: rdn and effrt 5f out: chsd main gp ldrs but wl off the pce over 3f out: carried lft and plugged on same pce fr over 1f out* **12/1**

2- **8** *1 ½* **Rajik (IRE)**[23] 2368 5-9-0 **92**....................(t) JPO'Brien(7) 2 94+
(C F Swan, Ire) *hld up wl off the pce towards rr: rdn and kpt on fr over 2f out: nvr trbld ldrs* **11/1**

0060 **9** *2* **Ocean's Minstrel**[11] 2708 4-9-3 **91**.................... AdamKirby 5 91
(J Ryan) *stdd and dropped in bhd after s: hld up in last pair: rdn and sme hdwy over 2f out: nvr trbld ldrs* **66/1**

0-51 **10** *½* **Perfect Shot (IRE)**[17] 2549 4-9-4 **92**.................... MartinDwyer 13 91
(J L Dunlop) *hld up wl in rr: nt clr run 4f out: rdn and sme hdwy over 2f out: kpt on fnl f: nvr trbld ldrs* **11/1**

122- **11** *6* **Tyrrells Wood (IRE)**[321] 4417 5-9-7 **92**.................... StevieDonohoe 9 85
(Jane Chapple-Hyam) *hld up in midfield: rdn and no prog 3f out: nvr trbld ldrs* **8/1**[2]

/60- **12** *¾* **Enjoy The Moment**[241] 6851 7-9-5 **90**.................... TomQueally 10 83
(J A Osborne) *hld up towards rr: hdwy 6f out: rdn and no prog ent fnl 3f: n.d* **33/1**

30-0 **13** *9* **Unleashed (IRE)**[10] 1220 5-9-10 **95**....................(bt) PaulHanagan 19 79
(C J Mann) *hld up wl off the pce towards rr: rdn and no prog over 3f out: nvr on terms* **66/1**

20-4 **14** *19* **Woolfall Treasure**[44] 1736 5-9-3 **88**....................(b) RyanMoore 4 53
(G L Moore) *chsd wnr for 4f and again 7f out: rdn and lost 2nd over 3f out: sn wknd: wl btn and eased fnl f* **11/1**

30/0 **15** *6* **Colloquial**[38] 1902 9-9-3 **88**....................(v) FergusSweeney 1 47
(H Candy) *chsd ldrs tl wknd u.p 5f out: wl bhd fr over 2f out: eased ins fnl f* **25/1**

50-0 **16** *8* **Bon Spiel**[46] 946 6-9-0 **85**.................... DaneO'Neill 17 36
(C Gordon) *hld up wl off the pce towards rr: short-lived effrt u.p on outer 4f out: wl bhd fr over 2f out: eased ins fnl f* **100/1**

06-0 **17** *5* **Som Tala**[41] 1821 7-9-1 **86**....................(v) RichardHughes 20 32
(M R Channon) *in tch: drvn and struggling 4f out: wl bhd fr over 2f out: virtually p.u ins fnl f* **12/1**

1-23 **18** *44* **Lucky Punt**[41] 1829 4-9-2 **90**.................... GeorgeBaker 6 —
(B G Powell) *chsd ldrs tl wknd qckly over 4f out: t.o and eased fnl 2f* **33/1**

365 **19** *22* **Mister Green (FR)**[36] 1974 4-9-7 **95**....................(t) EddieAhern 11 —
(K McAuliffe) *in tch tl wknd rapidly 5f out: wl t.o eased fr wl over 2f out* **66/1**

0-41 **20** *57* **Callisto Moon**[42] 1798 6-9-3 **88**....................(p) NeilCallan 18 —
(F J Brennan) *chsd ldrs tl wnt 2nd after 4f tl 7f out: sn dropped out: wl t.o fnl 3f: virtually p.u fr over 1f out* **20/1**

4m 23.92s (2.92) **Going Correction** +0.20s/f (Good) **20** Ran SP% **128.5**
WFA 4 from 5yo+ 3lb
Speed ratings (Par 109): **102,100,99,99,99 99,98,98,97,97 94,94,91,83,81 77,75,58,49,26**
Tote Swingers: 1&2 £36.30, 1&3 £21.10, 2&3 £102.80 CSF £118.41 CT £1907.17 TOTE £8.60: £2.20, £4.40, £3.60; EX 171.00 Trifecta £5358.90 Pool: £9,414.40 - 1.30 winning units. PL: Dayia £2.50, Ghimaar £1.00.
Owner Middleham Park Racing LI **Bred** P C Green **Trained** Nicholashayne, Devon

FOCUS

A typically wide-open running of this decent staying handicap. A high draw again proved an advantage and it was run at a true test. Junior is rated to a best view of his old form, with the third a solid guide.

NOTEBOOK

Junior made all for a decisive success. He had looked unwilling over jumps earlier this year (despite winning twice), but this was his first outing for new connections and, more importantly, he was making his debut for David Pipe, who had saddled runners to be placed here in the last two seasons and whose father Martin also won it twice in 2002/03. He had to be vigorously ridden through the early parts to get in front, but was soon in a nice rhythm having been allowed a fairly easy lead. He began to wind up the tempo around 5f out and went for everything off the home turn. It was clear nearing the final furlong he was going to collect and he has now been successful on four of his last five outings on the Flat. A crack at the valuable Cesarewitch will surely now come into consideration as further improvement in this sphere is entirely possible. (op 8-1 tchd 9-1 and 10-1 in places)
Elyaadi, a winner over 1m6f on her return to the Flat 16 days earlier, was racing off a 13lb higher mark and had a stiff task under her big weight. Ridden right out the back to get this longer distance, she was staying on stoutly in the home straight and ran a career-best in defeat. (op 16-1)
Aaim To Prosper(IRE) likes this venue and deserves credit as he fared best of those drawn wide. He is high enough in the handicap at present, but could still be found a winning turn back over a slightly sharper test. (op 12-1)
Dayia(IRE) was 5lb higher and only just failed to confirm her last-time-out form with the third. She rates a sound benchmark and will be suited by a return to slightly easier ground. (op 14-1)
Ghimaar ◆ came good over hurdles at the second attempt nine days earlier and proved very popular for this return to the Flat, despite his trainer not having the best of past records in the race. There was a good chance he was still nicely handicapped on some of his previous form when trained in Ireland and held decent claims of seeing out the trip. He ran well considering he had to come wide with his challenge around 6f out, and it will be surprising were he not placed to advantage at some point this summer. (op 14-1)
Rangefinder ◆, representing last year's winning stable, was equipped with first-time cheekpieces. He got a nice sit through the race on the inside and was keeping on respectably in the home straight to think he can be found an opening in the coming weeks. (op 18-1)
Sleepy Hollow, another returning from hurdling, kept on without landing a serious blow. (op 14-1)
Perfect Shot(IRE) also stayed on late. He was 10lb higher for his recent Haydock success over 1m6f, but would've probably had more of a say under a more positive ride. (tchd 10-1)
Enjoy The Moment, somewhat of a standing dish in this race, was found to have finished lame. (tchd 50-1 in a place)
Woolfall Treasure Official explanation: jockey said gelding had no more to give
Som Tala Official explanation: vet said gelding finished lame
Callisto Moon Official explanation: jockey said gelding stopped quickly

3051 WINDSOR CASTLE STKS (LISTED RACE) 5f

5:35 (5:36) (Class 1) 2-Y-O

£28,385 (£10,760; £5,385; £2,685; £1,345; £675) **Stalls** Centre

Form RPR

1 **1** **Marine Commando**[22] 2376 2-9-3 0.................... PaulHanagan 2 101+
(R A Fahey) *chsd ldrs: rdn over 1f out: cl 3rd whn nt clr run ins fnl f: swtchd lft 110yds out: str run to ld cl home* **9/2**[2]

2 *nk* **Petronius Maximus (IRE)**[33] 2061 2-9-3 0.................... JMurtagh 5 100
(A P O'Brien, Ire) *niggled along in rr: rdn and hdwy over 1f out: hung rt and r.o strly ins fnl f: fin wl* **20/1**

01 **3** *nse* **Excello**[13] 2638 2-8-12 0.................... IanMongan 1 95
(M S Saunders) *broke wl: chsd ldrs: rdn and hung rt fr jst over 1f out: led ins fnl f: hdd cl home* **14/1**

2 **4** *2* **Stone Of Folca**[22] 2397 2-9-3 0.................... RobertWinston 9 93
(J R Best) *gd spd to chse ldrs: led jst over 2f out: rdn over 1f out: hdd ins fnl f: no ex fnl 50yds* **10/1**

212 **5** *1* **Chilworth Lad**[19] 2468 2-9-3 0.................... RyanMoore 14 89
(M R Channon) *dwlt: bhd: swtchd rt whn rdn and hdwy over 1f out: styd on ins fnl f: nt pce to rch ldrs* **11/2**[3]

3154 **6** *3 ½* **Style And Panache (IRE)**[10] 2757 2-8-12 0.................... CathyGannon 10 71
(P D Evans) *in tch: rdn 2f out: nt qckn: kpt on same pce fnl f* **66/1**

6 **7** *1 ½* **Sonoran Sands (IRE)**[15] 2594 2-9-3 0.................... JimmyFortune 15 71
(J S Moore) *hld up: rdn over 1f out: kpt on ins fnl f: no imp on ldrs* **25/1**

424 **8** *2* **Diamond Geezah (IRE)**[40] 1835 2-9-3 0.................... MichaelHills 12 64
(B W Hills) *midfield: rdn 2f out: outpcd over 1f out: nvr able to get on terms* **25/1**

9 *1 ¼* **Metropolitan Man (USA)**[54] 2-9-3 0....................(bt) ElvisTrujillo 7 59
(Wesley A Ward, U.S.A) *gd spd w ldr to 2f out: rdn and wknd qckly wl over 1f out* **9/4**[1]

10 *hd* **Speightowns Kid (USA)** 2-9-3 0.................... GrahamGibbons 3 59
(F J Brennan) *dwlt: towards rr: hdwy 3f out: sn in midfield: effrt to chse ldrs over 1f out: no imp ins fnl f* **100/1**

11 *2 ¾* **Oor Jock (IRE)**[8] 2826 2-9-3 0.................... PJSmullen 4 49
(D K Weld, Ire) *hld up: rdn 2f out: nvr able to chal* **7/1**

2134 **12** *1 ¾* **Meandmyshadow**[20] 2436 2-8-12 0.................... FrannyNorton 8 37
(A D Brown) *in tch: rdn and outpcd 2f out: hung rt and wknd over 1f out* **66/1**

511 **13** *3 ¼* **Boundless Spirit**[17] 2525 2-9-3 0.................... TomEaves 6 31
(B Smart) *led: hdd jst over 2f out: rdn and wknd over 1f out* **9/1**

01 **14** *9* **Roche Des Vents**[39] 1871 2-9-3 0.................... RichardHughes 11 —
(R Hannon) *sn dropped to midfield: outpcd over 2f out: bhd over 1f out: eased whn btn fnl f* **20/1**

61.09 secs (0.59) **Going Correction** +0.125s/f (Good) **14** Ran SP% **123.8**
Speed ratings (Par 101): **100,99,99,96,94 89,86,83,81,81 76,73,68,54**
Tote Swingers: 1&2 £19.90, 1&3 £13.70, 2&3 £54.80 CSF £98.31 CT £840.71 TOTE £6.80: £2.40, £4.30, £3.60; EX 120.40 Trifecta £3182.90 Pool: £7,226.18 - 1.68 winning units. Place 6: £134.06 Place 5: £94.40..
Owner M Wynne **Bred** L J Vaessen **Trained** Musley Bank, N Yorks

FOCUS

A smaller field than of late for the Windsor Castle, but a decent renewal. The pace was strong and the picture changed rapidly inside the final furlong. The front three were clear and the form looks sound.

NOTEBOOK

Marine Commando was the sole unbeaten domestic runner, successful first time out in a Carlisle maiden auction. Chasing the pace, he hung in behind the two leaders inside the last but quickened up well to lead once his rider pulled his whip through and switched him. There are no immediate plans for the colt, who should get another furlong. (op 15-2)
Petronius Maximus(IRE) ran a startling race, some way off the pace in rear for much of the trip before picking up under pressure. Still only fifth or sixth passing the furlong pole, he then flew home near the stands' rail to grab second on the line despite hanging with his rider. A Coventry entry too, and dropped in trip after running over 7f last time, he needs further than this and connections will try to win a maiden with him before raising him in grade again. (op 16-1)
Excello, a Kempton Polytrack winner, wore down the leader to lead in the final half furlong and seemed set to become the first filly to win this since Autumnal ten years ago, but she could not hold on and was relegated two places in the dying stages. More success should come her way, perhaps back against her own sex. (tchd 16-1)
Stone Of Folca ◆'s yard is always to be respected in this; Best had the first and third with Flashmans Papers and Mullionmileanhour two years ago and sent out Kingsgate Native to finish second in 2007. The colt travelled very strongly up with the pace before taking a definite lead, and was only worried out of it in the last half furlong. Still a maiden, he should soon put that right and the Molecomb at Goodwood could suit him. (tchd 11-1)
Chilworth Lad, runner-up in this grade in the National Stakes at Sandown latest, was slowly away for the third time in four starts. Switched back to the outside of the field, he stayed on well through the final furlong without managing to trouble the principals. (op 13-2)
Style And Panache(IRE) was the most experienced in the line-up and this tough filly ran her race, lending substance to the form.
Sonoran Sands(IRE) made modest late gains without getting involved. He may be ready for a return to 6f. (op 40-1)
Diamond Geezah(IRE), reported to have been held up with sore shins since Chester, passed a few rivals late on without getting involved.

Metropolitan Man(USA)'s trainer made a big splash at the Royal meeting 12 months ago, winning with two juveniles including Strike The Tiger in this race. The American handler's only runner this year, he had made a winning debut on Polytrack at Keeneland and broke well here, clearly knowing what was required, but had competiton for the lead and was in trouble by halfway. His rider was of the opinion that the gelding didn't try. Official explanation: trainer's rep said, that the gelding was unsuited by the track. (tchd 2-1)
Speightowns Kid(USA) did not shape without promise following a slow start on this debut.
Oor Jock(IRE), a recent Naas winner, was never in the hunt. (op 6-1)
Meandmyshadow, already beaten at this level, is in need of 6f again.
Boundless Spirit 's Beverley form wasn't boosted by Chiswick Bey's Coventry effort. He has bags of pace, but was taken on by Stone Of Folca and Metropolitan Man and was beaten with two to run. (op 10-1)
Roche Des Vents showed a bit of early dash but was struggling by halfway. (op 16-1)
T/Jkpt: £14,200 to a £1 stake. Pool: £50,000.00 - 2.50 winning tickets T/Plt: £251.00 to a £1 stake. Pool: £400,213.88 - 1,163.79 winning tickets T/Qpdt: £45.60 to a £1 stake. Pool: £20,304.88 - 329.01 winning tickets SP

[2779] BRIGHTON (L-H)

Tuesday, June 15

OFFICIAL GOING: Good to firm (watered; 8.6)
Wind: Fresh, behind Weather: Fine

3052 LEISURE BOXER H'CAP — 5f 59y

6:30 (6:31) (Class 6) (0-60,60) 3-Y-O+ — **£2,201** (£655; £327; £163) **Stalls** Low

Form				RPR
40-2	**1**		**Multahab**[28] 2196 11-9-11 **60**.....(t) MarcHalford 1 (M Wigham) *trckd ldr and sn clr of rest: allowed to drift to nr side in st and racd alone there: def advantage fnl f: styd on wl* **5/1**	69
1622	**2**	*2 ½*	**Spic 'n Span**[89] 913 5-9-9 **58**.....(b) LukeMorris 4 (R A Harris) *taken down early: led: clr of gp fr 3f out: lost ld and edgd rt fnl f* **7/2**[2]	59
1624	**3**	*1 ½*	**Bookiesindex Boy**[8] 2809 6-9-4 **53**.....(b) StephenCraine 5 (J R Jenkins) *mostly in 4th: effrt to go 3rd bhd far side ldr 1f out: clsng whn sltly checked ins fnl f: no imp after* **11/2**	48
2066	**4**	*½*	**Caribbean Coral**[8] 2809 11-9-9 **58**..... RobertHavlin 3 (A B Haynes) *settled in last trio and wl off the pce: rdn 2f out: fnlly styd on fnl f: no ch* **16/1**	52
3002	**5**	*nk*	**Bobs Dreamflight**[3] 2964 4-9-6 **60**..... MarkCoumbe(5) 6 (D K Ivory) *settled in last trio and wl off the pce: rdn 2f out: fnlly styd on ins fnl f: no ch* **9/4**[1]	53
0260	**6**	*¾*	**Best One**[9] 2779 6-9-3 **52**.....(b) ChrisCatlin 2 (R A Harris) *racd in 3rd: no imp on far side ldr 2f out: fdd fnl f* **4/1**[3]	42
0000	**7**	*1 ¼*	**Joan's Legacy**[15] 2588 3-8-4 **46**.....(b) FrankieMcDonald 7 (J C Fox) *s.i.s: a wl off the pce in last trio: no prog fnl f* **33/1**	29

60.41 secs (-1.89) **Going Correction** -0.325s/f (Firm)
WFA 3 from 4yo+ 7lb — **7** Ran SP% **113.9**
Speed ratings (Par 101): **102,98,95,94,94 93,91**
Tote Swingers: 1&2 £5.10, 1&3 £5.40, 2&3 £2.80 CSF £22.57 CT £98.62 TOTE £3.40: £1.20, £1.60; EX 13.70.
Owner Mrs Roxanne Simms **Bred** Shadwell Estate Company Limited **Trained** Newmarket, Suffolk

FOCUS
Not a bad race for the grade, although the clear-cut winner raced alone against the stands' rail in the straight. He is rated to last year's best.

3053 EUROPEAN BREEDERS' FUND MAIDEN STKS — 5f 213y

7:00 (7:00) (Class 5) 2-Y-O — **£3,238** (£963; £481; £240) **Stalls** Low

Form				RPR
U25	**1**		**Kojak (IRE)**[11] 2687 2-9-3 0..... PatDobbs 7 (R Hannon) *mde virtually all: drew clr fr 2f out: pushed out fnl f* **4/1**[3]	81
33	**2**	*3 ¼*	**Battle Of Britain**[14] 2621 2-9-0 0..... AhmedAjtebi(3) 8 (Mahmood Al Zarooni) *wnt rt s: trckd wnr after 1f: chal and upsides over 2f out: nt qckn and hung in bhd over 1f out: n.d after: clung on for 2nd* **11/8**[1]	71
3	**3**	*nk*	**Freckenham (IRE)**[35] 1999 2-8-12 0..... HayleyTurner 1 (M L W Bell) *dwlt: hld up in last trio: plld out and effrt 1/2-way: rn green but prog to go 3rd over 1f out: styd on and nrly tk 2nd* **10/3**[2]	65
0	**4**	*3 ¾*	**Fantasy Fry**[14] 2621 2-9-3 0..... TravisBlock 4 (H Morrison) *t.k.h after 2f and snatched up on inner: shkn up 2f out: no imp on ldrs* **22/1**	60+
262	**5**	*1 ¾*	**Indian Narjes**[12] 2677 2-8-12 0..... ChrisCatlin 6 (M R Channon) *trckd wnr 1f: outpcd fr 2f out: pushed along and one pce over 1f out: fdd* **7/1**	49
60	**6**	*1 ½*	**Whitby Jet (IRE)**[28] 2216 2-9-3 0..... LiamKeniry 5 (E F Vaughan) *dwlt: mostly in last trio: rdn over 2f out: n.d* **100/1**	49
44	**7**	*shd*	**Diamond Vine (IRE)**[11] 2687 2-9-3 0..... LukeMorris 3 (R A Harris) *t.k.h: hld up in rr: drvn 2f out: no real prog* **12/1**	49
	8	*8*	**Newstarmcgrath** 2-9-3 0..... DavidProbert 2 (Miss Gay Kelleway) *a in last trio: wknd 2f out* **50/1**	25

68.84 secs (-1.36) **Going Correction** -0.325s/f (Firm) — **8** Ran SP% **112.7**
Speed ratings (Par 93): **96,91,91,86,83 81,81,71**
Tote Swingers: 1&2 £1.70, 1&3 £2.80, 2&3 £1.60 CSF £9.58 TOTE £5.90: £2.90, £1.30, £1.10; EX 11.20.
Owner Mrs J Wood **Bred** Tally-Ho Stud **Trained** East Everleigh, Wilts

FOCUS
Just a fair juvenile maiden, although the time was good, being 0.39 seconds quicker than the later Class 5 handicap for older horses. They all stayed far side this time.

NOTEBOOK
Kojak(IRE) had not looked straightforward on his first three starts, but he was more professional this time and showed himself capable of fair form. Front-running tactics suited, and so too did having a rail to run against when coming under just hands-and-heels pressure. He jinked slightly once or twice, but maintained his momentum and never looked in danger. The suspicion is he remains one to tread carefully with, but equally he's obviously not one to underestimate, especially during the nursery season. (op 5-1 tchd 7-2)
Battle Of Britain's recent third at Leicester received a boost earlier in the day when the winner, Roayh, finished third in the Coventry Stakes at Royal Ascot, but this one couldn't justify favouritism. He simply didn't handle the track as well as the winner, edging left into the rail late on. (op 15-8)
Freckenham(IRE) ruined her chance by hanging right when first coming under pressure early in the straight, and as such, couldn't build sufficiently on her debut third at Warwick. (op 9-4)
Fantasy Fry finished closer to Battle Of Britain than when around 8l behind that rival on debut, but having been keen at around halfway, he never really threatened. (op 16-1)
Indian Narjes was one paced under pressure and ran below form, perhaps not appreciating the track. (tchd 6-1 and 8-1)

3054 LEISURE BOXER BRIGHTON H'CAP — 7f 214y

7:30 (7:30) (Class 6) (0-65,65) 4-Y-O+ — **£2,201** (£655; £327; £163) **Stalls** Low

Form				RPR
-600	**1**		**Monashee Rock (IRE)**[69] 1171 5-9-2 **60**..... LiamKeniry 4 (Matthew Salaman) *mounted on crse: cl up: trckd ldr 1/2-way: rdn to chal over 1f out: led ins fnl f: drvn rt out* **6/1**[3]	68
1322	**2**	*½*	**Yourgolftravel Com**[9] 2781 5-9-1 **59**..... StephenCraine 1 (M Wigham) *stdd s: t.k.h: hld up and mostly last: swtchd to outer and smooth prog 2f out: c to chal ins fnl f: drvn and nt qckn* **5/4**[1]	66+
-054	**3**	*½*	**Cordell (IRE)**[47] 1634 5-9-2 **60**.....(t) SebSanders 8 (Jim Best) *led: drvn 2f out: hdd ins fnl f: kpt on* **11/4**[2]	66
0203	**4**	*4 ½*	**Dichoh**[21] 2415 7-9-4 **62**.....(v) GeorgeBaker 7 (M Madgwick) *hld up in last trio: effrt over 2f out: sn outpcd and btn* **8/1**	58
2410	**5**	*½*	**Justcallmehandsome**[56] 1458 8-8-11 **60**.....(v) SophieDoyle(5) 2 (D J S Ffrench Davis) *trckd ldr to 1/2-way: cl up over 2f out: shkn up and wknd over 1f out* **8/1**	55
000-	**6**	*3*	**Motor Home**[260] 6333 4-8-9 **53**..... HayleyTurner 5 (C P Morlock) *dwlt: t.k.h: hld up in last trio: prog on outer and cl up 3f out: wknd 2f out* **33/1**	41

1m 35.13s (-0.87) **Going Correction** -0.325s/f (Firm) — **6** Ran SP% **110.6**
Speed ratings (Par 101): **91,90,90,85,85 82**
Tote Swingers: 1&2 £5.10, 1&3 £3.00, 2&3 £1.80 CSF £13.61 CT £23.19 TOTE £9.20: £2.60, £1.10; EX 20.70.
Owner Mrs P G Lewin & D Grieve **Bred** M J Lewin And D Grieve **Trained** Upper Lambourn, Berks

FOCUS
Just a modest handicap and they didn't seem to go that quick. Muddling form, rated around the third.

3055 BOB CHAMPION 60:60 CHALLENGE H'CAP — 1m 1f 209y

8:00 (8:01) (Class 6) (0-65,65) 3-Y-O — **£2,201** (£655; £327; £163) **Stalls** High

Form				RPR
0001	**1**		**Captain John Nixon**[6] 2853 3-8-7 **51** 6ex..... AndreaAtzeni 10 (Pat Eddery) *trckd ldng pair: wnt 2nd 3f out: gng easily over 1f out: nudged along to ld ins fnl f: cosily* **2/1**[2]	61+
60-4	**2**	*¾*	**Luck Of The Draw (IRE)**[10] 2753 3-9-2 **60**..... SebSanders 5 (Sir Mark Prescott) *mde most: kicked on over 3f out: drvn 2f out: narrowly hdd ins fnl f: styd on but no ch w wnr* **15/8**[1]	66
0044	**3**	*shd*	**Denton Ryal**[5] 2909 3-7-13 **50**..... AdamBeschizza(7) 4 (M E Rimmer) *hld up in midfield: shkn up and prog fr 3f out: drvn to chal 1f out: styd on but no ch w wnr* **17/2**	56
00-4	**4**	*3*	**Optimistic Duke (IRE)**[42] 1796 3-8-12 **56**..... DavidProbert 2 (W R Muir) *trckd ldng trio: rdn 4f out: stl chsng ldrs u.p 2f out: fdd fnl f* **8/1**[3]	56
0-00	**5**	*nk*	**Consider Yourself (USA)**[33] 2042 3-9-6 **64**..... HayleyTurner 9 (M L W Bell) *hld up in tch: effrt on outer 3f out: rdn and in tch 2f out: sn no ex* **14/1**	63
0000	**6**	*3 ¼*	**Electric City (IRE)**[18] 2503 3-8-11 **55**..... AdamKirby 7 (M G Quinlan) *settled in rr: rdn 4f out: no imp or prog over 2f out* **33/1**	48
621	**7**	*1 ¾*	**D'Urberville**[24] 2336 3-9-3 **61**..... StephenCraine 8 (J R Jenkins) *trckd ldrs: effrt 3f out: chsng ldrs 2f out: wknd sn after* **14/1**	50
-460	**8**	*2 ¾*	**Catbells (IRE)**[39] 1861 3-8-12 **63**..... NatashaEaton(7) 1 (A Bailey) *hld up in last pair: rdn 3f out: no real prog* **12/1**	47
0-00	**9**	*6*	**Donair**[24] 2336 3-8-10 **54**..... ChrisCatlin 6 (P F I Cole) *chsd ldr to 3f out: wknd rapidly* **50/1**	26
-350	**10**	*¾*	**Jennerous Blue**[10] 2753 3-8-5 **49**..... EddieCreighton 3 (D K Ivory) *dwlt: a in last pair: rdn 1/2-way: struggling fnl 3f* **66/1**	19

2m 0.92s (-2.68) **Going Correction** -0.325s/f (Firm) — **10** Ran SP% **117.2**
Speed ratings (Par 97): **97,96,96,93,93 91,89,87,82,82**
Tote Swingers: 1&2 £1.60, 1&3 £4.60, 2&3 £5.10 CSF £6.11 CT £24.54 TOTE £4.60: £1.20, £1.10, £1.70; EX 6.70.
Owner Paul Dean **Bred** Patrick Eddery Ltd **Trained** Nether Winchendon, Bucks

FOCUS
A moderate contest, but it was well run and an unexposed pair finished 1-2. The form is rated through the third to her recent best.

3056 FROSTS JAGUAR H'CAP — 6f 209y

8:30 (8:33) (Class 6) (0-65,65) 4-Y-O+ — **£2,201** (£655; £327; £163) **Stalls** Centre

Form				RPR
2312	**1**		**Eager To Bow (IRE)**[28] 2198 4-9-2 **60**..... GeorgeBaker 6 (P R Chamings) *hld up: last 3f out: weaved through fr over 2f out: urged along and led jst ins fnl f: styd on* **1/1**[1]	71+
-140	**2**	*¾*	**Art Market (CAN)**[66] 1224 7-9-7 **65**.....(p) IanMongan 11 (Miss Jo Crowley) *disp ld to 2f out: nt qckn u.p: kpt on to take 2nd again ins fnl f* **8/1**[3]	69
4-05	**3**	*1 ¼*	**Crystallize**[11] 2727 4-9-5 **63**..... RobertHavlin 3 (A B Haynes) *trckd ldrs: effrt against rail over 2f out: cl enough jst over 1f out: kpt on same pce* **10/1**	64
00-0	**4**	*nse*	**Novastasia (IRE)**[21] 2417 4-8-2 **46** oh1..... LukeMorris 8 (D K Ivory) *disp ld: narrow advantage u.p 2f out: hdd & wknd jst ins fnl f* **66/1**	46
600-	**5**	*2*	**Phluke**[222] 7250 9-9-0 **61**..... PatrickHills(3) 10 (Eve Johnson Houghton) *disp ld 2f: cl up after: rdn over 2f out: one pce and hld in 5th whn nt clr run and eased nr fin* **8/1**[3]	59+
2-06	**6**	*1 ¾*	**Connor's Choice**[13] 2647 5-8-11 **60**..... SimonPearce(5) 12 (Andrew Turnell) *trckd ldrs: cl enough on outer 2f out: pushed along and sn outpcd: hanging lft fnl f* **13/2**[2]	50
5000	**7**	*shd*	**Cheveyo (IRE)**[14] 2629 4-8-0 **51**.....(t) AdamBeschizza(7) 7 (Patrick Morris) *hld up: effrt on outer 3f out: cl enough 2f out: sn outpcd and btn* **20/1**	41
6004	**8**	*2 ¾*	**Prince Valentine**[19] 2456 9-7-10 **47**.....(p) HarryBentley(7) 5 (G L Moore) *wl in tch to 2f out: steadily wknd* **16/1**	30
50-0	**9**	*3 ¾*	**Mr Loire**[34] 2021 6-8-2 **46** oh1.....(p) FrankieMcDonald 4 (M F Harris) *dwlt: hld up in last pair: effrt on wd outside 3f out: wknd 2f out* **50/1**	19
-000	**10**	*20*	**Admiral Sandhoe (USA)**[11] 2727 4-8-13 **57**.....(be[1]) PatCosgrave 9 (Mrs A J Perrett) *wl in tch tl wknd 2f out: virtually p.u fnl f* **16/1**	—

1m 21.53s (-1.57) **Going Correction** -0.325s/f (Firm) — **10** Ran SP% **114.6**
Speed ratings (Par 101): **95,94,92,92,90 88,88,85,80,57**
Tote Swingers: 1&2 £2.00, 1&3 £5.60, 2&3 £12.60 CSF £9.12 CT £53.05 TOTE £2.00: £1.30, £2.00, £3.30; EX 8.70.
Owner Mrs J E L Wright **Bred** Stone Ridge Farm **Trained** Baughurst, Hants

The Form Book, Raceform Ltd, Compton, RG20 6NL

FOCUS
A moderate but reasonably competitive handicap, and the pace seemed fair enough. The winner was the only one on the upgrade and rates a bit better than the bare form.

3057 FROSTS LOTUS H'CAP 5f 213y
9:00 (9:00) (Class 5) (0-70,73) 3-Y-O+ £2,849 (£847; £423; £211) **Stalls** Low

Form RPR

0-54 **1** **Choreography**[9] 2783 7-10-0 **69**.....(b) PatDobbs 1 77
(Jim Best) *mde all: rdn 2f out: fended off chalrs fnl f: drvn out* **4/1**[2]

4020 **2** *1* **Highland Harvest**[11] 2719 6-9-9 **64**..... StevieDonohoe 3 69
(Jamie Poulton) *cl up: rdn to chse wnr over 1f out: tried to chal fnl f: nt qckn* **4/1**[2]

0211 **3** *nk* **Piazza San Pietro**[8] 2808 4-9-13 **73** 6ex..... AmyBaker(5) 6 77
(A B Haynes) *hld up in 5th: prog on outer 2f out: urged along to throw down chal 1f out: nt qckn* **7/2**[1]

6100 **4** *shd* **Titus Gent**[22] 2385 5-9-8 **63**..... LukeMorris 4 67
(R A Harris) *pressed ldng pair: nt qckn and lost pl over 1f out: kpt on again u.p ins fnl f* **11/1**

6050 **5** *½* **Bateleur**[15] 2590 6-9-2 **57**..... CathyGannon 8 59
(M R Channon) *hld up in 6th: effrt on inner over 2f out: rdn and cl up after but nvr any ch of clr run: one pce ins fnl f* **7/2**[1]

234 **6** *2½* **Ask Jenny (IRE)**[10] 2751 8-8-12 **60**..... AdamBeschizza(7) 9 54
(Patrick Morris) *mostly chsd wnr to over 1f out on outer: wknd ins fnl f* **10/1**[3]

3100 **7** *1½* **Radiator Rooney (IRE)**[18] 2485 7-9-0 **55**..... StephenCraine 7 44
(Patrick Morris) *s.s: nvr rcvrd any of lost grnd and a last* **10/1**[3]

69.23 secs (-0.97) **Going Correction** -0.325s/f (Firm)
WFA 3 from 4yo+ 8lb **7 Ran SP% 111.0**
Speed ratings (Par 103): **93,91,91,91,90 87,85**
Tote Swingers: 1&2 £3.10, 1&3 £3.10, 2&3 £1.90 CSF £19.03 CT £57.34 TOTE £3.60: £1.30, £2.80; EX 21.90 Place 6: £21.90 Place 5:£5.51.
Owner Bill Wallace **Bred** Cheveley Park Stud Ltd **Trained** Lewes, E Sussex

FOCUS
A modest sprint handicap. The winner is rated to last year's best.
T/Plt: £11.60 to a £1 stake. Pool: £59,570.35 - 3,734.51 winning tickets T/Qpdt: £5.50 to a £1 stake. Pool: £5,513.87 - 731.64 winning tickets JN

2391 THIRSK (L-H)
Tuesday, June 15

OFFICIAL GOING: Good (9.4)
Wind: Light half against Weather: Fine and dry

3058 TURFTV (S) STKS 6f
2:15 (2:15) (Class 4) 2-Y-O £4,274 (£1,271; £635; £317) **Stalls** High

Form RPR

351 **1** **Hayley Cropper**[7] 2836 2-8-13 0..... MichaelGeran(3) 6 66+
(D Nicholls) *mde most: rdn clr over 1f out: kpt on wl* **11/4**[2]

53 **2** *1* **Alhoni**[6] 2848 2-8-4 0..... IanBrennan(5) 7 55
(J J Quinn) *in tch: rdn along and outpcd 1/2-way: styng on whn n.m.r over 2f out: swtchd lft to outer and styd on wl u.p ins fnl f* **15/2**

03 **3** *1* **Captain Dimitrios**[12] 2677 2-8-11 0..... AndrewHeffernan(3) 11 57
(P D Evans) *cl up: effrt 2f out: sn rdn and ev ch tl drvn appr fnl f and kpt on same pce* **6/1**[3]

0 **4** *1¼* **Beyaz Villas**[22] 2376 2-8-9 0..... BillyCray(5) 3 53
(D Nicholls) *chsd ldrs: rdn along over 2f out: drvn over 1f out and sn one pce* **14/1**

05 **5** *nse* **Dark Times (IRE)**[21] 2420 2-8-9 0..... AndrewElliott 10 48
(J R Weymes) *towards rr: hdwy wl over 2f out: chsd ldrs wl over 1f out: sn rdn and kpt on same pce* **80/1**

0055 **6** *1¼* **Dispol Snapper (IRE)**[15] 2605 2-9-0 0..... PhillipMakin 9 49
(P T Midgley) *bmpd sltly s: hld up towards rr: hdwy 2f out: sn rdn and kpt on appr fnl f: nrst fin* **50/1**

2 **7** *2¾* **Thakeham (IRE)**[4] 2939 2-8-11 0..... MartinLane(3) 13 41
(P D Evans) *cl up: rdn along over 2f out: sn wknd* **7/4**[1]

8 *7* **Memimajic** 2-8-9 0..... RoystonFfrench 2 15
(C W Fairhurst) *s.i.s: a towards rr* **50/1**

5 **9** *1* **Ad Value (IRE)**[15] 2577 2-9-0 0..... PJMcDonald 1 17
(G A Swinbank) *wnt bdly lft and lost many l s: a bhd* **12/1**

10 *5* **Forever Vienna** 2-9-0 0..... PaulMulrennan 8 —
(J Howard Johnson) *chsd ldrs: rdn along over 2f out: sn wknd* **28/1**

400 **11** *nk* **Mrs Nisbett (IRE)**[6] 2848 2-8-4 0.....(p) DeclanCannon(5) 4 —
(A J McCabe) *sn chsng ldrs: rdn along over 2f out: sn wknd* **80/1**

00 **12** *nk* **No Explanation**[9] 2785 2-9-0 0..... DuranFentiman 5 —
(D W Thompson) *chsd ldrs: rdn along over 2f out: sn wknd* **150/1**

1m 13.63s (0.93) **Going Correction** -0.20s/f (Firm) **12 Ran SP% 113.9**
Speed ratings (Par 95): **85,83,82,80,80 78,75,65,64,57 57,57**
Tote Swingers: 1&2 £4.50, 1&3 £7.40, 2&3 £8.40. CSF £21.95 TOTE £3.30: £1.20, £2.70, £2.30; EX 19.10.There was no bid for the winner.
Owner Mrs Jackie Love & David Nicholls **Bred** R J & S A Carter **Trained** Sessay, N Yorks

FOCUS
This was a modest seller with several dropping to this grade for the first time.

NOTEBOOK
Hayley Cropper, the only previous winner in the field following her convincing success in a Redcar maiden claimer seven days earlier, made full use of her experience under a positive ride. She had quickened into a decisive advantage well over a furlong from home and will have more options open to her with the nurseries just around the corner. (op 5-2 tchd 9-4)
Alhoni was back up in trip, but even so she soon became outpaced and was under strong pressure at halfway. She finished to good effect to run on into second, but the winner was home and hosed and on this evidence she will be suited by a step up to 7f. (op 13-2)
Captain Dimitrios, back on turf, was never far away and kept on to the line. He has a race like this in him. (op 7-1)
Beyaz Villas improved for the extra furlong and drop in grade and can be given extra credit as he saw plenty of daylight on the wide outside. Official explanation: jockey said gelding hung left (op 16-1)
Dark Times(IRE) improved on previous efforts over this extra furlong, but will need to progress again if she is to win a race. (op 66-1)
Thakeham(IRE), second of 19 in a valuable York seller on his debut for the yard four days earlier, was disappointing as he had every chance against the stands' rail but dropped away tamely. (op 2-1 tchd 85-40 in a place)
Ad Value(IRE) was fortunate not to decapitate himself when jumping straight up into the top of the stalls as the gate opened and then almost ran off the track. This can be ignored. (tchd 14-1)

3059 EUROPEAN BREEDERS' FUND UNDERWOOD NOVICE STKS 5f
2:50 (2:50) (Class 4) 2-Y-O £5,569 (£1,657; £828; £413) **Stalls** High

Form RPR

16 **1** **Jamesway (IRE)**[10] 2757 2-9-5 0..... TonyHamilton 3 89+
(R A Fahey) *trckd ldrs gng wl: hdwy over 1f out: qcknd to ld ins fnl f: styd on strly* **8/1**

01 **2** *2* **Waking Warrior**[9] 2785 2-9-5 0..... WilliamBuick 4 83+
(K A Ryan) *towards rr and keen early: hdwy 2f out: nt clr run over 1f out: rdn and kpt on ins fnl f* **9/2**[3]

014 **3** *1¼* **Lord Avon**[29] 2177 2-9-2 0..... JackDean(3) 8 78
(W G M Turner) *cl up: rdn to ld 1f out: sn drvn and edgd rt: hdd and one pce ins fnl f* **9/2**[3]

61 **4** *½* **Sacrosanctus**[29] 2183 2-9-2 0..... PaulMulrennan 9 73
(J A Glover) *led: rdn 2f out: hdd 1/2f out: sn drvn and wknd fnl f* **33/1**

21 **5** *½* **Mappin Time (IRE)**[62] 1292 2-9-2 0..... DavidAllan 6 76+
(T D Easterby) *trckd ldrs on rail: effrt 2f out and sn nt clr run: swtchd lft ins fnl f and kpt on towards fin* **3/1**[1]

1 **6** *½* **Sergeant Suzie**[21] 2420 2-8-9 0..... PatrickDonaghy(5) 5 67
(M Dods) *towards rr: hdwy to chse ldrs after 2f: rdn and cl up wl over 1f out: sn edgd lft and wknd ent fnl f* **14/1**

521 **7** *1¼* **Dolly Parton (IRE)**[31] 2130 2-8-11 0..... MichaelGeran(3) 2 63
(D Nicholls) *cl up: rdn 2f out and ev ch tl drvn: edgd lft and wknd appr fnl f* **4/1**[2]

4 **8** *1* **Ingleby Exceed (IRE)**[31] 2130 2-8-9 0..... PhillipMakin 1 54
(T D Barron) *sn rdn along and cl up on outer: lost pl bef 1/2-way and sn towards rr* **7/1**

3251 **9** *6* **Molly Mylenis**[25] 2292 2-8-11 0..... AndrewHeffernan(3) 7 37
(P D Evans) *cl up: rdn along 1/2-way: grad wknd* **33/1**

59.71 secs (0.11) **Going Correction** -0.20s/f (Firm) **9 Ran SP% 117.5**
Speed ratings (Par 95): **91,87,85,85,84 83,81,79,70**
Tote Swingers: 1&2 £8.50, 1&3 £6.90, 2&3 £6.10 CSF £44.69 TOTE £9.60: £4.00, £2.60, £1.40; EX 43.60.
Owner Middleham Park Racing Xix **Bred** Yeomanstown Stud **Trained** Musley Bank, N Yorks
■ Stewards' Enquiry : Paul Mulrennan three-day ban: careless riding (Jun 29-Jul 1)

FOCUS
A fair novice event in which eight of the nine runners were previous winners. The bulk of the action unfolded closer to the stands' rail.

NOTEBOOK
Jamesway(IRE) may have found the ground too quick at Musselburgh last time after having beaten Mappin Time on his Fibresand debut, but he bounced back to form on this good ground. Never far away, the gap appeared just when he needed it and he shot through it to hit the front inside the last furlong. He looks capable of winning something even better provided the ground isn't too fast. (op 9-1)
Waking Warrior was given a bit to do and didn't have a lot of room to play with when trying to get closer, but he ran on well once in the clear. He may need an easier surface or an extra furlong now. (tchd 10-3 and 5-1)
Lord Avon had every chance and was in front over a furlong out, but he couldn't cope with the winner. This was a fair effort considering he couldn't dominate this time. (op 7-2)
Sacrosanctus tried to make full use of the rails draw and made the early running, but he started to hang badly and lost the advantage over a furlong out. He is worth another chance on an easier surface or back on Polytrack.
Mappin Time(IRE) had to be niggled along to go the early pace, but was in a good position at halfway. However, he got no sort of run when trying to squeeze between the hanging Sacrosanctus and the stands' rail and it's best to forgive him this. (op 6-1)
Sergeant Suzie, who made all on her Ripon debut, couldn't repeat the feat in this better race and was behind early. She did manage to put herself in with every chance a furlong out before fading again, but she still has scope for further improvement. (tchd 12-1)

3060 PORRITT'S STRIPE H'CAP 1m 4f
3:25 (3:25) (Class 4) (0-80,79) 4-Y-O+ £5,569 (£1,657; £828; £413) **Stalls** Low

Form RPR

03-1 **1** **Hel's Angel (IRE)**[25] 2277 4-9-2 **77**..... BarryMcHugh(3) 9 84
(Mrs A Duffield) *trckd ldrs: hdwy on wd outside over 2f out: rdn and hung lft over 1f out: led ent fnl f: sn drvn and edgd lft: kpt on gamely towards fin* **7/1**[3]

30-6 **2** *nk* **High Ambition**[10] 2739 7-9-5 **77**..... TonyHamilton 10 84
(R A Fahey) *hld up in rr: hdwy over 3f out: nt clr run wl over 1f out: swtchd rt and rdn to chal ins fnl f: drvn and no ex towards fin* **10/1**

2131 **3** *hd* **Destinys Dream (IRE)**[22] 2395 5-9-4 **79**..... KellyHarrison(3) 4 86
(Miss Tracy Waggott) *hld up in rr: hdwy 3f out: effrt whn nt clr run over 1f out: rdn to chal ent fnl f and ev ch tl drvn and no ex nr fin* **4/1**[2]

-660 **4** *2* **Hurlingham**[15] 2579 6-8-7 **65**.....(b) DavidAllan 7 68
(M W Easterby) *hld up in tch: hdwy over 2f out: rdn and ch wl over 1f out: drvn and one pce ent fnl f* **3/1**[1]

5350 **5** *½* **Kames Park (IRE)**[6] 2857 8-9-4 **76**..... PaulEddery 1 79
(R C Guest) *stdd s and hld up in rr: hdwy over 2f out: effrt wl over 1f out and sn rdn to chse ldrs: no imp fnl f* **10/1**

65-2 **6** *nk* **Bergonzi (IRE)**[25] 2276 6-9-3 **75**.....(p) PaulMulrennan 2 77
(J Howard Johnson) *trckd ldr: hdwy 3f out: led over 2f out and sn rdn: drvn and hdd ent fnl f: grad wknd* **3/1**[1]

2005 **7** *nse* **River Ardeche**[25] 2276 5-8-8 **71**..... PatrickDonaghy(5) 6 73
(B M R Haslam) *trckd ldrs: hdwy to chse ldng pair over 5f out: chal over 2f out: sn rdn and hung lft wl over 1f out: drvn and wkng whn n.m.r ins fnl f* **33/1**

26/0 **8** *6* **Pertemps Networks**[11] 2723 6-8-2 **65**..... JamesSullivan(5) 8 58
(M W Easterby) *led: rdn along over 3f out: hdd over 2f out and sn wknd* **40/1**

0-36 **9** *6* **Lyra's Daemon**[15] 2586 4-9-1 **73**..... WilliamBuick 5 56
(W R Muir) *chsd ldng pair: effrt 3f out: rdn over 2f out: sn drvn and wknd* **8/1**

2m 33.73s (-2.47) **Going Correction** -0.20s/f (Firm) **9 Ran SP% 117.2**
Speed ratings (Par 105): **100,99,99,98,98 97,97,93,89**
Tote Swingers: 1&2 £7.10, 1&3 £4.80, 2&3 £6.10 CSF £75.28 CT £320.25 TOTE £11.70: £4.00, £3.80, £2.90; EX 72.30.
Owner Mrs H Baines & Middleham Park Racing VII **Bred** S White **Trained** Constable Burton, N Yorks

FOCUS
A fair handicap, but the early pace set didn't seem that strong. As a result a couple raced keenly early and several still held every chance over a furlong out. The form is rated around the runner-up.

3061 FAIRFAX ARMS, GILLING H'CAP (DIV I) 7f
4:05 (4:05) (Class 5) (0-70,70) 3-Y-0+ £3,950 (£1,175; £587; £293) Stalls Low

Form RPR
0006 1 **Silly Gilly (IRE)**[12] 2670 6-8-9 51 oh3 PatrickMathers 4 62
(R E Barr) *mid-div: drvn along 3f out: styd on to ld last 100yds: kpt on wl* 16/1

-500 2 1 ½ **Darcey**[24] 2331 4-9-4 65 IanBrennan[(5)] 7 72
(Miss Amy Weaver) *hld up in rr: hdwy on ins 3f out: edgd lft and wnt 2nd last 50yds: no ex* 25/1

0436 3 nk **Spavento (IRE)**[11] 2705 4-9-2 58 (p) DavidAllan 5 64
(E J Alston) *t.k.h in midfield: hdwy over 2f out: nt clr run over 1f out: styd on ins fnl f: tk 3rd nr fin* 13/2[3]

/602 4 1 ¾ **Tawzeea (IRE)**[18] 2504 5-10-0 70 JoeFanning 1 71
(J D Bethell) *sn trcking ldrs: upsides over 1f out: styd on same pce: wl hld whn n.m.r towards fin* 7/1

0005 5 nk **Nacho Libre**[11] 2700 5-9-9 70 (b) JamesSullivan[(5)] 8 71
(M W Easterby) *t.k.h: led: edgd rt over 1f out: hdd and no ex ins fnl f* 12/1

-235 6 1 ¾ **Chushka**[18] 2502 3-8-13 65 (v[1]) RoystonFfrench 2 57
(B Smart) *chsd ldrs: wknd 1f out* 17/2

-366 7 2 ½ **Clumber Place**[6] 2875 4-8-12 54 PaulEddery 13 43
(R C Guest) *sn chsng ldrs: hung lft over 1f out: sn wknd* 28/1

-441 8 1 ¾ **Just The Tonic**[7] 2834 3-8-5 60 6ex KellyHarrison[(3)] 6 40
(Mrs Marjorie Fife) *chsd ldrs: one pce fnl 2f* 6/1[2]

5-00 9 2 ½ **Eastern Hills**[6] 2864 5-9-0 61 (v) LanceBetts[(5)] 10 39
(J S Wainwright) *s.i.s: sme hdwy over 2f out: nvr on terms* 25/1

4004 10 2 ¾ **He's A Humbug (IRE)**[8] 2817 6-8-13 60 JamesO'Reilly[(5)] 9 30
(J O'Reilly) *t.k.h towards rr: nvr a factor* 20/1

0064 11 6 **Peter's Gift (IRE)**[9] 2791 4-9-4 60 (b) WilliamBuick 3 14
(K A Ryan) *mid-div: wknd over 1f out: sn eased* 14/1

-212 12 2 ¾ **Spin Again (IRE)**[91] 892 5-9-8 69 MichaelO'Connell[(3)] 12 16
(D Nicholls) *awkward s: sn chsng ldrs: drvn over 3f out: sn wknd* 11/1

5002 13 2 ½ **Glenridding**[17] 2531 6-9-13 69 (p) PaulMulrennan 14 9
(J G Given) *mid-div on outside: lost pl over 4f out: hung bdly lft and bhd 2f out* 4/1[1]

0240 U **Toby Tyler**[10] 2764 4-9-9 65 (p) PhillipMakin 11 —
(P T Midgley) *hld up towards rr: stmbld and uns rdr bnd over 4f out* 14/1

1m 25.11s (-2.09) **Going Correction** -0.20s/f (Firm)
WFA 3 from 4yo+ 10lb 14 Ran SP% **121.8**
Speed ratings (Par 103): **103,101,100,98,98 96,93,91,88,85 78,75,72,—**
Tote Swingers: 1&2 £53.30, 1&3 £45.80, 2&3 £36.10 CSF £377.56 CT £2861.87 TOTE £20.50: £4.80, £8.60, £2.00; EX 435.80.
Owner D Thomson **Bred** Barronstown Stud **Trained** Seamer, N Yorks

FOCUS
A modest handicap in which the early pace was strong and the principals came from off the pace. The time was similar to division two and the winner is rated close to last year's best.
Glenridding Official explanation: jockey ran flat

3062 FAIRFAX ARMS, GILLING H'CAP (DIV II) 7f
4:40 (4:40) (Class 5) (0-70,70) 3-Y-0+ £3,950 (£1,175; £587; £293) Stalls Low

Form RPR
0412 1 **Imperial Djay (IRE)**[10] 2764 5-9-9 65 PJMcDonald 3 81
(Mrs R A Carr) *dwlt and towards rr: smooth hdwy 3f out: chal on bit wl over 1f out: rdn and qcknd to ld appr fnl f: sn clr* 15/8[1]

U00- 2 4 ½ **Mad Millie (IRE)**[259] 6354 3-8-6 58 SilvestreDeSousa 13 58
(D O'Meara) *led to 1/2-way: cl up: rdn to ld again 2f out: drvn and hdd over 1f out: kpt on u.p fnl f: no ch w wnr* 8/1

-350 3 shd **Could It Be Magic**[15] 2587 3-9-0 69 (v) JackDean[(3)] 7 69
(W G M Turner) *dwlt and towards rr: hdwy on wd outside over 2f out: rdn to chse ldrs over 1f out: edgd lft and kpt on same pce ins fnl f* 9/2[2]

621 4 ¾ **Crocodile Bay (IRE)**[12] 2670 7-9-0 56 PaulEddery 9 58
(R C Guest) *hld up: hdwy 3f out: sltly hmpd: swtchd rt and effrt over 2f out: rdn to chse ldrs over 1f out: sn edgd lft and one pce* 13/2[3]

0/ 5 1 **Island Home**[587] 4-9-11 70 Louis-PhilippeBeuzelin[(3)] 1 69
(B J Meehan) *towards rr: hdwy wl over 2f out: rdn to chse ldrs over 1f out: kpt on same pce ins fnl f* 20/1

0301 6 2 ¼ **Soto**[11] 2699 7-9-2 63 (b) JamesSullivan[(5)] 2 56
(M W Easterby) *cl up on inner: led 1/2-way: rdn and hdd 2f out: sn drvn and grad wknd* 12/1

-055 7 hd **Royal Patriot (IRE)**[25] 2288 3-8-12 64 PhillipMakin 5 52
(Paul Green) *chsd ldrs: rdn alongand hung rt wl over 2f out: grad wknd* 25/1

5436 8 nse **Cool Art (IRE)**[22] 2378 4-8-4 51 (p) LanceBetts[(5)] 8 43
(J S Wainwright) *chsd ldrs on inner: rdn along 3f out: sn wknd* 16/1

5-00 9 4 **Captainrisk (IRE)**[14] 2635 4-9-13 69 (tp) JerryO'Dwyer 6 50
(Mrs C A Dunnett) *a in rr* 20/1

6310 10 1 ¾ **The History Man (IRE)**[13] 2647 7-9-5 61 (p) KirstyMilczarek 11 38
(B D Leavy) *prom: rdn along whn sltly hmpd over 2f out: sn wknd* 12/1

-000 11 ½ **Sea Salt**[12] 2671 7-9-9 65 TonyHamilton 12 40
(R E Barr) *chsd ldrs: pushed along whn hmpd over 2f out: sn rdn and wknd* 16/1

0-00 12 7 **Celestial Tryst**[13] 2656 3-8-13 70 PatrickDonaghy[(5)] 4 22
(G M Moore) *s.i.s: a bhd* 50/1

1m 24.95s (-2.25) **Going Correction** -0.20s/f (Firm)
WFA 3 from 4yo+ 10lb 12 Ran SP% **119.9**
Speed ratings (Par 103): **104,98,98,97,96 94,93,93,89,87 86,78**
Tote Swingers: 1&2 £3.20, 1&3 £6.50, 2&3 £3.50 CSF £16.50 CT £63.10 TOTE £2.20: £1.10, £3.40, £2.30; EX 18.50.
Owner Hollinbridge Partnership **Bred** D Veitch And Musagd Abo Salim **Trained** Huby, N Yorks

FOCUS
Another modest handicap, though the pace was good and the winning time was 0.16 seconds faster than the first division. A clear personal best from the winner.
Celestial Tryst Official explanation: jockey said filly finished distressed

3063 EUROPEAN BREEDERS' FUND FILLIES' H'CAP 1m
5:15 (5:16) (Class 3) (0-90,90) 3-Y-0+ £10,102 (£3,006; £1,502; £750) Stalls Low

Form RPR
0314 1 **Gobama**[13] 2652 3-8-0 78 KierenFox[(5)] 3 88
(J W Hills) *plld hrd: trckd ldng pair: nt clr run and swtchd lft 2f out: rdn to ld ent fnl f: styd on strly* 5/2[2]

00-0 2 4 **Arabian Mirage**[38] 1899 4-9-6 85 Louis-PhilippeBeuzelin[(3)] 6 89
(B J Meehan) *led: rdn over 2f out: drvn over 1f out: hdd ent fnl f: one pce* 8/1

1045 3 1 **She's In The Money**[20] 2428 4-9-0 83 LeeTopliss[(7)] 8 85+
(R A Fahey) *s.i.s and bhd: hdwy and in tch 1/2-way: effrt and n.m.r 2f out: sn swtchd lft and rdn to chse ldrs over 1f out: kpt on same pce ins fnl f* 14/1

-332 4 ¾ **Off Chance**[21] 2423 4-10-0 90 DuranFentiman 9 90+
(T D Easterby) *dwlt: hld up in rr: hdwy on wd outside over 2f out: rdn to chse ldrs over 1f out: sn hung lft and no imp ins fnl f* 7/4[1]

0-51 5 2 ¼ **Path Of Peace**[18] 2502 3-8-2 75 JoeFanning 7 70+
(J D Bethell) *chsd ldrs: rdn along whn hmpd and snatched up 2f out: one pce after* 11/2[3]

626- 6 hd **Diamond Daisy (IRE)**[259] 6365 4-8-7 72 BarryMcHugh[(3)] 4 66
(Mrs A Duffield) *chsd ldrs: rdn along over 2f out: grad wknd* 16/1

-454 7 ½ **Avonrose**[31] 2110 3-8-2 75 RoystonFfrench 5 66
(M Johnston) *a towards rr* 10/1

2-25 8 1 ¼ **Wishformore (IRE)**[19] 2473 3-8-0 73 SilvestreDeSousa 1 63+
(J S Moore) *chsd ldrs on inner: rdn along whn hmpd 2f out: bhd after* 28/1

6005 9 ½ **Carcinetto (IRE)**[13] 2651 8-9-7 88 RichardEvans[(5)] 10 77
(P D Evans) *cl up: effrt to chal 3f out: sn rdn: drvn 2f out and sn wknd* 22/1

1m 38.51s (-1.59) **Going Correction** -0.20s/f (Firm)
WFA 3 from 4yo+ 11lb 9 Ran SP% **120.9**
Speed ratings (Par 104): **99,95,94,93,91 90,90,89,88**
Tote Swingers: 1&2 £3.90, 1&3 £8.40, 2&3 £21.10 CSF £24.37 CT £243.27 TOTE £2.50: £1.02, £3.10, £4.20; EX 22.10.
Owner W Y Chen **Bred** Newsells Park Stud Limited **Trained** Upper Lambourn, Berks
■ Stewards' Enquiry : Kieren Fox three-day ban: careless riding (Jun 29-Jul 1)

FOCUS
A valuable fillies' handicap which has been won by some decent types in recent years, not least the subsequent top-class miler Peeress in 2004, but this year's renewal was spoiled to a degree by a very pedestrian early pace which cause several to take a grip. It therefore paid to be handy. Slightly muddling form.

NOTEBOOK
Gobama, who probably ran better than her finishing position of fourth would suggest at Nottingham last time, was one of those to take a hold early, but despite getting slightly outpaced 2f from home she quickened up well when switched to the inside rail to hit the front a furlong from home. She was 8lb above her last winning mark, so she looks progressive. (op 4-1 tchd 9-2 in places)
Arabian Mirage, lightly raced and disappointing since finishing fourth in last year's Nell Gwyn, was down another 4lb and ran a fine race from the front, but may have been helped by being up there given the way the race was run. (op 9-1 tchd 15-2)
She's In The Money, disappointing at Ayr last time, was very slowly away and raced keenly out the back before running on late. This was a fair effort considering she was weak in the market, but she is yet to win over this far. (op 9-1)
Off Chance is very consistent, but another 4lb rise meant that she was off an 11lb higher mark than for her last win. She gave away ground at the start and was taken wider than ideal around the turn, but still looked the likely winner when looming up on the wide outside in the straight before her effort flattened out. Things didn't go her way here. (tchd 6-4 and 15-8 and 2-1 in places)
Path Of Peace, put up 8lb for her convincing success on her handicap debut stepped up to this trip at Newcastle last month, was badly hampered by the winner towards the inside over 2f from home and she in turn squeezed out Wishformore. She can be given another chance. (op 13-2 tchd 7-1)
Avonrose Official explanation: jockey said filly was slow away

3064 STONEACRE FORD H'CAP 5f
5:50 (5:51) (Class 6) (0-65,65) 3-Y-0+ £3,070 (£906; £453) Stalls High

Form RPR
01U3 1 **Mey Blossom**[9] 2791 5-9-7 61 MichaelStainton[(3)] 20 77
(R M Whitaker) *racd stands' side: dwlt: pushed along early: hdwy and swtchd lft 2f out: led overall 1f out: sn clr: v readily: 1st of 9 that gp* 3/1[1]

0330 2 3 **Dispol Kylie (IRE)**[6] 2849 4-10-0 65 PhillipMakin 4 70
(P T Midgley) *racd far side: in tch: hdwy over 1f out: edgd lft and styd on wl to ld that gp nr fin: 1st of 7 that gp* 7/1[2]

2353 3 nk **Punching**[39] 1884 6-9-7 61 BarryMcHugh[(3)] 2 65
(C R Dore) *racd far side: chsd ldr: led that gp ins fnl f: kpt on same pce: 2nd of 7 that gp* 7/1[2]

2040 4 1 **Sands Crooner (IRE)**[14] 2622 7-10-0 65 (vt) PaulMulrennan 14 65
(J G Given) *racd stands' side: chsd ldrs: wnt 2nd that gp 1f out: no ch w wnr: 2nd of 9 that gp* 12/1

42-0 5 ½ **Bertie Southstreet**[11] 2695 7-9-6 62 (v) JamesO'Reilly[(5)] 8 61
(J O'Reilly) *racd far side: led that gp tl ins fnl f: no ex: 3rd of 7 that gp* 16/1

/406 6 3 ½ **Socceroo**[10] 2741 5-9-3 54 RoystonFfrench 19 40
(D C Griffiths) *racd stands' side: chsd ldrs: one pce fnl 2f: 3rd of 9 that gp* 40/1

30-2 7 ½ **Arriva La Diva**[25] 2278 4-8-10 52 IanBrennan[(5)] 10 36
(J J Quinn) *swtchd rt and racd stands' side: chsd ldrs: fdd appr fnl f: 4th of 9 that gp* 11/1

0-10 8 nk **Micky Mac (IRE)**[42] 1805 6-9-10 64 AndrewHeffernan[(3)] 18 47
(C J Teague) *racd stands' side: chsd ldrs: outpcd fnl 2f: 5th of 9 that gp* 20/1

46-5 9 ½ **Cayman Fox**[12] 2669 5-9-10 61 (e) LeeVickers 15 42
(James Moffatt) *racd stands' side: chsd ldrs: hung lft and wknd over 1f out: 6th of 9 that gp* 8/1[3]

3404 10 ¾ **Trick Or Two**[11] 2721 4-8-11 53 (b) JamesSullivan[(5)] 11 32
(Mrs R A Carr) *overall ldr stands' side: hdd & wknd 1f out: 7th of 9 that gp* 9/1

0-55 11 1 **Lady Vivien**[15] 2581 4-9-2 53 PJMcDonald 7 28
(D H Brown) *racd far side: dwlt: sn chsng ldrs: lost pl over 1f out: 4th of 7 that gp* 14/1

0606 12 shd **Guto**[14] 2622 7-9-6 60 KellyHarrison[(3)] 5 35
(W J H Ratcliffe) *racd far side: chsd ldrs: lost pl over 1f out: 5th of 7 that gp* 16/1

-000 13 ½ **Russian Rocket (IRE)**[38] 1915 8-8-11 53 KierenFox[(5)] 6 26
(Mrs C A Dunnett) *racd far side: hld up: effrt 2f out: sn wknd: 6th of 7 that gp* 33/1

006 14 4 ½ **Future Gem**[9] 2790 4-9-12 63 (p) DanielTudhope 1 20
(A Dickman) *racd far side: in rr: edgd rt fnl f: nvr on terms: last of 7 that gp* 66/1

230- 15 3 ¾ **Elsie Jo (IRE)**[459] 831 4-8-10 52 TobyAtkinson[(5)] 17 —
(M Wigham) *swtchd rt and racd stands' side: sn bhd: hung lft over 1f out: 8th of 9 that gp* 20/1

00-0 16 11 **Keep Dancing (IRE)**[32] 2087 4-9-9 60 (p) PatrickMathers 12 —
(R E Barr) *racd stands' side: s.s: sn wl bhd: last of 9 that gp* 50/1

58.60 secs (-1.00) **Going Correction** -0.20s/f (Firm) 16 Ran SP% **123.9**
Speed ratings (Par 101): **100,95,94,93,92 86,85,85,84,83 81,81,80,73,67 50**
CSF £21.10 CT £147.74 TOTE £3.70: £1.30, £2.80, £1.10, £3.90; EX 34.10.
Owner Waz Developments Ltd **Bred** Hellwood Stud Farm **Trained** Scarcroft, W Yorks

The Form Book, Raceform Ltd, Compton, RG20 6NL

FOCUS
A competitive if modest sprint handicap in which they soon split into two groups with nine coming stands' side headed by Trick Or Two, whilst seven raced up the far side headed by Bertie Southstreet. The result suggests there was little between the two groups and the front five pulled well clear. The form looks solid, with the winner the bset guide.
Keep Dancing(IRE) Official explanation: jockey said filly missed the break

3065 STATION WHIN H'CAP 6f
6:20 (6:21) (Class 4) (0-85,85) 3-Y-O+ **£5,569** (£1,657; £828; £413) **Stalls** High

Form				RPR
2426	**1**		**Cornus**[3] 2957 8-8-7 **68**......(be) DeclanCannon(5) 10 *(A J McCabe) towards rr: hdwy 1/2-way: sn pushed along: swtchd lft and rdn over 1f out: led ent fnl f and sn clr* **28/1**	83
5431	**2**	2 3/4	**Legal Eagle (IRE)**[11] 2696 5-9-2 **77**...... JamesSullivan(5) 15 (Paul Green) *led: pushed along and hdd 1/2-way: rdn wl over 1f out: kpt on ins fnl f* **12/1**	84
5500	**3**	1/2	**Red Cape (FR)**[10] 2748 7-9-5 **80**...... IanBrennan(5) 12 (Mrs R A Carr) *cl up: led 1/2-way: rdn 2f out: drvn and hdd ent fnl f: sn edgd lft and wknd towards fin* **7/2**[2]	85
-000	**4**	1	**Hamoody (USA)**[19] 2465 6-9-9 **84**...... BillyCray(5) 4 (D Nicholls) *chsd ldrs: hdwy 2f out: rdn and ch over 1f out: sn drvn and one pce fnl f* **20/1**	86+
1-41	**5**	nk	**Gap Princess (IRE)**[25] 2275 6-9-3 **73**...... PJMcDonald 11 (G A Harker) *chsd ldrs: rdn along 2f out: drvn and kpt on same pce appr fnl f* **16/1**	74
1253	**6**	1/2	**Leonid Glow**[6] 2856 5-9-8 **78**...... PhillipMakin 16 (M Dods) *trckd ldrs on inner: effrt and nt clr run 2f out: swtchd lft and rdn over 1f out: no imp fnl f* **3/1**[1]	78
2130	**7**	1/2	**Discanti (IRE)**[24] 2346 5-9-13 **83**......(t) DavidAllan 1 (T D Easterby) *swtchd to r alone far side: prom: rdn wl over 1f out and kpt on same pce* **10/1**	81
10-6	**8**	hd	**Turnkey**[61] 1332 8-9-5 **80**...... MichaelO'Connell(5) 8 (D Nicholls) *nvr bttr than midfield* **14/1**	77
0242	**9**	hd	**Indian Skipper (IRE)**[6] 2856 5-9-7 **77**......(be) PaulEddery 9 (R C Guest) *s.i.s: a in rr* **10/1**	74
-334	**10**	1/2	**Mandalay King (IRE)**[15] 2578 5-8-8 **69**...... DeanHeslop(5) 13 (Mrs Marjorie Fife) *dwlt: a in rr* **12/1**	64
2325	**11**	nk	**Wotashirtfull (IRE)**[53] 1506 5-9-8 **81**...... MichaelGeran(3) 7 (D Nicholls) *chsd ldrs: rdn along 2f out: sn wknd* **25/1**	75
00-1	**12**	1/2	**Beat Baby (IRE)**[39] 1868 3-9-7 **85**...... PaulMulrennan 14 (J Howard Johnson) *chsd ldrs: rdn 2f out: sn wknd* **9/1**[3]	78
-315	**13**	10	**Just Sam (IRE)**[15] 2578 5-8-13 **72**...... BarryMcHugh(3) 3 (R E Barr) *prom: rdn along 1/2-way: wknd over 2f out* **18/1**	33
3-00	**14**	12	**Waveband**[44] 1732 3-9-7 **85**...... RoystonFfrench 6 (M Johnston) *prom: rdn along 1/2-way: sn wknd* **33/1**	7

1m 10.65s (-2.05) **Going Correction** -0.20s/f (Firm)
WFA 3 from 4yo+ 8lb **14 Ran SP% 123.6**
Speed ratings (Par 105): **105,101,100,99,98 98,97,97,97,96 96,95,82,66**
CSF £330.44 CT £1490.43 TOTE £37.80: £9.00, £3.60, £2.20; EX 326.80 Place 6: £208.40 Place 5: £111.23..
Owner Triple A Partnership **Bred** G Russell **Trained** Averham Park, Notts

FOCUS
A better sprint handicap than the previous contest, but this time only one horse was taken to race solo against the far rail. The pace was generous and the winner is rated back to last year's best.
Indian Skipper(IRE) Official explanation: jockey said gelding was slow away
Just Sam(IRE) Official explanation: jockey said mare was never travelling
T/Plt: £690.90 to a £1 stake. Pool: £46,946.52 - 49.60 winning tickets T/Qpdt: £252.90 to a £1 stake. Pool: £3,555.32 - 329.01 winning tickets JR

3046 ASCOT (R-H)
Wednesday, June 16

OFFICIAL GOING: Good to firm (good in places; stands' side 9.4, centre 9.3, far side 9.6; round course 9.4)
Round course rail positioned 3m out from the inside line from about 9f to home straight increasing Old Mile by 6yds, 110f by 9yd and 12f and over by 12yds
Wind: Fresh behind

3066 JERSEY STKS (GROUP 3) 7f
2:30 (2:31) (Class 1) 3-Y-O
£45,416 (£17,216; £8,616; £4,296; £2,152; £1,080) **Stalls** Centre

Form				RPR
12	**1**		**Rainfall (IRE)**[18] 2537 3-8-12 103...... RyanMoore 10 (M Johnston) *chsd ldr: rdn to ld over 1f out: kpt finding more whn pressed wl ins fnl f: hld on wl* **8/1**	115
-102	**2**	hd	**Red Jazz (USA)**[18] 2546 3-9-1 113...... MichaelHills 6 (B W Hills) *led: rdn and hdd over 1f out: coninued to chal: rallied gamely u.p towards fin* **13/2**	117
0634	**3**	3 3/4	**Rock Jock (IRE)**[33] 2075 3-9-1 105...... PShanahan 12 (Tracey Collins, Ire) *hld up: hdwy 3f out: rdn over 2f out: chsd front pair and hung rt fr over 1f out: no imp ins fnl f* **28/1**	107
1-04	**4**	1 1/2	**Freeforaday (USA)**[25] 2316 3-9-1 91...... SteveDrowne 2 (J R Best) *hld up in rr: rdn and hdwy 2f out: chsd ldrs over 1f out: styd on ins fnl f: nt pce to rch ldrs* **66/1**	103
0-51	**5**	2 1/2	**Field Of Dream**[18] 2546 3-9-1 110...... J-PGuillambert 13 (L M Cumani) *racd keenly: hld up: pushed along over 4f out: rdn into midfield 2f out: kpt on one pce ins fnl f: nt pce to chal ldrs* **14/1**	96
16-1	**6**	1 1/4	**Shakespearean (IRE)**[12] 2712 3-9-4 112......(t) FrankieDettori 7 (Saeed Bin Suroor) *prom: rdn over 2f out: wknd over 1f out* **3/1**[1]	96
-612	**7**	nk	**Free Judgement (USA)**[25] 2354 3-9-4 115...... KJManning 3 (J S Bolger, Ire) *midfield: effrt over 3f out: sn chsd ldrs: outpcd u.p over 1f out: sn btn* **9/2**[2]	95
-125	**8**	shd	**Meezaan (IRE)**[31] 2159 3-9-1 111...... RichardHills 5 (J H M Gosden) *hld up in midfield: clsd to trck ldrs 5f out: rdn and nt qckn 2f out: wknd 1f out* **5/1**[3]	92
-413	**9**	3 1/2	**Rodrigo De Torres**[18] 2546 3-9-1 104...... TomQueally 8 (H R A Cecil) *racd keenly: trckd ldrs: rdn 2f out: wknd over 1f out* **14/1**	82
-014	**10**	1	**Kaptain Kirkup (IRE)**[12] 2712 3-9-1 105...... PhillipMakin 11 (M Dods) *in tch: lost pl over 5f out: sn in rr div: u.p over 2f out: nvr able to get on terms after* **28/1**	79
-665	**11**	nse	**Lucky General (IRE)**[12] 2712 3-9-1 105...... RichardHughes 1 (R Hannon) *hld up: rdn over 2f out: nvr picked-up* **25/1**	79
-303	**12**	11	**Mon Cadeaux**[12] 2712 3-9-1 100...... JimmyFortune 9 (A M Balding) *hld up in midfield: lost pl over 4f out: bhd fnl 3f: eased whn btn ins fnl f* **20/1**	50
13-0	**13**	5	**Quarrel (USA)**[18] 2537 3-9-1 108...... JMurtagh 4 (W J Haggas) *trckd ldrs: rdn and lost pl 4f out: struggling and bhd after* **16/1**	36

1m 24.94s (-3.06) **Going Correction** -0.15s/f (Firm) course record **13 Ran SP% 120.5**
Speed ratings (Par 109): **111,110,106,104,101 100,100,100,96,94 94,82,76**
toteswingers:1&2:£9.20, 1&3:£55.50, 2&3:£48.00 CSF £56.19 CT £1458.80 TOTE £11.30: £3.10, £2.50, £14.80; EX 52.00 Trifecta £7398.80 Part won. Pool: £9,998.38 - 0.32 winning units..
Owner Sheikh Hamdan Bin Mohammed Al Maktoum **Bred** Barouche Stud Ireland Ltd **Trained** Middleham Moor, N Yorks
■ Rainfall became the first filly to win this race since 1991. No mean feat considering 46 others have tried and failed since then.

FOCUS
This looked a typically competitive Jersey Stakes, but the first two were in the front two throughout and very few were ever involved. Plus the proximity of the 91-rated fourth, for now at least, seems to limit the form. The track record was lowered by 0.95 seconds (64th race over the distance since the redevelopment, and the 35th for 3-y-os or above), but Ryan Moore was quoted as saying "there was a huge tailwind and if it was athletics it would be illegal." That also explains the lack of closers. They raced up the middle of the track.

NOTEBOOK
Rainfall(IRE) ◆ had impressed when winning her maiden over this trip, before keeping on well to be second in a 6f Listed event at Haydock, and the return to this distance suited. She benefited from a good ride from Ryan Moore, who was happy to take a lead off the runner-up, before timing his run just about right. Once in front she didn't manage to get away from Red Jazz, possibly idling and nearly letting that rival back in close to the line, but she just held on. There are no immediate plans for her, but she's obviously an exciting filly, seeing as she has loads of speed, yet has breeding that suggests she may get even further in time. (op 15-2 tchd 7-1)
Red Jazz(USA) had this as his main target after winning the Free Handicap at the Craven Meeting and he ran a terrific race. Considering the tailwind, he was obviously in the right place up front, leading at a fair pace, but even so there was much to like about the way he stuck on once headed, very nearly getting back up. It's possible he'll now be stepped back up to 1m, a trip he shaped as though he'll get, although he did have the wind to help him. In the longer term, he is said to be likely to go to Hong Kong to race next year. (tchd 7-1)
Rock Jock(IRE) looked well exposed coming into this, with a record of 1-12, but he did at least have an official mark of 105 and he emerges with a deal of credit, faring best of those who raced off the pace. Apparently he could go back to Dubai next year, with the Golden Shaheen a possible target. (op 33-1 tchd 40-1 in places)
Freeforaday(USA), the only one of these not officially rated in the 100s, seems to limit the form, although in fairness this was his first try beyond a sprint trip. The step up in distance obviously suited and it will be interesting to see whether he can confirm this apparent improvement next time.
Field Of Dream had Red Jazz 1/2l behind when winning a Listed race over this trip on his previous start, but he was never seriously involved this time, shaping as though he might be worth another try over 1m. (tchd 12-1)
Shakespearean(IRE) won a Listed race at Epsom on his debut for this yard/reappearance, but this was tougher, especially under the 3lb penalty for last year's success in the Solario Stakes. Plus this probably came soon enough for him. (op 7-2 tchd 4-1 in places and 9-2 in a place)
Free Judgement(USA) proved a major disappointment, even allowing for his 3lb penalty. Although only 3l behind Canford Cliffs when runner-up in the Irish Guineas last time, the winner was much the best that day and the suspicion is that the bare form of that race is rank ordinary for the level. (op 6-1)
Meezaan(IRE) looked an ideal type for this race when winning a hot 3-y-o handicap at Newbury on his reappearance, and he ran creditably to be fifth in the French Guineas latest, so this was hugely disappointing. (op 11-2 tchd 6-1 in places)
Rodrigo De Torres was too keen early on. (op 12-1 tchd 16-1 in places and 10-1 in places)

3067 WINDSOR FOREST STKS (GROUP 2) (F&M) 1m (S)
3:05 (3:05) (Class 1) 4-Y-O+
£70,962 (£26,900; £13,462; £6,712; £3,362; £1,687) **Stalls** Centre

Form				RPR
14-1	**1**		**Strawberrydaiquiri**[45] 1725 4-8-12 113...... RyanMoore 1 (Sir Michael Stoute) *t.k.h: mde all: rdn and jnd 2f out: clr w runner-up over 1f out: hld on v gamely u.p fnl f* **9/2**[2]	117
03-3	**2**	shd	**Spacious**[45] 1725 5-8-12 112...... JMurtagh 2 (J R Fanshawe) *t.k.h: trckd ldng pair: chsd wnr ent over 2f out: sn ev ch: rdn over 1f out: sustained chal u.p thrght fnl f: jst hld* **13/2**	116
1-1	**3**	3	**Antara (GER)**[11] 2744 4-8-12 116...... FrankieDettori 6 (Saeed Bin Suroor) *in tch: swtchd rt and rdn ent fnl 2f: chsd clr ldng pair u.p over 1f out: kpt on trying but no imp: eased nr fin* **7/2**[1]	109
42-1	**4**	3/4	**Alsace Lorraine (IRE)**[39] 1899 5-8-12 100...... JamieSpencer 3 (J R Fanshawe) *stdd s: hld up in last: swtchd lft and effrt u.p towards stands' side wl over 1f out: kpt on fnl f: nvr gng pce to rch ldrs* **10/1**	107+
0-62	**5**	1	**Golden Stream (IRE)**[39] 1908 4-8-12 103...... WilliamBuick 5 (Sir Michael Stoute) *t.k.h: hld up in last pair: swtchd sharply rt and bmpd rival 2f out: sn rdn: kpt on u.p but nvr gng pce to threaten ldrs* **20/1**	105
-111	**6**	6	**Shamwari Lodge (IRE)**[25] 2355 4-8-12 107...... RichardHughes 4 (R Hannon) *t.k.h: hld up in tch: rdn and unable qck ent fnl 2f: drvn and wl btn over 1f out* **5/1**[3]	91
2245	**7**	2 1/2	**Aspectoflove (IRE)**[11] 2744 4-8-12 102...... TedDurcan 10 (Saeed Bin Suroor) *stdd s: hld up in tch on outer: effrt and rdn ent fnl 2f: no prog and btn whn edgd rt u.p ent fnl f* **33/1**	86
213-	**8**	5	**Sahpresa (USA)**[206] 7498 5-9-3 118...... OlivierPeslier 9 (Rod Collet, France) *stdd s: t.k.h: hld up wl in tch: rdn whn bdly bmpd and lost pl 2f out: no ch after* **5/1**[3]	79
30-3	**9**	3 1/2	**Super Sleuth (IRE)**[46] 1693 4-8-12 105...... MartinDwyer 7 (B J Meehan) *racd keenly: chsd ldrs: rdn and unable qck over 2f out: sn struggling: wl bhd fnl f* **16/1**	66
11-1	**10**	8	**Pyrrha**[39] 1908 4-8-12 105...... AlanMunro 8 (C F Wall) *racd keenly: chsd wnr tl ent fnl 2f: sn rdn and struggling: wl bhd fnl f* **12/1**	48

1m 38.04s (-2.56) **Going Correction** -0.15s/f (Firm) course record **10 Ran SP% 117.4**
Speed ratings (Par 115): **106,105,102,102,101 95,92,87,84,76**
toteswingers:1&2:£7.10, 1&3:£3.00, 2&3:£7.90 CSF £34.19 CT £117.44 TOTE £4.40: £1.80, £2.40, £1.90; EX 32.50 Trifecta £107.50 Pool: £8,171.68 - 56.21 winning units..
Owner Mrs R J Jacobs **Bred** Newsells Park Stud Limited **Trained** Newmarket, Suffolk
■ Stewards' Enquiry : William Buick one-day ban: careless riding (Jul 2)

FOCUS
This Group 2 for older fillies has only a short history but has been won by top-class fillies such as Peeress and Soviet Song. The first four winners had all scored or went on to score at the highest level but the last two both failed to win subsequently.

NOTEBOOK

Strawberrydaiquiri ◆ is a really progressive filly, and came into this having won five of her seven starts, scoring at Group 3 level on her previous start. She had finished behind Sahpresa and today's runner-up at the end of last season but reversed those placings in the gamest fashion. She was very keen early and was soon in front, then showed terrific courage to hold off last year's winner in a sustained duel to the line. She looks capable of making the step up to the highest class now, with the Falmouth possibly next on the agenda. However, she had a hard race here and might be given more time to recover, with the Prix Rothschild (formerly Prix d'Astarte) at Deauville in early August a possible, and then another crack at the Sun Chariot later in the season. (op 4-1)

Spacious won this race last season and has twice been Group 1 placed. She had the beating of the winner on Sun Chariot form and looked likely to confirm it when coming to challenge approaching the final furlong, but could not get past the winner hard as she tried. She will presumably renew rivalry later in the season.

Antara(GER), a 1m2f Group 3 winner in Germany, won a similar contest over an extended mile at Epsom on her return and first run for this stable. Stepping up in grade, she tracked the leaders from the start and tried to chase the principals through the last quarter-mile, but made no real impression. She could step back up in trip now, and connections have given her an entry in the Nassau Stakes at the end of next month. (op 4-1 tchd 5-1, 11-2 in a place and 3-1 in a palce)

Alsace Lorraine(IRE) ◆, a stable companion of the runner-up, goes well here, having won a Listed race last time and finished runner-up on her other two other starts on the track. She had conditions to suit but was held up in a race where it paid to be handy and, although she stayed on well enough in the closing stages, never got near enough to pose a threat. She looks up to winning a Group race. (op 12-1 tchd 14-1 in a place)

Golden Stream(IRE), a dual Listed winner, had gained all her wins at 7f and had finished runner-up to Pyrrha at Lingfield, having also finished second in the Sandringham Handicap over this trip at the meeting last year. She had a bit to find and ran as well as could have been expected. (op 16-1)

Shamwari Lodge(IRE), another progressive filly, completed the hat-trick when scoring at the Curragh to gain her first success in Group 3 company. She had beaten two of today's rivals when scoring at Goodwood before that and had conditions to suit, so was a trifle disappointing despite confirming that form. She tracked the leaders early and was close enough over 2f out but could not respond to pressure and was allowed to come home in her own time when beaten. She had looked better than this but it may be that a turning track suits her best. The Oak Tree Stakes at Goodwood appeals as a possible target, although it will entail a drop back to 7f. (tchd 11-2 and 6-1 in places)

Aspectoflove(IRE), a Listed winner in Ireland on easy ground but narrowly beaten in two Group 3s at Meydan early in the year, had finished behind Shamwari Lodge at Goodwood and Antara at Epsom this season, so it was no surprise she was held in this better grade. (op 50-1 tchd 28-1)

Sahpresa(USA), the winner of last season's Group 1 Sun Chariot Stakes from Ghanaati with Spacious and Strawberrydaiquiri behind, was carrying a 5lb penalty for that and had not run since finishing third in Japan in November. She had conditions to suit though, and has gone well fresh in the past but failed to fire, having been held up off the pace. She was already beaten when slightly hampered and her trainer's somewhat negative quote proved accurate, so a much better effort can be expected next time, possibly in the Prix Rothschild. (op 13-2)

Super Sleuth(IRE), still a maiden despite finishing third in the 2009 1,000 Guineas, is arguably best on easier ground and had a bit to find on this season's form. She was the first under pressure and dropped away, so perhaps a confidence booster in an ordinary maiden might be on the cards for her. (op 20-1)

Pyrrha, yet another progressive filly, had completed the hat-trick when beating Golden Stream at Lingfield on her first try in Group 3 company. Having her first try at 1m, she had made the running on two of her three previous outings but was not allowed to do so here, and faded out of contention some way from home. (cthd 14-1 in a place)

3068 PRINCE OF WALES'S STKS (GROUP 1) 1m 2f

3:50 (3:50) (Class 1) 4-Y-O+

£255,465 (£96,840; £48,465; £24,165; £12,105; £6,075) **Stalls** High

Form				RPR
4-12	**1**		**Byword**[24] 2374 4-9-0 124 ... MaximeGuyon 8 (A Fabre, France) *trckd ldrs: qcknd up on outer to ld jst over 1f out: rdn out and r.o ins fnl f: a looked in control towards fin* **5/2**[1]	123+
13-0	**2**	½	**Twice Over**[81] 1027 5-9-0 123 ... TomQueally 7 (H R A Cecil) *hld up: nt clr run briefly jst over 2f out: rdn and hdwy whn edgd rt over 1f out: r.o to take 2nd fnl 75yds: clsng on wnr towards fin but nvr gng to get there* **11/2**[2]	122+
6-22	**3**	¾	**Tazeez (USA)**[20] 2470 6-9-0 114 ... TadhgO'Shea 4 (J H M Gosden) *led: rdn over 1f out: sn hdd: styd on u.p ins fnl f but a hld* **40/1**	120
54-6	**4**	1 ½	**Stimulation (IRE)**[32] 2118 5-9-0 110 ... JMurtagh 12 (H Morrison) *in tch: rdn 2f out: nt qckn over 1f out: kpt on wl towards fin: nt pce to mount serious chal* **40/1**	117
14-3	**5**	nse	**Wiener Walzer (GER)**[24] 2374 4-9-0 120 ... ADeVries 2 (J Hirschberger, Germany) *chsd ldr: rdn to chal 2f out: stl ch over 1f out: styd on same pce fnl 100yds* **20/1**	117
2-13	**6**	1 ½	**Glass Harmonium (IRE)**[20] 2470 4-9-0 114 ... RyanMoore 9 (Sir Michael Stoute) *racd keenly: hld up: nt clr run 2f out: sn rdn and nt qckn: prog and styd on wl fnl 100yds: nt pce to rch ldrs* **10/1**	114+
-001	**7**	hd	**Debussy (IRE)**[41] 1832 4-9-0 114 ... WilliamBuick 11 (J H M Gosden) *racd keenly: chsd ldrs: wnt 2nd briefly and ev ch over 1f out: no ex and fdd fnl 100yds* **25/1**	114
11-2	**8**	nk	**Shalanaya (IRE)**[45] 1747 4-8-11 119 ... Christophe-PatriceLemaire 6 (M Delzangles, France) *hld up: sme hdwy over 1f out: one pce and no imp on ldrs ins fnl f* **7/1**[3]	110
1055	**9**	1 ¾	**Presvis**[31] 2154 6-9-0 119 ... KierenFallon 10 (L M Cumani) *s.i.s: pushed along early: in rr: rdn and sme hdwy over 1f out: one pce and no imp on ldrs fnl 100yds* **9/1**	110
112-	**10**	nse	**Mawatheeq (USA)**[242] 6850 5-9-0 121 ... RichardHills 5 (M P Tregoning) *hld up: effrt over 2f out: hung rt whn no imp over 1f out: nvr a danger* **7/1**[3]	109
1143	**11**	6	**Allybar (IRE)**[81] 1027 4-9-0 119 ... AhmedAjtebi 1 (Mahmood Al Zarooni) *racd keenly on outer in midfield: pushed along over 3f out: wknd 2f out* **25/1**	97
-055	**12**	12	**Cavalryman**[12] 2709 4-9-0 118 ... FrankieDettori 3 (Saeed Bin Suroor) *in tch: rdn 2f out: wknd qckly wl over 1f out* **8/1**	73

2m 5.35s (-1.65) **Going Correction** +0.20s/f (Good) **12** Ran SP% **116.5**

Speed ratings (Par 117): **114,113,113,111,111 110,110,110,108,108 103,94**

toteswingers:1&2:£3.40, 1&3:£22.60, 2&3:£33.80 CSF £14.09 CT £429.03 TOTE £2.80: £1.40, £2.50, £11.60; EX 12.30 Trifecta £423.20 Pool: £18,160.62 - 31.75 winning units..

Owner K Abdulla **Bred** Juddmonte Farms Ltd **Trained** Chantilly, France

■ This was a third French winner in the last four years, and a second for Andre Fabre. It was Maxime Guyon's first ride in Britain.

■ Stewards' Enquiry : J Murtagh caution: careless riding

FOCUS

This looked an ordinary running of the Prince of Wales's beforehand, with no obvious standout performer, and plenty of these with something to prove, and that impression seemed to be borne out. The pace looked modest early on, before gradually increasing into just a fair enough gallop, and unsurprisingly it seemed to pay to race prominently.

NOTEBOOK

Byword was sent off favourite on account of his close second to subsequent Queen Anne winner Goldikova in the Prix D'Ispahan, for although he was race-fit that day, while the great mare was making her reappearance, that looked the strongest recent form on offer, and so it proved. Always beautifully placed by his young jockey, he produced a sustained effort in the straight to lead inside the final furlong, and built up a sufficient advantage to hold off the runner-up's late challenge. Andre Fabre seems to doubt whether this colt will get 1m4f and, as such, may keep him to 1m-1m2f, with the Prix Jacques le Marois mentioned as a possible target. (op 3-1 tchd 10-3 in places and 7-2 in a place)

Twice Over, too free when caught out wide in a steadily run Dubai World Cup on his only previous start this year, returned to form with a fine effort in second, improving on last season's fourth in this race, despite not having things go his way. In a race where running room was at a premium, he had a lot to do turning into the straight - he was around 3l off the winner - and got going too late after being switched into the clear around 2f out. He did, though, by some way fare best of those who raced off the pace. It's possible he'll now go for the Eclipse, a race he managed only seventh in last year, and in the longer term Henry Cecil would apparently like to win a second Champion Stakes with him. (op 5-1 tchd 6-1 in places)

Tazeez(USA) fared better than when fifth in this race last year, although his proximity seems to confirm the bare form of this season's running is nothing out of the ordinary, and he did have the run of the race. John Gosden suggested this 6-y-o he could now go for the Group 2 York Stakes on July 24, a race in which he managed only sixth last year. (tchd 50-1 in places)

Stimulation(IRE), winless since taking the 2008 Challenge Stakes over 7f, although having only his fourth run since then, performed better than could have been expected on his first try at this trip. (tchd 66-1 in a place)

Wiener Walzer(GER), a German challenger, had the ground to suit and ran better than when 10l behind Byword in the Prix D'Ispahan, but he still found this an insufficient test of stamina. He was sensibly given a forward ride, but was outpaced from early in the straight and should be capable of better when going back up to 1m4f.

Glass Harmonium(IRE) was short of room 2f out, but was not quickening at the time. Just as when a beaten favourite in the Brigadier Gerard Stakes on his previous start, he looked to be feeling the quick ground under pressure, and also again shaped as though in need of a step up to 1m4f. The Princess of Wales's Stakes at the July course on July 8 could be the race for him, especially as the stiff track there could help him if conditions are fast.

Debussy(IRE), a Group 3 winner at Chester on his previous start, looked set to place when produced with every chance 2f out, but he was inclined to edge left and lost several places when tiring quite quickly. (tchd 20-1)

Shalanaya(IRE) was set a lot to do and her rider didn't seem to get serious until inside the final 2f. She made some progress, but her effort flattened out late on and a stronger gallop would probably have suited better. (op 15-2 tchd 8-1 in places)

Presvis needed to be driven along early and showed little. Luca Cumani had mentioned the Eclipse as a possible target pre-race, but this gelding has long shaped as though he'd appreciate 1m4f. Whatever, he might have been feeling the effects of a busy year. (op 8-1 tchd 10-1 in places)

Mawatheeq(USA) came into this off an interrupted preparation, having suffered a setback (fetlock injury) during the winter, and he didn't run his race, hanging right when trying to make ground from well back out wide in the straight. (op 8-1)

Allybar(IRE) was too keen through the early stages, proving unable to get cover from stall one, with the ordinary early pace not helping. Unsurprisingly, he was well below the form he showed in Dubai on Tapeta earlier in the year. (op 18-1)

Cavalryman, fifth in the Coronation Cup last time, was reported to have lost his action. He probably wants 1m4f on easy ground. Official explanation: jockey said colt lost its action (op 9-1 tchd 15-2)

3069 ROYAL HUNT CUP (HERITAGE H'CAP) 1m (S)

4:25 (4:28) (Class 2) 3-Y-O+

£62,310 (£18,660; £9,330; £4,670; £2,330; £1,170) **Stalls** Centre

Form				RPR
0-44	**1**		**Invisible Man**[20] 2472 4-8-9 95 ... (b[1]) FrankieDettori 23 (Saeed Bin Suroor) *racd far side: hld up wl bhd: stl plenty to do 2f out: gd hdwy and switching rt over 1f out: drvn to ld fnl 150yds: kpt on wl* **28/1**	107
10-3	**2**	½	**Riggins (IRE)**[46] 1697 6-9-0 100 ... JimmyFortune 22 (A M Balding) *racd far side: hld up in midfield: shuffled bk towards rr 3f out: hdwy and nt clr run briefly 2f out: gd hdwy jst over 1f out: str run ins fnl f to go 2nd fnl 50yds: nt rch wnr* **12/1**	111+
5-32	**3**	1	**St Moritz (IRE)**[19] 2508 4-8-7 93 ... JoeFanning 32 (M Johnston) *racd far side: chsd ldr tl led wl over 2f out: sn rdn: kpt on wl u.p tl hdd fnl 150yds: no ex and lost 2nd fnl 75yds* **12/1**	101
230-	**4**	1	**Tryst**[31] 5-8-5 91 ... HayleyTurner 29 (J E Hammond, France) *racd far side: hld up in midfield: rdn wl over 2f out: switching lft and hdwy 2f out: styng on whn nt clr run ent fnl f tl jst ins fnl f: r.o wl fnl 100yds: nt rch ldrs* **12/1**	97+
-005	**5**	hd	**Proponent (IRE)**[21] 2444 6-8-11 97 ... RichardMullen 17 (R Charlton) *racd far side: wl in tch: rdn and effrt ent fnl 2f: chsd ldrs and drvn over 1f out: styd on same pce fnl 150yds* **50/1**	103
534	**6**	½	**Noble Citizen (USA)**[39] 1900 5-8-6 92 ... (be) WilliamBuick 14 (D M Simcock) *racd far side: in tch: rdn to chse ldrs and unable qck wl over 1f out: drvn and edgd rt 1f out: no ex fnl 150yds* **25/1**	96
-205	**7**	1 ½	**Forgotten Voice (IRE)**[81] 1022 5-9-13 113 ... (v[1]) JMurtagh 20 (J Noseda) *racd far side: wl in tch: rdn ent fnl 2f: edging rt u.p but hdwy to chse ldr over 1f out tl 1f out: wknd fnl 100yds* **20/1**	114
63-4	**8**	1 ¾	**Acrostic**[34] 2057 5-9-3 103 ... KierenFallon 25 (L M Cumani) *racd far side: in tch in midfield: effrt and rdn over 2f out: chsd ldrs and drvn over 1f out: styng on same pce and btn whn short of room ins fnl f* **10/1**[2]	103+
1356	**9**	hd	**December Draw (IRE)**[21] 2444 4-8-13 99 ... ShaneKelly 27 (W J Knight) *racd far side: rdn and effrt over 2f out: nt clr run and swtchd lft wl over 1f out: kpt on u.p fnl f: unable to rch ldrs* **66/1**	95
3116	**10**	4 ½	**Lovelace**[18] 2539 6-9-6 106 ... AdrianNicholls 24 (D Nicholls) *racd far side: hld up towards rr: swtchd out lft and effrt over 2f out: chsd ldrs and drvn wl over 1f out: no hdwy after and wl btn 1f out* **16/1**	92
1-01	**11**	¾	**Fareer**[34] 2057 4-9-7 107 ... RichardHills 16 (E A L Dunlop) *chsd ldng pair: rdn 2f out: plugging on same pce whn n.m.r wl over 1f out: btn 1f out: eased ins fnl f* **11/1**[3]	91
-040	**12**	1	**Al Muheer (IRE)**[33] 2100 5-9-3 103 ... (b) SebSanders 21 (C E Brittain) *racd far side: hld up towards rr: rdn and effrt ent fnl 2f: no prog over 1f out and n.d fnl f* **40/1**	85
6220	**13**	1 ¼	**Mia's Boy**[18] 2539 6-9-5 105 ... EddieAhern 28 (C A Dwyer) *racd far side: chsd ldrs: rdn and unable qck jst over 2f out: hrd drvn: edgd rt and wknd over 1f out: wl btn and eased ins fnl f* **33/1**	84+
-240	**14**	nk	**Stoic (IRE)**[111] 713 4-9-4 104 ... RyanMoore 10 (J Noseda) *racd in centre: rdn 3f out: midfield and plenty to do whn gps merged over 2f out: no threat to ldrs after* **16/1**	83
1-00	**15**	¾	**Manassas (IRE)**[39] 1900 5-8-12 98 ... MartinDwyer 15 (B J Meehan) *crossed to r in far side gp: overall ldr tl wl over 2f out: wknd u.p wl over 1f out: eased whn btn ins fnl f* **33/1**	75

0341 **16** *hd* **Moynahan (USA)**[25] 2322 5-8-5 **91**............ TadhgO'Shea 30 67+
(P F I Cole) *racd far side: stdd s: hld up in rr: hdwy on far rail 2f out: styng on but stl plenty to do whn bdly hmpd and snatched up jst over 1f out: no ch and nt pushed after* **28/1**

-050 **17** *1* **Docofthebay (IRE)**[20] 2472 6-8-6 **92**............(b) RobertWinston 7 66
(J A Glover) *racd in centre: s.i.s: bhd: rdn and sme hdwy 3f out: no ch w ldrs whn gps merged over 2f out* **25/1**

6332 **18** *1/2* **Balcarce Nov (ARG)**[14] 2651 5-9-3 **103**............ JamieSpencer 33 76+
(T P Tate) *racd far side: hld up wl in rr: rdn and sme prog on far rail but stl plenty to do whn bdly hmpd over 1f out: no ch and nt pushed after* **16/1**

02-0 **19** *nk* **Spectait**[35] 2027 8-8-8 **94**............ JimCrowley 26 66
(Jonjo O'Neill) *racd far side: midfield: u.p 1/2-way: nvr trbld ldrs* **66/1**

-504 **20** *1/2* **Please Sing**[11] 2744 4-8-6 **92**............ AlanMunro 31 63
(M R Channon) *racd far side: hld up towards rr: hdwy over 2f out: rdn and in tch wl over 1f out: btn over 1f out: eased ins fnl f* **20/1**

0-1 **21** *1/2* **Dandy Boy (ITY)**[39] 1900 4-9-0 **100**............ CO'Donoghue 5 70
(David Marnane, Ire) *racd in centre: chsd ldr tl led that gp over 3f out: sn rdn: midfield and struggling whn gps merged over 2f out: sn wknd and no ch over 1f out: eased ins fnl f* **8/1**[1]

05-4 **22** *7* **Smokey Oakey (IRE)**[81] 1008 6-8-11 **97**............ MichaelHills 18 51
(M H Tompkins) *racd far side: a bhd: lost tch over 2f out: eased ins fnl f* **50/1**

0124 **23** *2* **King Jock (USA)**[17] 2570 9-9-7 **107**............ PShanahan 19 56
(Tracey Collins, Ire) *racd far side: stdd s: hld up in midfield: rdn and btn over 2f out: wl bhd and eased ins fnl f* **25/1**

-023 **24** *2 1/2* **Marajaa (IRE)**[39] 1900 8-8-9 **95**............ TomQueally 8 38
(W J Musson) *racd in centre: hld up towards rr: n.d: no ch fr over 2f out: eased ins fnl f* **20/1**

0-13 **25** *1/2* **Shavansky**[21] 2444 6-8-6 **92**............ ChrisCatlin 6 34
(B R Millman) *racd in centre: a in rr: no ch whn gps merged over 2f out: eased ins fnl f* **20/1**

-305 **26** *hd* **Mull Of Killough (IRE)**[12] 2708 4-8-10 **96**............ SteveDrowne 11 38
(J L Spearing) *racd in centre: u.p 1/2-way: wl bhd whn gps merged over 2f out: eased ins fnl f* **10/1**[2]

4-01 **27** *2* **Tiger Reigns**[31] 2141 4-8-12 **98**............ PhillipMakin 2 35
(M Dods) *racd in centre: prom in that gp: rdn over 3f out: no ch whn gps merged over 2f out: eased ins fnl f* **25/1**

2-00 **28** *1/2* **Axiom**[117] 626 6-9-4 **104**............ Christophe-PatriceLemaire 4 40
(L M Cumani) *racd in centre: stdd s: hld up in rr: sme hdwy over 3f out: no bttr than midfield whn gps merged over 2f out: sn wl bhd: eased ins fnl f* **22/1**

510- **29** *25* **Supaseus**[243] 6812 7-9-8 **108**............ TravisBlock 13 —
(H Morrison) *racd in centre: led that gp tl over 3f out: sn struggling: wl bhd whn gps merged over 2f out: virtually p.u fnl f* **50/1**

1m 37.16s (-3.44) **Going Correction** -0.15s/f (Firm) course record **29** Ran SP% **141.2**
Speed ratings (Par 109): **111,110,109,108,108 107,106,104,104,99 99,98,96,96,95 95,94,94,93,93 92,85,83,81,80 80,78,78,**
toteswingers:1&2:£51.50, 1&3:£73.20, 2&3:£40.90 CSF £296.49 CT £4309.14 TOTE £35.80: £7.00, £4.00, £3.20, £4.00; EX 895.00 Trifecta £10097.80 Part won. Pool: £13,645.74 - 0.70 winning units..
Owner Godolphin **Bred** Darley **Trained** Newmarket, Suffolk
■ Stewards' Enquiry : Jimmy Fortune one-day ban: used whip in incorrect place (Jul 2)

FOCUS
A typically ultra-competitive renewal of this major mile handicap. In the previous ten seasons winners have come from all parts of the track, but since the course was realigned the draw has tended to favour those drawn nearer the stands' side. However, this was not the case on this occasion as the vast majority of the field immediately went far side and the nine that raced centre-to-stands' side had no chance as the race panned out, being well behind at halfway. The time narrowly beat the previous track record, further evidence of how fast the track was riding, at least partly due to the following wind.

NOTEBOOK
Invisible Man, a three-time winner over this trip on fast ground last season for John Gosden, had been held on both starts in lower-grade handicaps since joining Godolphin this year. However, tried in blinkers for the first time - full-cup blinkers at that - he came from the rear to score in good style. He was held up well off the pace on the far side, being near the back crossing the junction with the round course, but picked up well when asked and avoided traffic problems to hit the front inside the last furlong. (tchd 33-1 in a place)
Riggins(IRE), a lightly raced gelding, had finished third over 1m1f on his seasonal debut at Newmarket behind a subsequent winner. He travelled well some way off the pace but ahead of the winner, and picked up nicely but not as quickly at the winner, although he was closing that rival down at the line. He is arguably best on slightly easier ground and looks capable of picking up a similar contest before the season is out, with the Cambridgeshire appealing as a race that could suit. (tchd 14-1 in a place)
St Moritz(IRE), a dual winner on Polytrack at 7f, had run well in two handicaps at 7f and 1m on turf and put up another bold show, having raced up with the pace throughout. He deserves to win one of these now, and the Bunbury Cup, or possibly the big mile handicap at Goodwood in July, could be on the agenda now. (op 14-1)
Tryst, a 7f winner for Sir Michael Stoute last season, has also been placed over 1m2f. Sold for a relatively cheap 24,000gns last autumn after finishing behind in Cambridgeshire, he had won a small race at Nantes for John Hammond last month. Tracking the leaders on the far rail, he got outpaced at around the intersection with the round course and encountered some trouble in running before staying on in the closing stages. He was not unlucky though and might just need to step back up in trip on ground this fast. (op 14-1)
Proponent(IRE) has won over 1m1f and on fast ground but his last three wins were all at Newmarket. He ran a fine race only to fade in the closing stages and he is another who might have the Cambridgeshire as his target. (op 40-1)
Noble Citizen(USA) ◆ ran well when close fourth behind Dandy Boy in the Victoria Cup and had a weight pull. He ran another good race, tracking the leaders on the outer of the far-side group and only weakening late on. All his wins have been at 7f and he could be the sort to make his mark in the Bunbury Cup. (op 33-1)
Forgotten Voice(IRE) was unbeaten when winning this in 2009 but was 12lb higher now and had not scored since, although he had raced mainly in Group company. He was returning from a break after reasonable efforts on Tapeta at Meydan earlier in the year but has gone well fresh. Wearing a visor for the first time, he ran a solid race under his welter burden, only backing out of things late on, although his rider reported that the gelding hung right. Official explanation: jockey said gelding hung right (op 25-1)
Acrostic, 5lb better off with Fareer for a 3½l beating at York, had run well in big-field handicaps before. He came to challenge inside the last quarter-mile but his effort petered out. (op 11-1 tchd 12-1 in places)
December Draw(IRE), had gained all his wins on Polytrack at up to 1m2f but had been placed over trip and ground from limited turf starts. He was doing his best work in the closing stages and will benefit from the return to a longer trip. (op 50-1)
Lovelace, a dual winner this season, including a Listed race at 7f, was ninth in this last season and nearly matched that. He has been held on all four tries in big-field handicaps here. (op 20-1 tchd 25-1 in a place)
Fareer won the Britannia Handicap at this meeting last season when held up, but had been successful on his seasonal return when making all in a Listed race at York. Now 15lb higher compared with last year, he raced up with the early pace before fading, and a return to waiting tactics in future may be of benefit. (op 12-1)
Stoic(IRE) ◆ was progressive on fast ground and Polytrack last summer but was 14lb higher than for his last win. Having his first run since February, he was one of the nine that raced towards the stands' side and did by far the best of them. He can be rated better than the bare form and is one to bear in mind. (tchd 20-1 in a place)
Manassas(IRE), 11th in this last season and well beaten in the Victoria Cup last month, ran really well under a positive ride before fading and reportedly hanging right. He might be best suited by a flat track. Official explanation: jockey said gelding hung right
Docofthebay(IRE) had not won since August 2007 but finished runner-up in this in 2008. He ran well with blinkers reapplied for the first time since March 2009, but was another hampered by a low draw and racing towards the stands' side early on. (op 22-1)
Dandy Boy(ITY) gained his wins in Ireland on Polytrack and soft ground but had won the Victoria Cup here last month on good ground. Having only his second try at this trip, he raced in the stands' side group early but his rider realised at about the halfway mark that they were well behind those on the far side and went in pursuit, edging across as he did so. However, he paid for the effort in the closing stages and is another who can be rated better than the bare form. (tchd 10-1, 11-1 in places)
Marajaa(IRE) had no chance after racing in the centre, a part of the track that was unfavoured. (tchd 25-1 in a place)
Mull Of Killough(IRE) did not have a great draw and suffered as a result. (op 14-1 tchd 16-1 in a place)
Tiger Reigns had no chance of making any impact from stall 2. (op 22-1)

3070 QUEEN MARY STKS (GROUP 2) (FILLIES) 5f
5:00 (5:02) (Class 1) 2-Y-O

£51,093 (£19,368; £9,693; £4,833; £2,421; £1,215) **Stalls** Centre

Form RPR

1 **1** **Maqaasid**[27] 2251 2-8-12 0............ RichardHills 18 107+
(J H M Gosden) *racd on far side: hld up: nt clr run and hdwy 2f out: r.o wl to ld fnl 110yds: rdn out* **9/4**[1]

2 *nk* **Meow (IRE)**[27] 2266 2-8-12 0............(t) JMurtagh 17 106
(David Wachman, Ire) *racd on far side: led: rdn over 1f out: hdd fnl 110yds: r.o u.p but a jst hld* **7/2**[2]

1 **3** *nk* **Ladies Are Forever**[18] 2522 2-8-12 0............ TomEaves 16 105
(G R Oldroyd) *racd towards far side: a.p: chal 2f out: rdn and nt qckn over 1f out: edgd lft ins fnl f: r.o u.p towards fin but hld* **10/1**

41 **4** *5* **Serena's Pride**[25] 2330 2-8-12 0............ KierenFallon 15 87
(A P Jarvis) *racd on far side: prom: rdn to chal 2f out: nt qckn over 1f out: styd on same pce but outpcd by ldng trio ins fnl f* **50/1**

23 **5** *nk* **Catalinas Diamond (IRE)**[15] 2616 2-8-12 0............ TadhgO'Shea 12 86
(B W Duke) *racd towards far side: hld up in midfield: hdwy 2f out: rdn to chse ldrs over 1f out: styd on ins fnl f: nt pce of ldrs* **100/1**

2 **6** *1* **Purple Glow (IRE)**[9] 2826 2-8-12 0............ KJManning 14 82
(J S Bolger, Ire) *stdd s: hld up towards far side: rdn 2f out: hdwy over 1f out: styd on ins fnl f: nt pce to get to ldrs* **20/1**

7 *1 1/4* **Moonlit Garden (IRE)**[24] 2365 2-8-12 0............ PJSmullen 1 78+
(D K Weld, Ire) *racd in isolation towards nr side: in tch: at least 4 l off pce 1/2-way: kpt on but a fighting losing battle against ldrs on far side* **8/1**

21 **8** *1/2* **Dress Up (IRE)**[41] 1835 2-8-12 0............ JimmyFortune 13 78+
(S Kirk) *racd towards far side: prom: effrt to chal 2f out: edgd lft over 1f out: keeping on u.p but hld whn n.m.r and hmpd fnl 100yds: eased towards fin* **33/1**

131 **9** *1 3/4* **Primo Lady**[33] 2095 2-8-12 0............(v) DavidProbert 3 70+
(Miss Gay Kelleway) *in tch: swtchd to centre of trck after 1f: rdn and wknd over 1f out* **16/1**

51 **10** *1* **Swiss Dream**[17] 2561 2-8-12 0............ RyanMoore 10 66
(D R C Elsworth) *racd towards far side: hld up in midfield: effrt to chse ldrs 2f out: one pce and no imp ins fnl f* **11/2**[3]

11 *hd* **Saskia's Dream** 2-8-12 0............ ShaneKelly 4 65+
(Jane Chapple-Hyam) *racd in cente of trck: midfield: rdn and wknd over 1f out* **100/1**

161 **12** *2* **The Sydney Arms (IRE)**[33] 2074 2-8-12 0............ RichardHughes 7 58+
(R Hannon) *racd in centre of trck: prom: rdn over 2f out: wknd over 1f out* **25/1**

1 **13** *3/4* **Penny's Pearl (IRE)**[62] 1324 2-8-12 0............ FrankieDettori 2 56+
(R Hannon) *racd in centre of trck: bhd: rdn 2f out: nvr on terms* **16/1**

21 **14** *1 1/4* **Marlinka**[21] 2440 2-8-12 0............ SteveDrowne 6 51+
(R Charlton) *gd spd and prom in centre of trck: rdn and wknd over 1f out* **20/1**

4 **15** *3 3/4* **Overwhelm**[30] 2176 2-8-12 0............ TomQueally 11 38
(Andrew Reid) *racd towards far side: bhd: effrt and pushed along 2f out: no imp on ldrs: outpcd over 1f out* **100/1**

1 **16** *1 1/4* **Masaya**[30] 2176 2-8-12 0............ ChrisCatlin 9 33+
(C E Brittain) *racd in centre of trck: in tch: rdn and outpcd over 2f out: n.d after* **66/1**

2431 **17** *3/4* **Yarooh (USA)**[20] 2474 2-8-12 0............ NeilCallan 8 30+
(C E Brittain) *racd in cente of trck: hld up: rdn and outpcd over 1f out* **66/1**

40 **18** *3* **Cerejeira (IRE)**[5] 2936 2-8-12 0............ SilvestreDeSousa 5 20+
(E J Alston) *s.i.s: racd in centre of trck: a bhd* **200/1**

59.17 secs (-1.33) **Going Correction** -0.15s/f (Firm) 2y crse rec **18** Ran SP% **125.1**
Speed ratings (Par 102): **104,103,103,95,94 92,90,90,87,85 85,82,81,79,73 71,69,65**
toteswingers:1&2:£2.60, 1&3:£9.80, 2&3:£9.40 CSF £8.83 CT £69.89 TOTE £3.80: £1.80, £1.70, £3.70; EX 12.10 Trifecta £96.50 Pool: £9,940.65 - 76.21 winning units..
Owner Hamdan Al Maktoum **Bred** Shadwell Estate Company Limited **Trained** Newmarket, Suffolk

FOCUS
The draw played a huge part in this year's Queen Mary (the Hunt Cup earlier on the card had suggested that would be the case), with the main action taking place towards the far side, and eight of the first ten finishers emerged from a double-figure draw. Indeed, the first four finishers came from the top four boxes. The bias was massively disappointing for such a high-class meeting. Thanks to quick ground and a tailwind, the juvenile track record was lowered by 0.60 seconds, the third to fall on the straight track on this card. Tricky form to pin down and it is unwise to take it too literally with the first three racing more towards the far rail, although the winner has more to offer.

NOTEBOOK
Maqaasid had to overcome trouble in running, having been stuck in behind the runner-up until just over 1f out when going well, but the general feeling afterwards was that she benefited from having her run delayed, as she looks to have only a short burst of acceleration and probably does little in front. That said, John Gosden feels this Sandown maiden winner will get 6f in due course and has one eye on the Cheveley Park. The winner is obviously pretty smart, but she was on the best ground, close to the far rail throughout, and also she's entitled to be an early type seeing as she's a January foal. (op 11-4 tchd 3-1 in places)

Meow(IRE), a 7l maiden winner at Tipperary on her second start, had a tongue-tie fitted for the first time and showed loads of natural speed on the best part of the track, before finding only one too strong. According to David Wachman she may now go for a Listed race in Ireland before stepping back up in class. (op 4-1 tchd 3-1 and 9-2 in places)

Ladies Are Forever, a 6l winner of an ordinary Beverley maiden on debut, produced a fine effort. Well clear of the remainder, she should be up to getting plenty more black type. (op 12-1 tchd 9-1)

Serena's Pride, off the mark over 6f at Lingfield on her second start, lacked the pace of the front three on this drop in trip but still ran well. (op 40-1)

Catalinas Diamond(IRE) ◆ had shaped with a deal of promise when running green (noticeably so first time up) on her first two starts, including in good company last time, and she ran a blinder on this step up in class. She didn't travel as well as some of these, but kept on admirably for pressure and gives the impression she'll improve again for this experience. It should take a very useful one to deny her a maiden victory next time and she ought to be competitive when returned to pattern company.

Purple Glow(IRE) raced further back than the front five and had little chance considering the tailwind. She shapes as though in need of 6f. (op 16-1)

Moonlit Garden(IRE) ◆, an impressive maiden winner over 6f at the Curragh on debut, is one to take from the race. She faced an impossible task from the worst draw, racing alone towards the nearside, and it's to her credit she finished as close as seventh. It's likely she's a smart filly in the making. (op 7-1 tchd 9-1 in places)

Dress Up(IRE) wasn't quite up to this class but still ran well and would have been slightly closer with a clearer run. (tchd 40-1 in places)

Primo Lady, a Listed winner at York last time, had little chance from stall three, racing towards the middle after gradually edging across.

Swiss Dream, a 5f maiden winner at Newmarket, was caught a little wider than ideal and lacked the pace of some these. (op 8-1)

Saskia's Dream, a half-sister to a moderate 1m winner, showed a deal of ability on debut and must have delighted her connections. Already faced with a stiff task first time out, stall four only made things tougher and she ran with real credit in the circumstances.

Penny's Pearl(IRE) struggled from a poor draw. She was said to have got sick after making a good impression when winning a decent maiden at Newmarket on debut. (op 18-1 tchd 20-1)

3071 SANDRINGHAM H'CAP (LISTED RACE) (FILLIES) 1m (S)

5:35 (5:37) (Class 1) (0-110,107) 3-Y-O

£28,385 (£10,760; £5,385; £2,685; £1,345; £675) Stalls Centre

Form	Pos	Dist	Horse / Trainer / Comment	Jockey	RPR
-420	1		**Timepiece**[12] 2711 3-9-5 **105** (H R A Cecil) *in tch: shkn up and hung lft over 2f out: swtchd rt and rdn 2f out: led over 1f out: kpt on wl u.p fnl f* 5/1[2]	TomQueally 17	113
-200	2	1 ¼	**Blue Maiden**[24] 2370 3-9-5 **105** (P J McBride) *chsd ldrs: pushed along and outpcd over 3f out: rallied u.p over 1f out: chsd wnr fnl f: r.o wl but a hld* 8/1[3]	KierenFallon 12	110
3-41	3	2 ¾	**Safina**[40] 1861 3-8-10 **96** (Sir Michael Stoute) *stdd s: hld up in rr: effrt u.p over 2f out: hdwy but hanging rt and swtchd lft over 1f out: chsd ldng pair ins fnl f: kpt on but nvr gng pce to rch ldrs* 10/3[1]	RyanMoore 6	95
10	4	1 ¼	**Lolly For Dolly (IRE)**[24] 2370 3-9-7 **107** (T Stack, Ire) *in tch in midfield: rdn and lost pl wl over 2f out: styd on u.p ent fnl f: nvr gng pce to threaten ldrs* 9/1	WMLordan 9	103
4256	5	¾	**Kinky Afro (IRE)**[18] 2543 3-8-13 **99** (J S Moore) *stdd s: hld up in rr: effrt on far rail over 2f out: no prog u.p over 1f out: wl hld fnl f* 40/1	LiamKeniry 13	93
02-3	6	shd	**Sweet Sonnet (USA)**[33] 2098 3-9-0 **100** (Saeed Bin Suroor) *in tch: rdn and lost pl wl over 2f out: bhd and no ch w ldrs wl over 1f out: plugged on past btn horses ins fnl f* 16/1	FrankieDettori 5	94
61-1	7	2	**Miss Zooter (IRE)**[32] 2120 3-8-7 **93** oh5 (R M Beckett) *hld up in rr: swtchd rt and effrt over 2f out: chsng ldrs and pushed rt 2f out: no prog after and wl btn fnl f* 12/1	JimCrowley 4	82
4-52	8	½	**Dubai Media (CAN)**[32] 2120 3-8-7 **93** oh14 (D M Simcock) *t.k.h: chsd ldr after 1f: led ent fnl 2f: hung lft and sn hdd: continued to hang bdly lft and wknd fnl f* 50/1	ShaneKelly 7	81
0-54	9	hd	**Mudaaraah**[28] 2224 3-8-13 **99** (J L Dunlop) *dwlt: sn in tch in midfield: rdn and edgd rt over 2f out: sn outpcd and no ch wl over 1f out* 14/1	RichardHills 11	87
4310	10	¾	**Marie De Medici (USA)**[12] 2711 3-9-2 **102** (M Johnston) *led tl ent fnl 2f: wknd qckly over 1f out: wl btn fnl f* 9/1	JoeFanning 15	88
4-34	11	½	**Berg Bahn (IRE)**[111] 709 3-9-0 **100** (G M Lyons, Ire) *hld up towards rr: rdn and effrt over 2f out: chsng ldrs and carried rt 2f out: wknd qckly jst over 1f out* 25/1	KLatham 14	85
16-0	12	1 ½	**Song Of My Heart (IRE)**[24] 2370 3-9-2 **102** (David Wachman, Ire) *towards rr: rdn 1/2-way: struggling and bhd wl over 2f out: plugged on and hung rt over 1f out* 16/1	JMurtagh 3	83
1450	13	¾	**Clairvoyance (IRE)**[12] 2712 3-8-7 **93** oh5 (J H M Gosden) *chsd ldrs: rdn and ev ch ent fnl 2f: drvn and btn over 1f out: wknd qckly fnl f* 16/1	WilliamBuick 10	73
3-13	14	1	**Miss Mittagong (USA)**[20] 2466 3-8-7 **93** oh10 (v[1]) (R M Beckett) *in tch in midfield: rdn and unable qck over 2f out: wknd and wl btn over 1f out* 33/1	AlanMunro 8	70
512-	15	1 ½	**Za Za Zoom (IRE)**[235] 7033 3-8-10 **96** (B W Hills) *hld up in rr: rdn and no rspnse ent fnl 2f: wl btn and eased fnl f* 14/1	MichaelHills 1	70
1365	16	16	**Siyaadah**[17] 2575 3-9-2 **102** (Mahmood Al Zarooni) *t.k.h early: in tch in midfield: rdn and struggling whn sltly hmpd over 2f out: sn wl bhd* 25/1	AhmedAjtebi 16	39
1-03	17	11	**Pollenator (IRE)**[33] 2076 3-9-5 **105** (R Hannon) *t.k.h early: in tch: drvn and btn over 2f out: wl bhd and eased fnl f: t.o* 11/1	RichardHughes 2	17

1m 38.53s (-2.07) **Going Correction** -0.15s/f (Firm) **17** Ran SP% **132.9**

Speed ratings (Par 104): **104,102,100,98,98 97,95,95,95,94 93,92,91,90,89 73,62**

toteswingers:1&2:£15.50, 1&3:£5.30, 2&3:£8.90 CSF £46.59 CT £166.34 TOTE £6.20: £1.80, £2.80, £1.60, £2.40; EX 55.50 Trifecta £239.70 Pool: £7,322.56 - 22.60 winning units. Place 6 £171.31; Place 5 £24.18.

Owner K Abdulla **Bred** Juddmonte Farms Ltd **Trained** Newmarket, Suffolk

FOCUS

This Listed fillies' handicap for 3-y-os has usually fallen to an improver. It normally attracts a field in the teens and the draw has tended to favour those berthed on the flanks rather than centre-field. Despite the clear bias towards the far side demonstrated in earlier races, the jockeys raced up the centre of the track for most of the way. The time was slowest of the three over the trip on the card but respectable, as those races were for older horses. The race was dominated by fillies dropping in grade having contested Classics.

NOTEBOOK

Timepiece had finished ninth in the Oaks last time following a close second in the Lingfield Oaks Trial so this was a big drop in trip. She handled it well though, tracking the leaders before going on over a furlong out and then finding more when the runner-up drew alongside. She should be capable of winning Group races at around this trip or even over 1m2f. (tchd 7-1 in places)

Blue Maiden, narrowly beaten in the Nell Gwyn on her seasonal debut, had since been well held in both the English and Irish 1,000 Guineas. Suited by the drop in grade, she was held up before coming through strongly to challenge the winner inside the last and looked like winning before her rival found more. She has recently been purchased and may continue her racing career in the USA. (op 12-1)

Safina was stepping up in both trip and grade but was sent off favourite. She was dropped out early from her single-figure draw but got quite a way off the pace, and by the time she was brought with her effort the first two had gone beyond recall. She can be given another chance at this level. (tchd 4-1 in places)

Lolly For Dolly(IRE) was another dropping in grade, having finished ahead of today's runner-up when eighth in the Irish 1,000 Guineas on her previous start. She was also settled out the back and ran on late, delivering her challenge towards the far rail. Her previous form suggests easier ground suits her best. (op 11-1 tchd 17-2)

Kinky Afro(IRE) had finished runner-up in a Listed race in Germany and fifth in the German 1,000 Guineas this season. Dropping in trip having been well beaten over 1m2f last time, she bounced back to form and stayed on in the closing stages, without ever looking likely to trouble the principals. She might be best suited by easier ground or artificial surfaces. (op 33-1)

Sweet Sonnet(USA) was placed in Listed company at this trip on her return. She ran a reasonable race and stayed on having been left behind when the winner kicked. She might be worth a try over further but will do well to score at this level.

Miss Zooter(IRE) has looked progressive but was stepping up in both trip and grade, but was racing from 5lb out of the handicap. She confirmed form with Dubai Media but looked out of her depth in this grade. (op 14-1)

Dubai Media(CAN) ran a decent race under a positive ride despite being a stone out of the handicap. She ran close to previous form with Miss Zooter although she was worse off at the weights, so might have ruined her handicap mark. At least she has the option of maidens.

Marie De Medici(USA), another who finished well beaten in the Oaks, looked to have conditions to suit on this drop back in trip, and had already won over 1m2f. She set off in front but the response under pressure was less than expected and she dropped away tamely. This race may have come too soon. (op 12-1)

Za Za Zoom(IRE) was reportedly unsuited by the ground. Official explanation: jockey said gelding was unsuit by good to firm (good in places) (tchd 12-1)

Pollenator(IRE) was another to disappoint, although she was not helped by a low draw. A Group 2 winner last season, she had run well in a Listed race over 1m2f last time but failed to perform on ground that should have suited. She may well be retired now. (op 12-1 tchd 14-1)

T/Jkpt: Not won. T/Plt: £129.60 to a £1 stake. Pool:£435,305.19 - 2,450.92 winning tickets T/Qpdt: £20.60 to a £1 stake. Pool:£22,936.96 - 822.99 winning tickets SP

2854 HAMILTON (R-H)

Wednesday, June 16

OFFICIAL GOING: Good to firm (watered)

Rail realignment around the loop reduced distances on round course by about 8yds.

Wind: Almost nil Weather: Cloudy, warm

3072 EUROPEAN BREEDERS' FUND MAIDEN STKS 6f 5y

2:20 (2:21) (Class 5) 2-Y-O £3,626 (£1,079; £539; £269) Stalls Low

Form	Pos	Dist	Horse / Trainer / Comment	Jockey	RPR
2	1		**Dr Noverre (IRE)**[13] 2667 2-9-3 0 (K A Ryan) *w ldr: led 1/2-way: rdn and hrd pressed fnl f: jst hld on* 8/15[1]	StephenCraine 5	73
2320	2	shd	**Roodee Queen**[4] 2951 2-8-7 0 (Patrick Morris) *trckd ldrs: rdn and str chal fnl f: kpt on: jst hld* 16/1	JamesSullivan(5) 3	68
43	3	7	**Night Singer**[21] 2427 2-9-3 0 (J Howard Johnson) *trckd ldrs tl rdn and wknd 1f out* 7/2[2]	PaulMulrennan 1	54
	4	7	**Crabbies Bay** 2-8-9 0 (Mrs L Williamson) *half rrd s: bhd and sn outpcd: nvr on terms* 50/1	PJMcDonald 2	23
0	5	12	**Glitter Bug (IRE)**[21] 2427 2-9-3 0 (M Johnston) *led to 1/2-way: sn rdn: wknd over 1f out* 7/1[3]	GregFairley 4	—

1m 11.41s (-0.79) **Going Correction** -0.30s/f (Firm) **5** Ran SP% **107.8**

Speed ratings (Par 93): **93,92,83,74,58**

CSF £9.88 TOTE £1.40: £1.02, £6.90; EX 8.50.

Owner Dr Marwan Koukash **Bred** J F Tuthill **Trained** Hambleton, N Yorks

FOCUS

This was an ordinary juvenile maiden.

NOTEBOOK

Dr Noverre(IRE) made hard work of winning, especially as the runner-up is now winless in eight attempts. He had shaped with a good deal of promise when second over C&D on debut, and probably failed to improve on that despite winning. It's likely he will improve for the step up to 7f and handicaps will surely be next. (op 1-2 tchd 4-7)

Roodee Queen is well exposed, but she clearly appreciated the extra furlong and turned in an improved effort. She deserves to find a race. (op 14-1 tchd 12-1)

Night Singer failed to reproduce his Ayr form, but is sure to do better once contesting nurseries. (op 5-1)

Crabbies Bay, half-sister to several 7f winners, was a bit awkward leaving the stalls and quickly became outpaced. She will learn from this and it's still early days. (op 40-1)

Glitter Bug(IRE), well backed prior to showing little on his debut at Ayr (behind Night Singer), showed bright early speed, but he dropped away very quickly and still has it all to prove. (op 5-1)

3073 NEILSLAND AND EARNOCK H'CAP 1m 65y

2:55 (2:56) (Class 6) (0-60,60) 3-Y-O £1,942 (£578; £288; £144) Stalls High

Form	Pos	Dist	Horse / Trainer / Comment	Jockey	RPR
445-	1		**Cross Key (IRE)**[301] 5146 3-9-1 **57** (R A Fahey) *midfield: rdn over 3f out: gd hdwy wl over 1f out: led ins fnl f: kpt on strly* 7/2[2]	PaulHanagan 15	66+
0542	2	1 ¼	**Destiny's Dancer**[8] 2838 3-8-3 **50** (B M R Haslam) *in tch: rdn to chse wnr over 2f out: kpt on fnl f: nt pce of wnr* 3/1[1]	PatrickDonaghy(5) 11	56
-630	3	¾	**High Resolution**[23] 2380 3-8-10 **55** (p) (Miss L A Perratt) *hld up: hdwy over 2f out: kpt on fnl f: nrst fin* 8/1	BarryMcHugh(3) 12	59
6500	4	1 ½	**Barnstorm**[12] 2700 3-9-4 **60** (M Johnston) *t.k.h: led: rdn and clr over 3f out: hdd ins fnl f: no ex* 16/1	GregFairley 5	61
6031	5	1 ¼	**Hathaway (IRE)**[32] 2132 3-9-2 **58** (W M Brisbourne) *chsd ldrs: wnt 2nd over 3f out to 2f out: one pce over 1f out* 5/1[3]	GrahamGibbons 16	56
3-00	6	7	**Anna's Boy**[21] 2432 3-8-5 **47** (A Berry) *bhd: rdn 4f out: kpt on fnl f: nvr on terms* 50/1	AndrewMullen 14	29
0023	7	hd	**Broctune Papa Gio**[19] 2503 3-8-0 **47** (K G Reveley) *hld up: rdn and outpcd over 4f out: kpt on fnl f: nvr rchd ldrs* 5/1[3]	PaulPickard(5) 13	28
0-00	8	3	**Acol**[19] 2501 3-8-1 **48** (A G Foster) *unruly bef s: dwlt: bhd: shortlived effrt over 2f out: nvr rchd ldrs* 50/1	JamesSullivan(5) 9	22
-550	9	2	**Ochilview Warrior (IRE)**[29] 2209 3-8-8 **50** (b) (R Bastiman) *t.k.h: hld up: outpcd over 3f out: nvr on terms* 25/1	TonyHamilton 3	20

4210 **10** *5* **Dispol Kabira**[12] 2700 3-8-8 **50** PatrickMathers 4 8
(D W Thompson) *in tch: swtchd lft over 4f out: rdn and wknd fr 3f out* **20/1**

00-5 **11** *3* **Newtons Cradle (IRE)**[33] 2072 3-8-11 **58** IanBrennan(5) 1 9
(J Howard Johnson) *in tch: carried lft over 4f out: sn rdn and lost pl* **22/1**

0-00 **12** *1 ½* **Sydney Bridge**[47] 1667 3-8-6 **48** PJMcDonald 10 —
(J Barclay) *in tch tl rdn and wknd over 3f out* **50/1**

00-0 **13** *13* **Woodhouse Mill (IRE)**[37] 1971 3-8-1 **46** oh1 KellyHarrison(3) 6 —
(N Tinkler) *bhd: drvn 1/2-way: nvr on terms* **100/1**

14 *4 ½* **Snore No More (IRE)**[8] 1563 3-8-8 **57** LeeTopliss(7) 7 —
(W S Colthերd) *hld up: struggling 1/2-way: nvr on terms* **100/1**

-300 **15** *hd* **Welcome Bounty**[23] 2377 3-8-11 **53** PaulMulrennan 8 —
(Miss L A Perratt) *chsd ldr tl rdn and wknd over 3f out* **66/1**

1m 44.54s (-3.86) **Going Correction** -0.45s/f (Firm) **15** Ran SP% **119.9**
Speed ratings (Par 97): **101,99,99,97,96 89,89,86,84,79 76,74,61,57,56**
toteswingers:1&2:£4.20, 1&3:£7.70, 2&3:£6.50 CSF £13.02 CT £79.37 TOTE £3.30: £1.10, £2.10, £3.20; EX 16.50.
Owner Ballinlough Castle Racing **Bred** Airlie Stud And Mrs A Nugent **Trained** Musley Bank, N Yorks

FOCUS
A low-grade handicap, but it was well run and the time seems quick. The form has been rated to face value around the runner-up.

3074 HAMILTON-PARK.CO.UK FILLIES' H'CAP (QUALIFIER FOR THE SCOTTISH TROPHY HANDICAP SERIES FINAL) 1m 1f 36y

3:35 (3:36) (Class 5) (0-70,69) 3-Y-O+ **£3,238** (£963; £481; £240) **Stalls** High

Form RPR

406- **1** **Belle Noverre (IRE)**[9] 2825 6-9-3 **63** JohnFahy(5) 7 71
(Shaun Harley, Ire) *in tch: smooth hdwy to chse ldr over 3f out: led over 1f out: drvn clr fnl f* **9/2[3]**

-646 **2** *3 ¼* **Tia Juana (IRE)**[16] 2606 3-8-8 **60** (p) PaulMulrennan 8 60
(B M R Haslam) *hld up: hdwy over 2f out: edgd rt over 1f out: chsd wnr ins fnl f: no imp* **16/1**

2-24 **3** *1* **Graceful Descent (FR)**[12] 2703 5-9-11 **69** GaryBartley(3) 4 68
(J S Goldie) *hld up: rdn and hung rt fr 4f out: styd on wl fr over 1f out: nvr able to chal* **4/1[2]**

-450 **4** *1* **Damietta (USA)**[26] 2289 3-9-3 **69** (b[1]) GregFairley 6 65
(M Johnston) *t.k.h: led: clr after 3f: hdd over 1f out: nt qckn* **14/1**

065 **5** *5* **Casino Night**[11] 2766 5-9-2 **62** DeanHeslop(5) 10 48
(R Johnson) *dwlt: hld up: rdn and hung rt over 3f out: no imp fnl 2f* **15/2**

-645 **6** *3 ¾* **Papa's Princess**[13] 2670 6-8-9 **50** oh4 PJMcDonald 3 27
(James Moffatt) *chsd ldr to over 3f out: wknd over 2f out* **16/1**

2-61 **7** *nk* **Al Shababiya (IRE)**[30] 2189 3-8-8 **63** MartinLane(3) 5 39
(D M Simcock) *prom: drvn over 3f out: wknd wl over 1f out* **10/3[1]**

0005 **8** *11* **Stateside (CAN)**[16] 2583 5-8-12 **53** (b[1]) PaulHanagan 2 5
(R A Fahey) *cl up: chsd ldr over 4f out to 3f out: sn btn* **9/2[3]**

502- **9** *16* **Madame Excelerate**[229] 7157 3-9-3 **69** GrahamGibbons 1 —
(W M Brisbourne) *hld up: drvn over 4f out: sn struggling* **33/1**

1m 55.49s (-4.21) **Going Correction** -0.45s/f (Firm)
WFA 3 from 4yo+ 11lb **9** Ran SP% **112.6**
Speed ratings (Par 100): **100,97,96,95,90 87,87,77,63**
toteswingers:1&2:£16.00, 1&3:£5.40, 2&3:£12.40 CSF £70.32 CT £307.88 TOTE £5.40: £1.40, £5.30, £1.10; EX 99.60.
Owner Lough Derg Syndicate **Bred** Rozelle Bloodstock **Trained** Letterkenny, Co. Donegal

FOCUS
This was run at a decent clip. Weakish form, but sound enough.

3075 CASH FOR KIDS NIGHT NEXT WEEK CLAIMING STKS 5f 4y

4:10 (4:10) (Class 6) 3-Y-O+ **£1,942** (£578; £288; £144) **Stalls** Low

Form RPR

0-63 **1** **Artsu**[20] 2453 5-9-0 68 PJMcDonald 5 57+
(M Dods) *t.k.h: cl up: rdn to ld ins fnl f: edgd lft: hld on wl* **5/4[2]**

0046 **2** *nk* **Rothesay Dancer**[21] 2431 7-9-0 74 KellyHarrison(3) 2 59+
(J S Goldie) *t.k.h: stdd in tch: smooth hdwy over 1f out: chsd wnr and rdn ins fnl f: kpt on but a hld* **4/6[1]**

30-0 **3** *2 ½* **Angelofthenorth**[29] 2213 8-8-7 47 AndrewElliott 4 40
(C J Teague) *trckd ldrs: effrt over 2f out: kpt on same pce ins fnl f* **20/1[3]**

660 **4** *½* **Mr Rooney (IRE)**[13] 2669 7-8-5 35 MarkCoumbe(5) 1 41
(A Berry) *led tl hung rt and hdd ins fnl f: kpt on same pce* **100/1**

0-00 **5** *1 ¾* **Balzarine**[15] 2629 4-8-5 43 (b[1]) PatrickMathers 3 30
(C J Teague) *awkward s: sn chsng ldrs: drvn over 2f out: wknd 1f out* **66/1**

60.35 secs (0.35) **Going Correction** -0.30s/f (Firm) **5** Ran SP% **111.7**
Speed ratings (Par 101): **85,84,80,79,76**
CSF £2.43 TOTE £3.00: £1.40, £1.10; EX 2.70.
Owner N A Riddell & Partners **Bred** Lady Whent **Trained** Denton, Co Durham
■ Stewards' Enquiry : Mark Coumbe three-day ban: uswed whip with excessive frequency without giving gelding time to respond (Jun 30-Jul 2)

FOCUS
A muddling claimer. The 'big' two fought out the finish, though the other runners finished close enough to hold the form down.

3076 SAM COLLINGWOOD-CAMERON H'CAP 6f 5y

4:45 (4:45) (Class 5) (0-75,72) 3-Y-O+ **£3,238** (£963; £481; £240) **Stalls** Low

Form RPR

0-01 **1** **Arjemis**[12] 2698 4-8-12 **61** IanBrennan(5) 6 69
(C R Wilson) *in tch: pushed along briefly 1/2-way: hdwy over 1f out: led ins fnl f: pushed out* **9/2[3]**

06-0 **2** *nk* **Dark Moment**[18] 2531 4-10-0 **72** (p) DanielTudhope 7 79
(A Dickman) *t.k.h: cl up: led over 1f out to ins fnl f: kpt on towards fin* **8/1**

3-00 **3** *1* **Distant Sun (USA)**[11] 2756 6-9-6 **67** BarryMcHugh(3) 3 71
(Miss L A Perratt) *racd keenly: w ldrs: rdn over 1f out: kpt on same pce ins fnl f* **15/2**

0011 **4** *½* **Musical Bridge**[13] 2669 4-10-0 **72** (b) TonyHamilton 2 74
(Mrs L Williamson) *t.k.h: led to over 1f out: kpt on same pce fnl f* **2/1[1]**

1003 **5** *5* **Monte Mayor One**[13] 2669 3-8-6 **57** PJMcDonald 1 43
(P Monteith) *trckd ldrs tl rdn and wknd appr fnl f* **9/1**

5-54 **6** *1 ¾* **Optical Illusion (USA)**[20] 2454 6-8-4 **55** LeeTopliss(7) 4 36
(R A Fahey) *s.i.s: hld up last but in tch: rdn over 2f out: wknd over 1f out* **11/4[2]**

1m 11.64s (-0.56) **Going Correction** -0.30s/f (Firm)
WFA 3 from 4yo+ 7lb **6** Ran SP% **111.1**
Speed ratings (Par 103): **91,90,89,88,81 79**
toteswingers:1&2:£3.70, 1&3:£4.90, 2&3:£7.30 CSF £37.00 TOTE £4.10: £1.60, £7.30; EX 28.60.
Owner David Bartlett **Bred** Mrs Andrea Bartlett **Trained** Manfield, N Yorks
■ Stewards' Enquiry : Daniel Tudhope caution: careless riding.

FOCUS
A modest enough handicap. The form is rated around the runner-up.

3077 SATURDAYS AT HAMILTON PARK NEXT WEEK MEDIAN AUCTION MAIDEN STKS 1m 1f 36y

5:20 (5:20) (Class 6) 3-5-Y-O **£2,388** (£705; £352) **Stalls** High

Form RPR

46 **1** **Line Of Duty (IRE)**[14] 2658 3-9-1 0 AndrewElliott 2 79
(G A Swinbank) *mde all: rdn and edgd lft over 2f out: edgd rt over 1f out: hld on wl* **12/1[3]**

2 **2** *1 ¾* **Cockney (IRE)**[9] 2812 3-9-1 0 GregFairley 3 75
(M Johnston) *coltish in paddock: dwlt: sn chsng wnr: rdn and edgd lft over 2f out: effrt and edgd rt over 1f out: kpt on same pce ins fnl f* **1/5[1]**

6 **3** *1 ¼* **Maid Of Meft**[20] 2463 3-8-7 0 BarryMcHugh(3) 6 67
(Miss L A Perratt) *s.i.s: hld up in tch: rdn over 3f out: styd on fnl f: nrst fin* **7/1[2]**

46-2 **4** *7* **Urban Clubber**[19] 2499 3-8-10 66 IanBrennan(5) 1 57
(J Howard Johnson) *hld up in tch: drvn and outpcd over 3f out: no imp fnl 2f* **14/1**

5 *16* **Fantastic Storm** 3-9-1 0 TonyHamilton 5 21
(R Bastiman) *trckd ldrs tl rdn and wknd over 3f out* **66/1**

1m 55.62s (-4.08) **Going Correction** -0.45s/f (Firm) **5** Ran SP% **111.7**
Speed ratings (Par 101): **100,98,97,91,76**
CSF £15.71 TOTE £7.70: £2.00, £1.10; EX 10.50.
Owner J N Swinbank **Bred** Olive O'Connor And Raymond Gaffney **Trained** Melsonby, N Yorks
■ Stewards' Enquiry : Greg Fairley two-day ban: used whip causing minor weals (Jun 30-Jul 1)

FOCUS
A weak maiden which has not been rated too positively.

3078 TURFTV IN YOUR BETTING SHOP APPRENTICE H'CAP (ROUND 1) 1m 4f 17y

5:50 (5:51) (Class 6) (0-60,60) 4-Y-O+ **£2,047** (£604; £302) **Stalls** High

Form RPR

52- **1** **Sovento (GER)**[44] 1790 6-9-0 **55** JohnFahy 9 61
(Shaun Harley, Ire) *trckd ldrs: hld up: rdn over 2f out: edgd rt over 1f out: sn strly pressed: kpt on wl fnl f: all out* **4/1[3]**

40-6 **2** *nse* **Regent's Secret (USA)**[16] 2583 10-8-9 **50** (v) IanBrennan 10 56
(J S Goldie) *hld up: hdwy and prom over 3f out: effrt and str chal fnl f: kpt on wl: jst hld* **11/4[1]**

5033 **3** *nk* **Without Equal**[10] 2786 4-8-2 **46** oh1 SoniaEaton(3) 6 51
(A Dickman) *hld up: hdwy on outside 3f out: effrtt over 1f out: kpt on fnl f but a hld* **9/1**

-164 **4** *1* **Shekan Star**[19] 2500 8-9-1 **56** LeeTopliss 3 60
(K G Reveley) *hld up: rdn over 3f out: no imp tl hdwy over 1f out: kpt on ins fnl f: nvr able to chal* **5/1**

5-03 **5** *3* **Ballade De La Mer**[8] 2833 4-8-2 **46** oh1 AdamCarter(3) 1 45
(A G Foster) *chsd ldrs: rdn over 4f out: rallied: no ex appr fnl f* **25/1**

2525 **6** *3 ¼* **Lisbon Lion (IRE)**[19] 2500 5-8-4 **52** DavidSimmonson(7) 8 46
(James Moffatt) *hld up: hdwy and in tch 3f out: edgd rt and outpcd fr 2f out* **10/3[2]**

-002 **7** *31* **Media Stars**[8] 2833 5-8-2 **48** oh1 ow2 (p) AnthonyBetts(5) 7 —
(R Johnson) *cl up: led after 4f to over 4f out: wknd fr 3f out: t.o* **18/1**

000 **8** *14* **Siberian Sunset (IRE)**[15] 2627 4-8-13 **54** JohnCavanagh 2 —
(G A Swinbank) *in tch: drvn over 4f out: wknd over 3f out: t.o* **12/1**

9 *36* **Mobus Wan (FR)**[9] 2825 7-9-5 **60** (p) DavidKenny 5 —
(Shaun Harley, Ire) *rn wout declared tongue-tie: led 4f: cl up tl wknd qckly over 4f out: t.o* **16/1**

2m 33.82s (-4.78) **Going Correction** -0.45s/f (Firm) **9** Ran SP% **119.1**
Speed ratings (Par 101): **97,96,96,96,94 91,71,61,37**
toteswingers:1&2:£3.40, 1&3:£10.30, 2&3:£9.90 CSF £15.99 CT £94.85 TOTE £7.60: £2.80, £1.10, £4.10; EX 25.00 Place 6 £40.66; Place 5 £28.55.
Owner Lough Derg Syndicate **Bred** Achim Stahn **Trained** Letterkenny, Co. Donegal
■ Stewards' Enquiry : John Fahy four-day ban: used whip with excessive frequency (Jun 30-Jul 1,2,4)

FOCUS
A competitive apprentices' handicap but only modest form, with the fifth close enough from 9lb wrong.
Sovento(GER) Official explanation: trainer's rep said, regarding apparent improvement in form, that the gelding was better suited by faster conditions.
T/Plt: £24.10 to a £1 stake. Pool:£32,961.51 - 996.86 winning tickets T/Qpdt: £7.90 to a £1 stake. Pool:£2,426.20 - 226.76 winning tickets RY

2866 KEMPTON (A.W) (R-H)

Wednesday, June 16

OFFICIAL GOING: Standard
Wind: Strong, half against Weather: Sunny

3079 KEMPTON.CO.UK APPRENTICE H'CAP 1m 2f (P)

6:10 (6:11) (Class 4) (0-80,77) 4-Y-O+ **£4,209** (£1,252; £625; £312) **Stalls** High

Form RPR

-212 **1** **Speed Dating**[12] 2723 4-9-4 **74** (b[1]) RosieJessop(3) 9 87+
(Sir Mark Prescott) *s.s: hld up in last pair: plenty to do whn effrt 2f out: drvn and rapid prog over 1f out: r.o to ld last 50yds* **1/1[1]**

0355 **2** *¾* **Mons Calpe (IRE)**[12] 2723 4-8-12 **68** (b) DuilioDaSilva(3) 6 73
(P F I Cole) *trckd ldr after 1f: chal over 2f out and sn clr of rest: rdn to ld 1f out: styd on: hdd and outpcd last 50yds* **10/1**

1 **3** *1 ¾* **Quarante Deux (USA)**[148] 226 4-9-5 **75** (t) TobyAtkinson(3) 4 77+
(G A Butler) *towards rr: rdn 3f out: prog u.p 2f out: styd on to take 3rd nr fin* **9/2[2]**

0030 **4** *2* **Zerzura**[12] 2723 4-9-0 **67** KierenFox 1 65
(P Howling) *led: pressed over 2f out and sn clr of rest: hdd 1f out: wknd* **33/1**

0500 **5** *3 ½* **Dream Of Fortune (IRE)**[4] 2966 6-8-12 **65** (t) RichardEvans 8 56
(P D Evans) *hld up in last trio: rdn 2f out: plugged on to pass wkng rivals fnl f* **8/1[3]**

0515 **6** *1 ½* **Expensive Problem**[28] 2236 7-9-1 **73** NathanAlison(5) 3 61
(R J Smith) *s.s: hld up in last pair: plenty to do 2f out: rdn and no real prog* **25/1**

2240 **7** *1 ¾* **Dinner Date**[14] 2653 8-9-8 **75** RossAtkinson 10 59
(T Keddy) *hld up towards rr: rdn over 2f out: no prog and sn btn* **16/1**

2400 **8** *¾* **Formidable Guest**[61] 1346 6-9-5 **72** SimonPearce 2 55
(J Pearce) *trckd ldrs: outpcd 2f out: wnt 3rd briefly over 1f out: sn wknd* **14/1**

-054 **9** *½* **Apex**[22] 2411 9-8-12 **65** MatthewDavies 7 47
(M Hill) *chsd ldr 1f: racd in 3rd after: outpcd 2f out: wknd over 1f out* **25/1**

/12- 10 *14* **Penton Hook**[230] 7134 4-9-10 **77** AshleyMorgan 5 31
(P Winkworth) *t.k.h: trckd ldrs tl wknd rapidly over 2f out: t.o* **12/1**

2m 6.80s (-1.20) **Going Correction** -0.05s/f (Stan) **10** Ran SP% **119.3**
Speed ratings (Par 105): **102,101,100,98,95 94,93,92,92,80**
toteswingers:1&2:£3.80, 1&3:£2.00, 2&3:£8.70 CSF £12.36 CT £35.45 TOTE £2.60: £1.70, £3.30, £1.20; EX 16.50.
Owner Cheveley Park Stud **Bred** Cheveley Park Stud Ltd **Trained** Newmarket, Suffolk

FOCUS
It was reported that 30mm of water was put on the track during the day in order to lessen the kickback. An ordinary handicap for apprentice riders. The winner, third and fourth had met over 1m4f at Wolverhampton earlier in the month and upheld that form. The pace was fairly steady and the winner was value for extra.
Formidable Guest Official explanation: jockey said mare hung right on final bend

3080 BARNES RUGBY CLUB MAIDEN FILLIES' STKS 1m 2f (P)
6:40 (6:43) (Class 5) 3-Y-0+ **£2,590** (£770; £385; £192) **Stalls** High

Form RPR
5-2 **1** **Mirror Lake**[12] 2718 3-8-12 0 TomQueally 10 91+
(Mrs A J Perrett) *trckd ldrs: effrt on inner to ld over 2f out: sn clr: pushed out* **6/5**[1]
4 **2** *6* **Sumerian**[25] 2334 3-8-12 0 SebSanders 2 79
(Sir Mark Prescott) *trckd ldng pair after 3f: chal over 2f out: chsd wnr after: outpcd and hanging sltly wl over 1f out: styd on but no ch* **7/1**
3 *4* **Miss Jean Brodie (USA)** 3-8-5 0 AntiocoMurgia(7) 8 71+
(Mahmood Al Zarooni) *dwlt: mostly in last trio: wl off the pce whn hung bdly lft bnd 2f out: rdn and styd on strly after: tk 3rd nr fin* **33/1**
4 *1 3/4* **Minikin (IRE)** 3-8-12 0 SteveDrowne 6 67
(H Morrison) *s.i.s: pushed up into midfield after 2f: effrt fr 3f out: outpcd by ldrs fr 2f out: kpt on* **33/1**
64 **5** *1/2* **Medici Palace**[21] 2434 3-8-12 0 EddieAhern 9 66
(J R Fanshawe) *hld up in 10th and off the pce: rapid prog on wd outside fr 4f out to press ldrs over 2f out: outpcd in 3rd over 1f out: fdd* **10/1**
5 **6** *4* **Olympic Medal**[27] 2255 3-8-12 0 RichardKingscote 4 58
(R Charlton) *trckd ldrs: rdn and cl enough over 2f out: sn outpcd and btn* **16/1**
2 **7** *2 3/4* **Librettista (AUS)**[20] 2473 4-9-7 0 J-PGuillambert 3 50
(L M Cumani) *a in midfield: pushed along firmly 3f out: sn outpcd: no ch after* **11/2**[2]
30 **8** *nse* **Derecho**[40] 1882 3-8-12 0 AdamKirby 7 52
(C G Cox) *broke wl but sn settled bk into 9th: pushed along and outpcd fr over 2f out: nvr on terms after* **14/1**
0 **9** *13* **Now What**[45] 1735 3-8-12 0 PatCosgrave 1 26
(J G Portman) *w ldr: led over 3f out to over 2f out: wknd rapidly: t.o* **100/1**
10 *1* **La Divina (IRE)** 3-8-12 0 RichardMullen 12 24
(Sir Michael Stoute) *trckd ldrs in abt 6th: pushed along firmly 3f out: sn wknd: t.o* **13/2**[3]
0- **11** *8* **Smirfys Copper (IRE)**[329] 4187 3-8-12 0 SilvestreDeSousa 11 8
(Mrs D J Sanderson) *sn last: nvr a factor: t.o* **66/1**
00 **12** *6* **Jasmin Rai**[20] 2473 3-8-12 0 AndreaAtzeni 5 —
(D Donovan) *mostly in last trio: outpcd and reminder over 3f out: wknd: t.o* **66/1**
0-56 **13** *8* **Tammela**[53] 1514 3-8-12 62 NeilCallan 14 —
(A P Jarvis) *mde most to over 3f out: wknd rapidly: sn t.o* **50/1**

2m 7.16s (-0.84) **Going Correction** -0.05s/f (Stan)
WFA 3 from 4yo+ 12lb **13** Ran SP% **120.1**
Speed ratings (Par 100): **101,96,93,91,91 88,85,85,75,74 68,63,56**
toteswingers:1&2:£2.20, 1&3:£15.00, 2&3:£29.40 CSF £9.65 TOTE £2.20: £1.10, £2.90, £13.20; EX 11.20.
Owner K Abdulla **Bred** Millsec Limited **Trained** Pulborough, W Sussex

FOCUS
An interesting fillies' maiden which should throw up some winners in ordinary company. The pace seemed solid but the time was marginally slower than the earlier apprentice handicap, which had been hand-timed. Improvement from the first two.

3081 DIGIBET H'CAP 1m 2f (P)
7:10 (7:10) (Class 4) (0-85,84) 3-Y-0 **£4,209** (£1,252; £625; £312) **Stalls** High

Form RPR
-120 **1** **Mawaddah (IRE)**[45] 1734 3-8-13 **76** RichardHughes 5 85
(R Hannon) *trckd ldng pair: effrt on outer to ld over 1f out: sn rdn clr* **7/2**[2]
-512 **2** *2 1/2* **Buffett**[23] 2386 3-9-0 **77** KierenFallon 7 81
(L M Cumani) *trckd ldng pair on inner: effrt over 1f out: rdn to chse wnr ent fnl f: no imp* **4/6**[1]
1300 **3** *1 1/4* **Whippers Love (IRE)**[35] 2033 3-9-6 **83** JoeFanning 2 85
(M Johnston) *trckd ldr: effrt to ld v briefly over 1f out: sn wl outpcd* **25/1**
2-03 **4** *1 1/2* **Be A Devil**[14] 2644 3-8-13 **76** DaneO'Neill 3 75
(W R Muir) *settled in 6th: rdn 3f out: tried to cl u.p over 1f out: outpcd but plugged on* **8/1**[3]
0-26 **5** *1 1/4* **Song To The Moon (IRE)**[28] 2225 3-8-11 **74** DavidProbert 6 70
(A M Balding) *led to over 1f out: wknd rapidly* **20/1**
610 **6** *nse* **My Nan Nell (IRE)**[14] 2652 3-8-12 **75** NeilCallan 4 71
(M Botti) *hld up in 5th: gng wl enough on inner 2f out: no prog over 1f out: wknd fnl f* **16/1**
1-00 **7** *5* **Elspeth's Boy (USA)**[18] 2542 3-9-7 **84** TedDurcan 1 70
(J R Best) *restrained s: plld hrd and hld up in last: rdn 3f out: sn lost tch* **25/1**

2m 6.76s (-1.24) **Going Correction** -0.05s/f (Stan) **7** Ran SP% **111.7**
Speed ratings (Par 101): **102,100,99,97,96 96,92**
toteswingers:1&2:£1.10, 1&3:£10.40, 2&3:£11.00 CSF £5.87 TOTE £5.40: £2.30, £1.10; EX 7.10.
Owner Malih L Al Basti **Bred** J Beckett **Trained** East Everleigh, Wilts

FOCUS
The third race of the night over 1m2f, and it was run in a similar time to the earlier two. The form looks sound.

3082 EUROPEAN BREEDERS' FUND MAIDEN FILLIES' STKS 7f (P)
7:40 (7:43) (Class 5) 2-Y-0 **£3,302** (£982; £491; £245) **Stalls** High

Form RPR
5 **1** **Sceal Nua (IRE)**[11] 2749 2-9-0 0 RichardHughes 13 75+
(R Hannon) *mde virtually all: jnd 2f out: shkn up over 1f out: styd on to gain upper hand last 100yds* **9/2**[3]
2 *1/2* **Pencarrow** 2-9-0 0 TedDurcan 10 74+
(Mahmood Al Zarooni) *dwlt: sn trckd ldng pair: wnt 2nd 3f out: jnd wnr 2f out: upsides tl no ex last 100yds* **15/2**
3 *1/2* **Dubai Moon (USA)** 2-8-11 0 AhmedAjtebi(3) 2 73+
(Mahmood Al Zarooni) *hld up in rr on outer: prog over 2f out: wnt 3rd ent fnl f: clsd on ldng pair fin* **25/1**
2 **4** *1 1/2* **Jetfire**[14] 2641 2-9-0 0 KierenFallon 3 69
(P F I Cole) *trckd ldrs in 6th: effrt to dispute 3rd 2f out: rdn and nt qckn over 1f out: styd on* **2/1**[1]
6 **5** *1 1/4* **Jolah**[25] 2330 2-9-0 0 NeilCallan 9 66
(C E Brittain) *t.k.h: cl up in 5th: wnt 3rd wl over 2f out: no imp on ldng pair: fdd ins fnl f* **16/1**
6 *nk* **The Shrew** 2-9-0 0 WilliamBuick 12 65
(J H M Gosden) *hld up towards rr: lost grnd bhd struggling rival 1/2-way: effrt on inner over 2f out: chsd ldrs over 1f out: one pce after* **10/1**
7 *1 1/2* **Indian Wish (USA)** 2-9-0 0 JamieSpencer 8 62+
(M L W Bell) *trckd ldng trio on outer: lost pl bnd 3f out: squeezed out over 2f out: tried to rally over 1f out: one pce* **4/1**[2]
8 *2 1/4* **Dubai Glory** 2-9-0 0 JimCrowley 6 56+
(E A L Dunlop) *dwlt: pushed along in rr after 3f: outpcd over 2f out: kpt on steadily* **50/1**
0 **9** *3 3/4* **Wanchai Minx**[19] 2498 2-9-0 0 TomQueally 7 46
(A P Jarvis) *dwlt: midfield on inner: awkward bnd 1/2-way and lost grnd: fdd over 2f out* **100/1**
10 *12* **Twin Soul (IRE)** 2-9-0 0 JimmyFortune 4 16
(A M Balding) *dwlt: a wl in rr: t.o* **20/1**
44 **11** *hd* **Veil Of Night**[24] 2358 2-9-0 0 DaneO'Neill 1 16
(D Haydn Jones) *a wl in rr: t.o* **66/1**
65 **12** *6* **Sister June (IRE)**[15] 2630 2-9-0 0 EddieCreighton 5 —
(E J Creighton) *trckd wnr to 3f out: wknd rapidly: t.o* **66/1**

1m 26.48s (0.48) **Going Correction** -0.05s/f (Stan) **12** Ran SP% **112.8**
Speed ratings (Par 90): **95,94,93,92,90 90,88,86,81,68 67,61**
toteswingers:1&2:£8.40, 1&3:£27.80, 2&3:£35.80 CSF £33.93 TOTE £4.10: £1.70, £4.80, £5.00; EX 30.50.
Owner Mrs Clodagh Mitchell **Bred** Kevin Mitchell **Trained** East Everleigh, Wilts
■ Stewards' Enquiry : Kieren Fallon one-day ban: careless riding (Jun 30)

FOCUS
An ordinary fillies' maiden, one of the first juvenile races of the year over 7f. The pace was sound enough. The first two were locked together from the two-pole

NOTEBOOK
Sceal Nua(IRE) put her previous experience to good use, just edging ahead of the runner-up in the final half-furlong and showing a pleasing attitude. The step up in trip suited and she was always to the fore from the inside stall. (op 5-1 tchd 4-1)
Pencarrow was travelling strongly turning in but did not find quite as much as she had promised when let down and eventually had to give best to the winner after a good tussle. A 260,000gns buy and a half-sister to a useful performer in Fireside, she should soon be going one better in similar company. (op 12-1)
Dubai Moon(USA), the yard's second-string, was not as well drawn as her stablemate and found herself in rear, but she stayed on relentlessly down the outer in the straight and was closing in on the first two close home. Acquired for $200,000, she is a sister to a Grade 1 winner in the States and the dam is a half-sister to Washington International winner Vanlandingham.
Jetfire, runner-up over 6f here on her debut, probably ran to a similar level on her second start and saw the extra yardage out well enough. (op 13-8 tchd 9-4 in places)
Jolah again showed ability but more is needed if she is to win one of these. The seventh furlong just seemed to find her out. (op 14-1)
The Shrew, whose dam won the Chesham Stakes, stayed on nicely enough despite looking a little green and ought to make the grade. (tchd 11-1)
Indian Wish(USA), a half-sister to no fewer than seven winners in the US, came in for plenty of support. After chasing the pace she looked held when she was hampered just before the two-pole, but it is probably too soon to be writing her off. (op 9-2 tchd 7-2)
Dubai Glory is a half-sister to several winners and showed enough on her debut to suggest that she will pay her way in time. (op 40-1)

3083 DIGIBET.COM H'CAP 7f (P)
8:10 (8:14) (Class 4) (0-85,86) 3-Y-0+ **£4,209** (£1,252; £625; £312) **Stalls** High

Form RPR
-201 **1** **All The Nines (IRE)**[20] 2475 4-9-11 **82** SilvestreDeSousa 9 90
(Mrs D J Sanderson) *chsd ldr's str pce: clsd to ld over 1f out: hrd pressed ins fnl f clung on: all out* **25/1**
1100 **2** *shd* **Jake The Snake (IRE)**[32] 2129 9-10-0 **85** NeilCallan 4 93
(A W Carroll) *settled in abt 7th: rdn and prog over 2f out: wnt 2nd ins fnl f: chal last 100yds: jst failed* **5/1**[3]
110- **3** *hd* **Gold Express**[299] 5221 7-9-9 **80** TedDurcan 2 87
(P J O'Gorman) *dropped in fr wd draw and hld up: wl off the pce in last trio: stdy prog fr over 2f out: clsd on ldrs fnl f: chal last 75yds: jst hld* **33/1**
-431 **4** *3/4* **Cape Rock**[7] 2872 5-10-1 **86** 6ex JimCrowley 5 91
(W J Knight) *chsd ldrs in 6th: rdn fr 1/2-way: struggling over 2f out: styd on stoutly fnl f: nrst fin* **9/2**[2]
4-55 **5** *1/2* **Hurricane Spirit (IRE)**[44] 1767 6-9-12 **83** SteveDrowne 8 87
(J R Best) *trckd ldrs in 5th: rdn and effrt over 2f out: clsd over 1f out: ch ins fnl f on inner: no ex last 150yds* **8/1**
3300 **6** *1 1/4* **Tamasou (IRE)**[36] 1990 5-9-3 **74** SimonWhitworth 7 74
(F J Brennan) *off the pce in 9th: pushed along over 2f out: reminders over 1f out: styd on steadily fnl f: nvr nr ldrs* **50/1**
3223 **7** *nk* **Tiradito (USA)**[23] 2394 3-9-2 **82** (p) WilliamBuick 14 78
(M Botti) *off the pce in 10th: rdn and no prog wl over 1f out: styd on fnl f: n.d* **12/1**
05-0 **8** *2 1/4* **Hurricane Hymnbook (USA)**[49] 1625 5-9-12 **83** TomQueally 11 83+
(Stef Higgins) *chsd ldng pair: rdn over 2f out: tried to cl wl over 1f out: nt pce to hold position whn trapped bhd wkng rival 1f out and lost any ch* **11/4**[1]
115- **9** *nse* **Arteus**[180] 7801 4-9-4 **82** (b) LewisWalsh(7) 13 75
(Jane Chapple-Hyam) *led at v str pce: clr over 2f out: wandering after: wknd and hdd over 1f out* **14/1**
1000 **10** *3/4* **Arachnophobia (IRE)**[20] 2472 4-10-0 **85** DaneO'Neill 1 76
(Pat Eddery) *dropped in fr wd draw and hld up in detached last: nudged along over 2f out: nvr remotely involved: nrst fin* **25/1**
5406 **11** *2* **Ilie Nastase (FR)**[32] 2124 6-9-8 **79** RichardHughes 6 65
(C R Dore) *a wl in rr: shkn up and no prog wl over 2f out* **25/1**
0-00 **12** *3/4* **Pravda Street**[16] 2595 5-9-9 **80** (b) JimmyFortune 10 64
(P F I Cole) *chsd ldng pair: rdn over 2f out: wknd wl over 1f out* **10/1**
-100 **13** *10* **Print (IRE)**[36] 2009 4-9-0 **71** SamHitchcott 12 28
(M R Channon) *rrd s: a towards rr: u.str.p 3f out: sn bhd* **25/1**
-020 **14** *dist* **Monsieur Fillioux (USA)**[69] 1185 4-9-6 **77** AdamKirby 3 —
(J R Fanshawe) *dropped in fr wd draw: hld up in last trio: virtually p.u fnl 2f* **20/1**

1m 25.59s (-0.41) **Going Correction** -0.05s/f (Stan)
WFA 3 from 4yo+ 9lb **14** Ran SP% **121.1**
Speed ratings (Par 105): **100,99,99,98,98 96,96,93,93,92 90,89,78,—**
toteswingers:1&2:£23.20, 1&3:£9.40, 2&3:£30.80 CSF £138.04 CT £4271.54 TOTE £23.00: £7.40, £2.50, £12.80; EX 228.00.
Owner R J Budge **Bred** Deerpark Stud **Trained** Wiseton, Notts

The Form Book, Raceform Ltd, Compton, RG20 6NL

FOCUS
Quite a competitive handicap, run at a strong pace. The form looks pretty solid.
Hurricane Hymnbook(USA) Official explanation: jockey said gelding was denied a clear run
Monsieur Fillioux(USA) Official explanation: jockey said gelding lost its action final bend

3084 DIGIBET CASINO H'CAP 2m (P)
8:40 (8:41) (Class 6) (0-65,65) 4-Y-0+ **£2,047** (£604; £302) **Stalls** High

Form RPR
2/32 **1** **Ultimate Quest (IRE)**[20] 2476 5-9-4 **62** .... SebSanders 4 71+
(Sir Mark Prescott) *dwlt: hld up tl prog to ld after 6f: rdn over 3f out: jnd wl over 1f out: styd on wl* **15/8**[1]
2243 **2** *1 1/4* **Where's Susie**[23] 2402 5-9-0 **58** .... RobertHavlin 14 65
(M Madgwick) *wl in tch: 7th over 3f out: hmpd and snatched up on inner wl over 2f out: rallied over 1f out: wnt 2nd ins fnl f: unable to chal* **16/1**
5116 **3** *1* **Mountain Forest (GER)**[44] 1758 4-8-11 **55** .... JimmyQuinn 2 61
(H Morrison) *t.k.h early: hld up in midfield: gng wl in 5th over 3f out: prog to press wnr over 2f out: upsides wl over 1f out: rdn and nt qckn: fdd ins fnl f* **7/1**[3]
6043 **4** *shd* **Purely By Chance**[34] 1283 5-8-4 **53** ....(v) SimonPearce(5) 5 59
(J Pearce) *rn in snatches: prog fr rr on outer 4f out: 6th over 3f out: nt qckn over 2f out: styd on again fr over 1f out* **16/1**
21-4 **5** *1 1/4* **Saute**[35] 2023 4-9-6 **64** .... AdamKirby 12 68
(W R Swinburn) *prom: rdn to chse ldng pair over 3f out to over 2f out: nt qckn: renewed effrt over 1f out: one pce fnl f* **11/4**[2]
4346 **6** *2* **Naheell**[7] 2880 4-8-12 **56** .... SaleemGolam 3 58
(G Prodromou) *hld up in last trio: sme prog fr 4f out: hrd rdn over 2f out: kpt on: n.d* **66/1**
6150 **7** *2* **Two Oclock John**[16] 2597 4-9-7 **65** .... JackMitchell 6 64
(H J Collingridge) *hld up in last trio: rapid prog on inner fr 3f out to chse ldrs over 1f out: effrt petered out sn after* **33/1**
-243 **8** *8* **Wightgold**[30] 2169 4-9-0 **58** .... RichardHughes 8 48
(H J L Dunlop) *mostly in ldng trio: rdn in 2nd over 3f out: wknd over 2f out* **14/1**
/0-5 **9** *5* **Jocheski (IRE)**[14] 2645 6-8-13 **57** .... DaneO'Neill 13 41
(A G Newcombe) *settled in 9th: rdn and effrt over 3f out: sn no prog: wknd over 2f out* **25/1**
4101 **10** *2* **Coda Agency**[44] 1768 7-9-7 **65** .... NeilCallan 7 46
(D W P Arbuthnot) *led 5f: styd prom: rdn in 4th over 3f out: wknd over 2f out* **12/1**
66-0 **11** *8* **Command Marshal (FR)**[10] 198 7-8-11 **55** .... PatCosgrave 11 27
(M J Scudamore) *a wl in rr: u.p and struggling in last trio 4f out: t.o* **66/1**
451/ **12** *4* **Mvuto**[42] 6909 5-9-7 **65** .... WilliamBuick 10 32
(Mrs L Wadham) *prom: led after 5f to after 6f: rdn over 5f out: wknd 4f out: t.o* **8/1**
0-60 **13** *16* **Lilly Royal (IRE)**[14] 2645 4-8-8 **57** ....(p) DeclanCannon(5) 1 5
(B Palling) *settled in midfield: wknd over 4f out: t.o* **66/1**

3m 28.17s (-1.93) **Going Correction** -0.05s/f (Stan) **13** Ran SP% **122.4**
Speed ratings (Par 101): **102,101,100,100,100 99,98,94,91,90 86,84,76**
toteswingers:1&2:£6.60, 1&3:£2.30, 2&3:£7.30 CSF £35.58 CT £182.70 TOTE £2.80: £1.70, £3.60, £2.80; EX 44.10.
Owner Syndicate 2006 **Bred** T W Bloodstock Ltd **Trained** Newmarket, Suffolk
FOCUS
A modest staying handicap. Sound form, and although the winner did not need to improve he is capable of doing so.
Where's Susie Official explanation: jockey said mare was denied a clear run

3085 BOOK NOW FOR BEST OF BRITISH NIGHT H'CAP 6f (P)
9:10 (9:12) (Class 4) (0-85,85) 3-Y-0 **£4,209** (£1,252; £625; £312) **Stalls** High

Form RPR
0-12 **1** **Addictive Dream (IRE)**[34] 2052 3-8-13 **77** .... ShaneKelly 3 89+
(W R Swinburn) *a gng wl: hld up in 5th: prog over 2f out: pushed into ld over 1f out: sn clr: decisively* **15/8**[2]
2-21 **2** *2* **Strictly Dancing (IRE)**[25] 2340 3-9-7 **85** .... JimmyFortune 4 90
(A M Balding) *sn trckd ldr: pushed into ld 2f out: hdd and rdn over 1f out: styd on but readily outpcd* **5/1**[3]
4234 **3** *2* **Night Trade (IRE)**[20] 2475 3-9-0 **78** .... SilvestreDeSousa 2 77
(Mrs D J Sanderson) *settled in 6th: rdn over 2f out: prog on outer to take 3rd jst over 1f out: kpt on but outpcd* **20/1**
6-52 **4** *2* **Gojeri (IRE)**[7] 2868 3-8-6 **70** ow1 .... JackMitchell 6 63+
(M A Jarvis) *pushed along in last: prog and swtchd to inner 2f out: wl outpcd in 4th fnl f* **7/4**[1]
1-61 **5** *2* **Glen Shiel (USA)**[20] 2450 3-9-3 **81** .... JoeFanning 1 67
(M Johnston) *forced to r wd early: trckd ldng pair to over 2f out: nt qckn and lost pl: n.d after* **15/2**
2141 **6** *3/4* **Maoi Chinn Tire (IRE)**[15] 2617 3-8-12 **76** ....(p) RichardHughes 5 60
(J S Moore) *reluctant to enter stalls: led to 2f out: wknd over 1f out* **16/1**
1020 **7** *14* **Candyfloss Girl**[39] 1913 3-8-13 **77** .... DavidProbert 7 16
(H J L Dunlop) *reluctant to go to post: chsd ldrs tl wknd over 2f out: t.o* **33/1**

1m 11.57s (-1.53) **Going Correction** -0.05s/f (Stan) **7** Ran SP% **113.2**
Speed ratings (Par 101): **108,105,102,100,97 96,77**
toteswingers:1&2:£2.90, 1&3:£4.50, 2&3:£13.80 CSF £11.51 TOTE £3.10: £1.40, £4.00; EX 8.80 Place 6 £57.37; Place 5 £45.89.
Owner Caveat Emptor Partnership **Bred** Eugene Matthews **Trained** Aldbury, Herts
FOCUS
An interesting little handicap which was truly run. The favourite disappointed but the time was good and the form looks solid.
Candyfloss Girl Official explanation: vet said mare was in season
T/Plt: £113.70 to a £1 stake. Pool:£47,538.50 - 305.11 winning tickets T/Qpdt: £32.70 to a £1 stake. Pool:£3,904.17 - 88.30 winning tickets JN

2654 RIPON (R-H)
Wednesday, June 16
OFFICIAL GOING: Good (8.3)
Wind: almost nil Weather: fine and sunny, very warm

3086 TOTEPLACEPOT APPRENTICE (S) STKS 6f
6:50 (6:51) (Class 6) 3-4-Y-0 **£2,590** (£770; £385; £192) **Stalls** Low

Form RPR
-406 **1** **Suzie Quw**[6] 2904 4-9-2 71 ....(v[1]) NeilFarley 3 59
(J R Weymes) *unruly s: chsd ldrs: outpcd 3f out: hdwy over 1f out: styd on wl on ins to ld nr fin* **9/2**[3]
0014 **2** *nk* **Newbury Street**[13] 2668 3-9-5 67 .... MarzenaJeziorek 1 66
(R A Fahey) *w ldrs: led over 2f out: edgd rt ins fnl f: hdd nr fin* **11/4**[2]
500- **3** *2 1/2* **Needy McCredie**[275] 5948 4-8-11 44 .... ShaneBKelly(5) 6 50
(J R Turner) *chsd ldrs: kpt on ins fnl f: tk 3rd nr fin* **25/1**
2332 **4** *hd* **Powerful Pierre**[12] 2722 3-8-9 70 ....(v) LanaChambers(5) 5 52
(Jedd O'Keeffe) *led tl over 2f out: wknd fnl 75yds* **2/1**[1]
4406 **5** *1 1/2* **Kinigi (IRE)**[4] 2965 4-9-2 47 .... JakePayne 9 45
(R A Harris) *outpcd and lost pl after 2f: hdwy over 1f out: kpt on same pce: nvr nr to chal* **7/1**
0600 **6** *2 3/4* **Mandhooma**[10] 2779 4-8-11 44 .... IanBurns(5) 10 36
(P W Hiatt) *w ldrs: wknd fnl f* **25/1**
-000 **7** *hd* **Lieu Day Louie (IRE)**[20] 2449 3-8-9 52 .... ShirleyTeasdale(5) 7 38
(N Wilson) *chsd ldrs: wknd fnl f* **20/1**
-654 **8** *4 1/2* **Thewinnatakesitall**[91] 906 3-8-9 53 .... NoraLooby 11 19
(N Tinkler) *wnt rt s: in tch: drvn after 2f: lost pl over 1f out* **14/1**
0-00 **9** *1 1/2* **Woldgate**[16] 2609 3-8-9 54 .... GarethEdwards(5) 2 19
(G R Oldroyd) *outpcd and bhd after 2f: kpt on fnl f: nvr on terms* **50/1**
10 *1/2* **Tipperary Tickle** 3-8-9 0 .... LukeStrong 4 12
(J R Weymes) *s.s: a bhd* **40/1**
-005 **11** *9* **Infinity World**[10] 2787 3-8-9 53 ....(p) NatashaEaton 8 —
(G R Oldroyd) *sn outpcd and bhd: edgd rt 2f out* **25/1**

1m 13.04s (0.04) **Going Correction** -0.125s/f (Firm)
WFA 3 from 4yo 7lb **11** Ran SP% **118.0**
Speed ratings (Par 101): **94,93,90,90,88 84,84,78,76,75 63**
toteswingers:1&2:£3.40, 1&3:£17.50, 2&3:£29.90 CSF £15.88 TOTE £6.00: £2.20, £2.20, £5.40; EX 13.70.There was no bid for the winner. Newbury Street was claimed by P. F. Holmes for £6,000.
Owner Aricabeau Racing Limited **Bred** The National Stud **Trained** Middleham Moor, N Yorks
■ Stewards' Enquiry : Marzena Jeziorek two-day ban: used whip with excessive frequency without giving gelding time to respond (Jun 30-Jul 1)
FOCUS
After a dry night the official ground description was changed to good. An ordinary apprentice selling race. It was run at a good pace and there was an exciting finish between two of the three main form contenders. The form is sound overall, best judged around the runner-up.

3087 CHARLIE WALLER MEMORIAL MEDIAN AUCTION MAIDEN STKS 5f
7:20 (7:21) (Class 5) 2-Y-0 **£2,914** (£867; £433; £216) **Stalls** Low

Form RPR
22 **1** **Defence Council (IRE)**[16] 2577 2-9-3 0 .... PaulMulrennan 8 81
(J Howard Johnson) *racd stands' side: overall ld: edgd lft fnl f: hld on towards fin* **2/1**[1]
252 **2** *nk* **Whisper Louise (IRE)**[9] 2813 2-8-12 0 .... MickyFenton 10 75
(Mrs P Sly) *racd stands' side: chsd ldrs: wnt 2nd that gp 1f out: sn chalng: no ex towards fin: 2nd of 9 that gp* **11/4**[2]
4U **3** *2 1/2* **Novalist**[12] 2693 2-8-10 0 .... MatthewLawson(7) 4 71
(R Bastiman) *racd stands' side: chsd ldrs: edgd rt and kpt on same pce fnl f: 3rd of 9 that gp* **100/1**
0325 **4** *1/2* **Belle Bayardo (IRE)**[13] 2680 2-9-3 0 .... LukeMorris 17 69
(R A Harris) *racd far side: chsd ldrs: edgd lft over 1f out: led that gp ins fnl f: kpt on same pce: 1st of 6 that gp* **8/1**
5 *1/2* **Blaze Of Thunder (IRE)** 2-9-3 0 .... PaulHanagan 13 67
(R A Fahey) *racd far side: s.i.s: hdwy over 2f out: wnt 2nd that gp ins fnl f: kpt on same pce: 2nd of 6 that gp* **8/1**
4 **6** *1 1/4* **Hortensis**[14] 2654 2-8-12 0 .... DavidAllan 3 58+
(T D Easterby) *s.i.s: racd stands' side: hdwy over 2f out: kpt on fnl f: 4th of 9 that gp* **4/1**[3]
0 **7** *1/2* **Welsh Inlet (IRE)**[24] 2358 2-8-9 0 .... WilliamCarson(3) 12 56
(S C Williams) *led 5 others far side: hdd ins fnl f: sn wknd: 3rd of 6 that gp* **50/1**
3 **8** *1 1/2* **Shy Bird**[16] 2577 2-8-12 0 .... LeeVickers 15 51
(J A Glover) *racd far side: towards rr: kpt on fnl 2f: nvr a factor: 4th of 6 that gp* **50/1**
9 *1/2* **The Oboist (IRE)** 2-8-12 0 .... RoystonFfrench 5 49
(M Johnston) *uns rdr bef s: racd stands' side: in tch: outpcd over 2f out: 5th of 9 that gp* **25/1**
10 *3/4* **Paragons Folly (IRE)** 2-9-3 0 .... GrahamGibbons 14 51
(J J Quinn) *racd far side: chsd ldrs: wknd over 1f out: 5th of 6 that gp* **25/1**
11 *1/2* **Amazing Amoray (IRE)** 2-9-3 0 .... DaraghO'Donohoe 9 49
(T D Barron) *racd stands' side: chsd ldrs: wknd over 1f out: 6th of 9 that gp* **40/1**
00 **12** *2 1/2* **Aprication (IRE)**[19] 2498 2-9-0 0 .... MartinLane(3) 16 40
(J R Weymes) *racd far side: chsd ldrs: lost pl over 1f out: last of 6 that gp* **150/1**
13 *4* **Mimi's Princess** 2-8-12 0 .... StevieDonohoe 7 21
(K A Ryan) *racd stands' side: s.i.s: a bhd: 7th of 9 that gp* **25/1**
0 **14** *19* **Good Faith**[61] 1359 2-9-3 0 .... FrannyNorton 2 —
(G M Moore) *racd stands' side: sn bhd: t.o 2f out: 8th of 9 that gp* **40/1**
15 *26* **Pride Of Tagula** 2-8-12 0 .... DuranFentiman 1 —
(N Wilson) *s.v.s: racd stands' side: sn t.o: last of 9 that gp* **100/1**

59.94 secs (-0.76) **Going Correction** -0.125s/f (Firm) **15** Ran SP% **125.2**
Speed ratings (Par 93): **101,100,96,95,94 92,92,89,88,87 86,82,76,46,4**
toteswingers:1&2:£2.10, 1&3:£29.10, 2&3:£18.70 CSF £7.16 TOTE £2.80: £1.10, £1.30, £10.60; EX 9.40.
Owner Transcend Bloodstock LLP **Bred** Chris Glynn **Trained** Billy Row, Co Durham
FOCUS
A fair maiden. They split into two groups but the strongly supported favourite and the other main contender pulled clear of the rest and the form looks solid, rated around the front pair.
NOTEBOOK
Defence Council(IRE) had leading claims on his very narrow odds-on defeat by an expensive and well-backed Richard Fahey-trained newcomer in a 5f Carlisle maiden on his second run last month. Always travelling well near the stands' rail, he hit the front approaching the dip and had enough left to fight off his main market rival. The 55,000gns son of Kheleyf has plenty of natural speed and some scope for physical progression. He should be able to win more races. (op 15-8 tchd 7-4 and 9-4)
Whisper Louise(IRE) had a solid chance on her second to a useful type in a 6f Pontefract maiden last week and gave it a good try to run down the winner but couldn't quite get there. She should not have too much trouble winning a slightly less competitive event. (op 3-1 tchd 10-3 and 5-2)
Novalist bucked and unseated his rider after the saddle slipped soon after the start at Catterick last time but he bounced back from that unfortunate experience to confirm the promise of his 100-1 debut fourth.
Belle Bayardo(IRE) ran a solid enough race and did best of those on the far side. He is fairly exposed after five runs but seems a consistent and willing type who is good value at 3,000 euros. (op 15-2 tchd 13-2)
Blaze Of Thunder(IRE) put in a promising effort in the far group on debut. He is a £26,000 first foal of an unplaced half-sister to Wixoe Express, a triple 6f-1m winner at three and later a Listed winner in US. (op 7-1)

Hortensis never looked like justifying a big market move but she stayed on nicely against the near rail and has probably built on her 7l fourth here on debut. A return to 6f will suit. (op 14-1)

3088 NORMAN WELLS MEMORIAL CHALLENGE TROPHY H'CAP 6f

7:50 (7:51) (Class 3) (0-95,88) 3-Y-O **£7,569** (£2,265; £1,132; £566; £282) **Stalls** Low

Form RPR

2311 **1** **Kellys Eye (IRE)**[14] 2656 3-9-6 **87** .... GrahamGibbons 3 101+
(D H Brown) *chsd ldrs: sn pushed along: squeezed through appr fnl f: led last 150yds: styd on wl* **10/11**[1]

0221 **2** *3* **Flaneur**[26] 2287 3-8-13 **80** .... (b) DavidAllan 7 84
(T D Easterby) *led: crossed stands' side rail after 1f: hdd jst ins fnl f: no ex* **11/4**[2]

00-1 **3** *3/4* **Little Scotland**[25] 2309 3-9-7 **88** .... PaulHanagan 2 90+
(R A Fahey) *chsd ldrs: sn drvn along: hmpd over 2f out: kpt on same pce fnl f* **14/1**

10-5 **4** *2 3/4* **Makbullet**[26] 2275 3-8-10 **77** .... PaulMulrennan 4 70
(J Howard Johnson) *chsd ldr: wknd fnl f* **33/1**

4 **5** *1 1/4* **Schoolboy Champ**[30] 2179 3-7-12 **70** .... SophieDoyle(5) 1 59
(Patrick Morris) *chsd ldrs on ins: outpcd and lost pl after 2f: hdwy and swtchd wd over 1f out: one pce* **25/1**

5431 **6** *nk* **Fly Silca Fly (IRE)**[17] 2565 3-9-1 **82** .... CathyGannon 5 70
(M R Channon) *chsd ldrs: wknd fnl f* **12/1**

-205 **7** *6* **Edgewater (IRE)**[39] 1913 3-9-6 **87** .... (p) MickyFenton 6 56
(J Akehurst) *lost off-fore shoe on way to s: dwlt: sn chsng ldrs on outside: hung rt and wknd over 1f out* **7/1**[3]

1m 11.68s (-1.32) **Going Correction** -0.125s/f (Firm) **7 Ran SP% 112.7**
Speed ratings (Par 103): **103,99,98,94,92 92,84**
toteswingers:1&2:£1.10, 2&3:£3.10, 1&3:£1.50 CSF £3.39 TOTE £1.90: £1.10, £1.50; EX 3.60.
Owner Ron Hull **Bred** Michael Downey And Roalso Ltd **Trained** Maltby, S Yorks

FOCUS
Four last-time-out winners lined up for this decent handicap. The pace wasn't particularly strong but the hot favourite romped clear to complete a hat-trick. This was another personal best from him.

NOTEBOOK
Kellys Eye(IRE) was a stylish winner in C&D handicaps the last twice. The progressive performer missed the cut in the Reg Griffin Memorial Trophy at York on Saturday but was retargeted to this less-demanding race and powered clear from just off the pace to defy a 7lb rise and maintain his unbeaten record at this track. He can need a bit of stoking up but there is no sign of his improvement levelling out and his style and pedigree suggest he should stay an extra furlong. His next assignment could be in a 6f handicap for three-year-olds at the Newmarket July meeting. (op Evens tchd 5-6)
Flaneur showed a good attitude to win a 0-80 classified event at Haydock last time. The consistent gelding ran a solid race under a prominent ride off 3lb higher back in a handicap but was no match for the improving winner. (op 4-1)
Little Scotland had to work hard to justify odds-on favouritism and beat an 18lb lower rated rival in a four-runner Chester maiden last time. Much more was needed on her belated handicap debut but she finished quite strongly after not getting much luck. She rates a bit better than the form implies and the former Windsor Castle fourth could be one to keep an eye on. (op 12-1 tchd 11-1)
Makbullet couldn't sustain his effort on his second run back from a layoff. He looks a bit high in the weights on the balance of his form. (op 20-1)
Schoolboy Champ could find only a short-lived effort from off the pace. He has been a bit disappointing since his Haydock maiden auction win on debut last June and has been a non-runner four times since his Windsor reappearance last month. (op 20-1)
Edgewater(IRE) weakened quickly after racing wide for most of the way. He was reported to have run on three shoes after losing one on the way to the start. (op 6-1)

3089 BETFAIR H'CAP 1m 1f 170y

8:20 (8:20) (Class 4) (0-85,85) 4-Y-O+ **£4,533** (£1,348; £674; £336) **Stalls** High

Form RPR

05-4 **1** **Tepmokea (IRE)**[16] 2579 4-9-1 **79** .... PaulHanagan 2 88
(R A Fahey) *led: qcknd 4f out: hld on gamely fnl f: all out* **11/8**[1]

4310 **2** *nk* **Bollin Dolly**[16] 2579 7-8-11 **75** .... DavidAllan 4 83
(T D Easterby) *chsd wnr: drvn over 3f out: kpt on fnl f: a jst hld* **11/4**[2]

-630 **3** *1 1/2* **Persian Peril**[7] 2857 6-9-3 **81** .... PJMcDonald 1 86
(G A Swinbank) *trckd ldrs: effrt over 3f out: styd on same pce fnl f* **7/2**[3]

-534 **4** *4* **Veiled Applause**[11] 2761 7-8-12 **76** .... (v[1]) GrahamGibbons 6 73
(J J Quinn) *trckd ldrs: drvn over 3f out: fdd over 1f out* **8/1**

0-00 **5** *11* **Wigwam Willie (IRE)**[64] 1272 8-9-7 **85** .... (tp) PaulMulrennan 3 59
(K A Ryan) *dwlt: in last: drvn and outpcd over 3f out: sn lost tch* **11/1**

2m 1.10s (-4.30) **Going Correction** -0.30s/f (Firm) **5 Ran SP% 110.4**
Speed ratings (Par 105): **105,104,103,100,91**
CSF £5.43 TOTE £1.90: £1.10, £1.50; EX 5.50.
Owner Keep Racing **Bred** J H A Baggen **Trained** Musley Bank, N Yorks

FOCUS
An interesting handicap. It became quite tactical and the first two filled the same positions throughout. The form is rated around the third, with steps up from the front two.

3090 ATTHERACES.COM ROYAL ASCOT MEGASITE H'CAP 1m 4f 10y

8:50 (8:51) (Class 5) (0-75,73) 4-Y-O+ **£2,914** (£867; £433; £216) **Stalls** High

Form RPR

0/64 **1** **Ubi Ace**[6] 2881 4-9-4 **70** .... GrahamGibbons 7 78
(T D Walford) *sn trcking ldrs: led over 1f out: hld on gamely* **14/1**

-506 **2** *1* **Bollin Greta**[27] 2243 5-9-3 **69** .... DavidAllan 6 75
(T D Easterby) *chsd ldrs: drvn over 3f out: chal over 1f out: no ex wl ins fnl f* **7/2**[1]

20-0 **3** *nk* **Bavarian Nordic (USA)**[36] 1996 5-9-1 **70** .... (v[1]) BarryMcHugh(3) 5 76
(Mrs A Duffield) *hld up: hdwy over 3f out: kpt on to take cl 3rd 1f out: styd on same pce* **20/1**

6421 **4** *1 1/2* **Inspirina (IRE)**[29] 2199 6-9-5 **71** .... PaulHanagan 9 74
(R Ford) *led: t.k.h: qcknd 4f out: hdd over 1f out: wknd towards fin* **11/2**[2]

4-62 **5** *1 1/4* **Cotillion**[7] 2860 4-9-7 **73** .... StevieDonohoe 3 74+
(Ian Williams) *hld up in rr: drvn and wl outpcd over 4f out: styd on fnl 2f* **7/2**[1]

-040 **6** *1/2* **French Applause (IRE)**[11] 2739 4-9-3 **69** .... MickyFenton 2 69+
(T P Tate) *stdd s: t.k.h detached in last: hdwy 3f out: kpt on: nt rch ldrs* **12/1**

0123 **7** *2* **Maslak (IRE)**[6] 2881 6-8-13 **68** .... WilliamCarson(3) 8 65
(P W Hiatt) *trckd ldr: one pce whn checked 2f out: sn wknd* **7/2**[1]

-003 **8** *13* **Safebreaker**[13] 2672 5-8-11 **68** .... (p) AmyRyan(5) 1 44
(K A Ryan) *hld up: drvn and outpcd 4f out: sn lost pl: bhd fnl 2f* **6/1**[3]

2m 34.9s (-1.80) **Going Correction** -0.30s/f (Firm) **8 Ran SP% 115.5**
Speed ratings (Par 103): **94,93,93,92,91 90,89,80**
toteswingers:1&2:£12.30, 1&3:£9.90, 2&3:£20.70 CSF £63.22 CT £997.37 TOTE £23.20: £6.50, £2.30, £4.60; EX 105.70.
Owner N J Maher **Bred** Steel's Thoroughbred Breeding **Trained** Sheriff Hutton, N Yorks

FOCUS
An ordinary handicap. It was run at a stop-start gallop and they finished in a bit of a bunch. The form is rated around the fourth.

3091 SIS LIVE MAIDEN STKS 6f

9:20 (9:20) (Class 5) 3-Y-O **£2,914** (£867; £433; £216) **Stalls** Low

Form RPR

1 **Supreme Spirit (IRE)** 3-8-12 0 .... FrannyNorton 6 70
(D Nicholls) *chsd ldrs: wnt 2nd over 1f out: styd on to ld nr fin* **20/1**

50 **2** *nk* **Bahamian Jazz (IRE)**[36] 1991 3-8-10 0 .... MatthewLawson(7) 3 74
(R Bastiman) *t.k.h: trckd ldrs: led after 1f: edgd rt fnl f: hdd nr fin* **66/1**

00 **3** *4 1/2* **Offspring**[23] 2393 3-8-12 0 .... DavidAllan 1 55
(T D Easterby) *w ldrs: one pce appr fnl f* **11/2**[3]

2-60 **4** *1 1/4* **Olney Lass**[19] 2517 3-8-7 70 .... PaulPickard(5) 10 51
(W J H Ratcliffe) *chsd ldrs: wl outpcd and in rr over 3f out: hdwy 2f out: kpt on one pce* **14/1**

3232 **5** *1 1/4* **Nimue (USA)**[28] 2227 3-8-12 80 .... GrahamGibbons 12 47
(P F I Cole) *chsd ldrs on outer: rdn over 2f out: wknd over 1f out* **8/13**[1]

000 **6** *2 1/4* **Hail Bold Chief (USA)**[27] 2242 3-9-3 67 .... PJMcDonald 9 45
(G A Swinbank) *in tch: outpcd and lost pl over 3f out: kpt on fnl 2f: nvr on terms* **25/1**

34 **7** *3/4* **Blue Moon**[82] 997 3-8-12 0 .... PaulHanagan 4 37
(K A Ryan) *mid-div: hrd drvn and outpcd 3f out: sme hdwy and edgd rt over 1f out: nvr a factor* **5/1**[2]

00 **8** *2* **Marteau**[19] 2517 3-9-3 0 .... PaulMulrennan 8 36
(K A Ryan) *led 1f: chsd ldrs: edgd lft 2f out: sn wknd* **50/1**

0-0 **9** *3/4* **House Point**[36] 2003 3-8-9 0 .... WilliamCarson(3) 11 29
(S C Williams) *s.i.s: wl outpcd and bhd: sme hdwy 2f out: nvr on terms* **20/1**

0 **10** *4 1/2* **Happy The Man (IRE)**[12] 2706 3-9-3 0 .... DuranFentiman 5 19
(T D Easterby) *prom: lost pl 2f out* **80/1**

0 **11** *1/2* **Lord Lansing (IRE)**[18] 2530 3-9-3 0 .... AndrewElliott 7 18
(J R Weymes) *dwlt: short of room sn after s: sn wl bhd* **100/1**

1m 12.49s (-0.51) **Going Correction** -0.125s/f (Firm) **11 Ran SP% 119.7**
Speed ratings (Par 99): **98,97,91,89,88 85,84,81,80,74 73**
toteswingers:1&2:£37.70, 1&3:£41.80, 2&3:£54.80 CSF £883.20 TOTE £17.40: £3.50, £10.30, £1.60; EX 573.60 Place 6 £71.83; Place 5 £26.09.
Owner Mrs C C Regalado-Gonzalez **Bred** Jill Finnegan And Noel Cogan **Trained** Sessay, N Yorks

FOCUS
The first two pulled a long way clear in this maiden but the hot favourite was very disappointing. Modest form.
T/Plt: £1,088.60 to a £1 stake. Pool:£56,593.45 - 37.95 winning tickets T/Qpdt: £233.10 to a £1 stake. Pool:£4,536.28 - 14.40 winning tickets WG

3092 - 3098a (Foreign Racing) - See Raceform Interactive

3014 CHANTILLY (R-H)
Wednesday, June 16

OFFICIAL GOING: Turf: good to soft

3099a PRIX LA MOSKOWA (LISTED RACE) (4YO+) (TURF) 1m 7f

2:40 (12:00) 4-Y-O+ **£23,008** (£9,203; £6,902; £4,601; £2,300)

RPR

1 **Opinion Poll (IRE)**[12] 2716 4-9-1 0 .... PhilipRobinson 11 101
(M A Jarvis) *racd in midfield on outside: moved forward bef end of bk st: rdn early in st: qcknd wl u.p 2f out: grabbed ld 1 1/2f out: r.o wl ins fnl f* **7/2**[2]

2 *3/4* **Aizavoski (IRE)**[41] 1856 4-9-4 0 .... AnthonyCrastus 5 103
(E Lellouche, France) **5/2**[1]

3 *1 1/2* **Green Tango (FR)**[24] 2375 7-9-1 0 .... RonanThomas 6 98
(P Van De Poele, France) **43/10**[3]

4 *hd* **Redesignation (IRE)**[46] 5-8-11 0 .... ThierryJarnet 9 94
(R Pritchard-Gordon, France) **33/1**

5 *1 1/2* **Americain (USA)**[237] 5-8-11 0 .... GeraldMosse 3 92
(A De Royer-Dupre, France) **73/10**

6 *4* **Babyla**[453] 4-8-8 0 .... Pierre-CharlesBoudot 7 84
(A Fabre, France) **11/1**

7 *2* **The Diamond (FR)**[43] 4-8-11 0 .... FlavienPrat 2 84
(D Bressou, France) **14/1**

8 *nk* **Hekatompylos (FR)**[23] 5-8-11 0 .... IoritzMendizabal 8 84
(Mme Pia Brandt, France) **20/1**

9 *3/4* **Mont Joux (FR)**[58] 8-8-11 0 .... FredericSpanu 4 83
(H Billot, France) **20/1**

10 *2* **Refik (FR)**[21] 2447 7-8-11 0 .... DominiqueBoeuf 10 80
(M Cesandri, France) **26/1**

11 **Quartz Jem (IRE)**[12] 6-8-11 0 .... JohanVictoire 1 —
(Mme Pia Brandt, France) **30/1**

3m 11.2s (-4.90) **11 Ran SP% 116.1**
WIN (incl. 1 euro stake): 4.40. PLACES: 1.60, 1.30, 1.60. DF: 8.10. SF: 13.30.
Owner Sheikh Ahmed Al Maktoum **Bred** Darley **Trained** Newmarket, Suffolk

NOTEBOOK
Opinion Poll(IRE), up in trip and back on his favoured softish surface, moved up rounding the final turn, took up the running approaching the final furlong and stayed on well. The Goodwood Cup is a possibility next, providing the ground is suitable.

3066 ASCOT (R-H)
Thursday, June 17

OFFICIAL GOING: Good to firm (good in places; stands' side 9.9, centre 9.8, far side 10.0; round course 9.2)
Round course rail positioned 3m out from the inside line from about 9f to home straight increasing Old Mile by 6yds, 110f by 9yd and 12f and over by 12yds
Wind: light across Weather: sunny

3100 NORFOLK STKS (GROUP 2) 5f

2:30 (2:33) (Class 1) 2-Y-O

£51,093 (£19,368; £9,693; £4,833; £2,421; £1,215) **Stalls** Centre

Form RPR

314 **1** **Approve (IRE)**[12] 2743 2-9-1 0 .... EddieAhern 2 107
(W J Haggas) *in tch: rdn and effrt 2f out: hdwy u.p over 1f out: str run to ld fnl 100yds: r.o wl* **16/1**

61 **2** 1¼ **Reckless Reward (IRE)**[23] 2413 2-9-1 0.......................... RyanMoore 6 103
(R Hannon) *led tl 3f out: rdn and sltly outpcd 2f out: rallied u.p ent fnl f: r.o wl to go 2nd wl ins fnl f* **16/1**

11 **3** ½ **Excel Bolt**[12] 2757 2-9-1 0.. TomEaves 1 101
(B Smart) *racd alone on stands' rail: a.p: rdn ent fnl 2f: kpt on same pce u.p ins fnl f* **7/1**

24 **4** nk **Stone Of Folca**[2] 3051 2-9-1 0... KierenFallon 5 100
(J R Best) *stdd s: t.k.h: hld up in rr: gd hdwy on bit to ld over 1f out: sn rdn: hdd fnl 100yds: wknd towards fin* **18/1**

11 **5** ½ **Zebedee**[50] 1612 2-9-1 0... RichardHughes 9 98
(R Hannon) *w ldrs: ev ch and rdn wl over 1f out: hrd drvn and unable qck 1f out: one pce and btn fnl 100yds* **11/2**[3]

11 **6** ½ **Dinkum Diamond (IRE)**[21] 2468 2-9-1 0......................... DaneO'Neill 4 96
(H Candy) *t.k.h: hld up in tch: effrt and rdn 2f out: unable qck and styd on same pce u.p fnl f* **11/4**[1]

0 **7** hd **Emperor Hadrian (IRE)**[6] 2942 2-9-1 0............................(v) JMurtagh 3 96
(A P O'Brien, Ire) *s.i.s: sn outpcd in rr: rdn 1/2-way: hdwy u.p and edging rt over 1f out: kpt on fnl f: nvr gng pce to rch ldrs* **25/1**

12 **8** 1 **Arctic Feeling (IRE)**[62] 1359 2-9-1 0............................ PaulHanagan 10 92
(R A Fahey) *in tch in midfield: rdn and unable qck 2f out: styd on same pce after: nvr gng pce to threaten ldrs* **16/1**

31 **9** shd **Al Aasifh (IRE)**[7] 2882 2-9-1 0....................................... FrankieDettori 12 92
(Saeed Bin Suroor) *in tch in midfield: effrt to chse ldrs ent fnl 2f: sn rdn: struggling u.p over 1f out: wknd ins fnl f* **4/1**[2]

12 **10** 2½ **Dubawi Gold**[12] 2743 2-9-1 0... PhillipMakin 8 83
(M Dods) *dwlt: sn pressing ldrs: rdn and unable qck 1/2-way: wknd u.p over 1f out: no ch fnl f* **8/1**

31 **11** 1¾ **Black Moth (IRE)**[13] 2687 2-9-1 0.................................... MartinDwyer 7 76
(B J Meehan) *w ldrs: led 3f out tl drvn and hdd over 1f out: wknd jst over 1f out: fdd ins fnl f* **33/1**

1 **12** 4½ **Little Lion Man**[17] 2598 2-9-1 0...................................... WilliamBuick 11 60+
(P W Chapple-Hyam) *a outpcd and sn pushed along in rr: wl btn and eased ins fnl f* **25/1**

60.14 secs (-0.36) **Going Correction** -0.10s/f (Good) **12 Ran SP% 119.2**
Speed ratings (Par 105): **98,96,95,94,93 93,92,91,91,87 84,77**
toteswingers:1&2 £31.80, 2&3 £18.10, 1&3 £25.50 CSF £244.27 CT £1984.28 TOTE £27.90: £6.80, £4.00, £2.50; EX 230.50 Trifecta £5475.30 Pool: £12578.58 - 1.70 winning units..
Owner Highclere Thoroughbred Racing (Bahram) **Bred** Abbeville And Meadow Court Partners **Trained** Newmarket, Suffolk

FOCUS
The GoingStick reading on the stands' side was 9.9, while it was 9.8 up centre and 10.0 on the far side. The round course had a reading of 9.2. Since 2000, every winner of this race had won on their previous start, and none of them had been out of the first three in any of their outings. Only Johannesburg in the last ten renewals had not been a distance winner, so this year's victor managed to overturn to some fairly strong statistics. Interestingly, also since 2000, only Radiohead has gone on to land a race as a 3-y-o, a 1m dirt allowance race at Gulfstream Park in February this year. That said, Dutch Art performed creditably the following season, finishing third in the 2000 Guineas and second in the July Cup. The form looks reasonable but nothing appeals as a significant improver.

NOTEBOOK
Approve(IRE), a fair fourth in the 6f Woodcote Stakes last time (behind Dubawi Gold after finding little room over 1f out), needed a reminder at the 2f marker and a few more before the 1f pole, but responded well and stayed on strongly. It's impressive that he won a Group 2 over this distance seeing as he looks sure to be most effective over a furlong further. Races like the July Stakes, Richmond Stakes and Gimcrack all look logical targets later in the year. (op 20-1)
Reckless Reward(IRE) chased home Dinkum Diamond on his first outing and then secured his first victory on Polytrack at Lingfield. He broke well and seemed a little keen in front, but after getting outpaced for a few strides, he kept on nicely again. A move up in trip, possibly for the July Stakes at Newmarket, should also help this son of Royal Ascot winner Choisir. (op 14-1 tchd 18-1 in places)
Excel Bolt came into this unbeaten over 5f in two races at Musselburgh, and his jockey made a bold move to take his mount towards the stands'-side rail - said to be quicker than the middle of the track according to the GoingStick - away from all of his rivals. He wasn't beaten far after finishing well, but never looked like winning from 2f out. (op 13-2)
Stone Of Folca, a respectable fourth in the Windsor Castle on two days earlier, got stirred up in the paddock and was walked to the start. The horse was slowly away but seemed a likely winner just over a furlong out once hitting the front, before being caught by the fast finishers inside the final half-furlong. It was a fine effort and any ordinary maiden can be won with him before trying his luck at this level again. (op 20-1 tchd 16-1)
Zebedee came from a stable that was enjoying a great time at the Royal meeting, and his two wins from two starts record, the latter coming over C&D, made him look an ideal candidate for success. He was one of the last to come off the bridle and looks all speed, although he probably needs his sights lowering a little. The Molecomb Stakes at Goodwood next month could be the right race for him, although connections suggested afterwards that they felt 6f is what he needs. (op 9-2 tchd 6-1 in places)
Dinkum Diamond(IRE), unbeaten in two starts and the winner of the National Stakes at Sandown, was disappointing, as he was off the bridle by halfway. He ran on inside the final furlong but seemed to lack pace over this trip at Group 2 level. (op 3-1 tchd 10-3 in places and 7-2 in places)
Emperor Hadrian(IRE), off the mark on his previous start when wearing headgear for the first time, was held up towards the rear looking a bit keen under restraint and never reached a challenging position. (op 20-1)
Arctic Feeling(IRE) was a Fibresand winner on debut in March before finishing a neck second on his only other start. (op 20-1)
Al Aasifh(IRE), a wide-margin winner over 6f at Haydock recently, made little impression and wasn't up to this class at this stage of his career. (op 13-2 tchd 7-1 in places)
Dubawi Gold, dropping to 5f for the first time, finished ahead of Approve at Epsom last time but did not get home in this after being prominent in the early stages. (op 9-1 tchd 10-1)
Black Moth(IRE), off the mark at Bath last time, was up with the leaders early but seemed to edge left under pressure in the final stages as he weakened. (tchd 25-1)
Little Lion Man, whose trainer Peter Chapple-Hyam was 2-3 in the race, never featured and was readily left behind. (op 20-1 tchd 28-1 in a place)

3101 RIBBLESDALE STKS (GROUP 2) (FILLIES) 1m 4f
3:05 (3:05) (Class 1) 3-Y-O

£70,962 (£26,900; £13,462; £6,712; £3,362; £1,687) **Stalls** High

Form RPR

1-03 **1** **Hibaayeb**[25] 2373 3-8-12 110...(t) FrankieDettori 7 109
(Saeed Bin Suroor) *midfield: swtchd lft and hdwy over 3f out: rdn to ld wl over 1f out: r.o wl to draw clr ins fnl f: pushed out and wl in command fnl 110yds* **4/1**[1]

6-1 **2** 3¾ **Eldalil**[63] 1329 3-8-12 85... TadhgO'Shea 6 103+
(Sir Michael Stoute) *hld up in rr: pushed along 3f out: hdwy whn swtchd lft to r arnd the field over 2f out: gd prog over 1f out: r.o to take 2nd fnl 120yds: gng on at the fin: could nt trble wnr* **12/1**

-065 **3** ¾ **Gallic Star (IRE)**[11] 2800 3-8-12 96................................... RyanMoore 9 102
(M R Channon) *racd keenly: hld up: rdn and hdwy whn sltly hmpd 2f out: styd on and stdy prog fr over 1f out: kpt on towards fin: nt gng pce to mount serious chal* **16/1**

-341 **4** 1½ **Principal Role (USA)**[34] 2076 3-8-12 108......................... TomQueally 8 99
(H R A Cecil) *trckd ldrs: rdn to ld 2f out: hdd wl over 1f out: sn outpcd by wnr: lost 2nd fnl 120yds: sn no ex* **4/1**[1]

-122 **5** ¾ **Middle Club**[18] 2575 3-8-12 108.................................. RichardHughes 12 98
(R Hannon) *chsd ldr: led 3f out: rdn over 2f out: sn hdd: continued to chse ldrs u.p over 1f out: one pce and btn ins fnl f* **7/1**[3]

2-12 **6** 1¾ **Fatanah (IRE)**[34] 2076 3-8-12 107................................... RichardHills 10 95
(M P Tregoning) *trckd ldrs: effrt whn swtchd rt 2f out: nt qckn over 1f out: fdd ins fnl f* **8/1**

-115 **7** 8 **Gertrude Bell**[13] 2711 3-8-12 104..................................... WilliamBuick 2 83
(J H M Gosden) *trckd ldrs: rdn over 3f out: outpcd whn carried lft 2f out: n.d after* **5/1**[2]

0 **8** hd **Awe Inspiring (IRE)**[13] 2711 3-8-12 95................................ JMurtagh 3 82
(A P O'Brien, Ire) *hld up: pushed along over 3f out: gng nowhere whn hmpd 2f out: n.d* **20/1**

0-00 **9** 15 **Cabaret (IRE)**[13] 2711 3-8-12 103.. PJSmullen 4 58
(A P O'Brien, Ire) *hld up in midfield: lost pl 5f out: bhd over 4f out: toiling and n.d after* **33/1**

2450 **10** ¾ **Bikini Babe (IRE)**[13] 2711 3-8-12 97.................................. KierenFallon 5 57+
(M Johnston) *in tch: clipped heels and lost pl over 6f out: pushed along 4f out: outpcd and no imp whn carried wd 2f out: dropped rt away* **10/1**

0-21 **11** 4½ **Acquainted**[28] 2244 3-8-12 102.. MichaelHills 1 50
(B W Hills) *led: hdd 3f out: rdn and wknd jst over 2f out* **16/1**

2m 31.18s (-1.32) **Going Correction** +0.10s/f (Good) **11 Ran SP% 116.5**
Speed ratings (Par 108): **108,105,105,104,103 102,97,96,86,86 83**
toteswingers:1&2 £14.80, 2&3 £30.30, 1&3 £12.80 CSF £52.78 CT £695.81 TOTE £3.20: £1.20, £5.20, £5.20; EX 51.40 Trifecta £741.70 Pool: £10394.52 - 10.36 winning units..
Owner Godolphin **Bred** Rabbah Bloodstock Limited **Trained** Newmarket, Suffolk
■ Stewards' Enquiry : Tadhg O'Shea three-day ban: careless riding (Jul 1,2,4)

FOCUS
A decent renewal of the Ribblesdale with three previous Group winners and three Listed winners amongst the 11 fillies. Three of the past ten winners had previously contested the Oaks and four of these came into the race after running in the Epsom classic. The best recent record as far as trainers are concerned belongs to Saeed Bin Suroor, who had won the race four times since 1998, and he further enhanced that here. The pace looked only ordinary but the winner looks up to scratch for the race, while the improved runner-up can do even better in future.

NOTEBOOK
Hibaayeb was the only Group 1 winner in the field having taken the Fillies' Mile at Ascot last September on her final start for Clive Brittain, and she ran much better than she had in the 1000 Guineas when third behind the subsequent Prix de Diane winner Sarafina in the Prix Saint-Alary at Longchamp last month. She was expected to improve for this extra quarter-mile and that is how it proved. Settled against the inside rail off the pace early, she made her ground smoothly entering the last half-mile before being switched out to make her run over 2f from. She quickened up pretty smartly too, and once in front over a furlong out she quickly powered clear. There is more to come from her over this trip and she will now take her chance in the Irish Oaks. (op 5-1)
Eldalil ◆, the least exposed in the field and stepping up 5f in trip after winning a Newmarket maiden in April that has worked out well, is bred to be suited by this sort of trip. She was deserted by Richard Hills in favour of Fatanah, but did better than that filly and this was a smart effort as she was switched right off out the back of the field and still had plenty to do turning in. She made up a lot of late ground to take second, but was never in the same parish as the winner. She still has plenty of scope and is in the right hands to exploit any further improvement. (tchd 14-1, 16-1 in a place)
Gallic Star(IRE), a staying-on fifth in a Chantilly Group 3 over this trip 11 days earlier, was another to make up a lot of late ground from off the pace and she could be the type for the Park Hill over an extra 2.5f at Doncaster in September. (op 25-1 tchd 14-1)
Principal Role(USA), up in trip after just getting the better of Fatanah following a protracted tussle in a 1m2f Listed event at Newbury last month, travelled nicely just behind the leader and had every chance when hitting the front inside the last 2f, but the winner soon cut her down on her outside and she didn't seem to get home. She may need hanging on to a little longer or a returned to a shorter trip. (op 9-2)
Middle Club had been shaping as though this longer trip would suit, especially when failing by a short-head to get up in the Italian Oaks over a furlong shorter last month. Always up there, she made her move to hit the front rounding the home bend but she didn't last very long and did not see her race out. (op 6-1 tchd 15-2)
Fatanah(IRE), the choice of Richard Hills over the runner-up, was keen enough early but still looked a danger when switching to the inside rail 2f from home before flattening out. She didn't seem to stay. (tchd 9-1)
Gertrude Bell, winner of the Cheshire Oaks last month before faring best of the four fillies in this race to have contested the Epsom Oaks by finishing fifth, was never far away but she seemed to hang off the final bend and was beaten when slightly inconvenienced by the runner-up 2f from home. This race may have come soon enough, but she may also be better going left-handed. (op 11-2 tchd 9-2, 6-1 in a place)
Awe Inspiring(IRE), beaten a long way when 11th of the 15 runners in the Oaks, looked the stable's first string but she never got into the race and was held when hampered 2f out. She may need softer ground. Official explanation: jockey said filly suffered interference in running
Cabaret(IRE), very disappointing since winning twice in Ireland last summer, was beaten over half a mile from home. (tchd 28-1)
Bikini Babe(IRE), regularly in the frame in Listed/Group company and eighth in the Oaks, almost came down when getting hampered over 6f from home and lost a hind shoe, but she was already well beaten when getting badly interfered with passing the 2f pole. A record of 1-12 is modest for a filly of her ability. Official explanation: jockey said filly suffered interference in running and was struck into from behind losing a shoe (op 14-1)
Acquainted, easy winner of a weak Haydock maiden after chasing home Gertrude Bell in the Cheshire Oaks, tried to make all the running but had no more to give after being headed 3f from home. (op 11-1)

3102 GOLD CUP (GROUP 1) 2m 4f
3:50 (3:51) (Class 1) 4-Y-O+

£141,925 (£53,800; £26,925; £13,425; £6,725; £3,375) **Stalls** High

Form RPR

1 **Rite Of Passage**[92] 7261 6-9-2 0... PJSmullen 13 122
(D K Weld, Ire) *chsd ldng pair: swtchd lft arnd wkng rival over 4f out: chsd ldr and edgd rt 4f out: rdn 3f out: drvn to chal over 1f out: led jst ins fnl f: kpt on and a holding runner-up after* **20/1**

2-22 **2** nk **Age Of Aquarius (IRE)**[18] 2571 4-9-0 117........................... JMurtagh 5 122
(A P O'Brien, Ire) *chsd ldr tl led gng wl over 5f out: 2 l clr and rdn 3f out: jnd and drvn over 1f out: hdd jst ins fnl f: kpt on: a hld after* **8/1**

3-02 **3** 6 **Purple Moon (IRE)**[34] 2097 7-9-2 112............................... KierenFallon 6 116
(L M Cumani) *t.k.h: chsd ldrs tl midfield 10f out: hdwy and rdn along 5f out: chsd ldrs u.p 3f out: wnt 3rd over 1f out: no prog and btn ent fnl f: plugged on* **12/1**

/36- **4** *13* **Bannaby (FR)**[25] 9005 7-9-2 115 .... ChristopheSoumillon 4 103
(M Delcher-Sanchez, Spain) *t.k.h early: hld up in last trio: hdwy over 5f out: chsd ldrs wl over 3f out: rdn to chse ldng pair over 2f out: wknd over 1f out: wl btn fnl f* **20/1**

131- **5** *11* **Ask**[235] 7047 7-9-2 121 .... RyanMoore 12 92
(Sir Michael Stoute) *t.k.h: hld up wl in tch: rdn to chse ldrs 4f out: wkng qckly whn short of room ent fnl 2f: eased fnl f* **11/4**[1]

3-22 **6** *2 ½* **Kasbah Bliss (FR)**[25] 2375 8-9-2 118 .... ThierryThulliez 3 90
(F Doumen, France) *hld up towards rr: rdn and struggling over 4f out: sn lost tch w ldrs: no ch fnl 3f* **13/2**

12-1 **7** *8* **Kite Wood (IRE)**[25] 2375 4-9-0 116 .... FrankieDettori 11 82
(Saeed Bin Suroor) *hld up in midfield: swtchd lft and rdn 7f out: no prog 5f out: 7th and no ch over 3f out: eased fnl f: t.o* **6/1**[3]

0-02 **8** *hd* **Tastahil (IRE)**[43] 1821 6-9-2 111 .... TadhgO'Shea 2 81
(B W Hills) *hld up towards rr: rdn and struggling 6f out: no ch fnl 4f: eased ins fnl f: t.o* **50/1**

21-3 **9** *30* **Darley Sun (IRE)**[21] 2469 4-9-0 109 .... WilliamBuick 1 51
(Saeed Bin Suroor) *t.k.h: chsd ldrs tl lost pl qckly over 5f out: wl t.o fnl 3f* **12/1**

3-21 **10** *½* **Manifest**[34] 2097 4-9-0 117 .... TomQueally 9 51
(H R A Cecil) *hld up in midfield: hdwy on outer 6f out: chsd ldrs and rdn over 4f out: 6th and wkng qckly 3f out: eased fr over 2f out: virtually p.u fnl f: t.o* **7/2**[2]

-001 **11** *102* **Akmal**[21] 2469 4-9-0 111 .... RichardHills 8 —
(J L Dunlop) *led tl over 5f out: struggling whn barging match w wnr ent fnl 4f: sn wl bhd: wl t.o and eased fr over 2f out* **16/1**

0245 **12** *79* **Montaff**[21] 2469 4-9-0 104 .... AlanMunro 10 —
(M R Channon) *stdd s: a last: nudged along 12f out: lost tch 6f out: sn wl t.o: virtually p.u fnl 3f* **100/1**

4m 16.92s (-4.08) **Going Correction** +0.10s/f (Good)
WFA 4 from 5yo+ 2lb **12** Ran SP% **121.4**
Speed ratings (Par 117): **112,111,109,104,99 98,95,95,83,83 —,—**
toteswingers:1&2 £16.80, 2&3 £15.30, 1&3 £31.70 CSF £171.29 CT £2031.46 TOTE £23.80: £6.30, £2.60, £3.80; EX 164.10 Trifecta £1630.60 Pool: £18283.87 - 8.29 winning units..
Owner Dr R Lambe **Bred** Newsells Park Stud **Trained** The Curragh, Co Kildare
■ Stewards' Enquiry : J Murtagh three-day ban: used whip with excessive frequency (Jul 1,2,4)
P J Smullen four-day ban: careless riding (Jul 1,2,4,5)

FOCUS

For the first time in five years this historic staying contest did not include Yeats, who is now happily enjoying himself as a stallion. Plenty of these had their stamina to prove, and although the early pace did not seem frenetic, resulting is some of the runners taking quite a grip under restraint, the course record was lowered, suggesting this was still a serious stamina test. Indeed, somewhat ironically considering how the winner was campaigned over the winter, the field came home like 2m4f hurdlers. The winner recorded a personal best while the third is rated close to his former level.

NOTEBOOK

Rite Of Passage, given a break since finishing third in the Neptune Investement Management Novices' Hurdle, had loads to find on his Flat form considering his BHA mark, and his last victory in this sphere came in the 2009 Irish November Handicap. However, his trainer, a master under any code, is renowned for his stayers on the level, so the success of his horse in the premier staying event of the season should probably not come as a shock. That said, few could have foreseen the winner and runner-up pulling so far clear of classy, but ultimately non-staying rivals. Always well placed under Pat Smullen, Rite Of Passage had ground to make up on the second turning in, but responded nicely to a strong ride and battled hard for a narrow success. The Melbourne Cup had been on his connections' mind even before this victory (Dermot Weld also has the well-fancied Profound Beauty), and he may not be handed a stopping weight if going for it this year, as this will be the 150th running of that contest and many smart types are either already out in Australia (Alandi, a top stayer over here last season, was purchased by an Australian owner) or heading there. Very much unexposed, Rite Of Passage has the potential to emulate Yeats in winning multiple runnings of this great race. In the shorter term, the Irish St Leger seems the obvious target before any trip down under. (op 16-1)

Age Of Aquarius(IRE) had given the impression throughout his career that a test of stamina was going to suit. It was heartening to see him shape so nicely behind an in-form sort at Chester on his reappearance, but it was slightly disappointing to see him easily brushed aside by the aforementioned Profound Beauty on her return in the Listed Saval Beg Stakes over 1m6f. He was on his toes prior to the off but still produced an immensely creditable performance, as Murtagh rode him positively and managed to gain an advantage on his rivals into the home straight. The winner was just too strong in the final stages, but there was no hint that Aidan O'Brien's colt shirked the issue and he has plenty of time to make his mark at this level over extended distances. Perhaps the Goodwood Cup will be the race for him - that's where Yeats went after his first Gold Cup. (op 6-1)

Purple Moon(IRE)had been beaten by wide margins on his two outings this season. He looked to be going nowhere quickly heading to the home bend but, under a strong ride, he kept going nicely at the one pace. The step up in trip on going he thrives on brought out the best in him, and he is likely to stick to staying trips. According to Luca Cumani he could aimed at races likes the Goodwood Cup and the Lonsdale Cup, although the Ebor (which he won in 2007) has been mentioned as an alternative, and he'll probably be entered for the Melbourne Cup again as well. (op 18-1 tchd 20-1 in places)

Bannaby(FR) was an interesting participant for a trainer who tasted Royal Ascot success with Equiano a couple of years ago, not least considering he won the Prix Du Cadran in 2008 (Kasbah Bliss and Yeats behind), although he had been fairly lightly raced since. The signs had been promising in his three starts this season (his 1-10 defeat could easily be excused), but it was a little surprising to see him held up when considering his obvious stamina reserves. He made impressive headway as others started to drop away (he touched 2 on Betfair) but looked seriously one paced off the bridle, and easier ground, as well as a more prominent ride, will probably suit better in future.

Ask ran a fine race coming home in fifth, but as was the worry before the off, he had nothing left in the latter stages. He had taken a keen hold in midfield and was still travelling too strongly 6f out when others were being pushed along. It was worth the experiment, but one would imagine he will be running over shorter distances in the future. Moore reported that he felt the ground was too quick for his mount. (op 4-1 tchd 5-1 in a place)

Kasbah Bliss(FR) had thrived since having his attentions solely concentrated on the Flat, and there should have been no issues with his stamina running out over this trip, as his fine effort in the Prix Du Cadran behind Alandi proved last year. However, he never really featured and proved disappointing. (op 7-1 tchd 8-1)

Kite Wood(IRE) was given every chance once the tempo lifted, albeit he was forced wide, but he struggled to get involved. He had got very warm beforehand, something he did on occasions last year, and that probably compromised his chance. (op 13-2)

Tastahil(IRE) bounced back to form in the Chester Cup after a disappointing start to his season, and ran as well as connections could have been realistically hoping for.

Darley Sun(IRE) made impressive progress last season under the care of David Simcock, which ended in a 5l success over the improved Mamlook in Cesarewitch. Now with Godolphin, and the second string on jockey bookings, he had made a respectable start to the season behind Akmal at Sandown but was seemingly exposed at this level after racing prominently. (op 14-1 tchd 16-1 in places)

Manifest sprung to prominence and to the top of the betting for this race after demolishing his rivals in the Yorkshire Cup, looking every inch a top-notch stayer in the making. A lightly raced sort related to some horses effective over at least 1m6f, he was wide of his rivals throughout, looking a little keen, and simply ran like a horse who did not stay, an opinion backed up by Queally afterwards. He is certainly not one to give up on, and this effort can easily be forgiven. Official explanation: vet said colt lost a shoe (left fore) (op 4-1)

Akmal looked the most likely of these to dominate, as he returned to his best in the Blue Square Henry II Stakes after connections tried holding him up in the Sagaro Stakes at this course. He was afforded an easy lead, one that he held until the runner-up ranged alongside him, and wasn't totally done with when hampered by the winner coming to the home bend. His rider eased off quickly once he was barged and his final position is not a true reflection of his performance.

3103 BRITANNIA STKS (HERITAGE H'CAP) (C&G) 1m (S)

4:25 (4:30) (Class 2) (0-105,103) 3-Y-O

£62,310 (£18,660; £9,330; £4,670; £2,330; £1,170) **Stalls** Centre

Form RPR

1-12 **1** **Ransom Note**[19] 2544 3-8-10 **92** .... MichaelHills 27 103+
(B W Hills) *racd on far side: midfield: rdn and hdwy 3f out: led overall wl over 1f out: r.o wl: 1st of 16 in gp* **9/1**[2]

-622 **2** *½* **Invincible Soul (IRE)**[37] 2002 3-8-4 **86** .... FrankieMcDonald 2 96
(R Hannon) *racd on stands' side: midfield: hdwy 3f out: led gp fnl 150yds: r.o but nt get to far side wnr: 1st of 11 in gp* **33/1**

1205 **3** *nk* **Greyfriarschorista**[21] 2471 3-9-2 **98** .... JoeFanning 4 107+
(M Johnston) *racd stands' side: prom: led gp 3f out: rdn and hdd fnl 150yds: r.o u.p: hld after: 2nd of 11 in gp* **40/1**

6221 **4** *hd* **Secretive**[27] 2288 3-7-13 **81** ....(b) AndrewMullen 10 90
(M Johnston) *racd on stands' side: in tch: rdn to chal in gp over 1f out: r.o u.p ins fnl f: hld towards fin: 3rd of 11 in gp* **33/1**

3-22 **5** *2 ¼* **King Of Reason**[27] 2288 3-8-1 **83** .... PaulHanagan 1 86
(D M Simcock) *racd on stands' side: in rr: hdwy over 1f out: r.o ins fnl f: nt rch ldrs: 4th of 11 in gp* **25/1**

3-40 **6** *½* **Audacity Of Hope**[47] 1699 3-9-6 **102** ....(t) ChristopheSoumillon 18 104
(P J McBride) *racd on far side: hld up: hdwy 3f out: nt qckn over 1f out: styd on same pce ins fnl f: 2nd of 16 in gp* **25/1**

-015 **7** *½* **One Good Emperor (IRE)**[19] 2544 3-7-12 **85** ow4 .... KierenFox(5) 16 86
(J R Best) *racd on far side: prominnent: rdn to chal 2f out: kpt on same pce ins fnl f: 3rd of 16 in gp* **33/1**

-511 **8** *nse* **Sea Lord (IRE)**[12] 2737 3-8-13 **95** .... FrankieDettori 31 96+
(M Johnston) *racd on far side: trckd ldrs: rdn over 1f out: n.m.r brielfly sn after: kpt on same pce: 4th of 16 in gp* **7/1**[1]

6-21 **9** *¾* **Fireback**[40] 1913 3-8-2 **84** .... DavidProbert 8 83
(A M Balding) *racd stands' side: led gp to 3f out: edgd rt over 1f out: no ex ins fnl f: 5th of 11 in gp* **20/1**

-420 **10** *1 ¾* **High Twelve (IRE)**[26] 2324 3-8-12 **94** .... WilliamBuick 28 89
(J H M Gosden) *racd on far side: in rr: rdn and hdwy over 1f out: kpt on one pce ins fnl f: nt gng pce to chal ldrs: 5th of 16 in gp* **14/1**[3]

12-6 **11** *¾* **Pleasant Day (IRE)**[35] 2045 3-9-6 **102** ....(b) KierenFallon 26 95+
(B J Meehan) *racd on far side: towards rr: pushed along over 4f out: swtchd lft and hdwy over 1f out: styd on ins fnl f: nt gng pce to rch ldrs: 6th of 16 in gp* **25/1**

3121 **12** *shd* **Balducci**[26] 2324 3-9-0 **96** .... JimmyFortune 15 89
(A M Balding) *racd on far side: hld up: hdwy over 3f out: chsd ldrs over 1f out: styd on same pce ins fnl f: 7th of 16 in gp* **7/1**[1]

-402 **13** *½* **White Devil**[15] 2644 3-7-13 **81** .... FrannyNorton 30 73+
(A M Balding) *racd on far side: in tch: rdn 2f out: nt qckn: styd on ins fnl f: no imp on ldrs: 8th of 16 in gp* **25/1**

3-10 **14** *¾* **Cumulus Nimbus**[21] 2471 3-8-8 **90** .... RichardHughes 3 80
(R Hannon) *stdd s: racd on stands' side: hld up: pushed along and outpcd over 2f out: nvr a danger: 6th of 11 in gp* **33/1**

130- **15** *2 ¾* **Layline (IRE)**[237] 6993 3-8-9 **91** .... JimCrowley 32 75
(R M Beckett) *racd on far side: midfield: rdn 2f out: sn outpcd: 9th of 16 in gp* **20/1**

0003 **16** *½* **Kona Coast**[47] 1703 3-8-4 **86** ....(p) NickyMackay 25 69
(J H M Gosden) *racd on far side: prom: overall ldr 4f out: hdd overall wl over 1f out: wknd ins fnl f: 10th of 16 in gp* **16/1**

-142 **17** *1 ¼* **Hypnotized (USA)**[29] 2225 3-8-9 **91** ....(p) JamieSpencer 17 71+
(M L W Bell) *racd on far side: towards rr: nt clr run on inner over 1f out: sme prog over 1f out: no imp on ldrs on: 11th of 16 in gp* **7/1**[1]

3031 **18** *3 ¼* **Navajo Chief**[19] 2542 3-9-4 **100** .... TomQueally 29 73
(A P Jarvis) *racd on far side: w ldrs: pushed along 4f out: wknd over 1f out: 12th of 16 in gp* **16/1**

0320 **19** *hd* **Al Farahidi (USA)**[13] 2713 3-8-12 **94** ....(v[1]) GregFairley 23 66
(M Johnston) *racd on far side: racd keenly: overall ldr: hdd 4f out: remained prom tl wknd over 1f out: 13th of 16 in gp* **33/1**

105- **20** *½* **Suffolk Punch (IRE)**[295] 5347 3-8-6 **88** .... LiamKeniry 24 59
(A M Balding) *racd on far side: trckd ldrs: rdn and wknd 2f out: 14th of 16 in gp* **40/1**

0043 **21** *1* **Ongoodform (IRE)**[5] 2970 3-7-13 **86** ow3 .... JohnFahy(5) 5 55
(P W D'Arcy) *racd on stands' side: hld up: rdn and outpcd over 1f out: 7th of 11 in gp* **66/1**

-022 **22** *¾* **Excellent Guest**[19] 2545 3-8-2 **84** .... JimmyQuinn 22 51
(G G Margarson) *racd on far side: midfield: u.p and wknd 2f out 15th of 16 in gp* **25/1**

1-30 **23** *9* **Carnaby Street (IRE)**[38] 1985 3-9-7 **103** .... RyanMoore 6 49
(R Hannon) *racd stands' side: prom: rdn and wknd over 2f out: 8th of 11 in gp* **25/1**

5403 **24** *4* **Black Snowflake (USA)**[26] 2324 3-8-12 **97** .... AhmedAjtebi(3) 13 34
(Mahmood Al Zarooni) *swtchd lft to r on stands' side: in tch: rdn and wknd 3f out: 9th of 11 in gp* **25/1**

4-20 **25** *¾* **Azizi**[47] 1703 3-9-2 **98** .... TadhgO'Shea 7 33
(W J Haggas) *racd stands' side: midfield: rdn and wknd 2f out: 10th of 11 in gp* **40/1**

-211 **26** *3 ¾* **Dherghaam (IRE)**[26] 2348 3-9-4 **100** .... RichardHills 14 27
(E A L Dunlop) *swtchd lft to r on stands' side: chsd ldrs tl rdn and wknd over 2f out: 11th of 11 in gp* **18/1**

1-20 **27** *15* **Zaahy (USA)**[21] 2471 3-9-1 **97** .... JMurtagh 12 —
(P W Chapple-Hyam) *racd on far side: dwlt: in rr: pushed along and wl outpcd 3f out: lost tch: 16th of 16 in gp* **33/1**

1m 37.82s (-2.78) **Going Correction** -0.10s/f (Good) course record **27** Ran SP% **134.1**
Speed ratings (Par 105): **109,108,108,108,105 105,104,104,103,102 101,101,100,100,97 96,95,92,92,91 90,89,80,76,76 72,5**
toteswingers: 1&2 £106.80, 1&3 £247.30, 2&3 £308.20 CSF £279.33 CT £10981.07 TOTE £8.90: £2.10, £10.50, £10.70, £9.90; EX 389.90 TRIFECTA Not won..
Owner H R Mould **Bred** Rabbah Bloodstock Limited **Trained** Lambourn, Berks
■ Stewards' Enquiry : Christophe Soumillon one-day ban: used whip down shoulder in the forehand (Jul 1)
Andrew Mullen three-day ban: used whip with excessive frequency (Jul 1,2,4)

FOCUS
A typically ultra-competitive Britannia. A group of 11 horses decided to come nearside whilst the larger group of 16 raced up the far side, and that bunch seemed to hold an advantage of a good 5l passing the 3f pole, but there wasn't much between the two sides at the line, as although the winner was drawn high, the next four home were all drawn low. The form looks sound enough and should work out well.

NOTEBOOK
Ransom Note had been put up 6lb since a narrow defeat when favourite at Newmarket last month, but this result proved that the Handicapper was more than justified. His supporters may have been worried as he didn't seem to be going at all well at halfway, but the further they went the better he was travelling, and he skipped clear of the others in the far-side group over 1f from home. As it turned out, his nearest challengers emerged from the nearside group, but he was always holding them. Connections believe he could be a Group horse in the making. (op 8-1 tchd 10-1)
Invincible Soul(IRE), just in front of a subsequent winner when runner-up off 2lb lower at Warwick last month, finished well up the nearside to just emerge the best of that group. He has a good prize in him, even though he will face another rise for this. (op 25-1)
Greyfriarschorista hadn't made the same impact in two starts on turf as he did on Polytrack earlier in the year (though one of those was in the 2000 Guineas) but this was much more like it. He was sent to the front of the nearside group passing the 3f pole and battled on well to hold on to third. (op 33-1)
Secretive ◆, raised 7lb for his all-the-way success from King Of Reason at Haydock last month, stayed on really well in the nearside group and he remains progressive.
King Of Reason ◆, in the frame all five starts to date but yet to win, was closely matched with Secretive on last month's Haydock running and, although behind him again here, he deserves plenty of credit as he was dropped right out in the nearside group before making up plenty of late ground. It can only be a matter of time before he breaks his duck. (op 33-1)
Audacity Of Hope, outclassed in the 2000 Guineas though he also lost a shoe, ran on late in the far-side group to finish second on his side and this was better returned to handicap company. He may not be the easiest to place, however. (op 33-1)
One Good Emperor(IRE) ◆, who found that the ground had turned against him when unplaced at Newmarket last month, appreciated the return to a quicker surface and ran well for a long way in the far-side group, especially as he carried 4lb overweight. There are more handicaps to be won with him at a slightly lower level. (tchd 40-1 in a place)
Sea Lord(IRE), up 4lb in his bid for a hat-trick, was another to stay on late towards the far side, but the Handicapper may have his measure now. (op 8-1 tchd 13-2, 9-1 in a place)
Fireback, 6lb higher than when making all to easily beat a subsequent winner at Lingfield last month, tried the same tactics in the nearside group but was in trouble once headed passing the 3f pole.
High Twelve(IRE) stayed on under pressure in the far-side bunch, but although never a threat this was better than when tailed off in the Betfred Silver Bowl at Haydock last month. (op 16-1)
Pleasant Day(IRE) ◆, closely matched with Carnaby Street and Audacity Of Hope on last autumn's Horris Hill running, ran poorly when last of six on his Newmarket reappearance, but this was better as he was given an awful lot to do in the far-side group and made up a fair amount of late ground. (tchd 28-1)
Balducci, bumped up 12lb for his convincing success in the Betfred Silver Bowl last month, made a brief effort coming to the last 2f but his run then flattened out. His middle draw probably wouldn't have been ideal so he is worth another chance. (op 10-1)
White Devil, in the frame a few times but still to get his head in front, didn't run badly on the far side and has the ability to win races.
Cumulus Nimbus, disappointing in Listed company last time after winning a classified event over a furlong further on his Goodwood reappearance, was making his handicap debut but could never get competitive in the nearside bunch, and may need to drop a few pounds. (op 40-1)
Layline(IRE), the least exposed in the field, hadn't been seen since October but he did win first time up at two. This was a tough race in which to make his reappearance, however, so he is worth another chance.
Kona Coast, who put some modest efforts behind him when splitting Balducci and Hypnotized at Newmarket last month, was 15lb better off with the former and 7lb better off with the latter. He made much of the running in the far-side group, but couldn't see his race out.
Hypnotized(USA) ◆, clear of a subsequent winner when just beaten over a furlong further at Goodwood last time, was put up 7lb for that and had cheekpieces on for the first time. He never got into the race, but didn't have much room to play with so is worth another chance. (op 8-1)
Navajo Chief, raised 6lb for beating a decent sort at Haydock last month, was a springer in the market and showed up for a long way in the far-side group but didn't get home. (op 25-1)
Zaahy(USA) Official explanation: jockey said colt hung left

3104 HAMPTON COURT STKS (LISTED RACE) 1m 2f
5:00 (5:04) (Class 1) 3-Y-O

£28,385 (£10,760; £5,385; £2,685; £1,345; £675) **Stalls** High

Form RPR

211 **1** **Afsare**[12] 2738 3-9-5 110 KierenFallon 8 112+
(L M Cumani) *broke wl: stdd and hld up in tch: rdn and effrt 2f out: drvn and ev ch over 1f out: led jst ins fnl f: sn edgd rt u.p and hdd: hrd drvn to ld again last stride* **9/4**[1]

2-21 **2** *shd* **Quadrille**[35] 2045 3-9-2 108 RichardHughes 16 109
(R Hannon) *chsd ldng pair: rdn to chse ldr over 2f out: drvn and ev ch over 1f out: led and edgd rt ins fnl f: kpt on wl tl hdd last stride* **4/1**[2]

-122 **3** *nk* **Wigmore Hall (IRE)**[12] 2738 3-9-2 101 JamieSpencer 14 111+
(M L W Bell) *t.k.h: hld up towards rr: hdwy 4f out: nt clr run over 2f out tl swtchd rt 2f out: sn rdn and hanging rt: running on whn swtchd lft ent fnl f: r.o strly and clsng qckly at fin* **12/1**[3]

1 **4** *1 ½* **Film Score (USA)**[20] 2507 3-9-2 0 FrankieDettori 10 105+
(Mahmood Al Zarooni) *hld up in midfield: rdn and unable qck 3f out: c wd and drvn 2f out: styd on wl u.p ins fnl f: nvr gng pce to chal ldrs* **12/1**[3]

5-30 **5** *¾* **Critical Moment (USA)**[42] 1833 3-9-2 105 MichaelHills 5 107+
(B W Hills) *led and crossed to rail: rdn ent fnl 2f: hrd pressed over 1f out: hdd jst ins fnl f: looking btn whn hmpd and snatched up sn after: nt rcvr* **25/1**

2-00 **6** *shd* **Fencing Master**[26] 2354 3-9-2 115 JMurtagh 13 104
(A P O'Brien, Ire) *racd in midfield: rdn wl over 2f out: swtchd lft ent fnl 2f: hdwy u.p to chse ldrs jst over 1f out: styd on fnl f: nvr gng pce to rch ldrs* **4/1**[2]

-104 **7** *½* **Lord Zenith**[21] 2471 3-9-7 103 WilliamBuick 15 108
(A M Balding) *hld up wl in tch: rdn and effrt over 2f out: kpt on same pce u.p fnl f* **33/1**

2-10 **8** *2 ¾* **Fair Trade**[47] 1699 3-9-2 104 JimmyFortune 2 97+
(D R C Elsworth) *stdd and dropped in bhd after s: plld v hrd in rr: hmpd and pushed wd bnd after 2f: kpt on wl u.p fr over 1f out: nvr trbld ldrs* **12/1**[3]

31-0 **9** *½* **Mont Agel**[63] 1327 3-9-2 93 TomQueally 11 96
(M L W Bell) *stdd s: hld up in rr: hmpd bnd after 2f: rdn and hdwy over 2f out: keeping on same pce whn n.m.r jst over 1f out: no imp ins fnl f* **40/1**

1353 **10** *2 ¼* **Miss Starlight**[19] 2543 3-8-11 99 DaneO'Neill 3 87
(P J McBride) *stdd s: hld up in rr: hmpd and pushed wd bnd after 2f: rdn and effrt on outer over 2f out: no imp over 1f out: nvr trbld ldrs* **50/1**

2-12 **11** *shd* **The Rectifier (USA)**[21] 2471 3-9-2 102 MickyFenton 4 92
(Stef Higgins) *t.k.h: chsd ldrs tl wknd u.p wl over 1f out* **33/1**

0003 **12** *2 ¾* **Dubai Miracle (USA)**[12] 2738 3-9-2 95 MartinDwyer 1 86
(D M Simcock) *hld up towards rr: rdn and effrt on outer 3f out: no real prog n.d whn n.m.r ent fnl f* **40/1**

2-10 **13** *9* **Lion Mountain**[32] 2160 3-9-2 92 AhmedAjtebi 6 68
(Mahmood Al Zarooni) *chsd ldr: hanging lft bnd wl over 2f out: lost 2nd over 2f out: wknd and edgd lft over 1f out* **66/1**

-214 **14** *1 ¾* **Alrasm (IRE)**[19] 2543 3-9-2 102 RichardHills 12 65+
(M A Jarvis) *stdd s: plld v hrd and hld up in rr: wnt lft bnd after 2f and racd wd after: hdwy to chse ldrs 4f out: wknd 2f out: wl btn whn nt clr run and swtchd rt over 1f out* **14/1**

221- **15** *3 ½* **Champagne Style (USA)**[244] 6811 3-9-5 103 RyanMoore 7 61
(B J Meehan) *v awkward leaving stalls: plld v hrd and racd v awkwardly towards rr: veered lft bnd after 2f: a bhd: lost tch over 2f out* **16/1**

2m 6.22s (-0.78) **Going Correction** +0.10s/f (Good) **15 Ran SP% 124.5**
Speed ratings (Par 107): **107,106,106,105,104 104,104,102,101,100 99,97,90,89,86**
toteswingers: 1&2 £3.10, 1&3 £9.80, 2&3 £12.10 CSF £10.29 CT £94.12 TOTE £3.70: £1.80, £1.90, £5.10; EX 12.50 Trifecta £133.50 Pool: £6786.02 - 37.60 winning units..
Owner Sheikh Mohammed Obaid Al Maktoum **Bred** Darley **Trained** Newmarket, Suffolk
■ Stewards' Enquiry : Kieren Fallon two-day ban: careless riding (Jul1-2)

FOCUS
An open-looking contest on paper that had its fair share of trouble in running, with there being early scrimmaging as the field started to settle into positions. Plenty of these are on the upgrade though, with the runner-up setting the standard.

NOTEBOOK
Afsare, unraced at two, has improved immeasurably from his first start, and was raised a whopping 20lb after winning a Doncaster conditions event on his previous outing. This was obviously a step up in class for him, but he travelled like a good horse and battled on well when asked to get to the front despite edging right. Connections intend watching the race again after the dust has settled, but are sure the horse will get 1m4f in due course. There are no specific plans for him, although it is felt he needs a galloping track to be at his best. (op 5-2 tchd 11-4 in places and 3-1 in a place)
Quadrille, like the winner, was given a positive ride and gave little away under pressure. He was undoubtedly intimidated as the Cumani horse came towards him, but it is difficult to argue that it cost him the race, even though it was such a close finish. A fantastically consistent sort, he has yet to finish out of the first two. (op 5-1)
Wigmore Hall(IRE) ran better than when hammered by Afsare last time, with the bigger field and stronger pace helping, and one even got the impression that he was an unlucky loser as he endured a troubled trip in the straight.
Film Score(USA) made a great start to his career when winning on debut from a smart but very frustrating performer last month and ran a cracker when considering his lack of experience. He hit a flat spot about 2f out but kept on well in the final stages. (op 11-1)
Critical Moment(USA) ran with promise in the Craven Stakes but failed miserably to build on it when upped to 1m4f in the Chester Vase. He was allowed to get to the front quite easily here and dictate a pace to suit him, but he was starting to weaken when hampered by Quadrille. It may have cost him one place, but nothing more. (op 20-1)
Fencing Master was taking a fair drop in grade after running in both the English and Irish 2000 Guineas, but he failed to capitalise on it. He took a long time to hit top gear before staying on. (op 11-2 tchd 13-2)
Lord Zenith, trying 1m2f for the first time, was far from disgraced in the 2000 Guineas (he was a place in front of St James's Palace third Hearts Of Fire) and then ran into an improver in a hot Sandown handicap. He was never far away and plugged on under pressure. (op 25-1)
Fair Trade was poorly drawn, pulled hard and was badly hampered in the early stages. Little went right for him and his effort can be upgraded. (op 9-1)
Mont Agel was another who got caught up in the early scrimmaging and can be rated better than his final position suggests. (op 33-1)
The Rectifier(USA), who was in front of Lord Zenith last time, sat quite handy and had every chance coming to the final furlong before weakening, failing to prove himself over the trip. (op 25-1 tchd 50-1 in a place)
Lion Mountain tracked the leader turning into the home straight but dropped away steadily once asked to quicken. (op 50-1)
Alrasm(IRE) Official explanation: jockey said colt ran to free
Champagne Style(USA) Official explanation: jockey said colt did not handle bend

3105 KING GEORGE V STKS (H'CAP) 1m 4f
5:35 (5:36) (Class 2) (0-105,99) 3-Y-O

£31,155 (£9,330; £4,665; £2,335; £1,165; £585) **Stalls** High

Form RPR

-111 **1** **Dandino**[12] 2742 3-8-13 **91** PaulMulrennan 18 102+
(J G Given) *broke wl: led for 1f: trckd ldrs after: rdn to ld ent fnl f: r.o gamely to the line* **7/1**[3]

51-1 **2** *¾* **London Stripe (IRE)**[46] 1730 3-8-10 **88** RyanMoore 3 98+
(Sir Michael Stoute) *chsd ldr: rdn to chal 2f out: led over 1f out: hdd ent fnl f: continued to chal: nt qckn towards fin* **5/1**[2]

04-1 **3** *2* **Caucus**[27] 2281 3-8-7 **85** SteveDrowne 13 92
(H Morrison) *in tch: effrt to chse ldrs over 2f out: nt qckn 1f out: swtchd lft fnl 110yds: styd on towards fin: nt gng pce to chal front pair* **33/1**

4231 **4** *hd* **Bay Willow (IRE)**[24] 2390 3-8-7 **85** GregFairley 19 91
(M Johnston) *led after 1f: rdn and hdd over 1f out: kpt on u.p ins fnl f: no ex cl home* **10/1**

3-11 **5** *nse* **Berling (IRE)**[34] 2079 3-8-9 **87** EddieAhern 20 99+
(J L Dunlop) *hld up: nt clr run 2f out: sn swtchd lft and c arnd field 2f out: r.o ins fnl f: gng on at fin* **3/1**[1]

1-01 **6** *1 ¼* **Christopher Wren (USA)**[27] 2289 3-8-3 **81** JimmyQuinn 7 85
(J R Best) *midfield: rdn and sme hdwy over 2f out: styd on same pce fr over 1f out* **33/1**

1-43 **7** *2 ¼* **Contract Caterer (IRE)**[36] 2033 3-9-1 **93** KierenFallon 5 94+
(Pat Eddery) *midfield: rdn over 2f out: hdwy over 1f out: kpt on: one pce whn eased fnl 100yds* **12/1**

24-1 **8** *½* **Tactician**[61] 1386 3-8-11 **89** HayleyTurner 10 89
(M L W Bell) *racd keenly: trckd ldrs: rdn and nt qckn 2f out: kpt on one pce fr over 1f out* **12/1**

1-30 **9** *hd* **Rashaad (USA)**[29] 2226 3-9-7 **99** RichardHills 16 99
(B W Hills) *hld up: rdn and hdwy over 1f out: styd on ins fnl f: one pce fnl 100yds nt gng pce to get to ldrs* **25/1**

4-16 **10** *1 ½* **Rawnaq (IRE)**[26] 2323 3-8-3 **81** TadhgO'Shea 15 78
(M Johnston) *missed break: in rr: rdn 2f out: hdwy over 1f out: nt clr run briefly ins fnl f: no imp sn after* **33/1**

2215 **11** *2* **Dancing Dude (IRE)**[34] 2101 3-8-0 **78** FrannyNorton 9 72
(M Johnston) *towards rr: niggled along over 4f out: outpcd over 2f out: sn swtchd rt: nvr able to rch ldrs* **33/1**

12 *nk* **Bright Horizon**[13] 2732 3-9-1 **93** JMurtagh 17 87
(A P O'Brien, Ire) *midfield: pushed along over 2f out: one pce fr over 1f out* **8/1**

5-14 **13** *½* **Hayzoom**[28] 2254 3-8-2 **80** DavidProbert 11 73
(P W Chapple-Hyam) *hld up in midfield: rdn over 2f out: wnt lft over 1f out: one pce and no imp after* **20/1**

-132 **14** 1 ¼ **Life And Soul (IRE)**[12] 2742 3-8-4 **82**............................ PaulHanagan 6 73
(Mrs A J Perrett) *hld up: hmpd whn nt clr run 2f out: nvr able to get on terms* **20/1**

1-11 **15** 1 ½ **Agent Archie (USA)**[28] 2254 3-8-1 **84**............................ KierenFox(5) 4 72
(J R Best) *midfield: rdn 2f out: wknd over 1f out* **16/1**

300- **16** 1 ½ **Top Spin (IRE)**[13] 2732 3-8-7 **85**.................................. JamieSpencer 1 71
(John Joseph Murphy, Ire) *prom: rdn over 2f out: wknd over 1f out* **33/1**

-260 **17** 1 ½ **Right Step**[18] 2562 3-8-9 **87**.............................. TomQueally 12 71
(A P Jarvis) *midfield: rdn over 2f out: wknd over 1f out* **40/1**

1-25 **18** 12 **Bowdler's Magic**[12] 2758 3-8-4 **82**................................ JoeFanning 8 46
(M Johnston) *trckd ldrs: rdn and wkng whn n.m.r and hmpd 2 out: wl btn after* **20/1**

2m 30.51s (-1.99) **Going Correction** +0.10s/f (Good) **18** Ran SP% **130.9**
Speed ratings (Par 105): **110,109,108,108,108 107,105,105,105,104 102,102,102,101,100 99,98,90**
toteswingers: 1&2 £6.40, 1&3 £71.50, 2&3 £50.50 CSF £38.99 CT £1140.82 TOTE £8.20: £1.80, £1.30, £8.00, £3.00; EX 25.10 Trifecta £901.00 Pool: £7752.66 - 6.36 winning units. Place 6: £4566.07 Place 5: £728.43 .
Owner Elite Racing Club **Bred** Elite Racing Club **Trained** Willoughton, Lincs
■ Stewards' Enquiry : David Probert three-day ban: careless riding (Jul 1,2,4)
Paul Mulrennan one-day ban: used whip with excessive frequency (Jul 1)

FOCUS
One gelding against 17 colts and a race that is usually won by a progressive staying 3-y-o. Typically this year's renewal featured several coming into the race at the top of their game. The pace was very ordinary, however, and it paid to be handy with the first four finishers up there from the start. Despite that, the winning time was still 0.67 seconds faster than the Ribblesdale and the form looks sound rated around the first four with the first two progressing.

NOTEBOOK
Dandino, 9lb higher in his bid for a four-timer, was trying this trip for the first time. Always close to the pace, he worked hard to force his head in front inside the last furlong and saw his race out in game style. He is likely to be aimed at the St Leger, and is probably going to run in a trial such as the Gordon Stakes or the Great Voltigeur on the way.
London Stripe(IRE) ◆, raised 5lb for his Newmarket reappearance success, was another trying this trip for the first time and his awkward wide draw meant that he had to cover a fair bit of ground to get across and take up a handy position. He had his chance when leading over a furlong from home, but the winner was soon pressing him and, although he rallied well, he was always just being held. This was a decent effort under the circumstances and he still has plenty of scope. (op 4-1 tchd 11-2)
Caucus ◆, making his handicap debut after beating an odds-on shot in a six-runner Chepstow maiden on his first start for the yard last month, was another to race handily and battled on well after coming off the bridle turning in. The best of him is still to be seen and he shapes as though he will get further. (op 28-1)
Bay Willow(IRE) ◆, making his handicap debut after making all to win a maiden over a similar trip at Leicester last month, was given another positive ride and made a good fist of it until headed over furlong from home. He did enjoy the run of the race here, but considering he didn't see the racecourse at two he is entitled to carry on improving. (op 11-1)
Berling(IRE) was held up amongst horses in a steadily run race and never saw any daylight when he needed it rounding the home turn. He had to be switched extremely wide and took off when in the clear, but he faced a hopeless task. Although he was off a 9lb higher mark here, he deserves compensation for this, although it's worth bearing in mind that he did show a quirky side despite winning at Newbury last month. (op 9-2 tchd 5-1 in places)
Christopher Wren(USA) ◆, raised 6lb for his Haydock success last month, was trying this trip for the first time but he ran well having been close to the pace throughout and can win more races at a slightly lower level.
Contract Caterer(IRE) ◆, another trying this trip for the first time, was possibly unlucky at York last time but was put up 8lb for that. He can be rated better than his finishing position here too, as he was always trapped out wide off the pace and had to come very wide to make his effort after turning in. He made up plenty of late ground and is one to keep an eye on.
Tactician, making his handicap debut after winning an ordinary Newbury maiden on his reappearance, had his chance turning in but lacked a turn of foot under pressure. This was only his fourth start so he is likely to still have improvement in him. (op 11-1)
Rashaad(USA), making his handicap debut after hanging his chance away behind Rewilding in a Listed contest at Goodwood last month, did himself few favours by racing keenly out the back in a steadily run race, so he did well to finish where he did. He doesn't look that well handicapped off a mark of 99 on this evidence, however. Official explanation: jockey said colt ran to free
Bright Horizon, raised 8lb in his bid for a hat-trick, was well backed beforehand but he made no impression from off the pace and was disappointing. (op 14-1)
Agent Archie(USA), up in trip and 5lb higher in his bid for a four-timer, was admittedly kept wide the whole way round but he faded very tamely and was another to disappoint. (op 18-1 tchd 20-1 in a place)
T/Jkpt: Not won. T/Plt: 2,689.70 to a £1 stake. Pool: £419,494.78 - 113.85 winning tickets. T/Qpdt: £116.00 to a £1 stake. Pool: £25,443.32 - 162.22 winning tickets. SP

2848 BEVERLEY (R-H)
Thursday, June 17

OFFICIAL GOING: Good to firm (9.3)
Wind: Light, half-behind. Weather: Fine and dry

3106 BEVERLEY-RACECOURSE.CO.UK MAIDEN AUCTION STKS 7f 100y
6:30 (6:32) (Class 5) 2-Y-O **£2,729** (£806; £403) **Stalls** High

Form RPR

24 **1** **Last Destination (IRE)**[19] 2522 2-9-3 0.................. SilvestreDeSousa 4 72
(N Tinkler) *trckd ldrs: hdwy 3f out: led 1 1/2f out and sn rdn: drvn ins fnl f: jst hld on* **2/1**[1]

003 **2** shd **Kissing Clara (IRE)**[21] 2457 2-8-12 0.............................. LukeMorris 12 67
(J S Moore) *led: rdn along and jnd over 2f out: hdd 1 1/2f out and sn drvn: rallied u.p and ev ch ins fnl f: kpt on* **3/1**[2]

000 **3** 4 ½ **Market Maker (IRE)**[9] 2832 2-9-3 0.................................. DavidAllan 8 61+
(T D Easterby) *in rr: pushed along 3f out: hdwy on inner 2f out: kpt on ins fnl f: nrest at fin* **33/1**

062 **4** 1 ¼ **Lady Morganna (IRE)**[8] 2867 2-8-7 0.............................. IanBrennan(5) 1 53
(Miss Gay Kelleway) *towards rr: pushed along 1/2-way: hdwy over 2f out: sn rdn and kpt on same pce* **13/2**[3]

0 **5** 4 ½ **Mr Shifter**[20] 2498 2-9-3 0.. LNewman 6 48
(Mrs L Stubbs) *cl up: effrt to chal 3f out: rdn along over 2f out: drvn wl over 1f out and sn wknd* **14/1**

040 **6** 1 ¼ **Mirror Lad**[24] 2376 2-9-3 0.. RichardSmith 7 45
(Tom Dascombe) *s.i.s and in rr: hdwy over 2f out: sn rdn and no imp* **12/1**

0 **7** 1 ¼ **Adzing (IRE)**[13] 2687 2-9-3 0.. DanielTudhope 3 42
(R A Harris) *in tch: effrt over 2f out: sn rdn and n.d* **100/1**

8 shd **Caramella Brownie** 2-8-7 0....................................... LanceBetts(5) 10 37
(T D Easterby) *dwlt: a towards rr* **16/1**

0023 **9** nse **Henrys Air**[11] 2785 2-9-3 0.. DavidNolan 2 41
(D G Bridgwater) *cl up on outer: rdn along 3f out: drvn 2f out and sn wknd* **12/1**

00 **10** 2 ½ **Miss Cosette (IRE)**[16] 2623 2-8-7 0............................ DeanHeslop(5) 11 31
(T D Barron) *a towards rr* **12/1**

0 **11** 11 **Bathwick Siesta**[9] 2839 2-9-3 0...................................... PatCosgrave 5 10
(J G Portman) *cl up: rdn along over 3f out: sn wknd* **7/1**

12 4 ½ **Henry Bond** 2-9-3 0... LeeVickers 9 —
(S A Harris) *a in rr: bhd and drvn along 3f out* **66/1**

1m 32.81s (-0.99) **Going Correction** -0.25s/f (Firm) **12** Ran SP% **125.2**
Speed ratings (Par 93): **95,94,89,88,83 81,80,80,80,77 64,59**
Tote Swingers:1&2:£2.40, 2&3:£29.90, 1&3:£23.40 CSF £8.22 TOTE £1.80: £1.02, £2.40, £19.10; EX 8.60.
Owner Killoran Civil Engineering Ltd **Bred** Pier House Stud **Trained** Langton, N Yorks
■ Stewards' Enquiry : Silvestre De Sousa two-day ban: used whip down shoulder in the forehand (Jul 1-2)

FOCUS
A fair pace and a stiff stamina test for these juveniles, none of whom had raced beyond 6f before, but no better than modest form overall and fairly limited.

NOTEBOOK
Last Destination(IRE) put his modest effort here last time from a poor draw well behind him with a game effort and, as expected, proved suited by the increased test of stamina, seeing out the trip gamely despite being firmly pressed. His future lies in modest staying nurseries, and he'd probably be one to take on if getting less of a test than he had here. (op 7-2)
Kissing Clara(IRE) confirmed that her last run had not flattered her by turning in another improved effort, always to the fore on the far rail and rallying gamely after being headed. Staying is clearly her game, and she can win one of these at around this trip while stamina remains at a premium. (op 11-4 tchd 7-2)
Market Maker(IRE) never really seemed to be racing on an even keel but still left his previous form behind despite a troubled run, staying on late to take a remote third. He has something of a pronounced knee action, and might be seen to better effect on an easier surface. (op 50-1)
Lady Morganna(IRE) is starting to look exposed and, while seeming to see out the extra distance, can't have been said to have benefited from it. (op 5-1)
Mr Shifter had been keen to post and perhaps that told on the climb to the line as he faded. Nonetheless, this was still an improvement on his debut run.
Mirror Lad, who reared leaving the stalls, plugged on for sixth without ever threatening, and didn't seem to benefit as much as seemed likely from the extra distance. Official explanation: jockey said colt reared as gates opened (op 14-1)
Henrys Air might be a bit flattered by his Wolverhampton second but wasn't helped here by racing wide throughout and left the impression 6f will suit him better. (op 11-1 tchd 14-1)
Bathwick Siesta was backed at long odds but dropped away before stamina became an issue. (op 11-1)

3107 HEARING DOGS FOUNDER BEATRICE WRIGHT CENTENARY H'CAP 7f 100y
7:00 (7:01) (Class 4) (0-80,80) 4-Y-O+ **£4,533** (£1,348; £674; £336) **Stalls** High

Form RPR

-402 **1** **Amethyst Dawn (IRE)**[8] 2850 4-8-8 **67**.............................. DavidAllan 1 74
(T D Easterby) *cl up: effrt to chal wl over 2f out: rdn wl over 1f out: styd on to ld ins fnl f: drvn and kpt on wl towards fin* **3/1**[1]

1-42 **2** nk **Ancient Cross**[19] 2532 6-9-7 **80**.............................(t) GrahamGibbons 5 86+
(M W Easterby) *hld up in rr: hdwy 3f out: swtchd lft and effrt to chse ldrs wl over 1f out: drvn to chal ent fnl f and ev ch tl nt qckn nr fin* **10/3**[2]

20U1 **3** ½ **Samarinda (USA)**[29] 2235 7-9-0 **73**.............................. TonyCulhane 2 78
(Mrs P Sly) *led: rdn along over 2f out: jnd wl over 1f out: sn drvn: hdd ins fnl f: wknd towards fin* **16/1**

1/34 **4** nse **Fadhb Ar Bith (IRE)**[37] 1997 5-8-10 **69**............................ PatCosgrave 4 74
(John A Harris) *stdd s: plld hrd and hld up in rr: hdwy on inner over 2f out: rdn to chse ldrs over 1f out: swtchd lft and drvn ins fnl f: nrest at fin* **20/1**

0051 **5** 3 **Summer Dancer (IRE)**[19] 2524 6-9-7 **80**.......................... PhillipMakin 6 77
(P T Midgley) *plld hrd: hld up in tch: effrt and sme hdwy 3f out: rdn wl over 1f out: no imp* **10/1**

0404 **6** nk **Mujaadel (USA)**[6] 2937 5-9-0 **76**............................(p) MichaelGeran(3) 7 73
(D Nicholls) *hld up in rr: hdwy over 2f out: swtchd lft and rdn wl over 1f out: sn no imp* **7/2**[3]

-316 **7** 2 ¼ **Just Five (IRE)**[43] 1826 4-9-2 **80**.......................... PatrickDonaghy(5) 9 71
(M Dods) *trckd ldrs: hdwy 3f out: rdn along 2f out: sn drvn and wkng whn n.m.r over 1f out* **11/1**

00-5 **8** 2 ¾ **Boy Blue**[45] 1754 5-8-7 **71**.. TobyAtkinson(5) 3 55
(P Salmon) *chsd ldrs: rdn along wl over 2f out: sn wknd* **7/1**

3451 **9** 3 ¼ **Apache Ridge (IRE)**[17] 2578 4-9-0 **73**..................(b) SilvestreDeSousa 8 49
(K A Ryan) *chsd ldng pair on inner: swtchd lft and hdwy wl over 2f out: rdn wl over 1f out and sn wknd* **12/1**

1m 31.05s (-2.75) **Going Correction** -0.25s/f (Firm) **9** Ran SP% **118.6**
Speed ratings (Par 105): **105,104,104,104,100 100,97,94,90**
Tote Swingers: 1&2 £2.20, 1&3 £10.00, 2&3 £9.80 CSF £13.55 CT £138.89 TOTE £3.70: £1.40, £1.70, £7.40; EX 11.00.
Owner D A West **Bred** W Kane **Trained** Great Habton, N Yorks

FOCUS
A fair handicap and despite the bunched finish probably decent form as a case can be made for each of the first four being well handicapped right now. The pace was just a fair one initially, and it was an advantage to be prominent and the form is a bit muddling.
Apache Ridge(IRE) Official explanation: trainers rep said gelding bled from nose

3108 SEE OUR OFFERS AT NEWBET.CO.UK CONDITIONS STKS 5f
7:30 (7:30) (Class 3) 3-Y-O+ **£6,799** (£2,023; £1,011; £505) **Stalls** High

Form RPR

000- **1** **Group Therapy**[259] 6427 5-9-0 100.................................... ShaneKelly 5 112
(J Noseda) *hmpd s: cl up: led over 3f out: rdn clr ent fnl f: kpt on strly* **6/1**[3]

0-50 **2** 3 ¼ **Enderby Spirit (GR)**[24] 2400 4-9-0 98.............................(v[1]) TomEaves 4 100
(B Smart) *hmpd s and towards rr: hdwy over 2f out: swtchd lft and rdn over 1f out: kpt on same pce u.p ins fnl f:* **16/1**

3211 **3** 1 **Hamish McGonagall**[12] 2759 5-9-0 105............................ DavidAllan 6 97
(T D Easterby) *awkward and wnt lft s: trckd ldng pair on inner: chsd wnr fr 1/2-way: rdn wl over 1f out and ev ch tl drvn and wknd ent fnl f* **10/11**[1]

-100 **4** ¾ **Wi Dud**[26] 2325 6-9-4 102.. PhillipMakin 2 98
(K A Ryan) *sltly hmpd s: hld up in rr: hdwy 2f out: sn rdn and no imp appr fnl f* **20/1**

-461 **5** 1 ¾ **Look Busy (IRE)**[19] 2526 5-8-10 102.............................. MarkCoumbe(5) 1 89
(A Berry) *trckd ldng pair: effrt over 2f out: rdn wl over 1f out: sn wknd* **3/1**[2]

-354 **6** 19 **Judge 'n Jury**[12] 2745 6-9-0 99 LukeMorris 3 19
(R A Harris) *led: hdd over 3f out: rdn along 1/2-way: sn wknd* **15/2**

60.47 secs (-3.03) **Going Correction** -0.375s/f (Firm) **6** Ran SP% **114.1**
Speed ratings (Par 107): **109,103,102,101,98 67**
Tote Swingers: 1&2:£10.70, 2&3:£2.50, 1&3:£2.50 CSF £84.18 TOTE £11.40: £6.10, £14.20; EX 104.00.
Owner Franconson Partners **Bred** Stratford Place Stud **Trained** Newmarket, Suffolk

FOCUS
A good conditions event run at a decent pace but, despite that, once again it proved difficult to come from off the pace. The winner looks Group class on this evidence, although these races are not always reliable.

NOTEBOOK
Group Therapy ◆ had looked better than a handicapper when winning a hot 5f handicap at Ascot last summer before his form tailed off, but he's clearly come back a better horse for the switch to Jeremy Noseda and looked a potential Listed/Group winner in the making with an very authoritative defeat of some useful rivals, never more impressive than inside the last when scooting away. Best at 5f, he'd take some catching if heading for the Listed Toteswinger City Wall Stakes at Chester next month. (op 11-2 tchd 5-1)
Enderby Spirit(GR) showed signs of revival in first-time headgear, albeit staying on only when the race was all but over. He'll be suited by return to 6f, though this trip is probably still fine for him on easier ground than he encountered here. (op 14-1)
Hamish McGonagall's last two wins have seen his official rating rise to 105 but he's going to struggle to be competitive off that if this is any guide, looking second best from a long way out before surrendering that position late as the runner-up found his stride. He's probably best on an easier track than he had here. (op 6-4)
Wi Dud had plenty to prove after a couple of tame efforts and proved once again that he isn't easy to catch right, always behind, though in his defence his task ast the weights wasn't an easy one. (tchd 25-1)
Look Busy(IRE) had won all of her four races over C&D but ran poorly for little obvious reason. She's usually reliable and will bounce back. (op 5-2 tchd 9-4)
Judge 'n Jury didn't last as long as he usually does and left the impression that something was amiss with his rider looking down when easing him off. Official explanation: jockey said gelding was unsuited by good to firm going (op 11-2)

3109 LUCKY IN LOVE NIGHT H'CAP 2m 35y
8:00 (8:03) (Class 5) (0-70,70) 4-Y-O+ **£2,914** (£867; £433; £216) **Stalls** High

Form RPR
-001 **1** **Andorn (GER)**[9] 2833 6-8-0 **54** JamesSullivan(5) 4 61
(P A Kirby) *trckd ldng pair: hdwy wl over 2f out: sn swtchd lft and rdn to chal: kpt on to ld appr fnl f: drvn out* **14/1**
2013 **2** ¾ **They All Laughed**[21] 2464 7-8-1 **55** ow1 (p) DeanHeslop(5) 3 61
(Mrs Marjorie Fife) *hld up: hdwy 5f out: led over 3f out: rdn 2f out: drvn and hdd jst over 1f out: kpt on* **11/2**[3]
-111 **3** shd **Tillietudlem (FR)**[4] 2995 4-7-13 **53** IanBrennan(5) 2 59+
(J S Goldie) *trckd ldr: rdn along: outpcd and lost pl 4f out: hdwy on outer 2f out: sn drvn: kpt on u.p fnl f* **8/15**[1]
-302 **4** 11 **Moonbeam Dancer (USA)**[22] 2445 4-9-4 **70** MartinLane(3) 1 63
(D M Simcock) *set stdy pce: rdn and qcknd 4f out: hdd over 3f out: drvn 2f out and sn wknd* **7/2**[2]

3m 39.25s (-0.55) **Going Correction** -0.25s/f (Firm) **4** Ran SP% **109.5**
Speed ratings (Par 103): **91,90,90,85**
CSF £71.40 TOTE £18.50; EX 48.20.
Owner Preesall Garage **Bred** Gestut Schlenderhan **Trained** Castleton, N Yorks

FOCUS
A modest handicap that was run at a steady pace and developed into a sprint from the home turn. The form promises to be unreliable.

3110 MATCH YOUR PADLOCK AND KEY H'CAP 1m 1f 207y
8:30 (8:30) (Class 6) (0-60,60) 4-Y-O+ **£2,104** (£626; £312; £156) **Stalls** High

Form RPR
-000 **1** **Bollin Freddie**[20] 2500 6-8-2 **51** ShaneBKelly(7) 5 64
(A J Lockwood) *mde most: rdn along and hdd briefly over 2f out: drvn to ld again wl over 1f out: clr ins fnl f: kpt on strly* **9/2**[3]
-445 **2** 3 ¼ **Rowan Lodge (IRE)**[24] 2377 8-8-13 **60** (b) IanBrennan(5) 6 67+
(Ollie Pears) *t.k.h early: hld up in rr: swtchd lft and hdwy 2f out: rdn over 1f out: drvn and kpt on ins fnl f* **7/1**
-061 **3** ½ **Highland Love**[8] 2851 5-9-2 **58** 6ex TonyCulhane 4 64
(Jedd O'Keeffe) *trckd wnr: hdwy to chal 3f out: rdn to ld briefly over 2f out: drvn and hdd wl over 1f out: kpt on same pce appr fnl f* **5/2**[1]
-004 **4** 2 ¼ **Tivers Song (USA)**[15] 2653 6-7-11 **46** oh1 (b) SoniaEaton(7) 8 47
(John A Harris) *trckd ldrs on inner: swtchd lft and hdwy wl over 2f out: rdn wl over 1f out: sn drvn and one pce* **9/1**
3000 **5** ½ **Starburst**[7] 2902 5-9-4 **60** GrahamGibbons 9 60
(Miss Gay Kelleway) *dwlt: sn chsng ldng pair: rdn along wl over 2f out: drvn over 1f out: sn one pce* **16/1**
2102 **6** 4 ½ **Blackstone Vegas**[8] 2880 4-8-4 **53** ow2 (v) LeeTopliss(7) 1 44
(D Shaw) *hld up in tch: pushed along and lost pl 4f out: effrt on outer wl over 2f out: sn rdn and no hdwy* **3/1**[2]
/50- **7** hd **Dr Light (IRE)**[472] 567 6-8-4 **46** oh1 LukeMorris 3 37
(M A Peill) *dwlt: a in rr* **33/1**
3443 **8** 1 ½ **Magic Haze**[28] 2259 4-9-0 **56** TomEaves 2 44
(Miss S E Hall) *chsd ldrs: rdn along wl over 2f out: sn wknd* **8/1**

2m 4.27s (-2.73) **Going Correction** -0.25s/f (Firm) **8** Ran SP% **114.2**
Speed ratings (Par 101): **100,97,97,95,94 91,91,89**
Tote Swingers:1&2:£5.00, 2&3:£5.00, 1&3:£2.40 CSF £35.57 CT £94.66 TOTE £6.20: £2.60, £1.30, £1.70; EX 18.80.
Owner Highgreen Partnership **Bred** Sir Neil & Exors Of Late Lady Westbrook **Trained** Brawby, N Yorks

FOCUS
A modest handicap where once again the early pace wasn't strong and it proved a huge advantage to race handily. The first three ran close to recent marks and the form looks sound.
Blackstone Vegas Official explanation: jockey said gelding hung right handed in straight

3111 BUSES INTO TOWN AFTER RACING MAIDEN STKS 5f
9:00 (9:01) (Class 5) 3-4-Y-O **£2,590** (£770; £385; £192) **Stalls** High

Form RPR
-400 **1** **Mercers Row**[23] 2426 3-9-3 62 DanielTudhope 10 66
(A Dickman) *mde all: rdn clr wl over 1f out: kpt on* **14/1**
25-6 **2** 1 ¼ **Melundy**[61] 1402 3-8-7 70 JamesSullivan(5) 9 57+
(Mrs L Stubbs) *towards rr: hdwy 2f out: swtchd ins and rdn wl over 1f out: styd on strly ins fnl f* **11/1**
4 **3** nk **Panama Jack**[17] 2609 3-9-0 0 BarryMcHugh(3) 8 60
(R A Fahey) *in tch: hdwy 2f out: rdn to chse wnr ins fnl f: drvn and one pce towards fin* **11/4**[3]
-253 **4** nk **Ravenfield (IRE)**[13] 2695 3-9-3 68 PhillipMakin 5 59+
(D H Brown) *in tch: effrt 2f out: rdn and n.m.r wl over 1f out: swtchd rt and styd on ins fnl f: nrest at fin* **2/1**[1]
2205 **5** ¾ **Fine Silk (USA)**[12] 2751 4-8-13 64 (p) TobyAtkinson(5) 2 54
(M G Quinlan) *chsd ldrs on outer: rdn along 2f out: drvn and one pce ent fnl f* **16/1**
442 **6** 1 ¼ **Gold Gleam (USA)**[12] 2741 3-9-3 70 ShaneKelly 4 52
(J Noseda) *cl up: rdn along 2f out: sn drvn and wknd ent fnl f* **9/4**[2]
-6 **7** 1 **Red Roar (IRE)**[19] 2530 3-8-7 0 MarkCoumbe(5) 7 44
(A Berry) *a towards rr* **66/1**
440- **8** 9 **Menediva**[313] 4800 3-8-12 48 DuranFentiman 3 11
(L A Mullaney) *chsd ldng pair: rdn along 2f out: sn drvn and wknd* **100/1**
0 **9** 1 **Best Known Secret (IRE)**[19] 2535 4-9-4 0 TomEaves 6 10
(C C Bealby) *chsd ldrs on inner: rdn along 2f out: sn drvn and wknd over 1f out* **50/1**
10 1 ¼ **Tombellini (IRE)** 3-9-0 0 MichaelGeran(3) 1 8
(D Nicholls) *swvd bdly lft s: a in rr* **20/1**
11 2 ¼ **J'Amour Dance** 3-9-3 0 PatrickMathers 11 —
(C J Teague) *s.i.s: a in rr* **50/1**

62.73 secs (-0.77) **Going Correction** -0.375s/f (Firm)
WFA 3 from 4yo 6lb **11** Ran SP% **122.8**
Speed ratings (Par 103): **91,89,88,88,86 84,83,68,67,65 61**
Tote Swingers:1&2:£13.20, 2&3:£6.60, 1&3:£15.20 CSF £157.28 TOTE £20.10: £4.40, £2.70, £1.80; EX 132.90 Place 6: £2562.92 Place 5: £1502.45.
Owner Allan Dickman - Keith Fitzsimons **Bred** Heather Raw **Trained**

FOCUS
Not much between the first seven at the end of a modest maiden, and not form to be getting carried away with. Once again, the winner made all the running and, with the third and fourth disappointing, the runner-up is probably the best guide to the form.
Mercers Row Official explanation: trainer had no explanation for the apparent improvement in form
Panama Jack Official explanation: trainers rep said gelding bled from nose
T/Plt: £1,679.70 to a £1 stake. Pool: £42,454.50 - 18.45 winning tickets. T/Qpdt: £680.00 to a £1 stake. Pool: £2,756.85 - 3.00 winning tickets. JR

2957 LEICESTER (R-H)
Thursday, June 17

OFFICIAL GOING: Good to firm (good in places; 8.7)
Wind: Light, half-against. Weather: Sunny

3112 GREENSHIRES MAIDEN STKS 7f 9y
6:40 (6:40) (Class 4) 2-Y-O **£5,180** (£1,541; £770; £384) **Stalls** Low

Form RPR
5 **1** **Stentorian (IRE)**[24] 2389 2-9-0 0 RoystonFfrench 8 76+
(M Johnston) *w ldr: rdn over 2f out: drvn over 1f out: edgd rt fnl f: styd on to ld fnl 75yds* **15/2**[2]
52 **2** ½ **Greek Islands (IRE)**[16] 2621 2-9-0 0 TedDurcan 6 75
(Mahmood Al Zarooni) *trckd ldr: rdn over 2f out: led over 1f out: edgd rt and hdd fnl 75yds* **4/11**[1]
6 **3** 5 **Il Battista**[13] 2701 2-9-0 0 JamesDoyle 3 62
(A J McCabe) *hld up: rdn over 2f out: kpt on wl fnl f: tk 3rd nr line* **66/1**
0 **4** shd **Windward Islands**[35] 2059 2-8-7 0 AntiocoMurgia(7) 7 62
(Mahmood Al Zarooni) *led: rdn over 2f out: hdd over 1f out: no ex fnl f: rdr dropped hands nr fin and ct for 3rd nr line* **12/1**
0 **5** 2 ¾ **Bankroller**[34] 2077 2-9-0 0 SaleemGolam 2 55
(J G Portman) *trckd ldr: rdn over 2f out: sn one pce* **80/1**
6 6 **Josie's Dream (IRE)** 2-9-0 0 KevinGhunowa 5 39
(F J Brennan) *trckd ldr: rdn over 2f out: sn wknd* **50/1**
0 **7** 5 **Canada Fleet (CAN)**[19] 2547 2-9-0 0 DaraghO'Donohoe 4 26
(E A L Dunlop) *hld up: chsd along 1/2-way: sn no imp* **10/1**[3]
8 8 **Jeeran** 2-9-0 0 ChrisCatlin 1 —
(C E Brittain) *chsd along 1/2-way: sn wknd* **16/1**

1m 27.27s (1.07) **Going Correction** +0.05s/f (Good) **8** Ran SP% **112.4**
Speed ratings (Par 95): **95,94,88,88,85 78,72,63**
Tote Swingers: 1&2 £1.30, 1&3 £12.60, 2&3 £7.40 CSF £10.31 TOTE £6.10: £1.70, £1.02, £12.70; EX 13.20.
Owner Sheikh Hamdan Bin Mohammed Al Maktoum **Bred** Ceka Ireland Limited **Trained** Middleham Moor, N Yorks
■ Stewards' Enquiry : Antioco Murgia ten-day ban: failed to ride out for 3rd (Jul 1-10)

FOCUS
A dry night and warm day and it was no surprise conditions were on the quick side. An uncompetitive maiden where the first two finished clear of the field and the runner-up sets the level.

NOTEBOOK
Stentorian(IRE) ◆, too green to do himself justice over 6f at this track on his debut, was easy to back but showed much improved form and a good attitude to get off the mark over this longer trip. He'll be suited by 1m in due course, is in good hands and is the type to progress again. (op 6-1 tchd 8-1)
Greek Islands(IRE), up in trip, looked the one to beat on his run at this track behind subsequent Coventry third Roayh and, although well backed, failed to build on that after racing keenly and showing a tendency to edge right. He pulled clear of the remainder and, while this was a bit disappointing, he remains capable of picking up a similar event. Easier conditions may be more to his liking. (op 4-9, tchd 1-2 in places)
Il Battista bettered the form of his racecourse debut over this longer trip. He will be suited by further still but will be of more interest in ordinary nursery company granted a sufficient test of stamina. (op 50-1)
Windward Islands had the run of the race and bettered the form shown in stronger company on his debut, despite his rider seemingly taking things easy and getting caught for third in the last stride. Run-of-the-mill nurseries will be the way forward with him. (tchd 10-1)
Bankroller again hinted at ability at a moderate level but, while he is likely to remain vulnerable in this type of race, he may do better in nurseries or when dropped to selling or claiming company. (op 66-1)

3113 SYTNERS (S) STKS 1m 1f 218y
7:10 (7:10) (Class 6) 3-Y-O **£1,942** (£578; £288; £144) **Stalls** High

Form RPR
3064 **1** **Dane Cottage**[21] 2460 3-8-12 55 ChrisCatlin 6 68
(Miss Gay Kelleway) *midfield: hdwy 3f out: shkn up to ld wl over 1f out: sn clr: easily* **5/1**[2]
33-0 **2** 11 **Admiral Breese**[16] 2619 3-9-3 54 (p) JerryO'Dwyer 11 51
(R Hollinshead) *trckd ldr: hdwy to chal over 3f out: no match for wnr fnl 2f* **15/2**
4003 **3** 1 ¾ **Danceintothelight**[13] 2724 3-9-3 63 StevieDonohoe 5 48
(K A Ryan) *midfield: hdwy over 3f out: rdn to chal over 2f out: one pce* **5/1**[2]

5265 **4** *2* **Battle Study (IRE)**[13] 2704 3-8-12 61 DeclanCannon(5) 8 44
(A J McCabe) *hld up: chsd along over 4f out: rdn and hdwy 2f out: sn one pce* **11/2**[3]
0-00 **5** *1 1/2* **Suzi's Challenger**[14] 2675 3-8-12 45 (v[1]) KirstyMilczarek 3 36
(H J Collingridge) *s.i.s: rdn along over 3f out: mod late hdwy* **50/1**
4664 **6** *shd* **Baggsy (IRE)**[13] 2724 3-8-12 48 (v[1]) CathyGannon 13 35
(Miss J Feilden) *sn led: rdn along 4f out: hdd wl over 1f out: sn wknd* **16/1**
4560 **7** *2 1/2* **Hill Of Miller (IRE)**[9] 2844 3-9-3 60 (t) TedDurcan 1 35
(Rae Guest) *midfield: brief hdwy over 3f out: sn rdn and no imp* **10/1**
0001 **8** *nk* **Fasette**[8] 2878 3-8-7 54 AshleyMorgan(5) 4 30
(M H Tompkins) *hld up: hdwy towards outer over 3f out: sn drvn and no imp* **11/4**[1]
500 **9** *28* **Yorksters Prince (IRE)**[21] 2477 3-9-8 58 (v[1]) AdamKirby 2 —
(G Prodromou) *trckd ldrs: rdn over 3f out: sn wknd: eased fnl 2f* **20/1**
-400 **10** *1/2* **Springwell Giant (IRE)**[30] 2221 3-8-11 53 ow1 ConorQuish(7) 12 —
(A J McCabe) *w ldr: rdn over 4f out: edgd lft and wknd fnl 3f* **33/1**
-443 **11** *51* **Shercon (IRE)**[11] 2787 3-9-3 49 DaraghO'Donohoe 7 —
(N Tinkler) *t.o 1/2-way* **18/1**

2m 5.73s (-2.17) **Going Correction** -0.275s/f (Firm) **11 Ran SP% 117.0**
Speed ratings (Par 97): **97,88,86,85,84 83,81,81,59,58 18**
Tote Swingers: 1&2 £12.50, 1&3 £9.90, 2&3 £12.60 CSF £41.29 TOTE £12.60: £3.60, £3.30, £3.00; EX 36.40.There was no bid for the winner. Danceintothelight was claimed by M. D. Hammond for £7,000.
Owner Holistic Racing Ltd **Bred** Winterbeck Manor Stud **Trained** Exning, Suffolk
■ Stewards' Enquiry : Kirsty Milczarek one-day ban: used whip down shoulder in the forehand (Jul 1)

FOCUS
A very ordinary seller but what had looked a fairly open event was turned into a procession by the wide-margin winner. The pace was reasonable and the form is rated at something like face value with the runner-up the best guide.
Baggsy(IRE) Official explanation: jockey said filly hung right
Shercon(IRE) Official explanation: jockey said gelding moved poorly throughout

3114 GREENSHIRES H'CAP 5f 2y
7:40 (7:40) (Class 4) (0-80,80) 3-Y-0+ **£6,308** (£1,888; £944; £472; £235) **Stalls Low**

Form RPR
0-10 **1** **Medici Time**[33] 2136 5-9-10 **76** (v) TedDurcan 10 91
(T D Easterby) *hld up in tch: led 1/2-way: r.o wl* **7/1**[3]
3102 **2** *3 1/2* **Solemn**[4] 2997 5-10-0 **80** (b) LiamKeniry 7 82
(J M Bradley) *chsd ldrs: rdn over 1f out: styd on same pce fnl f* **5/2**[1]
1410 **3** *hd* **Lucky Dan (IRE)**[5] 2982 4-9-11 **77** StevieDonohoe 11 79
(Paul Green) *hld up: outpcd 1/2-way: hdwy over 1f out: r.o: nt trble ldrs* **9/2**[2]
-600 **4** *1 1/4* **Triple Dream**[5] 2973 5-9-7 **76** (p) JackDean(3) 5 73
(J M Bradley) *hld up: rdn over 1f out: styd on: nrest at fin* **9/1**
250- **5** *shd* **Bahamian Ballet**[302] 5148 8-9-3 **69** RichardMullen 3 66
(E S McMahon) *chsd ldrs: rdn over 1f out: no ex fnl f* **25/1**
0004 **6** *1/2* **Mandurah (IRE)**[7] 2883 6-9-8 **74** J-PGuillambert 2 69
(B P J Baugh) *s.i.s: hdwy 1/2-way: rdn over 1f out: styd on same pce* **7/1**[3]
-534 **7** *1/2* **Our Piccadilly (IRE)**[27] 2280 5-9-8 **77** Louis-PhilippeBeuzelin(3) 6 70
(W S Kittow) *mid-div: outpcd 1/2-way: hdwy over 1f out: no ex fnl f* **8/1**
0640 **8** *1 1/4* **Incomparable**[5] 2973 5-9-12 **78** (bt) ChrisCatlin 1 67
(J A Glover) *led to 1/2-way: sn rdn: wknd fnl f* **14/1**
00- **9** *1/2* **Drifting Gold**[245] 6801 6-9-4 **70** (b) AdamKirby 4 57
(C G Cox) *hld up: hdwy u.p over 1f out: wknd fnl f* **25/1**
0361 **10** *nk* **Thoughtsofstardom**[10] 2809 7-8-4 **63** 6ex (be) LeonnaMayor(7) 8 49
(P S McEntee) *w ldr tl rdn 1/2-way: wknd fnl f* **33/1**
0315 **11** *1* **Perlachy**[19] 2528 6-9-4 **70** (v) KirstyMilczarek 9 52
(D Shaw) *prom: pushed along 1/2-way: wknd fnl f* **18/1**

59.54 secs (-0.46) **Going Correction** +0.05s/f (Good) **11 Ran SP% 115.4**
Speed ratings (Par 105): **105,99,99,97,96 96,95,93,92,92 90**
Tote Swingers: 1&2 £8.80, 1&3 £8.50, 2&3 £3.50 CSF £23.77 CT £88.44 TOTE £11.00: £3.50, £1.10, £1.50; EX 31.20.
Owner Mrs C A Hodgetts **Bred** Mrs Fiona Denniff **Trained** Great Habton, N Yorks

FOCUS
Exposed performers in a fair handicap. The gallop was reasonable but those held up were at a disadvantage, the placed horses are rated 5lb off their recent best and the form could be rated higher.
Perlachy Official explanation: jockey said gelding lost its action

3115 NEXT FILLIES' H'CAP 5f 218y
8:10 (8:10) (Class 5) (0-75,74) 3-Y-0+ **£3,238** (£963; £481; £240) **Stalls Low**

Form RPR
-666 **1** **Revue Princess (IRE)**[24] 2396 5-9-1 **57** (b) TedDurcan 1 64
(T D Easterby) *chsd ldr: led over 3f out: rdn and hdd over 1f out: rallied to ld nr fin* **11/1**
-501 **2** *3/4* **Cape Melody**[5] 2957 4-10-4 **74** 6ex (b) TravisBlock 9 78
(H Morrison) *s.i.s: sn pushed along in rr: rdn and r.o wl ins fnl f: nt quite get up* **3/1**[1]
5610 **3** *nse* **Plumage**[5] 2964 5-9-2 **63** LeeNewnes(5) 7 67
(Miss Tor Sturgis) *chsd ldrs: led over 1f out: rdn and hung rt ins fnl f: hdd nr fin* **12/1**
4362 **4** *nk* **Mrs Boss**[14] 2679 3-9-0 **66** JamesMillman(3) 5 67
(B R Millman) *chsd ldrs: rdn over 1f out: carried rt ins fnl f: r.o* **33/1**
1306 **5** *1/2* **Athboy Auction**[27] 2298 5-8-2 **51** oh5 NatashaEaton(7) 2 52
(H J Collingridge) *chsd ldrs: rdn over 1f out: r.o* **50/1**
0160 **6** *2* **White Shift (IRE)**[13] 2689 4-10-0 **70** J-PGuillambert 4 64
(P Howling) *led: hdd over 3f out: rdn over 1f out: no ex ins fnl f* **50/1**
020 **7** *3/4* **Ramamara (IRE)**[17] 2588 3-9-7 **70** JamesDoyle 8 59
(P D Evans) *hld up: rdn over 1f out: styd on ins fnl f: nvr trbld ldrs* **40/1**
4-14 **8** *1/2* **Rosedale**[18] 2566 3-9-0 **63** LiamKeniry 10 50
(J A R Toller) *hld up: shkn up over 2f out: nt clr run over 1f out: swtchd rt and r.o ins fnl f: nvr trbld ldrs* **7/2**[2]
-022 **9** *3/4* **Mrs Mogg**[17] 2588 3-9-1 **64** RichardKingscote 6 49
(Tom Dascombe) *trckd ldrs: rdn over 2f out: wknd ins fnl f* **5/1**
450- **10** *nk* **Sweet Gale (IRE)**[248] 6726 6-9-13 **69** AndreaAtzeni 11 55
(Mike Murphy) *hld up: rdn over 2f out: hdwy on outside over 1f out: wknd ins fnl f* **10/1**
-062 **11** *6* **Farmers Wish (IRE)**[7] 2904 3-9-7 **73** JackDean(3) 3 35
(J L Spearing) *chsd ldrs: rdn over 2f out: wknd fnl f* **9/2**[3]

1m 12.64s (-0.36) **Going Correction** +0.05s/f (Good)
WFA 3 from 4yo+ 7lb **11 Ran SP% 116.5**
Speed ratings (Par 100): **104,103,102,102,101 99,98,97,96,96 88**
Tote Swingers: 1&2 £11.00, 1&3 £20.90, 2&3 £22.10 CSF £42.91 CT £416.31 TOTE £17.50: £7.20, £1.70, £4.50; EX 72.30.
Owner S A Heley **Bred** Raymond Shanahan **Trained** Great Habton, N Yorks
■ Stewards' Enquiry : Lee Newnes two-day ban: careless riding (Jul 1-2)

FOCUS
No more than a fair fillies' handicap and one in which the gallop was reasonable. The form is modest but sound, with those in the frame behind the winner to their marks.

3116 VANTIS CORPORATE CHALLENGE MAIDEN STKS 1m 3f 183y
8:40 (8:41) (Class 5) 3-Y-0+ **£3,238** (£963; £481; £240) **Stalls High**

Form RPR
033 **1** **Najam**[50] 1627 3-8-5 75 ChrisCatlin 10 74
(C E Brittain) *mid-div: hdwy u.p over 2f out: styd on to ld nr fin* **20/1**
4 **2** *shd* **Fascination (IRE)**[55] 1501 3-8-5 0 HayleyTurner 2 74
(M L W Bell) *racd keenly and sn trcking ldrs: rdn to ld ins fnl f: hdd nr fin* **11/4**[2]
0-0 **3** *1 3/4* **Istidlaal**[45] 1757 3-8-10 0 RichardMullen 13 76
(Sir Michael Stoute) *sn prom: rdn over 3f out: styd on* **20/1**
3 **4** *hd* **Ceoil An Aith (IRE)**[12] 2767 4-9-5 0 RoystonFfrench 12 71
(M Johnston) *led: hdd over 5f out: sn rdn: styd on* **12/1**
23-3 **5** *nk* **Super Collider**[40] 1912 3-8-10 80 PhilipRobinson 4 75
(M A Jarvis) *a.p: chsd ldr over 3f out: led over 1f out: rdn and hdd ins fnl f: styd on same pce* **5/4**[1]
6 **6** *nk* **Charming Man**[27] 2290 3-8-3 0 AntiocoMurgia(7) 7 75+
(Mahmood Al Zarooni) *s.i.s: hld up: hdwy u.p fr over 2f out: edgd rt ins fnl f: styd on* **16/1**
05 **7** *1 1/2* **Najlaa**[21] 2463 3-8-5 0 TadhgO'Shea 1 67
(W J Haggas) *sn chsng ldr: led over 5f out: rdn and hdd over 1f out: no ex wl ins fnl f* **10/1**
5 **8** *2* **Kalamill (IRE)**[27] 2281 3-8-10 65 LiamKeniry 8 69
(S Lycett) *broke wl: sn stdd and lost pl: hdwy 3f out: nt clr run over 1f out: styd on: nvr nr to chal* **100/1**
00 **9** *19* **Four Quartets (GER)**[4] 2994 4-9-10 0 FrannyNorton 3 39
(D Shaw) *hld up: nvr on terms* **250/1**
0 **10** *5* **Kuantan Two (IRE)**[8] 2860 3-8-10 0 StevieDonohoe 5 31
(P F I Cole) *mid-div: rdn 1/2-way: wknd over 3f out* **80/1**
0-04 **11** *15* **Juwireya**[17] 2585 3-8-5 73 KirstyMilczarek 11 2
(M P Tregoning) *hld up: rdn over 6f out: bhd fnl 4f: t.o* **9/1**[3]
0-0 **12** *1 3/4* **Amylyn**[24] 2390 3-8-5 0 DaraghO'Donohoe 9 —
(J R Holt) *dwlt: a bhd: t.o* **300/1**

2m 30.67s (-3.23) **Going Correction** -0.275s/f (Firm)
WFA 3 from 4yo 14lb **12 Ran SP% 116.3**
Speed ratings (Par 103): **99,98,97,97,97 97,96,94,82,78 68,67**
Tote Swingers: 1&2 £12.70, 1&3 £22.50, 2&3 £13.10 CSF £72.16 TOTE £13.30: £3.20, £1.10, £5.10; EX 74.10.
Owner Saeed Manana **Bred** Rabbah Bloodstock Limited **Trained** Newmarket, Suffolk

FOCUS
No more than a fair maiden in which the gallop was an ordinary one and the first six finished in a bit of a heap. The form is rated at face value with the second and fourth to their debut form.
Kalamill(IRE) Official explanation: jockey said gelding hung right
Juwireya Official explanation: jockey said filly never travelled

3117 DAVID WILSON HOMES H'CAP 1m 60y
9:10 (9:10) (Class 4) (0-85,84) 3-Y-0+ **£5,828** (£1,734; £866; £432) **Stalls High**

Form RPR
4244 **1** **Heading To First**[51] 1608 3-8-4 **70** ow2 (p) ChrisCatlin 1 73
(C E Brittain) *racd keenly: led 7f out at stdy pce: qcknd over 2f out: rdn over 1f out: styd on gamely* **6/1**
-260 **2** *hd* **Chapter And Verse (IRE)**[21] 2472 4-9-10 **80** AndreaAtzeni 3 84
(Mike Murphy) *hld up in tch: rdn over 1f out: r.o* **9/2**[3]
4531 **3** *3/4* **Flowing Cape (IRE)**[5] 2959 5-9-6 **81** 6ex PaulPickard(5) 7 83
(R Hollinshead) *hld up: pushed along over 2f out: hdwy and nt clr run fr over 1f out tl swtchd rt and r.o wl ins fnl f: nt rch ldrs* **9/4**[1]
0-64 **4** *1* **Bold Cross (IRE)**[13] 2705 7-9-6 **76** PaulFitzsimons 4 76
(E G Bevan) *s.i.s: hld up: hdwy over 4f out: rdn over 2f out: edgd rt over 1f out: styd on* **9/2**[3]
0333 **5** *hd* **My Gacho (IRE)**[22] 2428 8-10-0 **84** (v) J-PGuillambert 2 84
(M Johnston) *chsd ldrs: rdn over 1f out: styd on* **4/1**[2]
000- **6** *2 1/4* **Flying Valentino**[230] 7158 6-9-4 **74** StevieDonohoe 5 68
(Ian Williams) *hld up in tch: rdn over 1f out: no ex wl ins fnl f* **40/1**
0065 **7** *2* **Negotiation (IRE)**[5] 2959 4-9-2 **72** FrannyNorton 6 62
(M Quinn) *led: hdd 7f out: chsd wnr: rdn over 2f out: wknd ins fnl f* **14/1**

1m 44.28s (-0.82) **Going Correction** -0.275s/f (Firm)
WFA 3 from 4yo+ 10lb **7 Ran SP% 110.5**
Speed ratings (Par 105): **93,92,92,91,90 88,86**
Tote Swingers:1&2:£6.00, 2&3:£3.90, 1&3:£3.60. CSF £30.58 TOTE £4.40: £1.60, £4.70; EX 36.40 Place 6: £140.25 Place 5: £116.68 .
Owner Saeed Manana **Bred** Darley **Trained** Newmarket, Suffolk

FOCUS
Exposed performers in a reasonable handicap but the steady pace, and the fact that several failed to settle means this race is not a reliable form-guide, despite the placed horses being to their turf marks.
Flowing Cape(IRE) ◆ Official explanation: jockey said gelding was denied a clear run
T/Plt: £195.00 to a £1 stake. Pool:£41,286.69 - 154.53 winning tickets. T/Qpdt: £21.50 to a £1 stake. Pool:£3,800.86 - 130.62 winning tickets. CR

3086 RIPON (R-H)
Thursday, June 17
OFFICIAL GOING: Good (good to firm in places; 8.5)
Wind: almost nil Weather: fine and sunny, very warm

3118 E B F BET BRITISH WITH TOTEPOOL MAIDEN STKS 6f
2:10 (2:10) (Class 5) 2-Y-0 **£3,885** (£1,156; £577; £288) **Stalls Low**

Form RPR
1 **Magic Casement** 2-9-3 0 AdrianNicholls 5 80+
(D Nicholls) *chsd ldrs: swtchd rt over 1f out: styd on to ld last 150yds: kpt on wl* **10/1**
6 **2** *2 1/2* **King Of Aquitaine (IRE)**[40] 1905 2-9-3 0 StephenCraine 6 72
(K A Ryan) *w ldr: led over 3f out: hdd and no ex ins fnl f* **10/1**
3 *4* **Misscomplacent** 2-8-9 0 BarryMcHugh(3) 8 55
(Mrs A Duffield) *chsd ldrs: one pce fnl f* **20/1**
40 **4** *2 1/4* **Mr Optimistic**[21] 2448 2-9-3 0 TonyHamilton 3 53+
(R A Fahey) *s.i.s: hdwy over 2f out: kpt on steadily fnl f* **22/1**
5 *1/2* **Reason To Believe (IRE)** 2-9-3 0 SebSanders 12 52
(B M R Haslam) *mid-div: effrt on outer over 2f out: chsng ldrs over 1f out: fdd* **33/1**
22 **6** *3 1/4* **Sea Flower (IRE)**[15] 2654 2-8-12 0 DavidAllan 4 37
(T D Easterby) *led: hdd over 2f out: wknd over 1f out* **10/11**[1]

2664 **7** 2 1/4 **Muse To Use**[8] [2848] 2-8-12 0 PatrickMathers 1 30
(I W McInnes) *mid-div: drvn over 2f out: nvr a factor* **125/1**

8 1/2 **Perignon (IRE)** 2-9-3 0 PJMcDonald 13 34
(G A Swinbank) *s.i.s: in rr: hdwy over 1f out: nvr nr ldrs* **33/1**

9 6 **Volcanic Ash (USA)** 2-9-3 0 AndrewElliott 2 16
(M Johnston) *chsd ldrs: reminders 3f out: sn wknd* **7/1**[3]

10 nk **Salagadoola** 2-8-7 0 LanceBetts[(5)] 10 10
(T D Easterby) *v.s.a: sme hdwy over 2f out: sn lost pl* **80/1**

11 3 1/2 **Countess Cheval (IRE)** 2-8-9 0 KellyHarrison[(3)] 9 —
(B M R Haslam) *hld up in rr: hmpd over 4f out: nvr on terms* **125/1**

12 3 **Slimline** 2-9-3 0 DuranFentiman 11 —
(T D Easterby) *s.i.s: a in rr* **80/1**

13 11 **Five To Five** 2-9-3 0 RobertWinston 7 —
(T P Tate) *sn drvn along towards rr: wnt rt and lost pl over 4f out: sn bhd: eased ins fnl f* **6/1**[2]

1m 12.86s (-0.14) **Going Correction** -0.25s/f (Firm) **13** Ran SP% **116.4**
Speed ratings (Par 93): **90,86,81,78,77 73,70,69,61,61 56,52,37**
toteswingers: 1&2 £13.10, 1&3 £23.90, 2&3 £33.40 CSF £95.65 TOTE £15.90: £2.90, £2.40, £5.80.
Owner Middleham Park Racing XXXVII **Bred** Fifehead Farms M C Denning **Trained** Sessay, N Yorks

FOCUS
An ordinary juvenile maiden and the front pair drew clear. The winner scored decisively but the form is rated around the averages with not much to go on.

NOTEBOOK
Magic Casement, an already gelded son of Proclamation who has suffered from sore shins, comes from a yard who can ready a newcomer and he picked up really well once switched, making a tidy winning debut. He should stay 7f before long, but looks best kept to this distance for the time being. (op 9-1 tchd 12-1)
King Of Aquitaine(IRE) improved on his debut effort when looking green at Haydock, showing good speed and keeping on to finish well clear of the third. He should progress again. (op 9-1)
Misscomplacent, related to a 6f 2-y-o scorer and representing a yard that had one win on its debut earlier in the week, showed enough to suggest she can find a race if improving. (op 12-1)
Mr Optimistic caught the eye staying on late and will be of obvious interest once contesting nurseries. (op 18-1)
Reason To Believe(IRE), bred to make a 2-y-o at about this trip, hinted at ability and should improve.
Sea Flower(IRE) proved bitterly disappointing. Runner-up on each of her first two starts (both at this course), she again showed good speed, but started to look vulnerable from halfway, and was beaten running into the final 2f. This clearly wasn't her form and she was reported to have run flat. Official explanation: jockey said filly ran flat (op Evens)
Volcanic Ash(USA), half-brother to a minor winner in the US, comes from a yard whose juveniles have yet to get going and he looked clueless. Better can be expected next time and he should improve for a longer trip. (op 15-2 tchd 8-1)

3119 BRENTWOOD DESIGN PARTNERSHIP H'CAP — 5f
2:45 (2:46) (Class 5) (0-75,72) 3-Y-O+ **£2,914** (£867; £433; £216) **Stalls** Low

Form — RPR

0343 **1** **Cape Royal**[16] [2622] 10-9-11 **69** (bt) PatCosgrave 6 78
(J M Bradley) *mde all: hung rt over 1f out: hld on wl towards fin* **14/1**

0-02 **2** 3/4 **Wicked Wilma (IRE)**[13] [2695] 6-8-12 **61** MarkCoumbe[(5)] 9 68
(A Berry) *chsd ldrs: edgd lft 1f out: kpt on same pce wl ins fnl f* **25/1**

0532 **3** 3/4 **Hazelrigg (IRE)**[3] [3024] 5-9-8 **66** (vt) DavidAllan 4 70
(T D Easterby) *mid-div: effrt and hung rt over 2f out: nt clr run: swtchd ins fnl f: kpt on* **8/11**[1]

0504 **4** 1 1/4 **The Tatling (IRE)**[16] [2622] 13-9-9 **70** JackDean[(3)] 12 70+
(J M Bradley) *in rr div: hdwy over 2f out: kpt on same pce ins fnl f* **16/1**

1600 **5** nk **Dispol Grand (IRE)**[19] [2528] 4-9-3 **66** PaulPickard[(5)] 13 64
(P T Midgley) *w wnr: n.m.r jst ins fnl f: kpt on same pce* **33/1**

1000 **6** 1 1/2 **Lord Of The Reins (IRE)**[19] [2528] 6-9-9 **67** SebSanders 5 65+
(J G Given) *bmpd sn after s: in rr div: hdwy over 2f out: keeping on same pce whn hmpd ins fnl f* **33/1**

-306 **7** 3/4 **Angelo Poliziano**[13] [2695] 4-9-5 **63** (b) StephenCraine 7 53+
(Mrs A Duffield) *swvd lft s: in rr: nt clr run on ins over 1f out: swtchd rt jst ins fnl f: nvr nr ldrs* **28/1**

22-0 **8** hd **Liberty Ship**[47] [1711] 5-9-9 **67** (bt) PJMcDonald 1 57
(J D Bethell) *mid-div: drvn over 2f out: nvr a factor: sddle slipped* **16/1**

2500 **9** nse **Kyzer Chief**[14] [2669] 5-9-1 **59** (v[1]) PatrickMathers 3 48
(R E Barr) *chsd ldrs: wknd over 1f out* **18/1**

2405 **10** 3 1/2 **Lucky Art (USA)**[16] [2626] 4-9-5 **68** (p) JamesSullivan[(5)] 8 45
(Mrs R A Carr) *chsd ldrs on wd outside: hung rt and lost pl over 1f out* **15/2**[3]

0-13 **11** nk **Sir Louis**[65] [1280] 3-9-0 **64** TonyHamilton 11 40
(R A Fahey) *wnt lft s: sn prom: lost pl over 1f out* **6/1**[2]

120/ **12** 6 **Gramm**[552] [7653] 7-8-6 **57** DavidSimmonson[(7)] 10 11
(G P Kelly) *hmpd sn after s: in rr: bhd fnl 2f* **66/1**

59.01 secs (-1.69) **Going Correction** -0.25s/f (Firm)
WFA 3 from 4yo+ 6lb **12** Ran SP% **122.3**
Speed ratings (Par 103): **103,101,100,98,98 95,94,94,94,88 88,78**
toteswingers: 1&2 £14.20, 1&3 £3.90, 2&3 £8.50 CSF £329.39 CT £588.16 TOTE £13.90: £3.40, £3.90, £1.10.
Owner E A Hayward **Bred** D R Brotherton **Trained** Sedbury, Gloucs
■ Stewards' Enquiry : Mark Coumbe one-day ban: careless riding (Jul 4)

FOCUS
A modest sprint handicap but straightforward form rated around the first two.
Hazelrigg(IRE) Official explanation: jockey said gelding hung badly right throughout
Lord Of The Reins(IRE) Official explanation: jockey said gelding was denied a clear run
Liberty Ship Official explanation: jockey said saddle slipped

3120 SIS OB SERVICES CLAIMING STKS — 6f
3:20 (3:20) (Class 5) 3-Y-O+ **£2,590** (£770; £385; £192) **Stalls** Low

Form — RPR

2011 **1** **Abbondanza (IRE)**[21] [2453] 7-9-2 79 AdrianNicholls 2 79
(D Nicholls) *trckd ldrs: drvn to ld jst ins fnl f: kpt on wl towards fin* **1/2**[1]

301 **2** 1/2 **Caprio (IRE)**[14] [2668] 5-9-8 84 PatCosgrave 3 83
(J R Boyle) *in rr: hdwy over 2f out: upsides ins fnl f: no ex* **11/4**[2]

5-15 **3** 1 1/2 **Ace Of Spies (IRE)**[24] [2378] 5-8-10 60 SilvestreDeSousa 5 66
(G A Harker) *led tl over 3f out: led over 2f out: hdd jst ins fnl f: kpt on same pce* **10/1**[3]

0-00 **4** 3 1/2 **Errigal Lad**[7] [2883] 5-9-0 75 (p) AndrewElliott 6 59
(J Balding) *w ldr: led over 3f out: hdd over 2f out: outpcd appr fnl f* **22/1**

5060 **5** 16 **Kheskianto (IRE)**[24] [2383] 4-8-8 52 (p) JackMitchell 7 2
(M C Chapman) *chsd ldrs: drvn over 3f out: hung lft and lost pl over 1f out: eased ins fnl f* **50/1**

1m 11.61s (-1.39) **Going Correction** -0.25s/f (Firm)
WFA 3 from 4yo+ 7lb **5** Ran SP% **108.7**
Speed ratings (Par 103): **99,98,96,91,70**
CSF £2.04 TOTE £1.60: £1.60, £1.10; EX 2.10.
Owner Middleham Park Racing XXXI **Bred** M Nolan **Trained** Sessay, N Yorks

FOCUS
Not a bad little claimer with the winner rated in line with recent for. The proximity of the third limits things though.

3121 LADIES DAY H'CAP — 1m 1f
4:00 (4:00) (Class 3) (0-90,90) 4-Y-O+
£7,477 (£2,239; £1,119; £560; £279; £140) **Stalls** High

Form — RPR

0112 **1** **Charlie Cool**[9] [2835] 7-9-5 **88** (b) RobertWinston 2 98+
(Mrs R A Carr) *hld up: effrt 3f out: r.o to ld last 75yds* **13/8**[1]

0311 **2** 1 3/4 **Templetuohy Max (IRE)**[21] [2452] 5-8-9 **78** (v) GrahamGibbons 5 84
(J D Bethell) *trckd ldrs: chal over 2f out: led over 1f out: sn rdn and hung rt: hdd and no ex wl ins fnl f* **7/1**[3]

1-10 **3** nse **Oneofapear (IRE)**[17] [2608] 4-9-4 **87** PJMcDonald 6 93+
(G A Swinbank) *hld up: effrt on ins over 3f out: nt clr run and swtchd lft over 1f out: r.o ins fnl f* **6/1**[2]

555- **4** 1/2 **Yorgunnabelucky (USA)**[255] [6535] 4-8-10 **79** AndrewElliott 10 84
(M Johnston) *chsd ldrs: drvn to chal 4f out: edgd rt over 1f out: kpt on same pce* **10/1**

2205 **5** 1/2 **Rosbay (IRE)**[6] [2937] 6-8-5 **79** LanceBetts[(5)] 7 83
(T D Easterby) *dwlt: in rr: drvn over 3f out: styd on fnl f* **8/1**

1-13 **6** 1 1/2 **Keys Of Cyprus**[7] [2885] 8-9-0 **83** AdrianNicholls 9 85+
(D Nicholls) *trckd ldrs: nt clr run on ins over 1f out: swtchd lft and styd on same pce: eased nr fin* **10/1**

-003 **7** 2 1/4 **Fastnet Storm (IRE)**[28] [2241] 4-9-7 **90** TonyHamilton 4 85
(T P Tate) *led: hdd over 1f out: sn fdd* **11/1**

50-0 **8** 3/4 **Bazergan (IRE)**[57] [1474] 5-9-3 **86** (bt) SebSanders 1 80
(C E Brittain) *s.i.s: hld up in rr: effrt on outer over 3f out: hung rt over 1f out: sn wknd* **16/1**

004 **9** 8 **Kidlat**[26] [2314] 5-8-11 **80** PatCosgrave 8 56
(A Bailey) *chsd ldrs: effrt over 3f out: lost pl over 1f out: eased ins fnl f* **25/1**

1m 50.83s (-3.87) **Going Correction** -0.25s/f (Firm) **9** Ran SP% **112.2**
Speed ratings (Par 107): **107,105,105,104,104 103,101,100,93**
toteswingers:1&2 £3.70, 2&3 £4.70, 1&3 £3.30 CSF £12.62 CT £53.32 TOTE £2.70: £1.40, £1.50, £1.20; EX 13.80.
Owner Middleham Park Racing Xxiv **Bred** Middle Park Stud Ltd **Trained** Huby, N Yorks
■ Stewards' Enquiry : Andrew Elliott one-day ban: careless riding (Jul 1)

FOCUS
A decent handicap run at a sound pace and the form makes sense at face value, rated around those in the frame behind the winner.

NOTEBOOK
Charlie Cool, who is due to be 7lb higher in future, stayed on strongly to assert inside the final half-furlong. The Cambridgeshire, a race he has been well beaten in before, is the long-term aim. (tchd 15-8)
Templetuohy Max(IRE), 4lb higher than when winning at Ayr, went ahead inside the final 2f, but couldn't stay on as strongly as Charlie Cool. (op 6-1)
Oneofapear(IRE) bounced back from a below-par effort at Redcar and just failed to get up for second. He was reported to have been denied a clear run, but whatever, he should be suited by a step back up to 1m2f. Official explanation: jockey said gelding was denied a clear run (op 15-2)
Yorgunnabelucky(USA) showed improved form on this seasonal debut and can win a small race at some stage. (op 11-1 tchd 9-1)
Rosbay(IRE) remains 5lb above his last winning mark. (op 10-1 tchd 13-2)
Keys Of Cyprus failed to improve for the longer trip, though was briefly short of room. He was duly reported to have been denied a clear run. Official explanation: jockey said gelding was denied a clear run (op 9-1 tchd 8-1)
Fastnet Storm(IRE) was a bit below par and remains too high in the handicap. (op 10-1)

3122 BEAUMONT ROBINSON LADIES' DERBY H'CAP (LADY AMATEUR RIDERS) — 1m 4f 10y
4:35 (4:35) (Class 6) (0-65,60) 4-Y-O+ **£2,498** (£774; £387; £193) **Stalls** High

Form — RPR

6/06 **1** **Maneki Neko (IRE)**[17] [2610] 8-10-2 **55** MissSBrotherton 11 71
(E W Tuer) *trckd ldrs: wnt 2nd over 3f out: led over 1f out: clr over 1f out: pushed out* **12/1**

03-5 **2** 4 1/2 **Golden Future**[3] [720] 7-9-4 **48** MissJoannaMason[(5)] 14 61+
(P D Niven) *mid-div: hdwy on ins whn nt clr run over 2f out: swtchd lft: n.m.r: styd on: wnt 2nd appr fnl f: could nt rch wnr* **7/4**[1]

3- **3** 2 1/4 **Choctaw Nation**[6] [4600] 6-10-2 **58** MissRJefferson[(3)] 5 63
(J M Jefferson) *hld up in rr: racd wd: hdwy over 3f out: styd on to take 3rd jst ins fnl f* **8/1**[3]

65-3 **4** 6 **Trumpstoo (USA)**[19] [2523] 4-10-2 **60** MrsVFahey[(5)] 6 55
(R A Fahey) *chsd ldrs: wknd fnl f* **6/1**[2]

3-00 **5** 3 **Regal Lyric (IRE)**[23] [2424] 4-10-2 **60** MissKECooper[(5)] 16 50+
(T P Tate) *steaded s: hld up and bnd: hdwy on ins over 3f out: nt clr run and swtchd lft over 2f out: nvr on terms* **11/1**

660- **6** 1/2 **Grethel (IRE)**[15] [6840] 6-9-1 **45** MissJRRichards[(5)] 15 35
(A Berry) *hld up in rr: hdwy on outer over 3f out: nvr nr ldrs* **66/1**

00-5 **7** nse **Hurricane Thomas (IRE)**[3] [3028] 6-10-0 **58** MissPhillipaTutty[(5)] 7 47
(R A Fahey) *led 1f: chsd ldrs: wknd 1f out* **12/1**

3-05 **8** nk **Front Rank (IRE)**[15] [1113] 10-9-4 **48** MissECSayer[(5)] 12 37
(Mrs Dianne Sayer) *mid-div: drvn to chse ldrs 3f out: wknd over 1f out* **25/1**

0322 **9** 4 **Amir Pasha (UAE)**[7] [2881] 5-9-11 **55** (v) MissEStead[(5)] 2 38
(Micky Hammond) *chsd ldr: wkng whn n.m.r on ins over 1f out* **8/1**[3]

0042 **10** 3/4 **Dispol Diva**[15] [2655] 4-9-7 **51** (v) MissWGibson[(5)] 10 32
(P T Midgley) *mid-div: r wd: hdwy over 3f out: sn chsng ldrs: hung rt wknd over 1f out* **8/1**[3]

000- **11** 6 **Danzig Fox**[9] [7085] 5-9-2 **46** MissMMullineaux[(5)] 17 18
(M Mullineaux) *mid-div: lost pl 6f out: wknd over 2f out* **100/1**

/00- **12** 1 1/2 **Skylarker (USA)**[247] [6769] 12-9-3 **47** MissHCuthbert[(5)] 3 16
(T A K Cuthbert) *led after 1f: clr 6f out: hdd over 2f out: sn wknd* **100/1**

6145 **13** 1/2 **Alloro**[12] [2765] 6-9-7 **46** MissLHorner 8 15
(A Kirtley) *chsd ldrs: racd wd: lost pl over 3f out* **20/1**

50-0 **14** 1 **Mceldowney**[13] [2694] 8-9-1 **45** MissRKneller[(5)] 1 12
(M C Chapman) *chsd ldrs: hrd rdn and lost pl 3f out* **125/1**

000 **15** 21 **Sri Kuantan (IRE)**[4] [2995] 6-10-7 **60** MissCharmaineO'Neill 13 —
(R C Guest) *rrd s: in rr: rn wd bnd over 4f out: short lived effrt over 3f out: sn bhd: virtually p.u: t.o* **40/1**

2m 34.66s (-2.04) **Going Correction** -0.25s/f (Firm) **15** Ran SP% **123.0**
Speed ratings (Par 101): **96,93,91,87,85 85,85,84,82,81 77,76,76,75,61**
toteswingers: 1&2 £10.30, 1&3 £30.60, 2&3 £6.30 CSF £32.62 CT £193.48 TOTE £17.00: £4.80, £1.30, £3.30; EX 93.90.
Owner Mr & Mrs C Tompkins & E Tuer **Bred** Mrs Orlagh Sherry **Trained** Great Smeaton, N Yorks

FOCUS
A really competitive ladies' handicap with the winner getting back to his old form and the third setting the level rated to his previous course form.

3123 HOUSE OF ELLIOT H'CAP 1m 4f 10y
5:10 (5:10) (Class 4) (0-85,80) 3-Y-O £4,533 (£1,348; £674; £336) Stalls High

Form RPR
-214 1 **Beat The Rush**[26] 2323 3-9-3 79 BarryMcHugh(3) 5 91
(Julie Camacho) *led: qcknd over 5f out: styd on strly fnl 2f: readily* 10/3[2]
-551 2 1 3/4 **Boss's Destination**[12] 2767 3-9-2 75 PJMcDonald 4 84
(G A Swinbank) *chsd ldng pair: chsd wnr over 2f out: kpt on same pce appr fnl f* 13/2
-021 3 nk **Boston Blue**[6] 2924 3-8-11 77 6ex HarryBentley(7) 6 86
(W J Knight) *rn in snatches in last: hdwy on outside 4f out: sn chsng ldrs: hung rt 2f out: kpt on same pce appr fnl f* 7/4[1]
-330 4 6 **Wild Rose**[12] 2758 3-9-7 80 JackMitchell 2 79
(M L W Bell) *dwlt: hld up: hdwy on ins 4f out: sn chsng ldrs: wknd fnl f* 9/1
0035 5 4 1/2 **Munaawer (USA)**[26] 2323 3-9-2 75 (p) GrahamGibbons 3 67
(J D Bethell) *chsd wnr: drvn over 4f out: wkng whn n.m.r 2f out* 7/1
05-5 6 2 3/4 **Sadler's Mark**[15] 2658 3-8-7 66 RobertWinston 1 54
(T P Tate) *hld up: effrt over 3f out: sn chsng ldrs: lost pl over 1f out: eased towards fin* 4/1[3]
2m 32.57s (-4.13) **Going Correction** -0.25s/f (Firm) 6 Ran SP% 115.3
Speed ratings (Par 101): **103,101,101,97,94 92**
toteswingers: 1&2 £2.10, 1&3 £1.70, 2&3 £3.60 CSF £25.21 TOTE £4.90: £2.20, £2.00; EX 18.60.
Owner Axom (XX) **Bred** David Brown & G B Turnbull Ltd **Trained** Norton, N Yorks

FOCUS
This had the look of a decent 3-y-o handicap with the first three progressive or unexposed and finishing clear of the remainder in a reasonable time for the grade.

3124 RACING AT REDCAR TOMORROW AND SATURDAY H'CAP 1m
5:40 (5:41) (Class 6) (0-65,65) 4-Y-O+ £2,590 (£770; £385; £192) Stalls High

Form RPR
-451 1 **Polish World (USA)**[8] 2850 6-8-7 56 6ex PaulPickard(5) 14 73
(P T Midgley) *trckd ldr: led 3f out: wnt clr over 1f out: eased fnl 100yds* 11/8[1]
-000 2 6 **Mississippian (IRE)**[13] 2714 6-8-6 50 DuranFentiman 2 53
(Mrs D J Sanderson) *chsd ldrs: hrd drvn and outpcd 4f out: styd on fnl 2f: tk 2nd nr fin* 50/1
0521 3 hd **Ninth House (USA)**[13] 2705 8-9-2 65 (t) JamesSullivan(5) 3 68+
(Mrs R A Carr) *rrd s: hdwy 4f out: wnt 2nd 1f out: kpt on same pce* 11/4[2]
5201 4 2 **Ivestar (IRE)**[8] 2854 5-9-3 64 6ex (v) KellyHarrison(3) 12 62+
(B M R Haslam) *s.s: hdwy on ins over 2f out: nt clr run and swtchd lft jst ins fnl f: nrst fin* 12/1
-450 5 1/2 **Nuit Sombre (IRE)**[19] 2527 10-8-10 59 ow1 (p) MichaelO'Connell(5) 11 56
(G A Harker) *set str pce: led tl 3f out: wknd ins fnl f* 20/1
0306 6 nse **Blue Charm**[8] 2850 6-9-5 63 PJMcDonald 10 60
(I W McInnes) *chsd ldrs: rdn 4f out: one pce fnl 2f* 16/1
000- 7 1/2 **Rainbow Zest**[244] 6817 7-8-3 47 oh1 ow1 AndrewElliott 13 43
(W Storey) *in rr: hdwy over 2f out: nvr a factor* 50/1
0000 8 1 1/4 **Carlitos Spirit (IRE)**[45] 1754 6-9-4 65 (v[1]) BarryMcHugh(3) 6 58
(I W McInnes) *chsd ldrs: wkng whn n.m.r on ins 1f out* 28/1
1005 9 1 1/4 **Flighty Fellow (IRE)**[91] 920 10-8-9 58 (p) KylieManser(5) 4 48
(Miss Olivia Maylam) *hld up in rr: effrt on outside over 2f out: hung rt: nvr a factor* 33/1
5-5 10 2 1/2 **Mister Maq**[24] 2382 7-7-9 46 (b) NeilFarley(7) 1 30
(A Crook) *s.i.s: in rr: sn pushed along: nvr on terms* 50/1
-020 11 23 **Hypnotist (UAE)**[92] 907 4-9-4 62 SebSanders 9 —
(C E Brittain) *chsd ldrs: drvn 4f out: wknd over 1f out: eased: t.o* 9/2[3]
1m 38.25s (-3.15) **Going Correction** -0.25s/f (Firm) 11 Ran SP% 117.6
Speed ratings (Par 101): **105,99,98,96,96 96,95,94,93,90 67**
toteswingers:1&2 £14.30, 2&3 £37.50, 1&3 £1.70 CSF £103.78 CT £177.83 TOTE £2.60: £1.30, £12.70, £1.30; EX 136.90 Place 6: £58.75 Place 5: £6.69.
Owner C R Green **Bred** Racehorse Management, Llc **Trained** Westow, N Yorks

FOCUS
A low-grade handicap in which few got involved. The first two set the level, while the third and fourth can be rated better than the bare form after missing the break.
Ninth House(USA) Official explanation: jockey said horse reared as gates opened
Ivestar(IRE) Official explanation: jockey said gelding missed the break
T/Plt: £163.20 to a £1 stake. Pool: £48,902.85 - 218.65 winning tickets T/Qpdt: £8.00 to a £1 stake. Pool: £4,578.27- 418.64 winning tickets WG

3028 WARWICK (L-H)
Thursday, June 17

OFFICIAL GOING: Good (good to firm in places; 7.2)
Wind: Light against Weather: Fine and sunny

3125 RACING UK ON CHANNEL 432 MAIDEN FILLIES' STKS 6f
1:50 (1:52) (Class 5) 3-Y-O+ £2,914 (£867; £433; £216)

Form RPR
32 1 **Beauty Pageant (IRE)**[22] 2441 3-9-0 0 RichardMullen 10 63
(E S McMahon) *chsd ldrs: led 1/2-way: drvn out* 85/40[1]
06- 2 3/4 **Elsie's Orphan**[253] 6582 3-9-0 0 RichardKingscote 12 60+
(P R Chamings) *s.s: hdwy over 4f out: rdn to chse wnr over 1f out: r.o* 5/1[3]
2 3 1 **Nativity**[17] 2590 4-9-7 55 SamHitchcott 9 59
(J L Spearing) *trckd ldrs: racd keenly: rdn over 1f out: r.o* 8/1
-4 4 3 1/2 **Bidruma**[28] 2249 3-9-0 0 FergusSweeney 12 46
(Mike Murphy) *hld up in tch: racd keenly: rdn over 1f out: styd on same pce* 12/1
5442 5 1/2 **Picnic Party**[13] 2688 3-9-0 68 PhilipRobinson 8 44
(D R C Elsworth) *sn pushed along in mid-div: hung rt: hdwy over 2f out: no ex fnl f* 3/1[2]
/6 6 2 **Croeso Mawr**[28] 2249 4-9-7 0 AdamKirby 11 40
(J L Spearing) *led 1f: sn rdn: n.m.r and outpcd 1/2-way: n.d after* 18/1
7 1/2 **Midnight M** 3-9-0 0 SaleemGolam 6 36
(Rae Guest) *s.i.s: sn pushed along in rr: nvr on terms* 33/1
60 8 2 1/4 **Patroller (USA)**[12] 2741 7-9-7 59 CathyGannon 4 31
(K A Ryan) *led 5f out: hdd 1/2-way: rdn over 1f out: wknd fnl f* 25/1
05 9 2 1/4 **Dilys Maud**[26] 2334 3-9-0 0 RobertHavlin 5 22
(R Ingram) *hld up: a in rr: wknd over 1f out* 18/1
10 9 **Miss Halfordbridge** 3-9-0 0 ChrisCatlin 1 —
(J Gallagher) *s.s: outpcd* 33/1
0 11 nse **Cinderella**[7] 2903 3-8-11 0 RussKennemore(3) 13 —
(Lucinda Featherstone) *s.i.s: sn pushed along in rr: hung rt and wknd wl over 2f out* 150/1
1m 12.9s (1.10) **Going Correction** +0.20s/f (Good)
WFA 3 from 4yo+ 7lb 11 Ran SP% 113.4
Speed ratings (Par 100): **100,99,97,93,92 89,89,86,83,71 70**
toteswingers: 1&2 £3.30, 1&3 £3.70, 2&3 £3.10 CSF £11.93 TOTE £2.40: £1.40, £2.60, £1.80.
Owner J C Fretwell **Bred** Mesnil, Mount Coote, New England Stud **Trained** Lichfield, Staffs

FOCUS
The going remained as good, good to firm in places. An ordinary looking maiden fillies sprint with a flip-start due to the stalls being held up in a road accident. The third is the best guide to the level.
Miss Halfordbridge Official explanation: jockey said, regarding running, that the filly was slowly away and this was its racecourse debut found himself inadvertently at the rear, having become so far detached he felt it prudent to to pressurise excessively, but to ride home by hands and heels.
Cinderella Official explanation: jockey said filly hung right throughout

3126 POPPLETON AND APPLEBY MEDIAN AUCTION MAIDEN STKS 5f
2:20 (2:20) (Class 5) 2-Y-O £2,914 (£867; £433; £216)

Form RPR
520 1 **Melodize**[31] 2176 2-8-12 0 RichardMullen 4 65
(W R Muir) *chsd ldrs: rdn over 1f out: r.o to ld wl ins fnl f* 9/2[3]
3 2 1/2 **Loki's Revenge**[17] 2598 2-9-3 0 ChrisCatlin 6 68
(W Jarvis) *prom: chsd ldr 1/2-way: led and j. path jst over 1f out: rdn: hung lft and hdd wl ins fnl f* 2/1[1]
3 3 **Mega Mount (IRE)** 2-9-3 0 GeorgeBaker 3 57
(R M Beckett) *mid-div: sn pushed along: rdn 1/2-way: hdwy over 1f out: r.o to go 3rd post* 3/1[2]
00 4 shd **Chester Deelyte (IRE)**[42] 1835 2-8-9 0 AndrewHeffernan(3) 1 52
(Mrs L Williamson) *sn pushed along to ld: rdn: hung lft and hdd over 1f out: no ex ins fnl f* 50/1
5 1/2 **Sugar Beet** 2-8-12 0 FergusSweeney 7 50+
(R Charlton) *s.i.s: hld up: rdn and hung lft over 1f out: r.o ins fnl f: could nt rch ldrs* 13/2
0 6 2 1/4 **Cinq Heavens (IRE)**[21] 2474 2-9-3 0 RichardKingscote 8 47
(Tom Dascombe) *in rr: rdn over 1f out: nvr on terms* 25/1
7 3 1/2 **Till Dawn (IRE)** 2-8-12 0 JamesDoyle 5 30
(A W Carroll) *prom: hung rt over 3f out: rdn 1/2-way: wknd over 1f out* 28/1
8 shd **Striking Love** 2-8-12 0 RichardThomas 9 29
(R Charlton) *s.s: bhd tl r.o wl ins fnl f: can do bttr* 20/1
9 nse **Piceno (IRE)** 2-9-3 0 J-PGuillambert 2 34
(L M Cumani) *sn pushed along in rr: sme hdwy 2f out: wknd fnl f* 7/1
00 10 44 **Danehill Deb**[61] 1375 2-8-12 0 (p) LukeMorris 10 —
(B De Haan) *in tch but sn pushed along: in rr fr 1/2-way: rdn and hung lft 2f out: bhd whn lost action crossing path jst over 1f out: eased: t.o* 100/1
62.20 secs (2.60) **Going Correction** +0.20s/f (Good) 10 Ran SP% 117.4
Speed ratings (Par 93): **87,86,81,81,80 76,71,71,71,—**
toteswingers: 1&2 £3.30, 1&3 £3.70, 2&3 £3.10 CSF £13.37 TOTE £3.10: £1.10, £2.30, £1.70.
Owner Foursome Thoroughbreds **Bred** Foursome Thoroughbreds **Trained** Lambourn, Berks

FOCUS
Another flip-start for this modest maiden auction that was run at a good pace. Only the three pacesetters ever got involved and the form is no more than fair, but solid enough.

NOTEBOOK
Melodize came out on top in a good tussle to the line, and in the process foiled a gamble. She had failed to build on a good effort on her second start when well held last time, but this was obviously much better. It remains early days but she could build on this. (op 4-1 tchd 5-1)
Loki's Revenge was all the rage beforehand after a promising debut at Leicester. He held every chance from over 1f out but could not quite get the upper-hand in a protracted duel with the winner. It was disappointing that he could not lose his maiden status at the second time of asking but he still showed a good attitude. (op 15-2)
Mega Mount(IRE) was not unfancied but ran green early on and could only stay on at the same pace in the straight. He did the best of the remainder from off the pace and hails from a yard in form, so should come on for this. (tchd 9-4)
Chester Deelyte(IRE) took them along at a fair pace before edging left and getting headed entering the distance. This seemed to be a much-improved effort on her previous performances but casts an overall shadow on the form as the two principals had to work quite hard to reel her in. (tchd 40-1)
Sugar Beet is related to several winners but could not get on terms from off the pace. She ought to do better in time, especially when upped in trip. (op 4-1)
Danehill Deb Official explanation: jockey said filly jumped the path and lost her action

3127 MOLSON COORS H'CAP 1m 6f 213y
2:55 (2:56) (Class 5) (0-75,72) 4-Y-O+ £3,238 (£963; £481; £240) Stalls Low

Form RPR
2525 1 **Yemeni Princess (IRE)**[26] 2341 4-8-13 67 RussKennemore(3) 2 75
(B G Powell) *s.i.s: sn hld up in tch: hung rt over 3f out: rdn and edgd lft over 2f out: led ins fnl f: styd on* 9/2[2]
313- 2 1/2 **Arab League (IRE)**[232] 7124 5-8-10 64 WilliamCarson(3) 7 71
(R J Price) *a.p: chsd ldr 4f out: led over 2f out: rdn and hdd ins fnl f: styd on* 11/2[3]
-304 3 2 1/2 **Hawridge King**[19] 2549 8-9-4 72 JamesMillman(3) 1 76
(W S Kittow) *chsd ldrs: rdn over 1f out: styd on same pce ins fnl f* 5/4[1]
-524 4 4 **Brad's Luck (IRE)**[10] 2810 4-8-2 53 oh2 LukeMorris 4 53
(M Blanshard) *chsd ldr tl rdn 4f out: no ex fnl f* 20/1
0553 5 1 1/2 **Divinatore**[22] 2445 4-8-5 56 (b) CathyGannon 8 53
(D Haydn Jones) *hld up: hdwy 8f out: outpcd 4f out: n.d after* 14/1
-410 6 10 **Cote D'Argent**[7] 2897 7-9-7 72 (t) ChrisCatlin 3 57
(C J Down) *led: racd keenly: rdn and hdd over 2f out: wknd over 1f out* 22/1
200- 7 2 **Warren Bank**[183] 7766 5-8-5 56 (b[1]) RichardKingscote 6 39
(Mrs Mary Hambro) *hld up: rdn over 4f out: wknd 3f out* 33/1
1-00 8 2 3/4 **Lombok**[19] 2549 4-9-2 67 (v[1]) GeorgeBaker 5 47
(M L W Bell) *hld up: rdn: hung lft and wknd 2f out* 9/2[2]
3m 19.23s (0.23) **Going Correction** -0.075s/f (Good) 8 Ran SP% 114.9
Speed ratings (Par 103): **96,95,94,92,91 86,85,83**
toteswingers:1&2:£4.00, 2&3:£2.50, 1&3:£2.70 CSF £28.50 CT £47.93 TOTE £6.30: £1.70, £1.10, £1.10; EX 30.00.
Owner Miss Juliet E Reed **Bred** P D Savill **Trained** Upper Lambourn, Berks

FOCUS
The stalls had arrived for this uncompetitive staying handicap, and they went just an ordinary gallop with the field spreading the width of the course in the straight. The form is a bit muddling although the first two are both rated slight improvers.

The Form Book, Raceform Ltd, Compton, RG20 6NL

Lombok Official explanation: jockey said colt had no more to give

3128 HARRISON BEALE AND OWEN LIMITED H'CAP 1m 2f 188y
3:35 (3:46) (Class 6) (0-55,61) 4-Y-O+ **£2,047** (£604; £302) **Stalls** Low

Form RPR
-065 **1** **Dark Ranger**[120] 588 4-8-13 **54**........ RobertHavlin 9 66
(T J Pitt) *hld up: hdwy over 3f out: rdn to ld over 1f out: styd on* **8/1**
-601 **2** 2 **Outland (IRE)**[7] 2897 4-9-6 **61** 6ex........ GeorgeBaker 11 69+
(M G Rimell) *broke wl: sn stdd into mid-div: hdwy over 2f out: rdn over 1f out: styd on* **2/1**[1]
0-30 **3** 2 **Filun**[8] 2870 5-8-0 **46** oh1........(t) BillyCray(5) 14 51
(A Middleton) *hld up: hdwy over 3f out: rdn and hung lft over 1f out: no ex ins fnl f* **20/1**
0002 **4** ¾ **Under Fire (IRE)**[5] 2955 7-8-4 **48**........ AndrewHeffernan(3) 8 51
(A W Carroll) *led 1f: chsd ldr tl led over 2f out: rdn and hdd over 1f out: no ex ins fnl f* **6/1**[2]
0260 **5** 1 ¼ **Corrib (IRE)**[55] 1507 7-8-2 **48**........(p) DeclanCannon(5) 4 49
(B Palling) *hld up: nt clr run over 3f out: hdwy over 2f out: sn rdn: no ex ins fnl f* **20/1**
5000 **6** 1 ½ **Shame The Devil (IRE)**[14] 1920 5-8-11 **52**........ FergusSweeney 10 50
(H J Evans) *s.i.s: hld up: hdwy over 1f out: r.o: nt rch ldrs* **20/1**
-053 **7** 2 ½ **Aspirational (IRE)**[25] 2360 4-8-9 **50**........ NeilChalmers 7 44
(B Palling) *led after 1f: rdn and hdd over 2f out: sn hung lft: wknd fnl f* **12/1**
-443 **8** ¾ **Iguacu**[8] 2870 6-8-4 **50**........ MatthewDavies(5) 13 42
(George Baker) *hld up in tch: rdn over 1f out: sn wknd* **7/1**[3]
4346 **9** ½ **Trysting Grove (IRE)**[17] 2604 9-8-6 **47**........ SaleemGolam 5 38
(E G Bevan) *pushed along in rr early: rdn over 2f out: n.d* **8/1**
-060 **10** 11 **Lucy's Perfect**[7] 2894 4-8-10 **51**........ ChrisCatlin 12 22
(B R Millman) *prom: rdn over 4f out: wknd 3f out* **16/1**
4223 **11** 1 ½ **Libre**[8] 2880 10-8-4 **50**........ AshleyMorgan(5) 17 18
(F Jordan) *hld up: hdwy over 4f out: rdn over 2f out: sn wknd* **20/1**
00-0 **12** ¾ **Laura Land**[38] 1983 4-8-8 **49**........ LiamJones 16 16
(W M Brisbourne) *prom: rdn over 3f out: wknd over 2f out* **33/1**
0000 **13** 3 ¼ **Firsaan (IRE)**[7] 2902 4-8-5 **46** oh1........ CathyGannon 15 7
(J R Norton) *chsd ldrs: rdn over 4f out: wknd over 3f out* **66/1**
46-0 **14** 1 ¾ **Rose Of Coma (IRE)**[5] 2955 4-8-7 **48**........ SamHitchcott 2 5
(A G Juckes) *prom: rdn over 3f out: wknd wl over 1f out* **33/1**
60-0 **15** 12 **Heart Of Tuscany**[45] 1755 4-8-2 **48**........ SimonPearce(5) 3 —
(J A T De Giles) *hld up: a in rr: bhd fnl 3f: t.o* **50/1**

2m 18.25s (-2.85) **Going Correction** -0.075s/f (Good) **15** Ran SP% **124.3**
Speed ratings (Par 101): **107,105,104,103,102 101,99,99,98,90 89,89,86,85,76**
toteswingers:1&2 £8.10, 2&3 £20.80, 1&3 £47.10 CSF £22.29 CT £331.29 TOTE £13.40: £4.40, £1.30, £7.80; EX 34.80.
Owner Recycled Products Limited **Bred** Thomas G N Burrage **Trained** Norton, N Yorks

FOCUS
A weak but open middle-distance handicap, but with New England breaking through the stalls and being withdrawn the field was reduced to 15. The pace was sound and the time was good for the grade, suggesting the form is solid.
Heart Of Tuscany Official explanation: jockey said filly was never travelling

3129 JOHN PANTON HAPPY 60TH BIRTHDAY H'CAP 7f 26y
4:10 (4:14) (Class 5) (0-70,70) 3-Y-O+ **£2,729** (£806; £403) **Stalls** Low

Form RPR
0-56 **1** **Piccolo Express**[13] 2726 4-8-9 **51** oh2........ J-PGuillambert 10 58
(B P J Baugh) *a.p: rdn and edgd lft over 1f out: r.o to ld post* **16/1**
2422 **2** shd **Gazboolou**[35] 2053 6-9-9 **65**........ FergusSweeney 8 72
(David Pinder) *w ldr: rdn over 1f out: led ins fnl f: hdd post* **9/2**[3]
010- **3** ¾ **Tudor Prince (IRE)**[208] 7496 6-10-0 **70**........ AdamKirby 7 75
(A W Carroll) *trckd ldrs: rdn and n.m.r over 1f out: r.o* **16/1**
6655 **4** ½ **Perfect Friend**[4] 3001 4-9-12 **68**........ JamesDoyle 1 72
(S Kirk) *led: rdn over 1f out: hdd and unable qck ins fnl f* **4/1**[2]
3342 **5** nse **Dickie Le Davoir**[10] 2817 6-9-6 **65**........(v) AndrewHeffernan(3) 5 68
(R C Guest) *hld up: hdwy over 1f out: r.o* **15/2**
3544 **6** nse **Billberry**[12] 2750 5-9-1 **57**........(t) GeorgeBaker 4 60
(S C Williams) *hld up: hdwy over 2f out: rdn and hung lft over 1f out: r.o* **3/1**[1]
0-00 **7** ½ **Song Of Praise**[36] 2026 4-8-9 **51** oh1........ NeilChalmers 9 53
(M Blanshard) *hld up: rdn over 1f out: r.o ins fnl f: could nt rch ldrs* **40/1**
06-0 **8** shd **Lily Wood**[17] 2590 4-8-9 **51** oh1........(v) LiamJones 6 53?
(J W Unett) *chsd ldrs: rdn over 2f out: styd on* **33/1**
000- **9** 1 ¾ **Stargazy**[183] 7768 6-8-4 **51** oh1........ MatthewDavies(5) 11 48?
(A J Lidderdale) *s.i.s: hld up: r.o ins fnl f: nrst fin* **50/1**
135 **10** hd **Belle Park**[13] 2722 3-8-4 **55**........ ChrisCatlin 3 48
(Karen George) *s.i.s: rdn over 1f out: styd on same pce fnl f* **25/1**
3-60 **11** 3 ¾ **Silver Guest**[13] 2689 5-9-13 **69**........ SamHitchcott 2 55
(M R Channon) *hld up: rdn over 2f out: sn rdn: wknd over 1f out* **11/2**

1m 25.46s (0.86) **Going Correction** -0.075s/f (Good)
WFA 3 from 4yo+ 9lb **11** Ran SP% **113.3**
Speed ratings (Par 103): **92,91,91,90,90 90,89,89,87,87 83**
toteswingers: 1&2 £12.10, 1&3 £14.80, 2&3 £13.40 CSF £81.20 CT £1181.01 TOTE £13.50: £3.30, £1.70, £2.60; EX 119.80.
Owner G B Hignett **Bred** G B Hignett **Trained** Audley, Staffs
■ Stewards' Enquiry : Fergus Sweeney three-day ban: used whip with excessive frequency (Jul 1-3)

FOCUS
A weak contest but plenty coming with chances in the straight. The form is rated around the runner-up to his latest turf form.
Stargazy Official explanation: jockey said gelding lost its action

3130 WARWICKRACECOURSE.CO.UK H'CAP 1m 22y
4:45 (4:46) (Class 5) (0-75,78) 4-Y-O+ **£2,914** (£867; £433; £216) **Stalls** Low

Form RPR
3261 **1** **Dr Wintringham (IRE)**[6] 2920 4-9-0 **68** 6ex........ JerryO'Dwyer 8 83
(Karen George) *hld up: hdwy over 2f out: led over 1f out: shkn up and sn clr* **4/1**[2]
-201 **2** 6 **Crazy Chris**[10] 2823 5-9-5 **78** 6ex........ DeclanCannon(5) 3 79
(B Palling) *prom: chsd ldr over 2f out: rdn and ev ch over 1f out: sn outpcd* **4/1**[2]
3540 **3** 1 **King Of The Moors (USA)**[4] 2991 7-8-12 **69**...(b) AndrewHeffernan(3) 1 68
(R C Guest) *hld up: rdn and hdd over 1f out: styd on same pce* **9/1**
-005 **4** ¾ **Outofoil (IRE)**[85] 975 4-9-0 **68**........(b) RichardKingscote 5 65
(R M Beckett) *stmbld s: hld up: rdn over 3f out: styd on ins fnl f: nvr nrr* **9/2**[3]
1014 **5** 2 ¼ **Very Well Red**[20] 2512 7-9-4 **75**........ WilliamCarson(3) 4 67
(P W Hiatt) *chsd ldr: rdn over 3f out: wknd over 1f out* **14/1**
000- **6** 1 **Theonebox (USA)**[102] 7759 5-9-4 **72**........ StevieDonohoe 6 62
(Ian Williams) *sn pushed along in rr: hdwy u.p over 3f out: wknd over 1f out* **20/1**
2240 **7** 1 ½ **Ermine Grey**[6] 2922 9-8-8 **62**........ KirstyMilczarek 7 48
(A W Carroll) *dwlt: outpcd* **12/1**
-621 **8** 10 **Golden Rock (IRE)**[31] 2167 4-9-5 **73**........ RichardMullen 2 46
(R Charlton) *trckd ldrs: rdn over 3f out: hung lft over 2f out: sn wknd* **9/4**[1]

1m 39.69s (-1.31) **Going Correction** -0.075s/f (Good) **8** Ran SP% **118.1**
Speed ratings (Par 103): **103,97,96,95,93 92,90,80**
toteswingers:1&2 £3.40, 2&3 £8.20, 1&3 £6.30 CSF £21.16 CT £138.05 TOTE £4.20: £1.50, £1.10, £4.10; EX 21.60.
Owner Mrs Isabel Fraser **Bred** Peter Molony **Trained** Higher Eastington, Devon

FOCUS
A competitive handicap run at a good pace with a decent time being set. The form is rated around the placed horses but could be a few pounds out either way.
Ermine Grey Official explanation: jockey said gelding was never travelling
Golden Rock(IRE) Official explanation: jockey said gelding stopped quickly

3131 TURFTV APPRENTICE H'CAP (DIV I) 1m 22y
5:20 (5:21) (Class 6) (0-60,61) 4-Y-O+ **£1,706** (£503; £252) **Stalls** Low

Form RPR
0-04 **1** **Bidable**[6] 2920 6-8-11 **55**........ DeclanCannon(3) 7 65
(B Palling) *hld up: pushed along over 3f out: hdwy over 2f out: led over 1f out: hung rt ins fnl f: rdn out* **6/1**[3]
0520 **2** 2 ½ **Grey Boy (GER)**[5] 2965 9-8-4 **52**........ GeorgeDowning(7) 5 56
(A W Carroll) *hld up: nt clr run: swtchd lft and hdwy over 1f out: rdn and edgd rt ins fnl f: styd on* **8/1**
0300 **3** 1 ½ **Mr Chocolate Drop (IRE)**[37] 1998 6-8-5 **46** oh1..(b) AshleyHamblett 10 47
(Miss M E Rowland) *hld up: plld hrd: hdwy 5f out: led 3f out: rdn and hdd over 1f out: styd on same pce ins fnl f* **33/1**
6500 **4** ½ **Lunar River (FR)**[5] 2966 7-8-11 **57**........(t) DavidKenny(5) 8 57
(David Pinder) *s.i.s: hld up: rdn and r.o ins fnl f: nrst fin* **12/1**
-060 **5** 1 ¼ **Indian Violet (IRE)**[27] 2274 4-8-12 **58**........ DuilioDaSilva(5) 6 55
(D W Thompson) *prom: racd keenly: rdn over 2f out: edgd lft over 1f out: styd on same pce u.p fnl f* **16/1**
-000 **6** 2 **Head Down**[15] 2643 4-9-2 **60**........(v[1]) MatthewDavies(3) 13 52
(M R Bosley) *prom: rdn over 2f out: wknd ins fnl f* **25/1**
331 **7** nk **Applaude**[8] 2859 5-9-6 **61** 6ex........(b) AndrewHeffernan 1 52
(R C Guest) *hld up: hdwy over 2f out: rdn over 1f out: no imp* **13/8**[1]
0-00 **8** 1 **Mr Loire**[2] 3056 6-8-2 **46** oh1........(p) SimonPearce(3) 14 35
(M F Harris) *s.i.s: hld up: hdwy over 3f out: rdn over 2f out: wknd over 1f out* **50/1**
0012 **9** hd **Shared Moment (IRE)**[27] 2279 4-9-1 **59**........(p) AmyRyan(3) 12 48
(J Gallagher) *hld up: hdwy 1/2-way: rdn and hung lft over 1f out: wknd ins fnl f* **7/2**[2]
-066 **10** 1 ¼ **Annes Rocket (IRE)**[21] 2456 5-8-9 **55**........ RyanClark(5) 4 41
(J C Fox) *s.s: bhd: nvr nrr* **17/2**
0660 **11** ½ **Hilbre Court (USA)**[111] 715 5-8-13 **57**........ BillyCray(3) 11 42
(B P J Baugh) *sn pushed along and prom: rdn over 3f out: wknd over 2f out* **10/1**
-006 **12** 8 **Pacific Bay (IRE)**[17] 1958 4-8-7 **53**........ JohnCavanagh(5) 3 19
(R Ford) *led: hdd 3f out: rdn and wknd over 1f out* **50/1**
000- **13** 2 ¼ **Da Bomber (IRE)**[185] 7754 5-8-9 **50**........ RussKennemore 2 11
(J W Unett) *chsd ldr tl rdn over 3f out: wknd over 1f out* **40/1**

1m 40.7s (-0.30) **Going Correction** -0.075s/f (Good) **13** Ran SP% **132.1**
Speed ratings (Par 101): **98,95,94,93,92 90,89,88,88,87 87,79,76**
toteswingers: 1&2 £9.50, 1&3 £32.60, 2&3 £20.00 CSF £57.36 CT £1522.65 TOTE £10.60: £3.40, £3.50, £15.00; EX 74.00.
Owner Flying Eight Partnership **Bred** W D Hodge **Trained** Tredodridge, Vale Of Glamorgan

FOCUS
The more competitive of the two divisions and it produced a strong gallop, although the very slightly slower time. The form is sound but modest rated around the principals.
Annes Rocket(IRE) Official explanation: jockey said horse was slowly away

3132 TURFTV APPRENTICE H'CAP (DIV II) 1m 22y
5:55 (5:58) (Class 6) (0-60,60) 4-Y-O+ **£1,706** (£503; £252) **Stalls** Low

Form RPR
065 **1** **Croeso Cusan**[8] 2880 5-8-11 **55**........ SophieDoyle(3) 13 64
(J L Spearing) *dwlt: hld up: hdwy over 1f out: led ins fnl f: r.o wl* **15/2**
0-30 **2** 2 ¾ **One Scoop Or Two**[19] 2527 4-8-3 **51**........ NicolaJackson(7) 11 54
(R Hollinshead) *led over 6f out: shkn up over 1f out: edgd lft and hdd ins fnl f: styd on same pce* **8/1**
214 **3** ¾ **Crocodile Bay (IRE)**[2] 3062 7-9-1 **56**........ AndrewHeffernan 6 57
(R C Guest) *led early: trckd ldrs: plld hrd: rdn to ld and edgd lft ins fnl f: sn hdd and no ex* **11/4**[1]
00-0 **4** 1 **Aggbag**[70] 1193 6-8-4 **50**........ AdamBeschizza(5) 1 49
(J Jay) *chsd ldrs: rdn over 1f out: styd on* **7/2**[2]
00-0 **5** 1 **Charlietoo**[17] 2590 4-8-11 **57**........(p) RyanClark(5) 2 53
(E G Bevan) *sn led: hdd over 6f out: chsd ldrs: rdn and ev ch over 1f out: no ex ins fnl f* **33/1**
4350 **6** ¾ **Kielty's Folly**[13] 2727 6-8-10 **54**........ BillyCray(3) 4 49
(B P J Baugh) *hld up: hdwy 2f out: sn rdn: no imp ins fnl f* **7/1**
0000 **7** 3 ½ **Dynamo Dave (USA)**[17] 2589 5-7-12 **46** oh1........(v) ThomasBrown(7) 8 33
(M D I Usher) *hld up: hdwy over 3f out: rdn and wknd over 1f out* **20/1**
05-5 **8** 1 ½ **Fitz**[45] 1772 4-8-11 **55**........(be[1]) RossAtkinson(3) 3 38
(Matthew Salaman) *hld up: hdwy over 2f out: rdn and wknd over 1f out* **6/1**[3]
0-05 **9** nk **Lytton**[20] 2487 5-8-12 **58**........ JohnCavanagh(5) 5 40
(R Ford) *s.i.s: hld up: hdwy over 3f out: hung rt and wknd over 2f out* **16/1**
000- **10** 6 **Bewdley**[439] 1131 5-7-12 **46** oh1........ HobieGill(7) 12 15
(R E Peacock) *jnd ldr over 6f out: wkng whn rdr dropped whip over 1f out* **66/1**

1m 40.59s (-0.41) **Going Correction** -0.075s/f (Good) **10** Ran SP% **113.6**
Speed ratings (Par 101): **99,96,95,94,93 92,89,87,87,81**
toteswingers:1&2 £14.10, 2&3 £6.70, 1&3 £5.50 CSF £62.98 CT £205.26 TOTE £10.10: £3.70, £3.00, £2.70; EX 95.80 Place 6: £32.63 Place 5: £20.60.
Owner Oxstalls Farm Stud **Bred** Richard Evans Bloodstock **Trained** Kinnersley, Worcs

FOCUS
The second division of the apprentice handicap was run at a similarly fast pace to the first leg and the time was marginally quicker. The winner is rated in line with her 2009 form backed up by the second.
T/Plt: £56.90 to a £1 stake. Pool: £30,705.22 - 393.26 winning tickets T/Qpdt: £17.60 to a £ stake. Pool: £2,504.59 - 104.84 winning tickets CR

3133 - 3140a (Foreign Racing) - See Raceform Interactive

3100 ASCOT (R-H)

Friday, June 18

OFFICIAL GOING: Good to firm (good in places: stands' side 10.2, centre 9.8, far side 10.2; round course 8.8)

Course at normal configuration and all distances as advertised.

3141 ALBANY STKS (GROUP 3) (FILLIES) 6f

2:30 (2:32) (Class 1) 2-Y-O

£39,739 (£15,064; £7,539; £3,759; £1,883; £945) **Stalls** Centre

Form RPR

1 **1** **Memory (IRE)**[30] 2223 2-8-12 0 RichardHughes 10 105+
(R Hannon) *dwlt: racd on stands' side: in rr: rdn and hdwy over 1f out: rn to ld towards fin: 1st of 10 in gp* **15/2**

11 **2** *hd* **Margot Did (IRE)**[17] 2630 2-8-12 0 HayleyTurner 3 104+
(M L W Bell) *racd on stands' side: midfield: rdn and hdwy 2f out: led overall over 1f out: edgd lft ins fnl f: hdd towards fin: 2nd of 10 in gp* **7/1**[3]

3 *2 1/2* **Tiz My Time (USA)**[21] 2-8-12 0 KierenFallon 8 97
(Kenneth McPeek, U.S.A) *racd on stands' side: prom: led overall 4f out: rdn and hdd over 1f out: styd on same pce ins fnl f: 3rd of 10 in gp* **16/1**

1 **4** *hd* **Radharcnafarraige (IRE)**[11] 2828 2-8-12 0 KJManning 6 96
(J S Bolger, Ire) *racd on stands' side: prom: rdn to chal over 1f out: nt qckn and styd on same pce fnl 100yds: 4th of 10 in gp* **4/1**[1]

431 **5** *1/2* **Emma's Gift (IRE)**[37] 2022 2-8-12 0 JimmyQuinn 21 95
(Miss J Feilden) *racd on far side: towards rr: pushed along 3f out: hdwy 2f out: r.o to ld gp fnl 110yds: sn hung lft: nt rch stands' side ldrs: 1st of 12 in gp* **50/1**

1 **6** *1* **Crying Lightening (IRE)**[17] 2616 2-8-12 0 MartinDwyer 16 92
(P W Chapple-Hyam) *racd on far side: hld up: pushed along over 2f out: rdn and hdwy over 1f out: r.o ins fnl f: gng on at fin but nt quite pce to get to ldrs: 2nd of 12 in gp* **12/1**

7 *1/2* **Queen Of Spain (IRE)**[14] 2728 2-8-12 0 JMurtagh 15 90
(A P O'Brien, Ire) *in tch and racd in centre: merged w far side gp 4f out: rdn 2f out: r.o ins fnl f: nt quite pce of stands' side ldrs: 3rd of 12 in gp* **16/1**

1 **8** *shd* **Hooray**[16] 2641 2-8-12 0 SebSanders 19 92
(Sir Mark Prescott) *racd keenly: prom on far side: led gp over 1f out: hdd fnl 110yds: keeping on but hld whn hmpd sn after: 4th of 12 in gp* **5/1**[2]

513 **9** *1 3/4* **Phoebs**[35] 2074 2-8-12 0 StevieDonohoe 7 84
(R A Mills) *racd on stands' side: in tch on outer in gp: rdn 2f out: one pce ins fnl f: 5th of 10 in gp* **33/1**

4 **10** *nse* **Grandmas Dream**[27] 2330 2-8-12 0 IanMongan 17 84
(G C Bravery) *led far side gp: rdn and hdd over 1f out: no ex ins fnl f: 5th of 12 in gp* **100/1**

10 **11** *3/4* **Turn The Tide**[35] 2095 2-8-12 0 DavidProbert 1 82
(A Bailey) *racd on stands' side: in rr: pushed along 2f out: kpt on ins fnl f: nt pce to chal: 6th of 10 in gp* **100/1**

14 **12** *3/4* **Twist Of Silver (USA)**[21] 2514 2-8-12 0 WilliamBuick 20 80
(J Noseda) *racd on far side: hld up in midfield: rdn over 1f out: no imp on ldrs: 6th of 12 in gp* **80/1**

03 **13** *1/2* **Juliet Capulet (IRE)**[11] 2828 2-8-12 0 (v[1]) RyanMoore 22 78
(A P O'Brien, Ire) *racd on far side: in rr: styd on and prog fr over 1f out: nt pce to rch ldrs: 7th of 12 in gp* **25/1**

1 **14** *nk* **Honeymead (IRE)**[18] 2577 2-8-12 0 PaulHanagan 23 77
(R A Fahey) *racd on far side: in tch: chalng 2f out: wknd u.p fnl 100yds: 8th of 12 in gp* **12/1**

31 **15** *3/4* **Bay Of Fires (IRE)**[10] 2832 2-8-12 0 JimCrowley 5 75
(D O'Meara) *racd on stands' side: in tch: rdn over 1f out: sn outpcd: n.d after: 7th of 10 in gp* **100/1**

1 **16** *hd* **Ladyanne (IRE)**[41] 1930 2-8-12 0 JimmyFortune 4 75
(S Kirk) *racd on stands' side: prom: rdn to chal 2f out: wknd ins fnl f: 8th of 10 in gp* **33/1**

17 *1* **Wave Of Applause**[40] 1948 2-8-12 0 WMLordan 14 72
(T Stack, Ire) *hld up in centre: merged w far side gp 4f out: rdn over 2f out: hdwy over 1f out: no ex ins fnl f: 9th of 12 in gp* **12/1**

01 **18** *4* **Al Sharood**[21] 2505 2-8-12 0 FrankieDettori 13 60
(Mahmood Al Zarooni) *prom: racd in centre tl merged w far side 4f out: rdn to chal 2f out: wknd over 1f out: 10th of 12 in gp* **9/1**

421 **19** *shd* **Hortensia (IRE)**[35] 2088 2-8-12 0 ChrisCatlin 2 59
(M R Channon) *racd on stands' side: led overall tl 4f out: remained prom: u.p over 2f out: hung rt and wknd over 1f out: 9th of 10 in gp* **40/1**

26 **20** *2 1/4* **Magic Stella**[41] 1901 2-8-12 0 TomQueally 18 53
(A P Jarvis) *gd spd in centre: merged w far side gp 4f out: pushed along 3f out: wknd over 1f out: 11th of 12 in gp* **66/1**

41 **21** *8* **Idiom (IRE)**[22] 2461 2-8-12 0 AhmedAjtebi 12 29
(Mahmood Al Zarooni) *in tch: racd in centre tl merged w far side gp 4f out: rdn and wknd 3f out: bhd fnl 2f: 12th of 12 in gp* **40/1**

2261 **22** *1 3/4* **Belle Royale (IRE)**[18] 2591 2-8-12 0 (v[1]) LukeMorris 9 23
(W M Brisbourne) *racd on stands' side: bhd: outpcd and struggling fnl 2f: 10th of 10 in gp* **200/1**

1m 13.7s (-0.70) **Going Correction** -0.075s/f (Good) 22 Ran SP% **128.5**
Speed ratings (Par 100): **101,100,97,97,96 95,94,94,92,91 90,89,89,88,87 87,86,80,80,77 67,64**
toteswingers:1&2:£13.50, 1&3:£27.90, 2&3:£63.80 CSF £56.78 CT £860.13 TOTE £8.10: £3.20, £3.10, £5.00; EX 54.40 Trifecta £728.40 Pool: £7,373.37 - 7.48 winning units..
Owner Highclere Thoroughbred Racing-Masquerade **Bred** Swordlestown Stud **Trained** East Everleigh, Wilts

FOCUS

The watering carried out was the same for a second straight day, with 6mm being put on the straight track, and 4mm applied on the round course, resulting in the ground remaining good to firm, good in places for day four of the meeting. Goingstick readings, for the first time this week, were the same on both the stands' side and far side of the course (10.2), while the centre remained slightly slower (10). The rail on the round course had been taken in a little in order to provide fresh ground, and not for the first time this week, there was a tailwind in the straight. This looked a wide-open contest, in contrast to the last few years when there has often been a red-hot favourite, with 14 of the 22 runners having won their previous start, half of which were unbeaten. Predictably the field split into two groups, and as suggested by the Goingstick readings, there appeared to be precious little in the draw, with the two fillies' who did come clear simply looking superior to the remainder of the field. The form looks fine with the fourth a length or so off her Irish form.

NOTEBOOK

Memory(IRE) was slow to find her stride on leaving the gates, as was the case when making a taking winning debut at Goodwood last month, and found herself right at the back of the field at halfway. Typical of Hughes, though, he didn't panic, and having been switched right to follow through the runner-up over 2f out, she really came good in the final furlong, running on strongly inside the last 75 yards and getting up in plenty of time. Not the biggest, her sluggish starting is a slight worry, but she doesn't always do a lot at home, which suggests she looks after herself a bit, and it's not hard to see her adding to this victory at a higher level at some point this season, with the Cherry Hinton, maybe followed by the Moyglare Stakes, being her targets. As for her longer-term prospects, her rider expects her to have no trouble with 1m, and she is a general 20-1 shot for next year's 1000 Guineas. (tchd 8-1)

Margot Did(IRE), having travelled strongly and readily come clear of the remainder, can count herself a bit unfortunate to have bumped into one too good. Pulled out to challenge over 2f out, she quickened nicely to assert 1.5f out, looking all over the winner, but as Memory began to close it became clear she was going to get worn down. She is clearly smart and shows enough speed to suggest she will be as effective at 5f , but the Cherry Hinton looks the target. (op 9-1)

Tiz My Time(USA), runner-up on both previous starts over shorter on Polytrack/dirt in the US, had shaped as though this stiffer test would suit, and having shown bright early speed to lead the stands' side group, it was no surprise to see her staying on again close home, having been headed just inside the final 2f. She will presumably return home now. (op 20-1 tchd 25-1 in a place)

Radharcnafarraige(IRE), representing connections of 2008 winner Cuis Ghaire, has been progressing with racing and put up a smart performance in easily winning a Group 3 at Naas just 11 days earlier. She travelled up strongly to challenge 2f out, but couldn't match the runner-up's acceleration and it was clear from well over 1f out that she wasn't going to be winning, getting run out of third close home. (op 9-2 tchd 5-1)

Emma's Gift(IRE) came out best of those on the far side. Held up early, she made her ground quite comfortably, but despite not being able to quicken when initially asked for her effort, she did stay on really well inside the final furlong, having ended up towards the far rail. This was her first run at 6f and she clearly improved for it. (op 66-1)

Crying Lightening(IRE), winner of a decent 5f Leicester maiden on debut (third Catalinas Diamond finished fifth in Wednesday's Queen Mary), was clearly in need of this extra furlong as she was found wanting for pace, staying on close home to take second in the far group. (op 9-1)

Queen Of Spain(IRE) had shown just fair form in two previous starts in Ireland, but as a close relation of Mastercraftsman (high-class at up to 1m2f), she seems likely to come good at some stage, and this effort strongly suggested she will improve once upped to 7f and 1m. (op 20-1)

Hooray, her trainer's first runner at the meeting in three years, had won nicely on her debut at Kempton and she went to the front of the far group over 1f out, but simply wasn't good enough. She was hampered by Emma's Gift close home, which may have cost her a place or two. (op 6-1 tchd 13-2)

Phoebs had plenty to find and ran about as well as could have been expected. (op 40-1 tchd 50-1 in a place)

Grandmas Dream showed plenty of pace in leading the far-side group before fading late on. (op 125-1)

Turn The Tide showed her York running to be all wrong (reportedly struck into), staying on late having been readily outpaced. (tchd 125-1 in a place)

Twist Of Silver(USA), whose yard won this in 2005 and 2006, hadn't achieved much in two previous starts and wasn't good enough. (op 100-1)

Juliet Capulet(IRE) offered a bit of encouragement in the first-time visor, though is clearly not one of Ballydoyle's stars.

3142 KING EDWARD VII STKS (GROUP 2) (C&G) 1m 4f

3:05 (3:05) (Class 1) 3-Y-O

£92,946 (£35,233; £17,633; £8,792; £4,404; £2,210) **Stalls** High

Form RPR

1121 **1** **Monterosso**[19] 2562 3-8-12 104 FrankieDettori 2 116
(M Johnston) *chsd ldng trio: rdn to ld 2f out: edgd rt but sn qcknd clr: r.o wl and in command fnl f: comf* **7/2**[2]

-131 **2** *2 1/4* **Arctic Cosmos (USA)**[9] 2869 3-8-12 78 WilliamBuick 3 113
(J H M Gosden) *dwlt and bustled along after s: wl in tch in midfield: rdn and effrt over 2f out: chsd clr wnr over 1f out: no imp on wnr but kpt on wl for clr 2nd* **14/1**

-040 **3** *2 1/4* **Buzzword**[13] 2746 3-8-12 111 AhmedAjtebi 6 109
(Mahmood Al Zarooni) *hld up in last pair: swtchd to outer and rdn wl over 1f out: styd on fnl f: wnt 3rd last strides: nvr trbld ldrs* **11/1**

232 **4** *hd* **At First Sight (IRE)**[13] 2746 3-8-12 116 JMurtagh 1 109
(A P O'Brien, Ire) *led: rdn and tried to qckn over 2f out: sn hrd pressed: hdd 2f out: carried sltly rt and nt pce of wnr wl over 1f out: 3rd and wl hld 1f out: lost 3rd fnl strides* **5/2**[1]

-111 **5** *2 1/2* **Green Moon (IRE)**[20] 2543 3-8-12 106 JamieSpencer 4 105
(H J L Dunlop) *chsd ldr: rdn to chal jst over 2f out: unable qck whn short of room and hmpd wl over 1f out: sn outpcd by wnr: wknd u.p and wl btn 1f out* **4/1**[3]

-210 **6** *2* **Bullet Train**[13] 2746 3-8-12 109 TomQueally 7 101
(H R A Cecil) *t.k.h: trckd ldrs: nt clr run over 2f out: swtchd rt and rdn 2f out: fnd nil and wl btn over 1f out* **5/1**

2-65 **7** *3 3/4* **Waseet**[30] 2226 3-8-12 103 RichardHills 8 95
(J L Dunlop) *dwlt and pushed along sn after s: t.k.h after 1f and hld up in last pair: rdn 3f out: no prog and wl btn fnl 2f* **20/1**

5-34 **8** *10* **Togiak (IRE)**[41] 1910 3-8-12 95 RyanMoore 5 79
(E A L Dunlop) *hld up wl in tch towards rr: rdn and struggling over 2f out: lost tch 2f out: wl btn and eased ins fnl f* **33/1**

2m 30.06s (-2.44) **Going Correction** +0.125s/f (Good) 8 Ran SP% **110.2**
Speed ratings (Par 111): **113,111,110,109,108 106,104,97**
toteswingers:1&2:£11.30, 1&3:£9.20, 2&3:£15.80 CSF £46.30 CT £453.19 TOTE £4.90: £1.70, £4.10, £2.90; EX 55.10 Trifecta £571.10 Pool: £13,059.20 - 16.92 winning units..
Owner Sheikh Hamdan Bin Mohammed Al Maktoum **Bred** Darley **Trained** Middleham Moor, N Yorks

FOCUS

This did not look a strong renewal on paper and there are one or two doubts about the form. However, the first two are progressive and the third is rated to his French Guineas form.

NOTEBOOK

Monterosso, whose only defeat in his previous five starts came when comfortably beaten by Green Moon over 1m2f at Newbury two starts back, was 6lb better off with that rival this time, and his style of running suggested he would improve for this longer trip. That was certainly the case as he quickened up well inside the final two, and drew nicely clear in the closing stages. He still showed some signs of inexperience out in front and there's more to come from him, with the Leger trip probably not out of the question, despite what his pedigree might suggest. He's 10-1 for the final Classic with Hills, but in the shorter term the Princess Of Wales's Stakes at Newmarket might be a suitable target. (tchd 9-2 and 4-1 in places)

Arctic Cosmos(USA) won a handicap at Kempton last time out off a mark of just 78 and, although he was quite impressive, this represented a huge step up in class. It said quite a lot that his trainer was prepared to blow a revised mark of 87 by running him in this race, though, and he justified the decision with a fine effort in second. He's clearly progressing fast and should be up to picking up a Listed contest before long. (op 16-1 tchd 12-1)

Buzzword was supplemented into the Derby but never really got competitive in that race. This track promised to give a better indication of whether he has the stamina for 1m4f, and having been given a patient ride out the back he did keep on well to just grab third. A strongly run race over shorter is likely to see him at his best, though, and as he's by Pivotal, so easier ground is also likely to suit. (op 12-1)
At First Sight(IRE), who was ostensibly the Ballydoyle pacemaker in the Derby, but having been allowed the run of things and stolen a march on his field rounding Tattenham Corner, kept on to take a surprising second place. Running on his own merits for the first time since winning his maiden last summer, he was again allowed a pretty easy time of it in front, but he wasn't allowed to get away from the rest this time, and from 2f down the writing was on the wall for him. This did come quite quick following his big run at Epsom, but the impression that there was an element of fluke about his Derby run remains. (op 3-1 tchd 9-4 and 10-3 in a place)
Green Moon(IRE), who was coltish beforehand, had been successful in each of his previous three starts this term, including in Listed company on his latest outing. This was another step up in grade, but he promised to be suited by the extra 2f. He couldn't confirm Newbury form with Monterosso though, and it was his inability to go with the Johnston horse 2f out that caused him to be squeezed up and to lose ground. It's possible the ground was on the fast side for him, but a return to 1m2f looks in order. (op 3-1 tchd 11-4)
Bullet Train, who didn't come down the hill at Epsom but had previously won the Lingfield Derby Trial, was disappointing. He raced a bit keenly but had a perfect position behind the leader on the rail throughout and simply didn't pick up under pressure. Although this was a quick run back after the Derby, he didn't look to have too hard a race there, and perhaps this was just one run too many on fast ground. (tchd 11-2)
Waseet sustained an injury after finishing second in the Royal Lodge last year and hasn't looked the same horse since. This ground would probably have been quicker than ideal too. (op 25-1 tchd 33-1 in a place)
Togiak(IRE) hadn't done anything in his previous starts this term to suggest he was up to winning in this grade, and he was never a danger. He needs to return to handicaps. (tchd 40-1)

3143 CORONATION STKS (GROUP 1) (FILLIES) 1m (R)
3:50 (3:51) (Class 1) 3-Y-O

£154,698 (£58,642; £29,348; £14,633; £7,330; £3,678) **Stalls** High

Form — RPR

10-5 **1** **Lillie Langtry (IRE)**[26] [2370] 3-9-0 109 ... JMurtagh 11 — 116
(A P O'Brien, Ire) *midfield: hdwy 3f out: chsd ldr wl over 1f out: led ins fnl f: edgd lft and r.o wl in full control towards fin* **7/2**[1]

5-30 **2** 1 1/4 **Gile Na Greine (IRE)**[26] [2370] 3-9-0 109 ... KJManning 8 — 113
(J S Bolger, Ire) *ponied to s: led: rdn over 2f out: hdd ins fnl f: nt qckn and hld towards fin* **25/1**

0-01 **3** 2 1/4 **Jacqueline Quest (IRE)**[47] [1726] 3-9-0 111 ... TomQueally 5 — 108
(H R A Cecil) *midfield: hdwy over 2f out: rdn to chse ldng pair and lugged rt over 1f out: edgd lft ins fnl f: styd on same pce fnl 100yds* **6/1**[3]

-163 **4** nk **Music Show (IRE)**[26] [2370] 3-9-0 110 ... RyanMoore 2 — 107+
(M R Channon) *hld up: hdwy on outer u.p 2f out: prog and styd on ins fnl f: unable to rch ldrs* **9/2**[2]

121 **5** 2 1/4 **Evading Tempete**[48] [1713] 3-9-0 107 ...(p) OlivierPeslier 6 — 102
(F Rohaut, France) *hld up: swtchd lft 2f out: sn rdn and nt qckn: prog ins fnl f: styd on fnl 100yds: nt pce to rch ldrs* **16/1**

3-36 **6** nk **Lady Of The Desert (USA)**[33] [2158] 3-9-0 113 ... KierenFallon 9 — 101
(B J Meehan) *ponied to s: hld up: rdn and hdwy 2f out: chsd ldrs over 1f out: edgd rt ins fnl f: one pce fnl 110yds* **11/1**

12 **7** 1 3/4 **Anna Salai (USA)**[26] [2370] 3-9-0 111 ... FrankieDettori 13 — 97
(Mahmood Al Zarooni) *hld up: rdn and hdwy 2f out: chsd ldng bunch over 1f out: nvr able to mount chal: no imp and no ex ins fnl f* **9/2**[2]

-020 **8** nk **Famous (IRE)**[26] [2370] 3-9-0 103 ...(v[1]) CO'Donoghue 3 — 97
(A P O'Brien, Ire) *bhd: pushed along over 3f out: rdn over 2f out: sme hdwy over 1f out: nvr able to get on terms w ldrs* **66/1**

14-4 **9** 3/4 **Sent From Heaven (IRE)**[47] [1726] 3-9-0 109 ... MichaelHills 7 — 95
(B W Hills) *dwlt: racd keenly: hld up in rr: pushed along over 2f out: nvr able to get on terms* **12/1**

42-1 **10** 1 1/2 **Puff (IRE)**[62] [1384] 3-9-0 108 ... JimCrowley 12 — 91
(R M Beckett) *racd keenly: prom: rdn to take 2nd over 2f out: lost 2nd wl over 1f out: wknd ins fnl f* **20/1**

113- **11** 9 **Tabassum (IRE)**[244] [6852] 3-9-0 108 ... RichardHills 1 — 71
(Sir Michael Stoute) *racd keenly: prom: rdn over 2f out: wknd over 1f out* **12/1**

65-1 **12** 1 1/2 **Chachamaidee (IRE)**[35] [2098] 3-9-0 105 ... EddieAhern 4 — 67
(H R A Cecil) *prom: pushed along over 3f out: wknd ent fnl 2f: eased whn btn over 1f out* **25/1**

21-5 **13** 26 **Electric Feel**[20] [2546] 3-9-0 99 ... MartinDwyer 10 — 7
(M Botti) *racd keenly: trckd ldrs: n.m.r whn wkng over 3f out: eased whn btn over 1f out: t.o* **66/1**

1m 39.69s (-1.01) **Going Correction** +0.125s/f (Good) **13 Ran SP% 117.9**
Speed ratings (Par 110): **110,108,106,106,103 103,101,101,100,99 90,88,62**
toteswingers:1&2:£28.80, 1&3:£6.10, 2&3:£40.60 CSF £101.67 CT £528.29 TOTE £4.80: £2.00, £7.40, £2.90; EX 123.70 Trifecta £893.70 Pool: £14,397.03 - 11.92 winning units..
Owner M Tabor, D Smith & Mrs John Magnier **Bred** K B Lynch **Trained** Ballydoyle, Co Tipperary

FOCUS
A race that has gone to some real top-notch fillies' in recent times, Crimplene, Banks Hill, Russian Rhythm and Attraction being about the pick of them, but for all that this season's renewal was an open one, it did lack the presence of either Special Duty (winner of the Newmarket and French 1000 Guineas), or Bethrah (winner of the Irish equivalent). None of the 13 runners had previously won at Group 1 level. The 1m fillies' classic picture has been a muddling one this season, with the massive draw bias controversy and demotion of Jacqueline's Quest at Newmarket being followed by trouble in running and a second Guineas being awarded to Special Duty by the stewards at Longchamp. However, on various form lines it's possible that, at last, we have found the best of the bunch in Lillie Langtry.

NOTEBOOK
Lillie Langtry(IRE), who has been slow to come to hand this term having injured her knee at last season's Breeders' Cup, but suggested she was up to challenging the best of her generation at the distance when a fast-finishing fifth (beaten 3/4l), in the Irish 1000 on her reappearance. With that run out of the way, it was easy to see why she was towards the head of the market, and Murtagh deserves much credit for being aware to the threat posed by the front-running Gile Na Griene, who caught the remainder out under a fine front-running ride. In fairness, it looked for a brief moment as though she wasn't going to be able to get past, but despite wandering to her left close home, she was ultimately well on top under a strong ride. She is likely to go up in trip now, with the Nassau Stakes looking the most likely target, though Aidan O'Brien did mention the Pretty Polly at the Curragh, so they clearly think she will get 1m2f, which judging by this performance she might. (tchd 4-1 and 9-2 in a place)
Gile Na Greine(IRE), racing on the heavily favoured stands' side when just failing to get up at Newmarket, failed to run a race at the Curragh, beating only two home, but her trainer was prepared to put a line through that effort, and under a well-judged front-running ride, she came right back to her best, if anything surpassing the level of form shown at Newmarket. She appeals as the type to keep on improving with racing, as many from the yard often do, and she will no doubt be contesting similar races to the winner in future, with a step up in trip likely. (op 33-1)
Jacqueline Quest(IRE), first past the post in the Guineas when a 66-1 shot, got a perfect tow through the race, but having been produced in the straight, she couldn't quicken on and then edged both ways under pressure, suggesting she was feeling the ground. The Falmouth Stakes could be her next target. (op 8-1)
Music Show(IRE), who 'won' her race on the far side at Newmarket and was beaten just 1/2l at the Curragh, had a low draw to overcome here. Despite a good start she couldn't get in and then lost her position, ending up with just one behind her as they straightened for home. Although she stayed on really well from over a furlong out, she faced a hopeless task and just failed to get up for third. She deserves a change in luck and the Falmouth Stakes looks the obvious next target, though connections are mulling a rise in distance for her. (op 5-1 tchd 11-2 in places)
Evading Tempete, who split Joanna and Special Duty in the Prix Imprudence back in April, comfortably won a Group 3 at Capannelle last time and ran well here despite lacking the pace to challenge. She continues to go the right way and a return to slower conditions will help. (op 14-1)
Lady Of The Desert(USA), in the same ownership as Music Show, looked unlucky in the French 1000, getting no run at a crucial stage, but that did little to prove her stamina for 1m (had looked very suspect beforehand). She was another who got too far back, not being helped by the weakening Electric Feel falling back into her lap as they turned for home, and she could make no impression on them from over 1f out. (op 9-1 tchd 14-1 in a place)
Anna Salai(USA), narrowly defeated by Bethrah at the Curragh (first run for connections having been switched from Andre Fabre), had to prove herself on quick ground a second time and the response was limited when Dettori asked her for an effort in the straight. (tchd 7-2, 5-1 in places and 6-1 in a place)
Famous(IRE) made modest late gains in the first-time visor. (tchd 50-1)
Sent From Heaven(IRE), fourth in the 1000 Guineas at Newmarket, was unable to get anywhere near the early lead this time having been slowly away. (op 16-1)
Puff(IRE), the Fred Darling winner, didn't get home having raced keenly, and can probably be given another chance.
Tabassum(IRE) isn't the biggest and her connections were far from convinced she would have improved from two to three. She didn't have much to find with Music Show on Rockfel form, but was keen on this first run in 244 days, and she slowly dropped away having been right there turning in. (op 11-1)
Chachamaidee(IRE), whose saddle slipped going to post, had only won a Listed race at York and she wasn't up to this. (op 20-1)
Electric Feel, the lowest-rated runner in the field, stopped very quickly and something was presumably amiss. (tchd 50-1)

3144 WOLFERTON H'CAP (LISTED RACE) 1m 2f
4:25 (4:25) (Class 1) (0-110,110) 4-Y-O+

£28,385 (£10,760; £5,385; £2,685; £1,345; £675) **Stalls** High

Form — RPR

11-2 **1** **Rainbow Peak (IRE)**[36] [2057] 4-9-4 **107** ... NeilCallan 16 — 116+
(M A Jarvis) *dwlt: sn in midfield: swtchd lft and effrt over 2f out: rdn to chal over 1f out: drvn to ld 1f out: r.o strly and drew clr fnl 150yds* **13/8**[1]

-145 **2** 2 1/4 **Kings Gambit (SAF)**[17] [2637] 6-9-2 **105** ... MickyFenton 12 — 109
(T P Tate) *chsd ldrs tl sltly hmpd and dropped to midfield bnd over 8f out: swtchd to outer and effrt 2f out: kpt on wl fnl f: edgd rt fnl 50yds: snatched 2nd last stride: no threat to wnr* **25/1**

3-05 **3** shd **Kingdom Of Fife**[43] [1832] 5-9-7 **110** ...(v) RyanMoore 15 — 114
(Sir Michael Stoute) *dwlt: sn pushed up to chse ldrs and t.k.h after 1f: rdn and chal between horses ent fnl 2f: drvn to ld over 1f out: hdd 1f out: nt pce of wnr ins fnl f: edgd lft and lost 2nd last stride* **15/2**[2]

-652 **4** 1 **Salute Him (IRE)**[35] [820] 7-9-2 **105** ... JMurtagh 14 — 107
(A J Martin, Ire) *t.k.h: hld up wl off the pce towards rr: rdn and hdwy ent fnl 2f: swtchd ins jst over 1f out: r.o wl fnl f: n.m.r cl home* **16/1**

2-40 **5** 1 1/4 **Three Moons (IRE)**[20] [2538] 4-8-13 **102** ... RichardHughes 11 — 102
(H J L Dunlop) *hld up in midfield: effrt u.p ent fnl 2f: styd on same pce and no imp fnl f* **33/1**

-524 **6** 3/4 **Indian Days**[18] [2593] 5-9-1 **104** ... PaulMulrennan 6 — 102
(J G Given) *led and set gd gallop: rdn ent fnl 2f: hdd over 1f out: no ex and btn ent fnl f: wknd fnl 150yds* **20/1**

0103 **7** 1 1/2 **Albaqaa**[18] [2608] 5-8-10 **99** ... PaulHanagan 9 — 94+
(R A Fahey) *v.s.a: wl bhd: rdn and effrt over 2f out: hdwy but hanging rt fr over 1f out: kpt on: nvr trbld ldrs* **10/1**

-045 **8** 1/2 **Traffic Guard (USA)**[18] [2593] 6-9-5 **108** ... JamieSpencer 3 — 102
(P F I Cole) *chsd ldrs: wnt 2nd over 8f out tl over 2f out: wknd u.p over 1f out* **16/1**

0001 **9** 1 **Fiery Lad (IRE)**[14] [2710] 5-9-7 **110** ... KierenFallon 7 — 102
(L M Cumani) *dwlt: niggled along and wl off the pce towards rr: sme hdwy on inner 2f out: no imp ins fnl f: n.d* **8/1**[3]

6015 **10** 1/2 **Beauchamp Xerxes**[14] [2707] 4-9-0 **103** ... DaneO'Neill 8 — 94
(G A Butler) *stdd s: hld up wl off the pce towards rr: rdn and effrt over 2f out: nvr trbld ldrs* **28/1**

-315 **11** nk **Antinori (IRE)**[14] [2710] 4-8-12 **101** ...(v) AhmedAjtebi 1 — 91
(Mahmood Al Zarooni) *hld up wl off the pce toward rr: pushed along and effrt ent fnl 2f: no prog u.p over 1f out: n.d* **20/1**

6211 **12** shd **Tartan Gigha (IRE)**[14] [2708] 5-9-1 **104** ... JoeFanning 4 — 94
(M Johnston) *racd keenly: chsd ldrs: rdn and struggling 3f out: wknd u.p 2f out* **14/1**

4-04 **13** 2 3/4 **Eastern Aria (UAE)**[40] [1956] 4-9-2 **105** ... FrankieDettori 2 — 90
(M Johnston) *t.k.h: chsd ldr tl over 8f out: rdn and wknd over 2f out: wl bhd fnl f* **14/1**

-465 **14** 3 1/2 **Steele Tango (USA)**[22] [2470] 5-9-5 **108** ... LiamKeniry 5 — 86
(R A Teal) *hld up in midfield: rdn and effrt on outer 3f out: no prog and btn 2f out: wl bhd fnl f* **28/1**

0540 **15** 8 **Halicarnassus (IRE)**[14] [2716] 6-9-5 **108** ... AlanMunro 10 — 70
(M R Channon) *s.i.s: a wl bhd: rdn 7f out: lost tch 3f out* **25/1**

2m 4.50s (-2.50) **Going Correction** +0.125s/f (Good) **15 Ran SP% 122.2**
Speed ratings (Par 111): **115,113,113,112,111 110,109,109,108,107 107,107,105,102,96**
toteswingers:1&2:£11.00, 1&3:£3.10, 2&3:£37.80 CSF £55.72 CT £262.03 TOTE £2.60: £1.50, £5.00, £2.00; EX 54.30 Trifecta £395.00 Pool: £6,621.49 - 12.40 winning units..
Owner P D Savill **Bred** P D Savill **Trained** Newmarket, Suffolk

FOCUS
Normally a competitive affair, but this year's race featured a hot favourite, and the market proved correct. The form looks solid with the winner progressive and the next four home close to their marks.

NOTEBOOK
Rainbow Peak(IRE) ◆, in contrast to most of his rivals, came here with an unexposed profile. He'd bagged the best draw and came here on the back of a fine effort in defeat at York over an inadequate trip. Talk of running him in a Group 3 after that race hinted at the regard in which he is held by his trainer, and he looked to have obvious claims in this Listed handicap off a mark of 107, 4lb higher than at York. The gallop was decent, he bagged a good position just off the pace and, once angled out in the straight, he picked up well for pressure and ran on resolutely to the line. He's a progressive 4-y-o and connections have ambitious plans for him, with a Group 1 race in Germany in their sights. Softer ground over there won't inconvenience him at all. (tchd 7-4, 15-8 in places)

Kings Gambit(SAF) got a little outpaced mid-race but came home really well down the outside in the straight. He's done most of his racing in recent times over 1m2f, but won a Group 1 in South Africa over 1m4f earlier in his career and his stamina came into play here. This was a good run but he's likely to remain a difficult horse to place. (tchd 22-1)

Kingdom Of Fife, dropping back in grade having been held in Group company on his last four starts, made the most of his favourable draw and got a good position tracking the pace on the rail. He had every chance in the straight and briefly gave the winner a race, but in reality had no chance against him at the weights. He's another who's difficult to find suitable opportunities for off his current mark. (op 8-1)

Salute Him(IRE), who finished well from off the pace to take third in this race last year off a 4lb lower mark, ran a similar race. Dropped in on the rail from his good draw, he got a clear run through in the straight, but the line was always going to come too soon for him. A longer straight suits his style of running better.

Three Moons(IRE), running in a handicap for the first time, was also ridden patiently with the benefit of the inside rail. She's likely to find things easier back against her own sex. (op 50-1)

Indian Days ran a brave race from the front considering how much use was made of him early and the decent gallop he set. He's an honest horse but as a result gives himself few chances with the Handicapper. (op 16-1)

Albaqaa faced a tough enough task off the same mark as when third in the Zetland Gold Cup last time. Slowly away and held up in last place, he just didn't pick up in the straight, and the way he was hanging suggests this ground was plenty quick enough for him. (op 12-1 tchd 14-1)

Traffic Guard(USA) was poorly drawn and, in trying to overcome that handicap, went too fast early to take up a position tracking the leader. He paid the price in the straight.

Fiery Lad(IRE), 5lb higher for his win at Epsom last time out, runs his best races when delivered late off a strong gallop. This race was run to suit him but he was never travelling this time and perhaps the race came too soon after his win on Oaks day. (op 10-1)

Tartan Gigha(IRE), winner of his last two starts in competitive handicaps, was another 4lb higher here. Poorly drawn, he was rushed up to take a prominent position but was caught wider than ideal and raced keenly. It was no surprise to see him weaken in the straight. (op 11-1)

Eastern Aria(UAE), who pulled too hard in a Group 2 in Germany last time, looked to have plenty on at the weights. Again keen, she had too much use made of her in crossing over from her unfavourable low draw. (op 12-1)

3145 QUEEN'S VASE (GROUP 3) 2m

5:00 (5:00) (Class 1) 3-Y-O

£39,739 (£15,064; £7,539; £3,759; £1,883; £945) **Stalls** High

Form				RPR
62-3	1		**Mikhail Glinka (IRE)**[61] 1414 3-9-1 110 .... JMurtagh 8 (A P O'Brien, Ire) *trckd ldrs: effrt 3f out: r.o to dipute ld fr jst ins fnl f: carried hd high: prevailed on the nod in driving fin* **2/1**[1]	107+
0-41	2	nse	**Theology**[43] 1851 3-9-1 86 .... WilliamBuick 11 (J Noseda) *hld up: hdwy on inner over 2f out: sn rdn: disp ld fr jst ins fnl f: jst denied in driving fin* **18/1**	107
2-41	3	2 ½	**Total Command**[43] 1847 3-9-1 85 .... RyanMoore 7 (Sir Michael Stoute) *racd keenly in midfield: gd hdwy to ld over 2f out: sn edgd rt: hdd jst ins fnl f: styd on u.p: no ex fnl 50yds* **8/1**[3]	104
1113	4	1 ¾	**Corsica (IRE)**[13] 2758 3-9-1 105 .... FrankieDettori 9 (M Johnston) *led: hdd over 5f out: remained prom: rdn and chalng fr 2f out: stl ev ch over 1f out: no ex fnl 150yds* **9/4**[2]	102+
-313	5	¾	**Moose Moran (USA)**[19] 2562 3-9-1 85 .... TomQueally 2 (H R A Cecil) *hld up: hdwy on outer over 4f out: chsd ldrs over 2f out: lugged rt bhd front quartet and one pce fnl 150yds* **20/1**	101
1223	6	3 ¼	**Chink Of Light**[43] 1833 3-9-1 98 ....(v) JimmyFortune 12 (A M Balding) *trckd ldrs: led and qcknd tempo over 5f out: sn swtchd to ins rail: rdn and hdd over 2f out: wknd over 1f out* **16/1**	97
-652	7	1 ¼	**Private Story (USA)**[27] 2323 3-9-1 95 .... RichardHughes 1 (R Hannon) *midfield: rdn over 2f out: no imp on ldrs over 1f out: one pce after* **25/1**	96
04-1	8	4	**Monterey (IRE)**[14] 2697 3-9-1 88 .... StevieDonohoe 3 (R A Mills) *hld up: struggling over 2f out: sn hung lft: nvr able to get on terms* **17/2**	91
6	9	3	**Troas (IRE)**[26] 2367 3-9-1 94 ....(p) FMBerry 4 (John M Oxx, Ire) *rrd s: in rr: niggled along over 6f out: struggling over 2f out: hung rt u.p over 1f out: nvr able to get on terms* **25/1**	87
624	10	nk	**Icon Dream (IRE)**[26] 2367 3-9-1 104 .... JamieSpencer 10 (David Wachman, Ire) *midfield: hdwy 3f out: rdn to chse ldrs over 2f out: wknd over 1f out: eased whn btn fnl f* **14/1**	91
	11	2 ½	**Alburj (USA)**[16] 2666 3-9-1 89 .... PJSmullen 5 (D K Weld, Ire) *hld up: struggling over 2f out: sn wl btn* **16/1**	87
3-	12	25	**Magic Prospect (FR)**[14] 3-9-1 82 .... OlivierPeslier 6 (E J O'Neill, France) *chsd ldr: lost pl over 5f out: gng bkwards whn n.m.r over 3f out: bhd after: t.o* **40/1**	54

3m 27.98s (-1.02) **Going Correction** +0.125s/f (Good) **12 Ran SP% 124.3**

Speed ratings (Par 109): **107,106,105,104,104 102,102,100,98,98 97,84**

toteswingers:1&2:£13.70, 1&3:£4.40, 2&3:£13.30 CSF £40.77 CT £258.65 TOTE £3.10: £1.30, £5.20, £2.00; EX 47.60 Trifecta £374.10 Pool: £10,236.94 - 20.24 winning units..

Owner Mrs John Magnier, M Tabor & D Smith **Bred** Paulyn Limited **Trained** Ballydoyle, Co Tipperary

FOCUS

Usually one of the more intriguing contests of the meeting, and a race that has produced a few high-class stayers in recent years, most notably last season's Gold Cup runner-up Patkai and St Leger winner Mastery. The pace was a stop-start one, but with so many promising middle-distance 3-y-os trying this sort of trip for the first time, you certainly needed to stay the trip well in order to win, and many of these didn't. The winner offer the best guide to the level.

NOTEBOOK

Mikhail Glinka(IRE), carrying the highest official rating of these on 110, had looked to be a Derby contender earlier in the year when chosen to contest the Ballysax Stakes, but he missed the Derrinstown the following month, and a step up to this sort of trip looked the right move, as he shaped like more of a stayer at two when finishing second in a heavy-ground 1m2f Group 1 at Saint-Cloud. Always ideally positioned under Murtagh, he tended to carry his head a tad high early in the straight, but one couldn't question his willingness, and his head was down when it mattered as they flashed across the line. The St Leger would be the obvious target for the son of Galileo, and he would appeal as one of the likelier winners at this stage, for all that he would need a truly run race back in distance. As for the longer term, connections feel he has the qualities to develop into a Gold Cup horse. (tchd 9-4 and 7-4 in places)

Theology, who finally got off the mark at the fourth attempt in a 1m4f maiden at Goodwood last time, stepped up massively on that form. Like the winner, a son of Galileo, he raced on the inside throughout and picked up really well to challenge inside the final furlong, but just lost out. He remains capable of better and will no doubt be aimed towards the St Leger also. (op 16-1)

Total Command raced keenly and showed a good change of pace to take over early in the straight, but his stamina appeared to fail him inside the final furlong. He, like the runner-up, had won a Goodwood maiden at the fourth attempt, and would appeal as one of the likelier St Leger winners at this stage, with something like the Great Voltigeur likely to be used as a trial race. (op 10-1)

Corsica(IRE), representing a yard responsible for five of the last nine winners of this race, doesn't have the stoutest of pedigrees, for all that he has been running as though he could get the trip, and he just couldn't see it out as well as the front three. This still represented a step up, and he's another who could be St Leger bound. (op 11-4 tchd 3-1 in places)

Moose Moran(USA), third behind King Edward winner Monterosso on his recent handicap debut, was up 6f in trip and challenged widest of all, but couldn't race on with the front four from over 1f out. This still represented a step forward and he remains capable of better back down in distance. (op 25-1 tchd 16-1)

Chink Of Light, third in the Chester Vase, injected some pace into the race with over 4f to run, but his stamina gave way in the straight.

Private Story(USA), second to a smart prospect at Haydock, was laboured in the straight and appeared not to stay. (op 20-1)

Monterey(IRE), who was well backed, never got into it having been held up and looked awkward under pressure in the straight. Official explanation: jockey said colt hung left home straight (op 16-1)

Icon Dream(IRE) was another who appeared not to stay. Official explanation: jockey said gelding was struck into behind (op 11-1)

Alburj(USA), who is still a maiden, never left the rear. (tchd 20-1)

3146 BUCKINGHAM PALACE H'CAP 7f

5:35 (5:35) (Class 2) (0-105,103) 3-Y-O+

£31,155 (£9,330; £4,665; £2,335; £1,165; £585) **Stalls** Centre

Form				RPR
-322	1		**Treadwell (IRE)**[14] 2713 3-8-10 98 .... FergusSweeney 27 (J A Osborne) *racd on far side: hld up bhd: hdwy and squeezed through wl over 1f out: rdn and str run ent fnl f: led fnl 75yds* **14/1**	105
4-02	2	½	**Himalya (IRE)**[19] 2563 4-9-10 103 .... RyanMoore 3 (J Noseda) *racd stands' side: stdd s: hld up towards rr: hdwy on stands' rail jst over 2f out: rdn wl over 1f out: led gp 1f out: ev ch overall ins fnl f: kpt on wl: 1st of 10 in gp* **7/1**[2]	112
3-10	3	nk	**Imperial Guest**[19] 2563 4-8-11 90 .... SebSanders 31 (G G Margarson) *racd far side: stdd s: hld up in midfield: hdwy over 2f out: rdn to chse ldrs over 1f out: ev ch ins fnl f: no ex towards fin: 2nd of 16 in gp* **50/1**	98
-510	4	1	**Hajoum (IRE)**[13] 2736 4-8-13 92 .... JoeFanning 23 (M Johnston) *racd far side: chsd ldrs tl led and overall ldr over 2f out: hung lft u.p over 1f out: hdd fnl 100yds: no ex: 3rd of 16 in gp* **50/1**	97
5-04	5	shd	**Webbow (IRE)**[29] 2241 8-8-11 90 .... JimmyFortune 6 (N Tinkler) *racd stands' side: stdd s: hld up towards rr: rdn and effrt ent fnl 2f: swtchd rt over 1f out: kpt on wl u.p fnl f: 2nd of 10 in gp* **16/1**	95
0-20	6	½	**Swift Gift**[113] 710 5-9-5 98 .... MartinDwyer 30 (B J Meehan) *racd far side: chsd ldrs: rdn over 2f out: edging lft u.p fr over 1f out: kpt on same pce ins fnl f: 4th of 16 in gp* **11/1**[3]	102
0264	7	1 ¾	**Wigram's Turn (USA)**[59] 1455 5-8-10 89 ....(v) DavidProbert 29 (A M Balding) *racd far side: in tch in midfield: rdn 3f out: unable qck and no hdwy 2f out: styd on again ins fnl f: nt pce to rch ldrs: 5th of 16 in gp* **40/1**	88
2-56	8	nse	**Mr Willis**[118] 635 4-8-6 90 .... KierenFox(5) 28 (J R Best) *racd far side: hld up wl in tch: rdn and effrt 2f out: unable qck and kpt on same pce fnl f: 6th of 16 in gp* **33/1**	89
4100	9	¾	**Everymanforhimself (IRE)**[13] 2748 6-9-6 99 ....(v) PJSmullen 2 (K A Ryan) *racd stands' side: chsd ldr in that gp: rdn over 2f out: swtchd lft over 1f out: wknd ent fnl f: 3rd of 10 in gp* **50/1**	96
5436	10	¾	**Light From Mars**[18] 2595 5-9-3 99 .... JamesMillman(3) 19 (B R Millman) *racd far side: in tch: rdn and unable qck over 2f out: styd on again ins fnl f: nvr gng pce to threaten ldrs: 7th of 16 in gp* **25/1**	94
-110	11	shd	**Spirit Of Sharjah (IRE)**[36] 2057 5-9-9 102 .... MichaelHills 11 (Miss J Feilden) *racd stands' side: t.k.h: hld up towards rr: rdn and effrt over 2f out: no hdwy 2f out and btn over 1f out: 4th of 10 in gp* **28/1**	97
0-10	12	hd	**Castles In The Air**[41] 1900 5-9-2 102 .... LeeTopliss(7) 1 (R A Fahey) *racd stands' side: clr ldr of that gp and w ldrs overall: rdn and hung rt fr 2f out: wknd 1f out: 5th of 10 in gp* **20/1**	96+
0-35	13	hd	**Nasri**[18] 2595 4-9-5 98 .... NeilCallan 25 (D M Simcock) *racd far side: in tch in midfield: rdn and unable qck over 2f out: styd on again ins fnl f: nvr gng pce to threaten ldrs: 8th of 16 in gp* **33/1**	91
6-03	14	nk	**Something (IRE)**[13] 2748 8-9-0 93 .... PaulQuinn 22 (D Nicholls) *racd far side: stdd s: hld up in rr: effrt 2f out: swtchd lft and hdwy u.p over 1f out: wknd ent fnl f: 9th of 16 in gp* **20/1**	86
1201	15	¾	**Dubai Dynamo**[21] 2508 5-9-6 99 .... HayleyTurner 4 (Mrs R A Carr) *racd stands' side: stdd s: hld up in rr: swtchd rt and effrt ent fnl 2f: no prog fr over 1f out: nvr trbld ldrs: 6th of 10 in gp* **20/1**	90
0/	16	1	**Bangalore Gold (IRE)**[27] 2351 4-9-7 100 .... FrankieDettori 18 (David Marnane, Ire) *racd far side: hld up in rr: swtchd lft and effrt 2f out: drvn and no prog over 1f out: n.d: 10th of 16 in gp* **11/2**[1]	88
0-43	17	2 ¼	**Al Khaleej (IRE)**[119] 626 6-9-7 100 .... TedDurcan 8 (E A L Dunlop) *racd stands' side: stdd s: hld up in rr: rdn and short-lived effrt over 2f out: n.d: 7th of 10 in gp* **20/1**	82
2-41	18	3	**Brae Hill (IRE)**[27] 2311 4-9-6 99 .... StevieDonohoe 20 (R A Fahey) *racd far side: mde most tl rdn and hdd over 2f out: wknd 2f out: wl btn ent fnl f: 11th of 16 in gp* **25/1**	73
12-0	19	shd	**Servoca (CAN)**[76] 1085 4-9-0 93 .... JimmyQuinn 17 (Mike Murphy) *racd far side: hld up in rr: rdn over 2f out: sn wl btn: 12th of 16 in gp* **80/1**	66
6636	20	nk	**Run For The Hills**[13] 2748 4-9-7 100 .... WilliamBuick 7 (J H M Gosden) *racd stands' side: hld up in tch: rdn and effrt to chse gp ldrs wl over 1f out: btn ent fnl f: eased fnl 100yds: 8th of 10 in gp* **14/1**	73
5401	21	2 ¼	**Kiwi Bay**[10] 2835 5-8-11 90 5ex .... PaulMulrennan 15 (M Dods) *racd stands' side: chsd ldrs: u.p 1/2-way: wknd over 2f out: wl bhd fnl f: 9th of 10 in gp* **16/1**	57
1-03	22	2	**Esoterica (IRE)**[35] 2100 7-8-13 92 ....(v) TomQueally 16 (J S Goldie) *racd far side: in tch: rdn 4f out: struggling 1/2-way: wl btn over 1f out: 10th of 10 in gp* **28/1**	53
3-12	23	3	**Dance And Dance (IRE)**[27] 2311 4-9-1 94 .... JimCrowley 26 (E F Vaughan) *racd far side: hld up in tch in midfield: rdn and effrt 2f out: hmpd and lost pl wl over 1f out: no ch after and eased fnl f: 13th of 16 in gp* **33/1**	47+
-620	24	3 ½	**Prime Exhibit**[41] 1900 5-9-2 95 .... PaulHanagan 13 (R A Fahey) *racd far side: in tch in midfield: struggling u.p 1/2-way: sn bhd: wl btn fnl 2f: 14th of 16 in gp* **20/1**	39
1-11	25	24	**Day Of The Eagle (IRE)**[13] 2736 4-8-13 92 .... KierenFallon 21 (L M Cumani) *racd far side: stdd strart: hld up in rr: stl in rr whn bdly hmpd wl over 1f out: virtually p.u after: t.o: 15th of 16 in gp* **11/2**[1]	—+

0-50 **26** *40* **Penny's Gift**[13] 2744 4-9-8 **101**....................(b) RichardHughes 24 —
(R Hannon) *racd far side: w ldr tl over 2f out: wkng whn bdly hmpd wl over 1f out: virtually p.u after: t.o: 16th of 16 in gp* **33/1**

1m 25.9s (-2.10) **Going Correction** -0.075s/f (Good)
WFA 3 from 4yo+ 9lb **26** Ran SP% **136.4**
Speed ratings (Par 109): **109,108,108,106,106 106,104,104,103,102 102,102,101,101,100 99,97,93,93,93 90,88,84,80,53 7**
toteswingers:1&2:£16.10, 1&3:£581.60, 2&3:£472.60 CSF £89.62 CT £4903.13 TOTE £15.60: £2.80, £2.20, £21.10, £20.60; EX 115.30 Trifecta £5408.60 Pool: £8,770.74 - 1.20 winning units. Place 6 £433.53; Place 5 £117.54.
Owner Mrs F Walwyn & A Taylor **Bred** Liberty Road Stables **Trained** Upper Lambourn, Berks

FOCUS
A typically competitive handicap; they split into two groups, with slightly more going far side. There was little in it at the finish, confirming the impression of the last two days that there was little bias between the two sides. The form looks solid with the first six all close to their marks.

NOTEBOOK
Treadwell(IRE) had shown steady improvement in each of his previous three starts this term, despite not winning and, although another 4lb higher than for his latest defeat at Epsom, this test promised to be right up his street. Well drawn towards the far side, he was buried in the pack and, as others wandered off it, he was angled towards the rail, and came with a strong finish to lead close home. The only 3-y-o in the field and the first of his age group to win this race, he's clearly a colt firmly on the upgrade, and the Bunbury Cup looks a logical next step.
Himalya(IRE) didn't get much luck in running over 6f at Newmarket last time but he's a notoriously frustrating type who tends to run on late when the race is over. The extra furlong here promised to help and he cannot be said to have done anything wrong this time as he was a good winner of the race on his side, having stuck limpet-like to the stands'-side rail. Another rise in the weights for this defeat isn't going to make things easier. (op 10-1)
Imperial Guest, well beaten last time out in the Newmarket race in which Himalya finished second, bounced back to form here. Drawn highest of all, he didn't come off the far rail until a furlong out. He battled on well under pressure and clearly saw out the extra furlong well. (op 40-1)
Hajoum(IRE) ran poorly at Doncaster last time out but had previously looked to be an improving colt. He tracked the two leaders on the far side and was the first to strike for home but didn't quite see it out. A more patient ride was perhaps required here, but similar tactics in a smaller field could well pay dividends and he remains one to be interested in.
Webbow(IRE) looked unlucky at Chester but his subsequent effort at Haydock suggested he might have been flattered by that view. Off the same mark as when seventh in this race last year when racing on the favoured side, he tracked Himalya through on the stands' side before being switched off the rail 1½f out. He finished well but was never quite getting there.
Swift Gift, who won the Victoria Cup over this C&D last year, followed up by finishing 11th, but fourth in his group, in this race. Racing off the same mark as last year, he again finished fourth on his side. It will be dangerous to assume that he will improve for this as he has gone well fresh in the past. (tchd 12-1 in a place)
Wigram's Turn(USA), better known as an AW performer, was well drawn and kept on well enough. He looks high enough in the weights at present, though. (op 33-1)
Mr Willis, another better known for his exploits on the Polytrack, ran a similar race to Wigram's Turn on the far side. (op 28-1)
Everymanforhimself(IRE) found this stiff track too much of a test but was still a fair third on his side.
Light From Mars raced further away from the far rail than most in that group, which might not have been ideal.
Spirit Of Sharjah(IRE) raced wider than most in the stands' side group, which probably didn't help. An easier 7f suits him better. (tchd 33-1 in a place)
Castles In The Air took them along on the stands' side but hung right into the centre of the track as he came under pressure approaching the 2f pole. He probably went a bit quicker than ideal early, but is also best served by easier conditions underfoot.
Something(IRE) races as often in sprints as he does over this distance but his record suggests that this is his best trip. Coming here on the back of a solid effort over 6f at Epsom, he got to race off a mark 2lb lower than when third on the wrong side in this race last year, but he proved a touch disappointing, failing to land a blow on the far side.
Dubai Dynamo had his Newmarket form boosted when the runner-up finished third in the Hunt Cup on Wednesday, but he failed to make any impression on the stands' side off a career-high mark.
Bangalore Gold(IRE), back over 7f after winning a big-field handicap over 1m at the Curragh last time out, had an awkward middle draw to overcome and struggled to make his presence felt. (tchd 15-2 in a place)
Al Khaleej(IRE), a lightly raced 6-y-o who was second in the Victoria Cup over this C&D back in 2008, was last seen running with credit out in Dubai in February, but he failed to reproduce that form back on turf, despite a record of going well fresh. (op 18-1)
Dance And Dance(IRE) Official explanation: jockey said colt suffered interference in running
Day Of The Eagle(IRE), a progressive sort chasing a four-timer off an 8lb higher mark than for his latest, narrow success, tends to finish his race off strongly, so it was most disappointing that, just as he was beginning to respond to pressure and stay on next to the far rail, he ran into the back of the weakening Penny's Gift. He would have finished closer with a clear run but the damage was done so far out that it's difficult to know where he would have finished. Official explanation: jockey said gelding suffered interference in running (tchd 13-2 in a place)
T/Jkpt: £21,534.20. Pool of £90,989.59 - 3 winning tickets. T/Plt: £613.50 to a £1 stake. Pool:£484,243.87 - 576.13 winning tickets T/Qpdt: £30.50 to a £1 stake. Pool:£24,694.12 - 597.41 winning tickets SP

2448 AYR (L-H)
Friday, June 18

OFFICIAL GOING: Good to firm (9.3)
Inside rail on round course moved out 2m and stands' side rail on straight course moved in 3m.
Wind: Breezy, half against Weather: Sunny, hot

3147 SAINTS AND SINNERS APPRENTICE H'CAP 1m
6:10 (6:12) (Class 6) (0-55,56) 4-Y-0+ **£2,266** (£674; £337; £168) **Stalls** Low

Form RPR

0-00 **1** **Glenluji**[9] 2854 5-8-0 **46**.................... NoraLooby(5) 11 53
(J S Goldie) *hld up and bhd: hdwy whn nt clr run briefly over 1f out: led ins fnl f: r.o* **20/1**

-060 **2** *½* **Catcher Of Dreams (IRE)**[21] 2500 4-8-5 **46** oh1.........(t) NathanAlison 4 52
(A G Foster) *led: rdn over 2f out: hdd ins fnl f: kpt on* **22/1**

00-0 **3** *¾* **Rain Stops Play (IRE)**[53] 1576 8-8-0 **46**.............. MarzenaJeziorek(5) 1 50
(N G Richards) *t.k.h: prom: effrt over 2f out: r.o fnl f: nrst fin* **8/1**

-404 **4** *2* **Chichen Daawe**[21] 2516 4-8-9 **50** ow1....................(p) DaleSwift 13 50
(B Ellison) *midfield: pushed along over 2f out: kpt on fnl f: nt rch ldrs* **11/2**[2]

-000 **5** *hd* **Primo Way**[15] 2670 9-8-0 **46** oh1.................... NeilFarley(5) 8 45
(D A Nolan) *hld up towards rr: hdwy over 2f out: one pce fnl f* **40/1**

0643 **6** *nse* **King's Jester (IRE)**[22] 2454 8-8-5 **53**................(b) DavidSimmonson(7) 7 52
(Lee Smyth, Ire) *awkward s: hld up: hdwy over 2f out: kpt on fnl f* **6/1**[3]

0025 **7** *2* **Fiefdom (IRE)**[9] 2850 8-9-0 **55**....................(p) AdamCarter 12 49
(I W McInnes) *prom: effrt over 2f out: outpcd appr fnl f* **8/1**

2-26 **8** *1¼* **Bed Fellow (IRE)**[9] 2858 6-8-7 **53**.................... LukeStrong(5) 5 46
(P Monteith) *t.k.h: hld up in midfield: effrt over 2f out: no ex whn n.m.r appr fnl f* **12/1**

-024 **9** *¾* **Anthemion (IRE)**[9] 2859 13-7-13 **47**.................... ShaneBKelly(7) 2 37
(Mrs J C McGregor) *t.k.h: cl up tl rdn and wknd over 1f out* **6/1**[3]

445/ **10** *¾* **Cheeky Chilli**[4] 3041 5-8-2 **46** oh1.................... JakePayne(3) 3 34
(Irene J Monaghan, Ire) *plld hrd: cl up tl rdn and wknd fnl f* **4/1**[1]

0001 **11** *3¾* **Chicamia**[25] 2382 6-8-7 **53**.................... JosephYoung(5) 6 32
(M Mullineaux) *slowly away and detached: bhd tl styd on fnl f: nvr on terms* **14/1**

0365 **12** *1* **Hettie Hubble**[15] 2671 4-8-7 **48**.................... SoniaEaton 10 25
(D W Thompson) *hld up on outside: shkn up 3f out: sn outpcd* **14/1**

/3-0 **13** *½* **Ten To The Dozen**[15] 2670 7-8-10 **56** ow4.................. PaulNorton(5) 14 32
(D W Thompson) *prom on outside: edgd lft and wknd over 2f out* **40/1**

00-0 **14** *5* **Suburbia (USA)**[35] 2072 4-8-11 **52**.................... MatthewLawson 9 16
(J Barclay) *loose bef s: cl up tl wknd fr 3f out* **20/1**

1m 40.47s (-3.33) **Going Correction** -0.60s/f (Hard) **14** Ran SP% **126.0**
Speed ratings (Par 101): **92,91,90,88,88 88,86,85,84,83 80,79,78,73**
toteswingers: 1&2 £165.70, 1&3 £77.60, 2&3 £96.10 CSF £399.47 CT £3881.67 TOTE £25.70: £6.10, £11.40, £4.00; EX 700.30.
Owner Jim Goldie Racing Club **Bred** Jim Goldie **Trained** Uplawmoor, E Renfrews

FOCUS
A poor handicap, run at a fair pace but by no means solid, with the fourth to his latest mark.
Anthemion(IRE) Official explanation: trainer said gelding lost a near-hind shoe
Hettie Hubble Official explanation: jockey said saddle slipped

3148 GLASGOW GALA CASINOS MAIDEN STKS 7f 50y
6:40 (6:40) (Class 5) 3-Y-0+ **£3,238** (£963; £481; £240) **Stalls** High

Form RPR

25-2 **1** **King Of Windsor (IRE)**[21] 2517 3-9-0 80.................... MartinLane(3) 1 79+
(R M Beckett) *hld up: hdwy and swtchd rt over 2f out: led over 1f out: qcknd clr: readily* **4/6**[1]

00 **2** *5* **Viking Warrior (IRE)**[25] 2393 3-9-3 0.................... PhillipMakin 6 66
(M Dods) *led: rdn over 2f out: hdd over 1f out: kpt on: no ch w wnr* **8/1**

-023 **3** *nk* **Antarctic Desert (IRE)**[25] 2393 3-9-3 74.................... PJMcDonald 3 65
(K A Ryan) *trckd ldrs gng wl: effrt over 2f out: one pce fr over 1f out* **3/1**[2]

4460 **4** *1¾* **Jack O'Lantern**[14] 2702 3-9-3 72.................... TonyHamilton 10 60
(R A Fahey) *hld up in tch: rdn over 2f out: edgd lft: no imp over 1f out* **7/1**[3]

/40 **5** *4½* **Rosbertini**[25] 2393 4-9-5 0.................... DaleSwift(7) 5 48
(Miss L A Perratt) *towards rr and sn pushed along: sme hdwy over 1f out: nvr rchd ldrs* **50/1**

03 **6** *nse* **Music Festival (USA)**[14] 2706 3-9-0 0.................... GaryBartley(3) 9 48
(J S Goldie) *dwlt: sn trcking ldrs: rdn over 2f out: wknd over 1f out* **12/1**

-000 **7** *1½* **Hotgrove Boy**[15] 2673 3-9-3 40....................(b[1]) DavidAllan 4 44
(A G Foster) *trckd ldr tl rdn and wknd over 2f out* **50/1**

8 *10* **Drumcomie** 3-8-9 0.................... KellyHarrison(3) 2 12
(J S Goldie) *s.i.s: a outpcd and bhd* **40/1**

1m 30.36s (-3.04) **Going Correction** -0.60s/f (Hard)
WFA 3 from 4yo 9lb **8** Ran SP% **122.7**
Speed ratings (Par 103): **93,87,86,84,79 79,78,66**
toteswingers: 1&2 £2.30, 1&3 £2.10, 2&3 £3.60 CSF £8.17 TOTE £1.90: £1.70, £1.40, £1.10; EX 8.20.
Owner Jones, Healy, Whitehead & Mitchell **Bred** Shadwell Estate Company Limited **Trained** Whitsbury, Hants

FOCUS
A modest maiden and the winner did not have to improve to score, with the third and fourth below their marks.
Drumcomie Official explanation: jockey said filly finished lame

3149 SCOTTISH DECORATORS/DECORATION MARINE SERVICES H'CAP 1m
7:15 (7:15) (Class 5) (0-70,68) 4-Y-0+ **£3,238** (£963; £481; £240) **Stalls** Low

Form RPR

6523 **1** **Daring Dream (GER)**[15] 2670 5-8-13 **63**.................... GaryBartley(3) 1 73
(J S Goldie) *prom: stdy hdwy over 2f out: plld out and rdn to ld 1f out: kpt on wl* **11/4**[2]

6032 **2** *1½* **El Dececy (USA)**[9] 2854 6-8-13 **60**.................... DavidAllan 3 67
(J Balding) *led 2f: cl up: led 2f out to 1f out: kpt on same pce ins fnl f* **9/2**[3]

63-5 **3** *1¼* **Talk Of Saafend (IRE)**[22] 2452 5-9-3 **64**.................... TonyHamilton 4 68
(P Monteith) *stdd in tch: effrt over 2f out: kpt on fnl f: nt pce to chal* **20/1**

6-51 **4** *1½* **King's Counsel (IRE)**[17] 2625 4-8-12 **59**....................(v) PJMcDonald 5 59
(D O'Meara) *sn drvn and led after 2f: hdd 2f out: rallied: outpcd fnl f* **11/4**[2]

0-41 **5** *22* **Liteup My World (USA)**[12] 2789 4-8-11 **65** 6ex.............. DaleSwift(7) 2 15
(B Ellison) *t.k.h: chsd ldrs: rdn and wknd over 2f out: t.o* **9/4**[1]

35-6 **6** *30* **Postman**[20] 2527 4-9-7 **68**.................... TomEaves 6 —
(B Smart) *trckd ldrs tl wknd over 2f out: eased whn no ch: t.o* **12/1**

1m 38.23s (-5.57) **Going Correction** -0.60s/f (Hard) **6** Ran SP% **114.7**
Speed ratings (Par 103): **103,101,100,98,76 46**
toteswingers: 1&2 £3.10, 1&3 £7.80, 2&3 £5.80 CSF £15.85 TOTE £3.30: £1.50, £2.70; EX 16.20.
Owner George Barclay & Graeme McGinlay **Bred** Gestut Auenquelle **Trained** Uplawmoor, E Renfrews

FOCUS
A moderate handicap but straightforward form and sound enough.
Liteup My World(USA) Official explanation: trainer said gelding was found to be lame
Postman Official explanation: jockey said gelding lost its action

3150 CLYDE COAST CONTRACTS H'CAP 7f 50y
7:45 (7:45) (Class 4) (0-85,85) 4-Y-0+ **£7,123** (£2,119; £1,059; £529) **Stalls** High

Form RPR

6020 **1** **Celtic Sultan (IRE)**[13] 2736 6-9-6 **84**....................(b) FrannyNorton 1 95
(T P Tate) *mde all: clr 1/2-way: rdn 2f out: kpt on wl fnl f* **3/1**[2]

4121 **2** *1½* **Imperial Djay (IRE)**[3] 3062 5-8-2 **71** 6ex.................... JamesSullivan(5) 6 78
(Mrs R A Carr) *hld up: stdy hdwy to chse (clr) wnr wl over 1f out: sn rdn and edgd lft: kpt on fnl f: nt pce to chal* **9/4**[1]

5510 **3** *2¼* **Opus Maximus (IRE)**[6] 2977 5-9-7 **85**.................... RoystonFfrench 2 86
(M Johnston) *prom: drvn 3f out: kpt on same pce fr 2f out* **5/1**[3]

0022 **4** *1½* **Stellite**[9] 2858 10-7-13 **66** oh1.................... KellyHarrison(3) 5 63
(J S Goldie) *hld up: shkn up and edgd lft 2f out: kpt on fnl f: no imp* **10/1**

6136 **5** *¾* **Come And Go (UAE)**[18] 2580 4-9-2 **80**.................... PJMcDonald 3 75
(G A Swinbank) *prom: pushed along over 2f out: edgd lft and sn no imp* **6/1**

0041 **6** *2* **La Zamora**[29] 2262 4-9-1 **79**.................... PhillipMakin 8 68
(T D Barron) *stdd s: hld up: n.m.r fr over 2f out: nvr able to chal* **16/1**

4-10 **7** *nk* **Deadly Encounter (IRE)**[49] 1672 4-9-6 **84**.................... TonyHamilton 7 73
(R A Fahey) *s.i.s: bhd: rdn 3f out: nvr rchd ldrs* **12/1**

1-00 **8** ¾ **Inheritor (IRE)**[24] 2423 4-9-6 **84**.. TomEaves 4 71
(B Smart) *chsd wnr: rdn over 3f out: edgd lft and wknd wl over 1f out* **9/1**

1m 28.29s (-5.11) **Going Correction** -0.60s/f (Hard) 8 Ran SP% **119.4**
Speed ratings (Par 105): **105,103,100,99,98 95,95,94**
toteswingers: 1&2 £3.70, 1&3 £3.10, 2&3 £3.10 CSF £10.75 CT £33.00 TOTE £5.20: £1.60, £1.10, £2.40; EX 11.00.

Owner Mrs Sylvia Clegg **Bred** Miss C Lyons **Trained** Tadcaster, N Yorks

FOCUS
A fair handicap with the time good and the winner rated back to last year's best. The runner-up was close to his latest form.

3151 AYR CENTRAL SHOPPING CENTRE H'CAP 6f
8:20 (8:22) (Class 4) (0-80,78) 3-Y-O **£7,123** (£2,119; £1,059; £529) **Stalls** Low

Form RPR

5164 **1** **Thrust Control (IRE)**[17] 2618 3-8-11 **75** ow2.................... DaleSwift(7) 7 81
(B Ellison) *cl up: effrt 2f out: led ins fnl f: styd on strly* **3/1**[2]

6313 **2** ¾ **Carrie's Magic**[17] 2628 3-8-12 **69**... TomEaves 2 73
(T D Barron) *led: rdn 2f out: hdd ins fnl f: kpt on u.p* **7/1**[3]

55-1 **3** *1* **Pepper Lane**[17] 2628 3-8-1 **63**..................................... JamesSullivan(5) 5 63
(D O'Meara) *hld up in tch: rdn and hdwy over 1f out: kpt on ins fnl f* **5/2**[1]

2335 **4** *1* **Boy The Bell**[17] 2628 3-8-2 **66**...................................... JosephYoung(7) 9 63
(M Mullineaux) *prom: effrt 2f out: kpt on same pce fnl f* **16/1**

0064 **5** *1* **Ruler's Honour (IRE)**[14] 2706 3-8-6 **63**...................... RoystonFfrench 3 57+
(T J Etherington) *dwlt: last but in tch: effrt over 1f out: kpt on fnl f: nvr rchd ldrs* **25/1**

1-01 **6** ¾ **Commanche Raider (IRE)**[13] 2768 3-9-7 **78**................. PhillipMakin 6 70
(M Dods) *t.k.h: cl up: rdn 2f out: btn fnl f* **5/2**[1]

05-4 **7** *1* **Weetentherty**[23] 2432 3-7-13 **59** oh3......................(b[1]) KellyHarrison(3) 8 47
(J S Goldie) *t.k.h: hld up in tch: rdn and edgd lft over 1f out: sn no imp* **12/1**

4-05 **8** *2* **Key Breeze**[13] 2762 3-8-6 **63**... PJMcDonald 1 45
(K A Ryan) *t.k.h: cl up on ins tl rdn and wknd over 1f out* **10/1**

1m 11.08s (-2.52) **Going Correction** -0.375s/f (Firm) 8 Ran SP% **121.2**
Speed ratings (Par 101): **101,100,98,97,96 95,93,91**
toteswingers: 1&2 £6.20, 1&3 £2.90, 2&3 £3.40 CSF £25.99 CT £62.10 TOTE £4.70: £1.80, £2.70, £1.10; EX 30.10.

Owner Dan Gilbert & Kristian Strangeway **Bred** Rathasker Stud **Trained** Norton, N Yorks

FOCUS
A moderate handicap with the runner-up close to his maiden form. The winner scored despite his rider carrying 2lb overweight.

3152 BETTOR.COM H'CAP 1m 5f 13y
8:50 (8:50) (Class 5) (0-75,72) 4-Y-O+ **£3,070** (£906; £453) **Stalls** Low

Form RPR

00-2 **1** **Forrest Flyer (IRE)**[28] 2295 6-8-12 **63**.............................. PhillipMakin 7 73
(J S Goldie) *chsd ldr: led 2f out: sn rdn: hrd pressed fnl f: hld on gamely* **4/5**[1]

1063 **2** *shd* **Wicked Daze (IRE)**[28] 2295 7-9-7 **72**.................................. TomEaves 2 82
(Miss L A Perratt) *led: rdn 3f out: hdd 2f out: rallied u.p: jst hld* **3/1**[2]

5-42 **3** *9* **Los Nadis (GER)**[13] 2430 6-8-6 **57**............................. RoystonFfrench 1 53
(P Monteith) *chsd ldrs tl outpcd wl over 2f out* **4/1**[3]

\- **4** *17* **Mcmurdo Sound (IRE)**[54] 1554 6-8-9 **60**...................(t) TonyHamilton 3 31
(Gordon Elliott, Ire) *prom: rdn over 3f out: sn btn* **6/1**

2m 50.38s (-3.62) **Going Correction** -0.60s/f (Hard) 4 Ran SP% **114.8**
Speed ratings (Par 103): **87,86,81,70**
CSF £3.86 TOTE £1.80; EX 4.80.

Owner Mrs Camille Macdonald **Bred** Philip Lau **Trained** Uplawmoor, E Renfrews

FOCUS
A modest handicap. The first two dominated and are rated to form.

3153 GUESTS OF PRINCESS ROYAL EVENTS CENTRE H'CAP 1m 2f
9:20 (9:20) (Class 6) (0-65,63) 3-Y-O **£2,047** (£604; £302) **Stalls** Low

Form RPR

640 **1** **Smarty Sam (USA)**[25] 2393 3-9-7 **63**.............................. PJMcDonald 2 69+
(G A Swinbank) *trckd ldrs: effrt and ev ch over 1f out: led wl ins fnl f: hld on wl* **9/4**[1]

000- **2** *hd* **Honoured (IRE)**[205] 7522 3-8-10 **52**.. TomEaves 7 58+
(Sir Mark Prescott) *cl up: rdn fr 3f out: rallied and led 1f out: hdd wl ins fnl f: r.o* **4/1**[2]

4525 **3** ¾ **Magic Millie (IRE)**[34] 2132 3-8-10 **52**................................ PhillipMakin 6 56
(D O'Meara) *in tch: smooth hdwy over 2f out: effrt and ev ch over 1f out: kpt on ins fnl f* **9/4**[1]

40-5 **4** *4* **Goodison Park**[15] 2673 3-9-0 **56**... DavidAllan 1 52
(A G Foster) *led: rdn 3f out: hdd 1f out: sn btn* **6/1**[3]

0600 **5** *1* **Light The City (IRE)**[10] 2838 3-8-0 **45**...................... KellyHarrison(3) 4 39
(Mrs R A Carr) *t.k.h: hld up in tch: effrt and edgd lft over 2f out: no imp fr over 1f out* **25/1**

0000 **6** 2¼ **Barastar**[10] 2838 3-8-5 **47**... RoystonFfrench 8 37
(N Tinkler) *t.k.h: hld up in tch: rdn over 2f out: wknd over 1f out* **14/1**

-530 **7** *hd* **Emeralds Spirit (IRE)**[10] 2838 3-8-1 **46** ow1................. MartinLane(3) 3 35
(J R Weymes) *slowly away: hdwy and cl up after 2f: rdn 3f out: wknd wl over 1f out* **8/1**

2m 8.41s (-3.59) **Going Correction** -0.60s/f (Hard) 7 Ran SP% **117.4**
Speed ratings (Par 97): **90,89,89,86,85 83,83**
toteswingers: 1&2 £6.20, 1&3 £2.90, 2&3 £3.40 CSF £12.18 CT £22.13 TOTE £3.30: £2.40, £2.70; EX 6.40 Place 6 £83.67; Place 5 £7.28.

Owner S S Anderson **Bred** Runnymede Farm Inc Et Al **Trained** Melsonby, N Yorks

FOCUS
A weak handicap where the first three came clear. The first two are improvers and the third is rated to her Nottingham form.

T/Plt: £148.20 to a £1 stake. Pool:£32,872.35 - 161.85 winning tickets T/Qpdt: £10.50 to a £1 stake. Pool:£3,602.57 - 251.95 winning tickets RY

2924 GOODWOOD (R-H)
Friday, June 18

OFFICIAL GOING: Straight course - good; round course - good to firm
First 2f of mile course dolled out 5yds but all distances as advertised.
Wind: Mild breeze Weather: Becoming overcast with heavy rain after 8.30

3154 IQUEST H'CAP 6f
5:50 (5:50) (Class 5) (0-75,75) 3-Y-O **£2,661** (£785; £393) **Stalls** Low

Form RPR

2355 **1** **R Woody**[11] 2824 3-9-7 **75**.. PatCosgrave 9 82
(D K Ivory) *trckd ldrs: swtchd to centre 2f out: str run to ld ent fnl f: r.o: rdn out* **12/1**

50-6 **2** ½ **Caldermud (IRE)**[49] 1661 3-9-5 **73**.............................. SteveDrowne 10 78
(J R Best) *prom: rdn to ld wl over 1f out: hdd ent fnl f: kpt on but no ex: jst hld on for 2nd* **6/1**[2]

6-05 **3** *nse* **One Hit Wonder**[10] 2844 3-8-6 **60**......................... FrankieMcDonald 5 65
(Mouse Hamilton-Fairley) *hld up last: pushed along and hdwy over 2f out: sn swtchd to centre: kpt on ins fnl f: jst failed to snatch 2nd* **12/1**

542 **4** 2¼ **Starwatch**[12] 2784 3-8-2 **56** oh1...................................... NeilChalmers 1 54
(J J Bridger) *led: rdn and hdd over 1f out: kpt on same pce* **16/1**

21-0 **5** 1¼ **Adventure Story**[11] 2824 3-9-7 **75**.. PatDobbs 7 69
(R Hannon) *squeezed up s: trckd ldrs: effrt 2f out: kpt on same pce fnl f* **15/2**[3]

6001 **6** 1¼ **Al Khimiya (IRE)**[9] 2871 3-9-1 **74** 6ex.............................. JohnFahy(5) 3 64
(S Woodman) *chsd ldrs: rdn over 2f out: sn outpcd* **14/1**

4604 **7** *hd* **Silvee**[36] 2052 3-7-13 **58**.. AmyBaker(5) 2 47
(J J Bridger) *cl up: outpcd whn nt clr run and swtchd lft 2f out: nvr bk on terms* **20/1**

3521 **8** 2½ **Sheer Force (IRE)**[23] 2441 3-9-6 **74**................................. ShaneKelly 8 55
(W J Knight) *prom: rdn and ev ch 2f out: wknd and eased fnl f* **4/5**[1]

3106 **9** 2¼ **Private Olley**[7] 2928 3-9-0 **67** ow1..................................... AdamKirby 4 42
(J Akehurst) *trckd ldrs: rdn 2f out: sn outpcd: wknd fnl f* **25/1**

0040 **10** *9* **Avongate**[16] 2648 3-9-0 **68**..(p) LukeMorris 6 13
(R A Harris) *prom: rdn and ev ch 2f out: wknd over 1f out* **25/1**

1m 11.8s (-0.40) **Going Correction** -0.05s/f (Good) 10 Ran SP% **122.0**
Speed ratings (Par 99): **100,99,99,96,94 92,92,89,86,74**
toteswingers:1&2:£7.90, 1&3:£16.20, 2&3:£9.40 CSF £83.86 CT £917.13 TOTE £17.50: £3.40, £2.40, £3.40; EX 86.60.

Owner Quintessential Thoroughbreds Solar Syn **Bred** R, D And M Close **Trained** Radlett, Herts

FOCUS
An ordinary handicap in which the principals tended to race down the centre of the track. The form is rated slightly positively, with the first three clear.

3155 CALLQUEST H'CAP 1m 1f 192y
6:20 (6:21) (Class 5) (0-70,73) 3-Y-O **£3,238** (£963; £481; £240) **Stalls** High

Form RPR

-450 **1** **Kerchak (USA)**[15] 2682 3-9-7 **70**... PatDobbs 6 76
(W Jarvis) *mid-div: hdwy 3f out: sn rdn: wnt 3rd over 1f out: str run fnl 100yds: led towards fin* **8/1**

1U55 **2** ¾ **Until The Man (IRE)**[27] 2321 3-9-3 **66**.............................(p) IanMongan 5 71
(Mrs L J Mongan) *trckd ldr: rdn wl over 2f out: hdd wl over 1f out: rallied gamely: led fnl 75yds: ct towards fin* **15/2**[3]

065 **3** 1¼ **Formulation (IRE)**[15] 2684 3-9-6 **69**................................. SteveDrowne 9 71+
(H Morrison) *little slowly away: sn trcking ldrs: swtchd rt to chal 2f out: sn led: rdn whn hung lft 1f out: hdd fnl 75yds: fdd* **5/4**[1]

5401 **4** *hd* **Onyx Of Arabia (IRE)**[4] 3039 3-9-10 **73** 6ex...................(b) EddieAhern 1 75
(B J Meehan) *hld up bhd: rdn and stdy prog fr over 2f out: styd on but nvr fining strly enough to rch ldrs* **3/1**[2]

6-00 **5** 3½ **Finch Flyer (IRE)**[27] 2336 3-8-2 **51** oh2................................. LukeMorris 8 46
(G L Moore) *mid-div: rdn over 3f out: prog 2f out: one pce fnl f* **25/1**

00-0 **6** 3¾ **Albeed**[62] 1394 3-8-9 **58**.. ShaneKelly 3 46
(J L Dunlop) *sme mod late prog but mainly towards rr* **11/1**

-306 **7** *2* **Double Fortune**[13] 2754 3-9-2 **65**................................(b[1]) PatCosgrave 4 49
(Jamie Poulton) *trckd ldrs: rdn over 3f out: wknd wl over 1f out* **40/1**

5050 **8** *11* **Madlool (IRE)**[10] 2844 3-9-2 **65**... LiamJones 2 27
(W J Haggas) *mid-div: rdn over 3f out: sn wknd* **16/1**

000 **9** 3¼ **Latent Light (USA)**[29] 2255 3-9-6 **69**.............................. GeorgeBaker 7 24
(E A L Dunlop) *a towards rr* **25/1**

24-0 **10** *7* **Resuscitator (USA)**[62] 1387 3-9-7 **70**............................... ChrisCatlin 10 11
(Mrs H S Main) *led tl over 5f out: pressed ldr: rdn over 3f out: wkng whn hmpd on rails 2f out* **14/1**

2m 8.87s (0.87) **Going Correction** -0.05s/f (Good) 10 Ran SP% **123.3**
Speed ratings (Par 99): **94,93,92,92,89 86,84,76,73,67**
toteswingers:1&2:£6.90, 1&3:£4.20, 2&3:£3.10 CSF £69.13 CT £127.52 TOTE £10.30: £2.70, £1.90, £1.40; EX 77.60.

Owner The Silverback Partnership **Bred** Dede McGehee Dvm **Trained** Newmarket, Suffolk

FOCUS
A fair handicap but one largely lacking progressive types and overall it looked a weak one for the track. The pace was only fair yet the winner was still able to come from some way off it. The favourite appeared to lose his action while the first two are both rated slight improvers.
Latent Light(USA) Official explanation: jockey said colt had no more to give

3156 CASEQUEST MAIDEN AUCTION FILLIES' STKS 6f
6:50 (6:51) (Class 4) 2-Y-O **£3,561** (£1,059; £529; £264) **Stalls** Low

Form RPR

2 **1** **Goodwood Treasure**[30] 2223 2-8-8 0................................. EddieAhern 5 70+
(J L Dunlop) *mde all: shkn up to qckn clr whn edgd rt ent fnl f: easily* **1/2**[1]

2 1½ **Methayel (IRE)** 2-8-13 0.. ChrisCatlin 6 67+
(C E Brittain) *s.i.s: last but in tch: hdwy over 1f out: kpt on wl fnl f: no ch w wnr* **14/1**

3 1¼ **Paco Belle (IRE)** 2-8-12 0.. PatCosgrave 1 62
(R Hannon) *jinked lft leaving stalls: trckd ldrs: rdn 2f out: kpt on ins fnl f* **5/1**[2]

0 **4** ½ **Mystica (IRE)**[13] 2749 2-8-13 0... LiamKeniry 2 61
(D J S Ffrench Davis) *trckd wnr: rdn over 2f out: kpt on same pce fnl f* **50/1**

5 *nk* **Look Twice** 2-8-11 0.. ShaneKelly 7 58+
(D M Simcock) *little slow away: cl 5th: effrt 2f out: kpt on same pce fnl f* **10/1**

6 ½ **So Choosy** 2-8-9 0.. PatDobbs 3 55
(R Hannon) *trckd ldrs: rdn over 2f out: kpt on same pce: no ex fnl 75yds* **13/2**[3]

0 7 30 **Fair Dame (IRE)**24 2407 2-8-2 0 AmyBaker(5) 4 —
(Mrs P N Dutfield) *sn pushed along in last pair: wknd 2f out: t.o* 80/1

1m 13.94s (1.74) **Going Correction** -0.05s/f (Good) 7 Ran SP% 115.6
Speed ratings (Par 92): **86,84,82,81,81 80,40**
toteswingers:1&2:£2.70, 1&3:£1.50, 2&3:£5.50 CSF £10.07 TOTE £1.40: £1.10, £5.70; EX 8.50.
Owner Goodwood Racehorse Owners Group (17)Ltd **Bred** Jeremy Green And Sons **Trained** Arundel, W Sussex

FOCUS
Just a fair maiden run at a fair pace but the winner did it as well as her form entitled her to and looks sure to on to better things. The level is fluid with little to go on, but the first two can rate higher.

NOTEBOOK
Goodwood Treasure looked to have an excellent chance even before Memory won the Albany Stakes at Royal Ascot earlier in the day, and she won with little fuss and plenty in hand, quickening smartly when asked to despite tending to drift towards the centre. She might not be as quite as good as her debut second to Memory makes her look, but she can probably win a novice event at least and her owners will no doubt be hoping she proves good enough for a crack at the Prestige Stakes here later in the summer. (tchd 4-5 in a place)
Methayel(IRE) ◆ is a half-sister to a couple of 1m2f winners and while she shaped as if she will be suited by further in time, it was inexperience and not the trip that cost her greatly here, bringing up the rear after a very slow start before running on strongly inside the last. It would be no surprise if she improved significantly next time. (op 12-1 tchd 11-1)
Paco Belle(IRE), out of a 2yo sprint winner, shaped encouragingly on her debut, racing closest to the rail throughout and keeping on well, showing a round action. She'll improve, and will stay 7f.
Mystica(IRE) improved significantly on her debut effort but was probably helped to some degree by the lack of early pace. She might not make the progress of some of these.
Look Twice, a filly by Royal Applause, didn't fare badly on her debut, travelling smoothly for a long way, and will improve. (op 9-1 tchd 8-1)
So Choosy, a half-sister to the dual 7f winner Night Kiss, looked her stable's first choice on jockey bookings but looked more in need of the experience than her stable companion. She looks to possess some scope, and ought to do a fair bit better in time. (op 11-2)

3157 TRACEQUEST MAIDEN FILLIES' STKS 1m 1f
7:25 (7:26) (Class 5) 3-Y-O+ £3,238 (£963; £481; £240) Stalls High

Form RPR
6-2 1 **Mazamorra (USA)**18 2603 3-9-0 0 ChrisCatlin 2 76
(M Botti) *trckd ldr: led over 2f out: sn rdn whn hrd pressed: styd on wl to assert fnl 100yds* 11/8[1]
63-0 2 1 ¾ **Queen's Envoy**22 2478 3-9-0 0 KirstyMilczarek 4 73
(L M Cumani) *travelled strly trcking ldrs: jnd ldrs wl over 2f out: rdn wl over 1f out: ev ch ent fnl f: no ex fnl 100yds* 7/4[2]
4-0 3 ¾ **Chicane**22 2478 3-9-0 0 LiamJones 5 71
(W J Haggas) *chsd ldrs: sltly outpcd over 2f out: hung lft ent fnl f: styd on fnl 100yds* 12/1
4 5 **Moresweets 'n Lace** 3-9-0 0 GeorgeBaker 1 63
(G L Moore) *racd green in 5th: rdn 3f out: slt bump 1f out: styd on same pce* 16/1
4-0 5 3 **Wajanaat**51 1620 3-9-0 0 PatDobbs 3 54
(M P Tregoning) *s.i.s: a bhd: rdn over 3f out: hung lft: no imp* 8/1[3]
0- 6 13 **Stargazing (IRE)**261 6390 4-9-11 0 EddieAhern 6 36
(B J Meehan) *led: rdn and hdd over 2f out: sn btn: eased fnl f* 8/1[3]

1m 58.23s (1.93) **Going Correction** -0.05s/f (Good)
WFA 3 from 4yo 11lb 6 Ran SP% 114.3
Speed ratings (Par 100): **89,87,86,82,79 68**
toteswingers:1&2:£1.20, 1&3:£3.80, 2&3:£4.60 CSF £4.16 TOTE £1.80: £1.10, £2.20; EX 4.20.
Owner J Barton & C Pizarro **Bred** Sarah S Farish **Trained** Newmarket, Suffolk

FOCUS
Little strength in depth to a fillies' maiden run at a steady pace. The winner sets the standard.

3158 CAPQUEST SOUTH AFRICA FILLIES' H'CAP 7f
7:55 (7:56) (Class 4) (0-85,84) 3-Y-O+ £4,209 (£1,252; £625; £312) Stalls High

Form RPR
23-3 1 **Fleeting Echo**8 2884 3-9-5 82 PatDobbs 2 90+
(R Hannon) *hld up: hdwy over 2f out: chal ent fnl f: led fnl 75yds: readily* 9/4[1]
0-35 2 1 ¼ **Cultured Pride (IRE)**21 2510 3-8-10 73 SteveDrowne 9 78
(R Hannon) *led: rdn in narrow advantage fr over 2f out: hdd fnl 75yds: no ex* 5/1[3]
-005 3 ½ **Spiritual Art**14 2719 4-8-5 66 HarryBentley(7) 4 73
(L A Dace) *trckd ldrs: rdn over 2f out: kpt on ins fnl f: nt pce to chal* 10/1
-000 4 1 ¾ **Seradim**22 2475 4-10-0 82 JimmyFortune 5 84
(P F I Cole) *chsd ldrs: jnd ldrs over 3f out: rdn 2f out: ev ch jst over 1f out: fdd fnl 100yds* 9/2[2]
0-1 5 1 ½ **Water Gipsy**30 2227 3-9-7 84 GeorgeBaker 7 79
(G L Moore) *s.i.s: hld up: hdwy 3f out: sn u.p: nvr gng pce to chal* 6/1
42-0 6 2 ¼ **Shibhan**34 2120 3-8-12 75 (p) KoseiMiura 8 64
(C E Brittain) *hld up in mid-div: hdwy 3f out: effrt 2f out: fdd ent fnl f* 16/1
230- 7 2 ¼ **Pictures (IRE)**217 7363 3-8-10 73 KirstyMilczarek 3 56
(L M Cumani) *racd keenly: prom: wkng whn hmpd over 2f out* 7/1
-001 8 3 ½ **Universal Circus**21 2491 3-8-12 75 ChrisCatlin 6 48
(M R Channon) *mid-div tl wknd 2f out* 10/1
6-00 9 nk **Secret Queen**19 2565 3-9-5 82 (b) EddieAhern 1 54
(B J Meehan) *prom: rdn over 2f out: wknd over 1f out* 16/1

1m 26.86s (-0.04) **Going Correction** -0.05s/f (Good)
WFA 3 from 4yo 9lb 9 Ran SP% 122.3
Speed ratings (Par 102): **101,99,99,97,95 92,90,86,85**
toteswingers:1&2:£4.10, 1&3:£7.50, 2&3:£11.90 CSF £14.56 CT £98.73 TOTE £3.50: £1.60, £1.80, £4.20; EX 18.50.
Owner P J & Mrs J P Haycock **Bred** P J Haycock **Trained** East Everleigh, Wilts

FOCUS
Quite a competitive fillies handicap run at a decent pace. The result looked the right one on the day, but the form is a little muddling and the runner-up is close to last year's form..
Cultured Pride(IRE) Official explanation: jockey said bit slipped through filly's mouth
Water Gipsy ◆ Official explanation: vet said filly finished sore

3159 CAPQUEST GROUP 25TH YEAR CELEBRATION H'CAP 1m 6f
8:30 (8:32) (Class 2) (0-100,91) 4-Y-O+
£9,969 (£2,985; £1,492; £747; £372; £187) Stalls High

Form RPR
0-40 1 **Woolfall Treasure**3 3050 5-9-6 88 (b) GeorgeBaker 6 97
(G L Moore) *slowly away: sn pushed along to chse ldrs: led 3f out: styd on wl: drvn out* 11/2
0-06 2 1 ½ **Hevelius**21 2509 5-9-5 87 AdamKirby 2 94
(W R Swinburn) *hld up in last pair: hdwy 5f out: rdn 3f out to chse wnr: styd on but a being hld fnl 2f* 8/1
16-4 3 2 ¾ **Rockfella**53 1579 4-8-7 75 CathyGannon 4 78
(D J Coakley) *prom: led after 2f: rdn and hdd 3f out: styd on same pce fnl 2f* 12/1
0-56 4 2 **Mykingdomforahorse**34 2126 4-8-4 72 ChrisCatlin 5 72
(M R Channon) *restrained in last s: hdwy on rails fr 3f out: rdn over 2f out: styd on same pce* 5/1[3]
130- 5 7 **Times Up**249 6734 4-9-9 91 EddieAhern 7 81
(J L Dunlop) *in tch tl dropped to last pair 5f out: rdn 4f out: no imp* 7/1
0-66 6 7 **Victoria Montoya**20 2538 5-9-8 90 (v) JimmyFortune 8 71
(A M Balding) *led for 2f: trckd ldrs: rdn over 4f out: sn btn* 7/2[1]
6-01 7 ½ **Rajeh (IRE)**13 2513 7-9-6 88 LiamJones 1 68
(J L Spearing) *trckd ldrs: rn wd on bnd after 2f: jnd ldr over 9f out tl rdn over 3f out: sn btn* 7/1
2-11 8 27 **Ermyn Lodge**41 1902 4-8-13 81 (v) IanMongan 3 23
(P M Phelan) *trckd ldrs: rdn over 4f out: dropped out tamely: eased fnl f* 4/1[2]

2m 59.66s (-3.94) **Going Correction** -0.05s/f (Good) 8 Ran SP% 118.1
Speed ratings (Par 109): **109,108,106,105,101 97,97,81**
toteswingers:1&2:£13.80, 1&3:£11.70, 2&3:£19.20 CSF £49.97 CT £511.89 TOTE £5.40: £2.00, £3.00, £3.90; EX 69.90.
Owner Andrew Bradmore **Bred** Serpentine Bloodstock Et Al **Trained** Lower Beeding, W Sussex

FOCUS
A useful handicap but one run at something of a muddling pace and possibly misleading form, with the two market leaders running well below their best. The first two set the level.

NOTEBOOK
Woolfall Treasure had finished well held in the Ascot Stakes on Tuesday but was well supported to put that behind him quickly and he returned to his best with a game effort, staying on well after being sent for home early. He's useful on his day, and is possibly ideally suited by fast ground. (op 8-1 tchd 5-1)
Hevelius had been shaping as if this first try at 1m6f would bring about some improvement, and he ran well to stay on strongly and pull clear of the rest. He's not got the best strike rate for one of his ability, but equally hasn't had many chances and is still unexposed as a stayer. (op 10-1 tchd 11-1)
Rockfella, up at a higher level than usual, seemed to see out the extra 2f without too much trouble but was beaten by two better-handicapped horses. He'll be of more interest next time back down in grade. (op 8-1)
Mykingdomforahorse was never nearer than at the finish after getting a long way behind and isn't easy to catch right but is another that will be better off back down in grade. (tchd 11-2)
Times Up had been a very progressive stayer last season and has a good record fresh, but he was very weak in the market and ran as if needing his first outing since October. He'll leave this form behind in due course. (tchd 8-1)
Victoria Montoya doesn't look to have trained on now she is in-foal, and it wouldn't be a surprise if connections decide to call it a day with her after this. (op 4-1)
Ermyn Lodge has been strongly progressive until now and was a major disappointment for little obvious reason, though his rider later reported that his mount was unsuited by not being allowed to make the running. Official explanation: jockey said gelding had been unsuited by the not being able to make the running (op 7-2)

3160 REQUEST H'CAP 1m 1f
9:00 (9:03) (Class 5) (0-70,70) 3-Y-O+ £3,238 (£963; £481; £240) Stalls High

Form RPR
-321 1 **Touch Of Style (IRE)**6 2952 6-8-6 53 6ex JohnFahy(5) 4 63+
(Matthew Salaman) *mid-div: rdn and hdwy over 2f out: styd on wl fnl f: led fnl 40yds* 4/1[1]
2004 2 ½ **Abhar (USA)**8 2906 3-8-5 63 KierenFox(5) 9 71
(J R Best) *trckd ldr: rdn 4f out: kpt on gamely to ld jst ins fnl f: hdd fnl 40yds* 14/1
605- 3 1 ¾ **Kings Troop**98 7428 4-9-12 68 FergusSweeney 15 73
(A King) *mid-div: outpcd 3f out: hdwy over 1f out: styd on fnl f* 25/1
0-03 4 nk **Mount Athos (IRE)**18 2587 3-8-8 64 PatrickHills(3) 13 69+
(J W Hills) *mid-div: outpcd 4f out: nt best of runs but hdwy 2f out: nt clr run and swtchd lft over 1f out: r.o whn swtchd to far side rails fnl f* 9/2[2]
3004 5 ¾ **Ivory Lace**14 2714 9-9-13 69 JimCrowley 5 72+
(S Woodman) *hld up towards rr: rdn and hdwy in centre fr over 2f out: edgd rt: styd on ins fnl f* 14/1
2464 6 ½ **Capeability (IRE)**26 2362 4-9-9 65 ChrisCatlin 11 67
(M R Channon) *trckd ldrs: rdn 3f out: kpt on same pce fnl 2f* 11/1
6006 7 1 **Trafalgar Square**18 2596 8-9-1 57 (v) GeorgeBaker 14 57
(M J Attwater) *s.i.s: in rr: hung rt fr over 2f out: styd on fnl f: nvr a threat* 13/2[3]
0000 8 ¾ **Dubai Gem**18 2597 4-8-13 55 IanMongan 2 53
(Jamie Poulton) *trckd ldrs: led 3f out: sn rdn: hdd jst ins fnl f: fdd* 20/1
0-33 9 nk **Jeremiah (IRE)**28 2279 4-9-8 64 (p) PatCosgrave 7 61
(J G Portman) *nvr bttr than mid-div* 12/1
0056 10 ½ **Lou Bear (IRE)**42 1873 3-8-4 57 KirstyMilczarek 10 52
(J Akehurst) *hld up towards rr: hdwy u.p over 2f out: fdd fnl f* 11/1
0-01 11 1 ¾ **Tilapia (IRE)**16 2645 6-9-11 67 AdamKirby 6 60
(Stef Higgins) *a towards rr* 20/1
0-04 12 1 ¼ **Gross Prophet**35 2080 5-9-12 68 (b) SteveDrowne 12 58
(A J Lidderdale) *sn led: clr 5f out: hdd 3f out: sn rdn: wknd ent fnl f* 7/1
1501 13 1 ¼ **Binnion Bay (IRE)**52 1591 9-8-9 51 (v) NeilChalmers 8 38
(J J Bridger) *s.i.s: a towards rr* 25/1
4634 14 15 **Trade Centre**32 2187 5-9-11 67 (p) LukeMorris 3 23
(R A Harris) *racd keenly: trckd ldrs: rdn 3f out: sn wknd* 20/1

1m 56.82s (0.52) **Going Correction** -0.05s/f (Good)
WFA 3 from 4yo+ 11lb 14 Ran SP% 123.7
Speed ratings (Par 103): **95,94,93,92,92 91,90,90,89,89 87,86,85,72**
toteswingers:1&2:£22.60, 1&3:£60.50, 2&3:£96.70 CSF £56.96 CT £1284.75 TOTE £5.40: £2.40, £5.30, £7.70; EX 92.00 Place 6 £79.79; Place 5 £15.76.
Owner Michael Barden **Bred** Yeomanstown Stud **Trained** Upper Lambourn, Berks

FOCUS
An ordinary handicap in very gloomy conditions to end proceedings. The pace was just fair but the field were soon well strung out. The form is modest and muddling.
Mount Athos(IRE) ◆ Official explanation: jockey said colt was denied a clear run
Gross Prophet Official explanation: jockey said gelding ran too freely

T/Plt: £325.00 to a £1 stake. Pool:£3,1122.30 - 69.90 winning tickets T/Qpdt: £11.40 to a £1 stake. Pool:£3,533.61 - 228.80 winning tickets TM

[2756]MUSSELBURGH (R-H)

Friday, June 18

OFFICIAL GOING: Good (good to firm in places; watered; 6.7)

Wind: Light across Weather: Bright and dry

3161 BALFOUR BEATTY ENGINEERING SERVICES H'CAP — 1m

1:50 (1:51) (Class 5) (0-70,70) 3-Y-O — £3,238 (£963; £481; £240) Stalls High

Form — RPR

0-46 **1** **Raleigh Quay (IRE)**[14] 2700 3-9-8 **69** .... PhillipMakin 10 — 76
(Micky Hammond) *trckd ldrs on inner: hdwy 3f out: swtchd lft and effrt 2f out: sn rdn: drvn ent fnl f: styd on to ld last 75yds* **5/1**[3]

6303 **2** *nk* **High Resolution**[2] 3073 3-8-8 **55** .... DavidAllan 7 — 61
(Miss L A Perratt) *dwlt and hld up in rr: hdwy 3f out: effrt on outer 2f out: sn rdn and ev ch tl drvn ins fnl f and no ex towards fin* **11/2**

5222 **3** *1 ¼* **Killing Moon (USA)**[28] 2296 3-9-6 **67** .... TonyHamilton 9 — 70
(K A Ryan) *sn led: pushed along 3f out: rdn 2f out: drvn over 1f out: hdd and no ex last 75yds* **9/4**[1]

-226 **4** *1* **Coolella (IRE)**[25] 2380 3-8-6 **56** .... KellyHarrison(3) 8 — 57
(J R Weymes) *trckd ldr: hdwy 3f out: pushed along 2f out: sn rdn: drvn and ev ch ins fnl f: no ex last 100yds* **9/1**

2450 **5** *4* **Chinese Democracy (USA)**[5] 3002 3-8-5 **55** .... MartinLane(3) 3 — 47
(P D Evans) *hld up: hdwy 3f out: rdn over 2f out: kpt on u.p fnl f: nt rch ldrs* **15/2**

00-4 **6** *6* **Thescottishsoldier**[13] 2762 3-8-5 **52** oh3 ow1 .... PJMcDonald 6 — 30
(A G Foster) *hld up towards rr: hdwy over 3f out: rdn to chse ldrs 2f out: sn drvn and wknd* **8/1**

5235 **7** *1 ¼* **Lord's Seat**[31] 2209 3-8-4 **51** oh2 .... FrannyNorton 2 — 26
(A Berry) *chsd ldrs: rdn along 3f out: sn wknd* **20/1**

40-1 **8** *hd* **Desert Forest (IRE)**[28] 2296 3-9-4 **70** .... JamesSullivan(5) 5 — 44
(J Howard Johnson) *trckd ldr: pushed along 3f out: rdn over 2f out and sn wknd* **4/1**[2]

6-00 **9** *12* **Lady Lube Rye (IRE)**[23] 2432 3-8-5 **52** .... RoystonFfrench 1 — —
(N Wilson) *a towards rr: pushed along 1/2-way: sn bhd* **25/1**

1m 38.88s (-2.32) **Going Correction** -0.30s/f (Firm) **9** Ran SP% **124.3**

Speed ratings (Par 99): **99,98,97,96,92 86,85,85,73**

toteswingers:1&2:£10.10, 1&3:£9.70, 2&3:£8.80 CSF £35.39 CT £81.44 TOTE £6.90: £1.90, £2.00, £1.40; EX 50.80.

Owner S T Brankin **Bred** S O'Sullivan **Trained** Middleham Moor, N Yorks

FOCUS

An ordinary handicap and the front four pulled well clear of the rest. Despite that the form is not rated too positively, although those in the frame behind the winner were close to their marks.

3162 LINKS NURSERIES - BEST POSSIBLE START E B F MAIDEN STKS — 7f 30y

2:20 (2:21) (Class 5) 2-Y-O — £3,885 (£1,156; £577; £288) Stalls High

Form — RPR

32 **1** **Falkland Flyer (IRE)**[8] 2882 2-9-3 0 .... SamHitchcott 2 — 74
(M R Channon) *mde all: rdn and qcknd 2f out: drvn ent fnl f: hld on gamely towards fin* **3/1**[2]

3 **2** *nk* **Polar Kite (IRE)**[21] 2493 2-9-3 0 .... TonyHamilton 4 — 73+
(R A Fahey) *trckd ldng pair: swtchd lft and hdwy 2f out: rdn to chal ent fnl f: sn drvn: kpt on towards fin* **1/1**[1]

2 **3** *1 ¾* **Residence And Spa (IRE)**[25] 2389 2-9-3 0 .... DavidAllan 1 — 69
(T D Easterby) *prom: trckd wnr fr 1/2-way: rdn and ev ch 2f out tl drvn and one pce ins fnl f* **7/2**[3]

4 *8* **Swift Alhaarth (IRE)** 2-9-3 0 .... RoystonFfrench 5 — 54+
(M Johnston) *s.i.s: green and in rr tl styd on fnl 2f* **8/1**

5 *5* **Domino Effect (IRE)** 2-9-3 0 .... PhillipMakin 6 — 36
(J Howard Johnson) *s.i.s: green and a in rr* **14/1**

00 **6** *1 ¼* **Rainbows Son**[33] 2138 2-9-3 0 .... PJMcDonald 3 — 33
(P T Midgley) *chsd ldrs: rdn along wl over 2f out and sn wknd* **50/1**

1m 28.39s (-0.61) **Going Correction** -0.30s/f (Firm) 2y crse rec **6** Ran SP% **117.0**

Speed ratings (Par 93): **98,97,95,86,80 79**

toteswingers:1&2:£1.10, 1&3:£2.20, 2&3:£1.40 CSF £6.78 TOTE £4.50: £2.70, £1.10; EX 8.40.

Owner Box 41 **Bred** Des Scott **Trained** West Ilsley, Berks

FOCUS

Only the front three ever figured in this maiden. The front three were clear but it is doubtful the form is any better than rated.

NOTEBOOK

Falkland Flyer(IRE), placed in his first two starts, is bred to be suited by this longer trip and he relished it under a positive ride. He looked likely to be picked off by the favourite coming to the last furlong, but he showed a really professional attitude to hold on and looks just the type for staying nurseries in the coming months. (tchd 7-2 in places)

Polar Kite(IRE), a very promising third on his Haydock debut last month, is also bred to have been suited by this extra furlong, but although he was always in a good position he was keen enough early. He looked likely to win when switched off the rail 2f from home, but though he tried his best he couldn't get the better of the winner. He is learning all the time and should win a race sooner rather than later. (tchd 5-6)

Residence And Spa(IRE), a 10l runner-up over 6f on his Leicester debut last month and another bred to be suited by this longer trip, was always up there and had every chance but he couldn't quicken sufficiently under pressure. He was just up against two better colts here. (op 4-1)

Swift Alhaarth(IRE), a 32,000gns half-brother to three winners at up to 1m2f including the smart sprinter Ooh Aah Camara, he became restless in the stalls and, after fluffing the start, he was fortunate not to come down when clipping heels after a furlong. He did show some ability late on, however, and is likely to have learnt plenty from this. Official explanation: jockey sasid colt stumbled shortly after start

3163 EDGEN MURRAY EUROPE LTD (S) STKS — 5f

2:55 (2:56) (Class 4) 2-Y-O — £6,476 (£1,927; £963; £481) Stalls Low

Form — RPR

6322 **1** **Madam Markievicz (IRE)**[9] 2848 2-8-9 0 ....(p) PhillipMakin 6 — 68+
(M Dods) *cl up: chal 2f out: sn led: rdn and styd on wl fnl f* **9/2**[2]

52 **2** *1 ½* **Crimson Knot (IRE)**[31] 2210 2-8-9 0 .... FrannyNorton 1 — 63+
(A Berry) *in tch: swtchd outside and hdwy wl over 1f out: rdn to chse wnr ins fnl f: kpt on* **6/1**[3]

310 **3** *6* **First Class Favour (IRE)**[23] 2436 2-9-0 0 .... DavidAllan 4 — 46
(T D Easterby) *led: rdn along 2f out and sn hdd: drvn and wknd appr fnl f* **4/5**[1]

4 *4 ½* **Eilean Mor** 2-9-0 0 .... SaleemGolam 7 — 30+
(J S Goldie) *green and sn outpcd in rr: swtchd rt and hdwy wl over 1f out: kpt on ins fnl f: nvr nr ldrs* **28/1**

025 **5** *1* **Kheya (IRE)**[14] 2693 2-8-9 0 .... PJMcDonald 3 — 23
(G M Moore) *chsd ldng pair: rdn along 2f out: sn wknd: eased nr fin* **6/1**[3]

3 **6** *2 ¾* **Gartsherrie**[70] 1198 2-8-4 0 .... PaulPickard(5) 2 — 11
(P T Midgley) *a towards rr* **18/1**

2510 **7** *1 ½* **Molly Mylenis**[3] 3059 2-8-11 0 .... MartinLane(3) 5 — 25
(P D Evans) *chsd ldng pair: rdn along over 2f out: sn drvn and wknd* **14/1**

59.63 secs (-0.77) **Going Correction** -0.20s/f (Firm) **7** Ran SP% **117.7**

Speed ratings (Par 95): **98,95,86,78,77 72,70**

toteswingers:1&2:£3.70, 1&3:£1.20, 2&3:£2.60 CSF £32.52 TOTE £7.00: £4.10, £4.20; EX 28.60.There was no bid for the winner.

Owner C A Lynch **Bred** Fragrant Partnership **Trained** Denton, Co Durham

FOCUS

The majority of these were dropping into a seller for the first time, but this was a valuable prize for a race of its type. The winner is progressing and the runner-up is rated to her mark.

NOTEBOOK

Madam Markievicz(IRE) wasn't one of those dropping in class as she had finished runner-up in a seller and a claimer in her last two starts, but she was still far too good for these. Always up with the pace, she took the measure of the favourite over a furlong out and saw her race out well. She seems to be progressing steadily. (op 4-1)

Crimson Knot(IRE) was dropping in class after chasing home the previous day's Norfolk Stakes third Excel Bolt at a respectful distance in a C&D maiden last month. She stayed on well when switched off the stands' rail over a furlong from home and pulled clear of the others, but couldn't get on terms with the winner. She can win a seller at the very least and may be worth stepping up to 6f. (early 10-1 in places)

First Class Favour(IRE), taking a big drop in class after finishing seventh in the Hilary Needler, tried to make all after bagging the stands' rail early, but she didn't put up much of a fight when headed by the winner and it's hard to know where she goes from here. (op Evens)

Eilean Mor, the only debutant and non-filly in the field, proved clueless early but he made some late headway to pass beaten horses. Out of a half-sister to a couple of winners, there is some ability there but his next start should tell us more. (op 25-1)

Molly Mylenis was dropping in class after finishing last of nine in a Thirsk novice event three days earlier. She was still battling for third when eased right off half a furlong from home suggesting that something may have been amiss. Her jockey felt that the filly had lost her action. Official explanation: jockey said filly had shortened its stride and lost its action approaching line and started pulling up (tchd 12-1)

3164 M&F FUNERAL SERVICES H'CAP — 7f 30y

3:35 (3:36) (Class 5) (0-70,69) 4-Y-O+ — £3,238 (£963; £481; £240) Stalls High

Form — RPR

4433 **1** **Smalljohn**[20] 2531 4-9-0 **69** ....(v) AdamCarter(7) 5 — 77
(B Smart) *disp ld on inner tl rdn along and outpcd wl over 2f out: swtchd lft and hdwy over 1f out: drvn to chal ent fnl f: styd on gamely to ld last 100yds* **6/4**[1]

1144 **2** *1 ¾* **Nufoudh (IRE)**[20] 2531 6-9-3 **68** .... KellyHarrison(3) 4 — 73
(Miss Tracy Waggott) *t.k.h: disp ld tl led 1/2-way: rdn 2f out and sn edgd rt: drvn ent fnl f: hdd last 100yds: hld whn n.m.r towards fin* **4/1**[3]

0364 **3** *¾* **Cold Quest (USA)**[15] 2670 6-7-12 **51** .... JamesSullivan(5) 2 — 52
(Miss L A Perratt) *hld up in rr: hdwy on outer over 2f out: rdn wl over 1f out: kpt on u.p fnl f to take 3rd nr fin* **11/2**

0200 **4** *½* **Hosanna**[9] 2854 4-8-5 **53** ow1 .... PJMcDonald 6 — 53
(J Barclay) *in tch: hdwy 3f out: rdn to chse ldrs 2f out: drvn and ch over 1f out: kpt on same pce fnl f* **25/1**

-251 **5** *4* **Mr Lu**[22] 2454 5-8-13 **64** .... GaryBartley(3) 8 — 53
(J S Goldie) *in tch: hdwy to chse ldng pair wl over 2f out: rdn wl over 1f out: sn drvn and wknd appr fnl f* **3/1**[2]

0000 **6** *4 ½* **Sendreni (FR)**[9] 2856 6-9-3 **65** ....(p) SamHitchcott 7 — 42
(Mrs J C McGregor) *chsd ldng pair: rdn along 3f out: drvn over 2f out and sn wknd* **50/1**

0-06 **7** *2 ¾* **Woodsley House (IRE)**[12] 2789 8-8-9 **57** ....(b[1]) DavidAllan 3 — 27
(A G Foster) *a in rr* **14/1**

6-36 **8** *30* **Al Wasef (USA)**[9] 2859 5-8-12 **60** .... PhillipMakin 1 — —
(J S Goldie) *chsd ldrs: rdn along and lost pl 3f out: sn bhd and eased wl over 1f out* **12/1**

1m 27.51s (-1.49) **Going Correction** -0.30s/f (Firm) **8** Ran SP% **120.6**

Speed ratings (Par 103): **103,101,100,99,95 89,86,52**

toteswingers:1&2:£2.30, 2&3:£6.60 CSF £8.44 CT £27.27 TOTE £2.50: £1.30, £1.10, £2.10; EX 8.10.

Owner B Smart **Bred** W H R John And Partners **Trained** Hambleton, N Yorks

FOCUS

They went a furious pace in this handicap with Smalljohn and Nufoudh duelling from the off. The form makes sense rated around the pair.

Al Wasef(USA) Official explanation: vet said gelding bled from the nose

3165 HBJ CLAIM SOLUTIONS H'CAP — 5f

4:10 (4:10) (Class 3) (0-90,90) 4-Y-O+

£9,346 (£2,799; £1,399; £700; £349; £175) Stalls Low

Form — RPR

3060 **1** **Rasaman (IRE)**[13] 2756 6-8-8 **80** ....(v) GaryBartley(3) 3 — 90
(J S Goldie) *sn outpcd in rr: hdwy wl over 1f out: styng on whn hung rt ent fnl f: sn drvn: hung bdly rt: kpt on to ld last 50yds* **11/1**

5026 **2** *hd* **The Nifty Fox**[13] 2759 6-9-2 **85** .... DavidAllan 1 — 94
(T D Easterby) *chsd ldrs: hdwy 2f out: rdn to ld 1f out: drvn and hdd fnl 50yds: kpt on* **9/4**[1]

4-40 **3** *3 ¼* **Grissom (IRE)**[23] 2431 4-8-8 **77** .... RoystonFfrench 6 — 74+
(A Berry) *in tch: hdwy wl over 1f out: styng on whn nt clr run and swtchd lft over 1f out: fining wl whn bdly hmpd ent fnl f: one pce after* **28/1**

1-62 **4** *1 ¾* **Lesley's Choice**[8] 2883 4-8-5 **74** ....(v) FrannyNorton 2 — 65
(F J Brennan) *prom on inner: rdn along 2f out: drvn and one pce appr fnl f* **7/2**[2]

1300 **5** *1 ½* **Le Toreador**[13] 2745 5-9-7 **90** ....(bt[1]) PhillipMakin 8 — 76
(K A Ryan) *wnt rt s: sn led: rdn wl over 1f out: hdd 1f out: wkng whn hmpd ins fnl f* **14/1**

-053 **6** *1 ¼* **Jargelle (IRE)**[34] 2135 4-9-2 **90** .... MichaelO'Connell(5) 4 — 71
(D Nicholls) *chsd ldr: rdn along wl over 1f out: drvn and wknd ent fnl f* **5/1**

1502 **7** *hd* **Ingleby Star (IRE)**[13] 2756 5-8-3 **75** ....(p) MartinLane(3) 5 — 55
(N Wilson) *chsd ldrs: rdn along 2f out: drvn and wkng whn hmpd ent fnl f* **7/1**

6350 **8** *6* **Indian Trail**[13] 2745 10-9-0 **83** ....(v) AdrianNicholls 7 — 42
(D Nicholls) *chsd ldrs on outer: rdn along 2f out: sn wknd* **4/1**[3]

58.41 secs (-1.99) **Going Correction** -0.20s/f (Firm) **8** Ran SP% **120.6**

Speed ratings (Par 107): **107,106,101,98,96 94,93,84**

toteswingers:1&2:£7.00, 1&3:£18.80, 2&3:£7.60 CSF £38.20 CT £714.09 TOTE £17.50: £3.90, £1.10, £5.80; EX 56.70.

Owner Paul Moulton **Bred** Rasana Partnership **Trained** Uplawmoor, E Renfrews

FOCUS

A decent sprint handicap, but the leaders went off far too fast and set it up for the closers. The first three horses home were well off the pace in the early stages. The winner is rated back to form with the second a solid guide.

NOTEBOOK

Rasaman(IRE) hadn't built on a promising reappearance and had looked in need of an extra furlong these days, but the furious pace played right into his hands. He was outpaced at the back of the field early, but the leaders were always likely to fall in a heap and he produced a strong run between horses to hit the front well inside the last furlong. He nearly threw it away by hanging out to his right in the closing stages, but he had done enough by then. He may turn out again at Carlisle next Wednesday or in the Gosforth Park Cup at Newcastle two days later.

The Nifty Fox, another suited by the strong pace, was brought to hold every chance a furlong out. He did little wrong, but was just denied and this was a good effort as he probably prefers an easier surface. (tchd 10-3 in places)

Grissom(IRE) ◆ is the one to take from the race and can be rated as having finished much closer. Another held up early, he was staying on when twice meeting traffic problems inside the last furlong, especially when badly hampered by the hanging winner. This ground would have been quick enough for him too, so he is very much one to note under more suitable conditions. (op 25-1)

Lesley's Choice, a good second off this mark on his return to turf at Haydock earlier this month when returning from a break, ran another solid race against the stands' rail and had every chance. (op 4-1)

Le Toreador, well held in a couple of higher-grade races in his last two starts, was off a 5lb lower mark here and had first-time blinkers on instead of cheekpieces alongside the usual tongue tie. However, he did far too much too soon and had run his race when hampered half a furlong out. (op 10-1)

Jargelle(IRE), without a win since landing the 2008 Weatherbys Super Sprint, was down to a new career-low mark on her debut for the yard. She was another to do too much too early, but her new yard will find the right opportunities for her. (op 4-1 tchd 11-2)

Ingleby Star(IRE), put up 2lb after a narrow defeat over C&D a fortnight earlier, was another to have run his race before reaching the furlong pole. (op 8-1)

Indian Trail usually likes to come late off a strong pace, but he never looked happy here. (op 7-2)

3166 SPECSAVERS 2 FOR 1 H'CAP — 1m 4f 100y

4:45 (4:45) (Class 5) (0-70,66) 4-Y-0+ £4,533 (£1,348; £674; £336) Stalls High

Form				RPR
0-05	1		**Amazing King (IRE)**[28] 2277 6-8-12 60 ... RussKennemore(3) 8 (P A Kirby) *led 2f: trckd ldr tl led wl over 2f out: rdn clr ent fnl f: styd on strly* **6/4**[1]	70+
4332	2	2 ¾	**Birkside**[15] 2672 7-9-1 60 ... PhillipMakin 5 (Miss L A Perratt) *trckd ldng pair: hdwy 3f out: rdn to chse wnr over 2f out: drvn over 1f out and sn one pce* **9/4**[2]	64
00-3	3	6	**Annibale Caro**[13] 2761 8-9-1 60 ... SaleemGolam 1 (J S Goldie) *hld up in rr: hdwy 3f out: rdn along 2f out: sn no imp* **7/2**[3]	54
3/S-	4	7	**Balwearie (IRE)**[340] 3911 9-8-7 52 ... PJMcDonald 6 (Miss L A Perratt) *t.k.h: chsd ldr tl led after 2f: rdn along 3f out: sn hdd & wknd over 2f out* **14/1**	35
1156	5	18	**Sudden Impulse**[21] 2516 9-9-4 63 ... FrannyNorton 7 (A D Brown) *hld up in rr: rdn along 3f out: sn lost pl and eased whn bhd* **6/1**	17

2m 43.29s (1.29) **Going Correction** -0.30s/f (Firm) 5 Ran SP% **113.9**

Speed ratings (Par 103): **83,81,77,72,60**

CSF £5.41 TOTE £2.90: £2.70, £1.10; EX 5.10.

Owner The New Venture Partnership **Bred** Kraemer Partnership **Trained** Castleton, N Yorks

FOCUS

A modest handicap, especially with the three non-runners, and they went no pace at all early. The winner is rated close to his best with the second to his latest mark.

3167 HBJ CLAIM SOLUTIONS APPRENTICE H'CAP — 5f

5:20 (5:21) (Class 5) (0-70,69) 3-Y-0 £3,238 (£963; £481; £240) Stalls Low

Form				RPR
-003	1		**Ya Boy Sir (IRE)**[23] 2432 3-8-7 52 ... JamesSullivan 2 (N Wilson) *trckd ldrs: hdwy and nt clr run over 1f out: sn swtchd rt and rdn to ld ent fnl f: kpt on strly* **11/2**	59
0122	2	2 ¾	**Lees Anthem**[13] 2768 3-9-4 63 ... LanceBetts 5 (C J Teague) *slt ld: rdn along 2f out: drvn and edgd lft wl over 1f out: hdd ent fnl f: kpt on same pce* **10/3**[3]	60
2114	3	2 ½	**Jigajig**[22] 2449 3-9-10 69 ... AmyRyan 7 (K A Ryan) *cl up: rdn and ev ch 2f out: sn edgd lft: drvn and one pce ent fnl f* **9/4**[1]	57
4600	4	1 ¼	**Reach For The Sky (IRE)**[30] 2235 3-8-6 54 ... JohnCavanagh(3) 8 (A Berry) *in tch: hdwy on outer 1/2-way: rdn along wl over 1f out: kpt on ins fnl f: nrst fin* **16/1**	38
0252	5	hd	**Drumpellier (IRE)**[6] 2962 3-8-12 57 ... PaulPickard 1 (P T Midgley) *s.i.s: sn chsng ldrs on inner: effrt and rdn whn n.m.r and hmpd over 1f out: sn btn* **11/4**[2]	40
2346	6	nse	**Dower Glen**[22] 2449 3-8-3 55 ... ShirleyTeasdale(7) 4 (N Wilson) *chsd ldrs: rdn along 2f out: sn no imp* **10/1**	38
0550	7	1 ¾	**Kristen Jane (USA)**[23] 2432 3-8-2 52 oh5 ow2 ... AnthonyBetts(5) 3 (Miss L A Perratt) *dwlt: a in rr* **25/1**	28
0-40	8	3 ¾	**Tai Hang (IRE)**[10] 2834 3-8-0 50 oh5 ... NatashaEaton(5) 6 (J S Goldie) *sn rdn along: outpcd and bhd fr 1/2-way* **25/1**	13

59.27 secs (-1.13) **Going Correction** -0.20s/f (Firm) 8 Ran SP% **118.6**

Speed ratings (Par 99): **101,96,92,90,90 90,87,81**

toteswingers:1&2:£3.40, 1&3:£3.90, 2&3:£2.50 CSF £25.17 CT £53.06 TOTE £7.80: £2.20, £2.30, £1.02; EX 24.70 Place 6 £19.37; Place 5 £12.03.

Owner David M Roan **Bred** Basil Brindley **Trained** Sandhutton, N Yorks

FOCUS

An ordinary apprentice handicap with the winner back to his early form and the runner-up to his latest mark.

T/Plt: £35.60 to a £1 stake. Pool:£33,562.48 - 687.61 winning tickets T/Qpdt: £12.80 to a £1 stake. Pool:£2,749.00 - 158.60 winning tickets JR

2560 NEWMARKET (July Course) (R-H)

Friday, June 18

OFFICIAL GOING: Good to firm (good in places; watered; 8.4)

First meeting of the year on July Course and stands' side track used.

Wind: Fresh half-behind Weather: Overcast with the odd spot of rain

3168 NEWMARKET NIGHTS APPRENTICE H'CAP — 1m

6:00 (6:00) (Class 5) (0-70,69) 4-Y-0+ £3,238 (£963; £481; £240) Stalls Low

Form				RPR
0545	1		**Sacrilege**[4] 3040 5-9-6 65 ... (p) SophieDoyle 5 (M C Chapman) *dwlt: hld up: hdwy over 1f out: sn edgd rt: rdn to ld ins fnl f: styd on* **10/1**	73
5603	2	¾	**Eastern Gift**[25] 2383 5-9-3 67 ... StephanieBancroft(5) 14 (Miss Gay Kelleway) *hld up: hdwy over 2f out: rdn and ev ch over 1f out: styd on* **16/1**	73
-003	3	1	**King Columbo (IRE)**[14] 2714 5-9-3 67 ... AdamBeschizza(5) 10 (Miss J Feilden) *hld up: hdwy over 3f out: led over 1f out: rdn and hdd ins fnl f: styd on same pce* **4/1**[1]	71
0200	4	¾	**Orpen Wide (IRE)**[6] 2961 8-9-3 65 ... (b) DavidKenny(3) 12 (M C Chapman) *chsd ldrs: led over 3f out: rdn and hdd 2f out: styd on same pce fnl f* **16/1**	67
4-25	5	¾	**Advertise**[36] 2053 4-9-5 69 ... FrancisHayes(5) 13 (A M Balding) *rrd in stalls: s.i.s: hdwy over 5f out: rdn over 1f out: styd on same pce* **9/2**[2]	70
0032	6	hd	**Tevez**[6] 2967 5-9-1 60 ... DeclanCannon 2 (D Donovan) *chsd ldrs: rdn to ld 2f out: edgd rt and sn hdd: no ex ins fnl f* **9/2**[2]	60
040/	7	1 ½	**Colinca's Lad (IRE)**[931] 6979 8-8-3 55 ... LeonnaMayor(7) 8 (P Charalambous) *stdd s: hld up: plld hrd: hdwy and swtchd rt over 2f out: no ex fnl f* **16/1**	52+
0000	8	8	**Greystoke Prince**[9] 2875 5-8-2 54 oh5 ow4 ... CarolineKelly(7) 7 (M D Squance) *prom: lost pl over 5f out: n.d after* **100/1**	32
5050	9	2 ½	**Whotsit (IRE)**[9] 2876 4-8-9 54 ... (b) AshleyMorgan 11 (Miss Amy Weaver) *hld up: a in rr* **25/1**	26
00-	10	2	**Clearing House**[254] 6587 5-8-2 52 ... LewisWalsh(5) 4 (J Ryan) *prom: racd keenly: wknd over 2f out* **18/1**	20
0-06	11	3 ¾	**Molly The Witch (IRE)**[38] 2012 4-8-1 51 ... RyanPowell(5) 3 (W J Musson) *led: hdd over 3f out: wknd over 2f out* **9/1**	10
2625	12	3 ½	**Land Hawk (IRE)**[9] 2866 4-9-8 67 ... (p) SimonPearce 1 (J Pearce) *prom: rdn over 2f out: wknd over 1f out* **6/1**[3]	18
00-4	13	10	**Ruwain**[121] 576 6-8-5 50 oh5 ... RossAtkinson 15 (P J McBride) *racd alone on stands' side: bhd fnl 3f* **33/1**	—

1m 39.31s (-0.69) **Going Correction** +0.075s/f (Good) 13 Ran SP% **120.4**

Speed ratings (Par 103): **106,105,104,103,102 102,101,93,90,88 84,81,71**

toteswingers:1&2:£48.30, 1&3:£36.00, 2&3:£20.10 CSF £158.95 CT £778.10 TOTE £14.00: £3.10, £6.40, £2.20; EX 119.60.

Owner F Michael **Bred** The National Stud **Trained** Market Rasen, Lincs

FOCUS

This was a comparatively small race for the track. It is hard to imagine more than the odd winner emerging from it, and the overall form appears modest, rated around the third and fourth.

Tevez Official explanation: jockey said gelding hung right-handed

3169 JULY COURSE MAIDEN STKS — 6f

6:30 (6:31) (Class 4) 2-Y-0 £5,180 (£1,541; £770; £384) Stalls Low

Form				RPR
	1		**Lord Of The Stars (USA)** 2-9-3 0 ... RichardKingscote 5 (R M Beckett) *sn led: hdd wl over 1f out: rallied to ld 1f out: r.o* **3/1**[1]	81+
	2	½	**The Paddyman (IRE)** 2-9-3 0 ... PhilipRobinson 7 (W J Haggas) *prom: rdn over 1f out: hung lft and r.o wl ins fnl f* **7/2**[2]	80+
	3	2 ¼	**Muzdahi (USA)** 2-9-3 0 ... TadhgO'Shea 6 (J L Dunlop) *chsd ldr 2f: remained handy: wnt 2nd again over 2f out: led wl over 1f out: hdd 1f out: no ex ins fnl f* **8/1**	73+
	4	½	**Peace And Calm (USA)** 2-8-10 0 ... AntiocoMurgia(7) 1 (Mahmood Al Zarooni) *prom: rdn over 1f out: styd on same pce ins fnl f* **9/2**[3]	72+
	5	9	**Marked Card (IRE)** 2-9-3 0 ... RichardMullen 2 (P W Chapple-Hyam) *s.s: hdwy over 3f out: rdn and wknd over 1f out: hung lft fnl f* **3/1**[1]	45
	6	¾	**Izzet** 2-8-12 0 ... AshleyMorgan(5) 4 (M H Tompkins) *s.i.s: in rr and pushed along 1/2-way: sme hdwy 2f out: sn wknd* **12/1**	42
60	7	shd	**Jamaica Grande**[5] 2990 2-9-3 0 ... JerryO'Dwyer 9 (P S McEntee) *prom: chsd wnr 4f out to over 2f out: wknd over 1f out* **22/1**	42

1m 13.49s (0.99) **Going Correction** +0.075s/f (Good) 7 Ran SP% **113.6**

Speed ratings (Par 95): **96,95,92,91,79 78,78**

toteswingers:1&2:£2.30, 1&3:£9.90, 2&3:£5.40 CSF £13.55 TOTE £4.70: £3.00, £2.50; EX 12.40.

Owner Mogeely Stud & Mrs Maura Gittins **Bred** JMJ Racing Stables LLC **Trained** Whitsbury, Hants

FOCUS

This juvenile maiden didn't appear to have a great deal of depth to it - and the time was nothing special - but a handful of winners are likely to emerge from it, with the first four finishing clear.

NOTEBOOK

Lord Of The Stars(USA), who cost $105,000 as a foal, possesses plenty of speed in his pedigree and it was no surprise he was able to make his mark over this trip. He was always to the fore and had enough in reserve to see off his long-time rival Muzdahi. He is entitled to improve for this debut and there should be further triumphs this summer. (op 9-2 tchd 11-2)

The Paddyman(IRE) is the first foal out of a dam who herself made a winning introduction over 6f as a juvenile, but other family members won over considerably further. He ran like he may be better suited by 7f in time, as he was momentarily outpaced before running on strongly in pleasing style. There is certainly a race to be won with him in the not-too-distant future. (op 3-1 tchd 11-4)

Muzdahi(USA) ◆ shaped like a really interesting prospect. He is a half-brother to a couple of horses, who have won over further, so it was pleasing to see him showing enough dash to dispute the lead for much of this. He was green, too, wandering around relatively early on and then appearing to become unbalanced in the Dip over 1f out. He looks sure to improve significantly on this and is worth close attention next time, especially over 7f. (op 6-1)

Peace And Calm(USA) is another who is likely to come on a lot for this debut. (op 4-1 tchd 7-2)

Marked Card(IRE)'s inexperience at the stalls gave him a mountain to climb. (op 7-2 tchd 4-1)

Izzet was also slowly away. (tchd 11-1)

Jamaica Grande's pedigree indicates that he wants time and a trip. This was his third start and his future looks likely to be in nurseries over further. (op 20-1)

3170 RACINGUK CLASSIFIED STKS — 1m 4f

7:05 (7:05) (Class 5) 3-Y-0 £3,238 (£963; £481; £240) Stalls Centre

Form				RPR
062-	1		**Calatrava Cape (IRE)**[267] 6232 3-9-0 69 ... TedDurcan 4 (J L Dunlop) *hld up: hdwy over 2f out: led over 1f out: styd on wl* **11/2**[3]	81+
-022	2	3 ¼	**Saggiatore**[8] 2901 3-9-0 70 ... RyanMoore 6 (E A L Dunlop) *prom: pushed along 4f out: rdn and hung lft over 1f out: styd on same pce* **11/8**[1]	73
3340	3	¾	**Corres (IRE)**[8] 2908 3-8-9 70 ... DeclanCannon(5) 8 (D R C Elsworth) *s.i.s: sn chsng ldrs: led over 4f out: rdn: hung lft and hdd over 1f out: styd on same pce* **6/1**	72
3-32	4	¾	**Sister Earth (IRE)**[25] 2390 3-9-0 68 ... WilliamBuick 7 (J H M Gosden) *chsd ldrs: rdn over 2f out: sn ev ch: hung lft over 1f out: no ex ins fnl f* **10/3**[2]	71
4-64	5	5	**Mausin (IRE)**[25] 2390 3-9-0 70 ... HayleyTurner 5 (H Morrison) *hld up: hdwy over 3f out: rdn and hung lft over 2f out: wknd over 1f out* **12/1**	63

3-00 **6** *18* **Knockdolian (IRE)**[14] 2717 3-9-0 70........................ RichardKingscote 3 34
(R Charlton) *chsd ldr: led over 10f out: hdd over 4f out: sn rdn and hung lft: wknd over 2f out* **12/1**

0-66 **7** *15* **Joe Rua (USA)**[52] 1606 3-9-0 43.....................................(t) RichardMullen 2 10
(J Ryan) *s.i.s: sn pushed along to ld: hdd over 10f out: chsd ldrs: rdn over 4f out: wknd 3f out: t.o* **80/1**

2m 31.51s (-1.39) **Going Correction** +0.075s/f (Good) **7** Ran SP% **111.5**
Speed ratings (Par 99): **107,104,104,103,100 88,78**
toteswingers:1&2:£2.20, 1&3:£2.90, 2&3:£2.40 CSF £12.82 TOTE £6.00: £2.70, £1.20; EX 15.10.
Owner Windflower Overseas Holdings Inc **Bred** Windflower Overseas **Trained** Arundel, W Sussex

FOCUS
A tight-knit race on paper. The pace appeared to be reasonably honest and the form looks sound, with those in the frame behind the winner close to their marks.

3171 TURFTV H'CAP 1m
7:35 (7:37) (Class 5) (0-75,75) 3-Y-O **£3,885** (£1,156; £577; £288) **Stalls** Low

Form RPR

0-05 **1** **Yabtree (IRE)**[25] 2398 3-9-1 **67**................................ RichardKingscote 12 74
(R Charlton) *a.p: chsd ldr over 3f out: led 2f out: r.o* **5/1**[2]

2642 **2** *2* **Marosh (FR)**[24] 2416 3-9-8 **74**.. FrankieDettori 8 76
(R M H Cowell) *hld up: hdwy over 1f out: r.o: nt rch wnr* **5/1**[2]

-440 **3** *hd* **Gifted Apakay (USA)**[29] 2256 3-9-5 **71**.............................. RyanMoore 9 73
(E A L Dunlop) *hld up: pushed along over 3f out: hdwy over 1f out: r.o* **8/1**

0035 **4** *3/4* **Eywa**[17] 2634 3-8-6 **58**.. AlanMunro 2 58
(W Jarvis) *prom: hmpd after 1f: rdn and ev ch 2f out: styd on same pce ins fnl f* **6/1**[3]

0-20 **5** *1/2* **Soho Theatre**[46] 1769 3-9-9 **75**.....................................(b[1]) WilliamBuick 11 74
(D R C Elsworth) *hld up: plld hrd: rdn over 2f out: hdwy and hung lft fnl f: nvr nrr* **25/1**

5635 **6** *1* **Bubbly Braveheart (IRE)**[49] 1666 3-9-3 **69**.................. KierenFallon 13 66
(A Bailey) *hld up: hdwy over 3f out: rdn over 1f out: styd on same pce* **10/1**

-056 **7** *2 3/4* **Inpursuitoffreedom**[14] 2702 3-8-6 **63**........................ TobyAtkinson(5) 3 53
(P J McBride) *hld up: hdwy u.p over 1f out: wknd ins fnl f* **12/1**

0111 **8** *7* **Collect Art (IRE)**[9] 2876 3-8-12 **64** 6ex......................(v) HayleyTurner 5 38
(M L W Bell) *hld up in tch: hmpd after 1f: rdn over 2f out: nt clr run sn after: wknd fnl f* **7/4**[1]

000 **9** *2 3/4* **Asterales**[22] 2478 3-8-9 **61**... JamieMackay 1 29
(W J Musson) *hld up: a in rr: bhd whn hung rt over 1f out* **66/1**

10 *10* **Alana Banana (IRE)**[63] 1370 3-8-6 **58**........................ SimonWhitworth 7 3
(J Akehurst) *plld hrd: trckd ldr: hung lft after 1f: wknd over 2f out* **50/1**

1-50 **11** *7* **Black Baccara**[19] 2566 3-8-7 **66**................................ LeonnaMayor(7) 6 —
(P S McEntee) *led: hung rt over 2f out: sn hdd: wknd over 1f out* **50/1**

1m 39.32s (-0.68) **Going Correction** +0.075s/f (Good) **11** Ran SP% **121.1**
Speed ratings (Par 99): **106,104,103,103,102 101,98,91,89,79 72**
toteswingers:1&2:£4.20, 1&3:£14.40, 2&3:£9.50 CSF £30.63 CT £202.38 TOTE £7.50: £2.10, £1.70, £2.80; EX 36.40.
Owner James D Wolfensohn **Bred** Kilfrush Stud **Trained** Beckhampton, Wilts

FOCUS
This was run in a fractionally slower time than the apprentice handicap and, while there are likely to be winners coming from it, this only left the impression of being an ordinary event. The third to six help set the level.

3172 HOME OF RACING H'CAP 7f
8:10 (8:11) (Class 3) (0-95,91) 3-Y-O+ **£9,066** (£2,697; £1,348; £673) **Stalls** Low

Form RPR

3-1 **1** **Man Of Action (USA)**[19] 2564 3-9-2 **88**........................ WilliamBuick 5 99+
(J H M Gosden) *chsd ldr tl led over 1f out: rdn out* **5/4**[1]

110- **2** *1* **Sarasota Sunshine**[293] 5432 4-9-1 **78**.......................(v[1]) RyanMoore 4 86
(J Noseda) *hld up in tch: rdn over 1f out: edgd lft ins fnl f: r.o* **10/1**

1540 **3** *hd* **Duellist**[14] 2713 3-8-11 **83**.. RichardHills 1 87
(M Johnston) *chsd ldrs: rdn over 2f out: outpcd over 1f out: r.o wl towards fin* **11/1**

6354 **4** *1/2* **Standpoint**[34] 2129 4-9-1 **78**.. GrahamGibbons 8 84
(R Hollinshead) *led: clr 1/2-way: rdn and hdd over 1f out: styd on* **16/1**

00-5 **5** *hd* **Big Noise**[41] 1900 6-9-10 **90**........................ Louis-PhilippeBeuzelin(3) 7 95
(Dr J D Scargill) *hmpd s: hld up: rdn over 2f out: swtchd lft and hdwy over 1f out: styd on same pce ins fnl f* **6/1**[2]

0-00 **6** *2* **Majuro (IRE)**[27] 2311 6-10-0 **91**.. TedDurcan 3 91
(C F Wall) *s.i.s: hld up: swtchd rt over 1f out: r.o: nt rch ldrs* **16/1**

0-51 **7** *3/4* **Dukes Art**[15] 2683 4-9-7 **84**... RobertHavlin 2 82
(J A R Toller) *prom: outpcd 1/2-way: rdn and hung lft over 1f out: no imp* **16/1**

212- **8** *4 1/2* **King's Colour**[205] 7516 5-9-7 **84**.................................... KierenFallon 10 70
(B R Johnson) *s.i.s: sn prom: rdn over 2f out: wknd over 1f out* **8/1**

0561 **9** *3 1/4* **Satwa Laird**[28] 2284 4-9-9 **86**.. FrankieDettori 6 63
(E A L Dunlop) *stmbld s: hld up: a in rr: eased over 1f out* **7/1**[3]

1m 24.92s (-0.78) **Going Correction** +0.075s/f (Good)
WFA 3 from 4yo+ 9lb **9** Ran SP% **117.4**
Speed ratings (Par 107): **107,105,105,105,104 102,101,96,92**
toteswingers:1&2:£4.00, 1&3:£3.00, 2&3:£30.70 CSF £15.37 CT £101.32 TOTE £2.30: £1.20, £3.50, £2.70; EX 17.00.
Owner H R H Princess Haya Of Jordan **Bred** Gainesway Thoroughbreds Ltd **Trained** Newmarket, Suffolk

FOCUS
A decent handicap and there is more to come from the winner, with the third and fourth rated to their recent turf marks.

NOTEBOOK
Man Of Action(USA) followed up his victory on the Rowley Mile course three weeks ago with a convincing success. He was always close to the decent pace set by Standpoint and was in the perfect position to take it up over 1f out. He lengthened upon meeting the rising ground, and created a favourable impression as he strode out to the line in a manner that suggested there is more to come. His action indicates that fast summer ground is what he wants, and he is on the way into making up into a smart performer. (op 13-8 tchd 11-10, 7-4 in places)
Sarasota Sunshine, wearing a visor for the first time after successfully sporting blinkers for her former yard, put up creditable opposition without threatening to master the winner. This was her first run for 293 days, and she is entitled to sharpen up for the experience and pay her way with her yard having run into good form of late. (tchd 11-1)
Duellist is gradually inching his way down the handicap towards a workable mark and wasn't beaten that far when seventh in a hot handicap at Epsom two weeks ago. He again ran with credit and could present each-way value in the near future. (op 9-1)
Standpoint led for a long way and to his credit didn't drop away after being headed. He has been running consistently and would be of real interest if eased a further couple of pounds or so. (op 12-1)
Big Noise received a slight bump as Satwa Laird stumbled upon leaving the stalls but wasn't overly inconvenienced. On the face of it, this was disappointing as he failed to pick up in his customary fashion and he may just be a shade high in the weights. (op 9-2)
Majuro(IRE) could never get competitive. (op 14-1)
Dukes Art was friendless in the market after being put up 4lb for a narrow victory over shorter at Sandown a fortnight previously. (op 11-1)
Satwa Laird just about lost all chance upon slipping badly immediately after breaking from the stalls and a line should be drawn through this effort. Official explanation: jockey said colt stumbled leaving stalls (tchd 10-1)

3173 NEWMARKETRACECOURSES.CO.UK MAIDEN STKS 1m 2f
8:40 (8:41) (Class 4) 3-Y-O **£5,180** (£1,541; £770; £384) **Stalls** Centre

Form RPR

32- **1** **Centurio**[253] 6617 3-9-3 0.. TedDurcan 6 79+
(R Charlton) *prom: led at stdy pce 7f out: qcknd 3f out: rdn and hdd ins fnl f: rallied to ld post* **5/2**[2]

2 *nse* **Nationalism** 3-9-3 0... RobertHavlin 10 79+
(J H M Gosden) *s.i.s: hld up: hdwy and swtchd lft 2f out: rdn to ld and hung lft ins fnl f: hdd post* **10/1**

30 **3** *2 3/4* **Weathervane**[29] 2255 3-9-3 0... WilliamBuick 8 74+
(J H M Gosden) *prom: lost pl 8f out: swtchd lft and hdwy over 1f out: sn rdn: styd on* **8/1**

6 **4** *1/2* **Surface Tension (IRE)**[34] 2115 3-9-3 0.......................... KierenFallon 3 73+
(L M Cumani) *trckd ldrs: plld hrd: nt clr run and swtchd rt over 1f out: r.o* **7/4**[1]

5 *3 1/2* **Dance Tempo** 3-9-3 0.. TravisBlock 7 66+
(H Morrison) *led: hdd over 8f out: chsd ldrs: nt clr run over 1f out: styd on same pce* **16/1**

06 **6** *2 1/2* **Tigranes The Great (IRE)**[9] 2860 3-9-3 0....................... JerryO'Dwyer 5 61
(M Botti) *chsd ldrs: rdn over 3f out: wknd fnl f* **33/1**

0-6 **7** *1 1/4* **Riccoche (IRE)**[8] 2891 3-8-12 0.. HayleyTurner 1 53
(E F Vaughan) *led over 8f out: hdd 7f out: chsd ldr: rdn over 2f out: wknd over 1f out* **33/1**

4 **8** *shd* **Tower**[71] 1186 3-8-10 0... RichardOld(7) 9 58?
(G Prodromou) *s.i.s: hld up: effrt and hmpd wl over 1f out: nvr on terms* **66/1**

0-00 **9** *1/2* **Wavertree Bounty**[17] 2633 3-8-12 48.................................. AlanMunro 2 52?
(J Ryan) *prom: rdn over 2f out: hung rt over 1f out: wknd fnl f* **100/1**

10 *1/2* **Sheklaan (USA)** 3-9-3 0.. RichardHills 4 56
(M A Jarvis) *s.i.s: hld up: hdwy over 3f out: wknd over 1f out* **4/1**[3]

2m 9.96s (4.46) **Going Correction** +0.075s/f (Good) **10** Ran SP% **119.4**
Speed ratings (Par 101): **85,84,82,82,79 77,76,76,76,75**
toteswingers:1&2:£6.30, 1&3:£4.10, 2&3:£18.20 CSF £27.91 TOTE £3.00: £1.10, £3.20, £2.60; EX 38.70.
Owner B E Nielsen **Bred** W And R Barnett Ltd **Trained** Beckhampton, Wilts

FOCUS
There was no pace through much of the race and it turned into something of a dash for home from over 3f out. The form is muddling and limited but the first five can all do better.

3174 NEWMARKETEXPERIENCE.CO.UK H'CAP 5f
9:10 (9:10) (Class 5) (0-75,75) 3-Y-O **£3,885** (£1,156; £577; £288) **Stalls** Low

Form RPR

1 **1** **Captain Coke (IRE)**[16] 2639 3-9-3 **69**............................. AndreaAtzeni 8 81
(Denis P Quinn, Ire) *trckd ldr: plld hrd: led 1f out: rdn and r.o wl* **5/1**[2]

1664 **2** *1 3/4* **Tom Folan**[14] 2688 3-8-6 **65**......................................(p) DavidKenny(7) 9 71
(Andrew Reid) *chsd ldrs: rdn over 1f out: r.o* **16/1**

4315 **3** *nse* **Liberty Lady (IRE)**[13] 2768 3-9-4 **75**........................ DeclanCannon(5) 1 81
(D Donovan) *chsd ldrs: rdn over 1f out: r.o* **8/1**

4-02 **4** *1/2* **Six Diamonds**[23] 2442 3-9-7 **73**.. RyanMoore 2 77
(H Morrison) *led: rdn and hdd 1f out: styd on same pce* **2/1**[1]

5133 **5** *1/2* **Flouncing (IRE)**[9] 2871 3-9-4 **70**................................... KierenFallon 3 72+
(W J Haggas) *s.i.s: hdwy 2f out: rdn and swtchd rt over 1f out: r.o wl: nvr able to chal* **6/1**[3]

2423 **6** *1 1/4* **Danzoe (IRE)**[7] 2931 3-9-4 **70**.......................................(b[1]) TedDurcan 4 68+
(Mrs C A Dunnett) *hld up: swtchd rt over 1f out: r.o ins fnl f: nvr nrr* **5/1**[2]

-035 **7** *3 1/4* **Imjin River (IRE)**[18] 2599 3-9-1 **72**.......................... AshleyMorgan(5) 7 58
(M H Tompkins) *hld up: hdwy over 1f out: wknd fnl f* **8/1**

1602 **8** *1/2* **Taborcillo**[22] 2449 3-8-13 **65**..................................(b) GrahamGibbons 6 49
(T D Barron) *prom: rdn 1/2-way: wknd over 1f out* **12/1**

223- **9** *8* **Excellent Thought**[211] 7453 3-9-7 **73**.......................... J-PGuillambert 5 28
(P Howling) *plld hrd and prom: rdn 1/2-way: wknd over 1f out* **16/1**

59.28 secs (0.18) **Going Correction** +0.075s/f (Good) **9** Ran SP% **122.6**
Speed ratings (Par 99): **101,98,98,97,96 94,89,88,75**
toteswingers:1&2:£14.30, 1&3:£13.40, 2&3:£27.40 CSF £85.23 CT £647.93 TOTE £6.40: £2.00, £4.50, £3.00; EX 145.50 Place 6 £71.51; Place 5 £25.25.
Owner Peter A Quinn **Bred** Fintan Walsh **Trained** Sixmilebridge, Co. Clare

FOCUS
An interesting handicap and the runner-up is rated to May form.
Taborcillo Official explanation: jockey said gelding suffered interference shortly after start
T/Plt: £72.80 to a £1 stake. Pool:£40,652.53 - 407.34 winning tickets T/Qpdt: £15.60 to a £1 stake. Pool:£3,526.97 - 167.28 winning tickets CR

2832 REDCAR (L-H)
Friday, June 18

OFFICIAL GOING: Good to firm (good in places) changing to good to firm after race 4 (4:00)
Wind: moderate 1/2 against Weather: fine

3175 BUY YOUR TICKETS ON-LINE @ REDCARRACING.CO.UK (S) STKS 7f
2:10 (2:10) (Class 6) 2-Y-O **£1,748** (£520; £260; £129) **Stalls** Centre

Form RPR

2532 **1** **Mica Mika (IRE)**[10] 2836 2-8-8 0.............................. BarryMcHugh(3) 9 61
(R A Fahey) *mid-div: hdwy 3f out: led 2f out: styd on wl* **15/8**[1]

532 **2** *3* **Alhoni**[3] 3058 2-8-1 0.. IanBrennan(5) 4 49
(J J Quinn) *hld up: hdwy 3f out: styd on fnl f: tk 2nd line* **15/8**[1]

00 **3** *nse* **Karafuse (IRE)**[7] 2939 2-8-6 0..................................(b[1]) DuranFentiman 7 48
(T D Easterby) *sn led: hdd 2f out: edgd lft and kpt on same pce ins fnl f* **16/1**

0 **4** *1 1/4* **Isitfridayyet (IRE)**[7] 2932 2-8-11 0.................................... LeeVickers 6 50
(J G Given) *w ldrs: 4th and styng on same pce whn hmpd ins fnl f* **25/1**

5430 **5** *1/2* **Sarandjam**[7] 2939 2-8-6 0.. MatthewDavies(5) 2 49
(M R Channon) *w ldrs: keeping on same pce whn edgd rt ins fnl f* **8/1**[3]

6 1 ½ **Lighthouse Keeper (IRE)** 2-8-11 0 TomEaves 1 45
(Miss Amy Weaver) *s.s and wnt lft s: hld up: hdwy over 2f out: edgd lft and kpt on fnl f* 33/1

530 7 4 **Look'N'Listen (IRE)**[39] 1978 2-8-6 0 SilvestreDeSousa 10 30
(A D Brown) *tk fierce hold: led early: w ldrs: lost pl over 1f out* 14/1

600 8 7 **Mercy Street**[7] 2939 2-8-11 0 (b[1]) AndrewElliott 5 18
(N Tinkler) *dwlt: hdwy 3f out: lost pl over 1f out* 66/1

005 9 4 ½ **Stevie Bee Party**[10] 2836 2-8-11 0 PatrickMathers 3 7
(I W McInnes) *t.k.h: trckd ldrs: wknd 2f out* 100/1

420 10 16 **Box Of Frogs (IRE)**[17] 2623 2-8-7 0 ow1 JamesDoyle 8 —
(A J McCabe) *mid-div: lost pl over 2f out: sn bhd: virtually p.u* 7/1[2]

1m 28.37s (3.87) **Going Correction** +0.175s/f (Good) 10 Ran SP% 115.0
Speed ratings (Par 91): **84,80,80,79,78 76,72,64,59,40**
toteswingers:1&2:£1.10, 1&3:£11.50, 2&3:£16.90 CSF £4.79 TOTE £2.40: £1.02, £1.10, £5.40; EX 5.60.There was no bid for the winner.
Owner Mrs Una Towell **Bred** Yeomanstown Stud **Trained** Musley Bank, N Yorks

FOCUS
A very modest event, run over five seconds outside the standard. The two joint favourites, both by the stallion Needwood Blade, had each finished second to the David Nicholls-trained Hayley Cropper on their most recent start and there was not much between them on a line through that filly. Not a race to be with although the winner scored decisively.

NOTEBOOK
Mica Mika(IRE) was closely matched with the runnner-up on previous form, but victory proved fairly comfortable. Dropping to this grade for the first time, he was ideally suited by the extra furlong and stayed on well after taking it up towards the stands' rail. (op 2-1 tchd 7-4)
Alhoni was under pressure by halfway and did not look to be enjoying herself or helping her jockey, but finally began to stay on inside the last and snatched second on the post. She saw out the seventh furlong fine but this may have come too soon for her after her run at Thirsk earlier in the week. (tchd 7-4 and 9-4)
Karafuse(IRE), fitted with blinkers for the first time, was another stepping up to 7f. After making the running she could not hold off the winner and was pipped for second on the post, but did confirm York superiority over a couple of these rivals. (op 25-1 tchd 28-1)
Isitfridayyet(IRE), quickly lowered to the basement level after finishing second-last in a Sandown maiden on his debut, was always up with the pace but already held when briefly snatched up late on. (op 16-1)
Sarandjam was not best drawn but looks fully exposed now.
Lighthouse Keeper(IRE) showed a hint of promise, keeping on late after running green. (tchd 28-1)
Box Of Frogs(IRE) is not progressing and was beaten too far out for the longer trip to be blamed. (op 11-2)

3176 REDCAR RACECOURSE FOR YOUR WEDDING VENUE MAIDEN STKS 1m 2f
2:45 (2:47) (Class 5) 3-Y-O+ **£2,396** (£712; £356; £177) **Stalls** Low

Form RPR
0-40 1 **Chain Of Events**[65] 1310 3-9-0 72 RobertWinston 8 72
(B W Hills) *hld up in mid-div: hdwy and swtchd outside over 2f out: edgd lft and led 1f out: drvn out* 5/2[2]

0-00 2 2 ¼ **Peaceful Rule (USA)**[16] 2658 4-9-9 63 MichaelGeran(3) 9 68
(D Nicholls) *led after 1f: hdd 1f out: no ex* 25/1

36 3 1 **Blazing Desert**[14] 2697 6-9-7 0 IanBrennan(5) 6 66
(J J Quinn) *hld up in rr: hdwy on outer 3f out: styd on to take 3rd ins fnl f* 20/1

52 4 1 ¼ **Tamarillo Grove (IRE)**[31] 2220 3-9-0 0 TomEaves 10 63
(B Smart) *t.k.h: trckd ldrs: effrt over 3f out: chsd wnr over 2f out: styd on same pce appr fnl f* 7/4[1]

04 5 2 ½ **Enchanting Smile (FR)**[62] 1380 3-8-9 0 JamesDoyle 2 53
(A J McCabe) *hld up in midfield: shkn up over 2f out: kpt on: nvr rchd ldrs* 25/1

6 6 1 ¾ **Farmers Glory**[38] 1991 3-9-0 0 AndrewElliott 1 55
(G A Swinbank) *sn mid-div: effrt over 3f out: kpt on one pce fnl 2f* 33/1

7 ½ **Tobernea (IRE)** 3-9-0 0 GregFairley 11 54
(M Johnston) *led 1f: chsd ldrs: one pce fnl 2f* 7/1

0 8 1 ¾ **Finellas Fortune**[14] 2697 5-9-2 0 PatrickDonaghy(5) 4 45
(G M Moore) *s.i.s: in rr: hdwy on ins over 3f out: swtchd rt ins fnl f: kpt on towards fin* 100/1

9 nse **Nephele (IRE)** 3-8-9 0 DuranFentiman 3 45
(T D Easterby) *sn chsng ldrs: wknd over 1f out* 100/1

10 9 **Hairy Maclary** 3-9-0 0 DavidNolan 7 32
(T D Easterby) *in rr: lost pl over 1f out* 66/1

2 11 3 ¼ **Mainland (USA)**[16] 2658 4-9-12 0 StephenCraine 12 25
(K A Ryan) *s.v.s: hdwy to trck ldrs after 2f: drvn over 3f out: hung rt and lost pl over 2f out* 4/1[3]

0 12 26 **Belvidera**[15] 2674 4-9-7 0 TonyCulhane 5 —
(Mrs C A Dunnett) *prom early: lost pl after 2f: wl bhd 6f out: eased over 1f out: t.o* 150/1

2m 6.88s (-0.22) **Going Correction** -0.075s/f (Good)
WFA 3 from 4yo+ 12lb 12 Ran SP% 117.0
Speed ratings (Par 103): **97,95,94,93,91 90,89,88,88,80 78,57**
toteswingers:1&2:£21.10, 1&3:£14.40, 2&3:£28.30 CSF £67.48 TOTE £2.70: £1.10, £12.00, £5.30; EX 61.00.
Owner Sir A Ferguson,Cavendish InvLtd,J Hanson **Bred** Bishop Wilton Stud **Trained** Lambourn, Berks

FOCUS
Just an ordinary maiden, run at an average pace. the winner is rated to form with the placed horses getting back to something like previous form.

3177 REDCAR RACECOURSE CONFERENCE & EVENTS VENUE H'CAP 1m 2f
3:20 (3:20) (Class 5) (0-70,68) 4-Y-O+ **£2,396** (£712; £356; £177) **Stalls** Low

Form RPR
0-20 1 **Smirfy's Silver**[18] 2602 6-9-7 **64** SilvestreDeSousa 5 75
(Mrs D J Sanderson) *mde all: shkn up over 2f out: styd on strly appr fnl f: v readily* 9/2[3]

-602 2 3 ¼ **Avitus**[17] 2625 4-8-13 **56** RobertWinston 9 61
(Micky Hammond) *hld up in rr: hdwy over 3f out: chsd wnr 2f out: styd on same pce appr fnl f* 9/4[1]

403 3 hd **Kyle Of Bute**[18] 2602 4-9-1 **58** TonyCulhane 2 62
(B P J Baugh) *trckd ldrs: effrt over 2f out: styd on same pce* 5/2[2]

62-0 4 2 ¾ **Miss Ferney**[34] 2109 6-8-10 **53** DuranFentiman 1 52
(A Kirtley) *in rr: dropped bk last 7f out: hdwy over 3f out: styd on fnl f* 11/1

-060 5 nk **Green Passion (USA)**[20] 2527 4-8-10 **53** GregFairley 7 51
(M Johnston) *chsd wnr: hung lft over 2f out: one pce* 14/1

-060 6 1 **Maybeme**[13] 2739 4-9-6 **63** LeeVickers 4 59
(N Bycroft) *trckd ldrs: effrt over 3f out: one pce fnl 2f* 8/1

45-0 7 12 **Tripbiyah (USA)**[25] 2378 4-9-3 **60** AndrewElliott 3 32
(G A Swinbank) *t.k.h: trckd ldrs: wknd 2f out: bhd whn eased ins fnl f* 11/1

000- 8 13 **Treetops Hotel (IRE)**[188] 7733 11-8-2 **45** AndrewMullen 6 —
(L R James) *s.i.s: drvn over 4f out: lost pl over 3f out: sn bhd* 100/1

2m 5.60s (-1.50) **Going Correction** -0.075s/f (Good) 8 Ran SP% 113.0
Speed ratings (Par 103): **103,100,100,98,97 97,87,77**
toteswingers:1&2:£1.90, 1&3:£2.60, 2&3:£1.40 CSF £14.66 CT £29.74 TOTE £4.10: £1.10, £1.40, £1.40; EX 18.90.
Owner Mrs Dian Plant **Bred** G S Shropshire **Trained** Wiseton, Notts

FOCUS
An uncompetitive handicap, and modest form, with the winner enjoying the run of the race in front. It was over a second quicker than the earlier maiden. The time was decent for the grade, the winner looks better than ever and the runner-up is rated to form.

3178 WIN A VIP DAY OUT @ REDCARRACING.CO.UK H'CAP 6f
4:00 (4:01) (Class 3) (0-95,91) 3-Y-O+ **£6,799** (£2,023; £1,011; £505) **Stalls** Centre

Form RPR
2420 1 **Indian Skipper (IRE)**[3] 3065 5-8-11 77 (be) AndrewHeffernan(3) 2 88
(R C Guest) *s.s: hdwy over 2f out: swtchd rt over 1f out: str run to ld 150yds out: hung lft and styd on strly* 5/1[2]

0451 2 2 ¼ **Five Star Junior (USA)**[23] 2431 4-10-0 91 LNewman 7 95
(Mrs L Stubbs) *led 1f: led 2f out: hdd and no ex ins fnl f* 13/2[3]

5003 3 ¾ **Red Cape (FR)**[3] 3065 7-8-12 80 IanBrennan(5) 8 81
(Mrs R A Carr) *chsd ldrs: drvn 3f out: edgd rt over 1f out: styd on ins fnl f* 5/2[1]

-160 4 ½ **Sunrise Safari (IRE)**[22] 2465 7-9-6 86 (v) BarryMcHugh(3) 4 86
(R A Fahey) *chsd ldrs: kpt on same pce appr fnl f* 14/1

0420 5 hd **Jarrow (IRE)**[27] 2316 3-9-6 90 GregFairley 10 87
(M Johnston) *s.i.s: hdwy to chse ldrs over 2f out: one pce appr fnl f* 8/1

1300 6 ½ **Discanti (IRE)**[3] 3065 5-9-6 83 (t) DuranFentiman 5 81
(T D Easterby) *t.k.h: hdwy over 2f out: n.m.r over 1f out: kpt on same pce* 7/1

5-62 7 ½ **Filligree (IRE)**[14] 2689 5-9-10 87 RobertWinston 1 83
(Rae Guest) *chsd ldrs: sn drvn along: one pce appr fnl f* 10/1

4666 8 6 **Tabaret**[5] 2992 7-9-7 87 MichaelStainton(3) 9 64
(R M Whitaker) *w ldr: wkng whn n.m.r over 1f out* 8/1

0420 9 ½ **Esprit De Midas**[16] 2657 4-9-13 90 (b) StephenCraine 3 65
(K A Ryan) *led after 1f: hdd 2f out: hung lft and nt run on* 20/1

1m 11.76s (-0.04) **Going Correction** +0.175s/f (Good)
WFA 3 from 4yo+ 7lb 9 Ran SP% 113.8
Speed ratings (Par 107): **107,104,103,102,102 101,100,92,92**
toteswingers:1&2:£3.10, 1&3:£4.30, 2&3:£4.60 CSF £36.81 TOTE £8.10: £3.90, £1.40, £1.10; EX 38.70.
Owner EERC **Bred** Calley House Syndicate **Trained** Stainforth, S Yorks

FOCUS
A decent sprint handicap and the form looks sound, although the pace did not look that strong. The winner is rated to his all-weather best.

NOTEBOOK
Indian Skipper(IRE) could not recover from his customary slow start at Thirsk on Tuesday but despite giving away several lengths leaving the stalls this time he was soon racing in touch. After being switched for a run he burst clear to win readily, hanging to the inside rail in the process. He was officially 3lb ahead of the Handicapper. (op 9-1)
Five Star Junior(USA) was dropping to 5f for the first time since his 2-y-o days when winning at Ayr, and he ran well back over his optimum trip from a 2lb higher mark. Having taken a slender lead, he could not prevent the winner from careering away. (op 9-2 tchd 4-1)
Red Cape(FR) finished in front of Indian Skipper when third at Thirsk and ran well again. He didn't have much room to work in for a time but did stay on despite drifting to his left. (op 4-1)
Sunrise Safari(IRE), who had excuses last time, travelled quite well but could have done with a stronger gallop. (op 9-1)
Jarrow(IRE), the only 3-y-o in the field, had his chance nearest the stands' side before fading through the final furlong. (op 7-1 tchd 9-1)
Discanti(IRE) finished between Red Cape and Indian Skipper on Tuesday after racing alone. Covered up here and taking a keen hold, he was never able to land a blow. (tchd 6-1 and 15-2)
Filligree(IRE), 3lb higher than when second at Bath, was dropped in from her outside draw and could never quite get into the action. She is most effective on turning tracks. (op 9-1 tchd 12-1)
Tabaret is largely consistent but has won just once in 25 attempts since landing this race two years ago. (op 15-2 tchd 13-2)

3179 RACING UK ON SKY 432 CLAIMING STKS 1m 2f
4:35 (4:35) (Class 6) 3-Y-O+ **£1,842** (£544; £272) **Stalls** Low

Form RPR
0521 1 **Guga (IRE)**[9] 2880 4-9-4 59 (b) GregFairley 3 69+
(Dr R D P Newland) *mde all: qcknd clr over 3f out: shkn up over 1f out: eased ins fnl f: unchal* 15/8[1]

14-2 2 3 ¾ **Night Knight (IRE)**[4] 3021 4-9-5 63 (p) BarryMcHugh(3) 2 62
(C Grant) *chsd ldrs: hung lft over 2f out: kpt on to take 2nd jst ins fnl f* 9/2

5152 3 nk **Atacama Sunrise**[22] 2477 4-9-3 60 TonyCulhane 5 56
(G Prodromou) *hld up off pce: wnt 2nd over 3f out: rdn 2f out: one pce fnl f* 3/1[3]

0-20 4 8 **Lucayan Dancer**[8] 2894 10-8-11 69 BillyCray(5) 4 39
(N Bycroft) *t.k.h in last: effrt on outside 3f out: wknd over 1f out* 2/1[2]

0 5 31 **Arkas**[16] 2658 4-8-11 0 SilvestreDeSousa 1 —
(C R Wilson) *sn chsng wnr: hung lft lost pl 3f out: sn bhd: t.o: virtually p.u* 50/1

2m 7.01s (-0.09) **Going Correction** -0.075s/f (Good) 5 Ran SP% 113.3
Speed ratings (Par 101): **97,94,93,87,62**
CSF £10.92 TOTE £1.70: £1.02, £7.80; EX 10.40.Guga was subject of a friendly claim £6,000. Arkas was subject a friendly claim £5,000
Owner C E Stedman, R J Corsan & J A Provan **Bred** Azienda Agricola Loreto Luciani **Trained** Claines, Worcs

FOCUS
The going was officially amended to good to firm all over before this race. This was a weak and uncompetitive claimer, and they were soon stretched out in single file behind the all-the-way winner. The form is rated around the first two.
Lucayan Dancer Official explanation: jockey said gelding never travelled
Arkas Official explanation: jockey said filly hung left-handed

3180 FOLLOW US ON FACEBOOK H'CAP 1m
5:10 (5:10) (Class 5) (0-75,73) 3-Y-O+ **£2,396** (£712; £356; £177) **Stalls** Centre

Form RPR
0-04 1 **Ting Ting (USA)**[39] 1970 3-8-2 56 AndrewMullen 3 62
(T P Tate) *in rr: sn pushed along: hdwy over 2f out: styd on wl appr fnl f: led towards fin* 11/4[1]

5442 **2** ½ **Classic Descent**[4] 3022 5-9-0 **58**.................(t) RobertWinston 5 65
(Mrs R A Carr) *dwlt: hld up: wnt 2nd over 2f out: led appr fnl f: hdd and no ex towards fin* **3/1**[2]

4-63 **3** 1 ¾ **Kings Point (IRE)**[13] 2760 9-9-9 **72**................. BillyCray(5) 7 75
(D Nicholls) *led tl appr fnl f: kpt on same pce* **8/1**

0045 **4** 4 **Coole Dodger (IRE)**[9] 2851 5-8-6 **53** oh1................. BarryMcHugh(3) 1 47
(B Ellison) *t.k.h: sn trcking ldrs: edgd rt over 1f out: sn wknd* **13/2**

04-2 **5** 4 ½ **Caracal**[121] 583 3-9-5 **73**................. GregFairley 8 54
(M Johnston) *sn trcking ldrs: drvn 3f out: wknd over 1f out* **9/2**[3]

03-3 **6** 5 **Ykikamoocow**[23] 2429 4-9-9 **67**................. SilvestreDeSousa 4 39
(G A Harker) *hld up: effrt and swtchd lft 3f out: wknd over 1f out* **6/1**

-320 **7** 5 **Rio Caribe (IRE)**[14] 2700 3-9-2 **70**................. DavidNolan 6 28
(T D Walford) *trckd ldrs: drvn 3f out: wknd 2f out* **16/1**

1m 39.1s (1.10) **Going Correction** +0.175s/f (Good)
WFA 3 from 4yo+ 10lb **7** Ran SP% **114.5**
Speed ratings (Par 103): **101,100,98,94,90 85,80**
toteswingers:1&2:£1.90, 1&3:£6.30, 2&3:£3.50 CSF £11.30 CT £56.80 TOTE £2.50: £1.10, £3.00; EX 8.50.
Owner Mrs Fitri Hay **Bred** Russell L Reinman Stable Inc **Trained** Tadcaster, N Yorks

FOCUS
A modest handicap rated through the third to his latest form.

3181 COME RACING TOMORROW ON LADIES' DAY MAIDEN H'CAP 5f
5:40 (5:42) (Class 5) (0-70,65) 3-Y-O+ **£2,396** (£712; £356; £177) **Stalls** Centre

Form RPR

6-00 **1** **Port Ronan (USA)**[25] 2378 4-8-3 **45**................. PatrickDonaghy(5) 2 50
(J S Wainwright) *led 1f: chsd ldr: styd on fnl f: led nr fin* **16/1**

6-03 **2** nk **Bronze Beau**[44] 1825 3-9-8 **65**.................(p) LNewman 5 67
(Mrs L Stubbs) *hmpd s: led after 1f: wnt 3 l clr appr fnl f: hung lft: hdd nr fin* **10/3**[1]

3-65 **3** 3 ½ **Reddy To Star (IRE)**[45] 1811 3-9-4 **64**.................(p) BarryMcHugh(3) 6 53
(Julie Camacho) *wnt lft s: sn chsng ldrs: effrt over 2f out: one pce* **9/2**[2]

-605 **4** 2 ¼ **Kirkby's Gem**[38] 1987 3-8-2 **45**.................(b[1]) PatrickMathers 1 26
(A Berry) *chsd ldrs: sn drvn along: outpcd fnl 2f* **50/1**

-440 **5** 2 ¾ **Greeley Bright (USA)**[23] 2434 3-9-5 **62**................. LeeVickers 3 33
(J G Given) *wnt rt s: sn chsng ldrs: drvn over 2f out: hung rt and wknd over 1f out: eased towards fin* **17/2**[3]

59.73 secs (1.13) **Going Correction** +0.175s/f (Good)
WFA 3 from 4yo 6lb **5** Ran SP% **59.6**
Speed ratings (Par 103): **97,96,90,87,82**
CSF £19.02 TOTE £13.00: £10.30, £1.10; EX 35.30 Place 6 £14.02; Place 5 £10.60.
Owner D R & E E Brown **Bred** Dr And Mrs M L Brosnan **Trained** Kennythorpe, N Yorks

FOCUS
Already a poor maiden handicap, this was weakened by the withdrawal at the start of Final Ovation, who sadly broke a leg after becoming upset in the stalls, and Star Twilight. The form is worth very little, even with the first two rated to last season's form.
T/Plt: £28.50 to a £1 stake. Pool:£33,796.46 - 864.89 winning tickets T/Qpdt: £4.50 to a £1 stake. Pool:£2,833.43 - 460.00 winning tickets WG

3182 - 3189a (Foreign Racing) - See Raceform Interactive

3141 ASCOT (R-H)
Saturday, June 19

OFFICIAL GOING: Good to firm (good in places; stands' side 10.1, centre 10.0, far side 10.3; round course 9.1)
Course at normal configuration and all distances as advertised.
Wind: Fresh, across Weather: Overcast, breezy

3190 CHESHAM STKS (LISTED RACE) 7f
2:30 (2:34) (Class 1) 2-Y-O
£28,385 (£10,760; £5,385; £2,685; £1,345; £675) **Stalls** Centre

Form RPR

1 **1** **Zaidan (USA)**[49] 1686 2-9-3 0................. SebSanders 13 104+
(C E Brittain) *stdd s: swtchd lft to r on stands' rail hld up towards rr: hdwy over 2f out: led wl over 1f out: sn rdn: r.o strly ins fnl f: drew clr fnl 150yds* **7/1**

21 **2** 3 **Sonning Rose (IRE)**[12] 2813 2-8-12 0................. AlanMunro 6 92
(M R Channon) *t.k.h: hld up in rr: n.m.r ent fnl 3f: nt clr run over 2f out tl swtchd lft ent fnl 2f: hung rt and hdwy 2f out: kpt wanting to hang rt after: r.o to go 2nd towards fin: no ch w wnr* **12/1**

3 ¾ **Casper's Touch (USA)**[58] 2-9-3 0.................(t) KierenFallon 7 95
(Kenneth McPeek, U.S.A) *restless in stalls: awkward and wnt rt s: sn in tch in midfield: rdn and effrt ent fnl 2f: hung rt fr 2f out: chsd wnr but continued to hang ins fnl f: btn fnl 100yds: lost 2nd towards fin* **9/1**

1 **4** 1 ½ **King Torus (IRE)**[26] 2384 2-9-3 0................. RichardHughes 11 91+
(R Hannon) *in tch in midfield on outer: effrt over 2f out: rdn to press wnr over 1f out: edgd rt and btn ins fnl f: wknd towards fin* **7/2**[2]

1 **5** 2 **Fanny May**[14] 2749 2-8-12 0................. RobertWinston 8 81
(D J Coakley) *stdd s: t.k.h: hld up towards rr: rdn and effrt ent fnl 2f: hung rt fr over 1f out: kpt on: nvr gng pce to threaten ldrs* **16/1**

5 **6** 2 **Slim Shadey**[11] 2839 2-9-3 0................. JamieSpencer 12 81
(J S Moore) *stdd and dropped in bhd after s: rdn and swtchd rt to outer over 2f out: no real prog and wl btn over 1f out: plugged on past btn horses fnl f* **33/1**

7 1 ½ **Jackaroo (IRE)**[48] 1738 2-9-3 0................. JMurtagh 3 77
(A P O'Brien, Ire) *chsd ldr: rdn to chal over 2f out: wknd u.p over 1f out: wl btn fnl f* **9/4**[1]

8 nk **Eskimo (IRE)**[30] 2264 2-9-3 0................. RyanMoore 5 77
(A P O'Brien, Ire) *chsd ldrs: rdn and nt qckning whn carried rt 2f out: sn wknd and wl btn fnl f* **5/1**[3]

434 **9** 4 **Straight Line (IRE)**[36] 2078 2-9-3 0................. TomQueally 2 67
(A P Jarvis) *led tl wl over 1f out: sn wknd and wl btn fnl f* **66/1**

3 **10** 2 ½ **Lexington Bay (IRE)**[28] 2312 2-9-3 0................. PaulHanagan 4 60
(R A Fahey) *dwlt: sn in midfield: rdn and struggling over 2f out: bhd fr wl over 1f out* **25/1**

12 **11** 8 **Clarke Lane (USA)**[22] 2514 2-9-3 0................. NeilCallan 9 40
(M A Jarvis) *chsd ldrs: rdn and wknd qckly ent fnl 2f: wl bhd and eased ins fnl f* **20/1**

0644 **12** nse **On Wings Of Love (IRE)**[7] 2958 2-8-12 0................. DavidProbert 10 35
(A Bailey) *in tch tl rdn and wknd qckly ent fnl 2f: wl bhd and eased ins fnl f* **80/1**

1m 27.51s (-0.49) **Going Correction** -0.05s/f (Good) **12** Ran SP% **120.0**
Speed ratings (Par 101): **100,96,95,94,91 89,87,87,82,79 70,70**
toteswingers: 1&2 £13.20, 1&3 £18.40, 2&3 £20.70 CSF £83.93 CT £781.08 TOTE £10.30: £3.10, £2.80, £3.40; EX 99.00 Trifecta £1062.60 Pool: £12,280.03 - 8.55 winning units..
Owner Saeed Manana **Bred** Stratford Place Stud **Trained** Newmarket, Suffolk

FOCUS
After just 1.2mm of rain overnight, the ground remained officially good to firm, good in places. First run in 1919 over 5f, the distance of the Chesham was changed from 6f to its current 7f in 1996 and is now restricted to two-year-olds whose sires were successful over further than 9.5f. The race hasn't produced anything that has gone on to do great things in recent years, seven of the past ten winners had won their only previous starts, which applied to four in this field, while two maidens were also successful, including last year's winner Big Audio, whose trainer Richard Hannon had taken the last two runnings. There is every reason to be optimistic that this year's renewal was won by an above-average juvenile.

NOTEBOOK
Zaidan(USA) could hardly have been more impressive. Taking a big step up in trip and class, having won a 5f Doncaster maiden on debut last month, he was switched left to drop in well off the pace from his high draw, but he travelled well and made smooth progress passing the 3f pole. A gap then appeared between Jackaroo and Straight Line, which he took even though his jockey said it meant he hit the front sooner than he wanted, but once through it he kept grinding away and was still putting daylight between himself and his rivals on reaching the line. The longer distance suited him and he was given a quote of 33-1 for the 2000 Guineas, but his trainer would like to aim him at the Kentucky Derby. (op 6-1 tchd 15-2)
Sonning Rose(IRE), runner-up in a hot Goodwood maiden on her debut before a comfortable success at Pontefract, was held up off the pace and she followed the winner through the gap inside the last 2f. She stayed on well to grab second and has a future, but she appeared to be hanging in the latter stages, so may be capable of even better on an easier surface. (op 10-1)
Casper's Touch(USA), the American challenger, had finished fourth to Metropolitan Man (ninth in Tuesday's Windsor Castle) on debut at Keeneland in April. He was awkward leaving the stalls and tracked the pace before making an effort passing the 2f pole. However, despite running on well, he tended to hang away to his right in the last furlong or so and may not have appreciated the quick ground. (op 15-2 tchd 11-1)
King Torus(IRE), whose trainer was looking for a hat-trick in the race, was an easy winner over 6f at Leicester on his debut last month, but he was kept wide from his high draw here and was always seeing plenty of daylight. Despite that, he still held every chance a furlong out and this was a creditable effort. (op 4-1)
Fanny May, the narrow winner of a 6f Lingfield fillies' maiden on debut this month from which the second and fifth have won since, could only find one pace over the last furlong or so, but she raced keenly through the early stages, so this wasn't a bad effort and there is more to come from her provided she settles better. (op 12-1)
Slim Shadey, a creditable fifth in a 6f Salisbury maiden auction event on debut 11 days earlier, was tucked in from his high draw but he struggled to go the pace in the first half of the contest. He couldn't make much impression when switched to the wide outside over 2f from home, but he can find easier opportunities than this. (op 40-1)
Jackaroo(IRE) was well backed, but they faded after racing up with the pace early. (op 7-2 tchd 2-1)
Eskimo(IRE), like his stable companion, was well backed, but also faded after racing up with the pace early. (op 8-1 tchd 9-2)
Straight Line(IRE), whose fourth to Strong Suit at Newbury last month looks better now, didn't seem to see out the 6f trip there, so it wasn't a great surprise when he dropped away after losing the advantage 2f from home. (op 50-1)
Lexington Bay(IRE) was a promising third from the worst draw over 6f at Chester on his debut, but the form of that race has taken a few knocks and he found this level too demanding. (op 20-1)
Clarke Lane(USA), who was comfortably beaten by Galtymore Lad (seventh in Tuesday's Coventry) at Pontefract last month, dropped away after showing up early and better might have been expected. (op 14-1)
On Wings Of Love(IRE), the most exposed in the field and yet to win after four previous attempts, was duly outclassed.

3191 HARDWICKE STKS (GROUP 2) 1m 4f
3:05 (3:06) (Class 1) 4-Y-O+
£70,962 (£26,900; £13,462; £6,712; £3,362; £1,687) **Stalls** High

Form RPR

3-11 **1** **Harbinger**[43] 1859 4-9-0 120................. RyanMoore 3 129+
(Sir Michael Stoute) *trckd ldrs: qcknd to ld over 2f out: edgd rt over 1f out: sn clr: r.o wl and in command thrght fnl f* **8/11**[1]

03-2 **2** 3 ½ **Duncan**[42] 1898 5-9-0 115................. WilliamBuick 11 123
(J H M Gosden) *hld up in rr: swtchd sltly lft whn effrt and hdwy 2f out: chsd wnr in vain fr over 1f out: edgd rt ins fnl f: styd on but no imp* **8/1**[2]

0-14 **3** 6 **Barshiba (IRE)**[21] 2538 6-8-11 110................. JimmyFortune 7 110
(D R C Elsworth) *racd keenly: led: hdd over 2f out: sn outpcd by wnr: rdn and lost 2nd over 1f out: one pce fnl f* **18/1**

3-66 **4** 1 ½ **Sans Frontieres (IRE)**[44] 1832 4-9-0 105.................(t) TomQueally 9 111
(J Noseda) *racd keenly: hld up: rdn over 2f out: hdwy whn n.m.r wl over 1f out: carried hd to one side: styd on ins fnl f: nvr gng pce to get to ldrs* **25/1**

0-20 **5** ¾ **Redwood**[44] 1832 4-9-0 113................. MichaelHills 4 110
(B W Hills) *midfield: dropped to rr after 3f: hdwy on outer 2f out: rdn whn styng on over 1f out: one pce fnl 100yds* **16/1**

2204 **6** 3 ¾ **Crowded House**[56] 1532 4-9-0 110.................(b[1]) KierenFallon 1 104
(B J Meehan) *prom: chalng on bnd 3f out: rdn and nt qckn 2f out: wknd fnl f* **12/1**

26/3 **7** 2 **Petara Bay (IRE)**[35] 2116 6-9-0 109................. StevieDonohoe 2 101
(R A Mills) *handy: pushed along and outpcd over 2f out: dropped away over 1f out* **66/1**

51-3 **8** 4 **Wajir (FR)**[36] 2097 4-9-0 115................. FrankieDettori 10 94
(Saeed Bin Suroor) *hld up: hdwy 3f out: rdn to chse ldrs over 2f out: wnt sltly lft wl over 1f out: sn wknd* **10/1**[3]

-010 **9** ¾ **Jukebox Jury (IRE)**[15] 2709 4-9-5 118.................(v) RoystonFfrench 6 98
(M Johnston) *racd keenly: in rr: impr into midfield after 2f: pushed along over 4f out: outpcd 3f out: struggling whn n.m.r 2f out: edgd rt u.p over 1f out: no imp and wl btn after* **12/1**

6331 **10** ¾ **Claremont (IRE)**[35] 2116 4-9-0 112.................(v) AhmedAjtebi 12 92
(Mahmood Al Zarooni) *in tch: lost pl over 3f out: rdn and outpcd 2f out: bhd after* **25/1**

-136 **11** 22 **South Easter (IRE)**[15] 2709 4-9-0 107.................(t) JMurtagh 8 57
(W J Haggas) *broke wl: prom: rdn along 4f out: wknd over 2f out: eased whn wl btn fnl f* **20/1**

2m 27.36s (-5.14) **Going Correction** -0.05s/f (Good) **11** Ran SP% **118.6**
Speed ratings (Par 115): **115,112,108,107,107 104,103,100,100,99 85**
toteswingers: 1&2 £2.00, 1&3 £7.10, 2&3 £12.50 CSF £6.55 CT £63.18 TOTE £1.70: £1.02, £2.70, £6.40; EX 6.60 Trifecta £67.50 Pool: £11,770.30 - 128.98 winning units..
Owner Highclere Thoroughbred Racing (Adm. Rous) **Bred** Mrs A K H Ooi **Trained** Newmarket, Suffolk

FOCUS
This Group 2 generally falls to genuine Group-race performers but rarely a horse out of the very top bracket. This year's line-up looked typical, although there were a couple of improving four-year-olds who had the potential to reach the top level.

NOTEBOOK

Harbinger ◆, after winning a Group 3 at Newbury on his seasonal reappearance, he had beaten subsequent Gold Cup runner-up Age Of Aquarius in the Ormonde next time. A well-backed odds-on favourite once his main rival Alainmaar was withdrawn in the morning, he won in straightforward fashion.Tracking the leaders early, he moved up on the approach to the straight and, once taking the lead 2f out, he set sail for home and the race was quickly over. He is worth stepping up to the top level, with the King George VI and Queen Elizabeth Stakes back here at the end of next month the obvious target. The trainer also has the Derby winner Workforce and possibly Ask for that race, but supplied the first three in last year's running. (tchd 4-5 in places)

Duncan, a C&D winner in a Listed race here in May 2009 and narrowly beaten by Barshiba in the same race this year, was sent off second favourite and ran his race, although no match for the winner. Held up early, he did not get the clearest of runs turning for home but went in pursuit of the winner from 2f out, although he was only eating into his rival's advantage gradually. He has yet to win above Listed level, but is capable of winning a Group race and gives the impression he will get a little further. (op 10-1)

Barshiba(IRE), a Group 2 winner against her own sex and fifth in this race in 2009, had beaten Duncan in a Listed race over C&D last month. Suited by fast ground, she made the running and, although no match for the first two, stuck on bravely for the minor placing. She can win more good races against her own sex, although she may also be aimed at the Melbourne Cup in November. (op 20-1)

Sans Frontieres(IRE) ◆ is lightly raced but acts on a sound surface and put up arguably his best effort. Stepping up in trip but with plenty of stamina in his pedigree, he was held up off the pace along with the runner-up and, despite taking a while to settle and getting involved in some buffeting off the home turn, picked up nicely in the straight. He is capable of winning a Group race if building on this. (op 20-1)

Redwood, another lightly raced colt, was a dual winner on fast ground at shorter trips and had finished ahead of Crowded House in a Group 3 at Sandown this season. He confirmed that form on this step up in trip, doing his best work late, having been held up at the back of the field. He is another who can win good races at around this distance. (op 14-1)

Crowded House has not won since beating Jukebox Jury in the Racing Post Trophy in 2008, although he had suffered a couple of long absences. He ran a couple of good races in Dubai early in the year but had finished behind Redwood when fourth in a Group 3 at Sandown on his return to action in Britain. Blinkered for the first time, he raced close to the pace but came under pressure in the straight and gradually faded. A return to 1m2f or even shorter looks likely. (tchd 14-1)

Petara Bay(IRE), third to Claremont in a Listed race on his return from almost 20 months off last month, stays further than this but could keep on at only one pace in the straight. A longer trip and a drop in grade might enable him to find a suitable opportunity.

Wajir(FR), winner of a Group 2 at 1m3f and a Group 3 at 1m7f when trained in France last season, finished a well-beaten third in the Yorkshire Cup on his first start for this yard and never posed a threat here. His form in France was on good ground or softer, and it would be no surprise to see him return to his former home or Germany in search of more suitable conditions. (op 11-1)

Jukebox Jury(IRE) is suited by this trip and ground but, after winning a sub-standard Jockey Club Stakes in a first-time visor, had been well beaten in the Coronation Cup. He never looked happy this time and, even though he carried a 5lb penalty, a more potent showing could have been expected. (op 14-1)

Claremont(IRE), well behind Jukebox Jury in the Jockey Club Stakes and behind Harbinger on his first start for this yard before that, had Petara Bay behind when winning a Listed race at Newbury over 1m5f in the first-time visor. He failed to make any impression over this shorter trip and in better grade.

3192 GOLDEN JUBILEE STKS (BRITISH LEG OF THE GLOBAL SPRINT CHALLENGE) (GROUP 1) 6f

3:50 (3:51) (Class 1) 3-Y-O+

£255,465 (£96,840; £48,465; £24,165; £12,105; £6,075) **Stalls** Centre

Form RPR

5 **1** **Starspangledbanner (AUS)**[38] 2030 4-9-4 117 JMurtagh 4 125
(A P O'Brien, Ire) *racd stands' side: broke wl: mde virtually all: rdn over 1f out: drvn and styd on strly fnl f: impressive* **13/2**[1]

0-12 **2** 1 3/4 **Society Rock (IRE)**[36] 2075 3-8-11 107 PatCosgrave 13 117
(J R Fanshawe) *racd stands' side: stdd and dropped in bhd s: t.k.h early: rdn and hdwy jst over 2f out: chsd ldrs and drvn ent fnl f: kpt on wl to go 2nd last strides: no threat to wnr: 2nd of 14 in gp* **50/1**

1 **3** *hd* **Kinsale King (USA)**[84] 1024 5-9-4 121 (bt) KierenFallon 9 119
(Carl O'Callaghan, U.S.A) *ponied to s: racd stands' side: chsd ldng pair: rdn and effrt to chse wnr 2f out: drvn and no imp over 1f out: kpt on same pce ins fnl f: lost 2nd last strides: 3rd of 14 in gp* **8/1**[2]

220- **4** 1/2 **Fleeting Spirit (IRE)**[224] 7306 5-9-1 118 RichardHughes 21 114
(J Noseda) *racd far side: wl in tch: rdn and effrt wl over 1f out: led far side gp 1f out: kpt on but no imp on wnr: 1st of 10 in gp* **13/2**[1]

1131 **5** *1* **Amico Fritz (GER)**[13] 2805 4-9-4 108 MaximeGuyon 2 114
(H-A Pantall, France) *racd stands' side: chsd ldrs: rdn and unable qck wl over 1f out: styd on same pce and no ch w wnr fnl f: 4th of 14 in gp* **66/1**

-154 **6** *nk* **War Artist (AUS)**[84] 1021 7-9-4 115 OlivierPeslier 23 113
(A De Royer-Dupre, France) *racd far side: hld up in rr: rdn and effrt on far rail 2f out: styd on wl fnl 150yds: nt rch ldrs: 2nd of 10 in gp* **12/1**

105- **7** *nk* **Balthazaar's Gift (IRE)**[259] 6503 7-9-4 115 AdamKirby 14 112
(C G Cox) *racd stands' side: stdd and swtchd lft after s: hld up wl bhd: hdwy and rdn ent fnl 2f: kpt on wl ins fnl f: nvr threatened ldrs: 5th of 14 in gp* **66/1**

21-4 **8** *shd* **Varenar (FR)**[41] 1955 4-9-4 121 Christophe-PatriceLemaire 17 112
(A De Royer-Dupre, France) *taken down early and led to post: racd far side: short of room and hmpd s: sn wl in tch: effrt and rdn 2f out: one pce ins fnl f: 3rd of 10 in gp* **25/1**

2411 **9** *nk* **Prime Defender**[38] 2030 6-9-4 111 RobertWinston 15 111
(B W Hills) *racd far side: broke wl and led far side gp tl over 2f out: sn rdn: led far side gp again over 1f out tl 1f out: styd on same pce u.p fnl f: 4th of 10 in gp* **33/1**

10-2 **10** *hd* **Serious Attitude (IRE)**[42] 1918 4-9-1 108 JimmyFortune 22 107
(Rae Guest) *racd far side: stdd s and hld up in rr: rdn ent fnl 2f: swtchd lft over 1f out: styd on wl ins fnl f: nvr trbld ldrs: 5th of 10 in gp* **40/1**

0-13 **11** *nse* **Marchand D'Or (FR)**[13] 2804 7-9-4 108 DavyBonilla 3 110+
(M Delzangles, France) *taken down early and led to post: stdd s: t.k.h: hld up in rr: nt clr run wl over 1f out: swtchd rt jst over 1f out: r.o fnl f: nvr trbld ldrs: 6th of 14 in gp* **11/1**[3]

0-34 **12** *1* **Lord Shanakill (USA)**[21] 2539 4-9-4 115 TomQueally 24 107
(H R A Cecil) *racd far side: chsd far side ldr tl led that gp over 2f out tl over 1f out: wknd ins fnl f: 6th of 10 in gp* **20/1**

/3-1 **13** 1/2 **Joy And Fun (NZ)**[34] 2153 7-9-4 118 (p) BrettDoyle 1 105
(D Cruz, Hong Kong) *racd stands: side: chsd ldrs: rdn and unable qck 2f out: one pce and btn 1f out: 7th of 14 in gp* **33/1**

1 **14** *1* **Alverta (AUS)**[91] 7-9-1 0 (b) TyeAngland 18 99
(Paul Messara, Australia) *racd far side: chsd ldrs: rdn ent fnl 2f: wknd u.p jst over 1f out: 7th of 10 in gp* **40/1**

0021 **15** 1/2 **Sir Gerry (USA)**[6] 2999 5-9-4 105 SteveDrowne 11 100
(J R Best) *racd stands' side: stdd and dropped in bhd: rdn and no prog ent fnl 2f: swtchd rt and styd on past btn horses fnl f: n.d: 8th of 14 in gp* **33/1**

21-0 **16** 1 1/2 **Regal Parade**[84] 1024 6-9-4 118 AdrianNicholls 12 96
(D Nicholls) *racd stands' side: in tch in midfield: rdn and struggling 1/2-way: n.d fr wl over 1f out: 9th of 14 in gp* **40/1**

42-1 **17** 3/4 **Triple Aspect (IRE)**[26] 2400 4-9-4 109 LiamJones 5 93
(W J Haggas) *racd stands' side: t.k.h: wl in tch: rdn and unable qck over 2f out: struggling wl over 1f out: wl btn ent fnl f: 10th of 14 in gp* **25/1**

-650 **18** *hd* **Total Gallery (IRE)**[4] 3047 4-9-4 116 (p) NeilCallan 20 93
(J S Moore) *racd far side: hld up in tch: rdn and effrt ent fnl 2f: no prog over 1f out: wl hld fnl f: 8th of 10 in gp* **50/1**

34-1 **19** *nk* **High Standing (USA)**[21] 2536 5-9-4 112 JamieSpencer 19 92
(W J Haggas) *racd far side: hld up in tch towards rr: rdn and no prog 2f out: drvn and wl btn jst over 1f out: eased fnl 100yds: 9th of 10 in gp* **11/1**[3]

41-0 **20** *1* **Sayif (IRE)**[38] 2030 4-9-4 115 RichardHills 6 88
(P W Chapple-Hyam) *racd stands' side: chsd wnr tl 2f out: wkng whn n.m.r over 1f out: eased fnl 100yds: 11th of 14 in gp* **25/1**

4-31 **21** 3/4 **Main Aim**[21] 2539 5-9-4 117 RyanMoore 16 86
(Sir Michael Stoute) *racd far side: in tch: rdn and effrt over 2f out: no hdwy and wknd u.p wl over 1f out: 10th of 10 in gp* **12/1**

2- **22** *7* **Happy Zero (AUS)**[34] 2153 6-9-4 119 DarrenBeadman 8 64
(J Moore, Hong Kong) *taken down early and led to post: racd stands' side: a towards rr: pushed along 1/2-way: rdn and btn ent fnl 2f: wl bhd and eased ins fnl f: 12th of 14 in gp* **8/1**[2]

502 **23** 1/2 **Fravashi (AUS)**[84] 1021 5-9-4 116 (b) FrankieDettori 10 62
(Saeed Bin Suroor) *racd stands' side: t.k.h: hld up in rr: rdn and no rspnse 2f out: wl btn and eased ins fnl f: 13th of 14 in gp* **33/1**

13-2 **24** *9* **Showcasing**[38] 2030 3-8-11 114 WilliamBuick 7 33
(J H M Gosden) *racd stands' side: dwlt: a towards rr: rdn and btn 2f out: wl bhd and eased ins fnl f: 14th of 14 in gp* **8/1**[2]

1m 12.57s (-1.83) **Going Correction** -0.05s/f (Good)

WFA 3 from 4yo+ 7lb **24** Ran SP% **134.3**

Speed ratings (Par 117): **110,107,107,106,105 105,104,104,104,103 103,102,101,100,99 97,96,96,96,94 93,84,83,71**

toteswingers: 1&2 £107.40, 1&3 £8.20, 2&3 £86.20 CSF £351.34 CT £2728.74 TOTE £7.20: £2.70, £20.80, £2.80; EX 1417.60 Trifecta £9533.00 Part won. Pool: £12,882.55 - 0.96 winning units..

Owner M Tabor/D Smith/Mrs Magnier/Mrs Massey **Bred** Emily Krstina (aust) Pty Ltd **Trained** Ballydoyle, Co Tipperary

FOCUS

Raised to Group 1 level in 2002 when it gained its current title, this race became part of the Global Sprint Challenge in 2005. In recent years the race has had a much more international feel, with the Australian-trained Choisir successful in 2003 (four days after winning the King's Stand) and the Hong Kong-trained Cape Of Good Hope winning (at York) in 2005. You couldn't get much more of an international line-up than this, with six countries represented, and it also featured the biggest field for many years. This was arguably the classiest sprint ever run in Britain, as half of the 24 runners had been successful at the highest level somewhere around the world. Although three-year-olds had won 13 of the last 30 runnings, including the last two, only two represented the Classic generation this year. The field predictably split into two, with 14 coming stands' side and ten racing far side. There wasn't a great deal to choose between the groups at the line, but the first three came up the stands' side.

NOTEBOOK

Starspangledbanner(AUS) ◆, a dual winner at this level in Australia, ran creditably on his debut for the yard when fifth under a 5lb penalty to Prime Defender in the Duke of York, but he needed to improve plenty on that to be a contender here. However, he had reportedly been working very well recently and he duly left that form well behind. Quickly away, he was able to bag the stands' rail in front in the early stages and made the best of his way home. It was obvious from some way out that he had his rivals on the nearside beaten off and the far-side group were behind too. He is likely to head for the July Cup and he must take all the beating there. (op 7-1 tchd 6-1 and 8-1 in places)

Society Rock(IRE), winner of three of his six starts including over C&D on his reappearance, was taking on Group company for the first time and covered himself in glory, especially as he had to be switched from his middle draw in order to tuck in towards the rear of the nearside group. However, he finished in great style and proved himself a genuine Group-class sprinter. Provided he comes out of this race all right, he may take on the winner again in the July Cup and, while he has ground to make up, he has the scope to improve.

Kinsale King(USA), winner of the Golden Shaheen at Meydan in March, was having his first start on turf. Always close up on the nearside, he kept on all the way to the line and he too is likely to head for the July Cup. (op 9-1 tchd 15-2 and 10-1 in a place)

Fleeting Spirit(IRE) ◆, third and second in the last two runnings of the King's Stand and a winner over this trip in last season's July Cup, has a fine record fresh, so her absence since finishing seventh in the Breeders' Cup Sprint in November was unlikely to be a problem. She was always travelling well behind the leaders in the far-side group and was produced to lead that flank at just the right time, but the race was unfolding on the opposite side. She is unlucky not to have won more top sprints, and she will surely win another big one before the end of the season. (op 7-1 tchd 15-2 and 8-1 in places)

Amico Fritz(GER) had been successful five times on the continent this year, but not above Group 3 level, and his ability to handle fast ground was also unproven. Under the circumstances he ran a blinder in the nearside group, and should win another Group sprint in Europe this year.

War Artist(AUS), placed in this race and the July Cup in 2008 for James Eustace, was making his debut for his yard after a three-month absence and he stayed on well to finish second in the far-side group. He may come on a bit for this run and can win again in Group company if he does. (op 20-1)

Balthazaar's Gift(IRE), running in the race for the third time (he was runner-up in 2006), was racing for the first time since October. Another who needed to be switched left from his central draw, he trailed the nearside group for much of the way but finished in good style. He seems better over further these days, but looks as good as ever.

Varenar(FR), who had Goldikova back in third when winning last season's Prix de la Foret, was a disappointing odds-on favourite in Germany on his reappearance. He had every chance in the far-side group, but had never raced over a trip this short and was done for pace. A return to further should help him win again. (op 28-1 tchd 33-1 and 40-1 in a place)

Prime Defender, who had four of these behind him when winning the Duke of York last month, made much of the running in the far-side group and, although only ninth overall, this still wasn't far short of a career-best effort.

Serious Attitude(IRE) was given plenty to do in the far-side group, but she was noted making some late progress. Lightly raced and mainly disappointing since winning the Cheveley Park at two, this suggests the engine is still there and she could be interesting from now on. Official explanation: jockey said filly hung left (op 50-1)

Marchand D'Or(FR), the dominant European sprinter of 2008, seems to have retained his ability since joining his current yard and was well backed, but although he made some late headway, he never looked like winning. However, a fourth success in the Prix Maurice de Gheest over an extra half-furlong at Deauville in August, especially on easier ground, would hardly be the biggest surprise. (op 18-1 tchd 20-1)

Lord Shanakill(USA), having his first try at the trip since winning the Mill Reef at two, had every chance in the far-side group but didn't get home. (op 25-1)

Joy And Fun(NZ), a winner at Meydan in March, dropped out tamely inside the last furlong after showing up for a long way and his rider felt he may have gone lame. Official explanation: vet said gelding finished lame

Alverta(AUS), winner of eight races in Australia at 6f to 1m including at Grade 1 level, faded entering the last furlong after showing pace on the far side, but her trainer had warned that she had travelled over poorly and that the July Cup was the more suitable race, so it will be interesting to see if she still turns out there. (op 33-1)

Total Gallery(IRE) hit the big time when beating Fleeting Spirit and War Artist in last season's Prix de l'Abbaye, but he had been below form in three previous starts this year, including when beating only one home in Tuesday's King's Stand. Wearing cheekpieces for the first time, he failed to spark here either and it looks a case of back to the drawing board. (tchd 100-1 in a place)

Happy Zero(AUS), a prolific winner in Hong Kong over 5f to 7f, didn't handle the conditions and this was too bad to be true. (op 15-2)

Showcasing was entitled to have come on from his half-length defeat by Prime Defender in the Duke of York when ahead of Starspangledbanner, but he dropped right out as though something was amiss. Official explanation: jockey said colt ran flat (op 7-1 tchd 10-1)

3193 WOKINGHAM STKS (HERITAGE H'CAP) 6f

4:25 (4:27) (Class 2) (0-110,108) 3-Y-O+

£62,310 (£18,660; £9,330; £4,670; £2,330; £1,170) **Stalls** Centre

Form RPR

316/ **1** **Laddies Poker Two (IRE)**[610] 6782 5-8-11 **95** JMurtagh 2 114+
(J Noseda) *racd on stands' side: hld up: swtchd rt and hdwy 2f out: r.o to ld overall ins fnl f: sn edgd rt: in command after: 1st of 16 in gp* **9/2**[1]

-242 **2** 2 ½ **Striking Spirit**[14] 2759 5-8-10 **94** AdrianNicholls 13 105
(D Nicholls) *racd on stands' side: a.p: led overall over 1f out: hdd ins fnl f: sn edgd rt: nt pce of wnr after: 2nd of 16 in gp* **16/1**

00-5 **3** 1 ¾ **Palace Moon**[6] 2999 5-9-7 **105** (t) KierenFallon 5 111
(W J Knight) *dwlt: racd on stands' side: in rr: swtchd rt hdwy over 1f out: r.o ins fnl f: gng on at fin: 3rd of 16 in gp* **16/1**

00-0 **4** ½ **Knot In Wood (IRE)**[6] 2999 8-9-3 **108** LeeTopliss(7) 15 112
(R A Fahey) *racd on stands' side: rdn and hdwy to chse ldrs over 1f out: styd on same pce fnl 75yds: 4th of 16 in gp* **66/1**

0-00 **5** ¾ **Golden Desert (IRE)**[42] 1900 6-9-2 **100** StevieDonohoe 3 102
(R A Mills) *racd on stands' side: midfield: swtchd rt and hdwy over 1f out: styd on ins fnl f: nt pce to rch ldrs: 5th of 16 in gp* **20/1**

03-4 **6** nk **Genki (IRE)**[48] 1727 6-9-5 **103** SteveDrowne 22 104+
(R Charlton) *racd on far side: in rr: swtchd on outer and hdwy 2f out: led gp over 1f out: hung rt ins fnl f: r.o but hld by stands' side ldrs: 1st of 11 in gp* **6/1**[2]

-431 **7** ½ **Noverre To Go (IRE)**[20] 2563 4-9-0 **98** 5ex (t) RichardKingscote 27 97+
(Tom Dascombe) *racd on far side: chsd ldrs: led gp briefly over 1f out: nt qckn ins fnl f: 2nd of 11 in gp* **11/1**

6-03 **8** ¾ **Edge Closer**[26] 2400 6-9-4 **102** RyanMoore 1 99
(R Hannon) *racd on stands' side: trckd ldrs: rdn over 1f out: kpt on same pce fnl 100yds: 6th of 16 in gp* **16/1**

2-13 **9** shd **Ingleby Lady**[14] 2759 4-8-13 **97** GrahamGibbons 6 93
(T D Barron) *racd on stands' side: trckd ldrs: rdn over 1f out: no ex fnl 75yds: 7th of 16 in gp* **8/1**[3]

-365 **10** ½ **Gallagher**[106] 817 4-9-6 **104** MartinDwyer 10 99
(B J Meehan) *racd on stands' side: midfield: rdn over 1f out: kpt on ins fnl f: nt pce to chal: 8th of 16 in gp* **20/1**

0013 **11** nse **Rileyskeepingfaith**[28] 2316 4-9-4 **102** (v) AlanMunro 31 97
(M R Channon) *racd on far side: towards rr: outpcd over 2f out: sswtchd lft and hdwy ins fnl f: r.o strly: gng on at fin: 3rd of 11 in gp* **20/1**

0-50 **12** nk **Valery Borzov (IRE)**[14] 2759 6-8-13 **97** JoeFanning 20 91
(R A Fahey) *racd on far side: midfield: effrt to chse ldrs 2f out: kpt on same pce ins fnl f: 4th of 11 in gp* **66/1**

3-10 **13** hd **Johannes (IRE)**[28] 2346 7-8-13 **100** BarryMcHugh(3) 19 93
(R A Fahey) *racd on far side: prom: rdn whn chalng and carried lft 2f out: styd on same pce ins fnl f: 5th of 11 in gp* **40/1**

1001 **14** nse **Medicean Man**[42] 1903 4-8-12 **96** (p) JimmyQuinn 12 89
(J R Gask) *s.s: racd on stands' side: midfield: rdn over 1f out: one pce and no imp ins fnl f: 9th of 16 in gp* **12/1**

1-13 **15** nse **Kaldoun Kingdom (IRE)**[21] 2526 5-9-4 **102** PaulHanagan 17 95
(R A Fahey) *racd on stands' side: in tch: rdn and outpcd over 1f out: 10th of 16 in gp* **20/1**

104 **16** ½ **Prohibit**[39] 2019 5-9-0 **98** PatCosgrave 30 89
(R M H Cowell) *racd on far side: chsd ldrs: effrt 2f out: kpt on same pce ins fnl f: 6th of 11 in gp* **25/1**

-040 **17** ¾ **Evens And Odds (IRE)**[42] 1906 6-9-2 **100** WilliamBuick 16 89
(D Nicholls) *racd on stands' side: prom: pushed along over 2f out: wknd ins fnl f: 11th of 16 in gp* **33/1**

2-14 **18** ½ **Masamah (IRE)**[14] 2759 4-8-13 **97** NeilCallan 7 84
(K A Ryan) *racd on stands' side: led overall: rdn and hdd over 1f out: wknd ins fnl f: 12th: of 16 in gp* **40/1**

-402 **19** 2 ¾ **Redford (IRE)**[42] 1906 5-9-4 **102** JamieSpencer 8 80
(K A Ryan) *racd on stands' side: a bhd: nvr on terms: 13th of 16 in gp* **12/1**

5-04 **20** 2 ¼ **Jimmy Styles**[6] 2999 6-9-7 **105** (p) FrankieDettori 24 76
(C G Cox) *racd on far side: midfield: rdn over 2f out: wknd over 1f out: eased whn btn ins fnl f: 7th of 11 in gp* **14/1**

0400 **21** nse **Mac Gille Eoin**[14] 2748 6-8-12 **96** RobertWinston 21 67
(J Gallagher) *racd on far side: led gp: rdn and hung lft 2f out: hdd over 1f out: wknd ins fnl f: 8th of 11 in gp* **66/1**

-550 **22** ½ **Sohraab**[28] 2346 6-8-10 **94** RichardHughes 11 63
(H Morrison) *racd on stands' side: chsd ldrs: rdn whn n.m.r and wknd over 1f out: 14th of 16 in gp* **33/1**

-420 **23** 1 ¾ **Damien (IRE)**[38] 2030 4-9-5 **103** MichaelHills 14 67
(B W Hills) *racd on stands' side: racd keenly in midfield: lost pl and outpcd over 3f out: n.d after: 15th of 16 in gp* **16/1**

0550 **24** 1 ¾ **Barney McGrew (IRE)**[48] 1727 7-9-4 **102** PhillipMakin 28 60
(M Dods) *racd on far side: midfield: rdn over 2f out: outpcd over 1f out: 9th of 11 in gp* **33/1**

-005 **25** ½ **Able Master (IRE)**[28] 2344 4-9-0 **98** (t) RoystonFfrench 23 54
(J R Gask) *rrd s: missed break: racd on far side: a bhd: 10th of 11 in gp* **33/1**

6030 **26** 7 **Judd Street**[6] 2999 8-9-7 **105** (v) TomQueally 18 39
(Eve Johnson Houghton) *racd on stands' side: racd keenly in midfield: rdn and wknd 2f out: 16th of 16 in gp* **66/1**

4032 **27** 20 **Marching (AUS)**[28] 2344 6-9-6 **107** AhmedAjtebi(3) 26 —
(Mahmood Al Zarooni) *racd on far side: towards rr: outpcd over 3f out: sn wl bhd: 11th of 11 in gp* **50/1**

1m 12.27s (-2.13) **Going Correction** -0.05s/f (Good) **27** Ran SP% **145.0**
Speed ratings (Par 109): **112,108,106,105,104 104,103,102,102,101 101,101,101,101,100 100,99,98,94,91 91,91,88,86,85 76**
toteswingers: 1&2 £30.70, 1&3 £31.70, 2&3 £244.30 CSF £73.09 CT £1147.13 TOTE £5.50: £1.80, £5.40, £4.20, £16.30; EX 135.40 Trifecta £2967.90 Pool: £77,834.41 - 26.11 winning units..
Owner D Smith, Mrs J Magnier, M Tabor **Bred** Jerry O'Sullivan **Trained** Newmarket, Suffolk

FOCUS

One of the hottest sprint handicaps of the season and, as usual, a big field. Those drawn high have a good record but it has been won from a low draw twice in recent runnings, although one of those was when the race was staged at York. This year the field split into two groups and those drawn low held the advantage. The time was a track record and was 0.30sec faster than the preceding Group 1 Golden Jubilee. As it turned out, what is usually a close race became a one-horse affair.

NOTEBOOK

Laddies Poker Two(IRE) ◆ was backed into a short-priced favourite from 25-1 at the beginning of the week and won in the style of a Group horse. The time suggests she would have gone very close to winning the preceding Group 1 had she taken part. A C&D winner off 24lb lower in September 2008 but absent since later that month, she acted on good ground back then but this was her first try on fast. She was held up at the back of the nearside group early before making smooth progress through the field, and it was clear even before she hit the front entering the final furlong that she would win. She drew away for a relatively cosy success but connections - who have entered her for the July Cup and the Stewards' Cup - have no definite plans at this stage. (op 5-1)

Striking Spirit ◆ ran a terrific race. A C&D winner last season, he has been running well this year and, having been up with the pace on the nearside from the start, went to the front inside the last quarter-mile, only to run into a Group horse in a handicap. He deserves to pick up one of these races and the Stewards' Cup could well be on the agenda, although he is likely to go up a few pounds for this.

Palace Moon ◆, suited by the trip and ground and a Listed winner last season, had won his only previous run in a handicap, albeit off a 17lb lower mark. Having his first run for the yard and loaded using a blanket, he was given a lot to do, being held up right at the back and still there at halfway and at least two lengths off the winner. He made good late headway and, although he would not have beaten the mare with a more positive ride, he would probably have finished closer.

Knot In Wood(IRE), a regular in these big handicaps and making his fourth appearance in the race, having been fourth in 2008 and tenth in 2007 and 2009, equalled his previous best aided by having a decent claimer up. He will appreciate slightly easier ground and is always one to consider in these big sprints.

Golden Desert(IRE) ◆ has won here over 7f and put up several other good efforts in big handicaps at the track. He did so again and tends to strike form from midsummer, so he is one to bear in mind for similar contests. (tchd 33-1 in places)

Genki(IRE) ◆, was first home on the far side. A dual course-and-distance winner who was well beaten in this race last season, he subsequently won the Stewards' Cup. He was 7lb higher here but ran a terrific race, and this should set him up nicely in his bid for a repeat success at Goodwood. (op 8-1 tchd 11-2 and 10-1 in a place)

Noverre To Go(IRE) beat the runner-up in the previous day's Buckingham Palace off a 5lb lower mark at Newmarket last time, and was another to run well on a track where he has won before. He was clear of the rest on the far side, and looks set to find another decent race before long. (op 14-1 tchd 16-1 in places)

Edge Closer looked on the way back when third for the second successive year in a Windsor Listed race last time. This was his first run in a handicap for the best part of two years and he ran well, having stuck to the stands' rail throughout. He has won on Newmarket's July course, so could head for the big meeting there next month.

Ingleby Lady has gained all her wins on fast ground and is suited by this trip. She ran well, having tracked the pace on the nearside from the start, and it would be no surprise were she aimed at the York Ebor meeting, as she has won at the course and flatter tracks suit. (op 14-1 tchd 16-1 in places)

Gallagher, a useful Group-class juvenile, has raced mainly over 7f and 1m since. Having his first start since running in Dubai during the winter, he found things happening too quickly and a return to further looks likely with this under his belt. (tchd 33-1 in places)

Rileyskeepingfaith, a 7f course winner last season, was struggling on the far side over 2f out but his stamina kicked in, and he ran on in the closing stages. He is another who will appreciate the return to further. (op 25-1)

Valery Borzov(IRE) had dropped back to his last winning mark but seems best on good or softer ground and ran quite well in the circumstances. His last win was in a visor and it has yet to be used by his current trainer, so he is one to bear in mind for when the headgear is reapplied.

Johannes(IRE), a progressive sprinter last season (won Stewards' Cup consolation race), has gone up 27lb in the handicap since the start of 2009 but scored off 5lb lower mark than this on his seasonal return. He showed plenty of speed on the far side until carried left 2f out, from which point he faded. He might be aimed at Goodwood again. (op 33-1 tchd 66-1 in a places)

Medicean Man, a C&D winner last time when Noverre To Go was behind, raced on the stands' side but failed to figure. He is arguably best on good or softer ground.

Kaldoun Kingdom(IRE) has hit form in the autumn in previous seasons but won on his seasonal return this year. He was another who failed to enter the argument on the stands' side but is arguably best suited by a flat track. (op 22-1)

Prohibit finished fifth in this race last year and has been in fair form this season. He came through to join the leaders on the far side entering the last quarter-mile but could not sustain the effort. (tchd 28-1)

Evens And Odds(IRE), runner-up to Genki in the Stewards' Cup last season, showed up early on the outside of the stands' side group before fading. (op 28-1)

Masamah(IRE) is usually a front-runner and made the pace up the stands' rail. He was headed 2f out and dropped away and will be seen to better effect back at the minimum trip.

Redford(IRE) was always at the back of the stands' side group and never improved his position.

Jimmy Styles, winner of Ayr Gold Cup last season but now 5lb higher, raced on the far side but was in trouble fully 2f from home. (op 16-1 tchd 18-1 and 20-1 in a place)

Mac Gille Eoin made the running on the far side but drifted left 2f out and weakened.

Able Master(IRE) was restive in the stalls and reared as they opened, which effectively cost him his chance. Official explanation: jockey said gelding reared at the stalls opening

Judd Street Official explanation: jockey said gelding hung right

Marching(AUS) Official explanation: jockey said horse ran flat

3194 DUKE OF EDINBURGH H'CAP 1m 4f

5:00 (5:00) (Class 2) (0-105,104) 3-Y-O+

£31,155 (£9,330; £4,665; £2,335; £1,165; £585) **Stalls** High

Form RPR

0-42 **1** **Cill Rialaig**[14] 2747 5-8-11 **91** SteveDrowne 12 102
(H Morrison) *hld up wl in tch and travelling wl: effrt to chse ldr 2f out: swtchd lft and rdn to ld over 1f out: clr ins fnl f: hld on* **16/1**

/2-1 **2** nk **Imposing**[38] 2027 4-9-6 **100** RyanMoore 15 111+
(Sir Michael Stoute) *broke okay but sn struggling to go pce and dropped to last trio after 2f: switching lft and effrt ent fnl 2f: gd hdwy on outer u.p over 1f out: chsd wnr fnl 100yds: clsng at fin but nvr quite getting to wnr* **7/4**[1]

-601 **3** 1 ¼ **Martyr**[22] 2509 5-8-12 **92** RichardHughes 11 101
(R Hannon) *t.k.h early: hld up wl in tch: rdn and effrt to chse ldng pair 2f out: kpt on same pce u.p fnl f* **9/1**[3]

42-0 **4** ¾ **Australia Day (IRE)**[15] 2710 7-9-1 **95** KierenFallon 18 103
(P R Webber) *led and set gd gallop: rdn jst over 2f out: hdd over 1f out and nt qckn w wnr: no ex and lost 2 pls fnl 100yds* **20/1**

3-12 **5** 1 **Sweet Lightning**[19] 2608 5-9-2 **96** PhillipMakin 14 102
(M Dods) *hld up in midfield: effrt and nt clr run briefly 2f out: sn rdn and chsng ldrs: no ex and one pce ent fnl f* **10/1**

-16 **6** ½ **Dangerous Midge (USA)**[36] 2096 4-9-3 **97** MartinDwyer 6 102
(B J Meehan) *t.k.h early: hld up in midfield on outer: rdn 4f out: sme hdwy and hanging rt over 1f out: swtchd lft 1f out: kpt on fnl f: nvr able to rch ldrs* **11/1**

-031 **7** ½ **Sandor**[24] 2444 4-8-12 **92** NeilCallan 19 97
(P J Makin) *plld hrd early: hld up in midfield: hmpd and lost pl bnd 8f out: rdn and effrt on inner over 2f out: drvn and kpt on fnl f: nvr gng pce to rch ldrs* **25/1**

1611 **8** ½ **Submariner (USA)**[17] 2640 4-9-0 **94** FrankieDettori 1 98
(M Johnston) *in tch: rdn and effrt 3f out: drvn and styd on same pce fr over 1f out* **13/2**[2]

4011 **9** nk **Just Lille (IRE)**[10] 2857 7-8-12 **95** (v) BarryMcHugh(3) 20 98
(Mrs A Duffield) *t.k.h early: chsd ldrs: rdn and chsd ldr jst over 2f out tl 2f out: drvn and unable qck wl over 1f out: wknd ent fnl f* **20/1**

0340 **10** 2 ¼ **Drill Sergeant**[36] 2096 5-9-7 **101** JoeFanning 8 101
(M Johnston) *chsd ldrs: rdn and effrt over 2f out: unable qck u.p 2f out: wknd over 1f out* **20/1**

0-03 **11** nk **Macarthur**[28] 2345 6-9-3 **97** (p) ShaneKelly 2 96
(Jane Chapple-Hyam) *stdd s: plld v hrd: hld up in rr: rdn and effrt 2f out: plugged on fnl f: nvr trbld ldrs* **28/1**

0-21 **12** shd **Final Victory**[28] 2317 4-8-11 **91** JimmyFortune 4 90
(A M Balding) *hld up towards rr: rdn and effrt wl over 2f out: no real prog: plugged on same pce fr over 1f out* **16/1**

-462 **13** 2 ¼ **Classic Vintage (USA)**[28] 2317 4-9-3 **97** (p) JMurtagh 22 92
(Mrs A J Perrett) *dwlt and bustled along early: a in rr: hrd rdn and no rspnse over 2f out: wl btn fnl 2f* **12/1**

2530 **14** 2 ¼ **Becausewecan (USA)**[48] 1724 4-9-0 **94** RobertWinston 13 86
(M Johnston) *hld up in midfield: rdn and nt qckn wl over 2f out: wl btn over 1f out* **40/1**

0-30 **15** ½ **Via Galilei (IRE)**[28] 2317 5-9-3 **97** GeorgeBaker 3 88
(G L Moore) *v.s.a: a in rr: rdn and no prog over 2f out: n.d* **66/1**

43/0 **16** 5 **Eradicate (IRE)**[23] 2469 6-9-10 **104** JamieSpencer 16 87
(N J Henderson) *t.k.h: chsd ldr tl jst over 2f out: drvn and wknd qckly wl over 1f out* **25/1**

0-03 **17** dist **Mystery Star (IRE)**[36] 2096 5-9-3 **97** (p) PatCosgrave 17 —
(M H Tompkins) *racd in midfield: pushed along 8f out: bhd and lost tch 3f out: virtually p.u fnl 2f* **16/1**

2m 29.64s (-2.86) **Going Correction** -0.05s/f (Good) **17** Ran SP% **131.8**
Speed ratings (Par 109): **107,106,105,105,104 104,104,103,103,102 101,101,100,98,98 95,—**
toteswingers: 1&2 £14.30, 1&3 £39.80, 2&3 £5.30 CSF £42.69 CT £303.13 TOTE £23.60: £3.70, £1.30, £2.20, £3.40; EX 69.80 Trifecta £295.60 Pool: £6,791.88 - 17.00 winning units..
Owner Pangfield Partners **Bred** T J Billington **Trained** East Ilsley, Berks
■ Stewards' Enquiry : Steve Drowne two-day ban: excessive use of whip (July 5-6)

FOCUS
A typically hot handicap which has been won by four-year-olds seven times in the past ten years and in that time no horse older than five had been successful. With a few established front-runners in the field, a decent pace was always likely and the draw played its part too, with the first five home all drawn in double figures.

NOTEBOOK
Cill Rialaig, 5lb above her last winning mark, beat all bar a progressive sort at Epsom on Derby day and stepped up on that effort here. This success was mainly due to her always holding a good position behind the leaders and, when sent to the front over a furlong out, she got first run on the favourite, which made all the difference. Already the winner of a Listed bumper at Cheltenham early last year, connections will now try to earn some black type on the Flat with her too. (op 14-1)
Imposing, raised 9lb after defying a 13-month absence to win at York last month, was upped to this trip for the first time. Held up near the back of the field, he wasn't in a great position turning in, as he was stuck in a pocket on the inside rail just as the leaders were setting sail for home. Pulled to the wide outside in order to get a run, he finished very strongly but, despite plenty of assistance from the saddle, he just failed to get up. Many of his supporters may feel aggrieved, but he apparently has to be ridden this way. Official explanation: jockey said colt was struck into on the right hind (op 2-1 tchd 9-4 in places)
Martyr was 5lb higher than when bouncing back to winning form over this trip at Newmarket last month and therefore 1lb higher than when third in this race last year. Always handy, he had every chance up the home straight but lacked a telling turn of foot and is likely to be stepped up to 1m6f. (op 10-1 tchd 17-2)
Australia Day(IRE), runner-up over C&D in his only previous try over the trip last September, was one of several in the field who likes to go from the front and he was the one who managed to bag the early lead. He stayed there until the winner headed him over a furlong from home and, considering he has won over hurdles, he does seem to get this trip well enough.
Sweet Lightning, whose trainer was worried about the ground being too quick, has been in fine form in two starts for his new yard this season and only ran in this as he didn't get into the Wolferton. He was never far away and had every chance coming to the last furlong, but couldn't go through with it. He did win over this trip as a 3-y-o, but does look better suited by 1m2f these days.
Dangerous Midge(USA), who didn't seem to stay this trip at the first attempt when bidding for a hat-trick at York last month, remains 9lb above his last winning mark and ran a rather strange race. After having raced keenly on the outside of the field early, he then looked lazy and had to be given a reminder passing the 5f pole. It seemed he would drop right out after hanging out to his left rounding the final turn, but once in line for home he stayed on again and was finishing well at the line. He doesn't look an easy ride, but could be of some interest back on a left-handed track. Official explanation: jockey said colt stumbled going down the hill towards swinley bottom (op 12-1 tchd 14-1 in places)
Sandor, raised 2lb for his narrow Ffos Las success, was doing his best work late up the inside rail but was never getting there in time. (op 20-1)
Submariner(USA), who didn't see the racecourse until April and had won three of his four starts, normally likes to be ridden positively but the outside draw made that a difficult task, so this wasn't a bad effort under the circumstances. He is likely to carry on improving. (op 7-1)
Just Lille(IRE) has been a revelation since the visor was applied and was bidding for a hat-trick off a 9lb higher mark, but although she ran well for a long way, she had gained her two recent wins from the front and couldn't get the early lead in this company. (op 18-1 tchd 16-1)
Final Victory, raised 7lb for his convincing success over Classic Vintage at Goodwood last month, never offered a threat but his trainer had voiced concerns over the quick ground, so it may be best to forgive him this effort.
Classic Vintage(USA), now 7lb above his last winning mark, had cheekpieces on for the first time but he never looked happy at any stage. (op 14-1)

3195 QUEEN ALEXANDRA STKS (CONDITIONS RACE) 2m 5f 159y
5:35 (5:36) (Class 2) 4-Y-0+

£31,155 (£9,330; £4,665; £2,335; £1,165; £585) Stalls High

Form RPR

2/5 **1** **Bergo (GER)**[35] 2116 7-9-2 105 RyanMoore 8 99
(G L Moore) *a.p: led over 2f out: edgd rt ins fnl f: styd on gamely and on top towards fin* **10/1**

1-26 **2** 1 ½ **Aajel (USA)**[28] 2345 6-9-2 106 RichardHills 1 98
(M P Tregoning) *racd wd of field early: handy: w ldr after 4f: led after 6f: rdn and hdd over 2f out: continued to press wnr: hld and no ex fnl 50yds* **11/1**

0-05 **3** 1 ¾ **Swingkeel (IRE)**[45] 1821 5-9-2 97 (p) JimmyFortune 18 96
(J L Dunlop) *midfield: rdn and hdwy 2f out: chsd front pair and edgd rt over 1f out: styd on and clsd ins fnl f: nt rch ldrs* **9/2**[2]

14-0 **4** 2 ½ **Caracciola (GER)**[28] 2345 13-9-5 102 AlanMunro 5 96
(N J Henderson) *in tch: pushed along over 3f out: effrt to cl over 2f out: chsd ldrs: over 1f out: styd on ins fnl f: one pce and no further imp fnl 75yds* **33/1**

6-35 **5** 1 ¼ **Starfala**[28] 2345 5-8-11 104 NeilCallan 13 87
(P F I Cole) *trckd ldrs: rdn and outpcd over 2f out: styd on to cl fnl 100yds: nt get to ldrs* **14/1**

100/ **6** ¾ **Sentry Duty (FR)**[93] 1916 8-9-2 99 KierenFallon 10 91
(N J Henderson) *midfield: rdn whn swtchd rt and hdwy 2f out: chsd ldrs over 1f out: no imp on ldrs: wknd fnl 75yds* **4/1**[1]

2 **7** 1 ¼ **Kid Charlemagne (IRE)**[44] 1851 7-9-2 0 TomQueally 6 90
(W J Greatrex) *handy: rdn to chse ldrs over 2f out: no further prog and one pce fnl f* **40/1**

8 hd **Ringaroses**[71] 9-9-2 0 (t) GeorgeBaker 2 90
(Jonjo O'Neill) *hld up: rdn and hdwy on outer over 2f out: kpt on ins fnl f: nvr able to chal ldrs* **10/1**

00-1 **9** 1 **Hollins**[37] 2060 6-9-2 78 SebSanders 16 89?
(Micky Hammond) *prom: rdn and nt qckn over 2f out: plugged on at one pce tl no ex ins fnl f* **20/1**

0-32 **10** 9 **Munsef**[28] 2345 8-9-2 107 JamieSpencer 15 80
(Ian Williams) *hld up: rdn and hdwy 2f out: no imp on ldrs: btn fnl f* **5/1**[3]

/05- **11** 2 **Deutschland (USA)**[20] 5824 7-9-2 101 JMurtagh 11 78
(W P Mullins, Ire) *midfield: pushed along over 5f out: rdn over 2f out: no real prog* **6/1**

20-5 **12** 4 **Baddam**[31] 1798 8-9-2 82 MartinDwyer 14 74
(Ian Williams) *led: hdd after 6f: remained w ldr: stl chalng 3f out: sn rdn: wknd over 1f out* **40/1**

0/0- **13** 2 ¼ **Midas Way**[22] 2994 10-9-2 87 (p) AdamKirby 9 72
(P R Chamings) *midfield: rdn 3f out: wknd 2f out* **66/1**

0406 **14** 2 **Sweetheart**[12] 2810 6-8-11 68 JoeFanning 3 65
(Jamie Poulton) *trckd ldrs: effrt over 3f out: rdn and wknd 2f out* **25/1**

0006 **15** 8 **Balkan Knight**[23] 2469 10-9-2 105 WilliamBuick 7 62
(D R C Elsworth) *hld up: rdn over 2f out: nvr on terms* **25/1**

406- **16** 6 **Casual Garcia**[25] 5917 5-9-2 63 (bt) NeilChalmers 12 56
(Mark Gillard) *hld up: rdn over 2f out: nvr on terms* **100/1**

0-50 **17** 1 ½ **Star Of Pompey**[44] 1849 6-8-11 50 RobertLButler 17 49
(M R Hoad) *hld up: toiling fr over 3f out: nvr on terms* **100/1**

1013 **18** 84 **Prince Picasso**[28] 2313 7-9-2 79 (b) PaulHanagan 4 —
(R A Fahey) *midfield: pushed along over 6f out: lost pl over 5f out: sn bhd: t.o: fin lame* **50/1**

4m 47.79s (-6.21) **Going Correction** -0.05s/f (Good) **18** Ran SP% **128.0**
Speed ratings (Par 109): **109,108,107,106,106 106,105,105,105,102 101,99,99,98,95 93,92,62**
toteswingers: 1&2 £19.70, 1&3 £15.50, 2&3 £16.30 CSF £111.15 CT £580.05 TOTE £13.90: £4.00, £3.90, £2.30; EX 121.20 Trifecta £1027.70 Pool: £8,634.19 - 6.21 winning units. Place 6 £340.19; Place 5 £44.26.
Owner S E Sangster **Bred** J Nickel **Trained** Lower Beeding, W Sussex

FOCUS
The closing race of the meeting and traditionally the longest Flat race of the season. A vast range of abilities were on show but there were still plenty in with a chance turning for home, despite the pace being good and the time being a course record.

NOTEBOOK
Bergo(GER), a multiple hurdle and chase winner but formerly Group-placed in Germany on the Flat, is suited by fast ground and put up a decent effort at Newbury in May. Given a no-nonsense ride, he tracked the leaders before making his effort off the home turn and responded to a strong ride from the champion jockey to just get the better of the long-time leader. He will presumably be put away for an autumn campaign over jumps. (op 8-1)
Aajel(USA) returned from nearly two years off to win a 2m handicap on fast ground at Yarmouth last season and was narrowly beaten in a Group 2 here on his return this year. He put his disappointing York effort last time behind him, making much of the running and galloping on bravely once headed. (tchd 12-1)
Swingkeel(IRE) put up a decent effort in the Chester Cup last time in first-time cheekpieces when he met trouble in running, and had also run well on both starts at this track. He was settled off the pace before staying on in the straight but could never get to the principals. (op 5-1 tchd 11-2 in places)
Caracciola(GER), formerly a useful hurdler, has become a good stayer on the Flat as a veteran, winning the Cesarewitch in 2008 and this race last season. Well beaten in both his starts since winning here last year, he bounced back to something like his old form, keeping on all the way to the line. (op 25-1)
Starfala has been Group and Listed-placed and has run well on this track, and this was her first run below Group/Listed level since October 2008. She tracked the leaders on the rail but did not immediately pick up when asked, only to find a second wind in the last furlong and finish as well as anything.
Sentry Duty(FR), a high-class hurdler and stablemate of the fourth, was a decent performer on the Flat in France. He was sent off favourite and travelled well enough in the pack behind the leaders. However, he had nothing in reserve in the straight and may have been beaten by a combination of lack of stamina and the fast ground. (tchd 9-2)
Kid Charlemagne(IRE) was a lightly raced dual bumper winner, the last of which was back in 2007, and had run well in a maiden over 1m4f on his Flat debut (winner of that touched off in Queen's Vase earlier in the week). He ran a terrific race and kept staying on under pressure, having never been far away.
Ringaroses, a useful staying hurdler/chaser out of a Stayers' Hurdle winner, was having his first run on the Flat. He goes well on a sound surface and was doing his best work in the closing stages, having been held up at the rear for most of the way. (tchd 9-1)
Hollins, another winning hurdler, had returned to the Flat to win ordinary 2m2f handicap on fast ground last time. He ran a fine race over this longer trip considering he had a lot to find on the ratings. (op 25-1)

Munsef, a smart middle-distance/stayer, goes well on fast ground but his only previous run beyond 1m6f was in last season's Melbourne Cup, so the trip was a big unknown. He travelled comfortably off the pace and had not been asked a question approaching the home turn. However, when his rider got serious, the tank was empty and he clearly did not stay. (op 13-2 tchd 7-1 in places)
Deutschland(USA), a useful hurdler chaser who has won on fast ground on the Flat, was another with a question mark over the trip. He was being ridden fully 4f out and stamina was the problem with him as well. (op 7-1)
Baddam, another who has been jumping of late and is a regular at the meeting, was attempting to repeat his success of 2006. He had a lot to do on the ratings but helped cut out the pace before dropping out in the straight.
Prince Picasso Official explanation: vet said gelding finsihed lame
T/Jkpt: Not won. T/Plt: £327.30 to a £1 stake. Pool: £457,107.09. 1,019.36 winning tickets.
T/Qpdt: £80.80 to a £1 stake. Pool: £20,670.00. 189.13 winning tickets. SP

3147 AYR (L-H)
Saturday, June 19

OFFICIAL GOING: Good to firm (9.6)
Inside rail on round course moved out 2m and stands' side rail on straight course moved in 3m.
Wind: Breezy, half against Weather: Sunny, hot

3196 SCOTTISH SUN H'CAP — 1m
2:25 (2:25) (Class 2) (0-100,100) 3-Y-O
£13,708 (£4,105; £2,052; £1,027; £512; £257) **Stalls** Low

Form				RPR
02-1	1		**Breakheart (IRE)**[28] 2334 3-8-2 **81** oh4 .... FrannyNorton 4 (A M Balding) *prom: rdn over 2f out: led ins fnl f: styd on wl* **10/1**	91
213-	2	1 ½	**Sand Skier**[238] 7013 3-8-8 **87** .... JimCrowley 1 (M Johnston) *chsd ldrs: drvn and outpcd 2f out: rallied ins fnl f: tk 2nd cl home* **6/1**[3]	94
1145	3	*nk*	**Hacienda (IRE)**[28] 2324 3-9-3 **96** .... GregFairley 8 (M Johnston) *chsd clr ldr: smooth hdwy to ld over 2f out: rdn 2 l clr wl over 1f out: hung lft and hdd ins fnl f: lost 2nd cl home* **9/2**[2]	102
-231	4	¾	**Finest Reserve (IRE)**[22] 2510 3-8-4 **83** oh2 ow2 ....(v) ChrisCatlin 6 (M R Channon) *bhd: rdn and outpcd 1/2-way: styd on wl fr 2f out: nrst fin* **10/1**	87
1	5	4 ½	**Qanoon (USA)**[21] 2548 3-8-8 **87** .... TadhgO'Shea 2 (W J Haggas) *s.s: bhd: rdn 3f out: nvr able to chal* **1/1**[1]	81+
1-01	6	1 ½	**Tres Coronas (IRE)**[23] 2466 3-8-4 **83** ow1 ....(b) PJMcDonald 7 (T D Barron) *led: clr after 3f: hdd over 2f out: sn btn* **13/2**	73
6-10	7	8	**No Hubris (USA)**[23] 2471 3-9-7 **100** .... PaulMulrennan 5 (P F I Cole) *in tch: rdn 3f out: wknd fr 2f out* **22/1**	72

1m 38.27s (-5.53) **Going Correction** -0.55s/f (Hard) 7 Ran SP% **118.3**
Speed ratings (Par 105): **105,103,103,102,97 96,88**
toteswingers:1&2:£3.50, 1&3:£3.70, 2&3:£2.60 CSF £70.42 CT £313.35 TOTE £12.90: £3.20, £3.10; EX 87.60 TRIFECTA Not won..
Owner J C Smith **Bred** Littleton Stud **Trained** Kingsclere, Hants

FOCUS
A useful handicap, despite the favourite blowing the start, contested by some horses who were eligible to tackle the Britannia. It was run at a good gallop with the lead changing hands several times.

NOTEBOOK
Breakheart(IRE) ◆'s reappearance win at Lingfield on the AW hadn't really been tested but he was clearly on a good mark going handicapping, despite being 4lb out of the weights back on turf. Being by Sakhee, he will probably remain ahead of the handicapper as he is stepped up in trip. He looks sure to win another handicap or two, and a more galloping track than this will probably suit him ideally as well. (op 11-1)
Sand Skier ◆, making his reappearance, looked potentially well treated on the form of his final run as a 2-y-o and ran creditably on his first run at the trip, keeping on well after being caught a bit flat-footed 2f out. He will stay further and should be sharper next time. (op 15-2)
Hacienda(IRE)'s form had a progressive look to it and, while he didn't run badly, left the impression that a return to 7f might suit him having looked the likely winner when moving smoothly to the front. That said, he tended to carry his head awkwardly and hang away from the rail once there, and might not be entirely straightforward. (op 11-2)
Finest Reserve(IRE) had got off the mark in a first-time visor last time, but this was a much warmer contest and, after stumbling early, it was only very late in the day that he got going. Out of a mare by Montjeu, he looks as if he's worth a try over further. (op 8-1)
Qanoon(USA) was all the rage after his ready Newmarket success, but he ruined all chance he had by rearing in the stalls and then starting very slowly. He threatened briefly to get back into contention in the straight, but was always fighting a losing battle on a tricky track for one still learning. He's well worth another chance to confirm debut promise. Official explanation: jockey said the colt reared as the stalls opened (tchd 5-4 in places)
Tres Coronas(IRE), 2-3 in blinkers and still improving coming into this, despite plenty of racing, is best when allowed to make the pace but he went off far too fast. (tchd 7-1)
No Hubris(USA) looked on a stiffish mark on his handicap debut despite two runs in much better grade, but never threatened and this was a second successive disappointing run. Official explanation: jockey said the colt hung right handed in the straight (op 25-1 tchd 20-1)

3197 SCOTTISH NEWS OF THE WORLD E B F LAND O'BURNS FILLIES' STKS (LISTED RACE) — 5f
3:00 (3:06) (Class 1) 3-Y-O+
£22,708 (£8,608; £4,308; £2,148; £1,076; £540) **Stalls** High

Form				RPR
10-3	1		**Tropical Treat**[42] 1918 3-8-11 94 .... JimCrowley 6 (R M Beckett) *prom: effrt over 1f out: led ins fnl f: drvn out* **11/2**[3]	95
-456	2	¾	**City Dancer (IRE)**[14] 2745 4-9-3 87 .... FrannyNorton 10 (D Nicholls) *hld up on ins: nt clr run over 2f out: effrt and gd hdwy ent fnl f: chsd wnr last 50yds: r.o* **15/2**	95
0-1	3	1	**Bewitched (IRE)**[21] 2537 3-9-1 105 .... WMLordan 1 (Charles O'Brien, Ire) *prom: effrt over 2f out: edgd rt and kpt on same pce fnl f* **3/1**[2]	93
2120	4	*shd*	**Glamorous Spirit (IRE)**[14] 2745 4-9-3 88 .... ChrisCatlin 11 (R A Harris) *t.k.h: led tl hdd ins fnl f: kpt on same pce* **10/1**	91
5243	5	1	**Feelin Foxy**[8] 2940 6-9-3 80 .... PaulMulrennan 5 (J G Given) *hld up: effrt on outside over 1f out: no imp ins fnl f* **33/1**	87?
-012	6	½	**Rose Blossom**[21] 2536 3-8-11 97 .... TonyHamilton 9 (R A Fahey) *chsd ldr: rdn over 2f out: no ex ins fnl f* **5/4**[1]	83
	7	1 ¼	**Miss Velocity**[15] 2730 3-8-11 88 .... GFCarroll 2 (Andrew Oliver, Ire) *in tch: checked and outpcd over 3f out: rallied on outside over 1f out: sn no imp* **25/1**	79
040-	8	3 ¼	**Swan Wings**[281] 5822 3-8-11 91 .... LiamKeniry 4 (A M Balding) *prom: rdn over 2f out: edgd lft and wknd over 1f out* **40/1**	67
-004	9	3 ½	**Impressible**[21] 2536 4-9-3 89 .... WilliamCarson 8 (S C Williams) *prom: n.m.r and lost pl over 2f out: sn rdn: btn over 1f out* **28/1**	56

58.16 secs (-1.94) **Going Correction** -0.225s/f (Firm)
WFA 3 from 4yo+ 6lb 9 Ran SP% **118.4**
Speed ratings (Par 108): **106,104,103,103,101 100,98,93,87**
toteswingers:1&2:£7.20, 1&3:£3.40, 2&3:£5.50 CSF £44.79 TOTE £8.00: £2.40, £1.60, £1.10; EX 21.60 Trifecta £259.00 Part won. Pool: £350.09 - 0.77 winning units..
Owner J C Smith **Bred** R J Cornelius **Trained** Whitsbury, Hants

FOCUS
A competitive Listed race for fillies loaded with front runners and, not surprisingly, the main action took place against the stands' rail. The proximity of the fifth just raises a doubt about the form.

NOTEBOOK
Tropical Treat doesn't take a lot of racing according to her trainer and was having her first run since an excellent reappearance when the ground was considered too soft. Ideally positioned on the rail and getting a good tow from the leader, she put her seal on the race quickly when asked and won with a bit in hand. She looks progressive and the Summer Stakes at York in three weeks' time might be next on the agenda. (op 6-1)
City Dancer(IRE) ◆, who had looked on the way back last time, followed up that run by finishing second in this race for the second year running having been held up some way off the pace before finishing strongly. She's going to go up in the weights for this, but looks a winner waiting to happen. (op 7-1)
Bewitched(IRE), unbeaten this year and boasting a defeat of the subsequent Jersey Stakes winner Rainfall at Haydock on her latest outing, was having her first run at 5f since winning on the AW at Dundalk last autumn. Her trainer had been reported as saying she would be even better back on quick ground, but she didn't look totally at ease on the very fast conditions and also left the impression that at this level she really needs an extra furlong. (tchd 11-4)
Glamorous Spirit(IRE) had always been as good on turf as the AW ahead of the improvement she showed over the winter, and proved she still is with a fine effort. (op 11-1 tchd 9-1)
Feelin Foxy appeared to have little chance at these weights despite being in good form in handicaps, but she ran well above herself and might even have finished a bit closer had she not been hampered. Her task in handicaps isn't going to be any easier after this. (tchd 25-1)
Rose Blossom has been much improved since dropped back to 5f and was allowed to stride on, but being drawn next to what must be the fastest filly in training at 4f didn't help her and she was never able to get into a rhythm. She's better than this, though a touch inconsistent too. (tchd 15-8 in a place)
Miss Velocity, a much-improved front-runner this season, couldn't assume her usual tactics from a wide draw and was also found out by the marked step up in class on her first run at 5f. (op 20-1)
Swan Wings hadn't been seen since bringing up the rear in the Flying Childers Stakes at Doncaster last autumn and once again showed she isn't really up to this level.
Impressible had come back to form at Haydock last time, but was suited by give in the ground then and found conditions here too fast. (op 25-1)

3198 SCOTTISH SUN MISS SCOTLAND H'CAP — 1m 5f 13y
3:30 (3:30) (Class 3) (0-95,94) 4-Y-O+ **£9,714** (£2,890; £1,444; £721) **Stalls** Low

Form				RPR
/01-	1		**Dirar (IRE)**[12] 7720 5-9-7 **94** .... WMLordan 2 (Gordon Elliott, Ire) *hld up in tch: hdwy over 2f out: led 1f out: rdn out* **11/4**[2]	107
0632	2	1	**Wicked Daze (IRE)**[1] 3152 7-7-11 **75** oh3 .... JamesSullivan(5) 4 (Miss L A Perratt) *led: rdn over 2f out: hdd 1f out: kpt on u.p* **11/1**	86
4112	3	¾	**Lady Eclair (IRE)**[10] 2857 4-8-5 **78** .... GregFairley 1 (M Johnston) *cl up: rdn over 3f out: rallied: kpt on ins fnl f* **2/1**[1]	88
15-0	4	5	**Chookie Hamilton**[30] 2243 6-7-9 **75** oh2 .... RyanPowell(7) 7 (N Wilson) *cl up: effrt and ch over 2f out: outpcd over 1f out: n.d after* **40/1**	78
0-05	5	1 ½	**Lochiel**[10] 2857 6-9-1 **88** .... PJMcDonald 5 (Mrs L B Normile) *hld up: effrt over 2f out: no imp over 1f out* **20/1**	88
130-	6	¾	**Buckie Boy (IRE)**[234] 7117 4-8-3 **76** .... ChrisCatlin 6 (J S Goldie) *hld up: effrt on ins over 2f out: nvr able to chal* **16/1**	75
43-0	7	1 ¼	**Cosmic Sun**[21] 2541 4-9-4 **91** .... TonyHamilton 3 (R A Fahey) *hld up in tch: effrt on outside over 2f out: edgd lft and wknd over 1f out* **9/2**[3]	88
-204	8	2 ½	**Cool Strike (UAE)**[22] 2509 4-9-1 **88** ....(v) LiamKeniry 8 (A M Balding) *cl up tl rdn and wknd fr 2f out* **5/1**	82

2m 46.28s (-7.72) **Going Correction** -0.55s/f (Hard) 8 Ran SP% **116.3**
Speed ratings (Par 107): **101,100,99,96,95 95,94,93**
toteswingers:1&2:£14.80, 1&3:£1.80, 2&3:£7.50 CSF £33.30 CT £72.70 TOTE £4.70: £1.10, £4.50, £2.20; EX 39.40.
Owner Mick White **Bred** His Highness The Aga Khan's Studs S C **Trained** Capranny, Co. Meath

FOCUS
A useful handicap but one that was run at something of an uneven pace and the form has a muddling look to it.

NOTEBOOK
Dirar(IRE) had improved substantially over hurdles since last seen winning on the Flat on the AW in December and carried that across to the turf with a win that is probably better than it looks on paper. He probably did well to get up and pull so far clear of those that were held up as he was entering the straight. He might be an interesting type for the Ebor, having looked a non-stayer in the Cesarewitch last autumn, but apparently has the Galway Hurdle as his first priority. (op 2-1)
Wicked Daze(IRE), 3lb out of the weights, had been touched off over this C&D the night before, and ran well in this much stronger contest. That said, he was helped by being able to dictate the gallop, and will find things tougher once reassessed. (op 9-1)
Lady Eclair(IRE) looked suited by being back up in trip after finishing clear of the rest behind a well-handicapped one last time, but she wasn't ridden with the same enterprise here and was made to look rather one-paced. She'll do better when her stamina is tested more. (op 3-1)
Chookie Hamilton hadn't shown much on his debut for a new yard last time and was 2lb out of the weights, but he shaped with more encouragement, albeit given less to do than some.
Lochiel hasn't been seen to best effect so far this year, but again left the impression that he is just starting to knock at the door. He would have preferred a stronger gallop. (op 14-1)
Buckie Boy(IRE), having just his second run for the yard, still looked on a stiffish mark on the balance of his form and never threatened after being dropped out in rear. (op 14-1)
Cosmic Sun, well held on his reappearance, was expected to be suited by the return to this quicker surface, but he ran moderately again down in lower grade than usual and has something to prove. (op 13-2)
Cool Strike(UAE) wasn't asked to lead on this occasion and turned in a rather moody display. Official explanation: jockey said that the gelding ran flat (op 11-2)

3199 REAL RADIO EUROPEAN BREEDERS' FUND MAIDEN STKS — 6f
4:05 (4:05) (Class 5) 2-Y-O **£3,238** (£963; £481; £240) **Stalls** High

Form				RPR
	1		**Wootton Bassett** 2-9-3 0 .... TonyHamilton 1 (R A Fahey) *trckd ldr: led over 2f out: hrd pressed and edgd lft ins fnl f: pushed out* **11/4**[2]	84+
	2	1 ¼	**Easy Ticket (IRE)** 2-9-3 0 .... RichardMullen 7 (D H Brown) *t.k.h: trckd ldrs: effrt over 1f out: chal and hung lft ins fnl f: kpt on same pce towards fin* **7/2**[3]	80+

5 **3** 5 **Jibaal (IRE)**[37] 2059 2-9-3 0 .... TadhgO'Shea 5 65+
(M Johnston) *dwlt: last and sn pushed along: hdwy and edgd lft over 2f out: outpcd over 1f out* **6/5**[1]

4 3 1/2 **Purkab** 2-9-0 0 .... GaryBartley(3) 3 55
(J S Goldie) *in tch tl rdn and wknd over 1f out* **25/1**

5 2 1/2 **Myjestic Melody (IRE)** 2-8-12 0 .... PaulMulrennan 2 42
(N Wilson) *trckd ldrs: rdn over 2f out: wknd over 1f out* **50/1**

4223 **6** 14 **Silca Conegliano (IRE)**[14] 2749 2-8-12 0 .... ChrisCatlin 4 —
(M R Channon) *led to over 2f out: sn rdn: wknd wl over 1f out* **13/2**

1m 11.2s (-2.40) **Going Correction** -0.225s/f (Firm) **6** Ran SP% **113.5**
Speed ratings (Par 93): **107,105,98,94,90 72**
toteswingers:1&2:£2.30, 1&3:£2.00, 2&3:£1.80 CSF £13.00 TOTE £3.70: £2.50, £2.80; EX 9.10.
Owner Frank Brady & The Cosmic Cases **Bred** Laundry Cottage Stud Farm **Trained** Musley Bank, N Yorks

FOCUS
Only six runners, but the first two both created big impressions and look potentially useful in coming so far clear. The winning time was very smart indeed.

NOTEBOOK
Wootton Bassett ◆ is bred to run as a 2-y-o, being a half-bother to the same yard's useful winners Mister Hardy and Mister Laurel (both of whom won first time out), and he looked a decent prospect in also making a winning debut. Soon travelling smoothly, he quickening smartly when asked and then kept a straighter course than the eventual runner-up. His trainer will probably be eyeing the Gimcrack at the big York August meeting. (op 5-2 tchd 3-1)
Easy Ticket(IRE) ◆, whose pedigree is a mix of speed and stamina, is from a yard that have struck with their youngsters this year and was interestingly short in the market. It was easy to see why once under way as he travelled strongly only to spoil his finishing effort by edging left. Not given a hard time thereafter, he should have little trouble going one better. (op 11-4 tchd 5-2)
Jibaal(IRE) had shown up for a long way in a good maiden on his debut at York, won by the subsequent Coventry second Elzaam, but he never travelled with the same fluency here after missing the break and was readily left behind by the first two. Mentally, he still looks like he has some growing up to do. (op 2-1 tchd Evens and 9-4 in places)
Purkab is a half-brother to several winners, but hails from a yard that tend to go quietly with their juveniles and, though never a factor, he left the impression that he has improvement in him. (op 20-1)
Myjestic Melody(IRE), a half-sister to a winning plater, never really threatened but is entitled to improve. Official explanation: jockey said that the filly was unsuited by the going (good to firm) (op 40-1)
Silca Conegliano(IRE) dropped away quickly after making the running. (op 5-1 tchd 7-1)

3200 SCOTTISH SUN SUPER GOALS H'CAP 6f
4:40 (4:40) (Class 5) (0-70,68) 3-Y-0+ **£2,914** (£867; £433; £216) **Stalls** High

Form RPR
0505 **1** **Bateleur**[4] 3057 6-9-3 **57** .... ChrisCatlin 5 64
(M R Channon) *hld up: hdwy over 1f out: squeezed through to ld ins fnl f: pushed out: comf* **5/2**[1]

-063 **2** 1 1/4 **Minturno (USA)**[15] 2699 4-9-9 **63** .... PaulMulrennan 2 66
(Mrs A Duffield) *pressed ldr: led over 1f out: hung lft and hdd ins fnl f: kpt on same pce* **3/1**[2]

0003 **3** 1 1/4 **Misterisland (IRE)**[18] 2629 5-8-2 **49** oh4 .... JosephYoung(7) 3 48
(M Mullineaux) *dwlt: sn prom: pushed along over 1f out: kpt on same pce ins fnl f* **12/1**

0035 **4** shd **Monte Mayor One**[3] 3076 3-8-10 **57** .... TonyHamilton 7 54
(P Monteith) *hld up: hdwy over 1f out: kpt on fnl f: nvr able to chal* **14/1**

-564 **5** 1 1/4 **Fantasy Fighter (IRE)**[13] 2790 5-8-10 **50** .... LiamKeniry 8 45
(J J Quinn) *t.k.h: trckd ldrs: effrt 2f out: outpcd fnl f* **13/2**

-062 **6** 1 3/4 **Classlin**[23] 2449 3-7-11 **51** .... RyanPowell(7) 6 38
(J S Goldie) *dwlt: bhd: effrt and swtchd lft over 1f out: sn outpcd: kpt on ins fnl f: nvr able to chal* **4/1**[3]

5020 **7** hd **Klynch**[12] 2817 4-9-9 **68** .... (b) JamesSullivan(5) 1 56
(Mrs R A Carr) *in tch on outside tl rdn and wknd over 1f out* **10/1**

6-50 **8** 1 3/4 **Hold On Tiger (IRE)**[43] 1869 3-9-7 **68** .... JimCrowley 4 49
(J Barclay) *led and crossed to stands' rail: rdn and hdd over 1f out: sn btn* **16/1**

000 **9** 2 1/4 **Maison Dieu**[5] 3026 7-8-10 **53** .... (b) GaryBartley(3) 9 29
(A Berry) *trckd ldrs tl rdn and wknd fr 2f out* **16/1**

1m 12.4s (-1.20) **Going Correction** -0.225s/f (Firm)
WFA 3 from 4yo+ 7lb **9** Ran SP% **122.1**
Speed ratings (Par 103): **99,97,95,95,93 91,91,88,85**
toteswingers:1&2:£2.40, 1&3:£12.40, 2&3:£13.00 CSF £10.81 CT £78.24 TOTE £3.70: £1.80, £1.10, £6.30; EX 12.30.
Owner Dave and Gill Hedley **Bred** G Hedley & Mike Channon Bloodstock Limited **Trained** West Ilsley, Berks

FOCUS
A modest handicap run at just a fair pace. The wining time was 1.2 secs slower than the preceding 2-y-o maiden.

3201 GLAM IN THE CITY H'CAP 5f
5:15 (5:15) (Class 4) (0-85,82) 3-Y-0+ **£5,828** (£1,734; £866; £432) **Stalls** High

Form RPR
2140 **1** **Ryan Style (IRE)**[36] 2073 4-9-6 **74** .... JimCrowley 8 83
(Mrs L Williamson) *in tch: drvn along 2f out: kpt on wl last 100yds: led nr fin* **16/1**

1233 **2** 3/4 **Ridley Didley (IRE)**[14] 2756 5-8-10 **67** .... WilliamCarson(3) 2 73
(N Wilson) *t.k.h: led at decent gallop: rdn over 1f out: kpt on fnl f: hdd nr fin* **7/4**[1]

0440 **3** 3/4 **Methaaly (IRE)**[19] 2578 7-7-7 **68** .... (be) JosephYoung(7) 3 71
(M Mullineaux) *bhd tl hdwy over 1f out: kpt on fnl f* **12/1**

-003 **4** shd **Distant Sun (USA)**[3] 3076 6-8-13 **67** .... TonyHamilton 1 70
(Miss L A Perratt) *bhd: hdwy over 1f out: r.o strly fnl f: nrst fin* **10/1**

1115 **5** shd **Chosen One (IRE)**[12] 2818 5-8-10 **69** .... JamesSullivan(5) 7 72
(Mrs R A Carr) *chsd ldr: drvn 2f out: kpt on same pce fnl f* **4/1**[2]

0-00 **6** nk **Crimea (IRE)**[14] 2745 4-10-0 **82** .... PaulQuinn 6 84
(D Nicholls) *trckd ldrs: effrt over 2f out: kpt on same pce fnl f* **8/1**

5400 **7** 2 1/2 **River Falcon**[14] 2759 10-9-9 **80** .... GaryBartley(3) 4 73
(J S Goldie) *sn towards rr on outside: pushed along 1/2-way: nvr able to chal* **9/2**[3]

0-00 **8** 3 **Smokey Ryder**[30] 2247 4-9-7 **75** .... ChrisCatlin 5 57
(R A Harris) *sn bhd and outpcd: struggling fr 1/2-way* **10/1**

58.26 secs (-1.84) **Going Correction** -0.225s/f (Firm) **8** Ran SP% **117.4**
Speed ratings (Par 105): **105,103,102,102,102 101,97,93**
toteswingers:1&2:£10.00, 1&3:£7.30, 2&3:£6.40 CSF £45.78 CT £371.49 TOTE £20.60: £4.50, £1.70, £3.20; EX 61.40.
Owner Bluegrass Racing Ltd **Bred** Johnny Kent **Trained** Saighton, Cheshire
■ Stewards' Enquiry : William Carson one-day ban; not keeping mount staight leaving stalls (4th) July

FOCUS
A fair handicap run at a cracking pace and the form looks reliable despite a slightly-bunched finish.

3202 BIZARRE H'CAP 1m 2f
5:45 (5:45) (Class 5) (0-75,75) 4-Y-0+ **£3,238** (£963; £481; £240) **Stalls** Low

Form RPR
-143 **1** **That'll Do Nicely (IRE)**[14] 2766 7-8-11 **65** .... JimCrowley 7 78
(N G Richards) *trckd ldr: led gng wl over 2f out: rdn clr over 1f out* **2/1**[1]

30-3 **2** 4 1/2 **Grand Diamond (IRE)**[50] 1669 6-8-11 **65** .... (p) ChrisCatlin 4 68
(J S Goldie) *t.k.h: prom: effrt and chsd wnr over 1f out: edgd lft: no imp fnl f* **13/2**

312- **3** 1 1/2 **Cool Baranca (GER)**[231] 7169 4-9-2 **75** .... JamesSullivan(5) 6 75+
(P Monteith) *t.k.h: hld up: effrt on outside over 2f out: kpt on fnl f: nvr able to chal* **7/1**

10-4 **4** 1 **Shy Glance (USA)**[23] 2452 8-9-3 **71** .... PaulMulrennan 1 69
(P Monteith) *hld up in tch: effrt over 2f out: no imp over 1f out* **13/2**

-603 **5** 8 **Starla Dancer (GER)**[23] 2452 4-9-7 **75** .... TonyHamilton 8 57
(R A Fahey) *led to over 2f out: rdn and wknd over 1f out* **5/2**[2]

-055 **6** 7 **King's Head (IRE)**[14] 2761 7-9-2 **70** .... LiamKeniry 2 38
(Miss L A Perratt) *chsd ldrs tl rdn and wknd fr over 2f out* **6/1**[3]

2m 7.34s (-4.66) **Going Correction** -0.55s/f (Hard) **6** Ran SP% **115.4**
Speed ratings (Par 103): **96,92,91,90,84 78**
toteswingers:1&2:£2.90, 1&3:£4.10, 2&3:£6.50 CSF £15.99 CT £76.20 TOTE £2.90: £1.70, £2.20; EX 13.90 Place 6 £151.77; Place 5 £22.39.
Owner J D Flood **Bred** J D Flood **Trained** Greystoke, Cumbria

FOCUS
A fair handicap run at just a steady pace. The form behind the winner, who did it easily, doesn't look strong.
King's Head(IRE) Official explanation: jockey said the gelding bled from the nose
T/Plt: £400.60 to a £1 stake. Pool:£53,736.98 - 97.90 winning tickets T/Qpdt: £37.60 to a £1 stake. Pool:£3,464.30 - 68.10 winning tickets RY

2881 HAYDOCK (L-H)
Saturday, June 19

OFFICIAL GOING: Good to firm (firm in places; 8.6)
Rail realignment increased advertised distances on round course by 25yds.
Wind: Moderate, half against Weather: Fine and sunny

3203 ARENA HOUSING GROUP H'CAP 1m 2f 95y
6:35 (6:36) (Class 5) (0-75,75) 4-Y-0+ **£2,914** (£867; £433; £216) **Stalls** High

Form RPR
-164 **1** **High Office**[14] 2766 4-9-5 **71** .... FranciscoDaSilva 7 82
(R A Fahey) *trckd ldrs: chal 3f out: led jst ins fnl f: hld on wl* **6/1**

5323 **2** 3/4 **Hawaana (IRE)**[22] 2492 5-9-6 **75** .... KellyHarrison(3) 2 85
(Miss Gay Kelleway) *t.k.h in rr: effrt on wd outside over 2f out: wnt 2nd 100yds out: kpt on* **2/1**[1]

-200 **3** 3 3/4 **Baltimore Jack (IRE)**[28] 2349 6-9-6 **72** .... DanielTudhope 4 74
(T D Walford) *led: hdd jst ins fnl f: fdd fnl 75yds* **3/1**[2]

2060 **4** 1 1/4 **Snow Dancer (IRE)**[56] 1512 6-9-7 **73** .... PatrickMathers 1 73
(H A McWilliams) *hld up: hdwy 4f out: one pce fnl 2f* **14/1**

-100 **5** 3/4 **Arashi**[12] 2821 4-8-8 **63** .... (p) AndrewHeffernan(3) 6 62
(Lucinda Featherstone) *trckd ldrs: t.k.h: hung lft over 1f out: one pce* **12/1**

110- **6** 7 **Denton (NZ)**[241] 6936 7-8-13 **70** .... (t) TobyAtkinson(5) 3 55
(J R Gask) *chsd ldr: chal 3f out: wknd jst ins fnl f: eased towards fin* **7/2**[3]

U056 **7** 4 **Bagutta Sun**[15] 2703 4-9-8 **74** .... RichardSmith 5 52
(Tom Dascombe) *chsd ldrs: drvn over 4f out: wl btn whn hmpd over 1f out: eased* **16/1**

2m 14.8s (-1.20) **Going Correction** +0.25s/f (Good) **7** Ran SP% **115.1**
Speed ratings (Par 103): **102,101,98,97,96 91,88**
toteswingers: 1&2 £2.90, 1&3 £3.90, 2&3 £2.80 CSF £18.71 TOTE £7.20: £4.30, £1.20; EX 18.60.
Owner R A Fahey **Bred** Genesis Green Stud Ltd **Trained** Musley Bank, N Yorks
■ Stewards' Enquiry : Andrew Heffernan two-day ban; careless riding (4th-5th) July

FOCUS
A modest handicap, run at a decent pace and the form is sound with the first two clear.

3204 ABACUS SECURITIES MAIDEN AUCTION STKS 5f
7:05 (7:05) (Class 5) 2-Y-0 **£2,914** (£867; £433; £216) **Stalls** High

Form RPR
64 **1** **Dubai Celebration**[26] 2376 2-8-7 0 .... PatrickDonaghy(5) 8 83
(Jedd O'Keeffe) *mde all: hung bdly lft over 1f out: kpt on: rdr lost iron after line and wnt abt anther 10f bef being p.u* **7/1**

2 1 1/2 **Ballinargh Girl (IRE)** 2-8-4 0 .... AndrewElliott 5 70
(R D Wylie) *hmpd s: t.k.h: sn prom: effrt over 2f out: styd on fnl f: tk 2nd nr fin* **28/1**

2263 **3** 1/2 **Master Macho (IRE)**[5] 3034 2-8-9 0 .... SamHitchcott 4 73
(M R Channon) *swvd lft s: chsd wnr: swtchd rt 1f out: kpt on same pce* **11/4**[1]

4 2 1/4 **Intrusion** 2-8-7 0 .... DavidAllan 13 63
(R A Fahey) *chsd ldrs stands' side: edgd lft and styd on same pce fnl f* **10/1**

3 **5** 5 **Barkston Ash**[21] 2540 2-8-9 0 .... FrannyNorton 3 47
(E J Alston) *sn chsng ldrs on outside: wknd over 1f out* **9/2**[2]

6 1/2 **Gottcher** 2-8-4 0 .... DeanHeslop(5) 11 45
(T D Barron) *chsd ldrs stands' side: wknd over 1f out* **16/1**

7 nse **Venus Empress** 2-8-3 0 ow3 .... DavidKenny(7) 10 46
(E S McMahon) *dwlt: in rr tl kpt on fnl 2f* **28/1**

0 **8** 1 1/2 **Lizzie (IRE)**[49] 1686 2-8-7 0 .... DuranFentiman 2 37
(T D Easterby) *chsd ldrs on wd outside: wknd over 1f out* **10/1**

3 **9** 1/2 **Mandy's Hero**[35] 2111 2-9-1 0 .... DanielTudhope 9 44
(R A Fahey) *mid-div: drvn over 2f out: lost pl over 1f out* **6/1**[3]

4 **10** 1 **Palindromic (IRE)**[17] 2638 2-8-7 0 .... TobyAtkinson(5) 7 37
(J R Gask) *hmpd s: mid-div: outpcd over 2f out: lost pl over 1f out* **16/1**

11 1 1/4 **Infectious (IRE)** 2-8-7 0 .... RichardMullen 12 27+
(D H Brown) *dwlt: sn outpcd and drvn along: bhd fnl 2f* **9/1**

12 3 **Running Water** 2-8-4 0 .... PatrickMathers 1 14
(H A McWilliams) *swtchd rt after s: in rr: bhd fnl 2f* **80/1**

61.10 secs (0.10) **Going Correction** -0.15s/f (Firm) **12** Ran SP% **119.7**
Speed ratings (Par 93): **93,90,89,86,78 77,77,74,74,72 70,65**
toteswingers: 1&2 £12.60, 1&3 £5.30, 2&3 £20.80 CSF £191.18 TOTE £9.10: £2.10, £7.20, £1.70; EX 439.60.
Owner Highbeck Racing **Bred** Wheelers Land Stud **Trained** Middleham Moor, N Yorks

FOCUS
An ordinary juvenile maiden and a decisive winner, but the third limits things.

NOTEBOOK

Dubai Celebration was at the sharp end throughout and rates value for further than the official verdict, his violent hanging left after his rider lost an iron a furlong out ensuring that he had to travel further than any of his rivals. Beaten less than 6l by subsequent Windsor Castle Stakes hero Marine Commando at Carlisle last time, connections couldn't wait to get him back to the track tonight and regard him as a decent prospect. Plans remain fluid for now. (tchd 6-1 and 8-1)

Ballinargh Girl(IRE), representing a yard not long back in action after several years' hiatus, knew her job first time and was keeping on to good effect close home. An ordinary fillies' maiden should prove within range on this showing. (op 25-1)

Master Macho(IRE) switched right as the winner careered across to the far side, but he was already beginning to lose the argument and his momentum was not checked. Placed in eight out of 11 starts and no longer improving, maybe a drop into claiming or selling company is going to be required to record that elusive first victory. (op 7-2)

Intrusion was nearest at the finish on debut. A half-sister to a 1m2f (and hurdles) winner and out of a winning miler, she is likely to want further sooner rather than later. (op 9-1)

Barkston Ash was still immature and noisy in the paddock despite this not being his first experience of a racecourse. He once again showed some reasonable early speed before fading out of things, and will be of more interest in handicaps after his next outing. (op 6-1 tchd 13-2)

Infectious(IRE) immediately let herself get outpaced and had to be chased along. She will surely prove better than this. (op 8-1)

3205 CRUK SUPPORTED BY BETFRED H'CAP — 6f

7:35 (7:36) (Class 5) (0-75,74) 3-Y-0+ £2,914 (£867; £433; £216) Stalls High

Form				RPR
4500	1		**Bosun Breese**[7] 2982 5-9-5 70 .... DeanHeslop(5) 9 (T D Barron) *edgd lft after s: chsd ldrs: chal over 1f out: edgd lft: styd on to ld towards fin* **12/1**	79
-005	2	*hd*	**Rainy Night**[12] 2817 4-8-9 60 .... (p) TobyAtkinson(5) 7 (R Hollinshead) *chsd ldr: led 2f out: edgd lft fnl f: hdd and no ex towards fin* **9/2**[2]	68
5-54	3	*1 ¾*	**Timber Treasure (USA)**[10] 2849 6-9-2 62 .... (b) FrannyNorton 1 (Paul Green) *hld up: effrt and edgd rt over 2f out: styd on fnl f* **3/1**[1]	64
-000	4	*2 ½*	**Forzarzi (IRE)**[10] 2864 6-8-9 55 oh7 .... PatrickMathers 4 (H A McWilliams) *mid-div: hdwy over 2f out: chsng ldrs over 1f out: styd on same pce* **50/1**	49
-200	5	*2 ½*	**Elegant Dancer (IRE)**[40] 1971 3-8-2 55 oh3 .... AndrewElliott 6 (Paul Green) *s.i.s: sme hdwy whn hung lft over 1f out: nvr nr ldrs* **14/1**	39
0000	6	*nse*	**Time Medicean**[9] 2883 4-9-3 63 .... TonyCulhane 3 (P T Midgley) *mid-div: drvn over 2f out: wknd over 1f out* **14/1**	49
0540	7	*1 ¼*	**Autocracy**[5] 3030 3-8-10 63 .... RichardMullen 5 (W J Haggas) *in rr and sn drvn along: nvr a factor* **8/1**	43
0030	8	*4 ½*	**Commander Wish**[19] 2581 7-8-6 55 oh7 .... (p) AndrewHeffernan(3) 8 (Lucinda Featherstone) *sn outpcd: hdwy over 3f out: hung lft and wknd 1f out: eased* **11/1**	23
0046	9	*¾*	**Mandurah (IRE)**[2] 3114 6-10-0 74 .... SaleemGolam 2 (B P J Baugh) *chsd ldrs: rdn and hung lft 2f out: wknd fnl f* **6/1**	39
0-50	10	*15*	**Francis Walsingham (IRE)**[5] 3037 4-9-5 68 .... (bt[1]) PatrickHills(3) 10 (H Morrison) *fast away: led and sn clr: swvd lft path after 1f: wknd rapidly and hdd 2f out: sn bhd: virtually p.u* **5/1**[3]	—

1m 14.36s (0.86) **Going Correction** -0.15s/f (Firm)

WFA 3 from 4yo+ 7lb **10 Ran SP% 116.6**

Speed ratings (Par 103): **88,87,85,82,78 78,77,71,70,50**

toteswingers: 1&2 £14.30, 1&3 £8.20, 2&3 £5.00 CSF £65.32 CT £211.98 TOTE £18.30: £4.80, £1.50, £1.50; EX 50.60.

Owner Estio Capital Racing **Bred** Lady Lonsdale **Trained** Maunby, N Yorks

■ Stewards' Enquiry : Dean Heslop one-day ban: careless riding (July 4)

FOCUS

A modest handicap with the runner-up to form and the fourth to this year's form.

Time Medicean Official explanation: jockey said gelding lost its action and hung left; trainer said gelding was found to be suffering from a corn

3206 DAVIS LANGDON LLP H'CAP — 1m 30y

8:05 (8:07) (Class 3) (0-90,90) 3-Y-0+ £9,066 (£2,697; £1,348; £673) Stalls Low

Form				RPR
1611	1		**Ezdeyaad (USA)**[9] 2885 6-10-0 90 .... PJMcDonald 4 (G A Swinbank) *chsd ldrs: swtchd rt over 3f out: nt clr run and swtchd outside wl over 1f out: r.o to ld last 150yds* **11/4**[1]	98
3-21	2	*1 ½*	**Harriet's Girl**[22] 2512 4-8-13 75 .... AndrewElliott 7 (J R Weymes) *chsd ldrs: chal over 2f out: led jst ins fnl f: sn hdd styd on same pce* **8/1**	80
5000	3	*nse*	**Moheebb (IRE)**[10] 2865 6-9-6 82 .... (b) RichardSmith 9 (Mrs R A Carr) *hld up in rr: effrt on outer 4f out: sn outpcd: hdwy over 2f out: abt to chal whn hmpd jst ins fnl f: r.o towards fin* **40/1**	90+
-535	4	*nk*	**Observatory Star (IRE)**[11] 2835 7-8-13 75 .... (bt) FrannyNorton 8 (T D Easterby) *mid-div: drvn over 2f out: hmpd over 1f out: styd on last 100yds* **9/2**[2]	80+
-250	5	*1 ¼*	**Sunnyside Tom (IRE)**[15] 2708 6-9-6 82 .... FranciscoDaSilva 6 (R A Fahey) *chsd ldrs: chal over 2f out: led over 1f out: edgd lft: hdd and fdd jst ins fnl f* **14/1**	83
1036	6	*1*	**Ginger Jack**[8] 2933 3-8-13 85 .... GregFairley 3 (M Johnston) *led 1f: chsd ldr: chal over 2f out: keeping on same pce whn bdly hmpd jst ins fnl f* **5/1**[3]	84+
0-03	7	*nk*	**Magaling (IRE)**[14] 2736 4-9-10 86 .... GrahamGibbons 5 (M W Easterby) *hld up in rr: hdwy on inner over 3f out: chsng ldrs whn nt clr run appr fnl f: swtchd rt: r.o fnl 50yds* **5/1**[3]	85+
0264	8	*3*	**Billy Dane (IRE)**[25] 2423 6-9-6 87 .... (p) MichaelO'Connell(5) 10 (F P Murtagh) *led after 1f: hdd over 1f out: one pce whn squeezed out jst ins fnl f* **6/1**	87+
6001	9	*16*	**Red Somerset (USA)**[66] 1301 7-9-7 83 .... RichardMullen 1 (Mike Murphy) *chsd ldrs: drvn 5f out: wknd 2f out: bhd whn eased fnl f: t.o* **16/1**	38
26-0	10	*26*	**Riqaab (IRE)**[9] 2885 5-8-9 71 oh1 .... DavidAllan 11 (M W Easterby) *in rr: drvn 4f out: wl bhd over 2f out: virtually p.u* **50/1**	—
-106	P		**Much Acclaimed (IRE)**[22] 2515 3-8-11 83 .... MickyFenton 2 (T P Tate) *s.i.s: in rr: heavily eased over 2f out: p.u over 1f out* **22/1**	—

1m 44.38s (-0.32) **Going Correction** +0.25s/f (Good)

WFA 3 from 4yo+ 10lb **11 Ran SP% 124.9**

Speed ratings (Par 107): **107,105,105,105,103 102,102,99,83,57 —**

toteswingers: 1&2 £4.90, 1&3 £23.20, 2&3 £19.70 CSF £27.32 CT £768.81 TOTE £4.00: £1.40, £2.80, £12.30; EX 17.00.

Owner B Boanson & M Wane **Bred** Caldara Farm **Trained** Melsonby, N Yorks

■ Stewards' Enquiry : Francisco Da Silva five-day ban; careless riding (3rd-8th) July

P J McDonald two-day ban; careless riding (6th-8th) July

FOCUS

A fair handicap, rated around the runner-up to her latest form.

NOTEBOOK

Ezdeyaad(USA) was switched to widest out in the centre of the course in good time, and kept on well to record a fourth win from his last five starts and third in a row over this C&D. Connections concede plans from now on may be contingent on how dim a view the assessor takes of this latest victory, but an entry in a conditions event at Hamilton in later on this week suggests a move out of handicaps may not be too far off. (op 9-2)

Harriet's Girl took her C&D record to 122, though places with the third may have been reversed had that one enjoyed a clearer passage. Her failure to pick up a win penalty here may have put paid to any Carlisle Bell aspirations, with ten above her in the weights needing to drop out. (op 15-2 tchd 7-1)

Moheebb(IRE) would have finished second had he not suffered the interference at a crucial stage. He remains of interest as long as his mark (back below his last winning one after failing to cope with a return to 1m2f the last twice) isn't marched up again after this luckless effort.

Observatory Star(IRE) is back down to his last winning mark, but never quite looked like getting there and was nearest at the finish. He remains pretty hard to win with. (op 9-1)

Sunnyside Tom(IRE), demoted when straying off a true line late on at Thirsk a month earlier, was just starting to lose the argument when again edging left and impeding some of those around him. He remains vulnerable off a mark 9lb above any he's successfully defied in handicaps (his win off 84 came in a claimer). Official explanation: trainer said gelding was found to have lost a hind shoe (op 10-1 tchd 9-1)

Magaling(IRE) ◆, ridden to stay the trip, was still staying on at the time and can't be written off over a mile yet just. (op 11-2 tchd 7-1 and 15-2 in places)

Much Acclaimed(IRE) Official explanation: jockey said gelding lost its action

3207 BULLOCK CONSTRUCTION LTD MAIDEN STKS — 1m 30y

8:35 (8:38) (Class 5) 3-Y-0+ £2,914 (£867; £433; £216) Stalls Low

Form				RPR
5-	1		**Thabit (USA)**[411] 1730 4-9-12 0 .... PhilipRobinson 8 (M A Jarvis) *restless in stalls: trckd ldrs: led 2f out: styd on wl fnl f: readily* **11/8**[1]	93
-223	2	*2 ¾*	**Spa's Dancer (IRE)**[21] 2544 3-8-13 80 .... PatrickHills(3) 9 (J W Hills) *chsd ldrs: chal 2f out: hung lft ins fnl f: no imp* **2/1**[2]	84
00	3	*7*	**Piddie's Power**[32] 2220 3-8-11 0 .... GrahamGibbons 12 (E S McMahon) *stdd and dropped to rr after 1f: hdwy 3f out: sn chsng ldrs: kpt on to take modest 3rd nr fin* **50/1**	62
	4	*¾*	**Pirate Coast** 3-9-2 0 .... DuranFentiman 4 (T D Easterby) *led: hdd over 2f out: one pce* **40/1**	65
3-43	5	*4 ½*	**Christmas Carnival**[19] 2603 3-9-2 80 .... RichardMullen 16 (B J Meehan) *chsd ldrs: wknd appr fnl f* **5/2**[3]	55
05-	6	*2*	**Major Monty (IRE)**[196] 7637 3-9-2 0 .... RichardKingscote 13 (Tom Dascombe) *in rr-div: hdwy over 3f out: one pce whn hung lft over 1f out* **33/1**	50
0-00	7	*2 ½*	**Fabled Dancer (IRE)**[9] 2881 4-9-12 47 .... (b[1]) FrannyNorton 3 (E J Alston) *s.i.s: hdwy over 2f out: nvr a factor* **28/1**	46
	8	*2*	**Barren Brook** 3-9-2 0 .... LeeVickers 11 (M W Easterby) *in rr: swtchd rt over 2f out: styd on steadily* **100/1**	39
000	9	*3 ½*	**Account Closed**[80] 1057 3-8-11 40 .... PJMcDonald 14 (M W Easterby) *awkward to load: in rr: sme hdwy over 2f out: nvr a factor* **100/1**	26
00	10	*½*	**Hannah Hawk**[10] 2860 3-8-8 0 .... AndrewHeffernan(3) 2 (Lucinda Featherstone) *chsd ldrs: hung rt bnd 6f out: wknd over 2f out* **100/1**	24
	11	*½*	**Johnston's Kiwi (IRE)**[263] 7-9-12 0 .... DavidAllan 15 (E J Alston) *chsd ldrs: led over 2f out: sn hdd & wknd* **25/1**	30
00/6	12	*4 ½*	**Inchmarlow (IRE)**[5] 3021 7-9-7 32 .... RossAtkinson(5) 7 (T H Caldwell) *chsd ldrs: rdn over 3f out: sn lost pl* **125/1**	19
	13	*1 ¼*	**Stephie**[41] 4-9-0 0 .... DavidSimmonson(7) 5 (M W Easterby) *s.s: a in rr* **100/1**	11
	14	*nk*	**Jubilant Lady (USA)** 3-8-11 0 .... GregFairley 1 (B Smart) *s.i.s: a in rr* **25/1**	9
0	15	*6*	**Pound Lane (IRE)**[39] 2003 4-9-12 0 .... VinceSlattery 10 (Miss T Spearing) *in rr: bhd fnl 3f* **100/1**	—
6	16	*10*	**Tender Appeal**[22] 2496 3-8-11 0 .... MickyFenton 6 (C W Moore) *chsd ldrs: wknd over 3f out: sn bhd: virtually p.u nr fin* **100/1**	—

1m 44.71s (0.01) **Going Correction** +0.25s/f (Good)

WFA 3 from 4yo+ 10lb **16 Ran SP% 129.2**

Speed ratings (Par 103): **105,102,95,94,90 88,85,83,80,79 79,74,73,72,66 56**

toteswingers: 1&2 £2.40, 1&3 £21.00, 2&3 £19.50 CSF £4.34 TOTE £3.60: £1.60, £1.10, £12.00; EX 4.90.

Owner Hamdan Al Maktoum **Bred** Green Gates Farm **Trained** Newmarket, Suffolk

FOCUS

No strength in depth here and the first pair came clear. There are doubts over the form due to the priximity of the third and fourth, and the runner-up looks the best guide.

Major Monty(IRE) Official explanation: jockey said gelding hung left-handed

3208 CRUDEN GROUP H'CAP — 1m 30y

9:05 (9:05) (Class 4) (0-80,77) 3-Y-0 £5,180 (£1,541; £770; £384) Stalls Low

Form				RPR
4-62	1		**Venutius**[22] 2510 3-9-9 77 .... GrahamGibbons 7 (E S McMahon) *mde all: shkn up 2f out: sn wnt clr: eased towards fin: unchal* **6/4**[1]	92
3100	2	*3 ½*	**Mejd (IRE)**[14] 2737 3-9-8 76 .... SamHitchcott 1 (M R Channon) *chsd wnr thrght: styd on same pce fnl 2f: nvr a real threat* **11/1**	83
44-2	3	*7*	**Woodford Belle (USA)**[43] 1882 3-9-9 77 .... RichardMullen 3 (B J Meehan) *sn chsng ldrs: rdn over 3f out: kpt on one pce* **3/1**[2]	68
0-06	4	*1 ¾*	**Bahamian Music (IRE)**[14] 2737 3-9-9 77 .... FranciscoDaSilva 8 (R A Fahey) *hld up in mid-div: effrt over 3f out: kpt on fnl f* **22/1**	64
00-3	5	*1 ½*	**Step In Time (IRE)**[28] 2348 3-9-9 77 .... GregFairley 9 (M Johnston) *chsd ldrs: drvn over 3f out: one pce* **7/1**	60
2-35	6	*5*	**Taste The Victory (USA)**[22] 2515 3-9-6 74 .... PJMcDonald 2 (G A Swinbank) *hld up in midfield: hdwy on ins to chse ldrs 4f out: outpcd on inner over 3f out: lost pl over 2f out* **5/1**[3]	46
0000	7	*2*	**Toga Tiger (IRE)**[9] 2884 3-9-2 70 .... TonyCulhane 4 (P T Midgley) *a last: drvn over 3f out: nvr on terms* **20/1**	37
2106	8	*2*	**Transmit (IRE)**[30] 2261 3-9-5 73 .... DavidAllan 5 (T D Easterby) *trckd ldrs: drvn and lost pl 4f out* **14/1**	36
20-0	9	*2*	**Quaker Parrot**[18] 2618 3-9-4 77 .... RossAtkinson(5) 6 (Tom Dascombe) *in rr: drvn and hung rt over 3f out: sn wknd* **33/1**	35

1m 43.87s (-0.83) **Going Correction** +0.25s/f (Good) **9 Ran SP% 121.2**

Speed ratings (Par 101): **109,105,98,96,95 90,88,86,84**

toteswingers: 1&2 £6.10, 1&3 £3.20, 2&3 £5.10 CSF £20.78 CT £48.42 TOTE £2.40: £1.10, £4.00, £2.40; EX 22.90 Place 6 £23.70, Place 5 £11.28.

Owner Mrs Fiona Williams **Bred** Mrs F S Williams **Trained** Lichfield, Staffs

FOCUS

A modest handicap where the winner comfortably dictated. It was a good winning time and the form is rated at face value through the runner-up.

T/Plt: £16.70 to a £1 stake. Pool: £59,207.50. 2,574.30 winning tickets. T/Qpdt: £6.30 to a £1 stake. Pool: £4,039.77. 473.94 winning tickets. WG

2963 LINGFIELD (L-H)

Saturday, June 19

OFFICIAL GOING: Turf course - good to firm (8.4); all-weather - standard

Wind: Light, against Weather: Fine but cloudy

3209 EDENBRIDGE MAIDEN AUCTION STKS — 7f

5:50 (5:52) (Class 6) 2-Y-O — **£2,388** (£705; £352) **Stalls** High

Form — RPR

5 **1** **Da Ponte**[42] 1930 2-8-11 0 MartinLane(3) 10 72+
(Pat Eddery) *w ldr and one off the rail: led wl over 1f out: rdn clr ent fnl f* **10/11**[1]

00 **2** *2* **Gower Rules (IRE)**[12] 2819 2-8-10 0 JackMitchell 13 63
(M D I Usher) *racd against rail: trckd ldng pair: rdn 3f out: plld out and effrt 2f out: wnt 2nd ins fnl f: no imp* **20/1**

04 **3** *shd* **Sheila's Star (IRE)**[31] 2223 2-8-10 0 LukeMorris 4 63
(J S Moore) *settled towards rr: u.p fr 3f out: prog over 1f out: styd on: nrly snatched 2nd* **9/2**[3]

00 **4** *3/4* **Stacey**[10] 2867 2-7-13 0 SophieDoyle(5) 5 55
(M Blanshard) *t.k.h early: trckd ldrs: rdn over 2f out: nt qckn over 1f out: kpt on* **33/1**

5 *1 1/4* **Bonniebridge** 2-8-4 0 JimmyQuinn 9 52+
(Miss J Feilden) *dwlt: hld up in last pair: nudged along over 2f out: keeping on whn one reminder 1f out: nrst fin* **25/1**

00 **6** *nk* **Irie Ute**[28] 2319 2-8-7 0 RichardRowe(7) 7 61
(S Kirk) *t.k.h: hld up towards rr against rail: pushed along fr 2f out: styd on ins fnl f: nt disgracd* **100/1**

0 **7** *nk* **Slumbering Sioux**[11] 2839 2-8-9 0 LiamJones 3 56
(H J L Dunlop) *hld up in tch on outer: rdn and no prog over 2f out: plugged on over 1f out* **12/1**

0 **8** *3/4* **Manchester Stanley**[11] 2839 2-8-12 0 IanMongan 12 57
(J A Osborne) *led against rail: rdn and hdd wl over 1f out: stl 2nd ent fnl f: wknd* **33/1**

0 **9** *4 1/2* **Arctic Reach**[16] 2677 2-8-5 0 KierenFox(5) 8 43
(G D Blake) *pushed along in last pair after 3f: detached over 2f out: kpt on fnl f* **50/1**

0 **10** *nk* **Foxy's Mint**[16] 2680 2-8-6 0 FrankieMcDonald 2 39
(R Hannon) *cl up on outer: shkn up over 2f out: wknd wl over 1f out* **33/1**

11 *1 1/4* **Soviet Spring (IRE)** 2-8-10 0 DavidProbert 6 40+
(A M Balding) *dwlt: hld up in last trio: pushed along over 2f out: wknd wl over 1f out: eased* **7/2**[2]

1m 25.66s (2.36) **Going Correction** +0.025s/f (Good) 11 Ran SP% **120.9**

Speed ratings (Par 91): **87,84,84,83,82 81,81,80,75,75 73**

toteswingers: 1&2 £5.30, 1&3 £3.30, 2&3 £18.10 CSF £27.93 TOTE £1.50: £1.10, £8.90, £1.50; EX 19.80.

Owner Mrs Bettine Evans **Bred** R P Williams **Trained** Nether Winchendon, Bucks

■

FOCUS

An ordinary maiden, run at a sound pace, and the form looks limited.

NOTEBOOK

Da Ponte was all the rage to improve for this step up in trip as his pedigree suggested he would, and he completed the task with a little more in hand than the bare margin suggests. He showed a much more professional attitude as a result of being able to get to the early pace and, from his decent draw, it was clear 2f out he would take the beating. He was idling from the furlong pole and this was another winner for his in-form stable. (op 11-8 tchd 13-8 in places, 6-4 in a place)

Gower Rules(IRE) had the plum draw and was soon tucked in behind the early leaders. He stayed on well without really looking like getting to the winner and this was by far his best effort yet over this suitably stiffer test. (op 22-1 tchd 25-1 and 16-1)

Sheila's Star(IRE) proved surprisingly easy to back considering the maiden she ran fourth in on her previous outing is now working out well. She appreciated the extra furlong, doing her best work towards the finish, and should find her feet when the nurseries begin. (op 4-1 tchd 6-1)

Stacey took time to settle early on, but still stayed on well for pressure and turned in her most encouraging effort yet. (op 28-1 tchd 25-1)

Bonniebridge Official explanation: jockey said filly was slowly away and ran green

Irie Ute ◆ was doing his best work too late in the day. He certainly wasn't given the hardest of times and appeals as one to look out for when switching to a nursery in due course. (tchd 80-1)

Soviet Spring(IRE) Official explanation: jockey said colt ran green

3210 BET US GOLF - BETDAQ MAIDEN STKS — 6f

6:20 (6:20) (Class 5) 3-Y-O+ — **£2,729** (£806; £403) **Stalls** High

Form — RPR

4-32 **1** **Poppy Seed**[28] 2340 3-8-9 80 RichardHughes 7 89+
(R Hannon) *racd against rail: mde virtually all: drew rt away fr 2f out: eased last 100yds* **1/6**[1]

-00 **2** *9* **Thalia Grace**[49] 1694 3-8-9 0 LukeMorris 9 57
(L Montague Hall) *trckd ldrs against rail: rdn to go 2nd 2f out: no ch w wnr* **33/1**

3 *1* **Mount Acclaim (IRE)** 4-9-2 0 IanMongan 4 56+
(J A Osborne) *detached in last after 2f: swtchd to outer and rdn 2f out: kpt on to take modest 3rd fnl f* **9/1**[2]

-560 **4** *3* **Patachou**[6] 2998 3-8-4 48 (v) KierenFox(5) 3 44
(R J Smith) *racd on outer: in tch: rdn and fnd nil over 2f out: wknd over 1f out* **50/1**

6000 **5** *2 3/4* **Aldorable**[16] 2675 3-8-2 49 AdamBeschizza(7) 8 36
(R A Teal) *rdn in 6th after 2f: nvr on terms: wknd 2f out* **25/1**

40 **6** *hd* **Well Overdue (IRE)**[7] 2968 4-9-2 0 SophieDoyle(5) 6 42
(J A Osborne) *cl up tl wknd over 2f out* **25/1**

00- **7** *3/4* **Grand Mary (IRE)**[277] 5966 3-8-9 0 DavidProbert 1 33
(P F I Cole) *w wnr tl wknd over 2f out* **14/1**[3]

1m 11.48s (0.28) **Going Correction** +0.025s/f (Good)

WFA 3 from 4yo 7lb 7 Ran SP% **115.0**

Speed ratings (Par 103): **99,87,85,81,78 77,76**

toteswingers: 1&2 £3.10, 1&3 £1.50, 2&3 £10.70 CSF £14.27 TOTE £1.10: £1.10, £11.00; EX 20.40.

Owner Lady Whent **Bred** Raffin Bloodstock **Trained** East Everleigh, Wilts

FOCUS

A weak and uncompetitive maiden, but the winner was still impressive.

Well Overdue(IRE) Official explanation: jockey said colt hung right throughout

3211 BURRIDGE RACING AND GOLF TROPHIES H'CAP — 5f

6:50 (6:50) (Class 5) (0-75,70) 3-Y-O+ — **£3,070** (£906; £453) **Stalls** High

Form — RPR

2020 **1** **Grudge**[18] 2622 5-9-13 70 (be) JimmyQuinn 8 80
(C R Dore) *taken down early: unable to grab ld against rail and dropped bk to 5th: prog on outer fr 2f out: rdn to go 2nd ent fnl f: styd on to ld last 100yds* **4/1**[2]

1232 **2** *1* **Wreningham**[29] 2301 5-8-10 60 RyanClark(7) 1 66
(S C Williams) *led and sn crossed fr wd draw to rail: rdn 2f out: hdd and one pce last 100yds* **9/2**[3]

3610 **3** *2* **Thoughtsofstardom**[2] 3114 7-8-11 61 LeonnaMayor(7) 5 60
(P S McEntee) *hld up in last trio: looking for room fr 2f out: styd on fnl f to take 3rd nr fin* **8/1**

0000 **4** *1/2* **Elusive Ronnie (IRE)**[25] 2417 4-8-3 51 oh3 (b) KierenFox(5) 6 48
(R A Teal) *sn pushed along in last pair: a struggling: styd on u.p fnl f: nrst fin* **9/1**

-600 **5** *1/2* **Edith's Boy (IRE)**[17] 2639 4-9-7 64 JackMitchell 2 60
(S Dow) *trckd ldrs against rail: cl enough over 1f out: rdn and nt qckn* **5/1**

405 **6** *2 3/4* **Colorus (IRE)**[7] 2954 7-9-5 69 (p) AdamBeschizza(7) 3 55
(W J H Ratcliffe) *dwlt: sn pushed along in last pair: a struggling: no real prog over 1f out on outer* **13/2**

22-0 **7** *1 1/4* **La Fortunata**[12] 2822 3-9-6 69 DaneO'Neill 7 52
(Mike Murphy) *nt that wl away but chsd ldr: wknd rapidly ent fnl f: eased* **7/2**[1]

0-00 **8** *9* **Morgans Choice**[33] 2179 3-8-13 65 (p) JackDean(3) 4 12
(J L Spearing) *chsd ldng pair to over 1f out: wknd v rapidly* **20/1**

58.58 secs (0.38) **Going Correction** +0.025s/f (Good)

WFA 3 from 4yo+ 6lb 8 Ran SP% **116.3**

Speed ratings (Par 103): **97,95,92,91,90 86,84,69**

toteswingers: 1&2 £2.90, 1&3 £9.60, 2&3 £5.70 CSF £22.78 CT £138.15 TOTE £4.70: £1.70, £1.20, £2.90; EX 18.30.

Owner Mrs Jennifer Marsh **Bred** D H Brailsford **Trained** Cowbit, Lincs

■ Stewards' Enquiry : Ryan Clark 4-day ban: careless riding (July 4-8)

FOCUS

This was always likely to be fast and furious, and it played out so. Everyone wanted the stands' rail.

3212 BET WORLD CUP FOOTBALL - BETDAQ H'CAP — 7f 140y

7:20 (7:21) (Class 5) (0-75,77) 3-Y-O+ — **£3,070** (£906; £453) **Stalls** Centre

Form — RPR

00-6 **1** **Roman Glory (IRE)**[29] 2284 4-10-0 75 RichardHughes 8 83
(B J Meehan) *racd against rail: chsd ldr 2f: styd handly: rdn 2f out: wnt 2nd jst over 1f out: styd on u.p to ld nr fin* **8/1**

1266 **2** *nk* **Purple Gallery (IRE)**[17] 2644 3-8-13 70 (p) HayleyTurner 6 74
(J S Moore) *sn led and grad crossed to rail: drvn over a l clr over 1f out: worn down nr fin* **25/1**

5142 **3** *1 1/4* **Tell Halaf**[20] 2566 3-9-1 72 JamieSpencer 2 78+
(M L W Bell) *dropped in fr wd draw: hld up in last of main gp against rail: prog 2f out: gng easily but nowhere to go thrght fnl f: unlucky* **9/2**[2]

5050 **4** *nk* **Khajaaly (IRE)**[19] 2587 3-8-8 65 JimmyQuinn 11 65
(E A L Dunlop) *hld up in rr: stdy prog fr over 2f out: tried to cl and n.m.r fr over 1f out: styd on* **33/1**

3233 **5** *hd* **High Importance (USA)**[30] 2242 3-9-1 72 (v[1]) TomQueally 3 72+
(J Noseda) *hld up in rr: swtchd lft and prog 2f out: drvn to cl on ldrs fnl f: nvr able to chal* **6/1**

6000 **6** *5* **Fault**[8] 2920 4-9-5 66 (t) SebSanders 7 56
(Stef Higgins) *pressed ldr after 2f: rdn to chal over 2f out: wknd over 1f out* **14/1**

1404 **7** *2 3/4* **Prince Of Sorrento**[9] 2888 3-8-13 70 DaneO'Neill 9 50
(J Akehurst) *a in midfield: shkn up and no prog over 2f out: wknd over 1f out* **11/4**[1]

-516 **8** *1 1/4* **Hobson**[21] 2531 5-9-5 73 AmyScott(7) 4 53
(Eve Johnson Houghton) *pressed ldrs on outer: stl in tch wl over 1f out: wknd* **10/1**

-055 **9** *1 3/4* **Ice Cool Lady (IRE)**[22] 2491 3-8-6 70 (v) AdamBeschizza(7) 10 43
(W R Swinburn) *rrd s: wl in tch on outer tl wknd over 2f out* **16/1**

/331 **10** *23* **Roshina (IRE)**[92] 931 4-9-7 68 IanMongan 5 —
(Miss Jo Crowley) *pressed ldrs towards outer: wkng whn hmpd 2f out: eased: t.o* **14/1**

0202 **11** *2 1/2* **My Learned Friend (IRE)**[11] 2846 6-9-9 77 ThomasBrown(7) 13 —
(A M Balding) *tried to sit down as stalls opened: stmbld and nrly uns rdr who lost his irons: t.o* **5/1**[3]

1m 31.72s (-0.58) **Going Correction** +0.025s/f (Good)

WFA 3 from 4yo+ 10lb 11 Ran SP% **122.0**

Speed ratings (Par 103): **103,102,101,101,100 95,93,91,90,67 64**

toteswingers: 1&2 £38.10, 1&3 £12.00, 2&3 £27.40 CSF £194.70 CT £1035.85 TOTE £13.00: £4.30, £8.90, £1.20; EX 333.30.

Owner Martin Doran **Bred** G Callanan **Trained** Manton, Wilts

■ Stewards' Enquiry : Tom Queally one-day: careless riding (date not yet known)

FOCUS

An open handicap in which the first four raced on the rail. The first five come clear and they were quite tightly bunched at the finish.

Roman Glory(IRE) Official explanation: jockey said gelding hung right

Tell Halaf ◆ Official explanation: jockey said colt was denied a clear run

My Learned Friend(IRE) Official explanation: jockey said gelding hit the starting gate causing the ridier to lose his irons

3213 SEVENOAKS (S) STKS — 1m 4f (P)

7:50 (7:50) (Class 6) 3-Y-O — **£2,047** (£604; £302) **Stalls** Low

Form — RPR

3035 **1** **Frameit (IRE)**[19] 2606 3-8-12 61 (b) RichardHughes 5 63
(J S Moore) *hld up in last trio: prog on inner fr 5f out: cl up 3f out: effrt to ld over 1f out: sn rdn clr* **3/1**[2]

-422 **2** *1 3/4* **Sassanian (IRE)**[12] 2820 3-8-12 65 ShaneKelly 2 60+
(Jane Chapple-Hyam) *hld up towards rr: prog 3f out: cl up 2f out: nt clr run over 1f out: wnt 2nd ins fnl f: styd on but wnr already gone* **7/4**[1]

0026 **3** *3 1/2* **Mnarani (IRE)**[10] 2878 3-8-12 63 (b) LukeMorris 4 54
(J S Moore) *pressed ldr: rdn to ld 2f out: hdd over 1f out: fdd* **9/1**

2640 **4** *3 3/4* **Rosewood Lad**[19] 2606 3-8-12 45 HayleyTurner 9 48
(J S Moore) *hld up last: effrt over 3f out: wl outpcd in 8th over 2f out: kpt on u.p to take 4th nr fin* **10/1**

-006 **5** *1 3/4* **Federal Reserve**[14] 2753 3-8-7 47 KierenFox(5) 1 46
(M Madgwick) *trckd ldng trio: rdn 4f out: chal and upsides 2f out: wknd over 1f out* **20/1**

-200 **6** 3 1/4 **Royal Etiquette (IRE)**[9] 2893 3-8-12 71........ SteveDrowne 10 46
(H J L Dunlop) *led: rdn and hdd 2f out: sn eased* **7/2**[3]
00-0 **7** 2 3/4 **Keep Silent**[40] 1976 3-8-7 38........ IvaMilickova 6 31
(John Berry) *trckd ldng pair tl wknd fr 3f out* **80/1**
-350 **8** 2 1/2 **Captain Clint (IRE)**[16] 2675 3-8-12 45........ PatCosgrave 8 32
(M H Tompkins) *hld up in last trio: effrt over 3f out: outpcd in 6th over 2f out: wknd over 1f out* **20/1**
0500 **9** 3 3/4 **Swain's Quest (USA)**[19] 2606 3-8-4 58........ MartinLane(3) 7 21
(Eve Johnson Houghton) *chsd ldrs: rdn over 4f out: sn dropped to rr and struggling: wl bhd 2f out* **20/1**
10 1 1/2 **Senator Logan (IRE)** 3-8-12 0........ KevinGhunowa 3 24
(F J Brennan) *racd wd in midfield: rdn 5f out: sn dropped to rr and struggling: bhd over 2f out* **50/1**

2m 34.31s (1.31) **Going Correction** +0.025s/f (Slow) **10** Ran SP% **120.2**
Speed ratings (Par 97): **96,94,92,90,88 86,84,83,80,79**
toteswingers: 1&2 £2.20, 1&3 £7.70, 2&3 £4.60 CSF £8.39 TOTE £3.90: £1.70, £1.50, £2.10; EX 11.70.There was no bid for the winner. Sassanian was claimed by Mr T. Vaughan for £6,000.
Owner Andrew Wright, Ernie Moore & Vic March **Bred** Liam Butler **Trained** Upper Lambourn, Berks

FOCUS
None of the runners had previously troubled the judge in this 3-y-o seller. It was run at an average pace and the form makes sense.
Royal Etiquette(IRE) Official explanation: jockey said gelding ran too free
Senator Logan(IRE) Official explanation: jockey said gelding hung left on the bends

3214 BETDAQ.CO.UK H'CAP 1m 2f (P)
8:20 (8:20) (Class 6) (0-60,60) 4-Y-0+ £2,047 (£604; £302) Stalls Low

Form RPR
3456 **1** **Ocean Of Peace (FR)**[18] 2636 7-8-4 46 oh1........ LukeMorris 6 54
(M R Bosley) *hld up in midfield: prog to trck ldrs 3f out: drvn and effrt over 1f out: edgd rt but led jst ins fnl f: kpt on* **10/1**
0222 **2** nk **Major Promise**[17] 2653 5-9-0 56........ ShaneKelly 11 63
(Jane Chapple-Hyam) *stdd s: hld up in last trio and racd wd: prog on wd outside 3f out: rdn over 2f out: styd on to take 2nd ins fnl f: clsd on wnr fin* **5/2**[1]
0-00 **3** 1 1/2 **Rowan Light**[18] 2632 4-8-13 55........ PatCosgrave 12 59
(J R Boyle) *trckd ldng trio: pushed along 1/2-way: effrt u.p to ld 2f out: hdd and one pce jst ins fnl f* **16/1**
666 **4** 3/4 **Drum Major (IRE)**[12] 2811 5-8-12 54........(b) RichardThomas 8 57
(Jim Best) *trckd ldng pair: cl up 2f out: rdn and nt qckn over 1f out: one pce after* **5/2**[1]
3066 **5** 3/4 **December**[10] 2870 4-8-10 52........(vt) SebSanders 10 53
(Mrs C A Dunnett) *dwlt: hld up in last trio: stdy prog over 2f out: chsd ldrs over 1f out: enough to do whn rdn ent fnl f: kpt on same pce* **6/1**[2]
0-60 **6** 1/2 **Red Willow**[16] 2674 4-7-13 46 oh1........ SophieDoyle(5) 2 46
(J E Long) *chsd ldrs: rdn on inner over 3f out: lost pl over 2f out: plugged on fnl f* **50/1**
112- **7** 1 1/4 **Recalcitrant**[256] 6565 7-9-4 60........ JamieSpencer 7 58
(S Dow) *pressed ldr: rdn to ld 3f out to 2f out: wknd fnl f* **6/1**[2]
4300 **8** 2 1/4 **Kings Topic (USA)**[57] 1507 10-8-7 54........(p) AmyBaker(5) 4 47
(A B Haynes) *reminders sn after s: mostly in last trio: u.p in last 3f out: n.d after* **20/1**
40-0 **9** 1 **D'Artagnans Dream**[17] 2645 4-8-12 54........ JimmyQuinn 1 45
(G D Blake) *a towards rr: effrt 3f out: wknd u.p 2f out* **16/1**
-530 **10** nk **Felicia**[53] 1591 5-8-6 48........ KirstyMilczarek 3 38
(J E Long) *led to 3f out: wknd 2f out* **16/1**
2-00 **11** 1/2 **Guiseppe Verdi (USA)**[17] 2645 6-9-0 56........ DaneO'Neill 9 45
(Miss Tor Sturgis) *nvr bttr than midfield: u.p over 3f out: wknd over 2f out* **7/1**[3]

2m 6.40s (-0.20) **Going Correction** +0.025s/f (Slow) **11** Ran SP% **131.7**
Speed ratings (Par 101): **101,100,99,98,98 97,96,95,94,94 93**
toteswingers: 1&2 £6.00, 1&3 £60.00, 2&3 £5.50 CSF £39.57 CT £434.20 TOTE £13.80: £3.40, £1.60, £6.40; EX 63.00 Place 6 £41.85, Place 5 £30.24.
Owner Mrs Jean M O'Connor **Bred** Raoul Rousset **Trained** Chalfont St Giles, Bucks

FOCUS
A weak handicap, run at a sound enough pace. The first five all ended up towards more stands side in the home straight.
T/Plt: £11.80 to a £1 stake. Pool: £44,255.95. 2,716.02 winning tickets. T/Qpdt: £12.00 to a £1 stake. Pool: £4,675.13. 286.84 winning tickets. JN

3168
NEWMARKET (July Course) (R-H)
Saturday, June 19

OFFICIAL GOING: Good to firm (good in places; 8.8)
Stands' side track used.
Wind: Fresh, half-behind Weather: Overcast with heavy showers

3215 32RED CASINO OF THE DECADE H'CAP 7f
2:10 (2:11) (Class 4) (0-85,84) 3-Y-O £6,476 (£1,927; £963; £481) Stalls High

Form RPR
-212 **1** **Suited And Booted (IRE)**[18] 2618 3-9-9 84........ PatDobbs 10 97
(R Hannon) *hld up: hdwy 1/2-way: rdn to ld and edgd lft fr over 1f out: r.o* **7/2**[1]
-221 **2** 3/4 **Tesslam**[15] 2706 3-9-7 82........ PhilipRobinson 6 93
(M A Jarvis) *chsd ldr: rdn and ev ch fr over 1f out: r.o* **7/1**
0-45 **3** 1/2 **State Gathering**[33] 2170 3-9-0 75........ DaneO'Neill 5 84
(H Candy) *chsd ldrs: rdn and ev ch whn carried lft over 1f out: edgd lft fnl f: styd on* **8/1**
56-1 **4** 1 1/2 **Rockabilly Rebel**[20] 2566 3-8-10 71........ EddieAhern 8 76
(B W Hills) *prom: rdn over 2f out: outpcd over 1f out: r.o ins fnl f* **5/1**[3]
52-1 **5** 1 **Illustrious Prince (IRE)**[73] 1164 3-9-7 82........ ShaneKelly 2 85
(J Noseda) *hld up: rdn over 2f out: r.o ins fnl f: nvr nrr* **9/2**[2]
331 **6** 1 1/4 **Feel The Heat**[19] 2609 3-9-3 78........ DavidAllan 3 77
(B Smart) *prom: rdn over 2f out: outpcd over 1f out: r.o towards fin* **10/1**
315 **7** shd **Ginger Ted (IRE)**[10] 2862 3-9-3 81........(p) AndrewHeffernan(3) 1 80
(R C Guest) *hld up: rdn over 2f out: nvr on terms* **16/1**
302 **8** 3/4 **Youm Jamil (USA)**[15] 2692 3-9-3 78........(b[1]) TedDurcan 9 75
(B J Meehan) *s.i.s: hld up: rdn over 1f out: nvr on terms* **8/1**
51 **9** 3/4 **Sailorman (IRE)**[26] 2393 3-9-3 78........ RobertHavlin 4 73
(M Johnston) *led: rdn: hung lft and hdd over 1f out: wknd ins fnl f* **8/1**

1m 23.39s (-2.31) **Going Correction** -0.20s/f (Firm) **9** Ran SP% **117.9**
Speed ratings (Par 101): **105,104,103,101,100 99,99,98,97**
toteswingers: 1&2 £2.90, 1&3 £21.50, 2&3 £11.60 CSF £28.97 CT £186.27 TOTE £4.60: £1.30, £2.50, £2.50; EX 23.70 Trifecta £379.90 Part won. Pool: £513.42 - 0.30 winning units..
Owner R Morecombe and D Anderson **Bred** Carpet Lady Partnership **Trained** East Everleigh, Wilts

FOCUS
An interesting handicap featuring some unexposed horses. They came up the centre of the track until spreading out approaching the 2f pole. The time was good and the form is rated positively with the fifth and sixth setting the level.
Youm Jamil(USA) Official explanation: jockey said colt had no more to give
Sailorman(IRE) Official explanation: jockey said colt hung left

3216 32RED.COM H'CAP 6f
2:45 (2:45) (Class 4) (0-80,80) 3-Y-0+ £6,476 (£1,927; £963; £481) Stalls High

Form RPR
0431 **1** **Joe Packet**[8] 2919 3-8-12 76........ JohnFahy(5) 12 87
(J G Portman) *hld up: hdwy 2f out: rdn to ld 1f out: hung lft: r.o* **4/1**[1]
5-31 **2** 1 1/4 **Pirate's Song**[29] 2297 3-8-9 68........(t) RobertHavlin 4 77+
(J A R Toller) *hld up: hdwy over 1f out: nt clr run ins fnl f: swtchd lft: r.o* **14/1**
4430 **3** hd **Dancing Maite**[14] 2736 5-9-3 72........ AshleyHamblett(3) 9 80
(S R Bowring) *chsd ldrs: rdn and ev ch over 1f out: styd on* **9/2**[2]
3610 **4** 1 **Elijah Pepper (USA)**[7] 2982 5-8-12 64........ DaneO'Neill 5 69
(T D Barron) *chsd ldrs: rdn over 1f out: styd on* **8/1**
4100 **5** 2 **Billy Red**[20] 2563 6-10-0 80........(b) FergusSweeney 2 78
(J R Jenkins) *led: clr 1/2-way: rdn and hdd 1f out: no ex* **25/1**
1050 **6** 3/4 **Rough Rock (IRE)**[7] 2957 5-8-8 63........ KellyHarrison(3) 3 59
(C A Dwyer) *chsd ldr: rdn over 1f out: no ex ins fnl f* **22/1**
1011 **7** 3 **Averoo**[7] 2982 5-9-12 78........(p) LukeMorris 13 64
(M D Squance) *mid-div: rdn over 2f out: wknd over 1f out* **6/1**[3]
0000 **8** nk **Resplendent Alpha**[19] 2590 6-8-9 61 oh7........ HayleyTurner 1 46
(P Howling) *hld up: rdn over 2f out: n.d* **28/1**
3425 **9** nk **Dickie Le Davoir**[2] 3129 6-8-13 68........(v) AndrewHeffernan(3) 10 52
(R C Guest) *hld up: sme hdwy over 1f out: sn rdn and wknd* **7/1**
4-11 **10** 3 1/2 **Top Bid**[42] 1915 6-9-2 68........(b) DavidAllan 7 41
(T D Easterby) *s.s: a in rr* **4/1**[1]
0400 **11** 3/4 **Onceaponatime (IRE)**[23] 2465 5-9-4 70........ KirstyMilczarek 8 41
(M D Squance) *s.i.s: outpcd* **25/1**
1606 **12** 9 **White Shift (IRE)**[2] 3115 4-9-4 78........ EddieAhern 11 12
(P Howling) *chsd ldrs: rdn over 2f out: wknd sn after* **25/1**

1m 10.96s (-1.54) **Going Correction** -0.20s/f (Firm)
WFA 3 from 4yo+ 7lb **12** Ran SP% **122.1**
Speed ratings (Par 105): **102,100,100,98,96 95,91,90,90,85 84,72**
toteswingers: 1&2 £11.90, 1&3 £4.60, 2&3 £18.30 CSF £57.96 CT £273.41 TOTE £5.40: £1.60, £4.30, £1.90; EX 49.70 Trifecta £364.80 Part won. Pool: £493.09 - 0.20 winning units..
Owner Stuart McPhee **Bred** Stuart McPhee Bloodstock Ltd **Trained** Compton, Berks

FOCUS
There were two 3-y-o in the field and they came out on top against some more exposed older horses. The form looks sound with the third and fourth close to their marks.
Averoo Official explanation: jockey said gelding was never travelling
Top Bid Official explanation: trainer's representative was unable to offer any explanation for the poor performance shown
Onceaponatime(IRE) Official explanation: jockey said gelding was unsuited by the Good to Firm, Good in places ground

3217 EUROPEAN BREEDERS' FUND 32RED FILLIES' H'CAP 1m
3:20 (3:20) (Class 4) (0-85,82) 3-Y-0+ £6,476 (£1,927; £963; £481) Stalls High

Form RPR
11 **1** **I'm A Dreamer (IRE)**[44] 1850 3-9-3 81........ HayleyTurner 1 94+
(D M Simcock) *stdd s: hld up: swtchd rt and hdwy over 1f out: shkn up to ld ins fnl f: r.o* **13/8**[1]
0434 **2** 1 3/4 **Baylini**[12] 2823 6-9-2 75........ SophieDoyle(5) 9 81
(Ms J S Doyle) *chsd ldrs: rdn over 1f out: r.o* **10/1**
4122 **3** 3/4 **Faithful One (IRE)**[23] 2475 3-9-4 82........ TedDurcan 4 84
(D R Lanigan) *led: hdd over 5f out: rdn to ld over 1f out: hdd and unable qck ins fnl f* **5/1**[3]
0-15 **4** nk **Sweet Clementine (IRE)**[30] 2256 3-9-2 80........ EddieAhern 5 82
(W J Knight) *chsd ldr tl wnt centre over 6f out: led over 5f out: c stands' side again 1/2-way: rdn and hdd over 1f out: styd on same pce ins fnl f* **16/1**
6023 **5** 1 1/4 **My Best Bet**[19] 2601 4-9-8 76........ JackMitchell 8 79+
(Stef Higgins) *hld up: swtchd lft over 2f out: nt clr run over 1f out: running on whn nt clr run ins fnl f: nvr able to chal* **20/1**
3166 **6** 1 **Flighty Frances (IRE)**[35] 2120 3-9-0 78........ DaneO'Neill 6 74
(D R C Elsworth) *chsd ldrs: rdn over 1f out: no ex fnl f* **12/1**
333- **7** 2 3/4 **Ethics Girl (IRE)**[203] 7583 4-9-7 75........ RobertHavlin 3 67
(John Berry) *prom: wnt centre over 6f out: c bk to stands' side 1/2-way: rdn over 1f out: sn wknd* **33/1**
-344 **8** 1 1/4 **Sakhee's Pearl**[30] 2262 4-9-7 82........ AdamBeschizza(7) 2 71
(Miss Gay Kelleway) *chsd ldrs: wnt centre over 6f out: c bk to stands' side 1/2-way: rdn and wknd over 1f out* **33/1**
1 **9** 6 **Bougainvilia (IRE)**[15] 2718 3-9-1 79........ PatDobbs 7 52
(R Hannon) *hld up in tch: plld hrd: rdn: hung lft and wknd over 1f out* **5/2**[2]

1m 39.12s (-0.88) **Going Correction** -0.20s/f (Firm)
WFA 3 from 4yo+ 10lb **9** Ran SP% **116.6**
Speed ratings (Par 102): **96,94,93,93,91 90,88,86,80**
toteswingers: 1&2 £4.50, 1&3 £2.30, 2&3 £9.50 CSF £19.15 CT £67.69 TOTE £2.40: £1.10, £2.70, £1.80; EX 18.40 Trifecta £275.20 Part won. Pool: £371.92 - 0.70 winning units..
Owner St Albans Bloodstock LLP **Bred** Sean Murphy **Trained** Newmarket, Suffolk

FOCUS
They didn't seem to go that quickly early on and the field split after a couple of furlongs as Sweet Clementine drifted out to the centre of the track, taking Sakhee's Pearl and Ethics Girl with her, while the majority raced up the stands' side. The three out wide rejoined the pack with 3f to run. The form is muddling but does not look bad, with those in the frame behind the winner close to their marks.
Bougainvilia(IRE) Official explanation: jockey said filly ran too free

3218 32RED CASINO H'CAP 5f
3:55 (3:55) (Class 2) (0-100,91) 3-Y-O
£11,215 (£3,358; £1,679; £840; £419; £210) Stalls High

Form RPR
0014 **1** **Russian Rock (IRE)**[21] 2545 3-9-1 88........ JohnFahy(5) 3 95
(R A Teal) *chsd ldrs: chal over 1f out: sn rdn: hung lft and led nr fin* **7/1**
-536 **2** 1/2 **Living It Large (FR)**[7] 2960 3-9-5 87........ RobertHavlin 2 92
(R F Fisher) *led: hdd over 3f out: led again over 1f out: sn rdn: hung lft and hdd nr fin* **20/1**
2313 **3** 3/4 **Confessional**[21] 2545 3-9-5 87........(p) DavidAllan 1 89
(T D Easterby) *hld up in tch: rdn over 1f out: r.o* **10/3**[2]
-610 **4** 1 3/4 **Magical Macey (USA)**[7] 2978 3-9-6 88........(b) DaneO'Neill 8 84
(T D Barron) *prom: jnd ldrs 1/2-way: rdn and edgd lft over 1f out: styd on same pce fnl f* **6/1**[3]

-420 **5** *2 1/4* **The Only Boss (IRE)**[7] 2978 3-9-9 **91** .... HayleyTurner 9 79
(W J Haggas) *hld up: rdn and nt clr run over 1f out: nt trble ldrs* **11/1**

35-0 **6** *hd* **High Spice (USA)**[29] 2287 3-8-10 **78** .... EddieAhern 5 65
(R M H Cowell) *chsd ldr tl led over 3f out: rdn and hdd over 1f out: wknd ins fnl f* **25/1**

-442 **7** *3/4* **Racy**[7] 2960 3-9-3 **88** .... Louis-PhilippeBeuzelin(3) 4 72
(Sir Michael Stoute) *prom: rdn 1/2-way: wknd fnl f* **13/8**[1]

-102 **8** *4* **The Strig**[37] 2046 3-8-9 **77** .... AndreaAtzeni 6 47
(S C Williams) *dwlt: hdwy 1/2-way: wknd over 1f out* **7/1**

57.64 secs (-1.46) **Going Correction** -0.20s/f (Firm) **8** Ran SP% **117.4**
Speed ratings (Par 105): **103,102,101,98,94 94,93,86**
toteswingers: 1&2 £15.50, 1&3 £5.20, 2&3 £9.80 CSF £131.67 CT £460.04 TOTE £11.90: £3.20, £4.90, £1.70; EX 123.50 Trifecta £267.40 Pool: £397.60 - 1.10 winning units..
Owner M Vickers **Bred** Barronstown Stud And Mrs T Stack **Trained** Ashtead, Surrey

FOCUS
The top weight weighed in 9lb below the ceiling for the race, so this was a 0-100 in name only. The three who raced widest of all, nearest the centre of the track finished 1-2-3. The form looks fair, rated through the fourth.

NOTEBOOK
Russian Rock(IRE), who ran well, doing best of the small group that raced on the far side, when fourth in a competitive heat over 6f on the Rowley Mile course last time out, promised to be suited by the drop back to the minimum trip as his two previous successes had come over the distance. He picked up well once they hit the rising ground and it wouldn't be a surprise to see him win a big-field handicap, where a strong pace will suit him ideally. (tchd 15-2)
Living It Large(FR), dropped 3lb since his last start, was prominent up the centre of the track throughout. He still looks high enough in the weights, though, and is likely to remain vulnerable to less-exposed rivals. (op 16-1)
Confessional would not have minded the shower that had fallen on the track as he ideally needs some dig in the ground to be seen at his best. The ground was probably still quicker than he'd like it, though. (op 4-1)
Magical Macey(USA), who set the pace up the stands' side, may have been at a disadvantage there, but this was still a return to form back over 5f. (op 5-1)
The Only Boss(IRE), who followed Magical Macey through next to the rail, didn't get the clearest of runs from over 2f out to a furlong out, but he didn't find a great deal once in the clear either. (op 8-1 tchd 12-1)
Racy ran below form and is perhaps a colt that needs to lead to be seen at his best. (op 15-8 tchd 2-1)

3219 32RED.COM MAIDEN STKS 7f
4:30 (4:31) (Class 4) 2-Y-O **£5,180** (£1,541; £770; £384) **Stalls** High

Form RPR

0 **1** **Liberty Cap (USA)**[32] 2216 2-9-3 0 .... (p) NickyMackay 11 78
(J H M Gosden) *led 3f: led again over 2f out: hdd over 1f out: rallied to ld ins fnl f: r.o* **20/1**

2 *1/2* **Introvert (IRE)** 2-8-10 0 .... AntiocoMurgia(7) 5 77
(Mahmood Al Zarooni) *chsd ldrs: rdn over 1f out: edgd lft ins fnl f: r.o* **14/1**

0 **3** *2 1/2* **Rutterkin (USA)**[28] 2319 2-9-3 0 .... TedDurcan 6 71
(Mahmood Al Zarooni) *trckd ldr: plld hrd: led 4f out: hdd over 2f out: led again over 1f out: hdd: hung lft and no ex ins fnl f* **2/1**[1]

0 **4** *1 1/2* **Ahlaain (USA)**[8] 2932 2-9-3 0 .... FergusSweeney 4 67
(D M Simcock) *chsd ldrs: rdn over 1f out: no ex fnl f* **40/1**

5 *2* **Riot Police (USA)** 2-9-3 0 .... RobertHavlin 10 62
(J H M Gosden) *hld up: hdwy 1/2-way: rdn and hung lft fr over 1f: wknd ins fnl f* **5/1**[3]

6 *2* **Dazzling Valentine** 2-8-12 0 .... MarcHalford 3 52
(A Bailey) *hld up: effrt over 2f out: wknd over 1f out* **25/1**

7 *1 3/4* **Star Surprise** 2-9-3 0 .... HayleyTurner 8 52
(M L W Bell) *trckd ldrs: racd keenly: rdn and wknd over 1f out* **5/2**[2]

0 **8** *6* **Cantonese Cat (IRE)**[8] 2932 2-9-3 0 .... EddieAhern 12 37
(B J Meehan) *hld up: rdn 1/2-way: wknd 2f out* **25/1**

9 *1/2* **Prince Freddie** 2-8-12 0 .... AshleyMorgan(5) 7 36
(M H Tompkins) *hld up: rdn and wknd over 2f out* **25/1**

10 *1 3/4* **Maratib (USA)** 2-9-3 0 .... DaneO'Neill 2 32
(D R Lanigan) *hld up: wknd over 2f out* **8/1**

11 *111* **Freehand (USA)** 2-9-3 0 .... DaraghO'Donohoe 1 —
(Mahmood Al Zarooni) *wnt rt s: outpcd* **16/1**

1m 25.8s (0.10) **Going Correction** -0.20s/f (Firm) **11** Ran SP% **121.0**
Speed ratings (Par 95): **91,90,87,85,83 81,79,72,71,69** —
toteswingers: 1&2 £54.30, 1&3 £15.80, 2&3 £3.10 CSF £261.19 TOTE £32.50: £6.90, £4.20, £1.10; EX 353.00.
Owner H R H Princess Haya Of Jordan **Bred** Randy Bloch Et Al **Trained** Newmarket, Suffolk

FOCUS
The whole field edged over to race more towards the centre of the track this time. A difficult race to rate, and the modest time and limited form of those to have previously run limits things.

NOTEBOOK
Liberty Cap(USA), in what was a field made up mostly of newcomers, put his previous experience to good use, making the running and responding well when challenged inside the final furlong. He'd finished a well-beaten last of 11 on his debut at Nottingham, but had clearly come on plenty for that and, with the benefit of cheekpieces on this time, showed dramatic improvement. (tchd 18-1)
Introvert(IRE), whose rider wore the owner's second colours, travelled well but showed his inexperience by running green when asked to go and win his race. He'll come on for this and should soon go one better. (tchd 11-1)
Rutterkin(USA) was the stable's first string according to the market and cap colour. Just like the winner, he tried to make the most of his previous experience by racing in the van throughout, but he didn't quite see his race out, despite his pedigree suggesting he'd appreciate the extra furlong. (op 3-1)
Ahlaain(USA), too green to do himself justice in a hot Sandown maiden on his debut, nevertheless showed the benefit of that run with a much-improved effort here. He'll be an interesting type for nurseries in time.
Riot Police(USA), who, like his winning stablemate, is a son of Street Cry, tracked him through for much of the race but betrayed his inexperience in the closing stages. He'll come on plenty of this. (op 9-2 tchd 4-1)
Dazzling Valentine, the only filly in the field, cost just 3,500gns at the sales. She kept on for pressure and looks to have a future.
Star Surprise, whose dam won a 1m2f Group 1 in Italy as a 3-y-o, ran well for along way and can be expected to see his race out better next time. (op 9-4 tchd 2-1)
Freehand(USA) Official explanation: jockey said colt was reluctant to race

3220 BET AT 32RED MAIDEN STKS 1m
5:05 (5:10) (Class 4) 3-Y-O **£5,180** (£1,541; £770; £384) **Stalls** High

Form RPR

3 **1** **Space War**[7] 2968 3-9-3 0 .... RobertHavlin 2 83+
(J H M Gosden) *mde all: rdn over 1f out: r.o* **5/2**[2]

2 *1 1/2* **Dhaamer (IRE)** 3-9-3 0 .... NickyMackay 7 79+
(J H M Gosden) *hld up: rdn over 3f out: hdwy 2f out: hung lft ins fnl f: r.o to go 2nd towards fin* **7/1**[3]

03 **3** *1/2* **Ertikaan**[20] 2564 3-9-3 0 .... PhilipRobinson 4 78+
(M A Jarvis) *chsd ldrs: rdn and ev ch over 1f out: styd on same pce ins fnl f: lost 2nd towards fin* **8/13**[1]

55 **4** *3 1/4* **Roose Blox (IRE)**[26] 2393 3-9-3 0 .... FergusSweeney 3 70?
(R F Fisher) *chsd wnr tl rdn over 1f out: wknd fnl f* **25/1**

5 *7* **Wallis** 3-8-12 0 .... KirstyMilczarek 1 48
(L M Cumani) *chsd ldrs: rdn and wknd over 1f out: sn hung rt* **16/1**

0 **6** *1 1/4* **Plan A (IRE)**[12] 2812 3-9-3 0 .... JerryO'Dwyer 5 50
(M G Quinlan) *s.i.s: hld up: rdn and wknd over 2f out* **66/1**

7 *3 1/2* **Chaqueta** 3-8-12 0 .... TedDurcan 9 37
(C F Wall) *wnt rt s: hld up: rdn and wknd over 2f out* **25/1**

1m 39.41s (-0.59) **Going Correction** -0.20s/f (Firm) **7** Ran SP% **118.1**
Speed ratings (Par 101): **94,92,92,88,81 80,77**
toteswingers: 1&2 £2.30, 1&3 £1.70, 2&3 £1.90 CSF £20.42 TOTE £3.90: £1.80, £2.80; EX 27.50.
Owner H R H Princess Haya Of Jordan **Bred** Shutford Stud And O F Waller **Trained** Newmarket, Suffolk

FOCUS
A fair maiden run at a muddling pace and the bare form is unlikely to prove reliable.

3221 32RED POKER H'CAP 1m 5f
5:40 (5:42) (Class 5) (0-75,72) 4-Y-O+ **£3,885** (£1,156; £577; £288) **Stalls** High

Form RPR

6303 **1** **Lastroseofsummer (IRE)**[9] 2897 4-8-3 **59** .... NoelGarbutt(7) 10 67
(Rae Guest) *a.p: chsd ldr over 5f out: rdn to ld over 1f out: r.o* **13/2**

2131 **2** *1 1/2* **Ghufa (IRE)**[9] 2881 6-9-2 **70** .... SimonPearce(5) 1 75
(J Pearce) *chsd ldrs: rdn and ev ch over 1f out: styd on* **3/1**[1]

00-3 **3** *nk* **Sheila's Castle**[20] 2560 6-8-11 **60** .... TedDurcan 6 65
(S Regan) *hld up: hdwy 3f out: rdn over 1f out: styd on* **7/2**[2]

2332 **4** *3/4* **My Mate Mal**[20] 2560 6-9-2 **70** .... JohnFahy(5) 5 74
(W B Stone) *led: rdn and hdd over 1f out: styd on same pce ins fnl f* **5/1**[3]

-453 **5** *hd* **Zaif (IRE)**[11] 2845 7-8-6 **55** .... RichardThomas 3 59
(D J S Ffrench Davis) *hld up: hdwy over 3f out: rdn over 1f out: styd on* **10/1**

3600 **6** *5* **Supernoverre (IRE)**[29] 2302 4-8-4 **53** oh1 .... KirstyMilczarek 2 49
(P Howling) *prom: rdn over 2f out: wknd over 1f out* **12/1**

4006 **7** *nse* **Dovedon Earl**[67] 1283 4-8-4 **53** oh2 .... NickyMackay 4 49
(T Keddy) *hld up: nt clr run over 2f out: n.d* **12/1**

0400 **8** *10* **Carnac (IRE)**[8] 2941 4-9-1 **64** .... (b[1]) JerryO'Dwyer 7 45
(J S Wainwright) *chsd ldr over 7f: rdn and wknd over 1f out* **33/1**

3-01 **9** *shd* **Marju King (IRE)**[26] 2402 4-9-9 **72** .... FergusSweeney 8 53
(W S Kittow) *hld up: hdwy over 3f out: rdn and wknd over 1f out: eased ins fnl f* **8/1**

1636 **10** *2 3/4* **Carlton Scroop (FR)**[15] 2723 7-9-2 **65** .... (b) AndreaAtzeni 9 42
(J Jay) *s.i.s: hld up: rdn over 3f out: wknd 2f out* **12/1**

2m 46.48s (2.48) **Going Correction** -0.20s/f (Firm) **10** Ran SP% **123.4**
Speed ratings (Par 103): **84,83,82,82,82 79,79,73,72,71**
toteswingers: 1&2 £7.10, 1&3 £5.20, 2&3 £4.40 CSF £27.99 CT £83.00 TOTE £10.00: £2.70, £1.60, £1.70; EX 37.70 Place 6 £121.24; Place 5 £50.12.
Owner E P Duggan **Bred** Mount Coote Stud **Trained** Newmarket, Suffolk

FOCUS
An ordinary middle-distance handicap with the runner-up and fourth to turf form.
Marju King(IRE) Official explanation: jockey said gelding no more to give
T/Plt: £185.40 to a £1 stake. Pool: £73,342.02. 288.68 winning tickets. T/Qpdt: £39.20 to a £1 stake. Pool: £3,919.57. 73.83 winning tickets. CR

3175 REDCAR (L-H)
Saturday, June 19

OFFICIAL GOING: Good to firm (8.9)
Wind: Strong, against Weather: Cloudy and blustery

3222 E B F MARKET CROSS JEWELLERS MAIDEN STKS 7f
2:20 (2:20) (Class 5) 2-Y-O **£3,302** (£982; £491; £245) **Stalls** Far side

Form RPR

62 **1** **Tinkertown (IRE)**[11] 2832 2-9-3 0 .... SilvestreDeSousa 9 79
(P F I Cole) *trckd ldrs: chsd along 1/2-way: rdn and hdwy to ld over 1f out: styd on wl u.p fnl f* **1/1**[1]

2 *1 3/4* **Next Edition (IRE)** 2-8-12 0 .... PatrickDonaghy(5) 3 75
(J Howard Johnson) *trckd ldrs: rdn over 2f out: styd on wl fnl f* **33/1**

43 **3** *3/4* **Local Singer (IRE)**[11] 2832 2-9-3 0 .... SamHitchcott 10 73
(M R Channon) *w ldr: led 1/2-way: hdd over 1f out: kpt on but a hld fnl f* **15/8**[2]

4 *1 1/4* **Mutajare (IRE)** 2-9-3 0 .... AndrewElliott 5 70+
(M Johnston) *led: hdd 1/2-way: remained prom tl rdn and hung lft over 1f out: one pce fnl f* **15/2**[3]

036 **5** *3 1/4* **Anddante (IRE)**[22] 2498 2-9-3 0 .... DuranFentiman 4 62
(T D Easterby) *trckd ldrs: rdn over 2f out: sn one pce* **11/1**

0 **6** *3/4* **Downtown Boy (IRE)**[22] 2498 2-9-3 0 .... MickyFenton 11 60
(T P Tate) *midfield: shkn up 1/2-way: kpt on: nvr rchd ldrs* **100/1**

5 **7** *3/4* **Finnker (IRE)**[15] 2701 2-8-12 0 .... IanBrennan(5) 7 58
(J J Quinn) *trckd ldrs: niggled and lost pl 1/2-way: sltly hmpd and swtchd rt over 1f out: kpt on nvr trble ldrs* **25/1**

8 *3/4* **Carrauntoohil (IRE)** 2-8-12 0 .... J-PGuillambert 1 51+
(Miss Amy Weaver) *hld up in midfield: shkn up over 2f out: kpt on: nvr rchd ldrs* **66/1**

9 *1 3/4* **Bollin Harry** 2-9-3 0 .... TomEaves 2 52+
(T D Easterby) *slowly away and wnt lft s: hld up: chsd along 1/2-way: hdwy over 2f out: wknd over 1f out* **22/1**

10 *4 1/2* **Land Bank** 2-8-12 0 .... LanceBetts(5) 6 41
(T D Easterby) *s.i.s: a towards rr* **50/1**

0 **11** *3 1/4* **Goodmanyourself**[8] 2936 2-9-3 0 .... TonyCulhane 8 32
(P T Midgley) *s.i.s: hld up: nvr a factor* **50/1**

1m 30.69s (6.19) **Going Correction** +0.35s/f (Good) **11** Ran SP% **122.4**
Speed ratings (Par 93): **78,76,75,73,70 69,68,67,65,60 56**
toteswingers:1&2:£13.10, 1&3:£1.10, 2&3:£15.10 CSF £50.82 TOTE £2.40: £1.10, £11.80, £1.10; EX 56.60.
Owner Mrs Fitri Hay **Bred** Corrin Stud **Trained** Whatcombe, Oxon

FOCUS
The ground was slightly easier than the previous day after 4mm of water was put on the home straight and the bends overnight, in addition to the 1.5mm of rain in the morning. There was also a strong headwind and that appears the reason why the time of this opener was over seven seconds over Racing Post standard. Experience came to the fore.

NOTEBOOK

Tinkertown(IRE) continued his progression to make it third time lucky and he relished the step up to 7f, seeing it out strongly and on both run style and pedigree he appears certain to get at least 1m next term. He isn't the smoothest of travellers, indeed he was being niggled along half a mile from home, but there is a chance it could still be down to greennness and there was nothing wrong with the way he saw out his race. Nurseries beckon, but he looks the type to continue improving for a while yet. (op 11-8)

Next Edition(IRE), difficult to assess on breeding given he is the first foal of an unraced dam and his second dam only had one runner, finished strongly down the middle of the track having taken time to find his stride. He won't need to improve too much on this to be a potent force next time.

Local Singer(IRE) has a similar profile to the winner having improved nicely on his second start and he saw out this extra furlong well enough to suggest the trip is fine for now. Although held by the winner, he looks up to winning his maiden soon, especially as he seems to be improving race by race. (tchd 5-2)

Mutajare(IRE) cost £80,000 as a yearling and he too shaped with promise having shown up well for a long way before running around under pressure and weakening. He's another entitled to improve considerably, both in terms of fitness and mentally. (op 17-2 tchd 7-1)

Anddante(IRE) travelled well for a long way and looks one to bear in mind when sent handicapping. (tchd 10-1)

Goodmanyourself Official explanation: jockey sasid colt reared as gates opened

3223 BUY YOUR TICKETS ON-LINE @ REDCARRACING.CO.UK H'CAP — 1m 6f 19y

2:55 (2:57) (Class 6) (0-60,58) 4-Y-O+ — **£1,748** (£520; £260; £129) **Stalls** Low

Form — RPR

4-13 **1** **Simple Jim (FR)**[6] 2995 6-9-3 57 ... SilvestreDeSousa 4 — 66+
(D O'Meara) *hld up in midfield: smooth hdwy 3f out: shkn up to ld over 1f out: kpt on wl* **15/8**[2]

4620 **2** 1 ¼ **Ocean Bright (USA)**[15] 2697 4-8-1 46 ... DeclanCannon(5) 6 — 53
(J G Given) *s.i.s: sn chsd ldrs: rdn and led narrowly over 2f out: edgd rt and hdd over 1f out: kpt on* **9/1**[3]

/6-5 **3** ½ **Stage Acclaim (IRE)**[8] 2285 5-9-1 55 ...(b) TomEaves 1 — 61
(Dr R D P Newland) *trckd ldrs: rdn and ev ch over 2f out: kpt on fnl f* **10/1**

550- **4** 2 ½ **Chateauneuf (IRE)**[184] 7374 4-8-5 50 ... PaulPickard(5) 5 — 53
(W M Brisbourne) *hld up: rdn over 3f out: hdwy 2f out: styd on: nvr rchd ldrs* **100/1**

60/1 **5** ¾ **Jeu De Roseau (IRE)**[14] 2765 6-9-1 55 ... MickyFenton 9 — 57
(C Grant) *in tch: rdn 4f out: sn one pce* **11/8**[1]

4660 **6** 1 ¼ **Haka Dancer (USA)**[21] 2533 7-8-6 46 ...(p) AndrewMullen 8 — 46
(P A Kirby) *midfield: effrt on outer over 3f out: sn no imp* **28/1**

0610 **7** ½ **Sea Land (FR)**[14] 2761 6-8-11 51 ... CathyGannon 2 — 50
(B Ellison) *hld up: hdwy on inner over 3f out: rdn and ev ch over 2f out: wknd over 1f out* **25/1**

60-0 **8** nk **Harcas (IRE)**[25] 1803 8-8-12 52 ...(v) TonyCulhane 11 — 51
(M Todhunter) *prom: led over 4f out: rdn over 3f out: hdd over 2f out: sn wknd* **25/1**

600/ **9** 1 ¾ **Pugnacity**[24] 6309 6-8-5 45 ... DuranFentiman 7 — 41
(Mrs Dianne Sayer) *prom: lost pl over 4f out: rdn over 3f out: sn wknd* **20/1**

2040 **10** 5 **Orkney (IRE)**[22] 2500 5-8-12 57 ...(v[1]) PatrickDonaghy(5) 12 — 46
(Julie Camacho) *v.s.a and lft 10 l s: a bhd* **16/1**

0-00 **11** 3 ½ **Prince Andjo (USA)**[33] 2184 4-8-0 47 ... NeilFarley(7) 10 — 32
(D Carroll) *led: hdd over 4f out: sn wknd* **50/1**

3m 5.89s (1.19) **Going Correction** +0.125s/f (Good) — **11** Ran SP% **120.7**
Speed ratings (Par 101): **101,100,100,98,98 97,97,96,95,93 91**
toteswingers:1&2:£4.00, 1&3:£4.50, 2&3:£7.00 CSF £18.01 CT £141.54 TOTE £2.00: £1.02, £3.90, £2.30; EX 12.10.

Owner R G Fell **Bred** Snc Haras Des Peltrais, Laurent Thibault **Trained** Nawton, N Yorks

■ The first training success for former jump jockey David O'Meara, who has taken over the licence from James Hetherton.

FOCUS

A weak handicap but it was run at a decent clip.

Orkney(IRE) Official explanation: jockey said gelding had been reluctant to race

3224 WIN A VIP DAY OUT @ REDCARRACING.CO.UK H'CAP — 7f

3:35 (3:36) (Class 3) (0-90,86) 4-Y-O+ — **£6,799** (£2,023; £1,011; £505) **Stalls** Centre

Form — RPR

-211 **1** **Tagseed (IRE)**[23] 2462 4-9-7 86 ... TonyCulhane 1 — 96
(W J Haggas) *w ldr: led narrowly 1/2-way: rdn 2f out: hld on gamely u.str.p fnl f* **8/11**[1]

0-04 **2** nk **Aldermoor (USA)**[28] 2322 4-9-5 84 ... SaleemGolam 4 — 93
(S C Williams) *trckd ldrs: hdwy to chal 2f out: sn drvn: kpt on wl: jst hld* **7/2**[2]

5034 **3** 1 ½ **Joseph Henry**[6] 2992 8-9-0 84 ... BillyCray(5) 2 — 89
(D Nicholls) *led: hdd 1/2-way: rdn over 2f out: remained w ev ch tl no ex fnl f* **5/1**[3]

-100 **4** 1 ¾ **Malcheek (IRE)**[21] 2532 8-9-0 79 ... TomEaves 3 — 79
(T D Easterby) *trckd pce: rdn over 2f out: edgd lft over 1f out: no imp* **14/1**

3150 **5** 5 **Just Sam (IRE)**[4] 3065 5-8-2 72 ... IanBrennan(5) 5 — 59
(R E Barr) *hld up: rdn over 2f out: wknd over 1f out* **12/1**

1m 28.94s (4.44) **Going Correction** +0.35s/f (Good) — **5** Ran SP% **111.2**
Speed ratings (Par 107): **88,87,85,83,78**
CSF £3.63 TOTE £1.20: £1.02, £3.00; EX 4.20.

Owner Hamdan Al Maktoum **Bred** Miss A R Byrne **Trained** Newmarket, Suffolk

FOCUS

There was a slow motion finish into strong headwind (all straight races slow) off a good pace.

NOTEBOOK

Tagseed(IRE) hasn't stopped improving this term and although he was ultimately made to work pretty hard for this third successive win, he dug deep and he outstayed Aldermoor in the final furlong. Unlike last time where he was allowed an easy lead and dictated at a steady pace, he wasn't able to dominate in similar style here as he had Joseph Henry for company on the front end. Having seen that rival off, he needed to pull out all the stops to hold off Aldermoor, which to his credit he did. Although very much going the right way, he'll probably need to improve again to defy another rise in the weights, but the handicapper can't do too much with his mark for this. (op 4-5)

Aldermoor(USA) has won over this trip, but the suspicion remains he is ideally suited by 6f. He looked a big danger to Tagseed a furlong out, but couldn't see his race out as well as that rival. Still, this was his second solid effort in defeat and he is now back down to his last winning mark. (op 9-2)

Joseph Henry served it up to Tagseed for a long way, but couldn't sustain his challenge despite being attractively treated on the pick of his form. (tchd 9-2 and 11-2)

Malcheek(IRE) had every chance, but wasn't good enough and isn't at his best right now. (op 9-1)

3225 H JARVIS 132ND ANNIVERSARY H'CAP — 5f

4:10 (4:10) (Class 4) (0-85,84) 3-Y-O — **£4,209** (£1,252; £625; £312) **Stalls** Centre

Form — RPR

0423 **1** **Ignatieff (IRE)**[12] 2822 3-9-2 79 ... DuranFentiman 3 — 84
(Mrs L Stubbs) *led: shkn up and edgd rt over 1f out: rdn and a in control fnl f* **3/1**[3]

241 **2** 1 ¾ **Philosophers Stone (FR)**[21] 2530 3-8-5 68 ... SilvestreDeSousa 2 — 67
(T D Barron) *s.i.s: chsd along towards rr 1/2-way: hdwy over 1f out: kpt on but a hld* **5/2**[2]

0-45 **3** ¾ **Danny's Choice**[12] 2822 3-9-7 84 ... J-PGuillambert 1 — 80
(R M Beckett) *in tch: rdn over 2f out: kpt on fnl f* **2/1**[1]

5235 **4** 1 ½ **Solstice**[17] 2656 3-9-4 81 ... TomEaves 5 — 72
(Julie Camacho) *in tch: hdwy to chse wnr 1/2-way: rdn 2f out: wknd fnl f* **4/1**

-400 **5** 4 **Dispol Keasha**[36] 2099 3-8-12 75 ... TonyCulhane 4 — 52
(P T Midgley) *in tch: rdn over 2f out: sn wknd* **20/1**

60.20 secs (1.60) **Going Correction** +0.35s/f (Good) — **5** Ran SP% **111.7**
Speed ratings (Par 101): **101,98,97,94,88**
CSF £11.02 TOTE £3.00: £1.10, £1.90; EX 8.90.

Owner P G Shorrock **Bred** Holborn Trust Co **Trained** Norton, N Yorks

FOCUS

Only five runners and an ordinary handicap for the grade with the winner looking fairly exposed.

3226 LAD'S NIGHT ON THURSDAY 1ST JULY CLAIMING STKS — 7f

4:45 (4:45) (Class 5) 3-Y-O+ — **£2,428** (£722; £361; £180) **Stalls** Centre

Form — RPR

0111 **1** **Abbondanza (IRE)**[2] 3120 7-9-2 79 ... MichaelGeran(3) 4 — 78
(D Nicholls) *cl up: rdn to ld over 1f out: kpt on wl* **13/8**[1]

0441 **2** 2 ½ **King's Sabre**[10] 2874 4-9-1 60 ...(e) PaulEddery 7 — 67
(R C Guest) *s.i.s: hld up: racd keenly: hdwy 2f out: rdn and kpt on wl fnl f* **20/1**

1400 **3** nse **Whispered Times (USA)**[18] 2628 3-8-7 64 ... AndrewMullen 5 — 65
(Miss Tracy Waggott) *chsd ldrs: rdn over 2f out: hung lft over 1f out: kpt on fnl f* **28/1**

000- **4** nse **White Deer (USA)**[210] 7492 6-9-1 80 ...(v) SilvestreDeSousa 10 — 67
(G A Harker) *hld up in midfield: hdwy on outer over 2f out: rdn and kpt on over 1f out* **6/1**

0020 **5** 3 ¼ **Luv U Noo**[11] 2834 3-7-13 56 ... CathyGannon 1 — 48
(B Ellison) *hld up: hdwy 2f out: kpt on fnl f but nvr threatened* **25/1**

3-00 **6** 1 ½ **San Cassiano (IRE)**[21] 2544 3-9-2 84 ... J-PGuillambert 8 — 61
(R M Beckett) *led: rdn over 2f out: hdd over 1f out: sn wknd* **12/1**

012 **7** 1 ¼ **Caprio (IRE)**[2] 3120 5-9-11 84 ... TomEaves 11 — 61
(J R Boyle) *hld up in midfield: hdwy over 2f out: rdn 2f out: sn no imp* **5/1**[3]

2155 **8** hd **Last Sovereign**[43] 1862 6-9-7 80 ... TonyCulhane 12 — 56
(Jane Chapple-Hyam) *w ldr: rdn over 2f out: wknd over 1f out* **11/4**[2]

00-0 **9** 3 ½ **Gadobout Dancer**[43] 1887 3-7-5 31 ... NeilFarley(7) 2 — 30
(D Carroll) *chsd ldrs: rdn along bef 1/2-way: sn wknd* **100/1**

10 1 ¼ **Feed The Goat (IRE)** 3-7-12 0 ...(t) BillyCray(5) 6 — 31
(Miss Amy Weaver) *sn chsd along towards rr: a bhd* **80/1**

0443 **11** hd **Vogarth**[30] 2263 6-8-7 45 ...(v) MarkCoumbe(5) 9 — 34
(M C Chapman) *s.i.s: sn chsd along towards rr: a bhd* **100/1**

4-33 **12** 9 **Pure Nostalgia (IRE)**[15] 2700 3-8-0 64 ... IanBrennan(5) 3 — 8
(J Howard Johnson) *trckd ldrs: rdn over 2f out: sn wknd: eased fnl f* **20/1**

1m 27.69s (3.19) **Going Correction** +0.35s/f (Good)
WFA 3 from 4yo+ 9lb — **12** Ran SP% **123.4**
Speed ratings (Par 103): **95,92,92,92,88 86,85,84,80,79 79,69**
toteswingers:1&2:£11.90, 1&3:£16.30, 2&3:£26.90 CSF £43.63 TOTE £2.20: £1.10, £4.70, £8.10; EX 28.40.

Owner Middleham Park Racing XXXI **Bred** M Nolan **Trained** Sessay, N Yorks

FOCUS

Quite a warm event for the grade though there were the usual doubts over a few.

3227 FOLLOW REDCAR RACING ON FACEBOOK MAIDEN STKS — 6f

5:20 (5:20) (Class 5) 3-Y-O+ — **£2,428** (£722; £361; £180) **Stalls** Centre

Form — RPR

00 **1** **Crianza**[9] 2899 4-8-9 0 ... NoraLooby(7) 8 — 56
(N Tinkler) *dwlt: hld up in rr: smooth hdwy 2f out: led ent fnl f: pushed out* **100/1**

06 **2** ½ **Clare Harrier (IRE)**[43] 1890 3-8-9 0 ... MarkCoumbe(5) 11 — 57
(A Berry) *hld up: rdn in rr 1/2-way: hdwy and edgd lft 2f out: drvn and styd on wl fnl f* **66/1**

00 **3** ¾ **Verluga (IRE)**[10] 2852 3-8-9 0 ... LanceBetts(5) 7 — 55
(T D Easterby) *hld up: hdwy over 2f out: rdn to ld over 1f out: hdd ent fnl f: kpt on* **66/1**

6- **4** 1 ½ **Nicholas Pocock (IRE)**[430] 1295 4-9-7 0 ... CathyGannon 4 — 52
(B Ellison) *dwlt: hld up: swtchd lft and hdwy on outer over 2f out: chal over 1f out: no ex fnl f* **16/1**

25 **5** ½ **Kielder (IRE)**[22] 2517 3-9-0 0 ... J-PGuillambert 10 — 48
(T D Barron) *cl up: effrt 2f out: edgd lft 1f out: no ex fnl f* **11/8**[1]

0-4 **6** 1 ½ **Times Ahead (USA)**[22] 2517 3-9-0 0 ... MickyFenton 3 — 43
(P W Chapple-Hyam) *w ldr: rdn over 2f out: wknd ins fnl f* **3/1**[3]

5 **7** 1 ¼ **Lady Anthracite**[15] 2706 3-8-9 0 ... TomEaves 2 — 34
(B Smart) *dwlt: sn in tch: hdwy to chal on outer 1/2-way: rdn and edgd rt over 1f out: wknd fnl f* **18/1**

4-32 **8** hd **North Central (USA)**[15] 2698 3-8-9 65 ... IanBrennan(5) 6 — 39
(J Howard Johnson) *led: rdn and hdd over 1f out: sn wknd* **5/2**[2]

4 **9** nse **Sammuramat (IRE)**[32] 2197 3-8-4 65 ... AmyRyan(5) 1 — 34
(M G Quinlan) *prom: rdn 1/2-way: already wkng whn n.m.r over 1f out* **12/1**

06 **10** 2 ¼ **Leolene Starlight**[11] 2837 5-9-2 0 ... SilvestreDeSousa 9 — 28
(D O'Meara) *chsd ldrs: rdn and ev ch 2f out: wknd appr fnl f* **20/1**

1m 15.64s (3.84) **Going Correction** +0.35s/f (Good)
WFA 3 from 4yo+ 7lb — **10** Ran SP% **123.3**
Speed ratings (Par 103): **88,87,86,84,83 81,80,79,79,76**
toteswingers:1&2:£119.10, 1&3:£56.00, 2&3:£66.40 CSF £2736.08 TOTE £76.40: £14.90, £14.60, £12.20; EX 862.70 Place 6 £328.14; Place 5 £266.51.

Owner Philip A Jarvis **Bred** Philip A Jarvis **Trained** Langton, N Yorks

FOCUS
A real Placepot buster with the first three home priced at 100-1, 66-1 and 66-1, but the time was slow and the form is hard to fathom.

3228 REDCARRACING.CO.UK H'CAP 5f
5:55 (6:03) (Class 6) (0-60,60) 3-Y-O £1,842 (£544; £272) Stalls Centre

Form				RPR
-000	1		**Arch Walker (IRE)**[75] 2426 3-9-1 60 MichaelStainton(3) 4 (Jedd O'Keeffe) *in tch: hdwy to chse ldr over 2f out: rdn over 1f out: styd on wl to ld ins fnl f* 12/1	68
45-0	2	1	**Oondiri (IRE)**[26] 2396 3-8-13 55 DavidNolan 2 (T D Easterby) *led: rdn 2f out: edgd lft over 1f out: hdd and no ex ins fnl f* 11/2[2]	59
0600	3	2 1/2	**Ignore**[75] 1118 3-8-4 46 oh1 SilvestreDeSousa 3 (Mrs R A Carr) *in tch: chsd along 1/2-way: hdwy over 1f out: kpt on take 3rd ins fnl 100yds* 12/1	41
1030	4	1 1/4	**Vilnius**[24] 2432 3-9-2 58 CathyGannon 1 (M R Channon) *chsd ldr: drvn 2f out: no ex ins fnl f* 8/1[3]	49
453-	5	1 1/4	**Whitby (IRE)**[190] 7705 3-8-10 57 (t) IanBrennan(5) 6 (M W Easterby) *hld up: outpcd bef 1/2-way: kpt on appr fnl f: nrst fin* 11/1	43
0203	6	2 3/4	**Duke Of Rainford**[19] 2582 3-8-11 53 JamieMackay 7 (M Herrington) *hld up: swtchd rt 2f out: kpt on tl eased fnl 100yds* 10/1	29
44-4	7	3 1/2	**Burnt Cream**[14] 2741 3-9-4 60 TomEaves 10 (B Smart) *in tch: rdn over 2f out: sn wknd* 11/4[1]	24
-043	8	1/2	**Media Jury**[39] 1987 3-8-5 52 (p) AmyRyan(5) 5 (J S Wainwright) *in tch: sltly hmpd and lost pl 1/2-way: sn rdn and no imp* 33/1	14
00-2	9	1 1/4	**Saucy Girl (IRE)**[63] 1390 3-8-9 56 LanceBetts(5) 9 (T D Easterby) *rrd and slowly away: sn outpcd in rr: a bhd* 11/4[1]	13
-506	10	3 1/2	**Camacho Flyer (IRE)**[14] 2768 3-8-8 55 (v) PaulPickard(5) 8 (P T Midgley) *chsd ldrs: rdn 1/2-way: sn wknd* 12/1	—

60.59 secs (1.99) **Going Correction** +0.35s/f (Good) **10** Ran SP% **123.3**
Speed ratings (Par 97): **98,96,92,90,88 84,78,77,75,70**
toteswingers:1&2:£20.30, 1&3:£16.50, 2&3:£12.30 CSF £81.10 CT £614.53 TOTE £18.20: £4.40, £2.70, £6.50; EX 153.70.
Owner A Walker **Bred** T Hirschfeld **Trained** Middleham Moor, N Yorks

FOCUS
Modest sprint handicap form.
Arch Walker(IRE) Official explanation: trainer said regarding the apparent improvement in form gelding was better suited by drop back to 5f and being dropped 5lb in the ratings.
Duke Of Rainford Official explanation: jockey sais that the gelding hung left in the final two furlongs
Saucy Girl(IRE) Official explanation: jockey said that the filly reared as the gates opened
T/Plt: £1,030.20 to a £1 stake. Pool:£39,402.56 - 27.92 winning tickets T/Qpdt: Part won. £1,463.30 to a £1 stake. Pool: £1,977.46 - 0.10 winning tickets. AS

3229 - 3235a (Foreign Racing) - See Raceform Interactive

2559 DUSSELDORF (R-H)
Saturday, June 19

OFFICIAL GOING: Turf: good

3236a PREIS DER HSBC TRINKAUS (EX BMW PREIS DUSSELDORF) (LISTED RACE) (3YO+ FILLIES & MARES) (TURF) 7f
3:30 (12:00) 3-Y-O+ £10,619 (£3,893; £2,123; £1,061)

			RPR
1		**Aslana (IRE)**[26] 2404 3-8-9 0 AStarke 1 (P Schiergen, Germany) 29/10[2]	91
2	1/2	**Magic Eye (IRE)**[21] 2559 5-9-2 0 THellier 5 (Andreas Lowe, Germany) 2/1[1]	91
3	1/2	**Devilish Lips (GER)**[26] 2404 3-8-9 0 (b) AndreBest 8 (Andreas Lowe, Germany) 91/10	89
4	2	**Pariala (GER)**[377] 2757 4-9-2 0 EFrank 6 (T Mundry, Germany) 32/5	84
5	nse	**Golden Whip (GER)**[33] 3-8-9 0 GregoryBenoist 11 (W Hickst, Germany) 89/10	83
6	nk	**Saldenart (GER)**[26] 4-9-2 0 AHelfenbein 2 (Uwe Ostmann, Germany) 159/10	83
7	2	**Penzena**[19] 2601 4-9-2 0 FilipMinarik 10 (A M Balding) *broke wl: trckd fast pce in 2nd: flattered briefly early in st but no ex ins fnl 1 1/2f: fdd* 63/10[3]	78
8	nse	**Marny (GER)**[26] 5-9-2 0 JiriPalik 9 (H Blume, Germany) 26/1	78
9	3	**Margie's World (GER)**[26] 6-9-2 0 EPedroza 3 (S Wegner, Germany) 34/1	70
10	nse	**Classic Summer (GER)**[26] 4-9-2 0 HenkGrewe 7 (Andreas Lowe, Germany) 28/1	70
11	shd	**Bella Platina (GER)**[26] 6-9-2 0 ADeVries 12 (U Stoltefuss, Germany) 106/10	69
12	10	**Marguerite Du Pre (GER)**[230] 3-8-9 0 WPanov 4 (M Figge, Germany) 41/1	41

1m 24.72s (84.72)
WFA 3 from 4yo+ 9lb **12** Ran SP% **133.1**
WIN (incl. 10 euro stake): 39. PLACES: 17, 14, 26. SF: 100.
Owner Stall Nizza **Bred** J Imm **Trained** Germany

NOTEBOOK
Penzena, beaten in a handicap at Leicester off 72 last time out, showed early speed but couldn't maintain her effort in the straight. It wasn't a bad effort on this big step up in class.

2813 PONTEFRACT (L-H)
Sunday, June 20

OFFICIAL GOING: Good to firm (good in places) changing to good to firm after race 2 (2.40)
There was a temporary rail 12ft from the original running rail over the last 6f.
Wind: Nil Weather: Fine and dry

3237 E B F TOTEPOOL A BETTER WAY TO BET MAIDEN FILLIES' STKS 6f
2:10 (2:13) (Class 5) 2-Y-O £3,885 (£1,156; £577; £288) Stalls Low

Form				RPR
3	1		**Zabeel Park (USA)**[18] 2641 2-9-0 0 FrankieDettori 2 (Saeed Bin Suroor) *sn led: pushed along over 2f out: rdn over 1f out: kpt on wl fnl f* 5/4[2]	86
2	2	2	**Mama Lulu (USA)**[15] 2740 2-9-0 0 JamieSpencer 11 (M L W Bell) *trckd ldng pair: effrt and cl up 1/2-way: rdn to chal 2f out: drvn over 1f out: hung persistently lft and one pce fnl f* 1/1[1]	81
0	3	8	**Princess Izzy**[19] 2616 2-9-0 0 KierenFallon 5 (M H Tompkins) *midfield: hdwy 3f out: rdn and kpt on fnl 2f: nvr nr ldng pair* 16/1	60+
0	4	3 1/2	**Cool In The Shade**[12] 2832 2-8-9 0 PaulPickard(5) 4 (P T Midgley) *chsd ldrs: rdn along over 2f out: drvn wl over 1f out and kpt on same pce* 66/1	46
0	5	4	**Kaifi (IRE)**[15] 2749 2-9-0 0 PhilipRobinson 10 (C E Brittain) *in tch: rdn along 3f out: grad wknd* 14/1[3]	34
0	6	1/2	**Livinadream**[23] 2498 2-9-0 0 SilvestreDeSousa 12 (N Tinkler) *dwlt and swtchd lft s: pushed along and outpcd in rr 1/2-way: sme hdwy wl over 1f out: nvr a factor* 80/1	32
60	7	2 1/4	**Georgina Bailey (IRE)**[15] 2740 2-8-9 0 DeclanCannon(5) 6 (A J McCabe) *cl up: rdn along 3f out: sn wknd* 100/1	25
	8	3	**Princess Gail** 2-9-0 0 EddieAhern 9 (W M Brisbourne) *a in rr* 66/1	16
	9	1	**Millies Folly** 2-9-0 0 DavidNolan 7 (D Carroll) *a in rr* 80/1	13

1m 17.04s (0.14) **Going Correction** -0.05s/f (Good) **9** Ran SP% **113.4**
Speed ratings (Par 90): **97,94,83,79,73 73,70,66,64**
Tote Swingers: 1&2 £1.20, 1&3 £2.70, 2&3 £3.00 CSF £2.66 TOTE £2.40: £1.20, £1.10, £1.90; EX 2.60 Trifecta £10.70 Pool: £425.64 - 29.35 winning units..
Owner Godolphin **Bred** Rathbarry Stud **Trained** Newmarket, Suffolk

FOCUS
Very little strength in depth to this fillies' maiden, they finished well spaced out and the front two pulled well clear.

NOTEBOOK
Zabeel Park(USA) looked really well beforehand and improved a good deal on the form she showed when third on Polytrack first time up. She showed the benefit of that initial experience, travelling well up front at a decent enough pace before keeping on strongly, albeit the runner-up didn't produce a particularly resolute challenge. This half-sister to Finsceal Beo looks useful and is open to further progression. (op 7-4 tchd 15-8 in a place)
Mama Lulu(USA), runner-up over 61/2f on debut, proved unsuited by the drop in trip. Stuck wider than the winner having started off from stall 11, she lacked that one's natural pace and, under pressure before the straight, she then compromised her chance by hanging left. It remains to be seen whether she's straightforward (also swished her tail before going in stalls on debut), or perhaps she just wants easier ground, but whatever, a longer trip should help. (op 10-11 tchd 11-10 and 6-5 in a place)
Princess Izzy did not seem to improve on the form she showed over 5f on debut.
Cool In The Shade is probably more of a nursery type. (tchd 80-1)
Kaifi(IRE) again showed only moderate form and seemingly needs more time. (op 16-1 tchd 12-1)

3238 BET TOTEPOOL AT TOTESPORT.COM FILLIES' H'CAP 1m 4y
2:40 (2:40) (Class 5) (0-70,68) 3-Y-O+ £3,238 (£963; £481; £240) Stalls Low

Form				RPR
-003	1		**Abu Dubai (IRE)**[9] 2920 4-8-11 51 JamieMackay 1 (J A Glover) *cl up on inner: led after 1f: rdn along over 1f out: drvn and hung bdly rt ins fnl f: jst hld on* 14/1	59
0-03	2	nk	**Rascal In The Mix (USA)**[11] 2874 4-8-7 52 (p) AmyRyan(5) 6 (R M Whitaker) *trckd ldrs on inner: hdwy over 2f out: rdn over 1f out: swtchd lft and styd on wl fnl f: jst hld* 16/1	59
600-	3	2 1/2	**Solitary**[274] 6120 4-10-0 68 SilvestreDeSousa 7 (G A Harker) *a cl up: rdn wl over 1f out: drvn ent fnl f and ev ch tl wknd last 100yds* 33/1	69
001	4	2 3/4	**Catawollow**[23] 2503 3-8-0 50 (e) PaulEddery 5 (R C Guest) *hld up: hdwy 1/2-way: chsd ldrs over 2f out: rdn wl over 1f out: sn one pce* 12/1	43
-066	5	3/4	**Akamon**[19] 2619 3-8-10 60 PaulHanagan 4 (E A L Dunlop) *hld up in midfield: effrt over 3f out: sn rdn along and n.m.r over 2f out: no imp* 2/1[1]	51
2124	6	1/2	**Whipma Whopma Gate (IRE)**[25] 2429 5-9-7 68 (v) NeilFarley(7) 3 (D Carroll) *towards rr: hdwy 3f out: sn rdn along swtchd rt wl over 1f out: sn drvn and kpt on ins fnl f: nt rch ldrs* 11/2[3]	60
50-5	7	2 1/2	**Ilkley**[10] 2899 3-7-12 53 oh1 ow4 JamesSullivan(5) 10 (M W Easterby) *chsd ldrs: rdn along 3f out: drvn and edgd rt wl over 1f out: sn wknd* 22/1	37
0-04	8	nse	**Location**[17] 2188 4-9-3 57 TadhgO'Shea 8 (Ian Williams) *a towards rr* 9/1	43
0101	9	1 1/2	**Buzz Bird**[14] 2787 3-8-7 57 JamieSpencer 11 (T D Barron) *chsd ldrs on wd outside: rdn along and lost pl after 2f: drvn along in rr 3f out: nvr a factor* 8/1	40
00-4	10	7	**Exopuntia**[11] 2874 4-8-9 52 MichaelStainton(3) 2 (Miss J Feilden) *s.i.s and sn rdn along to chse ldrs tl wknd wl over 3f out and sn bhd* 16/1	19
5264	11	7	**Crystal Feather**[19] 2625 4-9-7 61 JimmyFortune 9 (E F Vaughan) *trckd ldrs: effrt and cl up over 2f out: sn rdn and wknd wl over 1f out: eased ins fnl f* 7/2[2]	12

1m 45.32s (-0.58) **Going Correction** -0.05s/f (Good)
WFA 3 from 4yo+ 10lb **11** Ran SP% **125.5**
Speed ratings (Par 100): **100,99,97,94,93 93,90,90,89,82 75**
Tote Swingers: 1&2 £30.10, 1&3 £55.80, 2&3 £56.60 CSF £231.68 CT £7183.84 TOTE £19.60: £4.10, £5.50, £9.30; EX 249.70 TRIFECTA Not won..
Owner Paul J Dixon **Bred** Mohammad Al-Qatami **Trained** Babworth, Notts

FOCUS
Following this race the ground was changed to good to firm, from good to firm, good in places. This was just a modest fillies' handicap and they seemed to go an ordinary pace.
Akamon Official explanation: trainer was unable to offer any explination for poor run
Buzz Bird Official explanation: jockey said filly was unsuited by good to firm going

Crystal Feather Official explanation: jockey said filly was unsuited by good to firm going

3239 BET TOTEPOOL ON 0800 221 221 H'CAP — 1m 2f 6y
3:10 (3:11) (Class 3) (0-90,87) 3-Y-O+
£6,854 (£2,052; £1,026; £513; £256; £128) Stalls Low

Form			Horse	RPR
-025	1		**Arizona John (IRE)**[16] 2705 5-9-4 **77** .... StephenCraine 1 (J Mackie) *hld up: stdy hdwy 3f out: swtchd rt and rdn to chse ldr over 1f out: styd on to ld ins fnl f: r.o wl* **10/1**	89
5125	2	2 ¾	**Follow The Flag (IRE)**[20] 2608 6-9-7 **85** ....(p) DeclanCannon(5) 7 (A J McCabe) *trckd ldrs: hdwy 3f out: led 2f out: rdn over 1f out: edgd rt and hdd ins fnl f: kpt on same pce* **11/1**	91
-626	3	1 ½	**Changing The Guard**[20] 2608 4-9-11 **84** .... PaulHanagan 4 (R A Fahey) *trckd ldrs: hdwy on inner over 2f out: rdn and ch over 1f out: sn drvn and kpt on same pce* **5/2**[1]	87
-300	4	5	**Mister Angry (IRE)**[15] 2758 3-8-9 **80** .... GregFairley 3 (M Johnston) *chsd ldrs: rdn along 3f out: drvn wl over 1f out and kpt on same pce* **13/2**	73
2-36	5	9	**Profit's Reality (IRE)**[128] 526 8-9-8 **81** .... JamieSpencer 2 (M J Attwater) *mde most tl rdn along and hdd 2f out: sn wknd* **25/1**	56
0-00	6	1	**Bazergan (IRE)**[3] 3121 5-9-6 **86** ....(tp) DebraEngland(7) 10 (C E Brittain) *chsd ldrs: rdn along 3f out: drvn wl over 1f out and sn wknd* **16/1**	59
6-00	7	3 ¾	**Muftarres (IRE)**[9] 2937 5-9-2 **75** ....(t) TonyCulhane 6 (P T Midgley) *hld up: a in rr* **40/1**	41
200-	8	10	**Snoqualmie Boy**[239] 7018 7-9-13 **86** .... AdrianNicholls 8 (D Nicholls) *hld up: a in rr* **25/1**	32
1-63	9	7	**Luc Jordan**[18] 2640 4-10-0 **87** .... KierenFallon 5 (L M Cumani) *dwlt: a towards rr: rdn along over 3f out: sn bhd and heavily eased fnl f* **3/1**[2]	71
0003	P		**Kaolak (USA)**[9] 2934 4-9-13 **86** .... PhilipRobinson 9 (J Ryan) *cl up: rdn along over 3f out: wknd qckly 2f out: sn bhd: p.u ins fnl f and dismntd* **5/1**[3]	—

2m 10.95s (-2.75) **Going Correction** -0.05s/f (Good)
WFA 3 from 4yo+ 12lb — 10 Ran SP% **117.0**
Speed ratings (Par 107): **109,106,105,101,94 93,90,82,77,—**
Tote Swingers: 1&2 £9.40, 1&3 £6.80, 2&3 £7.60 CSF £111.68 CT £362.19 TOTE £11.10: £2.50, £3.20, £1.70; EX 147.80 Trifecta £373.60 Part won. Pool: £504.96 - 0.20 winning units..
Owner Derbyshire Racing **Bred** Abergwaun Farms **Trained** Church Broughton , Derbys

FOCUS
This looked just an ordinary handicap for the grade, but at least they went a decent gallop.

NOTEBOOK
Arizona John(IRE) ◆ was disappointing over 1m last time, but this step up in trip (furthest he has tried to date) really suited and he recorded a convincing success, having travelled well throughout. Unexposed over this sort of distance and, at the age of five, entitled to still be progressive, he can remain competitive. (op 8-1)
Follow The Flag(IRE) is holding his form tremendously well and this was another fine effort. He made a big move off the final bend to lead and kept on well for pressure, but the winner was simply the better handicapped of the pair. (op 9-1 tchd 8-1)
Changing The Guard looked the likeliest winner when moving well just behind the runner-up approaching the straight (touched 1.14 on Betfair), but he lost momentum briefly when denied a clear run between that rival and the inside rail. He could only find the one pace thereafter and failed to reverse recent Redcar form with Follow The Flag. (op 7-2 tchd 9-4)
Mister Angry(IRE) was extremely one paced on this drop in trip and offered little. (op 9-1 tchd 6-1)
Profit's Reality(IRE) couldn't sustain his challenge after setting a strong pace. He probably wasn't helped by being hassled up front by Kaolak. Official explanation: jockey said gelding was unsuited by good to firm going (op 22-1 tchd 20-1)
Luc Jordan looked an unlikely winner from the off, starting slowest of all and not really travelling with much enthusiasm. He probably didn't enjoy the quick ground. Official explanation: jockey said colt was unsuited by good to firm going (op 9-4)
Kaolak(USA) Official explanation: jockey said colt was unsuited by good to firm going

3240 TOTEPOOL PONTEFRACT CASTLE STKS (LISTED RACE) — 1m 4f 8y
3:40 (3:40) (Class 1) 4-Y-O+ £25,236 (£9,607; £4,810; £2,403; £1,201) Stalls Low

Form			Horse	RPR
/00-	1		**Prospect Wells (FR)**[412] 1762 5-9-1 105 .... PaulMulrennan 1 (J Howard Johnson) *trckd ldr: smooth hdwy 3f out: rdn to ld over 1f out and sn edgd lft: drvn and jnd ins fnl f: hld on gamely towards fin* **9/2**[2]	108
4-25	2	½	**Nanton (USA)**[37] 2097 8-9-1 107 .... KierenFallon 6 (J S Goldie) *hld up in tch: effrt and tk clsr order 3f out: rdn along 2f out: drvn to chse wnr ent fnl f: ev ch tl no ex towards fin* **8/11**[1]	107
3000	3	2 ¼	**Mojave Moon**[29] 2345 4-9-1 102 .... AhmedAjtebi 4 (Mahmood Al Zarooni) *led: rdn along over 2f out: hdd over 1f out: sn drvn and n.m.r ent fnl f: kpt on same pce* **7/1**[3]	103
05-5	4	6	**Hatton Flight**[43] 1898 6-9-1 99 .... JimmyFortune 7 (A M Balding) *hld up: effrt and rdn along over 4f out: n.d* **9/1**	94
0405	5	3 ¾	**Reve De Nuit (USA)**[15] 2747 4-9-1 86 .... JamieSpencer 5 (A J McCabe) *hld up: a in rr* **8/1**	88

2m 38.42s (-2.38) **Going Correction** -0.05s/f (Good) — 5 Ran SP% **109.7**
Speed ratings (Par 111): **105,104,103,99,96**
CSF £8.26 TOTE £5.30: £3.20, £1.10; EX 8.60.
Owner Andrea & Graham Wylie **Bred** Wertheimer & Frere **Trained** Billy Row, Co Durham
■ Stewards' Enquiry : Paul Mulrennan two-day ban: careless riding: excessive us of whip (July 4-6)

FOCUS
A weak Listed race and the pace was modest for much of the way, favouring those ridden prominently.

NOTEBOOK
Prospect Wells(FR) ◆, a Group 2 winner when trained in France by Andre Fabre, hadn't been seen since May 2009 (apparently nearly died following a castration operation), but he made a winning debut for his new connections. He looked fit enough in the paddock, but not a lot went right for him the race itself and, as such, he deserves extra credit. First up, he was plenty keen enough (probably through a combination of freshness and the steady pace), and then he looked to have handed the initiative to the runner-up when becoming unbalanced and colliding with the inside rail late on. He regained his momentum in time, but he did not look at all comfortable on the quick ground, displaying a significant knee action under pressure. All things considered this was a likeable return to action, and better can be expected in future seeing as he's entitled to be sharper next time. He will benefit from an easier surface. (op 10-3 tchd 5-1)
Nanton(USA), unsuited by the steady pace, had to work extremely hard to get into a challenging position. Eventually responding to the Fallon drive, he looked set to take advantage of the winner's waywardness, getting upsides inside the final furlong (touched 1.05 on Betfair), but he could find no extra near the line. (op 11-10)
Mojave Moon ran better than on his two previous starts in Britain, but he was allowed a soft lead in a weak race for the grade and probably still has some way to go to justify his current mark. (op 9-2)
Hatton Flight was never involved and probably would have preferred a stronger gallop. (op 11-1 tchd 12-1 in a place)
Reve De Nuit(USA), rated just 86, was predictably outclassed. (op 10-1 tchd 11-1)

3241 TOTESPORT.COM PONTEFRACT CUP H'CAP — 2m 1f 216y
4:10 (4:10) (Class 4) (0-85,83) 4-Y-O+ £4,533 (£1,348; £674; £336) Stalls Low

Form			Horse	RPR
020-	1		**Markington**[9] 7151 7-8-12 **70** ....(b) KierenFallon 7 (P Bowen) *hld up and bhd: tk clsr order 1/2-way: niggled along 5f out: gd hdwy 3f out: rdn to ld wl over 1f out and sn clr: drvn ins fnl f: hld on gamely* **15/8**[1]	78+
	2	nk	**Swinging Hawk (GER)**[192] 4-9-10 **83** .... EddieAhern 5 (Ian Williams) *in tch: hdwy and cl up 6f out: pushed along and n.m.r 2f out: sn rdn and hdwy to chse wnr over 1f out: drvn and styd on strly towards fin* **28/1**	91+
21-2	3	8	**Ambrose Princess (IRE)**[13] 2810 5-8-0 **63** oh5..........(p) IanBrennan(5) 1 (M J Scudamore) *in tch: hdwy 1/2-way: rdn along 4f out: drvn over 2f out: kpt on same pce* **16/1**	62
11-6	4	2 ¾	**Theola (IRE)**[43] 1902 4-9-3 **81** .... AshleyMorgan(5) 3 (M H Tompkins) *hld up: hdwy 1/2-way: trckd ldrs 4f out: led 2f out: rdn and hdd wl over 1f out: sn wknd* **2/1**[2]	77
6243	5	4	**Spiders Star**[13] 2814 7-8-0 **63** oh2..........(p) PaulPickard(5) 6 (S G West) *hld up in rr: hdwy 1/2-way: rdn to chse ldrs over 3f out: drvn 2f out and sn btn* **12/1**	55
1202	6	2 ¼	**Dan Buoy (FR)**[13] 2814 7-8-7 **70** ....(b) BillyCray(5) 4 (R C Guest) *led and sn wl clr: stdd 1/2-way: rdn and qcknd 5f out: drvn 3f out: hdd 2f out and sn wknd* **11/2**[3]	59
32-0	7	30	**Mith Hill**[22] 2541 9-9-6 **78** ....(p) TadhgO'Shea 2 (Ian Williams) *chsd clr ldr: tk clsr order 1/2-way: cl up over 5f out: rdn along 4f out: sn wknd and bhd fnl 2f* **8/1**	34

3m 54.62s (-1.58) **Going Correction** -0.05s/f (Good)
WFA 4 from 5yo+ 1lb — 7 Ran SP% **111.6**
Speed ratings (Par 105): **101,100,97,96,94 93,79**
Tote Swingers: 1&2 £6.40, 1&3 £5.50, 2&3 £7.70 CSF £47.34 TOTE £3.10: £2.20, £7.70; EX 55.70.
Owner Ron Stepney **Bred** Minster Enterprises Ltd **Trained** Little Newcastle, Pembrokes
■ Stewards' Enquiry : Kieren Fallon caution; use of whip
Eddie Ahern two-day ban: used whip without giving mount sufficient time to respond

FOCUS
A fair staying handicap run at a good pace, courtesy of Dan Buoy.
Mith Hill Official explanation: jockey said gelding finished lame

3242 BET ON WORLD CUP AT TOTESPORT.COM MAIDEN STKS — 1m 4f 8y
4:40 (4:42) (Class 5) 3-Y-O £2,914 (£867; £433; £216) Stalls Low

Form			Horse	RPR
5	1		**Rhyton (IRE)**[27] 2390 3-9-3 0 .... RichardMullen 2 (Sir Michael Stoute) *trckd ldrs: pushed along 4f out: rdn 3f out: outpcd 2f out: swtchd rt and drvn over 1f out: styd on strly ins fnl f: led on line* **6/4**[1]	67+
4020	2	nse	**Sharakti (IRE)**[7] 2993 3-8-12 57 .... DeclanCannon(5) 4 (A J McCabe) *trckd ldrs: hdwy on outer to ld over 2f out and sn rdn clr: drvn ins fnl f: hdd on line* **13/2**	67
0-02	3	8	**Yankee Bright (USA)**[16] 2697 3-8-12 70 .... PaulMulrennan 5 (J G Given) *trckd ldr: effrt and cl up 3f out: rdn to chse ldr wl over 1f out: drvn whn rdr dropped reins ent fnl f: sn one pce* **5/2**[2]	52
0	4	13	**Fuzzypeg (IRE)**[7] 2994 3-8-12 0 .... EddieAhern 7 (J R Fanshawe) *trckd ldrs: rdn along over 3f out and sn outpcd* **7/2**[3]	28
00	5	6	**Quitao (GER)**[16] 2697 3-9-3 0 .... GregFairley 3 (M Johnston) *led: rdn along over 3f out: hdd over 2f out and wknd qckly* **22/1**	24
0	6	30	**Tobermory Boy**[11] 2860 3-9-3 0 ....(p) LeeVickers 1 (J G Given) *s.i.s: a in rr: bhd fnl 3f* **40/1**	—
0	7	1 ¼	**Suleimah**[19] 2627 3-8-12 0 .... AndrewElliott 6 (C J Teague) *s.i.s: a in rr: bhd fnl 3f* **50/1**	—

2m 40.0s (-0.80) **Going Correction** -0.05s/f (Good) — 7 Ran SP% **112.9**
Speed ratings (Par 99): **100,99,94,85,81 61,61**
Tote Swingers: 1&2 £2.90, 1&3 £2.00, 2&3 £2.50 CSF £11.61 TOTE £2.60: £1.50, £3.50; EX 14.50.
Owner Ballymacoll Stud **Bred** Ballymacoll Stud Farm Ltd **Trained** Newmarket, Suffolk

FOCUS
A weak maiden and a couple of the more fancied contenders performed below expectations. If the runner-up, officially rated only 57, is a reliable guide then Rhyton only improved slightly on the moderate form he showed on debut.

3243 40 LIVE FOOTBALL MARKETS AT TOTESPORT.COM H'CAP — 6f
5:10 (5:10) (Class 5) (0-75,78) 3-Y-O £2,914 (£867; £433; £216) Stalls Low

Form			Horse	RPR
1630	1		**Tamarind Hill (IRE)**[6] 3030 3-8-2 **61** ....(b) DeclanCannon(5) 3 (A J McCabe) *led 2f: led again 1/2-way rdn wl over 1f out: drvn and hung rt ins fnl f: hld on gamely* **8/1**	64
-634	2	½	**We'll Deal Again**[15] 2768 3-8-6 **65** .... JamesSullivan(5) 9 (M W Easterby) *hld up in tch: hdwy 2f out: rdn and bmpd over 1f out: drvn to chal and hmpd ins fnl f: kpt on wl towards fin* **10/3**[2]	67
0-64	3	1	**Saxby (IRE)**[59] 1488 3-9-0 **68** ....(p) SilvestreDeSousa 1 (G A Harker) *cl up on inner: effrt 2f out: sn rdn and ev ch tl drvn: edgd rt and nt qckn wl ins fnl f* **4/1**[3]	67
4452	4	1	**Mon Brav**[13] 2824 3-9-10 **78** ....(v[1]) JamieSpencer 11 (D Carroll) *chsd ldrs: rdn along 2f out: drvn and edgd rt over 1f out: sn one pce* **15/8**[1]	73
4-00	5	¾	**Bubbelas**[16] 2702 3-8-0 **59** ow1..........(v[1]) IanBrennan(5) 4 (J J Quinn) *towards rr: hdwy on inner wl over 1f out: sn rdn and kpt on ins fnl f: nrst fin* **12/1**	52
6-00	6	3	**Fair Bunny**[16] 2700 3-8-6 **60** .... AndrewElliott 6 (A D Brown) *chsd ldrs: rdn along wl over 1f out: grad wknd* **20/1**	43
-000	7	1 ¾	**Scarboro Warning (IRE)**[12] 2834 3-8-9 **68** ow5.......... JamesO'Reilly(5) 7 (J O'Reilly) *a towards rr* **28/1**	46
3446	8	5	**Penrod Ballantyne (IRE)**[93] 932 3-8-6 **65** .... MarkCoumbe(5) 5 (A Berry) *dwlt a in rr* **50/1**	27
0350	9	8	**Bossy Kitty**[15] 2768 3-9-5 **73** .... EddieAhern 8 (N Tinkler) *in tch: effrt and sme hdwy over 2f out: sn rdn and wknd* **7/1**	9
360-	10	8	**On The Bounty**[283] 5795 3-9-0 **68** .... TonyCulhane 10 (P T Midgley) *cl up: led after 2f: hdd 1/2-way: cl up and rdn along over 2f out and sn wknd* **33/1**	—

1m 16.97s (0.07) **Going Correction** -0.05s/f (Good) — 10 Ran SP% **122.3**
Speed ratings (Par 99): **97,96,95,93,92 88,86,79,69,58**
Tote Swingers: 1&2 £9.00, 1&3 £9.10, 2&3 £5.30 CSF £35.46 CT £129.80 TOTE £10.00: £3.00, £1.70, £1.70; EX 45.10 Trifecta £160.60 Pool: £362.58 - 1.67 winning units.Place 6: £195.01 Place 5: £165.83.
Owner A C Timms **Bred** Ballylinch Stud **Trained** Averham Park, Notts
■ Stewards' Enquiry : Declan Cannon two-day ban; careless riding (4th-5th) July

FOCUS
A modest sprint handicap and only fractionally quicker the the 2-y-os.
Tamarind Hill(IRE) Official explanation: trainer said regarding apperent improvement gelding was suited by faster ground
T/Plt: £164.80 to a £1 stake. Pool:£65,512.94 - 290.05 winning tickets T/Qpdt: £8.90 to a £1 stake. Pool:£4,854.18 - 402.75 winning tickets JR

3244 - 3250a (Foreign Racing) - See Raceform Interactive

DORTMUND (R-H)
Sunday, June 20

OFFICIAL GOING: Turf: good

3251a GROSSER PREIS DER WIRTSCHAFT (GROUP 3) (3YO+) (TURF) 1m 2f
4:45 (4:50) 3-Y-O+
£28,318 (£9,734; £4,867; £2,654; £1,769; £1,327)

RPR
1 2 **Norderney (GER)**[42] 1956 4-9-2 0 AStarke 1 104
(P Schiergen, Germany) *racd in midfield: travelling smoothly: moved forward arnd fnl turn: r.o wl in st: hld on wl for 2nd ins fnl f: fin 2nd: plcd 1st* **3/1**[3]
2 nse **Scolari**[19] 5-9-1 0 ChristopheSoumillon 6 99
(T Mundry, Germany) *racd promly bhd ldrs: gd prog through fnl turn: qcknd wl in st on outside: running on wl and looked probable wnr whn suffering serious interference fr Illo ins fnl f: unlucky: fin 3rd: plcd 2nd* **2/1**[2]
3 **Illo (GER)**[42] 4-9-3 0 ADeVries 7 105
(J Hirschberger, Germany) *t.k.h in 3rd fr s: r.o wl in st: led 1 1/2f out: wandered off st line and interfered w Scolari ins fnl f: fin 1st: disqualified and plcd 3rd* **8/5**[1]
4 1 3/4 **Zaungast (IRE)**[333] 6-9-1 0 THellier 5 95
(W Hickst, Germany) *racd in 6th: shkn up ent st: r.o wl* **53/10**
5 nk **Alianthus (GER)**[22] 2559 5-9-1 0 SHellyn 9 95
(J Hirschberger, Germany) *broke wl and sn established clr ld: r.o wl in st but outpcd* **98/10**
6 2 **Il Divo (GER)**[42] 5-9-1 0 JBojko 4 91
(A Wohler, Germany) *broke wl: settled bhd ldr: hrd rdn in st but no imp clsng stages* **29/1**
7 1 1/2 **Serienhoehe (IRE)**[15] 4-9-0 0 FilipMinarik 3 87
(P Schiergen, Germany) *bkmarker fr s: nvr figured* **172/10**
8 7 **Torres (GER)**[70] 1251 4-9-1 0 (b) EFrank 2 74
(Frau E Mader, Germany) *a towards the rr: nvr figured* **35/1**

2m 3.10s (123.10) **8** Ran SP% **133.5**
WIN (incl. 10 euro stake): 40. PLACES: 10, 10, 10. SF: 245.
Owner Gestut Bona **Bred** Gestut Bona **Trained** Germany

3019 SAN SIRO (R-H)
Sunday, June 20

OFFICIAL GOING: Turf: very soft

3253a PREMIO PRIMI PASSI (GROUP 3) (2YO) (TURF) 6f
3:45 (12:00) 2-Y-O **£35,398** (£15,575; £8,495; £4,247)

RPR
1 **Blu Constellation (ITY)** 2-8-11 0 MircoDemuro 3 103
(Vittorio Caruso, Italy) *broke wl: w ldrs for 2f: lened to ld at 1/2-way: travelling wl ent fnl 2f: rdn fnl f: a in command* **5/2**[2]
2 1 1/4 **Avatar Day (USA)** 2-8-11 0 LManiezzi 7 99
(R Menichetti, Italy) *slowly away: settled in rr on outer: produced wd 3f out: prog to 4th at 2f mark: styd on u.p fnl f* **81/10**
3 2 1/4 **Step Up (ITY)**[18] 2-8-11 0 CDemuro 1 93
(A Candi, Italy) *stdd s on inner to trck eventual wnr: rdn and prog to move 2nd 2f out: hrd rdn and no rspnse fnl f* **21/10**[1]
4 2 1/2 **Free Winner (IRE)**[18] 2-8-11 0 DVargiu 6 85
(B Grizzetti, Italy) *broke wl to ld tl 1 1/2-way: rdn to stay in tch 2 1/2f out: no ex whn hrd rdn fnl f* **16/5**
5 8 **King's Omaha (IRE)** 2-8-11 0 SLandi 4 61
(A Peraino, Italy) *broke wl and prom for 2f: ct for pce 3 1/2f out: hrd rdn and no ex ent fnl 2f: eased fnl f* **15/1**
6 2 **Bolagio** 2-8-11 0 MEsposito 5 55
(Gabriele Miliani, Italy) *broke wl: stdd to r in rr: rdn 3 1/2f out and sn no ex: eased fnl 1 1/2f* **34/1**
7 10 **Way To Fly (IRE)**[18] 2-8-11 0 FabioBranca 8 25
(S Botti, Italy) *broke wl on outer to r w ldrs first 2f: rdn to stay in tch fnl 3f: hrd rdn and sn wknd: eased fnl 2f* **29/10**[3]

1m 14.0s (2.20) **7** Ran SP% **130.4**
WIN (incl. 1 euro stake): 3.50. PLACES: 1.58, 2.10, 1.37. DF: 12.14.
Owner Incolinx **Bred** Azienda Agricola Loreto Luciani **Trained** Italy

2918 CHEPSTOW (L-H)
Monday, June 21

OFFICIAL GOING: Good (good to firm in places; 8.2)
Wind: Mild breeze, across Weather: Fine and sunny

3254 WYVERN ICES H'CAP 6f 16y
6:50 (6:50) (Class 5) (0-70,68) 3-Y-O+ **£2,914** (£867; £433; £216) **Stalls High**

Form RPR
0000 1 **Blue Aura (IRE)**[12] 2866 7-8-10 **55** DeanHeslop(5) 1 65
(B G Powell) *sn prom: led over 2f out: sn hrd pressed and rdn: hld on wl fnl f: drvn out* **25/1**
3342 2 1/2 **Sermons Mount (USA)**[10] 2919 4-9-6 **60** (v1) TravisBlock 5 68
(Mouse Hamilton-Fairley) *untidy leaving stalls: sn led on stands' side rails: hdd over 2f out: sn rdn and kpt pressing wnr: kpt on but no ex ins fnl f* **9/2**[2]
3000 3 1 3/4 **Stamford Blue**[13] 2840 9-8-10 **57** (b) JakePayne(7) 12 59
(R A Harris) *chsd ldrs: rdn over 2f out: kpt on but nt pce to chal front pair* **22/1**
322 4 hd **Miss Firefly**[40] 2026 5-9-6 **60** GeorgeBaker 9 62
(R J Hodges) *hld up towards rr: hdwy u.p fr wl over 1f out: styd on same pce ins fnl f* **10/1**
-000 5 hd **Abhainn (IRE)**[21] 2589 4-9-0 **54** J-PGuillambert 13 55
(B Palling) *mid-div: rdn wl over 2f out: kpt on ins fnl f: nrst fin* **14/1**
6103 6 1 1/2 **Plumage**[4] 3115 5-9-4 **63** LeeNewnes(5) 14 59
(Miss Tor Sturgis) *hld up towards rr: rdn and hdwy over 1f out: styd on same pce fnl f* **15/2**
0054 7 1 **Avoncreek**[12] 2854 6-8-6 **49** oh4 KellyHarrison(3) 15 42
(B P J Baugh) *rrd leaving stalls: towards rr: nt clr run over 2f out and over 1f out: styd on fnl f: nvr a threat* **33/1**
23 8 hd **Nativity**[4] 3125 4-8-12 **55** JackDean(3) 11 47
(J L Spearing) *dwlt: bhd: hdwy into midfield 4f out: rdn and no further imp fr 2f out* **5/1**[3]
0465 9 3 **Namir (IRE)**[9] 2957 8-9-6 **60** (b) DuranFentiman 3 43
(H J Evans) *mid-div in centre: wknd fnl f* **25/1**
1004 10 2 **Titus Gent**[6] 3057 5-9-9 **63** RichardThomas 4 39+
(R A Harris) *in tch: rdn over 3f out: wknd fnl f* **33/1**
0000 11 1 **Affirmatively**[25] 2456 5-8-4 **49** oh4 SophieDoyle(5) 7 22
(A W Carroll) *mid-div: hmpd s: rdn over 2f out: wknd over 1f out* **100/1**
0024 12 3/4 **What Katie Did (IRE)**[15] 2779 5-9-3 **57** (p) SteveDrowne 8 28
(J M Bradley) *wnt sltly lft s: racd keenly in tch: rdn over 2f out: sn wknd* **16/1**
13 4 **Teilionn**[29] 2366 4-9-10 **64** KierenFallon 6 22
(John Joseph Murphy, Ire) *hmpd sn after s: sn trcking ldrs: rdn over 2f out: lost action and eased fr over 1f out* **2/1**[1]
-000 14 dist **Ghost Dancer**[19] 2647 6-9-5 **62** (p) RussKennemore(3) 10 —
(J M Bradley) *sn outpcd: a towards rr: virtually p.u fnl 2f* **33/1**

1m 10.92s (-1.08) **Going Correction** -0.10s/f (Good) **14** Ran SP% **123.4**
Speed ratings (Par 103): **103,102,100,99,99 97,96,95,91,89 87,86,81,—**
toteswingers: 1&2 £27.10, 1&3 £44.80, 2&3 £57.90 CSF £131.20 CT £2640.01 TOTE £46.20: £15.10, £1.10, £4.40; EX 322.10.
Owner D & J Newell **Bred** Miss Mary Davison **Trained** Upper Lambourn, Berks

FOCUS
Prominent runners dominated, with the first two disputing it throughout and the third never far behind them. The runner-up sets the level rated to previous his course mark.
Plumage Official explanation: jockey said that the mare missed the break
Avoncreek Official explanation: jockey said that the gelding reared up as the stalls opened
Namir(IRE) Official explanation: jockey said that the gelding clipped heels
Titus Gent Official explanation: jockey said that the gelding was denied a clear run
Teilionn Official explanation: jockey said that the gelding lost its action
Ghost Dancer Official explanation: vet said gelding was lame

3255 JAGGER AND WOODY'S REAL RADIO BREAKFAST 105-106FM H'CAP 5f 16y
7:20 (7:20) (Class 6) (0-60,63) 3-Y-O+ **£1,942** (£578; £288; £144) **Stalls High**

Form RPR
006- 1 **The Jailer**[342] 3948 7-8-8 **47** oh1 ow1 RussKennemore(3) 10 63
(J G M O'Shea) *trckd ldrs: rdn to ld jst over 1f out: r.o wl: readily* **66/1**
3031 2 3 1/4 **Comptonspirit**[7] 3024 6-9-13 **63** 6ex J-PGuillambert 2 67
(B P J Baugh) *in tch: rdn to chse ldrs over 2f out: kpt on to chse wnr jst ins fnl f but a wl hld* **7/2**[1]
0000 3 nk **Blessed Place**[17] 2720 10-8-8 **47** JackDean(3) 4 50
(D J S Ffrench Davis) *chsd ldrs: rdn over 2f out: disp 2nd ent fnl f: kpt on but no ex towards fin* **16/1**
4000 4 nk **Mazzola**[21] 2589 4-9-8 **58** (p) GeorgeBaker 1 60
(J M Bradley) *mid-div: rdn and hdwy 2f out: disp 2nd ent fnl f: no ex towards fin* **7/1**
0-02 5 hd **The Name Is Frank**[14] 2809 5-9-10 **60** (t) NeilChalmers 3 61
(Mark Gillard) *s.i.s: towards rr: rdn over 2f out: r.o fnl f: nrst fin* **6/1**
-002 6 3/4 **Island Legend (IRE)**[19] 2639 4-9-8 **58** (b) SteveDrowne 7 57
(J M Bradley) *little slowly away: sn led: rdn whn hdd jst over 1f out: one pce after* **11/1**
6222 7 1/2 **Spic 'n Span**[6] 3052 5-9-8 **58** (b) RichardThomas 8 55
(R A Harris) *t.k.h in mid-div: rdn 2f out: styng on but comf hld whn nt clr run towards fin* **11/2**[3]
60-0 8 1/2 **Wooden King (IRE)**[21] 2589 5-8-13 **49** (b1) MickyFenton 9 46
(M S Saunders) *s.i.s: towards rr: rdn 2f out: styng on but comf hld whn nt clr run towards fin* **17/2**
5305 9 3 3/4 **Ishipink**[21] 2584 3-7-13 **46** oh1 AmyBaker(5) 5 26
(R J Hodges) *mid-div: rdn over 2f out: wknd over 1f out* **33/1**
405 10 shd **Liel**[16] 2741 4-9-10 **60** KierenFallon 11 41
(B J Meehan) *sn struggling: a towards rr* **9/2**[2]
32-0 11 1 1/2 **Jolly Ranch**[164] 79 4-8-13 **52** KellyHarrison(3) 6 28
(A G Newcombe) *trckd ldr: ev ch whn hung lft 2f out: sn wknd* **18/1**

58.77 secs (-0.53) **Going Correction** -0.10s/f (Good)
WFA 3 from 4yo+ 6lb **11** Ran SP% **117.0**
Speed ratings (Par 101): **100,94,94,93,93 92,91,90,84,84 82**
toteswingers: 1&2 £49.10, 1&3 £39.70, 2&3 £17.40 CSF £286.99 CT £4019.42 TOTE £74.10: £18.70, £1.10, £8.60; EX 392.40.
Owner N G H Ayliffe **Bred** D R Tucker **Trained** Elton, Gloucs

FOCUS
Again, it proved hard to come from too far back in this low-grade contest, even though the pace was strong.
Wooden King(IRE) Official explanation: jockey said that the gelding was denied a clear run

3256 REAL RADIO 105-106FM MAIDEN STKS 1m 4f 23y
7:50 (7:51) (Class 5) 3-Y-O+ **£2,590** (£770; £385; £192) **Stalls Low**

Form RPR
4 1 **Emerging Artist (FR)**[12] 2860 4-9-12 0 KierenFallon 3 88+
(M Johnston) *mde all: rdn 3f out: styd on strly to assert over 1f out: comf* **2/1**[2]
0023 2 2 **Never Can Tell (IRE)**[10] 2924 3-8-2 **75** SophieDoyle(5) 1 79
(J A Osborne) *trckd ldrs: rdn to chal 3f out tl over 1f out: sn hung lft and hld but kpt on for clr 2nd* **7/1**[3]
3 2 3/4 **Royal Riviera**[198] 4-9-12 0 SteveDrowne 8 80
(J R Gask) *hld up bhd ldrs: hdwy 3f out: sn rdn: styd on to go 3rd ins fnl f: nvr trbld front pair* **12/1**
-622 4 3/4 **Bombadero (IRE)**[31] 2281 3-8-12 **82** IanMongan 9 79
(J L Dunlop) *trckd wnr: jnd wnr 5f out: rdn and ev ch 3f out: one pce fr wl over 1f out: lost 3rd ins fnl f* **1/1**[1]
5 9 **Mhilu (IRE)**[11] 8-9-9 0 (bt) RussKennemore(3) 5 64
(J G M O'Shea) *s.i.s: in tch: rdn over 3f out: wknd over 2f out* **25/1**
6 7 **Genes Of A Dancer (AUS)** 4-9-7 0 GeorgeBaker 6 48
(M Appleby) *trckd ldrs: rdn over 4f out: wknd over 2f out* **50/1**

5 7 *nk* **Shannon Falls (FR)**[124] 585 6-9-7 0 .... MickyFenton 10 48
(Miss Jo Crowley) *dwlt bdly: a last* **40/1**
2m 37.77s (-1.23) **Going Correction** -0.10s/f (Good)
WFA 3 from 4yo+ 14lb 7 Ran SP% **111.8**
Speed ratings (Par 103): **100,98,96,96,90 85,85**
toteswingers: 1&2 £2.20, 1&3 £5.90, 2&3 £5.60 CSF £15.18 TOTE £3.40: £2.70, £2.00; EX 10.00.
Owner Sheikh Hamdan Bin Mohammed Al Maktoum **Bred** Gainsborough Stud Management Ltd **Trained** Middleham Moor, N Yorks

FOCUS
A maiden containing some fair late-maturing types. The pace was modest, giving the winner the run of the race under a well-judged ride. The form is slightly muddling but is rated at face value through the runner-up to his latest mark.

3257 MOBILE CATERING GROUP H'CAP 1m 2f 36y
8:20 (8:21) (Class 5) (0-75,72) 4-Y-0+ **£3,238** (£963; £481; £240) **Stalls** Low

Form RPR
54-0 **1** **Sagredo (USA)**[18] 2685 6-9-4 **69** .... GeorgeBaker 1 80
(Jonjo O'Neill) *hld up: hdwy 3f out: rdn to chal over 1f out: led ins fnl f: styd on wl: rdn out* **15/2**
2 *1* **Born To Excel**[19] 2664 4-8-13 **64** .... KierenFallon 6 73
(John Joseph Murphy, Ire) *led: rn sltly wd ent st: rdn and edgd rt fr 2f out: hdd ins fnl f: no ex* **15/8**[1]
4314 **3** *2 ¾* **Sunny Future (IRE)**[17] 2690 4-9-5 **70** .... IanMongan 5 73
(M S Saunders) *hld up: rdn and hdwy over 2f out: briefly chal over 1f out: kpt on same pce* **2/1**[2]
03 **4** *3* **Ocean Transit (IRE)**[10] 2922 5-9-3 **71** .... RussKennemore(3) 4 68
(R J Price) *trckd ldrs: rdn over 2f out: sn one pce* **15/2**
3106 **5** *7* **Make Amends (IRE)**[10] 2922 5-9-6 **71** .... SteveDrowne 3 54
(R J Hodges) *s.i.s: pushed along and hdwy to trck ldr after 2f: rdn over 2f out: fdd over 1f out* **9/2**[3]
6300 **6** *1 ¾* **Mr Udagawa**[10] 2922 4-9-2 **67** .... MickyFenton 2 47
(B J Llewellyn) *chsd ldrs: rdn wl over 2f out: fdd over 1f out* **16/1**
2m 8.45s (-2.15) **Going Correction** -0.10s/f (Good) 6 Ran SP% **115.7**
Speed ratings (Par 103): **104,103,101,98,93 91**
toteswingers: 1&2 £8.20, 1&3 £1.10, 2&3 £1.60 CSF £22.93 TOTE £13.50: £9.80, £1.10; EX 17.20.
Owner John P McManus **Bred** Dr Catherine Wills **Trained** Cheltenham, Gloucs

FOCUS
A decent pace helped the hold-up runners but the long-time leader did well to hold on for second. The third is the best guide to the level.
Born To Excel Official explanation: jockey said that the gelding hung right throughout

3258 LINDLEY CATERING MAIDEN STKS 1m 14y
8:50 (8:51) (Class 5) 3-Y-0+ **£2,590** (£770; £385; £192) **Stalls** High

Form RPR
0- **1** **Cotswold Village (AUS)**[215] 7439 4-9-6 0 .... NeilChalmers 8 73
(M Appleby) *mde virtually all: hrd pressed fr over 2f out: kpt on gamely w narrow advantage: hld on wl: all out* **66/1**
06 **2** *hd* **Ancient Greece**[21] 2585 3-9-2 0 .... DaraghO'Donohoe 3 77
(George Baker) *pressed wnr: led briefly 3f out: rdn over 2f out: str chal thrght fnl f: kpt on: jst hld* **16/1**
5 **3** *2* **Wise Up**[23] 2548 3-9-2 0 .... GeorgeBaker 4 72
(B W Hills) *trckd ldrs: rdn 2f out: nt pce to mount chal: 3rd and hld whn hung rt towards fin* **13/8**[1]
0-36 **4** *2 ¼* **Lathaat**[21] 2603 3-8-11 77 .... TadhgO'Shea 5 62
(J L Dunlop) *w wnr: rdn over 2f out: sn one pce and btn* **7/2**[3]
5 *½* **Amity (IRE)** 3-8-11 0 .... KierenFallon 2 61
(M Johnston) *awkward leaving stalls: racd in 6th in tch: effrt 3f out: one pce fnl 2f* **2/1**[2]
00-0 **6** *14* **Little Buddy**[8] 2994 3-8-13 0 .... RussKennemore(3) 6 34
(R J Price) *restrained bhd ldrs: rdn 3f out: wknd 2f out* **80/1**
7 *6* **Dark Shines** 3-9-2 0 .... SteveDrowne 1 20
(B R Millman) *wnt lft and slowly away: racd green: a bhd* **10/1**
1m 39.84s (3.64) **Going Correction** -0.10s/f (Good)
WFA 3 from 4yo 10lb 7 Ran SP% **111.4**
Speed ratings (Par 103): **77,76,74,72,72 58,52**
toteswingers: 1&2 £21.10, 1&3 £15.50, 2&3 £5.50 CSF £774.79 TOTE £29.20: £9.80, £8.10; EX 128.30.
Owner Colin Rogers **Bred** C Rogers **Trained** Compton Verney, Warwicks

FOCUS
The second shock result on the card but the first two deserved their evening in the spotlight even though this looked a modest maiden. Some big owners had to be content with third, fourth and fifth places, with their representatives all beaten a surprisingly long way out. The form is rated negatively with the third to debut form.

3259 LINDLEY CATERING CLASSIFIED STKS 1m 14y
9:20 (9:20) (Class 5) 3-Y-0 **£2,914** (£867; £433; £216) **Stalls** High

Form RPR
-123 **1** **The Shuffler**[28] 2398 3-9-0 68 .... GeorgeBaker 8 72
(G L Moore) *trckd ldrs: rdn and r.o ent fnl f: led towards fin: hld on: all out* **6/4**[1]
4056 **2** *hd* **White Dart**[21] 2587 3-9-0 68 .... SamHitchcott 9 71
(M R Channon) *hld up: pushed along and no immediate imp 2f out: hrd rdn and prog ent fnl f: r.o wl fnl 100yds: jst failed* **7/2**[2]
4-00 **3** *½* **Wild Rockette**[11] 2888 3-9-0 70 .... (b[1]) TadhgO'Shea 7 70
(B J Meehan) *in tch: chal 3f out: sn rdn: led over 1f out: no ex whn hdd towards fin* **7/1**
444- **4** *1 ¾* **Santa Margherita**[249] 6786 3-9-0 68 .... MickyFenton 5 66
(H J L Dunlop) *sn led: rdn and hung lft fr 2f out: hdd over 1f out: kpt on same pce* **20/1**
5-56 **5** *3 ¼* **Al Jaadi**[18] 2674 3-9-0 70 .... J-PGuillambert 2 59
(W Jarvis) *plld v hrd: prom: rdn 3f out: wknd ins fnl f* **8/1**
4426 **6** *4* **Omaruru (IRE)**[21] 2607 3-9-0 70 .... KierenFallon 1 49
(M Johnston) *prom: rdn 3f out: wknd over 1f out* **6/1**[3]
44-3 **7** *25* **Ever So Bold**[17] 2725 3-8-9 67 .... (b) SophieDoyle(5) 4 —
(W R Muir) *squeezed up s: hld up in tch: rdn over 3f out: wknd over 2f out* **10/1**
1m 35.59s (-0.61) **Going Correction** -0.10s/f (Good) 7 Ran SP% **114.0**
Speed ratings (Par 99): **99,98,98,96,93 89,64**
toteswingers: 1&2 £4.60, 1&3 £2.20, 2&3 £9.10 CSF £6.78 TOTE £2.50: £1.90, £1.90; EX 10.30 Place 6 £2,714.91, Place 5 £552.28.
Owner Heart Of The South Racing **Bred** John And Caroline Penny **Trained** Lower Beeding, W Sussex

FOCUS
The seven runners were well matched on official ratings. There was a weak pace until halfway, with several hard pullers, then a significant increase that quickly had most off the bridle. The form rated through the runner-up to latest course form.
Ever So Bold Official explanation: jockey said that the gelding lost its action
T/Plt: £50,362.40 to a £1 stake. Pool: £72,439.16. 1.05 winning tickets. T/Qpdt: £263.60 to a £1 stake. Pool: £5,200.79. 14.60 winning tickets. TM

3209 LINGFIELD (L-H)
Monday, June 21

OFFICIAL GOING: Turf course - good to firm (firm in places; 8.9); all-weather: standard
Wind: Nil Weather: Overcast, warm

3260 EUROPEAN BREEDERS' FUND MAIDEN FILLIES' STKS 5f (P)
2:15 (2:16) (Class 5) 2-Y-0 **£3,561** (£1,059; £529; £264) **Stalls** High

Form RPR
44 **1** **Miss Clairton**[17] 2693 2-9-0 0 .... StevieDonohoe 4 76+
(Sir Mark Prescott) *mde all: rdn and c towards centre st: drvn ent fnl f: styd on wl and drew clr fnl 100yds: won gng away* **15/8**[2]
223 **2** *1 ¼* **Jambo Bibi (IRE)**[19] 2642 2-9-0 0 .... PatDobbs 2 71
(R Hannon) *trckd ldrs: chsd wnr wl over 1f out: effrt to chal and rdn 1f out: fnd little u.p and btn fnl 100yds* **4/6**[1]
3 *3 ¼* **Loved To Bits** 2-9-0 0 .... FergusSweeney 1 59+
(P J Makin) *s.i.s: hdwy into midfield after 1f: swtchd rt and rdn over 2f out: chsd ldng pair jst ins 1f out: no imp and wl hld after* **14/1**
00 **4** *2 ¾* **Alltherightmoves (IRE)**[9] 2958 2-9-0 0 .... (b[1]) TomQueally 8 49
(Eve Johnson Houghton) *chsd ldrs: wnt 2nd 3f out tl wl over 1f out: hung lft and btn 1f out: wknd fnl f* **33/1**
000 **5** *1* **Majestic Style (IRE)**[41] 1999 2-9-0 0 .... JimCrowley 5 46
(A P Jarvis) *chsd wnr tl 3f out: wknd qckly u.p ent fnl 2f: wl btn after* **40/1**
6 *hd* **Jameela Girl** 2-9-0 0 .... EddieAhern 7 45
(R M H Cowell) *s.i.s: racd in last pair: outpcd and wd bnd 2f out: kpt on ins fnl f: n.d* **14/1**
7 *½* **Arakova (IRE)** 2-9-0 0 .... NeilCallan 3 43
(Matthew Salaman) *s.i.s: sn rdn along and in midfield: struggling and lost tch over 2f out* **12/1**[3]
0 **8** *10* **Zafrina**[19] 2641 2-9-0 0 .... AdrianMcCarthy 6 7
(Peter Grayson) *s.i.s: sn rdn and flashing tail: a in rr: lost tch wl over 2f out* **66/1**
60.26 secs (1.46) **Going Correction** +0.275s/f (Slow) 8 Ran SP% **122.7**
Speed ratings (Par 90): **99,97,91,87,85 85,84,68**
toteswingers: 1&2 £1.20, 1&3 £3.90, 2&3 £2.90 CSF £3.71 TOTE £3.60: £1.20, £1.02, £3.30; EX 4.30 Trifecta £25.40 Pool: £763.96 - 22.23 winning units..
Owner Mrs June Rooney **Bred** Grove Farm Stud **Trained** Newmarket, Suffolk

FOCUS
The two market leaders pulled clear of the rest in this ordinary fillies' maiden. The runner-up is not progressing but remains the best guide to this.

NOTEBOOK
Miss Clairton, fourth in a pair of 5f maidens at Catterick, had a bit to find with the hot favourite but put in a feisty front-running display to get off the mark on her AW debut. A sister to smart seven-time 6f-7f winner Prince Aaron, she is steadily improving with practice and looks a genuine type. (op 5-2 tchd 3-1)
Jambo Bibi(IRE) set the standard on her three placed efforts in fair AW maidens. Things looked to be going smoothly for a long way dropped back to 5f but she didn't find as much as expected when ranging up alongside the pacesetter at the furlong pole and was comfortably outgunned. (op 8-13 tchd 8-11)
Loved To Bits showed signs of inexperience before doing some late work on debut. Her dam was placed at 5f-6f but her sire will have imparted some stamina and she should do better with time and distance. (op 16-1)
Alltherightmoves(IRE) lasted a bit longer dropped in trip on her AW debut with first-time blinkers tried. She is a half-sister to numerous winners at 5f-1m3f and this run suggests her trainer has something to work with. (op 40-1)
Jameela Girl was nibbled at in the betting and showed a glimmer of promise, staying on from a long way back on debut over a trip on the sharp side on pedigree. (op 16-1 tchd 12-1)
Arakova(IRE) attracted some support at big prices in the morning but she ran green and was never in the hunt on debut. (op 16-1 tchd 11-1)

3261 KIER H'CAP 5f (P)
2:45 (2:45) (Class 3) (0-90,89) 3-Y-0+ **£8,418** (£2,505; £1,251; £625) **Stalls** High

Form RPR
4116 **1** **Captain Carey**[10] 2940 4-10-0 **89** .... RobertWinston 7 99+
(M S Saunders) *in tch towards rr on outer: rdn along over 2f out: hung rt and wd bnd 2f out: hdwy ent fnl f: r.o wl to ld wl ins fnl f* **2/1**[1]
1200 **2** *½* **Bajan Tryst (USA)**[16] 2745 4-9-12 **87** .... NeilCallan 9 95
(K A Ryan) *chsd ldrs: rdn to chal over 1f out: led 1f out: hdd and no ex wl ins fnl f* **14/1**
1-11 **3** *½* **Sutton Veny (IRE)**[117] 679 4-9-7 **82** .... TomQueally 1 88
(J R Gask) *led: rdn over 1f out: hdd 1f out: kpt on but unable qck fnl 100yds* **7/1**
1130 **4** *¾* **Master Lightfoot**[18] 2681 4-9-3 **78** .... EddieAhern 5 81
(W R Swinburn) *wl in tch: rdn and no prog wl over 1f out: swtchd rt and kpt on ins fnl f* **13/2**
01-0 **5** *½* **Doric Lady**[50] 1727 5-9-6 **81** .... RobertHavlin 6 89+
(J A R Toller) *hld up wl in tch in last: hdwy ent fnl f: gap clsd and nt clr run ins fnl f tl swtchd lft wl ins fnl f: nt clr run again towards fin: nvr able to chal* **6/1**[3]
0-14 **6** *½* **Orange Pip**[29] 2364 5-9-5 **80** .... JimmyFortune 3 80
(P J Makin) *taken down early: w ldrs on outer: ev ch and rdn wl over 1f out: wknd ins fnl f: btn whn n.m.r wl ins fnl f* **7/1**
6066 **7** *½* **Garstang**[11] 2883 7-8-11 **72** .... (b) AlanMunro 4 70
(J Balding) *hld up wl in tch in last trio: rdn and effrt on inner to press ldrs over 1f out: no ex and btn ins fnl f* **20/1**
-303 **8** *5* **Russian Spirit**[8] 2997 4-9-8 **83** .... PhilipRobinson 2 63
(M A Jarvis) *w ldrs tl over 2f out: struggling ent fnl 2f: wl btn 1f out* **5/1**[2]
59.22 secs (0.42) **Going Correction** +0.275s/f (Slow) 8 Ran SP% **114.0**
Speed ratings (Par 107): **107,106,105,104,103 102,101,93**
toteswingers: 1&2 £8.50, 1&3 £2.90, 2&3 £10.50 CSF £32.70 CT £166.19 TOTE £2.30: £1.10, £7.30, £1.70; EX 34.80 Trifecta £329.30 Pool: £462.89 - 1.04 winning units..
Owner M S Saunders **Bred** B Walters **Trained** Green Ore, Somerset

FOCUS
A decent sprint handicap. They finished in a bunch and there was one hard-luck story but the form is probably reasonably sound with the placed horses close to their marks.

NOTEBOOK

Captain Carey was never dangerous in a hat-trick bid at York last time but nothing really got into that race from behind. The pace in this race was not particularly strong and he was forced wide for most of the way, but he found a sharp finishing burst in the closing stages to land a gamble and improve his career record to 6-17. This win will take his mark into the 90s and life will be tougher in a higher grade next time, but he is a likeable, powerfully built sprinter who may be able to strike again. (op 7-2)

Bajan Tryst(USA) put in a big run switched to slightly more patient tactics than usual. He is not the easiest to predict but hammered his rivals in a 6f Wolverhampton handicap in February and should be able to gain compensation for this close call. (op 9-1 tchd 16-1)

Sutton Veny(IRE) has been highly progressive under forcing tactics on Polytrack during the winter and completed a hat-trick in a Kempton handicap when last seen in February. She came up a bit short in her bid for a four-timer but she could never really dominate in a race littered with confirmed front-runners and emerges with credit on return from 117 days off. (op 11-2 tchd 5-1)

Master Lightfoot also put in a solid run under a fairly prominent ride. He has had a profitable time since November and is holding his form well. He was reported to have lost a left-fore shoe. Official explanation: vet said colt lost a left-fore shoe (op 8-1 tchd 9-1)

Doric Lady was trapped behind rivals for most of the final furlong and looked unlucky. Unexposed on AW, she has registered five 5f-6f wins in her last 15 starts and could get back in the groove if finding gaps next time. Official explanation: jockey said mare was denied a clear run (op 13-2 tchd 11-2)

Orange Pip was in the firing line for a long way before fading in the closing stages. Official explanation: jockey said mare ran too free (op 6-1 tchd 11-2)

Russian Spirit was one of the first under pressure and was left well behind by the leading group. (op 4-1)

3262 QUANTEM CONSULTING H'CAP — 7f (P)
3:15 (3:15) (Class 4) (0-80,79) 4-Y-O+ **£5,828** (£1,734; £866; £432) **Stalls** Low

Form / RPR

-446 **1** **Cativo Cavallino**[30] 2331 7-8-0 **61** NataliaGemelova(3) 3 — 70
(J E Long) *chsd ldr tl led 2f out: edgd rt u.p ent fnl f: hld on wl fnl 100yds* **25/1**

1256 **2** *nk* **Copperwood**[16] 2750 5-8-11 **69** NeilCallan 1 — 77
(M Blanshard) *stdd after s: hld up in tch in rr: hdwy on bit to trck ldrs ent fnl f: rdn to chal wnr ins fnl f: hld towards fin* **13/2**[3]

1-50 **3** *1 1/4* **Cape Quarter (USA)**[16] 2750 4-8-2 **65** JohnFahy(5) 7 — 70
(W J Haggas) *hld up wl in tch: n.m.r bnd ent fnl 2f: hdwy and barging match w rival 1f out: no imp and kpt on same pce fnl 100yds* **5/1**[2]

0-11 **4** *1/2* **Aegean Shadow**[15] 2783 4-9-7 **79** TomQueally 6 — 82+
(H R A Cecil) *dwlt: sn trcking ldrs: gng wl whn nt clr run and c off worse in barging match w rival 1f out: unable to rcvr and one pce fnl 100yds* **10/11**[1]

2530 **5** *hd* **Shaded Edge**[16] 2736 6-8-12 **70** EddieAhern 9 — 73
(D W P Arbuthnot) *chsd ldrs: rdn to chse wnr wl over 1f out: no ex and one pce ins fnl f* **16/1**

0003 **6** *1 3/4* **Lodi (IRE)**[9] 2959 5-8-12 **70** (tp) J-PGuillambert 8 — 68
(J Akehurst) *stdd s: t.k.h: hld up in tch in last pair: effrt to chse ldrs over 1f out: btn and eased wl ins fnl f* **9/1**

0013 **7** *3* **Lady Kent (IRE)**[13] 2840 4-9-0 **72** StephenCraine 5 — 62
(J R Boyle) *v.s.a and lost many ls: grad clsd and in tch 5f out: hdwy on outer to chse ldrs 3f out: wknd over 1f out* **14/1**

1106 **8** *nk* **Waterloo Dock**[18] 2678 5-8-6 **64** GregFairley 2 — 53
(M Quinn) *led: rdn and hdd 2f out: wknd ent fnl f* **20/1**

1m 26.1s (1.30) **Going Correction** +0.275s/f (Slow) 8 Ran SP% **113.5**
Speed ratings (Par 105): **103,102,101,100,100 98,95,94**
toteswingers: 1&2 £17.10, 1&3 £11.20, 2&3 £4.50 CSF £174.60 CT £969.14 TOTE £27.20: £3.90, £1.80, £1.60; EX 230.60 Trifecta £389.40 Part won. Pool: £526.22 - 0.50 winning units..
Owner P Saxon **Bred** Miss A M Rees **Trained** Caterham, Surrey
■ Stewards' Enquiry : Natalia Gemelova one-day ban: used whip with exessive frequenct (July 5th)

FOCUS
A fair handicap, but it was a messy race and the form probably shouldn't be taken literally. The runner-up is rated to his best and sets the standard.
Lady Kent(IRE) Official explanation: jockey said filly was slowly away

3263 CUNDALL SUSTAINABLE ENGINEERING H'CAP (DIV I) — 1m 1f
3:45 (3:48) (Class 6) (0-55,55) 3-Y-O+ **£2,047** (£604; £302) **Stalls** Low

Form / RPR

0024 **1** **Under Fire (IRE)**[4] 3128 7-9-2 **49** NeilCallan 8 — 55
(A W Carroll) *chsd ldrs: wnt 2nd 5f out: rdn to ld wl over 2f out: drvn ent fnl 2f: kpt on wl fnl f* **15/8**[1]

-405 **2** *1/2* **Flyinflyout**[16] 2753 3-8-8 **55** ow1 (p) RobertLButler(3) 1 — 59
(Miss Sheena West) *t.k.h: led for 1f: chsd ldr tl 5f out: styd handy: rdn wl over 1f out: pressed wnr fnl f: one pce and hld towards fin* **12/1**

4000 **3** *3/4* **Bookiebasher Babe (IRE)**[35] 2172 5-9-2 **49** JerryO'Dwyer 11 — 52
(M Quinn) *chsd ldrs: hdwy to press ldrs over 3f out: rdn and chsd wnr 2f out tl ins fnl f: one pce fnl 100yds* **20/1**

0/04 **4** *3/4* **Aah Haa**[111] 763 5-9-3 **50** JimCrowley 4 — 52
(N J Gifford) *t.k.h: hld up towards rr: rdn and hdwy jst over 2f out: chsd ldrs and drvn ent fnl f: one pce fnl 150yds* **8/1**[3]

6205 **5** *shd* **Al Rayanah**[9] 2966 7-9-6 **53** (p) SaleemGolam 14 — 54
(G Prodromou) *dwlt and bustled along early: towards rr: hdwy 4f out: rdn over 2f out: chsd ldrs and drvn over 1f out: one pce and hld fnl f* **8/1**[3]

0-00 **6** *2 1/4* **Burnbrake**[27] 2417 5-9-8 **55** PatDobbs 2 — 52
(L Montague Hall) *hld up in last pair: hdwy and swtchd rt arnd wkng rival over 1f out: pushed along and kpt on ins fnl f: nvr trbld ldrs* **16/1**

0540 **7** *1* **Holyfield Warrior (IRE)**[9] 2955 6-8-13 **46** oh1 StevieDonohoe 12 — 40
(R J Smith) *wl in tch in midfield: rdn and unable qck wl over 2f out: no prog and wl hld fr over 1f out* **11/2**[2]

5-00 **8** *1* **Herecomethegirls**[41] 2006 4-9-0 **50** JackDean(3) 9 — 42
(W G M Turner) *dwlt and pushed along early: racd towards rr: rdn and wanting to hang lft fr over 2f out: nvr threatened ldrs* **25/1**

0004 **9** *1 1/2* **Clerical (USA)**[12] 2876 4-8-13 **46** oh1 (p) EddieAhern 6 — 35
(R M H Cowell) *chsd ldrs: rdn ent fnl 2f: wknd u.p over 1f out* **14/1**

0602 **10** *1 1/4* **Sparkle Park**[29] 2359 3-8-3 **47** (b) TadhgO'Shea 5 — 32
(B J Meehan) *led after 1f tl rdn and hdd wl over 2f out: wknd over 1f out* **9/1**

0000 **11** *3 1/2* **Haasem (USA)**[20] 2636 7-9-0 **47** (t) StephenCraine 7 — 25
(J R Jenkins) *stdd s: hld up towards rr: rdn and no prog wl over 1f out: nvr trbld ldrs* **33/1**

0-40 **12** *3 1/2* **Glan Y Mor (IRE)**[109] 793 3-8-8 **52** (t) SimonWhitworth 13 — 22
(F J Brennan) *awkward leaving stalls and v.s.a: a in rr and tail swishing thrght: nvr on terms* **33/1**

04U0 **13** *3 1/4* **Bertie Smalls**[19] 2655 4-8-13 **46** oh1 TedDurcan 3 — 10
(M H Tompkins) *in tch tl rdn and lost pl qckly 3f out: wl btn fnl 2f* **25/1**

1m 57.65s (1.05) **Going Correction** -0.05s/f (Good)
WFA 3 from 4yo+ 11lb 13 Ran SP% **121.0**
Speed ratings (Par 101): **93,92,91,91,91 89,88,87,86,84 81,78,75**
toteswingers: 1&2 £8.60, 1&3 £14.20, 2&3 £42.30 CSF £24.55 CT £366.75 TOTE £3.10: £1.60, £3.30, £6.70; EX 35.40 TRIFECTA Not won..
Owner Marita Bayley and Trevor Turner **Bred** Mrs Marita Bayley **Trained** Cropthorne, Worcs

FOCUS
A modest handicap run at a fair pace but slower than the second division. The form looks weak.

3264 CUNDALL SUSTAINABLE ENGINEERING H'CAP (DIV II) — 1m 1f
4:15 (4:18) (Class 6) (0-55,61) 3-Y-O+ **£2,047** (£604; £302) **Stalls** Low

Form / RPR

0-00 **1** **Eye Of Eternity**[20] 2632 3-8-3 **45** DavidProbert 8 — 57
(Rae Guest) *squeezed for room s: sn rdn to chse ldr: rdn to ld ent fnl 2f: sn clr: styd on and in n.d after* **25/1**

0060 **2** *2 3/4* **James Pollard (IRE)**[9] 2955 5-9-0 **45** (t) StevieDonohoe 14 — 52
(B J Llewellyn) *hld up off the pce in midfield: rdn and effrt over 2f out: chsd clr wnr jst over 1f out: kpt on but no real imp* **11/1**

0641 **3** *shd* **Dane Cottage**[4] 3113 3-8-12 **61** 6ex AdamBeschizza(7) 11 — 67
(Miss Gay Kelleway) *towards rr: pushed along over 6f out: hdwy on inner and nt clr run over 1f out: rdn and chalng for 2nd jst ins fnl f: kpt on: no ch w wnr* **15/8**[1]

06-5 **4** *4* **Mr Maximas**[65] 1392 3-8-6 **53** DeclanCannon(5) 10 — 50
(B Palling) *t.k.h early: rdn and one pce over 2f out: nt clr run and lost pl over 1f out: swtchd rt and styd on ins fnl f: no ch w wnr* **9/1**

-005 **5** *1 1/4* **Summers Target (USA)**[12] 2874 4-9-8 **53** (t) EddieAhern 2 — 48
(S C Williams) *hld up wl off the pce in last trio: hdwy over 1f out: kpt on ins fnl f: no ch* **8/1**[3]

0602 **6** *1* **Orsett Lad (USA)**[8] 3002 3-8-13 **55** RobertWinston 6 — 46
(J R Best) *chsd ldrs: rdn 3f out: chsd clr wnr over 1f out tl jst over 1f out: no imp: wknd fnl f* **7/2**[2]

541 **7** *1/2* **Inquisitress**[15] 2781 6-9-4 **49** NeilChalmers 9 — 41
(J J Bridger) *short of room and bmpd s: hld up wl off the pce in rr: rdn and effrt in centre wl over 2f out: no imp fnl 2f* **9/1**

65-4 **8** *2* **Chantilly Dancer (IRE)**[31] 2299 4-9-4 **49** GregFairley 13 — 37
(M Quinn) *chsd ldrs: rdn and unable qck 3f out: wl btn over 1f out* **16/1**

0-00 **9** *2 3/4* **Mystic Touch**[31] 2303 4-9-6 **51** (v[1]) RobertHavlin 12 — 32
(A B Haynes) *racd freely: led tl rdn and hdd ent fnl 2f: sn outpcd by wnr: wknd qckly over 1f out: wl btn fnl f* **25/1**

000- **10** *1 1/4* **Square Of Gold (FR)**[290] 5632 4-9-3 **48** NeilCallan 7 — 27
(A W Carroll) *t.k.h: chsd ldrs: rdn to chse clr wnr wl over 1f out tl over 1f out: sn wknd* **16/1**

500- **11** *hd* **Michelle (IRE)**[448] 1036 4-8-12 **46** RobertLButler(3) 3 — 24
(P Butler) *hld up in last pair: rdn and no prog over 2f out: sn lost tch* **100/1**

600- **12** *3* **Frosty's Gift**[34] 2794 6-9-0 **45** (b[1]) PatDobbs 5 — 17
(J C Fox) *hld up in rr: short of room 7f out: rdn and no prog wl over 2f out: lost tch 2f out* **100/1**

1m 56.25s (-0.35) **Going Correction** -0.05s/f (Good)
WFA 3 from 4yo+ 11lb 12 Ran SP% **117.9**
Speed ratings (Par 101): **99,96,96,92,91 90,90,88,86,85 84,82**
toteswingers: 1&2 £7.70, 1&3 £33.60, 2&3 £17.00 CSF £271.50 CT £784.34 TOTE £45.00: £9.30, £2.00, £1.80; EX 427.30 TRIFECTA Not won..
Owner Light Valley Stud **Bred** Light Valley Stud **Trained** Newmarket, Suffolk

FOCUS
The second division of an ordinary handicap and run faster than the first. The winner finished clear of the placed horses who were a long way ahead of the rest. The form looks sound wnough with those in the frame behind the winner close to their marks.
Eye Of Eternity Official explanation: trainer said, regarding apparent improvement in form, the filly was having its first run in a handicap, had a cross noseband fitted, and improved for being ridden more prominently

3265 KIER REGIONAL H'CAP — 1m 2f
4:45 (4:46) (Class 3) (0-95,89) 3-Y-O+ **£8,418** (£2,505; £1,251; £625) **Stalls** Low

Form / RPR

2663 **1** **Jutland**[9] 2969 3-8-5 **78** GregFairley 2 — 91
(M Johnston) *mde all: set stdy gallop tl qcknd over 2f out: rdn clr but hanging lft over 1f out: wl in command fnl f: eased towards fin* **5/2**[1]

2112 **2** *3* **King's Masque**[10] 2922 4-9-3 **78** DavidProbert 4 — 84
(B J Llewellyn) *t.k.h: chsd wnr thrght: rdn and tried to chal over 2f out: nt pce of wnr over 1f out: no ch w wnr fnl f: kpt on to hold 2nd nr fin* **7/1**

-431 **3** *nk* **Jawaab (IRE)**[16] 2739 6-9-4 **79** TedDurcan 1 — 84
(Mark Buckley) *t.k.h: trckd ldrs: shkn up and nt qckn 2f out: no prog and swtchd rt 1f out: kpt on fnl 100yds: pressing for 2nd nr fin: no threat to wnr* **17/2**

4-23 **4** *1/2* **Norwegian Dancer (UAE)**[30] 2314 4-9-8 **83** NeilCallan 3 — 87
(E S McMahon) *hld up in tch: effrt to chse ldrs and rdn 2f out: nt pce of wnr over 1f out: plugged on same pce fnl f* **7/1**

15-5 **5** *3* **Navy List (FR)**[37] 2125 3-8-10 **86** AhmedAjtebi(3) 8 — 84
(Mahmood Al Zarooni) *hld up in tch: rdn and no prog over 3f out: hung lft ent fnl 2f: wl btn over 1f out* **5/1**[3]

45-0 **6** *1* **Seeking The Buck (USA)**[16] 2747 6-10-0 **89** JimCrowley 9 — 85
(R M Beckett) *t.k.h: hld up in tch: rdn and effrt 3f out: unable qck over 2f out: wl hld fr over 1f out* **3/1**[2]

-060 **7** *3* **Mark Twain (IRE)**[30] 2324 3-8-11 **84** StevieDonohoe 5 — 74
(D M Simcock) *a in last pair: rdn 4f out: wl btn fnl 3f* **16/1**

5125 **8** *11* **Officer In Command (USA)**[87] 990 4-9-7 **82** (p) JimmyFortune 7 — 50
(J S Moore) *niggled along after s: a in last pair: rdn and btn 3f out: wl bhd fnl 2f* **25/1**

2m 9.75s (-0.75) **Going Correction** -0.05s/f (Good)
WFA 3 from 4yo+ 12lb 8 Ran SP% **115.5**
Speed ratings (Par 107): **101,98,98,97,95 94,92,83**
toteswingers: 1&2 £5.60, 1&3 £6.20, 2&3 £5.50 CSF £20.86 CT £128.95 TOTE £3.80: £1.30, £1.40, £2.60; EX 20.70 Trifecta £142.40 Pool: £498.49 - 2.59 winning units..
Owner Sheikh Hamdan Bin Mohammed Al Maktoum **Bred** Darley **Trained** Middleham Moor, N Yorks

FOCUS
A good handicap. It was run at steady pace and the favourite did the job in emphatic style under a front-running ride. He is rated a 3lb improver with the next three home close to their marks.

NOTEBOOK
Jutland had been vulnerable in three runs off similar marks since just getting nailed at Thirsk in April but he ran his rivals into complete submission here, despite tilting his head to right in the closing stages. He did have the run of the race but looks a resolute galloper and his style suggests he could improve again switched back to a right-handed track. (op 3-1)

King's Masque just failed in his bid for a fourth win in the last five when clear second to an improver over 1m2f at Chepstow last time. He shadowed the winner for most of the way here and put in another creditable effort off 4lb higher. He should continue to run well but his improvement may have levelled out. (op 15-2 tchd 6-1)

Jawaab(IRE) increased his options when winning well over 1m4f at Doncaster last time. This contest didn't really set up for his hold-up style but he put in a respectable effort off 2lb higher in a more competitive race. (op 8-1)

Norwegian Dancer(UAE) plugged on but couldn't find the pace to pose a big threat. He is on his last winning mark but seems to save his very best form for Chester, the scene of both of his wins. (op 11-2 tchd 9-2 and 15-2)

Navy List(FR) couldn't respond when the pace quickened and also displayed a slightly high head carriage. (op 13-2)

Seeking The Buck(USA) found a very limited response out wide dropped back to what is arguably his best trip on a second run back from a layoff. (op 11-4 tchd 4-1)

3266 KIER MAIDEN FILLIES' STKS 1m 2f
5:15 (5:18) (Class 5) 3-Y-0+ £3,070 (£906; £453) Stalls Low

Form				RPR
00	1		**Anacopa (USA)**[17] 2718 3-8-7 0 ... AhmedAjtebi(3) 2 (Mahmood Al Zarooni) *led for 2f: chsd ldr after: rdn to chal 3f out: led over 1f out: wandered u.p wl ins fnl f: hld on cl home* 8/1	76
3	2	shd	**Pink Palace (USA)**[39] 2051 3-8-10 0 ... JimmyFortune 1 (Sir Michael Stoute) *chsd ldr tl led after 2f: rdn over 3f out: hdd over 1f out: one pce u.p: kpt on cl home: jst hld* 10/11[1]	76
5-6	3	¾	**Effervesce (IRE)**[59] 1501 3-8-10 0 ... NeilCallan 4 (Sir Michael Stoute) *trckd ldng pair: effrt to press ldrs over 3f out: rdn and nt qckn over 2f out: hld hd awkwardly and one pce fnl f* 9/4[2]	74
4	4	1½	**Invitee**[19] 2658 3-8-10 0 ... TedDurcan 3 (E A L Dunlop) *trckd ldng pair: rdn 3f out: outpcd by ldng trio 2f out: plugged on same pce fnl f* 13/2[3]	71
	5	114	**Beautiful One** 3-8-10 0 ... DavidProbert 5 (T D McCarthy) *virtually ref to r and set off a f bhd: rn v green* 66/1	—

2m 10.48s (-0.02) **Going Correction** -0.05s/f (Good) 5 Ran SP% **109.1**
Speed ratings (Par 100): **98,97,97,96,—**
CSF £15.77 TOTE £7.30: £2.00, £1.30; EX 17.20.
Owner Godolphin **Bred** Budget Stables & Kathryn Nikkel **Trained** Newmarket, Suffolk

FOCUS
An interesting fillies' event. A Godolphin runner was a springer in the market and just prevailed in a tight finish with the two Sir Michael Stoute-trained market leaders. The form is tricky to pin down but is best rated around the placed horses.

3267 MARRIOTT HOTEL & COUNTRY CLUB OFFICIAL OPENING H'CAP 1m 6f
5:45 (5:45) (Class 5) (0-70,69) 4-Y-0+ £3,238 (£963; £481; £240) Stalls High

Form				RPR
0343	1		**Dovedon Angel**[18] 2676 4-7-11 50 oh2 ... DeclanCannon(5) 7 (Miss Gay Kelleway) *stdd s: bhd: hdwy to trck ldrs 4f out: pushed up to chal ent fnl 3f: rdn ahd over 2f out: kpt on u.p and a holding runner-up fnl f* 9/1	56
5-64	2	¾	**Relative Strength (IRE)**[51] 1690 5-9-7 69 ...(v) JimmyFortune 8 (A M Balding) *chsd ldrs tl led 9f out: rdn and hdd over 2f out: kpt pressing wnr u.p: one pce and hld ins fnl f* 5/4[1]	74
06-2	3	¾	**Mohanad (IRE)**[15] 1183 4-8-11 62 ... RobertLButler(3) 5 (Miss Sheena West) *hld up in tch: rdn to chse ldng pair and hung lft ent fnl 2f: swtchd rt 1f out: kpt on wl ins fnl f: nt rch ldrs* 10/1	66
-143	4	6	**Locum**[24] 2495 5-9-4 66 ... TedDurcan 1 (M H Tompkins) *chsd ldrs: rdn and nt qckn w ldng pair 3f out: 4th and wl hld over 1f out: plugged on one pce fnl f* 6/1[3]	62
0505	5	5	**Valmari (IRE)**[55] 1609 7-9-6 68 ... SaleemGolam 3 (G Prodromou) *bustled along leaving stalls: hld up in tch: struggling on downhill run 4f out: rdn and no prog over 3f out: wl btn fnl 3f* 33/1	57
0	6	16	**Lindsay's Dream**[29] 2360 4-8-13 61 ... RobertHavlin 2 (A B Haynes) *mde most tl 9f out: chsd ldr after tl over 3f out: sn wknd u.p: wl btn fnl 2f* 33/1	27
-312	7	14	**Bedarra Boy**[14] 2811 4-8-3 51 ... NickyMackay 6 (D W P Arbuthnot) *chsd ldr tl 9f out: styd handy: pushed along over 5f out: rdn and wknd over 3f out: wl btn fnl 2f: t.o and eased ins fnl f* 11/4[2]	—
60/0	8	15	**Reload (IRE)**[9] 2966 7-9-4 66 ...(b[1]) JerryO'Dwyer 4 (Mrs S J Humphrey) *in tch towards rr: dropped to last and rdn over 4f out: lost tch 3f out: eased fr wl over 1f out: t.o* 33/1	—

3m 6.94s (-3.06) **Going Correction** -0.05s/f (Good) 8 Ran SP% **113.3**
Speed ratings (Par 103): **106,105,105,101,98 89,81,73**
toteswingers: 1&2 £3.60, 1&3 £7.80, 2&3 £3.70 CSF £20.37 CT £115.80 TOTE £13.40: £2.50, £1.10, £2.10; EX 28.70 Trifecta £100.40 Pool: £544.11 - 4.01 winning units. Place 6 £49.52, Place 5 £44.09.
Owner Whatley, Baber & Clark **Bred** M C Whatley **Trained** Exning, Suffolk

FOCUS
A minor staying handicap. The first three pulled a long way clear of the rest and the winner recorded a minor personal best, with the runner-up to his latest mark.

Bedarra Boy Official explanation: jockey said gelding lost a fore shoe

T/Jkpt: Not won. T/Plt: £71.20 to a £1 stake. Pool: £71,052.63. 728.07 winning tickets. T/Qpdt: £29.80 to a £1 stake Pool: £3,749.91. 92.96 winning tickets. SP

3034 WINDSOR (R-H)
Monday, June 21

OFFICIAL GOING: Good to firm (firm in places on intersection; 8.8)
Wind: Nil Weather: Fine, warm

3268 TOTESPORT.COM FILLIES' H'CAP 1m 2f 7y
6:40 (6:41) (Class 5) (0-70,70) 3-Y-0+ £2,729 (£806; £403) Stalls Low

Form				RPR
50/1	1		**Dolcetto (IRE)**[21] 2586 5-10-0 69 ... PaulMulrennan 2 (A King) *hld up towards rr: prog fr 4f out: trckd ldrs 2f out and towards outer: rdn to ld 1f out: styd on wl* 25/1	80+
-405	2	1	**Beauchamp Xiara**[9] 2956 4-9-11 66 ... FergusSweeney 3 (H Candy) *s.i.s: hld up wl in rr: prog over 3f out and followed wnr through: drvn over 1f out: wnt 2nd last 100yds: styd on but nvr really able to chal* 20/1	75
0252	3	2	**Broughtons Paradis (IRE)**[7] 3040 4-9-3 58 ... TonyCulhane 5 (W J Musson) *trckd ldrs: gng easily 3f out: effrt to ld 2f out: hdd 1f out: fdd last 100yds* 7/2[2]	63
0-21	4	nk	**Centime**[11] 2901 3-9-2 69 ... RobertWinston 7 (B J Meehan) *s.i.s: settled wl in rr: looking for room 3f out: swtchd out 2f out and drvn: styd on: nrst fin* 8/1	73+
61-6	5	1¼	**Avon Lady**[19] 2652 3-9-3 70 ... EddieAhern 10 (J R Fanshawe) *prom: chsd ldr over 6f out: led over 2f out to 2f out: fdd fnl f* 10/1	72
4632	6	7	**Pastello**[9] 2956 3-8-10 66 ... PatrickHills(3) 13 (R Hannon) *hld up wl in rr: effrt and wd fr 3f out: no hdwy over 1f out: wknd after* 20/1	54
0-00	7	2¾	**Madj's Baby**[9] 2956 3-7-8 54 oh3 ow3 ... RyanPowell(7) 1 (H S Howe) *led 2f: wd bnd over 6f out to over 4f out and lost pl: v wd in st: struggling fnl 2f* 100/1	36
-350	8	nk	**Alice Cullen**[28] 2398 3-9-2 69 ... AdamKirby 8 (W R Swinburn) *hld up in last: reminder wl over 3f out: properly rdn in last pair over 2f out: passed wkng rivals over 1f out* 18/1	51
5405	9	1	**Sheila Toss (IRE)**[11] 2886 3-9-1 68 ...(b[1]) PatDobbs 9 (R Hannon) *chsd ldrs: rdn and wknd jst over 2f out* 6/1[3]	48
01	10	2	**Shesells Seashells**[20] 2632 3-9-3 70 ... FrankieDettori 6 (M L W Bell) *led after 2f: styd against rail in st: hdd & wknd over 2f out* 9/4[1]	46
20-4	11	3¼	**Oriental Girl**[27] 2410 5-9-6 61 ...(p) StevieDonohoe 12 (J S Moore) *trckd ldrs: rdn 4f out: wknd over 2f out: eased* 25/1	30
6-50	12	1¼	**Lucky Score (IRE)**[7] 3040 4-9-7 62 ...(p) JimCrowley 4 (Mouse Hamilton-Fairley) *led 2f: chsd ldrs tl wknd 3f out* 66/1	29
443	13	3½	**White Finch (USA)**[32] 2255 3-9-1 68 ... DavidProbert 11 (A M Balding) *chsd ldrs: rdn 1/2-way: lost pl 4f out: last and eased 2f out* 18/1	28

2m 6.35s (-2.35) **Going Correction** -0.15s/f (Firm)
WFA 3 from 4yo+ 12lb 13 Ran SP% **117.7**
Speed ratings (Par 100): **103,102,100,100,99 93,91,91,90,88 86,85,82**
toteswingers: 1&2 £24.40, 1&3 £18.80, 2&3 £12.70 CSF £421.93 CT £2182.02 TOTE £30.10: £7.00, £6.50, £2.10; EX 276.20 Trifecta £871.00 Pool: £3,060.29 - 2.60 winning units..
Owner Mrs Lesley Field **Bred** Exors R E Sangster & Mrs S Magnier **Trained** Barbury Castle, Wilts

FOCUS
This modest fillies' handicap was run at an average sort of pace and there were a host of chances in the home straight. The form looks reasonable with the runner-up, fourth and fifth all running to previous marks.

Pastello Official explanation: jockey said filly hung left

Shesells Seashells Official explanation: trainer was unable to offer any explanation for the poor performance shown

Oriental Girl Official explanation: jockey said the mare was unsuited by the Good to Firm ground

3269 COOLMORE DUKE OF MARMALADE MAIDEN AUCTION STKS 6f
7:10 (7:10) (Class 5) 2-Y-0 £2,729 (£806; £403) Stalls High

Form				RPR
42	1		**Capaill Liath (IRE)**[11] 2895 2-8-11 0 ... MichaelHills 12 (B W Hills) *mde all: pushed along and drew away fr 2f out: edgd lft over 1f out* 10/11[1]	85+
32	2	4	**With Hindsight (IRE)**[13] 2839 2-9-2 0 ... PhilipRobinson 9 (C G Cox) *pressed wnr: rdn and lft bhd fr 2f out: hld on for 2nd* 10/3[2]	75
0	3	nk	**Nothing To Hide (IRE)**[13] 2839 2-8-9 0 ... JamesDoyle 13 (D J S Ffrench Davis) *cl up: outpcd fr 2f out: kpt on to hold 3rd fnl f* 66/1	67
6	4	1	**Arctic Mirage**[14] 2819 2-8-13 0 ... FergusSweeney 1 (M Blanshard) *chsd ldrs in 7th but nt on terms: pushed along and rn green over 2f out: veered lft over 1f out: kpt on fnl f* 12/1	68
4	5	3¼	**Laugh Or Cry**[12] 2867 2-8-9 0 ... JimCrowley 14 (P J Makin) *cl up against rail: shkn up over 2f out: wknd over 1f out* 8/1[3]	54
	6	¾	**Red Zeus (IRE)** 2-8-6 0 ... RyanPowell(7) 2 (J S Moore) *dwlt: wl off the pce in last quartet: brought wd fr 1/2-way: pushed along and sme prog over 1f out: nrst fin* 50/1	56
	7	1½	**Mr Perceptive (IRE)** 2-9-2 0 ... PatDobbs 7 (R Hannon) *dwlt: rn green in last quartet: pushed along and sme late prog: nvr a factor* 8/1[3]	55+
00	8	1¾	**Magical Star**[27] 2407 2-7-11 0 ... CharlesEddery(7) 8 (R Hannon) *chsd ldrs: rn green fr 1/2-way: wknd and hung lft over 1f out* 66/1	37
0	9	½	**Ad Vitam (IRE)**[70] 1263 2-8-9 0 ... RichardSmith 11 (S Kirk) *dwlt: off the pce in 9th: pushed along 2f out: no imp on ldrs but kpt on quite steadily* 50/1	41
0	10	1¾	**Snow Trooper**[14] 2819 2-8-9 0 ... EddieCreighton 3 (D K Ivory) *rn green in 8th and off the pce: no real prog fr 2f out* 100/1	36
040	11	1¾	**Blade Pirate**[12] 2873 2-8-9 0 ...(p) AlanMunro 6 (J Ryan) *cl up: rdn over 2f out: wkng whn hmpd over 1f out* 66/1	32
	12	2¼	**Indian Shuffle (IRE)** 2-8-13 0 ... EddieAhern 5 (J G Portman) *a in last quartet: detached fr 1/2-way: no prog* 25/1	28
00	13	shd	**Shesanindian (IRE)**[7] 3029 2-8-3 0 ... JohnFahy(5) 4 (A W Carroll) *scratchy to post: a in last quartet: nvr a factor* 100/1	22

1m 12.5s (-0.50) **Going Correction** -0.15s/f (Firm) 13 Ran SP% **119.6**
Speed ratings (Par 93): **97,91,91,89,85 84,82,80,79,77 74,71,71**
toteswingers: 1&2 £1.70, 1&3 £20.00, 2&3 £26.00 CSF £3.69 TOTE £1.80: £1.10, £2.00, £9.10; EX 5.30 Trifecta £153.50 Pool: £2,711.51 - 13.07 winning units..
Owner D Hanafin **Bred** Stanley Estate & Stud Co & Mount Coote Stud **Trained** Lambourn, Berks

FOCUS
A fair maiden rated around the first two with the winner quite impressive.

NOTEBOOK

Capaill Liath(IRE) made it third time lucky and won easily despite having got himself very warm beforehand. He was run out of it on softer ground at Nottingham 11 days previously, where he hung left under pressure, and he showed a tendency to want to edge that way again here despite being back on a quicker surface. He obviously has a decent engine, though, and it's a good bet more will be heard of him this season. He holds entries in two valuable sales races later on, both of which his stable has a good record in, and it wouldn't be surprising to see him run a bold race if pitched into that sort of company as expected. (op 7-4 tchd 15-8 in a place early)

With Hindsight(IRE) was firmly put in his place by the winner. He has now been placed on each of his three outings and deserves to get his head in front, but is clearly vulnerable in maidens. (op 5-2)

Nothing To Hide(IRE) stepped up big time and finished an awful lot closer to the runner-up than was the case on debut 13 days earlier. He should enjoy stepping up a furlong before long and is clearly progressing. (op 80-1)

Arctic Mirage was backed to step up on his debut form over C&D and did so from the outside stall, but never threatened. He still showed distinct signs of inexperience and looks more of one for nurseries. Official explanation: jockey said gelding ran very green (op 9-1)

Laugh Or Cry failed to improve as might have been expected on his debut run at Kempton 12 days earlier, but this was a stronger race. (op 6-1 tchd 9-1)

Red Zeus(IRE) was unconsidered in the betting and shaped as though this debut experience would be much to his benefit. (op 66-1)

Mr Perceptive(IRE) shaped as though this debut experience was badly needed. He kept on steadily under an educational ride and should be plenty sharper for the run. (op 15-2 tchd 17-2)

3270 PERTEMPS NETWORK H'CAP 6f
7:40 (7:41) (Class 4) (0-85,83) 3-Y-O £4,857 (£1,445; £722; £360) **Stalls** High

Form RPR
-225 1 **Gene Autry (USA)**[23] 2545 3-9-6 **82** JimmyFortune 6 96+
(R Hannon) *cl up against rail: wnt 2nd 1/2-way: gng easily tl led 1f out: shkn up and sn clr* **8/11**[1]
-313 2 4 **Bonheurs Art (IRE)**[22] 2565 3-8-10 **72** MichaelHills 2 73
(B W Hills) *led: rdn over 2f out: hdd 1f out: no ch w wnr but hung on for 2nd* **5/1**[3]
-321 3 *nk* **Vanilla Rum**[14] 2824 3-9-3 **79** FergusSweeney 3 79
(H Candy) *chsd ldng trio: rdn over 2f out: cl enough in 3rd jst over 1f out: sn outpcd* **10/3**[2]
0604 4 1 1/2 **Di Stefano**[14] 2815 3-9-6 **82** AlanMunro 5 77
(M R Channon) *hld up in last: outpcd after 2f: rdn and sme prog over 2f out: one pce over 1f out* **14/1**
6-00 5 10 **Footstepsofspring (FR)**[23] 2545 3-9-7 **83** TonyCulhane 1 46
(W J Musson) *mostly in 5th: shkn up and nt gng wl over 2f out: sn bhd* **28/1**
1-33 6 2 1/4 **Fazza**[145] 311 3-8-10 **72** DavidProbert 4 28
(D W P Arbuthnot) *chsd ldr to 1/2-way: wknd and sn bhd* **16/1**

1m 11.82s (-1.18) **Going Correction** -0.15s/f (Firm) 6 Ran SP% 113.6
Speed ratings (Par 101): **101,95,95,93,79 76**
toteswingers: 1&2 £1.20, 1&3 £1.10, 2&3 £2.10 CSF £5.04 TOTE £1.60: £1.10, £2.60; EX 3.60.
Owner Mrs J K Powell **Bred** Rankin, Freeman & McClinton **Trained** East Everleigh, Wilts

FOCUS
Not a bad little 3-y-o sprint handicap and they went a solid enough pace. The winner is the only one with potential while the placed horses set the level.
Footstepsofspring(FR) Official explanation: jockey said, regarding the running and riding, thathis instructions were to jump and if he showed good pace to make the running, but if outpaced hold on to him and do his best and that the colt had become tired inside the final furlong; the trainer confirmed these instructions.

3271 SUNLEY H'CAP 1m 67y
8:10 (8:10) (Class 4) (0-85,84) 3-Y-O £4,857 (£1,445; £722; £360) **Stalls** High

Form RPR
0-21 1 **Dance East**[41] 1991 3-9-6 **83** FrankieDettori 3 91+
(J Noseda) *trckd ldr 2f: cl up after: moved up to ld wl over 1f out gng bttr than rivals: rdn fnl f: jst hld on* **15/8**[1]
3113 2 *hd* **Kajima**[17] 2713 3-9-5 **82** JimmyFortune 5 89+
(R Hannon) *led: jnd after 2f: rdn and hdd wl over 1f out awkward hd carriage and hung lft fnl f but rallied wl: jst failed* **15/8**[1]
5-05 3 3 1/4 **Flip Flop (IRE)**[16] 2737 3-9-3 **80** MichaelHills 1 80
(B W Hills) *prog to join ldr after 2f to jst over 2f out: readily outpcd u.p* **10/1**
-15 4 1/2 **Fonterutoli (IRE)**[45] 1876 3-8-11 **74** TedDurcan 7 73
(M Botti) *hld up in last pair: nudged along and no prog over 2f out: shkn up and hdwy over 1f out: styd on: nrly tk 3rd* **9/1**[3]
0600 5 *hd* **Bell's Ocean (USA)**[12] 2879 3-7-9 **65** oh15 RyanPowell(7) 2 63?
(J Ryan) *hld up in last pair: stmbld bnd 5f out: drvn and effrt on outer over 2f out: ch of 3rd 1f out: outpcd and no ex* **100/1**
5052 6 2 1/2 **Osgood**[16] 2767 3-8-9 **72** AlanMunro 4 65
(M R Channon) *t.k.h: trckd ldrs: rdn over 2f out: easily outpcd fr over 1f out: fdd* **11/1**
5-00 7 1 1/2 **Desert Auction (IRE)**[30] 2324 3-9-7 **84** PatDobbs 8 73
(R Hannon) *scratchy to post: chsd ldrs: pushed along wl over 2f out: steadily wknd fr over 1f out* **8/1**[2]
0-50 8 2 1/2 **Krymian**[32] 2261 3-8-12 **75** RichardMullen 6 58
(Sir Michael Stoute) *chsd ldrs in 6th: rdn 3f out: wknd u.p 2f out* **33/1**

1m 43.38s (-1.32) **Going Correction** -0.15s/f (Firm) 8 Ran SP% 112.0
Speed ratings (Par 101): **100,99,96,96,95 93,91,89**
toteswingers: 1&2 £1.10, 1&3 £3.50, 2&3 £4.40 CSF £4.87 CT £24.02 TOTE £2.50: £1.10, £2.00, £3.00; EX 4.50 Trifecta £14.10 Pool: £688.83 - 36.00 winning units..
Owner Cheveley Park Stud **Bred** Cheveley Park Stud Ltd **Trained** Newmarket, Suffolk

FOCUS
The joint-favourites came clear in a driving finish in this modest handicap and the form should work out. The third sets the standard rated to this year's form.

3272 LADBROKES.COM MAIDEN STKS 1m 67y
8:40 (8:41) (Class 5) 3-Y-O £2,729 (£806; £403) **Stalls** High

Form RPR
24 1 **Rule Maker**[24] 2497 3-9-3 0 FrankieDettori 13 85+
(J Noseda) *trckd ldr: led 5f out: shkn up over 1f out: r.o and fully in command fnl f* **5/2**[2]
42 2 1 1/2 **Give Your Verdict (USA)**[13] 2842 3-9-3 0 RichardMullen 2 82+
(Sir Michael Stoute) *trckd ldng pair: wnt 2nd over 3f out: rdn over 2f out: styd on but nvr gng pce to threaten wnr seriously* **8/11**[1]
0-4 3 6 **Jubail (IRE)**[11] 2900 3-9-3 0 FergusSweeney 14 68+
(A King) *settled in 7th: in tch and gng wl: outpcd over 2f out: pushed along and styd on steadily to take 3rd nr fin* **20/1**
4 1/2 **Sunset Place** 3-9-3 0 AdamKirby 8 67
(C G Cox) *trckd ldng trio: pushed along and outpcd over 2f out: chsd clr ldng pair over 1f out: kpt on but lost 3rd nr fin* **50/1**
6 5 1 3/4 **Bernie's Moon (USA)**[22] 2564 3-8-12 0 JimmyFortune 12 58
(B J Meehan) *led 3f: shkn up and outpcd over 2f out: one pce after* **7/1**[3]
6 7 **Penshurst Lad (IRE)** 3-9-3 0 JimCrowley 7 46
(R T Phillips) *s.s: detached in last and wl bhd: pushed along and sme prog 2f out: passed wkng rivals fnl f: nrst fin* **66/1**
40 7 *hd* **Whisper Wind**[13] 2842 3-9-3 0 PatDobbs 1 46
(G L Moore) *chsd ldrs and in tch: pushed along 4f out: wl outpcd fr over 2f out: wknd* **40/1**
0-2 8 *hd* **Ocean Rosie (IRE)**[45] 1870 3-8-12 0 CathyGannon 4 41
(Miss J Feilden) *chsd ldrs in 6th: rdn 4f out: steadily wknd fr 3f out* **16/1**
9 1 **Namehim** 3-9-3 0 TedDurcan 10 43
(E F Vaughan) *rn green in 8th and sn off the pce: no prog fr 3f out* **50/1**
6 10 3/4 **Jakeys Girl**[7] 3038 3-8-7 0 KierenFox(5) 6 37
(P M Phelan) *sn wl off the pce in 9th: nvr a factor* **66/1**
0 11 2 3/4 **Final Try**[16] 2755 3-9-0 0 RobertLButler(3) 11 35
(P Butler) *dwlt: sn wl bhd in 10th: nvr a factor* **100/1**
12 1 3/4 **Weeza (IRE)** 3-8-12 0 IvaMilickova 9 26
(J Ryan) *dwlt: wl off the pce in 11th: no prog* **100/1**

1m 43.89s (-0.81) **Going Correction** -0.15s/f (Firm) 12 Ran SP% 120.9
Speed ratings (Par 99): **98,96,90,90,88 81,81,80,79,79 76,74**
toteswingers: 1&2 £1.20, 1&3 £12.70, 2&3 £6.00 CSF £4.55 TOTE £4.00: £1.40, £1.10, £5.40; EX 5.00 Trifecta £35.80 Pool: £1,038.38 - 21.46 winning units..
Owner Franconson Partners **Bred** Mr & Mrs G Middlebrook **Trained** Newmarket, Suffolk

FOCUS
Nothing got into this maiden from off the pace and it was another race that saw the market leaders dominate. The form is rated around the first two.

3273 TREASURE BEACH HOTEL, BARBADOS H'CAP 1m 3f 135y
9:10 (9:10) (Class 5) (0-75,74) 3-Y-O £2,729 (£806; £403) **Stalls** Low

Form RPR
406 1 **Montparnasse (IRE)**[18] 2684 3-9-4 **71** JimmyFortune 6 79
(B J Meehan) *hld up in last and detached: effrt over 2f out and swtchd to outer: hrd rdn to cl and led ins fnl f: styd on wl* **7/2**[2]
4121 2 1/2 **Leader Of The Land (IRE)**[26] 2439 3-9-6 **73** TedDurcan 7 80
(D R Lanigan) *trckd ldng trio: wnt 2nd 3f out: sn shkn up: clsd u.p to ld 1f out: hdd ins fnl f: styd on* **5/4**[1]
3025 3 1 1/4 **First Fandango**[17] 2717 3-9-4 **74** PatrickHills(3) 1 79
(J W Hills) *trckd ldng trio: carried wd 3f out: prog to dispute 2nd over 2f out: drvn to chal 1f out: no ex* **8/1**[3]
-532 4 1 1/4 **Baltimore Clipper (USA)**[15] 2782 3-9-5 **72** NeilCallan 3 75
(P F I Cole) *trckd ldng pair: rdn 3f out: sn nt qckn and lost pl: kpt on u.p fr over 1f out* **8/1**[3]
-453 5 3 1/2 **Whiepa Snappa (IRE)**[10] 2935 3-8-5 **63** KierenFox(5) 4 60
(P M Phelan) *trckd ldr: led over 5f out: kpt on u.p over 2f out: hdd 1f out and wknd* **7/2**[2]
-660 6 37 **Joe Rua (USA)**[3] 3170 3-7-9 **55** oh10 RyanPowell(7) 5 —
(J Ryan) *led to over 5f out: hung lft over 3f out: sn wknd rapidly: t.o* **66/1**

2m 27.45s (-2.05) **Going Correction** -0.15s/f (Firm) 6 Ran SP% 112.6
Speed ratings (Par 99): **100,99,98,98,95 71**
toteswingers: 1&2 £1.30, 1&3 £3.00, 2&3 £1.60 CSF £8.37 TOTE £4.00: £2.30, £1.70; EX 5.30 Place 6 £8.81, Place 5 £1.96.
Owner Lady Rothschild **Bred** Kincorth Investments Inc **Trained** Manton, Wilts

FOCUS
Despite this being run at a decent early pace there was still something of a bunched finish. The form is rated at face value around the third and fourth.
T/Plt: £9.10 to a £1 stake. Pool: £81,873.60. 6,535.84 winning tickets. T/Qpdt: £1.80 to a £1 stake. Pool: £5,408.65. 2,109.59 winning tickets. JN

2720 WOLVERHAMPTON (A.W) (L-H)
Monday, June 21

OFFICIAL GOING: Standard
Wind: Light, half-behind Weather: Fine and sunny

3274 EUROPEAN BREEDERS' FUND MAIDEN STKS 5f 216y(P)
2:30 (2:31) (Class 5) 2-Y-O £3,626 (£1,079; £539; £269) **Stalls** Low

Form RPR
0 1 **Silver Alliance**[28] 2384 2-9-3 0 AdamKirby 9 78
(W R Swinburn) *chsd ldr: rdn to ld ins fnl f: r.o* **12/1**
2 *nk* **Hokoumah (USA)** 2-9-3 0 FrankieDettori 6 77
(Saeed Bin Suroor) *chsd ldrs: rdn to ld over 1f out: hdd ins fnl f: r.o* **5/6**[1]
5 3 1 1/2 **Mishtaag**[82] 1066 2-9-3 0 KierenFallon 7 73
(C E Brittain) *chsd ldrs: shkn up over 2f out: r.o* **7/1**[3]
4 3/4 **Rock Ace (IRE)** 2-8-12 0 SilvestreDeSousa 4 66
(Mrs D J Sanderson) *prom: rdn over 2f out: styd on* **33/1**
04 5 3 1/2 **Pretium Sceleris**[28] 2384 2-9-3 0 AndreaAtzeni 8 60
(M Botti) *led: rdn and hdd over 1f out: wknd ins fnl f* **5/1**[2]
6 3 1/2 **Imperial Look** 2-9-3 0 AdrianNicholls 2 50
(E S McMahon) *mid-div: sn pushed along: rdn 1/2-way: outpcd fr over 2f out* **14/1**
7 3 3/4 **Carver County (IRE)** 2-9-3 0 RichardMullen 12 38
(K A Ryan) *sn drvn along in rr: nvr on terms* **33/1**
5 8 1 **Ridgeway Hawk**[45] 1871 2-9-0 0 ow2 LeeNewnes(5) 13 37
(M D I Usher) *prom: rdn over 2f out: sn wknd* **100/1**
4 9 *nk* **Hernando Torres**[15] 2785 2-8-12 0 JamesSullivan(5) 11 34
(M W Easterby) *mid-div: wknd 1/2-way* **25/1**
10 1/2 **Fabiello** 2-9-3 0 RichardKingscote 10 33
(Tom Dascombe) *s.i.s: sn pushed along and a in rr* **50/1**
11 17 **Princess Eliza** 2-8-12 0 VinceSlattery 3 —
(Miss Joanne Priest) *s.s: a bhd: t.o* **150/1**
12 106 **Black Annis Bower** 2-8-12 0 PaulMulrennan 1 —
(M W Easterby) *s.v.s and a t.o* **66/1**

1m 16.0s (1.00) **Going Correction** +0.10s/f (Slow) 12 Ran SP% 112.9
Speed ratings (Par 93): **97,96,94,93,88 84,79,77,77,76 54,—**
toteswingers: 1&2 £4.30, 1&3 £15.30, 2&3 £2.60 CSF £20.76 TOTE £18.80: £4.40, £1.02, £2.20; EX 34.70.
Owner In It To Win Partnership **Bred** Peter Harris **Trained** Aldbury, Herts

FOCUS
Only a fair maiden at best and one in which the gallop was just ordinary. The principals came down the centre in the straight and the form looks fairly decent.

NOTEBOOK
Silver Alliance ◆ was fairly easy to back but stepped up appreciably on debut form tackling this surface for the first time. He should have no problems with 7f and, although this was not a strong race, he has a bit of size and scope and is open to further improvement.
Hokoumah(USA), a well-backed first foal of a Prix Morny winner who was fourth to Speciosa in the 1000 Guineas in 2005, looked interesting on paper but, although he failed to justify the market support, he showed enough to suggest a similar race can be found. (op 5-4 tchd 4-5)
Mishtaag ◆, well beaten over 5f on Fibresand in March, turned in an improved effort on this Polytrack debut and first run since. His pedigree suggests the step up to 7f should suit better, he was not unduly knocked about and he will be one to take into nurseries granted a stiffer test. (op 9-2 tchd 8-1)
Rock Ace(IRE), a half-sister to Wokingham winner Laddies Poker Two, was on her toes and led round the paddock by two handlers but showed ability at a modest level on this racecourse debut. She is likely to remain vulnerable in this grade but should pick up a minor event. (op 25-1)
Pretium Sceleris had finished ahead of the winner on his previous start and looked the pick of those with previous experience. However, he proved disappointing after being allowed an uncontested lead on this AW debut and will have to better this to get off the mark. (op 11-2 tchd 9-2)
Imperial Look, a half-brother to fair maiden winner Look Whos Next, could never land a blow in a race where the leaders weren't stopping in the straight. He should be able to improve for this debut experience, and run-of-the-mill nurseries will be the way forward in due course. (op 12-1)

Fabiello Official explanation: jockey said that the colt ran green

3275 ENJOY THE PARTY PACK GROUP OFFER MEDIAN AUCTION MAIDEN STKS 1m 141y(P)
3:00 (3:02) (Class 5) 3-Y-O £2,456 (£725; £362) Stalls Low

Form RPR
2-2 **1** **Point Out (USA)**[88] 980 3-9-3 0 FrankieDettori 4 84+
(J H M Gosden) *s.i.s: sn trcking ldr: shkn up to ld over 2f out: clr over 1f out: eased ins fnl f* **1/2**[1]
2 *6* **Sweet Origin** 3-9-3 0 JimmyQuinn 6 65+
(M Botti) *hld up: hdwy over 2f out: r.o: no ch w wnr* **20/1**
4200 **3** *1* **Gra Adhmhar (IRE)**[40] 2025 3-9-3 72 KierenFallon 1 63
(D J Coakley) *sn led: rdn and hdd over 2f out: edgd lft over 1f out: styd on same pce* **6/1**[2]
0-4 **4** *nse* **Gwenllian (IRE)**[25] 2478 3-8-12 0 PJMcDonald 3 58
(Ian Williams) *w ldr: plld hrd: stdd to trck ldrs 7f out: rdn over 2f out: sn outpcd* **10/1**[3]
5 *1* **Marching Home** 3-9-3 0 AdamKirby 5 61
(W R Swinburn) *hld up in tch: rdn over 2f out: wknd fnl f* **16/1**
4 **6** *3/4* **Eastern Magic**[21] 2603 3-9-3 0 PhillipMakin 10 59
(R Hollinshead) *sn chsng ldr: rdn over 3f out: ev ch over 2f out: wknd over 1f out* **12/1**
00 **7** *1* **Defence Of Realm (GER)**[11] 2899 3-9-3 0 TonyCulhane 7 57
(George Baker) *s.i.s: hld up: nvr on terms* **100/1**
0 **8** *nk* **Converre**[8] 2998 3-8-12 0 JackMitchell 9 51
(G A Butler) *hld up: nvr on terms* **66/1**
00- **9** *11* **Gee Major**[257] 6591 3-9-3 0 LiamJones 8 31
(N J Vaughan) *mid-div: sn pushed along: rdn over 3f out: wknd over 2f out* **100/1**
0 **10** *3/4* **Monte Mayor Two (IRE)**[13] 2841 3-9-3 0 CathyGannon 11 29
(D Haydn Jones) *sn prom: rdn over 3f out: wknd over 2f out* **100/1**
0 **11** *12* **Daisy Dolittle**[25] 2478 3-8-12 0 RichardMullen 12 —
(J R Holt) *s.i.s: hdwy into mid-div 7f out: rdn 4f out: wknd sn after: t.o* **100/1**

1m 52.62s (2.12) **Going Correction** +0.10s/f (Slow) **11** Ran SP% **113.8**
Speed ratings (Par 99): **94,88,87,87,86 86,85,85,75,74 63**
CSF £17.97 TOTE £1.50: £1.10, £4.80, £1.50; EX 13.10.
Owner K Abdulla **Bred** Juddmonte Farms Inc **Trained** Newmarket, Suffolk

FOCUS
The betting suggested this was an uncompetitive event and that's how things turned out, with the short-priced market leader thrashing an ordinary field with more in hand than the official margin suggested. The gallop was a modest one and the winner raced towards the centre in the straight. The level is a bit fluid but the winner is value for more thn the official margin.

3276 BETDAQ THE BETTING EXCHANGE CLAIMING STKS 5f 216y(P)
3:30 (3:32) (Class 5) 3-Y-O £1,591 (£1,591; £362) Stalls Low

Form RPR
-660 **1** **Admin (IRE)**[13] 2840 3-8-9 75 RichardKingscote 12 67
(R M Beckett) *s.i.s: hld up: hdwy over 1f out: rdn and hung lft ins fnl f: r.o to join ldr post* **7/1**[3]
2-21 **1** *dht* **Bubbly Bellini (IRE)**[149] 276 3-8-3 75 ow1 (p) MatthewDavies(5) 10 66
(George Baker) *s.i.s: hld up: hdwy over 1f out: rdn to ld ins fnl f: jnd post* **4/1**[2]
2030 **3** *1 3/4* **Clear Ice (IRE)**[12] 2879 3-8-5 68 (b) PaulEddery 2 57
(R C Guest) *sn drvn along to ld: hung rt over 1f out: hdd and unable qck ins fnl f* **12/1**
03 **4** *hd* **Eviction (IRE)**[17] 2722 3-9-1 0 (b) RichardMullen 7 67
(E S McMahon) *hld up: hdwy 3f out: chsd ldr over 2f out: rdn and hung rt over 1f out: styng on same pce whn hung lft towards fin* **14/1**
3632 **5** *1* **Blue Zephyr**[15] 2787 3-8-5 57 (b) FrannyNorton 4 54
(W R Muir) *prom: sn pushed along: rdn over 1f out: styd on same pce ins fnl f* **14/1**
1341 **6** *1 1/4* **Anjomarba (IRE)**[17] 2722 3-7-13 64 (p) KierenFox(5) 11 49
(W G M Turner) *chsd ldrs: rdn over 1f out: styd on same pce* **16/1**
-625 **7** *1 1/4* **Stef And Stelio**[27] 2408 3-9-5 73 (bt) JackMitchell 6 60
(G A Butler) *prom: rdn over 2f out: styd on same pce fr over 1f out* **20/1**
0060 **8** *1/2* **Transfixed (IRE)**[16] 2762 3-8-6 68 CathyGannon 9 45
(P D Evans) *prom: rdn over 2f out: styd on same pce appr fnl f* **20/1**
1451 **9** *11* **Novay Essjay (IRE)**[55] 1594 3-9-3 70 VinceSlattery 1 21
(A G Juckes) *in tch: rdn and lost pl wl over 3f out: sn bhd* **12/1**
00 **10** *nk* **Bravo Tango**[45] 1872 3-8-5 0 FrankieMcDonald 8 8
(D W P Arbuthnot) *sn pushed along and a in rr* **150/1**
2031 **11** *1* **Il Forno**[55] 1604 3-8-11 75 (p) FrankieDettori 13 11
(Ian Williams) *prom: rdn over 2f out: wknd over 1f out* **11/4**[1]
0054 **12** *1 1/4* **Eight Hours**[15] 2787 3-8-6 57 ow4 (b) BarryMcHugh(3) 3 5
(R A Fahey) *dwlt: outpcd* **20/1**
3000 **13** *9* **Tres Amigos**[11] 2886 3-8-11 76 AdrianNicholls 5 —
(D Nicholls) *w ldr tl rdn over 2f out: wknd over 1f out* **11/1**

1m 15.7s (0.70) **Going Correction** +0.10s/f (Slow) **13** Ran SP% **117.0**
Speed ratings (Par 99): **99,99,96,96,95 93,91,91,76,76 74,73,61**
WIN: Admin £4.30, Bubbly Bellini £3.20; PL: A £2.60, BB £2.80, CI £5.60; CSF: A-BB £16.32, BB-A £14.91; EX: A-BB £16.32, BB-A £14.91; toteswingers: A & BB £16.10, A & CI £18.80, BB & CI £14.30.
Owner Mrs C E S Baker **Bred** J P Hand **Trained** Moreton Morrell, Warwicks
Owner The Anagram Partnership **Bred** M J Halligan **Trained** Whitsbury, Hants

FOCUS
A fair claimer in which the pace was sound. The dead-heaters raced in the centre and against the far rail in the straight. Not a race to rate too positively, with the fourth and fifth the best guides.
Bravo Tango Official explanation: jockey said that the gelding ran green throughout
Il Forno Official explanation: jockey said that the gelding hung right handed
Tres Amigos Official explanation: jockey said that the gelding hung right-handed

3277 BET WORLD CUP FOOTBALL - BETDAQ H'CAP 5f 20y(P)
4:00 (4:02) (Class 5) (0-75,74) 3-Y-O £2,456 (£725; £362) Stalls Low

Form RPR
1143 **1** **Jigajig**[3] 3167 3-8-11 69 AmyRyan(5) 3 74
(K A Ryan) *chsd ldr: pushed along 1/2-way: rdn and hung lft over 1f out: led ins fnl f: r.o* **9/2**
0-24 **2** *3/4* **Admirable Duchess**[19] 2648 3-8-9 67 BillyCray(5) 2 69
(D J S Ffrench Davis) *led: rdn over 1f out: hdd ins fnl f: r.o* **3/1**[2]
-533 **3** *shd* **Fear Nothing**[16] 2741 3-9-7 74 (b[1]) RichardMullen 4 76
(E S McMahon) *sn trcking ldrs: nt clr run over 1f out: swtchd rt: r.o* **7/2**[3]
3-30 **4** *3 1/2* **Lexi's Layla (IRE)**[17] 2722 3-8-10 63 PJMcDonald 1 52
(D M Simcock) *chsd ldrs: rdn over 1f out: no ex fnl f* **20/1**
1660 **5** *4 1/2* **Silver Linnet (IRE)**[12] 2868 3-8-10 63 FrankieMcDonald 8 36
(M G Quinlan) *sn pushed along in rr: nvr on terms* **16/1**
2-05 **6** *2* **Valmina**[26] 2442 3-9-5 72 (t) KierenFallon 7 38
(Andrew Turnell) *sn pushed along in rr: bhd fr 1/2-way* **7/1**
14-2 **7** *1 1/2* **Durham Express (IRE)**[24] 2494 3-9-6 73 PhillipMakin 6 34
(M Dods) *hld up: rdn 1/2-way: a in rr* **11/4**[1]
0-40 **8** *4 1/2* **Bombay Mist**[96] 906 3-8-2 55 oh10 PaulEddery 5 —
(R C Guest) *chsd ldrs: sn drvn along: wknd 1/2-way* **66/1**

62.80 secs (0.50) **Going Correction** +0.10s/f (Slow) **8** Ran SP% **116.7**
Speed ratings (Par 99): **100,98,98,93,85 82,80,73**
toteswingers: 1&2 £3.80, 1&3 £4.30, 2&3 £4.00 CSF £18.86 CT £52.65 TOTE £3.70: £1.10, £2.50, £1.20; EX 25.90.
Owner Mrs Maureen Eason **Bred** Miss D Fleming **Trained** Hambleton, N Yorks

FOCUS
An ordinary handicap but, although the gallop was a strong one, those up with the pace held the edge. The first three finished clear and the winner edged centre to far side in the closing stages. The placed horses set the level rated close to their marks.

3278 WOLVERHAMPTON HOLIDAY INN AMATEUR RIDERS' (S) STKS 1m 4f 50y(P)
4:30 (4:32) (Class 6) 4-Y-O+ £1,714 (£527; £263) Stalls Low

Form RPR
035- **1** **Pure Crystal**[26] 7557 4-10-2 51 (b) MrJMQuinlan(5) 10 61
(M G Quinlan) *chsd ldrs: outpcd over 2f out: rallied over 1f out: rdn to ld ins fnl f: r.o* **25/1**
0000 **2** *3 1/4* **Alternative Choice (USA)**[20] 2636 4-10-12 53 MrsEmmaLittmoden 6 61
(N P Littmoden) *hld up: hdwy 5f out: led over 2f out: rdn clr over 1f out: hdd and unable qck ins fnl f* **50/1**
20/0 **3** *1* **Rickety Bridge (IRE)**[19] 2645 7-10-7 60 MrNdeBoinville(5) 1 59
(P R Chamings) *hld up: hdwy over 1f out: sn rdn: styd on same pce ins fnl f* **8/1**
0/30 **4** *shd* **Dancing Sword**[68] 1303 5-10-5 60 MrLLewis-Salter(7) 2 59
(D Burchell) *hld up: hdwy over 2f out: rdn over 1f out: styd on same pce ins fnl f* **16/1**
-405 **5** *2* **Transvestite (IRE)**[15] 1439 8-10-5 71 MrTGarner(7) 8 56
(Miss Tor Sturgis) *led: rdn and hdd over 2f out: no ex fnl f* **20/1**
0006 **6** *1 3/4* **Resplendent Ace (IRE)**[35] 2182 6-10-12 62 MrJPFeatherstone(5) 7 58
(P Howling) *hld up: hdwy over 2f out: rdn over 1f out: wknd ins fnl f* **5/1**[2]
0-04 **7** *6* **Rebellious Spirit**[15] 2786 7-10-7 65 MissLCGriffiths(5) 11 43
(S Curran) *chsd ldr tl rdn over 2f out: sn wknd* **20/1**
5-40 **8** *3/4* **Lapina (IRE)**[30] 2341 6-10-2 57 (b) MissJodieHughes(5) 5 37
(A Middleton) *chsd ldrs: sddle slipped sn after s: rdn and wknd wl over 1f out* **11/1**
230- **9** *8* **Traphalgar (IRE)**[177] 7848 5-10-12 77 MrsEEvans 3 29
(P D Evans) *hld up: hdwy 5f out: rdn and wknd wl over 2f out* **5/4**[1]
1-63 **10** *nk* **Annambo**[19] 2645 10-10-5 61 MrAJones(7) 12 29
(Andrew Reid) *s.i.s: hld up and a in rr* **7/1**[3]
1140 **11** *4 1/2* **Lyrical Intent**[58] 1539 4-10-10 59 MrDDooyea(7) 9 27
(P Howling) *hld up: a iin rr* **33/1**
12 *34* **Lilly De Rome**[36] 7-10-4 0 ow2 MrJamieJenkinson(5) 4 —
(K G Wingrove) *s.s: hld up and a in rr: t.o* **80/1**

2m 44.8s (3.70) **Going Correction** +0.10s/f (Slow) **12** Ran SP% **118.4**
Speed ratings (Par 101): **91,88,88,88,86 85,81,81,75,75 72,49**
toteswingers: 1&2 £57.80, 1&3 £28.30, 2&3 £31.60 CSF £885.42 TOTE £26.90: £8.10, £11.70, £3.80; EX 671.90.There was no bid for the winner.
Owner T Manning **Bred** D B Clark And Elsdon Farms **Trained** Newmarket, Suffolk
■ Stewards' Enquiry : Mr T Garner two-day ban: used whip with excessive frequency (TBA)

FOCUS
A modest seller in which the market leader disappointed. The gallop was a reasonable one and the winner edged towards the far side in the straight. The form is not the most solid.
Traphalgar(IRE) Official explanation: vet said gelding finished sore

3279 BET ONE DAY CRICKET - BETDAQ H'CAP (DIV I) 7f 32y(P)
5:00 (5:01) (Class 6) (0-60,60) 3-Y-O+ £1,433 (£423; £211) Stalls High

Form RPR
-005 **1** **Yankee Storm**[9] 2965 5-9-12 59 (v) JimmyQuinn 2 80+
(H J Collingridge) *hld up in tch: chsd ldr 2f out: shkn up to ld ins fnl f: r.o wl* **7/1**
0016 **2** *2 1/4* **Dream Win**[20] 2625 4-9-5 59 DaleSwift(7) 6 74+
(B Ellison) *led: rdn over 1f out: hdd and unable qck ins fnl f* **9/2**[2]
2033 **3** *4 1/2* **Dimaire**[11] 2892 3-9-4 60 (b) CathyGannon 4 60
(D Haydn Jones) *chsd ldrs: rdn over 1f out: no ex ins fnl f* **3/1**[1]
0040 **4** *2* **Bob Stock (IRE)**[35] 2188 4-9-11 58 JamieMackay 9 55
(W J Musson) *hld up: hdwy u.p over 1f out: eased whn btn ins fnl f* **5/1**[3]
3003 **5** *1* **Mr Chocolate Drop (IRE)**[4] 3131 6-9-4 54 (b) AshleyHamblett(3) 7 49
(Miss M E Rowland) *s.i.s: hld up: hdwy over 2f out: rdn over 1f out: no imp fnl f* **16/1**
00-0 **6** *1/2* **Forshour**[49] 1753 3-9-2 58 AdrianNicholls 11 48
(E S McMahon) *s.i.s: bhd: last and plenty to do turning for home: rdn and r.o ins fnl f: nvr nrr* **25/1**
000 **7** *1 1/4* **Woolston Ferry (IRE)**[9] 2967 4-9-6 60 (p) DavidKenny(7) 12 50
(David Pinder) *sn pushed along in rr: styd on fnl f: nvr on terms* **50/1**
0000 **8** *2 3/4* **Cheveyo (IRE)**[6] 3056 4-8-13 51 (t) JamesSullivan(5) 1 34
(Patrick Morris) *hld up: nvr on terms* **20/1**
6644 **9** *3/4* **Carmenero (GER)**[11] 2896 7-9-10 60 BarryMcHugh(3) 3 41
(C R Dore) *chsd ldr tl over 5f out: remained handy: rdn over 2f out: wknd over 1f out* **13/2**
4001 **10** *nk* **Feet Of Fury**[17] 2727 4-9-8 55 LiamJones 8 35
(W M Brisbourne) *chsd ldrs: rdn over 2f out: wknd over 1f out* **14/1**
1-03 **11** *10* **Orangeleg**[42] 1967 4-9-13 60 AndreaAtzeni 10 13
(S C Williams) *prom: chsd ldr over 5f out: rdn over 2f out: wknd over 1f out* **11/2**

1m 29.3s (-0.30) **Going Correction** +0.10s/f (Slow)
WFA 3 from 4yo+ 9lb **11** Ran SP% **124.2**
Speed ratings (Par 101): **105,102,97,95,93 93,91,88,87,87 76**
toteswingers: 1&2 £10.00, 1&3 £5.60, 2&3 £4.60 CSF £40.08 CT £119.13 TOTE £6.40: £2.70, £2.20, £2.40; EX 48.40.
Owner Greenstead Hall Racing Ltd **Bred** Mark Johnston Racing Ltd **Trained** Exning, Suffolk

FOCUS
Division one of an open and moderate handicap. The gallop was a reasonable one and the first two, who raced in the centre, pulled clear. The form looks sound.
Feet Of Fury Official explanation: jockey said filly hung right-handed
Orangeleg Official explanation: vet said gelding finished lame on his left-fore

3280 BET ONE DAY CRICKET - BETDAQ H'CAP (DIV II) 7f 32y(P)
5:30 (5:31) (Class 6) (0-60,60) 3-Y-O+ £1,433 (£423; £211) Stalls High

Form RPR
3560 **1** **Bold Diva**[41] 1998 5-9-3 55 (v) BillyCray(5) 12 65
(A W Carroll) *hld up: hdwy over 1f out: r.o to ld nr fin* **20/1**

6062 **2** nk **El Libertador (USA)**[17] 2726 4-9-8 **60** KierenFox(5) 2 69
(E A Wheeler) *chsd ldrs: rdn over 2f out: hung lft and led wl ins fnl f: hdd nr fin* **5/2**[1]

0002 **3** 2 1/4 **Towy Boy (IRE)**[17] 2727 5-8-13 **51** (bt) AmyRyan(5) 3 54
(I A Wood) *chsd ldr over 5f out: led 1/2-way: clr 2f out: hdd and no ex wl ins fnl f* **12/1**

5000 **4** 3 **Pipers Piping (IRE)**[19] 2639 4-9-7 **57** MichaelStainton(3) 5 52
(P Howling) *mid-div: rdn 1/2-way: hdwy and hung lft over 1f out: nvr trbld ldrs* **4/1**[2]

641- **5** nk **Eliza Doolittle**[238] 7051 4-9-12 **59** FrannyNorton 6 53
(Matthew Salaman) *chsd ldrs: rdn to go 2nd over 2f out: wknd fnl f* **4/1**[2]

00-0 **6** 3 1/2 **Stargazy**[4] 3129 6-8-10 **50** AmyScott(7) 9 35+
(A J Lidderdale) *s.s: outpcd: nvr nrr* **20/1**

-053 **7** 3 1/2 **Crystallize**[6] 3056 4-9-13 **60** (v[1]) PhillipMakin 1 35
(A B Haynes) *trckd ldrs: racd keenly: rdn over 2f out: wknd over 1f out* **6/1**[3]

00-6 **8** 2 1/4 **Villaruz (IRE)**[19] 2646 4-9-12 **59** JackMitchell 11 28
(J W Unett) *hld up: rdn 1/2-way: n.d* **66/1**

2223 **9** 1 **Tag Team (IRE)**[115] 721 9-8-11 **49** MarkCoumbe(5) 8 15
(John A Harris) *chsd ldrs tl wknd over 2f out* **33/1**

2140 **10** 2 3/4 **Dhhamaan (IRE)**[17] 2726 5-9-2 **54** (b) JamesSullivan(5) 7 13
(Mrs R A Carr) *led to 1/2-way: sn rdn: wknd over 1f out* **16/1**

445- **11** 1 3/4 **Downhill Skier (IRE)**[212] 7480 6-9-13 **60** LiamJones 4 14
(W M Brisbourne) *hmpd leaving stalls: hld up: rdn over 2f out: a in rr* **14/1**

1m 30.73s (1.13) **Going Correction** +0.10s/f (Slow) 11 Ran SP% 117.1
Speed ratings (Par 101): **97,96,94,90,90 86,82,79,78,75 73**
toteswingers: 1&2 £12.10, 1&3 £36.00, 2&3 £5.50 CSF £67.45 CT £667.45 TOTE £23.70: £8.40, £1.40, £3.20; EX 126.60 Place 6 £103.14, Place 5 £80.37.
Owner Mrs P Izamis **Bred** Peter Balding **Trained** Cropthorne, Worcs

FOCUS
Division two of a moderate handicap and a reasonable gallop lifted passing halfway. The winner raced towards the centre in the straight and is rated in line with her best Polytrack form, while the runner-up ran his best race since February.
T/Plt: £119.20 to a £1 stake. Pool: £61,157.30. 374.38 winning tickets. T/Qpdt: £30.70 to a £1 stake. Pool: £3,576.36. 86.20 winning tickets. CR

3106 BEVERLEY (R-H)
Tuesday, June 22

OFFICIAL GOING: Good to firm (watered; 9.1)
Wind: Light against Weather: Sunny and dry

3281 RACING AGAIN ON FRIDAY 2 JULY MAIDEN AUCTION STKS 7f 100y
2:15 (2:15) (Class 6) 2-Y-O **£2,331** (£693; £346; £173) **Stalls High**

Form RPR

1 **Beyeh (IRE)** 2-8-6 0 AdrianNicholls 3 70
(C E Brittain) *dwlt: sn chsng ldrs: hdwy and cl up 4f out: rdn to ld jst over 1f out: drvn ins fnl f: edgd lft and hld on wl towards fin* **5/2**[2]

5 **2** nk **Spartic**[12] 2895 2-8-9 0 JamesDoyle 5 73
(A J McCabe) *t.k.h: cl up: led after 1f: hdd over 4f out: trckd ldng pair: swtchd lft and rdn to chal ent fnl f: sn drvn and ev ch tl no ex nr fin* **20/1**

43 **3** 4 1/2 **Paper Dreams (IRE)**[20] 2654 2-8-10 0 PaulMulrennan 2 63
(K A Ryan) *cl up: led over 4f out: rdn along 2f out: drvn and hdd appr fnl f: sn wknd* **1/1**[1]

40 **4** shd **Dark Dune (IRE)**[25] 2498 2-9-1 0 DavidNolan 4 68
(T D Easterby) *trckd ldrs: hdwy over 2f out: rdn wl over 1f out: kpt on same pce* **20/1**

5 2 3/4 **Laffraaj (IRE)** 2-8-9 0 TomEaves 7 55+
(Pat Eddery) *s.i.s: sn pushed along and green: a in rr* **9/2**[3]

0556 **6** 2 3/4 **Dispol Snapper (IRE)**[7] 3058 2-8-11 0 PhillipMakin 6 51
(P T Midgley) *t.k.h: led 1f: prom tl rdn along 3f out and sn wknd* **14/1**

1m 35.06s (1.26) **Going Correction** -0.225s/f (Firm) 6 Ran SP% 112.9
Speed ratings (Par 91): **83,82,77,77,74 71**
toteswingers:1&2:£7.70, 1&3:£2.00, 2&3:£3.50 CSF £44.26 TOTE £3.60: £2.00, £5.50; EX 56.40.
Owner Saeed Manana **Bred** Michael McGlynn **Trained** Newmarket, Suffolk
■ Stewards' Enquiry : James Doyle caution; excessive use of whip

FOCUS
On a hot sunny afternoon the watered ground was described as 'very fast'. A low-grade maiden auction race run over an extended 7f and the early pace was very steady. Those that had run were taking a step up in distance and were also racing around a bend for the first time. Modest form but it has been rated 3lb better than the pre-race figures suggest.

NOTEBOOK
Beyeh(IRE), one of two newcomers, is a close-coupled daughter of King's Best. Forced to race wide, she took plenty of driving to hit the front and in the end did just enough. She will need to improve a good deal to defy a penalty and nurseries look a better option. (op 9-4)
Spartic, who made his debut on soft ground, is a keen-going sort. Forced to pull three wide to make his final effort, in the end he was just found lacking. The step up in trip clearly suited him. (op 18-1)
Paper Dreams(IRE), whose two previous starts were over 6f, was very keen and pulled her way to the front. In the end the first two saw the extended trip out much the better and she looks to lack scope. Official explanation: jockey said filly hung left (op 5-4 tchd 6-5 in a place)
Dark Dune(IRE), quite a nice type, improved on his first two efforts, staying on in his own time all the way to the line. Nurseries now beckon. (tchd 22-1)
Laffraaj(IRE), initially coltish and with two handlers in the paddock, missed the break and looked clueless. Staying on when it was all over, this will have opened his eyes. (tchd 5-1)
Dispol Snapper(IRE), having his sixth start, had already been beaten in selling company. He raced very freely and dropped right away in the end. (op 12-1)

3282 ST JOHN AMBULANCE CLAIMING STKS 1m 4f 16y
2:45 (2:45) (Class 6) 3-Y-O+ **£2,331** (£693; £346; £173) **Stalls High**

Form RPR

3505 **1** **Kames Park (IRE)**[7] 3060 8-9-8 76 PaulEddery 6 69+
(R C Guest) *s.i.s: hld up and bhd: smooth hdwy over 3f out: cl up on bit over 2f out: led appr fnl f: sn shkn up and styd on* **1/1**[1]

0441 **2** 1 3/4 **Chocolate Caramel (USA)**[18] 2694 8-9-3 70 PaulHanagan 7 61
(R A Fahey) *trckd ldrs: hdwy on outer over 3f out: rdn to ld wl over 2f out: drvn and hdd appr fnl f: kpt on same pce* **5/2**[2]

0420 **3** 1/2 **Dispol Diva**[5] 3122 4-8-12 52 (v) PhillipMakin 5 55
(P T Midgley) *chsd ldr: rdn along 3f out: drvn wl over 1f out: kpt on u.p fnl f* **8/1**

3100 **4** 4 **Slip**[12] 2897 5-9-4 66 (b) BarryMcHugh(3) 2 58
(C R Dore) *trckd ldng pair: hdwy and cl up over 4f out: led wl over 2f out: sn rdn and hdd wl over 1f out: grad wknd* **5/1**[3]

500- **5** 5 **Kwami Biscuit**[295] 5519 3-8-3 45 SilvestreDeSousa 1 46
(G A Harker) *hld up in tch: hdwy over 3f out: rdn along over 2f out: sn btn* **28/1**

00-0 **6** 6 **Mujada**[27] 2434 5-9-1 39 LeeVickers 3 34
(M W Easterby) *led: rdn along over 4f out: hdd & wknd wl over 2f out* **100/1**

2m 38.95s (-0.85) **Going Correction** -0.225s/f (Firm)
WFA 3 from 4yo+ 14lb 6 Ran SP% 110.8
Speed ratings (Par 101): **97,95,95,92,89 85**
toteswingers:1&2:£1.90, 1&3:£2.70, 2&3:£1.90 CSF £3.59 TOTE £2.00: £1.10, £2.60; EX 4.30.
Owner Miss Vicki Shaw **Bred** Pat Beirne **Trained** Stainforth, S Yorks

FOCUS
A standard claimer with the first two clear of the rest on official ratings. The winner did not need to run to his recent best and the third, fifth and sixth are the best guide to the form.
Chocolate Caramel(USA) Official explanation: vet said gelding finished distressed

3283 SIEMENS CHEMICAL EXPRESS H'CAP 1m 1f 207y
3:15 (3:15) (Class 4) (0-80,80) 4-Y-O+ **£4,857** (£1,445; £722; £360) **Stalls High**

Form RPR

5162 **1** **Danehillsundance (IRE)**[22] 2579 6-9-7 **80** (t) RobertWinston 7 87+
(D H Brown) *hld up in tch: swtchd lft and hdwy over 2f out: rdn over 1f out: chal ent fnl f: drvn and kpt on to ld last 100yds* **9/4**[1]

4330 **2** 3/4 **Umverti**[11] 2941 5-8-3 **62** FrannyNorton 3 67
(N Bycroft) *cl up: led after 2f: rdn along 2f out: drvn over 1f out: hdd and no ex last 100yds* **8/1**

2316 **3** hd **Patavium (IRE)**[11] 2941 7-8-7 **66** PaulHanagan 8 71
(E W Tuer) *trckd ldng pair on inner: effrt 2f out: swtchd lft and rdn to chse ldr over 1f out: sn ev ch: drvn ins fnl f: no ex fnl 50yds* **4/1**[3]

2510 **4** 1 **General Tufto**[11] 2937 5-8-11 **75** (b) BillyCray(5) 2 78
(C Smith) *hld up in rr: tk cl order over 2f out: swtchd outside and rdn over 1f out: styd on ins fnl f: nrst fin* **11/1**

3000 **5** nk **Iron Out (USA)**[11] 2937 4-9-3 **76** PhillipMakin 1 78
(R Hollinshead) *led 2f: trckd ldr: effrt and cl up 3f out: rdn over 2f out: drvn and ch over 1f out: kpt on same pce ins fnl f* **12/1**

314 **6** 2 3/4 **Ahlawy (IRE)**[33] 2243 7-9-4 **77** (t) LeeVickers 6 74
(F Sheridan) *dwlt: hld up towards rr: effrt on inner: wl over 2f out: sn rdn and no imp appr fnl f* **14/1**

2144 **7** 3 **Fujin Dancer (FR)**[22] 2608 5-9-1 **79** (p) AmyRyan(5) 5 70
(K A Ryan) *trckd ldrs: hdwy 4f out: cl up 3f out: rdn along over 2f out: drvn and wknd over 1f out* **5/2**[2]

2m 4.61s (-2.39) **Going Correction** -0.225s/f (Firm) 7 Ran SP% 113.1
Speed ratings (Par 105): **100,99,99,98,98 96,93**
toteswingers:1&2:£6.40, 1&3:£2.70, 2&3:£4.10 CSF £20.23 CT £67.05 TOTE £3.90: £2.30, £4.10; EX 20.40.
Owner J P Hardiman **Bred** J P Hardiman **Trained** Maltby, S Yorks
■ Stewards' Enquiry : Franny Norton caution; using whip without giving mount time to respond

FOCUS
A fair 62-80 handicap run, at a sensible pace but the placed horses are not well treated at present and not a race to rate positively.

3284 YORKSHIRE RACING SUMMER FESTIVAL H'CAP 7f 100y
3:45 (3:46) (Class 5) (0-70,70) 3-Y-O+ **£2,914** (£867; £433; £216) **Stalls High**

Form RPR

4511 **1** **Polish World (USA)**[5] 3124 6-9-4 **63** 6ex BarryMcHugh(3) 8 70
(P T Midgley) *mde all: rdn clr wl over 1f out: drvn ins fnl f: jst hld on* **11/10**[1]

0010 **2** shd **Pretty Orchid**[15] 2817 5-8-9 **51** oh1 (p) RobertWinston 7 58
(P T Midgley) *hld up in midfield: swtchd lft and hdwy 2f out: effrt and nt clr run over 1f out: rdn and styd on strly ins fnl f: jst failed* **50/1**

3300 **3** nk **Fathey (IRE)**[13] 2880 4-8-8 **55** BillyCray(5) 12 61
(C Smith) *a.p: rdn 2f out: drvn over 1f out: styd on wl fnl f* **16/1**

0633 **4** nse **Northern Flyer (GER)**[13] 2850 4-9-1 **57** (p) PaulHanagan 6 63
(J J Quinn) *hld up in tch: hdwy over 2f out: rdn to chse ldrs over 1f out: edgd rt and sn drvn: kpt on* **9/2**[2]

4412 **5** 2 **King's Sabre**[3] 3226 4-9-4 **60** (e) PaulEddery 2 61
(R C Guest) *hld up towards rr: hdwy on wd outside 2f out: rdn over 1f out: styd on ins fnl f: nrst fin* **12/1**

560- **6** 2 1/4 **North Shadow**[204] 7597 3-8-8 **59** FrannyNorton 15 54
(A D Brown) *chsd wnr: rdn along over 2f out: drvn wl over 1f out: wknd appr fnl f* **20/1**

322 **7** 3/4 **Mister Jingles**[18] 2700 7-9-0 **59** (v) MichaelStainton(3) 14 53
(R M Whitaker) *chsd ldrs on inner: rdn along 2f out: drvn over 1f out: grad wknd* **8/1**[3]

3443 **8** 1 **Kladester (USA)**[16] 2788 4-8-9 **51** (p) PaulMulrennan 5 42
(M Herrington) *chsd ldrs: rdn along over 2f out: drvn and wknd over 1f out* **18/1**

5020 **9** 1 1/2 **Ansells Pride (IRE)**[13] 2850 7-9-5 **68** AdamCarter(7) 3 55
(B Smart) *hld up: hdwy on outer wl over 2f out: rdn to chse ldrs over 1f out: sn wknd* **9/1**

5602 **10** 1 3/4 **Shannon Golden**[10] 2957 4-8-6 **51** oh2 AshleyHamblett(3) 13 34
(S R Bowring) *a towards rr* **25/1**

/00- **11** 2 1/2 **Musca (IRE)**[27] 2235 6-9-8 **64** PJMcDonald 10 41
(J Wade) *s.i.s: a bhd* **66/1**

600- **12** 23 **The Midshipmaid**[295] 5526 3-8-3 **54** oh1 ow3 AdrianNicholls 11 —
(Lucinda Featherstone) *s.i.s: a bhd* **80/1**

1m 31.68s (-2.12) **Going Correction** -0.225s/f (Firm)
WFA 3 from 4yo+ 9lb 12 Ran SP% 119.0
Speed ratings (Par 103): **103,102,102,102,100 97,96,95,93,91 89,62**
toteswingers:1&2:£14.40, 1&3:£6.40, 2&3:£50.20 CSF £95.47 CT £636.16 TOTE £2.50: £1.40, £10.10, £3.50; EX 60.30.
Owner C R Green **Bred** Racehorse Management, Llc **Trained** Westow, N Yorks

FOCUS
A modest 51-70 handicap run at a strong pace and in the end a four-way photo finish. The form looks fine rated around the third andf fourth, with the time reasonable.
Shannon Golden Official explanation: jockey said gelding missed break
Musca(IRE) Official explanation: jockey said gelding missed break
The Midshipmaid Official explanation: jockey said filly missed break

3285 RACING UK ON SKY 432 MEDIAN AUCTION MAIDEN STKS 1m 100y
4:15 (4:15) (Class 5) 3-Y-O **£2,729** (£806; £403) **Stalls High**

Form RPR

5-05 **1** **Ajool (USA)**[14] 2842 3-8-12 68 TadhgO'Shea 7 74
(B W Hills) *trckd ldr: effrt wl over 2f out: sn rdn along and hung rt 2f out: drvn over 1f out: styd on ent fnl f to ld last 100yds* **5/2**[2]

4224 **2** 1 1/2 **Ezra Church (IRE)**[10] 2981 3-9-3 76 PhillipMakin 5 76
(T D Barron) *led: rdn along over 2f out: drvn and jnd over 1f out: hdd and no ex last 100yds* 4/7[1]
3 13 **Slinky Malinki (IRE)** 3-8-7 0 LanceBetts(5) 3 41
(T D Easterby) *s.i.s and bhd tl styd on fnl 2f: nvr a factor* 16/1
0 **4** 3 3/4 **Roydmore**[13] 2852 3-9-3 0 PaulHanagan 1 37
(R A Fahey) *s.i.s: a in rr* 14/1[3]
5 4 **Majic Mojo** 3-8-9 0 MichaelStainton(3) 6 23
(R M Whitaker) *t.k.h: in tch: pushed along over 3f out and sn outpcd* 33/1
0 **6** 6 **Presidium Galaxy**[96] 915 3-8-12 0 PJMcDonald 4 9
(G M Moore) *chsd ldng pair: rdn along wl over 3f out: sn wknd* 50/1

1m 45.1s (-2.50) **Going Correction** -0.225s/f (Firm) 6 Ran SP% **109.7**
Speed ratings (Par 99): **103,101,88,84,80 74**
CSF £4.02 TOTE £3.30: £1.40, £1.10; EX 4.20.
Owner Hamdan Al Maktoum **Bred** Shadwell Farm LLC **Trained** Lambourn, Berks

FOCUS
A very modest extended 1m maiden with just the first two under serious consideration. The runner-up sets the level.

3286 STARS OF THE FUTURE APPRENTICE H'CAP (DIV I) 5f
4:45 (4:46) (Class 6) (0-55,55) 3-Y-O+ **£2,007** (£597; £298; £149) **Stalls High**

Form RPR
520- **1** **Helping Hand (IRE)**[276] 6119 5-8-7 **50** NicolaJackson(7) 10 55
(R Hollinshead) *racd centre: mde most: rdn over 1f out: kpt on ins fnl f: jst hld on* 12/1
0062 **2** nk **Darcy's Pride (IRE)**[15] 2818 6-8-13 **54** NeilFarley(5) 14 58+
(P T Midgley) *chsd ldrs: hdwy 2f out: hmpd and carried lft wl over 1f out: swtchd rt and rdn ent fnl f: styd on strly towards fin* 7/4[1]
001 **3** nk **Port Ronan (USA)**[4] 3181 4-9-1 **51** 6ex RyanPowell 2 54
(J S Wainwright) *dwlt and towards rr: hdwy 2f out: nt clr run and swtchd rt over 1f out: sn rdn and styd on wl fnl f* 16/1
-040 **4** 1 **Rio Sands**[15] 2818 5-9-5 **55** SoniaEaton 5 54
(R M Whitaker) *in tch on outer: hdwy to chse ldrs 2f out: sn rdn and kpt on fnl f* 6/1[2]
0100 **5** 3 1/4 **Head To Head (IRE)**[130] 525 6-9-2 **52** (bt) RichardRowe 12 40
(A D Brown) *trckd ldrs: swtchd to ins and hdwy over 1f out: rdn and ch ent fnl f: sn wknd* 16/1
5466 **6** 1/2 **Turf Time**[8] 3026 3-8-11 **53** MatthewLawson 11 37
(J A Glover) *chsd ldrs: rdn along 2f out: n.m.r over 1f out and sn one pce* 9/1[3]
40-0 **7** 1 1/2 **Menediva**[5] 3111 3-8-6 **48** JamesRogers 8 27
(L A Mullaney) *chsd ldrs: rdn along wl over 1f out: grad wknd* 66/1
0300 **8** nse **Commander Wish**[3] 3205 7-8-7 **48** JosephYoung(5) 1 28
(Lucinda Featherstone) *a towards rr* 11/1
50-0 **9** 1/2 **Govenor Eliott (IRE)**[163] 113 5-8-6 **47** (b) ShaneBKelly(5) 6 26
(A J Lockwood) *towards rr tl sme late hdwy* 28/1
00-0 **10** hd **Calley Ho**[13] 2854 4-8-11 **52** NoraLooby(5) 4 30
(Mrs L Stubbs) *in rr and rdn along 1/2-way: swtchd rt and sme hdwy wl over 1f out: sn btn* 10/1
6300 **11** 4 1/2 **Fine And Dandie (IRE)**[78] 1118 3-8-5 **52** LukeStrong(5) 13 12
(D Nicholls) *prom: rdn along 2f out: wkng whn hmpd over 1f out* 16/1
4040 **12** 1 **Trick Or Two**[7] 3064 4-8-10 **53** (b) ShirleyTeasdale(7) 9 11
(Mrs R A Carr) *dwlt: sn chsng ldrs: rdn and hung bdly lft 2f out: sn wknd* 6/1[2]

63.33 secs (-0.17) **Going Correction** 0.0s/f (Good)
WFA 3 from 4yo+ 6lb 12 Ran SP% **122.6**
Speed ratings (Par 101): **101,100,100,98,93 92,90,89,89,88 81,80**
toteswingers:1&2:£8.80, 1&3:£27.40, 2&3:£7.20 CSF £34.32 CT £368.45 TOTE £12.10: £3.00, £1.70, £4.50; EX 56.10.
Owner N Chapman **Bred** P F Mulholland **Trained** Upper Longdon, Staffs

FOCUS
Part one of a divided rock bottom 48-55 apprentice riders' sprint handicap. The runner-up sets the level but the form is not solid.

3287 STARS OF THE FUTURE APPRENTICE H'CAP (DIV II) 5f
5:15 (5:17) (Class 6) (0-55,55) 3-Y-O+ **£2,007** (£597; £298; £149) **Stalls High**

Form RPR
40-0 **1** **Pinball (IRE)**[130] 525 4-8-11 **52** (v) HarryBentley(5) 14 60
(Mrs L Williamson) *cl up on inner: led 1/2-way: qcknd clr over 1f out: rdn ins fnl f: drvn out towards fin* 4/1[1]
0-26 **2** hd **Foreign Rhythm (IRE)**[32] 2278 5-9-1 **51** RyanPowell 9 58
(R E Barr) *in tch: hdwy to chse ldrs 2f out: rdn wl over 1f out: styd on to chse wnr ent fnl f: sn drvn and jst failed* 9/2[2]
5001 **3** 1/2 **Exceedingly Good (IRE)**[20] 2647 4-9-3 **53** SoniaEaton 5 58+
(S R Bowring) *towards rr: hdwy on wd outside wl over 1f out: sn rdn and styd on strly ins fnl f* 13/2[3]
3450 **4** 2 1/4 **Fashion Icon (USA)**[13] 2849 4-8-6 **47** ShaneBKelly(5) 4 44
(D O'Meara) *a chsng ldrs: rdn along wl over 1f out: drvn ent fnl f and kpt on same pce* 7/1
0600 **5** hd **Divine Spirit**[13] 2849 9-9-0 **55** FrancisHayes(5) 2 51
(M Dods) *stdd and swtchd rt s: hdwy on inner wl over 1f out: sn rdn and styd on ins fnl f: nrst fin* 14/1
2036 **6** shd **Duke Of Rainford**[3] 3228 3-8-11 **53** AdamCarter 8 47
(M Herrington) *towards rr: hdwy 2f out: swtchd rt and rdn over 1f out: kpt on ins fnl f: nrst fin* 15/2
0/ **7** 2 3/4 **Call The Law (IRE)**[45] 1936 4-8-9 **52** ChristyMews(7) 1 38
(Mrs P Sly) *in tch on wd outside: rdn along 2f out: no hdwy* 14/1
0430 **8** nk **Media Jury**[3] 3228 3-8-10 **52** RichardRowe 6 35
(J S Wainwright) *chsd ldrs: rdn along 2f out: grad wknd* 40/1
0056 **9** 1 1/4 **Sandy Toes**[37] 2161 3-8-4 **46** oh1 (p) MatthewLawson 7 25
(J A Glover) *dwlt: a towards rr* 22/1
00-2 **10** 2 3/4 **Azygous**[13] 2849 7-8-9 **52** DavidSimmonson(7) 13 23
(G P Kelly) *prom: rdn 2f out and sn wknd* 4/1[1]
00/0 **11** hd **Prigsnov Dancer (IRE)**[16] 2790 5-8-13 **54** AndrewYoxall(5) 10 24
(O Brennan) *chsd ldrs: rdn along 2f out: sn drvn and grad wknd* 18/1
00-0 **12** hd **Take That**[163] 112 5-8-5 **46** oh1 NoraLooby(5) 12 15
(S P Griffiths) *cl up: rdn along over 2f out: sn wknd* 50/1
00-0 **13** 1 **Molly Two**[18] 2695 5-8-8 **49** (be[1]) NeilFarley(5) 3 15
(L A Mullaney) *sn led: rdn along and hdd 1/2-way: wknd wl over 1f out* 25/1

63.42 secs (-0.08) **Going Correction** 0.0s/f (Good)
WFA 3 from 4yo+ 6lb 13 Ran SP% **127.0**
Speed ratings (Par 101): **100,99,98,95,94 94,90,89,87,83 83,82,81**
toteswingers:1&2:£6.10, 1&3:£6.70, 2&3:£7.10 CSF £22.46 CT £124.72 TOTE £5.90: £2.80, £1.40, £3.50; EX 28.10 Place 6 £19.17; Place 5 £4.48.
Owner D Manning, D Roycroft, P Kelly **Bred** John Morris **Trained** Saighton, Cheshire

FOCUS
Part two and a 46-55 handicap this time. The winner is rated to last year's form with the third to her latest mark.
Sandy Toes Official explanation: jockey said gelding was denied a clear run
Azygous Official explanation: trainer said gelding was found dehydrated after race
T/Plt: £28.00 to a £1 stake. Pool:£51,451.16 - 1,338.10 winning tickets T/Qpdt: £5.00 to a a £1 stake. Pool:£4,120.47 - 609.70 winning tickets JR

3052 BRIGHTON (L-H)
Tuesday, June 22

OFFICIAL GOING: Good to firm (watered; 8.6)
Wind: Moderate, against Weather: Sunny and warm

3288 BRAKES FOR FRESH IDEAS MAIDEN AUCTION STKS 5f 213y
2:30 (2:30) (Class 5) 2-Y-O **£2,849** (£847; £423; £211) **Stalls Low**

Form RPR
1 **Star Now** 2-8-7 SamHitchcott 6 74+
(M R Channon) *hld up: hdwy over 2f out: led over 1f out: rdn clr: comf* 15/2
32 **2** 3 1/4 **Stunning In Purple (IRE)**[28] 2413 2-8-0 AmyBaker(5) 5 62
(A B Haynes) *chsd ldng pair: wnt 2nd 1f out: nt pce of wnr* 3/1[3]
0 **3** nk **High On The Hog (IRE)**[31] 2319 2-8-13 NeilCallan 2 69
(J L Dunlop) *disp ld: slt ld over 3f out tl over 1f out: one pce* 2/1[1]
000 **4** 1 **Bendigedig**[19] 2677 2-8-7 LiamKeniry 3 60
(S Kirk) *towards rr: last and rdn 2f out: kpt on fr over 1f out: nt pce to chal* 66/1
403 **5** 3/4 **Comrade Bond**[13] 2867 2-8-11 TomQueally 1 62
(M H Tompkins) *in tch in 4th: rdn to press ldrs 2f out: no ex fnl f* 5/2[2]
054 **6** 1 **Moorland Boy**[10] 2951 2-8-13 FergusSweeney 4 61
(J A Osborne) *plld hrd: disp ld over 2f: prom tl outpcd wl over 1f out* 10/1

1m 11.67s (1.47) **Going Correction** +0.025s/f (Good) 6 Ran SP% **109.3**
Speed ratings (Par 93): **91,86,86,84,83 82**
toteswingers:1&2:£3.40, 1&3:£2.80, 2&3:£2.40 CSF £28.41 TOTE £9.60: £4.60, £1.10; EX 13.40.
Owner Jaber Abdullah **Bred** Baydon House Stud **Trained** West Ilsley, Berks

FOCUS
A modest juvenile maiden. The runner-up and sixth are the best guides to the form.

NOTEBOOK
Star Now, a half-sister to several winners, made an encouraging debut. Easy in the betting and looking in need of the run, she was not the quickest away and obliged to race wide. She showed good speed, though, and after leading 1f out was well in command at the finish. (op 11-2 tchd 5-1)
Stunning In Purple(IRE), in the frame in all four previous starts and receiving weight from each of her rivals, set only a modest standard but seemed to run her race. She was always prominent and stayed on gamely enough in the closing stages to indicate she can make a mark in nurseries. (op 2-1 tchd 15-8 and 10-3)
High On The Hog(IRE), slowly away when in midfield in a Goodwood maiden first time out, was much quicker from the stalls here. He got a nice rail position, too, so the fact that he was overhauled in the closing stages suggests he has only limited ability. Nurseries will probably be his metier too. (op 10-3 tchd 7-2 and 15-8)
Bendigedig, down the field in her three previous starts, appears to have shown slightly improved form in this. If she steps up again, a low-level contest, possibly in claiming or selling grade, should eventually come her way.
Comrade Bond, who showed improved form to be third on Polytrack on his most recent outing, fared less well on this return to turf. He was close up early on, but faded tamely in the final furlong. (op 7-2)
Moorland Boy, fourth over 5f here ten days previously, was very keen and used up too much energy to get home. (op 13-2)

3289 CRABBIES ALCOHOLIC GINGER BEER H'CAP 6f 209y
3:00 (3:00) (Class 5) (0-75,75) 3-Y-O+ **£2,849** (£847; £423; £211) **Stalls Centre**

Form RPR
0000 **1** **Seneschal**[29] 2383 9-9-1 **67** HobieGill(7) 1 84
(M Appleby) *mde virtually all: rdn clr fnl 2f: readily* 50/1
450- **2** 6 **Patavium Prince (IRE)**[243] 6964 7-10-0 **73** IanMongan 7 74
(Miss Jo Crowley) *mid-div: hdwy to dispute 2nd 2f out: kpt on to hold 2nd: nt pce of wnr* 10/1
6-13 **3** hd **Ocean Countess (IRE)**[16] 2783 4-9-12 **71** CathyGannon 6 71
(Miss J Feilden) *towards rr: rdn and dropped to last 4f out: rallied and r.o fnl f* 15/8[1]
01 **4** nk **Dashing Beauty (IRE)**[12] 2903 4-9-9 **68** AdamKirby 10 67
(M G Quinlan) *towards rr: rdn 3f out: hdwy to dispute 2nd 2f out: one pce* 10/1
5010 **5** 1 1/4 **Timeteam (IRE)**[16] 2783 4-9-6 **70** RichardEvans(5) 9 66
(P D Evans) *s.s: bhd: hrd rdn over 2f out: styd on fnl f* 25/1
-006 **6** 3/4 **Hi Shinko**[16] 2783 4-9-13 **72** JimCrowley 4 66
(B R Millman) *w wnr early: prom tl hrd rdn and wknd 2f out* 4/1[3]
-541 **7** 1 1/2 **Choreography**[7] 3057 7-10-2 **75** 6ex (b) PatDobbs 5 65
(Jim Best) *trckd ldrs in 4th tl hrd rdn and wknd 2f out* 13/2
0-46 **8** 1/2 **Desert Liaison**[64] 1431 3-8-13 **67** (v[1]) TomQueally 2 53
(J Noseda) *chsd ldng pair tl rdn and wknd 2f out* 7/2[2]

1m 22.15s (-0.95) **Going Correction** +0.025s/f (Good)
WFA 3 from 4yo+ 9lb 8 Ran SP% **114.3**
Speed ratings (Par 103): **106,99,98,98,97 96,94,94**
toteswingers:1&2:£22.30, 1&3:£13.80, 2&3:£4.20 CSF £473.86 CT £1441.47 TOTE £41.80: £6.60, £2.90, £1.10; EX 252.00 Trifecta £494.50 Part won. Pool: £668.30 - 0.83 winning units..
Owner Colin Rogers **Bred** Michael E Broughton **Trained** Compton Verney, Warwicks

FOCUS
Only an ordinary handicap, with the top weight rated 75, but it looked very competitive on paper. The winner is rated back to his best.

3290 MORGAN SINDALL H'CAP 1m 3f 196y
3:30 (3:30) (Class 6) (0-65,63) 4-Y-O+ **£2,072** (£616; £308; £153) **Stalls High**

Form RPR
303- **1** **Gulf President**[22] 4241 4-9-1 **60** AndrewHeffernan(3) 8 74
(Tim Vaughan) *drvn along in rr after 1f: on and off the bridle: rapid hdwy to join ldr 5f out: led 3f out: clr over 1f out* 5/1[3]
6430 **2** 8 **Rosy Dawn**[10] 2966 5-8-3 **45** NeilChalmers 5 46
(J J Bridger) *led: drvn along and hdd 3f out: outpcd by wnr fnl 2f* 16/1
6015 **3** 3 **Free Falling**[10] 2952 4-8-6 **48** (v) DavidProbert 1 44
(Miss Gay Kelleway) *dwlt: drvn along early: sn prom: rdn 1/2-way: one pce fnl 3f* 7/1

1346 **4** *nk* **Little Sark (IRE)**[12] 2897 5-8-10 **55**.......... MartinLane(3) 3 51
(P D Evans) *mid-div: rdn 6f out: mod effrt 4f out: no imp whn hung lft fnl 3f* **5/1**[3]

-F63 **5** *5* **Seaquel**[14] 611 4-8-0 **47**.......... (v) AmyBaker(5) 6 35
(A B Haynes) *in tch disputing 4th: rdn 6f out: wknd 3f out* **5/2**[2]

-000 **6** *hd* **Miss Jabba (IRE)**[43] 1958 4-8-3 **45**.......... (p) CathyGannon 2 32
(Miss J Feilden) *towards rr: sme hdwy and rdn in 4th over 4f out: wknd 3f out* **40/1**

3222 **7** *12* **Yourgolftravel Com**[7] 3054 5-9-7 **63**.......... StephenCraine 4 31
(M Wigham) *stdd s: hld up in rr: brief effrt on ins rail 5f out: wknd over 3f out* **9/4**[1]

-056 **8** *26* **Ledgerwood**[20] 2655 5-7-12 **45**.......... (p) DeclanCannon(5) 9 —
(A J Chamberlain) *chsd ldr tl wknd rapidly 5f out: sn wl bhd* **33/1**

2m 32.44s (-0.26) **Going Correction** +0.025s/f (Good) **8** Ran SP% **116.4**
Speed ratings (Par 101): **101,95,93,93,90 90,82,64**
toteswingers:1&2:£7.70, 1&3:£5.20, 2&3:£6.20 CSF £79.67 CT £562.50 TOTE £8.40: £2.80, £3.10, £1.90; EX 84.80 TRIFECTA Not won..
Owner Diamond Racing Ltd **Bred** Mrs J Gittins **Trained** Aberthin, Vale of Glamorgan
■ Stewards' Enquiry : Amy Baker one-day ban; careless riding (6th) July

FOCUS
A modest handicap, lacking depth, and weakened by the late absence of likely favourite Iceman George. The field finished well strung out and the runner-up is rated to her recent best.
Ledgerwood Official explanation: jockey said gelding lost its action

3291 SIS LIVE H'CAP — 7f 214y
4:00 (4:01) (Class 6) (0-55,55) 3-Y-O+ **£2,201** (£655; £327; £163) **Stalls** Low

Form — RPR

0-06 **1** **Stargazy**[1] 3280 6-8-9 **50**.......... AmyScott(7) 6 58
(A J Lidderdale) *s.s: bhd tl hdwy 3f out: styd on to ld ins fnl f* **20/1**

0-66 **2** *1½* **Fire King**[10] 2955 4-9-2 **50**.......... (p) NeilCallan 13 55
(A B Haynes) *chsd ldrs: led 2f out tl ins fnl f: nt qckn* **5/2**[1]

3003 **3** *½* **Foxtrot Bravo (IRE)**[16] 2781 4-8-12 **46** oh1.......... (b) NeilChalmers 1 49
(Miss S L Davison) *prom: led 3f out tl 2f out: styd on same pce* **10/1**

6000 **4** *shd* **The Mouse Carroll (IRE)**[112] 763 6-9-4 **52**.....(b) FrankieMcDonald 16 55
(S Curran) *dwlt: pushed along towards rr early: hdwy over 4f out: styd on fnl 2f* **14/1**

0040 **5** *½* **Prince Valentine**[7] 3056 9-8-13 **47**.......... (p) TomQueally 3 50+
(G L Moore) *hld up in midfield: rdn 3f out: hdwy on ins rail 2f out: disputing 3rd and hld whn n.m.r nr fin* **12/1**

56-0 **6** *¾* **Rebel Woman**[13] 2874 4-9-2 **50**.......... FergusSweeney 5 50
(J A Osborne) *hld up in rr: rdn and styng on whn swtchd rt 1f out: nrst fin* **25/1**

0004 **7** *½* **Easy Wonder (GER)**[13] 2875 5-8-12 **46** oh1.......... CathyGannon 7 45
(I A Wood) *towards rr: rdn and hdwy 2f out: nt rch ldrs* **40/1**

6-00 **8** *4½* **Dancing Poppy**[10] 2956 3-8-10 **54**.......... JimCrowley 10 41
(R A Farrant) *bhd tl sme late hdwy* **16/1**

004- **9** *1½* **Northern Genes (AUS)**[207] 7550 4-9-1 **50**.......... (p) GeorgeBaker 9 34
(M Appleby) *led tl 3f out: wknd 1f out* **16/1**

0000 **10** *½* **Baxter (IRE)**[26] 2480 3-8-5 **52**.......... (p) PatrickHills(3) 2 34
(J W Hills) *towards rr: hrd rdn 3f out: n.d* **66/1**

0035 **11** *1¼* **Bere Davis (FR)**[22] 2596 5-9-4 **55**.......... AndrewHeffernan(3) 14 36
(P D Evans) *in tch on outer: lost pl 5f out: btn whn hung lft over 1f out* **11/4**[2]

004- **12** *4* **Knowledgeable**[239] 7055 3-8-2 **46** oh1.......... DavidProbert 12 16
(B Palling) *in tch tl wknd 4f out* **9/1**[3]

0-60 **13** *9* **Auburn Place**[70] 1278 3-8-10 **54**.......... (b[1]) LiamKeniry 11 —
(E F Vaughan) *t.k.h: prom tl wknd 4f out* **20/1**

000 **14** *2½* **Yehonala (USA)**[56] 1590 3-8-6 **50**.......... KirstyMilczarek 15 —
(J R Best) *prom 4f* **50/1**

1m 36.25s (0.25) **Going Correction** +0.025s/f (Good)
WFA 3 from 4yo+ 10lb **14** Ran SP% **119.7**
Speed ratings (Par 101): **99,97,97,96,96 95,95,90,89,88 87,83,74,71**
toteswingers:1&2:£16.20, 1&3:£32.70, 2&3:£5.80 CSF £65.85 CT £571.47 TOTE £31.10: £8.40, £1.90, £2.00; EX 123.70 TRIFECTA Not won..
Owner C S J Beek **Bred** Bearstone Stud **Trained** Eastbury, Berks
■ Stewards' Enquiry : Neil Callan two-day ban; careless riding (6th-8th) July

FOCUS
A weak handicap that was soundly run and the form is taken at face value, with the runner-up and fourth close to their marks.
Stargazy Official explanation: jockey said gelding missed the break

3292 INSURECOM REAL-TIME PROPOSITION H'CAP — 5f 213y
4:30 (4:30) (Class 6) (0-60,60) 3-Y-O+ **£2,201** (£655; £327; £163) **Stalls** Low

Form — RPR

45-0 **1** **Forest Dane**[18] 2719 10-9-9 **58**.......... TomQueally 2 66
(Mrs N Smith) *in tch: hmpd and lost pl over 4f out: hdwy and nt clr run 2f out: r.o to ld fnl 50yds* **8/1**[3]

-042 **2** *hd* **Bermondsey Bob (IRE)**[12] 2896 4-9-6 **55**.......... SamHitchcott 11 62
(J L Spearing) *prom: slt ld 3f out: hrd rdn fnl f: hdd fnl 50yds: r.o* **8/1**[3]

0000 **3** *nk* **Top Flight Splash**[16] 2779 4-8-8 **46** oh1.......... MartinLane(3) 5 52
(P D Evans) *towards rr: effrt and hrd rdn 2f out: r.o fr over 1f out: clsng at fin* **17/2**

0-20 **4** *nk* **Maryolini**[21] 2635 5-9-6 **55**.......... NickyMackay 3 60
(T Keddy) *chsd ldrs: disp ld over 1f out tl ins fnl f: nt qckn* **20/1**

0-45 **5** *hd* **Super Frank (IRE)**[14] 2846 7-9-10 **59**.......... (p) J-PGuillambert 8 63
(J Akehurst) *rdn along towards rr: r.o fnl 2f: nrst fin* **8/1**[3]

3506 **6** *¾* **Dualagi**[16] 2779 6-9-2 **51**.......... GeorgeBaker 4 53+
(M R Bosley) *bhd: sme hdwy whn hmpd on rail and dropped to last over 4f out: r.o fr over 1f out: gng on at fin* **5/1**[1]

-003 **7** *nk* **Rio Royale (IRE)**[18] 2719 4-9-10 **59**.......... (p) JimCrowley 13 60
(Mrs A J Perrett) *prom tl no ex fnl f* **9/1**

161 **8** *¾* **Boldinor**[16] 2779 7-9-9 **58**.......... DavidProbert 14 57
(M R Bosley) *mid-div: effrt and hrd rdn over 2f out: styd on same pce: nvr able to chal* **13/2**[2]

06-0 **9** *hd* **One Cool Slash (IRE)**[21] 2632 3-8-8 **50**.......... LiamKeniry 6 46
(M J McGrath) *bhd tl shkn up and styd on fr over 1f out* **33/1**

4500 **10** *shd* **Hart Of Gold**[14] 2840 6-9-1 **50**.......... (p) RichardThomas 1 48
(R A Harris) *led tl 3f out: wknd fnl f* **12/1**

0-00 **11** *½* **Joss Stick**[36] 2178 5-8-7 **47**.......... SophieDoyle(5) 7 43
(R A Harris) *mid-div: hdwy and in tch 2f out: wknd fnl f* **40/1**

2423 **12** *2* **Bold Ring**[29] 2385 4-9-5 **54**.......... EddieCreighton 10 44
(E J Creighton) *towards rr: rdn over 2f out: n.d* **14/1**

0550 **13** *nk* **Come On Buckers (IRE)**[18] 2721 4-9-1 **50**.......... (b) AdamKirby 9 39
(E J Creighton) *prom tl wknd over 1f out* **14/1**

3045 **14** *6* **Speedyfix**[13] 2879 3-8-8 **50**.......... (bt[1]) AdrianMcCarthy 12 18
(Mrs C A Dunnett) *dwlt: hdwy over 4f out: hung bdly lft and wknd 2f out* **18/1**

00/0 **15** *8* **Jucebabe**[15] 2809 7-8-11 **46** oh1.......... (p) FergusSweeney 16 —
(John R Upson) *in tch on outer: wknd over 2f out: eased* **66/1**

1m 10.59s (0.39) **Going Correction** +0.025s/f (Good)
WFA 3 from 4yo+ 7lb **15** Ran SP% **121.8**
Speed ratings (Par 101): **98,97,97,96,96 95,95,94,94,93 93,90,90,82,71**
toteswingers:1&2:£12.40, 1&3:£20.50, 2&3:£15.60 CSF £68.81 CT £580.95 TOTE £8.80: £2.80, £2.90, £2.60; EX 75.40 TRIFECTA Not won..
Owner The Ember Partnership **Bred** Loan And Development Corporation **Trained** Bury, W Sussex
■ Stewards' Enquiry : Adam Kirby four-day ban; careless riding (6th-12th) July

FOCUS
A poor handicap and the first nine were covered by around three lengths, although the winner and placed horses ran close to recent marks.
Dualagi Official explanation: jockey said mare suffered interference in running

3293 4TH JULY MASCOT DERBY FAMILY RACEDAY H'CAP — 5f 59y
5:00 (5:02) (Class 6) (0-65,66) 3-Y-O+ **£2,072** (£616; £308; £153) **Stalls** Low

Form — RPR

0540 **1** **Littlemisssunshine (IRE)**[17] 2751 5-9-13 **63**.......... (t) LiamKeniry 2 71
(T B P Coles) *chsd ldrs: led over 1f out: drvn out* **5/2**[2]

0-21 **2** *1½* **Multahab**[7] 3052 11-9-11 **66** 6ex.......... (t) TobyAtkinson(5) 5 69
(M Wigham) *prom: c alone to centre in st: chsd wnr fnl f: nt qckn* **15/8**[1]

6000 **3** *¾* **Wanchai Whisper**[13] 2868 3-8-13 **58**.......... (p) AndrewHeffernan(3) 4 56
(P R Hedger) *hld up: hdwy to chse ldrs over 1f out: one pce fnl f* **20/1**

0340 **4** *1¾* **Nawaaff**[18] 2720 5-8-9 **45**.......... DavidProbert 7 39
(M Quinn) *in tch: outpcd and lost pl after 2f: styd on fnl f* **12/1**

0664 **5** *nse* **Caribbean Coral**[7] 3052 11-9-1 **58**.......... MarkPower(7) 6 52
(A B Haynes) *bhd tl styd on fr over 1f out* **12/1**

000 **6** *¾* **Morgans Choice**[3] 3211 3-9-9 **65**.......... (b[1]) SamHitchcott 3 56
(J L Spearing) *led tl over 1f out: wknd fnl f* **25/1**

-015 **7** *2¼* **Pressed For Time (IRE)**[15] 2809 4-9-3 **53**.......... (vt) EddieCreighton 1 36
(E J Creighton) *prom tl wknd over 1f out* **5/1**[3]

-504 **8** *8* **Kings Of Leo**[16] 2784 3-9-9 **65**.......... (be) StephenCraine 8 17
(J R Boyle) *sn prom: outpcd and lost pl 3f out: struggling after* **14/1**

62.80 secs (0.50) **Going Correction** +0.025s/f (Good)
WFA 3 from 4yo+ 6lb **8** Ran SP% **110.7**
Speed ratings (Par 101): **97,94,93,90,90 89,85,72**
toteswingers:1&2:£12.40, 1&3:£20.50, 2&3:£15.60 CSF £7.04 CT £64.68 TOTE £3.50: £1.40, £1.90, £4.40; EX 9.40 Trifecta £117.70 Place 6 £357.61; Place 5 £75.64. Pool: £652.18 - 4.10 winning units..
Owner T Coles & J Oakes **Bred** Swordlestown Stud **Trained** Newmarket, Suffolk

FOCUS
A moderate handicap and best rated around the principals.
T/Plt: £243.40 to a £1 stake. Pool:£78,477.34 - 235.36 winning tickets T/Qpdt: £51.60 to a £1 stake. Pool:£4,493.82 - 64.40 winning tickets LM

2887 NEWBURY (L-H)
Tuesday, June 22

OFFICIAL GOING: Good to firm (watering; 9.0)
Wind: modest, against Weather: warm and sunny

3294 PUMP TECHNOLOGY APPRENTICE H'CAP — 1m 3f 5y
6:20 (6:20) (Class 5) (0-70,70) 4-Y-O+ **£2,590** (£770; £385; £192) **Stalls** Low

Form — RPR

1312 **1** **Ghufa (IRE)**[3] 3221 6-9-10 **70**.......... SimonPearce 3 73
(J Pearce) *hld up wl off the pce towards rr: stdy prog fr over 2f out: swtchd rt 2f out: r.o wl to ld fnl 75yds: gng away fin* **9/2**[3]

02 **2** *1* **Contradiktive (IRE)**[22] 2604 4-8-5 **51** oh5.......... (b) JamesSullivan 5 52
(J R Boyle) *led tl over 4f out: styd handy: drvn and swtchd rt 2f out: rallied u.p to ld 1f out: hdd and no ex fnl 75yds* **9/1**

20/0 **3** *¾* **Black Coffee**[12] 2894 5-9-7 **67**.......... (p) KierenFox 4 67
(W M Brisbourne) *t.k.h: hld up in tch: rdn and effrt 3f out: drvn to ld over 1f out tl hdd 1f out: kpt on same pce ins fnl f* **14/1**

0-0 **4** *2¼* **Shooting Party (IRE)**[39] 2080 4-9-4 **67**.......... CharlesEddery(3) 6 63
(R Hannon) *chsd ldrs: rdn 4f out: pressing ldrs u.p 2f out: edgd rt and wknd ent fnl f* **33/1**

0623 **5** *¾* **Choral Festival**[8] 3040 4-8-8 **57**.......... (v) RyanClark(3) 11 51
(J J Bridger) *pressed ldr tl led over 4f out: edgd lft u.p jst over 2f out: hdd over 1f out: wknd jst ins fnl f* **12/1**

266- **6** *1½* **Force Group (IRE)**[213] 7475 6-9-8 **68**.......... AshleyMorgan 9 60
(M H Tompkins) *s.i.s: wl bhd: rdn over 3f out: no hdwy tl plugged on past btn horses fnl f: nvr trbld ldrs* **8/1**

3-4 **7** *hd* **Aegean King**[60] 1508 4-8-11 **62**.......... AdamBeschizza(5) 1 53
(M Wigham) *hld up wl off the pce towards rr: effrt and rdn over 3f out: no real hdwy and nvr trbld ldrs* **5/2**[1]

0633 **8** *¾* **Minder**[10] 2952 4-8-9 **55**.......... (p) JohnFahy 10 45
(J G Portman) *hld up off the pce towards rr: hdwy 3f out: rdn over 2f out: wknd u.p over 1f out: n.d fnl f* **4/1**[2]

-650 **9** *shd* **Princess Flame (GER)**[10] 2952 8-8-6 **52**.......... (v[1]) RossAtkinson 8 42
(B G Powell) *t.k.h: chsd ldrs: rdn and unable qck 3f out: wknd u.p wl over 1f out: no ch fnl f* **33/1**

04-4 **10** *16* **First To Call**[88] 996 6-9-5 **68**.......... DebraEngland(3) 7 29
(P J Makin) *racd in midfield: c centre over 4f out: rdn and no prog 3f out: wl btn fnl 2f: eased ins fnl f* **7/1**

36-0 **11** *3¾* **Attainable**[76] 1160 4-8-12 **63**.......... NathanAlison(5) 2 17
(J A B Old) *v awkward leaving stalls and lost many l s: a detached in last* **33/1**

2m 20.63s (-0.57) **Going Correction** -0.45s/f (Firm) **11** Ran SP% **123.5**
Speed ratings (Par 103): **84,83,82,81,80 79,79,78,78,67 64**
toteswingers:1&2:£9.20, 1&3:£13.50, 2&3:£23.50 CSF £46.50 CT £529.29 TOTE £5.10: £2.00, £3.60, £3.50; EX 57.40.
Owner Miss Emma Pearce **Bred** Shadwell Estate Company Limited **Trained** Newmarket, Suffolk

FOCUS
The watered ground was officially described as good to firm, with a GoingStick reading of 9.0. A modest apprentice handicap and not that competitive the time was moderate and the form looks unconvincing, with the winner the best guide.
First To Call Official explanation: jockey said gelding lost its action

Attainable Official explanation: jockey said filly was very slow away

3295 PUMP TECHNOLOGY & FRIENDS REMEMBER TONY PORTMAN MAIDEN AUCTION FILLIES' STKS 6f 8y

6:50 (7:12) (Class 4) 2-Y-O £4,533 (£1,348; £674; £336) Stalls High

Form				RPR
6	1		**Temptingfaith (IRE)**[45] 1930 2-8-6 0 AlanMunro 10 (M G Quinlan) *hld up in tch: swtchd lft and hdwy ent fnl 2f: rdn to ld 1f out: sn edgd rt u.p: r.o wl* 8/1	75
30	2	1	**Looksmart**[31] 2338 2-8-8 0 PatDobbs 12 (R Hannon) *stdd s: hld up wl bhd: hdwy jst over 2f out: chsng ldrs and n.m.r ent fnl f: swtchd lft and r.o wl to chse wnr fnl 75yds: nt rch wnr* 13/2[3]	74
562	3	1 1/4	**No Poppy (IRE)**[8] 3020 2-7-13 0 (b[1]) JamesSullivan(5) 14 (T D Easterby) *w ldrs: rdn to ld and edgd rt over 1f out: hdd 1f out: styd on same pce fnl f* 9/2[2]	66
	4	1 1/4	**Zamina (IRE)** 2-8-6 0 RichardMullen 11 (S Kirk) *s.i.s: bhd: hdwy jst over 1f out: swtchd lft ins fnl f and r.o wl fnl 100yds: snatched 4th last strides: gng on fin* 33/1	67+
	5	shd	**Park Ballet (IRE)** 2-8-6 0 SaleemGolam 6 (J G Portman) *s.i.s: towards rr: hdwy over 2f out: chsng ldrs whn nt clr run and swtchd rt ent fnl f: nvr enough room on stands' rail fnl f: kpt on but nvr able to chal* 20/1	69+
24	6	2	**Millyluvstobougie**[28] 2407 2-7-13 0 JohnFahy(5) 9 (C G Cox) *led after 1f tl hdd 2f out: wknd u.p fnl 150yds* 9/2[2]	56
00	7	1/2	**Water Ice**[10] 2958 2-8-10 0 RichardKingscote 7 (Tom Dascombe) *broke wl and led for 1f: w ldrs tl rdn and outpcd ent fnl 2f: plugged on same pce u.p fr over 1f out* 14/1	61
	8	1/2	**Ransom Request** 2-8-10 0 JamieSpencer 13 (E F Vaughan) *stdd after s: rn green and hld up in rr: hdwy 2f out: n.m.r ent fnl f: swtchd lft jst ins fnl f: edging bk rt and kpt on same pce fnl 150yds* 16/1	59+
	9	1 3/4	**Highcliffe** 2-8-8 0 SteveDrowne 5 (R Hannon) *s.i.s: bhd: hdwy but hanging lft 2f out: no prog ent fnl f* 16/1	52
	10	2 1/4	**Bouzy** 2-8-6 0 FrankieMcDonald 8 (P Winkworth) *in tch: rdn 3f out: outpcd ent fnl 2f: n.d after* 28/1	43
	11	3 3/4	**Mariyah** 2-8-6 0 JimmyQuinn 4 (M Blanshard) *s.i.s: in tch in midfield: rdn and struggling over 2f out: no ch fr wl over 1f out* 40/1	32
62	12	1	**Delira (IRE)**[10] 2951 2-8-4 0 LiamJones 15 (J G Portman) *w ldrs tl led 2f out: rdn and hdd over 1f out: struggling whn hmpd and snatched up 1f out: wl btn and nt pushed after* 4/1[1]	27
040	13	1 1/2	**I Scream (IRE)**[14] 2839 2-7-13 0 DeclanCannon(5) 2 (D R C Elsworth) *chsd ldrs tl wknd qckly u.p 2f out: wl bhd fnl f* 25/1	22
205	14	nk	**Lovat Lane**[10] 2951 2-8-4 0 CathyGannon 3 (Eve Johnson Houghton) *chsd ldrs: struggling u.p whn carried lft 2f out: wl btn over 1f out* 25/1	22
	15	2 3/4	**Wolf Slayer** 2-8-10 0 RichardSmith 1 (Tom Dascombe) *in tch in midfield on outer: rdn and hung lft ent fnl 2f: wknd wl over 1f out: continued to hang and wl bhd fnl f* 50/1	19+

1m 14.04s (1.04) **Going Correction** +0.15s/f (Good) 15 Ran SP% 120.6
Speed ratings (Par 92): **99,97,96,94,94 91,90,90,87,84 79,78,76,76,72**
toteswingers:1&2:£9.50, 1&3:£6.20, 2&3:£6.80 CSF £54.86 TOTE £10.30: £3.30, £2.90, £1.20; EX 63.60.
Owner Tommy Cummins **Bred** Rathdown Stud Ltd **Trained** Newmarket, Suffolk

FOCUS

This race, and for that matter every other race left on the card, was delayed by around 20 minutes due to part of the running rail in the straight being realigned. Following a runner in the Arab race, and a further two horses in the opening thoroughbred contest, appearing to jump a false patch of ground just inside the final furlong, the rail was pushed out the required distance for that area to be avoided. As such, the track was narrowed considerably at around the 1f pole, making for an unusual configuration. It's worth bearing in mind these inexperienced fillies were kept waiting in the paddock for much longer than ideal, especially considering it was a warm night. The form looks pretty average for the track and grade, but plenty of these shaped nicely.

NOTEBOOK

Temptingfaith(IRE) holds an entry in a Listed race this coming Saturday, which gave a fair hint to the regard in which she is held by her connections. She duly stepped up considerably on the form she showed at Warwick in May, having been supported in the market. She looked well beforehand and showed a professional attitude to gain a straightforward success. It's possible she'll now take up that Listed race engagement (trainer won the race in 2005), but while she'll probably have to leave this form well behind to figure, at least she goes there in good order. (op 12-1)

Looksmart was soon behind after a slow start and it's to her credit she stayed on for second, especially as she didn't get the clearest of runs through. She should be winning soon enough. (op 9-2)

No Poppy(IRE) had taken too long to get going on her first three starts, but she was lit up by first-time blinkers this time. At least she showed she's not as short on early speed as had appeared the case on her previous outing, far from it. (op 5-1)

Zamina(IRE), a 7,000euros half-sister to, among others, useful middle-distance/staying winner Castle Howard, fared best of the newcomers. This was a pleasing performance considering she was one of the slowest away and had to be niggled along to recover. (tchd 25-1)

Park Ballet(IRE) ◆would not have been at all far away with a clearer run. Representing the same trainer who saddled the beaten favourite, she was weak in the market but showed a deal of ability, looking to have plenty to offer when continually blocked inside the final 2f. Official explanation: jockey said filly was denied a clear run (op 25-1)

Millyluvstobougie seemed unsuited by the step up in trip and has yet to go on from an encouraging debut. (tchd 4-1 and 5-1)

Ransom Request ◆ looked to be going okay when having little room to make her move inside the final 2f, and as such she was not given anything like a hard time. She should leave this form well behind. For what it's worth, she seemed to have her tongue hanging out in the closing stages. Official explanation: jockey said filly was denied a clear run (op 14-1)

Delira(IRE) shaped as though the return to this trip would suit when runner-up at Bath last time, but she was disappointing. She was on the retreat when hampered against the near rail around 1f out, although that exaggerated the beaten margin. (tchd 5-1)

Wolf Slayer ◆ failed to beat a rival but there's reason to believe she'll be capable of better in time, probably over a longer trip on easier ground. A fine, scopey filly, she was nominated by co-owner Andrew Black as a horse to follow in a recent interview, and she showed up well to a point, before hanging badly left from halfway. As a consequence of her waywardness, she lost ground when having to be corrected around the rail realignment. Official explanation: jockey said filly hung left

3296 PUMPMATIC PUMP STATIONS BY PUMP TECHNOLOGY MAIDEN FILLIES' STKS 7f (S)

7:25 (7:48) (Class 4) 2-Y-O £4,533 (£1,348; £674; £336) Stalls High

Form				RPR
3	1		**Cape Dollar (IRE)**[25] 2505 2-9-0 0 RichardMullen 6 (Sir Michael Stoute) *hld up in tch: swtchd lft and smooth hdwy jst over 2f out: pushed into ld over 1f out: rdn and c clr ins fnl f: readily* 11/8[1]	82+
2	2	2 3/4	**Zanazzi (USA)**[20] 2642 2-9-0 0 RobertHavlin 13 (J H M Gosden) *led: hdd and rdn over 1f out: kpt on u.p but no ch w wnr fnl 100yds* 11/2[3]	75
	3	1 3/4	**Sahafh (USA)** 2-9-0 0 FrankieDettori 14 (Saeed Bin Suroor) *stdd s: hld up in tch on stands' rail: swtchd lft and hdwy 2f out: rdn to chse ldng pair jst over 1f out: outpcd fnl 150yds* 9/4[2]	71
	4	1 1/4	**Mortitia** 2-9-0 0 KierenFallon 2 (B J Meehan) *in tch in midfield on outer: hdwy to chse ldrs 2f out: rdn and unable qck jst over 1f out: outpcd ins fnl f* 25/1	68+
0	5	1 1/4	**Danzigs Grandchild (USA)**[30] 2358 2-9-0 0 LiamKeniry 9 (J S Moore) *hld up wl in tch: swtchd lft and hdwy ent fnl 2f: drvn and btn over 1f out: one pce and wl hld fnl f* 100/1	65+
	6	1/2	**Ponte Di Rosa** 2-9-0 0 FergusSweeney 10 (B G Powell) *s.i.s: bhd: swtchd lft and rdn along 2f out: styd on steadily fnl f: nvr trbld ldrs* 100/1	63+
	7	1 1/2	**Majestic Dubawi** 2-9-0 0 AlanMunro 3 (M R Channon) *chsd ldrs: effrt and rdn 2f out: btn over 1f out: wknd fnl f* 40/1	60
	8	3/4	**Celebrity** 2-9-0 0 PatDobbs 1 (R Hannon) *s.i.s: bhd and rn green: swtchd rt 3f out: edging lft and bhd a wall of horses and swtchd rt again 2f out: past btn horses fnl f: nvr a factor* 25/1	58+
	9	3 1/4	**Opera Dancer** 2-9-0 0 SteveDrowne 4 (S Kirk) *s.i.s: rn green in rr: sme modest hdwy wl over 1f out: no imp after: n.d* 33/1	50
	10	1/2	**Little Book** 2-9-0 0 JamieSpencer 5 (E F Vaughan) *hld up towards rr: swtchd lft to outer and short-lived effrt ent fnl 2f: edging lft and wl btn over 1f out* 50/1	48
	11	2 1/2	**Humdrum** 2-9-0 0 JimmyFortune 12 (R Hannon) *v.s.a: detached in last tl past btn rivals ins fnl f: nvr on terms* 14/1	42+
0	12	1	**Folly Drove**[22] 2594 2-8-9 0 JohnFahy(5) 11 (J G Portman) *chsd ldrs tl wnt 2nd 2f out tl over 1f out: wknd qckly and sn bhd* 25/1	40
0	13	nk	**Amistress**[19] 2677 2-9-0 0 SebSanders 7 (Eve Johnson Houghton) *chsd ldrs early: sn bustled along and dropping to midfield: wknd u.p 2f out: wl btn after* 100/1	39
00	14	6	**Seas Of Sorrow (IRE)**[31] 2338 2-8-9 0 SophieDoyle(5) 8 (B W Duke) *racd awkwardly: chsd ldr tl 2f out: sn dropped out bhd: bhd and wandering bdly jst ins fnl f* 100/1	24

1m 25.94s (0.24) **Going Correction** +0.15s/f (Good) 14 Ran SP% 117.8
Speed ratings (Par 92): **104,100,98,97,96 95,93,92,89,88 85,84,84,77**
toteswingers:1&2:£2.90, 1&3:£1.30, 2&3:£4.60 CSF £8.46 TOTE £2.50: £1.30, £1.70, £1.50; EX 10.20.
Owner Saeed Suhail **Bred** Rabbah Bloodstock Limited **Trained** Newmarket, Suffolk

FOCUS

Probably a decent fillies' maiden and the winner can do better still. The form is rated around the runner-up and the race averages.

NOTEBOOK

Cape Dollar(IRE) ◆ confirmed the promise she showed in a 6f Newmarket maiden on her debut with a tidy success, in the process providing her trainer with his first juvenile winner of the campaign. This daughter of Cape Cross, who is well suited by quick ground and expected to stay 1m, looks very useful. (op 7-4 tchd 15-8 in a place)

Zanazzi(USA) took them along for much of the way. She ran to a fair level when runner-up (albeit beaten favourite) over 6f on Polytrack on her debut and helps give the form a solid look. (op 5-1)

Sahafh(USA), a $475,000 half-sister to a 1m1/2f Stakes winner in the US, as well as three minor winners over sprint trips in that country, fared best of the newcomers. She couldn't muster the required speed once in the clear inside the final 2f, but this was still a respectable introduction. (tchd 11-4)

Mortitia ◆, who is out of a useful multiple sprint winner, hails from a stable whose juveniles usually need their first run and this was a pleasing start. Despite being pitched wider than ideal and coming under pressure around 3f out, she briefly looked set to get involved but simply got tired late on. There should be much better to come. (op 20-1)

Danzigs Grandchild(USA) stepped up on the form she showed on debut.

Ponte Di Rosa, who made little appeal on pedigree, showed ability.

Majestic Dubawi ◆ ran better than her finishing position indicates, showing up well for a long way before losing two of three positions when getting tired inside the final furlong. She should come on a good deal for this run. (op 33-1)

Celebrity ran green for much of the way and had to switch on more than one occasion when keeping on. (op 22-1 tchd 20-1)

Humdrum was never involved after losing several lengths at the start. Official explanation: jockey said regarding running and riding his instructions were to look after the filly adding filly did not move well in early stages and started very slow (op 16-1)

Seas Of Sorrow(IRE) Official explanation: trainer said filly was scoped pre-race and found to have a throat infection

3297 JUNG PUMPEN & PUMP TECHNOLOGY H'CAP 1m 7y(R)

7:55 (8:23) (Class 5) (0-70,70) 3-Y-O £3,238 (£963; £481; £240) Stalls Low

Form				RPR
-005	1		**Warning Song (USA)**[12] 2888 3-9-6 70 PatDobbs 4 (Mrs A J Perrett) *chsd ldrs: rdn to chal but wanting to hang lft over 1f out: led ins fnl f: styd on and asserted fnl 50yds* 10/1	76
2300	2	1	**Ginger Grey (IRE)**[23] 2566 3-9-3 67 (b) KierenFallon 2 (D R C Elsworth) *t.k.h: chsd ldr: rdn to chal 2f out: led wl over 1f out: hrd pressed over 1f out: drvn and hdd ins fnl f: no ex fnl 50yds* 10/1	71
3211	3	nk	**Kingsdine (IRE)**[14] 2844 3-9-3 67 FergusSweeney 10 (M S Saunders) *t.k.h: hld up in tch: hdwy and nt clr run wl over 1f out: swtchd rt and rdn to chal ent fnl f: no ex fnl 50yds* 5/1[3]	70
-500	4	1	**Ishtar Gate (USA)**[20] 2644 3-9-3 67 AlanMunro 12 (P F I Cole) *hld up in tch in rr: rdn and effrt 2f out: swtchd lft over 1f out: hanging rt u.p: kpt on but nvr quite gng pce to rch ldrs* 25/1	68
45-3	5	shd	**Beaumont's Party (IRE)**[12] 2888 3-9-3 70 PatrickHills(3) 9 (R Hannon) *t.k.h: trckd ldng pair: rdn and nt qckn whn n.m.r ent fnl f: one pce and no imp ins fnl f* 5/2[1]	71
-600	6	2 3/4	**Scottish Boogie (IRE)**[21] 2618 3-9-6 70 LiamKeniry 7 (S Kirk) *t.k.h: hld up in tch towards rr: rdn and effrt ent fnl 2f: plugged on one pce and n.d fnl f* 18/1	64
000	7	1 3/4	**Rocky Mood (IRE)**[17] 2755 3-9-4 68 TedDurcan 6 (W R Swinburn) *hmpd s and sn bustled along: rdn and effrt 3f out: wknd over 1f out* 20/1	58
-651	8	8	**Interakt**[26] 2459 3-9-2 66 SamHitchcott 5 (M R Channon) *led: rdn 2f out: hdd wl over 1f out: wknd and wl btn 1f out* 12/1	38
2331	F		**Volatilis (IRE)**[12] 2906 3-9-5 69 SebSanders 8 (J W Hills) *hld up wl in tch towards rr: swtchd lft 3f out: lost action and fell over 2f out: (fatally injured)* 4/1[2]	—

1204 U **First Post (IRE)**[29] 2398 3-9-5 **69** JimmyFortune 11 —
(D Haydn Jones) *t.k.h: stdd after s and hld up in last pair: last but wl in tch whn bdly hmpd and uns rdr over 2f out* **7/1**

1m 38.45s (98.45) **10** Ran SP% **117.5**
toteswingers:1&2:£16.40, 1&3:£17.60, 2&3:£12.10 CSF £106.26 CT £577.76 TOTE £15.80: £4.30, £2.30, £2.40; EX 118.70.
Owner G Harwood & G Bailey **Bred** Bloodstock Holdings Llc **Trained** Pulborough, W Sussex

FOCUS
There was a nasty incident in the straight when Volatilis fell over 2f from the finish and in the process badly hampered First Post, who then unseated his rider. The John Hills-trained runner sadly suffered a fatal injury. This was just a modest handicap and the pace didn't seem that strong while the winner and third help set the level. They came stands' side in the straight.

3298 ENJOY JUNIOR RUGBY WITH TADLEY TIGERS FILLIES' H'CAP 1m 2f 6y
8:30 (8:55) (Class 4) (0-85,85) 3-Y-O **£4,209** (£1,252; £625; £312) **Stalls** Low

Form RPR

1-11 **1** **Sea Of Heartbreak (IRE)**[14] 2843 3-9-7 **85** SteveDrowne 11 93+
(R Charlton) *hld up in last trio: hdwy and bhd wall of horses over 2f out: swtchd lft 2f out: sn rdn to chal: led jst ins fnl f: r.o strly* **7/4**[1]

1-43 **2** 1 ½ **Nafura**[26] 2479 3-9-7 **85** (v) FrankieDettori 10 90
(Saeed Bin Suroor) *led: clr tl stdd gallop after 2f: rdn ent fnl 2f: hdd over 1f out: edgd lft u.p ins fnl f: kpt on to go 2nd again nr fin* **10/1**

6-21 **3** ½ **Roxy Flyer (IRE)**[18] 2717 3-9-1 **79** JimmyQuinn 13 83
(Mrs A J Perrett) *chsd ldrs: wnt 2nd 3f out: upsides ldr 2f out: rdn to ld over 1f out: hdd jst ins fnl f: nt pce of wnr fnl 100yds: lost 2nd nr fin* **12/1**

41 **4** nk **Heavenly Dawn**[36] 2180 3-9-3 **81** RichardMullen 5 84
(Sir Michael Stoute) *hld up in midfield: rdn and effrt 2f out: ev ch over 1f out: one pce ins fnl f* **9/1**

41 **5** ½ **Akinoshirabe (JPN)**[26] 2463 3-9-2 **80** KierenFallon 9 84+
(L M Cumani) *hld up in tch in midfield: trckd ldrs over 2f out: rdn and effrt over 1f out: keeping on whn gap clsd and snatched up ins fnl f: swtchd lft and styd on fnl 100yds: nt rcvr* **4/1**[2]

1-2 **6** 8 **Namaskar**[40] 2047 3-9-5 **83** RobertHavlin 8 69
(J H M Gosden) *t.k.h: hld up in last trio: nt clr run over 2f out: pushed lft and lost pl 2f out: n.d after* **9/2**[3]

1140 **7** 6 **Bebopalula (IRE)**[17] 2758 3-9-3 **81** MichaelHills 1 55
(B W Hills) *hld up in last pair: rdn and effrt in centre over 2f out: struggling whn pushed lft 2f out: no ch after* **10/1**

4-23 **8** 2 ¼ **Woodford Belle (USA)**[3] 3208 3-8-13 **77** TedDurcan 6 47
(B J Meehan) *chsd ldr tl 3f out: wkng u.p whn pushed lft 2f out: wl bhd after* **14/1**

2150 **9** ¾ **Goodlukin Lucy**[13] 2869 3-8-10 **77** MartinLane(3) 7 45
(Pat Eddery) *s.i.s: a in rr: effrt and rdn in centre 4f out: no prog whn pushed lft 2f out: wl bhd after* **50/1**

2m 4.67s (-4.13) **Going Correction** -0.45s/f (Firm) **9** Ran SP% **119.0**
Speed ratings (Par 98): **98,96,96,96,95 89,84,82,82**
toteswingers:1&2:£3.50, 1&3:£6.10, 2&3:£27.80 CSF £21.92 CT £168.75 TOTE £3.20: £1.50, £1.70, £2.90; EX 24.10.
Owner D G Hardisty Bloodstock **Bred** D G Hardisty Bloodstock **Trained** Beckhampton, Wilts
■ Stewards' Enquiry : Ted Durcan two-day ban; careless riding (8th-10th) July

FOCUS
A decent fillies' handicap for the grade, although the gallop, which looked set to be quick, steadied noticeably early on. Once again they came stands' side in the straight. The second sets the standard, while the fifth could be rated as having finished second with a clear run.
Namaskar Official explanation: jockey said filly ran to freely

3299 SHREDDING FOR BEDDING H'CAP 5f 34y
9:00 (9:26) (Class 5) (0-70,70) 3-Y-O+ **£3,238** (£963; £481; £240) **Stalls** High

Form RPR

0053 **1** **You'relikemefrank**[18] 2721 4-8-9 **51** oh6 (p) AndrewElliott 3 56
(J Balding) *racd towards centre: mde all: rdn over 1f out: hld on gamely fnl f: all out* **16/1**

2114 **2** hd **Avrilo**[10] 2954 4-10-0 **70** FergusSweeney 14 75
(M S Saunders) *w wnr thrght: rdn over 1f out: kpt on u.p but a jst hld fnl f* **3/1**[1]

000- **3** ¾ **Volito**[318] 4783 4-9-8 **64** GeorgeBaker 9 66
(Jonjo O'Neill) *in tch: effrt to trck ldrs and nt clr run ent fnl f tl wl ins fnl f: kpt on u.p towards fin: unable to rch ldrs* **7/1**

0226 **4** nk **Peopleton Brook**[14] 2846 8-9-3 **59** (t) SteveDrowne 7 60
(B G Powell) *bhd: swtchd lft to outer and rdn 2f out: hdwy over 1f out: chsd ldrs ins fnl f: no imp and btn fnl 75yds* **7/1**

0030 **5** hd **Commandingpresence (USA)**[18] 2719 4-8-2 **51** oh5 RyanClark(7) 8 51
(J J Bridger) *w ldrs: rdn wl over 1f out: no ex and btn whn edgd lft u.p fnl 100yds* **14/1**

2643 **6** 2 **Captain Kallis (IRE)**[15] 2809 4-9-3 **59** AdamKirby 5 52
(D J S Ffrench Davis) *in tch: rdn and effrt wl over 1f out: unable qck and keeping on same pce whn n.m.r ins fnl f* **10/3**[2]

1103 **7** 1 ½ **West Leake (IRE)**[20] 2639 4-9-5 **61** LiamKeniry 10 48
(P Burgoyne) *in tch: rdn and unable qck 2f out: btn ent fnl f* **8/1**

4566 **8** ½ **Lithaam (IRE)**[10] 2954 6-9-4 **65** (p) SophieDoyle(5) 4 51
(J M Bradley) *chsd ldrs: rdn and unable qck over 1f out: wknd ent ins fnl f* **5/1**[3]

61.69 secs (0.29) **Going Correction** +0.15s/f (Good) **8** Ran SP% **113.4**
Speed ratings (Par 103): **103,102,101,101,100 97,95,94**
toteswingers:1&2:£12.90, 1&3:£24.50, 2&3:£3.20 CSF £62.77 CT £376.91 TOTE £19.70: £4.50, £1.90, £2.80; EX 79.30 Place 6 £149.48; Place 5 £40.83.
Owner Kate Barrett, Paul & David Clarkson **Bred** J R Mitchell **Trained** Scrooby, Notts
■ Stewards' Enquiry : Sophie Doyle one-day ban: exused whip when out of contention and horse showing no response 6th July

FOCUS
A modest but competitive sprint handicap, although the form is not the most solid.
T/Jkpt: Not won. T/Plt: £67.70 to a £1 stake. Pool:£82,950.96 - 893.21 winning tickets T/Qpdt: £10.90 to a £1 stake. Pool:£5,536.46 - 373.79 winning tickets SP

3300 - 3306a (Foreign Racing) - See Raceform Interactive

3099 CHANTILLY (R-H)
Tuesday, June 22

OFFICIAL GOING: Turf: good

3307a PRIX DE SYLVIE (CONDITIONS) (2YO FILLIES) (TURF) 6f
1:35 (12:00) 2-Y-O **£15,044** (£6,017; £4,513; £3,008; £1,504)

RPR

1 **Split Trois (FR)** 2-8-4 0 Pierre-CharlesBoudot(3) 6 86
(Y De Nicolay, France) **41/5**

2 1 **Lily Again**[20] 2642 2-9-0 0 ChristopheSoumillon 1 90
(P F I Cole) *awkward s: sn rcvrd to be prom: wnt 2nd after 1 1/2f: rdn to ld 2f out: hdd 150yds out: r.o wl but outpcd by wnr ins fnl f* **1/2**[1]

3 2 **Droit Devant (FR)**[20] 2-9-0 0 FredericSpanu 3 84
(D Prod'Homme, France) **12/1**

4 ¾ **Belle Aumone (FR)**[12] 2917 2-9-0 0 GregoryBenoist 2 82
(S Jesus, France) **7/1**[3]

5 nse **High Class (FR)**[66] 2-9-0 0 YohannGourraud 5 82
(C Gourdain, France) **9/2**[2]

6 ¾ **Union Des Brieres (FR)** 2-8-7 0 JohanVictoire 4 72
(F-X De Chevigny, France) **27/1**

1m 11.2s (-0.20) **6** Ran SP% **119.5**
WIN (incl. 1 euro stake): 9.20. PLACES: 2.80, 1.30. SF: 18.40.
Owner Christian Henry De Villeneuve **Bred** Nicholas J Hughes **Trained** France

NOTEBOOK
Lily Again, a good winner on Polytrack on her debut, came to win her race but found the winner too strong near the finish.

2950 BATH (L-H)
Wednesday, June 23

OFFICIAL GOING: Firm 9.6
Wind: modest, against Weather: warm and sunny

3308 FREE RACING WITH ODDSCHECKER.COM WEDNESDAY CLAIMING STKS 5f 11y
6:05 (6:06) (Class 6) 3-Y-O+ **£1,878** (£558; £279; £139) **Stalls** Centre

Form RPR

5304 **1** **Ocean Blaze**[10] 2997 6-9-3 80 GeorgeBaker 8 77
(B R Millman) *w ldr and a gng wl: led ent fnl 2f: pushed along and in command ins fnl f: comf* **8/11**[1]

-430 **2** 2 **Matterofact (IRE)**[21] 2639 7-8-9 62 SteveDrowne 2 61
(M S Saunders) *t.k.h: wl hld up in tch: nt clr run briefly over 2f out: hdwy to chse wnr 2f out: kpt on same pce ins fnl f* **9/2**[2]

0050 **3** 1 ½ **Talamahana**[23] 2590 5-8-5 45 (v) AmyBaker(5) 4 57
(A B Haynes) *s.i.s and short of room s: sn detached in last: rdn 1/2-way: styd on wl ins fnl f to go 3rd towards fin: no ch w wnr* **33/1**

3-00 **4** 1 **Green Lagonda (AUS)**[65] 1428 8-8-10 67 AndrewHeffernan(3) 6 56
(P D Evans) *taken down early: broke wl: sn stdd and hld up in tch: swtchd rt and effrt over 1f out: kpt on same pce u.p ins fnl f* **12/1**

5265 **5** 4 ½ **Desert Strike**[35] 2229 4-9-4 59 SamHitchcott 5 45
(P F I Cole) *short of room at s and s.i.s: sn bustled along and in midfield: n.m.r 1/2-way: sn swtchd rt and rdn ent fnl 2f: fnd little and racd awkwardly u.p: no ch ins fnl f* **14/1**

2220 **6** ½ **Spic 'n Span**[2] 3255 5-9-2 58 (b) LukeMorris 7 41
(R A Harris) *taken down early: chsd ldrs: rdn and nt qckn 2f out: edgd rt u.p and btn ent fnl f: wknd* **5/1**[3]

00- **7** ¾ **Orpen Lady**[317] 4860 4-8-10 0 JackMitchell 1 32
(J M Bradley) *led: rdn 1/2-way: hdd ent fnl 2f: wknd over 1f out* **100/1**

-000 **8** 5 **Joss Stick**[1] 3292 5-8-13 47 (p) RichardThomas 3 17
(R A Harris) *wnt rt s: in tch: rdn and wknd 2f out: wl bhd ins fnl f* **50/1**

0-00 **9** 3 ¼ **Miss California**[47] 1872 3-7-9 41 RyanPowell(7) 9 —
(Miss Tor Sturgis) *racd wd: in tch tl struggling 1/2-way: bhd fr wl over 1f out* **100/1**

61.94 secs (-0.56) **Going Correction** -0.125s/f (Firm)
WFA 3 from 4yo+ 6lb **9** Ran SP% **114.0**
Speed ratings (Par 101): **99,95,93,91,84 83,82,74,69**
toteswingers:1&2 £1.80, 2&3 £18.00, 1&3 £9.20 CSF £4.13 TOTE £1.80: £1.10, £1.60, £5.90; EX 4.40.
Owner Gary Hancock (Staffs) **Bred** Longdon Stud And Robin Lawson **Trained** Kentisbeare, Devon

FOCUS
A fair claimer, with the first two and the fourth setting a reasonable standard. The third limits the form while the winner did not need to be at her best.
Green Lagonda(AUS) Official explanation: jockey said gelding suffered interference leaving the stalls

3309 BATHWICK TYRES H'CAP 1m 5y
6:40 (6:40) (Class 5) (0-70,70) 4-Y-O+ **£2,396** (£712; £356; £177) **Stalls** Low

Form RPR

6010 **1** **Jewelled**[11] 2956 4-9-7 **70** (v) GeorgeBaker 3 78
(J W Hills) *hld up wl in tch: rdn and hdwy on inner to ld ent fnl f: r.o wl: eased nr fin* **4/1**[2]

626 **2** ¾ **Macanta (USA)**[11] 2967 4-8-11 **60** JackMitchell 1 66
(G A Butler) *stdd s: hld up wl in tch in last pair: nt clr run 2f out: swtchd lft and hdwy on inner ent fnl f: chsd wnr and drvn fnl 150yds: kpt on but a hld* **3/1**[1]

0/00 **3** 2 ¾ **Alright Chuck**[30] 2388 6-8-2 **51** oh6 RichardThomas 7 51
(P W Hiatt) *wl in tch in midfield on outer: rdn ent fnl 2f: chsd ldng pair and kpt on same pce ins fnl f* **40/1**

-503 **4** 1 **Second To Nun (IRE)**[11] 2956 4-7-11 **51** SophieDoyle(5) 2 49
(M Blanshard) *led at stdy gallop: rdn and hrd pressed over 2f out: hdd 1f out: wknd fnl 100yds* **3/1**[1]

000- **5** ¾ **Superstitious Me (IRE)**[219] 7417 4-7-12 **52** oh1 ow1 DeclanCannon(5) 5 48
(B Palling) *t.k.h: hld up wl in tch in midfield: nt clr run 2f out tl over 1f out: rdn and nt qckn ent fnl f: no ch w ldrs ins fnl f* **25/1**

0300 **6** ¾ **Ravi River (IRE)**[18] 2750 6-9-0 **66** (v) AndrewHeffernan(3) 8 60
(P D Evans) *t.k.h: stdd after s and hld up in last pair: rdn and effrt 2f out: swtchd rt and drvn over 1f out: no prog and wl hld fnl f* **16/1**

5002 **7** 1 ¾ **Darcey**[8] 3061 4-8-9 **65** AdamBeschizza(7) 6 55
(Miss Amy Weaver) *t.k.h early: w ldrs: rdn over 2f out: ev ch u.p 2f out: btn 1f out and wknd qckly fnl f* **5/1**[3]

1200 **8** 7 **Spinning Ridge (IRE)**[12] 2922 5-9-7 **70** (b) LukeMorris 4 44
(R A Harris) *sn w ldr: ev ch and rdn over 2f out: wknd qckly over 1f out: wl bhd ins fnl f* **11/2**

1m 40.47s (-0.33) **Going Correction** -0.125s/f (Firm) **8** Ran SP% **114.2**
Speed ratings (Par 103): **96,95,92,91,90 90,88,81**
toteswingers:1&2 £3.60, 2&3 £25.00, 1&3 £18.90 CSF £16.39 CT £412.44 TOTE £5.40: £1.80, £1.10, £11.80.
Owner J W Hills **Bred** Wyck Hall Stud Ltd **Trained** Upper Lambourn, Berks

FOCUS
The pace was poor until 3f from home, favouring those with a finishing kick. The form is weak with the third running from well out of the handicap.
Alright Chuck Official explanation: jockey said gelding did not handle the bend

Superstitious Me(IRE) Official explanation: jockey said filly was denied a clear run

3310 E B F AND BATHWICK TYRES BRISTOL MAIDEN STKS 5f 161y
7:10 (7:12) (Class 5) 2-Y-O **£3,238** (£963; £481; £240) **Stalls** Centre

Form				RPR
0	1		**Half Truth (IRE)**[14] 2861 2-8-5 0 AntiocoMurgia(7) 9	73
			(Mahmood Al Zarooni) *racd in last pair: rdn and effrt on outer 2f out: hdwy to chal 1f out: led fnl 100yds: kpt on* **9/2**[2]	
	2	*shd*	**Byronic (IRE)** 2-9-3 0 AdamKirby 2	78
			(C G Cox) *s.i.s: sn rdn along and in tch: nt clr run over 1f out: swtchd rt jst over 1f out: sn drvn and ev ch ins fnl f: jst hld* **10/1**	
43	3	*2*	**Diamond Charlie (IRE)**[20] 2680 2-9-3 0 AlanMunro 10	71
			(S Dow) *w ldrs: led over 1f out: sn rdn and hrd pressed 1f out: hdd fnl 100yds: wknd towards fin* **4/5**[1]	
00	4	*5*	**Country Waltz**[9] 3029 2-8-12 0 SamHitchcott 7	50
			(M R Channon) *t.k.h: hld up in tch: rdn ent fnl 2f: wknd jst over 1f out* **20/1**	
	5	*nk*	**Scommettitrice (IRE)** 2-8-12 0 LukeMorris 3	49
			(R A Harris) *broke wl: led tl 4f out: styd pressing ldr: ev ch and rdn 2f out: wknd ent fnl f* **40/1**	
0	6	*1 ½*	**Place And Chips**[22] 2621 2-9-3 0 RichardKingscote 4	49
			(Tom Dascombe) *s.i.s: hdwy to ld 4f out: rdn ent fnl 2f: hdd over 1f out: wknd qckly ent fnl f* **11/2**[3]	
0	7	*11*	**Compton Lass**[9] 3029 2-8-9 0 RussKennemore(3) 6	14
			(B G Powell) *s.i.s: a in rr: losing tch whn hmpd jst over 1f out: eased ins fnl f* **40/1**	
	U		**Blackleyf (IRE)** 2-9-3 0 RichardSmith 5	49+
			(Tom Dascombe) *in tch in midfield: rdn ent fnl 2f: losing pl whn hmpd: stmbld and uns rdr jst over 1f out* **33/1**	

1m 12.42s (1.22) **Going Correction** -0.125s/f (Firm) **8** Ran SP% **110.8**
Speed ratings (Par 93): **86,85,83,76,76 74,59,—**
toteswingers:1&2 £3.60, 2&3 £2.40, 1&3 £1.50 CSF £41.92 TOTE £3.80: £1.10, £2.30, £1.10; EX 27.10.
Owner Godolphin **Bred** Mrs Bernadette Hayden **Trained** Newmarket, Suffolk
■ Stewards' Enquiry : Adam Kirby five-day ban: careless riding (Jul 7, 9, 13-15)

FOCUS
Little experience on show, including four debutants, but it looked just an ordinary maiden.

NOTEBOOK
Half Truth(IRE) was green on her debut and again showed her inexperience, but she finished well enough to get up from the rear. She will need to improve greatly to be one of the stable's better performers, but at least she is off the mark. (tchd 4-1 and 5-1)

Byronic(IRE) ◆, a 29,000gns yearling Byron half-brother to several winners up to 7f, is out of a mare who won at 1m4f. After getting outpaced, he rallied well in the style of a youngster who should find a race, with 7f likely to suit before long. (op 8-1)

Diamond Charlie(IRE), though disappointing his supporters, has run well in all three maidens and still looks capable of winning one. However, nurseries are now an alternative option. (op 10-11 tchd 8-11)

Country Waltz, half-sister to a winning sprinter and a successful stayer, ran her best race yet but does not look good enough to win a maiden unless much more improvement is forthcoming. She will be more at home in nurseries from now on. (op 25-1 tchd 28-1 and 16-1)

Scommettitrice(IRE), daughter of the winning hurdler Hard To Lay, made a satisfactory debut especially considering she cost just 4,200gns as a yearling. (op 20-1)

Place And Chips, a Compton Place newcomer, is out of the decent 6f winner Our Sheila, so he is bred to be quick. Though some way short of living up to his pedigree, he stepped up on his debut run and should have improved again by the time he has qualified for nurseries. (op 7-1 tchd 8-1)

3311 CMS GURKHA WELFARE TRUST H'CAP 5f 11y
7:40 (7:44) (Class 4) (0-85,85) 3-Y-O **£4,338** (£1,291; £645; £322) **Stalls** Centre

Form				RPR
5-06	1		**High Spice (USA)**[4] 3218 3-9-0 **78** (p) JimCrowley 4	84
			(R M H Cowell) *chsd ldr tl led 1/2-way: rdn over 1f out: styd on wl ins fnl f* **14/1**	
-612	2	*1 ½*	**Humidor (IRE)**[16] 2822 3-8-13 **77** SteveDrowne 1	78
			(R Charlton) *reluctant to go to post and eventually led to s: t.k.h: chsd ldrs: wnt 2nd 2f out: rdn over 1f out: kpt on same pce u.p ins fnl f* **11/8**[1]	
4253	3	*1 ¾*	**Starlight Muse (IRE)**[16] 2824 3-8-9 **73** RichardMullen 5	67
			(E S McMahon) *s.i.s: racd in last pair: rdn and effrt over 1f out: kpt on to go 3rd ins fnl f: nvr gng pce to threaten ldng pair* **12/1**	
-603	4	*1 ¼*	**Secret Millionaire (IRE)**[11] 2960 3-9-7 **85** StephenCraine 6	75
			(Patrick Morris) *t.k.h: chsd ldrs: rdn over 2f out: edgd rt u.p and unable qck over 1f out: wknd ins fnl f* **5/1**[3]	
-400	5	*4 ½*	**Take Ten**[11] 2978 3-9-7 **85** J-PGuillambert 2	58
			(M Johnston) *sprawled bdly as stalls opened and v.s.a: clsd and in tch over 3f out: rdn and no prog 2f out: btn whn swtchd lft ent fnl f: eased wl ins fnl f* **5/2**[2]	
4034	6	*½*	**Leleyf (IRE)**[16] 2822 3-8-5 **69** SamHitchcott 3	40
			(M R Channon) *led tl 1/2-way: sn rdn and struggling: wknd and wl btn over 1f out* **9/1**	

61.66 secs (-0.84) **Going Correction** -0.125s/f (Firm) **6** Ran SP% **111.7**
Speed ratings (Par 101): **101,98,95,93,86 85**
toteswingers:1&2 £5.10, 2&3 £7.80, 1&3 £18.90 CSF £33.73 TOTE £14.10: £5.20, £2.90; EX 45.70.
Owner Khalifa Dasmal **Bred** Dell Ridge Farm Llc **Trained** Six Mile Bottom, Cambs

FOCUS
Some useful mid-ranking performers made up the small field, but the race was surprisingly uncompetitive in the closing stages. The runner-up is a solid guide based on his latest form.
Secret Millionaire(IRE) Official explanation: trainer said gelding banged his head leaving the stalls
Take Ten Official explanation: jockey said colt stumbled leaving the stalls

3312 BATHWICK TYRES CARDIFF MAIDEN STKS 1m 3f 144y
8:10 (8:10) (Class 5) 3-Y-O+ **£2,914** (£867; £433; £216) **Stalls** Low

Form				RPR
-203	1		**Miss Miracle**[13] 2891 3-8-8 80 (p) LukeMorris 1	69+
			(C G Cox) *t.k.h: led after 1f: qcknd 3f out: drvn 2f out: hdd over 1f out: edgd rt u.p jst ins fnl f: led again fnl 50yds: all out* **10/3**[3]	
4	2	*nse*	**Sensationally**[20] 2674 3-8-8 0 JimCrowley 4	69+
			(R M Beckett) *t.k.h early: chsd wnr 9f out: upsides and gng best ent fnl 2f: rdn to ld narrowly over 1f out: drvn 1f out: hdd and no ex fnl 50yds* **8/11**[1]	
60	3	*2 ¼*	**Peaceful Means (IRE)**[13] 2900 7-9-1 0 AdamBeschizza(7) 5	65
			(J Jay) *t.k.h early: led at slow gallop for 1f: chsd ldrs after: rdn and outpcd over 2f out: kpt on same pce ins fnl f* **16/1**	
	4	*7*	**Expressionist** 3-8-13 0 J-PGuillambert 2	63
			(M Johnston) *dwlt: sn niggled along and rn green: chsd ldrs: rdn and outpcd ent fnl 3f: lost tch 2f out* **3/1**[2]	

2m 31.52s (0.92) **Going Correction** -0.125s/f (Firm)
WFA 3 from 7yo 14lb **4** Ran SP% **111.9**
Speed ratings (Par 103): **91,90,89,84**
CSF £6.54 TOTE £2.90; EX 8.80.
Owner D J Burke & Peter Alderson **Bred** Whitley Stud **Trained** Lambourn, Berks

FOCUS
This was potentially a fascinating race, with the winner having run in the Cheshire Oaks, and the beautifully-bred runner-up having only her second outing. However, the end result, while producing an exciting finish, was rather unsatisfactory with the pace moderate.
Expressionist Official explanation: vet said colt was lame

3313 BATHWICK TYRES BRIDGEND CLASSIFIED STKS 5f 161y
8:40 (8:40) (Class 5) 3-Y-O **£2,460** (£732; £365; £182) **Stalls** Centre

Form				RPR
-500	1		**Grand Zafeen**[16] 2824 3-9-0 70 AlanMunro 3	68
			(M R Channon) *stdd s: racd in last: hdwy over 1f out: swtchd rt and rdn 1f out: qcknd and r.o wl to ld fnl 75yds* **3/1**[2]	
3062	2	*¾*	**Rainbow Six**[36] 2215 3-9-0 67 AndreaAtzeni 2	65
			(M Botti) *trckd ldrs: jnd ldr on bit wl over 1f out: shkn up to ld ins fnl f: immediately hrd pressed and fnd little u.p: hdd and nt qckn fnl 75yds* **11/10**[1]	
-20	3	*3 ½*	**Nollaig Shona (IRE)**[25] 2536 3-9-0 66 SteveDrowne 4	54
			(J W Mullins) *racd keenly: w ldr tl led over 2f out: sn rdn: hdd ins fnl f: wknd fnl 100yds* **7/2**[3]	
0000	4	*2 ½*	**King's Approach (IRE)**[14] 2868 3-9-0 62 (b) LukeMorris 1	45
			(R A Harris) *racd keenly: led tl rdn and hdd over 2f out: wknd jst over 1f out* **6/1**	

1m 11.64s (0.44) **Going Correction** -0.125s/f (Firm) **4** Ran SP% **109.1**
Speed ratings (Par 99): **92,91,86,83**
CSF £6.84 TOTE £4.00; EX 8.10.
Owner Jaber Abdullah **Bred** Rabbah Bloodstock Limited **Trained** West Ilsley, Berks

FOCUS
A disappointing turnout, but in theory the four runners were reasonably well matched on official ratings, with the winner best in by 3lb. The winner is rated to juvenile form with the runner-up close to recent marks.
Rainbow Six Official explanation: jockey said, regarding the running and riding, his instructions were to jump and go with them. He added the gelding travels well but tends to hang left-handed when in front. He further stated that he found himself left in front too soon today and the gelding found very little when he asked for an effort.

3314 BATHWICK TYRES NEWPORT H'CAP 1m 2f 46y
9:10 (9:10) (Class 6) (0-65,67) 4-Y-O+ **£1,774** (£523; £262) **Stalls** Low

Form				RPR
0-03	1		**Welsh Anthem**[11] 2961 4-9-7 **65** (p) GeorgeBaker 7	75
			(W R Muir) *chsd ldrs early: grad stdd and racd in last pair fr 7f out: hdwy on outer 2f out: rdn to chal jst ins fnl f: drvn to ld fnl 100yds: r.o wl* **5/1**[3]	
-066	2	*1*	**Parc Des Princes (USA)**[13] 2894 4-9-7 **65** (v) SamHitchcott 9	73
			(A M Balding) *s.i.s and rdn along early: detached in last and in tch 7f out: hdwy on inner 3f out: swtchd rt over 1f out: rdn to ld 1f out: hdd and no ex ins fnl f* **3/1**[1]	
6053	3	*3*	**Spinning Waters**[11] 2955 4-8-6 **50** (b) LukeMorris 6	52
			(Eve Johnson Houghton) *hld up in midfield: rdn and effrt on outer 2f out: edgd lft and plugged on same pce u.p ins fnl f* **5/1**[3]	
410	4	*hd*	**Noah Jameel**[11] 2955 8-8-3 **50** AndrewHeffernan(3) 8	52
			(A G Newcombe) *hld up in last trio: hdwy u.p ent fnl f: kpt on and pressing for 3rd at fin: no threat to ldng pair* **16/1**	
/0-1	5	*1 ¾*	**Cyril The Squirrel**[11] 2955 6-8-0 **51** AdamBeschizza(7) 2	49
			(Karen George) *stdd s: t.k.h: hdwy to chse ldrs after 1f: wnt 2nd 4f out: drvn and unable qck 3f out: wknd ent fnl f* **7/1**	
5211	6	*2*	**Guga (IRE)**[5] 3179 4-9-9 **67** 6ex (b) SteveDrowne 4	61
			(Dr R D P Newland) *led: rdn over 2f out: hdd 1f out: wknd ins fnl f* **7/2**[2]	
0502	7	*2 ½*	**Bramalea**[19] 2690 5-9-4 **62** AdamKirby 3	51
			(B W Duke) *taken down early: chsd ldrs: rdn and unable qck over 2f out: wknd jst over 1f out* **10/1**	
0025	8	*3 ¾*	**Hector Spectre (IRE)**[12] 2922 4-8-11 **58** (p) RussKennemore(3) 5	40
			(Mrs N S Evans) *in tch: effrt u.p over 2f out: wknd qckly over 1f out* **20/1**	
0000	9	*52*	**Warrior Nation (FR)**[19] 2691 4-8-2 **46** oh1 (b) AndreaAtzeni 1	—
			(A J Chamberlain) *t.k.h: chsd ldr tl 4f out: sn dropped out: t.o fnl 2f* **50/1**	

2m 8.56s (-2.44) **Going Correction** -0.125s/f (Firm) **9** Ran SP% **114.8**
Speed ratings (Par 101): **104,103,100,100,99 97,95,92,51**
toteswingers:1&2 £2.30, 2&3 £3.90, 1&3 £5.60 CSF £20.25 CT £78.38 TOTE £6.30: £1.70, £2.70, £2.60; EX 20.50 Place 6: £114.45 Place 5: £86.05.
Owner Usk Valley Stud **Bred** Usk Valley Stud **Trained** Lambourn, Berks
■ Stewards' Enquiry : Luke Morris caution: careless riding

FOCUS
A decent gallop set this up for the finishers. The time was good for the grade and the form looks pretty sound rated around the first three.
Guga(IRE) Official explanation: jockey said gelding ran too free
Hector Spectre(IRE) Official explanation: jockey said gelding lost its action
Warrior Nation(FR) Official explanation: jockey said gelding ran too free
T/Plt: £111.70 to a £1 stake. Pool:£44,162.72 - 288.41 winning tickets. T/Qpdt: £63.40 to a £1 stake. Pool: £4,361.85 - 50.85 winning tickets. SP

3020 CARLISLE (R-H)
Wednesday, June 23

OFFICIAL GOING: Good to firm (firm in places in home straight; 7.9)
Wind: Fresh, half against Weather: Cloudy

3315 EDMUNDSON ELECTRICAL MAIDEN AUCTION STKS 5f
1:25 (1:26) (Class 5) 2-Y-O **£3,238** (£963; £481; £240) **Stalls** High

Form				RPR
06	1		**Bold Bidder**[14] 2861 2-8-6 0 RoystonFfrench 9	77
			(K A Ryan) *pressed ldr: drvn to ld over 1f out: pushed clr ins fnl f* **25/1**	
2524	2	*3 ½*	**Tilliemint (IRE)**[12] 2936 2-8-4 0 (b) PJMcDonald 11	62
			(T D Easterby) *led to over 1f out: kpt on same pce ins fnl f* **11/4**[2]	
04	3	*¾*	**Sapphire Girl**[16] 2813 2-8-6 0 PaulHanagan 1	65+
			(R A Fahey) *towards rr on outside: hdwy 2f out: edgd rt: kpt on strly ins fnl f: nrst fin* **16/1**	
3	4	*2*	**Misscomplacent**[6] 3118 2-8-6 0 ow1 BarryMcHugh(3) 5	57
			(Mrs A Duffield) *trckd ldrs tl rdn and no ex appr fnl f* **8/1**	

405 **5** *nk* **Reposer (IRE)**[23] 2594 2-8-9 0 RobertWinston 2 56
(J R Best) *in tch: rdn over 2f out: no imp over 1f out* **15/8**[1]

60 **6** *1* **Witzend (IRE)**[15] 2832 2-8-9 0 EleanorMcGowan(7) 6 59
(Jedd O'Keeffe) *s.i.s: bhd and outpcd: hdwy over 1f out: kpt on: nvr able to chal* **25/1**

000 **7** *2 ¾* **Whats For Pudding (IRE)**[12] 2939 2-8-6 0 AndrewElliott 12 40
(D Carroll) *midfield: drvn and outpcd over 2f out: n.d after* **100/1**

32 **8** *6* **Saltergate**[55] 1646 2-8-9 0 SilvestreDeSousa 4 21
(N Tinkler) *chsd ldrs tl rdn and wknd over 1f out* **4/1**[3]

0 **9** *¾* **Running Water**[4] 3204 2-8-4 0 PatrickMathers 8 13
(H A McWilliams) *bhd and sn outpcd: nvr on terms* **125/1**

0 **10** *7* **Louis Vee (IRE)**[15] 2832 2-8-11 0 PaulMulrennan 7 —
(J G Given) *sn drvn along towards rr: no ch fr 1/2-way* **66/1**

0 **11** *4 ½* **Bonded Spirit**[29] 2420 2-8-11 0 TomEaves 10 —
(Mrs K Walton) *bhd on ins: struggling over 2f out: nvr on terms* **100/1**

12 *3* **Rothesay Chancer** 2-8-11 0 KierenFallon 3 —
(J S Goldie) *s.i.s: bhd and sn drvn along: nvr on terms* **14/1**

61.84 secs (1.04) **Going Correction** +0.225s/f (Good) **12** Ran SP% **117.1**
Speed ratings (Par 93): **100,94,93,90,89 87,83,73,72,61 54,49**
toteswingers: 1&2 £15.70, 1&3 £22.60, 2&3 £9.40 CSF £90.96 TOTE £30.80: £5.10, £1.10, £3.50; EX 123.10.
Owner T G & Mrs M E Holdcroft **Bred** Bearstone Stud And T Herbert Jackson **Trained** Hambleton, N Yorks

FOCUS
The ground had dried out a bit and was officially described as good to firm, firm in places in the home straight. An ordinary maiden and not that many got into it.

NOTEBOOK
Bold Bidder didn't seem to get home in her first two starts over 6f, but it was a different story on this drop in trip despite the stiff track. Quickly away, she was happy to get a lead from the runner-up but was in front again over a furlong out and she was soon clear. She looks just the type for nurseries. (op 16-1)
Tilliemint(IRE), the most experienced in the field and in the frame in three of her first four starts, was given a positive ride from her good draw but had no answer to the winner. There is a small race in her, but she looks exposed and remains vulnerable to an improver. (op 9-4)
Sapphire Girl shaped as though in need of further when fourth over 6f at Pontefract last time, so this drop in trip was a concern. Not surprisingly she was doing her best work late and fared best of those help up. She also could be interesting in a nursery back over further. (op 20-1)
Misscomplacent, a creditable third of 13 over 6f on her Ripon debut, was always up there and had every chance. A return to further may help her. (op 15-2)
Reposer(IRE), more exposed than most but beaten only around half a length when fifth in a Goodwood maiden last month that has worked out well, was always seeing plenty of daylight on the wide outside from his wide draw and is probably worth another chance. (op 5-2)
Witzend(IRE), unplaced in two 6f maidens, made up some late ground and is bred to stay much further than this. (op 28-1 tchd 33-1)
Rothesay Chancer, a half-brother to two winners including the stable's multiple-winner Rothesay Dancer, was the only newcomer in the field and looked clueless. (op 11-1)

3316 EUROPEAN BREEDERS' FUND MAIDEN STKS 5f 193y
2:00 (2:01) (Class 4) 2-Y-0 **£4,533** (£1,348; £674; £336) **Stalls** High

Form RPR

1 **Al Madina (IRE)** 2-8-12 0 RoystonFfrench 8 69+
(B Smart) *trckd ldrs: swtchd lft and hdwy to ld over 1f out: edgd rt and kpt on strly ins fnl f* **4/1**[3]

6 **2** *1 ¾* **Cotton Spirit**[13] 2882 2-9-3 0 TonyHamilton 1 69
(R A Fahey) *towards rr: pushed along 1/2-way: hdwy on outside over 1f out: edgd rt and kpt on ins fnl f: tk 2nd cl home* **20/1**

3 *hd* **Maverik** 2-9-3 0 PhillipMakin 3 68+
(M Dods) *dwlt: hld up in tch: nt clr run over 2f out and over 1f out: hdwy to chse wnr ins fnl f: kpt on: lost 2nd cl home* **4/1**[3]

3 **4** *1 ¾* **Dunmore Boy (IRE)**[14] 2855 2-9-3 0 PaulHanagan 5 63
(R A Fahey) *led to over 1f out: rdn and kpt on same pce fnl f* **3/1**[2]

5 *¾* **Deep Applause** 2-9-3 0 TomEaves 7 61
(M Dods) *prom: effrt over 1f out: no ex ins fnl f* **16/1**

6 *3 ¾* **Top Care (USA)** 2-9-3 0 KierenFallon 4 50+
(M Johnston) *t.k.h: w ldr tl wknd appr fnl f: bttr for r* **9/4**[1]

7 *nk* **Sandy Lonnen** 2-9-3 0 PaulMulrennan 2 49
(J Howard Johnson) *prom on outside: effrt over 2f out: wknd appr fnl f* **20/1**

8 *16* **Chin'n Tonic (IRE)** 2-9-3 0 PJMcDonald 6 —
(G A Swinbank) *bhd and sn outpcd: lost tch fr 1/2-way: t.o* **25/1**

1m 15.55s (1.85) **Going Correction** +0.225s/f (Good) **8** Ran SP% **115.0**
Speed ratings (Par 95): **96,93,93,91,90 85,84,63**
toteswingers: 1&2 £13.00, 1&3 £14.00, 2&3 £4.30 CSF £78.56 TOTE £5.50: £1.20, £4.00, £1.70; EX 87.90.
Owner A M A Al Shorafa **Bred** Forenaghts Stud **Trained** Hambleton, N Yorks

FOCUS
Not a bad maiden, with the one filly getting the better of the boys, and winners should emerge from it.

NOTEBOOK
Al Madina(IRE), a £26,000 half-sister to two winners at up to 1m, tracked the leaders on the inside early. She produced a decent turn of foot when pulled out to hit the front over a furlong from home and her rider took an age to pull her up after passing the post. Clearly held in high regard by her trainer, she looks to have a future and should have little trouble getting an extra furlong. (tchd 11-2)
Cotton Spirit, green when sixth of nine on his Haydock debut, had trouble going the pace in the early stages but stayed on nicely when pulled to the wide outside He is bred to need further than this and that is how he performed. (op 33-1)
Maverik, a 45,000gns colt, attracted market support but missed the break. He didn't have much room to play with at various stages when trying to make progress, but he stayed on well once in the clear. Out of a half-sister to a couple of useful middle-distance performances, he is another who will appreciate further in due course. (op 11-2 tchd 6-1)
Dunmore Boy(IRE), a well-beaten third of four on his Hamilton debut and a stable companion of the runner-up, helped force the pace but had little left when headed over a furlong out. (op 2-1 tchd 15-8)
Deep Applause, an £18,000 gelding and a stable companion of the third, travelled strongly behind the leaders but was inclined to run green when finally put under pressure. He is stoutly bred on the dam's side and needs more time and a stiffer test. (tchd 14-1)
Top Care(USA), a $50,000 half-brother to three winners at up to 1m4f including the useful Dream Lodge, went off well backed but, having shared the pace until over a furlong out, faded rather disappointingly. (op 7-2)

3317 LLOYD MOTOR GROUP CARLISLE BELL CONSOLATION (H'CAP) 7f 200y
2:30 (2:30) (Class 4) (0-80,76) 3-Y-0+ **£6,476** (£1,927; £963; £481) **Stalls** High

Form RPR

-041 **1** **Ailsa Craig (IRE)**[9] 3022 4-9-3 69 6ex TonyHamilton 4 80
(E W Tuer) *trckd ldr: rdn over 2f out: led over 1f out: styd on strly* **10/1**

053- **2** *1 ½* **Fishforcompliments**[184] 7832 6-9-10 76 PaulHanagan 15 83
(R A Fahey) *trckd ldrs: effrt over 2f out: chsd wnr over 1f out: kpt on ins fnl f* **11/1**

5012 **3** *¾* **Sedgwick**[18] 2739 8-9-9 75 SilvestreDeSousa 9 80+
(S A Harris) *bhd: hdwy on outside over 2f out: kpt on fnl f: nrst fin* **14/1**

4024 **4** *¾* **Veroon (IRE)**[12] 2934 4-9-8 74 (p) PaulMulrennan 8 77
(J G Given) *in tch: drvn over 2f out: kpt on u.p ins fnl f* **11/1**

6106 **5** *1 ¼* **Shadowtime**[10] 2991 5-9-6 72 AndrewMullen 10 72
(Miss Tracy Waggott) *midfield: rdn over 3f out: hdwy over 1f out: no imp ins fnl f* **8/1**[2]

2321 **6** *1* **Jonny Lesters Hair (IRE)**[23] 2580 5-9-6 72 PJMcDonald 5 70
(T D Easterby) *led: rdn over 2f out: hdd over 1f out: kpt on same pce* **15/2**[1]

0122 **7** *¾* **Chief Red Cloud (USA)**[26] 2512 4-9-1 70 BarryMcHugh(3) 3 66
(J R Weymes) *midfield: hdwy and in tch over 2f out: no ex over 1f out* **10/1**

1654 **8** *½* **Halsion Chancer**[20] 2683 6-9-10 76 RobertWinston 11 71
(J R Best) *midfield on ins: rdn and effrt over 2f out: no ex fnl f* **15/2**[1]

4523 **9** *½* **Bonnie Prince Blue**[46] 1923 7-9-5 76 JohnFahy(5) 12 70
(B Ellison) *bhd: reminders and drvn 1/2-way: hdwy over 1f out: nvr able to chal* **14/1**

0-02 **10** *3* **Jewelled Dagger (IRE)**[27] 2452 6-9-10 76 (v) KierenFallon 2 63
(J S Goldie) *prom tl rdn and wknd over 2f out* **9/1**[3]

5-40 **11** *½* **Toto Skyllachy**[76] 1185 5-9-5 76 JamesO'Reilly(5) 14 61
(J O'Reilly) *bhd: drvn 3f out: nvr rchd ldrs* **20/1**

3151 **12** *2 ¾* **Royal Straight**[14] 2858 5-9-4 70 TomEaves 6 49
(Miss L A Perratt) *towards rr: rdn over 2f out: nvr able to chal* **16/1**

000- **13** *2 ½* **Global**[254] 6731 4-9-2 75 DaleSwift(7) 13 48
(B Ellison) *bhd: drvn 1/2-way: nvr on terms* **20/1**

1246 **14** *1 ½* **Whipma Whopma Gate (IRE)**[3] 3238 5-8-9 68 (v) NeilFarley(7) 1 37
(D Carroll) *racd wd in midfield: rdn over 3f out: wknd over 2f out* **22/1**

-620 **15** *6* **Black N Brew (USA)**[20] 2685 4-9-6 72 NeilCallan 7 27
(J R Best) *towards rr: hrd rdn over 3f out: wknd over 2f out* **12/1**

1m 39.81s (-0.19) **Going Correction** +0.125s/f (Good) **15** Ran SP% **120.3**
Speed ratings (Par 105): **105,103,102,102,100 99,99,98,98,95 94,91,89,87,81**
toteswingers: 1&2 £10.80, 1&3 £35.60, 2&3 £13.80 CSF £111.20 CT £1585.73 TOTE £9.00: £3.20, £3.00, £6.20; EX 56.20.
Owner Far Distant Partnership **Bred** P J B O'Callaghan **Trained** Great Smeaton, N Yorks
■ Stewards' Enquiry : Paul Hanagan caution: careless riding
Kieren Fallon caution: careless riding

FOCUS
A competitive handicap run at a good pace and surprisingly the jockeys made for the stands' rail on reaching the home straight. The winner is rated a slight improver with the runner-up and fourth the best guides to the level.

3318 LLOYD MOTOR GROUP CARLISLE BELL (H'CAP) 7f 200y
3:05 (3:06) (Class 4) (0-80,84) 3-Y-0+ **£19,428** (£5,781; £2,889; £1,443) **Stalls** High

Form RPR

3121 **1** **Camerooney**[33] 2293 7-8-9 77 DaleSwift(7) 2 92
(B Ellison) *mde all: racd stands' side over 2f out: styd on strly ins fnl f* **18/1**

-321 **2** *1 ½* **Major Phil (IRE)**[10] 2991 4-9-9 84 6ex KierenFallon 17 95+
(L M Cumani) *s.i.s: drvn over 4f out: hdwy towards centre over 3f out: wnt 2nd jst ins fnl f: styd on same pce* **2/1**[1]

0000 **3** *1* **Smarty Socks (IRE)**[10] 2991 6-9-4 79 (e[1]) SilvestreDeSousa 11 88
(D O'Meara) *s.i.s: hdwy in centre over 2f out: in 5th 1f out: styd on wl* **33/1**

2241 **4** *½* **Sir George (IRE)**[32] 2328 5-9-1 79 BarryMcHugh(3) 9 87
(Ollie Pears) *in rr: hdwy on outside 3f out: chsng ldrs over 1f out: styd on same pce* **8/1**[3]

62 **5** *½* **Silver Rime (FR)**[23] 2580 5-9-5 80 PhillipMakin 16 87
(Miss L A Perratt) *chsd ldrs: wnt 2nd over 2f out: kpt on same pce ins fnl f* **22/1**

5003 **6** *3 ¾* **Raptor (GER)**[10] 2991 7-9-5 80 (b) NickyMackay 14 80
(M E Rimmer) *in tch: drvn over 3f out: one pce whn n.m.r outside over 1f out* **14/1**

0-00 **7** *4 ½* **Shotley Mac**[21] 2657 6-9-5 80 (b) FrannyNorton 13 67
(N Bycroft) *t.k.h: trckd ldrs: wknd appr fnl f* **20/1**

1-00 **8** *hd* **Espero (IRE)**[28] 2428 4-9-4 79 TomEaves 6 65
(Miss L A Perratt) *t.k.h in mid-div: effrt over 2f out: wknd over 1f out* **25/1**

55-4 **9** *2 ¼* **Yorgunnabelucky (USA)**[6] 3121 4-9-4 79 JoeFanning 10 60
(M Johnston) *chsd ldrs: drvn 3f out: lost pl over 1f out* **10/1**

5313 **10** *2* **Flowing Cape (IRE)**[6] 3117 5-8-12 78 PaulPickard(5) 4 54
(R Hollinshead) *hld up in mid-div: effrt over 2f out: wknd over 1f out* **10/1**

0200 **11** *½* **Handsome Falcon**[15] 2835 6-9-4 79 PaulHanagan 1 54
(R A Fahey) *prom: lost pl 2f out* **28/1**

0060 **12** *1* **Rainbow Mirage (IRE)**[18] 2736 6-9-2 77 RobertWinston 7 50
(E S McMahon) *hld up: hdwy on outside over 2f out: lost pl over 1f out* **12/1**

0402 **13** *¾* **Mount Hadley (USA)**[18] 2760 6-9-5 80 (p) TomQueally 5 51
(G A Butler) *chsd ldrs: wknd over 1f out* **14/1**

360 **14** *2 ½* **Mountain Cat (IRE)**[18] 2736 6-9-5 80 NeilCallan 12 45
(G A Swinbank) *chsd ldrs: wknd 2f out* **11/2**[2]

5-00 **15** *1 ¼* **Charlie Tipple**[60] 1513 6-9-3 78 (b) PaulMulrennan 8 40
(T D Easterby) *in rr: bhd whn hung lft over 2f out* **22/1**

040 **16** *13* **Kidlat**[6] 3121 5-9-5 80 (p) GregFairley 3 11
(A Bailey) *prom: effrt stands' side over 3f out: lost pl over 2f out: bhd whn eased clsng stages* **40/1**

1m 39.58s (-0.42) **Going Correction** +0.125s/f (Good) **16** Ran SP% **130.4**
Speed ratings (Par 105): **107,105,104,104,103 99,95,95,92,90 90,89,88,86,84 71**
toteswingers: 1&2 £14.00, 1&3 £98.90, 2&3 £37.20 CSF £53.15 CT £1350.17 TOTE £21.00: £3.10, £1.20, £6.40, £2.00.
Owner Mrs Jean Stapleton **Bred** Miss Dianne Hill **Trained** Norton, N Yorks
■ Stewards' Enquiry : Kieren Fallon caution: careless riding

FOCUS
A competitive and tight handicap with all bar Major Phil separated by just 3lb. They again came stands' side, but unlike in the consolation race they went a modest early pace even though the final winning time was 0.23 seconds faster. The third and fourth set the level.
Mount Hadley(USA) Official explanation: jockey said gelding had no more to give

3319 FANTAILS RESTAURANT CUMBERLAND PLATE (H'CAP) 1m 3f 107y
3:35 (3:36) (Class 4) (0-80,80) 3-Y-0+ **£19,428** (£5,781; £2,889; £1,443) **Stalls** Low

Form RPR

2241 **1** **Brushing**[23] 2579 4-9-6 78 KierenFallon 15 91
(M H Tompkins) *trckd ldr: rdn to ld over 2f out: hrd pressed fr over 1f out: kpt on gamely* **9/2**[2]

142 2 ½ **Pendragon (USA)**[60] 1512 7-9-0 75 BarryMcHugh(3) 5 87
(B Ellison) *t.k.h: prom: hdwy to chal over 1f out: kpt on ins fnl f: hld cl home* 10/1

2020 3 4 **Kingsdale Orion (IRE)**[42] 2031 6-9-6 78 PhillipMakin 17 84
(B Ellison) *prom: drvn along 3f out: rallied: kpt on same pce ins fnl f* 25/1

0/63 4 hd **Palomar (USA)**[67] 620 8-8-13 78 DaleSwift(7) 2 83
(B Ellison) *hld up: rdn over 3f out: hdwy over 1f out: kpt on: nvr able to chal* 12/1

-235 5 2 ¼ **Goodwood Starlight (IRE)**[26] 2506 5-9-2 77 RobertLButler(3) 10 79
(Miss Sheena West) *s.s: bhd tl hdwy over 3f out: rdn and kpt on fr 2f out: no imp* 33/1

3-51 6 1 ¼ **Some Sunny Day**[37] 2181 4-9-7 79 RobertWinston 4 78
(H Morrison) *hld up in tch: hdwy and ev ch over 1f out: rdn and drifted rt: btn ins fnl f* 9/1[3]

0-62 7 1 ½ **High Ambition**[8] 3060 7-9-5 77 PaulHanagan 6 74
(R A Fahey) *hld up: rdn over 3f out: hdwy over 1f out: n.d* 9/1[3]

150/ 8 ¾ **Boucheron**[685] 4784 5-9-7 79 TonyHamilton 12 75
(R A Fahey) *hld up: lost pl over 4f out: sn rdn: sme hdwy over 1f out: nvr able to chal* 25/1

6-11 9 hd **Agapanthus (GER)**[20] 2685 5-9-3 75 TomQueally 14 70
(B J Curley) *in tch: effrt over 3f out: wknd wl over 1f out* 11/4[1]

-401 10 ½ **Proud Times (USA)**[19] 2723 4-9-5 77 PJMcDonald 11 72
(G A Swinbank) *midfield: drvn over 3f out: outpcd fnl 2f* 14/1

2055 11 1 **Rosbay (IRE)**[6] 3121 6-9-2 79 LanceBetts(5) 1 72
(T D Easterby) *s.i.s: bhd: rdn over 4f out: nvr able to chal* 12/1

3200 12 4 **Daaweitza**[11] 2976 7-9-5 77 (b) TomEaves 8 63
(B Ellison) *led tl hdd over 2f out: sn wknd* 25/1

0-01 13 6 **Sir Royal (USA)**[67] 1398 5-9-7 79 NeilCallan 7 55
(G A Swinbank) *hld up: drvn over 3f out: nvr on terms* 14/1

-500 14 1 ¾ **Alsahil (USA)**[88] 1006 4-9-8 80 PaulMulrennan 13 54
(Micky Hammond) *midfield: drvn over 3f out: wknd 2f out* 66/1

2110 15 2 ¾ **Tropical Bachelor (IRE)**[10] 2995 4-8-11 74 JohnFahy(5) 3 43
(T J Pitt) *trckd ldrs: rdn over 3f out: wknd fnl 2f* 25/1

3366 16 22 **Mannlichen**[27] 2467 4-9-2 74 (b) JoeFanning 9 7
(M Johnston) *trckd ldrs tl wknd qckly over 3f out: t.o* 12/1

2m 24.25s (1.15) **Going Correction** +0.125s/f (Good) 16 Ran SP% **130.2**
Speed ratings (Par 105): **100,99,96,96,94 94,92,92,92,91 91,88,83,82,80 64**
toteswingers: 1&2 £12.00, 1&3 £41.40, 2&3 £107.40 CSF £48.85 CT £1064.11 TOTE £5.20: £1.70, £3.00, £7.30, £4.40; EX 53.60.
Owner Dullingham Park **Bred** Dullingham Park **Trained** Newmarket, Suffolk

FOCUS
Another competitive and tight handicap with just 6lb covering the 16 runners. The early pace was solid and again they came up the stands' side in the straight, but a few of these seemed to lose their footing at the crossing around 5f from home. The third to fifth set the level and the form seems sound enough.
Some Sunny Day Official explanation: jockey said filly hung right in the straight
Agapanthus(GER) Official explanation: trainer's rep said gelding lost the off fore shoe

3320 EUROPEAN BREEDERS' FUND FILLIES' H'CAP 6f 192y
4:10 (4:11) (Class 4) (0-85,80) 3-Y-O+ £6,476 (£1,927; £963; £481) **Stalls** High

Form RPR
1015 1 **Cheers For Thea (IRE)**[28] 2429 5-9-10 72 (bt) DuranFentiman 5 81
(T D Easterby) *trckd ldrs: effrt and drvn over 2f out: led ins fnl f: kpt on wl* 4/1[3]

6-16 2 1 ½ **Battlemaiden (IRE)**[27] 2466 3-9-9 80 JoeFanning 2 82
(M Johnston) *led: shkn up 2f out: hdd ins fnl f: kpt on* 9/1

1-26 3 2 ¾ **Elusive Sue (USA)**[38] 2140 3-9-8 79 PaulHanagan 1 74
(R A Fahey) *t.k.h: trckd ldr: effrt over 2f out: one pce ins fnl f* 6/5[1]

2-0 4 1 **Zubova**[14] 2871 3-9-2 73 (t) KierenFallon 4 65
(Rae Guest) *dwlt: hld up in tch: effrt over 1f out: no imp ins fnl f* 13/2

0-26 5 10 **Celtic Lynn (IRE)**[25] 2524 5-9-10 72 PhillipMakin 3 40
(M Dods) *prom tl rdn and wknd fr 2f out* 7/2[2]

1m 29.45s (2.35) **Going Correction** +0.125s/f (Good)
WFA 3 from 5yo 9lb 5 Ran SP% **111.0**
Speed ratings (Par 102): **91,89,86,85,73**
CSF £34.53 TOTE £3.70: £1.50, £4.60; EX 32.30.
Owner Ron George **Bred** Crone Stud Farms Ltd **Trained** Great Habton, N Yorks

FOCUS
A small field for this fillies' handicap and it became a tactical affair. Again they came stands' side. The winner is rated as recording a personal best but the form is not rock solid.

3321 WEATHERBYS BLOODSTOCK INSURANCE SPRINT H'CAP 5f
4:40 (4:40) (Class 4) (0-85,82) 3-Y-O+ £4,857 (£1,445; £722; £360) **Stalls** High

Form RPR
3026 1 **Atlantic Beach**[11] 2982 5-8-12 67 SilvestreDeSousa 5 76
(D O'Meara) *cl up: rdn to ld over 1f out: edgd lft: hld on wl ins fnl f* 9/4[1]

0123 2 1 ¼ **Noodles Blue Boy**[20] 2681 4-9-13 82 TonyHamilton 2 87
(Ollie Pears) *dwlt: sn in tch: effrt 2f out: chsd wnr ins fnl f: edgd rt: kpt on same pce towards fin* 4/1[2]

0034 3 ½ **Distant Sun (USA)**[4] 3201 6-8-12 67 PaulHanagan 8 72+
(Miss L A Perratt) *bhd: pushed along 1/2-way: hdwy whn nt clr run over 1f out to ins fnl f: kpt on fin* 7/1[3]

3060 4 hd **Angelo Poliziano**[6] 3119 4-8-5 63 (v) BarryMcHugh(3) 4 65
(Mrs A Duffield) *t.k.h: w ldrs tl rdn and kpt on same pce ins fnl f* 10/1

0462 5 nk **Rothesay Dancer**[7] 3075 7-9-5 74 KierenFallon 9 75+
(J S Goldie) *bhd: pushed along 1/2-way: hdwy and swtchd rt over 1f out: no imp ins fnl f* 12/1

2040 6 nk **Green Park (IRE)**[11] 2982 7-9-7 76 (b) DavidNolan 1 76
(D Carroll) *prom: effrt over 1f out: one pce ins fnl f* 14/1

0010 7 2 ¾ **Wyatt Earp (IRE)**[11] 2982 9-9-7 76 (p) GregFairley 3 66
(P Salmon) *disp ld to 1/2-way: no ex over 1f out* 8/1

0000 8 ½ **Bravely (IRE)**[13] 2883 6-8-12 67 PaulMulrennan 7 55
(T D Easterby) *hld up in tch: drvn 1/2-way: no imp fr over 1f out* 16/1

1155 9 1 ½ **Chosen One (IRE)**[4] 3201 5-9-0 69 TomEaves 6 52
(Mrs R A Carr) *slt ld to over 1f out: sn rdn and wknd* 7/1[3]

61.49 secs (0.69) **Going Correction** +0.225s/f (Good) 9 Ran SP% **116.2**
Speed ratings (Par 105): **103,101,100,99,99 98,94,93,91**
toteswingers: 1&2 £2.40, 1&3 £4.30, 2&3 £7.80 CSF £11.07 CT £54.23 TOTE £2.70: £1.20, £1.70, £3.00; EX 10.70.
Owner R Fell & K Everitt **Bred** D R Brotherton **Trained** Nawton, N Yorks

FOCUS
A competitive sprint handicap, run at a true pace, and again they came stands' side. The runner-up is rated to this year's improved form.

Distant Sun(USA) Official explanation: jockey said gelding was denied a clear run

3322 EDINBURGH WOOLLEN MILL HBLB H'CAP 5f 193y
5:15 (5:15) (Class 6) (0-60,60) 3-Y-O+ £2,047 (£604; £302) **Stalls** High

Form RPR
5533 1 **Sir Mozart (IRE)**[29] 2417 7-9-9 58 TomQueally 8 74+
(B J Curley) *hld up: nt clr run over 2f out: hdwy over 1f out: shkn up to ld ins fnl f: readily* 5/1[2]

0304 2 1 **Bentley**[9] 3027 6-8-12 47 (v) PaulMulrennan 7 55
(J G Given) *led: rdn over 2f out: hdd ins fnl f: kpt on: nt gng pce of wnr* 11/1

5-42 3 2 ½ **Red River Boy**[9] 3026 5-8-10 48 KellyHarrison(3) 13 48
(C W Fairhurst) *midfield: hdwy on outside over 1f out: kpt on ins fnl f* 13/2

6005 4 1 ¼ **Whatyouwoodwishfor (USA)**[27] 2454 4-9-9 58 (v[1]) PaulHanagan 15 54
(R A Fahey) *cl up: rdn over 2f out: hung lft over 1f out: one pce ins fnl f* 6/1[3]

4260 5 nk **Bollywood Style**[16] 2809 5-9-10 59 RobertWinston 11 54
(J R Best) *t.k.h: prom: outpcd over 2f out: rallied over 1f out: nt rch ldrs* 10/1

5-40 6 2 ½ **Weetentherty**[5] 3151 3-9-0 56 (v) KierenFallon 2 41+
(J S Goldie) *t.k.h: in tch: nt clr run and lost pl over 2f out: kpt on ins fnl f: nvr able to chal* 14/1

5-60 7 ½ **Firetrap**[63] 1465 3-8-11 56 BarryMcHugh(3) 5 39
(Mrs A Duffield) *t.k.h: prom tl edgd rt and no ex over 1f out* 10/1

5406 8 1 ¼ **Carnival Dream**[20] 2671 5-9-4 53 PatrickMathers 12 34
(H A McWilliams) *trckd ldrs tl rdn and no ex fr 2f out* 25/1

60-0 9 1 ¼ **Yungaburra (IRE)**[14] 2849 6-9-11 60 (b) LeeVickers 14 37
(T J Pitt) *bhd: pushed along over 2f out: nvr able to chal* 20/1

5532 10 2 **Piste**[9] 3027 4-9-8 57 TomEaves 6 28
(Miss T Jackson) *t.k.h: prom tl rdn and wknd over 1f out* 3/1[1]

-150 11 10 **Sonny G (IRE)**[15] 2844 3-9-0 56 NeilCallan 3 —
(J R Best) *cl up tl rdn and wknd fr over 2f out* 14/1

1m 14.76s (1.06) **Going Correction** +0.225s/f (Good)
WFA 3 from 4yo+ 7lb 11 Ran SP% **117.7**
Speed ratings (Par 101): **101,99,96,94,94 90,90,88,86,84 70**
toteswingers: 1&2 £6.40, 1&3 £12.30, 2&3 £12.70 CSF £59.12 CT £364.61 TOTE £6.80: £1.80, £2.90, £1.80; EX 64.90 Place 6: £2024.08 Place 5: £616.74.
Owner P A Byrne **Bred** Western Bloodstock **Trained** Newmarket, Suffolk
■ Stewards' Enquiry : Kelly Harrison caution: used whip down the shoulder in the forehand position

FOCUS
A modest sprint handicap, but still quite an interesting race. Once again they came stands' side. The form is rated around the placed horses.
Weetentherty Official explanation: jockey said gelding hung right-handed throughout
T/Jkpt: Not won. T/Plt: £728.00 to a £ stake. Pool:£53,108.74 - 53.25 winning ticket. T/Qpdt: £47.00 to a £1 stake. Pool:£4,395.91 - 69.20 winning tickets RY

3079 KEMPTON (A.W) (R-H)
Wednesday, June 23

OFFICIAL GOING: Standard
Wind: Almost Nil Weather: Sunny, very warm

3323 KEMPTON.CO.UK APPRENTICE H'CAP 1m (P)
5:50 (5:50) (Class 6) (0-60,60) 4-Y-O+ £2,047 (£604; £302) **Stalls** High

Form RPR
3 1 **Whispering Spirit (IRE)**[19] 2727 4-9-3 58 (v) AmyRyan 13 71
(Mrs A Duffield) *cl up: wnt 2nd over 2f out: pushed into ld over 1f out: sn clr: comf* 7/1[2]

5050 2 3 **Goodbye Cash (IRE)**[35] 2235 6-9-3 58 RichardEvans 5 64
(R J Smith) *chsd ldr: rdn over 3f out: lost 2nd over 2f out: kpt on again to chse wnr last 150yds: no imp* 20/1

0/00 3 ¾ **Beat Up**[21] 2643 4-9-4 59 RossAtkinson 10 63+
(G D Blake) *hld up wl in rr: prog into midfield over 3f out: styd on fr over 2f out to take 3rd nr fin* 14/1

3060 4 ¾ **Altimatum (USA)**[13] 2894 4-8-11 55 (b) DuilioDaSilva(3) 3 57
(P F I Cole) *cl up: rdn over 3f out: nt qckn over 2f out: kpt on to press for 2nd 1f out: one pce* 16/1

240- 5 2 ½ **Josr's Magic (IRE)**[196] 7693 6-9-3 58 MatthewDavies 7 54
(P R Hedger) *hld up in midfield: 6th 1/2-way: gng strly over 2f out: pushed along and kpt on same pce fnl 2f:* 8/1

2040 6 ¾ **Count Ceprano (IRE)**[23] 2596 6-9-0 55 SimonPearce 9 49
(J Pearce) *lost midfield pl sn after 1/2-way: in rr whn hmpd 3f out: kpt on u.p fnl 2f* 15/2[3]

0103 7 ½ **Batchworth Blaise**[11] 2967 7-9-4 59 KierenFox 6 52
(E A Wheeler) *dwlt: detached in last pair 1/2-way: styd on fnl 2f: nrst fin* 8/1

5334 8 1 **Sotik Star (IRE)**[47] 1877 7-9-4 59 (p) IanBrennan 11 50
(K A Morgan) *hld up wl in rr: sme prog on inner over 2f out: rdn and no imp over 1f out* 5/1[1]

3005 9 hd **Wrighty Almighty (IRE)**[31] 2362 8-8-12 58 HarryBentley(5) 8 48
(P R Chamings) *pressed ldrs: rdn 3f out: wknd rapidly jst over 1f out* 11/1

0300 10 ½ **Esteem Lord**[23] 2596 4-8-9 53 DavidKenny(3) 14 42
(Jamie Poulton) *led to over 1f out: wknd rapidly fnl f* 25/1

0066 11 nk **Gallego**[19] 2714 8-8-12 56 TobyAtkinson(3) 12 44
(R J Price) *s.s: detached in last and nvr a factor: keeping on at fin* 7/1[2]

5202 12 ½ **Grey Boy (GER)**[6] 3131 9-8-12 60 GeorgeDowning(7) 1 47
(A W Carroll) *hld up wl in rr: v wd bnd 3f out: no prog after* 10/1

0/0- 13 25 **Sienna Lake (IRE)**[255] 6699 4-8-11 55 RyanClark(3) 4 —
(T D McCarthy) *nvr beyond midfield: wknd 3f out: t.o* 100/1

003 14 6 **My Jeanie (IRE)**[51] 1772 6-8-5 46 oh1 BillyCray 2 —
(J C Fox) *racd wd: prom 3f: sn wknd and t.o* 18/1

1m 40.28s (0.48) **Going Correction** +0.075s/f (Slow) 14 Ran SP% **117.1**
Speed ratings (Par 101): **100,97,96,95,93 92,91,90,90,90 89,89,64,58**
toteswingers:1&2 £39.10, 2&3 £104.60, 1&3 £24.00 CSF £140.14 CT £1953.64 TOTE £9.90: £3.20, £7.30, £7.20; EX 189.90.
Owner Middleham Park Racing XLII **Bred** David Barry **Trained** Constable Burton, N Yorks
■ Stewards' Enquiry : Ian Brennan two-day ban: careless riding (Jul 8, 10)

FOCUS
A modest apprentice handicap. It was run at a good pace with the field soon well strung out but very few got involved from the back. The winner produced a 7lb personal best.
Gallego Official explanation: jockey said gelding was never travelling
Sienna Lake(IRE) Official explanation: jockey said filly lost her action

My Jeanie(IRE) Official explanation: jockey said mare failed to handle the bend

3324 BOOK KEMPTON TICKETS ON 0844 579 3008 H'CAP — 2m (P)
6:20 (6:20) (Class 6) (0-65,68) 4-Y-0+ — **£2,047** (£604; £302) **Stalls** High

Form — RPR

0233 **1** **Graylyn Ruby (FR)**[12] 2923 5-9-3 **61** ... JimmyQuinn 12 — 70
(R Dickin) *trckd ldrs: 4th 1/2-way: chsd ldng pair 4f out and sn clr of rest: drvn on inner to ld over 1f out: all out* **20/1**

6-53 **2** *nk* **Stage Acclaim (IRE)**[4] 3223 5-8-11 **55** ...(p) JamieSpencer 10 — 64
(Dr R D P Newland) *trckd ldr 2f: styd prom: wnt 2nd over 4f out: drvn to ld over 2f out: hdd over 1f out: kpt on wl ins fnl f: jst hld* **10/1**

/321 **3** *2* **Ultimate Quest (IRE)**[7] 3084 5-9-10 **68** 6ex ... SebSanders 4 — 75
(Sir Mark Prescott) *pressed ldr after 5f: led over 5f out and kicked on: hrd rdn and hdd over 2f out: one pce* **7/4**[1]

4001 **4** *1 ¾* **Uncle Keef (IRE)**[13] 2907 4-9-6 **64** ...(b) TadhgO'Shea 2 — 69
(M P Tregoning) *dwlt: hld up in 7th: gng easily over 4f out but ldrs drawing away: prog to modest 4th wl over 3f out: sn hrd rdn: kpt on: nrst fin and too much to do* **14/1**

0434 **5** *6* **Purely By Chance**[7] 3084 5-8-4 **53** ...(v) SimonPearce(5) 14 — 50+
(J Pearce) *hld up in abt 10th: effrt over 4f out but ldrs already gone: prog fr 3f out: no hope of getting into it* **6/1**[3]

251 **6** *5* **City Stable (IRE)**[9] 3028 5-8-13 **62** 6ex ... TobyAtkinson(5) 7 — 53+
(M Wigham) *hld up in last trio: gng wl enough but ldrs already gone whn trapped bhd struggling rivals 4f out: sme prog 3f out to 2f out: nt a ch* **11/4**[2]

0-34 **7** *¾* **Fulfilment (IRE)**[51] 1755 4-8-8 **52** ... StevieDonohoe 11 — 42
(W J Musson) *a abt same pl: wl outpcd fr over 4f out: no ch fnl 3f* **16/1**

-332 **8** *10* **Hassadin**[13] 2907 4-8-5 **49** ... NeilChalmers 1 — 27
(A B Haynes) *chsd ldr after 2f to after 5f: wknd over 4f out: sn bhd* **20/1**

642- **9** *3 ¼* **Night Orbit**[118] 7124 6-9-5 **63** ... CathyGannon 6 — 38
(Miss J Feilden) *rdn in last pair after 5f: a struggling: passed flagging rivals fnl 3f* **33/1**

0256 **10** *11* **Mister Frosty (IRE)**[13] 2907 4-8-2 **53** ... CharlotteKerton(7) 9 — 14
(G Prodromou) *led to over 5f out: wknd and sn bhd: t.o* **66/1**

0632 **11** *1* **Prickles**[20] 2676 5-8-7 **51** ow1 ... JerryO'Dwyer 13 — 11
(Karen George) *mostly in 6th tl wknd over 3f out: t.o* **28/1**

0-60 **12** *19* **Court Princess**[21] 2659 7-8-9 **58** ... MatthewDavies(5) 3 — —
(George Baker) *rdn in last pair after 5f: a struggling: t.o* **50/1**

53-3 **13** *2 ¼* **Dee Cee Elle**[27] 2476 6-7-13 **48** ow1 ...(p) KierenFox(5) 5 — —
(D Burchell) *s.s: a wl in rr: wknd over 4f out: t.o* **8/1**

3m 29.02s (-1.08) **Going Correction** +0.075s/f (Slow) **13** Ran SP% **124.2**
Speed ratings (Par 101): **105,104,103,102,99 97,97,92,90,84 84,74,73**
toteswingers:1&2 £40.10, 2&3 £5.50, 1&3 £12.50 CSF £202.65 CT £541.67 TOTE £16.10: £4.70, £3.30, £1.30; EX 141.30.
Owner Graham & Lynn Knight **Bred** Jonathan Jay **Trained** Atherstone on Stour, Warwicks

FOCUS
An interesting handicap featuring several in-form rivals. It was run at a strong pace and the form should work out well. The winner is rated back to last year's form.
Court Princess Official explanation: jockey said mare hung left
Dee Cee Elle Official explanation: jockey said mare was never travelling

3325 HBLB H'CAP — 7f (P)
6:50 (6:52) (Class 5) (0-70,70) 3-Y-O — **£2,661** (£785; £393) **Stalls** High

Form — RPR

4145 **1** **Honest Broker (IRE)**[62] 1488 3-9-2 **65** ... FrankieDettori 12 — 72
(M Johnston) *trckd ldrs in 6th: prog jst over 2f out: drvn between rivals to go 2nd ins fnl f: styd on wl to ld last strides* **10/3**[1]

-022 **2** *hd* **Primo De Vida (IRE)**[34] 2258 3-9-4 **70** ... MartinLane(3) 13 — 76
(R M Beckett) *led: kicked on over 2f out: drvn over 1f out: styd on: hdd last strides* **11/2**[2]

3-20 **3** *½* **Law Of Attraction (IRE)**[12] 2919 3-9-7 **70** ... JamieSpencer 10 — 75
(J R Gask) *pressed ldr: rdn 2f out: nt qckn over 1f out: kpt on: lost 2nd ins fnl f* **8/1**[3]

4003 **4** *3* **Texan Star (IRE)**[18] 2755 3-9-7 **70** ...(b) RobertHavlin 6 — 67
(J H M Gosden) *trckd ldng pair: rdn to dispute 2nd jst over 1f out: wknd last 150yds* **9/1**

05-0 **5** *1 ¼* **Sweet Secret**[19] 2718 3-8-13 **62** ... RichardHughes 1 — 56+
(R Hannon) *c across fr wd draw to chse ldng trio: rdn and nt qckn over 1f out: pushed along after: lost grnd ins fnl f* **16/1**

4544 **6** *1 ¾* **Barlaman (USA)**[26] 2491 3-9-2 **65** ...(t) SebSanders 11 — 54
(C E Brittain) *hld up in midfield: wnt 6th 2f out and cl enough: sn outpcd and reminders: fdd* **11/2**[2]

6-10 **7** *1 ½* **Durham Town (IRE)**[19] 2702 3-9-7 **70** ... FergusSweeney 3 — 55
(D K Ivory) *hld up in last quartet: plenty to do whn shkn up wl over 1f out: styd on whn r was over* **16/1**

0530 **8** *nse* **Chandrayaan**[22] 2633 3-8-5 **57** ...(v) NataliaGemelova(3) 4 — 42
(J E Long) *racd wdst of last quartet: struggling off bnd wl over 2f out: sme late prog* **20/1**

036- **9** *¾* **Sir William Orpen**[266] 6372 3-9-0 **68** ... KierenFox(5) 5 — 51
(P M Phelan) *stdd s: mostly in last and racd wd: nvr looked to be gng wl: pushed along and styd on ins fnl f* **20/1**

55-4 **10** *nk* **Irish Jugger (USA)**[57] 1602 3-9-2 **68** ... JamesMillman(3) 9 — 50
(B R Millman) *hld up in midfield: plenty to do whn reminders over 1f out: nvr a factor* **10/1**

1205 **11** *1 ¼* **Merorless**[141] 382 3-8-12 **61** ... KirstyMilczarek 2 — 40
(Miss Z C Davison) *racd wd: chsd ldrs in abt 7th: u.p and struggling over 2f out: fdd* **50/1**

644- **12** *1 ½* **Rich Boy**[209] 7538 3-9-7 **70** ... IanMongan 14 — 44
(Mrs L J Mongan) *trckd ldng quartet to 2f out: wknd* **20/1**

0500 **13** *4 ½* **Trelicia**[22] 2633 3-8-8 **57** ... EddieAhern 7 — 19
(S C Williams) *bmpd s: hld up in last quartet: shkn up and no prog 2f out* **33/1**

5-00 **14** *¾* **Many A Slip**[13] 2888 3-9-5 **68** ... JimmyQuinn 8 — 28
(J L Dunlop) *bmpd s: hld up in last quartet: couple of reminders wl over 1f out and no prog* **33/1**

1m 26.89s (0.89) **Going Correction** +0.075s/f (Slow) **14** Ran SP% **117.9**
Speed ratings (Par 99): **97,96,96,92,91 89,87,87,86,86 84,83,78,77**
toteswingers: 1&2 £5.60, 2&3 £10.00, 1&3 £8.50 CSF £17.89 CT £123.31 TOTE £4.40: £2.10, £3.00, £3.80; EX 22.50.
Owner F Towey **Bred** Frank Towey **Trained** Middleham Moor, N Yorks

FOCUS
A fair handicap, but one run at no more than a fair pace and it proved a big advantage to be ridden close up, with the first five on the home turn still the first five at the finish. The winner is generally progressive on the sand.
Sir William Orpen Official explanation: jockey said gelding did not face the kickback
Irish Jugger(USA) Official explanation: jockey said gelding missed the break
Many A Slip Official explanation: jockey said gelding suffered interference shortly after the start and was never travelling thereaftter

3326 DIGIBET MAIDEN STKS — 7f (P)
7:20 (7:21) (Class 4) 2-Y-O — **£3,497** (£1,040; £520; £259) **Stalls** High

Form — RPR

1 **Deep South** 2-9-3 0 ... FrankieDettori 12 — 87+
(Mahmood Al Zarooni) *trckd ldng pair: wnt 2nd 3f out: clsd to ld over 1f out: shkn up and sn clr* **9/2**[2]

2 *3 ¾* **U A E Storm (USA)** 2-9-3 0 ... ShaneKelly 8 — 78+
(D M Simcock) *chsd ldng trio: pushed along to go 3rd wl over 2f out: rdn and styd on ins fnl f to take 2nd last 50yds* **25/1**

3 *shd* **Tick Tock Lover** 2-9-3 0 ... FergusSweeney 2 — 77+
(Miss Jo Crowley) *veered lft s: t.k.h: hld up in rr: prog fr 1/2-way: reminder over 1f out: jst pushed along and styd on encouragingly ins fnl f: nrly snatched 2nd* **100/1**

32 **4** *¾* **Postscript (IRE)**[19] 2687 2-9-0 0 ... AhmedAjtebi(3) 14 — 76
(Mahmood Al Zarooni) *led: clr w 3 rivals after 3f: hdd over 1f out: no ch w wnr after: lost 2 pls last 50yds* **5/4**[1]

5 *3* **Diamond Penny (IRE)** 2-9-3 0 ... JamieSpencer 10 — 68
(P F I Cole) *awkward s: chsd ldng quartet but nt on terms: tried to cl fr over 2f out: no imp over 1f out* **9/2**[2]

6 *hd* **Handsome Jack (IRE)** 2-9-3 0 ... StevieDonohoe 5 — 68+
(R A Mills) *dwlt: virtually t.o in 12th much of r: picked up and weaved through fr 2f out: fin wl* **28/1**

7 *2 ¼* **Scottish Star** 2-9-3 0 ... SebSanders 9 — 62+
(J M P Eustace) *s.i.s: wl off the pce in rr: sme prog over 2f out: nvr a threat* **25/1**

0 **8** *1 ½* **Mediplomat**[26] 2493 2-9-3 0 ... JimmyQuinn 11 — 58
(M Botti) *chsd clr ldng quartet: tried to cl fr 3f out: rdn to go 4th over 1f out: sn wknd* **20/1**

9 *1* **Ya Hafed** 2-9-3 0 ... EddieAhern 7 — 56
(E A L Dunlop) *nvr bttr than midfield and a off the pce: n.d over 2f out* **33/1**

0 **10** *½* **Jibouti (IRE)**[88] 1017 2-9-3 0 ... KoseiMiura 4 — 54
(C E Brittain) *nvr bttr than abt 9th and a wl off the pce: no ch over 2f out* **14/1**[3]

0 **11** *11* **Futurism**[10] 3000 2-9-3 0 ... RichardHughes 6 — 30
(R Hannon) *chsd ldr: wnt wd bnd 3f out and lost 2nd: sn eased: t.o* **33/1**

12 *16* **Armagnac Rebel** 2-9-3 0 ... LiamKeniry 1 — —
(S C Burrough) *s.v.s: a t.o* **100/1**

0 **13** *1* **Castle Kirk (IRE)**[9] 3035 2-9-3 0 ... IanMongan 13 — —
(P M Phelan) *sn off the pce in abt 8th: wknd 3f out: t.o* **66/1**

1m 27.09s (1.09) **Going Correction** +0.075s/f (Slow) **13** Ran SP% **112.7**
Speed ratings (Par 95): **96,91,91,90,87 87,84,82,81,81 68,50,49**
toteswingers: 1&2 £19.10, 1&3 £37.50, 2&3 £100.80 CSF £110.53 TOTE £3.20: £1.10, £8.00, £13.90; EX 99.80.
Owner Godolphin **Bred** Meon Valley Stud **Trained** Newmarket, Suffolk

FOCUS
A three-horse race according to the market but a one-horse race as things turned out with the winner easily beating his better-fancied stablemate. The form should work out. The winning time was just 0.2sec lower than the preceding 3-y-o handicap.

NOTEBOOK
Deep South ◆, a well-related and expensive purchase, was sent off a surprisingly long price considering his breeding, the ordinary form of his stablemate and the fact that Dettori was on board. He could be called the winner some way out and, after quickening away inside the last, won easing up. He looks above average, though possibly not Pattern material just yet, and though he clearly knew his job he is entitled to improve. (op 3-1)
U A E Storm(USA), a half-brother to the quite useful 1m winner Charlotte Point, made a pleasing debut, never far away and staying on well. He looks likely to improve. (op 28-1)
Tick Tock Lover ◆ is modestly bred but ran an eyecatching first race and looks sure to improve and win a similar event. Soon behind after swerving left exiting his outside stall, he made good mid-race progress then carried that through all the way to the line without being given a hard time. (tchd 80-1)
Postscript(IRE) was sent off a very short price considering he'd had his limitations exposed at the minor tracks and could only plug on for fourth after being allowed to set his own pace. There's no guarantee he will find things any easier in nurseries. (op 2-1 tchd 11-10)
Diamond Penny(IRE) is related to several winners but was weak in the market and probably needed this first experience. He looks to have some scope and will probably do better in time. (op 3-1 tchd 11-4)
Handsome Jack(IRE) ◆ also caught the eye. He was in a hopeless position turning for home but the penny really dropped in the last furlong and he came home in good style. He seems sure to step up on this markedly. (op 25-1)
Scottish Star comes from a yard that don't normally rush their juveniles, so it was encouraging to see him make some headway early in the straight before flattening out. He'll be a different proposition next time.
Futurism Official explanation: jockey said colt lost its action

3327 EUROPEAN BREEDERS' FUND NOVICE STKS — 6f (P)
7:50 (7:51) (Class 4) 2-Y-O — **£4,533** (£1,348; £674; £336) **Stalls** High

Form — RPR

512 **1** **Bilko Pak (IRE)**[12] 2918 2-9-5 0 ... RichardHughes 2 — 88+
(R Hannon) *trckd ldr: led and qcknd 2f out: edgd rt over 1f out: shkn up and styd on wl* **5/2**[2]

3433 **2** *1 ¼* **Fifth Ave**[11] 2950 2-8-11 0 ... FergusSweeney 1 — 76
(J A Osborne) *hld up in last: effrt on outer 2f out: shkn up to dispute 2nd ins fnl f: no imp on wnr* **4/1**[3]

31 **3** *hd* **Coeus**[20] 2677 2-9-2 0 ... SebSanders 4 — 83+
(Sir Mark Prescott) *hld up in 3rd: effrt on inner 2f out: nt clr run over 1f out: jst pushed along ins fnl f and styd on same pce* **8/11**[1]

014 **4** *12* **Novabridge**[22] 2630 2-9-5 0 ... JamieSpencer 3 — 54
(A B Haynes) *led at mod pce: hdd 2f out: wkng whn sltly hmpd sn after* **25/1**

1m 14.57s (1.47) **Going Correction** +0.075s/f (Slow) **4** Ran SP% **110.3**
Speed ratings (Par 95): **93,91,91,75**
CSF £11.97 TOTE £4.60; EX 14.00.
Owner Middleham Park Racing XLIII **Bred** Stuart Weld **Trained** East Everleigh, Wilts
■ Stewards' Enquiry : Richard Hughes three-day ban: careless riding (Jul 8, 10, 12)

FOCUS
A fairly useful minor event but one that turned into something of a sprint for home. The runner-up helps set the level but the form promises to be unreliable.

NOTEBOOK
Bilko Pak(IRE) was the beneficiary of a no-nonsense ride and probably didn't have to do any more than give his running to win after getting first run from closer up to the steady pace than his two nearest rivals on form, drifting right late on. Nurseries rather than Listed events are probably the way forward with him. (op 7-2)

Fifth Ave looked likely to be suited by the step up in trip but this race didn't test stamina and he was the poorest placed of the quartet when the sprint began. (op 7-1)
Coeus didn't help himself by propping leaving the stalls, thereby conceding the initiative and pole rail position to Novabridge. Forced to sit and wait for a run after that, he was just beginning a challenge when forced to tighten up passing the cutaway, though he didn't pick up thereafter in the manner of one that looked particularly unlucky. It will be a surprise if he's not ridden with more urgency next time. (op 1-2)
Novabridge faced a very stiff task at the weights and was given every chance but looked quirky in the straight, jinking right. (op 18-1)

3328 DIGIBET CASINO FILLIES' H'CAP — 6f (P)
8:20 (8:21) (Class 4) (0-80,79) 3-Y-0+ **£4,209** (£1,252; £625; £312) **Stalls** High

Form / RPR

6213 **1** **Requisite**[9] 3037 5-9-9 **67**............(v) CathyGannon 6 — 80
(I A Wood) *hld up in 7th: shkn up on outer over 2f out: gd prog over 1f out: led last 150yds: sn clr* **7/2**[1]

55-1 **2** 2 1/4 **Pose (IRE)**[34] 2249 3-9-10 **75**............ RichardHughes 9 — 78
(R Hannon) *led 1f: cl up: effrt to ld wl over 1f out: styd on ins fnl f: hdd and outpcd last 150yds* **6/1**[2]

5030 **3** 1 **Sweet Applause (IRE)**[11] 2964 4-8-7 **58**............ CharlotteKerton(7) 2 — 59
(G Prodromou) *t.k.h: hld up in 4th: effrt to dispute 2nd over 1f out: urged along and outpcd ins fnl f* **25/1**

-000 **4** 1 3/4 **Song Of Praise**[6] 3129 4-9-2 **60**............ NeilChalmers 3 — 55
(M Blanshard) *c out of the stalls after the rest: hld up last: pushed along fr 2f out: styd on steadily to take 4th nr fin: nvr nr ldrs* **16/1**

4235 **5** 1 **Sulis Minerva (IRE)**[14] 2868 3-9-7 **72**............(t) JamieSpencer 8 — 61
(J R Gask) *sn restrained into 6th: effrt on inner 2f out: cl enough over 1f out: fdd ins fnl f* **6/1**[2]

-105 **6** shd **Key Light (IRE)**[24] 2565 3-9-9 **74**............ EddieAhern 4 — 63
(J W Hills) *racd wd in 5th: rdn over 2f out: steadily fdd fr over 1f out* **8/1**[3]

1-51 **7** 1 **Basle**[48] 1842 3-9-12 **77**............ DavidProbert 5 — 62
(Miss Gay Kelleway) *chsd ldr after 2f to 2f out: steadily fdd* **6/1**[2]

360 **8** 1 1/4 **Todber**[65] 1428 5-9-9 **67**............(v) TadhgO'Shea 10 — 54+
(M P Tregoning) *hld up in 8th: shuffled along on inner fnl 2f: no prog and nvr nr ldrs* **7/2**[1]

440- **9** 1 1/2 **Oriental Rose**[272] 6233 4-9-2 **60**............ JimmyQuinn 7 — 37
(D Shaw) *led after 1f to wl over 1f out: wknd* **16/1**

1m 13.3s (0.20) **Going Correction** +0.075s/f (Slow)
WFA 3 from 4yo+ 7lb — 9 Ran SP% **114.0**
Speed ratings (Par 102): **101,98,96,94,93 92,91,89,87**
toteswingers:1&2 £4.60, 2&3 £17.80, 1&3 £23.30 CSF £24.25 CT £450.45 TOTE £5.60: £2.20, £1.20, £6.30; EX 22.50.
Owner Paddy Barrett **Bred** Darley **Trained** Upper Lambourn, Berks

FOCUS
A 0-85 in name but just a fair handicap in reality in which the runners towards the bottom of the weights came to the fore. The pace seemed fairly solid and none of the field appeared to have any real excuses. The winner is rateed back towards her best.
Song Of Praise Official explanation: jockey said filly missed the break
Todber Official explanation: jockey said mare was denied a clear run

3329 DIGIBET.COM H'CAP — 1m 4f (P)
8:50 (8:50) (Class 4) (0-85,85) 4-Y-0+ **£4,209** (£1,252; £625; £312) **Stalls** Centre

Form / RPR

2121 **1** **Speed Dating**[7] 3079 4-8-10 **74**............(b) SebSanders 1 — 91+
(Sir Mark Prescott) *hld up in last pair: stl there 3f out: prog on outer 2f out: drvn and r.o wl to ld last 100yds: gng away fin* **11/10**[1]

2011 **2** 1 1/2 **Scamperdale**[11] 2961 8-9-2 **85**............ KierenFox(5) 7 — 96
(B P J Baugh) *hld up in 6th: smooth prog over 2f out: rdn to ld over 1f out: r.o wl: hdd and outpcd last 100yds* **12/1**

-305 **3** 3 3/4 **Incendo**[11] 2975 4-9-0 **78**............ JamieSpencer 2 — 83
(J R Fanshawe) *hld up in last pair: gng easily 3f out: effrt on inner 2f out: outpcd by ldrs over 1f out: kpt on to take 3rd* **4/1**[2]

5-05 **4** shd **Dakiyah (IRE)**[10] 2996 6-9-4 **82**............(p) IanMongan 8 — 87
(Mrs L J Mongan) *rousted along early: chsd ldng trio: wnt 2nd over 2f out and sn drvn upsides: nt qckn over 1f out: plugged on to press for 3rd nr fin* **25/1**

1-46 **5** nk **Grey Granite (IRE)**[11] 2975 4-8-12 **76**............ RichardHughes 3 — 81
(W Jarvis) *led after 2f to over 1f out: readily outpcd u.p* **5/1**[3]

2-30 **6** 3 1/2 **Foxhaven**[51] 1783 8-9-3 **81**............ DavidProbert 5 — 80
(P R Chamings) *trckd ldng pair: shkn up over 2f out: wknd over 1f out* **15/2**

2126 **7** 2 1/2 **Quinsman**[123] 636 4-9-0 **78**............ LiamKeniry 10 — 73
(J S Moore) *trckd ldng trio: rdn over 2f out: sn wknd* **25/1**

5/0- **8** 15 **Out Of Nothing**[414] 1775 7-8-2 **66** oh14............ CathyGannon 9 — 37
(D Burchell) *led 2f: chsd ldr to over 2f out: wknd rapidly: t.o* **66/1**

2m 32.5s (-2.00) **Going Correction** +0.075s/f (Slow) — 8 Ran SP% **112.9**
Speed ratings (Par 105): **109,108,105,105,105 102,101,91**
toteswingers:1&2 £3.00, 2&3 £7.30, 1&3 £1.20 CSF £15.63 CT £40.27 TOTE £2.40: £1.40, £2.30, £1.10; EX 15.90.
Owner Cheveley Park Stud **Bred** Cheveley Park Stud Ltd **Trained** Newmarket, Suffolk

FOCUS
An interesting handicap in which the two in-form runners pulled clear of the rest. The pace picked up after a steady first 2f but it still wasn't a proper test at the trip. The well-in winner is progressing.

3330 BOOK NOW FOR BEST OF BRITISH NIGHT H'CAP (LONDON MILE QUALIFIER) — 1m (P)
9:20 (9:21) (Class 4) (0-80,79) 3-Y-0+ **£4,209** (£1,252; £625; £312) **Stalls** High

Form / RPR

-134 **1** **Shamir**[11] 2970 3-9-6 **79**............ IanMongan 1 — 86
(Miss Jo Crowley) *hld up in last trio: prog on inner fr 2f out: drvn and r.o to ld ins fnl f: in command after* **8/1**

-560 **2** 1 1/4 **Kiss A Prince**[16] 2821 4-9-7 **70**............(b[1]) RichardHughes 2 — 75
(D K Ivory) *hld up wl in rr: looking for room 2f out: gd prog on inner jst over 1f out: r.o to take 2nd nr fin* **14/1**

205- **3** nk **Flapper (IRE)**[236] 7149 4-9-9 **72**............ EddieAhern 8 — 76
(J W Hills) *trckd ldr: poised to chal over 2f out gng wl: rdn to ld jst over 1f out: hdd and outpcd ins fnl f* **25/1**

5103 **4** 2 1/2 **Alqaahir (USA)**[35] 2236 8-9-7 **73**............ RobertLButler(3) 10 — 72
(P Butler) *pressed ldrs: effrt to chal 2f out: upsides jst over 1f out: wknd last 150yds* **20/1**

10/4 **5** 1/2 **Al Aqabah (IRE)**[21] 2643 5-9-1 **64**............ DavidProbert 4 — 61
(B Gubby) *hld up in rr: prog into midfield over 3f out: hdwy to chse ldrs over 1f out: one pce after* **16/1**

0304 **6** 1 3/4 **Zerzura**[7] 3079 4-8-13 **67**............ KierenFox(5) 12 — 60
(P Howling) *led to jst over 1f out: wknd* **20/1**

41-0 **7** nk **First Service (IRE)**[35] 2236 4-9-6 **69**............ JamieSpencer 6 — 62
(M J Attwater) *hld up last on outer: effrt over 2f out: shkn up and kpt on: nvr any ch* **33/1**

2000 **8** 4 1/2 **Sunshine Always (IRE)**[14] 2872 4-9-13 **76**............ KirstyMilczarek 7 — 58
(T D McCarthy) *trckd ldrs: prog on outer to go 3rd over 3f out: rdn 2f out: sn wknd* **20/1**

0-00 **9** hd **Smart Endeavour (USA)**[56] 1618 4-9-12 **75**............ ShaneKelly 9 — 57
(W R Swinburn) *prom: rdn and nt qckn over 2f out: wknd rapidly over 1f out* **15/2**[3]

2-0 **10** 1 **Fernando Torres**[47] 1875 4-9-4 **67**............(p) RobertHavlin 3 — 47+
(Matthew Salaman) *hld up in midfield: pushed along and in tch but making no prog whn hmpd over 1f out: no ch after* **16/1**

41-0 **11** 1 1/4 **Solicitor**[11] 2979 3-9-6 **79**............ FrankieDettori 14 — 54
(M Johnston) *wnt prom on inner after 2f: lost pl fr 1/2-way: no prog 2f out: sn btn* **13/8**[1]

-043 **12** 1 **North Cape (USA)**[26] 2512 4-9-10 **73**............ FergusSweeney 5 — 47
(H Candy) *towards rr and pushed along early: effrt over 2f out: sn no prog: fdd* **7/2**[2]

30-0 **13** 16 **Maswerte (IRE)**[26] 2508 4-10-0 **77**............ SebSanders 11 — 15
(M Wigham) *chsd ldng pair to over 3f out: wknd rapidly over 2f out: t.o* **25/1**

1m 39.78s (-0.02) **Going Correction** +0.075s/f (Slow)
WFA 3 from 4yo+ 10lb — **13** Ran SP% **126.5**
Speed ratings (Par 105): **103,101,101,98,98 96,96,91,91,90 89,88,72**
toteswingers:1&2 £27.70, 2&3 £9.90, 1&3 £24.10 CSF £107.32 CT £2780.60 TOTE £16.60: £5.30, £4.50, £22.00; EX 118.20 Place 6: £651.76 Place 5: £138.72.
Owner Kilstone Limited **Bred** Plantation Stud **Trained** Whitcombe, Dorset
■ Stewards' Enquiry : Kirsty Milczarek one-day ban: careless riding (Jul 8)

FOCUS
A very competitive finale run at a good pace. The form is rated around the third and fifth and seems likely to prove reliable.
Fernando Torres Official explanation: jockey said gelding suffered interference in running
Maswerte(IRE) Official explanation: jockey said gelding stopped quickly
T/Plt: £876.10 to a £1 stake. Pool: £47,756.65 - 39.79 winning tickets T/Qpdt: £108.80 to a £1 stake. Pool: £4,299.53 - 29.22 winning tickets JN

2996 SALISBURY (R-H)
Wednesday, June 23

OFFICIAL GOING: Good to firm (good in places from 4f out until 2f out)
Wind: virtually nil Weather: very warm and sunny

3331 E B F ASHBRITTLE STUD MAIDEN FILLIES' STKS — 5f
1:35 (1:35) (Class 4) 2-Y-O **£4,727** (£1,406; £702; £351) **Stalls** Centre

Form / RPR

1 **Perfect Tribute** 2-9-0 0............ LukeMorris 2 — 75+
(C G Cox) *wnt sltly rt but broke wl: trckd ldrs: qcknd up wl to ld ins fnl f: comf* **10/3**[2]

3404 **2** 2 1/2 **Darwin Star**[21] 2642 2-9-0 0............ JimmyQuinn 8 — 66
(D K Ivory) *sn led: rdn and hdd wl over 1f out: rallied to ld briefly jst ins fnl f: nt gng pce of wnr* **9/1**

3 3/4 **Best Be Careful (IRE)** 2-9-0 0............ LiamKeniry 3 — 63
(M D I Usher) *s.i.s: rcvrd to join ldr after 1f: rdn to ld wl over 1f out: drifted lft and hdd jst ins fnl f: no ex* **12/1**

4 3 **Chevise (IRE)** 2-9-0 0............ JimCrowley 5 — 53
(R M Beckett) *in tch: rdn over 2f out: kpt on same pce* **10/3**[2]

5 2 **Regal Rocket (IRE)** 2-9-0 0............ FrankieMcDonald 6 — 45
(R Hannon) *s.i.s: sn keen in tch: stmbld after 1f: rdn and one pce fnl 2f* **6/1**[3]

6 hd **Libertia** 2-9-0 0............ FergusSweeney 9 — 45
(A G Newcombe) *in tch: rdn over 2f out: sn one pce* **25/1**

7 1 1/2 **Porthgwidden Beach (USA)** 2-9-0 0............(t) SaleemGolam 1 — 39
(S C Williams) *awkward leaving stalls: in last pair: sme prog 2f out: fdd ins fnl f* **18/1**

8 3 3/4 **Silver Show (IRE)** 2-9-0 0............ AlanMunro 7 — 26
(M R Channon) *broke wl but sn outpcd and dropped in rr* **3/1**[1]

61.85 secs (0.85) **Going Correction** -0.125s/f (Firm) — 8 Ran SP% **112.2**
Speed ratings (Par 92): **88,84,82,78,74 74,72,66**
toteswingers: 1&2 £5.40, 2&3 £6.50, 1&3 not won. CSF £31.72 TOTE £5.20: £2.30, £1.20, £3.40; EX 34.50 Trifecta £231.40 Part won. Pool of £312.76 - 0.51 winning units..
Owner Mildmay Racing & D H Caslon **Bred** Mildmay Bloodstock **Trained** Lambourn, Berks

FOCUS
An average fillies' maiden that provided Clive Cox with his first juvenile winner of the season. The form is rated around the runner-up.

NOTEBOOK
Perfect Tribute hails from a stable whose past record in the race suggested a big run was on the cards, but it has found winners hard to come by of late and this filly was also reported to have got somewhat excited on the journey to the track. The money still came for her, though, and she ultimately ran out a convincing winner. Her pedigree suggests this trip would be plenty sharp enough for her, but she knew her job, showing decent early pace from her low draw, and there was a lot to like about her attitude when asked for everything. She should only improve when faced with another furlong and clearly has a good future. (op 9-2)
Darwin Star was the only one of these to have previously run and she set a moderate standard. Considering her experience it wasn't a surprise to see her lead early and she ran her race, so rates a sound benchmark. (op 11-2)
Best Be Careful(IRE) is speedily bred and, from a yard that won here with a 2-y-o earlier this month, came in for some support. She wasn't well away, but soon made her way to the front end and posted a pleasing debut display. (op 18-1)
Chevise(IRE), a half-sister to a juvenile winner at two, also attracted support. She was outpaced from an early stage and looks the type to come on for the run, with the step up to 6f promising to suit. (op 4-1)
Regal Rocket(IRE) has a pedigree that suggests speed and stamina. She proved easy to back and never threatened, but did enough to think she will get closer next time. (op 9-2)
Libertia wasn't disgraced and is another sure to enjoy stepping up in trip. (op 20-1)
Silver Show(IRE) cost 65,000gns and proved popular in the betting. She got hopelessly outpaced and was beaten after a furlong or so. (op 10-3)

3332 GEORGE SMITH HORSEBOXES MEDIAN AUCTION MAIDEN STKS — 6f
2:10 (2:11) (Class 5) 2-Y-O **£3,238** (£963; £481; £240) **Stalls** High

Form / RPR

22 **1** **Royal Exchange**[25] 2540 2-9-3 0............ RichardHughes 14 — 82+
(R Hannon) *mid-div: steadily clsd on ldrs fr over 2f out: shkn up to chse ldr ent fnl f: r.o to ld fnl 50yds* **8/11**[1]

0 **2** *shd* **Midnight Feast**[20] 2680 2-9-3 0 JimCrowley 3 82
(P Winkworth) *sn prom: led 4f out: rdn wl over 1f out: kpt on wl whn ct fnl 50yds* **50/1**

5 **3** *1 1/4* **Fight The Chance (IRE)**[13] 2887 2-9-3 0 AlanMunro 9 78
(M R Channon) *trckd ldr: rdn over 2f out: swtchd lft sn after: kpt on fnl f: nt quite gng pce to chal* **5/1**[2]

5 **4** *7* **St Oswald**[16] 2819 2-9-3 0 SteveDrowne 13 57
(R Charlton) *hld up towards rr: rdn and hdwy over 2f out: styd on: nvr gng pce to get on terms* **5/1**[2]

2 **5** *1/2* **Perfect Pastime**[16] 2819 2-9-3 0 AdamKirby 2 56
(W R Swinburn) *led for 2f: prom: rdn over 2f out: no pce of ldrs fr over 1f out: lost 4th nr fin* **13/2**[3]

6 *3 1/2* **Cape Rambler** 2-9-3 0 FergusSweeney 11 45
(H Candy) *outpcd in rr early: hdwy over 1f out: styd on ins fnl f: nrst fin* **25/1**

U **7** *1/2* **Manasha**[32] 2330 2-8-12 0 IanMongan 6 39
(J L Dunlop) *in tch: rdn over 2f out: hung rt and wknd ins fnl f* **25/1**

8 *3/4* **Bernie's Tune** 2-9-3 0 SamHitchcott 10 41
(J L Spearing) *rdn 3f out: nvr bttr than mid-div* **80/1**

9 *1/2* **Point Du Jour (FR)** 2-9-3 0 GeorgeBaker 5 40
(I A Wood) *in tch: rdn 3f out: wknd over 1f out* **66/1**

10 *3 3/4* **Areopagitica** 2-8-12 0 LukeMorris 12 24
(C G Cox) *a towards rr* **66/1**

0 **11** *1/2* **Little Oddy (IRE)**[41] 2059 2-9-0 0 AndrewHeffernan(3) 7 27
(P D Evans) *mid-div tl wknd 2f out* **66/1**

12 *2* **Dozy Joe** 2-9-3 0 RichardMullen 8 21
(I A Wood) *wnt rt s: sn outpcd: a in rr* **66/1**

13 *1 1/4* **Dew Reward (IRE)** 2-9-3 0 TonyCulhane 4 17
(Eve Johnson Houghton) *s.i.s: pushed along after 2f out: a towards rr* **80/1**

0 **14** *19* **Hazy Ridge**[18] 2749 2-8-12 0 RobertHavlin 1 —
(M Madgwick) *prom early: outpcd 3f out: wknd 2f out* **100/1**

1m 14.31s (-0.49) **Going Correction** -0.125s/f (Firm) **14** Ran SP% **123.7**
Speed ratings (Par 93): **98,97,96,86,86 81,80,79,79,74 73,70,69,43**
toteswingers: 1&2 £20.30, 1&3 £1.90, 2&3 £43.50 CSF £71.12 TOTE £1.80: £1.20, £13.50, £2.10; EX 71.50 Trifecta £383.20 Pool of £657.74 - 1.27 winning units..
Owner The Queen **Bred** The Queen **Trained** East Everleigh, Wilts
■ Stewards' Enquiry : Alan Munro one-day ban: used whip without giving colt time to respond (Jul 8)

FOCUS
There wasn't much strength in depth here and the first three came nicely clear.

NOTEBOOK
Royal Exchange was again all the rage despite having been turned over at odds-on last time out and he just got the job done, opening his account at the third attempt. He was made to work hard, though, and didn't look the easiest of rides when put under pressure, so the bang in-form Hughes again emerges with credit. The step up a furlong suited, however, and he does have a good engine, so it's worth giving him the benefit of the doubt at this stage. Connections later said they may step him up another furlong next time. (tchd 8-13 and 4-5 in a place)
Midnight Feast ◆'s proximity at first glance does little for the form, but along with the third he was well clear of two that had shown ability on their respective debuts and he rates a big improver. He only got reeled in late on, but deserves extra credit as he was moderately drawn, and he should not be long in winning (op 40-1)
Fight The Chance(IRE) was held by the first pair at the business end, but still stepped up on his Newbury debut as expected and showed a more professional attitude. He can be found an opening in the coming weeks. (op 11-2 tchd 13-2)
St Oswald lacked the pace to get seriously involved, but still reversed last-time-out form with Perfect Pastime. He may benefit from another furlong now. (op 6-1)
Perfect Pastime had his chance and ran well below his debut form. (op 7-1 tchd 8-1)
Cape Rambler was doing his best work too late in the day and it wouldn't be at all surprising to see him improve markedly next time out. (op 20-1)

3333 SMITH & WILLIAMSON MAIDEN FILLIES' STKS 6f 212y
2:45 (2:45) (Class 5) 3-Y-O £3,885 (£1,156; £577; £288) **Stalls** Centre

Form RPR

0-5 **1** **Starclass**[39] 2122 3-9-0 0 AdamKirby 4 81+
(W R Swinburn) *hld up: hdwy whn swtchd to centre 2f out: str run to ld ent fnl f: r.o wl: easily* **7/2**[2]

03 **2** *5* **Poppy Golightly**[15] 2841 3-9-0 0 RichardKingscote 5 67
(R J Hodges) *trckd ldrs: rdn wl over 2f out: kpt on to hold ev ch ent fnl f: sn outpcd by wnr: snatched 2nd fnl strides* **10/1**

0-3 **3** *nse* **Night Sky**[15] 2842 3-9-0 0 FergusSweeney 2 67
(P J Makin) *in tch: rdn to chal over 1f out: ev ch ent fnl f: sn nt gng pce of wnr: lost 2nd fnl strides* **11/4**[1]

0 **4** *3 3/4* **Lady Berta**[10] 2998 3-9-0 0 RichardHughes 1 57+
(R Hannon) *hld up bhd: pushed along and hdwy 2f out: styd on: nvr threatened ldrs* **6/1**

0-06 **5** *1 1/2* **Ellen Vannin (IRE)**[14] 2879 3-8-11 53 (p) PatrickHills(3) 6 53
(Eve Johnson Houghton) *led: rdn and hdd ent fnl f: wknd* **25/1**

4 **6** *3 3/4* **Laser Ruby**[15] 2841 3-9-0 0 LiamKeniry 7 43
(A M Balding) *little slowly away: sn mid-div: rdn 3f out: wknd over 1f out* **4/1**[3]

0- **7** *1 1/2* **Up At Last**[246] 6920 3-9-0 0 LiamJones 9 39
(W J Haggas) *trckd ldrs: n.m.r on far side rails after 1f: rdn over 3f out: wknd over 1f out* **16/1**

0 **8** *3 3/4* **Alnaseem (USA)**[68] 1355 3-9-0 0 RichardHills 8 29
(J L Dunlop) *trckd ldrs early: mid-div after early bustling match after 1f: pushed along 4f out: wknd wl over 2f out: eased ins fnl f* **8/1**

9 *8* **Into The Wind** 3-9-0 0 ow3 JamesMillman(3) 3 10
(B R Millman) *s.i.s: sn outpcd in rr* **25/1**

1m 26.63s (-2.37) **Going Correction** -0.125s/f (Firm) **9** Ran SP% **117.0**
Speed ratings (Par 96): **108,102,102,97,96 91,90,85,76**
toteswingers: 1&2 £8.00, 1&3 £2.90, 2&3 £4.60 CSF £38.81 TOTE £5.30: £2.10, £3.50, £1.10; EX 44.50 Trifecta £146.70 Pool £573.06 - 2.89 winning units..
Owner Borgatti & Moir **Bred** M E Broughton **Trained** Aldbury, Herts

FOCUS
A modest fillies' maiden but the form seems sound rated around the placed horses, with the fourth close to debut form.
Lady Berta ◆ Official explanation: jockey said filly stumbled coming down the hill

3334 MOLSON COORS NOEL CANNON MEMORIAL TROPHY H'CAP 1m
3:15 (3:15) (Class 2) (0-100,94) 3-Y-O+
£10,281 (£3,078; £1,539; £770; £384; £193) **Stalls** High

Form RPR

0000 **1** **Mahadee (IRE)**[12] 2934 5-9-5 85 (b) TedDurcan 8 99
(C E Brittain) *hld up towards rr: gd hdwy whn gap appeared on far side rail 2f out: rdn to ld jst ins fnl f: r.o strly* **9/1**

0000 **2** *2 3/4* **Benandonner (USA)**[27] 2472 7-9-4 84 AndreaAtzeni 3 92
(Mike Murphy) *in tch: rdn to ld 2f out: hdd jst ins fnl f: kpt on: sn hld by wnr* **16/1**

2154 **3** *2 1/2* **Gaily Noble (IRE)**[19] 2708 4-9-12 92 JimCrowley 5 94
(A B Haynes) *hld up towards rr: rdn and hdwy over 1f out: styd on ins fnl f* **8/1**

0-00 **4** *nse* **Nezami (IRE)**[20] 2683 5-9-7 87 SebSanders 7 89
(J Akehurst) *s.i.s: towards rr: swtchd to centre and stdy prog u.p fr 2f out: styd on ins fnl f* **10/1**

0413 **5** *1* **Vainglory (USA)**[19] 2708 6-9-11 94 MartinLane(3) 12 96
(D M Simcock) *trckd ldr: rdn over 3f out: trying to mount chal whn squeezed out over 1f out: no ch after but kpt on fnl 75yds* **10/3**[1]

0200 **6** *1* **Karaka Jack**[15] 2835 3-8-12 88 J-PGuillambert 1 83
(M Johnston) *trckd ldrs: rdn and ev ch 2f out: fdd ins fnl f* **5/1**[3]

1350 **7** *shd* **Highly Regal (IRE)**[21] 2640 5-9-2 82 (b) LiamKeniry 2 79
(R A Teal) *mid-div: sme hdwy in centre 3f out: wknd ins fnl f* **14/1**

1200 **8** *3* **Mujood**[19] 2708 7-10-0 94 RichardMullen 11 84
(Eve Johnson Houghton) *trckd ldrs tl u.p 4f out: grad fdd* **18/1**

0260 **9** *1 3/4* **Swift Chap**[19] 2710 4-9-2 82 AlanMunro 10 68
(B R Millman) *led tl 2f out: sn wknd* **11/2**

4311 **10** *2* **Avon River**[21] 2644 3-8-11 87 (b) RichardHughes 6 66
(R Hannon) *mid-div: rdn whn swtchd to centre 2f out: wknd fnl f* **9/2**[2]

1m 40.59s (-2.91) **Going Correction** -0.125s/f (Firm)
WFA 3 from 4yo+ 10lb **10** Ran SP% **121.3**
Speed ratings (Par 109): **109,106,103,103,102 101,101,98,96,94**
toteswingers: 1&2 £12.00, 1&3 £22.50, 2&3 £36.30 CSF £147.64 CT £1213.13 TOTE £12.00: £4.30, £6.70, £2.50; EX 247.20 TRIFECTA Not won..
Owner Saeed Manana **Bred** Darley **Trained** Newmarket, Suffolk

FOCUS
A 0-100 handicap but the top-weight was rated 6lb below the ceiling. There was a solid pace on and the third and fifth are rated close to their ltest Epsom form.

NOTEBOOK
Mahadee(IRE) travelled well in midfield on the inside but needed a gap to open up for him in the straight. It kindly did when Vainglory and Swift Chap edged off the rail, and he quickened up well to take advantage. Although a better horse on the AW, he was on a fair mark here judged on his running-on seventh from a poor draw at Newmarket two starts back over an inadequate 7f. Official explanation: trainer's rep had no explanation for the apparent improvement in form shown (op 10-1)
Benandonner(USA) has slipped to an attractive mark on turf, having won off a 10lb higher mark around this time last year. This was a return to form as he did by far the best of those that raced prominently. (op 25-1)
Gaily Noble(IRE), another 2lb higher than for his solid effort at Epsom last time, was held up and had to wait for a gap, but in truth he didn't pick up that well once in the clear. The Handicapper looks to be keeping up with his progress. (op 9-2)
Nezami(IRE) was ridden to get the trip but the final furlong saw him make no great impression. A drop back to 7f will be in his favour.
Vainglory(USA), racing off a career-high mark, was weakening when tightened up for room. He's another who the Handicapper has just about pegged for the time being. (op 9-2)
Karaka Jack likes to make the running but there was competition for that role here and he was denied the outright lead. Being a son of Pivotal, it's possible that this ground was also quicker than ideal. (op 7-1)
Avon River was reportedly unsuited by the ground. Official explanation: jockey said colt was unsuited by the good to firm ground (op 4-1)

3335 ASHBRITTLE STUD BIBURY CUP (H'CAP) 1m 4f
3:50 (3:50) (Class 3) (0-95,88) 3-Y-O
£8,723 (£2,612; £1,306; £653; £326; £163) **Stalls** High

Form RPR

6101 **1** **Vulcanite (IRE)**[30] 2386 3-9-2 83 JimCrowley 2 93+
(R M Beckett) *hld up last: smooth prog fr 3f out: led 2f out: sn rdn: styd on wl* **9/2**[3]

6-41 **2** *1 1/4* **Domination**[13] 2893 3-8-10 77 SteveDrowne 6 85+
(H Morrison) *trckd ldrs tl sltly flat-footed whn pce qcknd 3f out: swtchd lft 2f out: styd on ins fnl f: wnt 2nd fnl strides* **11/4**[1]

-511 **3** *nk* **Comedy Act**[22] 2619 3-8-8 75 SebSanders 5 83
(Sir Mark Prescott) *led after 1f: qcknd pce 3f out: hdd 2f out: kpt pressing wnr tl no ex ins fnl f: lost 2nd fnl strides* **9/2**[3]

126 **4** *1/2* **Tajaarub**[52] 1730 3-8-11 78 RichardHills 4 85
(B W Hills) *wnt lft s: hld up in last pair: hdwy over 3f out: sn rdn and edgd to centre: no imp tl styd on ins fnl f: clsng at fin* **9/2**[3]

0-21 **5** *3/4* **Mataaleb**[26] 2497 3-9-7 88 TadhgO'Shea 3 94
(M A Jarvis) *led for 1f: prom: rdn and ev ch 2f out: no ex fnl f* **12/1**

13 **6** *10* **Maxim Gorky (IRE)**[49] 1823 3-9-2 83 RichardMullen 1 73
(Sir Michael Stoute) *racd keenly early: trckd ldrs: effrt 3f out: wknd over 1f out: eased ins fnl f* **3/1**[2]

2m 34.21s (-3.79) **Going Correction** -0.325s/f (Firm) **6** Ran SP% **113.9**
Speed ratings (Par 103): **99,98,97,97,97 90**
toteswingers: 1&2 £3.60, 1&3 £2.90, 2&3 £3.70 CSF £17.62 TOTE £6.50: £2.20, £2.50; EX 18.50.
Owner Mrs Barbara Facchino **Bred** Barouche Stud Ireland Ltd **Trained** Whitsbury, Hants

FOCUS
A 3-y-o handicap which is always well contested and most of this year's field were open to improvement. There was a sound pace on and the first five all held every chance, with the third being the best guide to the level.

NOTEBOOK
Vulcanite(IRE) proved strongest and registered his third win from six career outings with a ready display. He bided his time out the back and moved up powerfully around 3f out. Once in front he was always doing enough and is obviously a fast-improving colt as he was 7lb higher this time. He promises to stay further down the line and something like the Melrose Handicap at York's Ebor meeting could suit, but there is a decent 1m4f handicap at Glorious Goodwood later this month that could well be on his radar in the meantime. (op 4-1 tchd 7-2)
Domination ◆ was popular despite being up in class and 10lb higher. He lost out by hitting a flat spot around 4f out, but was coming back strongly near the finish and the best of him has very likely still to be seen. (op 10-3 tchd 5-2)
Comedy Act was up another 7lb and unsurprisingly set out to make it a test. He was readily outpaced by the winner, but stuck on gamely and registered a career-best in defeat. (op 7-2)
Tajaarub was very well backed on this return to quicker ground. He had his chance more towards the centre of the track, but wasn't given too hard a time inside the final furlong and should go in when eased in grade. Official explanation: jockey said colt hung left (op 9-1)
Mataaleb was making his handicap debut under top weight in strong company. Never far away, he ran well and is entitled to improve still, but does look weighted to the hilt. (op 11-1 tchd 10-1)

Maxim Gorky(IRE) still showed his inexperience, but found nothing for pressure and was later reported to have been unsuited by the quick ground. Official explanation: jockey said colt was unsuited by the good to firm ground (op 11-4)

3336 NEW FOREST FARM MACHINERY/JOHN DEERE FILLIES' H'CAP 6f

4:20 (4:20) (Class 5) (0-70,70) 3-Y-O £3,238 (£963; £481; £240) Stalls High

Form RPR

2563 1 **Decency (IRE)**[14] 2879 3-8-10 **59** .... RichardHughes 1 67+
(E A L Dunlop) *confidently rdn: travelled wl thrght: hld up: crept clsr 2f out: nudged into ld wl ins fnl f: easily* 4/1[2]

0-03 2 ½ **Bathwick Xaara**[12] 2919 3-8-8 **57** .... RichardKingscote 9 59
(J G Portman) *led tl 3f out: pressed ldr: led over 1f out: readily hld by wnr whn hdd wl ins fnl f* 7/2[1]

0200 3 1 ½ **Ramamara (IRE)**[6] 3115 3-9-7 **70** .... (b[1]) JamesDoyle 10 67
(P D Evans) *chsd ldrs: rdn over 2f out: kpt on ins fnl f: nt gng pce to chal* 14/1

3624 4 ½ **Mrs Boss**[6] 3115 3-9-0 **66** .... JamesMillman(3) 5 62
(B R Millman) *hld up: rdn and nt clr run over 2f out and over 1f out: swtchd lft and r.o fnl 75yds: nvr able to chal* 7/1[3]

5031 5 ½ **Rathbawn Girl (IRE)**[17] 2784 3-8-3 **59** .... AdamBeschizza(7) 4 53
(Miss J Feilden) *t.k.h early: trckd ldrs: rdn and edgd lft over 2f out: one pce ins fnl f* 20/1

0-41 6 ½ **Sweet Pilgrim**[23] 2588 3-9-5 **68** .... JimCrowley 6 60
(M D I Usher) *prom: led 3f out tl u.p over 1f out: no ex fnl f* 7/2[1]

-000 7 ½ **Dream Number (IRE)**[13] 2892 3-9-5 **68** .... RichardMullen 3 59
(W R Muir) *trckd ldrs: rdn to chal over 2f out: one pce fnl f* 8/1

6040 8 ¾ **Silvee**[5] 3154 3-8-9 **58** .... LiamKeniry 8 46+
(J J Bridger) *chsd ldrs: rdn 3f out: cl enough whn squeezed out over 1f out: swtchd lft: running on whn knowhere to go ins fnl f* 8/1

00-0 9 4 ½ **Krysanthe**[15] 2841 3-8-9 **58** .... SteveDrowne 7 32
(M Blanshard) *s.i.s: in tch: a last* 22/1

1m 14.93s (0.13) **Going Correction** -0.125s/f (Firm) 9 Ran SP% **114.9**
Speed ratings (Par 96): **94,93,91,90,90 89,88,87,81**
toteswingers: 1&2 £3.50, 1&3 £10.20, 2&3 £10.10 CSF £18.33 CT £177.32 TOTE £4.90: £1.90, £2.20, £3.20; EX 20.50 Trifecta £94.20 Pool of £277.16 - 2.18 winning units..
Owner Highclere Thoroughbred Racing-St Simonll **Bred** Mohammed Al Sulaim **Trained** Newmarket, Suffolk

FOCUS
A moderate sprint handicap for fillies, run at a solid pace. The easy winner is value for further with the runner-up to his latest mark and the winner better than the bare form.
Silvee Official explanation: jockey said filly was denied a clear run
Krysanthe Official explanation: jockey said filly hung right

3337 SPORTINGBET.COM "COME ON ENGLAND" H'CAP 1m 1f 198y

4:55 (4:57) (Class 4) (0-80,79) 3-Y-O £4,533 (£1,348; £674; £336) Stalls High

Form RPR

0-11 1 **Sparkling Smile (IRE)**[55] 1652 3-9-4 **76** .... TedDurcan 1 90+
(D R Lanigan) *trckd ldrs: led 2f out: sn rdn 2 l clr: styd on: rdn out* 2/1[1]

4-21 2 1 **Grey Bunting**[22] 2627 3-9-5 **77** .... MichaelHills 4 87
(B W Hills) *hld up 5th: tk clsr order 3f out: sn rdn: stdy prog fr 2f out to chse wnr ins fnl f: styd on: clsng at fin* 15/2

0-23 3 4 **Raqeeb (USA)**[33] 2290 3-9-5 **77** .... RichardHills 5 79
(Sir Michael Stoute) *led: rdn and hdd 2f out: edgd lft whn no ex ins fnl f* 9/2[3]

00-1 4 6 **Valiant Knight (FR)**[44] 1976 3-9-6 **78** .... RichardHughes 6 68+
(R Hannon) *trckd ldrs tl dropped to last tamely over 3f out: passed wkng rivals fr over 2f out: nvr a threat after* 7/1

-106 5 4 ½ **Street Entertainer (IRE)**[40] 2079 3-9-5 **77** .... JimCrowley 3 58
(Mrs A J Perrett) *slowly away: sn pushed along in last: jnd gp for effrt over 3f out: wknd 2f out* 3/1[2]

6542 6 6 **Shades Of Grey**[22] 2619 3-8-12 **70** .... AdamKirby 2 39
(C G Cox) *trckd ldrs: rdn over 3f out: wknd 2f out* 15/2

2m 6.16s (-3.74) **Going Correction** -0.325s/f (Firm) 6 Ran SP% **112.5**
Speed ratings (Par 101): **101,100,97,92,88 83**
toteswingers:1&2 £3.00, 2&3 £2.90, 1&3 £2.60 CSF £17.46 CT £59.15 TOTE £3.00: £2.00, £1.40; EX 20.20 Trifecta £69.50 Pool of £320.29 - 3.41 winning units..
Owner Saif Ali & Saeed H Altayer **Bred** Georgestown Stud **Trained** Newmarket, Suffolk

FOCUS
Despite the two non-runners this was still a competitive 3-y-o handicap. The first two look ahead of their marks with the third to his maiden form.

3338 BOLLINGER CHAMPAGNE CHALLENGE SERIES H'CAP (FOR GENTLEMAN AMATEUR RIDERS) 6f 212y

5:30 (5:31) (Class 6) (0-65,64) 4-Y-O+ £2,810 (£871; £435; £217) Stalls Centre

Form RPR

0660 1 **Annes Rocket (IRE)**[6] 3131 5-10-12 **55** .... MrMSeston 3 64
(J C Fox) *hld up towards rr: smooth hdwy fr 3f out: wnt 2nd gng wl over 1f out: shkn up to ld ins fnl f: r.o: readily* 10/1

0030 2 1 ¼ **Eye For The Girls**[11] 2965 4-10-1 **51** .... MrCBishop(7) 4 57
(M R Channon) *mid-div: hdwy 3f out: led 2f out: sn rdn: hdd ins fnl f: no ex* 13/2[3]

5010 3 2 ¼ **Binnion Bay (IRE)**[5] 3160 9-10-5 **53** ow2 .... (b) MrJackSalmon(5) 7 53
(J J Bridger) *v.s.a: bhd: rdn and no imp fr 3f out: styd on strly ent fnl f: snatched 3rd line: nrst fin* 12/1

2034 4 nse **Dichoh**[8] 3054 7-11-5 **62** .... (p) MrSWalker 10 62
(M Madgwick) *mid-div: rdn wl over 2f out: swtchd to far side rails over 1f out: r.o ins fnl f* 9/2[2]

0033 5 nse **Foxtrot Bravo (IRE)**[1] 3291 4-9-13 **45** .... (b) MrDavidTurner(3) 5 45
(Miss S L Davison) *mid-div: hdwy 3f out: sn rdn: drifted rt but kpt on ins fnl f* 7/2[1]

0040 6 1 ¼ **Easy Wonder (GER)**[1] 3291 5-9-11 **45** .... MrCMartin(3) 2 41
(I A Wood) *hld up towards rr: hdwy in centre fr over 2f out: rdn over 1f out: kpt on same pce ins fnl f* 20/1

0300 7 2 ½ **Purus (IRE)**[18] 2750 8-11-3 **60** .... MrJoshuaMoore 6 50
(R A Teal) *trckd ldrs: rdn and ev ch over 2f out: wknd over 1f out* 12/1

0000 8 2 **Dynamo Dave (USA)**[6] 3132 5-9-11 **45** .... (b) MrJNewman(5) 11 29
(M D I Usher) *w ldr: rdn to ld after 3f out: hdd 2f out: fdd ins fnl f* 12/1

0062 9 ¾ **Admirals Way**[17] 2788 5-10-2 **48** .... MrRBirkett(3) 13 30
(C N Kellett) *trckd ldrs: rdn 3f out: wknd over 1f out* 8/1

-550 10 3 ½ **Lady Vivien**[8] 3064 4-10-3 **53** .... MrCGarroll(7) 8 26
(D H Brown) *a towards rr* 16/1

055 11 nk **Fine Silk (USA)**[6] 3111 4-11-2 **64** .... (p) MrJMQuinlan(5) 12 36
(M G Quinlan) *led tl rdn over 2f out: wknd ins fnl f* 12/1

000- 12 2 ½ **Like For Like (IRE)**[217] 7427 4-9-13 **47** .... MrPPrince(5) 14 12
(R J Hodges) *little slowly away: sn trcking ldrs: rdn 3f out: wknd over 1f out* 20/1

1m 27.91s (-1.09) **Going Correction** -0.125s/f (Firm) 12 Ran SP% **120.1**
Speed ratings (Par 101): **101,99,97,96,96 95,92,90,89,85 85,82**
toteswingers:1&2 £12.30, 2&3 £16.90, 1&3 £37.20 CSF £74.67 CT £793.23 TOTE £14.20: £4.40, £2.40, £4.30; EX 119.10 TRIFECTA Not won. Place 6: £161.70 Place 5: £42.39 .
Owner The Cross Keys Racing Club **Bred** S Coughlan **Trained** Collingbourne Ducis, Wilts

FOCUS
A typically open handicap of its type. There was a decent early pace on and it was run to suit the closers. The runner-up is rated back to form but overall the form is limited.
T/Plt: £210.80 to a £1 stake. Pool:£38,433.35 - 133.05 winning tickets. T/Qpdt: £36.30 to a £1 stake. Pool:£3,656.72 - 74.45 winning tickets. TM

3339 - 3345a (Foreign Racing) - See Raceform Interactive

3154 GOODWOOD (R-H)

Thursday, June 24

OFFICIAL GOING: Straight course - good; round course - good to firm (str 8.5, rnd 9.0)
The rail was dolled out 5yds for the first 2f of the 1m course, and the lower bend was also dolled out 3yds, increasing distances by 6yds.
Wind: Moderate, half against Weather: Fine becoming cloudy

3346 HAVE A HEART STKS (H'CAP) 7f

2:00 (2:03) (Class 4) (0-85,85) 4-Y-O+ £4,533 (£1,348; £674; £336) Stalls High

Form RPR

5-20 1 **Zero Money (IRE)**[40] 2113 4-8-13 **77** .... FergusSweeney 4 88
(R Charlton) *mde all: drvn over 1f out: edgd lft after: jnd nr fin: won on the nod* 9/1

1-42 2 nse **Santefisio**[13] 2926 4-9-7 **85** .... WilliamBuick 1 96+
(P J Makin) *hld up in last pair: threaded through fr 2f out: wnt 2nd ent fnl f: chal last 100yds: hrd rdn and upsides nr fin: jst pipped* 10/3[2]

2-53 3 ¾ **Truism**[13] 2926 4-9-7 **85** .... RyanMoore 6 94
(Mrs A J Perrett) *trckd ldng trio: prog to chse wnr 2f out: rdn and nt qckn over 1f out: lost 2nd ent fnl f: styd on u.p* 3/1[1]

404- 4 3 **Perfect Silence**[236] 7189 5-8-10 **79** .... (b) JohnFahy(5) 9 80
(C G Cox) *trckd ldng pair: rdn to dispute 2nd over 2f out: nt qckn wl over 1f out: outpcd after* 11/2[3]

-000 5 1 **Titan Triumph**[21] 2683 6-9-2 **80** .... (t) GeorgeBaker 5 78
(W J Knight) *hld up in 6th: prog on outer over 2f out: hanging u.p over 1f out: fdd* 25/1

1500 6 1 ¼ **Getcarter**[19] 2748 4-9-7 **85** .... RichardHughes 2 80
(R Hannon) *stdd s: hld up: nudged along in last over 1f out: nvr in contention: v modest late prog* 7/1

-066 7 nk **Woodcote Place**[13] 2926 7-9-5 **83** .... JimCrowley 8 77
(P R Chamings) *hld up in 5th: effrt on inner 2f out: rdn and cl enough over 1f out: wknd ins fnl f* 6/1

6000 8 7 **Pusey Street Lady**[13] 2929 6-9-1 **82** .... MartinLane(3) 3 57
(J Gallagher) *mostly chsd wnr tl wknd rapidly 2f out* 25/1

1m 26.91s (0.01) **Going Correction** -0.125s/f (Firm) 8 Ran SP% **107.9**
Speed ratings (Par 105): **97,96,96,92,91 90,89,81**
toteswingers: 1&2 £5.00, 2&3 £2.20, 1&3 not won. CSF £34.75 CT £98.16 TOTE £9.60: £2.30, £1.10, £1.50; EX 33.00.
Owner Ms Gillian Khosla **Bred** Carrigbeg Stud **Trained** Beckhampton, Wilts

FOCUS
A fair handicap. The qwinner made all under a good ride and the third is the best guide to the form.
Getcarter Official explanation: jockey said colt was unsuited by the good (good to firm places) ground

3347 MORE TH>N MAIDEN FILLIES' STKS 1m 4f

2:35 (2:38) (Class 5) 3-Y-O+ £3,238 (£963; £481; £240) Stalls Low

Form RPR

5-3 1 **Ship's Biscuit**[62] 1501 3-8-12 0 .... RyanMoore 6 79+
(Sir Michael Stoute) *trckd ldng pair after 4f: effrt over 2f out: rdn to ld over 1f out: styd on wl* 11/8[2]

-222 2 4 ½ **Scorn (USA)**[16] 2843 3-8-12 80 .... WilliamBuick 5 72
(J H M Gosden) *trckd ldr after 1f: led over 2f out: rdn and hdd over 1f out: fnd nil* 11/10[1]

0-43 3 3 ¼ **Best Intent**[28] 2463 3-8-12 74 .... RichardHughes 1 67
(M A Jarvis) *led after 1f: rdn and hdd over 2f out: steadily outpcd* 6/1[3]

65 4 2 ½ **Businessmoney Judi**[13] 2921 4-9-9 0 .... JamesMillman(3) 2 63
(B R Millman) *dwlt: detached in last early: in tch 1/2-way: wnt 4th 3f out: sn lft bhd* 50/1

54-4 5 ¾ **Zinjbar (USA)**[106] 849 3-8-12 65 .... KoseiMiura 4 62
(C E Brittain) *led 1f: stdd: rdn in 4th 4f out: last fr 3f out and struggling after* 33/1

2m 38.9s (0.50) **Going Correction** -0.125s/f (Firm)
WFA 3 from 4yo 14lb 5 Ran SP% **108.9**
Speed ratings (Par 100): **93,90,87,86,85**
CSF £3.13 TOTE £2.50: £1.50, £1.20; EX 3.20.
Owner Philip Newton **Bred** Philip Newton **Trained** Newmarket, Suffolk

FOCUS
Only three of these looked possible winners on paper, and the result was always going to be decided by which filly improved most for the step up from 1m2f to 1m4f. The race was steadily run with the runner-up and third the best guides to the winner's merit.

3348 INTERNATIONAL BUREAU OF AVIATION H'CAP 1m 6f

3:10 (3:11) (Class 6) (0-65,65) 4-Y-O+ £3,070 (£906; £453) Stalls Low

Form RPR

-040 1 **Sunny Spells**[72] 1283 5-8-12 **56** .... WilliamBuick 4 64
(S C Williams) *led after 1f: mde rest: kicked on 3f out: pressed ent fnl f: drvn and styd on wl* 8/1[3]

6-23 2 1 ¾ **Mohanad (IRE)**[3] 3267 4-9-4 **62** .... RyanMoore 11 68
(Miss Sheena West) *led 1f: sn in 3rd: rdn to go 2nd 2f out: threatened ent fnl f: no imp last 150yds* 7/4[1]

6241 3 ¾ **Seventh Hill**[20] 2691 5-9-7 **65** .... FergusSweeney 1 70+
(M Blanshard) *hld up in midfield in abt 7th: effrt on outer over 2f out: prog to go 3rd jst over 1f out: styd on: unable to chal* 9/1

000- 4 2 ¾ **Red Twist**[17] 2859 5-8-7 **51** .... HayleyTurner 3 52
(M Hill) *trckd ldng trio: rdn wl over 2f out: sn nt qckn and inclined to hang: kpt on ins fnl f* 8/1[3]

3-12 5 ¾ **Galiotto (IRE)**[36] 2232 4-9-1 **59** .... GeorgeBaker 2 59
(C F Wall) *trckd wnr after 2f to 2f out: steadily fdd* 4/1[2]

2430 **6** 1 1/4 **Wightgold**[8] 3084 4-9-0 **58** EddieAhern 8 56
(H J L Dunlop) *settled in midfield in abt 8th: effrt on inner over 2f out and one reminder: no prog over 1f out: fdd* **12/1**

6015 **7** 3/4 **Royal Premier (IRE)**[11] 2995 7-8-7 **56** SimonPearce(5) 7 53
(H J Collingridge) *hld up in last quartet: rdn 4f out and struggling: styd on ins fnl f* **16/1**

/205 **8** 1/2 **Byblos**[82] 1087 5-9-7 **65** (p) JimCrowley 6 62
(W J Greatrex) *hld up in last pair: effrt on outer fr over 4f out: drvn in chsng gp over 2f out: inclined to hang and steadily wknd* **40/1**

000/ **9** hd **Nesnaas (USA)**[14] 3945 9-8-8 **52** LukeMorris 13 48
(M G Rimell) *trckd ldrs in 5th: u.p and dropped to rr 4f out: no ch after: plugging on at fin* **40/1**

-126 **10** 3 1/2 **Winning Show**[160] 182 6-9-2 **60** (t) LiamKeniry 9 51
(C Gordon) *s.s: settled in last pair: sme limited prog 3f out: rdn and wknd 2f out* **33/1**

2505 **11** 12 **Silken Promise (USA)**[17] 2811 4-8-10 **54** (b) RichardHughes 5 29
(T B P Coles) *stdd s: hld up in last quartet: nursed along to rch 8th 2f out: wknd 1f out: virtually p.u* **14/1**

034/ **12** 2 1/4 **Eddie Dowling**[21] 6929 5-8-7 **51** (t) SamHitchcott 10 22
(M F Harris) *nvr bttr than midfield: dropped to rr and btn over 3f out: t.o* **66/1**

3m 6.74s (3.14) **Going Correction** -0.125s/f (Firm) **12** Ran SP% **118.1**
Speed ratings (Par 101): **86,85,84,83,82 81,81,81,81,79 72,70**
toteswingers: 1&2 £3.60, 1&3 £8.10, 2&3 £4.30 CSF £21.79 CT £134.06 TOTE £8.00: £1.20, £1.60, £2.40; EX 26.90.
Owner W E Enticknap **Bred** Whitsbury Manor Stud **Trained** Newmarket, Suffolk

FOCUS
An ordinary and steadily run handicap and not many got into it. The winner dictated the pace and is rated close to his AW best.

3349 CASCO MAIDEN AUCTION STKS 7f
3:45 (3:50) (Class 5) 2-Y-O **£3,238** (£963; £481; £240) **Stalls** High

Form RPR

1 **Sextons House (IRE)** 2-8-13 0 RyanMoore 10 79+
(R Hannon) *dwlt: settled in last trio: prog over 2f out: wnt 2nd 1f out: drvn ahd narrowly last 100yds: r.o wl* **7/2**[2]

0 **2** hd **Whodathought (IRE)**[16] 2839 2-8-11 0 RichardHughes 3 77
(R Hannon) *led: jnd over 2f out but stl gng wl: shkn up ent fnl f: hdd last 100yds: r.o: jst hld* **10/3**[1]

3 3 3/4 **Reillys Daughter** 2-8-4 0 LukeMorris 1 60+
(J S Moore) *dwlt: racd wd: rchd midfield by 1/2-way despite running green: effrt to press ldrs 2f out: drvn and outpcd over 1f out: styd on to take 3rd last stride* **33/1**

4 nse **Premium Coffee** 2-8-13 0 SamHitchcott 6 69
(M R Channon) *trckd ldrs: prog to go 2nd 3f out: upsides ldr over 2f out to jst over 1f out: sn outpcd* **14/1**

5 2 **Quite A Catch (IRE)** 2-9-0 0 JimCrowley 8 65+
(J G Portman) *settled in last: sme prog 2f out: pushed along and rn green over 1f out: kpt on: nt disgracd* **11/1**

0 **6** 1/2 **Valeo Si Vales (IRE)**[16] 2839 2-9-0 0 FergusSweeney 11 64
(J A Osborne) *hld up in midfield: taken to outer 3f out: prog to press ldrs 2f out: pushed along and steadily outpcd over 1f out* **9/2**[3]

7 1/2 **Barathea Dancer (IRE)** 2-8-1 0 ow2 JohnFahy(5) 5 55+
(R A Teal) *dwlt: mostly in last trio: pushed along over 2f out: nvr on terms: kpt on steadily fr over 1f out* **20/1**

8 1 1/4 **Bright Applause** 2-8-13 0 EddieAhern 7 59
(G L Moore) *trckd ldrs on inner: cl enough 2f out: wknd jst over 1f out* **7/1**

9 2 1/2 **Persian Herald** 2-8-11 0 NeilChalmers 9 50
(Pat Eddery) *late to post after last minute change of jockey: in tch towards rr: wknd 2f out* **11/1**

50 **10** 6 **Scatty (IRE)**[42] 2059 2-9-0 0 LiamKeniry 4 38
(S Kirk) *pressed ldng pair to 3f out: sn lost pl: wknd 2f out* **14/1**

0 **11** 2 **Minus Tolerance**[30] 2413 2-8-1 0 ow2 KierenFox(5) 2 25
(Miss S L Davison) *chsd ldr to 3f out: sn wknd* **50/1**

1m 29.68s (2.78) **Going Correction** -0.125s/f (Firm) **11** Ran SP% **115.6**
Speed ratings (Par 93): **81,80,76,76,74 73,73,71,68,61 59**
toteswingers: 1&2 £3.30, 1&3 £25.80, 2&3 £16.50 CSF £14.97 TOTE £4.60: £1.90, £1.50, £6.60; EX 11.00.
Owner Knockainey Stud **Bred** Davin Investments Ltd **Trained** East Everleigh, Wilts

FOCUS
No more than a fair maiden on paper, and it was the Richard Hannon-trained pair who came clear in the closing stages. It will take time before the true worth of the form is revealed.

NOTEBOOK
Sextons House(IRE), a half-brother to Sienna Lake, who also won over this trip at two, was given a patient ride before being angled to the inside of his stablemate approaching the final furlong. He showed a professional attitude when asked to go and win his race and, while he idled a little once he hit the front, he was always doing just enough. He should go on from this and will be interesting in nurseries. (op 4-1)
Whodathought(IRE) had the benefit of a previous run and it showed, as in contrast to his debut he was soon towards the fore and showed a good attitude under pressure. He would have been an easy winner had his stablemate not been in the race. (op 4-1)
Reillys Daughter, drawn worst of all, got trapped wide around the bend, didn't handle the downhill section very well and generally ran green. Despite all this she ran on to take third, and it's probably fair to assume she'll improve a lot for this. Although only a 1,000gns purchase, her dam is out of a sister to the Derby winner Commander In Chief. (op 50-1)
Premium Coffee has a speedy pedigree so it was a little surprising to see him make his debut over this distance. However, he ran a perfectly satisfactory race, and, as his trainer's juveniles invariably improve for a run, better can be expected next time. (op 8-1)
Quite A Catch(IRE), a half-brother to five-time sprint winner Golden Destiny, showed enough to suggest he has a future, probably in handicaps in due course. (op 10-1)
Valeo Si Vales(IRE) had his chance down the outside in the straight but he'd been plenty keen enough early and that cost him in the closing stages. (op 6-1)

3350 ALAN NORMAN 75TH BIRTHDAY CELEBRATION H'CAP 6f
4:20 (4:22) (Class 5) (0-70,70) 3-Y-O **£3,238** (£963; £481; £240) **Stalls** Centre

Form RPR

4-00 **1** **Slip Sliding Away (IRE)**[97] 934 3-8-9 **58** LiamKeniry 6 73
(P R Hedger) *stdd s: hld up last: stdy prog on outer fr 1/2-way: rdn to ld jst over 1f out: r.o wl and sn clr* **12/1**

5143 **2** 3 1/4 **Super Yellow**[27] 2491 3-9-6 **69** FergusSweeney 8 74
(J A Osborne) *trckd ldrs: prog to ld over 2f out on outer: rdn and hdd jst over 1f out: styd on: no ch w wnr* **7/2**[1]

2311 **3** 3 3/4 **Boogie Waltzer**[33] 2320 3-8-13 **69** (t) RyanClark(7) 9 62
(S C Williams) *chsd ldr: disp ld 1/2-way to over 2f out: outpcd and wl btn 3rd ins fnl f* **11/2**[2]

45-6 **4** 3/4 **Galatian**[13] 2931 3-9-4 **70** JamesMillman(3) 3 61
(B R Millman) *led to 1/2-way: outpcd fr 2f out: plugged on* **15/2**

424 **5** hd **Starwatch**[6] 3154 3-8-9 **58** NeilChalmers 1 48
(J J Bridger) *in tch: outpcd and rdn over 2f out: n.d after* **7/1**[3]

3060 **6** 3/4 **Ferris Wheel (IRE)**[22] 2644 3-9-5 **68** RyanMoore 4 56
(P F I Cole) *in tch: rdn and outpcd fr over 2f out: no ch after* **11/2**[2]

-200 **7** 2 1/2 **Kilmanseck**[23] 2618 3-9-4 **67** (b[1]) JimCrowley 5 47
(Eve Johnson Houghton) *chsd ldr: disp ld 1/2-way to over 2f out: wknd over 1f out* **12/1**

00-0 **8** 3/4 **Compton Way**[16] 2841 3-8-10 **59** WilliamBuick 7 36
(B W Hills) *hld up bhd ldrs: rdn over 2f out: sn struggling: wknd over 1f out* **8/1**

-356 **9** 3/4 **Slasl**[58] 1593 3-8-10 **59** KoseiMiura 10 34
(C E Brittain) *chsd ldrs: u.p by 1/2-way: wknd 2f out* **15/2**

1m 11.6s (-0.60) **Going Correction** -0.125s/f (Firm) **9** Ran SP% **115.5**
Speed ratings (Par 99): **99,94,89,88,88 87,84,83,82**
toteswingers: 1&2 £9.80, 1&3 £14.50, 2&3 £4.10 CSF £53.87 CT £262.77 TOTE £16.30: £4.00, £1.60, £1.10; EX 67.70.
Owner Bernard Keay & Partners **Bred** S Holt & A C Beggan & R J Beggan **Trained** Dogmersfield, Hampshire

FOCUS
A competitive sprint handicap on paper, but they finished quite strung out. The time was reasonable and the winner rates a clear personal best.

3351 RSA 300TH STKS (H'CAP) 1m 1f
4:55 (4:58) (Class 3) (0-95,89) 3-Y-O **£7,123** (£2,119; £1,059; £529) **Stalls** High

Form RPR

-421 **1** **Aattash (IRE)**[20] 2692 3-8-12 **80** SamHitchcott 9 99
(M R Channon) *mde all: clr fr 1/2-way: 4 l up and gng strly over 1f out: drvn out: unchal* **9/1**

21-0 **2** 2 3/4 **Start Right**[62] 1502 3-9-1 **83** J-PGuillambert 4 96+
(L M Cumani) *hld up in last pair: nightmare passage fr 3f out: fnlly got clr run over 1f out: drvn and hanging ent fnl f: kpt on to take 2nd last stride* **9/2**[2]

3-1 **3** shd **Sarrsar**[19] 2754 3-9-2 **84** JimCrowley 3 97
(M A Jarvis) *hld up in 5th: rdn to chse clr wnr 2f out: no imp: kpt on: lost 2nd post* **3/1**[1]

0202 **4** 4 **New Christmas (USA)**[12] 2969 3-9-1 **83** (b) EddieAhern 2 87
(B J Meehan) *hld up in last trio: effrt on outer over 2f out: nvr gng pce to threaten: plugged on* **9/2**[2]

-006 **5** 7 **Whistleinthewind (IRE)**[12] 2969 3-8-10 **78** (p) RyanMoore 6 67
(G L Moore) *trckd ldrs: disp 2nd briefly 3f out: struggling 2f out: wknd over 1f out* **11/2**[3]

1060 **6** 10 **Muwalla**[40] 2117 3-8-10 **78** (t) KoseiMiura 5 45
(C E Brittain) *hld up in last trio: no prog 2f out: wknd rapidly: t.o* **20/1**

3213 **7** 5 **Blues Music (IRE)**[13] 2927 3-8-10 **78** WilliamBuick 1 34
(B W Hills) *chsd ldng pair: wnt 2nd 3f out to 2f out: wkng whn hmpd over 1f out: eased: t.o* **7/1**

-204 **8** 2 1/2 **Strong Vigilance (IRE)**[19] 2737 3-8-9 **77** HayleyTurner 7 27
(M L W Bell) *chsd wnr: rdn 4f out: wknd 3f out: t.o* **6/1**

1m 54.01s (-2.29) **Going Correction** -0.125s/f (Firm) **8** Ran SP% **118.3**
Speed ratings (Par 103): **105,102,102,98,92 83,79,77**
toteswingers:1&2 £8.50, 2&3 £4.60, 1&3 £5.70 CSF £50.84 CT £154.16 TOTE £13.60: £3.30, £1.90, £1.30; EX 67.20 Place 6: £9.06 Place 5: £5.70.
Owner Sheikh Ahmed Al Maktoum **Bred** Oghill House Stud **Trained** West Ilsley, Berks
■ Stewards' Enquiry : J-P Guillambert three-day ban: careless riding (Jul 8,10,12)

FOCUS
The top-weight weighed in 6lb below the ceiling for the race, but this looked a fair 3-y-o handicap and it was won by a progressive sort. The form has been taken at face value.

NOTEBOOK
Aattash(IRE) made all to win his maiden at Bath last time and he successfully employed the same tactics here on his return to handicap company. The third winner on the day to make all on the round course, he no doubt benefited to a degree from the runner-up getting into trouble in behind, but he looked to win on merit, and there's probably even more to come now that connections have found the key to him. How he will react to being taken on in front remains to be seen, though. (op 10-1 tchd 11-1)
Start Right was held up out the back and got little luck in running in the straight. Denied a clear run until a furlong out, he kept on once in the clear but not perhaps as well as one might have expected. A strongly run race over 1m2f should see him at his best. (tchd 11-2)
Sarrsar, an easy winner of his maiden on Polytrack last time out, carried his owner's first colours. He kept on well without being able to get to the enterprisingly ridden winner, but is lightly raced and remains open to further improvement. (tchd 4-1)
New Christmas(USA) had the form of his recent Sandown second boosted when the third bolted up next time, but he didn't run so well this time, and perhaps the positive effect of the blinkers are beginning to wear off already. (tchd 4-1)
Whistleinthewind(IRE) continues to cut little ice in handicap company. (op 15-2 tchd 5-1)
Blues Music(IRE) failed to build on the promise of his third behind Treble Jig here 13 days earlier. He probably needs to revert to a longer trip. Official explanation: jockey said colt was unsuited by the good (good to firm places) ground (op 13-2 tchd 6-1)
Strong Vigilance(IRE) raced too keenly on this step up in trip and was in trouble some way out. (op 8-1)
T/Jkpt: Not won. T/Plt: £7.50 to a £1 stake. Pool: £65,305.20 - 6,319.49 winning tickets T/Qpdt: £6.60 to a £1 stake. Pool: £3,402.43 - 377.90 winning tickets JN

3072 HAMILTON (R-H)
Thursday, June 24

OFFICIAL GOING: Good to firm (9.8)
Wind: Fresh, across Weather: Cloudy

3352 HAMILTON PARK LADY AMATEUR RIDERS' H'CAP 1m 5f 9y
7:00 (7:01) (Class 6) (0-65,63) 4-Y-O+ **£1,977** (£608; £304) **Stalls** High

Form RPR

0-62 **1** **Regent's Secret (USA)**[8] 3078 10-9-8 **50** MrsCBartley 10 62
(J S Goldie) *s.i.s: hld up and bhd: smooth hdwy over 3f out: led over 1f out: rdn and edgd lft: kpt on strly* **2/1**[1]

-600 **2** 5 **Hi Dancer**[24] 2610 7-9-13 **60** MissCharlotteHolmes(5) 2 65
(B M R Haslam) *hld up in tch: hdwy over 3f out: outpcd over 2f out: styd on ins fnl f: tk 2nd cl home* **5/1**[3]

/-40 **3** shd **Perez (IRE)**[21] 2464 8-8-12 **45** (vt) MissLAlexander(5) 3 49
(W Storey) *cl up: led 4f out to over 1f out: kpt on same pce: lost 2nd cl home* **16/1**

061- **4** 1/2 **Zelos Diktator**[24] 6766 4-9-12 **57** (p) MissJCoward(3) 1 61
(Mrs R Dobbin) *prom: effrt over 3f out: kpt on same pce fr 2f out* **14/1**

00-6 **5** *4 1/2* **Yonder**[45] 164 6-10-0 **63**..(t) MissNDumelow(7) 6 60
(H Morrison) *hld up towards rr: shkn up on outside over 3f out: nvr able to chal* **7/2**[2]

0064 **6** *9* **Dulce Domum**[24] 2610 4-9-3 **45**.. MissEJJones 8 28
(A B Haynes) *midfield: outpcd 1/2-way: rallied and edgd rt over 2f out: nvr able to chal* **7/1**

60-6 **7** *2 1/2* **Grethel (IRE)**[7] 3122 6-8-12 **45**.......................... MissJoannaMason(5) 11 25
(A Berry) *cl up tl rdn and wknd fr 3f out* **16/1**

006/ **8** *2* **Troys Steps**[26] 6959 6-8-12 **45**.............................. MissPhillipaTutty(5) 9 22
(Miss S E Forster) *towards rr: pushed along over 3f out: sn btn* **50/1**

040- **9** *29* **Piermarini**[492] 578 5-9-3 **52**.. MissHDukes(7) 7 —
(P T Midgley) *led: clr 1/2-way: hdd 4f out: sn wknd: t.o* **12/1**

2m 49.96s (-3.94) **Going Correction** -0.275s/f (Firm) 9 Ran SP% **112.8**
Speed ratings (Par 101): **101,97,97,97,94 89,87,86,68**
toteswingers: 1&2 £3.30, 1&3 £11.60, 2&3 £11.90 CSF £11.75 CT £119.99 TOTE £3.50: £2.10, £3.50, £5.00; EX 11.00.
Owner Mrs M Craig **Bred** Adena Springs **Trained** Uplawmoor, E Renfrews

FOCUS
After 1.3mm overnight rain the ground was described as 'fast'. Races on the round course were over 8yds less than the advertised distance due to rail realignments. A low-grade 45-63 amateur riders' handicap run at a furious early pace. This rates the winner's best run since 2008.

3353 FAKE BAKE MAIDEN AUCTION STKS — 6f 5y
7:30 (7:35) (Class 6) 2-Y-0 — **£1,942** (£578; £288; £144) **Stalls** Low

Form RPR

3202 **1** **Roodee Queen**[8] 3072 2-8-6 0.. JoeFanning 1 68
(Patrick Morris) *t.k.h: mde all: shkn up and edgd rt over 1f out: hld on wl ins fnl f* **6/1**

24 **2** *1 1/4* **Sophie's Hero**[10] 3020 2-9-1 0.. PJMcDonald 3 73
(K A Ryan) *hld up in tch: effrt and plld out 2f out: hdwy to press wnr ins fnl f: kpt on: hld towards fin* **3/1**[3]

3 *nse* **Heartbreak** 2-8-11 0.. PaulHanagan 4 69
(R A Fahey) *trckd ldrs: effrt and chsd wnr over 1f out to ins fnl f: r.o* **13/8**[1]

325 **4** *3/4* **Coconut Ice**[50] 1819 2-8-5 0.. RossAtkinson(5) 2 66
(Tom Dascombe) *plld hrd: cl up: effrt over 1f out: kpt on same pce ins fnl f* **5/2**[2]

05 **5** *10* **Mr Shifter**[7] 3106 2-8-11 0.. DuranFentiman 5 37
(Mrs L Stubbs) *pressed wnr tl rdn and wknd over 1f out* **28/1**

1m 12.81s (0.61) **Going Correction** -0.025s/f (Good) 5 Ran SP% **109.4**
Speed ratings (Par 91): **94,92,92,91,77**
CSF £23.43 TOTE £9.90: £3.60, £1.30; EX 19.20.
Owner Chester Racing Club Ltd **Bred** Tom & Evelyn Yates **Trained** Tarporley, Cheshire

FOCUS
Just an average maiden auction race, and limited form. No one really wanted to lead and the pace for the first furlong or so was by no means strong, and both fillies pulled hard for their heads.

NOTEBOOK
Roodee Queen, having her ninth start, had almost certainly shown improved form when touched off here last week. She dropped anchor in front and, despite drifting away from the stands'-side rail, she did more than enough. She has a very willing attitude but will struggle to follow up outside nurseries. (tchd 11-2 and 15-2 in a place)
Sophie's Hero, who did too much too soon on easy ground on his second start at Carlisle, soon found himself being outpaced. He stuck to his guns, but in the end the filly was always holding him at bay. Nurseries now beckon. (op 4-1)
Heartbreak, by a leading first-season sire, is out of a Queen Mary winner. He travelled strongly on this debut but showed inexperience under pressure. Coming back for more at the line, this will have taught him plenty and he will be hard to beat at a similar level next time. (op 6-4 tchd 7-4 and 15-8 in places)
Coconut Ice, her trainer's first runner at this track, was back after a seven-week break. With a lack of early pace she was very keen but in the end was simply not good enough on the night. (op 9-4 tchd 11-4)
Mr Shifter, the rank outsider, ran over an extended seven furlongs last time. He was able to lay up due to the lack of early pace but in the end was very firmly put in his place. (op 33-1)

3354 EUROPEAN BREEDERS' FUND CONDITIONS STKS — 1m 65y
8:00 (8:02) (Class 3) 3-Y-0+ — **£8,742** (£2,601; £1,300; £649) **Stalls** High

Form RPR

1453 **1** **Hacienda (IRE)**[5] 3196 3-8-7 96.. JoeFanning 5 102
(M Johnston) *mde all: shkn up 2f out: keeping on strly whn rdr dropped whip ins fnl f: readily* **6/4**[2]

213- **2** *3 3/4* **Yamal (IRE)**[390] 2476 5-9-3 109.. FrankieDettori 1 95
(Saeed Bin Suroor) *prom: chsd wnr 4f out: effrt wl over 1f out: edgd rt: one pce ins fnl f* **5/6**[1]

1 **3** *2 1/2* **Inqaath (IRE)**[37] 2220 3-8-7 0.. RichardHills 4 87
(Sir Michael Stoute) *t.k.h: prom: effrt over 2f out: sn outpcd: no imp ins fnl f* **5/1**[3]

2350 **4** *21* **Lord's Seat**[6] 3161 3-8-7 49.. PatrickMathers 2 37
(A Berry) *chsd wnr to 4f out: rdn and wknd 3f out* **200/1**

60-0 **5** *52* **Ed's A Red**[26] 2535 3-8-4 33 ow2.. DuranFentiman 3 —
(A Berry) *unruly leaving paddock: dwlt: bhd: lost tch fr over 3f out* **200/1**

1m 44.63s (-3.77) **Going Correction** -0.275s/f (Firm)
WFA 3 from 5yo 10lb 5 Ran SP% **112.2**
Speed ratings (Par 107): **107,103,100,79,27**
CSF £3.15 TOTE £3.20: £1.70, £1.10; EX 3.40.
Owner Sheikh Hamdan Bin Mohammed Al Maktoum **Bred** Yeomanstown Stud **Trained** Middleham Moor, N Yorks

FOCUS
The first running of this Class 3 conditions race carrying £13,500 guaranteed prizemoney. Two no-hopers made up the field and the fact that one of them, rated just 49, was still in contention with 2f to race emphasises the lack of any pace. The form is best rated around the winner and third.

NOTEBOOK
Hacienda(IRE), unraced at two, was having his sixth start and his second in five days after finishing third in a handicap at Ayr from a mark of 96. Given a fine tactical ride from the front, he really wound up the gallop in the last 2f and was in total command when his rider lost his whip inside the final furlong. He is a typical improver from this yard, but if the Handicapper takes the form at face value he might struggle for further opportunities. (op 9-4 tchd 5-2 in places)
Yamal(IRE), a five-year-old rated 109, had 13lb in hand of the winner on official figures. Having his first outing for over a year, he looked fit and well and travelled equally as well as the winner. In the end he was put firmly in his place and his rider accepted defeat in the final 75 yards. Connections will be hoping it was just a case of ring-rust. (op Evens tchd 4-5)
Inqaath(IRE), winner of a modest Nottingham maiden last month on his only previous start, was not given a rating after that success. He was inclined to be quite keen then showed his inexperience when the dash for home began in earnest. Putting in some solid late work, he can now expect a mark of about 90. With that sort of rating he will need careful placing, but his trainer has no superior in seeking out suitable opportunities. (op 11-4)

Lord's Seat, a lowly-rated maiden after 17 previous starts, was able to lie up due to the lack of pace. In the end left well behind, he earned almost £650 for just turning up.

3355 PATERSONS OF GREENOAKHILL OPEN MAIDEN STKS — 1m 1f 36y
8:30 (8:31) (Class 5) 3-4-Y-0 — **£2,590** (£770; £385; £192) **Stalls** High

Form RPR

2246 **1** **I'm Super Too (IRE)**[13] 2935 3-9-0 73.. PJMcDonald 2 77
(G A Swinbank) *led: hdd briefly 3f out: sn rdn: hld on gamely ins fnl f* **7/2**[3]

22 **2** *1 3/4* **Cockney (IRE)**[8] 3077 3-9-0 0.. FrankieDettori 3 73
(M Johnston) *chsd wnr to over 3f out: sn rdn: wnt 2nd again ent fnl f: kpt on towards fin* **1/1**[1]

5-24 **3** *hd* **Logos Astra (USA)**[56] 1649 3-9-0 78.. PaulHanagan 7 73
(D R Lanigan) *trckd ldrs: hdwy and led briefly 3f out: lost 2nd ent fnl f: one pce* **9/4**[2]

63 **4** *8* **Maid Of Meft**[8] 3077 3-8-9 0.. PaulMulrennan 5 51
(Miss L A Perratt) *dwlt: hld up: hdwy over 3f out: edgd rt and wknd over 2f out* **20/1**

0 **5** *6* **Stoical (IRE)**[52] 1769 3-9-0 0.. LeeVickers 6 44
(W Jarvis) *hld up: shortlived effrt over 3f out: sn wknd* **40/1**

44 **6** *31* **Le Volcan D'Or (USA)**[53] 1721 3-9-0 0..(b[1]) JoeFanning 4 —
(M Johnston) *prom: struggling over 3f out: sn lost tch* **50/1**

1m 55.79s (-3.91) **Going Correction** -0.275s/f (Firm) 6 Ran SP% **112.2**
Speed ratings (Par 103): **106,104,104,97,91 64**
toteswingers:1&2 £1.10, 2&3 £1.10, 1&3 £1.20 CSF £7.42 TOTE £4.10: £1.60, £1.10; EX 8.60.
Owner David C Young **Bred** Norelands Bloodstock, J Hanly & H Lascelles **Trained** Melsonby, N Yorks

FOCUS
A fair maiden with three horses in line 2f out. The form has a sound look to it.

3356 IRN BRU SUPPORTS CASH FOR KIDS SPRINT H'CAP — 5f 4y
9:00 (9:00) (Class 4) (0-80,72) 3-Y-0+ — **£4,209** (£1,252; £625; £312) **Stalls** Low

Form RPR

-022 **1** **Wicked Wilma (IRE)**[7] 3119 6-8-10 **61**.. MarkCoumbe(5) 4 71
(A Berry) *cl up: led and edgd lft over 1f out: kpt on strly ins fnl f* **17/2**

5323 **2** *1 1/2* **Hazelrigg (IRE)**[7] 3119 5-9-6 **66**..(vt) PaulMulrennan 5 71
(T D Easterby) *in tch: hdwy over 1f out: chsd wnr and hung rt ins fnl f: fnd little* **2/1**[1]

6334 **3** *1 1/2* **Mandarin Spirit (IRE)**[19] 2756 10-9-6 **66**..(b) PaulHanagan 3 65
(Miss L A Perratt) *led to over 1f out: sn checked: kpt on same pce ins fnl f* **6/1**

46 **4** *1 1/4* **Ask Jenny (IRE)**[9] 3057 8-8-9 **60**.. RossAtkinson(5) 2 55
(Patrick Morris) *bhd and outpcd: hdwy over 1f out: kpt on ins fnl f: nvr rchd ldrs* **16/1**

2043 **5** *1* **Mr Wolf**[17] 2818 9-9-3 **68**..(p) IanBrennan(5) 1 59
(J J Quinn) *cl up: drvn 1/2-way: one pce fr over 1f out* **5/1**[3]

0114 **6** *1/2* **Musical Bridge**[8] 3076 4-9-12 **72**..(b) TomEaves 6 61
(Mrs L Williamson) *taken early to post: chsd ldrs tl edgd rt and wknd over 1f out* **5/2**[2]

-000 **7** *4 1/2* **Barraland**[19] 2756 5-8-10 **59**..(b[1]) GaryBartley(3) 7 32
(J S Goldie) *bhd and sn outpcd: struggling 2f out: n.d* **16/1**

59.21 secs (-0.79) **Going Correction** -0.025s/f (Good) 7 Ran SP% **115.1**
Speed ratings (Par 105): **105,102,100,98,96 95,88**
toteswingers:1&2 £2.20, 2&3 £2.50, 1&3 £6.10 CSF £26.34 TOTE £14.00: £5.80, £1.40; EX 35.80.
Owner Mrs Thelma White **Bred** Gerry O'Sullivan **Trained** Cockerham, Lancs

FOCUS
A modest 59-72 sprint handicap run at a furious pace. A small personal best from the winner.
Wicked Wilma(IRE) Official explanation: two-day ban: careless riding (Jul 8,10)

3357 HAMILTON PARK SUPPORTS CASH FOR KIDS H'CAP — 6f 5y
9:30 (9:31) (Class 6) (0-65,63) 4-Y-0+ — **£2,047** (£604; £302) **Stalls** Low

Form RPR

5664 **1** **Almaty Express**[20] 2720 8-8-0 **45**..(b) KellyHarrison(3) 2 54
(J R Weymes) *mde virtually all stands' rail: rdn and edgd rt ins fnl f: kpt on wl* **14/1**

5523 **2** *1/2* **Call Of Duty (IRE)**[10] 3022 5-8-12 **54**.. GregFairley 6 61
(Mrs Dianne Sayer) *cl up: effrt over 2f out: kpt on wl fnl f: a hld* **3/1**[1]

0632 **3** *2 1/2* **Minturno (USA)**[5] 3200 4-9-7 **63**..(p) PaulMulrennan 8 62
(Mrs A Duffield) *chsd ldrs: drvn and outpcd 2f out: styd on ins fnl f* **3/1**[1]

0003 **4** *shd* **Final Salute**[15] 2854 4-9-0 **56**..(v) TomEaves 5 55
(B Smart) *prom: effrt over 2f out: kpt on same pce ins fnl f* **5/1**[2]

-001 **5** *3/4* **Glenluji**[6] 3147 5-7-10 **45**.. NoraLooby(7) 12 42
(J S Goldie) *taken early to post: dwlt and wnt lft s: bhd and outpcd: gd hdwy over 1f out: kpt on: nvr rchd ldrs* **7/1**[3]

2004 **6** *1 3/4* **Welcome Approach**[21] 2669 7-8-9 **51**.. JoeFanning 9 42
(J R Weymes) *hld up in tch: effrt on outside 2f out: no imp appr fnl f* **8/1**

0-00 **7** *1 1/4* **Hitches Dubai (BRZ)**[51] 1805 5-9-4 **60**.. PaulHanagan 4 47
(G A Harker) *cl up tl edgd rt and outpcd 2f out: n.d after* **14/1**

000- **8** *8* **Lily Jicaro (IRE)**[251] 6824 4-8-2 **49** ow2..(t) IanBrennan(5) 10 10
(Mrs L Williamson) *hld up on outside: rdn over 2f out: wknd over 1f out* **40/1**

2004 **9** *1* **Hosanna**[6] 3164 4-8-8 **50**.. PJMcDonald 7 8
(J Barclay) *towards rr: drvn 1/2-way: nvr on terms* **16/1**

500- **10** *2* **Zabeel Tower**[222] 7403 7-9-6 **62**.. LeeVickers 1 14
(R Allan) *hld up in tch: rdn and wknd over 1f out* **20/1**

00- **11** *7* **Obe One**[266] 6414 10-8-3 **45**..(b) PatrickMathers 11 —
(A Berry) *missed break: sn wl bhd: nvr on terms* **40/1**

1m 11.4s (-0.80) **Going Correction** -0.025s/f (Good) 11 Ran SP% **119.1**
Speed ratings (Par 101): **104,103,100,99,98 96,94,84,82,80 70**
toteswingers:1&2 £7.90, 2&3 £2.60, 1&3 £15.60 CSF £55.74 CT £168.50 TOTE £28.10: £9.40, £1.40, £1.70; EX 61.00 Place 6: £24.27 Place 5: £14.04.
Owner Highmoor Racing & Miss K Buckle **Bred** P G Airey **Trained** Middleham Moor, N Yorks

FOCUS
A low-grade 45-63 sprint handicap. The winner is rated in line with this year's sand form.
T/Plt: £20.50 to a £1 stake. Pool of £50,801.29 - 1,803.08 winning tickets. T/Qpdt: £6.30 to a £1 stake. Pool of £4,078.52 - 474.54 winning tickets. RY

[3112] LEICESTER (R-H)

Thursday, June 24

OFFICIAL GOING: Good to firm (8.8)
Wind: virtually nil Weather: warm and muggy

3358 LANGHAM LADIES' H'CAP (LADY AMATEUR RIDERS) 5f 2y
6:40 (6:40) (Class 5) (0-70,70) 3-Y-0+ £2,498 (£774; £387; £193) Stalls Low

Form RPR
4403 1 **Methaaly (IRE)**[5] 3201 7-10-0 68 (be) MissMMullineaux(5) 8 76
(M Mullineaux) *dwlt: bhd: rdn and hdwy ent fnl 2f: chsd ldr u.p 1f out: kpt on wl to ld towards fin* 9/2[2]
3163 2 nk **Fromsong (IRE)**[70] 1320 12-9-3 59 MissECrossman(7) 1 66
(D K Ivory) *chsd ldr tl led wl over 2f out: pushed along and edgd rt ins fnl f: hdd and no ex towards fin* 20/1
5044 3 3/4 **The Tatling (IRE)**[7] 3119 13-10-0 70 MissHDavies(7) 6 74
(J M Bradley) *s.i.s: bhd: swtchd rt and hdwy on outer 2f out: chsd ldrs ent fnl f: kpt on wl: nt rch ldng pair* 17/2
0001 4 1 1/2 **Nomoreblondes**[20] 2695 6-10-2 70 (p) MissWGibson(5) 7 69
(P T Midgley) *chsd ldrs: rdn to chse ldr wl over 1f out tl 1f out: styd on same pce ins fnl f* 13/2
5034 5 1/2 **Magical Speedfit (IRE)**[27] 2485 5-9-13 69 MissKMargarson(7) 2 66
(G G Margarson) *chsd ldrs: pushed along and effrt over 1f out: edgd rt and no imp ins fnl f* 9/1
6103 6 1 3/4 **Thoughtsofstardom**[5] 3211 7-9-7 61 MrsJCO'Donohoe(5) 5 52
(P S McEntee) *in tch: n.m.r after s: hdwy to chse ldrs 2f out: rdn and unable qck over 1f out: wknd ent fnl f* 9/1
1604 7 2 3/4 **Short Cut**[20] 2727 4-9-2 51 (vt[1]) MissSBrotherton 9 32
(Ian Williams) *in tch: rdn wl over 1f out: sn struggling u.p: wknd and wl btn 1f out* 10/3[1]
-543 8 2 **Timber Treasure (USA)**[5] 3205 6-9-6 62 (b) MissACraven(7) 4 36
(Paul Green) *chsd ldrs: pushed along and struggling 2f out: wknd over 1f out* 5/1[3]
0000 9 3 3/4 **Town House**[19] 2751 8-8-11 51 oh6 MissAWallace(5) 10 11
(B P J Baugh) *broke wl: led and crossed towards stands' rail: hdd wl over 2f out: sn dropped out: wl bhd fr over 1f out* 28/1
006- 10 12 **Sam's Cross (IRE)**[176] 7879 5-9-4 60 (vt) MissKASmith(7) 3 —
(M R Bosley) *in tch to 1/2-way: sn bhd: t.o ins fnl f* 33/1

60.46 secs (0.46) **Going Correction** -0.15s/f (Firm) 10 Ran SP% 112.9
Speed ratings (Par 103): **90,89,88,85,85 82,77,74,68,49**
toteswingers: 1&2 £16.00, 1&3 £6.70, 2&3 £10.00 CSF £89.38 CT £748.13 TOTE £5.80: £2.30, £7.40, £1.60; EX 64.60.
Owner Noel Racing **Bred** Scuderia Golden Horse S R L **Trained** Alpraham, Cheshire

FOCUS
Few could be confidently discounted in this tricky contest. Modest form, rated around the third.

3359 STAPLEFORD (S) STKS 7f 9y
7:10 (7:11) (Class 6) 3-Y-O £1,942 (£578; £288; £144) Stalls Low

Form RPR
0-40 1 **Merchant Of Medici**[23] 2618 3-9-0 67 KierenFallon 13 66+
(W R Muir) *t.k.h: hld up in midfield: swtchd to outer and hdwy over 2f out: led wl over 1f out: edgd lft but pushed clr ent fnl f: eased towards fin: v easily* 5/2[1]
0305 2 2 1/4 **Sunrise Lyric (IRE)**[23] 2633 3-8-9 57 TedDurcan 10 55
(P F I Cole) *t.k.h: stdd s: hld up towards rr: swiching rt and n.m.r over 2f out: hdwy wl over 1f out: rdn to chse wnr jst ins fnl f: racd awkwardly and hung rt after: no imp* 6/1[3]
420- 3 nk **Alfalevva**[215] 7474 3-9-0 62 CathyGannon 11 59+
(M R Channon) *towards rr: rdn and n.m.r over 2f out: swtchd to outer and rdn ent fnl 2f: kpt on u.p fnl f to go 3rd fnl 50yds: no ch w wnr* 20/1
6665 4 1 3/4 **Magenta Strait**[12] 2962 3-8-9 51 TobyAtkinson(5) 14 54
(R Hollinshead) *hld up towards rr: rdn 1/2-way: hdwy to chse ldrs ent fnl 2f: styd on same pce u.p fr over 1f out* 22/1
U3-5 5 1 1/2 **Sarahthecarer (IRE)**[8] 3092 3-8-9 65 (b) TomQueally 6 45
(P M Mooney, Ire) *w ldrs tl led 4f out: hdd and rdn wl over 1f out: sn outpcd by wnr: wknd ins fnl f* 6/1[3]
0466 6 2 **Hounds Ditch**[14] 2903 3-9-0 58 ShaneKelly 1 45
(Eve Johnson Houghton) *midfield on stands' rail: effrt u.p and sme prog ent fnl 2f: no hdwy ent fnl f* 66/1
-250 7 1 **Madame Roulin (IRE)**[15] 2871 3-8-2 62 (v[1]) IanBurns(7) 8 37
(M L W Bell) *in tch in midfield: rdn 1/2-way: outpcd 2f out and wl hld after* 17/2
50-0 8 nse **Rainsborough**[23] 2619 3-8-9 57 (p) SophieDoyle(5) 7 42
(S Curran) *in tch in midfield: rdn and unable qck 4f out: drvn and sme prog ent fnl 2f: no prog and wl btn over 1f out* 28/1
5520 9 2 **Libertino (IRE)**[13] 2919 3-9-0 63 (b) FrannyNorton 17 37
(J Gallagher) *bhd: rdn and modest hdwy over 2f out: no hdwy fr wl over 1f out: n.d* 14/1
0426 10 2 3/4 **Lockantanks**[16] 2840 3-9-5 70 NeilCallan 9 34
(A B Haynes) *dwlt: sn in tch: rdn and edgd rt ent fnl 2f: sn wknd and wl btn 1f out* 4/1[2]
0-03 11 1/2 **Otterton**[79] 1144 3-8-9 45 JerryO'Dwyer 4 23
(R Hollinshead) *a towards rr: rdn and swtchd lft over 2f out: no hdwy and n.d* 50/1
0 12 1 1/2 **Tipperary Tickle**[8] 3086 3-8-9 0 JimmyQuinn 12 19
(J R Weymes) *s.i.s: a bhd: nvr a factor* 100/1
6006 13 7 **Proper Littlemadam**[30] 2418 3-8-9 50 (b[1]) SteveDrowne 15 —
(C N Kellett) *dwlt: sn rcvrd and chsd ldrs: wknd qckly u.p 3f out: wl bhd and eased ins fnl f* 50/1
0-00 14 nk **Naughty Norris**[15] 2878 3-9-0 33 (b[1]) NickyMackay 5 4
(R Bastiman) *led tl 4f out: wknd qckly u.p 3f out: wl bhd and eased ins fnl f* 100/1
0000 15 4 **Aim'Ees Star**[15] 2879 3-8-9 43 RoystonFfrench 16 —
(John A Harris) *chsd ldrs: rdn and struggling 1/2-way: wl bhd over 1f out: eased ins fnl f* 100/1
00-0 16 3 1/2 **Lady Compton**[37] 2217 3-8-2 42 (b[1]) MatthewLawson(7) 3 —
(R Bastiman) *w ldrs tl 1/2-way: sn struggling u.p: wl bhd over 1f out: eased ins fnl f* 80/1

1m 25.78s (-0.42) **Going Correction** -0.15s/f (Firm) 16 Ran SP% 116.5
Speed ratings (Par 97): **96,93,93,91,89 87,85,85,83,80 79,78,70,69,65 61**
CSF £15.18 TOTE £3.90: £2.00, £2.30, £9.20; EX 14.60.
Owner S Jones & R Haim **Bred** Cheveley Park Stud Ltd **Trained** Lambourn, Berks

FOCUS
A weak seller with doubts over most. The form is rated round the winner.

Proper Littlemadam Official explanation: jockey said filly suffered interference in running

3360 BRUNTINGTHORPE H'CAP 1m 3f 183y
7:40 (7:41) (Class 6) (0-65,65) 4-Y-0+ £2,590 (£770; £385; £192) Stalls High

Form RPR
2345 1 **Magnitude**[14] 2881 5-8-9 53 SteveDrowne 3 60
(B P J Baugh) *in tch in midfield: hdwy to chse ldrs 5f out: chsd ldr 3f out: rdn and ev ch over 1f out: led fnl 100yds: kpt on wl* 4/1[2]
2-40 2 nse **Chincoteague (IRE)**[24] 2597 4-9-7 65 KierenFallon 4 71
(B J Meehan) *chsd ldrs: wnt 2nd 7f out: led over 3f out: drvn ent fnl 2f: hdd fnl 100yds: kpt on: a jst hld* 7/2[1]
060- 3 1 1/4 **Marino Prince (FR)**[16] 4861 5-8-2 46 oh1 CathyGannon 6 50
(B D Leavy) *dwlt: hld up towards rr: pushed along and hdwy 4f out: rdn to chse ldng pair over 1f out: edgd rt u.p ent fnl f: styd on one pce fnl 150yds* 10/1
003- 4 3/4 **Astronomical (IRE)**[215] 7495 8-9-4 62 TomQueally 11 65
(R Hollinshead) *chsd ldrs: trcking ldng pair and n.m.r wl over 1f out tl jst over 1f out: rdn and unable qck 1f out: styd on same pce after* 4/1[2]
062 5 1 1/4 **Street Runner**[20] 2691 4-9-1 59 JerryO'Dwyer 7 59
(R Hollinshead) *hld up in tch in last trio: effrt and rdn over 2f out: edgd rt u.p and styd on same pce fr over 1f out* 5/1[3]
-563 6 1 1/4 **Quadrifolio**[14] 2902 4-8-2 46 oh1 NickyMackay 10 44
(Paul Green) *in tch in midfield: n.m.r over 2f out tl 2f out: edgd rt u.p and unable qck wl over 1f out: no threat to ldrs ins fnl f* 13/2
660- 7 2 **Miss Doodle**[299] 5430 4-8-11 55 SebSanders 8 51
(Eve Johnson Houghton) *in tch in midfield: nt clr run ent fnl 3f: swtchd arnd wkng rival over 2f out: keeping on same pce whn nt clr run again over 1f out: n.d after* 16/1
0-00 8 1/2 **Duke Of Normandy (IRE)**[15] 2874 4-8-2 46 oh1 JamieMackay 2 40
(B P J Baugh) *stdd and dropped in bhd after s: hld up in tch in rr: rdn and effrt over 2f out: no prog 2f out: and wl btn over 1f out* 25/1
/000 9 12 **Ernmoor**[15] 2874 8-8-2 46 oh1 JimmyQuinn 1 20
(A E Price) *hld up in last trio: pushed along and effrt 4f out: wknd u.p ent fnl 2f: wl bhd and eased ins fnl f* 28/1
006 10 dist **Annie Moyles**[24] 2600 4-8-2 46 oh1 FrannyNorton 5 —
(C N Kellett) *led tl over 3f out: sn wknd: wl t.o fnl 2f* 66/1

2m 31.6s (-2.30) **Going Correction** -0.15s/f (Firm) 10 Ran SP% 116.0
Speed ratings (Par 101): **101,100,100,99,98 97,96,96,88,—**
toteswingers:1&2 £3.50, 2&3 £18.50, 1&3 £11.40 CSF £18.01 CT £130.20 TOTE £3.60: £1.20, £2.10, £3.90; EX 18.60.
Owner J H Chrimes And Mr & Mrs G W Hannam **Bred** Cheveley Park Stud Ltd **Trained** Audley, Staffs

FOCUS
A weak event, with five runners out of the handicap, but the pace was solid and the form looks sound if limited.

Miss Doodle Official explanation: jockey said saddle slipped

3361 REMPSTONE FILLIES' H'CAP 7f 9y
8:10 (8:10) (Class 4) (0-85,83) 3-Y-O £4,209 (£1,252; £625; £312) Stalls Low

Form RPR
-161 1 **Maid In Heaven (IRE)**[23] 2618 3-9-7 83 ShaneKelly 6 95+
(W R Swinburn) *chsd ldrs: pushed along 2f out: rdn to chal ent fnl f: led fnl 150yds: r.o strly and drew clr after: readily* 9/4[1]
-621 2 2 3/4 **Love Match**[14] 2892 3-9-2 78 SteveDrowne 3 83
(R Charlton) *stdd s: hld up in rr: hdwy 2f out: chd a wall of horses and swtchd lft jst over 1f out: kpt on u.p ins fnl f to go 2nd nr fin: no threat to wnr* 7/1
6230 3 3/4 **The Hermitage (IRE)**[14] 2884 3-8-12 74 RoystonFfrench 7 77
(M Johnston) *chsd ldr: rdn to ld wl over 1f out: hdd fnl 150yds: nt gng pce of wnr after: lost 2nd nr fin* 18/1
3022 4 3/4 **Breathless Kiss (USA)**[10] 3023 3-9-4 80 NeilCallan 9 81
(K A Ryan) *t.k.h: hld up in tch: rdn and effrt 2f out: styd on same pce ins fnl f* 9/1
-000 5 nk **Hairspray**[34] 2283 3-9-4 80 CathyGannon 8 80
(M R Channon) *s.i.s: bhd early: hdwy into midfield 4f out: chsd ldrs and rdn wl over 1f out: unable qck ent fnl f: kpt on same pce* 33/1
0-40 6 9 **Dark Eyes (IRE)**[49] 1850 3-9-4 80 SebSanders 5 56
(D J Coakley) *led: rdn over 2f out: hdd wl over 1f out: wknd qckly over 1f out: eased wl ins fnl f* 12/1
-221 7 2 3/4 **Copper Penny**[29] 2434 3-9-2 78 TedDurcan 4 46
(D R Lanigan) *in tch in midfield: rdn and lost pl ent fnl 2f: hung rt and wl btn fr over 1f out* 9/2[3]
2-13 8 1 **Whirly Dancer**[49] 1850 3-9-6 82 TomQueally 2 48
(H R A Cecil) *dwlt: in tch towards rr: rdn and effrt on stands' rail over 2f out: no prog wl over 1f out: wl btn 1f out* 3/1[2]
215- 9 16 **Kai Mook**[186] 7824 3-8-13 75 KierenFallon 1 —
(P M Mooney, Ire) *chsd ldrs tl over 2f out: wknd qckly 2f out: wl bhd and eased ins fnl f* 28/1

1m 24.06s (-2.14) **Going Correction** -0.15s/f (Firm) 9 Ran SP% 115.8
Speed ratings (Par 98): **106,102,102,101,100 90,87,86,67**
toteswingers:1&2 £4.80, 2&3 £10.30, 1&3 £7.40 CSF £18.81 CT £228.89 TOTE £3.20: £1.10, £4.60, £4.80; EX 10.80.
Owner Delightful Dozen **Bred** Mrs C Hartery **Trained** Aldbury, Herts

FOCUS
A decent filies' handicap for the grade, with the top weight rated 83, and plenty could be fancied. The form appears sound.

Whirly Dancer Official explanation: jockey said filly never travelled

3362 OSBASTON MAIDEN AUCTION STKS 5f 218y
8:40 (8:41) (Class 5) 2-Y-O £2,914 (£867; £433; £216) Stalls Low

Form RPR
0256 1 **Colorado Gold**[21] 2680 2-8-13 0 TomQueally 4 85
(P F I Cole) *mde all: rdn over 1f out: styd on wl ins fnl f* 3/1[2]
60 2 2 **Sonoran Sands (IRE)**[9] 3051 2-8-13 0 KierenFallon 8 80
(J S Moore) *t.k.h early: hld up in midfield: effrt and n.m.r briefly 2f out: rdn to chse wnr over 1f out: hung lft and no imp ins fnl f* 4/5[1]
0 3 5 **Bajan Bear**[16] 2839 2-8-9 0 SteveDrowne 3 62+
(M Blanshard) *stdd s: bhd: rdn over 2f out: hdwy and swtchd rt over 1f out: kpt on to go modest 3rd ins fnl f: nvr trbld ldrs* 33/1
0624 4 3 1/4 **Lady Morganna (IRE)**[7] 3106 2-8-4 0 JimmyQuinn 2 45
(Miss Gay Kelleway) *in tch: rdn to chse wnr over 2f out tl over 1f out: drvn and wl btn 1f out: wknd ins fnl f* 7/1[3]
5 5 **Rylee Mooch** 2-8-9 0 PaulEddery 1 35
(R C Guest) *s.i.s: a bhd: nvr on terms* 33/1

0 **6** 1 3/4 **Mimi's Princess**[8] 3087 2-8-11 0 StevieDonohoe 7 32
(K A Ryan) *s.i.s: sn rcvrd and chsng ldrs: rdn and struggling 2f out: rn green and wknd qckly 2f out* **18/1**

7 5 **Romano (IRE)** 2-8-11 0 RoystonFfrench 6 17
(P T Midgley) *sn rdn along and a outpcd in rr* **22/1**

8 3 **Snow Legend (IRE)** 2-8-4 0 RichardSmith 5 —
(Tom Dascombe) *plld hrd and racd v awkwardly: chsd wnr tl over 2f out: sn hanging bdly rt and dropped out: wl bhd ins fnl f* **16/1**

1m 12.89s (-0.11) **Going Correction** -0.15s/f (Firm) **8** Ran SP% **114.4**
Speed ratings (Par 93): **94,91,84,80,73 71,64,60**
toteswingers:1&2 £1.70, 2&3 £6.90, 1&3 £13.20 CSF £5.61 TOTE £5.60: £2.50, £1.10, £10.00; EX 7.00.
Owner Goldswain,Jefferson,McLaughlan,Williams **Bred** Alan Parker **Trained** Whatcombe, Oxon

FOCUS
Just an ordinary maiden, but it provided an early test of Royal Ascot two-year-old form. The winner ran to his mark and the second to his Windsor Castle form.

NOTEBOOK
Colorado Gold, second at Bath in May and a solid sixth over this trip at Sandown three weeks ago, bolted up. Quickly away, he was soon close up against the stands' rail and led virtually throughout. He is bred stay further and may well be able to add to this victory.
Sonoran Sands(IRE), beaten little more than eight lengths when seventh in the Windsor Castle Stakes nine days previously, hardly franked that form. He was never far away, with his rider seemingly content to get a lead early on, but appeared to wander and duck in behind the winner when asked to mount a challenge. Perhaps the ground was too fast for him, or maybe this came too soon. (op 11-10)
Bajan Bear had shown little when down the field at Salisbury first time out, so this was an improvement. In rear early on, he stayed on well in the closing stages and looked as if he would handle a longer trip.
Lady Morganna(IRE), runner-up over this distance at Kempton two outings ago, did not match that form here. She was never closer than midfield and did not produce any obvious finishing kick. (op 11-2 tchd 5-1)
Rylee Mooch, a gelded newcomer, showed a glimpse of ability. Slowly away, he improved his position from halfway. (op 25-1)
Snow Legend(IRE) Official explanation: jockey said sheepskin nose band became loose partially blinding filly

3363 BOOTLEG BEATLES LIVE ON 24 AUGUST H'CAP 1m 60y
9:10 (9:10) (Class 5) (0-75,75) 3-Y-O **£2,914** (£867; £433; £216) **Stalls** High

Form RPR

-024 **1** **Dutiful**[27] 2503 3-8-10 **64** TedDurcan 5 71+
(M R Channon) *awkward leaving stalls and s.i.s: racd in last: rdn and hdwy jst over 1f out: rdn to ld fnl 100yds: r.o wl* **14/1**

-611 **2** 1 **Rock The Stars (IRE)**[11] 3002 3-8-8 **62** SebSanders 6 67+
(J W Hills) *racd in last pair: swtchd to outer over 3f out: rdn and effrt over 2f out: drvn and edgd rt ent fnl f: ev ch 1f out tl nt pce of wnr fnl 75yds* **4/5**[1]

-361 **3** 1/2 **Tamtara**[20] 2725 3-9-5 **73** NeilCallan 3 77
(Mrs A J Perrett) *chsd ldrs: rdn to chal ent fnl 2f: drvn and led 1f out: hdd and one pce fnl 100yds* **9/1**

1313 **4** 1 **Tribal Myth (IRE)**[29] 2438 3-8-10 **64** KierenFallon 2 66
(K A Ryan) *chsd ldr: upsides 4f out: rdn over 2f out: led wl over 1f out tl 1f out: one pce and btn fnl 100yds* **9/2**[2]

323 **5** 3 3/4 **Jay's Treaty (USA)**[30] 2425 3-9-7 **75** RoystonFfrench 7 68
(M Johnston) *led: jnd 4f out: rdn and hdd wl over 1f out: wknd ent fnl f* **11/2**[3]

0-30 **6** 1 1/4 **Swift Return**[13] 2935 3-9-0 **68** SteveDrowne 1 58
(S C Williams) *chsd ldrs: rdn and unable qck over 2f out: wknd over 1f out* **40/1**

-000 **7** 3/4 **The Human League**[13] 2933 3-9-5 **73** PaulEddery 4 61
(M R Channon) *in tch: rdn and n.m.r on rail over 2f out: wknd over 1f out* **33/1**

1m 45.09s (-0.01) **Going Correction** -0.15s/f (Firm) **7** Ran SP% **111.2**
Speed ratings (Par 99): **94,93,92,91,87 86,85**
toteswingers:1&2 £9.40, 2&3 £2.40, 1&3 £15.40 CSF £24.51 TOTE £21.80: £15.60, £4.30; EX 35.10 Place 6: £28.62 Place 5: £6.71.
Owner Wood Street Syndicate II **Bred** J Repard **Trained** West Ilsley, Berks

FOCUS
An interesting handicap, even though the top weight was rated just 75. The winner was 7lb well in but could not match his Salisbury win off this slower pace. The winner is generally progressive.
Jay's Treaty(USA) Official explanation: jockey said gelding hung badly left throughout
T/Plt: £44.40 to a £1 stake. Pool: £69,311.92 - 1,137.79 winning tickets. T/Qpdt: £4.90 to a £1 stake. Pool: £5,246.04 - 785.12 winning ticket. SP

2763 NEWCASTLE (L-H)
Thursday, June 24

OFFICIAL GOING: Good to firm (8.0)
Wind: Light against Weather: Cloudy and warm

3364 TRADERSBETTINGEXCHANGE.CO.UK NOVICE STKS 6f
2:10 (2:10) (Class 4) 2-Y-O **£3,497** (£1,040; £520; £259) **Stalls** High

Form RPR

1 **1** **Waltz Darling (IRE)**[22] 2654 2-9-5 0 PaulHanagan 3 87
(R A Fahey) *trckd ldng pair: hdwy 1/2-way: rdn to ld over 1f out: drvn ins fnl f: sn edgd rt: kpt on* **6/5**[1]

13 **2** 1 **On The High Tops (IRE)**[26] 2525 2-9-2 0 MickyFenton 1 81
(T P Tate) *led: rdn along over 2f out: drvn and hdd over 1f out: sn hung rt: keeping on whn n.m.r nr fin* **9/4**[2]

15 **3** nk **Dads Amigo**[27] 2514 2-9-2 0 PhillipMakin 5 80
(D H Brown) *in rr and pushed along 1/2-way: rdn 2f out: drvn and kpt on ins fnl f: nrst fin* **14/1**

21 **4** 2 3/4 **Lady Del Sol**[23] 2623 2-8-11 0 PJMcDonald 4 71+
(G R Oldroyd) *trckd ldr: effrt and cl up 2f out: sn rdn: drvn and hmpd ent fnl f: nt rcvr* **11/4**[3]

1m 16.31s (1.71) **Going Correction** +0.075s/f (Good) **4** Ran SP% **109.6**
Speed ratings (Par 95): **95,93,93,89**
CSF £4.25 TOTE £2.20; EX 3.50.
Owner Mike Browne **Bred** Ms Natalie Cleary **Trained** Musley Bank, N Yorks

FOCUS
A fair novice event but something of a slow-motion finish as the runners battled against a headwind. The runners came down the centre initially before ending up on the stand rail. Form that makes sense around the first two.

NOTEBOOK
Waltz Darling(IRE)'s debut form hadn't worked out particularly well, but he improved on that performance with a workmanlike victory that owed plenty to a willing attitude. Even on this stiff track he left the impression that 6f is very much a minimum for him and, a colt with plenty of scope, he looks sure to keep improving with both time and distance. (op 6-4 tchd 11-10)
On The High Tops(IRE) took the field along, but the winner always had his measure from the two-furlong pole and he didn't help himself by edging continually right despite his rider's efforts to correct him. For all he saw the trip out well, it's unlikely he improved as much for it as it seemed likely he might beforehand (op 7-4)
Dads Amigo looked to have plenty to find on figures but confirmed the promise of his Beverley debut when shaping as if this trip would suit. He was staying on steadily, albeit never a threat, and won't mind another furlong. (op 12-1 tchd 11-1)
Lady Del Sol is better than the result suggests as she was continually intimidated by the runner-up until forced to snatch up when disputing third inside the last. (op 7-2)

3365 COOPERS MARQUEES MEDIAN AUCTION MAIDEN STKS 6f
2:45 (2:45) (Class 5) 2-Y-O **£2,590** (£770; £385; £192) **Stalls** High

Form RPR

3324 **1** **Alfraamsey**[11] 2990 2-9-3 0 RobertWinston 7 75
(M R Channon) *qckly away and swtchd rt to stands' rail: mde all: rdn clr over 1f out: styd on wl* **7/2**[2]

2 3 1/4 **Piccoluck** 2-9-3 0 GregFairley 9 65
(Mrs D J Sanderson) *trckd ldrs on inner: hdwy 1/2-way: chsd wnr 2f out and sn rn green: kpt on ins fnl f: bttr for r* **10/1**

4 **3** 3 3/4 **Eland Ally**[27] 2498 2-9-3 0 MickyFenton 3 54
(T P Tate) *chsd wnr: rdn along 2f out: drvn and outpcd over 1f out: kpt on u.p towards fin* **7/2**[2]

4 3/4 **Talley Close** 2-9-3 0 PaulHanagan 4 52+
(R A Fahey) *trckd ldrs: hdwy to chse ldng pair wl over 1f out: sn rdn and one pce: lost 3rd nr fin* **11/4**[1]

6224 **5** 7 **Lady Royale**[16] 2832 2-8-9 0 (p) BarryMcHugh(3) 1 26+
(G R Oldroyd) *prom on outer: rdn along wl over 2f out: sn drvn and wknd wl over 1f out* **9/2**[3]

3 **6** 4 1/2 **Brian Sprout**[16] 2836 2-9-3 0 JoeFanning 8 17
(J R Weymes) *dwlt: t.k.h and chsd ldrs: pushed along over 2f out: sn outpcd* **12/1**

7 3/4 **Twennyshortkid** 2-9-3 0 TonyHamilton 6 15+
(P T Midgley) *a in rr: bhd fr 1/2-way* **40/1**

8 3/4 **Thunderway (IRE)** 2-8-7 0 PatrickDonaghy(5) 5 8
(M Dods) *s.i.s: a in rr: bhd fr 1/2-way* **20/1**

0 **9** 6 **Salagadoola**[7] 3118 2-8-7 0 LanceBetts(5) 2 —
(T D Easterby) *sn outpcd and bhd fr 1/2-way* **100/1**

1m 16.35s (1.75) **Going Correction** +0.075s/f (Good) **9** Ran SP% **114.3**
Speed ratings (Par 93): **95,90,85,84,75 69,68,67,59**
toteswingers: 1&2 £7.80, 1&3 £3.30, 2&3 £11.10 CSF £36.79 TOTE £5.00: £1.90, £2.80, £2.10; EX 43.70 Trifecta £149.80 Pool: £334.11 - 1.65 winning units..
Owner Lord Ilsley Racing (Harrow Syndicate) **Bred** G Hedley & Mike Channon Bloodstock Limited **Trained** West Ilsley, Berks

FOCUS
An ordinary juvenile maiden. The winner had the advantage of the rail and has only been rated to his mark.

NOTEBOOK
Alfraamsey had begun to look vulnerable in races of this nature, but his experience stood him in good stead up against some raw newcomers and he was always going to be hard to catch once he'd bagged pole position on the stand rail. The handicapper is likely to take a dim view of his winning margin and unless this represents much-improved form, it could be that he will struggle once going into nurseries. (op 3-1)
Piccoluck, a gelding by Piccolo with a sprint pedigree, hails from a yard in decent form and made an encouraging debut for all he had the benefit of the rail. He looked green when asked for his effort, but kept on well and seems a likely improver. (op 12-1)
Eland Ally again ran with promise and began to rally inside the last in a manner that suggests a step up to 7f will see him make more progress. (op 9-2)
Talley Close is out of a mare that won at up to 1m3f and he shaped as though he will do better over further in time, for all this debut wasn't without promise considering he looked in need of the experience. (op 3-1)
Lady Royale brought the best form into the contest but for all she was probably at a disadvantage racing more towards the outside, she looked a bit quirky tried in cheekpieces and dropped away inside the last. This was a second disappointing run in a row and her second place in a Listed race ensures she will be treated harshly in nurseries. Official explanation: trainer had no explanation for the poor form shown (op 10-3 tchd 11-4 in a place)

3366 S V RUTTER SEATON DELAVAL H'CAP 1m 3y(S)
3:20 (3:20) (Class 2) (0-100,99) 4-Y-O+
£12,462 (£3,732; £1,866; £934; £466; £234) **Stalls** High

Form RPR

5360 **1** **Tartan Gunna**[12] 2977 4-8-7 **85** (b[1]) PhilipRobinson 7 96
(M Johnston) *dwlt and in rr: stdy hdwy 1/2-way: swtchd lft and chsd ldrs 2f out: rdn to ld appr fnl f: kpt on strly* **5/2**[1]

0066 **2** 3 3/4 **Collateral Damage (IRE)**[16] 2835 7-9-0 **92** (t) DavidAllan 3 94
(T D Easterby) *trckd ldrs: pushed along and sltly outpcd 2f out: sn rdn: styd on ins fnl f: tk 2nd nr fin* **8/1**

-305 **3** 1/2 **Kay Gee Be (IRE)**[27] 2508 6-8-8 **86** JoeFanning 2 87
(W Jarvis) *led 2f: cl up tl led again 3f out: rdn along 2f out: drvn and hdd appr fnl f: sn one pce: lost 2nd nr fin* **9/2**[3]

5220 **4** 1 3/4 **Jordaura**[20] 2708 4-8-8 **86** GregFairley 8 83
(J R Holt) *trckd ldrs: hdwy 3f out: rdn along over 2f out: drvn and one pce fr over 1f out* **15/2**

00-1 **5** 3 3/4 **Justonefortheroad**[28] 2451 4-8-2 **80** PaulHanagan 1 69
(R A Fahey) *cl up: led after 2f: hdd 3f out and sn rdn along: drvn wl over 1f out and sn wknd* **5/1**

2010 **6** 8 **Dubai Dynamo**[6] 3146 5-9-7 **99** RobertWinston 5 69
(Mrs R A Carr) *hld up towards rr: effrt and sme hdwy 3f out: sn rdn and btn* **4/1**[2]

0-30 **7** 1 1/4 **Deadly Secret (USA)**[20] 2708 4-8-4 **82** PJMcDonald 6 49
(R A Fahey) *dwlt: in tch: rdn along 3f out: sn wknd* **16/1**

1m 41.31s (-2.09) **Going Correction** +0.075s/f (Good) **7** Ran SP% **112.2**
Speed ratings (Par 109): **101,97,96,95,91 83,82**
toteswingers:1&2 £4.80, 2&3 £7.30, 1&3 £2.80 CSF £22.17 CT £83.43 TOTE £3.20: £1.70, £3.80; EX 13.00 Trifecta £37.50 Pool: £429.35 - 8.45 winning units..
Owner Exors of the Late Mrs I Bird **Bred** Cheveley Park Stud Ltd **Trained** Middleham Moor, N Yorks

FOCUS
A good handicap, run at a decent pace. The winner is rated back to his best.

NOTEBOOK

Tartan Gunna had shown at York last month behind Imposing that he still retained plenty of ability and had dropped to a very tantalising mark after some lesser efforts since. Well backed down in trip in first-time blinkers, he came back to form in no uncertain fashion despite losing a couple of lengths at the start, forging clear inside the last. This trip is a minimum for him, but his immediate prospects rest in the hands of the handicapper, as he's bound to be raised to a mark after this similar to those from which he has come up short before. (op 3-1 tchd 10-3 and 7-2 in a place)
Collateral Damage(IRE) had been slow to find his form this season but he's dropped in the weights as a result and showed signs of a revival here. His turn might not be that fare away. (op 15-2 tchd 17-2)
Kay Gee Be(IRE)'s long winless streak defies a number of decent efforts and this was another with the return to 1m seeming to suit him.
Jordaura is as high now in the weights as she has ever been after two good seconds at this trip earlier this season and probably needs to drop down a grade or two again. (op 7-1)
Justonefortheroad had his own way in front when making a winning reappearance but that was in a weak 0-75 and he came up well short in this much stronger contest. He'll be of more interest back down a level or two and still looks to have the pace to be effective at 7f. (op 4-1)
Dubai Dynamo had a rare off day, never travelling, but even so his current career-high mark limits his options and he won't find adding to his three wins this season easy. Official explanation: jockey said gelding ran flat (op 5-1)

3367 LA TAXIS H'CAP — 2m 19y

3:55 (3:55) (Class 4) (0-80,78) 4-Y-O+ **£4,415** (£1,321; £660; £330; £164) **Stalls** Low

Form — RPR

1123 **1** **Lady Eclair (IRE)**[5] 3198 4-9-7 **78** .... JoeFanning 4 — 94
(M Johnston) *cl up: led 3f out: rdn wl over 1f out: drvn ins fnl f: kpt on wl* **5/4**[1]

-645 **2** ¾ **Simonside**[13] 2941 7-8-8 **65** .... TomEaves 3 — 79
(B Ellison) *led: pushed along and hdd 3f out: sn rdn: drvn and rallied over 1f out: chsd wnr ins fnl f: no imp towards fin* **5/2**[2]

12-0 **3** *9* **Bollin Judith**[26] 2549 4-8-11 **68** .... DavidAllan 2 — 71
(T D Easterby) *trckd ldng pair: hdwy 3f out: rdn wl over 1f out: drvn and no imp ins fnl f* **7/2**[3]

04-6 **4** *7* **Inchnadamph**[17] 2814 10-9-5 **76** ....(t) PaulHanagan 1 — 71
(T J Fitzgerald) *hld up in rr: effrt and sme hdwy over 3f out: rdn along wl over 2f out and nvr a factor* **12/1**

0024 **5** *9* **Planetarium**[10] 2672 5-8-9 **66** ....(p) TonyHamilton 6 — 50
(P Monteith) *trckd ldng pair: pushed along over 5f out: rdn along over 3f out and sn wknd* **11/1**

3m 34.22s (-5.18) **Going Correction** -0.175s/f (Firm) **5** Ran SP% **111.3**
Speed ratings (Par 105): **105,104,100,96,92**
CSF £4.70 TOTE £2.30: £1.20, £2.50.
Owner Netherfield House Stud **Bred** Lynch Bages Ltd & Samac Ltd **Trained** Middleham Moor, N Yorks

FOCUS
Another modest race for the grade, but the pace was a decent one and two came clear. The form is taken at face value.

3368 EUROPEAN BREEDERS' FUND HOPPINGS STKS (LISTED RACE) — 1m 2f 32y

4:30 (4:30) (Class 1) 3-Y-O+
£22,708 (£8,608; £4,308; £2,148; £1,076; £540) **Stalls** Centre

Form — RPR

5303 **1** **Pachattack (USA)**[19] 2744 4-9-5 101 ....(p) TomEaves 5 — 106
(G A Butler) *mde all: pushed along over 2f out: rdn over 1f out: drvn ins fnl f: kpt on gamely* **6/1**[3]

-561 **2** *2* **Lady Jane Digby**[10] 3031 5-9-9 104 .... GregFairley 4 — 106
(M Johnston) *trckd ldng pair: hdwy over 2f out: rdn to chal wl over 1f out: drvn and ev ch ent fnl f: kpt on same pce towards fin* **5/2**[2]

4246 **3** ½ **Honimiere (IRE)**[10] 3031 4-9-5 107 .... PJMcDonald 3 — 101
(G A Swinbank) *trckd ldrs: effrt on inner and n.m.r 2f out: swtchd rt and rdn ent fnl f: styd on wl towards fin* **8/1**

10 **4** 3½ **Sajjhaa**[20] 2711 3-8-7 91 .... PhilipRobinson 7 — 95
(M A Jarvis) *hld up: hdwy on outer 3f out: chal wl over 1f out: sn rdn and ev ch tl wknd jst ins fnl f* **5/6**[1]

611- **5** *1* **Supaverdi (USA)**[310] 5128 5-9-5 87 .... RobertWinston 1 — 93
(H Morrison) *trckd wnr: effrt 3f out: rdn and cl up 2f out: sn drvn and wknd appr fnl f* **22/1**

2516 **6** *6* **Dazzling Light (UAE)**[15] 2857 5-9-5 82 .... PhillipMakin 2 — 81
(J S Goldie) *hld up towards rr: effrt and sme hdwy 3f out: rdn along over 2f out: n.d* **33/1**

-560 **7** *7* **Cracking Lass (IRE)**[18] 2800 3-8-7 96 .... PaulHanagan 8 — 68
(R A Fahey) *dwlt and in rr: rdn along 1/2-way and sn outpcd* **20/1**

1144 **8** *5* **Island Sunset (IRE)**[55] 1665 4-9-5 91 .... JoeFanning 6 — 59
(W R Muir) *trckd ldrs: rdn along over 3f out: drvn over 2f out and sn wknd* **25/1**

2m 7.94s (-3.96) **Going Correction** -0.175s/f (Firm)
WFA 3 from 4yo+ 12lb **8** Ran SP% **124.4**
Speed ratings (Par 111): **108,106,106,103,102 97,92,88**
toteswingers:1&2 £3.30, 2&3 £4.00, 1&3 £3.90 CSF £22.42 TOTE £7.60: £1.70, £1.80, £1.70; EX 21.90 Trifecta £50.60 Pool: £386.39 - 5.65 winning units..
Owner M V Deegan **Bred** Dapple Broodmares 2004 **Trained** Newmarket, Suffolk

FOCUS
An up-to-scratch renewal of this Listed contest. It was run at a fair pace and the form makes sense at face value.

NOTEBOOK

Pachattack(USA) had run as well as ever on turf in a Group 3 over 8.5f at Epsom last time out, but she proved ideally suited by this longer trip and turned in a career-best effort. That was down to a much more positive ride than usual, able to steady the gallop in front turning for home before seeing it out stoutly. A similar ride would see her going close in something like the Lyric Stakes at York next month.
Lady Jane Digby lost nothing in defeat trying to win this race for the second year running. She's not quite up to winning a Group 3 in this country, but will continue to be a tough opponent at this level and continues to shape as if worth a try against her own sex at 1m4f. (tchd 11-4)
Honimiere(IRE) got closer to Lady Jane Digby than she had at Warwick last time and might have got closer still had she not been short of room at a vital stage, but she wasn't unlucky in any way. She ran well first time out this year on AW and there are several weak Listed races on that surface late in the year her connections may be eyeing. (op 16-1)
Sajjhaawas extremely short in the betting considering her bare form but ran much better than she did in the Oaks and perhaps paid for being set a bit to do relative to the more-experienced trio that beat her, though her trainer later reported she was unsuited by the fast ground. She's clearly held in high regard and looks like she can improve again with this experience behind her. Official explanation: jockey said filly was unsuited by the good to firm ground (op 11-10 tchd 6-5 and 4-5)
Supaverdi(USA) ran well for a long way but just left the impression she needed her first run for nearly a year. This was a big jump up in grade for her but she looked like she wasn't out of place in this company, which is just as well as she has probably blown her handicap mark. (op 20-1)
Cracking Lass(IRE) had had her limitations exposed up at a higher level than this the last twice but never went a yard, here ridden along virtually from the off. (op 22-1)
Island Sunset(IRE) Official explanation: jockey said filly was unsuited by the good to firm ground

3369 BORDER MINSTREL IS OPEN NOW H'CAP (DIV I) — 1m 2f 32y

5:05 (5:06) (Class 6) (0-55,60) 4-Y-O+ **£2,007** (£597; £298; £149) **Stalls** Centre

Form — RPR

660- **1** **Pattern Mark**[299] 5442 4-8-6 **47** .... BarryMcHugh(3) 2 — 58
(Ollie Pears) *hld up: tk cl order on inner 4f out: swtchd rt and smooth hdwy to join ldrs over 2f out: led over 1f out: rdn ins fnl f and kpt on* **4/1**[3]

5343 **2** ¾ **Dean Iarracht (IRE)**[10] 3025 4-9-0 **52** ....(p) AndrewMullen 8 — 62
(Miss Tracy Waggott) *hld up towards rr: hdwy 3f out: rdn to chse ldrs wl over 1f out: styd on ins fnl f* **11/1**

3123 **3** 3½ **Sharp Sovereign (USA)**[22] 2653 4-8-10 **53** .... DeanHeslop(5) 9 — 56
(T D Barron) *trckd ldrs: hdwy and cl up 3f out: led 2f out: sn rdn and hdd over 1f out: drvn and one pce ins fnl f* **10/3**[2]

6100 **4** 4½ **Sea Land (FR)**[5] 3223 6-8-8 **53** ow2 .... DaleSwift(7) 1 — 47
(B Ellison) *midfield: hdwy over 3f out: rdn to chse ldrs whn sltly hmpd over 2f out: drvn and wknd over 1f out* **6/1**

0651 **5** 1¾ **Dark Ranger**[7] 3128 4-9-3 **60** 6ex .... IanBrennan(5) 12 — 50
(T J Pitt) *hld up in rr: hdwy over 3f out: rdn along over 2f out: nvr nr ldrs* **11/4**[1]

0-03 **6** 1¾ **Rain Stops Play (IRE)**[6] 3147 8-8-3 **46** .... AmyRyan(5) 5 — 33
(N G Richards) *chsd ldrs: rdn along over 3f out: drvn over 2f out: grad wknd* **17/2**

06-0 **7** 3½ **Royal Applord**[18] 2789 5-8-9 **47** .... AndrewElliott 4 — 27
(N Tinkler) *chsd ldng pair: rdn along 3f out: drvn and over 2f out and sn wknd* **66/1**

000- **8** *24* **Flashy Max**[10] 4944 5-8-3 **46** oh1 ....(b) PatrickDonaghy(5) 11 — —
(Jedd O'Keeffe) *led: rdn along over 3f out: sn hdd & wknd* **66/1**

0300 **9** 3½ **Big Whitfield**[19] 2764 4-9-3 **55** .... PhillipMakin 7 — —
(M Dods) *a in rr: bhd fnl 3f* **28/1**

0-0 **10** 2½ **Napoletano (ITY)**[10] 3025 4-8-11 **49** .... TonyHamilton 10 — —
(R Johnson) *in tch: rdn along 4f out: sn wknd* **100/1**

560- **11** *8* **Broughtons Silk**[246] 6945 5-8-12 **50** .... DavidAllan 13 — —
(A C Whillans) *hld up: a towards rr: outpcd and bhd fnl 3f* **20/1**

5200 **12** *2* **Fitzwarren**[27] 2500 9-8-8 **46** oh1 ....(tp) RobertWinston 3 — —
(A D Brown) *cl up: led 3f out: rdn and hdd 2f out: wknd qckly* **25/1**

00/0 **F** **Merlins Dreams**[15] 2854 7-8-5 **48** oh1 ow2 ....(p) MarkCoumbe(5) 14 — —
(S A Harris) *s.i.s: sn rdn along and bhd: fell 1/2-way: broke leg: fatally injured* **100/1**

2m 9.20s (-2.70) **Going Correction** -0.175s/f (Firm) **13** Ran SP% **119.9**
Speed ratings (Par 101): **103,102,99,96,94 93,90,71,68,66 60,58,—**
toteswingers:1&2 £13.90, 2&3 £4.60, 1&3 £6.20 CSF £45.02 CT £164.65 TOTE £4.90: £1.40, £3.90, £1.30; EX 60.20 Trifecta £134.00 Pool: £268.01 - 1.48 winning units..
Owner David Scott and Co (Pattern Makers) Ltd **Bred** D Scott **Trained** Norton, N Yorks
■ Stewards' Enquiry : Barry McHugh one-day ban: careless riding (Jul 8)

FOCUS
A weak handicap, run at a strong pace to suit the closers. It was 0.81sec faster than division one. The winner produced a 4lb personal best.
Fitzwarren Official explanation: jockey said gelding had no more to give

3370 BORDER MINSTREL IS OPEN NOW H'CAP (DIV II) — 1m 2f 32y

5:40 (5:40) (Class 6) (0-55,57) 4-Y-O+ **£2,007** (£597; £298; £149) **Stalls** Centre

Form — RPR

0001 **1** **Bollin Freddie**[7] 3110 6-8-13 **57** 6ex .... ShaneBKelly(7) 10 — 69
(A J Lockwood) *trckd ldrs: hdwy 3f out: led over 2f out and sn clr: rdn ins fnl f: kpt on* **7/2**[1]

0-06 **2** *2* **Royal Composer (IRE)**[15] 2851 7-8-10 **47** .... DavidAllan 7 — 55
(T D Easterby) *trckd ldrs: pushed along 3f out: rdn over 2f out: chsd wnr ent fnl f: kpt on* **6/1**[2]

0600 **3** *6* **Tres Froide (FR)**[14] 2902 5-9-2 **53** ....(p) MickyFenton 11 — 49
(N Tinkler) *hld up towards rr: pushed along and hdwy 3f out: rdn wl over 1f out: styd on ins fnl f: nrst fin* **14/1**

-006 **4** ½ **Dechiper (IRE)**[19] 2765 8-8-13 **50** ....(p) PhillipMakin 1 — 45
(R Johnson) *dwlt and towards rr: hdwy into midfield 1/2-way: effrt 3f out: rdn to chse ldrs 2f out: drvn and one pce appr fnl f* **7/2**[1]

060- **5** 1¾ **Tae Kwon Do (USA)**[239] 5952 4-8-12 **49** .... TomEaves 3 — 41
(Julie Camacho) *prom: hdwy to chse ldr over 3f out: rdn and ev ch over 2f out: sn drvn and grad wknd appr fnl f* **8/1**

5-50 **6** 1¼ **Mister Maq**[7] 3124 7-8-9 **46** ....(v) AdrianNicholls 5 — 35
(A Crook) *dwlt and bhd: pushed along and hdwy over 3f out: rdn over 2f out: kpt on: nvr nr ldrs* **33/1**

50-0 **7** 3½ **Dr Light (IRE)**[7] 3110 6-8-8 **45** .... AndrewMullen 9 — 27
(M A Peill) *s.i.s and bhd tl sme late hdwy* **33/1**

05-0 **8** ½ **Marillos Proterras**[12] 2430 4-8-5 **45** ....(b[1]) BarryMcHugh(3) 4 — 26
(Mrs A Duffield) *led: rdn along 3f out: hdd over 2f out: sn drvn and wknd* **25/1**

0505 **9** *6* **Loyal Knight (IRE)**[15] 2876 5-8-3 **45** ....(t) PaulPickard(5) 2 — 14
(P T Midgley) *s.i.s and bhd: hdwy into midfield 1/2-way: sn rdn along and wknd 3f out* **20/1**

603 **10** *2* **Fitzolini**[18] 2789 4-9-3 **54** ....(p) RobertWinston 8 — 19
(A D Brown) *t.k.h: chsd ldrs: rdn along 3f out: sn wknd* **15/2**[3]

/040 **11** *10* **Custard Cream Kid (IRE)**[15] 2859 4-9-1 **52** ....(p) TonyHamilton 12 — —
(R A Fahey) *a towards rr* **8/1**

30-5 **12** *7* **Roman History (IRE)**[10] 3021 7-8-11 **48** ....(p) GregFairley 13 — —
(Miss Tracy Waggott) *midfield: rdn along 1/2-way: sn lost pl and bhd fnl 3f* **40/1**

00-0 **13** *21* **Rainbow Zest**[7] 3124 7-8-8 **45** .... AndrewElliott 6 — —
(W Storey) *chsd ldr: rdn along over 4f out: sn wknd: bhd and eased fnl 2f* **16/1**

2m 10.01s (-1.89) **Going Correction** -0.175s/f (Firm) **13** Ran SP% **122.2**
Speed ratings (Par 101): **100,98,93,93,91 90,88,87,82,81 73,67,50**
toteswingers:1&2 £4.70, 2&3 £16.00, 1&3 £14.10 CSF £23.17 CT £270.79 TOTE £4.70: £1.70, £2.50, £4.60; EX 29.00 Trifecta £141.70 Pool: £302.60 - 1.58 winning units..
Owner Highgreen Partnership **Bred** Sir Neil & Exors Of Late Lady Westbrook **Trained** Brawby, N Yorks

FOCUS
Arguably fewer in-form runners than in the first division but another race run at a frenetic pace and the hold-up horses came to the fore again. It was the slower division by 0.81sec. The winner is rated in line with the best view of his previous form.
Dr Light(IRE) Official explanation: jockey said gelding missed the break

Loyal Knight(IRE) Official explanation: jockey said gelding was denied a clear run

3371 GOSFORTH DECORATING AND BUILDING SERVICES H'CAP 7f
6:10 (6:10) (Class 5) (0-75,73) 3-Y-O **£2,590** (£770; £385; £192) **Stalls** High

Form RPR
4003 1 **Whispered Times (USA)**[5] 3226 3-8-12 **64**............(p) RobertWinston 11 80
(Miss Tracy Waggott) *trckd ldrs: hdwy on stands' rail to ld jst over 2f out: rdn clr over 1f out: kpt on strly* **3/1**[1]
0465 2 *10* **Vito Volterra (IRE)**[10] 2834 3-8-9 **64**...................... MichaelStainton(3) 12 53
(Michael Smith) *prom: chsd ldr 1/2-way: rdn over 2f out and ev ch: drvn over 1f out: kpt on: no ch w wnr* **11/2**[2]
00-U 3 *3/4* **Koo And The Gang (IRE)**[81] 1104 3-8-8 **67**.................... DaleSwift(7) 4 54
(B Ellison) *stdd s and sn swtchd rt: hdwy over 2f out and sn rdn: styd on u.p ins fnl f: tk 3rd nr fin* **20/1**
0341 4 *3/4* **Angel Of Fashion (IRE)**[23] 2624 3-9-1 **67**.................... AdrianNicholls 2 52
(D Nicholls) *hld up towards rr: hdwy 3f out: rdn to chse ldrs over 2f out: drvn over 1f out and sn one pce: lost 3rd nr line* **6/1**[3]
-066 5 *1 1/2* **Military Call**[19] 2762 3-8-12 **64**.. PhillipMakin 9 45
(A C Whillans) *sltly hmpd s and in rr: hdwy on outer wl over 2f out: sn rdn and kpt on ins fnl f: nvr a factor* **8/1**
-120 6 *shd* **Master Leon**[19] 2762 3-9-0 **73**....................................(v) AdamCarter(7) 10 54
(B Smart) *sn led: rdn along 3f out: hdd over 2f out: sn edgd lft and grad wknd* **6/1**[3]
0335 7 *9* **Refuse To Wait (IRE)**[31] 2379 3-8-10 **62**............................ DavidAllan 7 18
(T D Easterby) *wnt rt s: in tch: rdn along 1/2-way: sn drvn: lost pl and bhd* **3/1**[1]
1050 8 *2 1/4* **Always Dazzling**[23] 2628 3-8-11 **63**.................................... GregFairley 6 13
(M Johnston) *cl up: rdn along over 3f out: sn wknd* **12/1**
24-6 9 *1 1/4* **Olympic Ceremony**[173] 17 3-9-4 **70**.......................... TonyHamilton 5 17
(R A Fahey) *chsd ldrs: rdn along 1/2-way: sn wknd* **20/1**

1m 28.14s (-0.56) **Going Correction** +0.075s/f (Good) **9 Ran SP% 122.3**
Speed ratings (Par 99): **106,94,93,92,91 91,80,78,76**
toteswingers:1&2 £5.60, 2&3 £23.00, 1&3 £17.30 CSF £21.17 CT £283.44 TOTE £3.80: £1.10, £2.60, £8.30; EX 28.10 Trifecta £238.30 Part won. Pool of £322.12 - 0.20 winning units. Place 6: £47.20 Place 5: £21.03 .
Owner Michael Howarth **Bred** Hetrich-McCarthy Livestock **Trained** Spennymoor, Co Durham

FOCUS
The winner hacked up in this moderate handicap, being the one that stuck to the stands' rail. He is rated back to his best but it is probably unwise to take this form too literally.
T/Plt: £54.20 to a £1 stake. Pool: £53,886.59 - 725.61 winning tickets. T/Qpdt: £6.90 to a £1 stake. Pool: £4,227.89 - 447.10 winning tickets. JR

[3125]WARWICK (L-H)
Thursday, June 24

OFFICIAL GOING: Sprint course - good to firm (good in places) round course - good (good to firm in places)
Wind: Fresh behind Weather: Overcast

3372 TURFTV H'CAP 5f
2:20 (2:21) (Class 5) (0-70,66) 3-Y-O **£2,729** (£806; £403) **Stalls** Low

Form RPR
6642 1 **Tom Folan**[6] 3174 3-8-13 **65**.......................................(p) DavidKenny(7) 7 69
(Andrew Reid) *dwlt: hld up: swtchd lft and hdwy over 1f out: rdn to ld wl ins fnl f: r.o* **11/4**[2]
3232 2 *3/4* **Pherousa**[13] 2931 3-9-6 **65**.. SteveDrowne 6 66
(M Blanshard) *chsd ldrs: rdn to ld over 1f out: edgd lft and hdd wl ins fnl f* **2/1**[1]
3354 3 *2* **Boy The Bell**[6] 3151 3-9-7 **66**.. TomQueally 2 60
(M Mullineaux) *chsd ldrs: rdn over 1f out: styd on same pce ins fnl f* **3/1**[3]
4333 4 *1/2* **Annia Galeria (IRE)**[37] 2217 3-8-5 **50**.....................(b) DavidProbert 1 42
(C A Dwyer) *chsd ldr tl led over 3f out: rdn and hdd over 1f out: no ex ins fnl f* **9/2**
056- 5 *5* **The Two G'S**[191] 7757 3-7-13 **47**........................ AndrewHeffernan(3) 4 21
(R J Price) *led: hdd over 3f out: chsd ldr tl rdn over 1f out: wknd ins fnl f* **20/1**

59.38 secs (-0.22) **Going Correction** -0.15s/f (Firm) **5 Ran SP% 107.9**
Speed ratings (Par 99): **95,93,90,89,81**
CSF £8.29 TOTE £4.90: £3.30, £1.10.
Owner Dave Clayton **Bred** Chippenham Lodge Stud Ltd **Trained** Mill Hill, London NW7

FOCUS
Four of the five runners in this minor sprint handicap had finished in the frame on their latest start, but all looked pretty exposed. The winner is rated to her latest form.

3373 STERLING SOLUTIONS H'CAP 6f
2:55 (2:56) (Class 4) (0-80,80) 3-Y-O+ **£6,476** (£1,927; £963; £481) **Stalls** Low

Form RPR
5512 1 **Favourite Girl (IRE)**[13] 2940 4-9-12 **78**......................(v) TedDurcan 9 90
(T D Easterby) *mde all: rdn and edgd lft over 1f out: r.o* **5/1**[3]
1361 2 *1 1/4* **Alfresco**[24] 2592 6-9-4 **70**.......................................(b) KierenFallon 1 78
(J R Best) *trckd ldrs: racd keenly: wnt 2nd 4f out: rdn over 1f out: unable qck wl ins fnl f* **9/2**[2]
2010 3 *1* **Charles Darwin (IRE)**[14] 2896 7-8-13 **65**...................... FrannyNorton 11 70
(M Blanshard) *chsd ldrs: rdn over 2f out: r.o* **33/1**
21-0 4 *3/4* **Alice Alleyne (IRE)**[40] 2120 3-9-4 **77**.......................... RichardMullen 14 77
(Sir Michael Stoute) *prom: rdn over 2f out: r.o* **11/1**
215- 5 *hd* **Hand Painted**[283] 5937 4-9-10 **76**..................................... TravisBlock 13 78+
(P J Makin) *hld up in tch: rdn over 1f out: r.o* **16/1**
-061 6 *2 1/4* **Miss Hollybell**[49] 1843 4-9-8 **74**.. TadhgO'Shea 4 69
(J Gallagher) *sn pushed along in rr: rdn over 2f out: r.o ins fnl f: nvr nrr* **25/1**
2343 7 *nse* **Night Trade (IRE)**[8] 3085 3-9-5 **78**......................(p) SilvestreDeSousa 5 70
(Mrs D J Sanderson) *chsd ldrs: rdn over 2f out: edgd lft and no ex ins fnl f* **7/2**[1]
3000 8 *hd* **Vhujon (IRE)**[15] 2877 5-8-13 **70**.................................. RichardEvans(5) 8 64
(P D Evans) *hld up: rdn over 1f out: nvr on terms* **14/1**
-065 9 *1/2* **Barons Spy (IRE)**[24] 2592 9-9-11 **77**.................................... JamesDoyle 3 69
(R J Price) *chsd ldrs: rdn 1/2-way: wknd ins fnl f* **8/1**
6004 10 *1* **Triple Dream**[7] 3114 5-9-8 **74**....................................(p) SteveDrowne 10 63
(J M Bradley) *hld up: rdn over 2f out: n.d* **14/1**
-000 11 *4* **Baunagain (IRE)**[10] 3037 5-10-0 **80**...................................... AlanMunro 2 56
(P W Chapple-Hyam) *dwlt: sme hdwy into mid-div over 3f out: rdn and wknd 2f out* **8/1**

1m 10.03s (-1.77) **Going Correction** -0.15s/f (Firm) course record
WFA 3 from 4yo+ 7lb **11 Ran SP% 113.6**
Speed ratings (Par 105): **105,103,102,101,100 97,97,97,96,95 90**
toteswingers:1&2 £3.50, 2&3 £5.60, 1&3 £16.90 CSF £26.72 CT £676.25 TOTE £5.90: £2.10, £2.30, £9.30; EX 21.40.
Owner Peter C Bourke **Bred** Limestone And Tara Studs **Trained** Great Habton, N Yorks

FOCUS
A fair sprint handicap. The pace was decent but the two leaders dominated and nothing got into it from behind. The time was 0.47 seconds under standard, which was partly due to a tailwind. The form is rated at face value and seems sound amongst the principals.
Vhujon(IRE) Official explanation: jockey said gelding hung right

3374 STERLING SOLUTIONS MAIDEN STKS 7f 26y
3:30 (3:35) (Class 5) 3-Y-0+ **£2,914** (£867; £433; £216) **Stalls** Low

Form RPR
3- 1 **Parvaaz (IRE)**[240] 7099 3-9-3 0.. NeilCallan 6 64+
(M A Jarvis) *s.i.s: plld hrd and sn trcking ldrs: wnt 2nd 1/2-way: led over 1f out: edgd rt: shkn up and r.o* **4/6**[1]
-200 2 *1 3/4* **Rolling Hills (IRE)**[23] 2618 3-9-3 72................................ DaneO'Neill 12 59
(H Candy) *led over 5f out: rdn and hdd over 1f out: styd on same pce ins fnl f* **3/1**[2]
3 *3/4* **Wear 'Em Out Wilf** 3-9-3 0.. AlanMunro 5 57+
(P W Chapple-Hyam) *s.s: bhd: last turning for home: hdwy and edgd rt fr over 1f out: fin wl* **10/1**[3]
40 4 *3/4* **Ruby Dazzler**[47] 1932 3-8-12 0.. SebSanders 1 50
(S Lycett) *chsd ldrs: rdn over 2f out: styd on* **33/1**
0000 5 *1 1/4* **Red Dagger (IRE)**[18] 1236 4-9-9 42............... AndrewHeffernan(3) 10 55
(R J Price) *mid-div: hdwy u.p fr over 1f out: nt rch ldrs* **66/1**
6 *3 1/4* **Tt's Dream** 3-9-3 0... KierenFallon 11 43+
(A J Lidderdale) *hld up: styd on fr over 1f out: nvr nr to chal* **12/1**
0-4 7 *3 3/4* **Mahlak (IRE)**[76] 1211 3-8-12 0... TedDurcan 13 28+
(C E Brittain) *s.i.s: hld up: shkn up over 1f out: nvr nr to chal* **12/1**
0- 8 *1/2* **Filibuster**[266] 6423 3-9-3 0.. JackMitchell 9 32
(C F Wall) *s.s: hld up: rdn over 2f out: nvr on terms* **33/1**
0/60 9 *2 1/4* **Inchmarlow (IRE)**[5] 3207 7-9-12 32......................... StephenCraine 2 29
(T H Caldwell) *led: hdd over 5f out: chsd ldr to 1/2-way: sn rdn: wknd over 1f out* **100/1**
4-00 10 *15* **Ettrick Mill**[34] 2298 4-9-12 53.. FrannyNorton 4 —
(J M Bradley) *prom: racd keenly: rdn over 2f out: wknd over 1f out* **50/1**
00-0 11 *2 1/2* **Steeple Caster**[53] 1731 4-9-9 20......................................(p) JackDean(3) 8 —
(J M Bradley) *prom: rdn over 2f out: sn wknd* **200/1**

1m 25.38s (0.78) **Going Correction** -0.15s/f (Firm)
WFA 3 from 4yo+ 9lb **11 Ran SP% 120.3**
Speed ratings (Par 103): **89,87,86,85,83 80,75,75,72,55 52**
toteswingers: 1&2 £1.50, 1&3 £6.70, 2&3 £7.20 CSF £2.77 TOTE £1.90: £1.10, £1.10, £1.70; EX 3.00.
Owner Sheikh Ahmed Al Maktoum **Bred** Darley **Trained** Newmarket, Suffolk

FOCUS
There was very little strength in depth in this maiden. The hot favourite beat his main form rival but a 42-rated performer was not far away in fifth. It is likely that the winner did not need to match his debut form.
Rolling Hills(IRE) Official explanation: jockey said gelding hung right
Wear 'Em Out Wilf Official explanation: vet said colt finished distressed
Ettrick Mill Official explanation: jockey said gelding stopped quickly

3375 RACEHORSE WARWICK PUB AND RESTAURANT ETERNAL STKS (LISTED RACE) (FILLIES) 7f 26y
4:05 (4:05) (Class 1) 3-Y-O
£22,708 (£8,608; £4,308; £2,148; £1,076; £540) **Stalls** Low

Form RPR
3-01 1 **Seta**[31] 2387 3-8-12 107... KierenFallon 2 94+
(L M Cumani) *s.i.s: sn trcking ldrs: shkn up to ld and edgd rt over 1f out: rdn out* **10/11**[1]
-052 2 *1 1/2* **Bahati (IRE)**[25] 2565 3-8-12 85..................................... StephenCraine 10 90
(J G Portman) *hld up: hdwy and hung lft fr over 2f out: rdn and ev ch 1f out: styd on same pce ins fnl f* **40/1**
-111 3 *1/2* **Dever Dream**[15] 2868 3-8-12 90.. MichaelHills 3 89
(W J Haggas) *hld up: hdwy over 1f out: rdn and edgd rt ins fnl f: r.o* **3/1**[2]
226- 4 *1 1/4* **Virginia Hall**[286] 5825 3-8-12 105... SebSanders 4 85
(Sir Mark Prescott) *chsd ldrs: rdn and nt clr run over 1f out: styng on same pce whn nt clr run towards fin* **9/1**
4500 5 *1* **Clairvoyance (IRE)**[8] 3071 3-8-12 88............................ NickyMackay 5 83
(J H M Gosden) *hld up: hdwy over 1f out: sn rdn: nt rch ldrs* **12/1**
5-10 6 *nse* **Madam Macie (IRE)**[12] 2978 3-8-12 89................... SilvestreDeSousa 1 82
(D O'Meara) *led: hdd over 4f out: chsd ldr: rdn whn hmpd over 1f out: styd on same pce* **9/1**
-235 7 *hd* **Bella Swan**[36] 2224 3-8-12 99.. TedDurcan 8 88+
(W R Swinburn) *trckd ldrs: rdn whn hmpd over 1f out: nt rcvr* **8/1**[3]
20-4 8 *hd* **Chaussini**[25] 2565 3-8-12 79... RobertHavlin 6 81?
(J A R Toller) *hld up in tch: rdn over 1f out: no imp* **50/1**
-110 9 *3/4* **Kingston Acacia**[20] 2713 3-8-12 76...............................(v) DavidProbert 7 79
(A M Balding) *chsd ldr tl led over 4f out: rdn: hdd and hmpd over 1f out: wknd ins fnl f* **33/1**

1m 22.97s (-1.63) **Going Correction** -0.15s/f (Firm) **9 Ran SP% 123.5**
Speed ratings (Par 104): **103,101,100,99,98 98,97,97,96**
toteswingers: 1&2 £12.10, 1&3 £2.30, 2&3 £18.80 CSF £58.79 TOTE £2.00: £1.40, £10.40, £1.10; EX 49.00.
Owner Miss Sarah J Leigh **Bred** Sarah J Leigh And Robin S Leigh **Trained** Newmarket, Suffolk
■ Stewards' Enquiry : Kieren Fallon caution: careless riding.

FOCUS
An average fillies' Listed race. The pace was steady and there was not much covering the whole field in the end, but the main form contender did the job in fairly impressive style and should go on to better things. The form is a bit muddling.

NOTEBOOK
Seta bounced back from a disappointing run on the wrong side of the track in the 1,000 Guineas when beating a 96-rated rival with a bit in hand in a small-field fillies' 7f conditions race at Leicester last time. She set the standard on that win, and her third in the May Hill last year, and got the job done in good style. She still has some scope for physical development and is very useful filly who has a good cruising speed and decent turn of foot. She may be able to make a big impact in Group company at 7f/1m. (tchd Evens)
Bahati(IRE), a close second off a mark of 83 in a 6f Newmarket handicap last time, ran a big race to finish surrounded by classy rivals with much higher ratings in this Listed contest. (op 33-1)

Dever Dream made it three wins from four starts when winning with plenty in hand in a 6f Kempton handicap last time. This was a big leap up in grade and a step up in trip but the well bred filly put in a commendable staying-on effort down the centre of the track. (op 4-1)
Virginia Hall firmly entered the reckoning on a close call in a Group 3 7f race at Deauville last August. She never really posed a big threat and finished behind a couple of rivals with much lower BHA ratings but she may have needed the return from 286 days off and a Group 1 Falmouth Stakes entry suggests that bigger things are expected this season. (op 12-1)
Clairvoyance(IRE), well held off 93 in a 1m fillies' Listed handicap at Royal Ascot last time, was never dangerous back at 7f in a race where she had a tricky task on the figures. She was reported to have finished distressed. Official explanation: vet said filly finished distressed (op 10-1)
Madam Macie(IRE) didn't get an easy time up front and was comfortably overhauled on her first try in Listed company. (op 11-1)
Bella Swan attracted some support but she looked short of gears when the pace increased and then got involved in a bit of trouble. She has found life tough in four skirmishes in Listed/Group company and looks on a tough mark of 99 for handicaps. (op 11-1 tchd 12-1)

3376 SUNDERBET H'CAP — 1m 2f 188y
4:40 (4:40) (Class 5) 3-Y-O — **£2,914** (£867; £433; £216) **Stalls** Low

Form — RPR

-661 **1** **Home Advantage**[38] 2168 3-9-2 **65** .... SteveDrowne 10 — 70+
(R Charlton) *hld up: hdwy over 4f out: rdn over 2f out: led ins fnl f: r.o* **2/1**[1]

3536 **2** *hd* **Spice Fair**[14] 2893 3-8-11 **60** .... NeilCallan 7 — 65+
(M D I Usher) *stdd s: hld up: hmpd over 3f out: nt clr run and hmpd again over 2f out: hdwy over 1f out: rdn and ev ch ins fnl f: r.o* **9/2**[2]

065 **3** *1* **Candotoo (IRE)**[15] 2860 3-9-4 **67** .... TomQueally 3 — 70
(J Noseda) *hld up: hdwy 1/2-way: rdn to ld and hung rt over 1f out: hdd and unable qck ins fnl f* **5/1**[3]

01-0 **4** *1* **Sidney Melbourne (USA)**[41] 2089 3-9-7 **70** .... KierenFallon 4 — 71
(J R Best) *hld up: rdn and hung rt over 1f out: r.o ins fnl f: nt rch ldrs* **11/1**

3200 **5** *1* **Laverre (IRE)**[11] 2993 3-9-7 **70** .... TedDurcan 8 — 69
(T D Easterby) *chsd ldr after 1f to over 3f out: sn rdn: styd on same pce ins fnl f* **11/1**

054 **6** *shd* **Raktiman (IRE)**[59] 1586 3-9-2 **65** .... RichardKingscote 5 — 64
(Tom Dascombe) *prom: rdn over 2f out: styd on same pce ins fnl f* **33/1**

5253 **7** *1/2* **Magic Millie (IRE)**[6] 3153 3-8-3 **52** .... SilvestreDeSousa 6 — 50
(D O'Meara) *led 1f: chsd ldrs: rdn over 2f out: no ex ins fnl f* **5/1**[3]

-250 **8** *3 3/4* **Iron Condor**[35] 2252 3-9-5 **68** .... SebSanders 2 — 60
(J M P Eustace) *pushed along to ld after 1f: rdn and hdd over 1f out: wknd ins fnl f* **9/1**

2m 19.28s (-1.82) **Going Correction** -0.15s/f (Firm) — **8** Ran SP% **114.5**
Speed ratings (Par 99): **100,99,99,98,97 97,97,94**
toteswingers: 1&2 £3.30, 1&3 £4.20, 2&3 £4.90 CSF £11.04 CT £38.58 TOTE £2.30: £1.10, £1.80, £2.80.
Owner K Abdulla **Bred** Juddmonte Farms Ltd **Trained** Beckhampton, Wilts
■ Stewards' Enquiry : Neil Callan caution: used whip without giving gelding time to respond.

FOCUS
A minor middle-distance handicap. It was run at a stop-start gallop and there was not much between the first seven who were spread across the track. The form has been taken at something like face value.

3377 WARWICK APPRENTICE H'CAP — 1m 22y
5:15 (5:15) (Class 5) (0-70,70) 4-Y-O+ — **£2,729** (£806; £403) **Stalls** Low

Form — RPR

0655 **1** **Unlimited**[13] 2920 8-8-8 **57** .... LeeTopliss(3) 2 — 64
(A W Carroll) *racd keenly: trckd ldr 7f out: rdn to ld 1f out: styd on* **11/2**[3]

-300 **2** *3/4* **Maybe I Wont**[27] 2511 5-8-7 **56** .... DavidKenny(3) 4 — 61
(Lucinda Featherstone) *hld up: hdwy 1/2-way: rdn over 1f out: r.o* **12/1**

651 **3** *2 1/2* **Croeso Cusan**[7] 3132 5-8-13 **59** 6ex .... SophieDoyle 6 — 58
(J L Spearing) *stdd s: hld up: hdwy over 1f out: wnt 3rd post: nt rch ldrs* **5/1**[2]

6600 **4** *shd* **Hilbre Court (USA)**[7] 3131 5-8-11 **57** ....(p) DeclanCannon 1 — 56
(B P J Baugh) *led: rdn over 2f out: hung rt and hdd 1f out: styd on same pce: lost 3rd post* **14/1**

045 **5** *1 1/2* **Opera Prince**[17] 2821 5-9-7 **70** .... TobyAtkinson(3) 5 — 66
(Lady Herries) *chsd ldrs: rdn over 2f out: no ex ins fnl f* **11/8**[1]

0001 **6** *4 1/2* **Tanforan**[15] 2864 8-9-2 **62** .... BillyCray 9 — 47
(B P J Baugh) *prom: lost pl over 5f out: hdwy 1/2-way: rdn over 2f out: wknd ins fnl f* **15/2**

630/ **7** *15* **Woodcraft**[69] 5450 6-9-2 **65** .... JohnCavanagh(3) 7 — 16
(Mark Buckley) *hld up: wknd 1/2-way* **11/1**

0000 **8** *72* **Affirmatively**[3] 3254 5-8-0 **51** oh6 ....(p) RyanPowell(5) 8 — —
(A W Carroll) *prom: racd keenly: rdn and wknd over 4f out: t.o* **40/1**

1m 41.1s (0.10) **Going Correction** -0.15s/f (Firm) — **8** Ran SP% **111.1**
Speed ratings (Par 103): **93,92,89,89,88 83,68,—**
toteswingers:1&2 £10.90, 2&3 £6.90, 1&3 £4.60 CSF £63.62 CT £336.89 TOTE £5.00: £2.20, £3.60, £2.00; EX 69.90 Place 6: £16.14 Place 5: £10.85.
Owner M B Clarke **Bred** J Wise **Trained** Cropthorne, Worcs
■ Stewards' Enquiry : David Kenny one-day ban: used whip with excessive frequency (Jul 8)

FOCUS
A weak apprentice handicap. The pace was steady and the hold-up runners struggled to get involved. The form is rated around the runner-up.
Opera Prince Official explanation: jockey said gelding lost a shoe
Woodcraft Official explanation: jockey said gelding finished lame
Affirmatively Official explanation: jockey said mare ran too free
T/Plt: £10.10 to a £1 stake. Pool: £47,039.33 - 3,379.06 winning tickets. T/Qpdt: £3.80 to a £1 stake. Pool:£2,151.29 - 411.91 winning tickets. CR

3378 - 3385a (Foreign Racing) - See Raceform Interactive

[2309]CHESTER (L-H)
Friday, June 25

OFFICIAL GOING: Good to firm (watered; 8.4)
Wind: Nil Weather: Hot and Sunny

3386 TETLEY'S BITTER MAIDEN FILLIES' STKS — 7f 2y
6:40 (6:42) (Class 4) 2-Y-O — **£4,047** (£1,204; £601; £300) **Stalls** Low

Form — RPR

1 **Cheque Book** 2-9-0 0 .... MichaelHills 8 — 72+
(B W Hills) *midfield: rdn and hdwy over 1f out: edgd rt and led ins fnl f: r.o and in command towards fin* **15/2**

034 **2** *1 1/4* **Hoppy's Flyer (FR)**[23] 2641 2-9-0 0 .... RichardKingscote 1 — 69
(Tom Dascombe) *led: jnd fr jst over 4f out: rdn and hung rt fr over 1f out: hdd ins fnl f: nt pce of wnr towards fin* **4/1**[2]

35 **3** *hd* **Little Miss Take**[58] 1626 2-8-9 0 .... RossAtkinson(5) 7 — 68
(Tom Dascombe) *hld up: pushed along over 2f out: hdwy over 1f out: r.o ins fnl f: nvr gng to get there* **20/1**

6 **4** *nk* **Dazzling Valentine**[6] 3219 2-9-0 0 .... FrannyNorton 11 — 67+
(A Bailey) *towards rr: rdn and hdwy over 1f out: drifted rt ins fnl f: styd on: nt quite pce to get there* **16/1**

503 **5** *1 3/4* **Apazine (USA)**[13] 2958 2-9-0 0 .... WilliamBuick 5 — 63
(J H M Gosden) *chsd ldr: moved upsides over 4f out: rdn over 1f out: nt qckning whn carried rt jst ins fnl f: no ex fnl 100yds* **5/2**[1]

6 **6** *2 1/2* **My Elliemay**[24] 2616 2-9-0 0 .... SilvestreDeSousa 9 — 57+
(P D Evans) *missed break: in rr: pushed along 4f out: styd on steadily ins fnl f: nvr rchd ldrs* **16/1**

6 **7** *1* **Smart Red**[20] 2740 2-9-0 0 .... AlanMunro 4 — 54
(M R Channon) *chsd ldrs: rdn 3f out: one pce ins fnl f* **6/1**[3]

020 **8** *1 1/2* **Dancing Tara**[45] 1999 2-9-0 0 .... CathyGannon 6 — 50
(P D Evans) *racd on outer: chsd ldrs: pushed along over 3f out: rdn and wknd over 1f out* **66/1**

54 **9** *shd* **Al Andalyya (USA)**[20] 2749 2-9-0 0 .... ShaneKelly 10 — 50+
(D R Lanigan) *hld up: pushed along over 4f out: effrt and hdwy into midfield on outer over 2f out: no imp on ldrs: wknd over 1f out* **7/1**

1m 26.68s (0.18) **Going Correction** -0.20s/f (Firm) — **9** Ran SP% **105.1**
Speed ratings (Par 92): **90,88,88,88,86 83,82,80,80**
Tote Swingers: 1&2 £5.40, 1&3 £18.90, 2&3 £13.70 CSF £31.04 TOTE £6.70: £1.90, £1.30, £7.30; EX 30.30.Lexi's Princess was withdrawn. Price at time of withdrawal 6/1. Rule 4 applies to all bets. Deduction - 10p in the pound.
Owner Morecombe,Anderson,Netherthorpe & Mahal **Bred** Shortgrove Manor Stud **Trained** Lambourn, Berks
■ Lexi's Princess was withdrawn (6/1, unruly at s). R4 applies, deduct 10p in the £.

FOCUS
There was an ordinary gallop until halfway, but they were really racing after that, with the prize going to the only debutante. The field was compressed at the line and this is no more than fair form.

NOTEBOOK
Cheque Book, by Araafa out of a Desert Prince mare, took a while to get going but found a handy run reasonably close to the rail and won convincingly. This track provides a good test and education of an inexperienced juvenile, so she can be expected to improve quite a bit. (op 5-1)
Hoppy's Flyer(FR) made most until hanging right in the home straight but, while that was an inconvenience, it did not cost her the race. Having shown gradual improvement in maidens, she could probably still win one if connections decide not to go for a nursery. She just about got the 7f but a drop back to 6f would not be a problem. Official explanation: jockey said filly hung right-handed (op 5-1 tchd 7-2)
Little Miss Take, recovering late on after an awkward start, stayed the extra 2f well and could win a routine maiden. However, she is now qualified for nurseries. (op 25-1 tchd 18-1)
Dazzling Valentine, running well from the worst draw, had shown ability on her debut and looks likely to improve enough to win a race, this time showing that she stays 7f well. She will have a handicap mark after one more run.
Apazine(USA) was not helped when the runner-up carried her right-handed in the straight, but in no way was she unlucky. More relevantly, 6f probably suits her better at present. (op 11-4 tchd 3-1 and 10-3 in places)
My Elliemay has shown some ability in two maidens and will be more interesting when qualified for nurseries. (op 28-1)
Smart Red was no more convincing over this extra furlong than she had been at 6f on her debut, but what she needs more than anything is a handicap mark. (op 17-2)
Al Andalyya(USA), stuck wide all the way from a tough stall, ran pretty well in the circumstances and is one to consider if she switches to nurseries next time. (op 8-1)

3387 DOUBLETREE BY HILTON CHESTER H'CAP — 7f 122y
7:15 (7:15) (Class 5) (0-70,70) 3-Y-O — **£4,047** (£1,204; £601; £300) **Stalls** Low

Form — RPR

3456 **1** **Another Magic Man (USA)**[15] 2888 3-9-0 **68** .... KierenFox(5) 10 — 74
(J R Best) *chsd ldr: led over 5f out: mde rest: rdn whn hrd pressed over 1f out: plld out more and styd on gamely fnl 100yds* **13/2**[3]

0-23 **2** *1 1/4* **Rasselas (IRE)**[15] 2899 3-9-7 **70** .... MichaelHills 3 — 73+
(B W Hills) *awkward leaving stalls and s.i.s: racd in last pl: pushed along over 2f out: carried hd to one side: hdwy ent fnl f: fin strly: nt rch wnr* **7/2**[1]

-266 **3** *nk* **Jimmy The Poacher (IRE)**[17] 2834 3-9-4 **67** ....(b[1]) DavidNolan 11 — 69
(T D Easterby) *led: hdd over 5f out: continued to press wnr: rdn ent fnl f: nt qckn and lost battle w wnr 100yds out: no ex dying strides* **14/1**

3002 **4** *nse* **Dazeen**[17] 2834 3-9-2 **65** .... TonyCulhane 5 — 67
(P T Midgley) *hld up: rdn and hdwy over 1f out: hung lft ins fnl f: r.o u.p and gng on at fin* **12/1**

0315 **5** *1 3/4* **Hathaway (IRE)**[9] 3073 3-8-9 **58** .... ShaneKelly 1 — 56
(W M Brisbourne) *midfield: pushed along 5f out: outpcd over 2f out: styd on ins fnl f: no imp on ldrs: one pce fnl 50yds* **5/1**[2]

-014 **6** *3/4* **Ellies Image**[17] 2834 3-8-11 **60** .... J-PGuillambert 7 — 56
(B P J Baugh) *in tch: rdn and nt qckn over 1f out: fdd ins fnl f* **14/1**

-643 **7** *nk* **Saxby (IRE)**[5] 3243 3-9-5 **68** .... SilvestreDeSousa 6 — 63
(G A Harker) *chsd ldrs: pushed along 5f out: rdn over 2f out: no ex fnl 100yds* **8/1**

2005 **8** *3/4* **Elegant Dancer (IRE)**[6] 3205 3-8-3 **52** .... FrannyNorton 4 — 45
(Paul Green) *towards rr: rdn 2f out: kpt on ins fnl f: nvr able to trble ldrs* **14/1**

-002 **9** *1/2* **Pintura**[16] 2863 3-9-5 **68** .... StevieDonohoe 8 — 60
(D M Simcock) *towards rr: pushed along 4f out: kpt on ins fnl f: nt pce to trble ldrs* **7/1**

5004 **10** *3/4* **Barnstorm**[9] 3073 3-8-11 **60** .... JoeFanning 12 — 50
(M Johnston) *wnt rt s: ref to settle: chsd ldrs: rdn over 1f out: wknd ins fnl f* **14/1**

0600 **11** *4* **Transfixed (IRE)**[4] 3276 3-9-0 **68** ....(p) RichardEvans(5) 2 — 54
(P D Evans) *midfield: pushed along over 3f out: rdn and wknd over 1f out: eased whn btn ins fnl f* **16/1**

1m 31.91s (-1.89) **Going Correction** -0.20s/f (Firm) — **11** Ran SP% **116.1**
Speed ratings (Par 99): **101,99,99,99,97 96,96,95,95,94 90**
Tote Swingers: 1&2 £5.10, 1&3 £17.60, 2&3 £9.60 CSF £29.04 CT £315.48 TOTE £7.10: £2.00, £1.60, £4.00.
Owner Hucking Horses **Bred** Coronach Farm **Trained** Hucking, Kent

FOCUS
A weakish handicap. There was a good gallop but one of the two pacemakers still held on to win from a poor draw. There are one or two doubts over the form.
Rasselas(IRE) ◆ Official explanation: jockey said gelding missed the break
Saxby(IRE) Official explanation: jockey said gelding hung right-handed

Transfixed(IRE) Official explanation: jockey said filly hung right-handed

3388 EUROPEAN BREEDERS' FUND FILLIES' H'CAP 1m 2f 75y
7:45 (7:47) (Class 3) (0-90,89) 3-Y-0+ £9,714 (£2,890; £1,444; £721) Stalls High

Form RPR

3531 1 **Desert Kiss**[21] 2703 5-10-0 **89**.......... ShaneKelly 3 95
(W R Swinburn) *mde all: rdn over 1f out: r.o wl and in command ins fnl f* **5/2**[2]

0311 2 1 ¼ **Granny McPhee**[11] 3040 4-9-0 **75** 6ex.......... FrannyNorton 6 78
(A Bailey) *swtchd lft s: in rr: hdwy over 2f out: wnt 2nd 1f out: styd on ins fnl f but nvr a real threat to wnr* **11/2**[3]

0-22 3 1 ¼ **Sing Sweetly**[20] 2758 3-8-9 **82**.......... WilliamBuick 5 83
(G A Butler) *racd keenly: chsd wnr: rdn and hung lft whn nt qckn over 1f out: lost 2nd 1f out: kpt on same pce fnl 100yds* **5/6**[1]

0560 4 ¾ **Bagutta Sun**[6] 3203 4-8-13 **74**.......... RichardKingscote 2 73
(Tom Dascombe) *chsd ldrs: rdn and outpcd over 2f out: kpt on ins fnl f but no real imp* **16/1**

136 5 2 **Hollow Green (IRE)**[35] 2282 4-9-2 **82**.......... RichardEvans(5) 4 77
(P D Evans) *hld up: outpcd over 2f out: sn lft wl bhd* **11/1**

2m 9.87s (-2.33) **Going Correction** -0.20s/f (Firm)
WFA 3 from 4yo+ 12lb 5 Ran SP% **112.7**
Speed ratings (Par 104): **101,100,99,98,96**
CSF £16.16 TOTE £3.70: £1.40, £1.80; EX 10.30.
Owner The Capers **Bred** C R Mason **Trained** Aldbury, Herts

FOCUS
The pace was disappointing for the quality, helping the winner to make all. She recorded a length personal best.

NOTEBOOK
Desert Kiss dictated the modest tempo and was in control all the way, quickening it up in the last 4f and readily seeing off the late challenge of the runner-up. She has done particularly well since stepping up to 1m2f and, while she had the run of the race, she is indisputably progressive at the trip. (tchd 3-1)
Granny McPhee stays 1m4f, so the slack tempo would have been an inconvenience at this shorter trip. In the circumstances, although she never quite looked like overhauling the winner, it was a good effort under a 6lb penalty for winning by a neck last time. (op 4-1 tchd 6-1)
Sing Sweetly sat closest to the winner and was therefore in the best tactical position of the others in a modestly run race, but she was comfortably outpaced when the tempo quickened. She deserves one more chance with a stronger gallop, at either this trip or 1m4f, but it is possible that her handicap mark is too high. (op 6-5 tchd 5-4 in places)
Bagutta Sun, who has hardly been flying this year, ran quite a bit better than could have been expected. She may be finding some form at long last. (op 12-1)
Hollow Green(IRE) has been below her best on fast ground in her last two races. (op 10-1 tchd 12-1)

3389 FREEBETS.CO.UK H'CAP 7f 2y
8:20 (8:20) (Class 4) (0-85,85) 4-Y-0+ £4,533 (£1,348; £674; £336) Stalls Low

Form RPR

5103 1 **Opus Maximus (IRE)**[7] 3150 5-9-9 **85**.......... JoeFanning 8 93
(M Johnston) *trckd ldrs: effrt over 1f out: styd on to ld ins fnl f: a doing enough cl home* **6/1**[2]

6610 2 ½ **Bahamian Lad**[13] 2982 5-8-8 **70**..........(p) JerryO'Dwyer 2 76
(R Hollinshead) *w ldr: rdn to ld over 1f out: hdd ins fnl f: kpt on u.p: hld cl home* **15/2**[3]

3335 3 ½ **My Gacho (IRE)**[8] 3117 8-9-8 **84**.......... J-PGuillambert 11 89
(M Johnston) *in tch: outpcd 2f out: rdn 1f out: styd on ins fnl f: nt quite pce to get to front pair* **14/1**

4103 4 hd **Lucky Dan (IRE)**[8] 3114 4-9-0 **76**.......... FrannyNorton 3 83+
(Paul Green) *trckd ldrs: swtchd lft to chal over 1f out: sn n.m.r and hmpd: lost grnd: got gng again and rallied towards fin* **6/1**[2]

010 5 nse **Imprimis Tagula (IRE)**[11] 3037 6-8-5 **74**..........(v) NatashaEaton(7) 10 78
(A Bailey) *pushed along to sn ld: rdn and hdd over 1f out: continued to chal ins fnl f: nt qckn fnl 50yds* **20/1**

4206 6 shd **Rio Cobolo (IRE)**[15] 2885 4-8-9 **71**..........(v) SilvestreDeSousa 7 75
(Paul Green) *midfield: pushed along 3f out: rdn and hdwy over 1f out: kpt on towards fin: nt quite pce of ldrs* **8/1**

5443 7 1 ¼ **Fathsta (IRE)**[34] 2327 5-9-9 **85**.......... StevieDonohoe 13 86
(D M Simcock) *midfield: rdn and outpcd 2f out: styd on ins fnl f: nt pce to get to ldrs* **14/1**

0005 8 ½ **Desert Dreamer (IRE)**[15] 2885 9-8-12 **79**.......... RichardEvans(5) 4 80
(P D Evans) *s.i.s: in rr: pushed along over 3f out: rdn over 1f out: trying to prog whn nt clr run fnl 75yds: nvr a threat* **8/1**

-042 9 hd **Aldermoor (USA)**[6] 3224 4-9-8 **84**.......... AlanMunro 12 86
(S C Williams) *midfield: rdn over 1f out: keeping on whn n.m.r fnl 100yds: sn eased* **8/1**

0-00 10 ½ **Mr Macattack**[20] 2736 5-9-4 **80**..........(t) RichardKingscote 9 77
(Tom Dascombe) *dwlt: towards rr: effrt whn nt clr run over 1f out: styd on ins fnl f: nt trble ldrs* **14/1**

0000 11 ½ **Block Party**[16] 2872 4-8-9 **71**..........(v) WilliamBuick 1 69
(D M Simcock) *hld up: pushed along over 1f out: no imp whn eased fnl 75yds* **9/2**[1]

3005 12 14 **Bel Cantor**[16] 2877 7-9-1 **80**..........(p) KellyHarrison(3) 6 38
(W J H Ratcliffe) *w ldr: rdn and wknd 2f out* **33/1**

5040 13 20 **Jesse James (IRE)**[14] 2926 4-9-3 **79**..........(p) MichaelHills 5 —
(J R Gask) *towards rr: bhd 4f out: lost tch over 2f out* **12/1**

1m 24.15s (-2.35) **Going Correction** -0.20s/f (Firm) course record 13 Ran SP% **127.2**
Speed ratings (Par 105): **105,104,103,103,103 103,102,101,101,100 100,84,61**
Tote Swingers: 1&2 £11.10, 1&3 £16.50, 2&3 £22.70 CSF £54.18 CT £646.89 TOTE £6.60: £2.00, £3.00, £5.90; EX 72.80.
Owner Jim McGrath **Bred** Mrs Anne Marie Burns **Trained** Middleham Moor, N Yorks

FOCUS
A competitive race run at a good gallop. There was a bunch finish and several were denied clear runs. The form is rated around the second and third.
Lucky Dan(IRE) Official explanation: jockey said gelding suffered interference in home straight
Desert Dreamer(IRE) Official explanation: vet said gelding bled from the nose
Block Party Official explanation: jockey said gelding was denied a clear run

3390 HOLLYOAKS H'CAP 1m 2f 75y
8:50 (8:52) (Class 5) (0-70,70) 3-Y-0 £4,047 (£1,204; £601; £300) Stalls High

Form RPR

2123 1 **Layla's Lexi**[35] 2288 3-9-7 **68**.......... PaulMulrennan 1 73
(Ian Williams) *chsd ldrs: wnt 2nd 2f out: rdn to ld fnl 100yds: r.o wl towards fin* **7/1**[3]

-545 2 1 ½ **Sandy Shaw**[15] 2901 3-9-3 **64**.......... MichaelHills 3 67
(J W Hills) *led: rdn over 1f out: edgd lft ins fnl f: hdd fnl 100yds: no ex cl home* **13/2**[2]

3324 3 shd **Dazakhee**[21] 2702 3-9-0 **61**.......... TonyCulhane 14 63+
(P T Midgley) *dwlt: in rr: rdn and hdwy over 1f out: r.o ins fnl f: gng on at fin* **8/1**

6440 4 hd **New Code**[14] 2935 3-9-2 **63**.......... ShaneKelly 12 65
(W R Muir) *midfield: hdwy 2f out: chsd ldrs over 1f out: nt qckn fnl 100yds: sn swtchd rt: styd on towards fin* **16/1**

6-00 5 ¾ **Green Community (USA)**[62] 1537 3-8-13 **60**.......... J-PGuillambert 7 61
(E F Vaughan) *midfield: hdwy over 1f out: styd on ins fnl f: one pce cl home: nt get to ldrs* **25/1**

0011 6 ¾ **Princess Lexi (IRE)**[19] 2780 3-8-7 **54**.......... StevieDonohoe 5 58+
(Ian Williams) *chsd ldrs: rdn 3f out: pushed along over 2f out: prog to chal on inner whn n.m.r and hmpd 100yds out: sn eased* **13/2**[2]

3050 7 nk **Epic (IRE)**[18] 2816 3-9-5 **66**..........(b[1]) JoeFanning 11 65
(M Johnston) *racd keenly: towards rr: hdwy into midfield 7f out: rdn 2f out: kpt on fnl f: no imp on ldrstr* **14/1**

5-25 8 ¾ **Emerald Glade (IRE)**[30] 2438 3-8-6 **56**.......... KellyHarrison(3) 9 53
(T D Easterby) *s.i.s: bhd: pushed along over 4f out: rdn over 1f out: kpt on ins fnl f: nvr able to get on terms w ldrs* **16/1**

0042 9 1 **Abhar (USA)**[7] 3160 3-8-8 **60**.......... KierenFox(5) 10 55
(J R Best) *chsd ldr to 2f out: rdn over 1f out: wknd ins fnl f* **7/2**[1]

3653 10 hd **Sultan's Choice**[16] 2878 3-8-6 **53**..........(v) CathyGannon 13 48
(P D Evans) *towards rr: hdwy into midfield over 1f out: no imp fnl f* **20/1**

50-0 11 4 ½ **Lava Lamp (GER)**[15] 2884 3-9-9 **70**..........(v[1]) SilvestreDeSousa 6 56
(G A Harker) *dwlt: a bhd* **14/1**

6356 12 1 ¼ **Bubbly Braveheart (IRE)**[7] 3171 3-9-8 **69**..........(b) FrannyNorton 4 53
(A Bailey) *chsd ldrs: rdn over 2f out: wknd over 1f out* **15/2**

3160 13 8 **Posy Fossil (USA)**[16] 2871 3-9-2 **63**..........(t) AlanMunro 8 32
(S C Williams) *towards rr: struggling over 2f out: bhd fnl f* **25/1**

2m 10.03s (-2.17) **Going Correction** -0.20s/f (Firm) 13 Ran SP% **121.8**
Speed ratings (Par 99): **100,98,98,98,97 97,97,96,95,95 91,90,84**
Tote Swingers: 1&2 £8.50, 1&3 £14.40, 2&3 £7.70 CSF £51.73 CT £376.49 TOTE £6.70: £2.20, £2.60, £2.90; EX 65.70.
Owner Dr Marwan Koukash **Bred** Plantation Stud **Trained** Portway, Worcs

FOCUS
A strong early gallop soon had them stretched out by 15-20 lengths, although it did calm down a bit after the first 3f and the first two home were prominent throughout. Ordinary form, the winner rated up 4lb.

3391 CRUISE NIGHTSPOT H'CAP 7f 122y
9:20 (9:22) (Class 5) (0-70,69) 4-Y-0+ £4,047 (£1,204; £601; £300) Stalls Low

Form RPR

133- 1 **Feeling Fresh (IRE)**[321] 4772 5-9-1 **60**.......... SilvestreDeSousa 7 68
(Paul Green) *midfield: n.m.r and hmpd over 1f out: prog ins fnl f whn swtchd rt: r.o to ld fnl 100yds: rdr dropped hands briefly fnl strides: jst hld on* **8/1**

1-00 2 shd **Dragon Slayer (IRE)**[34] 2314 8-9-10 **69**.......... StevieDonohoe 15 77
(John A Harris) *missed break: swtchd lft s: bhd: hdwy over 1f out: str run ins fnl f: jst failed* **25/1**

3326 3 1 ½ **I Confess**[49] 1877 5-9-10 **69**..........(b) FrannyNorton 9 73
(Jim Best) *chsd ldrs: pushed along 3f out: rdn over 1f out: styd on ins fnl f: nt qckn cl home* **13/2**[3]

1302 4 hd **Saving Grace**[16] 2859 4-8-7 **55**.......... KellyHarrison(3) 13 59
(E J Alston) *midfield: rdn and hdwy over 1f out: styd on ins fnl f: nt rch ldrs* **12/1**

0020 5 2 **Glenridding**[10] 3061 6-9-10 **69**..........(p) PaulMulrennan 6 68
(J G Given) *led: rdn 2f out: hdd fnl 100yds: wknd cl home* **7/1**

-503 5 dht **Many Welcomes**[16] 2875 5-8-5 **55**.......... JemmaMarshall(5) 4 54
(B P J Baugh) *towards rr: effrt on wd outside wl over 2f out: hdwy over 1f out: styd on ins fnl f: nt get to ldrs* **8/1**

4363 7 nse **Spavento (IRE)**[10] 3061 4-8-13 **58**..........(p) ShaneKelly 3 57
(E J Alston) *chsd ldrs: pushed along over 3f out: rdn and nt qckn over 1f out: kpt on same pce ins fnl f* **7/2**[1]

1003 8 1 ¾ **Border Owl (IRE)**[25] 2580 5-9-6 **65**.......... GregFairley 11 59
(P Salmon) *pressed ldr: stl chalng over 1f out: wknd fnl 100yds* **16/1**

2510 9 hd **War And Peace (IRE)**[17] 2846 6-9-4 **68**.......... RichardEvans(5) 8 73+
(P D Evans) *midfield: hdwy whn n.m.r and hmpd over 1f out: styng on whn nt clr run fnl 75yds: sn eased* **14/1**

1000 10 2 ¼ **Portrush Storm**[14] 2920 5-8-1 **51** oh1 ow1..........(p) KierenFox(5) 14 39
(R E Peacock) *towards rr: rdn on wd outside wl over 2f out: nvr able to rch ldrs* **33/1**

-506 11 1 ¼ **Champain Sands (IRE)**[16] 2864 11-8-3 **53**.......... PaulPickard(5) 10 38
(E J Alston) *missed break: a bhd: nt clr run over 1f out: no imp* **33/1**

0310 12 4 ½ **Elusive Fame (USA)**[27] 2524 4-9-7 **66**..........(b) JoeFanning 1 40
(M Johnston) *chsd ldrs tl rdn and wknd 2f out* **5/1**[2]

6-00 13 9 **Lily Wood**[8] 3129 4-8-5 **50**..........(v) CathyGannon 5 —
(J W Unett) *chsd ldrs: rdn over 5f out: wknd over 2f out: eased whn btn over 1f out* **20/1**

1m 32.6s (-1.20) **Going Correction** -0.20s/f (Firm) 13 Ran SP% **121.7**
Speed ratings (Par 103): **98,97,96,96,94 94,94,92,92,89 88,84,75**
Tote Swingers: 1&2 £128.20, 1&3 £10.70, 2&3 £46.20 CSF £201.87 CT £1426.12 TOTE £7.60: £2.20, £7.00, £2.50; EX 234.30 Place 6: £527.52 Place 5: £180.48 .
Owner Paul Green (Oaklea) **Bred** J Mahon **Trained** Lydiate, Merseyside

FOCUS
The two front-runners, Border Owl and Glenridding, pelted off in front, going too fast in the process and setting the race up for the come-from-behind performers. The winner's best effort since he was a 3yo.
Lily Wood Official explanation: trainer said filly hung right, unsuited by the track and the good to firm ground
T/Jkpt: Not won. T/Plt: £650.10 to a £1 stake. Pool: £68,534.79 - 76.95 winning tickets T/Qpdt: £53.90 to a £1 stake. Pool: £4,212.96 - 57.78 winning tickets DO

2990 DONCASTER (L-H)
Friday, June 25

OFFICIAL GOING: Good (good to firm in places; 8.4)
Wind: Virtually nil Weather: Warm and dry

3392 CONSUMER AND PERSONAL INJURY SOLICITORS E B F MAIDEN FILLIES' STKS 6f
2:20 (2:24) (Class 5) 2-Y-0 £3,561 (£1,059; £529; £264) Stalls High

Form RPR

1 **Tanfeer** 2-9-0 0.......... FrankieDettori 1 77+
(Saeed Bin Suroor) *wnt lft s: sn trcking ldrs: smooth hdwy on outer over 2f out: led wl over 1f out: rdn and edgd lft ins fnl f: kpt on strly* **4/6**[1]

5 **2** 2 **Bakoura**[28] 2505 2-9-0 0 ...... RichardHills 2 65
(J L Dunlop) *a.p: effrt to dispute ld 2f out: sn rdn and ev ch tl one pce ins fnl f* **4/1**[2]

62 **3** 1 1/4 **Royal Liaison**[13] 2958 2-9-0 0 ...... HayleyTurner 6 61
(M L W Bell) *cl up: led after 1f: rdn along 2f out: sn hdd and kpt on same pce* **4/1**[2]

4 nse **Loukoumi** 2-9-0 0 ...... RoystonFfrench 4 61
(B Smart) *chsd ldrs: rdn along and outpcd over 2f out: kpt on u.p ins fnl f* **25/1**

65 **5** 3/4 **Evening Dress**[29] 2448 2-9-0 0 ...... JoeFanning 7 59
(M Johnston) *slt ld 1f: cl up tl rdn along over 2f out and grad wknd* **20/1**[3]

6 3 1/4 **Bilidn** 2-9-0 0 ...... NeilCallan 3 49
(C E Brittain) *dwlt and towards rr: hdwy 1/2-way and sn pushed along: rdn 2f out and sn no imp* **20/1**[3]

7 1/2 **Bigalo's Laura B (IRE)** 2-9-0 0 ...... (e[1]) DuranFentiman 5 48
(L A Mullaney) *chsd ldrs: rdn along wl over 2f out: sn wknd* **100/1**

8 9 **Deva Le Deva (IRE)** 2-9-0 0 ...... RichardKingscote 8 21
(Tom Dascombe) *dwlt: sn pushed along: bhd fr 1/2-way* **22/1**

1m 12.98s (-0.62) **Going Correction** -0.35s/f (Firm) **8** Ran SP% **118.7**
Speed ratings (Par 90): **90,87,85,85,84 80,79,67**
Tote Swingers: 1&2 £2.00, 2&3 £2.10 CSF £3.51 TOTE £1.80: £1.20, £1.20, £1.10; EX 4.70 Trifecta £7.80 Pool: £750.92 - 70.62 winning units..
Owner Godolphin **Bred** Shadwell Estate Co Ltd **Trained** Newmarket, Suffolk

FOCUS
An average juvenile fillies' maiden and a comfortable debut winner. It is debatable what strength in depth there was to the race.

NOTEBOOK
Tanfeer ran out an easy winner. This well-bred daughter of Dansili was backed as though defeat was not an option for this racecourse debut, and she was always in control after being asked to assert nearing the final furlong. She doesn't have much scope, but clearly does possess an engine and should only learn for the initial experience. (op 8-11 tchd 8-13)
Bakoura, fifth on debut at Newmarket 28 days earlier, still showed real signs of inexperience beforehand and in the race itself. She wasn't given a hard time when it became apparent her chance of winning had gone, but rates a clear second-best and she too should go forward again for the experience. (tchd 9-2)
Royal Liaison showed improved form when second in ordinary company at Leicester 13 days previously, but had finished one place behind the runner-up on debut and was never going to reverse that form. She ought to find her feet when the nurseries begin. (tchd 9-2)
Loukoumi ◆ is one to take from the race. She knew her job, but got badly outpaced as the race was getting serious. She stayed on with purpose late in the day, though, and looks sure to improve a deal for the outing. (op 20-1)
Evening Dress was having her third run and got readily outpaced when the first pair kicked 2f out.
Bilidn is bred to enjoy further in time and has scope. She proved very easy to back and ran accordingly. (op 16-1)

3393 TRADE UNIONS, DEFENDING RIGHTS AT WORK H'CAP 6f
2:50 (2:55) (Class 5) (0-70,70) 3-Y-O **£2,590** (£770; £385; £192) **Stalls** High

Form RPR

56-6 **1** **Dies Solis**[38] 2209 3-8-5 **54** ...... PaulHanagan 3 60
(N Wilson) *t.k.h: trckd ldrs: hdwy and cl up 1/2-way: rdn to ld 1 1/2f out: drvn ins fnl f: hld on wl* **8/1**

-040 **2** nk **Kings 'n Dreams**[26] 2566 3-9-5 **68** ...... (b[1]) RyanMoore 11 73
(D K Ivory) *hld up in tch: hdwy whn nt clr run and swtchd rt to stands' rail wl over 1f out: sn drvn and styd on strly ins fnl f: jst hld* **10/1**

0446 **3** 1/2 **Tislaam (IRE)**[24] 2634 3-8-6 **58** ...... (p) BarryMcHugh[(3)] 7 61
(J S Wainwright) *hld up in tch: hdwy over 2f out: rdn wl over 1f out: kpt on ins fnl f* **6/1**[2]

00-0 **4** hd **Swansea Jack**[31] 2425 3-8-2 **51** oh1 ...... (t) AndreaAtzeni 5 53
(S C Williams) *in tch: hdwy to chse ldrs 1/2-way: rdn 2f out: drvn and ev ch ent fnl f: no ex fnl 100yds* **13/2**[3]

3606 **5** 1 **Itsthursdayalready**[11] 3030 3-9-0 **63** ...... (b) PaulMulrennan 2 62
(J G Given) *hld up towards rr: hdwy over 2f out: sn rdn and kpt on ins fnl f: nrst fin* **10/1**

2525 **6** 2 1/4 **Drumpellier (IRE)**[7] 3167 3-8-6 **60** ...... PaulPickard[(5)] 10 52
(P T Midgley) *racd nr stands' rail: prom: effrt over 2f out: sn rdn and hung lft: drvn and one pce appr fnl f* **13/2**[3]

5-00 **7** 2 1/4 **On The Piste (IRE)**[24] 2628 3-8-8 **60** ...... GaryBartley[(3)] 6 45
(L A Mullaney) *prom: rdn along 1/2-way: drvn over 2f out and sn wknd* **40/1**

0224 **8** 1 **Bilash**[34] 2309 3-9-7 **70** ...... JerryO'Dwyer 4 52
(R Hollinshead) *led: rdn along over 2f out: hdd 1 1/2f out: sn drvn and wknd appr fnl f* **9/1**

5231 **9** 3 1/2 **Red Scintilla**[11] 3030 3-9-4 **67** 6ex ...... KierenFallon 1 37
(N Tinkler) *in tch: effrt and hdwy to chse ldrs on outer wl over 2f out: sn rdn and wknd* **9/4**[1]

60-0 **10** 8 **Daisy Brown**[13] 2962 3-8-0 **52** ...... KellyHarrison[(3)] 9 —
(N Tinkler) *chsd ldrs: rdn along bef 1/2-way: sn wknd and bhd* **40/1**

1m 11.62s (-1.98) **Going Correction** -0.35s/f (Firm) **10** Ran SP% **115.9**
Speed ratings (Par 99): **99,98,97,97,96 93,90,89,84,73**
Tote Swingers: 1&2 not won, 1&3 not won, 2&3 not won CSF £84.51 CT £523.14 TOTE £10.80: £3.10, £3.90, £3.20; EX 110.80 Trifecta £390.00 Part won. Pool: £527.06 - 0.66 winning units..
Owner A Gauley **Bred** Miss L A Perratt **Trained** Sandhutton, N Yorks

FOCUS
An open but modest sprint handicap. The field came more towards the stands' side and the first and second raced centre and on the rail respectively, so there was no bias. Slight improvement from the winner.
Red Scintilla Official explanation: jockey said filly ran flat
Daisy Brown Official explanation: jockey said filly ran too freely

3394 CW RACING CLUB H'CAP 7f
3:25 (3:28) (Class 4) (0-80,79) 3-Y-O **£4,533** (£1,348; £674; £336) **Stalls** High

Form RPR

-614 **1** **Brannagh (USA)**[29] 2466 3-9-5 **77** ...... (t) PaulHanagan 6 88
(J Noseda) *hld up: smooth hdwy to trck ldrs 1/2-way: effrt to ld 2f out: rdn and edgd rt appr fnl f: sn clr* **10/3**[3]

514 **2** 3 3/4 **Timeless Stride (IRE)**[23] 2656 3-9-3 **75** ...... RyanMoore 4 76
(Sir Michael Stoute) *trckd ldrs: hdwy to chse wnr wl over 1f out: sn drvn and no imp fnl f* **2/1**[1]

1P06 **3** 1/2 **Call To Arms (IRE)**[25] 2599 3-9-3 **75** ...... JoeFanning 1 75
(M Johnston) *cl up on outer: rdn to ld briefly 2 1/2f out: sn hdd and drvn: wknd over 1f out* **16/1**

4162 **4** 2 1/4 **Hot Spark**[15] 2884 3-9-6 **78** ...... (t) NeilCallan 2 72
(K A Ryan) *t.k.h: led: rdn along and hdd 2 1/2f out: drvn and edgd lft over 1f out: grad wknd* **3/1**[2]

1120 **5** 1/2 **Murura (IRE)**[42] 2069 3-9-1 **73** ...... PaulMulrennan 5 65
(J G Given) *chsd ldrs: rdn along over 2f out: sn wknd* **7/1**

12-0 **6** 5 **Sabatini (IRE)**[26] 2565 3-9-7 **79** ...... SaleemGolam 3 58
(J Pearce) *chsd ldrs: rdn along 3f out: sn wknd* **16/1**

30-0 **7** 14 **Pycian**[54] 1718 3-9-6 **78** ...... KierenFallon 7 19
(Mrs L Stubbs) *in tch: rdn along 1/2-way: sn outpcd and bhd* **20/1**

1m 25.22s (-1.08) **Going Correction** -0.35s/f (Firm) **7** Ran SP% **110.4**
Speed ratings (Par 101): **92,87,87,84,84 78,62**
Tote Swingers: 1&2 £1.80, 1&3 £8.70, 2&3 £6.30 CSF £9.67 TOTE £4.80: £2.60, £1.50; EX 9.70.
Owner Ms Gillian Khosla **Bred** Vimal Khosla, Gillian Khosla Et Al **Trained** Newmarket, Suffolk

FOCUS
A tight 3-y-o handicap. This time the runners kept towards the centre of the track and the form should work out. The race is rated around the runner-up.
Murura(IRE) Official explanation: jockey said colt hung left
Pycian Official explanation: jockey said gelding moved poorly throughout

3395 SIMPSONMILLAR.CO.UK SOLICITORS NOVICE STKS 7f
4:00 (4:05) (Class 3) 2-Y-O **£6,476** (£1,927; £963) **Stalls** High

Form RPR

5 **1** **Dffar (IRE)**[27] 2547 2-9-0 0 ...... NeilCallan 3 79+
(C E Brittain) *trckd ldng pair: swtchd rt and hdwy 3f out: qcknd to ld 2f out: styd on strly fnl f: comf* **2/1**[2]

321 **2** 2 **Falkland Flyer (IRE)**[7] 3162 2-9-5 0 ...... SamHitchcott 4 74
(M R Channon) *led: rdn along over 2f out: sn hdd and drvn: kpt on same pce fnl f* **9/2**[3]

41 **3** 4 **Whoateallthepius (IRE)**[11] 3035 2-8-9 0 ...... RyanMoore 2 54
(D K Ivory) *trckd ldr: hdwy and cl up 3f out: rdn 2f out and sn btn* **4/5**[1]

1m 26.08s (-0.22) **Going Correction** -0.35s/f (Firm) **3** Ran SP% **107.1**
Speed ratings (Par 97): **87,84,80**
CSF £8.35 TOTE £3.00; EX 8.80.
Owner Saif Ali **Bred** Rabbah Bloodstock Limited **Trained** Newmarket, Suffolk

FOCUS
A fair little novice event and the winner can rate higher than the bare form. Not an easy race to put a figure on.

NOTEBOOK
Dffar(IRE) showed promise when running green on his debut at Newmarket last month and this step up a furlong looked ideal on breeding. He relished the stiffer test, running out a taking winner, and rates value for a good bit further. That is down to him still running green when in front and idling, so there is a good bet he is a very useful performer in the making. His yard is having a great season with its juveniles and it wouldn't be that surprising to see him highly tried next time, with something like the Vintage Stakes at Glorious Goodwood a possible target. (op 5-2 tchd 11-4)
Falkland Flyer(IRE), a winner over this trip at Musselburgh a week earlier, set out to make all. He was a sitting duck for the winner and is flattered by his proximity to that rival, but was far from disgraced in giving him 5lb. (op 4-1 tchd 11-2)
Whoateallthepius(IRE) was bought by her new connections after sauntering home in a seller at Windsor 11 days earlier. She proved very popular for this step up a furlong in better company under Ryan Moore, despite looking the least likely of the three to appreciate the distance. She was ultimately held before the final furlong and looked a non-stayer, but it must be noted she got upset on the way to the start so it's hard to know just how that affected her performance. (op 8-11 tchd 8-13)

3396 CWU LEGAL SERVICES H'CAP 7f
4:35 (4:38) (Class 4) (0-80,80) 4-Y-O+ **£4,533** (£1,348; £674; £336) **Stalls** High

Form RPR

-032 **1** **Mac's Power (IRE)**[12] 2991 4-9-6 **79** ...... (t) AdamKirby 1 96+
(J R Fanshawe) *hld up in rr: smooth hdwy 3f out: chsd ldr over 1f out: rdn to ld ent fnl f: styd on strly* **11/8**[1]

3544 **2** 2 **Standpoint**[7] 3172 4-9-5 **78** ...... JackMitchell 5 87
(R Hollinshead) *trckd ldrs: hdwy 3f out: rdn to chse ldng pair over 1f out: kpt on u.p ins fnl f* **8/1**

0520 **3** 1 1/2 **Thunderball**[12] 2991 4-9-7 **80** ...... (b) PaulMulrennan 6 85
(J A Glover) *led: pushed clr 3f out: rdn 2f out: hdd ent fnl f and kpt on same pce* **20/1**

-400 **4** 2 1/4 **Toto Skyllachy**[2] 3317 5-8-12 **76** ...... JamesO'Reilly[(5)] 3 75
(J O'Reilly) *chsd ldrs on outer: rdn along wl over 2f out: plugged on same pce* **25/1**

0-46 **5** 1 3/4 **Poppet's Lovein**[25] 2601 4-9-4 **77** ...... KierenFallon 9 71
(A B Haynes) *chsd ldr: rdn along over 2f out: grad wknd* **16/1**

5045 **6** 1/2 **Legal Legacy**[29] 2462 4-9-2 **75** ...... PhillipMakin 11 68
(M Dods) *dwlt: keen and hld up in rr: sme hdwy fnl 2f: nvr a factor* **7/1**[3]

1212 **7** hd **Imperial Djay (IRE)**[7] 3150 5-8-12 **71** 6ex ...... RobertWinston 8 63
(Mrs R A Carr) *stdd and swtchd lft s: hld up in rr: rdn and sme hdwy fnl 2f: nvr a factor* **10/3**[2]

4161 **8** 1 3/4 **Kingswinford (IRE)**[17] 2840 4-9-3 **79** ...... AndrewHeffernan[(3)] 2 67
(P D Evans) *a towards rr* **14/1**

240U **9** 4 1/2 **Toby Tyler**[10] 3061 4-8-6 **65** ...... (p) RoystonFfrench 7 40
(P T Midgley) *chsd ldrs to 1/2-way: sn wknd* **66/1**

10-3 **10** 1 **Tudor Prince (IRE)**[8] 3129 6-8-6 **70** ...... KierenFox[(5)] 4 43
(A W Carroll) *chsd ldrs: rdn along 3f out: sn wknd* **18/1**

6/02 **11** nk **Chambers (IRE)**[35] 2274 4-7-11 **61** oh6 ...... PaulPickard[(5)] 10 33
(E J Alston) *racd alone towards stands' rail: in tch: rdn along 1/2-way: sn wknd* **50/1**

1m 22.92s (-3.38) **Going Correction** -0.35s/f (Firm) **11** Ran SP% **118.7**
Speed ratings (Par 105): **105,102,101,98,96 95,95,93,88,87 87**
Tote Swingers: 1&2 £3.70, 1&3 £8.30, 2&3 £21.30 CSF £12.92 TOTE £2.30: £1.10, £2.70, £4.30; EX 11.40 Trifecta £161.83 Pool: £685.35 - 4.30 winning units..
Owner Michael McDonnell **Bred** Ballyhane Stud **Trained** Newmarket, Suffolk

FOCUS
A modest handicap, run at a sound pace. The winner is worth a bit more than the bare form.
Poppet's Lovein Official explanation: jockey said filly had been unsuited by the good (good to firm places) ground
Legal Legacy Official explanation: jockey said gelding missed the break
Chambers(IRE) Official explanation: jockey said gelding hung left throughout

3397 MG LAW EDUCATION & SOCIAL CARE LAW MAIDEN STKS 6f
5:05 (5:07) (Class 5) 3-Y-O+ **£2,590** (£770; £385; £192) **Stalls** High

Form RPR

-432 **1** **Alkhataaf (USA)**[15] 2892 3-9-3 77 ...... RichardHills 4 83
(J L Dunlop) *trckd ldr: cl up 1/2-way: effrt 2f out: sn rdn and ev ch whn carried bdly lft fr over 1f out: kpt on gamely to ld nr fin* **11/10**[2]

-622 **2** shd **Engulf (IRE)**[20] 2762 3-9-3 78 ...... KierenFallon 5 83
(W J Haggas) *trckd ldrs: gd hdwy to ld over 2f out: rdn wl over 1f out and hung persistently lft: hdd and nt qckn nr fin* **1/1**[1]

3 8 **Henry Morgan** 3-9-3 0 ...... RoystonFfrench 2 57
(B Smart) *trckd ldng pair: effrt 3f out: sn rdn along and one pce fnl 2f* **20/1**[3]

00 **4** *8* **Happy The Man (IRE)**[9] 3091 3-8-12 0 LanceBetts(5) 6 31
(T D Easterby) *a in rr: rdn along 1/2-way: sn outpcd* **80/1**

6-4 **5** *3* **Nicholas Pocock (IRE)**[6] 3227 4-9-10 0 PaulMulrennan 1 22
(B Ellison) *led: rdn along and jnd 3f out: sn hdd & wknd* **28/1**

1m 11.52s (-2.08) **Going Correction** -0.35s/f (Firm)
WFA 3 from 4yo+ 7lb 5 Ran SP% **107.1**
Speed ratings (Par 103): **99,98,88,77,73**
CSF £2.32 TOTE £2.50: £1.40, £1.10; EX 2.30.
Owner Hamdan Al Maktoum **Bred** Shadwell Farm LLC **Trained** Arundel, W Sussex

FOCUS
Effectively a match. Just 1lb separated the two clear market leaders on official ratings here and they predictably fought out a very tight finish.

3398 ON-HOLIDAY-CLAIMS.CO.UK H'CAP — 1m 6f 132y
5:40 (5:41) (Class 4) (0-85,82) 4-Y-0+ **£4,533** (£1,348; £674; £336) **Stalls** Low

Form RPR

-221 **1** **Kazbow (IRE)**[28] 2495 4-9-4 **79** KierenFallon 2 92
(L M Cumani) *mde all: rdn along wl over 2f out: drvn clr over 1f out: styd on strly* **6/4**[1]

4-12 **2** *10* **My Mate Max**[28] 2495 5-9-4 **79** (p) AdamKirby 6 79
(R Hollinshead) *trckd ldng pair: chsd wnr 1/2-way: effrt 3f out: rdn over 2f out: drvn wl over 1f out and sn no imp* **5/2**[2]

4140 **3** *10* **Hallstatt (IRE)**[13] 2975 4-8-12 **73** SaleemGolam 3 60
(J Mackie) *trckd wnr on inner: pushed along 5f out: rdn wl over 3f out: drvn and outpcd fnl 2f* **17/2**[3]

1-20 **4** *12* **Twist Again (IRE)**[43] 2060 4-8-10 **76** JohnFahy(5) 4 47
(P Howling) *dwlt: hld up in rr: tk clsr order 1/2-way: effrt 4f out: rdn along 3f out: sn drvn and wknd 2f out* **5/2**[2]

3m 5.70s (-1.70) **Going Correction** +0.075s/f (Good) 4 Ran SP% **107.7**
Speed ratings (Par 105): **105,99,94,87**
CSF £5.44 TOTE £1.80; EX 4.20 Place 6: £34.88 Place 5: £32.53.
Owner Bruce Corman **Bred** Airlie Stud **Trained** Newmarket, Suffolk

FOCUS
A fair staying handicap and an improving winner. The first two were closely matched on their Haydock form and the winner is on the up.
Twist Again(IRE) Official explanation: jockey said filly was unsuited by the good (good to firm places) ground
T/Plt: £78.10 to a £1 stake. Pool: £59,547.86 - 556.10 winning tickets T/Qpdt: £10.70 to a £1 stake. Pool: £3,620.76 - 250.33 winning tickets JR

2807 FOLKESTONE (R-H)
Friday, June 25

OFFICIAL GOING: Good to firm (watered; 8.4)
Wind: virtually nil Weather: warm amd sunny

3399 COUNTRYSTYLE AGGREGATE RECYCLING MEDIAN AUCTION MAIDEN STKS — 7f (S)
2:30 (2:32) (Class 5) 2-Y-0 **£2,729** (£806; £403) **Stalls** Low

Form RPR

0 **1** **Spanish Pride (IRE)**[28] 2505 2-8-12 0 EddieAhern 2 66
(J L Dunlop) *trckd ldrs on stands' rail: swtchd rt and hdwy over 2f out: rdn to ld over 1f out: r.o wl fnl f* **11/8**[1]

3 **2** *1/2* **A Little Bit Dusty**[11] 3035 2-9-0 0 JackDean(3) 4 70
(W G M Turner) *in tch in midfield: pushed along 3f out: edgd rt and rdn ent fnl 2f: chsd wnr jst ins fnl f: kpt on wl but a hld* **10/1**

5 **3** *1* **Zakon (IRE)**[22] 2677 2-9-3 0 TomQueally 8 67
(D J Coakley) *restless in stalls: stdd s: t.k.h and hld up in last: stl last and swtchd rt over 1f out: gd hdwy to chse ldrs ent fnl f: edgd lft and one pce fnl f* **7/2**[3]

4 **4** *2* **Cathcart Castle**[18] 2819 2-9-3 0 TedDurcan 3 65+
(M R Channon) *stdd s: hld up in tch in last trio: swtchd rt and nt clr run wl over 1f out tl jst over 1f out: styd on same pce fnl f* **3/1**[2]

0 **5** *1/2* **Blaze On By**[33] 2358 2-8-12 0 SteveDrowne 5 56
(R Hannon) *led tl rdn and hdd over 1f out: wknd fnl 150yds* **18/1**

00 **6** *3* **Manchester Stanley**[6] 3209 2-9-3 0 FergusSweeney 7 53
(J A Osborne) *chsd ldr tl over 1f out: wknd u.p 1f out* **16/1**

7 *7* **Will Barrow** 2-9-3 0 StephenCraine 9 36
(J R Boyle) *chsd ldrs tl rdn and wknd qckly 2f out: wl bhd fnl f* **40/1**

8 *3 1/4* **Van Doesburg (IRE)** 2-9-3 0 LukeMorris 6 28
(J G Portman) *dwlt: in tch in last trio: pushed along 1/2-way: edgd rt and wknd qckly ent fnl 2f: wl bhd fnl f* **33/1**

1m 27.9s (0.60) **Going Correction** -0.10s/f (Good) 8 Ran SP% **114.9**
Speed ratings (Par 93): **92,91,90,88,87 84,76,72**
Tote Swingers: 1&2 £3.90, 1&3 £2.20, 2&3 £6.40 CSF £17.16 TOTE £2.30: £1.30, £3.10, £1.10; EX 17.30.
Owner Windflower Overseas Holdings Inc **Bred** Windflower Overseas Holdings Inc **Trained** Arundel, W Sussex

FOCUS
Probably just a modest maiden, but the race still ought to produce some winners. It was an unsatisfactory race in some respects and the form is rated 3lb or so lower than it might have been.

NOTEBOOK
Spanish Pride(IRE) was beaten a long way on her debut over 6f at Newmarket, but she caught the eye making late headway that day and is bred to be suited by longer trips. Nicely backed on this step up to 7f, she was always well placed and kept on strongly to build on that initial promise. Likely to stay even further, she should make a fair nursery type/handicapper. (op 6-4 tchd 5-4, 2-1 in a place)
A Little Bit Dusty improved on the form he showed when third in a 6f seller on debut, keeping on out wide to ensure the favourite had to work for her victory. He's evidently better than selling class. (op 9-1 tchd 8-1)
Zakon(IRE), well backed to improve on a moderate debut effort, was set a lot to do on a track that often favours pace and, although keeping on when in the clear over 1f out, he could make no impression, with his run flattening out late on. He can improve again. (tchd 4-1)
Cathcart Castle, fourth on debut over 6f, should have finished closer this time. Having been tucked away towards the near rail for much of the journey, he was continually denied a clear run when trying to make a move inside the final 2f, and the race was as good as over by the time he was in the open. Official explanation: jockey said colt was denied a clear run (tchd 11-4 and 7-2)

Blaze On By had the run of the race against the near rail but she looks limited. (op 25-1)

3400 COUNTRYSTYLE WASTE MANAGEMENT & RECYCLING CLAIMING STKS — 6f
3:05 (3:06) (Class 6) 3-Y-0+ **£2,047** (£604; £302) **Stalls** Low

Form RPR

1111 **1** **Abbondanza (IRE)**[6] 3226 7-9-2 79 BillyCray(5) 6 87
(D Nicholls) *chsd ldrs: wnt 2nd 1/2-way: rdn to ld over 1f out: r.o wl fnl f: asserted fnl 100yds* **6/4**[1]

2113 **2** *1 1/2* **Piazza San Pietro**[10] 3057 4-9-2 72 RobertHavlin 2 77
(A B Haynes) *chsd ldr tl 1/2-way: rdn and ev ch ent fnl f: no ex and btn fnl 75yds* **4/1**[3]

-500 **3** *1/2* **Cut The Cackle (IRE)**[11] 3037 4-8-7 73 LukeMorris 1 66
(P Winkworth) *chsd ldrs: rdn ent fnl 2f: edging rt and chsd ldrs ent fnl f: kpt on same pce u.p fnl 150yds* **11/4**[2]

-160 **4** *1 1/2* **Little Edward**[13] 2954 12-9-1 75 SteveDrowne 7 70
(R J Hodges) *stdd and dropped in bhd after s: hld up in last: pushed along and hdwy over 1f out: rdn and styd on same pce ins fnl f* **25/1**

2400 **5** *3 1/2* **Dusty Spirit**[18] 2824 3-8-9 72 (t) JackDean(3) 4 60
(W G M Turner) *in tch on outer: effrt u.p to chse ldrs wl over 1f out: btn and edgd lft jst ins fnl f* **14/1**

0006 **6** *1 1/4* **Fault**[6] 3212 4-9-3 66 (bt[1]) TomQueally 3 56
(Stef Higgins) *dwlt: sn rcvrd and led: hdd and rdn over 1f out: wknd qckly fnl f* **17/2**

1m 11.54s (-1.16) **Going Correction** -0.10s/f (Good)
WFA 3 from 4yo+ 7lb 6 Ran SP% **107.7**
Speed ratings (Par 101): **103,101,100,98,93 92**
Tote Swingers: 1&2 £1.40, 1&3 £1.30, 2&3 £3.60 CSF £7.09 TOTE £2.10: £1.10, £2.30; EX 6.90.
Owner Middleham Park Racing XXXI **Bred** M Nolan **Trained** Sessay, N Yorks

FOCUS
A fair claimer and sound form for the grade. The winner stepped up on his recent efforts.

3401 COUNTRYSTYLE GROUP FOLKESTONE HAMMER (A H'CAP) — 6f
3:40 (3:41) (Class 4) (0-85,84) 3-Y-0+ **£12,952** (£3,854; £1,926; £962) **Stalls** Low

Form RPR

4261 **1** **Cornus**[10] 3065 8-8-9 **74** 6ex (be) DeclanCannon(5) 2 91
(A J McCabe) *taken down early: bhd early: rdn and hdwy 1/2-way: chsd ldr over 1f out: led 1f out: sn clr: styd on wl* **9/1**

-615 **2** *2 1/2* **Glen Shiel (USA)**[9] 3085 3-9-0 **81** EddieAhern 1 87+
(M Johnston) *racd wl off the pce in midfield: hdwy on stands' rail over 1f out: swtchd rt ins fnl f: r.o wl to go 2nd fnl 100yds: no ch w wnr* **5/1**[1]

000- **3** *2 1/2* **Rash Judgement**[257] 6694 5-9-9 **83** IanMongan 6 84
(W S Kittow) *chsd ldrs: rdn and chsd clr ldr over 2f out tl over 1f out: keeping on but no ch w wnr whn pushed rt ins fnl f* **8/1**

0-34 **4** *3/4* **Victorian Bounty**[11] 3037 5-9-6 **80** TomQueally 4 82+
(Stef Higgins) *prom in main gp: rdn and effrt ent fnl 2f: styng on but stl plenty to do whn nt clr run 1f out tl ins fnl f: kpt on to go 4th nr fin: nvr trbld ldrs* **6/1**[2]

0602 **5** *1/2* **Lujeanie**[11] 3037 4-9-3 **77** FergusSweeney 3 74
(D K Ivory) *t.k.h early: hld up wl off the pce towards rr: hdwy over 2f out: rdn and chsng ldrs jst over 1f out: no prog and wl btn ins fnl f* **17/2**

1310 **6** *1/2* **Peter Island (FR)**[30] 2446 7-9-6 **83** (v) MartinLane(3) 8 78
(J Gallagher) *broke v fast: led and crossed to stands' rail: sn clr: 4 l clr 2f out: rdn over 1f out: hdd 1f out: sn btn: tired and lost 4 pls fnl 100yds* **25/1**

1612 **7** *3 1/2* **Beat The Bell**[33] 2364 5-9-5 **84** SophieDoyle(5) 11 68
(J A Osborne) *sltly hmpd: a off the pce in midfield: rdn and no prog ent fnl 2f: nvr trbld ldrs* **7/1**[3]

21- **8** *3 1/2* **Chat De La Burg (USA)**[246] 6971 3-8-11 **78** LukeMorris 5 51
(J R Best) *taken down early: racd off the pce in midfield: rdn and no rspnse ent fnl 2f: wl btn over 1f out* **16/1**

0-21 **9** *1/2* **Duster**[18] 2807 3-9-0 **81** SteveDrowne 12 50
(H Morrison) *chsd ldrs on outer but nvr on terms w ldr: rdn and btn wl over 1f out* **6/1**[2]

0004 **10** *3/4* **Hamoody (USA)**[10] 3065 6-9-5 **84** BillyCray(5) 14 53
(D Nicholls) *wl off the pce towards rr: hdwy over 2f out: nvr on terms and wl btn over 1f out* **14/1**

-030 **11** *4* **Beaver Patrol (IRE)**[14] 2926 8-9-8 **82** (v) RobertHavlin 13 38
(Eve Johnson Houghton) *a wl outpcd in rr: u.p 4f out: nvr a factor* **20/1**

3612 **12** *8* **Alfresco**[1] 3373 6-8-10 **70** (b) KirstyMilczarek 7 —
(J R Best) *chsd clr ldr tl over 2f out: sn dropped out: wl bhd over 1f out* **10/1**

5500 **13** *14* **Earlsmedic**[32] 2399 5-8-10 **77** (v) RyanClark(7) 9 —
(S C Williams) *racd in centre: nvr on terms: t.o fr wl over 1f out* **33/1**

1m 11.33s (-1.37) **Going Correction** -0.10s/f (Good)
WFA 3 from 4yo+ 7lb 13 Ran SP% **122.6**
Speed ratings (Par 105): **105,101,98,97,96 96,91,86,86,85 79,69,50**
Tote Swingers: 1&2 £10.20, 1&3 £23.70, 2&3 £11.70 CSF £53.74 CT £387.40 TOTE £16.00: £4.60, £1.80, £2.70; EX 61.50.
Owner Triple A Partnership **Bred** G Russell **Trained** Averham Park, Notts
■ Stewards' Enquiry : Eddie Ahern one-day ban: careless riding (Jul 10)

FOCUS
A fair sprint handicap run at an overly strong pace. The winner's best run for two years, with the form taken at something like face value amongst the principals.
Alfresco Official explanation: jockey said gelding ran flat after running day before

3402 COUNTRYSTYLE GOOD WITH WASTE H'CAP — 2m 93y
4:15 (4:15) (Class 4) (0-80,80) 4-Y-0+ **£5,180** (£1,541; £770) **Stalls** Low

Form RPR

111 **1** **On Terms (USA)**[18] 2810 4-9-2 **77** TomQueally 3 84+
(S Dow) *mde all: rdn over 2f out: a in command after: pushed out fnl f* **4/9**[1]

/3-0 **2** *3 1/4* **Black Jacari (IRE)**[14] 1720 5-9-1 **79** RussKennemore(3) 2 79
(P A Kirby) *t.k.h: hld up in tch: rdn 4f out: chsd wnr 3f out: kpt on same pce u.p fnl 2f* **13/2**[3]

6-40 **3** *10* **Act Of Kalanisi (IRE)**[16] 2857 4-9-5 **80** EddieAhern 1 68
(M Johnston) *chsd wnr: pushed along and tried to press wnr over 4f out: rdn and dropped to last 3f out: wl btn over 1f out: eased ins fnl f* **3/1**[2]

3m 42.04s (4.84) **Going Correction** +0.225s/f (Good) 3 Ran SP% **107.6**
Speed ratings (Par 105): **96,94,89**
CSF £3.53 TOTE £1.30; EX 2.60.
Owner S Dow **Bred** Juddmonte Farms Inc **Trained** Epsom, Surrey

FOCUS
A poor turnout numerically. The winner made all at a steady pace and is rated up another 7lb.

3403 COUNTRYSTYLE GOOD WITH WOOD WASTE H'CAP 1m 4f
4:45 (4:48) (Class 6) (0-60,66) 4-Y-0+ £2,047 (£604; £302) Stalls Low

Form RPR
051 1 **Amazing King (IRE)**[7] 3166 6-9-7 66 6ex.............. RussKennemore(3) 7 76+
(P A Kirby) *chsd ldrs: rdn and effrt 2f out: led ins fnl f: r.o strly and drew clr fnl 100yds* 7/4[1]
1000 2 2 **Vinces**[13] 2966 6-9-3 59.............. KirstyMilczarek 6 65
(T D McCarthy) *led: rdn and hrd pressed ent fnl 2f: hdd ins fnl f: nt pce of wnr fnl 100yds* 12/1
5331 3 ¾ **Dazzling Begum**[18] 2811 5-8-6 53.............. SimonPearce(5) 8 58+
(J Pearce) *hld up in rr: stl last and pushed along ent fnl 2f: hdwy and rdn over 1f out: swtchd lft 1f out: r.o wl fnl 150yds: nvr gng to rch wnr* 5/1[2]
22-4 4 1 ½ **Ubiquitous**[19] 2781 5-8-7 49..............(t) EddieAhern 3 51
(S Dow) *chsd ldr: rdn to chal 2f out: ev ch after tl ins fnl f: wknd fnl 100yds* 5/1[2]
0005 5 2 ½ **Starburst**[8] 3110 5-8-13 55.............. DavidProbert 2 53
(Miss Gay Kelleway) *hld up in rr: hdwy over 3f out: n.m.r 3f out: sn chsng ldrs and rdn: wknd over 1f out* 6/1[3]
2206 6 13 **Valkyrie (IRE)**[15] 982 4-8-4 46 oh1.............. LukeMorris 1 24
(N P Littmoden) *in tch: rdn and unable qck over 3f out: wknd ent fnl 2f* 5/1[2]
00/0 7 3 ¼ **Dora Explora**[18] 2811 6-8-8 53 ow1..............(p) RobertLButler(3) 5 25
(Mrs L C Jewell) *in tch towards rr: effrt and rdn on outer ent fnl 3f: wd bnd jst over 2f out: sn wknd* 40/1

2m 43.13s (2.23) **Going Correction** +0.225s/f (Good) 7 Ran SP% 110.8
Speed ratings (Par 101): **101,99,99,98,96 87,85**
Tote Swingers: 1&2 £5.40, 1&3 £2.60, 2&3 £6.80 CSF £22.97 CT £83.97 TOTE £3.00: £2.80, £6.80; EX 24.80.
Owner The New Venture Partnership **Bred** Kraemer Partnership **Trained** Castleton, N Yorks

FOCUS
A weak handicap and the pace was steady for much of the way, resulting in a slow time. The form is rated around the runner-up.

3404 COUNTRYSTYLE PLASTERBOARD DISPOSAL H'CAP 1m 1f 149y
5:15 (5:15) (Class 5) (0-75,74) 3-Y-0+ £3,238 (£963; £481; £240) Stalls Centre

Form RPR
1430 1 **Understory (USA)**[14] 2927 3-9-4 72.............. EddieAhern 4 77
(M Johnston) *led tl over 2f out: drvn to ld again over 1f out: styd on gamely fnl f* 3/1[2]
6233 2 ¾ **Buona Sarah (IRE)**[18] 2820 3-8-9 63.............. NickyMackay 2 66
(J R Boyle) *t.k.h: chsd ldrs: effrt and rdn to chal ent fnl 2f: ev ch tl no ex fnl 75yds* 3/1[2]
-254 3 1 ¾ **One Cool Poppy (IRE)**[24] 2620 3-8-0 54..............(t) LukeMorris 3 53
(H J L Dunlop) *chsd wnr tl led over 2f out: drvn ent fnl 2f: hdd over 1f out: stl ev ch tl no ex and btn ins fnl f* 4/1[3]
3-04 4 2 ¼ **Barliffey (IRE)**[37] 2233 5-10-0 70.............. TomQueally 6 65
(D J Coakley) *stdd s: t.k.h: hld up in last pair: rdn and unable qck over 2f out: kpt on u.p fnl f: nvr gng pce to chal ldrs* 11/4[1]
3306 5 1 **Goose Green (IRE)**[21] 2690 6-9-6 62.............. TravisBlock 5 55
(R J Hodges) *chsd ldrs: rdn and unable qck ent fnl 2f: styd on one pce u.p fr over 1f out* 16/1
2346 6 7 **Lago Indiano (IRE)**[15] 2892 3-9-6 74.............. SteveDrowne 1 52
(Mrs A J Perrett) *hld up in last pair: effrt and rdn over 2f out: no hdwy and wl btn wl over 1f out* 15/2

2m 7.07s (2.17) **Going Correction** +0.225s/f (Good)
WFA 3 from 5yo+ 12lb 6 Ran SP% 114.3
Speed ratings (Par 103): **100,99,98,96,95 89**
Tote Swingers: 1&2 £3.10, 1&3 £2.70, 2&3 £2.50 CSF £12.76 TOTE £5.40: £3.40, £3.50; EX 14.90 Place 6: £23.69 Place 5: £16.70.
Owner Sheikh Hamdan Bin Mohammed Al Maktoum **Bred** Darley **Trained** Middleham Moor, N Yorks

FOCUS
A modest handicap and form to treat with caution, as it was steadily run like the other two round-course races.
T/Plt: £53.60 to a £1 stake. Pool: £77,354.50 - 643.89 winning tickets T/Qpdt: £33.40 to a £1 stake. Pool: £3,163.87 - 70 winning tickets SP

3364 NEWCASTLE (L-H)
Friday, June 25

OFFICIAL GOING: Good to firm (8.0)
Wind: Breezy, half behind Weather: Cloudy, warm

3405 KB SHEET METAL & GDBS H'CAP 1m 2f 32y
6:50 (6:50) (Class 5) (0-70,71) 4-Y-0+ £3,885 (£1,156; £577; £288) Stalls Centre

Form RPR
1431 1 **That'll Do Nicely (IRE)**[6] 3202 7-9-4 71 6ex.............. IanBrennan(5) 5 83
(N G Richards) *hld up: smooth hdwy to ld over 1f out: sn rdn: kpt on strly fnl f* 15/8[2]
1004 2 2 ½ **Sea Land (FR)**[1] 3369 6-8-3 51.............. PaulHanagan 2 58
(B Ellison) *hld up and bhd: hdwy over 2f out: carried lft ins fnl f: sn chsng wnr: r.o* 17/2[3]
4112 3 2 **George Adamson (IRE)**[16] 2851 4-9-7 69.............. PJMcDonald 1 72
(G A Swinbank) *prom: stdy hdwy over 3f out: effrt and ev ch 2f out: edgd lft and one pce fnl f* 13/8[1]
-450 4 1 **Country Road (IRE)**[14] 2941 4-9-5 67..............(e1) LeeVickers 3 68
(M W Easterby) *hld up on ins: hdwy over 2f out: keeping on same pce whn hmpd ins fnl f* 10/1
-201 5 12 **Smirfy's Silver**[7] 3177 6-9-8 70 6ex.............. DuranFentiman 8 47
(Mrs D J Sanderson) *led to over 1f out: sn rdn and wknd* 10/1
0-40 6 3 ½ **Petsas Pleasure**[16] 2851 4-8-9 60.............. BarryMcHugh(3) 6 30
(Ollie Pears) *sn chsng ldr: rdn over 2f out: wknd over 1f out* 12/1
-002 7 39 **Peaceful Rule (USA)**[7] 3176 4-9-1 63.............. AdrianNicholls 7 —
(D Nicholls) *cl up tl rdn and wknd qckly over 2f out: eased whn no ch: t.o* 25/1

2m 9.32s (-2.58) **Going Correction** -0.175s/f (Firm) 7 Ran SP% 113.1
Speed ratings (Par 103): **103,101,99,98,89 86,55**
toteswingers: 1&2 £4.90, 1&3 £1.02, 2&3 £4.80. CSF £17.70 CT £29.76 TOTE £3.30: £3.20, £4.30; EX 18.50.
Owner J D Flood **Bred** J D Flood **Trained** Greystoke, Cumbria

FOCUS
The going was good to firm on a watered track. A competitive handicap run at a strong pace. The winner was impressive and notched another personal best. The form looks solid.

3406 TOTESPORT.COM GOSFORTH PARK CUP (H'CAP) 5f
7:25 (7:25) (Class 2) (0-105,102) 3-Y-0+
£12,462 (£3,732; £1,866; £934; £466; £234) Stalls High

Form RPR
-220 1 **Captain Dunne (IRE)**[20] 2745 5-9-9 100.............. DavidAllan 9 108
(T D Easterby) *pressed ldr: led and rdn over 1f out: kpt on wl fnl f: all out* 5/1[2]
-164 2 hd **Secret Asset (IRE)**[48] 1903 5-8-10 94.............. LewisWalsh(7) 7 101
(Jane Chapple-Hyam) *taken early to post: in tch: hdwy over 1f out: kpt on wl fnl f: jst failed* 4/1[1]
260- 3 1 ¼ **Skylla**[238] 7147 3-8-9 92.............. TonyHamilton 12 93
(R A Fahey) *led tl rdn and hdd over 1f out: kpt on same pce fnl f* 17/2
0000 4 1 ¼ **Ishetoo**[29] 2465 6-8-4 86..............(bt) IanBrennan(5) 6 84
(Ollie Pears) *bhd tl gd hdwy over 1f out: kpt on wl fnl f: nrst fin* 8/1
3012 5 1 **Fol Hollow (IRE)**[20] 2748 5-9-4 98.............. MichaelGeran(3) 10 93
(D Nicholls) *trckd ldrs: effrt 2f out: no ex ins fnl f* 7/1[3]
0301 6 2 ¾ **Hotham**[14] 2940 7-9-1 92.............. PaulHanagan 8 77
(N Wilson) *prom: drvn along over 2f out: no ex over 1f out* 10/1
0601 7 1 **Rasaman (IRE)**[7] 3165 6-8-6 86 6ex.............. GaryBartley(3) 2 67+
(J S Goldie) *racd alone in centre: rdn 1/2-way and nvr any ch w stands' side gp* 22/1
0262 8 2 ¾ **The Nifty Fox**[7] 3165 6-8-5 85.............. BarryMcHugh(3) 3 56
(T D Easterby) *hld up bhd ldng gp: drvn over 2f out: nvr able to chal* 8/1
2000 9 1 ½ **Green Manalishi**[20] 2759 9-9-1 92..............(p) PhillipMakin 5 58
(K A Ryan) *towards rr: drvn along 1/2-way: btn over 1f out* 22/1
4512 10 9 **Five Star Junior (USA)**[7] 3178 4-9-0 91.............. DuranFentiman 1 24
(Mrs L Stubbs) *bhd: drvn after 2f: no ch fr 1/2-way* 9/1
4100 11 99 **Buachaill Dona (IRE)**[42] 2100 7-9-11 102.............. AdrianNicholls 11 —
(D Nicholls) *virtually ref to r: t.o thrght* 15/2

58.94 secs (-2.16) **Going Correction** -0.175s/f (Firm)
WFA 3 from 4yo+ 6lb 11 Ran SP% 121.5
Speed ratings (Par 109): **107,106,104,102,101 96,95,90,88,73** —
toteswingers: 1&2 £9.80, 1&3 £15.20, 2&3 £13.90. CSF £26.25 CT £170.88 TOTE £7.80: £3.00, £1.70, £3.20; EX 32.40.
Owner Middleham Park Racing Xv **Bred** Ballybrennan Stud Ltd **Trained** Great Habton, N Yorks

FOCUS
Not the strongest of renewals of this historic handicap but it was still ultra-competitive. Most of the runners raced near the stands' rail. The form looks sound.

NOTEBOOK
Captain Dunne(IRE) went close on his first two starts this season before reportedly banging his head in the stalls at Epsom last time. He was always prominent from his good draw and showed plenty of determination to hold on. He does not have a great strike-rate (5-32) for a sprinter of his ability but has been as good as ever this year and should continue to be a powerful force in hot sprint handicaps. All of his wins have been at 5f but a easy 6f should not pose a problem and his next assignment could be in the Stewards' Cup. (op 4-1)
Secret Asset(IRE) finished well after being switched outside the winner in the final furlong but was just denied back at 5f on fast ground. He was a shock winner of a 6f Wolverhampton handicap on return from 17 months off in April but has mixed it well with some useful handicappers on turf since. He would be very interesting at a stiff 5f or back at 6f next time. (op 5-1)
Skylla, the only 3-y-o in the race, gave it a good shot under an attacking ride against the near rail on her return for a new yard after 238 days off. She ended her 2-y-o season on a low but was a progressive dual winner and Listed runner-up on her first four starts last season and looks set to resume her progress this year. (op 20-1)
Ishetoo gave a good hint of a revival with a tongue tie applied dropped back to 5f. He is very well treated on his York win off 7lb higher last May and is one to keep a close eye on. He was reported to have lost a shoe and finished lame on his near-fore. Official explanation: vet said gelding lost a shoe and was lame near-fore (op 9-1)
Fol Hollow(IRE) couldn't adopt a favoured prominent role after being squeezed out at an early stage but he blasted home from some way back to finish just behind the front four. (tchd 15-2)
Hotham posted a personal best when beating a subsequent winner in a 5f York handicap last time but the 7-y-o was well held off 5lb higher in his pursuit for the first back-to-back wins in his career. (op 9-1)
Rasaman(IRE) was always some way off the pace racing alone down the centre of the track. (op 25-1)
Five Star Junior(USA) was reported to have been struck into. Official explanation: trainer said gelding was struck into behind (op 10-1)
Buachaill Dona(IRE) lost all chance after a very slow start. (op 7-1)

3407 DELOITTE MAIDEN FILLIES' STKS 7f
7:55 (7:56) (Class 5) 3-Y-0+ £3,756 (£1,117; £558; £278) Stalls High

Form RPR
3005 1 **Dolly Royal (IRE)**[16] 2854 5-9-0 50.............. LeeTopliss(7) 8 60
(R Johnson) *prom: hdwy over 1f out: led wl ins fnl f: kpt on wl* 20/1
2 2 ½ **Jemima Nicholas**[35] 2297 3-8-12 0.............. LiamJones 5 56
(W J Haggas) *t.k.h: w ldr: rdn to ld over 1f out: hdd wl ins fnl f: kpt on* 9/2[3]
3 hd **Shethoughtshewas (IRE)** 3-8-12 0.............. PJMcDonald 6 55+
(G A Swinbank) *hld up: shkn up and hdwy over 1f out: kpt on wl fnl f: bttr for r* 16/1
6 4 ½ **Conciliatory**[34] 2334 3-8-12 0.............. PaulHanagan 2 54+
(Rae Guest) *hld up: hdwy on outside over 1f out: kpt on fnl f: no imp fnl 50yds* 4/1[2]
00 5 2 ¼ **Colamandis**[17] 2837 3-8-12 0.............. PatrickMathers 7 48
(H A McWilliams) *dictated stdy gallop: hdd over 1f out: no ex ins fnl f* 100/1
6 5 **Youm Al Mizayin** 3-8-12 0.............. PhillipMakin 4 34
(M R Channon) *missed break: hld up in tch: drvn and outpcd wl over 1f out: no imp fnl f* 9/2[3]
5 7 7 **Sayyedati Storm (USA)**[107] 843 3-8-12 0.............. RobertWinston 1 24
(B W Hills) *dwlt: t.k.h and sn trcking ldrs: rdn over 2f out: wknd appr fnl f* 6/4[1]
0 8 1 ¼ **Spirit Of Dixie**[20] 2741 3-8-12 0.............. LeeVickers 3 12
(J A Glover) *hld up in tch: drvn and outpcd over 2f out: sn btn* 40/1

1m 27.35s (-1.35) **Going Correction** -0.175s/f (Firm)
WFA 3 from 5yo 9lb 8 Ran SP% 110.4
Speed ratings (Par 100): **100,99,99,98,96 90,82,80**
toteswingers: 1&2 £10.90, 1&3 £8.30, 2&3 £9.40. CSF £100.17 TOTE £29.10: £6.90, £1.20, £8.10; EX 115.00.
Owner Robert Johnson **Bred** Miss Jane Hogan **Trained** Newburn, Tyne & Wear

FOCUS
A weak fillies' maiden. There was a very tight finish in which a 50-rated outsider prevailed, with rails runners again dominating. The form is rated around the runner-up and fifth.

Sayyedati Storm(USA) Official explanation: jockey said filly lost its action

3408 MORE WORLD CUP BETTING AT TOTESPORT.COM H'CAP 1m 3y(S)
8:30 (8:30) (Class 4) (0-85,83) 3-Y-O+ £4,415 (£1,321; £660; £330; £164) Stalls High

Form				RPR
0604	1		**Reel Buddy Star**[17] 2835 5-9-4 73 ... PJMcDonald 5 (G M Moore) *mde all at ordinary gallop: qcknd 2f out: kpt on strly fnl f: unchal* 11/2[3]	89
2214	2	3	**Secretive**[8] 3103 3-9-2 81 ...(b) RoystonFfrench 6 (M Johnston) *trckd ldrs: rdn and wnt 2nd 2f out: effrt ent fnl f: kpt on same pce last 100yds* 8/11[1]	88
40-5	3	2	**Rosko**[20] 2764 6-8-7 69 ... DaleSwift(7) 7 (B Ellison) *hld up in tch: hdwy to chse clr ldrs over 1f out: no imp fnl f* 8/1	73
1250	4	6	**Just Bond (IRE)**[17] 2835 8-9-11 83 ... BarryMcHugh(3) 1 (G R Oldroyd) *hld up in tch: drvn and outpcd over 2f out: passed btn horses ins fnl f: no ch w first three* 16/1	73
30-0	5	3 ¾	**Olympic Dream**[29] 2462 4-9-2 71 ... PaulHanagan 2 (R A Fahey) *t.k.h: cl up tl rdn and wknd over 1f out* 20/1	53
3112	6	2 ¾	**Templetuohy Max (IRE)**[8] 3121 5-9-9 78 ...(v) PhilipRobinson 3 (J D Bethell) *trckd ldrs: rdn over 2f out: wknd over 1f out* 5/1[2]	53

1m 38.49s (-4.91) **Going Correction** -0.175s/f (Firm)
WFA 3 from 4yo+ 10lb 6 Ran SP% **111.7**
Speed ratings (Par 105): **105,104,102,96,92 89**
toteswingers: 1&2 £1.60, 1&3 £11.80, 2&3 £1.80. CSF £9.90 TOTE £7.30: £3.20, £1.90; EX 10.10.
Owner J W Armstrong & M J Howarth **Bred** M Pennell **Trained** Middleham Moor, N Yorks

FOCUS
Just a fair handicap, with the favourite a bit disappointing. The pace was steady but they finished well strung out. Again the winner had the rail to race against.
Templetuohy Max(IRE) Official explanation: jockey said gelding ran flat

3409 SUNSHINE FUND H'CAP 6f
9:00 (9:00) (Class 5) (0-75,75) 3-Y-O+ £3,626 (£1,079; £539; £269) Stalls High

Form				RPR
0-00	1		**Lucy Brown**[13] 2959 4-9-4 69 ... PhillipMakin 9 (M W Easterby) *mde all stands' side: rdn and hrd pressed fnl f: jst hld on* 14/1	76
6-02	2	nse	**Dark Moment**[9] 3076 4-9-4 72 ...(p) BarryMcHugh(3) 13 (Ollie Pears) *prom: rdn over 2f out: hdwy to chal fnl f: kpt on: jst hld* 9/4[1]	79+
0-06	3	1	**Geojimali**[29] 2453 8-8-9 63 ...(p) GaryBartley(3) 1 (J S Goldie) *hld up bhd clr ldng pair far side: hdwy to ld that trio ent fnl f: kpt on wl: nt rch stands' side ldrs* 33/1	67+
-135	4	1 ¾	**Tadalavil**[16] 2856 5-9-3 68 ... PaulHanagan 5 (Miss L A Perratt) *w wnr stands' side: rdn 2f out: kpt on same pce ins fnl f* 9/1	66
0630	5	1	**Frognal (IRE)**[13] 2982 4-9-10 75 ... PJMcDonald 11 (Mrs R A Carr) *hld up stands' side: effrt and hung lft over 1f out: kpt on same pce ins fnl f* 5/1[3]	70
6024	6	5	**Tawzeea (IRE)**[10] 3061 5-9-5 70 ... PhilipRobinson 2 (J D Bethell) *chsd far side ldr: rdn over 2f out: outpcd fnl f* 7/2[2]	49
5664	7	1 ¾	**Slikback Jack (IRE)**[18] 2824 3-9-1 73 ... RobertWinston 3 (J A Glover) *wnt lft s: led far side gp: rdn over 1f out: hdd by farside gp ent fnl f: sn wknd* 13/2	44
-306	8	hd	**Distant Vision (IRE)**[22] 2669 7-8-5 56 oh9 ... PatrickMathers 8 (H A McWilliams) *trckd stands' side ldrs tl wknd over 1f out* 66/1	29
40-0	9	hd	**Twisted**[13] 2976 4-9-6 71 ... LeeVickers 7 (M W Easterby) *s.i.s: bhd stands' side: sme late hdwy: nvr on terms* 20/1	43
4060	10	8	**Carnival Dream**[2] 3322 5-8-0 58 oh3 ow2 ... DanielleMooney(7) 4 (H A McWilliams) *prom on outside of stands' side gp: rdn and wknd over 2f out* 33/1	4
2-55	11	2 ¾	**Embra (IRE)**[16] 2849 5-8-7 58 ... RoystonFfrench 6 (T J Etherington) *hld up in tch stands' side: struggling over 2f out: sn btn* 14/1	—

1m 13.47s (-1.13) **Going Correction** -0.175s/f (Firm)
WFA 3 from 4yo+ 7lb 11 Ran SP% **118.5**
Speed ratings (Par 103): **104,103,102,100,98 92,89,89,89,78 75**
toteswingers: 1&2 £4.40, 1&3 £88.50, 2&3 £13.20. CSF £44.78 CT £1081.01 TOTE £14.30: £4.40, £1.80, £7.70; EX 27.30.
Owner J T Brown **Bred** J T Brown **Trained** Sheriff Hutton, N Yorks

FOCUS
A minor handicap, and only one of the runners had finished placed on their previous start. Most of the runners raced near the stands' rail but the close third was in a breakaway group on the far side. The first five were a long way clear of the rest and the winner is rated back to his 3yo form.

3410 KEVIN LEE MEMORIAL H'CAP 5f
9:30 (9:32) (Class 5) (0-75,75) 3-Y-O £3,626 (£1,079; £539; £269) Stalls High

Form				RPR
0-16	1		**Perfect Blossom**[13] 2962 3-8-6 60 ... PJMcDonald 10 (K A Ryan) *pressed ldr: led after 2f: qcknd clr over 1f out: edgd lft: r.o strly* 15/8[1]	72
-661	2	2 ¼	**Patch Patch**[29] 2449 3-9-0 68 ... PhillipMakin 8 (M Dods) *plld hrd early: trckd ldrs: effrt and chsd wnr over 1f out: sn no imp* 5/1[3]	72
0626	3	4	**Classlin**[6] 3200 3-8-2 56 oh5 ... AdrianNicholls 9 (J S Goldie) *hld up: rdn and hdwy over 1f out: kpt on fnl f: no ch w first two* 14/1	46
1222	4	3 ¼	**Lees Anthem**[7] 3167 3-8-9 63 ... PatrickMathers 2 (C J Teague) *unruly bef s: cl up: rdn over 2f out: wknd ins fnl f* 12/1	41+
401-	5	1 ¼	**My One Weakness (IRE)**[280] 6048 3-9-0 75 ... DaleSwift(7) 4 (B Ellison) *bhd and outpcd: sme hdwy over 1f out: kpt on: nvr nr ldrs* 13/2	48
0031	6	2 ½	**Ya Boy Sir (IRE)**[7] 3167 3-8-2 56 oh4 ... PaulHanagan 7 (N Wilson) *chsd ldng gp: hung lft and effrt 2f out: wknd fnl f* 5/2[2]	20+
3000	7	20	**Fine And Dandie (IRE)**[3] 3286 3-8-2 56 oh4 ...(b) AndrewMullen 6 (D Nicholls) *led 2f: cl up tl wknd wl over 1f out: t.o* 33/1	—
20-6	8	18	**Six Wives**[153] 277 3-8-11 65 ... RobertWinston 3 (J A Glover) *towards rr and sn outpcd: lost tch fr 1/2-way* 20/1	—

60.33 secs (-0.77) **Going Correction** -0.175s/f (Firm) 8 Ran SP% **115.4**
Speed ratings (Par 99): **95,91,85,79,77 73,41,13**
toteswingers: 1&2 £1.80, 1&3 £12.30, 2&3 £6.10. CSF £11.90 CT £98.54 TOTE £3.10: £1.40, £2.00, £1.90; EX 10.60 Place 6: £92.95 Place 5: £32.03.
Owner Mrs Ann Morris **Bred** Mrs A Morris **Trained** Hambleton, N Yorks

FOCUS
Plenty of in-form runners lined up for this 0-75 handicap. The pace was not particularly strong and the well backed favourite hammered her rivals under a shrewd front-running ride. The form is taken at face value.
Ya Boy Sir(IRE) Official explanation: jockey said colt hung left throughout
Fine And Dandie(IRE) Official explanation: jockey said gelding hung both ways
Six Wives Official explanation: jockey said filly became upset in stalls
T/Plt: £73.60 to a £1 stake. Pool: £60,792.06 - 602.93 winning tickets T/Qpdt: £14.10 to a £1 stake. Pool: £4,754.61 - 249.22 winning tickets RY

3215 **NEWMARKET** (July Course) (R-H)
Friday, June 25
OFFICIAL GOING: Good to firm (good in places; 8.7)
Wind: Light across Weather: Overcast

3411 EUROPEAN BREEDERS' FUND MAIDEN FILLIES' STKS 6f
6:00 (6:01) (Class 4) 2-Y-O £5,180 (£1,541; £770; £384) Stalls Low

Form				RPR
2	1		**Sweet Cecily (IRE)**[14] 2930 2-9-0 0 ... RichardHughes 3 (R Hannon) *mde all: shkn up over 1f out: qcknd clr fnl f: impressive* 11/2[2]	88+
	2	6	**Ragsah (IRE)** 2-9-0 0 ... FrankieDettori 8 (Saeed Bin Suroor) *a.p: chsd wnr over 2f out: shkn up over 1f out: sn outpcd* 4/7[1]	70+
	3	1	**Wiqaaya (IRE)** 2-9-0 0 ... TadhgO'Shea 4 (E A L Dunlop) *chsd wnr to 1/2-way: rdn over 1f out: styd on same pce* 33/1	67+
	4	1 ¼	**Our Way Only (IRE)** 2-9-0 0 ... PatCosgrave 11 (R Hannon) *s.s: hld up: swvd rt 1/2-way: hdwy over 2f out: wknd ins fnl f* 50/1	63+
	5	1	**Spennymoor (IRE)** 2-9-0 0 ... AhmedAjtebi 5 (Mahmood Al Zarooni) *chsd ldrs: rdn over 2f out: edgd lft over 1f out: wknd fnl f* 20/1	60
	6	nk	**Istishaara (USA)** 2-9-0 0 ... DaneO'Neill 7 (J L Dunlop) *hld up: pushed along 1/2-way: n.d* 50/1	59+
	7	1	**Fakhuur** 2-9-0 0 ... SebSanders 1 (C E Brittain) *s.s: sme hdwy and hung lft over 1f out: n.d* 33/1	56+
3	8	hd	**Miss Moneypenni**[18] 2819 2-9-0 0 ... NeilCallan 12 (N P Littmoden) *racd wd: prom: chsd wnr 1/2-way to 2f out: sn rdn and hung lft: wknd fnl f* 16/1	56
	9	¾	**Empress Charlotte** 2-9-0 0 ... HayleyTurner 6 (M L W Bell) *s.s: hld up: rdn and wknd over 1f out* 20/1	54
	10	5	**Awesome Asset (USA)** 2-9-0 0 ... RyanMoore 9 (J Noseda) *sn pushed along in rr: bmpd 1/2-way: sn lost tch* 6/1[3]	39
	11	6	**Cometh** 2-9-0 0 ... MickyFenton 10 (N P Littmoden) *sn outpcd and bhd* 100/1	21
0	12	2 ¼	**Dallas Legend (IRE)**[11] 3029 2-9-0 0 ... MarcHalford 2 (J Ryan) *prom: rdn 1/2-way: wknd 2f out* 100/1	14

1m 13.8s (1.30) **Going Correction** +0.10s/f (Good) 12 Ran SP% **120.5**
Speed ratings (Par 92): **95,87,85,84,82 82,80,80,79,73 65,62**
Tote Swingers: 1&2 £1.50, 1&3 £25.00, 2&3 £14.70 CSF £8.60 TOTE £7.00: £2.00, £1.10, £8.60; EX 12.00 TRIFECTA .
Owner Mrs J Wood **Bred** Knocklong House Stud **Trained** East Everleigh, Wilts

FOCUS
Only three of these had previous racetrack experience including the winner, who impressed. The next two look likely maiden winners.

NOTEBOOK
Sweet Cecily(IRE), second over 5f at Sandown on her debut two weeks ago, had clearly tightened up mentally and physically for that as she dictated from the front in a race that very few got into. Her mother won at 5f and she has inherited plenty of speed with connections considering stepping her up into stakes company. That will be a totally different ball-game but if she can improve again then she can make her mark in better company. (op 4-1)
Ragsah(IRE) ◆ looked perfectly positioned to strike approaching the business end of the race, but was unable to go on with the winner. A half-sister to the brilliant Dubai Millennium among other winners, she will have learnt plenty from this experience and is likely to take the beating next time out. She is a nice type and will almost certainly get better as she matures and is upped in trip. (op 8-13 after early 8-11 and 4-5 in places)
Wiqaaya(IRE) ◆ was also well beaten but gave a good account of herself on her racetrack bow. From a fast family, she showed sufficient dash to suggest that she can go very close in a similar race next time, granted the usual level of development from a first run. (tchd 40-1)
Our Way Only(IRE) ◆ was slowly away and probably lost a little more ground in tacking over towards the far rail. As such, she did well to finish in the first four and on paper looks the type to get better with age and when slightly upped in distance.
Istishaara(USA) ◆ impressed on paddock inspection and enjoyed her racecourse introduction in a manner that suggested she'll go forward with this under her belt. She is from a family that has thrown up plenty of classy performers but is likely to be seen to better effect over 7f and beyond in the future.
Miss Moneypenni was a satisfactory third on debut at Windsor over this trip but didn't build on that here.
Awesome Asset(USA), a half-sister to plenty of winners, was relatively prominent in the market but never looked like getting a blow in. (op 7-1 tchd 5-1)
Cometh was very green.

3412 NEWMARKET NIGHTS H'CAP 1m
6:30 (6:30) (Class 5) (0-75,75) 3-Y-O+ £3,238 (£963; £481; £240) Stalls Low

Form				RPR
5451	1		**Sacrilege**[7] 3168 5-8-13 65 ...(p) MarkCoumbe(5) 5 (M C Chapman) *dwlt: hld up: hdwy over 1f out: swtchd rt wl ins fnl f: r.o to ld nr fin* 8/1	76
4-65	2	1 ¼	**Wilfred Pickles (IRE)**[18] 2823 4-9-12 73 ... DaneO'Neill 8 (Miss Jo Crowley) *hld up in tch: swtchd lft over 1f out: rdn to ld 1f out: hdd nr fin* 6/1	81
0033	3	1 ¾	**King Columbo (IRE)**[7] 3168 5-8-13 67 ... AdamBeschizza(7) 11 (Miss J Feilden) *hld up: hdwy 2f out: rdn and nt clr run over 1f out: r.o* 11/2[3]	71
35-0	4	hd	**Rock Anthem (IRE)**[74] 1265 6-9-7 75 ... BarryAdams(7) 3 (Mike Murphy) *hld up: hdwy and nt clr run over 2f out: styng on whn hmpd wl ins fnl f* 25/1	79
0500	5	1	**Emeebee**[18] 2823 4-9-9 70 ... RichardHughes 6 (W J Musson) *trckd ldrs: rdn over 1f out: styd on same pce ins fnl f* 9/1	71
6032	6	nk	**Eastern Gift**[7] 3168 5-9-6 67 ... RyanMoore 12 (Miss Gay Kelleway) *hld up: hdwy over 2f out: rdn and hung lft fr over 1f out: sn ev ch: no ex ins fnl f* 9/2[2]	68
4-23	7	1	**Saturn Way (GR)**[18] 2823 4-9-11 72 ... LiamKeniry 1 (P R Chamings) *prom: chsd ldr over 3f out: rdn to ld and edgd rt over 1f out: sn hdd: no ex ins fnl f* 3/1[1]	70
2004	8	1 ¾	**Orpen Wide (IRE)**[7] 3168 8-8-9 63 ...(b) DavidKenny(7) 4 (M C Chapman) *sn pushed along to ld: rdn and hdd over 1f out: wknd ins fnl f* 16/1	57

-001 9 11 **Aviso (GER)**[81] 1130 6-9-7 68 MickyFenton 10 37
(B J Curley) *plld hrd and sn trcking ldrs: rdn over 3f out: hmpd and wknd over 2f out* 16/1
0650 10 11 **Negotiation (IRE)**[8] 3117 4-9-9 70 SebSanders 7 14
(M Quinn) *chsd ldr to 1/2-way: wknd over 2f out* 16/1
1m 40.08s (0.08) **Going Correction** +0.10s/f (Good) 10 Ran SP% **115.5**
Speed ratings (Par 103): **103,101,100,99,98 98,97,95,84,73**
Tote Swingers: 1&2 £12.10, 1&3 £9.20, 2&3 £7.50 CSF £54.83 CT £294.25 TOTE £10.10: £2.90, £1.90, £2.30; EX 46.20.
Owner F Michael **Bred** The National Stud **Trained** Market Rasen, Lincs
■ Stewards' Enquiry : Mark Coumbe two-day ban: careless riding (Jul 12-13)

FOCUS
A competitive race of its type, but the time was ordinary. The form is rated through the runner-up.

3413 DANWOOD CLAIMING STKS 1m
7:00 (7:02) (Class 5) 3-Y-O **£3,238** (£963; £481; £240) **Stalls** Low

Form RPR
5000 1 **Calypso Star (IRE)**[11] 3039 3-8-11 70 (b) RichardHughes 8 70
(R Hannon) *hld up: hdwy 2f out: rdn to ld ins fnl f: r.o* 4/1[2]
0046 2 ¾ **Syrian**[13] 2970 3-9-13 84 JamieSpencer 12 84
(M L W Bell) *stdd s: hld up: hdwy 3f out: sn hung lft: led 2f out: rdn and hdd ins fnl f: styd on* 5/1[3]
-034 3 3 ¾ **On The Cusp (IRE)**[35] 2288 3-9-5 65 NeilCallan 10 67
(M A Jarvis) *hld up: hdwy over 3f out: rdn over 2f out: styd on same pce fnl f* 14/1
3402 4 1 ½ **Miami Gator (IRE)**[21] 2725 3-8-11 63 (v) AndrewElliott 1 56
(J R Weymes) *led: rdn and hdd 2f out: no ex fnl f* 12/1
6105 5 6 **Sternian**[15] 2906 3-8-4 57 (b[1]) JamieMackay 9 35
(M E Rimmer) *prom: chsd ldr over 3f out: rdn and ev ch 2f out: no ex fnl f* 40/1
0560 6 11 **Inpursuitoffreedom**[7] 3171 3-7-13 63 TobyAtkinson[(5)] 7 10
(P J McBride) *hld up: hdwy over 2f out: nt rcvr* 15/2
6005 7 4 **Bell's Ocean (USA)**[4] 3271 3-8-4 50 MarcHalford 3 —
(J Ryan) *hld up: hmpd over 2f out: n.d* 25/1
4000 8 ¾ **Marafong**[12] 2993 3-8-2 70 AdamBeschizza[(7)] 6 —
(Miss J Feilden) *chsd ldrs: wkng whn hmpd over 2f out* 66/1
610- 9 1 ½ **Chain Of Office**[248] 6923 3-8-9 73 RyanMoore 4 —
(W J Haggas) *trckd ldrs: plld hrd: hmpd and wknd over 2f out* 11/4[1]
0432 10 3 ½ **Brave Decision**[16] 2878 3-8-9 57 (p) HayleyTurner 2 —
(R M H Cowell) *prom: hung rt fnl 3f: wknd over 2f out* 10/1
0 11 6 **Embarkation**[53] 1769 3-9-3 0 PatCosgrave 11 —
(J R Fanshawe) *hld up: swtchd rt 3f out: bdly hmpd and eased sn after* 50/1
0050 12 7 **Highland Bridge**[26] 2566 3-8-9 63 DaneO'Neill 5 —
(D R C Elsworth) *chsd ldr tl rdn over 3f out: wknd over 2f out* 25/1
-602 F **Louisiana Gift (IRE)**[19] 2780 3-8-6 61 (p) PatrickHills[(3)] 13 —
(J W Hills) *hld up: hdwy 1/2-way: rdn whn hmpd and fell over 2f out* 14/1
1m 39.25s (-0.75) **Going Correction** +0.10s/f (Good) 13 Ran SP% **118.8**
Speed ratings (Par 99): **107,106,102,101,95 84,80,79,77,74 68,61,—**
Tote Swingers: 1&2 £4.90, 1&3 £10.80, 2&3 £14.10 CSF £23.08 TOTE £4.60: £2.10, £1.50, £3.90; EX 20.30.
Owner A C Pickford & N A Woodcock **Bred** Lisieux Stud **Trained** East Everleigh, Wilts

FOCUS
This was a most unsatisfactory race, with a serious incident occurring over 2f out that resulted in Louisiana Gift being brought down and a host of other horses being hampered. The form is rated around the winner.
Inpursuitoffreedom Official explanation: jockey said filly suffered interference in running
Chain Of Office Official explanation: jockey said filly was denied a clear run
Brave Decision Official explanation: jockey said gelding hung right throughout
Embarkation Official explanation: jockey said gelding suffered interference in running

3414 INVESCO PERPETUAL H'CAP 1m 4f
7:35 (7:35) (Class 4) (0-80,82) 3-Y-O **£4,857** (£1,445; £722; £360) **Stalls** Centre

Form RPR
0-14 1 **Trovare (USA)**[15] 2893 3-9-3 72 RyanMoore 2 83+
(Mrs A J Perrett) *chsd ldrs: led over 2f out: rdn and hung rt over 1f out: styd on u.p* 11/4[2]
62-1 2 nk **Calatrava Cape (IRE)**[7] 3170 3-9-6 75 6ex TedDurcan 4 86+
(J L Dunlop) *hld up: hdwy over 2f out: rdn: hung lft and ev ch fr over 1f out: styd on u.p* 11/8[1]
-000 3 2 ¼ **Higgy's Ragazzo (FR)**[16] 2869 3-9-5 74 RichardHughes 7 81
(R Hannon) *hld up: hdwy over 2f out: rdn and hung lft fr over 1f out: styd on* 10/1
1242 4 11 **Shelfah (IRE)**[21] 2704 3-9-9 78 FrankieDettori 1 67
(M A Jarvis) *sn led: hdd over 9f out: chsd clr ldr: tk clsr order over 3f out: rdn and ev ch over 2f out: wknd over 1f out* 10/3[3]
0-40 5 6 **Banana Republic (IRE)**[21] 2717 3-9-0 69 JamieSpencer 3 49
(P F I Cole) *hld up: plld hrd: hdwy to ld over 9f out: sn clr: rdn and edgd rt over 3f out: hdd over 2f out: sn wknd* 14/1
3-00 6 15 **Retrato (USA)**[23] 2658 3-8-7 62 DavidProbert 6 18
(Rae Guest) *hld up: hdwy u.p 3f out: hung rt and wknd 2f out: t.o* 28/1
2m 31.92s (-0.98) **Going Correction** +0.10s/f (Good) 6 Ran SP% **111.1**
Speed ratings (Par 101): **107,106,105,97,93 83**
Tote Swingers: 1&2 £1.90, 1&3 £3.70, 2&3 £4.30 CSF £6.78 TOTE £3.20: £1.80, £1.70; EX 7.70.
Owner John Connolly **Bred** James Heyward **Trained** Pulborough, W Sussex
■ Stewards' Enquiry : David Probert caution: used whip when out of contention.

FOCUS
The only two horses to take from the race for future consideration are the front pair, who look progressive. Sound form amongst the principals, who finished clear.
Banana Republic(IRE) Official explanation: jockey said gelding ran too free

3415 EUROPEAN BREEDERS' FUND FILLIES' CONDITIONS STKS 6f
8:05 (8:05) (Class 3) 3-Y-O+ **£9,066** (£2,697; £1,348; £673) **Stalls** Low

Form RPR
6-54 1 **Bounty Box**[28] 2508 4-8-12 93 TedDurcan 8 101
(C F Wall) *hld up: hdwy 2f out: hung lft over 1f out: rdn to ld wl ins fnl f* 10/3[2]
2- 2 ½ **Swiss Diva**[300] 5434 4-8-12 101 RyanMoore 7 99
(D R C Elsworth) *hld up in tch: jnd ldr 1/2-way: rdn and hung rt over 1f out: r.o* 7/4[1]
5-1 3 ½ **Flambeau**[41] 2122 3-8-8 82 DaneO'Neill 4 99
(H Candy) *trckd ldrs: racd keenly: led 1/2-way: rdn over 1f out: hdd wl ins fnl f* 10/3[2]
1211 4 3 ¾ **Rio Mist**[14] 2928 3-8-6 90 ow1 RichardHughes 6 85
(R Hannon) *trckd ldrs: rdn over 1f out: wknd ins fnl f* 7/2[3]
6302 5 11 **Angus Newz**[16] 2877 7-8-12 84 SebSanders 2 51
(M Quinn) *sn led: hdd 2f out: wknd over 1f out* 16/1
0-00 6 8 **Gessabelle**[16] 2878 3-7-12 42 (t) LeonnaMayor[(7)] 1 23
(P S McEntee) *chsd ldr tl rdn 1/2-way: wknd wl over 1f out* 100/1
000 7 1 ¾ **Slap And Tickle (IRE)**[16] 2876 4-8-5 48 CarolineKelly[(7)] 5 19
(M D Squance) *s.s: outpcd* 100/1
1m 12.36s (-0.14) **Going Correction** +0.10s/f (Good)
WFA 3 from 4yo+ 7lb 7 Ran SP% **112.6**
Speed ratings (Par 104): **104,103,102,97,83 72,70**
Tote Swingers: 1&2 £2.00, 1&3 £2.90, 2&3 £2.10 CSF £9.28 TOTE £4.20: £1.70, £2.00; EX 9.00.
Owner John E Sims **Bred** Farmers Hill Stud **Trained** Newmarket, Suffolk

FOCUS
A fair conditions event. The winner is rated back to her best and the race could turn out a bit better than rated.

NOTEBOOK
Bounty Box showed how she relishes the July Course with her third C&D victory. A stiff 6f seems to suit her and she only got on top as the line loomed. Connections feel she is a better filly on this track, but will consider heading to York for the Group 3 Summer Stakes on July 9. (op 4-1 tchd 3-1)
Swiss Diva ◆ was returning from a 300-day layoff. Best in on official figures, she may prefer an easier surface but shouldn't be too long in adding to her three career wins. (op 9-4 tchd 5-2 in places)
Flambeau ◆ had impressed when winning her maiden over 7f at Newbury last time and it looked indicative that her shrewd connections chose to run her in a race where the conditions meant she wasn't best treated at the weights. A powerful-moving filly with an action suited by fast ground, there probably wasn't enough early speed for her. She may have been better suited by bowling along out in front with that long stride rather seeking to get a tow into the contest. There are certainly more races to be won with her. (op 11-4 tchd 4-1)
Rio Mist arrived here with a progressive profile, having won her last two. But this was a marked step up in class and she was well beaten. She has been kept fairly busy through the early part of the season and may benefit from a break. (op 3-1 tchd 4-1)
Angus Newz, a once-prolific winner including at Listed level, is now on a long losing run that stretches back to September 2008. (op 14-1 tchd 12-1)

3416 JAMIE & ALI'S BIRTHDAY CELEBRATION H'CAP 1m 2f
8:40 (8:40) (Class 4) (0-80,80) 3-Y-O+
£4,673 (£1,399; £699; £350; £174; £87) **Stalls** Centre

Form RPR
12-0 1 **Sircozy (IRE)**[15] 2894 4-9-3 67 RyanMoore 7 77
(G L Moore) *hld up: hdwy wl over 1f out: sn rdn to chse ldr and hung rt: r.o to ld nr fin* 11/2[3]
1211 2 hd **Speed Dating**[2] 3329 4-10-2 80 6ex (b) SebSanders 1 90
(Sir Mark Prescott) *hld up: hdwy 1/2-way: rdn to ld and hung rt over 1f out: hdd nr fin* 10/11[1]
000 3 3 **Monte Cavallo (SAF)**[22] 2685 5-10-0 78 StephenCraine 2 82
(M Wigham) *s.i.s: hld up: hdwy and nt clr run fr over 2f out tl jst over 1f out: styd on same pce ins fnl f* 16/1
3102 4 2 ½ **Bollin Dolly**[9] 3089 7-9-11 75 TedDurcan 3 74+
(T D Easterby) *trckd ldrs: nt clr run fr over 2f out tl hmpd and lost pl over 1f out: r.o ins fnl f: nvr able to chal* 9/2[2]
-002 5 4 **Folio (IRE)**[25] 2602 10-8-11 61 JamieMackay 4 52
(W J Musson) *hld up: hdwy over 4f out: nt clr run briefly over 1f out: shkn up: nt trble ldrs* 12/1
5055 6 3 ¼ **Valmari (IRE)**[4] 3267 7-9-4 68 SaleemGolam 5 53
(G Prodromou) *chsd ldrs: rdn over 3f out: wkng whn hmpd over 1f out* 33/1
00-1 7 ¾ **Dancing Jest (IRE)**[37] 2233 6-9-2 66 DavidProbert 10 49
(Rae Guest) *chsd ldr: rdn over 2f out: sn ev ch: hmpd over 1f out: wknd fnl f* 14/1
441- 8 2 ¾ **Laish Ya Hajar (IRE)**[378] 2878 6-9-10 74 RichardHughes 8 60
(P R Webber) *led: hung lft and hdd over 1f out: eased* 16/1
600- 9 17 **Sonny Parkin**[212] 7512 8-8-11 66 (v) SimonPearce[(5)] 6 10
(J Pearce) *s.i.s: hld up: sme hdwy over 3f out: wknd over 2f out* 33/1
2m 6.41s (0.91) **Going Correction** +0.10s/f (Good) 9 Ran SP% **118.0**
Speed ratings (Par 105): **100,99,97,95,92 89,89,86,73**
Tote Swingers: 1&2 £2.20, 1&3 £17.30, 2&3 £6.50 CSF £11.09 CT £75.06 TOTE £7.00: £1.90, £1.10, £4.40; EX 13.10.
Owner A E Dean **Bred** Allevamento Pian Di Neve Srl **Trained** Lower Beeding, W Sussex
■ Stewards' Enquiry : Seb Sanders caution: careless riding; one-day ban: careless riding (Jul 10)

FOCUS
This was another somewhat messy affair but the front three were not too inconvenienced. A 4lb personal best from the winner.
Bollin Dolly Official explanation: jockey said mare was denied a clear run
Laish Ya Hajar(IRE) Official explanation: jockey said gelding lost its action

3417 TURFTV H'CAP 5f
9:10 (9:10) (Class 4) (0-85,84) 3-Y-O+ **£4,857** (£1,445; £722; £360) **Stalls** Low

Form RPR
11 1 **Captain Coke (IRE)**[7] 3174 3-8-13 75 6ex AndreaAtzeni 9 86+
(Denis P Quinn, Ire) *trckd ldrs: rdn to ld ins fnl f: r.o wl* 13/8[1]
4235 2 1 ½ **Brynfa Boy**[13] 2973 4-9-3 73 NeilCallan 8 80
(P W D'Arcy) *plld hrd and prom: rdn and swtchd lft over 1f out: styd on* 5/2[2]
0-41 3 hd **Steelcut**[13] 2973 6-9-3 76 RussKennemore[(3)] 3 83
(Andrew Reid) *chsd ldr tl led over 1f out: rdn and hdd ins fnl f: styd on same pce* 13/2
2146 4 shd **Diamond Johnny G (USA)**[13] 2972 3-8-11 73 (t) EddieCreighton 2 77
(E J Creighton) *led over 3f: sn rdn: ev ch ins fnl f: styd on* 16/1
0-00 5 1 ½ **Tony The Tap**[20] 2759 9-9-7 84 JamesRogers[(7)] 4 85
(W R Muir) *s.s: outpcd: r.o ins fnl f: nrst fin* 12/1
10-0 6 shd **Fleeting Star (USA)**[11] 3037 4-9-8 78 (v) RyanMoore 7 79
(J Noseda) *hld up: rdn over 1f out: no rspnse* 6/1[3]
00-0 7 2 ¼ **Tyrannosaurus Rex (IRE)**[14] 2940 6-9-4 74 DaneO'Neill 6 67
(D Shaw) *chsd ldrs: rdn over 1f out: no ex ins fnl f* 10/1
59.60 secs (0.50) **Going Correction** +0.10s/f (Good)
WFA 3 from 4yo+ 6lb 7 Ran SP% **117.0**
Speed ratings (Par 105): **100,97,97,97,94 94,90**
Tote Swingers: 1&2 £1.40, 1&3 £3.10, 2&3 £3.80 CSF £6.11 CT £19.98 TOTE £3.10: £2.40, £1.80 Place 6: £18.17 Place 5: £14.11 .
Owner Peter A Quinn **Bred** Fintan Walsh **Trained** Sixmilebridge, Co. Clare

FOCUS
The form of this sprint looks fairly solid, rated through the second and third.
T/Plt: £27.60 to a £1 stake. Pool: £56,767.33 - 1,500.35 winning tickets T/Qpdt: £8.20 to a £1 stake. Pool: £3,611.07 - 325.76 winning tickets CR

3418 - 3420a (Foreign Racing) - See Raceform Interactive

2728 CURRAGH (R-H)

Friday, June 25

OFFICIAL GOING: Straight course - good (good to firm in places); round course - good to firm

3421a BALLYGALLON STUD STKS (REGISTERED AS BALANCHINE STAKES) (LISTED RACE) (FILLIES) 6f

7:30 (7:30) 2-Y-O **£25,884** (£7,566; £3,584; £1,194)

			RPR
1		**Seeharn (IRE)**[21] 2728 2-8-12 .... DPMcDonogh 2 (Kevin Prendergast, Ire) *settled 3rd: 2nd and chal 1 1/2f out: led 1f out: r.o wl: comf* **3/1**[3]	99+
2	1	**Gatamalata (IRE)**[13] 2983 2-8-12 .... CDHayes 3 (Joseph G Murphy, Ire) *s.i.s and bhd: 8th and hdwy 1f out: r.o strly: nrst at fin* **20/1**	96+
3	1 1/4	**Moonlit Garden (IRE)**[9] 3070 2-8-12 .... PJSmullen 7 (D K Weld, Ire) *led: strly pressed fr 2f out: hdd 1f out: sn no ex* **9/4**[1]	92
4	1	**Galloping Queen (IRE)**[16] 2861 2-8-12 .... FMBerry 4 (M R Channon) *chsd ldrs: 7th 1/2-way: rdn over 2f out: 5th under 1f out: kpt on* **20/1**	89
5	shd	**Emerald Ring (IRE)**[18] 2828 2-8-12 .... WMLordan 9 (David Wachman, Ire) *trckd ldrs on outer: 5th 1/2-way: kpt on same pce fr 1 1/2f out* **8/1**	89
6	4	**Foot Perfect (IRE)**[18] 2828 2-8-12 .... CO'Donoghue 6 (David Marnane, Ire) *prom: 4th 1/2-way: no ex fr 1 1/2f out* **33/1**	77
7	1/2	**Khelino (IRE)**[12] 3003 2-8-12 .... BACurtis 5 (Rodger Sweeney, Ire) *towards rr: sme prog on outer 2f out: sn no ex* **33/1**	75
8	4	**Purple Glow (IRE)**[9] 3070 2-8-12 .... KJManning 1 (J S Bolger, Ire) *prom on stands' rail: 2nd 1/2-way: sn rdn: wknd fr 1 1/2f out* **8/1**	63
9	1 3/4	**Looking Lovely (IRE)**[8] 3133 2-8-12 .... JMurtagh 8 (A P O'Brien, Ire) *chsd ldrs in 6th: rdn 1/2-way: bhd whn eased fnl f* **11/4**[2]	58

1m 12.66s (-2.34) **Going Correction** -0.375s/f (Firm) 9 Ran SP% **120.1**
Speed ratings: **100,98,97,95,95 90,89,84,81**
CSF £65.02 TOTE £3.50: £1.10, £3.60, £2.00; DF 97.10.
Owner Norman Ormiston **Bred** Irish National Stud **Trained** Friarstown, Co Kildare
■ Stewards' Enquiry : P J Smullen severe caution: moved across before the marker poles

FOCUS
The winner improved on her good maiden win and can do better again. The form looks solid.

NOTEBOOK
Seeharn(IRE) ran out a gutsy winner of this competitive race, considering her trainer feels she hated the ground. Racing close to the pace and showing a nice bit of speed, she led over a furlong out and, while it took her most of the final furlong to beat off the challenge of the favourite, she showed resolution and gave the impression that an extra furlong would not trouble her. A good filly and improving, she is unlikely to be seen out again before the Moyglare Stud Stakes in late August. (op 3/1 tchd 11/4)
Gatamalata(IRE) is undoubtedly a good filly and was a shade unlucky. She fell out of the stalls and struggled to get into the race, but ran on really well inside the last, having had to manoeuvre to get a gap. Runs like this can often be flattering and time will tell, but this looks a filly who will come into her own over an extra furlong and has a bit of quality.
Moonlit Garden(IRE) showed some of the real speed in the race and battled it out with the winner from the 2f pole, but in the end she just ran out of steam. She's still capable of winning a nice race. (op 2/1)
Galloping Queen(IRE) fractionally missed the break but soon made up the ground and looked a serious threat when closing up 2f out. She was looking for racing room at that point but her effort began to peter out as the two leaders went on. It was a respectable effort.
Emerald Ring(IRE) never really had the pace to get involved but did stay on late and will get another furlong.
Foot Perfect(IRE) raced with plenty of dash but was ridden and beginning to struggle 2f out.
Purple Glow(IRE) disputed the lead to halfway before dropping away. (op 9/1)

3422 - 3424a (Foreign Racing) - See Raceform Interactive

2917 MAISONS-LAFFITTE (R-H)

Friday, June 25

OFFICIAL GOING: Turf: good

3425a PRIX HAMPTON (LISTED RACE) (3YO+) (TURF) 5f

2:35 (12:00) 3-Y-O+ **£23,008** (£9,203; £6,902; £4,601; £2,300)

			RPR
1		**Delvita (FR)**[19] 2804 6-9-2 0 .... GregoryBenoist 5 (J-V Toux, France) **4/1**[2]	103
2	shd	**Dam D'Augy (FR)**[39] 5-8-13 0 .... (b) ThierryJarnet 10 (Mlle S-V Tarrou, France) **8/1**[3]	100
3	1/2	**Moorhouse Lad**[20] 2745 7-9-2 0 .... TomEaves 2 (B Smart) *broke fast to ld: stl led at 1/2-way: rdn 2f out: hdd 1 1/2f out by eventual wnr: styd on wl* **8/1**[3]	101
4	1	**Orpen Shadow (IRE)**[77] 3-8-10 0 .... ChristopheSoumillon 6 (J-C Rouget, France) **9/5**[1]	95
5	nk	**Top Music**[36] 2271 3-8-10 0 .... OlivierPeslier 8 (A Fabre, France) **8/1**[3]	94
6	nse	**Tertio Bloom (SWE)**[19] 2804 5-9-8 0 .... ManuelMartinez 1 (Fredrik Reuterskiold, Sweden) **32/1**	102
7	snk	**Calrissian (GER)**[24] 6-9-5 0 .... MickaelBarzalona 13 (Fredrik Reuterskiold, Sweden) **56/1**	99
8	3/4	**Tiza (SAF)**[59] 1611 8-9-8 0 .... (p) GeraldMosse 11 (A De Royer-Dupre, France) **13/1**	99
9	1/2	**Kolokol (IRE)**[19] 2804 3-9-0 0 .... Christophe-PatriceLemaire 12 (D Prod'Homme, France) **17/1**	93
10	2	**Mood Music**[19] 2804 6-9-2 0 .... (b) MaximeGuyon 7 (Mario Hofer, Germany) **13/1**	84
0		**Manzila (FR)**[19] 2804 7-8-13 0 .... (p) CelineLaunay 3 (Mme C Barande-Barbe, France) **47/1**	—
0		**Best Joking (GER)**[40] 2157 5-9-2 0 .... JohanVictoire 4 (W Hefter, Germany) **57/1**	—

58.30 secs (58.30)
WFA 3 from 5yo+ 6lb 12 Ran SP% **117.5**
WIN (incl. 1 euro stake): 5.00. PLACES: 1.80, 2.70, 2.60. DF: 25.00. SF: 47.30.
Owner Raymond Choupeaux **Bred** Raymond Choupeaux **Trained** France

NOTEBOOK
Moorhouse Lad was quickly away and took the field along before being passed by the winner and runner-up at the furlong marker, where he stumbled. The King George Stakes at Goodwood, which he won in 2007, is now the target.

3386 CHESTER (L-H)

Saturday, June 26

OFFICIAL GOING: Good to firm (8.6)
Wind: Light, across Weather: Hot and Sunny

3426 TRAFFORD CENTRE ALWAYS AHEAD NOVICE STKS 5f 16y

2:05 (2:05) (Class 4) 2-Y-O **£4,857** (£1,445; £722; £360) **Stalls** Low

Form				RPR
221	1		**Leiba Leiba**[17] 2873 2-9-2 0 .... FrannyNorton 2 (M Botti) *racd keenly: trckd ldrs: nt clr run 2f out: wnt 2nd over 1f out: rdn to take narrow ld fnl 120yds: r.o on gamely in driving fin* **13/8**[1]	94
3021	2	nk	**The Thrill Is Gone**[14] 2963 2-8-11 0 .... SamHitchcott 1 (M R Channon) *led: rdn over 1f out: hdd narrowly fnl 120yds: stuck on gamely in driving fin* **9/2**[3]	88
23	3	6	**Lexi's Hero (IRE)**[30] 2448 2-9-0 0 .... TonyHamilton 3 (K A Ryan) *w ldr: rdn and lost 2nd over 1f out: no ch and outpcd by front pair ins fnl f* **7/4**[2]	69
0143	4	2 1/4	**Lord Avon**[11] 3059 2-9-2 0 .... JackDean(3) 5 (W G M Turner) *w ldrs racing 3 wd: effrt 2f out: u.p and nt qckning whn hung lft jst over 1f out: sn wknd* **13/2**	66
0023	5	22	**Fred Willetts (IRE)**[16] 2882 2-9-0 0 .... CathyGannon 4 (P D Evans) *outpcd: sn drvn along and wl bhd: eased whn wl btn ins fnl f* **20/1**	—

59.94 secs (-1.06) **Going Correction** -0.25s/f (Firm) 2y crse rec 5 Ran SP% **110.7**
Speed ratings (Par 95): **98,97,87,84,49**
toteswinger: 1&2 £3.80. CSF £9.30 TOTE £2.60: £1.50, £1.90; EX 5.70.
Owner Dachel Stud **Bred** Dachel Stud **Trained** Newmarket, Suffolk
■ Stewards' Enquiry : Franny Norton caution: used whip without giving colt time to respond
Sam Hitchcott caution: used whip without giving filly time to respond

FOCUS
This was a race badly reduced by four non-runners, who would have started from the four widest stalls. The remaining quintet provided a strongly run contest, with three disputing the lead from the off, and they broke the juvenile course record. The winner produced a big step up on his previous form.

NOTEBOOK
Leiba Leiba, easy winner of a weak Yarmouth maiden last time when long odds-on, travelled beautifully behind the pace-setters and a nice gap appeared when the leaders fanned out after the cutaway. He had to work hard to get the better of the runner-up and only hit the front close to the line, but he always gave the impression he was going to get there. He continues to progress and, on this evidence, will get another furlong. (op 2-1 tchd 9-4)
The Thrill Is Gone ◆, the only filly in the field, proved weak in the market, despite having the best of the draw, and got very sweaty beforehand. She showed good early speed, but was given little peace by two of her rivals and did really well to shake them off and then make the favourite work hard to get the better of her in the closing stages. There are more races to be won with her. (op 10-3 tchd 3-1)
Lexi's Hero(IRE), surrounded by subsequent winners when placed in his first two starts, raced in the centre of the leading trio in the early stages, but after coming off the bridle over a furlong from home was made to look very one-paced. (op 5-2)
Lord Avon, whose win came on Polytrack, is best when able to dominate on his own but was forced to cover more ground by racing widest of the three leaders from his outside draw. Once under pressure 2f from home, he started to hang and was soon completely left behind. (op 5-1 tchd 7-1)
Fred Willetts(IRE) seemed to find 6f on an easier surface stretching him at Haydock last time, but he missed the break here and was quickly left trailing. Official explanation: jockey said gelding never travelled (op 12-1)

3427 TRAFFORD CENTRE HIGH HEEL H'CAP 1m 4f 66y

2:35 (2:35) (Class 4) (0-85,85) 3-Y-O **£5,180** (£1,541; £770; £384) **Stalls** Low

Form				RPR
-250	1		**Bowdler's Magic**[9] 3105 3-9-5 **81** .... RoystonFfrench 2 (M Johnston) *chsd ldr for 3f: hld up: effrt and prog over 1f out: r.o to ld fnl 75yds: pushed out cl home* **5/2**[1]	90+
0-1	2	1/2	**Park View**[56] 1705 3-8-13 **75** .... PhilipRobinson 6 (B W Hills) *led: rdn over 1f out: edgd rt ins fnl f: hdd fnl 75yds: hld cl home* **4/1**[3]	83
-251	3	1 1/4	**Mujdeya**[16] 2891 3-9-9 **85** .... RobertHavlin 5 (J H M Gosden) *chsd ldrs: racd in 2nd pl after 3f tl 5f out: chsd ldr again over 2f out: rdn over 1f out: 1/2 l down and chalng for press whn n.m.r and squeezed out fnl 75yds: no imp after* **4/1**[3]	93+
024	4	6	**Ejteyaaz**[14] 2979 3-9-7 **83** .... TonyHamilton 4 (R A Fahey) *hld up: pushed along over 2f out: outpcd by ldrs over 1f out: no imp after* **5/1**	79
-521	5	38	**Widezain (IRE)**[29] 2499 3-9-6 **82** .... SamHitchcott 1 (M R Channon) *hld up: impr to chse ldr 5f out: pushed along over 3f out: lost 2nd over 2f out: wknd over 1f out: bhd and lost tch fnl f: t.o* **7/2**[2]	18

2m 36.09s (-3.81) **Going Correction** -0.25s/f (Firm) 5 Ran SP% **107.5**
Speed ratings (Par 101): **102,101,100,96,71**
toteswinger: 1&2 £6.60. CSF £11.89 TOTE £3.20: £1.70, £1.50; EX 11.00.
Owner Paul Dean **Bred** Miss K Rausing **Trained** Middleham Moor, N Yorks
■ Stewards' Enquiry : Philip Robinson caution: careless riding.

FOCUS
A fair 3-y-o handicap, though they didn't go much of a pace early. The winner did not need to match his May form here and the runner-up produced a clear personal best.
Widezain(IRE) Official explanation: jockey said colt lost its action

3428 TRAFFORD CENTRE LBD MIDSUMMER MAIDEN STKS 1m 2f 75y

3:10 (3:13) (Class 4) 3-Y-O+ **£5,180** (£1,541; £770; £384) **Stalls** High

Form				RPR
0-3	1		**Flotation (USA)**[14] 2974 3-8-10 0 .... FrannyNorton 2 (B W Hills) *chsd ldrs: rdn over 1f out: sn pressed: edgd lft 110yds out: r.o wl and on top after* **11/4**[2]	74
0-20	2	1 3/4	**Ellbeedee (IRE)**[17] 2860 3-8-10 **73** .... PhilipRobinson 5 (M A Jarvis) *chsd ldrs: wnt 2nd and chalng fr over 1f out: nt clr run and lost momentum briefly fnl 110yds: nt qckn after* **4/1**[3]	73+
4-	3	3	**Blissful Moment (USA)**[268] 6423 3-9-1 0 .... RichardMullen 8 (Sir Michael Stoute) *in tch: pushed along and outpcd over 2f out: styd on fr over 1f out: wnt 3rd fnl 110yds: nt rch front 2: eased whn no imp towards fin* **5/4**[1]	70+

3235 **4** 2 1/4 **Layla's Boy**[35] 2315 3-9-1 68 .... TonyHamilton 4 66
(Ian Williams) *chsd ldr tl rdn over 1f out: sn outpcd by ldrs: no ex fnl 100yds* **10/1**

50 **5** 3 3/4 **Quick Deal (USA)**[23] 2684 3-9-1 0 .... RobertHavlin 6 59
(J H M Gosden) *in tch: rdn over 1f out: no imp on ldrs and outpcd after* **10/1**

6 3 3/4 **Large Scotch** 3-8-7 0 .... RobertLButler[(3)] 7 46
(Paul Green) *in rr: pushed along 4f out: lft bhd over 2f out: nvr able to get on terms* **33/1**

5-4 **7** 1/2 **Peckforton Castle**[22] 2692 3-9-1 0 .... PaulMulrennan 1 51
(Patrick Morris) *racd keenly: chsd ldrs: rdn and wknd over 1f out* **33/1**

0 **8** 2 **Stephie**[7] 3207 4-9-1 0 .... DavidSimmonson[(7)] 3 42
(M W Easterby) *in rr: lft bhd over 2f out: eased whn n.d ins fnl f* **50/1**

2m 10.12s (-2.08) **Going Correction** -0.25s/f (Firm)
WFA 3 from 4yo 12lb **8** Ran SP% **117.1**
Speed ratings (Par 105): **98,96,94,92,89 86,86,84**
toteswingers: 1&2 £3.40, 1&3 £1.20, 2&3 £1.80. CSF £14.44 TOTE £3.60: £1.50, £1.50, £1.10; EX 15.10.
Owner K Abdulla **Bred** Juddmonte Farms Inc **Trained** Lambourn, Berks
■ Stewards' Enquiry : Franny Norton caution: careless riding.

FOCUS
A couple of interesting types in this maiden, but the pace was modest and not many got into it. The front pair look the best guides to the form.

3429 TRAFFORD CENTRE INSPIRED INTERIORS H'CAP 7f 2y

3:45 (3:46) (Class 2) (0-100,98) 3-Y-**£12,616** (£3,776; £1,888; £944; £470) **Stalls** Low

Form RPR

4304 **1** **Below Zero (IRE)**[17] 2862 3-9-1 **90** .... AdrianNicholls 7 98
(M Johnston) *mde all: rdn and qcknd 2f out: r.o wl and in command fnl f* **14/1**

4-11 **2** 2 3/4 **Cansili Star**[22] 2713 3-9-4 **93** .... PhilipRobinson 2 94+
(M A Jarvis) *chsd ldrs: wnt 2nd under 2f out: rdn and edgd rt ins fnl f: no imp on wnr* **13/8**[1]

4325 **3** 2 1/2 **William Morgan (IRE)**[17] 2863 3-8-4 **79** oh2 .... SilvestreDeSousa 4 73
(R A Fahey) *chsd ldrs: pushed along 5f out: rdn and outpcd 2f out: styd on ins fnl f: tk 3rd fnl 100yds: nt pce to rch front 2* **5/1**[3]

321 **4** 1 1/4 **Rule Breaker (IRE)**[17] 2852 3-8-13 **88** .... RoystonFfrench 1 78
(M Johnston) *chsd wnr tl rdn and nt qckn under 2f out: one pce fnl f* **5/2**[2]

0-66 **5** 1/2 **Hunting Tartan**[45] 2028 3-9-3 **92** .... RobertHavlin 3 81
(J H M Gosden) *upset in stalls bef r: s.i.s: hld up: rdn over 1f out: kpt on u.p ins fnl f: nvr able to chal* **8/1**

2230 **6** 2 1/2 **Tiradito (USA)**[10] 3083 3-8-6 **81** .... (p) FrannyNorton 6 63
(M Botti) *in rr: struggling 2f out: nvr on terms* **20/1**

-466 **7** 1 **Layla's Hero (IRE)**[22] 2712 3-9-9 **98** .... TonyHamilton 5 78
(D M Simcock) *towards rr: bhd and outpcd 2f out: nvr a threat* **14/1**

1m 24.19s (-2.31) **Going Correction** -0.25s/f (Firm) course record **7** Ran SP% **112.5**
Speed ratings (Par 105): **103,99,97,95,95 92,91**
toteswingers: 1&2 £5.70, 1&3 £8.00, 2&3 £2.20. CSF £36.18 TOTE £18.50: £7.20, £1.20; EX 54.20.
Owner Sheikh Hamdan Bin Mohammed Al Maktoum **Bred** Darley **Trained** Middleham Moor, N Yorks

FOCUS
A decent handicap and again it paid to race handily, with little getting into it. The fortm is rated a bit negatively through the winner.

NOTEBOOK
Below Zero(IRE), back up in trip and down another 3lb, looked the stable's second string behind Rule Breaker, but blew that theory apart under a particularly fine ride from Adrian Nicholls, who quickly managed to get him across to lead from the outside stall. An injection of pace rounding the home bend enabled him to put daylight between himself and his rivals and he never looked like getting caught. (op 10-1)
Cansili Star, who beat the subsequent Buckingham Palace Stakes winner Treadwell at Epsom last time, was bidding for a hat-trick off an 8lb higher mark. A little free in the early stages, he still had every chance to pick up the winner in the home straight had he been good enough, but although he pulled clear of the others he could make no impression on him. (tchd 11-8 and 7-4 in places)
William Morgan(IRE), 2lb wrong, was well backed but struggled to go the pace and didn't find his stride until it was too late. He did get himself warm beforehand but probably needs a more galloping track in any case. (op 8-1)
Rule Breaker(IRE), making his handicap debut after easily winning an ordinary Beverley maiden this month, seemed to be in a good position in the slipstream of his stable companion but found little when coming under maximum pressure. It may be that he needs a stiffer test or is badly handicapped. (op 11-4 tchd 10-3 in places)
Hunting Tartan, just behind three subsequent winners when a disappointing sixth of ten at York last month, got upset in the stalls and that may have contributed to him making little impression. (op 10-1 tchd 11-1)
Tiradito(USA), consistent so far this year, likes a turning left-handed track like this but was always at the back of the field and never figured. (op 16-1)
Layla's Hero(IRE) was 15lb higher than when winning a Haydock nursery last September. He didn't get the breaks when attempting this trip for the first time at Epsom earlier in the month but was weak in the market here, played up before the start, and made little impact. (op 9-1)

3430 TRAFFORD CENTRE SUMMER FASHION H'CAP 5f 16y

4:20 (4:21) (Class 3) (0-90,90) 3-Y-O-**£8,831** (£2,643; £1,321; £660; £329) **Stalls** Low

Form RPR

1401 **1** **Ryan Style (IRE)**[7] 3201 4-9-1 **78** .... BarryMcHugh[(3)] 1 86
(Mrs L Williamson) *prom: rdn to ld 1f out: r.o wl and sn edgd rt: kpt on cl home* **7/2**[2]

0406 **2** 1/2 **Green Park (IRE)**[3] 3321 7-9-2 **76** .... (v[1]) DavidNolan 3 82+
(D Carroll) *chsd ldrs: rdn over 1f out: nt clr run briefly ins fnl f: gd run fnl 50yds: nt quite get there* **15/2**

4131 **3** 1/2 **Lost In Paris (IRE)**[21] 2756 4-9-6 **80** .... (v) AdrianNicholls 9 84
(T D Easterby) *prom: chsd ldr 3f out: chalng 2f out: rdn and nt qckn over 1f out: styd on u.p cl home* **6/1**

1034 **4** 3/4 **Lucky Dan (IRE)**[1] 3389 4-9-2 **76** .... FrannyNorton 8 77+
(Paul Green) *towards rr: pushed along early: rdn and hdwy over 1f out: styd on towards fin: nt quite pce of ldrs* **5/1**[3]

403 **5** 3/4 **Grissom (IRE)**[8] 3165 4-9-1 **75** .... PaulMulrennan 10 74
(A Berry) *hld up: rdn over 1f out: prog and styd on ins fnl f: no imp cl home* **25/1**

3001 **6** 1 **Bertoliver**[21] 2745 6-10-0 **88** .... PhilipRobinson 4 83
(S C Williams) *led: rdn over 1f out: sn hdd: no ex fnl 75yds* **3/1**[1]

1600 **7** *hd* **Falasteen (IRE)**[14] 2978 3-9-10 **90** .... TonyHamilton 7 84
(R A Fahey) *chsd ldrs: rdn and nt qckn over 1f out: one pce ins fnl f* **12/1**

0010 **8** 1/2 **Memphis Man**[12] 3037 7-8-6 **73** .... MatthewCosham[(7)] 5 65
(P D Evans) *dwlt: racd keenly: hld up: rdn over 1f out: nvr able to chal* **33/1**

550- **9** 1/2 **Dancing Red Devil (IRE)**[308] 5274 3-8-8 **74** .... SilvestreDeSousa 6 65
(Paul Green) *dwlt: midfield: rdn over 1f out: sn outpcd* **14/1**

3000 **10** *hd* **Hoh Hoh Hoh**[21] 2745 8-9-11 **85** .... RoystonFfrench 2 75
(R J Price) *dwlt: hld up: rdn over 1f out: nt pce to chal* **12/1**

59.96 secs (-1.04) **Going Correction** -0.25s/f (Firm)
WFA 3 from 4yo+ 6lb **10** Ran SP% **118.8**
Speed ratings (Par 107): **98,97,96,95,94 92,92,91,90,90**
toteswingers: 1&2 £7.90, 1&3 £5.80, 2&3 £9.50. CSF £30.75 CT £157.96 TOTE £5.40: £2.10, £2.50, £1.90; EX 34.70.
Owner Bluegrass Racing Ltd **Bred** Johnny Kent **Trained** Saighton, Cheshire
■ Stewards' Enquiry : Barry McHugh caution: careless riding.

FOCUS
Fast and furious stuff early in this decent sprint handicap, but surprisingly the winning time was slightly slower than the 2-y-os in the opener. Straightforward Chester form.

NOTEBOOK
Ryan Style(IRE), raised 4lb for his Ayr success, had the best of the draw and was able to get a nice lead. Switched to the inside after the cutaway, he quickened up well to hit the front a furlong out and always had matters under control thereafter, despite edging away to his right late on. He didn't see the racecourse until February, so he could still have some improvement left in him. (op 4-1 tchd 9-2)
Green Park(IRE), who had a first-time visor replacing the blinkers and was well drawn, finished well from the middle of the field and may have finished even closer had he not become short of room when trying for a gap between Bertoliver and Lost In Paris entering the last furlong. This was a decent effort as he may be best on softer ground. (op 8-1 tchd 7-1)
Lost In Paris(IRE), winner of two of his previous three starts and up another 5lb, was always close to the pace and had every chance until well inside the last furlong. This was a good effort from his wide draw. (tchd 7-1)
Lucky Dan(IRE) ◆, an unlucky fourth of 13 over 7f here the previous evening, was another drawn high and was doing all his best work late up the inside rail. He is better known as a sprinter, but on this evidence needs further than this these days. (tchd 9-2)
Grissom(IRE) ◆, an unlucky third at Musselburgh eight days earlier, gave himself plenty to do and didn't pick up until it was too late, but he needs softer ground and had the worst of the draw so he remains one to watch out for under more suitable conditions. (tchd 28-1)
Bertoliver, raised 5lb for his success in the Investec Dash at Epsom on Derby day, showed his usual blinding early speed, but he couldn't get clear and had run his race entering the last furlong. He was 8lb higher than when runner-up in this race last year, so has little in hand of the handicapper. (op 4-1)
Falasteen(IRE), one of two 3-y-os in the field and the best horse in the race on official ratings, was always going to find it hard to dominate his elders in this field. (tchd 11-1)
Memphis Man was always struggling and needs further than this these days. (op 25-1)

3431 TRAFFORD CENTRE FASHION PARADE CLAIMING STKS 1m 2f 75y

4:50 (4:53) (Class 5) 3-Y-O+ **£4,047** (£1,204; £601; £300) **Stalls** High

Form RPR

0005 **1** **Lang Shining (IRE)**[21] 2760 6-9-6 84 .... PaulMulrennan 2 86
(J A Osborne) *racd keenly: sn trckd ldrs: wnt 2nd over 4f out: moved upsides gng wl 3f out: led over 2f out: rdn abt 2 l clr over 1f out: kpt up to work towards fin* **7/1**

4616 **2** 3/4 **Trip The Light**[14] 2976 5-9-13 90 .... (v) TonyHamilton 5 91
(R A Fahey) *sn chsd ldr: led over 5f out: hdd over 2f out: rdn and nt qckn over 1f out wth abt 2 l down: rallied u.p towards fin but a hld* **7/4**[1]

0050 **3** 2 1/4 **Carcinetto (IRE)**[11] 3063 8-8-12 84 .... CathyGannon 7 71
(P D Evans) *hld up: rdn over 4f out: plenty of work to do over 2f out: styd on fr over 1f out: wnt 3rd ins fnl f: nt rch front 2* **7/1**

00-0 **4** 7 **Snoqualmie Boy**[6] 3239 7-9-6 86 .... AdrianNicholls 4 66
(D Nicholls) *racd keenly: prom: lost pl after 1 1/2f: sn in last pl: clsd 5f out: chalng 3 wd 3f out: rdn over 2f out: outpcd over 1f out: wknd fnl f* **4/1**[3]

50 **5** 24 **General Eliott (IRE)**[14] 2977 5-9-13 93 .... (p) SilvestreDeSousa 6 27
(P F I Cole) *sn trckd ldrs: rdn over 4f out: outpcd by front trio over 3f out: wknd 2f out: eased whn wl btn ins fnl f* **11/4**[2]

6-00 **6** 34 **Riqaab (IRE)**[7] 3206 5-8-10 67 .... DavidSimmonson[(7)] 1 —
(M W Easterby) *led: hdd over 5f out: rdn and wknd over 3f out: eased fnl f: t.o* **33/1**

2m 9.44s (-2.76) **Going Correction** -0.25s/f (Firm) **6** Ran SP% **111.0**
Speed ratings (Par 103): **101,100,98,93,73 46**
toteswingers: 1&2 £2.40, 1&3 £4.70, 2&3 £3.80. CSF £19.31 TOTE £7.30: £3.00, £1.50; EX 18.90.
Owner A Taylor **Bred** Ballymacoll Stud Farm Ltd **Trained** Upper Lambourn, Berks

FOCUS
A rather messy claimer in which they finished well spread out. It was a decent race for the grade but only the first two showed their form.

3432 TRAFFORD CENTRE DINING DELIGHTS H'CAP 1m 3f 79y

5:25 (5:25) (Class 4) (0-85,81) 4-Y-O+ **£5,180** (£1,541; £770; £384) **Stalls** Low

Form RPR

4214 **1** **Inspirina (IRE)**[10] 3090 6-8-11 **71** .... TonyHamilton 1 81
(R Ford) *racd keenly: mde all: qcknd abt 4 l clr 2f out: rdn over 1f out: kpt on and a doing enough towards fin* **7/1**

1313 **2** 1 1/4 **Destinys Dream (IRE)**[11] 3060 5-9-3 **80** .... KellyHarrison[(3)] 7 91+
(Miss Tracy Waggott) *hld up: rdn over 2f out: nt clr run whn wl bk over 2f out: hdwy whn nt clr run over 1f out: sn swtchd lft: wnt 2nd ent fnl f: r.o and clsd on wnr towards fin: nvr gng to get there* **5/1**[3]

4132 **3** 4 **Visions Of Johanna (USA)**[14] 2961 5-9-0 **74** .... PhilipRobinson 6 75
(Ian Williams) *hld up: hdwy to chse ldrs over 2f out: racd in 2nd over 1f out tl ent fnl f: no ex fnl 100yds* **5/2**[1]

0061 **4** 2 1/2 **Brouhaha**[19] 2821 6-9-0 **81** .... SoniaEaton[(7)] 5 78
(Tom Dascombe) *stdd s: hld up in rr: rdn over 1f out: kpt on fnl f: unable to rch ldrs* **11/1**

3-11 **5** 1 **Hel's Angel (IRE)**[11] 3060 4-9-3 **80** .... BarryMcHugh[(3)] 3 75
(Mrs A Duffield) *in tch: effrt to chse ldrs over 2f out: one pce fnl f* **9/2**[2]

-650 **6** 1 1/4 **Tilos Gem (IRE)**[21] 2766 4-8-5 **65** .... RoystonFfrench 2 58
(M Johnston) *chsd wnr: rdn over 3f out: outpcd by wnr 2f out: lost 2nd over 1f out: wknd fnl f* **16/1**

2235 **7** 1 3/4 **Embsay Crag**[29] 2513 4-9-6 **80** .... PaulMulrennan 4 70
(Mrs K Walton) *chsd ldrs: lost pl over 3f out: outpcd and bhd fr over 1f out* **9/2**[2]

00-0 **8** 28 **Novikov**[13] 2996 6-9-2 **76** .... (tp) CathyGannon 8 18
(P D Evans) *chsd ldrs: rdn 4f out: wknd 3f out: eased whn wl btn fnl f* **28/1**

2m 22.44s (-4.16) **Going Correction** -0.25s/f (Firm) course record **8** Ran SP% **111.8**
Speed ratings (Par 105): **105,104,101,99,98 97,96,76**
toteswingers: 1&2 £5.80, 1&3 £4.80, 2&3 £2.40. CSF £39.79 CT £109.55 TOTE £9.10: £2.20, £1.60, £1.40; EX 51.50 Place 6: £22.06, Place 5: £11.77..
Owner Miss Gill Quincey **Bred** Mohammad Al-Qatami **Trained** Butterton, Staffs

FOCUS
A fair handicap, though the early pace looked ordinary. The winner is rated back to her best but the second may have been unlucky.
Brouhaha Official explanation: jockey said, regarding running and riding, that her orders were to make the running if she broke well, if not, get across and stay on rail, the gelding missed the break and suffered slight interference leaving it further back than she had wished, waited until a gap came close to the rails and made her effort in home straight.
T/Plt: £16.40 to a £1 stake. Pool: £66,980.92 - 2,964.50 winning tickets. T/Qpdt: £5.20 to a £1 stake. Pool: £3,308.51 - 470.50 winning tickets. DO

3392 DONCASTER (L-H)
Saturday, June 26

OFFICIAL GOING: Good to firm (good in places; 8.4)
Wind: Light half against Weather: Sunny and dry

3433 CROWNHOTEL-BAWTRY.COM MAIDEN STKS 7f
6:40 (6:41) (Class 5) 2-Y-O £2,590 (£770; £385; £192) **Stalls** High

Form RPR
2 **1** **Belgian Bill**[22] 2701 2-9-3 0 TonyCulhane 2 82+
(George Baker) *trckd ldng pair: hdwy and cl up 3f out: rdn to ld jst over 1f out: drvn and edgd rt ent fnl f: styd on strly* **11/4**[2]
2 **2** *3* **Jaahiz (IRE)**[13] 3000 2-9-3 0 PatCosgrave 9 75
(R Hannon) *cl up: effrt over 2f out: sn rdn and led briefly wl over 1f out tl hdd appr fnl f: sn drvn and n.m.r: kpt on same pce* **11/8**[1]
0 **3** *¾* **Memorabilia**[14] 2980 2-9-3 0 JoeFanning 10 73+
(M Johnston) *led: rdn along on inner over 2f out: hdd wl over 1f out: cl up tl drvn and hld whn n.m.r ent fnl f: sn swtchd lft and kpt on towards fin* **14/1**
4 *1* **Azrael** 2-9-3 0 JamesDoyle 7 70
(A J McCabe) *in tch on inner: rdn along and rn green 2f out: kpt on wl fnl f: nrst fin* **66/1**
5 *hd* **Mubtadi** 2-9-3 0 TedDurcan 8 69+
(D M Simcock) *dwlt: hld up towards rr: swtchd lft and hdwy 2f out: chsd ldrs 1f out: keeeping on whn n.m.r nr fin* **9/1**
5 **6** *nk* **My Single Malt (IRE)**[49] 1905 2-9-3 0 JamieSpencer 6 68
(T P Tate) *chsd ldrs: effrt over 2f out: sn rdn: kpt on same pce fnl f* **5/1**[3]
7 *½* **Cuban Quality (USA)** 2-9-3 0 RichardKingscote 1 71+
(Tom Dascombe) *in tch: pushed along and rn green 2f out: hdwy ent fnl f: keeping on whn n.m.r and hmpd towards fin* **14/1**
8 *9* **Whitby Warrior (USA)** 2-9-3 0 GrahamGibbons 4 45
(C Grant) *wnt lft s: sn rdn along and a outpcd in rr* **40/1**
9 *13* **Kalkan Bay** 2-8-12 0 (b[1]) PatrickDonaghy(5) 5 12
(Jedd O'Keeffe) *t.k.h: towards rr: rdn along and outpcd 1/2-way: sn bhd* **100/1**

1m 25.41s (-0.89) **Going Correction** -0.425s/f (Firm) **9** Ran SP% **113.7**
Speed ratings (Par 93): **88,84,83,82,82 82,81,71,56**
toteswingers: 1&2 £2.10, 1&3 £8.20, 2&3 £3.50. CSF £6.73 TOTE £3.60: £1.30, £1.10, £5.10; EX 7.10.
Owner Mr & Mrs D Heath **Bred** Wickfield Stud And Hartshill Stud **Trained** Moreton Morrell, Warwicks

FOCUS
After another very warm day the going had dried out since the previous afternoon and was described as 'quite quick'. This was quite an interesting 7f maiden.

NOTEBOOK
Belgian Bill had achieved a RPR of 73 when runner-up over 6f here three weeks earlier on his debut. A decent type, he edged right towards the stands' side rail after taking charge but won going away. He will have no difficulty getting a mile and can improve again. (op 7-2 tchd 4-1 and 5-2)
Jaahiz(IRE), who looks on the weak side, achieved a RPR of 75 when runner-up first time at Salisbury two weeks earlier. After taking charge he was pushed slightly sideways, but the winner proved much too strong. A drop back to 6f might be in his favour. (tchd 6-4)
Memorabilia, who showed little when beaten some way on his debut at York two weeks earlier, showed plenty of dash to take them along against the stands' side rail. He was left short of room and had to switch when the winner edged in. To his credit, he was coming back for more at the line and is sure to improve again, He looks sure to find an opening. (op 16-1)
Azrael, bred for speed rather than stamina, had to be given some sharp reminders soon after the start. He put in some solid late work and this will have taught him plenty.
Mubtadi, a decent type, is out of mare that has already produced four winners. Given a patient ride on his debut, he picked up nicely and looks capable of a fair bit better. (op 7-1 tchd 13-2)
My Single Malt(IRE) stuck on in the closing stages after being tapped for toe and will do better over a mile. (op 4-1 tchd 7-2)
Cuban Quality(USA) was staying on in good style late on when tightened up. He is another who will improve for this first taste of racecourse action. (op 25-1 tchd 12-1)

3434 SOCIETY LIFESTYLE AND LEISURE MAGAZINE FILLIES' H'CAP 7f
7:10 (7:11) (Class 5) (0-70,70) 3-Y-O+ £2,590 (£770; £385; £192) **Stalls** High

Form RPR
-660 **1** **Admire The View (IRE)**[16] 2892 3-9-9 70 TedDurcan 4 86+
(D R Lanigan) *hld up in rr: hdwy and swtchd rt to outer over 2f out: rdn and qckned to ld jst ins fnl f: sn clr: eased towards fin* **13/2**
60-3 **2** *2¾* **Bideeya (USA)**[93] 978 3-9-1 62 NeilCallan 5 67
(C E Brittain) *trckd ldrs: smooth hdwy 2f out: sn rdn and ev ch: drvn ent fnl f and kpt on same pce: tk 2nd nr fin* **9/1**
-043 **3** *hd* **Aleqa**[18] 2834 3-9-4 65 AlanMunro 1 69
(C F Wall) *cl up on outer: hdwy to ld 2f out: rdn and edgd rt over 1f out: hdd jst ins fnl f: sn drvn and kpt on same pce: lost 2nd nr fin* **15/2**
5121 **4** *2¼* **Sairaam (IRE)**[21] 2764 4-10-0 66 KirstyMilczarek 9 67
(C Smith) *racd wd: in tch: hdwy 2f out: sn cl up and ev ch tl rdn ent fnl f and kpt on same pce* **10/3**[1]
0102 **5** *6* **Pretty Orchid**[4] 3284 5-8-12 50 (p) TonyCulhane 7 35
(P T Midgley) *hld up: hdwy over 2f out: sn rdn and kpt on ins fnl f: nt rch ldrs* **5/1**[3]
40-0 **6** *½* **Venture Girl (IRE)**[18] 2834 3-8-8 55 DuranFentiman 2 36
(T D Easterby) *cl up: rdn along over 2f out: sn drvn and grad wknd* **40/1**
600 **7** *3¾* **Patroller (USA)**[9] 3125 7-9-3 55 JamieSpencer 8 29
(K A Ryan) *stmbld s: sn chsng ldrs and led after 1f: rdn along and hdd 2f out: grad wknd* **14/1**
/-04 **8** *2¾* **Frontline Girl (IRE)**[21] 2764 4-9-7 59 AndrewElliott 3 25
(J R Weymes) *led 1f: cl up tl rdn along wl over 2f out and grad wknd* **9/2**[2]
4000 **9** *1½* **Montego Breeze**[17] 2874 4-8-10 48 oh2 ow1 (p) PatCosgrave 6 10
(John A Harris) *chsd ldrs: rdn along over 3f out: sn wknd* **100/1**
001 **10** *2¼* **Crianza**[7] 3227 4-9-8 60 JoeFanning 11 16
(N Tinkler) *dwlt: a in rr* **14/1**
402/ **11** *15* **Manic**[1606] 262 8-8-2 47 oh1 DavidKenny(7) 10 —
(Andrew Reid) *chsd ldrs: rdn along wl over 2f out: sn wknd* **20/1**

1m 23.79s (-2.51) **Going Correction** -0.425s/f (Firm)
WFA 3 from 4yo+ 9lb **11** Ran SP% **114.5**
Speed ratings (Par 100): **97,93,93,91,84 83,79,76,74,71 54**
toteswingers: 1&2 £10.10, 1&3 £12.60, 2&3 £3.30. CSF £60.99 CT £447.75 TOTE £8.70: £2.30, £3.20, £1.80; EX 94.20.
Owner Saif Ali & Saeed H Altayer **Bred** Mountgrange Stud Ltd, T Stewart & A Stroud **Trained** Newmarket, Suffolk

FOCUS
A modest 55-66 fillies' only handicap but an easy winner.
Admire The View(IRE) Official explanation: trainer's rep said, regarding apparent improvement in form, that the filly benefited from both a drop in class and weights.
Montego Breeze Official explanation: caution: entered wrong stall

3435 JACK ISAACS MEMORIAL H'CAP 6f
7:45 (7:45) (Class 4) (0-85,85) 4-Y-O+ £4,533 (£1,348; £674; £336) **Stalls** High

Form RPR
0033 **1** **Red Cape (FR)**[8] 3178 7-8-10 79 IanBrennan(5) 10 87
(Mrs R A Carr) *cl up on stands' rail: led 2f out: sn rdn and hdd ent fnl f: sn led again: drvn: edgd lft and hld on gamely nr fin* **9/2**[2]
4130 **2** *nk* **Secret Witness**[21] 2748 4-9-5 83 (b) LukeMorris 7 90
(R A Harris) *sltly hmpd s: chsd ldrs: hdwy 2f out: rdn to chal over 1f out and ev ch ins fnl f tl drvn and nt qckn nr fin* **12/1**
4/0- **3** *1* **Go Nani Go**[310] 5203 4-9-6 84 RichardMullen 1 88
(B Smart) *in tch: hdwy over 2f out: rdn to chal on outer over 1f out: drvn and led ent fnl f: sn edgd rt and hdd: no ex last 100yds* **25/1**
/113 **4** *1½* **Tubby Isaacs**[26] 2592 6-8-13 77 NeilCallan 4 76+
(D K Ivory) *hld up towards rr: hdwy over 2f out: rdn to chse ldrs over 1f out: no imp ins fnl f* **10/3**[1]
3301 **5** *1½* **Lucky Numbers (IRE)**[16] 2883 4-9-7 85 SilvestreDeSousa 8 79
(Paul Green) *wnt lft s: cl up: rdn along over 2f out: drvn wl over 1f out and grad wknd* **13/2**[3]
3450 **6** *2* **Rowayton**[15] 2940 4-9-2 80 (p) GrahamGibbons 3 68
(J D Bethell) *t.k.h: led: rdn along and hdd 2f out: sn edgd rt and drvn: wknd ent fnl f* **17/2**
-044 **7** *nse* **Mrs Penny (AUS)**[22] 2689 6-9-3 81 (b) JamieSpencer 9 69
(J R Gask) *towards rr: effrt over 2f out: sn rdn and nvr nr ldrs* **8/1**
4031 **8** *1¾* **Methaaly (IRE)**[2] 3358 7-8-2 73 6ex (be) JosephYoung(7) 5 55
(M Mullineaux) *a towards rr* **12/1**
0-04 **9** *¾* **Go Go Green (IRE)**[15] 2940 4-9-7 85 PhillipMakin 6 65
(D H Brown) *sltly hmpd s: towards rr: hdwy 1/2-way: rdn along 2f out: sn btn* **9/2**[2]
0000 **10** *9* **Desert Falls**[17] 2877 4-8-2 66 oh1 PaulQuinn 11 17
(R M Whitaker) *chsd ldrs: rdn along 1/2-way: sn wknd* **40/1**

1m 10.2s (-3.40) **Going Correction** -0.425s/f (Firm) **10** Ran SP% **116.1**
Speed ratings (Par 105): **105,104,103,101,99 96,96,94,93,81**
toteswingers: 1&2 £9.30, 1&3 £23.20, 2&3 £31.20. CSF £57.02 CT £1240.53 TOTE £6.00: £2.40, £3.80, £4.20; EX 67.70.
Owner Middleham Park Racing LVI **Bred** Gilles And Mrs Forien **Trained** Huby, N Yorks

FOCUS
A tight 66-85 sprint handicap.
Rowayton Official explanation: jockey said filly hung right-handed from halfway

3436 DNSHOWCASE.CO.UK H'CAP 5f 140y
8:15 (8:15) (Class 4) (0-85,81) 3-Y-O £4,533 (£1,348; £674; £336) **Stalls** High

Form RPR
1333 **1** **Kakapuka**[15] 2928 3-9-0 73 JamieSpencer 8 80
(Mrs A L M King) *hld up in tch: hdwy wl over 1f out: squeezed through and rdn to ld ins fnl f: drvn out* **3/1**[1]
-134 **2** *1* **Kanaf (IRE)**[14] 2960 3-9-7 80 JoeFanning 11 84
(E A L Dunlop) *dwlt and swtchd lft to outer s: hdwy and cl up after 2f: effrt 2f out: sn rdn and ev ch tl drvn ins fnl f and no ex last 75yds* **7/2**[2]
2-41 **3** *½* **Drift And Dream**[15] 2931 3-9-3 76 TedDurcan 2 78
(C F Wall) *trckd ldrs: hdwy to ld wl over 1f out: drvn and edgd rt ent fnl f: sn hdd and drvn: kpt on same pce* **9/2**
2212 **4** *½* **Flaneur**[10] 3088 3-9-7 80 (b) DuranFentiman 4 81+
(T D Easterby) *trckd ldrs: effrt 2f out: sn rdn and n.m.r ent fnl f: sn drvn and kpt on* **4/1**[3]
-300 **5** *¾* **Gertmegalush (IRE)**[79] 1191 3-9-2 78 BarryMcHugh(3) 9 76
(John A Harris) *in tch: hdwy 2f out: sn swtchd rt and rdn over 1f out: kpt on u.p fnl f* **16/1**
4606 **6** *1¼* **Dancing Freddy (IRE)**[19] 2824 3-8-13 72 PaulMulrennan 3 66
(J G Given) *led: rdn along over 2f out: hdd wl over 1f out and grad wknd* **20/1**
3500 **7** *3¾* **Bossy Kitty**[6] 3243 3-9-0 73 KirstyMilczarek 1 55
(N Tinkler) *chsd ldrs: hdwy over 2f out: rdn to chal and ev ch tl drvn and hld whn n.m.r and wknd appr fnl f* **25/1**
1-0 **8** *shd* **Vested Interest**[14] 2982 3-8-11 75 IanBrennan(5) 10 56
(J S Wainwright) *towards rr: sme hdwy on stands' rails over 2f out: sn rdn and btn* **10/1**
-510 **9** *15* **Belinsky (IRE)**[19] 2815 3-9-1 74 J-PGuillambert 5 6
(N Tinkler) *cl up: rdn along over 2f out: sn drvn and wknd* **10/1**

66.82 secs (-1.68) **Going Correction** -0.425s/f (Firm) **9** Ran SP% **118.1**
Speed ratings (Par 101): **94,92,92,91,90 88,83,83,63**
toteswingers: 1&2 £2.90, 1&3 £3.00, 2&3 £5.60. CSF £13.96 CT £47.18 TOTE £4.50: £2.00, £1.10, £1.80; EX 15.80.
Owner Mrs E Mills & A Murphy **Bred** Paradime Ltd **Trained** Wilmcote, Warwicks

FOCUS
A tight 65-80 handicap run over the 'split' Portland distance.

3437 SCOUTING FOR GIRLS - AUGUST 14TH MAIDEN FILLIES' STKS 1m 2f 60y
8:50 (8:55) (Class 4) 3-Y-O+ £4,533 (£1,348; £674; £336) **Stalls** Low

Form RPR
3 **1** **Miss Jean Brodie (USA)**[10] 3080 3-8-12 0 AhmedAjtebi 10 84+
(Mahmood Al Zarooni) *hld up: hdwy on outer over 4f out: led 3f out: sn chal and rdn 2f out: drvn ent fnl f and styd on wl* **7/1**
42 **2** *1½* **Marywell**[16] 2890 3-8-12 0 RobertHavlin 7 82+
(J H M Gosden) *trckd ldrs: hdwy over 3f out: sn disp ld: rdn 2f out and ev ch tl drvn and one pce ins fnl f* **5/4**[1]
5- **3** *5* **Strictly Lambada**[249] 6920 3-8-12 0 NeilCallan 3 72
(J H M Gosden) *trckd ldrs: hdwy on outer over 3f out: rdn over 2f out: kpt on fnl f* **13/2**[3]
0- **4** *1* **Ertiyaad**[227] 7325 3-8-12 0 RichardMullen 2 70+
(Sir Michael Stoute) *hld up: hdwy 3f out: rdn along and slty outpcd 2f out: kpt on ins fnl f: n.d* **9/1**

4- **5** ½ **Knotgarden (IRE)**[364] 3379 4-9-10 0 PatCosgrave 8 69
(J R Fanshawe) *trckd ldng pair: effrt 3f out: sn rdn along: drvn wl over 1f out and grad wknd* **33/1**

6 2¼ **Sea Of Galilee** 3-8-12 0 FrankieMcDonald 11 65
(H Candy) *uns rdr and galloped loose to s: hld up in rr: hdwy wl over 2f out: kpt on ins fnl f: nrst fin* **66/1**

4 **7** 1¾ **Egmarey (IRE)**[13] 2998 3-8-12 0 TedDurcan 4 62
(D R Lanigan) *led: rdn along 4f out: hdd 3f out: wknd over 2f out* **4/1**[2]

8 3 **Blue Mamba** 3-8-12 0 GrahamGibbons 9 56
(R Hollinshead) *chsd ldr: cl up 4f out: rdn along over 3f out: sn wknd* **66/1**

5 **9** 1¾ **Sheikhtothemusic**[18] 2837 3-8-12 0 PaulMulrennan 1 53
(J G Given) *chsd ldrs on inner: rdn along over 3f out: wknd over 2f out* **50/1**

10 ¾ **Secret Sortie (IRE)**[425] 5-9-3 0 DaleSwift(7) 5 51
(T J Etherington) *a in rr* **100/1**

2 **11** ½ **Silvan Stream**[18] 2837 3-8-12 0 PJMcDonald 12 50
(J D Bethell) *hld up: a in rr* **20/1**

2m 9.33s (-0.07) **Going Correction** +0.075s/f (Good)
WFA 3 from 4yo+ 12lb **11** Ran SP% **113.9**
Speed ratings (Par 102): **110,108,104,104,103 101,100,98,96,96 95**
toteswingers: 1&2 £1.70, 1&3 £7.50, 2&3 £3.60. CSF £15.12 TOTE £9.40: £3.20, £1.10, £2.80; EX 19.50.
Owner Godolphin **Bred** Stonerside Stable **Trained** Newmarket, Suffolk

FOCUS
An ordinary maiden with little strength in depth. The start was delayed when Marywell proved mulish in the paddock and had to be led down to the start.

3438 DONCASTER RACECOURSE BOOK YOUR CHRISTMAS PARTY H'CAP 1m (R)
9:20 (9:21) (Class 4) (0-80,80) 4-Y-O+ **£4,533** (£1,348; £674; £336) **Stalls** Low

Form RPR

4004 **1** **Toto Skyllachy**[1] 3396 5-8-12 76 JamesO'Reilly(5) 7 81
(J O'Reilly) *trckd ldrs on outer: hdwy over 2f out: rdn and edgd lft over 1f out: drvn to ld jst ins fnl f: hld on gamely* **14/1**

0-40 **2** shd **Habshan (USA)**[23] 2683 10-9-7 80 AlanMunro 4 85+
(C F Wall) *hld up in rr: swtchd outside and hdwy wl over 1f out: sn rdn and styd on strly ins fnl f: jst failed* **10/1**

0-02 **3** 1¼ **Bold Diktator**[17] 2875 8-8-0 64 (v) AmyRyan(5) 2 66
(R M Whitaker) *trckd ldrs: hdwy 1/2-way: led 2f out and sn rdn: drvn over 1f out: hdd jst ins fnl f: no ex last 100yds* **25/1**

5213 **4** nse **Ninth House (USA)**[9] 3124 8-8-1 65 (t) JamesSullivan(5) 5 67+
(Mrs R A Carr) *dwlt and in rr: hdwy over 2f out: effrt whn nt clr run and hmpd 1 1/2f out: swtchd rt and rdn ins fnl f: fin strly* **9/2**[2]

0-61 **5** ½ **Roman Glory (IRE)**[7] 3212 4-9-6 79 JamieSpencer 9 80
(B J Meehan) *t.k.h: set stdy pce: hdd over 4f out: cl up: effrt over 2f out: sn rdn and ev ch tl drvn and one pce ins fnl f* **11/2**[3]

0650 **6** hd **Glenmuir (IRE)**[28] 2524 7-8-2 66 IanBrennan(5) 1 67+
(J J Quinn) *in tch: hdwy 3f out: rdn along to chse ldrs and n.m.r over 1f out: kpt on u.p ins fnl f* **14/1**

00-0 **7** 1 **Stevie Gee (IRE)**[35] 2328 6-9-2 75 JoeFanning 8 73
(Ian Williams) *t.k.h: cl up: rdn along wl over 2f out: n.m.r 1 1/2f out and one pce* **20/1**

4021 **8** ½ **Amethyst Dawn (IRE)**[9] 3107 4-8-10 69 DavidAllan 3 66
(T D Easterby) *dwlt and towards rr: rapid hdwy to ld over 4f out: rdn along and hdd 3f out: cl up tl drvn and wknd wl over 1f out* **9/4**[1]

1-00 **9** 1 **Truly Asia (IRE)**[23] 2683 4-9-2 75 TedDurcan 6 76+
(R Charlton) *trckd ldrs: effrt whn nt clr run and hmpd 1 1/2f out: nt rcvr and eased ins fnl f* **9/2**[2]

1m 39.24s (-0.46) **Going Correction** +0.075s/f (Good) **9** Ran SP% **113.5**
Speed ratings (Par 105): **105,104,103,103,103 102,101,101,100**
toteswingers: 1&2 £26.80, 1&3 £27.70, 2&3 £14.50. CSF £142.27 CT £3445.89 TOTE £21.90: £5.70, £4.20, £5.80; EX 263.30 Place 6: £474.50, Place 5: £346.31..
Owner Richard Walker **Bred** Mrs G Slater **Trained** Doncaster, S Yorks
■ Stewards' Enquiry : James O'Reilly three-day ban: used whip with excessive frequency down shoulder in forehand (Jul 10,12,13)

FOCUS
A 64-80 handicap run at a very steady pace until the final three furlongs and in the end there were plenty of hard-luck stories.
Ninth House(USA) Official explanation: jockey said horse was denied a clear run
Roman Glory(IRE) Official explanation: jockey said gelding hung right
Amethyst Dawn(IRE) Official explanation: jockey said filly ran too free
Truly Asia(IRE) Official explanation: jockey said gelding was denied a clear run
T/Plt: £168.40 to a £1 stake. Pool: £68,562.29 - 297.06 winning tickets. T/Qpdt: £33.40 to a £1 stake. Pool: £4,848.96 - 107.18 winning tickets. JR

3260 LINGFIELD (L-H)
Saturday, June 26

OFFICIAL GOING: Turf course - good to firm; all-weather - standard
Racing was put back half an hour after false patches of ground were found near the stands' rail.
Wind: Light, behind Weather: Sunny, hot

3439 EUROPEAN BREEDERS' FUND MAIDEN STKS 5f
5:50 (6:25) (Class 5) 2-Y-O **£3,626** (£1,079; £539; £269) **Stalls** High

Form RPR

320 **1** **Remotelinx (IRE)**[23] 2680 2-9-3 0 DaneO'Neill 1 78+
(J W Hills) *pressed ldr: led after 2f: clr over 1f out: shkn up and styd on: comf* **8/11**[1]

2 3¼ **Pearl Storm (IRE)** 2-9-3 0 LiamJones 2 67+
(W J Haggas) *dwlt: off the pce in 4th: pushed along after 2f: prog to go 2nd over 1f out: rn green but kpt on: no imp on wnr* **7/2**[2]

3 3¼ **My Love Fajer (IRE)** 2-8-10 0 CharlotteKerton(7) 6 55
(G Prodromou) *led 2f: rdn and outpcd fr 2f out* **40/1**

00 **4** 5 **Fairy Tales**[14] 2963 2-8-12 0 NeilChalmers 3 32
(J J Bridger) *chsd ldrs: disp 2nd fr 1/2-way to over 1f out: wknd rapidly* **100/1**

5 2 **Cheylesmore (IRE)** 2-9-3 0 SaleemGolam 4 30
(S C Williams) *dwlt and s.i.s: a last and struggling* **22/1**[3]

59.30 secs (1.10) **Going Correction** +0.075s/f (Good) **5** Ran SP% **87.9**
Speed ratings (Par 93): **94,88,83,75,72**
toteswinger: 1&2 £1.80. CSF £1.67 TOTE £1.40: £1.10, £1.10; EX 1.60.
Owner Prolinx Limited **Bred** Newtown Stud **Trained** Upper Lambourn, Berks

FOCUS
This didn't look too special a maiden even before the third and fourth favourites Zarazar (9/1) and Acclamazing (15/2) were withdrawn minutes before the off after giving problems at the stalls. Deduct 20p in the £ under R4.

NOTEBOOK
Remotelinx(IRE), a close second to subsequent Norfolk Stakes hero Approve on his penultimate start, barely had to turn a hair to get off the mark at the fourth time of asking. Soon able to track across to the stands' side from the worst draw, he required minimal assistance to keep the runner-up at bay. He holds an entry in next month's Weatherbys Super Sprint, but would need to improve again to rate among the leading players in that contest.
Pearl Storm(IRE) filled the eye in the preliminaries, but always had plenty to do after breaking less well than the winner and ran green late on. The first foal of a half-sister to juvenile winners at 5-6f, he is in good hands to find a race this summer. (op 9-2)
My Love Fajer(IRE), taken down early after getting agitated in the paddock, was readily outpaced before the final furlong. His one half-sibling to have won a race did so over 1m2f, so he is likely to need further in time. (op 33-1)
Fairy Tales once again appeared not to last the trip.
Cheylesmore(IRE), a 60,000gns yearling is a half-brother to a Group 3 7f winner and was always last after a slow start. He offered very little immediate promise. (op 20-1)

3440 CGG VERITAS H'CAP 5f
6:20 (6:50) (Class 5) (0-75,75) 3-Y-O+ **£3,070** (£906; £453) **Stalls** High

Form RPR

2060 **1** **Make My Dream**[12] 3037 7-9-8 70 MartinLane(3) 6 78
(J Gallagher) *chsd ldr: u.p over 2f out: styd on to ld ent fnl f: drvn out* **13/2**

1142 **2** ¾ **Avrilo**[4] 3299 4-9-11 70 IanMongan 7 75
(M S Saunders) *racd against rail: cl up: rdn over 1f out: kpt on to take 2nd ins fnl f: a hld* **7/2**[2]

0201 **3** nk **Grudge**[7] 3211 5-10-0 73 (be) JimmyQuinn 2 77
(C R Dore) *taken down early: dwlt: racd on outer in last trio: rdn over 2f out: styd on wl fnl f to take 3rd last 75yds* **6/1**

2322 **4** 1¼ **Wreningham**[7] 3211 5-8-8 60 RyanClark(7) 5 60
(S C Williams) *led: drvn over 1f out: hdd and fdd ent fnl f* **4/1**[3]

0-00 **5** nse **Wooden King (IRE)**[5] 3255 5-8-6 54 oh5 AndrewHeffernan(3) 4 54
(M S Saunders) *dwlt: rousted along to go prom on outer: hrd rdn over 1f out: fdd ins fnl f* **16/1**

3153 **6** 1½ **Liberty Lady (IRE)**[8] 3174 3-9-10 75 DaneO'Neill 8 67
(D Donovan) *dwlt: pushed along in last trio after 2f: tried to cl on ldrs over 1f out: no imp* **3/1**[1]

1000 **7** 1¾ **Step It Up (IRE)**[14] 2973 6-9-10 69 StephenCraine 3 57
(J R Boyle) *racd towards outer: hld up in tch: rdn and nt qckn over 1f out: eased whn no ch last 100yds* **11/1**

445- **8** 24 **Fiftyfourth Street**[316] 4990 4-9-12 71 TravisBlock 1 —
(P J Makin) *dwlt: a in last pair: hung rt and wknd 1/2-way: t.o* **33/1**

58.17 secs (-0.03) **Going Correction** +0.075s/f (Good)
WFA 3 from 4yo+ 6lb **8** Ran SP% **112.0**
Speed ratings (Par 103): **103,101,101,99,99 96,94,55**
toteswingers: 1&2 £8.70, 1&3 £7.70, 2&3 £3.70. CSF £28.25 CT £143.03 TOTE £8.00: £1.90, £1.20, £1.60; EX 38.20.
Owner Mrs Irene Clifford **Bred** The Valentines **Trained** Chastleton, Oxon

FOCUS
A reasonable handicap in which three were still vying for outright favouritism until the off.
Fiftyfourth Street Official explanation: jockey said gelding hung badly right

3441 SURREY ROYAL BRITISH LEGION FILLIES' H'CAP 7f
6:50 (7:25) (Class 5) (0-75,75) 3-Y-O **£3,070** (£906; £453) **Stalls** High

Form RPR

31- **1** **Cloud's End**[257] 6722 3-9-7 75 LiamJones 4 82+
(W J Haggas) *settled bhd ldrs: pushed along over 2f out: prog over 1f out: drvn ahd jst ins fnl f: styd on wl* **3/1**[1]

2250 **2** hd **Red Yarn**[16] 2888 3-8-11 65 (b[1]) PatDobbs 8 71
(G L Moore) *sn chsng ldrs: rdn wl over 2f out: prog 2f out on nr side: chal ent fnl f: styd on but jst hld* **9/2**[2]

50-0 **3** 2 **Perfect Ch'I (IRE)**[42] 2120 3-9-4 72 DaneO'Neill 2 73
(I A Wood) *racd on outer: mde most: rdn 2f out: hdd and fdd ent fnl f* **11/1**

0016 **4** ¾ **Al Khimiya (IRE)**[8] 3154 3-8-11 70 JohnFahy(5) 7 69
(S Woodman) *w ldrs: hrd rdn to dispute ld 2f out tl fdd ent fnl f* **9/1**

-250 **5** 2 **Wishformore (IRE)**[11] 3063 3-8-9 70 RyanPowell(7) 3 63
(J S Moore) *w ldrs to 1/2-way on outer: lost pl and sn rdn: no imp over 1f out* **20/1**

0365 **6** 3¾ **Blue Again**[17] 2871 3-9-1 69 AdamKirby 1 52
(W R Swinburn) *hld up bhd ldrs and racd wdst of all: effrt over 2f out: hanging and fnd nil sn after: wknd* **6/1**[3]

6021 **7** 8 **Miss Kitty Grey (IRE)**[17] 2875 3-8-6 60 NickyMackay 5 21
(J R Boyle) *w ldrs: shkn up over 2f out: wknd and eased* **8/1**

5-13 **8** 18 **Progress (IRE)**[89] 1045 3-9-3 71 ShaneKelly 6 —
(J Noseda) *w ldrs: shkn up over 2f out: wknd rapidly: eased: t.o* **3/1**[1]

1m 23.38s (0.08) **Going Correction** +0.075s/f (Good) **8** Ran SP% **116.7**
Speed ratings (Par 96): **102,101,99,98,96 92,82,62**
toteswingers: 1&2 £4.80, 1&3 £8.60, 2&3 £11.80. CSF £17.04 CT £131.71 TOTE £4.50: £2.70, £1.20, £6.70; EX 23.90.
Owner Manor Farm Stud & Miss S Hoare **Bred** R T And Mrs Watson **Trained** Newmarket, Suffolk

FOCUS
Barely three lengths covered the field with a quarter of a mile to run in this fillies' handicap.
Miss Kitty Grey(IRE) Official explanation: jockey said filly was unsuited by the good to firm (watered) ground
Progress(IRE) Official explanation: jockey said filly was unsuited by the good to firm (watered) ground

3442 SURREY BRITISH ARMED FORCES DAY (S) STKS 1m 4f (P)
7:25 (7:55) (Class 6) 3-Y-O+ **£2,047** (£604; £302) **Stalls** Low

Form RPR

1111 **1** **Timocracy**[21] 2752 5-9-13 70 SteveDrowne 11 60
(A B Haynes) *w ldr: led over 4f out: rdn whn pressed 2f out: asserted fnl f* **7/4**[1]

6404 **2** ¾ **Rosewood Lad**[7] 3213 3-8-8 49 StevieDonohoe 7 54
(J S Moore) *trckd ldng pair: rdn to chse wnr over 3f out to wl over 2f out: styd on inner in st: kpt on wl to take 2nd nr fin* **25/1**

0563 **3** nk **Sunset Boulevard (IRE)**[21] 2752 7-9-13 57 DaneO'Neill 6 59
(Miss Tor Sturgis) *hld up disputing 5th: prog to chse wnr wl over 2f out and sn chalng: nt qckn and hld fnl f: lost 2nd nr fin* **14/1**[3]

6132 **4** 3½ **Rapid City**[21] 2752 7-9-13 70 AdamKirby 9 53
(Jim Best) *hld up in last pair: prog fr 3f out to go 5th over 2f out but stl wl off the pce: rdn to take 4th over 1f out: nvr any ch* **7/4**[1]

0-42 **5** 3 ½ **Cactus King**72 1318 7-9-8 65 ... IanMongan 12 42
(P M Phelan) *hld up in last trio: prog 4f out to go 4th over 2f out: sn rdn and no rspnse: fdd* 8/1²

-005 **6** 3 ¼ **Suzi's Challenger**9 3113 3-8-3 45 ...(v) JimmyQuinn 10 32
(H J Collingridge) *dwlt: settled in last pair: rdn over 3f out: sme prog to take 6th 2f out: no hdwy after* 33/1

5-00 **7** 8 **Rainiers Girl**26 396 4-8-12 42 ... KierenFox(5) 1 19
(R A Teal) *in tch disputing 7th: shkn up 3f out: sn lft wl bhd* 66/1

-440 **8** 7 **Land Of Plenty (IRE)**21 2753 3-8-3 44 ... NickyMackay 8 8
(Jamie Poulton) *hld up disputing 7th: rdn 3f out: sn wknd* 66/1

9 11 **Beck's Bolero (IRE)**45 4-9-8 0 ... TomQueally 4 —
(J A Osborne) *led to over 4f out: wknd rapidly over 2f out* 33/1

0263 **10** 10 **Mnarani (IRE)**7 3213 3-8-8 60 ...(b) HayleyTurner 3 —
(J S Moore) *t.k.h: trckd ldng pair: lost pl and rdn 3f out: sn wknd: t.o* 8/1²

00 **11** 92 **Farmers Surprise**15 2921 3-8-0 0 ... AndrewHeffernan(3) 5 —
(H J Evans) *in tch disputing 5th tl wknd rapidly 1/2-way: sn wl t.o* 100/1

2m 35.39s (2.39) **Going Correction** +0.225s/f (Slow)
WFA 3 from 4yo+ 14lb 11 Ran SP% 115.3
Speed ratings (Par 101): **101,100,100,97,95 93,88,83,76,69 8**
toteswingers: 1&2 £9.20, 1&3 £5.20, 2&3 £16.30. CSF £55.87 TOTE £3.80: £1.60, £5.40, £2.10; EX 61.50.The winner was bought in for 8,000gns. Sunset Boulevard was claimed by Mr J J Best for £6,000.
Owner Ms C Berry **Bred** Gainsborough Stud Management Ltd **Trained** Limpley Stoke, Bath
■ Stewards' Enquiry : Steve Drowne one-day ban: failed to ride to draw (Jul 12)

FOCUS
An ordinary seller, in which three of the four market leaders posted disappointing efforts.
Land Of Plenty(IRE) Official explanation: jockey said filly was denied a clear run

3443 POPPYSHOP.ORG.UK MEDIAN AUCTION MAIDEN STKS 1m 2f (P)
7:55 (8:27) (Class 6) 3-4-Y-O £2,047 (£604; £302) Stalls Low

Form RPR

3 **1** **Viewing**50 1881 3-8-11 0 ... NickyMackay 10 70
(J H M Gosden) *prom: trckd ldr after 3f: led 3f out: kicked on 2f out: looked in command fnl f: drvn to hold on to dwindling ld nr fin* 8/11¹

6-3 **2** nk **Blitzed**19 2812 3-9-2 0 ... PatDobbs 5 75
(G L Moore) *restless in stalls: trckd ldrs: prog to chse wnr 2f out: styd on u.p fnl f: clsng at fin* 7/2²

050- **3** nk **Baralaka**260 6629 3-9-2 77 ... StevieDonohoe 11 74
(Sir Mark Prescott) *hld up in last trio: prog over 2f out: sn drvn: styd on to go 3rd fnl f: clsng steadily at fin* 4/1³

00 **4** 3 **Now What**10 3080 3-8-11 0 ... SaleemGolam 6 63
(J G Portman) *trckd ldrs: gng strly 3f out: rdn to go 3rd 2f out: no imp 1f out: sn fdd* 66/1

00 **5** 2 ¼ **Kuantan Two (IRE)**9 3116 3-9-2 0 ... TomQueally 1 64?
(P F I Cole) *hld up in midfield: bk of main gp over 2f out gng wl enough: rdn in 5th over 1f out: nt qckn* 33/1

00 **6** 3 **Budding Daffodil**23 2674 3-8-11 0 ... ShaneKelly 7 53
(W J Knight) *chsd ldr 3f: styd prom tl wknd 2f out* 10/1

0 **7** shd **Mandate**25 2632 3-9-2 0 ... HayleyTurner 3 57
(J A R Toller) *hld up in last pair: stl there 3f out: pushed along and no prog over 2f out: kpt on fr over 1f out* 25/1

00 **8** 6 **Marcus Antonius**12 3038 3-9-2 0 ... StephenCraine 12 45
(J R Boyle) *hld up towards rr: pushed along on outer over 4f out: in tch 3f out: sn lft bhd* 66/1

0 **9** 3 ½ **Melinoise**25 2632 3-8-8 0 ... WilliamCarson(3) 4 33
(Rae Guest) *mostly in last: rdn and struggling 1/2-way: no ch after* 66/1

0-00 **10** ¾ **Calm And Serene (USA)**23 2675 3-8-11 50 ... SteveDrowne 8 32
(Rae Guest) *led to 3f out: wknd rapidly 2f out* 66/1

2m 8.61s (2.01) **Going Correction** +0.225s/f (Slow)
WFA 3 from 4yo 12lb 10 Ran SP% 122.0
Speed ratings (Par 101): **100,99,99,97,95 92,92,88,85,84**
toteswingers: 1&2 £1.50, 1&3 £2.00, 2&3 £2.70. CSF £3.68 TOTE £2.00: £1.10, £1.10, £1.20; EX 4.00.
Owner Cheveley Park Stud **Bred** Cheveley Park Stud Ltd **Trained** Newmarket, Suffolk

FOCUS
Not much strength in depth to this maiden, but the right horses filled the frame and pulled out 3l and more on the remainder.

3444 CHRIS GUNAPALA 50TH BIRTHDAY CELEBRATION H'CAP 1m 4f (P)
8:25 (9:00) (Class 6) (0-60,60) 3-Y-O £2,047 (£604; £302) Stalls Low

Form RPR

0011 **1** **Captain John Nixon**11 3055 3-9-0 56 ... AndreaAtzeni 12 74+
(Pat Eddery) *mde virtually all: kicked on fr 3f out: clr over 1f out: in n.d after: comf* 11/8¹

0-12 **2** 1 ¾ **Corr Point (IRE)**31 2439 3-9-4 60 ...(t) TomQueally 4 72
(J A Osborne) *hld up in midfield: prog gng wl 3f out: rdn to chse wnr over 2f out: styd on but no imp fnl f* 7/2²

1063 **3** 2 ½ **Sheila's Bond**21 2753 3-8-7 56 ... RyanPowell(7) 15 64
(J S Moore) *hld up wl in rr: smooth prog 3f out: wnt 4th but nt on terms over 2f out: hrd rdn to go 3rd over 1f out: no ex fnl f* 16/1

0-03 **4** 3 ½ **Pleasant Way (IRE)**17 2853 3-9-1 57 ... DaneO'Neill 6 59+
(D R Lanigan) *hld up towards rr: gng wl enough whn hmpd 3f out: prog 2f out: styd on to take 4th fnl f: no ch* 8/1³

06-0 **5** 4 **Lyric Poet (USA)**27 2564 3-8-12 57 ... WilliamCarson(3) 1 53
(G C Bravery) *hld up wl in rr: stl there whn hmpd 3f out: drvn and kpt on fr 2f out: nrst fin* 66/1

-650 **6** ½ **Green Energy**15 2924 3-8-13 55 ... AdamKirby 10 50
(Mrs A J Perrett) *prom: rdn to chse wnr over 3f out to over 2f out: wknd quite qckly over 1f out* 25/1

00-0 **7** 3 ½ **Steely Bird**148 340 3-9-2 58 ... IanMongan 2 48
(Miss Jo Crowley) *hld up in detached last: stl there over 3f out gng wl: sme prog after: no hdwy fr midfield over 1f out* 66/1

600 **8** 3 **Technophobe (IRE)**14 2974 3-9-2 58 ...(p) ShaneKelly 16 43
(W J Knight) *wl in tch: chsng ldrs but outpcd over 2f out: rdn and wknd over 1f out* 25/1

-520 **9** 2 ¼ **Oak Leaves**23 2675 3-9-0 56 ... SaleemGolam 13 37
(J G Portman) *prom: rdn on outer over 3f out: stl chsng 2f out: wknd* 33/1

35-3 **10** 1 ¼ **Fine Lace (IRE)**25 2620 3-8-13 60 ... BillyCray(5) 7 39
(D J S Ffrench Davis) *towards rr: effrt on wd outside 3f out: no prog 2f out: wknd* 11/1

3044 **11** ½ **Red Amy**23 2675 3-9-0 56 ... HayleyTurner 11 34
(M L W Bell) *nvr bttr than midfield: rdn 3f out: sn btn* 8/1³

-000 **12** 2 **Happy Mood**16 2901 3-9-4 60 ... PatDobbs 14 35
(G L Moore) *racd wd: trckd ldrs: rdn 5f out: stl in tch 3f out: wknd over 2f out* 28/1

000 **13** 9 **Dolphin's Dream**16 2890 3-9-1 60 ...(b¹) Louis-PhilippeBeuzelin(3) 8 21
(B J Meehan) *t.k.h early: prom: rdn 5f out: wknd 3f out: t.o* 33/1

06-0 **14** 7 **Weliketobouggie**26 2603 3-9-1 57 ... SteveDrowne 3 —
(A M Hales) *in tch towards rr tl wknd over 3f out: t.o* 80/1

-355 **15** 11 **Astronomer's Dream**16 2909 3-9-0 59 ... MartinLane(3) 9 —
(E F Vaughan) *w wnr to over 3f out: wknd v rapidly: t.o* 16/1

2m 35.4s (2.40) **Going Correction** +0.225s/f (Slow) 15 Ran SP% 127.9
Speed ratings (Par 97): **101,99,98,95,93 92,90,88,87,86 85,84,78,73,66**
toteswingers: 1&2 £1.70, 1&3 £9.80, 2&3 £17.10. CSF £5.62 CT £60.56 TOTE £2.50: £1.40, £1.70, £3.70; EX 8.80 Place 6: £10.20, Place 5: £9.87..
Owner Paul Dean **Bred** Patrick Eddery Ltd **Trained** Nether Winchendon, Bucks
■ Stewards' Enquiry : Louis-Philippe Beuzelin three-day ban: careless riding (Jul 11-13)

FOCUS
This low-grade handicap was won in a time almost identical to that of the earlier seller, though that does belie the fact the comfortable winner was eased right down close home.
Dolphin's Dream Official explanation: jockey said filly hung right
T/Plt: £14.20 to a £1 stake. Pool: £48,613.79 - 2,492.93 winning tickets. T/Qpdt: £8.00 to a £1 stake. Pool: £4,147.52 - 382.18 winning tickets. JN

3405 NEWCASTLE (L-H)
Saturday, June 26

OFFICIAL GOING: Good to firm (7.8)
Wind: Breezy, half behind Weather: Sunny, hot

3445 TOTESPORT.COM CHIPCHASE STKS (GROUP 3) 6f
2:00 (2:00) (Class 1) 3-Y-O+
£36,900 (£13,988; £7,000; £3,490; £1,748; £877) Stalls High

Form RPR

5500 **1** **Barney McGrew (IRE)**7 3193 7-9-3 100 ... PhillipMakin 5 110
(M Dods) *dictated ordinary gallop: shkn up and qcknd 2f out: kpt on wl ins fnl f: unchal* 16/1

-022 **2** 2 ¼ **Himalya (IRE)**8 3146 4-9-3 107 ... EddieAhern 7 103
(J Noseda) *pressed wnr: rdn over 2f out: kpt on same pce ins fnl f* 15/8¹

42-0 **3** 2 ¾ **Bonnie Charlie**56 1700 4-9-3 104 ... NeilCallan 4 94
(W J Haggas) *sn prom: effrt over 2f out: rdn and one pce over 1f out* 4/1³

0-04 **4** 1 ¾ **Knot In Wood (IRE)**7 3193 8-9-3 107 ... PaulHanagan 1 88
(R A Fahey) *racd alone centre: prom: drvn over 2f out: kpt on same pce wl over 1f out* 3/1²

0210 **5** 2 **Sir Gerry (USA)**7 3192 5-9-3 107 ... RobertWinston 3 82
(J R Best) *stdd s: hld up: rdn over 2f out: hdwy over 1f out: nvr able to chal* 6/1

-620 **6** 9 **Filligree (IRE)**8 3178 5-9-0 86 ... DavidProbert 6 50
(Rae Guest) *hld up in tch: drvn and outpcd over 2f out: sn btn* 50/1

123F **7** 5 **Mister Hughie (IRE)**31 2437 3-8-10 99 ... ChrisCatlin 2 35
(M R Channon) *t.k.h: prom: rdn over 2f out: sn wknd* 10/1

1m 10.74s (-3.86) **Going Correction** -0.50s/f (Hard)
WFA 3 from 4yo+ 7lb 7 Ran SP% 111.0
Speed ratings (Par 113): **109,106,102,100,97 85,78**
toteswingers:1&2 £15.80, 2&3 £1.70, 1&3 £15.90 CSF £43.82 TOTE £15.90: £3.80, £1.40; EX 76.00.
Owner Andrew Tinkler **Bred** Mrs H B Raw **Trained** Denton, Co Durham
■ Micheal Dods's first Group winner.

FOCUS
A strong-looking contest, in which a few of these had taken their chance at Royal Ascot. However, very little happened once the winner got to the front soon after breaking from the stalls. The recorded time was 1min 10.74secs, which is just 0.1sec outside the course record, although the field did have the wind behind them.

NOTEBOOK
Barney McGrew(IRE) had been well beaten on his last two starts, albeit in big fields and on the wrong side, arguably, in the Wokingham. He hadn't won in this class before but his jockey made a decisive move leaving the stalls and came up the stands' rail at a good pace - his owner reported afterwards that they changed the tactics here after his lacklustre effort at Ascot. Nothing really looked like catching him once he changed gear and he was impressive in victory, although possibly slightly flattered by how the race fell into place for him under a great ride by Phillip Makin. Official explanation: trainer said, regarding apparent improvement in form, that the gelding had benefited from the change in tactics.
Himalya(IRE), lightly raced for his age, was fancied to go close in the Buckingham Palace Handicap at Ascot and only found the fast-finishing Treadwell, on the other side of the course, too good for him. He chased Barney McGrew from the off but could not close him down when the tempo increased. (op 2-1 tchd 7-4)
Bonnie Charlie ◆, absent since finishing a close eighth to Equiano in the Palace House Stakes, ran respectably and may well be sharper next time for this run. (op 13-2)
Knot In Wood(IRE), the winner of this race last year and an excellent fourth in the Wokingham on his previous outing, was bidding to give his trainer a third consecutive victory in this race. The horse has a great record in small-field races, but he may not have been favoured by racing away from his rivals down the centre of the course here, a fact proved throughout the day. (op 11-4 tchd 5-2)
Sir Gerry(USA) had run really well on his last three outings, and his fine effort in the Golden Jubilee Stakes the previous weekend looked the best of them. He also had a fair record in small-field races, but the way this race was run probably didn't suit him, and he got outpaced before keeping on. (op 5-1 tchd 9-2)
Filligree(IRE), the only mare in the contest, had little chance on official figures and never got involved. (op 33-1)
Mister Hughie(IRE) had been given a small break since falling at Beverley, but showed little sparkle in this. His jockey was not hard on him in the latter stages and perhaps the horse's confidence has been knocked. (op 8-1 tchd 12-1)

3446 TOTESCOOP6 H'CAP 6f
2:30 (2:30) (Class 2) (0-100,95) 3-Y-O+
£12,462 (£3,732; £1,866; £934; £466; £234) Stalls High

Form RPR

6022 **1** **Jonny Mudball**13 2992 4-9-9 90 ...(t) SebSanders 14 111
(Tom Dascombe) *mde all stands' rail: rdn clr over 1f out: kpt on strly ins fnl f: 1st of 7 in gp* 5/2¹

1-15 **2** 4 ½ **Poet's Place (USA)**13 2992 5-9-6 87 ... PhillipMakin 10 94+
(T D Barron) *dwlt: sn in tch stands' side: effrt over 2f out: chsd (clr) wnr ins fnl f: no imp: 2nd of 7 in gp* 4/1²

-000 **3** 3 ½ **Excusez Moi (USA)**13 2992 8-9-6 87 ... RobertWinston 9 83
(Mrs R A Carr) *slowly away: hld up stands' side: rdn and hdwy over 1f out: kpt on ins fnl f: no ch w first two: 3rd of 7 in gp* 16/1

-101 **4** 1 ½ **Medici Time**9 3114 5-9-4 85 ...(v) GrahamGibbons 8 76
(T D Easterby) *pressed wnr stands' side: rdn over 2f out: no ex and lost 2nd ins fnl f: sn btn: 4th of 7 in gp* 14/1

0343 **5** *1 ½* **Joseph Henry**[7] 3224 8-8-12 **84**........ BillyCray(5) 6 70
(D Nicholls) *led centre gp: rdn over 2f out: edgd rt and kpt on fnl f: nt pce of stands' side ldrs: 1st of 6 in gp* **25/1**

6-10 **6** *2 ¼* **Lenny Bee**[21] 2759 4-9-4 **92**........ DaleSwift(7) 2 71
(D H Brown) *chsd centre ldr: rdn over 2f out: one pce over 1f out: 2nd of 6 in gp* **11/1**

4000 **7** *nk* **River Falcon**[7] 3201 10-8-5 **77**........ IanBrennan(5) 4 55
(J S Goldie) *bhd centre: rdn and hung lft 2f out: kpt on ins fnl f: nvr rchd ldrs: 3rd of 6 in gp* **25/1**

0-00 **8** *2 ¼* **Roker Park (IRE)**[21] 2759 5-9-9 **90**........(p) NeilCallan 5 61
(K A Ryan) *in tch centre: drvn and outpcd over 2f out: no imp fr over 1f out: 4th of 6 in gp* **12/1**

1604 **9** *hd* **Sunrise Safari (IRE)**[8] 3178 7-8-11 **85**........(v) LeeTopliss(7) 12 55
(R A Fahey) *in tch stands' side: rdn over 2f out: btn over 1f out: 5th of 7 in gp* **16/1**

5-06 **10** *3* **Bond Fastrac**[28] 2542 3-9-0 **88**........ TomEaves 13 47
(G R Oldroyd) *chsd stands' side ldrs tl rdn and wknd fr 2f out: 6th of 7 in gp* **28/1**

5620 **11** *6* **Baldemar**[21] 2748 5-9-11 **92**........ PaulHanagan 3 33
(R A Fahey) *chsd centre ldrs: rdn over 2f out: sn wknd: 5th of 6 in gp* **17/2**[3]

0611 **12** *1 ¾* **Damika (IRE)**[30] 2465 7-10-0 **95**........ DaraghO'Donohoe 11 31
(R M Whitaker) *sn drvn towards rr stands' side: struggling 1/2-way: nvr on terms: last of 7 in gp* **9/1**

-210 **13** *12* **Atlantic Story (USA)**[15] 2940 8-9-6 **87**........(bt) DavidAllan 7 —
(M W Easterby) *hld up in tch centre: drvn over 2f out: sn wknd: last of 6 in gp* **10/1**

1m 10.58s (-4.02) **Going Correction** -0.50s/f (Hard) course record
WFA 3 from 4yo+ 7lb **13** Ran SP% **123.8**
Speed ratings (Par 109): **110,104,99,97,95 92,91,88,88,84 76,74,58**
toteswingers:1&2 £2.10, 2&3 £19.60, 1&3 £15.30 CSF £11.79 CT £138.98 TOTE £3.30: £1.30, £2.10, £3.90; EX 13.10 Trifecta £178.60 Pool: £1,259.94 - 5.22 winning units..
Owner Woodgate Family **Bred** Mrs P A Reditt And M J Reditt **Trained** Malpas, Cheshire

FOCUS
A typically tight sprint handicap, and most of them could have been given a chance of success if things fell right for them. However, it's fair to say that Joseph Henry, Lenny Bee, River Falcon (although he did catch the eye with the way he finished), last year's winner Roker Park,Baldemar and Atlantic Story might as well have stayed at home, because they had absolutely no chance of winning coming up the centre of the track against those who kept close to the stands' rail.

NOTEBOOK
Jonny Mudball ◆ was one of the least experienced in the field but had beaten Joseph Henry, Poet's Place and Excusez Moi last time when runner-up at Doncaster. His rider seemed keen to get to what looked a quicker strip of ground up the rail, and the combination won emphatically after setting the pace. The handicapper is sure to want to raise him significantly but hopefully he will take into account what looked a big bias, and not be too harsh on him. In any case, a step up to at least Listed class seems likely now, although connections mentioned the Stewards' Cup as a target, a race he should definitely make the cut when raised for this. His winning time was quicker than the one recorded for the preceding Group 3 Chipchase Stakes. (op 4-1)
Poet's Place(USA) ◆ has plenty of scope to improve again from this, and he may even get a bit further on this sort of ground when considering he appeared to get outpaced before staying on. Ultimately, he might be the sort of horse to pop up at the back-end of the season in a decent contest when there is ease in the ground, given his two victories came at Southwell. (op 7-2 tchd 9-2)
Excusez Moi(USA) got behind as he can do but finished well. He had no chance with the first two, however. (op 20-1)
Medici Time, raised 9lb for winning just over a week previously at Leicester, was brought over towards the stands' side on leaving the stalls, but could not live with the winner as he charged clear at about halfway. (tchd 12-1)
Joseph Henry did the best of those that came down the middle, but is basically not easy to win with.
Lenny Bee had no chance of winning coming down the middle of the course. (op 14-1)
River Falcon ◆ had no chance of winning from his draw, but did catch the eye in this group finishing well.
Damika(IRE), the winner of his last two races, including over C&D when his rider dropped his whip close home, was 5lb higher on his attempt at a hat-trick but was always finding the pace too quick for him. (tchd 17-2)

3447 JOHN SMITH'S NORTHUMBERLAND PLATE (HERITAGE H'CAP) 2m 19y
3:05 (3:07) (Class 2) 3-Y-0+

£107,887 (£32,480; £16,240; £8,102; £4,060; £2,047) **Stalls** Low

Form RPR

221- **1** **Overturn (IRE)**[49] 6734 6-8-7 **93**........ EddieAhern 21 103
(D McCain Jnr) *sn crossed over fr wd draw: mde all at ordinary gallop: qckng 3f out: kpt on strly ins fnl f: unchal* **14/1**

1153 **2** *2 ¾* **Drunken Sailor (IRE)**[26] 2593 5-9-7 **107**........(b) J-PGuillambert 14 114+
(L M Cumani) *t.k.h: hld up and bhd: weaved through fr over 2f out: styd on to take 2nd towards fin: no ch w wnr* **16/1**

00-6 **3** *½* **Desert Sea (IRE)**[52] 1821 7-8-8 **94** ow1........ NeilCallan 4 100
(D W P Arbuthnot) *hld up in midfield on ins: hdwy over 2f out: chsd wnr over 1f out: one pce ins fnl f: lost 2nd towards fin* **14/1**

-144 **4** *1* **Stanstill (IRE)**[28] 2541 4-8-7 **93**........ PJMcDonald 7 98+
(G A Swinbank) *hld up in tch: effrt over 2f out: disp 2nd pl over 1f out: one pce ins fnl f* **14/1**

-511 **5** *3 ½* **Deauville Flyer**[15] 2938 4-8-3 **89** 5ex........ RobertWinston 6 90+
(T D Easterby) *hmpd after 1f and after 2f: hld up in midfield: effrt and drvn over 3f out: kpt on fnl 2f: nvr able to chal* **3/1**[1]

3/02 **6** *nse* **La Vecchia Scuola (IRE)**[35] 2313 6-7-13 **90**........ IanBrennan(5) 13 91
(J S Goldie) *hld up in tch: effrt over 2f out: kpt on same pce over 1f out* **25/1**

-030 **7** *1* **Macarthur**[7] 3194 6-8-11 **97**........ PatCosgrave 16 96
(Jane Chapple-Hyam) *bhd: pushed along over 4f out: hdwy on ins over 2f out: kpt on same pce ins fnl f* **50/1**

-363 **8** *1* **Aaim To Prosper (IRE)**[11] 3050 6-7-11 **88**........(b) JamesSullivan(5) 17 86
(B J Meehan) *hld up in midfield: drvn over 4f out: plugged on same pce fnl 2f* **16/1**

-120 **9** *1* **Spirit Is Needed (IRE)**[14] 2976 4-8-6 **92**........ GregFairley 12 89
(M Johnston) *cl up: effrt and chsd wnr over 2f out to over 1f out: sn wknd* **22/1**

0-21 **10** *1 ¼* **Chiberta King**[42] 2126 4-9-2 **102**........ PhillipMakin 8 97
(A M Balding) *prom: drvn over 3f out: wknd over 1f out* **12/1**

31-0 **11** *2 ½* **Bernie The Bolt (IRE)**[52] 1821 4-8-8 **94**........ DavidProbert 9 86
(A M Balding) *hld up on ins: n.m.r over 4f out: effrt ent st: nvr able to chal* **13/2**[2]

0233 **12** *2 ¾* **Crackentorp**[14] 2976 5-8-6 **92**........ DavidAllan 2 81
(T D Easterby) *hld up in midfield on ins: hmpd after 1f: hrd drvn over 3f out: n.m.r and swtchd rt over 2f out: sn btn* **7/1**[3]

5300 **13** *12* **Becausewecan (USA)**[7] 3194 4-8-8 **94**........ LukeMorris 15 69
(M Johnston) *hld up on outside: struggling 5f out: sn btn* **66/1**

2-0 **14** *¾* **Rajik (IRE)**[11] 3050 5-8-6 **92**........(t) ChrisCatlin 3 66
(C F Swan, Ire) *bhd: struggling over 5f out: nvr on terms* **14/1**

5 **15** *1 ¼* **Zaralabad (IRE)**[20] 2799 6-8-6 **92**........ GrahamGibbons 11 64
(C F Swan, Ire) *midfield: drvn 4f out: no imp whn checked over 2f out: sn wknd* **40/1**

1-00 **16** *½* **Royal Diamond (IRE)**[42] 2126 4-8-7 **93** ow1........(p) TomEaves 20 65
(M Dods) *t.k.h: chsd wnr to over 2f out: sn rdn and wknd* **40/1**

4120 **17** *17* **Sabotage (UAE)**[30] 2469 4-9-10 **110**........ DaraghO'Donohoe 18 61
(Saeed Bin Suroor) *dwlt: sn midfield on outside: hdwy and cl up over 6f out: wkng whn hmpd over 2f out: eased* **50/1**

-333 **18** *12* **Halla San**[52] 1821 8-8-13 **99**........ PaulHanagan 19 36
(R A Fahey) *hld up: struggling over 5f out: btn ent st: eased whn no ch* **20/1**

/2-1 **19** *10* **Mamlook (IRE)**[52] 1821 6-9-0 **100**........ SebSanders 10 25
(D E Pipe) *dwlt: sn midfield: hmpd and lost pl after 1f: bhd: rdn whn n.m.r over 4f out: sn btn: eased fnl 3f* **10/1**

3m 28.05s (-11.35) **Going Correction** -0.50s/f (Hard) **19** Ran SP% **129.3**
Speed ratings (Par 109): **108,106,106,105,104 104,103,103,102,101 100,99,93,92,92 92,83,77,72**
toteswingers:1&2 £65.00, 2&3 £104.60, 1&3 £91.80 CSF £214.02 CT £3217.67 TOTE £18.60: £4.30, £3.10, £3.80, £4.30; EX 490.40 Trifecta £9699.60 Pool: £30,147.40 - 2.30 winning units..
Owner T G Leslie **Bred** Pendley Farm **Trained** Cholmondeley, Cheshire
■ Stewards' Enquiry : P J McDonald two-day ban: careless riding (Jul 14-15)

FOCUS
The draw is always perceived to be crucial to the outcome of the most valuable 2m handicap in the northern hemisphere, as only Archduke Ferdinand (stall 17) and Juniper Girl (stall 11) had won from double-figure draws since 1998 until this renewal. Only Bangalore (2002) had carried more than 8st 11lb to victory in the same period, and that statistic remained in place after this year's winner came home off 8st 7lb. This was also the first time since 2002 that the official going had the word firm in it.

NOTEBOOK
Overturn(IRE), much improved as a hurdler over the winter after having his breathing sorted out midway through it, got away smartly from the widest stall and managed to get across to the inside rail and the head of the field fairly readily. From that point, he assumed full control and was never seriously troubled, despite getting a strong ride, to hang on. If allowed his own way in front, he is always going to prove to be a difficult horse to pass over staying trips on the Flat. One would imagine a drop to 1m6f would not cause him any problems. His trainer is not too sure about future plans for Overturn, although he did suggest that the horse may have a break now before possibly coming back for another run on the Flat. He will, however, go back over jumps in the winter, and Donald McCain feels sure he will be a chaser in time. (op 12-1)
Drunken Sailor(IRE) ◆, who pulled very hard throughout the early stages, was taking a big step up in trip for this after running over 1m2f on his previous start (he had been tried over 1m6f in the past on the Flat), but the waiting tactics were probably slightly overdone on him here, as he was still taking a good grip turning into the home straight before finding a bit of trouble when making his way through the field. He may have made the winner work much harder for success had he been closer over 4f out. (op 25-1)
Desert Sea(IRE), absent since pulling too hard in the Chester Cup, and whose jockey was putting up 1lb overweight, ran yet another solid race and is a decent stayer when things go right for him. The plan is to head to the Ebor with him. (op 12-1)
Stanstill(IRE) ◆ is lightly raced but gave the impression that this trip stretched him on his only other try over it, which was last-time-out. However, that theory was dispelled with this run and he can develop into a serious Ebor contender back down in distance.
Deauville Flyer, 5lb higher than his win last time but still 6lb well in, was all the rage in the betting during the week for this and his rider had managed to get down to this weight. Tucked away towards the rear, he got outpaced as the tempo lifted before starting to stay on well. However, he ran into a wall of horses when making progress and needed to stop for a few strides to be pulled out into the clear. This was the end of his winning chance - if he had one at that stage- but he remains a stayer of some potential. (op 10-3 tchd 7-2 in a place)
La Vecchia Scuola(IRE) was produced to have every chance off her low weight but could not quicken when she needed to catch the front-runner.
Macarthur, placed in the 2008 Group 1 Coronation Cup, had the cheekpieces he wore last time removed (seemed to pull hard in them) and stayed on well up the inside rail after being well behind turning in.
Aaim To Prosper(IRE), with the blinkers back on, was a fine third to Junior in the 2m4f Ascot Stakes (Rajik behind him there) but hung under pressure down the home straight here. (op 20-1)
Spirit Is Needed(IRE) seemed to enjoy this step up in trip and was in second place up until 2f out. This was probably a bit too hot for him at this stage of his career, but he is sure to be well placed by his trainer to get back to winning ways.
Chiberta King ◆ has developed into a tough and reliable handicapper and was 8lb higher than last time after winning a decent handicap at Newmarket (1m6f). He was travelling well turning in, but didn't seem to get home. The Ebor seems a likely target for him. (op 14-1)
Bernie The Bolt(IRE) had little chance from his draw in the Chester Cup, but looked to have been given a chance here in a single-digit stall. However, he appeared to be hampered on a couple of occasions and can again be forgiven this effort. (op 8-1)
Crackentorp, back up in trip after catching the eye in a lady amateur riders' race at York, tended to run in snatches (he was also hampered early by his stablemate Deauville Flyer) which gave him no chance of getting involved. (op 9-1)
Royal Diamond(IRE) looked far too keen in the first-time cheekpieces and weakened accordingly early in the straight.
Mamlook(IRE) was bidding to become only the third horse in the last 100 years to do the Chester Cup/Northumberland Plate double in the same year (Attivo was the last in 1974), but had his chance ended even before they hit the home bend for the first time, as he got interfered with and lost many places as a result. At the rear turning in, he was hampered again so this effort can easily be forgotten. (op 8-1)

3448 TOTESPORT 0800 221 221 H'CAP 7f
3:40 (3:40) (Class 2) (0-100,99) 3-Y-0+

£12,462 (£3,732; £1,866; £934; £466; £234) **Stalls** High

Form RPR

1211 **1** **Camerooney**[3] 3318 7-8-7 **85** 6ex ow2........ DaleSwift(7) 11 95
(B Ellison) *mde all stands' side: styd on gamely ins fnl f: won gng away* **7/4**[1]

00-0 **2** *1 ¾* **Horatio Carter**[70] 1397 5-9-3 **88**........(p) NeilCallan 8 93
(K A Ryan) *chsd ldrs: wnt 2nd over 1f out: edgd lft to chal 1f out: kpt on wl: no ex last 100yds* **13/2**[3]

-030 **3** *¾* **Esoterica (IRE)**[8] 3146 7-9-3 **91**........(v) GaryBartley(3) 10 94
(J S Goldie) *in rr: hdwy stands' side over 2f out: styd on strly ins fnl f: fin wl* **9/1**

2150 **4** *1* **Osteopathic Remedy (IRE)**[22] 2708 6-9-3 **88**........ PhillipMakin 9 88+
(M Dods) *trckd ldrs: hmpd after 1f: effrt over 2f out: kpt on same pce ins fnl f* **8/1**

1013 **5** *3 ¾* **Game Lad**[30] 2462 8-8-12 **83**........(tp) DavidAllan 1 73
(T D Easterby) *hld up: swtchd rt after s to r stands' side: in rr: sme hdwy over 2f out: nvr a factor* **10/1**

-100 **6** ¾ **Deadly Encounter (IRE)**[8] 3150 4-8-11 **82**................(p) PaulHanagan 7 70
(R A Fahey) *chsd ldrs: one pce fnl 2f* **16/1**

-200 **7** 8 **Black Dahlia**[84] 1084 5-9-5 **90**... ChrisCatlin 3 57
(J A Glover) *in rr: bhd fnl 2f* **25/1**

5104 **8** 1 ¾ **Hajoum (IRE)**[8] 3146 4-9-8 **93**.. GregFairley 6 55
(M Johnston) *w wnr: drvn over 2f out: lost pl wl over 1f out* **4/1**[2]

01-0 **9** 2 ¼ **Golden Shaheen (IRE)**[19] 2815 3-8-5 **85**....................(v) AndrewElliott 5 38
(M Johnston) *s.i.s: in rr div: sme hdwy over 2f out: sn wknd* **25/1**

0-00 **10** 23 **Quanah Parker (IRE)**[14] 2971 4-9-0 **85**.................. DaraghO'Donohoe 4 —
(R M Whitaker) *dwlt: sn prom: drvn 3f out: sn wknd rapidly and t.o* **25/1**

1m 23.58s (-5.12) **Going Correction** -0.50s/f (Hard)
WFA 3 from 4yo+ 9lb **10** Ran SP% **117.3**
Speed ratings (Par 109): **109,107,106,105,100 99,90,88,86,59**
toteswingers:1&2 £2.40, 2&3 £13.00, 1&3 £5.70 CSF £13.15 CT £77.25 TOTE £3.00: £1.30, £1.90, £2.90; EX 18.10 Trifecta £101.50 Pool: £676.81 - 4.93 winning units..
Owner Mrs Jean Stapleton **Bred** Miss Dianne Hill **Trained** Norton, N Yorks

FOCUS
This looked a decent contest because most of those that took part could be given a chance but, as was the case throughout the day, bagging the stands'-side rail was seemingly the key to success. The course record for this distance was almost lowered by the winner.

NOTEBOOK
Camerooney, the winner of the 1m Carlisle Bell the previous Wednesday and carrying a 6lb penalty, was bounced out of the stalls to get the rails position and then made every yard of the running. His trainer reported afterwards that he doesn't know where the improvement the horse has shown will end, and would like to aim him towards next year's Lincoln all being well next March. (op 2-1)
Horatio Carter, 2lb lower than when winning this race last season, had been a little disappointing but shaped nicely here after tracking the pace-setter. This was only his second outing of the season, so he should have something to build on now. (tchd 6-1 and 7-1 in a place)
Esoterica(IRE), well behind Hajoum in the Buckingham Palace Stakes, looks a shade high in the weights, but he fought on well in this up the rail. (op 8-1)
Osteopathic Remedy(IRE), who was narrowly beaten by Horatio Carter in this race last season, edged left under pressure towards the centre of the course when in third, and possibly lost that position as a result. (op 9-1)
Game Lad, taking a step up in class for this, was going nowhere early but plugged on past a few rivals inside the final furlong. (op 7-1 tchd 6-1)
Hajoum(IRE) ran poorly after being up with the leader early. (op 11-2)
Quanah Parker(IRE) was found to have mucus on the lungs post race. Official explanation: trainer said gelding was found to have mucus on its lungs (tchd 33-1)

3449 E.B.F./TARMAC MAIDEN STKS 6f
4:15 (4:15) (Class 4) 2-Y-O **£5,046** (£1,510; £755; £377; £188) **Stalls** High

Form RPR

62 **1** **King Of Aquitaine (IRE)**[9] 3118 2-9-3 0............................. NeilCallan 9 80
(K A Ryan) *mde all stands' rail: set mod gallop: edgd lft and qcknd 2f out: kpt on wl ins fnl f* **7/2**[3]

2 2 ½ **Uptown Guy (USA)** 2-9-3 0... PhillipMakin 8 73+
(M Dods) *t.k.h early: trckd ldrs: effrt and chsd wnr over 1f out: kpt on same pce ins fnl f: bttr for r* **9/4**[2]

0 **3** 2 **Peters Spirit (IRE)**[14] 2980 2-8-12 0............................... PaulHanagan 4 62+
(R A Fahey) *prom: drvn along over 2f out: plugged on ins fnl f: nt gng pce of first two* **22/1**

0 **4** 1 **Perignon (IRE)**[9] 3118 2-9-3 0.. PJMcDonald 2 64
(G A Swinbank) *dwlt and wnt lft s: t.k.h early: hld up in tch: shkn up and stdy hdwy over 1f out: kpt on ins fnl f: nvr nr ldrs* **40/1**

22 **5** 8 **Dortmund**[16] 2887 2-9-3 0.. AhmedAjtebi 6 46+
(Mahmood Al Zarooni) *cl up tl rdn and wknd wl over 1f out* **6/4**[1]

524 **6** 1 ¾ **Arabian Star (IRE)**[13] 3000 2-9-3 0.................................. ChrisCatlin 5 40+
(M R Channon) *pressed wnr: rdn over 2f out: wknd over 1f out* **15/2**

7 5 **Kings Arms** 2-8-12 0.. JamesSullivan(5) 7 19
(M W Easterby) *dwlt: bhd: outpcd 1/2-way: no ch after* **50/1**

4 **8** 23 **Princess Dayna**[12] 3029 2-8-12 0..................................... SebSanders 1 —
(Tom Dascombe) *hld up towards rr: outpcd whn faltered over 2f out: sn btn: t.o* **25/1**

9 11 **Mayan Flight (IRE)** 2-9-3 0....................................... DaraghO'Donohoe 3 —
(R M Whitaker) *s.i.s: bhd: struggling over 3f out: t.o* **66/1**

1m 12.98s (-1.62) **Going Correction** -0.50s/f (Hard) **9** Ran SP% **118.8**
Speed ratings (Par 95): **94,90,88,86,76 73,67,36,21**
toteswingers:1&2 £4.30, 2&3 £14.90, 1&3 £30.90 CSF £11.72 TOTE £4.70: £1.60, £1.50, £3.80.

Owner Mrs Ger O'Driscoll **Bred** Cathal & Paul McCarthy **Trained** Hambleton, N Yorks

FOCUS
The odd decent performer has come out of this maiden in the past but, as with the previous races on the card, the result seemed influenced by the draw. The early pace did not seem strong. The winner improved but it is hard to gauge by how much.

NOTEBOOK
King Of Aquitaine(IRE) looked progressive and duly landed his first victory after his jockey intelligently made a dash for the rail. He was no doubt worthy of beating these rivals, but there is also little doubt that the route he took helped him stay out in front. (tchd 10-3)
Uptown Guy(USA) ♦, who cost 215,000gns at Craven breeze-up sale, seemed professional in his attitude just behind the winner and shaped with a lot of promise. (op 10-3)
Peters Spirit(IRE) stayed on nicely and seems sure to find her level in handicaps. (op 16-1)
Perignon(IRE), whose stable had a winner in this race back in 2007, finished nicely after getting a little outpaced. (op 33-1)
Dortmund was already starting to look one to take on after finishing runner-up on both his starts, especially as he was well backed to get off the mark on the second of those. He did not display any obvious signs of temperament (he was reported to have been unsuited by the going afterwards), but failed to make any impact in the final stages. Official explanation: jockey said colt was unsuited by the good to firm ground (op 7-4)
Arabian Star(IRE) looked a decent marker for all of his rivals to aim at, as he'd not been disgraced in any of his three previous outings, which also made him the most experienced horse in the line-up. Tracking the winner early, he stopped quickly inside the final furlong (already beaten at the time), as though something may have been amiss. (op 11-2)
Princess Dayna Official explanation: jockey said filly lost its action

3450 MORE WORLD CUP BETTING AT TOTESPORT.COM H'CAP 1m 2f 32y
4:45 (4:45) (Class 4) (0-85,83) 3-Y-O+ **£5,046** (£1,510; £755; £377; £188) **Stalls** Centre

Form RPR

-603 **1** **The Galloping Shoe**[17] 2865 5-9-6 **75**............................ SebSanders 4 86+
(A C Whillans) *hld up: smooth hdwy over 2f out: rdn to ld 1f out: sn clr* **9/1**

5-41 **2** 2 ¾ **Tepmokea (IRE)**[10] 3089 4-9-13 **82**............................ PaulHanagan 3 88
(R A Fahey) *t.k.h: cl up: led 2f out to 1f out: kpt on: no ch w wnr* **6/4**[1]

0260 **3** 1 **Prince Of Johanne (IRE)**[17] 2865 4-10-0 **83**.............. RobertWinston 6 87
(T P Tate) *hld up: hdwy over 2f out: chsd clr ldrs ins fnl f: kpt on fin* **16/1**

1-15 **4** 4 ½ **Judiciary (IRE)**[26] 2607 3-8-13 **80**.................................... AhmedAjtebi 2 75
(Mahmood Al Zarooni) *prom: drvn and outpcd over 2f out: no imp ins fnl f* **7/2**[2]

5-33 **5** 1 **Mason Hindmarsh**[19] 2816 3-7-12 **65**......................... AndrewMullen 10 58
(Karen McLintock) *led to 2f out: sn rdn: btn ins fnl f* **12/1**

1224 **6** 2 ¼ **Demonstrative (USA)**[73] 1297 3-8-13 **80**........................... GregFairley 9 69
(M Johnston) *in tch: drvn and outpcd over 4f out: n.d after* **12/1**

3046 **7** 1 ¼ **Desert Vision**[15] 2937 6-9-4 **78**...............................(vt) JamesSullivan(5) 7 65
(M W Easterby) *plld hrd: hld up in tch: drvn and outpcd 3f out: sn btn* **9/1**

2000 **8** 10 **Daaweitza**[3] 3319 7-9-1 **77**..(b) DaleSwift(7) 5 45
(B Ellison) *t.k.h: cl up tl wknd over 2f out* **8/1**[3]

2m 8.79s (-3.11) **Going Correction** -0.50s/f (Hard)
WFA 3 from 4yo+ 12lb **8** Ran SP% **114.6**
Speed ratings (Par 105): **92,89,89,85,84 82,81,73**
toteswingers:1&2 £1.70, 2&3 £6.70, 1&3 £24.80 CSF £23.05 CT £218.53 TOTE £8.20: £1.90, £1.40, £3.00; EX 20.90.
Owner G Brown & W Orr **Bred** Wood Hall Stud Limited **Trained** Newmill-On-Slitrig, Borders

FOCUS
This race was decimated by a spate of non-runners quite early in the day, so what had been a big-field handicap was more-or-less cut in half. The early pace seemed steady.

3451 BET ON LIVE FOOTBALL AT TOTESPORT.COM H'CAP 1m (R)
5:20 (5:20) (Class 4) (0-85,78) 3-Y-O **£5,046** (£1,510; £755; £377; £188) **Stalls** Low

Form RPR

4-34 **1** **Elmfield Giant (USA)**[29] 2515 3-9-1 **72**............................ PaulHanagan 3 77
(R A Fahey) *t.k.h early: trckd ldrs: plld out and chsd ldr over 1f out: styd on wl u.p ins fnl f: led nr fin* **4/1**[3]

4652 **2** nk **Vito Volterra (IRE)**[2] 3371 3-8-7 **64**................................ DavidProbert 5 68
(Michael Smith) *set stdy pce: rdn and qcknd over 2f out: kpt on ins fnl f: hdd nr fin* **15/2**

31 **3** 2 ½ **Law To Himself (IRE)**[32] 2425 3-9-7 **78**.......................... PJMcDonald 2 77
(G A Swinbank) *prom: rdn and outpcd over 2f out: kpt on ins fnl f: nt gng pce of first two* **2/1**[1]

-506 **4** nse **Antoniola (IRE)**[14] 2979 3-9-6 **77**......................................(t) DavidAllan 7 75
(T D Easterby) *t.k.h: hld up last: smooth hdwy over 2f out: rdn and hung bdly lft fr over 1f out: kpt on u.p ins fnl f* **9/4**[2]

0-35 **5** 2 ½ **Step In Time (IRE)**[7] 3208 3-9-3 **74**................................. GregFairley 6 67
(M Johnston) *trckd ldr: rdn over 2f out: lost 2nd over 1f out: btn ins fnl f* **7/1**

0-60 **6** 7 **Irish Eyes**[17] 2863 3-8-12 **69**.. AndrewMullen 1 46
(Jedd O'Keeffe) *in tch: drvn and outpcd 3f out: n.d after* **20/1**

1m 41.78s (-3.52) **Going Correction** -0.50s/f (Hard) **6** Ran SP% **113.1**
Speed ratings (Par 101): **97,96,94,94,91 84**
toteswingers:1&2 £6.30, 2&3 £3.90, 1&3 £2.40 CSF £32.70 TOTE £5.30: £2.00, £3.40; EX 28.50 Place 6: £77.77, Place 5: £37.29..
Owner Mike Browne **Bred** Brushwood Stable **Trained** Musley Bank, N Yorks

FOCUS
Not the strongest-looking handicap, as most of these had a negative or two to overcome to gain success, so this may not turn out to be reliable form, especially as the early pace was modest.
Antoniola(IRE) Official explanation: jockey said gelding hung left throughout and the bit slipped through its mouth
T/Jkpt: Not won. T/Plt: £379.20 to a £1 stake. Pool: £170,810.73 - 328.78 winning tickets.
T/Qpdt: £104.40 to a £1 stake. Pool:£8,269.69 58.60 winning tickets RY

3411

NEWMARKET (July Course) (R-H)
Saturday, June 26

OFFICIAL GOING: Good to firm changing to good to firm (firm in places) after race 3 (2.45)
Wind: Light across Weather: Sunny

3452 VIRGIN HOLIDAY CRUISES MAIDEN STKS 7f
1:45 (1:45) (Class 4) 2-Y-O **£4,857** (£1,445; £722; £360) **Stalls** High

Form RPR

1 **Zacynthus (IRE)** 2-8-10 0.................................. AntiocoMurgia(7) 3 81+
(Mahmood Al Zarooni) *a.p: rdn to ld over 1f out: r.o* **7/1**[3]

2 2 ¼ **Bowermaster (USA)** 2-9-3 0...................................... JamieSpencer 7 75
(Mahmood Al Zarooni) *led: rdn and hdd over 1f out: edgd rt and styd on same pce ins fnl f* **14/1**

3 nk **Maher (USA)** 2-9-3 0.. TomQueally 6 75+
(D M Simcock) *hld up: hdwy over 1f out: r.o* **33/1**

4 nk **Burj Hatta (USA)** 2-9-3 0......................................(t) TedDurcan 9 74
(Saeed Bin Suroor) *hld up: hdwy and hung lft fr over 1f out: r.o* **6/1**[2]

5 3 ¼ **Baransky** 2-9-3 0.. RichardHills 5 66
(Mahmood Al Zarooni) *chsd ldrs: rdn and ev ch over 1f out: wknd ins fnl f* **17/2**

0 **6** 4 **Jacobs Son**[15] 2932 2-9-3 0.. ShaneKelly 1 56
(R A Mills) *s.i.s and edgd lft s: hdwy and hung lft over 5f out: wknd over 1f out* **50/1**

7 ¾ **The Bells O Peover** 2-9-3 0... JoeFanning 8 54
(M Johnston) *chsd ldrs: pushed along 1/2-way: lft 2nd over 2f out: sn rdn: hung lft and wknd over 1f out* **8/1**

4 **P** **Cult Classic (IRE)**[16] 2887 2-9-3 0.............................. SteveDrowne 4 —
(R Hannon) *chsd ldr tl p.u and dismntd over 2f out* **10/11**[1]

1m 26.48s (0.78) **Going Correction** +0.10s/f (Good) **8** Ran SP% **112.4**
Speed ratings (Par 95): **99,96,96,95,92 87,86,—**
toteswingers: 1&2 £5.10, 1&3 £29.90, 2&3 £9.40 CSF £93.13 TOTE £7.90: £2.20, £3.30, £5.40; EX 73.10.
Owner Godolphin **Bred** Keatly Overseas Ltd **Trained** Newmarket, Suffolk

FOCUS
This was run at a just a fair pace with the runners well grouped for a long way and the field came up the centre. A 1-2-4 for Godolphin. With the favourite going wrong the form is rated around the race averages.

NOTEBOOK
Zacynthus(IRE), a half-brother to a winner at 1m in France, appeared to be the third pick on jockey bookings but he took the eye beforehand as a rangy type with scope and he ran out an emphatic winner, showing easily the best turn of foot. He'll improve, but this trip looks ideal for now, with something like the Superlative Stakes at the July meeting a likely target. (op 11-1 tchd 6-1)
Bowermaster(USA), a half-brother to some fair winners, made an encouraging debut, although he was at an advantage in being allowed to dictate at just a fair gallop. He's entitled to improve. (op 11-1 tchd 9-1)
Maher(USA) was expected to improve a lot for the run but shaped very well and made his effort from well back. For all his dam was a sprint winner in the US, there's some stamina in his pedigree and he'll probably be suited by a step up to 1m before the season is out. He can win a similar event. (op 25-1)

Burj Hatta(USA), a very costly yearling who is out of a winning half-sister to the Breeders' Cup Mile winner Val Royal, wore a tongue-tie on his debut, which isn't unusual where Godolphin are concerned bu he ended up racing with his tongue hanging out. He looked very green throughout but made some late headway. He should improve. Official explanation: trainer said colt hung left due to the good to firm ground (op 5-1 tchd 7-1)

Baransky ◆, a Green Desert half-brother to the useful duo Hunterview and Strobilus, both of them two-year-old 7f winners, ran as though he needed the race badly after travelling comfortably in the front rank. He took the eye beforehand and shaped as if he'll do better next time. (op 8-1 tchd 10-1)

Jacobs Son showed more than he did on his Sandown debut, but was never competitive.

The Bells O Peover, by Selkirk out of a very useful winning half-sister to the good sprinter Tante Rose, hails from a yard that have only recently got off the mark with their juveniles. He looked some way off the finished article and was coltish beforehand. (tchd 10-1)

Cult Classic(IRE) was representing a stable that has won this race five times since 2000, but went wrong at halfway and was pulled up. (tchd 4-5 and Evens)

3453 TOTESPORT.COM EMPRESS STKS (LISTED RACE) (FILLIES) 6f

2:15 (2:15) (Class 1) 2-Y-O

£15,327 (£5,810; £2,907; £1,449; £726; £364) **Stalls** High

Form RPR

2 **1** **Khor Sheed**[17] 2861 2-8-12 0 .... KierenFallon 6 94+
(L M Cumani) *s.i.s and edgd rt s: hld up: hdwy over 2f out: chsd ldr and edgd rt over 1f out: r.o to ld wl ins fnl f* **3/1**[2]

31 **2** *1* **Shoshoni Wind**[21] 2763 2-8-12 0 .... JamieSpencer 5 91
(K A Ryan) *led: rdn over 1f out: hung rt and hdd wl ins fnl f* **5/2**[1]

241 **3** *nk* **Imperialistic Diva (IRE)**[15] 2936 2-8-12 0 .... TedDurcan 9 90
(T D Easterby) *hld up: outpcd over 2f out: hdwy and hung lft fr over 1f out: r.o* **7/1**

1310 **4** *3 1/4* **Primo Lady**[10] 3070 2-9-1 0 ....(v) TomQueally 1 83
(Miss Gay Kelleway) *hld up: hdwy over 2f out: rdn over 1f out: no ex ins fnl f* **9/1**

0321 **5** *2 1/2* **Two Feet Of Snow (IRE)**[30] 2457 2-8-12 0 .... JoeFanning 8 73
(R Hannon) *chsd ldrs: wnt 2nd over 2f out: sn rdn: hung lft over 1f out: wknd ins fnl f* **14/1**

1 **6** *4* **Tipsy Girl**[34] 2358 2-8-12 0 .... ShaneKelly 7 61
(D J Coakley) *racd keenly: trckd ldr to over 4f out: remained handy tl rdn and wknd wl over 1f out* **6/1**[3]

11 **7** *nk* **Jollywood (IRE)**[14] 2950 2-8-12 0 .... SteveDrowne 2 60
(R Hannon) *prom: chsd ldr over 4f out to over 2f out: wknd over 1f out* **6/1**[3]

1m 13.23s (0.73) **Going Correction** +0.10s/f (Good) 7 Ran SP% **111.3**

Speed ratings (Par 98): **99,97,97,92,89 84,83**

toteswingers:1&2 £2.00, 2&3 £6.20, 1&3 £3.90 CSF £10.32 TOTE £3.80: £2.10, £2.70; EX 11.40 Trifecta £131.50 Pool: £576.05 - 3.24 winning units..

Owner Sheikh Mohammed Obaid Al Maktoum **Bred** Card Bloodstock **Trained** Newmarket, Suffolk

FOCUS

Traditionally one of the weaker juvenile Listed races and only Dixie Belle in recent years has gone on to won in higher grade. The pace wasn't strong and the runners came down the centre.

NOTEBOOK

Khor Sheed ◆ could have gone for a maiden, but left the form of her Haydock second (form working out nicely) well behind with an ultimately convincing success. She was allowed time to find her stride before staying on strongly once meeting the rising ground. In the short term, the Princess Margaret at Ascot seems a more realistic option than the Cherry Hinton, but she'll improve when stepped up to 7f. (op 7-2 tchd 11-4 and 4-1 in places)

Shoshoni Wind had looked open to more improvement when an impressive winner at Newcastle and ran well, albeit able to dictate and then getting first run. This looks her trip for now. (op 11-4 tchd 3-1)

Imperialistic Diva(IRE) had more on her plate than when winning at York last time, but promised to be suited by the return to 6f. She stayed on strongly to nearly grab second. (tchd 8-1)

Primo Lady, trying 6f for the first time and carrying a penalty for her Listed win at York, ran respectably ridden to get the trip, but left the impression that she didn't quite see it out. A return to 5f looks in order. (op 6-1 tchd 10-1)

Two Feet Of Snow(IRE) had to go to Brighton last time to get off the mark at the fourth attempt and looked a bit out of her depth here, although it wasn't a bad effort on figures. (op 16-1 tchd 20-1)

Tipsy Girl looked an interesting runner, having got up late to account for the subsequent Queen Mary fifth at Bath on her debut but seemed undone by inexperience. She made some modest late progress, though, and a step up to 7f will see her in a better light. (tchd 11-2 and 13-2)

Jollywood(IRE) was representing a yard which, surprisingly, haven't had much success in this race. She failed to give her running, despite the step up in trip looking like it would suit, dropping away from halfway. (op 13-2)

3454 BETFAIR FRED ARCHER STKS (LISTED RACE) 1m 4f

2:45 (2:45) (Class 1) 4-Y-O+ **£22,708** (£8,608; £3,228; £3,228; £1,076) **Stalls** Centre

Form RPR

1-32 **1** **Laaheb**[26] 2593 4-9-3 111 .... RichardHills 3 108+
(M A Jarvis) *chsd ldr tl led 3f out: rdn and edgd rt over 1f out: r.o* **5/2**[2]

1-14 **2** *1 1/4* **Whispering Gallery**[121] 712 4-9-0 115 .... TedDurcan 4 103+
(Saeed Bin Suroor) *led 9f: chsd wnr: rdn and swtchd lft over 1f out: styd on:* **13/8**[1]

541- **3** *2* **Man Of Iron (USA)**[232] 7281 4-9-3 116 .... KierenFallon 1 103
(L M Cumani) *chsd ldrs: swtchd lft over 3f out: sn rdn: hung lft and no ex ins fnl f* **5/2**[2]

13-4 **3** *dht* **Shahwardi (FR)**[35] 2345 4-9-3 99 .... SteveDrowne 5 103
(J R Gask) *hld up: hdwy 2f out: sn rdn: styd on: nt rch ldrs* **14/1**

1-10 **5** *9* **Highland Glen**[35] 2345 4-9-0 105 ....(t) JamieSpencer 2 86
(Saeed Bin Suroor) *hld up: plld hrd: rdn and wknd over 1f out* **10/1**[3]

2m 30.82s (-2.08) **Going Correction** +0.10s/f (Good) 5 Ran SP% **111.0**

Speed ratings (Par 111): **110,109,107,107,101**

CSF £7.07 TOTE £3.50: £1.80, £1.10; EX 6.30.

Owner Hamdan Al Maktoum **Bred** Darley **Trained** Newmarket, Suffolk

FOCUS

A closely-knit Listed event that featured the comeback of the Breeders' Cup Marathon winner Man Of Iron. The pace wasn't the breakneck one that the eventual second sometimes sets, and it wasn't quite the test of stamina it seemed it might be beforehand. Shahwardi sets the standard, with the first pair 8lb+ off their best and Man Of Iron a stone below his Breeders' Cup form.

NOTEBOOK

Laaheb had run right up to his best when third in a Listed race at Goodwood last month. He bettered that form here on his first run at 1m4f, proving suited by the relative test of speed, rather than a stamina test, after being given a canny ride. Things are going to be much tougher if he takes up a possible engagement in the Group 2 Princess Of Wales's Stakes. (op 3-1)

Whispering Gallery was back in trip after appearing not to stay 2m on the Tapeta when last seen in February. He might have fared better had his stamina been made more use of, rallying after the winner had got first run. He was really progressive last year and leaves the impression the best hasn't yet been seen of him for current connections. (op 15-8 tchd 2-1 in places)

Man Of Iron(USA) was having his first run since landing the Breeders' Cup Marathon on Pro-Ride at Santa Anita last autumn for Aidan O'Brien. The highest-rated, he left the impression he was a bit rusty but shaped well considering this was by far the toughest opposition he has faced on turf. He looks set for a good season. (op 2-1 tchd 15-8)

Shahwardi(FR) had pulled too hard at York on his debut for this yard and was a bit keen here, but this was a career-best effort. He'll improve again when settling better and getting his stamina tested more. (op 2-1 tchd 15-8)

Highland Glen, who had a tongue strap fitted for the first time, was troublesome at the stalls then too keen in the race, eventually eased off when his chance had gone. This was a second disappointing run in a row and he has something to prove now. (op 11-1 tchd 12-1)

3455 SUNLEY CRITERION STKS (GROUP 3) 7f

3:20 (3:20) (Class 1) 3-Y-O+

£36,900 (£13,988; £7,000; £3,490; £1,748; £877) **Stalls** High

Form RPR

1-50 **1** **Premio Loco (USA)**[127] 631 6-9-11 115 .... JackMitchell 5 121
(C F Wall) *hld up: hdwy over 2f out: rdn to ld and hung rt ins fnl f: r.o* **25/1**

1022 **2** *3/4* **Red Jazz (USA)**[10] 3066 3-8-8 113 .... MichaelHills 4 108
(B W Hills) *led 2f: chsd ldr tl led again over 2f out: rdn and hung rt over 1f out: hdd ins fnl f: styd on* **13/8**[1]

-342 **3** *1 1/4* **Doncaster Rover (USA)**[28] 2539 4-9-3 112 .... SteveDrowne 6 108
(D H Brown) *hld up: pushed along 1/2-way: hdwy u.p over 1f out: styd on same pce ins fnl f* **9/2**[3]

-214 **4** *2* **Fanunalter**[27] 2576 4-9-3 106 .... JamieSpencer 1 103
(M Botti) *prom: rdn and ev ch over 1f out: sn hung lft: no ex ins fnl f* **12/1**

0150 **5** *shd* **Beauchamp Xerxes**[8] 3144 4-9-3 103 .... HayleyTurner 8 102
(G A Butler) *edgd lft s: trckd ldrs: racd keenly: rdn over 1f out: styd on same pce* **25/1**

115- **6** *15* **Ashram (IRE)**[252] 6848 4-9-3 113 ....(v) TedDurcan 9 62
(Saeed Bin Suroor) *chsd ldr tl led 5f out: rdn and hdd over 2f out: wknd and eased fr over 1f out* **8/1**

-123 **7** *7* **Mabait**[22] 2707 4-9-3 108 .... KierenFallon 7 43
(L M Cumani) *hmpd s: trckd ldrs: plld hrd: rdn over 2f out: wknd over 1f out* **5/2**[2]

1m 24.74s (-0.96) **Going Correction** +0.10s/f (Good)

WFA 3 from 4yo+ 9lb 7 Ran SP% **111.3**

Speed ratings (Par 113): **109,108,106,104,104 87,79**

toteswingers:1&2 £12.10, 2&3 £1.80, 1&3 £34.60 CSF £62.93 TOTE £24.80: £5.60, £1.80; EX 70.00 Trifecta £565.80 Pool: £772.33 - 1.01 winning units..

Owner Bernard Westley **Bred** Kidder, Cole & Griggs **Trained** Newmarket, Suffolk

FOCUS

A competitive renewal that went to the highest-rated horse in the race. The pace picked up after a steady first 2f and once again the runners came up the centre, before edging back towards the rail. A personal best from the winner, above average for the grade, but the fifth limits the form to some effect.

NOTEBOOK

Premio Loco(USA) hadn't shown his form in Dubai earlier this year and looked to face a stiffish task conceding weight all round. Both his Group 2 wins before this were achieved abroad, but this performance suggests he is up to winning at that level here. (op 22-1 tchd 28-1)

Red Jazz(USA) ran a fine race turned out quickly after his runner-up effort in the Jersey Stakes but wasn't quite good enough at the weights. He saw the trip out well and might be worth another try back at 1m away from the very best company. (op 15-8 thd 2-1 in places)

Doncaster Rover(USA) had shown last time he had the form and stamina to go close, but ended up nearer the stands' rail than the rest. The Listed City of York Stakes at the Ebor meeting is presumably his late-summer target. (tchd 5-1)

Fanunalter had run respectably in a Group 2 in Italy last time, despite a slow start, but had a bit to find at the weights here. He didn't help by pulling too hard through the early stages. He stays 1m well and would have been better suited by a stronger gallop. (tchd 11-1)

Beauchamp Xerxes had plenty on at the weights and wasn't discredited. He travelled better than most for a long way, but being close up behind the uneven pace, might have flattered him a bit. (op 22-1 tchd 28-1)

Ashram(IRE) looked to have plenty in his favour if ready to run after a long break (gelded since last seen) but ran himself out after being allowed to stride on. He will be better with this run behind him. Official explanation: jockey said gelding had no more to give (op 9-1)

Mabait had looked to be going the right way, but was very keen early and lost his place quickly once the pace increased. This wasn't his running. Official explanation: jockey said colt ran flat (op 9-4 tchd 11-4)

3456 HALF MOON H'CAP 1m 2f

3:55 (3:55) (Class 2) (0-100,94) 3-Y-O+ **£11,656** (£3,468; £1,733; £865) **Stalls** Centre

Form RPR

4055 **1** **Reve De Nuit (USA)**[6] 3240 4-9-6 **86** .... TomQueally 7 95
(A J McCabe) *hld up: hdwy over 2f out: hit by rivals whip over 1f out: rdn to ld and hung rt ins fnl f: r.o* **9/1**

-502 **2** *1 1/4* **Classic Punch (IRE)**[24] 2640 7-10-0 **94** .... JamieSpencer 3 100
(D R C Elsworth) *led: pushed along 1/2-way: rdn over 1f out: hdd and unable qck ins fnl f* **6/1**

3042 **3** *2 1/2* **Ramona Chase**[22] 2710 5-9-3 **83** ....(t) NickyMackay 1 84
(M J Attwater) *dwlt: hld up: rdn over 2f out: swtchd lft 1f out: r.o: nt trble ldrs* **16/1**

0550 **4** *hd* **Kavachi (IRE)**[14] 2977 7-9-2 **82** .... ShaneKelly 8 83
(G L Moore) *chsd ldrs: rdn over 1f out: styd on: hung lft towards fin* **6/1**

3042 **5** *2* **Alcalde**[14] 2976 4-9-7 **87** .... JoeFanning 6 84
(M Johnston) *prom: rdn over 3f out: wknd ins fnl f* **7/2**[2]

1004 **6** *6* **Viva Vettori**[56] 1697 6-9-10 **90** .... KierenFallon 5 75
(D R C Elsworth) *hld up: plld hrd: hdwy over 6f out: rdn and edgd rt over 1f out: sn wknd* **9/4**[1]

0133 **7** *2 1/4* **Tinshu (IRE)**[22] 2703 4-9-5 **85** .... HayleyTurner 2 65
(D Haydn Jones) *chsd ldr: rdn whn hmpd over 1f out: sn wknd* **5/1**[3]

2m 4.12s (-1.38) **Going Correction** +0.10s/f (Good) 7 Ran SP% **114.1**

Speed ratings (Par 109): **109,108,106,105,104 99,97**

toteswingers:1&2 £10.20, 2&3 £7.10, 1&3 £21.70 CSF £60.44 CT £851.59 TOTE £10.70: £5.80, £2.10; EX 69.40.

Owner Jaber Ali Alsabah **Bred** Ecurie Du Haras De Meautry **Trained** Averham Park, Notts

FOCUS

A fairly useful handicap contested mostly by exposed sorts. It was run at a decent gallop with the field staying stands' side. The form looks sound.

NOTEBOOK

Reve De Nuit(USA) has been highly tried since switching to turf but this was a welcome drop in grade and he took full advantage. Always travelling well, the only question was whether he was going to find a clear run in time and when he did he responded well. This win will likely rule him out of this grade from next week, so things are set to get harder again. (tchd 8-1 and 10-1)

Classic Punch(IRE) has a good record here and built on his latest run with a good go from the front despite not always giving his rider much help. He's no sure thing to repeat this next time. (op 5-1)

Ramona Chase, off a 2lb higher mark than when running well from out of the weights at Epsom last time, was suited by the way the race developed, but hung right late and isn't easy to catch right. (op 14-1)
Kavachi(IRE) has dropped to a decent mark and got the decent gallop he needs, but he never threatened to finish any closer. He might be worth a try in headgear. (op 7-1 tchd 15-2)
Alcalde isn't the most reliable and couldn't build on his decent York effort last time back in trip. (tchd 10-3)
Viva Vettori stays this trip well but saw too much daylight and steadily dropped out of contention. He was later reported to have lost his action. Official explanation: jockey said horse was unsuited by the good to firm (firm in places) ground and lost its action (op 11-4)
Tinshu(IRE) usually gives her running, but was found out in this company on ground faster than ideal. (op 6-1 tchd 13-2)

3457 AGORA CARTERS CANCER CENTRE E B F FILLIES' H'CAP 1m
4:30 (4:31) (Class 3) (0-90,88) 3-Y-O+ £9,066 (£2,697; £1,348; £673) Stalls High

Form RPR
15-1 1 **Seasonal Cross**[14] 2956 5-8-9 69 HayleyTurner 3 81+
(S Dow) *stdd s: hld up: hdwy over 1f out: led ins fnl f: r.o wl* 16/1
0004 2 1 1/4 **Seradim**[8] 3158 4-9-6 80 KierenFallon 10 88
(P F I Cole) *chsd ldrs: rdn over 2f out: led ins fnl f: sn hdd: styd on same pce* 16/1
4-05 3 1 1/4 **Rafiqa (IRE)**[23] 2683 4-10-0 88 JackMitchell 7 93
(C F Wall) *hld up: hdwy over 1f out: sn rdn: styd on same pce ins fnl f* 7/1[3]
-361 4 shd **Ela Gorrie Mou**[12] 3036 4-9-0 74 EddieCreighton 6 80+
(P Charalambous) *hld up: hdwy and nt clr run over 1f out: swtchd rt: hmpd jst ins fnl f: r.o: nvr able to chal* 12/1
3141 5 1/2 **Gobama**[11] 3063 3-8-12 87 KierenFox(5) 8 89
(J W Hills) *chsd ldr tl led 2f out: rdn and hung lft over 1f out: hdd and no ex ins fnl f* 15/2
2112 6 nse **Night Lily (IRE)**[19] 2823 4-9-3 77 TonyCulhane 11 81
(P W D'Arcy) *led: hdd 2f out: sn rdn: no ex ins fnl f* 7/2[1]
342 7 3 **Baylini**[7] 3217 6-9-1 75 JamesDoyle 5 72
(Ms J S Doyle) *prom: rdn over 1f out: wknd ins fnl f* 8/1
-311 8 1/2 **Right Rave (IRE)**[37] 2256 3-8-7 77 ow1 ShaneKelly 1 70
(P J McBride) *prom: rdn and edgd rt over 1f out: wknd ins fnl f* 6/1[2]
6060 9 1 1/2 **Victoria Sponge (IRE)**[22] 2710 4-9-9 86 (t) WilliamCarson(3) 4 78
(S C Williams) *s.i.s: hld up: hdwy on outside over 2f out: sn rdn: wknd fnl f* 14/1
10-5 10 10 **Quiet**[28] 2542 3-9-1 85 SteveDrowne 9 52
(R Charlton) *trckd ldrs: rdn over 2f out: wknd over 1f out* 8/1
45-0 11 3/4 **Transvaal Sky**[51] 1834 3-8-11 86 RossAtkinson(5) 2 51
(Tom Dascombe) *chsd ldrs tl rdn and wknd 2f out* 10/1
1m 40.07s (0.07) **Going Correction** +0.10s/f (Good)
WFA 3 from 4yo+ 10lb 11 Ran SP% 118.2
Speed ratings (Par 104): **103,101,100,100,99 99,96,96,94,84 84**
toteswingers:1&2 £66.20, 2&3 £27.70, 1&3 £33.40 CSF £248.58 CT £1993.31 TOTE £17.50: £4.50, £4.60, £2.30; EX 264.90.
Owner Mrs Alicia Aldis **Bred** Adrienne And Michael Barnett **Trained** Epsom, Surrey
■ Stewards' Enquiry : Hayley Turner one-day ban: careless riding (Jul 10)
Kieren Fox caution: careless riding.

FOCUS
A fairly useful handicap won by a fast-improving filly. The field again came stands' side, and although three of the first four runners came from off the gallop, the pace didn't look a strong one with the runners still well bunched at halfway. A clear personal best from the winner.

NOTEBOOK
Seasonal Cross ◆ has now won four of her last five and, although up in grade, took this in the manner of one that had plenty more to give. Dropped right out, she found her way through blocked initially, but ultimately came through to win very smoothly. The handicapper still has some way to go before catching up with her, and she can win again. (op 14-1)
Seradim built on the promise she had shown at Goodwood last time. She has dropped to a very good mark on her best form and a similar event can come her way.
Rafiqa(IRE) had shaped very well off the same mark at Sandown last time and, held up as usual, ran creditably while leaving the impression she hasn't quite hit top form. She'll be interesting in a similar event if she gets more give in the ground. (op 9-2 tchd 15-2)
Ela Gorrie Mou ◆ had been progressing well on turf and this result didn't do her full justice, as she was twice stopped in her run before staying on well. She's eligible for lower grade races than this and can regain the winning thread.
Gobama wasn't discredited, but might have ended up seeing too much daylight. (op 7-1 tchd 6-1)
Night Lily(IRE) was another on an upward curve this year, but seemed to have no excuses having been allowed her own way on front on the rail, albeit up at a higher level than usual. (op 9-2)
Right Rave(IRE) Official explanation: jockey said filly was unsuited by the good to firm (firm in places) ground
Victoria Sponge(IRE), tried in a tongue-tie, failed to improve for the step back to 1m. (tchd 16-1)
Quiet, who possibly had soft ground as an excuse on her reappearance, left the impression that she had gone amiss, her rider looking down. (op 15-2 tchd 7-1)

3458 BRIDGES ASSET MANAGEMENT APPRENTICE H'CAP 7f
5:00 (5:02) (Class 5) (0-70,67) 4-Y-O+ £3,238 (£963; £481; £240) Stalls High

Form RPR
0003 1 **Hustle (IRE)**[21] 2750 5-9-4 66 AdamBeschizza(5) 5 76
(Miss Gay Kelleway) *chsd ldrs: led over 1f out: edgd lft and rdn clr ins fnl f* 7/4[1]
-340 2 4 1/2 **Russian Rave**[15] 2920 4-9-6 66 AshleyMorgan(3) 3 64
(J G Portman) *trckd ldrs: plld hrd: rdn over 1f out: styd on same pce* 6/1[3]
20-5 3 1 **Contemplate**[47] 1958 4-8-4 50 (b) KierenFox(3) 2 45
(Dr J D Scargill) *led: rdn and hdd over 1f out: no ex ins fnl f* 16/1
6016 4 6 **Learo Dochais (USA)**[14] 2959 4-9-7 67 (p) SimonPearce(3) 4 46
(M A Jarvis) *chsd ldrs: swtchd lft and racd alone over 5f out: rdn and wknd over 1f out* 9/2[2]
3240 5 4 **Fortezza**[16] 2896 4-8-1 49 (p) TobyAtkinson(5) 7 17
(A J McCabe) *hld up: drvn along 1/2-way: sme hdwy u.p over 2f out: sn wknd* 7/1
1m 27.32s (1.62) **Going Correction** +0.10s/f (Good) 5 Ran SP% 87.2
Speed ratings (Par 103): **94,88,87,80,76**
CSF £7.17 TOTE £1.80: £1.30, £2.00; EX 7.70 Place 6: £1,012.62, Place 5: £160.21..
Owner J Thompson, P Kerridge, Nightmare P'ship **Bred** Gigginstown House Stud **Trained** Exning, Suffolk
■ Cardinal was withdrawn (11/4, vet's advice). Deduct 25p in the £ under R4.

FOCUS
An uncompetitive handicap and not form to be getting carried away with. The winner is rated back to last season's form. The majority of the field stayed stands' side and the pace wasn't strong.
Learo Dochais(USA) Official explanation: jockey said gelding pulled off its off-fore shoe
T/Plt: £2,733.50 to a £1 stake. Pool: £86,313.69 - 23.05 winning tickets. T/Qpdt: £90.10 to a £1 stake. Pool £6,375.17 - 52.33 winning tickets. CR

3268 WINDSOR (R-H)
Saturday, June 26

OFFICIAL GOING: Good to firm
Wind: light breeze Weather: very warm

3459 BEST ODDS GUARANTEED AT TOTESPORT.COM MAIDEN STKS 6f
2:25 (2:28) (Class 5) 2-Y-O £2,729 (£806; £403) Stalls High

Form RPR
233 1 **Dr Green (IRE)**[26] 2594 2-9-3 0 PatDobbs 12 90+
(R Hannon) *a.p: led over 2f out: sn eased wl clr: unextended* 6/5[1]
2 8 **Harry Luck (IRE)** 2-9-3 0 DaneO'Neill 6 66+
(H Candy) *chsd ldrs: rdn over 2f out: swtchd lft to dispute 2nd ent fnl f: sn wnt clr 2nd but no ch w wnr* 9/2[2]
6 3 4 1/2 **Spirit Of Oakdale (IRE)**[23] 2677 2-9-3 0 AdamKirby 4 53
(W R Swinburn) *mid-div: rdn and stdy prog fr 2f out: styd on ins fnl f: wnt 3rd towards fin* 33/1
0 4 3/4 **Right Said Fred (IRE)**[25] 2621 2-9-3 0 JimCrowley 3 50
(R M Beckett) *prom: rdn over 2f out: kpt pressing for 2nd tl bmpd and no ex jst ins fnl f* 8/1
40 5 shd **Frankish Dynasty (GER)**[14] 2980 2-9-3 0 StevieDonohoe 9 50
(P F I Cole) *led tl rdn over 2f out: sn no ch w wnr: kpt holding on to narrow 2nd tl no ex ent fnl f* 20/1
6 1 1/4 **Clever Man** 2-9-3 0 AlanMunro 8 46+
(M R Channon) *chsd ldrs: rdn to dispute 2nd fr 2f out tl jst ins fnl f: fdd* 10/1
7 2 1/2 **High Avon** 2-9-3 0 JimmyQuinn 1 39+
(D K Ivory) *v.s.a: bhd: sme hdwy into midfield 2f out: no further imp after* 100/1
8 6 **Ocean Drift (USA)** 2-9-0 0 Louis-PhilippeBeuzelin(3) 11 21
(Mahmood Al Zarooni) *s.i.s: towards rr of midfield: wknd over 1f out* 15/2[3]
9 3 3/4 **Back For Tea (IRE)** 2-9-3 0 RichardKingscote 2 9
(Tom Dascombe) *chsd ldrs tl wknd over 2f out* 50/1
10 nse **Brave Battle** 2-9-0 0 PatrickHills(3) 7 9
(R Hannon) *s.i.s: towards rr: sme prog over 2f out: wknd over 1f out* 20/1
11 4 **Aquilifer (IRE)** 2-9-3 0 LiamJones 5 —
(W Jarvis) *s.i.s: a bhd* 33/1
12 24 **Windsor Knights** 2-9-3 0 MickyFenton 10 —
(A J Lidderdale) *s.i.s: sn outpcd: a detached: t.o* 80/1
1m 13.02s (0.02) **Going Correction** 0.0s/f (Good) 12 Ran SP% 115.2
Speed ratings (Par 93): **99,88,82,81,81 79,76,68,63,63 57,25**
toteswingers: 1&2 £3.30, 1&3 £14.30, 2&3 £22.60. CSF £5.55 TOTE £2.10: £1.10, £2.00, £9.70; EX 6.30 Trifecta £79.00 Pool:591.53 - 5.54 winning units..
Owner K T Ivory **Bred** John Morrin **Trained** East Everleigh, Wilts
■ Stewards' Enquiry : Dane O'Neill caution: careless riding.

FOCUS
Not much strength in depth here and the impressive winner bagged the favoured stands' side rail. He posted a clear step up on his previous sound efforts and this figure could underestimate him.

NOTEBOOK
Dr Green(IRE), who got very warm beforehand, was entitled to win this on the clear standard he set for the others and he had the plum draw in 12, but he still impressed in coming right away for his success. He had been placed on his three previous outings and was only just touched off in what is working out to be a decent Goodwood maiden last time, so this was much deserved. Despite this being just an average maiden, it has to rate an improved effort as he did the job without breaking sweat and will be high on confidence now. However, a likely reaction from the handicapper will probably dictate he is now forced to take a significant rise in class. (op 11-10 tchd 5-4)
Harry Luck(IRE) was going to put in a decent effort judged on market suppport and he finished a clear second-best, but found the winner in a different league. He is entitled to come on a deal for the run and, in good hands, evidently has a future. (op 11-2 tchd 4-1)
Spirit Of Oakdale(IRE), who could have been better drawn, has some scope and this rates a step up on his debut form at Lingfield this month. He left the impression he would go forward again for the experience.
Right Said Fred(IRE) was not helped by his low draw and was well held from 2f out, but still posted an improved effort on this second outing. He looks to need a bit more time and is one for nurseries in due course. (tchd 17-2)
Frankish Dynasty(GER), very easy to back, showed his previous York effort to be all wrong and is another to look out for in nurseries, for which he is now qualified. (op 16-1)
Clever Man, well bred, shaped as though he would come on a deal for this initial experience and be happier on easier ground. (op 11-1 tchd 12-1)
Ocean Drift(USA) Official explanation: jockey said colt missed the break

3460 ALL BETS ARE ON AT TOTESPORT.COM STKS (REGISTERED AS THE MIDSUMMER STAKES) (LISTED RACE) 1m 67y
2:55 (2:56) (Class 1) 3-Y-O+
£22,708 (£8,608; £4,308; £2,148; £1,076; £540) Stalls High

Form RPR
-120 1 **The Rectifier (USA)**[9] 3104 3-8-8 102 MickyFenton 6 108
(Stef Higgins) *mde all: slowed pce on bnd over 5f out: rdn to qckn 3f out: kpt on strly: rdn out* 7/2[2]
103 2 1 3/4 **Aldovrandi (IRE)**[30] 2471 3-8-8 102 AlanMunro 2 104
(M Botti) *hld up in last pair: racd keenly whn pce slowed over 5f out: hdwy 4f out: sn rdn: wnt 2nd over 1f out: kpt on but a being hld* 9/4[1]
4-16 3 1 1/2 **Party Doctor**[50] 1858 3-8-8 106 RichardKingscote 1 101
(Tom Dascombe) *chsd ldr: rdn over 2f out: unable to mount chal: kpt on same pce* 11/1
4-45 4 hd **Georgebernardshaw (IRE)**[28] 2539 5-9-4 105 StevieDonohoe 5 102
(D M Simcock) *chsd ldrs: rdn wl over 2f out: nt best of runs over 1f out: kpt on same pce* 8/1
-320 5 3 1/4 **Asset (IRE)**[91] 1021 7-9-4 107 (b) DaneO'Neill 4 95
(Saeed Bin Suroor) *hld up in last: effrt 3f out: nvr gng pce to get on terms* 7/2[2]
-626 6 3 1/2 **Ordnance Row**[22] 2707 7-9-4 106 PatDobbs 3 87
(R Hannon) *chsd ldr: rdn wl over 2f out: unable to mount chal: wknd ins fnl f* 9/2[3]
1m 42.45s (-2.25) **Going Correction** 0.0s/f (Good)
WFA 3 from 5yo+ 10lb 6 Ran SP% 112.8
Speed ratings (Par 111): **111,109,107,107,104 100**
toteswingers: 1&2 £2.30, 1&3 £13.60, 2&3 £4.90. CSF £11.95 TOTE £5.00: £2.40, £1.60; EX 15.10.
Owner Mrs Anne Cowley **Bred** Ceka Ireland Ltd **Trained** Lambourn, Berks
■ Stewards' Enquiry : Alan Munro caution: used whip without giving colt time to respond.

FOCUS
A tight Listed race, run at an uneven pace, that saw the 3-y-os dominate.

NOTEBOOK

The Rectifier(USA) was allowed to dictate as he pleased and made all. This well-backed colt proved free early on, but sensibly steadied things up after a couple of furlongs and was in the place to be against the rail entering the home straight. He kept on gamely after looking vulnerable 2f out and was well on top at the finish, becoming the first 3yo to take the race since its inception. Such tactics on this drop back in trip clearly worked the oracle and, while he is probably a touch flattered, there could still be more to come from this resolute galloper. (op 9-2)

Aldovrandi(IRE) ◆, out the back in the French Guineas two runs ago, pulled his way into midfield turning for home and likely would have preferred a more truly run race. He is well worth persevering with in this sort of grade as he has few miles on the clock. (op 10-3)

Party Doctor was returning from a 50-day break. He gave his all under a prominent ride and made it a 1-2-3 for the Classic generation. It wouldn't be surprising to see him fare a little better back over 1m2f now. (op 10-1)

Georgebernardshaw(IRE), who got himself warm beforehand, was another who would have enjoyed more of a test. He appreciated this lesser company, but is not simple to place. (op 15-2 tchd 7-1)

Asset(IRE), despite looking happier over shorter in the past, is yet another who would have likely benefited from a stronger pace. He is entitled to come on for the run, but he too is tricky to place successfully. (tchd 3-1)

Ordnance Row was disappointing, even allowing for the fact he did not get the best of runs on the stands' rail. He has a touch to prove at present. (op 3-1)

3461 BET ON WIMBLEDON AT TOTESPORT.COM H'CAP 6f

3:30 (3:30) (Class 2) (0-105,104) 3-Y-0+

£28,039 (£8,397; £4,198; £2,101; £1,048; £526) **Stalls** High

Form RPR

5015 **1** **Parisian Pyramid (IRE)**[21] 2748 4-8-13 **91**................ StephenCraine 13 102
(K A Ryan) *disp ld: outrt ldr 2f out: 2 l clr ent fnl f: kpt on wl: rdn out* **9/1**

1040 **2** *1* **Prohibit**[7] 3193 5-8-13 **96**....................(p) JohnFahy(5) 5 104
(R M H Cowell) *hld up towards rr: smooth hdwy in centre over 2f out: rdn over 1f out: chsd wnr jst ins fnl f: kpt on* **16/1**

-005 **3** *½* **Golden Desert (IRE)**[7] 3193 6-9-7 **99**.................... StevieDonohoe 10 105
(R A Mills) *trckd ldrs: rdn to chse wnr over 1f out tl jst ins fnl f: kpt on* **9/1**

6-02 **4** *½* **Signor Peltro**[26] 2595 7-9-8 **100**.................... DaneO'Neill 11 108+
(H Candy) *mid-div: nt clr run and lost pl 2f out: hdwy whn swtchd lft ins fnl f: r.o wl: nrst fin* **14/1**

-030 **5** *nk* **Edge Closer**[7] 3193 6-9-7 **102**.................... PatrickHills(3) 2 106+
(R Hannon) *restrained and swtchd rt sn after s: gng wl enough in rr but nt clr run fr over 2f out: weaved way through fr jst over 1f out: kpt on: nrst fin* **20/1**

-652 **6** *¾* **Iver Bridge Lad**[14] 2978 3-9-5 **104**....................(b) AlanMunro 7 103
(J Ryan) *mid-div: sltly outpcd u.p wl over 2f out: kpt on ins fnl f: nrst fin* **11/1**

0130 **7** *1* **Rileyskeepingfaith**[7] 3193 4-9-5 **102**....................(v) MatthewDavies(5) 6 100
(M R Channon) *mid-div: rdn wl over 2f out: chsd ldrs over 1f out: kpt on same pce* **9/1**

0-30 **8** *hd* **Olynard (IRE)**[21] 2748 4-8-13 **91**.................... JimCrowley 14 88
(R M Beckett) *disp ld tl 2f out: sn rdn: one pce ent fnl f* **7/1**[2]

4-01 **9** *1 ¼* **Northern Fling**[31] 2428 6-8-2 **83**.................... Louis-PhilippeBeuzelin(3) 3 76
(J S Goldie) *hld up towards rr: hdwy into midfield u.p over 2f out: no further imp fr over 1f out* **20/1**

6650 **10** *shd* **Lucky General (IRE)**[10] 3066 3-9-4 **103**....................(b[1]) PatDobbs 15 94
(R Hannon) *chsd ldrs: rdn over 2f out: one pce ent fnl f* **16/1**

0524 **11** *½* **Shifting Star (IRE)**[27] 2563 5-9-0 **92**.................... AdamKirby 1 83+
(W R Swinburn) *hld up towards rr: hdwy and gng okay whn nt clr run 2f out: nvr able to get on terms after* **20/1**

44-1 **12** *2* **Drawnfromthepast (IRE)**[22] 2689 5-8-4 **87**.................... SophieDoyle(5) 8 72
(J A Osborne) *in tch: rdn over 2f out: nt pce to get on terms whn bdly hmpd jst ins fnl f* **20/1**

2-00 **13** *hd* **Servoca (CAN)**[8] 3146 4-9-0 **92**.................... AndreaAtzeni 4 76
(Mike Murphy) *mid-div: rdn wl over 2f out: wknd ent fnl f* **40/1**

4103 **14** *nse* **Thebes**[26] 2595 5-9-3 **95**.................... JimmyQuinn 12 79
(M Johnston) *trckd ldrs: rdn wl over 2f out: keeping on at the same pce whn squeezed out and snatched up ins fnl f* **6/1**[1]

3-31 **15** *½* **Cockney Class (USA)**[43] 2090 3-8-2 **90**.................... MartinLane(3) 9 71
(B J Meehan) *mid-div: rdn over 3f out: wknd over 1f out: hmpd jst ins fnl f* **10/1**

-023 **16** *2 ¼* **Wildcat Wizard (USA)**[42] 2119 4-9-2 **94**....................(t) MickyFenton 16 87
(P F I Cole) *mid-div: rdn 3f out: wkng whn bdly hmpd jst ins fnl f* **8/1**[3]

1m 11.51s (-1.49) **Going Correction** 0.0s/f (Good) **16** Ran SP% **125.2**
WFA 3 from 4yo+ 7lb
Speed ratings (Par 109): **109,107,107,106,105 104,103,103,101,101 100,98,97,97,97 94**
toteswingers: 1&2 £69.50, 1&3 £33.10, 2&3 £63.00. CSF £136.88 CT £1408.82 TOTE £13.80: £3.00, £3.40, £2.70, £3.70; EX 312.90 TRIFECTA Not won..
Owner Dr Marwan Koukash **Bred** Illuminatus Investments **Trained** Hambleton, N Yorks

FOCUS

Competitive stuff. Unsurprisingly, the main action developed close to the stands' rail and there were plenty of hard-luck stories.

NOTEBOOK

Parisian Pyramid(IRE) was well drawn and showed real early pace to get across and help force the pace. Considering the way the two preceding races unfolded, it made sense that he held off his pursuers and his rider emerges with credit. He has now won two of his last three outings and is clearly now back at the top of his game. (op 10-1 tchd 11-1)

Prohibit ◆, in first-time cheekpieces, had run a fair race in the Wokingham at Royal Ascot a week earlier and, travelling strongly through the race here, ran better than the bare form. He comes out of this with plenty of credit as he was drawn poorly and his turn is surely nearing again. (op 25-1)

Golden Desert(IRE) finished well in front of the runner-up in the Wokingham, but he is something of an Ascot specialist and was better drawn there. He was also better housed in this, and he ran his race, helping to set the standard. Perhaps a return to 7f is now required and it wouldn't be surprising to see him find another winning turn back at his favourite venue before long.

Signor Peltro had plenty to do nearing the furlong pole, but the gaps opened up for him and he was motoring home late in the day. He is another back in top form and worth another go over 7f. Official explanation: jockey said gelding weas denied a clear run (op 11-1)

Edge Closer did well from his draw in stall two and this was a lot better, but consistency doesn't seem his strong suit.

Iver Bridge Lad fared best of the two 3-y-os and seems to have benefited for the recent application of blinkers. (op 14-1)

Olynard(IRE), who came into this 2-2 over C&D in handicap company, was well away and raced tight against the favoured stands' rail. His finishing effort was laboured, though. (op 5-1)

Shifting Star(IRE) must be given another chance. Official explanation: jockey said gelding was denied a clear run (op 22-1)

Drawnfromthepast(IRE) Official explanation: jockey said saddle slipped

Thebes was well backed and his chance had gone before meeting a little trouble. (op 8-1)

Wildcat Wizard(USA) was unable to lie up early on and, therefore, it wasn't at all surprising he failed to take advantage of his good draw. He was one of many who endured a troubled passage when trying to get through late on and this run is best forgiven. Official explanation: jockey said gelding had no more to give (op 15-2)

3462 BET ON WORLD CUP AT TOTESPORT.COM H'CAP 1m 3f 135y

4:00 (4:01) (Class 2) (0-100,100) 3-Y-0+ **£11,656** (£3,468; £1,733; £865) **Stalls** Low

Form RPR

2-62 **1** **The Fonz**[45] 2031 4-8-9 **84** oh2.................... Louis-PhilippeBeuzelin(3) 8 93+
(Sir Michael Stoute) *t.k.h early: trckd ldng pair: rdn wl over 2f out to cl on ldrs: tk narrow advantage jst ins fnl f: kpt on wl: drvn out* **2/1**[1]

-332 **2** *½* **Mildoura (FR)**[28] 2549 5-9-0 **86**.................... IanMongan 2 94
(Mrs L J Mongan) *led: 8 l clr 5f out: rdn 3f out: narrowly hdd ent fnl f: rallied v gamely: hld towards fin* **9/1**

5050 **3** *1 ½* **Record Breaker (IRE)**[17] 2857 6-9-1 **87**....................(v[1]) JimmyQuinn 6 92
(M Johnston) *chsd clr ldr: clsd on ldr fr 4f out: rdn over 2f out: ev ch ent fnl f tl fdd fnl 50yds* **7/2**[2]

434- **4** *4 ½* **Free Agent**[268] 6425 4-10-0 **100**.................... PatDobbs 3 98
(R Hannon) *hld up: rdn wl over 2f out: little imp on ldrs: wnt 4th nr fin* **11/1**

-100 **5** *1* **Dansili Dancer**[43] 2096 8-9-8 **99**.................... JohnFahy(5) 5 95
(C G Cox) *hld up: hdwy into 4th u.p over 2f out: nvr threatened ldrs: wknd ins fnl f* **5/1**[3]

060- **6** *3* **Magicalmysterytour (IRE)**[231] 7293 7-9-4 **90**............ StevieDonohoe 9 88+
(W J Musson) *hld up: rdn wl over 2f out: styng on at the same pce to mount chal for a n.d 4th whn hmpd ins fnl f* **11/2**

2-40 **7** *2* **Resplendent Light**[21] 2747 5-8-12 **84**....................(b[1]) DaneO'Neill 7 72
(W R Muir) *chsd ldrs: rdn wl over 2f out: wknd over 1f out* **18/1**

000- **8** *7* **Strategic Mount**[311] 5170 7-9-9 **95**.................... JimCrowley 1 71
(P F I Cole) *s.i.s: a last* **25/1**

2m 26.3s (-3.20) **Going Correction** 0.0s/f (Good) **8** Ran SP% **115.0**
Speed ratings (Par 109): **110,109,108,105,105 103,101,97**
toteswingers: 1&2 £3.90, 1&3 £1.80, 2&3 £4.70. CSF £21.41 CT £59.76 TOTE £2.70: £1.30, £2.60, £1.80; EX 19.60 Trifecta £64.10 Pool: £286.28 - 3.30 winning units..
Owner Anthony & David de Rothschild **Bred** Southcourt Stud **Trained** Newmarket, Suffolk

FOCUS

A good handicap, run at a strong early pace yet it still paid to race handily.

NOTEBOOK

The Fonz gained compensation for his narrow defeat to a subsequent winner at York on his previous outing 45 days earlier and was given a decent ride. He proved free early on, but his rider judged the pace to perfection in taking him back and getting him relaxed. The 4yo son of Oasis Dream knuckled down most gamely when asked to get to the front and is clearly progressing. His yard won the race with Warringah last year, who was then narrowly foiled on his next two outings before heading to the Ebor at York in August, and it wouldn't be surprising to see The Fonz follow the same path. (op 7-4 tchd 13-8)

Mildoura(FR) has now been placed on her four outings this term and certainly deserves a change of luck after this brave effort. She is most consistent and rates a good benchmark. (tchd 10-1)

Record Breaker(IRE) was the one who kept closest tabs on the winner through the first half of the race and shaped more encouragingly for the application of a first-time visor. (op 4-1)

Free Agent was making his handicap debut and having his first outing for 268 days. He is high enough in the weights but did best of those held up here and should improve a bundle for the run. (op 14-1 tchd 10-1)

Dansili Dancer (tchd 6-1)

Magicalmysterytour(IRE) ◆ finished second in the race last year off a 7lb higher mark and has a history of going well fresh, so it wasn't that surprising to see support. However, his supporters knew their fate a long way out, as he sat well out of his ground and his rider didn't get overly serious with him when attempting to make up ground in the home straight. He stays further and raced handily when missing out here last season, so it's baffling as to why he was held up this time. It was already over for him before he ran into the back of horses late on and he is no doubt better than he was able to show. (op 15-2)

3463 40 LIVE FOOTBALL MARKETS AT TOTESPORT.COM H'CAP 6f

4:35 (4:35) (Class 5) (0-70,70) 3-Y-0+ **£2,729** (£806; £403) **Stalls** High

Form RPR

0340 **1** **The Wee Chief (IRE)**[22] 2719 4-9-9 **65**.................... PatDobbs 5 77+
(J C Fox) *travelled wl in last but cl up: smooth hdwy to ld ent fnl f: idled but a enough in hand: rdn out: readily* **9/2**[2]

4236 **2** *¾* **Danzoe (IRE)**[8] 3174 3-9-6 **69**....................(b) StevieDonohoe 6 73
(Mrs C A Dunnett) *trckd ldr: led over 1f out: rdn and stmbld whn hdd ent fnl f: kpt on but a being hld by idling wnr* **7/1**

3614 **3** *2 ¾* **Dvinsky (USA)**[25] 2635 9-9-9 **65**....................(b) JimmyQuinn 2 62
(P Howling) *wnt v sltly lft s: sn prom: rdn 2f out: kpt on same pce fnl f* **5/1**[3]

3326 **4** *½* **Kyllachy Storm**[22] 2689 6-9-11 **70**....................(b) MichaelGeran(3) 4 66
(R J Hodges) *cl up: rdn 2f out: kpt on same pce* **10/1**

61 **5** *½* **Doctor Hilary**[14] 2964 8-9-10 **66**....................(v) JimCrowley 8 60
(M R Hoad) *led: rdn and hdd over 1f out: one pce after* **4/1**[1]

-003 **6** *nk* **George Thisby**[24] 2646 4-9-10 **69**.................... JamesMillman(3) 7 62
(B R Millman) *prom: rdn 2f out: sn one pce* **5/1**[3]

0-00 **7** *11* **Rigid**[26] 2587 3-8-0 **54**.................... JohnFahy(5) 3 10
(A W Carroll) *stdd s but cl up: effrt 3f out: sn hung lft: wknd over 1f out* **14/1**

-225 **8** *18* **Ginobili (IRE)**[68] 1428 4-9-9 **68**....................(t) RussKennemore(3) 1 —
(Andrew Reid) *little slowly away: sn prom: wknd 2f out* **5/1**[3]

1m 13.69s (0.69) **Going Correction** 0.0s/f (Good) **8** Ran SP% **116.4**
WFA 3 from 4yo+ 7lb
Speed ratings (Par 103): **95,94,90,89,89 88,73,49**
toteswingers: 1&2 £15.60, 1&3 £4.50, 2&3 £3.60. CSF £36.42 CT £165.07 TOTE £6.20: £2.20, £2.50, £1.60; EX 35.80 Trifecta £222.00 Part won. Pool: £300.03 - 0.86 winning units..
Owner R E Kavanagh **Bred** Dermot Kilmartin **Trained** Collingbourne Ducis, Wilts

■ Stewards' Enquiry : Stevie Donohoe four-day ban: hit gelding in annoyance cross win line (Jul 10, 12-14)

FOCUS

An ordinary sprint handicap and it was wide open. There were plenty of chances in the home straight.

3464 GET LIVE FOOTBALL STATS AT TOTESPORT.COM FILLIES' H'CAP 1m 67y

5:05 (5:05) (Class 5) (0-75,74) 3-Y-0+ **£2,729** (£806; £403) **Stalls** High

Form RPR

5304 **1** **Mellifera**[18] 2844 3-9-3 **65**....................(p) AdamKirby 1 73
(W R Swinburn) *hld up: rdn and hdwy fr 2f out: swtchd lft ent fnl f: led sn after: r.o: rdn out* **4/1**[3]

-352 **2** *1* **Cultured Pride (IRE)**[8] 3158 3-9-12 **74**.................... PatDobbs 2 80
(R Hannon) *trckd ldr: rdn to ld wl over 1f out: sn hrd pressed: hdd jst ins fnl f: kpt on but no ex* **7/2**[2]

-063 **3** ½ **Cat Hunter**[13] 3001 3-9-5 **67** ... JimCrowley 5 72
(Mrs A J Perrett) *trckd ldrs: rdn for str chal upsides fr 2f out: ev ch ins fnl f: no ex fnl 50yds* **7/2**[2]
0053 **4** ¾ **Spiritual Art**[8] 3158 4-10-0 **66** ... JamieMoore 6 71
(L A Dace) *led: rdn over 2f out: hdd wl over 1f out: kpt on* **6/1**
030 **5** 1 **Sula Two**[30] 2473 3-8-12 **63** ... MichaelGeran(3) 9 64
(R J Hodges) *disp 4th: rdn whn sltly outpcd over 2f out: hung lft fnl f: kpt on same pce* **25/1**
4/-0 **6** 3½ **On The Feather**[15] 2919 4-9-8 **63** ... JamesMillman(3) 3 57
(B R Millman) *hld up: hdwy fr 5f out to join ldrs briefly 4f out: rdn 3f out: wknd ent fnl f* **20/1**
0-35 **7** 9 **Tap Dance Way (IRE)**[27] 2564 3-9-2 **64** ... StevieDonohoe 4 36
(P R Chamings) *s.i.s: in last pair: t.k.h after 2f: rdn over 2f out: wknd over 1f out: eased fnl f* **10/3**[1]
50-0 **8** 19 **Tislimeen**[116] 758 3-9-3 **65** ... CoryParish 8 —
(M R Channon) *disp 4th: rdn over 3f out: wknd 2f out: t.o* **25/1**

1m 44.45s (-0.25) **Going Correction** 0.0s/f (Good)
WFA 3 from 4yo 10lb **8** Ran SP% **114.3**
Speed ratings (Par 100): **101,100,99,98,97 94,85,66**
toteswingers: 1&2 £3.20, 1&3 £2.80, 2&3 £1.60. CSF £17.85 CT £52.38 TOTE £5.60: £1.90, £1.50, £1.40; EX 22.60 Trifecta £37.30 Pool: £254.82 - 5.04 winning units. Place 6: £47.48, Place 5: £33.42..
Owner P W Harris **Bred** Pendley Farm **Trained** Aldbury, Herts

FOCUS
An ordinary fillies' handicap on paper in which there were several potential improvers. It was run at a decent pace and the form is rated slightly positively.
Tap Dance Way(IRE) Official explanation: jockey said filly hung left
T/Plt: £51.30 to a £1 stake. Pool: £62,680 - 891.90 winning tickets. T/Qpdt: £12.70 to a £1 stake. Pool: £4,606.60 - 268.20 winning tickets. TM

3465 - (Foreign Racing) - See Raceform Interactive

3418 CURRAGH (R-H)
Saturday, June 26

OFFICIAL GOING: Good to firm

3466a BALLYMACOLL STUD CELEBRATING 50 YEARS INTERNATIONAL STKS (GROUP 3) 1m 2f
1:45 (1:48) 3-Y-O+ **£37,389** (£10,929; £5,176; £1,725)

RPR
1 **Precious Gem (IRE)**[8] 3185 4-9-4 100 ... PJSmullen 5 101+
(D K Weld, Ire) *chsd ldr: clsd and travelling best fr bef st: led 2f out: styd on wl u.p fr over 1f out* **9/2**[3]
2 1¾ **Shintoh (USA)**[9] 3137 3-8-10 103 ... KJManning 2 101
(J S Bolger, Ire) *chsd ldrs in 3rd: pushed along to cl fr bef st: 2nd fr 2f out: no imp u.p and kpt on same pce ins fnl f* **4/1**[2]
3 3 **Grand Admiral (USA)**[7] 3232 4-9-7 90 ... (b[1]) JMurtagh 4 94
(A P O'Brien, Ire) *led and clr: rdn and reduced ld fr bef st: hdd 2f out: sn dropped to 3rd and no imp* **12/1**
4 5 **Recharge (IRE)**[16] 2913 4-9-7 109 ... CDHayes 1 84
(Kevin Prendergast, Ire) *racd in mod 4th: rdn fr bef st: no imp fr 2f out: eased ins fnl f tl shkn up to hold on to 4th* **8/13**[1]
5 shd **Carazam (IRE)**[366] 3326 3-8-10 ... WMLordan 3 85
(T Stack, Ire) *wl off pce in rr: no imp u.p st: jst failed to go 4th nr line* **16/1**

2m 5.94s (-6.66) **Going Correction** -0.75s/f (Hard)
WFA 3 from 4yo 12lb **5** Ran SP% **113.7**
Speed ratings: **106,104,102,98,98**
CSF £22.57 TOTE £4.60: £2.00, £2.60; DF 20.20.
Owner Mrs C L Weld **Bred** J Crowley,Crystal Blds, Ap & M **Trained** The Curragh, Co Kildare

FOCUS
The winning time was over two seconds slower than the Pretty Polly, and the race has been rated through the third to his best.

NOTEBOOK
Precious Gem(IRE) stepped further up in grade with a performance of some authority in this uncompetitive Group 3, but she's certainly going the right way and according to her trainer looks ready to take a step up in grade. Tracking the decent pace set by the eventual third, she quickened well to take up the slack inside the final quarter-mile and from there ran on well and didn't allow the runner-up to make any impression on her. She should be able to step up to 1m4f as well on this sort of evidence and should add to her tally in the coming months. (op 4/1)
Shintoh(USA) is useful but probably isn't the quickest. He looks a horse who would relish stepping up to 1m4f. Racing just behind the two leaders, he was unable to match the turn of foot shown by the winner to take her to the front, but he stayed on well and kept going to the line.
Grand Admiral(USA) was probably lit up to an extent by the first-time blinkers. He kept going until headed inside the 2f pole and was one paced from there. (op 10/1)
Recharge(IRE) was bitterly disappointing and ran a good stone below his best. Held up, he was being niggled coming down the hill into the straight and came under pressure soon after. He could make no impression and this effort can be safely forgotten. He was found to be blowing hard post-race. Official explanation: vet said colt was blowing hard and coughing post race (op 4/5)
Carazam(IRE) was in rear for the whole race and was never a factor, although he did pressure the off-colour favourite for fourth spot close home. (op 12/1)

3467a AUDI PRETTY POLLY STKS (GROUP 1) (FILLIES) 1m 2f
2:20 (2:21) 3-Y-O+
£106,194 (£33,628; £15,929; £5,309; £3,539; £1,769)

RPR
1 **Chinese White (IRE)**[34] 2369 5-9-9 113 ... PJSmullen 2 116
(D K Weld, Ire) *chsd clr ldr: clsd fr bef st: chal fr 2f out: led fr 1 1/2f out: styd on wl u.p* **4/1**[3]
2 1¼ **Flying Cloud (IRE)**[44] 2055 4-9-9 ... (t) FrankieDettori 1 113
(Saeed Bin Suroor) *chsd ldrs in mod 3rd: clsd fr bef st: styd on u.p fnl f: wnt 2nd wout troubling wnr last strides* **3/1**[2]
3 shd **Akdarena**[22] 2711 3-8-11 113 ... (bt) KJManning 9 113
(J S Bolger, Ire) *led and sn wl clr: reduced ld fr bef st: pressed fr 2f out: hdd fr 1 1/2f out: rallied fnl f: no ex and dropped to 3rd last strides* **5/1**
4 6 **Remember When (IRE)**[22] 2711 3-8-11 110 ... JMurtagh 5 101+
(A P O'Brien, Ire) *chsd ldrs in poor 4th: pushed along and sme improvement into st: no imp and kpt on same pce fr 2f out* **7/4**[1]
5 5 **Lolly For Dolly (IRE)**[10] 3071 3-8-11 107 ... WMLordan 4 91+
(T Stack, Ire) *racd in poor 5th: pushed along to be a little clsr into st: sn no imp and kpt on same pce* **14/1**
6 ½ **Crystal Gal (IRE)**[34] 2370 3-8-11 105 ... DPMcDonogh 3 90+
(Kevin Prendergast, Ire) *sn settled wl off pce towards rr: poor 7th for much: kpt on same pce u.p st* **20/1**
7 nk **Saphira's Fire (IRE)**[12] 3031 5-9-9 ... FMBerry 7 89+
(W R Muir) *racd in poor 6th for much: no imp u.p and kpt on same pce fr over 2f out* **25/1**
8 1¼ **Kinky Afro (IRE)**[10] 3071 3-8-11 ... LiamKeniry 6 87+
(J S Moore) *dwlt: wl off pce towards rr: nvr a factor* **66/1**
9 14 **Rose Hip (IRE)**[9] 3137 6-9-9 99 ... CDHayes 8 59+
(Joseph G Murphy, Ire) *wl off pce towards rr: no imp u.p fr bef st* **33/1**

2m 3.84s (-8.76) **Going Correction** -0.75s/f (Hard)
WFA 3 from 4yo+ 12lb **9** Ran SP% **117.7**
Speed ratings: **114,113,112,108,104 103,103,102,91**
CSF £16.17 TOTE £4.30: £1.30, £2.30, £1.30; DF 19.10.
Owner Lady O'Reilly **Bred** Skymarc Farm & Castlemartin St **Trained** The Curragh, Co Kildare

FOCUS
This was run at a good pace, but the winner probably didn't need to be at her best to score. The third has been rated to her best.

NOTEBOOK
Chinese White(IRE), in foal to Cape Cross, goes into retirement as a well-deserved Group 1 winner after a 14-race career that yielded seven wins as well as a fourth in the 2008 Irish Oaks and a third placing behind Fame And Glory in this year's Tattersalls Gold Cup. Her victory in last season's Blandford Stakes (Group 2) meant that she emulated her dam Chiang Mai, who was successful when it was a Group 3 race nine years earlier. Two previous Pattern wins for the daughter of Dalakhani had been gained on soft and heavy, and it is a tribute to her versatility that she handled quick conditions so effectively here. She displayed good battling qualities in seeing out the trip well after taking over from the front-runner around a furlong and a half down. She should make a really fine broodmare. (op 3/1)
Flying Cloud(IRE), last year's Ribblesdale winner, had her only previous run at this level in Italy last autumn. Her third behind Sariska and Midday in the Middleton Stakes was a solid effort, and the fillies' Pattern gives her plenty of opportunities. (op 7/2 tchd 3/1)
Akdarena set out to make all as she had done when winning the Blue Wind Stakes at Naas and when sixth in the Oaks. She did not have the resources to raise her effort when challenged by the winner, but rallied gamely and did not go down without a fight. At Group 3 level she would be hard to peg back in a race over this sort of trip. (op 11/2 tchd 6/1)
Remember When(IRE), in front of Akdarena in the Epsom Oaks, should really have been capable of better over this intermediate trip on the basis that she had finished fourth in the Irish 1,000 Guineas. She was being scrubbed along into the straight and never looked like making an impression. (op 7/4 tchd 2/1)
Lolly For Dolly(IRE) was comprehensively outclassed. Winner of the Athasi Stakes and fourth in the Sandringham Handicap, she did not find the rise in trip as suitable as might have been hoped.

3470a AT THE RACES CURRAGH CUP (GROUP 3) 1m 6f
4:00 (4:03) 3-Y-O+ **£34,513** (£10,929; £5,176; £1,725; £1,150)

RPR
1 **Tactic**[35] 2345 4-9-11 ... TadhgO'Shea 1 119
(J L Dunlop) *chsd ldr: clsd and led fr early st: strly pressed and jnd over 1f out: led again and styd on best fnl f* **5/1**[3]
2 2 **Profound Beauty (IRE)**[27] 2571 6-9-11 115 ... PJSmullen 3 116
(D K Weld, Ire) *chsd ldrs in 3rd: clsd travelling wl fr bef st: rdn to chal and on terms over 1f out: hdd and kpt on same pce ins fnl f* **9/10**[1]
3 3 **Roses For The Lady (IRE)**[62] 1560 4-9-8 110 ... FMBerry 4 109
(John M Oxx, Ire) *led and clr: reduced ld bef st and pushed along: sn narrowly hdd: dropped to 3rd and no imp fr under 2f out: kpt on same pce* **8/1**
4 12 **Popmurphy**[54] 1789 4-9-11 102 ... CDHayes 2 95
(P D Deegan, Ire) *racd wl off pce in rr: wnt poor 4th and kpt on same pce st* **33/1**
5 dist **Saptapadi (IRE)**[30] 2469 4-9-11 ... RyanMoore 5 —
(Sir Michael Stoute) *racd in mod 4th: pushed along appr st: sn dropped to last and virtually p.u* **5/2**[2]

2m 58.92s (-8.08) **Going Correction** -0.75s/f (Hard) **5** Ran SP% **111.9**
Speed ratings: **104,102,101,94,—**
CSF £10.28 TOTE £5.80: £1.80, £1.50; DF 10.70.
Owner Hamdan Al Maktoum **Bred** Shadwell Estate Company Limited **Trained** Arundel, W Sussex

FOCUS
The form looks solid rated around the winner and runner-up.

NOTEBOOK
Tactic ◆ looks to be a rapidly improving horse and followed up his runaway success over this trip at York the previous month with an arguably better performance here. Tracking the early leader at a proper gallop for such a small field, he moved up to challenge 2f out and when the favourite came to challenge, he responded well and won going away in the end. He would probably handle most ground conditions and would have to be considered a possibility to turn up for a race like the Irish St Leger in September. He certainly seems to be improving along those lines.
Profound Beauty(IRE) failed to win this race for the second straight year, but lost nothing in defeat. Given a patient ride, she was just ridden to close when the winner went on 2f out, but she came through on the outside to deliver her challenge in plenty of time. The winner just went away from her inside the last and the mare just looked as though she wasn't letting herself down on the quick ground inside the last furlong or so. Her rider did the right thing by not persevering when the winner found a bit more. (op 4/5 tchd 1/1)
Roses For The Lady(IRE), who went clear at one stage, kept on well enough and certainly wasn't disgraced. (op 10/1)
Popmurphy, held up off the pace, was well behind at halfway and never really got any closer.
Saptapadi(IRE) ran no race. Tracking the pace, he was under pressure to close turning into the straight but could make no impression and in the end dropped right away to finish a tailed-off last. He was found to be blowing hard post-race. Official explanation: jockey said gelding was unsuited by today's ground; vet said gelding was blowing hard post-race (op 5/2 tchd 3/1)

3471 - (Foreign Racing) - See Raceform Interactive

3331 SALISBURY (R-H)
Sunday, June 27

OFFICIAL GOING: Good to firm (firm in places; watered; 9.2)
Wind: virtually nil Weather: sunny

3472 E B F BLAGRAVE MAIDEN STKS 6f 212y
2:00 (2:00) (Class 4) 2-Y-O **£4,695** (£1,397; £698; £348) **Stalls** Centre

Form RPR
1 **Auld Burns** 2-9-0 0 ... DaneO'Neill 4 83+
(R Hannon) *a.p: led 2f out: kpt on wl fnl f: rdn out* **11/8**[1]
6 **2** ¾ **Waiter's Dream**[17] 2887 2-9-0 0 ... TadhgO'Shea 5 81
(B J Meehan) *led at modest pce: qcknd over 3f out: narrowly hdd 2f out: kpt on but hld ins fnl f* **6/4**[2]
0 **3** 11 **Knox Overstreet**[17] 2887 2-9-0 0 ... TonyCulhane 9 53+
(Tom Dascombe) *hld up in cl 5th: outpcd 3f out: wnt 3rd ent fnl f: no ch w ldng pair* **50/1**
4 2¾ **Roi Du Boeuf (IRE)** 2-9-0 0 ... PatCosgrave 6 44
(R Hannon) *s.i.s: sn trcking ldrs: outpcd 3f out: nt a danger after* **14/1**

5 *nk* **Green Pearl (IRE)** 2-9-0 0 .... JimCrowley 8 43
(R M Beckett) *trckd ldrs tl outpcd 3f out: lost 3rd ent fnl f* **6/1**[3]

6 *dist* **Pigeon Hollow** 2-9-0 0 .... ChrisCatlin 7 —
(M R Channon) *hld up: qckly lost tch 4f out: t.o* **25/1**

1m 30.09s (1.09) **Going Correction** -0.10s/f (Good) **6** Ran SP% **108.9**
Speed ratings (Par 95): **89,88,75,72,72** —
toteswingers:1&2:£1.10, 1&3:£8.50, 2&3:£8.30 CSF £3.44 TOTE £2.20: £1.10, £1.60; EX 4.20.
Owner P A Byrne **Bred** Simon Tindall **Trained** East Everleigh, Wilts

FOCUS
The horses ran up a fresh strip of ground on the straight course, although it was railed off by about a couple of yards between the six- and four-furlong markers to avoid firm ground. The jockeys who rode in this race said afterwards that it was riding on the fast side of good. Plenty of decent performers have taken this maiden in the past, so the winner is one worth keeping an eye on in the future. The pace was slow until it quickened in the final stages and the first two did well to pull so far clear.

NOTEBOOK
Auld Burns, said to be a bit coltish in the paddock, made a good start to his career with a workmanlike performance. A 160,000gns purchase at the sales, and a half-brother to Pickles, a triple 7f-1m winner as a three-year-old, and later a high-class miler in the US at 4, he should be better for this effort and can develop into a useful sort at the least. He holds entries in sales races later in the year. (op 11-10)
Waiter's Dream had experience on his side and got to the lead quite readily. He gave the winner plenty to think about and appeared to have come on from his debut. (op 7-4 tchd 15-8)
Knox Overstreet was having his second outing but still looked green. He does seem to have ability if it can be channelled in the right direction. (op 40-1)
Roi Du Boeuf(IRE), a stable companion of the winner, doesn't look the biggest and will need to improve from this to get involved in a finish next time. (op 16-1)
Green Pearl(IRE) is nicely bred (a half-brother to winning middle-distance performer Keenes Royale) but showed little in this. Official explanation: jockey said colt jumped the road crossing (op 13-2)
Pigeon Hollow lost touch by halfway. The suspicion was that he looked too green to do himself justice. (tchd 28-1)

3473 HOX BRASSERIE "OUTSTANDING INDIAN FOOD IN SALISBURY" H'CAP 1m 1f 198y
2:30 (2:32) (Class 5) (0-70,70) 4-Y-O+ **£3,238** (£963; £481; £240) **Stalls** High

Form RPR

-423 **1** **Rosco Flyer (IRE)**[30] 2511 4-9-4 **67** .... DaneO'Neill 1 77
(R A Teal) *racd in 4th: tk clsr order over 3f out: led 2f out: kpt on wl: rdn out* **11/4**[2]

450- **2** *1 ½* **Petomic (IRE)**[235] 7236 5-8-11 **60** .... TadhgO'Shea 5 67
(M Hill) *trckd ldrs: swtchd lft and rdn over 2f out: chal over 1f out: kpt on but no ex fnl f* **8/1**

3211 **3** *2 ½* **Touch Of Style (IRE)**[9] 3160 6-8-4 **58** .... JohnFahy(5) 3 60
(Matthew Salaman) *hld up in last pair but in tch: hdwy over 3f out: rdn to chse ldrs over 2f out: kpt on same pce* **6/4**[1]

5353 **4** *shd* **Alfredtheordinary**[17] 2894 5-8-6 **55** .... ChrisCatlin 2 57
(M R Channon) *little slow away: racd in last but in tch: rdn 4f out: styd on same pce: nvr threatened* **15/2**

0004 **5** *2 ¼* **Catholic Hill (USA)**[24] 2676 5-8-2 **51** oh3 .... NeilChalmers 7 48
(Mark Gillard) *led tl rdn 3f out: kpt chsng ldrs tl fdd ins fnl f* **25/1**

342- **6** *4 ½* **Merrymadcap (IRE)**[218] 7475 8-9-7 **70** .... JimCrowley 6 58
(Miss Tor Sturgis) *prom: rdn to ld 3f out tl 2f out: wknd fnl f* **6/1**[3]

2m 7.29s (-2.61) **Going Correction** -0.175s/f (Firm) **6** Ran SP% **107.7**
Speed ratings (Par 103): **103,101,99,99,97 94**
toteswingers:1&2:£4.10, 1&3:£1.80, 2&3:£3.40 CSF £21.80 TOTE £3.40: £1.60, £3.80; EX 25.30.
Owner Chris Simpson, Miss Elizabeth Ross **Bred** Ms Amy Mulligan **Trained** Ashtead, Surrey

FOCUS
Not a strong handicap as, apart from the favourite, all of these had something to prove, whether it was because they were returning from a break or just the ability to poke their head in front where it matters.

3474 K J PIKE & SONS LTD SENIORS' SPRINT H'CAP 5f
3:00 (3:00) (Class 4) (0-80,80) 6-Y-O+ **£6,476** (£1,927; £963; £481) **Stalls** High

Form RPR

-451 **1** **Brandywell Boy (IRE)**[15] 2954 7-8-1 **65** .... BillyCray(5) 10 76
(D J S Ffrench Davis) *cl up on rails: hdwy over 1f out: led jst ins fnl f: r.o strly* **7/2**[1]

3650 **2** *1 ¼* **Misaro (GER)**[19] 2846 9-8-13 **72** ....(b) DavidProbert 9 78
(R A Harris) *a.p: rdn and ev ch ent fnl f: kpt on but nt pce of wnr* **11/1**

3431 **3** *1* **Cape Royal**[10] 3119 10-9-0 **73** ....(bt) PatCosgrave 2 75
(J M Bradley) *led: rdn 2f out: edgd sltly lft whn hdd jst ins fnl f: no ex* **8/1**

3264 **4** *1* **Kyllachy Storm**[1] 3463 6-8-11 **70** ....(b) RichardKingscote 4 69
(R J Hodges) *hld up: swtchd to far rails and hdwy u.p over 1f out: kpt on fnl f* **6/1**[3]

056 **5** *hd* **Colorus (IRE)**[8] 3211 7-8-1 **67** ....(p) AdamBeschizza(7) 5 65
(W J H Ratcliffe) *mid-div: swtchd lft and hdwy over 2f out: r.o fnl f* **20/1**

0443 **6** *¾* **The Tatling (IRE)**[3] 3358 13-8-7 **69** .... JackDean(3) 8 64
(J M Bradley) *slowly away: towards rr: sme late prog: nvr a factor* **9/2**[2]

0-10 **7** *hd* **Efistorm**[24] 2681 9-9-4 **80** .... BarryMcHugh(3) 6 75
(C R Dore) *chsd ldrs: effrt whn swtchd lft over 2f out: one pce fr over 1f out* **10/1**

00-0 **8** *1 ¼* **Bold Argument (IRE)**[38] 2246 7-7-13 **63** ow1 .... SophieDoyle(5) 11 53
(Mrs P N Dutfield) *sn outpcd in rr: sme mod late prog: n.d* **25/1**

5660 **9** *½* **Lithaam (IRE)**[5] 3299 6-8-6 **65** ....(p) NickyMackay 7 53
(J M Bradley) *mid-div: rdn over 3f out: no imp* **20/1**

50-0 **10** *shd* **Sweet Gale (IRE)**[10] 3115 6-8-3 **67** .... JohnFahy(5) 1 55
(Mike Murphy) *rrd leaving stalls: reminders: a towards rr* **10/1**

0026 **11** *¾* **Even Bolder**[27] 2592 7-8-12 **76** .... KierenFox(5) 3 61
(E A Wheeler) *chsd ldrs: rdn over 2f out: wknd over 1f out* **7/1**

59.81 secs (-1.19) **Going Correction** -0.10s/f (Good) **11** Ran SP% **118.2**
Speed ratings: **105,103,101,99,99 98,97,95,95,95 93**
toteswingers:1&2:£9.00, 1&3:£3.70, 2&3:£15.80 CSF £41.88 CT £296.36 TOTE £4.00: £1.10, £3.80, £2.40; EX 33.70.
Owner P B Gallagher **Bred** Mountarmstrong Stud **Trained** Lambourn, Berks

FOCUS
Plenty of familiar faces for this sprint and, as is usual for these types of races, there is no guarantee the form will be repeated next time. It seemed to beneficial to race prominently.

3475 H S LESTER MEMORIAL H'CAP 1m 6f 21y
3:35 (3:35) (Class 4) (0-85,83) 4-Y-O+ **£4,857** (£1,445; £722; £360)

Form RPR

3-43 **1** **Drawn Gold**[13] 3028 6-8-2 **64** oh7 .... DavidProbert 5 67
(R Hollinshead) *mde all: 6 l clr over 3f out: styd on gamely: rdn out* **11/2**[3]

-564 **2** *¾* **Mykingdomforahorse**[9] 3159 4-8-8 **70** ....(v) ChrisCatlin 2 72+
(M R Channon) *hld up 4th: rdn over 2f out: no imp tl styd on to go 2nd ins fnl f: clsng on wnr at fin* **9/4**[1]

3031 **3** *1* **Lastroseofsummer (IRE)**[8] 3221 4-7-9 **64** oh1 .... NoelGarbutt(7) 1 65
(Rae Guest) *trckd wnr: rdn over 2f out: little imp on wnr but kpt on: lost 2nd ins fnl f* **4/1**[2]

2414 **4** *1 ½* **Satwa Gold (USA)**[50] 1902 4-9-7 **83** .... PatCosgrave 3 81
(Stef Higgins) *trckd ldng pair: rdn over 2f out: styd on same pce* **9/4**[1]

55-0 **5** *6* **Colonel Flay**[39] 2228 6-8-0 **67** .... SophieDoyle(5) 4 57
(Mrs P N Dutfield) *hld up last but in tch: rdn and drifted lft fr over 2f out: no imp* **8/1**

3m 10.43s (3.03) **Going Correction** -0.175s/f (Firm) **5** Ran SP% **108.0**
Speed ratings (Par 105): **84,83,83,82,78**
CSF £17.46 TOTE £5.90: £2.20, £1.70; EX 20.30.
Owner Tim Leadbeater **Bred** Longdon Stud Ltd **Trained** Upper Longdon, Staffs

FOCUS
This was a flag start and the runners followed each other in an orderly line for virtually all of the contest. The result is not going to be reliable.

3476 K J PIKE & SONS LTD AUCTION STKS (CONDITIONS RACE) 6f
4:10 (4:10) (Class 2) 2-Y-O **£8,100** (£2,425; £1,212; £607) **Stalls** High

Form RPR

1 **1** **Crown Prosecutor (IRE)**[27] 2594 2-8-6 0 .... TadhgO'Shea 4 94+
(B J Meehan) *trckd ldrs: swtchd lft over 1f out: bmpd but r.o wl ins fnl f: led fnl 50yds: readily* **5/6**[1]

31 **2** *1* **Avonmore Star**[36] 2319 2-8-8 0 .... DaneO'Neill 2 90
(R Hannon) *prom: rdn and ev ch fr 2f out: drifted sltly lft but kpt on ins fnl f: snatched 2nd fnl strides* **7/2**[3]

1 **3** *hd* **Ballista (IRE)**[29] 2540 2-8-8 0 .... RichardKingscote 1 89
(Tom Dascombe) *sn led: rdn over 1f out: hung lft ins fnl f: hdd fnl 50yds: no ex and lost 2nd fnl strides* **5/2**[2]

4332 **4** *7* **Fifth Ave**[4] 3327 2-7-13 0 .... FrankieMcDonald 6 59
(J A Osborne) *trckd ldrs: rdn 2f out: sn hung lft: wknd ins fnl f* **14/1**

1m 15.24s (0.44) **Going Correction** -0.10s/f (Good) **4** Ran SP% **112.0**
Speed ratings (Par 99): **93,91,91,82**
CSF £4.32 TOTE £1.70; EX 4.00.
Owner Sangster Families **Bred** Edmond And Richard Kent **Trained** Manton, Wilts

FOCUS
A race won by Derby winner Sir Percy and Dewhurst winner Milk It Mick in the recent past, along with a few other smart horses, and this was another good renewal. The early pace was not strong, which meant it developed into a messy finish. The winner produced a cracking effort and there is surely a good bit more to come.

NOTEBOOK
Crown Prosecutor(IRE) ◆ made a good start to his career when winning at Goodwood (winners have come out of that race) and there was talk afterwards that the Coventry Stakes was next for him, such is the regard he is held in seemingly. A nice looker, he travelled like a good horse here and, although taking a while to hit top gear, still got home comfortably in front even after getting a hefty bump from the runner-up. The exciting thing is that he seems sure to mentally progress for this and be better over another furlong so, like Sir Percy back in 2005, one would imagine he will head to the Vintage Stakes at Glorious Goodwood next all being well. (op Evens tchd 11-10 in a place)
Avonmore Star, a bit fractious before going into the stalls, was close up in the early part of the contest but edged left under pressure in the final stages, which took him into the winner. The weight he gave away to Crown Prosecutor made no difference to the result, but one would expect him to improve for a stiffer test at this distance. (op 4-1 tchd 3-1)
Ballista(IRE) ◆ represented a stable chasing a third consecutive win in this race after Orpen Grey and Classic Blade took the previous two renewals. He managed to turn over a 30/100 shot on his debut (who won next time out) and was almost forced to lead in this after nothing wanted to go on. His jockey tried to dictate the pace to suit, quickening things about 2f out, but could not hold off the winner as he eventually past. That said, he was not disgraced even though he was last of the three that came clear, and is a smart sort. Official explanation: jockey said colt hung left-handed (op 9-4 tchd 7-2)
Fifth Ave, the only filly in the field, was far more exposed than her rivals and was easily held when the sprint started. (op 11-1 tchd 10-1)

3477 BLACK GROUSE MAIDEN STKS 1m 1f 198y
4:45 (4:46) (Class 5) 3-Y-O+ **£3,885** (£1,156; £577; £288) **Stalls** High

Form RPR

1 **Balletlou (IRE)** 3-8-4 0 .... KierenFox(5) 10 79+
(J R Best) *s.i.s: racd green: bhd: gd hdwy fr over 3f out: led over 2f out: styd on strly: readily* **20/1**

0- **2** *6* **Sir Walter Raleigh**[235] 7244 3-8-11 0 .... Louis-PhilippeBeuzelin(3) 4 72+
(Sir Michael Stoute) *hld up towards rr: rdn over 3f out: stdy prog fr over 2f out: swtchd to far side rails ent fnl f: styd on: wnt 2nd towards fin: no ch w wnr* **5/2**[2]

3 **3** *½* **Eastern Paramour (IRE)**[24] 2674 5-9-4 0 .... JamesMillman(3) 9 66
(B R Millman) *trckd ldrs: jnd ldr travelling wl 3f out: rdn 2f out: styd on same pce: lost 2nd towards fin* **6/1**

04 **4** *nk* **Rio Tinto**[15] 2974 3-8-7 0 .... AntiocoMurgia(7) 5 70
(Mahmood Al Zarooni) *led after 2f: rdn and hdd over 2f out: styd on same pce* **2/1**[1]

-240 **5** *4* **Mavalenta (IRE)**[23] 2718 3-8-9 67 .... DaneO'Neill 6 57
(J W Hills) *hld up towards rr: hdwy over 3f out: sn rdn: wnt 4th over 2f out tl over 1f out: nvr rchd ldrs* **9/1**

6 *5* **Mutanaker** 3-9-0 0 .... TadhgO'Shea 3 52
(Sir Michael Stoute) *racd green: sn pushed along towards rr: nvr on terms* **4/1**[3]

0 **7** *8* **Rio Prince**[52] 1847 3-9-0 0 .... NeilChalmers 7 36
(J J Bridger) *mid-div: pushed along over 5f out: wknd 2f out* **100/1**

00- **8** *11* **Wee Bobbie**[250] 6911 3-8-4 0 .... SophieDoyle(5) 2 9
(Mrs P N Dutfield) *a towards rr* **100/1**

0 **9** *19* **Miss Tenacious**[19] 2842 3-8-9 0 .... RichardKingscote 1 —
(R J Hodges) *trckd ldrs tl rdn and wknd 3f out: t.o* **33/1**

0 **10** *6* **Distant Florin**[176] 18 5-9-7 0 .... NickyMackay 8 —
(M E Rimmer) *led for 2f: trckd ldr: rdn over 3f out: sn wknd: t.o* **100/1**

2m 7.51s (-2.39) **Going Correction** -0.175s/f (Firm)
WFA 3 from 5yo 12lb **10** Ran SP% **116.9**
Speed ratings (Par 103): **102,97,96,96,93 89,82,74,58,54**
toteswingers:1&2:£9.20, 1&3:£19.90, 2&3:£4.30 CSF £69.33 TOTE £20.30: £5.00, £2.20, £3.60; EX 116.20.
Owner S Malcolm M Winwright P Tindall **Bred** Irish National Stud **Trained** Hucking, Kent

FOCUS
An ordinary-looking maiden but an impressive winner.

3478 AXMINSTER CARPETS RACING EXCELLENCE APPRENTICE H'CAP (WHIPS SHALL BE CARRIED BUT NOT USED) 1m
5:20 (5:21) (Class 6) (0-60,60) 3-Y-O £2,914 (£867; £433; £216) Stalls High

Form RPR
0443 1 Denton Ryal[12] 3055 3-8-6 50 AdamBeschizza(3) 12 59
(M E Rimmer) *squeezed out s: mid-div: smooth hdwy travelling wl 3f out: led 2f out: sn clr: readily* 5/2[1]
-545 2 6 Catchanova (IRE)[26] 2620 3-9-4 59 CharlesEddery 8 54
(Eve Johnson Houghton) *prom: rdn to ld after 3f out: hdd 2f out: kpt on same pce* 4/1[2]
60-0 3 2 ½ Regal Rave (USA)[17] 2906 3-8-7 55 IanBurns(7) 1 45
(J R Best) *mid-div: rdn 3f out: hdwy over 1f out: styd on fnl f* 20/1
0-40 4 nk Truly Magic[41] 2168 3-8-12 56 RichardRowe(3) 2 45
(H J L Dunlop) *hld up towards rr: rdn and hdwy fr 2f out: styd on fnl f: n.d* 12/1
0-00 5 1 ½ Princess Seren[51] 1881 3-8-5 49 AntiocoMurgia(3) 3 35
(B R Millman) *hld up bhd: rdn and styd on fnl 2f: nvr trbld ldrs* 14/1
6043 6 nk Singingintherain (IRE)[14] 3002 3-8-10 56 MatthewCosham(5) 6 41
(R A Mills) *trckd ldrs: hung rt u.p 2f out: fdd fnl f* 6/1
0-66 7 hd Ridgeway Sapphire[40] 2200 3-7-12 46 oh1 ThomasBrown(7) 4 30
(M D I Usher) *hld up towards rr: styd on u.p fnl 2f: nvr a threat* 16/1
3040 8 1 ¾ Two Kisses (IRE)[23] 2725 3-9-5 60 DaleSwift 10 40
(B G Powell) *sn chsng ldrs: rdn 3f out: wknd over 1f out* 5/1[3]
000 9 7 Adoyen Spice[65] 1504 3-8-8 54 BarryAdams(5) 11 18
(Mike Murphy) *bmpd s: chsd ldrs: rdn over 3f out: wknd over 1f out* 25/1
0-00 10 10 Tudor Princess[26] 2634 3-8-13 57 JamesRogers(3) 7 —
(W R Muir) *mid-div tl wknd over 2f out* 20/1
0-00 11 3 ½ Thoughtful (IRE)[15] 2962 3-8-9 53 NathanAlison(3) 9 —
(J W Hills) *wnt rt s: led tl over 2f out: sn wknd* 10/1

1m 42.46s (-1.04) **Going Correction** -0.10s/f (Good) 11 Ran SP% **122.2**
Speed ratings (Par 97): **101,95,92,92,90 90,90,88,81,71 67**
toteswingers:1&2:£3.30, 1&3:£11.60, 2&3:£16.40 CSF £12.27 CT £172.61 TOTE £3.00: £1.50, £1.70, £7.20; EX 15.20 Place 6 £63.52; Place 6 £56.77.
Owner Clive Dennett **Bred** Clive Dennett **Trained** Newmarket, Suffolk

FOCUS
A moderate race.
T/Plt: £129.60 to a £1 stake. Pool:£43,617.16 - 245.60 winning tickets T/Qpdt: £32.50 to a £1 stake. Pool:£2,797.60 - 63.52 winning tickets TM

3459 WINDSOR (R-H)
Sunday, June 27

OFFICIAL GOING: Good to firm (watered; 7.8)
Wind: Light, behind Weather: Sunny, hot

3479 TOTEPLACEPOT H'CAP 1m 67y
2:20 (2:21) (Class 5) (0-70,68) 3-Y-O £2,729 (£806; £403) Stalls High

Form RPR
00-5 1 Al Joza[30] 2516 3-9-1 62 TedDurcan 4 70
(C E Brittain) *trckd ldr: led over 2f out: jnd fnl f: battled on wl* 10/1
005 2 hd Our Drama Queen (IRE)[19] 2841 3-9-4 65 PatDobbs 3 73
(R Hannon) *dwlt: hld up in last trio: prog on inner over 2f out: chsd wnr over 1f out: str chal and upsides fnl f: nt qckn nr fin* 5/2[1]
0060 3 4 Michael's Nook[19] 2844 3-8-10 57 FergusSweeney 7 56
(W S Kittow) *t.k.h: hld up in midfield: effrt on outer over 2f out and hanging lft: no imp over 1f out: kpt on to take 3rd nr fin* 15/2[3]
2400 4 hd Giulietta Da Vinci[33] 2416 3-9-4 65 GeorgeBaker 2 63
(S Woodman) *trckd ldng pair: cl enough 2f out: sn rdn and nt qckn: one pce* 25/1
-504 5 ¾ Pie Poudre[35] 2359 3-8-8 55 JackMitchell 9 52
(R Brotherton) *hld up in midfield: lost pl 3f out: effrt over 1f out: kpt on: n.d* 14/1
3043 6 1 ½ Rain On The Wind (IRE)[44] 2089 3-9-1 65 (t) WilliamCarson(3) 5 58
(S C Williams) *led to over 2f out: wknd over 1f out* 3/1[2]
5404 7 ½ Tregony Bridge[33] 2418 3-8-3 50 JimmyQuinn 6 42
(M Blanshard) *trckd ldng pair: lost pl and rdn over 2f out: no prog after* 20/1
0562 8 1 ¾ White Dart[6] 3259 3-9-7 68 SamHitchcott 8 56
(M R Channon) *awkward s: mostly in last pair: taken wd and rdn 3f out: no prog* 5/2[1]
050 9 22 Hope She Does (USA)[22] 2755 3-8-13 60 RobertWinston 10 —
(Mrs L C Jewell) *t.k.h: hld up in last trio: wd bnd over 4f out: wknd over 2f out: eased: t.o* 66/1

1m 43.74s (-0.96) **Going Correction** -0.125s/f (Firm) 9 Ran SP% **119.8**
Speed ratings (Par 99): **99,98,94,94,93 92,91,90,68**
toteswingers:1&2:£2.00, 1&3:£21.90, 2&3:£4.50 CSF £36.09 CT £208.33 TOTE £9.60: £3.00, £1.60, £1.80; EX 14.10.
Owner Saeed Manana **Bred** Rabbah Bloodstock Limited **Trained** Newmarket, Suffolk

FOCUS
A modest handicap, with the top weight rated 68.
White Dart Official explanation: trainer had no explanation for the poor form shown
Hope She Does(USA) Official explanation: jockey said filly lost its action

3480 TOTESWINGER FLEXI BETTING H'CAP 5f 10y
2:50 (2:51) (Class 5) (0-70,69) 3-Y-O £2,729 (£806; £403) Stalls High

Form RPR
0003 1 Wanchai Whisper[5] 3293 3-8-7 58 (p) AndrewHeffernan(3) 6 66
(P R Hedger) *hld up in 5th: prog and swtchd lft over 1f out: rdn to ld ins fnl f: sn clr* 8/1
0346 2 1 ½ Leleyf (IRE)[4] 3311 3-9-7 69 (v[1]) SamHitchcott 5 72
(M R Channon) *pressed ldr: led over 1f out: hdd and nt qckn ins fnl f: sn outpcd by wnr* 9/2[2]
2204 3 1 ½ Miss Polly Plum[18] 2879 3-8-3 51 JimmyQuinn 4 48
(C A Dwyer) *t.k.h in 4th: rdn and nt qckn 2f out: plugged on fnl f* 5/1[3]
1051 4 nk Lucky Flyer[23] 2688 3-9-7 69 LiamKeniry 8 65
(S Kirk) *led to over 1f out: steadily fdd* 3/1[1]
4425 5 1 Picnic Party[10] 3125 3-9-6 68 GeorgeBaker 3 61
(D R C Elsworth) *hld up in 6th: effrt on outer 2f out: hanging and nt qckn: n.d after* 3/1[1]
0465 6 1 ½ Itwasonlyakiss (IRE)[16] 2931 3-8-10 58 (t) LiamJones 1 45
(J W Hills) *awkward s: settled in last: pushed along and no real prog fr 2f out* 8/1
2246 7 1 Papageno[59] 1639 3-8-10 58 FergusSweeney 7 42
(J R Jenkins) *trckd ldng pair: rdn 2f out: sn wknd* 10/1

59.73 secs (-0.57) **Going Correction** -0.125s/f (Firm) 7 Ran SP% **116.2**
Speed ratings (Par 99): **99,96,94,93,92 89,88**
toteswingers:1&2:£2.70, 1&3:£44.67, 2&3:£8.70 CSF £44.67 CT £200.72 TOTE £11.40: £4.50, £2.60; EX 60.10 Trifecta £68.10 Pool: £157.45 - 1.71 winning units..
Owner Koo's Racing Club **Bred** Mike Smith **Trained** Dogmersfield, Hampshire

FOCUS
Another modest contest, but with more depth than the first on the card.

3481 TOTEQUADPOT H'CAP 1m 2f 7y
3:25 (3:25) (Class 3) (0-90,85) 3-Y-O £8,095 (£2,408; £1,203; £601) Stalls Low

Form RPR
31- 1 Con Artist (IRE)[225] 7390 3-9-2 80 TedDurcan 1 89+
(Saeed Bin Suroor) *mde all: shkn up over 1f out: styd on wl fnl f* 6/4[1]
0-14 2 ¾ Valiant Knight (FR)[4] 3337 3-9-0 78 PatDobbs 4 86
(R Hannon) *trckd wnr: plld out and effrt over 1f out: styd on but a hld* 7/2[3]
6-40 3 6 Aerodynamic (IRE)[36] 2324 3-9-7 85 AndreaAtzeni 3 81
(Pat Eddery) *hld up last: effrt over 2f out: chsd ldng pair wl over 1f out: no imp at all* 13/8[2]
51-0 4 25 Jibrrya[80] 1182 3-9-3 81 SamHitchcott 5 27
(M R Channon) *t.k.h: sn trckd ldng pair: disp 2nd over 3f out to over 2f out: wknd rapidly: t.o* 7/1
600- 5 7 Professor John (IRE)[236] 7218 3-8-11 75 CathyGannon 2 7
(I A Wood) *plld hrd: sn restrained into 4th: rdn over 3f out: sn wknd: t.o* 20/1

2m 5.97s (-2.73) **Going Correction** -0.125s/f (Firm) 5 Ran SP% **117.6**
Speed ratings (Par 103): **105,104,99,79,74**
CSF £7.82 TOTE £3.20: £1.90, £1.70; EX 6.60.
Owner Godolphin **Bred** Airlie Stud **Trained** Newmarket, Suffolk

FOCUS
A decent handicap.

NOTEBOOK
Con Artist(IRE), a smooth winner on Polytrack at Lingfield last November, demonstrated he is just as much at home on turf. Fastest away, he led from the start and scored gamely. He was challenged from the 2f pole, but kept responding to driving and never looked likely to be overhauled. He should remain competitive, even after the handicapper has reassessed him. (op 5-4 tchd 2-1)

Valiant Knight(FR), a C&D maiden winner in May, had cut little ice on his first dip into a handicap, but ran much better this time. Always chasing the winner, he came to deliver a challenge approaching the 1f marker, but could not quite get alongside. (op 4-1)

Aerodynamic(IRE), sixth in Royal Ascot's Chesham Stakes last season, had been dropped 5lb after two moderate runs this term but it was not nearly enough in this company. Held up in rear early on, he made progress from 3f out, but could not close on the first two when they kicked hard for home. (op 9-4 tchd 6-4)

Jibrrya, gelded since flopping in a Leicester handicap in April, was again disappointing. Close up early and second 3f out, he faded in the closing stages. (op 8-1)

Professor John(IRE), who has changed stables since last season, was making his first appearance for 236 days and, perhaps a bit fresh, pulled hard early on. He did not negotiate the home turn well and was left behind when the pace quickened in the straight. (op 16-1)

3482 E B F TOTEEXACTA FLEXI BETTING FILLIES' CONDITIONS STKS 5f 10y
4:00 (4:00) (Class 2) 2-Y-O
£11,215 (£3,358; £1,679; £840; £419; £210) Stalls High

Form RPR
210 1 Marlinka[11] 3070 2-8-12 0 SteveDrowne 7 89
(R Charlton) *fast away: mde all: in full command over 1f out: pushed out* 9/4[2]
315 2 1 ¾ Golden Shine[44] 2074 2-8-12 0 SamHitchcott 3 83
(M R Channon) *chsd ldng pair: shkn up 2f out: wnt 2nd over 1f out: no imp on wnr* 12/1
041 3 hd Eucharist (IRE)[24] 2680 2-8-9 0 PatDobbs 5 79
(R Hannon) *hld up in 5th: effrt over 1f out: r.o to take 3rd ins fnl f: clsng on runner-up fin* 11/2[3]
013 4 1 ¾ Excello[12] 3051 2-8-9 0 RobertWinston 1 73
(M S Saunders) *t.k.h: chsd wnr: rdn and nt qckn 2f out: sn lost 2nd: wknd ins fnl f* 1/1[1]
013 5 1 Rosina Grey[56] 1733 2-8-12 0 AndreaAtzeni 2 72
(B R Millman) *chsd ldng trio: rdn and no prog 2f out: fdd* 22/1
6 shd Fettuccine (IRE) 2-8-7 0 TomQueally 4 67
(J Noseda) *a last: shkn up and no prog 2f out* 10/1

59.45 secs (-0.85) **Going Correction** -0.125s/f (Firm) 6 Ran SP% **117.3**
Speed ratings (Par 96): **101,98,97,95,93 93**
toteswingers:1&2:£3.20, 1&3:£1.80, 2&3:£7.00 CSF £28.77 TOTE £3.40: £2.10, £10.90; EX 64.20.
Owner Elite Racing Club **Bred** Elite Racing Club **Trained** Beckhampton, Wilts

FOCUS
A fascinating juvenile fillies' event, providing two tests of Royal Ascot form. Excello was below par, but Marlinka had an easier time in the Queen Mary and ran a personal best here.

NOTEBOOK
Marlinka, a Ffos Las winner who raced in the unfavoured centre of the track when well adrift in the Queen Mary, found this an easier assignment. Fast away, she established a useful lead by halfway and ran on far too strongly for her rivals. She should stay another furlong and may be capable of making an impact in Listed grade. (op 3-1)

Golden Shine, successful in a three-runner Warwick maiden in May but beaten in a Class 3 event since, ran as well as could be expected. Racing in third for much of the race, she took second when the fourth faded in the closing stages. (op 20-1)

Eucharist(IRE) showed improved form to take a Sandown maiden on her latest outing and seemed to run to a similar level here. Held up early, she stayed on late without threatening to get to grips with the smooth winner. (op 9-2)

Excello, beaten a neck and a nose when third in the Windsor Castle Stakes, ran poorly and is not the first from that contest to let the form down. Keen from the outset and sweating heavily under a breastgirth, she held her head high and back-tracked in the closing stages. It is possible this came too soon, but the early evidence relating to the Windsor Castle has not been encouraging. The race came too soon according to Malcolm Saunders afterwards. (op 11-10)

Rosina Grey, winner of a Bath maiden in April, was predictably outclassed. She was never closer than fourth. (op 20-1 tchd 25-1)

Fettuccine(IRE), a first-time-out daughter of a multiple sprint winner, ran green. She was outpaced early on and, although she made late ground, this can be considered no more than a satisfactory debut. (op 15-2)

3483 TOTETRIFECTA FLEXI BETTING H'CAP 1m 67y
4:35 (4:42) (Class 3) (0-90,90) 3-Y-0+ **£7,447** (£2,216; £1,107; £553) **Stalls** High

Form RPR

-100 **1** **Guilded Warrior**[15] 2971 7-9-10 **86** FergusSweeney 4 96
(W S Kittow) *mde all at decent pce: rdn over 2f out: kpt on wl u.p fr over 1f out* **14/1**

-114 **2** 2 1/4 **Play It Sam**[17] 2885 4-9-7 **83** AdamKirby 1 88
(W R Swinburn) *tried to match strides w wnr but forced to chse: rdn over 2f out: a hld fr over 1f out: nrly ct napping for 2nd* **2/1**[1]

-013 **3** *nse* **South Cape**[36] 2322 7-9-10 **86** GeorgeBaker 6 91
(G L Moore) *settled in 4th: rdn to chse ldng pair 3f out: nt qckn and no imp 2f out: styd on fnl f: nrly snatched 2nd* **3/1**[3]

-000 **4** 2 1/2 **The Which Doctor**[36] 2322 5-9-9 **85** TomQueally 8 84
(J Noseda) *hld up in last pair: pushed along over 3f out: no prog over 2f out: kpt on fr over 1f out* **11/4**[2]

-600 **5** *11* **Cyflymder (IRE)**[15] 2971 4-10-0 **90** PatDobbs 2 64
(R Hannon) *hld up in last pair: shkn up over 2f out: no prog and wl btn after* **6/1**

1006 **6** *7* **The Scorching Wind (IRE)**[58] 1662 4-8-11 **76** (t) WilliamCarson(3) 3 34
(S C Williams) *drvn to chse ldng pair after 2f: wknd rapidly 3f out: t.o and fin tired* **5/1**

1m 42.17s (-2.53) **Going Correction** -0.125s/f (Firm) **6** Ran SP% **122.6**
Speed ratings (Par 107): **107,104,104,102,91 84**
toteswingers:1&2:£13.50, 1&3:£4.60, 2&3:£1.10 CSF £46.58 CT £114.65 TOTE £17.70: £8.00, £1.10; EX 80.70 Trifecta £129.70 Pool: £229.71 - 1.31 winning units..

Owner The Racing Guild **Bred** Manor Farm Packers Ltd **Trained** Blackborough, Devon

FOCUS
A decent handicap featuring several runners with a record of forcing the pace. The start was delayed for more than five minutes by the antics of Everybody Knows, who broke through the front of his stall before running loose and being withdrawn (9/2, deduct 15p in the £ under R4). A new market was formed.

NOTEBOOK
Guilded Warrior, well beaten in two starts since scoring at Leicester in April, came back to form with a bang. Quickly away, he was allowed an easy lead early on and had established a clear advantage by halfway. The second attempted to mount a challenge from the 3f pole, but Guilded Warrior showed admirable resolution under pressure and was well on top at the finish. (old market op 20-1 tchd 25-1)

Play It Sam, who made all at Ascot and Newbury before losing ground at the start last time out, could not dominate here either. He chased the winner from the start and tried to cut down his lead in the last 3f, but was tiring at the finish and only just held on to claim the runner-up spot. (old market op 10-3)

South Cape, successful at Ascot and third at Goodwood on his last two starts, was probably a little below his best. He raced in fourth for much of the race and made only limited late progress. (old market op 4-1 tchd 5-1)

The Which Doctor was on the same mark as when scoring at Newbury in September, but his form this term has been disappointing and he never showed with a chance. His finishing position was the best he managed throughout. (old market op 4-1 tchd 9-2)

Cyflymder(IRE), 2lb higher than for his most recent victory at Sandown last July, was never in the hunt. He is well below last summer's form. (old market op 10-1)

The Scorching Wind(IRE), 13lb lower than when scoring on Polytrack in January, is clearly not as effective on turf. He raced in third for much of the race, but faded in the closing stages. (old market op 13-2, new market tchd 9-2)

3484 BET TOTEPOOL ON ALL UK RACING MAIDEN FILLIES' STKS 1m 67y
5:05 (5:10) (Class 5) 3-5-Y-0 **£2,729** (£806; £403) **Stalls** High

Form RPR

5 **1** **Akhmatova**[14] 2998 3-8-10 0 TomQueally 11 69
(G A Butler) *mde most: wd bnd 5f out: racd awkwardly and reminder 4f out: jnd over 2f out: edgd lft but battled on wl fnl f* **5/4**[1]

0-60 **2** 1/2 **Profligate (IRE)**[15] 2974 3-8-10 0 SteveDrowne 2 68
(W Jarvis) *trckd wnr: rdn to chal and upsides over 2f out: nt qckn ent fnl f: hld nr fin* **7/1**[3]

0 **3** 4 1/2 **Miss Flash Dancer**[31] 2478 4-9-6 0 SamHitchcott 9 58
(C C Bealby) *sn chsd ldng quartet: outpcd fr over 2f out: kpt on to take 3rd over 1f out* **40/1**

4 *1* **Pebble Beech (IRE)** 3-8-10 0 LiamJones 1 55
(W J Haggas) *dwlt: hld up in 6th: effrt over 3f out: outpcd over 2f out: kpt on but n.d* **7/1**[3]

00 **5** *5* **Barberhoney**[55] 1782 3-8-10 0 PatDobbs 7 44
(J R Jenkins) *dwlt: hld up in rr: outpcd fr 3f out: pushed along and sme late hdwy* **25/1**

6 1 1/2 **Trendy Way (IRE)** 3-8-10 0 LiamKeniry 10 40
(P R Chamings) *chsd ldng pair: outpcd over 2f out: wknd over 1f out* **12/1**

03 **7** *hd* **Dreamacha**[87] 1075 3-8-10 0 SaleemGolam 5 40
(S C Williams) *hld up in rr: rdn over 3f out: steadily lost tch* **12/1**

0 **8** *9* **Spirit Of Darley (USA)**[131] 570 3-8-10 0 TedDurcan 6 19
(C E Brittain) *chsd ldng trio tl wknd rapidly over 2f out* **7/2**[2]

0- **9** 1 1/2 **Natalie N G**[232] 7289 3-8-10 0 FergusSweeney 8 16
(J R Jenkins) *a wl in rr: detached in last 3f out* **66/1**

10 4 1/2 **Jenny Dawson (IRE)** 4-9-6 0 IvaMilickova 4 5
(John Berry) *s.i.s: a in last trio: lost tch fr 3f out* **50/1**

1m 44.58s (-0.12) **Going Correction** -0.125s/f (Firm)
WFA 3 from 4yo 10lb **10** Ran SP% **116.8**
Speed ratings (Par 100): **95,94,90,89,84 82,82,73,71,67**
toteswingers:1&2:£4.70, 1&3:£31.30, 2&3:£85.00 CSF £10.47 TOTE £2.00: £1.20, £1.90, £8.40; EX 11.30 Trifecta £266.70 Part won. Pool: £360.50 - 0.82 winning units. Place 6 £214.36; Place 5 £89.93.

Owner Trevor C Stewart **Bred** Sunny Days Ltd **Trained** Newmarket, Suffolk

FOCUS
A weak fillies' maiden, lacking depth.

Natalie N G Official explanation: jockey said filly ran too freely

T/Plt: £179.30 to a £1 stake. Pool:£53,265.99 - 216.85 winning tickets T/Qpdt: £13.10 to a £1 stake. Pool:£3,390.08 - 190.96 winning tickets JN

3465 CURRAGH (R-H)
Sunday, June 27

OFFICIAL GOING: Good to firm

3486a DUBAI DUTY FREE SAPPHIRE STKS (GROUP 3) 5f
2:15 (2:20) 3-Y-0+
£34,513 (£10,929; £5,176; £1,725; £1,150; £575)

RPR

1 **Glamorous Spirit (IRE)**[8] 3197 4-9-2 KierenFallon 1 105
(R A Harris) *mde all: rdn fr 1 1/2f out: kpt on wl ins fnl f* **16/1**

2 1/2 **Reverence**[266] 6522 9-9-8 WJSupple 4 109
(E J Alston) *chsd ldrs: 5th 2f out: sn rdn: 4th 1f out: kpt on wl ins fnl f: nt rch wnr* **33/1**

3 1 1/2 **Elnawin**[14] 2999 4-9-5 RyanMoore 2 101
(R Hannon) *towards rr: mod 9th and rdn 1 1/2f out: styd on strly ins fnl f: nvr nrr* **11/2**[2]

4 *shd* **Piccadilly Filly (IRE)**[21] 2804 3-8-10 EddieCreighton 7 95
(E J Creighton) *chsd ldr in 2nd: rdn fr 2f out: dropped to 3rd 1f out: no ex* **12/1**

5 *nk* **Spin Cycle (IRE)**[12] 3047 4-9-5 RichardMullen 3 99
(B Smart) *chsd ldrs: rdn fr 2f out: 5th 1f out: sn no ex* **9/2**[1]

6 1 1/2 **Sole Power**[20] 2827 3-8-13 106 JMurtagh 6 92
(Edward Lynam, Ire) *chsd ldrs: 5th 1/2-way: cl 4th and rdn 1 1/2f out: no ex ins fnl f* **8/1**

7 *3* **Look Busy (IRE)**[10] 3108 5-9-2 PatrickMathers 10 80
(A Berry) *towards rr: rdn fr 1/2-way: kpt on same pce ins fnl f* **14/1**

8 1 1/2 **Rain Delayed (IRE)**[20] 2827 4-9-5 109 KLatham 9 78
(G M Lyons, Ire) *sn mid-div: rdn and no imp fr 2f out* **8/1**

9 *2* **Benbaun (IRE)**[36] 2325 9-9-8 (b) PJSmullen 12 73
(K A Ryan) *chsd ldrs in 4th: rdn after 1/2-way: mod 7th 1f out: no ex* **6/1**[3]

10 1 1/4 **Arctic (IRE)**[268] 6450 3-9-2 116 PShanahan 5 67
(Tracey Collins, Ire) *hld up: rdn fr 1/2-way: sn no imp* **6/1**[3]

11 *2* **Judge 'n Jury**[10] 3108 6-9-5 (t) LukeMorris 8 59
(R A Harris) *chsd ldrs: rdn fr 1/2-way: sn no imp* **20/1**

12 3 1/2 **Miss Gorica (IRE)**[17] 2912 6-9-2 106 WMLordan 11 43
(Ms Joanna Morgan, Ire) *towards rr: no imp fr 1/2-way* **10/1**

57.85 secs (-4.65) **Going Correction** -0.625s/f (Hard)
WFA 3 from 4yo+ 6lb **12** Ran SP% **121.4**
Speed ratings: **112,111,108,108,108 105,100,98,95,93 90,84**
CSF £460.53 TOTE £18.30: £4.10, £11.10, £2.20; DF 491.70.

Owner Robert Bailey **Bred** Carlo Soria **Trained** Earlswood, Monmouths
■ The first Group win for Ron Harris, and his first winner in Ireland.

FOCUS
Those drawn low were at an advantage in this. The runner-up has been rated to the best view of his recent win.

NOTEBOOK
Glamorous Spirit(IRE) showed the benefit of good early speed as it meant she had the perfect position throughout the race, and Fallon was able to keep enough up his sleeve for this game filly to keep it up all the way to the line. She's tough and honest and while she seemingly needed to find a good bit to win this, the way the race was run seemed to suit her ideally.

Reverence ran a fine race on his seasonal bow. He also had a good position on the inside rail with a clear path to mount his challenge, but he didn't pick up fully until inside the final furlong. It was still a fine effort by a horse racing on ground a good bit quicker than would have been thought ideal, and it augurs for a decent season ahead.

Elnawin hasn't won for two years and didn't really have the luck here. Perhaps he was outpaced a fraction early on, and from there he was stuck on the stands' rail and would need luck in running. He only had to switch once, but everywhere he went he had the runner-up in front of him and couldn't really stretch out. (op 7/1)

Piccadilly Filly(IRE) showed herself not to lack pace, although she was unable to sustain it inside the final half-furlong. She may still be able to win a decent sprint.

Spin Cycle(IRE) was held up just off the pace, but closed up with his chance a furlong out before his effort flattened out. (op 5/1)

Sole Power faded somewhat disappointingly inside the last, having improved over a furlong out and looked as though he would be a big danger. (op 8/1 tchd 9/1)

Look Busy(IRE) kept on without being a threat. (op 10/1)

Benbaun(IRE) showed his customary early dash before weakening inside the last furlong and a half. (op 5/1)

Arctic(IRE) Official explanation: trainer later said colt scoped badly post-race

3487a DUBAI DUTY FREE DOUBLE MILLIONAIRE H'CAP (PREMIER HANDICAP) 1m
2:45 (2:47) 3-Y-0+ **£35,951** (£10,508; £4,977; £1,659)

RPR

1 **Sea Lord (IRE)**[10] 3103 3-8-11 95 FrankieDettori 10 104
(M Johnston) *mde all: rdn clr over 1f out: kpt on wl ins fnl f* **4/1**[1]

2 1 1/4 **Scandal Sheet (IRE)**[49] 1950 4-8-12 86 (p) KJManning 15 93
(J S Bolger, Ire) *a.p: 3rd 3f out: sn rdn: kpt on same pce in 2nd ins fnl f* **16/1**

3 *nk* **Super Say (IRE)**[14] 3009 4-8-11 85 FMBerry 3 91
(Andrew Oliver, Ire) *a.p: rdn in 2nd 3f out: kpt on same pce fr 1 1/2f out* **20/1**

4 *shd* **Simla Sunset (IRE)**[23] 2733 4-8-1 78 oh4 (t) BACurtis(3) 17 84
(P J Prendergast, Ire) *mid-div: 7th 3f out: sn rdn: kpt on fr 1 1/2f out* **14/1**

5 *hd* **Royal Astronomer (IRE)**[10] 3138 5-9-0 88 PBBeggy 4 94
(Donal Kinsella, Ire) *s.i.s: sn mid-div on wd outside: rdn and hdwy fr 2f out: mod 4th 1f out: no ex* **10/1**[3]

6 *2* **Rock And Roll Kid (IRE)**[17] 2913 5-10-0 105 DEMullins(3) 18 106
(Anthony Mullins, Ire) *prom: rdn fr 3f out: no ex fr 1 1/2f out* **18/1**

7 *2* **Marias Dream (IRE)**[23] 2733 8-8-11 85 (b[1]) KierenFallon 11 81
(J G Coogan, Ire) *chsd ldrs: 5th 3f out: sn rdn: no ex over 1f out* **16/1**

8 *nk* **Castle Bar Sling (USA)**[10] 3138 5-8-3 82 (p) MACleere(5) 1 78
(T J O'Mara, Ire) *nvr bttr than mid-div: kpt on same pce fr 2f out* **16/1**

9 *hd* **Banna Boirche (IRE)**[63] 1552 4-8-12 89 GFCarroll(3) 7 84
(M Halford, Ire) *chsd ldrs: 4th 1/2-way: sn rdn: kpt on one pce fr 1 1/2f out* **20/1**

10 *shd* **Dahindar (IRE)**[20] 2831 5-8-10 84 DPMcDonogh 16 79
(Edward Lynam, Ire) *mid-div: no imp fr 3f out* **14/1**

11 1/2 **Sean Og Coulston (IRE)**[9] 3183 6-8-4 78 oh3 WMLordan 14 72
(John J Coleman, Ire) *nvr bttr than mid-div: kpt on same pce fr 2f out* **16/1**

12 *hd* **Ballivor (IRE)**[20] 2831 7-8-13 87 JAHeffernan 5 80
(W T Farrell, Ire) *nvr bttr than mid-div* **25/1**

13 ½ **Maggie The Cat**[1] 3468 4-7-13 78 oh3 KTO'Neill(5) 13 70
(Joseph G Murphy, Ire) *towards rr: no imp fr 3f out* **14/1**

14 1¾ **Charminamix (IRE)**[28] 2568 7-9-4 92 (t) JMurtagh 8 80
(W McCreery, Ire) *towards rr: no imp fr 3f out* **10/1**[3]

15 hd **Maundy Money**[36] 2351 7-9-8 96 (t) CO'Donoghue 6 84
(David Marnane, Ire) *mid-div: wknd fr 3f out* **10/1**[3]

16 1¼ **Broad Meaning**[70] 1413 4-9-9 97 (t) PJSmullen 19 82
(D K Weld, Ire) *chsd ldrs: rdn and wknd fr 3f out* **13/2**[2]

17 1¾ **Lord Kenmare (USA)**[28] 2568 4-9-1 92 (p) ShaneFoley(3) 9 73
(M Halford, Ire) *mid-div on outer: wknd fr 3f out* **10/1**[3]

18 1 **Money Trader (IRE)**[10] 3134 3-8-6 90 CDHayes 2 67
(J T Gorman, Ire) *a bhd* **16/1**

19 4½ **Mountain Pride (IRE)**[17] 2568 5-8-10 89 (t) MHarley(5) 12 57
(Paul Nolan, Ire) *a bhd* **33/1**

20 17 **Dul Ar An Ol (IRE)**[84] 717 9-8-4 78 oh3 DJMoran 20 —
(John C McConnell, Ire) *a towards rr: no imp fr 3f out: eased over 1f out* **16/1**

1m 37.21s (-8.79) **Going Correction** -1.075s/f (Hard)
WFA 3 from 4yo+ 10lb **20** Ran SP% **146.6**
Speed ratings: **101,99,99,99,99 97,95,94,94,94 94,93,93,91,91 90,88,87,82,65**
CSF £79.54 CT £1283.10 TOTE £4.10: £1.40, £4.80, £6.10, £4.20; DF 108.00.

Owner Sheikh Hamdan Bin Mohammed Al Maktoum **Bred** Darley **Trained** Middleham Moor, N Yorks

FOCUS

The winning time was poor and the first five finished pretty close together. It has been rated through the third and fourth to slight PBs, and the fifth as just off his best.

NOTEBOOK

Sea Lord(IRE) was given a fine front-running ride by his jockey, who gradually upped the tempo and had all of his rivals on the stretch by the intersection. He might have expected something to come from off the pace and challenge but really nothing did and the horse won with a degree of comfort. He looks a bit better than a handicapper. (op 5/1)

Scandal Sheet(IRE) has been lightly raced since he bolted up in a Gowran nursery two years back, and this was by far his best effort since then. He was ridden positively and raced handily, and having been caught perhaps for tactical speed briefly, he stayed on to good effect once again inside the last. This was a very encouraging effort.

Super Say(IRE) was almost certainly better suited by this almost straight mile than being on the turn on his last two starts. He also raced with a good bit of zest and travelled well in the slipstream of the winner until that horse started to really stretch them over two furlongs out. He couldn't match that but did keep on well at the same pace.

Simla Sunset(IRE) was one of only a couple that came from off the pace, closing up on the outside at the 2f pole while being under pressure to do so. She flattened out inside the last but it was still a fine effort.

Royal Astronomer(IRE) never looked like getting on terms. He kept on well under pressure inside the last to be nearest at the finish. (op 10/1 tchd 12/1)

Rock And Roll Kid(IRE) has often been ridden from well off the pace but was much more prominent here before fading inside the last. (op 16/1)

Dul Ar An Ol(IRE) Official explanation: jockey said gelding may have not handled today's ground

3488a LADBROKES.COM RAILWAY STKS (GROUP 2) 6f

3:15 (3:17) 2-Y-O

£53,097 (£16,814; £7,964; £2,654; £1,769; £884)

RPR

1 **Formosina (IRE)**[14] 2990 2-9-1 RyanMoore 1 105+
(J Noseda) *chsd ldrs: cl 4th and nt clr run 1 1/2f out: styd on strly ins fnl f: led on line* **7/2**[3]

2 shd **Samuel Morse (IRE)**[12] 3049 2-9-1 JMurtagh 6 105
(A P O'Brien, Ire) *prom: led fr 1/2-way: sn rdn: strly pressed ins fnl f: hdd on line* **5/2**[1]

3 nk **Clondinnery (IRE)**[14] 3004 2-9-1 KLatham 4 104
(G M Lyons, Ire) *led: hdd 1/2-way: sn rdn: kpt on wl ins fnl f: no ex cl home* **7/2**[3]

4 1½ **Chilworth Lad**[12] 3051 2-9-1 KierenFallon 5 101
(M R Channon) *dwlt: sn chsd ldrs: nt clr run under 2f out: 4th 1f out: kpt on wout threatening ins fnl f* **12/1**

5 1½ **High Award (IRE)**[22] 2743 2-9-1 WMLordan 7 95
(T Stack, Ire) *prom tl rdn fr 2f out: wknd ins fnl f* **12/1**

6 2 **Oor Jock (IRE)**[12] 3051 2-9-1 PJSmullen 3 89
(D K Weld, Ire) *in rr: rdn and no imp fr 2f out* **16/1**

7 nk **Longhunter**[28] 2569 2-9-1 DPMcDonogh 8 88+
(Kevin Prendergast, Ire) *dwlt and hld up: 6th 1/2-way: sn rdn: no imp fr 2f out* **11/4**[2]

1m 10.77s (-4.23) **Going Correction** -0.625s/f (Hard) **7** Ran SP% **120.9**
Speed ratings: **103,102,102,100,98 95,95**
CSF £13.76 TOTE £4.50: £2.30, £1.80; DF 13.70.

Owner Daniel Pittack **Bred** Oak Lodge Bloodstock **Trained** Newmarket, Suffolk

■ Formosina is the first British-trained winner of this since Daylight In Dubai in 1996.

FOCUS

The form is best rated around the fifth and sixth, and looks pretty solid for the grade.

NOTEBOOK

Formosina(IRE) ◆ took the step up to Group company in his stride. Tracking the pace, it looked as though he wouldn't be able to find room, but inside the last he picked up well and just got his nose in front to inflict a rare defeat on a Ballydoyle juvenile in this race. He would have been a very unlucky loser, and is a progressive colt that will get further. He could go for the Vintage Stakes at Goodwood. (op 3/1)

Samuel Morse(IRE) didn't shirk the issue inside the last furlong when coming under pressure but was just touched off by a better colt on the day. How much further he'll get will be interesting to see, but he's not short of pace and the Phoenix Stakes would look to be an obvious target. (op 7/2 tchd 4/1)

Clondinnery(IRE) was attempting a hat-trick and is improving. He had the benefit of the stands' rail while helping to set the formidable gallop and he stuck to his task well inside the final furlong when the big guns challenged. Whether he's just a sprinter, time will tell, but like the runner-up the Phoenix Stakes does look a natural target as he has proved himself up to this level. (op 7/2 tchd 4/1)

Chilworth Lad missed the break by a fraction and was struggling to find racing room a furlong or so from the finish. He ran on quite nicely inside the last in a race where most things went wrong for him.

High Award(IRE) showed his fair share of early speed but faded inside the last and may not be quite up to this level. (op 10/1)

Oor Jock(IRE) was never a factor.

Longhunter, most impressive on his Leopardstown debut over a furlong further, travelled well to halfway here and looked as though he was going to throw down a challenge on the outside but, from 1½f down he just failed to pick up and was eased inside the last. He may not have let himself down on the quick ground, but he hasn't turned into a bad horse overnight. He was blowing hard post race. Official explanation: vet said colt was found to be blowing very hard post race (op 3/1)

3489a NATIONAL LOTTERY SWEEPSTAKES RACE (REGISTERED AS THE SCURRY) (PREMIER H'CAP) 6f 63y

3:50 (3:53) 3-Y-0+

£51,548 (£17,035; £8,185; £2,876; £1,991; £1,106)

RPR

1 **Invincible Ash (IRE)**[14] 3006 5-9-3 92 (p) GFCarroll(3) 1 102
(M Halford, Ire) *led and disp: led over 1f out: sn clr: styd on wl: easily* **20/1**

2 5 **Brushed Aside**[46] 2036 3-8-11 90 (b) PJSmullen 3 82
(D K Weld, Ire) *chsd ldrs on stands' side: rdn fr 2f out: mod 5th 1f out: kpt on to go 2nd wout threatening easy wnr cl home* **9/1**[2]

3 ½ **Hawkeyethenoo (IRE)**[22] 2745 4-9-6 92 KierenFallon 18 84+
(J S Goldie) *chsd ldrs on far side: rdn fr 2f out: 3rd 1f out: kpt on same pce* **5/2**[1]

4 1 **Novellen Lad (IRE)**[36] 2327 5-9-7 93 WJSupple 19 82+
(E J Alston) *chsd ldrs on far side: rdn 2f out: 4th 1f out: no ex ins fnl f* **12/1**[3]

5 ¾ **Lough Mist (IRE)**[16] 2943 4-9-1 87 PShanahan 17 74+
(Tracey Collins, Ire) *led and disp on far side gp: hdd over 1f out: no ex ins fnl f* **14/1**

6 1½ **Toufan Express**[20] 2831 8-8-12 84 DPMcDonogh 20 66+
(Adrian McGuinness, Ire) *towards rr: hdwy fr 2f out: kpt on wout threatening ins fnl f* **22/1**

7 1½ **Arganil (USA)**[43] 2135 5-9-13 99 KLatham 16 76+
(K A Ryan) *in tch: kpt on same pce fr 2f out* **25/1**

8 hd **Ishiadancer**[36] 2326 5-9-1 90 DEMullins(3) 23 67+
(E J Alston) *mid-div on far side: kpt on same pce fr 2f out* **25/1**

9 nk **Arcadian Dream (IRE)**[23] 2729 3-8-6 85 (t) PBBeggy 2 59
(Edward Lynam, Ire) *chsd ldrs on stands' side: no imp fr 1 1/2f out* **20/1**

10 nk **Duff (IRE)**[17] 2913 7-10-0 107 (t) JPO'Brien(7) 4 82
(Edward Lynam, Ire) *prom on stands' side: rdn 2f out: 6th 1f out: no ex* **12/1**[3]

11 1¼ **Flipando (IRE)**[22] 2748 9-9-12 98 GrahamGibbons 9 69
(T D Barron) *nvr bttr than mid-div on stands' side: no ex fr 2f out* **12/1**[3]

12 1 **Air Chief Marshal (IRE)**[20] 2829 3-9-12 105 JMurtagh 5 70
(A P O'Brien, Ire) *chsd ldrs on stands' rail: rdn after 1/2-way: sn no imp* **12/1**[3]

13 shd **Hotham**[2] 3406 7-9-6 92 CDHayes 11 59
(N Wilson) *chsd ldrs: no imp fr 2f out* **20/1**

14 1 **Miss Velocity**[8] 3197 3-8-2 88 RPWhelan(7) 8 50
(Andrew Oliver, Ire) *prom on stands' side: no imp fr 2f out* **33/1**

15 nk **Douze Points (IRE)**[20] 2831 4-9-0 86 (p) JAHeffernan 7 49
(Joseph G Murphy, Ire) *towards rr on stands' side: kpt on same pce fr 2f out* **25/1**

16 3 **Oldjoesaid**[22] 2745 6-9-5 91 RichardMullen 22 44
(K A Ryan) *chsd ldrs: wknd fr 1/2-way* **14/1**

17 1¼ **Cape Vale (IRE)**[20] 2831 5-8-7 86 SHJames(7) 21 35
(Kevin Prendergast, Ire) *nvr bttr than mid-div* **25/1**

18 1 **Calm Bay (IRE)**[16] 2943 4-9-1 94 (t) DCByrne(7) 10 40
(H Rogers, Ire) *prom in centre gp: wknd fr 2f out* **50/1**

19 2 **Royal Intruder**[32] 2431 5-9-2 88 RyanMoore 25 28
(S Donohoe, Ire) *a towards rr on far side* **25/1**

20 3 **Mountain Coral (IRE)**[42] 2145 6-9-5 91 NGMcCullagh 15 21
(F Oakes, Ire) *a bhd* **33/1**

21 1¼ **Three Way Stretch (IRE)**[98] 956 4-9-4 90 (p) KJManning 24 16
(J T Gorman, Ire) *a towards rr* **50/1**

22 1 **Copper Dock (IRE)**[16] 2943 6-9-2 91 (p) BACurtis(3) 6 14
(T G McCourt, Ire) *a towards rr on stands' side* **25/1**

23 nk **Hitchens (IRE)**[247] 6994 5-9-13 99 JamieSpencer 12 21
(T D Barron) *nvr bttr than mid-div: wknd fr 2f out* **9/1**[2]

24 3 **Tornadodancer (IRE)**[212] 7566 7-8-11 88 (b) MHarley(5) 14 —
(T G McCourt, Ire) *mid-div in centre gp: wknd fr 1/2-way* **33/1**

25 dist **Jembatt (IRE)**[4] 3345 3-9-5 98 FMBerry 13 —
(Edward Lynam, Ire) *chsd ldrs in centre: brought to stands' side bef 1/2-way: wknd fr 2f out: eased fnl f* **12/1**[3]

1m 13.08s (-5.52) **Going Correction** -0.625s/f (Hard)
WFA 3 from 4yo+ 7lb **25** Ran SP% **154.8**
Speed ratings: **111,104,103,102,101 99,97,97,96,96 94,93,93,91,91 87,85,84,81,77 76,74,74,70,—**
CSF £195.30 TOTE £28.30: £5.20, £1.40, £1.40, £4.40; DF 110.40.

Owner P J Condron **Bred** Mrs Sandra Maye **Trained** Doneany, Co Kildare

FOCUS

The inaugural running of this race and a maximum field given race restrictions, with seven British-trained raiders. Those racing on the stands' side dominated and enjoyed perhaps a 14-18lb advantage over those racing on the far side.

NOTEBOOK

Invincible Ash(IRE) produced a blistering performance to make a mockery of her mark back in handicap company. She has generally been struggling in Pattern races until running well at Cork last time and everything went right for her here. Drawn nearest the stands' rail, she made virtually all among the posse on the stands' side and was still travelling easily with 2f to go. With the rail to help, she had the race in safe-keeping well over a furlong out, and if anything she looked to be going away from them at the finish. Clearly she is Group class and it may be that she is a much better filly making the pace, as she has been generally held up prior to this. Maybe the cheekpieces that replaced her usual blinkers made a big difference, but there was likely more to it than that.

Brushed Aside was nicely placed on the stands' side and travelled quite well. She was well off the bridle from 2f out but ran on willingly with the rail to help. Only a 3-y-o, this was a storming effort for such a lightly raced horse and she deserves a try at Pattern level.

Hawkeyethenoo(IRE) raced quite keenly on the far side but came off the bridle with over 2f to go. He beat everything that had raced in the centre of the track with relative authority, but it is hard to think the draw beat him.

Novellen Lad(IRE) is an improver and ran a cracker on his 20th start. This was a big ask for him off easily his highest mark so far, but he more than justified the trip over.

Lough Mist(IRE) gave another brave pace-setting display in the centre of the track. She only gave best around a furlong out and has been a credit to her trainer.

Toufan Express was drawn 20 but ended up tacking over towards the stands' side and this rather exposed performer ran with credit and easily his best race of the season.

Arganil(USA) had plenty on his plate here off 99 but ran well.

Duff(IRE) disputed for a period with the winner but was fighting a losing battle from well over 2f out and he is surely too high in the weights for handicaps.

3491a DUBAI DUTY FREE IRISH DERBY (GROUP 1) 1m 4f

5:10 (5:10) 3-Y-O

£641,592 (£210,176; £99,557; £33,185; £22,123; £11,061)

RPR

1 **Cape Blanco (IRE)**[21] 2802 3-9-0 115 JMurtagh 3 122+
(A P O'Brien, Ire) *trckd ldrs: 4th 4f out: rdn in 2nd 2f out: led over 1f out: kpt on wl ins fnl f* **7/2**[2]

2 ½ **Midas Touch**[22] 2746 3-9-0 112 CO'Donoghue 5 121
(A P O'Brien, Ire) *trckd ldrs in 3rd: impr to ld ent st: sn rdn clr: hdd over 1f out: kpt on ins fnl f* **9/2**

3 1 ½ **Jan Vermeer (IRE)**[22] 2746 3-9-0 119 JAHeffernan 1 119
(A P O'Brien, Ire) *dwlt and sn brought towards rail at rr: clsr in 8th 4f out: sn rdn: 4th 2f out: 3rd over 1f out: kpt on same pce* **4/1**[3]

4 1 **Monterosso**[9] 3142 3-9-0 FrankieDettori 7 117
(M Johnston) *trckd ldrs: outpcd and pushed along in mod 5th 5f out: 4th under 2f out: kpt on one pce ins fnl f* **3/1**[1]

5 3 **At First Sight (IRE)**[9] 3142 3-9-0 118 JPO'Brien 9 113
(A P O'Brien, Ire) *trckd ldr in 2nd: 3rd 4f out: sn rdn: no imp fr 2f out* **20/1**

6 nk **Carraiglawn (IRE)**[23] 2731 3-9-0 104 DJMoran 10 112
(J S Bolger, Ire) *mid-div: 7th 5f out: sn rdn: kpt on one pce fr 2f out* **20/1**

7 5 ½ **Coordinated Cut (IRE)**[22] 2746 3-9-0 (t) JamieSpencer 4 103
(M L W Bell) *mid-div: 6th 1/2-way: rdn 4f out: no imp fr 3f out* **8/1**

8 ¾ **Puncher Clynch (IRE)**[70] 1414 3-9-0 105 KJManning 2 102
(J S Bolger, Ire) *a towards rr: rdn and wknd 5f out* **12/1**

9 8 **Dubawi Phantom**[50] 1910 3-9-0 AhmedAjtebi 8 89
(D M Simcock) *a towards rr: rdn and wknd 5f out* **40/1**

10 1 ¼ **Bright Horizon**[10] 3105 3-9-0 92 SMLevey 6 87
(A P O'Brien, Ire) *led and sn clr: hdd and rdn ent st: sn wknd* **100/1**

2m 28.68s (-10.42) **Going Correction** -0.55s/f (Hard) 10 Ran SP% **117.2**
Speed ratings: **112,111,110,110,108 107,104,103,98,97**
CSF £18.98 TOTE £3.80: £1.90, £2.00, £2.40; DF 25.40.
Owner Derrick Smith **Bred** Jack Ronan & Des Vere Hunt Far **Trained** Ballydoyle, Co Tipperary

FOCUS
Aidan O'Brien's domination of the race continued, making it five in a row, and seven from the last ten. He also saddled a 1-2-3. With five of the ten runners in the line-up this was a predictable scenario, even though the supplemented King Edward VII winner Monterosso was sent off favourite. The winner looked to score with a bit in hand, while the third and eighth set the standard.

NOTEBOOK
Cape Blanco(IRE) bounced back from his below-par effort in the Prix du Jockey Club to give a performance that one could more readily reconcile with his handsome victory over the Derby winner Workforce in the Dante. The Galileo colt responded well for Murtagh as the three Ballydoyle principals slogged it out through the last furlong. With what O'Brien described as the "blip" of Chantilly behind him, it is perfectly realistic to think in terms of a showdown with Workforce in the King George. (op 11/4)
Midas Touch was able to benefit from being ridden closer to the pace than Jan Vermeer, who had finished one place in front of him at Epsom. He is not far off the best in the middle-distance division. (op 4/1)
Jan Vermeer(IRE) tried to challenge up the far rail on the inside of his stablemate, but was a bit one-paced when it mattered. He had gone to Epsom with hopes high that he might prove an able deputy for St Nicholas Abbey, but is beginning to slip in the pecking order. (op 9/2 tchd 5/1)
Monterosso, a 78-rated AW handicapper during the winter, has come a very long way in a short time. Supplemented for this, he emerged with plenty of credit in the end, having looked as if he was making heavy weather of it more than half a mile out. He could well be a St Leger horse. (op 7/2 tchd 11/4)
At First Sight(IRE) improved on a moderate effort behind Monterosso at Royal Ascot to take fifth place for Aidan O'Brien.
Carraiglawn(IRE), the outsider of two runners for Jim Bolger, was an honourable sixth, giving rise to the prospect of sustained improvement, though he has a fair way to go before being considered a Group 1 horse.
Dubawi Phantom's rider revealed that the colt lost his balance early in the race and clipped himself behind, and there was blood coming out of his hind legs after. The jockey was not hard on his mount in the straight.

3492a DUBAI TENNIS CHAMPIONSHIP EUROPEAN BREEDERS FUND H'CAP (PREMIER HANDICAP) 1m 4f

5:50 (5:51) 3-Y-O+ £43,141 (£12,610; £5,973; £1,991)

RPR

1 **Bay Willow (IRE)**[10] 3105 3-8-4 87 JoeFanning 10 99
(M Johnston) *sn led and mde most: rdn clr fr 2f out: kpt on wl ins fnl f: comf* **3/1**[2]

2 4 ½ **Gimli's Rock (IRE)**[35] 2368 4-9-0 83 (b) FMBerry 14 88
(Mrs John Harrington, Ire) *mid-div: 6th 1/2-way: rdn in 5th 3f out: mod 3rd 1f out: kpt on wout threatening to go 2nd wout threatening wnr on line* **5/1**[3]

3 shd **Tovaria**[14] 3012 6-9-5 88 JamesMcDonald 7 93
(Edward P Harty, Ire) *in rr of mid-div: prog into 7th 4f out: sn rdn: mod 4th 1f out: kpt on wout threatening to go mod 3rd on line* **16/1**

4 shd **Mid Mon Lady (IRE)**[7] 3247 5-9-0 90 (b) DCByrne(7) 9 95
(H Rogers, Ire) *in rr of mid-div on inner: prog into mid-div 1/2-way: 6th 4f out: travelling wl in 3rd ent st: rdn in 2nd 2f out: no imp on wnr ins fnl f: dropped to 4th on line* **16/1**

5 4 ½ **Ballyhaunis**[212] 5620 5-9-3 89 (t) GFCarroll(3) 16 86
(W P Mullins, Ire) *trckd ldrs: lost pl and dropped to 9th 4f out: checked sltly ent st: kpt on wout threatening st* **12/1**

6 1 ¼ **Behtarini (IRE)**[72] 1373 3-8-6 89 NGMcCullagh 17 84
(John M Oxx, Ire) *prom: rdn 4f out: no imp fr 2 1/2f out* **11/4**[1]

7 1 ¾ **Lancetto (FR)**[2] 3420 5-7-13 73 oh5 KTO'Neill(5) 3 66
(James J Hartnett, Ire) *chsd ldrs on outer: cl 2nd ent st: sn rdn: no imp fr 2f out* **14/1**

8 ½ **Righteous Man (IRE)**[36] 2350 3-8-1 87 oh1 (b) ShaneFoley(3) 1 79
(Mrs John Harrington, Ire) *s.i.s and reminders early in rr: sme modest late hdwy st* **16/1**

9 nk **Celtic Dane (IRE)**[8] 3232 6-9-3 93 SHJames(7) 11 84
(Kevin Prendergast, Ire) *in rr of mid-div: no imp fr 4f out* **16/1**

10 hd **Northgate (IRE)**[8] 3232 5-9-12 95 PJSmullen 4 86
(Joseph G Murphy, Ire) *towards rr: rdn and no imp fr 4f out* **12/1**

11 8 **Ceannline (IRE)**[15] 2988 4-9-4 87 KJManning 12 65
(J S Bolger, Ire) *mid-div: wknd fr 4f out: eased ins fnl f* **12/1**

12 4 ½ **Vivacious Vivienne (IRE)**[7] 3247 4-9-6 89 PBBeggy 5 60
(Donal Kinsella, Ire) *in rr of mid-div: wknd fr 4f out* **14/1**

13 7 **Baracas (FR)**[8] 3232 5-8-10 79 DPMcDonogh 15 39
(Eoin Griffin, Ire) *disp ld early: hdd after 3f: wknd fr 4f out* **20/1**

14 1 ¼ **Whispering Wind (IRE)**[271] 5689 7-8-10 79 WMLordan 2 37
(Ms Joanna Morgan, Ire) *a bhd: wknd 5f out* **33/1**

15 1 **Holyrood**[14] 3012 4-8-11 83 (p) BACurtis(3) 6 39
(T G McCourt, Ire) *chsd ldrs: rdn and wknd fr 5f out: eased over 1f out* **33/1**

2m 29.93s (-9.17) **Going Correction** -0.55s/f (Hard)
WFA 3 from 4yo+ 14lb 15 Ran SP% **138.9**
Speed ratings: **108,105,104,104,101 101,99,99,99,99 93,90,86,85,84**
CSF £21.36 CT £230.72 TOTE £3.80: £1.60, £2.00, £5.30; DF 19.70.
Owner Sheikh Hamdan Bin Mohammed Al Maktoum **Bred** Philip Brady **Trained** Middleham Moor, N Yorks

FOCUS
Yet another winner from the front. The runner-up and fourth have been rated to their recent best and the winner and third to small PBs.

NOTEBOOK
Bay Willow(IRE) came here having been a close enough fourth in a strong renewal of the King George V Stakes at Royal Ascot. That looked the best form on offer and so it proved. Bay Willow was always well placed, settled well and took it up travelling easily before they turned into the straight. His rider started niggling before the 2f pole, but the winner was never in any trouble and found plenty under pressure. This was only his sixth run and he is better than this level. He has a very uncomplicated way about him and ran as straight as a gun barrel under pressure. He looks well worth a try at a higher level and there could be more to come. (op 5/2)
Gimli's Rock(IRE) has been holding his form well and basically ran into a handicap blot. He never looked like winning but did nothing wrong and his presence as runner-up leaves little doubt about the truth of the form. Against that, he will again be hard to win with as he continues, without winning, to go up the weights. However, he showed guts to emerge best in a blanket finish for second.
Tovaria was quite a smooth winner at Roscommon last time in weaker company and ran very well. She was racing off a career-high mark here but is ground-versatile and can pick up another handicap.
Mid Mon Lady(IRE) looked a big danger to the winner at one stage, travelling best of all in clear second over 2f out. However, she did not find a great deal under pressure and only finished fourth. This trip probably stretches her stamina but she will be interesting next time if held on to a little longer, as she has dropped down to a mark off which she is competitive. (op 14/1)
Ballyhaunis was one to possibly take out of the race. He was always close up and shaped well on his first start since November and only his second since September 2008. This run off a mark of 89 implies that he was well worth keeping in training. (op 12/1 tchd 14/1)
Behtarini(IRE), gelded since going down in a maiden at Dundalk last time, was a shade keen just off the lead but was ultimately one of the first beaten. In light of that, he plugged on willingly. (op 4/1)
T/Jkpt: @5,000.00. Pool of @20,000.00 - 3 winning units. T/Plt: @469.20. Pool of @27,697.00 - 44.27 winning units. II

3490 - 3492a (Foreign Racing) - See Raceform Interactive

2735 SAINT-CLOUD (L-H)

Sunday, June 27

OFFICIAL GOING: Turf: good to soft

3493a ABU DHABI PRIX DE MALLERET (GROUP 2) (3YO FILLIES) (TURF) 1m 4f

1:35 (12:00) 3-Y-O £75,663 (£29,203; £13,938; £9,292; £4,646)

RPR

1 **Never Forget (FR)**[21] 2800 3-8-11 0 AnthonyCrastus 1 105
(E Lellouche, France) *racd in 3rd on rail: qcknd wl whn swtchd off rail to chse ldr 2 1/2f out: chal for ld 2f out: grabbed ld 1 1/2f out: r.o strly: comf* **14/1**

2 ¾ **Shamanova (IRE)**[34] 3-8-11 0 Christophe-PatriceLemaire 2 104
(A De Royer-Dupre, France) *racd in 4th: failed to qckn immediately 2 1/2f out: chsd ldrs and qcknd wl 1 1/2f out and r.o strly ins fnl f to take 2nd in clsng strides* **15/8**[1]

3 snk **Lady's Purse**[21] 2800 3-8-11 0 GeraldMosse 4 104
(H-A Pantall, France) *led fr s: rdn 2 1/2f out and hld clr ld: r.o wl but ct and hdd 1 1/2f out: r.o wl but lost 2nd clsng strides* **5/2**[2]

4 2 **Peacoat**[24] 2686 3-8-11 0 MaximeGuyon 6 101
(A Fabre, France) *racd in 2nd early stages: rdn early in st: outpcd fr 2f out: styd on wl but no threat to ldrs* **7/2**[3]

5 2 ½ **Pearl Away (FR)**[21] 2800 3-8-11 0 OlivierPeslier 5 97
(Y De Nicolay, France) *racd in 5th fr s and failed to prog in st* **11/2**

6 1 ½ **Oekaki (FR)**[21] 2800 3-8-11 0 DavyBonilla 3 94
(Y Barberot, France) *s.i.s and a in rr: no prog in st* **33/1**

2m 34.6s (-5.80) **Going Correction** -0.275s/f (Firm) 6 Ran SP% **110.6**
Speed ratings: **108,107,107,106,104 103**
WIN (incl. 1 euro stake): 11.80. PLACES: 3.50, 1.40. SF: 43.90.
Owner Claude Cohen **Bred** C Cohen & E Lellouche **Trained** Lamorlaye, France

NOTEBOOK
Never Forget(FR) preferred this flatter track and less testing ground, and quickened up well when asked, scoring comfortably in the end. She provided her sire Westerner with his first Group race success, and will now be given a break before being aimed at the Prix Vermeille.
Shamanova(IRE) finished her race off well and would undoubtedly have preferred a stronger pace. She remains progressive.
Lady's Purse was a reluctant leader and didn't settle in front. She'll be seen to better effect when more patient tactics are employed.

3494a GRAND PRIX DE SAINT-CLOUD (GROUP 1) (4YO+) (TURF) 1m 4f

2:45 (12:00) 4-Y-O+ £202,265 (£80,920; £40,460; £20,212; £10,123)

RPR

1 **Plumania**[34] 2403 4-8-13 0 OlivierPeslier 8 116
(A Fabre, France) *racd in 2nd on settling: qcknd to ld 2 1/2f out: r.o wl: caused minor interference to rival on her ins: r.o strly: jst hld on* **7/1**[3]

2 nse **Youmzain (IRE)**[23] 2709 7-9-2 0 RichardHughes 5 119
(M R Channon) *settled in rr and stl last ent st: rdn 2f out: qcknd wl 1 1/2f out: fin strly ins fnl f and jst failed on line* **4/1**[2]

3 snk **Daryakana (FR)**[34] 2403 4-8-13 0 Christophe-PatriceLemaire 4 115
(A De Royer-Dupre, France) *racd in 3rd: qcknd wl fr 2 1/2f out: c to chal ldr 1f out: r.o strly fnl f: no ex fnl strides* **5/4**[1]

4 1 **Celimene (IRE)**[34] 2403 4-8-13 0 YannLerner 3 114
(C Lerner, France) *racd in 5th fr s: qcknd wl 2f out: styd on wl wout threatening ldrs* **10/1**

5 nk **Pouvoir Absolu**[21] 2803 5-9-2 0 (b) AnthonyCrastus 1 116
(E Lellouche, France) *led fr s: chal and hdd 2 1/2f out: r.o: suffered minor interference 1 1/2f out and had to be checked: rdn and fin wl* **16/1**

6 2½ **Mores Wells**[32] 2447 6-9-2 0..(b) DavyBonilla 6 112
(R Gibson, France) *racd in 6th fr s: rdn early in st on wd outside: fnd no ex ins fnl 1 1/2f: r.o* **20/1**

7 hd **High Heeled (IRE)**[23] 2709 4-8-13 0.............................. WilliamBuick 7 109
(J H M Gosden) *racd in 4th fr s: rdn early in st: styd on* **4/1**[2]

2m 34.4s (-6.00) **Going Correction** -0.275s/f (Firm) **7** Ran SP% **116.7**
Speed ratings: **109,108,108,108,108 106,106**
WIN (incl. 1 euro stake): 7.10. PLACES: 1.40, 1.30, 1.10. DF: 15.00. SF: 42.70.
Owner Wertheimer & Frere **Bred** Wertheimer Et Frere **Trained** Chantilly, France
■ The winner had to survive a 20-minute stewards' inquiry.

FOCUS
With the likes of Montjeu, Helissio, El Condor Pasa, Pride and Alkaased among the rollcall of recent winners there is no doubt that the Grand Prix de Saint-Cloud often figures among the top middle-distance races for older horses in Europe. This year, however, it was hard to argue that this was a competitive Group 1, with just two of the seven-strong field, Youmzain and Daryakana, boasting winning form at the highest level. The form is rated through the fourth and sixth.

NOTEBOOK
Plumania had been found wanting on each of her four previous tries in Group 1 company, her best effort before this coming when she had Celimene and Daryakana in behind in a Group 2 over 1½f shorter here last time. On that occasion she was receiving 2lb and 5lb from the pair respectively while beating them by 1½l and a short head. She confirmed that running here, getting the better of them as the trio faced up again at level weights. This was the first time she had raced out of fillies' only races, and on her favoured quicker ground she showed that she is still improving. She is likely to race against her own sex again next in the Prix Vermeille.
Youmzain(IRE) gets plenty of credit for finishing so close considering the lack of pace early on suited the prominently ridden winner. Having been steadied at the start, he was slightly detached from the field just before they turned for home and got going late on to just narrowly fail. He has now gone 11 races without wining - his last win came in this race two years ago - but showed that he retains all his enthusiasm for racing. This is now an incredible seventh second in Group 1 races and, while some have questioned him in the past, it is not possible to knock this effort. On the evidence of this it is worth leaving the visor off in the hope to build on his Group 1 record of two wins in 21 races but, with the likes of Workforce and Fame And Glory likely to be up against him in the King George and Arc, you can't help but feel he will again find at least one too good.
Daryakana(FR) looked like an interesting runner coming into this but was ultimately a tad disappointing, finishing third for the second time since her win in Hong Kong in December. She raced towards the front of the field throughout, but never looked like getting to the front. Both defeats this year have come going left-handed and connections admitted beforehand that they had a concern about going this way round. She would be of more interest in the future if she is seen going right-handed again.
Celimene(IRE) raced in mid-division and, after looking one-paced, kept on again. This was her first start over this trip and another try looks well worth it, particularly as this ground would have been plenty quick enough for her.
Pouvoir Absolu was gifted an easy lead. He was done no favours by the winner late on, but was up against it here and would have been unlikely to trouble the front three even with a trouble-free passage.
Mores Wells ran as well as could be expected in this company, particularly as he was unsuited by the steady pace early on and used up unnecessary energy pulling.
High Heeled(IRE) had run a good race on her debut for her new trainer last time when finishing third, one place in front of Youmzain, in the Coronation Cup. She never really got into this and there is a suspicion that she found the ground too quick.

3253 SAN SIRO (R-H)
Sunday, June 27

OFFICIAL GOING: Turf: good

3495a PREMIO MARIO INCISA DELLA ROCCHETTA (GROUP 3) (3YO FILLIES) (TURF) 1m 2f
4:30 (12:00) 3-Y-O **£44,247** (£19,469; £10,619; £5,309)

RPR

1 **Tech Exceed (GER)**[40] 3-8-11 0.. EPedroza 3 97
(A Wohler, Germany) *broke wl: settled in 2nd for 3f: 4th ent ent st: 3rd ent fnl 3f: hrd rdn 2 1/2f out: prog fnl f to catch ldr on line* **11/5**[2]

2 nse **Lolamar (ITY)**[49] 3-8-11 0.. SLandi 1 97
(S Botti, Italy) *broke wl to ld: set stdy pce for 5f: lened wl to go 6 l clr ent fnl 3f: rdn and stl 4 l clr ent fnl f: wandered under hrd ride fnl 100yads and ct on line* **19/10**[1]

3 1¾ **Hosiba (GER)**[35] 3-8-11 0... MircoDemuro 4 94
(R Rohne, Germany) *stdy prog to trck ldrs after 4f: clr 2nd ent fnl 3 1/2f: hrd rdn and rallied fnl f: hmpd by eventual 2nd fnl 50yds* **8/1**

4 ¾ **Aoife Alainn (IRE)**[71] 3-8-11 0...(b) NPinna 5 92
(M Guarnieri, Italy) *racd towards rr for 6f: prog ent st on inner: moved 4th ent fnl 2f: styd on wl fnl f* **43/10**[3]

5 1¼ **Cronsa (GER)**[28] 2575 3-8-11 0.................................. UmbertoRispoli 2 90
(S Botti, Italy) *settled midfield on inner for 6f: rdn to go 4th ent fnl 3f: hrd rdn fnl 2f: styd on* **19/10**[1]

6 1½ **Monblue**[28] 2575 3-8-11 0... DVargiu 11 87
(B Grizzetti, Italy) *s.i.s first f: rdn to r midfield tl ent st and in tch w chsng gp ent fnl 3f: hrd rdn and no ex fnl f* **15/2**

7 5½ **Paloma Varga (IRE)**[57] 1713 3-8-11 0.............................. MEsposito 10 76
(Gabriele Miliani, Italy) *stdd to r nr rr tl 1/2-way: rdn to stay in tch fnl 3f: no imp and sn wknd: eased fnl f* **39/1**

8 nk **Blessed Luck (IRE)**[28] 2575 3-8-11 0................................. CDemuro 7 74
(S Botti, Italy) *racd midfield: 6th ent st: n.m.r whn rdn 4f out: hrd rdn fnl 3f: no imp: eased fnl f* **11/1**

9 6 **Letizia Relco (IRE)**[21] 3-8-11 0... SUrru 9 62
(B Grizzetti, Italy) *s.i.s first f: settled towards rr on inner: rdn and no imp ent fnl 3f* **38/1**

10 3 **Wedding Fair**[35] 3-8-11 0.. FabioBranca 6 56
(E Botti, Italy) *hld up in rr: effrt 4f out: sn wknd* **71/10**

11 1¼ **Sadowa Destination**[28] 2575 3-8-11 0................................ CColombi 8 53
(B Grizzetti, Italy) *broke wl: plld hrd for 2f: stdd to trck ldrs and 3rd ent st: hrd rdn 3f out: sn wknd* **15/2**

2m 1.50s (-5.20) **11** Ran SP% **179.5**
WIN (incl. 1 euro stake): 3.20. PLACES: 1.71, 5.39, 2.82. DF: 50.03.
Owner Gestut Wittekindshof **Bred** Gestut Wittekindshof **Trained** Germany

3161 MUSSELBURGH (R-H)
Monday, June 28

OFFICIAL GOING: Good to firm changing to good (good to firm in places) after race 3 (7:55)
Wind: Light across Weather: Overcast and raining

3496 BOLLINGER CHAMPAGNE CHALLENGE SERIES H'CAP (GENTLEMAN AMATEUR RIDERS) 2m
6:55 (6:55) (Class 6) (0-65,65) 4-Y-0+ **£1,873** (£581; £290; £145) **Stalls** Low

Form RPR

-423 1 **Los Nadis (GER)**[10] 3152 6-10-11 **55**................................ MrSWalker 5 69
(P Monteith) *trckd ldrs: smooth hdwy to ld 3f out: rdn clr wl over 1f out: kpt on strly* **11/4**[1]

0011 2 7 **Andorn (GER)**[11] 3109 6-10-11 **55**.................................... MrMSeston 7 59
(P A Kirby) *hld up towards rr: hdwy over 3f out: rdn to chse wnr wl over 1f out: sn drvn and no imp* **4/1**[2]

466- 3 2¼ **Summer Soul (IRE)**[26] 7170 8-11-0 **65**.................(p) MrGJCockburn(7) 1 66
(Miss Lucinda V Russell) *hld up in rr: hdwy to trck ldrs after 5f: effrt to chse wnr 3f out: sn rdn and kpt on same pce fnl 2f* **9/2**[3]

4-00 4 2 **Kyber**[41] 2214 9-9-11 **46** oh1.. MrJMQuinlan(5) 6 45
(J S Goldie) *prom: rdn along and outpcd 3f out: plugged on u.p fr over 1f out* **12/1**

0-42 5 hd **Sand Repeal (IRE)**[14] 3028 8-10-8 **55**............................ MrRBirkett(3) 9 53
(Miss J Feilden) *prom: rdn along 3f out: drvn over 2f out and plugged on same pce* **15/2**

0606 6 2¼ **Maybeme**[10] 3177 4-10-11 **60**...................................... MrSebSpencer(5) 4 56
(N Bycroft) *hld up and bhd: hdwy on inner wl over 2f out: sn rdn and nvr a factor* **12/1**

6606 7 15 **Haka Dancer (USA)**[9] 3223 7-10-2 **46** oh1...................(p) MrSDobson 10 24
(P A Kirby) *sn led and clr: rdn along over 5f out: hdd 3f out: sn drvn and grad wknd* **15/2**

0020 8 17 **Media Stars**[12] 3078 5-9-11 **46** oh1.................................... MrJNewman(5) 8 3
(R Johnson) *chsd ldrs: rdn along and lost pl over 7f out: sn bhd* **40/1**

-240 9 shd **Merrion Tiger (IRE)**[84] 1113 5-10-6 **57**............................ MrMEnnis(7) 3 14
(A G Foster) *hld up in rr: hdwy over 5f out: rdn along to chse ldrs 3f out: sn drvn and wknd* **20/1**

032/ 10 30 **Devilfishpoker Com**[885] 83 6-9-11 **46**............................ MrCAHarris(5) 2 —
(S A Harris) *midfield: pushed along 1/2-way: sn lost pl and bhd* **33/1**

3m 32.19s (-1.31) **Going Correction** -0.025s/f (Good) **10** Ran SP% **113.9**
Speed ratings (Par 101): **102,98,97,96,96 95,87,79,79,64**
toteswingers:1&2:£2.30, 1&3:£3.80, 2&3:£8.80 CSF £12.82 CT £46.62 TOTE £3.00: £1.50, £2.30, £1.60; EX 16.50.
Owner Ian G M Dalgleish **Bred** Stiftung Gestut Fahrhof **Trained** Rosewell, Midlothian
■ Stewards' Enquiry : Mr Seb Spencer three-day ban: used whip with excessive force without giving filly time to respond (tbn)

FOCUS
Despite a dry and sunny day, there was a downpour at the course not long before racing began and it would have certainly taken any jar out of the ground. This was a typically open-looking staying handicap of its type, run at a sound pace. The winning rider, Simon Walker, said afterwards it was "good ground". Los Nadis is rated back to last year's Flat best.

3497 MATRIX H'CAP 5f
7:25 (7:25) (Class 6) (0-65,65) 4-Y-0+ **£1,942** (£578; £288; £144) **Stalls** Low

Form RPR

0012 1 **Silvanus (IRE)**[24] 2720 5-9-3 **61**....................................... PaulHanagan 7 71
(P T Midgley) *trckd ldrs: swtchd rt and hdwy over 1f out: rdn to ld ins jst fnl f: styd on strly* **6/1**[3]

0-06 2 2¼ **Speedy Senorita (IRE)**[55] 1805 5-9-5 **63**.................. GrahamGibbons 1 65
(J J Quinn) *cl up on inner: rdn wl over 1f out: led briefly ent fnl f: sn hdd and one pce* **5/1**[2]

5-02 3 1 **Sandwith**[25] 2669 7-9-2 **60**.. LNewman 3 58
(A G Foster) *cl up: rdn and ev ch over 1f out tl drvn and one pce ins fnl f* **10/3**[1]

5323 4 nk **Fasliyanne (IRE)**[14] 3024 4-8-12 **56**........................(v) PaulMulrennan 5 53
(K A Ryan) *cl up: rdn along 2f out: drvn and one pce appr fnl f* **6/1**[3]

-340 5 2 **Raccoon (IRE)**[24] 2695 10-9-7 **65**.................................... PhillipMakin 2 55
(Mrs R A Carr) *led: rdn 2f out: drvn and hdd appr fnl f: sn wknd* **13/2**

410 6 shd **The Bear**[25] 2669 7-9-3 **64**... BarryMcHugh(3) 9 54
(Miss L A Perratt) *rrd s and in rr tl styd on appr fnl f: nrst fin* **14/1**

040- 7 1 **Bees River (IRE)**[271] 6379 4-7-9 **46** oh1........................ NoraLooby(7) 4 32
(J S Goldie) *in tch: rdn along over 2f out: no hdwy* **11/1**

0-10 8 1 **Green Poppy**[19] 2849 4-9-2 **60**... TomEaves 8 42
(B Smart) *chsd ldrs: rdn along over 2f out: sn wknd* **20/1**

5051 9 1¾ **Bateleur**[9] 3200 6-9-3 **61**... ChrisCatlin 10 37
(M R Channon) *a in rr* **8/1**

60.06 secs (-0.34) **Going Correction** -0.025s/f (Good) **9** Ran SP% **112.5**
Speed ratings (Par 101): **101,97,95,95,92 91,90,88,85**
toteswingers:1&2:£8.80, 1&3:£5.00, 2&3:£5.30 CSF £34.89 CT £115.84 TOTE £7.10: £2.30, £1.30, £1.10; EX 38.00.
Owner Colin Alton **Bred** Barronstown Stud And Mrs T Stack **Trained** Westow, N Yorks

FOCUS
A low-grade sprint handicap, but it was competitive for the class. It was run at a solid tempo and only the winner came from off the pace. He is rated back to his early 2009 form.

3498 MATRIX EUROPEAN BREEDERS' FUND MAIDEN STKS 5f
7:55 (7:55) (Class 5) 2-Y-O **£3,885** (£1,156; £577; £288) **Stalls** Low

Form RPR

1 **Alben Star (IRE)** 2-9-3 0.. PaulHanagan 7 87+
(R A Fahey) *sn trcking ldrs: hdwy 1/2-way: led 1 1/2f out: sn rdn and hung lft ent fnl f: drvn and kpt on wl* **3/1**[2]

2 ¾ **Earl Wild (IRE)** 2-9-3 0... PaulMulrennan 8 82+
(J Howard Johnson) *cl up: rdn to ld briefly 2f out: hdd 1 1/2f out: n.m.r and hmpd ent fnl f: swtchd rt and kpt on wl towards fin* **20/1**

3 3 ½ **Miss Mediator (USA)**[17] 2936 2-8-12 0................................ PhillipMakin 3 77+
(M Dods) *chsd ldrs on inner: rdn and swtchd rt wl over 1f out: sn rdn and styd on to chal ins fnl f: drvn and no ex last 100yds* **11/8**[1]

2633 4 6 **Master Macho (IRE)**[9] 3204 2-9-3 0.................................. ChrisCatlin 6 59
(M R Channon) *sn led: rdn along and hdd 2f out: drvn and wkng whn n.m.r ent fnl f* **13/2**

04 5 ¾ **Golden Taurus (IRE)**[17] 2930 2-9-3 0..................................... TomEaves 4 56
(J W Hills) *in tch: rdn along over 2f out: no imp* **16/1**

06 **6** 1 3/4 **Fleet Captain**[16] 2980 2-9-3 0 .... GrahamGibbons 1 53
(K A Ryan) *cl up on inner: rdn and ev ch 2f out: wkng whn n.m.r and hmpd ent fnl f: eased after* **4/1**[3]

4 **7** nse **Eilean Mor**[10] 3163 2-9-0 0 .... GaryBartley[(3)] 2 50
(J S Goldie) *a towards rr* **50/1**

36 **8** nk **Gartsherrie**[10] 3163 2-8-9 0 .... BarryMcHugh[(3)] 9 44
(P T Midgley) *a in rr* **100/1**

0 **9** 3/4 **Marina Belle**[30] 2522 2-8-12 0 .... JoeFanning 5 41
(M Johnston) *prom: rdn along bef 1/2-way: sn wknd* **33/1**

10 11 **Georgian Silver** 2-8-12 0 .... LNewman 10 1
(A G Foster) *wnt rt s: racd wd: a towards rr* **80/1**

60.38 secs (-0.02) **Going Correction** -0.025s/f (Good) **10** Ran SP% **118.2**
Speed ratings (Par 93): **99,97,97,87,86 83,83,82,81,64**
toteswingers:1&2:£11.50, 1&3:£1.30, 2&3:£10.20 CSF £63.79 TOTE £5.30: £1.90, £5.70, £1.50; EX 70.40.
Owner J K Shannon & M A Scaife **Bred** Rathasker Stud **Trained** Musley Bank, N Yorks
■ Stewards' Enquiry : Paul Hanagan one-day ban: careless riding (Jul 12)

FOCUS
The first three came nicely clear in this decent juvenile maiden and the form looks solid. The runners were kicking up the turf as the race went on.

NOTEBOOK
Alben Star(IRE) was popular in the betting for this racecourse debut and he rewarded his supporters with a determined effort. A 2-y-o with strength and scope, he responded positively when asked to get involved from 2f out and, despite hanging over to the rail late on, was always finding enough after hitting the front. He is the sort his trainer excels with, is bred to be useful and looks sure to come on for this experience. (op 5-2 tchd 9-4 and 7-2 in places)
Earl Wild(IRE) was backed at fancy prices and knew his job from the gates, soon racing near the leaders. He kept on gamely and wasn't beaten far, but was always being held by the winner. Stepping up a furlong should be in his favour and he soon ought to be winning. (op 50-1)
Miss Mediator(USA) set the standard on her debut third at York 17 days earlier. She set out against the rail just off the pace, but lost ground when having to switch more towards the centre with her challenge and is better than the bare form. Winning a maiden against her own sex should be well within her compass. (op 6-4 tchd 13-8 and 7-4 in places)
Master Macho(IRE) came into this having failed to place in only one of his previous seven outings (when well behind the third at York), so obviously rates the benchmark here. (op 7-1 tchd 8-1 in places)
Golden Taurus(IRE) took a keen hold and is clearly still learning his trade. (op 14-1 tchd 20-1)
Fleet Captain produced a tame effort. He showed speed against the stands' rail but had found nothing for pressure before meeting trouble. Perhaps he wants genuinely quick ground. (op 5-1)

3499 NAIRN'S OATCAKES H'CAP — 1m 4f 100y
8:25 (8:25) (Class 5) (0-70,70) 4-Y-0+ **£3,885** (£1,156; £577; £288) **Stalls** High

Form RPR

1433 **1** **Park's Prodigy**[34] 2424 6-8-12 **61** .... SilvestreDeSousa 3 68
(G A Harker) *trckd ldng pair: hdwy to chse ldr 5f out: rdn along over 2f out: styd on to ld ins fnl f: sn drvn and edgd lft: kpt on gamely* **3/1**[2]

1510 **2** 3/4 **Royal Straight**[5] 3317 5-9-4 **70** .... BarryMcHugh[(3)] 4 76
(Miss L A Perratt) *hld up in rr: tk clsr order over 3f out: hdwy on outer 2f out: sn rdn: drvn over 1f out: edgd rt and kpt on u.p ins fnl f* **5/1**[3]

2153 **3** 3/4 **Hydrant**[28] 2579 4-9-1 **69** .... BillyCray[(5)] 6 75+
(P Salmon) *led 1f: trckd ldr: rdn along 3f out: drvn 2f out: kpt on ins fnl f: n.m.r towards fin* **2/1**[1]

0-32 **4** hd **Grand Diamond (IRE)**[9] 3202 6-9-2 **65** .... (p) PaulHanagan 5 70
(J S Goldie) *hld up in tch: hdwy 3f out: rdn over 2f out and sltly outpcd: drvn and styng on whn nt clr run ins fnl f: swtchd lft and kpt on towards fin* **3/1**[2]

/S-4 **5** 1 1/4 **Balwearie (IRE)**[10] 3166 9-8-3 **52** oh1 ow1 .... ChrisCatlin 1 55
(Miss L A Perratt) *led after 1f: rdn clr 3f out: drvn wl over 1f out: hdd ins fnl f: no ex* **28/1**

0030 **6** 30 **Safebreaker**[12] 3090 5-9-4 **67** .... (p) PaulMulrennan 2 25
(K A Ryan) *chsd ldrs: rdn along wl over 3f out: drvn over 2f out: sn wknd and eased* **9/1**

2m 41.69s (-0.31) **Going Correction** -0.025s/f (Good) **6** Ran SP% **113.4**
Speed ratings (Par 103): **100,99,99,98,98 78**
toteswingers:1&2:£2.10, 1&3:£2.20, 2&3:£3.10 CSF £18.37 TOTE £3.00: £1.50, £2.00; EX 21.10.
Owner John J Maguire **Bred** P D And Mrs Player **Trained** Thirkleby, N Yorks

FOCUS
The ground was officially changed to good, good to firm in places after the maiden. A moderate handicap which was run at a fair enough pace, but the first five finished in a heap and the form may be worth treating with a little caution. The winner rates a small personal best.
Safebreaker Official explanation: jockey said gelding hung right throughout

3500 NCB STOCKBROKERS H'CAP — 1m
8:55 (8:55) (Class 6) (0-65,65) 3-Y-0+ **£1,942** (£578; £288; £144) **Stalls** High

Form RPR

0015 **1** **Glenluji**[4] 3357 5-9-1 **52** .... PaulHanagan 9 59
(J S Goldie) *t.k.h early: hld up: hdwy wl over 2f out: rdn over 1f out: drvn and styd on on ins fnl f: led last 50yds* **7/1**

4-03 **2** 1 **San Silvestro (IRE)**[19] 2858 5-9-11 **65** .... (p) BarryMcHugh[(3)] 6 70
(Mrs A Duffield) *led: rdn along 2f out: drvn and edgd lft ent fnl f: sn hdd: rallied wl towards fin* **9/1**

030 **3** 1/2 **Queen's Scholar (USA)**[15] 2998 3-9-3 **64** .... JoeFanning 5 66
(M Johnston) *cl up: rdn along over 2f out: drvn and ev ch over 1f out tl one pce wl ins fnl f* **4/1**[2]

00-0 **4** 3/4 **Zabeel Tower**[4] 3357 7-9-11 **62** .... TomEaves 10 64
(R Allan) *trckd ldrs: hdwy on inner 2f out: rdn over 1f out: styd on to ld insd fnl f: drvn: hdd & wknd last 50yds* **20/1**

6334 **5** 2 1/4 **Northern Flyer (GER)**[6] 3284 4-9-6 **57** .... GrahamGibbons 8 54
(J J Quinn) *trckd ldrs: hdwy 3f out: rdn 2f out: drvn over 1f out and sn no imp* **7/4**[1]

3643 **6** 3 1/4 **Cold Quest (USA)**[10] 3164 6-9-0 **51** .... PhillipMakin 7 40
(Miss L A Perratt) *hld up in rr: hdwy wl over 2f out: sn rdn and one pce* **13/2**[3]

-005 **7** 1 1/2 **Barataria**[32] 2451 8-9-2 **60** .... MatthewLawson[(7)] 2 46
(R Bastiman) *rrd s and s.i.s: a in rr* **50/1**

0605 **8** 6 **Indian Violet (IRE)**[11] 3131 4-9-5 **56** .... PatrickMathers 1 28
(D W Thompson) *chsd ldrs on outer: rdn along 3f out: drvn over 2f out and sn wknd* **33/1**

4646 **9** 1/2 **Capeability (IRE)**[10] 3160 4-9-12 **63** .... ChrisCatlin 4 34
(M R Channon) *a in rr: rdn along and bhd fr 1/2-way* **7/1**

1m 41.18s (-0.02) **Going Correction** -0.025s/f (Good)
WFA 3 from 4yo+ 10lb **9** Ran SP% **114.4**
Speed ratings (Par 101): **99,98,97,96,94 91,89,83,83**
toteswingers:1&2:£11.70, 1&3:£4.90, 2&3:£17.00 CSF £65.31 CT £287.78 TOTE £6.60: £1.80, £2.90, £2.00; EX 41.90.
Owner Jim Goldie Racing Club **Bred** Jim Goldie **Trained** Uplawmoor, E Renfrews
■ Stewards' Enquiry : Matthew Lawson caution: used whip when out of contention.

FOCUS
There was no hanging about in this modest handicap, but again it saw the principals fight out a blanket finish. The runner-up sets the standard.
Barataria Official explanation: jockey said gelding missed the break

3501 MATRIX GROUP H'CAP — 7f 30y
9:25 (9:25) (Class 6) (0-55,55) 3-Y-O **£1,942** (£578; £288; £144) **Stalls** High

Form RPR

4200 **1** **Choc'A'Moca (IRE)**[20] 2834 3-8-2 **50** .... (v[1]) NeilFarley[(7)] 2 53
(D Carroll) *cl up: rdn to chal over 2f out: drvn over 1f out: styd on u.p to ld last 100yds: jst hld on* **14/1**

5505 **2** shd **Rescent**[35] 2380 3-8-5 **46** oh1 .... (p) SilvestreDeSousa 6 49
(Mrs R A Carr) *led: rdn along 2f out: drvn over 1f out: hdd last 100yds: rallied wl towards fin: jst hld* **6/1**

-003 **3** 1/2 **Monsieur Pontaven**[14] 3026 3-8-0 **48** .... MatthewLawson[(7)] 10 49+
(R Bastiman) *s.i.s and bhd: gd hdwy on inner wl over 2f out: chsd ldrs over 1f out: swtchd lft ins fnl f and sn drvn: styd on strly towards fin* **6/1**

2264 **4** 4 **Coolella (IRE)**[10] 3161 3-9-0 **55** .... ChrisCatlin 7 46
(J R Weymes) *hld up towards rr: hdwy 1/2-way: rdn to chse ldng pair 2f out: drvn over 1f out: sn one pce* **9/4**[1]

-000 **5** 3/4 **Acol**[12] 3073 3-8-8 **49** ow1 .... PaulMulrennan 8 38
(A G Foster) *t.k.h: chsd ldrs: rdn along wl over 2f out: drvn wl over 1f out and sn one pce* **16/1**

2100 **6** nk **Dispol Kabira**[12] 3073 3-8-8 **49** .... PatrickMathers 1 37
(D W Thompson) *hld up towards rr: effrt and sme hdwy 3f out: sn rdn and no imp fnl 2f* **20/1**

0030 **7** 2 3/4 **Lady Vyrnwy (IRE)**[20] 2834 3-8-9 **50** .... PaulHanagan 3 30
(R A Fahey) *chsd ldrs: rdn along 3f out: sn wknd* **5/1**[3]

-406 **8** 2 **Weetentherty**[5] 3322 3-8-10 **54** .... (v) GaryBartley[(3)] 4 29
(J S Goldie) *plld hrd: chsd ldrs: rdn wl over 2f out: sn btn* **3/1**[2]

1m 29.49s (0.49) **Going Correction** -0.025s/f (Good) **8** Ran SP% **118.3**
Speed ratings (Par 97): **96,95,95,90,89 89,86,84**
toteswingers:1&2:£6.30, 1&3:£6.60, 2&3:£4.90 CSF £97.88 CT £574.43 TOTE £16.50: £3.80, £2.20, £4.20; EX 99.40 Place 6 £95.41; Place 5 £71.51.
Owner John Milburn - Andrew Stephenson **Bred** Yeomanstown Stud **Trained** Sledmere, E Yorks

FOCUS
A poor 3yo handicap in which winning form was thin on the ground. It was run at a strong pace and there was little covering the first three at the finish. Not form to take too positively.
Weetentherty Official explanation: trainer had no explanation for the poor form shown
T/Plt: £51.30 to a £1 stake. Pool:£61,384.01 - 872.00 winning tickets T/Qpdt: £13.90 to a £1 stake. Pool:£4,990.14 - 264.32 winning tickets JR

3237 PONTEFRACT (L-H)
Monday, June 28

OFFICIAL GOING: Good to firm (firm in places; watered; 9.0)
Temporary dolling in place over last 6f, 12ft from original running rail.
Wind: moderate 1/2 behind Weather: fine and sunny, very warm

3502 PONTEFRACT LADIES' H'CAP (LADY AMATEUR RIDERS) — 1m 2f 6y
2:15 (2:15) (Class 5) (0-70,70) 3-Y-O+ **£3,123** (£968; £484; £242) **Stalls** Low

Form RPR

0514 **1** **Haljaferia (UAE)**[20] 2845 4-10-0 **68** .... MissLAllan[(5)] 8 84
(D R C Elsworth) *t.k.h: trckd ldrs: led over 2f out: drvn wl clr fnl f* **5/2**[1]

000- **2** 9 **Winged Farasi**[30] 1276 6-9-0 **54** oh4 ow3 .... MissJFoster[(5)] 5 52
(Miss J E Foster) *mid-div: hdwy on ins 4f out: kpt on to take modest 2nd ins fnl f* **20/1**

5232 **3** 1 1/2 **Call Of Duty (IRE)**[4] 3357 5-9-0 **54** .... MissECSayer[(5)] 11 49
(Mrs Dianne Sayer) *t.k.h: w ldrs: led after 3f: hdd over 2f out: kpt on same pce* **7/2**[2]

-005 **4** 1 1/2 **Regal Lyric (IRE)**[11] 3122 4-9-4 **58** .... MissKECooper[(5)] 9 50
(T P Tate) *hld up towards rr: hdwy over 1f out: kpt on ins fnl f* **4/1**[3]

1-60 **5** 1 1/4 **Edas**[16] 2976 8-10-0 **68** .... MissHCuthbert[(5)] 3 58
(T A K Cuthbert) *hld up in rr: hdwy 4f out: kpt on same pce fnl 2f* **15/2**

4-22 **6** shd **Night Knight (IRE)**[10] 3179 4-10-0 **63** .... (p) MissLHorner 12 52
(C Grant) *hld up in rr: hdwy on outside 5f out: one pce fnl 2f* **7/1**

0010 **7** 2 1/4 **Chicamia**[10] 3147 6-9-0 **52** .... MissMMullineaux[(3)] 7 37
(M Mullineaux) *dwlt: in rr: drvn 4f out: sme hdwy and edgd rt over 1f out: nvr on terms* **28/1**

6114 **8** 6 **Bernix**[39] 2240 8-9-4 **60** .... (p) MissLWilson[(7)] 13 33
(N Tinkler) *swtchd lft after s: led 3f: wknd over 1f out* **12/1**

0000 **9** 3 1/2 **Amber Ridge**[27] 2625 5-9-9 **65** oh6 ow14 .... MissStefaniaGandola[(7)] 4 31
(B P J Baugh) *mid-div: t.k.h: hdwy 5f out: wknd over 1f out* **100/1**

1-50 **10** 15 **Sitwell**[82] 1177 4-9-4 **60** .... MissCBell[(7)] 1 —
(I W McInnes) *w ldrs: lost pl 2f out: sn bhd* **16/1**

000- **11** 20 **Play To Win (IRE)**[389] 2635 4-9-0 **54** .... MissWGibson[(5)] 6 —
(P T Midgley) *in rr: drvn 4f out: t.o 2f out* **33/1**

2m 13.24s (-0.46) **Going Correction** -0.025s/f (Good) **11** Ran SP% **120.8**
Speed ratings (Par 103): **100,92,91,90,89 89,87,82,79,67 51**
toteswingers:1&2:£13.30, 1&3:£2.50, 2&3:£12.20 CSF £60.72 CT £182.71 TOTE £3.10: £1.20, £6.40, £1.90; EX 66.90.
Owner The Howarting's Partnership **Bred** Darley **Trained** Newmarket, Suffolk

FOCUS
A typically modest handicap for female amateur riders and the pace was strong from the off. The form is rated around the clear winner.

3503 ALFIE MILLS - A LIFETIME IN RACING FILLIES' H'CAP — 1m 4y
2:45 (2:46) (Class 5) (0-70,70) 3-Y-O+ **£2,914** (£867; £433; £216) **Stalls** Low

Form RPR

4406 **1** **Nurai**[25] 2675 3-8-0 **50** .... FrannyNorton 2 57+
(P W D'Arcy) *s.i.s: hdwy 4f out: chal on ins over 2f out: led over 1f out: sn clr: pushed out* **9/4**[1]

-000 **2** 2 **Wiseman's Diamond (USA)**[61] 1628 5-9-9 **68** .... PaulPickard[(5)] 3 71
(P T Midgley) *chsd ldrs: wandered and kpt on same pce fnl f: tk 2nd nr fin* **11/1**

0061 **3** shd **Silly Gilly (IRE)**[13] 3061 6-9-2 **56** .... PaulHanagan 7 59
(R E Barr) *chsd ldrs: drvn over 2f out: sn outpcd: kpt on fnl f: tk 3rd nr line* **5/1**[3]

0031 **4** 1/2 **Abu Dubai (IRE)**[8] 3238 4-8-11 **58** 6ex .... LeeTopliss[(7)] 4 60
(J A Glover) *led: hdd over 1f out: kpt on same pce: lost 2 pls nr line* **11/4**[2]

3202 **5** 6 **Tomintoul Star**[22] 2789 4-9-0 **54** .... PaulMulrennan 8 42
(Mrs R A Carr) *hld up in rr: effrt over 2f out: lost pl over 1f out* **11/2**

04-0 **6** *5* **Verity Lane (USA)**[56] 1769 3-9-6 **70** NeilCallan 6 44
(R M H Cowell) *chsd ldrs: effrt over 2f out: wknd appr fnl f: eased towards fin* **15/2**
0-00 **7** *16* **Woodhouse Mill (IRE)**[12] 3073 3-7-13 **49** oh4 (p) DuranFentiman 5 —
(N Tinkler) *chsd ldrs: reminders after 1f: hung rt and lost pl over 2f out: bhd whn eased ins fnl f* **80/1**
1m 45.36s (-0.54) **Going Correction** -0.025s/f (Good)
WFA 3 from 4yo+ 10lb **7** Ran SP% **110.8**
Speed ratings (Par 100): **101,99,98,98,92 87,71**
toteswingers:1&2:£5.20, 1&3:£3.00, 2&3:£5.80 CSF £25.66 CT £105.93 TOTE £2.90: £1.50, £6.20; EX 28.70.
Owner K Snell **Bred** New England Stud, Lord Derby And P Vela **Trained** Newmarket, Suffolk

FOCUS
A smallish field for this modest fillies' handicap but it was a case of gamble landed. The form appears sound.
Tomintoul Star Official explanation: jockey said filly was unsuited by the good to firm (firm patches) ground

3504 SPINDRIFTER CONDITIONS STKS 6f
3:15 (3:15) (Class 2) 2-Y-O
£9,346 (£2,799; £1,399; £700; £349; £175) **Stalls** Low

Form RPR
213 **1** **Premier Clarets (IRE)**[23] 2743 2-8-10 0 PaulHanagan 3 92+
(R A Fahey) *trckd ldrs: effrt over 2f out: carried rt fnl f: styd on to ld nr fin* **10/11**[1]
11 **2** *nk* **Drawing Board**[45] 2082 2-8-12 0 RichardMullen 5 93+
(K A Ryan) *led: edgd rt fnl f: hdd nr fin* **4/1**[2]
51 **3** *4* **Minch Man**[39] 2238 2-8-10 0 AndrewElliott 6 79
(J R Weymes) *chsd ldrs on outer: drvn over 2f out: hung rt and styd on same pce appr fnl f* **10/1**
221 **4** *hd* **Defence Council (IRE)**[12] 3087 2-8-10 0 PaulMulrennan 7 79
(J Howard Johnson) *chsd ldrs: effrt over 2f out: hung rt and one pce appr fnl f* **9/1**
010 **5** *1* **Planet Waves (IRE)**[13] 3049 2-8-12 0 (t) NeilCallan 4 78
(C E Brittain) *dwlt: t.k.h: sn trcking ldrs: outpcd and edgd lft 2f out: rallied 1f out: kpt on same pce* **6/1**[3]
130 **6** *5* **Saucy Buck (IRE)**[23] 2743 2-8-12 0 SamHitchcott 2 66
(M R Channon) *hld up in rr: outpcd whn hmpd on ins 2f out: hdwy over 1f out: wknd and eased last 100yds* **20/1**
1m 17.16s (0.26) **Going Correction** -0.025s/f (Good) **6** Ran SP% **110.5**
Speed ratings (Par 99): **97,96,91,91,89 83**
toteswingers:1&2:£1.80, 1&3:£2.60, 2&3:£4.90 CSF £4.60 TOTE £1.60: £1.50, £1.40; EX 4.40.
Owner The Matthewman Partnership **Bred** Killarkin Stud **Trained** Musley Bank, N Yorks

FOCUS
A decent prize for this juvenile conditions stakes and several progressive types in the line-up. It produced a good finish between the market leaders. Straightforward, solid form, and the first two can rate higher.

NOTEBOOK
Premier Clarets(IRE) pulled too hard when third in the Woodcote last time, and the form of that race has since been boosted by the victory of the fourth at Royal Ascot. He settled better this time but had to work quite hard to get to the leader and only wore him down near the finish. His pedigree doesn't suggest he will get much further, but possibly York next month might be on the agenda now. (op Evens tchd 11-10)
Drawing Board came into this unbeaten in two starts, although neither race looked particularly strong. He ran a fine race from the front, and stuck on well under pressure, only to be worn down near the line. (tchd 9-2)
Minch Man won the other division of the maiden in which today's winner broke his duck at Haydock last month. This was his first outing since but he ran fairly close to what the comparative times that day suggested he should. His rider reported that he hung right. Official explanation: jockey said colt hung left-handed (op 12-1)
Defence Council(IRE) had gone close twice before scoring over 5f at Ripon. He had run over this trip previously and stayed on pretty well in the straight, but his chance was compromised by racing on the outside of his rivals for most of the way, and his rider also reported that the colt hung right. (op 8-1)
Planet Waves(IRE) was well beaten in the Coventry Stakes from a poor draw last time, but previously had beaten four subsequent winners when taking his maiden. He was held up after slightly missing the break, but did not appear to handle the bend that well, and was always struggling from that point. (op 9-2)
Saucy Buck(IRE) had finished well behind the winner in the Woodcote and finished further back here, never getting out of last place. (op 25-1)

3505 E B F PARK SUITE FILLIES' H'CAP 6f
3:45 (3:45) (Class 3) (0-90,88) 3-Y-O+
£6,854 (£2,052; £1,026; £513; £256; £128) **Stalls** Low

Form RPR
-604 **1** **Pretty Bonnie**[17] 2929 5-9-5 **82** NataliaGemelova(3) 6 89
(A E Price) *mde all: hld on gamely* **5/1**[2]
4612 **2** *hd* **Misplaced Fortune**[16] 2982 5-9-10 **84** KirstyMilczarek 2 90
(N Tinkler) *trckd ldrs: effrt over 2f out: chal last 100yds: no ex nr fin* **3/1**[1]
-130 **3** *2* **Diapason (IRE)**[32] 2475 4-9-2 **76** (t) RichardKingscote 4 76+
(Tom Dascombe) *s.i.s: swtchd lft after s: effrt and nt clr run over 1f out: swtchd ins and sn chsng ldrs: kpt on same pce fnl 100yds* **7/1**
0401 **4** *2* **Kerrys Requiem (IRE)**[17] 2929 4-10-0 **88** (v) SamHitchcott 1 81
(M R Channon) *t.k.h: hdwy over 2f out: kpt on same pce fnl f* **11/2**[3]
-431 **5** *¾* **Emerald Girl (IRE)**[14] 3023 3-8-8 **75** TonyHamilton 7 64
(R A Fahey) *chsd ldrs on outside: edgd lft and one pce fnl f* **3/1**[1]
4115 **6** *nk* **Yawary**[61] 1613 3-9-5 **86** (t) NeilCallan 3 74
(C E Brittain) *trckd ldrs: chal on ins over 2f out: wknd fnl 75yds* **9/1**
2RR- **R** **Rafta (IRE)**[302] 5471 4-9-3 **77** JamieMackay 5 —
(W G Harrison) *ref to r: tk no part* **14/1**
1m 17.0s (0.10) **Going Correction** -0.025s/f (Good)
WFA 3 from 4yo+ 7lb **7** Ran SP% **111.2**
Speed ratings (Par 104): **98,97,95,92,91 91,—**
toteswingers:1&2:£4.20, 1&3:£8.30, 2&3:£5.60 CSF £19.20 TOTE £5.50: £2.00, £1.60; EX 25.50.
Owner Mrs P Field **Bred** P And Mrs A G Venner & Alpha Bloodstock Ltd **Trained** Leominster, H'fords

FOCUS
A decent fillies' sprint handicap but several of the runners had questions to answer and it wasn't a strong race for the grade. The time was only fractionally faster than the preceding juvenile contest.

NOTEBOOK
Pretty Bonnie finished behind the top weight at Goodwood but was 8lb better off, and was well backed to reverse the placings. She made all the running and battled on gamely when the runner-up drew alongside. A stiff track suits her well and she might go for a similar race over 7f at Ascot in just under a fortnight. (op 13-2)
Misplaced Fortune is a consistent mare and is well suited by fast ground. She got a good lead into the race and, when delivering her challenge, looked likely to score but the winner refused to give way. (tchd 11-4 and 10-3)
Diapason(IRE) ◆, dropping in trip on this return to turf and wearing a tongue tie for the first time, looked a little unlucky. Held up at the back, she had to wait for a run early in the straight and then finished best of all. She seemed to handle the fast ground and may have more to offer on this surface. (op 8-1)
Kerrys Requiem(IRE) had beaten the winner at Goodwood but was worse off at the weights, and could not pick up having raced keenly early. (op 4-1)
Emerald Girl(IRE) was prominent form the start but had to race wide and was struggling from the home turn. She likes a stiff track but two of her wins were gained when going the other way around. (tchd 11-4 and 10-3)
Yawary gained both her wins this season over 7f on Fibresand. She was quite keen on this drop in trip, and paid for it in the straight. (tchd 17-2)
Rafta(IRE) refused to race for the third successive time and might well be off to the paddocks, as she has clearly lost interest in racing. (tchd 16-1)

3506 WAYNE CONWAY MEMORIAL H'CAP 1m 4f 8y
4:15 (4:15) (Class 5) (0-70,67) 3-Y-O
£3,238 (£963; £481; £240) **Stalls** Low

Form RPR
012 **1** **Lauberhorn**[16] 2953 3-9-7 **67** NeilCallan 3 75
(Eve Johnson Houghton) *hld up wl in tch: effrt over 2f out: edgd lft and led last 100yds: styd on wl* **10/3**[2]
4354 **2** *3½* **Sheiling (IRE)**[25] 2673 3-9-3 **63** TonyHamilton 2 65
(R A Fahey) *prom: effrt 4f out: hrd rdn over 1f out: styd on to take 2nd last 75yds* **9/2**[3]
-500 **3** *2¼* **Henry Havelock**[23] 2606 3-8-5 **58** LeeTopliss(7) 7 57
(C Grant) *chsd ldrs: outpcd and edgd lft over 2f out: styd on same pce fnl f* **25/1**
132 **4** *½* **Meetings Man (IRE)**[14] 2673 3-8-13 **64** PatrickDonaghy(5) 4 62
(Micky Hammond) *chsd ldr on outside: kpt on same pce fnl f* **3/1**[1]
0-03 **5** *½* **The Mighty Mod (USA)**[117] 775 3-8-5 **51** RoystonFfrench 8 48
(M Johnston) *s.i.s: in rr and drvn 6f out: hdwy over 3f out: hung lft over 1f out: styd on wl last 150yds* **8/1**
-032 **6** *nk* **High Rolling**[48] 1989 3-9-2 **62** DuranFentiman 9 59
(T D Easterby) *led: hdd last 100yds: fdd* **9/1**
060 **7** *5* **Fantastic Favour**[34] 2425 3-8-12 **63** MichaelO'Connell(5) 10 52
(Jedd O'Keeffe) *chsd ldrs: rdn over 4f out: wknd jst ins fnl f* **33/1**
050 **8** *hd* **Fantastic Sam (IRE)**[32] 2463 3-9-0 **60** AndrewElliott 6 48
(Mrs K Walton) *hld up in last: pushed along 6f out: nvr on terms* **25/1**
00-0 **9** *3* **Cheyenne Chant**[37] 2336 3-8-4 **50** KoseiMiura 1 34
(Sir Mark Prescott) *chsd ldrs: drvn over 4f out: wkng whn hmpd on ins over 2f out* **11/2**
2m 40.83s (0.03) **Going Correction** -0.025s/f (Good) **9** Ran SP% **113.4**
Speed ratings (Par 99): **98,95,94,93,93 93,89,89,87**
toteswingers:1&2:£4.70, 1&3:£14.10, 2&3:£12.50 CSF £17.91 CT £313.63 TOTE £4.80: £2.00, £1.50, £4.80; EX 21.60.
Owner R F Johnson Houghton **Bred** Grasshopper 2000 Ltd **Trained** Blewbury, Oxon

FOCUS
A modest 3-y-o handicap but a fairly interesting contest. The winner is rated up another 4lb with the next two close to their marks.

3507 WILFRED UNDERWOOD MEMORIAL MEDIAN AUCTION MAIDEN STKS 6f
4:45 (4:46) (Class 5) 3-4-Y-O
£3,238 (£963; £481; £240) **Stalls** Low

Form RPR
255 **1** **Kielder (IRE)**[9] 3227 3-9-0 72 (t) RoystonFfrench 2 70
(T D Barron) *dwlt: drvn and hdwy over 2f out: wnt 2nd 1f out: styd on to ld last 50yds* **1/1**[1]
4006 **2** *1¼* **Pelmanism**[28] 2609 3-9-0 65 (b[1]) TonyHamilton 5 66
(K A Ryan) *swvd rt s: led: 4l clr over 2f out: hdd and no ex wl ins fnl f* **7/2**[2]
-065 **3** *2¼* **Ellen Vannin (IRE)**[5] 3333 3-8-6 53 (p) PatrickHills(3) 1 54
(Eve Johnson Houghton) *chsd ldrs: wknd fnl f* **4/1**[3]
062 **4** *1¾* **Clare Harrier (IRE)**[9] 3227 3-8-9 60 MarkCoumbe(5) 6 53
(A Berry) *hmpd s: sn outpcd and bhd: hdwy over 1f out: kpt on* **8/1**
/0-0 **5** *½* **Harley Fern**[39] 2249 4-8-11 41 PatrickDonaghy(5) 3 47?
(T T Clement) *sn outpcd and in rr: drvn over 3f out: kpt on fnl 2f: nvr a factor* **50/1**
0 **6** *10* **J'Amour Dance**[11] 3111 3-9-0 0 LeeVickers 4 20
(C J Teague) *chsd ldrs: wknd 2f out: sn bhd* **66/1**
1m 17.68s (0.78) **Going Correction** -0.025s/f (Good)
WFA 3 from 4yo 7lb **6** Ran SP% **106.8**
Speed ratings (Par 103): **93,91,88,86,85 72**
toteswingers:1&2:£1.70, 1&3:£1.50, 2&3:£2.20 CSF £4.18 TOTE £1.90: £1.10, £2.80; EX 4.80.
Owner Mrs J Hazell **Bred** Sandra Russell **Trained** Maunby, N Yorks

FOCUS
A moderate and uncompetitive older-horse maiden that was run at a sound gallop. The time was the slowest of the three over the trip on the day. Sound enough form.
Ellen Vannin(IRE) Official explanation: jockey said filly was unsuited by the good to firm (firm patches) ground

3508 BEST UK RACECOURSES ON TURFTV H'CAP 1m 4y
5:15 (5:15) (Class 5) (0-75,73) 3-Y-O+
£2,914 (£867; £433; £216) **Stalls** Low

Form RPR
3220 **1** **Desert Hunter (IRE)**[14] 3022 7-8-6 **53** PatrickDonaghy(5) 1 62
(Micky Hammond) *chsd ldrs: styd on to ld appr fnl f: drvn clr* **11/4**[1]
00-5 **2** *3¼* **Betteras Bertie**[31] 2512 7-9-9 **65** FrannyNorton 5 67
(M Brittain) *dwlt: in rr: effrt over 2f out: styd on to take 2nd last 100yds* **9/1**
4540 **3** *3* **Avonrose**[13] 3063 3-9-7 **73** RoystonFfrench 3 66
(M Johnston) *t.k.h in rr: drvn over 3f out: styd on to take 3rd nr fin* **7/2**[3]
00-0 **4** *nk* **Lujano**[19] 2864 5-9-13 **69** TonyHamilton 8 63
(Ollie Pears) *swtchd lft after s: led: hdd appr fnl f: wknd last 150yds* **10/1**
26-6 **5** *12* **Diamond Daisy (IRE)**[13] 3063 4-10-0 **70** KoseiMiura 4 36
(Mrs A Duffield) *prom: hdwy to chse ldrs 4f out: lost pl over 1f out* **3/1**[2]
5540 **6** *2¼* **Daniel Thomas (IRE)**[18] 2894 8-9-12 **68** (b[1]) SamHitchcott 6 29
(Mrs A L M King) *chsd ldrs: wknd over 1f out* **6/1**
0000 **7** *13* **Peter Tchaikovsky**[16] 2982 4-10-0 **70** DuranFentiman 2 —
(B S Rothwell) *sn drvn along: sn chsng ldrs: lost pl over 2f out: bhd whn eased ins fnl f* **14/1**
5330 **8** *29* **Ancient Times (USA)**[15] 2994 3-8-11 **70** DavidKenny(7) 7 —
(Joss Saville) *chsd ldrs: drvn and wknd 3f out: sn bhd: t.o* **25/1**
1m 45.01s (-0.89) **Going Correction** -0.025s/f (Good)
WFA 3 from 4yo+ 10lb **8** Ran SP% **117.8**
Speed ratings (Par 103): **103,99,96,96,84 82,69,40**
toteswingers:1&2:£5.10, 1&3:£3.20, 2&3:£5.20 CSF £29.07 CT £90.60 TOTE £3.30: £1.10, £4.30, £2.40; EX 31.40 Place 6 £15.29; Place 5 £8.72.
Owner Big Bull Partnership **Bred** Meridian Stud **Trained** Middleham Moor, N Yorks

 The Form Book, Raceform Ltd, Compton, RG20 6NL

FOCUS
A tightly knit handicap with the majority of the field closely matched on official ratings, and it was dominated by the pair who fought out the finish in 2009. Modest form overall.
Diamond Daisy(IRE) Official explanation: jockey said filly was unsuited by the good to firm (firm patches) ground
Ancient Times(USA) Official explanation: jockey said gelding was unsuited by the good to firm (firm patches) ground
T/Plt: £69.70 to a £1 stake. Pool:£62,750.35 - 656.35 winning tickets T/Qpdt: £10.80 to a £1 stake. Pool:£4,015.36 - 274.10 winning tickets WG

3479 WINDSOR (R-H)
Monday, June 28

OFFICIAL GOING: Good to firm (watered; 7.8)
Straight at normal configuration. Top bend dolled out 6yds from innermost line, adding 12yds to races of one mile and over.
Wind: Behind, light, races 1-5; moderate, race 6 Weather: Sunny and hot becoming cloudy and cooler by race 4

3509 ALL BETS ARE ON AT TOTESPORT.COM FILLIES' MEDIAN AUCTION MAIDEN STKS 5f 10y
6:40 (6:41) (Class 5) 2-Y-O £2,729 (£806; £403) Stalls High

Form RPR
6 **1** **Instructress**[14] 3029 2-9-0 0 EddieAhern 9 73
(R M H Cowell) *s.i.s: sn trckd ldng pair: wnt 2nd 1/2-way: rdn to chal over 1f out: narrow ld nr fin: hld on* **7/1**[3]
00 **2** *hd* **Welsh Inlet (IRE)**[12] 3087 2-9-0 0 JimCrowley 10 72
(S C Williams) *led against rail: hrd pressed over 1f out: narrowly hdd nr fin: kpt on* **10/1**
3 *1 1/2* **Golden Tempest (IRE)** 2-9-0 0 ShaneKelly 6 67+
(W R Swinburn) *settled in 7th: pushed along and prog fr 1/2-way: shkn up and kpt on fnl f to take 3rd nr fin* **8/1**
03 **4** *hd* **Second Encore**[23] 2763 2-9-0 0 LiamKeniry 2 66
(J S Moore) *wl in tch in 4th: chsd ldng pair 2f out: no imp over 1f out: kpt on but lost 3rd nr fin* **4/1**[1]
202 **5** *4 1/2* **Never Can Stop**[16] 2963 2-8-9 0 JohnFahy(5) 3 50
(J G Portman) *chsd ldrs in 6th: outpcd and no prog on outer 2f out: n.d after* **9/2**[2]
6 *1* **Choral** 2-9-0 0 DaneO'Neill 4 46
(R Hannon) *dwlt: rn green in last pair: effrt on wd outside 1/2-way: hanging and nvr on terms* **15/2**
5 **7** *nk* **Regal Rocket (IRE)**[5] 3331 2-9-0 0 PatDobbs 1 45
(R Hannon) *s.i.s: off the pce in last trio: rdn and no prog 2f out* **7/1**[3]
6 **8** *1* **Amber Mist**[16] 2963 2-9-0 0 FergusSweeney 8 42
(David Pinder) *chsd ldng quartet: outpcd fr 2f out: fdd* **15/2**
54 **9** *4* **Sirens**[16] 2963 2-9-0 0 (t) DavidProbert 5 30
(P S McEntee) *chsd ldr to 1/2-way: wknd rapidly: eased ins fnl f* **16/1**
00 **10** *7* **Romany Gypsy**[27] 2621 2-9-0 0 CathyGannon 7 —
(P D Evans) *a struggling in last pair: bhd fnl 2f* **66/1**

60.45 secs (0.15) **Going Correction** -0.075s/f (Good) 10 Ran SP% 114.3
Speed ratings (Par 90): **95,94,92,91,84 83,82,81,74,63**
toteswingers:1&2:£7.30, 1&3:£17.20, 2&3:£44.30 CSF £73.22 TOTE £8.20: £2.90, £3.80, £2.50; EX 62.60 Trifecta £723.70 Pool: £2,444.97 - 2.50 winning units..
Owner B & F Partnership **Bred** Bottisham Heath Stud **Trained** Six Mile Bottom, Cambs

FOCUS
An ordinary fillies' maiden and pretty modest form for the track. The first two were always prominent from high draws and hardly anything got into it from behind. The first four finished a long way clear of the rest.

NOTEBOOK
Instructress got a bit upset in stalls when a never-nearer sixth in a similar race at Warwick on debut this month. A big market mover in the morning, she broke with much more urgency this time and showed plenty of natural pace and a good attitude to get off the mark for a trainer who was also on target with her half-sisters Smooch and Regal Step in the first half of their 2-y-o seasons. (op 8-1 tchd 13-2)
Welsh Inlet(IRE) gave it a good shot under a positive ride against the stands' rail but was just overhauled. She looks a speedy type and this represents a step forward on her fifth when racing on the wrong side in a Ripon maiden last time. (op 9-1)
Golden Tempest(IRE) travelled quite well in mid-division and stayed on steadily to be nearest at the finish. This was a very promising debut from a late foal who is a 12,000gns half-sister to 6f-1m winners by Titus Livius. (op 12-1)
Second Encore was well backed but a bit keen when third in a 6f Newcastle maiden auction on her second run. The drop back to 5f looked a potential positive and she ran a respectable race from a tough draw but couldn't quite find the gears to get into the firing line with the front two. (op 9-2)
Never Can Stop, second to a fair sort on good to soft at Lingfield last time, was forced wide for most of the way but put in a very lacklustre effort back on fast ground. Official explanation: jockey said filly was unsuited by the good to firm ground (op 5-1)
Choral, a big market drifter, looked inexperienced and was never anywhere near the leaders on debut. (op 5-1 tchd 8-1)
Sirens Official explanation: jockey said filly was unsuited by the good to firm ground

3510 BET ON WIMBLEDON AT TOTESPORT.COM (S) STKS 6f
7:10 (7:10) (Class 6) 3-Y-O+ £1,910 (£564; £282) Stalls High

Form RPR
0105 **1** **Timeteam (IRE)**[6] 3289 4-9-3 70 RichardEvans(5) 7 71
(P D Evans) *taken down early: rel to r: sn in tch in last quartet: swtchd sharply lft wl over 1f out and prog: rdn and r.o to ld ins fnl f: sn clr* **8/1**
03-0 **2** *1 3/4* **Baby Rock**[19] 2875 5-9-3 55 GeorgeBaker 9 60
(C F Wall) *trckd ldng trio: gng wl 1/2-way: prog to chal over 1f out: nt qckn ent fnl f: edgd lft but kpt on* **7/1**[3]
3064 **3** *1 1/4* **Desert Pride**[17] 2919 5-9-3 50 FergusSweeney 11 56
(W S Kittow) *mde most against rail: hrd pressed over 1f out: hdd and outpcd ins fnl f* **9/2**[2]
-035 **4** *nse* **Frank Street**[26] 2646 4-9-3 63 (t) LiamKeniry 4 56
(Eve Johnson Houghton) *chsd ldng pair: losing pl u.p whn hmpd 2f out: styd on wl again fnl f* **8/1**
-506 **5** *nk* **Feeling Fragile (IRE)**[35] 2385 3-8-10 62 AndreaAtzeni 10 53
(Pat Eddery) *taken down early: chsd ldr: rdn to chal 2f out: nt qckn jst over 1f out: fdd* **8/1**
6223 **6** *1* **Fazbee (IRE)**[18] 2904 4-8-12 68 (b) KierenFox(5) 2 52
(P W D'Arcy) *trckd ldng quartet: cl enough over 1f out: nt qckn and fdd fnl f* **7/4**[1]
0004 **7** *3 1/4* **Elusive Ronnie (IRE)**[9] 3211 4-9-8 48 (b) JackMitchell 6 46
(R A Teal) *wl in rr: struggling in last bef 1/2-way: effrt on wd outside u.p over 2f out: no hdwy 1f out: wknd* **33/1**
0564 **8** *2 1/4* **Equinity**[40] 2234 4-9-3 52 (t) DaneO'Neill 8 34
(J Pearce) *taken down early: nvr bttr than midfield: no prog u.p 2f out: wknd fnl f* **16/1**
0520 **9** *3 1/4* **Sovereignty (JPN)**[129] 615 8-9-3 55 PatCosgrave 5 24
(D K Ivory) *taken down early: a in last quartet: no prog 2f out: wknd* **50/1**
06-0 **10** *7* **Bush Master**[56] 1784 3-8-10 64 (b[1]) StephenCraine 1 —
(J R Boyle) *wl in rr: effrt on wd outside u.p over 2f out: sn wknd and eased* **33/1**
3000 **11** *10* **Roybuoy**[34] 2418 3-8-10 48 (p) DavidProbert 3 —
(H J L Dunlop) *a towards rr: wknd over 2f out: eased and t.o* **50/1**

1m 12.17s (-0.83) **Going Correction** -0.075s/f (Good)
WFA 3 from 4yo+ 7lb 11 Ran SP% **116.1**
Speed ratings (Par 101): **102,99,98,97,97 96,91,88,84,75 61**
toteswingers:1&2:£5.20, 1&3:£5.70, 2&3:£5.50 CSF £60.52 TOTE £4.50: £1.90, £2.90, £2.30; EX 54.10 Trifecta £271.30 Pool: £2,423.66 - 6.61 winning units..There was no bid for the winner.
Owner Roger Ambrose & William Reilly **Bred** R N Auld **Trained** Pandy, Monmouths
■ Stewards' Enquiry : Richard Evans two-day ban: careless riding (Jul 12-13)

FOCUS
A modest seller run at a decent pace. The third looks the best guide.
Feeling Fragile(IRE) Official explanation: jockey said gelding had no more to give
Fazbee(IRE) Official explanation: jockey said filly hung right

3511 BET ON THE WORLD CUP AT TOTESPORT.COM MAIDEN STKS 6f
7:40 (7:40) (Class 5) 3-4-Y-O £2,729 (£806; £403) Stalls High

Form RPR
23 **1** **Blackdown Boy**[42] 2164 3-9-0 0 JamesMillman(3) 8 68
(B R Millman) *prom: chsd clr ldr 1/2-way: rdn to cl over 1f out: led ins fnl f: drvn out* **15/8**[2]
0-00 **2** *2* **Compton Way**[4] 3350 3-9-3 59 (b[1]) GeorgeBaker 10 62
(B W Hills) *led and sn 4 l clr: rdn and pressed over 1f out: hdd ins fnl f: styd on* **12/1**
5-0 **3** *nk* **Scottish Glen**[16] 2968 4-9-10 0 LiamKeniry 11 63
(P R Chamings) *chsd ldr to 1/2-way: nt qckn over 2f out: kpt on fnl f to take 3rd last strides* **25/1**
5460 **4** *hd* **Master Mylo (IRE)**[29] 2566 3-9-3 68 PatCosgrave 3 60
(D K Ivory) *taken down early: sltly awkward s: prog fr rr on outer 1/2-way: hrd rdn and cl enough 1f out: kpt on* **5/1**[3]
00 **5** *1/2* **Picansort**[16] 2968 3-9-3 0 EddieAhern 7 58
(B R Johnson) *hld up in 6th: gng strly 1/2-way: prog to dispute 3rd 1f out and cl enough: pushed along and one pce* **25/1**
62-4 **6** *5* **Hooligan Sean**[20] 2842 3-8-10 83 AmyScott(7) 5 42
(H Candy) *hld up in 8th: pushed along over 2f out: no real prog: nvr a threat* **6/4**[1]
5000 **7** *1 1/2* **Trading Nation (USA)**[28] 2589 4-9-10 54 JimCrowley 2 40
(P W Hiatt) *taken down early: pushed up to chse ldng trio after 2f: lost pl u.p 2f out: wknd* **66/1**
8 *8* **Mushy Peas (IRE)** 3-9-3 0 CathyGannon 4 12
(P D Evans) *s.i.s: mostly last: wl bhd fnl 2f: t.o* **20/1**
9 *1 1/2* **Bilbaray (IRE)** 4-9-5 0 TravisBlock 13 —
(W J H Ratcliffe) *a wl in rr: lost tch over 2f out: t.o* **25/1**

1m 12.27s (-0.73) **Going Correction** -0.075s/f (Good)
WFA 3 from 4yo 7lb 9 Ran SP% **116.9**
Speed ratings (Par 103): **101,98,97,97,97 90,88,77,75**
toteswingers:1&2:£6.50, 1&3:£10.70, 2&3:£22.60 CSF £21.82 TOTE £3.20: £1.50, £2.40, £5.00; EX 19.10 Trifecta £174.00 Pool: £545.80 - 2.32 winning units..
Owner Roy Brooke **Bred** Brookridge Timber Ltd **Trained** Kentisbeare, Devon

FOCUS
There was not much strength in depth in this maiden. The favourite was disappointing and the close second was rated 59, and the winner didn't need to improve on his debut form.
Hooligan Sean Official explanation: trainer said gelding was unsuiited by trip 7f to 6f.

3512 40 LIVE FOOTBALL MARKETS AT TOTESPORT.COM H'CAP 1m 2f 7y
8:10 (8:11) (Class 4) (0-80,79) 3-Y-O+ £4,857 (£1,445; £722; £360) Stalls Low

Form RPR
3630 **1** **Archie Rice (USA)**[17] 2937 4-9-6 **72** SteveDrowne 3 79
(T Keddy) *trckd ldr 3f and again 3f out: rdn to chal over 1f out: led ent fnl f: styd on wl* **8/1**
-212 **2** *2* **Megalala (IRE)**[18] 2894 9-9-2 **68** NeilChalmers 2 71
(J J Bridger) *led: rdn over 2f out: hdd and one pce ent fnl f* **11/2**[2]
-013 **3** *1 1/4* **Resentful Angel**[73] 1346 5-9-8 **74** AndreaAtzeni 6 75
(Pat Eddery) *hld up in last: rdn 3f out: prog on wd outside over 2f out: wandering but tk 3rd jst over 1f out: kpt on* **11/4**[1]
0-00 **4** *2* **Never Ending Tale**[30] 2549 5-9-11 **77** (b[1]) LiamKeniry 4 74
(E F Vaughan) *trckd ldng trio: wnt 3rd over 2f out: sn rdn and stuck hd in air: nt run on* **14/1**
-063 **5** *2* **Uncle Fred**[32] 2467 5-9-13 **79** JimCrowley 7 72
(P R Chamings) *t.k.h: hld up in 6th: looking for room on inner over 2f out and swtchd lft: shkn up and no prog over 1f out* **11/4**[1]
44-1 **6** *2 3/4* **Ebiayn (FR)**[96] 971 4-9-9 **75** EddieAhern 1 62
(A King) *trckd ldr after 3f to 3f out: steadily wknd* **6/1**[3]
5000 **7** *28* **Franco Is My Name**[26] 2640 4-9-11 **77** DaneO'Neill 5 —
(P R Hedger) *settled in 5th: u.p and struggling 3f out: sn wknd and t.o* **7/1**

2m 6.64s (-2.06) **Going Correction** -0.075s/f (Good) 7 Ran SP% **113.3**
Speed ratings (Par 105): **105,103,102,100,99 97,74**
toteswingers:1&2:£6.80, 1&3:£3.40, 2&3:£4.70 CSF £49.66 TOTE £11.90: £6.20, £2.10; EX 57.10.
Owner Andrew Duffield **Bred** Baltusrol Thoughbreds Llc Et Al **Trained** Newmarket, Suffolk

FOCUS
A competitive but ordinary handicap. The pace was decent but the first two were always prominent and the hold-up performers found it tough to get involved.

3513 CLIC SARGENT CHARITY FILLIES' H'CAP 1m 3f 135y
8:40 (8:40) (Class 5) (0-70,70) 3-Y-O+ £2,729 (£806; £403) Stalls Low

Form RPR
-030 **1** **Milnagavie**[18] 2893 3-8-10 **66** DaneO'Neill 6 77
(R Hannon) *mde virtually all: rdn and jnd by 3rd 2f out: jnd again by runner-up over 1f out: fought on wl* **17/2**
1-5 **2** *3/4* **Fastback (IRE)**[25] 2685 4-10-0 **70** JimCrowley 3 80
(R M Beckett) *a in ldng quartet: rdn to chal over 2f out: upsides over 1f out tl last 100yds: no ex* **2/1**[1]
6235 **3** *3* **Choral Festival**[6] 3294 4-9-4 **60** (v) EddieAhern 2 65
(J J Bridger) *trckd ldng trio: wnt 2nd 1/2-way: rdn to chal on inner and upsides 2f out: fdd over 1f out* **11/1**
0-05 **4** *1 3/4* **Shianda**[17] 2925 3-7-13 **55** ow1 JimmyQuinn 1 57
(G L Moore) *chsd ldrs and disp 5th: effrt over 3f out: 4th 2f out: no imp on ldrs* **10/1**

4055 **5** ¾ **Leaving Alone (USA)**[16] 2953 3-8-7 **63** .... PatDobbs 8 64
(R Hannon) *hld up in last pair: stl there 3f out: sme prog and rdn over 1f out: styd on fnl f: nvr nrr* **20/1**

604- **6** *hd* **Little Oz (IRE)**[236] 7244 3-8-5 **61** .... HayleyTurner 10 61
(E A L Dunlop) *hld up in last pair: pushed along over 2f out: sme prog and shkn up over 1f out: nvr nr ldrs* **9/2**[2]

6450 **7** 6 **Love In The Park**[28] 2586 5-9-6 **62** .... PatCosgrave 9 52
(R Brotherton) *hld up disputing 7th: shkn up 3f out: no prog 2f out: wknd* **20/1**

4-05 **8** 2 **Top Tigress**[27] 2632 3-8-4 **63** .... Louis-PhilippeBeuzelin(3) 7 50
(Sir Michael Stoute) *hld up disputing 5th: rdn 3f out: no prog 2f out: wknd* **11/1**

6413 **9** 2¼ **Dane Cottage**[7] 3264 3-8-9 **65** .... DavidProbert 4 48
(Miss Gay Kelleway) *rousted along early: disp 7th: effrt on outer over 3f out: no prog over 2f out: wknd* **13/2**[3]

0-36 **10** 4½ **Queen Of Wands**[56] 1778 3-8-9 **65** .... SteveDrowne 5 40
(H Morrison) *chsd wnr to 1/2-way: disp 2nd again over 3f out: wknd rapidly over 2f out* **16/1**

2m 26.76s (-2.74) **Going Correction** -0.075s/f (Good)
WFA 3 from 4yo+ 14lb **10** Ran SP% **116.5**
Speed ratings (Par 100): **106,105,103,102,101 101,97,96,94,91**
toteswingers:1&2:£4.00, 1&3:£16.20, 2&3:£6.60 CSF £25.80 CT £188.41 TOTE £10.20: £2.80, £1.50, £2.70; EX 30.80 Trifecta £186.70 Pool: £557.68 - 2.21 winning units..
Owner Mrs R Ablett **Bred** Darley **Trained** East Everleigh, Wilts

FOCUS
An ordinary fillies' handicap that favoured those who raced near the pace. The winner is rated back to her early maiden form.
Milnagavie Official explanation: trainer had no explanation for the apparent improvement in form

3514 PLAY ROULETTE AT TOTESPORT.COM H'CAP 1m 67y
9:10 (9:10) (Class 5) (0-70,70) 3-Y-O+ **£2,729** (£806; £403) **Stalls** High

Form RPR
0-04 **1** **Bramshill Lady (IRE)**[28] 2587 3-8-10 **62** .... AndreaAtzeni 9 68
(Pat Eddery) *t.k.h early: hld up in midfield: clsd steadily fr 2f out: drvn and r.o to ld last 100yds: styd on wl* **11/2**[3]

4-00 **2** ½ **Storm Hawk (IRE)**[15] 2993 3-8-7 **62** .... (v) MartinLane(3) 5 67
(Pat Eddery) *trckd ldng trio: drvn to chal fr over 1f out: upsides ins fnl f: nt qckn last 50yds* **16/1**

2225 **3** *hd* **Sunley Spinalonga**[82] 1159 3-8-5 **62** .... DeclanCannon(5) 2 66
(D R C Elsworth) *hld up towards rr: looking for room fr over 2f out: swtchd out wd jst over 1f out: r.o fnl f: nt quite get there* **4/1**[2]

1650 **4** 1½ **French Art**[21] 2823 5-10-0 **70** .... (p) EddieAhern 10 73
(N Tinkler) *cl up in 3rd: drvn to chal 2f out: narrow ld over 1f out: hdd & wknd last 100yds* **5/2**[1]

5 3¼ **Miss Bounty**[222] 5-9-8 **64** .... DaraghO'Donohoe 8 59
(George Baker) *mostly trckd ldr: rdn to chal 2f out: disp ld over 1f out: wknd fnl f* **6/1**

4-00 **6** ½ **Jasmeno**[18] 2901 3-8-8 **60** .... SteveDrowne 3 52
(H Morrison) *hld up towards rr: prog on outer over 2f out: tried to cl on ldrs over 1f out: wknd fnl f* **14/1**

0056 **7** 1¼ **Kyleene**[19] 2866 4-9-11 **67** .... (p) RobertHavlin 1 58
(M D I Usher) *led to over 1f out: wknd fnl f* **20/1**

1400 **8** 3¾ **Wunder Strike (USA)**[21] 2821 4-9-8 **64** .... (p) NickyMackay 6 47
(J R Boyle) *hld up in 9th: shkn up and no prog over 2f out: wknd over 1f out* **20/1**

300- **9** 1 **My Shadow**[292] 5780 5-9-12 **68** .... HayleyTurner 7 49
(S Dow) *t.k.h: hld up in midfield: rdn 3f out: sn lost pl and btn* **13/2**

000- **10** 24 **Upstairs**[21] 3421 6-8-9 **51** oh1 .... FrankieMcDonald 4 —
(Paul Henderson) *s.s: hld up in last: wknd over 2f out: eased: t.o* **50/1**

1m 43.84s (-0.86) **Going Correction** -0.075s/f (Good)
WFA 3 from 4yo+ 10lb **10** Ran SP% **115.6**
Speed ratings (Par 103): **101,100,100,98,95 95,93,90,89,65**
toteswingers:1&2:£11.70, 1&3:£4.90, 2&3:£17.00 CSF £84.90 CT £397.55 TOTE £5.60: £2.50, £5.30, £1.30; EX 68.20 TRIFECTA Not won. Place 6 £535.13; Place 5 £122.31.
Owner Devenish, Eddery, Hancock and Mathews **Bred** Tom Kindregan **Trained** Nether Winchendon, Bucks

FOCUS
A modest handicap. The pace was fairly steady and there was a tight finish but the three market leaders finished in the first four and the form could work out.
T/Jkpt: Not won. T/Plt: £876.50 to a £1 stake. Pool:£91,734.74 - 76.40 winning tickets T/Qpdt: £59.50 to a £1 stake. Pool:£7,311.59 - 90.85 winning tickets JN

3274 WOLVERHAMPTON (A.W) (L-H)
Monday, June 28

OFFICIAL GOING: Standard
Wind: Fresh behind Weather: Fine and sunny

3515 BET WORLD CUP FOOTBALL - BETDAQ H'CAP 5f 216y(P)
2:30 (2:31) (Class 6) (0-65,64) 3-Y-O **£1,774** (£523; £262) **Stalls** Low

Form RPR
-023 **1** **Fleetwoodsands (IRE)**[14] 3027 3-9-3 **60** .... TomQueally 6 71
(Ollie Pears) *chsd ldr over 2f: remained handy: rdn to go 2nd again over 1f out: r.o to ld wl ins fnl f* **9/4**[1]

-555 **2** 1 **Faithful Duchess (IRE)**[19] 2875 3-9-0 **57** .... HayleyTurner 4 65+
(E A L Dunlop) *s.i.s: hld up: hdwy over 1f out: r.o to go 2nd wl ins fnl f: nt rch wnr* **13/2**[3]

0450 **3** 1¼ **Speedyfix**[6] 3292 3-8-7 **50** .... (vt[1]) DavidProbert 13 54
(Mrs C A Dunnett) *sn led: rdn and hdd wl ins fnl f: no ex* **16/1**

000 **4** 2¼ **Serious Matters (IRE)**[23] 2741 3-9-2 **59** .... AdamKirby 10 56
(W R Swinburn) *prom: chsd ldr over 3f out tl rdn and hung rt over 1f out: styng on same pce whn hung lft ins fnl f* **8/1**

034 **5** 3 **Lady Brickhouse**[69] 1456 3-8-3 **46** .... LukeMorris 1 33
(M D Squance) *mid-div: sn pushed along: nt clr run 1/2-way: r.o ins fnl f: nvr nrr* **10/1**

53-5 **6** ½ **Whitby (IRE)**[9] 3228 3-8-7 **55** .... (t) JamesSullivan(5) 3 41
(M W Easterby) *prom: rdn over 2f out: wknd over 1f out* **6/1**[2]

0640 **7** *hd* **Force To Spend**[17] 2931 3-8-11 **54** .... JamesDoyle 12 39
(N P Littmoden) *mid-div: rdn over 3f out: no imp fnl 2f* **33/1**

-050 **8** 3 **Key Breeze**[10] 3151 3-9-1 **58** .... (t) PJMcDonald 9 33
(K A Ryan) *prom: rdn over 2f out: wknd over 1f out* **6/1**[2]

006 **9** *shd* **Boragh Jamal (IRE)**[25] 2679 3-9-3 **63** .... Louis-PhilippeBeuzelin(3) 8 38
(B J Meehan) *s.i.s: hdwy over 3f out: nt clr run over 2f out: rdn and wknd over 1f out* **33/1**

305- **10** 1 **Bond Together**[343] 4153 3-8-11 **54** .... JimmyQuinn 11 26
(R E Peacock) *s.i.s: a in rr* **33/1**

6-10 **11** 3¾ **Royal Cheer**[16] 2962 3-8-7 **50** .... JackMitchell 2 10
(Mrs A Duffield) *chsd ldrs: rdn whn nt clr run 1/2-way: wknd over 2f out* **14/1**

0000 **12** 2 **Strike Shot**[14] 3030 3-8-12 **55** .... (b) StevieDonohoe 5 8
(W R Muir) *sn pushed along in rr: bhd fr 1/2-way* **25/1**

1m 15.69s (0.69) **Going Correction** +0.10s/f (Slow) **12** Ran SP% **118.1**
Speed ratings (Par 97): **99,97,96,93,89 88,88,84,83,82 77,74**
toteswingers:1&2:£4.70, 1&3:£8.50, 2&3:£21.20 CSF £15.75 CT £185.31 TOTE £2.90: £1.10, £3.10, £6.10; EX 16.30 Trifecta £172.30 Pool: £251.46 - 1.08 winning units..
Owner Ian Bishop **Bred** Gary O'Reilly **Trained** Norton, N Yorks

FOCUS
A moderate handicap, and sound if limited form.
Boragh Jamal(IRE) Official explanation: jockey said filly missed the break

3516 GREAT OFFERS AT WOLVERHAMPTON-RACECOURSE.CO.UK (S) STKS 5f 20y(P)
3:00 (3:00) (Class 6) 3-Y-O+ **£1,774** (£523; £262) **Stalls** Low

Form RPR
400 **1** **Triskaidekaphobia**[24] 2721 7-9-5 **46** .... (t) PaulFitzsimons 7 55
(Miss J R Tooth) *mde all: rdn over 1f out: edgd rt ins fnl f: jst hld on* **20/1**

2030 **2** *hd* **Romantic Queen**[40] 2234 4-8-9 **60** .... (t) MatthewDavies(5) 4 49+
(George Baker) *dwlt: hld up: hdwy over 1f out: rdn and r.o wl ins fnl f: jst failed* **9/4**[2]

1621 **3** 1½ **Chjimes (IRE)**[40] 2234 6-9-10 **66** .... HayleyTurner 6 54
(C R Dore) *chsd ldrs: rdn over 1f out: styd on* **7/4**[1]

2606 **4** 1 **Best One**[13] 3052 6-9-5 **51** .... (b) LukeMorris 2 45
(R A Harris) *chsd wnr: rdn over 1f out: no ex ins fnl f* **7/1**

6500 **5** 7 **Southwark Newshawk**[19] 2879 3-8-3 **46** .... KierenFox(5) 5 13
(Mrs C A Dunnett) *mid-div: rdn over 3f out: wknd 1/2-way* **25/1**

-600 **6** *shd* **Riggs (IRE)**[21] 2809 4-9-5 **30** .... AdamKirby 9 20
(Peter Grayson) *sn pushed along in rr: nvr on terms* **100/1**

0-00 **7** 1¾ **Yungaburra (IRE)**[5] 3322 6-9-0 **75** .... (b) JohnFahy(5) 3 13
(T J Pitt) *prom: rdn 1/2-way: wknd over 1f out* **3/1**[3]

62.72 secs (0.42) **Going Correction** +0.10s/f (Slow)
WFA 3 from 4yo+ 6lb **7** Ran SP% **114.2**
Speed ratings (Par 101): **100,99,97,95,84 84,81**
toteswingers:1&2:£7.70, 1&3:£4.30, 2&3:£2.30 CSF £64.99 TOTE £17.90: £7.10, £1.50; EX 105.70 Trifecta £274.10 Part won. Pool: £370.41 - 0.50 winning units..There was no bid for the winner.
Owner Raymond Tooth And Steve Gilbey **Bred** K Bowen **Trained** Upper Lambourn, Berks

FOCUS
A poor seller, and improved form from the winner at face value.

3517 EUROPEAN BREEDERS' FUND MAIDEN STKS 7f 32y(P)
3:30 (3:31) (Class 5) 2-Y-O **£3,302** (£982; £491; £245) **Stalls** High

Form RPR
U **1** **Toolain (IRE)**[17] 2932 2-9-3 0 .... FrankieDettori 9 79+
(M A Jarvis) *a.p: chsd ldr over 2f out: led on bit over 1f out: shkn up and edgd rt ins fnl f: comf* **2/5**[1]

2 1¼ **Askaud (IRE)** 2-8-12 0 .... PJMcDonald 7 68+
(J A Glover) *trckd ldrs: racd keenly: outpcd over 2f out: rallied over 1f out: r.o to go 2nd post* **33/1**

03 **3** *shd* **Rutterkin (USA)**[9] 3219 2-9-3 0 .... AhmedAjtebi 1 73
(Mahmood Al Zarooni) *sn led: rdn and hdd over 1f out: styd on same pce ins fnl f: eased last stride and lost 2nd post* **3/1**[2]

5 **4** ½ **Merjaan**[89] 1065 2-9-3 0 .... AdrianNicholls 2 72
(C E Brittain) *sn pushed along to chse ldr: rdn 1/2-way: outpcd over 1f out: rallied ins fnl f: r.o* **12/1**[3]

0 **5** 5 **Lexi's Boy (IRE)**[33] 2427 2-9-3 0 .... (b[1]) StevieDonohoe 5 60+
(K A Ryan) *hld up: pushed along over 2f out: r.o ins fnl f: nvr nrr* **50/1**

0 **6** 2¾ **Maratib (USA)**[9] 3219 2-9-3 0 .... TedDurcan 12 53
(D R Lanigan) *s.i.s: in rr: pushed along 3f out: nvr nr to chal* **18/1**

0 **7** 1 **Major Return (IRE)**[77] 1256 2-8-12 0 .... DeclanCannon(5) 10 50
(A J McCabe) *mid-div: rdn over 2f out: sn wknd* **50/1**

0 **8** 17 **Elusive Vine (IRE)**[36] 2358 2-8-12 0 .... LukeMorris 6 4
(R A Harris) *prom: rdn 1/2-way: wknd over 2f out* **100/1**

9 5 **Green With Envy (IRE)** 2-9-3 0 .... TonyCulhane 8 —
(George Baker) *sn pushed along in rr: sme hdwy 1/2-way: wknd sn after* **66/1**

10 20 **Complicate** 2-8-9 0 .... RussKennemore(3) 4 —
(Andrew Reid) *sn outpcd* **66/1**

1m 31.36s (1.76) **Going Correction** +0.10s/f (Slow) **10** Ran SP% **120.2**
Speed ratings (Par 93): **93,91,91,90,85 82,80,61,55,32**
toteswingers:1&2:£12.00, 1&3:£1.20, 2&3:£15.50 CSF £29.67 TOTE £1.60: £1.10, £7.70, £1.10; EX 32.80 Trifecta £54.20 Pool: £757.66 - 10.33 winning units..
Owner Sheikh Ahmed Al Maktoum **Bred** Darley **Trained** Newmarket, Suffolk
■ Stewards' Enquiry : Ahmed Ajtebi seven-day ban: failed to ride out for 2nd (Jul 12-18)
Stevie Donohoe three-day ban: careless riding (Jul 15-17)

FOCUS
An interesting maiden run at only a fair pace with the front four certainly looking capable of upholding the form, although the time of the race was 4secs outside standard. The winner did not need to match the form of his debut.

NOTEBOOK
Toolain(IRE) made immediate amends for depositing his rider when looking the winner on racecourse debut at Sandown last time. He again showed signs of greenness when taking the lead over a furlong out and had to be nudged out but never looked like being collared and scored with plenty in hand. Well regarded, he looks to have a bright future. (tchd 4-9)
Askaud(IRE) made a very encouraging debut and should be off the mark before long as she was a little unfortunate to bump into such a decent prospect. She was a little keen tracking the leaders early on but stuck to her task gamely in the straight to snatch second on the line. (op 40-1)
Rutterkin(USA) settled better in the lead than when pulling quite hard at Newmarket last time and this was another step in the right direction. He is improving with experience. (op 11-4)
Merjaan shaped with more promise than when outpaced over 5f on debut and saw out this extra 2f well. He's going the right way and should be capable of finding an opportunity. (op 14-1)
Lexi's Boy(IRE) stepped up on debut when not unfancied and was trying blinkers on only his second start. As with his debut he again missed the break and, although, he did best of the ones racing off the pace, he could never get to the principals.

3518 WOLVERHAMPTON HOLIDAY INN APPRENTICE CLAIMING STKS 7f 32y(P)
4:00 (4:00) (Class 6) 4-Y-O+ **£1,774** (£523; £262) **Stalls** High

Form RPR
030 **1** **Orpenindeed (IRE)**[45] 2091 7-9-1 **87** .... AntiocoMurgia(5) 1 78
(M Botti) *mde all: shkn up and c clr fnl f* **1/1**[1]

0300 **2** *6* **By Command**[14] 3022 5-8-12 65....(b) AmyRyan 8 53
(K A Ryan) chsd wnr: rdn and ev ch over 2f out: styd on same pce appr fnl f **12/1**

0-00 **3** *½* **Bold Hawk**[39] 2258 4-8-10 45....(tp) KierenFox 11 50
(Mrs C A Dunnett) sn pushed along in rr: hdwy over 1f out: r.o: nt rch ldrs **100/1**

4065 **4** *¾* **Kinigi (IRE)**[12] 3086 4-8-5 52.... JohnFahy 9 43
(R A Harris) prom: chsd wnr briefly over 1f out: styd on same pce **50/1**

3006 **5** *2 ¾* **Ravi River (IRE)**[5] 3309 6-8-5 69....(v) MatthewCosham(5) 12 41
(P D Evans) hld up: r.o ins fnl f: nvr nrr **20/1**

-340 **6** *3 ½* **Southandwest (IRE)**[38] 2284 6-9-6 78.... RossAtkinson 10 41
(J S Moore) prom: rdn over 3f out: wknd over 2f out **15/2**[3]

0 **7** *1 ¼* **Johnston's Kiwi (IRE)**[9] 3207 7-9-10 0.... SimonPearce 3 42
(E J Alston) chsd ldrs: rdn over 2f out: wknd over 1f out **66/1**

2030 **8** *¾* **Fol Liam**[14] 3033 4-8-12 70....(p) DeclanCannon 4 28
(A J McCabe) prom: plld hrd: rdn over 2f out: sn wknd **4/1**[2]

3145 **9** *5* **Flores Sea (USA)**[48] 1997 6-8-12 72....(b) JamesSullivan 7 14
(Mrs R A Carr) hld up: rdn 1/2-way: a in rr **9/1**

10 *2 ½* **Ginger Jalapeno**[27] 4-8-4 0.... JohnCavanagh(3) 6 —
(E G Bevan) s.i.s: sn in tch: wknd 1/2-way **100/1**

203 **U** **Landucci**[26] 2643 9-8-12 65....(p) MatthewDavies 2 —
(S Curran) stmbld and uns rdr s **14/1**

1m 30.33s (0.73) **Going Correction** +0.10s/f (Slow) 11 Ran SP% **116.3**
Speed ratings (Par 101): **99,92,91,90,87 83,82,81,75,72** —
.Orpenindeed was claimed by Diamond Racing Ltd for £10,000\n\x\x
Owner Giuliano Manfredini **Bred** A Pereira **Trained** Newmarket, Suffolk

FOCUS
An uncompetitive claimer in which Landucci stumbled and unseated his rider on leaving the stalls then proceeded to hamper debutant Ginger Jalapeno after a couple of furlongs. The easy winner did not need to match his winter form.
Fol Liam Official explanation: jockey said gelding was hampered by loose horse

3519 BET WIMBLEDON TENNIS - BETDAQ H'CAP — 1m 4f 50y(P)
4:30 (4:31) (Class 4) (0-80,80) 3-Y-O — £4,209 (£1,252; £625; £312) Stalls Low

Form — RPR

0312 **1** **Yashrid (USA)**[18] 2893 3-9-4 77.... FrankieDettori 3 85+
(M A Jarvis) chsd ldrs: led over 1f out: edgd rt: rdn out **5/4**[1]

3-50 **2** *½* **Cloudy City (USA)**[17] 2935 3-8-11 70.... GregFairley 5 77+
(M Johnston) s.i.s: hld up: hdwy over 1f out: rdn and r.o wl **28/1**

2-04 **3** *1 ½* **Plato (JPN)**[61] 1627 3-9-7 80.... TomQueally 4 85
(H R A Cecil) prom: rdn over 2f out: styd on **11/1**

2-35 **4** *1 ¼* **Magnetic Force (IRE)**[19] 2869 3-8-11 70....(v¹) JimmyQuinn 10 73
(Sir Michael Stoute) hld up: hdwy over 2f out: rdn and no ex wl ins fnl f **6/1**[3]

2-40 **5** *hd* **Tiger Star**[39] 2254 3-9-0 73.... LukeMorris 8 76
(J M P Eustace) a.p: chsd ldr over 2f out: rdn and ev ch over 1f out: edgd lft and styd on same pce ins fnl f **14/1**

5512 **6** *1* **Boss's Destination**[11] 3123 3-9-2 75.... PJMcDonald 12 76
(G A Swinbank) chsd ldr tl led over 5f out: rdn and hdd over 1f out: no ex ins fnl f **11/2**[2]

1434 **7** *3 ½* **Beneath**[28] 2607 3-9-3 79.... MartinLane(3) 11 74
(Pat Eddery) prom: rdn over 4f out: wknd ins fnl f **7/1**

6224 **8** *7* **Port Hill**[82] 1158 3-7-12 62.... DeclanCannon(5) 2 46
(W M Brisbourne) hld up: rdn and nt clr run 2f out: nvr on terms **40/1**

5324 **9** *6* **Musical Mark**[45] 2101 3-9-1 74....(b) AdamKirby 9 49
(M Botti) hld up: rdn over 2f out: a bhd **33/1**

-560 **10** *11* **Tukitinyasok (IRE)**[18] 2884 3-8-9 68.... TedDurcan 7 25
(R F Fisher) led: hdd over 5f out: chsd ldr tl rdn over 2f out: sn wknd: t.o **66/1**

1320 **11** *22* **Parhelion**[18] 2893 3-9-0 73....(t) StevieDonohoe 1 —
(Tim Vaughan) hld up: hdwy over 6f out: wknd and eased over 2f out: t.o **11/2**[2]

2m 40.74s (-0.36) **Going Correction** +0.10s/f (Slow) 11 Ran SP% **127.3**
Speed ratings (Par 101): **105,104,103,102,102 102,99,95,91,83 69**
toteswingers:1&2:£13.80, 1&3:£5.50, 2&3:£34.50 CSF £54.12 CT £317.60 TOTE £2.90: £1.20, £9.20, £3.70; EX 60.50 Trifecta £384.00 Part won. Pool: £518.96 - 0.82 winning units..
Owner Sheikh Ahmed Al Maktoum **Bred** Darley **Trained** Newmarket, Suffolk

FOCUS
A competitive 61-80 handicap run at an ordinary pace. The form looks sound.
Musical Mark Official explanation: jockey said gelding suffered interference shortly after start
Parhelion Official explanation: jockey said colt hung left-handed throughout

3520 BACK & LAY AT BETDAQ H'CAP (DIV I) — 1m 141y(P)
5:00 (5:01) (Class 6) (0-60,60) 3-Y-O+ — £1,433 (£423; £211) Stalls Low

Form — RPR

0162 **1** **Dream Win**[7] 3279 4-9-5 59.... DaleSwift(7) 1 79+
(B Ellison) edgd rt s: mde all: clr whn hung rt over 1f out: rdn out **11/4**[3]

0655 **2** *3 ½* **Star Addition**[14] 3025 4-9-3 50.... TedDurcan 4 62
(E J Alston) prom: racd keenly: rdn over 3f out: styd on to go 2nd nr fin: nt trble wnr **16/1**

31 **3** *¾* **Whispering Spirit (IRE)**[5] 3323 4-9-6 58....(v) AmyRyan(5) 7 68
(Mrs A Duffield) chsd wnr over 2f: wnt 2nd again over 4f out: rdn over 2f out: styd on same pce ins fnl f: lost 2nd nr fin **5/2**[2]

4 *1 ½* **Aragall (GER)**[281] 5-9-9 56.... TonyCulhane 8 63
(George Baker) hld up: hdwy over 2f out: rdn over 1f out: no ex fnl f **9/4**[1]

5320 **5** *4* **Novillero**[55] 1795 3-8-6 50.... JimmyQuinn 10 47
(J C Fox) hld up: hdwy over 2f out: nvr trbld ldrs **20/1**

3050 **6** *2* **Golden Ratio (IRE)**[18] 2886 3-8-13 57.... LukeMorris 11 49
(J R Gask) sn pushed along in rr: hung lft 4f out: nvr nrr **33/1**

553- **7** *¾* **Emperor's Well**[242] 7142 11-8-11 49.... JamesSullivan(5) 9 40
(M W Easterby) hld up: bhd 1/2-way: nvr nrr **33/1**

0605 **8** *3 ½* **Green Passion (USA)**[10] 3177 4-9-13 60.... GregFairley 6 43
(M Johnston) prom tl rdn and wknd over 2f out **20/1**

0060 **9** *1* **Frontline Phantom (IRE)**[24] 2702 3-8-11 58....(t) MartinLane(3) 3 38
(J R Weymes) hmpd s: bhd: hdwy over 7f out: rdn over 3f out: wknd over 2f out **6/1**

00-0 **10** *14* **Da Bomber (IRE)**[11] 3131 5-9-1 48.... StevieDonohoe 2 —
(J W Unett) hmpd s: sn prom: chsd wnr 6f out to over 4f out: rdn over 2f out: wknd over 1f out: t.o **50/1**

1m 50.93s (0.43) **Going Correction** +0.10s/f (Slow) 10 Ran SP% **123.5**
WFA 3 from 4yo+ 11lb
Speed ratings (Par 101): **102,98,98,96,93 91,90,87,86,74**
toteswingers:1&2:£8.00, 1&3:£2.70, 2&3:£7.40 CSF £43.42 CT £131.85 TOTE £4.00: £1.20, £5.60, £1.30; EX 57.40 Trifecta £166.20 Pool: £435.89 - 1.94 winning units..
Owner Koo's Racing Club **Bred** Juddmonte Farms Ltd **Trained** Norton, N Yorks

FOCUS
The first division of the 46-60 mile handicap was the quicker of the two, although only an ordinary pace was set. The winner is rated back to his best.

3521 BACK & LAY AT BETDAQ H'CAP (DIV II) — 1m 141y(P)
5:30 (5:30) (Class 6) (0-60,60) 3-Y-O+ — £1,433 (£423; £211) Stalls Low

Form — RPR

1600 **1** **Provost**[22] 2788 6-9-9 56....(b) PJMcDonald 9 66
(M W Easterby) dwlt: hld up: hdwy over 2f out: r.o to ld post **18/1**

1251 **2** *nse* **The City Kid (IRE)**[24] 2726 7-9-12 59.... SaleemGolam 5 69
(G D Blake) chsd ldrs: led wl over 1f out: sn rdn: hdd post **7/2**[1]

0110 **3** *2 ¾* **Dabbers Ridge (IRE)**[17] 2937 8-9-6 60.... DaleSwift(7) 4 64
(I W McInnes) hld up: hdwy over 1f out: rdn and edgd lft ins fnl f: styd on **15/2**

5400 **4** *shd* **Holyfield Warrior (IRE)**[7] 3263 6-9-5 52.... StevieDonohoe 1 55
(R J Smith) hld up: swtchd lft and r.o wl ins fnl f: nt rch ldrs **14/1**

0650 **5** *2 ½* **Mojeerr**[15] 2995 4-8-8 46....(v) DeclanCannon(5) 8 44
(A J McCabe) prom: racd keenly: chsd ldr over 2f out: sn rdn and ev ch: no ex ins fnl f **7/1**

0-04 **6** *1 ½* **Aggbag**[11] 3132 6-9-2 49.... MickyFenton 3 43
(J Jay) hld up in tch: rdn and lost pl over 3f out: n.d after **8/1**

0011 **7** *¾* **True Pleasure (IRE)**[24] 2724 3-9-2 60.... JimmyQuinn 6 52
(J D Bethell) hld up: hdwy over 2f out: rdn over 1f out: edgd lft and wknd ins fnl f **4/1**[2]

0-44 **8** *¾* **Optimistic Duke (IRE)**[13] 3055 3-8-11 55....(b¹) HayleyTurner 2 45
(W R Muir) chsd ldr to over 5f out: remained handy: rdn over 2f out: wknd over 1f out **5/1**[3]

060 **9** *3 ½* **Vertumnus**[42] 2174 3-9-0 58.... JamesDoyle 10 40
(N P Littmoden) mid-div: hdwy over 5f out: chsd ldr over 4f out tl led over 3f out: rdn and hdd wl over 1f out: wknd fnl f **11/1**

0000 **10** *20* **All About You (IRE)**[22] 2789 4-9-10 57.... J-PGuillambert 7 —
(P Howling) led: rdn and hdd over 3f out: wknd over 2f out: t.o **28/1**

1m 52.24s (1.74) **Going Correction** +0.10s/f (Slow)
WFA 3 from 4yo+ 11lb 10 Ran SP% **118.0**
Speed ratings (Par 101): **96,95,93,93,91 89,89,88,85,67**
toteswingers:1&2:£17.40, 1&3:£26.00, 2&3:£5.70 CSF £81.26 CT £546.56 TOTE £27.40: £7.90, £1.70, £2.00; EX 161.20 Trifecta £383.90 Part won. Pool: £518.84 - 0.50 winning units. Place 6 £35.60; Place 5 £17.81.
Owner A G Black **Bred** Charlie Wyatt **Trained** Sheriff Hutton, N Yorks

FOCUS
The second division of the 46-60 mile handicap was run at similar pace to the previous division, but resulted in the slower time. The runner-up looks the best guide.
Provost Official explanation: trainer said, regarding apparent improvement in form, that the gelding is inconsistent and difficult to predict.
All About You(IRE) Official explanation: jockey said gelding stopped quickly
T/Plt: £32.10 to a £1 stake. Pool:£66,653.13 - 1,511.59 winning tickets T/Qpdt: £3.90 to a £1 stake. Pool:£4,563.72 - 861.80 winning tickets CR

3288 BRIGHTON (L-H)
Tuesday, June 29

OFFICIAL GOING: Good to firm (firm in places; 9.1)
Rail dolled out from 4.5f to 2f adding circa 30yds to advertised distances.
Wind: Fresh, against Weather: Sunny

3522 BRIGHTON FAMILY FUNDAY SUNDAY 4TH JULY H'CAP — 1m 3f 196y
2:30 (2:30) (Class 5) (0-70,67) 3-Y-O+ — £2,719 (£809; £404; £202) Stalls High

Form — RPR

-461 **1** **Goldtrek (USA)**[26] 2675 3-9-1 67.... SteveDrowne 3 77
(R Charlton) sn led: mde virtually all: rdn clr 1f out: styd on wl **5/4**[1]

00-6 **2** *3 ¼* **Allannah Abu**[19] 2909 3-8-7 59.... SebSanders 2 63
(Sir Mark Prescott) cl up disputing 3rd: hrd rdn over 2f out: kpt on same pce to take 2nd nr fin **3/1**[2]

64/0 **3** *nk* **Celtic Dragon**[17] 2961 5-10-0 66.... JimCrowley 7 69
(Mrs A J Perrett) cl up disputing 3rd: drvn to chse wnr over 1f out: one pce: lost 2nd nr fin **18/1**

6-04 **4** *4* **Affirmable**[22] 2812 3-8-13 65.... HayleyTurner 5 62
(J W Hills) chsd wnr: hrd rdn 2f out: wknd over 1f out **13/2**[3]

-030 **5** *1 ¾* **Tom Wade (IRE)**[23] 2792 3-8-7 59.... JackMitchell 6 53
(M A Jarvis) in tch in 5th: rdn 3f out: no imp: fdd fr over 1f out **8/1**

6360 **6** *10* **Carlton Scroop (FR)**[10] 3221 7-9-10 62....(b) AndreaAtzeni 1 39
(J Jay) s.s: bhd: rdn 4f out: n.d fnl 3f **18/1**

3466 **7** *10* **Naheell**[13] 3084 4-8-12 50 oh2.... SaleemGolam 4 11
(G Prodromou) s.i.s and rdn along early: a in rr: no ch fnl 3f **9/1**

2m 32.79s (0.09) **Going Correction** +0.125s/f (Good)
WFA 3 from 4yo+ 14lb 7 Ran SP% **114.4**
Speed ratings (Par 103): **104,101,101,98,97 91,84**
toteswingers:1&2:£2.20, 1&3:£4.60, 2&3:£6.70 CSF £5.10 TOTE £2.00: £1.10, £2.50; EX 6.90.
Owner AXOM (XVII) **Bred** Kenneth Lejeune & Charles Simon **Trained** Beckhampton, Wilts

FOCUS
Over the previous five days 30mm of water had been put on the track, but following a dry night the going remained as advertised, Good to Firm, Firm in places (watered). The rail had been dolled out 4yds from between 4.5f to 2f from home, adding approximately 30yds to race distances. This was a modest handicap, run at a moderate pace, and the order hardly changed during the contest. Not bad form for the grade, with the front pair improvers.
Carlton Scroop(FR) Official explanation: jockey said gelding never travelled

3523 INNER WHEEL DISTRICT 25 MAIDEN STKS — 1m 1f 209y
3:00 (3:03) (Class 5) 3-Y-O+ — £2,719 (£809; £404; £202) Stalls High

Form — RPR

42 **1** **Sumerian**[13] 3080 3-8-9....[1] SebSanders 3 73+
(Sir Mark Prescott) trckd ldr: led over 3f out: hung rt fr over 1f out: hld on fnl f **2/1**[2]

3 **2** *1* **Bitter Fortune (USA)**[24] 2754 3-9-0.... GeorgeBaker 1 76
(J Noseda) chsd ldng pair: hrd rdn over 2f out: chal and carried rt by wnr fr over 1f out: nt qckn fnl 50yds **5/2**[3]

-252 **3** *1 ¾* **Plus Ultra (IRE)**[15] 3039 3-9-0 72.... TomQueally 4 73
(H R A Cecil) led tl over 3f out: hung rt over 1f out: one pce ins fnl f **13/8**[1]

40 **4** *14* **Tower**[11] 3173 3-9-0.... SaleemGolam 5 45
(G Prodromou) dwlt: a 4th: lost tch over 3f out **66/1**

5 *hd* **Officer Lily (USA)** 3-8-9.... SteveDrowne 2 39
(J R Best) dwlt: a last: rdn and n.d fnl 4f **16/1**

2m 4.16s (0.56) **Going Correction** +0.125s/f (Good) 5 Ran SP% **107.4**
Speed ratings (Par 103): **102,101,99,88,88**
CSF £6.97 TOTE £2.90: £1.10, £3.30; EX 6.80.
Owner Dr Catherine Wills **Bred** St Clare Hall Stud **Trained** Newmarket, Suffolk

FOCUS
A routine maiden run at a modest pace. The front three edged over to the stands' rail after the cutaway, but it didn't look to be a predetermined manoeuvre. The winner and third ran to form.

3524 JOHN SMITHS RACEDAY 4TH AUGUST H'CAP — 7f 214y
3:30 (3:30) (Class 6) (0-60,60) 4-Y-0+ — £2,047 (£604; £302) Stalls Low

Form — RPR
0502 1 **Goodbye Cash (IRE)**[6] 3323 6-8-11 56 .... AndrewHeffernan(3) 11 — 65
(R J Smith) *mde all: hrd rdn and hung lft 2f out: hld on gamely u.p* 10/1
021 2 1 1/4 **Lady Lam**[33] 2456 4-9-0 56 .... GeorgeBaker 7 — 62
(S Kirk) *towards rr: rdn and hdwy over 2f out: chsd wnr over 1f out: hung lft: kpt on* 7/2[2]
0335 3 1/2 **Foxtrot Bravo (IRE)**[6] 3338 4-7-13 46 oh1 ....(b) AmyBaker(5) 2 — 52+
(Miss S L Davison) *towards rr: hdwy on rail to chse ldrs whn nt clr run 1f out: swtchd rt: styd on* 15/2
-306 4 1 **Rock Relief (IRE)**[15] 3025 4-9-4 60 ....(b[1]) SebSanders 10 — 63
(Sir Mark Prescott) *in tch in 5th: effrt on outer and hrd rdn over 2f out: hung lft and one pce appr fnl f* 9/4[1]
0004 5 1 1/4 **The Mouse Carroll (IRE)**[7] 3291 6-8-10 52 ....(b) JamesDoyle 9 — 52
(S Curran) *chsd ldrs: drvn along and outpcd over 2f out: kpt on fnl f* 7/1[3]
0406 6 shd **Easy Wonder (GER)**[6] 3338 5-8-4 46 oh1 .... CathyGannon 1 — 46
(I A Wood) *prom: hrd rdn over 2f out: no ex jst over 1f out* 25/1
0200 7 hd **Hypnotist (UAE)**[12] 3124 4-9-4 60 ....(b) JackMitchell 8 — 59
(C E Brittain) *chsd wnr: rdn and edgd lft 2f out: wknd 1f out* 16/1
-061 8 nk **Stargazy**[7] 3291 6-8-7 56 6ex .... AmyScott(7) 3 — 54
(A J Lidderdale) *dwlt: bhd: sme hdwy into midfield 4f out: hrd rdn over 2f out: no imp over 1f out* 12/1
-000 9 1 1/4 **Mr Loire**[12] 3131 6-7-13 46 oh1 ....(p) SimonPearce(5) 4 — 42
(M F Harris) *a towards rr: rdn and nt pce to chal fnl 3f* 50/1
-000 10 56 **Some Time Good (IRE)**[20] 2870 4-8-7 49 ....(b[1]) FrankieMcDonald 6 — —
(Miss J S Davis) *s.s: sn in midfield: rdn and lost pl 4f out: sn wl bhd* 10/1
1m 36.88s (0.88) **Going Correction** +0.125s/f (Good) 10 Ran SP% **114.8**
Speed ratings (Par 101): **100,98,98,97,96 95,95,95,94,38**
toteswingers:1&2:£5.60, 1&3:£11.40, 2&3:£5.60 CSF £44.29 CT £288.76 TOTE £9.70: £2.30, £1.20, £3.30; EX 31.90 Trifecta £369.00 Part won. Pool £498.74 - 0.81 winning units..
Owner Kevin Old **Bred** Mrs A C Peters **Trained** Epsom, Surrey
■ Stewards' Enquiry : Jack Mitchell two-day ban: careless riding (Jul 13-14)

FOCUS
A moderate handicap, though the pace seemed solid. The field looked likely to head towards the stands' rail or stay in the centre of the track coming to the last 2f, but after the cutaway they all dived over to the inside rail. Four of these met here the previous week.
Lady Lam Official explanation: jockey said filly lost a front shoe
Foxtrot Bravo(IRE) Official explanation: jockey said gelding suffered interference
Some Time Good(IRE) Official explanation: jockey said gelding did not face the blinkers

3525 BRIGHTON RACECOURSE LADIES DAY 5TH AUGUST H'CAP — 6f 209y
4:00 (4:00) (Class 5) (0-70,69) 3-Y-0 — £2,719 (£809; £404; £202) Stalls Centre

Form — RPR
5446 1 **Barlaman (USA)**[6] 3325 3-9-3 65 ....(t) NeilCallan 5 — 69
(C E Brittain) *in tch: effrt over 2f out: styd on to ld ins fnl f: rdn out* 13/2
4505 2 1 1/4 **Chinese Democracy (USA)**[11] 3161 3-8-2 53..... AndrewHeffernan(3) 7 — 53
(P D Evans) *in tch: effrt over 2f out: drvn to press ldrs 1f out: styd on to take 2nd nr fin* 4/1[2]
6510 3 1/2 **Interakt**[7] 3297 3-9-4 66 .... CathyGannon 3 — 65
(M R Channon) *prom: disp ld 3f out: hrd rdn and hdd ins fnl f: one pce* 7/2[1]
0004 4 1/2 **King's Approach (IRE)**[6] 3313 3-9-0 62 ....(b) LukeMorris 2 — 60
(R A Harris) *led tl over 3f out: disp ld after: hrd rdn over 1f out: no ex 100yds* 16/1
54-0 5 1 **Gypsy Boy (USA)**[18] 2925 3-9-5 67 .... SimonWhitworth 8 — 64+
(F J Brennan) *chsd ldr: led briefly over 3f out: hrd rdn and cl up whn n.m.r on stands' rail ins fnl f: disputing 4th and hld whn tightened up fnl 50yds* 6/1[3]
0533 6 4 **Mini Max**[23] 2780 3-8-8 56 ....(b) JimCrowley 6 — 40
(B W Duke) *dwlt: hld up towards rr on outer: sltly hmpd 5f out: hrd rdn 2f out: nt pce to chal* 7/2[1]
2003 7 6 **Ramamara (IRE)**[6] 3336 3-9-7 69 .... JamesDoyle 11 — 37
(P D Evans) *hld up in rr: rdn over 3f out: n.d* 11/1
50-0 8 6 **James Barrymore**[15] 3030 3-9-1 63 ....(bt[1]) PaulFitzsimons 4 — 15
(Miss J R Tooth) *dwlt: sn chsng ldrs: hrd rdn and wknd over 2f out* 16/1
0000 9 8 **Paphos**[15] 3030 3-8-2 50 oh2 ....(t) NickyMackay 9 — —
(S C Williams) *chsd ldrs tl tried to jump road after 1f: lost pl: rdn and wknd over 3f out: no ch and eased fnl 2f* 16/1
1m 24.06s (0.96) **Going Correction** +0.125s/f (Good) 9 Ran SP% **118.0**
Speed ratings (Par 99): **99,97,97,96,95 90,83,77,67**
toteswingers:1&2:£6.50, 1&3:£5.60, 2&3:£5.20 CSF £33.47 CT £108.22 TOTE £6.70: £2.10, £1.60, £2.30; EX 36.70 Trifecta £175.80 Pool £411.10 - 1.73 winning units..
Owner Saeed Manana **Bred** W S Farish **Trained** Newmarket, Suffolk
■ Stewards' Enquiry : Cathy Gannon one-day ban: careless riding (Jul 13)

FOCUS
An ordinary handicap, though with three disputing the early pace the tempo was solid enough. On this occasion the runners came over to the stands' rail. The third is the best guide to this modest form.
James Barrymore Official explanation: jockey said gelding made a noise

3526 BRAKES FRESH IDEAS H'CAP — 5f 213y
4:30 (4:30) (Class 6) (0-55,55) 3-Y-0+ — £2,183 (£644; £322) Stalls Low

Form — RPR
6006 1 **Mandhooma**[13] 3086 4-8-8 46 oh1 .... WilliamCarson(3) 6 — 57
(P W Hiatt) *hld up towards rr: rdn and hdwy fr 2f out: hung lft fnl f: styd on to ld fnl 100yds* 16/1
-004 2 1/2 **Rosiliant (IRE)**[17] 2962 3-8-3 50 ....(b) JohnFahy(5) 12 — 57
(C G Cox) *bhd: hdwy 2f out: led 1f out: hung lft and hdd fnl 100yds: kpt on* 6/1[3]
0630 3 2 1/4 **Avonlini**[15] 3026 4-9-0 49 .... JackMitchell 1 — 51
(B P J Baugh) *mde most tl 1f out: one pce* 18/1
5066 4 1 1/2 **Dualagi**[7] 3292 6-9-2 51 .... GeorgeBaker 8 — 48
(M R Bosley) *bhd: rdn and hdwy 2f out: chsd ldrs over 1f out: styd on same pce* 11/4[1]
06-1 5 1 3/4 **The Jailer**[8] 3255 7-8-13 51 6ex .... RussKennemore(3) 11 — 43
(J G M O'Shea) *cl up: jnd ldrs on outside rail 3f out: wknd over 1f out* 5/1[2]
0-00 6 2 **Queen Of Thebes (IRE)**[17] 2967 4-9-6 55 ....(t) HayleyTurner 4 — 40
(S Kirk) *dwlt: bhd: hdwy towards far side to press ldrs 2f out: wknd over 1f out* 16/1
0400 7 hd **Briannsta (IRE)**[17] 2965 8-8-6 46 ....(b) SophieDoyle(5) 7 — 31
(J E Long) *prom: hrd rdn over 2f out: sn outpcd* 25/1
3065 8 2 3/4 **Athboy Auction**[12] 3115 5-8-7 49 .... NatashaEaton(7) 3 — 25
(H J Collingridge) *dwlt: sn in midfield: outpcd fnl 2f* 17/2
4500 9 2 **Lucky Diva**[16] 3002 3-8-11 53 .... LiamKeniry 2 — 21
(S Kirk) *in tch: outpcd 2f out: sn btn* 16/1
5000 10 1 3/4 **Hart Of Gold**[7] 3292 6-9-1 50 ....(b) LukeMorris 5 — 14
(R A Harris) *chsd ldr tl drvn along and wknd over 2f out* 15/2
0-04 11 8 **Novastasia (IRE)**[14] 3056 4-8-11 46 oh1 .... SebSanders 10 — —
(D K Ivory) *chsd ldrs tl wknd 2f out* 10/1
1m 10.69s (0.49) **Going Correction** +0.125s/f (Good)
WFA 3 from 4yo+ 7lb 11 Ran SP% **115.8**
Speed ratings (Par 101): **101,100,97,95,93 90,90,86,83,81 70**
toteswingers:1&2:£15.80, 1&3:£34.10, 2&3:£22.60 CSF £107.44 CT £1784.93 TOTE £24.50: £5.30, £2.10, £6.80; EX 183.90 TRIFECTA Not won..
Owner P W Hiatt **Bred** Shadwell Estate Company Limited **Trained** Hook Norton, Oxon

FOCUS
A moderate handicap and these sprinters used the whole of the width of the track, first coming stands' side after the cutaway and then hanging back towards the inside rail. The 11 runners were almost in a line across the track over a furlong from home with barely a length between them. The winner is rated in line with the best of this year's form.

3527 BRIGHTON ROCKET RACEDAY FRIDAY 6TH AUGUST H'CAP — 5f 59y
5:00 (5:00) (Class 5) (0-70,69) 3-Y-0+ — £2,719 (£809; £404; £202) Stalls Low

Form — RPR
0202 1 **Highland Harvest**[14] 3057 6-9-8 64 .... StevieDonohoe 1 — 71
(Jamie Poulton) *chsd ldrs: effrt 2f out: drvn to ld ins fnl f* 9/2[3]
533 2 3/4 **Green Velvet**[24] 2751 5-9-4 60 .... SebSanders 4 — 64
(P J Makin) *sn outpcd in rr: hdwy over 1f out: edgd lft and r.o fnl f* 7/2[2]
-212 3 shd **Multahab**[7] 3293 11-9-9 65 ....(t) MarcHalford 5 — 69
(M Wigham) *mde most tl ins fnl f: one pce* 5/1
00-0 4 1 1/4 **Drifting Gold**[12] 3114 6-9-9 65 ....(b) AdamKirby 2 — 64
(C G Cox) *in tch: rdn to press ldrs 2f out: one pce fnl f* 11/4[1]
-004 5 nk **Green Lagonda (AUS)**[6] 3308 8-9-8 67 .... AndrewHeffernan(3) 6 — 65
(P D Evans) *chsd ldrs: drvn along 2f out: rdr dropped whip ins fnl f: one pce* 11/1
-226 6 12 **Tiger Trail (GER)**[17] 2964 6-9-1 57 ....(b[1]) TomQueally 7 — 13
(Mrs N Smith) *s.i.s: hdwy to join ldr 3f out: wknd over 1f out* 9/2[3]
62.97 secs (0.67) **Going Correction** +0.125s/f (Good) 6 Ran SP% **110.3**
Speed ratings (Par 103): **99,97,97,95,95 75**
toteswingers::1&2:£2.90, 1&3:£3.70, 2&3:£3.70 CSF £19.63 TOTE £7.10: £4.20, £1.30; EX 26.00 Place 6 £79.01, Place 5 £66.22..
Owner J Wotherspoon **Bred** John Wotherspoon **Trained** Lewes, E Sussex

FOCUS
Another modest sprint handicap and this time all six runners made for the stands' side after the cutaway. Straightforward form.
T/Plt: £209.50 to a £1 stake. Pool:£73,986.03 - 257.72 winning tickets T/Qpdt: £37.90 to a £1 stake. Pool:£4,464.04 - 87.10 winning tickets LM

3352 HAMILTON (R-H)
Tuesday, June 29

OFFICIAL GOING: Good to firm (good in places; 9.9)
Rail realignment around the loop reduced distances on round course by about 8yds.
Wind: Fresh, half against Weather: Cloudy, warm

3528 WEATHERBYS BANK MAIDEN STKS — 5f 4y
2:15 (2:15) (Class 5) 2-Y-0 — £2,729 (£806; £403) Stalls Low

Form — RPR
2 1 **Mayson**[18] 2936 2-9-3 0 .... PaulHanagan 5 — 84+
(R A Fahey) *mde all: shkn up and qcknd clr fnl f: readily* 1/7[1]
0 2 5 **Baby Driver**[27] 2654 2-9-3 0 .... TonyHamilton 3 — 60
(J Howard Johnson) *s.i.s: rn green in rr: hdwy over 1f out: chsd clr ldr ins fnl f: no imp* 25/1[3]
5 3 2 **Countrywide Flame**[31] 2540 2-9-3 0 .... SilvestreDeSousa 4 — 53
(K A Ryan) *cl up: rdn over 2f out: edgd rt over 1f out: no imp fnl f* 15/2[2]
00 4 1/2 **Roman Ruler (IRE)**[21] 2832 2-9-3 0 .... PhillipMakin 1 — 51
(C W Fairhurst) *cl up: rdn 2f out: outpcd fnl f* 66/1
05 5 22 **Glitter Bug (IRE)**[13] 3072 2-9-3 0 .... GregFairley 2 — —
(M Johnston) *t.k.h: cl up: rdn over 2f out: wknd qckly wl over 1f out* 33/1
60.15 secs (0.15) **Going Correction** +0.025s/f (Good) 5 Ran SP% **107.5**
Speed ratings (Par 93): **99,91,87,87,51**
toteswingers:1&2:£6.10 CSF £6.32 TOTE £1.10: £1.10, £7.20; EX 6.60.
Owner David W Armstrong **Bred** Highfield Farm Llp **Trained** Musley Bank, N Yorks

FOCUS
No strength in depth here and the winner was much too good. The form is rated conservatively around the time and the third.

NOTEBOOK
Mayson capitalised on a golden opportunity to get his head in front. After showing ability on his debut at York, he was never far off the pace here, and won with the minimum of fuss to keep up the fine run of his stable. (tchd 1-8 and 1-5 in a place)
Baby Driver, who failed to beat a rival on his debut over 6f, stayed on late in the day after looking green early. He should continue to progress and can make his mark in due course.
Countrywide Flame also got the hang of things late on and will be of interest in a nursery, especially over 6f. (op 13-2 tchd 6-1)
Roman Ruler(IRE) appears to be going the right way, this being his third start. (op 50-1 tchd 40-1)
Glitter Bug(IRE), warm beforehand, was quickly of the bridle and can only be watched at present. (tchd 25-1)

3529 SCOTTISH RACING CLAIMING STKS — 5f 4y
2:45 (2:45) (Class 6) 3-5-Y-0 — £2,047 (£604; £302) Stalls Centre

Form — RPR
-006 1 **Crimea (IRE)**[10] 3201 4-9-13 80 .... AdrianNicholls 2 — 90
(D Nicholls) *mde all: rdn and qcknd clr fnl f: eased towards fin* 15/8[1]
-320 2 7 **North Central (USA)**[10] 3227 3-8-9 65 .... PaulHanagan 4 — 51
(J Howard Johnson) *cl up: drvn and outpcd over 1f out: styd fnl f to take 2nd cl home: no ch w wnr* 7/1
-631 3 nk **Artsu**[13] 3075 5-9-3 68 .... PhillipMakin 6 — 54
(M Dods) *t.k.h: prom on outside: swtchd bhd horses 1/2-way: hmpd wl over 1f out: rallied 1f out: wnt 2nd briefly wl ins fnl f: no imp* 3/1[3]
3250 4 1/2 **Wotashirtfull (IRE)**[14] 3065 5-9-4 77 ....(p) MichaelO'Connell(5) 5 — 58
(D Nicholls) *chsd wnr: rdn 1/2-way: no imp fnl f: lost two pls last 50yds* 2/1[2]

5500 **5** 2 3/4 **Kristen Jane (USA)**[11] 3167 3-7-12 44 ow2............ JamesSullivan(5) 1 32
(Miss L A Perratt) *upset in stalls: prom: rdn 1/2-way: wknd over 1f out* **80/1**

59.53 secs (-0.47) **Going Correction** +0.025s/f (Good)
WFA 3 from 4yo+ 6lb 5 Ran SP% **106.9**
Speed ratings (Par 101): **104,92,92,91,87**
toteswingers:1&2:£5.40 CSF £13.69 TOTE £3.30: £1.10, £3.30; EX 12.90.North Central was claimed by J S Goldie for £8,000.
Owner Middleham Park Racing Xvi **Bred** Lodge Park Stud **Trained** Sessay, N Yorks

FOCUS
A modest claimer and an easy winner, but it is most likely only he showed his form.
Wotashirtfull(IRE) Official explanation: trainer's rep said gelding finished distressed

3530 WEATHERBYS BANK H'CAP 1m 65y
3:15 (3:15) (Class 5) (0-70,66) 3-Y-O £2,914 (£867; £433; £216) **Stalls** High

Form RPR
2223 **1** **Killing Moon (USA)**[11] 3161 3-9-7 66.................... TonyHamilton 5 71
(K A Ryan) *trckd ldrs: effrt and rdn over 1f out: styd on wl to ld fnl 50yds* **15/8**[1]
0006 **2** 3/4 **Hail Bold Chief (USA)**[13] 3091 3-9-4 63.................... PJMcDonald 2 66
(G A Swinbank) *led: rdn over 2f out: hung lft ins fnl f: hdd last 50yds: kpt on* **10/1**
3032 **3** 1/2 **High Resolution**[11] 3161 3-8-12 57....................(b[1]) PaulHanagan 6 59
(Miss L A Perratt) *t.k.h: hld up in tch: effrt over 1f out: ev ch ins fnl f: hld towards fin* **2/1**[2]
4504 **4** 5 **Damietta (USA)**[13] 3074 3-9-7 66.................... GregFairley 4 57
(M Johnston) *s.i.s: last but in tch: effrt on outside over 2f out: edgd rt and outpcd fnl f* **4/1**[3]
3504 **5** 3 1/4 **Lord's Seat**[5] 3354 3-8-4 49 ow1.................... PatrickMathers 1 32
(A Berry) *chsd ldr: rdn over 3f out: wknd wl over 1f out* **22/1**
040 **6** 7 **Affordable (IRE)**[21] 2840 3-9-3 62.................... SamHitchcott 3 29
(M R Channon) *t.k.h: cl up tl rdn and wknd fr 2f out* **14/1**

1m 47.55s (-0.85) **Going Correction** -0.275s/f (Firm) 6 Ran SP% **108.2**
Speed ratings (Par 99): **93,92,91,86,83 76**
toteswingers:1&2:£3.40, 1&3:£1.40, 2&3:£4.00 CSF £18.78 TOTE £2.40: £1.10, £7.60; EX 25.20.
Owner Mrs J Ryan **Bred** Stonehaven Farm LLC **Trained** Hambleton, N Yorks

FOCUS
A moderate handicap. The form makes sense at face value.

3531 WEATHERBYS BLOODSTOCK INSURANCE H'CAP (SCOTTISH TROPHY QUALIFIER) 1m 1f 36y
3:45 (3:45) (Class 5) (0-75,73) 3-Y-O+ £3,238 (£963; £481; £240) **Stalls** High

Form RPR
-323 **1** **Gritstone**[39] 2289 3-9-6 73.................... PaulHanagan 6 88+
(R A Fahey) *trckd ldrs on ins: nt clr run over 2f out tl gap appeared and qcknd to ld 1f out: sn clr: eased ins fnl f: readily* **10/11**[1]
3215 **2** 3 **Finsbury**[20] 2858 7-9-11 67.................... PhillipMakin 7 71
(Miss L A Perratt) *hld up on ins: effrt and swtchd lft over 1f out: styd on fnl f: wnt 2nd last 50yds: no ch w easy wnr* **16/1**
/405 **3** 1/2 **Rosbertini**[11] 3148 4-9-3 59.................... TomEaves 9 62+
(Miss L A Perratt) *hld up in tch: rdn over 3f out: effrt whn nt clr run 2f out: styd on fnl f: nrst fin* **66/1**
5231 **4** 1/2 **Daring Dream (GER)**[11] 3149 5-9-8 67.................... GaryBartley(3) 8 69
(J S Goldie) *prom: hdwy to ld briefly over 1f out: one pce ins fnl f* **3/1**[2]
3-53 **5** nk **Talk Of Saafend (IRE)**[11] 3149 5-9-7 63.................... TonyHamilton 3 64
(P Monteith) *hld up: hdwy and swtchd lft over 1f out: kpt on fnl f: no imp* **8/1**[3]
0-44 **6** 3 1/4 **Shy Glance (USA)**[10] 3202 8-9-9 70.................... MichaelO'Connell(5) 1 64
(P Monteith) *hld up on ins: effrt and swtchd lft over 1f out: kpt on fnl f: nvr able to chal* **20/1**
4-25 **7** nk **Caracal**[11] 3180 3-9-3 70.................... GregFairley 2 62
(M Johnston) *pressed ldr tl rdn and wknd over 1f out* **12/1**
0240 **8** shd **Anthemion (IRE)**[11] 3147 13-8-9 51 oh4.................... AndrewMullen 4 44
(Mrs J C McGregor) *led to over 1f out: sn rdn and wknd* **33/1**
0005 **9** 3 1/4 **Primo Way**[11] 3147 9-8-4 51 oh6.................... JamesSullivan(5) 5 37
(D A Nolan) *towards rr on outside: struggling over 2f out: sn btn* **66/1**

1m 56.44s (-3.26) **Going Correction** -0.275s/f (Firm)
WFA 3 from 4yo+ 11lb 9 Ran SP% **112.8**
Speed ratings (Par 103): **103,100,99,99,99 96,96,95,93**
toteswingers:1&2:£4.50, 1&3:£9.60 , 2&3:£18.50 CSF £17.17 CT £554.55 TOTE £1.70: £1.02, £6.20, £12.00; EX 16.80.
Owner David W Armstrong **Bred** D W Armstrong **Trained** Musley Bank, N Yorks

FOCUS
An ordinary handicap, run at a fair pace. The form seems sound overall.

3532 RACING UK SKY 432 H'CAP 1m 4f 17y
4:15 (4:15) (Class 6) (0-65,65) 3-Y-O £2,266 (£674; £337; £168) **Stalls** High

Form RPR
-632 **1** **Dubawi King**[20] 2853 3-8-8 52.................... PaulHanagan 4 57+
(N Tinkler) *hld up: drvn and outpcd over 3f out: plenty to do over 2f out: hung lft u.p: str run fr over 1f out: led towards fin* **2/1**[1]
1446 **2** nk **Vittachi**[26] 2673 3-8-9 53.................... TomEaves 5 57
(A C Whillans) *cl up: led over 2f out: sn rdn: kpt on fnl f: hdd towards fin* **20/1**
6200 **3** 2 **Il Portico**[19] 2909 3-8-13 57.................... SamHitchcott 8 57
(M R Channon) *prom: effrt over 2f out: kpt on same pce ins fnl f* **11/1**
424 **4** hd **Cat O' Nine Tails**[25] 2697 3-9-7 65.................... GregFairley 9 65
(M Johnston) *chsd ldr: lft in ld home bnd over 5f out: hdd over 2f out: rallied: no ex ins fnl f* **5/1**[3]
6005 **5** 2 **Light The City (IRE)**[11] 3153 3-7-13 46 oh1............ KellyHarrison(3) 3 43
(Mrs R A Carr) *hld up towards rr: effrt over 2f out: no imp fr over 1f out* **40/1**
6401 **6** 3 1/2 **Smarty Sam (USA)**[11] 3153 3-9-7 65.................... PJMcDonald 10 56
(G A Swinbank) *prom: effrt over 2f out: wknd appr fnl f* **3/1**[2]
0006 **7** 9 **Barastar**[11] 3153 3-8-2 46 oh1.................... SilvestreDeSousa 1 23
(N Tinkler) *hld up: drvn and outpcd over 3f out: nvr able to chal* **33/1**
0-00 **8** 1 **Star Of Kalani (IRE)**[20] 2853 3-7-11 46 oh1............(b) PaulPickard(5) 2 21
(R D Wylie) *t.k.h: hld up on outside: rdn and wandered 3f out: nvr on terms* **6/1**
66U0 **9** 18 **On The Right Path**[28] 2627 3-8-3 52.................... PatrickDonaghy(5) 7 —
(Paul Murphy) *led tl hung bdly lft and hdd home bnd over 5f out: sn lost pl and eased* **100/1**

2m 36.34s (-2.26) **Going Correction** -0.275s/f (Firm) 9 Ran SP% **108.8**
Speed ratings (Par 97): **96,95,94,94,93 90,84,84,72**
toteswingers:1&2:£4.70, 1&3:£6.00, 2&3:£11.50 CSF £43.27 CT £311.53 TOTE £3.90: £2.20, £5.40, £2.00; EX 35.40.
Owner D Bloy & P Beecroft **Bred** Cliveden Stud Ltd **Trained** Langton, N Yorks

FOCUS
A weak 3-y-o handicap which looked sound run. The form is rated around those in the frame behind the winner.

3533 WEATHERBYS BETTRENDS WORLD CUP SERVICE H'CAP 5f 4y
4:45 (4:46) (Class 5) (0-75,70) 3-Y-O+ £2,914 (£867; £433; £216) **Stalls** Centre

Form RPR
0343 **1** **Distant Sun (USA)**[6] 3321 6-9-8 66.................... PhillipMakin 3 75
(Miss L A Perratt) *prom: effrt and hdwy to ld ent fnl f: edgd lft u.p: hld on wl* **7/2**[1]
0005 **2** hd **Tournedos (IRE)**[15] 3024 8-8-6 55....................(b) JamesSullivan(5) 2 63
(Mrs R A Carr) *hld up in tch: hdwy over 1f out: chsd wnr ins fnl f: r.o: jst hld* **9/2**[2]
106 **3** 2 3/4 **The Bear**[1] 3497 7-9-1 64.................... MichaelO'Connell(5) 1 62
(Miss L A Perratt) *rdr slow to remove blindfold: dwlt: sn prom: effrt and ev ch 1f out: kpt on same pce fnl f* **14/1**
4625 **4** 3/4 **Rothesay Dancer**[6] 3321 7-9-9 70.................... KellyHarrison(3) 4 66
(J S Goldie) *bhd and outpcd: hdwy ent fnl f: r.o: nvr able to chal* **7/1**
6-50 **5** 1 1/4 **Cayman Fox**[14] 3064 5-9-1 59....................(e) LeeVickers 5 50
(James Moffatt) *led to 1/2-way: cl up tl wknd ins fnl f* **11/2**[3]
3343 **6** 1 **Mandarin Spirit (IRE)**[5] 3356 10-9-8 66....................(b) TonyHamilton 7 54
(Miss L A Perratt) *hld up: rdn 1/2-way: no imp fnl f* **9/2**[2]
0221 **7** 4 1/2 **Wicked Wilma (IRE)**[5] 3356 6-9-6 69 6ex.................. MarkCoumbe(5) 6 40
(A Berry) *w ldrs: led 1/2-way to ent fnl f: sn wknd* **7/2**[1]

59.94 secs (-0.06) **Going Correction** +0.025s/f (Good) 7 Ran SP% **115.4**
Speed ratings (Par 103): **101,100,96,95,93 91,84**
toteswingers:1&2:£6.30, 1&3:£6.30, 2&3:£13.10 CSF £19.78 TOTE £4.30: £1.70, £5.00; EX 30.30.
Owner Ken McGarrity **Bred** Forging Oaks Llc **Trained** East Kilbride, South Lanarks

FOCUS
Plenty of track form on offer here. It was run at a furious pace, with the race developing down the centre of the track, but in the end, the first two ended up under the stands'-side rail. The winner is rated to last year's form.
Rothesay Dancer Official explanation: jockey said, regarding running and riding, that her orders were to ride the mare as normal, having ridden it many times, it is always well behind and usually creeps into the race at the end, but it didn't come down the hill well and became further behind than she would have liked.
Wicked Wilma(IRE) Official explanation: jockey said mare ran too free early stages

3534 FAMILY NIGHT WITH STARS FROM XFACTOR H'CAP 6f 5y
5:15 (5:15) (Class 6) (0-65,63) 3-Y-O+ £2,388 (£705; £352) **Stalls** Centre

Form RPR
-153 **1** **Ace Of Spies (IRE)**[12] 3120 5-10-0 63.................... SilvestreDeSousa 9 74
(G A Harker) *trckd ldrs: rdn to ld over 1f out: hung lft ins fnl f: drvn out* **11/2**[3]
4006 **2** 3/4 **Botham (USA)**[20] 2856 6-9-1 57.................... PaulNorton(7) 6 66
(J S Goldie) *bhd and sn outpcd: hdwy over 1f out: swtchd lft and styd on wl fnl f: nt rch wnr* **13/2**
0260 **3** 3/4 **Two Turtle Doves (IRE)**[20] 2854 4-9-7 56.................... AndrewElliott 5 62
(M Mullineaux) *trckd ldrs: rdn over 2f out: kpt on u.p ins fnl f* **5/1**[2]
3003 **4** 1/2 **Fathey (IRE)**[7] 3284 4-9-6 55.................... PhillipMakin 4 60
(C Smith) *prom: rdn over 2f out: kpt on same pce fnl f* **10/3**[1]
0354 **5** 1/2 **Monte Mayor One**[10] 3200 3-8-13 55.................... TonyHamilton 1 56
(P Monteith) *hld up: hdwy wl over 1f out: kpt on fnl f: nt pce to chal* **20/1**
-200 **6** 3/4 **Cross Of Lorraine (IRE)**[20] 2850 7-8-10 52............(b) LeeTopliss(7) 10 53
(J Wade) *led to over 1f out: sn no ex* **12/1**
0510 **7** 3/4 **Bateleur**[1] 3497 6-9-12 61.................... SamHitchcott 3 59
(M R Channon) *in tch: effrt over 1f out: wknd ins fnl f* **15/2**
4645 **8** 1 1/4 **Aqua Vitae (IRE)**[15] 3030 3-9-1 57.................... GregFairley 2 49
(M Johnston) *sn drvn towards rr: outpcd 1/2-way: n.d after* **8/1**
0-0 **9** 20 **Obe One**[5] 3357 10-8-5 45....................(b) PatrickDonaghy(5) 8 —
(A Berry) *dwlt: sn in tch: rdn over 2f out: sn wknd* **80/1**
-442 **10** 2 1/4 **Tongalooma**[29] 2581 4-9-4 53.................... LeeVickers 7 —
(James Moffatt) *missed break: t.k.h and in tch: rdn 2f out: sn btn* **17/2**

1m 12.11s (-0.09) **Going Correction** +0.025s/f (Good)
WFA 3 from 4yo+ 7lb 10 Ran SP% **115.6**
Speed ratings (Par 101): **101,100,99,98,97 96,95,94,67,64**
toteswingers:1&2:£9.10, 1&3:£7.30, 2&3:£8.90 CSF £40.75 CT £190.41 TOTE £5.80: £1.60, £1.50, £2.60; EX 38.70 Place 6 £19.87, Place 5 £17.55.
Owner A S Ward **Bred** Gainsborough Stud Management Ltd **Trained** Thirkleby, N Yorks

FOCUS
A furious gallop to this wide-open 6f handicap. The winner is rated back towards his best early form.
Tongalooma Official explanation: jockey said filly stopped quickly
T/Plt: £68.00 to a £1 stake. Pool:£49,958.57 - 535.75 winning tickets T/Qpdt: £66.30 to a £1 stake. Pool:£3,288.28 - 36.70 winning tickets RY

3058 THIRSK (L-H)
Tuesday, June 29

OFFICIAL GOING: Good to firm (9.6)
Wind: Light 1/2 behind Weather: Fine and sunny

3535 BETFAIR RACING EXCELLENCE APPRENTICE TRAINING SERIES H'CAP 2m
6:30 (6:30) (Class 6) (0-60,60) 4-Y-O+ £3,070 (£906; £453) **Stalls** Low

Form RPR
1113 **1** **Tillietudlem (FR)**[12] 3109 4-9-3 58.................... DebraEngland 6 68+
(J S Goldie) *w ldrs: upsides 8f out: led over 3f out: hdd over 2f out: styd on wl to ld last 50yds* **1/1**[1]
6002 **2** 1/2 **Hi Dancer**[5] 3352 7-8-12 60.................... GerardGalligan(7) 2 69
(B M R Haslam) *bmpd s: trckd ldrs: led over 2f out: hung lft: hdd and no ex towards fin* **7/2**[2]
3220 **3** 4 **Amir Pasha (UAE)**[12] 3122 5-9-0 58....................(v) AdamCarter(3) 1 62
(Micky Hammond) *wnt rt s: led 1f: t.k.h: trckd ldrs: wnt 3rd over 2f out: one pce* **9/2**[3]
0333 **4** 8 **Without Equal**[13] 3078 4-8-4 48.................... SoniaEaton(3) 7 43
(A Dickman) *s.s: hld up towards rr: effrt over 3f out: nvr nr ldrs* **8/1**
-160 **5** 4 **Spruzzo**[27] 2659 4-8-9 50.................... DaleSwift 8 40
(C W Thornton) *led after 1f: hdd over 3f out: lost pl over 1f out* **12/1**

0-00 6 1 3/4 **Mceldowney**[12] 3122 8-8-0 **46** oh1 ....(p) HobieGill(5) 5 34
(M C Chapman) *sn in rr: drvn 7f out: nvr on terms* **50/1**

3m 33.07s (0.27) **Going Correction** -0.05s/f (Good) **6** Ran SP% **111.2**
Speed ratings (Par 101): **97,96,94,90,88 87**
toteswingers:1&2:£1.10, 1&3:£1.60, 2&3:£2.40 CSF £4.63 CT £9.33 TOTE £1.50: £1.10, £2.80; EX 5.50.
Owner Mr & Mrs C J Smith **Bred** Bernard Ducasse **Trained** Uplawmoor, E Renfrews
■ Without Equal was Allan Dickman's final runner as a trainer.
■ Stewards' Enquiry : Hobie Gill caution: used whip when out of contention

FOCUS
Following 6mm of recent rain, the ground was officially described as good to firm with a GoingStick reading of 9.6. Only two horses really counted, but they are reasonably types for the grade, particularly the winner, who looks better than the bare form. The second looks the best guide. The pace was modest for the first mile or so.

3536 EBF BUCK INN THORNTON WATLASS MAIDEN STKS 6f
7:00 (7:00) (Class 5) 2-Y-O **£4,209** (£1,252; £625; £312) **Stalls** High

Form RPR

00 1 **Lizzie (IRE)**[10] 3204 2-8-12 0 ....(b1) GrahamGibbons 6 73+
(T D Easterby) *in rr: gd hdwy over 1f out: led jst ins fnl f: sn clr* **11/2**

332 2 2 **Battle Of Britain**[14] 3053 2-9-3 0 ....(v1) AhmedAjtebi 1 69
(Mahmood Al Zarooni) *led after 2f and sn qcknd: rdn over 1f out: hdd and fnd little jst ins fnl f* **1/1**[1]

0 3 2 1/2 **Volcanic Ash (USA)**[12] 3118 2-9-3 0 .... JoeFanning 5 62
(M Johnston) *s.i.s: hdwy to chse ldrs after 2f: drvn over 2f out: kpt on same pce appr fnl f* **4/1**[3]

0 4 2 1/2 **Bernisdale**[21] 2832 2-8-12 0 .... RoystonFfrench 7 49
(G M Moore) *in rr: swtchd lft over 1f out: styd on fnl 100yds* **50/1**

0 5 1/2 **Guinea Seeker**[66] 1517 2-8-12 0 .... LanceBetts(5) 3 53
(T D Easterby) *chsd ldrs: drvn over 2f out: wknd fnl f* **50/1**

6 1 3/4 **Sleights Boy (IRE)** 2-9-3 0 .... PatrickMathers 4 47
(I W McInnes) *s.i.s: effrt on outside over 2f out: nvr nr ldrs* **40/1**

7 2 3/4 **Irelandisuperman** 2-9-3 0 .... AdrianNicholls 2 39
(D Nicholls) *led 2f: drvn over 2f out: lost pl over 1f out* **7/2**[2]

0 8 6 **Pinotage**[31] 2522 2-9-0 0 .... MichaelStainton(3) 8 21
(R M Whitaker) *s.i.s: a outpcd and bhd* **40/1**

1m 12.59s (-0.11) **Going Correction** -0.05s/f (Good) **8** Ran SP% **116.4**
Speed ratings (Par 93): **98,95,92,88,88 85,82,74**
toteswingers:1&2:£2.30, 1&3:£3.10, 2&3:£1.60 CSF £11.62 TOTE £11.20: £3.10, £1.10, £1.10; EX 16.20.
Owner Mrs Jean P Connew **Bred** L Mulryan **Trained** Great Habton, N Yorks

FOCUS
An ordinary juvenile maiden run at a strong pace and the runner-up sets the level. The winner improved in the blinkers.

NOTEBOOK
Lizzie(IRE) benefited considerably from the combination of a step up in trip and fitting of blinkers for the first time. The decent gallop also suited and she stayed on well to win tidily after getting behind early on. She should make a fair nursery type. (op 11-1)
Battle Of Britain, fitted with a visor for the first time, showed good speed to lead against the near rail having started from the widest draw, and he had most of these in trouble by about halfway. However, he carried his head high throughout and found the winner too strong. Despite being a half-brother to French Derby winner Lawman, he shapes as though a drop back to 5f may suit, and there ought to be a race in him, but he makes no appeal as one to follow. (op 8-11 tchd 4-6)
Volcanic Ash(USA) improved significantly on his debut effort and should come on again for this. He gradually recovered from a sluggish start, but didn't see his race out and is still learning. (op 6-1)
Bernisdale made encouraging late headway and this was a major improvement on her first outing. There should be more to come. (op 40-1)
Guinea Seeker, gelded since his only previous start over two months earlier, could make no impression but this was still an improvement. He should progress again but may be more of a nursery or handicap type. (op 66-1)
Sleights Boy(IRE), already gelded, missed the break and was never involved, but he made moderate late progress. (op 50-1)
Irelandisuperman, another already gelded, was supported in the market but dropped out after showing early speed and looked to find the ground quicker than ideal. (op 3-1 tchd 5-1)

3537 CARLETON FURNITURE H'CAP 1m
7:30 (7:30) (Class 4) (0-85,83) 3-Y-O+ **£5,180** (£1,541; £770; £384) **Stalls** Low

Form RPR

6041 1 **Reel Buddy Star**[4] 3408 5-9-10 **79** 6ex .... TomEaves 1 87
(G M Moore) *led after 1f: rdn 3f out: edgd rt fnl f: hld on gamely* **11/4**[1]

0003 2 3/4 **Moheebb (IRE)**[10] 3206 6-9-13 **82** ....(b) PaulHanagan 7 88+
(Mrs R A Carr) *mid-div: effrt on outer over 2f out: hung lft: styd on wl fnl f* **5/1**[3]

1365 3 1 1/2 **Come And Go (UAE)**[11] 3150 4-9-10 **79** .... PJMcDonald 6 82
(G A Swinbank) *trckd ldng pair: t.k.h: styd on same pce fnl f* **7/1**

5354 4 1 1/2 **Observatory Star (IRE)**[10] 3206 7-9-6 **75** ....(tp) FrannyNorton 2 74
(T D Easterby) *trckd ldrs: effrt on ins 3f out: kpt on same pce fnl f* **7/2**[2]

2504 5 1 **Just Bond (IRE)**[4] 3408 8-9-11 **83** .... BarryMcHugh(3) 5 80
(G R Oldroyd) *dwlt: t.k.h in rr: hung rt over 2f out: styd on fnl f* **11/1**

-142 6 1 **Turn Me On (IRE)**[25] 2696 7-10-0 **83** .... GrahamGibbons 9 78
(T D Walford) *hld up in rr: effrt over 3f out: kpt on fnl 2f: nvr a threat* **16/1**

024- 7 shd **Fantastic Strike (IRE)**[295] 5715 3-8-7 **72** .... JoeFanning 3 65
(M Johnston) *dwlt: t.k.h in midfield: drvn along over 4f out: styd on wl last 150yds* **17/2**

-633 8 1 **Kings Point (IRE)**[11] 3180 9-9-3 **72** .... AdrianNicholls 4 64
(D Nicholls) *led 1f: chsd wnr: wknd fnl f* **9/1**

1m 38.76s (-1.34) **Going Correction** -0.05s/f (Good)
WFA 3 from 4yo+ 10lb **8** Ran SP% **112.8**
Speed ratings (Par 105): **104,103,101,100,99 98,98,97**
toteswingers:1&2:£4.40, 1&3:£6.80, 2&3:£8.40 CSF £16.21 CT £85.09 TOTE £3.30: £1.10, £3.00, £2.00; EX 13.80.
Owner J W Armstrong & M J Howarth **Bred** M Pennell **Trained** Middleham Moor, N Yorks

FOCUS
A fair handicap in which the winner showed his Newcastle win didn't flatter him.

3538 BLACK SHEEP BREWERY H'CAP 1m
8:00 (8:02) (Class 6) (0-55,55) 3-Y-O+ **£3,070** (£906; £453) **Stalls** Low

Form RPR

-032 1 **Rascal In The Mix (USA)**[9] 3238 4-8-12 **52** ....(p) AmyRyan(5) 5 61+
(R M Whitaker) *s.i.s: mid-div: hdwy on outside over 2f out: hung bdly lft and led over 1f out: hld on towards fin* **5/1**[2]

5640 2 1/2 **Green Agenda**[20] 2859 4-9-6 **55** .... JoeFanning 9 62
(M Johnston) *chsd ldrs: kpt on wl ins fnl f: no ex nr fin* **9/2**[1]

5060 3 nse **Champain Sands (IRE)**[4] 3391 11-8-13 **53** .... PaulPickard(5) 13 60+
(E J Alston) *s.i.s: in rr: hdwy on outside and hung lft over 1f out: edgd lft and styd on wl ins fnl f* **12/1**

0002 4 3/4 **Mississippian (IRE)**[12] 3124 6-9-1 **50** .... DuranFentiman 11 55
(Mrs D J Sanderson) *chsd ldrs: kpt on same pce fnl f* **14/1**

-302 5 1/2 **One Scoop Or Two**[12] 3132 4-9-2 **51** .... GrahamGibbons 4 55
(R Hollinshead) *in rr: hdwy on inner over 2f out: chsng ldrs 1f out: kpt on same pce* **6/1**[3]

53-0 6 1 1/2 **Emperor's Well**[1] 3520 11-8-9 **49** .... JamesSullivan(5) 6 50
(M W Easterby) *s.i.s: hdwy on outer over 2f out: one pce fnl f* **9/1**

-440 7 2 1/2 **Fyodorovich (USA)**[36] 2381 5-8-8 **46** oh1 ....(v) BarryMcHugh(3) 7 41
(J S Wainwright) *in rr: effrt on outer over 2f out: n.m.r over 1f out: kpt on: nvr rchd ldrs* **9/1**

0605 8 2 1/4 **Kheskianto (IRE)**[12] 3120 4-8-10 **50** .... MarkCoumbe(5) 2 40
(M C Chapman) *prom: effrt over 2f out: one pce* **40/1**

00-3 9 3/4 **Needy McCredie**[13] 3086 4-9-2 **51** .... PaddyAspell 8 39
(J R Turner) *led after 1f: hdd over 2f out: wknd fnl f* **28/1**

3400 10 1 1/4 **Dream Express (IRE)**[29] 2589 5-9-4 **53** .... PaulHanagan 14 38
(D W Thompson) *led 1f: chsd ldrs: led over 2f out: hdd over 1f out: sn wknd* **20/1**

4360 11 2 **Cool Art (IRE)**[14] 3062 4-9-1 **50** ....(p) RoystonFfrench 1 30
(J S Wainwright) *chsd ldrs: wknd over 1f out* **18/1**

0066 12 shd **Redwater River**[25] 2699 6-8-10 **50** ....(b) DeanHeslop(5) 16 30
(Mrs R A Carr) *chsd ldrs: wknd over 1f out* **25/1**

604- 13 3 1/2 **There We Go (IRE)**[332] 4531 4-8-11 **46** oh1 .... PJMcDonald 3 18
(G A Swinbank) *s.i.s: a in rr* **10/1**

14 nk **Suor Angelica (IRE)**[180] 5-8-6 **46** oh1 .... MatthewDavies(5) 15 17
(George Baker) *swtchd lft after s: a in rr* **20/1**

0-40 15 1/2 **Karate Queen**[20] 2854 5-8-11 **46** oh1 .... PatrickMathers 10 16
(R E Barr) *in rr: effrt on outer over 2f out: sn btn* **40/1**

1m 39.66s (-0.44) **Going Correction** -0.05s/f (Good) **15** Ran SP% **119.5**
Speed ratings (Par 101): **100,99,99,98,98 96,94,91,91,89 87,87,84,84,83**
toteswingers:1&2:£5.30, 1&3:£23.60 , 2&3:£16.90 CSF £24.62 CT £263.79 TOTE £4.60: £2.60, £1.60, £6.10; EX 25.40.
Owner One-Six-One Partnership **Bred** Robert Hunter **Trained** Scarcroft, W Yorks

FOCUS
A moderate but reasonably competitive handicap, and they seemed to go a decent enough pace. There was a bunch finish but the form does look sound.

3539 WHITE SWAN AMPLEFORTH H'CAP 7f
8:30 (8:31) (Class 5) (0-75,75) 3-Y-O+ **£3,885** (£1,156; £577; £288) **Stalls** Low

Form RPR

/020 1 **Chambers (IRE)**[4] 3396 4-8-8 **55** .... PaulPickard(5) 7 62
(E J Alston) *led: qcknd clr bnd over 4f out: hmpd by loose horse and swtchd rt over 1f out: jst hld on* **6/1**

0-10 2 nk **Loveinthesand (IRE)**[59] 1709 3-9-7 **72** .... JoeFanning 5 75+
(M Johnston) *chsd ldrs: outpcd and lost pl over 4f out: hung lft and swtchd outside over 1f out: styd on wl: nt quite rch wnr* **8/1**

2335 3 1/2 **High Importance (USA)**[10] 3212 3-9-7 **72** ....(v) PaulHanagan 6 74
(J Noseda) *trckd ldr: t.k.h: drvn 3f out: styd on fnl f* **13/8**[1]

2120 4 1/2 **Spin Again (IRE)**[14] 3061 5-9-10 **66** .... AdrianNicholls 2 69
(D Nicholls) *hld up in rr: hdwy over 3f out: styd on same pce fnl f* **8/1**

1442 5 9 **Nufoudh (IRE)**[11] 3164 6-9-12 **68** .... AndrewMullen 8 47
(Miss Tracy Waggott) *rrd and stmbld s: in rr: hdwy u.p over 2f out: wknd over 1f out: eased nr fin* **4/1**[2]

0233 U **Antarctic Desert (IRE)**[11] 3148 3-9-7 **72** .... TomEaves 3 —
(K A Ryan) *lunged and uns rdr s* **5/1**[3]

1m 27.24s (0.04) **Going Correction** -0.05s/f (Good)
WFA 3 from 4yo+ 9lb **6** Ran SP% **111.3**
Speed ratings (Par 103): **97,96,96,95,85** —
toteswingers:1&2:£6.40, 1&3:£2.80, 2&3:£3.10 CSF £48.82 CT £109.05 TOTE £7.10: £3.70, £3.90; EX 64.80.
Owner Geoff & Astrid Long **Bred** Darley **Trained** Longton, Lancs

FOCUS
This was a really messy race and the form needs treating with caution. First, Antarctic Desert unseated his rider with an awkward start, and independently Nufoudh nearly did exactly the same thing. In the latter stages the loose horse almost cost the winner the race, drifting slightly in his path late on and costing him momentum. The form is rated around the winner and third.
Nufoudh(IRE) Official explanation: jockey said gelding reared as stalls opened

3540 HELMSLEY CASTLE H'CAP 5f
9:00 (9:00) (Class 4) (0-85,84) 3-Y-O+ **£5,180** (£1,541; £770; £384) **Stalls** High

Form RPR

1U31 1 **Mey Blossom**[14] 3064 5-8-8 **69** .... MichaelStainton(3) 3 78
(R M Whitaker) *chsd ldrs: outpcd over 3f out: hdwy 2f out: led jst ins fnl f: r.o wl* **15/8**[1]

5166 2 1 **Mullglen**[28] 2626 4-9-2 **74** ....(tp) GrahamGibbons 6 79
(T D Easterby) *hld up: effrt over 2f out: nt clr run and edgd lft over 1f out: edgd rt and styd on to chse wnr ins fnl f: no imp* **10/3**[2]

1260 3 1 **Sir Geoffrey (IRE)**[28] 2622 4-9-2 **74** ....(b) PaulHanagan 2 76
(J A Glover) *wnt lft s: sn chsng ldrs: drvn over 2f out: kpt on same pce fnl f* **7/2**[3]

-000 4 1/2 **Secret Venue**[25] 2695 4-8-9 **67** .... TonyHamilton 4 67
(Jedd O'Keeffe) *led: hdd and sltly hmpd jst ins fnl f: no ex* **8/1**

4050 5 nk **Lucky Art (USA)**[12] 3119 4-8-2 **65** .... JamesSullivan(5) 5 64
(Mrs R A Carr) *chsd ldr: kpt on same pce appr fnl f* **4/1**

58.48 secs (-1.12) **Going Correction** -0.05s/f (Good) **5** Ran SP% **111.2**
Speed ratings (Par 105): **106,104,102,102,101**
toteswingers: 1&2:£6.90 CSF £8.46 TOTE £2.50: £2.00, £1.20; EX 9.20 Place 6 £32.71, Place 5 £27.36..
Owner Waz Developments Ltd **Bred** Hellwood Stud Farm **Trained** Scarcroft, W Yorks

FOCUS
Only five runners, but a fair little sprint handicap. Straightforward form.

T/Plt: £104.70 to a £1 stake. Pool £59,123.00 - 411.89 winning tickets T/Qpdt: £34.90 to a £1 stake. Pool £4,873.91 -103.15 winning tickets. WG

[2693] CATTERICK (L-H)

Wednesday, June 30

OFFICIAL GOING: Good to firm (8.7)

Wind: Virtually nil Weather: Fine and dry

3549 EUROPEAN BREEDERS' FUND MAIDEN FILLIES' STKS 5f
2:30 (2:31) (Class 5) 2-Y-O £3,302 (£982; £491; £245) Stalls Low

Form RPR

202 1 **Orchid Street (USA)**[26] [2693] 2-8-11 0 .... BarryMcHugh(3) 7 76+
(Mrs A Duffield) *cl up: led 1/2-way: rdn and qcknd clr over 1f out: comf* **7/4**[1]

53 2 3 **Lady Kildare (IRE)**[26] [2693] 2-8-9 0 .... PatrickDonaghy(5) 9 65
(Jedd O'Keeffe) *trckd ldrs: hdwy to chse wnr over 2f out: rdn over 1f out: kpt on same pce* **11/2**[3]

3 2 3/4 **Normandy Maid** 2-9-0 0 .... PaulHanagan 6 55
(R A Fahey) *in tch: hdwy 2f out: sn pushed along and styd on ins fnl f: tk 3rd nr line* **6/1**

5 4 hd **Empress Royal**[54] [1879] 2-9-0 0 .... PhillipMakin 10 55
(M Dods) *dwlt: hdwy on outer to chse ldrs 1/2-way: rdn wl over 1f out: sn edgd lft and kpt on same pce: lost 3rd nr line* **17/2**

0 5 4 1/2 **Royal Hush**[46] [2130] 2-9-0 0 .... FrannyNorton 4 42+
(K A Ryan) *dwlt and in rr: swtchd rt and hdwy over 1f out: sme hdwy ins fnl f* **9/2**[2]

6 2 3/4 **Holy Arrangement (IRE)** 2-9-0 0 .... StephenCraine 3 28
(Patrick Morris) *chsd ldrs on inner: rdn along over 2f out: sn wknd* **40/1**

5 7 1 1/4 **Tancred Spirit**[40] [2272] 2-9-0 0 .... TonyHamilton 8 24
(P T Midgley) *led: rdn along and hdd 1/2-way: sn wknd* **16/1**

420 P **Miserere (IRE)**[35] [2436] 2-9-0 0 .... PJMcDonald 2 —
(J S Wainwright) *in tch whn p.u injured after 2f: fatally injured* **9/1**

59.12 secs (-0.68) **Going Correction** -0.225s/f (Firm) 8 Ran SP% **113.1**
Speed ratings (Par 90): **96,91,86,86,79 74,72,—**
toteswingers: 1&2 £2.80, 1&3 £2.90, 2&3 £5.20 CSF £11.31 TOTE £3.00: £1.80, £1.10, £2.90; EX 8.30 Trifecta £16.80 Pool: £362.23 - 15.92 winning units..
Owner David & Carole McMahon **Bred** H Allen Poindexter **Trained** Constable Burton, N Yorks

FOCUS
A fair fillies' maiden which was dominated by those with experience. The fourth is among those to help with the standard.

NOTEBOOK
Orchid Street(USA) was just beaten here at the beginning of the month when Lady Kildare was close behind. However, ridden more positively this time by the winning rider that day, she was sent to the front a good way from home and galloped on strongly to the line. She should be competitive in nurseries and gives the impression another furlong would not be beyond her. (tchd 15-8 and 2-1 in a place)
Lady Kildare(IRE), who got involved in a duel for the lead when behind today's winner here last time, was ridden more patiently this time. However, she could not go with her old rival when she went for home. She has been behind that filly on all three starts, and connections will be hoping to avoid her in nurseries, for which she also qualifies. (op 5-1 tchd 9-2)
Normandy Maid, from the family of smart sprinters Corrybrough and Artie amongst others, was making her debut and showed ability, chasing the pace and keeping on steadily under pressure. She should get another furlong and will be better for the experience.
Empress Royal was backed late and stepped up on her debut effort. She was drawn on the outside which did not help, and can be expected to build on this again next time. (op 12-1)
Royal Hush got upset at the start before her debut and had a handler at the start this time. She behaved much better but missed the break slightly before staying on nicely in the closing stages. (op 5-1)
Holy Arrangement(IRE) showed some early pace on this debut.
Tancred Spirit took them along before fading and does not appear to be getting home in her races. (op 18-1 tchd 20-1)

3550 YORKSHIRE4X4.COM ADVENTURE ACTIVITIES MEDIAN AUCTION MAIDEN STKS 5f 212y
3:00 (3:01) (Class 5) 2-Y-O £2,331 (£693; £259; £259) Stalls Low

Form RPR

433 1 **Local Singer (IRE)**[11] [3222] 2-9-3 0 .... SamHitchcott 2 79
(M R Channon) *cl up: rdn along over 2f out: styd on to ld ent fnl f: sn drvn and edgd lft: kpt on wl* **5/2**[2]

3 2 1 **Cathedral Spires**[18] [2980] 2-9-3 0 .... PhillipMakin 1 76
(J Howard Johnson) *sn led on inner and set str pce: rdn along wl over 1f out: drvn and hdd ent fnl f: kpt on u.p: n.m.r towards fin* **5/4**[1]

4 3 2 1/2 **Intrusion**[11] [3204] 2-8-12 0 .... PaulHanagan 5 63
(R A Fahey) *chsd ldrs: rdn along 3f out: drvn over 1f out: kpt on ins fnl f* **7/2**[3]

46 3 dht **Hortensis**[14] [3087] 2-8-7 0 .... LanceBetts(5) 6 63
(T D Easterby) *trckd ldrs on inner: hdwy 2f out: rdn to chse ldng pair over 1f out: sn drvn and kpt on same pce* **25/1**

5623 5 1/2 **No Poppy (IRE)**[8] [3295] 2-8-12 0 ....(b) DavidAllan 8 62+
(T D Easterby) *racd wd: stdd after 1f: hdwy on outer over 2f out: sn rdn and kpt on appr fnl f: nrst fin* **15/2**

0 6 3 3/4 **Countess Cheval (IRE)**[13] [3118] 2-8-12 0 .... AndrewElliott 4 50
(B M R Haslam) *dwlt and in rr: rdn along 1/2-way: sme late hdwy* **100/1**

7 1/2 **Better Self** 2-8-12 0 .... StephenCraine 7 49
(Mrs A Duffield) *towards rr: effrt and sme hdwy over 2f out: sn rdn and wknd* **50/1**

8 2 3/4 **Grazeon Again (IRE)** 2-9-3 0 .... GrahamGibbons 9 46
(J J Quinn) *dwlt: sn rdn along and a in rr* **18/1**

9 1/2 **Better Offer (IRE)** 2-9-3 0 .... MickyFenton 3 44
(Miss Amy Weaver) *chsd ldng pair: rdn along 2f out: sn wknd* **66/1**

1m 13.53s (-0.07) **Going Correction** -0.225s/f (Firm) 9 Ran SP% **120.6**
Speed ratings (Par 93): **91,89,86,86,85 80,80,76,75**PL: Hortensis £2.30, Intrusion £1.30. toteswingers: 1&2 £2.10, 1&H £5.70, 1&I £1.50, 2&H £3.60, 2&I £1.50 TRI: Local Singer/Cathedral Spires/ Hortensia £49.90, LS/CP/Intrusion £11.90 CSF £6.24 TOTE £3.40: £1.10, £2.20; EX 7.70 TRIFECTA Pool: £375.66 - 2.727 Owner.

FOCUS
An ordinary median auction maiden that was dominated by the market leaders.

NOTEBOOK
Local Singer(IRE) did not appear to get home over an extra furlong last time and the drop back in distance here suited. He was never far away and proved too strong for the favourite in the last furlong. Nurseries await but much will depend on the mark he gets. (op 3-1)
Cathedral Spires was sent off favourite on the basis of his good effort in a York maiden on his debut. However, he was keen to post and the saddle slipped, which resulted in him overshooting the start. He was quite free in the race too, and made the running, but could not respond when challenged by the winner entering the last furlong. He can be given another chance. (op 7-4)
Intrusion ran pretty well on this step up in distance but was one paced in the closing stages and will appreciate even further in time. (op 4-1)
Hortensis has shown a fair measure of ability in all three starts now and kept on steadily having tracked the pace throughout. She could be of interest once competing in nurseries. (op 4-1)
No Poppy(IRE) was drawn towards the outside and proved too keen under restraint, not helping herself by running wide on the bend. She stayed on late and a return to a more conventional track should help. (op 6-1)
Countess Cheval(IRE) improved considerably on her debut effort but will need to do so again before she is competitive.
Better Offer(IRE) showed fair early pace on this first start before fading, and should improve for the experience.

3551 WE RACE AGAIN NEXT WEDNESDAY H'CAP 5f 212y
3:30 (3:30) (Class 4) (0-80,80) 3-Y-O+ £4,209 (£1,252; £625; £312) Stalls Low

Form RPR

-415 1 **Gap Princess (IRE)**[15] [3065] 6-9-7 73 .... SilvestreDeSousa 5 86
(G A Harker) *hld up in tch: hdwy on inner 2f out: rdn to ld jst ins fnl f: kpt on wl* **7/2**[1]

1013 2 2 1/2 **Sir Nod**[26] [2696] 8-9-11 77 .... PaulHanagan 4 82
(Julie Camacho) *led: rdn along over 2f out: edgd rt and drvn over 1f out: hdd jst ins fnl f: kpt on same pce* **8/1**

2303 3 3/4 **The Hermitage (IRE)**[6] [3361] 3-9-1 74 .... JoeFanning 8 75
(M Johnston) *cl up: rdn to chal 2f out: drvn over 1f out: kpt on same pce ins fnl f* **7/2**[1]

-011 4 nk **Arjemis**[14] [3076] 4-8-8 65 .... IanBrennan(5) 6 67
(C R Wilson) *hld up in rr: hdwy on outer 2f out: rdn wl over 1f out: kpt on u.p ins fnl f: nrst fin* **8/1**

3000 5 nk **Orpsie Boy (IRE)**[41] [2247] 7-9-10 76 .... PJMcDonald 1 77
(Mrs R A Carr) *in rr: hdwy on inner 2f out: sn rdn and kpt on ins fnl f: nrst fin* **9/2**[2]

0111 6 1 1/4 **Ryedane (IRE)**[16] [3026] 8-9-3 69 ....(b) DavidAllan 2 66
(T D Easterby) *chsd ldng pair: effrt over 2f out: swtchd rt wl over 1f out and sn rdn: drvn and wknd ent fnl f* **11/2**[3]

0540 7 nk **Baybshambles (IRE)**[23] [2818] 6-8-12 64 .... PatrickMathers 3 60
(R E Barr) *sn chsng ldrs: rdn along over 2f out: grad wknd* **14/1**

0-00 8 29 **Galpin Junior (USA)**[32] [2534] 4-10-0 80 .... AdrianNicholls 7 —
(D Nicholls) *chsd ldrs: rdn over 2f out: sn wknd and eased* **8/1**

1m 11.88s (-1.72) **Going Correction** -0.225s/f (Firm)
WFA 3 from 4yo+ 7lb 8 Ran SP% **118.0**
Speed ratings (Par 105): **102,98,97,97,96 95,94,56**
CSF £33.20 CT £106.92 TOTE £5.90: £1.40, £1.80, £1.90; EX 27.10 Trifecta £222.50 Pool: £ 303.78 - 1.01 winning units..
Owner Northumbria Leisure Ltd C H McGhie **Bred** D Veitch And Musagd Abo Salim **Trained** Thirkleby, N Yorks

FOCUS
A competitive-looking sprint handicap featuring several in-form sprinters, run faster than standard and 1.65secs quicker than the preceding juvenile maiden.

3552 BOOK RACEDAY HOSPITALITY ON 01748 810165 H'CAP 1m 3f 214y
4:00 (4:00) (Class 6) (0-65,65) 4-Y-O+ £2,047 (£604; £302) Stalls Low

Form RPR

2050 1 **Film Festival (USA)**[16] [2705] 7-8-13 64 .... DaleSwift(7) 3 76
(B Ellison) *trckd ldng pair: hdwy to chse ldr 5f out: rdn 2f out: drvn to chal wl over 1f out: styd on u.p ins fnl f to ld last 50yds* **5/1**[2]

-026 2 3/4 **Drop The Hammer**[34] [2464] 4-8-5 49 .... SilvestreDeSousa 2 60
(D O'Meara) *led: rdn along over 2f out: jnd and drvn over 1f out: hdd and no ex last 50yds* **9/2**[1]

6022 3 2 1/4 **Avitus**[12] [3177] 4-8-12 56 .... PhillipMakin 7 63
(Micky Hammond) *hld up towards rr: stdy hdwy over 3f out: rdn to chse ldrs 2f out: drvn over 1f out: kpt on same pce ins fnl f* **13/2**

/061 4 3 **Maneki Neko (IRE)**[13] [3122] 8-9-2 65 .... JamesSullivan(5) 6 67
(E W Tuer) *hld up in rr: hdwy over 3f out: rdn to chse ldrs 2f out: edgd lft and no imp appr fnl f* **5/1**[2]

-606 5 4 1/2 **Classic Contours (USA)**[30] [2277] 4-9-2 65 .... IanBrennan(5) 4 60
(J J Quinn) *trckd ldrs: effrt and hdwy over 3f out: rdn 2f out: sn drvn and wknd* **10/1**

5-02 6 1/2 **Castlebury (IRE)**[26] [2694] 5-9-5 63 ....(b) PJMcDonald 1 57
(G A Swinbank) *trckd ldrs on inner: hdwy over 4f out: rdn along 3f out: drvn over 2f out and sn wknd* **14/1**

5-34 7 3 1/4 **Trumpstoo (USA)**[13] [3122] 4-8-13 57 .... PaulHanagan 8 46
(R A Fahey) *hld up towards rr: rdn along over 4f out: nvr a factor* **11/2**[3]

3-52 8 21 **Noche De Reyes**[16] [3025] 5-8-9 53 ....(p) DavidAllan 10 9
(E J Alston) *cl up: rdn along 5f out: sn wknd* **9/2**[1]

0-40 9 30 **Kendalewood**[36] [2424] 4-8-13 57 ....(b[1]) GrahamGibbons 5 —
(T D Walford) *reminders s and sn prom: pushed along 1/2-way: rdn and wknd over 5f out: sn bhd* **50/1**

2m 33.76s (-5.14) **Going Correction** -0.225s/f (Firm) 9 Ran SP% **116.1**
Speed ratings (Par 101): **108,107,106,104,101 100,98,84,64**
toteswingers: 1&2 £5.80, 1&3 £10.60, 2&3 £5.20 CSF £27.95 CT £148.30 TOTE £8.40: £2.20, £1.90, £2.50; EX 34.90 Trifecta £114.10 Pool: £178.86 - 1.16 winning units..
Owner Koo's Racing Club **Bred** Jim Ryan And Geraldine Ryan **Trained** Norton, N Yorks

FOCUS
This very modest handicap was run at a decent pace but very few got into it.
Trumpstoo(USA) Official explanation: trainer had no explanation for the poor form shown
Noche De Reyes Official explanation: trainer said gelding was unsuited by the good to firm ground

3553 CATTERICKBRIDGE.CO.UK H'CAP 7f
4:30 (4:31) (Class 4) (0-80,79) 3-Y-O+ £4,209 (£1,252; £625; £312) Stalls Low

Form RPR

4425 1 **Nufoudh (IRE)**[1] [3539] 6-9-3 68 .... AndrewMullen 2 75
(Miss Tracy Waggott) *mde all: rdn over 2f out: drvn over 1f out: kpt on gamely u.p ins fnl f* **15/2**

3340 2 3/4 **Mandalay King (IRE)**[15] [3065] 5-8-11 67 .... IanBrennan(5) 6 72
(Mrs Marjorie Fife) *hld up and bhd: hdwy over 2f out: swtchd outside and rdn wl over 1f out: styd on strly ins fnl f* **8/1**

1004 3 hd **Malcheek (IRE)**[11] [3224] 8-9-12 77 .... DavidAllan 5 81
(T D Easterby) *prom: chsd wnr 2f out: drvn over 1f out: kpt on u.p ins fnl f* **17/2**

6305 4 nk **Frognal (IRE)**[5] [3409] 4-9-10 75 .... PJMcDonald 1 79
(Mrs R A Carr) *s.i.s and in rr: hdwy on outer over 2f out: rdn to chse ldrs over 1f out: drvn and edgd lft ins fnl f: kpt on* **5/1**[3]

2200 5 3/4 **Magic Omen (USA)**[25] [2762] 3-8-13 73 .... JoeFanning 3 72
(M Johnston) *chsd ldrs on inner: rdn along 2f out: drvn over 1f out: one pce whn n.m.r wl ins fnl f* **9/1**

2066 6 2 **Rio Cobolo (IRE)**[5] [3389] 4-9-1 71 ....(v) JamesSullivan(5) 8 67
(Paul Green) *hld up in tch: effrt and hdwy 2f out: rdn over 1f out and sn no imp* **7/2**[2]

0515 **7** ½ **Summer Dancer (IRE)**[13] 3107 6-10-0 **79**.......................... PhillipMakin 4 74
(P T Midgley) *trckd ldrs: effrt 2f out: sn rdn and wknd over 1f out* **8/1**

0205 **8** 11 **Glenridding**[5] 3391 6-9-4 **69**..(p) PaulHanagan 7 34
(J G Given) *chsd wnr: rdn along over 2f out: sn wknd and in rr whn eased over 1f out* **3/1**[1]

1m 25.13s (-1.87) **Going Correction** -0.225s/f (Firm)
WFA 3 from 4yo+ 9lb **8** Ran SP% **118.4**
Speed ratings (Par 105): **101,100,99,99,98 96,95,83**
toteswingers:1&2 £12.20, 2&3 £14.00, 1&3 £7.70 CSF £67.46 CT £529.53 TOTE £5.70: £2.20, £2.80, £3.80; EX 87.10 TRIFECTA Not won..
Owner H Conlon **Bred** Swordlestown Stud **Trained** Spennymoor, Co Durham

FOCUS
Another tight little handicap run at a sound gallop and it produced a good finish.
Glenridding Official explanation: jockey said gelding was unable to dominate

3554 ZETLAND MEDIAN AUCTION MAIDEN STKS 7f
5:00 (5:01) (Class 6) 3-4-Y-O **£2,047** (£604; £302) **Stalls** Low

Form				RPR
0	**1**		**Barren Brook**[11] 3207 3-9-3 0..................... PhillipMakin 3 (M W Easterby) *trckd ldrs: smooth hdwy on outer over 1f out: qcknd to ld ins fnl f: sn clr* **15/2**[2]	74+
2-40	**2**	3	**Quite Sparky**[22] 2837 3-9-3 75..................... MickyFenton 5 (T P Tate) *led: rdn along over 2f out: drvn wl over 1f out: hdd ins fnl f: one pce* **5/4**[1]	66
003	**3**	hd	**Offspring**[14] 3091 3-8-12 62..................... DavidAllan 6 (T D Easterby) *cl up: effrt to chal over 2f out: sn rdn and ev ch tl drvn and one pce ins fnl f* **5/4**[1]	60
	4	3 ¼	**Spread Boy (IRE)** 3-9-3 0..................... PatrickMathers 2 (A Berry) *in rr and rdn along 1/2-way: sme late hdwy* **40/1**	56
0	**5**	4 ½	**Hairy Maclary**[12] 3176 3-8-12 0..................... LanceBetts(5) 1 (T D Easterby) *chsd ldng pair on inner: rdn along over 2f out: drvn wl over 1f out and sn wknd* **25/1**[3]	44
0	**6**	22	**Octaviana**[22] 2837 3-8-12 0..................... PaulHanagan 4 (E J Alston) *a in rr* **28/1**	—

1m 25.87s (-1.13) **Going Correction** -0.225s/f (Firm) **6** Ran SP% **110.4**
Speed ratings (Par 101): **97,93,93,89,84 59**
toteswingers:1&2 £1.90, 2&3 £1.10, 1&3 £2.20 CSF £16.97 TOTE £10.40: £2.90, £1.30; EX 25.40 Place 6: £37.39 Place 5: £25.08.
Owner David Scott **Bred** David Allan **Trained** Sheriff Hutton, N Yorks

FOCUS
An uncompetitive 3-y-o maiden run in a time 0.74secs slower than the preceding handicap.
T/Plt: £28.80 to a £1 stake. Pool: £52,458.37 - 1,328.92 winning tickets. T/Qpdt: £23.10 to a £1 stake. Pool: £2,766.81 - 88.45 winning tickets. JR

3254 CHEPSTOW (L-H)
Wednesday, June 30

OFFICIAL GOING: Good to firm
Wind: mild breeze Weather: fine and sunny

3555 E.B.F./LINDLEY GROUP MAIDEN STKS 6f 16y
6:40 (6:46) (Class 5) 2-Y-O **£3,238** (£963; £481; £240) **Stalls** High

Form				RPR
3	**1**		**Rossetti**[44] 2171 2-9-3 0..................... PatDobbs 3 (R Hannon) *trckd ldr: rdn to ld over 1f out: r.o wl* **10/3**[2]	74+
50	**2**	1 ¼	**Kyncraighe (IRE)**[27] 2680 2-8-10 0..................... AmyScott(7) 10 (Eve Johnson Houghton) *led: rdn and hdd over 1f out: kpt on but a being hld ins fnl f* **9/1**	70
	3	¾	**The Long Game** 2-9-0 0..................... Louis-PhilippeBeuzelin(3) 1 (B J Meehan) *little slow away: sn pushed along to be in tch: rdn over 2f out: swtchd lft ent fnl f: styd on* **13/2**[3]	68+
3	**4**	2 ½	**Mega Mount (IRE)**[13] 3126 2-9-3 0..................... JimCrowley 5 (R M Beckett) *trckd ldrs: effrt in cl 3rd over 2f out: kpt on same pce fr over 1f out* **11/8**[1]	61
	5	4	**Token Gift** 2-9-0 0..................... AndrewHeffernan(3) 4 (P D Evans) *s.i.s: towards rr: sme late prog: nvr trbld ldrs* **25/1**	49
	6	1 ¾	**Jack's Revenge (IRE)** 2-9-3 0..................... TonyCulhane 6 (George Baker) *s.i.s: towards rr: hung lft u.p over 2f out: wknd over 1f out* **14/1**	43
	7	nse	**Suave Character** 2-9-3 0..................... NeilChalmers 8 (M Blanshard) *broke wl: t.k.h early: trckd ldrs: pushed along whn losing pl over 3f out: nvr bk on terms: wknd ins fnl f* **66/1**	43
	8	2	**Shaabek (IRE)** 2-9-3 0..................... ChrisCatlin 7 (M R Channon) *s.i.s: a outpcd in rr* **12/1**	37
	9	10	**Dreams Of Glory** 2-9-3 0..................... GeorgeBaker 2 (R J Hodges) *chsd ldrs: edging lft whn pushed along 4f out: wknd 2f out* **33/1**	7+

1m 13.74s (1.74) **Going Correction** -0.15s/f (Firm) **9** Ran SP% **111.2**
Speed ratings (Par 93): **82,80,79,76,70 68,68,65,52**
toteswingers: 1&2 £5.40, 1&3 £2.40, 2&3 £5.50 CSF £30.91 TOTE £4.40: £1.40, £2.30, £1.70; EX 29.20.
Owner Geoff Howard-Spink **Bred** Bricklow Ltd **Trained** East Everleigh, Wilts

FOCUS
Probably just an ordinary maiden at best, with a number of these too green to do themselves justice. The form is rated around the fourth. It was run on good to firm ground which had been watered, and was perhaps not riding as quick as advertised.

NOTEBOOK
Rossetti was always up with the pace and settled better than he had when third of four on his debut over 5f at Leicester. Ridden to lead approaching the final furlong, he was always holding the runner-up. A light-framed colt, he may not have a great deal of improvement in him. (tchd 3-1 and 4-1)
Kyncraighe(IRE), the most experienced in the line-up having run twice before, represented last season's winning stable. Upped in trip, he was drawn closest to the stands' rail and made the running, but could not hold off the winner. He is eligible for nurseries now. (op 7-1)
The Long Game, whose connections won this two years ago with the smart Gallagher, is a speedily bred half-brother to several decent sprinters. Drawn widest of all and a bit slow to find his stride, he came through to chase the first two but lacked the pace to get to them. The experience will have sharpened him up, although on this evidence his big-race entries look somewhat optimistic. (op 9-1 tchd 6-1)
Mega Mount(IRE) was doing his best work at the finish on his Warwick debut and promised to be suited by the extra furlong, but after chasing the pace he faded inside the last. He might not have handled the track. (tchd 5-4 and 6-4)
Token Gift, a half-brother to three winning juveniles, missed the break and was under pressure a good way out before making modest late gains. (op 20-1)
Jack's Revenge(IRE) Official explanation: jockey said colt hung left-handed
Shaabek(IRE) was very slowly away and beat just one home, but gave the impression he can improve considerably on this, granted time and a stiffer test. (tchd 10-1)
Dreams Of Glory Official explanation: jockey said colt was unsuited by the track

3556 NESTLE PROFESSIONAL H'CAP 6f 16y
7:10 (7:13) (Class 6) (0-65,64) 3-Y-O+ **£2,266** (£674; £337; £168) **Stalls** High

Form				RPR
0422	**1**		**Bermondsey Bob (IRE)**[8] 3292 4-9-1 **55**..................... JackDean(3) 9 (J L Spearing) *a.p: rdn over 2f out: led ent fnl f: hrd pressed: jst hld on: all out* **3/1**[1]	62
3230	**2**	hd	**Cwmni**[41] 2246 4-9-6 **57**..................... DavidProbert 14 (B Palling) *s.i.s: towards rr: rdn and hdwy fr over 2f out: chsng ldrs whn edgd lft ent fnl f: r.o wl: jst failed* **8/1**[3]	63
0001	**3**	nk	**Blue Aura (IRE)**[9] 3254 7-9-5 **61** 6ex..................... DeanHeslop(5) 10 (B G Powell) *prom: led after 1f: rdn and hdd ent fnl f: kpt pressing wnr: no ex whn lost 2nd nr fin* **6/1**[2]	66
0003	**4**	1 ½	**Stamford Blue**[9] 3254 9-9-6 **57**..................... (b) LukeMorris 11 (R A Harris) *sn pushed along towards rr: rdn 3f out: nt clr run 2f out: sn swtchd rt and hdwy: r.o ins fnl f: nt rch ldrs* **9/1**	58
-025	**5**	nk	**The Name Is Frank**[9] 3255 5-9-9 **60**..................... (t) NeilChalmers 2 (Mark Gillard) *chsd ldrs: rdn over 3f out: kpt on same pce ins fnl f* **14/1**	60
04-0	**6**	½	**Northern Genes (AUS)**[8] 3291 4-8-13 **50**..................... JimmyQuinn 13 (M Appleby) *mid-div: effrt over 2f out: kpt on same pce ins fnl f* **20/1**	48
0540	**7**	1	**Avoncreek**[9] 3254 6-8-5 **45**..................... KellyHarrison(3) 5 (B P J Baugh) *s.i.s: sn pushed along towards rr: rdn over 2f out: stdy prog wl over 1f out: kpt on same pce ins fnl f* **14/1**	40
0-05	**8**	nk	**Charlietoo**[13] 3132 4-9-3 **54**..................... (p) SaleemGolam 7 (E G Bevan) *little slow away: mid-div: outpcd 3f out: styd on ins fnl f: nvr a threat* **33/1**	48
0-30	**9**	½	**Emiratesdotcom**[19] 2919 4-8-9 **49**..................... WilliamCarson(3) 3 (J M Bradley) *racd centre wdst of all fr over 3f out: nvr bttr than mid-div* **9/1**	41
0040	**10**	1	**Titus Gent**[9] 3254 5-9-8 **62**..................... Louis-PhilippeBeuzelin(3) 6 (R A Harris) *mid-div: pushed along over 4f out: rdn over 3f out: wknd ent fnl f* **22/1**	51
1036	**11**	½	**Plumage**[9] 3254 5-9-8 **64**..................... LeeNewnes(5) 4 (Miss Tor Sturgis) *mid-div: rdn over 3f out: wknd ins fnl f* **12/1**	51
0526	**12**	2 ¾	**Interchoice Star**[110] 869 5-9-10 **61**..................... ChrisCatlin 12 (R Hollinshead) *led for 1f: prom: rdn over 2f out: wknd over 1f out* **16/1**	40
-066	**13**	3 ½	**Connor's Choice**[15] 3056 5-9-7 **58**..................... GeorgeBaker 8 (Andrew Turnell) *mid-div: rdn over 3f out: wknd over 1f out* **12/1**	25
00-0	**14**	16	**Swirl Tango**[41] 2249 4-8-3 **45**..................... AshleyMorgan(5) 1 (F Jordan) *wnt sltly lft s: sn outpcd towards rr: wknd over 2f out* **100/1**	—

1m 11.81s (-0.19) **Going Correction** -0.15s/f (Firm) **14** Ran SP% **118.0**
Speed ratings (Par 101): **95,94,94,92,91 91,89,89,88,87 86,83,78,57**
toteswingers: 1&2 £5.70, 1&3 £3.40, 2&3 £6.30 CSF £24.39 CT £137.80 TOTE £3.80: £2.10, £2.20, £1.90; EX 17.80.
Owner A A Campbell **Bred** Pier House Stud **Trained** Kinnersley, Worcs

FOCUS
A very modest handicap but the form appears sound enough.

3557 JOHN SMITH'S NO NONSENSE (S) STKS 7f 16y
7:40 (7:41) (Class 6) 3-5-Y-O **£1,942** (£578; £288; £144) **Stalls** High

Form				RPR
5-54	**1**		**Invincible Prince (IRE)**[33] 2510 3-8-10 72..................... (b) JimCrowley 1 (R M Beckett) *trckd ldr in centre: led that gp over 2f out: sn rdn: overall ldr over 1f out: idled and drifted rt ins fnl f: fnd enough whn chal fnl 100yds* **15/8**[1]	58
4064	**2**	nk	**Lindoro**[23] 2808 5-9-2 77..................... WilliamCarson(3) 8 (M G Quinlan) *chsd ldrs on stands' side: rdn over 2f out: r.o and drifted lft ent fnl f: ev ch fnl 100yds: hld nr fin* **3/1**[2]	60
0242	**3**	3 ¾	**Liberty Trail (IRE)**[29] 2624 4-9-2 68..................... AndrewHeffernan(3) 5 (P D Evans) *overall ldr on stands' side: rdn over 2f out: hdd jst over 1f out: rallying whn squeezed out ins fnl f: no ch after* **7/2**[3]	53
5000	**4**	¾	**Daddy's Gift (IRE)**[23] 2823 4-9-0 67..................... PatDobbs 4 (R Hannon) *chsd ldrs in centre: rdn wl over 2f out: nvr gng pce to get on terms* **6/1**	43
00-0	**5**	1 ½	**Bewdley**[13] 3132 5-9-0 37..................... JimmyQuinn 10 (R E Peacock) *towards rr on stands' side: rdn wl over 2f out: sme late prog: nvr a factor* **66/1**	39
405-	**6**	1 ½	**We'Re Delighted**[14] 4941 5-9-5 66..................... (t) LukeMorris 3 (Michael Blake) *s.i.s: bhd and sn rdn in centre: hdwy into midfield over 3f out: no further imp fr over 1f out* **25/1**	40
00-0	**7**	6	**Doric Echo**[16] 3036 4-9-5 64..................... IanMongan 6 (C P Morlock) *sn swtchd to centre and led gp but prom overall: rdn over 3f out: wknd over 1f out* **33/1**	24
0-00	**8**	4 ½	**Rainsborough**[6] 3359 3-8-5 57..................... (p) SophieDoyle(5) 7 (S Curran) *s.i.s: a towards rr in centre* **33/1**	9
50	**9**	2 ¼	**Mujdy (IRE)**[23] 2812 3-9-1 0 ow10..........(p) GemmaGracey-Davison(5) 11 (Miss Z C Davison) *little slowly away: a towards rr in centre* **100/1**	13
0005	**10**	10	**Aroundthebay**[23] 2808 4-9-0 70..................... (p) ChrisCatlin 2 (H J L Dunlop) *chsd ldrs in centre gp tl wknd 2f out* **16/1**	—

1m 22.96s (-0.24) **Going Correction** -0.15s/f (Firm)
WFA 3 from 4yo+ 9lb **10** Ran SP% **114.4**
Speed ratings (Par 101): **95,94,90,89,87 86,79,74,71,60**
toteswingers:1&2 £2.10, 2&3 £3.20, 1&3 £2.60 CSF £7.08 TOTE £2.80: £1.70, £1.10, £1.30; EX 7.30.The winner was bought in for 6,500gns.
Owner R Roberts **Bred** Lady Legard & Sir Tatton Sykes **Trained** Whitsbury, Hants

FOCUS
Just a fair seller in which they split into two groups, with four racing near the stands' rail and the other seven down the centre. The pace was on the fence.

3558 SHIRE FOODS DOT COM H'CAP 1m 14y
8:10 (8:11) (Class 5) (0-75,75) 3-Y-O+ **£3,561** (£1,059; £529; £264) **Stalls** High

Form				RPR
10-6	**1**		**You've Been Mowed**[19] 2920 4-8-11 **61**..................... WilliamCarson(3) 8 (R J Price) *wnt sltly rt s: racd alone on stands' side: mde virtually all: r.o strly fr over 1f out: heavily eased towards fin* **15/2**	77
3340	**2**	5	**Yes Chef**[20] 2888 3-9-2 **73**..................... ChrisCatlin 5 (J Gallagher) *hmpd and snatched up s: hdwy to ld centre gp after 1f: overall prom: rdn 3f out: no ch w wnr fr over 1f out: edgd rt ins fnl f* **8/1**	74
-255	**3**	1 ½	**Advertise**[12] 3168 4-9-7 **68**..................... (p) DavidProbert 2 (A M Balding) *s.i.s: towards rr: rdn 4f out: hdwy 3f out: edgd rt: styd on ins fnl f: wnt 3rd nr fin: nvr threatened* **3/1**[1]	67

0000 **4** *hd* **Cheam Forever (USA)**[23] 2823 4-9-10 **71**............(v) RichardKingscote 1 70
(R Charlton) *led centre gp for over 1f: prom: rdn 3f out: kpt on same pce fnl 2f* **4/1**[2]

6000 **5** *3/4* **Aflaam (IRE)**[76] 1323 5-10-0 **75**........................... LukeMorris 7 72
(R A Harris) *jnd centre gp after 1f: mid-div: hdwy 3f out: sn rdn: wnt 3rd over 1f out: no ex ins fnl f* **16/1**

3140 **6** *8* **Magroom**[23] 2823 6-9-11 **72**........................... GeorgeBaker 3 50
(R J Hodges) *hld up in centre: rdn 3f out: nvr gng pce to get on terms: wknd ent fnl f* **5/1**[3]

05/0 **7** *2 1/2* **Acheekyone (IRE)**[39] 2339 7-9-11 **75**.......... Louis-PhilippeBeuzelin(3) 6 48
(B J Meehan) *mid-div of centre gp: effrt 3f out: wknd over 1f out* **7/1**

-650 **8** *4 1/2* **Cadeaux Fax**[37] 2383 5-8-11 **61** ow1.................. JamesMillman(3) 9 23
(B R Millman) *unruly befhand: s.i.s: sn swtchd to rr of centre gp: wknd over 3f out* **8/1**

150- **9** *5* **Lordship (IRE)**[230] 7350 6-9-10 **71**..................... VinceSlattery 4 22
(A W Carroll) *wnt rt s: sn prom in centre tl wknd qckly 4f out* **40/1**

1m 33.68s (-2.52) **Going Correction** -0.15s/f (Firm)
WFA 3 from 4yo+ 10lb **9** Ran SP% **116.5**
Speed ratings (Par 103): **106,101,99,99,98 90,88,83,78**
toteswingers: 1&2 £11.30, 1&3 £4.70, 2&3 £7.00 CSF £66.34 CT £221.83 TOTE £8.80: £2.50, £3.30, £1.80; EX 45.90.
Owner Mrs K Oseman **Bred** T E Pocock **Trained** Ullingswick, H'fords
■ Stewards' Enquiry : David Probert one-day ban: used whip with excessive frequency (Jul 14)

FOCUS
A fair handicap which saw a clear-cut winner. All bar the winner raced down the centre of the course.

3559 ROBERT MONDAVI H'CAP — 1m 2f 36y
8:40 (8:40) (Class 6) (0-65,65) 4-Y-O+ £2,266 (£674; £337; £168) Stalls Low

Form RPR

2605 **1** **Corrib (IRE)**[13] 3128 7-8-2 **46**........................(p) NeilChalmers 4 55
(B Palling) *plld hrd in midfield: nt clr run over 3f out: pushed along and hdwy fr over 2f out: cl 4th whn nt clr run ent fnl f: r.o whn gap appeared: led fnl stride* **16/1**

025- **2** *hd* **Urban Space**[284] 6116 4-9-3 **64**..................... WilliamCarson(3) 14 73
(J L Flint) *trckd ldrs: rdn to ld over 2f out: styd on u.p: hdd fnl stride* **9/1**

0602 **3** *1 1/4* **James Pollard (IRE)**[9] 3264 5-8-2 **46** oh1.................. JimmyQuinn 2 52
(B J Llewellyn) *hld up towards rr: hdwy fr 3f out: rdn over 2f out: chsd ldrs fr over 1f out: styd on* **16/1**

12-0 **4** *1/2* **Recalcitrant**[11] 3214 7-9-1 **59**..................... SaleemGolam 13 64
(S Dow) *plld hrd: prom: led over 4f out: rdn and hdd over 2f out: kpt pressing ldr: ev ch ent fnl f: no ex fnl 100yds* **8/1**[3]

0662 **5** *2 1/4* **Parc Des Princes (USA)**[7] 3314 4-9-7 **65**..............(v) DavidProbert 5 66
(A M Balding) *mid-div: hdwy 3f out: sn rdn: cl 3rd 2f out: styng on at same pce whn bmpd ent fnl f: no ex* **15/8**[1]

021 **6** *2 1/2* **Duneen Dream (USA)**[96] 995 5-8-2 **49**........... AndrewHeffernan(3) 10 45
(Mrs N S Evans) *t.k.h: trckd ldrs: rdn wl over 2f out: one pce fr over 1f out* **20/1**

5-00 **7** *1* **Transfer**[16] 3032 5-9-2 **60**..................... IanMongan 9 54
(C P Morlock) *hld up towards rr: stdy prog u.p fr over 2f out: nvr threatened ldrs* **8/1**[3]

3411 **8** *1 1/4* **King Zeal (IRE)**[20] 2902 6-8-12 **63**.................. JamesRogers(7) 6 54
(B D Leavy) *mid-div: effrt 3f out but unable to get on trems: fdd ins fnl f* **7/2**[2]

2204 **9** *5* **Great Bounder (CAN)**[18] 2955 4-8-10 **54**..............(p) JimCrowley 3 35
(Michael Blake) *led tl over 4f out: sn rdn: fdd fr over 2f out* **12/1**

06/0 **10** *1/2* **Royal Indulgence**[16] 3032 10-8-1 **48**........... Louis-PhilippeBeuzelin(3) 1 28
(W M Brisbourne) *dwlt bdly: detached tl jnd rr of gp after 3f: midfield u.p 4f out: wknd 2f out* **50/1**

11 *1* **Finzi Contini (FR)**[102] 6-9-0 **58**..................... ChrisCatlin 8 36
(Tim Vaughan) *s.i.s: sn in tch: rdn over 4f out: wknd over 2f out* **33/1**

0000 **12** *7* **Devon Diva**[57] 1797 4-7-9 **46** oh1.................. RichardRowe(7) 7 10
(M Hill) *stdd s: a towards rr* **80/1**

300- **13** *dist* **Rowaad**[302] 5549 5-8-2 **46**..................... LukeMorris 11 —
(A E Price) *plld hrd in tch: rdn over 4f out: wknd over 2f out: sn eased: virtually p.u* **66/1**

2m 8.65s (-1.95) **Going Correction** -0.15s/f (Firm) **13** Ran SP% **121.1**
Speed ratings (Par 101): **101,100,99,99,97 95,94,93,89,89 88,83,—**
toteswingers:1&2:£35.30, 2&3:£34.90, 1&3:£13.20 CSF £149.63 CT £2360.90 TOTE £25.60: £6.10, £3.90, £4.80; EX 127.70.
Owner Bryn Palling **Bred** Dr John Waldron **Trained** Tredodridge, Vale Of Glamorgan

FOCUS
A moderate handicap. It was run at a steady pace until they were in the home straight, and a number pulled hard as a consequence. Not form to take too seriously.

3560 COCA-COLA CLASSIC H'CAP — 1m 4f 23y
9:10 (9:11) (Class 6) (0-60,66) 4-Y-O+ £2,266 (£674; £337; £168) Stalls Low

Form RPR

-034 **1** **Shy**[16] 3040 5-9-0 **59**..................... JamesMillman(3) 5 68
(B R Millman) *trckd ldrs: led wl over 2f out: sn rdn: styd on strly: comf* **9/2**[2]

3036 **2** *2 1/2* **Party Palace**[13] 2363 6-8-5 **47**..................... JimmyQuinn 1 52
(H S Howe) *trckd ldr tl rdn 4f out: styd chsng ldrs: regained 2nd over 1f out: a being comf hld* **16/1**

0533 **3** *2 3/4* **Spinning Waters**[7] 3314 4-8-8 **50**..................(b) LukeMorris 4 51
(Eve Johnson Houghton) *mid-div: rdn and hdwy 3f out: styd on same pce: snatched 3rd line: nvr trbld ldng pair* **9/2**[2]

2043 **4** *nse* **Carter**[16] 3032 4-9-4 **60**..................... JimCrowley 3 61
(W M Brisbourne) *trckd ldrs: led over 4f out: rdn and hdd wl over 2f out: styd on same pce: lost 3rd line* **7/1**[3]

5-05 **5** *2* **Robbmaa (FR)**[20] 2199 5-7-13 **45** oh1..................(b[1]) SophieDoyle(5) 2 43
(A W Carroll) *mid-div: rdn over 3f out: little imp tl styd on ins fnl f* **66/1**

5466 **6** *3 1/4* **Swiss Art (IRE)**[20] 1995 4-9-0 **56**..................... ChrisCatlin 6 48
(Mrs A M Thorpe) *t.k.h in midfield: rdn 3f out: styd on same pce fnl 2f* **25/1**

330/ **7** *3* **Berry Hill Lass (IRE)**[25] 7667 6-8-10 **52**..................(v) TonyCulhane 7 39
(J G M O'Shea) *towards rr: rdn over 3f out: styd on past btn horses fnl 2f: nvr a factor* **50/1**

03-1 **8** *8* **Gulf President**[8] 3290 4-9-7 **66** 6ex..................... AndrewHeffernan(3) 8 41
(Tim Vaughan) *nvr travelling in rr: drvn and sme prog into midfield 4f out: wknd over 1f out* **6/4**[1]

3460 **9** *10* **Trysting Grove (IRE)**[13] 3128 9-8-4 **46** oh1..............(p) SaleemGolam 10 5
(E G Bevan) *s.i.s: a towards rr: eased ins fnl f* **14/1**

/00- **10** *13* **Croon**[46] 6584 8-9-4 **60**..................(b[1]) GeorgeBaker 9 —
(Andrew Turnell) *a towards rr: eased fr over 1f out* **33/1**

5050 **11** *6* **Silken Promise (USA)**[6] 3348 4-8-12 **54**..................(p) IanMongan 11 —
(T B P Coles) *led: swtchd to centre whn racd alone and hdd over 4f out: rdn 3f out: wknd 2f out: virtually p.u ins fnl f* **14/1**

2m 37.25s (-1.75) **Going Correction** -0.15s/f (Firm) **11** Ran SP% **118.3**
Speed ratings (Par 101): **99,97,95,95,94 91,89,84,77,69 65**
toteswingers:1&2 £8.00, 2&3 £10.70, 1&3 £4.60 CSF £71.26 CT £346.25 TOTE £4.70: £1.30, £3.80, £1.70; EX 68.70 Place 6: £145.73 Place 5: £62.43.
Owner Mrs Jenny Willment **Bred** Mrs Jenny Willment **Trained** Kentisbeare, Devon

FOCUS
A low-grade handicap, and not form to take too positively. The pace was ordinary and not many got into it.
Gulf President Official explanation: jockey said gelding never travelled
Croon Official explanation: jockey said gelding had no more to give
T/Plt: £242.00 to a £1 stake. Pool:£72,541.26 - 218.75 winning tickets. T/Qpdt: £54.70 to a £1 stake. Pool:£5,806.65 - 78.50 winning tickets. TM

3323 KEMPTON (A.W) (R-H)
Wednesday, June 30

OFFICIAL GOING: Standard
Wind: Light, half behind Weather: Fine, very warm

3561 DAY TIME, NIGHT TIME, GREAT TIME H'CAP — 5f (P)
6:20 (6:21) (Class 5) (0-75,75) 3-Y-O £2,590 (£770; £385; £192) Stalls High

Form RPR

0060 **1** **Boragh Jamal (IRE)**[2] 3515 3-8-9 **63**..................(b) MartinDwyer 6 71
(B J Meehan) *chsd ldng trio: prog to go 2nd over 1f out: rdn and narrow ld ins fnl f: asserted nr fin* **16/1**

2-00 **2** *nk* **La Fortunata**[11] 3211 3-8-13 **67**..................... AndreaAtzeni 1 74
(Mike Murphy) *swtg: fast away fr wd draw: led: rdn over 1f out: hdd ins fnl f: kpt on: hld nr fin* **12/1**

3113 **3** *1 1/4* **Boogie Waltzer**[6] 3350 3-9-1 **69**..................(t) RyanMoore 2 72
(S C Williams) *chsd ldng pair: cl up on inner over 1f out: nt qckn ent fnl f: kpt on* **9/4**[1]

5314 **4** *1 3/4* **Special Quality (USA)**[19] 2931 3-9-5 **73**..................... FrankieDettori 3 69
(R M H Cowell) *chsd ldr to over 1f out: grad fdd* **9/4**[1]

2120 **5** *hd* **Freddie's Girl (USA)**[105] 901 3-9-7 **75**..................... AdamKirby 4 70
(Stef Higgins) *lw: sn in 5th: outpcd by ldrs over 1f out: n.d after: keeping on at fin* **11/2**[2]

-056 **6** *1 1/2* **Valmina**[9] 3277 3-9-4 **72**..................(t) RichardHughes 7 62
(Andrew Turnell) *hld up in last pair: pushed along 2f out: no prog* **14/1**

3002 **7** *1 3/4* **Exceed Power**[30] 2584 3-8-1 **58**..................(b[1]) MartinLane(3) 5 42
(D M Simcock) *s.i.s: last early: prog to chse ldrs 1/2-way: wknd over 1f out* **8/1**[3]

0260 **8** *7* **Avonside (IRE)**[27] 2682 3-8-1 **60**..................... DeclanCannon(5) 8 19
(J J Bridger) *last and struggling after 2f: t.o* **14/1**

60.71 secs (0.21) **Going Correction** 0.0s/f (Stan) **8** Ran SP% **114.9**
Speed ratings (Par 99): **98,97,95,92,92 90,87,76**
toteswingers: 1&2 £24.60, 1&3 £9.00, 2&3 £7.00 CSF £188.08 CT £604.99 TOTE £22.70: £7.80, £3.70, £1.10; EX 173.30.
Owner Miceal Martin Sammon **Bred** James Burns And A Moynan **Trained** Manton, Wilts

FOCUS
There were some reasonable-quality performers in the line-up, so it was surprising that the prize should go to a runner with minimal form.
Boragh Jamal(IRE) Official explanation: trainer said, regarding apparent improvement in form, that the filly was better suited by the shorter distance.
Avonside(IRE) Official explanation: jockey said gelding was outpaced all the way

3562 EUROPEAN BREEDERS' FUND MAIDEN FILLIES' STKS — 7f (P)
6:50 (6:51) (Class 5) 2-Y-O £3,302 (£982; £491; £245) Stalls High

Form RPR

1 **Jaaryah (IRE)** 2-9-0 0..................... PhilipRobinson 5 85+
(M A Jarvis) *leggy: athletic: lw: nt that wl away: prog arnd field to chse ldrs 3f out: wnt 3rd 2f out: couple of reminders and clsd to ld last 150yds: r.o wl: promising* **5/1**[3]

2 *2* **Najoum (USA)** 2-9-0 0..................... FrankieDettori 8 80
(Saeed Bin Suroor) *w'like: athletic: led: shkn up 2f out: styd on wl but hdd and outpcd last 150yds* **9/4**[1]

24 **3** *1* **Jetfire**[14] 3082 2-9-0 0..................... RyanMoore 2 77
(P F I Cole) *leggy: spd fr wd draw to chse ldr: rdn to chal 2f out: hld and lost 2nd ent fnl f: styd on* **11/2**

66 **4** *3 1/4* **Byrony (IRE)**[44] 2163 2-8-11 0..................... PatrickHills(3) 10 69
(R Hannon) *w'like: str: in tch on inner: sme prog over 2f out: wnt 4th over 1f out: easily outpcd by ldng trio* **18/1**

3 **5** *2 1/4* **Paco Belle (IRE)**[12] 3156 2-9-0 0..................... RichardHughes 9 63
(R Hannon) *w'like: str: trckd ldng pair: shkn up over 2f out: sn lost 3rd: grad fdd* **4/1**[2]

6 *1* **Romantic Wish** 2-9-0 0..................... StevieDonohoe 12 61+
(R A Mills) *w'like: towards rr: effrt and n.m.r 1/2-way: 9th 2f out: styd on steadily ins fnl f* **66/1**

7 *1 1/4* **Huwayit (IRE)** 2-9-0 0..................... NeilCallan 14 60+
(C E Brittain) *w'like: leggy: bit bkwd: mostly in midfield on inner: briefly n.m.r over 3f out and over 2f out: no prog* **22/1**

6 **8** *1 1/2* **Sukhothai (USA)**[28] 2641 2-9-0 0..................... TomQueally 3 54
(H R A Cecil) *w'like: chsd ldrs: rdn over 2f out: sn wknd* **10/1**

9 *2* **Toms River Tess (IRE)** 2-9-0 0..................... SteveDrowne 7 49
(B W Hills) *unf: chsd ldrs on outer to 1/2-way: losing pl over 2f out: n.d after* **16/1**

10 *1 1/4* **Gay Gallivanter** 2-9-0 0..................... RobertHavlin 6 46+
(J H M Gosden) *w'like: dwlt: plld hrd early: hld up in rr: effrt and limited prog over 2f out: no hdwy over 1f out* **20/1**

11 *1* **Red Lite (IRE)** 2-9-0 0..................... MartinDwyer 4 43
(B J Meehan) *unf: scope: chsd ldng trio to over 2f out: wknd* **50/1**

12 *2 1/4* **One Lucky Lady** 2-9-0 0..................... SebSanders 11 38
(B W Hills) *unf: lw: a abt same pl: rdn and no prog 3f out* **33/1**

00 **13** *12* **I Dreamed A Dream**[16] 3035 2-9-0 0..................... FergusSweeney 13 8
(D K Ivory) *leggy: dwlt: a in last pair: struggling fr 1/2-way: t.o* **100/1**

00 **14** *7* **Maxiyow (IRE)**[39] 2330 2-8-9 0..................... DeclanCannon(5) 1 —
(B Palling) *neat: dwlt: racd wd and a in last trio: t.o* **100/1**

1m 26.46s (0.46) **Going Correction** 0.0s/f (Stan) **14** Ran SP% **120.5**
Speed ratings (Par 90): **97,94,93,89,87 86,84,83,80,79 78,75,61,53**
toteswingers: 1&2 £2.90, 1&3 £6.60, 2&3 £4.00 CSF £15.77 TOTE £5.60: £1.60, £1.80, £1.30; EX 17.40.
Owner Sheikh Ahmed Al Maktoum **Bred** Darley **Trained** Newmarket, Suffolk

FOCUS
The 7f trip provided a good test of stamina for juveniles at this stage of the season even though the pace was ordinary. Decent, sound form, with the first three clear.

NOTEBOOK
Jaaryah(IRE), by Halling out of a Sinndar mare, made a taking debut and did particularly well because she was wide throughout and had to make ground from midfield off a run-of-the-mill pace. She clearly stays well and the way she finished suggests she will get 1m later in the season. (op 7-1 tchd 15-2)
Najoum(USA), a Giant's Causeway half-sister to five winners in the US, showed she gets 7f without quite having the finishing power of the winner. She was also favoured by helping to dictate an unspectacular gallop. However, she showed enough to indicate she can take a similar event. (op 11-4 tchd 2-1)
Jetfire had already run twice, unlike the pair who finished ahead of her. She has done enough to suggest she can win a maiden, either at this trip or 6f, but to date she has only raced on the Kempton Polytrack. (op 4-1 tchd 6-1)
Byrony(IRE), reported not to have enjoyed firm ground in her previous race, kept on in the style of a filly who needs at least this trip. However, it was quite hard work and she looks more of a nursery type. (tchd 16-1 and 20-1)
Paco Belle(IRE) had run better than this over 6f first time out and did not convince over the extra furlong. (tchd 7-2 and 9-2)
Romantic Wish, a Hawk Wing debutante, got going too late but appears to need more experience and possibly even further as the season progresses.

3563 DIGIBET MAIDEN STKS — 1m 4f (P)
7:20 (7:22) (Class 5) 3-Y-O+ — **£2,590** (£770; £385; £192) **Stalls** Centre

Form — RPR

1 **Vita Nova (IRE)** 3-8-7 0 — EddieAhern 5 — 74+
(H R A Cecil) *w'like: scope: lengthy: trckd ldrs: wnt 3rd 1/2-way: shkn up 2f out: clsd to ld 1f out: pushed out: readily* **16/1**

3 **2** 2 **Royal Riviera**[9] 3256 4-9-12 0 — SteveDrowne 8 — 76
(J R Gask) *str: lw: mostly in 6th: rdn on outer over 3f out: styd on fr 2f out: clsd ins fnl f to take 2nd last stride* **4/1**[2]

4-4 **3** shd **Dynamic Idol (USA)**[59] 1735 3-8-12 0 — RyanMoore 14 — 78+
(M A Magnusson) *str: trckd ldrs on inner: 4th fr 1/2-way: effrt over 2f out: trapped over 1f out: styd on ins fnl f to take 3rd last stride* **5/1**[3]

2 **4** shd **Marching Song (USA)**[16] 3038 4-9-12 0 — RichardHughes 13 — 76
(Andrew Turnell) *str: lw: led: kicked on over 2f out: rdn and hdd 1f out: lost 2 pls last stride* **9/1**

5 **5** 2 **Zigato**[91] 1059 3-8-12 0 — FrankieDettori 7 — 72
(J H M Gosden) *w'like: lw: dwlt: rousted along to press ldr: led after 3f to 1/2-way: rdn and nt qckn 2f out: lost 2nd over 1f out: wknd last 150yds* **9/4**[1]

6 ½ **Thistle Stikk** 3-8-12 0 — MartinDwyer 1 — 72
(R Charlton) *leggy: scope: tall: bit bkwd: mostly in 5th: shkn up over 2f out: tried to cl on ldrs over 1f out: wknd last 100yds* **40/1**

7 6 **Honest Strike (USA)** 3-8-12 0 — TomQueally 9 — 62+
(H R A Cecil) *w'like: athletic: awkward s: mostly in rr: outpcd in 9th wl over 2f out and rn green: sme modest late prog* **15/2**

6 **8** nk **Deejan (IRE)**[19] 2921 5-9-2 0 — DeclanCannon(5) 11 — 57
(B Palling) *w'like: nvr bttr than midfield: outpcd fr over 2f out* **50/1**

0- **9** 4 **Cheerfully**[242] 7182 3-8-7 0 — RobertHavlin 12 — 50
(J H M Gosden) *str: bit bkwd: dwlt: sn in tch on inner: 7th 3f out: hung bdly lft sn after and wknd* **10/1**

5 **10** hd **Royal Dalakhani (IRE)**[17] 2994 3-8-7 0 — LiamJones 6 — 50
(P W D'Arcy) *w'like: str: sn last: nvr a factor: wl btn in 10th 3f out* **20/1**

11 ¾ **Desert Emerald (USA)** 3-8-12 0 — (be[1]) StevieDonohoe 3 — 54
(D M Simcock) *leggy: s.s: a wl in rr and rn green: swishing tail in last over 3f out* **40/1**

- **12** 23 **Respective Way**[99] 5-9-12 0 — LiamKeniry 10 — 17
(P R Chamings) *w'like: a towards rr: wknd 3f out: t.o* **100/1**

13 19 **Boomtown Kat**[419] 6-9-7 0 — EamonDehdashti(5) 4 — —
(Karen George) *w'like: leggy: chsd ldrs and racd wd: wknd wl over 3f out: t.o* **66/1**

2m 33.55s (-0.95) **Going Correction** 0.0s/f (Stan)
WFA 3 from 4yo+ 14lb — **13** Ran SP% **118.3**
Speed ratings (Par 103): **103,101,101,101,100 99,95,95,93,92 92,77,64**
toteswingers:1&2 £14.40, 2&3 £4.50, 1&3 £12.70 CSF £75.45 TOTE £20.50: £5.30, £2.80, £1.20; EX 103.30.
Owner H E Sheikh Sultan Bin Khalifa Al Nahyan **Bred** Paget Bloodstock **Trained** Newmarket, Suffolk

FOCUS
A fair maiden for late developers, but nothing special. The pace was modest, and it helped to race handily.
Honest Strike(USA) Official explanation: jockey said colt hung right

3564 DIGIBET.COM H'CAP — 1m 4f (P)
7:50 (7:52) (Class 6) (0-65,65) 3-Y-O — **£2,047** (£604; £302) **Stalls** Centre

Form — RPR

0111 **1** **Captain John Nixon**[4] 3444 3-9-4 **62** 6ex — AndreaAtzeni 10 — 84+
(Pat Eddery) *trckd ldr after 2f: led wl over 2f out and sn clr: unchal after* **8/11**[1]

-042 **2** 7 **Apache Kid (IRE)**[20] 2909 3-9-3 **61** — TomQueally 13 — 69
(D M Simcock) *swtg: trckd ldrs: wnt 4th 5f out: rdn to chse wnr jst over 2f out: hanging and no ch: kpt on to draw clr of rest* **15/2**[3]

4300 **3** 6 **Larkrise Star**[22] 2844 3-9-5 **63** — FergusSweeney 2 — 61
(D K Ivory) *prom: wnt 3rd 5f out: rdn to dispute 2nd over 2f out: sn easily outpcd* **50/1**

0351 **4** 1 ½ **Frameit (IRE)**[11] 3213 3-9-5 **63** — (b) LiamKeniry 7 — 59
(J S Moore) *chsd ldrs: wl outpcd fr 3f out: plugged on to take modest 4th 1f out* **20/1**

003 **5** ¾ **Best Of Broadway (IRE)**[24] 2792 3-8-11 **55** — (b) TedDurcan 6 — 50
(D R Lanigan) *hld up in last: wnt v wd bnd 3f out: rdn and kpt on past toiling rivals last 2f* **12/1**

066 **6** 3 ¼ **Tigranes The Great (IRE)**[12] 3173 3-9-7 **65** — JerryO'Dwyer 12 — 55
(M Botti) *stdd s: hld up in last trio: pushed along and prog into midfield over 3f out: wl outpcd and shkn up over 2f out: no ch after* **22/1**

350 **7** 2 ¼ **Business Bay (USA)**[37] 2401 3-9-6 **64** — JamieSpencer 1 — 50
(E F Vaughan) *rousted along fr wd draw to ld after 1f: hdd & wknd wl over 2f out* **40/1**

-430 **8** 3 ¾ **Rose Alba (IRE)**[19] 2935 3-9-5 **63** — MartinDwyer 3 — 43
(J L Dunlop) *wl in rr: wnt sharply lft after 3f: rdn over 3f out: no real prog* **25/1**

5000 **9** 15 **Bethlehem (IRE)**[36] 2412 3-8-13 **57** — SteveDrowne 11 — 13
(H Morrison) *lw: nvr gng wl and a in rr: lft bhd fr over 3f out: t.o* **50/1**

0-00 **10** ½ **High Holborn (IRE)**[22] 1522 3-9-1 **59** — SebSanders 8 — 14
(D E Pipe) *settled in midfield: rdn 4f out: downed tools completely over 2f out: t.o* **20/1**

2146 **11** 5 **Captain Cool (IRE)**[28] 2650 3-9-0 **58** — RichardHughes 9 — 5
(R Hannon) *lw: chsd ldrs: rdn over 4f out: wknd over 2f out: virtually p.u over 1f out: t.o* **13/2**[2]

00-0 **12** 34 **Sirri**[103] 930 3-9-1 **59** — NeilCallan 14 — —
(C E Brittain) *led 1f: wknd rapidly 5f out: sn wl t.o* **66/1**

2m 33.67s (-0.83) **Going Correction** 0.0s/f (Stan) — **12** Ran SP% **116.3**
Speed ratings (Par 97): **102,97,93,92,91 89,88,85,75,75 72,49**
toteswingers:1&2 £3.00, 2&3 £61.50, 1&3 £20.20 CSF £5.18 CT £150.61 TOTE £2.30: £2.00, £1.30, £7.70; EX 6.60.
Owner Paul Dean **Bred** Patrick Eddery Ltd **Trained** Nether Winchendon, Bucks

FOCUS
A generally modest handicap with a rapidly improving winner. The pace was slack, favouring the prominent runners.
Apache Kid(IRE) Official explanation: vet said colt lost a front shoe
Best Of Broadway(IRE) Official explanation: jockey said gelding ran in snatches
Captain Cool(IRE) Official explanation: jockey said gelding's stride shortened in straight

3565 DIGIBET CASINO H'CAP (LONDON MILE QUALIFIER) — 1m (P)
8:20 (8:21) (Class 4) (0-85,85) 3-Y-O+ — **£4,209** (£1,252; £625; £312) **Stalls** High

Form — RPR

-202 **1** **Clockmaker (IRE)**[21] 2872 4-9-8 **81** — FrankieDettori 11 — 95+
(J H M Gosden) *lw: dwlt: wl in rr: 10th 1/2-way: gd prog on outer over 2f out: led over 1f out: in command ins fnl f: pushed out* **6/4**[1]

0010 **2** 3 **Red Somerset (USA)**[11] 3206 7-9-12 **85** — AndreaAtzeni 3 — 92
(Mike Murphy) *sn midfield: rdn in 8th 1/2-way: prog over 2f out and cl up wl over 1f out: outpcd by wnr: wnt 2nd ins fnl f and kpt on* **33/1**

0235 **3** ¾ **My Best Bet**[11] 3217 4-9-6 **79** — TomQueally 4 — 84
(Stef Higgins) *hld up in last quartet and wl off the pce: gd prog on wd outside over 2f out w wnr: nt qckn over 1f out: kpt on* **11/1**

-510 **4** hd **Dukes Art**[12] 3172 4-9-11 **84** — RobertHavlin 13 — 89+
(J A R Toller) *sn trckd ldng trio in strly run r: clsd to ld over 2f out: hdd over 1f out: no ex* **6/1**[2]

-555 **5** 3 ¾ **Hurricane Spirit (IRE)**[14] 3083 6-9-10 **83** — SteveDrowne 2 — 79
(J R Best) *hld up in last pair: shuffled along fr over 2f out: kpt on steadily: nvr nr ldrs* **9/1**[3]

4060 **6** nk **Ilie Nastase (FR)**[14] 3083 6-9-4 **77** — LiamKeniry 8 — 72
(C R Dore) *settled in 9th: clsd as pack gped over 2f out: nt qckn over 1f out: fdd ins fnl f* **25/1**

6066 **7** 1 ¾ **Totally Focussed (IRE)**[21] 2872 5-9-6 **79** — HayleyTurner 10 — 70+
(S Dow) *s.s: wl in rr: 11th 1/2-way: tried to cl and nt clr run over 2f out: plugged on fr over 1f out: n.d* **16/1**

-150 **8** 1 **Striding Edge (IRE)**[67] 1530 4-9-5 **78** — MartinDwyer 1 — 67
(W R Muir) *hld up and sn last: nudged along over 2f out: nvr remotely involved* **14/1**

04 **9** 7 **L'Hirondelle (IRE)**[19] 2926 6-9-8 **81** — NeilCallan 12 — 54
(M J Attwater) *chsd ldrs in 6th: effrt on inner and hmpd over 2f out: tried to rally wl over 1f out: sn wknd* **20/1**

115- **10** 4 ½ **Bea Menace (USA)**[242] 7181 4-9-11 **84** — JamieSpencer 9 — 46
(P F I Cole) *in tch in 7th: no prog over 2f out: sn wknd and bhd* **12/1**

0012 **11** 1 ½ **Calahonda**[16] 3036 4-9-2 **75** — LiamJones 6 — 34
(P W D'Arcy) *lw: chsd ldng pair: n.m.r wl over 2f out: sn wknd: t.o* **10/1**

6026 **12** 10 **Bomber Command (USA)**[16] 3036 7-9-10 **83** — (v) SebSanders 7 — 19
(J W Hills) *chsd ldng quartet: pushed along 1/2-way: effrt u.p to chal jst over 2f out: stl cl up over 1f out: wknd rapidly and heavily eased: t.o* **12/1**

4-00 **13** 1 ¼ **Leverage (IRE)**[21] 2872 4-9-5 **78** — NickyMackay 5 — 11
(M Wigham) *noseband wnt awry sn after s: pushed up on wd outside to go 2nd after 2f: rdn 1/2-way: wknd rapidly over 2f out: t.o* **50/1**

3100 **14** 1 **Elusive Fame (USA)**[5] 3391 4-9-5 **85** — (b) CharlesPerkins(7) 14 — 16
(M Johnston) *led at suicidal pce to over 2f out: wknd rapidly: t.o* **33/1**

1m 39.08s (-0.72) **Going Correction** 0.0s/f (Stan) — **14** Ran SP% **126.1**
Speed ratings (Par 105): **103,100,99,99,95 95,93,92,85,80 79,69,68,67**
toteswingers: 1&2 £8.50, 1&3 £6.10, 2&3 £159.50 CSF £77.52 CT £468.92 TOTE £2.10: £1.40, £8.50, £3.70; EX 55.00.
Owner H R H Princess Haya Of Jordan **Bred** Lemongrove Stud & Brendan Arthur **Trained** Newmarket, Suffolk

FOCUS
A strong gallop set this up for the come-from-behind performers.
Bomber Command(USA) Official explanation: jockey said gelding stopped quickly
Leverage(IRE) Official explanation: jockey said gelding had no more to give

3566 BOOK NOW FOR BEST OF BRITISH NIGHT H'CAP — 2m (P)
8:50 (8:50) (Class 3) (0-90,90) 4-Y-O+
£6,542 (£1,959; £979; £490; £244; £122) **Stalls** High

Form — RPR

-001 **1** **Phoenix Flight (IRE)**[19] 2341 5-8-12 **81** — RichardHughes 12 — 89
(H J Evans) *stdd s: t.k.h: hld up in detached last: stl there 3f out: threaded through fr over 2f out: wl timed effrt to ld last 100yds: hld on wl* **7/1**[3]

40-0 **2** hd **Keenes Day (FR)**[46] 2126 5-9-7 **90** — RoystonFfrench 5 — 98
(M Johnston) *hld up bhd ldrs: tapped for toe whn pce lifted 4f out and drvn: lost pl 3f out: rallied over 1f out: r.o to press wnr nr fin: jst hld* **16/1**

-514 **3** 1 **Dayia (IRE)**[15] 3050 6-9-2 **90** — SimonPearce(5) 4 — 97
(J Pearce) *lw: t.k.h: trckd ldrs: rdn whn pce lifted 4f out: nt qckn over 2f out: styd on fr over 1f out: tk 3rd nr fin* **9/2**[2]

36-0 **4** ½ **Rugell (ARG)**[19] 2938 5-9-1 **84** — AdamKirby 9 — 90
(C G Cox) *led at mod pce: hdd 4f out: led again over 2f out: kpt on tl hdd and folded last 100yds* **20/1**

0600 **5** 1 ¼ **Ocean's Minstrel**[15] 3050 4-9-5 **88** — AlanMunro 7 — 92
(J Ryan) *hld up towards rr: prog on inner over 2f out: nt qckn over 1f out: kpt on same pce* **12/1**

2-05 **6** 1 **Featherweight (IRE)**[33] 2509 4-8-10 **79** — SebSanders 6 — 82
(B W Hills) *wl in tch: sltly outpcd 4f out and wd bnd 3f out: renewed effrt over 2f out and sn chalng: fdd ins fnl f* **16/1**

-406 **7** 1 **Rangefinder**[15] 3050 6-9-2 **85** — (p) FrankieDettori 8 — 87
(Jane Chapple-Hyam) *disp 2nd pl to over 4f out: lost pl and rdn whn pce lifted sn after: rallied u.p 2f out: fdd ins fnl f* **5/2**[1]

6243 **8** shd **Rose Row**[95] 1020 6-8-9 **78** — HayleyTurner 11 — 80
(Mrs Mary Hambro) *s.s: t.k.h: hld up in last trio tl allowed to stride foward fr 6f out to ld 4f out: hdd over 2f out: fdd over 1f out* **12/1**

-601 **9** ¾ **Brett Vale (IRE)**[42] 2228 4-9-2 **85** — DaneO'Neill 2 — 86
(P R Hedger) *t.k.h: hld up in last trio: gng strly over 3f out: prog over 2f out: sn rdn and nt qckn* **9/1**

51-0 **10** 7 **Just Like Silk (USA)**[18] 2976 4-9-2 **85**........................(p) JackMitchell 10 78
(G A Butler) *wl in tch in midfield: rdn 4f out: wknd over 2f out* **12/1**
-420 **11** 2 3/4 **Highland Legacy**[18] 2975 6-9-0 **83**................................ JamieSpencer 1 72
(M L W Bell) *b: lw: disp 2nd pl to over 4f out: sn rdn: wknd 2f out* **15/2**
0665 **12** 9 **December**[11] 3214 4-7-9 **71** oh20................................(vt) RyanPowell(7) 3 50
(Mrs C A Dunnett) *t.k.h: wl in tch tl wknd over 3f out: t.o* **80/1**
3m 32.24s (2.14) **Going Correction** 0.0s/f (Stan) 12 Ran SP% **121.9**
Speed ratings (Par 107): **94,93,93,93,92 92,91,91,91,87 86,81**
toteswingers: 1&2 £21.20, 1&3 £5.30, 2&3 £7.60 CSF £116.81 CT £568.62 TOTE £11.70: £3.30, £4.80, £1.30; EX 128.60.
Owner D Ross **Bred** Airlie Stud And Sir Thomas Pilkington **Trained** Broadwas, Worcs

FOCUS
The pace was pretty weak until increasing at the end of the back straight, so it was remarkable that the winner was deliberately dropped out in a detached last place.

NOTEBOOK
Phoenix Flight(IRE) ◆ was given a peach of a ride by Richard Hughes, who was still last turning for home but oozing confidence as he pounced late. He is in the form of his life and must have a good chance of winning again next time. (tchd 13-2 and 15-2 and 8-1 in a place)
Keenes Day(FR) gets 2m well, so the steady pace would not have helped him. He was staying on strongly close home, almost depriving the winner, and will be a factor in similar races, on turf as well as sand, from now on. (op 20-1)
Dayia(IRE) is higher in the weights this year but her recent form shows why. This was another excellent run and, though this is a tough mark, she may yet win off it granted a stronger pace. (tchd 5-1)
Rugell(ARG), who looked a decent stayer in the making in August and September last year, returned to form after a poor run on easy ground earlier in the month. Though helped by dictating a weak pace, he seemed to enjoy making the running and can win off this mark if he goes on from here. (op 16-1)
Ocean's Minstrel, having another crack at a much longer trip, was more convincing this time, admittedly in an easier race. He continues to drop in the weights and is now well handicapped if he returns to anything like his best, but he was still some way short here. (op 14-1)
Featherweight(IRE), trying a longer trip, nearly got home, but another attempt with a better gallop is needed to make sure she stays. (op 11-1)
Rangefinder continues to get found out at the end of these stamina tests, but he can hardly be said to be a non-stayer as he nearly got 2m4f last time. However, he was caught out when the tempo quickened, so may well have appreciated a more solid pace. (op 7-2)
Rose Row tried to increase the tempo with a sudden move at the end of the back straight, but those heroics ended up as a gallant failure. (tchd 14-1)

3567 KEMPTON.CO.UK APPRENTICE H'CAP 6f (P)
9:20 (9:21) (Class 5) (0-75,75) 3-Y-0+ **£2,590** (£770; £385; £192) **Stalls** High

Form RPR
6600 **1** **Simple Rhythm**[22] 2846 4-8-4 **56** oh1........................ NatashaEaton(5) 11 65
(J Ryan) *trckd ldng pair: led on inner over 1f out: shuffled along ins fnl f: comf* **16/1**
2131 **2** 1 1/2 **Requisite**[7] 3328 5-10-0 **75** 6ex....................................(v) JamesSullivan 9 79
(I A Wood) *hld up in last pair: prog 2f out: wnt 2nd 1f out: no imp on wnr last 100yds* **11/10**[1]
0-55 **3** hd **Midnight Fantasy**[20] 2904 4-9-6 **72**................................ NoelGarbutt(5) 6 76
(Rae Guest) *dwlt: hld up in last trio: rdn over 2f out: styd on fr over 1f out to take 3rd nr fin* **13/2**[3]
0106 **4** nk **Do More Business (IRE)**[21] 2868 3-8-5 **62**........... AdamBeschizza(3) 5 63
(P M Phelan) *in tch in 4th: effrt over 1f out: chsd ldng pair ins fnl f: kpt on but lost 3rd nr fin* **15/2**
0505 **5** 2 3/4 **Spinning Bailiwick**[19] 2929 4-9-9 **75**........................ HarryBentley(5) 7 69+
(G L Moore) *rrd bdly s: rcvrd into 5th: rdn 2f out: chal for a pl 1f out: fdd* **16/1**
0315 **6** 1 **Avow (USA)**[71] 1449 3-9-0 **68**.......................................(b) DeclanCannon 4 57
(J J Bridger) *pressed ldr: upsides over 2f out to over 1f out: hanging and fnd nil: wknd ins fnl f* **33/1**
45 **7** 2 1/4 **Lethal**[44] 2178 7-9-1 **62**... SimonPearce 8 45
(Andrew Reid) *led: jnd over 2f out: hdd over 1f out: wknd ins fnl f* **7/1**
1003 **8** 1/2 **Teen Ager (FR)**[21] 2866 6-8-11 **61**................................ RyanPowell(3) 10 43
(P Burgoyne) *settled in last: effrt on inner 2f out: sn no prog* **12/1**
1514 **9** 1 1/4 **Knightfire (IRE)**[21] 2868 3-9-6 **74**..................................(t) IanBrennan 2 50
(W R Swinburn) *nvr bttr than midfield: wknd over 2f out and sn last* **6/1**[2]
1m 13.09s (-0.01) **Going Correction** 0.0s/f (Stan)
WFA 3 from 4yo+ 7lb 9 Ran SP% **121.9**
Speed ratings (Par 103): **100,98,97,97,93 92,89,88,87**
toteswingers:1&2 £21.30, 1&3 £4.80, 2&3 £11.50 CSF £36.10 CT £143.53 TOTE £32.80: £8.80, £1.10, £4.10; EX 84.90 Place 6: £54.64 Place 5: £20.72.
Owner J Ryan **Bred** P Quinlan **Trained** Newmarket, Suffolk

FOCUS
A decent gallop gave everyone a chance.
T/Plt: £48.00 to a £1 stake. Pool: £58,336.26 - 885.89 winning tickets. T/Qpdt: £15.80 to a £1 stake. Pool: £5,193.37 - 242.70 winning tickets. JN

3568 - 3570a (Foreign Racing) - See Raceform Interactive

3092 FAIRYHOUSE (R-H)
Wednesday, June 30

OFFICIAL GOING: Good to firm

3571a IRISH STALLION FARMS EUROPEAN BREEDERS FUND BROWNSTOWN STKS (GROUP 3) (F&M) 7f
7:30 (7:31) 3-Y-0+ **£46,017** (£13,451; £6,371; £2,123)

RPR
1 **Berg Bahn (IRE)**[14] 3071 3-8-11 99.. KLatham 8 101
(G M Lyons, Ire) *settled bhd ldrs: 6th 1/2-way: rdn in 5th 2f out: swtchd out and prog under 2f out: 3rd 1 1/2f out: 2nd 1f out: styd on to ld fnl 100yds: kpt on wl* **14/1**
2 1 1/4 **Velvet Flicker (IRE)**[20] 2912 3-8-11 98.......................... DPMcDonogh 4 98
(Kevin Prendergast, Ire) *hld up towards rr: hdwy in 6th 2f out: rdn into 4th 1 1/2f out: 3rd 1f out: kpt on ins fnl f to 2nd cl home* **25/1**
3 1/2 **Miss Gorica (IRE)**[3] 3486 6-9-6 106............................... WMLordan 6 100
(Ms Joanna Morgan, Ire) *led: rdn and kpt on fr over 1f out: hdd last 100yds and no ex: lost 2nd cl home* **12/1**
4 1 **Distinctive**[20] 2912 3-9-0 .... TomEaves 3 97+
(B Smart) *settled bhd ldrs: 5th 1/2-way: rdn in 7th 2f out: 6th 1 1/2f out: styd on in 5th 1f out: kpt on wl ins fnl f* **9/2**[2]
5 4 **Sent From Heaven (IRE)**[12] 3143 3-9-0 .... MichaelHills 9 86
(B W Hills) *s.i.s: drvn to chse ldrs and t.k.h: 3rd 1/2-way: rdn 2f out: sltly bmpd and swished tail under 2f out: no ex in 5th 1 1/2f out: kpt on one pce* **5/4**[1]
6 4 1/2 **Bewitched (IRE)**[11] 3197 3-8-11 105.. JMurtagh 7 71
(Charles O'Brien, Ire) *chsd ldr in 2nd: rdn 1 1/2f out: 4th and no ex 1f out: sn eased* **5/1**[3]
7 3 **Kitty Kiernan**[23] 2829 3-8-11 106... KJManning 5 63
(J S Bolger, Ire) *chsd ldrs: 4th 1/2-way: rdn 2f out: sn no ex and wknd* **5/1**[3]
8 10 **Queen Of Troy (IRE)**[17] 3006 3-8-11 94.......................... JAHeffernan 1 36
(A P O'Brien, Ire) *a towards rr: rdn and no imp ent st* **25/1**
1m 28.15s (-2.35)
WFA 3 from 4yo+ 9lb 8 Ran SP% **118.0**
CSF £297.72 TOTE £18.00: £3.40, £5.80, £2.60; DF 186.20.
Owner Anamoine Limited **Bred** Windflower Overseas Holdings Inc **Trained** Dunsany, Co. Meath

FOCUS
A race that was run at the pace of a sprint, and in that regard perhaps it was a surprise that sprinters filled two of the first three places over this trip.

NOTEBOOK
Berg Bahn(IRE) was stepping back in distance from a mile but quickened up well to score. Held up off the pace, she had to be switched towards the centre of the track to make her challenge, causing a concertina effect on her outside. However, she picked up really well inside the last and won well, giving the impression she would have found more if challenged. It was a good performance and it will be interesting to see where she goes next. (op 20/1)
Velvet Flicker(IRE) made her challenge late and ran on well enough inside the last, but couldn't threaten the winner. It's a run that does open up more options for this filly.
Miss Gorica(IRE) doesn't have too many runs left as she's in foal to Dylan Thomas, but she ran another cracker here. Setting off at six-furlong pace, she was still travelling well turning in and had most of her rivals off the bridle, but she was unable to last it out.
Distinctive ◆ didn't have much luck. Racing reasonably handily, she was being ridden to close when getting a bump from the winner, which saw her forced out quite wide. She ran on pretty well from that position and might have been more involved but for that. (op 9/2 tchd 4/1)
Sent From Heaven(IRE) missed the break and was then ridden up to take a prominent position, but once getting there she was too keen and had to be restrained. She was under pressure and not making any obvious impression when she swished her tail and jinked left when the winner was switched out. There didn't seem to be much contact between them and it was a run that leaves some question marks about her temperament. (op 2/1)
Bewitched(IRE) tracked the leader and was travelling as well as anything turning in, but once she was asked over a furlong out she faded tamely and her rider didn't appear exactly happy with her as she was eased inside the last. Official explanation: jockey said filly made a respiratory noise in running (op 9/2)
Kitty Kiernan ran no real race, weakening tamely inside the final furlong. Official explanation: jockey said filly slipped on leaving the stalls and was never comfortable thereafter (op 7/2)

3572 - 3574a (Foreign Racing) - See Raceform Interactive

2742 EPSOM (L-H)
Thursday, July 1

OFFICIAL GOING: Good to firm (firm in places in back straight; 9.0)
Rails at innermost configuration and all distances as advertised.
Wind: Moderate, across (towards stands') Weather: Fine but cloudy

3576 RACING FOR RESEARCH H'CAP 1m 4f 10y
6:20 (6:26) (Class 5) (0-75,75) 4-Y-0+ **£3,885** (£1,156; £577; £288) **Stalls** Centre

Form RPR
/1-4 **1** **Silent Applause**[34] 2506 7-8-13 **67**...................................... LiamKeniry 1 74
(Dr J D Scargill) *hld up last of main gp: wnt 5th st: eased out and drvn 2f out: sn chsd ldng pair: clsd fnl f: led post* **8/1**[3]
1230 **2** hd **Maslak (IRE)**[15] 3090 6-8-13 **67**...................................... ChrisCatlin 6 74
(P W Hiatt) *led: hrd pressed fr over 1f out: kpt on wl u.p: hdd post* **9/1**
4035 **3** shd **Rowan Tiger**[20] 2934 4-9-3 **71**... PatCosgrave 5 78
(J R Boyle) *hld up: prog 1/2-way: 4th st: chsd ldr over 2f out: grad clsd fr over 1f out: nrly upsides nr fin but lost 2nd on post* **7/4**[1]
6-50 **4** 7 **Norman The Great**[45] 2181 6-9-7 **75**................................ DaneO'Neill 7 70
(A King) *cl up: trckd ldng pair after 4f: rdn and fnd nil over 2f out: grad wknd* **4/1**[2]
1216 **5** 1/2 **Penang Cinta**[18] 2996 7-8-13 **72**.................................. RichardEvans(5) 3 67
(P D Evans) *trckd ldr after 3f to over 2f out: grad wknd* **10/1**
0300 **6** 32 **Indian Ghyll (IRE)**[23] 2845 4-9-0 **68**................................ ShaneKelly 2 11
(R A Teal) *chsd ldr 3f: 6th and wkng st: t.o and eased: lame* **33/1**
40-5 **7** 47 **Gloucester**[23] 2845 7-9-4 **72**.. GeorgeBaker 8 —
(M J Scudamore) *sed abt 25l bhd rest: no ch to rcvr and allowed to complete in own time* **4/1**[2]
2m 37.53s (-1.37) **Going Correction** -0.075s/f (Good) 7 Ran SP% **109.5**
Speed ratings (Par 103): **101,100,100,96,95 74,43**
Tote Swingers:1&2:£9.90, 2&3:£4.10, 1&3:£3.70 CSF £68.40 CT £167.72 TOTE £10.00: £3.20, £3.90; EX 74.20.
Owner J P T Partnership **Bred** R A Dalton **Trained** Newmarket, Suffolk

FOCUS
The ground appeared to be riding very quick following a dry, breezy day, with it officially being described as good to firm, firm in places down the back straight. There wasn't much pace on in this modest handicap and that resulted in a tight finish, the front three being separated by about a neck. The form is rated around the runner-up.
Indian Ghyll(IRE) Official explanation: vet said colt pulled up lame left-fore
Gloucester Official explanation: jockey said gelding was very slowly away giving away approximately 30 lengths

3577 BRIGHT SPARKS E B F MEDIAN AUCTION MAIDEN STKS 7f
6:50 (6:52) (Class 4) 2-Y-O **£4,533** (£1,348; £674; £336) **Stalls** Low

Form RPR
02 **1** **Whodathought (IRE)**[7] 3349 2-9-3 0.................................... PatDobbs 6 75+
(R Hannon) *mde virtually all: jnd 3f out: sn pushed along: gained upper hand jst over 1f out: nt hrd pressed after* **2/5**[1]
65 **2** 1 1/4 **Presto Volante (IRE)**[20] 2932 2-9-3 0.............................. ShaneKelly 1 70+
(Mrs A J Perrett) *hld up in tch: 5th st: rdn and nt qckn over 2f out: sn chsd ldng pair: r.o fnl f to take 2nd last strides* **10/3**[2]
3 nk **Highlife Dancer** 2-9-3 0... CoryParish 3 69+
(M R Channon) *s.s: last tl quick move along inner to join wnr 3f out: stl upsides over 1f out: no ex fnl f: lost 2nd last strides* **20/1**[3]
4 4 1/2 **Rowan Ridge** 2-9-3 0... PatCosgrave 5 58
(J R Boyle) *sn trckd ldng pair and racd wd: nt qckn over 2f out: grad wknd* **20/1**[3]
0 **5** 3/4 **Dew Reward (IRE)**[8] 3332 2-9-3 0.................................... LiamKeniry 4 56
(Eve Johnson Houghton) *chsd wnr to 3f out: wknd 2f out* **50/1**

00 **6** ¾ **Canada Fleet (CAN)**[14] 3112 2-9-3 0 .... DaraghO'Donohoe 2 54
(E A L Dunlop) *t.k.h early: restrained bhd ldrs: 4th st: wknd over 2f out* **20/1**[3]

1m 25.82s (2.52) **Going Correction** -0.075s/f (Good) 6 Ran SP% **110.8**
Speed ratings (Par 96): **82,80,80,75,74 73**
Tote Swingers: 1&2 £3.00, 1&3 £3.00, 2&3 £1.10 CSF £1.72 TOTE £1.50: £1.10, £1.40; EX 2.00.

Owner Mrs Philip Snow **Bred** Meadowlands Stud **Trained** East Everleigh, Wilts

FOCUS
An ordinary maiden run at a slow tempo, and not an easy race to pitch the level of the form.

NOTEBOOK
Whodathought(IRE) set the standard having lost out narrowly at Goodwood last week and, though making hard enough work of it, was ultimately well on top at the line. It will presumably be nurseries next. (op 1-2 tchd 8-15)
Presto Volante(IRE) didn't look totally at ease on the track, but he finished to very good effect in getting up for second, and will be of particular interest once handicapping. (op 3-1 tchd 4-1)
Highlife Dancer, whose pedigree is a blend of speed and stamina, showed plenty of toe against the rail to narrowly take over the running approaching the final 2f, but couldn't race on with the winner in the final 100 yards and lost second close home. This was a promising start. (op 16-1)
Rowan Ridge, a half-brother to numerous middle-distance winners, has a bit of speed on his sire's side and he shaped pleasingly back in fourth. (op 14-1)
Dew Reward(IRE) looks in need of more time and can be expected to fare better once handicapping down the line.
Canada Fleet(CAN) was keen early and looks in need of more time. He can also be expected to fare better once handicapping. (tchd 22-1)

3578 TOTESPORT H'CAP 6f
7:25 (7:26) (Class 3) (0-95,92) 3-Y-O+ £6,476 (£1,927; £963; £481) Stalls High

Form RPR
-030 **1** **Something (IRE)**[13] 3146 8-9-13 **92** .... DaraghO'Donohoe 1 99
(D Nicholls) *hld up: sn detached in last and abt 12l down ent st: prog on outer fr jst over 2f out: rdn and r.o wl fnl f: led post* **9/2**[3]
-204 **2** *nse* **We Have A Dream**[26] 2748 5-9-9 **88** .... GeorgeBaker 3 95
(W R Muir) *led 100yds: chsd ldr: led wl over 1f out but hrd pressed: styd on wl: hdd post* **6/1**
5-50 **3** *1* **King's Wonder**[26] 2748 5-9-4 **86** .... MichaelGeran(3) 5 90
(D Nicholls) *trckd ldng trio: rdn to chal 2f out: chsd ldr wl over 1f out: edging lft and nt qckn: lost 2nd nr fin* **7/2**[2]
30-0 **4** ¾ **Aye Aye Digby (IRE)**[54] 1903 5-9-11 **90** .... PatCosgrave 2 91
(J R Boyle) *trckd ldng pair to over 2f out: effrt on inner and drvn over 1f out: kpt on same pce* **20/1**
4205 **5** 1 ¼ **Jarrow (IRE)**[13] 3178 3-9-4 **89** .... RoystonFfrench 10 85
(M Johnston) *chsd ldng quartet: lost pl and rdn 2f out: struggling after: styd on nr fin* **9/1**
0220 **6** *hd* **Abraham Lincoln (IRE)**[26] 2748 6-9-11 **90** .... JackMitchell 4 87
(R A Harris) *dwlt: hld up in 7th: prog on outer over 2f out: tried to cl on ldrs but hanging bdly lft and no imp* **3/1**[1]
1005 **7** *shd* **Billy Red**[12] 3216 6-8-12 **77** .... (b) LiamKeniry 8 73
(J R Jenkins) *led after 100yds at scorching pce: hdd wl over 1f out: sn lost pl and no ex* **16/1**
2100 **8** *4* **Rocker**[19] 2973 6-8-11 **76** .... ShaneKelly 6 75+
(G L Moore) *hld up in 6th: looking for room fr 2f out: keeping on but nt threatening ldrs whn hmpd jst ins fnl f: eased* **14/1**
2050 **9** 2 ½ **Edgewater (IRE)**[15] 3088 3-9-0 **85** .... (p) DaneO'Neill 9 61
(J Akehurst) *outpcd and sn pushed along in 8th: nvr on terms: wl bhd fnl 2f* **8/1**

68.21 secs (-1.19) **Going Correction** -0.075s/f (Good)
WFA 3 from 5yo+ 6lb 9 Ran SP% **118.1**
Speed ratings (Par 107): **104,103,102,101,99 99,99,94,90**
Tote Swingers:1&2:£2.60, 2&3:£5.10, 1&3:£8.80 CSF £32.45 CT £107.05 TOTE £6.30: £2.10, £1.90, £1.60; EX 11.60.

Owner Middleham Park Racing LIII **Bred** Newlands House Stud **Trained** Sessay, N Yorks
■ Stewards' Enquiry : Jack Mitchell three-day ban: careless riding (Jul 15-17)

FOCUS
This was always likely to be run at a fast pace with Billy Red blazing off in customary fashion. A competitive handicap and the form makes sense at face value.

NOTEBOOK
Something(IRE) produced a remarkable performance to get up in the final stride. Soon behind, he became further detached in last place as his rider attempted to restrain him running down hill, but as the pace collapsed in the straight, he began to unwind with a sustained run out wide, and got there in the nick of time to win his first race in 15 months. He had beaten the runner-up by a similarly narrow margin when third in a valuable C&D handicap on Derby Day, and this again showed he needs a proper test to win at this distance. (op 4-1 tchd 6-1)
We Have A Dream often goes well here and he got a nice tow off the front-running Billy Red. He looked the winner having battled his way to the front, but as had been the case here on Derby Day, he couldn't quite hang on. This was a cracking effort from a career-high mark. (op 4-1 tchd 7-2)
King's Wonder, representing the same connections as the winner, was nicely backed and travelled really strongly, but didn't look overly straightforward under pressure, and certainly didn't knuckle down as well as the front pair. He hadn't looked in love with the track on Derby Day, so this has to go down as a good effort. (op 7-1)
Aye Aye Digby(IRE) produced a much better effort and, though still a little high in the handicap, ran well enough to suggest he is up to winning off this sort of mark. (op 14-1 tchd 12-1)
Jarrow(IRE) was outpaced from over 2f out, but did stay on well close home. (tchd 10-1)
Abraham Lincoln(IRE), with no cheekpieces this time, was backed in the expectation that he would do much better than when behind several of these last time, but he didn't, hanging noticeably under pressure late on. Official explanation: jockey said horse hung left (op 5-1)
Billy Red was forced to go faster than he would have liked with We Have A Dream in opposition, so was never going to last. (op 14-1)
Rocker was travelling extremely well when forced to switch off the rail inside the final 2f, and he then found disappointingly little. Official explanation: jockey said gelding suffered interference in running (op 12-1)

3579 BGC H'CAP 7f
7:55 (7:56) (Class 4) (0-85,85) 3-Y-O+ £5,180 (£1,541; £770; £384) Stalls Low

Form RPR
-021 **1** **Space Station**[26] 2750 4-9-4 **75** .... (b) ShaneKelly 12 87
(S Dow) *hld up in rr: 9th st: prog on outer over 2f out: rdn to ld over 1f out: sn in command: styd on wl* **4/1**[2]
2-30 **2** 2 ½ **Belle Des Airs (IRE)**[20] 2929 4-10-0 **85** .... JackMitchell 10 90
(R M Beckett) *dwlt: settled in last: rdn 3f out: edging lft but prog on outer fr 2f out: styd on to take 2nd fnl f: no imp* **16/1**
-560 **3** ½ **Dubai Set**[19] 2969 3-9-4 **83** .... (b) PatDobbs 4 84
(R Hannon) *sn pressed ldr: rdn and nt qckn over 2f out: disp 2nd over 1f out: kpt on* **13/2**
03-0 **4** *nk* **Twilight Star (IRE)**[68] 1530 6-8-13 **70** .... DaneO'Neill 1 73
(R A Teal) *trckd ldrs gng wl: wnt 3rd st: effrt against rail 2f out: disp 2nd over 1f out: kpt on same pce* **25/1**
6241 **5** *nse* **My Kingdom (IRE)**[20] 2926 4-9-13 **84** .... (t) GeorgeBaker 8 87+
(H Morrison) *hld up: 8th st: hmpd sn after: trapped bhd rivals fr 2f out tl last 100yds: r.o and nrly snatched a pl* **11/2**[3]
5156 **6** ½ **Buxton**[17] 3033 6-9-0 **71** .... (t) LiamKeniry 9 73
(R Ingram) *hld up in rr: 11th st: plld out and prog 2f out: styd on same pce: nvr rchd ldrs* **20/1**
20-0 **7** *1* **Leadenhall Lass (IRE)**[20] 2926 4-8-8 **70** .... JemmaMarshall(5) 5 69
(P M Phelan) *chsd ldrs: 5th st: cl enough 2f out: nt qckn after* **16/1**
6152 **8** 1 ¼ **Glen Shiel (USA)**[6] 3401 3-9-2 **81** .... RoystonFfrench 2 74+
(M Johnston) *awkward s: wl in rr: 10th st: rdn and nt handling trck over 2f out and dropped to last: styd on ins fnl f* **3/1**[1]
2-06 **9** ½ **Shibhan**[13] 3158 3-8-8 **73** .... (p) ChrisCatlin 3 64
(C E Brittain) *led: drvn and hdd over 1f out: wknd fnl f* **40/1**
0-20 **10** *1* **Salient**[54] 1933 6-9-7 **78** .... PatCosgrave 6 69
(M J Attwater) *chsd ldrs: 6th st: rdn and grad lost pl fr 2f out* **20/1**
2020 **11** 1 ¾ **My Learned Friend (IRE)**[12] 3212 6-8-13 **77** .... FrancisHayes(7) 11 64
(A M Balding) *settled in midfield: 7th st: stmbld on inner over 2f out: no prog after: fdd* **25/1**
1403 **12** *7* **Fivefold (USA)**[28] 2682 3-8-12 **77** .... AlanMunro 7 42
(J Akehurst) *w ldr early: 4th and sing to lose pl st: wknd 2f out* **7/1**

1m 21.74s (-1.56) **Going Correction** -0.075s/f (Good)
WFA 3 from 4yo+ 8lb 12 Ran SP% **117.6**
Speed ratings (Par 105): **105,102,101,101,101 100,99,98,97,96 94,86**
Tote Swingers:1&2:£16.10, 2&3:£27.20, 1&3:£9.90 CSF £59.24 CT £417.63 TOTE £4.50: £1.60, £4.40, £1.90.

Owner Mr & Mrs Chua, Moore & Jurd **Bred** Juddmonte Farms Ltd **Trained** Epsom, Surrey

FOCUS
A competitive-looking handicap. The winner improved, the form is rated around the second, and the fifth was arguably unlucky.
Belle Des Airs(IRE) Official explanation: jockey said, regarding running and riding, that the filly was slow away as blind had become snagged on the halter which was attached to the bridle.
My Kingdom(IRE) ◆ Official explanation: jockey said gelding was denied a clear run
Glen Shiel(USA) Official explanation: jockey said gelding stumbled on leaving stalls
My Learned Friend(IRE) Official explanation: jockey said gelding stumbled badly 2f out
Fivefold(USA) Official explanation: trainer said colt was unsuited by the track

3580 BGC CLAIMING STKS 1m 114y
8:30 (8:32) (Class 5) 3-Y-O+ £3,412 (£1,007; £504) Stalls Low

Form RPR
0051 **1** **Lang Shining (IRE)**[5] 3431 6-9-8 84 .... SophieDoyle(5) 3 86
(J A Osborne) *rrd s: hld up in 5th: prog over 2f out: pushed into ld on inner jst over 1f out: rdn out nr fin* **15/8**[1]
0035 **2** 1 ¼ **Blue Noodles**[30] 2624 4-8-13 64 .... ShaneKelly 4 69
(P D Evans) *trckd ldng pair: prog to ld over 2f out: rdn and hdd jst over 1f out: styd on but a hld* **10/1**[3]
3002 **3** *4* **Ginger Grey (IRE)**[9] 3297 3-8-2 67 .... (b) DeclanCannon(5) 6 63
(D R C Elsworth) *pressed ldr: rdn and nt qckn over 2f out: steadily outpcd fr over 1f out* **4/1**[2]
1113 **4** *6* **Royal Dignitary (USA)**[22] 2858 10-9-2 80 .... MichaelGeran(3) 2 53
(D Nicholls) *hld up in 4th: rdn 3f out: nt gng wl after: wl btn fnl 2f* **15/8**[1]
3000 **5** *11* **Purus (IRE)**[8] 3338 8-8-13 60 .... DaneO'Neill 5 23
(R A Teal) *led to over 2f out: wknd rapidly* **14/1**
00-R **6** *31* **Grand Vista**[160] 259 6-8-13 80 .... AmirQuinn 7 —
(G L Moore) *ref to r tl others had gone over 100yds: trailed rnd* **33/1**

1m 43.32s (-2.78) **Going Correction** -0.075s/f (Good)
WFA 3 from 4yo+ 10lb 6 Ran SP% **108.3**
Speed ratings (Par 103): **109,107,104,99,89 61**
Tote Swingers:1&2:£3.60, 2&3:£3.40, 1&3:£2.40. CSF £20.07 TOTE £3.10: £1.40, £2.80.

Owner A Taylor **Bred** Ballymacoll Stud Farm Ltd **Trained** Upper Lambourn, Berks

FOCUS
A decent little claimer, but the favourite ran poorly so it proved straightforward for the winner.
Royal Dignitary(USA) Official explanation: jockey said gelding hit its head on stalls

3581 GEORGE'S APPEAL BEATS NEUROBLASTOMA H'CAP 1m 2f 18y
9:00 (9:03) (Class 4) (0-80,84) 3-Y-O+ £5,180 (£1,541; £770; £384) Stalls Low

Form RPR
6631 **1** **Jutland**[10] 3265 3-9-7 **84** 6ex .... RoystonFfrench 4 96
(M Johnston) *trckd ldng pair: led on inner over 2f out: sn drvn: maintained gallop and a looked in command* **6/5**[1]
-154 **2** *1* **Flying Destination**[20] 2927 3-8-13 **76** .... ShaneKelly 9 86
(W J Knight) *led: rdn and hdd over 2f out: styd on wl to press wnr but a hld* **7/1**[3]
4501 **3** *3* **Kerchak (USA)**[13] 3155 3-8-10 **73** .... PatDobbs 1 77
(W Jarvis) *hld up in last pair: prog fr 3f out: chsd ldng pair over 1f out: styd on but no imp* **5/1**[2]
-644 **4** *3* **Bold Cross (IRE)**[14] 3117 7-9-8 **74** .... PaulFitzsimons 3 72
(E G Bevan) *hld up in midfield: 6th st: prog to chse ldng pair over 2f out to over 1f out: one pce* **16/1**
-130 **5** 2 ½ **Addwaitya**[35] 2467 5-10-0 **80** .... (p) IanMongan 7 73
(Mrs L J Mongan) *s.i.s and pushed along early: chsd ldrs: disp 4th st: rdn and outpcd fr over 2f out* **12/1**
4640 **6** ½ **Potentiale (IRE)**[26] 2747 6-9-9 **78** .... (p) PatrickHills(3) 2 70
(J W Hills) *s.s: hld up in last pair: rdn and effrt on outer over 2f out: nt qckn and no imp on ldrs* **7/1**[3]
32-5 **7** *2* **Inner Angel**[28] 2674 3-8-7 **70** .... LiamKeniry 5 58
(R A Teal) *trckd ldrs: disp 4th st: no prog over 2f out: sn lost pl and btn* **14/1**
00-4 **8** *12* **Integria**[20] 2922 4-9-1 **67** .... DaneO'Neill 6 31
(Miss Venetia Williams) *a in rr: 7th st: sn struggling: bhd fnl 2f* **25/1**
2045 **9** *20* **Thundering Home**[17] 3039 3-8-4 **67** .... (t) NickyMackay 8 —
(M J Attwater) *pushed up to chse ldr: wknd 3f out: t.o* **25/1**

2m 7.19s (-2.51) **Going Correction** -0.075s/f (Good)
WFA 3 from 4yo+ 11lb 9 Ran SP% **115.1**
Speed ratings (Par 105): **107,106,103,101,99 99,97,87,71**
Tote Swingers:1&2:£3.50, 2&3:£6.10, 1&3:£2.20 CSF £10.02 CT £30.27 TOTE £2.10: £1.10, £2.50, £1.70; EX 11.80 Place 6: £176.10, Place 5: £12.23..

Owner Sheikh Hamdan Bin Mohammed Al Maktoum **Bred** Darley **Trained** Middleham Moor, N Yorks

FOCUS
A fair handicap and the pace was sound. The form is taken at face value.
T/Plt: £111.00 to a £1 stake. Pool:£52,894.96 - 347.72 winning tickets. T/Qpdt: £15.70 to a £1 stake. Pool:£4,301.81 - 201.54 winning tickets. JN

The Form Book, Raceform Ltd, Compton, RG20 6NL

3203 HAYDOCK (L-H)

Thursday, July 1

OFFICIAL GOING: Good to firm (8.2)

Inner sprint course used. Rail realignment on round course increased advertised distances by 10yds.

Wind: Fresh, across Weather: Overcast

3582 RITEC CLEAR-SHIELD H'CAP — 1m 2f 95y

2:00 (2:00) (Class 5) (0-70,70) 3-Y-O+ £2,590 (£770; £385; £192) Stalls High

Form RPR

-034 1 **Mount Athos (IRE)**[13] 3160 3-8-11 64 MichaelHills 7 91+
(J W Hills) *led for 2f: remained handy: regained ld over 3f out: clr ent fnl 2f: eased down ins fnl f* 3/1[2]

33-0 2 11 **Grams And Ounces**[27] 2702 3-8-9 62 TomEaves 3 63
(Miss Amy Weaver) *hld up in tch: rdn and outpcd over 2f out: styd on fr over 1f out: prog to take 2nd cl home: no ch w wnr* 13/2[3]

-041 3 ½ **Ting Ting (USA)**[13] 3180 3-8-7 60 JamieSpencer 4 60
(T P Tate) *cl up: lost pl 6f out: sn pushed along: rallied to chse ldrs over 2f out: chsd wnr in vain over 1f out: no ch and lost 2nd cl home* 15/8[1]

033 4 3 ¼ **Kyle Of Bute**[13] 3177 4-9-2 58 RobertWinston 5 52
(B P J Baugh) *racd keenly on outer: in tch: chsd wnr and pushed along over 3f out: lost 2nd over 2f out: sn outpcd by wnr over 1f out: wknd ins fnl f* 9/1

5001 5 1 ¾ **Harare**[17] 3032 9-9-7 63 (v) JamesDoyle 2 54
(R J Price) *hdwy to ld after 2f: hdd 7f out: rdn and wknd over 2f out* 16/1

2152 6 4 ½ **Finsbury**[2] 3531 7-9-11 67 DavidAllan 9 49
(Miss L A Perratt) *s.i.s: in rr: swtchd rt and pushed along over 2f out: carried hd high: no imp: hung lft ins fnl f: nvr a danger* 9/1

0-60 7 3 ½ **Highland Jewel (IRE)**[22] 2871 3-8-9 62 LukeMorris 8 37
(C G Cox) *racd keenly: in rr: struggling over 4f out: hung lft whn n.d 3f out: nvr on terms* 28/1

4040 8 51 **Prohibition (IRE)**[18] 2991 4-10-0 70 (b[1]) EddieAhern 6 —
(W J Haggas) *racd keenly: hld up in tch: plld his way into ld 7f out: hdd over 3f out: sn wknd: eased whn wl btn ins fnl f: t.o* 17/2

2m 12.78s (-3.22) **Going Correction** -0.125s/f (Firm)
WFA 3 from 4yo+ 11lb 8 Ran SP% 113.0
Speed ratings (Par 103): **95,86,85,83,81 78,75,34**
toteswingers: 1&2 £4.00, 1&3 £2.30, 2&3 £2.80 CSF £22.21 CT £44.37 TOTE £4.60: £1.40, £2.20, £1.50; EX 28.50.
Owner Corinthian **Bred** David Magnier And Cobra Bloodstock **Trained** Upper Lambourn, Berks

FOCUS

Races of 1m and upwards were on the stands' side course, with the bend out of the back straight on Line 3, so the distance from the 1m start to the winning post was 1m 40yds. The winning jockey described the ground as good to firm, with a little cut on top. A modest handicap, but it was sound run. The winner did it easily but there was little depth to the race.

Prohibition(IRE) Official explanation: jockey said gelding lost its action

3583 E B F RONNIE BERLYNE MEMORIAL NOVICE FILLIES' STKS — 6f

2:30 (2:31) (Class 4) 2-Y-O £4,533 (£1,348; £674; £336) Stalls Low

Form RPR

22 1 **Madany (IRE)**[30] 2623 2-8-12 0 MichaelHills 2 82+
(B W Hills) *hld up: effrt on outer 2f out: led jst over 1f out: pushed out and in full control fnl 100yds* 8/11[1]

4210 2 2 **Hortensia (IRE)**[13] 3141 2-9-3 0 RyanMoore 3 81
(M R Channon) *led: pushed along and hdd jst over 1f out: nt qckn ins fnl f: wl hld fnl 100yds* 2/1[2]

30 3 1 ¾ **Elkmait**[29] 2641 2-8-12 0 NeilCallan 5 71
(C E Brittain) *briefly got upset in stalls bef s: ref to settle: racd cl up in 2nd pl: u.p and lost 2nd wl over 1f out: styd on same pce: no imp ins fnl f* 6/1[3]

0 4 shd **Wolf Slayer**[9] 3295 2-8-12 0 RichardKingscote 1 70
(Tom Dascombe) *cl up: rdn over 1f out: styd on same pce ins fnl f: nt gng pce to chal* 33/1

1m 14.03s (0.53) **Going Correction** -0.125s/f (Firm) 4 Ran SP% 108.5
Speed ratings (Par 93): **91,88,86,85**
CSF £2.44 TOTE £1.40; EX 2.40.
Owner Hamdan Al Maktoum **Bred** Mesnil Investments Ltd **Trained** Lambourn, Berks

FOCUS

A small field but an interesting contest nonetheless. The standard is set around the second and third.

NOTEBOOK

Madany(IRE) was turned over at odds-on last time but she'd run well behind the more experienced Hortensia on her debut, and a 5lb pull in the weights proved more than sufficient to reverse that form. She did this nicely, quickening up from off the pace, and was well on top at the finish. There's more to come from her, and given the stamina on her dam's side, she should get 7f in time, especially now that the riding tactics have changed. (op 4-5 tchd 5-6 in places)

Hortensia(IRE) is likely to want 7f sooner rather than later. She enjoyed the run of things out in front here but lacked the acceleration of the winner, although there was no disgrace in her performance strictly at the weights. (op 7-2)

Elkmait again failed to settle through the early stages, which wouldn't have helped her chance. Nurseries are now open to her. (op 3-1)

Wolf Slayer, well beaten on her debut, looked to face a stiff task but ran well, especially as she was rather trapped near the far rail throughout the closing stages. She's clearly improved plenty for her first effort, though, and might be able to find a little race. (op 25-1)

3584 VISTA PANELS H'CAP — 6f

3:00 (3:01) (Class 4) (0-80,80) 3-Y-O+ £4,533 (£1,348; £674; £336) Stalls Low

Form RPR

1411 1 **King Of Eden (IRE)**[28] 2671 4-9-4 70 DavidAllan 9 86+
(E J Alston) *bhd: hdwy over 1f out: r.o to ld fnl 150yds: edgd lft: pushed out cl to home* 11/4[1]

-033 2 1 ½ **Tyfos**[19] 2982 5-9-10 76 RobertWinston 11 84
(B P J Baugh) *hld up: hdwy 1/2-way: rdn and chalng 1f out: nt gng pce of wnr fnl 75yds* 9/2[2]

4312 3 1 **Legal Eagle (IRE)**[16] 3065 5-9-11 77 JamieSpencer 5 82
(Paul Green) *led: rdn over 1f out: hdd fnl 150yds: kpt on same pce cl home* 5/1[3]

035 4 1 **Grissom (IRE)**[5] 3430 4-9-9 75 JoeFanning 4 77
(A Berry) *chsd ldrs: rdn over 1f out: trying to chal over 1f out: nt qckn ins fnl f* 12/1

0052 5 ½ **Rainy Night**[12] 3205 4-8-7 62 (p) KellyHarrison[(3)] 13 62
(R Hollinshead) *chsd ldrs: rdn 2f out: styd on same pce ins fnl f* 22/1

0053 6 1 ½ **Coleorton Choice**[21] 2883 4-9-9 80 PaulPickard[(5)] 7 75
(R Hollinshead) *midfield: hdwy to chse ldrs over 2f out: rdn over 1f out: one pce ins fnl f* 14/1

2000 7 ½ **Pearly Wey**[18] 2991 7-9-9 75 TomEaves 10 69
(I W McInnes) *missed break: bhd: rdn over 1f out: prog and hung lft ins fnl f: nt gng pce to trble ldrs* 20/1

0022 8 shd **Silver Wind**[24] 2808 5-9-8 77 (v) MartinLane[(3)] 3 70
(P D Evans) *midfield: rdn 4f out: outpced 1/2-way: hdwy u.p over 1f out: no imp on ldrs ins fnl f* 20/1

0U30 9 nk **Northern Bolt**[19] 2982 5-9-9 75 (v) PatrickMathers 1 67
(I W McInnes) *s.i.s: outpcd: rdn and sme hdwy over 1f out: unable to rch ldrs* 28/1

540- 10 2 ¼ **Commando Scott (IRE)**[299] 5673 9-8-8 67 NeilFarley[(7)] 8 52
(D Carroll) *midfield: effrt 2f out: no imp on ldrs: wknd over 1f out* 28/1

5001 11 hd **Bosun Breese**[12] 3205 5-9-7 73 GrahamGibbons 14 57
(T D Barron) *prom: rdn over 1f out: sn wknd* 14/1

-050 12 1 **Northern Dare (IRE)**[18] 2992 6-10-0 80 (b[1]) StevieDonohoe 6 61
(R A Fahey) *prom: rdn 2f out: wknd over 1f out* 7/1

0103 13 1 ¼ **Charles Darwin (IRE)**[7] 3373 7-8-13 65 FrannyNorton 2 42
(M Blanshard) *midfield: pushed along and wknd 2f out* 20/1

1m 11.89s (-1.61) **Going Correction** -0.125s/f (Firm) 13 Ran SP% 120.6
Speed ratings (Par 105): **105,103,101,100,99 97,97,96,96,93 93,91,90**
toteswingers: 1&2 £3.50, 1&3 £3.80, 2&3 £4.00 CSF £12.67 CT £60.74 TOTE £3.60: £1.70, £1.40, £2.00; EX 18.30.
Owner The Grumpy Old Geezers **Bred** Gainsborough Stud Management Ltd **Trained** Longton, Lancs

FOCUS

Quite a competitive handicap on paper, but it was won in pretty ready fashion by the favourite, who can do better still. The second and third give the form a solid look.

3585 TUFFX CONSERVATORY ROOF GLASS H'CAP — 1m 30y

3:30 (3:31) (Class 3) (0-95,94) 3-Y-O+ £8,095 (£2,408; £1,203; £601) Stalls Low

Form RPR

0366 1 **Ginger Jack**[12] 3206 3-8-8 83 JoeFanning 1 94
(M Johnston) *led for 2f: remained prom: rdn to regain ld 2f out: r.o gamely for press: on top cl home* 4/1[3]

0002 2 ½ **Benandonner (USA)**[8] 3334 7-9-4 84 AndreaAtzeni 7 95
(Mike Murphy) *racd keenly: prom: led after 2f: rdn and hdd 2f out: r.o and continued to chal for press: hld cl home* 8/1

1252 3 2 ¼ **Follow The Flag (IRE)**[11] 3239 6-9-0 85 (p) DeclanCannon[(5)] 5 91
(A J McCabe) *chsd ldrs: effrt over 2f out: ch over 1f out: no ex fnl 75yds* 6/1

1-35 4 ½ **Rumool**[61] 1703 3-9-1 90 NeilCallan 9 92
(C E Brittain) *hld up: effrt to chse ldrs wl over 2f out: sn hung lft u.p: styd on same pce ins fnl f: no imp on ldrs* 7/2[2]

6003 5 nk **Kyllachy Star**[19] 2971 4-9-8 88 StevieDonohoe 8 92
(R A Fahey) *hld up: pushed along over 2f out: kpt on u.p ins fnl f: nt gng pce to chal ldrs* 8/1

6111 6 1 **Ezdeyaad (USA)**[12] 3206 6-10-0 94 PJMcDonald 4 96
(G A Swinbank) *in tch: pushed along and nt qckn 3f out: kpt on u.p bhd ldrs: fdd fnl 50yds* 11/4[1]

2-00 7 15 **Leceile (USA)**[27] 2710 4-9-7 87 RyanMoore 2 54
(W J Haggas) *hld up in rr: u.p 2f out: lft bhd over 1f out* 9/1

1m 42.1s (-2.60) **Going Correction** -0.125s/f (Firm)
WFA 3 from 4yo+ 9lb 7 Ran SP% 115.4
Speed ratings (Par 107): **103,102,100,99,99 98,83**
toteswingers: 1&2 £5.20, 1&3 £10.60, 2&3 £8.40 CSF £35.65 CT £190.07 TOTE £5.70: £3.10, £6.20; EX 37.60.
Owner Sheikh Hamdan Bin Mohammed Al Maktoum **Bred** Darley **Trained** Middleham Moor, N Yorks

FOCUS

The quickest of tyhe three C/D times, and the first two were always prominent in this decent handicap.

NOTEBOOK

Ginger Jack had been a little disappointing on his previous two starts, but he went too quick up front on his last visit here and was ridden more conservatively this time, taking a lead from Benandonner. His third to stablemate Sea Lord at Doncaster last month looked solid form and he returned to that sort of level to score off a 2lb lower mark. (op 11-2)

Benandonner(USA), who would not have been helped by the rain that had fallen, was officially 3lb well in at the weights following his good second at Salisbury eight days earlier. Keen to lead, he ran a solid race, but things will be tougher off his new mark. (op 9-1)

Follow The Flag(IRE) was given every chance but over this shorter trip he just lacked the required pace in the closing stages. He'll appreciate a return to 1m2f. (tchd 11-2)

Rumool carried his head high, hung left under pressure and didn't look to be putting it all in at the finish. (op 4-1 tchd 9-2)

Kyllachy Star has never won over a trip this far but he looked worth another go over 1m when running on well at the finish over 7f at Sandown last time. A stronger-run race here would have suited him better. (op 15-2)

Ezdeyaad(USA), chasing a C&D four-timer, didn't look to have been handicapped out of things off just a 4lb higher mark, but he proved disappointing. (op 5-2)

3586 ULTRAFRAME MAIDEN STKS (DIV I) — 1m 30y

4:00 (4:01) (Class 5) 3-Y-O+ £2,266 (£674; £337; £168) Stalls Low

Form RPR

0 1 **Green Destiny (IRE)**[59] 1769 3-9-0 0 MichaelHills 12 80
(W J Haggas) *chsd ldrs: rdn to chal 2f out: led jst over 1f out: all out towards fin* 14/1

2-50 2 hd **Official Style**[50] 2033 3-9-0 81 RyanMoore 4 80+
(Sir Michael Stoute) *midfield: nt clr run 2f out: hdwy over 1f out: rn to take 2nd fnl 110yds: fin wl: jst failed* 11/8[1]

22 3 1 ¼ **City Ground (USA)**[19] 2968 3-9-0 0 NeilCallan 10 77
(M A Jarvis) *midfield: pushed along and hdwy 2f out: effrt to chse ldrs over 1f out: nt qckn fnl 100yds* 7/2[2]

04 4 nse **Khandaq (USA)**[54] 1927 3-9-0 0 JoeFanning 1 77
(M Johnston) *led: rdn and hdd jst over 1f out: continued to chal tl no ex fnl 50yds* 25/1

5 1 **Jet Away** 3-9-0 0 EddieAhern 7 74+
(H R A Cecil) *dwlt: hld up: nt clr run over 1f out: kpt on under hands and heels riding ins fnl f: nt quite rch ldrs: promising* 8/1

23- 6 2 ¾ **No Mean Trick (USA)**[193] 7826 4-9-9 0 LukeMorris 6 70
(C G Cox) *chsd ldr: rdn to chal 2f out: nt qckn u.p over 1f out: one pce ins fnl f* 33/1

0- 7 1 ½ **Satwa Excel**[334] 4542 3-8-6 0 AshleyHamblett[(3)] 2 60
(E A L Dunlop) *chsd ldrs: pushed along over 2f out: rdn and wknd over 1f out* 100/1

06- **8** 1 3/4 **Montelissima (IRE)**[243] 7183 3-8-9 0 .... JimmyQuinn 8 60+
(E A L Dunlop) *trckd ldrs: nt clr run 2f out: shkn up over 1f out: wknd ins fnl f* **50/1**

2 **9** 3 1/2 **Captivator**[30] 2632 3-8-9 0 .... JamieSpencer 9 47
(J R Fanshawe) *racd keenly in midfield: effrt over 2f out: no imp: wknd ins fnl f* **4/1**[3]

/03 **10** 6 **Cheddar George**[21] 2900 4-9-9 0 .... RobertWinston 5 41
(B J Meehan) *racd keenly: hld up: pushed along over 2f out: outpcd over 1f out* **25/1**

11 4 1/2 **Norville (IRE)** 3-9-0 0 .... JamesDoyle 11 28
(P D Evans) *dwlt: in rr: struggling fnl 2f: nvr on terms* **150/1**

6 **12** 3 1/2 **Gracie May**[21] 2900 3-8-4 0 .... PaulPickard(5) 3 15
(R Hollinshead) *racd keenly: towards rr: pushed along over 3f out: bhd fnl 2f* **100/1**

1m 43.09s (-1.61) **Going Correction** -0.125s/f (Firm)
WFA 3 from 4yo 9lb **12** Ran SP% **117.3**
Speed ratings (Par 103): **98,97,96,96,95 92,91,89,86,80 75,72**
toteswingers: 1&2 £6.50, 1&3 £8.90, 2&3 £2.80 CSF £32.51 TOTE £20.20: £3.50, £1.10, £1.90; EX 67.60.
Owner Saleh Al Homaizi & Imad Al Sagar **Bred** Mubkera Syndicate **Trained** Newmarket, Suffolk

FOCUS
A messy race run at a steady early pace, and the favourite looked unlucky not to get up following a troubled passage. The form makes a fair bit of sense overall.
Montelissima(IRE) Official explanation: trainer's rep said filly was unsuited by the good to firm ground

3587 SAINT-GOBAIN PLANITHERM MAIDEN STKS (DIV II) 1m 30y
4:30 (4:30) (Class 5) 3-Y-O+ **£2,266** (£674; £337; £168) **Stalls** Low

Form RPR

43-0 **1** **Munsarim (IRE)**[33] 2544 3-9-0 79 .... JamieSpencer 1 86+
(J L Dunlop) *mde all: qcknd pce over 3f out: clr under 2f out: eased down fnl 100yds* **15/8**[2]

00 **2** 11 **Mont Ras (IRE)**[21] 2900 3-9-0 0 .... JamesMcDonald 6 58
(E A L Dunlop) *chsd wnr: outpcd over 2f out: kpt on in vain pursuit after: no ch* **80/1**

3 1 1/4 **Swiftly Done (IRE)** 3-9-0 0 .... JoeFanning 4 55
(J Noseda) *s.s: hld up bhd: hdwy and hung lft u.p over 1f out to move into 3rd: no imp after* **12/1**[3]

00- **4** 2 3/4 **Carnival Time (IRE)**[322] 4933 3-9-0 0 .... LukeMorris 11 49
(C G Cox) *hld up: rdn and outpcd over 3f out: kpt on and edgd lft over 1f out: nt trble ldrs* **80/1**

5 1/2 **Tasza (USA)** 3-8-9 0 .... JamesDoyle 10 42
(A J McCabe) *s.s: sn in midfield: rdn to chse ldrs over 2f out: wknd over 1f out* **50/1**

202- **6** 2 1/2 **Paradise Spectre**[341] 4306 3-9-0 83 .... NeilCallan 8 42
(J R Weymes) *chsd ldrs: rdn over 2f out: wknd over 1f out* **20/1**

00 **7** 4 1/2 **Kayaan**[30] 2632 3-9-0 0 .... MichaelHills 3 31
(W J Haggas) *s.i.s: ref to settle: trckd ldrs: rdn and wknd 3f out* **16/1**

2 **8** 19 **Warm Memories**[23] 2841 3-9-0 0 .... RyanMoore 7 —
(Sir Michael Stoute) *ref to settle: trckd ldrs tl pushed along and wknd 2f out* **8/11**[1]

9 12 **Tek A Deek**[776] 6-9-9 0 .... LeeVickers 5 —
(James Moffatt) *s.s: a bhd: rdn 4f out: nvr on terms* **100/1**

1m 42.8s (-1.90) **Going Correction** -0.125s/f (Firm)
WFA 3 from 6yo 9lb **9** Ran SP% **116.4**
Speed ratings (Par 103): **100,89,87,85,84 82,77,58,46**
toteswingers:1&2 £14.80, 2&3 £30.10, 1&3 £3.40 CSF £148.13 TOTE £2.70: £1.30, £9.40, £2.30; EX 139.30.
Owner Hamdan Al Maktoum **Bred** Shadwell Estate Company Limited **Trained** Arundel, W Sussex

FOCUS
The quicker of the two divisions by 0.29sec, but it looked the weaker race overall with the favourite flopping. The form is rated around the winner.

3588 GLASS TIMES STAYERS' H'CAP 1m 6f
5:00 (5:00) (Class 4) (0-85,85) 4-Y-O+ **£4,533** (£1,348; £674; £336) **Stalls** Low

Form RPR

1231 **1** **Lady Eclair (IRE)**[7] 3367 4-9-6 84 6ex .... JoeFanning 4 95+
(M Johnston) *trckd ldrs: wnt 2nd 4f out: rdn to ld 2f out: hld on gamely cl home* **10/3**[2]

2-24 **2** hd **Plymouth Rock (IRE)**[22] 2865 4-9-5 83 ....(v[1]) RyanMoore 1 94
(J Noseda) *hld up: hdwy to chse ldrs over 3f out: wnt 2nd fnl 75yds: styd on strly to cl on wnr cl home* **15/8**[1]

6322 **3** 1 1/2 **Wicked Daze (IRE)**[12] 3198 7-8-12 76 .... TomEaves 3 85
(Miss L A Perratt) *led: rdn and hdd 2f out: hung rt u.p over 1f out: no ex towards fin* **11/1**

13-2 **4** 1 1/4 **Arab League (IRE)**[14] 3127 5-8-3 67 .... LukeMorris 7 74
(R J Price) *hld up: rdn 3f out: hdwy to chse ldrs u.p 2f out: hung lft over 1f out: styd on ins fnl f: nt rch ldrs* **10/1**

0-03 **5** 1 1/2 **Bavarian Nordic (USA)**[15] 3090 5-8-8 72 ....(v) JamieSpencer 8 77
(Mrs A Duffield) *hld up: rdn and hdwy over 2f out: one pce fnl 100yds* **20/1**

-604 **6** 1/2 **Bollin Felix**[20] 2938 6-9-2 80 ....(b) DavidAllan 2 84
(T D Easterby) *hld up: pushed along 2f out: kpt on ins fnl f: nt gng pce to rch ldrs* **9/2**[3]

1/41 **7** 5 **Just Rob**[61] 1690 5-9-7 85 .... EddieAhern 10 82
(Ian Williams) *in tch: effrt to chse ldrs 3f out: wknd 2f out* **12/1**

050 **8** 21 **Kimberley Downs (USA)**[20] 2938 4-8-11 75 ....(v) JimmyQuinn 6 43
(N Wilson) *chsd ldrs: lost pl over 4f out: wknd 2f out* **40/1**

3350 **9** 1 3/4 **Hindu Kush (IRE)**[40] 2313 5-8-10 74 .... StevieDonohoe 9 40
(Ian Williams) *chsd ldr to 4f out: sn wknd: eased and t.o fnl 2f* **12/1**

3m 0.58s (-0.62) **Going Correction** -0.125s/f (Firm) **9** Ran SP% **116.1**
Speed ratings (Par 105): **105,104,104,103,102 102,99,87,86**
toteswingers:1&2 £3.50, 2&3 £3.30, 1&3 £6.40 CSF £10.03 CT £60.05 TOTE £4.60: £1.40, £1.50, £2.20; EX 11.90 Place 6: £39.30 Place 5: £30.58.
Owner Netherfield House Stud **Bred** Lynch Bages Ltd & Samac Ltd **Trained** Middleham Moor, N Yorks

Just Rob Official explanation: trainer's rep said gelding was unsuited by the good to firm ground
T/Plt: £57.10 to a £1 stake. Pool:£52,194.26 - 667.11 winning tickets. T/Qpdt: £13.90 to a £1 stake. Pool: £3,523.28 - 187.51 winning tickets. DO

3294 NEWBURY (L-H)
Thursday, July 1

OFFICIAL GOING: Good to firm (7.5)
Rail realignment increased races on round course by 15metres.
Wind: Virtually nil Weather: Warm and muggy

3589 INKERMAN LONDON APPRENTICE H'CAP 1m 3f 5y
6:30 (6:30) (Class 5) (0-70,68) 4-Y-O+ **£2,590** (£770; £385; £192) **Stalls** Low

Form RPR

-063 **1** **Sgt Schultz (IRE)**[27] 2690 7-9-2 65 .... RyanPowell(5) 7 71
(J S Moore) *sn restrained bk into 5th: swtchd rt to centre and hdwy over 2f out: led ent fnl f: styd on wl: rdn out* **3/1**[2]

05-3 **2** 3/4 **Kings Troop**[13] 3160 4-9-10 68 .... SimonPearce 1 73
(A King) *trckd ldr: led 2f out: sn rdn: hdd ent fnl f: styd on: no ex towards fin* **15/2**

2122 **3** 1 1/4 **Megalala (IRE)**[3] 3512 9-9-10 68 .... AshleyMorgan 2 71
(J J Bridger) *led tl over 7f out: prom: led on bit wl over 3f out: rdn and hdd 2f out: ev ch ent fnl f: no ex fnl 100yds* **11/4**[1]

2113 **4** 1 **Touch Of Style (IRE)**[4] 3473 6-8-11 58 .... DavidKenny(3) 5 59
(Matthew Salaman) *trckd ldrs: effrt in cl 3rd 2f out: styd on same pce fnl f* **7/2**[3]

1252 **5** 1 1/2 **What's Up Doc (IRE)**[35] 2455 9-9-4 65 .... GemmaGracey-Davison(3) 3 63
(Mrs Lawney Hill) *trckd ldr: led over 7f out: hdd wl over 3f out: sn rdn: styd on same pce fnl 2f* **7/2**[3]

660/ **6** 23 **Hail The King (USA)**[53] 4733 10-8-5 49 oh4 .... MatthewDavies 6 8
(R Curtis) *stdd s: a last: rdn 4f out: wknd over 2f out* **33/1**

2m 20.12s (-1.08) **Going Correction** -0.10s/f (Good) **6** Ran SP% **110.8**
Speed ratings (Par 103): **99,98,97,96,95 79**
toteswingers: 1&2 £3.30, 1&3 £1.90, 2&3 £5.50. CSF £23.93 TOTE £4.60: £2.10, £2.40; EX 10.60.
Owner Jim Barnes **Bred** Frank Dunne **Trained** Upper Lambourn, Berks
■ Stewards' Enquiry : Gemma Gracey-Davison two-day ban: used whip with excessive frequency (Jul 15-16)

FOCUS
A fairly tight handicap for apprentice riders, and ordinary form. The race is rated around the fourth.

3590 DENFORD STUD E B F MAIDEN FILLIES' STKS 6f 8y
7:05 (7:08) (Class 4) 2-Y-O **£3,885** (£1,156; £577; £288) **Stalls** High

Form RPR

1 **Admirable Spirit** 2-9-0 0 .... RichardHughes 7 86+
(R Hannon) *trckd ldrs: pushed along 2f out: chal 1f out: rdn to ld fnl 120yds: rn green: drifted lft: in command whn veered lft nr fin* **7/1**

3 **2** 1 **Florestans Match**[18] 3000 2-9-0 0 .... JimCrowley 8 83+
(R M Beckett) *disp ld: overall ldr wl over 1f out: sn rdn: hdd fnl 120yds: kpt on but nt pce of wnr* **13/8**[1]

5 **3** 2 **Eshoog (IRE)**[38] 2397 2-9-0 0 .... WilliamBuick 3 77
(C E Brittain) *trckd ldrs: rdn over 2f out: ev ch over 1f out: kpt on but nt pce of front 2 fnl f* **11/2**[3]

4 4 **Apace (IRE)** 2-9-0 0 .... RyanMoore 2 65+
(Sir Michael Stoute) *broke wl: sn pushed along in mid-div: nt pce to cl whn squeezed up wl over 1f out: swtchd rt ins 1f out: styd on* **9/2**[2]

5 1 3/4 **Storm Tide** 2-8-9 0 .... MatthewDavies(5) 4 60
(G D Blake) *sn pushed along in mid-div: rdn 3f out: no imp tl styd on ins fnl f* **100/1**

5 **6** nk **Star Today**[30] 2616 2-9-0 0 .... MartinDwyer 11 59
(B J Meehan) *disp ld tl rdn wl over 1f out: kpt on same pce: fading whn lost 2 pls fnl 100yds* **10/1**

7 3/4 **Adelina Patti** 2-9-0 0 .... AdamKirby 9 57
(W R Swinburn) *mid-div: rdn over 2f out: nt pce to get on terms* **22/1**

8 nk **Azlaa** 2-9-0 0 .... SteveDrowne 10 60+
(R Hannon) *sn outpcd in last pair: drifted lft fnl f: n.d* **16/1**

9 3 **Make My Mark (IRE)** 2-8-11 0 .... MartinLane(3) 5 47+
(Pat Eddery) *little slowly away whn squeezed out s: sn pushed along towards rr: sme prog over 2f out: fdd ins fnl f* **66/1**

10 2 1/4 **Boogie Down (IRE)** 2-9-0 0 .... TedDurcan 6 40
(W R Swinburn) *s.i.s: a outpcd in rr* **28/1**

5 **11** 6 **Mabsam**[26] 2740 2-9-0 0 .... RichardHills 1 22
(E A L Dunlop) *trckd ldrs: rdn over 2f out: wknd over 1f out* **15/2**

1m 12.56s (-0.44) **Going Correction** -0.10s/f (Good) **11** Ran SP% **121.2**
Speed ratings (Par 93): **98,96,94,88,86 85,84,84,80,77 69**
toteswingers: 1&2 £3.50, 1&3 £11.90, 2&3 £4.40. CSF £18.94 TOTE £8.70: £2.40, £1.40, £2.20; EX 26.30.
Owner Longview Stud & Bloodstock Ltd **Bred** Wyck Hall Stud Ltd **Trained** East Everleigh, Wilts

FOCUS
This should work out to be an above-average juvenile fillies' maiden and several winners should emerge from it. There should be more to come from the winner.

NOTEBOOK
Admirable Spirit ◆ was representing the juvenile-winning machine that is the Hannon/Hughes combination and surprisingly proved easy to back for this racecourse debut. She knew her job, though, and ultimately ran out a taking winner. She travelled strongly just behind the early leaders and it was apparent soon after she was asked to get on top she was going to win the race. Her pedigree suggests a mix of both speed and stamina, and when looking at the stable's two previous winners of this maiden in the past decade, Indian Ink and Full Mandate, there is every reason to think she could be smart. (op 11-2)
Florestans Match, third on her debut, proved all the rage to get off the mark. She travelled kindly on the front end and held every chance, but simply met a classier filly in the winner. Switching to one of the smaller tracks should see her go one better. (op 3-1)
Eshoog(IRE), another that attracted support, looked in need of the outing when fifth in novice company on her debut 38 days earlier. She was never far away and had her chance, but eventually paid for doing too much early on over this extra furlong. More patient handling over this trip, or more likely a drop back to 5f, should do the trick for this speedily bred filly. (op 9-2)
Apace(IRE) ◆ is another with a pedigree that mixes speed with stamina. Easy to back for her debut, she got badly outpaced early on and behind. She was staying on strongly once the penny dropped, however, and is sure to improve for the experience. Remembering her leading connections sent out Red Bloom to get beaten on debut in this race back in 2003 and that one went on to take the Fillies' Mile, this clearly rates a promising effort. (op 4-1 tchd 7-2)
Storm Tide produced an encouraging debut effort and she appeals as one to improve a deal for the outing.

Star Today showed bright early pace, but was done with before the final furlong and failed to see out the longer trip under such tactics.

3591 CHILDREN IN CROSSFIRE CONDITIONS STKS 7f (S)
7:35 (7:37) (Class 3) 3-Y-O+ **£6,542** (£1,959; £979; £490) **Stalls** High

Form RPR

2-12 **1** **Yaa Wayl (IRE)**[27] 2712 3-8-6 100 ow1 ... PhilipRobinson 1 107+
(M A Jarvis) *led for 2f at stdy pce: trckd ldr: led 2f out: sn qcknd pce: r.o strly to assert fnl 75yds: rdn out* **10/11**[1]

1-14 **2** *1 1/4* **Dafeef**[33] 2546 3-8-5 102 ... TedDurcan 3 103
(Saeed Bin Suroor) *awkward leaving stalls: sn trcking ldng pair: qcknd up wl w wnr 2f out: ev ch whn rdn ent fnl f: hld whn edgd lft fnl 75yds* **5/4**[2]

2000 **3** *8* **Mujood**[8] 3334 7-8-13 94 ... (v) WilliamBuick 2 84
(Eve Johnson Houghton) *trckd ldrs: rdn and ch 2f out: sn outpcd* **10/1**[3]

0610 **4** *13* **Stargazy**[2] 3524 6-8-6 50 ... AmyScott(7) 4 49
(A J Lidderdale) *s.i.s: hdwy to ld and qckn pce after 2f: rdn and hdd 2f out: qckly btn* **100/1**

1m 25.52s (-0.18) **Going Correction** -0.10s/f (Good)
WFA 3 from 4yo+ 8lb **4** Ran SP% **106.9**
Speed ratings (Par 107): **97,95,86,71**
CSF £2.26 TOTE £1.70; EX 1.90.
Owner Sheikh Ahmed Al Maktoum **Bred** Ballylinch Stud **Trained** Newmarket, Suffolk

FOCUS
The defection of Lord Shanakill took a lot of interest away from this conditions event and ensured it was a match between the two 3-y-os. The pair predictably dominated and the progressive winner looks the best guide to the form.

NOTEBOOK
Yaa Wayl(IRE) wasn't suited by the stop-start pace in Listed company at Epsom on Oaks day earlier this month, and was very well backed on this drop back down in grade. He again got a bit warm beforehand and, having set out to make all, had to be content to give up that spot as the outclassed Stargazy made his way to the front. That may well have helped him, though, as he got a nice lead and was perfectly placed 2f out. He had to work to fend off the runner-up, but always looked to be doing enough from the furlong marker and it should be noted that rival was rated 2lb his superior. His jockey also put up 1lb overweight and, while there is still some doubt over his temperament, he is well worth another crack at a Listed prize. (op Evens tchd 11-10)
Dafeef was very closely matched on previous form with the winner, having been tried in a Listed race last time out, and has few miles on the clock. Not for the first time, though, he was sluggish from the gates and took time to settle. He also showed a tendency to hang and looked to be feeling the quick ground, so probably did very well to finish so close in the end. Returning to an easier surface should prove much more to his liking, but he isn't simple to place off 102. (op 11-10 tchd Evens)
Mujood, a tough and very useful handicapper at his best, had a fair bit to find with the first pair at these weights. He still ran below expectations, though, and is currently struggling for form. Perhaps a return to his beloved Goodwood later this month will spark a revival. (op 12-1)

3592 SUN FILLIES' H'CAP 7f (S)
8:10 (8:12) (Class 4) (0-80,79) 3-Y-O+ **£4,533** (£1,348; £674; £336) **Stalls** High

Form RPR

10-2 **1** **Sarasota Sunshine**[13] 3172 4-9-13 79 ... (v) RyanMoore 1 93+
(J Noseda) *trckd ldrs: led travelling smoothly wl over 1f out: clr ent fnl f: rdn fnl 75yds: comf* **10/11**[1]

6554 **2** *1 1/2* **Perfect Friend**[14] 3129 4-9-2 68 ... StephenCraine 4 75
(S Kirk) *mid-div: hdwy over 2f out: sn rdn to chse ldrs: styd on to go 2nd ins fnl f but a being hld by wnr* **20/1**

-065 **3** *nse* **Kurtanella**[19] 2970 3-9-4 78 ... RichardHughes 5 82
(R Hannon) *trckd ldrs: rdn 3f out: styd on to chal for 2nd ins fnl f but a being hld by wnr* **8/1**[2]

0014 **4** *3 1/4* **Ken's Girl**[18] 3001 6-9-2 68 ... AdamKirby 3 66
(W S Kittow) *led: rdn and hdd wl over 1f out: sn hld by wnr: no ex whn lost 2nd ins fnl f* **10/1**[3]

-613 **5** *nk* **Scarcity (IRE)**[31] 2588 3-8-7 67 ... TedDurcan 8 61
(E A L Dunlop) *jinked leaving stalls: hld up: rdn over 2f out: styd on ins fnl f: nvr trbld ldrs* **8/1**[2]

3052 **6** *1 3/4* **Steel Free (IRE)**[18] 3001 4-9-2 68 ... RobertHavlin 7 61
(M Madgwick) *trckd ldrs: rdn over 2f out: sn one pce* **10/1**[3]

30-0 **7** *1 1/2* **Pictures (IRE)**[13] 3158 3-8-12 72 ... TomQueally 6 58
(L M Cumani) *s.i.s: sn mid-div: hdwy over 2f out: sn hrd rdn: wknd fnl f* **10/1**[3]

0-50 **8** *hd* **Romancea (USA)**[18] 2998 3-8-11 71 ... (b1) WilliamBuick 10 56
(E F Vaughan) *hld up towards rr: rdn over 2f out: little imp* **25/1**

-206 **9** *3/4* **Tarita (IRE)**[17] 3023 3-9-1 75 ... JimCrowley 9 58
(R Hannon) *dwlt: rdn over 2f out: a towards rr* **33/1**

10-0 **10** *5* **Netta (IRE)**[64] 1618 4-9-11 77 ... SteveDrowne 2 49
(P J Makin) *trckd ldr tl rdn over 2f out: sn wknd* **22/1**

0/5 **11** *1/2* **Island Home**[16] 3062 4-9-3 69 ... MartinDwyer 11 40
(B J Meehan) *s.i.s: sn hung lft: a towards rr* **20/1**

1m 24.23s (-1.47) **Going Correction** -0.10s/f (Good)
WFA 3 from 4yo+ 8lb **11** Ran SP% **122.5**
Speed ratings (Par 102): **104,102,102,98,98 96,94,94,93,87 87**
toteswingers: 1&2 £9.20, 1&3 £4.30, 2&3 £15.10. CSF £29.38 CT £110.21 TOTE £1.80: £1.10, £4.60, £2.60; EX 26.90.
Owner Franconson Partners **Bred** London Thoroughbred S'Vces Ltd & West Bl **Trained** Newmarket, Suffolk

FOCUS
The runners kept to the centre of the track in this modest fillies' handicap and they went a sound enough pace. The winner is value for a bit extra.

3593 HUMPHREY BUTLER LTD FINE JEWELLERY MAIDEN STKS 1m 4f 5y
8:40 (8:41) (Class 4) 3-Y-O+ **£3,885** (£1,156; £577; £288) **Stalls** Low

Form RPR

33 **1** **Heart Of Hearts**[20] 2921 3-8-9 0 ... TomQueally 7 76+
(H R A Cecil) *trckd ldr: led 2f out: sn rdn: fnd more and hld on wl whn chal ins fnl f: rdn out* **11/4**[2]

5 **2** *1/2* **Dance Tempo**[13] 3173 3-9-0 0 ... SteveDrowne 8 80+
(H Morrison) *mid-div: hdwy over 2f out: sn rdn: pressed wnr ins fnl f: hld towards fin* **16/1**

5324 **3** *3/4* **Baltimore Clipper (USA)**[10] 3273 3-9-0 72 ... RichardHughes 2 79
(P F I Cole) *mid-div: hdwy over 2f out: rdn in cl 4th over 1f out: kpt on ins fnl f:* **12/1**

3 **4** *3 1/4* **Mascarene (USA)**[54] 1932 3-8-9 0 ... RyanMoore 9 69
(Sir Michael Stoute) *led: rdn and hdd 2f out: kpt on tl no ex fnl 150yds* **6/4**[1]

-03 **5** *3 1/4* **Old Hundred (IRE)**[18] 2994 3-9-0 0 ... AdamKirby 10 69
(J R Fanshawe) *hld up towards rr: hdwy 3f out: sn rdn: hung lft fr over 1f out: styd on same pce* **11/1**[3]

-040 **6** *hd* **Juwireya**[14] 3116 3-8-9 71 ... (b1) RichardHills 3 63
(M P Tregoning) *hld up towards rr of midfield: rdn over 3f out: little imp tl styd on fnl f* **20/1**

6 **7** *5* **Genes Of A Dancer (AUS)**[10] 3256 4-9-9 0 ... NeilChalmers 1 56
(M Appleby) *hld up towards rr: sme prog u.p into midfield 3f out: wknd over 1f out* **80/1**

06 **8** *2 1/2* **Lamps**[19] 2974 3-9-0 0 ... MartinDwyer 13 56
(B J Meehan) *trckd ldrs: rdn over 3f out: wknd 2f out* **25/1**

00- **9** *19* **Another Character (USA)**[229] 7400 3-9-0 0 ... (v1) TravisBlock 11 26
(M D I Usher) *mid-div: rdn over 3f out: wknd over 2f out* **150/1**

0- **10** *10* **Pivotal Express (IRE)**[262] 6741 4-9-13 0 ... MattieBatchelor 5 10
(J F Panvert) *s.i.s: bmpd over 6f out: a towards rr* **125/1**

11 *11* **Loupy Loups**[16] 4-9-5 0 ... RussKennemore(3) 12 —
(B G Powell) *s.i.s: sn in tch: effrt 4f out: wknd over 2f out* **100/1**

2m 37.0s (1.50) **Going Correction** -0.10s/f (Good)
WFA 3 from 4yo 13lb **11** Ran SP% **100.9**
Speed ratings (Par 105): **91,90,90,88,85 85,82,80,68,61 54**
toteswingers: 1&2 £11.10, 1&3 £5.30, 2&3 £9.50. CSF £28.19 TOTE £2.80: £1.10, £3.10, £4.20; EX 35.40.
Owner K Abdulla **Bred** Juddmonte Farms Ltd **Trained** Newmarket, Suffolk
■ Fluter Phil (100/1) and Mountain Hiker (4/1) were withdrawn; refused to enter stalls. Rule 4 applies, deduction 20p in the £.

FOCUS
The refusal of Mountain Hiker to enter the stalls took a little away from this maiden and there was just an average pace on. The form is still fair but the winner may not have had to match her early efforts.

3594 TOTESPORT.COM H'CAP 1m 4f 5y
9:10 (9:10) (Class 4) (0-85,85) 3-Y-O **£4,533** (£1,348; £674; £336) **Stalls** Low

Form RPR

-016 **1** **Christopher Wren (USA)**[14] 3105 3-9-3 81 ... SteveDrowne 6 92+
(J R Best) *hld up in last pair in tch: bit slipped completely through mouth 4f out: clsd on ldrs and nt best of runs on rails fr over 2f out: swtchd rt ent fnl f: rdn to ld fnl 75yds: hld on: drvn out* **5/2**[1]

31-4 **2** *shd* **Valid Reason**[64] 1624 3-9-1 79 ... TedDurcan 3 89
(Mrs A J Perrett) *trckd ldrs: nt clr run jst over 2f out: sn swtchd rt: str run jst ins fnl f to hold ev ch fnl 75yds: jst hld* **9/1**

1-05 **3** *1 1/2* **Fine Sight**[26] 2742 3-9-2 80 ... RichardHughes 8 88
(R Hannon) *racd keenly: sn led: rdn wl over 1f out: hdd fnl 75yds: no ex* **5/1**

0003 **4** *5* **Higgy's Ragazzo (FR)**[6] 3414 3-8-10 74 ... RyanMoore 4 74
(R Hannon) *trckd ldrs: rdn to chal 3f out: one pce fr over 1f out* **9/2**[3]

-002 **5** *11* **Meglio Ancora**[27] 2717 3-8-13 77 ... StephenCraine 2 59
(J G Portman) *stdd s: hld up in last: swtchd rt over 3f out: hdwy sn after: rdn and ev ch jst over 2f out: wknd over 1f out* **14/1**

2441 **6** *1* **Heading To First**[14] 3117 3-8-7 71 ... (p) AhmedAjtebi 1 52
(C E Brittain) *trckd ldr: rdn and ev ch over 2f out: wknd over 1f out* **14/1**

4-1 **7** *1 1/4* **Countess Comet (IRE)**[31] 2585 3-9-7 85 ... JimCrowley 7 64
(R M Beckett) *cl up: effrt 3f out: btn 2f out* **11/4**[2]

2m 33.43s (-2.07) **Going Correction** -0.10s/f (Good) **7** Ran SP% **113.4**
Speed ratings (Par 102): **102,101,100,97,90 89,88**
toteswingers: 1&2 £13.80, 1&3 £4.10, 2&3 £9.00. CSF £24.78 CT £103.64 TOTE £3.90: £3.00, £5.90; EX 37.50 Place 6: £65.71, Place 5: £16.13..
Owner Kingsgate Racing **Bred** Rod D'Elia **Trained** Hucking, Kent
■ Stewards' Enquiry : Ted Durcan caution: used whip without giving colt time to respond.

FOCUS
A fair middle-distance handicap. It was run at an uneven pace, but the first three still came nicely clear. The form looks sound.
T/Plt: £67.60 to a £1 stake. Pool:£49,971.60 - 539.10 winning tickets. T/Qpdt: £13.20 to a £1 stake. Pool:£3,844.67 - 215.30 winning tickets. TM

3222 REDCAR (L-H)
Thursday, July 1

OFFICIAL GOING: Good to firm (8.9)
Wind: Moderate,half-behind. Weather: overcast, shower after race 2

3595 CHALLENGE DARTS LEGEND BOBBY GEORGE TONIGHT APPRENTICE CLAIMING STKS 7f
6:10 (6:11) (Class 5) 3-Y-O+ **£3,399** (£1,011; £505; £252) **Stalls** Centre

Form RPR

4505 **1** **Nuit Sombre (IRE)**[14] 3124 10-9-1 57 ... (p) MichaelO'Connell(3) 11 66
(G A Harker) *mde all: hrd rdn and hld on wl whn towards fin* **28/1**

0054 **2** *3/4* **Bold Marc (IRE)**[22] 2864 8-9-6 68 ... PatrickDonaghy(3) 7 69
(J R Weymes) *trckd ldrs: effrt over 2f out: chal jst ins fnl f: no ex towards fin* **11/1**

1111 **3** *shd* **Abbondanza (IRE)**[6] 3400 7-9-10 79 ... BillyCray(3) 2 73
(D Nicholls) *trckd ldrs: drvn 3f out: hrd rdn over 1f out: styd on towards fin* **4/7**[1]

4422 **4** *2 1/4* **Classic Descent**[13] 3180 5-9-2 60 ... (t) JamesSullivan(3) 3 59
(Mrs R A Carr) *s.s: hdwy over 3f out: kpt on fnl f* **6/1**[3]

0065 **5** *4 1/2* **Ravi River (IRE)**[3] 3518 6-8-13 66 ... (v) KevinLundie(5) 6 46
(P D Evans) *sn drvn along: mid-div: reminders 4f out: hung lft 2f out: nvr nr ldrs* **20/1**

6-10 **6** *2 1/4* **Maison Brillet (IRE)**[19] 2979 3-9-0 74 ... IanBrennan(3) 12 43
(J Howard Johnson) *mid-div: drvn 4f out: one pce* **11/2**[2]

5500 **7** *2 3/4* **Ochilview Warrior (IRE)**[15] 3073 3-8-3 48 ... (b) MatthewLawson(5) 9 27
(R Bastiman) *chsd ldrs: wkng whn hmpd 2f out* **100/1**

00 **8** *2 1/2* **Stephie**[5] 3428 4-9-6 0 ... LeeTopliss(3) 4 30
(M W Easterby) *dwlt: a towards rr* **100/1**

-000 **9** *6* **Sydney Bridge**[15] 3073 3-8-3 45 ... AdamCarter(5) 1 4
(J Barclay) *chsd ldrs: rdn and lost pl 3f out* **100/1**

10 *2 1/2* **Binglybonglyboo** 4-9-6 0 ... LanceBetts(3) 10 7
(L A Mullaney) *s.i.s: bhd and reminders 4f out* **66/1**

3-00 **11** *hd* **Ten To The Dozen**[13] 3147 7-9-1 50 ... AmyRyan(3) 5 2
(D W Thompson) *s.v.s: a wl bhd* **100/1**

1m 22.44s (-2.06) **Going Correction** -0.20s/f (Firm)
WFA 3 from 4yo+ 8lb **11** Ran SP% **115.3**
Speed ratings (Par 103): **103,102,102,99,94 91,88,85,78,76 75**
Tote Swingers: 1&2 £15.50, 1&3 £6.80, 2&3 £3.20 CSF £289.73 TOTE £48.10: £8.60, £3.60, £1.02; EX 235.50.
Owner P I Harker **Bred** M P B Bloodstock Ltd **Trained** Thirkleby, N Yorks
■ Stewards' Enquiry : Michael O'Connell one-day ban: used whip with excessive frequency (Jul 15)
Billy Cray caution: used whip with excessive frequency.

FOCUS
Few of these made any impact, with the field soon strung out and all bar the first three under pressure by halfway. The form of this modest claimer is rated around the front pair.
Binglybonglyboo Official explanation: jockey said gelding missed the break

3596 GLANBIA NUTRITIONALS NURSERY 6f
6:40 (6:40) (Class 4) 2-Y-O £4,533 (£1,348; £674; £336) Stalls Centre

Form				RPR
14	1		**Majestic Myles (IRE)**50 2032 2-9-4 77 PaulHanagan 5 (R A Fahey) *in rr and sn drvn along: swtchd outside over 2f out: edgd rt and styd on wl to ld appr fnl f: sn drew clr* 6/4[1]	86+
31	2	3 1/4	**Azzurra Du Caprio (IRE)**52 1964 2-8-11 73 KellyHarrison(3) 8 (B M R Haslam) *t.k.h: trckd ldrs: hdwy to chal over 1f out: kpt on same pce: tk 2nd ins fnl f* 10/1	72
215	3	1 1/4	**Mappin Time (IRE)**16 3059 2-9-2 80 LanceBetts(5) 2 (T D Easterby) *w ldrs: led over 2f out: hdd appr fnl f: styd on same pce* 5/1[2]	76
4053	4	1/2	**Lady Platinum Club**35 2461 2-8-8 70 BarryMcHugh(3) 9 (G R Oldroyd) *s.i.s: hdwy over 2f out: styd on fnl f* 16/1	64
033	5	nk	**Captain Dimitrios**16 3058 2-7-12 57 oh1 CathyGannon 1 (P D Evans) *chsd ldrs: kpt on same pce fnl 2f* 17/2	50
3254	6	3 1/4	**Coconut Ice**7 3353 2-9-2 75 RichardKingscote 11 (Tom Dascombe) *led tl over 2f out: wknd over 1f out* 16/1	58
0146	7	nk	**Prophet In A Dream**45 2177 2-8-10 69 SamHitchcott 3 (M R Channon) *mid-div: effrt over 2f out: wknd fnl f* 28/1	51
614	8	8	**Sacrosanctus**16 3059 2-9-5 78 PhillipMakin 12 (J A Glover) *sn chsng ldrs: lost pl over 1f out* 20/1	36
643	9	2 1/2	**Surely This Time (IRE)**51 1986 2-8-12 71 GrahamGibbons 6 (K A Ryan) *in rr and sn drvn along: lost pl 2f out: sn bhd* 10/1	22
3511	10	1 1/2	**Hayley Cropper**16 3058 2-8-9 68 AdrianNicholls 4 (D Nicholls) *led tl over 2f out: lost pl over 1f out* 7/1[3]	14

69.98 secs (-1.82) **Going Correction** -0.20s/f (Firm) 10 Ran SP% **117.8**
Speed ratings (Par 96): **104,99,98,97,96 92,92,81,78,76**
Tote Swingers: 1&2 £6.50, 1&3 £1.90, 2&3 £4.60 CSF £18.07 CT £65.54 TOTE £1.80: £1.10, £5.70, £3.50; EX 13.10.
Owner James Gaffney **Bred** Arctic Tack Stud **Trained** Musley Bank, N Yorks

FOCUS
The 'official' ratings shown next to each horse are estimated and for information purposes only. There was a field of reasonable size and quality for this nursery but the favourite proved far too good. He can rate higher, and the form has a solid feel.

NOTEBOOK
Majestic Myles(IRE), well backed, appreciated the step up to 6f but, even so, found the early pace too fast on this firm ground. However, he recovered to win well, with connections feeling that he had benefited from a short break. He will go up for this, so his next engagement is likely to be at Pontefract next Tuesday, where the stiffish track should suit him. (op 2-1 tchd 5-4)
Azzurra Du Caprio(IRE), whose two previous races had been at 5f, got the extra furlong well and was only beaten by a progressive type. She looks capable of winning a nursery over this trip. (op 9-1 tchd 11-1)
Mappin Time(IRE), who coped with the step up to 6f but who would not be inconvenienced by a return to 5f, put in a creditable performance. A decent juvenile who should find another winning opportunity, he was only beaten by two other useful types. (op 6-1 tchd 13-2)
Lady Platinum Club had not been convincing at 6f on her first attempt at the trip, but this suggested that the extra furlong does suit her after all. (op 12-1)
Captain Dimitrios, who ran well in a seller last time, was just run out of third. However, he was not out of place on this first attempt in handicap company. (op 14-1)
Coconut Ice had run one decent race over this trip but, particularly ridden like this, she may still be best at 5f. (op 14-1)
Hayley Cropper Official explanation: trainer had no explanation for the poor form shown

3597 WIN A VIP DAY OUT @ REDCARRACING.CO.UK (S) STKS 1m
7:15 (7:15) (Class 5) 3-4-Y-O £3,582 (£1,057; £529) Stalls Centre

Form				RPR
0-00	1		**Cono Zur (FR)**22 2863 3-8-7 73 AdrianNicholls 2 (M Johnston) *chsd ldrs: drvn to ld 3f out: rdn wl clr appr fnl f: eased fnl strides* 11/4[2]	76
4125	2	9	**King's Sabre**9 3284 4-9-8 60 (e) PaulEddery 10 (R C Guest) *hld up in rr: effrt on ins over 2f out: styd on to take modest 2nd jst ins fnl f* 9/2[3]	64
3650	3	3	**Hettie Hubble**13 3147 4-8-8 48 BarryMcHugh(3) 12 (D W Thompson) *led tl 3f out: fdd fnl 150yds* 20/1	46
6630	4	2 1/2	**Fortunate Bid (IRE)**22 2850 4-8-11 59 JamesSullivan(5) 9 (Mrs L Stubbs) *trckd ldrs: effrt over 2f out: one pce* 5/2[1]	45
0046	5	nk	**Scooby Dee**23 2838 3-8-2 45 PaulQuinn 8 (R M Whitaker) *trckd ldrs: outpcd over 3f out: kpt on fnl 2f* 14/1	38
20-3	6	2 3/4	**Alfalevva**7 3359 3-8-7 62 SamHitchcott 1 (M R Channon) *sn chsng ldrs on outside: drvn over 3f out: wknd 2f out* 11/2	36
3-05	7	3/4	**Melkatant**23 2833 4-8-11 42 GrahamGibbons 4 (N Bycroft) *dwlt: sme hdwy 3f out: sn wknd* 16/1	32
066	8	1	**Hong Kong Island (IRE)**55 1868 3-8-2 65 IanBrennan(5) 3 (J Barclay) *dwlt: t.k.h: effrt over 3f out: nvr a factor* 14/1	32
6540	9	hd	**Thewinnatakesitall**15 3086 3-7-9 50 NoraLooby(7) 13 (N Tinkler) *chsd ldrs: lost pl over 3f out* 33/1	27

1m 34.55s (-3.45) **Going Correction** -0.20s/f (Firm)
WFA 3 from 4yo 9lb 9 Ran SP% **115.7**
Speed ratings (Par 103): **109,100,97,94,94 91,90,89,89**
Tote Swingers: 1&2 £2.90, 1&3 £7.60, 2&3 £1.70 CSF £15.70 TOTE £4.60: £2.20, £1.30, £6.30; EX 14.80.The winner was sold to David W Chapman for £9,500.
Owner T T Bloodstocks **Bred** Jean-Pierre-Joseph Dubois **Trained** Middleham Moor, N Yorks

FOCUS
A routine seller on the whole, but the winner was rated a respectable 73 and he duly routed his rivals in a fast time for the grade.

3598 MARKET CROSS JEWELLERS NURSERY 5f
7:45 (7:46) (Class 6) 2-Y-O £2,729 (£806; £403) Stalls Centre

Form				RPR
331	1		**Bachelor Knight (IRE)**46 2139 2-8-10 65 PaulHanagan 2 (R A Fahey) *sn outpcd and drvn along: hdwy 2f out: edgd rt and chsd ldrs appr fnl f: styd on to ld nr fin* 10/3[2]	66
665	2	nse	**Wild Hysteria (IRE)**28 2667 2-7-13 54 JamieMackay 8 (T P Tate) *mid-div: sn drvn along: hdwy on ins over 1f out: styd on wl ins fnl f: jst failed* 6/1	55
3221	3	nk	**Madam Markievicz (IRE)**13 3163 2-8-13 68 (p) PhillipMakin 9 (M Dods) *w ldrs: led after 2f: hung lft over 2f out: hdd nr fin* 3/1[1]	68
3346	4	1	**Johnny Hancocks (IRE)**17 3035 2-8-3 58 CathyGannon 3 (P D Evans) *wnt rt and bmpd s: led 2f: styd on same pce appr fnl f* 14/1	54
41	5	nk	**Puddle Duck**55 1886 2-9-1 70 GrahamGibbons 6 (K A Ryan) *hmpd s: in rr and drvn along: hdwy on ins over 1f out: styd on ins fnl f* 5/1[3]	67
064	6	3/4	**Press Release**44 2210 2-8-11 66 (t) RichardKingscote 5 (Tom Dascombe) *n.m.r s: trckd ldrs: effrt over 2f out: kpt on same pce appr fnl f* 8/1	59
051	7	1 1/2	**Mini Bon Bon**41 2300 2-7-12 60 NatashaEaton(7) 7 (A Bailey) *wnt lft s: chsd ldrs: one pce fnl 2f* 20/1	47
000	8	4 1/2	**Sky Booster**17 3035 2-7-12 53 oh3 (b[1]) PaulQuinn 4 (W J Haggas) *carried lft s: chsd ldrs: rdn and hung rt over 1f out: sn lost pl* 16/1	24
01	9	1 1/4	**Las Verglas Star (IRE)**83 1198 2-9-0 76 LeeTopliss(7) 1 (R A Fahey) *wnt lft s: sn outpcd in rr: nvr on terms* 12/1	43

58.23 secs (-0.37) **Going Correction** -0.20s/f (Firm) 9 Ran SP% **115.1**
Speed ratings (Par 92): **94,93,93,91,91 90,87,80,78**
Tote Swingers: 1&2 £10.10, 1&3 £3.50, 2&3 £3.10 CSF £23.65 CT £65.87 TOTE £4.80: £2.30, £3.10, £1.10; EX 35.50.
Owner Lets Go Racing 1 **Bred** Angelo Robiati **Trained** Musley Bank, N Yorks

FOCUS
A flat-out sprint gallop set this up for the finishers, with the two involved in the photo just getting there in time. The 'official' ratings shown next to each horse are estimated and for information purposes only.

NOTEBOOK
Bachelor Knight(IRE), on his toes in the paddock, won a 6f seller last time and just about got away with the drop to 5f. However, he showed himself to be well at home in nursery company and should do even better if he steps back up in trip. (op 5-1)
Wild Hysteria(IRE), unspectacular in three maidens, has come into handicaps on a low mark and nearly made it pay. Though beaten twice at 6f, he looked as if a slightly longer trip would suit, but he is likely to go up significantly for this. (op 5-1 tchd 9-2)
Madam Markievicz(IRE) helped to set a blazing pace and did well to go so close to hanging on, though the fast conditions helped a lot. Her speed will be a useful asset in similar races, with these tactics likely to prove best on similar ground. (tchd 11-4)
Johnny Hancocks(IRE), who has been tried in a seller and a claimer, had to show plenty of pace to dispute the lead. Very effective on firm ground, he looks well at home in nurseries. (op 25-1)
Puddle Duck, the paddock pick, ran with credit on this nursery debut and looks capable of handling a step up to 6f. Official explanation: jockey said colt never travelled (op 9-2)
Press Release looked effective being asked to use his early speed, and is only a few pounds too high. (op 10-1)

3599 PSYCHE DEPARTMENT STORE H'CAP 6f
8:20 (8:21) (Class 4) (0-85,85) 3-Y-O £5,180 (£1,541; £770; £384) Stalls Centre

Form				RPR
1523	1		**Esuvia (IRE)**29 2656 3-9-3 81 TomEaves 2 (B Smart) *w ldrs on outside: led over 2f out: edgd rt over 1f out: hld on towards fin* 11/4[1]	94
5-13	2	nk	**Pepper Lane**13 3151 3-7-11 66 oh3 JamesSullivan(5) 9 (D O'Meara) *hmpd after 1f: sn towards rr: hdwy on ins 2f out: swtchd lft and styd on wl ins fnl frurlong: no ex nr fin* 11/2[3]	78
-000	3	4	**Waveband**16 3065 3-8-13 77 JoeFanning 5 (M Johnston) *led tl over 2f out: kpt on same pce appr fnl f* 14/1	76
54-4	4	2 3/4	**Sunnandaeg**60 1718 3-9-7 85 PhillipMakin 10 (N Wilson) *in tch: hmpd after 1f: outpcd over 2f out: kpt on fnl f* 9/2[2]	75
5606	5	nk	**Comedy Hall (USA)**24 2815 3-9-7 85 AdrianNicholls 14 (M Johnston) *w ldrs stands' side: edgd lft over 1f out: kpt on same pce* 13/2	74
254-	6	2 1/4	**Briary Mac**240 7217 3-8-2 66 oh4 PaulQuinn 11 (N Bycroft) *w ldrs: edgd lft after 1f: wknd over 1f out* 33/1	48
0-54	7	1 1/4	**Makbullet**15 3088 3-8-5 74 IanBrennan(5) 13 (J Howard Johnson) *s.i.s: in rr: sme late hdwy* 11/1	52
4-20	8	3	**Durham Express (IRE)**10 3277 3-8-9 73 PJMcDonald 4 (M Dods) *rrd s: bhd: hung lft over 1f out: nvr a factor* 14/1	42
-500	9	1	**Hold On Tiger (IRE)**12 3200 3-7-9 66 oh5 NeilFarley(7) 3 (J Barclay) *chsd ldrs: wknd 2f out* 40/1	31
2412	10	3 1/4	**Philosophers Stone (FR)**12 3225 3-8-4 68 GrahamGibbons 8 (T D Barron) *mid-div: effrt over 2f out: sn lost pl: lame* 9/2[2]	23

1m 10.3s (-1.50) **Going Correction** -0.20s/f (Firm) 10 Ran SP% **118.8**
Speed ratings (Par 102): **102,101,96,92,92 89,87,83,82,77**
Tote Swingers: 1&2 £4.80, 1&3 £10.70, 2&3 £18.80 CSF £18.35 CT £187.68 TOTE £2.60: £1.10, £2.40, £5.60; EX 23.40.
Owner Ceffyl Racing **Bred** Round Hill Stud **Trained** Hambleton, N Yorks

FOCUS
They went a good gallop, so the winner deserves extra credit for having been prominent all the way. This might not have taken that much winnng though, with the second 3lb wrong.
Durham Express(IRE) Official explanation: jockey said gelding reared as stalls opened
Philosophers Stone(FR) Official explanation: vet said gelding finished lame

3600 YORKSHIRE SUMMER RACING FESTIVAL 17TH - 25TH JULY H'CAP 1m 6f 19y
8:50 (8:50) (Class 5) (0-70,65) 4-Y-O+ £3,399 (£1,011; £505; £252) Stalls Low

Form				RPR
2203	1		**Amir Pasha (UAE)**2 3535 5-9-0 58 (p) TomEaves 10 (Micky Hammond) *trckd ldrs: wnt 2nd over 3f out: led over 1f out: hung lft: all out* 10/1	65
05-3	2	nk	**Zefooha (FR)**31 2610 6-9-2 60 GrahamGibbons 6 (T D Walford) *trckd ldr: led over 4f out: hdd over 1f out: rallied ins fnl f: jst hld* 11/4[2]	67
-131	3	hd	**Simple Jim (FR)**12 3223 6-9-1 62 BarryMcHugh(3) 3 (D O'Meara) *hld up in rr: stdy hdwy over 3f out: wnt 3rd 2f out: styd on fnl f* 11/8[1]	68+
-235	4	1 3/4	**Smugglers Bay (IRE)**29 2659 6-9-4 62 (b) PhillipMakin 4 (T D Easterby) *dwlt: in rr: hdwy 9f out: wnt 4th 2f out: kpt on same pce* 17/2	66+
5034	5	4	**What A Day**17 3028 4-8-6 50 PaulHanagan 8 (J J Quinn) *trckd ldrs: t.k.h: effrt over 3f out: wknd 2f out* 7/1[3]	48
-050	6	5	**Obara D'Avril (FR)**23 2610 8-7-11 46 oh1 (p) PaulPickard(5) 2 (S G West) *in rr: drvn over 4f out: nvr on terms* 33/1	37
25-0	7	27	**Everaard (USA)**20 1028 4-9-4 65 (p) KellyHarrison(3) 9 (Mrs K Walton) *mid-div: effrt over 4f out: sn lost pl: wl bhd whn eased ins fnl f: t.o* 20/1	18
001/	8	23	**Banquet (IRE)**582 5399 5-9-1 59 (p) DuranFentiman 5 (T D Walford) *led: reminders sn after s: hdd over 4f out: lost pl 3f out: sn bhd: virtually p.u 1f out: wl t.o* 20/1	—

3m 5.08s (0.38) **Going Correction** +0.125s/f (Good) 8 Ran SP% **113.4**
Speed ratings (Par 103): **103,102,102,101,99 96,81,68**
Tote Swingers: 1&2 £3.70, 1&3 £4.10, 2&3 £1.02 CSF £36.49 CT £61.68 TOTE £11.10: £1.40, £1.10, £1.60; EX 39.80.
Owner J McAllister **Bred** Darley **Trained** Middleham Moor, N Yorks

FOCUS
After a decent gallop around the first bend, the pace steadied along the back straight before increasing again off the final turn. The form is rated around the front pair.

3601 REDCARRACING.CO.UK FILLIES' H'CAP — 1m 2f
9:20 (9:20) (Class 5) (0-70,70) 3-Y-O+ — £3,399 (£1,011; £505; £252) Stalls Low

Form — RPR

1242 **1** **Marjury Daw (IRE)**[21] 2902 4-9-11 **60** ... BarryMcHugh(3) 7 — 71+
(J G Given) *trckd ldrs: nt clr run over 3f out: shkn up to ld over 1f out: styd on wl* **5/1**[2]

2-04 **2** 3 **Miss Ferney**[13] 3177 6-8-13 **50** ... PaulPickard(5) 6 — 54
(A Kirtley) *hld up in tch: hdwy to trck ldrs 6f out: effrt 3f out: styd on wl ins fnl f: snatched 2nd on line* **15/2**

45-1 **3** shd **Cross Key (IRE)**[15] 3073 3-9-8 **65** ... PaulHanagan 1 — 69
(R A Fahey) *trckd ldr: drvn over 4f out: narrow ld over 2f out: edgd rt over 1f out: sn hdd: kpt on same pce* **8/11**[1]

324 **4** 3/4 **Kathlatino**[23] 2837 3-9-8 **70** ... IanBrennan(5) 2 — 73
(Micky Hammond) *led: qcknd over 4f out: hdd over 2f out: hmpd over 1f out: kpt on one pce* **9/1**

0464 **5** 3 **Cygnet Committee (IRE)**[23] 2838 3-8-5 **48** ow3 ... (b) PJMcDonald 3 — 45
(J S Wainwright) *dwlt: hld up in rr: hdwy over 5f out: n.m.r on ins over 3f out: outpcd over 2f out* **20/1**

6462 **6** 4 1/2 **Tia Juana (IRE)**[15] 3074 3-9-3 **60** ... (p) PhillipMakin 4 — 48
(B M R Haslam) *trckd ldrs: effrt 3f out: hung rt and wknd over 1f out* **13/2**[3]

2m 8.49s (1.39) **Going Correction** +0.125s/f (Good)
WFA 3 from 4yo+ 11lb — 6 Ran SP% **114.4**
Speed ratings (Par 100): **99,96,96,95,93 89**
Tote Swingers:1&2:£2.20, 2&3:£3.30, 1&3:£1.10 CSF £40.83 CT £56.55 TOTE £5.00: £2.30, £1.60; EX 25.00 Place 6 £11.30, Place 5 £7.80..
Owner Danethorpe Racing Partnership **Bred** Mulhime Ltd Marston Stud & D Bonnycastle **Trained** Willoughton, Lincs

FOCUS
The pace was sedate, and the race only began to take shape 3f from home. Weak fillies' form, and not too solid.
Tia Juana(IRE) Official explanation: jockey said filly hung right-handed in straight
T/Plt: £14.10 to a £1 stake. Pool:£50,587.67 - 2,606.22 winning tickets. T/Qpdt: £6.70 to a £1 stake. Pool:£3,666.75 - 404.30 winning tickets. WG

2903 YARMOUTH (L-H)
Thursday, July 1

OFFICIAL GOING: Good to firm
Wind: slight breeze across Weather: hot and sunny

3602 E.B.F./PREMIER RACING FREE £100 BET IN 4.40 MAIDEN STKS — 6f 3y
2:10 (2:10) (Class 5) 2-Y-O — £3,406 (£1,019; £509; £254; £126) Stalls High

Form — RPR

2 **1** **The Paddyman (IRE)**[13] 3169 2-9-3 0 ... PhilipRobinson 2 — 87+
(W J Haggas) *led centre eight and travelling strly: led overall over 3f out: rdn clr over 1f out: v easily* **1/2**[1]

2 8 **Albaasil (IRE)** 2-9-3 0 ... RichardHills 3 — 63+
(Sir Michael Stoute) *t.k.h chsng ldrs: wnt 2nd and rdn over 1f out where wnr was surging clr* **3/1**[2]

3 3 1/4 **Formal Demand** 2-9-3 0 ... RichardMullen 7 — 53
(E F Vaughan) *last away: racd awkwardly in rr: kpt on over 1f out: edgd rt: nvr plcd to chal* **12/1**[3]

4 1 1/2 **Piccarello** 2-9-3 0 ... PatCosgrave 4 — 49
(M H Tompkins) *sn rdn: midfield: struggling 2f out: plugged on* **20/1**

5 1 1/4 **Algurayn (IRE)** 2-9-3 0 ... SaleemGolam 8 — 45
(G Prodromou) *rdn 1/2-way: sn btn: plugged on ins fnl f* **66/1**

6 2 1/4 **Nettis** 2-9-3 0 ... SebSanders 5 — 38
(G Prodromou) *chsd ldr in centre tl rdn and lost pl qckly over 1f out* **33/1**

0 **7** hd **Sammy Alexander**[24] 2819 2-9-3 0 ... MarcHalford 6 — 38
(G G Margarson) *centre gp tl swtchd rt to chse one horse on stands' rails over 3f out: rdn and fdd over 2f out* **66/1**

0 **8** 3/4 **Time For Applause**[52] 1972 2-8-12 0 ... HayleyTurner 1 — 30
(E A L Dunlop) *chsd ldrs and t.k.h: rdn and btn over 2f out* **12/1**[3]

00 **9** 27 **Knudstrup Noble (IRE)**[21] 2905 2-8-10 0 ... (b[1]) LeonnaMayor(7) 9 — —
(P S McEntee) *racd alone in ld on stands' rail tl over 3f out: rapidly downed tools and sn t.o* **100/1**

1m 14.74s (0.34) **Going Correction** +0.15s/f (Good) — 9 Ran SP% **118.7**
Speed ratings (Par 94): **103,92,88,86,84 81,81,80,44**
toteswingers: 1&2 £1.30, 1&3 £3.20, 2&3 £3.70 CSF £2.21 TOTE £1.70: £1.10, £1.60, £1.30; EX 2.10 Trifecta £6.90 Pool: £557.99 - 59.12 winning units..
Owner Mr & Mrs R Scott **Bred** Mr & Mrs R & P Scott **Trained** Newmarket, Suffolk

FOCUS
The course had 5mm of water put on in the morning and the ground was Good to Firm, with firm places in the back straight. The full course layout was in use and the runners had a slight breeze across to contend with. This maiden threw up two good winners in 2008 and 2009 in Khor Dubai and Showcasing. This year's renewal looked a match according to the market but impressive winner The Paddyman was much too strong. He is likely to rate in the 90s.

NOTEBOOK
The Paddyman(IRE) ran out a very easy winner. Always in the front rank, he led from halfway and came well clear from over a furlong out. His pedigree would suggest that a longer trip ought to be well within his capabilities and he can make his mark in a higher grade. He will apparently now be aimed at the Listed Rose Bowl Stakes at Newbury on July 16th. (op 8-13)
Albaasil(IRE) took the eye in the parade ring with his athletic walk. His yard's 2-y-o debutantes tend to benefit from a run and he showed signs of greeness in the preliminaries and also during the race. He gave vain chase to the winner from over 1f out and without making any impression he kept on to finish a clear second best. He will improve for the experience and is capable of taking a maiden. (op 5-2)
Formal Demand wasn't best away and took a fair grip early on when held up towards the rear. He carried his head rather awkwardly and didn't look entirely straightforward when asked for his effort. It's perfectly possible that he found this ground plenty quick enough for his debut. (op 14-1)
Piccarello looked far from wound up and was the first off the bridle. He kept plugging away without being anything like competitive in the final half of the race. He will come on for the run and a longer trip looks imperative. (op 25-1)
Algurayn(IRE), a smallish type, will need to come on a fair bit for this to get competitive. (op 100-1)
Nettisa big strong, backward sort, was on his toes in the preliminaries. Like his stablemate, he will need to come on a fair bit for this to get competitive

3603 PREMIER RACING FREE £100 BET IN 4.40 (S) STKS — 6f 3y
2:40 (2:40) (Class 6) 2-Y-O — £1,554 (£462; £231; £115) Stalls High

Form — RPR

1 **My Lord** 2-8-8 0 ... JackDean(3) 1 — 60
(W G M Turner) *cl up: led over 2f out: clr and u.p ins fnl f: hld on wl* **16/1**

6 **2** 1 **Lighthouse Keeper (IRE)**[13] 3175 2-8-11 0 ... JerryO'Dwyer 9 — 57
(Miss Amy Weaver) *last away: rn green: wnt lft whn rdn and prog over 1f out: tk 2nd ins fnl f: nt rch wnr* **11/2**[2]

60 **3** nk **Livia Quarta (IRE)**[17] 3035 2-8-7 0 ow1 ... EddieCreighton 3 — 52
(E J Creighton) *hld up and bhd: rdn and hdwy over 1f out: racd awkwardly: kpt on cl home: unable to chal* **33/1**

05 **4** 1 1/2 **Liberty Ess (IRE)**[41] 2292 2-8-6 0 ... RichardMullen 6 — 47
(K A Ryan) *plld hrd: chsd ldrs: rdn over 2f out: edgd lft: one pce and no ex 1f out* **6/1**[3]

04 **5** 1 3/4 **River Blade**[23] 2836 2-8-11 0 ... PatCosgrave 2 — 46
(W M Brisbourne) *prom: rdn over 2f out: btn 1f out* **8/1**

6 nk **Milk Maid (IRE)** 2-7-13 0 ... IanBurns(7) 5 — 40
(W G M Turner) *midfield: sn bmpd along: unco-ordinated and btn over 1f out* **33/1**

422 **7** 2 1/4 **Artic Rose (IRE)**[21] 2905 2-8-3 0 ... WilliamCarson(3) 4 — 34
(S C Williams) *t.k.h and prom: rdn and lost pl over 1f out* **1/1**[1]

6640 **8** 3/4 **Muse To Use**[14] 3118 2-8-6 0 ... SaleemGolam 7 — 31
(I W McInnes) *led tl rdn and hdd over 2f out: sn lost pl* **12/1**

0 **9** 3/4 **Shot Silk**[19] 2958 2-8-6 0 ... HayleyTurner 8 — 29
(N P Littmoden) *bhd: rdn and struggling over 2f out* **33/1**

1m 16.9s (2.50) **Going Correction** +0.15s/f (Good) — 9 Ran SP% **113.2**
Speed ratings (Par 92): **89,87,87,85,82 82,79,78,77**
toteswingers:1&2 £7.30, 2&3 £22.80, 1&3 £35.40 CSF £97.49 TOTE £17.30: £3.80, £1.50, £6.90; EX 93.20 TRIFECTA Not won..The winner was bought in for £5,600.
Owner Mrs M S Teversham **Bred** Mrs Monica Teversham **Trained** Sigwells, Somerset
■ Stewards' Enquiry : Jack Dean one-day ban: used whip with excessive frequency (Jul 15)

FOCUS
This race was run in a time 2.16 seconds slower than the earlier maiden. The early pacesetters all dropped away over 1f out and, with only 8l covering the whole field at the finish, it was probably a weak event. A fair start from the winner.

NOTEBOOK
My Lord made a winning debut. He went to the front travelling well just over 2f from home and kept on well inside the final furlong. Life will be harder under a penalty, but connections feel a little more cut in the ground and a longer trip will help. They went to 5,660gns to retain him. (op 20-1)
Lighthouse Keeper(IRE) ran a similar race to his debut effort which was over a furlong further. He was well behind early and only made headway over 1f out. A mile already looks within his stamina capabilities. (op 9-1)
Livia Quarta(IRE) also stayed on under strong pressure in the final furlong. She is gradually going in the right direction but probably needs a little more before scoring. (tchd 28-1)
Liberty Ess(IRE) edged left under pressure and never got competitive. (op 4-1)
River Blade did best of the early pacesetters but was ultimately disappointing on his debut in this grade. A drop to the minimum trip may help. (op 13-2)
Artic Rose(IRE) failed to give her running having been keen early. This was disappointing. (op 11-10 tchd 10-11 and 6-5 and 5-4 and 11-8 in a place)

3604 "COLONEL" HAS JOINED PREMIER RACING SERVICES H'CAP — 7f 3y
3:10 (3:10) (Class 5) (0-75,74) 3-Y-O+ — £2,201 (£655; £327; £163) Stalls High

Form — RPR

111- **1** **Kuanyao (IRE)**[201] 7729 4-9-11 **71** ... SebSanders 3 — 81+
(P J Makin) *mde all: rdn over 1f out: a holding chalrs ins fnl f: bit in hand* **7/2**[2]

0506 **2** 3/4 **Rough Rock (IRE)**[12] 3216 5-9-1 **61** ... JerryO'Dwyer 6 — 67
(C A Dwyer) *chsd ldrs: drvn over 1f out: kpt on to go 2nd fnl 50yds: nt quite rch wnr* **14/1**

5160 **3** 1 **Hobson**[12] 3212 5-9-13 **73** ... RichardMullen 4 — 76
(Eve Johnson Houghton) *pressed wnr: rdn over 2f out: no imp over 1f out: lost 2nd clsng stages* **13/2**

2605 **4** 2 3/4 **Defector (IRE)**[22] 2872 4-9-11 **71** ... TonyCulhane 1 — 67
(W R Muir) *chsd ldrs tl rdn and outpcd over 1f out* **12/1**

1423 **5** nk **Tell Halaf**[12] 3212 3-9-6 **74** ... HayleyTurner 8 — 66
(M L W Bell) *bhd: brief effrt 2f out: nvr gng wl enough to get involved: btn over 1f out* **11/8**[1]

645 **6** 1 1/4 **Medici Palace**[15] 3080 3-8-12 **66** ... (v[1]) PatCosgrave 5 — 55
(J R Fanshawe) *reluctant to set off and lost 10l s: plld hrd and sn in tch: rdn wl over 1f out: nt run on and sn btn* **11/2**[3]

6500 **7** 8 **Negotiation (IRE)**[6] 3412 4-9-4 **67** ... (v[1]) WilliamCarson(3) 7 — 37
(M Quinn) *rdn and sn swtchd rt to r alone on stands' rails: cl up: drvn over 2f out: lost pl qckly* **20/1**

1m 27.06s (0.46) **Going Correction** +0.15s/f (Good)
WFA 3 from 4yo+ 8lb — 7 Ran SP% **112.2**
Speed ratings (Par 103): **103,102,101,97,97 96,86**
toteswingers: 1&2 £6.20, 1&3 £3.50, 2&3 £10.60 CSF £46.54 CT £301.08 TOTE £4.40: £2.40, £6.10; EX 47.70 Trifecta £195.00 Pool: £348.00 - 1.32 winning units..
Owner D M Ahier **Bred** Newlands House Stud **Trained** Ogbourne Maisey, Wilts

FOCUS
The gallop here was only steady in the early stages. The winner was value for a bit extra but the favourite disappointed and the form is modest.
Tell Halaf Official explanation: jockey said colt hung left

3605 OPEN AN ACCOUNT TODAY WITH PREMIER RACING H'CAP — 5f 43y
3:40 (3:40) (Class 6) (0-60,60) 3-Y-O+ — £1,683 (£501; £250; £125) Stalls High

Form — RPR

6R66 **1** **Greek Secret**[22] 2849 7-8-12 **54** ... (b) JamesO'Reilly(5) 7 — 63
(J O'Reilly) *s.i.s: hdwy over 1f out: drvn and ins fnl f: kpt on wl* **9/2**[2]

-350 **2** 2 1/4 **Pocket's Pick (IRE)**[58] 1799 4-9-9 **60** ... IanMongan 1 — 60
(Jim Best) *taken down early: led at brisk pce: rdn and hdd 200yds out: nt qckn* **11/2**

1036 **3** 1 **Thoughtsofstardom**[7] 3358 7-9-2 **60** ... LeonnaMayor(7) 2 — 57
(P S McEntee) *chsd ldr: rdn over 2f out: lost 2nd over 1f out: kpt gng gamely* **5/1**[3]

23-1 **4** 2 1/4 **Mansii**[27] 2721 5-8-13 **55** ... (t) TobyAtkinson(5) 9 — 44
(P J McBride) *chsd ldrs: rdn over 1f out: sn fnd nil* **5/2**[1]

3404 **5** 3/4 **Nawaaff**[9] 3293 5-8-6 **46** oh1 ... WilliamCarson(3) 6 — 32
(M Quinn) *midfield: rdn and btn over 1f out* **17/2**

60-0 **6** 3/4 **Andrasta**[25] 2791 5-8-11 **48** ... FrankieMcDonald 8 — 31
(S A Harris) *s.s: sn rdn: nvr on terms* **18/1**

30-0 **7** 2 3/4 **Elsie Jo (IRE)**[16] 3064 4-8-13 **50** ... StephenCraine 4 — 23
(M Wigham) *s.i.s: last and struggling over 2f out* **18/1**

1202 **8** *hd* **Tanley**[155] 312 5-9-3 54 SebSanders 5 27
(I W McInnes) *chsd ldrs: drvn and fdd over 1f out: eased ins fnl f* **11/2**
63.35 secs (0.65) **Going Correction** +0.15s/f (Good) 8 Ran SP% **115.2**
Speed ratings (Par 101): **96,92,90,87,86 84,80,80**
toteswingers: 1&2 £6.30, 1&3 £6.30, 2&3 £5.70 CSF £29.61 CT £128.83 TOTE £6.80: £1.90, £1.70, £2.80; EX 36.50 Trifecta £182.90 Pool: £252.16 - 1.02 winning units..
Owner The Boot & Shoe Ackworth Partnership **Bred** James Clark **Trained** Doncaster, S Yorks

FOCUS
A modest sprint handicap but the pace was strong from the outset. The winner is the best guide.
Andrasta Official explanation: jockey said mare was slowly away
Tanley Official explanation: jockey said gelding stopped quickly

3606 PREMIER RACING SERVICES IN BECCLES H'CAP 1m 1f
4:10 (4:12) (Class 5) (0-75,72) 3-Y-O £2,201 (£655; £327; £163) Stalls Low

Form RPR
03-1 **1** **Aktia (IRE)**[21] 2886 3-9-7 72 J-PGuillambert 2 86+
(L M Cumani) *trckd ldrs: effrt to go 2nd 350yds out: rdn to ld over 1f out: styd on wl* **6/5**[1]
-553 **2** *1* **Granite Girl**[27] 2725 3-8-12 68 TobyAtkinson(5) 1 78
(P J McBride) *cl up: 4th and chsng ldrs over 2f out: swtchd rt and effrt 1f out: wnt 2nd 120yds out: nt rch wnr* **10/1**
0134 **3** *2* **Al Dafa (USA)**[17] 3039 3-9-7 72 (v) HayleyTurner 9 78
(M L W Bell) *bhd and drvn and racing v lazily: prog fnl 2f: styng on wl ins fnl f: wnt 3rd 50yds out: gave himself too much to do* **11/2**[3]
0-10 **4** *2 1/4* **On Her Way**[23] 2843 3-9-7 72 (be) IanMongan 3 73
(H R A Cecil) *taken down early: plld hrd: prom: led over 2f out: sn drvn: put hd in air and hdd over 1f out: nt run on: lost two pls ins fnl 120yds* **9/1**
-603 **5** *2 3/4* **Charpoy Cobra**[21] 2906 3-8-4 55 (v[1]) SaleemGolam 10 50
(J A R Toller) *t.k.h early: chsd ldrs: 5th and rdn 4f out: one pce and no imp after* **20/1**
003- **6** *3* **Mme De Stael**[239] 7244 3-8-10 61 SebSanders 7 49
(Sir Mark Prescott) *rdn in stable yard bef r and looked a proper madam in preliminaries: arrived at s rdrless: immediately rdn to r promly: led 4f out tl hdd over 2f out: immediately lost interest and dropped out fast* **9/2**[2]
000 **7** *1* **Wavertree Bounty**[13] 3173 3-7-11 53 oh5 AmyBaker(5) 8 39
(J Ryan) *bhd: struggling 4f out* **80/1**
004 **8** *5* **Nelson's Bounty**[19] 2968 3-9-4 69 TonyCulhane 4 44
(P W D'Arcy) *bhd: detached last st: racd awkwardly and all at sea after* **33/1**
2-46 **9** *1/2* **Faith Jicaro (IRE)**[21] 2901 3-9-6 71 MickyFenton 11 45
(N J Vaughan) *sn lost gd pl: in rr after 4f: wl btn 4f out* **33/1**
522- **10** *16* **Edward Whymper**[212] 7604 3-9-3 68 RichardMullen 6 —
(M H Tompkins) *towards rr: struggling bdly 4f out: t.o* **20/1**
-500 **11** *32* **Black Baccara**[13] 3171 3-8-2 60 LeonnaMayor(7) 5 —
(P S McEntee) *led: hdd 4f out: lost pl rapidly: bdly t.o* **100/1**
1m 53.81s (-1.99) **Going Correction** -0.175s/f (Firm) 11 Ran SP% **115.7**
Speed ratings (Par 100): **101,100,98,96,93 91,90,85,85,71 42**
toteswingers: 1&2 £4.30, 1&3 £2.50, 2&3 £8.70 CSF £12.98 CT £51.32 TOTE £2.30: £1.40, £2.20, £1.50; EX 15.20 Trifecta £45.70 Pool: £502.47 - 8.12 winning units..
Owner Mrs M Marinopoulos **Bred** Swordlestown Stud **Trained** Newmarket, Suffolk

FOCUS
An interesting 3-y-o handicap in which they went a good gallop from the off. The winner was value for a bit extra but there is a bit of doubt over the form.
Nelson's Bounty Official explanation: trainer said, gelding was unsuited by the good to firm (firm in places back straight) ground
Edward Whymper Official explanation: trainer's rep said, gelding was unsuited by the good to firm (firm in places back straight) ground

3607 PREMIER RACING SERVICES IN HALESWORTH H'CAP 1m 2f 21y
4:40 (4:41) (Class 5) (0-70,70) 3-Y-O+ £2,201 (£655; £327; £163) Stalls Low

Form RPR
-505 **1** **Seattle Speight (USA)**[28] 2675 3-7-9 55 (v[1]) HarryBentley(7) 3 63
(W J Knight) *cl up in 3rd: rdn over 3f out: led over 1f out: duelled for ld tl asserted cl home* **8/1**
-001 **2** *3/4* **Eye Of Eternity**[10] 3264 3-7-5 51 6ex NoelGarbutt(7) 2 58
(Rae Guest) *led: pushed along 2f out: hdd over 1f out: kpt on gamely tl no ex fnl 50yds* **85/40**[1]
500 **3** *1 3/4* **Abu Wathab**[28] 2684 3-8-9 62 RichardMullen 8 65
(P W Chapple-Hyam) *awkward at s: t.k.h and pressed ldrs: rdn 3f out: wl hld over 1f out* **12/1**
0-13 **4** *7* **Saviour Sand (IRE)**[118] 814 6-9-6 67 (t) KylieManser(5) 5 57
(Miss Olivia Maylam) *plld hrd in midfield: brief effrt over 3f out: sn btn* **12/1**
4421 **5** *3 1/2* **Rocky's Pride (IRE)**[38] 2388 4-10-0 70 TonyCulhane 4 53
(W J Musson) *bhd: detached last st: v unbalanced whn rdn 3f out: sn floundering* **11/2**[3]
05-5 **6** *1* **Before The War (USA)**[31] 2603 3-9-1 68 J-PGuillambert 6 49
(L M Cumani) *w ldr tl drvn over 3f out: steadily lost pl* **3/1**[2]
20-4 **7** *13* **Power Of Dreams (IRE)**[51] 1992 3-9-0 67 SebSanders 7 24
(M H Tompkins) *hld up in rr: struggling 4f out: t.o* **6/1**
2m 7.76s (-2.74) **Going Correction** -0.175s/f (Firm)
WFA 3 from 4yo+ 11lb 7 Ran SP% **113.2**
Speed ratings (Par 103): **103,102,101,95,92 91,81**
toteswingers: 1&2 £5.40, 1&3 £10.90, 2&3 £5.90 CSF £24.90 CT £203.99 TOTE £14.40: £5.60, £2.20; EX 31.60 Trifecta £249.10 Part won. Pool: £336.72 - 0.61 winning units..
Owner Bluehills Racing Limited **Bred** Blue Mountain Equine **Trained** Patching, W Sussex

FOCUS
A modest handicap which was well run. The form is rated around the runner-up.
Seattle Speight(USA) Official explanation: trainer said, regarding apparent improvement in form, that the filly had benefited from wearing a first time visor.

3608 PREMIER RACING SERVICES IN OULTON BROAD "HANDS AND HEELS" APPRENTICE SERIES H'CAP 1m 3f 101y
5:10 (5:10) (Class 6) (0-65,65) 4-Y-O+ £1,554 (£462; £231; £115) Stalls Low

Form RPR
65-0 **1** **Mistoffelees**[47] 2109 4-9-3 65 TalibHussain(5) 1 78+
(L M Cumani) *trckd ldrs gng wl: plld off rail and effrt wl over 1f out: led jst ins fnl f: qcknd clr* **5/2**[2]
0411 **2** *3 1/4* **Iceman George**[41] 2303 6-9-5 62 (v) AdamBeschizza 6 67
(G C Bravery) *t.k.h trcking ldrs: led 3f out: rdn and hdd jst ins fnl f: immediately outpcd* **11/4**[3]
022 **3** *2 3/4* **Contradiktive (IRE)**[9] 3294 4-8-3 46 (b) NathanAlison 5 46
(J R Boyle) *sn led: rdn and hdd 3f out: btn 1f out* **7/4**[1]
2645 **4** *1 1/2* **Quince (IRE)**[31] 2604 7-8-9 55 (v) SophieSilvester(3) 4 53
(J Pearce) *hld up: pushed along 3f out: sn carrying hd high and finding nthing* **15/2**
0000 **5** *12* **Greystoke Prince**[13] 3168 5-8-4 52 oh1 ow6 (t) CarolineKelly(5) 2 29
(M D Squance) *led for 100yds: pressed ldr tl 4f out: lost tch 3f out: t.o* **28/1**
/00- **6** *1 1/2* **Renege The Joker**[15] 5483 7-7-12 46 oh1 LeonnaMayor(5) 8 21
(S Regan) *s.i.s: effrt on outside 3f out: rdn and wkng sn after: t.o* **66/1**
2m 30.0s (1.30) **Going Correction** -0.175s/f (Firm) 6 Ran SP% **108.3**
Speed ratings (Par 101): **88,85,83,82,73 72**
toteswingers:1&2 £2.10, 2&3 £1.40, 1&3 £2.00 CSF £9.04 CT £11.77 TOTE £3.10: £1.80, £2.70; EX 10.40 Trifecta £29.50 Pool: £284.12 - 7.11 winning units. Place 6: £117.52 Place 5: £106.83.
Owner Mrs Luca Cumani **Bred** The Kingwood Partnership **Trained** Newmarket, Suffolk

FOCUS
Another modest race on paper but a very comprehensive winner. Improvement from the winner with the second the best guide.
Mistoffelees Official explanation: trainer's rep said, regarding apparent improvement in form, that the colt had benefited from being dropped in and ridden more patiently.
T/Plt: £833.50 to a £1 stake. Pool:£52,182.46 - 45.70 winning tickets. T/Qpdt: £81.20 to a £1 stake. Pool:£4,172.33 - 38.00 winning tickets. IM

3609 - (Foreign Racing) - See Raceform Interactive

[3281] BEVERLEY (R-H)
Friday, July 2

OFFICIAL GOING: Good to firm (9.3)
Wind: light 1/2 against Weather: fine and sunny

3610 RACING AGAIN TOMORROW (S) STKS 7f 100y
6:20 (6:20) (Class 6) 3-Y-O+ £2,266 (£674; £337; £168) Stalls High

Form RPR
421 **1** **Bajan Pride**[18] 3025 6-9-8 67 PaulHanagan 9 70
(R A Fahey) *chsd ldrs: wnt 2nd 2f out: led last 75yds: jst hld on* **6/4**[1]
3414 **2** *nse* **Angel Of Fashion (IRE)**[8] 3371 3-8-4 67 BillyCray(5) 4 62
(D Nicholls) *mid-div: hdwy 6f out: chsng ldrs 4f out: wnt 3rd 2f out: styd on to chal ins fnl f: jst failed* **4/1**[3]
0000 **3** *1* **Carlitos Spirit (IRE)**[15] 3124 6-9-0 63 (v) BarryMcHugh(3) 3 62
(I W McInnes) *swtchd rt after s: led: hdd wl ins fnl f: no ex* **11/1**
1252 **4** *nk* **King's Sabre**[1] 3597 4-9-3 60 (e) JamesSullivan(5) 11 67
(R C Guest) *hld up in rr: gd hdwy over 2f out: kpt on same pce fnl f* **7/2**[2]
6050 **5** *1 1/2* **Kheskianto (IRE)**[3] 3538 4-8-5 50 DavidKenny(7) 10 53
(M C Chapman) *mid-div: effrt on outside over 2f out: kpt on one pce fnl f* **20/1**
4400 **6** *7* **Fyodorovich (USA)**[3] 3538 5-8-12 45 (b) LanceBetts(5) 5 40
(J S Wainwright) *t.k.h in mid-div: kpt on fnl 2f: nvr nr ldrs* **25/1**
-000 **7** *nk* **Eastern Hills**[17] 3061 5-9-3 58 (v) TomEaves 7 40
(J S Wainwright) *in tch: hung rt over 1f out: sn wknd* **12/1**
0000 **8** *1 3/4* **Peter Tchaikovsky**[4] 3508 4-9-3 70 (b[1]) RobertWinston 2 35
(B S Rothwell) *dwlt: bhd tl kpt on fnl 2f: nvr a factor* **16/1**
0-00 **9** *hd* **Govenor Eliott (IRE)**[10] 3286 5-8-10 47 (b) ShaneBKelly(7) 8 35
(A J Lockwood) *chsd ldrs: wkng whn hmpd 2f out* **80/1**
0-00 **10** *2* **Union Jack Jackson (IRE)**[43] 2257 8-8-13 49 ow1 (b) JamesO'Reilly(5) 6 31
(John A Harris) *chsd ldrs: hung rt and wknd over 1f out* **33/1**
0505 **11** *5* **Favouring (IRE)**[59] 571 8-9-0 44 (vt) RobertLButler(3) 12 17
(M C Chapman) *in rr: bhd whn reminders over 3f out* **100/1**
60-0 **12** *1 1/4* **Home Before Dark**[31] 2624 4-9-0 37 MichaelStainton(3) 1 14
(R M Whitaker) *t.k.h in midfield: lost pl over 3f out: sn bhd* **125/1**
1m 32.05s (-1.75) **Going Correction** -0.125s/f (Firm)
WFA 3 from 4yo+ 8lb 12 Ran SP% **118.7**
Speed ratings (Par 101): **105,104,103,103,101 93,93,91,91,88 83,81**
Tote Swingers: 1&2 £2.10, 1&3 £2.20, 2&3 £10.70 CSF £7.02 TOTE £2.00: £1.10, £2.10, £3.20; EX 5.90.There was no bid for the winner. Angel of Fashion was claimed by P. Charalambous for £6,000.
Owner R A Fahey **Bred** Plantation Stud **Trained** Musley Bank, N Yorks
■ Stewards' Enquiry : Paul Hanagan caution: used whip with excessive frequency

FOCUS
An ordinary seller contested mostly by out-of form horses. The pace was fair and the form looks sound.

3611 E B F WILLIAM JACKSON BAKERY NOVICE STKS 5f
6:50 (6:51) (Class 4) 2-Y-O £5,180 (£1,541; £770; £384) Stalls High

Form RPR
310 **1** **Black Moth (IRE)**[15] 3100 2-9-0 0 (b[1]) JamesSullivan(5) 5 93
(B J Meehan) *trckd ldrs: plld outside over 1f out: led jst ins fnl f: edgd lft: hld on towards fin* **7/2**[2]
120 **2** *nk* **Arctic Feeling (IRE)**[15] 3100 2-9-5 0 PaulHanagan 3 92
(R A Fahey) *trckd ldrs: led appr fnl f: hdd and edgd lft jst ins fnl f: no ex towards fin* **8/11**[1]
3 *9* **Malgoof (IRE)** 2-9-0 0 TomEaves 1 55+
(B Smart) *dwlt: sn w ldr: hung rt and kpt on same pce appr fnl f* **13/2**
1 **4** *1* **Clipthorne**[28] 2693 2-8-11 0 BarryMcHugh(3) 4 51+
(Ollie Pears) *dwlt: outpcd and reminders after 1f: hdwy over 1f out: kpt on same pce* **9/2**[3]
1 **5** *2* **Tro Nesa (IRE)**[18] 3020 2-8-11 0 JackMitchell 2 41+
(Mrs A Duffield) *swvd lft s: led: reminders over 2f out: hdd apprloaching fnl f: wknd fnl 150yds* **20/1**
62.70 secs (-0.80) **Going Correction** -0.15s/f (Firm) 5 Ran SP% **116.4**
Speed ratings (Par 96): **100,99,85,83,80**
CSF £6.96 TOTE £5.30: £3.10, £1.10; EX 7.80.
Owner Sangster Families **Bred** Victor Stud Bloodstock & Brendan Cummins **Trained** Manton, Wilts

FOCUS
A fairly useful novice event that pitted two down the field in the Norfolk Stakes against two once-raced unbeaten youngsters and a well-regarded newcomer. The Ascot pair produced useful efforts to pull well clear.

NOTEBOOK
Black Moth(IRE) had finished behind Arctic Feeling at Royal Ascot but had made some of the running that day and reversed the form in first-time blinkers under a more patient ride, settling well before showing plenty of determination as the first two drew clear despite edging left. He's probably entitled to go for a Listed race after this. (tchd 10-3)
Arctic Feeling(IRE) set the standard but still turned in an improved effort despite failing to land the odds. He looked in pole position when eased to the front with under 2f to run, but didn't quite have enough to fend off the winner despite running on strongly. He, too, looks Listed class and his trainer will probably be eyeing the Roses Stakes at York. (op 11-10)
Malgoof(IRE) had clearly impressed at the Breeze-Ups judging by his sale price and, representing a yard going well with their 2yos this year, must have been showing something to have started so short in the market. He was left behind when the first two powered away, but he'd shown good mid-race speed to recover from a slow start. With improvement likely, he should have little trouble winning a maiden. (op 11-2 tchd 7-1)

Clipthorne had finished ahead of two subsequent winners when making a winning debut at Catterick but was still too inexperienced for her own good here, finding herself with too much to do up before making some late progress. She'll have more time to get organised over 6f, and is sure to do better again. (tchd 6-1)
Tro Nesa(IRE) was back in trip after winning a Carlisle maiden on softish ground on her debut but that form doesn't look strong in hindsight and she was readily left behind after making the early running. She'll be better off back up in trip in nurseries. (op 16-1)

3612 AUNT BESSIE'S YORKSHIRE PUDDING H'CAP — 7f 100y
7:25 (7:25) (Class 4) (0-80,77) 3-Y-O — £4,857 (£1,445; £722; £360) Stalls High

Form — RPR

126 **1** **Don't Call Me (IRE)**[48] 2110 3-9-5 **75**.................................(t) TomEaves 8 — 81
(B Smart) *chsd ldrs: nt clr run over 1f out: styd on strly fnl f: led nr fin* **5/1**[3]

-233 **2** ½ **Raqeeb (USA)**[9] 3337 3-9-7 **77**.............................(v[1]) RichardMullen 9 — 82
(Sir Michael Stoute) *led: hdd and no ex towards fin* **85/40**[1]

-034 **3** ¾ **Be A Devil**[16] 3081 3-9-5 **75**.. PhillipMakin 4 — 78+
(W R Muir) *hld up in rr: effrt over 2f out: swtchd outside and hdwy over 1f out: fin strly* **10/1**

4 1½ **Christmas Light**[300] 5684 3-9-4 **74**................................ DuranFentiman 6 — 73
(D O'Meara) *chsd ldrs: chal over 2f out: one pce fnl f* **18/1**

-145 **5** nk **Mighty Clarets (IRE)**[19] 2993 3-8-13 **69**........................ PaulHanagan 3 — 67
(R A Fahey) *chsd ldrs: drvn over 2f out: one pce* **6/1**

6342 **6** nk **We'll Deal Again**[12] 3243 3-8-4 **65**........................... JamesSullivan[(5)] 1 — 63
(M W Easterby) *swvd lft s: t.k.h: sn trcking ldrs: wd bnd 4f out: drvn on outer over 2f out: hung rt: kpt on ins fnl f* **8/1**

00-0 **7** 1 **Fardyieh**[38] 2416 3-9-2 **72**... JackMitchell 2 — 67
(C E Brittain) *chsd ldrs: wandered over 1f out: wknd fnl f* **16/1**

0031 **8** 1¾ **Whispered Times (USA)**[8] 3371 3-8-13 **69** 6ex.......(p) RobertWinston 5 — 60
(Miss Tracy Waggott) *s.i.s: detached last and sn drvn along: nvr on terms* **7/2**[2]

3000 **9** 2½ **Jupiter Fidius**[23] 2863 3-8-11 **70**..............................(p) KellyHarrison[(3)] 7 — 55
(Mrs K Walton) *dwlt: sn in tch: hdwy on inner over 3f out: n.m.r over 1f out: sn wknd* **25/1**

1m 32.37s (-1.43) **Going Correction** -0.125s/f (Firm) — **9** Ran SP% **120.4**
Speed ratings (Par 102): **103,102,101,99,99 99,98,96,93**
Tote Swingers: 1&2 £9.30, 1&3 £7.80, 2&3 £4.00 CSF £16.79 CT £106.33 TOTE £7.20: £1.90, £1.60, £3.10; EX 22.60.
Owner H E Sheikh Rashid Bin Mohammed **Bred** Darley **Trained** Hambleton, N Yorks

FOCUS
A fair handicap run at a decent pace but, as at recent meetings here on fast ground, it still proved an advantage to race handily. The winner was back to his penultimate Redcar form.
Whispered Times(USA) Official explanation: jockey said gelding never travelled

3613 NATWEST AGRICULTURAL TEAM H'CAP — 1m 1f 207y
7:55 (7:55) (Class 5) (0-75,75) 3-Y-O+ — £3,238 (£963; £481; £240) Stalls High

Form — RPR

422 **1** **Pendragon (USA)**[9] 3319 7-9-7 **75**..................................... DaleSwift[(7)] 9 — 83+
(B Ellison) *chsd ldrs: nt clr run 2f out: swtchd lft appr fnl f: styd on wl to ld last 100yds* **10/11**[1]

-055 **2** 1 **Snowed Under**[20] 2961 9-9-11 **72**.. PhillipMakin 1 — 78
(J D Bethell) *trckd ldr: chal 3f out: led over 1f out: hdd and no ex ins fnl f* **12/1**

5104 **3** ½ **General Tufto**[10] 3283 5-9-10 **74**..............................(b) BarryMcHugh[(3)] 2 — 79
(C Smith) *in tch: hdwy on ins over 2f out: plld wd 1f out: edgd lft and styd on wl* **17/2**

1005 **4** 1¼ **Arashi**[13] 3203 4-9-0 **61**..(p) LiamJones 5 — 63
(Lucinda Featherstone) *t.k.h in rr: hdwy on outer over 2f out: styd on wl: hmpd ins fnl f* **14/1**

2-16 **5** shd **Saint Thomas (IRE)**[41] 2315 3-8-10 **68**................................ TomEaves 4 — 70
(J Mackie) *swvd lft s: trckd ldrs: t.k.h: n.m.r 2f out: edgd rt ins fnl f: one pce* **14/1**

3-01 **6** 1½ **City Vaults Girl (IRE)**[35] 2516 3-9-1 **73**.......................... PaulHanagan 6 — 72
(R A Fahey) *led: hdd over 1f out: wknd fnl 150yds* **8/1**[3]

3302 **7** 2¼ **Umverti**[10] 3283 5-9-1 **62**... DavidAllan 3 — 57
(N Bycroft) *hmpd and slipped s: sn chsng ldrs on outside: chal over 2f out: wknd over 1f out* **7/1**[2]

8 2¾ **Descaro (USA)**[154] 6195 4-9-0 **61**................................. DuranFentiman 7 — 50
(D O'Meara) *in rr: shkn up over 4f out: drvn 3f out: sn btn* **50/1**

2233 **9** 1¼ **Blue Spinnaker (IRE)**[21] 2937 11-9-4 **70**................. JamesSullivan[(5)] 8 — 57
(M W Easterby) *s.i.s: a last: nvr on terms* **9/1**

2m 4.79s (-2.21) **Going Correction** -0.125s/f (Firm)
WFA 3 from 4yo+ 11lb — **9** Ran SP% **119.5**
Speed ratings (Par 103): **103,102,101,100,100 99,97,95,94**
Tote Swingers: 1&2 £3.50, 1&3 £16.10, 2&3 £4.50 CSF £14.43 CT £65.85 TOTE £1.80: £1.10, £4.50, £2.40; EX 13.00.
Owner Dan Gilbert & Kristian Strangeway **Bred** Flaxman Holdings Ltd **Trained** Norton, N Yorks

FOCUS
Plenty of in-form horses in this fair handicap and it looks likely to represent reliable form, for all that it wasn't easy to get involved from off the pace. The well-in winner did not need to match his Carlisle form.
Umverti Official explanation: jockey said mare slipped on leaving stalls

3614 FERGUSON FAWSITT ARMS H'CAP — 1m 4f 16y
8:30 (8:30) (Class 6) (0-60,60) 3-Y-O+ — £2,590 (£770; £385; £192) Stalls High

Form — RPR

3432 **1** **Dean Iarracht (IRE)**[8] 3369 4-9-6 **52**............................ RobertWinston 4 — 60
(Miss Tracy Waggott) *hld up in midfield: stdy hdwy over 2f out: led jst ins fnl f: hld on wl* **2/1**[1]

4452 **2** ¾ **Rowan Lodge (IRE)**[15] 3110 8-9-9 **60**........................(b) IanBrennan[(5)] 8 — 67+
(Ollie Pears) *hld up in rr: hdwy and nt clr run over 1f out: swtchd outside: styd on wl: nt quite rch wnr* **9/2**[3]

2520 **3** 1½ **Pedasus (USA)**[44] 2232 4-10-0 **60**..................................(p) TomEaves 3 — 64
(T Keddy) *hld up in midfield: hdwy 6f out: nt clr run over 1f out: kpt on same pce ins fnl f* **16/1**

00-0 **4** ¾ **Chichina (USA)**[35] 2503 3-8-4 **49**.. GregFairley 1 — 52
(M Johnston) *sn w ldr: led 3f out: hdd and no ex jst ins fnl f* **12/1**

-062 **5** nse **Royal Composer (IRE)**[8] 3370 7-9-1 **47**............................... DavidAllan 2 — 50
(T D Easterby) *trckd ldrs: drvn over 2f out: one pce appr fnl f* **3/1**[2]

-300 **6** 1¼ **Dimashq**[33] 2560 8-9-4 **50**... PaulHanagan 5 — 51
(P T Midgley) *hld up in rr: gd hdwy to chal 2f out: one pce* **7/1**

000 **7** 2 **Massachusetts**[22] 2899 3-7-11 **47** oh1 ow1............. JamesSullivan[(5)] 10 — 45
(B J Meehan) *chsd ldrs: effrt on ins over 2f out: wknd appr fnl f* **14/1**

0560 **8** 1¼ **French Seventyfive**[24] 2838 3-8-2 **47**............................. DuranFentiman 9 — 45
(T D Walford) *led: hdd 3f out: hung bdly lft and lost pl over 1f out: bit slipped and eased* **16/1**

050/ **9** 1½ **Parchment (IRE)**[687] 5003 8-8-7 **46**................................ ShaneBKelly[(7)] 7 — 40
(A J Lockwood) *t.k.h towards rr: hdwy on outside over 2f out: sn chsng ldrs: wknd appr fnl f* **14/1**

2m 44.15s (4.35) **Going Correction** -0.125s/f (Firm)
WFA 3 from 4yo+ 13lb — **9** Ran SP% **121.8**
Speed ratings (Par 101): **84,83,82,82,81 81,79,78,77**
Tote Swingers: 1&2 £3.80, 1&3 £11.20, 2&3 £11.90 CSF £12.06 CT £117.53 TOTE £3.30: £1.40, £1.10, £3.10; EX 12.40.
Owner Michael Howarth **Bred** Ken Carroll **Trained** Spennymoor, Co Durham

FOCUS
Three-year-olds have a decent record in this race but the trio fielded here had little form to speak of and the finish was fought out by two exposed sorts at the end of a steadily-run race. The form is sound enough.
French Seventyfive Official explanation: jockey said bit slipped through gelding's mouth

3615 COCKTAILS AND CALYPSO NIGHT H'CAP — 5f
9:00 (9:00) (Class 6) (0-65,63) 3-Y-O+ — £2,266 (£674; £337; £168) Stalls High

Form — RPR

0052 **1** **Tournedos (IRE)**[3] 3533 8-8-13 **55**.......................(b) JamesSullivan[(5)] 13 — 67
(Mrs R A Carr) *wnt lft s: chsd ldrs: styd on wl to ld last 100yds* **15/8**[1]

2-05 **2** 1 **Bertie Southstreet**[17] 3064 7-9-5 **61**.......................(v) JamesO'Reilly[(5)] 15 — 69
(J O'Reilly) *led: hdd and no ex last 100yds* **7/1**[2]

5645 **3** ½ **Fantasy Fighter (IRE)**[13] 3200 5-8-10 **47**............................ PaulHanagan 9 — 54
(J J Quinn) *chsd ldrs: edgd lft 1f out: styd on wl* **14/1**

-000 **4** nk **Hitches Dubai (BRZ)**[8] 3357 5-9-9 **60**......................... DanielTudhope 12 — 66
(G A Harker) *hmpd s: in rr: hdwy and edgd rt 2f out: styd on wl fnl f* **14/1**

0622 **5** nk **Darcy's Pride (IRE)**[10] 3286 6-8-12 **54**........................ PaulPickard[(5)] 10 — 58
(P T Midgley) *mid-div: hdwy on outer over 1f out: styd on wl* **7/1**[2]

4504 **6** 1 **Fashion Icon (USA)**[10] 3287 4-8-5 **47**.............................. IanBrennan[(5)] 1 — 48
(D O'Meara) *wnt rt s: w ldrs: one pce fnl f* **20/1**

0155 **7** ¾ **Wotatomboy**[18] 3026 4-8-5 **47**.. AmyRyan[(5)] 16 — 45
(R M Whitaker) *chsd ldrs: fdd fnl 75yds* **8/1**[3]

0000 **8** shd **City For Conquest (IRE)**[43] 2263 7-8-5 **45**.............(b) KellyHarrison[(3)] 7 — 43
(John A Harris) *in rr: effrt on ins whn hmpd 2f out: kpt on fnl f* **50/1**

5014 **9** ½ **Lake Chini (IRE)**[18] 3026 8-9-1 **59**..................................(b) DavidAllan 11 — 55
(M W Easterby) *in rr: hdwy over 1f out: nvr nr ldrs* **9/1**

3000 **10** 1½ **Commander Wish**[10] 3286 7-8-10 **47**..............................(p) LiamJones 8 — 38
(Lucinda Featherstone) *in rr: effrt on outer over 2f out: lost pl over 1f out* **25/1**

013 **11** 1¼ **Port Ronan (USA)**[10] 3286 4-8-4 **46**........................ PatrickDonaghy[(5)] 4 — 32
(J S Wainwright) *dwlt: effrt on outside over 2f out: sn wknd* **16/1**

3016 **12** 6 **Soto**[17] 3062 7-9-12 **63**...(b) RobertWinston 14 — 27
(M W Easterby) *rrd s: sn chsng ldrs: wknd over 1f out* **9/1**

0-00 **13** 4 **Take That**[10] 3287 5-8-1 **45**.. NoraLooby[(7)] 5 — —
(S P Griffiths) *hld up in midfield: lost pl 2f out: sn bhd* **50/1**

62.60 secs (-0.90) **Going Correction** -0.15s/f (Firm)
WFA 3 from 4yo+ 5lb — **13** Ran SP% **122.6**
Speed ratings (Par 101): **101,99,98,98,97 96,94,94,93,91 89,79,73**
Tote Swingers: 1&2 £4.50, 1&3 £11.00, 2&3 £23.40 CSF £14.53 CT £153.95 TOTE £3.20: £1.90, £1.50, £4.00; EX 18.30 Place 6: £6.23 Place 5: £4.43 .
Owner David W Chapman **Bred** Pat Grogan **Trained** Huby, N Yorks

FOCUS
A modest sprint but one run at a good pace that soon had the field well strung out. The form looks basically sound among the principals.
T/Plt: £10.80 to a £1 stake. Pool:£50,820.79 - 3,428.34 winning tickets. T/Qpdt: £7.80 to a £1 stake. Pool:£4,204.40 - 397.60 winning tickets. WG

3433 DONCASTER (L-H)
Friday, July 2

OFFICIAL GOING: Good to firm (9.1)
Wind: Virtually nil Weather: Fine and dry

3616 SOCIETY LIFESTYLE & LEISURE MAGAZINE CLAIMING STKS — 1m (S)
2:00 (2:04) (Class 5) 4-Y-O+ — £2,729 (£806; £403) Stalls High

Form — RPR

2340 **1** **Moody Tunes**[20] 2977 7-9-0 81.. AndrewElliott 4 — 76
(J R Weymes) *mde all: rdn 1 1/2f out: drvn ins fnl f: hld on wl* **10/11**[1]

5044 **2** shd **Bolodenka (IRE)**[27] 2760 8-9-1 73...........................(p) PaulHanagan 6 — 77
(R A Fahey) *trckd wnr: effrt to chal wl over 1f out: sn rdn and ev ch tl drvn ins fnl f: edgd lft and no ex nr line* **7/4**[2]

1203 **3** 4 **Plush**[36] 2477 7-8-12 74.. RossAtkinson[(5)] 1 — 70
(Tom Dascombe) *hld up: hdwy to trck ldng pair 1/2-way: effrt over 2f out: rdn to chal wl over 1f out and ev ch tl drvn and wknd ent fnl f* **5/1**[3]

0 **4** 30 **True Union (USA)**[100] 971 4-9-1 0.................................... JoeFanning 5 — —
(A P Jarvis) *trckd ldng pair: pushed along 1/2-way: sn rdn and outpcd: bhd and eased fnl 2f* **33/1**

1m 39.22s (-0.08) **Going Correction** -0.225s/f (Firm) — **4** Ran SP% **108.4**
Speed ratings (Par 103): **91,90,86,56**
CSF £2.77 TOTE £1.70; EX 2.70.
Owner Mrs Elaine M Burke **Bred** Llety Stud **Trained** Middleham Moor, N Yorks

FOCUS
A fair standard for the grade. The form is rated around the front pair.

3617 RODGER GOOSEMAN AND LUCY WALKER CARDSAVE H'CAP — 1m 4f
2:30 (2:30) (Class 5) (0-70,68) 4-Y-O+ — £2,590 (£770; £385; £192) Stalls Low

Form — RPR

0-04 **1** **Fantino**[18] 3032 4-8-13 **60**... PaulHanagan 5 — 76
(J Mackie) *mde all: rdn and qcknd clr 3f out: styd on strly* **3/1**[3]

03-4 **2** 7 **Astronomical (IRE)**[8] 3360 8-9-1 **62**........................(p) RobertWinston 3 — 67
(R Hollinshead) *trckd wnr: rdn along over 3f out: drvn to chse wnr 2f out: sn no imp* **11/4**[2]

6-45 **3** ¾ **Madamlily (IRE)**[29] 2672 4-8-11 **63**............................ IanBrennan[(5)] 4 — 67
(J J Quinn) *hld up in rr: pushed along 4f out: rdn and outpcd 3f out: styd on u.p fnl 2f* **7/1**

3451 **4** 6 **Magnitude**[8] 3360 5-8-12 **59** 6ex............................(v) GrahamGibbons 2 — 53
(B P J Baugh) *trckd ldrs: rdn along and outpcd over 3f out: sn drvn and n.d* **9/4**[1]

0406 **5** 14 **French Applause (IRE)**[16] 3090 4-9-5 **66**............................ JoeFanning 1 — 38
(T P Tate) *dwlt: sn trcking ldng pair: hdwy to chse wnr over 4f out: rdn along 3f out and sn wknd* **11/2**

2m 30.63s (-4.27) **Going Correction** -0.225s/f (Firm) — **5** Ran SP% **110.3**
Speed ratings (Par 103): **105,100,99,95,86**
CSF £11.56 TOTE £4.80: £2.90, £2.40; EX 10.90.
Owner Norman A Blyth **Bred** Norman A Blyth **Trained** Church Broughton , Derbys

FOCUS
A modest handicap but it looked fairly competitive on paper. A clear personal best from the winner.

3618 ATTEYS SOLICITORS H'CAP 1m 4f
3:00 (3:01) (Class 4) (0-85,83) 3-Y-O+ **£3,885** (£1,156; £577; £288) **Stalls** Low

Form RPR

-111 **1** **Sparkling Smile (IRE)**[9] 3337 3-9-0 **82** 6ex................. RichardMullen 1 90+
(D R Lanigan) *trckd ldrs on inner: hdwy 3f out: led over 2f out: rdn wl over 1f out: drvn ins fnl f: hld on gamely* **11/10**[1]

542- **2** *nse* **Indochina**[270] 6533 3-8-3 **71**.................................... JoeFanning 4 79+
(M Johnston) *led: rn green: hung rt and rdn along 3f out: hdd over 2f out and sn drvn: rallied to chal over 1f out: ev ch ins fnl frurlong: kpt on gamely: jst hld* **11/2**[3]

00-4 **3** *3/4* **Union Island (IRE)**[29] 2685 4-9-10 **79**.................................... NeilCallan 6 86
(A King) *trckd ldrs: hdwy on wd outside 3f out: rdn 2f out: drvn and ch ent fnl f: kpt on* **13/2**

-243 **4** *3* **Graceful Descent (FR)**[16] 3074 5-8-13 **68**...................... PaulHanagan 3 70
(J S Goldie) *trckd ldr: hdwy and cl up 3f out: sn trdn: drvn wl over 1f out and sn one pce* **9/1**

3121 **5** *1/2* **Ghufa (IRE)**[10] 3294 6-9-2 **71**.......................... RobertWinston 2 72
(J Pearce) *hld up in tch: hdwy 3f out: rdn along over 2f out: swtchd rt and drvn over 1f out: sn no imp* **4/1**[2]

55-6 **6** *7* **Amanda Carter**[135] 224 6-9-7 **83**.................................... LeeTopliss(7) 7 73
(R A Fahey) *s.i.s: a in rr* **16/1**

2m 30.69s (-4.21) **Going Correction** -0.225s/f (Firm)
WFA 3 from 4yo+ 13lb 6 Ran SP% **112.2**
Speed ratings (Par 105): **105,104,104,102,102 97**
Tote Swingers: 1&2 £2.70, 1&3 £2.30, 2&3 £6.80 CSF £7.62 TOTE £1.90: £1.20, £1.60; EX 7.80.
Owner Saif Ali & Saeed H Altayer **Bred** Georgestown Stud **Trained** Newmarket, Suffolk

FOCUS
Not a bad little handicap, and the form looks solid for the grade. The progressive winner is rated to form.

3619 PAUL LOUGHNANE AND ALEXIS CALLAN CARDSAVE H'CAP 7f
3:35 (3:36) (Class 3) (0-95,95) 3-Y-O+ **£6,476** (£1,927; £963; £481) **Stalls** High

Form RPR

0001 **1** *hd* **Mahadee (IRE)**[9] 3334 5-9-10 **91** 6ex...............................(b) NeilCallan 3 101
(C E Brittain) *dwlt: smooth hdwy to trck ldrs 1/2-way: nt clr run over 1f out: swtchd lft and rdn to ld jst ins fnl f: hdd whn bmpd and carried lft nr fin: fin 2nd, hd: awrdd rr* **7/1**

-422 **2** **Ancient Cross**[15] 3107 6-9-0 **81**...............................(t) GrahamGibbons 4 91
(M W Easterby) *towards rr: gd hdwy over 2f out: nt clr run and swtchd rt over 1f out: squeezed through and rdn ent fnl f: qcknd to ld and hung bdly lft wl ins fnl f: fin 1st: disq and plcd 2nd* **9/2**[1]

0303 **3** *2 1/4* **Esoterica (IRE)**[6] 3448 7-9-10 **91**...............................(v) PaulHanagan 8 97+
(J S Goldie) *in tch: hdwy 3f out: rdn and ev ch whn hmpd over 1f out: rallied ins fnl f: kpt on* **5/1**[2]

0003 **4** *1 1/2* **Excusez Moi (USA)**[6] 3446 8-9-6 **87**.......................... RobertWinston 5 86
(Mrs R A Carr) *in tch: hdwy to join ldrs over 2f out: rdn to ld briefly appr fnl f: sn hdd and kpt on same pce* **9/1**

0420 **5** *1* **Aldermoor (USA)**[7] 3389 4-9-3 **87**.......................... WilliamCarson(3) 11 84
(S C Williams) *chsd clr ldr: hdwy over 2f out and sn cl up: rdn and edgd lft and rt over 1f out: sn drvn and one pce* **5/1**[2]

6110 **6** *nk* **Damika (IRE)**[6] 3446 7-9-11 **95**.......................... MichaelStainton(3) 10 91
(R M Whitaker) *prom: hdwy 1/2-way: rdn to ld 2f out: drvn over 1f out: hdd appr fnl f: wknd* **14/1**

-040 **7** *nse* **Colonel Mak**[20] 2978 3-8-13 **88**.......................... PhillipMakin 7 81
(T D Barron) *dwlt and hmpd s: in rr tl sme late hdwy* **7/1**

0135 **8** *4 1/2* **Game Lad**[6] 3448 8-9-2 **83**...............................(tp) DavidAllan 1 67
(T D Easterby) *a in rr* **12/1**

0201 **9** *8* **Celtic Sultan (IRE)**[14] 3150 6-9-9 **90**...............................(b) MickyFenton 9 52
(T P Tate) *wnt lft s: sn led and clr: rdn along and hdd 2f out: sn wknd* **6/1**[3]

4-00 **10** *30* **Mirrored**[55] 1900 4-10-0 **95**...............................(e[1]) AdrianNicholls 6 —
(D Nicholls) *sltly hmpd s: sn chsng ldrs: rdn along 1/2-way: sn wknd and bhd whn eased fnl 2f* **25/1**

1m 24.49s (-1.81) **Going Correction** -0.225s/f (Firm)
WFA 3 from 4yo+ 8lb 10 Ran SP% **119.0**
Speed ratings (Par 107): **100,101,98,96,95 95,94,89,80,46**
Tote Swingers: 1&2 £6.90, 1&3 £3.80, 2&3 £5.10 CSF £39.41 CT £178.64 TOTE £8.20: £2.80, £1.50, £2.30; EX 37.30 Trifecta £129.70 Pool: £415.41 - 2.37 winning units..
Owner Saeed Manana **Bred** Darley **Trained** Newmarket, Suffolk

■ Stewards' Enquiry : Graham Gibbons two four-day bans: careless riding (16-23 July)

FOCUS
An open handicap run at a strong pace. Sound form, with a 5lb best from the disqualified Ancient Cross.

NOTEBOOK
Mahadee(IRE) was 3lb well in at the weights under his penalty for winning at Salisbury nine days earlier, but he was dropping back a furlong in distance. The strong pace helped to counter that, though, and given the interference he suffered close home it's easy to see why the stewards reversed the placings. Official explanation: jockey said gelding hung left final furlong (tchd 6-1)

Ancient Cross was travelling well 2f out but was behind a wall of horses. He went for an ambitious gap between horses near the rail, making room for himself and doing no favours to Esoterica in the process, and then quickened up well to edge ahead, at which point he hung left and gave Mahadee a fairly hefty bump close to the line. In the subsequent stewards' enquiry he lost the race to Mahadee, but he looked the best horse in the race, and is fully capable of making amends soon, although he does need a strong pace to run off and, as was demonstrated here, does not like to be in front too long. (op 5-1 tchd 7-2)

Esoterica(IRE) would have finished closer had he not been badly hampered next to the rail a furlong out. His current mark doesn't make things easy for him, though. (op 9-2)

Excusez Moi(USA), who hinted at a return to form at Newcastle last time, has dropped to a fair mark and ran a solid race. (op 12-1)

Aldermoor(USA) chased the strong pace set by Celtic Sultan and didn't see out the trip. He might be worth dropping back to 6f. (op 7-1 tchd 8-1)

Damika(IRE), who is on a stiff mark now, also had too much use made of him in chasing the fast pace set by the leader. (op 16-1)

Colonel Mak failed to improve for the step up to 7f and is beginning to look pretty exposed. (op 10-1)

Celtic Sultan(IRE) went off fast, indeed too fast, and simply set it up for the closers. (op 5-1)

3620 MICHAEL LIPOSITS AND LAUREN POPE CARDSAVE MAIDEN FILLIES' STKS 7f
4:10 (4:11) (Class 4) 3-Y-O+ **£3,885** (£1,156; £577; £288) **Stalls** High

Form RPR

0 **1** **Fleeting Glance (IRE)**[19] 2998 3-8-12 0.......................... ShaneKelly 8 74
(B J Meehan) *trckd ldrs: hdwy over 2f out: rdn to ld over 1f out: drvn and hdd ins fnl f: kpt on and led towards fin* **9/2**[3]

0- **2** *3/4* **Fashionable Gal (IRE)**[289] 5980 3-8-12 0.......................... SebSanders 7 75+
(Sir Mark Prescott) *towards rr: pushed along 1/2-way: hdwy 2f out: rdn to chse ldr over 1f out: drvn and slt ld ins fnl f: hung bdly rt and hdd fnl 40yds* **12/1**

2325 **3** *3 3/4* **Nimue (USA)**[16] 3091 3-8-12 77.......................... NeilCallan 2 62
(P F I Cole) *rrd s: in tch: hdwy to chse ldrs over 2f out: rdn wl over 1f out: drvn and one pce ent fnl f* **9/4**[1]

5 **4** *1/2* **Amity (IRE)**[11] 3258 3-8-12 0.......................... JoeFanning 9 61
(M Johnston) *cl up: disp ld 1/2-way: rdn over 2f and sn hung lft: drvn over 1f out: sn one pce* **4/1**[2]

-44 **5** *nk* **Bidruma**[15] 3125 3-8-12 0.......................... RobertWinston 5 60
(Mike Murphy) *t.k.h: hld up in rr: hdwy 3f out and sn rdn along: kpt on fnl 2f: nrst fin* **11/1**

60- **6** *1/2* **Asaab (IRE)**[350] 4047 3-8-12 0.......................... RichardMullen 1 59
(C E Brittain) *trckd ldrs: effrt over 2f out: sn rdn and wknd appr fnl f* **12/1**

7 *10* **Topaze Star** 3-8-12 0.......................... IvaMilickova 6 32
(Jane Chapple-Hyam) *chsd ldrs to 1/2-way: sn wknd* **33/1**

0-45 **8** *6* **Mighty Aphrodite**[32] 2609 3-8-12 64.......................... PaulHanagan 4 15
(Rae Guest) *led: rdn along 3f out: hdd 2f out and sn wknd* **5/1**

1m 26.01s (-0.29) **Going Correction** -0.225s/f (Firm)
WFA 3 from 4yo 8lb 8 Ran SP% **112.3**
Speed ratings (Par 102): **92,91,86,86,85 85,73,67**
Tote Swingers: 1&2 £11.30, 1&3 £3.60, 2&3 £5.50 CSF £53.73 TOTE £4.20: £2.30, £3.70, £1.10; EX 62.60 TRIFECTA Not won..
Owner Sangster Family & Mrs J Magnier **Bred** Swettenham Stud **Trained** Manton, Wilts

FOCUS
There was a dramatic finish to this fillies' maiden.

3621 1STSECURITYSOLUTIONS.CO.UK MAIDEN STKS 7f
4:45 (4:46) (Class 4) 3-Y-O **£3,885** (£1,156; £577; £288) **Stalls** High

Form RPR

033 **1** **Ertikaan**[13] 3220 3-9-3 82.......................... RichardHills 1 84+
(M A Jarvis) *t.k.h: led after 1f: shkn up and qcknd clr wl over 1f out: easily* **4/6**[1]

2 *6* **Self Employed** 3-9-3 0.......................... RobertWinston 5 68
(G Woodward) *rrd s and in rr: hdwy 1/2-way: chsd wnr wl over 2f out: sn rdn and no imp* **25/1**

20- **3** *1* **Serhaal (IRE)**[261] 6781 3-9-3 0.......................... RichardMullen 4 65
(Sir Michael Stoute) *led 1f: cl up: rdn along wl over 2f out: drvn and one pce fr wl over 1f out* **3/1**[2]

4 *2* **Sraab** 3-9-3 0.......................... NeilCallan 2 60
(C E Brittain) *prom: rdn along over 2f out: sn wknd* **9/1**[3]

5 *13* **Fear Factor (IRE)** 3-9-3 0...............................(p) TomQueally 3 36
(G A Butler) *chsd ldrs: rdn along over 3f out: sn outpcd and bhd* **9/1**[3]

1m 26.34s (0.04) **Going Correction** -0.225s/f (Firm) 5 Ran SP% **108.8**
Speed ratings (Par 102): **90,83,82,79,64**
CSF £17.57 TOTE £1.30: £1.10, £10.60; EX 16.60.
Owner Hamdan Al Maktoum **Bred** Floors Farming And Dominic Burke **Trained** Newmarket, Suffolk

FOCUS
This proved a straightforward task for the 82-rated winner but there are doubts over what he beat in this slightly muddling event.

3622 FIRST TRANSPENNINE EXPRESS FILLIES' H'CAP 5f
5:15 (5:15) (Class 4) (0-80,84) 4-Y-O+ **£3,885** (£1,156; £577; £288) **Stalls** High

Form RPR

5121 **1** **Favourite Girl (IRE)**[8] 3373 4-9-11 **84** 6ex...............................(v) DavidAllan 1 93
(T D Easterby) *wnt lft s: racd centre: cl up: rdn to ld ent fnl f: sn drvn and edgd lft: kpt on* **5/2**[1]

0260 **2** *hd* **Milton Of Campsie**[25] 2818 5-8-11 **70**.......................... AndrewElliott 2 78
(J Balding) *sn trcking wnr centre: hdwy whn nt clr run and swtchd rt ent fnl f: sn rdn and styd on strly towards fin* **16/1**

-350 **3** *1* **Hypnosis**[21] 2940 7-9-1 **74**.......................... PhillipMakin 6 78
(N Wilson) *qckly away and led towards stands' rail: rdn along 2f out: hung bdly lft and hdd ent fnl f: sn drvn and one pce* **15/2**

2435 **4** *2* **Feelin Foxy**[13] 3197 6-9-7 **80**.......................... TomQueally 7 77
(J G Given) *chsd ldr towards stands' rail: effrt 2f out: sn rdn and one pce appr fnl f* **7/2**[2]

-062 **5** *1/2* **Speedy Senorita (IRE)**[4] 3497 5-7-13 **63**.......................... IanBrennan(5) 3 58
(J J Quinn) *trckd ldrs: effrt 2f out: sn rdn and one pce appr fnl f* **13/2**

2614 **6** *shd* **Poppy's Rose**[25] 2818 6-8-8 **74** ow5.......................... DaleSwift(7) 4 69
(T J Etherington) *chsd ldrs: rdn along 2f out and sn no imp* **4/1**[3]

3302 **7** *2 1/2* **Dispol Kylie (IRE)**[17] 3064 4-8-1 **65**.......................... PaulPickard(5) 5 51
(P T Midgley) *dwlt: a in rr* **15/2**

58.73 secs (-1.77) **Going Correction** -0.225s/f (Firm) 7 Ran SP% **113.5**
Speed ratings (Par 102): **105,104,103,99,99 98,94**
Tote Swingers: 1&2 £4.90, 1&3 £5.40, 2&3 £12.50 CSF £41.75 TOTE £2.40: £1.20, £9.40; EX 30.50 Place 6:£17.08 Place 5: £8.83 .
Owner Peter C Bourke **Bred** Limestone And Tara Studs **Trained** Great Habton, N Yorks

FOCUS
A tight little sprint handicap. The winner is getting close to her old form.

Hypnosis Official explanation: jockey said mare hung badly left

Feelin Foxy Official explanation: jockey said mare hung badly left

T/Plt: £13.00 to a £1 stake. Pool:£58,457.33 - 3,276.05 winning tickets. T/Qpdt: £5.40 to a £1 stake. Pool:£3,545.51 - 480.84 winning tickets. JR

[3582]HAYDOCK (L-H)

Friday, July 2

OFFICIAL GOING: Sprint course - good to firm; round course - good (good to firm in places)

Inner sprint course used and rail realignment on round course increased advertised distances by 10yds.

Wind: Breeze, half - against Weather: Sunny

3623 BETDAQ RACING EXCELLENCE APPRENTICE TRAINING SERIES H'CAP 5f
6:40 (6:40) (Class 5) (0-75,68) 3-Y-O+ £2,590 (£770; £385; £192) Stalls Low

Form RPR

0604 1 **Angelo Poliziano**[9] 3321 4-9-11 60..............................(p) RosieJessop 3 71
(Mrs A Duffield) *hld up bhd ldrs: impr to ld over 1f out: rdn ins fnl f: kpt on wl* 5/2[1]

0531 2 1 1/2 **You'relikemefrank**[10] 3299 4-8-11 51 6ex................(p) FrancisHayes(5) 7 56
(J Balding) *trckd ldrs: rdn to take 2nd and chalng fr over 1f out: edgd lft ins fnl f: nt qckn fnl 50yds* 11/4[2]

-335 3 2 1/4 **First Swallow**[115] 832 5-9-5 61..............................(t) ClaireMurray(7) 4 58
(D H Brown) *plld hrd: led: shkn up and hdd over 1f out: no ex fnl 100yds* 7/1

0404 4 1/2 **Rio Sands**[10] 3286 5-9-6 55.................................... JohnCavanagh 2 50
(R M Whitaker) *w ldr: rdn whn chalng over 1f out: nt qckn ent fnl f: kpt on at one pce after* 3/1[3]

64 5 2 1/4 **Ask Jenny (IRE)**[8] 3356 8-9-3 59......................... DavidSimmonson(7) 6 46
(Patrick Morris) *hld up in rr: pushed along over 1f out: outpcd fnl f* 5/1

62.11 secs (1.11) **Going Correction** +0.225s/f (Good)
WFA 3 from 4yo+ 5lb 5 Ran SP% **109.4**
Speed ratings (Par 103): **100,97,94,93,89**
CSF £9.50 TOTE £4.00: £1.30, £1.60; EX 10.10.
Owner Middleham Park Racing XXVIII **Bred** Bumble Bs, C Liesack & Mrs S Nicholls **Trained** Constable Burton, N Yorks

FOCUS
A small field as sprint handicaps go, the early pace also much steadier than is often the case in these events, and doubtful the form is anything out of the ordinary. The winner is rated in line with this year's efforts.

3624 E B F RACING UK £20 PER MONTH MAIDEN STKS 6f
7:10 (7:14) (Class 5) 2-Y-O £3,238 (£963; £481; £240) Stalls Low

Form RPR

5 1 **Blaze Of Thunder (IRE)**[16] 3087 2-9-3 0.................... TonyHamilton 8 78
(R A Fahey) *trckd ldrs: rdn over 1f out: r.o to ld fnl 100yds: on top at fin* 8/1

53 2 1 1/4 **Fight The Chance (IRE)**[9] 3332 2-9-3 0...................... SamHitchcott 3 74
(M R Channon) *a.p: rdn to ld wl over 1f out: hdd fnl 100yds: hld cl home* 6/1

55 3 1/2 **Red Marling (IRE)**[22] 2882 2-9-3 0.................................... PaulEddery 1 73
(B W Hills) *towards rr: hdwy 2f out: rdn to chse ldrs over 1f out: styd on but nt quite pce of front 2* 33/1

2 4 2 **Restless Bay (IRE)**[19] 2990 2-9-3 0............................. GeorgeBaker 15 68
(R Hollinshead) *midfield: pushed along 2f out: nt qckn whn n.m.r over 1f out: hdwy and styd on ins fnl f: nt rch ldrs* 5/1[3]

0 5 hd **My Mate Jake (IRE)**[20] 2980 2-9-3 0............................ MickyFenton 14 66
(J G Given) *chsd ldrs: rdn over 1f out: styd on same pce ins fnl f* 50/1

0 6 nk **Elusivity (IRE)**[22] 2882 2-9-3 0.. SebSanders 2 65
(R Hannon) *a.p: rdn to chal over 1f out: no ex fnl 75yds* 10/1

7 1 **C P Joe (IRE)** 2-9-3 0.. FrannyNorton 10 64+
(Paul Green) *rn green in rr: styd on and prog ins fnl f: under hand ride fnl 50yds whn unable to get to ldrs* 66/1

3 8 hd **Squires Gate (IRE)**[97] 1009 2-9-3 0.............................. MichaelHills 16 61
(B W Hills) *dwlt: hld up: hdwy 1/2-way: effrt over 1f out: kpt on u.p: one pce fnl 100yds* 4/1[1]

9 1 **King Kurt (IRE)** 2-9-3 0.. NeilCallan 6 58+
(K A Ryan) *sn pushed along in midfield: outpcd and lost pl 1/2-way: styd on and edgd rt ins fnl f: nt pce to trble ldrs* 28/1

10 nse **Hoot (IRE)** 2-9-3 0... TedDurcan 9 58+
(Saeed Bin Suroor) *missed break: hld up: hdwy 1/2-way: rdn to chse ldrs over 1f out: no ex fnl 100yds* 7/1

44 11 1 1/4 **Indian Ballad (IRE)**[22] 2882 2-9-3 0......................... GrahamGibbons 11 55
(E S McMahon) *led: rdn and hdd wl over 1f out: wknd ins fnl f* 25/1

0 12 2 **The Oboist (IRE)**[16] 3087 2-8-12 0................................... JoeFanning 13 44+
(M Johnston) *w ldrs: u.p and losing pl whn n.m.r and hmpd over 1f out: n.d after* 50/1

13 2 3/4 **Say A Prayer** 2-8-12 0... AdrianNicholls 12 35
(T D Easterby) *towards rr and rn green: sn pushed along: nvr on terms* 50/1

00 14 1 3/4 **Ad Vitam (IRE)**[11] 3269 2-9-3 0.................................... JamesDoyle 4 35
(S Kirk) *midfield: rdn over 1f out: sn wknd* 100/1

4223 15 11 **Bunce (IRE)**[21] 2930 2-9-3 0...................................... RichardHughes 7 2
(R Hannon) *racd w ldrs: pushed along 2f out: rdn and wknd over 1f out* 9/2[2]

16 4 1/2 **Lady Of The Knight (IRE)** 2-8-12 0......................... PatrickMathers 17 —
(H A McWilliams) *missed break: a bhd* 100/1

1m 14.42s (0.92) **Going Correction** +0.225s/f (Good) 16 Ran SP% **121.4**
Speed ratings (Par 94): **102,100,99,97,96 96,95,94,93,93 91,89,85,83,68 62**
Tote Swingers: 1&2 £14.60, 1&3 £83.50, 2&3 £84.70 CSF £52.07 TOTE £10.70: £4.00, £1.60, £10.30; EX 78.80.
Owner G Brogan **Bred** Miss Caterina Dargan **Trained** Musley Bank, N Yorks

FOCUS
A big field of juveniles and probably best to view the form fairly positively for the time being, for all a few performed below expectations. The runner-up and the time help with the level.

NOTEBOOK
Blaze Of Thunder(IRE) had shaped well on his debut at Ripon (raced on unfavoured side) and duly came on from that, impressing with how he travelled in behind and responding willingly to get on top inside the last. His yard continues in excellent form and there will doubtless be more to come, nurseries the obvious next port of call.
Fight The Chance(IRE) ran to a similar level as at Salisbury and should bag a race at some stage, though he could always be a little vulnerable to progressive sorts in maidens. (op 13-2 tchd 7-1)
Red Marling(IRE) will get a higher nursery mark than might have been the case but this was an encouraging effort, travelling well under restraint for much of the way, and he should have further improvement in him. (op 40-1)
Restless Bay(IRE) confirmed he has a fair level of ability, possibly ridden from a bit further back than ideal the way things went but his Gimcrack entry looks ambitious. (op 13-2)
My Mate Jake(IRE) stepped up on his debut effort and will have nurseries as an option after this. (op 66-1)
Elusivity(IRE) is another who stepped up on his debut effort and can now run in nurseries after this. (op 12-1)
C P Joe(IRE) was too green to do himself full justice but showed ability as the penny finally dropped. He should be all the sharper next time. (tchd 80-1)
Squires Gate(IRE) had been absent since a promising third in the Brocklesby but there was confidence behind him in the market and this has to go down as slightly disappointing.
Hoot(IRE) showed his inexperience with a slow start and is another who should do better next time. (op 5-1)
Bunce(IRE) has a had a few chances but can't have been right here, weakening from prominence before stamina should have been an issue on his first start beyond 5f. Official explanation: jockey said colt stopped very quickly (op 4-1)

3625 HALLIWELL JONES BMW "JOY" (S) STKS 6f
7:45 (7:52) (Class 4) 2-Y-O £4,533 (£1,348; £674; £336) Stalls Low

Form RPR

5210 1 **Dolly Parton (IRE)**[17] 3059 2-8-11 0............................ AdrianNicholls 4 65
(D Nicholls) *mde all: rdn over 1f out: pressed ins fnl f: kpt on and jst doing enough cl home* 8/11[1]

04 2 hd **Beyaz Villas**[17] 3058 2-8-11 0... FrannyNorton 5 64
(D Nicholls) *hld up bhd ldrs: effrt and hdwy 2f out: wnt 2nd over 1f out: chalng and ev ch ins fnl f: kpt on: jst hld* 11/2[3]

4442 3 2 1/4 **Crown Ridge (IRE)**[18] 3035 2-8-11 0............................ SamHitchcott 8 58
(M R Channon) *w wnr: pushed along 2f out: lost 2nd whn rdn over 1f out: styd on same pce u.p ins fnl f* 7/1

05 4 1 3/4 **Blaze On By**[7] 3399 2-8-8 0 ow2................................ RichardHughes 10 49
(R Hannon) *racd keenly: hld up: pushed along 2f out: rdn over 1f out: failed to pick up: nvr able to chal* 9/2[2]

4 5 2 1/2 **Painters Easel (IRE)**[18] 3035 2-8-4 0............................ RyanPowell(7) 2 45
(J S Moore) *s.i.s: racd freely: prom after 1f: rdn and hung lft 2f out: lost grnd and sn on far rail: no imp on front quartet fnl f* 10/1

00 6 11 **Buon Compleanno (IRE)**[28] 2693 2-8-6 0............... PatrickMathers 11 7
(A Berry) *in rr: niggled along after 1f: sn hung lft: lft wl bhd over 1f out* 100/1

1m 15.45s (1.95) **Going Correction** +0.225s/f (Good) 6 Ran SP% **114.1**
Speed ratings (Par 96): **96,95,92,90,87 72**
Tote Swingers: 1&2 £1.60, 1&3 £1.90, 2&3 £5.30 CSF £5.51 TOTE £1.90: £1.20, £2.10; EX 5.70.There was no bid for the winner.
Owner Mrs Love and Mrs Barker **Bred** I W Glenton **Trained** Sessay, N Yorks

FOCUS
A glut of non-runners made this seller much less competitive than it looked initially. It is still better than average form for the grade, best rated around the third.

NOTEBOOK
Dolly Parton(IRE) was the clear pick on her Thirsk maiden success and almost certainly didn't reproduce that form in scraping home. She should continue to hold her own if kept to this sort of level. Speed looks her main forte at present and a drop back to 5f certainly wouldn't inconvenience. (op 5-6 tchd 10-11 and evens in places)
Beyaz Villas only just failed to peg back his stable companion. He's bred to be suited by 7f and, having improved with every start to date, should get his head in front before long if his sights aren't set too high. (op 8-1)
Crown Ridge(IRE) had no excuses and simply doesn't look to be progressing. (op 11-2)
Blaze On By already looks one of her stable's lesser lights. (tchd 4-1)
Painters Easel(IRE) showed a bit on his debut at Windsor last month but spoiled his chance here by hanging badly left under pressure. His wayward tendencies will have to be curbed if he's to go the right way. (op 9-1 tchd 8-1)
Buon Compleanno(IRE) Official explanation: trainer's rep said filly was unsuited by the good to firm ground

3626 CHESHIRE OAKS DESIGNER OUTLET H'CAP 1m 6f
8:15 (8:16) (Class 5) (0-70,70) 3-Y-O £2,590 (£770; £385; £192) Stalls Low

Form RPR

-521 1 **Motrice**[22] 2908 3-9-7 70.. SebSanders 5 84+
(Sir Mark Prescott) *hld up: swtchd rt 4f out: hdwy over 3f out: moved upsides on bit 2f out: led wl over 1f out: sn clr: r.o wl: eased down cl home* 10/11[1]

0-05 2 5 **High Ransom**[32] 2585 3-9-7 70..(p) NeilCallan 4 73
(M A Jarvis) *chsd ldrs: rdn to chal 2f out: coninued to chal for 2nd whn wnr asserted over 1f out: prevailed for 2nd pl cl home whn no ch w wnr* 12/1

-453 3 hd **Pena Dorada (IRE)**[30] 2650 3-9-4 67............................(p) AndrewElliott 2 70
(J R Weymes) *chsd ldr: led 3f out: rdn and hdd wl over 1f out: sn no ch w wnr: pressed for 2nd after: lost that position cl home* 16/1

00-5 4 1 3/4 **Straversjoy**[23] 2853 3-8-2 51 oh4..................................... LukeMorris 6 52
(R Hollinshead) *hld up in midfield: rdn 2f out: no imp on ldrs: plugged on at one pce after* 33/1

6-26 5 2 1/2 **Escape Artist**[23] 2853 3-8-4 53 ow1............................ GrahamGibbons 8 51
(T D Easterby) *chsd ldrs: effrt 3f out: chalng 2f out: wknd ins fnl f: eased whn btn fnl 100yds* 3/1[2]

4314 6 15 **Dubara Reef (IRE)**[23] 2853 3-8-7 56.............................. FrannyNorton 1 32+
(Paul Green) *hld up: pushed along over 3f out: effrt to chse ldrs over 2f out: wknd over 1f out: eased whn btn after* 8/1[3]

-604 7 1 **Aalya (IRE)**[21] 2924 3-8-13 62.. TedDurcan 9 37
(J L Dunlop) *s.i.s: in rr: effrt over 3f out: wknd 2f out: eased whn btn fnl f* 18/1

1-20 8 22 **Fairy Flight (USA)**[22] 2893 3-9-7 70................................ ShaneKelly 10 14
(W J Knight) *sn led: rdn and hdd 3f out: wknd 2f out: t.o* 8/1[3]

3m 3.31s (2.11) **Going Correction** +0.225s/f (Good) 8 Ran SP% **121.4**
Speed ratings (Par 100): **111,108,108,107,105 97,96,83**
Tote Swingers: 1&2 £5.80, 1&3 £6.10, 2&3 £10.40 CSF £15.56 CT £121.10 TOTE £2.10: £1.10, £2.80, £5.10; EX 11.40.
Owner Miss K Rausing **Bred** Miss K Rausing **Trained** Newmarket, Suffolk

FOCUS
A one-sided handicap. The winner was value for extra and the form is rated around the third and fifth.

3627 BETFRED WORLD CUP BUS H'CAP 1m 2f 95y
8:50 (8:51) (Class 4) (0-85,85) 3-Y-O+ £4,533 (£1,348; £674; £336) Stalls High

Form RPR

0604 1 **Snow Dancer (IRE)**[13] 3203 6-8-13 70......................... PatrickMathers 9 82
(H A McWilliams) *s.i.s: hld up: hrd at work over 3f out: hdwy over 2f out: r.o ins fnl f to ld fnl 110yds: pushed out cl home* 40/1

3216 2 3/4 **Jonny Lesters Hair (IRE)**[9] 3317 5-9-1 72.............. GrahamGibbons 7 83
(T D Easterby) *racd keenly: led: clr after 2f: reduced advantage fr 3f out: rdn over 1f out: hdd fnl 110yds: hld cl home* 11/2

3003 **3** 2 **Whippers Love (IRE)**[16] 3081 3-8-9 **77** JoeFanning 2 84
(M Johnston) *chsd ldr: rdn 2f out: chalng 1f out: no ex fnl 75yds* **14/1**
2-01 **4** 1 ¼ **Kindest**[21] 2937 4-9-8 **79** GeorgeBaker 1 84
(C F Wall) *chsd ldrs: rdn and tried to chal over 1f out: hung lft ins fnl f: one pce fnl 100yds* **5/2**[1]
6263 **5** 3 ¼ **Changing The Guard**[12] 3239 4-9-13 **84** TonyHamilton 8 83
(R A Fahey) *chsd ldrs: rdn 2f out: hung lft u.p over 1f out: one pce ins fnl f* **4/1**[3]
3-12 **6** 4 **Music Of The Moor (IRE)**[38] 2422 3-8-11 **79** MickyFenton 5 70
(T P Tate) *bhd: rdn and lugged lft 2f out: failed to pick up* **7/2**[2]
13-0 **7** 2 ¼ **Wing Play (IRE)**[21] 2934 5-10-0 **85** (p) ShaneKelly 10 72
(H Morrison) *midfield: nt clr run 2f out: sn swtchd rt and carried hd high u.p: btn over 1f out* **14/1**
12-3 **8** 2 **Cool Baranca (GER)**[13] 3202 4-9-4 **75** RichardHughes 4 58
(P Monteith) *midfield: effrt over 2f out: no real imp on ldrs: wknd ins fnl f* **12/1**
2-00 **9** 19 **Cygnet**[50] 2044 4-9-11 **82** J-PGuillambert 6 29
(L M Cumani) *hld up: dropped to last pl over 4f out: sn struggling: lost tch ent fnl 2f* **12/1**

2m 13.95s (-2.05) **Going Correction** +0.225s/f (Good)
WFA 3 from 4yo+ 11lb **9** Ran SP% **117.3**
Speed ratings (Par 105): **105,104,102,101,99 96,94,92,77**
Tote Swingers: 1&2 £23.90, 1&3 £23.10, 2&3 £12.20 CSF £250.59 CT £3269.41 TOTE £20.90: £6.70, £2.00, £4.40; EX 259.50.
Owner Mrs L Wohlers **Bred** Liam Queally **Trained** Pilling, Lancs

FOCUS
A fair handicap, though there's no reason to believe the form is anything out of the ordinary for the level. The form is rated around the front-running second, who set a good pace.
Music Of The Moor(IRE) Official explanation: jockey said gelding hung left-handed in the straight

3628 TURFTV FILLIES' H'CAP — 1m 30y
9:20 (9:21) (Class 5) (0-75,75) 3-Y-O **£2,590** (£770; £385; £192) **Stalls** Low

Form RPR
305 **1** **Law Of The Range**[56] 1882 3-9-6 **74** SebSanders 11 82
(M Botti) *chsd ldr: led narrowly 2f out: continually pressed: rdn over 1f out: kpt finding for press towards fin* **12/1**
5-05 **2** ½ **Sweet Secret**[9] 3325 3-8-8 **62** RichardHughes 5 69
(R Hannon) *led: rdn and hdd narrowly 2f out: continued to chal: no ex fnl strides* **7/2**[3]
0-00 **3** nse **Ashkalara**[19] 3001 3-8-3 **57** JoeFanning 4 64
(H S Howe) *racd keenly in midfield: hyeadway over 2f out: rdn to chse ldrs and edgd rt over 1f out: r.o to chal fnl strides: jst hld* **16/1**
1-16 **4** 2 ½ **Hulcote Rose (IRE)**[50] 2042 3-9-5 **73** GeorgeBaker 7 74
(S Kirk) *hld up: hdwy over 2f out: rdn to chse ldrs over 1f out: lugged lft ins fnl f: kpt on but nt pce to chal ldrs* **10/1**
4362 **5** ½ **Easy Terms**[19] 2998 3-9-1 **72** JamesMillman(3) 1 72
(B R Millman) *chsd ldrs: rdn over 2f out: one pce fnl 110yds* **10/3**[2]
025 **6** 4 ½ **Tafawut**[57] 1850 3-9-7 **75** LukeMorris 3 65
(C G Cox) *racd keenly: hld up in rr: rdn over 2f out: hung lft over 1f out: kpt on but no imp on ldrs* **11/4**[1]
02-2 **7** 2 ¼ **Jozafeen**[35] 2503 3-8-1 **62** MatthewLawson(7) 6 47
(R Bastiman) *chsd ldrs: rdn over 2f out: wknd over 1f out* **8/1**
0-00 **8** 3 ¾ **Quaker Parrot**[13] 3208 3-9-4 **72** RichardKingscote 8 48
(Tom Dascombe) *hld up: rdn over 1f out: nvr on terms* **33/1**
0-06 **9** 1 ¾ **Les Yeux Bleus (IRE)**[19] 3001 3-9-5 **73** J-PGuillambert 2 45
(L M Cumani) *midfield: pushed along over 2f out: wknd over 1f out* **16/1**
0010 **10** shd **Universal Circus**[14] 3158 3-9-6 **74** SamHitchcott 9 46
(M R Channon) *midfield tl pushed along and wknd over 3f out* **25/1**

1m 45.99s (1.29) **Going Correction** +0.225s/f (Good) **10** Ran SP% **118.4**
Speed ratings (Par 97): **98,97,97,94,94 89,87,83,82,82**
Tote Swingers: 1&2 £13.60, 1&3 £41.70, 2&3 £14.60 CSF £54.70 CT £710.51 TOTE £12.40: £3.50, £2.00, £5.00; EX 82.30 Place 6: £455.47 Place 5: £294.44.
Owner Christopher McHale **Bred** Brookside Breeders Club **Trained** Newmarket, Suffolk

FOCUS
They went a steady gallop and it paid to race handily with the front pair always 1-2. The form is rated at face value, with the winner up 10lb.
T/Plt: £651.80 to a £1 stake. Pool:£61,840.04 - 69.25 winning tickets. T/Qpdt: £77.50 to a £1 stake. Pool:£5,174.44 - 49.40 winning tickets. DO

2969 SANDOWN (R-H)
Friday, July 2

OFFICIAL GOING: Round course - good (good to firm in places); sprint course - good to firm
Rails out 3yds from 7f to 3f creating a drop in and increasing distances on round course by 4yds.
Wind: Moderate, against Weather: Fine, very warm

3629 BLUEFIN H'CAP — 5f 6y
2:20 (2:22) (Class 3) (0-95,94) 3-Y-O+ **£6,476** (£1,927; £963; £481) **Stalls** High

Form RPR
4450 **1** **Piscean (USA)**[21] 2940 5-8-13 **81** AdamKirby 4 89
(T Keddy) *hld up in 8th: plenty to do whn plld to outer and effrt over 1f out: prog to press ldng pair last 100yds: r.o to ld post* **16/1**
2523 **2** shd **Rocket Rob (IRE)**[27] 2745 4-9-3 **85** RyanMoore 5 93
(M Botti) *settled in 7th: effrt wl over 1f out: squeezed through ent fnl f: drvn to ld last 100yds: hdd post* **5/2**[2]
0-12 **3** hd **Osiris Way**[29] 2681 8-9-5 **87** JimCrowley 6 94
(P R Chamings) *hld up bhd ldrs: plld to outer and prog over 1f out: rdn to ld jst ins fnl f: hdd last 100yds: kpt on* **8/1**[3]
-026 **4** 1 ¼ **Rapid Water**[19] 2997 4-8-12 **80** (b¹) LiamKeniry 8 82
(A M Balding) *hld up bhd ldng trio against rail: gng easily 2f out: gap appeared and effrt jst over 1f out: styd on but ldng trio already gone on outer* **12/1**
1642 **5** 1 ½ **Secret Asset (IRE)**[7] 3406 5-9-5 **94** LewisWalsh(7) 10 91
(Jane Chapple-Hyam) *mde most against far rail: hung lft over 1f out: hdd & wknd jst ins fnl f: sddle slipped* **2/1**[1]
2-36 **6** ¾ **Excellerator (IRE)**[21] 2929 4-9-5 **92** (t) MatthewDavies(5) 1 86
(George Baker) *racd wd in rr: a struggling to go the pce: styd on u.p fnl f* **25/1**
0-10 **7** 2 **Fathom Five (IRE)**[27] 2745 6-9-12 **94** AlanMunro 7 81
(C F Wall) *racd three off rail: pressed ldr to jst over 1f out: wknd* **8/1**[3]
00 **8** shd **Cheveton**[19] 2992 6-9-7 **89** PhilipRobinson 9 76
(R J Price) *pressed ldr to over 1f out: wknd* **12/1**
-005 **9** hd **Tony The Tap**[7] 3417 9-9-2 **84** MartinDwyer 2 70
(W R Muir) *stdd s and swtchd to r against rail: effrt fr last trio whn nt clr run and snatched up 2f out: no real prog after* **25/1**
3025 **10** 3 ½ **Angus Newz**[7] 3415 7-9-2 **84** (v) ChrisCatlin 3 57
(M Quinn) *chsd ldrs on outer: rdn 1/2-way: wknd over 1f out* **33/1**

60.63 secs (-0.97) **Going Correction** 0.0s/f (Good) **10** Ran SP% **116.0**
Speed ratings (Par 107): **107,106,106,104,102 100,97,97,97,91**
Tote Swingers: 1&2 £7.60, 1&3 £21.40, 2&3 £3.50 CSF £54.82 CT £356.95 TOTE £25.50: £5.60, £1.40, £2.80; EX 85.10.
Owner Andrew Duffield **Bred** Connie And John Iacuone **Trained** Newmarket, Suffolk

FOCUS
The sprint track was at its full width, and not in 3yds as had been advertised, to allow the dolling off of a false patch of ground caused by a burst on the irrigation system at around the 2f pole. On the round course the rail had been moved out 3yds from the 7f start to the 3f marker, creating a drop-in at that point and adding 4yds to race distances. The ground was officially described as good, good to firm patches on the round course and good to firm on the sprint track. A decent sprint handicap, but although the pace was ordinary it still favoured those held up. The form is sound.

NOTEBOOK
Piscean(USA), without a win in over a year, was held up as usual but, with the pace far from breakneck, he was able to stay in touch and travelled well. Making his effort up the final climb, he finished with a real flourish to hit the front right on the line and gain his first win on turf away from Goodwood. He should not go up much for this so would still be of interest if turning out at the Glorious meeting.
Rocket Rob(IRE), successful in his last two starts over C&D, has been running well off this mark without winning in his last few outings. He didn't do much wrong on this occasion either, being delivered with his effort at just the right time and having the race snatched from him right on the line. (op 11-4 tchd 3-1)
Osiris Way, back to form this season, was put up another 2lb for his narrow defeat over C&D last month. After travelling well behind the leaders, he quickened up when pulled out to hit the front inside the last furlong before being run out of it. (tchd 10-1)
Rapid Water, well held on his first attempt at the minimum trip last time, had blinkers on for the first time. He tracked the leader, travelling well, and looked to be handed a golden opportunity when the leader hung left a furlong out, leaving him with an inviting gap up the rail, but he didn't find as much as had seemed likely. He may need a return to 6f. (op 17-2)
Secret Asset(IRE), due to go up 3lb following his narrow defeat in the Gosforth Park Cup seven days earlier, had the run of the race out in front against the rail, but he hung away to his left entering the last furlong and threw his chance away. His saddle was reported to have slipped.
Official explanation: jockey said saddle slipped (op 5-2 tchd 15-8, 11-4 in places)
Excellerator(IRE), still without a win since her racecourse debut, was soon totally outpaced and saw far too much daylight on the wide outside, so this can probably be ignored. (op 33-1)
Fathom Five(IRE) showed up until weakening inside the last furlong and seems best caught fresh these days. (op 7-1)
Tony The Tap ◆, who hinted at a return to form last time, missed the break but was trying to make some progress when running into trouble over a furlong from home. He is already due to drop another 3lb, so is worth keeping an eye on. (op 28-1)

3630 DRAGON STKS (LISTED RACE) — 5f 6y
2:50 (2:50) (Class 1) 2-Y-O **£14,192** (£5,380; £2,692; £1,342; £672) **Stalls** High

Form RPR
115 **1** **Zebedee**[15] 3100 2-9-2 0 RichardHughes 5 100+
(R Hannon) *trckd ldrs and a gng wl: led ent fnl f: shkn up and drew away last 100yds* **8/15**[1]
0212 **2** 1 ¼ **The Thrill Is Gone**[6] 3426 2-8-11 0 RyanMoore 1 88
(M R Channon) *led and styd away fr far rail: rdn and hdd ent fnl f: kpt on same pce* **10/1**
161 **3** 1 ¾ **Jamesway (IRE)**[17] 3059 2-9-2 0 TonyHamilton 3 87
(R A Fahey) *t.k.h: hld up in last: rdn and effrt wl over 1f out: wnt 3rd fnl f: no imp* **9/2**[2]
5130 **4** 6 **Phoebs**[14] 3141 2-8-11 0 StevieDonohoe 4 60
(R A Mills) *chsd ldr to over 1f out: wknd* **7/1**[3]
01 **5** 4 **Believe It Or Not (IRE)**[18] 3034 2-9-2 0 LiamKeniry 2 51
(J S Moore) *chsd ldrs tl wknd rapidly wl over 1f out: t.o* **33/1**

61.49 secs (-0.11) **Going Correction** 0.0s/f (Good) **5** Ran SP% **107.9**
Speed ratings (Par 102): **100,98,95,85,79**
CSF £6.37 TOTE £1.50: £1.10, £2.70; EX 5.10.
Owner Mrs J Wood **Bred** Hascombe & Valiant Studs **Trained** East Everleigh, Wilts

FOCUS
All five contesting this Listed event were previous winners, but it was obvious from some way out that this was a one-horse race. Zebedee stepped up slightly on his Ascot form and the race could be rated up to 6lb higher.

NOTEBOOK
Zebedee, beaten under 3l into fifth in the Norfolk last time, opened up a short price but that didn't stop the money from piling in on him. Even though he wasn't best away, he was soon travelling powerfully against the inside rail and was still on the bridle when hitting the front a furlong out. He took a little time to respond when finally shaken up, but soon powered clear and had much more in hand at the line than the margin would suggest. He shapes as though another furlong won't be any problem at all, but it seems that he will stay at around this trip for the time being with the Molecomb, Prix Robert Papin and Roses Stakes all possible targets. (op 8-11 tchd 4-5)
The Thrill Is Gone, upped in class, was soon in front from the outside stall and did her best, but she was completely outclassed by the winner inside the last furlong. This was another decent effort in defeat. (op 15-2)
Jamesway(IRE), successful from seven other previous winners at Thirsk last time, pulled too hard in the early stages here and although he stayed on, he was never a threat. He doesn't want the ground too quick and probably isn't up to this level in any case. (tchd 11-2)
Phoebs, back in trip after finishing well beaten over the extra furlong in the Albany, ran fast for a long way but was done with over a furlong from home. (op 11-2 tchd 5-1)
Believe It Or Not(IRE), up in class after a narrow success in a Windsor maiden, saw quite a bit of daylight on the wide outside and was struggling well over a furlong from home. (op 22-1 tchd 20-1)

3631 EUROPEAN BREEDERS' FUND MAIDEN STKS — 7f 16y
3:25 (3:26) (Class 4) 2-Y-O **£5,180** (£1,541; £770; £384) **Stalls** High

Form RPR
1 **Roman Eagle (IRE)** 2-9-3 0 PhilipRobinson 14 81
(M A Jarvis) *t.k.h early: trckd ldng pair: wnt 2nd jst over 1f out: sustained chal fnl f to ld last strides* **4/1**[2]
2 hd **Jehanbux (USA)** 2-9-3 0 RichardHughes 6 81+
(R Hannon) *trckd ldr: led 2f out: hrd pressed and kpt on fnl f: hdd last strides* **11/2**[3]
2 **3** 1 ½ **Introvert (IRE)**[13] 3219 2-9-3 0 AhmedAjtebi 10 77
(Mahmood Al Zarooni) *t.k.h: trckd ldng trio: effrt to chal 2f out: wandered and nt qckn over 1f out: kpt on* **5/2**[1]
6 **4** 3 ½ **El Mansour (USA)**[19] 3000 2-9-3 0 AdamKirby 11 68
(C G Cox) *chsd ldng quartet: shkn up 3f out: kpt on to take 4th ins fnl f: n.d* **20/1**

The Form Book, Raceform Ltd, Compton, RG20 6NL

0 **5** *1* **Star Surprise**[13] 3219 2-9-3 0 .... JamieSpencer 3 66
(M L W Bell) *chsd ldrs in 6th but nt on terms: shkn up over 2f out: no imp over 1f out* **12/1**

03 **6** *2 1/4* **Jamhoori**[21] 2932 2-9-3 0 .... ChrisCatlin 1 60
(C E Brittain) *dwlt: off the pce in 7th: rdn wl over 2f out: no prog tl kpt on ins fnl f* **20/1**

4 **7** *nk* **Mutajare (IRE)**[13] 3222 2-9-3 0 .... RoystonFfrench 8 59
(M Johnston) *led at decent pce to 2f out: steadily wknd* **12/1**

8 *3/4* **Menadati (USA)** 2-9-3 0 .... TedDurcan 7 58+
(D R Lanigan) *sed slowest of all: wl bhd in 12th: pushed along over 2f out and same pl: styd on in encouraging style fnl f* **25/1**

9 *1/2* **Control Chief** 2-9-3 0 .... JimCrowley 9 56
(R M Beckett) *sn off the pce in 9th: shkn up 3f out: no prog or imp: plugged on nr fin* **20/1**

10 *nse* **Orange Ketchup (IRE)** 2-9-3 0 .... AlanMunro 2 56
(P F I Cole) *sn wl bhd in 11th: nvr a factor: plugged on fnl f* **50/1**

11 *1 3/4* **Chain Lightning** 2-9-3 0 .... RyanMoore 4 52+
(R Hannon) *dwlt: off the pce in 10th: shkn up and sme prog on outer over 2f out: no hdwy over 1f out: wknd* **4/1**[2]

12 *6* **Al Furat (USA)** 2-9-3 0 .... IanMongan 5 37
(D R Lanigan) *sn off the pce in 8th: shkn up and no prog 3f out: wknd over 1f out* **66/1**

13 *36* **Rasteau (IRE)** 2-9-3 0 .... NickyMackay 13 —
(T Keddy) *sn wl bhd in last: t.o bef 1/2-way* **100/1**

1m 29.76s (0.26) **Going Correction** -0.10s/f (Good) **13** Ran SP% **121.9**
Speed ratings (Par 96): **94,93,92,88,86 84,84,83,82,82 80,73,32**
Tote Swingers: 1&2 £6.70, 2&3 £3.90 CSF £24.78 TOTE £5.90: £1.90, £2.60, £1.50; EX 34.30.
Owner A D Spence **Bred** Longueville B'Stk & H Lascelles B'Stk **Trained** Newmarket, Suffolk
■ Stewards' Enquiry : Richard Hughes two-day ban: careless riding (Jul 16-17)

FOCUS
A decent maiden which has been one by the likes of No Excuse Needed, Scintillo and Zacinto within the past ten years. The pace was very generous and the field were soon well spread out, but on this occasion it paid to race handily. It provided a thrilling finish between two newcomers who should both go on to better things. Not an easy race to put a figure on.

NOTEBOOK
Roman Eagle(IRE) ◆, a 90,000gns half-brother to four winners including a Grade 2 winner in the US, was never far away and made his effort between horses entering the last 2f. He looked held by the runner-up throughout the last furlong but, with Robinson giving it everything, he battled on against the rail to hit the front close home. He obviously knows how to fight and should go on from here. (op 7-2 tchd 9-2)
Jehanbux(USA) ◆, an 80,000gns 2-y-o and a half-brother to five winners including a 1m stakes winner in the US, was keen enough early in a handy position before hitting the front 2f from home. He battled on gamely and gave his all, but was inched out close to the line. He shouldn't take long in going one better. (op 13-2)
Introvert(IRE), who ran green but was only narrowly beaten over this trip on his Newmarket debut last month, had the edge in experience on the front pair but he still pulled like a train early, so he probably did well to hang in there and keep on for as long as he did. He will win races when he learns to settle. (op 9-4 tchd 2-1)
El Mansour(USA), sixth of 12 on his Salisbury debut, is bred to appreciate this extra furlong and was always in about the same place. An ordinary maiden should come his way. (op 22-1 tchd 16-1)
Star Surprise, around 10l behind Introvert on his Newmarket debut, ran with credit but is likely to come into his own over further in due course. (tchd 14-1)
Jamhoori, a well-beaten third of 15 over C&D on his second start last month, didn't improve here but now qualifies for nurseries and may have more success there.
Mutajare(IRE), just behind a subsequent winner when fourth of 11 over this trip on his Redcar debut, did far too much too soon and didn't get home. Official explanation: jockey said colt suffered interference in running (op 10-1 tchd 14-1)
Menadati(USA) ◆, a 28,000gns 2-y-o out of a Listed winner in Chile who was later successful in the US, completely missed the break and trailed the field early but he did show a little ability late on without being knocked about. He can be expected to improve. (op 22-1)
Orange Ketchup(IRE) ◆, a 65,000gns colt out of a half-sister to a very useful performer in Germany, made some modest late progress and is bred to appreciate further in due course. (tchd 66-1)
Chain Lightning, a 55,000euros Hurricane Run colt, is speedily bred on the dam's side. He gave himself little chance by missing the break and then having to come very wide in order to make his effort after turning for home. That took its toll, but he is likely much better than this effort would suggest. (op 6-1 tchd 15-2 in places)

3632 MOUTON CADET GALA STKS (LISTED RACE) 1m 2f 7y
4:00 (4:00) (Class 1) 3-Y-O+
£21,004 (£7,962; £3,984; £1,986; £995; £499) **Stalls** High

Form / RPR

-401 **1** **Stotsfold**[36] 2470 7-9-11 116 .... AdamKirby 10 121
(W R Swinburn) *hld up in 6th: prog fr 3f out to trck ldr over 2f out: rdn to chal over 1f out: hrd drvn to ld last 150yds* **9/2**[3]

12-4 **2** *1/2* **Prince Siegfried (FR)**[36] 2470 4-9-5 114 .... TedDurcan 1 114
(Saeed Bin Suroor) *trckd ldng trio: prog on outer to ld over 2f out: pressed over 1f out: hanging rt after: hdd last 150yds: styd on* **3/1**[1]

0450 **3** *3 1/4* **Traffic Guard (USA)**[14] 3144 6-9-5 105 .... JamieSpencer 3 108
(P F I Cole) *hld up in 5th: rdn to chse ldng pair 2f out but nt on terms: kpt on u.str.p but no imp* **13/2**

4650 **4** *1 3/4* **Steele Tango (USA)**[14] 3144 5-9-5 104 .... LiamKeniry 2 104
(R A Teal) *hld up in 9th: rdn and prog to dispute 3rd 2f out: nt on terms w ldng pair: plugged on* **16/1**

-514 **5** *6* **Once More Dubai (USA)**[56] 1859 5-9-8 110 .... (bt) AlanMunro 8 95
(Saeed Bin Suroor) *hld up in 8th: rdn and prog to dispute 3rd 2f out but nt on terms w ldng pair: hanging and wknd rapidly jst over 1f out* **22/1**

2-00 **6** *3* **Poet**[134] 609 5-9-5 116 .... PhilipRobinson 6 86
(C G Cox) *chsd ldr: upsides 3f out: sn lost pl and btn* **12/1**

6-06 **7** *3 1/4* **Confront**[69] 1531 5-9-5 114 .... RyanMoore 4 80
(Sir Michael Stoute) *hld up in 7th: rdn 3f out: no prog and struggling bdly 2f out: no ch after* **7/2**[2]

2456 **8** *3* **Laudatory**[25] 2821 4-9-5 78 .... ChrisCatlin 7 74
(W R Swinburn) *sn led and set str pce: hdd & wknd over 2f out* **125/1**

-126 **9** *5* **Fatanah (IRE)**[15] 3101 3-8-5 107 ow2 .... MartinDwyer 9 61
(M P Tregoning) *mostly in 3rd tl wknd rapidly 3f out* **6/1**

034/ **P** **Bouguereau**[703] 4505 5-9-5 106 .... RichardHughes 5 —
(P W Chapple-Hyam) *wl bhd whn p.u after 3f: dismntd* **25/1**

2m 5.14s (-5.36) **Going Correction** -0.10s/f (Good)
WFA 3 from 4yo+ 11lb **10** Ran SP% **115.6**
Speed ratings (Par 111): **117,116,114,112,107 105,102,100,96,—**
Tote Swingers: 1&2 £4.10, 1&3 £9.30, 2&3 £5.20 CSF £17.91 TOTE £6.60: £2.10, £1.50, £2.40; EX 16.20.
Owner P W Harris **Bred** Pendley Farm **Trained** Aldbury, Herts
■ Stewards' Enquiry : Martin Dwyer three-day ban: weighed-in 2lb heavy (Jul 16,18)

FOCUS
A Listed race that had been won by a 3-y-o five times in the past eight years, but only one represented the Classic generation this time around. The pace was good and this is strong form for the grade.

NOTEBOOK
Stotsfold, carrying a 6lb penalty on account of his narrow success in the Group 3 Brigadier Gerard Stakes over C&D last time, was down to this level for the first time in almost three years. He travelled very well off the strong pace until making his move over 3f out, but though he had to fight hard to get up the inside of the runner-up, he showed plenty of guts to get there well inside the last furlong. He will now head for the Skybet York Stakes at the end of the month before another tilt at the Arlington million, in which he was third last year. (op 4-1 tchd 5-1)
Prince Siegfried(FR), just over 3l behind Stotsfold in the Brigadier Gerard and 6lb better off, duly got closer this time and looked like winning until his old rival cut him down near the line. There are more Pattern races to be won with him either here or abroad. (tchd 11-4, 10-3 in a place)
Traffic Guard(USA) had every chance on the outside passing the 2f pole and this was a good effort, but he is hard to win with and is now 2-31 since winning his first two starts as a juvenile. (op 14-1)
Steele Tango(USA), well held in four previous starts this year and behind Stotsfold and Prince Siegfried in the Brigadier Gerard, made some late headway from the back of the field but never looked like winning. (op 22-1)
Once More Dubai(USA), a well-beaten fourth of six behind Harbinger in the Ormonde last time, tried to get into the race passing the 2f pole but he then hung away to his right and had no more to offer. He has done all his winning over further. (op 16-1)
Poet, marginally best in on adjusted official ratings and a Group 3 winner for Aidan O'Brien last September, showed nothing in two starts for different trainers at Meydan earlier in the year. Making his debut for yet another new yard after five months off, he raced close to the pace until weakening inside the last 2f and is entitled to come on for this.
Confront, whose only previous try over 1m2f was when fourth of seven behind Kirklees in this race last year, made a token effort on the wide outside coming to the last 2f, but it came to nothing and he wouldn't have won this at any trip. (op 11-4)
Laudatory set the pace for Stotsfold, but although he had to work to get to the front he did a good job once there until folding 2f out.
Fatanah(IRE), the only 3-y-o in the field, was back over the same C&D as for her maiden success having failed to see out the extra 2f in the Ribblesdale. She showed up for a long way, but faded very tamely coming to the last quarter-mile and didn't even beat the pacemaker. Her rider was banned after weighing in 2lb heavy. (op 7-1 tchd 15-2, 8-1 in a place)

3633 MOORCROFT H'CAP 1m 2f 7y
4:35 (4:35) (Class 2) (0-100,97) 3-Y-O+
£9,346 (£2,799; £1,399; £700; £349; £175) **Stalls** High

Form / RPR

-103 **1** **Verdant**[27] 2742 3-8-10 90 .... RyanMoore 7 103+
(Sir Michael Stoute) *trckd ldng pair: wnt 2nd 3f out: pushed along and clsd to ld wl over 1f out: edgd rt u.p fnl f: styd on* **5/6**[1]

2-04 **2** *3* **Australia Day (IRE)**[13] 3194 7-9-12 95 .... MartinDwyer 4 103
(P R Webber) *led and sn at least 3l clr: hdd and rdn wl over 1f out: keeping on but looked hld whn hmpd 150yds out* **5/1**[2]

-120 **3** *3 1/4* **Aurorian (IRE)**[27] 2747 4-9-3 86 .... RichardHughes 5 87
(R Hannon) *dwlt: hld up in 5th: pushed along over 2f out: rdn to go 3rd fnl f: nvr nr to chal* **14/1**

-220 **4** *1* **Safari Sunup (IRE)**[32] 2593 5-10-0 97 .... JimCrowley 1 96
(P Winkworth) *dwlt: hld up in 4th: rdn 3f out: no prog* **16/1**

3601 **5** *nk* **Tartan Gunna**[8] 3366 4-9-8 91 6ex .... (b) PhilipRobinson 6 89+
(M Johnston) *s.s: hld up in last: effrt over 2f out: hanging rt and trapped bhd rival after: pushed along and no ch* **5/1**[2]

-100 **6** *nk* **Brunston**[41] 2317 4-9-7 90 .... JamieSpencer 2 87
(R Charlton) *dwlt: hld up in 6th: effrt on outer over 2f out: shkn up and no prog* **12/1**[3]

003P **7** *nk* **Kaolak (USA)**[12] 3239 4-9-3 86 .... (v) ChrisCatlin 3 83
(J Ryan) *chsd ldr to 3f out: sn outpcd: wknd fnl f* **33/1**

2m 7.19s (-3.31) **Going Correction** -0.10s/f (Good)
WFA 3 from 4yo+ 11lb **7** Ran SP% **111.1**
Speed ratings (Par 109): **109,106,104,103,102 102,102**
Tote Swingers: 1&2 £2.60, 1&3 £3.60, 2&3 £4.80 CSF £4.95 TOTE £1.60: £1.60, £3.80; EX 4.60.
Owner K Abdulla **Bred** Juddmonte Farms Ltd **Trained** Newmarket, Suffolk

FOCUS
A good handicap, but although the pace set by Australia Day looked decent the winning time was over 2secs slower than the Listed race. The form is rated around the runner-up.

NOTEBOOK
Verdant, the only 3-y-o in the field, was successful over C&D in his only previous visit here and had been put up 1lb after finishing third behind the subsequent Royal Ascot winner Dandino at Epsom. He travelled well in a handy position until taking over from the runner-up 2f from home, but once there he hung away to his right before pulling clear. He still has scope, but doesn't look entirely straightforward. (op Evens tchd 5-4 in a place, 6-5 in a place and 11-10 in places)
Australia Day(IRE), a confirmed front-runner back to a more suitable trip, had gained his last two Flat successes over this C&D. He was able to establish an uncontested lead and held a clear advantage at one stage, but couldn't respond when the favourite headed him passing the 2f pole and looked held when hampered as his rival hung across him. He still finished clear of the rest and can win more races like this if avoiding progressive sorts. (op 4-1)
Aurorian(IRE) lacked the pace to threaten the front pair and his best form has come over further. (op 16-1)
Safari Sunup(IRE) raced in the middle of the field, but didn't find a great deal when put under maximum pressure. He is without a win since September 2008, but is still 11lb higher. (op 14-1 tchd 18-1)
Tartan Gunna, carrying a 6lb penalty for his Newcastle success in first-time blinkers last month but still 1lb well in compared with his new mark, can be forgiven this to a degree as he totally missed the break and then didn't have much room to play with when trying to make progress in the last couple of furlongs. He has made the frame a few times over this trip, but is yet to win over it. (tchd 11-2)
Brunston, twice well beaten since his shock 40-1 win in the Newbury Spring Cup on his reappearance, seemed to travel well enough off the pace but found very little off the bridle and was again disappointing. (tchd 11-1)
Kaolak(USA) is effective from the front, but with Australia Day in the field that was always going to be difficult and, after racing prominently, he gradually faded out of it up the home straight. Official explanation: vet said colt returned lame left-hind

3634 HOUSE OF FRASER H'CAP 1m 6f
5:05 (5:06) (Class 4) (0-85,85) 3-Y-O+ **£6,476** (£1,927; £963; £481) **Stalls** High

Form / RPR

0/00 **1** **Colloquial**[17] 3050 9-10-0 85 .... (v) RyanMoore 1 92
(H Candy) *sn chsd ldr: drvn ahd over 2f out: mde v hrd work of it but styd on fnl 2f* **5/1**[3]

2-01 **2** *1 3/4* **Outrageous Request**[20] 2975 4-9-9 80 .... AndreaAtzeni 3 85
(Pat Eddery) *trckd ldng pair: rdn and nt qckn wl over 2f out and lost pl: styd on again fr over 1f out: wnt 2nd last 150yds: no real imp* **9/2**[2]

10 **3** 3/4 **Ugalla**[23] 2869 3-8-3 **75** .... MartinDwyer 2 79
(W J Knight) *led: drvn and hdd over 2f out: chsd wnr after but hld: lost 2nd fnl 150yds* **10/1**

-324 **4** 1 **Curaco**[44] 2228 4-9-6 **77** .... JimCrowley 5 79
(Mrs A J Perrett) *trckd ldng trio: effrt on outer 3f out: tried to cl 2f out: one pce u.p after* **13/2**

5-24 **5** 3 1/4 **Ragdollianna**[32] 2586 6-9-0 **71** .... LiamKeniry 7 69
(M J McGrath) *hld up in 7th: effrt 3f out: sme prog over 2f out: one pce over 1f out: fdd fnl f* **33/1**

1-52 **6** 3 3/4 **Crocus Rose**[20] 2975 4-9-7 **78** .... RichardHughes 4 70
(H J L Dunlop) *hld up in 6th: rdn and no prog wl over 2f out: fdd over 1f out* **10/1**

2150 **7** shd **Dancing Dude (IRE)**[15] 3105 3-8-3 **75** .... RoystonFfrench 6 67
(M Johnston) *rn in snatches and mostly in last: weaving arnd u.p fnl 3f and no prog* **6/1**

2 **8** 8 **Swinging Hawk (GER)**[12] 3241 4-9-12 **83** .... JamieSpencer 8 64
(Ian Williams) *t.k.h: hld up in 5th: dropped to last and btn bef 2f out: t.o* **9/4**[1]

3m 1.12s (-3.38) **Going Correction** -0.10s/f (Good)
WFA 3 from 4yo+ 15lb **8** Ran SP% **114.4**
Speed ratings (Par 105): **105,104,103,103,101 99,98,94**
Tote Swingers: 1&2 £4.70, 1&3 £7.90, 2&3 £9.60 CSF £27.71 CT £215.44 TOTE £5.70: £1.70, £1.10, £4.40; EX 35.20 Place 6:£21.26 Place 5: £6.22.
Owner Mrs David Blackburn & M Blackburn **Bred** Mrs M J Blackburn **Trained** Kingston Warren, Oxon

FOCUS
They went an even pace in this staying handicap and this was another contest which favoured those who raced handily. It was also a race where the betting market spoke volumes. The winner showed his best form in over two years.
Swinging Hawk(GER) Official explanation: trainer had no explanation for the poor form shown
T/Plt: £19.80 to a £1 stake. Pool:£72,877.73 - 2,679.16 winning tickets. T/Qpdt: £9.80 to a £1 stake. Pool:£4,044.31 - 304.70 winning tickets. JN

3372 WARWICK (L-H)

Friday, July 2

OFFICIAL GOING: Good to firm (firm in places; 8.3)
Wind: Light behind Weather: Cloudy with sunny spells

3635 RACING UK MAIDEN STKS 7f 26y
2:10 (2:11) (Class 5) 3-4-Y-O **£2,590** (£770; £385; £192) **Stalls** Low

Form RPR

4 **1** **Pirate Coast**[13] 3207 3-9-3 0 .... DuranFentiman 2 73
(T D Easterby) *mde all: rdn and hung rt fr over 1f out: r.o* **6/1**[3]

5-0 **2** 1 3/4 **Hierarch (IRE)**[67] 1581 3-9-3 0 .... PatDobbs 13 68
(R Hannon) *chsd ldrs: lost pl 1/2-way: hdwy over 1f out: r.o: wnt 2nd post: nt rch wnr* **5/2**[2]

43 **3** hd **Danehill Sunset (IRE)**[56] 1870 3-9-3 0 .... FrannyNorton 10 68
(B W Hills) *hld up: racd keenly: hdwy 1/2-way: rdn over 1f out: r.o* **15/8**[1]

0- **4** nk **Millden**[201] 7736 3-8-10 0 .... AmyScott(7) 8 67
(H Candy) *s.i.s: sn chsng wnr: pushed along 3f out: hung lft 2f out: rdn and nt clr run over 1f out: styd on* **14/1**

404 **5** 1 **Ruby Dazzler**[8] 3374 3-8-12 0 .... DaneO'Neill 9 59
(S Lycett) *chsd ldrs: rdn over 2f out: styd on* **16/1**

5 **6** 3/4 **Grand Piano (IRE)**[66] 1590 3-9-3 0 .... NeilChalmers 11 62
(A M Balding) *prom: outpcd over 2f out: rallied over 1f out: styd on same pce ins fnl f* **14/1**

0 **7** 1 1/4 **Crimson Queen**[22] 2899 3-8-12 0 .... PatCosgrave 7 54
(R Brotherton) *chsd ldrs: rdn 3f out: no ex fnl f* **150/1**

8 3 1/2 **Kargarann (IRE)** 3-9-3 0 .... JackMitchell 14 49
(Stef Higgins) *s.i.s: hld up: rdn over 2f out: nvr on terms* **18/1**

0 **9** 1 1/4 **Jovial (IRE)**[27] 2754 3-9-3 0 .... EddieAhern 4 46
(D J Coakley) *mid-div: lost pl 1/2-way: n.d after* **20/1**

0 **10** 12 **Miss Halfordbridge**[15] 3125 3-8-9 0 .... AndrewHeffernan(3) 3 9
(J Gallagher) *hld up: hung rt 1/2-way: n.d* **80/1**

11 hd **River Tease** 3-9-0 0 .... RussKennemore(3) 5 13
(J S Moore) *dwlt: outpcd* **40/1**

12 6 **Pre Raphaelite** 3-9-3 0 .... CathyGannon 12 —
(J S Moore) *s.s: outpcd* **25/1**

1m 23.46s (-1.14) **Going Correction** -0.10s/f (Good) **12** Ran SP% **115.1**
Speed ratings (Par 103): **102,100,99,99,98 97,96,92,90,76 76,69**
Tote Swingers: 1&2 £3.90, 1&3 £3.90, 2&3 £1.10 CSF £19.83 TOTE £4.60: £1.40, £1.40, £1.10; EX 25.30.
Owner Mrs E J Wills **Bred** The Hon Mrs E J Wills **Trained** Great Habton, N Yorks

FOCUS
A modest maiden which has been rated around the runner-up. The pace was fairly steady and there was not much distance covering the first seven. The time was just over two seconds above standard.

3636 BUDBROOKE NOVICE AUCTION STKS 7f 26y
2:40 (2:41) (Class 5) 2-Y-O **£2,590** (£770; £385; £192) **Stalls** Low

Form RPR

45 **1** **Wotsthehurry**[86] 1173 2-8-6 0 .... CoryParish 3 70
(M R Channon) *trckd ldrs: rdn to ld and edgd rt ins fnl f: r.o* **20/1**[3]

0032 **2** 1 1/4 **Kissing Clara (IRE)**[15] 3106 2-8-6 0 .... LukeMorris 2 67
(J S Moore) *w ldr tl led 1/2-way: rdn and hung rt fr over 1f out: hdd and unable qck ins fnl f* **4/6**[1]

16 **3** 1 1/4 **Malice Or Mischief (IRE)**[20] 2950 2-9-1 0 .... JackMitchell 6 75
(R M Beckett) *led to 1/2-way: sn rdn: ev ch whn hmpd over 1f out: stl ev ch whn hmpd ins fnl f: nt rcvr* **7/4**[2]

006 **4** 5 **Lady On Top (IRE)**[38] 2407 2-8-1 0 .... SophieDoyle(5) 4 52
(Mrs P N Dutfield) *chsd ldrs: rdn over 2f out: wknd over 1f out* **20/1**[3]

1m 24.5s (-0.10) **Going Correction** -0.10s/f (Good) **4** Ran SP% **105.9**
Speed ratings (Par 94): **96,94,93,87**
CSF £34.12 TOTE £11.40; EX 29.60.
Owner John & Zoe Webster **Bred** Azienda Agricola Mediterranea **Trained** West Ilsley, Berks
■ The first winner in Britain for New Zealand rider Cory Parish.
■ Stewards' Enquiry : Luke Morris two-day ban: careless riding (Jul 16-17); five-day ban: careless riding (Jul 18-22)

FOCUS
An ordinary novice stakes. Things got a bit rough between the two market leaders and there was a 20-1 winner. She has been rated up 9lb, with the form behind fitting in.

NOTEBOOK
Wotsthehurry was an encouraging fourth in a decent 5f Lingfield fillies' maiden on debut in March but she finished tailed off in a novice stakes event on soft ground the following month and a selling entry this week was not encouraging for her prospects in this company. However, after getting a bit worked up at the start she settled well behind the duelling leaders and found a sustained run to get off the mark on her return from three months off. This was a likeable effort from a filly who has quite a bit of stamina on the dam's side of her pedigree but the favourite was disappointing and the third looked unlucky, so the form should not be taken too literally. (op 16-1)
Kissing Clara(IRE) had shown a marked step up in level of form the last twice, the latest when giving the favourite a scare in a 7.5f Beverley maiden auction. She had strong form claims and was heavily backed but found a limited response under a positive ride and gave the third-placed horse several bumps as she shifted right in the last 2f. (op 5-6 tchd 10-11)
Malice Or Mischief(IRE) was disappointing at Bath last time but he entered the reckoning on his 9-1 debut win at Chepstow. He was always prominent but couldn't get any momentum together as the favourite kept hanging into his path. He should be worth another chance if faced with a feasible opportunity next time. (op 6-4 tchd 11-8)
Lady On Top(IRE) had plenty to find and got only marginally closer to the third than she did at Chepstow last time. (op 22-1)

3637 STRATFORD FILLIES' H'CAP 5f 110y
3:10 (3:10) (Class 5) (0-70,69) 3-Y-O+ **£2,590** (£770; £385; £192) **Stalls** Low

Form RPR

0312 **1** **Comptonspirit**[11] 3255 6-9-7 **61** .... J-PGuillambert 2 70
(B P J Baugh) *chsd ldrs: led over 1f out: rdn and edgd rt ins fnl f: r.o* **3/1**[1]

6661 **2** 3/4 **Revue Princess (IRE)**[15] 3115 5-9-6 **60** ....(b) DuranFentiman 5 67
(T D Easterby) *led to 1/2-way: chsd ldrs: hrd rdn and edgd lft ins fnl f: r.o* **7/1**

0031 **3** hd **Wanchai Whisper**[5] 3480 3-9-1 **64** 6ex........(p) AndrewHeffernan(3) 7 68
(P R Hedger) *s.i.s: hld up: hdwy over 1f out: r.o* **4/1**[3]

0000 **4** 1 1/2 **Red Rosanna**[39] 2396 4-9-12 **66** .... JerryO'Dwyer 3 67
(R Hollinshead) *w ldr tl led 1/2-way: rdn and hdd over 1f out: no ex ins fnl f* **14/1**

3334 **5** 1 1/4 **Annia Galeria (IRE)**[8] 3372 3-8-1 **50** ....(b) KellyHarrison(3) 10 45
(C A Dwyer) *mid-div: hdwy 1/2-way: rdn and hung lft over 1f out: no ex ins fnl f* **14/1**

6060 **6** 2 3/4 **White Shift (IRE)**[13] 3216 4-9-8 **67** .... KierenFox(5) 8 54
(P Howling) *s.i.s: outpcd: nvr nrr* **16/1**

0656 **7** 1/2 **Ajara (IRE)**[27] 2751 4-9-9 **63** ....(p) RichardKingscote 9 49
(Tom Dascombe) *mid-div: rdn 1/2-way: wknd fnl f* **11/1**

5401 **8** 2 **Littlemisssunshine (IRE)**[10] 3293 5-10-1 **69** 6ex........(t) EddieAhern 4 48
(T B P Coles) *chsd ldrs tl rdn and wknd over 1f out* **7/2**[2]

0000 **9** hd **A Pocketful Of Rye (IRE)**[18] 3030 3-8-10 **56** .... PatCosgrave 6 32
(P Howling) *s.i.s: outpcd* **16/1**

65.48 secs (-0.42) **Going Correction** -0.10s/f (Good)
WFA 3 from 4yo+ 5lb **9** Ran SP% **113.2**
Speed ratings (Par 100): **98,97,96,94,93 89,88,86,85**
Tote Swingers: 1&2 £1.90, 1&3 £3.30, 2&3 £8.10 CSF £23.86 CT £83.83 TOTE £4.20: £1.70, £1.80, £1.90; EX 21.30.
Owner G B Hignett **Bred** Mrs F Wilson **Trained** Audley, Staffs

FOCUS
A modest but competitive fillies' handicap run at a fair pace. The first pair improved slighty on their recent wins.

3638 WARWICK FOR ALL YOUR OUTSIDE EVENTS H'CAP 6f
3:45 (3:45) (Class 4) (0-80,79) 3-Y-O **£6,152** (£1,830; £914; £456) **Stalls** Low

Form RPR

U0-4 **1** **Spanish Acclaim**[27] 2754 3-8-9 **67** .... NeilChalmers 6 74
(A M Balding) *edgd lft s: set stdy pce tl qckned clr over 3f out: rdn and hung rt over 1f out: unchal* **16/1**

0620 **2** 1 1/4 **Farmers Wish (IRE)**[15] 3115 3-8-12 **73** .... JackDean(3) 1 76
(J L Spearing) *chsd wnr: rdn over 1f out: styd on* **5/1**[3]

-312 **3** 1 **Pirate's Song**[13] 3216 3-8-11 **69** ....(t) RobertHavlin 5 69+
(J A R Toller) *hmpd s: hld up: hdwy u.p over 1f out: r.o: nt rch ldrs* **9/4**[1]

3551 **4** 1/2 **R Woody**[14] 3154 3-9-7 **79** .... PatCosgrave 4 77
(D K Ivory) *chsd ldrs: rdn over 1f out: styd on u.p* **8/1**

-200 **5** nk **Fawley Green**[25] 2824 3-9-2 **74** .... EddieAhern 7 71
(W R Muir) *chsd ldrs: rdn over 1f out: edgd rt ins fnl f: styd on same pce* **8/1**

-001 **6** 1 **Slip Sliding Away (IRE)**[8] 3350 3-8-6 **64** 6ex........ LukeMorris 8 58
(P R Hedger) *s.i.s: hld up: rdn over 2f out: nvr on terms* **11/4**[2]

6206 **7** 1/2 **Nubar Boy**[22] 2884 3-9-0 **72** ....(t) CathyGannon 2 64
(P D Evans) *hld up: plld hrd: rdn over 1f out: n.d* **15/2**

1m 10.88s (-0.92) **Going Correction** -0.10s/f (Good) course record **7** Ran SP% **114.0**
Speed ratings (Par 102): **102,100,99,98,97 96,95**
Tote Swingers: 1&2 £8.80, 1&3 £3.00, 2&3 £3.60 CSF £91.76 CT £252.00 TOTE £15.20: £4.70, £3.30; EX 94.50.
Owner The Farleigh Court Racing Partnership **Bred** Farleigh Court Racing Partnership **Trained** Kingsclere, Hants

FOCUS
A fair handicap for 3-y-os but the pace was fairly steady and the outsider seemed to steal it under an enterprising ride. The runner-up was always in second.

3639 1707 RESTAURANT H'CAP 1m 6f 213y
4:20 (4:21) (Class 5) (0-70,61) 3-Y-O+ **£2,590** (£770; £385; £192) **Stalls** Low

Form RPR

-122 **1** **Corr Point (IRE)**[6] 3444 3-8-10 **60** ....(t) EddieAhern 1 71+
(J A Osborne) *chsd ldrs: led and j. path over 1f out: hung rt and hdd ins fnl f: styd on to ld nr fin* **8/11**[1]

1504 **2** nk **Sir Sandicliffe (IRE)**[19] 2995 6-8-13 **51** .... KierenFox(5) 2 59
(W M Brisbourne) *a.p: rdn over 2f out: led and edgd lft ins fnl f: hmpd sn after: hdd nr fin* **8/1**[3]

0-40 **3** 3 1/2 **Almutaham (USA)**[43] 2248 3-8-1 **54** .... Louis-PhilippeBeuzelin(3) 5 57
(J L Dunlop) *hld up: hdwy over 3f out: rdn over 1f out: styd on: nt trble ldrs* **5/1**[2]

0625 **4** 4 **Street Runner**[8] 3360 4-9-12 **59** .... JerryO'Dwyer 3 57
(R Hollinshead) *hld up: hdwy over 2f out: sn rdn: wknd fnl f* **14/1**

0-00 **5** 1/2 **Laura Land**[15] 3128 4-8-12 **45** .... PatCosgrave 7 42
(W M Brisbourne) *chsd ldr tl led 4f out: rdn and hdd over 1f out: wknd ins fnl f* **33/1**

0130 **6** 1 **Spiritonthemount (USA)**[12] 2810 5-9-1 **48** .... LukeMorris 4 44
(P W Hiatt) *sn pushed along in rr: nvr on terms* **14/1**

40-0 **7** 3 1/2 **Present**[18] 1283 6-8-12 **45** .... DaneO'Neill 6 36
(Miss Diana Weeden) *led 11f: rdn and wknd over 1f out* **40/1**

6436 **8** 3 **War Of The Roses (IRE)**[38] 2424 7-10-0 **61** .... J-PGuillambert 9 48
(R Brotherton) *hld up: rdn over 2f out: a in rr* **16/1**

/0-6 9 hd **Synonymy**[21] 2923 7-8-12 45......(b) FrannyNorton 8 32
(M Blanshard) *prom: drvn along thrght tl wknd wl over 1f out* **12/1**
3m 16.16s (-2.84) **Going Correction** -0.10s/f (Good)
WFA 3 from 4yo+ 17lb 9 Ran SP% **118.0**
Speed ratings (Par 103): **103,102,100,98,98 98,96,94,94**
Tote Swingers: 1&2 £2.80, 1&3 £2.20, 2&3 £3.80 CSF £7.64 CT £19.71 TOTE £2.10: £1.30, £1.90, £1.70; EX 8.20.
Owner J Duddy & R A Pegum **Bred** T J Pabst And Newtown Stud **Trained** Upper Lambourn, Berks
FOCUS
The top weight had a rating 9lb below the ceiling for this 0-70 staying handicap. The favourite had to work a lot harder than looked likely 2f out but there was a freakish incident and he looks a progressive sort who rates better than the winning margin implies. Moderate form overall.
Street Runner Official explanation: jockey said gelding was unsuited by the good to firm (firm in places) ground
War Of The Roses(IRE) Official explanation: jockey said gelding lost a left-fore shoe

3640 WARWICK (S) STKS 1m 2f 188y
4:55 (4:56) (Class 6) 3-Y-O £2,047 (£604; £302) Stalls Low

Form RPR
4130 1 **Dane Cottage**[4] 3513 3-8-6 65...... AdamBeschizza(7) 9 53+
(Miss Gay Kelleway) *hld up: hdwy to ld and edgd lft over 1f out: rdn out* **6/5**[1]
4042 2 1 ¼ **Rosewood Lad**[6] 3442 3-8-10 49...... RussKennemore(3) 2 51
(J S Moore) *chsd ldr: rdn to ld wl over 1f out: sn hdd: styd on u.p* **3/1**[2]
00 3 nk **Embarkation**[7] 3413 3-8-13 0...... PatCosgrave 5 50+
(J R Fanshawe) *hld up: hdwy over 1f out: styd on* **10/1**
1030 4 ¾ **Kathindi (IRE)**[19] 3002 3-9-4 63...... LukeMorris 8 54
(J S Moore) *chsd ldrs: rdn over 1f out: styd on same pce ins fnl f* **9/2**[3]
00-0 5 6 **Priestley (IRE)**[32] 2606 3-8-8 42...... DeclanCannon(5) 6 39
(J G Given) *mid-div: rdn over 2f out: hdwy over 1f out: wknd ins fnl f* **20/1**
00-0 6 1 ½ **Silvermine Bay (IRE)**[35] 2503 3-8-8 47...... RichardKingscote 10 31
(A P Jarvis) *hld up: hdwy over 3f out: sn rdn: swtchd rt over 1f out: wknd fnl f* **28/1**
560- 7 3 ¼ **Pollan Bay (IRE)**[266] 6639 3-8-8 53...... SophieDoyle(5) 1 31
(Ms J S Doyle) *mid-div: plld hrd: effrt over 2f out: wknd over 1f out* **20/1**
6006 8 1 ½ **Oh Two**[22] 2908 3-8-8 48...... EddieAhern 3 23
(S C Williams) *led: rdn over 2f out: hdd wl over 1f out: wknd fnl f* **16/1**
4000 9 1 **Clayton Flick (IRE)**[3] 2418 3-8-8 50......(p) AmyBaker(5) 4 27
(A B Haynes) *chsd ldrs: rdn over 2f out: wknd over 1f out* **33/1**
2m 20.22s (-0.88) **Going Correction** -0.10s/f (Good) 9 Ran SP% **119.5**
Speed ratings (Par 98): **99,98,97,97,92 91,89,88,87**
Tote Swingers: 1&2 £6.50, 1&3 £2.20, 2&3 £4.50 CSF £4.75 TOTE £2.00: £1.20, £1.80, £2.60; EX 7.10.The winner was sold to Nick Shutts for 4,700gns.
Owner Holistic Racing Ltd **Bred** Winterbeck Manor Stud **Trained** Exning, Suffolk
FOCUS
An ordinary seller. It was run at an ordinary pace and the clear form pick was value for a bit more than the winning margin. The first four finished a long way clear of the rest and the form is rated around the runner-up.

3641 TURFTV APPRENTICE H'CAP 1m 4f 134y
5:25 (5:27) (Class 6) (0-60,60) 4-Y-O+ £1,706 (£503; £252) Stalls Low

Form RPR
3313 1 **Dazzling Begum**[7] 3403 5-8-4 53...... SophieSilvester(8) 2 60
(J Pearce) *broke wl: sn stdd and lost pl: hdwy over 4f out: rdn over 1f out: styd on to ld post* **9/4**[1]
-303 2 shd **Filun**[15] 3128 5-8-5 46 oh1...... RichardRowe 10 53
(A Middleton) *chsd ldrs: rdn to ld wl ins fnl f: hdd post* **9/1**
22-6 3 1 **It's Josr**[18] 3028 5-8-9 50......(b) MatthewLawson 12 55
(I A Wood) *led: hdd over 6f out: led again 4f out: rdn clr over 2f out: edgd rt and hdd wl ins fnl f* **11/2**[3]
300/ 4 8 **Garafena**[12] 6395 7-8-13 54......(p) NathanAlison 1 47
(R Lee) *hld up: rdn over 3f out: nvr trbld ldrs* **20/1**
-425 5 1 ½ **Sand Repeal (IRE)**[4] 3496 8-8-11 55...... AdamBeschizza(3) 7 46
(Miss J Feilden) *chsd ldr 3f: remained handy: rdn over 2f out: sn outpcd* **7/2**[2]
0006 6 7 **Shame The Devil (IRE)**[15] 3128 5-8-9 50...... SoniaEaton 4 30
(H J Evans) *s.i.s: hld up and a in rr: rdn and wknd over 2f out* **6/1**
0-62 7 4 **Looks The Business (IRE)**[20] 2952 9-8-8 59...... MarkPower(10) 3 33
(A B Haynes) *prom: chsd ldr over 9f out: led over 6f out: hdd 4f out: rdn and wknd over 2f out* **13/2**
2m 42.21s (-2.39) **Going Correction** -0.10s/f (Good) 7 Ran SP% **110.8**
Speed ratings (Par 101): **103,102,102,97,96 92,89**
Tote Swingers: 1&2 £5.70, 1&3 £3.10, 2&3 £5.30 CSF £21.63 CT £93.21 TOTE £3.20: £1.60, £5.50; EX 28.40 Place 6:£299.12 Place 5: £257.29 .
Owner Macniler Racing Partnership **Bred** Ian Bryant **Trained** Newmarket, Suffolk
FOCUS
A low-grade apprentice handicap run at a strong pace. There was a tight finish but the first three pulled a long way clear of the rest. Muddling form, rated around the front two. Nouailhas burst through the stalls and was withdrawn.
T/Jkpt: £32,687.50 to a £1 stake. Pool:£46,038.86 - 1 winning ticket. T/Plt: £527.70 to a £1 stake. Pool:£46,920.78 - 64.90 winning tickets. T/Qpdt: £5.40 to a £1 stake. Pool:£3,545.51 - 480.84 winning tickets. CR

3642 - 3644a (Foreign Racing) - See Raceform Interactive

3133 LEOPARDSTOWN (L-H)
Thursday, July 1

OFFICIAL GOING: Good to firm

3645a GOLDEN FLEECE STKS (LISTED RACE) 7f
7:30 (7:31) 2-Y-O £23,008 (£6,725; £3,185; £1,061)

RPR
1 **Zoffany (IRE)**[16] 3049 2-9-1...... JAHeffernan 4 101+
(A P O'Brien, Ire) *hld up bhd ldrs: 4th 1/2-way: hdwy in 3rd 1 1/2f out: pushed out to chal 1f out: led last 200yds: sn asserted: comf* **4/7**[1]
2 2 **Stentorian (IRE)**[14] 3112 2-9-1...... FMBerry 5 96
(M Johnston) *led: rdn and chal 1f out: hdd last 200yds: no ex and kpt on same pce* **10/3**[2]
3 3 **Free Art**[7] 3380 2-9-1 ...... WJSupple 2 89
(P D Deegan, Ire) *chsd ldr in 2nd: rdn 1 1/2f out: no ex in 3rd 1f out: kpt on same pce fnl f* **16/1**
4 3 **Sydney Harbour (IRE)**[4] 3485 2-9-1 ......(p) MACleere 1 81
(David Wachman, Ire) *hld up bhd ldrs: 3rd 1/2-way: rdn in 4th 2f out: sn no ex* **5/1**[3]
1m 27.89s (-0.81) **Going Correction** -0.10s/f (Good) 4 Ran SP% **109.3**
Speed ratings: **100,97,94,90**
CSF £2.83 TOTE £1.50; DF 2.90.
Owner Michael Tabor **Bred** Epona Bloodstock Ltd **Trained** Ballydoyle, Co Tipperary
FOCUS
The winner posted an effort in keeping with his Naas win, with an improved effort from the second.
NOTEBOOK
Zoffany(IRE) won impressively. Ridden like a good horse, he was held up off the strong pace set by the runner-up, but didn't seem to handle the bend into the straight too well. When asked to pick up he quickened up well and left his rivals pretty much for dead. Stiffer tests undoubtedly await but he has earned the right to take on much better opposition. (op 8/13 tchd 8/15)
Stentorian(IRE) gradually increased the tempo. He certainly ran his race but just came up against a juvenile that was a class better than him. (op 3/1 tchd 7/2)
Free Art tracked the leader and travelled well enough to the straight but once the pace really quickened he was found out. He's still good enough to win at least an ordinary maiden. (op 14/1)
Sydney Harbour(IRE) raced too keenly early on while his rider tried to get plenty of cover but he was under pressure turning into the straight and was a spent force from there. (op 9/2)

3646 - 3656a (Foreign Racing) - See Raceform Interactive

3610 BEVERLEY (R-H)
Saturday, July 3

OFFICIAL GOING: Good to firm (9.1)
Wind: Light, half against Weather: Fine and dry

3657 AWARD WINNING COACHMAN CARAVANS MEDIAN AUCTION MAIDEN STKS 7f 100y
2:10 (2:12) (Class 5) 2-Y-O £2,729 (£806; £403) Stalls High

Form RPR
52 1 **Spartic**[11] 3281 2-9-3 0...... JamesDoyle 4 69
(A J McCabe) *mde all: rdn wl over 1f out: drvn ent fnl f: edgd rt and kpt on wl* **11/2**[3]
404 2 ¾ **Dark Dune (IRE)**[11] 3281 2-9-3 0...... DuranFentiman 7 67
(T D Easterby) *in tch: hdwy over 2f out: rdn along wl over 1f out: styd on strly ins fnl f* **12/1**
0 3 ½ **Dubai Glory**[17] 3082 2-8-12 0...... JamesMcDonald 15 63+
(E A L Dunlop) *hld up towards rr: swtchd outside and hdwy over 2f out: rdn over 1f out: styd on strly ins fnl f* **9/4**[2]
44 4 1 **Cathcart Castle**[8] 3399 2-9-3 0...... SamHitchcott 12 64
(M R Channon) *trckd ldrs: hdwy on inner over 2f out: effrt and ch over 1f out: sn rdn and one pce* **13/8**[1]
0 5 ¾ **Kalkan Bay**[7] 3433 2-9-3 0......(b) TonyHamilton 3 62
(Jedd O'Keeffe) *cl up: rdn along over 2f out: drvn wl over 1f out: grad wknd* **100/1**
5 6 4 ½ **Domino Effect (IRE)**[15] 3162 2-9-3 0...... LeeVickers 1 51
(J Howard Johnson) *in tch: hdwy to chse ldrs 3f out: rdn along wl over 1f out: wknd appr fnl f* **28/1**
7 2 ¼ **Pockett Rockett** 2-8-12 0...... SilvestreDeSousa 13 41
(D O'Meara) *towards rr: hdwy 3f out: rdn over 2f out: no imp appr fnl f* **11/1**
8 9 **Newport Arch** 2-8-12 0...... IanBrennan(5) 8 25
(J J Quinn) *midfield: effrt and rdn along over 2f out: n.d* **12/1**
0 9 4 ½ **Romano (IRE)**[9] 3362 2-9-3 0...... TonyCulhane 5 14
(P T Midgley) *a towards rr* **66/1**
000 10 1 ¼ **No Explanation**[18] 3058 2-9-3 0...... NickyMackay 6 11
(D W Thompson) *plld hrd: hdwy to chse ldrs after 1f: rdn along wl over 2f out: sn wknd* **100/1**
11 shd **Gothic Chick** 2-8-12 0...... JamieMackay 14 6
(Miss Amy Weaver) *dwlt: a bhd* **50/1**
12 1 **Logans Rose** 2-9-3 0...... FrannyNorton 2 9
(A D Brown) *s.i.s: a bhd* **33/1**
13 ½ **Milly Filly** 2-8-12 0...... StevieDonohoe 11 3
(Miss Amy Weaver) *a in rr* **28/1**
0 14 3 **Land Bank**[14] 3222 2-9-0 0...... KellyHarrison(3) 9 1
(T D Easterby) *s.i.s: a bhd* **66/1**
1m 34.52s (0.72) **Going Correction** -0.275s/f (Firm) 14 Ran SP% **124.7**
Speed ratings (Par 94): **84,83,82,81,80 75,72,62,57,56 55,54,54,50**
toteswingers: 1&2 £7.90, 1&3 £3.90, 2&3 £13.10 CSF £68.66 TOTE £7.70: £2.20, £2.70, £1.70; EX 47.40.
Owner Derek Buckley **Bred** D J Buckley **Trained** Averham Park, Notts
FOCUS
A modest maiden auction event.
NOTEBOOK
Spartic kept finding off the front for an all-the-way success. Just run out of it late on when second over C&D last time, he saw it out better this time and showed a most willing attitude, one which will serve him well once handicapping. (op 9-2)
Dark Dune(IRE), almost five lengths behind the winner latest, improved to run his best race yet and is another likely sort for nurseries. (op 11-1)
Dubai Glory, who had shaped well at Kempton on debut, had what looked a good draw, but got too far back and, despite running on well late in the day, the race was all over by the time she really got going. She can be rated better than the bare form. (op 9-2)
Cathcart Castle held an ideal sit, but couldn't quicken when asked and was always held inside the final furlong. He may fare better over 1m in nurseries. (op 11-8 tchd 5-4)
Kalkan Bay improved markedly on his debut effort and shows enough speed to think he will be effective at 6f. (tchd 80-1)

3658 EBF LEISURE FURNISHINGS MAIDEN STKS 5f
2:45 (2:46) (Class 5) 2-Y-O £3,885 (£1,156; £577; £288) Stalls High

Form RPR
23 1 **Ahtoug**[36] 2498 2-9-3 0...... AhmedAjtebi 1 78
(Mahmood Al Zarooni) *chsd ldrs on outer: hdwy 1/2-way: rdn to ld 1f out: edgd rt and kpt on* **3/1**[2]
2 1 **El Viento (FR)** 2-8-13 0...... TonyHamilton 10 73+
(R A Fahey) *trckd ldrs on inner: n.m.r and swtchd lft 2f out: effrt and nt clr run over 1f out: swtchd rt and rdn ent fnl f: styd on wl* **9/2**
2245 3 ½ **Lady Royale**[9] 3365 2-8-9 0...... BarryMcHugh(3) 9 68
(G R Oldroyd) *wnt lft s: sn trcking ldrs: effrt and n.m.r over 1f out: sn swtchd lft and rdn to chse wnr ins fnl f: kpt on same pce towards fin* **11/4**[1]
5 4 2 ¾ **Close To The Edge (IRE)**[22] 2936 2-8-7 0...... PatrickDonaghy(5) 3 58
(J S Wainwright) *cl up: rdn along over 2f out: drvn over 1f out: grad wknd* **10/1**

44 **5** *1 1/4* **Brave Dream**[31] 2649 2-9-3 0 .... StevieDonohoe 8 60+
(K A Ryan) *sltly hmpd s and towards rr: hdwy 2f out: rdn over 1f out: kpt on ins fnl f: nrst fin* **20/1**

452 **6** *2* **Good Morning Dubai (IRE)**[19] 3029 2-8-7 0 .... JamesSullivan(5) 4 46
(B J Meehan) *t.k.h: trckd ldrs: hdwy to ld 2f out: sn rdn: drvn and hdd 1f out: wknd* **7/2**[3]

40 **7** *1* **Finn's Rainbow**[20] 2990 2-9-3 0 .... SilvestreDeSousa 6 47
(K A Ryan) *led: rdn along 1/2-way: hdd 2f out: drvn and wknd over 1f out* **18/1**

60 **8** *1/2* **Another Wise Kid (IRE)**[25] 2832 2-9-3 0 .... TonyCulhane 2 46
(P T Midgley) *prom: rdn along 2f out: wknd over 1f out* **50/1**

9 *1 3/4* **Yachtmaster (IRE)** 2-8-8 0 .... IanBrennan(5) 11 35
(J J Quinn) *s.i.s: a in rr* **16/1**

10 *1* **Bonne Millie** 2-8-8 0 .... PJMcDonald 7 27
(R A Fahey) *hmpd s: a in rr* **25/1**

64.35 secs (0.85) **Going Correction** +0.125s/f (Good) **10 Ran SP% 122.9**
Speed ratings (Par 94): **98,96,95,91,89 86,84,83,80,79**
toteswingers: 1&2 £4.10, 1&3 £2.40, 2&3 £5.60 CSF £17.73 TOTE £3.80: £1.30, £2.90, £1.40; EX 19.80.
Owner Godolphin **Bred** Darley **Trained** Newmarket, Suffolk

FOCUS
An ordinary sprint maiden.

NOTEBOOK
Ahtoug, dropping to 5f for the first time, had disappointed at Newcastle latest and was drawn widest of all here, but he showed plenty of pace and stayed on strongly to score. He should prove just as effective back at 6f and it will be interesting to see what mark he gets for nurseries. (op 7-2)

El Viento(FR), closely related to a couple of useful sprinters, was certainly unlucky not to give the winner more of a race, as having been short of room and forced to switch, he was then denied a run and, though staying on for second, he couldn't match the winner. (op 4-1)

Lady Royale bounced back from a poor effort in cheekpieces at Newcastle. She didn't get the clearest of runs, but couldn't be called unlucky. (op 9-2)

Close To The Edge(IRE) showed pace before fading and ran close to her debut form.

Brave Dream got behind having been slightly impeded before running on late. It will be nurseries now for him. (op 14-1)

Good Morning Dubai(IRE) was most disappointing, racing keenly and stopping quickly having been headed over 1f out. Official explanation: jockey said filly stumbled leaving stalls and ran too free early stages

3659 ELTHERINGTON H'CAP — 7f 100y
3:15 (3:19) (Class 4) (0-80,79) 4-Y-O+ **£4,209** (£1,252; £625; £312) **Stalls High**

Form RPR

-060 **1** **Stonehaugh (IRE)**[19] 3022 7-8-3 **66** .... (t) IanBrennan(5) 11 75
(J Howard Johnson) *mde all: rdn along 2f out: drvn ent fnl f: edgd lft and hld on gamely* **8/1**

5150 **2** *hd* **Summer Dancer (IRE)**[3] 3553 6-9-7 **79** .... TonyCulhane 6 87+
(P T Midgley) *hld up in rr: hdwy over 2f out: swtchd lft and rdn over 1f out: styd on strly ins fnl f: jst hld* **13/2**

0210 **3** *1 1/4* **Amethyst Dawn (IRE)**[7] 3438 4-8-11 **69** .... DuranFentiman 3 74
(T D Easterby) *trckd ldrs: hdwy over 2f out: rdn to chse wnr over 1f out: sn drvn and ev ch tl nt qckn wl ins fnl f* **9/4**[1]

2000 **4** *hd* **Handsome Falcon**[10] 3318 6-9-5 **77** .... TonyHamilton 8 81
(R A Fahey) *trckd ldrs on inner: swtchd lft and hdwy 2f out: rdn to chse ldrs over 1f out: drvn and kpt on ins fnl f* **15/2**

4331 **5** *1/2* **Smalljohn**[15] 3164 4-8-7 **72** .... (v) AdamCarter(7) 2 75
(B Smart) *cl up: effrt over 2f out: sn rdn and ch tl drvn and one pce appr fnl f* **7/2**[2]

-615 **6** *3/4* **Roman Glory (IRE)**[7] 3438 4-9-2 **79** .... JamesSullivan(5) 1 80
(B J Meehan) *wnt lft s: hld up in rr: hdwy on outer 2f out: rdn to chse ldrs over 1f out: drvn and one pce ent fnl f* **9/2**[3]

0000 **7** *1/2* **Violent Velocity (IRE)**[40] 2392 7-8-4 **69** .... ShaneBKelly(7) 10 69
(J J Quinn) *trckd ldrs: effrt on inner 2f out: rdn and n.m.r over 1f out: sn one pce* **14/1**

6540 **8** *4* **Carnivore**[44] 2241 8-9-2 **74** .... AndrewMullen 9 64
(T D Barron) *dwlt: a in rr* **14/1**

1m 31.89s (-1.91) **Going Correction** -0.275s/f (Firm) **8 Ran SP% 120.7**
Speed ratings (Par 105): **99,98,97,97,96 95,95,90**
toteswingers: 1&2 £8.80, 1&3 £8.00, 2&3 £4.30 CSF £61.89 CT £159.98 TOTE £10.20: £2.80, £2.10, £1.20; EX 71.90.
Owner J Howard Johnson **Bred** Yakup Demir Tokdemir **Trained** Billy Row, Co Durham

FOCUS
An ordinary handicap where two came clear late on. The first of three winners on the round course to make all, but the form makes some sense at face value.

Stonehaugh(IRE) Official explanation: trainer's rep said, regarding apparent improvement in form, that the gelding was suited by being allowed to dominate.

Carnivore Official explanation: jockey said gelding never travelled

3660 COACHMAN CARAVANS QUALITY H'CAP — 5f
3:50 (3:50) (Class 4) (0-85,82) 3-Y-O+ **£6,476** (£1,927; £963; £481) **Stalls High**

Form RPR

0261 **1** **Atlantic Beach**[10] 3321 5-9-1 **71** .... SilvestreDeSousa 5 83
(D O'Meara) *trckd ldr on inner: swtchd lft after 1f: effrt and cl up 2f out: rdn over 1f out: qcknd to ld ins fnl f: kpt on* **5/4**[1]

1232 **2** *2 1/4* **Noodles Blue Boy**[10] 3321 4-9-12 **82** .... TonyHamilton 4 86
(Ollie Pears) *qckly away and led: rdn over 1f out: drvn and hdd ins fnl f: kpt on same pce* **7/4**[2]

1662 **3** *shd* **Mullglen**[4] 3540 4-9-4 **74** .... (tp) DuranFentiman 3 78
(T D Easterby) *trckd ldrs whn n.m.r after 1f: hdwy wl over 1f out: swtchd lft and rdn ent fnl f: kpt on* **7/1**[3]

3150 **4** *2 1/4* **Perlachy**[16] 3114 6-8-8 **67** .... (v) KellyHarrison(3) 1 63
(D Shaw) *hld up: hdwy 2f out: sn rdn and no imp appr fnl f* **16/1**

2254 **5** *1/2* **Select Committee**[19] 3024 5-8-8 **69** .... (v) IanBrennan(5) 2 63
(J J Quinn) *chsd ldrs: rdn along wl over 1f out: sn drvn and wknd over 1f out* **7/1**[3]

63.40 secs (-0.10) **Going Correction** +0.125s/f (Good) **5 Ran SP% 111.7**
Speed ratings (Par 105): **105,101,101,97,96**
CSF £3.78 TOTE £2.30: £1.80, £1.10; EX 3.10.
Owner R Fell & K Everitt **Bred** D R Brotherton **Trained** Nawton, N Yorks
■ Stewards' Enquiry : Silvestre De Sousa two-day ban: careless riding (Jul 17-18)

FOCUS
A competitive enough sprint handicap, but the time was relatively slow. The form is taken at something like face value.

3661 C.G.I. H'CAP — 1m 100y
4:25 (4:25) (Class 4) (0-80,80) 3-Y-O **£5,180** (£1,541; £770; £384) **Stalls High**

Form RPR

1002 **1** **Mejd (IRE)**[14] 3208 3-9-6 **79** .... SamHitchcott 3 86
(M R Channon) *cl up: led after 2f: rdn along over 2f out: drvn over 1f out: styd on wl* **8/1**

3134 **2** *1 1/4* **Tribal Myth (IRE)**[9] 3363 3-8-5 **64** .... SilvestreDeSousa 4 68
(K A Ryan) *led 2f: prom on inner: rdn along 2f out: swtchd lft and drvn ent fnl f: styd on* **9/2**[3]

-221 **3** *1* **Cabal**[29] 2702 3-9-6 **79** .... FrannyNorton 5 81
(Sir Michael Stoute) *trckd ldng pair: hdwy to chse wnr 1/2-way: rdn 2f out: drvn over 1f out: wknd ins fnl f* **11/10**[1]

00-0 **4** *1 1/4* **Marsh Warbler**[45] 2225 3-9-7 **80** .... AndrewMullen 2 79
(M Johnston) *in tch: hdwy on outer to chse ldrs 1/2-way: rdn along over 2f out: drvn wl over 1f out: kpt on same pce* **10/1**

-016 **5** *3 3/4* **Count Bertoni (IRE)**[23] 2898 3-9-2 **75** .... (v[1]) StevieDonohoe 7 65
(S Gollings) *in tch: pushed along bef 1/2-way: sn rdn and outpcd fr wl over 2f out* **25/1**

2461 **6** *1 1/4* **I'm Super Too (IRE)**[9] 3355 3-9-4 **77** .... PJMcDonald 6 64
(G A Swinbank) *hld up in tch: pushed along on inner wl over 2f out: sn rdn and n.d* **9/4**[2]

1m 44.27s (-3.33) **Going Correction** -0.275s/f (Firm) **6 Ran SP% 120.6**
Speed ratings (Par 102): **105,103,102,101,97 96**
toteswingers: 1&2 £3.80, 1&3 £2.80, 2&3 £2.00 CSF £46.11 TOTE £9.70: £3.20, £3.00; EX 37.20.
Owner M Al-Qatami & K M Al-Mudhaf **Bred** Michael Dalton **Trained** West Ilsley, Berks

FOCUS
A fair little handicap and it was another winner who raced handily. The form is rated around the second, with surprise improvement from the winner.

3662 POWERPART FILLIES' H'CAP — 1m 1f 207y
5:00 (5:03) (Class 5) (0-70,68) 3-Y-O **£3,885** (£1,156; £577; £288) **Stalls High**

Form RPR

2530 **1** **Magic Millie (IRE)**[9] 3376 3-8-4 **51** .... SilvestreDeSousa 1 58
(D O'Meara) *trckd ldrs: hdwy over 2f out: rdn to ld over 1f out: drvn out* **11/8**[1]

045 **2** *1 3/4* **Enchanting Smile (FR)**[15] 3176 3-9-7 **68** .... JamesDoyle 2 70
(A J McCabe) *trckd ldr: effrt and cl up 3f out: led over 2f out: sn rdn and hdd over 1f out: drvn and one pce ins fnl f* **11/2**[3]

0-06 **3** *1 1/4* **Venture Girl (IRE)**[7] 3434 3-8-3 **53** .... KellyHarrison(3) 5 53+
(T D Easterby) *t.k.h: hld up in rr: hdwy over 2f out: rdn over 1f out: styd on ins fnl f: tk 3rd nr fin* **9/1**

60-0 **4** *1/2* **Quality Mover (USA)**[37] 2478 3-9-7 **68** .... NickyMackay 4 67
(D M Simcock) *hld up in tch: hdwy 3f out: rdn to chse ldrs wl over 1f out: sn no imp: lost 3rd nr fin* **7/2**[2]

-000 **5** *3* **Calm And Serene (USA)**[7] 3443 3-8-2 **49** oh4 .... (bt[1]) FrannyNorton 3 42
(Rae Guest) *hld up in rr: hdwy over 3f out: rdn over 2f out: sn no imp* **22/1**

2-03 **6** *4* **Brink**[36] 2499 3-8-13 **60** .... StevieDonohoe 8 45
(T J Pitt) *led: rdn along 3f out: hdd over 2f out and sn wknd* **7/1**

00-0 **7** *2* **Footsie (IRE)**[34] 2564 3-9-4 **65** .... LeeVickers 7 46
(J G Given) *chsd ldrs on inner: rdn along over 3f out: sn wknd* **10/1**

1055 **8** *57* **Sternian**[8] 3413 3-8-8 **55** .... (b) JamieMackay 6 —
(M E Rimmer) *t.k.h: in tch: sddle slipped 1/2-way: lost pl and bhd over 2f out: sn eased* **8/1**

2m 4.75s (-2.25) **Going Correction** -0.275s/f (Firm) **8 Ran SP% 126.8**
Speed ratings (Par 97): **98,96,95,95,92 89,88,42**
toteswingers: 1&2 £2.40, 1&3 £4.00, 2&3 £12.40 CSF £10.99 CT £56.33 TOTE £2.30: £1.60, £1.80, £1.70; EX 10.80.
Owner R Fell & K Everitt **Bred** John C Little **Trained** Nawton, N Yorks

FOCUS
A moderate fillies' handicap which was sound run. The winner looks the best guide.

Sternian Official explanation: jockey said saddle slipped

3663 COACHMAN MAIDEN STKS — 5f
5:35 (5:36) (Class 5) 3-Y-O+ **£3,561** (£1,059; £529; £264) **Stalls High**

Form RPR

50- **1** **Alis Aquilae (IRE)**[382] 3003 4-9-1 0 .... DaleSwift(7) 11 83
(T J Etherington) *prom: chsd ldr over 2f out: rdn over 1f out: kpt on to ld last 75yds* **22/1**

2022 **2** *1 1/2* **Sharp Eclipse**[24] 2879 3-9-3 69 .... SilvestreDeSousa 14 75
(K A Ryan) *stmbld s: sn led: rdn over 1f out: drvn ins fnl f: hdd and one pce last 75yds* **8/11**[1]

4463 **3** *6* **Tislaam (IRE)**[8] 3393 3-8-12 58 .... (v) IanBrennan(5) 2 54
(J S Wainwright) *swtchd rt after 1f: in tch: hdwy wl over 1f out: sn rdn and kpt on fnl f: nrst fin* **14/1**

5 **4** *1 1/4* **Rare Tern (IRE)**[44] 2249 3-8-12 0 .... StevieDonohoe 7 44
(Sir Mark Prescott) *dwlt and swtchd rt to rails shortly after s: in rr tl hdwy 2f out: swtchd lft and rdn over 1f out: kpt on ins fnl f: nrst fin* **5/1**[2]

054- **5** *1* **Residency (IRE)**[196] 7815 4-9-1 62 .... AdamCarter(7) 6 47
(B Smart) *in tch: hdwy to chse ldrs 2f out: swtchd lft and drvn over 1f out: sn no imp* **16/1**

5-62 **6** *1/2* **Melundy**[16] 3111 3-8-7 68 .... JamesSullivan(5) 10 39
(Mrs L Stubbs) *midfield: swtchd lft and hdwy 2f out: rdn to chse ldrs on outer whn sltly hmpd over 1f out: n.d* **7/1**[3]

2-3 **7** *1/2* **Praesepe**[38] 2441 3-8-12 0 .... KoseiMiura 1 37
(W J Haggas) *in rr: sme hdwy on wd outside whn hmpd over 1f out: n.d* **7/1**[3]

4300 **8** *7* **Media Jury**[11] 3287 3-9-3 48 .... PaddyAspell 12 17
(J S Wainwright) *chsd ldr: rdn along 1/2-way: drvn wl over 1f out and grad wknd* **80/1**

9 *4 1/2* **Toms Return** 3-8-12 0 .... KierenFox(5) 9 —
(J R Best) *swtchd rt s: nvr bttr than midfield* **12/1**

0-00 **10** *2 1/2* **Daisy Brown**[8] 3393 3-8-9 49 .... KellyHarrison(3) 13 —
(N Tinkler) *chsd ldrs to 1/2-way: sn wknd* **40/1**

0- **11** *1* **Grant Me A Wish**[260] 6823 4-9-8 0 .... AndrewMullen 5 —
(S P Griffiths) *chsd ldrs to 1/2-way: sn wknd* **80/1**

62.75 secs (-0.75) **Going Correction** +0.125s/f (Good)
WFA 3 from 4yo 5lb **11 Ran SP% 129.1**
Speed ratings (Par 103): **111,108,99,97,95 94,93,82,75,71 69**
toteswingers: 1&2 £8.00, 1&3 £26.00, 2&3 £4.60 CSF £41.87 TOTE £38.80: £8.60, £1.10, £3.40; EX 92.40 Place 6 £63.03, Place 5 £23.88.
Owner R Hogton R Bradley Training at Woldhouse **Bred** Ballyhane Stud **Trained** Norton, N Yorks

The Form Book, Raceform Ltd, Compton, RG20 6NL

FOCUS
A moderate sprint maiden with doubts over several. The runner-up looks the best guide.
Rare Tern(IRE) Official explanation: jockey said filly reared as stalls opened
Grant Me A Wish Official explanation: jockey said gelding bolted to post
T/Plt: £71.90 to a £1 stake. Pool: £50,965.08. 516.95 winning tickets. T/Qpdt: £32.50 to a £1 stake. Pool: £3,046.71. 69.30 winning tickets. JR

3315 CARLISLE (R-H)
Saturday, July 3

OFFICIAL GOING: Good to firm (firm in places; 7.9)
Wind: Breezy, across Weather: Fine, sunny

3664 NORTHERN SECURITY APPRENTICE H'CAP — 5f 193y
6:55 (6:55) (Class 5) (0-75,74) 4-Y-O+ — £2,388 (£705; £176; £176) — Stalls High

Form				RPR
33-1	1		**Feeling Fresh (IRE)**[8] 3391 5-9-0 **64**........ PatrickDonaghy 6	75
			(Paul Green) *s.i.s: hdwy in centre over 2f out: led ins fnl f: drvn out* **4/1**[2]	
-022	2	2 ½	**Dark Moment**[8] 3409 4-9-10 **74**........(p) MatthewDavies 3	77
			(Ollie Pears) *sn outpcd and drvn along: hdwy over 1f out: styd on wl fnl f: tk 2nd cl home: nt rch wnr* **5/1**[3]	
4510	3	½	**Apache Ridge (IRE)**[16] 3107 4-9-9 **73**........(b) AmyRyan 5	74
			(K A Ryan) *prom: drvn fr 1/2-way: led over 1f out to ins fnl f: kpt on same pce: lost 2nd cl home* **7/1**	
1116	3	dht	**Ryedane (IRE)**[3] 3551 8-9-5 **69**........(b) LanceBetts 4	70
			(T D Easterby) *w ldr: drvn and outpcd wl over 1f out: r.o fnl f: no imp* **5/1**[3]	
0-15	5	½	**Secret City (IRE)**[23] 2896 4-8-6 **61**........(b) MatthewLawson(5) 8	61
			(R Bastiman) *cl up: drvn and outpcd 1/2-way: no imp fr over 1f out* **15/2**	
3054	6	5	**Frognal (IRE)**[3] 3553 4-9-9 **73**........(b¹) DeanHeslop 1	57
			(Mrs R A Carr) *t.k.h: led to over 1f out: sn wknd* **2/1**[1]	

1m 13.74s (0.04) **Going Correction** +0.10s/f (Good) **6** Ran SP% **110.9**
Speed ratings (Par 103): **103,99,99,99,98 91**
TRICAST: FF-DM-AR £63.96, FF-DM-R £47.98; toteswingers: 1&2 £1.70, 1&3 (AR) £1.50, 1&3 (R) £2.60, 2&3 (AR) £3.10, 2&3 (R) £1.10 CSF £23.09 TOTE £3.30: £1.10, £2.70; EX 12.70.
Owner Paul Green (Oaklea) **Bred** J Mahon **Trained** Lydiate, Merseyside
■ Stewards' Enquiry : Dean Heslop one-day ban: careless riding (Jul 17)
Amy Ryan one-day ban: used whip with excessive frequency (Jul 17)

FOCUS
The pace was strong thanks to Frognal, who is normally held up but was lit up by first-time blinkers, and that brought the proven stamina of Feeling Fresh into play. He recorded a small personal best.
Apache Ridge(IRE) Official explanation: jockey said gelding started to gurgle approaching line

3665 STORY CONSTRUCTION MAIDEN AUCTION STKS — 5f 193y
7:25 (7:27) (Class 5) 2-Y-O — £2,266 (£674; £337; £168) — Stalls High

Form				RPR
	1		**Alaskan Spirit (IRE)** 2-8-13 0........ BarryMcHugh(3) 7	79+
			(Mrs A Duffield) *coltish in paddock: trckd ldr: rdn to ld over 1f out: styd on wl fnl f* **8/1**	
40	2	2	**Boundaries**[56] 1930 2-8-11 0........ DavidAllan 3	68
			(T D Easterby) *plld hrd: hld up: effrt on outside 2f out: chsd wnr ins fnl f: r.o* **8/1**	
242	3	nk	**Sophie's Hero**[9] 3353 2-9-2 0........ TonyHamilton 2	73
			(K A Ryan) *trckd ldrs: effrt and rdn 2f out: kpt on same pce fnl f* **3/1**[2]	
30	4	1 ¼	**Philharmonic Hall**[19] 3020 2-8-9 0........ PaulHanagan 5	61+
			(R A Fahey) *in tch: rdn over 2f out: no imp fr over 1f out* **9/2**[3]	
3	5	shd	**Ajaafa**[19] 3020 2-8-10 0 ow1........ PhillipMakin 11	62
			(J G Given) *led tl rdn and hdd over 1f out: kpt on same pce* **11/4**[1]	
35	6	1 ½	**Dotty Darroch**[24] 2873 2-8-6 0........ GregFairley 4	53
			(R Bastiman) *t.k.h: prom: rdn along 2f out: sn no imp* **11/1**	
0	7	½	**Green Pastures (IRE)**[36] 2498 2-8-11 0........ PatrickMathers 1	57
			(J Howard Johnson) *hld up in midfield on ins: drvn over 3f out: nvr able to chal* **50/1**	
0	8	nk	**Dance For Livvy (IRE)**[20] 2990 2-8-8 0........ AndrewElliott 9	53+
			(B M R Haslam) *bhd: drvn over 3f out: nvr rchd ldrs* **33/1**	
	9	5	**Beer Flush (IRE)** 2-8-8 0........ PatrickDonaghy(5) 10	43
			(Jedd O'Keeffe) *s.s: a outpcd and bhd* **20/1**	
56	10	hd	**Louis Girl**[19] 3020 2-8-1 0........ MarzenaJeziorek(7) 8	37
			(R A Fahey) *s.i.s: pushed along towards rr over 2f out: sn wknd* **28/1**	

1m 15.38s (1.68) **Going Correction** +0.10s/f (Good) **10** Ran SP% **113.5**
Speed ratings (Par 94): **92,89,88,87,87 85,84,84,77,77**
toteswingers: 1&2 £10.70, 1&3 £3.30, 2&3 £6.70 CSF £65.04 TOTE £7.60: £1.70, £2.00, £1.40; EX 54.40.
Owner John Gatenby **Bred** Mountarmstrong Stud **Trained** Constable Burton, N Yorks

FOCUS
A modest maiden.

NOTEBOOK
Alaskan Spirit(IRE) is clearly well thought of and the son of Kodiac looks set for a plenty more success having seen off some decent yardsticks here on debut. You wouldn't have known this was the colt's first run because he was thoroughly professional, breaking well and showing good speed before moving smoothly through to take over well over a furlong out and keep on stoutly. Well in command at the line, this was a promising performance and he's one to keep an eye on. (tchd 7-1 and 9-1)
Boundaries deserves credit for keeping on into second having raced far too freely early on and he's of interest now qualified for nurseries.
Sophie's Hero kept on for yet another solid placed effort and, while he is capable of winning an ordinary maiden, he is clearly vulnerable to anything with potential. (op 11-4)
Philharmonic Hall took a step in the right direction at least and looks one who can improve when handicapping (op 7-2 tchd 11-4)
Ajaafa showed good speed to lead but was readily left behind by the winner and probably hasn't improved on his fairly encouraging debut. (op 3-1 tchd 4-1)

3666 ANDERSONS DENTON HOLME LTD (S) STKS — 7f 200y
7:55 (7:56) (Class 6) 3-Y-O — £1,706 (£503; £252) — Stalls High

Form				RPR
0050	1		**Bell's Ocean (USA)**[8] 3413 3-8-7 55........ PaulHanagan 3	57
			(J Ryan) *trckd ldrs: styd far side ent st: rdn and chal over 1f out: led ins fnl f: all out* **5/2**[2]	
4024	2	shd	**Miami Gator (IRE)**[8] 3413 3-9-3 62........(v) AndrewElliott 2	67
			(J R Weymes) *led: rdn and styd far side ent st: hdd ins fnl f: rallied: jst hld* **7/4**[1]	
6-24	3	8	**Urban Clubber**[17] 3077 3-8-12 63........ TonyHamilton 1	42
			(J Howard Johnson) *cl up: racd centre ent st: outpcd by first two fr 2f out: no imp whn edgd rt fnl f* **5/1**[3]	
-006	4	2	**Anna's Boy**[17] 3073 3-8-12 46........ DavidAllan 4	37
			(A Berry) *plld hrd: in tch: c centre ent st: sn btn* **16/1**	
0	5	9	**Feed The Goat (IRE)**[14] 3226 3-8-9 0........(t) BarryMcHugh(3) 7	14
			(Miss Amy Weaver) *in tch: effrt and styd far side ent st: sn rdn and wknd* **12/1**	
5-00	6	9	**Miss Lauz**[43] 2273 3-8-7 41........(b) PatrickMathers 5	—
			(A Berry) *hld up: rdn and racd centre ent st: sn btn* **80/1**	

1m 40.87s (0.87) **Going Correction** +0.10s/f (Good) **6** Ran SP% **96.4**
Speed ratings (Par 98): **99,98,90,88,79 70**
toteswingers: 1&2 £1.10, 1&3 £2.20, 2&3 £1.60 CSF £5.19 TOTE £2.60: £1.30, £1.20; EX 6.20.There was no bid for the winner.
Owner Ocean Trailers Ltd **Bred** Brereton C Jones **Trained** Newmarket, Suffolk

FOCUS
Not much of a race, but a ding-dong finish as Bell's Ocean and Miami Gator pulled clear up the far side. The form is rated around the runner-up.

3667 STOBART SILVER CUP H'CAP — 7f 200y
8:25 (8:26) (Class 3) (0-90,89) 3-Y-O+ — £9,714 (£2,890; £1,444; £721) — Stalls High

Form				RPR
12	1		**Capponi (IRE)**[44] 2261 3-9-5 **89**........ AdrianNicholls 6	96+
			(M Johnston) *t.k.h: broke wl but sn stdd on outside: effrt and hdwy 3f out: led on wd outside ins fnl f: styd on wl* **3/1**[1]	
-023	2	nk	**Ithinkbest**[30] 2683 4-9-11 **86**........ RichardMullen 10	94
			(Sir Michael Stoute) *prom: effrt over 2f out: ev ch on outside ins fnl f: kpt on: jst hld* **4/1**[2]	
2505	3	nk	**Sunnyside Tom (IRE)**[14] 3206 6-9-5 **80**........ PaulHanagan 2	87
			(R A Fahey) *pressed ldr: led and hung lft into centre over 1f out: hdd ins fnl f: rallied: hld towards fin* **11/2**	
0032	4	1 ½	**Moheebb (IRE)**[4] 3537 6-9-7 **82**........(b) PhillipMakin 4	86
			(Mrs R A Carr) *hld up: hdwy on ins over 1f out: kpt on fnl f: nt rch centre ldrs* **5/1**[3]	
-006	5	1	**Medici Pearl**[21] 2977 6-9-10 **85**........ DavidAllan 3	86
			(T D Easterby) *hld up: hdwy over 1f out: no imp fnl f* **14/1**	
0-00	6	¾	**Stevie Gee (IRE)**[7] 3438 6-8-12 **73**........ TonyHamilton 8	72
			(Ian Williams) *in tch: rdn over 2f out: no imp over 1f out* **14/1**	
2640	7	nse	**Billy Dane (IRE)**[14] 3206 6-9-3 **85**........(p) LeeTopliss(7) 9	84
			(F P Murtagh) *led tl hung lft and hdd over 1f out: kpt on same pce* **5/1**[3]	
-212	8	2 ¼	**Harriet's Girl**[14] 3206 4-9-0 **75**........ AndrewElliott 1	75
			(J R Weymes) *prom: effrt on outside over 2f out: one pce whn hmpd over 1f out* **14/1**	
1440	9	1	**Fujin Dancer (FR)**[11] 3283 5-8-12 **78**........(p) AmyRyan(5) 7	70
			(K A Ryan) *hld up towards rr: drvn 3f out: wknd over 1f out* **18/1**	

1m 39.71s (-0.29) **Going Correction** +0.10s/f (Good)
WFA 3 from 4yo+ 9lb **9** Ran SP% **119.0**
Speed ratings (Par 107): **105,104,104,102,101 101,101,98,97**
toteswingers: 1&2 £2.80, 1&3 £6.60, 2&3 £5.20 CSF £15.50 CT £64.25 TOTE £5.30: £2.30, £2.10, £2.90; EX 14.10.
Owner Sheikh Hamdan Bin Mohammed Al Maktoum **Bred** Darley **Trained** Middleham Moor, N Yorks
■ Stewards' Enquiry : Lee Topliss one-day ban: careless riding (Jul 17)
Adrian Nicholls caution: used whip down shoulder in the forehand.

FOCUS
A competitive handicap in which they were spread right across the track but the three on the near side asserted in the final half furlong. Solid form.

NOTEBOOK
Capponi(IRE) stayed on strongly up the stands' rail to make a winning turf debut. Although nudged up 4lb for his good second at Southwell last time, the unexposed colt took another step forward here in beating a group of more experienced rivals and, given he is closely related to high-class miler No Excuse Needed, he has the potential to improve a good deal more and it would be no surprise if he was a Pattern class performer by the end of the season. (op 4-1)
Ithinkbest ran another fine race in defeat and he's surely going to be going one better soon. (tchd 7-2)
Sunnyside Tom(IRE) has yet to get his head in front this term but this was yet another solid effort in defeat and he is 4lb below his last winning mark, so it will be a surprise if he doesn't find a winning opportunity this summer. Official explanation: jockey said gelding hung left-handed throughout (tchd 5-1)
Moheebb(IRE) stayed on well up the far rail and is crying out for some easier ground. He looks one for the notebook. (tchd 9-2)
Medici Pearl has done all her winning on ground with give in it and this was an encouraging effort in the circumstances. (op 12-1)
Stevie Gee(IRE) is a well handicapped horse at the moment and he appears to be slowly working his way to the boil. (op 8-1)
Billy Dane(IRE) got the lead to himself but couldn't maintain his effort and was a little below par. (op 9-1 tchd 10-1)

3668 CARLISLE TOURISM PARTNERSHIP H'CAP — 6f 192y
8:55 (8:56) (Class 5) (0-70,67) 3-Y-O — £2,590 (£770; £385; £192) — Stalls High

Form				RPR
003	1		**Verluga (IRE)**[14] 3227 3-8-12 **58**........ DavidAllan 6	63+
			(T D Easterby) *in tch: effrt and hdwy over 1f out: chal ins fnl f: styd on u.p to ld nr fin* **7/2**[3]	
3120	2	shd	**So Bazaar (IRE)**[23] 2886 3-9-5 **65**........ PJMcDonald 7	70
			(G A Swinbank) *led: rdn 2f out: hrd pressed ins fnl f: hdd nr fin* **11/4**[2]	
0323	3	1 ¼	**High Resolution**[4] 3530 3-8-11 **57**........(p) PaulHanagan 3	59
			(Miss L A Perratt) *t.k.h: hld up in tch: effrt and hdwy over 1f out: chsd ldrs ins fnl f: hld nr fin* **7/4**[1]	
1006	4	7	**Dispol Kabira**[5] 3501 3-8-3 **49**........ PatrickMathers 1	32
			(D W Thompson) *hld up: rdn over 2f out: hdwy 1f out: nvr able to chal* **20/1**	
-330	5	1 ½	**Pure Nostalgia (IRE)**[14] 3226 3-9-4 **64**........ TonyHamilton 4	43
			(J Howard Johnson) *cl up: drvn over 2f out: wknd over 1f out* **12/1**	
00-0	6	8	**Monalini (IRE)**[70] 1511 3-9-7 **67**........ GregFairley 8	24
			(B Smart) *t.k.h: chsd ldr: rdn over 2f out: edgd rt and wknd appr fnl f* **16/1**	
-005	7	10	**Bubbelas**[13] 3243 3-8-11 **57**........(v) PhillipMakin 2	—
			(J J Quinn) *hld up: rdn 3f out: btn wl over 1f out* **8/1**	

1m 28.3s (1.20) **Going Correction** +0.10s/f (Good) **7** Ran SP% **114.7**
Speed ratings (Par 100): **97,96,95,87,85 76,65**
toteswingers: 1&2 £2.40, 1&3 £1.10, 2&3 £1.40 CSF £13.67 CT £21.47 TOTE £4.00: £2.00, £1.50; EX 15.60.
Owner Habton Farms **Bred** Derek Veitch And Saleh Ali Hammadi **Trained** Great Habton, N Yorks
■ Stewards' Enquiry : P J McDonald caution: used whip with excessive frequency.

FOCUS
A weak race in which the front three finished clear. The form is rated around the second.

3669 LLOYD MOTOR GROUP MAIDEN H'CAP — 2m 1f 52y
9:25 (9:25) (Class 6) (0-65,60) 4-Y-0+ — £1,706 (£503; £252) Stalls High

Form — RPR

-332 **1** **Petella**[28] 2765 4-8-6 **48** — KellyHarrison(3) 11 — 56
(C W Thornton) *hld up towards rr: hdwy over 3f out: led on outside 2f out: kpt on strly fnl f* **9/2**[2]

-460 **2** 1 **Bandanaman (IRE)**[8] 1150 4-9-7 **60** — PJMcDonald 9 — 66
(G A Swinbank) *hld up: hdwy over 2f out: styd on fnl f: wnt 2nd cl home: nt rch wnr* **12/1**

0-53 **3** nk **Knock Three Times (IRE)**[38] 2430 4-8-1 **45** — JamesSullivan(5) 13 — 51
(W Storey) *midfield: hdwy and ev ch over 2f out: sn chsng wnr: kpt on fnl f: lost 2nd cl home* **16/1**

6202 **4** 7 **Ocean Bright (USA)**[14] 3223 4-8-10 **49** ow2 — PhillipMakin 3 — 47
(J G Given) *prom: effrt and ev ch over 2f out: sn rdn and one pce* **15/2**

3200 **5** 2 ½ **Arisea (IRE)**[19] 506 7-8-7 **46** — PatrickMathers 8 — 41
(James Moffatt) *dwlt: hld up: hdwy on ins over 2f out: no further imp appr fnl f* **16/1**

00-6 **6** 2 ¾ **Favours Brave**[20] 2995 4-9-5 **58** — (e[1]) DavidAllan 12 — 49
(T D Easterby) *t.k.h: chsd ldr: led over 3f out to 2f out: sn outpcd* **7/1**[3]

0/0- **7** hd **Flying Doctor**[3] 252 7-8-6 **45** — (b[1]) TonyHamilton 7 — 36
(E J Cooper) *hld up in midfield: drvn and outpcd over 3f out: n.d after* **13/8**[1]

004/ **8** ½ **Word Of Warning**[13] 4905 6-9-4 **57** — PaulHanagan 2 — 47
(M Todhunter) *hld up in midfield: hdwy on outside and cl up over 3f out: wknd over 1f out* **10/1**

00-0 **9** ½ **Strevelyn**[19] 1199 4-8-5 **47** ow2 — (e[1]) BarryMcHugh(3) 6 — 37
(Mrs A Duffield) *t.k.h: trckd ldrs tl wknd wl over 1f out* **50/1**

50-4 **10** 3 **Chateauneuf (IRE)**[14] 3223 4-8-7 **49** — PaulPickard(3) 1 — 35
(W M Brisbourne) *hld up: drvn on outside 4f out: btn fnl 2f* **20/1**

5636 **11** 2 ½ **Quadrifolio**[9] 3360 4-8-2 **46** ow1 — PatrickDonaghy(5) 4 — 29
(Paul Green) *hld up: drvn over 3f out: sn n.d* **33/1**

500- **12** 25 **Sea Cove**[19] 4848 10-8-6 **45** — GregFairley 10 — —
(Mrs Dianne Sayer) *led to over 3f out: sn rdn and wknd: t.o* **40/1**

3m 52.51s (-0.49) **Going Correction** +0.10s/f (Good) — 12 Ran SP% **121.2**
Speed ratings (Par 101): **105,104,104,101,99 98,98,98,96 95,83**
toteswingers: 1&2 £12.50, 1&3 £6.00, 2&3 £33.00 CSF £56.72 CT £809.63 TOTE £5.50: £1.70, £4.30, £3.40; EX 47.10 Place 6 £79.26, Place 5 £35.15.
Owner A Crute & Partners **Bred** C And Mrs Wilson **Trained** Middleham Moor, N Yorks

FOCUS
A very weak maiden handicap.
T/Plt: £33.70 to a £1 stake. Pool: £60,731.83. 1,315.05 winning tickets. T/Qpdt: £12.40 to a £1 stake. Pool: £4,397.40. 262.40 winning tickets. RY

3623 HAYDOCK (L-H)
Saturday, July 3

OFFICIAL GOING: Good to firm (7.8)
Inner sprint course used and rail realignment on round course increased advertised distances by 16yds.
Wind: Light, half-against Weather: Cloudy with sunny intervals turning fine

3670 BET365.COM H'CAP — 1m 3f 200y
2:15 (2:16) (Class 2) (0-100,96) 3-Y-0 — £14,571 (£4,335; £2,166; £1,082) Stalls High

Form — RPR

12-5 **1** **Anhar (USA)**[63] 1702 3-9-7 **96** — (t) TedDurcan 2 — 103+
(Saeed Bin Suroor) *awkward leaving stalls: hld up: eased to outer 2f out: effrt and hdwy over 1f out: led ins fnl f: r.o and on top towards fin* **10/1**[3]

2501 **2** 1 ½ **Bowdler's Magic**[7] 3427 3-8-9 **84** — JoeFanning 3 — 89+
(M Johnston) *chsd ldr: rdn 2f out: stl chalng for press ins fnl f: nt qckn fnl 75yds* **11/2**[2]

03-1 **3** 1 **Mecox Bay (IRE)**[26] 2812 3-8-2 **77** oh1 — DavidProbert 5 — 80
(A M Balding) *led: rdn and hdd 2f out: stl chalng u.p ins fnl f: kpt on same pce fnl 100yds* **16/1**

-115 **4** hd **Berling (IRE)**[16] 3105 3-9-0 **89** — EddieAhern 7 — 92
(J L Dunlop) *chsd ldrs: led 2f out: rdn whn pressed over 1f out: hdd ins fnl f: rdr stopped riding for a stride sn after: no ex towards fin* **2/5**[1]

-010 **5** 8 **Nurture (IRE)**[23] 2889 3-9-4 **93** — (p) GeorgeBaker 6 — 83
(R M Beckett) *hld up: pushed along over 3f out: rdn over 1f out: no imp and outpcd: eased whn btn ins fnl f* **20/1**

2m 35.09s (1.09) **Going Correction** +0.05s/f (Good) — 5 Ran SP% **106.5**
Speed ratings (Par 106): **95,94,93,93,87**
CSF £54.93 TOTE £8.30: £3.40, £2.10; EX 38.30.
Owner Godolphin **Bred** Daylesford Stud **Trained** Newmarket, Suffolk

FOCUS
The ground was changed to good to firm all round before the start of racing, and there were a plethora of non-runners throughout the afternoon. The jockeys reported there was no jar. This good handicap featured only a small field and, with no guaranteed pacemaker, the gallop was steady before picking up off the home turn. The first pair can rate higher for a stiffer test.

NOTEBOOK
Anhar(USA) had good juvenile form, being touched off in Zetland Stakes, and had put up a fair effort in a minor Listed race on his reappearance. Stepping up in trip for this handicap debut, he was held up after going left at the start but found much the best pace when switched to the outside to win cosily. He looks up to running creditably back at Listed level after this, although a quote of 20-1 for the St Leger does not look particularly generous at this stage. (op 15-2)
Bowdler's Magic finished last in King George V Handicap and had a lot to find with the favourite on that, especially as he had won since and was 2lb higher. He was never far away and battled on under pressure to get back up for second, but was no match for the winner. (tchd 5-1)
Mecox Bay(IRE) progressed to narrowly win a 1m2f maiden at Folkestone but was up in trip for this handicap debut. He dictated a steady pace before pushing on off the bend, but could never get away, although he did keep going despite being done no favours by the runner-up. (op 14-1)
Berling(IRE) won two handicaps this season before his strong-finishing fifth in the King George V Handicap at Royal Ascot. With the fourth and sixth having both won since, he went off a short-priced favourite. He went to the front narrowly at the quarter-mile pole but could not get away and was very one-paced under pressure inside the last furlong. This was disappointing but maybe a stronger pace and/or longer trip might suit him better. (op 8-15 early in places)
Nurture(IRE) has well beaten in Listed company since her maiden win earlier in the season. Stepping up in trip for this handicap debut, she was struggling as soon as the pace picked up. (op 14-1)

3671 BET365 LANCASHIRE OAKS (GROUP 2) (F&M) — 1m 3f 200y
2:50 (2:51) (Class 1) 3-Y-0+
£52,512 (£19,906; £9,962; £4,967; £2,488; £1,248) Stalls High

Form — RPR

-143 **1** **Barshiba (IRE)**[14] 3191 6-9-5 108 — HayleyTurner 9 — 112+
(D R C Elsworth) *racd keenly: hdwy to ld after 2f: mde rest: rdn whn pressed wl over 1f out: r.o gamely ins fnl f: in control whn jinked rt cl home* **7/2**[2]

2-42 **2** ¾ **Polly's Mark (IRE)**[35] 2538 4-9-5 104 — RichardHughes 12 — 110
(C G Cox) *hld up: hdwy over 3f out: styd on to take 2nd fnl 110yds: clsng but nvr gng to get there whn carried rt by wnr cl home* **3/1**[1]

5612 **3** 1 ½ **Lady Jane Digby**[9] 3368 5-9-5 104 — GregFairley 6 — 108
(M Johnston) *led for 2f: chsd wnr: rdn to chal 2f out: lost 2nd fnl 110yds: keeping on but hld whn intimidated and skipped cl home* **11/1**

1-21 **4** 4 **Les Fazzani (IRE)**[35] 2538 6-9-5 108 — PaulHanagan 4 — 102
(K A Ryan) *midfield: hdwy 3f out: rdn to chse ldrs 2f out: chalng over 1f out: one pce fnl 110yds* **13/2**[3]

-331 **5** nk **Grace O'Malley (IRE)**[20] 3007 4-9-5 101 — PJSmullen 11 — 101
(D K Weld, Ire) *trckd ldrs: rdn to chal fr over 2f out: nt qckn ins fnl f: wknd fnl 100yds* **8/1**

0-02 **6** 1 **Cassique Lady (IRE)**[19] 3031 5-9-5 101 — EddieAhern 8 — 100
(Mrs L Wadham) *hld up: rdn over 2f out: kpt on fnl f: nt pce to threaten ldrs* **33/1**

12-3 **7** nse **Rosika**[35] 2538 4-9-5 97 — RichardMullen 7 — 99
(Sir Michael Stoute) *trckd ldrs: pushed along and lost pl over 3f out: no imp after* **15/2**

-213 **8** ½ **Tinaar (USA)**[50] 2071 4-9-5 97 — PhillipMakin 1 — 99
(G A Butler) *broke wl: chsd ldrs: outpcd 2f out: dropped away over 1f out* **17/2**

0-30 **9** 15 **Champagnelifestyle**[29] 2711 3-8-6 101 — MichaelHills 3 — 84
(B W Hills) *hld up: rdn over 2f out: toiling over 1f out: eased whn wl btn ins fnl f bhd* **10/1**

0331 **10** 2 ¾ **Najam**[16] 3116 3-8-6 79 — ChrisCatlin 5 — 70
(C E Brittain) *midfield: pushed along 3f out: wknd over 2f out* **50/1**

2m 30.85s (-3.15) **Going Correction** +0.05s/f (Good)
WFA 3 from 4yo+ 13lb — 10 Ran SP% **116.3**
Speed ratings (Par 115): **109,108,107,104,104 103,103,103,93,91**
Tote Swingers: 1&2 £3.50, 1&3 £12.00, 2&3 £14.20 CSF £14.39 TOTE £4.50: £1.60, £1.60, £3.00; EX 17.60 Trifecta £137.20 Pool: £5,391.62 - 29.07 winning units..
Owner J C Smith **Bred** Littleton Stud **Trained** Newmarket, Suffolk
■ Barshiba is the firfst dual winner of this race, which was opened up to older fillies and mares in 1991.

FOCUS
This Group 2 has been pretty evenly shared by the age groups 3-5 in recent seasons but this year there were two 6-y-os who entered the argument. Pretty solid form, with the winner close to her best.

NOTEBOOK
Barshiba(IRE) has been in good form this season and ran well when third at Ascot behind Harbinger. With conditions to suit, she went on after a furlong or so when it was clear nothing else was going to make it, and then kept finding in the straight, eventually scoring slightly cosily. She jinked slightly near the line but the result was not affected. (tchd 4-1)
Polly's Mark(IRE) is a consistent sort at Listed level and was closely match with today's fourth on previous course form although 3lb worse off. She had handled fast going in the past but had avoided it of late and, after getting to the heels of the winner 2f out, took a long while to pick up and probably found the ground too quick. (op 9-2)
Lady Jane Digby scored at Warwick recently and had won a Group 3 at 1m3f last year. The ground was in her favour but she had a bit to find at this level and, although running her race, could find no extra in the final furlong. (op 9-1)
Les Fazzani(IRE) is a game multiple Listed winner who has won over C&D but all her best form has been with cut in the ground, and she had never previously run on fast. She came to have every chance but her effort flattened out in the final furlong, and a return to easier conditions will see her in a more favourable light. (op 6-1)
Grace O'Malley(IRE) won a Cork Group 3 at this sort of trip in both of the last two years. She acts on this ground but had a bit to find on form and, after having every chance in the straight, faded in the closing stages. (op 15-2 tchd 7-1)
Cassique Lady(IRE), a Listed winner at an extended 1m2f, handles most ground and was closely matched with today's third on Warwick form. She ran on from the rear in the straight but never really got competitive. (op 28-1)
Rosika won a handicap off 86 at this trip last autumn but had something to find with Les Fazzani and Polly's Mark on previous course form, and she faded under pressure. (op 8-1 tchd 17-2 and 9-1 in a place)
Tinaar(USA), a progressive handicapper who won off 90 earlier in the season, was stepping up in grade and dropped away after being close enough turning in. Her best form has been on good and easy ground, so she might be worth a try at Listed level when the going suits better. (tchd 8-1 and 9-1)

3672 BET365 OLD NEWTON CUP (HERITAGE H'CAP) — 1m 3f 200y
3:25 (3:28) (Class 2) 4-Y-0+
£56,079 (£16,794; £8,397; £4,203; £2,097; £1,053) Stalls High

Form — RPR

-166 **1** **Dangerous Midge (USA)**[14] 3194 4-8-10 **96** — MartinDwyer 13 — 112
(B J Meehan) *chsd ldrs: wnt 2nd 4f out: led 2f out: drew clr ins fnl f: in command and r.o wl* **17/2**

-304 **2** 8 **Demolition**[21] 2977 6-8-6 **92** — PaulHanagan 5 — 95
(R A Fahey) *chsd ldrs: nt qckn 3f out: rdn 2f out: styd on ins fnl f to take 2nd fnl 110yds: n.d to wnr* **16/1**

0010 **3** ½ **Fiery Lad (IRE)**[15] 3144 5-9-10 **110** — J-PGuillambert 4 — 112+
(L M Cumani) *hld up: hdwy over 2f out: chsd ldrs under driving over 1f out: styd on towards fin: nt pce to chal* **16/1**

0-25 **4** 1 ½ **Almiqdaad**[58] 1831 4-9-0 **100** — (b[1]) TadhgO'Shea 1 — 100
(M A Jarvis) *led: abt 5 l clr 1/2-way: rdn and hdd 2f out: continued to chse wnr u.p: outpcd ins fnl f: lost 2nd fnl 110yds: no ex cl home* **10/1**

0551 **5** 1 **Reve De Nuit (USA)**[7] 3456 4-7-13 **90** — DeclanCannon(5) 15 — 88
(A J McCabe) *chsd ldrs: rdn over 2f out: kpt on same pce u.p after* **33/1**

-210 **6** nk **Final Victory**[14] 3194 4-8-5 **91** — LiamKeniry 7 — 89
(A M Balding) *in tch: pushed along and outpcd 3f out: edgd lft over 1f out: styd on towards fin but nt pce to chal: sddle slipped* **25/1**

6110 **7** ¾ **Submariner (USA)**[14] 3194 4-8-6 **92** — JoeFanning 11 — 89
(M Johnston) *chsd ldr to 4f out: rdn over 3f out: sn outpcd by ldrs: wknd fnl f: eased whn wl hld towards fin* **11/2**[2]

0-06 **8** ½ **Red Merlin (IRE)**[29] 2716 5-8-9 **100**.......(v) JohnFahy(5) 10 96
(C G Cox) *missed break: hld up: rdn 2f out: kpt on ins fnl f: nvr able to get on terms w ldrs* **16/1**

1-21 **9** *hd* **Hanoverian Baron**[50] 2096 5-8-2 **88**....... DavidProbert 12 84
(A G Newcombe) *midfield: clipped heels and stmbld after 2f: u.p over 2f out: no imp on ldrs: plugged on at one pce ins fnl f* **10/3**[1]

-320 **10** 3¾ **Munsef**[14] 3195 8-9-7 **107**.......(p) EddieAhern 14 97
(Ian Williams) *midfield: rdn 2f out: sn outpcd: btn over 1f out* **20/1**

-621 **11** 1¾ **The Fonz**[7] 3462 4-7-13 **88**....... Louis-PhilippeBeuzelin(3) 6 75
(Sir Michael Stoute) *midfield: pushed along 3f out: no imp on ldrs: plugged on at one pce tl wknd ins fnl f: eased whn wl btn fnl 75yds* **7/1**[3]

1-13 **12** 1 **Thin Red Line (IRE)**[29] 2710 4-8-9 **95**....... PhillipMakin 8 80
(M Dods) *midfield: lost pl 3f out: u.p and gng nowhere over 2f out: n.d after* **14/1**

1200 **13** 7 **Spirit Is Needed (IRE)**[7] 3447 4-8-4 **90**....... GregFairley 16 64
(M Johnston) *bhd: pushed along 5f out: nvr on terms* **25/1**

2-41 **14** 23 **Hillview Boy (IRE)**[50] 2071 6-8-12 **98**....... RichardHughes 2 35
(J S Goldie) *midfield: lost pl 5f out: eased whn wl btn over 2f out: t.o* **8/1**

2m 28.66s (-5.34) **Going Correction** +0.05s/f (Good) **14** Ran SP% **121.4**
Speed ratings (Par 109): **117,111,111,110,109 109,108,108,108,106 104,104,99,84**
Tote Swingers: 1&2 £53.80, 1&3 £47.60, 2&3 £68.40 CSF £131.52 CT £2145.47 TOTE £9.80: £3.30, £4.90, £6.10; EX 202.20 Trifecta £2130.70 Pool: £16,988.08 - 5.90 winning units..
Owner Iraj Parvizi **Bred** Tony Holmes & Dr Walter Zent **Trained** Manton, Wilts

FOCUS
A typically competitive renewal of this high-class handicap and the time was 2.19sec faster than the preceding Group 3, but very few got involved from off the pace. A 6lb personal best from the winner, with the form rated around the runner-up.

NOTEBOOK
Dangerous Midge(USA), lightly raced and with form at 1m2f, had to prove he truly stayed this far. However, he was ridden as if stamina was no problem, being close to the pace throughout. When he was asked to go to the front, he quickly put daylight between himself and the rest and scored impressively. He will go up a fair amount for this but his target is reportedly the Ebor, and on this showing the longer trip should not be a problem. (op 9-1)
Demolition stays the trip and handles the ground but was 10lb above his last winning mark. He was another who was close to the pace most of the way, and he picked up well after reportedly running lazily in the straight, but had no chance with the winner. (tchd 20-1)
Fiery Lad(IRE) ◆, a last-gasp winner at the Epsom Derby meeting before a fair effort in Listed company at Royal Ascot, was stepping up in trip. He was held up at the back before making headway in the straight and, although he was unable to pose a threat to the winner, can be given extra credit as he was the only one in the frame to come from the back.
Almiqdaad won a big handicap last season but his best form was at around 1m2f. He was unproven at the trip and 7lb higher than for his last win, and after going to the front he got rather lit up in blinkers for the first time, going clear at about halfway. It was to his credit that he stuck to his task under pressure and he will be of interest if he settles better next time. (op 11-1 tchd 12-1)
Reve De Nuit(USA), a 1m2f winner on fast last time, was 4lb higher and ran his race despite being a little keen early and racing on the outside of the pack.
Final Victory had gained all his wins on good and easy ground and was 7lb above his last winning mark. He ran with credit but could not trouble the principals on this surface, and his rider reported that the saddle slipped. Official explanation: jockey said saddle slipped (tchd 28-1)
Submariner(USA), a 1m4f winner on his debut who had won at shorter since, showed up for a good way until fading once the winner went on. (op 13-2)
Red Merlin(IRE) last year's winner, had not won since and was 8lb higher. He did not help his chances by missing the break, from which point he never got competitive. (op 14-1)
Hanoverian Baron came into this a progressive sort who handles fast ground. However, he was tracking the leaders when stumbling and losing his place in the early stages, and could never get back into it. The vet reported that the gelding had been struck into. Official explanation: jockey said gelding clipped heels and lost early position; vet said gelding was struck into (op 4-1 tchd 9-2)
Munsef, runner-up in this last season, was wearing cheekpieces for the first time but was another who was forced to race on the outside of his field and was beaten fairly early in the straight. (op 16-1)
The Fonz, 4lb higher for his win in lower grade last time, had a bit to find with the winner on previous form and, after tracking the leaders, was unable to respond under pressure. (op 13-2)
Thin Red Line(IRE), who was narrowly beaten in the opening race on this day last year and finished third behind Fiery Lad at Epsom, never improved from the rear having been held up. (op 12-1)
Hillview Boy(IRE) won a Listed race over this trip last time but his best form came on good or softer ground, and he had a bit to prove on this surface. He was keen under restraint early but was eased in the straight as if something was amiss but was later reported as being unsuited by the ground. Official explanation: trainer said gelding was unsuited by the good to firm ground (op 9-1)

3673 POKER AT BET365 H'CAP 6f
4:00 (4:01) (Class 2) (0-100,96) 3-Y-O **£12,952** (£3,854; £1,926; £962) **Stalls** Low

Form RPR

11 **1** **Bated Breath**[26] 2815 3-9-6 **95**....... RichardHughes 5 111+
(R Charlton) *hld up bhd ldrs: smooth hdwy to ld 1f out: sn qcknd away: pushed out: smart prospect* **4/5**[1]

-412 **2** 3 **Little Garcon (USA)**[24] 2862 3-8-13 **88**....... MartinDwyer 7 94+
(M Botti) *hld up in rr: hdwy on outer whn carried rt 1f out: styd on to take 2nd fnl 120yds: no ch w wnr* **11/2**[3]

6034 **3** 3¼ **Secret Millionaire (IRE)**[10] 3311 3-8-10 **85**....... StephenCraine 3 81
(Patrick Morris) *in rr: hdwy 2f out: chsd ldrs and ev ch over 1f out: sn rdn: one pce ins fnl f* **28/1**

5362 **4** 1¾ **Living It Large (FR)**[14] 3218 3-9-0 **89**....... TedDurcan 6 79
(R F Fisher) *w ldr: rdn 2f out: u.p whn n.m.r 1f out: sn lost pl: one pce after* **12/1**

3133 **5** 2 **Confessional**[14] 3218 3-8-12 **87**.......(p) DavidAllan 8 71
(T D Easterby) *led: rdn whn hung rt and hdd 1f out: sn wknd* **5/1**[2]

0-05 **6** *hd* **Tasmeem (IRE)**[58] 1836 3-8-8 **83**....... PaulHanagan 10 66
(R A Fahey) *chsd ldrs: pushed along over 2f out: sn outpcd: wknd ins fnl f* **17/2**

44- **7** 12 **Rahya Cass (IRE)**[267] 6651 3-9-6 **95**.......(t) SteveDrowne 2 40
(J R Gask) *prom tl rdn and wknd over 1f out* **33/1**

1m 12.82s (-0.68) **Going Correction** +0.05s/f (Good) **7** Ran SP% **112.2**
Speed ratings (Par 106): **106,102,97,95,92 92,76**
Tote Swingers: 1&2 £1.90, 1&3 £6.00, 2&3 £10.20 CSF £5.39 CT £63.01 TOTE £1.80: £1.20, £3.20; EX 5.40.
Owner K Abdulla **Bred** Juddmonte Farms Ltd **Trained** Beckhampton, Wilts

FOCUS
A good 3-y-o sprint handicap in which there had been no obvious draw advantage in recent runnings, and they raced up the centre of the track. The time compared favourably with the following conditions race for older horses. The winner looks to have Group potential and the second is progressive too.

NOTEBOOK
Bated Breath ◆ had won a decent maiden and a handicap, both at Pontefract, and retained his unbeaten record in the style of a potential Group horse. Always going well in the wake of the leaders, he came through smoothly and scored without being extended. Listed races are probably next on the agenda, although connections indicated that heritage handicaps might be preferred, as the prizemoney is better. The long-term aim is the Sprint Cup back here next season. (tchd 10-11)
Little Garcon(USA), a dual Polytrack winner, was held up at the back and was making headway when hampered by the long-time leader entering the last furlong. He recovered to keep on well, but would not have beaten the winner, even with a clear passage. (tchd 5-1 and 6-1)
Secret Millionaire(IRE) has been running creditably in handicaps this season off similar marks and sets the standard. He came from off the pace and, although unable to contend with the first two, looks the best guide to the form. (op 25-1)
Living It Large(FR) showed plenty of pace but is best at 5f and faded entering the final furlong. (op 10-1)
Confessional, another consistent sort, set the pace but had just been headed when jinking right about a furlong from home, hampering the runner-up. (op 7-1 tchd 9-2)
Tasmeem(IRE) was struggling by the quarter-mile pole and has yet to recapture his juvenile form since joining his current yard. (op 8-1 tchd 15-2)

3674 BET365.COM CONDITIONS STKS 6f
4:35 (4:36) (Class 2) 3-Y-O+
£14,019 (£4,198; £2,099; £1,050; £524; £263) **Stalls** Low

Form RPR

3-46 **1** **Genki (IRE)**[14] 3193 6-8-11 103.......(b[1]) SteveDrowne 1 109+
(R Charlton) *racd keenly: hld up: hdwy over 1f out: led ins fnl f: r.o and fnd more towards fin* **13/8**[1]

1300 **2** *nk* **Rileyskeepingfaith**[7] 3461 4-8-11 101.......(v) AlanMunro 9 108
(M R Channon) *midfield: rdn and hdwy over 1f out: str chal and ev ch ins fnl f: r.o but looked hld towards fin* **7/1**

-100 **3** *hd* **Castles In The Air**[15] 3146 5-8-11 100....... PaulHanagan 2 107
(R A Fahey) *hld up: hdwy over 1f out: rdn to mount str chal and ev ch ins fnl f: nt qckn fnl strides* **9/2**[3]

-502 **4** 2¾ **Enderby Spirit (GR)**[16] 3108 4-8-11 97.......(v) RichardMullen 4 99
(B Smart) *hld up: rdn and hdwy over 1f out: sn hung lft u.p: one pce and no imp on ldrs fnl 100yds* **20/1**

0305 **5** 1¼ **Edge Closer**[7] 3461 6-8-11 102....... RichardHughes 10 99+
(R Hannon) *led: rdn over 1f out: hdd ins fnl f and sn n.m.r and hmpd: lost grnd: n.d fnl 100yds* **4/1**[2]

3044 **6** *hd* **Fitz Flyer (IRE)**[35] 2526 4-8-11 100....... PhillipMakin 6 94
(D H Brown) *racd keenly: prom: rdn over 1f out: wkng whn forced lft fnl 150yds* **25/1**

2201 **7** ½ **Captain Dunne (IRE)**[8] 3406 5-9-2 104....... DavidAllan 11 97
(T D Easterby) *prom: rdn over 1f out: n.m.r whn wkng ins fnl f* **10/1**

-116 **8** 1¾ **Global City (IRE)**[120] 817 4-9-2 106.......(t) TedDurcan 3 92
(Saeed Bin Suroor) *in tch: rdn to chal over 1f out: wknd ent fnl f* **10/1**

1m 12.7s (-0.80) **Going Correction** +0.05s/f (Good) **8** Ran SP% **115.6**
Speed ratings (Par 109): **107,106,106,102,101 100,100,97**
Tote Swingers: 1&2 £3.40, 1&3 £3.50, 2&3 £4.80 CSF £13.99 TOTE £3.00: £1.40, £2.10, £1.70; EX 14.40.
Owner Ms Gillian Khosla **Bred** Rathbarry Stud **Trained** Beckhampton, Wilts
■ Stewards' Enquiry : Alan Munro one-day ban: used whip without giving gelding time to respond (Jul 17)

FOCUS
A high-class and tightly knit conditions sprint run 0.12secs faster than the preceding handicap. The form makes a good deal of sense.

NOTEBOOK
Genki(IRE) is a pretty reliable performer who competes in most of the top-class sprint handicaps, and came into this off the back of a good effort in the Wokingham. Wearing blinkers for the first time, he was quite keen under restraint early but travelled well into the race and found enough to score slightly more comfortably than the official margin suggests. Presumably the winner will be on course for Glorious Goodwood, where he will attempt to win a second Stewards' Cup at the end of the month. He is quoted as short as 8-1 for that race, and connections might try a visor to enable the gelding to see more. (op 2-1 tchd 5-4 and 9-4 in a place)
Rileyskeepingfaith ◆ finished behind the winner in the Wokingham but was 1lb worse off and did well to give him a race. He has been running well all season and looks capable of picking up a decent prize before long. (tchd 8-1)
Castles In The Air is better known as a 7f performer but three of his four wins have been at this trip. He came from off the pace to challenge and only went down narrowly. He could be the sort for a race like the Ayr Gold Cup. (op 6-1 tchd 13-2)
Enderby Spirit(GR) had a bit to find at the weights but ran reasonably, although drifting away from the action to the far rail did not help his chance in the last furlong. (op 14-1)
Edge Closer, who finished between today's first two in the Wokingham, made the running but was just fading out of things when hampered inside the last furlong. He is running reasonably but needs to step up, and connections might consider trying headgear in view of how it worked on today's winner. (op 5-1)
Fitz Flyer(IRE) ran his race but is arguably best at 5f. (op 20-1)
Captain Dunne(IRE) was another who is best suited by the minimum trip and faded in the closing stages. (op 8-1)
Global City(IRE) was returning from a break and looked a threat 2f out, but he faded as if the run was needed. Official explanation: jockey said colt had no more to give (op 15-2)

3675 CASINO AT BET365.COM H'CAP 5f
5:10 (5:11) (Class 4) (0-80,80) 3-Y-O+ **£5,504** (£1,637; £818; £408) **Stalls** Low

Form RPR

3232 **1** **Hazelrigg (IRE)**[9] 3356 5-9-0 **68**.......(bt[1]) DavidAllan 6 81
(T D Easterby) *hld up in rr: hdwy wl over 1f out: wnt 2nd sn after: rdn to ld fnl 100yds: carried hd high: jst lasted* **2/1**[1]

00-1 **2** *nk* **Foxy Music**[32] 2622 6-9-12 **80**....... RichardHughes 1 92
(E J Alston) *led: rdn ins fnl f: hdd fnl 100yds: rallied and pushed wnr to line* **3/1**[2]

0650 **3** 2½ **Haajes**[31] 2657 6-9-10 **78**....... PhillipMakin 2 81
(P T Midgley) *hld up: rdn over 1f out: styd on to chse front pair fnl 100yds: no imp* **7/2**[3]

6502 **4** *nk* **Misaro (GER)**[6] 3474 9-9-4 **72**.......(b) JoeFanning 8 74
(R A Harris) *chsd ldr: rdn 2f out: lost 2nd over 1f out: kpt on same pce ins fnl f* **6/1**

0-00 **5** *hd* **Tyrannosaurus Rex (IRE)**[8] 3417 6-9-3 **71**....... PaulHanagan 7 72
(D Shaw) *hld up: rdn ins fnl f: styd on u.p fnl 100yds: nt pce to mount serious chal* **7/1**

0100 **6** 2¼ **Memphis Man**[7] 3430 7-8-12 **73**....... MatthewCosham(7) 5 66
(P D Evans) *chsd front pair tl over 2f out: sn pushed along and outpcd: n.d after* **16/1**

60.61 secs (-0.39) **Going Correction** +0.05s/f (Good) **6** Ran SP% **113.2**
Speed ratings (Par 105): **105,104,100,100,99 96**
Tote Swingers: 1&2 £1.70, 1&3 £2.30, 2&3 £2.80 CSF £8.38 CT £18.47 TOTE £2.60: £1.70, £2.10; EX 8.00.
Owner The Senators **Bred** Rathbarry Stud **Trained** Great Habton, N Yorks

■ Stewards' Enquiry : David Allan one-day ban: used whip without giving gelding time to respond (Jul 17)

FOCUS
An ordinary sprint handicap and the field came to race on the stands' side. The winner is rated to last year's best.

3676 FINANCIALS AT BET365.COM H'CAP — 1m 30y
5:45 (5:45) (Class 5) (0-75,75) 3-Y-0+ £4,857 (£1,445; £722; £360) Stalls Low

Form / RPR

1166 **1** **Sir Frank Wappat**[64] 1663 3-9-2 72 .... JoeFanning 4 77
(M Johnston) *mde all: rdn over 1f out: sn hung lft: kpt on gamely ins fnl f* **8/1**[3]

6552 **2** ¾ **Star Addition**[5] 3520 4-8-9 56 oh6 .... TedDurcan 6 62
(E J Alston) *trckd ldrs: chal 2f out: sn rdn: wnt 2nd 1f out: kpt on u.p towards fin but hld* **14/1**

5100 **3** ¾ **War And Peace (IRE)**[8] 3391 6-9-7 68 .... GeorgeBaker 7 72
(P D Evans) *a.p: rdn to chal 2f out: nt qckn over 1f out: kpt on u.p ins fnl f: hld clsng stages* **8/1**[3]

2134 **4** 2¾ **Ninth House (USA)**[7] 3438 8-9-4 65 ....(t) EddieAhern 12 63+
(Mrs R A Carr) *hld up: hmpd 6f out: hdwy on outer over 2f out: rdn whn chsng ldrs over 1f out: styd on same pce fnl 110yds* **5/2**[2]

-051 **5** ½ **Yabtree (IRE)**[15] 3171 3-9-1 71 .... SteveDrowne 11 66+
(R Charlton) *midfield: rdn and hdwy 3f out: chsd ldrs 2f out: no ex fnl 75yds* **2/1**[1]

-400 **6** 2½ **Music Maestro (IRE)**[23] 2892 3-9-2 72 .... MichaelHills 3 61
(B W Hills) *hld up: pushed along 4f out: effrt bhd ldrs 3f out: one pce over 1f out* **11/1**

05-6 **7** 2¾ **Major Monty (IRE)**[14] 3207 3-8-2 58 .... HayleyTurner 2 40
(Tom Dascombe) *racd keenly: trckd ldrs: rdn and nt qckn over 2f out: btn over 1f out* **20/1**

-205 **8** 3½ **Soho Theatre**[15] 3171 3-9-3 73 ....(b) ChrisCatlin 10 47
(D R C Elsworth) *racd keenly: hld up: hmpd 6f out: rdn over 2f out: nvr on terms* **16/1**

5430 **9** 13 **Timber Treasure (USA)**[9] 3358 6-9-0 61 ....(b) RichardHughes 9 8
(Paul Green) *midfield: pushed along 2f out: dropped away over 1f out* **16/1**

1m 45.08s (0.38) **Going Correction** +0.05s/f (Good)
WFA 3 from 4yo+ 9lb 9 Ran SP% **115.7**
Speed ratings (Par 103): **95,94,93,90,90 87,85,81,68**
Tote Swingers: 1&2 £7.80, 1&3 £10.50, 2&3 £13.60 CSF £112.00 CT £925.72 TOTE £9.10: £2.50, £2.80, £2.10; EX 87.10 Place 6 £127.10, Place 5 £19.99.
Owner Paul Dean **Bred** Itchen Valley Stud **Trained** Middleham Moor, N Yorks
■ Stewards' Enquiry : Steve Drowne two-day ban: careless riding (Jul 17-18)

FOCUS
A run-of-the-mill handicap in which the majority were closely matched judged on official marks. It proved difficult to come from behind and the first three were in the first quartet throughout. The form is a bit muddling but the second and third were close to their marks.
T/Plt: £349.70 to a £1 stake. Pool: £120,391.23. 251.30 winning tickets. T/Qpdt: £46.40 to a £1 stake. Pool: £6,677.81. 106.35 winning tickets. DO

3358 LEICESTER (R-H)
Saturday, July 3

OFFICIAL GOING: Good to firm (firm in places; 8.6)
Wind: Light, behind Weather: Cloudy with sunny spells

3677 JOHN SMITH'S FILLIES' H'CAP — 5f 218y
1:55 (1:56) (Class 5) (0-70,70) 3-Y-O £3,238 (£963; £481; £240) Stalls Centre

Form / RPR

-002 **1** **Thalia Grace**[14] 3210 3-8-5 54 .... KirstyMilczarek 11 62
(L Montague Hall) *trckd ldrs: rdn to ld over 1f out: r.o* **16/1**

1600 **2** 1½ **Posy Fossil (USA)**[8] 3390 3-8-8 60 ....(vt[1]) WilliamCarson(3) 3 63
(S C Williams) *led: rdn and hdd over 1f out: styd on same pce ins fnl f* **12/1**

5001 **3** 1 **Grand Zafeen**[10] 3313 3-9-7 70 .... AlanMunro 4 70+
(M R Channon) *hld up: rdn 1/2-way: hdwy over 1f out: r.o to go 3rd nr fin: nt rch ldrs* **9/1**

0000 **4** 1 **Dream Number (IRE)**[10] 3336 3-9-2 65 .... NeilCallan 5 62
(W R Muir) *chsd ldrs: rdn over 1f out: styd on same pce fnl f: lost 3rd nr fin* **8/1**

1335 **5** nk **Flouncing (IRE)**[15] 3174 3-9-6 69 .... PatCosgrave 10 65+
(W J Haggas) *hld up: hdwy over 1f out: r.o: nt trble ldrs* **4/1**[2]

5631 **6** ½ **Decency (IRE)**[10] 3336 3-9-3 66 .... PatDobbs 12 60+
(E A L Dunlop) *s.s: hld up: r.o ins fnl f: nvr nrr* **3/1**[1]

6244 **7** 1½ **Mrs Boss**[10] 3336 3-8-13 65 .... JamesMillman(3) 8 54
(B R Millman) *chsd ldrs: rdn over 2f out: no ex fnl f* **13/2**[3]

43-0 **8** nse **Kenyan Cat**[33] 2588 3-9-5 68 .... DaraghO'Donohoe 6 57
(George Baker) *sn outpcd: styd on ins fnl f: nvr nrr* **28/1**

0050 **9** 1½ **Elegant Dancer (IRE)**[8] 3387 3-8-5 54 oh1 ow3 .... RichardKingscote 2 38
(Paul Green) *w ldr: rdn over 2f out: wknd over 1f out* **10/1**

6-00 **10** 2¼ **Gibraltar Lass (USA)**[29] 2702 3-8-2 51 oh1 .... CathyGannon 7 28
(H J Collingridge) *mid-div: pushed along 1/2-way: rdn and wknd over 1f out* **25/1**

40 **11** 2½ **Sammuramat (IRE)**[14] 3227 3-8-10 59 .... JerryO'Dwyer 1 28
(M G Quinlan) *hld up in tch: rdn over 2f out: wknd over 1f out* **20/1**

00-0 **12** 2 **Grand Mary (IRE)**[14] 3210 3-8-2 51 oh2 .... FrankieMcDonald 9 14
(P F I Cole) *hld up: hdwy over 2f out: wknd wl over 1f out* **50/1**

1m 11.47s (-1.53) **Going Correction** -0.225s/f (Firm) 12 Ran SP% **116.1**
Speed ratings (Par 97): **101,99,97,96,95 95,93,93,91,88 84,82**
Tote Swingers: 1&2 £71.90, 1&3 £31.80, 2&3 £50.00 CSF £182.30 CT £1860.37 TOTE £15.50: £6.40, £4.70, £3.40; EX 301.40 TRIFECTA Not won..
Owner The Gracie Partnership **Bred** Bob Pain **Trained** Epsom, Surrey

FOCUS
An interesting sprint fillies' handicap run ito it and the form is rated around the runner-up.

3678 JOHN SMITH'S EXTRA SMOOTH (S) STKS — 5f 218y
2:30 (2:30) (Class 6) 2-Y-O £1,942 (£578; £288; £144) Stalls Centre

Form / RPR

4550 **1** **Silly Billy (IRE)**[22] 2939 2-8-11 0 .... PatDobbs 11 60
(S Kirk) *hld up: hdwy 1/2-way: led over 1f out: rdn out* **11/1**

00 **2** nk **Lord Of The Storm**[31] 2638 2-8-8 0 .... JackDean(3) 2 59
(W G M Turner) *a.p: rdn and ev ch whn hung rt ins fnl f: styd on* **40/1**

60 **3** 1¼ **Barista (IRE)**[77] 1389 2-8-11 0 .... PaulEddery 10 55
(M R Channon) *stdd s: hld up: hdwy over 1f out: sn rdn: styd on* **10/1**[3]

005 **4** 5 **Majestic Style (IRE)**[12] 3260 2-8-6 0 .... RichardKingscote 9 35
(A P Jarvis) *chsd ldrs: rdn over 2f out: wknd fnl f* **22/1**

6441 **5** 1¼ **Nellie Ellis (IRE)**[24] 2848 2-8-11 0 .... NeilCallan 4 39
(K A Ryan) *chsd ldr: led 2f out: sn rdn and hdd: hld whn hmpd and wknd ins fnl f* **8/11**[1]

00 **6** ¾ **Bert And Ernie**[19] 3035 2-8-6 0 .... MatthewDavies(5) 3 34+
(M R Channon) *sn drvn along in rr: styd on ins fnl f: nvr nrr* **33/1**

20 **7** 1¾ **Thakeham (IRE)**[18] 3058 2-8-11 0 .... PatCosgrave 6 29
(P D Evans) *led: racd keenly: hdd 2f out: wknd fnl f* **7/2**[2]

2022 **8** 7 **Calormen**[43] 2300 2-8-11 0 .... VinceSlattery 7 8
(A G Juckes) *sn prom: rdn over 2f out: wknd wl over 1f out* **12/1**

046 **9** 2 **Nalany**[47] 2183 2-8-6 0 .... FrankieMcDonald 1 —
(D Haydn Jones) *sn pushed along in rr: wknd 2f out* **50/1**

1m 11.98s (-1.02) **Going Correction** -0.225s/f (Firm) 9 Ran SP% **116.9**
Speed ratings (Par 92): **97,96,94,88,86 85,83,73,71**
Tote Swingers: 1&2 £35.10, 1&3 £7.60, 2&3 £45.30 CSF £362.09 TOTE £17.20: £4.00, £7.20, £2.90; EX 184.20 TRIFECTA Not won..There was no bid for the winner.
Owner Lady Davis **Bred** Sir E J Loder **Trained** Upper Lambourn, Berks

FOCUS
A weak seller with only one winner in the field beforehand but run at a good clip, with the front three pulling clear of the remainder.

NOTEBOOK
Silly Billy(IRE) has moderate form in maidens and fared no better when dropped to this grade last time, but this was a weak affair and so he had some claims. He stuck on well when challenged from over 1f out to win driven out. There was no bid at the auction and it remains to be seen if he can build on this. (op 9-1)

Lord Of The Storm is a half-brother to Avonbridge but had shown precious little in two runs and was dropping into selling company on his first try at the trip. He held every chance throughout the final furlong but could not get on top. His trainer does well in this type of race so he should find a similarly weak affair. Official explanation: jockey said gelding hung right (op 50-1)

Barista(IRE) had been well beaten on both starts on the AW and on turf but was having his first run for Mick Channon and showed a degree of promise. Coming from the rear to chase the leaders over a furlong out, he kept on without laying down a serious threat. (op 16-1)

Majestic Style(IRE) is exposed as moderate and was being dropped to this grade. She could never get involved off the early pace, although staying on best of the rest. (op 14-1)

Nellie Ellis(IRE) was a little awkward leaving the stalls but was a warm order. She was being upped in trip and appeared not to see it out after holding every chance when stopping quickly entering the final furlong. (op 11-10 after 11-8 in a place)

Bert And Ernie was a no-show in similar company last time and was struggling to get on terms from a fair way out. He stayed on in the latter stages and might benefit form a step up in distance but looks moderate.

3679 JOHN SMITH'S EUROPEAN BREEDERS' FUND FILLIES' H'CAP — 1m 1f 218y
3:00 (3:00) (Class 4) (0-80,80) 3-Y-O+ £6,308 (£1,888; £944; £472; £235) Stalls High

Form / RPR

1024 **1** **Bollin Dolly**[8] 3416 7-9-11 77 .... DavidNolan 1 86
(T D Easterby) *mde all: led at stdy pce tl qcknd over 2f out: rdn over 1f out: eased towards fin* **2/1**[1]

33-0 **2** 3 **Ethics Girl (IRE)**[14] 3217 4-9-9 75 .... IvaMilickova 5 78
(John Berry) *a.p: rdn over 2f out: chsd wnr fnl f: styd on same pce* **10/1**

-532 **3** 1 **Tut (IRE)**[26] 2816 3-9-2 79 .... AndrewElliott 3 80
(J R Weymes) *chsd wnr: rdn over 2f out: lost 2nd 1f out: styd on same pce* **5/2**[2]

0000 **4** 2¾ **Caster Sugar (USA)**[19] 3031 4-10-0 80 .... PatDobbs 2 76
(R Hannon) *chsd ldrs: rdn over 2f out: wknd over 1f out* **7/2**[3]

3112 **5** 7 **Granny McPhee**[8] 3388 4-9-3 76 .... NatashaEaton(7) 7 58
(A Bailey) *s.v.s: hdwy over 6f out: rdn over 3f out: wknd over 2f out* **9/2**

2m 5.57s (-2.33) **Going Correction** -0.10s/f (Good)
WFA 3 from 4yo+ 11lb 5 Ran SP% **111.4**
Speed ratings (Par 102): **105,102,101,99,94**
CSF £20.70 TOTE £2.20: £1.40, £2.90; EX 27.60 TRIFECTA Not won..
Owner Sir Neil Westbrook **Bred** Sir Neil And Lady Westbrook **Trained** Great Habton, N Yorks

FOCUS
A much-depleted field for this tight-looking fillies' middle-distance handicap run at a muddling pace. The form is rated around the winner, who made all.

3680 JOHN SMITH'S EXTRA COLD RATING RELATED MAIDEN STKS — 7f 9y
3:35 (3:35) (Class 5) 3-Y-O £2,590 (£770; £385; £192) Stalls Centre

Form / RPR

2034 **1** **Goolagong (IRE)**[21] 2956 3-8-12 70 .... JackMitchell 10 77
(R M Beckett) *hld up: hdwy over 2f out: led and edgd lft fr over 1f out: rdn out* **6/1**[3]

3-64 **2** 1¾ **Sir Bruno (FR)**[47] 2170 3-9-1 70 .... AndreaAtzeni 6 75
(B Palling) *hld up: hdwy 1/2-way: rdn to chse wnr over 1f out: styd on* **12/1**

2663 **3** 3¾ **Jimmy The Poacher (IRE)**[8] 3387 3-9-1 67 ....(b) DavidNolan 8 65
(T D Easterby) *chsd ldrs: rdn over 2f out: ev ch over 1f out: styd on same pce fnl f* **9/1**

4-20 **4** 3 **Redden**[39] 2416 3-9-1 70 .... PatCosgrave 12 57
(W J Haggas) *hld up in tch: led over 2f out: rdn and hdd over 1f out: wknd ins fnl f* **9/1**

5-35 **5** 1¾ **Beaumont's Party (IRE)**[11] 3297 3-9-1 70 .... PatDobbs 1 52
(R Hannon) *hld up: rdn over 2f out: styd on ins fnl f: nvr nrr* **5/1**[2]

0343 **6** ¾ **On The Cusp (IRE)**[8] 3413 3-9-1 65 .... NeilCallan 11 50
(M A Jarvis) *chsd ldrs: rdn 1/2-way: wknd wl over 1f out* **9/1**

-232 **7** ¾ **Rasselas (IRE)**[8] 3387 3-9-1 71 .... PaulEddery 2 48
(B W Hills) *stdd s: hld up: rdn over 2f out: no rspnse* **15/8**[1]

-003 **8** ¾ **Wild Rockette**[12] 3259 3-8-9 69 ....(b) PatrickHills(3) 3 43
(B J Meehan) *hld up: hdwy 1/2-way: hung rt and wknd over 1f out* **12/1**

-060 **9** 12 **Quaestor (IRE)**[82] 1269 3-9-1 70 .... RichardKingscote 5 14
(Tom Dascombe) *chsd ldrs tl rdn and wknd over 2f out* **50/1**

4604 **10** 9 **Jack O'Lantern**[15] 3148 3-9-1 69 ....(b[1]) PaulMulrennan 4 —
(R A Fahey) *sn led: hdd & wknd over 2f out* **25/1**

1m 23.14s (-3.06) **Going Correction** -0.225s/f (Firm) 10 Ran SP% **116.9**
Speed ratings (Par 100): **108,106,101,98,96 95,94,93,80,69**
Tote Swingers: 1&2 £11.70, 1&3 £61.80, 2&3 £17.90 CSF £75.63 TOTE £10.10: £2.50, £3.30, £3.00; EX 97.00 TRIFECTA Not won..
Owner R A Pegum **Bred** Swordlestown Stud **Trained** Whitsbury, Hants

FOCUS
A competitive but ordinary maiden in which most of them were closely matched. It was strongly run and has been rated around the runner-up.

3681 JOHN SMITH'S NO NONSENSE H'CAP 7f 9y
4:10 (4:10) (Class 3) (0-95,93) 3-Y-0+
£7,477 (£2,239; £1,119; £560; £279; £140) **Stalls** Centre

Form RPR
0-02 **1** **Arabian Mirage**[18] 3063 4-9-6 **85** .... PatCosgrave 5 96
(B J Meehan) *a.p: led 3f out: rdn and hung rt ins fnl f: r.o* **10/1**
3130 **2** *1 ½* **Flowing Cape (IRE)**[10] 3318 5-9-1 **80** .... JackMitchell 6 87
(R Hollinshead) *prom: outpcd 1/2-way: rallied over 1f out: swtchd rt ins fnl f: r.o* **17/2**
2212 **3** *1 ½* **Tesslam**[14] 3215 3-8-13 **86** .... NeilCallan 2 86
(M A Jarvis) *led: hdd over 5f out: chsd ldr: rdn and ev ch over 1f out: edgd rt and styd on same pce ins fnl f* **15/8**[1]
0-55 **4** *½* **Big Noise**[15] 3172 6-9-11 **90** .... MickyFenton 8 92
(Dr J D Scargill) *hld up: hdwy over 2f out: rdn over 1f out: edgd rt and no ex ins fnl f* **5/2**[2]
-004 **5** *½* **Nezami (IRE)**[10] 3334 5-9-7 **86** .... PatDobbs 1 86
(J Akehurst) *chsd ldr tl led over 5f out: hdd 3f out: sn rdn: styd on same pce fr over 1f out* **11/1**
4201 **6** *1 ¼* **Indian Skipper (IRE)**[15] 3178 5-9-3 **85** ....(be) AndrewHeffernan(3) 3 82
(R C Guest) *dwlt: hdwy 1/2-way: rdn 2f out: styd on same pce* **14/1**
1040 **7** *2* **Hajoum (IRE)**[7] 3448 4-10-0 **93** .... PaulMulrennan 7 84
(M Johnston) *chsd ldrs: rdn 1/2-way: wknd fnl f* **11/2**[3]

1m 23.26s (-2.94) **Going Correction** -0.225s/f (Firm)
WFA 3 from 4yo+ 8lb **7** Ran SP% **113.4**
Speed ratings (Par 107): **107,105,103,103,102 101,98**
Tote Swingers: 1&2 £3.60, 1&3 £7.50, 2&3 £4.70 CSF £86.74 CT £228.37 TOTE £8.30: £3.40, £2.30; EX 73.70 Trifecta £143.20 Pool: £272.89 - 1.41 winning units..
Owner David F O'Rourke **Bred** Minster Stud **Trained** Manton, Wilts

FOCUS
A small field for this competitive handicap run at a strong pace in a time a fraction under the RP Standard. Sound form with a clear personal best from the winner.

NOTEBOOK
Arabian Mirage has been lightly campaigned since finishing fourth in the Nell Gwyn last year but was back on track when second at Thirsk last time when things fell into place. Always up with the pace, she had enough to repel the late thrust of the runner-up inside the distance to be a game winner. The drop back to 7f clearly suited and there should be more opportunities as she has scope for improvement. (op 9-1 tchd 11-1)
Flowing Cape(IRE), a winner over C&D three runs back who needs a bit of luck when coming with a late rattle, had a small field to his benefit but could not quite reel in the winner. He has been in good order this season, and this was another good effort off a fair mark. (op 9-1 tchd 10-1 and 8-1)
Tesslam set off to make this a good test but could only keep on at the same pace when headed. A second decent effort in handicaps and he can remain competitive, although he has become rather expensive to follow. (op 9-4 tchd 5-2 in places)
Big Noise, winner of this last year, had come into the race showing he remains in good heart after a couple of decent efforts in competitive handicaps. He had the pace to suit but, after looking threatening at the 2f marker, could not find the pace to get on terms. (op 3-1 tchd 7-2)
Nezami(IRE) has been lightly raced since finishing second in the Victoria Cup at Royal Ascot last season but was returning to this trip after tackling a couple of competitive handicaps over 1m. He figured prominently for a long way before running on at the same pace from over 1f out. (op 9-1 tchd 17-2)
Hajoum(IRE) raced prominently for 5f but dropped out tamely, this being the second time he has done so after a decent effort in a hot contest at Royal Ascot that seems to have left its mark. (tchd 5-1 and 6-1)

3682 JOHN SMITH'S SPRINT H'CAP 5f 2y
4:45 (4:46) (Class 5) (0-70,70) 3-Y-0
£2,590 (£770; £385; £192) **Stalls** Low

Form RPR
1-40 **1** **Melody In The Mist (FR)**[28] 2768 3-9-7 **70** .... NeilCallan 4 77
(T D Barron) *chsd ldr tl led 1/2-way: rdn and hung rt ins fnl f: r.o* **3/1**[2]
2322 **2** *¾* **Pherousa**[9] 3372 3-9-2 **65** .... FergusSweeney 7 69
(M Blanshard) *chsd ldrs: rdn and edgd rt ins fnl f: styd on same pce* **15/8**[1]
2043 **3** *2 ¾* **Miss Polly Plum**[6] 3480 3-8-2 **51** .... CathyGannon 8 45
(C A Dwyer) *a.p: rdn over 1f out: no ex ins fnl f* **6/1**[3]
0315 **4** *4* **Rathbawn Girl (IRE)**[10] 3336 3-8-1 **57** .... AdamBeschizza(7) 3 37
(Miss J Feilden) *mid-div: rdn 1/2-way: hung rt ins fnl f: nt trble ldrs* **14/1**
543 **5** *1 ¾* **Boy The Bell**[9] 3372 3-8-8 **64** .... JosephYoung(7) 2 38
(M Mullineaux) *dwlt: outpcd: hung rt and r.o ins fnl f: nrst fin* **15/2**
00-6 **6** *½* **Satin Princess (IRE)**[33] 2584 3-7-11 **51** oh6........ AmyBaker(5) 5 23
(A M Hales) *hld up: rdn 1/2-way: nvr on terms* **40/1**
056 **7** *3* **Baby Judge (IRE)**[24] 2876 3-7-9 **51** oh3........ RyanPowell(7) 1 12
(M C Chapman) *sn outpcd: hrd rdn 1/2-way: nvr on terms* **22/1**
56-5 **8** *1 ¼* **The Two G'S**[9] 3372 3-7-13 **51** oh6........(b[1]) AndrewHeffernan(3) 6 8
(R J Price) *led to 1/2-way: wknd over 1f out* **14/1**
0550 **9** *4 ½* **Royal Patriot (IRE)**[18] 3062 3-8-13 **62** .... PatCosgrave 10 2
(Paul Green) *chsd ldrs: rdn 1/2-way: wknd 2f out: eased fnl f* **9/1**

58.79 secs (-1.21) **Going Correction** -0.225s/f (Firm) **9** Ran SP% **116.0**
Speed ratings (Par 100): **100,98,94,88,85 84,79,77,70**
Tote Swingers: 1&2 £1.40, 1&3 £3.90, 2&3 £2.50 CSF £9.06 CT £30.74 TOTE £3.60: £1.40, £1.40, £2.00; EX 10.30 Trifecta £17.90 Pool: £233.56 - 9.60 winning units..
Owner P D Savill **Bred** Ballykilbride Stud **Trained** Maunby, N Yorks

FOCUS
A fairly exposed field for this 51-70 sprint handicap. The winner is rated back towards her initial 2yo form.

3683 JOHN SMITH'S H'CAP 1m 60y
5:20 (5:20) (Class 6) (0-65,65) 3-Y-0+
£2,590 (£770; £385; £192) **Stalls** High

Form RPR
6262 **1** **Macanta (USA)**[10] 3309 4-9-11 **62** ....(p) JackMitchell 10 70
(G A Butler) *hld up: hdwy over 3f out: led over 2f out: drvn out* **7/2**[2]
0504 **2** *½* **Khajaaly (IRE)**[14] 3212 3-9-5 **65** .... JamesMcDonald 9 70
(E A L Dunlop) *hld up: hdwy over 1f out: sn rdn: styd on* **13/2**[3]
5034 **3** *2 ¾* **Second To Nun (IRE)**[10] 3309 4-8-11 **51** .... WilliamCarson(3) 13 52
(M Blanshard) *chsd ldrs: rdn 2f out: outpcd over 1f out: styd on to go 3rd towards fin* **7/1**
310 **4** *¾* **Applaude**[16] 3131 5-9-7 **61** ....(b) AndrewHeffernan(3) 14 60
(R C Guest) *chsd ldrs: hmpd over 2f out: rdn and ev ch over 1f out: no ex ins fnl f* **7/1**
-041 **5** *1 ¼* **Bidable**[16] 3131 6-9-9 **60** .... NeilCallan 12 56
(B Palling) *chsd ldrs: rdn over 3f out: hung rt and no ex ins fnl f* **3/1**[1]
0040 **6** *½* **Orpen Wide (IRE)**[8] 3412 8-9-7 **63** ....(p) MarkCoumbe(5) 11 58
(M C Chapman) *chsd ldrs: rdn over 2f out: hung rt and no ex fnl f* **11/1**
00-5 **7** *4* **Superstitious Me (IRE)**[10] 3309 4-8-13 **50** .... NeilChalmers 4 36
(B Palling) *hld up: rdn over 2f out: nvr on terms* **20/1**
0120 **8** *½* **Shared Moment (IRE)**[16] 3131 4-9-8 **59** ....(b[1]) FergusSweeney 3 43
(J Gallagher) *hld up: hdwy over 1f out: wknd ins fnl f* **10/1**
6000 **9** *2 ¾* **Chadwell Spring (IRE)**[29] 2714 4-9-4 **62** .... AdamBeschizza(7) 1 40
(Miss J Feilden) *sn led: hdd 5f out: rdn whn hmpd over 2f out: sn wknd* **22/1**
4-10 **10** *2* **Munich (IRE)**[103] 965 6-9-12 **63** ....(p) AndreaAtzeni 7 37
(R Curtis) *hld up: rdn over 3f out: a in rr* **14/1**
00-5 **11** *10* **Nomoretaxes (BRZ)**[30] 2678 8-10-0 **65** ....(bt) JAlKaabi 2 16
(Miss D Mountain) *chsd ldr tl led 5f out: clr 4f out: rdn: hdd and hung lft over 2f out: sn wknd* **33/1**

1m 43.79s (-1.31) **Going Correction** -0.10s/f (Good)
WFA 3 from 4yo+ 9lb **11** Ran SP% **121.7**
Speed ratings (Par 101): **102,101,98,98,96 96,92,91,89,87 77**
Tote Swingers: 1&2 £6.30, 1&3 £8.20, 2&3 £12.20 CSF £27.00 CT £156.13 TOTE £3.80: £1.20, £2.40, £2.50; EX 22.20 Trifecta £89.70 Part won. Pool: £121.31 - 0.41 winning units. Place 6 £6,134.98, Place 5 £902.29.
Owner Beetle N Wedge Partnership **Bred** March Thoroughbreds **Trained** Newmarket, Suffolk

FOCUS
A low-grade affair but quite open, with a good pace. The form is not rated too positively.
T/Plt: £6,480.50 to a £1 stake. Pool £59,035.54. 6.65 winning tickets. T/Qpdt: £84.60 to a £1 stake. Pool: £5,423.75. 47.40 winning tickets. CR

2895 NOTTINGHAM (L-H)
Saturday, July 3

OFFICIAL GOING: Good to firm (firm in places; 7.5)
Rail out 2m from 2nd dog leg to 1m2f start adding 14yds to advertised distances on round course.
Wind: Light, half against Weather: Fine

3684 AJA LADIES' FEGENTRI WORLD CHAMPIONSHIP INVITATION H'CAP (FOR LADY AMATEUR RIDERS) 1m 2f 50y
6:10 (6:12) (Class 6) (0-60,56) 3-Y-0+
£1,648 (£507; £253) **Stalls** Low

Form RPR
4 **1** **Aragall (GER)**[5] 3520 5-10-7 **56** .... MissRJefferson 5 69+
(George Baker) *s.i.s: hld up in last: stdy hdwy 3f out: led 2f out: rdn clr fnl f* **6/5**[1]
0-50 **2** *3 ½* **Hurricane Thomas (IRE)**[16] 3122 6-10-6 **55** .... MissPhillipaTutty 7 58
(R A Fahey) *led 1f: chsd ldrs: wnt 2nd over 1f out: no imp* **5/1**[3]
2000 **3** *1 ¼* **Desert Fairy**[19] 3032 4-9-10 **45** .... MissTinaHenriksson 6 46
(J W Unett) *sn w ldr: led over 4f out: hdd 2f out: kpt on same pce* **20/1**
2100 **4** *1 ¼* **Nayessence**[49] 2109 4-10-6 **55** ....(t) MissJoannaMason 3 54
(M W Easterby) *chsd ldrs: outpcd over 2f out: kpt on fnl f* **7/2**[2]
0055 **5** *½* **Starburst**[8] 3403 5-10-4 **53** ....(v[1]) MissPaulineBoisgontier 2 51
(Miss Gay Kelleway) *hld up: hdwy on ins to chse ldrs over 3f out: hmpd over 2f out: one pce* **9/1**
6003 **6** *4* **Tres Froide (FR)**[9] 3370 5-10-2 **51** ....(p) MissCBurri 4 41
(N Tinkler) *hld up in tch: effrt over 2f out: sn wknd* **8/1**
0-0 **7** *13* **Apurna**[33] 2600 5-10-2 **51** .... MissNinaWagner 1 16
(John A Harris) *led after 1f: hdd over 4f out: lost pl over 2f out: sn bhd* **40/1**

2m 12.77s (1.07) **Going Correction** -0.075s/f (Good) **7** Ran SP% **112.7**
Speed ratings (Par 101): **92,89,88,87,86 83,73**
toteswingers: 1&2 £1.80, 1&3 £5.00, 2&3 £5.00 CSF £7.36 TOTE £2.80: £1.40, £1.50; EX 8.80.
Owner Mrs Natalie Heath **Bred** Stiftung Gestut Fahrhof **Trained** Moreton Morrell, Warwicks

FOCUS
Due to problems with a pump, watering was limited for this meeting. However, 7mm had been put on the home straight on the previous day and 7mm on the back straight during the morning of this fixture. Racing began with a weak event in which the top weight was rated just 56.

3685 KONICA MINOLTA EAST (S) STKS 6f 15y
6:40 (6:42) (Class 6) 3-4-Y-0
£1,706 (£503; £252) **Stalls** Low

Form RPR
1051 **1** **Timeteam (IRE)**[5] 3510 4-9-2 69 .... RichardEvans(5) 1 70
(P D Evans) *s.s: hdwy over 2f out: r.o to ld last 75yds: readily* **15/8**[1]
-440 **2** *1 ¼* **Frontline Boy (IRE)**[29] 2722 3-8-10 64 ....(t) NeilCallan 12 60
(J R Weymes) *led: hdd wl ins fnl f: no ex* **13/2**[3]
3416 **3** *1 ½* **Anjomarba (IRE)**[12] 3276 3-8-7 62 ....(p) JackDean(3) 7 55
(W G M Turner) *w ldrs: kpt on same pce fnl f* **13/2**[3]
3200 **4** *1 ½* **Rio Caribe (IRE)**[15] 3180 3-8-10 68 ....(b[1]) GrahamGibbons 4 50
(T D Walford) *s.i.s: hdwy to chse ldrs over 2f out: hung bdly lft over 1f out: one pce* **10/1**
-030 **5** *2 ¾* **Otterton**[9] 3359 3-8-5 40 .... PaulEddery 9 37
(R Hollinshead) *dwlt: in rr: wnt lft and sme hdwy 2f out: nvr nr ldrs* **50/1**
4666 **6** *nk* **Hounds Ditch**[9] 3359 3-8-10 55 .... LiamKeniry 6 41
(Eve Johnson Houghton) *mid-div: reminders sn after s: rdn and hung lft 2f out: one pce* **25/1**
0250 **7** *¾* **Macroy**[19] 3030 3-8-10 62 ow3........ JamesMillman(3) 10 41
(B R Millman) *chsd ldrs: sn pushed along: one pce fnl 2f* **9/1**
0-00 **8** *2* **Wigan Lane**[155] 346 3-8-2 56........ Louis-PhilippeBeuzelin(3) 11 27
(P Howling) *chsd ldrs: hung lft and lost pl over 1f out* **25/1**
6065 **9** *½* **Itsthursdayalready**[8] 3393 3-8-10 62........(b) PaulMulrennan 8 30
(J G Given) *w ldr: t.k.h: hung lft and lost pl over 1f out* **10/3**[2]
006- **10** *13* **Taeping (IRE)**[197] 7793 3-8-3 47 .... NicolaJackson(7) 2 —
(R Hollinshead) *rrd s: sn chsng ldrs on outside: wknd over 2f out: sn bhd* **40/1**
0000 **11** *10* **Aim'Ees Star**[9] 3359 3-8-0 38 .... DeclanCannon(5) 3 —
(John A Harris) *chsd ldrs: lost pl over 3f out: bhd whn hung lft and eased 2f out* **100/1**

1m 14.15s (-0.75) **Going Correction** -0.075s/f (Good)
WFA 3 from 4yo 6lb **11** Ran SP% **116.7**
Speed ratings (Par 101): **102,100,98,96,92 92,91,88,87,70 57**
toteswingers: 1&2 £4.90, 1&3 £3.20, 2&3 £7.30 CSF £13.79 TOTE £4.20: £2.10, £1.60, £1.30; EX 13.20.There was no bid for the winner.
Owner Roger Ambrose & William Reilly **Bred** R N Auld **Trained** Pandy, Monmouths

FOCUS
A modest seller, lacking depth.
Rio Caribe(IRE) Official explanation: jockey said gelding hung left

Aim'Ees Star Official explanation: trainer said filly was unsuited by the good to firm (firm in places) ground

3686 GOLDEVA MAIDEN AUCTION FILLIES' STKS — 5f 13y

7:10 (7:11) (Class 5) 2-Y-O — **£2,590** (£770; £385; £192) **Stalls** High

Form				RPR
034	1		**Second Encore**[5] 3509 2-8-8 0 ... LiamKeniry 10 (J S Moore) *mde all stands' side: rdn 1f out: kpt on wl: readily* **6/4**[1]	72+
	2	2 1/4	**Ishbelle** 2-8-1 0 ow2 ... JohnFahy(5) 1 (R M Beckett) *s.s and wnt lft s: bhd tl hdwy on outer over 2f out: styd on to take 2nd clsng stages* **6/1**	62+
3	3	3/4	**Best Be Careful (IRE)**[10] 3331 2-8-4 0 ... LukeMorris 3 (M D I Usher) *chsd ldrs on outer: outpcd over 2f out: hrd rdn and chsng ldrs over 1f out: one pce* **7/2**[2]	57
0	4	1 1/4	**Venus Empress**[14] 3204 2-8-8 0 ... GrahamGibbons 8 (E S McMahon) *chsd ldrs: kpt on same pce appr fnl f* **15/2**	57
33	5	hd	**Kokojo (IRE)**[21] 2963 2-8-8 0 ... FergusSweeney 7 (B G Powell) *chsd ldrs: kpt on same pce fnl 2f* **5/1**[3]	56
00	6	3/4	**Key To The Motion (IRE)**[24] 2873 2-8-4 0 ... DuranFentiman 2 (P T Midgley) *wnt lft s: hld up in rr: hdwy over 1f out: nvr nr ldrs* **66/1**	49
53	7	shd	**Slatey Hen (IRE)**[31] 2649 2-8-7 0 ... DeclanCannon(5) 5 (A J McCabe) *chsd ldrs: sddle sn slipped: 4th whn eased clsng stages* **16/1**	60+
	8	3 1/2	**Alhoralhora (IRE)** 2-8-8 0 ... PaulMulrennan 4 (J G Given) *s.i.s: a in rr* **25/1**	40+
030	9	2 3/4	**My Mate Al**[31] 2638 2-8-4 0 ... RichardKingscote 6 (Tom Dascombe) *chsd ldrs: lost pl over 1f out* **33/1**	26

60.51 secs (-0.49) **Going Correction** -0.075s/f (Good) **9** Ran SP% **119.1**
Speed ratings (Par 91): **100,96,95,93,92 91,91,85,81**
toteswingers: 1&2 £3.90, 1&3 £2.50, 2&3 £5.10 CSF £11.46 TOTE £2.30: £1.10, £2.30, £1.90; EX 16.10.
Owner G V March **Bred** D A Yardy **Trained** Upper Lambourn, Berks

FOCUS
A moderate auction maiden.

NOTEBOOK
Second Encore, well backed on each of her last two starts, was again supported and this time scored snugly. Always close up, she established a useful position close to the stands' rail and stayed on much too strongly for her rivals. She was going further clear in the closing stages and may stay another furlong. A nursery looks likely to be her next assignment. (op 3-1)
Ishbelle ◆, a newcomer related to juvenile winners, made an encouraging start to her career. Slowly away, awkward from the stalls and outpaced early on, she had made up a good deal of ground by halfway and launched a late challenge on the wide outside. She had no chance with the winner, but showed enough to suggest she can win a race this season. (op 5-1)
Best Be Careful(IRE) had shown promise when third on her debut ten days previously and again ran creditably. In midfield early on, she plugged on gamely in the closing stages. (op 3-1 tchd 4-1)
Venus Empress had started slowly on her only previous run, but was faster out of the stalls here. She chased the pace from the start, racing in fifth or sixth, and stayed on without ever really promising to make the first three. (op 8-1 tchd 9-1)
Kokojo(IRE), third on both her previous outings, seemed to take a step backwards. She figured prominently to halfway, but lost ground in the closing stages. (op 7-2)
Slatey Hen(IRE), third in this class over the C&D last time out, can be forgiven this as her saddle slipped soon after the start and her rider was hanging on for dear life. Official explanation: jockey said saddle slipped (op 14-1)

3687 MATTHEWS & TANNERT H'CAP — 5f 13y

7:40 (7:40) (Class 5) (0-70,68) 3-Y-O+ — **£2,266** (£674; £337; £168) **Stalls** High

Form				RPR
50-5	1		**Bahamian Ballet**[16] 3114 8-9-13 **67** ... GrahamGibbons 6 (E S McMahon) *trckd ldrs gng wl: hdwy to ld 1f out: pushed out* **7/2**[2]	78
-500	2	1/2	**Francis Walsingham (IRE)**[14] 3205 4-9-9 **63** ...(bt) RobertWinston 10 (H Morrison) *s.s: hdwy stands' side over 2f out: styd on to take 2nd last 50yds* **10/1**	72
-100	3	1 1/2	**Micky Mac (IRE)**[18] 3064 6-9-8 **62** ... NeilCallan 9 (C J Teague) *chsd ldrs: led over 1f out: hung lft: sn hdd and no ex* **14/1**	66
0121	4	hd	**Silvanus (IRE)**[5] 3497 5-9-13 **67** 6ex ... PaulMulrennan 4 (P T Midgley) *stdd s: hld up in rr: swtchd lft and hdwy 2f out: upsides 1f out: kpt on same pce* **9/4**[1]	70
0000	5	3/4	**Vhujon (IRE)**[9] 3373 5-9-9 **68** ... RichardEvans(5) 8 (P D Evans) *in rr: hdwy over 1f out: nt clr run and swtchd lft ins fnl f: hung rt and kpt on: nt rch ldrs* **6/1**[3]	72+
6000	6	1 3/4	**King Of Swords (IRE)**[26] 2818 6-9-6 **60** ...(p) DaraghO'Donohoe 2 (N Tinkler) *towards rr: hdwy on outer over 2f out: chsng ldrs 1f out: kpt on same pce* **17/2**	54
0-02	7	hd	**Baby Queen (IRE)**[28] 2751 4-9-8 **62** ... J-PGuillambert 11 (B P J Baugh) *led on stands' side tl over 1f out: sn wknd* **7/1**	55
0303	8	nse	**Sweet Applause (IRE)**[10] 3328 4-8-8 **55** ... CharlotteKerton(7) 3 (G Prodromou) *in rr-div and sn urged along: nvr a factor* **12/1**	48
003	9	3/4	**Blessed Place**[12] 3255 10-8-4 **49** oh2 ... BillyCray(5) 1 (D J S Ffrench Davis) *racd wd towards centre: w ldr: wknd appr fnl f* **14/1**	39
-000	10	nse	**On The Piste (IRE)**[8] 3393 3-8-12 **57** ... DuranFentiman 5 (L A Mullaney) *chsd ldrs on outer: hung lft and fdd fnl f* **33/1**	47

60.20 secs (-0.80) **Going Correction** -0.075s/f (Good)
WFA 3 from 4yo+ 5lb **10** Ran SP% **123.4**
Speed ratings (Par 103): **103,102,99,99,98 95,95,95,93,93**
toteswingers: 1&2 £6.10, 1&3 £11.60, 2&3 £20.60 CSF £41.13 CT £453.35 TOTE £3.50: £1.30, £5.00, £4.70; EX 42.70.
Owner B N Toye **Bred** B N And Mrs Toye **Trained** Lichfield, Staffs

FOCUS
A run-of-the-mill handicap, with the top weight rated 68.
Micky Mac(IRE) Official explanation: jockey said gelding hung left
Vhujon(IRE) Official explanation: jockey said gelding hung right and was denied a clear run
Blessed Place Official explanation: trainer said gelding was unsuited by the good to firm (firm in places) ground

3688 HAPPY LADIES' NIGHT FROM DG TAXIS H'CAP — 1m 2f 50y

8:10 (8:11) (Class 4) (0-80,79) 3-Y-O+ — **£3,885** (£1,156; £577; £288) **Stalls** Low

Form				RPR
P-00	1		**Geneva Geyser (GER)**[42] 2314 4-9-12 **77** ... MickyFenton 8 (J M P Eustace) *reminders after s: drvn to ld: qcknd over 3f out: styd on: drvn rt out: unchal* **16/1**	90
3232	2	5	**Hawaana (IRE)**[14] 3203 5-9-7 **79** ... AdamBeschizza(7) 6 (Miss Gay Kelleway) *hld up in r: hdwy to trck ldrs 6f out: wnt 2nd 1f out: no imp* **4/1**[3]	83
3552	3	2 3/4	**Mons Calpe (IRE)**[17] 3079 4-9-6 **71** ...(b) NeilCallan 4 (P F I Cole) *awkward to load: t.k.h: trckd ldrs: reminder 4f out: kpt on same pce to take n.d 3rd 1f out* **11/2**	69
1500	4	3 1/4	**Jeer (IRE)**[22] 2937 6-9-11 **76** ...(b) GrahamGibbons 1 (M W Easterby) *t.k.h: trckd ldr: drvn over 3f out: wknd 1f out* **13/2**	68
6662	5	15	**Admirable Duque (IRE)**[26] 2821 4-9-8 **73** ...(p) RobertWinston 2 (D J S Ffrench Davis) *stdd s: hld up in rr: drvn 4f out: hung rt and lost pl over 2f out: sn bhd* **7/2**[2]	37
4301	6	14	**Understory (USA)**[8] 3404 3-8-13 **75** ... JoeFanning 9 (M Johnston) *w ldrs: drvn over 3f out: sn wknd: wl bhd whn eased ins fnl f* **7/4**[1]	12

2m 9.54s (-2.16) **Going Correction** -0.075s/f (Good)
WFA 3 from 4yo+ 11lb **6** Ran SP% **113.2**
Speed ratings (Par 105): **105,101,98,96,84 73**
toteswingers: 1&2 £5.60, 1&3 £13.00, 2&3 £3.90 CSF £78.18 CT £403.43 TOTE £26.10: £10.40, £1.40; EX 45.40.
Owner J C Smith **Bred** Graf And Grafin Von Stauffenberg **Trained** Newmarket, Suffolk

FOCUS
A fair handicap, despite the depleted field, and most seemed to hold solid chances.
Geneva Geyser(GER) Official explanation: trainer said, regarding apparent improvement in form, that his horses had been out of form recently, but were now coming back.
Understory(USA) Official explanation: trainer's rep had no explanation for the poor form shown

3689 THINK TAXI, THINK DG CARS - 0115 9607607 H'CAP — 1m 2f 50y

8:40 (8:40) (Class 5) (0-75,74) 3-Y-O — **£2,266** (£674; £337; £168) **Stalls** Low

Form				RPR
45-5	1		**Mushreq (USA)**[23] 2900 3-9-5 **72** ... TadhgO'Shea 3 (Sir Michael Stoute) *mde all: tk gd grip: drvn 3f out: styd on strly: eased towards fin: unchal* **3/1**[2]	84+
6031	2	3 1/4	**Crunched**[20] 2993 3-9-7 **74** ... HayleyTurner 5 (M L W Bell) *trckd wnr: drvn over 2f out: no imp* **7/4**[1]	77
-440	3	1 1/4	**Skyrider (IRE)**[23] 2901 3-9-7 **74** ... TedDurcan 2 (R Charlton) *s.i.s: sn trcking ldrs: drvn over 3f out: wnt 3rd over 1f out: one pce* **9/2**[3]	75
1-06	4	3/4	**Shoot The Pot (IRE)**[19] 3039 3-8-9 **62** ... RichardKingscote 7 (R M Beckett) *hld up in last: hdwy over 4f out: effrt 3f out: edgd lft and tk 4th over 1f out: one pce* **9/2**[3]	61
-355	5	9	**Step In Time (IRE)**[7] 3451 3-9-5 **72** ... JoeFanning 6 (M Johnston) *hld up in tch: hdwy to chse ldrs over 4f out: drvn over 3f out: wknd over 1f out: sn bhd and eased* **13/2**	54

2m 11.76s (0.06) **Going Correction** -0.075s/f (Good) **5** Ran SP% **111.1**
Speed ratings (Par 100): **96,93,92,91,84**
CSF £8.78 TOTE £2.70: £1.10, £2.40; EX 3.60.
Owner Hamdan Al Maktoum **Bred** W S Farish **Trained** Newmarket, Suffolk

FOCUS
An ordinary handicap, but competitive on paper, despite three withdrawals.

3690 LIFE&STYLE MAGAZINE H'CAP — 1m 75y

9:10 (9:10) (Class 5) (0-70,70) 3-Y-O+ — **£2,266** (£674; £337; £168) **Stalls** Centre

Form				RPR
2003	1		**Baltimore Jack (IRE)**[14] 3203 6-10-0 **70** ... GrahamGibbons 2 (T D Walford) *mde all: qcknd over 2f out: hld on gamely* **5/4**[1]	77
0326	2	1/2	**Eastern Gift**[8] 3412 5-9-5 **68** ... StephanieBancroft(7) 5 (Miss Gay Kelleway) *hld up in rr: hdwy over 4f out: chal 100yds out: no ex nr fin* **9/2**[2]	74
0016	3	1/2	**Tanforan**[9] 3377 8-9-6 **62** ... RobertWinston 8 (B P J Baugh) *trckd ldrs: drvn on inner and n.m.r over 2f out: kpt on same pce fnl 75yds* **8/1**	67
4224	4	3 1/2	**Vaultage (USA)**[23] 2903 3-8-13 **64** ... HayleyTurner 6 (E A L Dunlop) *hld up in rr: effrt and plld wd 2f out: edgd lft and kpt on one pce fnl f* **9/2**[2]	59
143	5	1	**Crocodile Bay (IRE)**[16] 3132 7-9-0 **56** ... PaulEddery 7 (R C Guest) *trckd wnr: drvn over 2f out: wknd fnl f* **7/1**[3]	51
/003	6	shd	**Alright Chuck**[10] 3309 6-8-9 **51** oh4 ... LukeMorris 3 (P W Hiatt) *chsd ldrs: drvn over 3f out: one pce fnl 2f* **16/1**	45
2055	7	3 1/2	**Al Rayanah**[12] 3263 7-8-3 **52** ...(p) CharlotteKerton(7) 1 (G Prodromou) *t.k.h in rr: hdwy over 4f out: sn drvn: wknd over 1f out* **16/1**	38

1m 45.95s (0.35) **Going Correction** -0.075s/f (Good)
WFA 3 from 4yo+ 9lb **7** Ran SP% **116.2**
Speed ratings (Par 103): **95,94,94,90,89 89,85**
toteswingers: 1&2 £2.80, 1&3 £3.50, 2&3 £12.00 CSF £7.44 CT £31.70 TOTE £3.00: £1.30, £2.40; EX 9.40 Place 6 £56.74, Place 5 £42.21.
Owner D Swales **Bred** P Monaghan, J Collins & G Dillon **Trained** Sheriff Hutton, N Yorks
■ In separate incidents, a racegoer and a dog got onto the course during this race.

FOCUS
A modest handicap, though few could be discounted.
T/Plt: £108.50 to a £1 stake. Pool: £48,813.13. 328.33 winning tickets. T/Qpdt: £51.80 tto a £1 stake. Pool: £3,799.50. 54.20 winning tickets. WG

3629 SANDOWN (R-H)

Saturday, July 3

OFFICIAL GOING: Good to firm (round 8.4; sprint 8.6)
Rails at innermost configuration and all distances as advertised.
Wind: Virtually nil Weather: Warm and sunny

3691 CORAL CHARGE STKS (REGISTERED AS THE SPRINT STAKES) (GROUP 3) — 5f 6y

2:00 (2:01) (Class 1) 3-Y-O+
£34,062 (£12,912; £6,462; £3,222; £1,614; £810) **Stalls** High

Form				RPR
2-10	1		**Triple Aspect (IRE)**[14] 3192 4-9-3 109 ... LiamJones 7 (W J Haggas) *sn niggled along in last: hdwy 1/2-way: chsd ldrs and swtchd lft over 1f out: rdn and edgd lft ent fnl f: edgd rt and chal fnl 100yds: edgd lft again u.p but styd on wl to ld nr fin* **15/8**[1]	114+
00-1	2	1/2	**Group Therapy**[16] 3108 5-9-3 103 ... ShaneKelly 6 (J Noseda) *taken down early and ponied to s: t.k.h: trckd ldrs: effrt and pushed into ld jst ins ins fnl f: hrd pressed and drvn fnl 100yds: kpt on wl tl hdd and no ex nr fin* **3/1**[2]	112
24-5	3	2 1/4	**Bould Mover**[18] 3047 3-8-12 110 ... GrahamGibbons 4 (F J Brennan) *chsd ldr tl led 1/2-way: rdn over 1f out: hdd jst ins fnl f: nt pce of ldng pair fnl 100yds* **10/3**[3]	102
2113	4	1 1/2	**Hamish McGonagall**[16] 3108 5-9-3 105 ... RyanMoore 2 (T D Easterby) *chsd ldrs: outpcd and n.m.r 2f out: kpt on again ins fnl f but no threat to ldrs* **11/2**	99

The Form Book, Raceform Ltd, Compton, RG20 6NL

6-42 **5** 3 1/4 **Reignier**[21] 2972 3-8-12 95 ... JimCrowley 3 85
(J R Weymes) *hld up in last pair: swtchd lft and effrt ent fnl 2f: no prog and wknd u.p ent fnl f* **16/1**

2103 **6** 2 1/4 **Moorhouse Lad**[8] 3425 7-9-3 100 ... TomEaves 1 79
(B Smart) *led tl 1/2-way: wknd u.p over 1f out: wl hld fnl f* **14/1**

59.47 secs (-2.13) **Going Correction** -0.125s/f (Firm)
WFA 3 from 4yo+ 5lb **6** Ran SP% **110.8**
Speed ratings (Par 113): **112,111,107,105,100 96**
toteswingers: 1&2 £2.00, 1&3 £2.00, 2&3 £3.50 CSF £7.49 TOTE £3.10: £1.80, £2.10; EX 7.00.
Owner Tony Bloom **Bred** Noel O'Callaghan **Trained** Newmarket, Suffolk
■ Stewards' Enquiry : Shane Kelly one-day ban: careless riding (Jul 17)

FOCUS
3mm of water was put on overnight, but not on the home bend, and the going was given as Good to Firm all over. The going stick measured 8.4 on the round course and 8.6 on the 5f track. The winning time was quicker than Racing Post standard but the form looks ordinary for the grade, although there are grounds for rating it a little higher.

NOTEBOOK
Triple Aspect(IRE) avenged his narrow defeat in this last year to collect his third victory over C&D. However, it was a success that looked unlikely early, as he was outpaced for at least a furlong and a half before catching his rivals. His jockey took the brave route up the far-side rail, and luckily found the gaps open when they were required. The horse looked quirky once manoeuvred into a challenging position, but he stuck on well and improved his already impressive win-to-runs record. It goes without saying that this course evidently suits him well, but it was also interesting to hear afterwards that his connections reported that he is more sound now than he's ever been. The nominated target is the Group 2 Goldene Peitsche at Baden-Baden in late August over 6f. (op 9-4)
Group Therapy, who was ponied down to the start, made a winning debut for this trainer last time and had a good record in small-field events. He played up a little before going into the stalls but showed a good attitude during the race and ran right up to his best. (tchd 7-2)
Bould Mover had decent form as a juvenile and then ran a cracker on his seasonal return in the King's Stand Stakes, only being beaten just over two lengths into fifth. Quickly away, he showed good pace to lead and only started to falter significantly about a furlong out. This appeared to confirm his Ascot effort was no fluke and that he has trained on. He does have an entry in the Nunthorpe Stakes and it's easy to see him running well in that, although he will have other front-runners to take him on, but, like many in this field, his ideal target before that should be the King George Stakes at Glorious Goodwood. (tchd 3-1 and 7-2)
Hamish McGonagall had been beaten a similar distance last time by Group Therapy at Beverley but had a bit of an excuse this time as, even though he was being ridden at the time, he was squeezed for room over 2f out. Once gathered together again, he kept on well. (op 6-1 tchd 5-1)
Reignier, up slightly in class, was a bit keen just in behind the leaders and could not accelerate when his jockey asked for maximum effort. (tchd 14-1)
Moorhouse Lad showed speed but could not quicken about a furlong from home and was soundly held. (op 12-1)

3692 CORAL CHALLENGE STKS (HERITAGE H'CAP) 1m 14y
2:35 (2:37) (Class 2) 3-Y-0+
£46,732 (£13,995; £6,997; £3,502; £1,747; £877) **Stalls** High

Form RPR

40-0 **1** **Black Spirit (USA)**[63] 1703 3-8-8 **97** ... (t) LukeMorris 6 106
(C G Cox) *in tch: rdn ent fnl 3f: hdwy and carried sltly lft ent fnl f: str run to ld fnl 75yds: r.o wl* **33/1**

3-40 **2** 1/2 **Acrostic**[17] 3069 5-9-7 **101** ... KierenFallon 2 111+
(L M Cumani) *hld up wl bhd: effrt and rdn over 2f out: kpt edging rt but gd hdwy over 1f out: chsd ldrs jst ins fnl f: ev ch fnl 75yds: kpt on* **6/1**[2]

2303 **3** 1 **Dunn'o (IRE)**[37] 2472 5-8-13 **93** ... PhilipRobinson 15 100
(C G Cox) *taken down early: led: rdn over 2f out: kpt on gamely finding ex tl hdd and one pce fnl 75yds* **10/1**

-302 **4** 2 3/4 **Oratory (IRE)**[21] 2977 4-9-0 **94** ... JMurtagh 16 95
(R Hannon) *bustled along early and sn chsng ldng pair: wnt 2nd and rdn jst over 2f out: pressed wnr u.p 2f out: edgd rt and btn jst ins fnl f* **5/1**[1]

5-06 **5** 1 1/4 **Desert Creek (IRE)**[64] 1665 4-8-11 **91** ... RyanMoore 13 89
(Sir Michael Stoute) *t.k.h: chsd ldrs: swtchd lft and rdn over 2f out: edgd lft u.p and btn ent fnl f* **16/1**

3410 **6** 1/2 **Moynahan (USA)**[17] 3069 5-8-11 **91** ... TomQueally 9 88
(P F I Cole) *hld up wl bhd: stdy hdwy on inner ent fnl 2f: nt clr run over 1f out tl ent fnl f: styd on wl fnl 150yds: nvr able to chal* **20/1**

00-2 **7** hd **Set The Trend**[29] 2708 4-9-2 **96** ... JimmyFortune 4 93
(A M Balding) *hld up wl off the pce towards rr: rdn and effrt on outer over 2f out: hdwy but edging rt fr over 1f out: no imp ins fnl f: nvr trbld ldrs* **6/1**[2]

1031 **8** 1 1/2 **Opus Maximus (IRE)**[8] 3389 5-8-9 **89** ... RoystonFfrench 19 82
(M Johnston) *t.k.h: in tch: rdn and unable qck ent fnl 2f: edgd rt and plugged on same pce fr over 1f out* **25/1**

1121 **9** 1/2 **Charlie Cool**[16] 3121 7-9-1 **95** ... (b) RobertWinston 1 87
(Mrs R A Carr) *stdd s: hld up wl bhd: rdn and effrt jst over 2f out: styd on past btn horses fnl f: nvr trbld ldrs* **11/1**

0662 **10** 1 3/4 **Collateral Damage (IRE)**[9] 3366 7-8-12 **92** ... (t) GrahamGibbons 7 80
(T D Easterby) *hld up towards rr: sme modest late hdwy: n.d* **16/1**

0/15 **11** nse **Coasting**[21] 2971 5-9-2 **96** ... JimCrowley 5 84
(Mrs A J Perrett) *t.k.h: hld up wl off the pce in midfield: rdn and unable qck over 2f out: wl hld fnl 2f* **17/2**[3]

2053 **12** 2 1/4 **Greyfriarschorista**[16] 3103 3-9-0 **103** ... RichardHills 10 84
(M Johnston) *s.i.s: a wl bhd: rdn and no prog ent fnl 2f: n.d* **9/1**

-430 **13** nk **Al Khaleej (IRE)**[15] 3146 6-9-5 **99** ... AdamKirby 8 81+
(E A L Dunlop) *taken down early: stdd s: hld up in rr: rdn and no prog 2f out: n.d* **33/1**

-560 **14** 3 1/4 **Mr Willis**[15] 3146 4-8-10 **90** ... LiamJones 12 64
(J R Best) *t.k.h: hld up in rr: rdn and no prog over 2f out: n.d* **25/1**

2110 **15** 5 **Tartan Gigha (IRE)**[15] 3144 5-9-10 **104** ... WilliamBuick 18 67
(M Johnston) *a towards rr: rdn and no real prog over 2f out: no ch whn nt clr run over 1f out: n.d* **20/1**

0400 **16** 2 1/4 **Al Muheer (IRE)**[17] 3069 5-9-7 **101** ... (b) SebSanders 11 59
(C E Brittain) *in tch in midfield: rdn and hanging rt over 2f out: wknd and wl btn 2f out: eased ins fnl f* **33/1**

4531 **17** 7 **Hacienda (IRE)**[9] 3354 3-8-7 **96** ... AdrianNicholls 3 36
(M Johnston) *chsd ldr: tl over 2f out: hung rt and wknd qckly wl over 1f out: heavily eased ins fnl f* **11/1**

1m 39.65s (-3.65) **Going Correction** -0.225s/f (Firm)
WFA 3 from 4yo+ 9lb **17** Ran SP% **129.3**
Speed ratings (Par 109): **109,108,107,104,103 103,102,101,100,99 99,96,96,93,88 85,78**
toteswingers: 1&2 £60.70, 1&3 £106.00, 2&3 £13.60 CSF £218.15 CT £2238.46 TOTE £58.20: £10.20, £2.10, £2.80, £1.80; EX 540.20 Trifecta £2749.20 Part won. Pool: £3,715.17 - 0.10 winning units..
Owner A D Spence **Bred** Arundel Farm Llc **Trained** Lambourn, Berks

FOCUS
A competitive handicap run at a sound gallop in a fast time. Little bar the second got involved from the rear. The form is rated around the third.

NOTEBOOK
Black Spirit(USA) looked very much the stable's second string but, as a 3-y-o who had only run four times previously, he came into this completely unexposed. It turns out that he'd had a breathing operation since he last ran, and, with the tongue tie which was missing on his reappearance back in place, he posted a career-best effort to take this valuable handicap. He was under pressure quite early on in the straight, but responded well to a strong ride and stayed on really well to score. On this evidence he'll appreciate a step up to 1m2f, although in the short term he could go for the totesport Mile at Goodwood. Official explanation: trainer's rep said, regarding apparent improvement in form, that the colt benefited from the refitting of a tongue strap.
Acrostic, last year's winner, had more on his plate this time around off a 7lb higher mark, but he ran really well in defeat, only finding the well-handicapped youngster too strong. Any further rise in the weights will leave him vulnerable to similar types. (op 7-1 tchd 8-1)
Dunn'o(IRE) had a good draw and made the most of it, quickly taking up his favoured front-running role. He was a shade keen, but when he quickened things up approaching the 2f pole he looked as though he might just see them all off. He just couldn't hang on in the closing stages, but it was another fine effort at his favourite track, where his record now reads three wins and three thirds from six starts. (tchd 9-1)
Oratory(IRE), also well drawn, took up a good position tracking the leader on the rail but seemed to hang in behind him when asked to quicken. He'll probably edge a little further up the handicap for this, which won't help matters. (op 8-1 tchd 9-1 in a place)
Desert Creek(IRE) pulled for his head in the early stages while tracking the leaders but soon settled and looked dangerous at the top of the straight. He didn't quite have enough in the closing stages but the drop back from 1m2f was definitely in his favour. (op 14-1)
Moynahan(USA) again didn't enjoy the clearest of runs, but his style of running does tend to lend itself to finding trouble.
Set The Trend, who raced wider than most from his low draw, would have preferred more cover as he was a little keen. He never got close enough to land a challenge. (op 7-1 tchd 15-2)
Opus Maximus(IRE) looked to find this stiff mile too much of a test. An easier track or return to shorter should suit him. (op 22-1)
Charlie Cool, 7lb higher than for his win at Ripon last time, was keeping on at the finish but was never really involved. (op 14-1)
Coasting didn't help his chance of seeing out this longer trip by racing keenly early. (op 10-1 tchd 8-1)
Greyfriarschorista faced a stiff task off a mark of 103 and never got much closer than he was at the finish. Richard Hills later reported that the colt anticipated the start and hit his head on the gate. Official explanation: jockey said colt anticipated start and hit its head on the gate (op 8-1)
Al Khaleej(IRE) Official explanation: jockey said gelding missed the break
Hacienda(IRE) had too much use made of him in crossing over from stall five to dispute the early lead with Dunn'o. (op 12-1 tchd 14-1)

3693 CORAL-ECLIPSE (GROUP 1) 1m 2f 7y
3:10 (3:15) (Class 1) 3-Y-0+ **£283,850** (£107,600; £53,850; £26,850; £13,450) **Stalls** High

Form RPR

3-02 **1** **Twice Over**[17] 3068 5-9-7 123 ... TomQueally 5 119+
(H R A Cecil) *w ldr tl led 7f out: rdn and qcknd over 3f out: 3 l clr over 1f out: rdn ins fnl f: being ct towards fin but a holding rivals* **13/8**[1]

0-10 **2** 1/2 **Sri Putra**[37] 2470 4-9-7 111 ... PhilipRobinson 1 118
(M A Jarvis) *stdd after s and racd in last: swtchd lft and rdn over 2f out: no imp after tl hdwy to chse wnr ins fnl f: styd on wl fnl 100yds and clsng at fin: nvr quite getting to wnr* **33/1**

2035 **3** 1/2 **Viscount Nelson (USA)**[27] 2802 3-8-10 114 ... (v) JMurtagh 3 117
(A P O'Brien, Ire) *in tch: rdn and unable qck over 2f out: edging rt u.p and chsd clr wnr jst over 1f out tl ins fnl f: styd on fnl 100yds: nvr able to rch wnr* **4/1**[3]

53-1 **4** 5 **Dar Re Mi**[98] 1026 5-9-4 120 ... WilliamBuick 2 104
(J H M Gosden) *led tl 7f out: w wnr after tl rdn and nt pce of wnr ent fnl 3f: lost 2nd jst over 1f out: wknd fnl f* **7/2**[2]

0-04 **5** 21 **Zacinto**[18] 3046 4-9-7 119 ... RyanMoore 6 65
(Sir Michael Stoute) *t.k.h: trckd ldrs: rdn and unable qck wl over 2f out: wl btn over 1f out: eased fnl f* **6/1**

2m 4.64s (-5.86) **Going Correction** -0.225s/f (Firm)
WFA 3 from 4yo+ 11lb **5** Ran SP% **97.5**
Speed ratings (Par 117): **114,113,113,109,92**
CSF £32.07 TOTE £2.10: £1.10, £4.10; EX 16.30.
Owner K Abdulla **Bred** Juddmonte Farms Ltd **Trained** Newmarket, Suffolk
■ Henry Cecil's first Eclipse winner since Gunner B in 1978. Mawatheeq withdrawn, 5/1, deduct 15p in the £ under R4.
■ Stewards' Enquiry : Philip Robinson caution: used whip with excessive frequency without giving colt time to respond.

FOCUS
It would take something special from the five that took part here to top what happened to the runners in this race last year afterwards. Not only did the imperious Sea The Stars start to stamp his authority on the 2009 season when beating Rip Van Winkle but, including those two, the whole field have already won 17 subsequent races, including nine at Group 1 level. The lack of runners gave this year's renewal a below-par look, especially as four of them did not manage a place on their previous outing, so it was really disappointing when the mulish Mawatheeq refused to go into the stalls, reducing the field to only five, the smallest amount of runners since Hawk Wing outclassed four rivals in 2002. Marcus Tregoning's horse had a handler at the start to help but he was having none of it and never looked like going in. He will now need to pass a stalls test before running again. Twice Over is rated 5lb off his best in this below-par renewal, with improvement from Sri Putra.

NOTEBOOK
Twice Over, a well-beaten seventh in this last season when starting at 14-1, showed grim determination to hang on. Possibly a bit unlucky in the Prince Of Wales's Stakes after getting behind, a change of tactics were employed this time and he helped to share the pace before going on quite a way out, something that both the trainer and jockey reportedly discussed prior to the race to prevent it being a sprint. Tom Queally stretched his rivals just over 3f from home and gained enough of an advantage at that point to claim a second Group 1 success for the horse. He will have all the major 1m2f races as targets, presumably starting with the Juddmonte International at York in mid-August, but the trainer would also love to win the Dubai World Cup with him, as he felt nothing went right for his horse in that race this year. (op 7-4 tchd 15-8 and 2-1 in places)
Sri Putra, from a stable in flying form, almost pulled off quite a shock. Very warm in the paddock and in the parade, without looking irritated this time (he reportedly got very coltish in the stables at this course last time before running badly), his form this season did not suggest he was about to win one of the most prestigious races of the Flat season, although a closer inspection of his success in the Group 2 Prix Guillaume D'ornano at Deauville last August, where he had Byword held behind, gave him every chance. Connections have always felt he is a decent sort when at his best, and as he has stallion potential, will try and find races, possibly abroad, from 1m2f-1m4f to further enhance his profile.
Viscount Nelson(USA), whose trainer has a good record in this race, had a visor fitted for the first time. He was hard-ridden to keep going after sitting just off the gallop, but never really looked like winning at any stage and arguably looked a little quirky in the headgear, although the ground may not have been to his liking. He does give a line to this year's 3-y-os so, judged on this effort, one would imagine that the Classic generation aren't that far behind their elders, if at all. (op 13-2 tchd 7-1)

Dar Re Mi, having her first outing since winning the Sheema Classic in March, was always going to want a true test at this distance, even on a course this stiff, but one got the impression that she was doing a bit too much in a prominent position, even allowing for the fact that the winner was along side for a lot of the contest. She weakened quickly once under strong pressure, but it will surely bring her on and she should head to the King George VI and Queen Elizabeth Stakes at Ascot later this month with every chance, over arguably a more suitable distance. (op 10-3 tchd 3-1 and 4-1 in places)

Zacinto, wearing a noseband, has not really progressed from three to four and even though he ran respectably in the Queen Anne, he must be considered disappointing this year. His pedigree did look as though it gave hope for him staying the extra 2f, but he put up a lacklustre performance and the distance was probably irrelevant. (op 5-1)

3694 CORAL DISTAFF (LISTED RACE) — 1m 14y

3:40 (3:43) (Class 1) 3-Y-O

£21,004 (£7,962; £3,984; £1,986; £995; £499) **Stalls** High

Form				RPR
26-4	1		**Virginia Hall**[9] 3375 3-8-12 105 SebSanders 2	107
			(Sir Mark Prescott) *mde all: pushed along and drew clr over 2f out: rdn and styd on wl fr over 1f out: rdn out* **11/2**[3]	
-011	2	3	**Fontley**[22] 2933 3-8-12 88 TomQueally 3	100
			(Eve Johnson Houghton) *racd in last pair: niggled along 6f out: rdn over 2f out: hdwy over 1f out: kpt on gamely u.p fnl f to go 2nd towards fin: no ch w wnr* **15/2**	
-064	3	½	**Lady Darshaan (IRE)**[23] 2889 3-8-12 106 JimmyFortune 4	99
			(J S Moore) *ponied to s: t.k.h: chsd ldng pair: swtchd lft and rdn jst over 2f out: chsd clr wnr over 1f out: kpt on same pce u.p after: lost 2nd towards fin* **11/8**[1]	
1-10	4	3 ¼	**Totally Ours**[62] 1729 3-8-12 85 JimCrowley 1	91
			(W R Muir) *racd in midfield: rdn and unable qck wl over 2f out: no ch w wnr fnl 2f* **22/1**	
2350	5	nse	**Bella Swan**[9] 3375 3-8-12 97 AdamKirby 6	91
			(W R Swinburn) *chsd wnr: rdn and nt pce of wnr over 2f out: lost 2nd over 1f out: wknd ins fnl f* **12/1**	
3100	6	½	**Marie De Medici (USA)**[17] 3071 3-9-1 101 KierenFallon 8	93
			(M Johnston) *racd in midfield: rdn 4f out: no prog and wl hld whn edgd rt over 1f out* **4/1**[2]	
1103	7	2 ½	**Srda (USA)**[58] 1836 3-8-12 86 RyanMoore 5	84
			(C E Brittain) *stdd and dropped in bhd after s: a in rr: rdn and no prog fr over 2f out* **10/1**	

1m 40.42s (-2.88) **Going Correction** -0.225s/f (Firm) 7 Ran SP% **110.4**
Speed ratings (Par 108): **105,102,101,98,98 97,95**
toteswingers: 1&2 £4.30, 1&3 £2.30, 2&3 £2.90 CSF £41.87 TOTE £6.20: £2.60, £2.70; EX 28.20 Trifecta £98.20 Pool: £484.66 - 3.65 winning units..
Owner C G Rowles Nicholson **Bred** Limestone And Tara Studs **Trained** Newmarket, Suffolk

FOCUS

This didn't look a particularly strong Listed contest on paper, and the winning time was 0.77sec slower than the heritage handicap earlier on the card, but it was won in convincing style. The winner looks the best guide to the form.

NOTEBOOK

Virginia Hall set out to make all, drew nicely clear approaching the furlong pole and had more than enough in hand from then on. Apparently a little fresh on her reappearance when fourth behind Seta at Warwick, she was back to her best here, and deserves to return to Group company next. She was placed in a French Group 3 last summer, acts on easier ground, and there should be plenty of opportunities for her to pick up more black type this season. (op 5-1)

Fontley is an improving filly with a liking for this track and she posted a career-best in defeat. The quick ground was a concern but she coped with it pretty well and stayed on well from off the pace to grab valuable black type. This performance won't have done her handicap mark any good, especially when it comes to chasing the big bonus here on Variety Club day, but there could yet be further improvement to come from her when stepped up to 1m2f. (op 6-1 tchd 8-1)

Lady Darshaan(IRE), who was officially best in at the weights, was happier back over a mile, but she undoubtedly would have preferred an easier surface. (op 6-4 tchd 5-4 and 7-4 in a place and 13-8 in places)

Totally Ours had an excuse last time as she was apparently poorly afterwards. This race still required a big step up from her, though, and she wasn't up to it. (op 20-1 tchd 16-1)

Bella Swan has now run below her best in her last three starts and is becoming disappointing. (op 10-1)

Marie De Medici(USA) was ridden differently this time but again failed to sparkle. She could probably do with a rest now. (op 5-1)

Srda(USA) promised to be suited by the return to a mile but she didn't look at all comfortable on the ground and never got involved. (op 8-1)

3695 CORAL MARATHON STKS (REGISTERED AS THE ESHER STAKES) (LISTED RACE) — 2m 78y

4:15 (4:15) (Class 1) 4-Y-O+

£21,004 (£7,962; £3,984; £1,986; £995; £499) **Stalls** Centre

Form				RPR
5-14	1		**King Of Wands**[29] 2716 4-9-0 105 WilliamBuick 8	112
			(J H M Gosden) *hld up in tch in midfield: rdn and effrt ent fnl 2f: drvn to ld over 1f out: edgd rt u.p but styd on wl fnl f* **8/1**	
4314	2	¾	**Illustrious Blue**[37] 2469 7-9-5 107 JimCrowley 7	116
			(W J Knight) *stdd s: t.k.h: hld up in last: effrt on outer ent fnl 2f: hdwy u.p ent fnl f: swtchd rt ins fnl f: chsd wnr fnl 75yds: no imp after* **14/1**	
-131	3	¾	**Opinion Poll (IRE)**[17] 3099 4-9-3 110 PhilipRobinson 4	113
			(M A Jarvis) *hld up in last pair: rdn and effrt on outer over 2f out: hdwy u.p over 1f out: chsd wnr briefly ins fnl f: kpt on same fnl 100yds* **11/2**[2]	
312/	4	2 ¼	**Samuel**[728] 3743 6-9-0 110 RobertHavlin 5	109+
			(J H M Gosden) *t.k.h: sn chsng ldrs: trckd ldr 4f out: wnt upsides ldr gng wl 3f out: shkn up to ld 2f out: rdn and hdd over 1f out: keeping on one pce and btn whn hmpd fnl 100yds: eased after* **16/1**	
13-2	5	2 ¼	**Manighar (FR)**[29] 2716 4-9-0 114 KierenFallon 3	105
			(L M Cumani) *t.k.h: hld up in tch in midfield: effrt and edging rt jst over 2f out: chsd ldrs ent fnl f: btn ins fnl f: fdd fnl 100yds* **4/5**[1]	
-262	6	9	**Aajel (USA)**[14] 3195 6-9-0 106 RichardHills 6	98
			(M P Tregoning) *led: jnd 3f out: rdn and hdd 2f out: btn jst over 1f out: eased ins fnl f* **7/1**[3]	
0	7	39	**Ringaroses**[14] 3195 9-9-0 0 (t) SebSanders 1	47
			(Jonjo O'Neill) *chsd ldr tl 4f out: wkng whn sltly hmpd wl over 2f out: virtually p.u fnl f: t.o* **33/1**	

3m 29.86s (-8.84) **Going Correction** -0.225s/f (Firm) course record 7 Ran SP% **110.0**
Speed ratings (Par 111): **113,112,112,111,110 105,86**
toteswingers: 1&2 £6.90, 1&3 £4.70, 2&3 £5.50 CSF £97.77 TOTE £9.30: £3.50, £3.70; EX 74.20.
Owner R J H Geffen **Bred** Normandie Stud Ltd **Trained** Newmarket, Suffolk

FOCUS

The course record set by Sadeem 21 years previously was broken in this sound run race. The winner may yet do better but the favourite was disappointing.

NOTEBOOK

King Of Wands, trying this trip for the first time, and running over 4f further than he did on his previous start, kept on really well after sitting in midfield and was a fully deserved winner. Lightly raced, he ought to have more to come and should probably head towards the Goodwood Cup next, as his handicap opportunities are going to be limited. He was purchased by the owner to go hurdling, interestingly from the connections of the fourth here, and that option is still very much on the horizon.

Illustrious Blue is another that may head towards the Goodwood race when considering his record at that course. He has made the leap to the staying division with surprising ease for a horse that won plenty of times between 7f-1m2f, and would have gone even closer here had he not got squeezed for room in the latter stages. (op 12-1)

Opinion Poll(IRE), the winner of a 1m7f contest on Good to Soft ground at Chantilly last time, moved up going well but gave the impression that he was finding the ground too firm for him, which would make sense considering his best form. Connections may need to head abroad for more suitable going, or wait until the autumn in the hope of rain. Official explanation: jockey said colt hung right (op 13-2)

Samuel, absent with a leg since finishing runner-up in this race to Distinction back in 2008, and stable companion of the winner, travelled with purpose throughout - indeed his jockey had a quick look behind him just over 2f out - but unsurprisingly tired a little in the final stages. The late interference he suffered when the runner-up came across him did not affect his final position. (op 12-1)

Manighar(FR) was disappointing for a couple of reasons. He was almost Group 1 standard last season for different connections, but was easily held here, albeit after travelling well. Also, he was really well treated with the winner and third on their meeting in the Tapster Stakes at Goodwood last month. It is almost certain that we will see the best of him when he can race on much easier ground. (op 5-6 tchd 8-1, 10-11 and evens in places)

Aajel(USA) ran a great race in the Queen Alexandra last time over 5f further so he was always going to ensure a proper gallop here. He did a fine job out in front, so much so that the winner broke the course record, but unfortunately, that may have compromised his chance at the end, as he had no more to give once joined. (op 15-2 tchd 13-2)

Ringaroses ran no sort of race. (op 20-1)

3696 CORAL.CO.UK H'CAP — 7f 16y

4:50 (4:52) (Class 3) (0-95,95) 3-Y-O

£7,477 (£2,239; £1,119; £560; £279; £140) **Stalls** High

Form				RPR
0-21	1		**Kakatosi**[21] 2968 3-8-8 **82** KierenFallon 10	92+
			(A M Balding) *t.k.h: chsd ldrs: rdn to ld over 1f out: drvn ins fnl f: hld on cl home* **2/1**[1]	
211-	2	hd	**Mass Rally (IRE)**[224] 7494 3-9-1 **89** WilliamBuick 3	99+
			(J H M Gosden) *stdd s: bhd: stl last ent fnl 2f: rdn and hdwy over 1f out: str run ins fnl f: chsd wnr fnl 75yds: jst hld* **16/1**	
10-4	3	1 ¾	**Oil Strike**[30] 2682 3-8-10 **84** JimCrowley 1	89
			(P Winkworth) *racd keenly: chsd ldrs: rdn over 2f out: ev ch and drvn over 1f out tl ins fnl f: one pce and btn fnl 75yds* **11/1**	
-011	4	½	**Imperial Delight**[30] 2682 3-8-8 **82** DaneO'Neill 2	86
			(H Candy) *chsd ldr tl rdn to ld jst over 2f out: drvn and hdd over 1f out: styd on same pce u.p fnl f* **7/1**[3]	
612	5	¾	**Eton Forever (IRE)**[35] 2542 3-9-5 **93** PhilipRobinson 6	95
			(M A Jarvis) *in tch in midfield: effrt on outer over 2f out: drvn to press ldrs ent fnl f: wknd fnl 100yds* **9/4**[2]	
6-06	6	1	**Haadeeth**[77] 1376 3-8-13 **87** RichardHills 8	86
			(M P Tregoning) *bhd: rdn over 2f out: no hdwy tl styd on steadily ins fnl f: nvr trbld ldrs* **20/1**	
0-20	7	2 ½	**Unshakable Will (IRE)**[42] 2324 3-8-8 **82** TomEaves 5	74
			(B Smart) *led and crossed over to rail: rdn and hdd jst over 2f out: wknd u.p ent fnl f* **12/1**	
5403	8	½	**Duellist**[15] 3172 3-8-10 **84** RoystonFfrench 7	75
			(M Johnston) *racd in midfield: rdn and unable qck 3f out: drvn 2f out: no hdwy and wl hld fnl f* **14/1**	
0-15	9	4	**Water Gipsy**[15] 3158 3-8-9 **83** RyanMoore 9	63
			(G L Moore) *racd in midfield: rdn and no prog ent fnl 2f: no ch over 1f out* **20/1**	
0300	10	2 ½	**Duplicity**[21] 2972 3-9-7 **95** JimmyFortune 4	68
			(R Hannon) *hld up wl off the pce in last pair: effrt on inner wl over 2f out: no prog and wl hld fnl 2f* **20/1**	

1m 27.51s (-1.99) **Going Correction** -0.225s/f (Firm) 10 Ran SP% **119.5**
Speed ratings (Par 104): **102,101,99,99,98 97,94,93,89,86**
toteswingers: 1&2 £9.40, 1&3 £10.30, 2&3 £12.70 CSF £35.38 CT £286.54 TOTE £3.10: £1.40, £3.80, £3.40; EX 36.90.
Owner Robert E Tillett **Bred** T E Pocock **Trained** Kingsclere, Hants

FOCUS

The market spoke loudly in favour of two of these beforehand, especially the winner who was on a fair mark for this debut. The form looks sound.

NOTEBOOK

Kakatosi was supported into favouritism in the moments before the race. Running in a handicap for the first time, he was a little keen early but Kieren Fallon soon got him settled and, when asked to go and win his race in the straight, he picked up well, before holding off the late challenge of the runner-up. He's an improving 3-y-o, capable of defying a rise in the handicap, but it's worth noting that Andrew Balding expressed concerns beforehand that the ground might be quicker than ideal here, so he might need a slightly easier surface as he moves up in grade and takes on stronger opposition. (op 3-1 tchd 10-3 and 7-2 in a place)

Mass Rally(IRE) ran a cracker on his seasonal reappearance. He looked to improve for a switch to Polytrack last autumn, but showed here that he can be just as effective on turf, and, with this run under his belt, he'll take some beating in similar company next time. (op 14-1)

Oil Strike ran well considering he was drawn worst of all. He carried his head a little high under pressure but kept on pretty well, and he remains open to further improvement, having had only the five starts to date. (op 12-1 tchd 14-1)

Imperial Delight, 4lb higher for his narrow win in a lower-grade contest over C&D last time out, was never too far away and looks to have run right up to his best. He's probably not a bad guide to the level of the form. (op 8-1 tchd 6-1)

Eton Forever(IRE), whose stable can do little wrong at present, was seen as the main danger to the winner by the market. He had his chance down the outside but tended to hang right under pressure and perhaps he was feeling the ground. He can do better back on an easier surface. (op 5-2 tchd 2-1)

Haadeeth did not show any great improvement for the return to 7f and simply looks held off his current mark. (op 25-1)

Unshakable Will(IRE) was given a positive ride back over his best trip, but was headed and beaten before the 2f marker.

Duellist looks pretty exposed now, especially compared to some of the rivals he was taking on here. (op 9-1)

3697 CORAL TV H'CAP 1m 2f 7y
5:25 (5:25) (Class 4) (0-85,85) 3-Y-O **£6,476** (£1,927; £963; £481) **Stalls** High

Form				RPR
131	**1**		**Beachfire**[21] 2969 3-9-7 **85** WilliamBuick 8 (J H M Gosden) *bhd: rdn and effrt on inner ent fnl 2f: swtchd lft ent fnl f: drvn to chse ldng pair jst ins fnl f: r.o strly to ld wl ins fnl f* **13/8**[1]	97+
31-5	**2**	*nk*	**Revered**[21] 2969 3-9-5 **83** RyanMoore 6 (Sir Michael Stoute) *chsd ldng trio: rdn over 2f out: chsd ldr over 1f out: flashed tail u.p but kpt to ld wl ins fnl f: sn hdd and no ex towards fin* **4/1**[2]	94
-462	**3**	*1*	**Hidden Glory**[22] 2927 3-8-11 **78** (p) MartinLane(3) 7 (Pat Eddery) *pressed ldr on inner tl led 4f out: rdn ent fnl 2f: clr over 1f out: hdd and no ex wl ins fnl f* **7/1**	87
-020	**4**	*3*	**Essexbridge**[50] 2079 3-9-0 **78** DaneO'Neill 1 (R Hannon) *in tch in midfield: effrt u.p over 2f out: chsd ldrs ent fnl f: no prog and btn fnl 150yds* **10/1**	82
5122	**5**	*4*	**Buffett**[17] 3081 3-9-2 **80** KierenFallon 3 (L M Cumani) *in tch in midfield: n.m.r ent fnl 2f tl wl over 1f out: sn rdn and no real prog whn n.m.r again over 1f out: wl btn after* **9/2**[3]	76
0606	**6**	*4 ½*	**Muwalla**[9] 3351 3-8-11 **75** (bt[1]) SebSanders 2 (C E Brittain) *chsd ldrs: chsd ldr over 2f out tl over 1f out: sn wknd* **33/1**	62
2-11	**7**	*6*	**Lovers Causeway (USA)**[164] 240 3-9-0 **78** RoystonFfrench 5 (M Johnston) *sn led: pushed along and hdd 4f out: wandered and wknd ent fnl 2f* **11/1**	54
0-41	**8**	*4*	**Veni Vedi Veci (IRE)**[33] 2603 3-9-0 **78** JimmyFortune 4 (A M Balding) *stdd and dropped to last pair after 1f: rdn and no hdwy wl over 2f out: eased ins fnl f* **14/1**	46

2m 6.77s (-3.73) **Going Correction** -0.225s/f (Firm) **8** Ran SP% **115.8**
Speed ratings (Par 102): **105,104,103,101,98 94,89,86**
toteswingers: 1&2 £2.50, 1&3 £3.70, 2&3 £6.90 CSF £8.28 CT £35.11 TOTE £2.50: £1.20, £1.70, £2.80; EX 9.10 Place 6 £1,124.27, Place 5 £770.94.
Owner H R H Princess Haya Of Jordan **Bred** Bridgewater Equine Ltd **Trained** Newmarket, Suffolk

FOCUS
An interesting 3-y-o handicap which should throw up future winners. The time was a respectable 2.13sec slower than the Eclipse and the first two looked progressive and unexposed. The form is rated fairly positively.
Veni Vedi Veci(IRE) Official explanation: jockey said filly lost its action
T/Jkpt: Not won. T/Plt: £1,026.10 to a £1 stake. Pool: £158,189.69. 112.54 winning tickets. T/Qpdt: £90.10 to a £1 stake. Pool: £7,261.97. 59.60 winning tickets. SP

3698 - 3702a (Foreign Racing) - See Raceform Interactive

[3045]LONGCHAMP (R-H)
Saturday, July 3

OFFICIAL GOING: Turf: soft

3703a PRIX DAPHNIS (GROUP 3) (3YO COLTS & GELDINGS) (TURF) 1m 1f 55y
1:35 (12:00) 3-Y-O **£35,398** (£14,159; £10,619; £7,079; £3,539)

			RPR
1		**Emerald Commander (IRE)**[20] 3016 3-8-11 0 FrankieDettori 2 (Saeed Bin Suroor) *led tl settled in 2nd after 2f: rdn 2f out: qcknd wl: grabbed ld 1 1/2f out: r.o wl* **3/1**[2]	102
2	*½*	**Wealthy (IRE)**[31] 3-8-11 0 Pierre-CharlesBoudot 1 (A Fabre, France) *racd in 3rd fr s: short of room 2f out: qcknd wl 1 1/2f out whn fnd clr run: fin wl* **6/1**[3]	101
2	*dht*	**Mellon Martini (USA)**[29] 2735 3-8-11 0 GeraldMosse 5 (A De Royer-Dupre, France) *settled last: c wd into st: rdn 2f out: fin wl to dead-heat for 2nd on line* **13/10**[1]	101
4	*½*	**Green Rock (FR)**[27] 2802 3-8-11 0 ChristopheSoumillon 3 (Mme M Bollack-Badel, France) *racd in 5th fr s: rdn 2f out: r.o wl ins fnl f* **8/1**	100
5	*nk*	**Pink Gin (FR)**[17] 3-8-11 0 OlivierPeslier 4 (J-M Beguigne, France) *racd in 2nd: rdn to ld after 2f: led tl 2f out: hdd and no ex fnl f* **6/1**[3]	99
6	*4*	**Kenmour (FR)**[20] 3-8-11 0 (p) AnthonyCrastus 6 (P Demercastel, France) *racd in 4th fr s: wnt 3rd at dist: rdn 1 1/2f out: no ex ins fnl f* **12/1**	91

2m 0.72s (5.42) **Going Correction** +0.85s/f (Soft) **6** Ran SP% **115.9**
Speed ratings: **109,108,108,108,107 104**
WIN (incl. 1 euro stake): 2.60 (Emerald Commander coupled with Wealthy). PLACES: 1.50, 1.30, 1.10. SF (Emerald Commander - Mellon Martini): 5.00; (Emerald Commander - Wealthy): 6.60.
Owner Godolphin **Bred** Grangecon Stud **Trained** Newmarket, Suffolk

NOTEBOOK
Emerald Commander(IRE) was happy to get a lead from Pink Gin before leading over a furlong out and then saw his race out in game style. His trainer stated that the morning rain was a help, as he likes cut, and he will now be aimed at the Prix Eugene Adam on July 25.

3704a PRIX DE LA PORTE MAILLOT (GROUP 3) (3YO+) (TURF) 7f
2:40 (12:00) 3-Y-O+ **£35,398** (£14,159; £10,619; £7,079; £3,539)

			RPR
1		**Joanna (IRE)**[27] 2801 3-8-10 0 ChristopheSoumillon 11 (J-C Rouget, France) *racd towards rr: prog early in st: qcknd wl 1 1/2f out: grabbed ld 150yds out: r.o wl* **6/4**[1]	104
2	*nk*	**Salut L'Africain (FR)**[28] 2778 5-9-2 0 (p) IoritzMendizabal 6 (Robert Collet, France) *prom early: styd on wl fr 300yds out: fin wl* **9/1**	104
3	*nk*	**Lovelace**[17] 3069 6-9-2 0 DominiqueBoeuf 3 (D Nicholls) *racd in 6th tl st: short of room in st: fin wl whn in clr* **34/1**	103
4	*¾*	**Flash Dance (IRE)**[33] 2615 4-8-13 0 MaximeGuyon 2 (H-A Pantall, France) *lost several l at s and stl in rr ent st: qcknd wl fr dist: r.o wl* **24/1**	98
5	*¾*	**Reggane**[28] 2744 4-8-13 0 GeraldMosse 8 (A De Royer-Dupre, France) *prom tl early in st: rdn: fnd no ex* **5/1**[2]	96
6	*2 ½*	**The Cheka (IRE)**[29] 2707 4-9-2 0 Christophe-PatriceLemaire 4 (Eve Johnson Houghton) *racd midfield: nvr threatened in st along rail: styd on* **10/1**	92
7	*1 ½*	**Pietra Santa (FR)**[19] 4-8-13 0 OlivierPeslier 7 (J-M Beguigne, France) *prom: one of ldrs ent st: rdn and wknd fr dist* **78/10**	85
8	*1*	**Indomito (GER)**[27] 2805 4-9-2 0 ThierryThulliez 9 (P Vovcenko, Germany) *towards rr fr s: nvr threatened: styd on* **28/1**	86
9	*5*	**Poet's Voice**[48] 2159 3-8-8 0 FrankieDettori 5 (Saeed Bin Suroor) *broke wl and sn led: maintaining ld early in st: rdn 2f out: fnd no ex: wknd towards rr* **58/10**[3]	69
10	*6*	**Slickly Royal (FR)**[20] 3017 6-9-2 0 (b) AnthonyCrastus 1 (P Demercastel, France) *prom tl 2f out: fdd* **19/1**	56
11		**Blue And Gold (FR)**[28] 2778 4-8-13 0 YannLerner 10 (C Lerner, France) *nvr figured* **88/1**	53

1m 24.23s (3.53) **Going Correction** +0.85s/f (Soft)
WFA 3 from 4yo+ 8lb **11** Ran SP% **118.3**
Speed ratings: **113,112,112,111,110 107,106,104,99,92 92**
WIN (incl. 1 euro stake): 2.50. PLACES: 1.40, 2.20, 5.30. DF: 11.40. SF: 17.60.
Owner Hamdan Al Maktoum **Bred** Giovanni Faldutto **Trained** Pau, France

NOTEBOOK
Joanna(IRE) quickened up nicely to hit the front inside the final furlong and proved tough in the finish. Highly regarded by her trainer, she now goes for the Prix Maurice De Gheest on August 8.
Lovelace ran well and according to his jockey may have been a bit unlucky as he was stuck in traffic for a while in the home straight.
The Cheka(IRE) was always in about the same place and never got in an effective challenge.
Poet's Voice tried to make all, but faded rapidly once headed.

[3196]AYR (L-H)
Sunday, July 4

OFFICIAL GOING: Good (good to soft in places; 9.1)
Straight course stands' rail moved in 3yds. Round course straights moved out 4m and bends 2m increasing round course distances by about 6yds.
Wind: Strong, half against Weather: Cloudy

3705 UNISON'S AYRSHIRE & ARRAN HEALTH BRANCH MEDIAN AUCTION MAIDEN STKS 7f 50y
2:10 (2:14) (Class 5) 2-Y-O **£2,590** (£770; £385; £192) **Stalls** High

Form				RPR
4240	**1**		**Diamond Geezah (IRE)**[19] 3051 2-9-3 0 FrannyNorton 2 (B W Hills) *trckd ldr: rdn to ld over 1f out: kpt on wl fnl f* **7/4**[1]	86+
2	**2**	*2 ¼*	**Next Edition (IRE)**[15] 3222 2-9-3 0 TomEaves 4 (J Howard Johnson) *dictated ordinary gallop: rdn and hdd over 1f out: kpt on same pce ins fnl f* **3/1**[2]	80
	3	*½*	**Goldenveil (IRE)** 2-8-12 0 TonyHamilton 1 (R A Fahey) *t.k.h: trckd ldrs: effrt 2f out: kpt on same pce fnl f* **16/1**	74+
353	**4**	*8*	**Little Miss Take**[9] 3386 2-8-7 0 RossAtkinson(5) 7 (Tom Dascombe) *stdd in tch: rdn over 3f out: wknd fr over 2f out* **8/1**[3]	55
0	**5**	*3*	**Arctic Cat (IRE)**[21] 2990 2-9-3 0 AndrewElliott 5 (G A Swinbank) *hld up in tch: rdn 3f out: sn wknd* **22/1**	52
44	**6**	*1 ¾*	**Golden Blaze**[31] 2667 2-9-3 0 RoystonFfrench 6 (James Moffatt) *hld up in tch: outpcd over 3f out: btn fnl 2f* **50/1**	48

1m 32.51s (-0.89) **Going Correction** -0.20s/f (Firm) **6** Ran SP% **84.7**
Speed ratings (Par 94): **97,94,93,84,81 79**
Tote Swingers: 1&2 £1.10, 1&3 £2.60, 2&3 £3.60 CSF £3.67 TOTE £1.90: £1.10, £1.30; EX 3.70.
Owner Rebel Racing **Bred** Camogue Stud Ltd **Trained** Lambourn, Berks
■ Cotton Spirit was withdrawn after getting loose before the start (5/2, deduct 25p in the £ under R4).

FOCUS
The course had 12mm of rain in the early hours of the morning and the ground was officially eased to good, good to soft in places. There was also a strong wind blowing half across the track just prior to this opening juvenile maiden and it looked hard work for the runners.

NOTEBOOK
Diamond Geezah(IRE) had been outclassed in the Windsor Castle on his previous outing and so this was obviously a lot easier for him. His stable also has a great record at this venue, but the step up to this trip was a question mark. He answered positively, though, coming away readily nearing the final furlong and clearly stays very well. It is likely to be nurseries now for him. (op 2-1)
Next Edition(IRE), an encouraging second over this trip at Redcar on debut, took the field along at an average pace and tried to make it a test. He was a sitting duck for the winner, but kept on all the way to the line once headed and is sure to win a race or two this year. He will also get another furlong without much fuss. (op 7-2 tchd 4-1)
Goldenveil(IRE), whose better-fancied stablemate Cotton Spirit was withdrawn after unseating his rider and running loose down at the start, posted a very pleasing debut effort. She missed the break, but was soon racing handy and took a keen hold. She kept on gamely for a debutante considering the strong wind and should soon be winning.
Little Miss Take was never seriously on terms with the principals and may not have enjoyed the easing ground. (op 13-2)

3706 TOTEPLACEPOT H'CAP 7f 50y
2:40 (2:40) (Class 5) (0-70,68) 3-Y-O+ **£2,590** (£770; £385; £192) **Stalls** High

Form				RPR
000	**1**		**Signore Momento (IRE)**[38] 2462 4-9-11 **68** (tp) GFCarroll(3) 1 (Miss Amy Weaver) *prom: effrt over 1f out: led ins fnl f: rdn and hld on wl* **4/1**[2]	76
0040	**2**	*nk*	**Hosanna**[10] 3357 4-8-9 **49** RoystonFfrench 5 (J Barclay) *trckd ldr: led over 1f out to ins fnl f: kpt on u.p* **33/1**	56
0224	**3**	*¾*	**Stellite**[16] 3150 10-9-8 **65** GaryBartley(3) 8 (J S Goldie) *hld up: hdwy over 1f out: kpt on fnl f: no ex towards fin* **6/1**	70+
0601	**4**	*2 ½*	**Prime Circle**[22] 2965 4-9-6 **60** (p) FrannyNorton 6 (A D Brown) *in tch: rdn and edgd lft over 2f out: sn outpcd: kpt on ins fnl f: nt pce to chal* **7/1**	59
2515	**5**	*½*	**Mr Lu**[16] 3164 5-9-10 **64** PaulHanagan 9 (J S Goldie) *trckd ldrs: effrt over 2f out: edgd lft over 1f out: one pce fnl f* **13/2**	61
3630	**6**	*½*	**Spavento (IRE)**[9] 3391 4-9-5 **59** (p) DavidAllan 4 (E J Alston) *midfield: drvn over 2f out: no imp fr over 1f out* **11/4**[1]	55
0040	**7**	*2 ¾*	**Barnstorm**[9] 3387 3-8-11 **59** (b[1]) JoeFanning 2 (M Johnston) *t.k.h: led tl edgd rt and hdd over 1f out: sn btn* **9/2**[3]	45
000-	**8**	*6*	**Santiago Atitlan**[226] 7171 8-9-1 **55** TonyHamilton 3 (P Monteith) *hld up: rdn over 2f out: wknd wl over 1f out* **50/1**	28
00-0	**9**	*34*	**Defi (IRE)**[63] 1719 8-8-9 **49** oh4 (bt) PatrickMathers 7 (D A Nolan) *bhd: struggling 1/2-way: sn btn* **100/1**	—

1m 32.27s (-1.13) **Going Correction** -0.20s/f (Firm)
WFA 3 from 4yo+ 8lb **9** Ran SP% **110.9**
Speed ratings (Par 103): **98,97,96,93,93 92,89,82,43**
Tote Swingers: 1&2 £22.40, 1&3 £6.90, 2&3 £16.20 CSF £113.03 CT £753.20 TOTE £6.10: £1.70, £5.20, £1.90; EX 123.90.
Owner White, Bringloe, Warner and Murphy **Bred** P J Moloney **Trained** Newmarket, Suffolk
■ Stewards' Enquiry : Gary Bartley one-day ban: careless riding (Jul 18)

FOCUS
An ordinary handicap, run at a solid pace and the first three came clear late on.
Signore Momento(IRE) Official explanation: trainer said, regarding apparent improvement in form, that the gelding benefited from the application of first time cheek pieces and first time tongue strap and the yard is coming into form.
Barnstorm Official explanation: jockey said gelding hung badly right

3707 TOTESWINGER FLEXI BETTING H'CAP 1m 1f 20y
3:10 (3:14) (Class 6) (0-65,65) 4-Y-0+ **£1,942** (£578; £288; £144) **Stalls** Low

Form				RPR
4-40	**1**		**Red Skipper (IRE)**[32] 1576 5-8-7 **51** ... DavidAllan 1 (N Wilson) *mde all: rdn clr over 1f out: hld on wl fnl f* **11/4**[2]	59
-324	**2**	½	**Grand Diamond (IRE)**[6] 3499 6-9-4 **65** ...(p) GaryBartley(3) 4 (J S Goldie) *hld up on ins: effrt whn nt clr run over 2f out: hdwy to chse wnr ins fnl f: r.o but a hld* **9/4**[1]	72
3024	**3**	2 ½	**Saving Grace**[9] 3391 4-8-8 **55** ... KellyHarrison(3) 6 (E J Alston) *cl up: rdn over 2f out: chsd wnr over 1f out to ins fnl f: kpt on same pce* **5/1**[3]	57
6456	**4**	¾	**Papa's Princess**[18] 3074 6-8-2 **46** oh1 ... FrannyNorton 11 (James Moffatt) *hld up: hdwy on outside 2f out: edgd lft and kpt on fnl f: no imp* **20/1**	46
5-00	**5**	½	**Marillos Proterras**[10] 3370 4-8-2 **46** oh1 ...(b) DuranFentiman 9 (Mrs A Duffield) *hld up: rdn 3f out: hdwy over 1f out: kpt on: nvr able to chal* **40/1**	45
0050	**6**	¾	**Primo Way**[5] 3531 9-8-6 **50** oh1 ow4 ...(be) PatrickMathers 5 (D A Nolan) *bhd tl hdwy over 1f out: nrst fin* **40/1**	48
3002	**7**	¾	**Maybe I Wont**[10] 3377 5-9-0 **58** ...(p) JoeFanning 13 (Lucinda Featherstone) *prom: rdn over 2f out: nt qckn appr fnl f* **10/1**	54
655	**8**	¾	**Casino Night**[18] 3074 5-8-8 **59** ... LeeTopliss(7) 10 (R Johnson) *in tch: rdn over 2f out: sn one pce* **16/1**	53
13-0	**9**	4 ½	**Social Rhythm**[47] 2207 6-9-1 **59** ... TomEaves 2 (A C Whillans) *prom: rdn over 2f out: wknd over 1f out* **14/1**	44
1050	**10**	4 ½	**Wrongwayround (IRE)**[31] 2670 4-9-6 **64** ... AndrewElliott 3 (G A Swinbank) *towards rr: struggling 3f out: sn btn* **11/1**	40
-260	**11**	1 ¼	**Bed Fellow (IRE)**[16] 3147 6-8-8 **52** ... TonyHamilton 12 (P Monteith) *pressed wnr: rdn and edgd lft over 2f out: wknd over 1f out* **25/1**	25
0-00	**12**	¾	**Suburbia (USA)**[16] 3147 4-8-5 **49** ... RoystonFfrench 8 (J Barclay) *towards rr: drvn over 3f out: sn struggling* **50/1**	20

1m 56.25s (-2.15) **Going Correction** -0.20s/f (Firm) **12** Ran SP% **119.5**
Speed ratings (Par 101): **101,100,98,97,97 96,95,95,91,87 86,85**
Tote Swingers: 1&2 £2.20, 1&3 £3.50, 2&3 £4.00 CSF £8.86 CT £29.51 TOTE £3.30: £1.20, £1.10, £1.80; EX 9.70.
Owner The Sandburn Racing Partnership **Bred** Keith Moran **Trained** Sandhutton, N Yorks

FOCUS
An open-looking handicap in which there was no hanging about early on.

3708 CAMPBELTOWN BAR STEWART SCOTT MEMORIAL H'CAP 1m
3:40 (3:41) (Class 4) (0-85,84) 3-Y-0+ **£4,792** (£1,425; £712; £355) **Stalls** Low

Form				RPR
25	**1**		**Silver Rime (FR)**[11] 3318 5-10-0 **80** ... PhillipMakin 6 (Miss L A Perratt) *dwlt: hld up: smooth hdwy on outside over 2f out: rdn to ld ins fnl f: r.o* **11/2**	88
-000	**2**	¾	**Espero (IRE)**[11] 3318 4-9-10 **76** ... GrahamGibbons 3 (Miss L A Perratt) *trckd ldrs gng wl: led and rdn over 1f out: edgd rt and hdd ins fnl f: kpt on* **15/2**	82
2314	**3**	1 ¼	**Daring Dream (GER)**[5] 3531 5-8-12 **67** ... GaryBartley(3) 4 (J S Goldie) *hld up: nt clr run and swtchd rt over 2f out: effrt over 1f out: kpt on ins fnl f* **9/4**[1]	70+
4146	**4**	¾	**Bin Shamardal (IRE)**[25] 2863 3-9-2 **77** ... FrannyNorton 5 (B W Hills) *prom: effrt over 2f out: kpt on same pce fnl f* **5/1**[3]	77
-535	**5**	6	**Talk Of Saafend (IRE)**[5] 3531 5-8-11 **63** ... TonyHamilton 9 (P Monteith) *dwlt: hld up: pushed along over 2f out: sn outpcd* **18/1**	51
-102	**6**	4 ½	**Loveinthesand (IRE)**[5] 3539 3-8-11 **72** ... JoeFanning 2 (M Johnston) *in tch: drvn and outpcd 1/2-way: no imp fr over 2f out* **3/1**[2]	48
-020	**7**	½	**Jewelled Dagger (IRE)**[11] 3317 6-9-9 **75** ... TomEaves 1 (J S Goldie) *led tl rdn and wknd over 1f out: sn wknd* **11/1**	51
062	**8**	12	**Hail Bold Chief (USA)**[5] 3530 3-8-2 **63** ... AndrewElliott 7 (G A Swinbank) *pressed ldr tl rdn and wknd over 2f out* **16/1**	10

1m 41.12s (-2.68) **Going Correction** -0.20s/f (Firm)
WFA 3 from 4yo+ 9lb **8** Ran SP% **119.1**
Speed ratings (Par 105): **105,104,103,102,96 91,91,79**
Tote Swingers: 1&2 £5.10, 1&3 £4.50, 2&3 £5.80 CSF £47.82 CT £120.66 TOTE £5.80: £1.20, £5.70, £1.10; EX 36.70.
Owner Ken McGarrity **Bred** Jean-Philippe Dubois **Trained** East Kilbride, South Lanarks
■ Stewards' Enquiry : Graham Gibbons caution: careless riding.

FOCUS
This modest handicap was another race run at a decent early tempo.

3709 TOTEEXACTA FLEXI BETTING H'CAP 1m 5f 13y
4:10 (4:11) (Class 5) (0-70,70) 4-Y-0+ **£2,590** (£770; £385; £192) **Stalls** Low

Form				RPR
S-45	**1**		**Balwearie (IRE)**[6] 3499 9-8-2 **51** oh1 ... FrannyNorton 7 (Miss L A Perratt) *t.k.h: cl up: led over 7f out: qckned over 2f out: hld on wl fnl f* **12/1**	62
363	**2**	nk	**Blazing Desert**[16] 3176 6-9-3 **66** ... GrahamGibbons 3 (J J Quinn) *tk keen hold: prom: effrt and chsd wnr over 1f out: r.o u.p fnl f* **5/1**[3]	77
0-21	**3**	1	**Forrest Flyer (IRE)**[16] 3152 6-9-4 **67** ... PhillipMakin 2 (J S Goldie) *trckd ldrs: effrt over 2f out: kpt on u.p ins fnl f* **11/8**[1]	76
02	**4**	4	**Hunters Belt (IRE)**[23] 2941 6-9-4 **67** ... TomEaves 9 (N Wilson) *hld up in tch: effrt over 2f out: edgd lft and outpcd over 1f out* **7/2**[2]	70
5256	**5**	¾	**Lisbon Lion (IRE)**[18] 3078 5-8-1 **53** ow2 ... KellyHarrison(3) 5 (James Moffatt) *hld up: stdy hdwy over 2f out: rdn wl over 1f out: sn no ex* **15/2**	55
4-04	**6**	3 ½	**Snowberry Hill (USA)**[24] 2907 7-8-2 **51** oh6 ... JoeFanning 4 (Lucinda Featherstone) *led to over 7f out: rdn and wknd fr 2f out* **14/1**	48
000-	**7**	6	**Oh Landino (GER)**[32] 4529 5-7-11 **51** oh6 ... JamesSullivan(5) 6 (P Monteith) *t.k.h: hld up: rdn over 3f out: nvr on terms* **66/1**	39
-446	**8**	½	**Shy Glance (USA)**[5] 3531 8-9-7 **70** ... TonyHamilton 1 (P Monteith) *prom tl rdn and wknd over 2f out* **16/1**	57

2m 54.01s (0.01) **Going Correction** -0.20s/f (Firm) **8** Ran SP% **114.5**
Speed ratings (Par 103): **91,90,90,87,87 85,81,81**
Tote Swingers: 1&2 £8.20, 1&3 £5.80, 2&3 £3.00 CSF £70.68 CT £135.99 TOTE £18.30: £4.30, £2.30, £1.10; EX 77.90.
Owner Ken McGarrity **Bred** Ms Amy Mulligan **Trained** East Kilbride, South Lanarks

FOCUS
A moderate staying handicap. Nothing got involved from off the pace as the first three dominated.

3710 TOTETRIFECTA FLEXI BETTING H'CAP 6f
4:40 (4:43) (Class 6) (0-60,60) 3-Y-0 **£1,942** (£578; £288; £144) **Stalls** Centre

Form				RPR
3545	**1**		**Monte Mayor One**[5] 3534 3-8-13 **55** ... TonyHamilton 3 (P Monteith) *prom: effrt over 1f out: rdn to ld ins fnl f: hld on wl towards fin* **14/1**	66
6-61	**2**	shd	**Dies Solis**[9] 3393 3-9-0 **56** ... DuranFentiman 2 (N Wilson) *led: rdn over 1f out: hdd ins fnl f: r.o* **15/8**[1]	67
4060	**3**	5	**Weetentherty**[6] 3501 3-8-12 **54** ...(v) TomEaves 5 (J S Goldie) *hld up: hdwy over 1f out: kpt on fnl f: nt rch first two* **18/1**	49
63-0	**4**	4 ½	**Chookie Avon**[44] 2296 3-9-4 **60** ... DavidAllan 1 (N Wilson) *prom tl rdn and outpcd over 1f out* **18/1**	41
5256	**5**	½	**Drumpellier (IRE)**[9] 3393 3-9-3 **59** ... PhillipMakin 10 (P T Midgley) *hld up in tch: pushed along 2f out: nvr able to chal* **6/1**[3]	38
6004	**6**	1	**Reach For The Sky (IRE)**[16] 3167 3-8-3 **52** ... CharlotteKerton(7) 6 (A Berry) *dwlt: bhd: rdn over 2f out: nvr on terms* **33/1**	28
0-00	**7**	nk	**Hot Rod Mamma (IRE)**[20] 3027 3-8-5 **47** ow1 ... RoystonFfrench 8 (Mrs Dianne Sayer) *prom tl rdn and wknd over 1f out* **50/1**	22
-600	**8**	1 ½	**Firetrap**[11] 3322 3-8-8 **53** ...(b[1]) BarryMcHugh(3) 11 (Mrs A Duffield) *hld up in tch: rdn over 2f out: edgd lft and wknd over 1f out* **7/1**	23
6263	**9**	3	**Classlin**[9] 3410 3-8-3 **50** ... IanBrennan(5) 7 (J S Goldie) *dwlt and wnt rt s: a bhd: no ch fr over 2f out* **11/1**	10
60-6	**10**	1 ¼	**North Shadow**[12] 3284 3-9-2 **58** ...(p) FrannyNorton 9 (A D Brown) *chsd ldrs: drvn over 2f out: wknd wl over 1f out* **3/1**[2]	14

1m 13.2s (-0.40) **Going Correction** -0.10s/f (Good) **10** Ran SP% **117.0**
Speed ratings (Par 98): **98,97,91,85,84 83,82,80,76,75**
Tote Swingers: 1&2 £6.30, 1&3 £20.20, 2&3 £8.20 CSF £40.70 CT £438.50 TOTE £13.80: £4.20, £1.10, £7.70; EX 52.50 TRIFECTA Not won..
Owner The Dregs Of Humanity **Bred** Mrs D J Hughes **Trained** Rosewell, Midlothian
■ Stewards' Enquiry : Duran Fentiman one-day ban: used whip with excessive frequency (Jul 18)

FOCUS
The first two came right away in this poor sprint handicap and fought out a bobbing finish. The field kept to the middle of the track throughout.
Reach For The Sky(IRE) Official explanation: jockey said filly hung left throughout
North Shadow Official explanation: trainer said gelding lost a shoe

3711 TOTEPOOL A BETTER WAY TO BET AMATEUR RIDERS' H'CAP 5f
5:10 (5:11) (Class 6) (0-60,61) 4-Y-0+ **£1,977** (£608; £304) **Stalls** Centre

Form				RPR
0-20	**1**		**Arriva La Diva**[19] 3064 4-10-2 **51** ... MissJCoward(3) 9 (J J Quinn) *prom: hdwy over 1f out: shkn up and led ins fnl f: r.o wl* **4/1**[2]	62
-262	**2**	¾	**Foreign Rhythm (IRE)**[12] 3287 5-10-1 **52** ... MissVBarr(5) 1 (R E Barr) *led: rdn and 2 l clr over 1f out: hdd ins fnl f: r.o* **8/1**	60
6041	**3**	hd	**Angelo Poliziano**[2] 3623 4-10-10 **61** ...(b) MrJMQuinlan(5) 10 (Mrs A Duffield) *hld up: hdwy over 1f out: chsng ldrs whn hung lft ins fnl f: r.o* **7/4**[1]	69
40-0	**4**	2 ½	**Bees River (IRE)**[6] 3497 4-10-0 **46** oh1 ... MrsCBartley 11 (J S Goldie) *stdd s: hld up: effrt over 1f out: kpt on fnl f: nrst fin* **6/1**[3]	45
0033	**5**	shd	**Misterisland (IRE)**[15] 3200 5-9-11 **46** ...(p) MissMMullineaux(3) 7 (M Mullineaux) *bhd: drvn 1/2-way: hdwy over 1f out: nvr rchd ldrs* **12/1**	44
6005	**6**	3 ½	**Handsinthemist (IRE)**[128] 716 5-10-0 **46** oh1 ... MissSBrotherton 2 (Anthony Mulholland, Ire) *pressed ldr: rdn over 2f out: wknd over 1f out* **16/1**	32
6005	**7**	1 ½	**Spirit Of Coniston**[30] 2695 7-10-7 **58** ... MissWGibson(5) 6 (P T Midgley) *in tch: shkn up whn n.m.r wl over 1f out: sn outpcd* **10/1**	38
6300	**8**	hd	**Officer Mor (USA)**[25] 2854 4-9-9 **46** oh1 ... MissECSayer(5) 5 (Mrs Dianne Sayer) *s.i.s: hld up: effrt whn carried lft wl over 1f out: sn wknd* **20/1**	26
0-00	**9**	1	**Thunder Bay**[44] 2278 5-9-13 **50** ... MissKECooper(5) 4 (R E Barr) *in tch on outside tl wknd wl over 1f out* **18/1**	26
0-00	**10**	1 ¼	**Obe One**[5] 3534 10-9-7 **46** oh1 ...(b) MissDLenge(7) 3 (A Berry) *in tch: rdn and hung lft wl over 1f out: sn btn* **66/1**	17

61.41 secs (1.31) **Going Correction** -0.10s/f (Good) **10** Ran SP% **115.9**
Speed ratings (Par 101): **85,83,83,79,79 73,71,71,69,67**
Tote Swingers: 1&2 £7.90, 1&3 £3.20, 2&3 £4.00 CSF £35.87 CT £76.50 TOTE £5.40: £2.00, £2.30, £1.30 Place 6: £17.12 Place 5: £14.97 .
Owner Allan Stennett **Bred** Mickley Stud, Stennett, Hillside Racing **Trained** Settrington, N Yorks

FOCUS
A typically weak handicap for amateur riders and once again the main action developed down the centre of the track, with the first three pulling well clear.
T/Plt: £23.80 to a £1 stake. Pool: £68,219.045. 2,085.59 winning tickets. T/Qpdt: £4.70 to a £1 stake. Pool: £4,450.66. 688.48 winning tickets. RY

3522 BRIGHTON (L-H)
Sunday, July 4

OFFICIAL GOING: Firm (good to firm in places; 9.4)
Rail dolled out from 4.5f to 2f increasing advertised distances by about 30yds.
Wind: Fresh, against Weather: Bright and Breezy

3712 EUROPEAN BREEDERS' FUND BET365 MEDIAN AUCTION MAIDEN STKS 5f 213y
2:30 (2:31) (Class 5) 2-Y-0 **£3,154** (£944; £472; £236; £117) **Stalls** Low

Form				RPR
602	**1**		**Sonoran Sands (IRE)**[10] 3362 2-9-3 0 ... LiamKeniry 5 (J S Moore) *mde all: nudged clr 2f out: sn wl clr: eased towards fin: v easily* **8/11**[1]	83+
60	**2**	9	**Smart Red**[9] 3386 2-8-12 0 ... SamHitchcott 2 (M R Channon) *chsd ldng pair: rdn and wl outpcd by wnr 2f out: wl btn after: wnt modest 2nd jst ins fnl f* **13/2**[3]	48
06	**3**	2 ¼	**Cinq Heavens (IRE)**[17] 3126 2-9-3 0 ... RichardKingscote 4 (Tom Dascombe) *w wnr tl c towards stands' side fr 3f out: outpcd by wnr 2f out and wl btn after: lost modest 2nd jst ins fnl f* **8/1**	46
	4	4 ½	**Surprise (IRE)** 2-8-12 0 ... AhmedAjtebi 1 (Mahmood Al Zarooni) *s.i.s: sn rcvrd and chsd ldrs: rdn and btn ent fnl 2f: wknd fnl f* **3/1**[2]	33

6 5 1 3/4 **Pigeon Hollow**[7] 3472 2-9-3 0 ChrisCatlin 3 28
(M R Channon) *s.i.s and reminders sn after s: a deatached in last: lost tch 1/2-way* **40/1**

1m 11.25s (1.05) **Going Correction** +0.20s/f (Good) **5** Ran SP% **109.8**
Speed ratings (Par 94): **101,89,86,80,77**
CSF £6.06 TOTE £1.70: £1.10, £2.80; EX 5.50.
Owner Ernest H Moore **Bred** Lynn Lodge Stud **Trained** Upper Lambourn, Berks

FOCUS
There had been no rain at the track for three weeks, but 30mm of water had been put down in that period to keep the ground safe. It was described as firm, good to firm in places (9.4). The rail was dolled out from the 4.5f point to the 2f pole, adding approximately 30 yards to race distances. A modest maiden won by the form choice.

NOTEBOOK
Sonoran Sands(IRE) finished seventh in the Windsor Castle Stakes two starts back but let odds-on backers down at Leicester subsequently. He made no mistake here, though, was soon in front and proceeded to make every yard. He drew right away in the closing stages but beat very little and connections will be hoping the handicapper doesn't take too much action. Nevertheless, they might opt to turn him out quickly as he's already entered in a nursery at Newmarket on Friday. (tchd 4-6 and 4-5)

Smart Red was dropping back a furlong in distance, which wasn't sure to suit on pedigree. Her best chance will lie in nurseries in due course. (op 15-2 tchd 6-1)

Cinq Heavens(IRE) drifted over towards the middle of the track and then towards the stands' side. He's another for whom handicaps will present better opportunities. (op 12-1)

Surprise(IRE), whose sales price shot up from 21,000gns as a yearling to 160,000gns as a two-year-old at the breeze-ups, is a half-sister to five winners at up to 7f, including smart sprinter Triple Aspect. Her stable is in form, but this is not an easy track for a juvenile to make its racecourse debut and she ran pretty green. She should come on a deal for the experience. (op 5-2)

3713 BET365 MAIDEN STKS 7f 214y
3:00 (3:00) (Class 5) 3-Y-O £2,590 (£770) **Stalls** Low

Form RPR
-225 1 **King Of Reason**[17] 3103 3-9-3 83 ShaneKelly 3 89+
(D M Simcock) *chsd rival: cruised upsides over 2f out: led on bit wl over 1f out: sn clr: nt extended* **4/7**[1]

4-35 2 16 **Lay Claim (USA)**[31] 2682 3-9-3 77 (v[1]) RyanMoore 2 70
(Sir Michael Stoute) *led: rdn over 2f out: drvn and hdd wl over 1f out: immediately btn: eased fnl f* **11/8**[2]

1m 38.1s (2.10) **Going Correction** +0.20s/f (Good) **2** Ran SP% **105.8**
Speed ratings (Par 100): **97,81**
TOTE £1.20.
Owner Saeed Manana **Bred** Darley **Trained** Newmarket, Suffolk

FOCUS
A poor turnout for this maiden.

3714 BET365 H'CAP 1m 1f 209y
3:30 (3:30) (Class 5) (0-70,69) 3-Y-O £2,460 (£732; £365; £182) **Stalls** High

Form RPR
4425 1 **Celestial Girl**[61] 1796 3-8-7 55 ChrisCatlin 1 62
(H Morrison) *t.k.h: hld up in tch towards rr: rdn and effrt on inner ent fnl 2f: led ent fnl f: spooked by seagulls on crse and sn hung bdly rt: styd on wl fnl f* **10/1**

2502 2 2 **Red Yarn**[8] 3441 3-9-7 69 (b) RyanMoore 8 72
(G L Moore) *stdd s: t.k.h: hld up in last: rdn and c to stands' rail ent fnl 2f: hdwy u.p over 1f out: chsd wnr ins fnl f: no imp fnl 75yds* **5/2**[1]

4535 3 1/2 **Whiepa Snappa (IRE)**[13] 3273 3-8-7 60 KierenFox[(5)] 5 63
(P M Phelan) *chsd ldrs: hdwy to chal over 2f out: rdn to ld over 1f out: hdd: pushed rt and bdly hmpd ent fnl f: nt rcvr and kpt on same pce fnl f* **7/2**[2]

4431 4 3 3/4 **Denton Ryal**[7] 3478 3-7-9 50 LeonnaMayor[(7)] 3 45
(M E Rimmer) *pressed ldr: ev ch and rdn ent fnl 2f: keeping on same pce whn hmpd ent fnl f: wknd fnl f* **7/2**[2]

U552 5 1/2 **Until The Man (IRE)**[16] 3155 3-9-5 67 (p) IanMongan 4 61
(Mrs L J Mongan) *led: jnd and rdn over 2f out: hdd over 1f out: stl ev ch whn hmpd ent fnl f: wknd fnl f* **9/2**[3]

0-64 6 1 1/4 **Vadition (IRE)**[28] 2782 3-8-2 50 oh5 NeilChalmers 9 41
(J J Bridger) *chsd ldrs tl wknd u.p over 1f out: wl btn fnl f* **100/1**

0-45 7 1/2 **Fancy Star**[29] 2754 3-9-3 65 MichaelHills 7 55
(B W Hills) *stdd s: t.k.h: hld up in rr: hdwy to trck ldrs 3f out: n.m.r over 2f out: rdn and nt qckn wl over 1f out: wknd ent fnl f* **11/1**

2m 5.67s (2.07) **Going Correction** +0.20s/f (Good) **7** Ran SP% **109.6**
Speed ratings (Par 100): **99,97,97,94,93 92,92**
Tote Swingers: 1&2 £2.50, 1&3 £13.20, 2&3 £3.80 CSF £32.38 CT £97.74 TOTE £6.40: £4.20, £2.20; EX 28.00 Trifecta £41.40 Pool: £136.30 - 2.43 winning units..
Owner Helena Springfield Ltd **Bred** Meon Valley Stud **Trained** East Ilsley, Berks

FOCUS
A modest handicap.

3715 BET365.COM H'CAP 7f 214y
4:00 (4:00) (Class 6) (0-65,65) 3-Y-O+ £2,072 (£616; £308; £153) **Stalls** Low

Form RPR
5410 1 **Inquisitress**[13] 3264 6-8-12 49 NeilChalmers 3 56
(J J Bridger) *t.k.h early: hld up in tch: hdwy to trck ldrs 3f out: pushed ahd ent fnl f: edgd rt u.p but battled on gamely fnl f* **12/1**[3]

-662 2 1/2 **Fire King**[12] 3291 4-8-13 50 (p) SebSanders 8 56
(A B Haynes) *chsd ldng pair: wnt 2nd over 4f out: upsides ldr travelling wl 3f out: rdn wl over 1f out: stl ev ch and hrd drvn 1f out: edgd rt and a jst hld fnl f* **9/4**[1]

4066 3 2 1/2 **Easy Wonder (GER)**[5] 3524 5-8-9 46 oh1 CathyGannon 2 46
(I A Wood) *hld up in rr: rdn and effrt over 2f out: kpt on u.p fnl f: nt pce to chal ldng pair* **16/1**

0405 4 1 3/4 **Prince Valentine**[12] 3291 9-8-9 46 (p) RyanMoore 7 42
(G L Moore) *t.k.h early: hld up in tch: rdn and unable qck ent fnl 2f: kpt on u.p ins fnl f: nt pce to threaten ldrs* **6/1**[2]

0543 5 2 1/2 **Cordell (IRE)**[19] 3054 5-9-12 63 (t) IanMongan 5 53
(Jim Best) *led: rdn ent fnl 2f: hrd drvn and hdd jst over 1f out: n.m.r and sltly hmpd 1f out: sn wknd* **6/1**[2]

0000 6 nk **Mr Loire**[5] 3524 6-8-4 46 oh1 (b) SimonPearce[(5)] 4 36
(M F Harris) *s.i.s: t.k.h: hld up in tch towards rr: n.m.r and hmpd over 4f out: effrt u.p 2f out: no prog and btn whn short of room jst over 1f out* **25/1**

5200 7 6 **Libertino (IRE)**[10] 3359 3-9-0 60 (b) ChrisCatlin 10 34
(J Gallagher) *hld up in tch: hdwy to chse ldrs over 3f out: drvn and nt qckn ent fnl 2f: wknd over 1f out* **16/1**

-002 8 4 1/2 **Lady Florence**[32] 2456 5-9-10 61 MichaelHills 1 42
(A B Coogan) *awkward leaving stalls: sn chsng ldr tl over 4f out: rdn and lost pl over 2f out: wl btn 1f out* **9/4**[1]

1m 37.38s (1.38) **Going Correction** +0.20s/f (Good)
WFA 3 from 4yo+ 9lb **8** Ran SP% **113.4**
Speed ratings (Par 101): **101,100,98,96,93 93,87,82**
Tote Swingers: 1&2 £4.70, 1&3 £8.30, 2&3 £3.80 CSF £38.72 CT £444.15 TOTE £11.10: £2.20, £1.40, £3.70; EX 41.50 TRIFECTA Not won..
Owner C Marshall T Wallace J J Bridger **Bred** A Saccomando **Trained** Liphook, Hants

FOCUS
A low-grade handicap.

3716 CASINO AT BET365 H'CAP 6f 209y
4:30 (4:30) (Class 5) (0-75,75) 3-Y-O+ £2,460 (£732; £365; £182) **Stalls** Centre

Form RPR
3353 1 **High Importance (USA)**[5] 3539 3-9-3 72 (v) RyanMoore 4 81
(J Noseda) *chsd clr ldng trio: pushed along: swtchd rt and clsd wl over 2f out: swtchd rt again and drvn ahd ent fnl f: kpt up to work and drew clr fnl f* **5/4**[1]

50-2 2 8 **Patavium Prince (IRE)**[12] 3289 7-9-12 73 IanMongan 6 63
(Miss Jo Crowley) *stdd s: hld up in last pair: clsd and in tch over 2f out: rdn wl over 1f out: wl outpcd by wnr 1f out: wnt modest 2nd fnl 150yds* **5/1**[3]

-133 3 2 3/4 **Ocean Countess (IRE)**[12] 3289 4-9-10 71 CathyGannon 2 54
(Miss J Feilden) *s.i.s: nvr gng wl in rr: reminders sn after s: clsd u.p 3f out: wl outpcd over 1f out and wl btn after* **5/1**[3]

-350 4 hd **Berbice (IRE)**[26] 2840 5-10-0 75 (e) PatDobbs 5 57
(S Kirk) *racd keenly: led for 1f: styd upsides ldrs tl rdn to ld over 1f out: hdd ent fnl f: immediately btn: fdd fnl f* **11/1**

-455 5 13 **Super Frank (IRE)**[12] 3292 7-8-12 59 (p) SebSanders 3 6
(J Akehurst) *w ldrs: led over 4f out: tl over 1f out: sn wknd: wl btn and eased wl ins fnl f* **4/1**[2]

5336 6 6 **Mini Max**[5] 3525 3-8-1 56 NickyMackay 1 —
(B W Duke) *dwlt: sn rcvrd to press ldrs: led after 1f tl 4f out: wkng whn n.m.r over 2f out: wl bhd fr over 1f out: eased wl ins fnl f* **12/1**

1m 22.37s (-0.73) **Going Correction** +0.20s/f (Good)
WFA 3 from 4yo+ 8lb **6** Ran SP% **113.8**
Speed ratings (Par 103): **112,102,99,99,84 77**
Tote Swingers: 1&2 £2.30, 1&3 £2.40, 2&3 £3.30 CSF £8.15 TOTE £2.30: £1.40, £2.60; EX 8.80.
Owner Saeed Suhail **Bred** River Bend Farm Inc **Trained** Newmarket, Suffolk

FOCUS
The leaders went off too quick and set the race up for those ridden more patiently.

3717 POKER AT BET365 H'CAP 5f 59y
5:00 (5:00) (Class 6) (0-55,56) 3-Y-O+ £2,072 (£616; £308; £153) **Stalls** Low

Form RPR
0061 1 **Mandhooma**[5] 3526 4-9-0 51 6ex ChrisCatlin 5 58
(P W Hiatt) *bhd and sn niggled along: rdn over 2f out: str run u.p ins fnl f to ld towards fin* **5/2**[2]

-204 2 1/2 **Maryolini**[12] 3292 5-9-4 55 NickyMackay 3 60
(T Keddy) *stdd s: t.k.h: hld up in tch: effrt on inner and rdn ent fnl 2f: drvn ahd ins fnl f: hdd and no ex towards fin* **9/4**[1]

6-15 3 nse **The Jailer**[5] 3526 7-9-2 56 RussKennemore[(3)] 4 61
(J G M O'Shea) *chsd ldr tl led 3f out: c towards stands' rail and rdn over 2f out: hrd drvn over 1f out: hdd ins fnl f: kpt on same pce towards fin* **11/2**

0305 4 nse **Commandingpresence (USA)**[12] 3299 4-8-6 48 KierenFox[(5)] 6 53
(J J Bridger) *chsd ldrs: rdn and effrt to chal wl over 1f out: ev ch after tl no ex fnl 50yds* **11/2**

6645 5 2 1/2 **Caribbean Coral**[12] 3293 11-9-4 55 SebSanders 2 51
(A B Haynes) *chsd ldrs: effrt and rdn ent fnl 2f: ev ch fr over 1f out tl wknd ins fnl f* **5/1**[3]

-050 6 10 **Louie's Lad**[46] 2229 4-8-9 46 (p) NeilChalmers 1 18
(J J Bridger) *led tl 3f out: wknd u.p 2f out: wl btn and eased ins fnl f* **20/1**

63.21 secs (0.91) **Going Correction** +0.20s/f (Good) **6** Ran SP% **111.5**
Speed ratings (Par 101): **100,99,99,99,95 79**
Tote Swingers: 1&2 £2.00, 1&3 £3.20, 2&3 £3.30 CSF £8.44 TOTE £3.30: £1.90, £1.50; EX 7.10 Place 6: £16.60 Place 5: £11.54.
Owner P W Hiatt **Bred** Shadwell Estate Company Limited **Trained** Hook Norton, Oxon

FOCUS
There was a tight finish to this sprint handicap.
The Jailer Official explanation: jockey said mare hung right
Louie's Lad Official explanation: jockey said gelding was unsuited by the ground
T/Plt: £73.10 to a £1 stake. Pool: £60,102.65. 599.80 winning tickets. T/Qpdt: £38.90 to a £1 stake. Pool: £4,546.168. 86.31 winning tickets. SP

3307 CHANTILLY (R-H)
Sunday, July 4

OFFICIAL GOING: Turf: good to soft

3718a PRIX DU BOIS (GROUP 3) (2YO) (TURF) 5f
1:35 (12:00) 2-Y-O £35,398 (£14,159; £10,619; £7,079; £3,539)

RPR
1 **Keratiya (FR)**[32] 2-8-8 0 Christophe-PatriceLemaire 8 105
(J-C Rouget, France) *towards rr: mde gd prog on wd outside over 1 1/2f out: qcknd wl to chal for ld 50yds out: got up on line* **3/1**[1]

2 nse **Irish Field (IRE)**[28] 2-8-11 0 OlivierPeslier 1 108
(M Delcher-Sanchez, Spain) *prom early along rail: drifted away fr rail and qcknd wl to grab ld over 1 1/2f out: r.o wl but ct on line* **6/1**[3]

3 2 **Lone Cat (FR)**[24] 2917 2-8-9 0 ow1 ChristopheSoumillon 3 99
(Y De Nicolay, France) *racd bhd ldrs: swtchd to rail 2f out: r.o wl to go 3rd ins fnl 100yds* **11/1**

4 nk **Captain Chop (FR)**[24] 2917 2-8-11 0 FlavienPrat 5 100
(D Guillemin, France) *settled bhd ldrs: short of room over 1 1/2f out: qcknd wl whn in clr: r.o wl* **10/1**

5 snk **Miss Liberty (FR)**[24] 2917 2-8-8 0 MaximeGuyon 6 96
(Mme Pia Brandt, France) *racd bhd ldrs on outside: qcknd wl 2f out: wnt 3rd 1 1/2f out: outpcd in fnl f* **10/3**[2]

6 4 **Dream Catcher (FR)**[44] 2-8-11 0 PhilippeSogorb 7 85
(D Guillemin, France) *prom: rdn and failed to qckn 2f out: fdd* **3/1**[1]

7 2 **Lady Jak (FR)**[16] 2-8-8 0 DominiqueBoeuf 2 75
(J-V Toux, France) *a in rr: rdn 2f out: no ex* **33/1**

8 2 ½ **Magic Potion (FR)**[24] 2917 2-8-8 0 .... GregoryBenoist 4 66
(P Bary, France) *led fr s: stl prom 2f out whn sltly hmpd by drifting rival 1 1/2f out: wknd fnl f* **8/1**

59.10 secs (1.00) **Going Correction** +0.225s/f (Good) **8 Ran SP% 118.8**
Speed ratings: **101,100,97,97,97 90,87,83**
WIN (incl. 1 euro stake): 3.70. PLACES: 1.80, 2.50, 2.70. DF: 20.90. SF: 25.50.

Owner H H Aga Khan **Bred** H H Aga Khan **Trained** Pau, France

NOTEBOOK
Keratiya(FR) showed a decent turn of foot to get up right on the line, though it took some time for the result to be confirmed in the photo. Her trainer doesn't think she will get any further than 6f and she will be aimed at the Prix Morny next month, though if she recovers from this race well enough she may take in the Prix Robert Papin on July 25 along the way.

3719a PRIX JEAN PRAT (GROUP 1) (3YO COLTS & FILLIES) (TURF) 1m
2:42 (12:00) 3-Y-O **£202,265** (£80,920; £40,460; £20,212; £10,123)

RPR

1 **Dick Turpin (IRE)**[19] 3048 3-9-2 0 .... RichardHughes 4 124+
(R Hannon) *racd in 3rd fr s: cruised to ld 2f out: qcknd clr: easily* **5/1**[2]

2 4 **Siyouni (FR)**[19] 3048 3-9-2 0 .... Christophe-PatriceLemaire 8 115
(A De Royer-Dupre, France) *racd in 5th: rdn early in st: qcknd wl to chse ldr 1 1/2f out: r.o wl* **5/1**[2]

3 hd **Xtension (IRE)**[43] 2354 3-9-2 0 .... GeraldMosse 2 114
(C G Cox) *racd in 4th: qcknd wl 2f out: wnt 3rd ent fnl f: r.o wl* **16/1**[3]

4 2 **Hearts Of Fire**[19] 3048 3-9-2 0 .... OlivierPeslier 1 110
(Pat Eddery) *settled towards rr: proged early in st: r.o wl u.p: no ex fnl f* **5/1**[2]

5 1 ½ **Frozen Power (IRE)**[41] 2405 3-9-2 0 .... FrankieDettori 7 106
(Mahmood Al Zarooni) *settled towards rr: mde late prog and fin wl ins fnl f* **33/1**

6 hd **Sormiou (FR)**[21] 3016 3-9-2 0 .... AlexandreRoussel 6 106
(C Diard, France) *settled towards rr: rdn but failed to qckn 2f out: styd on* **40/1**

7 3 **Altair Star (IRE)**[16] 3-9-2 0 .... MickaelBarzalona 3 99
(P Schiergen, Germany) *led at fast pce: wknd fr 2f out: eased* **150/1**

8 1 ½ **Lope De Vega (IRE)**[28] 2802 3-9-2 0 .... MaximeGuyon 8 95
(A Fabre, France) *racd in 2nd: assumed ld 2 1/2f out: rdn but failed to qckn and sn fdd: eased* **1/1**[1]

1m 36.3s (-1.70) **Going Correction** +0.225s/f (Good) **8 Ran SP% 111.9**
Speed ratings: **117,113,112,110,109 109,106,104**
WN (incl. 1 euro stake): 8.30. PLACES: 2.60, 2.50, 8.10. DF: 15.50. SF: 30.70.

Owner John Manley **Bred** John McEnery **Trained** East Everleigh, Wilts

NOTEBOOK
Dick Turpin(IRE), after finishing runner-up in three consecutive Group 1s, finally gained success at the highest level and did it in some style, quickening up impressively and soon pulling clear in effortless fashion. His trainer believes he could getr further, but his owner nominated the Sussex Stakes and later in the season the Prix de la Foret or Prix du Moulin as possible targets.

Siyouni(FR) was never in the same parish as the winner, but his trainer was still delighted by this effort.

Xtension(IRE) ran yet another fine race at Group 1 level and his trainer was making no excuses.

Hearts Of Fire, unlucky when just behind Dick Turpin in the St James's Palace, was put firmly in his place by his old rivals this time and seemed to have no excuses.

Lope De Vega(IRE) had looked exceptional in winning the French Guineas (when beating Dick Turpin) and French Derby, but he found nothing for pressure after taking the lead from his pacemaker and this was hugely disappointing. There must have been a reason for this dismal effort.

3720a PRIX CHLOE (GROUP 3) (3YO FILLIES) (TURF) 1m 1f
3:22 (12:00) 3-Y-O **£35,398** (£14,159; £10,619; £7,079; £3,539)

RPR

1 **Lily Of The Valley (FR)**[46] 2237 3-8-11 0 .... ChristopheSoumillon 3 102
(J-C Rouget, France) *settled in 6th: proged early in st in mid-trck: qcknd wl 1f out to grab ld and go clr: easily* **13/8**[1]

2 1 ½ **Fadela Style (FR)**[47] 2222 3-8-11 0 .... FranckBlondel 5 99
(F Rossi, France) *racd bhd eventual wnr fr s: mde gd prog 2 1/2f out on wd outside: wnt 2nd 1f out and r.o wl* **12/1**

3 2 **Mahamaya (GER)**[41] 2404 3-8-11 0 .... Christophe-PatriceLemaire 2 95
(A Trybuhl, Germany) *prom early: one of ldrs early in st: outpcd 2f out but styd on wl fnl f to maintain 3rd pl* **11/1**

4 ½ **Shining Sea (FR)**[36] 3-8-11 0 .... Francois-XavierBertras 6 94
(F Rohaut, France) *towards rr tl st: mde move along rail 2f out: fin wl ins fnl f* **12/1**

5 ½ **Plain Vanilla (FR)**[26] 3-8-11 0 .... RonanThomas 8 93
(P Van De Poele, France) *towards rr on rail tl st: proged wl in mid-trck and styd on wl wout threatening* **10/1**

6 1 ½ **Skia (FR)**[31] 2686 3-8-11 0 .... OlivierPeslier 9 90
(C Laffon-Parias, France) *settled at rr of field: early prog in st: rdn but no ex fnl 2f: nvr threatened* **11/2**[2]

7 snk **Banderille (IRE)**[34] 3-8-11 0 .... AnthonyCrastus 4 89
(E Lellouche, France) *prom early: rdn early in st: failed to qckn: no ex fr 1f out* **9/1**

8 5 **Carioca (IRE)**[28] 2801 3-8-11 0 .... FrankieDettori 7 79
(M Botti) *led: racing freely: stl prom 2f out: rdn but fnd no ex clsng stages* **7/1**[3]

9 ¾ **Green Ridge (FR)**[46] 2237 3-8-11 0 .... ThierryThulliez 1 77
(J Van Handenhove, France) *prom early: fnd no ex in st: wknd* **12/1**

1m 51.4s (0.30) **Going Correction** +0.225s/f (Good) **9 Ran SP% 116.5**
Speed ratings: **107,105,103,103,103 101,101,97,96**
WIN (incl. 1 euro stake): 1.90. PLACES: 1.40, 2.40, 2.40. DF: 11.40. SF: 14.10.

Owner Bernard Barsi **Bred** Dunmore Stud Limited **Trained** Pau, France

NOTEBOOK
Lily Of The Valley(FR) quickened up well to win this in comfortable style. She looks a progressive filly, but her trainer is undecided whether to go up to 1m2f or down to 1m with her as there are few races for her over this intermediate trip.

Carioca(IRE), up in trip, did too much too soon and gave herself little chance of seeing it out. She is yet to prove that she is up to this level.

3308 BATH (L-H)
Monday, July 5

OFFICIAL GOING: Firm
Wind: Brisk across Weather: Sunny spells

3721 E. B. F. & GREAT WESTERN WINE MAIDEN STKS 5f 11y
2:30 (2:33) (Class 5) 2-Y-O **£3,238** (£963; £481; £240) **Stalls** Centre

Form RPR

322 1 **Stunning In Purple (IRE)**[13] 3288 2-8-12 0 .... NeilCallan 5 66
(A B Haynes) *mde all: rdn and styd on wl ins fnl f* **5/1**

04 2 1 ¼ **Fantasy Fry**[20] 3053 2-9-3 0 .... RichardHughes 3 68
(H Morrison) *stdd s: in rr but in tch: hdwy 2f out: styng on whn sltly hmpd and veered rt over 1f out: rallied and r.o wl ins fnl f to take 2nd cl home: no imp on wnr* **3/1**[2]

5 3 nk **Scommettitrice (IRE)**[12] 3310 2-8-12 0 .... LukeMorris 1 60
(R A Harris) *unruly in paddock: chsd wnr: rdn over 1f out and no imp: lost 2nd cl home* **16/1**

504 4 shd **Sarangoo**[21] 3034 2-8-12 0 .... RobertWinston 4 60
(M S Saunders) *chsd ldrs: drvn along fr 1/2-way: styd on to dispute 2nd fr over 1f out: no imp on wnr and one pce ins fnl f: lost two pls cl home* **9/4**[1]

405 5 nk **Frankish Dynasty (GER)**[9] 3459 2-9-3 0 .... ChrisCatlin 6 64
(P F I Cole) *sn trcking ldrs: rdn appr fnl f: styd on cl home but nvr a threat to wnr* **12/1**

U 6 1 **Blackleyf (IRE)**[12] 3310 2-9-3 0 .... RichardKingscote 7 60
(Tom Dascombe) *unruly paddock: reluctant to stalls: sn pushed along: styng on same pce on outside whn carried bdly rt over 1f out: kpt on again fnl 100yds* **28/1**

0 7 6 **Local Diktator**[26] 2867 2-9-3 0 .... DavidProbert 8 39
(R A Harris) *chsd ldrs: rdn over 2f out: hung rt and wknd over 1f out* **50/1**

46 8 nk **Maggie's Treasure (IRE)**[42] 2397 2-9-3 0 .... TadhgO'Shea 2 38
(J Gallagher) *outpcd* **7/2**[3]

63.55 secs (1.05) **Going Correction** +0.175s/f (Good) **8 Ran SP% 113.6**
Speed ratings (Par 94): **98,96,95,95,94 93,83,83**
toteswingers: 1&2 £3.00, 1&3 £6.90, 2&3 £8.00 CSF £20.13 TOTE £4.00: £1.10, £2.10, £4.10; EX 19.90 Trifecta £359.50 Part won. Pool of £485.92- 0.97 winning units..

Owner Mrs Barbara Fuller **Bred** Ms C Corrigan **Trained** Limpley Stoke, Bath

FOCUS
There had been just 2mm of rain the previous day and the ground was described as firm, with a GoingStick reading of 9.5. A modest juvenile maiden and the pace did not look that strong for a sprint. Limited form, best viewed around the time and the winner.

NOTEBOOK
Stunning In Purple(IRE) benefited from a shrewd front-running ride and showed a good attitude under pressure to record her first success at the sixth attempt. She's only modest, but is certainly game enough and should hold her own in nurseries. (op 4-1)

Fantasy Fry, too keen over 6f last time, was possibly a bit unlucky on this drop in trip as, having raced towards the rear (presumably to help him settle), he was forced out extremely wide by a wayward rival, just as he was looking to make his move inside the final 2f. The impression is that he's still learning and he might do well in nurseries in due course. (op 5-1)

Scommettitrice(IRE) was always well placed and posted a respectable effort to improve on her debut showing.

Sarangoo had been progressing nicely but she never really looked to be going all that well this time and proved a little disappointing. Perhaps the ground was quicker than ideal. (op 3-1 tchd 2-1)

Frankish Dynasty(GER) tried hard enough but he could find only the one pace, giving the impression he might do a bit better given time. (op 9-1)

Blackleyf(IRE), who played up beforehand, looked held when carried right late on. (op 40-1 tchd 25-1)

Local Diktator Official explanation: jockey said colt hung right on the firm ground

Maggie's Treasure(IRE) seemed to show fair form at Windsor on his previous start, but he was nowhere near that level this time. He didn't look totally comfortable on the track, but perhaps something was amiss. (op 5-2)

3722 NOBLE LOCKS H'CAP 5f 11y
3:00 (3:00) (Class 6) (0-65,64) 3-Y-O+ **£1,942** (£578; £288; £144) **Stalls** Centre

Form RPR

645 1 **Ask Jenny (IRE)**[3] 3623 8-9-6 **58** .... RichardHughes 10 66
(Patrick Morris) *in rr: hdwy 2f out: rdn and str run ins fnl f to ld last stride* **8/1**

00-3 2 nse **Volito**[13] 3299 4-9-12 **64** .... GeorgeBaker 3 72
(Jonjo O'Neill) *chsd ldrs: rdn and styd on wl ins fnl f: slt advantage fnl 20yds: ct last stride* **11/4**[1]

4302 3 nk **Matterofact (IRE)**[12] 3308 7-9-10 **62** .... RobertWinston 7 69
(M S Saunders) *chsd ldrs: rdn to ld 1f out: narrowly hdd fnl 20yds and no ex* **3/1**[2]

0255 4 1 ¼ **The Name Is Frank**[5] 3556 5-9-7 **59** ....(t) NeilChalmers 2 61
(Mark Gillard) *chsd ldrs: rdn and one pce 2f out: rallied and styd on again ins fnl f: nvr a threat* **5/1**[3]

6600 5 1 ½ **Lithaam (IRE)**[8] 3474 6-9-10 **62** ....(p) PatCosgrave 4 59
(J M Bradley) *chsd ldr: rdn 2f out: wknd ins fnl f* **33/1**

2206 6 1 ½ **Spic 'n Span**[12] 3308 5-9-5 **57** ....(b) LukeMorris 1 49
(R A Harris) *led tl hdd 1f out: sn wknd* **9/1**

0004 7 nk **Mazzola**[14] 3255 4-9-5 **57** ....(p) DaneO'Neill 6 48
(J M Bradley) *in tch: sme hdwy 2f out: wknd over 1f out* **12/1**

0-01 8 ½ **Pinball (IRE)**[13] 3287 4-9-2 **54** ....(v) ChrisCatlin 8 43
(Mrs L Williamson) *s.i.s: outpcd most of way* **6/1**

63.14 secs (0.64) **Going Correction** +0.175s/f (Good)
WFA 3 from 4yo+ 5lb **8 Ran SP% 114.4**
Speed ratings (Par 101): **101,100,100,98,96 93,93,92**
toteswingers: 1&2 £6.40, 1&3 £3.20, 2&3 £6.30 CSF £30.34 CT £81.89 TOTE £9.40: £2.70, £1.60, £1.10; EX 26.70 Trifecta £70.50 Pool: £333.51 - 3.50 winning units..

Owner W J Crosbie **Bred** Mrs J Costelloe **Trained** Tarporley, Cheshire

FOCUS
A modest sprint handicap run at a strong pace. Straightforward form.

3723 ENPURE H'CAP 1m 2f 46y
3:30 (3:31) (Class 5) (0-65,64) 3-Y-O+ **£1,942** (£578; £288; £144) **Stalls** Low

Form RPR

0241 1 **Under Fire (IRE)**[14] 3263 7-9-10 **52** .... NeilCallan 7 60
(A W Carroll) *chsd ldrs: led 2f out: rdn and styd on ins fnl f* **8/1**[3]

0546 2 1 ½ **Raktiman (IRE)**[11] 3376 3-9-11 **64** .... RichardKingscote 8 69
(Tom Dascombe) *in rr: in tch: gd hdwy over 3f out: chsd wnr ins fnl 2f: kpt on u.p: a hld* **14/1**

6-06 **3** 1 ½ **Rebel Woman**[13] 3291 4-9-7 **49** .... RichardHughes 10 51
(J A Osborne) *hld up in rr and wl off pce tl impr 3f out: hdwy on outside to chse ldrs ins fnl f but sn fnd no ex* **11/1**

0633 **4** nse **Sheila's Bond**[9] 3444 3-8-11 **57** .... RyanPowell(7) 1 59+
(J S Moore) *trckd ldrs: hdwy on ins: n.m.r and swtchd rt ins fnl 3f: stl nt clr run and swtchd lft over 1f out: kpt on fnl f but nvr gng pce to trble ldng duo* **3/1**[2]

0-00 **5** 1 ¾ **Red Eddie**[32] 2675 3-8-13 **52** .... ShaneKelly 9 50
(S Dow) *hld up in rr and wl off pce: pushed along and hdwy over 2f out: hung lft over 1f out and fnd no ex ins fnl f* **22/1**

5066 **6** 1 **Highland Cadett**[22] 3002 3-9-2 **55** ....(v[1]) TadhgO'Shea 2 51
(B R Millman) *chsd ldrs: rdn over 2f out: wknd ins fnl f* **12/1**

0000 **7** 5 **Bethlehem (IRE)**[5] 3564 3-9-4 **57** ....(b[1]) RobertWinston 5 43
(H Morrison) *drvn along fr stalls: towards rr but in tch: mid-div whn hrd drvn over 2f out: wknd sn after* **22/1**

043- **8** 4 ½ **Forty Thirty (IRE)**[20] 4730 4-10-0 **56** .... DaneO'Neill 3 33
(Miss Sheena West) *sn chsng ldr: led ins fnl 3f: hdd 2f out and sn btn* **6/4**[1]

4040 **9** 8 **Tregony Bridge**[8] 3479 3-8-11 **50** .... FrannyNorton 6 11
(M Blanshard) *in rr: rdn and sme hdwy over 3f out: nvr rchd ldrs and sn wknd* **20/1**

0000 **10** 3 ¾ **Warrior Nation (FR)**[12] 3314 4-9-3 **45** ....(b) NeilChalmers 4 —
(A J Chamberlain) *led tl hdd & wknd ins fnl 3f* **100/1**

2m 8.91s (-2.09) **Going Correction** -0.125s/f (Firm)
WFA 3 from 4yo+ 11lb **10** Ran SP% **113.3**
Speed ratings (Par 103): **103,101,100,100,99 98,94,90,84,81**
toteswingers: 1&2 £10.00, 1&3 £5.10, 2&3 £8.90 CSF £102.19 CT £1225.13 TOTE £7.90: £2.20, £4.00, £2.90; EX 56.10 TRIFECTA Not won..
Owner Marita Bayley and Trevor Turner **Bred** Mrs Marita Bayley **Trained** Cropthorne, Worcs

FOCUS
A modest handicap which was sound run. The winner built on his Lingfield win.

3724 WESSEX GRID PARTNERSHIP H'CAP 1m 3f 144y
4:00 (4:00) (Class 5) (0-75,75) 3-Y-O **£2,590** (£770; £385; £192) **Stalls** Low

Form RPR

6611 **1** **Home Advantage**[11] 3376 3-9-3 **71** .... RichardHughes 1 85+
(R Charlton) *racd in 3rd: hdwy fr 4f out: led ins fnl 2f: rdn whn pressed ins fnl f: asserted fnl 100yds* **Evs**[1]

5113 **2** 2 **Comedy Act**[12] 3335 3-9-7 **75** .... SebSanders 2 86
(Sir Mark Prescott) *hld up in last pl: hdwy 3f out: pushed along 2f out and sn chsng wnr: effrt to chal u.p ins fnl f: sn outpcd* **Evs**[1]

0-50 **3** 7 **Ocean Club**[26] 2860 3-8-2 **56** oh1 .... FrannyNorton 3 55
(B W Hills) *led after 2f: hdd over 2f out and sn wknd* **33/1**[3]

3514 **4** ½ **Frameit (IRE)**[5] 3564 3-8-2 **63** ....(b) RyanPowell(7) 4 61
(J S Moore) *led 2f: styd chsng ldr: led briefly over 2f out: hdd sn after: wandered and wknd qckly* **25/1**[2]

2m 27.88s (-2.72) **Going Correction** -0.125s/f (Firm) **4** Ran SP% **106.8**
Speed ratings (Par 100): **104,102,98,97**
CSF £2.18 TOTE £2.00; EX 2.30.
Owner K Abdulla **Bred** Juddmonte Farms Ltd **Trained** Beckhampton, Wilts

FOCUS
Only two of these mattered, but at least they're both fair, progressive types. Despite the small field, the time was 1.72 seconds under standard, and the form has been taken at face value.

3725 WESSEX FOR WEST AFRICA H'CAP 1m 5y
4:30 (4:30) (Class 5) (0-75,75) 3-Y-O+ **£2,590** (£770; £385; £192) **Stalls** Low

Form RPR

0051 **1** **Warning Song (USA)**[13] 3297 3-9-2 **72** .... PatDobbs 7 76+
(Mrs A J Perrett) *t.k.h: chsd ldrs tl rn wd and lost pl bnd ins fnl 5f: hdwy over 2f out: chsd ldr 1f out: kpt on u.p to ld last strides* **11/4**[2]

-652 **2** hd **Wilfred Pickles (IRE)**[10] 3412 4-10-0 **75** .... DaneO'Neill 4 81
(Miss Jo Crowley) *in tch: hdwy on ins over 2f out: led over 1f out: rdn and kpt on ins fnl f: hdd last strides* **5/2**[1]

-000 **3** 3 **Smart Endeavour (USA)**[12] 3330 4-9-11 **72** .... ShaneKelly 2 71
(W R Swinburn) *sn led: jnd 4f out to 3f out: rdn over 2f out: hdd over 1f out: wknd ins fnl f* **15/2**

6210 **4** 2 ¾ **Golden Rock (IRE)**[18] 3130 4-9-10 **71** ....(v) RichardHughes 3 64
(R Charlton) *t.k.h: chsd ldrs: wd bnd ins fnl 5f: styd prom: jnd ldr 4f out to 3f out: rdn over 2f out: wknd ins fnl f* **4/1**[3]

6551 **5** nk **Unlimited**[11] 3377 8-9-0 **61** .... NeilCallan 6 53
(A W Carroll) *plld hrd: chsd ldrs: wd bnd ins fnl 5f: styd prom tl wknd u.p ins fnl 2f* **10/1**

-243 **6** 3 **Logos Astra (USA)**[11] 3355 3-9-5 **75** ....(b[1]) ChrisCatlin 5 58
(D R Lanigan) *drvn to chse ldrs tl rn v wd and lost pl bnd ins fnl 5f: sn rdn again and nvr any ch fr 3f out* **6/1**

006- **7** 7 **My Red Kite**[243] 7235 3-8-6 **62** ....(e[1]) SaleemGolam 1 29
(G D Blake) *a in rr* **40/1**

1m 40.64s (-0.16) **Going Correction** -0.125s/f (Firm)
WFA 3 from 4yo+ 9lb **7** Ran SP% **112.8**
Speed ratings (Par 103): **95,94,91,89,88 85,78**
toteswingers: 1&2 £2.00, 1&3 £5.10, 2&3 £4.40 CSF £9.79 TOTE £5.10: £2.40, £1.50; EX 10.30.

Owner G Harwood & G Bailey **Bred** Bloodstock Holdings Llc **Trained** Pulborough, W Sussex

FOCUS
A modest handicap, and with the pace just ordinary early on, a few of these were a bit keen. The form is rated around the runner-up, with the winner a bit better than the bare form.
Golden Rock(IRE) Official explanation: jockey said gelding ran too freely
Logos Astra(USA) Official explanation: jockey said colt hung right on the bend

3726 WATERAID H'CAP 5f 161y
5:00 (5:00) (Class 5) (0-75,73) 3-Y-O **£2,590** (£770; £385; £192) **Stalls** Centre

Form RPR

3-00 **1** **Panpiper**[27] 2844 3-8-10 **62** .... DaneO'Neill 5 67
(G L Moore) *in rr: pushed along over 3f out: hdwy over 1f out: str run thrght ins fnl f to ld last strides* **20/1**

6065 **2** nk **Yurituni**[28] 2807 3-9-7 **73** .... TonyCulhane 4 77
(Eve Johnson Houghton) *chsd ldrs: chal fr 2f out tl slt advantage appr fnl f: kpt on tl hdd last strides* **5/2**[2]

0220 **3** 1 **Mrs Mogg**[18] 3115 3-8-12 **64** .... RichardKingscote 3 65
(Tom Dascombe) *chsd ldrs: chal over 2f out: sn slt ld: narrowly hdd appr fnl f: styd pressing ldr tl outpcd fnl 100yds* **5/1**

0622 **4** 4 ½ **Rainbow Six**[12] 3313 3-9-1 **67** .... NeilCallan 1 53
(M Botti) *t.k.h: chsd ldrs: sltly hmpd on ins over 3f out: wknd over 1f out* **6/4**[1]

-002 **5** 4 **Compton Way**[7] 3511 3-8-3 **55** ....(b) FrannyNorton 2 28
(B W Hills) *drvn fr stalls and sn led: hdd 2f out: sn btn* **4/1**[3]

1m 12.19s (0.99) **Going Correction** +0.175s/f (Good) **5** Ran SP% **110.0**
Speed ratings (Par 100): **100,99,98,92,86**
CSF £68.32 TOTE £17.20: £5.40, £1.50; EX 58.80.
Owner Pillar To Post Racing (IV) **Bred** Pillar To Post Racing **Trained** Lower Beeding, W Sussex

FOCUS
An ordinary sprint handicap run a strong gallop. Weakish form, rated around the third.
Panpiper ◆ Official explanation: trainer said, regarding apparent improvement in form, that the gelding had taken time to come to itself having suffered an injury.

3727 WATER FOR LIFE H'CAP 5f 161y
5:30 (5:31) (Class 6) (0-55,55) 3-Y-O+ **£1,942** (£578; £288; £144) **Stalls** Centre

Form RPR

-300 **1** **Emiratesdotcom**[5] 3556 4-8-13 **49** .... RichardKingscote 12 57
(J M Bradley) *trckd ldr: chal ins fnl 2f: led over 1f out: edgd lft ins fnl f: hld on wl* **6/1**[3]

0503 **2** 1 **Talamahana**[12] 3308 5-8-11 **52** ....(v) AmyBaker(5) 4 57
(A B Haynes) *mid-div: hdwy 2f out: nt clr run over 1f out: styd on wl ins fnl f to take 2nd cl home: nt rch wnr* **16/1**

-005 **3** hd **Wooden King (IRE)**[9] 3440 5-9-0 **50** .... TonyCulhane 6 54
(M S Saunders) *s.i.s: in rr: rdn and hdwy over 1f out: styd on strly ins fnl f: gng on cl home* **11/2**[2]

-660 **4** nse **Ridgeway Sapphire**[8] 3478 3-7-13 **46** oh1 ....(v[1]) BillyCray(5) 2 49
(M D I Usher) *in rr: hdwy on outside over 1f out: styd on strly ins fnl f: fin wl* **33/1**

620 **5** ¾ **Loyal Royal (IRE)**[35] 2590 7-9-0 **50** ....(bt) PatCosgrave 11 51
(J M Bradley) *chsd ldrs: rdn 2f out: styd on fnl f to dispute 2nd: no ex cl home* **17/2**

20-1 **6** nk **Helping Hand (IRE)**[13] 3286 5-9-2 **52** .... DaneO'Neill 3 52
(R Hollinshead) *led tl hdd over 1f out: hmpd jst ins fnl f: no ex nr fin* **7/1**

6455 **7** hd **Caribbean Coral**[1] 3717 11-9-5 **55** .... NeilCallan 15 55
(A B Haynes) *stdd s: sn in tch: chsd ldrs 2f out: disp 2nd ins fnl f: wknd cl home* **14/1**

8 hd **D'Allziance (IRE)**[659] 4-9-5 **55** .... GeorgeBaker 16 54
(Jonjo O'Neill) *chsd ldrs: rdn 2f out: styd on same pce ins fnl f* **22/1**

0046 **9** 1 ½ **Welcome Approach**[11] 3357 7-9-0 **50** .... LukeMorris 9 47+
(J R Weymes) *chsd ldrs: rdn over 2f out: wknd ins fnl f: eased whn n.m.r fnl 120yds* **9/1**

0340 **10** 2 **Dolly Will Do**[123] 788 3-8-4 **46** oh1 .... FrankieMcDonald 5 33
(N P Mulholland) *s.i.s: in rr: rdn and styd on fr over 1f out: nvr in contention* **66/1**

5-60 **11** 3 **Dilli Dancer**[29] 2779 5-8-10 **46** oh1 ....(e) SaleemGolam 8 24
(G D Blake) *chsd ldrs over 3f* **16/1**

0/00 **12** 1 ½ **Turtle Dove**[29] 2779 5-9-2 **52** ....(b[1]) NeilChalmers 1 25
(Mark Gillard) *outpcd most of way* **66/1**

00-0 **13** ¾ **Lily Jicaro (IRE)**[11] 3357 4-8-3 **46** ....(t) JosephYoung(7) 7 16
(Mrs L Williamson) *chsd ldrs to 1/2-way* **50/1**

6104 **14** 4 ½ **Stargazy**[4] 3591 6-8-10 **53** .... CarolineKelly(7) 17 8+
(A J Lidderdale) *v.s.a and detached after 1f: nt rcvr* **25/1**

00-2 **15** 1 ¾ **French Fantasy**[63] 1760 3-8-12 **54** .... RobertWinston 14 —
(H Morrison) *chsd ldrs tl rdn 2f out: sn hung bdly rt and eased whn no ch ins fnl f* **11/4**[1]

1m 12.25s (1.05) **Going Correction** +0.175s/f (Good)
WFA 3 from 4yo+ 6lb **15** Ran SP% **123.9**
Speed ratings (Par 101): **100,98,98,98,97 96,96,96,94,91 87,85,84,78,76**
toteswingers:1&2 £28.90, 2&3 £19.90, 1&3 £11.00 CSF £94.46 CT £581.08 TOTE £9.00: £2.90, £5.60, £2.00; EX 137.50 Trifecta £337.00 Part won. Pool of £455.53 - 0.85 winning units. Place 6: £137.11 Place 5: £49.95.
Owner Ms S Howell **Bred** Newsells Park Stud Limited **Trained** Sedbury, Gloucs

FOCUS
A moderate contest and straightforward form.
Dolly Will Do Official explanation: jockey said filly missed the break
French Fantasy Official explanation: jockey said filly hung right-handed and the bit slipped through its mouth
T/Plt: £676.10 to a £1 stake. Pool:£67,325.08 - 72.69 winning tickets. T/Qpdt: £213.10 to a £1 stake. Pool: £4,595.03 - 15.95 winning tickets. ST

3118 RIPON (R-H)
Monday, July 5

OFFICIAL GOING: Good to firm (8.9)
Rail from back straight into home straight moved out 4m adding 9yd to races on round course.
Wind: Moderate across Weather: Cloudy, sunny periods

3728 SIS LIVE (S) STKS 1m 1f 170y
6:50 (6:52) (Class 6) 3-Y-O **£2,729** (£806; £403) **Stalls** High

Form RPR

3005 **1** **Market Puzzle (IRE)**[27] 2838 3-8-12 51 .... TedDurcan 2 53
(W M Brisbourne) *hld up in rr: stdy hdwy over 3f out: swtchd outside and effrt 2f out: rdn to ld appr fnl f: styd on* **11/2**[3]

0-00 **2** 1 ¼ **Reel Love**[63] 1760 3-8-7 43 .... JamesSullivan(5) 5 50
(Mrs L Stubbs) *in tch: hdwy over 3f out: rdn 2f out: hmpd and sltly outpcd over 1f out: drvn and styd on ins fnl f* **40/1**

6530 **3** nk **Sultan's Choice**[10] 3390 3-8-7 52 ....(v) SilvestreDeSousa 3 45
(P D Evans) *trckd ldrs: smooth hdwy 3f out: cl up 2f out: sn rdn and edgd rt over 1f out: ev ch tl drvn and one pce ins fnl f* **13/8**[1]

4320 **4** 2 ½ **Minortransgression (USA)**[58] 1927 3-8-12 73 ....(t) PaulHanagan 4 44
(T J Pitt) *trckd ldr: hdwy and cl up 4f out: led 3f out: rdn along wl over 1f out: drvn and hdd appr fnl f: sn wknd* **3/1**[2]

4645 **5** 8 **Cygnet Committee (IRE)**[4] 3601 3-8-5 45 ow1...(b) BarryMcHugh(3) 10 24
(J S Wainwright) *in tch: effrt and hdwy 3f out: rdn 2f out and sn one pce* **6/1**

0- **6** 3 ½ **Pobs Trophy**[10] 7420 3-8-12 0 .... PaulEddery 12 20
(R C Guest) *trckd ldrs on inner: pushed along over 3f out: rdn over 2f out: sn btn* **20/1**

7 ¾ **Dark Gem**[21] 3-8-4 0 ....(p) PaulPickard(3) 1 14
(S G West) *dwlt and bhd: rdn along 1/2-way: sme late hdwy* **100/1**

5300 **8** 4 **Emeralds Spirit (IRE)**[17] 3153 3-8-7 42 ....(b[1]) JoeFanning 11 5
(J R Weymes) *in tch: led: rdn along 4f out: hdd 3f out and sn wknd* **8/1**

0-00 **9** 17 **Patricks Lodge**[26] 2853 3-8-12 42 ....(v[1]) GrahamGibbons 6 —
(J D Bethell) *chsd ldrs: rdn along over 4f out: sn lost pl and bhd* **33/1**

00- **10** *nk* **Areeg (IRE)**[279] 6363 3-8-7 0 PatrickMathers 9 —
(A Berry) *a in rr: rdn along 1/2-way and sn bhd* **100/1**

2m 4.98s (-0.42) **Going Correction** -0.175s/f (Firm) **10** Ran SP% **116.0**
Speed ratings (Par 98): **94,93,92,90,84 81,80,77,64,63**
toteswingers: 1&2 £43.50, 1&3 £2.70, 2&3 £24.60 CSF £200.76 TOTE £6.60: £1.80, £9.60, £1.10; EX 312.00.There was no bid for the winner.
Owner G & S & S & M Racing **Bred** Yeomanstown Stud **Trained** Great Ness, Shropshire

FOCUS
The rail from the back straight into the home straight was moved out by four metres adding nine yards to races on the round course. An uncompetitive seller. The clear form pick was disappointing and the winner had a BHA rating of just 51. The form is rated through him.

3729 PLAY CROQUET AT RIPON SPA HOTEL MAIDEN AUCTION FILLIES' STKS 6f

7:20 (7:22) (Class 5) 2-Y-O **£2,914** (£867; £433; £216) **Stalls Low**

Form RPR

4 **1** **Rock Ace (IRE)**[14] 3274 2-8-10 0 SilvestreDeSousa 8 74
(Mrs D J Sanderson) *trckd ldrs edging rt: hdwy 1/2-way: rdn to chal over 1f out: hung bdly rt and drvn ins fnl f: styd on to ld last 50yds* **5/4**[1]

226 **2** *shd* **Sea Flower (IRE)**[18] 3118 2-8-7 0 DavidAllan 7 71
(T D Easterby) *cl up: led after 2f: rdn along 2f out: drvn over 1f out: hdd last 50yds: kpt on* **9/4**[2]

66 **3** *1/2* **Mother Jones**[66] 1668 2-8-10 0 PaulHanagan 3 72
(D H Brown) *trckd ldrs: hdwy 1/2-way: rdn over 1f out and sn ev ch: drvn and kpt on wl towards fin* **6/1**[3]

4 *1 1/4* **Maggie Mey (IRE)** 2-8-5 0 ow1 GrahamGibbons 6 63
(D O'Meara) *led 2f: cl up tl rdn along and sltly outpcd over 2f out: kpt on ins fnl f* **15/2**

0 **5** *1 3/4* **Deva Le Deva (IRE)**[10] 3392 2-8-10 0 RichardSmith 5 63
(Tom Dascombe) *chsd ldrs: pushed along 1/2-way: rdn wl over 2f out and sn one pce* **33/1**

44 **6** *3 3/4* **Peppercorn Rent (IRE)**[48] 2202 2-8-4 0 (e[1]) DuranFentiman 9 46
(T D Easterby) *prom: rdn along bef 1/2-way: grad wknd fr over 2f out* **16/1**

0 **7** *nse* **Princess Gail**[15] 3237 2-8-1 0 PaulPickard(3) 2 46+
(W M Brisbourne) *s.i.s and bhd: sme hdwy 1/2-way: kpt on appr fnl f* **66/1**

8 *14* **Mini's Destination** 2-8-4 0 NickyMackay 4 4
(J R Holt) *dwlt: a in rr: bhd fr 1/2-way* **33/1**

0 **9** *3* **Willow's Wish**[33] 2654 2-8-2 0 PatrickDonaghy(5) 1 —
(G M Moore) *s.i.s: a bhd* **33/1**

1m 12.83s (-0.17) **Going Correction** -0.175s/f (Firm) **9** Ran SP% **117.5**
Speed ratings (Par 91): **94,93,93,91,89 84,84,65,61**
toteswingers: 1&2 £1.50, 1&3 £1.90, 2&3 £2.70 CSF £4.12 TOTE £2.10: £1.10, £1.10, £3.00; EX 5.00.
Owner R J Budge **Bred** Jerry O'Sullivan **Trained** Wiseton, Notts
■ Stewards' Enquiry : David Allan two-day ban: used whip with excessive frequency (Jul 19-20)

FOCUS
A fair fillies' maiden. The two market leaders dominated and the form looks best viewed around the runner-up and sixth.

NOTEBOOK
Rock Ace(IRE) finished a prominent 33-1 fourth in a 6f Wolverhampton maiden on debut. She had a bit to find on form but was heavily backed and showed a good attitude to get the job done, despite racing wide for most of the way and edging right under pressure. This represents a reasonable step forward from the 14,000euros half-sister to Wokingham winner Laddies Poker Two. She still has a bit to learn but looks a nice type who should go on to better things. (op 9-4)
Sea Flower(IRE) was an odds-on flop here last time, but she set the target for the others to aim at on her two previous runner-up efforts at this track and put in a creditable run in her bid to redeem herself. She looks very speedy and should be able to win similar race, possibly back at 5f. (op 7-4 tchd 5-2)
Mother Jones was reported to have been in season when disappointing as 13-8 favourite in a Musselburgh maiden on her second start. She had a bit to prove but the spark returned and she gave it a decent try to reel in the front pair. Out of a triple sprint winner and closely related to seven-time 5f-6f winner Fast Freddie, she looks a willing character who should be able to win races. (op 9-2)
Maggie Mey(IRE) attracted some support but she looked a bit inexperienced and couldn't land a blow on her more streetwise rivals. However, this was a promising first run from a 4,500euros purchase whose siblings include three sprint winners. (op 9-1)
Deva Le Deva(IRE) did some late work from the back and has found quite a bit of improvement on her debut effort. She is the first foal of an unraced sister to several winners at up to 1m6f, and should do better over a stiffer test in nurseries later on.

3730 KPMG H'CAP 1m 4f 10y

7:50 (7:50) (Class 4) (0-80,77) 3-Y-O **£4,209** (£1,252; £625) **Stalls High**

Form RPR

3004 **1** **Mister Angry (IRE)**[15] 3239 3-9-7 **77** JoeFanning 2 89+
(M Johnston) *trckd ldng pair: hdwy over 3f out: swtchd lft and effrt to ld 2f out: rdn clr over 1f out: eased last 75yds* **5/4**[1]

2005 **2** *13* **Laverre (IRE)**[11] 3376 3-8-12 **68** TedDurcan 1 68
(T D Easterby) *trckd ldr: hdwy 4f out: led 3f out: sn rdn and hdd 2f out: wl hld whn eased ins fnl f* **5/2**[3]

3410 **3** *8* **Firehawk**[25] 2893 3-8-2 **58** PaulHanagan 5 46
(P D Evans) *led: rdn along 4f out: hdd 3f out: sn wknd and eased wl over 1f out* **15/8**[2]

2m 33.9s (-2.80) **Going Correction** -0.175s/f (Firm) **3** Ran SP% **107.8**
Speed ratings (Par 102): **102,93,88**
CSF £4.39 TOTE £1.80; EX 4.60.
Owner The Originals **Bred** Darley **Trained** Middleham Moor, N Yorks

FOCUS
All three of the runners in this handicap had been well held on their latest start. They finished well strung out and the form should be treated with a bit of caution.

3731 ATTHERACES.COM BE A VIRTUAL OWNER H'CAP 6f

8:20 (8:21) (Class 3) (0-90,87) 3-Y-O **£7,569** (£2,265; £1,132; £566; £282) **Stalls Low**

Form RPR

0200 **1** **Lowdown (IRE)**[23] 2978 3-9-7 87 JoeFanning 7 94
(M Johnston) *prom: hdwy and cl up 1/2-way: rdn to ld over 1f out: drvn ins fnl f: edgd rt and hld on wl towards fin* **5/1**[3]

2060 **2** *1* **Nubar Boy**[3] 3638 3-8-6 72 (v[1]) SilvestreDeSousa 8 76
(P D Evans) *hld up in rr: hdwy 1/2-way: chsd ldrs 2f out: rdn ent fnl f and ev ch tl drvn: edgd rt and nt qckn last 50yds* **10/1**

1431 **3** *1 1/2* **Jigajig**[14] 3277 3-8-1 72 AmyRyan(5) 4 71
(K A Ryan) *led: rdn along and jnd 2f out: drvn and hdd over 1f out: kpt on same pce ins fnl f* **10/1**

1624 **4** *1 1/4* **Hot Spark**[10] 3394 3-8-12 78 (t) GrahamGibbons 6 73
(K A Ryan) *cl up: rdn along over 2f out: ev ch tl drvn and one pce ent fnl f* **6/1**

0-13 **5** *nk* **Little Scotland**[19] 3088 3-9-7 87 PaulHanagan 5 81
(R A Fahey) *chsd ldrs: hdwy and cl up 1/2-way: rdn and ev ch 2f out: drvn over 1f out: wknd ent fnl f* **4/1**[2]

2124 **6** *1 1/2* **Flaneur**[9] 3436 3-9-0 80 (b) DavidAllan 2 69
(T D Easterby) *trckd ldrs on inner: effrt over 2f out: rdn wl over 1f out and wknd appr fnl f* **7/2**[1]

6044 **7** *1 3/4* **Di Stefano**[14] 3270 3-8-13 79 SamHitchcott 9 63
(M R Channon) *chsd ldrs on outer: rdn along over 2f out: grad wknd* **8/1**

0-05 **8** *nk* **Coin From Heaven (IRE)**[39] 2450 3-8-11 80 BarryMcHugh(3) 3 63
(R A Fahey) *a towards rr* **11/1**

-060 **9** *3 1/4* **Bond Fastrac**[9] 3446 3-9-4 84 TomEaves 1 56
(G R Oldroyd) *dwlt: a towards rr* **16/1**

1m 11.34s (-1.66) **Going Correction** -0.175s/f (Firm) **9** Ran SP% **116.7**
Speed ratings (Par 104): **104,102,100,99,98 96,94,93,89**
toteswingers:1&2 £7.50, 2&3 £14.40, 1&3 £10.40 CSF £54.31 CT £487.03 TOTE £7.10: £2.40, £4.50, £2.60; EX 47.10.
Owner Sheikh Hamdan Bin Mohammed Al Maktoum **Bred** A Stroud And J Hanly **Trained** Middleham Moor, N Yorks

FOCUS
A decent sprint handicap and the runner-up looks the key to the form. Hardly anything got into it from off the pace.

NOTEBOOK
Lowdown(IRE) suffered a big downturn in form in hot handicaps the last twice but he burst back to action to land a gamble under a positive ride. An inconsistent 12-race profile makes him a slightly risky one but he looks a very genuine type who is equally effective on fast turf and Polytrack and should be able to win more races. Official explanation: trainer's rep had no explanation for the apparent improvement in form (op 13-2 tchd 7-1 and 9-2)
Nubar Boy was never dangerous at Warwick three days earlier but he bounced back with a decent staying-on effort with a tongue tie removed and a visor tried. He has some quirks but deserves credit for doing best of the hold-up runners and could find something more with his newly acquired headgear next time. (op 12-1 tchd 14-1)
Jigajig recorded three wins in the spring and got back in the groove off 3lb lower at Wolverhampton last time. He couldn't shake off his rivals here but gave it a fair shot in a bid to make it five wins from his last eight. His mark has shot up 26lb since the start of the season and the handicapper may almost have him but the tough front-runner should continue to go well and would be interesting if sent back to Wolverhampton next time where he is 4-4 in sprint contests. (op 8-1)
Hot Spark kept plugging away but could never land a blow back in trip against some 6f specialists. The reliable type will be suited by returning to 7f but he may not have much leeway off a current mark 7lb higher than when winning at Doncaster in May. (op 11-2 tchd 7-1)
Little Scotland ran respectably but she has found things tough in two handicaps since working hard to justify favouritism in a Chester maiden in May. (op 11-4)
Flaneur, the most exposed runner in the line-up, was sent off favourite but couldn't make any inroads on the leaders. He is a consistent type but has come up short in three runs since winning a 0-80 classified at Haydock in May and control may have shifted to the handicapper. (op 9-2)

3732 YORKSHIRE RACING SUMMER FESTIVAL COMING SOON H'CAP 1m

8:50 (8:51) (Class 5) (0-70,70) 3-Y-O+ **£2,914** (£867; £433; £216) **Stalls High**

Form RPR

0030 **1** **Border Owl (IRE)**[10] 3391 5-9-4 **65** TobyAtkinson(5) 9 73
(P Salmon) *in tch w ldng pair: hdwy 3f out: swtchd lft and effrt 2f out: rdn to ld over 1f out: kpt on* **11/2**[3]

4224 **2** *3/4* **Classic Descent**[4] 3595 5-8-13 **60** (t) JamesSullivan(5) 3 66
(Mrs R A Carr) *hld up in tch: hdwy over 2f out: rdn wl over 1f out: styd on ins fnl f* **5/2**[2]

5111 **3** *1 1/4* **Polish World (USA)**[13] 3284 6-9-11 **70** PaulPickard(3) 8 73+
(P T Midgley) *led: rdn along over 2f out: drvn and hdd over 1f out: wknd ins fnl f* **2/1**[1]

3005 **4** *7* **Wovoka (IRE)**[48] 2204 7-9-4 **65** (tp) AmyRyan(5) 2 52
(K A Ryan) *hld up in rr: hdwy over 2f out: sn rdn and no imp appr fnl f* **7/1**

30-0 **5** *1 1/2* **Turf Trivia**[41] 2422 3-8-4 **60** PatrickDonaghy(5) 7 41
(G M Moore) *hld up: a in rr* **16/1**

5403 **6** *3/4* **King Of The Moors (USA)**[18] 3130 7-9-5 **68** (b) DaleSwift(7) 5 50
(R C Guest) *chsd ldr: cl up whn hung lft bnd after 2f: rdn 3f out: sn drvn and wknd over 2f out* **7/1**

060 **7** *9* **Leolene Starlight**[16] 3227 5-8-13 **55** SilvestreDeSousa 4 16
(D O'Meara) *in tch: rdn along over 3f out: sn wknd* **16/1**

1m 39.25s (-2.15) **Going Correction** -0.175s/f (Firm)
WFA 3 from 5yo+ 9lb **7** Ran SP% **114.1**
Speed ratings (Par 103): **103,102,101,94,92 91,82**
toteswingers:1&2 £3.50, 2&3 £2.60, 1&3 £3.80 CSF £19.56 CT £36.29 TOTE £8.30: £3.70, £2.40; EX 16.50.
Owner Viscount Environmental **Bred** Gainsborough Stud Management Ltd **Trained** Kirk Deighton, West Yorks

FOCUS
A competitive handicap run at a fast pace. The first three finished a long way clear of the rest. The winner is rated to last year's best.

3733 TOTEEXACTA MAIDEN STKS 1m

9:20 (9:20) (Class 5) 3-Y-O+ **£2,914** (£867; £433; £216) **Stalls High**

Form RPR

354 **1** **Squall**[51] 2128 3-9-3 74 PaulHanagan 14 77+
(J Noseda) *trckd ldrs on inner: hdwy over 2f out: swtchd lft and rdn to chal over 1f out: drvn ins fnl f: kpt on wl to ld last 50yds* **9/4**[2]

30 **2** *1/2* **Bursary (CAN)**[36] 2564 3-9-3 0 JoeFanning 11 76
(M Johnston) *set stdy pce: qcknd 3f out: rdn 2f out: drvn ent fnl f: hdd and no ex last 50yds* **11/4**[3]

3 *3* **Broadway Dancer** 3-8-9 0 BarryMcHugh(3) 10 64+
(R A Fahey) *midfield: hdwy on inner over 3f out: swtchd lft and rdn wl over 1f out: kpt on ins fnl f: nrst fin* **20/1**

3-2 **4** *3* **Mureb (USA)**[24] 2925 3-9-3 0 (t) TedDurcan 2 62
(Saeed Bin Suroor) *hld up in tch: hdwy on outer 3f out: rdn along 2f out: drvn and edgd rt over 1f out: sn btn* **5/4**[1]

05 **5** *3 3/4* **Hairy Maclary**[5] 3554 3-8-12 0 LanceBetts(5) 7 54
(T D Easterby) *t.k.h: prom: cl up 4f out: rdn along 3f out: grad wknd fr over 1f out* **33/1**

00-0 **6** *9* **Singing Scott (IRE)**[25] 2900 3-8-10 42 MatthewLawson(7) 3 33
(R Bastiman) *t.k.h: prom on outer: rdn along over 3f out: wknd over 2f out* **100/1**

7 *2 3/4* **March Forth** 3-9-3 0 RichardSmith 8 27
(Tom Dascombe) *s.i.s: a in rr* **33/1**

8 *3 1/2* **Sandgate Story** 4-9-2 0 JamesSullivan(5) 4 16
(N Wilson) *s.i.s: a in rr* **100/1**

9 *6* **The Nifty Belle** 4-9-7 0 PatrickMathers 5 —
(N Wilson) *chsd ldrs: rdn along over 3f out: sn wknd* **100/1**

06 **10** 2 1/4 **Presidium Galaxy**[13] 3285 3-8-7 0 PatrickDonaghy(5) 6 —
(G M Moore) *dwlt: a in rr* **100/1**

1m 39.76s (-1.64) **Going Correction** -0.175s/f (Firm)
WFA 3 from 4yo 9lb **10** Ran SP% **116.5**
Speed ratings (Par 103): **101,100,97,94,90 81,79,75,69,67**
toteswingers:1&2 £2.10, 2&3 £7.00, 1&3 £4.80 CSF £8.57 TOTE £3.90: £1.50, £1.10, £3.50; EX 10.10 Place 6: £59.01 Place 5: £32.79.
Owner Sir Robert Ogden & Lady Lloyd-Webber **Bred** Breeding Capital, Watership Down, Farish **Trained** Newmarket, Suffolk

FOCUS
There was not much strength in depth in this steadily run maiden. The favourite was disappointing but the second and third in the market fought out a tight finish and pulled clear of the rest, so the form looks solid enough. The winner produced a length personal best.
T/Plt: £99.60 to a £1 stake. Pool: £76,710.31 - 561.97 winning tickets. T/Qpdt: £69.30 to a £1 stake. Pool: £5,199.21 - 55.50 winning tickets. JR

3509 WINDSOR (R-H)
Monday, July 5

OFFICIAL GOING: Good to firm (firm in places; 8.4)
Stands' rail dolled out 7yds at 6f and 1yd at winning post. Top bend dolled out 9yds from innermost line, adding 24yds to races of one mile and over.
Wind: Moderate, half behind Weather: Fine, very warm

3734 SPORTINGBET.COM APPRENTICE H'CAP 6f
6:40 (6:45) (Class 5) (0-75,74) 4-Y-O+ £2,729 (£806; £403) Stalls High

Form RPR
1132 **1** **Piazza San Pietro**[10] 3400 4-9-8 **72** AndreaAtzeni 7 80
(A B Haynes) *trckd ldrs: rdn over 2f out: styd on against rail to ld jst over 1f out: drvn out* **7/2**[3]

413 **2** 1 1/2 **Headache**[21] 3033 5-9-3 **70** (bt) SophieDoyle(3) 2 73
(B W Duke) *t.k.h: hld up bhd ldrs: effrt on outer 2f out: styd on one pce to take 2nd ins fnl f* **10/3**[2]

6001 **3** 1 1/4 **Simple Rhythm**[5] 3567 4-9-0 **71** 6ex JoshCrane(7) 1 70+
(J Ryan) *t.k.h: prog on outer to join ldrs after 2f: led 1/2-way: gng bttr than rest 2f out: hdd and pushed along jst over 1f out: nt qckn* **12/1**

5024 **4** 3/4 **Misaro (GER)**[2] 3675 9-9-5 **72** (b) JohnFahy(3) 9 69
(R A Harris) *led to 1/2-way: rdn and nt qckn over 2f out: grad fdd ins fnl f* **7/2**[3]

4221 **5** 5 **Bermondsey Bob (IRE)**[5] 3556 4-8-12 **62** 6ex JackDean 6 46
(J L Spearing) *pressed ldr over 2f out: swtchd lft and rdn 2f out: sn wknd: eased ins fnl f* **3/1**[1]

0-00 **6** shd **Bold Argument (IRE)**[8] 3474 7-8-12 **62** JamesMillman 8 42
(Mrs P N Dutfield) *mostly in last: outpcd fr over 2f out: no ch after* **13/2**

1m 11.2s (-1.80) **Going Correction** -0.225s/f (Firm) **6** Ran SP% **113.5**
Speed ratings (Par 103): **103,101,99,98,91 91**
toteswingers: 1&2 £3.30, 1&3 £4.10, 2&3 £9.90 CSF £15.79 CT £122.50 TOTE £5.50: £2.10, £2.70; EX 23.00 Trifecta £135.60 Pool: £2915.77 - 15.91 winning units..
Owner K Corke **Bred** T E Pocock **Trained** Limpley Stoke, Bath
■ Sermons Mount (5/2) withdrawn (burst out of stalls); deduct 25p in £ from bets struck before new market formed.
■ Stewards' Enquiry : Sophie Doyle one-day ban: used whip with excessive frequency (Jul 19)

FOCUS
The going was changed to good to firm, firm in places before racing started, due to a lack of rain and despite nearly an inch of water having been applied in the last week. The stands' rail was dolled out from the winning post to the 6f marker. The top bend was dolled out 9yds, adding 24yds to the distance of races of 1m plus. A modest sprint handicap for apprentices, but there was a delay as the favourite Sermons Mount played up and burst out of the stalls, causing him to be withdrawn and resulting in a 25p deduction to those bets placed before the new market was formed. The form is rated around the runner-up.

3735 E B F SPORTINGBET.COM MAIDEN STKS 6f
7:10 (7:11) (Class 5) 2-Y-O £3,238 (£722; £722; £240) Stalls High

Form RPR
2 **1** **Byronic (IRE)**[12] 3310 2-9-3 0 AdamKirby 4 78
(C G Cox) *pressed ldrs: led jst over 2f out: hrd rdn over 1f out: edgd lft: styd on wl* **6/1**[3]

2 2 **Morache Music** 2-9-3 0 FergusSweeney 6 72+
(P J Makin) *hld up in midfield: lft bhd by ldrs fr 2f out: nt clr run over 1f out: pushed along and r.o strly ins fnl f* **66/1**

2 dht **Regal Approval** 2-9-3 0 RyanMoore 3 72
(H Morrison) *sn pressed ldrs: rdn to chal fr 2f out: nrly upsides ent fnl f: no ex* **7/1**

00 **4** nk **Velvet Underground (IRE)**[38] 2493 2-9-3 0 JimmyFortune 11 71
(B J Meehan) *mde most to jst over 2f out: cl enough over 1f out: one pce* **15/2**

5 1 **Lord Of Persia (USA)** 2-9-3 0 JimCrowley 10 68
(R M Beckett) *chsd ldrs: outpcd by ldng trio fr 2f out: styd on ins fnl f* **9/1**

6 2 **Majestic Dream (IRE)** 2-9-3 0 ShaneKelly 2 62+
(W R Swinburn) *s.s: rn green in last trio: sme prog over 2f out: pushed along and r.o wl ins fnl f: nrst fin* **33/1**

0 **7** 1/2 **Piceno (IRE)**[18] 3126 2-9-3 0 KierenFallon 13 61
(L M Cumani) *t.k.h: hld up bhd ldrs: nt qckn and outpcd fr 2f out: pushed along and nt on terms after* **20/1**

0 **8** 1/2 **Aldwick Bay (IRE)**[22] 3000 2-9-3 0 RichardHughes 15 59
(R Hannon) *chsd ldrs against rail: outpcd 2f out: pushed along and no imp after* **11/2**[2]

9 5 **Mirradores** 2-9-3 0 MartinDwyer 14 47
(W R Muir) *s.i.s: sn in tch chsng ldrs: wknd fr 2f out* **33/1**

3 **10** nk **Spokesperson (USA)**[31] 2715 2-9-3 0 AhmedAjtebi 16 43
(Mahmood Al Zarooni) *nvr beyond midfield: struggling towards rr over 2f out: sn no ch* **15/8**[1]

11 nk **Sea The Flames (IRE)** 2-9-3 0 PatDobbs 8 42
(M P Tregoning) *rn green and a in rr: no ch fr over 2f out* **33/1**

12 1 1/4 **Putin (IRE)** 2-9-3 0 TadhgO'Shea 5 41+
(D Haydn Jones) *a towards rr: lft bhd fr 2f out: wl bhd whn hmpd nr fin* **80/1**

0 **13** hd **Will Barrow**[10] 3399 2-9-3 0 StephenCraine 1 38
(J R Boyle) *hld up in last trio: pushed along and no prog 2f out: bhd after* **100/1**

14 nse **Striking Box** 2-9-0 0 JamesMillman(3) 7 40
(B R Millman) *s.i.s: early reminder: rn v green and a wl in rr* **100/1**

06 **15** nk **Robber Stone**[23] 2951 2-9-3 0 CoryParish 9 37
(M R Channon) *chsd ldrs: wknd rapidly fr over 2f out* **66/1**

1m 12.94s (-0.06) **Going Correction** -0.225s/f (Firm) **15** Ran SP% **118.5**
Speed ratings (Par 94): **91,88,88,87,86 83,83,82,75,75 75,73,73,73,72**PL: Morache Music £17.70, Regal Approve £2.10. EX: Byronic/MM £138.60. B/RA £16.00 CSF: B/MM £184.05 B/RA £21.76 toteswingers: 1&2 £73.80, 1&3 £7.20, 2&3 £62.70 CSF £21.76 TOTE £4.00: £1.90; EX 138.60 Trifecta £185.70 Part won. Pool: £1455.92 - 2.90 winning units..

FOCUS
An interesting maiden run 1.74s slower than the opening handicap. It was quite a messy race and the favourite disappointed, but the favourite ran to form.

NOTEBOOK
Byronic(IRE), a 29,000gns half-brother to several winners up to 7f, had been touched off on his debut and gained compensation here. He broke well from his low draw and was soon at the head of affairs, then stuck on well under pressure and was drawing away in the closing stages. He looks capable of going on again from this. (op 5-1 tchd 9-2)
Morache Music ◆, unfancied in the market, was the eyecatcher. He tracked the leaders for most of the way but had to be switched to get a run over a furlong out and then finished best of all. He is bred to be effective at this trip and will know more next time. Official explanation: jockey said colt was denied a clear run (op 6-1 tchd 15-2)
Regal Approval, whose sales price rose from 800gns as a foal to 100,000gns at the breeze-ups, holds a Gimcrack entry. He ran well on this debut but got tired in the closing stages. He should have no trouble winning a similar race if going the right way from this. (op 6-1 tchd 15-2)
Velvet Underground(IRE) got the rails from the start and appeared to run his race. He now qualifies for nurseries and might find his niche in that sphere. (op 8-1)
Lord Of Persia(USA) cost $55,000 and showed ability on this debut without ever looking likely to score. (op 6-1)
Majestic Dream(IRE) ◆ is related to winners at 7f and 1m. After missing the break from his low draw, was switched to the inside rail at the back of the field. He was noted making steady late headway and should improve considerably for the experience. (op 50-1)
Piceno(IRE) ran reasonably but is likely to be seen to better effect in handicaps over further. (op 14-1)
Aldwick Bay(IRE) was another who ran reasonably close to the rail but is also likely to be seen to better effect in handicaps over further. (op 15-2 tchd 8-1)
Spokesperson(USA) was the big disappointment of the race. He had run with promise behind a stablemate on his debut and had the rail draw. However, he could not hold his place near the rail after a modest start and never got into the race. The disappointing thing was that he failed to pick up at all and finished towards the rear, while less experienced horses went past him. (op 5-2 tchd 13-8)
Striking Box Official explanation: jockey said colt ran green

3736 SPORTINGBET.COM H'CAP 5f 10y
7:40 (7:40) (Class 4) (0-85,81) 3-Y-O+ £4,857 (£1,445; £722; £360) Stalls High

Form RPR
122- **1** **Desert Poppy (IRE)**[234] 7372 3-9-2 **76** ShaneKelly 10 83
(W R Swinburn) *mde virtually all: hung lft fr over 1f out w hd at awkward angle: drvn out and hld on wl* **6/1**[2]

1022 **2** 1/2 **Solemn**[18] 3114 5-9-12 **81** (b) RyanMoore 7 88
(J M Bradley) *cl up: rdn to chse wnr wl over 1f out: chal and edgd lft fnl f: nt qckn last 100yds* **9/4**[1]

0601 **3** nk **Make My Dream**[9] 3440 7-9-4 **73** TadhgO'Shea 5 79
(J Gallagher) *hld up bhd ldrs: gng wl 2f out: taken to outer and shkn up over 1f out: styd on ins fnl f: nrst fin* **12/1**

413 **4** hd **Steelcut**[10] 3417 6-9-0 **76** DavidKenny(7) 9 81
(Andrew Reid) *hld up bhd ldrs: looking for room over 1f out: rdn and styd on ins fnl f: nvr able to chal* **12/1**

0040 **5** 1/2 **Triple Dream**[11] 3373 5-9-3 **72** (p) LiamKeniry 1 75
(J M Bradley) *settled in last: stl there 2f out: rdn and styd on wl ins fnl f: nrst fin* **16/1**

0045 **6** nse **Green Lagonda (AUS)**[6] 3527 8-8-7 **65** MartinLane(3) 6 68+
(P D Evans) *towards rr: effrt and nt clr run 1f out: styd on ins fnl f: nrst fin* **33/1**

5340 **7** 3/4 **Our Piccadilly (IRE)**[18] 3114 5-9-6 **75** FergusSweeney 3 76
(W S Kittow) *settled in rr: shkn up and no prog 2f out: kpt on same pce ins fnl f* **14/1**

4000 **8** 3/4 **Equuleus Pictor**[24] 2940 6-9-8 **80** JackDean(3) 8 78
(J L Spearing) *pressed wnr to wl over 1f out: fdd and lost pls ins fnl f* **7/1**

3041 **9** hd **Ocean Blaze**[12] 3308 6-9-8 **77** TomQueally 4 74
(B R Millman) *sn pressed ldrs towards outer: shkn up 2f out: losing pl whn sltly impeded ins fnl f* **7/1**

4621 **10** 1 1/2 **Riflessione**[28] 2818 4-9-6 **75** (b) KierenFallon 2 67
(R A Harris) *w.w: taken to wd outside 1/2-way: no prog over 1f out: fdd* **13/2**[3]

59.10 secs (-1.20) **Going Correction** -0.225s/f (Firm)
WFA 3 from 4yo+ 5lb **10** Ran SP% **114.3**
Speed ratings (Par 105): **100,99,98,98,97 97,96,95,94,92**
toteswingers: 1&2 £2.80, 1&3 £14.30, 2&3 £10.50 CSF £19.40 CT £159.64 TOTE £6.20: £2.00, £1.10, £3.80; EX 17.90 Trifecta £593.70 Part won. Pool of £802.35 - 0.82 winning units..
Owner Oasis Dreamers **Bred** Kildaragh Stud **Trained** Aldbury, Herts
■ Stewards' Enquiry : David Kenny caution: careless riding; 2nd incident one-day ban: careless riding (Jul 19)

FOCUS
A fair sprint and the whole field drifted across the track in the closing stages, and a couple looked to have hard-luck stories. Fairly sound form, with the winner posting a clear personal best.
Riflessione Official explanation: jockey said gelding lost its action

3737 E B F SPORTINGBET.COM H'CAP 1m 2f 7y
8:10 (8:10) (Class 4) (0-85,83) 3-Y-O+ £4,857 (£1,445; £722; £360) Stalls Low

Form RPR
61 **1** **Abergavenny**[150] 421 3-8-12 **75** GregFairley 1 85+
(M Johnston) *trckd ldr: forced to switch lft over 3f out to centre: chal and upsides 1f out: drvn ahd nr fin* **8/1**

-001 **2** shd **Geneva Geyser (GER)**[2] 3688 4-10-3 **83** 6ex MickyFenton 2 93
(J M P Eustace) *rousted along to ld at str pce: frequently looked awkward: urged along and wnt wd to centre over 3f out: jnd 1f out: styd on: hdd nr fin* **4/1**[2]

0520 **3** 3 **Resurge (IRE)**[24] 2934 5-10-0 **80** FergusSweeney 3 84
(W S Kittow) *trckd ldng pair to 4f out: cl up whn forced to switch lft over 3f out: rdn to press ldng pair in centre 2f out: no ex ins fnl f* **11/4**[1]

-504 **4** 3 **Sequillo**[22] 2996 4-10-0 **80** RichardHughes 4 78
(R Hannon) *hld up last: styd against nr side rail fr 3f out: no imp on ldrs after* **7/1**

-425 **5** nk **Effigy**[22] 2991 6-9-13 **79** DaneO'Neill 5 76
(H Candy) *hld up disputing 4th: rdn in 5th wl over 3f out: c centre sn after: no imp over 2f out* **13/2**[3]

6226 **6** 1 ¼ **Penchesco (IRE)**[24] 2934 5-9-11 77 .... RyanMoore 6 72
(Mrs A J Perrett) *hld up disputing 4th: wnt cl 3rd 4f out: led pair against nr side rail 3f out: nt on terms after: wknd ins fnl f* **11/4**[1]

2m 5.85s (-2.85) **Going Correction** -0.15s/f (Firm)
WFA 3 from 4yo+ 11lb **6** Ran SP% **110.3**
Speed ratings (Par 105): **105,104,102,100,99 98**
CSF £37.81 TOTE £4.90: £2.70, £2.80; EX 20.20.
Owner Sheikh Hamdan Bin Mohammed Al Maktoum **Bred** Mrs J Gittins **Trained** Middleham Moor, N Yorks

FOCUS
A tightly knit handicap despite the small field and it produced a good finish. The majority of the field raced up the centre of the track from the intersection, and they had the advantage over those that stayed on the rail, something that had been hinted at by the results of the earlier races. The form makes sense around the first two.

3738 SPORTINGBET.COM MAIDEN FILLIES' STKS 1m 67y
8:40 (8:45) (Class 5) 3-4-Y-0 **£2,593** (£765; £383) **Stalls** High

Form RPR
432 **1** **Belgique (IRE)**[49] 2180 3-9-0 79 .... RichardHughes 6 78+
(R Hannon) *trckd ldr: led 3f out: in command and shkn up jst over 1f out: pushed out: cosily* **7/4**[1]
2 ¾ **Entitled** 3-9-0 0 .... RyanMoore 5 75+
(Sir Michael Stoute) *trckd ldrs: pushed up to chse wnr over 1f out: readily hld ins fnl f: clsd at fin* **7/4**[1]
3 1 ½ **Snow Magic (IRE)** 3-9-0 0 .... PatCosgrave 7 72+
(J R Fanshawe) *trckd ldrs in 6th: pushed along on outer over 2f out: styd on steadily to take 3rd over 1f out* **28/1**
0 **4** 1 ¾ **Chasse Coeur**[27] 2842 3-9-0 0 .... DavidProbert 1 67
(A M Balding) *trckd ldrs: outpcd over 2f out: rdn and kpt on fr over 1f out* **28/1**
5 *nk* **Mexican Deb** 3-9-0 0 .... DaneO'Neill 3 67
(W R Muir) *trckd ldng pair: rdn and outpcd fr over 2f out: kpt on* **40/1**
6 6 **Bill's Story** 3-9-0 0 .... CoryParish 9 52+
(M R Channon) *rrd bdly s and lost many l: ct up at rr after 3f: rdn and outpcd over 2f out: plugged on past wkng rivals* **50/1**
7 ¾ **Queen Ranavola (USA)** 3-8-9 0 .... KierenFox(5) 11 50
(J R Best) *s.s: in tch at rr after 3f: outpcd over 2f out: plugged on* **50/1**
0 **8** 1 **Into The Wind**[12] 3333 3-8-12 0 ow1 .... JamesMillman(3) 2 49
(B R Millman) *nvr beyond midfield: rdn over 3f out: no imp over 2f out: wknd* **100/1**
60 **9** *nk* **Jakeys Girl**[14] 3272 3-9-0 0 .... IanMongan 8 47
(P M Phelan) *settled in last trio: shkn up 3f out: sn outpcd: wknd over 1f out* **100/1**
65 **10** ¾ **Bernie's Moon (USA)**[14] 3272 3-9-0 0 .... MartinDwyer 4 46+
(B J Meehan) *led to 3f out: wknd rapidly wl over 1f out* **10/1**[2]
11 *shd* **Hotfoot** 3-9-0 0 .... IvaMilickova 12 45
(John Berry) *a towards rr: shkn up 3f out: sn outpcd: wknd over 1f out* **80/1**
0-5 **12** ½ **Lady Of Garmoran (USA)**[67] 1639 3-9-0 0 .... KierenFallon 14 44
(P F I Cole) *in tch in midfield: drvn 4f out: wknd over 2f out* **20/1**[3]

1m 47.37s (2.67) **Going Correction** -0.15s/f (Firm) **12** Ran SP% **103.1**
Speed ratings (Par 100): **80,79,77,76,75 69,68,67,67,66 66,66**
toteswingers:1&2 £1.10, 2&3 £6.50, 1&3 £5.20 CSF £3.04 TOTE £2.30: £1.10, £1.10, £5.10; EX 3.50 Trifecta £30.40 Pool: £566.61 - 13.75 winning units..
Owner Philip F Myerscough **Bred** Philip And Mrs Jane Myerscough **Trained** East Everleigh, Wilts
■ Fun Affair (11/2) and Spirit Of Darley (33/1) withdrawn (refused to enter stalls). Rule 4 apples to all bets, deduction 15p in £.

FOCUS
Some major yards were represented in this fillies' maiden but the market was only about four, and one of those was withdrawn after rearing up and losing her rider at the start. The pace was stop-start and the market leaders dominated. Just fair form, rated around the winner.
Bill's Story Official explanation: jockey said filly reared as gates opened and was slowly away

3739 BMS SOLUTIONS H'CAP 1m 67y
9:10 (9:10) (Class 5) (0-70,70) 3-Y-0 **£2,593** (£765; £383) **Stalls** High

Form RPR
0420 **1** **Abhar (USA)**[10] 3390 3-8-11 65 .... KierenFox(5) 3 72
(J R Best) *trckd ldr: rdn to chal towards centre over 2f out: led over 1f out: styd on wl* **9/1**
-044 **2** 1 ¼ **Fire Raiser**[22] 3002 3-8-11 60 .... JimmyFortune 4 64+
(A M Balding) *hld up in 8th: effrt over 2f out: drvn and r.o fr over 1f out: tk 2nd nr fin* **6/1**[3]
-153 **3** *nk* **Flag Of Glory**[22] 2993 3-9-7 70 .... GeorgeBaker 10 73
(C F Wall) *led at decent pce: drvn against rail over 2f out: hdd over 1f out: edgd lft and one pce ins fnl f: lost 2nd nr fin* **9/2**[1]
0010 **4** 1 **Cereal Killer (IRE)**[25] 2888 3-9-6 69 ....(b) RichardHughes 13 70
(R Hannon) *chsd ldng pair: reminders 1/2-way: styd cl up u.p 2f out: kpt on same pce* **12/1**
3520 **5** 1 ½ **Edition**[26] 2863 3-9-4 67 .... LiamKeniry 7 65
(J R Gask) *trckd ldng trio: rdn 3f out: no imp u.p 2f out* **13/2**
-605 **6** *nk* **Cuckoo Rock (IRE)**[39] 2460 3-8-4 58 ow2 ....(b[1]) JohnFahy(5) 11 55
(J G Portman) *trckd ldrs in 5th: gng wl enough over 2f out: sn rdn and no prog: fdd over 1f out* **25/1**
0633 **7** 2 ¾ **Cat Hunter**[9] 3464 3-9-4 67 .... JimCrowley 6 58+
(Mrs A J Perrett) *hld up in last: pushed along 3f out: modest prog 2f out: shkn up whn no ch fnl f* **17/2**
3041 **8** ¾ **Mellifera**[9] 3464 3-9-5 68 ....(p) AdamKirby 2 57+
(W R Swinburn) *hld up in last pair: rdn and no prog over 3f out: struggling over 2f out* **5/1**[2]
5-40 **9** 1 **Irish Jugger (USA)**[12] 3325 3-8-13 65 .... JamesMillman(3) 9 52+
(B R Millman) *hld up in 7th: rdn 3f out: no prog and btn 2f out* **33/1**
0-32 **10** 1 ½ **Bideeya (USA)**[9] 3434 3-9-1 64 ....(p) RyanMoore 8 47+
(C E Brittain) *hld up in 9th: rdn over 3f out: no prog and struggling over 2f out* **9/2**[1]
01-5 **11** 11 **Empress Leizu (IRE)**[63] 1775 3-8-11 60 .... TomQueally 5 18
(A W Carroll) *chsd ldrs in 6th: wknd u.p over 3f out: t.o* **25/1**

1m 43.82s (-0.88) **Going Correction** -0.15s/f (Firm) **11** Ran SP% **119.5**
Speed ratings (Par 100): **98,96,96,95,93 93,90,90,89,87 76**
toteswingers:1&2 £14.00, 2&3 £5.40, 1&3 £9.70 CSF £61.92 CT £286.16 TOTE £14.20: £3.50, £2.50, £2.60; EX 112.10 Trifecta £339.50 Part won. Pool of £458.88 - 0.30 winning units. Place 6: £273.88 Place 5: £127.01 .
Owner Ian Beach & John Fletcher **Bred** Brambly Lane Farm **Trained** Hucking, Kent
■ Stewards' Enquiry : Jimmy Fortune two-day ban: careless riding (Jul 19-20)

FOCUS
This modest 3-y-o handicap was run 3.55sec faster than the preceding fillies' maiden. There were some disappointing performances among the market leaders and again not much got into it from the rear. The winner is rated back to form.
Cat Hunter Official explanation: jockey said filly suffered interference leaving stalls and never travelled
T/Jkpt: Not won. T/Plt: £229.90 to a £1 stake. Pool:£114,824.67 - 364.49 winning tickets. T/Qpdt: £15.90 to a £1 stake. Pool: £7,700.27 - 357.30 winning tickets. JN

3740 - 3747a (Foreign Racing) - See Raceform Interactive

2161 LES LANDES
Sunday, July 4

OFFICIAL GOING: Firm

3748a THE SUPPORTERS SPRINT (H'CAP) 7f
4:15 (4:15) 3-Y-0+ **£1,460** (£525; £315)

RPR
1 **Fast Freddie**[16] 6-9-6 .... MattieBatchelor 5 —
(Mrs A Malzard, Jersey) **5/2**[3]
2 10 **Peopleton Brook**[12] 3299 8-10-5 ....(t) WilsonRenwick 3 —
(B G Powell) **7/4**[1]
3 2 **Majestical (IRE)**[16] 8-9-1 ....(p) JemmaMarshall 6 —
(J S O Arthur, Jersey) **7/2**
4 3 ½ **Toggle**[16] 6-9-2 ....(p) MarkLawson 1 —
(Mrs A Corson, Jersey) **15/8**[2]
R **Athania (IRE)**[34] 4-10-12 ....(p) AntonyProcter 7 —
(J S O Arthur, Jersey) **4/1**

1m 28.0s (-2.00) **5** Ran SP% **141.9**
Owner The Crawford Family **Bred** New Hall Stud **Trained** St Ouen, Jersey

NOTEBOOK
Peopleton Brook

3502 PONTEFRACT (L-H)
Tuesday, July 6

OFFICIAL GOING: Last 6f - good to firm; remainder - good to firm (firm in places) (9.0)
Temporary dolling in place over last 6f and positioned 12ft from original running rail.
Wind: Moderate, behind. Weather: Sunny periods

3749 DIANNE NURSERY 6f
2:30 (2:31) (Class 4) 2-Y-0 **£3,885** (£1,156; £577; £288) **Stalls** Low

Form RPR
141 **1** **Majestic Myles (IRE)**[5] 3596 2-9-12 84 6ex .... PaulHanagan 2 86
(R A Fahey) *t.k.h: trckd ldrs: smooth hdwy on inner wl over 1f out: led appr fnl f: shkn up and r.o wl last 100yds* **4/9**[1]
606 **2** *nk* **Witzend (IRE)**[13] 3315 2-8-9 67 .... TonyHamilton 4 69
(Jedd O'Keeffe) *hld up in rr: hdwy wl over 1f out: swtchd rt and rdn to chse wnr ins fnl f: styd on wl towards fin* **20/1**
145 **3** 1 ½ **Orientalist**[38] 2525 2-9-2 74 .... KierenFallon 6 71
(Eve Johnson Houghton) *t.k.h: cl up on outer: effrt 2f out: rdn to ld briefly 1 1/2f out: sn hdd: drvn and kpt on same pce ins fnl f* **14/1**
3241 **4** 9 **Alfraamsey**[12] 3365 2-9-7 79 .... RobertWinston 3 49
(M R Channon) *led: rdn along 2f out: hdd 1 1/2f out: sn drvn: wknd ent fnl f and eased* **9/2**[2]
032 **5** 13 **Loves Theme (IRE)**[45] 2347 2-9-2 74 .... JoeFanning 5 5
(A Bailey) *t.k.h: cl up: rdn along 2f out: drvn and wknd wl over 1f out* **10/1**[3]

1m 17.93s (1.03) **Going Correction** 0.0s/f (Good) **5** Ran SP% **108.0**
Speed ratings (Par 96): **93,92,90,78,61**
CSF £10.32 TOTE £1.40: £1.10, £3.80; EX 9.60.
Owner James Gaffney **Bred** Arctic Tack Stud **Trained** Musley Bank, N Yorks
■ The 'official' ratings shown next to each horse are estimated and for information purposes only.

FOCUS
The third nursery of the current campaign. The first three were clear and the winner is rated to his mark.

NOTEBOOK
Majestic Myles(IRE), who comfortably took the first nursery of the season at Redcar last week, proved all the rage to follow up under his penalty. He completed the task and, now a winner of three of his four outings, is value for further than the bare margin but was workmanlike in winning. Looking at the manner in which he held his head high when sent to the front, he was probably feeling this quicker surface and should be happier back with a little ease, so it will be very interesting to see how he copes once the handicapper reassesses him. (tchd 2-5)
Witzend(IRE), who failed to reach the frame in three maidens previously, bided his time out the back and was suited by doing so as the leaders went off quick early on. He stayed on strongly from the furlong marker, but the winner got first run and the line was always coming that bit too soon. This step up a furlong was evidently much to his liking and, despite the fact he will be going up for this, he looks capable of winning one of these in the coming weeks. (op 22-1 tchd 18-1)
Orientalist shaped better for this return to 6f and switch to a nursery. He wasn't helped by having to race wide and fared best of the three that forced the early pace. (tchd 16-1)
Alfraamsey won easily at the sixth attempt at Newcastle 12 days earlier, but everything went his way there and he looked high enough for this nursery debut. He ultimately paid for doing too much on the front end, but does need some respite from the handicapper. He was later reported to have hung right. Official explanation: jockey said colt hung right (tchd 5-1)
Loves Theme(IRE) ran a career-best when just held in a moderate York maiden on her previous outing in May. She was close up early, but faded tamely before the final furlong and something may have been amiss. (op 17-2)

3750 YORKSHIRE RACING SUMMER FESTIVAL H'CAP 1m 2f 6y
3:00 (3:01) (Class 5) (0-75,75) 3-Y-0+ **£3,238** (£963; £481; £240) **Stalls** Low

Form RPR
6220 **1** **Monkton Vale (IRE)**[45] 2315 3-9-1 73 .... PaulHanagan 2 81
(R A Fahey) *mde all: rdn 2f out: drvn over 1f out: edgd rt ins fnl f: kpt on gamely* **15/8**[1]
0050 **2** *nk* **River Ardeche**[21] 3060 5-9-4 70 .... PatrickDonaghy(5) 5 77+
(B M R Haslam) *hld up in tch: hdwy over 2f out: swtchd rt and rdn over 1f out: styd on strly ins fnl f: jst hld* **14/1**

5-56 **3** 2 1/2 **Sadler's Mark**[19] 3123 3-8-6 **64** .... JamieSpencer 6 66
(T P Tate) *trckd ldrs: hdwy over 3f out: effrt to chal over 2f out: sn rdn and ev ch tl drvn and one pce ins fnl f* **9/2**[3]
146- **4** 1 1/2 **Autumn Harvest**[217] 2698 6-10-0 **75** .... SilvestreDeSousa 7 74
(G A Harker) *stdd s and hld up in rr: hdwy 3f out: rdn to chse ldrs wl over 1f out: no imp ins fnl f* **15/2**
610- **5** 3 1/4 **Knight's Victory (IRE)**[308] 5551 4-9-7 **71** .... MichaelStainton(3) 1 64
(Michael Smith) *trckd ldrs on inner: hdwy 3f out: rdn along 2f out: drvn and wknd over 1f out* **12/1**
5000 **6** 7 **Alsahil (USA)**[13] 3319 4-9-11 **72** .... TomEaves 3 51
(Micky Hammond) *prom: rdn along over 3f out: sn wknd* **10/1**
0500 **7** 5 **Epic (IRE)**[11] 3390 3-8-6 **64** .... (b) JoeFanning 9 33
(M Johnston) *prom: rdn along over 3f out: sn wknd* **4/1**[2]
00/ **8** 8 **Jackson (BRZ)**[156] 8-10-0 **75** .... PaddyAspell 4 28
(R C Guest) *a in rr: rdn along 3f out: sn outpcd* **16/1**

2m 12.93s (-0.77) **Going Correction** 0.0s/f (Good)
WFA 3 from 4yo+ 11lb **8** Ran SP% **114.1**
Speed ratings (Par 103): **103,102,100,99,96 91,87,80**
Tote Swingers:1&2:£6.30, 2&3:£8.10, 1&3:£3.10 CSF £30.54 CT £104.92 TOTE £2.80: £1.50, £3.30, £2.00; EX 28.70.
Owner B Plows P M Watson J Owen **Bred** P Bergin **Trained** Musley Bank, N Yorks

FOCUS
A tricky looking handicap. There was just a routine early pace on and the first pair were clear at the finish. A 6lb personal best from the winner.

3751 HARWORTH ESTATES H'CAP 5f
3:30 (3:30) (Class 5) (0-75,75) 3-Y-O **£3,238** (£963; £481; £240) **Stalls** Low

Form RPR
-161 **1** **Perfect Blossom**[11] 3410 3-8-13 **67** .... PaulHanagan 8 73+
(K A Ryan) *mde all: rdn wl over 1f out: drvn ins fnl f: kpt on wl* **11/4**[1]
41-3 **2** 3/4 **Jack Luey**[31] 2768 3-8-8 **65** .... AndrewHeffernan(3) 3 68
(L A Mullaney) *in tch: hdwy 2f out: swtchd rt and effrt whn sltly hmpd over 1f out: drvn and styd on strly fnl f* **7/1**[3]
-300 **3** nk **Tillys Tale**[24] 2960 3-9-4 **75** .... PaulPickard(3) 1 77
(P T Midgley) *trckd ldng pair on inner: hdwy 2f out: swtchd rt and rdn to chse wnr over 1f out: sn drvn and edgd lft: kpt on* **25/1**
3355 **4** 1 1/2 **Flouncing (IRE)**[3] 3677 3-9-1 **69** .... KierenFallon 6 66
(W J Haggas) *dwlt and in rr: hdwy 2f out on outer wl over 1f out: sn rdn and kpt on ins fnl f* **7/2**[2]
2533 **5** 3/4 **Starlight Muse (IRE)**[13] 3311 3-8-11 **72** .... DavidKenny(7) 4 71+
(E S McMahon) *s.i.s and in rr: sme hdwy on inner whn hmpd over 1f out: nvr a factor* **12/1**
3132 **6** 1 1/4 **Carrie's Magic**[18] 3151 3-9-3 **71** .... PhillipMakin 7 60
(T D Barron) *chsd ldrs: rdn along 2f out: sn drvn and no imp* **7/2**[2]
3462 **7** 3 1/4 **Leleyf (IRE)**[9] 3480 3-8-13 **67** .... (v) ChrisCatlin 5 45
(M R Channon) *cl up: rdn over 2f out: drvn and edgd rt over 1f out: sn wknd* **8/1**
4320 **8** shd **Song Of Parkes**[26] 2883 3-9-2 **70** .... EddieAhern 2 47
(E J Alston) *a towards rr* **7/1**[3]

63.53 secs (0.23) **Going Correction** 0.0s/f (Good) **8** Ran SP% **118.8**
Speed ratings (Par 100): **98,96,96,93,92 90,85,85**
Tote Swingers:1&2:£4.40, 2&3:£19.30, 1&3:£6.80 CSF £23.71 CT £407.47 TOTE £3.30: £1.10, £2.90, £5.50; EX 30.90.
Owner Mrs Ann Morris **Bred** Mrs A Morris **Trained** Hambleton, N Yorks
■ Stewards' Enquiry : Paul Pickard three-day ban: careless riding (Jul 20-22)

FOCUS
Modest handicap form. The progressive winner stepped forward again.
Carrie's Magic Official explanation: jockey said filly was unsuited by the good to firm ground
Song Of Parkes Official explanation: jockey said filly was unsuited by the good to firm ground

3752 WEATHERBYS BANK PIPALONG STKS (LISTED RACE) (F&M) 1m 4y
4:00 (4:00) (Class 1) 4-Y-O+
£22,432 (£8,540; £4,276; £2,136; £1,068; £536) **Stalls** Low

Form RPR
3324 **1** **Off Chance**[21] 3063 4-8-12 89 .... DuranFentiman 2 102
(T D Easterby) *hld up in rr: gd hdwy over 2f out: nt clr run and swtchd rt ent fnl f: rdn and qcknd wl to ld last 75yds* **8/1**
5040 **2** 3/4 **Please Sing**[20] 3069 4-8-12 95 .... ChrisCatlin 4 100
(M R Channon) *trckd ldr: effrt 2f out: sn rdn and ev ch ins fnl f: drvn and kpt on wl towards fin* **11/1**
0-61 **3** 1 1/4 **Tropical Paradise (IRE)**[36] 2595 4-8-12 102 .... JimCrowley 1 97+
(P Winkworth) *hld up towards rr: hdwy 3f out: swtchd rt and rdn to chal wl over 1f out: led appr fnl f: drvn and hdd last 75yds* **15/2**[3]
0-41 **4** 3/4 **Flora Trevelyan**[40] 2472 4-8-12 98 .... TedDurcan 10 96
(W R Swinburn) *trckd ldrs: hdwy on outer 3f out: chal 2f out: rdn to ld briefly 1 1/2f out: sn hdd and drvn: ev ch tl n.m.r and wknd wl ins fnl f* **4/6**[1]
1-00 **5** hd **Good Again**[59] 1899 4-8-12 93 .... HayleyTurner 3 97+
(G A Butler) *trckd ldrs on inner: effrt whn nt clr run and hmpd over 1f out: swtchd rt and nt clr run ins fnl f: swtchd lft and kpt on towards fin* **16/1**
0110 **6** 1 3/4 **Just Lille (IRE)**[17] 3194 7-8-12 94 .... (v) BarryMcHugh 7 91
(Mrs A Duffield) *led: rdn along over 2f out: drvn and hdd 1 1/2f out: sn hung lft and grad wknd* **7/1**[2]
1-03 **7** 5 **Theatrical Award (NOR)**[35] 2637 5-8-12 107 .... CarlosLopez 6 80
(Michael Taylor, Norway) *in tch on outer: rdn along 3f out: sn btn* **16/1**
00-0 **8** 3 1/4 **King's Starlet**[45] 2326 4-8-12 89 .... FrankieDettori 9 72
(H Morrison) *hld up: a towards rr* **40/1**
5-00 **9** 1 1/4 **Sarah Park (IRE)**[31] 2744 5-8-12 92 .... KierenFallon 8 69
(B J Meehan) *trckd ldng pair: rdn along wl over 2f out: sn wknd* **25/1**

1m 43.94s (-1.96) **Going Correction** 0.0s/f (Good) **9** Ran SP% **121.7**
Speed ratings (Par 111): **109,108,107,106,106 104,99,96,94**
Tote Swingers: 1&2 £10.10, 1&3 £13.20, 2&3 £7.10 CSF £96.33 TOTE £11.30: £3.30, £3.00, £1.90; EX 89.40.
Owner L B Holliday **Bred** Cleaboy Farms Co **Trained** Great Habton, N Yorks
■ Stewards' Enquiry : Barry McHugh three-day ban: careless riding (Jul 20-22)

FOCUS
The seventh running of this Listed prize for fillies, which had been moved to a month or so later this year than is normally the case, in a bid to avoid clashing with Royal Ascot. It attracted just an average field for the grade, though, and there was something of a bunched finish. The form is rated around the runner-up, with a 5lb personal best from the winner.

NOTEBOOK
Off Chance, ponied down to the start, relished the decent early tempo and motored home from off the pace to score with something left up her sleeve. She did very well to win as she did after having to be switched wide with her effort around the furlong marker, and it rates by far her best effort so far, being officially rated just 89 coming into this. (op 12-1)
Please Sing, out the back in the Hunt Cup last time, returned to the sort of form that saw her finish fourth in a Group 3 last month and was only caught by the winner near the line. She deserves to find another winning turn. (op 14-1)
Tropical Paradise(IRE), officially rated 102, was up in class and trip. She is bred to get this far and, on this showing does stay the trip fine, but she probably found the ground quicker than she cares for. (op 7-1)
Flora Trevelyan hosed up at Sandown 40 days earlier, for which she was hiked up 11lb, and was backed to the exclusion of her rivals on this return to Listed company. She wasn't helped by the draw, though, and after making a bold move around the final turn her early exploits told where it mattered most. (op 5-6)
Good Again, a previous C&D winner, had run well below-par in two previous runs this term. Her yard is in decent fettle at present, however, and this was a definite return to form for her. She would have been closer had she not been hampered approaching the final furlong and deserves another chance in this class.
Just Lille(IRE), second in the race last term, unsurprisingly set out to make this a test yet was a sitting duck turning for home and needs further now. (op 8-1)
Theatrical Award(NOR), a dual Classic winner in her native Norway, was allotted the highest BHB mark of these for her British debut on 107. Another ponied to the start, she found this too sharp and is evidently flattered by her official rating. (op 12-1)
Sarah Park(IRE) was later reported to have been unsuited by the ground. Official explanation: jockey said mare was unsuited by the good to firm (firm in places) ground (tchd 28-1)

3753 KING RICHARD III H'CAP 6f
4:30 (4:31) (Class 3) (0-90,89) 3-Y-O+
£6,231 (£1,866; £933; £467; £233; £117) **Stalls** Low

Form RPR
2611 **1** **Cornus**[11] 3401 8-9-5 **81** .... (be) JamesDoyle 8 91
(A J McCabe) *in tch: hdwy 2f out: rdn to chse ldrs over 1f out: styd on ins fnl f to ld last 100yds* **9/1**
0331 **2** 1 1/2 **Red Cape (FR)**[10] 3435 7-9-1 **82** .... IanBrennan(5) 7 87+
(Mrs R A Carr) *cl up on outer: effrt to chal 2f out: rdn over 1f out: slt ld jst ins fnl f: sn drvn: hdd and nt qckn last 100yds* **5/1**[3]
3005 **3** 1 **Gertmegalush (IRE)**[10] 3436 3-8-5 **76** .... BarryMcHugh(3) 9 77
(John A Harris) *towards rr: hdwy 2f out: sn rdn and kpt on ins fnl f: nrst fin* **16/1**
1101 **4** 3/4 **Tangerine Trees**[27] 2856 5-9-5 **81** .... TomEaves 1 80+
(B Smart) *led: rdn along 2f out: drvn and hdd jst ins fnl f: grad wknd* **3/1**[1]
2016 **5** shd **Indian Skipper (IRE)**[3] 3681 5-9-9 **85** .... (be) KierenFallon 4 84
(R C Guest) *dwlt and in rr: hdwy 2f out: rdn and kpt on ins fnl f: nrst fin* **5/1**[3]
0203 **6** 10 **Doctor Parkes**[23] 2992 4-9-10 **86** .... EddieAhern 6 53
(E J Alston) *cl up: ev ch 2f out: sn rdn and wknd* **9/2**[2]
4250 **7** 1 **Dickie Le Davoir**[17] 3216 6-8-5 **70** oh4 .... (v) AndrewHeffernan(3) 3 34
(R C Guest) *dwlt: a towards rr* **9/1**
0050 **8** 2 3/4 **Bel Cantor**[11] 3389 7-8-13 **78** .... (v[1]) KellyHarrison(3) 5 33
(W J H Ratcliffe) *cl up: rdn along over 2f out and sn wknd* **20/1**
0000 **9** 2 **Green Manalishi**[11] 3406 9-9-13 **89** .... (p) PaulHanagan 2 38
(K A Ryan) *chsd ldrs: rdn along 1/2-way: sn wknd* **7/1**

1m 16.71s (-0.19) **Going Correction** 0.0s/f (Good)
WFA 3 from 4yo+ 6lb **9** Ran SP% **119.7**
Speed ratings (Par 107): **101,99,97,96,96 83,81,78,75**
Tote Swingers: 1&2 £6.10, 1&3 £16.80, 2&3 £17.00 CSF £55.50 CT £549.22 TOTE £8.70: £3.20, £2.00, £5.60; EX 29.20.
Owner Triple A Partnership **Bred** G Russell **Trained** Averham Park, Notts

FOCUS
A fair sprint handicap, run at a frantic early tempo. The winner showed his best form since his early 3yo career.

NOTEBOOK
Cornus got up late on to register a hat-trick off a 7lb higher mark. That latest rise took him to a perch 25lb higher than when winning on his return to turf back in April and, despite now being an 8-y-o, this has to officially rate as a career-best success. He was well suited by the way the race developed and was going away at the finish, so ruling out further improvement while he remains in such form would be unwise. (op 13-2)
Red Cape(FR), back to winning ways at Doncaster ten days previously, was up 3lb and proved easy to back in this bid to improve on his second in the race last season. He was one of the four that forced the strong early pace, racing on the outside, and kept on bravely in the home straight. (tchd 13-2)
Gertmegalush(IRE) attracted support and ran a solid race taking on his elders for the first time. The recent change of scenery has clearly done him some good. (op 12-1)
Tangerine Trees was bidding to win his fourth race from five outings since resuming this year. Racing off a 4lb higher mark, he was unable to dictate as he prefers and could offer no more nearing the business end. (op 4-1)
Indian Skipper(IRE) got taken off his feet early on. The early pace helped his cause, but he was never a serious player. (op 8-1)
Doctor Parkes did far too much early on over a trip too stiff and probably needs dropping back to the minimum distance. (tchd 4-1 and 5-1)
Dickie Le Davoir was chasing a hat-trick in the race, but this ground was too quick for his needs. (op 10-1 tchd 8-1)
Green Manalishi never got involved on this drop in class. (op 9-1 tchd 6-1)

3754 BOOK ONLINE AT PONTEFRACT-RACES.CO.UK MAIDEN STKS 1m 4f 8y
5:00 (5:01) (Class 5) 3-Y-O+ **£2,914** (£867; £433; £216) **Stalls** Low

Form RPR
0- **1** **Lajidaal (USA)**[298] 5831 3-8-13 0 .... RichardHills 6 81
(M P Tregoning) *chsd ldrs: rdn along whn n.m.r and swtchd rt 2f out: hdwy over 1f out: drvn to chse ldr ins fnl f: led last 100yds and styd on strly* **7/2**[3]
42 **2** 2 3/4 **Fascination (IRE)**[19] 3116 3-8-8 0 .... JamieSpencer 8 71
(M L W Bell) *led: rdn clr 2f out: drvn over 1f out: hdd and no ex wl ins fnl f* **11/8**[1]
66 **3** 4 1/2 **Charming Man**[19] 3116 3-8-13 0 .... FrankieDettori 11 69
(Mahmood Al Zarooni) *chsd ldng pair: hdwy over 3f out: rdn along and edgd lft 2f out: drvn wl over 1f out and sn one pce* **5/2**[2]
05 **4** 1/2 **Stoical (IRE)**[12] 3355 3-8-13 0 .... LeeVickers 2 68
(W Jarvis) *dwlt: sn in tch: hdwy on inner to chse ldrs 4f out and sn rdn: drvn over 2f out: sn one pce* **50/1**
0-50 **5** 3 1/4 **Baibars (USA)**[23] 2994 3-8-13 75 .... (p) HayleyTurner 5 63
(G A Butler) *chsd ldr: rdn along 3f out: drvn wl over 1f out and grad wknd* **16/1**
00 **6** 2 **Finellas Fortune**[18] 3176 5-9-2 0 .... PatrickDonaghy(5) 12 55
(G M Moore) *dwlt and bhd: hdwy 4f out: rdn and kpt on fnl 2f: nvr nr ldrs* **80/1**
0044 **7** 10 **Tivers Song (USA)**[19] 3110 6-9-9 43 .... (b) BarryMcHugh(3) 3 44
(John A Harris) *midfield: rdn along over 4f out: nvr a factor* **40/1**

43 **8** *28* **Hidden**[66] 1705 4-9-12 0 ...... KierenFallon 1 —
(B J Meehan) *chsd ldrs: rdn along over 4f out: sn wknd and bhd: eased fnl 2f* **10/1**

00 **9** *2 3/4* **Benamy Boy**[23] 2994 4-9-12 0 ...... ChrisCatlin 9 —
(N Bycroft) *dwlt: a bhd: t.o fnl 3f* **100/1**

50 **10** *dist* **National Theatre (USA)**[106] 963 4-9-7 0 ......(p) KylieManser(5) 10 —
(Miss Olivia Maylam) *a bhd: t.o fnl 3f* **100/1**

2m 40.29s (-0.51) **Going Correction** 0.0s/f (Good) **10** Ran SP% **115.5**
WFA 3 from 4yo+ 13lb
Speed ratings (Par 103): **101,99,96,95,93 92,85,67,65,—**
Tote Swingers: 1&2 £2.60, 1&3 £3.00, 2&3 £1.70 CSF £8.58 TOTE £5.00: £1.90, £1.40, £1.40; EX 11.30.
Owner Hamdan Al Maktoum **Bred** Shadwell Farm LLC **Trained** Lambourn, Berks

FOCUS
There was no hanging about in this ordinary middle-distance maiden. The second and third are rated a few pounds off their recent Leicester form.

3755 RED SHIRT NIGHT ON FRIDAY 16TH JULY H'CAP 1m 4y
5:30 (5:30) (Class 5) (0-70,69) 3-Y-O **£2,914** (£867; £433; £216) **Stalls** Low

Form RPR

6522 **1** **Vito Volterra (IRE)**[10] 3451 3-9-1 **66** ...... MichaelStainton(3) 3 72
(Michael Smith) *set stdy pce: rdn and qcknd wl clr 2f out: eased towards fin* **3/1**[2]

0241 **2** *3 1/4* **Dutiful**[12] 3363 3-9-7 **69** ...... TedDurcan 6 67
(M R Channon) *hld up in tch: hdwy over 2f out: rdn wl over 1f out: sn drvn and kpt on same pce* **7/4**[1]

0033 **3** *hd* **Danceintothelight**[19] 3113 3-9-0 **62** ...... TomEaves 5 60
(Micky Hammond) *trckd ldng pair: rdn and hdwy to chse wnr 2f out: drvn wl over 1f out and kpt on same pce* **5/1**[3]

1550 **4** *28* **Sixties Rock**[32] 2700 3-8-6 **54** ...... ChrisCatlin 7 —
(J A Glover) *hld up in rr: effrt over 2f out: sn rdn and nvr a factor* **6/1**

043 **5** *1 1/4* **Director General (USA)**[28] 2837 3-9-0 **65** ...... BarryMcHugh(3) 8 —
(Julie Camacho) *trckd wnr: rdn along 3f out: drvn and wknd 2f out* **5/1**[3]

1m 45.6s (-0.30) **Going Correction** 0.0s/f (Good) **5** Ran SP% **109.0**
Speed ratings (Par 100): **101,97,97,69,68**
CSF £8.50 TOTE £3.90: £2.20, £1.10; EX 6.00 Place 6 £ 91.09, Place 5 £66.90..
Owner Ace Racing **Bred** O McElroy **Trained** Kirkheaton, Northumberland
■ Michael Smith's first Flat winner.

FOCUS
This was a moderate 3-y-o handicap. The winner had an easy lead and is rated back to his 2yo best.
T/Jkpt: £27,719.50 to a £1 stake. Pool:£58,562.52 - 1.50 winning tickets. T/Plt: £53.60 to a £1 stake. Pool:£76,114,.17 - 1,034.93 winning tickets. T/Qpdt: £28.30 to a £1 stake. Pool:£4,498.95 - 117.51 winning tickets. JR

2785 SOUTHWELL (L-H)
Tuesday, July 6

OFFICIAL GOING: Standard
Wind: Light, half-against. Weather: overcast and humid

3756 EUROPEAN BREEDERS' FUND MAIDEN STKS 5f (F)
6:40 (6:40) (Class 5) 2-Y-O **£3,480** (£1,027; £514) **Stalls** High

Form RPR

1 **Berberana (IRE)** 2-8-12 0 ...... DavidAllan 5 78+
(T D Easterby) *chsd ldr: rdn 2f out: r.o to ld jst ins fnl f: styd on strly* **7/2**[2]

2 *3 3/4* **Nine Before Ten (IRE)** 2-8-12 0 ...... SilvestreDeSousa 4 63+
(Mrs D J Sanderson) *chsd ldrs: swtchd rt jst ins fnl f: kpt on to take 2nd last 50yds* **8/1**

6 **3** *1 1/4* **Key Lago (IRE)**[40] 2448 2-9-3 0 ...... PhillipMakin 3 64
(M Dods) *led: hdd jst ins fnl f: wknd fnl 75yds* **5/2**[1]

32 **4** *1* **Loki's Revenge**[19] 3126 2-9-3 0 ...... MickyFenton 12 60
(W Jarvis) *dwlt: sn chsng ldrs: kpt on same pce appr fnl f* **4/1**[3]

6 **5** *2 1/4* **Imperial Look**[15] 3274 2-9-3 0 ...... AdrianNicholls 10 52
(E S McMahon) *sn drvn along: chsd ldrs: outpcd over 2f out: kpt on fnl f* **9/1**

64 **6** *nk* **Fast Shot**[46] 2292 2-9-3 0 ...... DuranFentiman 2 51
(T D Easterby) *dwlt: in midfield on wd outside: kpt on fnl 2f: nvr nr ldrs* **22/1**

7 *hd* **Winning Draw (IRE)** 2-8-12 0 ...... TonyCulhane 9 45+
(P T Midgley) *hmpd s: bhd tl styd on wl appr fnl f* **100/1**

8 *3 1/2* **Wandering Lad** 2-9-3 0 ...... DavidNolan 6 38
(D Carroll) *dwlt: sn drvn along and outpcd: nvr a factor* **40/1**

30 **9** *nse* **Shy Bird**[20] 3087 2-8-12 0 ...... PaulHanagan 13 32
(J A Glover) *mid-div: outpcd over 2f out* **16/1**

40 **10** *2 1/4* **Hernando Torres**[15] 3274 2-8-12 0 ...... JamesSullivan(5) 11 29
(M W Easterby) *sn wl outpcd and in rr* **25/1**

0 **11** *hd* **Carver County (IRE)**[15] 3274 2-9-3 0 ...... RichardMullen 7 29
(K A Ryan) *wnt rt s: sn wl outpcd and in rr* **20/1**

3 **12** *5* **My Love Fajer (IRE)**[10] 3439 2-9-3 0 ...... SaleemGolam 1 11
(G Prodromou) *prom: outpcd over 2f out: sn wknd* **40/1**

60.70 secs (1.00) **Going Correction** +0.15s/f (Slow) **12** Ran SP% **116.6**
Speed ratings (Par 94): **98,92,90,88,84 84,84,78,78,74 74,66**
Tote Swingers: 1&2 £6.70, 1&3 £2.90, 2&3 £7.00 CSF £28.28 TOTE £4.40: £1.60, £2.40, £1.10; EX 46.20.
Owner D A West **Bred** Patrick F Kelly And M J Foley **Trained** Great Habton, N Yorks

FOCUS
A fair maiden auction in which the action took place down the centre of the track. The pace was good and the field was soon strung out. The standard is set around the fifth and sixth.

NOTEBOOK
Berberana(IRE), an early foal out of a winning sprinter in Germany, was well backed to make a winning debut and ultimately did so quite readily, taking time to assert but never stronger than at the finish. She knew her job well but still seems sure to improve. (op 7-1)
Nine Before Ten(IRE), a Captain Rio half-sister to quite useful 6f/7f winner All The Nines (who was a winner on Fibresand), is bred to handle this surface and made a promising debut for her in-form yard, not looking unlucky for all she had to be switched around the fading third late on. She'll improve, and should be just as effective at 6f. (op 7-1 tchd 17-2)
Key Lago(IRE) had suffered from sore shins, according to his trainer, since his debut at Ayr when behind two subsequent winners. Well away, he showed good speed, travelling comfortably, until found out by lack of a recent outing at 5f. All speed, he will improve again and looks the sort who might do well in 5f nurseries. (op 11-4 tchd 9-4)
Loki's Revenge had looked only modest beforehand but might not have been at his best having his first run away from turf, seeming ill at ease off the bridle on the surface and not making any impression, albeit not hard-ridden either. He'll be better off in nurseries at 6f or more. (op 5-2)
Imperial Look shaped quite well considering he was back in trip on his Fibresand debut. He was staying on at the end and needs a return to further. (op 11-1)
Fast Shot had hinted at promise in turf maidens and did so again on his final run before nurseries. He'll do better at a modest level in that sphere, or perhaps dropped into a seller. (op 25-1)
Winning Draw(IRE) was soon on the back foot after a slow start and never got competitive, but was noted staying on well along the stands' rail. She's bred to need further and ought to improve.

3757 BET IN RUNNING - BETDAQ (S) STKS 5f (F)
7:10 (7:10) (Class 6) 2-Y-O **£1,774** (£523; £262) **Stalls** High

Form RPR

6 **1** **Hereselle (IRE)**[36] 2605 2-8-6 0 ...... GrahamGibbons 3 55
(T D Barron) *wnt rt s: w ldrs: led over 1f out: hld on towards fin* **3/1**[1]

054 **2** *1/2* **Liberty Ess (IRE)**[5] 3603 2-8-6 0 ......(p) PaulHanagan 8 53
(K A Ryan) *w ldrs: kpt on fnl f: no ex towards fin* **6/1**[3]

5300 **3** *1/2* **Look'N'Listen (IRE)**[18] 3175 2-8-6 0 ...... SilvestreDeSousa 9 51
(A D Brown) *led tl over 1f out: styd on same pce ins fnl f* **16/1**

5060 **4** *1 1/2* **Blind Stag (IRE)**[28] 2836 2-8-11 0 ...... TonyCulhane 4 51
(P T Midgley) *hmpd s: hld up in midfield stands' side: effrt over 1f out: sn rdn: kpt on: nt rch ldrs* **10/1**

50 **5** *hd* **Ridgeway Hawk**[15] 3274 2-8-13 0 ow2 ...... MickyFenton 1 52
(M D I Usher) *dwlt: outpcd in rr far side: hdwy 2f out: kpt on: nvr rchd ldrs* **5/1**[2]

6263 **6** *2* **Crazy In Love**[36] 2591 2-8-3 0 ......(b) JackDean(3) 7 38
(W G M Turner) *sn drvn along and outpcd stands' side: kpt on fnl f: nvr nr ldrs* **5/1**[2]

4200 **7** *4* **Box Of Frogs (IRE)**[18] 3175 2-8-1 0 ......(b[1]) DeclanCannon(5) 5 23
(A J McCabe) *bmpd s and s.i.s: sn drvn and outpcd: nvr on terms* **17/2**

05 **8** *5* **Tufty**[57] 1978 2-8-6 0 ...... JamesSullivan(5) 2 10
(M W Easterby) *chsd ldrs: lost pl over 2f out* **5/1**[2]

0 **9** *1/2* **Columba's Boy**[22] 3035 2-8-11 0 ...... EddieCreighton 6 8
(D K Ivory) *s.i.s: sn outpcd and bhd* **50/1**

61.94 secs (2.24) **Going Correction** +0.15s/f (Slow) **9** Ran SP% **116.7**
Speed ratings (Par 92): **88,87,86,84,83 80,74,66,65**
Tote Swingers: 1&2 £4.10, 1&3 £16.10, 2&3 £5.80 CSF £21.53 TOTE £6.90: £3.20, £4.70, £3.20; EX 36.60.There was no bid for the winner.
Owner D Pryde & J Cringan **Bred** E Byrne & C Roker **Trained** Maunby, N Yorks

FOCUS
A poor seller with several of the field already exposed at this level, and not form to be with at all. The action again unfolded down the centre of the track and the first three dominated from the off.

NOTEBOOK
Hereselle(IRE) was representing a yard with a good record in these races here and showed some of the dash that was presumably responsible for her starting favourite on her turf debut, gradually asserting and comfortably on top at the end. The slow surface probably suited her well looking at the way she moves, and whether she's got much of a future outside of sellers (there was no bid) remains to be seen. (op 7-2)
Liberty Ess(IRE) had had her limitations exposed in this grade last time but, back at 5f and on her Fibresand debut, gave her running, and was always thereabouts in the first-time cheekpieces. She's not any better than this. (op 7-2 tchd 13-2)
Look'N'Listen(IRE) is another who has already been beaten in sellers, but she took to the surface well at the first attempt and benefited from being allowed to stride on returned to 5f, posting an improved effort. (op 12-1)
Blind Stag(IRE) has become disappointing and again found less than looked likely having travelled well to halfway. This is his level nowadays. (op 12-1 tchd 14-1)
Ridgeway Hawk was well backed dropped in grade but lost his chance with a slow start. He made some late progress (without looking unlucky) and leaves the impression he has a bit more to give at this level. (op 12-1)
Crazy In Love sets the standard on form and might have been expected to have done better given her dam won on Fibresand, but she started slowly and was soon outpaced on the stands' rail. She's proving very inconsistent. (op 4-1 tchd 7-2)

3758 BETDAQ.CO.UK MAIDEN H'CAP 1m (F)
7:40 (7:42) (Class 6) (0-60,60) 3-Y-O+ **£2,320** (£685; £342) **Stalls** Low

Form RPR

2025 **1** **Tomintoul Star**[8] 3503 4-9-0 **54** ...... JamesSullivan(5) 13 64+
(Mrs R A Carr) *swtchd lft after s: hld up: hdwy over 2f out: chsd ldr 1f out: r.o to ld towards fin* **7/2**[1]

-005 **2** *1/2* **Green Community (USA)**[11] 3390 3-9-1 **59** ...... TomQueally 8 66
(E F Vaughan) *trckd ldrs: led over 1f out: edgd rt: hdd and no ex towards fin* **7/1**[3]

2-00 **3** *2* **Dandarrell**[43] 2380 3-8-10 **57** ...... BarryMcHugh(3) 6 59
(Julie Camacho) *chsd ldrs: led over 2f out: hdd over 1f out: kpt on same pce* **14/1**

3-56 **4** *10* **Whitby (IRE)**[8] 3515 3-8-11 **55** ......(t) PhillipMakin 14 34
(M W Easterby) *chsd ldrs on outside: wknd over 1f out* **9/1**

000 **5** *1/2* **Tinseltown**[23] 2995 4-9-3 **52** ...... MickyFenton 9 32
(B S Rothwell) *lost pl and swtchd outside after 1f: hdwy over 4f out: sn chsng ldrs: wknd over 1f out* **33/1**

0606 **6** *1* **Miereveld**[140] 570 3-8-10 **54** ...... StevieDonohoe 12 30
(Sir Mark Prescott) *chsd ldrs: outpcd over 2f out: wknd over 1f out* **14/1**

0-06 **7** *nk* **Forshour**[15] 3279 3-8-10 **54** ...... AdrianNicholls 11 29
(E S McMahon) *s.i.s: hdwy on outside to chse ldrs over 3f out: wknd over 2f out* **20/1**

0604 **8** *4 1/2* **Altimatum (USA)**[13] 3323 4-9-4 **53** ......(bt) PaulHanagan 3 20
(P F I Cole) *hld up in rr: effrt over 2f out: hmpd over 1f out: nvr a factor* **6/1**[2]

24-5 **9** *2 1/4* **Barbarian**[26] 291 4-9-11 **60** ...... GrahamGibbons 5 22
(A D Brown) *led 1f: sn drvn along: lost pl over 4f out* **22/1**

000 **10** *2 1/2* **Marteau**[20] 3091 3-8-9 **53** ......(p) JamieSpencer 7 —
(K A Ryan) *led after 1f: hdd over 2f out: wkng whn hung lft over 1f out: sn eased* **9/1**

4320 **11** *9* **Brave Decision**[11] 3413 3-8-8 **55** ...... WilliamCarson(3) 4 —
(R M H Cowell) *chsd ldrs on ins: sn drvn along: lost pl over 3f out* **8/1**

0602 **12** *1/2* **Catcher Of Dreams (IRE)**[18] 3147 4-9-1 **50** ......(t) LNewman 10 —
(A G Foster) *chsd ldrs: lost pl over 2f out* **16/1**

00 **13** *1* **Mackintosh (IRE)**[39] 2490 4-9-1 **50** ...... StephenCraine 2 —
(Patrick Morris) *s.i.s: mid-div: lost pl over 2f out* **20/1**

406 **14** *22* **Elle Est**[32] 2706 3-9-2 **60** ...... DavidAllan 1 —
(E J Alston) *s.i.s: sn drvn along: lost pl over 4f out: sn bhd: virtually p.u: t.o* **33/1**

1m 43.66s (-0.04) **Going Correction** +0.025s/f (Slow) **14** Ran SP% **119.1**
WFA 3 from 4yo 9lb
Speed ratings (Par 101): **101,100,98,88,88 87,86,82,79,77 68,67,66,44**
Tote Swingers: 1&2 £9.10, 1&3 £13.40, 2&3 £29.10 CSF £24.26 CT £313.48 TOTE £2.70: £1.20, £3.10, £4.40; EX 28.10.
Owner Michael Hill **Bred** Millsec Limited **Trained** Huby, N Yorks

FOCUS
Little convincing recent form on show in an uncompetitive heat. The pace was only fair early, with the leaders keen to avoid the rail until the home turn. The first three finished clear but this is not form to take too literally.

Marteau Official explanation: jockey said colt lost its action
Brave Decision Official explanation: jockey said gelding would not face the kick-back

3759 TRY BETDAQ FOR AN EXCHANGE CLAIMING STKS 1m (F)
8:10 (8:15) (Class 5) 3-Y-O £2,456 (£725; £362) Stalls Low

Form RPR
-04 1 **Zubova**[13] 3320 3-8-7 66 (t) WilliamCarson(3) 12 73
(Rae Guest) *chsd ldrs: wnt 2nd over 4f out: chal over 2f out: led over 1f out: styd on wl ins fnl f* **11/1**
5000 2 1 ½ **Takajan (IRE)**[26] 2892 3-8-4 67 Louis-PhilippeBeuzelin(3) 5 67
(S Kirk) *t.k.h: trckd ldrs: wnt 4th 2f out: kpt on fnl f to take 2nd nr fin* **12/1**
-203 3 ½ **Law Of Attraction (IRE)**[13] 3325 3-8-11 73 JamieSpencer 8 69
(J R Gask) *led: qcknd 3f out: edgd rt and hdd over 1f out: kpt on same pce* **11/4**[2]
1010 4 ½ **Buzz Bird**[16] 3238 3-9-0 67 GrahamGibbons 13 71
(T D Barron) *chsd ldrs on outside: drvn 4f out: wnt 3rd over 2f out: kpt on same pce fnl f* **9/4**[1]
10-0 5 14 **Chain Of Office**[11] 3413 3-9-0 72 LiamJones 9 39
(W J Haggas) *in rr: hdwy over 3f out: c wd and sn lost pl: no ch after* **11/1**
0000 6 4 ½ **Baileys Vision**[24] 2962 3-8-0 50 AndreaAtzeni 7 15
(C A Dwyer) *chsd ldrs: drvn 5f out: wknd over 2f out* **66/1**
1002 7 2 **Juicy Pear (IRE)**[35] 2617 3-8-10 73 (v) IanBurns(7) 10 27
(M L W Bell) *chsd ldrs: drvn over 3f out: wknd over 1f out* **5/1**[3]
0 8 1 **Gilderoy**[33] 2684 3-9-0 0 BillyCray(5) 14 27
(D J S Ffrench Davis) *in rr: hdwy over 3f out: wknd over 2f out* **100/1**
0000 9 4 **Scarboro Warning (IRE)**[16] 3243 3-9-4 60 JamesO'Reilly(5) 4 22
(J O'Reilly) *s.i.s: lost pl over 4f out: sn bhd* **50/1**
00 10 4 ½ **Labretella (IRE)**[35] 2633 3-8-4 48 (b[1]) SilvestreDeSousa 11 —
(S A Harris) *prom: drvn over 4f out: lost pl over 3f out* **33/1**
1565 11 10 **Tiger Hawk (USA)**[7] 1995 3-8-11 60 (b) StevieDonohoe 1 —
(P D Evans) *sn drvn along and bhd: t.o 3f out* **20/1**
0064 12 2 ¼ **Dispol Kabira**[3] 3668 3-8-2 49 PatrickMathers 6 —
(D W Thompson) *mid-div: drvn and lost pl over 4f out: t.o 2f out* **40/1**

1m 43.77s (0.07) **Going Correction** +0.025s/f (Slow) **12** Ran SP% **113.0**
Speed ratings (Par 100): **100,98,98,97,83 79,77,76,72,67 57,55**
Tote Swingers: 1&2 £7.80, 1&3 £3.80, 2&3 £7.40 CSF £120.22 TOTE £10.50: £3.30, £2.70, £1.10; EX 97.40.Takajan was claimed by Mark Brisbourne for £4,000.
Owner J M Duggan & T P Duggan **Bred** D A Yardy **Trained** Newmarket, Suffolk

FOCUS
An uncompetitive claimer with the majority of runners struggling for form. The pace was fair, with the principals again staying clear of the inside rail. The first four finished clear and the winner is rated back to her best.
Baileys Vision Official explanation: jockey said filly never travelled

3760 ALKANE ENERGY PLC H'CAP 1m 6f (F)
8:40 (8:43) (Class 6) (0-65,65) 4-Y-O+ £2,047 (£604; £302) Stalls Low

Form RPR
2516 1 **City Stable (IRE)**[13] 3324 5-9-7 65 PaulHanagan 12 77+
(M Wigham) *hld up in mid-div: smooth hdwy on outer over 5f out: shkn up to ld appr fnl f: rdn ins fnl f: hld on towards fin* **5/1**[1]
-140 2 ¾ **Three Boars**[26] 2907 8-8-13 57 (b) JamieSpencer 4 65
(S Gollings) *hld up in rr: hdwy on wd outside over 6f out: rdn over 2f out: styd on to take 2nd towards fin* **14/1**
0-35 3 ½ **Benozzo Gozzoli**[41] 2445 4-8-11 55 NickyMackay 10 62
(H Morrison) *led: hdd appr fnl f: styd on same pce ins fnl f* **13/2**[2]
20/5 4 hd **Mutadarrej (IRE)**[41] 2430 6-8-9 53 SaleemGolam 1 60
(Ian Williams) *w ldrs: chal 2f out: kpt on same pce appr fnl f* **9/1**
614/ 5 3 **Zed Candy (FR)**[563] 5559 7-8-3 52 JamesSullivan(5) 9 55
(R Ford) *t.k.h in midfield: hdwy to trck ldrs over 4f out: effrt over 2f out: hung lft and one pce* **20/1**
5312 6 shd **Silent Lucidity (IRE)**[23] 2995 6-8-10 54 (p) TonyHamilton 11 56
(P D Niven) *chsd ldrs: one pce appr fnl f* **5/1**[1]
0646 7 1 **Dulce Domum**[12] 3352 4-7-12 47 DeclanCannon(5) 6 48
(A B Haynes) *chsd ldrs: one pce fnl 2f* **14/1**
2400 8 21 **Merrion Tiger (IRE)**[8] 3496 5-8-13 57 LNewman 3 29
(A G Foster) *chsd ldrs: drvn 5f out: wknd over 2f out* **7/1**[3]
0120 9 10 **Red Wine**[23] 2995 11-8-5 52 KellyHarrison(3) 14 10
(J A Glover) *t.k.h in rr: hdwy on outer over 5f out: effrt and chsng ldrs 3f out: sn wknd* **18/1**
61/ 10 6 **Hareem (IRE)**[119] 5754 6-9-0 65 JamesRogers(7) 5 14
(W R Muir) *s.i.s: in rr: bhd and drvn 6f out: t.o over 3f out* **18/1**
-250 11 ¾ **Act Three**[32] 2691 6-8-8 52 (t[1]) FergusSweeney 13 —
(Mouse Hamilton-Fairley) *s.i.s: in rr: hdwy 7f out: lost pl over 4f out: t.o 3f out* **20/1**
05 12 7 **Dream Risk (FR)**[25] 2085 4-8-6 55 IanBrennan(5) 8 —
(Mrs K Walton) *chsd ldrs: drvn over 4f out: wknd 3f out* **20/1**
-010 13 47 **Tilapia (IRE)**[18] 3160 6-9-6 64 TomQueally 7 —
(Stef Higgins) *mid-div: drvn 7f out: lost pl over 4f out: sn bhd and eased: t.o: virtually p.u* **7/1**[3]

3m 11.88s (3.58) **Going Correction** +0.025s/f (Slow) **13** Ran SP% **119.8**
Speed ratings (Par 101): **90,89,89,89,87 87,86,74,69,65 65,61,34**
Tote Swingers: 1&2 £23.60, 1&3 £8.00, 2&3 £12.70 CSF £74.40 CT £454.08 TOTE £6.30: £2.40, £4.60, £2.40; EX 62.00.
Owner G Swan **Bred** Ballymacoll Stud Farm Ltd **Trained** Newmarket, Suffolk

FOCUS
A fair staying handicap, although the pace wasn't strong and that meant, unusually for a race of this type here, there were several still in with a chance at the distance. The form is rated around the third and the winner is value for a bit extra.
Tilapia(IRE) Official explanation: jockey said gelding failed to face the kick-back

3761 DAIRY WORLD LTD H'CAP 6f (F)
9:10 (9:13) (Class 5) (0-70,70) 3-Y-O+ £2,729 (£806; £403) Stalls Low

Form RPR
2620 1 **Westwood**[64] 1779 5-9-5 62 DaneO'Neill 7 77
(D Haydn Jones) *mde all: rdn clr over 1f out: eased towards fin* **9/1**
6243 2 7 **Bookiesindex Boy**[21] 3052 6-9-13 70 (b) JamieSpencer 9 63
(J R Jenkins) *chsd wnr thrght: hung lft and kpt on same pce fnl 2f* **9/1**
0550 3 ½ **Elusive Warrior (USA)**[67] 1653 7-9-4 68 (p) ConorQuish(7) 5 59
(A J McCabe) *chsd ldng pair: kpt on same pce fnl 2f* **25/1**
0-41 4 3 **Efisio Princess**[30] 2790 7-9-11 68 RichardThomas 10 49
(J E Long) *prom: effrt on outer over 2f out: one pce* **11/1**
1432 5 ½ **Super Yellow**[12] 3350 3-9-7 70 FergusSweeney 2 49
(J A Osborne) *prom: wknd over 1f out* **9/2**[1]
0010 6 1 **Figaro Flyer (IRE)**[34] 2639 7-9-7 64 J-PGuillambert 14 41+
(P Howling) *in rr: kpt on fnl 2f: nvr a factor* **22/1**
1265 7 nk **Charles Parnell (IRE)**[36] 2589 7-9-8 68 MichaelStainton(3) 6 44+
(S P Griffiths) *s.i.s: hdwy over 3f out: nvr nr ldrs* **8/1**
20-0 8 2 ¼ **This Ones For Eddy**[27] 2850 5-9-10 67 AndrewElliott 11 35+
(J Balding) *in rr: sme hdwy 2f out: nvr on terms* **16/1**
1330 9 3 ¾ **Fuzzy Cat**[26] 2896 4-8-12 60 DeanHeslop(5) 13 16
(T D Barron) *in rr: effrt on wd outside over 2f out: sn rdn and carried hd high: nvr a factor* **5/1**[2]
2-13 10 3 **Ambrogina**[166] 247 3-8-13 67 TobyAtkinson(5) 4 13
(M Botti) *s.i.s: nvr on terms* **11/1**
0-00 11 nk **Twisted**[11] 3409 4-9-5 67 JamesSullivan(5) 8 13
(M W Easterby) *s.i.s: a towards rr* **28/1**
5 12 2 **Schoolboy Champ**[20] 3088 3-9-5 68 StephenCraine 12 6
(Patrick Morris) *in rr and sn drvn along: nvr on terms* **16/1**
0-01 13 6 **Mayoman (IRE)**[59] 1929 5-9-6 63 (b) DavidNolan 3 —
(D Carroll) *stmbld s: chsd ldrs: lost pl 2f out* **6/1**[3]
60-0 14 4 **On The Bounty**[16] 3243 3-9-2 65 TonyCulhane 1 —
(P T Midgley) *t.k.h on ins: hmpd and lost pl after 1f* **66/1**

1m 15.88s (-0.62) **Going Correction** +0.025s/f (Slow)
WFA 3 from 4yo+ 6lb **14** Ran SP% **121.8**
Speed ratings (Par 103): **105,95,95,91,90 89,88,85,80,76 76,73,65,60**
Tote Swingers: 1&2 £50.60, 1&3 £49.90, 2&3 £75.80 CSF £85.47 CT £1975.41 TOTE £8.70: £2.40, £4.20, £13.90; EX 102.10 Place 6 £219.69, Place 5 £162.12..
Owner Merry Llewelyn And Runeckles **Bred** D Llewelyn & J Runeckles **Trained** Efail Isaf, Rhondda C Taff

FOCUS
A modest finale. The pace was good but nothing remotely threatened to get into the race from behind and the first three held the same positions throughout. The winner is rated back to his post-2yo best.
Fuzzy Cat Official explanation: jockey said gelding never travelled
Mayoman(IRE) Official explanation: jockey said gelding stumbled leaving stalls
T/Plt: £343.10 to a £1 stake. Pool:£65,249.76 - 138.80 winning tickets. T/Qpdt: £80.00 to a £1 stake. Pool:£5,913.97 - 54.70 winning tickets. WG

3515 WOLVERHAMPTON (A.W) (L-H)
Tuesday, July 6

OFFICIAL GOING: Standard
Wind: Fresh, behind. Weather: Overcast

3762 BET WORLD CUP FOOTBALL - BETDAQ H'CAP (DIV I) 5f 216y(P)
2:15 (2:19) (Class 6) (0-60,60) 3-Y-O+ £1,364 (£403; £201) Stalls Low

Form RPR
4305 1 **Athaakeel (IRE)**[42] 2409 4-9-8 60 LukeMorris 4 69
(R A Harris) *hld up: hdwy and nt clr run over 1f out: rdn to ld and edgd lft ins fnl f: r.o* **25/1**
023 2 2 ¾ **Towy Boy (IRE)**[15] 3280 5-8-13 51 (bt) CathyGannon 7 51
(I A Wood) *w ldr tl led 5f out: hdd over 3f out: rdn to ld over 1f out: hdd and unable qck ins fnl f* **13/2**[3]
4223 3 ½ **Divertimenti (IRE)**[24] 2957 6-8-12 53 (b) AshleyHamblett(3) 2 52
(S R Bowring) *w ldr tl led over 3f out: rdn and hdd over 1f out: styd on same pce ins fnl f* **5/1**[1]
0004 4 shd **Song Of Praise**[13] 3328 4-9-6 58 DaneO'Neill 12 56
(M Blanshard) *s.i.s: sn pushed along in rr: hdwy u.p over 1f out: r.o: nrst fin* **11/1**
550 5 1 **Lucas Pitt**[109] 936 3-9-0 58 PatCosgrave 6 52
(M J Scudamore) *prom: pushed along 1/2-way: rdn and swtchd rt over 1f out: styd on same pce ins fnl f* **9/1**
5640 6 nk **Equinity**[8] 3510 4-9-4 56 (t) FergusSweeney 1 50
(J Pearce) *hld up: hdwy u.p over 1f out: nvr trbld ldrs* **12/1**
3-00 7 nse **Mata Hari Blue**[59] 1929 4-9-5 57 JerryO'Dwyer 11 51
(J R Holt) *hld up: rdn over 2f out: r.o ins fnl f: nvr nrr* **25/1**
0632 8 1 ½ **Albero Di Giuda (IRE)**[30] 2791 5-9-1 58 (bt) BillyCray(5) 3 47
(F Sheridan) *dwlt: sn pushed along in rr: rdn over 1f out: n.d* **11/2**[2]
0530 9 1 ½ **Crystallize**[15] 3280 4-9-5 57 TomQueally 13 41
(A B Haynes) *mid-div: hdwy u.p over 2f out: wknd over 1f out* **11/1**
-006 10 ½ **Queen Of Thebes (IRE)**[7] 3526 4-9-3 55 (t) StephenCraine 9 38
(S Kirk) *prom: rdn over 2f out: wknd over 1f out* **33/1**
-503 11 ½ **Mr Skipiton (IRE)**[32] 2726 5-9-7 59 JackMitchell 5 40
(B J McMath) *sn pushed along in rr: swtchd rt wl over 1f out: n.d* **5/1**[1]
4066 12 ½ **Socceroo**[21] 3064 5-9-1 53 MartinDwyer 8 33
(D C Griffiths) *led 1f: chsd ldrs: rdn over 2f out: wknd over 1f out* **33/1**
40-0 13 2 ¾ **Oriental Rose**[13] 3328 4-9-5 57 JimmyQuinn 10 28
(D Shaw) *hld up: a in rr: rdn 1/2-way: wknd over 2f out* **25/1**

1m 14.5s (-0.50) **Going Correction** 0.0s/f (Stan)
WFA 3 from 4yo+ 6lb **13** Ran SP% **113.8**
Speed ratings (Par 101): **103,99,98,98,97 96,96,94,92,92 91,90,87**
Tote Swingers: 1&2 £5.40, 1&3 £29.60, 2&3 £24.40 CSF £164.38 CT £952.96 TOTE £37.40: £9.60, £2.60, £2.10; EX 166.70 Trifecta £314.90 Part won. Pool £425.66 - 0.41 winning units..
Owner Ridge House Stables Ltd **Bred** Shadwell Estate Company Limited **Trained** Earlswood, Monmouths

FOCUS
A moderate sprint handicap, but run at a fast pace with Towy Boy and Divertimenti going at it hammer and tongs. Fairly sound form.
Mr Skipiton(IRE) Official explanation: trainer said gelding ran flat

3763 BET WORLD CUP FOOTBALL - BETDAQ H'CAP (DIV II) 5f 216y(P)
2:45 (2:47) (Class 6) (0-60,60) 3-Y-O+ £1,364 (£403; £201) Stalls Low

Form RPR
0302 1 **Romantic Queen**[8] 3516 4-9-3 60 (t) MatthewDavies(5) 12 70
(George Baker) *s.i.s: hld up: nt clr run wl over 1f out: hdwy sn after: shkn up to ld and hung lft wl ins fnl f: sn clr* **12/1**
4122 2 2 ½ **Cavitie**[50] 2186 4-9-1 56 RussKennemore(3) 11 58
(Andrew Reid) *chsd ldrs: rdn over 1f out: unable qck wl ins fnl f* **4/1**[1]
3100 3 shd **The History Man (IRE)**[21] 3062 7-9-6 58 (p) KirstyMilczarek 9 60
(B D Leavy) *led: rdn over 1f out: hdd and unable qck wl ins fnl f* **14/1**
000 4 nse **Ever Cheerful**[118] 845 9-9-3 55 (p) AndreaAtzeni 4 57
(A B Haynes) *mid-div: rdn over 2f out: hdwy u.p over 1f out: edgd lft and r.o ins fnl f* **20/1**
0013 5 2 **Exceedingly Good (IRE)**[14] 3287 4-8-12 53 AshleyHamblett(3) 13 48
(S R Bowring) *chsd ldrs: rdn over 1f out: no ex ins fnl f* **11/2**[2]
2655 6 ½ **Desert Strike**[13] 3308 4-8-12 57 DuilioDaSilva(7) 3 51
(P F I Cole) *prom: rdn over 1f out: no ex fnl f* **12/1**
45-0 7 1 **Downhill Skier (IRE)**[15] 3280 6-9-1 58 KierenFox(5) 7 48
(W M Brisbourne) *hld up: rdn over 2f out: r.o ins fnl f: nvr nrr* **12/1**

0550 **8** *nk* **Cookie Galore**[24] 2962 3-8-13 57 .... RoystonFfrench 2 45
(J A Glover) *hld up: rdn 1/2-way: hdwy over 1f out: wknd ins fnl f* **14/1**

0654 **9** *nse* **Kinigi (IRE)**[8] 3518 4-8-9 52 .... JohnFahy(5) 10 41
(R A Harris) *mid-div: rdn over 2f out: nt clr run wl over 1f out: n.d* **13/2**[3]

0006 **10** *2 ¾* **Silver Hotspur**[22] 3024 6-9-5 57 .... DaneO'Neill 6 37
(D Shaw) *s.s: a in rr* **33/1**

0-02 **11** *1 ¼* **Double Carpet (IRE)**[32] 2721 7-9-0 57 .... RossAtkinson(5) 5 33
(G Woodward) *chsd ldr: rdn and ev ch over 1f out: wknd ins fnl f* **8/1**

2545 **12** *2* **Calmdownmate (IRE)**[30] 2791 5-9-1 58 .... JamesSullivan(5) 8 28
(Mrs R A Carr) *plld hrd and prom: rdn 1/2-way: wknd wl over 1f out* **12/1**

1005 **13** *hd* **Head To Head (IRE)**[14] 3286 6-8-13 51 ....(bt) JimmyQuinn 1 28
(A D Brown) *hld up: a in rr: rdn over 2f out: swtchd lft over 1f out: eased whn btn ins fnl f* **16/1**

1m 14.53s (-0.47) **Going Correction** 0.0s/f (Stan)
WFA 3 from 4yo+ 6lb **13 Ran SP% 117.5**
Speed ratings (Par 101): **103,99,99,99,96 96,94,94,94,90 89,86,86**
Tote Swingers: 1&2 £6.90, 1&3 £33.00, 2&3 £13.20 CSF £58.41 CT £523.51 TOTE £17.70: £4.00, £1.20, £5.40; EX 39.50 Trifecta £145.80 Part won. Pool £197.10 - 0.10 winning units..
Owner The Betfair Radioheads **Bred** G B Turnbull Ltd **Trained** Moreton Morrell, Warwicks

FOCUS
They didn't seem to go as quickly early on in this division, but the winning time was only 3/100ths of a second slower. Ordinary form.
Downhill Skier(IRE) Official explanation: jockey said gelding was slowly away
Silver Hotspur Official explanation: jockey said gelding missed the break
Calmdownmate(IRE) Official explanation: jockey said gelding hung badly right

3764 NEAL WOOD FIRST ANNIVERSARY MEMORIAL H'CAP 1m 4f 50y(P)
3:15 (3:16) (Class 5) (0-75,75) 3-Y-O+ £2,388 (£705; £352) Stalls Low

Form RPR

524 **1** **Reality Show (IRE)**[23] 2994 3-9-1 75 .... AhmedAjtebi 7 84
(Mahmood Al Zarooni) *trckd ldrs: swtchd lft wl over 3f out: rdn and hung lft over 1f out: r.o to ld post* **5/1**[2]

4-26 **2** *hd* **Wulfrida (IRE)**[49] 2219 3-9-1 75 ....[1] PatCosgrave 2 83
(J R Fanshawe) *hld up: hdwy 2f out: rdn to ld wl ins fnl f: hdd post* **8/1**

-035 **3** *1 ¾* **Bavarian Nordic (USA)**[5] 3588 5-9-9 75 ....(p) RosieJessop(5) 12 80
(Mrs A Duffield) *hld up: hdwy over 5f out: led over 1f out: rdn and hdd wl ins fnl f* **14/1**

13 **4** *nk* **Quarante Deux (USA)**[20] 3079 4-10-0 75 .... TomQueally 6 80+
(G A Butler) *hld up: pushed along 3f out: hdwy wl over 1f out: nt clr run 1f out: r.o: nt rch ldrs* **6/1**

30-0 **5** *½* **Kansai Spirit (IRE)**[27] 2860 4-10-0 75 .... NickyMackay 4 79+
(J H M Gosden) *hld up: hdwy and hung lft over 1f out: r.o: nt rch ldrs* **11/1**

3324 **6** *4 ½* **My Mate Mal**[17] 3221 6-9-4 70 .... JohnFahy(5) 8 67
(W B Stone) *led: rdn and hdd over 1f out: wknd ins fnl f* **14/1**

4-4 **7** *2 ¼* **Starkat**[32] 2723 4-9-11 72 .... IvaMilickova 1 65
(Jane Chapple-Hyam) *chsd ldrs: hmpd and lost pl wl over 3f out: n.d after* **11/2**[3]

1115 **8** *1 ¾* **Bivouac (UAE)**[56] 1996 6-10-0 75 .... AndrewElliott 10 66
(G A Swinbank) *hld up in tch: tk clsr order over 5f out: rdn and ev ch over 2f out: wknd over 1f out* **12/1**

1266 **9** *3* **Leyte Gulf (USA)**[39] 2495 7-9-5 66 .... DaneO'Neill 11 52
(C C Bealby) *s.i.s: hdwy 4f out: wknd 2f out* **20/1**

1-40 **10** *1 ¾* **Shifting Gold (IRE)**[25] 2941 4-9-1 67 ....(b) AmyRyan(5) 5 50
(K A Ryan) *s.i.s: hld up: rdn over 3f out: a in rr* **33/1**

-023 **11** *17* **Red Kestrel (USA)**[45] 2349 5-9-13 74 .... JimmyFortune 3 30
(K A Ryan) *chsd ldr over 7f: wknd wl over 2f out* **4/1**[1]

2m 40.7s (-0.40) **Going Correction** 0.0s/f (Stan)
WFA 3 from 4yo+ 13lb **11 Ran SP% 114.5**
Speed ratings (Par 103): **101,100,99,99,99 96,94,93,91,90 79**
Tote Swingers: 1&2 £9.60, 1&3 £11.20, 2&3 £24.70 CSF £43.51 CT £523.12 TOTE £5.60: £1.70, £3.40, £3.60; EX 37.90 TRIFECTA Not won..
Owner Godolphin **Bred** Highfort Stud **Trained** Newmarket, Suffolk

FOCUS
A fair handicap run at an ordinary pace, but a graveyard for in-running players with four different leaders in the final 2f and the runner-up was matched at 1.01 to decent money a few yards from the line. It was a fair race for the grade and the form should work out.
Quarante Deux(USA) ◆ Official explanation: jockey said gelding was unsuited by the slow pace
Red Kestrel(USA) Official explanation: jockey said gelding moved poorly

3765 STAY AT THE WOLVERHAMPTON HOLIDAY INN (S) STKS 1m 141y(P)
3:45 (3:46) (Class 6) 3-Y-O+ £1,706 (£503; £252) Stalls Low

Form RPR

3025 **1** **One Scoop Or Two**[7] 3538 4-9-5 51 .... RussKennemore(3) 13 69
(R Hollinshead) *mde virtually all: rdn over 1f out: styd on wl* **12/1**

00-6 **2** *1* **Flying Valentino**[19] 3117 6-9-3 70 .... StevieDonohoe 3 62
(Ian Williams) *a.p: chsd wnr over 2f out: rdn and ev ch over 1f out: hung lft: styd on same pce ins fnl f* **11/4**[1]

2260 **3** *½* **Full Victory (IRE)**[26] 2885 8-9-8 65 .... LiamKeniry 9 66
(R A Farrant) *a.p: rdn to go 3rd over 1f out: styd on* **4/1**[2]

0300 **4** *5* **Fol Liam**[8] 3518 4-9-9 70 ....(p) DeclanCannon(5) 7 60
(A J McCabe) *hld up: racd keenly: hdwy over 2f out: rdn over 1f out: wknd ins fnl f* **8/1**

-260 **5** *1* **Man In The Mirror (IRE)**[26] 2909 3-8-9 52 ....(p) AshleyHamblett(3) 12 51
(P L Gilligan) *prom: rdn over 2f out: wknd over 1f out* **16/1**

0003 **6** *½* **Bookiebasher Babe (IRE)**[15] 3263 5-9-3 52 .... PatCosgrave 6 46
(M Quinn) *mid-div: nt clr run and lost pl over 3f out: r.o ins fnl f: nvr trbld ldrs* **16/1**

6340 **7** *1 ¼* **Trade Centre**[18] 3160 5-9-8 65 ....(p) LukeMorris 8 48
(R A Harris) *chsd wnr tl rdn over 2f out: wknd over 1f out* **9/2**[3]

1450 **8** *2 ½* **Flores Sea (USA)**[8] 3518 6-9-9 72 ....(b) JamesSullivan(5) 10 48
(Mrs R A Carr) *s.i.s: hdwy over 3f out: rdn over 2f out: sn wknd* **12/1**

-500 **9** *1* **Angelena Ballerina (IRE)**[72] 1542 3-8-7 57 ....(p) JamieMackay 11 34
(Karen George) *hld up: rdn over 2f out: a in rr* **25/1**

4/0 **10** *1 ½* **Broughtons Dream**[33] 2678 4-9-3 0 .... FergusSweeney 2 31
(W J Musson) *hld up: a in rr* **25/1**

00 **11** *20* **Avaricious**[46] 2297 3-8-7 0 .... JackMitchell 5 —
(C F Wall) *prom: drvn along 1/2-way: wknd over 3f out: eased fr over 1f out: t.o* **8/1**

12 *½* **Pushy Princess** 5-9-3 0 .... FrankieMcDonald 1 —
(C N Kellett) *sn outpcd: t.o* **100/1**

1m 49.88s (-0.62) **Going Correction** 0.0s/f (Stan)
WFA 3 from 4yo+ 10lb **12 Ran SP% 122.9**
Speed ratings (Par 101): **102,101,100,96,95 94,93,91,90,89 71,71**
Tote Swingers:1&2:£10.10, 2&3:£5.30, 1&3:£8.30 CSF £46.10 TOTE £12.20: £1.90, £2.70, £1.60; EX 62.90 TRIFECTA Not won..There was no bid for the winner.
Owner Showtime Ice Cream Concessionaire **Bred** S And R Ewart **Trained** Upper Longdon, Staffs

FOCUS
A moderate seller and not a race to dwell on. Few ever got into it and this was another reminder that official ratings mean less at this lowly level. The front three pulled well clear and the winner rates a personal best.

3766 ENJOY THE PARTY PACK GROUP OFFER MEDIAN AUCTION MAIDEN STKS 1m 141y(P)
4:15 (4:18) (Class 6) 3-4-Y-O £1,706 (£503; £252) Stalls Low

Form RPR

44-4 **1** **Miss Antonia (IRE)**[49] 2220 3-8-12 70 .... TomQueally 13 79
(H R A Cecil) *hld up: hdwy 1/2-way: edgd rt over 1f out: rdn to ld wl ins fnl f* **8/1**[3]

02- **2** *1* **Fourth Generation (IRE)**[263] 6821 3-9-3 0 .... AndrewElliott 1 82
(G A Swinbank) *chsd ldrs: rdn to ld ins fnl f: sn hdd and unable qck* **12/1**

4020 **3** *1 ¼* **White Devil**[19] 3103 3-9-3 81 .... JimmyFortune 3 79
(A M Balding) *chsd ldr: rdn and ev ch fr over 1f out tl no ex wl ins fnl f* **4/6**[1]

0 **4** *3 ½* **Aldo**[31] 2755 3-9-3 0 .... MartinDwyer 7 71
(A J Lidderdale) *hld up: hdwy over 1f out: nvr nr to chal* **66/1**

5- **5** *¾* **Mr Money Maker**[260] 6903 3-9-3 0 .... DavidProbert 10 69
(B Palling) *led: rdn over 1f out: hdd & wknd ins fnl f* **14/1**

0-2 **6** *2* **Battle Honour**[52] 2128 3-9-3 0 .... DaneO'Neill 6 64
(H Candy) *s.i.s: hdwy over 7f out: rdn over 2f out: wknd over 1f out* **5/2**[2]

00 **7** *14* **Converre**[15] 3275 3-8-12 0 .... JackMitchell 8 27
(G A Butler) *s.i.s: a in rr* **66/1**

0/ **8** *5* **Amba**[682] 5256 4-9-8 0 .... JimmyQuinn 12 17
(D Shaw) *sn outpcd* **100/1**

00-0 **9** *1 ¾* **The Midshipmaid**[14] 3284 3-8-9 50 ....(p) RussKennemore(3) 4 12
(Lucinda Featherstone) *mid-div: rdn over 5f out: wknd over 3f out* **100/1**

03 **10** *1* **Miss Flash Dancer**[9] 3484 4-9-8 0 .... FergusSweeney 11 10
(C C Bealby) *prom: rdn over 3f out: wknd over 2f out* **50/1**

11 *2 ¾* **Bedouin Princess (IRE)** 3-8-9 0 .... AshleyHamblett(3) 5 —
(Lucinda Featherstone) *s.i.s: a in rr* **100/1**

00 **12** *4 ½* **Monte Mayor Two (IRE)**[15] 3275 3-9-3 0 .... FrankieMcDonald 2 —
(D Haydn Jones) *mid-div: pushed along 5f out: wknd 3f out* **100/1**

1m 49.18s (-1.32) **Going Correction** 0.0s/f (Stan)
WFA 3 from 4yo 10lb **12 Ran SP% 122.9**
Speed ratings (Par 101): **105,104,103,99,99 97,85,80,79,78 75,71**
Tote Swingers: 1&2 £6.00, 1&3 £2.70, 2&3 £3.80 CSF £100.46 TOTE £5.70: £1.70, £2.60, £1.10; EX 69.90 Trifecta £568.00 Pool £959.58 - 1.25 winning units..
Owner Gestut Ammerland **Bred** Ammerland Verwaltung Gmbh **Trained** Newmarket, Suffolk

FOCUS
This was a fairly uncompetitive maiden, but it did feature a couple of interesting sorts. The market suggested it was a straight match between the pair, but it didn't turn out that way. They went a good pace and the winning time was 0.7 seconds faster than the seller. The form is best judged around the front pair.
Miss Flash Dancer Official explanation: jockey said filly had no more to give

3767 BET MULTIPLES - BETDAQ MAIDEN AUCTION STKS (DIV I) 7f 32y(P)
4:45 (4:46) (Class 6) 2-Y-O £2,047 (£604; £302) Stalls High

Form RPR

1 **Fifth Dimension (IRE)** 2-8-13 0 .... FergusSweeney 7 71+
(J A Osborne) *hld up: nt clr run wl over 1f out: hdwy sn after: edgd lft and r.o to ld wl ins fnl f* **10/1**

0 **2** *¾* **Fabiello**[15] 3274 2-8-10 0 .... RichardKingscote 6 66
(Tom Dascombe) *hld up: hdwy to ld over 1f out: sn rdn: hdd wl ins fnl f* **14/1**

004 **3** *½* **Stacey**[17] 3209 2-8-4 0 .... NeilChalmers 3 59
(M Blanshard) *pushed along in rr early: hdwy over 2f out: rdn over 1f out: r.o* **9/1**

0 **4** *2* **Ya Hafed**[13] 3326 2-8-9 0 .... PatCosgrave 10 59
(E A L Dunlop) *chsd ldrs: rdn over 2f out: hung lft fr over 1f out: no ex wl ins fnl f* **7/2**[2]

0 **5** *4 ½* **Amore Et Labore**[61] 1845 2-8-13 0 .... LiamKeniry 2 52
(S Kirk) *chsd ldrs: rdn over 1f out: wknd ins fnl f* **25/1**

6 *1 ¾* **Miss Toldyaso (IRE)** 2-8-3 0 ow1 .... WilliamCarson(3) 1 41
(M G Quinlan) *s.i.s: sn rcvrd to ld: rdn over 2f out: edgd rt and hdd over 1f out: wknd ins fnl f* **18/1**

0 **7** *¾* **Indian Shuffle (IRE)**[15] 3269 2-8-12 0 .... JimmyFortune 4 45
(J G Portman) *chsd ldr: rdn and edgd rt over 2f out: nt clr run and wknd over 1f out* **18/1**

00 **8** *½* **Louis Vee (IRE)**[13] 3315 2-8-10 0 .... TomQueally 5 42
(J G Given) *chsd ldrs: n.m.r 6f out: rdn 1/2-way: wknd wl over 1f out* **25/1**

002 **9** *½* **Gower Rules (IRE)**[17] 3209 2-8-10 0 .... JackMitchell 9 40
(M D I Usher) *mid-div: pushed along 1/2-way: wkng whn nt clr run wl over 1f out* **13/2**[3]

05 **10** *1 ¼* **Guinea Seeker**[7] 3536 2-8-4 0 .... LanceBetts(5) 11 36
(T D Easterby) *prom: rdn over 2f out: wknd over 1f out* **20/1**

11 *1 ¾* **Inca Chief** 2-8-12 0 .... RoystonFfrench 8 35
(Mrs A Duffield) *hld up: a in rr: rdn over 1f out: wkng whn hung lft fnl f* **2/1**[1]

1m 31.74s (2.14) **Going Correction** 0.0s/f (Stan) **11 Ran SP% 117.6**
Speed ratings (Par 92): **87,86,85,83,78 76,75,74,74,72 70**
Tote Swingers: 1&2 £27.10, 1&3 £10.60, 2&3 £21.50 CSF £136.86 TOTE £15.80: £3.60, £4.60, £2.20; EX 174.60 TRIFECTA Not won..
Owner Hearn, Durkan & Pennick **Bred** Rathbarry Stud **Trained** Upper Lambourn, Berks

FOCUS
A modest maiden auction event in which the pace was decent thanks to Indian Shuffle and Miss Toldyaso disputing the early advantage, but they probably did too much and set it up for the closers. Limited form.

NOTEBOOK
Fifth Dimension(IRE), a 15,000gns half-brother to a winner at up to 1m1f, was held up well off the pace early but, with the leaders falling in a heap in the home straight, he put in a power-packed finish down the centre of the track to prevail. The form may not be totally reliable, but he should continue to progress. (tchd 9-1)
Fabiello, a well-beaten tenth of 12 in a 6f maiden here last month after missing the break, was being ridden along in last place turning in but he enjoyed a clear run up the inside rail and finished well. He is another that may have been helped by the leaders going off too quick, but this was still a big improvement. (op 20-1)
Stacey, about a length behind Gower Rules at Lingfield last time when not as favourably drawn, was better berthed than her rival this time and she was another to do her best work late. She has had more chances than most and may be worth a try in a nursery. (op 8-1)
Ya Hafed, a never-nearer ninth of 13 in a Kempton maiden last month, did best of those that raced up with the pace from the off so he deserves some credit for that alone. (tchd 4-1)
Amore Et Labore, a well-beaten last of 11 on his Goodwood debut, raced handily throughout and, though well beaten at the line, this was still a small step forward. (op 28-1 tchd 20-1)

Gower Rules(IRE), who left his previous form behind when runner-up in a 7f turf maiden at Lingfield last time, ran no sort of race here and added credence to the belief that his improved Lingfield effort was down to a track bias. (op 4-1)
Inca Chief, a 15,000gns 2-y-o and half-brother to the Polytrack winner Havanavich, was all the rage in the market but he barely went a yard. He must have been showing something at home.
Official explanation: trainer said colt was found to be lame (op 3-1)

3768 BETDAQ ON 0870 178 1221 H'CAP — 7f 32y(P)
5:15 (5:16) (Class 6) (0-65,65) 3-Y-O+ — £1,706 (£503; £252) Stalls High

Form				RPR
435	1		**Crocodile Bay (IRE)**[3] 3690 7-9-5 **56** ... PaulEddery 8 (R C Guest) *sn chsng ldr: rdn to ld over 1f out: r.o* 13/2[2]	65
5064	2	2 3/4	**Guildenstern (IRE)**[32] 2726 8-9-4 **55** ... JimmyQuinn 3 (P Howling) *hld up: hdwy over 2f out: rdn to chse wnr ins fnl f: r.o* 8/1	57
6020	3	1 3/4	**Shannon Golden**[14] 3284 4-8-13 **53** ... AshleyHamblett(3) 1 (S R Bowring) *a.p: rdn over 1f out: sn edgd rt: styd on: hung lft towards fin* 12/1	50
0-30	4	nse	**Decree Absolute (USA)**[26] 2888 3-9-4 **63** ...(b[1]) PaulFitzsimons 5 (Miss J R Tooth) *s.i.s: hld up: hdwy u.p over 1f out: r.o* 20/1	57
6030	5	1/2	**Via Mia**[35] 2625 4-9-3 **54** ...(b[1]) StevieDonohoe 6 (John A Harris) *led: rdn and hdd over 1f out: no ex ins fnl f* 14/1	50
5601	6	1	**Bold Diva**[15] 3280 5-9-3 **59** ...(v) BillyCray(5) 11 (A W Carroll) *hld up: hdwy 2f out: sn rdn: r.o: nt trble ldrs* 7/1[3]	52
0622	7	1 1/4	**El Libertador (USA)**[15] 3280 4-9-7 **63** ... KierenFox(5) 7 (E A Wheeler) *prom: rdn over 2f out: edgd lft and no ex fr over 1f out* 3/1[1]	52
	8	1 1/4	**Home Sweet Home (GER)**[72] 3-9-6 **65** ... AhmedAjtebi 12 (E A L Dunlop) *s.i.s: hld up: rdn over 1f out: nvr on terms* 11/1	48
0000	9	3 1/2	**Sapphire Prince (USA)**[27] 2866 4-9-8 **59** ...(bt) LukeMorris 9 (J R Best) *hld up: rdn 1/2-way: a in rr* 25/1	36
3002	10	4	**By Command**[8] 3518 5-9-9 **65** ...(bt) AmyRyan(5) 4 (K A Ryan) *hdwy over 5f out: rdn over 2f out: sn wknd* 7/1[3]	31
260-	11	12	**Anagram**[236] 7353 4-10-0 **65** ... MartinDwyer 10 (J G Given) *hld up: rdn and wknd over 2f out* 16/1	—
210-	12	2 1/4	**Sands Of Dee (USA)**[291] 6071 3-9-5 **64** ... JimmyFortune 2 (J A Glover) *prom: lost pl over 5f out: wknd 1/2-way* 16/1	—

1m 29.1s (-0.50) **Going Correction** 0.0s/f (Stan)
WFA 3 from 4yo+ 8lb — **12** Ran SP% **117.5**
Speed ratings (Par 101): **102,98,96,96,96 95,93,92,88,83 69,67**
Tote Swingers: 1&2 £8.30, 1&3 £24.40, 2&3 £22.10 CSF £57.23 CT £624.01 TOTE £9.90: £3.50, £1.40, £5.40; EX 53.30 TRIFECTA Not won..
Owner Stan Wright **Bred** James And Joe Brannigan **Trained** Stainforth, S Yorks

FOCUS
A modest handicap, but they went a strong pace and the runners were soon well spread out. The form has not been rated too positively.
Anagram Official explanation: jockey said filly moved poorly; vet said filly was lame

3769 BET MULTIPLES - BETDAQ MAIDEN AUCTION STKS (DIV II) — 7f 32y(P)
5:45 (5:48) (Class 6) 2-Y-O — £2,047 (£604; £302) Stalls High

Form				RPR
6	1		**Handsome Jack (IRE)**[13] 3326 2-8-12 0 ... RichardKingscote 5 (R A Mills) *a.p: rdn over 1f out: qcknd to ld wl ins fnl f* 5/4[1]	71+
6244	2	1 1/4	**Lady Morganna (IRE)**[12] 3362 2-8-0 0 ... KierenFox(5) 2 (Miss Gay Kelleway) *chsd ldr tl led over 1f out: rdn and hdd wl ins fnl f* 8/1[3]	59
4	3	4	**Not So Bright (USA)**[27] 2855 2-8-12 0 ... PatCosgrave 1 (J G Given) *led: rdn and hdd over 1f out: no ex ins fnl f* 10/1	56
0	4	3 1/4	**Eduardo**[43] 2384 2-8-10 0 ... JackMitchell 4 (Jedd O'Keeffe) *hld up: r.o ins fnl f: nrst fin* 100/1	46
	5	hd	**Echos Of Motivator** 2-8-12 0 ... LukeMorris 6 (R A Harris) *s.s: hld up: hdwy over 1f out: nvr nrr* 33/1	48
000	6	1 1/2	**Ad Vitam (IRE)**[4] 3624 2-8-9 0 ...(t) LiamKeniry 7 (S Kirk) *chsd ldr tl rdn over 2f out: wknd over 1f out* 40/1	41
5	7	shd	**Bonniebridge**[17] 3209 2-8-4 0 ... JimmyQuinn 3 (Miss J Feilden) *s.i.s: hld up: hdwy over 2f out: rdn and wknd over 1f out* 20/1	36
5	8	1/2	**Quite A Catch (IRE)**[12] 3349 2-8-13 0 ... JimmyFortune 9 (J G Portman) *prom: rdn over 2f out: wknd over 1f out* 3/1[2]	44
0	9	2 1/4	**Lucky Tricks**[71] 1577 2-8-4 0 ... RichardSmith 8 (S Kirk) *hld up: a in rr* 66/1	29
	10	nk	**Run Daisy Run** 2-8-6 0 ... MartinDwyer 11 (B J Meehan) *s.s: a in rr* 12/1	30
34	11	2 1/2	**Mollyow (IRE)**[56] 1999 2-8-6 0 ... DavidProbert 10 (B Palling) *hld up in tch: rdn 1/2-way: sn wknd* 12/1	24

1m 31.66s (2.06) **Going Correction** 0.0s/f (Stan) — **11** Ran SP% **117.7**
Speed ratings (Par 92): **88,86,82,78,78 76,76,75,73,72 69**
Tote Swingers: 1&2 £4.20, 1&3 £5.40, 2&3 £7.80 CSF £11.72 TOTE £3.30: £1.50, £1.20, £3.10; EX 10.10 Trifecta £69.50 Pool £384.57 - 4.09 winning units. Place 6 £307.60, Place 5 £114.68..
Owner Exors Of The Late T G Mills **Bred** Louis A Walshe **Trained** Headley, Surrey

FOCUS
They finished well spread out in this and the winning time was 8/100ths of a second faster than the first division. The runner-up and sixth set the very modest level.

NOTEBOOK
Handsome Jack(IRE), who finished an eyecatching sixth of 13 on his Kempton debut last month, came off the bridle just after halfway but that may still have been due to greenness as the further they went, the better he was going. After having hit the front well inside the last furlong, he eventually won this with some authority and, as he seems to be held in some regard, he should go on from here. (op 11-10 tchd Evens and 11-8)
Lady Morganna(IRE), whose best previous effort came on Polytrack, was by far the most experienced in the field and seemed to have timed it just right when hitting the front over a furlong out, but the winner's turn of foot proved too much. She is starting to look a bit exposed, so may need a switch to nurseries in order to avoid less-exposed types. (op 11-1)
Not So Bright(USA), a well-beaten last of four over shorter on his Hamilton debut last month, attempted to make all but he had little left to offer once headed by the runner-up over a furlong out, though he still finished clear of the rest. He may be worth a return to 6f for the time being. (op 12-1 tchd 9-1)
Eduardo seemed to be going nowhere at the back of the field at halfway, but he did make some late progress and this was a step up from finishing a tailed-off last of 11 on his Leicester debut.
Echos Of Motivator, a 14,000euros half-brother to two winners including the multiple Polytrack winner Ravi River, missed the break and raced near the back of the field early, but he did show a little ability later on and may need a bit more time. (op 25-1 tchd 40-1)
Quite A Catch(IRE), green when fifth of 11 on his Goodwood debut last month, was sent off a well-backed second favourite but having raced prominently for a long way, he didn't get home. He is obviously thought capable of better. (op 6-1 tchd 7-1)
T/Plt: £215.50 to a £1 stake. Pool:£73,626.24 - 249.38 winning tickets. T/Qpdt: £23.00 to a £1 stake. Pool:£4,953.25 - 158.94 winning tickets. CR

3549 CATTERICK (L-H)
Wednesday, July 7

OFFICIAL GOING: Good to firm (firm in places; 9.1)
Wind: Fresh 1/2 against Weather: Overcast and very breezy, sharp shower race 4

3770 YORKSHIRE4X4.COM ADVENTURE ACTIVITIES (S) STKS — 5f
2:15 (2:15) (Class 6) 2-Y-O — £1,706 (£503; £252) Stalls Low

Form				RPR
3464	1		**Johnny Hancocks (IRE)**[6] 3598 2-8-11 0 ... CathyGannon 1 (P D Evans) *fast away: mde all: rdn and edgd rt over 1f out: forged clr ins fnl f: v readily* 6/4[1]	64
004	2	6	**Chester Deelyte (IRE)**[20] 3126 2-8-6 0 ... RoystonFfrench 5 (Mrs L Williamson) *chsd ldrs: hung lft: hmpd and chsd wnr 1f out: no imp* 9/2[2]	37
0	3	2 3/4	**Forever Vienna**[22] 3058 2-8-11 0 ... PaulMulrennan 4 (J Howard Johnson) *chsd wnr: drvn over 2f out: kpt on same pce appr fnl f* 25/1	33
0	4	3/4	**Bigalo's Laura B (IRE)**[12] 3392 2-8-6 0 ...(e) DuranFentiman 8 (L A Mullaney) *chsd ldrs: sn drvn along: one pce fnl 2f* 5/1[3]	25
	5	3	**Cruise Racer (IRE)** 2-8-11 0 ... StephenCraine 3 (Patrick Morris) *s.i.s: sn chsng ldrs: lost pl over 1f out* 12/1	19
6400	6	3/4	**Muse To Use**[6] 3603 2-8-7 0 ow1 ... TomEaves 6 (I W McInnes) *t.k.h: trckd ldrs: effrt 2f out: sn rdn and wknd* 10/1	12
550	7	14	**Ever Roses**[53] 2130 2-8-6 0 ... PaulHanagan 2 (P T Midgley) *outpcd and lost pl over 2f out: bhd whn eased ins fnl f* 5/1[3]	—

59.90 secs (0.10) **Going Correction** -0.20s/f (Firm) — **7** Ran SP% **112.1**
Speed ratings (Par 92): **91,81,77,75,71 69,47**
toteswingers: 1&2 £2.40, 1&3 £9.70, 2&3 £16.40 CSF £8.08 TOTE £3.50: £2.10, £2.20; EX 9.60.There was no bid for the winner.
Owner Shropshire Wolves 3 **Bred** Mountarmstrong Stud **Trained** Pandy, Monmouths

FOCUS
A very ordinary seller which was run at a sound pace. An improved effort from the winner but the form is rated conservatively.

NOTEBOOK
Johnny Hancocks(IRE), a very speedy sort, lacks size but did this well and should remain competitive in similarly ordinary company. (op 13-8 tchd 15-8)
Chester Deelyte(IRE), having her fourth start, had shown ability last time at Warwick and again suggested there is a similar race within her grasp. (op 4-1 tchd 7-2)
Forever Vienna, well held on his debut in similar company at Thirsk, appears to be going the right way. Although not one to take a short-price about next time, if he keeps progressing, he can win a similar event. (tchd 28-1)
Bigalo's Laura B(IRE) couldn't take advantage of the drop into selling company. (op 6-1 tchd 9-2)

3771 BOOK TICKETS ON-LINE AT CATTERICKBRIDGE.CO.UK H'CAP — 7f
2:50 (2:50) (Class 5) (0-75,73) 3-Y-O — £2,266 (£674; £337; £168) Stalls Low

Form				RPR
4410	1		**Just The Tonic**[22] 3061 3-8-3 **60** ... IanBrennan(5) 4 (Mrs Marjorie Fife) *trckd ldrs: outpcd over 2f out: hdwy on wd outside 1f out: fin wl to ld nr fin* 4/1[2]	67
0100	2	nk	**Skyfire**[48] 2242 3-9-7 **73** ... GregFairley 7 (M Johnston) *sn w ldrs: drvn along 3f out: edgd lft and styd on to ld wl ins fnl f: hdd fnl strides* 7/1	79
-401	3	hd	**Merchant Of Medici**[13] 3359 3-9-1 **67** ... PaulHanagan 3 (W R Muir) *trckd ldrs: t.k.h: narrow advantage over 1f out: hdd and no ex fnl 50yds* 6/4[1]	72
5052	4	1 1/2	**Chinese Democracy (USA)**[8] 3525 3-8-2 **56** oh3...(p) CathyGannon 2 (P D Evans) *trckd ldrs: t.k.h: upsides over 1f out: keeping on same pce whn short of room and eased nr fin* 9/2[3]	55
2000	5	2 1/4	**Kilmanseck**[13] 3350 3-8-12 **64** ... AndreaAtzeni 6 (Eve Johnson Houghton) *w ldrs: wknd jst ins fnl f* 11/1	59
0-10	6	2	**Desert Forest (IRE)**[19] 3161 3-9-4 **70** ...(p) PaulMulrennan 1 (J Howard Johnson) *led: shkn up and qcknd 3f out: hdd and hung rt over 1f out: wknd fnl 150yds* 8/1	60

1m 27.13s (0.13) **Going Correction** -0.20s/f (Firm) — **6** Ran SP% **110.1**
Speed ratings (Par 100): **91,90,90,88,86 83**
toteswingers: 1&2 £3.10, 1&3 £1.30, 2&3 £3.70 CSF £29.37 TOTE £4.10: £1.80, £5.20; EX 27.90.
Owner R W Fife **Bred** West Dereham Abbey Stud **Trained** Stillington, N Yorks

FOCUS
This 3-y-o handicap for horses rated 56-75 was run at a sound pace and the handicapper had done his job, with all six runners holding some sort of chance entering the final furlong. The overall time was slow, suggesting they stopped in front, and the form is not rated too positively.
Just The Tonic Official explanation: trainer said, regarding apparent improvement in form, that the filly had benefitted from a three week break.
Desert Forest(IRE) Official explanation: jockey said gelding hung right-handed

3772 5TH REGIMENT ROYAL ARTILLERY "TURMERIC" H'CAP — 1m 7f 177y
3:20 (3:20) (Class 4) (0-85,77) 3-Y-O+ — £3,885 (£1,156; £577; £288) Stalls Low

Form				RPR
5-26	1		**Bergonzi (IRE)**[22] 3060 6-9-11 **74** ... PaulMulrennan 1 (J Howard Johnson) *led 1f: trckd ldrs: led over 2f out: jnd over 1f out: all out* 10/3[3]	85
-502	2	shd	**Cloudy City (USA)**[9] 3519 3-8-2 **70** ... AndrewMullen 4 (M Johnston) *trckd ldrs: effrt over 4f out: nt clr run over 2f out: upsides over 1f out: jst hld* 9/4[2]	81
-403	3	7	**Act Of Kalanisi (IRE)**[12] 3402 4-10-0 **77** ... GregFairley 3 (M Johnston) *led after 1f: jnd over 5f out: hdd over 2f out: wknd appr fnl f* 12/1	79
3-53	4	7	**Architrave**[33] 2697 3-8-4 **72** ... PaulHanagan 6 (Sir Mark Prescott) *s.i.s: sn trcking ldrs: upsides over 5f out: sn hrd drvn: hung lft and lost pl over 1f out* 7/4[1]	66
5-04	5	40	**Bijou Dan**[30] 2814 9-9-0 **63** ... PJMcDonald 5 (G M Moore) *s.i.s: a last: drvn 8f out: t.o 3f out: lame* 8/1	9

3m 26.14s (-5.86) **Going Correction** -0.20s/f (Firm)
WFA 3 from 4yo+ 19lb — **5** Ran SP% **109.0**
Speed ratings (Par 105): **106,105,102,98,78**
toteswinger: 1&2 £5.20. CSF £10.97 TOTE £2.50: £1.10, £4.40; EX 12.90.
Owner Transcend Bloodstock LLP **Bred** Deer Forest Stud **Trained** Billy Row, Co Durham

FOCUS
A 2m handicap open to horses rated 66-85, with the top weight 8lb below the ceiling rating. They went a good pace and the form is sound enough.
Architrave Official explanation: jockey said gelding hyung left-handed throughout

Bijou Dan Official explanation: vet said gelding finished lame left-fore

3773 CALL 01748 810165 TO BOOK RACEDAY HOSPITALITY H'CAP 5f 212y
3:55 (3:56) (Class 5) (0-75,75) 3-Y-O **£2,266** (£674; £337; £168) **Stalls** Low

Form RPR

3-50 **1** **Thinking**[32] 2768 3-8-4 **58** .... DuranFentiman 6 63
(T D Easterby) *chsd ldrs: styd on ins fnl f: led last stride* **7/1**

3033 **2** *nse* **The Hermitage (IRE)**[7] 3551 3-9-7 **75** .... GregFairley 3 79
(M Johnston) *led: qcknd over 2f out: hdd post* **85/40**[2]

0046 **3** *3 ¼* **Reach For The Sky (IRE)**[3] 3710 3-7-13 **56** oh4 .... PaulPickard(3) 1 50
(A Berry) *chsd ldrs: one pce fnl 2f* **14/1**

0645 **4** *2 ½* **Ruler's Honour (IRE)**[19] 3151 3-8-7 **61** .... RoystonFfrench 5 47
(T J Etherington) *chsd ldrs: outpcd 4f out: kpt on one pce ins fnl f* **12/1**

2534 **5** *½* **Ravenfield (IRE)**[20] 3111 3-8-9 **70** ow2 .... DaleSwift(7) 2 54
(D H Brown) *chsd ldrs: drvn over 2f out: one pce* **2/1**[1]

-040 **6** *½* **Regal Emperor (IRE)**[61] 1890 3-8-3 **62** .... BillyCray(5) 4 45
(D Nicholls) *t.k.h: trckd ldrs: drvn and outpcd 4f out: hdwy on wd outside 2f out: nvr a factor* **25/1**

0062 **7** *5* **Pelmanism**[9] 3507 3-8-11 **65** ....(b) PaulHanagan 7 32
(K A Ryan) *chsd ldrs: effrt on outer and hung rt over 3f out: lost pl over 1f out* **5/1**[3]

1m 12.37s (-1.23) **Going Correction** -0.20s/f (Firm) **7** Ran SP% **112.7**
Speed ratings (Par 100): **100,99,95,92,91 90,84**
toteswingers: 1&2 £4.50, 1&3 £11.50, 2&3 £7.20 CSF £21.66 TOTE £10.50: £5.40, £2.40; EX 24.30.
Owner Habton Farms **Bred** L T Roberts **Trained** Great Habton, N Yorks

FOCUS
A sound pace for this 3-y-o 56-75 handicap. A 5lb personal best from the winner.
Thinking Official explanation: trainer said, regarding apparent improvement in form, that the gelding benefitted from a 31-day break.
Pelmanism Official explanation: jockey said gelding never travelled and hung right final bend

3774 YORKSHIRE RACING SUMMER FESTIVAL H'CAP (DIV I) 7f
4:30 (4:31) (Class 6) (0-65,65) 3-Y-O+ **£1,706** (£503; £252) **Stalls** Low

Form RPR

1400 **1** **Dhhamaan (IRE)**[16] 3280 5-8-11 **53** ....(b) JamesSullivan(5) 9 61
(Mrs R A Carr) *mde all: kpt on wl ins fnl f: decisively* **9/1**

2323 **2** *1 ½* **Call Of Duty (IRE)**[9] 3502 5-9-7 **58** .... PaulHanagan 8 62
(Mrs Dianne Sayer) *chsd wnr 4f out: styd on same pce ins fnl f: no imp* **7/4**[1]

0-30 **3** *¾* **Needy McCredie**[8] 3538 4-9-0 **51** .... PaddyAspell 5 53
(J R Turner) *chsd ldrs: kpt on same pce ins fnl f* **16/1**

0114 **4** *2* **Arjemis**[7] 3551 4-9-9 **65** .... IanBrennan(5) 3 62+
(C R Wilson) *in rr: hdwy on ins over 2f out: tk n.d 4th jst ins fnl f* **5/1**[3]

0034 **5** *1 ½* **Fathey (IRE)**[8] 3534 4-8-13 **55** .... BillyCray(5) 1 47
(C Smith) *chsd ldrs: outpcd over 3f out: hung rt and one pce fnl 2f* **7/2**[2]

0/00 **6** *nse* **Prigsnov Dancer (IRE)**[15] 3287 5-8-12 **49** .... DavidAllan 2 41
(O Brennan) *tk fierce hold in rr: kpt on fnl 2f: nvr nr ldrs* **33/1**

440 **7** *½* **Braille**[28] 2849 5-9-3 **54** .... DuranFentiman 10 45
(T D Walford) *chsd ldrs: outpcd over 3f out: hung lft and one pce fnl 2f* **14/1**

5640 **8** *13* **Straight Face (IRE)**[31] 2783 6-9-8 **64** ....(b) RichardEvans(5) 4 20
(P D Evans) *rrd s and hood removed v late: slowly away: a detached in rr* **9/1**

600- **9** *nk* **Camomile**[12] 7796 4-8-9 **46** oh1 .... AndrewMullen 6 —
(Miss Tracy Waggott) *mid-div: drvn over 4f out: slipped bnd and lost pl over 3f out: sn bhd* **33/1**

320- **10** *3 ¼* **Neva A Mull Moment (IRE)**[307] 5599 4-9-11 **62** .... PatrickMathers 11 —
(R E Barr) *t.k.h: stdd on outside and lost pl after 1f: bhd fnl 3f* **28/1**

1m 25.6s (-1.40) **Going Correction** -0.20s/f (Firm)
WFA 3 from 4yo+ 8lb **10** Ran SP% **117.1**
Speed ratings (Par 101): **100,98,97,95,93 93,92,77,77,73**
toteswingers:1&2 £4.70, 2&3 £7.50, 1&3 £16.30 CSF £24.86 CT £253.17 TOTE £13.70: £4.40, £1.80, £6.10; EX 31.60.
Owner S B Clark **Bred** D Veitch And Musagd Abo Salim **Trained** Huby, N Yorks
■ Stewards' Enquiry : Richard Evans caution: used whip when out of contention.

FOCUS
An ordinary 46-65 handicap. It was run at a sound pace and favoured those racing up with the pace, but the form makes some sense at face value.
Fathey(IRE) Official explanation: jockey said gelding hung right-handed throughout
Straight Face(IRE) Official explanation: jockey said, regarding late removal of blindfold, that the gelding had been restless in the stalls and had reared up, when the gates opened it sat back causing the delay.
Camomile Official explanation: jockey said filly slipped on bend

3775 YORKSHIRE RACING SUMMER FESTIVAL H'CAP (DIV II) 7f
5:05 (5:05) (Class 6) (0-65,65) 3-Y-O+ **£1,706** (£503; £252) **Stalls** Low

Form RPR

0146 **1** **Ellies Image**[12] 3387 3-8-13 **58** .... PaulHanagan 10 61
(B P J Baugh) *chsd ldr: led 2f out: wandered: hld on nr fin* **9/2**[3]

-032 **2** *½* **San Silvestro (IRE)**[9] 3500 5-9-11 **65** ....(b) BarryMcHugh(3) 9 70
(Mrs A Duffield) *in rr-div: hdwy 4f out: effrt on outside over 2f out: edgd lft and styd on wl ins fnl f: jst hld* **4/1**[2]

00-0 **3** *½* **Ursus**[33] 2699 5-9-2 **53** ....(p) PaddyAspell 7 56
(C R Wilson) *t.k.h: trckd ldr: styd on same pce ins fnl f* **33/1**

5400 **4** *nk* **Baybshambles (IRE)**[7] 3551 6-9-6 **64** .... DaleSwift(7) 1 66
(R E Barr) *trckd ldrs: nt clr run on inner and rdr lost whip 1f out: hld whn squeezed out nr line* **7/1**

5051 **5** *1* **Nuit Sombre (IRE)**[6] 3595 10-9-6 **57** ....(p) SilvestreDeSousa 2 57
(G A Harker) *led: hdd 2f out: fading whn n.m.r fnl 50yds* **2/1**[1]

220 **6** *2 ¼* **Mister Jingles**[15] 3284 7-9-3 **59** ....(b) AmyRyan(5) 8 53
(R M Whitaker) *chsd ldrs: rdn over 2f out: one pce* **5/1**

4000 **7** *8* **Dream Express (IRE)**[8] 3538 5-9-2 **53** .... PhillipMakin 5 25
(D W Thompson) *t.k.h in rr: hung rt and bhd fnl 3f* **16/1**

46-0 **8** *3 ¼* **Rainbow Bay**[33] 2699 7-8-9 **46** ....(p) AndrewMullen 3 9
(Miss Tracy Waggott) *dwlt: hdwy over 4f out: sn outpcd and lost pl: sme hdwy on outer 2f out: sn wknd* **25/1**

-004 **9** *1 ½* **Its Beyond Me**[23] 3021 6-8-9 **46** oh1 ....(tp) PJMcDonald 6 5
(F P Murtagh) *s.v.s: a detached in last* **80/1**

1m 25.52s (-1.48) **Going Correction** -0.20s/f (Firm)
WFA 3 from 5yo+ 8lb **9** Ran SP% **114.6**
Speed ratings (Par 101): **100,99,98,98,97 94,85,81,80**
toteswingers: 1&2 £4.20, 1&3 £13.50, 2&3 £12.60. CSF £22.34 CT £523.51 TOTE £7.00: £1.80, £1.10, £4.60; EX 20.50.
Owner F Gillespie **Bred** Miss S M Potts **Trained** Audley, Staffs
■ Stewards' Enquiry : Paul Hanagan caution: careless riding.

FOCUS
Six of the nine runners had been successful at the track, making this look more competitive than the first division. It was also run at a sound pace and it proved hard to come off the pace. The winner probably only had to run to form.
Dream Express(IRE) Official explanation: jockey said gelding hung right-handed

3776 WE RACE AGAIN NEXT WEDNESDAY MEDIAN AUCTION MAIDEN STKS 1m 3f 214y
5:40 (5:41) (Class 5) 3-4-Y-O **£2,266** (£674; £337; £168) **Stalls** Low

Form RPR

5 **1** **Nezhenka**[57] 1993 3-8-9 0 .... PaulHanagan 7 85+
(Sir Mark Prescott) *trckd ldrs: wnt 2nd 4f out: chal over 2f out: edgd lft and led appr fnl f: sn drew clr: readily* **11/4**[2]

34 **2** *4* **Ceoil An Aith (IRE)**[20] 3116 4-9-8 0 .... GregFairley 4 78
(M Johnston) *led: hdd appr fnl f: kpt on same pce* **1/1**[1]

634 **3** *14* **Maid Of Meft**[13] 3355 3-8-9 67 .... PhillipMakin 3 56
(Miss L A Perratt) *s.i.s: sn chsng ldrs: drvn over 5f out: kpt on to take poor 3rd appr fnl f* **11/2**[3]

50 **4** *3 ¾* **Sheikhtothemusic**[11] 3437 3-8-9 0 .... PaulMulrennan 9 50
(J G Given) *t.k.h: in tch: drvn 4f out: wnt modest 3rd 2f out: wknd appr fnl f* **14/1**

5 *3 ½* **Maxi Moo (IRE)** 3-9-0 0 .... SilvestreDeSousa 2 49
(G A Harker) *s.s: sn mid-div: drvn over 5f out: sn lost pl: kpt on fnl 2f* **15/2**

66-0 **6** *10* **New World Symphony (IRE)**[33] 2697 3-9-0 55 .... TomEaves 5 33
(J Howard Johnson) *chsd ldrs: wknd over 2f out* **25/1**

600- **7** *8* **Convitezza**[257] 6997 4-9-8 37 .... PatrickMathers 1 16
(M E Sowersby) *chsd ldrs: drvn over 4f out: wd bnd and lost pl 3f out* **200/1**

05 **8** *86* **Arkas**[19] 3179 4-9-8 0 .... PaddyAspell 6 —
(C R Wilson) *hld up towards rr: drvn over 5f out: sn lost pl and bhd: t.o 3f out: eventually completed* **125/1**

2m 35.12s (-3.78) **Going Correction** -0.20s/f (Firm)
WFA 3 from 4yo 13lb **8** Ran SP% **115.6**
Speed ratings (Par 103): **104,101,92,89,87 80,75,17**
toteswingers: 1&2 £3.20, 1&3 £3.60, 2&3 £1.50. CSF £5.91 TOTE £2.70: £1.10, £1.10, £1.10; EX 6.40 Place 6: £82.90, Place 5: £55.10..
Owner Miss K Rausing **Bred** Miss K Rausing **Trained** Newmarket, Suffolk

FOCUS
Plenty of dead wood in this ordinary maiden. It was run at an even pace and the first two pulled well clear of the remainder. Improvement from the first two, who could have rated higher.
Maid Of Meft Official explanation: jockey said filly never travelled
T/Plt: £185.50 to a £1 stake. Pool:£38,116.02 - 149.97 winning tickets. T/Qpdt: £11.50 to a £1 stake. Pool:£2,901.43 - 186.50 winning tickets. WG

[3561]KEMPTON (A.W) (R-H)
Wednesday, July 7

OFFICIAL GOING: Standard
Wind: Moderate behind Weather: Overcast

3777 KEMPTON.CO.UK APPRENTICE H'CAP 7f (P)
6:20 (6:21) (Class 5) (0-70,70) 4-Y-O+ **£2,320** (£685; £342) **Stalls** High

Form RPR

5003 **1** **Cut The Cackle (IRE)**[12] 3400 4-9-10 **70** .... AshleyMorgan 4 79
(P Winkworth) *towards rr tl hdwy over 2f out: qcknd out to ld appr fnl f: styd on strly* **16/1**

2100 **2** *1 ¼* **Army Of Stars (IRE)**[43] 2415 4-9-9 **69** ....(p) SophieDoyle 9 75
(J A Osborne) *t.k.h: chsd ldrs: pushed along and qcknd to chal over 1f out: styd on wl fnl f but nt pce of wnr* **20/1**

3022 **3** *¾* **Harting Hill**[28] 2866 5-8-12 **63** .... KatiaScallan(5) 1 67
(M P Tregoning) *in tch: racd on outside: pushed along and styd on fr over 1f out: kpt on ins fnl f: nt rch ldrs* **13/2**[3]

3554 **4** *hd* **Pha Mai Blue**[25] 2967 5-8-8 **59** ....(v) NathanAlison(5) 12 62
(J R Boyle) *awkward s: towards rr tl gd hdwy fr over 2f out to press ldrs over 1f out: outpcd ins fnl f* **8/1**

0-01 **5** *1 ¼* **Hazytoo**[29] 2846 6-9-7 **70** .... DebraEngland(3) 8 70+
(P J Makin) *stdd s: in rr: stl last wl over 1f out: str run sn after and fin strly: gng on cl home* **12/1**

0-30 **6** *3* **Tudor Prince (IRE)**[12] 3396 6-9-7 **70** .... AnthonyFreeman(3) 5 62
(A W Carroll) *sn chsng ldr: slt ld towards outer fr 2f out: hdd appr fnl f: wknd ins fnl f* **14/1**

0250 **7** *¾* **Kipchak (IRE)**[27] 2896 5-9-2 **69** ....(p) MarkPower(7) 11 59
(C R Dore) *led tl hdd 2f out: stl rt there over 1f out: wknd fnl f* **20/1**

-503 **8** *nk* **Cape Quarter (USA)**[16] 3262 4-9-5 **65** ....(t) JohnFahy 13 54
(W J Haggas) *chsd ldrs: rdn and ev ch over 1f out: sn wknd* **2/1**[1]

0030 **9** *1 ¼* **Teen Ager (FR)**[7] 3567 6-9-1 **61** .... RossAtkinson 6 46
(P Burgoyne) *in rr: sme hdwy and edgd rt over 1f out: nvr anywhere nr ldrs* **33/1**

50 **10** *1 ½* **Lethal**[7] 3567 7-8-13 **62** .... DavidKenny(3) 14 43
(Andrew Reid) *chsd ldrs: rdn over 2f out: wknd over 1f out* **25/1**

5542 **11** *1 ¾* **Perfect Friend**[6] 3592 4-9-0 **65** .... RichardRowe(5) 10 42
(S Kirk) *in rr: sme prog whn n.m.r over 1f out and stmbld sn after: nvr in contention after* **6/1**[2]

-520 **12** *¾* **Ede's Dot Com (IRE)**[66] 1737 6-9-1 **61** .... KierenFox 2 36
(P M Phelan) *wnt rt s: a in rr* **10/1**

1m 25.42s (-0.58) **Going Correction** -0.025s/f (Stan) **12** Ran SP% **117.7**
Speed ratings (Par 103): **102,100,99,99,98 94,93,93,92,90 88,87**
toteswingers: 1&2 £34.80, 1&3 £19.90, 2&3 £25.30 CSF £302.79 CT £2316.50 TOTE £17.10: £5.40, £7.50, £1.70; EX 211.90.
Owner P Winkworth **Bred** Mountarmstrong Stud **Trained** Chiddingfold, Surrey

FOCUS
An ordinary handicap but one that took less winning than seemed likely with the market leader disappointing. The gallop was a reasonable one, the first five pulled clear and the winner came down the centre in the straight. Straightforward form.
Lethal Official explanation: vet said gelding lost a right-hind shoe

3778 EUROPEAN BREEDERS' FUND MAIDEN FILLIES' STKS 6f (P)
6:50 (6:53) (Class 5) 2-Y-O **£3,108** (£924; £462; £230) **Stalls** High

Form RPR

1 **Tale Untold (USA)** 2-9-0 0 .... RichardHughes 2 84+
(R Hannon) *s.i.s: sn trcking ldrs: led wl over 1f out: pushed clr: easily* **4/5**[1]

40 **2** *5* **Overwhelm**[21] 3070 2-8-11 0 .... RussKennemore(3) 6 67
(Andrew Reid) *led: rdn edgd lft and hdd wl over 1f out: sn no ch w wnr but hld on wl for 2nd* **13/2**[2]

3 ½ **Out Of The Storm** 2-9-0 0 SebSanders 12 65+
(S Dow) *in rr: stl plenty to do ins fnl 2f: gd prog fnl f: fin wl to cl on 2nd nr fin but nvr any ch w wnr* **16/1**

04 4 1¼ **Mystica (IRE)**[19] 3156 2-9-0 0 LiamKeniry 4 61
(D J S Ffrench Davis) *chsd ldrs: rdn and edgd rt over 1f out: styd on same pce fnl f* **9/1**

5 hd **Spring Bouquet (IRE)** 2-9-0 0 ChrisCatlin 1 61
(M R Channon) *s.i.s: sn prom: rdn and one pce 3f out: styd on again fnl f: nvr a threat* **20/1**

6 6 2¼ **Jameela Girl**[16] 3260 2-9-0 0 EddieAhern 3 54
(R M H Cowell) *chsd ldrs on outside: rdn 2f out: btn wl over 1f out* **12/1**

7 1 **Talkhees (IRE)** 2-9-0 0 TadhgO'Shea 5 51
(B J Meehan) *rdn over 3f out: a outpcd* **7/1**[3]

0 8 shd **Thank You Joy**[28] 2867 2-9-0 0 JimmyQuinn 7 51
(J R Jenkins) *in rr: pushed along over 3f out: sme late prog* **40/1**

0 9 2¼ **Arakova (IRE)**[16] 3260 2-9-0 0 NeilCallan 9 44
(Matthew Salaman) *chsd ldr: rdn over 2f out: wknd sn after* **16/1**

5 10 10 **Molly Piccles**[62] 1838 2-9-0 0 StevieDonohoe 10 14
(M S Tuck) *slowly away: a bhd* **66/1**

00 11 1 **Dallas Legend (IRE)**[12] 3411 2-9-0 0 MarcHalford 11 11
(J Ryan) *sn rdn: a outpcd* **50/1**

1m 14.01s (0.91) **Going Correction** -0.025s/f (Stan) **11** Ran SP% **121.5**
Speed ratings (Par 91): **92,85,84,83,82 79,78,78,75,61 60**
toteswingers: 1&2 £3.70, 1&3 £10.70, 2&3 £9.20 CSF £6.44 TOTE £2.00: £1.50, £1.30, £5.20; EX 8.30.
Owner Trevor Stewart & Anna Doyle **Bred** Newtown Stud Ltd & Joseph Stewart Inv **Trained** East Everleigh, Wilts

FOCUS
Not a competitive fillies' race and those with previous experience looked modest at best, but the well-touted winner looks potentially useful. The gallop was a fair one and the winner raced close to the inside rail in the straight. The second and fourth help with the form.

NOTEBOOK
Tale Untold(USA) ◆, a 26,000gns half-sister to dual Polytrack winner I'm In Love, was very well supported throughout the day and created a favourable impression on her debut. While the bare form of this race is not strong, she is open to plenty of improvement and appeals as the type to hold her own in stronger company. (op Evens tchd 11-10 and 6-5 in a place)
Overwhelm, out of her depth in the Queen Mary and upped to this trip on sand for the first time, was suited by the drop in grade and ran to a similar level as on her debut. She shouldn't mind the return to 5f and is capable of picking up a race away from the better types in this grade or when switched to ordinary nursery company. (tchd 6-1 and 7-1)
Out Of The Storm, the first foal of the yard's former 6f-1m2f winner Night Storm, was noticeably green on this debut but caught the eye with the amount of ground she made up in the closing stages. She will be of more interest over further when qualified for a mark.
Mystica(IRE) was not disgraced but failed to build on the improved form she showed at Goodwood. She leaves the impression the step up to 7f will be to her liking and ordinary nurseries will be the way forward with her. (op 8-1)
Spring Bouquet(IRE), who has winners from 7f-1m2f in her pedigree, hinted at ability on this debut. She should improve for this experience and shaped here as though a stiffer test of stamina would suit ideally. (op 25-1)
Talkhees(IRE) has winners in her pedigree but was far too green to do herself justice on this debut. (op 13-2 tchd 11-2)

3779 DIGIBET H'CAP 6f (P)
7:20 (7:22) (Class 4) (0-80,80) 3-Y-O+ £3,885 (£1,156; £577; £288) Stalls High

Form RPR

0-00 1 **Crown (IRE)**[53] 2120 3-9-5 80 IanMongan 7 88
(Miss Jo Crowley) *chsd ldrs: drvn 2f out: led fnl 120yds: all out* **50/1**

1014 2 hd **Quasi Congaree (GER)**[28] 2872 4-9-6 75 (t) NeilCallan 2 83
(I A Wood) *wnt rt s: t.k.h: in tch: hdwy over 1f out: str chal fr ins fnl f but a jst hld* **14/1**

-000 3 1 **Tagula Night (IRE)**[23] 3037 4-9-9 78 (vt) ShaneKelly 10 83
(W R Swinburn) *sn led: rdn over 2f out: hdd and no ex fnl 120yds* **9/2**[1]

3413 4 1 **Lastkingofscotland (IRE)**[36] 2624 4-9-3 72 (b) LiamKeniry 6 74
(C R Dore) *in rr: pushed along over 2f out: hdwy appr fnl f: fin wl but nvr any ch w ldng trio* **7/1**[3]

4524 5 ½ **Mon Brav**[17] 3243 3-9-2 77 (v) DavidNolan 9 76
(D Carroll) *chsd ldrs: rdn 2f out: wknd over 1f out* **10/1**

-303 6 1¼ **Bold Tie**[29] 2846 4-9-6 75 RichardHughes 1 71+
(R Hannon) *in rr and racd wd: styd on fr over 1f out: nvr a threat* **12/1**

-553 7 nk **Midnight Fantasy**[7] 3567 4-9-3 72 SaleemGolam 12 67
(Rae Guest) *s.i.s: in rr: sme hdwy fr over 1f out but nvr a threat* **7/1**[3]

3-10 8 hd **Felsham**[47] 2283 3-9-2 77 DaneO'Neill 8 71
(H Candy) *chsd ldr: rdn 2f out: sn wknd* **9/2**[1]

3006 9 1½ **Tamasou (IRE)**[21] 3083 5-9-4 73 FrankieMcDonald 3 63
(F J Brennan) *hmpd s: in rr: styd on fr over 1f out but nvr a threat* **20/1**

5600 10 3½ **Hellbender (IRE)**[28] 2872 4-9-3 72 JimmyFortune 11 51
(S Kirk) *chsd ldrs: rdn 2f out and sn btn* **14/1**

21-0 11 5 **Chat De La Burg (USA)**[12] 3401 3-9-2 77 SteveDrowne 4 39
(J R Best) *wnt lft s: t.k.h: in tch on outside: rdn 3f out: wknd sn after* **16/1**

1312 U **Requisite**[7] 3567 5-9-4 73 (v) GeorgeBaker 5 —
(I A Wood) *uns rdr s* **5/1**[2]

1m 12.86s (-0.24) **Going Correction** -0.025s/f (Stan)
WFA 3 from 4yo+ 6lb **12** Ran SP% **120.8**
Speed ratings (Par 105): **100,99,98,97,96 94,94,94,92,87 80,—**
toteswingers: 1&2 £73.50, 1&3 £61.80, 2&3 £17.50 CSF £650.08 CT £3831.41 TOTE £77.80: £26.10, £4.90, £1.40; EX 322.40.
Owner Kilstone Limited **Bred** Shortgrove Manor Stud **Trained** Whitcombe, Dorset

FOCUS
A fair handicap in which the in-form Requisite parted company with her rider leaving the stalls. Although the gallop was reasonable, those held up were at a disadvantage and the first two raced in the centre in the straight. The winner is rated back to her 2yo best but this form may not be too solid.
Crown(IRE) Official explanation: trainer's rep said, regarding apparent improvement in form, that the filly was better suited by a drop back to 6f and positive tactics on its first run on the all-weather.
Chat De La Burg(USA) Official explanation: jockey said gelding ran too free

3780 DIGIBET.COM H'CAP 2m (P)
7:50 (7:50) (Class 5) (0-75,75) 4-Y-O+ £2,320 (£685; £342) Stalls High

Form RPR

1-50 1 **Saborido (USA)**[35] 2659 4-8-13 67 JimCrowley 9 76
(Mrs A J Perrett) *chsd ldrs: wnt 2nd 3f out: led ins fnl 2f: hdd ins fnl f: rallied gamely to ld again last strides* **11/1**

0-33 2 nk **Sheila's Castle**[18] 3221 6-8-4 58 JimmyQuinn 10 67
(S Regan) *in rr tl stdy hdwy fr 4f out: swtchd rt towards ins over 2f out: str run to ld ins fnl f: hdd and no ex last strides* **12/1**

3-46 3 nse **Alnwick**[124] 811 6-9-7 75 DaneO'Neill 12 84+
(P D Cundell) *towards rr: hdwy fr 3f out: styd on wl fr 2f out and clsng on ldrs thrght fnl f but a jst hld* **7/1**[2]

1443 4 5 **Broughtons Point**[27] 2907 4-8-3 57 JamieMackay 8 60+
(W J Musson) *in rr: plenty to do whn styd on fr over 2f out: hung rt sn after: styd on but nvr a threat* **10/1**[3]

3213 5 hd **Ultimate Quest (IRE)**[14] 3324 5-8-12 66 (b[1]) SebSanders 6 68
(Sir Mark Prescott) *chsd ldr after 4f: slt ld fr 1/2-way: rdn and styd on fr 3f out: hdd ins fnl 2f: wknd fnl f* **11/10**[1]

13/0 6 8 **Pocketwood**[73] 8-8-3 62 ow3 (b) JohnFahy(5) 3 55
(A J Lidderdale) *in rr: styd on fnl 2f but nvr anywhere nr ldrs* **20/1**

615- 7 9 **Kokkokila**[104] 7124 6-8-5 59 KirstyMilczarek 14 41
(Lady Herries) *chsd ldrs: rdn 3f out: wknd ins fnl 3f* **25/1**

41-0 8 3 **Perception (IRE)**[62] 1849 4-8-11 65 FergusSweeney 4 43
(A King) *sn slt ld: jnd after 4f: narrowly hdd 1/2-way but styd upsides tl 4f out: lost 2nd and wknd 3f out* **20/1**

500/ 9 3½ **Red Lancer**[357] 981 9-9-2 70 LiamJones 2 44
(J A T De Giles) *chsd ldrs tl wknd 4f out* **50/1**

400/ 10 8 **Lyes Green**[473] 6614 9-8-2 56 oh2 (p) FrankieMcDonald 7 21
(O Sherwood) *chsd ldrs: rdn 1/2-way: wknd 5f out* **18/1**

010 11 13 **Coda Agency**[21] 3084 7-8-10 64 NeilCallan 13 13
(D W P Arbuthnot) *chsd ldrs tl wknd over 4f out* **11/1**

055- 12 13 **Double Whammy**[308] 5578 4-8-13 67 PatCosgrave 1 —
(Jamie Poulton) *a towards rr* **33/1**

-00 13 dist **Pass The Port**[27] 2897 9-9-7 75 HayleyTurner 5 —
(D Haydn Jones) *a in rr: eased and t.o fr over 2f out* **33/1**

3m 27.55s (-2.55) **Going Correction** -0.025s/f (Stan) **13** Ran SP% **120.0**
Speed ratings (Par 103): **105,104,104,102,102 98,93,92,90,86 79,73,—**
toteswingers: 1&2 £15.20 1&3 £15.50, 2&3 £9.70 CSF £123.76 CT £1001.71 TOTE £10.50: £1.60, £4.50, £2.80; EX 166.60.
Owner Tracey, Cotton, James, Slade **Bred** R D Hubbard And R Masterson **Trained** Pulborough, W Sussex

FOCUS
An ordinary handicap in which the pace was fair and the first three, who raced centre to far side in the straight, pulled clear in the closing stages. The form is rated around the third.

3781 DIGIBET CASINO H'CAP 1m 3f (P)
8:20 (8:21) (Class 4) (0-80,80) 3-Y-O+ £3,885 (£1,156; £577; £288) Stalls High

Form RPR

0133 1 **Resentful Angel**[9] 3512 5-9-7 74 MartinLane(3) 7 86
(Pat Eddery) *in rr: hdwy and hung rt over 2f out: str run u.p to ld fnl 50yds: hld on wl* **7/1**[3]

1204 2 ½ **Dromore (IRE)**[28] 2869 3-9-4 80 JimmyFortune 9 91
(A M Balding) *mid-div: rdn and hdwy over 2f out: str run fr over 1f out: fin wl to take 2nd fnl 30yds: a jst hld by wnr* **5/2**[1]

10-6 3 ½ **Denton (NZ)**[18] 3203 7-9-0 69 (t) SimonPearce(5) 12 79
(J R Gask) *t.k.h: trckd ldrs: led over 1f out: shkn up fnl f: hdd and no ex fnl 50yds* **14/1**

0004 4 2¾ **Aurora Sky (IRE)**[25] 2966 4-8-11 61 SebSanders 5 66
(J Akehurst) *chsd ldrs: led jst ins fnl 3f: rdn 2f out: hdd over 1f out: wknd ins fnl f* **16/1**

-043 5 13 **Wiggy Smith**[24] 2996 11-10-0 78 DaneO'Neill 6 60
(H Candy) *in rr: rdn and sme hdwy fr over 2f out: mod prog into wl btn 5th wl ins fnl f* **20/1**

4006 6 shd **Eseej (USA)**[57] 1996 5-9-3 67 ChrisCatlin 11 49
(P W Hiatt) *led tl hdd ins fnl 3f: wknd 2f out* **14/1**

4-01 7 2¾ **Sagredo (USA)**[16] 3257 6-9-10 74 GeorgeBaker 3 51
(Jonjo O'Neill) *in rr: mod late prog* **9/1**

-520 8 8 **Trachonitis (IRE)**[82] 1348 6-9-13 77 RichardHughes 14 39
(J R Jenkins) *in tch: chsd ldrs and rdn 3f out: wknd sn after* **20/1**

4000 9 5 **Formidable Guest**[21] 3079 6-9-6 70 PatCosgrave 2 23
(J Pearce) *a towards rr* **33/1**

2-06 10 1 **Manshoor (IRE)**[61] 1863 5-9-13 77 EddieAhern 8 28
(Mrs L Wadham) *in tch: rdn: wd and wknd 3f out* **10/1**

3/2- 11 2½ **Fleurissimo**[446] 1329 4-9-12 76 WilliamBuick 10 23
(J H M Gosden) *t.k.h: chsd ldrs tl wknd ins fnl 3f* **7/1**[3]

35-3 12 2½ **Penangdouble O One**[39] 2548 3-8-10 72 JimCrowley 13 14
(R M Beckett) *chsd ldrs: rdn 5f out: btn 4f out* **6/1**[2]

1104 13 14 **Turjuman (USA)**[51] 2181 5-9-11 75 StevieDonohoe 4 —
(W J Musson) *bhd fr 1/2-way* **14/1**

2m 18.86s (-3.04) **Going Correction** -0.025s/f (Stan)
WFA 3 from 4yo+ 12lb **13** Ran SP% **125.3**
Speed ratings (Par 105): **110,109,109,107,97 97,95,89,86,85 83,81,71**
toteswingers: 1&2 £5.40, 1&3 £51.50, 2&3 £63.70 CSF £25.33 CT £253.91 TOTE £7.10: £2.90, £1.50, £5.00; EX 31.30.
Owner P J J Eddery **Bred** Patrick Eddery Ltd **Trained** Nether Winchendon, Bucks

FOCUS
A fair handicap although the two least-exposed runners proved disappointing on their respective handicap debuts. The gallop was a reasonable one and the winner raced close to the inside rail in the straight. The time was good for the grade and the form has been rated postively.
Manshoor(IRE) Official explanation: jockey said gelding resented the kickback
Fleurissimo Official explanation: jockey said filly stopped quickly

3782 MIX BUSINESS WITH PLEASURE H'CAP (LONDON MILE QUALIFIER) 1m (P)
8:50 (8:50) (Class 4) (0-80,79) 3-Y-O+ £3,885 (£1,156; £577; £288) Stalls High

Form RPR

-453 1 **State Gathering**[18] 3215 3-9-2 78 DaneO'Neill 14 89+
(H Candy) *chsd ldrs: wnt 2nd 2f out: led appr fnl f: pushed out: readily* **7/2**[1]

5602 2 1¾ **Kiss A Prince**[14] 3330 4-9-3 70 (b) RichardHughes 4 77
(D K Ivory) *in rr: hdwy fr 2f out: styd on thrght fnl f to take 2nd cl home but nt imp on wnr* **6/1**[3]

2220 3 nk **West Emirates (USA)**[61] 1883 4-9-1 73 (b[1]) JohnFahy(5) 6 79
(C G Cox) *led: rdn 2f out: hdd appr fnl f: styd on same pce: ct for 2nd cl home* **7/1**

1-40 4 3¼ **At Wits End**[26] 2934 4-9-7 74 KirstyMilczarek 2 73
(J A R Toller) *in rr and racd wd: styd on fr 2f out: kpt on same pce u.p fnl f* **9/1**

1034 5 nk **Alqaahir (USA)**[14] 3330 8-9-2 72 RobertLButler(3) 9 70
(P Butler) *in tch early: dropped to rr 1/2-way: rdn and hdwy over 2f out: nvr a threat and one pce fnl f* **20/1**

411- 6 1¾ **Mustakmil (IRE)**[203] 7769 4-9-11 78 HayleyTurner 12 72
(S Dow) *in tch: racd on outer: pushed along 3f out: styd on same pce fnl 2f* **13/2**

0506 **7** *6* **Johnmanderville**[37] 2133 4-9-5 **72**.................................... SebSanders 3 52
(A W Carroll) *chsd ldrs towards outside: rdn and wknd 2f out* **11/1**

05-3 **8** *2 1/4* **Flapper (IRE)**[14] 3330 4-9-5 **72**.. EddieAhern 8 47
(J W Hills) *s.i.s: sn chsng ldrs: wknd 2f out* **11/2**[2]

-013 **9** *nk* **Kilburn**[23] 3036 6-9-4 **71**.. SteveDrowne 11 45
(A J Lidderdale) *chsd ldrs: wknd over 2f out* **7/1**

-000 **10** *22* **Red Suede Shoes**[23] 3036 4-9-7 **74**............................(p) SaleemGolam 5 —
(J Pearce) *mid-div and rdn 3f out: sn wknd* **28/1**

1m 38.66s (-1.14) **Going Correction** -0.025s/f (Stan)
WFA 3 from 4yo+ 9lb **10** Ran SP% **116.8**
Speed ratings (Par 105): **104,102,101,98,98 96,90,88,88,66**
toteswingers: 1&2 £7.20, 1&3 £6.00, 2&3 £11.70 CSF £24.29 CT £143.55 TOTE £5.40: £3.00, £2.20, £2.40; EX 19.40.
Owner Six Too Many **Bred** Mrs R D Peacock **Trained** Kingston Warren, Oxon

FOCUS
Four non-runners but still a fair handicap in which the gallop was just an ordinary one. The winner ended up towards the inside rail in the closing stages. He is rated up 5lb and value for a bit extra.
Flapper(IRE) Official explanation: jockey said filly ran too free

3783 BEST OF BRITISH NIGHT NEXT WEDNESDAY H'CAP 1m (P)
9:20 (9:20) (Class 6) (0-58,58) 3-Y-O+ **£1,637** (£483; £241) **Stalls** High

Form RPR

0404 **1** **Bob Stock (IRE)**[16] 3279 4-9-3 **56**.................................... TonyCulhane 7 67+
(W J Musson) *towards rr: stdy hdwy over 2f out: str run fr over 1f out: rdn to ld fnl 50yds: styd on strly* **7/1**[3]

-330 **2** *1* **Jeremiah (IRE)**[19] 3160 4-8-12 **56**................................(b[1]) JohnFahy(5) 8 65
(J G Portman) *chsd ldr: rdn to ld jst ins fnl f: hdd and no ex fnl 50yds* **9/1**

40-5 **3** *2 1/4* **Josr's Magic (IRE)**[14] 3323 6-9-4 **57**.................................. DaneO'Neill 2 61
(P R Hedger) *led: rdn over 2f out: hdd jst ins fnl f: sn outpcd* **10/1**

212 **4** *2* **Lady Lam**[8] 3524 4-9-3 **56**... RichardHughes 5 55
(S Kirk) *chsd ldrs: rdn wl over 2f out: styd wl there tl wknd fnl f* **4/1**[1]

2020 **5** *nk* **Grey Boy (GER)**[14] 3323 9-8-12 **58**........................ GeorgeDowning(7) 12 57
(A W Carroll) *s.i.s: in rr: pushed along and hdwy fr 2f out: kpt on fnl f but nvr a threat* **16/1**

0000 **6** *1* **Pab Special (IRE)**[25] 2967 7-8-13 **57**................................ KierenFox(5) 6 53
(B R Johnson) *chsd ldrs towards outside: rdn fr 3f out: wknd ins fnl 2f* **16/1**

3534 **7** *1 1/4* **Alfredtheordinary**[10] 3473 5-9-2 **55**................................... ChrisCatlin 1 48
(M R Channon) *in tch on outside: rdn 3f out: one pce fnl 2f* **8/1**

0050 **8** *2* **Flighty Fellow (IRE)**[20] 3124 10-8-12 **56**...................... KylieManser(5) 11 45+
(Miss Olivia Maylam) *s.i.s: in rr: mod late prog* **40/1**

6620 **9** *3* **Signora Frasi (IRE)**[25] 2956 5-9-3 **56**...................... FergusSweeney 14 38
(A G Newcombe) *towards rr most of way* **4/1**[1]

2400 **10** *1/2* **Ermine Grey**[20] 3130 9-9-2 **55**... NeilCallan 10 36
(A W Carroll) *towards rr most of way* **13/2**[2]

0103 **11** *3/4* **Binnion Bay (IRE)**[14] 3338 9-9-3 **56**.............................(b) NeilChalmers 13 35
(J J Bridger) *s.i.s: a towards rr* **14/1**

0010 **12** *nse* **Feet Of Fury**[16] 3279 4-9-2 **55**..(p) LiamJones 4 34
(W M Brisbourne) *chsd ldrs: rdn 3f out: wknd qckly over 2f out* **25/1**

5-50 **13** *hd* **Fitz**[20] 3132 4-9-4 **57**..(p) LiamKeniry 9 35
(Matthew Salaman) *in tch whn n.m.r on ins and lost pl after 2f: hdwy on ins 3f out: sn rdn: wknd over 2f out* **16/1**

1m 39.65s (-0.15) **Going Correction** -0.025s/f (Stan) **13** Ran SP% **126.6**
Speed ratings (Par 101): **99,98,95,93,93 92,91,89,86,85 84,84,84**
toteswingers: 1&2 £6.60, 1&3 £14.10, 2&3 £28.50 CSF £73.11 CT £650.20 TOTE £10.90: £2.70, £3.10, £3.60; EX 96.00 Place 6 £324.17, Place 5 £44.69..
Owner B N Fulton **Bred** Hugo Merry And Khalid Al-Mudhaf **Trained** Newmarket, Suffolk

FOCUS
A moderate but tightly knit handicap in which the gallop was an ordinary one. The winner raced towards the centre in the straight and is rated back to his best form at this trip.
T/Plt: £772.00 to a £1 stake. Pool:£54,465.13 - 51.50 winning tickets. T/Qpdt: £180.40 to a £1 stake. Pool:£5,856.25 - 24.02 winning tickets. ST

3439 LINGFIELD (L-H)
Wednesday, July 7

OFFICIAL GOING: Turf course - firm (good to firm in places; 10.0); all-weather - standard
Wind: Fresh, behind Weather: Fine but cloudy, warm

3784 "OUR MUM IN A MILLION" NURSERY 5f (P)
2:25 (2:26) (Class 5) 2-Y-O **£3,238** (£963; £481; £240) **Stalls** High

Form RPR

3254 **1** **Belle Bayardo (IRE)**[21] 3087 2-9-7 **75**................................ LukeMorris 1 77+
(R A Harris) *disp ld on inner: hrd rdn to gain advantage over 1f out: kpt on wl: all out* **7/4**[1]

665 **2** *3/4* **Ruby Alexander (IRE)**[51] 2183 2-8-0 **57**..................(p) MartinLane(3) 4 56
(R M Beckett) *trckd ldng trio: rdn over 2f out: kpt on to take 2nd last 100yds: clsng at fin: a hld* **5/2**[2]

0646 **3** *1 1/2* **Press Release**[6] 3598 2-8-8 **67**................................(vt[1]) RossAtkinson(5) 6 61
(Tom Dascombe) *t.k.h: jnd ldng pair after 1f: stl upsides and drvn 2f out: nt qckn over 1f out: lost 2nd last 100yds* **5/1**

600 **4** *1* **Jamaica Grande**[19] 3169 2-7-12 **59**.................................. LeonnaMayor(7) 2 49
(P S McEntee) *sn pushed along in last pair: effrt over 1f out: kpt on: n.d* **16/1**

004 **5** *nk* **Triple Agent (IRE)**[26] 2939 2-8-5 **64**........................(v) DeclanCannon(5) 5 53
(A Bailey) *sn pushed along in last pair: plugged on fr over 1f out: nvr gng pce to threaten* **9/2**[3]

050 **6** *4* **Battenberg**[23] 3035 2-7-12 **52** oh8..................................(b) NickyMackay 3 27
(Miss Amy Weaver) *disp ld: rdn bef 1/2-way: lost pl 2f out: wknd* **16/1**

60.86 secs (2.06) **Going Correction** +0.175s/f (Slow) **6** Ran SP% **111.5**
Speed ratings (Par 94): **90,88,86,84,84 77**
toteswingers: 1&2 £2.40, 1&3 £2.10, 2&3 £2.50 CSF £6.26 TOTE £1.90: £1.02, £2.40; EX 6.70.
Owner William Jones **Bred** L Mulryan **Trained** Earlswood, Monmouths

FOCUS
The 'official' ratings shown next to each horse are estimated and for information purposes only. A very weak nursery, with the only one of the sextet to have been placed before prevailing. Not form to dwell on, although it is sound enough.

NOTEBOOK
Belle Bayardo(IRE) had a good chance at the weights and made up for being on the wrong side at Ripon last time to score in workmanlike fashion, despite the bit slipping through his mouth on the home turn. Nurseries won't come much weaker than this, though. (op 13-8 tchd 6-4 and 2-1)
Ruby Alexander(IRE) probably showed a bit of improvement tried in cheekpieces coming back from a break and might have been a bit closer (without looking unlucky) after having to switch entering the straight. She shapes as if she will stay 6f. (op 4-1)
Press Release has already been beaten in a nursery and though he fared a bit better here in a first-time visor, looking a bit less quirky, he's starting to look exposed. Sellers or claimers will be more his level. (op 4-1 tchd 3-1)
Jamaica Grande is clearly only modest but isn't bred to shine at 5f and was noted making some modest late headway. Longer trips will see him in a better light. (op 12-1)
Triple Agent(IRE) had run his best race when fourth in a 6f seller last time and left the impression that he found the drop back to 5f against him, struggling to hold his place from an early stage. (tchd 5-1)
Battenberg had little realistic chance from 8lb out of the handicap and was beaten turning for home. (op 25-1tchd 33-1 in places)

3785 BET WORLD CUP FOOTBALL - BETDAQ MAIDEN AUCTION STKS 6f (P)
3:00 (3:00) (Class 6) 2-Y-O **£2,047** (£604; £302) **Stalls** Low

Form RPR

1 **Cochabamba (IRE)** 2-8-7 0.. JackMitchell 11 80+
(R A Teal) *sn midfield: pushed along 1/2-way: prog 2f out: rdn to ld jst over 1f out: edgd rt but drew rt away* **12/1**

03 **2** *4* **Nothing To Hide (IRE)**[16] 3269 2-8-9 0.......................... JamesDoyle 4 70
(D J S Ffrench Davis) *pressed ldr: upsides 2f out: drifted rt over 1f out: readily outpcd ins fnl f: kpt on* **5/1**[2]

02 **3** *1/2* **Midnight Feast**[14] 3332 2-8-12 0... LukeMorris 12 72
(P Winkworth) *trckd ldrs and racd wd: prog to go 3rd jst over 2f out: drvn over 1f out: styd on but wl outpcd* **1/1**[1]

4 *3 3/4* **Catalyze** 2-8-9 0...(t) LiamKeniry 6 57+
(A M Balding) *trckd ldrs gng wl: pushed along on inner 2f out: reminder jst over 1f out: wl outpcd after but kpt on steadily* **8/1**[3]

6 **5** *3/4* **Red Zeus (IRE)**[16] 3269 2-8-8 0.. RyanPowell(7) 1 61
(J S Moore) *dwlt: hld up in last quartet: c wd bnd 2f out: str reminder and veered lft over 1f out: styd on: nrst fin* **12/1**

6 **6** *3/4* **Avalon Bay**[28] 2867 2-8-9 0... MartinLane(3) 5 56
(Pat Eddery) *led: drvn and styd on inner in st: hdd & wknd jst over 1f out* **17/2**

06 **7** *1 1/2* **Valeo Si Vales (IRE)**[13] 3349 2-8-10 0....................... SophieDoyle(5) 3 54
(J A Osborne) *hld up towards rr: nudged along fr 2f out: nvr nr ldrs: do bttr* **10/1**

0 **8** *1/2* **Back For Tea (IRE)**[11] 3459 2-8-7 0.......................... RossAtkinson(5) 7 50
(Tom Dascombe) *chsd ldng pair to jst over 2f out: wknd* **33/1**

9 *6* **Ignore The Advice (IRE)** 2-8-9 0................................. PatCosgrave 10 29
(J S Moore) *pushed along in midfield after 2f: a struggling to stay in tch: no ch fnl 2f* **25/1**

0 **10** *9* **Mariyah**[15] 3295 2-8-4 0.. WilliamCarson(3) 9 —
(M Blanshard) *a wl in rr: shkn up over 3f out: sn btn: t.o* **66/1**

11 *nk* **Jelyvator** 2-8-9 0.. StevieDonohoe 8 1
(Ms E L McWilliam) *dwlt: outpcd in last: a struggling: t.o* **100/1**

05 **12** *3/4* **Bankroller**[20] 3112 2-8-9 0... SaleemGolam 2 —
(J G Portman) *chsd ldng pair to 1/2-way: wknd rapidly: t.o* **40/1**

1m 12.74s (0.84) **Going Correction** +0.175s/f (Slow) **12** Ran SP% **124.5**
Speed ratings (Par 92): **101,95,95,90,89 88,86,85,77,65 64,63**
toteswingers: 1&2 £2.20, 1&3 £13.40, 2&3 £4.40 CSF £72.69 TOTE £20.40: £4.60, £1.40, £1.50; EX 119.50 Trifecta £157.70 Part won. Pool: £213.19 - 0.62 winning units..
Owner The Rat Racers **Bred** Shortgrove Manor Stud **Trained** Ashtead, Surrey

FOCUS
A fair maiden auction in which the field were well bunched to the home turn, so the winning margin reflects plenty of credit on the winner. The third and the time set the level.

NOTEBOOK
Cochabamba(IRE) has something of a mixed pedigree, being by Hurricane Run (whose first winner she is) out of a mare that has already produced a dual 2yo 5f winner, but she didn't look short of speed in making quite a taking debut and was nowhere more impressive than in the last furlong when waltzing away. Her yard don't get many first-time-out winners, so she could prove quite useful, and 7f will not be a problem. (op 10-1)
Nothing To Hide(IRE) ran well while continuing to shape as though he will be suited by a step up to 7f. He'll be better off in nurseries than maidens from now on. (op 9-2)
Midnight Feast was a disappointment but didn't look ideally suited by the track, hanging right on the final bend and never really threatening to pick up. His Salisbury run shows he's better than this, but it also suggests he might find life tough in nurseries if the handicapper assesses him literally through the winner. (op 6-4)
Catalyze, by a brother to Giant's Causeway, shaped quite well on his debut tried tongue tied, looking threatening on the turn but then seeming to just need the run. He'll be suited by a step up to 7f in time. (op 10-1 tchd 11-1)
Red Zeus(IRE) ◆, who was quickly on the back foot after missing the start, wasn't helped by being taken back on the home turn. He finished well and appeals as an interesting type for nurseries along the line.
Avalon Bay broke smartly and showed plenty of pace before fading noticeably inside the last, again shaping as though he might be worth dropping to 5f. (op 7-1 tchd 10-1)
Valeo Si Vales(IRE) seemed unsuited by the drop in trip and never threatened. Nurseries will soon be a more appealing option. (op 12-1)

3786 HAMMERWOOD MEDIAN AUCTION MAIDEN STKS 6f (P)
3:30 (3:31) (Class 6) 3-4-Y-O **£2,047** (£604; £302) **Stalls** Low

Form RPR

-330 **1** **Lutine Bell**[29] 2834 3-9-3 70..(b[1]) StevieDonohoe 5 72
(Sir Mark Prescott) *slowest away: pushed along and prog arnd field to ld after 2f: clr 1/2-way: hrd rdn over 1f out: all out but nvr gng to be ct* **7/2**[2]

2 **2** *1* **Valencha**[48] 2249 3-8-12 0... NeilCallan 3 64
(H Morrison) *pushed along in 5th bef 1/2-way and struggling to keep up: sn outpcd: styd on fr over 1f out: wnt 2nd last strides* **7/4**[1]

-450 **3** *hd* **Yarra River**[43] 2416 3-9-3 70... LiamKeniry 4 68
(A M Balding) *chsd ldr 2f: rdn to chse clr wnr 2f out: grad clsd ins fnl f but lost 2nd last strides* **9/2**[3]

0400 **4** *2 3/4* **Silvee**[14] 3336 3-8-12 55... NeilChalmers 2 54
(J J Bridger) *pushed along in 6th bef 1/2-way: sn outpcd and no ch: kpt on fr over 1f out* **20/1**

3000 **5** *1 3/4* **Esteem Lord**[14] 3323 4-9-6 50.....................................(b) MartinLane(3) 8 55
(Jamie Poulton) *led 2f: chsd wnr to 2f out: wknd* **25/1**

222 **6** *7* **Pippbrook Ministar**[127] 759 3-8-12 72................................ PatCosgrave 9 26
(J R Boyle) *cl up: outpcd fr 1/2-way: wknd over 1f out: t.o* **5/1**

55 **7** *1* **Mush Mir (IRE)**[61] 1878 3-9-3 0... JackMitchell 1 28
(J R Boyle) *wl bhd by 1/2-way: t.o* **14/1**

00 **8** *4* **Lilli Palmer (IRE)**[25] 2968 3-8-12 0.................................. PaulFitzsimons 7 10
(Miss J R Tooth) *wl bhd by 1/2-way: t.o* **50/1**

05 **9** *4 1/2* **Sparkys Gift (IRE)**[132] 692 3-9-3 0... IanMongan 6 1
(P M Phelan) *wl bhd by 1/2-way: t.o* **66/1**

1m 12.78s (0.88) **Going Correction** +0.175s/f (Slow)
WFA 3 from 4yo 6lb **9** Ran SP% **112.2**
Speed ratings (Par 101): **101,99,99,95,93 84,82,77,71**
toteswingers:1&2 £2.90, 2&3 £2.60, 1&3 £2.50 CSF £9.35 TOTE £4.70: £1.80, £1.10, £1.90; EX 11.70 Trifecta £22.30 Pool: £333.17 - 11.03 winning units..

Owner Tom Wilson/Nicholas Jones **Bred** Coln Valley Stud **Trained** Newmarket, Suffolk

FOCUS

A maiden lacking strength in depth. It was steadily run, with the winner allowed to pinch it, and the form promises to be unreliable. The winner sets the standard.

Lilli Palmer(IRE) Official explanation: jockey said filly was unsuited by the kickback

3787 BLACKBERRY LANE (S) STKS — 1m 2f

4:05 (4:05) (Class 6) 3-Y-0+ — **£2,047** (£604; £302) **Stalls** Low

Form — RPR

060/ **1** — **Domino Dancer (IRE)**[21] 4749 6-9-6 83 ....(b) IanMongan 4 — 75
(Jim Best) *mde all: rdn and drew clr fr 2f out: wl in command after* **9/4**[2]

2006 **2** *4 1/2* **Royal Etiquette (IRE)**[18] 3213 3-8-9 69 .... LiamKeniry 3 — 66
(H J L Dunlop) *t.k.h: trckd ldng trio: rdn over 2f out: styd on to take 2nd 1f out: no imp on wnr* **12/1**

1-00 **3** *1 1/2* **Just Like Silk (USA)**[7] 3566 4-9-6 85 ....(p) NickyMackay 9 — 63
(G A Butler) *hld up in 5th: drvn wl over 2f out: kpt on fr 2f out to take 3rd ent fnl f: n.d* **11/8**[1]

1045 **4** *3 1/4* **Golden Prospect**[45] 2360 6-9-12 60 .... PaulFitzsimons 1 — 63
(Miss J R Tooth) *chsd wnr: rdn and no imp over 2f out: wknd and lost 2nd 1f out* **20/1**

1523 **5** *nk* **Atacama Sunrise**[19] 3179 4-9-0 58 .... CharlotteKerton(7) 2 — 57
(G Prodromou) *settled in 6th: shkn up over 2f out: plugged on but n.d* **14/1**

0054 **6** *1 1/2* **Outofoil (IRE)**[20] 3130 4-9-6 65 ....(b) JackMitchell 7 — 53
(R M Beckett) *trckd ldng pair: hrd rdn and fnd nil over 2f out: wknd* **4/1**[3]

0600 **7** *1 3/4* **Escardo (GER)**[21] 2788 7-9-6 48 ....(b) DavidNolan 8 — 49
(D G Bridgwater) *mostly in last: struggling u.p over 2f out: no prog* **100/1**

00 **8** *15* **Snow White Feet (IRE)**[26] 2921 3-8-4 0 .... LukeMorris 5 — 14
(H J L Dunlop) *a in last pair: pushed along 1/2-way: wknd over 3f out: t.o* **50/1**

2m 9.07s (-1.43) **Going Correction** -0.25s/f (Firm)
WFA 3 from 4yo+ 11lb — 8 Ran SP% **114.9**
Speed ratings (Par 101): **95,91,90,87,87 86,84,72**
toteswingers:1&2 £6.90, 2&3 £4.30, 1&3 £1.90 CSF £28.30 TOTE £3.20: £1.10, £2.20, £1.50; EX 36.10 Trifecta £80.30 Pool: £511.17 - 4.71 winning units..The winner was bought in for 5,200gns.
Owner Derek Westley & Colin Pullen **Bred** D And Mrs D Veitch **Trained** Lewes, E Sussex

FOCUS

A seller not without interest, despite the widely differing abilities on show. The winner dictated and did not need to get close to his old form.

Royal Etiquette(IRE) Official explanation: jockey said gelding slipped on bend
Escardo(GER) Official explanation: jockey said gelding slipped on the bend
Snow White Feet(IRE) Official explanation: jockey said filly slipped on bend

3788 BET ASIAN H'CAPS - BETDAQ HANDICAP — 1m 1f

4:40 (4:41) (Class 6) (0-60,60) 3-Y-0 — **£2,047** (£604; £302) **Stalls** Low

Form — RPR

04-0 **1** — **Explorator (IRE)**[61] 1872 3-9-3 59 .... TonyCulhane 2 — 70+
(George Baker) *settled in last trio: urged along and looked in trble 5f out: gd prog on inner over 2f out: led over 1f out: sn clr: pushed out* **11/8**[1]

600 **2** *2 1/2* **Amends (USA)**[42] 2441 3-8-13 60 .... KierenFox(5) 6 — 63
(J R Best) *settled in last trio: rdn and prog fr 3f out: squeezed through 2f out: tk 2nd ent fnl f: kpt on but no ch w wnr* **15/2**[3]

0-03 **3** *3/4* **Regal Rave (USA)**[10] 3478 3-8-13 55 .... SteveDrowne 10 — 56
(J R Best) *settled in midfield: rdn over 2f out: prog to chal over 1f out: kpt on same pce* **8/1**

0043 **4** *1/2* **Miss Whippy**[29] 2838 3-8-11 53 .... J-PGuillambert 9 — 53
(P Howling) *mde most w much tail swishing: hdd and nt qckn over 1f out* **11/1**

-000 **5** *5* **Brave Ghurka**[25] 2962 3-8-10 52 .... RichardMullen 7 — 41
(S Kirk) *in tch towards rr: rdn on outer and nt qckn over 2f out: sn outpcd: plugged on past wkng rivals ins fnl f* **33/1**

-150 **6** *2* **Cool Kitten (IRE)**[24] 3002 3-8-13 55 ....(v[1]) NeilCallan 11 — 40
(W J Knight) *wl in tch: rdn over 2f out: wknd quite qckly over 1f out* **7/1**[2]

040- **7** *1/2* **Ermyntrude**[213] 7654 3-8-5 52 .... JemmaMarshall(5) 14 — 36
(P M Phelan) *racd wd: wl in tch: rdn fr 3f out: no prog 2f out: sn wknd qckly* **33/1**

000 **8** *3* **Ayam Zainah**[33] 2718 3-9-1 57 .... PaulEddery 13 — 40
(M R Channon) *mostly chsd ldr to wl over 1f out: wknd rapidly and eased* **25/1**

0000 **9** *1 1/4* **Paphos**[8] 3525 3-8-3 48 ....(v[1]) WilliamCarson(3) 3 — 22
(S C Williams) *pressed ldng pair: rdn over 2f out: wknd rapidly over 1f out* **33/1**

0-60 **10** *1/2* **Lily Rio (IRE)**[27] 2901 3-9-3 59 ....(b[1]) GeorgeBaker 12 — 32
(W R Muir) *cl up: rdn wl over 2f out: wknd rapidly over 1f out* **25/1**

4052 **11** *1 3/4* **Flyinflyout**[16] 3263 3-8-11 56 ....(p) RobertLButler(3) 8 — 25
(Miss Sheena West) *hld up bhd ldrs: in tch whn nt clr run bnd over 3f out: no prog 2f out: wknd rapidly sn after* **8/1**

0-00 **12** *14* **Southern Breeze**[152] 421 3-8-13 55 .... LiamKeniry 5 — —
(S Kirk) *sltly hmpd after 2f and dropped to rr: no prog 3f out: sn bhd and eased: t.o* **50/1**

600 **13** *hd* **Appledore (IRE)**[86] 1268 3-8-9 51 ....(p) StevieDonohoe 1 — —
(A G Newcombe) *a in last trio: wknd 4f out: t.o* **33/1**

4503 **U** — **Little Meadow (IRE)**[46] 2336 3-8-0 47 .... AmyBaker(5) 4 — —
(Miss J Feilden) *cl up whn sddle slipped and uns rdr after 2f* **16/1**

1m 55.89s (-0.71) **Going Correction** -0.25s/f (Firm) — 14 Ran SP% **124.2**
Speed ratings (Par 98): **93,90,90,89,85 83,83,80,79,78 77,64,64,—**
toteswingers:1&2 £5.20, 2&3 £8.60, 1&3 £5.60 CSF £11.22 CT £69.67 TOTE £2.70: £1.50, £1.70, £2.10; EX 18.30 Trifecta £112.90.
Owner Kismet Partnership **Bred** Joseph Stewart Investments **Trained** Moreton Morrell, Warwicks

FOCUS

A very modest handicap dominated by two unexposed sorts. The fourth looks the best guide. The pace was only fair and that makes the winner's performance all the more impressive.

Flyinflyout Official explanation: jockey said filly suffered interference on final bend

3789 BETDAQ THE BETTING EXCHANGE FILLIES' H'CAP — 1m 3f 106y

5:15 (5:16) (Class 5) (0-70,73) 3-Y-0+ — **£2,388** (£705; £352) **Stalls** High

Form — RPR

4611 **1** — **Goldtrek (USA)**[8] 3522 3-9-6 73 6ex .... SteveDrowne 1 — 83+
(R Charlton) *trckd ldr: led gng easily 3f out: pushed along and wl in command 2f out: one reminder over 1f out: comf* **8/11**[1]

4-23 **2** *1 3/4* **Astral Flower**[33] 2704 3-9-1 68 .... RichardMullen 3 — 74
(Sir Michael Stoute) *hld up in 4th: sltly awkward downhill 4f out: rdn to dispute 2nd over 2f out: nvr able to threaten wnr* **4/1**[3]

031 **3** *1/2* **Welsh Anthem**[14] 3314 4-10-0 69 ....(p) GeorgeBaker 5 — 74
(W R Muir) *hld up in last: prog to dispute 2nd over 2f out: sn rdn: no real threat to wnr* **7/2**[2]

4302 **4** *1* **Rosy Dawn**[15] 3290 5-8-10 51 oh6 .... NeilChalmers 2 — 54
(J J Bridger) *mde most to 3f out: sn wknd* **25/1**

2332 **5** *2* **Buona Sarah (IRE)**[12] 3404 3-8-11 64 .... PatCosgrave 7 — 64
(J R Boyle) *trckd ldng pair: wknd wl over 2f out* **12/1**

2m 28.53s (-2.97) **Going Correction** -0.25s/f (Firm)
WFA 3 from 4yo+ 12lb — 5 Ran SP% **111.7**
Speed ratings (Par 100): **100,98,98,97,96**
toteswinger: 1&2 £6.00. CSF £4.13 TOTE £2.40: £3.10, £1.60; EX 3.30 Place 6: £2.57, Place 5: £1.96..
Owner AXOM (XVII) **Bred** Kenneth Lejeune & Charles Simon **Trained** Beckhampton, Wilts

FOCUS

A fair handicap. The pace was decent considering the small field and the result looks the right one. The winner continues on the upgrade and the third sets the standard.

T/Plt: £7.50 to a £1 stake. Pool:£41,809.53 - 4,036.71 winning tickets. T/Qpdt: £4.20 to a £1 stake. Pool:£3,074.69 - 540.77 winning tickets. JN

3452 NEWMARKET (July Course) (R-H)

Wednesday, July 7

OFFICIAL GOING: Good to firm (8.0)

Far side of July course utilised on ground not used since August 2009. An Arab race was run between the last two thoroughbred races on the card.

Wind: Light, across Weather: Warm, overcast

3790 CHAMPAGNE LANSON E B F FILLIES' H'CAP — 7f

1:30 (1:30) (Class 2) (0-100,94) 3-Y-0

£24,924 (£7,464; £3,732; £1,868; £932; £468) **Stalls** High

Form — RPR

-010 **1** — **Folly Bridge**[39] 2545 3-9-2 87 .... SteveDrowne 1 — 94
(R Charlton) *hld up in tch in midfield: hdwy on far rail over 2f out: drvn to chal ins fnl f: r.o wl to ld fnl 50yds* **17/2**

-212 **2** *nk* **Strictly Dancing (IRE)**[21] 3085 3-9-2 87 .... JimmyFortune 3 — 93
(A M Balding) *led and set stdy gallop: rdn and qcknd ent fnl 2f: hdd over 1f out: carried rt after but led again ins fnl f tl hdd and no ex fnl 50yds* **8/1**[3]

1-04 **3** *1/2* **Alice Alleyne (IRE)**[13] 3373 3-8-8 79 ow3 .... RyanMoore 2 — 83
(Sir Michael Stoute) *t.k.h: cl up: wnt 2nd ent fnl 2f: rdn to ld over 1f out: kpt edging rt u.p: hdd ins fnl f: styd on same pce fnl 100yds* **9/1**

-154 **4** *1/2* **Sweet Clementine (IRE)**[18] 3217 3-8-9 80 .... WilliamBuick 8 — 86+
(W J Knight) *t.k.h: hld up in tch towards rr: effrt and nt clr run wl over 1f out: swtchd rt and barged rival over 1f out: rdn and swtchd rt again 1f out: r.o wl fnl 150yds: gng on fin: nvr able to chal ldrs* **12/1**

4316 **5** *3/4* **Fly Silca Fly (IRE)**[21] 3088 3-8-11 82 .... AlanMunro 12 — 83
(M R Channon) *t.k.h: hld up in tch towards rr: hdwy and chsng ldrs 3f out: rdn and kpt on same pce fr over 1f out* **33/1**

60-2 **6** *3/4* **Dylanesque**[34] 2682 3-8-9 80 .... PhilipRobinson 13 — 79
(M A Jarvis) *t.k.h: chsd ldrs: wnt 2nd 4f out tl 2f out: styd on same pce u.p ins fnl f* **10/1**

1-10 **7** *1/2* **Miss Zooter (IRE)**[21] 3071 3-9-3 88 .... JimCrowley 4 — 86+
(R M Beckett) *s.i.s: hld up in last pair: pushed along and nt clr run wl over 1f out tl jst ins fnl f: r.o fnl 100yds: gng on at fin but nvr able to chal* **5/1**[2]

1611 **8** *nse* **Maid In Heaven (IRE)**[13] 3361 3-9-7 92 .... ShaneKelly 6 — 89+
(W R Swinburn) *t.k.h: hld up in tch in midfield: rdn and effrt 2f out: no real hdwy: kpt on ins fnl f but nvr gng pce to threaten ldrs* **11/4**[1]

3-31 **9** *3/4* **Fleeting Echo**[19] 3158 3-9-2 87 .... PatDobbs 5 — 82
(R Hannon) *plld hrd: hld up wl in tch in midfield: rdn and unable qck wl over 1f out: no imp fr over 1f out* **14/1**

06-0 **10** *1/2* **Don't Tell Mary (IRE)**[44] 2404 3-9-0 85 .... RichardKingscote 7 — 79
(Tom Dascombe) *stdd s: hld up in tch towards rr: rdn and unable qck wl over 1f out: n.d* **25/1**

1 **11** *3 1/4* **Chica Whopa (IRE)**[29] 2842 3-8-12 83 .... RichardHughes 9 — 68
(R Hannon) *t.k.h: rdn and unable qck ent fnl 2f: wknd ent fnl f* **11/1**

4315 **12** *1 1/4* **Yer Woman (IRE)**[54] 2090 3-9-6 94 .... PatrickHills(3) 10 — 76
(R Hannon) *stdd s: hld up in last pair: rdn and no prog wl over 1f out: n.d* **66/1**

0-00 **13** *4* **Seeking Dubai**[26] 2929 3-9-0 85 .... KierenFallon 11 — 72
(E F Vaughan) *t.k.h: chsd ldrs: rdn and effrt over 2f out: keeping on same pce whn pushed bdly rt over 1f out: nt rcvr and wl btn after* **33/1**

1m 25.43s (-0.27) **Going Correction** 0.0s/f (Good) — 13 Ran SP% **118.0**
Speed ratings (Par 103): **101,100,100,99,98 97,97,97,96,95 92,90,86**
toteswingers: 1&2 £20.80, 1&3 £17.50, 2&3 £13.80 CSF £71.73 CT £461.48 TOTE £11.20: £3.70, £2.80, £3.00; EX 103.00 Trifecta £464.50 Pool: £1,450.01 - 2.31 winning units..
Owner D J Deer **Bred** The National Stud Never Say Die Club Ltd **Trained** Beckhampton, Wilts
■ Stewards' Enquiry : William Buick three-day ban: careless riding (Jul 21-23)

FOCUS

The racing took place on the far-side track, which had not been used since the previous August, and the GoingStick readings suggested the ground was riding fairly even across its width. A good 3-y-o fillies' handicap in which the best recent winners were the Stoute-trained pair, Peeress and Heaven Sent. This year's running did not look that strong, with the majority stepping up in grade and few obvious improvers. The fifth sets the standard, with minor improvement from the first three. The field raced close to the far-side rail early on before drifting more towards the centre of the track in the closing stages and the first three, who were always close to the pace, came from the three lowest stalls.

NOTEBOOK

Folly Bridge, a dual winner at 6f on a sound surface, was racing off 7lb higher than her last winning mark and was back up in trip. However, she represented a yard in terrific form and, never far away, she came through to challenge and proved strongest on the climb to the line. Connections believe she will get a mile and they will look for a Listed handicap for her. (op 11-1 tchd 12-1)

Strictly Dancing(IRE), a 6f winner on fast turf who appeared to stay this trip on her only previous try, made the running and battled back after being headed over a furlong out, only to be unable to hold the winner's challenge late on. This was a creditable effort and she can pick up a similar contest before long.

Alice Alleyne(IRE), a 7f winner on Polytrack but well behind Miss Zooter on her only run over the trip on turf, had a bit to find, especially with Moore putting up 3lb overweight. However, she ran really well, having been in the firing line throughout. She took a slight advantage over a furlong out but the runner-up got back past her inside the last. This was a step up on her previous form this year. (op 8-1)

Sweet Clementine(IRE) ◆, a 1m winner on Polytrack on her seasonal debut, had been racing at that trip since. She was held up early but had trouble getting a run over a furlong out and her rider had to force her through, doing Seeking Dubai no favours and earning himself a three-day ban in the process. She finished well widest of all and proved she is as effective over this trip as further. (op 16-1)

Fly Silca Fly(IRE), a three-time winner at up to 6f, had finished well beaten on her previous tries at the trip and was 4lb above her last winning mark. She was keen under restraint in the early stages but, after being ridden to challenge 2f out, could only keep on at the one pace in the last furlong.

Dylanesque, a 6f winner on fast ground at two, had since been beaten in three handicaps at this trip, although she ran better on her seasonal debut last time. She raced close to the pace early but saw plenty of daylight on the outside of the pack and faded late on. (op 9-1)

Miss Zooter(IRE) was up 7lb for her last success but down in class, having been out of her depth in Listed handicap at Ascot when she raced from 5lb out of the handicap. She compromised her chance here with a tardy start and, although running on, never got close enough to pose a threat. Official explanation: jockey said filly was denied a clear run (op 11-2)

Maid In Heaven(IRE), came into this having won three of her four starts on turf, the last two over 7f. Although 9lb higher than for her last success and up in grade, she was sent off favourite. She was hampered slightly in the early stages but made ground to race on the heels of the leaders over 2f from home, only to find less than expected when asked. (op 10-3 tchd 7-2 in places)

Chica Whopa(IRE), a 7f maiden winner on good ground on her first start for the yard, was making her handicap debut and was up in grade. However, she was far too keen early on and faded out of things up the hill. (op 10-1)

3791 TOTESPORT.COM STKS (HERITAGE H'CAP) 6f

2:00 (2:00) (Class 2) (0-105,104) 3-Y-O

£62,310 (£18,660; £9,330; £4,670; £2,330; £1,170) **Stalls** High

Form RPR

-210 **1** **Fireback**[20] 3103 3-8-1 **84** DavidProbert 10 95
(A M Balding) *chsd ldrs: rdn and effrt ent fnl 2f: chsd ldr over 1f out: led ins fnl f: hld on wl u.p fnl 100yds* **12/1**

2-20 **2** ¾ **Bagamoyo**[39] 2545 3-8-13 **96** EddieAhern 4 105
(J R Fanshawe) *stdd s: hld up in tch in midfield: hdwy ent fnl 2f: drvn to chal ins fnl f: kpt on: a hld fnl 100yds* **12/1**

2251 **3** ½ **Gene Autry (USA)**[16] 3270 3-8-9 **92** JimmyFortune 6 99
(R Hannon) *dwlt: hld up in midfield: rdn and effrt ent fnl 2f: hdwy u.p and swtchd rt ent fnl f: r.o wl to go 3rd nr fin: nvr quite gng pce to rch ldng pair* **10/1**[3]

4005 **4** *nk* **Take Ten**[14] 3311 3-8-2 **85** JoeFanning 13 91
(M Johnston) *chsd ldrs tl led 2f out: sn rdn: drvn and hdd ins fnl f: styd on same pce fnl 100yds* **22/1**

6526 **5** *2* **Iver Bridge Lad**[11] 3461 3-9-7 **104** (b) AlanMunro 18 104
(J Ryan) *dwlt: bhd: rdn and hdwy ent fnl 2f: barging match w rival and pushed rt fr over 1f out tl jst ins fnl f: styd on u.p fnl 100yds: nvr able to chal* **20/1**

0141 **6** ½ **Russian Rock (IRE)**[18] 3218 3-8-4 **92** JohnFahy[(5)] 15 90
(R A Teal) *chsd ldrs: rdn and unable qck ent fnl 2f: kpt on u.p but no threat to ldrs fr over 1f out* **20/1**

3111 **7** ¾ **Kellys Eye (IRE)**[21] 3088 3-8-13 **96** RobertWinston 9 92
(D H Brown) *in tch in midfield: rdn 3f out: edging lft and outpcd over 1f out: styd on same pce and no threat to ldrs ins fnl f* **10/1**[3]

-321 **8** ½ **Deacon Blues**[28] 2877 3-8-7 **90** JamieSpencer 5 84+
(J R Fanshawe) *stdd s: hld up wl off the pce towards rr: stl plenty to do but gng wl 2f out: hdwy: nt clr run and trying to force way out fr over 1f out tl jst ins fnl f: kpt on but no ch w ldrs* **15/2**[1]

23F0 **9** 1¾ **Mister Hughie (IRE)**[11] 3445 3-9-2 **99** RyanMoore 12 87
(M R Channon) *dwlt: sn pushed along and struggling to go pce: sme hdwy u.p whn n.m.r over 1f out: nvr trbld ldrs* **16/1**

-204 **10** *hd* **Pastoral Player**[25] 2978 3-8-13 **96** SteveDrowne 7 84+
(H Morrison) *rrd and lost many l s: detached in last tl styd on past btn horses fr over 1f out: n.d* **10/1**[3]

0220 **11** *hd* **Excellent Guest**[20] 3103 3-8-0 **83** JimmyQuinn 1 70
(G G Margarson) *hld up in midfield on far side: effrt u.p 2f out: no prog and wl hld fnl f* **12/1**

2-61 **12** 3¼ **Robinson Cruso**[40] 2517 3-8-3 **86** ow1 (p) MartinDwyer 14 63
(M A Jarvis) *w ldrs tl led over 3f out tl 2f out: wknd u.p over 1f out: wl btn ins fnl f* **16/1**

60-3 **13** ½ **Skylla**[12] 3406 3-8-9 **92** TonyHamilton 11 67
(R A Fahey) *led tl over 3f out: wkng u.p whn hmpd over 1f out: wl btn ins fnl f* **25/1**

3041 **14** *nk* **Below Zero (IRE)**[11] 3429 3-8-13 **96** AdrianNicholls 8 70
(M Johnston) *chsd ldrs: struggling u.p over 2f out: wknd and wl btn over 1f out* **18/1**

-011 **15** 1½ **Kingsgate Choice (IRE)**[30] 2822 3-8-7 **90** KierenFallon 16 59
(J R Best) *sn bustled along and off the pce towards rr: hdwy and in tch 3f out: wknd u.p wl over 1f out* **8/1**[2]

-310 **16** *1* **Cockney Class (USA)**[11] 3461 3-8-7 **90** LiamJones 2 56
(B J Meehan) *a struggling to go pce on far side: rdn and btn 1/2-way* **28/1**

2055 **17** *shd* **Jarrow (IRE)**[6] 3578 3-8-6 **89** RichardHills 20 55
(M Johnston) *s.i.s: a wl off the pce in rr and sn rdn along: n.d* **40/1**

5610 **18** 1¼ **Swilly Ferry (USA)**[25] 2978 3-9-6 **103** MichaelHills 17 65
(B W Hills) *a off the pce towards rr and sn niggled along: hung lft u.p and wl btn 2f out* **20/1**

5-10 **19** ¾ **Palisades Park**[24] 2997 3-8-5 **88** WilliamBuick 3 47
(R Hannon) *hld up off the pce in midfield: clsd and rdn 2f out: sn hung lft and btn ins fnl f* **50/1**

2043 **20** 2½ **Singeur (IRE)**[25] 2978 3-9-3 **100** FrankieDettori 19 51
(R Bastiman) *nvr gng pce and sn rdn along in rr: nvr on terms* **12/1**

1m 10.81s (-1.69) **Going Correction** 0.0s/f (Good) **20** Ran SP% **128.3**
Speed ratings (Par 106): **111,110,109,108,106 105,104,103,101,101 101,96,96,95,93 92,92,90,89,86**
toteswingers: 1&2 £26.30, 1&3 £22.60, 2&3 £24.90 CSF £135.59 CT £1525.75 TOTE £11.20: £3.20, £2.80, £2.50, £5.20; EX 153.20 Trifecta £831.60 Pool: £1,638.87 - 1.45 winning units..
Owner Kennet Valley Thoroughbreds VII **Bred** M Pennell **Trained** Kingsclere, Hants
■ Stewards' Enquiry : Eddie Ahern one-day ban: used whip in incorrect place (Jul 21)

FOCUS

A red-hot 3-y-o handicap which has been won by some smart sprinters in recent times, including Tax Free in 2005 and the subsequent Prix de l'Abbaye winner Total Gallery last year. Despite the field size, they stayed together as one group in an arrowhead formation up the centre of the track. The early pace was relentless. The form reads sound enough and the winner rates a 10lb personal best.

NOTEBOOK

Fireback was down to this trip for the first time since his racecourse debut, after having led the stands' side group for 5f before fading into ninth in the Britannia last time. Always close to the pace, he came off the bridle 2f out but, with stamina on his side, he responded to pressure up the hill to hit the front inside the final furlong. His trainer still considers him to be unfurnished and believes he will really come into his own as a sprint handicapper next year, not that this prize was to be sniffed at. (op 18-1)

Bagamoyo, over 5l behind Swilly Ferry on the Rowley Mile last time, put in a strong challenge from over 1f out, but could never quite get there. Not for the first time he gives the impression that he may be worth a try at 7f. (op 16-1)

Gene Autry(USA), raised 10lb for his Windsor cakewalk last month, finished strongly up the hill and seemed to cope better with these undulations than he did on the Rowley Mile in May. On this evidence he isn't handicapped out of things just yet. (op 11-1 tchd 12-1)

Take Ten ◆, yet to fire so far this season despite a slipping mark, came right back to form here. Having stalked the pace early, he moved smoothly to the front over 2f from home, but couldn't get clear and, despite battling on gamely, was run out of it inside the final furlong. He looks very capable of winning off this sort of mark. (op 25-1)

Iver Bridge Lad, back against his own age-group and in front of four of these when runner-up in the Reg Griffin Memorial Trophy at York two starts ago, ran a blinder under top weight and, after getting bumped over 1f from home, he stayed on strongly up the stands' rail in the closing stages. The problem is that he is on a stiff mark now and this effort won't give the handicapper much reason to drop him. (op 16-1)

Russian Rock(IRE), up 4lb for his narrow success here last month, came off the bridle over 2f from home and stayed on up the hill. This was another decent effort at the trip, but all three of his successes have come over the minimum.

Kellys Eye(IRE), up another 9lb in his bid for a four-timer following three successes at Ripon, ran creditably enough having come under pressure over 2f from home, but he might be held off this mark now, and he also may not want the ground quite as quick as this. (op 9-1)

Deacon Blues ◆, raised 9lb after his easy win over his elders at Yarmouth last time, can be considered to have run better than his final position as he was looking for room passing the 2f pole and then ran into traffic problems. He is worth another chance. Official explanation: jockey said colt was denied a clear ru (op 13-2 tchd 6-1)

Mister Hughie(IRE) showed little sparkle when a well-beaten last of seven in a Newcastle Group 3 last time, but although this was better, he is still to prove that his previous Beverley tumble hasn't left its mark. (op 20-1)

Pastoral Player has been known to start slowly, but he gave away a good 6l this time and was soon detached. In a race of this competitiveness that was always going to be fatal, so under the circumstances he did incredibly well to run on into the middle of the field. He is much better than this, but his tardiness at the stalls will remain a concern. Official explanation: jockey said gelding reared as stalls opened

Excellent Guest, a non-stayer in the Britannia last time but 3lb better off for a length beating by Swilly Ferry over this trip on the Rowley Mile the time before, made a short-lived effort towards the far side of the track passing the 2f pole, but it came to little. (op 16-1)

Kingsgate Choice(IRE), 9lb higher in his bid for a hat-trick after two wins at 5f, has won over this trip on Polytrack, but he never looked happy at any stage and faded right out of it from over a furlong out. Official explanation: jockey said colt lost its action (op 9-1)

Swilly Ferry(USA) was very disappointing at York last time, but his previous success on the Rowley Mile off 7lb lower when ahead of seven of today's rivals has been well boosted since. However, his supporters soon knew their fate and he looks one just to watch for the time being.

3792 IRISH THOROUGHBRED MARKETING CHERRY HINTON STKS (GROUP 2) (FILLIES) 6f

2:35 (2:35) (Class 1) 2-Y-O

£39,739 (£15,064; £7,539; £3,759; £1,883; £945) **Stalls** High

Form RPR

11 **1** **Memory (IRE)**[19] 3141 2-8-12 0 RichardHughes 4 111+
(R Hannon) *wnt rt and stdd after s: in tch towards rr: pushed along 2f out: nt clr run wl over 1f out tl swtchd rt ins fnl f: qcknd wl to ld to fnl 50yds: in command at fin* **5/4**[1]

1 **2** ¾ **Soraaya (IRE)**[28] 2855 2-8-12 0 RyanMoore 7 105
(M R Channon) *hmpd and pushed rt s: sn rcvrd and in tch: rdn and unable qck ent fnl 2f: rallied u.p ins fnl f: r.o wl to go 2nd towards fin* **10/1**

10 **3** ½ **Hooray**[19] 3141 2-8-12 0 SebSanders 3 104
(Sir Mark Prescott) *stdd s: t.k.h and hld up in tch in last: rdn and gd hdwy on far rail over 1f out: led ins fnl f: edgd rt u.p and hdd fnl 50yds: no ex* **9/2**[2]

14 **4** 1½ **Radharcnafarraige (IRE)**[19] 3141 2-8-12 0 KJManning 6 99
(J S Bolger, Ire) *t.k.h: chsd ldng pair: rdn and effrt wl over 1f out: drvn to ld ent fnl f: hdd ins fnl f: carried rt and outpcd fnl 100yds* **5/1**[3]

12 **5** ½ **Lily Again**[15] 3307 2-8-12 0 JamieSpencer 1 98
(P F I Cole) *in tch: effrt and n.m.r over 1f out tl ins fnl f swtchd rt fnl 150yds: kpt on: nvr able to chal* **25/1**

414 **6** *1* **Serena's Pride**[21] 3070 2-8-12 0 KierenFallon 2 95
(A P Jarvis) *led for 1f: pressed ldr after: ev ch and drvn over 1f out: unable qck and btn whn n.m.r ins fnl f* **22/1**

1 **7** ½ **Tanfeer**[12] 3392 2-8-12 0 FrankieDettori 5 93
(Saeed Bin Suroor) *swvd rt s: rcvrd and led after 1f tl rdn and hdd ent fnl f: edgd rt and wknd fnl 150yds* **5/1**[3]

1m 12.44s (-0.06) **Going Correction** 0.0s/f (Good) **7** Ran SP% **113.2**
Speed ratings (Par 103): **100,99,98,96,95 94,93**
toteswingers: 1&2 £4.00, 1&3 £2.30, 2&3 £6.70 CSF £14.94 TOTE £2.60: £1.80, £3.50; EX 10.50.
Owner Highclere Thoroughbred Racing-Masquerade **Bred** Swordlestown Stud **Trained** East Everleigh, Wilts

FOCUS

This Group 2 juvenile fillies' contest has produced variable subsequent results for its winner in recent times. The best filly to win it this century was the subsequent dual 1000 Guineas winner Attraction, while Donna Blini went on to take the Cheveley Park. This year's line-up offered plenty of interest, with three unbeaten fillies competing. The field raced towards the far side, the pace was steady until halfway, and the time was 1.63secs slower than the preceding 3-y-o handicap. The form is far from special for the grade but Memory was impressive and can definitely rate higher. The fourth is the best guide to the race.

NOTEBOOK

Memory(IRE) ◆ was an uneasy favourite beforehand but broke much better this time, unlike on her previous starts. However, she was stuck behind a wall of horses over 1f out and had a lot to do in a short time, but her rider switched to the outside and she picked up so well he could sit still in the last few strides. She is clearly a top-class filly and her change of gear is a potent weapon. She will go next for the Moyglare Stud Stakes over an extra furlong and her pedigree suggests she should stay a mile. She was quoted at between 5/1 and 10/1 for next year's 1000 Guineas after this performance. (op 4-5 tchd 11-8 in places)

Soraaya(IRE), a sturdily built 55,000gns yearling and a half-sister to two winning juveniles, including Declaration of War, made a winning debut over 6f at Hamilton and coped well with this step up in grade. She came to challenge entering the final furlong but the winner blitzed her for speed. She looks capable of winning a Group race though, and can do so if avoiding today's winner. The Lowther Stakes is her target. (op 12-1 tchd 9-1)

Hooray, a half-sister to Hypnotic, a useful triple 7f-1m winner at two, won a Polytrack maiden on her debut but finished well behind Memory at Ascot from a bad draw. She was keen early but got a good run up the rail to lead entering the last furlong and, although she drifted right under pressure, hung on under vigorous riding to secure some valuable black type. (op 7-1)

Radharcnafarraige(IRE), a Group 3 winner at Naas over 6f, had been well held by Memory in the Albany Stakes. She came to have every chance, much as she did at Ascot, but could only keep on at the one pace and was beaten about the same distance by the winner as last time. (op 15-2)

Lily Again, a half-sister to the quite useful dual 7f winner Pravda Street, had won on her debut over 6f on Polytrack but was narrowly beaten in a conditions stakes at Chantilly next time. Taking a step up in grade, she lead early before being settled then, like the winner, did not get much room over a furlong out before staying on late. She has a bit more scope than some of these and another furlong might be in her favour now. (op 33-1)

Serena's Pride had won a 6f Lingfield maiden on her second start before finishing a good fourth in Queen Mary. She was keen under restraint early and then picked up the pace from halfway but could not respond when the challenges arrived. A drop to Listed level might be in her favour. (op 25-1 tchd 20-1)

Tanfeer, a well-bred daughter of Dansili from the family of Almutawakel, had made a winning debut over 6f at Doncaster at the end of last month beating more experienced rivals. She made the running after a furlong and tried to pick up the pace with the sixth, but she had nothing more to offer on the climb to the line and her rider was not hard on her once her chance had gone. She can win again at a lower level. (op 6-1)

3793 ETIHAD AIRWAYS FALMOUTH STKS (GROUP 1) (F&M) 1m

3:10 (3:11) (Class 1) 3-Y-O+

£105,024 (£39,812; £19,924; £9,934; £4,976; £2,497) **Stalls** High

Form RPR

1634 **1** **Music Show (IRE)**[19] 3143 3-8-10 110 RichardHughes 1 119+
(M R Channon) *stdd s: hld up in last pair: clsd gng wl 2f out: nt clr run and swtchd rt 1f out: rdn and r.o wl to ld ins fnl f: gng away at fin* **13/2**

3-32 **2** *2* **Spacious**[21] 3067 5-9-5 113 KierenFallon 6 116
(J R Fanshawe) *ponied to s: w ldr tl led and qcknd gallop over 5f out: edgd lft ent fnl 3f: rdn 2f out: battled on gamely u.p tl hdd and nt gng pce of wnr ins fnl f* **9/1**

121 **3** *¾* **Rainfall (IRE)**[21] 3066 3-8-10 111 FrankieDettori 2 112
(M Johnston) *stdd after s: hld up in last trio: outpcd 5f out: pushed along and hdwy 3f out: chsd ldr u.p ent fnl f: nt gng pce of wnr fnl 75yds* **15/2**

4-11 **4** *1* **Strawberrydaiquiri**[21] 3067 4-9-5 114 RyanMoore 5 114+
(Sir Michael Stoute) *led tl over 5f out: sltly hmpd and rdn ent fnl 3f: lost 2nd 2f out: styd on to press ldrs 1f out: keeping on gamely but one pce whn nt clr run and swtchd rt ins fnl f* **6/1**[3]

0-51 **5** *1 ¾* **Lillie Langtry (IRE)**[19] 3143 3-8-10 118 JMurtagh 4 106
(A P O'Brien, Ire) *chsd ldrs: rdn to chse ldr 2f out tl ent fnl f: wknd fnl 150yds* **9/4**[1]

-302 **6** *7* **Gile Na Greine (IRE)**[19] 3143 3-8-10 115 KJManning 8 90
(J S Bolger, Ire) *ponied to s: in tch in midfield: outpcd 5f out: rdn 1/2-way: sme hdwy over 2f out: wknd qckly over 1f out* **16/1**

-322 **7** *8* **Special Duty**[52] 2158 3-8-10 117 TomQueally 7 71
(Mme C Head-Maarek, France) *plld hrd: chsd ldrs: outpcd 1/2-way: rdn and effrt over 2f out: wknd qckly and wl btn over 1f out: eased ins fnl f* **3/1**[2]

-660 **8** *21* **Lahaleeb (IRE)**[52] 2154 4-9-5 114 WilliamBuick 3 25
(G A Butler) *ponied to s: a bhd: rdn and lost tch over 2f out: t.o fr over 1f out* **33/1**

1m 36.76s (-3.24) **Going Correction** 0.0s/f (Good)
WFA 3 from 4yo+ 9lb 8 Ran SP% **114.0**
Speed ratings (Par 117): **116,114,113,112,110 103,95,74**
toteswingers: 1&2 £8.10, 1&3 £6.10, 2&3 £7.80 CSF £62.04 TOTE £9.90: £2.20, £3.00, £2.40; EX 62.60 Trifecta £1647.80 Pool: £9,241.43 - 4.15 winning units..
Owner Jaber Abdullah **Bred** Darley **Trained** West Ilsley, Berks

FOCUS

Seven of the eight fillies in this year's renewal had been successful at Group level (Gile Na Greine being the exception, though she had twice been placed in Group 1 company), whilst three of those had previously been successful at the highest level (Lahaleeb won a Grade 1 in Canada). The score was 5-5 between the 3-y-os and the older fillies over the previous ten years. They seemed to go a decent pace with Strawberrydaiquiri setting the early fractions before Spacious was sent on at halfway. Music Show is entitled to rate the leading 3yo miling filly so far, but the form is not rated as positively as it might have been.

NOTEBOOK

Music Show(IRE) had appeared to just be found wanting in three previous tries at this level - in both the English and Irish 1,000 Guineas and Coronation Stakes - but more accurately she hadn't enjoyed much in the way of luck. Everything went smoothly for her here, however, as she travelled beautifully well off the early pace and was still on the bridle when reaching the heels of the leaders passing the 2f pole. She had to be switched out wide by Hughes in order to get a clear run, but she quickened up smartly once there and hit the front around half a furlong from home. She richly deserved this first success at the top level and her trainer would like to keep her to the Group 1 races confined to fillies and mares over this trip until the end of the season, with races like the Prix Rothschild (where she may meet Goldikova) mentioned as possible targets. He would also like to keep her in training next year and then step her up to 1m2f to contest races like the Nassau. (op 8-1)

Spacious, beaten a length when third behind Goldikova in this race last year and just edged out by Strawberrydaiquiri in the Windsor Forest last time, was given every possible chance to win this. Always handy, she was sent to the front by Fallon at halfway and edged across to bag the inside rail. She kept battling hard and held most of her rivals at bay, but the winner's turn of foot proved too much for her inside the last furlong. She will now be aimed at the Matron Stakes and has made the frame five times from seven attempts at Group 1 level, but she keeps finding success at this grade just beyond her. (op 10-1)

Rainfall(IRE), by far the least exposed in the field, was taking a big step up in class on this first try at 1m following her game success in the Jersey Stakes. Held up early, she made her move entering the last 2f and tried hard to get to the front up the hill, but she couldn't quite go through with it. Stamina didn't appear to be an issue, though she may be better suited by an easier mile, and as she still has scope for further improvement, she shouldn't have too much trouble winning a Group 2 contest at the very least. (op 8-1 tchd 9-1)

Strawberrydaiquiri, winner of six of her last seven starts but only fourth in last season's Sun Chariot in her only previous try at this level, set the early pace but was already being niggled when the runner-up headed her and then hung across her passing the 3f pole. She stayed in contention for a long time after that, but lacked the pace to put in another challenge and she shapes as though she may benefit from a return to further. (op 5-1 tchd 13-2)

Lillie Langtry(IRE), who proved herself a genuine Group 1 filly when winning the Coronation Stakes, needs a strong pace to run at and she certainly got that, but having moved into a challenging position entering the last 2f she faded disappointingly up the hill. Her rider reported that she had run flat. Official explanation: jockey said filly ran flat (tchd 2-1)

Gile Na Greine(IRE), a close third behind Special Duty in the 1,000 Guineas and runner-up to Lillie Langtry in the Coronation Stakes, came off the bridle over 3f from home and gradually dropped right away. Despite her fine effort at Ascot, she may prefer an easier surface. Official explanation: jockey said filly never travelled (tchd 20-1)

Special Duty was awarded both the English and French 1,000 Guineas' in the stewards' room, so she was trying to pass the post in front for the first time since winning the Cheveley Park last October. However, the filly looked a pale shadow of herself here, and having taken a keen hold just behind the leaders early, she folded very tamely under pressure coming to the last 2f. She had reportedly been working well before the race, but her trainer wasn't happy with the way she was walking afterwards, although she was reported fine the following day. The jury is now out on her and it will be interesting to see where she reappears next, if at all. Official explanation: trainer had no explanation for the poor form shown (op 7-2)

Lahaleeb(IRE), a high-class filly for Mick Channon in her first two seasons, has been on her travels of late with her last eight runs having been in six different countries. Making her debut for Gerard Butler and back down in trip, she came under pressure in last place at halfway and soon lost touch with her rivals.

3794 EUROPEAN BREEDERS' FUND MAIDEN STKS 7f

3:45 (3:47) (Class 2) 2-Y-O **£9,714** (£2,890; £1,444; £721) **Stalls** High

Form RPR

1 **Native Khan (FR)** 2-9-3 0 KierenFallon 12 93+
(E A L Dunlop) *travelled strly: wl in tch: pushed along and effrt to ld over 1f out: rdn and styd on strly ins fnl f: drew wl clr fnl 100yds: readily* **14/1**

5 **2** *3 ¼* **Baransky**[11] 3452 2-9-3 0 AhmedAjtebi 6 85
(Mahmood Al Zarooni) *hld up in tch in midfield: hdwy on far side 2f out: rdn to chal and edgd rt over 1f out: chsd wnr but wl outpcd ins fnl f* **12/1**

2 **3** *1* **Bowermaster (USA)**[11] 3452 2-9-3 0 FrankieDettori 8 82
(Mahmood Al Zarooni) *led and set stdy gallop: rdn and qcknd wl over 1f out: hdd over 1f out: lost 2nd 1f out: plugged on same pce and no ch w wnr after* **11/4**[1]

4 *½* **El Muqbil (IRE)** 2-9-3 0 RichardHills 10 83+
(B J Meehan) *in tch in midfield tl shuffled bk towards rr 1/2-way: hdwy and rdn over 1f out: kpt on steadily ins fnl f: nvr gng pce to trble wnr* **7/1**[3]

5 *2 ½* **Major Art** 2-9-3 0 RyanMoore 7 75
(R Hannon) *stdd s: t.k.h: hld up wl in tch: rdn and edgd rt wl over 1f out: sn outpcd and edgd lft ent fnl f: n.d but kpt on ins fnl f* **16/1**

6 *nk* **Yair Hill (IRE)** 2-9-3 0 TedDurcan 11 74+
(J L Dunlop) *stdd s: t.k.h: hld up in tch towards rr: pushed along and hdwy 2f out: edgd lft and plugged on steadily fnl f: nvr trbld ldrs* **6/1**[2]

7 *1* **Bloodsweatandtears** 2-9-3 0 JimCrowley 9 73+
(W J Knight) *t.k.h: hld up and rn green towards rr: rdn: hmpd and lost pl over 1f out: no ch w ldrs but kpt on ins fnl f* **8/1**

8 *¾* **Flodden (USA)** 2-9-3 0 JamieSpencer 13 69+
(P F I Cole) *s.i.s: rn green and sn pushed along detached last: styd on past btn horses ins fnl f: nvr trbld ldrs* **40/1**

9 *1 ¼* **Pisco Sour (USA)** 2-9-3 0 JMurtagh 4 66
(H Morrison) *dwlt: sn in tch in midfield: rdn and no hdwy 3f out: no ch w ldrs fr wl over 1f out* **16/1**

10 *shd* **Enabling (IRE)** 2-9-3 0 RichardHughes 2 66
(R Hannon) *in tch in midfield: rdn and effrt ent fnl 2f: edgd lft and wl btn over 1f out* **8/1**

0 **11** *2* **Scottish Star**[14] 3326 2-9-3 0 SebSanders 1 61
(J M P Eustace) *a in rr: rdn and struggling 1/2-way: no ch fnl 2f* **25/1**

03 **12** *1 ½* **Volcanic Ash (USA)**[8] 3536 2-9-3 0 JoeFanning 3 57
(M Johnston) *chsd ldrs tl wknd qckly u.p over 1f out: fdd ins fnl f* **33/1**

13 *1 ¼* **Power Punch (IRE)** 2-9-3 0 RobertWinston 14 54
(B W Hills) *in tch in midfield: rdn and struggling 1/2-way: wl btn fnl 2f* **66/1**

14 *¾* **Sole Danser (IRE)** 2-9-3 0 MichaelHills 5 52
(B W Hills) *in tch: hdwy to chse ldrs and rdn over 2f out: wknd qckly wl over 1f out: wl bhd fr over 1f out* **12/1**

1m 25.81s (0.11) **Going Correction** 0.0s/f (Good) **14** Ran SP% **120.2**
Speed ratings (Par 100): **99,95,94,93,90 90,89,88,86,86 84,82,81,80**
toteswingers: 1&2 £40.90, 1&3 £12.90, 2&3 £8.10 CSF £167.49 TOTE £20.90: £5.70, £4.00, £1.50; EX 328.50 Trifecta £564.60 Part won. Pool: £763.03 - 0.10 winning units..
Owner V I Araci **Bred** Aliette Forien And Gilles Forien **Trained** Newmarket, Suffolk

FOCUS

A valuable maiden that has produced some high-class performers in recent seasons. Dubai Destination took this in 2001 before going on to win at the highest level, while the last three winners, Rio De La Plata, Soul City, and Elusive Pimpernel either won or were placed in Group 1s. Very few of the runners in this year's renewal had previous racecourse experience, but the pace was a reasonable one, the field ended up racing in the centre of the track, and the time was just 0.38secs slower than the 3-y-o fillies in the opener. The winner impressed and the form has been positively rated, around the third, the time and the race averages.

NOTEBOOK

Native Khan(FR) ◆, whose price increased from 70,000euros as a yearling to 180,000gns at the breeze-ups, is from a speedy French family. He knew his job on this debut, and was always close up before proving too strong for the Godolphin pair in the final furlong, powering clear. Connections have nothing specific in mind, except that the colt will be given a light campaign this season in order that he has time to develop. (op 16-1)

Baransky, 4l behind Bowermaster here on his debut over C&D, is a half-brother to juvenile winners at this trip. Despite still carrying condition, he improved past his stable companion with that run under his belt, coming from off the pace to challenge and sticking on up the hill. He should be able to win a similar race if going on again from this. (tchd 14-1)

Bowermaster(USA), a $100,000 half-brother to some fair winners, had run well in a C&D maiden at the end of last month, when today's runner-up was behind. He was ridden positively, but proved one paced once headed as they met the rising ground, and did not really seem to have built on that debut effort. (op 10-3)

El Muqbil(IRE) ◆, a 450,000gns half-brother to last season's high-class juvenile Arcano and with other speedy juveniles in family, put up a promising effort on this racecourse debut, despite looking in need of the experience. He was doing his best work late and should come on a lot for the outing. (op 13-2)

Major Art ◆'s price rose from 35,000gns as a yearling to 98,000gns at the breeze-ups. A half-brother to the stayer Ermyn Lodge, he was green in the parade ring but showed up well early on this debut before losing his place, then running on again when meeting the rising ground. His sire was a sprinter, so there are mixed messages regarding what his ideal trip will be, but he looks sure to benefit from the run. (op 14-1)

Yair Hill(IRE) ◆, a brother to the useful Jedburgh and half-brother to winners at longer trips, was held up early before staying on quite well in the closing stages, despite carrying his head awkwardly. He is another who can be expected to do better next time. (op 7-1 tchd 15-2)

Bloodsweatandtears, a £16,000 yearling from a speedy family, was backed on the exchanges in the morning prior to this debut, so had clearly shown ability at home. However, he was green beforehand and ran pretty green in the race, missing the break and then getting hampered prior to staying on up the hill. (op 9-1)

Flodden(USA), a $170,000 yearling from a good US family, was another to miss the break and looked like finishing at the rear before getting the idea late on. He should benefit considerably for the experience. (op 50-1)

Pisco Sour(USA), a 100,000gns second foal from a good US family, was another to miss a beat at the start. He soon made up the ground to race just behind the leaders, but was being niggled along and gradually lost his place from the halfway point.

Enabling(IRE), an 80,000euros yearling related to winners at 5f-1m from the family of Golden Opinion and Optimistic Lass, was the choice of the stable jockey. He ended up racing on the outside of his field and wandered towards the far rail, away from the rest, on meeting the rising ground. (op 7-1)

Sole Danser(IRE), a powerfully built 60,000euros half-brother to a middle-distance winner, was quite keen early and showed up well until around the 2f pole. He got very tired from that point and dropped away to finish last, but showed enough to suggest he can do better in time. (tchd 14-1)

3795 THREE CHIMNEYS MAIDEN STKS 1m 2f
4:20 (4:21) (Class 3) 3-Y-O £9,714 (£2,890; £1,444; £721) Stalls Centre

Form				RPR
0	1		**Cotton Mill**[40] 2507 3-9-3 0 ... JoeFanning 2 *(W Jarvis) s.i.s: hld up wl bhd: pushed along and clsd 2f out: rdn to chal ins fnl f: led fnl 75yds: r.o wl* 66/1	92+
2	2	1/2	**Nationalism**[19] 3173 3-9-3 0 ... WilliamBuick 3 *(J H M Gosden) hld up wl off the pce in midfield: hdwy 4f out: rdn and clsd on ldr wl over 1f out: drvn to ld ins fnl f: hdd and unable qck fnl 75yds* 7/2[2]	91+
-223	3	5	**Sing Sweetly**[12] 3388 3-8-12 82 ... HayleyTurner 12 *(G A Butler) racd keenly: led: clr after 1f: wl clr fr 8f out: rdn 2f out: hdd ins fnl f: wknd fnl 100yds* 5/1[3]	76
-302	4	3/4	**Mata Keranjang (USA)**[40] 2507 3-9-3 104 ...(t) JamieSpencer 9 *(P F I Cole) handy in main gp: rdn to chse clr ldr over 2f out: clsd and ch over 1f out: sn edgd lft u.p and btn 1f out* 15/8[1]	80
	5	nk	**Short Break** 3-8-12 0 ... TomQueally 4 *(H R A Cecil) hld up wl off the pce towards rr: effrt on outer and hung lft 3f out: no real prog tl kpt on steadily ins fnl f: nvr trbld ldrs* 12/1	74+
0	6	1 1/4	**Sheklaan (USA)**[19] 3173 3-9-3 0 ... RichardHills 10 *(M A Jarvis) led chsng gp tl over 2f out: sn rdn: styng on same pce whn n.m.r over 1f out: btn whn nt clr run and swtchd lft ins fnl f: eased towards fin* 8/1	76+
	7	4 1/2	**Sea Change (IRE)** 3-9-3 0 ... RyanMoore 5 *(J Noseda) s.i.s: wl bhd: hdwy into midfield of main gp 7f out: rdn and no prog over 3f out: nvr on terms* 14/1	67
53-0	8	2	**Ultravox (USA)**[83] 1335 3-9-3 82 ... MartinDwyer 1 *(B J Meehan) handy in main gp tl struggling u.p over 3f out: wl btn fnl 2f* 33/1	63
032	9	3	**Norse Dame**[27] 2891 3-8-12 72 ... JimmyFortune 7 *(D R C Elsworth) stdd s: hld up wl off the pce towards rr: hdwy into midfield of main gp 1/2-way: rdn and btn over 3f out: wl btn fnl 2f* 22/1	52
5	10	2 3/4	**Kitty Wells**[27] 2891 3-8-12 0 ... KierenFallon 8 *(L M Cumani) chsd ldrs in main gp tl wknd u.p wl over 3f out: wl bhd fnl 2f* 14/1	47
	11	8	**Tranquil Waters (IRE)** 3-9-3 0 ... MichaelHills 6 *(B W Hills) s.i.s and short of room s: a towards rr of main gp: rdn and toiling over 4f out: wl bhd fnl 3f* 50/1	36
0	12	10	**Weeza (IRE)**[16] 3272 3-8-12 0 ... IvaMilickova 11 *(J Ryan) a wl bhd: rdn and lost tch 5f out: t.o fnl 2f* 200/1	11

2m 5.86s (0.36) **Going Correction** 0.0s/f (Good) 12 Ran SP% 117.0
Speed ratings (Par 104): **98,97,93,93,92 91,88,86,84,81 75,67**
toteswingers:1&2 £35.80, 2&3 £4.70, 1&3 £39.80 CSF £280.73 TOTE £125.20: £17.70, £2.20, £1.70; EX 473.10 TRIFECTA Not won..
Owner Ali Saeed **Bred** W And R Barnett Ltd **Trained** Newmarket, Suffolk

FOCUS
Some well-bred 3-y-os lined up for this maiden and the pace was strong thanks to the free-running Sing Sweetly, but this proved a complete boil-over for punters. The front pair pulled well clear. The form could be rated higher but the favourite disappointed again and it is doubtful if the third matched her previous form.

NOTEBOOK
Cotton Mill had disappointed when finishing well behind Mata Keranjang on his debut on the Rowley Mile in May, but this a half-brother to eight winners, including the top-class Pure Grain, is bred to be better than that and he proved it here. Ridden with plenty of patience, he made his progress gradually down the centre of the track and sustained his effort by getting up just a few yards from the line. Still considered a 'big baby' by connections, he should stay further and may improve for a bit of cut in the ground, but whatever he does this term they consider that he will be a better horse next year. (op 100-1)
Nationalism, a half-brother to several winners, including the high-class Sleeping Indian, was beaten a nose on his debut over C&D last month and found one too good again. He was keen enough early, but was ridden to the front in plenty of time and pulled clear of the others, but the winner just outstayed him. A maiden like this should be a formality. (op 11-4 tchd 4-1 in places)
Sing Sweetly, placed four times from five starts in maiden/handicap company, took a keen grip early and went off at a rate of knots. She soon held a healthy advantage which she maintained to the last 2f, but her stride began to shorten up the hill and she was cut down inside the last furlong. Currently rated 82, she has already run well over further than this and can win a race if ridden with a little more restraint. (op 6-1 tchd 9-2)
Mata Keranjang(USA), officially rated 104 and already placed six times in Group/Listed company, including in an Italian Group 1 at two, again found one too good when dropped into maiden company on the Rowley Mile last time. He was always in a good position and had every chance when the leader started to falter, but didn't find a great deal under pressure. This trip again looked beyond him, but he is rapidly running out of excuses and doesn't appeal as a betting proposition. (op 9-4 tchd 5-2 in places)
Short Break ◆ ran green when asked to take closer order coming to the last 3f and hung out into the centre of the track, but she did stay on in pleasing fashion over the last furlong or so. From the family of high-class performers Polish Summer, Meteor Storm, Sunshack and Raintrap, she should have learnt plenty from this. (op 16-1)
Sheklaan(USA), the first foal of Oaks winner Eswarah, was too green when a long way behind Nationalism on his debut over C&D last month and it was a similar story here. He showed an awkward head-carriage when put under pressure coming to the last 3f, and having met a bit of trouble was then inclined to hang all over the place. He looks to still need more time. (tchd 9-1)
Sea Change(IRE), a 290,000gns half-brother to six winners, was by no means knocked about and may be capable of better.

3796 FRESSSH BATHROOMS H'CAP 1m
5:30 (5:37) (Class 3) (0-90,90) 3-Y-O+ £9,714 (£2,890; £1,444; £721) Stalls High

Form				RPR
2121	1		**Suited And Booted (IRE)**[18] 3215 3-9-6 90 ... RichardHughes 6 *(R Hannon) hld up towards rr: pushed along and hdwy ent fnl 2f: gng wl and nt clr run over 1f out tl ent fnl f: rdn to chse ldr ins fnl f: r.o wl to ld towards fin* 9/1[3]	100+
-621	2	shd	**Venutius**[18] 3208 3-9-3 87 ... GrahamGibbons 16 *(E S McMahon) hld up towards rr: rdn and gd hdwy ent fnl 2f: led over 1f out: drvn ent fnl f: hdd towards fin: kpt on* 11/1	95
2523	3	3/4	**Follow The Flag (IRE)**[6] 3585 6-9-10 85 ...(p) JamesDoyle 10 *(A J McCabe) hld up towards rr: swtchd lft and rdn wl over 2f out: hdwy u.p to chse ldrs and hrd drvn ent fnl f: kpt on same pce fnl 100yds* 22/1	93
2142	4	2	**Secretive**[12] 3408 3-9-2 86 ...(b) FrankieDettori 8 *(M Johnston) in tch: effrt u.p to press ldrs over 2f out: styd pressing ldrs tl no ex and btn fnl 75yds* 9/2[2]	87
5610	5	1 1/4	**Satwa Laird**[19] 3172 4-9-11 86 ... RyanMoore 15 *(E A L Dunlop) hld up bhd: rdn and swtchd rt wl over 1f out: styd on fnl f: nvr gng pce to rch ldrs* 25/1	87
3332	6	1	**Sweet Child O'Mine**[40] 2515 3-8-9 79 ... FrannyNorton 11 *(R C Guest) in tch: rdn and effrt to press ldrs over 2f out: wknd u.p jst ins fnl f* 12/1	75
4314	7	3/4	**Cape Rock**[21] 3083 5-9-11 86 ... JimCrowley 14 *(W J Knight) chsd ldr: rdn over 2f out: ev ch 2f out tl wknd u.p jst over 1f out* 20/1	83
-322	8	nk	**Directorship**[34] 2683 4-9-7 82 ... KierenFallon 7 *(P R Chamings) stdd s: hld up in rr: hdwy 1/2-way: rdn to chse ldrs on far side over 2f out: drvn and unable qck over 1f out: wknd jst ins fnl f* 12/1	78
31	9	3 1/2	**Space War**[18] 3220 3-9-2 86 ... WilliamBuick 19 *(J H M Gosden) racd in stands' side pair tl converged w main gp 1/2-way: in tch in midfield: rdn and effrt over 2f out: edgd lft and wknd jst over 1f out* 11/1	72+
-006	10	4	**Majuro (IRE)**[19] 3172 6-10-0 89 ... AlanMunro 17 *(C F Wall) a towards rr: rdn and no real prog 3f out: nvr trbld ldrs* 16/1	68
5-1	11	2 1/4	**Thabit (USA)**[18] 3207 4-9-12 87 ... RichardHills 4 *(M A Jarvis) in tch: hdwy to ld wl over 2f out: rdn ent fnl 2f: hdd over 1f out: sn wknd* 3/1[1]	60
5203	12	3 3/4	**Thunderball**[12] 3396 4-9-5 80 ...(b) Jean-BaptisteHamel 1 *(J A Glover) racd alone on far side tl 1/2-way: overall ldr tl wl over 2f out: wknd 2f out: wl bhd fnl f* 20/1	45
10-3	13	2	**Gold Express**[21] 3083 7-9-7 82 ... TedDurcan 18 *(P J O'Gorman) stdd s: hld up in rr: nvr a factor* 25/1	42
0030	14	4	**Fastnet Storm (IRE)**[20] 3121 4-10-0 89 ... MickyFenton 20 *(T P Tate) racd in stands' side pair tl converged w main gp 1/2-way: chsd ldrs tl rdn over 2f out: wknd qckly ent fnl 2f* 25/1	40
-000	15	11	**Captain Macarry (IRE)**[25] 2971 5-9-6 81 ...(v) JoeFanning 3 *(J J Quinn) chsd ldrs tl rdn and lost pl 3f out: t.o fnl f* 50/1	7

1m 38.44s (-1.56) **Going Correction** 0.0s/f (Good)
WFA 3 from 4yo+ 9lb 15 Ran SP% 118.5
Speed ratings (Par 107): **107,106,106,104,102 101,101,100,97,93 91,87,85,81,70**
toteswingers: 1&2 £12.50, 1&3 £40.40, 2&3 £41.50. CSF £91.27 CT £2158.67 TOTE £6.70: £2.20, £3.30, £5.90; EX 101.40 Trifecta £1177.20 Part won. Pool: £1,590.92 - 0.30 winning units. Place 6: £537.23, Place 5: £162.15..
Owner R Morecombe and D Anderson **Bred** Carpet Lady Partnership **Trained** East Everleigh, Wilts
■ Hurricane Hymnbook (16/1) was withdrawn (burst out of stalls). Rule 4 does not apply.

FOCUS
A decent and competitive 1m handicap that was dominated by older, battle-hardened horses in the early years of the century, but was won by 3-y-os twice in the previous four years and their record was improved this time. The big field was reduced with four non-runners, but there was a false start when Hurricane Hymnbook burst the stalls and was withdrawn, reducing the field to 15. The field raced right across the track in the early stages, but converged soon after halfway and the principals raced more towards the far side. The time was 1.65secs slower than the feature race. Solid form, with the progressive winner a bit better than the bare figure.

NOTEBOOK
Suited And Booted(IRE) ◆, a 1m winner on easy ground and 7f winner on fast at this track, had been raised 6lb for that, but he defied it under a patient ride from Hughes, who continues in great form. Held up off the pace, he got a good lead into the race from the fourth and found enough under pressure to collar the runner-up near the line. He is clearly on the upgrade and looks one to keep on-side. (op 8-1)
Venutius, a dual winner at 1m on Polytrack and fast turf, had beaten a subsequent winner last time, but was raised 10lb as a result. He ran a terrific race, never being far away and going on over 1f out. He ran on bravely but was just caught by another progressive sort. He looks capable of gaining compensation if the Handicapper does not put him up again. (op 10-1)
Follow The Flag(IRE) is a consistent performer at 1m2f but effective at this trip. Although 3lb above his last winning mark, he ran his race again and looks the best guide to the level of the form. He also deserves to pick up a race before long. (tchd 25-1)
Secretive, with conditions to suit, was beaten by subsequent winner last time, but had been fourth in Britannia at Ascot previously. He made headway to challenge 2f out, but could not find any extra once taken on. He has had several hard races recently and might need a break. (op 7-1)
Satwa Laird, a 1m winner on fast ground but last of nine here last time, ran much better, staying on from well back, though without ever looking likely to threaten. (op 28-1)
Sweet Child O'Mine, placed in all three starts on turf at up to 1m2f and narrowly beaten over this trip on her last start, was 2lb higher here but ran creditably, although only able to keep on at the one pace in the last 2f. (op 14-1)
Cape Rock, both of whose wins have been at 7f, was 6lb higher than for his last success and this was his first run at 1m since October 2007. He made the running but gradually faded after being headed at around the 2f pole.
Directorship, a 1m winner on fast ground, has been running well this season, but has gone up the handicap as a result and on this evidence could do with some respite from the assessor. Official explanation: jockey said gelding was unsuited by the good to firm ground (op 14-1)
Space War, another lightly raced colt, was a C&D winner the previous month on his turf debut. Making his handicap debut, he raced behind one other away from the rest centre to near side, but never really got involved at the business end. (op 15-2 tchd 7-1)
Thabit(USA), a lightly raced 4-y-o, had been a winner over 1m on his sole start on turf. He was sent off favourite for this handicap debut but was a little keen early and faded before being eased once beaten. (op 7-2)
T/Jkpt: Not won. T/Plt: £1,237.40 to a £1 stake. Pool:£172,564.38 - 101.80 winning tickets. T/Qpdt: £44.80 to a £1 stake. Pool: £9,901.32 - 163.44 winning tickets. SP

3797 - 3803a (Foreign Racing) - See Raceform Interactive

3616 DONCASTER (L-H)
Thursday, July 8

OFFICIAL GOING: Good to firm (8.8)
Wind: Light against Weather: Cloudy and warm

3804 BETFAIR RACING EXCELLENCE APPRENTICE TRAINING SERIES H'CAP 2m 110y
6:35 (6:35) (Class 6) (0-65,64) 4-Y-O+ £2,729 (£806; £403) Stalls Low

Form				RPR
1131	1		**Tillietudlem (FR)**[9] 3535 4-9-12 64 6ex ... DebraEngland 5 *(J S Goldie) trckd ldrs: hdwy to chse ldr over 7f out: led wl over 4f out: jnd and pushed along over 1f out: styd on: cheekily* 4/6[1]	73+
00-6	2	1/2	**Haldibari (IRE)**[32] 1768 6-8-12 50 ... DaleSwift 3 *(S Lycett) chsd ldrs: pushed along 1/2-way: rdn along wl over 3f out: chal 2f out and sn ev ch: drvn ent fnl f: kpt on* 9/2[2]	54
6-05	3	4 1/2	**Ingenue**[30] 2218 4-8-7 52 ...(b) LauraSimpson(7) 2 *(P Howling) hld up towards rr: hdwy 1/2-way: trckd wnr 4f out: shkn up 3f out: rdn along over 2f out and sn one pce* 25/1[3]	51
40-0	4	8	**Piermarini**[14] 3352 5-8-12 50 ... LeeTopliss 6 *(P T Midgley) hld up in rr: hdwy over 7f out: trckd ldrs 4f out: effrt over 2f out: sn rdn and btn* 28/1	39

500/ **5** *30* **Lawaaheb (IRE)**53 3705 9-8-3 **46** LukeStrong(5) 4 —
(T D Walford) *chsd ldrs: rdn along 1/2-way: lost pl 6f out: bhd fnl 3f* **9/2**2

0-06 **6** *30* **Mujada**16 3282 5-8-4 **45** AdamCarter(3) 1 —
(M W Easterby) *led: rdn along 1/2-way: sn hdd: wknd 5f out: t.o fnl 3f* **66/1**

-006 **7** *30* **Riqaab (IRE)**4 3431 5-9-3 **62** (bt1) DavidSimmonson(7) 8 —
(M W Easterby) *t.k.h: chsd ldr to 1/2-way: wknd qckly and t.o fr over 4f out* **40/1**

3m 34.9s (-5.50) **Going Correction** -0.30s/f (Firm) 7 Ran SP% **107.6**
Speed ratings (Par 101): **100,99,97,93,79 65,51**
Tote Swingers: 1&2 £1.10, 1&3 £3.10, 2&3 £5.10 CSF £3.25 CT £25.54 TOTE £1.80: £1.20, £2.40; EX 4.90.
Owner Mr & Mrs C J Smith **Bred** Bernard Ducasse **Trained** Uplawmoor, E Renfrews

FOCUS
A very ordinary staying handicap, confined to apprentice riders. The bang in-form winner is value for a deal further. The form is rated around the runner-up.

3805 CROWNHOTEL-BAWTRY.COM MAIDEN STKS 6f
7:10 (7:12) (Class 5) 2-Y-O £2,590 (£770; £385; £192) **Stalls** High

Form RPR

1 **Georges Lane** 2-9-3 0 PaulHanagan 8 88+
(R A Fahey) *trckd ldng pair: hdwy 1/2-way: cl up 2f out: rdn over 1f out: led and edgd lft ins fnl f and rdr dropped reins: drvn: hung lft and kpt on wl towards fin* **11/4**2

5 **2** *3/4* **Cadeaux Pearl**34 2715 2-9-3 0 PatDobbs 3 86+
(R Hannon) *led: rdn along 2f out: drvn over 1f out: hdd and carried lft ins fnl f: hmpd and no ex nr fin* **6/5**1

3 *5* **Hammer Home (USA)** 2-9-3 0 JamieSpencer 2 71+
(B J Meehan) *trckd ldng pair: effrt 2f out: sn rdn and kpt on same pce fr over 1f out* **11/2**3

6 **4** *1* **Top Care (USA)**15 3316 2-9-3 0 JoeFanning 7 68
(M Johnston) *cl up: rdn along 2f out: sn drvn and wknd over 1f out* **7/1**

5 *1 1/2* **Hal Of A Lover** 2-9-3 0 TonyHamilton 1 63
(R A Fahey) *in tch: pushed along wl over 2f out: sn rdn and wknd* **28/1**

6 *1 3/4* **Bearheart (IRE)** 2-9-3 0 TomQueally 6 58
(E A L Dunlop) *dwlt: sn in tch: pushed along 1/2-way: rdn 2f out and sn outpcd* **14/1**

7 *30* **Be My Spy** 2-8-12 0 TomEaves 4 —
(P Salmon) *s.i.s: a outpcd and bhd fr 1/2-way* **66/1**

1m 12.01s (-1.59) **Going Correction** -0.30s/f (Firm) 7 Ran SP% **111.6**
Speed ratings (Par 94): **98,97,90,89,87 84,44**
Tote Swingers: 1&2 £1.02, 1&3 £2.30, 2&3 £3.60 CSF £6.08 TOTE £3.70: £1.50, £1.10; EX 8.50.
Owner David W Armstrong **Bred** David Jamison Bloodstock **Trained** Musley Bank, N Yorks
■ Stewards' Enquiry : Paul Hanagan one-day ban: careless riding (Jul 22)

FOCUS
This could work out to be a fair juvenile maiden and the first pair came nicely clear. The winner can rate considerably higher.

NOTEBOOK
Georges Lane, another scopey newcomer from his stable, made a winning debut despite showing real inexperience. He moved somewhat free to post and took time to settle through the early parts of the race. He moved up stylishly at the 2f pole, though, and looked set to go about his business. Once given a smack, however, he drifted left and caused Paul Hanagan to momentarily lose his reins. He then went even more markedly left when given another to get on top and drifted right over to the middle of the track, doing the battling Cadeaux Pearl no favours at all. If he had kept a straight line he would have probably run out a clearcut winner and this was surely down to greenness, so it's a good bet this speedily bred colt has a deal more to offer. (op 7-2)
Cadeaux Pearl ran very green on his debut at Goodwood, but was well backed here with his stable remaining in cracking form and raced a lot more professionally through the early parts. He gave his all under pressure and was obviously hampered by the winner hanging, but he was always just being held. It shouldn't be long before he gains compensation. (op 10-11tchd 5-4 in places)
Hammer Home(USA) cost $145,000 and has a Gimcrack entry. That would look unrealistic at this stage, but debutants from this stable very often improve plenty for their initial outings and he showed plenty of ability. (op 6-1 tchd 13-2)
Top Care(USA) showed early speed but got readily outpaced 2f out and will surely benefit for a stiffer test. (op 8-1 tchd 9-2)
Hal Of A Lover was very much the second string, but posted a fair debut effort over a trip plenty sharp enough.
Bearheart(IRE) is bred to enjoy longer trips and shaped very much as though this debut experience was needed. (op 20-1)

3806 EASTSIDE IS 21 FILLIES' H'CAP 1m (R)
7:45 (7:45) (Class 4) (0-85,82) 3-Y-O+ £4,094 (£1,209; £604) **Stalls** Low

Form RPR

6601 **1** **Admire The View (IRE)**12 3434 3-9-3 **80** TedDurcan 1 89+
(D R Lanigan) *hld up in tch: smooth hdwy 3f out: qcknd to ld wl over 1f out: edgd lft and clr ins fnl f: kpt on* **4/1**3

0042 **2** *1* **Seradim**12 3457 4-10-0 **82** JamieSpencer 6 91
(P F I Cole) *hld u[p in rr: swtchd outside and hdwy 2f out: sn rdn and str run to chse wnr ent fnl f: sn hung lft and no imp towards fin* **7/2**2

4403 **3** *2 3/4* **Gifted Apakay (USA)**20 3171 3-8-8 **71** JackMitchell 3 74+
(E A L Dunlop) *trckd ldng pair on inner: effrt and nt clr run 2f out: swtchd rt and rdn over 1f out: styd on ins fnl f: tk 3rd nr line* **7/1**

-064 **4** *hd* **Bahamian Music (IRE)**19 3208 3-8-12 **75** PaulHanagan 7 75
(R A Fahey) *t.k.h: chsd ldrs: hdwy 3f out: cl up over 2f out: sn rdn and ev ch tl drvn and one pce ent fnl f: lost 3rd nr line* **14/1**

-114 **5** *1* **Aegean Shadow**17 3262 4-9-11 **79** TomQueally 5 79
(H R A Cecil) *hld up in tch: hdwy on outer 3f out: rdn wl over 1f out: sn drvn and one pce appr fnl f* **2/1**1

0002 **6** *2 1/2* **Wiseman's Diamond (USA)**10 3503 5-8-11 **68** PaulPickard(3) 4 62
(P T Midgley) *chsd ldr: hdwy and cl up over 3f out: rdn along over 2f out: sn drvn and wknd over 1f out* **16/1**

00-3 **7** *3 1/4* **Solitary**18 3238 4-8-13 **67** SilvestreDeSousa 2 54
(G A Harker) *led: rdn along and jnd 3f out: drvn over 2f out: hdd wl over 1f out and sn wknd* **7/1**

1m 39.65s (-0.05) **Going Correction** -0.30s/f (Firm)
WFA 3 from 4yo+ 9lb 7 Ran SP% **113.1**
Speed ratings (Par 102): **88,87,84,84,83 80,77**
Tote Swingers: 1&2 £2.10, 1&3 £9.20, 2&3 £5.20 CSF £17.94 TOTE £6.50: £2.70, £2.70; EX 20.80.
Owner Saif Ali & Saeed H Altayer **Bred** Mountgrange Stud Ltd, T Stewart & A Stroud **Trained** Newmarket, Suffolk

FOCUS
A modest fillies' handicap. There was just an ordinary pace on early and that resulted in the field being fanned across the track around 2f out. The winner is rated back to her 2yo best.

Bahamian Music(IRE) Official explanation: jockey said gelding missed the break

3807 REGIONAL MAGAZINE COMPANY H'CAP 1m 4f
8:15 (8:15) (Class 4) (0-80,79) 3-Y-O+ £3,885 (£1,156; £577; £288) **Stalls** Low

Form RPR

3163 **1** **Patavium (IRE)**16 3283 7-9-6 **67** PaulHanagan 2 74
(E W Tuer) *sn led and set stdy pce: qcknd 4f out: rdn over 2f out: drvn over 1f out: styd on strly fnl f* **9/2**

5051 **2** *1 1/2* **Kames Park (IRE)**16 3282 8-10-0 **75** PaulEddery 6 80
(R C Guest) *hld up in rr: hdwy wl over 2f out: rdn wl over 1f out: styd on to chse wnr ins fnl f: no imp towards fin* **6/1**

-154 **3** *2 1/4* **Judiciary (IRE)**12 3450 3-9-5 **79** AhmedAjtebi 5 80
(Mahmood Al Zarooni) *t.k.h: trckd ldrs on inner: hdwy 3f out: effrt to chse wnr 2f out: sn rdn and one pce ent fnl f* **9/4**1

121 **4** *3/4* **Lauberhorn**10 3506 3-8-8 **73** 6ex JohnFahy(5) 4 73+
(Eve Johnson Houghton) *trckd ldrs: hdwy over 3f out: rdn along 2f out: drvn wl over 1f out and sn one pce* **11/4**2

30-6 **5** *3 1/2* **Buckie Boy (IRE)**19 3198 4-9-11 **72** TomQueally 1 66
(J S Goldie) *trckd wnr: effrt 3f out: rdn along over 2f out: sn drvn and wknd* **4/1**3

2m 34.47s (-0.43) **Going Correction** -0.30s/f (Firm)
WFA 3 from 4yo+ 13lb 5 Ran SP% **109.9**
Speed ratings (Par 105): **90,89,87,87,84**
CSF £28.82 TOTE £5.30: £3.10, £7.50; EX 25.20.
Owner J A Nixon **Bred** M Channon **Trained** Great Smeaton, N Yorks

FOCUS
This modest handicap didn't begin in earnest until 4f out due to the uneven pace on and the winner dictated. He rates a small personal best, but there are doubts over the form.

3808 RMC WINNER SANDRA DONNELLY MAIDEN STKS 6f
8:50 (8:51) (Class 5) 3-Y-O+ £2,729 (£806; £403) **Stalls** High

Form RPR

26 **1** **Qudwah (IRE)**62 1861 3-8-12 0 TadhgO'Shea 9 87+
(M A Jarvis) *cl up: smooth hdwy to ld wl over 1f out: qcknd clr appr fnl f: easily* **5/6**1

2 **2** *8* **Oh So Spicy**28 2903 3-8-12 0 JackMitchell 4 62+
(C F Wall) *chsd ldrs: rdn along and outpcd over 2f out: drvn wl over 1f out: kpt on to go 2nd ins fnl f: no ch w wnr* **3/1**2

2240 **3** *3* **Bilash**13 3393 3-9-3 68 JerryO'Dwyer 8 57
(R Hollinshead) *cl up: effrt over 2f out and ev ch tl rdn and hung lft wl over 1f out: sn one pce* **11/1**

502 **4** *3 1/4* **Bahamian Jazz (IRE)**22 3091 3-8-10 77 MatthewLawson(7) 6 47+
(R Bastiman) *rrd s: s.i.s and rdn along in rr: drvn and hdwy 1/2-way: nvr nr ldrs* **11/2**3

0-05 **5** *1 1/4* **Rio's Girl**40 2530 3-8-9 40 MichaelStainton(3) 3 38
(R M Whitaker) *led: rdn along over 2f out: drvn and hdd wl over 1f out and sn wknd* **66/1**

0624 **6** *1 1/2* **Clare Harrier (IRE)**10 3507 3-9-3 60 PatrickMathers 5 38
(A Berry) *towards rr: rdn along 1/2-way: nvr a factor* **40/1**

0 **7** *6* **Shamarlane**28 2903 3-8-12 0 StephenCraine 10 14
(M Wigham) *v.s.a: a bhd* **50/1**

0- **8** *6* **Sue And Sue**297 5934 3-8-12 0 TomEaves 7 —
(G Woodward) *chsd ldrs: rdn along 1/2-way: sn wknd* **100/1**

0 **9** *hd* **Tombellini (IRE)**21 3111 3-8-12 0 BillyCray(5) 2 —
(D Nicholls) *sn outpcd and a bhd* **33/1**

1m 11.1s (-2.50) **Going Correction** -0.30s/f (Firm) 9 Ran SP% **113.1**
Speed ratings (Par 103): **104,93,89,85,83 81,73,65,65**
Tote Swingers: 1&2 £2.10, 1&3 £3.80, 2&3 £1.10 CSF £3.24 TOTE £1.80: £1.10, £1.10, £4.00; EX 3.10.
Owner Hamdan Al Maktoum **Bred** Mrs S O'Riordan **Trained** Newmarket, Suffolk

FOCUS
An uncompetitive and modest maiden and an easy winner. The runner-up sets the level.
Bilash Official explanation: jockey said colt hung left throughout
Shamarlane Official explanation: jockey said, regarding running and riding, that his orders were to see how the filly broke and do his best, but it missed the break again, became detached but stayed on towards the end.

3809 EASTSIDE PRIDE OF DONCASTER H'CAP 5f
9:20 (9:21) (Class 5) (0-75,75) 3-Y-O+ £2,590 (£770; £385; £192) **Stalls** High

Form RPR

0404 **1** **Sands Crooner (IRE)**23 3064 7-9-3 **64** (vt) PaulMulrennan 10 71
(J G Given) *in tch: hdwy 2f out: swtchd rt and rdn to chal ent fnl f: qckd to ld and edgd lft last 100yds: kpt on* **10/3**1

0546 **2** *nk* **Frognal (IRE)**5 3664 4-9-7 **73** (b) JamesSullivan(5) 1 79
(Mrs R A Carr) *in tch: hdwy on outer 2f out: rdn over 1f out: drvn and kpt on ins fnl f: ev ch whn edgd rt and nt qckn last 75yds* **11/2**3

4313 **3** *3/4* **Cape Royal**11 3474 10-9-12 **73** (bt) PatCosgrave 3 77+
(J M Bradley) *cl up: effrt 2f out: sn rdn and ev ch: drvn ins fnl f and cl 3rd but hld whn n.m.r nr fin* **9/1**

0014 **4** *nk* **Nomoreblondes**14 3358 6-9-9 **70** (p) TonyHamilton 7 72
(P T Midgley) *cl up: led 1/2-way: rdn wl over 1f out: drvn ent fnl f: hdd and one pce last 100yds: n.m.r nr fin* **12/1**

-423 **5** *nk* **Red River Boy**15 3322 5-8-4 **54** oh6 KellyHarrison(3) 5 55
(C W Fairhurst) *chsd ldrs: rdn along and sltly outpcd wl over 1f out: styd on u.p ins fnl f: nrst fin* **17/2**

U311 **6** *1* **Mey Blossom**9 3540 5-9-11 **75** 6ex MichaelStainton(3) 4 72+
(R M Whitaker) *stmbld s: hdwy and in tch 1/2-way: rdn to chse ldrs whn n.m.r ent fnl f: sn one pce* **4/1**2

-000 **7** *2 1/4* **Mythical Blue (IRE)**25 2997 4-9-11 **72** PaulHanagan 6 61
(J M Bradley) *led to 1/2-way: sn rdn and cl up tl drvn and wknd appr fnl f* **6/1**

-004 **8** *2 1/4* **Errigal Lad**21 3120 5-9-1 **62** (p) AndrewElliott 2 43
(J Balding) *dwlt and sltly hmpd s: sn outpcd and a bhd* **12/1**

0006 **9** *4 1/2* **Guest Connections**29 2854 7-8-6 **58** (v) BillyCray(5) 9 23
(D Nicholls) *s.i.s: a bhd* **12/1**

58.47 secs (-2.03) **Going Correction** -0.30s/f (Firm)
WFA 3 from 4yo+ 5lb 9 Ran SP% **116.4**
Speed ratings (Par 103): **104,103,102,101,101 99,96,92,85**
Tote Swingers: 1&2 £5.20, 1&3 £5.10 CSF £21.97 CT £152.07 TOTE £4.50: £1.80, £2.80, £2.10; EX 22.80 Place 6: £55.40 Place 5: £44.72.
Owner Danethorpe Racing Partnership **Bred** Peter Molony **Trained** Willoughton, Lincs
■ Stewards' Enquiry : Paul Mulrennan one-day ban: careless riding (Jul 22)

FOCUS
This moderate sprint handicap was predictably run at a frantic pace and there were plenty of chances. The main action was down the middle of the track and things got a bit tight late on. The form is sound among the principals.
Red River Boy Official explanation: jockey said she lost an iron leaving stalls

Mey Blossom Official explanation: jockey said mare was denied a clear run
Guest Connections Official explanation: jockey said gelding missed the break
T/Plt: £28.30 to a £1 stake. Pool: £67,684.75 - 1,745.90 winning units. T/Qpdt: £15.30 to a £1 stake. Pool: £5,381.34 - 259.74 winning units. JR

3576 EPSOM (L-H)

Thursday, July 8

OFFICIAL GOING: Good to firm (good in places; 8.6 overall 8.2 home straight)
Wind: Light, across Weather: Fine, warm

3810 BROTHERS PEAR CIDER APPRENTICE H'CAP — 1m 2f 18y
6:20 (6:26) (Class 5) (0-75,74) 4-Y-O+ — **£3,238** (£963; £481; £240) **Stalls** Low

Form				RPR
0430	**1**		**North Cape (USA)**[15] 3330 4-9-4 **73** ... AmyScott(5) 7	80
			(H Candy) *pressed ldr: shkn up to ld jst over 2f out: jnd over 1f out: styd on wl* **15/8**[1]	
-126	**2**	*1 ½*	**The Hague**[30] 2845 4-9-7 **71** ... AndrewHeffernan 4	75
			(P D Evans) *t.k.h: hld up last: gng wl 3f out: wnt 2nd wl over 1f out and sn chalng: hung lft and nt qckn 1f out* **15/8**[1]	
0020	**3**	*8*	**Peaceful Rule (USA)**[13] 3405 4-9-4 **68** ... MichaelGeran 3	56
			(D Nicholls) *led to jst over 2f out: steadily wknd* **12/1**[3]	
-425	**4**	*2 ¾*	**Cactus King**[12] 3442 7-8-11 **64** ... KierenFox(3) 1	47
			(P M Phelan) *hld up in 3rd: rdn 3f out: sn struggling* **5/1**[2]	

2m 9.05s (-0.65) **Going Correction** -0.025s/f (Good) — 4 Ran SP% **93.9**
Speed ratings (Par 103): **101,99,93,91**
CSF £4.08 TOTE £2.00; EX 4.00.
Owner Henry Candy **Bred** W S Farish **Trained** Kingston Warren, Oxon

FOCUS
The going was good to firm, good in places on a watered track. The clerk of the course reported that the good patches were mainly in the home straight. All of the runners in this weak apprentice handicap had been beaten 7 lengths plus on their previous start. The pace was steady and the first two pulled clear of the rest. The winner ran to form. Laish Ya Hajar (11/2) was withdrawn after bolting and unseating his rider on the way to the start. Deduct 15p in the £ under R4.

3811 CHAMPAGNE LANSON 250TH ANNIVERSARY MAIDEN AUCTION STKS — 6f
6:50 (6:50) (Class 4) 2-Y-O — **£3,885** (£1,156; £577) **Stalls** High

Form				RPR
4	**1**		**Premium Coffee**[14] 3349 2-8-11 0 ... ChrisCatlin 1	77
			(M R Channon) *led: awkward bnd over 3f out: shkn up and hdd over 1f out: rallied u.p to ld nr fin* **7/4**[2]	
24	**2**	*hd*	**Cocohatchee**[35] 2680 2-8-9 0 ... LukeMorris 2	74
			(P M Phelan) *hld up in 2nd: chal over 2f out: wanting to hang lft and nursed into narrow ld over 1f out: hrd rdn fnl f: hdd nr fin* **1/2**[1]	
6	**3**	*2 ½*	**Upark Flyer**[70] 1646 2-8-0 0 ow1 ... KierenFox(5) 3	63
			(Patrick Morris) *cl up in 3rd: pushed along over 2f out: upsides jst over 1f out: fdd* **20/1**[3]	

1m 12.23s (2.83) **Going Correction** -0.025s/f (Good) — 3 Ran SP% **107.8**
Speed ratings (Par 96): **80,79,76**
CSF £3.11 TOTE £3.00; EX 2.60.
Owner Jaber Abdullah **Bred** Miss E J Wright And T D Galer **Trained** West Ilsley, Berks

FOCUS
There were only three runners but there was a very exciting finish in this steadily run 6f maiden auction. The time was over four seconds above standard. Despite the muddling pace the form is taken at face value.

NOTEBOOK
Premium Coffee was a promising 14-1 fourth in a 7f Goodwood maiden on debut last month. He had a bit to find with the hot favourite and there were early warning signs as he got unbalanced around the turn but he knuckled down in the straight and displayed a low head carriage and a very willing attitude to get off the mark on the second attempt. The slow time and the fact that he was allowed a soft lead are potential negatives regarding the form but he is out of a smart 5f-6f performer and should have learned a lot from this run. (op 5-4)
Cocohatchee finished in the frame in a pair of 5f maidens at Folkestone and Sandown. He was sent off at odds-on and gave it a decent enough try in a muddling race, particularly as he was a bit keen early on and couldn't find a sustained burst because he was inclined to hang left on the camber. His trainer reported that he had a lung problem and a bit of trouble in preparation for this race but things have cleared up now, and he looks a fair type who should be able to cash in on a similar opportunity in a more strongly run race on a less idiosyncratic track. (op 8-11)
Upark Flyer, a distant last of six at 40-1 in a 5f Redcar maiden on debut in April, showed a lot more speed and ability on her second run. She is related to several winners and could improve again next time. (op 16-1)

3812 FLEMING RUSSELL STENT H'CAP — 1m 4f 10y
7:25 (7:28) (Class 4) (0-80,80) 4-Y-O+ — **£5,180** (£1,541; £770) **Stalls** Centre

Form				RPR
20-2	**1**		**Run For Ede's**[52] 2181 6-9-4 **77** ... IanMongan 1	85
			(P M Phelan) *hld up in 3rd: wnt 2nd ent st: led over 2f out: hung lft over 1f out: styd on to draw clr* **4/6**[1]	
-365	**2**	*3 ¾*	**Profit's Reality (IRE)**[18] 3239 8-9-4 **77** ... LukeMorris 2	80
			(M J Attwater) *led at mod pce: shkn up and hdd over 2f out: hld whn hung lft and nrly hit rail 1f out* **4/1**[3]	
2-31	**3**	*41*	**Peace Corps**[81] 468 4-9-2 **75** ... (v) DaneO'Neill 5	—
			(J R Boyle) *trckd ldr tl dropped to last ent st: shkn up and wknd rapidly 3f out: eased and t.o* **11/4**[2]	

2m 42.53s (3.63) **Going Correction** -0.025s/f (Good) — 3 Ran SP% **106.7**
Speed ratings (Par 105): **86,83,56**
CSF £3.42 TOTE £1.50; EX 3.10.
Owner Ede's (uk) Ltd **Bred** Mrs James Wigan & London TB Services Ltd **Trained** Epsom, Surrey

FOCUS
Another very tactical affair run at a slow pace, and it turned into a match. The winner is generally progressive.
Peace Corps Official explanation: jockey said gelding had a breathing problem

3813 TOTEPOOL FLEXI BETTING H'CAP — 1m 114y
7:55 (7:55) (Class 4) (0-85,85) 3-Y-O+ — **£6,476** (£1,927; £963; £481) **Stalls** Low

Form				RPR
12-0	**1**		**King's Colour**[20] 3172 5-9-11 **82** ... GeorgeBaker 4	88
			(B R Johnson) *sn trckd ldng trio: prog to 2nd 2f out: rdn to ld ent fnl f: a holding on* **7/1**[3]	
61	**2**	*nk*	**Hear The Roar (IRE)**[27] 2925 3-8-11 **78** ... NickyMackay 3	88+
			(J R Boyle) *sn shuffled bk to 5th: dropped to 6th ent st and rdn: effrt whn hung lft wl over 1f out: r.o fnl f to take 2nd and cl on wnr fin* **15/8**[1]	
0066	**3**	*¾*	**Hi Shinko**[16] 3289 4-8-13 **70** ... DavidProbert 2	74
			(B R Millman) *trckd ldr: led over 2f out: hdd ent fnl f: one pce* **10/1**	
0123	**4**	*1 ¾*	**Sedgwick**[15] 3317 8-9-5 **76** ... ChrisCatlin 7	76+
			(S A Harris) *hld up last: awkward downhill 4f out: pushed along fr 3f out: looked ill at ease and no real prog tl styd on wl fnl f: nrst fin* **9/1**	
1-00	**5**	*shd*	**Young Dottie**[165] 284 4-8-9 **66** ... CathyGannon 6	66
			(P M Phelan) *hld up in 6th: pushed up to go 5th st: rdn over 2f out: kpt on but no real imp on ldrs* **14/1**	
3353	**6**	*4 ½*	**My Gacho (IRE)**[13] 3389 8-10-0 **85** ... (v) HayleyTurner 5	75
			(M Johnston) *wnt lft s: hld up in 7th: rdn and no prog over 2f out: wl btn whn hung lft 1f out* **7/1**[3]	
3-04	**7**	*7*	**Twilight Star (IRE)**[7] 3579 6-8-13 **70** ... DaneO'Neill 8	44
			(R A Teal) *pressed ldng pair: wknd over 2f out* **15/2**	
1360	**8**	*6*	**Tudor Key (IRE)**[25] 2991 4-9-11 **82** ... JimCrowley 1	43
			(Mrs A J Perrett) *led to over 2f out: wknd rapidly over 1f out* **9/2**[2]	

1m 44.63s (-1.47) **Going Correction** -0.025s/f (Good)
WFA 3 from 4yo+ 10lb — 8 Ran SP% **115.5**
Speed ratings (Par 105): **105,104,104,102,102 98,92,86**
Tote Swingers: 1&2 £20.70, 2&3 £7.00 CSF £20.80 CT £133.19 TOTE £6.70: £1.80, £1.10, £3.20; EX 24.60.
Owner Tann Racing **Bred** Cheveley Park Stud Ltd **Trained** Ashtead, Surrey

FOCUS
A decent handicap. The pace was just fair and this was another muddling race. The winner is rated to his AW best and the second shaped better than the bare form.

3814 BROTHERS STRAWBERRY CIDER CLAIMING STKS — 1m 2f 18y
8:30 (8:32) (Class 5) 3-Y-O+ — **£3,238** (£963; £481; £240) **Stalls** Low

Form				RPR
0511	**1**		**Lang Shining (IRE)**[7] 3580 6-9-9 85 ... SophieDoyle(5) 2	91+
			(J A Osborne) *hld up in 4th: cruised into 2nd over 2f out and into ld jst over 1f out: sn clr: easily* **11/8**[1]	
311-	**2**	*3 ½*	**Kaleo**[278] 6470 6-9-9 80 ... HayleyTurner 4	74
			(S Dow) *led: hrd rdn and hdd jst over 1f out: no ch w wnr* **5/2**[2]	
6406	**3**	*3*	**Potentiale (IRE)**[7] 3581 6-10-0 78 ... (p) SebSanders 3	73
			(J W Hills) *hld up last: nt gng wl fr 6f out: hrd rdn 3f out: kpt on to take 3rd 1f out: no ch* **9/2**[3]	
2525	**4**	*4 ½*	**What's Up Doc (IRE)**[7] 3589 9-9-6 65 ... DaneO'Neill 5	56
			(Mrs Lawney Hill) *mostly chsd ldr to over 2f out: hanging lft and wknd over 1f out* **16/1**	
-054	**5**	*8*	**Ogre (USA)**[38] 2601 5-9-2 75 ... (t) AndrewHeffernan(3) 1	39
			(P D Evans) *cl up in 3rd: rdn over 2f out: sn wknd rapidly* **11/2**	

2m 8.14s (-1.56) **Going Correction** -0.025s/f (Good) — 5 Ran SP% **110.1**
Speed ratings (Par 103): **105,102,99,96,89**
CSF £5.06 TOTE £2.50: £1.10, £2.20; EX 4.30.
Owner A Taylor **Bred** Ballymacoll Stud Farm Ltd **Trained** Upper Lambourn, Berks

FOCUS
Four of the five runners had BHA ratings between 75 and 85 in this decent claimer. The early pace was steady but it increased significantly at around the halfway point. The winner impressed and might have been rated higher.

3815 TOTEPOOL A BETTER WAY TO BET H'CAP — 6f
9:00 (9:00) (Class 4) (0-80,78) 3-Y-O+ — **£5,180** (£1,541; £770; £384) **Stalls** High

Form				RPR
0005	**1**		**Hairspray**[14] 3361 3-9-8 **78** ... ChrisCatlin 7	85
			(M R Channon) *pressed ldng pair on outer: chal over 2f out: narrow ld ent fnl f: drvn out* **14/1**	
4265	**2**	*½*	**Another Try (IRE)**[24] 3037 5-8-11 **66** ... MatthewDavies(5) 3	72
			(A P Jarvis) *mde most: hrd pressed fr over 2f out: hdd ent fnl f: kpt on* **15/2**	
0332	**3**	*½*	**Tyfos**[7] 3584 5-9-12 **76** ... RobertWinston 5	80
			(B P J Baugh) *t.k.h early: pressed ldr: upsides over 2f out tl ent fnl f: nt qckn* **7/4**[1]	
15-5	**4**	*1 ¼*	**Hand Painted**[14] 3373 4-9-11 **75** ... TravisBlock 4	75
			(P J Makin) *hld up in 5th: effrt to chse ldng trio 2f out: kpt on but no real imp* **7/1**[3]	
1000	**5**	*1 ½*	**Rocker**[7] 3578 6-9-12 **76** ... GeorgeBaker 6	72
			(G L Moore) *stdd s: hld up in 6th: rdn over 2f out: no real prog* **12/1**	
0-00	**6**	*2*	**Leadenhall Lass (IRE)**[7] 3579 4-9-6 **70** ... (v) IanMongan 1	59
			(P M Phelan) *chsd ldng trio: rdn and nt qckn over 2f out: fdd over 1f out* **15/2**	
0113	**7**	*4*	**Poppanan (USA)**[26] 2954 4-9-6 **77** ... AdamBeschizza(7) 2	53
			(S Dow) *hld up last: rdn over 2f out: wknd over 1f out* **11/4**[2]	

69.71 secs (0.31) **Going Correction** -0.025s/f (Good)
WFA 3 from 4yo+ 6lb — 7 Ran SP% **113.4**
Speed ratings (Par 105): **96,95,94,93,91 88,83**
Tote Swingers: 1&2 £0.00, 2&3 £5.60 CSF £109.00 TOTE £14.60: £8.00, £2.30; EX 72.90 Place 6: £272.31 Place 5: £141.28.
Owner John Breslin **Bred** J Breslin **Trained** West Ilsley, Berks

FOCUS
They went a steady pace in this sprint handicap and the first three filled those positions throughout. The winner is rated back close to her 2yo form.
Poppanan(USA) Official explanation: jockey said gelding ran flat
T/Plt: £342.50 to a £1 stake. Pool: £56,399 - 120.20 winning units. T/Qpdt: £104.00 to a £1 stake. Pool: £4,103 - 29.17 winning units. JN

3399 FOLKESTONE (R-H)

Thursday, July 8

OFFICIAL GOING: Good to firm (firm in places; 8.0)
Wind: light, across Weather: warm and sunny

3816 CORAL.CO.UK MAIDEN STKS — 7f (S)
2:10 (2:12) (Class 5) 3-Y-O — **£2,729** (£806; £403) **Stalls** Low

Form				RPR
	1		**Daboos (USA)** 3-9-3 0 ... ChrisCatlin 7	77+
			(M P Tregoning) *racd in last trio: swtchd rt ent fnl 2f: pushed along and gd hdwy over 1f out: r.o wl under hands and heels riding to ld fnl 100yds: sn clr: readily* **9/2**[3]	
2002	**2**	*2 ¼*	**Rolling Hills (IRE)**[14] 3374 3-9-3 72 ... DaneO'Neill 3	71
			(H Candy) *led: rdn 2f out: sn hrd pressed: kpt battling on wl tl hdd and nt pce of wnr fnl 100yds* **5/2**[2]	
3-00	**3**	*shd*	**Pytheas (USA)**[27] 2935 3-8-12 71 ... (p) JemmaMarshall(5) 1	71
			(M J Attwater) *trckd ldrs and travelling wl: wnt 2nd over 2f out: rdn and ev ch fr over 1f out tl nt pce of wnr fnl 100yds* **8/1**	
0433	**4**	*3*	**Aleqa**[12] 3434 3-8-12 67 ... SebSanders 6	69+
			(C F Wall) *chsd ldrs: rdn and effrt on stands' rail wl over 1f out: nt clr run fr over 1f out tl hmpd ins fnl f: nt rcvr and nvr able to chal* **11/8**[1]	

50-6 **5** *12* **Rose Aurora**[58] 2004 3-8-5 0 KatiaScallan(7) 9 26
(M P Tregoning) *a wl off the pce in last trio: lost tch over 2f out* **28/1**

0- **6** *8* **Clifton Encore (USA)**[260] 6932 3-8-7 0 RossAtkinson(5) 5 —
(Tom Dascombe) *dwlt: sn pushed along in rr: a wl bhd: lost tch 4f out* **33/1**

-530 **7** *11* **Great Intrigue (IRE)**[28] 2892 3-9-3 68 (p) IanMongan 2 —
(J S Moore) *chsd ldr tl over 2f out: wknd rapidly wl over 1f out: eased fnl f: t.o* **9/1**

00- **8** *45* **Lutine Lady**[416] 2135 3-8-12 0 LukeMorris 8 —
(P Winkworth) *chsd ldrs tl dropped out rapidly 1/2-way: virtually p.u fnl 2f: wl t.o* **33/1**

1m 26.32s (-0.98) **Going Correction** -0.075s/f (Good) **8** Ran SP% **119.3**
Speed ratings (Par 100): **102,99,99,95,82 73,60,9**
Tote Swingers: 1&2 £2.90, 1&3 £7.40, 2&3 £3.50 CSF £16.73 TOTE £3.80: £1.60, £1.40, £1.90; EX 15.40 Trifecta £72.20 Pool: £422.97 - 4.33 winning units..
Owner Hamdan Al Maktoum **Bred** Gainesway Thoroughbreds Ltd **Trained** Lambourn, Berks

FOCUS
A fairly uncompetitive maiden which was quite well run. A nice start from the winner and the favourite is rated a length second.
Aleqa Official explanation: jockey said filly was denied a clear run
Lutine Lady Official explanation: jockey said filly had a breathing problem

3817 EUROPEAN BREEDERS' FUND MAIDEN FILLIES' STKS 5f
2:45 (2:45) (Class 5) 2-Y-O **£3,076** (£915; £457; £228) **Stalls** Low

Form RPR

2546 **1** **Coconut Ice**[7] 3596 2-8-9 0 RossAtkinson(5) 6 71+
(Tom Dascombe) *mde all: rdn wl clr over 1f out: edgd rt ins fnl f: easily* **8/13**[1]

0 **2** *5* **Silver Show (IRE)**[15] 3331 2-9-0 0 ChrisCatlin 1 53+
(M R Channon) *chsd wnr tl pushed along and dropped to last over 2f out: plugged on to chse clr wnr again ins fnl f: no ch w wnr* **7/2**[2]

U0 **3** *3 ½* **Manasha**[15] 3332 2-9-0 0 IanMongan 3 40
(J L Dunlop) *wnt rt s: chsd ldng pair: effrt to chse wnr over 2f out: rdn wl over 1f out: btn and edgd rt jst over 1f out: lost 2nd and wknd ins fnl f* **9/2**[3]

0 **4** *shd* **Magic Cross**[40] 2547 2-9-0 0 LukeMorris 5 40
(P J McBride) *dwlt: bhd: hdwy and rdn to dispute 2nd 2f out: edgd rt and wl btn ent fnl f: wknd* **9/1**

60.07 secs (0.07) **Going Correction** -0.075s/f (Good) **4** Ran SP% **112.3**
Speed ratings (Par 91): **96,88,82,82**
CSF £3.31 TOTE £1.60; EX 3.10.
Owner Timeform Betfair Racing Club Ltd **Bred** Jenny Hall Bloodstock Ltd **Trained** Malpas, Cheshire

FOCUS
This looked a golden opportunity for the warm favourite Coconut Ice to get off the mark, which proved just to be the case. She did not need to improve.

NOTEBOOK
Coconut Ice, breaking well and soon taking the lead on the favoured stands'-side rail, used her experience to good effect and scored with plenty in hand. Coupled with her superior form, the drop back to the minimum proved just the ticket after not quite seeing out the extra furlong the last twice, but this was a weak race. (op 8-11)
Silver Show(IRE) was well backed on debut but was readily outpaced from an early stage. She again found the pace a little hot at the 2f pole, but stayed on to regain second entering the distance, although never looking any threat. This was a step in the right direction and, although she still has a way to go, a step up in trip should hold her in a better light. (op 4-1 tchd 10-3)
Manasha got injured on debut but showed good speed over 6f last time and did so again here, dropping back to the minimum. Her effort petered out entering the distance, however. (op 4-1 tchd 5-1)
Magic Cross was another dropping back to 5f after not figuring in a Newmarket maiden last time. She showed good early speed after an untidy start but had no more to give entering the final furlong. (op 17-2 tchd 8-1 and 10-1)

3818 JEWSON H'CAP 5f
3:20 (3:22) (Class 5) (0-70,70) 3-Y-O+ **£2,729** (£806; £403) **Stalls** Low

Form RPR

30-4 **1** **Luminous Gold**[26] 2973 5-9-11 69 SebSanders 5 80
(C F Wall) *broke wl: sn stdd and travelled strly trcking ldrs: effrt to chse ldr jst over 1f out: rdn to ld ins fnl f: r.o strly* **13/8**[1]

6005 **2** *2* **Edith's Boy (IRE)**[19] 3211 4-8-11 62 AdamBeschizza(7) 4 66
(S Dow) *sn led: rdn over 1f out: hdd ins fnl f: nt pce of wnr fnl 100yds: hld on for 2nd* **13/2**

0363 **3** *nk* **Thoughtsofstardom**[7] 3605 7-9-1 59 (be) RobertWinston 6 62
(P S McEntee) *stdd and swtchd lft s: hld up in tch towards rr: nt clr run 2f out: swtchd rt and rdn over 1f out: kpt on ins fnl f: no threat to wnr* **8/1**

0013 **4** *nk* **Simple Rhythm**[3] 3734 4-9-7 65 MarcHalford 1 67
(J Ryan) *chsd ldr: rdn and unable qck over 1f out: styd on same pce u.p fnl f* **11/4**[2]

3500 **5** *½* **Watch Chain (IRE)**[29] 2879 3-7-11 51 oh1 SimonPearce(5) 8 49
(M H Tompkins) *sn outpcd in last: hdwy jst over 1f out: styd on wl ins fnl f: nt rch ldrs* **33/1**

30-6 **6** *1 ½* **Jimmy Ryan (IRE)**[31] 2808 9-9-4 62 (t) LukeMorris 8 57
(T D McCarthy) *taken down early and led to s: in tch: hdwy to chse ldrs 1/2-way: rdn over 1f out: wknd u.p fnl 150yds* **28/1**

2020 **7** *10* **Ten Down**[34] 2721 5-8-5 54 SophieDoyle(5) 10 13
(M Quinn) *restless stalls: a towards rr: struggling ent fnl 2f: wl btn fnl f* **25/1**

1422 **8** *¾* **Avrilo**[12] 3440 4-9-9 70 AndrewHeffernan(3) 9 26
(M S Saunders) *chsd ldrs tl rdn and wknd qckly over 1f out: wl bhd and eased ins fnl f* **11/2**[3]

59.19 secs (-0.81) **Going Correction** -0.075s/f (Good)
WFA 3 from 4yo+ 5lb **8** Ran SP% **114.8**
Speed ratings (Par 103): **103,99,99,98,98 95,79,78**
Tote Swingers: 1&2 £2.90, 1&3 £7.40, 2&3 £3.50 CSF £12.70 CT £65.36 TOTE £2.60: £1.60, £1.10, £2.20; EX 15.80 Trifecta £69.00 Pool: £548.77 - 5.88 winning units..
Owner Dr Philip Brown **Bred** Darley **Trained** Newmarket, Suffolk

FOCUS
A few with claims made this a competitive 51-70 sprint handicap. Straightforward form.
Avrilo Official explanation: trainer said filly finished lame

3819 MORGAN SINDALL H'CAP 2m 93y
3:55 (3:56) (Class 6) (0-60,60) 4-Y-O+ **£2,047** (£604; £302) **Stalls** Low

Form RPR

4353 **1** **Calzaghe (IRE)**[13] 2455 6-9-4 60 IanMongan 6 67
(Jim Best) *stdd s and hld up in last pair: pushed along and clsd 3f out: swtchd lft and chsd ldr 2f out: rdn to ld over 1f out: styd on wl fnl f* **4/1**[2]

4345 **2** *2* **Purely By Chance**[15] 3324 5-8-5 52 (v) SimonPearce(5) 2 57
(J Pearce) *in tch in midfield: pushed along over 2f out: rdn and hdwy over 1f out: chsd wnr jst ins fnl f: no imp fnl 100yds* **15/8**[1]

5244 **3** *1 ¼* **Brad's Luck (IRE)**[21] 3127 4-8-7 49 LukeMorris 3 53
(M Blanshard) *chsd ldng pair: reminder after 4f and pushed along at times: rdn to chse ldr 3f out tl 2f out: plugged on same pce u.p fr over 1f out* **5/1**[3]

35-1 **4** *1* **Pure Crystal**[17] 3278 4-8-7 54 (b) TobyAtkinson(5) 5 56
(M G Quinlan) *bhd: pushed along over 3f out: hdwy ent fnl 2f: styd on same pce u.p and no imp fnl f* **10/1**

0153 **5** *3 ½* **Free Falling**[16] 3290 4-8-5 47 ChrisCatlin 4 45
(Miss Gay Kelleway) *led: rdn over 2f out: drvn and hdd over 1f out: wknd fnl 150yds* **11/2**

-500 **6** *17* **Star Of Pompey**[19] 3195 6-8-8 50 RobertWinston 1 28
(M R Hoad) *chsd ldr tl 3f out: wknd u.p over 1f out: eased fnl f* **11/2**

3m 40.25s (3.05) **Going Correction** -0.075s/f (Good) **6** Ran SP% **111.3**
Speed ratings (Par 101): **89,88,87,86,85 76**
Tote Swingers: 1&2 £8.40, 1&3 £8.40, 2&3 £4.60 CSF £11.75 TOTE £3.30: £1.10, £1.90; EX 17.10.
Owner Chipstead Racehorse Owners Club **Bred** Wentworth Racing Pty Ltd **Trained** Lewes, E Sussex

FOCUS
A run-of-the-mill 0-60 staying handicap run at a muddling pace. The form is rated around the second and third.
Star Of Pompey Official explanation: trainer said mare did not handle the track and was eased down, later found to be in season

3820 J & J RECRUITMENT H'CAP 1m 4f
4:30 (4:30) (Class 5) (0-70,70) 3-Y-O **£2,729** (£806; £403) **Stalls** Low

Form RPR

0341 **1** **Mount Athos (IRE)**[7] 3582 3-9-7 70 6ex SebSanders 1 84+
(J W Hills) *chsd ldrs: hdwy to ld gng wl over 2f out: rdn clr 2f out: in n.d after: easily* **1/4**[1]

3243 **2** *3 ¼* **Baltimore Clipper (USA)**[7] 3593 3-9-7 70 ChrisCatlin 6 79
(P F I Cole) *led after 1f: rdn and hdd over 2f out: no ch w wnr fr over 1f out: kpt on for clr 2nd* **6/1**[2]

2003 **3** *11* **Il Portico**[9] 3532 3-8-8 57 RobertWinston 4 48
(M R Channon) *v.s.a: rdn along thrght and nvr gng wl in last: lost tch over 2f out: kpt on to go modest 3rd ins fnl f* **7/1**[3]

4400 **4** *1 ¾* **Land Of Plenty (IRE)**[12] 3442 3-7-9 51 oh6 RyanPowell(7) 5 40
(Jamie Poulton) *chsd ldrs: rdn to chse ldng pair over 2f out: sn wl outpcd and no ch: lost modest 3rd ins fnl f* **33/1**

60-0 **5** *½* **Pollan Bay (IRE)**[6] 3640 3-7-13 53 (b1) SophieDoyle(5) 2 41
(Ms J S Doyle) *t.k.h: hld up in last pair: rdn and wl outpcd by ldng pair over 2f out: pressing for modest 3rd fnl 2f: one pce fnl f* **50/1**

0000 **6** *25* **Baxter (IRE)**[16] 3291 3-8-2 51 oh2 LukeMorris 3 —
(J W Hills) *led for 1f: w ldr after tl drvn and wknd qckly over 2f out: wl bhd and eased ins fnl f* **50/1**

2m 39.18s (-1.72) **Going Correction** -0.075s/f (Good) **6** Ran SP% **113.6**
Speed ratings (Par 100): **102,99,92,91,91 74**
Tote Swingers: 1&2 £1.02, 1&3 £1.30, 2&3 £1.40 CSF £2.40 TOTE £1.30: £1.10, £1.30; EX 2.10.
Owner Corinthian **Bred** David Magnier And Cobra Bloodstock **Trained** Upper Lambourn, Berks

FOCUS
An uncompetitive handicap but it was quite sound run. The winner did not need to match his Haydock figure.
Il Portico Official explanation: jockey said gelding was slowly away

3821 LIPSCOMB.CO.UK FILLIES' H'CAP 1m 1f 149y
5:05 (5:06) (Class 5) (0-70,69) 3-Y-O+ **£2,729** (£806; £403) **Stalls** Centre

Form RPR

2-44 **1** **Ubiquitous**[13] 3403 5-8-4 50 oh4 (t) SimonPearce(5) 6 56
(S Dow) *led for 1f: chsd ldrs after: rdn and effrt on inner wl over 1f out: led fnl 75yds: kpt on* **11/1**

0012 **2** *¾* **Eye Of Eternity**[7] 3607 3-8-1 53 LukeMorris 4 57
(Rae Guest) *led after 1f and set stdy gallop: qcknd ent fnl 2f: rdn over 1f out: hung lft ins fnl f: hdd and no ex fnl 75yds* **3/1**[2]

4052 **3** *¾* **Beauchamp Xiara**[17] 3268 4-10-0 69 DaneO'Neill 2 72
(H Candy) *in tch: rdn and effrt ent fnl 2f: chsd ldr wl over 1f out: carried lft and styd on same pce fnl f* **5/2**[1]

-320 **4** *¾* **Markhesa**[84] 1323 4-9-3 63 MatthewDavies(5) 7 64
(J R Boyle) *hld up in tch: nt clr run and swtchd lft over 1f out: keeping on but nt pce to rch ldrs whn sltly hmpd and swtchd rt ins fnl f* **8/1**

44-4 **5** *1 ½* **Santa Margherita**[17] 3259 3-9-0 66 SebSanders 3 64
(H J L Dunlop) *stdd s: hld up in last pair: swtchd lft and rdn over 1f out: no imp fnl f* **6/1**[3]

5532 **6** *1 ¾* **Granite Girl**[7] 3606 3-8-11 68 TobyAtkinson(5) 1 62
(P J McBride) *stdd s: hld up in last pair: rdn and c wd bnd ent st: no prog* **3/1**[2]

0045 **7** *hd* **Ivory Lace**[20] 3160 9-9-13 68 IanMongan 5 62
(S Woodman) *chsd ldr over 7f out tl wl over 1f out: wknd jst over 1f out* **12/1**

2m 6.33s (1.43) **Going Correction** -0.075s/f (Good)
WFA 3 from 4yo+ 11lb **7** Ran SP% **120.0**
Speed ratings (Par 100): **91,90,89,89,88 86,86**
Tote Swingers: 1&2 £2.40, 2&3 £8.00 CSF £46.78 TOTE £13.50: £3.20, £3.30; EX 55.90 Place 6:£27.08 Place 5: £9.76. .
Owner T Staplehurst **Bred** T Staplehurst **Trained** Epsom, Surrey

■ Stewards' Enquiry : Luke Morris sixteen-day ban (two-days for Folkestone and fourteen-days under totting up procedure): Jul 30 - Aug 10 (4-days deferred to Oct 11)

FOCUS
A tight but very modest fillies' handicap run at just an ordinary pace. The winner is rated back to her best.

T/Plt: £41.60 to a £1 stake. Pool: £46,503 - 814.67 winning units. T/Qpdt: £9.60 to a £1 stake. Pool: £3,470 - 265.85 winning units. SP

[3790]NEWMARKET (R-H)

Thursday, July 8

OFFICIAL GOING: Good to firm (7.6)

Far side of July course utilised.

Wind: Light across Weather: Coudy with sunny spells

3822 BAHRAIN TROPHY (GROUP 3) 1m 5f

1:30 (1:33) (Class 1) 3-Y-O

£34,062 (£12,912; £6,462; £3,222; £1,614; £810) **Stalls** Centre

Form RPR

1134 **1** **Corsica (IRE)**[20] 3145 3-9-0 105 FrankieDettori 1 112
(M Johnston) *chsd ldr: wnt centre and led that gp 4f out: rdn over 1f out: hung rt and styd on u.p to ld overall wl ins fnl f* **15/8**[1]

-121 **2** ¾ **Harris Tweed**[33] 2758 3-9-0 96 LiamJones 4 111
(W J Haggas) *lw: pushed along to ld: lft to r alone 4f out: remained in command: rdn over 1f out: hdd wl ins fnl f* **5/2**[2]

4-13 **3** 5 **Caucus**[21] 3105 3-9-0 87 JamieSpencer 2 103
(H Morrison) *prom: wnt centre 4f out: rdn sn after: styd on same pce fr over 1f out: hung rt and styd on u.p ins fnl f: wnt 3rd towards fin* **14/1**

-344 **4** 1 **Simenon (IRE)**[33] 2738 3-9-0 100 JimmyFortune 7 102
(A M Balding) *racd in 3rd: wnt centre and chsd ldr of that gp 4f out: rdn over 2f out: edgd lft and no ex fnl f: lost 3rd towards fin* **25/1**

2-31 **5** ½ **Very Good Day (FR)**[29] 2860 3-9-0 105 RyanMoore 5 101
(M R Channon) *s.i.s: hld up: wnt centre 4f out: rdn over 2f out: r.o ins fnl f: nt trble ldrs* **5/1**[3]

1-5 **6** 7 **Kithonia (FR)**[28] 2889 3-8-11 93 TomQueally 3 87
(H R A Cecil) *hld up in tch: racd keenly: wnt centre 4f out: rdn over 2f out: wknd over 1f out* **10/1**

-624 **7** 3 **Prizefighting (USA)**[25] 3014 3-9-0 106 (b[1]) WilliamBuick 6 86
(J H M Gosden) *hld up: wnt centre 4f out: rdn over 2f out: hung lft and wknd over 1f out* **15/2**

2m 43.51s (-0.49) **Going Correction** -0.075s/f (Good) **7** Ran SP% **111.4**
Speed ratings (Par 110): **98,97,94,93,93 89,87**
Tote Swingers: 1&2 £1.02, 1&3 £7.70, 2&3 £8.60 CSF £6.33 TOTE £2.60: £1.70, £1.90; EX 6.20.

Owner Sheikh Hamdan Bin Mohammed Al Maktoum **Bred** Epona Bloodstock Ltd And P A Byrne **Trained** Middleham Moor, N Yorks

FOCUS

There had been minimal rain, but the going had eased to good to firm, good in places after 6mm of water was applied to the track the previous evening. GoingStick readings suggested the centre was again riding quickest (7.8), with there being little between the stands' side (7.5) and far side (7.4). The far-side course was again in use. A race that has worked out well in recent years, producing high-class performers such as Youmzain and Kite Wood, as well as multiple pattern scorer Tranquil Tiger. Upgraded to a Group 3 contest last season, this year's renewal didn't look the strongest, with four of the seven runners having only a maiden win to their name, and it was the two most progressive individuals in the field who came clear. Corsica probably didn't need to improve to beat Harris Tweed at the weights but is rated close to his best. The second and fourth are both rated up 6-7lb.

NOTEBOOK

Corsica(IRE) has been most progressive and, although beaten 5l by Harris Tweed in a valuable Musselburgh handicap two starts back, he had an 18lb swing at the weights, and had since run creditably to finish fourth in the Queen's Vase, when appearing to find the 2m trip beyond him. A fine, big, galloping sort, the stiff uphill finish suited him well and the St Leger will presumably be on connections' minds now, with the Great Voltigeur likely to be the chosen trial. (op 9-4)

Harris Tweed may have won had he headed centre-field with the rest of the runners with 4f to run, as he ended up staying on what was the slowest ground, and was eventually worn down by old rival Corsica. He showed much-improved form when ridden more aggressively at Musselburgh and was expected to have no trouble with the extra furlong. He again set off in front and very much had the run of things, but probably did himself no favours in hugging the stands' side rail and was eventually worn down. This still represented a big step forward, considering he was significantly worse off at the weights with the winner, and he too is entitled to take in a St Leger trial. (tchd 11-4 in places)

Caucus, rated 18lb inferior to the winner, showed he is most progressive when third in the King George V Handicap latest, and he very much looked a stayer in the making here, being the first off the bridle before staying on under strong pressure for third. (op 12-1 tchd 16-1)

Simenon(IRE) has been coming up well short in smart company all season and this first try beyond 1m3f failed to spark any real improvement, losing out on third close home. (op 22-1)

Very Good Day(FR), a player on his earlier Goodwood third behind Rewilding, produced a rather laboured effort on this step back up in grade. The way he plugged on suggests he may ultimately be a stayer. (op 6-1)

Kithonia(FR) was unable to improve on her reappearance effort, racing keenly, and would appear to need her sights lowering. (op 12-1)

Prizefighting(USA), who wore blinkers for the first time, had finished ahead of a couple of these at Goodwood on his penultimate start, but ran poorly. (op 6-1)

3823 TNT JULY STKS (GROUP 2) (C&G) 6f

2:00 (2:00) (Class 1) 2-Y-O **£39,739** (£15,064; £7,539; £3,759; £1,883) **Stalls** Low

Form RPR

1 **1** **Libranno**[40] 2547 2-8-12 0 RyanMoore 3 109
(R Hannon) *w'like: athletic: edgd rt s: mde all: shkn up over 1f out: rdn and r.o* **10/1**

21 **2** ¾ **Neebras (IRE)**[34] 2715 2-8-12 0 FrankieDettori 5 107
(Mahmood Al Zarooni) *lw: s.i.s: hld up: hdwy to chse wnr over 1f out: rdn and edgd lft ins fnl f: r.o* **10/3**[2]

12 **3** 3 ¼ **Elzaam (AUS)**[23] 3049 2-8-12 0 RichardHills 4 97
(M A Jarvis) *trckd ldrs: wnt 2nd over 3f out: rdn and hung lft fr over 1f out: no ex ins fnl f* **4/7**[1]

3141 **4** 2 ¼ **Approve (IRE)**[21] 3100 2-9-1 0 EddieAhern 2 93
(W J Haggas) *chsd wnr to over 3f out: rdn and hung lft over 1f out: wknd ins fnl f* **9/1**[3]

5 2 **Marston Moor (USA)** 2-8-12 0 AhmedAjtebi 1 84
(Mahmood Al Zarooni) *str: prom tl rdn and wknd over 1f out* **50/1**

1m 11.37s (-1.13) **Going Correction** -0.075s/f (Good) **5** Ran SP% **107.8**
Speed ratings (Par 106): **104,103,98,95,93**
CSF £40.06 TOTE £19.40: £2.60, £1.80; EX 19.40.

Owner Mcdowell Racing **Bred** O Mcdowell **Trained** East Everleigh, Wilts

FOCUS

Despite the small field this looked a solid Group 2 on paper, featuring as it did the Norfolk Stakes winner and Coventry Stakes runner-up, not to mention a couple of very interesting maiden winners from the Godolphin and Hannon camps. Elzaam and Approve were clearly below form though and this is a tricky race to assess, which could have been pitched several pounds higher or lower. The first two are both capable of improvement.

NOTEBOOK

Libranno was a shock winner when he made all to beat Ecliptic on his debut, but that form has worked out really well and he fully deserved to take his chance at this level. His stable had a good line to the level of the opposition through Strong Suit and, while once again pretty well dismissed in the betting, he repeated his debut performance and made every yard. He quickened up well from the front and, when challenged by Neebras inside the last, found a little bit more, sticking his head out willingly near the line. He's not fashionably bred but clearly has plenty of ability and has now proved on two occasions that he is a very tough horse to pass. Whether the watered ground helped his style of running, and whether he will be as good when taken on in front remains to be seen, but the bookmakers seemed rather underwhelmed, with Hills offering a best price 33-1 for the 2000 Guineas. His owner, who had the beaten favourite Scarteen Fox (later renamed Best Light) in the 1999 Racing Post Trophy, nominated the Doncaster Group 1 as the end-of-season target for this colt. (op 9-1 tchd 11-1)

Neebras(IRE) was second to Guineas favourite Strong Suit on his debut before winning his maiden easily next time on his debut for Godolphin. Given a patient ride and tracking Elzaam through, he came to have every chance as they hit the rising ground, but the winner kept pulling out more and was always just being held. He looks well up to winning a Group race and should have no trouble staying another furlong. (op 7-2)

Elzaam(AUS) set a strong standard on his narrow defeat to Strong Suit at Royal Ascot, and was well backed to get back to winning ways. He didn't run up to that form, though, hanging and failing to pick up at all in the closing stages. Perhaps the watered ground didn't suit him as he's surely a lot better than this. The Ballydoyle colts who ran fourth and sixth in the Coventry have already given the Ascot race a boost by running well since, and it might be hasty to start doubting the value of that form based on this under-par performance. Official explanation: trainer had no explanation for the poor form shown (op 8-13 tchd 8-15)

Approve(IRE), winner of the Norfolk Stakes last time out, faced a stiff task carrying a 3lb penalty in a stronger race over an extra furlong. Like the third he too hung left as he came under pressure, and he might not prove the easiest to place now. The Gimcrack looks a suitable target, though, as it'll probably be a weaker race than this. Official explanation: jockey said colt hung left (op 15-2)

Marston Moor(USA), whose sales price went up from $77,000 as a yearling to $375,000 as a juvenile, is by a high-class sprinter in the US out of a half-sister to French 1m1f Group 3 2yo winner Naval Officer. It goes without saying that he was pushed in at the deep end in making his debut in this class of race, and in the circumstances he ran a perfectly good race. A maiden should be a formality before a return to better company. (op 33-1)

3824 SPORTINGBET.COM HERITAGE H'CAP 1m 2f

2:35 (2:37) (Class 2) (0-105,103) 3-Y-O

£49,848 (£14,928; £7,464; £3,736; £1,864; £936) **Stalls** Centre

Form RPR

2-35 **1** **Circumvent**[56] 2056 3-9-7 **103** TomQueally 19 112
(P F I Cole) *s.i.s: sn rcvrd to chse ldrs: led over 7f out: rdn and pressed fr over 1f out: styd on gamely* **40/1**

2-11 **2** nk **Breakheart (IRE)**[19] 3196 3-8-3 **85** FrannyNorton 20 93
(A M Balding) *hld up in tch: rdn over 1f out: edgd lft: r.o* **20/1**

6610 **3** shd **Arlequin**[33] 2742 3-8-7 **89** GrahamGibbons 18 97+
(J D Bethell) *hld up in tch: rdn and hung lft over 1f out: r.o* **20/1**

13-2 **4** nse **Sand Skier**[19] 3196 3-8-5 **87** JoeFanning 4 95
(M Johnston) *lw: a.p: rdn and ev ch fr over 1f out: r.o* **11/1**

-330 **5** 1 **Hot Prospect**[33] 2746 3-9-5 **101** PhilipRobinson 9 107+
(M A Jarvis) *lw: hld up: nt clr run 2f out: hdwy and hmpd over 1f out: nt clr run and swtchd lft ins fnl f: r.o: nt rch ldrs* **14/1**

-430 **6** 1 **Contract Caterer (IRE)**[21] 3105 3-8-10 **92** FrankieDettori 12 96
(Pat Eddery) *lw: hld up in tch: rdn over 1f out: styd on same pce ins fnl f* **13/2**[3]

-121 **7** nk **Ransom Note**[21] 3103 3-9-4 **100** MichaelHills 8 103
(B W Hills) *hld up: hdwy 3f out: rdn over 1f out: no ex wl ins fnl f* **5/1**[1]

1-02 **8** 2 **Start Right**[14] 3351 3-8-2 **84** HayleyTurner 2 83+
(L M Cumani) *plld hrd and prom: rdn over 1f out: no ex ins fnl f* **16/1**

4030 **9** hd **Aquarian Spirit**[33] 2758 3-7-13 **81** JimmyQuinn 6 83+
(R A Fahey) *mid-div: hdwy over 2f out: rdn whn hmpd and lost pl over 1f out: r.o towards fin: nt trble ldrs* **40/1**

0-42 **10** 1 ¾ **Red Badge (IRE)**[40] 2543 3-9-4 **100** JimmyFortune 7 95
(R Hannon) *hld up: hdwy u.p over 1f out: wknd ins fnl f* **16/1**

-131 **11** 1 **Gold Rules**[38] 2607 3-8-8 **90** KierenFallon 17 83+
(L M Cumani) *swtg: hld up: rdn over 2f out: styd on ins fnl f: nvr nrr* **10/1**

2-60 **12** 2 **Pleasant Day (IRE)**[21] 3103 3-9-3 **99** (b) MartinDwyer 1 88
(B J Meehan) *hld up: hdwy u.p over 1f out: wknd ins fnl f* **20/1**

2-10 **13** nk **Constant Contact**[33] 2742 3-8-8 **90** LiamKeniry 13 79
(A M Balding) *prom: jnd ldr over 6f out: rdn wknd 2f out* **33/1**

-110 **14** 2 **Agent Archie (USA)**[21] 3105 3-8-0 **87** ow3 KierenFox(5) 15 72
(J R Best) *chsd ldrs: rdn over 2f out: wknd over 1f out* **16/1**

0030 **15** ¾ **Dubai Miracle (USA)**[21] 3104 3-8-10 **95** MartinLane(3) 11 78
(D M Simcock) *hld up: rdn over 4f out: a in rr* **50/1**

1-51 **16** 4 ½ **Treble Jig (USA)**[27] 2927 3-8-7 **89** ow1 RyanMoore 3 63
(Sir Michael Stoute) *lw: mid-div: rdn over 2f out: sn wknd* **11/2**[2]

2-21 **17** ½ **Point Out (USA)**[17] 3275 3-8-5 **87** WilliamBuick 14 60
(J H M Gosden) *mid-div: rdn over 3f out: wknd over 2f out* **16/1**

-112 **18** 1 ¼ **Caldercruix (USA)**[39] 2562 3-8-10 **92** JamieSpencer 10 63+
(T P Tate) *led: hdd over 7f out: remained handy: rdn and ev ch 2f out: wknd over 1f out* **9/1**

1030 **19** 3 ½ **Doctor Zhivago**[33] 2742 3-8-6 **88** GregFairley 16 52
(M Johnston) *hld up: a in rr: rdn over 3f out: sn lost tch* **33/1**

2m 4.65s (-0.85) **Going Correction** -0.075s/f (Good) **19** Ran SP% **130.0**
Speed ratings (Par 106): **100,99,99,99,98 98,97,96,96,94 93,92,92,90,89 86,85,84,82**
Tote Swingers: 1&2 £66.60, 1&3 £106.60, 2&3 £70.10 CSF £696.02 CT £15250.56 TOTE £52.70: £9.40, £5.20, £6.30, £3.40; EX 818.00 Trifecta £2248.20 Part won. Pool: £3,038.10 - 0.60 winning units..

Owner The Fairy Story Partnership **Bred** Deepwood Farm Stud **Trained** Whatcombe, Oxon

FOCUS

This looked a hot handicap and it's likely to throw up plenty of winners in the coming weeks, but they didn't go a strong gallop in front and on this watered ground it proved very difficult to make up ground from off the pace. The first three home were drawn in the highest three boxes and the field finished compressed. A 5lb personal best from the winner.

NOTEBOOK

Circumvent ran poorly on quick ground in the Dante when last seen (apparently pulled a muscle) but he'd previously run with credit in a French Group 3, and despite apparently facing a stiff task off top weight, he had a few things go his way. The well-watered ground was to his liking, he was well drawn to get a prominent early pitch - he likes to make the running - and he didn't have to go too fast in the early stages, which meant he had energy in reserve to rally when strongly tackled inside the final 2f. A rise in the weights is unlikely to bother connections as the gelding looks sure to be on his travels abroad again soon in search of Group-race honours. (op 50-1)

Breakheart(IRE) came into the race with some stamina doubts as he's a half-brother to the sprinter Dark Missile and there's plenty of speed on the dam's side. He is by Sakhee, though, and after tracking the pace he stayed on strongly once they hit the rising ground. Clearly he gets the trip without any problem, and it was interesting that, despite being 4lb worse off at the weights, he confirmed Ascot form with Sand Skier. He's an improving sort and should soon be winning again. (op 16-1)

The Form Book, Raceform Ltd, Compton, RG20 6NL

Arlequin didn't really act around Epsom last time but he'd previously won narrowly at York, with Contract Caterer back in third. He was 4lb worse off at the weights with that rival this time but readily confirmed the form. (op 18-1)
Sand Skier, running off the same mark as when posting a promising reappearance behind Breakheart at Ascot, looked sure to be suited by this extra 2f but, having been brought to have every chance, didn't quite see the trip out as strongly as one or two others. He didn't settle as well as some through the early stages and that probably cost him in the end, but he can win a similar race given a stronger all-round gallop. (op 12-1)
Hot Prospect, returning to handicap company after finishing towards the rear in the Derby, looked to have plenty on at the weights, but he ran well, especially considering that the race was dominated by horses who raced quite prominently, while he was held up out the back. He was also denied a clear run and hampered as he went for a gap approaching the furlong pole. (op 16-1)
Contract Caterer(IRE), seventh in the King George V Handicap last time out, lacked a little pace in the closing stages, but kept on well up once he hit the rising ground, and a return to 1m4f should suit him. (op 8-1)
Ransom Note, who won the Britannia last time out, was stepping up 2f in distance but his pedigree - dam is a half-sister to Arc winner Marienbard - gave hope that he would cope with it. He stayed well enough but didn't improve for the longer trip. (tchd 11-2 and 6-1 in places)
Start Right, who had a poor draw, pulled hard in the early stages and could have done with getting cover. He can do better held up in a stronger-run race. (tchd 20-1 in places)
Aquarian Spirit would have finished a bit closer had he not been hampered approaching the furlong pole, but he looks likely to remain vulnerable to less-exposed types. (op 50-1)
Red Badge(IRE) didn't have an easy task having been put up 8lb for finishing second to Green Moon last time out.
Gold Rules sweated up beforehand and raced keenly under restraint. He wasn't seen to best effect the way this race was run. (op 9-1 tchd 17-2)
Constant Contact didn't stay and needs dropping back to 1m. (tchd 40-1 in a place)
Treble Jig(USA), who holds a Great Voltigeur entry, was the biggest disappointment of the race, and there looked no obvious explanation. (op 6-1)
Point Out(USA) has a dirt pedigree and had done all his previous racing on Polytrack, so there was a question mark next to his name regarding the switch to turf. It was a little off-putting to see him put his head in the air once asked to pick up.
Caldercruix(USA), last seen finishing second to Monterosso over this trip on the Rowley Mile course, has since been put up 5lb, but that looked fair enough considering what the winner has gone on to do, not to mention the third, who finished fifth in the Queen's Vase next time out. He was well placed towards the head of affairs for much of the race but dropped out tamely from 1½f out and was eased right off. (op 12-1 tchd 14-1 in a place)

3825 PRINCESS OF WALES'S SPORTINGBET.COM STKS (GROUP 2) 1m 4f

3:10 (3:11) (Class 1) 3-Y-O+

£53,931 (£20,444; £10,231; £5,101; £2,555; £1,282) **Stalls** Centre

Form				RPR
-664	1		**Sans Frontieres (IRE)**[19] 3191 4-9-2 105 (tp) TomQueally 4 *(J Noseda) hld up: hdwy to ld over 1f out: rdn and r.o wl* **14/1**	121
-205	2	2½	**Redwood**[19] 3191 4-9-2 113 MichaelHills 7 *(B W Hills) a.p: rdn over 1f out: styd on to go 2nd ins fnl f: no imp on wnr* **16/1**	117
-223	3	2¼	**Tazeez (USA)**[22] 3068 6-9-2 120 RichardHills 5 *(J H M Gosden) lw: led: rdn: hung rt and hdd over 1f out: no ex ins fnl f* **5/1**[3]	113
42-3	4	¾	**Spanish Moon (USA)**[103] 1026 6-9-2 122 RyanMoore 6 *(Sir Michael Stoute) lw: trckd ldrs: rdn over 1f out: wknd ins fnl f* **11/8**[1]	112
31-1	5	1½	**Holberg (UAE)**[34] 2716 4-9-2 115 FrankieDettori 3 *(Saeed Bin Suroor) lw: chsd ldr: rdn and ev ch over 2f out: edgd rt over 1f out: wknd fnl f* **5/2**[2]	110
-252	6	3½	**Nanton (USA)**[18] 3240 8-9-2 107 JimmyFortune 1 *(J S Goldie) hld up: rdn over 2f out: wknd fnl f* **40/1**	104
2046	7	8	**Crowded House**[19] 3191 4-9-2 103 (b) MartinDwyer 8 *(B J Meehan) chsd ldrs: rdn over 1f out: sn hung lft and wknd* **20/1**	91
41-3	8	3¾	**Man Of Iron (USA)**[12] 3454 4-9-2 107 KierenFallon 2 *(L M Cumani) hld up: hdwy 7f out: rdn over 3f out: wknd wl over 1f out* **12/1**	85

2m 30.34s (-2.56) **Going Correction** -0.075s/f (Good) **8** Ran SP% **114.8**
Speed ratings (Par 115): **105,103,101,101,100 98,92,90**
Tote Swingers: 1&2 £22.70, 1&3 £17.20, 2&3 £34.60 CSF £207.63 TOTE £28.60: £4.50, £3.50, £1.50; EX 208.90 Trifecta £1197.40 Pool: £16,052.27 - 9.92 winning units..
Owner Sir Robert Ogden **Bred** The Lavington Stud **Trained** Newmarket, Suffolk

FOCUS
Perhaps not the strongest running of this race, and certainly not as competitive as it can sometimes be, with only Spanish Moon and Crowded House having previously won a this level or better, and the latter's Racing Post Trophy victory seeming a distant memory. The pace really lifted from over 4f out, and unlike in the earlier races on the card, the winner came from off the pace.

NOTEBOOK
Sans Frontieres(IRE) finished fourth in what is working out to be a good Hardwicke last month (third Barshiba since won Lancashire Oaks, and fifth Redwood chased him home here), and he burst through to lead over 1f out before staying on strongly to record his first victory since his 2-y-o debut in 2008. Third in last season's Dante, there had been excuses for his earlier defeats this season, and the tongue tie seemed to have a positive effect last time, so combined with the first-time cheekpieces, it enabled him to produce the sort of form his trainer has always thought him capable of. It's doubtful whether he would be up to mixing it with the elite middle-distance performers, but he may be forced into Group 1 company following this, as he will now be saddled with a penalty. (tchd 16-1)
Redwood made a promising reappearance at Sandown but had failed to make an impact in two subsequent outings, although he had excuses. He failed to show the same acceleration as the winner, but chased him through inside the final furlong for second, and it's hoped that he now goes on from this and lands a first success at Group level, with something like the Rose Of Lancaster Stakes at Haydock next month looking an ideal target.
Tazeez(USA), who recorded a career-best when third in the Prince Of Wales's Stakes at Royal Ascot, was trying this trip for the first time and looked potentially dangerous if allowed an easy time of things in front. He was forced to increase the tempo sooner than Richard Hills would have liked, though, and for all that he ran on under pressure, he was beaten by stronger stayers at the distance. He's another possible for the Rose Of Lancaster, a race his owner has a good record in. (tchd 6-1 in places)
Spanish Moon(USA) was racing for the first time in Britain since 2008, having been banned due to his bad behaviour at the starting stalls. Representing Sir Michael Stoute, responsible for four of the last ten winners of the race, he hadn't run since finishing third in the Sheema Classic back in March, but goes well fresh and set a very high standard for the others to aim at. The slight ease in the ground should have suited, so it was therefore disappointing to see him beaten so readily, failing to pick up for strong pressure. This clearly wasn't his best form and he's left with a bit to prove now. (tchd 6-4 in places)
Holberg(UAE), a former Queen's Vase winner, made a taking winning debut for Godolphin in a Listed race at Goodwood (race not working out). He had his chance but didn't race with the same zest as he had done on his reappearance, and was made to look rather slow. He was disappointing, but undoubtedly deserves another chance. (op 3-1 tchd 10-3 in places)
Nanton(USA) isn't up to this level, for all that he was second in a weak Group 2 earlier in the season. (op 50-1)
Crowded House ended up well beaten in the first-time blinkers at Ascot, and again dropped right away here. He is no betting proposition. Official explanation: trainer's rep said colt lost both front shoes
Man Of Iron(USA) had shaped well on his recent reappearance in a Listed race over C&D but this was a big step back. (tchd 11-1)

3826 EUROPEAN BREEDERS' FUND CONDITIONS STKS 6f

3:45 (3:45) (Class 2) 2-Y-O **£12,952** (£3,854; £1,926; £962) **Stalls** Low

Form				RPR
15	1		**Casual Glimpse**[33] 2743 2-9-1 0 RyanMoore 4 *(R Hannon) lw: hld up: hdwy over 1f out: shkn up to ld ins fnl f: r.o wl* **7/1**[3]	98+
1	2	2½	**Lord Of The Stars (USA)**[20] 3169 2-9-1 0 JimCrowley 3 *(R M Beckett) unf: scope: trckd ldr: led on bit over 1f out: rdn: edgd lft and hdd ins fnl f: unable qck* **8/1**	91
513	3	2¼	**Roayh (USA)**[23] 3049 2-9-1 0 FrankieDettori 2 *(Saeed Bin Suroor) led: rdn and hdd over 1f out: edgd lft and no ex ins fnl f* **1/1**[1]	84
	4	2¼	**Fityaan** 2-8-13 0 RichardHills 5 *(B W Hills) str: hld up: rdn over 1f out: wknd ins fnl f* **12/1**	77+
521	5	2¾	**Extra Power (IRE)**[27] 2930 2-9-1 0 KierenFallon 6 *(M R Channon) chsd ldrs: rdn and ev ch over 1f out: edgd lft and wknd fnl f* **14/1**	69
1	6	11	**Major Dude**[31] 2819 2-8-13 0 JimmyFortune 1 *(R Hannon) w'like: chsd ldrs: rdn over 2f out: wknd over 1f out* **7/2**[2]	34

1m 12.65s (0.15) **Going Correction** -0.075s/f (Good) **6** Ran SP% **110.2**
Speed ratings (Par 100): **96,92,89,86,83 68**
Tote Swingers: 1&2 £3.40, 1&3 £2.20, 2&3 £1.70 CSF £55.52 TOTE £8.50: £3.30, £3.00; EX 55.80.
Owner Sir Robert Ogden **Bred** Wickfield Farm Partnership **Trained** East Everleigh, Wilts

FOCUS
An interesting little conditions race, won last year by subsequent Middle Park winner Awzaan.

NOTEBOOK
Casual Glimpse put up a performance that marks him down as a very useful juvenile. Well fancied when disappointing in the Woodcote Stakes at Eposm (not handle track/race working out really well), he looked a likely improver for the switch to a more conventional course and, having picked up well to lead inside the final furlong, he always looked to be doing enough, despite hanging a little under pressure. He has already won at Goodwood, so it would be no surprise to see him take his place in the Richmond Stakes at the Glorious meeting later this month, though connections may consider supplementing him for the Gimcrack. (tchd 15-2)
Lord Of The Stars(USA) lost his unbeaten record but there was still plenty to like about his performance as he travelled really strongly before getting outstayed by the winner inside the final furlong. He may be as effective at 5f and remains capable of better. (op 15-2)
Roayh(USA), following on from the disappointment of Elzaam earlier in the afternoon, dealt the form of the Coventry a further blow by finishing well held back in third. It's clear he failed to reproduce that form, with the watered ground appearing against him, but none the less he now has plenty to prove. (op 10-11)
Fityaan, the sole newcomer in the field, is a 100,000gns Gimcrack entrant. He was plenty keen enough under restraint and briefly looked set to be involved racing inside the final 2f, but those earlier exertions ultimately took their toll. This was a promising start and he should be up to winning a standard maiden. (op 10-1 tchd 14-1)
Extra Power(IRE) faced a stiff task and ended up well held having emptied inside the final furlong. (op 11-1)
Major Dude had won at Windsor on debut and clearly failed to run up to expectations on this rise in grade. (op 5-1)

3827 PORTLAND PLACE PROPERTIES CONDITIONS STKS 1m

4:20 (4:21) (Class 2) 3-Y-O

£12,462 (£3,732; £1,866; £934; £466; £234) **Stalls** Low

Form				RPR
-305	1		**Critical Moment (USA)**[21] 3104 3-8-12 105 MichaelHills 5 *(B W Hills) chsd ldr tl led over 3f out: rdn and edgd rt over 1f out: r.o u.p* **11/4**[1]	102+
100	2	1	**Fair Trade**[21] 3104 3-8-12 104 JimmyFortune 1 *(D R C Elsworth) lw: stdd s: hld up: racd keenly: hdwy over 1f out: hrd rdn ins fnl f: r.o* **11/4**[1]	99+
6222	3	nk	**Invincible Soul (IRE)**[21] 3103 3-8-12 92 RyanMoore 3 *(R Hannon) hld up in tch: rdn and edgd lft over 1f out: r.o* **7/2**[2]	99
2-36	4	hd	**Sweet Sonnet (USA)**[22] 3071 3-8-7 98 TedDurcan 8 *(Saeed Bin Suroor) hld up: hdwy over 2f out: rdn and edgd rt over 1f out: r.o* **7/1**[3]	93
-100	5	½	**Cumulus Nimbus**[21] 3103 3-8-12 88 PatDobbs 7 *(R Hannon) hld up: rdn over 2f out: r.o ins fnl f: nt trble ldrs* **20/1**	97
-163	6	1¼	**Party Doctor**[12] 3460 3-8-12 103 RichardKingscote 4 *(Tom Dascombe) led over 4f: rdn and edgd rt over 1f out: no ex ins fnl f* **9/1**	94
1-53	7	nk	**Mufarrh (IRE)**[56] 2045 3-8-12 95 RichardHills 6 *(J L Dunlop) trckd ldrs: racd keenly: rdn: nt clr run and hung lft over 1f out: styd on same pce fnl f* **10/1**	93
6	8	14	**Tt's Dream**[14] 3374 3-8-12 0 GregFairley 2 *(A J Lidderdale) prom: pushed along 3f out: wknd 2f out* **200/1**	60?
-006	9	17	**Gessabelle**[13] 3415 3-8-7 42 (t) LeonnaMayor 9 *(P S McEntee) hld up: racd keenly: hung rt and wknd over 2f out: bhd whn swvd lft over 1f out: t.o* **200/1**	14

1m 38.16s (-1.84) **Going Correction** -0.075s/f (Good) **9** Ran SP% **112.9**
Speed ratings (Par 106): **106,105,104,104,104 102,102,88,71**
Tote Swingers: 1&2 £1.70, 1&3 £3.90, 2&3 £2.20 CSF £10.00 TOTE £3.70: £1.40, £1.50, £1.50; EX 8.10 TRIFECTA Pool: £1,646.72 - 33.64 winning units..
Owner K Abdulla **Bred** Juddmonte Farms Inc **Trained** Lambourn, Berks

FOCUS
A good-quality conditions race in which the class horses came to the fore.

NOTEBOOK
Critical Moment(USA), who ran a career-best when fifth in the Hampton Court latest (had run of the race/hampered late on), was never going to have any trouble with the shorter trip, having finished third in the Craven earlier in the season, and just as had been the case at Ascot, he got first run on Fair Trade. A likeable sort, he could be good enough to win a minor Listed race, although on the whole isn't going to be the easiest to place. (op 7-2)
Fair Trade didn't have things go right at Ascot. He was hampered early and got well behind before staying on once the race was all over, but it was surprising to see him not made more use of on this drop in trip, as for all that he picked up well when asked to hold every chance inside the final furlong, this out-and-out galloper lacked a finishing kick. He has plenty of scope to develop into a smart older horse, though, and remains one to keep on side. (tchd 3-1 and 10-3 in places)
Invincible Soul(IRE), the Britannia runner-up, had a bit to find with the front two at the weights, but conditions were in his favour and it was no surprise to see him run a big race. He has yet to win this season, but can put that right in a similar contest. (tchd 3-1)
Sweet Sonnet(USA) misbehaved before the race, getting loose and as a result beginning to sweat, so it's possible she's done well in finishing fourth. Connections will presumably go in search of more black-type with her now. (op 6-1)

Cumulus Nimbus stood little chance at the weights and ran about as well as could have been expected, staying on late. (tchd 18-1)
Party Doctor was readily brushed aside and ran most disappointingly, considering he had returned to something like his best at Windsor last time. (op 8-1 tchd 10-1)
Mufarrh(IRE) again failed to settle and then didn't get much of a run when asked for his effort.

3828 WAREHOUSE SOLUTIONS H'CAP — 5f
4:55 (4:56) (Class 3) (0-95,93) 3-Y-O+ **£9,714** (£2,890; £1,444; £721) **Stalls** Low

Form — RPR
-026 **1** **Astrophysical Jet**[26] 2978 3-9-10 **93** .... GrahamGibbons 3 — 106
(E S McMahon) *lw: trckd ldrs: a gng wl: led over bit over 1f out: shkn up and r.o wl* **9/2**[1]
5120 **2** *2 ½* **Five Star Junior (USA)**[13] 3406 4-9-13 **91** .... KierenFallon 10 — 95
(Mrs L Stubbs) *swtg: sn pushed along in rr: hdwy: nt clr run and swtchd rt over 1f out: rdn and hung lft ins fnl f: r.o: no ch w wnr* **8/1**
0045 **3** *nk* **Invincible Lad (IRE)**[27] 2940 6-9-6 **84** .... RyanMoore 4 — 87
(E J Alston) *chsd ldrs: rdn over 1f out: r.o* **13/2**[3]
1014 **4** *1 ¼* **Medici Time**[12] 3446 5-9-7 **85** ....(v) TedDurcan 6 — 83
(T D Easterby) *s.i.s: outpcd: r.o ins fnl f: nrst fin* **9/1**
0061 **5** *½* **Crimea (IRE)**[9] 3529 4-9-8 **86** 6ex .... AdrianNicholls 11 — 83
(D Nicholls) *sn led: rdn and hdd over 1f out: no ex ins fnl f* **8/1**
6660 **6** *nk* **Tabaret**[20] 3178 7-9-6 **84** ....(p) MichaelHills 12 — 80
(R M Whitaker) *chsd ldrs: rdn over 1f out: styd on same pce* **12/1**
6010 **7** *½* **Rasaman (IRE)**[13] 3406 6-9-3 **84** ....(v) GaryBartley(3) 1 — 78
(J S Goldie) *mid-div: rdn over 1f out: nt trble ldrs* **20/1**
3500 **8** *¾* **Indian Trail**[20] 3165 10-9-4 **82** ....(v) FrannyNorton 2 — 73
(D Nicholls) *hld up: sme hdwy over 1f out: nvr on terms* **20/1**
5500 **9** *½* **Sohraab**[19] 3193 6-10-0 **92** .... GeorgeBaker 9 — 81
(H Morrison) *chsd ldrs: rdn and edgd lft over 1f out: wknd ins fnl f* **6/1**[2]
-106 **10** *8* **Lenny Bee**[12] 3446 4-9-13 **91** .... PhillipMakin 7 — 51
(D H Brown) *chsd ldrs tl rdn and wknd over 1f out* **13/2**[3]
1-05 **11** *7* **Doric Lady**[17] 3261 5-9-1 **79** .... FrankieDettori 5 — 14
(J A R Toller) *dwlt: outpcd* **7/1**

57.79 secs (-1.31) **Going Correction** -0.075s/f (Good)
WFA 3 from 4yo+ 5lb — **11** Ran SP% **121.1**
Speed ratings (Par 107): **107,103,102,100,99 99,98,97,96,83 72**
Tote Swingers: 1&2 £11.40, 1&3 £3.90, 2&3 £6.20 CSF £41.73 CT £238.19 TOTE £5.80: £1.90, £2.90, £2.50; EX 63.20 Trifecta £361.70 Pool: £1,628.06 - 3.33 winning units. Place 6:£1,111.93 Place 5: £821.08..
Owner Ladas **Bred** Grangecon Stud **Trained** Lichfield, Staffs

FOCUS
A competitive sprint handicap on paper, but there was one horse in the race open to more improvement than the rest, and she was not only backed into favouritism but justified the support in tremendous style.

NOTEBOOK
Astrophysical Jet did best of the pace-setters in the Reg Griffin Memorial Trophy last time out, and got to race off a 1lb lower mark here. The only 3-y-o in the field and the least exposed runner in the race, the question was whether she would cope with the drop back to 5f. Not only did she cope with it, but she improved significantly, travelling comfortably up with the pace and quickening up smartly as she hit the rising ground. She had plenty in hand at the finish and will surely take a big hike in the weights, but now that her best trip has been found there should be further improvement to come, and connections will no doubt be keen to return her to Pattern company before long, in search of some valuable black type. (op 6-1 tchd 7-1)
Five Star Junior(USA), apparently struck into last time out, bounced back to form, picking up well from off the pace and running on to take second. He was unlucky to bump into a well-handicapped rival in the winner, but he again showed he can be just as effective over 5f as 6f.
Invincible Lad(IRE) got a nice tow into the race and put up another solid effort, but the handicapper is just about keeping up with him. (tchd 6-1)
Medici Time didn't run badly considering he was slowly away and detached along with Doric Lady early on. He picked up well once he hit the rising ground, but his current mark doesn't make things easy. (op 10-1)
Crimea(IRE), 1lb wrong at the weights under his penalty for winning a claimer at Hamilton last time out, showed good pace throughout but the winner was cruising all over him approaching the furlong pole and he weakened in the closing stages. (tchd 7-1)
Tabaret won off a 2lb higher mark on his reappearance but hasn't been in the same form recently, and the drop back to 5f here didn't do the trick. (tchd 14-1 in places)
Rasaman(IRE) struggled to land a blow.
Indian Trail remains on a long losing run. (op 16-1)
Lenny Bee Official explanation: trainer's rep said gelding finished distressed
Doric Lady, who endured a nightmare run at Lingfield last time, got to race off a 2lb lower mark here, back on turf. She missed the break badly, though, and never got into the race. Official explanation: jockey said mare missed the break (op 13-2 tchd 15-2)
T/Jkpt: Not won. T/Plt: £905.30 to a £1 stake. Pool: £151,461 - 122.12 winning units. T/Qpdt: £119.80 to a £1 stake. Pool: £10,043 - 62.02 winning units. CR

3635 WARWICK (L-H)
Thursday, July 8

OFFICIAL GOING: Good to firm (8.2)
Wind: Virtually nil Weather: Bright

3829 LODGE SERVICE MAIDEN STKS — 1m 2f 188y
2:20 (2:22) (Class 5) 3-Y-O+ **£2,590** (£770; £385; £192) **Stalls** Low

Form — RPR
2-24 **1** **Opera Gal (IRE)**[33] 2758 3-8-9 79 .... DavidProbert 9 — 81+
(A M Balding) *mde all: pressed ins fnl 3f: drvn and asserted 2f out: c stands' side and r.o strly fr over 1f out and sn clr* **1/1**[1]
00 **2** *10* **Jewellery (IRE)**[45] 2390 3-8-9 0 .... PatCosgrave 1 — 63
(J R Fanshawe) *chsd ldrs: drvn along 4f out: styd on to dispute 2nd 1f out: chsd wnr ins fnl f but nvr any ch* **33/1**
42 **3** *1 ¼* **Sensationally**[15] 3312 3-8-9 0 .... JackMitchell 3 — 61
(R M Beckett) *chsd wnr: drvn to chal ins fnl 3f: sn no imp and outpcd fr 2f out: one pce and lost 2nd ins fnl f* **5/1**[2]
4 *½* **My Galway Man (IRE)** 3-9-0 0 .... RoystonFfrench 4 — 65
(M Johnston) *chsd ldrs: rdn and one pce over 3f out: styd on again fr over 1f out but nvr any ch w wnr* **20/1**
44 **5** *3 ¾* **Invitee**[17] 3266 3-8-9 0 .... TadhgO'Shea 7 — 53
(E A L Dunlop) *t.k.h: towards rr but in tch: rdn 4f out and nvr gng pce to get nr to ldrs* **14/1**[3]
6 *1 ¼* **Stitchnick (IRE)**[23] 5-9-12 0 .... FergusSweeney 2 — 56?
(W S Kittow) *in rr but in tch: rdn and styd on to go modest 4th 3f out: wknd fr ins fnl 2f* **80/1**
00 **7** *12* **Pound Lane (IRE)**[19] 3207 4-9-9 0 .... RobertLButler(3) 6 — 34
(Miss T Spearing) *in rr: lost tch fr 4f out* **200/1**
000 **8** *6* **Defence Of Realm (GER)**[17] 3275 3-9-0 62 .... TonyCulhane 8 — 23
(George Baker) *pushed along sn after s: a in rr: lost tch 4f out* **66/1**

2m 18.21s (-2.89) **Going Correction** -0.20s/f (Firm)
WFA 3 from 4yo+ 12lb — **8** Ran SP% **84.3**
Speed ratings (Par 103): **102,94,93,93,90 89,81,76**
Tote Swingers: 1&2 £4.70, 1&3 £1.02, 2&3 £12.00 CSF £21.59 TOTE £1.40: £1.10, £5.50, £1.10; EX 33.40.
Owner J C Smith **Bred** Littleton Stud **Trained** Kingsclere, Hants

FOCUS
An ordinary older-horse maiden in which there was little strength in depth. It was straightforward for the winner, who may not have needed to match her previous form.
Pound Lane(IRE) Official explanation: jockey said gelding hung right-handed
Defence Of Realm(GER) Official explanation: jockey said gelding was unsuited by the good to firm (good in places) ground

3830 EUROPEAN BREEDERS' FUND FILLIES' H'CAP — 7f 26y
2:55 (2:55) (Class 4) (0-80,80) 3-Y-O+ **£6,152** (£1,830; £914; £456) **Stalls** Low

Form — RPR
-465 **1** **Poppet's Lovein**[13] 3396 4-9-10 **75** .... StevieDonohoe 3 — 86
(A B Haynes) *awkward stalls: in rr: plenty to do whn c to r stands' side and gd hdwy fr 2f out to take narrow ld 1f out: drvn out fnl f and in command nr fin* **7/1**
1126 **2** *1 ½* **Night Lily (IRE)**[12] 3457 4-9-12 **77** .... TonyCulhane 8 — 84
(P W D'Arcy) *in rr: rdn and hdwy fr 2f out: styd on to chal 1f out: kpt on ins fnl f but nt pce of wnr* **5/2**[1]
0151 **3** *hd* **Cheers For Thea (IRE)**[15] 3320 5-9-10 **75** ....(bt) DavidAllan 2 — 81
(T D Easterby) *s.i.s: sn rcvrd to chse ldrs: rdn 2f out: chal 1f out: kpt on same pce ins fnl f* **7/2**[2]
2611 **4** *¾* **Dr Wintringham (IRE)**[21] 3130 4-9-11 **76** .... JerryO'Dwyer 9 — 80
(Karen George) *in rr: stl plenty to do whn hdwy ins fnl 2f: qcknd between horses over 1f out and sn chsng ldrs: no imp ins fnl f* **6/1**[3]
0020 **5** *2 ¼* **Darcey**[15] 3309 4-9-2 **67** .... CathyGannon 7 — 65
(Miss Amy Weaver) *chsd ldrs: rdn along 3f out: chsng ldrs but one pce whn edgd lft ins fnl f: sn wknd* **18/1**
0503 **6** *¾* **Carcinetto (IRE)**[12] 3431 8-9-9 **79** ....(v) RichardEvans(5) 5 — 75
(P D Evans) *sn chsng ldr at str pce: rdn 2f out: wknd appr fnl f* **8/1**
-162 **7** *½* **Battlemaiden (IRE)**[15] 3320 3-9-7 **80** .... RoystonFfrench 1 — 72
(M Johnston) *led at str pce: rdn over 2f out: hdd & wknd qckly 1f out* **15/2**
0200 **8** *4* **Candyfloss Girl**[22] 3085 3-9-2 **75** .... DavidProbert 4 — 59
(H J L Dunlop) *chsd ldrs: rdn 2f out: sn flashing tail and wknd qckly sn after* **40/1**
0416 **9** *3 ¼* **La Zamora**[20] 3150 4-10-0 **79** .... ShaneKelly 6 — 54
(T D Barron) *in rr: rdn and mod prog on inner over 2f out: nvr rchd ldrs and sn wknd* **18/1**

1m 22.27s (-2.33) **Going Correction** -0.20s/f (Firm)
WFA 3 from 4yo+ 8lb — **9** Ran SP% **113.4**
Speed ratings (Par 102): **105,103,103,102,99 98,98,93,89**
Tote Swingers: 1&2 £6.00, 1&3 £2.80, 2&3 £4.10 CSF £24.38 CT £71.75 TOTE £9.70: £3.40, £1.10, £1.60; EX 29.20.
Owner Mr and Mrs G Robinson **Bred** G And Mrs Robinson **Trained** Limpley Stoke, Bath

FOCUS
A pretty competitive fillies' handicap on paper and the early pace was good. Solid form, with the winner back to her best.
Poppet's Lovein Official explanation: trainer said, regarding apparent improvement in form, that the filly was suited by the less competition and the way it was run.
Battlemaiden(IRE) Official explanation: jockey said filly ran too freely

3831 SISK GROUP CONSTRUCTION H'CAP — 7f 26y
3:30 (3:32) (Class 5) (0-75,73) 3-Y-O **£2,590** (£770; £385; £192) **Stalls** Low

Form — RPR
0524 **1** **Chinese Democracy (USA)**[1] 3771 3-8-2 **54** oh1 .....(p) CathyGannon 4 — 58
(P D Evans) *t.k.h: in tch: hdwy: n.m.r and swtchd lft over 1f out: str run u.p ins fnl f to ld fnl 30yds* **5/1**
3-35 **2** *hd* **Plutocraft**[45] 2383 3-9-2 **68** ....(e[1]) PatCosgrave 2 — 72
(J R Fanshawe) *chsd ldrs in 3rd: drvn to dispute 2nd ins fnl 2f: slt ld ins fnl f: hdd and outpcd fnl 30yds* **5/2**[1]
-323 **3** *¾* **Kilt Rock (IRE)**[62] 1873 3-9-4 **70** .... StevieDonohoe 6 — 72
(R A Mills) *chsd ldr: jnd for 2nd ins fnl 2f: stl rt there and u.p fnl f: kpt on cl home but nt pce of wnr* **7/2**[2]
4-00 **4** *1 ¾* **Resuscitator (USA)**[20] 3155 3-8-13 **65** .... TadhgO'Shea 8 — 62
(Mrs H S Main) *led: rdn and kpt narrow advantage fr 2f out tl hdd ins fnl f: wknd fnl 120yds* **33/1**
4040 **5** *1* **Prince Of Sorrento**[19] 3212 3-9-2 **68** .... JackMitchell 7 — 62
(J Akehurst) *s.i.s: in rr: rdn and edgd lft ins fnl 2f: swtchd lft and rdn sn after: no ex ins fnl f* **9/2**[3]
00-4 **6** *1 ½* **State Fair**[29] 2852 3-9-6 **72** .... TomEaves 3 — 62
(Julie Camacho) *chsd ldrs tl shkn up and lost position bnd 3f out: rdn and styd on again fr 2f out: nvr a threat and wknd fnl f* **8/1**
4-05 **7** *¾* **Gypsy Boy (USA)**[9] 3525 3-9-1 **67** .... SimonWhitworth 5 — 55
(F J Brennan) *s.i.s: rdn over 2f out: a towards rr* **7/1**

1m 23.37s (-1.23) **Going Correction** -0.20s/f (Firm) — **7** Ran SP% **112.2**
Speed ratings (Par 100): **99,98,97,95,94 93,92**
Tote Swingers: 1&2 £8.80, 1&3 £1.70, 2&3 £1.10 CSF £17.22 CT £48.01 TOTE £5.00: £2.40, £2.60; EX 21.80.
Owner Mrs I M Folkes **Bred** Hurstland Farm **Trained** Pandy, Monmouths
■ Stewards' Enquiry : Cathy Gannon caution: used whip with excessive frequency; three-day ban: improper conduct during enquiry (Jul 22,23,25)

FOCUS
A modest 3-y-o handicap run in a time 1.10secs slower than the preceding fillies' contest. The winner was pretty exposed and it is doubtful she had to improve.

3832 EUROPEAN BREEDERS' FUND MEDIAN AUCTION MAIDEN STKS — 7f 26y
4:05 (4:08) (Class 5) 2-Y-O **£3,238** (£963; £481; £240) **Stalls** Low

Form — RPR
0 **1** **Ocean Drift (USA)**[12] 3459 2-9-3 0 .... TadhgO'Shea 12 — 77+
(Mahmood Al Zarooni) *mde virtually all: stl green and high hd carriage but c clr over 1f out: easily* **9/1**
05 **2** *2 ¾* **Danzigs Grandchild (USA)**[16] 3296 2-8-12 0 .... FergusSweeney 5 — 65
(J S Moore) *chsd ldrs: wnt 2nd 3f out: rdn over 2f out: styd on but nvr any ch w easy wnr* **13/2**[3]
5 **3** *½* **Sky Falcon (USA)**[33] 2763 2-9-3 0 .... RoystonFfrench 9 — 69
(M Johnston) *chsd ldrs: rdn and styd on same pce fnl 2f* **8/1**
5 **4** *2 ¾* **Diamond Penny (IRE)**[15] 3326 2-9-3 0 .... StevieDonohoe 10 — 62+
(P F I Cole) *hdwy on outside to chse ldrs over 4f out: rdn: green and outpcd over 2f out: styd on again ins fnl f but nvr a threat* **5/1**[2]

4 **5** 3/4 **Degly Bo (IRE)**[35] 2677 2-9-3 0 .... RichardMullen 2 62+
(P W Chapple-Hyam) *in tch whn awkward ins fnl 4f and lost position: rdn over 2f out and styd on fr over 1f out but nvr anywhere nr ldrs* **5/1**[2]

3 **6D** 3/4 **Highlife Dancer**[7] 3577 2-9-3 0 .... SamHitchcott 1 58
(M R Channon) *in rr: awkward ins fnl 4f: rdn along fr 3f out and nvr gng pce to get into contention: fin 6th, disq: (prohibit substance in sample)* **7/2**[1]

03 **6** nk **Knox Overstreet**[11] 3472 2-9-3 0 .... TonyCulhane 11 57
(Tom Dascombe) *in rr tl rapid hdwy on outside to chse ldrs 4f out: rdn over 2f out and sn btn: fin 7th, plcd 6th* **14/1**

7 1/2 **Educated Son** 2-9-3 0 .... ShaneKelly 6 56
(W R Muir) *plld hrd: stdd ins fnl 4f: rdn and sme prog over 2f out: nvr in contention and sn btn: fin 8th, plcd 7th* **12/1**

0 **8** 6 **Captain Sharpe**[49] 2245 2-9-3 0 .... DavidProbert 7 41+
(H J L Dunlop) *chsd ldrs: rdn and n.m.r bnd ins fnl 3f: sn wknd: plcd 8th* **33/1**

9 1/2 **High Fallutin (IRE)** 2-8-12 0 .... CathyGannon 4 35+
(Eve Johnson Houghton) *s.i.s: green: a in rr* **25/1**

0 **10** 1 1/4 **Bernie's Tune**[15] 3332 2-9-0 0 .... JackDean(3) 3 37
(J L Spearing) *awkward bnd ins fnl 4f: a in rr: fin 11th, plcd 10th* **33/1**

00 **11** hd **Arctic Reach**[19] 3209 2-9-3 0 .... SaleemGolam 8 36
(G D Blake) *reluctant to load: a in rr: fin 12th, plcd 11th* **100/1**

1m 24.11s (-0.49) **Going Correction** -0.20s/f (Firm) 12 Ran SP% **115.1**
Speed ratings (Par 94): **94,90,90,87,86 85,85,84,77,77 75,75**
Tote Swingers: 1&2 £23.80, 1&3 £23.80, 2&3 £18.90 CSF £62.61 TOTE £13.10: £3.40, £1.80, £3.70; EX 87.00.
Owner Godolphin **Bred** Stoneside Stable **Trained** Newmarket, Suffolk

FOCUS
A decent-sized field for this maiden but the time was not surprisingly, as they were juveniles, much slower than the preceding races over the trip. The principals were close up throughout. The form is ordinary but solid.

NOTEBOOK
Ocean Drift(USA), from a good American family that produced Van Nistelrooy, lost his race at the start on his debut. Drawn on the wide outside, he went right at the start but was soon at the head of affairs. He went clear over 1f out and won easily, despite running green and carrying his head high in the closing stages. (op 11-1)
Danzigs Grandchild(USA), a half-sister to six winners from the family of Doctor Dino, improved on her debut effort last time and stepped up again here. She showed up throughout and did enough to suggest she will be competitive in handicaps, now she is qualified. (tchd 11-2 and 8-1)
Sky Falcon(USA), a half-brother to Capercaillie, had reared at the start and ran green on his debut but had learnt from that race, and showed up throughout before sticking on all the way to the line. He can progress again. (op 15-2 tchd 9-1)
Diamond Penny(IRE) built on his Polytrack debut despite still looking green and not appearing particularly happy on this fast turf. (op 4-1)
Degly Bo(IRE), a half-brother to four winners including the very useful Nashmiah, finished well held in an ordinary maiden on his debut. He was held up before getting carried back due to scrimmaging ahead of him on the home turn, then had to switch to towards the inside of the track to get a run. He can be given another chance. (tchd 11-2)
Highlife Dancer, who ran with promise in an Epsom maiden on his debut, was held up early but then did not handle the bend that well and failed to pick up in the straight. The rider reported that the gelding ran green and ran too freely. Official explanation: jockey said gelding ran green and too freely. The gelding was subsequently disqualified after testing postive for morphine. (tchd 11-4)
Educated Son, whose stable's juveniles have been running promisingly of late, was another to hint at ability, showing early pace before getting hampered turning in. (op 16-1)

3833 FESTIVAL OF THE HORSE, STONELEIGH PARK H'CAP — 6f
4:40 (4:42) (Class 4) (0-85,82) 3-Y-O+
£5,919 (£1,772; £886; £443; £221; £111) **Stalls** Low

Form RPR
15-0 **1** **Arteus**[22] 3083 4-9-6 **82** ....(b) LewisWalsh(7) 3 94
(Jane Chapple-Hyam) *sn pressing ldrs: pushed along to ld jst ins fnl f: readily* **7/2**[1]

3106 **2** 2 **Peter Island (FR)**[13] 3401 7-9-13 **82** ....(v) TadhgO'Shea 4 88
(J Gallagher) *sn led: rdn 2f out: hdd jst ins fnl f: styd on same pce* **7/2**[1]

3213 **3** 2 **Vanilla Rum**[17] 3270 3-9-3 **78** .... FergusSweeney 8 77
(H Candy) *sn chsng ldrs: rdn over 2f out: hung lft fr over 1f out: nvr gng pce to trble ldng duo* **9/2**[3]

0-41 **4** nk **Spanish Acclaim**[6] 3638 3-8-12 **73** 6ex .... NeilChalmers 6 71
(A M Balding) *reluctant to load: sn pressing ldrs: c to stands' side and rdn over 2f out: wknd appr fnl f* **4/1**[2]

1006 **5** nk **Memphis Man**[5] 3675 7-9-0 **74** ow1 .... RichardEvans(5) 1 72
(P D Evans) *chsd ldrs: rdn fr 1/2-way: wknd fnl f* **14/1**

0000 **6** 6 **Baunagain (IRE)**[14] 3373 5-9-8 **77** .... PatCosgrave 5 55
(P W Chapple-Hyam) *s.i.s: in rr: rdn along 1/2-way: a outpcd* **6/1**

330- **7** 4 **Outshine**[312] 5478 3-8-9 **70** .... JerryO'Dwyer 7 35
(Karen George) *in tch: rdn 3f out: wknd wl over 2f out* **12/1**

1m 10.56s (-1.24) **Going Correction** -0.20s/f (Firm) course record
WFA 3 from 4yo+ 6lb 7 Ran SP% **111.3**
Speed ratings (Par 105): **100,97,94,94,93 85,80**
Tote Swingers: 1&2 £2.80, 1&3 £1.50, 2&3 £1.40 CSF £14.99 CT £52.49 TOTE £5.00: £3.10, £1.90; EX 19.50.
Owner Norcroft Park Stud **Bred** Norcroft Park Stud **Trained** Dalham, Suffolk

FOCUS
A fair sprint handicap and a tight betting heat. There were several front runners in the race but they did not appear to go totally flat out. A personal best for the winner with the second to his Brighton win.

3834 WARWICK FOR CONFERENCES H'CAP — 5f
5:15 (5:15) (Class 5) (0-75,75) 3-Y-O **£2,590** (£770; £385; £192) **Stalls** Low

Form RPR
-024 **1** **Six Diamonds**[20] 3174 3-9-4 **72** .... NickyMackay 2 77
(H Morrison) *trckd ldrs: drvn to chal over 1f out: led ins fnl f: drvn out* **9/2**

006 **2** 1/2 **Morgans Choice**[16] 3293 3-8-6 **60** ....(b) SamHitchcott 5 63
(J L Spearing) *sn led: c to stands' side: rdn over 2f out: jnd over 1f out: narrowly hdd ins fnl f: styd on same pce* **25/1**

4313 **3** 2 **Jigajig**[3] 3731 3-8-13 **72** ....(p) AmyRyan(5) 7 68
(K A Ryan) *chsd ldrs: rdn and effrt fr 2f out: nvr quite upsides and kpt on same pce ins fnl f* **4/1**[3]

0313 **4** 1 1/4 **Wanchai Whisper**[6] 3637 3-8-8 **62** 6ex ....(p) FergusSweeney 4 53
(P R Hedger) *in rr but in tch: rdn over 2f out: edgd lft over 1f out and no imp on ldng trio* **9/2**

0652 **5** 1 1/4 **Yurituni**[3] 3726 3-9-5 **73** .... TonyCulhane 3 60
(Eve Johnson Houghton) *in tch whn rdn over 2f out: sn outpcd* **5/2**[1]

5333 **6** 5 **Fear Nothing**[17] 3277 3-9-7 **75** ....(b) RichardMullen 1 44
(E S McMahon) *rdn along in rr 1/2-way: edgd lft over 2f out and fnd nthing sn after* **7/2**[2]

58.54 secs (-1.06) **Going Correction** -0.20s/f (Firm) 6 Ran SP% **111.0**
Speed ratings (Par 100): **100,99,96,94,92 84**
Tote Swingers: 1&2 £0.00, 2&3 £1.10 CSF £83.94 TOTE £5.50: £4.90, £10.10; EX 139.20 Place 6:£164.70 Place 5: £141.28. .
Owner A J Struthers And Mrs Julia Scott **Bred** Mrs S F Dibben **Trained** East Ilsley, Berks

FOCUS
A fair 3-y-o sprint run in a decent time, and it paid to race up with the pace. The winner is rated up to her best.
T/Plt: £171.80 to a £1 stake. Pool: £46,093 - 195.75 winning units. T/Qpdt: £120.50 to a £1 stake. Pool: £2,688 - 16.50 winning units. ST

3835 - 3841a (Foreign Racing) - See Raceform Interactive

3190 ASCOT (R-H)
Friday, July 9

OFFICIAL GOING: Good to firm (firm in places on straight course; str 8.7, rnd 8.2)
Rail realignment added circa 25ds to 2m race, 20yds to 12 &10f races and 10yds to Round Mile.
Wind: Virtually nil Weather: very warm

3842 HELICAL BAR E B F MAIDEN STKS — 6f
2:25 (2:26) (Class 3) 2-Y-O **£7,771** (£2,312; £1,155; £577) **Stalls** Low

Form RPR
3 **1** **The Long Game**[9] 3555 2-9-0 0 .... Louis-PhilippeBeuzelin(3) 7 82+
(B J Meehan) *wnt rt s: in tch: hdwy to chal ent fnl 2f: rdn to ld over 1f out: edgd lft ent fnl f: drew wl clr fnl 150yds: easily* **4/5**[1]

0 **2** 4 1/2 **Shaabek (IRE)**[9] 3555 2-9-3 0 .... ChrisCatlin 5 69
(M R Channon) *chsd ldng pair: rdn and ev ch ent fnl 2f tl over 1f out: wl outpcd by wnr ins fnl f* **33/1**

3 4 **Golden Creek (USA)** 2-9-3 0 .... JimCrowley 2 57+
(R M Beckett) *led tl hdd and rdn over 1f out: wknd ent fnl f* **11/4**[2]

0 **4** 2 1/4 **Dr Darcey**[28] 2932 2-9-3 0 .... PatDobbs 4 50
(R Hannon) *chsd ldr tl over 2f out: rdn and wknd qckly wl over 1f out: wl btn fnl f* **5/1**[3]

5 2 1/2 **Oetzi** 2-8-12 0 .... MatthewDavies(5) 1 42+
(A P Jarvis) *s.i.s: sn rdn along and rn green in rr: lost tch over 2f out* **66/1**

6 1 1/4 **Matavia Bay (IRE)** 2-9-3 0 .... NeilCallan 6 39
(A P Jarvis) *dwlt: sn pushed along: in tch tl rdn and wknd qckly ent fnl 2f* **25/1**

7 1/2 **Sabot D'Or** 2-9-3 0 .... TomQueally 3 37
(R Ingram) *in tch: pushed along and no prog over 2f out: wl bhd fr wl over 1f out* **33/1**

1m 16.77s (2.37) **Going Correction** +0.20s/f (Good) 7 Ran SP% **110.1**
Speed ratings (Par 98): **92,86,80,77,74 72,72**
Tote Swingers:1&2:£6.80, 2&3:£8.40, 1&3:£1.10 CSF £33.55 TOTE £1.80: £1.30, £4.90; EX 18.60.
Owner Sangster Families **Bred** Manor Farm Stud (rutland) **Trained** Manton, Wilts

FOCUS
A hot sunny day and the going was given as good to firm, firm in places on the straight course (8.7) and good to firm (8.2) on the round course. It's questionable how strong the form of this maiden is but the winner improved on his debut and the form could be rated 5lb higher.

NOTEBOOK
The Long Game ◆ drew nicely clear in the closing stages and went a little way to justifying his big-race entries. Racing widest out, he took a while to assert but the further he went the better he looked and there looks to be better to come from him as he gathers more experience. (op 10-11 tchd 8-11)
Shaabek(IRE) finished ten lengths behind The Long Game on his debut at Chepstow, but he clearly needed that and, as is common with most juveniles from his yard, improved on this second start.
Golden Creek(USA) ◆ shaped with a deal of promise on this debut and looks the one to take out of the race. A $180,000 purchase, he made much of the running before tiring inside the last, and should last longer next time. (tchd 10-3)
Dr Darcey, who finished in mid-division behind Ecliptic in a hot Sandown maiden on his debut, was dropping back a furlong and that might have been against him. He looks the type for nurseries once qualified. (op 9-2 tchd 4-1)
Oetzi was very green. (tchd 50-1)
Matavia Bay(IRE) was coltish in the preliminaries. (op 16-1)

3843 ICAP H'CAP — 2m
3:00 (3:03) (Class 3) (0-95,95) 3-Y-O+
£6,542 (£1,959; £979; £490; £244; £122) **Stalls** High

Form RPR
6013 **1** **Martyr**[20] 3194 5-9-12 **93** .... PatDobbs 3 99
(R Hannon) *t.k.h: led for 1f: stdd and chsd ldrs after: rdn to ld ent fnl 2f: kpt on wl fnl f and asserted fnl 75yds* **15/2**

020 **2** 3/4 **Bow To No One (IRE)**[27] 2976 4-9-6 **87** .... NeilCallan 7 92
(A P Jarvis) *stdd s: t.k.h: hld up towards rr: nt clr run over 2f out: hdwy and edging rt over 1f out: chsng ldrs and n.m.r ent fnl f: wnt between horses and chsd wnr ins fnl f: no ex* **12/1**

4144 **3** nse **Satwa Gold (USA)**[12] 3475 4-9-2 **83** .... MickyFenton 4 88
(Stef Higgins) *stdd s: t.k.h: hld up in rr: swtchd lft and effrt on outer ent fnl 2f: hdwy to chse ldrs and drvn 1f out: kpt on wl* **33/1**

6005 **4** hd **Ocean's Minstrel**[9] 3566 4-9-7 **88** .... AlanMunro 5 93
(J Ryan) *hld up in tch: hdwy to chse ldrs 5f out: rdn and ev ch 2f out: edgd rt u.p ent fnl f: no ex fnl 100yds* **20/1**

-062 **5** 1/2 **Hevelius**[21] 3159 5-9-9 **90** .... ChrisCatlin 10 94
(W R Swinburn) *t.k.h: hld up in tch: nt clr run ent fnl 3f tl swtchd lft 2f out: hdwy on outer over 1f out: styd on wl fnl f: nt rch ldrs* **12/1**

3311 **6** 1 **Desert Recluse (IRE)**[27] 2976 3-8-3 **92** .... MartinLane(3) 8 95
(Pat Eddery) *hld up in tch in midfield: rdn and short of room 2f out: sn swtchd lft and drvn: edgd rt and hdwy over 1f out: kpt on fnl f but nt gng pce to rch ldrs* **9/2**[1]

10-1 **7** 3 1/4 **Dazinski**[76] 1525 4-9-6 **87** .... GeorgeBaker 12 86
(M H Tompkins) *hld up in tch: rdn and unable qck ent fnl 2f: nt clr run and swtchd lft over 1f out: plugged on but no theat to ldrs fnl f* **5/1**[2]

-655 **8** 1 1/4 **Topolski (IRE)**[41] 2541 4-9-2 **83** ....(p) DavidProbert 13 81
(A M Balding) *chsd ldrs: rdn 3f out: unable qck u.p ent fnl 2f: plugged on same pce and wl hld after* **5/1**[2]

0-02 **9** 3 1/2 **Keenes Day (FR)**[9] 3566 5-9-9 **90** ....(b[1]) RoystonFfrench 6 83
(M Johnston) *s.i.s: sn pushed along and nvr gng wl: rdn and dropped to last 7f out: wl btn fnl 2f: plugged on past btn horses fnl f* **10/1**

111 **10** *1 ¾* **On Terms (USA)**[14] 3402 4-9-0 **81** ..... TomQueally 9 72
(S Dow) *led: pushed along over 3f out: rdn and hdd ent fnl 2f: sn wknd* **7/1**[3]

3024 **11** *2* **Epsom Salts**[27] 2975 5-8-11 **78** ..... IanMongan 2 67
(P M Phelan) *in tch: hdwy to chse ldrs 7f out: rdn and ev ch over 2f out tl 2f out: wknd qckly* **16/1**

10-0 **12** *4* **Urban Poet (USA)**[41] 2541 4-10-0 **95** ..... (b[1]) TadhgO'Shea 1 79
(Saeed Bin Suroor) *chsd ldr after 1f tl wl over 2f out: sn wknd and wl btn whn edgd lft 2f out* **25/1**

6010 **13** *12* **Brett Vale (IRE)**[9] 3566 4-9-4 **85** ..... FergusSweeney 11 55
(P R Hedger) *stdd s: hld up in rr: rdn and short-lived effrt over 3f out: wl btn 2f out: eased ins fnl f* **50/1**

3m 29.55s (0.55) **Going Correction** +0.20s/f (Good)
WFA 3 from 4yo+ 19lb **13** Ran SP% **119.6**
Speed ratings (Par 107): **106,105,105,105,105 104,103,102,100,99 98,96,90**
Tote Swingers: 1&2 £28.20, 1&3 £73.20, 2&3 £81.80 CSF £90.43 CT £2798.10 TOTE £8.40: £2.40, £5.10, £8.30; EX 103.80 TRIFECTA Not won..
Owner Highclere Thoroughbred Racing (Delilah) **Bred** D Maroun **Trained** East Everleigh, Wilts

FOCUS
A competitive staying handicap which got a bit messy and resulted in a tight finish. The first two ran to form.

NOTEBOOK
Martyr ◆ was completely unexposed over this trip, having never previously run beyond 1m4f. He did have good track form, though, having finished third in the Duke Of Edinburgh Handicap at the Royal meeting for the past two seasons, and off just a 1lb higher mark than for that latest run, he saw this 2m distance out strongly, winning with a bit up his sleeve. He looks one to keep on side in staying events and could well run a big race in the Ebor, which is his next target. (op 8-1 tchd 7-1)
Bow To No One(IRE) ◆, proven over this C&D, travelled well and didn't get the clearest of runs in the straight. She remains on a mark she can win off. (op 10-1)
Satwa Gold(USA), who is due to be dropped 2lb, was closely matched with Bow To No One on C&D form from May, and ran another fine race. A consistent sort, he's the best guide to the level of the form. (op 25-1)
Ocean's Minstrel ◆, another due to be dropped 2lb, hinted at a return to form last time out and built on that. He has fallen to a workable mark and is one to keep in mind for a similar race. (op 25-1)
Hevelius, up 2f in distance, got the trip well as he was never nearer than at the finish. The handicapper is just about still in charge, though. (op 14-1 tchd 16-1)
Desert Recluse(IRE), the only 3-y-o in the field, was chasing a hat-trick, but an 11lb higher mark than for his last win made things difficult. It's true that he was trying 2m for the first time, but it wasn't lack of stamina that beat him in the end. (op 4-1)
Dazinski didn't enjoy the clearest of runs, but he wouldn't have won anyway. This was disappointing as he looked to have conditions in his favour. Official explanation: jockey said gelding was denied a clear run (op 11-2 tchd 4-1)
Topolski(IRE) enjoyed a nice trip through the race, but found little in the straight. He ran like a blatant non-stayer. (op 8-1)
Keenes Day(FR) ran poorly and the market seemed to know that he would run a stinker in the first-time blinkers. (tchd 12-1)
Urban Poet(USA) Official explanation: jockey said colt finished lame

3844 BOURNE CAPITAL NOVICE STKS 6f 110y
3:35 (3:37) (Class 4) 2-Y-O **£6,476** (£1,927; £963; £481) **Stalls** Low

Form RPR
56 **1** **Slim Shadey**[20] 3190 2-9-0 0 ..... LiamKeniry 3 88
(J S Moore) *t.k.h: pressed ldrs: rdn ent fnl 2f: ev ch ent fnl f: kpt on wl to ld last stride* **9/2**[2]

4340 **2** *shd* **Straight Line (IRE)**[20] 3190 2-9-0 0 ..... NeilCallan 6 88
(A P Jarvis) *wnt rt s: sn stdd and swtchd lft: t.k.h: hld up in tch: rdn 2f out: drvn and ev ch ent fnl f: led ins fnl f tl hdd last stride* **6/1**[3]

2331 **3** *1* **Dr Green (IRE)**[13] 3459 2-9-5 0 ..... PatDobbs 4 90
(R Hannon) *t.k.h: chsd ldrs: rdn to chse ldr 2f out: drvn to ld 1f out: hdd ins fnl f: no ex and btn fnl 75yds* **6/5**[1]

4 *1 ¾* **Custom House (IRE)** 2-8-11 0 ..... PatrickHills(3) 1 80+
(R Hannon) *s.i.s: bhd: swtchd rt and pushed along 2f out: rdn and unable qck over 1f out: kpt on same pce ins fnl f* **20/1**

140 **5** *nse* **Twist Of Silver (USA)**[21] 3141 2-8-11 0 ..... TomQueally 5 77
(J Noseda) *wnt rt s: sn rcvrd and led over 4f out: rdn over 1f out: hdd 1f out: wknd ins fnl f* **9/2**[2]

3212 **6** *12* **Falkland Flyer (IRE)**[14] 3395 2-9-5 0 ..... ChrisCatlin 2 52
(M R Channon) *led tl over 4f out: styd w ldrs tl rdn and lost pl qckly ent fnl 2f: hung rt and wl btn over 1f out* **10/1**

1m 21.41s (0.21) **Going Correction** +0.20s/f (Good) **6** Ran SP% **110.0**
Speed ratings (Par 96): **106,105,104,102,102 88**
Tote Swingers: 1&2 £3.80, 1&3 £33.30, 2&3 £1.50 CSF £29.13 TOTE £5.30: £2.40, £3.60; EX 34.10.
Owner Phil Cunningham **Bred** P M Cunningham **Trained** Upper Lambourn, Berks
■ Stewards' Enquiry : Neil Callan two-day ban: used whip with excessive frequency (Jul 23,25)

FOCUS
A tight finish to this novice event, which was dominated by Dr Green in the betting but proved much more competitive in reality. The fourth is rated around the third and the time.

NOTEBOOK
Slim Shadey finished sixth in the Chesham last time out and the fourth (King Torus) had given that race a timely boost by winning the Superlative Stakes at Newmarket. He got outpaced over 2f out, but kept battling away next to the stands' rail and with his stamina coming into play inside the last, he stayed on just the best. Sure to be suited by a return to 7f, his trainer has ambitious plans for him and is targeting the Group 2 Vintage Stakes at Goodwood next. (op 8-1)
Straight Line(IRE), ninth in the Chesham, could not reverse form with Slim Shadey, but he appreciated being ridden with more restraint and posted a career-best in defeat. (op 12-1)
Dr Green(IRE) comes out of the race as the best horse in the line-up, as he gave 5lb to the first two, but considering he went off a short-priced favourite some might say he was disappointing. He had every chance, but didn't quite see the race out as well as the other two. (op 5-6 tchd 4-5)
Custom House(IRE) ◆, a 50,000gns newcomer from the all-conquering Hannon stable, shaped with a deal of promise against some useful rivals. He shouldn't have too much trouble winning a maiden. (tchd 25-1)
Twist Of Silver(USA) showed pace to 1½f out, but then fell in a hole somewhat and it might be worth dropping her back in distance. (op 4-1 tchd 5-1)
Falkland Flyer(IRE) faced a stiff task carrying a 5lb penalty, but he dropped out very tamely from 2f out while hanging right, and perhaps all was not fine. (op 9-1 tchd 12-1)

3845 JAMES TAYLOR GROUP H'CAP 6f
4:10 (4:11) (Class 3) (0-90,87) 3-Y-0+ **£6,799** (£2,023; £1,011; £505) **Stalls** Low

Form RPR
4311 **1** **Joe Packet**[20] 3216 3-8-11 **81** ..... JohnFahy(5) 2 97
(J G Portman) *trckd ldrs and a gng wl: led on bit over 1f out: pushed clr 1f out and in command after: comf* **3/1**[1]

-306 **2** *2 ¾* **Gramercy (IRE)**[35] 2713 3-9-5 **84** ..... GeorgeBaker 4 91
(M L W Bell) *stdd and wnt rt s: hld up in last trio: swtchd rt and hdwy over 2f out: chsd ldrs and rdn over 1f out: nt pce of wnr 1f out: wnt 2nd ins fnl f* **4/1**[3]

-503 **3** *1 ¼* **King's Wonder**[8] 3578 5-9-10 **86** ..... MichaelGeran(3) 3 90
(D Nicholls) *wnt lft s: hld up in tch: pushed along and hdwy wl over 1f out: rdn to chse wnr over 1f out: btn 1f out: lost 2nd ins fnl f* **7/2**[2]

11-4 **4** *1* **Fantasy Gladiator**[30] 2877 4-9-2 **75** ..... LiamKeniry 11 76
(R M H Cowell) *stdd and wnt rt s: hld up in last: pushed along and hdwy over 1f out: kpt on fnl f: no ch w wnr* **11/1**

5012 **5** *2* **Cape Melody**[22] 3115 4-9-4 **77** ..... (b) TravisBlock 5 71
(H Morrison) *pushed rt and hmpd s: bhd: hdwy ent fnl 2f: rdn and no prog over 1f out: plugged on fnl f* **16/1**

-344 **6** *7* **Victorian Bounty**[14] 3401 5-9-6 **79** ..... MickyFenton 9 51
(Stef Higgins) *led tl rdn and hdd over 1f out: sn wknd: wl btn and eased ins fnl f* **15/2**

-050 **7** *½* **Desert Icon (IRE)**[28] 2926 4-9-1 **74** ..... NeilCallan 10 44
(W J Knight) *chsd ldr tl 2f out: sn wknd u.p: wl btn fnl f* **14/1**

4-10 **8** *2 ½* **Drawnfromthepast (IRE)**[13] 3461 5-10-0 **87** ..... (t) FergusSweeney 7 49
(J A Osborne) *wnt rt s: sn chsng ldrs: rdn and effrt over 2f out: wknd qckly over 1f out and sn wl btn* **10/1**

0-06 **9** *2 ¼* **Fleeting Star (USA)**[14] 3417 4-9-2 **75** ..... (b[1]) TomQueally 6 30
(J Noseda) *pushed rt s: t.k.h: hld up in tch in midfield: rdn and nt qckn wl over 1f out: wl btn over 1f out* **16/1**

6206 **10** *5* **Filligree (IRE)**[13] 3445 5-9-13 **86** ..... DavidProbert 8 25
(Rae Guest) *in tch in midfield: pushed along 1/2-way: rdn and unable qck over 2f out: wknd wl over 1f out: sn wl btn* **22/1**

1m 14.51s (0.11) **Going Correction** +0.20s/f (Good)
WFA 3 from 4yo+ 6lb **10** Ran SP% **119.2**
Speed ratings (Par 107): **107,103,101,100,97 88,87,84,81,74**
Tote Swingers: 1&2 £3.20, 1&3 £3.60, 2&3 £4.50 CSF £15.41 CT £44.27 TOTE £3.80: £1.60, £1.90, £1.90; EX 20.20 Trifecta £60.40 Pool £731.54 - 8.95 winning units..
Owner Stuart McPhee **Bred** Stuart McPhee Bloodstock Ltd **Trained** Compton, Berks

FOCUS
They edged over to race towards the centre of the track in this sprint handicap. The progressive winner took another step forward.

NOTEBOOK
Joe Packet ◆ defied a 5lb rise in the weights for his win at Newmarket last time and looks to be a colt firmly on the upgrade. It was noticeable how strongly he travelled, and that he was last off the bridle, and it wouldn't be a surprise to see him land a four-timer granted a fair rise from the handicapper. (op 7-2 tchd 4-1 in places)
Gramercy(IRE) made it a one-two for the two 3-y-os in the line-up. Ridden patiently out the back, he was putting in his best work at the finish, as one would expect of a colt dropping back from 7f, and he was simply unlucky to bump into a very progressive rival. (op 7-2 tchd 9-2)
King's Wonder had shown improved form on each of his previous three starts for this stable, and was nicely backed. He came up short but it was only the less-exposed 3-y-os who proved too good for him, and this was another solid effort. (op 11-2 tchd 6-1)
Fantasy Gladiator picked up well from off the pace but, by the time he got rolling, the winner had flown. He raced more handily when successful twice last season. (op 12-1 tchd 10-1)
Cape Melody has improved for the fitting of blinkers recently, but she had a career-high mark to overcome in a stronger race and wasn't up to it. (op 12-1)
Victorian Bounty showed good early speed, but is probably ideally suited by a sharper track. (op 7-1 tchd 8-1)

3846 LONDON AND REGENT CONSTRUCTION H'CAP 1m (R)
4:45 (4:45) (Class 3) (0-95,91) 3-Y-0+ **£6,799** (£2,023; £1,011; £505) **Stalls** High

Form RPR
3053 **1** **Kay Gee Be (IRE)**[15] 3366 6-9-8 **85** ..... AlanMunro 6 92
(W Jarvis) *mde all: rdn over 2f out: edgd lft u.p jst over 1f out: battled on gamely and forged ahd ins fnl f* **5/2**[2]

5442 **2** *1* **Standpoint**[14] 3396 4-9-4 **81** ..... LiamKeniry 2 86
(R Hollinshead) *chsd ldr: jnd wnr 2f out: rdn and edgd lft jst over 1f out: unable qck u.p ins fnl f* **5/1**[3]

1330 **3** *¾* **Tinshu (IRE)**[13] 3456 4-9-8 **85** ..... TomQueally 7 88
(D Haydn Jones) *stdd after s: hld up in last pair: swtchd lft and effrt 2f out: rdn to press ldrs over 1f out: kpt on same pce u.p fnl f* **10/1**

15 **4** *½* **Qanoon (USA)**[20] 3196 3-9-1 **87** ..... RichardHills 8 87
(W J Haggas) *sn bustled along to trck ldng pair: swtchd lft and rdn jst over 2f out: unable qck u.p wl over 1f out: edgd rt fnl f: kpt on again fnl 100yds* **6/4**[1]

420 **5** *¾* **Baylini**[13] 3457 6-8-7 **75** ..... SophieDoyle(5) 3 75
(Ms J S Doyle) *hld up in tch: rdn and unable qck 2f out: styd on same pce and no imp fr over 1f out* **8/1**

3020 **6** *6* **Wise Dennis**[37] 2640 8-9-5 **82** ..... NeilCallan 1 68
(A P Jarvis) *stdd s: hld up in last: rdn and no rspnse over 2f out: wl btn over 1f out* **7/1**

1m 41.51s (0.81) **Going Correction** +0.20s/f (Good)
WFA 3 from 4yo+ 9lb **6** Ran SP% **117.9**
Speed ratings (Par 107): **103,102,101,100,100 94**
Tote Swingers:1&2:£3.20, 2&3:£6.40, 1&3:£6.70 CSF £16.23 CT £107.86 TOTE £3.70: £1.90, £2.60; EX 15.00 Trifecta £52.90 Pool £424.84 - 5.94 winning units..
Owner The KGB Partnership **Bred** Pursuit Of Truth Syndicate **Trained** Newmarket, Suffolk
■ Stewards' Enquiry : Alan Munro one-day ban: used whip without giving gelding time to respond (Jul 23)

FOCUS
A 0-95 in name only as the highest rated horse in the race was the 87-rated Qanoon. The pace was decent. The form looks pretty ordinary, but sound enough.

NOTEBOOK
Kay Gee Be(IRE), who last won a race in October 2007, took full advantage of the fact that nothing else wanted to go on, and set out to make all. He proved brave when tackled in the straight, and stayed on well to score, but this race probably didn't take much winning and he doesn't look an obvious choice to follow up. (op 3-1)
Standpoint, who mainly races over 7f, had every chance entering the straight but the winner saw the trip out that bit better. He is proving very consistent this season. (op 6-1)
Tinshu(IRE) has never won over a trip as short as this and could have done with a much stronger all-round pace. Official explanation: jockey said filly hung left (op 12-1)
Qanoon(USA) had his excuses last time, but this performance is harder to overlook. He made little progress under pressure, and simply looks to have been overrated for his maiden win, which hasn't worked out at all well. (tchd 7-4)
Baylini remains winless from 23 starts on turf. (op 9-1 tchd 10-1)

The Form Book, Raceform Ltd, Compton, RG20 6NL

Wise Dennis remains firmly on the downgrade.

3847 DELANCEY APPRENTICE H'CAP 1m 4f
5:20 (5:20) (Class 4) (0-85,83) 4-Y-0+ £6,476 (£1,927; £963; £481) Stalls High

Form RPR

3413 1 **Peintre D'Argent (IRE)**[28] 2941 4-8-0 **64** ..... HarryBentley(7) 7 73+
(W J Knight) *chsd ldr untl 5f out: styd chsng ldrs: rdn over 2f out: ev ch whn squeezed and hmpd ent fnl f: rallied gamely u.p and r.o wl to ld fnl 75ds: won gng away* **3/1**[2]

0614 2 1 ¼ **Brouhaha**[13] 3432 6-9-5 **81** ..... SoniaEaton(5) 6 87
(Tom Dascombe) *stdd s: t.k.h: hld up in tch in last pair: hdwy on inner and pushed along over 1f out: led ins fnl f: hdd and nt pce of wnr fnl 75yds* **18/1**

5-01 3 ¾ **Mistoffelees**[8] 3608 4-8-7 **71** 6ex ..... TalibHussain(7) 5 76
(L M Cumani) *stdd s: hld up in last: c wd and urged along over 2f out: edgd lft and no prog 2f out: styd on ins fnl f: nt rch ldrs* **5/4**[1]

4313 4 ¾ **Jawaab (IRE)**[18] 3265 6-9-8 **79** ..... MarcHalford 4 83
(Mark Buckley) *t.k.h: chsd ldng pair: wnt 2nd 5f out: rdn to ld jst over 2f out: hdd ins fnl f: one pce and btn ins fnl f* **7/1**

0-50 5 ½ **Brooklyn Spirit**[27] 2975 4-8-8 **68** ..... (p) JohnFahy(3) 1 71
(C G Cox) *led: edgd lft and reminder after 1f: rdn and hdd over 2f out: one pce and btn ins fnl f* **5/1**[3]

0631 6 5 **Sgt Schultz (IRE)**[8] 3589 7-8-9 **71** 6ex ..... RyanPowell(5) 3 66
(J S Moore) *t.k.h: in tch: rdn and unable qck ent fnl 2f: wknd over 1f out* **8/1**

2m 36.18s (3.68) **Going Correction** +0.20s/f (Good) **6** Ran SP% **115.0**
Speed ratings (Par 105): **95,94,93,93,92 89**
Tote Swingers:1&2:£23.70, 2&3:£4.70, 1&3:£1.10 CSF £49.07 TOTE £3.60: £1.60, £5.60; EX 64.40 Place 6 £300.59, Place 5 £183.65..
Owner The Pro-Claimers **Bred** D Couper Snr **Trained** Patching, W Sussex

FOCUS
Some in-form horses contested this apprentice handicap, but it was run at a steady early pace. Muddling form, with the favourite disappointing.
T/Plt: £3,334.50 to a £1 stake. Pool: £74,685.51 - 16.35 winning units. T/Qpdt: £173.40 to a £1 stake. Pool: £5,694.35 - 24.30 winning units. SP

3555 CHEPSTOW (L-H)
Friday, July 9

OFFICIAL GOING: Good to firm (good in places; 7.5)
Wind: Fresh, across. Weather: fine and sunny

3848 TOTEPLACEPOT APPRENTICE H'CAP 1m 4f 23y
6:30 (6:31) (Class 5) (0-70,65) 4-Y-0+ £2,590 (£770; £385; £192) Stalls Low

Form RPR

0-02 1 **Vertueux (FR)**[28] 2923 5-8-12 **53** ..... DebraEngland 4 62
(A W Carroll) *mid-div: stdy prog on rails fr over 2f out: shkn up to ld ent fnl f: pushed clr: readily* **6/4**[1]

00/4 2 2 ½ **Garafena**[7] 3641 7-8-10 **54** ..... (p) NathanAlison(3) 3 59
(R Lee) *trckd ldr: led wl over 3f out: rdn over 2f out: hdd ent fnl f: kpt on but sn hld* **22/1**

25-2 3 3 ¼ **Urban Space**[9] 3559 4-9-4 **64** ..... MatthewCosham(5) 6 64
(J L Flint) *trckd ldrs: hung lft whn rdn over 2f out: chal over 1f out: kpt on same pce fnl f* **3/1**[2]

-005 4 1 ½ **Laura Land**[7] 3639 4-7-12 **46** oh1 ..... IanBurns(7) 10 44
(W M Brisbourne) *trckd ldr: narrow ld over 4f out: rdn and hdd wl over 3f out: one pce fnl 2f* **18/1**

6320 5 1 ¼ **Prickles**[16] 3324 5-8-5 **49** ..... AdamBeschizza(3) 7 45
(Karen George) *led tl narrowly hdd over 4f out: rdn over 3f out: one pce fnl 2f* **11/2**[3]

-055 6 2 ½ **Robbmaa (FR)**[9] 3560 5-8-5 **46** oh1 ..... (b) DavidKenny 5 38
(A W Carroll) *slowly away: sn mid-div: rdn 3f out: hung lft over 1f out: little imp* **18/1**

0 7 3 ¼ **Finzi Contini (FR)**[9] 3559 6-9-0 **58** ..... RichardRowe(3) 2 44
(Tim Vaughan) *dwlt: a in rr* **40/1**

2050 8 4 **Byblos**[15] 3348 5-9-7 **62** ..... (p) CharlesEddery 8 42
(W J Greatrex) *s.i.s: towards rr: hdwy over 3f out: sn rdn: nt pce to get on terms: wknd ent fnl f* **12/1**

506 9 10 **Sirdave**[32] 2812 4-9-7 **65** ..... JamesRogers(3) 1 29
(P W Hiatt) *little slowly away: a towards rr* **14/1**

2m 36.29s (-2.71) **Going Correction** -0.15s/f (Firm) **9** Ran SP% **112.1**
Speed ratings (Par 103): **103,101,99,98,97 95,93,90,84**
Tote Swingers: 1&2 £10.00, 1&3 £1.10, 2&3 £20.70 CSF £37.94 CT £89.35 TOTE £2.30: £1.10, £5.90, £1.80; EX 45.00.
Owner John Rutter **Bred** Roger Baudouin **Trained** Cropthorne, Worcs

FOCUS
A seller in all but name but the gallop was strong thanks to Prickles. The winner was potentially well treated on his old Flat form.

3849 E.B.F./TOTESWINGER NOVICE STKS 5f 16y
7:00 (7:00) (Class 4) 2-Y-0 £5,342 (£1,589; £794; £396) Stalls High

Form RPR

2541 1 **Belle Bayardo (IRE)**[2] 3784 2-9-2 0 ..... ChrisCatlin 4 89+
(R A Harris) *mde virtually all: rdn and hrd pressed over 2f out: r.o strly to assert jst over 1f out: comf* **3/1**[3]

0126 2 4 **Inagh River**[44] 2436 2-8-11 0 ..... PatDobbs 3 70
(R Hannon) *pressed wnr most of way: rdn to ld briefly over 2f out: kpt on but nt pce of wnr fr jst over 1f out* **11/10**[1]

62 3 1 **Zarazar**[39] 2598 2-8-11 0 ..... AndrewHeffernan(3) 2 69
(P D Evans) *trckd ldrs: rdn over 2f out: frequently changed legs: kpt on ins fnl f: nvr gng pce to chal* **14/1**

0341 4 1 **Second Encore**[6] 3686 2-8-11 0 ..... TadhgO'Shea 1 62
(J S Moore) *little awkward leaving stalls: trckd ldrs: rdn over 2f out: nvr gng pce to chal* **2/1**[2]

60.31 secs (1.01) **Going Correction** -0.05s/f (Good) **4** Ran SP% **112.6**
Speed ratings (Par 96): **89,82,81,79**
CSF £7.09 TOTE £4.90; EX 9.40.
Owner William Jones **Bred** L Mulryan **Trained** Earlswood, Monmouths

FOCUS
This developed into a match. The winner showed massive improvement on the face of things, but the form has been rated quite consevatively.

NOTEBOOK
Belle Bayardo(IRE) looks game as a pebble and he battled back to the front at the distance before storming away from his main rival. That's two wins in three days which isn't bad for a horse who cost just 3,000euros and Ron Harris said afterwards he'll give him a small break now before having a crack at another nursery. (op 100-30 tchd 7-2)
Inagh River poked her head in front at the 2f pole, but was readily left behind in the final furlong. She has a bit to prove now. (tchd 11-8)
Zarazar kept on at the one pace and looks the type to fare better when upped in trip in nurseries, for which he is now qualified. (op 11-1)
Second Encore, who looked quite decent when dominating at Nottingham last time, wasn't able to do so here and never got in a blow. (op 5-2 tchd 15-8)

3850 TOTEQUADPOT SPRINT STKS (H'CAP) 6f 16y
7:35 (7:36) (Class 2) (0-100,93) 3-Y-0+ £10,361 (£3,083; £1,540; £769) Stalls High

Form RPR

-300 1 **Olynard (IRE)**[13] 3461 4-9-9 **89** ..... JackMitchell 8 98
(R M Beckett) *little awkward leaving stalls: sn in tch: rdn 2f out: r.o wl whn gap appeared jst ins fnl f: led fnl 75yds: edgd lft: drvn out* **9/2**[2]

2042 2 hd **We Have A Dream**[8] 3578 5-9-8 **88** ..... GeorgeBaker 9 96
(W R Muir) *led: rdn over 2f out: sn hrd pressed: hdd fnl 75yds: kpt on gamely* **3/1**[1]

650 3 1 ¾ **Barons Spy (IRE)**[15] 3373 9-8-6 **75** ..... AndrewHeffernan(3) 10 77
(R J Price) *trckd ldr: rdn and ev ch over 1f out: kpt on but no ex towards fin* **10/1**

0-64 4 3 ¼ **Spanish Bounty**[39] 2595 5-9-8 **88** ..... SaleemGolam 6 80
(J G Portman) *trckd ldrs: rdn and ev ch over 1f out: kpt on tl no ex fnl 100yds* **9/1**

5240 5 1 ½ **Shifting Star (IRE)**[13] 3461 5-9-11 **91** ..... PatDobbs 5 78
(W R Swinburn) *stdd s: hld up: rdn and stdy prog fr over 2f out: styd on but nvr threatened ldrs* **9/2**[2]

4000 6 1 ½ **Mac Gille Eoin**[20] 3193 6-9-8 **91** ..... MartinLane(3) 7 73
(J Gallagher) *s.i.s: sn pushed along: chsd ldrs after 2f: rdn 3f out: one pce fnl 2f* **11/1**

2206 7 1 ½ **Abraham Lincoln (IRE)**[8] 3578 6-9-10 **90** ..... (p) TadhgO'Shea 4 68
(R A Harris) *mid-div: hdwy to trck ldrs 4f out: effrt over 2f out: wknd fnl f* **7/1**[3]

4014 8 2 ¼ **Kerrys Requiem (IRE)**[11] 3505 4-9-8 **88** ..... (v) ChrisCatlin 3 58
(M R Channon) *sn outpcd: a in rr* **14/1**

0230 9 1 **Wildcat Wizard (USA)**[13] 3461 4-9-13 **93** ..... (t) GregFairley 2 60
(P F I Cole) *mid-div: rdn over 3f out: wknd over 1f out* **7/1**[3]

1m 10.95s (-1.05) **Going Correction** -0.05s/f (Good) **9** Ran SP% **120.5**
Speed ratings (Par 109): **105,104,102,98,96 94,92,89,87**
Tote Swingers: 1&2 £5.10, 1&3 £22.80, 2&3 £12.30 CSF £19.32 CT £122.79 TOTE £5.20: £1.30, £1.90, £3.30; EX 18.50.
Owner R Roberts **Bred** Redmyre Bloodstock & John Cullinan **Trained** Whitsbury, Hants

FOCUS
A competitive event on paper but not a lot got into it and those who raced wide were ultimately well beaten, suggesting the stands rail was the place to be.

NOTEBOOK
Olynard(IRE) was a bit sluggish from the stalls but he managed to get a good tow through the race in behind long time leader We Have A Dream and, having travelled smoothly, the gap came in the nick of time. He picked up well to collar We Have A Dream close home under a well-judged ride to take advantage of his slip down the handicap. He is well suited to coming off a strong pace and the cards hadn't really dropped right for him so far this season. (op 4-1 tchd 5-1)
We Have A Dream ran a blinder in defeat, showing bright speed to bag the stands rail and gallop on strongly only to be collared close home. He has been running with great credit in defeat all season and deserves to find success. (op 7-2 tchd 4-1 in places)
Barons Spy(IRE) hasn't shown a great deal this year, but this was a major step forward and he is very well handicapped (8lb below last winning mark). (op 14-1 tchd 16-1)
Spanish Bounty dropped away having been close up, but he may not have been well served by racing wide of the main protagonists. (op 8-1)
Shifting Star(IRE) kept on from off the pace without getting in a blow. (op 13-2)
Abraham Lincoln(IRE) kept pitching away for a long way out wide before crying enough in the final furlong. (tchd 6-1and 15-2 in places)

3851 TOTEEXACTA H'CAP 7f 16y
8:05 (8:06) (Class 4) (0-85,85) 3-Y-0+ £5,180 (£1,541; £770; £384) Stalls High

Form RPR

510 1 **Sailorman (IRE)**[20] 3215 3-8-11 **76** ..... GregFairley 5 91+
(M Johnston) *broke wl: mde all: forged clr ent fnl f: v easily* **13/8**[1]

0660 2 5 **Woodcote Place**[15] 3346 7-9-10 **81** ..... GeorgeBaker 3 79
(P R Chamings) *hld up bhd ldrs: rdn and prog fr over 2f out: wnt 2nd over 1f out: kpt on to draw clr of remainder: nvr any ch w wnr* **5/1**[3]

-302 3 6 **Belle Des Airs (IRE)**[8] 3579 4-9-9 **85** ..... JohnFahy(5) 4 67
(R M Beckett) *trckd ldrs: swtchd out for effrt u.p over 2f out: fdd fnl f* **5/2**[2]

0001 4 1 ½ **Seneschal**[17] 3289 9-8-13 **77** ..... LucyBarry(7) 1 55
(M Appleby) *racd alone towards centre: prom: rdn over 2f out: wknd over 1f out* **14/1**

2644 5 3 ¼ **Kyllachy Storm**[12] 3474 6-8-12 **69** ..... (b) ChrisCatlin 2 38
(R J Hodges) *hld up bhd ldrs: rdn over 3f out: nvr any imp* **10/1**

2562 6 dist **Copperwood**[18] 3262 5-8-9 **66** ..... TadhgO'Shea 6 —
(M Blanshard) *rrd and v.s.a: detached and nvr rcvrd: cantered bk* **6/1**

1m 21.46s (-1.74) **Going Correction** -0.05s/f (Good)
WFA 3 from 4yo+ 8lb **6** Ran SP% **113.4**
Speed ratings (Par 105): **107,101,94,92,89** —
Tote Swingers: 1&2:£2.00, 1&3:£2.00 , 2&3:£2.60 CSF £10.43 TOTE £2.30: £1.20, £3.50; EX 11.60.
Owner Sheikh Hamdan Bin Mohammed Al Maktoum **Bred** 6c Racing Ltd **Trained** Middleham Moor, N Yorks

FOCUS
This was turned into a procession by the winner.

3852 BET TOTEPOOL AT TOTESPORT.COM FILLIES' H'CAP 1m 14y
8:40 (8:41) (Class 5) (0-70,70) 3-Y-0 £2,914 (£867; £433; £216) Stalls High

Form RPR

640 1 **Sooraah**[35] 2718 3-9-2 **70** ..... JohnFahy(5) 9 80+
(W J Haggas) *hld up: hdwy 4f out: travelling ok waiting for gap fr 2f out: qcknd up wl to ld jst ins fnl f: r.o wl: readily* **5/2**[1]

6-04 2 1 ¼ **My Sister**[29] 2901 3-8-10 **59** ow1 ..... PatDobbs 5 63
(M D I Usher) *w ldr: rdn over 2f out: ev ch ent fnl f: kpt on to snatch 2nd nr fin but nt pce of wnr* **10/1**

-645 3 hd **Mausin (IRE)**[21] 3170 3-9-4 **67** ..... GeorgeBaker 8 71
(H Morrison) *led: rdn ahd 2f out: hdd jst ins fnl f: nt pce of wnr: lost 2nd nr fin* **5/2**[1]

0305 4 hd **Sula Two**[13] 3464 3-8-8 **60** ..... WilliamCarson(3) 6 63+
(R J Hodges) *trckd ldrs tl outpcd over 2f out: hdwy whn swtchd lft over 1f out: styd on ins fnl f* **11/1**

0432 5 1 ½ **Leitzu (IRE)**[31] 2844 3-9-1 **64** ..... ChrisCatlin 7 64+
(M R Channon) *s.i.s: towards rr: swtchd lft 2f out: effrt sn after: kpt on same pce* **9/2**[2]

3500 **6** ¾ **Alice Cullen**[18] 3268 3-9-1 **64**........(v[1]) JackMitchell 10 62
(W R Swinburn) *s.i.s: hld up: rdn over 2f out: sme late prog: nvr gng pce to get on terms* **11/2**[3]

-004 **7** 3¾ **Ravens Rose**[39] 2600 3-8-6 **55**........ SaleemGolam 1 44
(J G Portman) *in tch: effrt over 2f out: wknd fnl f* **22/1**

3155 **8** 3 **Hathaway (IRE)**[14] 3387 3-8-8 **57**........ TadhgO'Shea 3 39
(W M Brisbourne) *s.i.s: towards rr: struggling 4f out: wknd over 1f out* **14/1**

006 **9** 2 **Better Be Blue (IRE)**[42] 2487 3-7-13 **51** oh6........ AndrewHeffernan(3) 2 29
(A W Carroll) *awkward leaving stalls: racd keenly: sn prom: rdn over 2f out: sn wknd* **40/1**

1m 36.16s (-0.04) **Going Correction** -0.05s/f (Good) 9 Ran SP% **121.6**
Speed ratings (Par 97): **98,96,96,96,94 94,90,87,85**
Tote Swingers: 1&2:£8.20, 1&3:£4.20, 2&3:£8.20 CSF £31.74 CT £71.59 TOTE £3.90: £1.10, £2.70, £1.40; EX 38.70.
Owner Mohammed Jaber **Bred** C R Mason **Trained** Newmarket, Suffolk

FOCUS
An ordinary fillies' handicap.

3853 BET TOTEPOOL ON 0800 221 221 H'CAP 1m 14y
9:10 (9:11) (Class 5) (0-70,70) 3-Y-0+ **£2,914** (£867; £433; £216) **Stalls** High

Form RPR

0415 **1** **Bidable**[6] 3683 6-8-13 **60**........ DeclanCannon(5) 10 67
(B Palling) *cl up on stands' side rails: rdn to chse ldr fr 2f out: kpt on wl ins fnl f: led towards fin: rdn out* **9/2**[3]

0-1 **2** ½ **Cotswold Village (AUS)**[18] 3258 4-9-13 **69**........ NeilChalmers 8 75
(M Appleby) *broke wl: led: rdn clr over 2f out: sn edgd lft: kpt on but no ex whn hdd towards fin* **14/1**

5-62 **3** 2 **Quiquillo (USA)**[45] 2410 4-9-8 **67**........(b) AndrewHeffernan(3) 9 68
(P D Evans) *s.i.s: hld up: rdn over 2f out: hdwy wl over 1f out: styd on fnl f: nt rch ldrs* **8/1**

0001 **4** 1¾ **Calypso Star (IRE)**[14] 3413 3-9-3 **68**........(b) PatDobbs 1 63+
(R Hannon) *wnt lft leaving stalls: hld up: swtchd lft and hdwy over 2f out: sn rdn: styd on: nvr trbld ldrs* **9/4**[1]

0005 **5** 2¾ **Red Dagger (IRE)**[15] 3374 4-8-10 **52**........ JackMitchell 5 43+
(R J Price) *hld up: rdn over 2f out: sme late prog but nvr gng pce to get involved* **20/1**

3006 **6** 1 **Mr Udagawa**[18] 3257 4-9-8 **64**........(p) GregFairley 2 53
(B J Llewellyn) *sn pushed into prom position: rdn 3f out: one pce fnl 2f* **10/1**

455 **7** 2¾ **Opera Prince**[15] 3377 5-9-9 **70**........ JohnFahy(5) 6 52
(Lady Herries) *hld up: sme prog u.p 2f out: wknd over 1f out* **5/2**[2]

0000 **8** 10 **Portrush Storm**[14] 3391 5-8-9 **51** oh3........ ChrisCatlin 4 10
(R E Peacock) *racd keenly trcking ldrs: struggling over 3f out: wknd 2f out* **33/1**

00-0 **9** 8 **Square Of Gold (FR)**[18] 3264 4-8-6 **51** oh6........ WilliamCarson(3) 7 —
(A W Carroll) *plld hrd trcking ldrs: rdn over 2f out: sn wknd: eased ins fnl f* **20/1**

1m 35.11s (-1.09) **Going Correction** -0.05s/f (Good)
WFA 3 from 4yo+ 9lb 9 Ran SP% **116.9**
Speed ratings (Par 103): **103,102,100,98,96 95,92,82,74**
Tote Swingers: 1&2 £12.40, 1&3 £9.10, 2&3 £3.90 CSF £62.59 CT £388.44 TOTE £7.10: £2.90, £3.80, £2.30; EX 41.50 Place 6 £90.00, Place 5 £63.52..
Owner Flying Eight Partnership **Bred** W D Hodge **Trained** Tredodridge, Vale Of Glamorgan

FOCUS
Not much strength in depth here and the front pair had the race between them from the furlong marker.
T/Plt: £187.00 to a £1 stake. Pool £60,627.54 - 236.60 winning units. T/Qpdt: £23.70 to a £1 stake. Pool £5,423.26 - 168.70 winning units. TM

3426 CHESTER (L-H)
Friday, July 9

OFFICIAL GOING: Good to firm (8.3)
Rail out 5y from 6f to top of home straight (where false rail ends) adding 12yds to advertised distances.
Wind: Light, half-against. Weather: Overcast

3854 BREAST CANCER CARE PINK MILE (A PRO-AM LADY RIDERS' FILLIES' H'CAP) 7f 122y
6:10 (6:10) (Class 5) (0-70,70) 4-Y-0+ **£4,047** (£1,204; £601; £300) **Stalls** Low

Form RPR

0321 **1** **Rascal In The Mix (USA)**[10] 3538 4-9-12 **61** 6ex........(p) AmyRyan 8 69
(R M Whitaker) *hld up: pushed along over 2f out: swtchd rt and hdwy over 1f out: r.o to ld fnl 150yds: in command after* **11/2**[2]

5035 **2** 2¼ **Many Welcomes**[14] 3391 5-9-6 **55**........ JemmaMarshall 10 57
(B P J Baugh) *midfield: effrt on outer 2f out: prog ins fnl f: r.o to take 2nd post: nt pce to trble wnr* **8/1**

0040 **3** shd **Piquante**[34] 2764 4-10-2 **65**........ KirstyMilczarek 2 67
(N Tinkler) *trckd ldrs: struggling to qckn whn bmpd over 1f out: r.o u.p ins fnl f to chal for pls: nt pce of wnr* **6/1**[3]

3660 **4** hd **Clumber Place**[24] 3061 4-9-4 **53**........ MissSBrotherton 1 55
(R C Guest) *chsd ldrs: effrt on inner to chal over 1f out: nt qckn fnl 50yds* **6/1**[3]

0-61 **5** 1½ **You've Been Mowed**[9] 3558 4-10-4 **67** 6ex........ KellyHarrison 5 65
(R J Price) *led: rdn over 1f out: hdd fnl 150yds: no ex fnl 75yds: eased whn hld after* **2/1**[1]

2603 **6** 3 **Two Turtle Doves (IRE)**[10] 3534 4-9-7 **56**........ MissMMullineaux 9 46
(M Mullineaux) *in tch: rdn 2f out: effrt to chse ldrs over 1f out: one pce fnl 100yds* **16/1**

-504 **7** 3½ **Astrodonna**[39] 2580 5-9-13 **67**........ MissNMcCaffrey(5) 6 49
(M H Tompkins) *bhd: pushed along over 1f out: nvr able to get on terms w ldrs fnl f* **10/1**

1025 **8** hd **Pretty Orchid**[13] 3434 5-8-12 **52**........(p) MissWGibson(5) 3 33
(P T Midgley) *towards rr: struggling 3f out: outpcd after* **16/1**

1505 **9** nk **Just Sam (IRE)**[20] 3224 5-10-2 **70**........ MissVBarr(5) 4 50
(R E Barr) *pressed ldr: rdn over 2f out: lost 2nd over 1f out: wknd ins fnl f* **16/1**

1m 33.38s (-0.42) **Going Correction** -0.025s/f (Good) 9 Ran SP% **115.1**
Speed ratings (Par 100): **101,98,98,98,96 93,90,90,89**
Tote Swingers: 1&2 £6.10, 1&3 £5.40, 2&3 £7.10 CSF £48.59 CT £274.83 TOTE £5.30: £1.40, £2.20, £2.40; EX 66.40.
Owner One-Six-One Partnership **Bred** Robert Hunter **Trained** Scarcroft, W Yorks
■ All the jockeys wore basically pink colours in this race for charity.

FOCUS
An ordinary handicap, albeit not many were obviously in form coming into the race. The pace was good and the winner was able to come from the rear.

3855 SEAKING ELECTRICAL H'CAP 7f 2y
6:40 (6:41) (Class 5) (0-70,69) 3-Y-0+ **£4,047** (£1,204; £601; £300) **Stalls** Low

Form RPR

6334 **1** **Gemma's Delight (IRE)**[25] 3030 3-8-3 **52**........(p) KirstyMilczarek 1 62
(J W Unett) *racd keenly: chsd ldrs: effrt over 2f out: r.o to ld fnl 150yds: in command towards fin* **18/1**

6104 **2** 2½ **Elijah Pepper (USA)**[20] 3216 5-9-7 **62**........ PhillipMakin 10 68+
(T D Barron) *hld up: swtchd lft s: hld up: rdn and hdwy over 1f out: r.o ins fnl f: fin wl to take 2nd cl home: nt rch wnr* **12/1**

2050 **3** ½ **Glenridding**[9] 3553 6-10-0 **69**........(p) PaulMulrennan 4 74
(J G Given) *led: rdn over 1f out: hdd fnl 150yds: nt pce of wnr: no ex and lost 2nd cl home* **8/1**[3]

4351 **4** 1¾ **Crocodile Bay (IRE)**[3] 3768 7-9-7 **62** 6ex........ PaulEddery 3 62
(R C Guest) *chsd ldr to 5f out: regained 2nd 3f out: outpcd and lost 2nd 1f out: rdn ins fnl f whn nt qckn: no ex fnl 75yds* **5/1**[2]

0525 **5** shd **Rainy Night**[8] 3584 4-9-4 **62**........(p) KellyHarrison(3) 5 62
(R Hollinshead) *midfield: hdwy 2f out: rdn to chse ldrs ins fnl f: styd on: nt pce to chal ldrs* **17/2**

1003 **6** ¾ **War And Peace (IRE)**[6] 3676 6-9-8 **68**........ RichardEvans(5) 8 66
(P D Evans) *midfield: sn pushed along: effrt over 1f out: swtchd rt ins fnl f: styd on u.p towards fin: nt rch ldrs* **8/1**[3]

6143 **7** ½ **Dvinsky (USA)**[13] 3463 9-9-9 **64**........(b) JimmyQuinn 6 60+
(P Howling) *slow removal of blindfold and awkward s: midfield: rdn and hdwy to chse ldrs over 1f out: styd on same pce ins fnl f* **14/1**

3-11 **8** 2¼ **Feeling Fresh (IRE)**[6] 3664 5-9-9 **64**........ SilvestreDeSousa 12 54+
(Paul Green) *bhd: u.p over 1f out: kpt on ins fnl f: nt pce to threaten ldrs* **10/3**[1]

0055 **9** 1½ **Nacho Libre**[24] 3061 5-10-0 **69**........(b) GrahamGibbons 7 55
(M W Easterby) *chsd ldrs: rdn and nt qckn over 1f out: u.p and no imp whn bmpd ins fnl f: n.d after* **12/1**

-561 **10** 1½ **Piccolo Express**[22] 3129 4-8-13 **54**........ J-PGuillambert 9 36
(B P J Baugh) *midfield: pushed along and wknd over 1f out* **20/1**

0335 **11** 2 **Misterisland (IRE)**[5] 3711 5-8-9 **50** oh4........ AndrewElliott 11 27
(M Mullineaux) *a bhd* **66/1**

0201 **12** 13 **Chambers (IRE)**[10] 3539 4-9-6 **61** 6ex........ WJSupple 2 3
(E J Alston) *chsd ldrs: 2nd 5f out tl 3f out: pushed along over 2f out: wknd over 1f out* **8/1**[3]

-600 **13** 1¼ **Silver Guest**[22] 3129 5-9-12 **67**........ SamHitchcott 13 5
(M R Channon) *s.i.s: sn swtchd lft: a bhd: nvr on terms: eased whn wl btn ins fnl f* **25/1**

1m 25.84s (-0.66) **Going Correction** -0.025s/f (Good)
WFA 3 from 4yo+ 8lb 13 Ran SP% **121.0**
Speed ratings (Par 103): **102,99,98,96,96 95,95,92,90,89 86,71,70**
Tote Swingers: 1&2 £52.80, 1&3 £39.60, 2&3 £33.60 CSF £217.49 CT £1939.12 TOTE £20.60: £4.30, £3.80, £3.60; EX 388.80.
Owner Miss Ciara Doyle **Bred** John Doyle **Trained** Tedsmore Hall, Shropshire

FOCUS
A competitive handicap but it wasn't run at the end-to-end strong pace that seemed likely given the number of potential front-runners in opposition and it proved very hard to come from off the pace.
Dvinsky(USA) Official explanation: jockey said blindfold got stuck at start
Feeling Fresh(IRE) Official explanation: jockey said horse ran flat
Chambers(IRE) Official explanation: jockey said gelding lost its action

3856 ENVIROSIPS H'CAP 5f 16y
7:10 (7:11) (Class 3) (0-95,95) 3-Y-0 **£8,200** (£2,454; £1,227; £613; £305) **Stalls** Low

Form RPR

1464 **1** **Diamond Johnny G (USA)**[14] 3417 3-8-2 **76** oh3........(t) JimmyQuinn 4 77
(E J Creighton) *mde all: rdn whn pressed ins fnl f: edgd rt: kpt on gamely and kpt finding for press towards fin* **10/1**

1226 **2** nk **Diman Waters (IRE)**[30] 2862 3-8-6 **80**........ WJSupple 5 79
(E J Alston) *a.p: rdn and nt qckn over 1f out: r.o u.p to press wnr towards fin but a looked hld* **7/2**[1]

5-05 **3** hd **Tawaabb**[27] 2972 3-9-7 **95**........(v[1]) SamHitchcott 1 94
(M R Channon) *in rr: rdn and hdwy over 1f out: chalng whn hung lft fnl 100yds: hld fnl strides* **7/2**[1]

50-0 **4** ¾ **Dancing Red Devil (IRE)**[13] 3430 3-8-2 **76** oh4........ SilvestreDeSousa 2 72
(Paul Green) *chsd ldrs: pushed along over 2f out: nt qckn over 1f out: keeping on for press whn n.m.r 75yds out: nt quite pce of ldrs clsng stages* **14/1**

1110 **5** nse **Hoof It**[27] 2978 3-9-5 **93**........ GrahamGibbons 9 89+
(M W Easterby) *bhd: outpcd over 2f out: prog whn swtchd rt ins fnl f: fin wl* **11/2**[3]

0343 **6** 1¼ **Secret Millionaire (IRE)**[6] 3673 3-8-11 **85**........ StephenCraine 3 76
(Patrick Morris) *midfield: effrt and hdwy over 1f out sn chalng: no ex fnl 100yds* **9/2**[2]

6104 **7** shd **Magical Macey (USA)**[20] 3218 3-8-13 **87**........(b) PhillipMakin 6 78
(T D Barron) *hld up in rr: u.p over 1f out: kpt on towards fin: nt pce to chal* **11/2**[3]

6000 **8** 1¼ **Falasteen (IRE)**[13] 3430 3-9-0 **88**........ TonyHamilton 7 74
(R A Fahey) *in tch: pushed along and outpcd 2f out: nvr able to chal* **12/1**

60.55 secs (-0.45) **Going Correction** -0.025s/f (Good) 8 Ran SP% **116.8**
Speed ratings (Par 104): **102,101,101,100,99 97,97,95**
Tote Swingers: 1&2 £8.10, 1&3 £11.70, 2&3 £3.70 CSF £46.00 CT £151.41 TOTE £12.00: £3.30, £1.80, £2.50; EX 51.00.
Owner John Griffin Owen Mullen **Bred** B & B Thoroughbreds Llc **Trained** Wormshill, Kent
■ Stewards' Enquiry : Jimmy Quinn one-day ban: used whip with excessive frequency (Jul 23)

FOCUS
A useful handicap run seemingly at a good clip but once again the best place to be was out in front.

NOTEBOOK
Diamond Johnny G(USA) has often been highly tried and was well weighted relative to Tawaabb on their running in a Sandown Listed race last month, but he's only a fair handicapper and probably not much better than this either given things dropped kindly on a track more suited to this style of running than Newmarket last time. He'll be vulnerable after a rise in the weights. (op 8-1)
Diman Waters(IRE) has run well here before and did so again. Well placed as the race was run, he had every chance if good enough from the final turn but couldn't get past the winner. He's plenty of size about him, though, and might well be the sort that will appreciate a more galloping or straight 5f. He's almost certainly got more improvement in him. (op 9-2)
Tawaabb, third in the Norfolk last year and a close fifth in Listed race at Sandown on his latest start, was having his first run in a handicap and was wearing a visor for the first time. He wasn't well away so couldn't make the best use of his plum draw but rallied well late on despite hanging to his left. He's capable of winning off this mark. (op 9-2 tchd 5-1)

Dancing Red Devil(IRE), a C&D winner last year, ran better than on her reappearance despite struggling to hold her position throughout and might be worth another try at 6f. (op 10-1 tchd 9-1)
Hoof It ◆ was a fast improver back in the spring and left the impression he's still unexposed. Usually a prominent racer, he had to settle in behind from his wide draw and was poorly positioned as a consequence turning in, but he fairly motored home and hasn't stopped winning yet. (op 6-1 tchd 5-1)
Secret Millionaire(IRE) was well backed all day, but had every chance as the race developed and clearly has nothing in hand of the handicapper. (op 4-1 tchd 5-1)
Magical Macey(USA) likes to race at or near the front, but was soon poorly placed running on a round track for the first time. (op 7-1)
Falasteen(IRE) is most effective racing prominently, but had his chance compromised by being forced wide from the off. (op 11-1 tchd 14-1)

3857 GRAND-NATIONAL.ME.UK H'CAP — 1m 2f 75y
7:45 (7:45) (Class 4) (0-85,83) 3-Y-O — £5,180 (£1,541; £770; £384) Stalls High

Form — RPR
4210 1 — **Cultivar**[27] 2979 3-9-7 83 ... SebSanders 3 — 88
(B W Hills) *sn chsd ldr: upsides 2f out: rdn to ld 1f out: kpt on gamely whn pressed towards fin* **15/8**[1]
1231 2 hd **Dolphin Rock**[30] 2863 3-9-2 78 ... PhillipMakin 2 — 83+
(T D Barron) *a.p: rdn and nt qckn whn swtchd rt over 1f out: r.o ins fnl f: str chal towards fin: jst hld* **9/4**[2]
-460 3 2 **Faith Jicaro (IRE)**[8] 3606 3-8-9 71 ... GrahamGibbons 5 — 72
(N J Vaughan) *led: rdn and hdd 1f out: no ex fnl 50yds* **14/1**
1231 4 3½ **Layla's Lexi**[14] 3390 3-8-10 72 ... PaulMulrennan 4 — 66
(Ian Williams) *racd keenly: hld up: clsd on outer 3f out: sn chalng: rdn and outpcd over 1f out: wl hld fnl f* **5/2**[3]
002- 5 ½ **Flipping**[214] 7669 3-8-11 73 ... FrannyNorton 1 — 66
(W S Kittow) *s.i.s: hld up: rdn over 1f out: nvr able to chal* **10/1**

2m 12.91s (0.71) **Going Correction** -0.025s/f (Good) 5 Ran SP% **109.9**
Speed ratings (Par 102): **96,95,94,91,91**
CSF £6.38 TOTE £2.90: £1.50, £1.70; EX 8.60.
Owner K Abdulla **Bred** Juddmonte Farms Ltd **Trained** Lambourn, Berks

FOCUS
A fair handicap run at a steady pace and all of the first four were still in with a chance turning for home.
Layla's Lexi Official explanation: jockey said filly ran too freely

3858 TETLEY BITTER CONDITIONS STKS — 5f 16y
8:15 (8:17) (Class 2) 2-Y-O — £8,200 (£2,454; £1,227; £613; £305) Stalls Low

Form — RPR
2144 1 — **Scarlet Rocks (IRE)**[27] 2950 2-8-9 0 ... SilvestreDeSousa 1 — 88
(P D Evans) *mde most: rdn over 1f out: pressed thrght fnl f: kpt finding for press: hld on wl* **7/2**[3]
2211 2 nk **Leiba Leiba**[13] 3426 2-9-0 0 ... SebSanders 3 — 92
(M Botti) *racd keenly: trckd ldrs: effrt to chal 1f out: pressed wnr ins fnl f: r.o u.p: looked hld cl home* **6/4**[1]
33 3 2¼ **Miss Mediator (USA)**[11] 3498 2-8-6 0 ... TomEaves 6 — 76
(M Dods) *hld up: wnt prom over 3f out: 2nd over 2f out: rdn whn chalng over 1f out: sn lost 2nd: kpt on same pce and no answer to front pair fnl 100yds* **9/2**
233 4 ¾ **Malpas Missile (IRE)**[44] 2436 2-8-6 0 ... RichardKingscote 5 — 73
(Tom Dascombe) *towards rr: pushed along 2f out: effrt bhd ldrs over 1f out: kpt on but nt pce to chal* **11/4**[2]
0 5 8 **Furiosa (IRE)**[37] 2638 2-8-6 0 ... JimmyQuinn 4 — 45
(E J Creighton) *s.i.s: in rr: u.p over 1f out: nvr able to get on terms w ldrs* **100/1**
0300 6 7 **My Mate Al**[6] 3686 2-8-6 0 ... RichardSmith 2 — 19
(Tom Dascombe) *w ldr for 1f: remained prom tl rdn and wknd over 1f out* **50/1**

61.62 secs (0.62) **Going Correction** -0.025s/f (Good) 6 Ran SP% **110.0**
Speed ratings (Par 100): **94,93,89,88,75 64**
Tote Swingers:1&2:£1.30, 2&3:£1.40, 1&3:£2.60 CSF £8.80 TOTE £5.10: £2.30, £1.30; EX 9.80.
Owner Nick Shutts **Bred** Mountarmstrong Stud **Trained** Pandy, Monmouths

FOCUS
Quite an interesting conditions event, but it developed into something of a tactical affair and once again the winner made all the running. She had the number one stall so it remains to be seen whether she can replicate this 9lb improvement.

NOTEBOOK
Scarlet Rocks(IRE) gained her third win of the year under a good front-running ride despite tending to hang away from the inside rail. Having already come up short at Listed level, she'll likely struggle under a penalty in a similar event. (op 5-1)
Leiba Leiba was arguably a bit unlucky as she had to be heavily restrained during the middle of the race when the winner steadied the gallop and hung off the rail. The winner pinched a length or so off her turning in and she though she was gaining steadily all the way to the line, she couldn't quite reduce the deficit. (op 11-8 tchd 5-4)
Miss Mediator(USA) ran well last time when third behind two who have Gimcrack entries. She was forced to race wide here after diving right leaving her outside stall and ended up pulling too hard into the bargain, having little left when the race began in earnest. She's a good looker and has an ordinary 5f maiden in the North at her mercy. (op 10-3)
Malpas Missile(IRE) is clearly well thought of, steering clear of maiden company for the second time in a row, but she still looked in need of the experience and found herself tapped for toe at various stages before staying on. A step up to 6f and a drop into a maiden might enable her to get off the mark. (op 7-2)
Furiosa(IRE) never threatened and was probably well out of her depth. (op 66-1)
My Mate Al probably needs a drop into sellers. (op 25-1)

3859 ASTBURY WREN NURSERY — 6f 18y
8:50 (8:51) (Class 4) 2-Y-O — £5,439 (£1,618; £808; £404) Stalls Low

Form — RPR
415 1 — **Puddle Duck**[8] 3598 2-9-0 71 ... PaulMulrennan 2 — 74
(K A Ryan) *s.i.s: in rr: effrt over 2f out: hdwy on inner over 1f out: r.o to ld wl ins fnl f: kpt on wl cl home* **9/2**[2]
2610 2 ½ **Belle Royale (IRE)**[21] 3141 2-8-8 65 ... FrannyNorton 3 — 67
(W M Brisbourne) *racd keenly: chsd ldr tl over 3f out: remained prom: rdn to chal over 1f out: ev ch ins fnl f: r.o u.p: nt quite pce of wnr* **15/2**
322 3 nse **With Hindsight (IRE)**[18] 3269 2-9-3 74 ... PhilipRobinson 1 — 75
(C G Cox) *led: rdn over 1f out: hdd wl ins fnl f: hld fnl strides* **10/11**[1]
2102 4 2¾ **Hortensia (IRE)**[8] 3583 2-9-7 78 ... SamHitchcott 6 — 71
(M R Channon) *hld up: hdwy over 3f out: rdn whn chsng ldrs 2f out: kpt on same pce ins fnl f: no imp fnl 100yds* **11/2**[3]
2021 5 2½ **Roodee Queen**[15] 3353 2-8-13 70 ... StephenCraine 4 — 56
(Patrick Morris) *chsd ldrs: wnt 2nd over 3f out: ev ch 2f out: rdn and lost 2nd over 1f out: wknd fnl f* **9/1**
5150 6 26 **Little Libretto (IRE)**[65] 1819 2-8-10 67 ... SilvestreDeSousa 5 — —
(P D Evans) *in tch: niggled along most of way: dropped to last 3f out: lft bhd 2f out* **12/1**

1m 15.41s (1.61) **Going Correction** -0.025s/f (Good) 6 Ran SP% **115.4**
Speed ratings (Par 96): **88,87,87,83,80 45**
Tote Swingers:1&2:£7.60, 2&3:£1.70, 1&3:£2.70 CSF £37.28 TOTE £4.40: £2.10, £2.60; EX 33.40.
Owner Mrs S J Barker **Bred** Cecil And Miss Alison Wiggins **Trained** Hambleton, N Yorks

FOCUS
A competitive nursery despite the small field and little in it at the line. The third was allowed to dictate an ordinary pace. The form looks modest but should prove reliable enough.

NOTEBOOK
Puddle Duck had seemed likely to be suited by a step up to this trip last time yet still deserves credit for managing to overcome a slow start and a relatively modest position 2f out to lead close home. The winning margin undervalues him, and he can improve again given a more galloping 6f. He reportedly goes to the big Goodwood meeting next. (op 4-1 tchd 7-2 and 5-1 in places)
Belle Royale(IRE) had been out of her depth at Royal Ascot last time, but ran well. She was a bit uneasy round the turns but battled on well in the straight and this probably ranks as a career-best effort. (op 7-1)
With Hindsight(IRE) was allowed to set his own pace in front and didn't really have any excuses, but is at least proving consistent and is clearly on a fair mark. (op 5-4 tchd 11-8)
Hortensia(IRE) wasn't done any favours by his outside stall, but probably needs to drop in the weights a bit. (tchd 5-1 and 13-2)
Roodee Queen had seemed to improve at Hamilton last time but had the run of things that day in a messy race and she looked far from good enough off this mark, for all she wasn't helped by being forced a bit wide early on when Belle Royale veered off her racing line. (op 8-1 tchd 12-1)
Little Libretto(IRE) again didn't last long here on her first run for over two months and presumably needs very soft conditions to show her form. (op 10-1)

3860 GO-STYLE.CO.UK H'CAP — 1m 4f 66y
9:20 (9:20) (Class 5) (0-75,75) 3-Y-O+ — £4,047 (£1,204; £601; £300) Stalls Low

Form — RPR
5230 1 — **Oriental Cavalier**[28] 2937 4-9-11 72 ... (v) GrahamGibbons 1 — 82
(R Hollinshead) *chsd ldrs: wnt 2nd 6f out: led 2f out: kicked clr over 1f out: r.o wl and in command ins fnl f* **11/2**[2]
2141 2 2¾ **Inspirina (IRE)**[13] 3432 6-10-0 75 ... TonyHamilton 10 — 81+
(R Ford) *hld up: hdwy 2f out: r.o ins fnl f: tk 2nd fnl 50yds: nt rch wnr* **7/1**
2302 3 ½ **Maslak (IRE)**[8] 3576 6-9-6 67 ... PhillipMakin 2 — 72
(P W Hiatt) *led for 1f: chsd ldr to 6f out: rdn and nt qckn over 2f out: styd on to take 2nd 1f out: no imp on wnr: lost 2nd fnl 50yds* **3/1**[1]
0436 4 hd **Valdan (IRE)**[39] 2597 6-9-1 67 ... RichardEvans(5) 5 — 71+
(P D Evans) *midfield: rdn and hdwy whn swtchd lft over 1f out: r.o ins fnl f to chal for pls: nvr a threat to wnr* **11/2**[2]
1533 5 1¾ **Hydrant**[11] 3499 4-9-10 71 ... SebSanders 7 — 73
(P Salmon) *midfield: hdwy 3f out: rdn and hung lft whn chsd ldrs over 1f out: one pce fnl 75yds* **6/1**[3]
1434 6 2 **Locum**[18] 3267 5-8-12 64 ... AshleyMorgan(5) 9 — 62
(M H Tompkins) *hld up: u.p over 1f out: styd on fnl f: nvr able to trble ldrs* **8/1**
412- 7 5 **Kind Heart**[33] 6570 4-9-4 65 ... PaulMulrennan 4 — 55
(D McCain Jnr) *rushed up to ld after 1f: rdn and hdd 2f out: wknd fnl f* **8/1**
0015 8 ½ **Harare**[8] 3582 9-9-2 63 ... (v) StephenCraine 8 — 53
(R J Price) *hld up: pushed along over 2f out: nvr able to get on terms* **33/1**
4514 9 22 **Magnitude**[7] 3617 5-8-11 58 oh3 ... J-PGuillambert 3 — 12
(B P J Baugh) *in tch: pushed along after 4f: wknd 2f out: eased whn wl btn ins fnl f* **14/1**
-060 10 dist **Dove Cottage (IRE)**[26] 2996 8-9-5 66 ... FrannyNorton 6 — —
(W S Kittow) *chsd ldrs after 2f: pushed along 5f out: sn wknd: t.o 3f out: eased whn btn fnl f* **12/1**

2m 38.47s (-1.43) **Going Correction** -0.025s/f (Good) 10 Ran SP% **122.1**
Speed ratings (Par 103): **103,101,100,100,99 98,94,94,79,—**
Tote Swingers:1&2:£7.30, 2&3:£4.80, 1&3:£4.60 CSF £46.04 CT £140.20 TOTE £7.30: £2.20, £3.10, £2.10; EX 48.10 Place 6 £180.68, Place 5 £65.36..
Owner The Three R'S **Bred** Mrs Claire Massey **Trained** Upper Longdon, Staffs

FOCUS
A fair handicap but not one that developed as seemed likely, for all the winner won it well, with the three usual front runners restrained and several ending up being set too much to do.
T/Plt: £254.10 to a £1 stake. Pool £65,543.54 - 188.25 winning units. T/Qpdt: £21.10 to a £1 stake. Pool £4,926.60 - 172.10 winning units. DO

3589 NEWBURY (L-H)
Friday, July 9

OFFICIAL GOING: Good to firm (8.2)
Rail realignment increased advertised distances on round course by 25yds.
Wind: Virtually nil Weather: Bright, warm

3861 CHRISTAL MANAGEMENT EBF MAIDEN FILLIES' STKS — 7f (S)
6:20 (6:22) (Class 4) 2-Y-O — £4,533 (£1,348; £674; £336) Stalls High

Form — RPR
1 — **Date With Destiny (IRE)** 2-9-0 0 ... RichardHughes 14 — 84+
(R Hannon) *mid-div: hdwy fr 2f out: shkn up to ld jst ins fnl f: asserted fnl 100yds: readily* **9/2**[3]
22 2 1½ **Zanazzi (USA)**[17] 3296 2-9-0 0 ... NickyMackay 6 — 78
(J H M Gosden) *led: rdn 2f out: hdd jst ins fnl f: kpt on but nt pce of wnr* **9/2**[3]
0 3 ½ **Opera Dancer**[17] 3296 2-9-0 0 ... JamesDoyle 3 — 77
(S Kirk) *chsd ldrs: rdn and kpt on to press ldrs over 1f out: styd on same pce ins fnl f* **33/1**
4 4 10 **Mortitia**[17] 3296 2-9-0 0 ... MartinDwyer 11 — 52
(B J Meehan) *chsd ldrs: rdn and hung lft 2f out: sn wknd over 1f out* **4/1**[2]
5 hd **Rosa Midnight (USA)** 2-9-0 0 ... HayleyTurner 9 — 51
(M L W Bell) *in rr: pushed along 1/2-way: styd on fnl 2f but nvr any threat* **18/1**
0 6 ½ **Ventose**[74] 1577 2-9-0 0 ... CoryParish 10 — 50
(M R Channon) *chsd ldrs: rdn 2f out: ev ch 1f out: wknd qckly* **50/1**
0 7 2¾ **Ellie In The Pink (IRE)**[37] 2642 2-8-9 0 ... MatthewDavies(5) 7 — 43
(A P Jarvis) *chsd ldrs: rdn 3f out: wknd over 2f out* **50/1**
8 nk **Summer Jasmine** 2-9-0 0 ... DavidProbert 13 — 42
(H J L Dunlop) *in rr tl sme hdwy fr over 1f out* **66/1**
66 9 2¼ **My Elliemay**[14] 3386 2-9-0 0 ... CathyGannon 15 — 37
(P D Evans) *a in rr* **40/1**
10 ¾ **Strictly Rhythm** 2-8-11 0 ... PatrickHills(3) 4 — 35
(R Hannon) *s.i.s: in rr: sme hdwy 1/2-way: hung lft and wknd 2f out* **40/1**

11 *nk* **Erythrina (IRE)** 2-9-0 0 .... FergusSweeney 8 34
(B G Powell) *in tch 4f* **100/1**

0 12 ½ **Highcliffe**[17] 3295 2-9-0 0 .... JimmyFortune 1 33
(R Hannon) *bhd fr 1/2-way* **11/1**

2 13 1 ½ **Pencarrow**[23] 3082 2-9-0 0 .... AhmedAjtebi 2 29
(Mahmood Al Zarooni) *pressed ldrs: rdn over 3f out: sn btn* **2/1**[1]

14 2 ¼ **Levantera (IRE)** 2-9-0 0 .... IanMongan 12 24
(C G Cox) *a in rr* **20/1**

1m 26.73s (1.03) **Going Correction** 0.0s/f (Good) 14 Ran SP% **122.3**
Speed ratings (Par 93): **94,92,91,80,80 79,76,76,73,72 72,71,69,67**
Tote Swingers: 1&2 £4.30, 1&3 £31.80, 2&3 £25.60 CSF £24.08 TOTE £4.10: £2.30, £2.00, £9.40; EX 16.60.

Owner Mrs J Wood **Bred** Azienda Agricola Loreto Luciani **Trained** East Everleigh, Wilts

FOCUS

A dry night and very warm day so conditions not surprisingly remained on the quick side. The rail was moved out so the Round course was 24m further than usual. The two previous runnings of this fillies' race have produced a couple of decent types in Minor Vamp and Middle Club and this year's renewal has thrown up another potentially smart sort. The gallop was just ordinary (into a headwind) but the first three finished a long way clear. Form to be positive about, with more to come from the winner.

NOTEBOOK

Date With Destiny(IRE) ◆, the only progeny of ill-fated George Washington and a half-sister to a French Group 3 winner, was easy to back beforehand but created a most favourable impression on this racecourse debut to maintain the unbeaten record of her trainer in this race. She travelled noticeably strongly and, although green when initially asked to quicken, she lengthened in good style to beat a reliable yardstick with a fair bit in hand and she appeals strongly as the type to hold her own in stronger company. (op 7-2 tchd 5-1)

Zanazzi(USA) also proved easy in the market just before the off but this fair and consistent sort again gave it her best shot and looks the best guide to the worth of this form. She has had the misfortune to bump into a couple of potentially very useful sorts but she should have no problem with a bit further and she is more than capable of picking up a race of this nature. (op 3-1 tchd 11-4)

Opera Dancer, who has several smart winners in her pedigree, was too green to do herself justice on this racecourse debut but shaped with considerably more promise this time and finished a good deal closer to the runner-up. She pulled a long way clear of the remainder, should have no problems with 1m and is capable of winning races. (op 66-1)

Mortitia had shown promise over this course and distance on her debut but failed to build on that and finished further behind the runner-up this time. However, she did not look entirely happy on this quick ground and will be worth another chance in ordinary company. (tchd 3-1)

Rosa Midnight(USA), the first foal of a 1m1f Polytrack winner, showed ability at a modest level on this racecourse debut. She shaped as though the step up to 1m would be more to her liking and she will be of interest when qualified for a nursery mark. (op 20-1 tchd 16-1)

Ventose fared a little better than the bare result suggests after showing up well for a long way on this first outing since April and on this first run over this trip. Run-of-the-mill-nurseries will be the way forward with her in due course. (op 66-1)

Pencarrow, who had shown promise on her debut at Kempton but who folded tamely on this first run on turf after racing on the outside of the field, was the disappointment of the race. She too will be worth another chance. Official explanation: jockey said filly hung right throughout (op 7-2)

3862 AXMINSTER CARPETS H'CAP 1m 2f 6y

6:50 (6:53) (Class 5) (0-70,70) 4-Y-0+ **£3,238** (£963; £481; £240) **Stalls** Low

Form RPR

0406 1 **Count Ceprano (IRE)**[16] 3323 6-7-11 **51** .... SimonPearce(5) 11 58
(J Pearce) *in rr: rdn and hdwy on outside fr over 2f out to take narrow advantage wl over 1f out: drvn out fnl f* **14/1**

0534 2 1 **Spiritual Art**[13] 3464 4-9-3 **66** .... RichardHughes 5 71
(L A Dace) *in rr tl stdy hdwy fr 3f out: travelling wl whn chal fr 2f out: rdn 1f out: nt pce of wnr ins fnl f* **7/1**[3]

0-10 3 ¾ **Dancing Jest (IRE)**[14] 3416 6-9-2 **65** .... MartinDwyer 4 69
(Rae Guest) *slt ld tl hdd 5f out: styd on far rail and styd chalng fr over 3f out: stl ev ch appr fnl f: nt qckn* **9/1**

2036 4 ½ **Having A Ball**[67] 1772 6-8-2 **51** oh2 .... NickyMackay 2 54
(P D Cundell) *chsd ldrs: rdn to chal fr 2f out tl outpcd ins fnl f* **14/1**

-134 5 ½ **Saviour Sand (IRE)**[8] 3607 6-8-13 **67** ....(t) KylieManser(5) 9 69+
(Miss Olivia Maylam) *stdd s: in rr: hdwy and nt clr run fr over 2f out: rdn and styd on fnl f but nvr gng pce to rch ldrs* **25/1**

3450 6 1 **Bolanderi (USA)**[25] 3036 5-9-7 **70** .... TomQueally 12 70
(Andrew Turnell) *in tch: rdn and hdwy on outside fr 3f out: hung lft u.p over 1f out and styd on same pce* **15/2**

2353 7 ½ **Choral Festival**[11] 3513 4-8-3 **59** ....(v) RyanClark(7) 8 58
(J J Bridger) *chsd ldrs on outer: led wl over 2f out tl hdd wl over 1f out: wknd fnl f* **15/2**

1001 8 1 **Beaubrav**[27] 2966 4-9-2 **65** ....(t) JimmyFortune 3 62+
(M Madgwick) *in rr: rdn and hdwy fr 3f out: n.m.r over 2f out: sme prog over 1f out: no imp and eased whn no ch wl ins fnl f* **11/4**[1]

0002 9 1 ¾ **Vinces**[14] 3403 6-8-9 **58** .... HayleyTurner 10 51
(T D McCarthy) *led tl hdd 5f out: styd chalng tl wknd appr fnl 2f* **15/2**

124 10 *nk* **Lady Lam**[2] 3783 4-8-7 **56** .... DavidProbert 7 48
(S Kirk) *in tch: rdn to chse ldrs 3f out: u.p but stl wl there whn n.m.r over 1f out: wknd: qckly sn after* **13/2**[2]

006- 11 3 ½ **Mt Kintyre (IRE)**[205] 7101 4-9-5 **68** .... AlanMunro 6 53
(M R Channon) *chsd ldrs 6f* **14/1**

2m 8.23s (-0.57) **Going Correction** 0.0s/f (Good) 11 Ran SP% **121.6**
Speed ratings (Par 103): **102,101,100,100,99 99,98,97,96,96 93**
Tote Swingers: 1&2 £18.20, 1&3 £48.30, 2&3 £15.00 CSF £112.44 CT £951.31 TOTE £24.80: £5.60, £2.60, £3.90; EX 169.10.

Owner Mrs Louise Marsh **Bred** Pendley Farm **Trained** Newmarket, Suffolk

FOCUS

Mainly exposed types in a moderate handicap. The gallop was no more than ordinary.

Beaubrav Official explanation: jockey said gelding was denied a clear run

3863 GARDNER MECHANICAL SERVICES H'CAP 1m (S)

7:25 (7:27) (Class 4) (0-80,80) 3-Y-0+ **£5,180** (£1,541; £770; £384) **Stalls** High

Form RPR

204U 1 **First Post (IRE)**[17] 3297 3-8-6 **69** .... CathyGannon 15 77
(D Haydn Jones) *trckd ldr: rdn: hung lft and led wl over 1f out: styd on strly ins fnl f* **12/1**[3]

-100 2 1 **Signor Verdi**[50] 2254 3-9-1 **78** .... MartinDwyer 14 84
(B J Meehan) *in tch: rdn over 2f out: hdwy u.p over 1f out: hung lft ins fnl f: tk 2nd cl home but no imp on wnr* **20/1**

0600 3 *nk* **Rainbow Mirage (IRE)**[16] 3318 6-9-6 **74** ....(t) TomQueally 12 81
(E S McMahon) *chsd ldrs: rdn 2f out: hung lft but kpt on ins fnl f to press for 2nd but no imp on wnr and one pce into 3rd cl home* **9/1**[2]

2232 4 ¾ **Spa's Dancer (IRE)**[20] 3207 3-9-0 **80** .... PatrickHills(3) 9 84
(J W Hills) *led: shkn up and hdd wl over 1f out: hung lft u.p and one pce fnl f* **9/2**[1]

2220 5 *nk* **Yourgolftravel Com**[17] 3290 5-8-9 **63** .... NickyMackay 8 68
(M Wigham) *hld up in rr: shkn up and styd on wl fr over 1f out: gng on cl home* **16/1**

0526 6 *shd* **Osgood**[18] 3271 3-8-7 **70** .... AlanMunro 13 73
(M R Channon) *in rr: pushed along and hdwy fr 2f out: kpt on fnl f: gng on cl home* **16/1**

0-51 7 2 **Starclass**[16] 3333 3-9-2 **79** .... ShaneKelly 11 77+
(W R Swinburn) *t.k.h: hld up in tch: hdwy to chse ldrs 2f out: wknd ins fnl f* **9/2**[1]

-036 8 *hd* **Basra (IRE)**[56] 2093 7-9-4 **72** .... FergusSweeney 7 72
(Miss Jo Crowley) *in rr: hdwy and n.m.r over 2f out: styd on fr over 1f out: one pce ins fnl f* **20/1**

5-04 9 1 **Rock Anthem (IRE)**[14] 3412 6-9-6 **74** .... AndreaAtzeni 6 71
(Mike Murphy) *in tch: rdn and effrt over 2f out: nvr quite rchd ldrs and wknd fnl f* **14/1**

1605 10 3 ½ **King's Caprice**[31] 2840 9-9-0 **73** .... RossAtkinson(5) 10 62
(J C Fox) *chsd ldrs: wknd u.p appr fnl 2f* **50/1**

-120 11 ½ **Our Boy Barrington (IRE)**[51] 2225 3-9-0 **77** .... RichardHughes 4 63
(R Hannon) *hld up: shkn up over 2f out: a in rr* **9/2**[1]

0036 12 4 **George Thisby**[13] 3463 4-8-11 **68** ow1 .... JamesMillman(3) 1 47
(B R Millman) *bhd fr 1/2-way* **25/1**

0401 13 *nk* **Maze (IRE)**[35] 2700 5-9-6 **74** .... NeilCallan 3 52
(A W Carroll) *t.k.h: chsd ldrs tl wknd qckly 2f out* **20/1**

1-14 14 10 **Compton Blue**[48] 2339 4-9-10 **78** ....(b) JimmyFortune 5 33
(R Hannon) *in tch: shkn up and wknd 2f out* **9/1**[2]

00-0 15 12 **Isphahan**[36] 2683 7-9-5 **80** ....(v) ThomasBrown(7) 2 8
(A M Balding) *chsd ldrs to 1/2-way: sn wknd: eased fnl f* **28/1**

1m 38.52s (-1.18) **Going Correction** 0.0s/f (Good)
WFA 3 from 4yo+ 9lb 15 Ran SP% **124.2**
Speed ratings (Par 105): **105,104,103,102,102 102,100,100,99,95 95,91,91,81,69**
Tote Swingers: 1&2 £56.50, 1&3 £26.90, 2&3 £54.40 CSF £242.57 CT £1422.37 TOTE £18.20: £4.80, £4.70, £3.60; EX 297.60.

Owner Llewelyn, Runeckles **Bred** D Llewelyn & J Runeckles **Trained** Efail Isaf, Rhondda C Taff

FOCUS

Progressive performers were in a minority but this was a fair handicap and one run at a reasonable gallop.

Spa's Dancer(IRE) Official explanation: jockey said colt hung left

Yourgolftravel Com Official explanation: jockey said gelding was denied a clear run

Our Boy Barrington(IRE) Official explanation: jockey said colt was unsuited by the good to firm ground

Compton Blue Official explanation: jockey said colt was unsuited by the good to firm ground

3864 GT EXHIBITIONS 10TH ANNIVERSARY (S) STKS 6f 110y

7:55 (7:56) (Class 4) 2-Y-O **£6,476** (£1,927; £963; £481) **Stalls** High

Form RPR

0335 1 **Captain Dimitrios**[8] 3596 2-9-0 0 .... CathyGannon 11 65
(P D Evans) *mde all: drvn clr fnl f: styd on wl* **7/1**[3]

0 2 2 ¼ **Pahente**[25] 3035 2-9-0 0 .... LukeMorris 9 59
(J S Moore) *chsd ldrs: rdn over 2f out: styd on to go 2nd fnl 120yds but no ch w wnr* **40/1**

1 3 3 **My Lord**[8] 3603 2-9-2 0 .... JackDean(3) 8 56
(W G M Turner) *t.k.h: chsd wnr: rdn 2f out: no imp over 1f out: one pce and lost 2nd fnl 120yds* **7/1**[3]

451 4 1 **Wotsthehurry**[7] 3636 2-8-9 0 .... MatthewDavies(5) 6 48
(M R Channon) *t.k.h in rr: hdwy fr 2f out: rdn and keeping on same pce whn hung lft fnl 120yds* **3/1**[1]

0 5 1 ¼ **Striking Love**[22] 3126 2-8-9 0 .... RichardThomas 7 43
(R Charlton) *chsd ldrs: hung lft over 2f out: styng on whn hmpd over 1f out and lost position: kpt on fnl f but nvr any ch* **8/1**

0004 6 2 **Bendigedig**[17] 3288 2-8-9 0 .... JamesDoyle 5 34
(S Kirk) *chsd ldrs: rdn over 2f out: wknd ins fnl f: btn whn carried lft fnl 120yds* **16/1**

3225 7 7 **Russian Ice**[28] 2939 2-8-9 0 .... EddieCreighton 2 15
(D K Ivory) *rdn 1/2-way: a outpcd* **6/1**[2]

063 8 1 ¼ **Chilworth Lass (IRE)**[29] 2905 2-8-9 0 .... NeilCallan 1 12+
(M R Channon) *trckd ldrs: rdn 2f out: hung bdly rt wl over 1f out and sn no ch: eased* **8/1**

5340 9 1 **Kodiac Star (IRE)**[27] 2963 2-8-9 0 .... FergusSweeney 3 9
(J A Osborne) *in tch whn hmpd over 2f out: no ch after* **7/1**[3]

00 10 9 **Foxy's Mint**[20] 3209 2-8-9 0 .... RichardHughes 4 —
(R Hannon) *a in rr* **10/1**

1m 21.16s (1.86) **Going Correction** 0.0s/f (Good) 10 Ran SP% **116.4**
Speed ratings (Par 96): **89,86,83,81,80 78,70,68,67,57**
Tote Swingers:1&2:£31.50, 2&3:£24.60, 1&3:£5.90. CSF £238.85 TOTE £7.80: £1.80, £11.00, £2.50; EX 389.50.The winner was bought in for 5,500gns.

Owner Bathwick Gold Partnership **Bred** W G H Barrons **Trained** Pandy, Monmouths

FOCUS

No more than a modest seller but the most valuable race on the card, and the first seller at Newbury for many years. The gallop was an ordinary one and those held up were at a disadvantage. High draws dominated and the winner produced a decent effort for the grade.

NOTEBOOK

Captain Dimitrios had the run of the race and turned in an improved effort returned to selling company. He should prove equally effective over 7f and is just the type to win again for current connections (bought in). (op 6-1)

Pahente, soundly beaten in a seller on his debut, fared a good deal better this time. He will be suited by a stiffer test of stamina and, as this was only his second start, he may be capable of a little better. (op 50-1)

My Lord, successful on his debut at Yarmouth this month, took a good hold but wasn't disgraced over this slightly longer trip after conceding weight all round. He may be capable of better, especially if he learns to settle better. Official explanation: jockey said gelding ran too freely (op 6-1)

Wotsthehurry, edgy and sweaty beforehand, looked to have good claims on his novice win but he wasn't seen to best effect after meeting trouble in a race that suited those right up with the pace. He will be worth another chance when a better overall gallop looks likely. (tchd 7-2)

Striking Love, quickly dropped into this grade, failed to travel with much fluency and had her limitations exposed after running into trouble at a crucial stage. She again shaped as though a stiffer test of stamina would have suited. Official explanation: jockey said filly suffered interference in running (op 9-1 tchd 10-1)

Chilworth Lass(IRE) Official explanation: jockey said filly hung badly right

The Form Book, Raceform Ltd, Compton, RG20 6NL

Kodiac Star(IRE) Official explanation: jockey said filly ran too freely

3865 RIDGEWAY H'CAP — 1m 5f 61y

8:30 (8:30) (Class 5) (0-75,70) 4-Y-O+ — **£3,238** (£963; £481; £240) **Stalls** Low

Form — RPR

-041 **1** — **Fantino**[7] 3617 4-9-3 **66** 6ex .... DavidProbert 3 — 75
(J Mackie) *trckd ldrs: rdn to chal 3f out: led wl over 2f out: sn rdn: a doing enough thrght fnl f* — **7/2**[2]

5642 **2** *1* — **Mykingdomforahorse**[12] 3475 4-9-7 **70** ....(v) RichardHughes 7 — 78
(M R Channon) *hld up in rr: hdwy on ins and nt clr run 3f out tl wl over 2f out: styd on to chse wnr appr fnl f: kpt on u.p but a hld* — **11/8**[1]

2413 **3** *1 1/2* — **Seventh Hill**[15] 3348 5-9-3 **66** .... FergusSweeney 2 — 71
(M Blanshard) *in rr tl hdwy 3f out: swtchd rt and styd on fr 2f out: kpt on fnl f but nvr gng pce to rch ldng duo* — **8/1**

5020 **4** *2 1/4* — **Bramalea**[16] 3314 5-8-12 **61** .... TomQueally 4 — 63
(B W Duke) *hld up in tch: smooth hdwy to trck ldrs travelling wl 3f out: rdn ins fnl 2f: wknd fnl f* — **22/1**

00-4 **5** *7* — **Red Twist**[15] 3348 5-8-2 **51** oh3 .... HayleyTurner 5 — 42
(M Hill) *in tch: swtchd sharply rt to outside over 3f out: sn hrd drvn: wknd ins fnl 2f* — **11/1**

32-3 **6** *8* — **Meirig's Dream (IRE)**[67] 1755 4-8-9 **58** .... PaulFitzsimons 6 — 37
(Miss N A Lloyd-Beavis) *chsd ldrs: drvn to take slt ld ins fnl 3f: hdd u.p wl over 2f out: sn wknd* — **16/1**

500 **7** *10* — **Sleep Over**[26] 2994 5-8-11 **60** .... NeilCallan 9 — 24
(D Morris) *sn led: narrowly hdd over 4f out: styd pressing ldrs and upsides ins fnl 3f tl wknd qckly 2f out* — **20/1**

4/03 **8** *8* — **Celtic Dragon**[10] 3522 5-9-3 **66** ....(b[1]) JimCrowley 8 — 18
(Mrs A J Perrett) *trckd ldr tl slt advantage over 4f out: hdd ins fnl 3f: sn wknd* — **5/1**[3]

2m 50.76s (-1.24) **Going Correction** 0.0s/f (Good) — **8** Ran SP% **115.4**
Speed ratings (Par 103): **103,102,101,100,95 90,84,79**
Tote Swingers:1&2:£2.00, 2&3:£2.70, 1&3:£4.60 CSF £8.79 CT £34.38 TOTE £4.60: £1.70, £1.10, £2.00; EX 7.10.
Owner Norman A Blyth **Bred** Norman A Blyth **Trained** Church Broughton , Derbys

FOCUS
A modest handicap in which the gallop was just ordinary.

3866 CRYSTAL BALL FILLIES' H'CAP — 7f (S)

9:00 (9:02) (Class 5) (0-75,75) 3-Y-O — **£3,238** (£963; £481; £240) **Stalls** High

Form — RPR

0052 **1** — **Our Drama Queen (IRE)**[12] 3479 3-8-11 **65** .... RichardHughes 2 — 74+
(R Hannon) *stdd s and swtchd rt to stands' rail: hdwy 2f out: travelling wl whn nt clr run appr fnl f: swtchd lft and qcknd ins fnl f: led fnl 75yds: readily* — **6/4**[1]

0-01 **2** *1/2* — **Lenkiewicz**[59] 2003 3-9-4 **75** .... JamesMillman(3) 4 — 79
(B R Millman) *chsd ldrs: rdn and str chal ins fnl f: upsides fnl 100yds: outpcd by wnr fnl 50yds* — **20/1**

5103 **3** *hd* — **Interakt**[10] 3525 3-8-12 **66** .... CathyGannon 12 — 69
(M R Channon) *trckd ldr tl led over 3f out: rdn and kpt on whn chal fnl f: hdd and no ex fnl 75yds* — **16/1**

-140 **4** *1/2* — **Rosedale**[22] 3115 3-8-8 **62** .... SteveDrowne 6 — 64+
(J A R Toller) *in rr: stl plenty to do whn rdn and hdwy over 1f out: swtchd lft and styd on strly ins fnl f: edgd lft: gng on cl home* — **10/1**

4-23 **5** *3 1/4* — **Shaluca**[25] 3023 3-9-0 **68** .... NeilCallan 11 — 61
(E S McMahon) *t.k.h: in tch: rdn 2f out: styd on same pce u.p fr over 1f out* — **13/2**[2]

220- **6** *1/2* — **Falling Angel**[385] 3086 3-9-6 **74** .... JimmyFortune 8 — 66
(P F I Cole) *t.k.h: towards rr tl hdwy fr 3f out: effrt fr 2f out but nvr quite on terms: wkng whn sltly hmpd wl ins fnl f* — **7/1**[3]

-032 **7** *1 1/4* — **Bathwick Xaara**[16] 3336 3-8-5 **59** .... HayleyTurner 10 — 48
(J G Portman) *chsd ldrs: drvn along fr 3f out: stl rt there over 1f out: sn wknd* — **14/1**

-164 **8** *shd* — **Hulcote Rose (IRE)**[7] 3628 3-9-5 **73** .... DavidProbert 5 — 61
(S Kirk) *chsd ldrs: rdn along fr 3f out: wknd over 1f out* — **12/1**

256 **9** *1/2* — **Tafawut**[7] 3628 3-9-7 **75** .... LukeMorris 7 — 62
(C G Cox) *chsd ldrs: rdn 3f out: wknd over 1f out* — **16/1**

-500 **10** *2 1/2* — **Silver Symphony (IRE)**[57] 2049 3-9-2 **70** .... TomQueally 3 — 50
(P F I Cole) *towards rr most of way* — **25/1**

6020 **11** *2 1/2* — **Sparkle Park**[18] 3263 3-7-13 **56** oh9 ....(v) Louis-PhilippeBeuzelin(3) 1 — 29
(B J Meehan) *chsd ldrs on outside: rdn over 3f out sn btn* — **40/1**

032 **12** *14* — **Poppy Golightly**[16] 3333 3-9-1 **69** .... AlanMunro 13 — —
(R J Hodges) *led tl hdd & wknd over 3f out* — **12/1**

1m 26.25s (0.55) **Going Correction** 0.0s/f (Good) — **12** Ran SP% **119.8**
Speed ratings (Par 97): **96,95,95,94,90 90,88,88,88,85 82,66**
Tote Swingers:1&2:£9.50, 2&3:£24.50, 1&3:£8.70 CSF £39.80 CT £376.56 TOTE £2.50: £1.60, £6.00, £4.20; EX 42.10 Place 6 £678.42, Place 5 £256.14 ..
Owner Patrick Wilmott & Martin White **Bred** Swettenham Stud **Trained** East Everleigh, Wilts

FOCUS
A fair fillies' handicap in which the pace was a reasonable one. The first four finished clear of the remainder.
Sparkle Park Official explanation: jockey said saddle slipped
T/Plt: £1,768.30 to a £1 stake. Pool £68,432.02 - 28.25 winning units. T/Qpdt: £146.70 to a £1 stake. Pool £ 5,274.68 - 26.60 winning units. ST

3822

NEWMARKET (July Course) (R-H)

Friday, July 9

OFFICIAL GOING: Good to firm (8.3)
Far side of July course utilised.
Wind: Fresh, half-behind. Weather: Cloudy

3867 32RED CASINO H'CAP — 1m

1:30 (1:31) (Class 2) (0-100,101) 3-Y-O — **£24,924** (£7,464; £3,732; £1,868; £932; £468) **Stalls** Low

Form — RPR

1101 **1** — **Sea Lord (IRE)**[12] 3487 3-9-9 **101** 6ex .... AmyRyan(5) 3 — 112
(M Johnston) *mde all: rdn over 1f out: edgd lft: styd on gamely* — **13/2**[3]

0233 **2** *nk* — **First Cat**[28] 2933 3-8-7 **80** .... FrankieMcDonald 11 — 91
(R Hannon) *hld up: hdwy 2f out: rdn and ev ch ins fnl f: styd on* — **33/1**

-211 **3** *1/2* — **Dance East**[18] 3271 3-9-2 **89** .... RichardHughes 4 — 98
(J Noseda) *trckd ldrs: rdn and ev ch whn hung lft ins fnl f: unable qck nr fin* — **13/2**[3]

5-21 **4** *hd* — **King Of Windsor (IRE)**[21] 3148 3-8-10 **83** .... WilliamBuick 8 — 92
(R M Beckett) *hld up: rdn over 2f out: edgd lft and r.o ins fnl f: nt rch ldrs* — **14/1**

0-21 **5** *1 1/4* — **Highland Knight (IRE)**[34] 2755 3-9-0 **87** ....(t) JimmyFortune 10 — 93
(A M Balding) *chsd ldrs: rdn over 1f out: styd on same pce ins fnl f* — **3/1**[1]

2314 **6** *1 1/2* — **Finest Reserve (IRE)**[20] 3196 3-8-8 **81** ....(v) KierenFallon 9 — 84
(M R Channon) *hld up: rdn over 2f out: styd on ins fnl f: nt trble ldrs* — **5/1**[2]

5-35 **7** *1* — **Colepeper**[29] 2898 3-9-6 **93** .... GregFairley 7 — 93
(M Johnston) *chsd ldrs: rdn over 1f out: no ex ins fnl f* — **28/1**

0-46 **8** *2 1/2* — **Musaafer (IRE)**[69] 1703 3-9-9 **96** .... RichardHills 6 — 91
(M A Jarvis) *s.i.s: hld up: hdwy 1/2-way: rdn over 1f out: wknd fnl f* — **15/2**

2006 **9** *8* — **Karaka Jack**[16] 3334 3-8-13 **86** .... FrankieDettori 2 — 62
(M Johnston) *prom: rdn over 2f out: wknd over 1f out* — **11/1**

-042 **10** *1 3/4* — **Mr Irons (USA)**[28] 2933 3-8-8 **81** .... RyanMoore 5 — 53
(Sir Michael Stoute) *chsd ldrs: rdn over 2f out: wknd over 1f out* — **8/1**

-100 **11** *7* — **No Hubris (USA)**[20] 3196 3-9-8 **95** ....(b[1]) JamieSpencer 12 — 51
(P F I Cole) *hld up: a in rr: rdn and wknd wl over 1f out* — **40/1**

1m 37.98s (-2.02) **Going Correction** -0.05s/f (Good) — **11** Ran SP% **115.0**
Speed ratings (Par 106): **108,107,107,107,105 104,103,100,92,91 84**
Tote Swingers:1&2:£17.00, 2&3:£16.50, 1&3:£4.50 CSF £200.83 CT £1465.05 TOTE £8.20: £2.50, £6.50, £2.60; EX 202.00 Trifecta £769.90 Pool £1,144,52 - 1.10 winning units..
Owner Sheikh Hamdan Bin Mohammed Al Maktoum **Bred** Darley **Trained** Middleham Moor, N Yorks

FOCUS
This was a decent, competitive 3-y-o handicap, but rather surprisingly the pace was not that strong. The main action took place up the middle of the track. The progressive winner made all but the form might not be as strong as it could have been.

NOTEBOOK
Sea Lord(IRE) made all under an astute ride. He was carrying a penalty (2lb well in) for his recent front-running success in a big field at the Curragh, but his rider's claim helped to negate that somewhat, and he also benefited considerably from being allowed to set modest fractions. He looks the type to go on improving, and may eventually stay further, but on this occasion everything went his way. Mark Johnston said afterwards that this son of Cape Cross could soon be contesting Group races, but he holds an entry in the totesport Mile, for which he has picked up a 3lb penalty, putting him on a mark of 106, and is around 12-1 for that Goodwood handicap. (op 7-1 tchd 6-1)

First Cat did well to finish so close at the finish seeing as, not only did he come into the race looking exposed, but he completely blew the start, losing several lengths. It's to his credit he stayed on for second, even briefly looking as though he might go by the winner, although he did carry his head at an angle under pressure. (op 28-1)

Dance East, the only filly in the line up, had given the impression that 1m1/2f stretched her when just holding on at Windsor last time, and she couldn't defy a 6lb rise on this stiffer track. She travelled well, but didn't see her race out quite as well as the front pair, not helping herself by edging left under pressure, and may appreciate a drop back to 7f. (op 5-1)

King Of Windsor(IRE) won his maiden over 7f at Ayr last time, but he seemed to find this modestly run 1m an insufficient test in this tougher company (handicap debut). He travelled okay to a point, but was being niggled along over 3f out and simply took too long to get going. A stronger pace should suit better, and he might stay further. (op 16-1)

Highland Knight(IRE), reported to have hung left on his first two starts, before winning his maiden convincingly on his first try around a left-handed track, once again seemed inclined to hang in that direction (through the early stages, before coming under pressure) on his return to a straight course. He ran straight enough for much of the time when off the bridle late on, but could make no impression and edged left near the line. (tchd 11-4)

Finest Reserve(IRE) is a fine big horse, and he looked in good nick beforehand but he never threatened, possibly being unsuited by the lack of pace in the race. (op 6-1)

Mr Irons(USA) should have run better considering he had today's runner-up 1/2l behind him when second at Sandown last time. (op 17-2 tchd 9-1)

3868 32RED.COM SUPERLATIVE STKS (GROUP 2) — 7f

2:00 (2:00) (Class 1) 2-Y-O
£39,739 (£15,064; £7,539; £3,759; £1,883; £945) **Stalls** Low

Form — RPR

14 **1** — **King Torus (IRE)**[20] 3190 2-9-0 0 .... RichardHughes 2 — 104
(R Hannon) *led: hdd over 5f out: chsd ldr tl rdn to ld ins fnl f: hung rt towards fin: jst hld on* — **7/2**[2]

21 **2** *nk* — **Ecliptic (USA)**[28] 2932 2-9-0 0 .... AhmedAjtebi 6 — 104
(Mahmood Al Zarooni) *plld hrd: w ldr tl led at stdy pce over 5f out: qcknd over 2f out: rdn: swvd rt and hdd ins fnl f: sn hung lft: r.o* — **5/1**[3]

115 **3** *2 1/4* — **Klammer**[24] 3049 2-9-0 0 .... ShaneKelly 1 — 98
(Jane Chapple-Hyam) *chsd ldrs: rdn and ev ch over 1f out: styd on same pce ins fnl f* — **6/1**

00 **4** *shd* — **Emperor Hadrian (IRE)**[22] 3100 2-9-0 0 ....(v) JMurtagh 5 — 98
(A P O'Brien, Ire) *hld up: rdn over 1f out: styd on: nvr able to chal* — **8/1**

3 **5** *nk* — **Ocean Bay**[86] 1309 2-9-0 0 .... MichaelHills 4 — 97+
(J Ryan) *hld up: rdn over 1f out: styd on: nvr trbld ldrs* — **25/1**

311 **6** *nk* — **Formosina (IRE)**[12] 3488 2-9-3 0 .... RyanMoore 3 — 99
(J Noseda) *trckd ldrs: rdn over 1f out: styd on same pce ins fnl f* — **11/8**[1]

1m 26.24s (0.54) **Going Correction** -0.05s/f (Good) — **6** Ran SP% **110.2**
Speed ratings (Par 106): **94,93,91,90,90 90**
Tote Swingers:1&2:£2.40, 2&3:£3.40, 1&3:£3.50 CSF £20.06 TOTE £4.20: £2.50, £2.50; EX 20.80.
Owner Sir Robert Ogden **Bred** Whisperview Trading Ltd **Trained** East Everleigh, Wilts

FOCUS
A juvenile race with a mixed tradition, only Dubawi and the ill-fated Horatio Nelson really catching the eye of previous winners in the past decade. It was the smallest field since Redback won in 2001 when it was of Listed status and, perhaps therefore unsurprisingly, it was a tactical affair with an uneven pace set until the halfway stage. The first pair came clear late on, though, and the form looks straightforward enough. The first two can rate higher and the next pair provided minor boosts to Royal Ascot form.

NOTEBOOK
King Torus(IRE) failed to shine when well backed in the Chesham Stakes at Royal Ascot last month, a race that often has a bearing on this event. He was equipped with the chifney bridle here in an attempt to stop him hanging and was popular with his stable continuing to fire in the winners. Never far away, he was ideally placed as the race became serious around 3f out and kept on resolutely up the climbing finish, just doing enough to hand his yard a fourth juvenile success at the meeting. Despite his new tack, however, he still veered to his right nearing the business end, but that wasn't down to getting a smack and it was probably just a sign of inexperience, this being only his third outing to date. Where the winner goes from here is not certain, though connections did mention the Group 1 Dewhurst later on, but he has the scope to rate a bit higher and ought to have no trouble getting 1m down the line. Whether he gets a bit further than that is open to debate looking at his pedigree, though. (op 4-1)

Ecliptic(USA) was flattered by his winning margin at Sandown last month, but his debut form was given a big boost thanks to the previous day's July Stakes winner Libranno. He was the only one of these to have previously won over the distance and took time to settle here, looking a reluctant leader when pulling his way to the front. He was certainly suited by being on the front end, though, and like the winner he was perfectly placed when the tempo increased. However, after looking like taking advantage nearing the furlong marker, he hung badly right when given a reminder and lost vital ground. He came back across when his rider switched his whip hand and only just lost out, so the percentage call is to think he would have won had he kept a true line. That is not totally conclusive as the winner may well have pulled out more, but he looks a winner waiting to happen in Pattern company should he learn as expected for this added experience. The Vintage Stakes at Glorious Goodwood later this month looks an obvious next step for him and he may well prove happier for racing around a bend once more. (op 11-2 tchd 9-2)
Klammer, fifth in the Coventry Stakes last time, looked sure to appreciate this extra furlong on breeding. He was the other that raced near the lead, but failed to see it out like the first pair and ultimately looked to find the stiffer test coming soon enough at this stage of his career. He remains a horse of potential, but a drop down in grade looks on the cards. (op 13-2 tchd 7-1)
Emperor Hadrian(IRE) really caught the eye motoring home from off the pace in the Norfolk Stakes over 5f last time out and stepping up to this trip looked a decent move. He never seriously threatened under a waiting ride, but could have likely done with a more truly run race and is a little better than he was able to show. That said, however, he is one of his powerful operation's lesser lights and evidently not the most straightforward.
Ocean Bay ◆, whose connections took this race with Silver Grecian last year, ran most pleasingly. He was having just his second outing (debut form working out well) and jumping up 2f in trip, but is bred to enjoy this sort of test at two. He was reported to have had an interrupted prep for this and was still showing distinct signs of greenness in the preliminaries. Considering he was at a disadvantage in being held up here, it was a massive run in defeat and connections obviously have another promising colt on their hands. Winning a maiden should prove a formality. (tchd 20-1)
Formosina(IRE), who broke the stranglehold of Ballydoyle when just getting up in the Group 2 Railway Stakes in Ireland on his previous outing 12 days earlier, proved most disappointing. He was carrying a 3lb penalty, but only one horse has attempted to win under one since Redback's win and none since the race became a Group 2. He looked in top shape, but was ultimately beaten before stamina for the extra furlong became a serious issue and really the run looked to come too soon. (tchd 6-4)

3869 32RED TROPHY (HERITAGE H'CAP) (FORMERLY KNOWN AS THE BUNBURY CUP) 7f

2:35 (2:36) (Class 2) 3-Y-0+

£49,848 (£14,928; £7,464; £2,800; £2,800; £936) **Stalls** Low

Form	Pos	Dist	Horse / details	RPR
-323	1		**St Moritz (IRE)**[23] 3069 4-9-1 **96** FrankieDettori 16 (M Johnston) *racd stands' side tl gps merged 3f out: mde all: rdn over 1f out: r.o wl* **4/1**[1]	106
0-53	2	*nk*	**Palace Moon**[20] 3193 5-9-10 **105** (t) KierenFallon 5 (W J Knight) *racd centre tl gps merged 3f out: hld up: hdwy 2f out: rdn and hung rt fr over 1f out: ev ch ins fnl f: r.o* **8/1**[2]	114
4360	3	*2*	**Light From Mars**[21] 3146 5-8-13 **97** JamesMillman(3) 9 (B R Millman) *racd centre tl gps merged 3f out: chsd ldrs: rdn over 1f out: edgd rt ins fnl f: styd on* **14/1**	101
0230	4	*nk*	**Marajaa (IRE)**[23] 3069 8-9-0 **95** JamieMackay 10 (W J Musson) *racd centre tl gps merged 3f out: hld up: swtchd rt and hdwy over 1f out: r.o* **22/1**	98
1031	4	*dht*	**Crown Choice**[27] 2971 5-8-12 **93** JamieSpencer 6 (W R Swinburn) *racd centre tl gps merged 3f out: hld up: gd hdwy over 2f out: hrd rdn fr over 1f out: edgd rt ins fnl f: styd on same pce* **9/1**[3]	96
-024	6	*½*	**Signor Peltro**[13] 3461 7-9-5 **100** DaneO'Neill 15 (H Candy) *racd stands' side tl gps merged 3f out: hld up: hdwy over 2f out: rdn over 1f out: edgd rt and styd on same pce ins fnl f* **8/1**[2]	101
1100	7	*½*	**Spirit Of Sharjah (IRE)**[21] 3146 5-9-5 **100** MichaelHills 17 (Miss J Feilden) *racd stands' side tl gps merged 3f out: hld up: hdwy 2f out: rdn and hung lft over 1f out: kpt on* **22/1**	100
63-4	8	*nse*	**Captain Brilliance (USA)**[37] 2651 5-9-7 **102** (v) RyanMoore 18 (J Noseda) *racd stands' side tl gps merged 3f out: chsd wnr: rdn and hmpd over 1f out: styng on same pce whn n.m.r wl ins fnl f* **9/1**[3]	102
4030	9	*¾*	**Advanced**[62] 1900 7-8-13 **99** AmyRyan(5) 7 (K A Ryan) *led centre gp tl gps merged 3f out: remained handy: rdn over 1f out: styng on same pce whn n.m.r ins fnl f* **18/1**	97
3650	10	*shd*	**Gallagher**[20] 3193 4-9-8 **103** MartinDwyer 3 (B J Meehan) *racd in centre tl gps merged 3f out: prom: rdn over 1f out: r.o* **16/1**	101
-410	11	*½*	**Brae Hill (IRE)**[21] 3146 4-9-3 **98** RichardMullen 14 (R A Fahey) *racd centre tl gps merged 3f out: hld up: rdn 2f out: sn hung rt and outpcd: r.o wl ins fnl f: nt trble ldrs* **25/1**	94
0400	12	*hd*	**Evens And Odds (IRE)**[20] 3193 6-9-0 **98** WilliamCarson(3) 8 (D Nicholls) *racd centre tl gps merged 3f out: chsd ldrs: rdn over 2f out: outpcd over 1f out: styd on ins fnl f* **25/1**	94
-103	13	*1 ¾*	**Imperial Guest**[21] 3146 4-8-12 **93** RichardHughes 20 (G G Margarson) *racd stands' side tl gps merged 3f out: hld up: rdn over 1f out: nvr on terms* **14/1**	84
-000	14	*nk*	**Axiom**[23] 3069 6-9-2 **102** IanBrennan(5) 1 (L M Cumani) *racd centre tl gps merged 3f out: hld up: hdwy u.p over 1f out: hung rt and wknd ins fnl f* **33/1**	92
0106	15	*nk*	**Dubai Dynamo**[15] 3366 5-9-4 **99** HayleyTurner 13 (Mrs R A Carr) *racd centre tl gps merged 3f out: prom: rdn over 2f out: styd on same pce appr fnl f* **33/1**	88
1000	16	*6*	**Everymanforhimself (IRE)**[21] 3146 6-9-3 **98** (v) StevieDonohoe 19 (K A Ryan) *racd stands' side tl gps merged 3f out: chsd ldrs: rdn over 2f out: wknd over 1f out* **33/1**	71
5346	17	*1*	**Noble Citizen (USA)**[23] 3069 5-8-11 **92** (be) WilliamBuick 2 (D M Simcock) *rc alone towards far side tl latched on to centre gp 3f out: chsd ldrs: rdn and wknd over 1f out* **9/1**[3]	63
1300	18	*nk*	**Autumn Blades (IRE)**[27] 2971 5-9-3 **98** (v) PatCosgrave 12 (A Bailey) *racd centre tl gps merged 3f out: hld up in tch: plld hrd: rdn over 2f out: wknd over 1f out* **66/1**	68
-044	19	*6*	**Freeforaday (USA)**[23] 3066 3-8-13 **102** RobertWinston 11 (J R Best) *racd centre tl gps merged 1/2-way: plld hrd and prom: rdn and wknd over 1f out* **20/1**	53

1m 23.75s (-1.95) **Going Correction** -0.05s/f (Good)
WFA 3 from 4yo+ 8lb **19** Ran SP% **128.2**
Speed ratings (Par 109): **109,108,106,106,106 105,104,104,103,103 103,103,101,100,100 93,92,92,85**
4th place tote: Marajaa £2.90, Crown Choice £1.30. Tote Swingers:1&2:£5.60, 2&3:£32.00, 1&3:£16.60 CSF £30.07 CT £439.01 TOTE £4.20: £1.60, £2.40, £4.30; EX 27.30 Trifecta £545.40 Pool £2,930.04 - 3.97 winning units..
Owner Mrs R J Jacobs **Bred** Newsells Park Stud Limited **Trained** Middleham Moor, N Yorks
■ A change of title for this historic event.

FOCUS
A typically competitive running of this famous handicap, but the GoingStick readings suggested that those drawn low were at a disadvantage (far side 8.0, compared to 8.5 centre, and 8.4 stands' side). The field split into two groups early on, with six runners, including the winner, racing towards the stands' side (albeit off the rail), while the majority were towards the middle, but they joined up late on. Not many got involved and the bare form was not as strong as it might have been.
NOTEBOOK
St Moritz(IRE) just failed to see his race out when third off a 3lb lower mark in the Hunt Cup last time and this stiff 7f proved ideal. Allowed to dominate throughout towards the nearside, he was strongly pressed by the runner-up late on but kept responding to pressure to see off that one's challenge. This was only his seventh start, so he should keep progressing, and he ran as though he'll get 1m better than he has done so far in due course, which will give him more options. The logical target now would seem to be the International Stakes at Ascot on July 24, and he'll look fairly treated under a 3lb penalty. He's in the totesport Mile as well, for which he's also picked up a 3lb penalty, and he is a best-price 10-1 shot for that race with both the sponsors and Stan James. However, Mark Johnston said afterwards that, seeing as the owners are breeders, they would like him to go for pattern races before long. (op 11-2)
Palace Moon ◆, off the same mark as when third in the Wokingham on his debut for this yard, ran a tremendous race in defeat considering stall five meant he did much of his racing towards the unfavoured far side. Although he raced up the centre through the middle part of the contest, he had started off far side, and that's where he made his move before hanging badly right inside the final furlong. He briefly looked the winner when ending up alongside St Moritz near the line, but he could find no extra in the final strides. All things considered, it's clear he got this trip well, but it's unlikely he would want to go any further and he will surely be fine back over 6f, making him a player for the Stewards' Cup, for which he is a best-price 10-1. (tchd 15-2)
Light From Mars wasn't at his best in the Buckingham Palace Stakes at Royal Ascot, but he had dropped to a mark only 3lb higher than when a clear-cut winner over this trip at York last October and returned to form with a decent effort. (op 16-1)
Crown Choice ◆, poorly drawn, was dropped in and gradually switched towards the centre of the track which meant he was on the best ground, but on the downside the track had been favouring prominent racers throughout this meeting. He travelled well and made good headway, but didn't quite see his race out off a 5lb higher mark than when winning at Sandown last time. Probably better than the beaten margin suggests, he looks one to keep onside, and the impression is he might even be worth a try over a stiff 6f one day. (op 20-1)
Marajaa(IRE), who looked well beforehand, lost his place slightly when short of room at around halfway and took too long to get going. (op 20-1)
Signor Peltro, 4lb higher than when seventh in this race last year, is probably better than he showed as he was held up well off the pace on a track that throughout the meeting seemed to be favouring speed. (op 13-2)
Spirit Of Sharjah(IRE) looks high enough in the weights. (tchd 25-1)
Captain Brilliance(USA), 4lb higher than when a close second in this race last year, had only been seen out once this season when well held in a Nottingham conditions race, and he couldn't make a telling impression despite having been well placed. He was short of room on a couple of occasions in the latter stages, but was finding only the one pace. (tchd 17-2)
Advanced, returning from two months off, was held when short of room near the line. (op 25-1)
Gallagher did not really improve for the return to 7f, although his draw was no help.
Axiom had the worst draw of all and did his racing towards the outer of the group up the middle, before ending up near the far rail, so this is easily excused.
Noble Citizen(USA), having started from stall two, raced on the slowest ground towards the far side for most of the journey and should have the run ignored. (op 12-1)

3870 DARLEY JULY CUP (BRITISH LEG OF THE GLOBAL SPRINT CHALLENGE) (GROUP 1) 6f

3:10 (3:13) (Class 1) 3-Y-0+

£227,080 (£86,080; £43,080; £21,480; £10,760; £5,400) **Stalls** Low

Form	Pos	Dist	Horse / details	RPR
51	1		**Starspangledbanner (AUS)**[20] 3192 4-9-5 120 JMurtagh 11 (A P O'Brien, Ire) *prom: swtchd lft to grab far side rail 5f out: chsd ldr: rdn to ld wl ins fnl f: r.o* **2/1**[1]	125
1121	2	*nk*	**Equiano (FR)**[24] 3047 5-9-5 117 MichaelHills 10 (B W Hills) *led in centre tl wnt far side 1/2-way: rdn and hdd wl ins fnl f: r.o* **12/1**	124
10	3	*¾*	**Alverta (AUS)**[20] 3192 7-9-2 112 (b) TyeAngland 14 (Paul Messara, Australia) *racd in centre: chsd ldrs: rdn over 1f out: edgd lft: r.o* **66/1**	119
6-16	4	*¾*	**Kingsgate Native (IRE)**[24] 3047 5-9-5 116 RyanMoore 2 (Sir Michael Stoute) *trckd ldrs on far side: hmpd wl over 4f out: swtchd rt over 1f out: sn rdn: r.o* **14/1**	119
20-4	5	*½*	**Fleeting Spirit (IRE)**[20] 3192 5-9-2 116 FrankieDettori 12 (J Noseda) *trckd ldrs on far side: rdn over 1f out: r.o* **7/2**[2]	115
1-40	6	*½*	**Varenar (FR)**[20] 3192 4-9-5 118 GeraldMosse 3 (A De Royer-Dupre, France) *racd far side: hld up: hmpd wl over 4f out: swtchd rt and hdwy over 2f out: nt clr run over 1f out: r.o: nvr able to chal* **16/1**	116+
-122	7	*2 ½*	**Society Rock (IRE)**[20] 3192 3-8-13 115 PatCosgrave 6 (J R Fanshawe) *racd far side: hld up: rdn over 2f out: r.o ins fnl f: nvr nrr* **16/1**	108
05-0	8	*1*	**Balthazaar's Gift (IRE)**[20] 3192 7-9-5 115 PhilipRobinson 5 (C G Cox) *racd far side: hld up: hmpd wl over 4f out: sn bhd: r.o ins fnl f: nvr nrr* **66/1**	105+
-130	9	*½*	**Marchand D'Or (FR)**[20] 3192 7-9-5 109 DavyBonilla 7 (M Delzangles, France) *racd far side: hld up: hmpd wl over 4f out: rdn over 2f out: nvr on terms* **16/1**	103+
4	10	*1*	**Nicconi (AUS)**[24] 3047 5-9-5 117 (v) DamienOliver 8 (David Hayes, Australia) *racd far side: mid-div: racd keenly: hmpd wl over 4f out: rdn over 2f out: n.d* **17/2**	100
4110	11	*2 ¼*	**Prime Defender**[20] 3192 6-9-5 111 RobertWinston 9 (B W Hills) *racd far side: carried lft 5f out: prom: rdn over 2f out: wknd fnl f* **50/1**	93
13	12	*hd*	**Kinsale King (USA)**[20] 3192 5-9-5 119 (bt) KierenFallon 13 (Carl O'Callaghan, U.S.A) *racd centre tl jnd far side over 3f out: chsd ldrs: rdn over 2f out: wknd fnl f* **7/1**[3]	92
3-20	13	*6*	**Showcasing**[20] 3192 3-8-13 114 (b[1]) WilliamBuick 1 (J H M Gosden) *s.i.s: sn prom: bdly hmpd and lost pl wl over 4f out: bhd fr 1/2-way* **28/1**	73+
0-20	14	*nk*	**Serious Attitude (IRE)**[20] 3192 4-9-2 108 JimmyFortune 4 (Rae Guest) *racd far side: mid-div: hmpd wl over 4f out: rdn over 2f out: sn wknd* **66/1**	69

69.81 secs (-2.69) **Going Correction** -0.05s/f (Good)
WFA 3 from 4yo+ 6lb **14** Ran SP% **120.5**
Speed ratings (Par 117): **115,114,113,112,111 111,107,106,105,104 101,101,93,92**
Tote Swingers: 1&2 £8.10, 1&3 £40.60, 2&3 £146.80 CSF £27.56 TOTE £2.70: £1.40, £4.40, £14.70; EX 28.50 Trifecta £923.10 Pool £12,791.04 - 10.25 winning units..
Owner M Tabor/D Smith/Mrs Magnier/Ms Massey **Bred** Emily Krstina (aust) Pty Ltd **Trained** Ballydoyle, Co Tipperary
■ Stewards' Enquiry : J Murtagh six-day ban: careless riding (Jul 23-28)

The Form Book, Raceform Ltd, Compton, RG20 6NL

FOCUS

A cracking running of this top sprinting prize, with little covering the runners on official figures and plenty attracting support in the market. Despite those drawn low in the preceding handicap looking at a disadvantage, the far side proved the place to be here as the pace setters blazed their way over there through the first furlong. Starspangledbanner confirmed his status as top sprinter and Equiano ran as well as ever. Again not many got involved, but for which the form could rate a bit higher.

NOTEBOOK

Starspangledbanner(AUS) followed up his Golden Jubilee win with a most game display to fend off the front-running Equiano, who had landed the King's Stand for a second time at Royal Ascot last month, so the form looks rock-solid despite this being a contest where racing handily was a must. Aidan O'Brien's colt was having his third outing since arriving from his native Australia and his improvement since running fourth on his British debut at York in May has been most taking. While there was solid reasoning for thinking he may have been flattered to have raced against the stands' side at Royal Ascot, he did have the race sewn up a fair way out that day and further progression was firmly on the cards. Johnny Murtagh was intent on crossing right over to the far rail in the early parts and that saw the majority of his rivals follow him across after they initially went to the middle of the track. That did cause interference -Murtagh was suspended six days - but only Showcasing was badly affected. The winner couldn't dominate, though, as the runner-up showed his customary early dash, and this conclusively proves he can be versatile on that front. He did again have the benefit of a rail, though, and that would have aided him inside the final furlong. He had to dig really deep in order to repel Equiano up the climbing finish and he showed real guts to emerge on top. This stiffer finish was, if anything, to his liking (won over 1m in Australia) and he really is a very classy operator. Connections later decided he is to continue his racing career and targets could include the Coolmore Nunthorpe at York and the Sprint Cup at Haydock, and with his devastating early pace he would no doubt go off a warm order in the former. (op 15-8 tchd 9-4 and 5-2 in places)

Equiano(FR) emerges with any amount of credit for this brave effort in defeat and turned in a career-best. He led for most of the race, electing to go far side later than the winner, and is obviously not just a 5f specialist these days. It wouldn't be surprising to see him renew rivalry with the winner at some stage, but should that rival opt out of the Nunthorpe, surely he would take all the beating in that. He was just eighth in the race last season, but is a much better horse this year. (tchd 11-1)

Alverta(AUS) was reported to have travelled badly prior to her British debut in the Golden Jubilee, when finishing down the field. This was a lot more like it from this very tough mare, however, and while she was another suited by racing near the lead, she deserves credit as she raced alone down the middle of the track for most of the race. Connections intend her last race before heading off to the paddocks to be in the Prix Maurice De Gheest.

Kingsgate Native(IRE), fifth in the race in 2008, finished a deal closer to Equiano than was the case in the King's Stand and continued his profile of an in-and-out performer. He could be another that heads for another crack at the Nunthorpe, which he won as a juvenile in 2007. (tchd 16-1)

Fleeting Spirit(IRE) came out on top of those racing on the far side when fourth behind the winner in the Golden Jubilee. She was never a serious threat this time, but ran to her previous level and there should still be other days for her. (op 4-1)

Varenar(FR) ◆, who was walked down to the start early, was something of an eye-catcher in the Golden Jubilee when two places behind Fleeting Spirit on the far side. He got a little closer to that rival this time and left the impression he would have been a deal better off under a more positive ride. There is still a big pay-day in this colt and surely the Prix Maurice De Gheest will be next for him (fourth last year). (op 18-1 tchd 20-1)

Society Rock(IRE) ◆ was better than the bare form when finishing second to Starspangledbanner on his previous outing. The suspicion was that he was an Ascot horse coming into this, but he hampered his cause here by getting behind after a sluggish start and finished strongly, albeit far too late in the day. He remains one to follow and should be winning again when dropped in class. (op 14-1)

Balthazaar's Gift(IRE) got badly outpaced and did meet interference when the winner came across early on. He finished his race encouragingly in the circumstances and this was a much-improved effort. Reverting to 7f should only help.

Marchand D'Or(FR), another walked down early to the start, also met some trouble as a result of the winner's early manoeuvre. He finished mid-field in the Golden Jubilee and did so here, still looking some way off the horse that won this in 2008.

Nicconi(AUS) finished fourth to Equiano in the King's Stand, when looking in need of a stiffer test, and does boast a verdict over Starspangledbanner earlier this year in Austrailia. Damien Oliver was brought over to renew their association, but while being held up here was a disadvantage, this was a rather laboured effort over the extra furlong. (op 11-1 after early 16-1 in places)

Prime Defender, who beat the winner over 5f at York in May, has been put in his place by that rival on level terms the last twice now. He has yet to finish in the frame in four appearances in this race, but he reportedly returned lame.

Kinsale King(USA) was a big disappointment. He looked a shadow of the horse that finished third in the Golden Jubilee and perhaps the different track wasn't for him. (op 9-1)

Showcasing, sporting first-time blinkers, was badly hampered 4f out as the majority came across to join him on the far side. That obviously didn't help, but he wasn't looking keen prior to that and, on the evidence of his last two outings, is going badly the wrong way. Official explanation: jockey said colt suffered interference shortly after start (op 20-1 tchd 33-1)

Serious Attitude(IRE) didn't run too badly on the far side at Royal Ascot, but she failed to fire here and now has something to prove. (op 50-1)

3871 EARL OF EUSTON E B F MAIDEN FILLIES' STKS — 6f

3:45 (3:47) (Class 2) 2-Y-O — £9,714 (£2,890; £1,444; £721) Stalls Low

Form	Pos	Dist	Horse	Jockey	RPR
	1		**Catfish (IRE)** 2-9-0 0 (Miss Gay Kelleway) *led: hdd over 3f out: remained w ldr tl led again 2f out: drvn out* **40/1**	JimmyFortune 2	79
2	2	nk	**Ragsah (IRE)**[14] 3411 2-9-0 0 (Saeed Bin Suroor) *hld up: hdwy over 2f out: rdn to chse wnr over 1f out: edgd lft: r.o* **5/4**[1]	FrankieDettori 9	78+
	3	2 1/4	**Our Gal** 2-9-0 0 (M G Quinlan) *chsd ldr tl led over 3f out: hdd 2f out: sn rdn: styd on same pce fnl f* **12/1**	WilliamCarson 6	71
	4	1 1/2	**Layla Jamil (IRE)** 2-9-0 0 (M R Channon) *prom: rdn over 2f out: outpcd over 1f out: styd on ins fnl f* **8/1**[3]	KierenFallon 1	67
	5	shd	**Sodashy (IRE)** 2-9-0 0 (Miss Amy Weaver) *s.i.s: hdwy over 3f out: rdn over 1f out: styd on* **100/1**	JerryO'Dwyer 10	66
4	6	1 1/4	**Our Way Only (IRE)**[14] 3411 2-9-0 0 (R Hannon) *chsd ldrs: rdn over 1f out: wknd and edgd rt ins fnl f* **4/1**[2]	RichardHughes 8	63
	7	2	**Chinook Wind (IRE)** 2-9-0 0 (B W Hills) *chsd ldrs: rdn over 1f out: wknd fnl f: hmpd towards fin* **25/1**	RobertWinston 11	58+
5035	8	nk	**Apazine (USA)**[14] 3386 2-9-0 0 (J H M Gosden) *chsd ldrs: rdn over 1f out: sn wknd* **12/1**	(b[1]) WilliamBuick 7	56
	9	1	**Theyskens' Theory (USA)** 2-9-0 0 (B J Meehan) *s.s: hdwy over 2f out: wknd over 1f out* **12/1**	MartinDwyer 13	53+
	10	1	**Apticanti (USA)** 2-9-0 0 (B W Hills) *hld up: hmpd over 3f out: a in rr* **10/1**	MichaelHills 3	50
	11	17	**Dualite (IRE)** 2-9-0 0 (J L Dunlop) *s.i.s: hld up: rdn and wknd over 2f out: hung lft over 1f out* **25/1**	RichardMullen 12	—

1m 12.77s (0.27) **Going Correction** -0.05s/f (Good) **11** Ran SP% **118.8**

Speed ratings (Par 97): **96,95,92,90,90 88,86,85,84,83 60**

Tote Swingers: 1&2 £12.90, 1&3 £50.10, 2&3 £6.50 CSF £90.17 TOTE £38.50: £5.80, £1.10, £3.20; EX 95.80 TRIFECTA Not won..

Owner Raymond Tooth **Bred** Castellane Partnership **Trained** Exning, Suffolk

FOCUS

This is sometimes a quality fillies' maiden, with Gossamer and Fantasia the most notable winners in recent years, but it remains to be seen just how strong the bare form is this time around. The winner did it well but along with the third and fourth had the far rail to help.

NOTEBOOK

Catfish(IRE), who had a sheepskin noseband fitted, "can be tricky at home" according to Gay Kelleway, but she showed a fine attitude in the race, including when strongly challenged by the more experienced runner-up late on, in the process displaying a fluent, fast-ground action. A 22,000gns half-sister to dual 1m-1m1f winner Tempsford Flyer, she's obviously pretty useful and will surely go up in grade now, with her trainer mentioning that she could be off to Deauville. (tchd 33-1)

Ragsah(IRE), beaten 6l into second when sent off 4-7 over C&D on debut, had no apparent excuse. She raced towards the outer of the main bunch, but was simply unable to reel in the winner. This half-sister to Dubai Millennium has yet to live up to market expectations, but it wouldn't surprise to see her do better in due course. (tchd 11-8 and 6-4 in places)

Our Gal, a half-sister to, among others, 6f juvenile winner Bow Wave, showed up well for a long way but couldn't go with the front pair late on. Quite a leggy filly, she's open to improvement. (op 9-1)

Layla Jamil(IRE), a 60,000euros half-sister to 5f debut winner Pelican Key, kept on after being outpaced inside the final 2f. She should be sharper next time. (op 10-1)

Sodashy(IRE) twice failed to find a buyer at 4,500gns and was dismissed in the betting ahead of this debut, but she evidently has ability. She raced off the pace after missing the break, but kept on and should improve.

Our Way Only(IRE) seemed well fancied to at least get a lot closer to Ragsah than when over 2l behind that rival on debut, but that wasn't the case, with her finding little after showing early speed. (op 9-2)

Chinook Wind(IRE), a smartly bred 125,000gns purchase, ran green and wasn't given a hard time, so much better can be expected. (tchd 28-1)

Theyskens' Theory(USA) ◆ looked badly in need of the experience through the opening stages and was wide throughout. (op 16-1 tchd 20-1 in places)

3872 WEATHERBYS NURSERY — 7f

4:20 (4:22) (Class 2) 2-Y-O — £12,952 (£3,854; £1,926; £962) Stalls Low

Form	Pos	Dist	Horse	Jockey	RPR
414	1		**Memen (IRE)**[28] 2918 2-8-11 **81** (P F I Cole) *hld up: hdwy over 1f out: rdn to ld ins fnl f: r.o wl* **12/1**	JimmyFortune 7	90
10	2	2	**Amwell Pinot**[24] 3049 2-9-0 **84** (A Bailey) *hld up in tch: rdn to ld wl over 1f out: sn hdd: ev ch ins fnl f: styd on same pce: edgd rt towards fin* **5/1**[2]	FrankieDettori 5	88
31	3	3/4	**Rerouted (USA)**[42] 2493 2-9-2 **86** (B W Hills) *hld up: hdwy over 2f out: led over 1f out: rdn and hdd ins fnl f: no ex and hung rt nr fin* **15/8**[1]	MichaelHills 12	88
51	4	2 1/4	**Sceal Nua (IRE)**[23] 3082 2-8-2 **72** (R Hannon) *chsd ldrs: rdn over 2f out: edgd lft and wknd wl ins fnl f* **6/1**	FrankieMcDonald 11	69
6062	5	1	**Witzend (IRE)**[3] 3749 2-7-12 **68** oh1 (Jedd O'Keeffe) *s.i.s: sn chsng ldrs: led 2f out: sn rdn and hdd: wknd wl ins fnl f* **14/1**	JamieMackay 1	62
043	6	shd	**Sheila's Star (IRE)**[20] 3209 2-7-12 **68** oh1 (J S Moore) *prom: racd keenly early: outpcd 1/2-way: rallied over 1f out: wknd ins fnl f* **22/1**	DuranFentiman 2	62
310	7	6	**Singapore Lilly (IRE)**[34] 2743 2-8-5 **75** (M R Channon) *chsd ldr: rdn over 2f out: ev ch over 1f out: wknd fnl f* **16/1**	AdrianNicholls 3	54
01	8	3/4	**Liberty Cap (USA)**[20] 3219 2-9-0 **84** (J H M Gosden) *chsd ldrs tl rdn and wknd over 1f out* **12/1**	(p) WilliamBuick 10	61
410	9	7	**Idiom (IRE)**[21] 3141 2-9-7 **91** (Mahmood Al Zarooni) *chsd ldrs: rdn over 2f out: wknd wl over 1f out* **25/1**	AhmedAjtebi 6	50
51	10	7	**Breathless Storm (USA)**[54] 2138 2-8-12 **82** (T P Tate) *hld up in tch: wknd over 2f out* **11/2**[3]	JamieSpencer 8	24

1m 24.88s (-0.82) **Going Correction** -0.05s/f (Good) **10** Ran SP% **117.2**

Speed ratings (Par 100): **102,99,98,96,95 95,88,87,79,71**

Tote Swingers:1&2:£10.80, 2&3:£3.20, 1&3:£4.40 CSF £71.43 CT £169.05 TOTE £14.90: £3.10, £2.30, £1.10; EX 106.40 Trifecta £280.21 Pool £1,173.85 - 3.10 winning units..

Owner Jared Sullivan **Bred** Keatly Overseas Ltd **Trained** Whatcombe, Oxon

FOCUS

A decent nursery, and the time was 1.36 seconds quicker than the earlier Group 2 Superlative Stakes, although that race was steadily run. The majority of these raced up the centre of the track. Strong form, as is usual for this nursery.

NOTEBOOK

Memen(IRE) proved suited by the step up in trip on this handicap debut and picked up really well from off the pace to win convincingly. Connections said afterwards that he could now go for a nursery at Goodwood, provided he makes the cut. (tchd 14-1)

Amwell Pinot, a Chester maiden winner before finishing down the field in the Coventry, ran a solid race in defeat and could pick up a similar event. (op 8-1)

Rerouted(USA) couldn't follow up his recent 6f Haydock maiden success, failing to justify good market support. He didn't run badly, though, and could yet do better. (op 5-2 tchd 7-4)

Sceal Nua(IRE) found this tougher than the Polytrack maiden she won over this trip last time. (op 11-2)

Witzend(IRE), 1lb out of the weights, recovered from a slow start but failed to convince that he got the trip. (op 10-1)

Sheila's Star(IRE) is better than she showed as she was keen early and raced towards the far rail for most of the way - the slowest ground according to the GoingStick. (op 16-1)

Breathless Storm(USA) came into this off the back of a win in a 6f maiden at Ripon, but he ran poorly this time and presumably something was amiss. Official explanation: jockey said colt hung right (op 8-1)

3873 EGERTON HOUSE STABLES H'CAP — 1m 4f

4:55 (4:55) (Class 3) (0-90,93) 3-Y-O+ — £9,714 (£2,890; £1,444; £721) Stalls Centre

Form	Pos	Dist	Horse	Jockey	RPR
30-5	1		**Times Up**[21] 3159 4-10-0 **89** (J L Dunlop) *a.p: rdn over 1f out: led ins fnl f: r.o wl* **9/1**	JamieSpencer 4	99+
3141	2	2 1/4	**Bay Willow (IRE)**[12] 3492 3-9-5 **93** 6ex (M Johnston) *sn led: rdn over 1f out: hdd and unable qck ins fnl f* **11/10**[1]	FrankieDettori 3	100+
0031	3	1	**Ouster (GER)**[26] 2996 4-9-11 **86** (D R C Elsworth) *chsd ldrs: nt clr run over 2f out: rdn over 1f out: styd on* **9/1**	JimmyFortune 10	91

00-0 **4** *hd* **Strategic Mount**[13] 3462 7-9-13 **88** RichardHughes 2 93
(P F I Cole) *s.i.s: hld up: hdwy over 5f out: hmpd over 3f out: rdn over 1f out: edgd lft ins fnl f: styd on* **28/1**

2112 **5** *1 1/4* **Speed Dating**[14] 3416 4-9-10 **85** (b) KoseiMiura 12 88+
(Sir Mark Prescott) *hld up: hdwy u.p on outside over 1f out: no ex wl ins fnl f* **13/2**[2]

100- **6** *nse* **Overrule (USA)**[63] 4769 6-9-5 **87** DaleSwift(7) 6 90+
(B Ellison) *hld up: rdn over 3f out: styd on ins fnl f: nvr rchd ldrs* **33/1**

5166 **7** *2 3/4* **Dazzling Light (UAE)**[15] 3368 5-9-5 **80** WilliamBuick 1 78
(J S Goldie) *chsd ldrs: rdn and ev ch over 2f out: edgd lft over 1f out: wknd ins fnl f* **16/1**

0-00 **8** *2* **Bon Spiel**[24] 3050 6-9-5 **80** (p) DaneO'Neill 13 75
(C Gordon) *hld up: hdwy over 2f out: sn rdn: wknd fnl f* **66/1**

-102 **9** *3 3/4* **Bugaku**[28] 2934 5-9-11 **86** RyanMoore 11 75
(Sir Michael Stoute) *chsd ldrs: rdn and ev ch over 2f out: wknd fnl f* **8/1**[3]

60-6 **10** *1 1/4* **Magicalmysterytour (IRE)**[13] 3462 7-9-12 **87** StevieDonohoe 9 74
(W J Musson) *hld up: hdwy over 5f out: lost pl over 3f out: n.d after* **11/1**

-000 **11** *1 3/4* **Pevensey (IRE)**[34] 2747 8-9-5 **85** (p) IanBrennan(5) 7 69
(J J Quinn) *s.i.s: sn pushed along into mid-div: rdn over 2f out: wknd over 1f out* **33/1**

0430 **U** **Mull Of Dubai**[27] 2976 7-9-10 **85** AdrianNicholls 5 —
(D Nicholls) *hld up: plld hrd: hdwy over 6f out: w ldrs whn wnt wrong and uns rdr over 3f out* **25/1**

2m 33.21s (0.31) **Going Correction** -0.05s/f (Good)
WFA 3 from 4yo+ 13lb **12** Ran SP% **120.9**
Speed ratings (Par 107): **96,94,93,93,92 92,91,89,87,86 85,—**
Tote Swingers:1&2:£4.10, 2&3:£3.50, 1&3:£12.70 CSF £18.83 CT £100.84 TOTE £12.20: £3.00, £1.10, £3.10; EX 28.40 Trifecta £103.90 Pool £1,296.82 - 9.22 winning units. Place 6 £92.01, Place 5 £21.75..
Owner Mrs I H Stewart-Brown & M J Meacock **Bred** I Stewart-Brown And M Meacock **Trained** Arundel, W Sussex

FOCUS
This was a decent middle-distance handicap, but Frankie Dettori was able to dictate a muddling pace on the well-backed Bay Willow and that made it into a messy sort of race. The form may not prove too reliable, but the first two are progressive.

NOTEBOOK
Times Up did well to come from midfield and get up on this drop back to a suitably sharper test. He had clearly improved a bundle for his seasonal return three weeks earlier and this success is made more meritorious as he was conceding weight all around. His course form figures now read 311 and both those wins have been over C&D. (op 8-1 tchd 15-2)
Bay Willow(IRE) was penalised for his clear-cut success at the Curragh 12 days previously and proved all the rage to gain a third career success. He unsurprisingly set out to make all and had it very much his own way, slowing things right down after turning for home and causing most to take a keen hold. However, looking at the way he kept on up the rising finish, he may well have been better off going quicker. (op 7-4)
Ouster(GER), 5lb higher, raced just off the early leader and travelled well. He got outpaced when switched to the stands' rail, but would have no doubt enjoyed a stiffer test and remains in good form.
Strategic Mount was settled in last place early on after a slow start and proved keen. He crept into things going strongly around 3f out when hampered, but finished well. This was a decent effort considering the uneven pace and was much his best for some time. (op 20-1)
Speed Dating was 5lb higher than when just held over 1m2f here last time out. It wasn't surprising to see him held onto for longer here and he was another not helped by the stop-start pace, but his promising finishing effort did rather flatten out late on. The handicapper may well now be in charge. (op 7-1)
Overrule(USA) was last seen tailing off on his chase debut 63 days earlier and so this was obviously much more encouraging as he was another that came from well back. (op 25-1)
Bugaku was well enough placed when the race began to hot up and faded when it mattered. (op 13-2)
Magicalmysterytour(IRE) ◆ was again given plenty to do in a race where it was an advantage to be handy and shaped better than the bare form. His season could well revolve around another crack at the Ebor and he is one to keep an eye on. (op 12-1 tchd 14-1)
T/Jkpt: Not won. T/Plt: £104.80 to a £1 stake. Pool: £175,369.03 - 1,221.03 winning units. T/Qpdt: £6.30 to a £1 stake. Pool: £12,712.44 - 1,481.98 winning units. CR

2976 YORK (L-H)
Friday, July 9

OFFICIAL GOING: Good to firm (8.0)
Wind: Moderate, half-behind. Weather: Cloudy and warm

3874 CAKEMARK E B F MAIDEN STKS 7f
2:15 (2:16) (Class 3) 2-Y-O **£6,929** (£2,061; £1,030; £514) **Stalls** Low

Form RPR

32 **1** **Polar Kite (IRE)**[21] 3162 2-9-3 0 PaulHanagan 7 82
(R A Fahey) *trckd ldr: hdwy and cl up 3f out: led wl over 1f out: rdn ins fnl f and kpt on* **10/11**[1]

3 **2** *2 1/4* **King Of The Celts (IRE)**[26] 2990 2-9-3 0 DavidAllan 8 76
(T D Easterby) *in tch: hdwy 3f out: rdn to chse wnr over 1f out: edgd lft and one pce ins fnl f* **4/1**[3]

6 **3** *2 3/4* **Lady Gar Gar**[26] 2990 2-8-12 0 PaulMulrennan 1 65
(G R Oldroyd) *sn trcking ldrs: effrt 3f out: rdn over 2f out: kpt on same pce* **14/1**

6004 **4** *1 1/4* **Jamaica Grande**[2] 3784 2-9-3 0 JoeFanning 2 66
(P S McEntee) *led: rdn along 3f out: drvn 2f out: sn hdd and grad wknd* **50/1**

52 **5** *3 3/4* **Tokum (IRE)**[46] 2384 2-9-3 0 ChristopheSoumillon 9 59+
(J Noseda) *trckd ldrs: effrt 3f out: rdn over 2f out and sn btn* **11/4**[2]

00 **6** *6* **Goodmanyourself**[20] 3222 2-9-3 0 PJMcDonald 3 42
(P T Midgley) *a towards rr* **100/1**

0 **7** *4 1/2* **Kings Arms**[13] 3449 2-8-12 0 JamesSullivan(5) 5 31
(M W Easterby) *a towards rr* **66/1**

06 **8** *8* **Livinadream**[19] 3237 2-8-12 0 SilvestreDeSousa 6 6
(N Tinkler) *chsd ldrs: rdn along after 3f and sn wknd* **50/1**

1m 24.67s (-0.63) **Going Correction** -0.175s/f (Firm) **8** Ran SP% **112.1**
Speed ratings (Par 98): **96,93,90,88,84 77,72,63**
Tote Swingers: 1&2 £1.40, 1&3 £3.90, 2&3 £6.20 CSF £4.70 TOTE £2.00: £1.20, £1.40, £2.10; EX 4.80.
Owner Mr And Mrs J D Cotton **Bred** Holborn Trust Co **Trained** Musley Bank, N Yorks

FOCUS
Just 14mm rain in the month since the last meeting here. The course had been well watered and the ground was described as 'lovely ground, just on the quick side of good'. The time was fast and the winner is rated up 8lb.

NOTEBOOK
Polar Kite(IRE), who has plenty of size and scope, had finished third and second, beaten a neck at Musselburgh, on his two previous outings. He had the leader covered and had only to be kept up to his work for a most convincing success. He already looks very professional and nurseries now beckon. He should continue to give a good account of himself. (tchd Evens and 6-5 in a place)
King Of The Celts(IRE), a well-beaten third at Doncaster first time, is a decent sort but he sweated up at the start. He kept on to take second inside the final furlong, and should improve and make his mark. (op 7-2 tchd 9-2 in a place)
Lady Gar Gar, who is not very big, kept on despite showing a marked tendency to hang right, and ending up under the stands' side rail. Official explanation: jockey said filly hung right final 2f (op 12-1)
Jamaica Grande, who habitually swished his tail beforehand, was having his second start in just three days. With a provisional official rating of just 58, he led on sufferance but was quickly put in his place by the first two. (op 40-1)
Tokum(IRE) is only small. Runner-up behind King Torus at Leicester on his second start, he had no excuse here and does not look to be progressing. (op 3-1 tchd 7-2 in a place)

3875 CUISINE DE FRANCE SUMMER STKS (GROUP 3) (F&M) 6f
2:45 (2:48) (Class 1) 3-Y-O+ **£38,519** (£14,566; £7,280; £3,640) **Stalls** High

Form RPR

0126 **1** **Rose Blossom**[20] 3197 3-8-10 95 PaulHanagan 6 109
(R A Fahey) *mde all: rdn and qcknd wl over 1f out: drvn ins fnl f: edgd lft and hld on wl towards fin* **8/1**

0-31 **2** *nk* **Tropical Treat**[20] 3197 3-8-10 94 RichardKingscote 11 108+
(R M Beckett) *trckd ldrs: hdwy 2f out: rdn to chal ent fnl f and ev ch tl drvn and nt qckn towards fin* **13/2**[3]

-211 **3** *2 1/2* **Gilt Edge Girl**[29] 2912 4-9-4 105 LukeMorris 7 103
(C G Cox) *trckd ldrs: hdwy 2f out: sn rdn to chal and ev ch tl drvn and one pce ins fnl f* **13/2**[3]

-541 **4** *3/4* **Bounty Box**[14] 3415 4-9-2 93 TedDurcan 2 99+
(C F Wall) *hld up in rr: hdwy 2f out: sn rdn and styd on ins fnl f: nrst fin* **17/2**

5 *1/2* **Letteratura (IRE)**[29] 4-9-2 97 ChristopheSoumillon 10 97+
(J-C Rouget, France) *in rr and pushed along 1/2-way: hdwy on stands' rail wl over 1f out: sn rdn and kpt on ins fnl f: nrst fin* **9/2**[1]

3250 **6** *1/2* **Jaconet (USA)**[34] 2745 5-9-2 93 (b) PhillipMakin 5 95
(T D Barron) *chsd wnr: rdn along over 2f out: grad wknd* **14/1**

-2 **7** *2 1/4* **Swiss Diva**[14] 3415 4-9-2 100 PaulMulrennan 4 88
(D R C Elsworth) *prom: rdn along 2f out: grad wknd* **5/1**[2]

4562 **8** *3/4* **City Dancer (IRE)**[20] 3197 4-9-2 88 FrannyNorton 8 86
(D Nicholls) *dwlt: towards rr: rdn along 2f out: n.d* **10/1**

6150 **9** *nk* **Look Busy (IRE)**[12] 3486 5-9-2 100 PatrickMathers 1 85
(A Berry) *prom on outer: rdn along over 2f out: drvn and wknd wl over 1f out* **25/1**

1-20 **10** *2 3/4* **Golden Destiny (IRE)**[62] 1918 4-9-2 100 (p) SebSanders 3 76
(P J Makin) *in tch on wd outside: hdwy to chse ldrs over 2f out: sn rdn and wknd wl over 1f out* **16/1**

69.75 secs (-2.15) **Going Correction** -0.05s/f (Good)
WFA 3 from 4yo+ 6lb **10** Ran SP% **108.6**
Speed ratings (Par 113): **112,111,108,107,106 105,102,101,101,97**
Tote Swingers:1&2:£9.60, 2&3:£8.30, 1&3:£9.10 CSF £50.06 TOTE £9.30: £2.20, £2.40, £2.10; EX 58.80 Trifecta £396.00 Part won. Pool £535.20 - 0.20 winning units..
Owner Highclere Thoroughbred Racing (Blossom) **Bred** J R Mitchell **Trained** Musley Bank, N Yorks

FOCUS
A Group 3 for fillies and mares. The winner reversed Ayr form with the runner-up and posted a small personal best. The second is progressive.

NOTEBOOK
Rose Blossom, all-the-way winner of a Class 2 5f fillies' race here in May, repeated the dose in this better event over 6f. Given an uncontested lead, she saw out the extra furlong in game fashion. The Nunthorpe is under consideration, but she is unlikely to be able to dominate in Group 1 company. (tchd 15-2)
Tropical Treat improved from the rear under a patient ride. After looking a serious threat, she was held near the line and 5f may suit her slightly better. (tchd 6-1 and 7-1)
Gilt Edge Girl, carrying just a 2lb penalty, had 8lb on hand of the winner on official figures. She threw down a strong challenge, but hard as she tried she could not get the better of the game winner and, in the end, had to settle for third spot. (op 9-2 tchd 4-1)
Bounty Box, narrow conqueror of Swiss Diva at Newmarket, stayed on after struggling to go the pace. (op 8-1)
Letteratura(IRE), a French challenger, was run off her feet and was last soon after the halfway mark. She made considerable late ground and may need more give. Official explanation: jockey said filly was unsuited by the good to firm ground (op 11-2)
Jaconet(USA), unable to dominate, is better suited by Polytrack. (op 16-1)
Swiss Diva, fourth in this race last year and closely matched with Bounty Box on Newmarket running, raced far too keenly and dropped right out of contention in the end. Official explanation: jockey said filly ran too free (op 13-2 tchd 7-1)

3876 GLOBAL TRADING UK RESPONSIBLE PACKAGING (H'CAP) 7f
3:20 (3:21) (Class 4) (0-85,85) 3-Y-O+ **£6,540** (£1,946; £972; £485) **Stalls** Low

Form RPR

153 **1** **Avenuesnalleyways (IRE)**[53] 2170 3-9-1 **78** RichardKingscote 12 96+
(R M Beckett) *broke wl: sn led: rdn clr wl over 1f out: edgd lft ins fnl f: kpt on strly* **7/1**[2]

53-2 **2** *5* **Fishforcompliments**[16] 3317 6-9-9 **78** PaulHanagan 1 83
(R A Fahey) *stall opened early and led for 100yds: stdd to trck wnr: effrt over 2f out: rdn wl over 1f out: kpt on: no ch w wnr* **6/1**[1]

0003 **3** *3/4* **Smarty Socks (IRE)**[16] 3318 6-9-11 **80** (e) SilvestreDeSousa 8 83+
(D O'Meara) *s.i.s and bhd: hdwy over 2f out: sn rdn and kpt on ins fnl f: nrst fin* **8/1**[3]

-006 **4** *3/4* **Zomerlust**[63] 1862 8-9-11 **80** (v) GrahamGibbons 6 81
(J J Quinn) *midfield: rdn along over 2f out: styd on u.p appr fnl f: nrst fin* **12/1**

4304 **5** *1/2* **Istiqdaam**[27] 2982 5-9-4 **73** (b) PhillipMakin 10 73
(M W Easterby) *in tch: rdn along to chse ldrs over 2f out: drvn wl over 1f out: kpt on same pce* **11/1**

3402 **6** *3/4* **Mandalay King (IRE)**[9] 3553 5-8-12 **67** PJMcDonald 13 65
(Mrs Marjorie Fife) *towards rr: hdwy over 2f out: sn rdn and kpt on ins fnl f: nrst fin* **20/1**

-004 **7** *1 3/4* **Euston Square**[44] 2428 4-9-10 **79** AndrewMullen 5 72
(D Nicholls) *bhd: hdwy over 2f out: sn rdn and kpt on appr fnl f: nvr nr ldrs* **25/1**

1-00 **8** *1/2* **Golden Shaheen (IRE)**[13] 3448 3-9-5 **82** (b[1]) JoeFanning 11 71
(M Johnston) *prom: rdn along 3f out: grad wknd* **16/1**

0041 **9** *hd* **Toto Skyllachy**[13] 3438 5-9-5 **79** JamesO'Reilly(5) 17 70
(J O'Reilly) *bhd: rdn along and hdwy 2f out: styd on u.p ins fnl f: nvr rchd ldrs* **20/1**

1350 **10** 1¾ **Game Lad**[7] 3619 8-9-13 **82**........(tp) DavidAllan 16 68
(T D Easterby) *bhd tl styd on fnl 2f: nvr a factor* **28/1**
4046 **11** ¾ **Mujaadel (USA)**[22] 3107 5-9-7 **76**........(p) PaulMulrennan 3 60
(D Nicholls) *chsd ldrs on inner: rdn along over 2f out: sn drvn and grad wknd* **16/1**
4-44 **12** ½ **Sunnandaeg**[8] 3599 3-9-8 **85**........ SteveDrowne 14 65
(N Wilson) *chsd ldrs on outer: rdn along 1/2-way: sn wknd* **25/1**
0300 **13** ½ **Salerosa (IRE)**[39] 2580 5-8-13 **68**........ JimmyQuinn 7 50
(Mrs A Duffield) *nvr bttr than midfield* **33/1**
3253 **14** hd **William Morgan (IRE)**[13] 3429 3-9-0 **77**........ TonyHamilton 4 55
(R A Fahey) *midfield: rdn along over 3f out: n.d* **9/1**
6-65 **15** 1 **Diamond Daisy (IRE)**[11] 3508 4-8-12 **70**........ BarryMcHugh(3) 2 48
(Mrs A Duffield) *a towards rr* **33/1**
-010 **16** 5 **Northern Fling**[13] 3461 6-10-0 **83**........ TedDurcan 19 48
(J S Goldie) *a in rr* **14/1**
4303 **17** 2¾ **Dancing Maite**[20] 3216 5-9-1 **73**........ RussKennemore(3) 15 30
(S R Bowring) *chsd ldrs: rdn along 3f out: grad wknd* **16/1**
0-10 **18** 2¼ **Steel Stockholder**[103] 1030 4-9-1 **70**........ FrannyNorton 9 21
(M Brittain) *prom: rdn along wl over 2f out: sn drvn and wknd* **33/1**
1-44 **19** 10 **Saharia (IRE)**[29] 2884 3-9-4 **81**........ SebSanders 20 —
(J Noseda) *chsd ldrs on wd outside: rdn along 3f out: sn wknd* **17/2**

1m 22.56s (-2.74) **Going Correction** -0.175s/f (Firm)
WFA 3 from 4yo+ 8lb **19** Ran SP% **128.3**
Speed ratings (Par 105): **108,102,101,100,100 99,97,96,96,94 93,92,92,92,90 85,82,79,68**
Tote Swingers:1&2:£7.80, 2&3:£6.60, 1&3:£12.50 CSF £44.43 CT £360.89 TOTE £8.40: £2.30, £1.50, £2.00, £3.20; EX 36.60.
Owner Tony Perkins & James D Cameron **Bred** P G Lyons **Trained** Whitsbury, Hants

FOCUS
On paper a highly competitive 67-83 handicap, but very few got into it and those who chose to race towards the stands' side rail seemed to be at a major disadvantage. The unexposed winner did it easily but had the run of the race.
Euston Square Official explanation: jockey said gelding hung right throughout
Steel Stockholder Official explanation: trainer said colt had not let himself down on the good to firm ground
Saharia(IRE) Official explanation: trainer had no explanation for the poor form shown

3877 CARAVAN CHAIRMAN'S CHARITY CUP (H'CAP) 1m 4f
3:55 (3:56) (Class 2) (0-100,97) 3-Y-O+ **£10,361** (£3,083; £1,540; £769) **Stalls** Centre

Form RPR
2/1- **1** **La De Two (IRE)**[245] 7278 4-10-0 **97**........(t) TedDurcan 1 113+
(Saeed Bin Suroor) *trckd ldrs on inner: hdwy 3f out: led 2f out: sn rdn and clr ent fnl f: styd on strly* **3/1**[2]
41 **2** 5 **Emerging Artist (FR)**[18] 3256 4-9-3 **86**........ JoeFanning 5 94+
(M Johnston) *led 3f: chsd ldr tl led again over 3f out and sn rdn: hdd 2f out and sn drvn: kpt on same pce u.p fnl f* **9/2**
2330 **3** 2¼ **Crackentorp**[13] 3447 5-9-8 **91**........ GrahamGibbons 2 95
(T D Easterby) *hld up in tch: smooth hdwy to trck ldrs over 3f out: rdn to chse ldng pair wl over 1f out: sn drvn and no imp* **5/2**[1]
3-00 **4** 3¼ **Cosmic Sun**[20] 3198 4-9-5 **88**........ PaulHanagan 4 87
(R A Fahey) *trckd ldrs: hdwy 4f out: effrt and cl up 3f out: rdn over 2f out: sn drvn and wknd wl over 1f out* **4/1**[3]
6162 **5** nk **Trip The Light**[13] 3431 5-9-3 **89**........(v) BarryMcHugh(3) 3 88
(R A Fahey) *hld up in tch: hdwy 3f out: rdn over 2f out: sn drvn and n.d* **11/1**
2603 **6** 4½ **Prince Of Johanne (IRE)**[13] 3450 4-8-13 **82**........ SteveDrowne 6 74
(T P Tate) *hld up in rr: sme hdwy over 3f out: sn rdn and nvr a factor* **16/1**
-000 **7** 3¾ **Royal Diamond (IRE)**[13] 3447 4-9-7 **90**........ TomEaves 7 76
(M Dods) *t.k.h: chsd ldr tl led after 3f: rdn along 4f out: hdd 3f out and sn wknd* **20/1**

2m 29.85s (-3.35) **Going Correction** -0.05s/f (Good) 7 Ran SP% **110.7**
Speed ratings (Par 109): **109,105,104,102,101 98,96**
Tote Swingers:1&2:£3.00, 2&3:£4.00, 1&3:£1.80 CSF £15.72 TOTE £4.00: £2.20, £2.60; EX 11.50.
Owner Godolphin **Bred** Airlie Stud And Sir Thomas Pilkington **Trained** Newmarket, Suffolk

FOCUS
A competitive 82-97 handicap run at a fair pace and the first two were unexposed, lightly-raced sorts. This looks form to be positive about, with the third the best guide.

NOTEBOOK
La De Two(IRE) an imposing individual, had taken a weak maiden in a canter at Wolverhampton in November after finishing runner-up behind Kite Wood at Doncaster on his sole backend outing at two. He travelled strongly and, after taking charge, came home a most decisive wide-margin winner. Rated 97 here, he looks ready to step up to Listed class. (tchd 11-4 and 10-3 in a place)
Emerging Artist(FR), who did not see a racetrack until finishing fourth at Haydock last month, took a maiden in ready fashion at Chepstow two weeks later. Rated 86 here, he finished clear second-best. He deserves plenty of credit for this and deserves to go one better in handicap company. (tchd 5-1)
Crackentorp, who had no luck in running in the Northumberland Plate, ran right up to his best but came across two unexposed types. (op 11-4 tchd 3-1)
Cosmic Sun, on the same mark as when he took this a year ago, has not sparkled now in three outings this time. (tchd 7-2 and 5-1 in a place)
Trip The Light, who has run in claimers in two of his last three starts, is now 2lb higher than his last handicap success. (op 10-1 tchd 9-1)
Prince Of Johanne(IRE) ran a moody type of race and may be worth a try over much further. (op 14-1)
Royal Diamond(IRE) was a shade keen and dropped right out when challenged. He is slipping back to a more realistic mark, but may appreciate some give underfoot these days. (op 16-1)

3878 MRS PEEK'S STKS (H'CAP) 1m 6f
4:30 (4:33) (Class 3) (0-95,85) 3-Y-O **£6,799** (£2,023; £1,011; £505) **Stalls** Low

Form RPR
5211 **1** **Motrice**[7] 3626 3-9-0 **76** 6ex........ SebSanders 2 88+
(Sir Mark Prescott) *hld up in rr: smooth hdwy on inner over 3f out: effrt to ld and edgd rt wl over 1f out: rdn and kpt on strly fnl f* **4/7**[1]
2113 **2** 2½ **Atlantic Tiger (IRE)**[50] 2252 3-9-9 **85**........ JoeFanning 1 91+
(M Johnston) *trckd ldr: effrt 3f out: rdn along 2f out and ev ch whn squeezed out over 1f out: rallied to take 2nd ins fnl f* **9/4**[2]
0-12 **3** 1¼ **Park View**[13] 3427 3-9-0 **76**........ FrannyNorton 4 79
(B W Hills) *led: rdn along 3f out: drvn: edgd lft and hdd wl over 1f out: sn one pce* **8/1**[3]
0244 **4** 8 **Ejteyaaz**[13] 3427 3-9-6 **82**........ PaulHanagan 3 74
(R A Fahey) *trckd ldng pair: hdwy 4f out: rdn along 3f out and sn wknd* **16/1**

3m 1.96s (1.76) **Going Correction** -0.05s/f (Good) 4 Ran SP% **111.4**
Speed ratings (Par 104): **92,90,89,85**
CSF £2.23 TOTE £1.70; EX 2.20.
Owner Miss K Rausing **Bred** Miss K Rausing **Trained** Newmarket, Suffolk

FOCUS
A 76-85 stayers' handicap run at just a steady pace until the final half-mile. The form is rated around the third and the first pair were unable to show their best.

NOTEBOOK
Motrice, an easy winner from a mark of 59 at Yarmouth, defied an 11lb higher mark with a facile success at Haydock. Raised 16lb for that, she defied a 6lb penalty in most decisive fashion in the end. She will need to raise her game again if she is to defy the handicapper from her new rating. (tchd 1-2, 8-13 and 8-11 in places)
Atlantic Tiger(IRE), another progressive type, was the meat in the sandwich when the winner and Park View came together. He shapes like a true stayer and would have appreciated a stronger gallop. We still have not seen the best of him. (op 7-2 tchd 4-1)
Park View, who lacks size and scope, quickened it up once in line for home but in the end came up some way short. Narrowly beaten from a 1lb lower mark at Chester, the tighter the track the better. (op 7-1 tchd 9-1)
Ejteyaaz, taking another step up in trip, was readily shaken off and his trainer is struggling with this one. (op 11-1)

3879 WARBURTONS, BAKERS BORN & BRED APPRENTICE STKS (H'CAP) 5f
5:05 (5:06) (Class 4) (0-80,77) 3-Y-O+ **£5,180** (£1,541; £770; £384) **Stalls** High

Form RPR
2320 **1** **Brierty (IRE)**[48] 2327 4-9-10 **77**........ NeilFarley(4) 4 86
(D Carroll) *trckd ldng pair: pushed along and sltly outpcd 1/2-way: hdwy over 1f out: swtchd lft and rdn to ld ins fnl f: kpt on* **9/2**[3]
2332 **2** ¾ **Ridley Didley (IRE)**[20] 3201 5-9-5 **68**........ DeanHeslop 5 74
(N Wilson) *led: rdn along 2f out: drvn ent fnl f: sn hung rt and hdd: no ex last 100yds* **2/1**[1]
2-00 **3** shd **Liberty Ship**[22] 3119 5-9-2 **65**........(bt) AshleyMorgan 8 71
(J D Bethell) *trckd ldrs: hdwy 2f out: rdn to chal over 1f out and ev ch whn bmpd ins fnl f: no ex after* **13/2**
-132 **4** 1½ **Pepper Lane**[8] 3599 3-8-9 **63**........ JamesSullivan 6 62
(D O'Meara) *in tch: effrt 2f out: sn rdn and hung lft over 1f out: one pce* **11/4**[2]
2120 **5** ½ **Highland Warrior**[56] 2073 11-9-7 **70**........ PaulPickard 7 69
(P T Midgley) *in rr: hdwy 2f out: sn rdn and no imp appr fnl f* **14/1**
0000 **6** 2¾ **Bravely (IRE)**[16] 3321 6-9-1 **64**........ LanceBetts 3 53
(T D Easterby) *chsd ldr: rdn along 2f out: sn wknd* **15/2**
652- **7** 13 **Alacity (IRE)**[247] 7241 4-8-9 **58** oh1........ BillyCray 2 —
(N Bycroft) *rrd s and s.i.s: hdwy 1/2-way: rdn 2f out and sn wknd* **16/1**

58.56 secs (-0.74) **Going Correction** -0.05s/f (Good)
WFA 3 from 4yo+ 5lb 7 Ran SP% **115.8**
Speed ratings (Par 105): **103,101,101,99,98 94,73**
Tote Swingers:1&2:£2.70, 2&3:£3.00, 1&3:£5.10 CSF £14.35 CT £57.92 TOTE £5.30: £2.30, £1.90; EX 13.40 Place 6 £46.86, Place 5 £34.74..
Owner G P Clarke **Bred** Fortbarrington Stud **Trained** Sledmere, E Yorks
■ Stewards' Enquiry : Dean Heslop caution: careless riding.

FOCUS
A modest 58-77 apprentice riders' sprint handicap and straightforward form.
Alacity(IRE) Official explanation: jockey said filly reared up leaving stalls
T/Plt: £20.70 to a £1 stake. Pool: £91,357.40 - 3,214.91 winning units. T/Qpdt: £7.10 to a £1 stake. Pool: £3,818.56 - 392.80 winning units. JR

3880 - 3885a (Foreign Racing) - See Raceform Interactive

3842 ASCOT (R-H)
Saturday, July 10

OFFICIAL GOING: Good to firm (firm in places on straight course; str 8.4; rnd 8.0)
Rail realignment added 20yds to 12 &10f races and 10yds to Round Mile.
Wind: Virtually nil Weather: hot and sunny

3886 TOTESCOOP6 H'CAP 7f
1:45 (1:48) (Class 2) 3-Y-O
£31,155 (£9,330; £4,665; £2,335; £1,165; £585) **Stalls** Low

Form RPR
-465 **1** **Side Glance**[28] 2978 3-8-8 **90**........ DavidProbert 2 101
(A M Balding) *stdd s: hld up in tch in rr: hdwy ent fnl 2f: rdn to chal over 1f out: kpt edging rt u.p: led ins fnl f: styd on wl to draw clr fnl 75yds* **9/2**[3]
3-11 **2** 2¼ **Man Of Action (USA)**[22] 3172 3-9-0 **96**........ WilliamBuick 9 101
(J H M Gosden) *in tch: hdwy to ld 2f out: sn rdn and hrd pressed: hdd ins fnl f: wknd fnl 50yds: hld on for 2nd cl home* **7/2**[1]
-112 **3** shd **Haatheq (USA)**[35] 2737 3-8-5 **87**........ RichardHills 3 95+
(J L Dunlop) *hld up in tch towards rr: rdn whn n.m.r and outpcd 2f out: swtchd lft wl over 1f out: kpt on wl u.p ins fnl f: pressing for 2nd at fin but no threat to wnr* **4/1**[2]
2122 **4** nk **Bohemian Melody**[28] 2970 3-8-3 **85**........ JimmyQuinn 10 89
(M Botti) *stdd s: t.k.h: hld up in tch in rr: hdwy and n.m.r ent fnl 2f: swtchd rt and rdn 2f out: chsd ldng pair over 1f out: kpt on same pce u.p fnl f* **14/1**
1034 **5** 2 **Burghley**[57] 2090 3-8-2 **84**........ AndreaAtzeni 4 83
(M L W Bell) *t.k.h: chsd ldrs: rdn and unable qck 2f out: drvn and plugged on same pce fnl f* **25/1**
1641 **6** 1¼ **Thrust Control (IRE)**[22] 3151 3-7-12 **80** oh1........ CathyGannon 11 75
(B Ellison) *taken down early: awkward leaving stalls: stdd and hld up in rr: hdwy over 2f out: rdn 2f out: no prog and kpt on same pce fr over 1f out* **22/1**
0400 **7** 2¾ **Colonel Mak**[8] 3619 3-8-5 **87**........ SamHitchcott 8 75
(T D Barron) *hld up in tch towards rr: rdn and unable qck over 2f out: no prog and wl hld fr over 1f out* **33/1**
0530 **8** 2¾ **Greyfriarschorista**[7] 3692 3-9-7 **103**........ JoeFanning 5 83
(M Johnston) *chsd ldr: rdn to ld ent fnl 2f: sn hdd: wknd qckly over 1f out: wl btn fnl f* **11/2**
0310 **9** 6 **Navajo Chief**[23] 3103 3-9-3 **99**........ JimmyFortune 6 63
(A P Jarvis) *chsd ldrs: rdn and struggling 3f out: wl btn fr wl over 1f out: eased ins fnl f* **14/1**
3214 **10** 5 **Rule Breaker (IRE)**[14] 3429 3-8-4 **86**........ AdrianNicholls 1 37
(M Johnston) *sn led: rdn and hdd ent fnl 2f: wkng whn sltly hmpd 2f out: wl bhd over 1f out: eased ins fnl f* **20/1**

1m 28.22s (0.22) **Going Correction** +0.20s/f (Good) **10** Ran SP% **105.0**
Speed ratings (Par 106): **106,103,103,102,100 99,96,92,86,80**
Tote Swingers: 1&2:£3.80, 1&3:£3.80, 2&3:£1.40 CSF £15.82 CT £50.39 TOTE £4.60: £1.60, £1.60, £1.40; EX 18.00 Trifecta £28.50 Pool: £1,105.42 - 28.63 winning units..
Owner Kingsclere Racing CLub **Bred** Kingsclere Stud **Trained** Kingsclere, Hants
■ Citrus Star was withdrawn (7/1, ref to enter stalls). Deduct 10p in the £ under R4.

FOCUS
The jockeys agreed the ground was riding fast, but with no jar. A good 3yo handicap, and solid form. The runners came down the centre of the track and the time was nearly a second and a half outside the RP standard. A clear personal best from the winner and the first four can all improve again.

NOTEBOOK
Side Glance had produced sound efforts in a couple of handicaps over a furlong shorter while giving every indication that a return to 7f would be in his favour. So it proved as, after racing on the near side of the bunch, but tending to edge to his right, he came through to lead inside the last and was pulling away at the line. He is a consistent, professional gelding with more to offer, and on this evidence should get a mile. (op 13-2)
Man Of Action(USA), on a hat-trick, but 8lb higher than when winning at Newmarket, was let down to lead moving well but could not hold off the winner. His stride was shortening late on and he would have been only fourth with slightly further to run. (op 3-1 tchd 4-1 in a place)
Haatheq(USA), ridden less prominently than usual, improved from the rear with a quarter of a mile left and was running on well at the line, requiring another stride to grab second. A stiffer test at this trip might prove ideal.
Bohemian Melody ◆ travelled strongly but the gaps weren't there when he needed them, although he wouldn't have won in any case. He stayed on once switched out and, still relatively unexposed on turf, has further improvement in him. (tchd 12-1)
Burghley's trainer won this event a year ago. Back up in trip, the gelding raced rather keenly through the early parts and lacked the requisite pace in the latter stages. He carried his head just a shade high and this ground might have been a little fast for him. (op 22-1)
Thrust Control(IRE), back up to 7f but effectively 5lb higher than when winning at Ayr, went to post early. He stayed on from the rear on the far side of the bunch but never posed a realistic threat to the principals. (op 28-1 tchd 20-1)
Greyfriarschorista blew the start at Sandown the previous Saturday but was well away this time. After tracking his stablemate Rule Breaker, he dropped away when things became serious. (op 7-1 tchd 15-2)

3887 KELLY GROUP NURSERY — 6f
2:20 (2:21) (Class 4) 2-Y-O — **£6,476** (£1,927; £963; £481) **Stalls** Low

Form — RPR

541 **1** **Major Conquest (IRE)**[27] 3000 2-9-2 **80** ... RichardHills 9 — 83
(J W Hills) *stdd s: in tch towards rr: hdwy to trck ldrs 2f out: pushed into ld jst over 1f out: rdn 1f out: carried lft ins fnl f: wandered lft u.p fnl 100yds: fnd ex and hld on towards fin* **9/2**[3]

634 **2** *nk* **Royal Opera**[47] 2389 2-8-5 **69** ... JimmyQuinn 5 — 71
(B R Millman) *slowly stride: sn bustled along in rr: hdwy u.p over 1f out: swtchd rt ins fnl f: ev ch fnl 50yds: nt quite rch wnr* **25/1**

5501 **3** *nk* **Silly Billy (IRE)**[7] 3678 2-8-0 **64** ... DavidProbert 8 — 65
(S Kirk) *in tch in midfield: rdn and effrt to ld over 1f out: sn hung lft and hdd: ev ch but kpt hanging lft fnl f: kpt on same pce fnl 100yds* **18/1**

413 **4** *2* **Whoatealthepius (IRE)**[15] 3395 2-9-0 **78** ... AlanMunro 7 — 73
(D K Ivory) *in tch in midfield: rdn and effrt ent fnl 2f: unable qck u.p over 1f out: keeping on same pce and hld whn swtchd lft wl ins fnl f* **14/1**

01 **5** *shd* **Silver Alliance**[19] 3274 2-8-13 **77** ... EddieAhern 1 — 72
(W R Swinburn) *pressed ldrs and travelling wl: rdn and unable qck wl over 1f out: styd on same pce after and hld whn n.m.r wl ins fnl f* **3/1**[1]

421 **6** *nk* **Capaill Liath (IRE)**[19] 3269 2-9-7 **85** ... MichaelHills 2 — 79
(B W Hills) *sn pressing ldr: ev ch and rdn wl over 1f out: keeping on same pce and btn whn nt clr run: hmpd and swtchd rt wl ins fnl f* **3/1**[1]

6432 **7** *5* **Rojo Boy**[28] 2980 2-8-13 **77** ... JimmyFortune 3 — 56
(A M Balding) *a towards rr: u.p and no prog 1/2-way: wl btn over 1f out* **4/1**[2]

306 **8** *½* **Saucy Buck (IRE)**[12] 3504 2-8-13 **77** ... TonyCulhane 4 — 55
(M R Channon) *a towards rr: rdn and no rspnse 2f out: wl btn over 1f out* **25/1**

0135 **9** *1 ½* **Rosina Grey**[13] 3482 2-8-10 **74** ... AndreaAtzeni 6 — 48
(B R Millman) *sn led: rdn and hdd over 1f out: wkng whn sltly hmpd sn after: sn wl btn* **20/1**

1m 15.49s (1.09) **Going Correction** +0.20s/f (Good) — **9** Ran SP% **112.6**
Speed ratings (Par 96): **100,99,99,96,96 96,89,88,86**
Tote Swingers: 1&2 £7.20, 1&3 £51.20, 2&3 £18.10 CSF £108.41 CT £1821.60 TOTE £4.80: £2.10, £5.80, £2.20; EX 124.40 Trifecta £711.60 Part won. Pool: £961.74 - 0.30 winning units..
Owner T J W Ellis **Bred** Deer Forest Stud **Trained** Upper Lambourn, Berks
■ Stewards' Enquiry : David Probert two-day ban: careless riding (Jul 25-26)

FOCUS
An ordinary nursery for the course and a pretty messy race, so there are one or two doubts over the form, although it does make some sense. The field made their way towards the far side of the track.

NOTEBOOK
Major Conquest(IRE) needed to be pushed along to pick up from the rear but was travelling well again when striking the front. He hung to his left inside the last and the winning margin was tight in the end, but he looked to have more in hand than that and it may be that he was in front soon enough. He holds a Gimcrack entry, which might be flying rather high but does indicate that he is held in some regard. (op 7-2)
Royal Opera, one of only two maidens in the field, was at the back for much of the trip, but stayed on well for pressure nearest the far rail as the leaders edged to their left and was only narrowly denied.
Silly Billy(IRE)'s Leicester win was only in a seller and he had been beaten in that grade previously, so his proximity does not enhance the form. From the yard that won this two years ago, the colt ran well, but he hung to his left when the pressure was on, which ended what chance he had. (op 16-1)
Whoatealthepius(IRE), another selling winner and last of three when odds-on for her debut for the yard last time, could not land an effective challenge but kept on late to confirm she has the necessary stamina for this trip. (op 10-1)
Silver Alliance, a Wolverhampton winner last time, did best of the three greys who cut out the running but was held when the first pair went across him slightly late on. (op 5-1)
Capaill Liath(IRE), another who helped push the pace, was already beaten when losing momentum inside the last. (op 7-2 tchd 11-4)
Rojo Boy was in trouble by halfway but did make modest late gains. Official explanation: trainer had no explanation for the poor form shown (op 7-2)
Rosina Grey Official explanation: jockey said filly ran too free

3888 TOTESPORT.COM SUMMER MILE STKS (GROUP 2) — 1m (R)
2:50 (2:53) (Class 1) 4-Y-0+
£56,770 (£21,520; £10,770; £5,370; £2,690; £1,350) **Stalls** High

Form — RPR

-501 **1** **Premio Loco (USA)**[14] 3455 6-9-1 119 ... GeorgeBaker 8 — 122+
(C F Wall) *stdd s: hld up in last trio: effrt on inner and squeezed through jst over 1f out: rdn to ld and edgd lft fnl 75yds: r.o strly* **4/1**[2]

-542 **2** *1* **Vertigineux (FR)**[27] 3017 6-9-1 113 ... (t) PhilippeSogorb 10 — 118
(Mme C Dufreche, France) *stdd s: hld up in last trio: hdwy wl over 1f out: rdn and ev ch ent fnl f tl nt pce of wnr fnl 75yds: kpt on* **15/2**

0-33 **3** *nk* **Dream Eater (IRE)**[25] 3046 5-9-1 117 ... (t) JimmyFortune 9 — 117
(A M Balding) *stdd s: hld up in last trio: hdwy jst over 2f out: rdn to ld over 1f out: drvn ent fnl f: hdd and no ex fnl 75yds* **5/2**[1]

2-20 **4** *2 ¼* **Ouqba**[25] 3046 4-9-1 119 ... RichardHills 1 — 113+
(B W Hills) *hld up in midfield: rdn to chal wl over 1f out: stl ev ch but keeping on same pce whn hmpd fnl 100yds: nt rcvr and btn after* **9/2**[3]

2050 **5** *4* **Forgotten Voice (IRE)**[24] 3069 5-9-1 111 ... (v) FrankieDettori 5 — 103
(J Noseda) *t.k.h: chsd ldrs: wnt 2nd ent fnl 3f: led over 2f out: rdn 2f out: hdd over 1f out: c off worse in barging match w rival and lost pl jst over 1f out: no ch w ldrs fnl f* **9/2**[3]

-010 **6** *9* **Fareer**[24] 3069 4-9-1 107 ... TadhgO'Shea 2 — 82
(E A L Dunlop) *led for 1f: chsd ldr after tl ent fnl 3f: rdn and ev ch over 2f out: wknd rapidly wl over 1f out: eased ins fnl f* **11/1**

5-14 **7** *10* **King Of Dixie (USA)**[49] 2318 6-9-1 109 ... JimCrowley 3 — 59
(W J Knight) *broke wl: stdd and hld up in tch after 1f: nt clr run bhd wkng rival over 2f out: swtchd lft and rdn 2f out: immediately hung rt and btn: eased fr over 1f out* **14/1**

0305 **8** *6* **Dingaan (IRE)**[26] 3033 7-9-1 77 ... NeilChalmers 4 — 46
(A M Balding) *awkward leaving stalls: sn rdn along and hdwy to ld after 1f: hdd wl over 2f out: sn wknd: eased fnl f: t.o* **100/1**

1m 40.43s (-0.27) **Going Correction** +0.20s/f (Good) — **8** Ran SP% **112.7**
Speed ratings (Par 115): **109,108,107,105,101 92,82,76**
Tote Swingers: 1&2:£7.70, 1&3:£2.50, 2&3:£3.60 CSF £32.71 TOTE £5.50: £1.80, £1.80, £1.30; EX 31.30 Trifecta £98.80 Pool: £1,873.53 - 14.02 winning units..
Owner Bernard Westley **Bred** Kidder, Cole & Griggs **Trained** Newmarket, Suffolk
■ Stewards' Enquiry : George Baker 1st incident: four-day ban: careless riding (Jul 25-27,29); 2nd: caution: careless riding.

FOCUS
Rail alignments meant the race was run over ten yards further than a mile. The fourth running of this event. Paco Boy was ruled out in the week because of the ground and Pressing and Alexandros were a pair of significant non-runners on the day, but it was still a decent renweal. The pace was solid and the first three all came from the rear to fight out a fine finish. Sound form, with the winner rated slightly better than the bare figures.

NOTEBOOK
Premio Loco(USA) won twice at this level in Germany last September and landed the Group 3 Criterion Stakes over 7f at Newmarket on his previous start. Held up at the back with only the runner-up behind him on straightening up, he was switched inside and squeezed through a narrow gap past Forgotten Voice on the rail before reaching the front inside the last. The winner on merit, although his rider picked up a suspension for careless riding, he deserves a try in a Group 1 now and has several options at that level. (op 3-1)
Vertigineux(FR), a French challenger, was the only runner other than the winner to have scored at this level. Last into the straight, he ran on really well down the outside but no sooner had he collared the third than the winner claimed him. He is smart and consistent and well at home in easier ground too. (op 13-2 tchd 8-1)
Dream Eater(IRE) was third behind Goldikova and Paco Boy in the Queen Anne over the straight mile here at the royal meeting. He travelled strongly into contention, but after easing to the front could not fight off challengers on either side. He has failed to win in 15 tries in Group company now but has made the frame in nine of those runs and thoroughly deserves to get his head in front again. (op 3-1)
Ouqba was runner-up to Paco Boy in the Lockinge before finishing only seventh in the Queen Anne. After taking a bit of time to slot in from his outside draw he came through to hold every chance in the straight but was just held when he was slightly hampered in the final half-furlong. (op 4-1 tchd 7-2)
Forgotten Voice(IRE), back in Group company after trying a first-time visor in the Royal Hunt Cup here, raced keenly before leading going into the home turn. He had just been headed when he was bumped by the winner, who was challenging on his inside, losing momentum and costing him any chance he may have had of getting back into the race. Official explanation: jockey said gelding suffered interference in running (op 13-2 tchd 4-1 in places)
Fareer had plenty to find with most of his rivals and dropped away quickly in the straight after chasing the pace. (op 12-1 tchd 14-1)
King Of Dixie(USA) was steadied back through the field early on. He was still close enough in the straight, albeit in need of racing room, but found nothing when let down. Official explanation: jockey said gelding hung right throughout (op 16-1)
Dingaan(IRE) is only a fair handicapper but made a decent fist of pacemaking for the favourite. (op 80-1)

3889 EURO EARTHWORKS H'CAP — 1m 2f
3:30 (3:30) (Class 3) (0-90,90) 3-Y-0+ — **£6,476** (£1,927; £963; £481) **Stalls** High

Form — RPR

0-00 **1** **Greylami (IRE)**[38] 2640 5-10-0 **90** ... EddieAhern 2 — 98+
(R A Mills) *hld up in tch: hdwy and jnd ldrs on bit 2f out: pushed ahd over 1f out: rdn and a finding enough fnl f* **11/2**[2]

-511 **2** *1 ¼* **Jo'Burg (USA)**[29] 2934 6-9-3 **86** ... DavidKenny(7) 1 — 92
(Lady Herries) *s.i.s and dropped in bhd after s: hld up in last: rdn and hdwy on outer over 2f out: chsd wnr 1f out: kpt on but no imp fnl 150yds* **7/1**[3]

33-4 **3** *1* **Elvira Madigan**[29] 2935 3-7-12 **71** oh2 ... DavidProbert 3 — 75
(A M Balding) *dwlt: hld up towards rr: rdn and effrt on outer 3f out: edging rt but hdwy u.p to chse ldng pair 1f out: no imp after* **10/1**

5-10 **4** *3 ¾* **Shernando**[69] 1730 3-8-10 **83** ... JoeFanning 9 — 84+
(M Johnston) *chsd ldng pair: nt clr run 2f out tl jst over 1f out: no ch w ldrs and plugged on same pce fnl f* **17/2**

-220 **5** *1* **Mabuya (UAE)**[27] 2996 4-9-8 **84** ... NeilCallan 4 — 78
(P J Makin) *t.k.h: hdwy to ld after 1f: jnd and rdn jst over 2f out: hdd over 1f out: wknd ent fnl f* **11/2**[2]

0251 **6** *½* **Arizona John (IRE)**[20] 3239 5-9-7 **83** ... WilliamBuick 7 — 76
(J Mackie) *t.k.h: hld up in tch: rdn and unable qck over 2f out: one pce and no threat to ldrs fnl 2f* **3/1**[1]

0-04 **7** *½* **Snoqualmie Boy**[14] 3431 7-9-4 **80** ... AdrianNicholls 10 — 72
(D Nicholls) *led for 1f: chsd ldr after: rdn and ev ch jst over 2f out: wknd u.p over 1f out* **20/1**

5504 **8** *6* **Kavachi (IRE)**[14] 3456 7-9-4 **80** ... GeorgeBaker 5 — 60
(G L Moore) *t.k.h: chsd ldrs: rdn and unable qck 3f out: wl btn fnl 2f* **8/1**

1621 **9** *nse* **Danehillsundance (IRE)**[18] 3283 6-9-8 **84** ... (t) JimmyFortune 8 — 64
(D H Brown) *t.k.h: hld up in tch in midfield: lost pl and dropped towards rr 6f out: rdn and btn over 2f out* **15/2**

2m 9.43s (2.43) **Going Correction** +0.20s/f (Good)
WFA 3 from 4yo+ 11lb — **9** Ran SP% **115.5**
Speed ratings (Par 107): **98,97,96,93,92 92,91,86,86**
Tote Swingers: 1&2:£9.80, 1&3:£10.60, 2&3:£14.40 CSF £43.62 CT £375.59 TOTE £6.40: £2.20, £2.30, £2.60; EX 34.90 Trifecta £679.50 Part won. Pool: £918.33 - 0.80 winning units..
Owner J Humphreys, Exors Of The Late T G Mills,B Ecclest **Bred** Barouche Stud Ireland Ltd **Trained** Headley, Surrey

FOCUS
Rail alignments added 25 yards to the distance of this decent handicap, in which the pace was fairly steady. Sound form, with the winner rated to last year's best.

NOTEBOOK

Greylami(IRE) travelled strongly, as he often does, before being eased into the lead with more than 1f left. He was probably in front sooner than was desirable, but was always holding the runner-up. Two of his three previous wins were over 1m3f and that is his optimum trip, according to connections, but there are not all that many races over that distance. (op 6-1 tchd 5-1)

Jo'Burg(USA) was on a hat-trick after a pair of wins at Sandown, for which he had gone up a total of 11lb. Not as slowly away as usual but still at the back of the field entering the straight, he then came with a sustained run down the outside that took him past all his rivals bar the winner. He gave the impression that he can win again off this sort of mark and would appear likely to head for Sandown's Variety Club meeting next month. (op 5-1)

Elvira Madigan ran well from 2lb out of the weights, staying on from the rear of the field for third and finishing clear of the remainder. There was not much wrong with her head carriage this time but she did edge to her right. (op 12-1 tchd 14-1 in a place)

Shernando ◆, having only fourth start, was tackling fast ground for the first time. He was momentarily outpaced by the leaders in the straight but was attempting to pick up when he was repeatedly denied a clear run. While it did not cost him a winning chance, he would have finished closer had a gap appeared for him. A step up to 1m4f will be right up his street and he is one to keep a close eye on. (op 7-1 tchd 9-1)

Mabuya(UAE), last year's runner-up, was back down in trip and had the headgear left off. He pulled his way to the front after 1f and could not hold on in the straight. This was a respectable effort but he is not easy to win with. (op 7-1)

Arizona John(IRE) won well on his first try over this trip at Pontefract but he was up 6lb in this stronger race and could never really make his presence felt. (op 4-1)

Snoqualmie Boy has been given a chance by the handicapper and showed up well for a long way, but he remains without a win since taking the Hampton Court Stakes at the royal meeting here more than four years ago. (tchd 16-1)

Kavachi(IRE) is without a win since scoring at York in June last year. He is currently operating off 6lb lower but is running nowhere near well enough to take advantage. (op 15-2)

Danehillsundance(IRE), a Beverley winner off 4lb lower, was found wanting in this better grade. (op 7-1)

3890 NORMAN COURT STUD FILLIES' H'CAP — 7f

4:05 (4:06) (Class 3) (0-90,90) 3-Y-O+ **£7,123** (£2,119; £1,059; £529) **Stalls** Low

Form					RPR
0003	**1**		**Waveband**[9] 3599 3-8-3 **75** ... JoeFanning 1 (M Johnston) *mde all and racd towards stands' rail: rdn and qcknd clr wl over 1f out: in n.d fnl f: eased towards fin* **12/1**[3]		93
0-21	**2**	*6*	**Sarasota Sunshine**[9] 3592 4-9-8 **86** ... (v) FrankieDettori 7 (J Noseda) *stdd s: t.k.h: hld up in rr towards centre: rdn and hdwy over 1f out: chsd clr wnr and hung lft 1f out: no imp* **4/5**[1]		91+
3440	**3**	*1*	**Sakhee's Pearl**[21] 3217 4-9-0 **78** ... MichaelHills 4 (Miss Gay Kelleway) *hld up towards rr: rdn and effrt ent fnl 2f: no ch w wnr fr over 1f out: kpt on to snatch 3rd last strides* **14/1**		80
1223	**4**	*hd*	**Faithful One (IRE)**[21] 3217 3-8-10 **82** ... EddieAhern 5 (D R Lanigan) *chsd wnr and racd in centre: rdn ent fnl 2f: outpcd and no ch w wnr fr over 1f out: lost 2 pls fnl f* **3/1**[2]		81+
5420	**5**	*4*	**Perfect Friend**[3] 3777 4-8-7 **71** oh1 ... DavidProbert 8 (S Kirk) *in tch: rdn and struggling over 2f out: wl btn over 1f out* **16/1**		62+
5-20	**6**	*2 ½*	**Penzena**[21] 3236 4-8-13 **77** ... (p) JimmyFortune 3 (A M Balding) *t.k.h: chsd ldrs tl rdn and btn ent fnl 2f* **12/1**[3]		61
650-	**7**	*7*	**Iasia (GR)**[234] 7431 4-9-12 **90** ... AndreaAtzeni 6 (Jane Chapple-Hyam) *in tch: rdn and btn over 2f out: wl bhd and eased ins fnl f* **33/1**		55+

1m 27.25s (-0.75) **Going Correction** +0.20s/f (Good)
WFA 3 from 4yo 8lb **7** Ran SP% **111.4**
Speed ratings (Par 104): **112,105,104,103,99 96,88**
Tote Swingers:1&2:£3.70, 1&3:£16.90, 2&3:£4.10 CSF £21.13 CT £139.11 TOTE £10.00: £3.60, £1.10; EX 28.40 Trifecta £555.90 Pool: £1,667.76 - 2.22 winning units..
Owner Sheikh Hamdan Bin Mohammed Al Maktoum **Bred** Stratford Place Stud **Trained** Middleham Moor, N Yorks

FOCUS

A fair distaff handicap, but it hinged on tactics and the form may not be all that solid. The winner is rated back to her 2yo best but may be flattered.

NOTEBOOK

Waveband ran out a clear winner in a tactical race. She was drawn one and her jockey made the decision to keep her near to the stands' side, whereas the runners in the earlier races on the straight course had all made for the centre. The tactic paid off and, after she had moved right over to the fence in the last quarter-mile or so, she came away to win decisively. She had run a better race at Redcar on her previous start and the step back up to 7f was a plus. (op 9-1)

Sarasota Sunshine was second to first-race runner-up Man Of Action on her reappearance before accounting for Perfect Friend at Newbury. Now 7lb higher, she travelled well last of the quartet who raced down the centre but when it became obvious that the leader on the stands' side wasn't stopping, Dettori switched her towards the rail. She kept on for second despite appearing to hang, but she never had a chance with Waveband. (op 5-6 tchd 8-11 and 10-11 in places)

Sakhee's Pearl, who has been dropped 4lb, stayed on for a well-held third down the stands' side. She may have been flattered by this. (tchd 16-1)

Faithful One(IRE) remained down the centre and was at a disadvantage as a result. This consistent filly still ran her race and probably remains in good form. (op 4-1)

Perfect Friend, well beaten on sand three days earlier, never looked like reversing Newbury form with Sarasota Sunshine, despite a 4lb pull. (op 14-1 tchd 20-1)

Penzena, tried in first-time cheekpieces, raced in the stands' side trio but still ended up well beaten. (op 10-1)

3891 RITZ CLUB CASINO H'CAP — 5f

4:40 (4:41) (Class 2) (0-105,102) 3-Y-O+
£9,346 (£2,799; £1,399; £700; £349; £175) **Stalls** Low

Form					RPR
-540	**1**		**Rowe Park**[70] 1700 7-9-8 **98** ... AlanMunro 2 (Mrs L C Jewell) *pushed rt s: in tch: switching rt and hdwy wl over 1f out: rdn to chal ent fnl f: led ins fnl f: hld on wl towards fin* **10/1**		106
-151	**2**	*nk*	**Monsieur Joe (IRE)**[28] 2960 3-9-2 **97** ... GeorgeBaker 8 (W R Swinburn) *in tch towards rr: pushed along 2f out: nt clr run briefly and swtchd rt over 1f out: drvn to press ldrs ins fnl f: one pce towards fin* **9/2**[3]		102
0402	**3**	*hd*	**Prohibit**[14] 3461 5-9-8 **98** ... (p) FrankieDettori 6 (R M H Cowell) *hld up in rr: hdwy wl over 1f out: nt clr run ent fnl f: swtchd lft 1f out: rdn and pressed ldrs fnl 100yds: kpt on* **10/3**[2]		104
3005	**4**	*1 ¾*	**Le Toreador**[22] 3165 5-8-11 **87** ... (tp) NeilCallan 7 (K A Ryan) *led: rdn and hdd ins fnl f: wknd u.p fnl 100yds* **20/1**		87
0-00	**5**	*2 ½*	**Sonny Red (IRE)**[82] 1423 6-9-7 **97** ... AdrianNicholls 4 (D Nicholls) *stdd after s: hld up in last pair: niggled along 1/2-way: rdn ent fnl 2f: plugged on fnl f but no ch w ldrs* **11/2**		88
40-0	**6**	*3 ½*	**Swan Wings**[21] 3197 3-8-4 **85** ... DavidProbert 5 (A M Balding) *chsd ldrs: rdn over 2f out: wkng and towards rr whn sltly hmpd wl over 1f out: no ch w ldrs after* **16/1**		61
0300	**7**	*1 ¼*	**Judd Street**[21] 3193 8-9-12 **102** ... (v) WilliamBuick 3 (Eve Johnson Houghton) *short of room s and s.i.s: sn in midfield: rdn and effrt towards centre 2f out: wknd u.p over 1f out* **33/1**		76
04-1	**8**	*1*	**Archers Road (IRE)**[64] 1860 3-9-1 **96** ... JimCrowley 1 (T D Barron) *wnt bdly rt s: chsd ldr tl over 1f out: wknd qckly ent fnl f* **13/2**		64
1-01	**9**	*9*	**Present Alchemy**[27] 2997 4-8-11 **87** ... (t) JimmyFortune 10 (H Morrison) *wnt rt s: rcvrd to chse ldrs after 1f: rdn and unable qck over 2f out: wknd wl over 1f out* **3/1**[1]		25

60.34 secs (-0.16) **Going Correction** +0.20s/f (Good)
WFA 3 from 4yo+ 5lb **9** Ran SP% **117.7**
Speed ratings (Par 109): **109,108,108,105,101 95,93,92,77**
Tote Swingers: 1&2:£13.00, 1&3:£9.60 , 2&3:£3.70 CSF £55.63 CT £186.89 TOTE £14.00: £3.10, £2.00, £1.80; EX 89.40 Trifecta £278.10 Pool: £1,301.70 - 3.46 winning units..
Owner Mrs Sue Ashdown **Bred** J Baker **Trained** Sutton Valence, Kent

FOCUS

A good sprint handicap, run over a second quicker than the following 66-85 race. The main action took place on the stands' side. The winner is rated close to last year's course-and-distance form.

NOTEBOOK

Rowe Park had not been seen since finishing down the field in the Group 3 Palace House Stakes in early May. Drawn 2, but obliged to issue his challenge a little way off the stands' rail, he edged ahead inside the last and held off a pair of closers. He will go back up the weights now and will probably return to Group company in the Audi (King George) Stakes at Glorious Goodwood. (tchd 11-1)

Monsieur Joe(IRE), a progressive 3yo, was another 6lb higher but ran a big race against these established sprinters, running on well through the final furlong. This was a fine effort from what proved an unfavourable draw and he should pay to follow. (op 11-2 tchd 6-1 in a place)

Prohibit, dropped in trip, travelled strongly in rear and ran on well once switched to the rail. He usually acquits himself well at Ascot and this was no exception. (op 7-2 tchd 3-1)

Le Toreador ◆ grabbed the lead and tacked over to the rail, conceding defeat only inside the last. He showed more zip here than of late and could be about to find his form again. (op 16-1 tchd 22-1)

Sonny Red(IRE), last year's winner, has been running over further recently and has dropped to a handy mark. Soon steadied at the back, he stayed on late without ever managing to get into the race. (op 6-1 tchd 7-1)

Swan Wings was put up just a pound for his win at the Chester May meeting and was drawn closest to the rail. He showed decent pace but faded in the final furlong.\n (tchd 20-1)

Archers Road(IRE) was put up just a pound for his win at the Chester May meeting and was drawn closest to the rail. He showed decent pace but faded in the final furlong. (op 6-1 tchd 15-2)

Present Alchemy had a progressive look about him and a 7lb rise for his Slaisbury win seemed fair. After diving right from the stalls he was soon chasing the leaders on the outer but had been seen off before the final furlong. He had the worst of the draw but this was still disappointing.
Official explanation: jockey said colt lost its action (op 100-30 tchd 7-2)

3892 IVAN THE TERRIBLE H'CAP — 5f

5:15 (5:19) (Class 4) (0-85,85) 3-Y-O+ **£3,885** (£1,156; £577; £288) **Stalls** Low

Form					RPR
4511	**1**		**Brandywell Boy (IRE)**[13] 3474 7-8-8 **72** ... BillyCray[(5)] 1 (D J S Ffrench Davis) *chsd ldrs: rdn to chal over 1f out: led jst ins fnl f: r.o wl and forged ahd fnl 75yds* **7/1**		81
0405	**2**	*1 ¼*	**Triple Dream**[5] 3736 5-8-10 **72** ... (p) JackDean[(3)] 3 (J M Bradley) *led: rdn ent fnl 2f: edgd rt u.p ent fnl f: hdd jst ins fnl f: kpt on same pce fnl 100yds* **11/2**[3]		76
0264	**3**	*1 ¼*	**Rapid Water**[8] 3629 4-9-7 **80** ... (b) JimmyFortune 2 (A M Balding) *rrd s: t.k.h: hld up wl in tch: swtchd lft and rdn over 1f out: kpt on u.p ins fnl f: nt rch ldrs* **11/4**[1]		80
3504	**4**	*nse*	**Berbice (IRE)**[6] 3716 5-9-2 **75** ... (e) GeorgeBaker 6 (S Kirk) *awkward s and s.i.s: hld up in last: effrt and switching rt over 1f out: nt clr run and swtchd lft jst ins fnl f: kpt on fnl 100yds: nvr able to chal* **16/1**		74
1-10	**5**	*hd*	**Clifton Bridge**[87] 1315 3-9-3 **81** ... JimCrowley 5 (R M Beckett) *chsd ldr: rdn and unable qck wl over 1f out: carried rt ent fnl f: one pce fnl 100yds* **10/3**[2]		78+
2352	**6**	*nk*	**Brynfa Boy**[15] 3417 4-9-0 **73** ... (t) TonyCulhane 9 (P W D'Arcy) *t.k.h: hld up wl in tch: hdwy to press ldrs ent fnl 2f: ev ch and rdn over 1f out: wknd fnl 100yds* **13/2**		71
0-00	**7**	*¾*	**Safari Mischief**[35] 2745 7-9-7 **85** ... AshleyMorgan[(5)] 7 (P Winkworth) *t.k.h: pressed ldrs: ev ch and drvn over 1f out: wknd ins fnl f* **15/2**		80
0514	**8**	*½*	**Lucky Flyer**[13] 3480 3-7-12 **69** ... RyanPowell[(7)] 8 (S Kirk) *stdd s: t.k.h: hld up in tch: rdn and effrt ent fnl 2f: nt clr run and swtchd rt ent fnl f: kpt on but nvr gng pce to threaten ldrs* **20/1**		60
0260	**9**	*2 ¼*	**Even Bolder**[13] 3474 7-8-11 **75** ... LeeNewnes[(5)] 10 (E A Wheeler) *stdd s: t.k.h: hld up in tch: hdwy to chse ldrs and rdn wl over 1f out: wknd 1f out* **20/1**		60

61.47 secs (0.97) **Going Correction** +0.20s/f (Good)
WFA 3 from 4yo+ 5lb **9** Ran SP% **118.1**
Speed ratings (Par 105): **100,98,96,95,95 95,93,93,89**
Tote Swingers: 1&2 £10.20, 1&3 £4.10, 2&3 £4.90 CSF £46.30 CT £124.50 TOTE £6.70: £2.10, £2.60, £1.60; EX 59.80 Trifecta £185.50 Pool: £1,539.68 - 6.14 winning units. Place 6 £113.87, Place 5 £86.32..
Owner P B Gallagher **Bred** Mountarmstrong Stud **Trained** Lambourn, Berks

FOCUS

They went no pace in the early stages of this ordinary sprint handicap and the form, rated around the third, may prove a little suspect. The winner ran his best race on turf for four years at face value. In the end, those drawn in the three lowest stalls filled the first three places.

Triple Dream Official explanation: jockey said gelding hung right throughout

T/Plt: £61.80 to a £1 stake. Pool: £153,005.45 - 1,806.72 winning tickets. T/Qpdt: £10.80 to a £1 stake. Pool: £8,053.18 - 550.60 winning tickets. SP

3854 CHESTER (L-H)

Saturday, July 10

OFFICIAL GOING: Good to firm (8.2)

Rail out 7yds from 6f to top of home straight adding 15yds to advertised distances.

Wind: Breeze, across Weather: Overcast

3893 TOTEPOOL CITY PLATE (LISTED RACE) — 7f 2y

2:15 (2:16) (Class 1) 3-Y-O+
£21,004 (£7,962; £3,984; £1,986; £995; £499) **Stalls** Low

Form					RPR
-340	**1**		**Lord Shanakill (USA)**[21] 3192 4-9-2 113 ... TomQueally 4 (H R A Cecil) *hld up: clsd 3f out: wnt 2nd 2f out: r.o to ld wl ins fnl f: pushed out: comf* **8/13**[1]		108+

6130 **2** ¾ **Dunelight (IRE)**[63] 1900 7-9-5 105..............................(v) PhilipRobinson 2 109
(C G Cox) *led: rdn over 1f out: hdd wl ins fnl f: hld by wnr cl home* **5/1**[2]
4450 **3** 8 **Ishiadancer**[13] 3489 5-8-11 88.. WJSupple 3 79
(E J Alston) *hld up bhd ldrs: effrt over 2f out: outpcd by front duo fnl f* **33/1**
15-6 **4** nk **Ashram (IRE)**[14] 3455 4-9-2 113......................................(v) FrannyNorton 6 84
(Saeed Bin Suroor) *chsd ldrs: wnt 2nd over 5f out and sn w ldr: lost 2nd 2f out: rdn and wknd over 1f out* **13/2**[3]
-454 **5** 3¾ **Georgebernardshaw (IRE)**[14] 3460 5-9-2 103........... StephenCraine 1 73
(D M Simcock) *a little trblesme in stalls bef s: missed break: in rr: rdn over 1f out: no imp: wl btn ins fnl f* **9/1**
20-1 **6** 8 **Bow Beaver (USA)**[64] 1865 3-8-8 100.................................. DavidAllan 5 49
(J Howard Johnson) *racd keenly: chsd ldr tl over 5f out: niggled along and lost grnd over 4f out: toiling fnl 2f* **14/1**
1m 25.72s (-0.78) **Going Correction** +0.125s/f (Good)
WFA 3 from 4yo+ 8lb **6** Ran SP% **111.5**
Speed ratings (Par 111): **109,108,99,98,94 85**
Tote Swingers: 1&2 £1.10, 1&3 £6.50, 2&3 £19.00 CSF £4.03 TOTE £1.60: £1.10, £2.50; EX 3.40.
Owner Mogeely Stud & Mark T Gittins **Bred** Vimal Khosla, Gillian Khosla Et Al **Trained** Newmarket, Suffolk

FOCUS
The third running of this race as a Listed contest and a weak race for the grade. It was run at a good gallop thanks to the runner-up and the front pair pulled right away. The winner did not even need to match this year's best.

NOTEBOOK
Lord Shanakill(USA), a Group 1 winner and joint best-in at the weights, was taking a big drop in class and he proved more than up to it. He didn't enjoy the best of trips, however, and had to circle his rivals in order to get into a challenging position, but he still travelled smoothly and picked off the runner-up inside the last furlong with his rider never having to go for the whip. This was seen as a confidence-boosting exercise, a policy which certainly did his stable-companion Twice Over no harm, and it will be interesting to see where he goes next. The Prix Maurice De Gheest over 6.5f at Deauville next month is one possibility. (op 10-11 tchd evens in places)
Dunelight(IRE) hadn't been at his very best this year, but he still had a 3lb penalty to contend with on account of his success in a Listed race on Polytrack in March. Given his usual aggressive ride, he set a decent pace and tried to run the finish out of his rivals from the home turn, but the winner was running all over him. This was his best effort on turf this year, but he isn't the easiest horse to place.
Ishiadancer faced a very tall order on these terms, but not for the first time this year she outran her official rating in Listed company, despite taking a keen hold early. She will remain hard to place until her handicap mark returns to where it was at the start of the year, but that doesn't seem likely in the immediate future after this. (op 25-1)
Ashram(IRE) had an equal chance to the winner on official ratings and was successful the last time he competed at this level, but he was very weak in the market. He tried to serve it up to the leader from some way out, but came off the bridle inside the last 2f and gradually dropped away. Connections had suggested that they would have preferred some rain for him, but even that doesn't explain this modest effort and he looks worth treating with caution for the time being. (op 9-2)
Georgebernardshaw(IRE) got upset in the stalls and completely missed the break. He soon managed to get within striking distance of his rivals, but never offered a threat. He remains without a win in well over two years and ideally needs much softer conditions than these. (op 8-1)
Bow Beaver(USA), the only 3-y-o in the field, was up in class after beating two much higher-rated rivals in a 6f conditions event on his reappearance at Hamilton in May. He broke well enough, but was being ridden along at halfway and gradually dropped right out. He is another that is likely to prove hard to place in the near future off a mark of 100. (op 10-1)

3894 TOTEPOOL FLEXI BETTING H'CAP 1m 2f 75y
2:45 (2:46) (Class 4) (0-80,79) 4-Y-0+ **£5,180** (£1,541; £770; £384) **Stalls** High

Form RPR
1125 **1** **Granny McPhee**[7] 3679 4-9-4 76.. FrannyNorton 8 83
(A Bailey) *s.i.s: hld up: rdn and hdwy over 1f out: r.o ins fnl f to ld towards fin* **6/1**[3]
6041 **2** ½ **Snow Dancer (IRE)**[8] 3627 6-9-3 75........................... PatrickMathers 3 81
(H A McWilliams) *midfield: hdwy 3f out: lugged lft whn effrt over 1f out: sn led: hdd and nt pce of wnr towards fin* **10/1**
1122 **3** 1 **King's Masque**[19] 3265 4-9-3 78........................... AndrewHeffernan(3) 9 82
(B J Llewellyn) *chsd ldrs: chalng whn n.m.r briefly 1f out: nt qckn fnl 75yds* **4/1**[2]
6515 **4** ¾ **Dark Ranger**[16] 3369 4-8-2 60.. LukeMorris 1 63
(T J Pitt) *a.p: effrt on inner over 1f out: sn n.m.r briefly: styd on u.p: no imp towards fin* **13/2**
0434 **5** nse **Carter**[10] 3560 4-8-2 60 oh2.................................... DuranFentiman 4 63
(W M Brisbourne) *led: rdn over 1f out: sn hdd: continued to chse ldrs: no ex fnl 75yds* **9/1**
6444 **6** nk **Bold Cross (IRE)**[9] 3581 7-9-0 72................................ PaulFitzsimons 5 74
(E G Bevan) *missed break: hld up: rdn and hdwy over 1f out: styd on ins fnl f: nt quite pce to rch ldrs* **12/1**
-002 **7** 2 **Dragon Slayer (IRE)**[15] 3391 8-8-11 72...................... GaryBartley(3) 10 70
(John A Harris) *missed break: hld up: rdn over 1f out: kpt on ins fnl f: nvr able to chal* **12/1**
5036 **8** 1¾ **Carcinetto (IRE)**[2] 3830 8-9-7 79.. PatCosgrave 2 74
(P D Evans) *in tch: pushed along over 4f out: outpcd 2f out: no imp after* **9/1**
0244 **9** nse **Veroon (IRE)**[17] 3317 4-9-2 74....................................(p) PaulMulrennan 7 69
(J G Given) *chsd ldr: effrt over 1f out: sn n.m.r and lost pl: wknd ins fnl f* **3/1**[1]
2m 11.51s (-0.69) **Going Correction** +0.125s/f (Good) **9** Ran SP% **117.1**
Speed ratings (Par 105): **107,106,105,105,105 104,103,101,101**
Tote Swingers: 1&2 £10.30, 1&3 £3.70, 2&3 £4.60 CSF £64.89 CT £270.28 TOTE £5.70: £1.80, £2.70, £1.80; EX 66.40.
Owner Middleham Park Racing XXVI & Alan Bailey **Bred** Sugar Puss Corporation **Trained** Newmarket, Suffolk

FOCUS
A fair handicap, but the early pace was only modest and the principals finished in a bit of a heap. The race was a bit muddling but the winner is rated back to her best old form.

3895 TOTESPORT 0800 221 221 CITY WALL STKS (LISTED RACE) 5f 16y
3:20 (3:21) (Class 1) 3-Y-0+
£21,004 (£7,962; £3,984; £1,986; £995; £499) **Stalls** Low

Form RPR
1300 **1** **Blue Jack**[25] 3047 5-9-0 109...................................(v[1]) RichardKingscote 9 108+
(Tom Dascombe) *missed break: hld up: nt clr run 2f out: hdwy to chse ldr over 1f out: r.o ins fnl f: led fnl stride* **10/1**
2010 **2** shd **Captain Dunne (IRE)**[7] 3674 5-9-0 104.............................. DavidAllan 6 108
(T D Easterby) *chsd ldr: led 2f out: qcknd abt 3 l clr over 1f out: hrd pressed fnl 75yds: ct fnl stride* **9/1**
-233 **3** nk **Borderlescott**[25] 3047 8-9-0 112.. TomQueally 1 107
(R Bastiman) *chsd ldrs: rdn and nt qckn over 1f out: r.o ins fnl f: gng on at fin but nt quite pce to get there* **8/13**[1]
-140 **4** 4½ **Masamah (IRE)**[21] 3193 4-9-0 96..............................(t) PaulMulrennan 3 91+
(K A Ryan) *awkward s: in rr: outpcd 3f out: hdwy over 1f out: styd on ins fnl f: nt pce to trble front trio* **7/1**[3]
10-2 **5** 1¼ **Reverence**[13] 3486 9-9-0 107.. WJSupple 5 86
(E J Alston) *chsd ldrs: rdn and outpcd over 1f out: no imp fnl f* **12/1**
-005 **6** 1 **Star Rover (IRE)**[64] 1860 3-8-9 98..................................... PatCosgrave 4 81
(P D Evans) *chsd ldrs: sn pushed along: rdn and outpcd over 1f out: n.d after* **25/1**
0660 **7** 6 **Socceroo**[4] 3762 5-8-9 53.......................................(e[1]) AndrewHeffernan 7 56?
(D C Griffiths) *chsd ldrs: pushed along 2f out: wknd wl over 1f out* **100/1**
2041 **8** 7 **Glamorous Spirit (IRE)**[13] 3486 4-9-2 103......................... LukeMorris 2 38
(R A Harris) *led: rdn and hdd 2f out: wknd and eased whn btn ins fnl f:* **13/2**[2]
60.21 secs (-0.79) **Going Correction** +0.125s/f (Good)
WFA 3 from 4yo+ 5lb **8** Ran SP% **119.4**
Speed ratings (Par 111): **111,110,110,103,101 99,89,78**
Tote Swingers: 1&2 £15.40, 1&3 £3.20, 2&3 £3.00 CSF £98.65 TOTE £9.70: £2.10, £2.50, £1.20; EX 145.10 Trifecta £390.70 Pool: £1,251.40 - 2.37 winning units..
Owner A Black & M Owen **Bred** Miss S N Ralphs **Trained** Malpas, Cheshire

FOCUS
A decent Listed sprint and, as would be expected, there was no hanging about with Glamorous Spirit setting a strong pace from stall two. The two non-runners would have started from stalls eight and ten, yet the winner came from stall nine. There are one or two doubts over the form, which is rated around the runner-up. The winner didn't need to match his early-season form.

NOTEBOOK
Blue Jack has been successful in blinkers before, but this was his first try in a visor. He was down in class here having found Group company just beyond him since winning a Newbury handicap on his reappearance, but this level proved within his grasp. He was weak in the market beforehand and his chances didn't look that great when he missed the break from the outside stall, which looked a major handicap at this level, but he travelled well nonetheless and, having been taken right over to the inside rail after the intersection, produced a telling turn of foot to cut down the clear leader near the line. He may now be aimed at a Group 3 contest at the Curragh at the end of next month. (op 7-1)
Captain Dunne(IRE), back down to his best trip, had a few pounds to find with the best of these, but one thing he possesses is blistering early pace, which is a big asset around here. Although not asked to lead, he was handy from the off and looked likely to win when sent into a clear advantage after taking it up over a furlong from home, but his stride began to shorten in the closing stages and he was cut down close to the line. This was a smart effort. (op 10-1)
Borderlescott, last year's winner when favourably drawn in stall two, had the plum draw this time, and again the race conditions were very much in his favour. He travelled well enough behind the leaders and though he had a few lengths to find on the runner-up turning in, it still looked as though he might get up. However, he didn't find quite as much as had looked likely. His trainer had warned that not all of his horses had been running up to their best lately, so he shouldn't be judged too harshly on this and it would be a brave person who would bet against him completing a hat-trick of Nunthorpes next month. (op 4-6 tchd 8-11 in places)
Masamah(IRE) had a bit to find on these terms, but he attracted decent market support earlier in the day, and again on course, and had already shown that he is effective around here. Sporting a first-time tongue tie, he ran a very strange race, soon dropping himself out and looking very reluctant, but he eventually decided to run on into fourth. He has plenty of ability, but also has a few questions marks against him after this. Official explanation: jockey said gelding missed the break (op 10-1)
Reverence enjoyed an 8lb pull with Glamorous Spirit for a half-length beating at the Curragh last month and reversed that form, but he could never pick up and he would have found this ground too quick. (op 11-1)
Star Rover(IRE), the only 3-y-o in the field, is effective around here but he had a bit to do at the weights and, although he raced prominently early, he never looked like winning.
Socceroo had no chance in this company and even the first-time eyeshield wasn't going to change that.
Glamorous Spirit(IRE) faced a stiff task under a 7lb penalty for her success at the Curragh last month, but she likes a turning 5f and was successful in a handicap over C&D a year ago. However, after setting a furious pace she had run herself into the ground before the furlong pole. (op 6-1)

3896 BET ON LIVE GOLF AT TOTESPORT.COM H'CAP 1m 7f 195y
3:55 (4:20) (Class 4) (0-85,79) 3-Y-0+ **£5,180** (£1,541; £770; £384) **Stalls** Low

Form RPR
1-64 **1** **Theola (IRE)**[20] 3241 4-10-0 79.. PatCosgrave 3 86
(M H Tompkins) *hld up: pushed along 5f out: hrd at work 2f out: hdwy over 1f out: r.o ins fnl f to ld towards fin* **10/3**[3]
6452 **2** hd **Simonside**[16] 3367 7-9-5 70.. DavidAllan 4 77
(B Ellison) *chsd ldr: led after 4f: rdn and edgd rt ent fnl f: hdd towards fin* **3/1**[2]
6-00 **3** 1 **Command Marshal (FR)**[24] 3084 7-8-4 60 oh9.............. KierenFox(5) 5 66
(M J Scudamore) *in tch: pushed along 5f out: lost pl over 4f out: outpcd 3f out: rallied ins fnl f: r.o towards fin: nt get to front pair* **40/1**
3-24 **4** nk **Arab League (IRE)**[9] 3588 5-8-13 67......................... WilliamCarson(3) 1 72
(R J Price) *led: hdd after 4f: remained prom: rdn over 1f out: styd on u.p ins fnl f: one pce cl home* **11/2**
-312 **5** 1¾ **Rare Ruby (IRE)**[30] 2897 6-9-8 73...................................... TomQueally 2 76
(Jennie Candlish) *chsd ldrs: wnt 2nd 9f out: nt qckn u.p and lost 2nd over 1f out: fdd fnl 75yds* **11/2**
0003 **6** 1½ **Monte Cavallo (SAF)**[15] 3416 5-9-13 78....................... StephenCraine 6 80
(M Wigham) *stdd s: hld up in rr: stl gng wl 2f out: rdn over 1f out: failed to pick up and nt trble ldrs* **11/4**[1]
4-64 **7** ½ **Inchnadamph**[16] 3367 10-9-7 72................................(t) PaulMulrennan 7 73
(T J Fitzgerald) *stdd s: hld up: hdwy over 4f out: rdn to chse ldrs over 1f out: fdd ins fnl f* **16/1**
3m 31.87s (3.87) **Going Correction** +0.125s/f (Good) **7** Ran SP% **113.8**
Speed ratings (Par 105): **95,94,94,94,93 92,92**
CSF £13.65 TOTE £5.20: £2.40, £2.40; EX 15.40.
Owner E Buddle **Bred** Richard Klay And Dr M Klay **Trained** Newmarket, Suffolk
■ This race was delayed due to medical emergencies in the crowd.

FOCUS
They only went a very modest pace, so this wasn't the test of stamina that it might have been and it developed into a sprint. There wasn't that much covering the seven runners at the line. The form is sound enough despite the steady pace and the proximity of the third.

3897 ALL BETS ARE ON AT TOTESPORT.COM MAIDEN AUCTION STKS 5f 16y
4:30 (4:45) (Class 5) 2-Y-0 **£4,047** (£1,204; £601; £300) **Stalls** Low

Form RPR
6334 **1** **Master Macho (IRE)**[12] 3498 2-8-4 0............................. MatthewDavies(5) 5 73
(M R Channon) *hld up: rdn and hdwy over 1f out: hung lft and r.o to ld wl ins fnl f: on top at fin* **5/1**[3]

2 **2** ½ **Earl Wild (IRE)**[12] 3498 2-9-2 0 PaulMulrennan 8 78
(J Howard Johnson) *sn racd 3 wd w ldrs: str chal fr over 1f out: nt qckn and nt pce of wnr towards fin* **3/1**[1]

522 **3** *nk* **Crimson Knot (IRE)**[22] 3163 2-8-4 0 FrannyNorton 2 65
(A Berry) *bustled along to ld: rdn and hrd pressed fr over 1f out: hdd wl ins fnl f: hld fnl strides* **11/2**

34 **4** *4* **Dunmore Boy (IRE)**[17] 3316 2-9-2 0 FranciscoDaSilva 1 63
(R A Fahey) *chsd ldrs: rdn over 1f out: one pce and n.d to front trio ins fnl f* **15/2**

35 **5** *4* **Barkston Ash**[21] 3204 2-8-9 0 WJSupple 9 44+
(E J Alston) *bhd: intimidated by horse parting company w jockey after 1f: kpt on ins fnl f: nt pce to rch ldrs* **22/1**

5242 **6** *2¾* **Tilliemint (IRE)**[17] 3315 2-8-4 0 (b) DuranFentiman 4 26
(T D Easterby) *bmpd s and s.i.s: outpcd and bhd: nvr on terms w ldrs* **11/2**

002 **7** *3* **Welsh Inlet (IRE)**[12] 3509 2-8-5 0 WilliamCarson(3) 3 20
(S C Williams) *racd w ldr 2 wd: lost pl wl over 1f out: sn wknd and hung rt: eased whn btn ins fnl f* **7/2**[2]

30 **U** **Chestival (IRE)**[28] 2951 2-8-1 0 AndrewHeffernan(3) 6 —
(Patrick Morris) *towards rr: stmbld bdly and uns rdr after 1f* **33/1**

62.00 secs (1.00) **Going Correction** +0.125s/f (Good) **8** Ran SP% **113.7**
Speed ratings (Par 94): **97,96,95,89,82 78,73,—**
Tote Swingers: 1&2 £4.20, 1&3 £5.60, 2&3 £4.00 CSF £20.16 TOTE £6.80: £1.90, £1.50, £2.00; EX 30.20.
Owner Lord Ilsley Racing (Hylands Syndicate) **Bred** Kevin Blake **Trained** West Ilsley, Berks

FOCUS
A modest maiden, but a dramatic race with a thrilling three-horse finish and another one unseating her rider having clipped heels after a furlong. Sound form with the exposed winner rated to his mark.

NOTEBOOK
Master Macho(IRE) had already had far more chances than his rivals and was well behind Earl Wild at Musselburgh last time. However, this was his day as he travelled well off the pace and always looked like getting up when brought with his effort after the cutaway. The fact that he was getting off the mark at the 13th attempt doesn't suggest that this is strong form, but he should have a future in nurseries. (op 15-2)

Earl Wild(IRE) may not have been helped by getting caught on the outside of a three-horse battle for the early lead, so he may have done well to keep on going right to the line. There should be an ordinary maiden in him. (op 7-2)

Crimson Knot(IRE), runner-up in her last two starts at Musselburgh, firstly behind the smart Excel Bolt and then in a valuable seller, tried to make all from her good draw and wasn't worn down until late. She looks the type for nurseries. (op 9-2)

Dunmore Boy(IRE), who didn't get home in two starts over a stiff 6f, had the plum draw but although he showed some early pace, he couldn't make the most of his stall and seemed to hang about in the home straight. He may be worth another chance back on a more conventional track, especially as he now qualifies for nurseries. (op 13-2)

Barkston Ash was hampered when Chestival unseated her rider after a furlong and never recovered.

Tilliemint(IRE), runner-up three times from five previous starts, had shaped as though this sharp 5f would suit, but she was short of room after missing the break and was soon playing catch-up. (op 5-1 tchd 9-2)

Welsh Inlet(IRE), narrowly beaten on her third start at Windsor last time, was involved in the battle for the early lead but she faded very tamely well over a furlong from home.

3898 40 LIVE FOOTBALL MARKETS AT TOTESPORT.COM H'CAP 6f 18y
5:05 (5:22) (Class 4) (0-80,79) 3-Y-O+ **£5,180** (£1,541; £770; £384) **Stalls** Low

Form RPR

1550 **1** **Last Sovereign**[21] 3226 6-10-0 **79** PatCosgrave 7 88
(Jane Chapple-Hyam) *chsd ldrs: effrt over 1f out: r.o to ld ins fnl f: gamely doing enough towards fin* **14/1**

4062 **2** ½ **Green Park (IRE)**[14] 3430 7-9-12 **77** (v) DavidNolan 2 84
(D Carroll) *chsd ldrs: effrt whn n.m.r briefly over 1f out: str chal ins fnl f: r.o under driving: hld fnl strides* **5/1**[3]

4006 **3** *nk* **Viking Spirit**[26] 3037 8-10-0 **79** TomQueally 3 85
(W R Swinburn) *midfield: plld out and hdwy over 1f out: r.o ins fnl f: gng on at fin but nt quite pce to get there* **8/1**

105 **4** ½ **Imprimis Tagula (IRE)**[15] 3389 6-9-2 **74** (v) NatashaEaton(7) 8 79
(A Bailey) *racd in midfield on outer: effrt over 1f out: prog and styd on towards fin: nt quite pce to chal* **12/1**

6102 **5** *1* **Bahamian Lad**[15] 3389 5-9-7 **72** (p) JerryO'Dwyer 4 74
(R Hollinshead) *w ldr: led 2f out: lugged lft over 1f out: hdd ins fnl f: no ex fnl 75yds* **7/2**[2]

0065 **6** *hd* **Memphis Man**[2] 3833 7-8-13 **71** MatthewCosham(7) 5 72
(P D Evans) *hld up: rdn over 1f out: styd on ins fnl f: gd prog towards fin: nt pce to rch ldrs* **20/1**

3123 **7** *nk* **Legal Eagle (IRE)**[9] 3584 5-9-12 **77** (p) FrannyNorton 1 77
(Paul Green) *led: hdd 2f out: sn rdn: continued to chal: no ex fnl 75yds* **9/4**[1]

0100 **8** *1* **Wyatt Earp (IRE)**[17] 3321 9-9-5 **75** (p) TobyAtkinson(5) 9 72
(P Salmon) *hld up: rdn over 1f out: nvr able to rch chalng position* **16/1**

5335 **9** ½ **Starlight Muse (IRE)**[4] 3751 3-9-1 **72** GrahamGibbons 13 67+
(E S McMahon) *s.i.s: towards rr: rdn whn n.m.r and hmpd over 1f out: no imp after* **20/1**

0000 **10** *2½* **The Human League**[16] 3363 3-8-12 **69** PaulEddery 10 56
(M R Channon) *in rr: kpt on ins fnl f: nvr able to chal* **33/1**

01-5 **11** ½ **My One Weakness (IRE)**[15] 3410 3-9-3 **74** PaulMulrennan 12 60
(B Ellison) *midfield: pushed along whn n.m.r over 1f out: sn btn: eased ins fnl f* **20/1**

3315 **12** *6* **Whitechapel**[30] 2884 3-9-3 **74** WJSupple 11 40
(E J Alston) *squeezed out s: towards rr: rdn over 2f out: sn lft bhd* **14/1**

1m 14.17s (0.37) **Going Correction** +0.125s/f (Good)
WFA 3 from 5yo+ 6lb **12** Ran SP% **124.9**
Speed ratings (Par 105): **102,101,100,100,98 98,98,96,96,92 92,84**
Tote Swingers: 1&2 £14.90, 1&3 £15.60, 2&3 £8.00 CSF £82.77 CT £621.77 TOTE £15.70: £4.60, £2.40, £3.20; EX 157.30 TRIFECTA Not won..
Owner Howard Spooner **Bred** Gestut Hof Ittlingen & Cheveley Park Stud Ltd **Trained** Dalham, Suffolk
■ Stewards' Enquiry : Tom Queally three-day ban: careless riding (Jul 25-27)

FOCUS
Quite a competitive sprint handicap run at a strong pace, which favoured those who raced handily, and the high-drawn horses never figured. Sound form amongst the principals.

Whitechapel Official explanation: jockey said gelding was unsuited by the track

3899 BET ON WORLD CUP AT TOTESPORT.COM APPRENTICE H'CAP 7f 122y
5:40 (5:50) (Class 4) (0-80,82) 3-Y-O **£5,180** (£1,541; £770; £384) **Stalls** Low

Form RPR

0021 **1** **Mejd (IRE)**[7] 3661 3-9-9 **82** MatthewDavies 4 87
(M R Channon) *trckd ldrs: rdn to ld over 1f out: r.o wl: eased whn in command towards fin* **7/2**[2]

-135 **2** *1* **Red Gulch**[39] 2618 3-9-4 **77** AshleyHamblett 5 79
(E A L Dunlop) *hld up: rdn and hdwy over 1f out: styd on to take 2nd wl ins fnl f: edgd lft towards fin: nt pce to shake up wnr* **7/2**[2]

0602 **3** *hd* **Nubar Boy**[5] 3731 3-8-4 **70** (v) MatthewCosham(7) 7 71
(P D Evans) *s.i.s: bhd: u.p 2f out: hdwy over 1f out: hung rt fr ent fnl f: styd on towards fin but hld* **7/1**

4561 **4** *1¾* **Another Magic Man (USA)**[15] 3387 3-8-12 **71** KierenFox 3 68
(J R Best) *racd keenly: w ldr: led 2f out: sn rdn: hdd over 1f out: no ex fnl 100yds* **11/4**[1]

0-03 **5** *1¾* **Perfect Ch'l (IRE)**[14] 3441 3-8-13 **72** WilliamCarson 2 64
(I A Wood) *midfield: pushed along to go pce over 3f out: clsd 2f out: rdn whn chsng ldrs over 1f out: one pce fnl 100yds* **11/2**[3]

-250 **6** *3¼* **Caracal**[11] 3531 3-8-6 **65** MartinLane 1 49
(M Johnston) *bustled along to ld: rdn and hdd 2f out: stl in contention but u.p over 1f out: hld whn n.m.r and bmpd ins fnl f: dropped away* **11/2**[3]

1m 34.41s (0.61) **Going Correction** +0.125s/f (Good) **6** Ran SP% **114.4**
Speed ratings (Par 102): **101,100,99,98,96 93**
Tote Swingers: 1&2 £2.60, 1&3 £3.40, 2&3 £4.30 CSF £16.49 TOTE £4.70: £2.40, £2.50; EX 17.20 Place 6 £42.06, Place 5 £36.76..
Owner M Al-Qatami & K M Al-Mudhaf **Bred** Michael Dalton **Trained** West Ilsley, Berks

FOCUS
An ordinary apprentice handicap, but they went a furious pace and there was soon a big gap between the front three and the last trio. The form makes sense.
T/Plt: £56.90 to a £1 stake. Pool: £88,889.74 - 1,139.07 winning tickets. T/Qpdt: £12.80 to a £1 stake. Pool: £5,178.66 - 298.80 winning tickets. DO

3528 HAMILTON (R-H)
Saturday, July 10

OFFICIAL GOING: Good (good to firm; 9.4)
Wind: Almost nil Weather: Overcast, dull

3900 TWO FOR ONE ADMISSION NEXT THURSDAY APPRENTICE RIDERS' H'CAP (ROUND 2) 6f 5y
6:00 (6:00) (Class 6) (0-60,59) 3-Y-O+ **£2,388** (£705; £352) **Stalls** Centre

Form RPR

0504 **1** **Angaric (IRE)**[115] 912 7-8-12 **53** PeterSword(7) 8 62
(B Smart) *t.k.h: chsd ldr: led and hung lft over 1f out: pushed out fnl f* **6/1**[3]

0062 **2** ¾ **Botham (USA)**[11] 3534 6-9-6 **59** PaulNorton(5) 7 66
(J S Goldie) *n.m.r s: sn bhd: plenty to do 1/2-way: gd hdwy over 1f out: chsd wnr last 100yds: r.o* **1/1**[1]

00-0 **3** ½ **Santiago Atitlan**[6] 3706 8-9-0 **55** DavidSimmonson(7) 5 60
(P Monteith) *bhd: rdn 1/2-way: edgd rt and hdwy over 1f out: r.o ins fnl f* **33/1**

6503 **4** *3* **Hettie Hubble**[9] 3597 4-8-13 **47** LeeTopliss 1 43
(D W Thompson) *prom: rdn and edgd rt fr 1/2-way: kpt on same pce ins fnl f* **11/4**[2]

-100 **5** *2¼* **Royal Cheer**[12] 3515 3-8-7 **50** (p) JamesRogers(3) 4 38
(Mrs A Duffield) *led to over 1f out: wknd ins fnl f* **28/1**

0-00 **6** *1¼* **Calley Ho**[18] 3286 4-8-10 **49** NoraLooby(5) 3 34
(Mrs L Stubbs) *prom: effrt over 2f out: wknd ins fnl f* **10/1**

0006 **7** *14* **Sendreni (FR)**[22] 3164 6-9-0 **55** (p) GerardGalligan(7) 6 —
(Mrs J C McGregor) *hmpd s: sn chsng ldrs: hung rt and wknd fr 1/2-way: t.o* **18/1**

1m 13.88s (1.68) **Going Correction** 0.0s/f (Good)
WFA 3 from 4yo+ 6lb **7** Ran SP% **111.7**
Speed ratings (Par 101): **88,87,86,82,79 77,59**
Tote Swingers: 1&2 £1.70, 1&3 £9.90, 2&3 £8.40 CSF £11.86 CT £174.70 TOTE £4.70: £1.30, £1.60; EX 13.30.
Owner B Smart **Bred** Humphrey Okeke **Trained** Hambleton, N Yorks
■ Stewards' Enquiry : James Rogers three-day ban: careless riding (Jul 25-27)

FOCUS
Hard to escape the conclusion that this wasn't a strong handicap and it'll be a surprise if too many winners emerge from it in the coming weeks. Given the size of the field they were quite well spread across the track from an early stage, the winner sticking more towards the centre.

3901 TURFTV CLAIMING STKS 1m 3f 16y
6:30 (6:30) (Class 6) 4-Y-O+ **£2,388** (£705; £352) **Stalls** High

Form RPR

2434 **1** **Graceful Descent (FR)**[8] 3618 5-8-6 67 GregFairley 5 64+
(J S Goldie) *pressed ldr: rdn 3f out: led over 1f out: drew clr fnl f* **5/4**[1]

/00- **2** *7* **Orpen Bid (IRE)**[10] 2816 5-7-13 40 ow1 KellyHarrison(3) 6 47
(A M Crow) *led: rdn 3f out: hdd over 1f out: edgd lft: kpt on same pce fnl f* **100/1**

0556 **3** *hd* **King's Head (IRE)**[21] 3202 7-9-2 68 TomEaves 2 61
(Miss L A Perratt) *hld up towards rr: effrt and hdwy over 2f out: kpt on u.p fnl f: nrst fin* **10/1**

4 *hd* **La Bacouetteuse (FR)**[28] 5-9-0 0 LNewman 11 58
(A G Foster) *in tch: effrt u.p 3f out: hung lft over 1f out: kpt on same pce fnl f* **40/1**

-035 **5** *2* **Ballade De La Mer**[24] 3078 4-7-13 43 JamesSullivan(5) 4 45
(A G Foster) *hld up in tch: effrt over 2f out: kpt on same pce fr over 1f out* **20/1**

4460 **6** *4½* **Shy Glance (USA)**[6] 3709 8-8-11 67 TonyHamilton 3 44
(P Monteith) *midfield: rdn over 2f out: sn no imp* **7/1**[3]

5100 **7** *1½* **Sand Tiger (IRE)**[36] 2710 4-9-2 82 BarryMcHugh(3) 7 49
(R A Fahey) *prom: drvn over 3f out: wknd fr 2f out* **9/4**[2]

5000 **8** *2¾* **Lava Steps (USA)**[37] 2218 4-8-4 52 PaulPickard(3) 1 32
(P T Midgley) *s.i.s: hld up: rdn over 3f out: nvr on terms* **40/1**

000- **9** ½ **Wilmington**[9] 5947 6-7-13 45 ShaneBKelly(7) 8 30
(Mrs J C McGregor) *chsd ldrs: rdn over 3f out: wknd over 2f out* **66/1**

10 *2¼* **Why So Serious**[28] 4-8-6 0 (b) AndrewElliott 10 26
(D W Whillans) *bhd: drvn over 4f out: sn struggling* **50/1**

11 *6* **Claude Carter**[38] 6-8-6 0 ..... DeanHeslop(5) 9 20
(A C Whillans) *dwlt: bhd: drvn over 4f out: nvr on terms* **20/1**

2m 24.77s (-0.83) **Going Correction** 0.0s/f (Good) **11** Ran SP% **115.6**
Speed ratings (Par 101): **103,97,97,97,96 92,91,89,89,87 83**
Tote Swingers: 1&2 £52.30, 1&3 £4.70, 2&3 £24.00 CSF £189.11 TOTE £2.10: £1.10, £23.40, £3.40; EX 176.90.
Owner Eric Nisbet & Stan Moffat **Bred** Castleton Group **Trained** Uplawmoor, E Renfrews
■ Stewards' Enquiry : James Sullivan two-day ban: used whip with excessive frequency (Jul 25-26))
L Newman one-day ban: careless riding (Jul 25)

FOCUS
Only a few of these could be given a realisitic chance beforehand, and with a couple of those running below expectations, this claimer took little winning.

3902 HAMILTON-PARK.CO.UK H'CAP — 5f 4y
7:00 (7:02) (Class 4) (0-80,77) 3-Y-0+ **£5,180** (£1,541; £770; £384) **Stalls** Centre

Form | | | | RPR

6503 **1** **Haajes**[7] [3675] 6-9-11 **77** ..... PaulPickard(3) 3 92
(P T Midgley) *bhd and sn pushed along: gd hdwy over 1f out: led ins fnl f: sn clr* **3/1**[1]

-624 **2** *3* **Lesley's Choice**[22] [3165] 4-9-6 **74** .....(b) JamesSullivan(5) 2 78
(F J Brennan) *chsd ldrs: rdn over 2f out: ev ch and hung rt ins fnl f: kpt on: no ch w wnr* **5/1**[3]

1354 **3** *1* **Tadalavil**[15] [3409] 5-9-4 **67** ..... TomEaves 4 68
(Miss L A Perratt) *dwlt: sn pushed along towards rr: hdwy over 1f out: kpt on fnl f: nrst fin* **6/1**

1063 **4** *1 1/4* **The Bear**[11] [3533] 7-8-13 **62** ..... TonyHamilton 6 58
(Miss L A Perratt) *set str pce: rdn 2f out: hdd ins fnl f: no ex* **8/1**

1151 **5** *1 3/4* **La Capriosa**[66] [1827] 4-9-9 **72** ..... LeeVickers 5 62
(J A Glover) *trckd ldr: rdn over 2f out: wknd ins fnl f* **16/1**

-110 **6** *1 1/4* **Top Bid**[21] [3216] 6-9-2 **68** .....(b) KellyHarrison(3) 7 53
(T D Easterby) *dwlt: bhd: effrt on outside 2f out: wknd ins fnl f* **4/1**[2]

0310 **7** *1/2* **Methaaly (IRE)**[14] [3435] 7-9-0 **70** .....(be) JosephYoung(7) 8 54
(M Mullineaux) *bhd and pushed along: shortlived effrt 2f out: sn btn* **8/1**

0010 **8** *1* **Bosun Breese**[9] [3584] 5-9-4 **72** .....(t) DeanHeslop(5) 1 52
(T D Barron) *racd towards stands' side and away fr main gp: towards rr: drvn 1/2-way: sn outpcd* **7/1**

59.33 secs (-0.67) **Going Correction** 0.0s/f (Good) **8** Ran SP% **116.6**
Speed ratings (Par 105): **105,100,98,96,93 91,91,89**
Tote Swingers: 1&2 £4.80, 1&3 £4.50, 2&3 £6.90 CSF £18.60 CT £84.77 TOTE £3.40: £1.20, £3.10, £3.00; EX 12.40.
Owner N Lomas, A Taylor Snr, A Taylor Jnr **Bred** Irish National Stud **Trained** Westow, N Yorks

FOCUS
The front two here were both potentially well treated and it's probably best to view the form in a reasonably positive light for the time being.
Top Bid Official explanation: jockey said gelding missed the break

3903 RACING UK MAIDEN (S) STKS — 5f 4y
7:35 (7:36) (Class 6) 3-Y-0+ **£2,047** (£604; £302) **Stalls** Centre

Form | | | | RPR

-032 **1** **Bronze Beau**[22] [3181] 3-8-9 65 .....(t) JamesSullivan(5) 1 68+
(Mrs L Stubbs) *mde all: pushed along and r.o strly fnl f: comf* **11/8**[1]

54-5 **2** *2 1/2* **Residency (IRE)**[7] [3663] 4-9-5 61 ..... TomEaves 9 61
(B Smart) *chsd ldrs: drvn and outpcd wl over 1f out: rallied to chse wnr ins fnl f: no imp* **7/2**[2]

5005 **3** *1* **Kristen Jane (USA)**[11] [3529] 3-8-9 43 ..... GregFairley 6 50
(Miss L A Perratt) *towards rr and sn pushed along: hdwy over 1f out: kpt on same pce fnl f* **40/1**

3060 **4** *4* **Distant Vision (IRE)**[15] [3409] 7-9-0 47 ..... PatrickMathers 7 38
(H A McWilliams) *sn rdn bhd ldng gp: effrt 2f out: sn no imp* **10/1**

6000 **5** *hd* **Firetrap**[6] [3710] 3-8-9 53 .....(v) AmyRyan(5) 2 40
(Mrs A Duffield) *cl up: effrt and ev ch over 1f out: edgd lft: wknd ins fnl f* **13/2**

6054 **6** *2* **Kirkby's Gem**[22] [3181] 3-8-6 40 ..... PaulPickard(3) 10 28
(A Berry) *in tch on outside: rdn and outpcd fr 2f out* **50/1**

0-04 **7** *1/2* **Bees River (IRE)**[6] [3711] 4-8-11 45 .....(p) GaryBartley(3) 4 28
(J S Goldie) *upset in stalls: cl up tl wknd over 1f out* **11/2**[3]

8 *6* **Salamera (IRE)**[573] 4-9-0 0 ..... LeeVickers 5 7
(F J Brennan) *dwlt: bhd and rdn along: nvr on terms* **25/1**

-005 **9** *3* **Balzarine**[24] [3075] 4-9-0 33 .....(b) AndrewElliott 8 —
(C J Teague) *cl up tl wknd fr 2f out* **50/1**

0-00 **10** *1 1/2* **Rightcar Dominic**[91] [1234] 5-9-5 39 .....(b) TonyHamilton 3 —
(Peter Grayson) *sn: a bhd and outpcd* **50/1**

59.89 secs (-0.11) **Going Correction** 0.0s/f (Good)
WFA 3 from 4yo+ 5lb **10** Ran SP% **114.3**
Speed ratings (Par 101): **100,96,94,88,87 84,83,74,69,66**
Tote Swingers: 1&2 £14.10, 1&3 £2.50, 2&3 £13.30 CSF £5.69 TOTE £2.00: £1.02, £1.10, £15.90; EX 5.80.There was no bid for the winner.
Owner D Arundale **Bred** Meon Valley Stud **Trained** Norton, N Yorks

FOCUS
A weak race, even by selling standards, this one open only to maidens, and it was plain sailing for the favourite.

3904 JOHN SMITH'S FAIR FRIDAY NEXT WEEK H'CAP — 6f 5y
8:05 (8:05) (Class 5) (0-75,75) 3-Y-O **£2,914** (£867; £433; £216) **Stalls** Centre

Form | | | | RPR

0220 **1** **Besty**[26] [3024] 3-9-5 **73** ..... TomEaves 6 80
(B Smart) *cl up: rdn to ld over 1f out: hrd pressed ins fnl f: kpt on gamely towards fin* **5/2**[1]

5451 **2** *1/2* **Monte Mayor One**[6] [3710] 3-8-7 **61** 6ex ow1 ..... TonyHamilton 4 66
(P Monteith) *in tch: hdwy over 1f out: rdn and str chal ins fnl f: hld cl home* **9/2**[3]

-002 **3** *1 3/4* **Loss Leader (IRE)**[42] [2530] 3-7-13 **56** oh2 ..... KellyHarrison(3) 1 56
(T D Easterby) *hld up in tch: hdwy over 1f out: kpt on ins fnl f* **3/1**[2]

520 **4** *1 1/2* **Coolree Star (IRE)**[98] [1086] 3-9-7 **75** ..... LeeVickers 2 70
(J A Glover) *prom: edgd rt and outpcd 2f out: rallied ins fnl f: no imp* **10/1**

4402 **5** *1 1/4* **Frontline Boy (IRE)**[7] [3685] 3-8-10 **64** .....(t) AndrewElliott 5 55
(J R Weymes) *fly-jmpd s: sn cl up: rdn and edgd rt over 1f out: sn outpcd* **11/2**

-004 **6** *3 1/2* **Tartufo Dolce (IRE)**[26] [3023] 3-8-3 **62** ..... AmyRyan(5) 3 42
(J G Given) *led to over 1f out: sn rdn and wknd* **6/1**

1m 12.23s (0.03) **Going Correction** 0.0s/f (Good) **6** Ran SP% **110.5**
Speed ratings (Par 100): **99,98,96,94,92 87**
Tote Swingers: 1&2 £3.00, 1&3 £2.30, 2&3 £2.10 CSF £13.51 TOTE £4.20: £1.70, £2.30; EX 13.60.
Owner A Turton & P Langford **Bred** Argosy Ltd **Trained** Hambleton, N Yorks

FOCUS
No real depth to this handicap.

3905 TOTEPOOL FLEXI BETTING H'CAP (QUALIFIER FOR THE SCOTTISH TROPHY HANDICAP SERIES FINAL) — 1m 65y
8:40 (8:40) (Class 5) (0-75,72) 3-Y-0+ **£2,914** (£867; £433; £216) **Stalls** High

Form | | | | RPR

2243 **1** **Stellite**[6] [3706] 10-9-6 **65** ..... GaryBartley(3) 5 73
(J S Goldie) *hld up: hdwy on outside over 2f out: styd on wl fnl f: led nr fin* **13/2**

2600 **2** *hd* **Bed Fellow (IRE)**[6] [3707] 6-8-5 **52** ..... JamesSullivan(5) 4 59
(P Monteith) *t.k.h: in tch: hdwy on outside to ld over 1f out: kpt on fnl f: hdd towards fin* **28/1**

5102 **3** *2* **Royal Straight**[12] [3499] 5-9-7 **70** ..... DaleSwift(7) 9 72
(Miss L A Perratt) *hld up: hdwy 3f out: ev ch over 1f out: kpt on u.p ins fnl f* **11/4**[1]

-335 **4** *1 1/2* **Mason Hindmarsh**[14] [3450] 3-8-11 **65** ..... KellyHarrison(3) 1 62
(Karen McLintock) *led 3f: cl up: drvn over 3f out: ev ch over 1f out* **4/1**[3]

0542 **5** *3/4* **Bold Marc (IRE)**[9] [3595] 8-9-11 **67** ..... AndrewElliott 2 64
(J R Weymes) *trckd ldrs: drvn over 2f out: kpt on same pce fnl f* **12/1**

-461 **6** *1 1/4* **Raleigh Quay (IRE)**[22] [3161] 3-9-7 **72** ..... TomEaves 8 64
(Micky Hammond) *in tch: drvn and outpcd over 2f out: no imp fr over 1f out* **7/2**[2]

6513 **7** *2 1/4* **Croeso Cusan**[16] [3377] 5-8-13 **60** ..... AmyRyan(5) 3 49
(J L Spearing) *dwlt: t.k.h: hld up: hdwy to ld after 3f: rdn over 2f out: hdd over 1f out: sn btn* **8/1**

60-0 **8** *3/4* **Funky Munky**[31] [2864] 5-9-3 **59** ..... GregFairley 6 47
(A C Whillans) *hld up: drvn over 2f out: edgd rt and sn outpcd* **16/1**

4053 **9** *130* **Rosbertini**[11] [3531] 4-9-3 **59** ..... TonyHamilton 7 —
(Miss L A Perratt) *plld hrd: cl up tl rdn and wknd over 3f out: eased whn no ch over 1f out* **10/1**

1m 48.41s (0.01) **Going Correction** 0.0s/f (Good)
WFA 3 from 4yo+ 9lb **9** Ran SP% **119.4**
Speed ratings (Par 103): **99,98,96,95,94 93,91,90,—**
Tote Swingers: 1&2 £8.30, 1&3 £5.00, 2&3 £37.60 CSF £167.91 CT £623.26 TOTE £9.30: £3.10, £6.00, £1.10; EX 240.00 Place 6: £14.60 Place 5: £9.60.
Owner M Mackay, S Bruce, J S Goldie **Bred** Cheveley Park Stud Ltd **Trained** Uplawmoor, E Renfrews

FOCUS
Very much run-of-the-mill fare. The pace was steady until Croeso Cusan pulled her way to the head of affairs after two furlongs or so.
Rosbertini Official explanation: jockey said gelding hung left throughout
T/Plt: £10.30 to a £1 stake. Pool £50,906 - 3,597.99 winning tickets. T/Qpdt: £6.70 to a £1 stake. Pool £4,278 - 467.20 winning tickets. RY

3684 NOTTINGHAM (L-H)
Saturday, July 10

OFFICIAL GOING: Good to firm (7.4)
All races on outer track and rail moved out 2m from 2nd dog leg to 10f start adding about 14yds to advertised distances on round course.
Wind: Light against Weather: Sunny

3906 DOH! SIMPSONS VISIT TWINLAKES 3RD AUGUST EUROPEAN BREEDERS' FUND MAIDEN FILLIES' STKS — 6f 15y
2:05 (2:09) (Class 5) 2-Y-O **£3,561** (£1,059; £529; £264) **Stalls** High

Form | | | | RPR

1 **Nordic Spruce (USA)** 2-9-0 0 ..... IanMongan 3 73+
(H R A Cecil) *s.i.s: sn prom: swtchd lft 2f out: sn rdn: r.o to ld wl ins fnl f* **4/1**[2]

2 *nk* **Royalorien** 2-9-0 0 ..... MartinDwyer 10 72+
(W J Knight) *s.i.s: outpcd: edgd rt and hdwy 2f out: nt clr run and swtchd rt wl ins fnl f: r.o wl* **14/1**

260 **3** *1/2* **Magic Stella**[22] [3141] 2-8-9 0 ..... MatthewDavies(5) 6 71
(A P Jarvis) *w ldr: rdn over 1f out: r.o* **8/1**

235 **4** *nk* **Catalinas Diamond (IRE)**[24] [3070] 2-9-0 0 ..... JamesDoyle 9 70
(B W Duke) *led: rdn over 1f out: edgd lft and hdd wl ins fnl f* **10/11**[1]

0 **5** *5* **Empress Charlotte**[15] [3411] 2-9-0 0 ..... SaleemGolam 1 55
(M L W Bell) *sn pushed along in rr: hdwy over 2f out: rdn and wknd over 1f out* **22/1**

6 *hd* **Scantily Clad (IRE)** 2-9-0 0 ..... RichardMullen 5 54+
(E S McMahon) *chsd ldrs: shkn up and ev ch 2f out: wknd over 1f out* **9/2**[3]

00 **7** *8* **Time For Applause**[9] [3602] 2-9-0 0 ..... DaraghO'Donohoe 7 30
(E A L Dunlop) *stdd s: hld up: bhd fr 1/2-way* **80/1**

8 *1/2* **Silent Serenade** 2-9-0 0 ..... DaneO'Neill 4 29
(W R Swinburn) *prom: pushed along 1/2-way: wknd 2f out* **16/1**

00 **9** *4 1/2* **Laugia**[28] [2963] 2-9-0 0 ..... SimonWhitworth 8 15
(J R Jenkins) *s.i.s and hmpd s: sn prom: wkng whn hmpd 2f out* **100/1**

1m 14.44s (-0.46) **Going Correction** -0.10s/f (Good) **9** Ran SP% **120.8**
Speed ratings (Par 91): **99,98,97,97,90 90,79,79,73**
Tote Swingers: 1&2 £15.90, 1&3 £2.20, 2&3 £21.30 CSF £59.16 TOTE £4.90: £1.60, £4.10, £2.30; EX 38.10.
Owner Gestut Ammerland **Bred** Gestut Ammerland **Trained** Newmarket, Suffolk

FOCUS
The runners all came stands' side. A fair maiden that produced a tight finish. The first pair are likely to do a good deal better.

NOTEBOOK
Nordic Spruce(USA), who is by Dynafomer out of a mare that won at up to 6.5f, made a very encouraging debut, not least considering she is bred to do better over further. Always travelling well, she looked very green once switched widest of all but still did it a touch readily wiithout her rider getting anywhere near the bottom of her. There's every likelihood she'll improve quite significantly. (op 5-2)
Royalorien ◆ caught the eye in second and seems sure to improve and win a similar event. Soon on the back foot after a slow start, she had to weave a passage through, having a troubled run at one point, but she continued to run on strongly. She has some stamina in her pedigree and also be suited by 7f. Official explanation: jockey said filly hung right
Magic Stella found Royal Ascot too hot last time but probably ran somewhere near the level of her previous 5f form, always to the fore and battling on well. (op 15-2 tchd 7-1)
Catalinas Diamond(IRE) had an outstanding chance on form and has to be considered disappointing, not least considering she also had the benefit of the stand rail. She might be better going back to 5f for time being, but she's going to remain vulnerable in races like this and is unlikely to be well handicapped in nurseries. Official explanation: jockey said filly hung left (op 7-4)
Empress Charlotte probably improved a little on her recent Newmarket debut but never threatened and might be more one for nurseries later in the season. (op 20-1)

The Form Book, Raceform Ltd, Compton, RG20 6NL

Scantily Clad(IRE), from a yard that does well with its juveniles and out of a winner over 7f, took the eye beforehand but left the impression she needed the race badly. She promises to be a different proposition next time. (tchd 5-1)
Time For Applause Official explanation: trainer's rep said filly was in season and unsuited by the good to firm ground
Silent Serenade, who gave some trouble at the stalls, is a late foal and isn't bred to shine this early in season. She dropped away from halfway and has some growing up to do.

3907 PEPPA VISITS WHEELGATE 27TH JULY, OINK H'CAP 6f 15y
2:35 (2:36) (Class 6) (0-65,65) 3-Y-O **£1,619** (£481; £240; £120) **Stalls** High

Form RPR
-300 **1** **Batgirl**[31] 2879 3-8-10 **54**........................ DaneO'Neill 8 67+
(John Berry) *chsd ldr: swtchd lft 2f out: rdn to ld over 1f out: r.o wl* **9/2**[2]
000- **2** *3 1/2* **Master Of Song**[207] 7757 3-8-3 **47** oh1 ow1..........(p) RichardThomas 1 47
(S R Bowring) *s.i.s: outpcd: swtchd lft over 1f out: r.o to go 2nd towards fin: no ch w wnr* **33/1**
0042 **3** *1* **Rosiliant (IRE)**[11] 3526 3-8-5 **54**.........................(b) JohnFahy[(5)] 2 51
(C G Cox) *dwlt: sn drvn along in rr: hdwy over 1f out: wnt 2nd briefly wl ins fnl f: one pce* **7/4**[1]
0060 **4** *1 3/4* **Barastar**[11] 3532 3-8-2 **46** oh1.........................(v[1]) KirstyMilczarek 4 37
(N Tinkler) *s.i.s: outpcd: hung lft and r.o ins fnl f: nrst fin* **14/1**
650- **5** *nk* **Kate Skate**[269] 6775 3-8-8 **59**........................ AdamBeschizza[(7)] 6 49
(Miss Gay Kelleway) *dwlt: sn prom: led over 4f out: rdn and hdd over 1f out: hung lft and no ex ins fnl f* **7/1**
000- **6** *2* **Rosetta Hill**[264] 6903 3-8-7 **51**........................ SimonWhitworth 9 35
(J R Jenkins) *s.i.s: in rr: hdwy over 2f out: rdn over 1f out: wknd ins fnl f* **16/1**
00-4 **7** *11* **Musical Delight**[81] 1449 3-8-9 **53**........................ RichardMullen 7 —
(A P Jarvis) *led: hdd over 4f out: sn pushed along: rdn and wknd wl over 1f out: eased* **11/1**
-000 **8** *17* **Many A Slip**[17] 3325 3-9-7 **65**.........................(b[1]) IanMongan 5 —
(J L Dunlop) *prom: rdn over 2f out: wknd and eased wl over 1f out* **13/2**[3]
650 **U** **Music Lover**[32] 2841 3-9-0 **61**........................ RobertLButler[(3)] 3 —
(R A Harris) *uns rdr sn after leaving stalls* **8/1**

1m 14.69s (-0.21) **Going Correction** -0.10s/f (Good) **9** Ran SP% **115.3**
Speed ratings (Par 98): **97,92,91,88,88 85,70,48,—**
Tote Swingers: 1&2 £44.80, 1&3 £1.10, 2&3 £24.70 CSF £132.16 CT £355.24 TOTE £5.70: £1.70, £7.90, £1.10; EX 105.90.
Owner Tony Fordham **Bred** Mrs M L Parry & P M Steele-Mortimer **Trained** Newmarket, Suffolk

FOCUS
A very weak race, with the favourite disappointing, and form to treat with caution with the eventual second and third badly impeded by a loose horse early on. The runners again stayed stands' side.
Musical Delight Official explanation: trainer said gelding was unsuited by the good to firm ground
Many A Slip Official explanation: trainer's rep said gelding was unsuiited by the good to firm ground

3908 HORRIBLE HAPPENINGS THIS HALLOWEEN AT TWINLAKES H'CAP 5f 13y
3:10 (3:11) (Class 5) (0-70,68) 3-Y-O+ **£2,388** (£705; £352) **Stalls** High

Form RPR
0005 **1** **Vhujon (IRE)**[7] 3687 5-9-7 **68**........................ RichardEvans[(5)] 7 81+
(P D Evans) *trckd ldrs: shkn up to ld ins fnl f: readily* **7/4**[1]
-020 **2** *2* **Baby Queen (IRE)**[7] 3687 4-9-3 **59**........................ JackMitchell 6 63
(B P J Baugh) *w ldr tl led 2f out: rdn over 1f out: hdd: edgd lft and unable qck ins fnl f* **4/1**[3]
0006 **3** *hd* **King Of Swords (IRE)**[7] 3687 6-9-1 **57**....................(p) KirstyMilczarek 1 60
(N Tinkler) *stdd s: hld up: hdwy over 1f out: sn rdn: styd on* **11/2**
5260 **4** *1 1/2* **Interchoice Star**[10] 3556 5-9-4 **60**.........................(p) DaneO'Neill 4 58
(R Hollinshead) *s.i.s: sn prom: rdn over 1f out: no ex ins fnl f* **7/1**
0006 **5** *nk* **Lord Of The Reins (IRE)**[23] 3119 6-9-11 **67**................ RichardMullen 2 64
(J G Given) *s.i.s: sn pushed along in rr: rdn over 1f out: no imp* **10/1**
0134 **6** *6* **Simple Rhythm**[2] 3818 4-9-9 **65**........................ MarcHalford 5 40
(J Ryan) *led 3f: sn rdn: wknd and eased fnl f* **3/1**[2]
0000 **7** *8* **Town House**[16] 3358 8-8-7 **49** oh4........................ LiamJones 3 —
(B P J Baugh) *w ldrs tl rdn 1/2-way: wknd over 1f out* **33/1**

60.09 secs (-0.91) **Going Correction** -0.10s/f (Good) **7** Ran SP% **121.3**
Speed ratings (Par 103): **103,99,99,97,96 87,74**
Tote Swingers: 1&2 £1.60, 1&3 £5.40, 2&3 £5.30 CSF £10.04 CT £33.49 TOTE £2.50: £1.10, £3.80; EX 15.90.
Owner Nick Shutts **Bred** Robert Berns **Trained** Pandy, Monmouths

FOCUS
An uncompetitive handicap with few bang-in-form runners. The gallop seemed a decent one, the runners again staying stands' side. The form is rated around the runner-up.
Simple Rhythm Official explanation: trainer said filly was unsuited by the good to firm ground

3909 COMING SOON WHEELGATE'S NEW ANIMAL FARM H'CAP 1m 6f 15y
3:45 (3:45) (Class 4) (0-80,80) 3-Y-O **£6,476** (£1,927; £963; £481) **Stalls** Low

Form RPR
4061 **1** **Montparnasse (IRE)**[19] 3273 3-9-3 **76**........................ MartinDwyer 1 88
(B J Meehan) *hld up: racd keenly: hdwy and nt clr run over 3f out: swtchd rt: rdn over 1f out: led ins fnl f: styd on u.p* **9/2**[3]
1-04 **2** *3/4* **Sidney Melbourne (USA)**[16] 3376 3-8-11 **70**................... LiamJones 4 81
(J R Best) *chsd ldrs: pushed along 1/2-way: drvn over 4f out: led over 2f out: edgd rt and hdd ins fnl f: styd on* **6/1**
0213 **3** *nk* **Boston Blue**[23] 3123 3-9-6 **79**........................ LiamKeniry 5 89
(W J Knight) *hld up: rdn 5f out: hdwy over 3f out: hung lft and rt fr over 1f out: kpt on* **3/1**[2]
1166 **4** *15* **Keenes Royale**[31] 2869 3-9-1 **74**.........................(t) JackMitchell 3 63
(R M Beckett) *chsd ldr tl led over 3f out: rdn and hdd over 2f out: wknd over 1f out* **9/1**
0-03 **5** *3* **Istidlaal**[23] 3116 3-9-7 **80**........................ RichardMullen 6 65
(Sir Michael Stoute) *chsd ldrs: pushed along 6f out: rdn over 4f out: wknd 3f out* **7/1**
-221 **6** *hd* **Dream Spinner**[38] 2650 3-9-0 **73**........................ DaneO'Neill 2 58
(J L Dunlop) *led: rdn and hdd over 3f out: wknd over 2f out* **2/1**[1]

3m 4.06s (-3.24) **Going Correction** -0.10s/f (Good) **6** Ran SP% **113.3**
Speed ratings (Par 102): **105,104,104,95,94 94**
Tote Swingers: 1&2 £22.50, 1&3 £5.20, 2&3 £8.30 CSF £30.90 TOTE £4.90: £2.80, £4.30; EX 19.60.
Owner Lady Rothschild **Bred** Kincorth Investments Inc **Trained** Manton, Wilts

FOCUS
A fair handicap run at a decent gallop considering the small field. The first three, who finished clear, were progressive and unexposed.
Dream Spinner Official explanation: trainer's rep said gelding was unsuited by the good to firm ground

3910 WALKING IN A WINTER WONDERLAND, TWINLAKES (S) STKS 1m 75y
4:20 (4:21) (Class 6) 3-4-Y-O **£1,706** (£503; £252) **Stalls** Centre

Form RPR
0354 **1** **Frank Street**[12] 3510 4-9-7 60........................(t) LiamKeniry 11 58
(Eve Johnson Houghton) *prom: chsd clr ldr over 4f out: sn rdn: styd on u.p to ld ins fnl f* **10/3**[2]
6654 **2** *1/2* **Magenta Strait**[16] 3359 3-8-13 55........................ JackMitchell 4 56
(R Hollinshead) *s.i.s: hld up: hdwy over 3f out: sn rdn: ev ch ins fnl f: unable qck nr fin* **7/1**[3]
0000 **3** *1 3/4* **Marafong**[15] 3413 3-8-5 60........................ AdamBeschizza[(7)] 9 51
(Miss J Feilden) *prom: outpcd 1/2-way: rallied over 1f out: styd on* **9/1**
2116 **4** *1 1/4* **Guga (IRE)**[17] 3314 4-9-13 67.........................(b) DaneO'Neill 10 56
(Dr R D P Newland) *s.i.s: sn rcvrd to ld: clr 5f out: rdn over 1f out: wknd and hdd ins fnl f* **4/6**[1]
00 **5** *3/4* **Tipperary Tickle**[16] 3359 3-8-7 0........................ LiamJones 7 41
(J R Weymes) *sn pushed along in rr: styd on fr over 1f out: nvr nrr* **66/1**
-000 **6** *2* **Wigan Lane**[7] 3685 3-8-7 53........................ RichardMullen 5 37
(P Howling) *led early: settled to chse ldrs: rdn over 3f out: no ex fr over 1f out* **20/1**
00 **7** *hd* **Lord Lansing (IRE)**[24] 3091 3-8-7 0........................ PatrickDonaghy[(5)] 8 41
(J R Weymes) *mid-div: racd keenly: hdwy over 3f out: sn rdn: no ex fr over 1f out* **25/1**
0060 **8** *20* **Annie Moyles**[16] 3360 4-9-2 27........................ TomMcLaughlin 2 —
(C N Kellett) *hld up: a in rr: bhd fr 1/2-way* **66/1**
9 *37* **Silverwort**[15] 4-9-7 0........................ RichardThomas 1 —
(M E Sowersby) *plld hrd and trckd ldr tl rdn over 4f out: wknd over 3f out: t.o* **40/1**

1m 47.62s (2.02) **Going Correction** -0.10s/f (Good)
WFA 3 from 4yo 9lb **9** Ran SP% **119.6**
Speed ratings (Par 101): **85,84,82,81,80 78,78,58,21**
Tote Swingers: 1&2 £3.40, 1&3 £4.30, 2&3 £7.20 CSF £25.77 TOTE £4.40: £1.80, £1.90, £3.40; EX 25.70.The winner was bought in for 4,500gns.
Owner R F Johnson Houghton **Bred** R F Johnson Houghton **Trained** Blewbury, Oxon

FOCUS
A very weak seller. The eventual fourth went off a shade too fast and helped set things up for the closers. The winner did not need to match even this year's form.

3911 ALL YEAR, ALL WEATHER FUN, WHEELGATE H'CAP 1m 75y
4:55 (4:56) (Class 5) (0-70,69) 3-Y-O+ **£2,266** (£674; £337; £168) **Stalls** Centre

Form RPR
3262 **1** **Eastern Gift**[7] 3690 5-9-6 **68**........................ AdamBeschizza[(7)] 8 74
(Miss Gay Kelleway) *s.i.s: hld up: hdwy over 3f out: rdn to ld over 1f out: styd on* **6/1**[3]
0000 **2** *1/2* **Montego Breeze**[14] 3434 4-8-9 **50** oh5..............(p) DaraghO'Donohoe 12 55
(John A Harris) *chsd ldrs: rdn to ld 2f out: hdd over 1f out: styd on* **66/1**
/30- **3** *1* **Talayeb**[335] 4822 5-10-0 **69**........................ RichardMullen 7 72
(M P Tregoning) *hld up: hdwy over 2f out: sn rdn and hung lft: nt run on* **9/2**[2]
2242 **4** *hd* **Classic Descent**[5] 3732 5-9-5 **60**.........................(t) TomMcLaughlin 2 62
(Mrs R A Carr) *s.i.s: sn pushed into mid-div: hdwy 1/2-way: rdn over 2f out: styd on* **7/2**[1]
0163 **5** *2* **Tanforan**[7] 3690 8-9-7 **62**........................ JackMitchell 11 59
(B P J Baugh) *s.i.s: in rr: pushed along 1/2-way: styd on fr over 1f out: nt trble ldrs* **7/1**
0501 **6** *3/4* **Bell's Ocean (USA)**[7] 3666 3-8-5 **55**........................ MarcHalford 9 49
(J Ryan) *hld up: rdn over 2f out: styd on ins fnl f: nvr nrr* **10/1**
6004 **7** *1/2* **Hilbre Court (USA)**[16] 3377 5-8-13 **54**....................(p) LiamJones 5 49
(B P J Baugh) *broke wl: sn lost pl: rdn 1/2-way: kpt on ins fnl f: nt trble ldrs* **25/1**
6504 **8** *hd* **French Art**[12] 3514 5-10-0 **69**.........................(p) KirstyMilczarek 3 63
(N Tinkler) *chsd ldrs: nt clr run over 2f out: sn shkn up: no ex fnl f* **8/1**
2200 **9** *1/2* **Diamond Twister (USA)**[50] 2285 4-9-7 **62**....................(t) LiamKeniry 10 55
(J R Best) *led early: chsd ldrs: rdn over 3f out: styd on same pce fr over 1f out* **8/1**
0620 **10** *10* **Admirals Way**[17] 3338 5-8-5 **51** oh2 ow1.................... MarkCoumbe[(5)] 6 21
(C N Kellett) *w ldr: racd keenly: rdn and ev ch 3f out: wknd wl over 1f out* **50/1**
0-04 **11** *2 3/4* **Lujano**[12] 3508 5-9-7 **67**........................ PatrickDonaghy[(5)] 1 31
(Ollie Pears) *sn led: rdn and hdd over 2f out: wknd over 1f out* **17/2**
1-00 **12** *6* **Kildare Sun (IRE)**[36] 2705 8-9-5 **60**.........................(p) SaleemGolam 4 10
(J Mackie) *hld up in tch: rdn and wknd over 2f out* **16/1**

1m 46.84s (1.24) **Going Correction** -0.10s/f (Good)
WFA 3 from 4yo+ 9lb **12** Ran SP% **122.2**
Speed ratings (Par 103): **89,88,87,87,85 84,84,83,83,73 70,64**
Tote Swingers: 1&2 £11.40, 2&3 £40.30 CSF £365.09 CT £1991.76 TOTE £8.70: £2.50, £13.40, £3.20; EX 868.30.
Owner P Crook, N Palgrave Brown **Bred** P And Mrs A G Venner **Trained** Exning, Suffolk

FOCUS
A modest handicap containing a smattering of in-form rivals. The pace was decent with the two early leaders possibly doing too much in front. The form is rated around the winner, but the second is a worry.
Admirals Way Official explanation: jockey said gelding ran too free

3912 NOTTINGHAM POST APPRENTICE H'CAP 1m 2f 50y
5:30 (5:30) (Class 5) (0-75,74) 4-Y-O+ **£2,266** (£674; £337; £168) **Stalls** Low

Form RPR
2421 **1** **Marjury Daw (IRE)**[9] 3601 4-9-3 **67**........................ AdamCarter 1 73+
(J G Given) *chsd ldr tl led over 4f out: rdn over 1f out: styd on* **7/4**[1]
3541 **2** *1/2* **Bavarica**[30] 2894 8-9-9 **73**........................ AdamBeschizza 2 78
(Miss J Feilden) *a.p: rdn and ev ch fr over 1f out: styd on* **10/3**[3]
0406 **3** *1/2* **Orpen Wide (IRE)**[7] 3683 8-8-8 **61**........................(v) SophieSilvester[(3)] 3 65
(M C Chapman) *led: edgd rt fr over 6f out: hdd over 4f out: stl ev ch fr over 1f out: kpt on* **4/1**
4511 **4** *33* **Sacrilege**[15] 3412 5-8-13 **70**.........................(p) LeonnaMayor[(7)] 5 11
(M C Chapman) *s.i.s: sn chsng ldrs: shkn up over 4f out: nt run on and sn t.o* **5/2**[2]

2m 13.04s (1.34) **Going Correction** -0.10s/f (Good) **4** Ran SP% **108.0**
Speed ratings (Par 103): **90,89,89,62**
CSF £7.60 TOTE £1.90; EX 4.00 Place 6 £211.79, Place 5 £62.60..
Owner Danethorpe Racing Partnership **Bred** Mulhime Ltd Marston Stud & D Bonnycastle **Trained** Willoughton, Lincs

FOCUS
A modest finale that wasn't strongly run and turned into something of a tactical affair. The winner more than confirmed her Redcar improvement.

Sacrilege Official explanation: trainer said gelding was unsuited by the track
T/Plt: £320.30 to a £1 stake. Pool: £39,416 - 89.82 winning units. T/Qpdt: £35.60 to a £1 stake. Pool: £3,439 - 71.40 winning units. CR

3472 SALISBURY (R-H)

Saturday, July 10

OFFICIAL GOING: Good to firm (watered; 9.0)
Rail erected up to 16ft off permanent far side rail between 1f and 6f.
Wind: virtually nil Weather: fine and sunny

3913 BATHWICK TYRES NOVICE AUCTION STKS 6f
6:15 (6:15) (Class 5) 2-Y-O **£3,561** (£1,059; £529; £264) **Stalls** High

Form RPR
312 **1** **Avonmore Star**[13] 3476 2-9-2 0 .... PatDobbs 3 90+
(R Hannon) *racd keenly upsides ldr: led 2f out: shkn up ent fnl f: kpt on wl: comf* **4/9**[1]
4 **2** *1 ½* **Chevise (IRE)**[17] 3331 2-8-1 0 ow2 .... JohnFahy(5) 2 76
(R M Beckett) *s.i.s: sn trcking ldng pair: rdn over 2f out: kpt on to go 2nd jst ins fnl f: a being hld by wnr* **12/1**[3]
21 **3** *1 ½* **Goodwood Treasure**[22] 3156 2-8-11 0 .... EddieAhern 4 76
(J L Dunlop) *led tl hdd 2f out: sn rdn and hld: keeping on at same pce whn lost 2nd jst ins fnl furlng* **5/2**[2]
4 *12* **Minety Lass** 2-7-13 0 .... SimonPearce(5) 5 33
(M Appleby) *racd green in tch: outpcd 1/2-way: wknd ent fnl f* **66/1**
006 **5** *20* **Marmaduke**[26] 3034 2-8-11 0 .... (b[1]) NeilChalmers 1 —
(J J Bridger) *chsd ldrs: rdn 3f out: sn wknd* **80/1**

1m 14.72s (-0.08) **Going Correction** -0.10s/f (Good) 5 Ran SP% **108.2**
Speed ratings (Par 94): **96,94,92,76,49**
Tote Swingers: 1&2 £5.10, 1&3 £21.10, 2&3 £19.10 CSF £6.88 TOTE £1.50: £1.10, £4.00; EX 5.90.
Owner Ken Geering **Bred** Miss J R Tooth **Trained** East Everleigh, Wilts

FOCUS
After a very warm, dry week, during which extensive watering had been carried out, a further 3mm was applied to the last 2f of the course at lunchtime on raceday. The meeting began with a fair novice stakes, especially interesting because it was won in 2009 by Dick Turpin. Straightforward form, the winner perhaps value for a little extra.

NOTEBOOK
Avonmore Star, successful at Goodwood in May and runner-up behind a smart prospect here last time out, set a standard too high for his rivals. Quickly away, he was soon close up in second, racing a bit keenly. He had more or less settled by halfway, however, and once sent into the lead at the 2f marker, he had the race in the bag. He seemed to idle close home, but won with something in hand and will surely step up into a higher grade next time. He does not look in the same league as stablemate Dick Turpin, who took this last year, but should win again. His trainer feels he would not mind a drop back to 5f. (tchd 8-15 in places)
Chevise(IRE) had shown a modicum of promise on her only previous outing and stepped up on that form. She wasn't the fastest out the stalls and took a little while to make up the lost ground, but engaged top gear in the last 2f and was going on at the finish. She ought to find a suitable opening. (op 10-1)
Goodwood Treasure, easy winner of a weak maiden at Goodwood three weeks previously, was disappointing. She led from the start, gaining a pitch near the inside rail, but had no response when the winner went past. (tchd 9-4 and 11-4)
Minety Lass, an inexpensively bought newcomer, showed little. Last early on, she gained a place in the closing stages, but did nothing like enough to suggest she can take a maiden at this stage of her career. (op 40-1)
Marmaduke, well beaten previously in 5f maidens, failed to improve for the extra distance and addition of blinkers. Never in the hunt, he finished tailed off.

3914 BATHWICK TYRES SALISBURY H'CAP 6f
6:45 (6:45) (Class 5) (0-75,76) 3-Y-O+ **£3,238** (£963; £481; £240) **Stalls** High

Form RPR
11-1 **1** **Kuanyao (IRE)**[9] 3604 4-10-1 **76** .... FergusSweeney 3 91+
(P J Makin) *mde all: rdn clr over 1f out: r.o wl: readily* **4/1**[2]
0-36 **2** *3 ½* **Pragmatist**[36] 2719 6-8-12 **62** .... JamesMillman(3) 9 66
(B R Millman) *in tch: trckd ldrs 2f out: sn rdn: kpt on ins fnl f: wnt 2nd towards fin: no ch w wnr* **9/2**[3]
0302 **3** *nk* **Eye For The Girls**[17] 3338 4-8-9 **56** oh4 .... SamHitchcott 5 59
(M R Channon) *trckd wnr: rdn 2f out: nt pce to chal but kpt on: lost 2nd towards fin* **20/1**
-001 **4** *¾* **Lucy Brown**[15] 3409 4-9-11 **72** .... EddieAhern 7 73
(M W Easterby) *trckd ldrs: rdn 2f out: swtchd lft over 1f out: kpt on same pce* **14/1**
3401 **5** *1 ¾* **The Wee Chief (IRE)**[14] 3463 4-9-8 **69** .... PatDobbs 6 64+
(J C Fox) *s.i.s: towards rr: t.k.h fr over 3f out tl over 2f out: nt clr run on rails sn after: hdwy ent fnl f but nt pce to get on terms* **7/2**[1]
0-00 **6** *nk* **Sweet Gale (IRE)**[13] 3474 6-9-4 **65** .... AndreaAtzeni 2 59
(Mike Murphy) *little slowly away: hld up: rdn wl over 1f out: little imp* **8/1**
5100 **7** *2* **Bateleur**[11] 3534 6-8-13 **60** .... CathyGannon 8 48
(M R Channon) *t.k.h: hld up: rdn 2f out: nt pce to get involved* **18/1**
6-31 **8** *8* **Erebus (IRE)**[46] 2408 3-9-2 **69** .... FrankieDettori 1 31
(S Kirk) *fly-leapt and wnt lft leaving stalls: sn in tch: effrt over 2f out: slty hmpd whn wkng over 1f out* **4/1**[2]
0511 **9** *5* **Timeteam (IRE)**[7] 3685 4-9-7 **73** .... RichardEvans(5) 4 19+
(P D Evans) *rel to r: bhd: clsd on rr of gp over 3f out: wknd 2f out: eased fnl f* **12/1**

1m 14.23s (-0.57) **Going Correction** -0.10s/f (Good)
WFA 3 from 4yo+ 6lb 9 Ran SP% **115.9**
Speed ratings (Par 103): **99,94,93,92,90 90,87,76,70**
Tote Swingers: 1&2 £5.10, 1&3 £21.10, 2&3 £19.10 CSF £22.49 CT £321.73 TOTE £3.30: £1.10, £2.30, £4.90; EX 24.80.
Owner D M Ahier **Bred** Newlands House Stud **Trained** Ogbourne Maisey, Wilts

FOCUS
Just an ordinary sprint handicap, with the top weight rated 76, but it looked competitive on paper.

3915 E B F BATHWICK TYRES MAIDEN STKS 6f 212y
7:20 (7:22) (Class 4) 2-Y-O **£4,209** (£1,252; £625; £312) **Stalls** Centre

Form RPR
1 **Measuring Time** 2-9-3 0 .... FergusSweeney 2 84+
(R Hannon) *mid-div: swtchd lft over 2f out: carried lft briefly but gd hdwy sn after: led over 1f out: drifted rt: r.o wl: readily* **9/2**
2 *1 ¾* **Marzante (USA)** 2-9-3 0 .... GeorgeBaker 4 77
(R Charlton) *in tch: hdwy to join ldrs 2f out: rdn and ev ch over 1f out: kpt on but nt pce of wnr* **7/2**[2]
3 *½* **Perfect Cracker** 2-9-3 0 .... DavidProbert 13 76
(C G Cox) *s.i.s: sn trcking ldrs: rdn and ev ch over 1f out: kpt on but nt pce of wnr* **10/3**[1]
4 *3* **Coachlight** 2-9-3 0 .... EddieAhern 14 68
(J L Dunlop) *squeezed up sn after s: in tch: rdn 3f out: kpt on same pce fnl 2f* **12/1**
5 *3* **Noonenose** 2-9-3 0 .... JimCrowley 1 61+
(W J Knight) *s.i.s: racd green in rr: styd on fr jst over 1f out: nvr trbld ldrs* **14/1**
0 **6** *2 ¼* **Van Doesburg (IRE)**[15] 3399 2-8-12 0 .... JohnFahy(5) 5 55
(J G Portman) *led: rdn over 2f out: hdd over 1f out: fdd ins fnl f* **80/1**
5 **7** *½* **Token Gift**[10] 3555 2-9-3 0 .... CathyGannon 9 53
(P D Evans) *trckd ldr: rdn 3f out: wknd jst over 1f out* **28/1**
5 **8** *1 ¼* **Sir Rocky (IRE)**[82] 1429 2-9-3 0 .... PatDobbs 3 50
(R Hannon) *trckd ldr: bit sn slipped through mouth: effrt and hung lft over 2f out: wknd jst over 1f out* **4/1**[3]
9 *3 ¼* **All The Evil (IRE)** 2-9-3 0 .... JimmyFortune 7 42
(B J Meehan) *s.i.s: a towards rr* **11/1**
10 *15* **Princesse Fleur** 2-8-12 0 .... AmirQuinn 11 —
(M J Scudamore) *unsettled stalls: v.s.a: a in rr* **100/1**
11 *2 ½* **Gamesmanship** 2-9-3 0 .... TadhgO'Shea 6 —
(J L Dunlop) *s.i.s: racd v green: a in rr* **18/1**

1m 29.67s (0.67) **Going Correction** -0.10s/f (Good) 11 Ran SP% **117.1**
Speed ratings (Par 96): **92,90,89,86,82 80,79,78,74,57 54**
Tote Swingers: 1&2 £5.40, 1&3 £5.80, 2&3 £4.20 CSF £20.40 TOTE £7.20: £2.30, £1.10, £2.70; EX 24.80.
Owner Woodcote Stud Ltd **Bred** Woodcote Stud Ltd **Trained** East Everleigh, Wilts

FOCUS
Not much public form to go on, but several well-bred newcomers from major stables in this interesting juvenile maiden. Not easy form to gauge.

NOTEBOOK
Measuring Time is bred to stay middle-distances next year, so victory here suggests a bright future. Held up in midfield early on, he began to take closer order 3f out and was pulled wide to make his challenge two from home. He quickened smartly and was going away at the finish in the manner of a colt capable of taking a step up in grade. A robust sort, with a long stride, he looks a useful prospect. (op 13-2 tchd 4-1)
Marzante(USA), a gelded newcomer with a decent pedigree, was feisty beforehand. He had calmed down by the time he got out on to the track and it was noticeable that he was backed while going to post. He ran well, too, figuring prominently from the start and staying on gamely in the closing stages. He seems sure to improve, if his temperament holds up, and should soon win. (op 9-2)
Perfect Cracker, the first foal of a fair 6/7f performer, was another to make an encouraging debut. Always chasing the pace, he plugged on resolutely and looks capable of finding an opening this term. (tchd 4-1)
Coachlight, from the yard that took this race with a newcomer in 2009, also showed enough to be worth watching in future. He lacked the finishing kick of those in front of him - and changed his legs when initally asked a question - but performed creditably and will stay longer trips than this. (op 10-1)
Token Gift, who missed the break over 6f on his only previous start, ran better here and should win races, albeit most likely in handicaps. Official explanation: jockey said colt hung right-handed
Sir Rocky(IRE) does not appear to be progressing, however. Sent off favourite when fifth of seven on his only previous outing, he ran too keenly here and, after racing in second early on, faded tamely when push came to shove. (op 7-2)

3916 BATHWICK TYRES ANDOVER H'CAP 1m
7:50 (7:51) (Class 4) (0-85,84) 3-Y-O **£4,209** (£1,252; £625; £312) **Stalls** High

Form RPR
1 **1** **Rock N Roll Ransom**[30] 2899 3-9-6 **83** .... MartinDwyer 5 92+
(L M Cumani) *broke wl to ld briefly early: trckd ldr: rdn 2f out: chal jst ins fnl f: kpt on gamely to ld towards fin* **13/8**[1]
241 **2** *hd* **Rule Maker**[19] 3272 3-9-7 **84** .... FrankieDettori 4 93+
(J Noseda) *sn led: rdn jst over 1f out: sn hrd pressed: kpt on but no ex whn hdd towards fin* **15/8**[2]
5603 **3** *8* **Dubai Set**[9] 3579 3-9-6 **83** .... (b) PatDobbs 1 73
(R Hannon) *hld up 5th: rdn over 2f out: wnt 2rd over 1f out: styd on same pce: nvr trbld ldng pair* **11/2**[3]
-005 **4** *2 ¾* **Blakey's Boy**[29] 2927 3-9-4 **81** .... WilliamBuick 3 65
(J L Dunlop) *hld up 4th: tk clsr order over 3f out: effrt 2f out: sn hung rt: wknd over 1f out* **11/2**[3]
00-5 **5** *9* **Professor John (IRE)**[13] 3481 3-8-4 **67** .... CathyGannon 2 30
(I A Wood) *trckd ldrs: rdn over 3f out: wknd 2f out* **28/1**

1m 41.86s (-1.64) **Going Correction** -0.10s/f (Good) 5 Ran SP% **107.1**
Speed ratings (Par 102): **104,103,95,93,84**
CSF £4.65 TOTE £2.10: £1.10, £2.10; EX 3.30.
Owner Castle Down Racing **Bred** Meon Valley Stud **Trained** Newmarket, Suffolk

FOCUS
A small field but, with two unexposed contenders, still an interesting handicap.

3917 PICADOR CHEVROLET H'CAP 1m 4f
8:25 (8:27) (Class 5) (0-75,73) 3-Y-O+ **£3,238** (£963; £481; £240) **Stalls** High

Form RPR
0341 **1** **Shy**[10] 3560 5-9-6 **65** .... JamesMillman(3) 2 73
(B R Millman) *trckd ldr: clr 2nd over 7f out: led over 3f out: styd on gamely: rdn out* **7/2**[2]
0034 **2** *nk* **Higgy's Ragazzo (FR)**[9] 3594 3-9-4 **73** .... PatDobbs 1 80
(R Hannon) *hld up: rdn and stdy prog fr over 2f out: styd on fnl f: wnt 2nd fnl strides: nrst fin* **7/2**[2]
4535 **3** *shd* **Zaif (IRE)**[21] 3221 7-8-8 **55** .... BillyCray(5) 4 62
(D J S Ffrench Davis) *hld up: swtchd to centre and stdy prog u.p fr over 2f out: chsd wnr ins fnl f: styd on: lost 2nd fnl strides* **16/1**
4106 **4** *2 ½* **Cote D'Argent**[23] 3127 7-10-0 **70** .... (t) FergusSweeney 3 73
(C J Down) *led: clr 7f out: rdn whn hdd over 3f: kpt chsng wnr tl no ex ins fnl f* **20/1**
5523 **5** *1 ½* **Mons Calpe (IRE)**[7] 3688 4-10-0 **70** .... (b) WilliamBuick 8 71
(P F I Cole) *trckd ldrs: rdn over 2f out: sn one pce* **7/1**
-402 **6** *½* **Chincoteague (IRE)**[16] 3360 4-9-11 **67** .... JimmyFortune 6 67
(B J Meehan) *trckd ldrs: rdn 3f out: kpt on same pce fr over 1f out* **4/1**[3]
52- **7** *11* **Cast Of Stars (IRE)**[213] 7683 3-9-1 **70** .... JimCrowley 5 52
(R M Beckett) *trckd ldrs: rdn 3f out: sn hld: wknd over 1f out* **11/4**[1]

2m 35.74s (-2.26) **Going Correction** -0.10s/f (Good)
WFA 3 from 4yo+ 13lb 7 Ran SP% **114.3**
Speed ratings (Par 103): **103,102,102,101,100 99,92**
Tote Swingers: 1&2 £5.40, 1&3 £13.60, 2&3 £6.50 CSF £16.13 CT £169.34 TOTE £4.40: £1.40, £3.30; EX 22.10.
Owner Mrs Jenny Willment **Bred** Mrs Jenny Willment **Trained** Kentisbeare, Devon

FOCUS
A run-of-the-mill handicap, with the top weight rated 70.

3918 EUROPEAN BREEDERS' FUND LADIES EVENING FILLIES' H'CAP — 1m
8:55 (8:56) (Class 3) (0-95,86) 3-Y-O £8,723 (£2,612; £1,306; £653) Stalls High

Form RPR

1-2 **1** **Field Day (IRE)**38 2652 3-9-7 86 ....(t) MartinDwyer 4 97+
(B J Meehan) *trckd ldng pair: wnt 2nd 2f out: shkn up to ld jst ins fnl f: edgd rt: r.o: readily* 5/6[1]

-621 **2** 1 1/2 **Frances Stuart (IRE)**27 2998 3-8-13 78 .... JimmyFortune 1 83
(A M Balding) *led: rdn 2f out: hdd jst ins fnl f: kpt on but sn hld* 5/2[2]

-005 **3** 1 3/4 **Sunarise (IRE)**38 2652 3-8-12 77 .... PatDobbs 5 78
(R Hannon) *trckd ldr tl 2f out: sn rdn: kpt on same pce* 12/1

6212 **4** 2 1/4 **Love Match**16 3361 3-9-2 81 .... WilliamBuick 3 77
(R Charlton) *hld up in cl 4th: rdn 2f out: nt pce to chal* 9/2[3]

1m 43.75s (0.25) **Going Correction** -0.10s/f (Good) 4 Ran SP% **109.0**
Speed ratings (Par 101): **94,92,90,88**
CSF £3.20 TOTE £1.70; EX 3.30 Place 6: £21.60 Place 5: £15.49.
Owner Ballymacoll Stud **Bred** Ballymacoll Stud Farm Ltd **Trained** Manton, Wilts

FOCUS
A fair fillies' handicap, despite the small turnout.

NOTEBOOK
Field Day(IRE), a Newmarket maiden winner last term and a solid second on her only subsequent outing, outclassed her rivals. Held up in third in the early stages, she closed on the front-running second over 2f out and quickened impressively inside the last to win without coming under serious pressure. Successful off a mark of 86 here, she will surely go up 7lb or more, which suggests connections have realistic hopes of gaining black type this season. Once considered a Classic prospect, but slow to come to hand this year, she is a fine, big filly and should make a smart broodmare. (tchd evens in a place)
Frances Stuart(IRE), who beat a 72-rated rival when scoring over C&D last time, again performed creditably. She led shortly after the start, setting a sound gallop, and tried to quicken the pace from 3f out. She had no answer when the winner swept past, but stayed on gamely nonetheless. Provided the Handicapper is not severe, she should remain competitive. (op 11-4 tchd 10-3)
Sunarise(IRE), whose only previous victory came in an ordinary all-weather maiden last season, was not disgraced. She raced in second for much of the contest, but was demoted to third when the winner made her move and could not quicken in the closing stages. (op 8-1)
Love Match had been raised 3lb since finishing second at Leicester 16 days earlier and found the extra too much of a burden. Always last, she never got into contention. (tchd 4-1 and 5-1)
T/Plt: £37.80 to a £1 stake. Pool £55,865 - 1,076.86 winning tickets. T/Qpdt: £14.50 to a £1 stake. Pool £4,328 - 220.70 winning tickets. TM

3874 YORK (L-H)
Saturday, July 10

OFFICIAL GOING: Good to firm (8.0)
Wind: Moderate 1/2 behind Weather: fine

3919 JOHN SMITH'S STKS (H'CAP) — 6f
2:00 (2:03) (Class 3) (0-95,95) 3-Y-O+ £7,771 (£2,312; £1,155; £577) Stalls High

Form RPR

0160 **1** **Hotham**13 3489 7-9-6 91 .... BarryMcHugh(3) 13 101
(N Wilson) *v awkward to load: dwlt: hdwy 2f out: styd on to ld last strides* 20/1

3006 **2** shd **Discanti (IRE)**22 3178 5-8-13 81 ....(t) TedDurcan 9 91
(T D Easterby) *hmpd after 1f: in rr stands' side: hdwy 2f out: r.o wl ins fnl f: jst failed* 11/1

4151 **3** 1/2 **Gap Princess (IRE)**10 3551 6-8-12 80 .... SilvestreDeSousa 4 88
(G A Harker) *chsd ldrs: led ins fnl f: hdd post* 10/1

0300 **4** 1 1/4 **Courageous (IRE)**38 2657 4-9-5 87 ....(v1) TomEaves 10 91
(B Smart) *led tl ins fnl f: edgd rt and fdd* 16/1

2060 **5** shd **Internationaldebut (IRE)**35 2736 5-9-4 86 .... MickyFenton 14 90
(P T Midgley) *in rr: hdwy stands' side over 1f out: swtchd lft and styd on wl clsng stages* 12/1

6111 **6** 1/2 **Cornus**4 3753 8-9-0 87 6ex ....(be) DeclanCannon(5) 7 89
(A J McCabe) *mid-div: hdwy over 1f out: styng on same pce whn n.m.r ins fnl f* 8/1[2]

3312 **7** 3/4 **Red Cape (FR)**4 3753 7-9-0 82 .... RobertWinston 2 82
(Mrs R A Carr) *chsd ldrs: styd on same pce fnl 150yds* 5/1[1]

1413 **8** 1 1/4 **Tiddliwinks**105 1014 4-9-11 93 .... JamieSpencer 5 89
(K A Ryan) *hood removed v late: dwlt: hdwy on wd outside over 2f out: sn chsng ldrs: hung lft and wknd ins fnl f* 8/1[2]

2100 **9** 1/2 **Atlantic Story (USA)**14 3446 8-9-3 85 ....(bt) KierenFallon 12 79
(M W Easterby) *chsd ldrs: wnt lft after 1f: edgd lft and wknd ins fnl f* 12/1

2055 **10** 1/2 **Saucy Brown (IRE)**35 2736 4-9-7 89 .... PaulQuinn 15 82
(D Nicholls) *in rr: drvn over 2f out: nvr a factor* 10/1

-263 **11** 1/2 **Elusive Sue (USA)**17 3320 3-8-4 78 .... PaulHanagan 6 69
(R A Fahey) *chsd ldrs: wknd fnl f* 11/1

0000 **12** nk **River Falcon**14 3446 10-8-8 76 oh1 .... ChrisCatlin 8 66
(J S Goldie) *sn outpcd and in rr: nvr on terms* 16/1

165/ **13** 8 **Marvellous Value (IRE)**659 6069 5-9-6 88 .... PhillipMakin 1 52
(M Dods) *chsd ldrs: wknd over 1f out: eased towards fin* 12/1

1-11 **14** 22 **Harlech Castle**151 474 5-9-0 82 ....(b) RyanMoore 3 —
(J R Boyle) *s.i.s: sn outpcd and drvn along: wl bhd fnl 2f: virtually p.u: t.o* 9/1[3]

1m 10.43s (-1.47) **Going Correction** -0.05s/f (Good)
WFA 3 from 4yo+ 6lb 14 Ran SP% **123.3**
Speed ratings (Par 107): **107,106,106,104,104 103,102,101,100,99 99,98,88,58**
Tote Swingers: 1&2 £81.00, 1&3 £58.80, 2&3 £36.10 CSF £230.71 CT £2411.51 TOTE £29.80: £7.70, £4.90, £3.90; EX 365.10 Trifecta £300.20 Pool: £1,217.30 - 3 winning units..
Owner Far 2 Many Sues **Bred** Capt J H Wilson **Trained** Sandhutton, N Yorks

FOCUS
A typically wide-open sprint handicap on the Knavesmire. Sound form, with further improvement from the winner.

NOTEBOOK
Hotham was on a going day, running on strongly close home and getting up to record his second win of the season. \n\x\x Last month's victory had also been at the course, over 5f, and the winner showed his versatility and toughness with this display. This was the highest mark he has ever won off, though, so it remains to be seen whether he will be capable of going in again anytime soon.
Discanti(IRE) is still 5lb above his last winning mark, but he remains perfectly capable off this sort of rating and the result may have been different if he hadn't suffered early interference. He picked up well more towards the stands' side without being able to stay on quite as well as the winner. (op 12-1)
Gap Princess(IRE) was up in the weights and grade, but showed she is in the form of her life with a cracking effort in defeat, just being run out of it close home. (op 17-2 tchd 11-1)
Courageous(IRE) showed plenty of pace in the first-time visor and briefly looked like holding on over a furlong out, but got a bit weary as he started to edge right, and in the end was run out of the places. (op 20-1)
Internationaldebut(IRE) is on a good mark and looks to have benefited from a short break, staying on well inside the final furlong and just missing out on fourth. (op 14-1 tchd 16-1)
Cornus, seeking a four-timer following his Pontefract win earlier in the week, faced a stiffer task in this under a penalty and he couldn't muster the speed to challenge.
Red Cape(FR), another in-form sprinter who had finished second to Cornus at Pontefract, had his chance and was entitled to do better. (op 7-1 tchd 15-2)
Tiddliwinks, whose hood was removed late, on this return from a 105-day absence. All five wins have come on the AW, but his turf rating is 10lb lower as a result and, given this was just his fourth run on it, it's reasonable to expect him to improve. (op 7-1)
Marvellous Value(IRE) was well backed on this return from a 659-day absence, but he ended up well held having been eased once beaten. (op 20-1 tchd 11-1)
Harlech Castle was one of the first beaten and shaped with no obvious promise for the immediate future, coming home in his own time. Official explanation: jockey said gelding was unsuited by the good to firm ground (op 7-1)

3920 JOHN SMITH'S RACING STKS (H'CAP) — 1m
2:30 (2:33) (Class 2) (0-100,95) 3-Y-O+ £11,656 (£3,468; £1,733; £865) Stalls Low

Form RPR

121 **1** **Capponi (IRE)**7 3667 3-9-2 92 .... GregFairley 3 105+
(M Johnston) *chsd ldr: chal over 2f out: led over 1f out: styd on strly* 3/1[1]

-030 **2** 2 1/4 **Magaling (IRE)**21 3206 4-8-13 85 .... JamesSullivan(5) 12 92
(M W Easterby) *rr-div: hdwy 2f out: styd on wl to take 2nd clsng stages: no imp* 18/1

1210 **3** 1 3/4 **Charlie Cool**7 3692 7-10-0 95 ....(b) RobertWinston 11 98
(Mrs R A Carr) *prom: effrt over 2f out: kpt on wl fnl f* 10/1

-045 **4** hd **Webbow (IRE)**22 3146 8-9-10 91 .... SilvestreDeSousa 7 94
(N Tinkler) *mid-div: hdwy on ins over 2f out: hung lft and styd on same pce fnl f* 6/1

4010 **5** 1 1/4 **Kiwi Bay**22 3146 5-9-12 93 .... TomEaves 6 93
(M Dods) *rr-div: effrt 3f out: styd on: nt rch ldrs* 22/1

0-15 **6** nk **Justonefortheroad**16 3366 4-8-13 80 .... PaulHanagan 1 79
(R A Fahey) *sn trcking ldrs: led 2f out: sn hdd: fdd fnl f* 10/1

0460 **7** 6 **Mujaadel (USA)**1 3876 5-8-9 76 ....(p) AndrewMullen 4 61
(D Nicholls) *chsd ldrs: hung lft and lost pl over 1f out* 50/1

1504 **8** 1/2 **Osteopathic Remedy (IRE)**14 3448 6-9-7 88 .... PhillipMakin 13 72
(M Dods) *t.k.h in mid-div: effrt on outside over 2f out: wknd over 1f out* 22/1

6400 **9** 1/2 **Billy Dane (IRE)**7 3667 6-9-2 83 ....(p) RoystonFfrench 2 66
(F P Murtagh) *led tl hdd & wknd 2f out* 20/1

-110 **10** nk **Day Of The Eagle (IRE)**22 3146 4-9-11 92 .... KierenFallon 10 74
(L M Cumani) *s.i.s: effrt on outside 3f out: edgd lft: lost pl over 1f out* 5/1[3]

0410 **11** shd **Toto Skyllachy**1 3876 5-8-12 79 .... ChrisCatlin 8 61
(J O'Reilly) *s.i.s: sme hdwy on ins over 2f out: lost pl over 1f out* 40/1

0321 **12** 1/2 **Mac's Power (IRE)**15 3396 4-9-6 87 ....(t) RyanMoore 9 68
(J R Fanshawe) *hld up in rr: effrt on outer over 2f out: no imp whn n.m.r over 1f out: sn wknd* 7/2[2]

-136 **13** 4 **Keys Of Cyprus**23 3121 8-9-2 83 .... PaulQuinn 5 55
(D Nicholls) *t.k.h: trckd ldrs: lost pl 2f out* 28/1

1m 36.24s (-2.56) **Going Correction** -0.05s/f (Good)
WFA 3 from 4yo+ 9lb 13 Ran SP% **122.9**
Speed ratings (Par 109): **110,107,106,105,104 104,98,97,97,96 96,96,92**
Tote Swingers: 1&2 £28.50, 1&3 £20.10, 2&3 £7.90 CSF £55.23 CT £515.42 TOTE £4.70: £1.90, £5.80, £2.70; EX 94.80 TRIFECTA Not won..
Owner Sheikh Hamdan Bin Mohammed Al Maktoum **Bred** Darley **Trained** Middleham Moor, N Yorks

FOCUS
A decent handicap run at a searching gallop. Solid form, with the winner progressive and the third and fourth helping with the level.

NOTEBOOK
Capponi(IRE) galloped on relentlessly having taken over, winning in the style of a rapidly progressive 3-y-o. The only member of the younger generation in the field, he was nicely backed beforehand and may soon find himself forced into Pattern company as he was winning here off a mark of 92. Connections will wait and see what the handicapper does, but the Cambridgeshire was mentioned as a possible long-term aim. (op 9-2 tchd 5-1)
Magaling(IRE), unlucky not to get closer at Haydock last time, got a good pace to chase and stayed on late for second, but Capponi was not for catching. He's on a decent mark and could find a race before long. (op 12-1)
Charlie Cool ran here instead of the John Smith's Cup. He bounced back from a below-par effort at Sandown last week, boxing on in third, but was another who couldn't get near the winner. (op 16-1)
Webbow(IRE), narrowly beaten in the race last season, couldn't get close enough to challenge and it's almost three years now since his last success. (op 13-2 tchd 11-2)
Kiwi Bay is 8lb higher than when winning on his penultimate start and he failed to pick up well enough when asked down the straight. (op 16-1)
Justonefortheroad was soon tracking the early pace and those early exertions ultimately took their toll. (op 11-1 tchd 12-1)
Day Of The Eagle(IRE), eased right off having been badly hampered at Royal Ascot, wasn't the best away and didn't pick up when asked for an effort by Fallon, eventually dropping out. (op 4-1)
Mac's Power(IRE) had won well off 8lb lower at Doncaster but failed to run a race this time, already looking beaten when a bit short of room. Official explanation: jockey said gelding had no more to give (op 4-1)

3921 51ST JOHN SMITH'S CUP (HERITAGE H'CAP) — 1m 2f 88y
3:05 (3:07) (Class 2) 3-Y-O+ £97,140 (£28,905; £14,445; £7,215) Stalls Low

Form RPR

1223 **1** **Wigmore Hall (IRE)**23 3104 3-8-2 101 .... MartinLane(3) 13 111+
(M L W Bell) *dwlt: hld up: hdwy on ins 3f out: led jst ins fnl f: edgd rt: veered rt nr line: jst hld on* 5/1[2]

1452 **2** shd **Kings Gambit (SAF)**22 3144 6-9-6 105 .... JamieSpencer 2 115
(T P Tate) *chsd ldrs: led over 2f out: hdd ins fnl f: crowded: carried rt and rallied nr line: jst failed* 14/1

3042 **3** 1 1/2 **Demolition**7 3672 6-8-7 92 .... PaulHanagan 4 99
(R A Fahey) *w ldrs: chal over 2f out: styd on same pce fnl f* 9/1

-410 **4** 3/4 **Hillview Boy (IRE)**7 3672 6-8-13 98 .... ChrisCatlin 22 104+
(J S Goldie) *in rr: hdwy on ins over 2f out: styd on wl fnl f* 50/1

0310 **5** 1 **Sandor**21 3194 4-8-7 92 .... RobertWinston 5 98+
(P J Makin) *t.k.h: trckd ldrs: nt clr run and swtchd lft over 1f out: styd on wl ins fnl f* 25/1

2-12 **6** 1/2 **Imposing**21 3194 4-9-1 100 .... RyanMoore 7 103
(Sir Michael Stoute) *trckd ldrs: tk quite t.k.h: drvn 3f out: one pce over 1f out* 3/1[1]

5246 **7** 2 **Indian Days**22 3144 5-8-12 104 .... DaleSwift(7) 17 103
(J G Given) *chsd ldrs on outside: c wd over 3f out: kpt on fnl f* 20/1

-203 **8** *1* **Dream Lodge (IRE)**[28] 2977 6-9-3 **105** BarryMcHugh(3) 3 102
(R A Fahey) *in rr: hdwy on ins over 2f out: nvr rchd ldrs* **20/1**

-125 **9** *hd* **Sweet Lightning**[21] 3194 5-8-11 **96** PhillipMakin 11 93
(M Dods) *hld up in mid-div: smooth hdwy over 2f out: sn trcking ldrs: wknd over 1f out* **12/1**

00-5 **10** *½* **Royal Destination (IRE)**[28] 2977 5-8-11 **96** MickyFenton 12 92
(J Noseda) *hld up in rr: hdwy on outside over 2f out: nvr trbld ldrs* **14/1**

5311 **11** *4 ½* **Desert Kiss**[15] 3388 5-8-9 **94** 5ex ShaneKelly 18 81
(W R Swinburn) *t.k.h: led: drvn over 3f out: hdd over 2f out: sn wknd* **28/1**

-141 **12** *nk* **Forte Dei Marmi**[40] 2608 4-8-13 **98** KierenFallon 1 85
(L M Cumani) *mid-div: hdwy to chal over 2f out: wknd over 1f out* **13/2**[3]

1-21 **13** *2* **Emirates Champion**[142] 605 4-9-3 **102** (t) AhmedAjtebi 16 85
(Saeed Bin Suroor) *in rr: drvn over 3f out: nvr a factor* **20/1**

5600 **14** *2* **Extraterrestrial**[36] 2708 6-8-12 **97** TomEaves 9 76+
(R A Fahey) *mid-div: effrt over 3f out: wknd 2f out* **66/1**

1030 **15** *1 ½* **Albaqaa**[22] 3144 5-9-0 **99** TonyHamilton 19 75
(R A Fahey) *prom on outside: lost pl over 2f out* **28/1**

6003 **16** *1* **Porgy**[65] 1831 5-8-5 **90** RoystonFfrench 14 64
(R A Fahey) *hld up in rr: nvr on terms* **33/1**

0046 **17** *22* **Viva Vettori**[14] 3456 6-8-0 **90** DeclanCannon(5) 21 22
(D R C Elsworth) *dwlt: t.k.h: sn trcking ldrs: lost pl over 3f out: virtually p.u: t.o* **50/1**

22-3 **18** *7* **Sopranist**[135] 4-9-3 **102** TedDurcan 8 21
(Saeed Bin Suroor) *prom: lost pl over 3f out: virtually p.u: t.o* **14/1**

3300 **19** *4* **Shadows Lengthen**[28] 2976 4-8-0 **90** (b) JamesSullivan(5) 6 2
(M W Easterby) *t.k.h: in tch: stmbld 8f out: lost pl 4f out: sn bhd: virtually p.u: t.o* **50/1**

2m 8.65s (-3.85) **Going Correction** -0.05s/f (Good)
WFA 3 from 4yo+ 11lb **19** Ran SP% **128.0**
Speed ratings (Par 109): **113,112,111,111,110 109,108,107,107,106 103,103,101,99,98 97,80,74,71**
Tote Swingers: 1&2 £20.50, 1&3 £12.70, 2&3 £19.30 CSF £65.30 CT £638.25 TOTE £6.80: £2.10, £3.20, £1.90, £10.40; EX 101.70 Trifecta £1241.90 Pool: £47,602.58 - 28.36 winning units..
Owner M B Hawtin **Bred** K And Mrs Cullen **Trained** Newmarket, Suffolk
■ Stewards' Enquiry : Martin Lane one-day ban: careless riding (Jul 25)

FOCUS
A typically competitive running of what is one of the most prestigious handicaps of the season. Scheduled topweight Distant Memories (9-10) was a non-runner. There wasn't much of an early pace on, and as a result quite a few were noted racing keenly in behind. The field came centre-track having straightened for home. Sound form, with the winner not needing to quite match his Royal Ascot effort. The winner kept the race after a stewards' enquiry and the runner-up's connections are to appeal.

NOTEBOOK
Wigmore Hall(IRE), the only member of the younger generation in this contest, came out on top by the narrowest of margins under his young claimer, though connections would have been nervous during the stewards' enquiry as Martin Lane (received one-day ban for careless riding) did have his whip in the incorrect hand when the interference occurred. Michael Bell's colt, due to race off 7lb higher in future, ran so well to finish third having met trouble in the Hampton Court at Royal Ascot, and being able to make ground through runners in this big field on a spacious track certainly suited this strong-travelling hold-up performer. He didn't get as fast a pace as he would have liked, having to work harder to make ground, but was always going forward and, having got to the front inside the final furlong, was just able to hold on. He has now won both starts in handicaps, but having taken this off 101, he will now have to return to Pattern company, where he is far less likely to get a double-figure field which suits so well. (op 9-2 tchd 11-2)
Kings Gambit(SAF) ◆ was off the same mark as when second to many people's banker of the week Rainbow Peak in the Wolferton at Royal Ascot. Due to be 1lb higher in future, he was asked for his effort over three furlongs out and didn't give in without a fight, being done no favours by Wigmore Hall close home. He has only won a conditions race since joining connections, but looks well up to winning a Group race on this evidence. (op 12-1)
Demolition, representing a yard responsible for three of the last eight winners, and with five representatives this time round. He was never far away and held every chance alongside the runner-up inside the final three furlongs but was just found wanting for acceleration. (op 10-1 tchd 17-2)
Hillview Boy(IRE) had reportedly been unsuited by the fast ground when running a shocker at Haydock the previous weekend but seemed to get on okay with it here, staying on well inside the final two furlongs over a trip short of his best. In an ideal world he wouldn't have got so far back, but his draw left him with little chance but to be dropped right out. (tchd 66-1 in a place)
Sandor ran creditably in the Duke of Edinburgh at Royal Ascot and he may have been a length or so closer had he not been denied a clear run two furlongs out. A return to 1m4f should suit and he is due to race off 1lb lower in future.
Imposing, 9lb higher than when wining over the course and distance on his reappearance, should really have followed up in the Duke of Edinburgh at Royal Ascot, just failing to get up having got too far back, and he looked a major player, especially as he is due to race off 3lb higher in future. The one concern was the drop in trip, however, and his lack of necessary pace was evident inside the final two furlongs, keeping on at just the one speed having been close enough if good enough. (tchd 4-1 in a place)
Indian Days, not ridden as positively as usual, got caught a bit wide round the bend, but he did keep on at the same pace, though that is often his problem – the lack of a change of pace. (op 28-1)
Dream Lodge(IRE) often goes well here and had been targeted at the race, but he got too far back and couldn't get close enough to seriously challenge. (op 16-1)
Sweet Lightning moved ominously well, so it was disappointing to see him produce little off the bridle. (op 11-1)
Royal Destination(IRE) got too far back early on.
Forte Dei Marmi has looked smart on both occasions he's won this season, but he was below-par behind Imposing over course and distance off 5lb lower in May, and this was a most disappointing effort. He's clearly better than this and perhaps an easier surface is preferable. Official explanation: jockey said gelding lost its action (tchd 9-1 in a place)
Shadows Lengthen Official explanation: jockey said gelding clipped heels

3922 JOHN SMITH'S SILVER CUP (H'CAP) (LISTED RACE) 1m 6f
3:40 (3:40) (Class 1) (0-110,110) 3-Y-O+**£23,704** (£8,964; £4,480; £2,240) **Stalls** Low

Form RPR

34-4 **1** **Free Agent**[14] 3462 4-9-1 **98** RyanMoore 1 107+
(R Hannon) *trckd ldrs: effrt over 3f out: styd on wl to ld ins fnl f: won gng rt away* **15/2**

1532 **2** *1 ½* **Drunken Sailor (IRE)**[14] 3447 5-9-13 **110** (b) KierenFallon 2 117
(L M Cumani) *s.i.s: hld up: smooth hdwy over 3f out: drvn to ld 2f out: edgd rt: hdd and wl btn ins fnl f* **9/4**[1]

5115 **3** *3 ¾* **Deauville Flyer**[14] 3447 4-8-13 **96** oh3 RobertWinston 3 98
(T D Easterby) *trckd ldrs: pushed along over 4f out: edgd lft over 1f out: swtchd lft and styd on ins fnl f* **11/4**[2]

6- **4** *4* **Moon Indigo**[265] 6885 4-8-13 **96** oh3 PaulHanagan 4 92
(J Howard Johnson) *trckd ldrs: drvn 4f out: outpcd over 2f out: kpt on fnl f* **16/1**

0003 **5** *2* **Mojave Moon**[20] 3240 4-9-5 **102** AhmedAjtebi 6 95
(Mahmood Al Zarooni) *tk fierce hold: trckd ldrs: effrt 4f out: slt advantage over 2f out: sn hdd: wkng whn sltly hmpd over 1f out* **16/1**

1200 **6** *1 ¾* **Sabotage (UAE)**[14] 3447 4-9-11 **108** TedDurcan 7 99
(Saeed Bin Suroor) *hld up: effrt over 3f out: wknd 2f out* **11/1**

-210 **7** *1 ½* **Chiberta King**[14] 3447 4-9-5 **102** PhillipMakin 5 91
(A M Balding) *led: qcknd 4f out: hdd over 2f out: sn wknd* **7/2**[3]

2m 59.89s (-0.31) **Going Correction** -0.05s/f (Good) **7** Ran SP% **111.5**
Speed ratings (Par 111): **98,97,95,92,91 90,89**
Tote Swingers: 1&2 £3.20, 1&3 £2.60, 2&3 £2.30 CSF £23.55 TOTE £9.20: £3.20, £1.60; EX 28.00.
Owner The Queen **Bred** The Queen **Trained** East Everleigh, Wilts

FOCUS
The front two drew a few lengths clear in this Listed handicap, despite it appearing to have been run at an ordinary gallop until the tempo lifted rounding for home. The first two rate improvers but the form may not be all that solid.

NOTEBOOK
Free Agent struggled to make an impact as a 3-y-o, having won the Chesham as a juvenile, but he shaped as though this trip may suit when fourth off a mark of 100 on his reappearance at Windsor, and really came strong inside the final furlong, readily picking off Drunken Sailor and winning with a bit in hand. He remains an interesting horse, this being just his ninth start, and connections will presumably look for another Listed of Group 3 race now, though Ryan Moore later mentioned the Ebor. (op 8-1)
Drunken Sailor(IRE) looked all over the likely winner when driven to the front over 2f out. However, he was unable to put the race to bed, and once he started to edge right, it was clear he was going to be claimed. He doesn't always do much once getting to the front, and his rider will no doubt be wishing he had held on to him a bit longer.
Deauville Flyer, twice hampered early when fifth as the favourite for the Northumberland Plate, was 3lb out of the handicap, as which made things tricky, but he still ran well and got closer to the runner-up than he had done at Newcastle. He's only four and still has more to offer as a stayer. (op 9-4)
Moon Indigo, another 3lb 'wrong' at the weights, was formerly with Aidan O'Brien and he made a pleasing enough start considering this would have been the fastest ground he has tackled to date. (op 20-1)
Mojave Moon pulled hard and simply wasn't up to the task. (op 12-1)
Sabotage(UAE) continued his regression. (op 12-1)
Chiberta King, who looked a non-stayer in the Northumberland Plate, again made the running but was joined soon on straightening and his finishing effort was weak. (op 4-1 tchd 9-2)

3923 JOHN SMITH'S MEDIAN AUCTION MAIDEN STKS 6f
4:15 (4:19) (Class 3) 2-Y-O **£6,605** (£1,965; £982; £490) **Stalls** High

Form RPR

22 **1** **Jaahiz (IRE)**[14] 3433 2-9-3 0 RyanMoore 6 80
(R Hannon) *led over 1f: trckd ldrs: swtchd rt 2f out: hung lft and led over 1f out: rdn rt and styd on wl* **13/8**[1]

3 **2** *3 ¾* **Maverik**[17] 3316 2-9-3 0 PhillipMakin 8 69
(M Dods) *dwlt: hld up in midfield: effrt 2f out: kpt on to take n.d 2nd last 50yds* **6/1**[3]

042 **3** *1 ¾* **Beyaz Villas**[8] 3625 2-9-0 0 MichaelGeran(3) 10 64
(D Nicholls) *sn chsng ldr: led over 4f out: hung bdly lft 2f out: hdd over 1f out: kpt on same pce* **12/1**

34 **4** *1 ½* **Nicola's Dream**[28] 2980 2-8-12 0 PaulHanagan 4 54
(R A Fahey) *chsd ldrs on outer: chal 2f out: one pce* **6/1**[3]

5 *2* **Another Citizen (IRE)** 2-9-3 0 TedDurcan 1 53+
(T D Easterby) *s.i.s: in rr: kpt on fnl f: will improve* **7/1**

6 *1* **Pitkin** 2-9-3 0 SilvestreDeSousa 5 54+
(M W Easterby) *s.s: outpcd and in rr: kpt on fnl 2f* **25/1**

005 **7** *½* **Bellemere**[28] 2980 2-8-12 0 JamieSpencer 7 44
(M W Easterby) *chsd ldrs: lost pl over 1f out* **9/1**

8 *2 ½* **Set Me Free (IRE)** 2-9-3 0 KierenFallon 3 41
(L M Cumani) *sn chsng ldrs on outside: hung lft and outpcd over 2f out: sn wknd* **11/2**[2]

9 *4* **Hartforth** 2-9-3 0 RoystonFfrench 9 29
(J D Bethell) *s.i.s: sn pushed along: nvr wnt pce* **40/1**

06 **10** *16* **Silver Writer**[29] 2939 2-9-3 0 ChrisCatlin 2 —
(M W Easterby) *prom early: lost pl after 2f: sn bhd: virtually p.u: t.o* **50/1**

1m 12.22s (0.32) **Going Correction** -0.05s/f (Good) **10** Ran SP% **120.5**
Speed ratings (Par 98): **95,90,87,85,83 81,81,77,72,51**
Tote Swingers:1&2:£3.70, 1&3:£5.40, 2&3:£9.40 CSF £11.99 TOTE £2.60: £1.30, £2.10, £3.30; EX 13.20.
Owner Jaber Abdullah **Bred** Watership Down Stud **Trained** East Everleigh, Wilts

FOCUS
An ordinary juvenile maiden, with the third having finished second in a seller last time. The decisive winner showed slightly improved form.

NOTEBOOK
Jaahiz(IRE) had bumped into useful sorts on both previous starts and took advantage of this easier opportunity returned to 6f. He had to switch right when the third cut across him two furlongs out, but ran on strongly for pressure despite still looking a bit green, and he will presumably go down the nursery route now. (op 2-1 tchd 9-4)
Maverik confirmed the promise of his debut effort, staying on well for second without threatening the winner having allowed him a bit too much rope. (tchd 11-2 and 7-1)
Beyaz Villas has twice run well at selling level and does cast doubts over the form, but he knows his job well and should soon be winning a small race. Official explanation: jockey said gelding hung left throughout (tchd 16-1)
Nicola's Dream finished a close fourth behind a highly regarded stablemate over course and distance last time and probably failed to reproduce that form here. She is at least qualified for nurseries now. (op 9-2)
Another Citizen(IRE) kept on nicely late and should improve quite a bit. (op 12-1)
Pitkin had been given a positive mention by his trainer beforehand. An already gelded half-brother to a couple of 5f juvenile winners, he was very slow to break, but recovered to make good ground past halfway before fading, and he should be a different proposition altogether next time. (op 18-1 tchd 16-1)
Set Me Free(IRE), whose sales price increased several times to 62,000gns, offered little immediate promise, but he is in good hands and should improve. (op 9-2 tchd 6-1)

3924 JOHN SMITH'S FILLIES' STKS MAIDEN FILLIES 7f
4:50 (4:50) (Class 4) 3-4-Y-O **£6,540** (£1,946; £972; £485) **Stalls** Low

Form RPR

4 **1** **Christmas Light**[8] 3612 3-9-0 74 SilvestreDeSousa 4 80
(D O'Meara) *chsd ldrs: rdn to ld over 2f out: hdd jst ins fnl f: led again last 50yds: all out* **3/1**[2]

-520 **2** *¾* **Dubai Media (CAN)**[24] 3071 3-9-0 85 PaulHanagan 2 78
(E A L Dunlop) *t.k.h in rr: smooth hdwy over 3f out: shkn up to ld jst ins fnl f: jinked rt and hdd clsng stages* **4/6**[1]

3 *6* **Forever Hope** 3-9-0 0 .... DanielTudhope 5 62
(T D Walford) *in rr: hdwy over 3f out: kpt on to take modest 3rd ins fnl f* **33/1**

04 4 *1/2* **Lady Berta**[17] 3333 3-9-0 0 .... RyanMoore 7 61
(R Hannon) *trckd ldrs: effrt over 2f out: one pce* **7/1**[3]

54-6 5 *2 1/4* **Briary Mac**[9] 3599 3-9-0 60 .... PaulQuinn 3 55
(N Bycroft) *led tl over 2f out: wknd over 1f out* **28/1**

6 6 *2 1/2* **Youm Al Mizayin**[15] 3407 3-9-0 0 .... ChrisCatlin 6 48
(M R Channon) *dwlt: hld up: effrt over 3f out: wknd 2f out* **18/1**

54 7 *3* **Amity (IRE)**[8] 3620 3-9-0 0 .... RoystonFfrench 1 40
(M Johnston) *s.i.s: sn chsng ldrs: drvn over 3f out: lost pl 2f out* **14/1**

1m 23.59s (-1.71) **Going Correction** -0.175s/f (Firm) 7 Ran SP% **115.8**
Speed ratings (Par 102): **102,101,94,93,91 88,84**
Tote Swingers: 1&2:£1.40, 1&3:£8.10, 2&3:£7.40 CSF £5.48 TOTE £4.60: £1.90, £1.10; EX 6.40.

Owner Mrs Lynne Lumley **Bred** Rabbah Bloodstock Limited **Trained** Nawton, N Yorks

FOCUS
The first pair came well clear in this modest fillies' maiden. The form is rated around the first two and the fourth.

3925 JOHN SMITH'S SPRINT (NURSERY) 5f
5:25 (5:26) (Class 3) 2-Y-O **£7,123** (£2,119; £1,059; £529) **Stalls** High

Form RPR

2453 1 **Lady Royale**[7] 3658 2-9-2 **74** .... (b[1]) SilvestreDeSousa 1 81
(G R Oldroyd) *trckd ldr: hung lft and led over 1f out: kpt on* **7/1**

2153 2 *1* **Mappin Time (IRE)**[9] 3596 2-9-7 **79** .... TedDurcan 2 82
(T D Easterby) *chsd ldrs: drvn over 2f out: hrd rdn and styd on to take 2nd ins fnl f: nt rch wnr* **3/1**[2]

2021 3 *2 1/4* **Orchid Street (USA)**[10] 3549 2-9-5 **77** .... RoystonFfrench 5 72
(Mrs A Duffield) *dwlt: sn drvn along: hdwy 2f out: styd on to take 3rd clsng stages* **9/4**[1]

61 4 *1 1/4* **Instructress**[12] 3509 2-9-5 **77** .... KierenFallon 6 67
(R M H Cowell) *dwlt: effrt over 2f out: nvr nr ldrs* **9/2**

3311 5 *3/4* **Bachelor Knight (IRE)**[9] 3598 2-8-11 **69** .... PaulHanagan 3 57
(R A Fahey) *chsd ldrs: drvn over 2f out: one pce* **7/2**[3]

6430 6 *2 1/4* **Surely This Time (IRE)**[9] 3596 2-8-10 **68** .... (b[1]) JamieSpencer 4 48
(K A Ryan) *led: edgd rt after s: hung lft and hdd over 1f out: wknd rapidly fnl 150yds* **10/1**

58.98 secs (-0.32) **Going Correction** -0.05s/f (Good) 6 Ran SP% **117.8**
Speed ratings (Par 98): **100,98,94,92,91 88**
Tote Swingers: 1&2:£3.10, 1&3:£3.60, 2&3:£1.90 CSF £29.69 TOTE £9.80: £3.70, £1.80; EX 31.20 Place 6 £209.21, Place 5 £22.88.
Owner R C Bond **Bred** Bond Thoroughbred Corporation **Trained** Brawby, N Yorks
■ Stewards' Enquiry : Ted Durcan one-day ban: used whip without giving colt time to respond (Jul 25)

FOCUS
A modest nursery, run at a strong pace. The winner is rated to form but the race could have been pitched maybe 4lb better.

NOTEBOOK
Lady Royale, sporting blinkers for the first time, found more than enough to hold on having gone to the front and taken a couple of lengths out the field over a furlong out. Having her seventh start, the daughter of Monsieur Bond had finished runner-up in the Hilary Needler earlier in the season, but her subsequent efforts had been well below that, and it took the application of blinkers to get her head in front. She showed tons of pace but her future prospects very much depend on whether the headgear continues to have the same effect. (tchd 13-2)
Mappin Time(IRE), runner-up over 6f on his nursery debut, couldn't go the early pace, but he did keep on well for second and looks capable of winning a nursery at some stage. (op 11-2)
Orchid Street(USA), the cosy winner of a Catterick maiden last week, was quickly outpaced on this nursery debut but did start to run on inside the final two furlongs, brought more towards the rail, and looks ready for an extra furlong now. (op 3-1 tchd 7-2)
Instructress, narrow winner of a Windsor maiden, kept on late without really posing a threat, shaping as though 6f will help. (op 100-30)
Bachelor Knight(IRE), who got up in the dying stride to win a 5f nursery at Redcar last time, got too far behind here and could only plod on at the one pace inside the final furlong. He has won a seller over 6f and looks in need of a return to that trip, or even further. (op 3-1 tchd 11-4)
Surely This Time(IRE) burnt himself out in the first-time blinkers. (op 8-1)
T/Jkpt: Not won. T/Plt: £214.70 to a £1 stake. Pool £199,267.39 - 677.22 winning tickets. T/Qpdt: £8.80 to a £1 stake. Pool:£9,251.21 - 770.12 winning tickets. WG

3926 - 3932a (Foreign Racing) - See Raceform Interactive

3609 DEAUVILLE (R-H)
Saturday, July 10

OFFICIAL GOING: Turf: good to firm; fibresand: standard

3933a PRIX DU HARAS DE LA HUDERIE (LISTED RACE) (3YO COLTS & GELDINGS) (TURF) 1m (R)
12:50 (12:00) 3-Y-O **£24,336** (£9,734; £7,300; £4,867; £2,433)

RPR

1 **Royal Bench (IRE)**[34] 2802 3-8-11 0 .... IoritzMendizabal 7 103
(Robert Collet, France) **23/10**[2]

2 *1* **Lochinver (USA)**[32] 3-8-11 0 .... MickaelBarzalona 1 101
(A Fabre, France) **5/1**[3]

3 *1/2* **Semos (FR)**[18] 3-8-11 0 .... ChristopheSoumillon 5 100
(A De Royer-Dupre, France) **2/1**[1]

4 *nk* **Don Bosco (FR)**[43] 3-8-11 0 .... GregoryBenoist 9 99
(D Smaga, France) **13/1**

5 *3/4* **Vagabond Shoes (IRE)** 3-8-11 0 .... OlivierPeslier 2 97
(Y Durepaire, Spain) **14/1**

6 *1 1/2* **Mont Agel**[23] 3104 3-8-11 0 .... ThierryThulliez 4 94
(M L W Bell) *settled 3rd: moved 2nd bef st: u.p 2f out: fnd no ex: styd on fnl f* **39/1**

7 *nk* **High Link (FR)**[38] 3-8-11 0 .... Roberto-CarlosMontenegro 10 93
(X Thomas-Demeaulte, France) **59/1**

8 *1 1/2* **Ramble On (FR)**[27] 3016 3-8-11 0 .... StephanePasquier 3 90
(G Botti, Italy) **44/5**

9 *3* **Dibir (FR)**[53] 2222 3-8-11 0 .... GeraldMosse 8 83
(J-C Rouget, France) **9/1**

1m 41.2s (0.40) 9 Ran SP% **118.5**
WIN (incl. 1 euro stake): 3.30. PLACES: 1.40, 1.50, 1.40. DF: 9.20. SF: 14.30.
Owner R C Strauss **Bred** Kilfrush Stud **Trained** Chantilly, France

NOTEBOOK
Mont Agel hasn't really built on the promise of his maiden win at two, but might benefit from a drop into handicaps.

HAMBURG (R-H)
Saturday, July 10

OFFICIAL GOING: Turf: good

3934a FRANZ-GUNTHER VON GAERTNER-GEDACHTNISRENNEN (HAMBURGER MEILE) (GROUP 3) (3YO+) (TURF) 1m
4:00 (4:17) 3-Y-O+ **£28,318** (£9,734; £4,867; £2,654; £1,769; £1,327)

RPR

1 **Earl Of Fire (GER)**[42] 2559 5-9-2 0 .... DominiqueBoeuf 10 104
(W Baltromei, Germany) *wnt st to ld: mde all: r.o wl in st: saw off all chals in fnl f* **87/10**

2 *1/2* **Sehrezad (IRE)**[42] 2559 5-9-6 0 .... JiriPalik 5 107
(Andreas Lowe, Germany) *hmpd by rdrless horse: grad manoeuvred through field: swtchd to wd outside in st: r.o strly: flew home in fnl f: unlucky* **84/10**

3 *nk* **Win For Sure (GER)**[41] 2576 5-9-6 0 .... EPedroza 4 106
(A Wohler, Germany) *racd in midfield: hmpd by rdrless horse: mde gd move in st: r.o wl: no threat to first two* **6/5**[1]

4 *1/2* **Abbashiva (GER)**[42] 2559 5-9-6 0 .... EFrank 2 105
(T Mundry, Germany) *racd in midfield: failed to qckn early in st: styd on wl* **87/10**

5 *nk* **Noble Alpha (IRE)**[27] 3016 3-8-11 0 .... THellier 9 104
(Mario Hofer, Germany) *racd in 4th: avoided rdrless horse: flattered briefly at top of st: styd on but no ex fnl f* **81/10**[3]

6 *2 1/2* **Sanjii Danon (GER)**[42] 2559 4-9-4 0 .... APietsch 11 96
(W Hickst, Germany) *racd in midfield: bdly hmpd by rdrless horse: r.o in st but no imp fnl 2f* **121/10**

7 *1/2* **Tertullus (FR)**[39] 2637 7-9-6 0 .... EspenSki 3 97
(Rune Haugen, Norway) *racd in midfield: briefly flattered early in st: failed to qckn: wknd* **157/10**

8 *shd* **Quilboquet (BRZ)**[60] 2020 7-9-2 0 .... FilipMinarik 8 93
(Lennart Reuterskiold Jr, Sweden) *racd towards rr: hmpd by rdrless horse: nvr showed in st* **43/1**

9 *4* **Alianthus (GER)**[20] 3251 5-9-4 0 .... ADeVries 7 86
(J Hirschberger, Germany) *a.p: trcking ldr: wknd qckly in st* **114/10**

10 *26* **Le Big (GER)**[42] 2559 6-9-2 0 .... AStarke 1 24
(U Stoltefuss, Germany) *broke wl: bdly hmpd by rdrless horse: almost brought to a halt: lost all ch* **145/10**

U **Kite Hunter (IRE)**[47] 2405 3-8-11 0 .... StefanieHofer 6 —
(Mario Hofer, Germany) *sddle slipped and uns rdr sn after s* **61/10**[2]

1m 35.6s (95.60)
WFA 3 from 4yo+ 9lb 11 Ran SP% **132.2**
WIN (incl. 10 euro stake): 97. PLACES: 20, 18, 11. SF: 500..
Owner Frau M Haller **Bred** Frau M Haller **Trained** Germany

3044 HOLLYWOOD PARK (L-H)
Saturday, July 10

OFFICIAL GOING: Cushion track: fast

3935a TRIPLE BEND H'CAP (GRADE 1) (3YO+) (CUSHION TRACK) 7f
11:41 (11:47) 3-Y-O+ **£83,333** (£27,777; £16,666; £8,333; £2,777)

RPR

1 **E Z's Gentleman (USA)**[35] 5-8-4 **0** .... (b) MPedroza 1 112
(Bob Baffert, U.S.A) **39/10**[3]

2 *3 1/4* **Sangaree (USA)**[27] 5-8-4 **0** .... (b) MGarcia 6 103
(Bob Baffert, U.S.A) **58/10**

3 *1* **Gayego (USA)**[105] 1024 5-8-10 **0** .... RBejarano 4 107
(Saeed Bin Suroor) **6/4**[1]

4 *1 1/4* **M One Rifle (USA)**[35] 4-8-5 **0** .... MESmith 3 98
(Bruce Headley, U.S.A) **5/2**[2]

5 *1* **New Bay (USA)**[196] 4-8-2 **0** .... TBaze 8 92
(Mike Mitchell, U.S.A) **121/10**

6 *2 1/4* **Fantasy Free (USA)**[35] 5-8-4 **0** ow2 .... (b) OBerrio 2 88
(A C Avila, U.S.A) **28/1**

7 *1 3/4* **Bestdressed (USA)**[76] 6-8-2 **0** .... VEspinoza 5 82
(John W Sadler, U.S.A) **176/10**

1m 21.11s (81.11) 7 Ran SP% **120.1**
PARI-MUTUEL (all including $2 stake): WIN 9.80; PLACE (1-2) 4.80, 4.80; SHOW (1-2-3) 3.20, 2.60, 2.40; DF 28.60; SF 45.80.
Owner Arnold Zetcher LLC **Bred** Dixiana Stables Inc **Trained** USA

NOTEBOOK
Gayego(USA), who had to give weight all round, was entitled to need this, his first outing since finishing down the field in the Golden Shaheen back in March.

3936 - 3938a (Foreign Racing) - See Raceform Interactive

3378 TIPPERARY (L-H)
Sunday, July 11

OFFICIAL GOING: Good (good to firm in places)

3939a DANEHILL DANCER TIPPERARY STKS (LISTED RACE) 5f
3:45 (3:48) 2-Y-O **£25,884** (£7,566; £3,584; £1,194)

RPR

1 **Anadolu (IRE)**[34] 2828 2-8-12 84 .... PShanahan 5 95
(Tracey Collins, Ire) *a.p: rdn along in cl 2nd 2f out: led ins fnl f: styd on wl* **14/1**

2 *1/2* **Moonlit Garden (IRE)**[16] 3421 2-8-12 94 .... PJSmullen 1 93
(D K Weld, Ire) *sn led: rdn 1 1/2f out: sn strly pressed: hdd ins fnl f: no ex cl home* **4/5**[1]

3 *3/4* **Cloneylass (IRE)**[9] 3649 2-8-12 .... FMBerry 3 90
(Mrs John Harrington, Ire) *hld up in tch: rdn 2f out: 4th 1 1/2f out: 3rd 1f out: styd on wl fnl f* **7/1**[3]

4 *1 1/4* **Mr Man In The Moon (IRE)**[22] 3229 2-9-1 95 .... PBBeggy 4 89
(Paul W Flynn, Ire) *prom: rdn in 3rd 2f out: sn no ex* **5/1**[2]

5 2 **Waking Warrior**[26] 3059 2-9-1 .... DPMcDonogh 6 85
(K A Ryan) *prom on outer: rdn 1/2-way: no imp fr 2f out* **10/1**

6 4 ½ **Lightening Thief (IRE)**[50] 2352 2-9-1 90.............................. JMurtagh 2 71
(W McCreery, Ire) *in tch bhd ldrs on far rail: cl 4th and pushed along whn bdly checked over 1f out: eased and virtually p.u* **5/1**[2]

59.13 secs (0.13) **6** Ran SP% **117.1**
CSF £27.51 TOTE £26.50: £3.30, £1.30; DF 22.20.
Owner Selman Tasbek **Bred** Suleyman Selman Tasbek **Trained** The Curragh, Co Kildare
■ Stewards' Enquiry : P B Beggy two-day ban: careless riding (Jul 26-27)

FOCUS
All six runners in this Listed event were winners.

NOTEBOOK
Anadolu(IRE), back to the trip over which she won her maiden at Down Royal, did the job nicely. Soon disputing the lead, she edged ahead early in the final furlong and kept on well. Trainer Tracey Collins believes 5f is her optimum trip. She said: "She didn't stay 6f when she ran in a Group 3 last time. We've always thought a lot of her and we'll look for more suitable races for her over the distance." (op 10/1)
Moonlit Garden(IRE), successful over 6f on her debut at the Curragh before performing creditably from an unfavourable draw when dropped to 5f in the Queen Mary Stakes, had not helped her chance by racing quite keenly back over 6f at the Curragh on her previous start. She ran fast here next to the rail and appeared to touch the front briefly 1f out. She kept on when headed but the winner was always holding her. (op 4/5 tchd 9/10)
Cloneylass(IRE), successful over the trip on her previous start at Bellewstown, chased the leaders and ran on quite well inside the final furlong to be nearest at the finish. (op 6/1)
Mr Man In The Moon(IRE), placed on his first three starts before getting off the mark over this trip at Down Royal last month, led and disputed and, after coming under pressure 2f out, was unable to raise his effort from over 1f out where he edged left. (op 7/1)
Waking Warrior, a winner over the trip at Southwell before finishing second at Thirsk, raced close up towards the centre of the course but was struggling to make any impression from almost 2f out. (op 7/1)
Lightening Thief(IRE) was chasing the leaders and making little impression when he was tightened for room and hampered over 1f out, after which he was immediately eased. (op 9/2)

3940 - 3942a (Foreign Racing) - See Raceform Interactive

3934 HAMBURG (R-H)
Sunday, July 11

OFFICIAL GOING: Turf: good

3943a H.H. SHEIKH HAMDAN BIN RASHID AL MAKTOUM TROPHY (HAMBURGER STUTENPREIS) (GROUP 3) (3YO FILLIES) 1m 3f
4:10 (4:15) 3-Y-O
£28,318 (£9,734; £4,867; £2,654; £1,769; £1,327)

RPR
1 **Miss Starlight**[24] 3104 3-9-2 0... THellier 5 101
(P J McBride) *broke slowly: settled towards rr: mde gd prog arnd fnl turn: swtchd to outer: qckn wl: grabbed ld 150yds out: r.o wl* **127/10**

2 1 **Elle Shadow (IRE)**[49] 2372 3-9-2 0..................................... AStarke 2 99
(P Schiergen, Germany) *settled midfield: mde move on inner ent st: qcknd u.p: chsd wnr to line* **11/5**[2]

3 1 **Ovambo Queen (GER)**[40] 3-9-2 0.................................. HenkGrewe 4 97
(Dr A Bolte, Germany) *a.p: racing bhd ldrs: kpt on wl for 3rd in st* **49/10**[3]

4 1 **Nianga (GER)**[36] 3-9-2 0... ADeVries 1 95
(P Schiergen, Germany) *in rr fr s: mde move on inner ent st: short of room: fin wl whn in clr* **116/10**

5 1 ½ **Waldjagd**[49] 2372 3-9-2 0... EPedroza 8 93
(A Wohler, Germany) *settled midfield: rdn early in st: flattered briefly: wknd fnl f* **17/10**[1]

6 1 ¼ **Glady Romana (GER)**[51] 3-9-2 0............................... DominiqueBoeuf 3 90
(W Baltromei, Germany) *broke wl: racd freely bhd two ldrs: flattered early in st: no ex* **68/10**

7 2 **Tuiga (IRE)**[41] 3-9-2 0... FilipMinarik 7 87
(P Schiergen, Germany) *in rr fr s: proged in centre of trck early in st: no ex: styd on* **225/10**

8 3 **Pragelata (GER)** 3-9-2 0.. JBojko 6 81
(A Wohler, Germany) *racd in 2nd fr s: moved into ld early in bk st: led into st: fdd* **28/1**

9 9 **Kaya Belle (GER)**[41] 3-9-2 0.. EFrank 9 65
(T Mundry, Germany) *led fr s: settled in 2nd in bk st: rdn early in st: no ex: wknd* **94/10**

2m 21.27s (-3.43) **9** Ran SP% **130.6**
WIN (incl. 10 euro stake): 137. PLACES: 35, 16, 22. SF: 589.
Owner Maelor Racing **Bred** T J Cooper **Trained** Newmarket, Suffolk

NOTEBOOK
Miss Starlight didn't have much go her way at Ascot last time but ran better than her finishing position suggested. Up a furlong in distance and back on easier ground, she was held up at the back of the field befort quickening well once switched to the outside in the straight.

3944 - (Foreign Racing) - See Raceform Interactive

3705 AYR (L-H)
Monday, July 12

OFFICIAL GOING: Good (good to firm in places on straight course; 9.1)
Wind: Slight, half against Weather: Cloudy

3945 BET AT VICTOR CHANDLER ON 08000 78 78 78 MEDIAN AUCTION MAIDEN STKS 6f
2:00 (2:06) (Class 5) 2-Y-O **£2,719** (£809; £404; £202) **Stalls** High

Form RPR
3 1 **Bahamian Sunset**[41] 2623 2-8-12 0.............................. TonyHamilton 8 75
(R A Fahey) *trckd ldrs: drvn and led appr fnl f: r.o wl* **15/8**[1]

6 2 ¾ **Calypso Magic (IRE)**[55] 2210 2-8-12 0........................ IanBrennan(5) 9 78
(J Howard Johnson) *led: rdn and hdd appr fnl f: kpt on u.p ins fnl f* **33/1**

0 3 ½ **Point Du Jour (FR)**[19] 3332 2-9-3 0....................... SilvestreDeSousa 13 76
(I A Wood) *t.k.h: cl up: effrt over 1f out: edgd lft ins fnl f: kpt on same pce towards fin* **66/1**

4 2 ¼ **Jack Smudge** 2-9-3 0.. PaulMulrennan 3 70+
(J G Given) *cl up: rdn over 2f out: hung lft over 1f out: one pce ins fnl f* **66/1**

5 2 ¾ **Teriyaki (IRE)**[15] 3485 2-9-3 0.. RPCleary 6 61
(Daniel Mark Loughnane, Ire) *in tch: drvn and outpcd over 2f out: no imp fr over 1f out* **16/1**

6 3 ¼ **Prince Of Passion (CAN)** 2-9-3 0............................... PhillipMakin 14 52+
(M Dods) *hld up in tch: drvn over 2f out: sn no imp* **11/1**

53 7 nk **Jibaal (IRE)**[23] 3199 2-9-3 0.. TadhgO'Shea 10 51
(M Johnston) *in tch: drvn 1/2-way: outpcd fr 2f out* **9/4**[2]

8 1 **Rocky Coast** 2-9-3 0.. TomEaves 12 48
(B Smart) *s.i.s: bhd: drvn over 3f out: sme late hdwy: nvr on terms* **16/1**

605 9 4 **West Stand**[33] 2861 2-8-12 0................................ RoystonFfrench 7 31
(Mrs K Walton) *prom tl rdn and wknd over 2f out* **33/1**

10 10 **Punt Road (IRE)** 2-8-12 0.................................. JamesSullivan(5) 11 6
(Lee Smyth, Ire) *missed break: bhd: struggling whn hung lft 1/2-way: nvr on terms* **100/1**

11 13 **Magnini (IRE)** 2-8-10 0.. JPO'Brien(7) 5 —
(K A Ryan) *dwlt and wnt lft s: sn cl up: rdn and drifted lft to far rail wl over 2f out: sn struggling* **15/2**[3]

1m 11.84s (-1.76) **Going Correction** -0.375s/f (Firm) **11** Ran SP% **107.3**
Speed ratings (Par 94): **96,95,94,91,87 83,82,81,76,62 45**
toteswingers:1&2:£8.20, 1&3:£19.70, 2&3:£41.00 CSF £69.88 TOTE £2.80: £1.10, £7.60, £15.80; EX 45.50.
Owner The National Stud Never Say Die Club Ltd **Bred** The National Stud Never Say Die Club Ltd **Trained** Musley Bank, N Yorks

FOCUS
An ordinary maiden. Tricky form to pin down, with a big step up from the second.

NOTEBOOK
Bahamian Sunset improved enough on her debut effort to score, leading inside the final furlong and staying on in the manner of a horse likely to be suited by 7f before too long. It will presumably be nurseries next. (tchd 2-1 in a place)
Calypso Magic(IRE) found it all happening too quickly over 5f on his debut, but he proved a different proposition this time, staying on right the way to the line without quite being able to match the winner.
Point Du Jour(FR), comfortably held on his debut at Salisbury, knew a lot more this time and was soon chasing the speed. He stayed on well to challenge inside the final 2f, but couldn't race on with the winner inside the final 150 yards. This represented a big step forward and he should be capable of winning a standard maiden with a little further progress.
Jack Smudge, a half-brother to numerous winners, fared best of the newcomers in fourth, challenging wide and keeping on despite still showing signs of greenness. He should learn from this. (op 50-1)
Teriyaki(IRE), third at 100/1 in a Curragh maiden latest, was unable to take a further step forward and will do better once handicapping.
Prince Of Passion(CAN), a 25,000gs yearling, looked in need of the experience and is sure to come on for the outing. (tchd 12-1)
Jibaal(IRE) had disappointed at the course last time when only third at 6-5, and it was much of the same here, being unable to quicken. He is clearly in need of a greater test and could prove a different proposition once upped in distance and contesting handicaps. (tchd 2-1)
Magnini(IRE) Official explanation: jockey said colt was keen to post and hung badly left throughout

3946 BEST ODDS GUARANTEED AT VICTOR CHANDLER H'CAP 5f
2:30 (2:33) (Class 6) (0-65,65) 3-Y-O+ **£2,047** (£604; £302) **Stalls** High

Form RPR
0634 1 **The Bear**[2] 3902 7-9-9 **62**....................................... TonyHamilton 6 74
(Miss L A Perratt) *mde all: sn crossed to stands' rail: rdn 2f out: drew clr fnl f* **6/1**[3]

0625 2 5 **Speedy Senorita (IRE)**[10] 3622 5-9-10 **63**.................. GrahamGibbons 2 57
(J J Quinn) *cl up: rdn over 2f out: edgd rt and kpt on fnl f: no ch w wnr* **4/1**[1]

3436 3 nk **Mandarin Spirit (IRE)**[13] 3533 10-9-11 **64**........................(b) TomEaves 5 57
(Miss L A Perratt) *hld up in tch: smooth hdwy 2f out: rdn and kpt on same pce ins fnl f* **13/2**

1003 4 2 ½ **Micky Mac (IRE)**[9] 3687 6-9-9 **62**.........................(p) SilvestreDeSousa 12 46
(C J Teague) *in tch: drvn over 2f out: n.m.r briefly ent fnl f: kpt on: no imp* **11/2**[2]

-023 5 ½ **Sandwith**[14] 3497 7-9-5 **58**.. LNewman 3 40
(A G Foster) *trckd ldrs: rdn over 2f out: no ex over 1f out* **11/2**[2]

6006 6 3 ½ **Riggs (IRE)**[14] 3516 4-8-7 **46** oh1............................... RoystonFfrench 4 16
(Peter Grayson) *cl up: rdn over 2f out: wknd over 1f out* **100/1**

6/06 7 ½ **Cutting Comments**[57] 2144 4-9-12 **65**............................... PhillipMakin 10 33
(M Dods) *chsd ldrs: n.m.r and lost pl over 3f out: effrt over 2f out: wknd over 1f out* **6/1**[3]

2630 8 hd **Classlin**[8] 3710 3-8-1 **50**... IanBrennan(5) 7 15
(J S Goldie) *dwlt: bhd: rdn and effrt on outside over 2f out: wknd over 1f out* **12/1**

0005 9 1 **Miacarla**[63] 1965 7-8-7 **46** oh1.................................. PatrickMathers 11 9
(H A McWilliams) *t.k.h: hld up bhd ldng gp: n.m.r over 2f out: sn rdn: wknd wl over 1f out* **40/1**

0/0- 10 shd **Red Humour (IRE)**[28] 3043 4-8-9 **48**...................................(b) RPCleary 1 11
(M McDonagh, Ire) *prom on outside: rdn 1/2-way: wknd wl over 1f out* **12/1**

04 11 6 **Mr Rooney (IRE)**[26] 3075 7-8-7 **46** oh1.......................(b) AdrianNicholls 9 —
(A Berry) *dwlt: bhd: struggling over 2f out: nvr on terms* **40/1**

58.07 secs (-2.03) **Going Correction** -0.375s/f (Firm)
WFA 3 from 4yo+ 5lb **11** Ran SP% **113.9**
Speed ratings (Par 101): **101,93,92,88,87 82,81,81,79,79 69**
toteswingers:1&2:£6.70, 1&3:£8.30, 2&3:£8.70 CSF £28.99 CT £160.41 TOTE £6.30: £2.40, £2.00, £3.30; EX 27.70.
Owner Cincinnati Club **Bred** P G Airey And R R Whitton **Trained** East Kilbride, South Lanarks

FOCUS
Few got into this sprint handicap. The winner had a fairly easy lead and is rated back to something like his post-2yo best.
Micky Mac(IRE) Official explanation: jockey said gelding suffered interference in running and lost a near hind shoe
Riggs(IRE) Official explanation: jockey said gelding hung left final 2f

3947 WATCH LIVE RACING AT VICTORCHANDLER.COM FILLIES' H'CAP 6f
3:00 (3:04) (Class 4) (0-85,84) 3-Y-O+ **£5,180** (£1,541; £770; £384) **Stalls** High

Form RPR
0-00 1 **Ursula (IRE)**[30] 2982 4-9-6 **75**.. AndrewElliott 5 85
(J R Weymes) *in tch: niggled along 1/2-way: hdwy over 1f out: led ent fnl f: r.o strly* **8/1**

1-61 2 1 ½ **Jeannie Galloway (IRE)**[37] 2762 3-9-7 **82**.......................... TonyHamilton 6 86
(R A Fahey) *trckd ldr: effrt and ev ch 1f out: kpt on u.p ins fnl f* **7/2**[1]

312U 3 ¾ **Requisite**[5] 3779 5-9-6 **75**.....................................(v) SilvestreDeSousa 7 78
(I A Wood) *rrd s: hld up in tch: effrt on outside over 1f out: kpt on same pce wl ins fnl f* **11/2**[3]

4354 4 hd **Feelin Foxy**[10] 3622 6-9-11 **80**.. PaulMulrennan 3 82
(J G Given) *led and sn crossed to stands' rail: rdn 2f out: hdd ent fnl f: kpt on same pce* **11/1**

-115 **5** *hd* **Timeless Elegance (IRE)**[28] 3023 3-8-11 **77**................ IanBrennan(5) 1 78
(J Howard Johnson) *trckd ldrs: rdn over 2f out: effrt over 1f out: kpt on same pce ins fnl f* **5/1**[2]

2536 **6** *nk* **Leonid Glow**[27] 3065 5-9-8 **77**.................................... PhillipMakin 8 78
(M Dods) *hld up in tch: hdwy whn nt clr run appr fnl f: styd on ins fnl f nrst fin* **7/2**[1]

6254 **7** *1* **Rothesay Dancer**[13] 3533 7-8-13 **71**........................ KellyHarrison(3) 9 72+
(J S Goldie) *hld up: hdwy whn nt clr run and swtchd lft over 1f out: keeping on whn nt clr run last 50yds: no imp* **14/1**

1303 **8** *6* **Diapason (IRE)**[14] 3505 4-9-6 **75**...............................(t) RichardSmith 10 53
(Tom Dascombe) *hld up bhd ldng gp: drvn over 2f out: wknd over 1f out* **11/1**

1m 11.61s (-1.99) **Going Correction** -0.375s/f (Firm)
WFA 3 from 4yo+ 6lb **8** Ran SP% **110.9**
Speed ratings (Par 102): **98,96,95,94,94 94,92,84**
toteswingers:1&2:£5.40, 1&3:£8.80, 2&3:£4.30 CSF £33.95 CT £160.97 TOTE £9.30: £2.70, £1.70, £1.40; EX 44.50.
Owner The Ursula Partnership **Bred** Rathbarry Stud **Trained** Middleham Moor, N Yorks
■ Stewards' Enquiry : Ian Brennan one-day ban: careless riding (Jul 26)

FOCUS
A competitive sprint handicap run at a strong pace. The winner is rated back to her turf berst with the runner-up close to form.
Ursula(IRE) Official explanation: trainer said, regarding apparent improvement in form, that the filly was suited by the faster pace.
Rothesay Dancer Official explanation: jockey said mare was denied a clear run

3948 PLAY POKER AT VICTORCHANDLER.COM H'CAP 7f 50y
3:30 (3:30) (Class 6) (0-65,65) 3-Y-0+ **£2,047** (£604; £302) **Stalls** High

Form RPR

-040 **1** **Frontline Girl (IRE)**[16] 3434 4-9-6 **57**............................ AndrewElliott 12 73
(J R Weymes) *hld up on outside: rdn over 3f out: gd hdwy over 1f out: led ins fnl f: sn clr* **8/1**[3]

0402 **2** *3 ¾* **Hosanna**[8] 3706 4-8-12 **49**.. RoystonFfrench 8 55
(J Barclay) *hld up in tch: effrt over 2f out: hdwy to chse wnr ins fnl f: kpt on: no imp* **8/1**[3]

0003 **3** *1 ½* **Carlitos Spirit (IRE)**[10] 3610 6-9-2 **60**...........................(v) DaleSwift(7) 4 62
(I W McInnes) *led: rdn over 2f out: hdd ins fnl f: kpt on same pce* **4/1**[1]

5155 **4** *1 ¾* **Mr Lu**[8] 3706 5-9-6 **64**.. PaulNorton(7) 3 61
(J S Goldie) *hld up: effrt and shkn up over 2f out: hdwy appr fnl f: r.o fin* **4/1**[1]

0665 **5** *nk* **Military Call**[18] 3371 3-9-3 **62**... LNewman 5 55
(A C Whillans) *in tch: effrt over 2f out: rdn and kpt on same pce fr over 1f out* **7/1**[2]

60-6 **6** *½* **Secret Hero**[28] 3043 4-8-10 **52**................................(b) JamesSullivan(5) 9 47
(Lee Smyth, Ire) *midfield: rdn over 2f out: kpt on ins fnl f: nvr able to chal* **14/1**

6565 **7** *½* **Captain Imperial (IRE)**[36] 2779 4-8-2 **46**...........(t) MatthewLawson(7) 6 40
(R Bastiman) *trckd ldrs: drvn over 2f out: wknd ins fnl f* **11/1**

60-0 **8** *shd* **Broughtons Silk**[18] 3369 5-8-10 **47**.................................... TomEaves 1 40
(A C Whillans) *trckd ldrs: rdn over 2f out: wknd appr fnl f* **12/1**

4-00 **9** *½* **Charity Fair**[52] 2296 3-8-0 **48** ow2.............................. KellyHarrison(3) 14 37
(A Berry) *s.i.s: bhd tl hdwy over 1f out: kpt on: nvr able to chal* **50/1**

030- **10** *shd* **Pont De Nuit**[243] 7333 3-9-6 **65**.. PhillipMakin 10 54
(A B Haynes) *sn pushed along towards rr: sme hdwy over 1f out: nvr on terms* **25/1**

005- **11** *1* **Only A Splash**[320] 5332 6-8-13 **50**.................................. PaulMulrennan 7 39
(Mrs R A Carr) *prom: rdn over 2f out: wknd wl over 1f out* **20/1**

0004 **12** *nk* **Forzarzi (IRE)**[23] 3205 6-8-11 **48**.................................. PatrickMathers 2 36
(H A McWilliams) *hld up in midfield on ins: drvn over 2f out: wknd over 1f out* **22/1**

0-46 **13** *7* **Thescottishsoldier**[24] 3161 3-8-4 **49** ow1.................. AdrianNicholls 13 15
(A G Foster) *hld up towards rr: reminders after 2f: hdwy and cl up over 2f out: wknd over 1f out* **14/1**

000 **14** *16* **Boundless Applause**[66] 1884 4-8-9 **46**..............(b) SilvestreDeSousa 11 —
(I A Wood) *midfield: drvn along 3f out: wknd fr 2f out: t.o* **25/1**

1m 31.47s (-1.93) **Going Correction** -0.275s/f (Firm)
WFA 3 from 4yo+ 8lb **14** Ran SP% **122.8**
Speed ratings (Par 101): **100,95,94,92,91 91,90,90,89,89 88,88,80,61**
toteswingers:1&2:£13.10, 1&3:£7.80, 2&3:£4.20 CSF £67.20 CT £308.62 TOTE £8.70: £3.40, £2.20, £1.80; EX 80.90.
Owner M A Roden **Bred** J Donnelly **Trained** Middleham Moor, N Yorks

FOCUS
Another race run at a good gallop, and the form reads sound.
Frontline Girl(IRE) Official explanation: trainer said, regarding apparent improvement in form, that the filly had come to hand and the yard's runners are in better form.
Thescottishsoldier Official explanation: jockey said gelding finished lame right-hind

3949 PLAY CASINO AT VICTORCHANDLER.COM H'CAP 1m
4:00 (4:00) (Class 4) (0-85,82) 3-Y-0 **£5,180** (£1,541; £770; £384) **Stalls** Low

Form RPR

1261 **1** **Don't Call Me (IRE)**[10] 3612 3-9-4 **79**...............................(t) TomEaves 6 90
(B Smart) *hld up: rdn over 3f out: hdwy 2f out: led ins fnl f: r.o wl* **13/8**[1]

136 **2** *½* **Lord Raglan (IRE)**[32] 2886 3-8-6 **67**................................ AndrewElliott 8 77
(J R Weymes) *cl up: led 2f out: sn rdn: hdd ins fnl f: r.o* **9/1**

4-34 **3** *2 ¼* **Layla's Dancer**[73] 1658 3-9-2 **77**...................................... TonyHamilton 4 82
(R A Fahey) *in tch: effrt over 2f out: drvn and styd on fnl f: nt rch first two* **10/3**[2]

-105 **4** *1 ¼* **Master Of Dance (IRE)**[31] 2933 3-8-13 **74**.................. PaulMulrennan 9 76
(J G Given) *hld up: effrt whn nt clr run on ins over 2f out: kpt on fnl f: no imp* **20/1**

6553 **5** *1 ¾* **Amenable (IRE)**[37] 2762 3-8-13 **74**.............................. AdrianNicholls 5 72
(D Nicholls) *led tl rdn and hdd 2f out: kpt on same pce over 1f out* **5/1**[3]

51-5 **6** *1 ¼* **Starry Mount**[65] 1921 3-8-12 **73**... PhillipMakin 2 68
(A B Haynes) *trckd ldrs tl rdn and wknd over 1f out* **10/1**

0-1 **7** *7* **Staff Sergeant**[77] 1143 3-9-7 **82**.. LNewman 1 61
(J S Goldie) *t.k.h: trckd ldrs: rdn over 2f out: sn wknd* **10/1**

1m 41.01s (-2.79) **Going Correction** -0.275s/f (Firm) **7** Ran SP% **110.8**
Speed ratings (Par 102): **102,101,99,98,96 95,88**
toteswingers:1&2:£3.50, 1&3:£2.30, 2&3:£4.00 CSF £16.09 CT £40.87 TOTE £3.40: £2.30, £4.50; EX 20.50.
Owner H E Sheikh Rashid Bin Mohammed **Bred** Darley **Trained** Hambleton, N Yorks

FOCUS
A fair 3-y-o handicap. The winner and runner-up both stepped forward.

3950 JAMES HALSTEAD PLC H'CAP 1m 2f
4:30 (4:30) (Class 5) (0-70,70) 3-Y-0+ **£2,719** (£809; £404; £202) **Stalls** Low

Form RPR

4211 **1** **Marjury Daw (IRE)**[2] 3912 4-9-11 **67**............................... PaulMulrennan 9 80+
(J G Given) *trckd ldrs: smooth hdwy to ld over 2f out: rdn clr fr over 1f out: eased nr fin* **7/2**[2]

5355 **2** *4 ½* **Talk Of Saafend (IRE)**[8] 3708 5-9-6 **62**......................... TonyHamilton 6 66
(P Monteith) *s.i.s: hld up: hdwy over 2f out: chsd wnr ins fnl f: r.o* **11/1**

-523 **3** *½* **Highkingofireland**[48] 2421 4-9-5 **61**............................... AndrewElliott 7 64
(J R Weymes) *hld up: hdwy and prom over 2f out: rdn and kpt on same pce fnl f* **6/1**

640 **4** *hd* **Holiday Cocktail**[33] 2851 8-9-2 **58**............................(p) GrahamGibbons 4 61
(J J Quinn) *in tch: rdn over 2f out: nt qckn appr fnl f* **7/1**

0-53 **5** *½* **Chantilly Pearl (USA)**[45] 2516 4-9-6 **62**...................... RoystonFfrench 10 64
(J G Given) *hld up: hdwy on outside over 2f out: rdn wl over 1f out: no ex ins fnl f* **11/2**[3]

3242 **6** *hd* **Grand Diamond (IRE)**[8] 3707 6-9-6 **65**........................(p) GaryBartley(3) 2 66
(J S Goldie) *trckd ldrs: ev ch over 2f out: sn rdn: no ex appr fnl f* **3/1**[1]

000- **7** *3 ¾* **Real Desire**[285] 6385 4-8-4 **51** oh1.......................... JamesSullivan(5) 5 45
(P Monteith) *cl up: effrt and ev ch over 2f out: wknd over 1f out* **50/1**

546/ **8** *7* **Deal Clincher**[28] 3043 4-8-9 **51** oh5............................ AdrianNicholls 8 31
(M McDonagh, Ire) *bhd: drvn over 3f out: sn btn* **66/1**

0/ **9** *6* **Fikrah**[25] 3138 5-10-0 **70**.. RPCleary 3 38
(Daniel Mark Loughnane, Ire) *hld up: rdn along over 3f out: nvr on terms* **40/1**

20-5 **10** *½* **Dream Of Olwyn (IRE)**[42] 2602 5-9-13 **69**......................... TomEaves 1 36
(J G Given) *led to over 2f out: sn rdn and wknd* **9/1**

2m 8.58s (-3.42) **Going Correction** -0.275s/f (Firm) **10** Ran SP% **113.6**
Speed ratings (Par 103): **102,98,98,97,97 97,94,88,83,83**
toteswingers:1&2:£8.20, 1&3:£4.20, 2&3:£7.30 CSF £39.99 CT £222.12 TOTE £3.00: £1.10, £4.30, £1.60; EX 46.40.
Owner Danethorpe Racing Partnership **Bred** Mulhime Ltd Marston Stud & D Bonnycastle **Trained** Willoughton, Lincs

FOCUS
A modest handicap. Another clear personal best from the winner with the next two to form.

3951 BET NOW AT VICTORCHANDLER.COM APPRENTICE H'CAP 1m 2f
5:00 (5:01) (Class 6) (0-65,62) 3-Y-0 **£2,183** (£644; £322) **Stalls** Low

Form RPR

3-02 **1** **Grams And Ounces**[11] 3582 3-9-10 **62**................................ JPO'Brien 3 67
(Miss Amy Weaver) *cl up: led over 3f out: clr over 1f out: hld on wl fnl f* **6/4**[1]

0006 **2** *1 ¾* **Electric City (IRE)**[27] 3055 3-8-9 **52**............................ NeilFarley(5) 6 54
(M G Quinlan) *in tch: effrt and chsd wnr over 2f out: kpt on ins fnl f* **16/1**

036 **3** *4 ½* **Music Festival (USA)**[24] 3148 3-9-4 **61**......................... PaulNorton(5) 5 54
(J S Goldie) *hld up: hdwy over 2f out: sn no imp* **7/1**

00-1 **4** *1* **Valantino Oyster (IRE)**[34] 2838 3-9-1 **53**........................ DaleSwift 2 44
(J Howard Johnson) *cl up: ev ch over 3f out: sn rdn: lost 2nd and wknd over 2f out* **7/4**[2]

6066 **5** *44* **Miereveld**[6] 3758 3-9-2 **54**.. RosieJessop 1 —
(Sir Mark Prescott) *led to over 3f out: sn rdn and wknd qckly* **5/1**[3]

2m 9.83s (-2.17) **Going Correction** -0.275s/f (Firm) **5** Ran SP% **111.4**
Speed ratings (Par 98): **97,95,92,91,56**
CSF £22.63 TOTE £1.90: £1.10, £8.90; EX 13.20 Place 6 £68.61; Place 5 £30.64.
Owner Miss A Weaver **Bred** Brook Stud Bloodstock Ltd **Trained** Newmarket, Suffolk
■ The first winner outside Ireland for Jospeh O'Brien, son of Aidan.

FOCUS
This was a weak handicap, although the pace was reasonable. With the favourite disappointing the winner had little to beat.
T/Jkpt: Not won. T/Plt: £41.40 to a £1 stake. Pool:£73,184.20 - 1,289.16 winning tickets T/Qpdt: £14.10 to a £1 stake. Pool:£5,408.68 - 282.62 winning tickets RY

2440 FFOS LAS (L-H)
Monday, July 12

OFFICIAL GOING: Good to firm (watered; 8.3)
Wind: Nil Weather: Sunny

3952 O.J. WILLIAMS MAIDEN FILLIES' STKS 6f
2:20 (2:21) (Class 5) 3-Y-0+ **£2,266** (£674; £252; £252) **Stalls** High

Form RPR

4-24 **1** **Pin Cushion**[31] 2928 3-8-12 79.. MartinDwyer 3 71+
(B J Meehan) *ponied to s: mde all: shkn up to stretch clr fnl f: easily* **30/100**[1]

-242 **2** *6* **Admirable Duchess**[21] 3277 3-8-7 68.............................. BillyCray(5) 5 52
(D J S Ffrench Davis) *plld hrd: prom: u.p and outpcd over 2f out: kpt on to take 2nd fnl 120yds: no ch w wnr* **9/2**[2]

/66 **3** *1* **Croeso Mawr**[25] 3125 4-9-4 0.. SebSanders 1 49
(J L Spearing) *dwlt: hld up in rr: rdn 2f out: effrt whn hung lft over 1f out: plugged on but no real threat* **16/1**

-000 **3** *dht* **Thoughtful (IRE)**[15] 3478 3-8-12 48.............................. JimmyFortune 2 49
(J W Hills) *prom: pushed along 2f out: outpcd by wnr over 1f out: lost 2nd fnl 120yds: one pce towards fin* **25/1**

3 **5** *¾* **Mount Acclaim (IRE)**[23] 3210 4-9-4 0........................ FergusSweeney 4 46
(J A Osborne) *hld up: effrt 2f out: hung lft over 1f out whn chsng ldrs: one pce and no imp ins fnl f* **10/1**[3]

1m 10.9s (1.20) **Going Correction** -0.15s/f (Firm)
WFA 3 from 4yo 6lb **5** Ran SP% **113.9**
Speed ratings (Par 100): **86,78,76,76,75**
CSF £2.27 TOTE £1.20: £1.10, £1.70; EX 2.20.
Owner Lady Rothschild **Bred** Kincorth Investments Inc **Trained** Manton, Wilts

FOCUS
A very ordinary maiden, and it was easy for the winner with the runner-up below form.

3953 OWEN FUELS MEDIAN AUCTION MAIDEN STKS 1m 4f (R)
2:50 (2:51) (Class 5) 3-4-Y-0 **£2,266** (£674; £337; £168) **Stalls** Low

Form RPR

-230 **1** **Woodford Belle (USA)**[20] 3298 3-8-8 75....................(b[1]) MartinDwyer 1 78
(B J Meehan) *hld up bhd ldrs: pushed along and outpcd over 3f out: clsd u.p 2f out: led and hung rt fr over 1f out: tail flashed and pressed ins fnl f: kpt on* **9/1**

5- **2** 1 ½ **Western Pearl**[235] 7451 3-8-1 0 ... HarryBentley(7) 4 76
(W J Knight) *prom: pushed along 3f out: rdn to chal 2f out: cl 2nd whn intimidated by wnr and wnt wd over 1f out: ev ch ins fnl f: keeping on whn checked cl home* **11/2**3

0253 **3** 4 **First Fandango**[21] 3273 3-8-13 74 ... SebSanders 5 75
(J W Hills) *prom: lft in ld over 6f out: rdn whn hrd pressed over 2f out: hdd over 1f out: no ex ins fnl f* **2/1**2

4 **4** 3 ¼ **Tweedledrum**[35] 2820 3-8-8 0 ... DavidProbert 2 64
(A M Balding) *hld up: clsd to take 2nd 4f out: rdn 3f out: sn upsides: edgd rt u.p ent fnl 2f: btn over 1f out* **8/1**

222 **P** **Cockney (IRE)**[18] 3355 3-8-13 75 ... JoeFanning 3 —
(M Johnston) *led: wnt wrong and hdd over 6f out: sn p.u* **6/4**1

2m 32.99s (-3.81) **Going Correction** -0.15s/f (Firm) 5 Ran SP% **109.8**
Speed ratings (Par 103): **106,105,102,100,—**
CSF £52.51 TOTE £12.80: £7.00, £5.70; EX 35.00.

Owner Catesby W Clay **Bred** Runnymede Farm Inc Et Al **Trained** Manton, Wilts

FOCUS
The complexion of this middle-distance maiden totally changed when the favourite was pulled up. That slowed up the tempo as he was in front at the time, but the form still looks straightforward enough with the first two coming clear. Modest form.

Cockney(IRE) Official explanation: vet said colt pulled up lame

3954 GULF OIL H'CAP 1m 2f (R)
3:20 (3:20) (Class 5) (0-70,70) 3-Y-0+ **£2,266** (£674; £337; £168) **Stalls** Low

Form RPR

-003 **1** **Shabak Hom (IRE)**[32] 2886 3-9-8 68 ... JoeFanning 5 76+
(D M Simcock) *chsd ldrs: led over 2f out: qcknd up over 1f out: r.o wl and in command fnl f* **4/1**2

41 **2** 2 **Aragall (GER)**[9] 3684 5-9-9 63 ... MatthewDavies(5) 3 67+
(George Baker) *hld up: swtchd rt 2f out: hdwy over 1f out: chsd wnr fnl f but no imp* **11/4**1

1301 **3** 1 **Dane Cottage**[10] 3640 3-8-10 63 ... AdamBeschizza(7) 1 65
(P D Evans) *dwlt: hld up: pushed along 3f out: hdwy over 2f out: rdn to chse ldrs over 1f out: kpt on ins fnl f but nt quite pce of front 2* **14/1**

3664 **4** 1 **Pullyourfingerout (IRE)**[30] 2953 3-9-7 67 ... FergusSweeney 7 67
(B G Powell) *led: rdn and hdd over 2f out: nt qckn over 1f out: kpt on same pce ins fnl f* **11/1**

0-65 **5** ½ **Fame Is The Spur**[54] 2225 3-9-10 70 ... SebSanders 8 69
(J W Hills) *chsd ldr: ev ch over 2f out: outpcd by wnr and lost 2nd 1f out: no ex fnl 100yds* **15/2**

0442 **6** ½ **Fire Raiser**[7] 3739 3-9-0 60 ... JimmyFortune 4 58
(A M Balding) *racd keenly in tch: rdn over 2f out: outpcd over 1f out: n.d after* **11/4**1

050 **7** hd **Sounds Of Thunder**[53] 2250 3-9-5 65 ... MartinDwyer 2 63
(H J L Dunlop) *midfield: rdn over 2f out: no imp: outpcd over 1f out: no imp after* **25/1**

6023 **8** ½ **James Pollard (IRE)**[12] 3559 5-8-12 47 ... (t) DavidProbert 6 44
(B J Llewellyn) *hld up in midfield: rdn over 2f out: wknd fnl f* **7/1**3

2m 7.08s (-1.32) **Going Correction** -0.15s/f (Firm)
WFA 3 from 5yo 11lb 8 Ran SP% **116.4**
Speed ratings (Par 103): **99,97,96,95,95 95,94,94**
toteswingers:1&2:£3.70, 1&3:£8.90, 2&3:£8.50 CSF £15.78 CT £139.53 TOTE £7.80: £1.80, £1.10, £5.20; EX 19.70 Trifecta £128.40 Pool: £310.66 - 1.79 winning units..

Owner Ahmed Ali **Bred** Rabbah Bloodstock Limited **Trained** Newmarket, Suffolk

FOCUS
There was a sound early pace on in this moderate handicap and the form looks sound rated around the placed horses. Another small step up from the winner.

Pullyourfingerout(IRE) Official explanation: jockey said colt hung right

3955 O.J. WILLIAMS HEATING OIL H'CAP 1m 6f (R)
3:50 (3:50) (Class 3) (0-90,89) 4-Y-0+ **£6,476** (£1,927; £963; £481) **Stalls** Low

Form RPR

2311 **1** **Lady Eclair (IRE)**[11] 3588 4-9-7 89 ... JoeFanning 3 97+
(M Johnston) *prom: racd in 2nd pl after 2f tl over 3f out: pushed along whn nt clr run briefly over 2f out: swtchd rt ent fnl 2f: wnt 2nd over 1f out: str chal ins fnl f: nosed ahd fnl 110yds: r.o gamely* **15/8**2

441- **2** hd **Excelsior Academy**[340] 4709 4-8-11 79 ... NickyMackay 4 86
(B J Meehan) *hld up in rr: hdwy to ld over 2f out: rdn over 1f out: narrowly hdd fnl 110yds: r.o u.p* **8/1**

2040 **3** 3 ½ **Cool Strike (UAE)**[23] 3198 4-9-5 87 ... (v) JimmyFortune 2 90
(A M Balding) *led: rdn and hdd over 2f out: stl in cl contention but u.p over 1f out: no ex fnl 100yds: eased whn btn cl home* **10/3**3

0-11 **4** 19 **Lady Hestia (USA)**[56] 2165 5-8-5 73 ... MartinDwyer 5 59
(M P Tregoning) *chsd ldr tl after 2f: u.p fr 5f out: regained 2nd over 3f out: bmpd and lost 2nd over 2f out: sn wknd: eased whn wl btn over 1f out* **6/4**1

2m 58.61s (-5.19) **Going Correction** -0.15s/f (Firm) 4 Ran SP% **109.0**
Speed ratings (Par 107): **108,107,105,95**
CSF £14.07 TOTE £3.00; EX 11.10.

Owner Netherfield House Stud **Bred** Lynch Bages Ltd & Samac Ltd **Trained** Middleham Moor, N Yorks

FOCUS
With three potential front-runners in attendance this good little staying handicap was always going to be fair test. The first two came clear late on. The winner progressed again but the form does not look that solid.

NOTEBOOK
Lady Eclair(IRE) just did enough to make it six wins from her ten career starts, making it 2-2 over C&D in the process. She was up another 5lb and conceding weight all round, but travelled really well in the race. She took time to hit top gear, and had to wait before making her effort around 2f out, but always looked like getting on top at the business end. Unraced as a juvenile, further improvement is impossible to rule out yet and no doubt the Ebor will now come under real consideration for her next month. She does also have a Listed entry at Leopardstown on Thursday and takes her racing very well, so it wouldn't be that surprising to see her make the journey for that. (op 7-4)

Excelsior Academy was having his first run since winning over a shorter trip at Haydock last August. He was resuming off 6lb higher for this return to a winning distance and was the outsider of the field, but his yard had twice won races earlier on the card. He ran a massive race, only just losing out at the finish, and could be the sort to rate higher as a 4-y-o. (op 12-1)

Cool Strike(UAE) was allowed his own way out in front as he seems to prefer. He ensured a fair gallop and gave his all, but was a sitting duck from 2f out and failed to get home like the first pair over this stiffer test. (op 7-2 tchd 4-1 and 3-1)

Lady Hestia(USA) was returning from a 56-day break in this quest to make it six wins from her last eight outings, and got well backed. She was the first beaten, however, and dropped out too early for this to be her true form. Official explanation: jockey said mare ran flat (op 11-8 tchd 5-4)

3956 O.J. WILLIAMS LUBRICANTS H'CAP 1m (R)
4:20 (4:20) (Class 2) (0-100,100) 3-Y-0+ **£9,462** (£2,832; £1,416; £708) **Stalls** Low

Form RPR

1110 **1** **Dajen**[32] 2885 4-8-2 81 oh2 ... LauraPike(7) 2 87+
(D M Simcock) *hld up bhd ldrs: hdwy to ld over 1f out: r.o wl: in command fnl 100yds* **5/1**3

-046 **2** 2 **Aspectus (IRE)**[40] 2651 7-10-0 100 ... FergusSweeney 3 101
(J A Osborne) *sn led: rdn and hdd over 1f out: nt pce of wnr fnl 100yds* **5/1**3

0310 **3** 1 ¼ **Opus Maximus (IRE)**[9] 3692 5-9-3 89 ... JoeFanning 5 87
(M Johnston) *chsd ldr tl c u.p 2f out: outpcd over 1f out: kpt on to take 3rd towards fin: nt pce of ldrs* **9/4**2

-000 **4** nk **Manassas (IRE)**[26] 3069 5-9-10 96 ... MartinDwyer 1 93
(B J Meehan) *racd keenly: hld up bhd ldrs: rdn over 1f out: failed to pick up: no imp* **5/4**1

1m 37.41s (-3.09) **Going Correction** -0.15s/f (Firm) 4 Ran SP% **108.5**
Speed ratings (Par 109): **109,107,105,105**
CSF £25.38 TOTE £6.00; EX 17.10.

Owner Tick Tock Partnership **Bred** Miss D Fleming **Trained** Newmarket, Suffolk

FOCUS
A decent little handicap that was run at a respectable pace. The form is best rated around the runner-up, with the front pair in the market both disappointing.

NOTEBOOK
Dajen, 2lb out of the handicap, bounced back to winning ways and obviously gets on very well with his claiming rider, as the pair have now been successful in three out of four outings. The quick ground was of some concern beforehand, but he handled it without fuss and there was a good bit to like about the manner in which he completed the task. Official explanation: trainer said, regarding apparent improvement of form of the colt, compared with its last run, that on that occasion it was caught wide and ran too freely. (op 11-2 tchd 9-2)

Aspectus(IRE) stepped up nicely on his disappointing run at Nottingham 40 days earlier with a sound effort from the front. This former German Group 3 winner is entitled go forward again from this run, and will probably appreciate getting back on some easier ground. (op 11-2 tchd 13-2 and 9-2)

Opus Maximus(IRE) came under pressure 2f out and was well held by the first pair. This was better than his previous outing at Sandown, but the handicapper probably has him where he wants him at present. (op 13-8)

Manassas(IRE) was faced with an easier assignment than he usually encounters and was strongly supported with his yard in such good form. He was very disappointing, however, and now could be the time to experiment with some form of headgear. Official explanation: vet said gelding was found to have lost its right-fore shoe (op 6-4 tchd 13-8 and 7-4 in places)

3957 BETFAIR RACING EXCELLENCE APPRENTICE TRAINING SERIES H'CAP 1m (R)
4:50 (4:50) (Class 6) (0-65,65) 3-Y-0 **£1,910** (£564; £282) **Stalls** Low

Form RPR

6006 **1** **Scottish Boogie (IRE)**[20] 3297 3-9-7 65 ... AdamBeschizza(3) 3 68
(S Kirk) *in tch: clsd to chse ldr 2f out: r.o to chal ins fnl f: led towards fin* **11/4**1

5452 **2** nk **Catchanova (IRE)**[15] 3478 3-9-2 57 ... AmyScott 5 59
(Eve Johnson Houghton) *led: rdn over 1f out: hrd pressed ins fnl f: worn down towards fin* **4/1**3

-005 **3** 1 ¾ **Princess Seren**[15] 3478 3-8-9 50 ow1 ... DebraEngland 7 48
(B R Millman) *hld up in tch: rdn and nt qckn over 1f out: styd on ins fnl f: nt pce to get to front pair* **8/1**

2224 **4** 1 ¾ **Celtic Ransom**[41] 2619 3-9-3 61 ... HollyHall(3) 2 55
(J W Hills) *s.i.s: hld up: swtchd rt 2f out: hdwy to chse ldrs over 1f out: one pce and no further imp fnl 100yds* **3/1**2

0-00 **5** 1 ½ **Diamondgeezer Luke (IRE)**[42] 2587 3-9-2 62 ... BarryAdams(5) 6 53
(Patrick Morris) *prom: rdn and nt qckn over 2f out: fdd ins fnl f* **5/1**

-404 **6** ¾ **Truly Magic**[15] 3478 3-8-10 54 ... NathanAlison(3) 4 43
(H J L Dunlop) *hld up in rr: rdn over 2f out: no imp on ldrs fnl f* **15/2**

04-0 **7** 8 **Knowledgeable**[20] 3291 3-8-2 46 oh1 ... JamesRogers(3) 1 16
(B Palling) *prom: rdn over 2f out: wknd wl over 1f out* **16/1**

1m 39.82s (-0.68) **Going Correction** -0.15s/f (Firm) 7 Ran SP% **117.1**
Speed ratings (Par 98): **97,96,94,93,91 90,82**
toteswingers:1&2:£3.60, 1&3:£6.80, 2&3:£6.80 CSF £14.71 TOTE £5.00: £2.70, £1.90; EX 21.70 Place 6 £648.74; Place 5 £605.02.

Owner J C Smith **Bred** Littleton Stud **Trained** Upper Lambourn, Berks

■ Stewards' Enquiry : Nathan Alison seven-day ban: used whip in the forehand, contravention of conditions (tbn)

FOCUS
A weak handicap, confined to apprentice riders. The runner-up looks the best guide.
T/Plt: £495.70 to a £1 stake. Pool:£58,136.68 - 85.61 winning tickets T/Qpdt: £75.70 to a £1 stake. Pool:£4,915.28 - 48.04 winning tickets DO

3734 WINDSOR (R-H)
Monday, July 12

OFFICIAL GOING: Good to firm (watered; 8.5)
Wind: Moderate, behind Weather: Fine

3958 TRAILFINDERS TRAVEL EXPERTS APPRENTICE H'CAP 5f 10y
6:10 (6:10) (Class 5) (0-75,73) 3-Y-0+ **£2,729** (£806; £403) **Stalls** High

Form RPR

00 **1** **Caledonia Princess**[33] 2849 4-9-3 62 ... RossAtkinson 1 70
(F J Brennan) *hld up bhd ldrs: prog over 2f out to ld over 1f out: edgd lft but styd on wl* **33/1**

1056 **2** 1 **Key Light (IRE)**[19] 3328 3-9-9 73 ... PaulPickard 2 75
(J W Hills) *settled in last: pushed along after 2f: prog u.p over 1f out: wnt 2nd fnl f: nvr able to chal* **9/2**2

4052 **3** 1 **Triple Dream**[2] 3892 5-9-13 72 ... (p) SimonPearce 9 72
(J M Bradley) *led: hdd and nt qckn over 1f out: kpt on fnl f* **7/2**1

0-04 **4** 1 ½ **Drifting Gold**[13] 3527 6-9-3 62 ... (b) JohnFahy 3 57
(C G Cox) *t.k.h: hld up in tch: prog to chal over 1f out: nt qckn and fdd fnl f* **9/2**2

0456 **5** ¾ **Green Lagonda (AUS)**[7] 3736 8-9-1 64 ... MatthewCosham(4) 6 56
(P D Evans) *pressed ldng pair on wd outside: chal over 1f out: wknd fnl f* **6/1**3

4436 **6** shd **The Tatling (IRE)**[15] 3474 13-9-10 69 ... AshleyMorgan 10 61
(J M Bradley) *chsd ldrs: rdn and outpcd 2f out: plugged on fnl f* **9/1**

0345 **7** 2 ½ **Magical Speedfit (IRE)**[18] 3358 5-9-7 **68**..................... RyanPowell(2) 5 51
(G G Margarson) *towards rr: styd alone against nr side rail fr 1/2-way: nt on terms fr over 1f out* **13/2**

0-50 **8** ¾ **Harry Up**[51] 2310 9-8-12 **59**..................................(tp) DavidKenny(2) 8 39
(Andrew Reid) *w ldr to 2f out: wknd rapidly fnl f* **9/1**

0- **9** 8 **Elhamri**[334] 4907 6-9-10 **73**........................ RichardRowe(4) 4 24
(S Kirk) *propped leaving stalls: rdr lost an iron and nvr regained it: in tch over 3f* **20/1**

59.42 secs (-0.88) **Going Correction** -0.10s/f (Good)
WFA 3 from 4yo+ 5lb **9** Ran SP% **113.9**
Speed ratings (Par 103): **103,101,99,97,96 96,92,90,78**
toteswingers:1&2:£25.30, 1&3:£27.80, 2&3:£2.80 CSF £173.57 CT £669.65 TOTE £42.60: £6.90, £2.50, £1.60; EX 249.10 TRIFECTA Not won..
Owner Isla & Colin Cage **Bred** Mrs I M Cage And C J Cage **Trained** Lambourn, Berks

FOCUS
Unusually, all but one of the field came up the middle of the track, probably because this was an apprentice race rather than any great tactical relevance. The only runner on the stands' rail, Magical Speedfit, never looked likely to win. Moderate form, rated around the runner-up.
Elhamri Official explanation: jockey said he lost an iron

3959 E B F SPORTINGBET.COM MAIDEN STKS 5f 10y
6:40 (6:42) (Class 4) 2-Y-O **£4,209** (£1,252; £625; £312) **Stalls** High

Form RPR

600 **1** **Roman Dancer (IRE)**[42] 2594 2-9-3 0.............................. TomQueally 6 77
(J Gallagher) *pressed ldng pair: rdn to ld ent fnl f: edgd lft but hld on wl* **28/1**

40 **2** ½ **Grandmas Dream**[24] 3141 2-8-12 0.............................. IanMongan 10 70
(G C Bravery) *led 1f against rail: led again 1/2-way: drvn and hdd ent fnl f: edgd lft but kpt on* **11/4**[1]

3 shd **Supercharged (IRE)** 2-8-12 0.............................. AlanMunro 2 70+
(C F Wall) *settled in 9th: prog fr 2f out on outer: clsd on wnr ins fnl f: no ex nr fin* **11/2**[3]

25 **4** ½ **Perfect Pastime**[19] 3332 2-9-3 0.............................. ShaneKelly 4 73
(W R Swinburn) *settled in 7th: pushed along and prog fr 2f out: shkn up and clsd on ldrs fnl f: nvr quite able to chal* **16/1**

4042 **5** 4 ½ **Darwin Star**[19] 3331 2-8-12 0.............................. FrankieDettori 3 52
(D K Ivory) *wnt lft s: gd spd fr wd draw to ld after 1f: hdd 1/2-way: fdd over 1f out* **11/1**

6 **6** nk **Cheers**[34] 2839 2-8-12 0.............................. PatDobbs 8 54+
(R Hannon) *squeezed out sn after s: mostly in last: pushed along and prog fr 2f out: n.d but kpt on* **9/1**

2232 **7** shd **Jambo Bibi (IRE)**[21] 3260 2-8-12 0.............................. RyanMoore 11 50
(R Hannon) *fractious bef ent stalls: tried to match strides w ldr but unable to do so: struggling 2f out: fdd* **5/1**[2]

600 **8** 2 ½ **Ree's Rascal (IRE)**[28] 3034 2-9-3 0.............................. PatCosgrave 5 46
(J R Boyle) *stdd s: mostly in last trio: taken to outer 1/2-way: nvr on terms* **50/1**

06 **9** nse **Place And Chips**[19] 3310 2-9-3 0.............................. RichardKingscote 13 46
(Tom Dascombe) *stmbld s: settled in 8th: effrt and reminder over 1f out: no imp on ldrs* **40/1**

10 1 ¼ **Urban Kode (IRE)** 2-9-3 0.............................. CathyGannon 12 42
(P D Evans) *a wl in rr: shkn up and no prog 2f out* **66/1**

0 **11** 1 ½ **Speightowns Kid (USA)**[27] 3051 2-9-3 0.............. FrankieMcDonald 7 39+
(F J Brennan) *pushed along in 5th: no imp 2f out: wknd and eased fnl f* **5/1**[2]

12 1 ¼ **Pineapple Pete (IRE)** 2-9-3 0.............................. KierenFallon 9 36+
(P F I Cole) *pushed along in 6th: rn green and steadily wknd fr 1/2-way* **12/1**

50 **13** 1 ½ **Regal Rocket (IRE)**[14] 3509 2-8-12 0.............................. DaneO'Neill 1 21
(R Hannon) *a wl in rr: no prog on outer 1/2-way* **33/1**

59.84 secs (-0.46) **Going Correction** -0.10s/f (Good) **13** Ran SP% **119.6**
Speed ratings (Par 96): **99,98,98,97,90 89,89,85,85,83 80,78,76**
toteswingers:1&2:£17.90, 1&3:£19.10, 2&3:£6.70 CSF £102.11 TOTE £21.60: £5.40, £1.10, £3.60; EX 179.30 Trifecta £1030.50 Pool: £2,367.38 - 1.70 winning units..
Owner C R Marks (banbury) **Bred** F Sheedy **Trained** Chastleton, Oxon

FOCUS
More traditionally compared with the first race, the field raced middle-to-stands' side. The first four finished clear, with the rest looking more like nursery types than potential maiden winners. Solid but limited form.

NOTEBOOK
Roman Dancer(IRE), down the field in three previous maidens on good-quality tracks, continued in maiden company rather than heading to nurseries, and it paid dividends, as did the return to 5f. The fact that he had been gelded following his previous run may also have been significant, and connections may now aim high - with the Solario Stakes at Sandown a possible target. (op 33-1)
Grandmas Dream, though not quite able to live up to favouritism, has done well enough in her three races to suggest she can soon make amends. She is now eligible for a handicap mark, but a routine maiden is still within reach. (op 10-3 tchd 7-2 and 5-2)
Supercharged(IRE) ◆, a 28,000gnsIffraaj half-sister to a 7f winner, impressed on the way to post and won plenty of admirers in the race, too. This was a debut full of promise, and she ought to win soon. (op 13-2 tchd 15-2 and 8-1 in a place)
Perfect Pastime finished close enough to suggest that he could still win a maiden, though the drop to 5f looked a bit sharp for him. However, he is now able to run in nurseries and that provides another option. (op 14-1)
Darwin Star continues to show some ability, this time from an unhelpful stall, and would be interesting in a nursery. (op 9-1)
Cheers looks to be one for nurseries over a slightly longer trip when she is qualified. (op 15-2 tchd 7-1)
Jambo Bibi(IRE), making a belated turf debut, has not looked a strong finisher, but to be fair she is being pushed to the limit in maidens and deserves a chance in nurseries. (op 9-2 tchd 11-2 in a place)
Place And Chips Official explanation: jockey said colt stumbled leaving stalls
Speightowns Kid(USA) was never going but is capable of better if his debut was any guide. Official explanation: trainer's rep said colt was unsuited by the good to firm ground (op 7-1 tchd 9-1 in a place)

3960 TRAILFINDERS, TAILORMADE TRAVEL WORLDWIDE (S) STKS 1m 3f 135y
7:10 (7:10) (Class 6) 3-4-Y-O **£1,910** (£564; £282) **Stalls** Centre

Form RPR

3003 **1** **Larkrise Star**[12] 3564 3-8-4 59 ow3.......................... WilliamCarson(3) 13 51+
(D K Ivory) *hld up in midfield on inner: 6th over 4f out: gng much bttr than rest whn prog 3f out: drvn to chal fnl f: hung rt and led nr fin* **8/1**[3]

00-0 **2** nk **Rockweiller**[63] 1977 3-8-9 54..................................(b) WilliamBuick 6 53
(C R Egerton) *mostly pressed ldr: cajoled along to chal over 2f out: narrow ld over 1f out: hdd nr fin and bmpd twice* **16/1**

2004 **3** 1 **Playful Asset (IRE)**[76] 1606 4-9-8 50.............................. KierenFallon 3 51
(P Howling) *hld up towards rr: prog to 7th over 4f out: drvn to cl on ldrs over 1f out: nrly upsides ent fnl f: nt qckn* **16/1**

-000 **4** 2 ¼ **Duke Of Normandy (IRE)**[18] 3360 4-9-8 43..............(p) TomQueally 10 47
(B P J Baugh) *led: hrd pressed fr over 2f out: narrowly hdd over 1f out: losing pl whn sltly squeezed out jst ins fnl f* **28/1**

5144 **4** dht **Frameit (IRE)**[7] 3724 3-9-0 62..(b) LiamKeniry 1 52+
(J S Moore) *hld up towards rr: 11th over 4f out: prog over 2f out: str reminders over 1f out: swtchd to rail and styd on: nrst fin* **8/1**[3]

0000 **6** hd **Massachusetts**[10] 3614 3-8-9 44..............................(b[1]) PatCosgrave 16 47
(B J Meehan) *trckd ldng pair: rdn over 3f out: styd chsng ldrs u.p: kpt on* **40/1**

304 **7** 3 **Kathindi (IRE)**[10] 3640 3-9-0 60.............................. RyanMoore 2 47
(J S Moore) *trckd ldrs: 4th over 4f out: drvn to chal over 2f out: upsides over 1f out: wknd rapidly fnl f* **8/1**[3]

5200 **8** ¾ **Oak Leaves**[16] 3444 3-8-1 53 ow2.............................. JohnFahy(5) 7 37
(J G Portman) *trckd ldng quartet: rdn 4f out: steadily fdd fr 2f out* **11/1**

0-05 **9** 1 **Pollan Bay (IRE)**[4] 3820 3-8-4 50.............................. SophieDoyle(5) 11 39
(Ms J S Doyle) *hld up in last trio: rdn 3f out: v modest late prog* **66/1**

5604 **10** ½ **Bagutta Sun**[17] 3388 4-9-3 72.............................. RichardKingscote 14 33
(Tom Dascombe) *nvr bttr than midfield: 9th over 4f out: rdn and no prog 3f out* **11/4**[1]

0-06 **11** 2 **Silvermine Bay (IRE)**[10] 3640 3-8-4 44 ow5............. RossAtkinson(5) 4 34
(A P Jarvis) *hld up: 10th over 4f out: sn rdn: struggling over 2f out* **100/1**

0065 **12** 3 ¼ **Federal Reserve**[23] 3213 3-8-9 47.............................. NeilChalmers 8 29
(M Madgwick) *a in last quartet: rdn and no prog 3f out* **66/1**

-064 **13** ¾ **Shoot The Pot (IRE)**[9] 3689 3-8-9 60........................(b[1]) JimCrowley 12 28
(R M Beckett) *hld up in midfield: 8th over 4f out: gng wl enough over 3f out: sn shkn up and wknd* **4/1**[2]

5303 **14** 6 **Sultan's Choice**[7] 3728 3-8-4 52..............................(b[1]) CathyGannon 15 12
(P D Evans) *a in last quartet: struggling over 3f out: sn bhd* **9/1**

00 **15** 19 **Belvidera**[24] 3176 4-8-10 0.............................. RyanPowell(7) 9 —
(Mrs C A Dunnett) *a wl in rr: dropped to last and lost tch 5f out: t.o* **66/1**

2m 30.34s (0.84) **Going Correction** -0.05s/f (Good)
WFA 3 from 4yo 13lb **15** Ran SP% **121.5**
Speed ratings (Par 101): **95,94,94,92,92 92,90,90,89,89 87,85,85,81,68**
toteswingers:1&2:£26.60, 1&3:£15.40, 2&3:£102.90 CSF £125.44 TOTE £10.90: £3.00, £4.80, £2.90; EX 135.40 TRIFECTA Not won..There was no bid for the winner. Bagutta Sun was claimed by B Leavy. Frameit was claimed by T Vaughan. Massachusetts was claimed by B Powell. Rockweiller was claimed by P D Evans. Shoot The Pot was claimed by D Penman. All above claimed for £5,000.
Owner Dean Ivory **Bred** D K Ivory **Trained** Radlett, Herts
■ Stewards' Enquiry : William Carson three-day ban: careless riding (Jul 26,27,29)

FOCUS
There was a medium pace, which steadied a bit around the bend until quickening again 4f out. The race then culminated in a rough finish, with the first-past-the-post carrying the runner-up left-handed and bumping him near the finish, so an inquiry was inevitable. Though it was possible to make a case for reversing the placings, the margin of a neck will have helped make up the stewards' minds in allowing the result to stand. Unconvincing and weak form.

3961 SPORTINGBET.COM MAIDEN STKS 6f
7:40 (7:41) (Class 5) 2-Y-O **£2,729** (£806; £403) **Stalls** High

Form RPR

4 **1** **Face The Problem (IRE)**[59] 2077 2-9-3 0.......................... MichaelHills 3 78
(B W Hills) *dwlt: tk fierce hold: led after 2f: in command and pushed along over 1f out: hung bdly lft fnl f: ld dwindling qckly at fin* **4/1**[3]

2 ¾ **Ardour (IRE)** 2-9-3 0.............................. RyanMoore 5 76+
(R Hannon) *t.k.h: trckd ldng trio: shkn up 2f out: styd on wl to take 2nd ins fnl f: clsng at fin* **4/1**[3]

2 **3** 1 **Harry Luck (IRE)**[16] 3459 2-9-3 0.............................. DaneO'Neill 13 73
(H Candy) *led 2f: rdn and nt qckn over 2f out: styd on wl again fnl f* **11/4**[2]

2 **4** nk **Hokoumah (USA)**[21] 3274 2-9-3 0.............................. FrankieDettori 10 72
(Saeed Bin Suroor) *prom: chsd wnr 1/2-way: rdn over 2f out: no imp over 1f out: one pce* **9/4**[1]

5 1 ¾ **Mon Visage** 2-8-12 0.............................. AlanMunro 8 62+
(C F Wall) *chsd ldrs in 6th: pushed along and no imp 2f out: kpt on steadily fnl f* **20/1**

6 1 ½ **Hero From Zero (IRE)** 2-9-3 0.............................. PatCosgrave 7 62
(B J Meehan) *trckd ldng quartet: rdn over 2f out: stl chsng and in tch over 1f out: fdd* **40/1**

0 **7** 4 ½ **Sea The Flames (IRE)**[7] 3735 2-9-3 0.............................. PatDobbs 16 49+
(M P Tregoning) *chsd ldrs in 7th: rdn bef 1/2-way: outpcd over 2f out* **50/1**

34 **8** ¾ **Mega Mount (IRE)**[12] 3555 2-9-3 0.............................. JimCrowley 2 46
(R M Beckett) *dwlt: off the pce and wl in rr: no ch fr over 2f out* **16/1**

9 2 ¼ **Blue Vinney** 2-8-10 0.............................. KatiaScallan(7) 9 40
(M P Tregoning) *a towards rr: pushed along and wl outpcd fr over 2f out: no ch after* **40/1**

10 3 ½ **Only Ten Per Cent (IRE)** 2-8-10 0.............................. RyanPowell(7) 4 29
(J S Moore) *scratchy to post: dwlt: wl bhd in last pair: v modest late prog* **100/1**

11 2 ¼ **Dances With Words (IRE)** 2-9-3 0.............................. IanMongan 6 22
(R A Farrant) *nvr on terms w ldrs: wl outpcd fr over 2f out: no ch after* **80/1**

12 nk **Iwantobreakfree** 2-9-3 0.............................. CathyGannon 12 21
(P D Evans) *a wl in rr and struggling fr 1/2-way* **66/1**

13 3 **Appyjack** 2-9-3 0.............................. LiamKeniry 15 12
(J S Moore) *s.v.s: a in last pair and wl bhd* **50/1**

14 ¾ **Ishikawa (IRE)** 2-9-3 0.............................. TomQueally 11 10
(A King) *dwlt: rchd abt 8th after 2f but nvr on terms: wknd 2f out* **40/1**

1m 13.0s **Going Correction** -0.10s/f (Good) **14** Ran SP% **123.0**
Speed ratings (Par 94): **96,95,93,93,90 88,82,81,78,74 71,70,66,65**
toteswingers:1&2:£5.70, 1&3:£4.70, 2&3:£5.40 CSF £19.71 TOTE £5.20: £1.70, £2.10, £1.90; EX 23.30 Trifecta £79.90 Pool: £608.01 - 5.63 winning units..
Owner Sir A Ferguson,Cavendish InvLtd,J Hanson **Bred** J Joyce **Trained** Lambourn, Berks

FOCUS
Even though the winner soon ensured a good gallop, it proved impossible to come from behind and prominent runners dominated. However, they were probably just the best horses in the race. A good second effort from the winner and a nice debut by the runner-up. The favourite was a bit below form.

NOTEBOOK
Face The Problem(IRE) had shown promise on his debut and he looks progressive, since he was too headstrong early on and hung across the track in the last furlong. When he gets his act completely together, he should develop into a useful juvenile. Jockey Michael Hills, pleased that he had overcome his low stall, reported that he "needs to come on and has to get up the ladder" to justify his Gimcrack entry, but that he is "very quick and a nice horse for the future". (op 6-1)

Ardour(IRE), a 100,000gns Danehill Dancer newcomer, is bred to be a speedy juvenile and this was a promising start to his career. He is comfortably capable of winning a maiden but he is in the right hands to have a tilt at something a bit more ambitious. (op 7-2 tchd 10-3)

Harry Luck(IRE), putting in his second sound run in two attempts, has chased home some potentially smart sorts. He is good enough to win a maiden, and success of some sort should come soon. (op 3-1 tchd 5-2)

Hokoumah(USA) followed up his encouraging debut on Polytrack with a solid first performance on turf. He is unlikely to be a stable star but should win races. (op 5-2 tchd 3-1 in a place)

Mon Visage, a 40,000gns Ishiguru debutante and the only filly in the field, made a satisfactory debut. She can do better with experience.

Hero From Zero(IRE), a 40,000euros son of Invincible Spirit, showed something for the future considering there are winners from 7f-1m4f in the family, so he is likely to improve with time. (op 50-1)

3962 TF FOR EXCEPTIONAL VALUE HOLIDAYS FILLIES' H'CAP — 1m 67y

8:10 (8:10) (Class 4) (0-80,80) 3-Y-O+ — **£4,533** (£1,348; £674; £336) **Stalls** High

Form — RPR

0-1 **1** **Hidden Fire**[73] 1661 3-9-3 **73** ... KierenFallon 7 — 80+
(D R C Elsworth) *cl up: pushed along over 3f out: effrt on outer over 2f out: led over 1f out: drvn and a holding off rivals* **11/2**[3]

2353 **2** 3/4 **My Best Bet**[12] 3565 4-10-0 **75** ... TomQueally 6 — 82
(Stef Higgins) *hld up in tch: effrt gng strly over 2f out: drvn to chse wnr ent fnl f: styd on but a hld* **9/2**[2]

3614 **3** shd **Ela Gorrie Mou**[16] 3457 4-9-13 **74** ... RobertWinston 5 — 81
(P Charalambous) *prom: wnt 2nd 5f out: led over 2f out: rdn and hdd over 1f out: hung lft but styd on* **15/8**[1]

3402 **4** 2 1/2 **Russian Rave**[16] 3458 4-8-13 **65** ... JohnFahy(5) 4 — 66
(J G Portman) *stdd s: t.k.h: hld up in 6th: prog to go 3rd over 3f out: rdn to chal 2f out: nt qckn over 1f out: fdd* **16/1**

0000 **5** 1 1/4 **Dubai Gem**[24] 3160 4-8-9 **56** oh4 ... DaneO'Neill 8 — 54
(Jamie Poulton) *trckd ldr to 5f out: styd in tch: shkn up over 2f out: grad outpcd* **12/1**

641- **6** 6 **Levitation (IRE)**[196] 7863 4-9-7 **68** ... FergusSweeney 3 — 53
(W S Kittow) *led: hdd and shkn up over 2f out: wknd and eased* **16/1**

5022 **7** 1 3/4 **Red Yarn**[8] 3714 3-8-13 **69** ... (b) RyanMoore 1 — 48
(G L Moore) *hld up in last pair: rdn 3f out: no prog and sn btn* **9/2**[2]

321- **8** 6 **Vegas Palace (IRE)**[242] 7351 3-9-8 **78** ... RichardKingscote 2 — 43
(Tom Dascombe) *fractious to post: hld up in last pair: shkn up 3f out: sn dropped out* **10/1**

1m 44.47s (-0.23) **Going Correction** -0.05s/f (Good)
WFA 3 from 4yo 9lb — **8** Ran SP% **115.1**
Speed ratings (Par 105): **99,98,98,95,94 88,86,80**
toteswingers:1&2:£4.60, 1&3:£3.10, 2&3:£2.40 CSF £30.61 CT £63.06 TOTE £4.70: £2.70, £2.70, £1.10; EX 33.90 Trifecta £91.20 Pool: £548.48 - 4.44 winning units..

Owner J C Smith **Bred** Littleton Stud **Trained** Newmarket, Suffolk

FOCUS

The modest pace would not have been ideal for the winner, so she deserves extra credit for overcoming that disadvantage. The form makes sense, with the winner up 6lb.

Red Yarn Official explanation: jockey said filly hung badly right

3963 TRAILFINDERS AWARD WINNING SERVICE H'CAP — 1m 2f 7y

8:40 (8:40) (Class 5) (0-75,75) 3-Y-O — **£2,729** (£806; £403) **Stalls** Centre

Form — RPR

-104 **1** **On Her Way**[11] 3606 3-9-2 **70** ... IanMongan 8 — 83
(H R A Cecil) *led 2f: pressed ldr: led over 3f out: shkn up over 2f out: pushed along and styd on stoutly fr over 1f out* **9/1**

2253 **2** 1 1/4 **Sunley Spinalonga**[14] 3514 3-8-8 **62** ... DaneO'Neill 5 — 72
(D R C Elsworth) *hld up in tch: prog over 2f out: rdn to chse wnr over 1f out: styd on but no imp* **8/1**

5362 **3** hd **Spice Fair**[18] 3376 3-8-11 **65** ... JimCrowley 3 — 75
(M D I Usher) *hld up last: stl there but gng easily 3f out: prog wl over 1f out to take 3rd fnl f: styd on* **11/4**[1]

3613 **4** 4 1/2 **Tamtara**[18] 3363 3-9-7 **75** ... PatCosgrave 6 — 76
(Mrs A J Perrett) *cl up: disp 2nd over 2f out u.p: wknd over 1f out* **14/1**

0-43 **5** 1/2 **Jubail (IRE)**[21] 3272 3-9-0 **68** ... FergusSweeney 1 — 68
(A King) *hld up in tch and racd wd: prog to press ldrs over 3f out: chsd wnr over 2f out to over 1f out: wknd* **9/2**[3]

4014 **6** 3 3/4 **Onyx Of Arabia (IRE)**[24] 3155 3-9-6 **74** ... (b) KierenFallon 7 — 67
(B J Meehan) *awkward s: hld up in tch: hmpd over 2f out: lft bhd sn after and no ch* **3/1**[2]

1-30 **7** 3/4 **If I Were A Boy (IRE)**[59] 2079 3-9-1 **69** ... (p) RyanMoore 9 — 60
(D J S Ffrench Davis) *cl up: shkn up over 2f out: steadily wknd* **11/1**

4-00 **8** 23 **Dashing Doc (IRE)**[28] 3039 3-9-4 **72** ... RobertWinston 10 — 17
(D R C Elsworth) *pushed up to ld after 2f at mod pce: rdn and hdd over 3f out: hanging and losing pl qckly whn hmpd over 2f out: virtually p.u fnl f* **14/1**

0000 **9** 34 **Rocky Mood (IRE)**[20] 3297 3-8-12 **66** ... ShaneKelly 2 — —
(W R Swinburn) *prom on outer: lost pl over 4f out: in rr whn veered wildly lft 2f out: virtually p.u after* **20/1**

2m 8.00s (-0.70) **Going Correction** -0.05s/f (Good) — **9** Ran SP% **117.4**
Speed ratings (Par 100): **100,99,98,95,94 91,91,72,45**
toteswingers:1&2:£10.30, 1&3:£6.40, 2&3:£6.90 CSF £79.76 CT £253.00 TOTE £11.10: £4.00, £2.40, £1.10; EX 96.10 Trifecta £350.20 Pool: £520.62 - 1.10 winning units. Place 6 £112.00; Place 5 £53.65.

Owner Malih L Al Basti **Bred** Whatton Manor Stud **Trained** Newmarket, Suffolk

FOCUS

The pace was weak, and the winner was in the right place when the tempo increased 3f out. Ordinary form, rated around the second and third.

Onyx Of Arabia(IRE) Official explanation: jockey said colt suffered interference in running and never travelled

If I Were A Boy(IRE) Official explanation: jockey said filly suffered interference and never travelled

T/Plt: £192.50 to a £1 stake. Pool:£91,833.38 - 348.17 winning tickets T/Qpdt: £35.10 to a £1 stake. Pool:£7,461.57 - 156.94 winning tickets JN

3762 WOLVERHAMPTON (A.W) (L-H)

Monday, July 12

OFFICIAL GOING: Standard changing to standard to fast after race 1 (6:20)

Wind: Light against Weather: Overcast

3964 EQUINE RESCUE SERVICES MAIDEN AUCTION STKS — 5f 216y(P)

6:20 (6:22) (Class 5) 2-Y-O — **£2,388** (£705; £352) **Stalls** Low

Form — RPR

1 **Tedsmore Dame** 2-8-8 0 ... LukeMorris 4 — 76+
(J W Unett) *chsd ldrs: rdn and hung lft over 1f out: r.o to ld and hung lft wl ins fnl f* **20/1**

2 1 **Major Muscari (IRE)** 2-8-13 0 ... JamesDoyle 5 — 78+
(A J McCabe) *led: hdd over 4f out: chsd ldr: led again over 1f out: rdn and hdd wl ins fnl f* **6/1**[3]

3 **3** 1 **Heartbreak**[18] 3353 2-8-11 0 ... JimmyQuinn 6 — 73+
(R A Fahey) *chsd ldr: led over 4f out: rdn and hdd over 1f out: styd on same pce ins fnl f* **7/4**[1]

24 **4** 3 1/2 **Restless Bay (IRE)**[10] 3624 2-8-13 0 ... JackMitchell 8 — 65
(R Hollinshead) *mid-div: hdwy over 2f out: rdn over 1f out: styd on same pce* **2/1**[2]

5 3 1/2 **Microlight** 2-8-9 0 ... DavidAllan 10 — 50+
(T D Easterby) *in rr: hdwy over 2f out: wknd fnl f* **33/1**

6 nk **Polar Auroras** 2-8-4 0 ... AndreaAtzeni 13 — 49+
(Pat Eddery) *sn outpcd: styd on fr over 1f out: nvr nrr* **33/1**

40 **7** 2 3/4 **Palindromic (IRE)**[23] 3204 2-8-11 0 ... JamieSpencer 12 — 43
(J R Gask) *chsd ldrs: rdn over 2f out: wknd over 1f out* **14/1**

8 1/2 **Imaginary World (IRE)** 2-8-8 0 ... RichardMullen 9 — 38
(E S McMahon) *s.i.s: hdwy 5f out: wknd over 2f out* **12/1**

5 **9** 1 **Bradbury (IRE)**[66] 1886 2-8-11 0 ... FrannyNorton 1 — 38
(J D Bethell) *prom: pushed along 1/2-way: wknd over 2f out* **28/1**

10 1/2 **King Cobra (IRE)** 2-8-9 0 ... SimonWhitworth 2 — 35
(J W Hills) *s.i.s: outpcd* **66/1**

11 1 **May's Boy** 2-8-9 0 ... HayleyTurner 7 — 32
(M D I Usher) *rn green and sn outpcd* **100/1**

12 3 3/4 **Near The Mark (IRE)** 2-8-11 0 ... StephenCraine 3 — 23
(M Wigham) *chsd ldrs tl wknd over 2f out* **50/1**

0 **13** 22 **Our Folly**[69] 1793 2-8-9 0 ... ChrisCatlin 11 — —
(W S Kittow) *sn outpcd: t.o* **66/1**

1m 13.97s (-1.03) **Going Correction** -0.25s/f (Stan) — **13** Ran SP% **118.4**
Speed ratings (Par 94): **96,94,93,88,84 83,79,79,77,77 75,70,41**
toteswingers:1&2:£20.40, 1&3:£11.10, 2&3:£4.60 CSF £129.01 TOTE £19.10: £6.90, £1.10, £1.40; EX 169.30.

Owner Guyzance Hall Ltd **Bred** Bearstone Stud And T Herbert Jackson **Trained** Tedsmore Hall, Shropshire

FOCUS

Probably just an ordinary maiden which was run at an even pace, with the first two home both debutants. The form is rated around the third, the fourth and the race averages.

NOTEBOOK

Tedsmore Dame, easy to back beforehand, stayed on strongly close home after travelling well throughout. Bought for £22,000 in April, she should stay 7f in due course and can go on from this pleasing performance. (op 25-1)

Major Muscari(IRE) attracted support in the betting, and he also ran with promise. Although he looked to know his job here, he can go one better next time, in similar company. (op 8-1 tchd 10-1)

Heartbreak, from a stable bang among the winners, travelled well throughout and looks to have a future. Coming from a speedy pedigree, he might be worth a try back at 5f. (op 15-8 tchd 2-1 and 11-8)

Restless Bay(IRE), who had shown ability on both starts before this, never appeared happy on this surface. He can be forgiven this and would still appeal in a modest nursery later in the season. (op 7-4 tchd 13-8 and 5-2)

Microlight, also coming from a yard going well, got the hang of things late on after running green, and showed he has ability and can make his mark at some point.

Polar Auroras didn't help himself with a slow start. (op 40-1)

3965 SPONSOR A RACE BY CALLING 01902 390000 H'CAP — 1m 5f 194y(P)

6:50 (6:55) (Class 6) (0-65,71) 4-Y-O+ — **£1,706** (£503; £252) **Stalls** Low

Form — RPR

3306 **1** **Moscow Oznick**[8] 2966 5-9-3 **61** ... (v) AndreaAtzeni 1 — 67
(D Donovan) *sn led: hdd wl over 10f out: chsd ldrs: wnt 2nd again over 5f out: rdn to ld over 1f out: styd on u.p* **20/1**

1-45 **2** 1/2 **Saute**[26] 3084 4-9-5 **63** ... ChrisCatlin 5 — 69
(W R Swinburn) *chsd ldrs: pushed along 4f out: rdn over 2f out: styd on u.p to go 2nd nr fin* **5/2**[1]

1500 **3** 1/2 **Two Oclock John**[26] 3084 4-9-2 **60** ... JackMitchell 3 — 65
(H J Collingridge) *chsd ldrs: rdn and ev ch over 1f out: styd on: lost 2nd nr fin* **8/1**

-046 **4** 1/2 **Snowberry Hill (USA)**[8] 3709 7-8-6 **50** ... JimmyQuinn 7 — 54
(Lucinda Featherstone) *hld up: hdwy to ld over 10f out: rdn and hdd over 1f out: styd on same pce ins fnl f* **14/1**

2565 **5** 3/4 **Lisbon Lion (IRE)**[8] 3709 5-8-7 **51** ... FrannyNorton 10 — 54
(James Moffatt) *dwlt: sn latched on to the rr of the field: hld up: hdwy over 3f out: rdn over 1f out: styd on same pce ins fnl f* **7/2**[2]

6254 **6** 3 1/4 **Street Runner**[10] 3639 4-8-13 **57** ... (p) JerryO'Dwyer 4 — 56
(R Hollinshead) *hld up: rdn over 3f out: styd on ins fnl f: nvr nrr* **12/1**

5042 **7** 3/4 **Sir Sandicliffe (IRE)**[10] 3639 6-8-6 **55** ... KierenFox(5) 8 — 53
(W M Brisbourne) *broke wl: sn stdd to chse ldrs: outpcd over 3f out: rdn and hung lft over 1f out: n.d after* **8/1**

3-30 **8** 3/4 **Dee Cee Elle**[19] 3324 6-8-3 **47** ... (p) LukeMorris 12 — 44
(D Burchell) *s.s: hld up: rdn over 2f out: n.d* **20/1**

6/00 **9** 4 **Pertemps Networks**[27] 3060 6-8-10 **61** ... DavidSimmonson(7) 9 — 52
(M W Easterby) *plld hrd: w ldr: led wl over 10f out: sn hdd: chsd ldr to over 5f out: rdn and wknd over 2f out* **20/1**

5161 **10** nk **City Stable (IRE)**[6] 3760 5-9-13 **71** 6ex ... JamieMackay 13 — 62
(M Wigham) *hld up: a in rr: eased over 1f out* **4/1**[3]

3m 2.32s (-3.68) **Going Correction** -0.25s/f (Stan) — **10** Ran SP% **121.7**
Speed ratings (Par 101): **100,99,99,99,98 96,96,96,93,93**
totewingers:1&2:£4.10, 1&3:£25.00, 2&3:£5.80 CSF £71.06 CT £444.45 TOTE £19.60: £5.40, £1.02, £4.90; EX 84.70.

Owner W P Flynn **Bred** Llety Stud **Trained** Newmarket, Suffolk

The Form Book, Raceform Ltd, Compton, RG20 6NL

FOCUS
The going was changed from standard to fast before this run-of-the-mill 46-65 handicap. The early pace was steady to say the least and the first five home were well clear of the remainder. The winner is rated back to his January form.

3966 ENJOY THE PARTY PACK GROUP OFFER (S) STKS 5f 20y(P)
7:20 (7:22) (Class 6) 3-4-Y-O £1,706 (£503; £252) Stalls Low

Form RPR
5605 1 **Avonvalley**[38] 2688 3-8-9 69 TomMcLaughlin 5 64
(M S Saunders) *led: hdd over 4f out: chsd ldrs: rdn to ld ins fnl f: r.o* **5/1**[2]
3021 2 1 **Romantic Queen**[6] 3763 4-9-0 58 (t) MatthewDavies(5) 11 67
(George Baker) *hld up: hdwy over 1f out: sn rdn: r.o* **9/4**[1]
6556 3 2 ½ **Desert Strike**[6] 3763 4-8-12 57 DuilioDaSilva(7) 2 58
(P F I Cole) *trckd ldrs: rdn over 1f out: r.o: wnt 3rd nr fin* **7/1**
0650 4 hd **Itsthursdayalready**[9] 3685 3-9-0 60 (b) FrannyNorton 1 56
(J G Given) *hld up: hdwy over 1f out: r.o* **6/1**[3]
0150 5 hd **Pressed For Time (IRE)**[20] 3293 4-9-5 53 (vt) EddieCreighton 7 57
(E J Creighton) *prom: chsd ldr over 3f out: rdn to ld over 1f out: hdd and unable qck ins fnl f: lost 2 pls nr fin* **16/1**
-000 6 1 ½ **Mata Hari Blue**[6] 3762 4-9-0 57 JerryO'Dwyer 8 47
(J R Holt) *mid-div: hdwy 1/2-way: rdn over 1f out: hung lft and styd on same pce fnl f* **14/1**
0630 7 2 ¼ **Imperial House**[65] 1923 4-9-10 65 (b) LukeMorris 4 49
(R A Harris) *hld up: rdn 1/2-way: styd on ins fnl f: nrst fin* **25/1**
0366 8 2 **Duke Of Rainford**[20] 3287 3-9-5 55 JamieSpencer 9 39
(M Herrington) *s.i.s: hld up: swtchd rt over 1f out: nvr on terms* **14/1**
6325 9 ¾ **Blue Zephyr**[21] 3276 3-9-0 57 (b) EddieAhern 3 32
(W R Muir) *prom: rdn 2f out: wknd fnl f* **8/1**
06 10 ½ **Octaviana**[12] 3554 3-8-9 0 DavidAllan 13 25
(E J Alston) *s.i.s: hld up: nvr on terms* **100/1**
11 ½ **Wizzacus** 3-8-9 0 JamesDoyle 10 23
(P D Evans) *s.i.s: sn outpcd* **66/1**
/05- 12 2 **Makaykla**[357] 4137 4-9-0 55 LeeVickers 12 18
(M W Easterby) *s.i.s: sn pushed along: wknd 1/2-way* **50/1**
0400 13 ¾ **Trick Or Two**[20] 3286 4-9-5 53 (b) JimmyQuinn 6 20
(Mrs R A Carr) *led over 4f out: rdn and hdd over 1f out: wknd ins fnl f* **12/1**

60.81 secs (-1.49) **Going Correction** -0.25s/f (Stan)
WFA 3 from 4yo 5lb 13 Ran SP% **120.5**
Speed ratings (Par 101): **101,99,95,95,94 92,88,85,84,83 82,79,78**
toteswingers:1&2:£3.50, 1&3:£11.30, 2&3:£4.20 CSF £16.45 TOTE £7.50: £2.80, £2.10, £1.80; EX 19.30.The winner was sold to George Baker for 5,750gns.
Owner Chris Scott **Bred** Ercan Dogan **Trained** Green Ore, Somerset

FOCUS
Three previous course winners in this sprint seller, which was run at a furious pace. It's unlikely to throw up many future winners but the form makes sense.

3967 STAY AT THE WOLVERHAMPTON HOLIDAY INN CLASSIFIED CLAIMING STKS 1m 4f 50y(P)
7:50 (7:50) (Class 6) 3-Y-0+ £1,706 (£503; £252) Stalls Low

Form RPR
0002 1 **Alternative Choice (USA)**[21] 3278 4-9-8 53 GeorgeBaker 11 61
(N P Littmoden) *stdd s: hld up: hdwy on outside over 2f out: rdn to ld wl ins fnl f* **14/1**
0-10 2 nk **Gamesters Lady**[74] 1635 7-9-9 56 (b) EddieAhern 5 61
(Jim Best) *led over 6f: chsd ldr tl led again over 1f out: sn rdn and edgd lft: hdd wl ins fnl f* **9/4**[1]
2040 3 hd **Great Bounder (CAN)**[12] 3559 4-8-10 53 RyanClark(7) 8 55
(Michael Blake) *chsd ldr tl led over 5f out: rdn and hdd over 1f out: r.o* **12/1**
0066 4 shd **Resplendent Ace (IRE)**[21] 3278 6-9-5 60 JimmyQuinn 6 57
(P Howling) *hld up: hdwy and hmpd over 2f out: rdn over 1f out: r.o* **10/1**
4004 5 nk **Holyfield Warrior (IRE)**[14] 3521 6-8-13 52 KierenFox(5) 2 55
(R J Smith) *mid-div: hdwy over 3f out: rdn and swtchd lft over 1f out: r.o* **12/1**
-630 6 ½ **Annambo**[21] 3278 10-9-0 58 (v) RussKennemore(3) 7 54
(Andrew Reid) *hld up: hdwy over 2f out: rdn over 1f out: r.o* **14/1**
-014 7 shd **Othello (IRE)**[32] 2908 3-8-12 57 (b[1]) ChrisCatlin 10 61+
(E F Vaughan) *s.i.s: sn pushed along into mid-div: rdn and hmpd over 2f out: r.o ins fnl f* **9/1**[3]
5053 8 1 ½ **Royal Torbo (ISR)**[105] 1054 3-8-4 57 MatthewDavies(5) 3 56
(George Baker) *chsd ldrs: rdn over 2f out: edgd rt over 1f out: styd on* **16/1**
5-14 9 ¾ **Pure Crystal**[4] 3819 4-9-5 54 (b) JerryO'Dwyer 4 52
(M G Quinlan) *hld up: rdn over 2f out: styd on fr over 1f out: nt trble ldrs* **4/1**[2]
0546 10 1 ¼ **Back To Paris (IRE)**[57] 2142 8-9-3 57 (t) AndrewMullen 9 48
(P A Kirby) *trckd ldrs: racd keenly: rdn over 1f out: btn whn hmpd ins fnl f* **10/1**
0/6 11 ½ **Gold Ring**[37] 2752 10-8-13 60 (t) MichaelStainton(3) 1 46
(Mark Gillard) *hld up: rdn over 2f out: nvr on terms* **28/1**
-600 12 5 **Lilly Royal (IRE)**[26] 3084 4-9-0 52 (v[1]) DeclanCannon(5) 12 41
(B Palling) *prom: rdn over 2f out: wkng whn hung lft over 1f out* **40/1**

2m 39.77s (-1.33) **Going Correction** -0.25s/f (Stan)
WFA 3 from 4yo+ 13lb 12 Ran SP% **119.4**
Speed ratings (Par 101): **94,93,93,93,93 93,93,92,91,90 90,87**
toteswingers:1&2:£11.50, 1&3:£35.10, 2&3:£14.90 CSF £45.85 TOTE £27.80: £6.80, £1.10, £8.20; EX 73.80.
Owner A A Goodman **Bred** Gainesway Thoroughbreds Ltd **Trained** Newmarket, Suffolk
■ Stewards' Enquiry : Matthew Davies one-day ban: careless riding (Jul 26)

FOCUS
A wide open 0-60 classified claiming stakes which was run at an even pace. The first seven home were only a couple of lengths apart but the form does make some sense.

3968 COMPTON HOSPICE ROOF RAISER H'CAP 1m 141y(P)
8:20 (8:21) (Class 6) (0-60,60) 3-Y-0+ £1,706 (£503; £252) Stalls Low

Form RPR
1103 1 **Dabbers Ridge (IRE)**[14] 3521 8-9-9 60 DanielTudhope 10 72
(I W McInnes) *hld up: hdwy over 1f out: led ins fnl f: r.o* **9/1**
05-4 2 1 **Cottonfields (USA)**[48] 2417 4-9-7 58 (p) EddieAhern 6 68
(Mrs H S Main) *chsd ldrs: rdn and ev ch whn hung lft ins fnl f: styd on same pce* **5/1**[3]
5021 3 2 ½ **Goodbye Cash (IRE)**[13] 3524 6-9-6 60 AndrewHeffernan(3) 2 64+
(R J Smith) *led: hdd over 7f out: chsd ldr: rdn to ld again wl over 1f out: hdd and hmpd ins fnl f: no ex* **6/1**
5004 4 2 **Lunar River (FR)**[25] 3131 7-9-3 59 (t) BillyCray(5) 1 58
(David Pinder) *s.s: hld up: hdwy over 1f out: nt rch ldrs* **3/1**[1]
0100 5 ¾ **Feet Of Fury**[5] 3783 4-9-4 55 (p) LiamJones 8 53
(W M Brisbourne) *hld up: hdwy over 2f out: sn rdn: styd on same pce appr fnl f* **16/1**
4430 6 2 ½ **Kladester (USA)**[20] 3284 4-9-5 56 (p) TonyCulhane 5 48
(M Herrington) *led over 7f out: rdn and hdd wl over 1f out: wknd ins fnl f* **9/2**[2]
0-00 7 5 **Fiancee (IRE)**[54] 2231 4-9-7 58 GeorgeBaker 4 38
(R Brotherton) *chsd ldrs: rdn over 2f out: wknd fnl f* **25/1**
-520 8 shd **Noche De Reyes**[12] 3552 5-9-2 53 DavidAllan 11 33
(E J Alston) *hld up: hdwy over 2f out: rdn and wknd over 1f out* **5/1**[3]
21-6 9 3 ¼ **Why Nee Amy**[159] 396 4-9-1 57 KylieManser(5) 9 30
(Miss Olivia Maylam) *s.i.s: hld up: rdn over 2f out: a in rr* **14/1**

1m 48.8s (-1.70) **Going Correction** -0.25s/f (Stan) 9 Ran SP% **117.2**
Speed ratings (Par 101): **97,96,93,92,91 89,84,84,81**
toteswingers:1&2:£12.40, 1&3:£5.60, 2&3:£9.00 CSF £54.32 CT £298.16 TOTE £11.10: £4.80, £2.10, £4.30; EX 68.20.
Owner G Parkinson **Bred** Franco Castelfranci **Trained** Catwick, E Yorks

FOCUS
Recent good form was hard to find in this 46-60 handicap and the winner did not need to match this year's turf form. It was run at a furious pace.
Lunar River(FR) Official explanation: jockey said mare missed the break

3969 BELVOIR LETTINGS H'CAP 7f 32y(P)
8:50 (8:52) (Class 3) (0-95,94) 3-Y-0+ £6,308 (£1,888; £944; £472; £235) Stalls High

Form RPR
6200 1 **Prime Exhibit**[24] 3146 5-9-4 94 LeeTopliss(7) 3 106
(R A Fahey) *sn led: rdn and edgd lft over 1f out: clr fnl f: r.o* **7/2**[2]
2-01 2 1 **Mr Rainbow**[28] 3033 4-9-6 89 NeilCallan 2 98
(G A Swinbank) *chsd ldrs: rdn to chse wnr and edgd lft over 1f out: edgd rt ins fnl f: r.o* **3/1**[1]
1302 3 1 **Flowing Cape (IRE)**[9] 3681 5-9-5 88 JackMitchell 12 94
(R Hollinshead) *hld up: hdwy over 2f out: rdn over 1f out: r.o: nt rch ldrs* **8/1**
2000 4 1 ¼ **Black Dahlia**[16] 3448 5-9-7 90 ChrisCatlin 8 93
(J A Glover) *hld up: nt clr run over 2f out: hdwy over 1f out: nt clr run and swtchd lft ins fnl f: r.o: nvr able to chal* **8/1**
-103 5 1 **Street Power (USA)**[33] 2877 5-9-7 90 JamieSpencer 11 90
(J R Gask) *s.i.s: hld up: hdwy on outside over 2f out: rdn and hung lft fnl f: no imp* **7/1**[3]
3000 6 ¾ **One Way Or Another (AUS)**[29] 2992 7-9-6 89 HayleyTurner 4 87
(J R Gask) *chsd ldr tl rdn over 1f out: no ex fnl f* **15/2**
-100 7 ¾ **Bond City (IRE)**[29] 2992 8-9-2 85 JimmyQuinn 9 81
(G R Oldroyd) *chsd ldrs: rdn over 1f out: styd on same pce* **20/1**
2-00 8 1 ½ **Spectait**[26] 3069 8-9-9 92 GeorgeBaker 5 84
(Jonjo O'Neill) *s.i.s: bhd tl styd on fnl f: nvr nrr* **12/1**
1000 9 3 ½ **Elusive Fame (USA)**[12] 3565 4-8-9 85 (b) CharlesPerkins(7) 10 68
(M Johnston) *s.i.s: sn prom: rdn over 2f out: wknd over 1f out* **40/1**
3315 10 ¾ **Mr Hichens**[40] 2640 5-9-4 87 TedDurcan 6 68
(Karen George) *prom: rdn over 2f out: wknd over 1f out* **9/1**

1m 26.66s (-2.94) **Going Correction** -0.25s/f (Stan) 10 Ran SP% **118.6**
Speed ratings (Par 107): **106,104,103,102,101 100,99,97,93,92**
toteswingers:1&2:£3.70, 1&3:£10.50, 2&3:£3.90 CSF £14.73 CT £80.88 TOTE £6.40: £3.80, £1.10, £7.40; EX 18.40.
Owner Dab Hand Racing **Bred** Matthews Breeding And Racing Ltd **Trained** Musley Bank, N Yorks

FOCUS
Seven previous course winners made this a very interesting 76-95 handicap. It was run at a sound pace and it proved hard to make up ground from the back. The form seems sound.

NOTEBOOK
Prime Exhibit has not had many starts for his respected yard and showed a willing attitude for his 7lb claimer, who looks good value for his allowance in these types of races. The handicapper will have his say but will remain of interest for this in-form yard. (op 4-1 tchd 3-1)
Mr Rainbow, a winner of his maiden over course and distance in October, was 5lb higher for his recent Warwick success. He ran a solid race and as he is lightly raced he should continue to progress. (tchd 9-4)
Flowing Cape(IRE), who has been busy of late, appeared to run bang up to form. Twice a course winner, he can continue to pay his way. (op 12-1)
Black Dahlia could do with some help from the handicapper as she is 15lb higher than her last winning mark. (op 12-1 tchd 16-1)
Street Power(USA) could never land a blow. (tchd 8-1)
Spectait, a four times course winner over further, was always struggling over this trip. (op 11-1 tchd 10-1 and 14-1)
Mr Hichens Official explanation: jockey said gelding had no more to give

3970 HOTEL & CONFERENCING AT WOLVERHAMPTON H'CAP 7f 32y(P)
9:20 (9:21) (Class 5) (0-75,75) 3-Y-0+ £2,388 (£705; £352) Stalls High

Form RPR
0051 1 **Yankee Storm**[21] 3279 5-9-6 67 (v) JimmyQuinn 1 78+
(H J Collingridge) *hld up: swtchd rt and hdwy over 1f out: hmpd 1f out: rdn to ld wl ins fnl f: r.o* **9/4**[1]
2113 2 1 ¼ **Kingsdine (IRE)**[20] 3297 3-8-12 67 TomMcLaughlin 7 72
(M S Saunders) *chsd ldrs: led over 1f out: rdn hung rt and hdd wl ins fnl f* **5/1**[2]
4134 3 nk **Lastkingofscotland (IRE)**[5] 3779 4-9-9 70 (b) HayleyTurner 11 77
(C R Dore) *hld up in tch: rdn and hung rt 1f out: sn hung lft: r.o* **13/2**
000 4 1 **Leverage (IRE)**[12] 3565 4-10-0 75 StephenCraine 2 79
(M Wigham) *hld up: hdwy over 2f out: rdn and ev ch whn hung rt ins fnl f: styd on same pce* **40/1**
6054 5 3 **Defector (IRE)**[11] 3604 4-9-13 74 EddieAhern 3 70
(W R Muir) *hld up: hdwy over 2f out: rdn over 1f out: no ex ins fnl f* **10/1**
5005 6 ½ **Emeebee**[17] 3412 4-9-7 68 TonyCulhane 4 63
(W J Musson) *hld up: shkn up over 1f out: nvr nr to chal* **12/1**
U300 7 2 ¾ **Northern Bolt**[11] 3584 5-9-7 68 (v) DanielTudhope 6 55
(I W McInnes) *prom: chsd ldr over 2f out: rdn and ev ch over 1f out: wknd ins fnl f* **40/1**
05-6 8 1 ½ **We'Re Delighted**[12] 3557 5-9-3 64 (t) LukeMorris 8 47
(Michael Blake) *hld up: rdn over 1f out: n.d* **66/1**
3320 9 ½ **Rubenstar (IRE)**[58] 2123 7-9-10 71 GeorgeBaker 12 53
(Patrick Morris) *stdd and swtchd lft s: hld up: hdwy over 1f out: wknd fnl f* **16/1**
034 10 4 **Eviction (IRE)**[21] 3276 3-9-1 70 (b) ChrisCatlin 10 38
(Miss M E Rowland) *chsd ldr tl led over 5f out: rdn and hdd over 1f out: wknd fnl f* **25/1**
4105 11 ¾ **Justcallmehandsome**[27] 3054 8-9-7 73 (v) BillyCray(5) 9 42
(D J S Ffrench Davis) *hld up: a in rr* **10/1**

3235 **12** *5* **Jay's Treaty (USA)**[18] 3363 3-9-4 **73**...............................(b[1]) GregFairley 5 26
(M Johnston) *led: hdd over 5f out: chsd ldr tl rdn over 2f out: wknd over 1f out* **11/2**[3]

1m 27.21s (-2.39) **Going Correction** -0.25s/f (Stan)
WFA 3 from 4yo+ 8lb **12** Ran SP% **118.1**
Speed ratings (Par 103): **103,101,101,100,96 96,92,91,90,86 85,79**
toteswingers:1&2:£3.20, 1&3:£2.60, 2&3:£3.40 CSF £12.46 CT £65.56 TOTE £2.10: £1.02, £2.00, £2.40; EX 14.90 Place 6 £48.22; Place 5 £26.77.
Owner Greenstead Hall Racing Ltd **Bred** Mark Johnston Racing Ltd **Trained** Exning, Suffolk

FOCUS
A furious gallop for this 56-75 handicap, in which very few landed any sort of blow. Solid form, with the winner back to his best.
Justcallmehandsome Official explanation: jockey said gelding never travelled
T/Plt: £31.80 to a £1 stake. Pool:£72,231.78 - 1,658.05 winning tickets T/Qpdt: £7.50 to a £1 stake. Pool:£6,484.38 - 633.08 winning tickets CR

3657 BEVERLEY (R-H)

Tuesday, July 13

OFFICIAL GOING: Good to firm (watered; 9.4)
Around the bottom bend the rail was moved out to provide a fresh strip of ground.
Wind: moderate 1/2 against Weather: overcast

3971 RACING UK ON SKY 432 MAIDEN AUCTION STKS 5f
2:00 (2:00) (Class 5) 2-Y-O **£3,238** (£963; £481; £240) **Stalls** High

Form RPR

1 **Katell (IRE)** 2-8-11 0.. TomEaves 2 73
(Mrs L Stubbs) *sn w ldrs: led over 2f out: hung lft and hdd over 1f out: styd on to ld fnl 75yds* **8/1**

320 **2** *1 ¼* **Saltergate**[20] 3315 2-8-9 0......................................(p) SilvestreDeSousa 11 67
(N Tinkler) *w ldrs: led after 2f: sn hdd: led over 1f out: hung bdly lft and hdd wl ins fnl f* **9/2**[3]

4U3 **3** *3* **Novalist**[27] 3087 2-8-2 0... MatthewLawson(7) 9 56
(R Bastiman) *led 2f: kpt on same pce fnl f* **4/1**[2]

0 **4** *hd* **Thirteen Shivers**[32] 2939 2-8-4 0.. JamesSullivan(5) 5 58+
(M W Easterby) *sn outpcd: hdwy and nt clr run over 1f out: styd on ins fnl f* **7/2**[1]

3 **5** *1* **Hawk Moth (IRE)**[34] 2873 2-8-6 0.. JackDean(3) 6 51
(J L Spearing) *chsd ldrs: outpcd 2f out: kpt on fnl f* **5/1**

0 **6** *2 ¾* **Bonne Millie**[10] 3658 2-8-6 0.. PaulHanagan 10 38
(R A Fahey) *chsd ldrs: drvn over 2f out: fdd fnl f* **7/1**

7 *1* **Moral Issue** 2-8-11 0.. TonyHamilton 4 40
(Jedd O'Keeffe) *wnt lft s: sn outpcd and in rr: kpt on fnl f: nvr a factor* **20/1**

8 *1* **None Sweeter** 2-8-6 0.. DavidAllan 1 31
(T D Easterby) *outpcd and lost pl over 3f out: sn in rr* **12/1**

9 *¾* **Lakota** 2-8-4 0.. RoystonFfrench 7 27
(J A Glover) *dwlt: mid-div: hung lft and lost pl over 1f out* **28/1**

62.16 secs (-1.34) **Going Correction** -0.35s/f (Firm) **9** Ran SP% **116.6**
Speed ratings (Par 94): **96,94,89,88,87 82,81,79,78**
toteswingers:1&2:£9.00, 1&3:£9.00, 2&3:£4.00 CSF £44.32 TOTE £10.80: £2.40, £1.30, £1.40; EX 60.90.
Owner D Arundale **Bred** Barouche Stud (ire) Ltd **Trained** Norton, N Yorks

FOCUS
This looked just an ordinary maiden.

NOTEBOOK
Katell(IRE), a 10,500gns already gelded half-brother to, among others, 1m-1m2f winner Ricci De Mare, made a nice debut. He seemed reasonably well educated, showing good speed from the off, but he took a while to respond when first coming under pressure, initially carrying his head at a slight angle, before running on well up the middle of the track. He's a big gelding with plenty of scope and could progress into a useful type. (op 15-2 tchd 17-2)
Saltergate, fitted with cheekpieces for the first time after disappointing at Carlisle on his previous start, displayed loads of pace but he stuck more towards the far rail than the winner for much of the closing stages, which might not have been ideal. (op 4-1)
Novalist, who went to post early, showed good early pace but was under pressure by halfway. He may be more of a nursery type. (tchd 9-2 and 5-1 in a place)
Thirteen Shivers lacked the speed of some of these but ran on quite nicely in the closing stages, including when switched towards the possibly unfavoured far rail late on. He should have more to offer. (tchd 4-1)
Hawk Moth(IRE) didn't build on the form he showed on debut at Yarmouth. (tchd 11-2 in a place)

3972 AUNTY EVE APPLE PIE CLAIMING STKS 7f 100y
2:30 (2:33) (Class 5) 3-Y-O **£2,590** (£770; £385; £192) **Stalls** High

Form RPR

0000 **1** **Jupiter Fidius**[11] 3612 3-8-7 65...................................(p) JamesSullivan(5) 3 70
(Mrs K Walton) *squeezed s: trckd ldr: bmpd over 2f out: sn led: kpt on wl ins fnl f* **8/1**[3]

-001 **2** *1 ¼* **Cono Zur (FR)**[12] 3597 3-9-4 73.. PaulHanagan 6 72
(Mrs R A Carr) *led: rdn: hung bdly lft and bmpd over 2f out: sn hdd: kpt on same pce ins fnl f* **8/11**[1]

6430 **3** *3 ¾* **Saxby (IRE)**[18] 3387 3-8-11 67.................................... SilvestreDeSousa 4 56
(G A Harker) *hld up in midfield: effrt 3f out: styd on same pce fnl f* **7/2**[2]

560 **4** *7* **Baby Judge (IRE)**[10] 3682 3-8-4 47 ow3.................... JamesRogers(7) 7 39
(M C Chapman) *bolted abt 4f gng to s: chsd ldrs: lost pl over 1f out* **66/1**

4000 **5** *3 ¾* **Springwell Giant (IRE)**[26] 3113 3-8-0 50........................ DeclanCannon(5) 1 23
(A J McCabe) *swvd lft s: sn chsng ldrs: lost pl 2f out* **50/1**

0606 **6** *1* **Ferris Wheel (IRE)**[19] 3350 3-8-8 65.. TomEaves 5 24
(P F I Cole) *in rr: nvr on terms* **9/1**

0-0 **7** *hd* **Both Ends Burning (IRE)**[49] 2425 3-8-4 42.................... LanceBetts(5) 9 24
(J S Wainwright) *hld up in rr: nvr a factor* **80/1**

0142 **8** *5* **Newbury Street**[27] 3086 3-8-10 67.. GrahamGibbons 2 13
(P F Holmes) *swvd lft s: mid-div: lost pl over 4f out* **9/1**

06-0 **9** *22* **Taeping (IRE)**[10] 3685 3-8-0 45.. NicolaJackson(7) 8 —
(R Hollinshead) *trckd ldrs: sddle sn slipped: dropped bk over 3f out: eased and sn bhd: virtually p.u: t.o* **80/1**

1m 31.66s (-2.14) **Going Correction** -0.35s/f (Firm) **9** Ran SP% **117.2**
Speed ratings (Par 100): **98,96,92,84,80 78,78,72,47**
toteswingers:1&2:£2.70, 1&3:£4.70, 2&3:£1.90 CSF £14.58 TOTE £10.90: £2.40, £1.10, £1.60; EX 16.90.
Owner Tennant, Sharpe & Boston **Bred** A C Birkle **Trained** Middleham Moor, N Yorks

FOCUS
It paid to race prominently in this modest claimer, and the main action was up the middle of the track in the straight. It was well run and the form is rated around the first two.
Taeping(IRE) Official explanation: jockey said saddle slipped

3973 HAPPY BIRTHDAY PHILIP MEGGINSON H'CAP 1m 100y
3:00 (3:00) (Class 4) (0-80,77) 3-Y-O+ **£4,727** (£1,406; £702; £351) **Stalls** High

Form RPR

1065 **1** **Shadowtime**[20] 3317 5-9-8 71.. AndrewMullen 5 83
(Miss Tracy Waggott) *stmbld sltly s: t.k.h: trckd ldrs: led 2f out: hld on wl u.p* **5/2**[1]

5403 **2** *1 ¼* **Avonrose**[15] 3508 3-8-12 70.. RoystonFfrench 7 77
(M Johnston) *chsd ldrs: drvn over 3f out: styd on to chse wnr appr fnl f: no real imp* **8/1**

3544 **3** *2 ½* **Observatory Star (IRE)**[14] 3537 7-9-11 74..........(vt[1]) GrahamGibbons 3 78
(T D Easterby) *dwlt: hdwy 4f out: styd on same pce fnl 2f* **11/2**

211 **4** *hd* **Bajan Pride**[11] 3610 6-9-4 67.. TonyCulhane 6 70
(P T Midgley) *w ldrs: chal over 2f out: kpt on same pce fnl f* **10/1**

00-0 **5** *¾* **Global**[20] 3317 4-9-9 72.. TomEaves 4 74
(B Ellison) *hld up in rr: hdwy 2f out: hung lft: styd on ins fnl f* **16/1**

4036 **6** *1 ¾* **King Of The Moors (USA)**[8] 3732 7-9-5 68.........(b) SilvestreDeSousa 1 66
(R C Guest) *stmbld s: racd wd: t.k.h: led after 1f: hdd 2f out: wknd fnl f* **16/1**

0004 **7** *¾* **Handsome Falcon**[10] 3659 6-10-0 77.................................... PaulHanagan 9 73
(R A Fahey) *led 1f: chsd ldrs: wknd fnl f* **5/1**[3]

1344 **8** *1* **Ninth House (USA)**[10] 3676 8-8-10 64.................(t) JamesSullivan(5) 10 58
(Mrs R A Carr) *in rr-div: sme hdwy 4f out: lost pl 2f out* **4/1**[2]

2524 **9** *5* **King's Sabre**[11] 3610 4-9-0 63..(e) PaulEddery 8 46
(R C Guest) *s.s: t.k.h in rr: nvr on terms: eased towards fin* **16/1**

1m 44.72s (-2.88) **Going Correction** -0.35s/f (Firm)
WFA 3 from 4yo+ 9lb **9** Ran SP% **118.5**
Speed ratings (Par 105): **100,98,96,96,95 93,92,91,86**
toteswingers:1&2:£6.90, 1&3:£4.60, 2&3:£6.00 CSF £24.13 CT £104.00 TOTE £3.70: £1.30, £2.10, £2.50; EX 32.10.
Owner H Conlon **Bred** Darley **Trained** Spennymoor, Co Durham

FOCUS
A fair handicap run at a reasonable gallop. The principals avoided the far rail in the straight. Straightforward form.
Ninth House(USA) Official explanation: jockey said horse ran flat

3974 125TH YEAR OF WATT MEMORIAL H'CAP 2m 35y
3:30 (3:31) (Class 4) (0-85,85) 3-Y-O+ **£11,656** (£3,468; £1,733; £865) **Stalls** High

Form RPR

20-1 **1** **Markington**[23] 3241 7-9-1 76.......................................(b) RobertWinston 7 84+
(P Bowen) *in rr: drvn over 4f out: gd hdwy on wd outside over 1f out: str run to ld towards fin* **4/1**[2]

1311 **2** *1 ¼* **Tillietudlem (FR)**[5] 3804 4-8-4 65.................................... PaulHanagan 10 71+
(J S Goldie) *trckd ldrs: pushed along 5f out: rdn over 2f out: led jst ins fnl f: edgd rt: hdd towards fin* **15/8**[1]

/634 **3** *¾* **Palomar (USA)**[20] 3319 8-8-10 78.. DaleSwift(7) 9 83
(B Ellison) *sn trcking ldrs: upsides 7f out: no ex ins fnl f* **10/1**

3320 **4** *½* **Royal Trooper (IRE)**[32] 2938 4-8-10 71.................................... PaulMulrennan 6 76
(J G Given) *led: edgd lft 3f out: hdd jst ins fnl f: kpt on same pce* **10/1**

-122 **5** *1 ¼* **My Arch**[45] 2541 8-9-5 85.. IanBrennan(5) 1 88
(Ollie Pears) *hld up in midfield: effrt over 4f out: hdwy on ins to chse ldrs over 2f out: kpt on same pce fnl f* **5/1**[3]

0132 **6** *1 ¾* **They All Laughed**[26] 3109 7-7-13 60 oh4 ow1......(b) SilvestreDeSousa 8 61
(Mrs Marjorie Fife) *chsd ldrs: drvn 9f out: outpcd over 3f out: one pce fnl 2f* **16/1**

50/0 **7** *3 ½* **Boucheron**[20] 3319 5-9-2 77.. TonyHamilton 11 74
(R A Fahey) *trckd ldr: wknd over 1f out* **16/1**

0011 **8** *¾* **Phoenix Flight (IRE)**[13] 3566 5-9-10 85.................................... TonyCulhane 3 81
(H J Evans) *swtchd rt after s: hld up in rr: effrt 3f out: hung rt: nvr nr ldrs* **12/1**

2354 **9** *4* **Smugglers Bay (IRE)**[12] 3600 6-8-0 61...................(b) DuranFentiman 4 52
(T D Easterby) *hld up in rr: hdwy on outside 9f out: chsng ldrs 5f out: lost pl over 1f out* **18/1**

0203 **10** *14* **Kingsdale Orion (IRE)**[20] 3319 6-9-3 78.................................... TomEaves 2 52
(B Ellison) *mid-div: drvn 6f out: lost pl over 3f out: sn bhd* **22/1**

3m 31.75s (-8.05) **Going Correction** -0.35s/f (Firm) **10** Ran SP% **118.7**
Speed ratings (Par 105): **106,105,105,104,104 103,101,101,99,92**
toteswingers:1&2:£3.50, 1&3:£9.30, 2&3:£6.80 CSF £12.11 CT £70.79 TOTE £5.60: £2.00, £1.30, £3.60; EX 12.90.
Owner Ron Stepney **Bred** Minster Enterprises Ltd **Trained** Little Newcastle, Pembrokes

FOCUS
Excellent prize money was rewarded with a good race for the grade, and they seemed to go an even gallop. Again, the principals raced up the middle of track in the straight. A slightly muddling feel to the form, with the sixth close enough, but a clear personal best from the winner.

3975 TOTEPOOL A BETTER WAY TO BET H'CAP 7f 100y
4:00 (4:02) (Class 6) (0-65,65) 3-Y-O **£2,428** (£722; £361; £180) **Stalls** High

Form RPR

0205 **1** **Luv U Noo**[24] 3226 3-8-11 55.. TonyCulhane 4 65
(B Ellison) *hld up in rr: gd hdwy on wd outside over 1f out: styd on strly to ld last 50yds* **16/1**

003 **2** *¾* **Piddie's Power**[24] 3207 3-9-6 64.. GrahamGibbons 10 72+
(E S McMahon) *chsd ldrs: hung lft and led over 1f out: hdd and no ex wl ins fnl f* **7/2**[1]

3052 **3** *4* **Sunrise Lyric (IRE)**[19] 3359 3-8-13 57.................................... PaulHanagan 5 55
(P F I Cole) *prom: hmpd bnd over 5f out: hdwy on outer over 1f out: styd on same pce* **8/1**

2654 **4** *½* **Battle Study (IRE)**[26] 3113 3-8-10 59...................(b[1]) DeclanCannon(5) 3 56
(A J McCabe) *s.i.s: in rr: hdwy over 2f out: styd on fnl f* **16/1**

-542 **5** *1* **Green For Luck (IRE)**[42] 2633 3-9-2 60.................................... RobertWinston 6 54
(S Gollings) *w ldrs: led 3f out: hdd over 1f out: kpt on same pce* **6/1**[3]

0062 **6** *1 ¾* **Gazamali (IRE)**[29] 3030 3-8-4 53.. JohnFahy(5) 12 43
(H J Evans) *swvd lft s: t.k.h in rr: hdwy on ins over 2f out: sn chsng ldrs: wknd ins fnl f* **16/1**

0031 **7** *1 ¼* **Verluga (IRE)**[10] 3668 3-9-4 62.. DavidAllan 14 49
(T D Easterby) *in tch: drvn 6f out: hdwy over 3f out: one pce fnl 2f* **4/1**[2]

5052 **8** *nk* **Rescent**[15] 3501 3-8-3 47...(p) SilvestreDeSousa 9 33
(Mrs R A Carr) *in tch: drvn over 3f out: one pce fnl 2f* **14/1**

3426 **9** *2* **We'll Deal Again**[11] 3612 3-9-7 65.................................... PaulMulrennan 1 46
(M W Easterby) *mid-div: drvn and lost pl over 1f out* **12/1**

1664 **10** *1 ½* **Sophie's Beau (USA)**[31] 2957 3-9-1 62.................................... RobertLButler(3) 11 39
(M C Chapman) *mid-div: hung lft bnd over 5f out: effrt over 3f out: wknd over 1f out* **28/1**

0-00 11 4 1/2 **William Arnold**[39] 2700 3-8-2 46 oh1 PaulQuinn 13 12
(C W Fairhurst) *gave problems in stalls: dwlt: reminders after s: a in rr* 66/1

-653 12 4 **Reddy To Star (IRE)**[25] 3181 3-9-2 60 TomEaves 8 16
(Julie Camacho) *chsd ldrs: lost pl over 1f out* 25/1

0000 13 2 1/4 **Scarboro Warning (IRE)**[7] 3759 3-9-2 60 TonyHamilton 2 11
(J O'Reilly) *led: hdd 3f out: lost pl over 1f out* 33/1

0231 14 16 **Fleetwoodsands (IRE)**[15] 3515 3-9-2 65 IanBrennan(5) 7 —
(Ollie Pears) *prom: outpcd and drvn 5f out: wknd over 2f out: bhd whn eased 1f out: virtually p.u: t.o* 8/1

1m 31.9s (-1.90) **Going Correction** -0.35s/f (Firm) 14 Ran SP% 122.5
Speed ratings (Par 98): **96,95,90,90,88 86,85,85,82,81 75,71,68,50**
toteswingers:1&2:£20.10, 1&3:£23.90, 2&3:£7.50 CSF £70.56 CT £516.69 TOTE £25.10: £6.30, £1.80, £2.50; EX 121.40.
Owner Phones Direct Partnership **Bred** Richard Hunt **Trained** Norton, N Yorks
■ Stewards' Enquiry : Paul Quinn caution; used whip when out of contention

FOCUS
A modest handicap and a lower-grade race than it used to be, but competitive nonetheless. They went a good gallop from the start and were spread right across the track in the straight, with the principals racing more towards the stands' side, following the earlier trend. Solid form, best rated through the third.
Sophie's Beau(USA) Official explanation: jockey said gelding hung left
Fleetwoodsands(IRE) Official explanation: vet said gelding scoped dirty post race

3976 YORKSHIRE RACING SUMMER FESTIVAL STARTS SATURDAY H'CAP (DIV I) 5f
4:30 (4:30) (Class 6) (0-60,60) 3-Y-O+ £1,942 (£578; £288; £144) Stalls High

Form RPR

2540 1 **Miss Daawe**[43] 2581 6-8-13 57 DaleSwift(7) 2 68
(B Ellison) *chsd ldrs on wd outside: styd on to ld last 50yds: hld on nr fin* 8/1

4650 2 3/4 **Namir (IRE)**[22] 3254 8-9-3 59 (vt) JohnFahy(5) 7 67
(H J Evans) *led to s: in rr: hdwy wd outside over 1f out: styd on wl to take 2nd nr fin* 15/2

5000 3 nk **Kyzer Chief**[26] 3119 5-9-5 56 (v) SilvestreDeSousa 10 63
(R E Barr) *wnt lft s: w ldrs centre: led and edgd lft 3f out: hdd wl ins fnl f: no ex* 6/1[3]

0135 4 1 1/4 **Exceedingly Good (IRE)**[7] 3763 4-8-13 53 AshleyHamblett(3) 9 56
(S R Bowring) *hmpd s: sn trcking ldrs: styd on same pce ins fnl f* 11/2[2]

0460 5 2 1/4 **Welcome Approach**[8] 3727 7-8-13 50 PaulMulrennan 12 44
(J R Weymes) *chsd ldrs: kpt on same pce appr fnl f* 10/1

0000 6 3/4 **City For Conquest (IRE)**[11] 3615 7-8-4 46 oh1 (b) TobyAtkinson(5) 6 38
(John A Harris) *in rr: hdwy on outside over 1f out: styd on wl fnl 100yds* 50/1

0521 7 1 3/4 **Tournedos (IRE)**[11] 3615 8-9-4 60 (b) JamesSullivan(5) 8 45
(Mrs R A Carr) *prom early: effrt over 2f out: kpt on: nvr trbld ldrs* 5/2[1]

5500 8 3/4 **Lady Vivien**[20] 3338 4-8-13 50 GrahamGibbons 13 33
(D H Brown) *w ldr towards far side: edgd lft over 2f out: fdd fnl f* 14/1

6225 9 shd **Darcy's Pride (IRE)**[11] 3615 6-9-3 54 TonyHamilton 3 36
(P T Midgley) *chsd ldrs: hung rt over 1f out: sn wknd* 14/1

4006 10 nk **Fyodorovich (USA)**[11] 3610 5-8-4 46 oh1 (b) LanceBetts(5) 14 27
(J S Wainwright) *racd far side: led 2f: lft to r alone: wknd ins fnl f* 20/1

2020 11 8 **Tanley**[12] 3605 5-9-3 54 (p) RoystonFfrench 15 6
(I W McInnes) *racd far side: swtchd lft and lost pl after 1f: bhd fnl 2f* 28/1

R661 12 10 **Greek Secret**[12] 3605 7-9-9 60 (b) RobertWinston 11 —
(J O'Reilly) *s.s: a in rr: bhd and eased over 1f out* 12/1

61.98 secs (-1.52) **Going Correction** -0.35s/f (Firm)
WFA 3 from 4yo+ 5lb 12 Ran SP% 121.4
Speed ratings (Par 101): **98,96,96,94,90 89,86,85,85,84 72,56**
toteswingers:1&2:£12.50, 1&3:£10.40, 2&3:£9.40 CSF £67.21 CT £401.08 TOTE £9.80: £3.10, £2.90, £2.90; EX 77.20.
Owner Mrs Andrea M Mallinson **Bred** N R C Trading Ltd **Trained** Norton, N Yorks
■ Stewards' Enquiry : Ashley Hamblett one-day ban; excessive use of whip (27 july)

FOCUS
A moderate sprint handicap, and a middle-to-low draw was an advantage, with the main action taking place towards the stands' rail. The time was 0.41 seconds slower than the second division. The form is rated to face value.
Tanley Official explanation: trainer said gelding scoped dirty on return
Greek Secret Official explanation: jockey said gelding slipped leaving stalls and moved poorly throughout

3977 YORKSHIRE RACING SUMMER FESTIVAL STARTS SATURDAY H'CAP (DIV II) 5f
5:00 (5:02) (Class 6) (0-60,60) 3-Y-O+ £1,942 (£578; £288; £144) Stalls High

Form RPR

0004 1 **Hitches Dubai (BRZ)**[11] 3615 5-9-8 59 SilvestreDeSousa 9 72
(G A Harker) *mid-div: hdwy 2f out: styd on wl to ld last 100yds: sddle slipped* 3/1[1]

3353 2 1 1/4 **First Swallow**[11] 3623 5-9-9 60 (t) GrahamGibbons 15 68
(D H Brown) *led: hdd ins fnl f: no ex* 13/2[3]

3030 3 1 **Shakespeare's Son**[119] 896 5-8-6 48 JohnFahy(5) 7 52
(H J Evans) *hld up in mid-div: effrt 2f out: edgd rt: styd on same pce last 150yds* 9/1

5046 4 1/2 **Fashion Icon (USA)**[11] 3615 4-8-4 46 oh1 JamesSullivan(5) 14 49
(D O'Meara) *chsd ldrs: rdn over 2f out: kpt on same pce fnl f* 9/2[2]

6005 5 nk **Divine Spirit**[21] 3287 9-8-12 54 PatrickDonaghy(5) 10 56+
(M Dods) *sn in rr: hdwy and edgd rt over 1f out: kpt on same pce ins fnl f* 12/1

0130 6 1 **Port Ronan (USA)**[11] 3615 4-8-13 50 DanielTudhope 8 48
(J S Wainwright) *chsd ldrs: drvn over 2f out: kpt on same pce* 18/1

3234 7 1 **Fasliyanne (IRE)**[15] 3497 4-8-12 54 (v) AmyRyan(5) 5 48
(K A Ryan) *towards rr stands' side: effrt over 2f out: kpt on: nvr nr ldrs* 7/1

0-16 8 8 **Helping Hand (IRE)**[8] 3727 5-9-1 52 RoystonFfrench 11 18
(R Hollinshead) *chsd ldrs: lost pl over 1f out* 7/1

-000 9 1 3/4 **Take That**[11] 3615 5-8-6 46 oh1 (b[1]) MichaelStainton(3) 12 5
(S P Griffiths) *mid-div: lost pl over 1f out* 66/1

-100 10 2 1/4 **Green Poppy**[15] 3497 4-9-6 57 TonyHamilton 3 8
(B Smart) *chsd ldrs: edgd rt and wknd over 1f out* 14/1

0-00 11 nk **Oriental Rose**[7] 3762 4-9-6 57 RobertWinston 6 7
(D Shaw) *w ldrs: drvn over 2f out: wknd over 1f out* 20/1

650- 12 7 **Captain Royale (IRE)**[251] 7241 5-9-2 53 AndrewMullen 1 —
(Miss Tracy Waggott) *mid-div: lost pl over 2f out* 14/1

0-20 U **Azygous**[21] 3287 7-8-8 52 DavidSimmonson(7) 4 —
(G P Kelly) *stmbld bdly and uns rdr s* 20/1

61.57 secs (-1.93) **Going Correction** -0.35s/f (Firm)
WFA 3 from 4yo+ 5lb 13 Ran SP% 128.8
Speed ratings (Par 101): **101,99,97,96,96 94,92,80,77,73 73,62,—**
toteswingers:1&2:£6.80, 1&3:£12.90, 2&3:£19.80 CSF £23.81 CT £175.27 TOTE £5.80: £2.10, £3.60, £4.00; EX 33.30.
Owner Miss K Watson **Bred** Haras Valente **Trained** Thirkleby, N Yorks

FOCUS
The time was 0.41 seconds quicker than the first division, and the middle of the track was the place to be this time. The runner-up is the key to the form.

3978 LADY JANE BETHELL MEMORIAL LADY RIDERS' H'CAP (FOR LADY AMATEUR RIDERS) 1m 1f 207y
5:30 (5:38) (Class 6) (0-65,65) 3-Y-O+ £2,029 (£629; £314; £157) Stalls High

Form RPR

334 1 **Kyle Of Bute**[12] 3582 4-9-13 57 MissSBrotherton 7 68
(B P J Baugh) *hld up in midfield: hdwy over 3f out: str run on inner to ld 1f out: styd on wl* 7/1[1]

0625 2 2 1/2 **Royal Composer (IRE)**[11] 3614 7-8-13 48 MissRKneller(5) 1 54
(T D Easterby) *hld up towards rr: hdwy over 3f out: styng on whn carried lft ins fnl f: tk n.d 2nd nr line* 14/1

4504 3 nk **Country Road (IRE)**[18] 3405 4-10-7 65 (e) MissJCoward 2 70
(M W Easterby) *chsd ldr: hung bdly lft and kpt on same pce fnl f* 7/1[1]

3006 4 1/2 **Dimashq**[11] 3614 8-8-13 48 MissWGibson(5) 10 52
(P T Midgley) *hld up towards rr: swtchd rt after 1f: hdwy over 2f out: edgd lft and styd on same pce fnl f* 14/1

-502 5 hd **Hurricane Thomas (IRE)**[10] 3684 6-9-6 55 MissPhillipaTutty(5) 4 59
(R A Fahey) *in tch: effrt 3f out: styng on whn hmpd and swtchd rt ins fnl f* 17/2[2]

1004 6 nse **Nayessence**[10] 3684 4-9-4 53 (t) MissJoannaMason(5) 14 57
(M W Easterby) *gave problems in stalls: chsd ldrs: one pce fnl f* 10/1[3]

0314 7 4 **Abu Dubai (IRE)**[15] 3503 4-9-12 56 (p) MissEJJones 16 52
(J A Glover) *led: hdd 1f out: sn wknd* 10/1[3]

014- 8 3 3/4 **Bateau Bleu**[277] 6639 3-9-3 63 MissCharlotteHolmes(5) 12 51
(B M R Haslam) *t.k.h towards rr: sme hdwy over 2f out: nvr a factor* 12/1

3-06 9 1 **Emperor's Well**[14] 3538 11-8-10 47 MissSMStaveley(7) 13 33
(M W Easterby) *in rr: hdwy over 3f out: chsng ldrs over 2f out: sn wknd* 22/1

0-00 10 2 **Masterofceremonies**[39] 2714 7-9-10 61 (p) MissALMurphy(7) 15 43
(W M Brisbourne) *s.i.s: effrt on outer over 1f out: hung rt and sn wknd* 25/1

024 11 1 1/4 **Rub Of The Relic (IRE)**[34] 2851 5-9-11 62 (be) MissHDukes(7) 17 42
(P T Midgley) *chsd ldrs: lost pl 2f out* 12/1

-000 12 3 1/2 **Dancing Poppy**[21] 3291 3-8-8 56 ow5 MissCEReid(7) 8 29
(R A Farrant) *t.k.h in rr: hdwy on outside over 4f out: wknd over 2f out* 22/1

-500 13 10 **Sitwell**[15] 3502 4-9-8 59 MissCBell(7) 5 12
(I W McInnes) *racd wd in midfield: sme hdwy 3f out: wknd over 1f out: eased whn bhd ins fnl f* 40/1

2m 6.54s (-0.46) **Going Correction** -0.35s/f (Firm)
WFA 3 from 4yo+ 11lb 13 Ran SP% 97.4
Speed ratings (Par 101): **87,85,84,84,84 84,80,77,77,75 74,71,63**
toteswingers:1&2:£9.20, 1&3:£6.90, 2&3:£13.70 CSF £60.11 CT £315.08 TOTE £6.20: £2.30, £3.80, £1.80; EX 68.40 Place 6 £45.53; Place 5 £15.29.
Owner J H Chrimes And Mr & Mrs G W Hannam **Bred** Chippenham Lodge Stud Ltd **Trained** Audley, Staffs

FOCUS
This race was delayed by over eight minutes following three withdrawals. They were spread out across the track in the closing stages, and Kyle Of Bute became the only winner on this eight-race card to make his move against the far rail in the straight, but the form of amateur races often needs treating with caution. The form is rated around the first two. Coole Dodger (10/1, bolted circ bef s), Tropical Duke (5/1F, unruly in stalls) & Acquavella (8/1, ref to ent stalls) were withdrawn. Deduct 25p in the £ under R4.
Rub Of The Relic(IRE) Official explanation: caution; used whip when out of contention
T/Jkpt: Not won. T/Plt: £184.60 to a £1 stake. Pool:£74,330.13 - 293.80 winning tickets T/Qpdt: £56.10 to a £1 stake. Pool:£4,648.60 - 61.30 winning tickets WG

3712 BRIGHTON (L-H)
Tuesday, July 13

OFFICIAL GOING: Good (watered; 8.2)
Wind: light, half against Weather: overcast, dry

3979 HARDINGS CATERING H'CAP 5f 59y
2:10 (2:10) (Class 6) (0-55,53) 3-Y-O+ £2,266 (£674; £337; £168) Stalls Low

Form RPR

6064 1 **Best One**[15] 3516 6-9-2 51 (b) ChrisCatlin 6 57
(R A Harris) *dwlt: hld up in last trio: rdn and hdwy over 1f out: rdn to chal ins fnl f: led fnl 50yds: kpt on* 12/1

0053 2 nk **Wooden King (IRE)**[8] 3727 5-9-1 50 TomMcLaughlin 10 55
(M S Saunders) *prom: rdn to chse ldr wl over 1f out: drvn and ev ch ent fnl f: no ex u.p towards fin* 11/2[2]

6320 3 shd **Albero Di Giuda (IRE)**[7] 3762 5-9-4 53 (bt) LeeVickers 3 58
(F Sheridan) *taken down early: chsd ldr tl led 3f out: rdn and hrd pressed ent fnl f: hdd and no ex fnl 50yds* 10/1

5032 4 1 1/2 **Talamahana**[8] 3727 5-9-3 52 (v) NeilCallan 2 51
(A B Haynes) *s.i.s: bhd: rdn and effrt on inner 2f out: chsd ldrs jst ins fnl f: no imp fnl 100yds* 6/1[3]

0003 5 nk **Top Flight Splash**[21] 3292 4-8-11 46 (p) ShaneKelly 4 44
(P D Evans) *in tch in midfield: swtchd lft and drvn over 1f out: one pce and no imp ins fnl f* 4/1[1]

6641 6 1 1/4 **Almaty Express**[19] 3357 8-8-13 51 (b) KellyHarrison(3) 7 45
(J R Weymes) *w ldrs: rdn 2f out: wknd u.p fnl 150yds* 7/1

0404 7 1/2 **Sharp Shoes**[45] 2530 3-8-13 53 (p) TomQueally 9 43
(Mrs A Duffield) *restless in stalls: s.i.s: bhd and sn bustled along: drvn over 1f out: kpt on fnl f: nvr trbld ldrs* 7/1

3054 8 1/2 **Commandingpresence (USA)**[9] 3717 4-8-8 48 KierenFox(5) 5 38
(J J Bridger) *in tch in midfield: rdn 2f out: nt clr run over 1f out tl jst ins fnl f: nvr able to chal* 6/1[3]

0000 9 2 1/4 **Joss Stick**[20] 3308 5-8-5 45 SophieDoyle(5) 8 28
(R A Harris) *in tch in midfield: rdn 2f out: wkng whn short of room and hmpd over 1f out: n.d fnl f* 14/1

0506 **10** *nk* **Louie's Lad**[9] 3717 4-8-11 **46**....(v[1]) NeilChalmers 1 28
(J J Bridger) *led tl 3f out: btn over 1f out: wknd fnl f* **40/1**

63.69 secs (1.39) **Going Correction** +0.10s/f (Good)
WFA 3 from 4yo+ 5lb **10** Ran SP% **114.8**
Speed ratings (Par 101): **92,91,91,88,88 86,85,84,81,80**
toteswingers:1&2:£10.60, 1&3:£14.50, 2&3:£10.40 CSF £75.50 CT £706.66 TOTE £12.10: £3.20, £2.50, £4.30; EX 87.70 Trifecta £141.80 Part won. Pool: £191.68 - 0.42 winning units..
Owner The Govin Partnership **Bred** Darley **Trained** Earlswood, Monmouths

FOCUS
The going had eased to good, having been good to firm, following 12.5mm of overnight rain. This was just a moderate sprint handicap and the time was slow. The winner is rated to this year's form.

3980 3663 FIRST FOR FOOD SERVICE H'CAP 5f 213y
2:40 (2:40) (Class 5) (0-75,75) 3-Y-O+ **£2,590** (£770; £288; £288) **Stalls** Low

Form RPR
0611 **1** **Mandhooma**[9] 3717 4-8-10 **58** 6ex.... ChrisCatlin 2 63
(P W Hiatt) *bhd: rdn and c towards stands' side over 2f out: drvn ent fnl f: edgd lft u.p but r.o wl to ld wl ins fnl f* **8/1**

1321 **2** *hd* **Piazza San Pietro**[8] 3734 4-9-10 **72**.... NeilCallan 5 76
(A B Haynes) *t.k.h: trckd ldrs: effrt to chal over 1f out: rdn ent fnl f: led fnl 100yds: sn hdd and no ex towards fin* **11/8**[1]

06-0 **3** *nk* **Comadoir (IRE)**[106] 1044 4-9-11 **73**.... IanMongan 6 76
(Miss Jo Crowley) *led: rdn over 1f out: drvn ent fnl f: hdd fnl 100yds: kpt on wl tl no ex towards fin* **9/2**[3]

014 **3** *dht* **Dashing Beauty (IRE)**[21] 3289 4-9-3 **68**.... WilliamCarson[(3)] 4 71
(M G Quinlan) *jostled leaving stalls: in tch: rdn and effrt to chal over 1f out: ev ch fnl f: kpt on tl no ex towards fin* **6/1**

5-01 **5** *6* **Forest Dane**[21] 3292 10-8-12 **60**.... TomQueally 7 44
(Mrs N Smith) *chsd ldr tl over 1f out: wknd u.p ent fnl f* **3/1**[2]

1m 11.44s (1.24) **Going Correction** +0.10s/f (Good) **5** Ran SP% **110.7**
Speed ratings (Par 103): **95,94,94,94,86**
CSF £19.78 TOTE £9.60: £4.90, £1.10; EX 10.30.
Owner P W Hiatt **Bred** Shadwell Estate Company Limited **Trained** Hook Norton, Oxon
■ Stewards' Enquiry : Chris Catlin three-day ban; careless riding (27-30 july)

FOCUS
They went an ordinary gallop for this 6f handicap. It produced a desperately close finish, with the front four separated by a head and a neck. The winner is rated back to her best, but the form is not that solid.

3981 CATERING SERVICES INTERNATIONAL MEDIAN AUCTION MAIDEN STKS 5f 213y
3:10 (3:10) (Class 6) 2-Y-O **£2,590** (£770; £385; £192) **Stalls** Low

Form RPR
30 **1** **Miss Moneypenni**[18] 3411 2-8-12 0.... JimCrowley 5 64
(N P Littmoden) *w ldr tl pushed ahd ent fnl 2f: hung lft u.p ent fnl f: styd on wl* **5/2**[2]

602 **2** *1 ¾* **Smart Red**[9] 3712 2-8-12 0.... SamHitchcott 6 59
(M R Channon) *chsd ldrs: rdn and c stands' side wl over 2f out: chsd wnr jst ins fnl f: hung lft and no imp after* **5/1**[3]

4 **3** *1* **Surprise (IRE)**[9] 3712 2-8-5 0.... AntiocoMurgia[(7)] 3 56
(Mahmood Al Zarooni) *racd in last pair: pushed along and effrt in centre 2f out: kpt on same pce u.p fnl f* **11/2**

03 **4** *1 ¼* **High On The Hog (IRE)**[21] 3288 2-9-3 0.... NeilCallan 2 57
(J L Dunlop) *led: c stands' side wl over 2f out: hdd 2f out: wknd u.p jst ins fnl f* **13/8**[1]

5 *8* **Miss Nimbus** 2-8-7 0.... MatthewDavies[(5)] 1 32
(George Baker) *s.i.s: sn pushed along in rr: hung lft and lost tch 2f out* **11/1**

1m 12.3s (2.10) **Going Correction** +0.10s/f (Good) **5** Ran SP% **107.1**
Speed ratings (Par 92): **90,87,86,84,74**
CSF £13.83 TOTE £3.50: £2.80, £2.80; EX 9.50.
Owner R D Hartshorn **Bred** Miss H M A Omersa **Trained** Newmarket, Suffolk

FOCUS
It was no surprise to see the field head stands' side in the straight for this maiden auction. Weak form, the winner probably not needing to improve.

NOTEBOOK
Miss Moneypenni held on well for an all-the-way success. She held strong claims on the form of her debut third at Windsor, and showed her latest Newmarket running to be all wrong with this victory. It will presumably be nurseries next. (tchd 9-4)
Smart Red, a well-beaten second on firm ground at the course last time, stayed on well for second to record her best effort so far. (op 9-2 tchd 7-2)
Surprise(IRE) stayed more centre-track and improved on her initial effort, but was unable to reverse form with Smart Red. She surely won't be sporting the Godolphin silks for much longer. (op 7-1)
High On The Hog(IRE), whose dam was placed up to 2m, is now qualified for nurseries and should fare better in that sphere, with a longer trip certain to suit. (tchd 9-4 2-1 in a place)
Miss Nimbus looked green and couldn't race on with the front four. Official explanation: jockey said filly hung left (op 9-1 tchd 12-1)

3982 IT FIRST H'CAP 7f 214y
3:40 (3:41) (Class 6) (0-60,60) 3-Y-O+ **£2,590** (£770; £385; £192) **Stalls** Low

Form RPR
6622 **1** **Fire King**[9] 3715 4-9-1 **50**....(p) NeilCallan 10 58
(A B Haynes) *t.k.h: hld up in tch: hdwy to trck ldr over 1f out: rdn to ld ins fnl f: r.o wl: comf* **9/4**[1]

1403 **2** *1 ¼* **Motty's Gift**[42] 2633 3-8-11 **55**....(v) ShaneKelly 11 58
(W R Swinburn) *led: rdn over 2f out: drvn ent fnl f: hdd and nt pce of wnr ins fnl f* **8/1**

4101 **3** *2 ¾* **Inquisitress**[9] 3715 6-9-6 **55** 6ex.... NeilChalmers 6 54
(J J Bridger) *stdd s: hld up in last trio: hdwy and n.m.r wl over 1f out: swtchd lft and rdn to chse ldng pair 1f out: no imp fnl 100yds* **9/1**

4054 **4** *2* **Prince Valentine**[9] 3715 9-8-11 **46**....(p) FergusSweeney 7 40
(G L Moore) *t.k.h: chsd ldrs tl stdd in midfield 1/2-way: effrt u.p to chse ldrs over 1f out: wknd fnl f* **20/1**

6136 **5** *¾* **Musical Script (USA)**[41] 2643 7-9-11 **60**....(b) LiamKeniry 2 52
(Mouse Hamilton-Fairley) *stdd s: hld up in rr: swtchd lft and effrt in centre over 1f out: no prog and kpt on same pce fnl f* **15/2**[3]

0-0 **6** *½* **Clearing House**[25] 3168 5-8-6 **48**.... LewisWalsh[(7)] 8 39
(J Ryan) *t.k.h: hld up in rr: rdn and hdwy over 1f out: styd on same pce ins fnl f: nvr gng pce to rch ldrs* **25/1**

0354 **7** *1 ¾* **Eywa**[25] 3171 3-8-12 **56**.... JimCrowley 5 41
(W Jarvis) *t.k.h: chsd ldrs tl wknd qckly u.p jst over 1f out: wl btn fnl f* **7/2**[2]

0663 **8** *1 ¼* **Easy Wonder (GER)**[9] 3715 5-8-6 **46** oh1.... SophieDoyle[(5)] 12 30
(I A Wood) *in tch in midfield: rdn and unble to qckn ent fnl 3f: wknd over 1f out* **18/1**

0050 **9** *4 ½* **Foreign Investment (IRE)**[71] 1762 4-9-8 **60**....(v) AndrewHeffernan[(3)] 4 34
(P D Evans) *short of room s: hld up in rr: swtchd lft and rdn wl over 1f out: sn hung lft u.p and wl btn 1f out* **14/1**

0044 **10** *nk* **King's Approach (IRE)**[14] 3525 3-9-2 **60**....(p) LukeMorris 9 31
(R A Harris) *plld hrd: sn chsng ldr tl over 1f out: sn wknd: wl btn and eased ins fnl f* **14/1**

1m 36.45s (0.45) **Going Correction** +0.10s/f (Good)
WFA 3 from 4yo+ 9lb **10** Ran SP% **113.1**
Speed ratings (Par 101): **101,99,97,95,94 93,92,90,86,85**
toteswingers:1&2:£3.20, 1&3:£3.80, 2&3:£8.70 CSF £20.07 CT £136.50 TOTE £3.20: £1.20, £4.00, £4.00; EX 20.90 Trifecta £40.00 Pool: £368.68 - 6.81 winning units..
Owner Dr J M Leigh, T Suttle & S Wicks **Bred** Dr J M Leigh **Trained** Limpley Stoke, Bath

FOCUS
A moderate handicap in which the runners again came stands' side. The runner-up sets the standard.

3983 HARDINGSCATERING.CO.UK H'CAP 1m 1f 209y
4:10 (4:10) (Class 6) (0-60,61) 3-Y-O+ **£2,590** (£770; £385; £192) **Stalls** High

Form RPR
4251 **1** **Celestial Girl**[9] 3714 3-9-9 **61** 6ex.... ChrisCatlin 5 73+
(H Morrison) *t.k.h: hld up in midfield: hdwy over 2f out: chsd ldng pair 2f out: swtchd lft ent fnl f: rdn to ld ins fnl f: r.o wl: eased towards fin: comf* **13/8**[1]

3024 **2** *3 ¼* **Rosy Dawn**[6] 3789 5-9-4 **45**.... NeilChalmers 7 50
(J J Bridger) *sn led: clr over 8f out: rdn over 2f out: hdd ins fnl f: nt pce of wnr after but kpt on gamely for 2nd* **13/2**[3]

0-40 **3** *1 ¾* **Mayfair's Future**[34] 2870 5-9-11 **52**.... IanMongan 3 54
(J R Jenkins) *chsd ldr: rdn and clsd u.p 2f out: lost 2nd jst over 1f out: kpt on same pce fnl f* **9/1**

104 **4** *6* **Noah Jameel**[20] 3314 8-9-8 **49**.... FergusSweeney 10 39
(A G Newcombe) *hld up towards rr: rdn and effrt over 2f out: wnt modest 4th over 1f out: nvr threatened ldrs* **13/2**[3]

2411 **5** *2 ¼* **Under Fire (IRE)**[8] 3723 7-10-3 **58** 6ex.... NeilCallan 2 43
(A W Carroll) *prom in main gp tl wknd u.p 2f out: wl btn over 1f out* **5/1**[2]

4042 **6** *3 ¾* **Farncombe (IRE)**[29] 3032 4-9-13 **54**.... TomQueally 4 32
(M J Scudamore) *racd in midfield: pushed along 4f out: rdn and btn over 2f out: wl bhd over 1f out* **11/1**

046- **7** *3 ¾* **Autumn Morning (IRE)**[377] 3502 4-9-8 **49**.... ShaneKelly 8 19
(P D Evans) *stdd and dropped in bhd after s: hld up in rr: pushed along and no prog over 3f out: wl bhd fnl 2f* **22/1**

/044 **8** *1 ¼* **Aah Haa**[22] 3263 5-9-8 **49**.... JimCrowley 9 17
(N J Gifford) *prom in main gp: rdn and wknd over 2f out: wl bhd over 1f out* **8/1**

2m 3.38s (-0.22) **Going Correction** +0.10s/f (Good)
WFA 3 from 4yo+ 11lb **8** Ran SP% **115.2**
Speed ratings (Par 101): **104,101,100,95,93 90,87,86**
toteswingers:1&2:£4.80, 1&3:£4.20, 2&3:£8.40 CSF £12.77 CT £72.95 TOTE £2.10: £1.10, £3.10, £2.10; EX 15.50 Trifecta £89.90 Pool: £263.74 - 2.17 winning units..
Owner Helena Springfield Ltd **Bred** Meon Valley Stud **Trained** East Ilsley, Berks

FOCUS
A low-grade handicap which was well run. Celestial Gold won in good style and is rated up 10lb.

3984 BLAKES BUTCHERS APPRENTICE H'CAP 1m 3f 196y
4:40 (4:40) (Class 6) (0-65,62) 4-Y-O+ **£2,266** (£674; £337; £168) **Stalls** High

Form RPR
6-14 **1** **Le Corvee (IRE)**[31] 2952 8-8-9 **50**.... KierenFox[(3)] 6 55
(A W Carroll) *chsd ldng pair: c stands' side and rdn wl over 2f out: drvn to ld over 1f out: styd on wl* **7/2**[3]

3353 **2** *1 ¼* **Foxtrot Bravo (IRE)**[14] 3524 4-8-3 **46**....(b) AdamBeschizza[(5)] 2 49
(Miss S L Davison) *chsd ldr tl c stands' side and lost pl over 3f out: sn rdn: rallied 1f out: styd on u.p to snatch 2nd on post* **3/1**[2]

3032 **3** *nse* **Filun**[11] 3641 5-8-5 **48**.... RichardRowe[(5)] 4 51
(A Middleton) *hld up in last pair: hdwy and c stands' side over 2f out: ev ch ent fnl f: no ex fnl 100yds: lost 2nd on line* **5/2**[1]

0205 **4** *3* **Turner's Touch**[46] 2489 8-8-0 **45**....(be) ChelseyBanks[(7)] 5 43
(G L Moore) *hld up in last: hdwy in centre 2f out: chsd ldrs and nudged along ent fnl f: one pce after* **16/1**

3464 **5** *¾* **Little Sark (IRE)**[21] 3290 5-8-8 **53**....(v[1]) MatthewCosham[(7)] 3 50
(P D Evans) *led and sn clr: styd centre and rdn over 2f out: hdd over 1f out: hung rt and btn 1f out* **9/2**

335- **6** *3 ¾* **Vita Mia**[272] 6784 4-9-3 **62**.... KevinLundie[(7)] 7 53
(P D Evans) *in tch in midfield: rdn and effrt over 2f out: no imp fr over 1f out: wl btn fnl f* **7/1**

2m 34.9s (2.20) **Going Correction** +0.10s/f (Good) **6** Ran SP% **112.4**
Speed ratings (Par 101): **96,95,95,93,92 90**
toteswingers:1&2:£2.30, 1&3:£2.80, 2&3:£2.20 CSF £14.39 TOTE £4.70: £2.40, £1.20; EX 15.00 Place 6 £100.63; Place 5 £23.73.
Owner A W Carroll **Bred** Forenaghts Stud And David O'Reilly **Trained** Cropthorne, Worcs

FOCUS
A competitive little handicap, but the form is weak.
T/Plt: £116.40 to a £1 stake. Pool:£72,821.26 - 456.52 winning tickets T/Qpdt: £18.20 to a £1 stake. Pool:£5,623.38 - 228.63 winning tickets SP

3496 MUSSELBURGH (R-H)
Tuesday, July 13

OFFICIAL GOING: Good to firm (7.5)
Wind: Moderate behind Weather: Cloudy but dry

3985 TOTEPLACEPOT MAIDEN AUCTION STKS 7f 30y
6:50 (6:51) (Class 5) 2-Y-O **£2,266** (£674; £337; £168) **Stalls** High

Form RPR
1 **Sensei (IRE)** 2-8-10 0.... PaulHanagan 3 84+
(M G Quinlan) *green in preliminaries and to post: trckd ldrs: swtchd outside and hdwy over 2f out: rdn: green whn effrt to chal wl over 1f out: led 1f out: edgd rt u.p ins fnl f: kpt on* **2/1**[2]

50 **2** *2* **Mullins Way (USA)**[28] 3049 2-8-9 0.... PhillipMakin 1 78
(F J Brennan) *trckd ldrs: smooth hdwy 1/2-way: led wl over 2f out: jnd and rdn wl over 1f out: drvn and hdd 1f out: n.m.r and kpt on same pce towards fin* **6/4**[1]

0 **3** *5* **Ransom Request**[21] 3295 2-8-7 0.... MartinLane[(3)] 7 66
(E F Vaughan) *trckd ldng pair on inner: hdwy 3f out: rdn: rn green and sltly outpcd wl over 1f out: sn swtchd lft and drvn: kpt on ins fnl f: tk 3rd nr fin* **5/1**[3]

402 **4** ½ **Boundaries**[10] 3665 2-8-12 0 DavidAllan 2 67
(T D Easterby) *led: rdn along 3f out: hdd over 2f out: sn drvn and kpt on same pce* **7/1**

5 1½ **Itzakindamagic (IRE)** 2-8-5 0 JoeFanning 4 56+
(M Johnston) *prom: pushed along over 3f out: rdn over 2f out: grad wknd* **16/1**

43 **6** 30 **Welsh Dresser (IRE)**[83] 1463 2-8-0 0 BillyCray(5) 6 —
(Peter Grayson) *dwlt: a in rr: rdn along and bhd fr 1/2-way* **40/1**

1m 28.14s (-0.86) **Going Correction** -0.35s/f (Firm) 2y crse rec **6** Ran SP% **110.8**
Speed ratings (Par 94): **90,87,82,81,79 45**
toteswingers: 1&2 £1.50, 1&3 £2.90, 2&3 £1.60. CSF £5.23 TOTE £2.60: £1.10, £1.20; EX 5.90.
Owner Burns Farm Racing **Bred** Burns Farm Stud **Trained** Newmarket, Suffolk

FOCUS
A dry night and day saw the ground changed to good to firm all over. The riders confirmed the ground was as the official. A fair maiden for the track and, although the gallop was an ordinary one, the first two pulled clear in the closing stages.

NOTEBOOK
Sensei(IRE) ◆, the first foal of an unraced half-sister to Flat winners Bea Menace and Sharp Reply (also won over hurdles and fences), was noticeably green on this racecourse debut but turned in a fairly useful performance to justify the market support. He will have no problems with 1m and, with this experience behind him looks the type to improve again and win more races. (op 5-2)
Mullins Way(USA) looked the one to beat on his eighth placing in the Coventry Stakes when tried blinkered but, although he failed to build on that effort over this longer trip with the headgear left off, he didn't do a lot wrong against a potentially decent sort. He pulled clear of the remainder and remains capable of winning a similar event. (op 7-4 tchd 11-8, 2-1 in places)
Ransom Request was easy to back beforehand on her first run over this trip but, although far from disgraced against a couple of useful sorts, she underlined her vulnerability in this type of event. She will be of more interest in nurseries granted a stiffer test of stamina. (op 4-1 tchd 11-2)
Boundaries, the most experienced of these, was readily brushed aside after having the run of the race over this longer trip. He too will be seen to better effect in run-of-the-mill nursery company in due course. (op 8-1)
Itzakindamagic(IRE), like several of her stablemates this year, seemed to need this debut. This half-sister to several winners over 6f-7f should be better for this run but she'll have to show a bit more before she is a solid betting proposition. (op 9-1)

3986 TOTEEXACTA NURSERY 5f
7:20 (7:20) (Class 4) 2-Y-0 **£3,885** (£1,156; £577; £288) **Stalls** Low

Form RPR
061 **1** **Bold Bidder**[20] 3315 2-9-7 **79** PaulHanagan 3 82+
(K A Ryan) *qckly away and sn led: jnd and rdn 2f out: drvn ins fnl f and kpt on wl* **8/15**[1]

2516 **2** 1½ **Lady Brookie**[60] 2095 2-8-11 **69** DavidNolan 4 67
(Peter Grayson) *sn cl up: effrt 2f out and ev ch: rdn over 1f out: drvn: edgd rt and one pce ins fnl f* **9/2**[2]

0042 **3** 3 **Chester Deelyte (IRE)**[6] 3770 2-8-1 **59** FrannyNorton 2 46
(Mrs L Williamson) *sn rdn along to chse ldng pair: hdwy 2f out and sn ev ch tl rdn and one pce appr fnl f* **12/1**

0215 **4** 4½ **Roodee Queen**[4] 3859 2-8-12 **70** JoeFanning 1 41
(Patrick Morris) *in tch: hdwy on outer 2f out: sn rdn and ev ch tl wknd appr fnl f and sn eased* **5/1**[3]

58.92 secs (-1.48) **Going Correction** -0.35s/f (Firm) **4** Ran SP% **107.8**
Speed ratings (Par 96): **97,94,89,82**
CSF £3.24 TOTE £2.00; EX 2.40.
Owner T G & Mrs M E Holdcroft **Bred** Bearstone Stud And T Herbert Jackson **Trained** Hambleton, N Yorks

FOCUS
Only four runners (all fillies) but three of them had previously won, and a decent gallop means this form should be reliable. The handicap marks are estimated and for information purposes only.

NOTEBOOK
Bold Bidder ◆, who was well backed, is a progressive performer who continued on the up and in the process showed a good attitude under pressure on this nursery debut. She shapes as though the return to 6f will suit and, although this was not the most competitive of races, this useful sort appeals as the type to win again. (op 4-6 tchd 8-11 in places)
Lady Brookie, far from disgraced in a Listed event at York on her previous start and having a first run for current connections, ran creditably in this more realistic grade. She looks well worth a try over 6f and may be capable of picking up a similar event away from the more progressive types. (op 7-2)
Chester Deelyte(IRE), the only one in this field not to have won a race, was not totally disgraced on this nursery debut. There will be easier races than this and she may be able to pick up a modest event in due course. (op 10-1 tchd 14-1)
Roodee Queen, well beaten on her nursery debut over further at Chester, was again a fair way below the form that saw her win a maiden. She looks fully exposed and will have to show a fair bit more before she is worth a bet again. (tchd 11-2)

3987 CANACCORD GENUITY H'CAP 1m
7:50 (7:50) (Class 3) (0-90,87) 3-Y-0+ **£7,771** (£2,312; £1,155; £577) **Stalls** High

Form RPR
3661 **1** **Ginger Jack**[12] 3585 3-9-5 **87** JoeFanning 5 98+
(M Johnston) *trckd ldr: pushed along and sltly outpcd 3f out: effrt and hdwy 2f out: squeezed through to ld 1 1/2f out: rdn out* **11/8**[1]

1360 **2** 1¼ **Keys Of Cyprus**[3] 3920 8-9-10 **83** AdrianNicholls 6 91
(D Nicholls) *hld up in rr: swtchd outside and hdwy over 2f out: rdn to chse wnr ent fnl f: sn edgd rt and no imp* **8/1**

0002 **3** 3½ **Espero (IRE)**[9] 3708 4-9-3 **76** TomEaves 2 76
(Miss L A Perratt) *trckd ldrs: smooth hdwy 3f out: rdn to ld briefly wl over 1f out: sn hdd and drvn: kpt on same pce* **3/1**[2]

0200 **4** 8 **Jewelled Dagger (IRE)**[9] 3708 6-9-2 **75** (v) PaulHanagan 4 57
(J S Goldie) *set str pce: rdn along 3f out: sn hdd and grad wknd* **7/1**

251 **5** 1¼ **Silver Rime (FR)**[9] 3708 5-9-13 **86** 6ex PhillipMakin 1 65
(Miss L A Perratt) *trckd ldng pair: hdwy to chse ldr over 3f out: led over 2f out and sn rdn: hdd wl over 1f out and wknd qckly* **9/2**[3]

1m 36.83s (-4.37) **Going Correction** -0.35s/f (Firm) course record
WFA 3 from 4yo+ 9lb **5** Ran SP% **108.9**
Speed ratings (Par 107): **107,105,102,94,93**
toteswinger: 1&2 £6.00. CSF £12.29 TOTE £2.00: £2.30, £6.10; EX 9.90.
Owner Sheikh Hamdan Bin Mohammed Al Maktoum **Bred** Darley **Trained** Middleham Moor, N Yorks

FOCUS
A couple of previous winners in a useful handicap and, although the early gallop appeared to be no more than an ordinary one, the winning time shaved nearly two seconds off the existing course record. A personal best from the progressive winner.

NOTEBOOK
Ginger Jack ◆ is a progressive sort who had to wait for a gap but once in the clear showed a fine attitude to register a career-best effort. Life will obviously be tougher after reassessment but he's the type to progress again for his in-form stable and he leaves the impression that he is well worth a try over 1m1f or 1m2f. (op 6-5 tchd 6-4 in a place)
Keys Of Cyprus put a below-par effort at York firmly behind him and, given his best form has been with plenty of give in the ground, he deserves plenty of credit for finishing as close as he did to a progressive rival, despite edging off a true line late on. He will be 1lb lower in future and will be of more interest when the ground eases. (op 9-1)
Espero(IRE) ran creditably to reverse recent Ayr placings with Silver Rime, especially as he raced with the choke out in the first half of the contest. Both his wins have been on Polytrack but he is capable of winning a race on grass away from the progressive or well-handicapped types. (op 10-3)
Jewelled Dagger(IRE) attracted support through the day but was again below the form that he showed at Musselburgh in May. He has undoubtedly slipped to a potentially decent mark but hasn't won since 2007 and doesn't look one for maximum faith. (op 8-1)
Silver Rime(FR) travelled strongly after being ridden closer to the pace than for his Ayr win but his response to pressure was limited and, although he will be 2lb lower in future, he may be one to watch rather than bet on next time. He was reportedly unsuited by the very quick ground. Official explanation: jockey said gelding was unsuited by good to firm going (op 5-1)

3988 TOTEQUADPOT CLAIMING STKS 5f
8:20 (8:20) (Class 6) 3-Y-0 **£2,266** (£674; £337; £168) **Stalls** Low

Form RPR
5-02 **1** **Oondiri (IRE)**[24] 3228 3-8-11 57 PaulHanagan 3 62
(T D Easterby) *qckly away and edgd lft to rails sn after s: mde all: rdn over 1f out and kpt on strly* **13/8**[2]

0053 **2** 2 **Kristen Jane (USA)**[3] 3903 3-8-6 43 FrannyNorton 2 50
(Miss L A Perratt) *sn cl up: effrt and ev ch 2f out: sn rdn and kpt on same pce ins fnl f* **10/1**[3]

0321 **3** 2½ **Bronze Beau**[3] 3903 3-8-13 65 (t) TomEaves 1 48
(Mrs L Stubbs) *n.m.r on inner and hmpd shortly after s: trckd ldng pair: effrt and nt clr run wl over 1f out and again appr fnl f: no imp* **10/11**[1]

2440 **4** 6 **Flow Chart (IRE)**[94] 1237 3-8-13 67 (b) DavidNolan 6 26
(Peter Grayson) *chsd ldrs: rdn along 1/2-way: sn wknd* **20/1**

6003 **5** ¾ **Ignore**[24] 3228 3-8-4 44 IanBrennan(5) 4 20
(Mrs R A Carr) *chsd ldrs: rdn along and lost pl after 1 1/2f: bhd fr 1/2-way* **12/1**

58.46 secs (-1.94) **Going Correction** -0.35s/f (Firm) **5** Ran SP% **112.0**
Speed ratings (Par 98): **101,97,93,84,83**
toteswinger: 1&2 £10.70. CSF £16.85 TOTE £2.50: £1.20, £4.80; EX 10.80.
Owner C H Stevens **Bred** Newlands House Stud **Trained** Great Habton, N Yorks

FOCUS
A modest and uncompetitive claimer and one that took less winning than looked likely with the market leader disappointing. The gallop was sound and the form is rated around the winner.

3989 SCOTTISH RACING YOUR BETTER BET H'CAP 1m 6f
8:50 (8:50) (Class 6) (0-65,63) 4-Y-0+ **£2,590** (£770; £385; £192) **Stalls** High

Form RPR
136- **1** **Beat The Shower**[31] 7425 4-9-0 **54** DavidAllan 5 61+
(P D Niven) *hld up: hdwy over 3f out: swtchd wd and rdn wl over 1f out: str run to ld ent fnl f: styd on* **7/2**[2]

6506 **2** 1½ **Tilos Gem (IRE)**[17] 3432 4-9-7 **61** JoeFanning 4 66
(M Johnston) *prom: hdwy to ld 2 1/2f out and sn rdn: drvn and hdd ent fnl f: kpt on* **9/2**[3]

0-00 **3** 2 **Harcas (IRE)**[2] 3223 8-8-9 **49** (b) PhillipMakin 7 51
(M Todhunter) *trckd ldrs: hdwy on inner 3f out: effrt and nt clr run 2f out: sn swtchd lft and rdn: kpt on same pce ent fnl f* **9/1**

61-4 **4** hd **Zelos Diktator**[19] 3352 4-9-2 **56** (p) TomEaves 1 58
(Mrs R Dobbin) *cl up: led after 2f: rdn along 3f out: sn hdd and ch tl drvn and one pce appr fnl f* **10/1**

-004 **5** nk **Kyber**[15] 3496 9-8-0 **45** IanBrennan(5) 3 46
(J S Goldie) *bhd: hdwy 3f out: rdn 2f out: swtchd lft and drvn over 1f out: styd on wl fnl f: nrst fin* **13/2**

0245 **6** ¾ **Planetarium**[19] 3367 5-9-6 **63** MartinLane(3) 2 63
(P Monteith) *trckd ldrs: chsd ldr 1/2-way: rdn and ev ch over 2f out: sn drvn and wknd* **11/2**

-533 **7** 4 **Knock Three Times (IRE)**[10] 3669 4-8-7 **47** PaulHanagan 6 42
(W Storey) *hld up: hdwy 1/2-way: chsd ldrs 3f out: rdn and ch over 2f out: drvn wl over 1f out and sn wknd* **11/4**[1]

-000 **8** 30 **Suburbia (USA)**[9] 3707 4-8-9 **49** FrannyNorton 8 —
(J Barclay) *led 2f: prom tl pushed along and lost pl 1/2-way: bhd fnl 4f* **28/1**

3m 1.30s (-4.00) **Going Correction** -0.35s/f (Firm) **8** Ran SP% **118.3**
Speed ratings (Par 101): **97,96,95,94,94 94,92,74**
toteswingers: 1&2 £4.30, 1&3 £6.10, 2&3 £11.50. CSF £20.47 CT £132.32 TOTE £6.30: £2.30, £2.90, £4.70; EX 25.10.
Owner Mrs Kate Young **Bred** C P E Brooks **Trained** Barton-le-Street, N Yorks

FOCUS
Exposed performers in a modest handicap. The gallop was an ordinary one and the form may not prove that reliable.
Knock Three Times(IRE) Official explanation: trainer was unable to offer any explanation to fillies below par run

3990 TOTESWINGER H'CAP 7f 30y
9:20 (9:20) (Class 5) (0-70,69) 3-Y-0+ **£3,238** (£963; £481; £240) **Stalls** High

Form RPR
3555 **1** **Step In Time (IRE)**[10] 3689 3-9-7 **69** JoeFanning 9 76+
(M Johnston) *sn led: rdn over 2f out: drvn clr appr fnl f: kpt on strly* **6/5**[1]

0-00 **2** 3 **Shunkawakhan (IRE)**[56] 2211 7-8-13 **53** PhillipMakin 7 55
(Miss L A Perratt) *trckd ldng pair: effrt on inner and n.m.r 2f out: sn rdn and styd on to chse wnr ins fnl f: no imp* **14/1**

0000 **3** 1¾ **Barraland**[19] 3356 5-8-12 **55** GaryBartley(3) 5 52
(J S Goldie) *hld up in rr: swtchd lft and hdwy 2f out: sn rdn and kpt on ins fnl f* **18/1**

0-04 **4** 2¼ **Zabeel Tower**[15] 3500 7-9-5 **59** (p) PaulHanagan 6 50
(R Allan) *trckd ldrs: hdwy over 3f out: rdn over 2f out and ch tl drvn and one pce fr over 1f out* **2/1**[2]

4022 **5** ¾ **Hosanna**[1] 3948 4-8-9 **49** DavidAllan 4 38
(J Barclay) *chsd wnr: effrt and cl up over 2f out: sn rdn and ch tl drvn and wknd wl over 1f out* **7/2**[3]

1m 27.54s (-1.46) **Going Correction** -0.35s/f (Firm)
WFA 3 from 4yo+ 8lb **5** Ran SP% **112.9**
Speed ratings (Par 103): **94,90,88,86,85**
toteswinger: 1&2 £4.70. CSF £18.06 TOTE £1.80: £1.10, £6.30; EX 22.10 Place 6: £27.26, Place 5: £22.94..
Owner S R Counsell **Bred** Orpendale **Trained** Middleham Moor, N Yorks

FOCUS
A depleted field and, although the gallop was an ordinary one, the winner won this with some authority. He is rated to his latter 2yo level, but the form is dubious.
T/Plt: £65.70 to a £1 stake. Pool:£56,407.50 - 625.94 winning tickets T/Qpdt: £21.90 to a £1 stake. Pool:£4,251.52 - 143.20 winning tickets JR

[3602]YARMOUTH (L-H)

Tuesday, July 13

OFFICIAL GOING: Good to firm

Wind: fresh against Weather: Overcast

3991 E B F AEROPAK MAIDEN STKS 7f 3y

6:30 (6:31) (Class 5) 2-Y-O £3,406 (£1,019; £509; £254; £126) Stalls High

Form RPR

4 **1** **Whaileyy (IRE)**[45] 2547 2-9-3 0 .... RyanMoore 4 75+
(Sir Michael Stoute) *mde all: modest pce early: rdn wl over 1f out: jst holding persistent rival through fnl f: all out* **4/9**[1]

04 **2** *hd* **Ahlaain (USA)**[24] 3219 2-9-3 0 .... WilliamBuick 1 75+
(D M Simcock) *s.i.s: sn pressing wnr: upsides 1/2-way: ev ch fnl f: rdn and kpt on wl: jst hld* **7/1**[2]

0 **3** *3 ½* **Regal Kiss**[47] 2461 2-8-12 0 .... RichardHills 10 61
(M Johnston) *cl up: rdn over 2f out: 3rd and no imp over 1f out* **10/1**[3]

5 **4** *1 ¾* **Algurayn (IRE)**[12] 3602 2-9-3 0 .... SaleemGolam 9 61
(G Prodromou) *hld up in rr: ungainly at 1/2-way: rdn and kpt on ins fnl f: nvr looked like chalng: snatched 4th* **66/1**

5 *¾* **Proper Charlie** 2-9-3 0 .... JamieSpencer 8 60
(W J Knight) *t.k.h in midfield: rdn over 2f out: btn wl over 1f out: lost modest 4th cl home* **10/1**[3]

6 *3 ¼* **Screenprint** 2-9-3 0 .... HayleyTurner 5 51
(M L W Bell) *t.k.h in midfield: btn wl over 1f out* **12/1**

7 *1 ½* **Loch Ordie** 2-9-3 0 .... JerryO'Dwyer 6 48
(M G Quinlan) *s.i.s: bhd: struggling fnl 3f* **66/1**

8 *hd* **Yahafedh Alaih** 2-9-3 0 .... SebSanders 2 47
(C E Brittain) *plld hrd and prom: drvn wl over 2f out: btn wl over 1f out* **25/1**

0 **9** *2 ¾* **Al Furat (USA)**[11] 3631 2-9-3 0 .... TedDurcan 7 40
(D R Lanigan) *last away: brief effrt 1/2-way: wknd over 2f out: eased fnl f* **33/1**

1m 26.9s (0.30) **Going Correction** -0.025s/f (Good) **9** Ran SP% **117.4**
Speed ratings (Par 94): **97,96,92,90,89 86,84,84,81**
toteswingers: 1&2 £1.20, 1&3 £3.20, 2&3 £4.00. CSF £4.11 TOTE £1.40: £1.02, £1.90, £2.70; EX 4.10.
Owner Saleh Al Homaizi & Imad Al Sagar **Bred** Iona Equine **Trained** Newmarket, Suffolk

FOCUS
An average juvenile maiden and the first pair dominated. Limited form but there should be more to come from the winner.

NOTEBOOK
Whaileyy(IRE) had finished fourth on his debut in a 6f Newmarket maiden working out well, but still looked as if this race would bring him on. He was quickly away, setting just a moderate pace, but soon joined by the runner-up and eventually had to work hard to land the odds. He needed strong driving to get his head in front close home and will have to do better if he is negotiate a step up in grade. (tchd 2-5)
Ahlaain(USA) had improved on his modest debut effort by taking fourth in a 7f Newmarket maiden 24 days earlier and may have taken another slight step forward here. He was slowly out of the stalls, but made up the lost ground quickly and was soon disputing the lead. He pushed the winner very hard inside the final furlong and will surely find a race, even if it requires a switch to nurseries, for which he now qualifies.
Regal Kiss, the only filly in the line-up, certainly improved on her modest debut run, but was a fair way off the first two at the finish and will need to progress again to land an ordinary maiden. She is bred to stay longer trips, though, so is no forlorn hope. (op 11-1 tchd 12-1)
Algurayn(IRE), a first-time-out half-brother to a smart miler, showed a hint of promise, racing close up most of the way before tiring late on.
Proper Charlie, a first-time-out half-brother to a smart miler, showed a hint of promise, racing close up most of the way before tiring late on. (op 11-1)
Screenprint, a newcomer from a good family, stayed on in the closing stages without ever threatening to make the frame. (op 14-1)

3992 FREEDERM (S) NURSERY 7f 3y

7:00 (7:00) (Class 6) 2-Y-O £1,554 (£462; £231; £115) Stalls High

Form RPR

002 **1** **Lord Of The Storm**[10] 3678 2-9-4 63 .... JackDean(3) 4 65
(W G M Turner) *towards rr: 5th and bit to do 1/2-way: wnt 2nd over 1f out: carried hd awkwardly and urged along: led cl home* **15/8**[1]

054 **2** *nse* **Majestic Style (IRE)**[10] 3678 2-8-1 50 .... HarryBentley(7) 2 52
(A P Jarvis) *chsd ldr: led over 2f out: rdn and hrd pressed fnl f: jst ct* **7/1**

6054 **3** *7* **Coolree Pearl (IRE)**[33] 2905 2-8-10 52 ow1 .... JamieSpencer 6 36
(A B Haynes) *last away: swtchd lft and effrt on outside over 2f out: chsd ldng pair vainly fr over 1f out* **9/2**[2]

603 **4** *6* **Livia Quarta (IRE)**[12] 3603 2-8-9 51 .... EddieCreighton 3 20
(E J Creighton) *chsd ldrs: pushed along after 3f: btn and wandering wl over 1f out* **9/2**[2]

005 **5** *¾* **No Peace (IRE)**[33] 2905 2-8-2 44 ....(p) HayleyTurner 7 12
(G G Margarson) *chsd ldrs: rdn over 3f out: fnd nil: drifting lft over 1f out* **9/1**

5654 **6** *nse* **Dancing With Fire**[42] 2631 2-8-2 44 .... AndreaAtzeni 5 11
(D Donovan) *bhd: rdn over 3f out: wl btn over 2f out* **13/2**[3]

0005 **7** *6* **Bold Deceiver**[75] 1632 2-8-2 44 .... JimmyQuinn 8 —
(P S McEntee) *plld hrd early: in midfield: rdn over 3f out: sn btn: t.o* **14/1**

650 **8** *2 ¼* **Sister June (IRE)**[27] 3082 2-8-2 44 ....(b[1]) NickyMackay 1 —
(E J Creighton) *led at brisk pce: rdn and hdd over 2f out: hanging rt and reluctant after: t.o* **33/1**

1m 27.78s (1.18) **Going Correction** -0.025s/f (Good) **8** Ran SP% **116.6**
Speed ratings (Par 92): **92,91,83,77,76 76,69,66**
toteswingers: 1&2 £2.60, 1&3 £2.50, 2&3 £2.90. CSF £16.20 CT £53.34 TOTE £3.50: £1.60, £3.20, £2.40; EX 20.10.There was no bid for the winner.
Owner Mrs M S Teversham **Bred** Mrs Monica Teversham **Trained** Sigwells, Somerset

FOCUS
A weak nursery but the form looks sound though. The 'official' ratings shown next to each horse are estimated and for information purposes only.

NOTEBOOK
Lord Of The Storm, beaten just a neck in a Leicester seller last time, just managed to get the job done this time. Held up in midfield early on, he began to make progress two furlongs out and knuckled down under pressure to assert close home. He does not appear to have much in hand over the handicapper, so may find it difficult to shrug off a rise in his rating. (op 5-2 tchd 11-4)
Majestic Style(IRE), more than six lengths behind Lord Of The Storm on her most recent run, got much closer on revised terms. She led from the start, setting a decent pace and, despite being headed briefly mid-race, battled on bravely. She lost out only on the nod and is clearly competitive from this mark. Life might get tough in handicaps, though. (tchd 6-1)
Coolree Pearl(IRE) has been running consistently at her level, but was left well behind in the closing stages here. She lost ground at the start and was carrying overweight, though, so can be counted a little better than the bare form. (tchd 7-2)
Livia Quarta(IRE), not beaten far when third in this grade here 12 days previously, fared less well on her return to the course. She was never closer than third and looked one-paced late on. (op 7-2 tchd 5-1)
No Peace(IRE) Official explanation: jockey said filly had no more to give
Dancing With Fire, fourth in an even weaker race of this type early in June, ran as well as could be expected. Last in the early stages, she made ground in the second half of the race. (op 9-1 tchd 6-1)
Bold Deceiver Official explanation: jockey said filly ran to free
Sister June(IRE) Official explanation: jockey said filly hung right

3993 BAZUKA H'CAP 6f 3y

7:30 (7:30) (Class 6) (0-60,60) 3-Y-0+ £1,554 (£462; £231; £115) Stalls High

Form RPR

0040 **1** **Clerical (USA)**[22] 3263 4-8-11 45 ....(p) J-PGuillambert 1 52
(R M H Cowell) *chsd ldrs: sn pushed along: sustained effrt over 1f out: sn disputing ld: led cl home: gamely* **14/1**

4550 **2** *nk* **Caribbean Coral**[8] 3727 11-9-7 55 .... JamieSpencer 11 61
(A B Haynes) *hmpd sn after s: wl bhd: gd prog 2f out: v narrow ld ins fnl f: drvn and r.o: hdd nr fin* **12/1**

0500 **3** *hd* **Always Dazzling**[19] 3371 3-9-6 60 .... RichardHills 12 64
(M Johnston) *hmpd sn after s: towards rr: prog wl over 1f out: ev ch 1f out: nt qckn fnl 75yds* **10/1**

1625 **4** *½* **Sirjosh**[16] 2964 4-9-7 55 .... AndreaAtzeni 9 59
(D Donovan) *last away and sn hmpd: stdy prog fnl 2f: kpt on wl ins fnl f: nvr quite able to chal* **9/2**[2]

5600 **5** *½* **Hill Of Miller (IRE)**[26] 3113 3-9-4 58 ....(bt[1]) HayleyTurner 14 59
(Rae Guest) *hmpd sn after s: sn midfield: hdwy over 1f out: styd on ins fnl f: nvr gng pce to chal* **10/1**

3030 **6** *nk* **Bahama Baileys**[36] 2808 5-8-9 46 .... KellyHarrison(3) 5 47
(C A Dwyer) *chsd ldrs: rdn and effrt over 2f out: w ldr over 1f out tl no ex fnl 100yds* **25/1**

230 **7** *1 ½* **Nativity**[22] 3254 4-9-6 54 .... SamHitchcott 4 50
(J L Spearing) *prom: rdn and wknd grad fr over 1f out* **10/3**[1]

0240 **8** *hd* **What Katie Did (IRE)**[22] 3254 5-9-8 56 ....(p) PatCosgrave 3 52
(J M Bradley) *led: rdn and hdd 1f out: sn btn* **15/2**[3]

000 **9** *3 ¾* **Rileys Crane**[42] 2632 3-9-1 55 .... TomMcLaughlin 2 38
(Mrs C A Dunnett) *chsd ldrs: rdn 3f out: btn over 1f out* **33/1**

3030 **10** *1 ½* **Sweet Applause (IRE)**[10] 3687 4-8-11 52 .... CharlotteKerton(7) 15 31
(G Prodromou) *wnt lft s and caused several problems: plld hrd: carted rdr to dispute ld 1/2-way: lost pl over 1f out* **14/1**

0-00 **11** *10* **Elsie Jo (IRE)**[12] 3605 4-9-0 48 .... StephenCraine 6 —
(M Wigham) *j. awkwardly fr stalls: labouring bdly wl over 2f out: t.o* **10/1**

0050 **12** *11* **Tigers Charm**[32] 2919 3-8-5 48 ....(b[1]) JackDean(3) 8 —
(J M Bradley) *plld hrd: chsd ldrs: wknd bdly over 2f out and nt keen: t.o* **12/1**

1m 13.99s (-0.41) **Going Correction** -0.025s/f (Good)
WFA 3 from 4yo+ 6lb **12** Ran SP% **115.8**
Speed ratings (Par 101): **101,100,100,99,99 98,96,96,91,89 76,61**
toteswingers: 1&2 £17.10, 1&3 £19.60, 2&3 £6.00. CSF £167.88 CT £1780.96 TOTE £17.20: £4.10, £3.20, £3.20; EX 231.70.
Owner J Sargeant **Bred** Walmac Stud Management Llc **Trained** Six Mile Bottom, Cambs
■ Stewards' Enquiry : Charlotte Kerton two-day ban; careless riding (27-29 july)

FOCUS
A modest handicap, with the top weight rated just 58 and a bunched finish. Sound if limited form.
Always Dazzling Official explanation: jockey said filly suffered interference at start

3994 4HEAD H'CAP 5f 43y

8:00 (8:00) (Class 5) (0-70,70) 3-Y-0+ £2,201 (£655; £327; £163) Stalls High

Form RPR

610 **1** **Desperate Dan**[39] 2689 9-9-12 70 ....(v) JamieSpencer 7 81
(A B Haynes) *taken down early: dropped out last: str run over 1f out: drvn along to ld w ears bk 75yds out: sn in command* **6/1**

3224 **2** *1 ¾* **Wreningham**[17] 3440 5-8-12 59 .... WilliamCarson(3) 1 64
(S C Williams) *led: rdn and hdd fnl 75yds: kpt on but no ch w qckning wnr* **9/2**[2]

3633 **3** *nse* **Thoughtsofstardom**[5] 3818 7-9-1 59 .... FrankieDettori 2 64
(P S McEntee) *pressed ldrs: rdn over 1f out: ev ch and r.o gamely tl wnr dashed by 75yds out* **4/1**[1]

062 **4** *¾* **Morgans Choice**[5] 3834 3-8-11 60 ....(b) SamHitchcott 9 60
(J L Spearing) *rather isolated on stands' rails: pressed ldrs: rdn w little rspnse over 1f out: edgd lft and plugged on* **11/2**[3]

5062 **5** *1 ½* **Rough Rock (IRE)**[12] 3604 5-9-5 63 .... JerryO'Dwyer 10 63+
(C A Dwyer) *bhd: rdn and btn over 2f out: sme late prog: snatched 5th* **15/2**

4426 **6** *nk* **Gold Gleam (USA)**[26] 3111 3-9-7 70 .... RyanMoore 5 64
(J Noseda) *sn rdn: midfield: btn over 1f out* **13/2**

0026 **7** *¾* **Island Legend (IRE)**[22] 3255 4-8-13 57 ....(p) PatCosgrave 6 50
(J M Bradley) *prom tl rdn and wknd over 1f out* **14/1**

446- **8** *2* **Imaginary Diva**[259] 7100 4-8-11 55 .... SebSanders 4 41
(G G Margarson) *prom: rdn and fdd fnl 300yds* **12/1**

0000 **9** *1* **Russian Rocket (IRE)**[28] 3064 8-8-0 51 oh1 .... LeonnaMayor(7) 8 33
(Mrs C A Dunnett) *chsd ldrs: rdn 1/2-way: btn over 2f out* **25/1**

0040 **10** *2 ¼* **Mazzola**[8] 3722 4-8-10 57 ....(b[1]) JackDean(3) 3 31
(J M Bradley) *last away: sn pressing ldrs: rdn and no rspnse and wknd over 1f out: eased* **16/1**

62.33 secs (-0.37) **Going Correction** -0.025s/f (Good)
WFA 3 from 4yo+ 5lb **10** Ran SP% **117.0**
Speed ratings (Par 103): **97,94,94,92,90 90,88,85,84,80**
toteswingers: 1&2 £4.60, 1&3 £5.40, 2&3 £3.00. CSF £33.32 CT £124.67 TOTE £8.20: £3.00, £1.20, £2.80; EX 39.60.
Owner Joe McCarthy **Bred** Sheikh Amin Dahlawi **Trained** Limpley Stoke, Bath

FOCUS
A competitive handicap for the grade, but still moderate form. It has been rated around the second and third.

3995 ADIOS H'CAP 1m 2f 21y

8:30 (8:30) (Class 4) (0-80,80) 3-Y-0+ £3,885 (£1,156; £577; £288) Stalls Low

Form RPR

5-40 **1** **Yorgunnabelucky (USA)**[20] 3318 4-9-12 78 ....(p) RichardHills 1 94
(M Johnston) *sn pushed into ld: rdn and jnd 2f out: asserted jst ins fnl f: kpt on stoutly* **5/2**[2]

001 **2** 2 1/2 **Anacopa (USA)**[22] 3266 3-9-0 77 FrankieDettori 2 88
(Mahmood Al Zarooni) *pressed ldr: rnged upsides 2f out: sn rdn: hdd jst ins fnl f: nt qckn* **9/2**[3]
33 **3** 2 1/2 **Dubai Bounty**[84] 1448 3-9-0 77 (p) NickyMackay 4 83+
(G A Butler) *chsd ldrs: rdn and outpcd over 2f out: plugged on into modest 3rd 1f out* **2/1**[1]
0036 **4** 1 3/4 **Raptor (GER)**[14] 3318 7-10-0 80 (b) JamieMackay 6 83
(M E Rimmer) *pressed ldng pair tl rdn and plodded on same pce fr over 2f out: lost 3rd 1f out* **10/1**
4215 **5** 1 1/4 **Rocky's Pride (IRE)**[12] 3607 4-9-2 68 RyanMoore 5 68
(W J Musson) *in tch tl rdn over 3f out: sn struggling: n.d fnl 2f* **7/1**
030- **6** 23 **Blaise Tower**[346] 4520 4-9-10 76 JamieSpencer 3 30
(A B Haynes) *bhd: drvn over 3f out: t.o 2f out: sn eased* **8/1**
2m 7.03s (-3.47) **Going Correction** -0.20s/f (Firm)
WFA 3 from 4yo+ 11lb **6 Ran SP% 112.8**
Speed ratings (Par 105): **105,103,101,99,98 80**
toteswingers: 1&2 £3.80, 1&3 £2.10, 2&3 £1.30. CSF £14.17 TOTE £4.00: £2.40, £2.50; EX 11.80.
Owner Mrs S J Brookhouse **Bred** March Thoroughbreds **Trained** Middleham Moor, N Yorks

FOCUS
A fair handicap, but run at just a middling pace until well into the home straight. The winner had a pretty easy lead and this is probably not form to rate too positively.
Blaise Tower Official explanation: jockey said gelding hung right

3996 IGLU GEL H'CAP 1m 6f 17y
9:00 (9:02) (Class 5) (0-70,58) 3-Y-O+ **£2,201** (£655; £327; £163) **Stalls** High

Form RPR
4434 **1** **Broughtons Point**[6] 3780 4-10-0 57 JamieMackay 6 62
(W J Musson) *settled 3rd: kpt on to ld 2f out: rdn over 1f out: hld on u.strer riding: all out* **9/4**[2]
404 **2** nk **Tower**[14] 3523 3-8-7 58 RichardOld(7) 2 63
(G Prodromou) *settled last: pushed along 4f out: sustained effrt fnl f: gaining nr fin* **40/1**
00-2 **3** 3/4 **Consult**[37] 2792 3-8-7 51 ow1 SebSanders 5 55
(Sir Mark Prescott) *pressed ldr but nt striding out and rdr sn appearing uneasy and cajoling along: drvn hrd 5f out: led over 4f out: hdd 2f out: hanging and fnd nil fnl f: eased cl home* **8/15**[1]
0150 **4** 2 3/4 **Royal Premier (IRE)**[19] 3348 7-9-5 53 SimonPearce(5) 3 53
(H J Collingridge) *hld up: struggling wl over 3f out: plugging on ins fnl f but no ch* **9/1**[3]
P00- **5** 17 **Rock Of Behistun (IRE)**[258] 7120 3-8-1 45 JimmyQuinn 4 21
(P L Gilligan) *led and t.k.h: hdd over 4f out: sn lost pl: t.o and eased* **66/1**
3m 5.53s (-2.07) **Going Correction** -0.20s/f (Firm)
WFA 3 from 4yo+ 15lb **5 Ran SP% 109.9**
Speed ratings (Par 103): **97,96,96,94,85**
toteswinger: 1&2 £21.50. CSF £50.26 TOTE £3.40: £1.50, £7.10; EX 45.60 Place 6: £113.62, Place 5: £99.09..
Owner Broughton Thermal Insulation **Bred** Broughton Bloodstock **Trained** Newmarket, Suffolk

FOCUS
A poor staying handicap with the first three coming clear. There was no great pace on and it is doubtful if the winner had to improve.
T/Plt: £234.00 to a £1 stake. Pool:£72,639.94 - 226.61 winning tickets T/Qpdt: £136.80 to a £1 stake. Pool:£5,048.80 - 27.30 winning tickets IM

3943 HAMBURG (R-H)
Tuesday, July 13

OFFICIAL GOING: Turf: good

4012a ROSSMANN-RENNEN (LANGER HAMBURGER) (GROUP 3) (4YO+) (TURF) 2m
6:30 (6:51) 4-Y-O+
£28,318 (£9,734; £4,867; £2,654; £1,769; £1,327)

RPR
1 **Tres Rock Danon (FR)**[44] 2574 4-9-2 0 APietsch 1 108
(W Hickst, Germany) *broke wl: a.p: gd prog into st: grabbed ld 2f out: wnt clr ins fnl f: easily* **9/10**[1]
2 3 1/2 **Brusco**[44] 4-9-0 0 EPedroza 8 102
(A Wohler, Germany) *broke wl: settled bhd ldr: tk ld early in st: r.o wl but no match for wnr* **17/5**[2]
3 3/4 **Northern Glory**[73] 7-9-0 0 KKerekes 6 101
(W Figge, Germany) *bkmarker fr s: racd freely: mde gd prog turning into st: fin wl on outside to take 3rd* **107/10**
4 2 **Caudillo (GER)**[44] 2574 7-9-0 0 HenkGrewe 5 99
(Dr A Bolte, Germany) *racd in midfield: effrt early in st: no ex: styd on* **73/10**
5 1 3/4 **Egon (IRE)**[373] 3670 4-9-0 0 ADeVries 7 97
(W Hickst, Germany) *racd in 4th: shkn up ent st: flattered briefly but no ex fnl 2f* **43/10**[3]
6 4 **Tarkheena Prince (USA)**[44] 2574 5-9-0 0 AStarke 4 93
(C Von Der Recke, Germany) *racd in midfield: effrt early in st: no ex: wknd* **67/10**
7 25 **Limatus (GER)**[55] 9-9-0 0 RJuracek 2 65
(P Vovcenko, Germany) *led fr s: set gd pce: hdd 2f out: briefly r.o but sn wknd* **209/10**
3m 28.51s (208.51) **7 Ran SP% 132.4**
WIN (incl. 10 euro stake): 19. PLACES: 11, 14, 19. SF: 78.
Owner Stall D'Angelo **Bred** Haras De Chevotel & Morton Bloodstock **Trained** Germany

3770 CATTERICK (L-H)
Wednesday, July 14

OFFICIAL GOING: Good (good to firm in places; 8.1)
Wind: Light across Weather: Cloudy and warm

4013 CATTERICKBRIDGE.CO.UK NOVICE AUCTION STKS 7f
2:20 (2:20) (Class 5) 2-Y-O **£2,266** (£674; £337) **Stalls** Low

Form RPR
310 **1** **Bay Of Fires (IRE)**[26] 3141 2-8-6 0 SilvestreDeSousa 1 68+
(D O'Meara) *mde virtually all: jnd and shkn up 2f out: pushed clr appr fnl f: easily* **2/5**[1]
50 **2** 1 3/4 **Bradbury (IRE)**[2] 3964 2-8-13 0 GrahamGibbons 3 71
(J D Bethell) *trckd ldng pair: effrt on inner 2f out: sn rdn and kpt on ins fnl f* **20/1**[3]
521 **3** 1/2 **Spartic**[11] 3657 2-8-11 0 JamesDoyle 4 67
(A J McCabe) *cl up: rdn and ev ch 2f out: one pce appr fnl f* **5/2**[2]
1m 29.36s (2.36) **Going Correction** +0.20s/f (Good) **3 Ran SP% 104.8**
Speed ratings (Par 94): **94,92,91**
CSF £6.32 TOTE £1.30; EX 5.60.
Owner P Bamford J M Binns R G Fell & K Everitt **Bred** Duncan A McGregor **Trained** Nawton, N Yorks

FOCUS
The favourite had a simple task with her market rival disappointing. Not form to take literally.

NOTEBOOK
Bay Of Fires(IRE) had run well in the Group 3 Albany Stakes at Royal Ascot and this represented a big drop in class. She duly won easily after gaining a decisive advantage on the home bend. One would imagine that connections will hope to find some black type for her in time, so possibly a race like the Firth Of Clyde Stakes at the Ayr Gold Cup meeting would be a target. She would need to drop a furlong on distance for that, though. (op 8-13)
Bradbury(IRE), giving weight away to rivals that had already won, and up to 7f for the first time, had shown little in two previous outings, so this seemed better because he kept on nicely under pressure after being held up. (op 16-1)
Spartic was disappointing on the face of it, as he was readily held coming to the furlong marker. There was no obvious reason for the disappointing effort. (op 7-4)

4014 YORKSHIRE4X4.COM ADVENTURE ACTIVITIES (S) STKS 5f 212y
2:50 (2:53) (Class 6) 3-Y-O+ **£1,706** (£503; £252) **Stalls** Low

Form RPR
2006 **1** **Cross Of Lorraine (IRE)**[15] 3534 7-8-7 50 (b) LeeTopliss(7) 8 64
(C Grant) *cl up on wd outside: chsd ldr after 2f: led over 2f out and sn rdn clr: drvn ins fnl f: kpt on* **6/1**
00-0 **2** hd **Musca (IRE)**[22] 3284 6-9-0 62 TonyHamilton 5 63
(C Grant) *dwlt and towards rr: hdwy 1/2-way: rdn to chse wnr over 1f out: drvn ins fnl f: kpt on wl towards fin* **22/1**
0642 **3** 1 1/4 **Lindoro**[14] 3557 5-9-0 75 (p) PhillipMakin 10 59
(M G Quinlan) *in rr: hdwy on outer over 2f out and sn rdn: drvn to chse ldrs over 1f out: sn drvn: edgd lft ins fnl f: kpt on* **9/4**[1]
3324 **4** nk **Powerful Pierre**[28] 3086 3-8-8 67 PaulHanagan 12 58
(Jedd O'Keeffe) *in rr: effrt and sme hdwy on outer 2f out: sn rdn and hung bdly lft over 1f out: kpt on ins fnl f: no imp towards fin* **4/1**[3]
0160 **5** 3 **Soto**[12] 3615 7-9-1 61 (p) JamesSullivan(5) 2 55
(M W Easterby) *chsd ldng pair: rdn along 2f out: drvn over 1f out: sn no imp* **5/2**[2]
3000 **6** 3 1/4 **Officer Mor (USA)**[10] 3711 4-9-0 44 (tp) AndrewElliott 1 38
(Mrs Dianne Sayer) *chsd ldrs on inner: rdn along wl over 2f out: sn one pce* **50/1**
3600 **7** 1 3/4 **Cool Art (IRE)**[15] 3538 4-8-9 47 (v[1]) IanBrennan(5) 11 33
(J S Wainwright) *led: rdn along 1/2-way: hdd over 2f out and grad wknd* **20/1**
-000 **8** 1 1/2 **Govenor Eliott (IRE)**[12] 3610 5-8-7 42 (b) ShaneBKelly(7) 4 28
(A J Lockwood) *a towards rr* **100/1**
20-0 **9** 7 **Neva A Mull Moment (IRE)**[7] 3774 4-8-7 62 (p) DaleSwift(7) 7 —
(R E Barr) *midfield: rdn along 1/2-way: sn wknd* **20/1**
040- **10** 8 **Wrens Hope**[345] 4596 4-8-9 40 JimmyQuinn 6 —
(N Bycroft) *chsd ldrs: rdn along 1/2-way: sn wknd* **80/1**
/600 **11** 2 **Inchmarlow (IRE)**[20] 3374 7-9-0 45 DuranFentiman 3 —
(T H Caldwell) *a in rr: bhd fr 1/2-way* **150/1**
1m 15.17s (1.57) **Going Correction** +0.20s/f (Good)
WFA 3 from 4yo+ 6lb **11 Ran SP% 112.3**
Speed ratings (Par 101): **97,96,95,94,90 86,84,82,72,62 59**
toteswingers: 1&2 £14.00, 1&3 £4.80, 2&3 £10.80 CSF £121.40 TOTE £7.30: £2.50, £4.70, £1.10; EX 102.30.There was no bid for the winner. Lindoro was claimed by Mr P. J. Raybould for £5,000.
Owner John Wade **Bred** Kildaragh Stud **Trained** Newton Bewley, Co Durham
■ A 1-2 for trainer Chris Grant and owner John Wade.

FOCUS
An ordinary-looking seller despite the number of runners. The front pair ran their best races for some time but this may not prove reliable form.

4015 YORKSHIRE RACING SUMMER FESTIVAL CLAIMING STKS 1m 3f 214y
3:20 (3:20) (Class 6) 3-Y-O+ **£2,047** (£604; £302) **Stalls** Low

Form RPR
0-23 **1** **Eijaaz (IRE)**[57] 2218 9-9-8 59 (p) SilvestreDeSousa 8 63
(G A Harker) *hld up towards rr: hdwy over 4f out: trckd ldrs over 2f out: effrt to chse wnr over 1f out: swtchd rt and rdn to ld ins fnl f* **9/2**[2]
0501 **2** 3/4 **Film Festival (USA)**[14] 3552 7-9-7 67 DaleSwift(7) 11 68
(B Ellison) *trckd ldr: led 1/2-way: rdn 2f out: drvn over 1f out: hdd and one pce ins fnl f: edgd lft nr fin* **15/8**[1]
0-00 **3** 1 **Cheyenne Chant**[16] 3506 3-7-12 47 (b[1]) JimmyQuinn 13 49
(Sir Mark Prescott) *a.p: chsd ldr over 4f out: rdn 2f out and ev ch tl drvn and one pce ins fnl f: hld whn n.m.r nr fin* **9/1**
4203 **4** 2 1/2 **Dispol Diva**[22] 3282 4-9-3 51 (v) PhillipMakin 12 51
(P T Midgley) *in tch: hdwy to chse ldrs over 3f out: rdn 2f out: sn drvn and kpt on same pce* **17/2**
-204 **5** 1 1/2 **Lucayan Dancer**[26] 3179 10-9-6 67 DanielTudhope 9 52
(N Bycroft) *hld up and bhd: hdwy 3f out: rdn wl over 1f out: kpt on: nt rch ldrs* **16/1**
03-0 **6** nk **Lady Norlela**[71] 1801 4-8-8 41 TimothyAyres(7) 3 46
(B S Rothwell) *midfield: hdwy 4f out: rdn along over 2f out: sn no imp* **100/1**
-026 **7** 1 1/2 **Castlebury (IRE)**[14] 3552 5-10-0 61 (b) TomEaves 10 57
(G A Swinbank) *in tch: hdwy to trck ldrs 5f out: effrt and chsd ldng pair over 3f out: rdn along 2f out: drvn and wknd over 1f out* **14/1**
4412 **8** 3 **Chocolate Caramel (USA)**[22] 3282 8-9-10 66 PaulHanagan 15 48
(R A Fahey) *hld up in rr: hdwy and in tch over 4f out: rdn over 3f out: sn btn* **5/1**[3]
50/0 **9** nk **Parchment (IRE)**[12] 3614 8-8-11 42 ShaneBKelly(7) 4 41
(A J Lockwood) *hld up: hdwy and in tch 4f out: rdn along 3f out: sn drvn and wknd fr wl over 1f out* **80/1**
0/ **10** 11 **Power Desert (IRE)**[45] 5903 5-9-4 0 PaddyAspell 14 24
(G A Harker) *a in rr* **50/1**
4024 **11** 23 **The Dial House**[52] 2361 4-10-0 60 DuranFentiman 1 —
(D W Thompson) *chsd ldrs: rdn along over 4f out: sn wknd* **20/1**
0000 **12** 1/2 **Firsaan (IRE)**[27] 3128 4-9-6 42 AndrewElliott 6 —
(J R Norton) *led to 1/2-way: sn rdn along and wknd 4f out* **150/1**

0055 **P** **Light The City (IRE)**[15] 3532 3-8-2 43 .... KellyHarrison(3) 5 —
(Mrs R A Carr) *racd wd: towards rr: sddle slipped after 4f: bhd whn p.u 2f out* **40/1**

2m 40.77s (1.87) **Going Correction** +0.20s/f (Good)
WFA 3 from 4yo+ 13lb **13** Ran SP% **114.8**
Speed ratings (Par 101): **101,100,99,98,97 96,95,93,93,86 71,70,—**
toteswingers: 1&2 £3.30, 1&3 £8.20, 2&3 £7.90 CSF £12.26 TOTE £6.20: £2.20, £1.10, £3.10; EX 14.60.Cheyenne Chant was claimed by Mr R. G. Fell for £2,000.
Owner A S Ward **Bred** Shadwell Estate Company Limited **Trained** Thirkleby, N Yorks
■ Stewards' Enquiry : Dale Swift caution: careless riding.

FOCUS
The early gallop looked slow, which counted against a few who were held up. An ordinary claimer with the winner not needing to be at his best.
Chocolate Caramel(USA) Official explanation: trainer had no explanation for the poor form shown
Light The City(IRE) Official explanation: jockey said saddle slipped

4016 AUGUST 13TH IS LADIES EVENING H'CAP 5f
3:50 (3:50) (Class 4) (0-85,83) 3-Y-O **£3,885** (£1,156; £577; £288) **Stalls** Low

Form RPR
1611 **1** **Perfect Blossom**[8] 3751 3-8-11 **73** 6ex .... PaulHanagan 1 82+
(K A Ryan) *led 1 1/2f: cl up tl led again 1 1/2f out: rdn and edgd lft ent fnl f: kpt on* **5/4**[1]
3003 **2** *1 ¾* **Tillys Tale**[8] 3751 3-8-10 **75** .... PaulPickard(3) 2 77
(P T Midgley) *chsd ldrs: pushed along and sltly outpcd 1/2-way: rdn and hdwy wl over 1f out: drvn to chse wnr ins fnl f: no imp towards fin* **7/2**[3]
061 **3** *5* **High Spice (USA)**[21] 3311 3-9-7 **83** ....(p) GrahamGibbons 3 74
(R M H Cowell) *dwlt and reminders s: hdwy to ld after 1f: rdn along and hdd 1 1/2f out: sn drvn and wknd ent fnl f* **85/40**[2]
4001 **4** *3 ¼* **Mercers Row**[27] 3111 3-8-11 **73** .... DanielTudhope 4 52
(N Wilson) *dwlt: hdwy and cl up 1/2-way: rdn along wl over 1f out and sn wknd* **12/1**

59.41 secs (-0.39) **Going Correction** -0.025s/f (Good) **4** Ran SP% **106.4**
Speed ratings (Par 102): **102,99,91,86**
CSF £5.65 TOTE £1.90; EX 4.50.
Owner Mrs Ann Morris **Bred** Mrs A Morris **Trained** Hambleton, N Yorks

FOCUS
A fair sprint. The progressive winner is rated up 7lb.

4017 RACINGUK.COM H'CAP 1m 3f 214y
4:20 (4:23) (Class 5) (0-70,65) 3-Y-O **£2,266** (£674; £337; £168) **Stalls** Low

Form RPR
0-62 **1** **Allannah Abu**[15] 3522 3-9-2 **60** .... PaulHanagan 3 68+
(Sir Mark Prescott) *mde all: rdn 3f out: c wd to stands' rail st: drvn over 1f out: kpt on* **11/8**[1]
0333 **2** *3 ¾* **Danceintothelight**[8] 3755 3-9-2 **60** .... TomEaves 5 62
(Micky Hammond) *trckd ldrs: hdwy to chse wnr 3f out: wd strraight and rdn over 2f out: drvn over 1f out: kpt on u.p fnl f* **11/1**[3]
5301 **3** *nk* **Magic Millie (IRE)**[11] 3662 3-8-12 **56** .... SilvestreDeSousa 10 57
(D O'Meara) *trckd ldng pair: hdwy to chse wnr 4f out: rdn along 3f out: drvn and ch over 1f out: wknd ins fnl f* **7/2**[2]
0-04 **4** *2 ¾* **Chichina (USA)**[12] 3614 3-8-5 **49** .... RoystonFfrench 2 46
(M Johnston) *chsd ldrs on inner: rdn along bef 1/2-way: drvn 3f out: plugged on same pce fnl 2f* **11/1**[3]
-035 **5** *4* **The Mighty Mod (USA)**[16] 3506 3-8-6 **50** .... GregFairley 9 41
(M Johnston) *sn chsng wnr: rdn along 4f out: racd alone far side in st: drvn 2f out and plugged on same pce* **12/1**
0-00 **6** *2 ¾* **Lava Lamp (GER)**[19] 3390 3-9-7 **65** ....(v) PaddyAspell 4 51
(G A Harker) *hld up towards rr: rdn along 4f out: drvn wl over 2f out: nvr a factor* **18/1**
00-5 **7** *1 ¼* **Tantsor (FR)**[30] 1466 3-7-13 **46** oh1 .... PaulPickard(3) 7 30
(P T Midgley) *a in rr: bhd fnl 3f* **100/1**
0000 **8** *16* **Marsh's Gift**[36] 2838 3-8-9 **53** .... PhillipMakin 11 12
(R E Barr) *hld up: a in rr: bhd fnl 3f* **33/1**
6U00 **P** **On The Right Path**[15] 3532 3-7-13 **48** .... JamesSullivan(5) 8 —
(Paul Murphy) *in tch: rdn along whn hung bdly rt, lost pl qckly and p.u 3f out* **100/1**

2m 40.76s (1.86) **Going Correction** +0.20s/f (Good) **9** Ran SP% **98.9**
Speed ratings (Par 100): **101,98,98,96,93 91,91,80,—**
toteswingers: 1&2 £3.10, 1&3 £1.60, 2&3 £4.50 CSF £12.58 CT £25.72 TOTE £2.30: £1.20, £3.50, £1.10; EX 12.00.
Owner Ennistown Stud **Bred** Miss K Rausing And Mrs S Rogers **Trained** Newmarket, Suffolk
■ Emerald Gale was withdrawn (9/2, ref to ent stalls). Deduct 15p in the £.

FOCUS
A moderate handicap. The winner only needed to reproduce her latest form.

4018 TURFTV MEDIAN AUCTION MAIDEN STKS 7f
4:50 (4:52) (Class 6) 3-Y-O **£2,047** (£604; £302) **Stalls** Low

Form RPR
20 **1** **George Benjamin**[40] 2702 3-9-3 74 .... AdrianNicholls 7 72
(D Nicholls) *prom: hdwy to chse ldr 1/2-way: rdn and cl up over 2f out: drvn over 1f out: kpt on ins fnl f to ld last 75yds* **2/1**[2]
002 **2** *¾* **Viking Warrior (IRE)**[26] 3148 3-9-3 73 .... PhillipMakin 9 70
(M Dods) *led: rdn and jnd over 2f out: drvn over 1f out: edgd lft ins fnl f: hdd and no ex last 75yds* **7/4**[1]
4633 **3** *5* **Tislaam (IRE)**[11] 3663 3-9-3 58 ....(v) PaulHanagan 1 56
(J S Wainwright) *trckd ldrs on inner: effrt to chse ldng pair 1/2-way: rdn over 2f out and sn one pce* **9/2**[3]
4 **4** *nk* **Spread Boy (IRE)**[14] 3554 3-8-12 0 .... MarkCoumbe(5) 5 56
(A Berry) *in tch: hdwy 1/2-way: rdn over 2f out: kpt on ins fnl f* **28/1**
005 **5** *11* **Colamandis**[19] 3407 3-8-12 58 .... PatrickMathers 3 21
(H A McWilliams) *chsd ldrs: rdn along 1/2-way: outpcd fnl 2f* **25/1**
6 *¾* **Mr Howe** 3-9-3 0 ....(t) TomEaves 8 24
(T J Fitzgerald) *dwlt: a in rr* **28/1**
7 *2 ¾* **Shamo Hill Theatre** 3-9-3 0 .... DavidNolan 10 17
(C J Teague) *dwlt: a in rr* **100/1**
00 **8** *6* **Daisy Dolittle**[23] 3275 3-8-12 0 .... GrahamGibbons 6 —
(J R Holt) *chsd ldrs: rdn along 1/2-way: sn wknd* **100/1**

1m 28.58s (1.58) **Going Correction** +0.20s/f (Good) **8** Ran SP% **100.6**
Speed ratings (Par 98): **98,97,91,91,78 77,74,67**
toteswingers: 1&2 £1.10, 1&3 £1.80, 2&3 £2.10 CSF £4.31 TOTE £2.10: £1.10, £1.20, £1.10; EX 4.10 Place 6 £5.49, Place 5 £3.96.
Owner C M & M A Scaife **Bred** Mascalls Stud **Trained** Sessay, N Yorks
■ Ruler's Honour was withdrawn (8/1, refused to ent stalls). Deduct 10p in the £ under R4.

FOCUS
A modest-looking maiden, despite a couple having official marks in the 70s. The form is rated around the front pair.

T/Plt: £10.20 to a £1 stake. Pool: £48,213.46. 3,430.16 winning tickets. T/Qpdt: £3.00 to a £1 stake. Pool: £2,738.84. 658.74 winning tickets. JR

3777 KEMPTON (A.W) (R-H)
Wednesday, July 14

OFFICIAL GOING: Standard
Wind: Fresh, behind Weather: Fine

4019 KEMPTON.CO.UK APPRENTICE H'CAP 1m 3f (P)
6:20 (6:22) (Class 4) (0-80,78) 4-Y-O+ **£3,885** (£1,156; £577; £288) **Stalls** High

Form RPR
4231 **1** **Rosco Flyer (IRE)**[17] 3473 4-9-4 **72** .... MatthewDavies 3 79
(R A Teal) *settled to dispute 4th: pushed along and prog over 2f out: led wl over 1f out: drvn out* **4/1**[2]
1305 **2** *½* **Addwaitya**[13] 3581 5-9-3 **78** .... CharlotteJenner(7) 6 84
(Mrs L J Mongan) *awkward s: hld up last and racd wd: v wd fr 4f out whn prog: clsd on ldrs 2f out: pushed along to press wnr fnl f: nt qckn* **9/1**
5141 **3** *½* **Haljaferia (UAE)**[16] 3502 4-9-9 **77** .... JohnFahy 4 82
(D R C Elsworth) *trckd ldng pair: rdn to chal 2f out: nt qckn over 1f out: styd on* **11/4**[1]
0000 **4** *2 ¼* **Formidable Guest**[7] 3781 6-8-11 **65** .... SimonPearce 1 66
(J Pearce) *hld up last: rdn and no prog over 2f out: styd on fnl f: n.d* **12/1**
6301 **5** *1* **Archie Rice (USA)**[16] 3512 4-9-5 **76** .... AdamBeschizza(3) 7 75
(T Keddy) *plld hrd early: trckd ldr: led over 2f out to wl over 1f out: wknd* **9/2**[3]
1000 **6** *nk* **Waahej**[32] 2961 4-8-10 **67** .... RyanClark(3) 8 66
(P W Hiatt) *hld up disputing 4th: rdn over 2f out: no prog over 1f out: fdd* **8/1**
0066 **7** *2 ¾* **Eseej (USA)**[7] 3781 5-8-8 **67** .... JamesRogers(5) 5 61
(P W Hiatt) *led at decent pce to over 2f out: sn btn* **13/2**

2m 21.22s (-0.68) **Going Correction** 0.0s/f (Stan) **7** Ran SP% **107.0**
Speed ratings (Par 105): **102,101,101,99,98 98,96**
toteswingers: 1&2:£5.50, 1&3:£1.50, 2&3:£6.80 CSF £33.39 CT £95.76 TOTE £3.60: £1.80, £5.80; EX 28.90.
Owner Chris Simpson, Miss Elizabeth Ross **Bred** Ms Amy Mulligan **Trained** Ashtead, Surrey
■ Theonebox was withdrawn (12/1, unruly in stalls and rider inj). Deduct 5p in the £ under R4.

FOCUS
A fair race of its type, with three last-time-out winners in the line-up, and few could be confidently discounted. The early pace was not especially fast. the form is bit muddling but rated around the placed horses to their marks.
Archie Rice(USA) Official explanation: vet said gelding lost a near-fore shoe

4020 DIGIBET.COM NURSERY 7f (P)
6:50 (6:51) (Class 5) 2-Y-O **£2,201** (£655; £327; £163) **Stalls** High

Form RPR
664 **1** **Byrony (IRE)**[14] 3562 2-9-3 **71** .... RyanMoore 2 77
(R Hannon) *trckd ldr after 2f: qcknd w him over 2f out: led wl over 1f out: rdn and styd on wl* **4/1**[3]
522 **2** *2 ¼* **Greek Islands (IRE)**[27] 3112 2-9-7 **75** .... WilliamBuick 4 75
(Mahmood Al Zarooni) *led after 1f at stdy pce: qcknd over 2f out: hdd wl over 1f out: steadily outpcd* **7/4**[1]
2442 **3** *1* **Lady Morganna (IRE)**[8] 3769 2-8-0 **59** .... KierenFox(5) 1 58+
(Miss Gay Kelleway) *fractious to post: stdd fr wd draw and hld up last: gd prog on inner over 2f out: wnt 3rd over 1f out: rdn and grad clsd on runner-up* **11/1**
1460 **4** *3 ½* **Prophet In A Dream**[13] 3596 2-8-7 **66** .... MatthewDavies(5) 7 55
(M R Channon) *hld up in tch: outpcd over 2f out: shkn up and no imp on ldrs after* **16/1**
006 **5** *shd* **Manchester Stanley**[19] 3399 2-8-5 **59** .... MartinDwyer 3 48
(J A Osborne) *trckd ldrs: outpcd over 2f out: disp modest 3rd wl over 1f out: fdd* **33/1**
030 **6** *3 ¼* **Uncle Dermot (IRE)**[34] 2887 2-9-1 **69** .... FergusSweeney 6 50
(B G Powell) *t.k.h: sn hld up in rr: outpcd over 2f out: wknd over 1f out* **12/1**
050 **7** *3* **Sky Diamond (IRE)**[42] 2654 2-8-7 **61** .... PaulMulrennan 5 34
(J G Given) *led 1f: rdn in midfield 1/2-way: sn struggling* **25/1**
4310 **8** *12* **Yarooh (USA)**[28] 3070 2-9-6 **74** .... NeilCallan 8 17
(C E Brittain) *t.k.h: trckd ldrs: wknd rapidly fr 2f out: eased: t.o* **3/1**[2]

1m 28.19s (2.19) **Going Correction** 0.0s/f (Stan) **8** Ran SP% **110.1**
Speed ratings (Par 94): **87,84,83,79,79 75,72,58**
toteswingers:1&2:£2.30, 1&3:£6.20, 2&3:£3.20 CSF £10.49 CT £62.50 TOTE £4.60: £1.90, £1.30, £1.70; EX 9.50.
Owner Axom XXIII **Bred** Mr & Mrs C Booth **Trained** East Everleigh, Wilts

FOCUS
Just an average nursery and a few looked over-rated. The pace was steady until the last 3f.

NOTEBOOK
Byrony(IRE), twice disappointing on turf but fourth over this C&D two weeks earlier, again showed her preference for Polytrack. She raced in second until the home straight, quickened with the runner-up two approaching out and then eased ahead for a comfortable victory. She is sure to be raised in the ratings after this, but it is debatable how much she needed to improve to score, so the Handicapper's response will be interesting. (op 7-2 tchd 11-4)
Greek Islands(IRE), runner-up last time out behind a subsequent Listed-race second, may have been overestimated on the strength of that run. He did nothing wrong here, leading early before trying to quicken away in the home straight, but was left behind once the winner engaged top gear. (op 6-4 tchd 2-1)
Lady Morganna(IRE), whose best previous runs had come on Polytrack, was another to show how much she enjoys this surface. Held up in rear early on, she made considerable late progress and will probably stay 1m in due course. Official explanation: vet said filly lost a near-fore shoe (op 12-1)
Prophet In A Dream was switched to this surface after a poor turf run in a Redcar nursery and, although this was an improvement, he never threatened to make a major impact. In midfield for most of the race, he stayed on at one pace in the home straight. (op 14-1)
Manchester Stanley, making his first appearance on an all-weather surface, coped okay with it, without showing enough to indicate he will soon break his duck. He was always in about the same position.

Yarooh(USA), a Wolverhampton winner whose last outing had been in the Queen Mary at Royal Ascot, appeared not to handle this longer trip. She was keen early on and, after racing prominently, faded in the closing stages. (op 4-1)

4021 EUROPEAN BREEDERS' FUND MAIDEN FILLIES' STKS 7f (P)
7:20 (7:20) (Class 4) 2-Y-O **£4,274** (£1,271; £635; £317) **Stalls** High

Form RPR

1 **Musharakaat (IRE)** 2-9-0 0 ... RichardHills 4 77+
(E A L Dunlop) *dwlt: in tch in rr: prog 1/2-way: swtchd lft over 2f out: pushed along and prog to ld jst over 1f out: shkn up and readily drew clr* **14/1**

3 2 2 1/4 **Sahafh (USA)**[22] 3296 2-9-0 0 ... TedDurcan 3 71+
(Saeed Bin Suroor) *slowest away and wnt lft: prog on wd outside to trck ldrs 1/2-way: hdwy and rdn to ld briefly over 1f out: outpcd by wnr after* **8/11**[1]

6 3 nk **Romantic Wish**[14] 3562 2-9-0 0 ... TomQueally 12 70
(R A Mills) *trckd ldrs: effrt on inner to chal wl over 1f out: styd on same pce fnl f* **15/2**[3]

64 4 1 1/2 **Dazzling Valentine**[19] 3386 2-9-0 0 ... RobertWinston 5 67
(A Bailey) *trckd ldng pair: rdn over 2f out: one pce fr over 1f out* **12/1**

5 nk **Soie De Chine** 2-9-0 0 ... PaulMulrennan 9 68+
(Sir Mark Prescott) *wl in tch bhd ldrs: pushed along 3f out: nvr gng pce to chal but kpt on steadily* **50/1**

6 4 1/2 **Daa'Iman** 2-9-0 0 ... NeilCallan 1 55
(C E Brittain) *dwlt: wl in rr: sme prog to midfield but outpcd 3f out: shkn up and kpt on: nt pce to threaten but nt disgracd* **33/1**

0 7 1/2 **One Lucky Lady**[14] 3562 2-9-0 0 ... MichaelHills 14 53
(B W Hills) *disp ld to over 1f out: wknd qckly* **25/1**

8 1 1/4 **Beach Babe** 2-9-0 0 ... JimCrowley 8 50
(J G Portman) *sn in last trio: outpcd fr 3f out: modest late prog* **66/1**

9 1/2 **Fly By White (IRE)** 2-9-0 0 ... RyanMoore 7 49
(R Hannon) *sn in last trio: outpcd fr 1/2-way: n.d after* **11/2**[2]

10 1 1/4 **Lady Barastar (IRE)** 2-9-0 0 ... ShaneKelly 10 46
(W R Swinburn) *bmpd s: n.m.r in midfield after 2f: outpcd over 2f out: no ch after* **33/1**

0 11 8 **Till Dawn (IRE)**[27] 3126 2-9-0 0 ... EddieAhern 6 26
(A W Carroll) *disp ld to 2f out: wknd v rapidly* **80/1**

12 7 **Slight Advantage (IRE)** 2-9-0 0 ... LukeMorris 11 8
(C G Cox) *bmpd s: squeezed out on inner after 2f and dropped to rr: struggling fr 3f out: sn wl bhd* **40/1**

13 31 **Brendan's Gift** 2-9-0 0 ... FergusSweeney 2 —
(B G Powell) *in tch to 3f out: wknd rapidly: wl t.o* **100/1**

1m 26.45s (0.45) **Going Correction** 0.0s/f (Stan) **13** Ran SP% **117.3**
Speed ratings (Par 93): **97,94,94,92,92 86,86,84,84,82 73,65,30**
toteswingers:1&2:£3.70, 1&3:£23.40, 2&3:£1.20 CSF £23.31 TOTE £22.30: £4.80, £1.02, £2.80; EX 35.90.
Owner Hamdan Al Maktoum **Bred** Mrs Mary Gallagher **Trained** Newmarket, Suffolk

FOCUS
Not much form to go on, but several well-bred newcomers added greatly to the interest. A nice start from the winner and the second ran to her pre-race level.

NOTEBOOK
Musharakaat(IRE), a half-sister to a useful juvenile winner, made an encouraging start to her career. Not the fastest away and then squeezed for room on the home turn, she tracked the runner-up into the straight and quickened smartly after being switched towards the near side. She seems sure to improve for this and may be able to hold her own in a higher grade. (op 16-1)
Sahafh(USA), who cost $475,000 and finished third at Newbury on her only previous start, was slowest to break and consequently obliged to race wide for much of the turn towards home. She came under pressure two out and, although she quickened slightly, it was not nearly enough to hold the winner's charge. (op 4-6 tchd 4-5 in a place)
Romantic Wish had stayed on nicely here when sixth on her debut two weeks earlier and almost certainly improved on that effort. Third virtually throughout, she plugged on gamely in the closing stages. (op 9-1 tchd 10-1 in a place)
Dazzling Valentine had taken a step forward when fourth at Chester last time out and, as she figured prominently from the outset, seems a feasible guide to the form. She may struggle to take a maiden, but looks reliable and now has the option of nurseries. (tchd 11-1)
Soie De Chine is bred to stay longer distances, so this was an encouraging start. Always in the leading group, she plugged on steadily in the home straight.
Daa'Iman, whose dam was a half-sister to Cherry Hinton winner Applaud, showed a glimpse of ability, staying on late without being unduly hard-pressed. (op 25-1)

4022 DIGIBET H'CAP (LONDON MILE QUALIFIER) 1m (P)
7:50 (7:53) (Class 5) (0-70,70) 3-Y-O **£2,320** (£685; £342) **Stalls** High

Form RPR

0-60 1 **Snoqualmie Star**[31] 2993 3-9-3 66 ... (b[1]) DaneO'Neill 3 73
(D R C Elsworth) *settled wl in rr early: rchd midfield by 1/2-way: prog through rivals fr 2f out: drvn ahd ins fnl f: styd on wl* **16/1**

-020 2 2 **Primary Colors**[55] 2250 3-9-7 70 ... (v[1]) RyanMoore 11 73
(C G Cox) *pushed up to go prom after 2f: drvn to go 2nd wl over 1f out: upsides ent fnl f: one pce* **6/1**[2]

40-5 3 nk **Pebblesonthebeach**[84] 1475 3-9-5 68 ... MichaelHills 9 70
(J W Hills) *hld up wl in rr: prog on wd outside over 2f out: styd on fr over 1f out: wnt 3rd nr fin* **12/1**

20-3 4 nk **Serhaal (IRE)**[12] 3621 3-9-7 70 ... RichardHills 8 71
(Sir Michael Stoute) *trckd ldr: led wl over 2f out: hdd and outpcd ins fnl f* **15/2**

-265 5 2 **Song To The Moon (IRE)**[28] 3081 3-9-7 70 ... LiamKeniry 2 67
(A M Balding) *settled towards rr: darted up inner over 2f out and sme prog: drvn and kpt on: no imp on ldrs* **10/1**

44-0 6 1 1/2 **Rich Boy**[21] 3325 3-9-5 68 ... IanMongan 6 61
(Mrs L J Mongan) *trckd ldrs and racd wd: wnt 2nd over 2f out to wl over 1f out: nt qckn: fdd fnl f* **33/1**

604 7 1 3/4 **Majestatic**[46] 2548 3-9-2 65 ... (t) SamHitchcott 5 56
(S W James) *racd wd in midfield: rdn over 2f out: keeping on in 6th but hld whn hmpd and snatched up 1f out* **40/1**

505 8 1 1/4 **Quick Deal (USA)**[18] 3428 3-9-1 64 ... WilliamBuick 14 50
(J H M Gosden) *awkward s: sn in tch in midfield on inner: nt qckn over 2f out: no imp on ldrs after* **7/1**[3]

0665 9 1 1/4 **Akamon**[24] 3238 3-9-0 63 ... EddieAhern 10 46+
(E A L Dunlop) *hld up wl in rr: nt clr run twice over 2f out: nvr able to make an impact after* **14/1**

-100 10 nse **Durham Town (IRE)**[21] 3325 3-9-5 68 ... JimCrowley 1 51
(D K Ivory) *hld up last: nt clr run wl over 2f out: rdn and sme prog fr 2f out: nvr involved* **25/1**

3560 11 3 **Bubbly Braveheart (IRE)**[19] 3390 3-9-3 66 ... RobertWinston 4 42
(A Bailey) *hld up wl in rr: rdn on outer over 2f out: hanging and no prog* **16/1**

00-2 12 1/2 **Claimant (IRE)**[39] 2754 3-9-4 67 ... PaulFitzsimons 7 42
(Miss J R Tooth) *wl in tch bhd ldrs: rdn over 2f out: wknd over 1f out* **16/1**

-550 13 6 **Golden Waters**[34] 2893 3-9-5 68 ... NeilCallan 13 30
(Eve Johnson Houghton) *trckd ldng pair: rdn over 2f out: wknd rapidly over 1f out* **20/1**

4 14 19 **Rezwaan**[34] 2886 3-9-5 68 ... ShaneKelly 12 —
(Jane Chapple-Hyam) *rdn to ld: hdd u.p wl over 2f out: dropped out rapidly* **3/1**[1]

1m 39.53s (-0.27) **Going Correction** 0.0s/f (Stan) **14** Ran SP% **118.6**
Speed ratings (Par 100): **101,99,98,98,96 94,93,91,90,90 87,87,81,62**
toteswingers::1&2:£30.20, 1&3:£89.30, 2&3:£17.10 CSF £103.39 CT £1243.26 TOTE £21.60: £6.20, £2.60, £4.10; EX 139.40.
Owner J C Smith **Bred** Littleton Stud **Trained** Newmarket, Suffolk
■ Stewards' Enquiry : Michael Hills one-day ban: careless riding (Jul 29)

FOCUS
Not the classiest of events, with the top weight rated only 70, but it looked very competitive. The pace was muddling and is rated around the third and fourth on their maiden form.
Snoqualmie Star Official explanation: trainer said, regarding apparent improvement in form, that the filly had benefited from being fitted with first time blinkers.

4023 DIGIBET CASINO H'CAP 1m (P)
8:20 (8:22) (Class 4) (0-85,85) 3-Y-O+ **£3,885** (£1,156; £577; £288) **Stalls** High

Form RPR

40 1 **L'Hirondelle (IRE)**[14] 3565 6-9-8 79 ... NeilCallan 6 90
(M J Attwater) *trckd ldng trio: wnt 3rd over 3f out and 2nd 2f out: clsd to ld over 1f out: edgd rt but drvn clr* **16/1**

3210 2 2 **Mishrif (USA)**[35] 2872 4-9-8 79 ... (b) RyanMoore 4 85
(J R Jenkins) *racd v wd 1st 3f: led after 1f at str pce: field strung out fr 3f out: hdd and one pce over 1f out* **10/1**

-500 3 1 1/2 **Licence To Till (USA)**[32] 2970 3-8-12 78 ... JoeFanning 9 79
(M Johnston) *chsd ldrs after 1f: clr in ldng trio 3f out: lost 2nd 2f out: tired but clung on for 3rd* **12/1**

0635 4 nk **Uncle Fred**[16] 3512 5-9-12 83 ... JimCrowley 11 85+
(P R Chamings) *settled wl in rr: wl off the pce over 3f out: shkn up and prog over 2f out: wnt 4th fnl f: nrst fin* **14/1**

1341 5 1 3/4 **Shamir**[21] 3330 3-9-3 83 ... FergusSweeney 7 79
(Miss Jo Crowley) *settled towards rr and off the pce: pushed along 3f out: sme prog to dispute modest 4th 1f out: no ex* **7/2**[1]

32-0 6 1 3/4 **Spirit Of A Nation (IRE)**[109] 1011 5-9-13 84 ... EddieAhern 12 78
(D H Brown) *chsd ldrs: rdn over 3f out: wl outpcd in 4th 2f out: wknd fnl f* **4/1**[2]

030- 7 1 3/4 **Cool Hand Jake**[294] 6209 4-9-9 80 ... WilliamBuick 1 70
(P J Makin) *racd wd in midfield: rdn 3f out: limited prog to dispute modest 4th over 1f out: wknd* **20/1**

314- 8 1 1/4 **Classically (IRE)**[153] 6977 4-8-12 72 ... RobertLButler(3) 3 59
(H Morrison) *racd wd and wl in rr: effrt on outer over 2f out: nvr on terms* **25/1**

12-3 9 1 3/4 **Miss Glitters (IRE)**[194] 6 5-9-11 82 ... SteveDrowne 10 65
(H Morrison) *pushed along in midfield after 3f: a struggling* **14/1**

1500 10 4 1/2 **Striding Edge (IRE)**[14] 3565 4-9-5 76 ... MartinDwyer 8 49
(W R Muir) *snatched up in rr after 1f: a off the pce after* **16/1**

0102 11 3 1/4 **Red Somerset (USA)**[14] 3565 7-10-0 85 ... AndreaAtzeni 13 50
(Mike Murphy) *rdn in midfield 1/2-way: brief effrt on inner over 2f out: sn wknd* **9/1**

0000 12 3/4 **Sunshine Always (IRE)**[21] 3330 4-9-2 73 ... KirstyMilczarek 5 37
(T D McCarthy) *nvr bttr than midfield: rdn over 3f out: lost pl and wknd 2f out* **25/1**

6031 13 1 3/4 **Cobo Bay**[30] 3021 5-9-13 84 ... (b) LiamKeniry 14 44
(C R Dore) *led 1f: chsd ldng pair to over 3f out: sn wknd rapidly* **15/2**[3]

35-0 14 16 **Gunslinger (FR)**[22] 2821 5-9-4 75 ... PatCosgrave 2 —
(M J Scudamore) *slowest away: in tch in rr to 1/2-way: wknd and t.o* **40/1**

1m 38.56s (-1.24) **Going Correction** 0.0s/f (Stan)
WFA 3 from 4yo+ 9lb **14** Ran SP% **120.8**
Speed ratings (Par 105): **106,104,102,102,100 98,96,95,93,89 86,85,83,67**
toteswingers:1&2:£11.40, 1&3:£77.90, 2&3:£13.90 CSF £160.89 CT £2005.91 TOTE £14.10: £4.40, £3.10, £4.40; EX 291.40.
Owner Canisbay Bloodstock **Bred** Gainsborough Stud Management Ltd **Trained** Epsom, Surrey

FOCUS
A decent handicap with the top-weight rated 85, and several held obvious claims. It paid to race handily and the winner is rated back to his best.
L'Hirondelle(IRE) Official explanation: trainer said, regarding apparent improvement in form, that on its previous run, the gelding suffered interference and was unable to get into the race.
Red Somerset(USA) Official explanation: jockey said gelding never travelled

4024 LEONARD CURTIS H'CAP 7f (P)
8:50 (8:51) (Class 5) (0-75,75) 3-Y-O+ **£2,320** (£685; £342) **Stalls** High

Form RPR

1002 1 **Army Of Stars (IRE)**[7] 3777 4-9-0 69 ... (p) SophieDoyle(5) 3 78
(J A Osborne) *trckd ldrs and racd wd: shkn up and effrt 2f out: clsd fnl f: r.o to ld last strides* **10/1**

-612 2 hd **Mambo Spirit (IRE)**[33] 2920 6-9-11 75 ... TomQueally 7 83
(Stef Higgins) *led after 1f: drvn 2f out: styd on u.p: hdd last strides* **5/1**[1]

5626 3 1 1/4 **Copperwood**[5] 3851 5-9-6 70 ... NeilCallan 11 75
(M Blanshard) *awkward and s.i.s: hld up in rr: prog over 2f out: drvn to cl on ldrs 1f out: styd on same pce* **9/1**

1-00 4 1 1/4 **First Service (IRE)**[21] 3330 4-9-3 67 ... LukeMorris 5 69
(M J Attwater) *hld up in last pair: gd prog over 2f out to chse ldrs over 1f out: hrd rdn and kpt on* **20/1**

600 5 shd **Todber**[21] 3328 5-9-3 67 ... (b[1]) PatDobbs 4 68
(M P Tregoning) *hld up in last pair: pushed along and stl there 2f out: styd on wl after: clst at fin* **16/1**

0036 6 nk **Lodi (IRE)**[23] 3262 5-9-4 68 ... (tp) GeorgeBaker 13 69
(J Akehurst) *t.k.h: prom: rdn to chse ldr 2f out to 1f out: wknd* **8/1**[3]

0606 7 1/2 **Ilie Nastase (FR)**[14] 3565 6-9-11 75 ... LiamKeniry 8 74
(C R Dore) *mostly in midfield: shkn up and no rspnse over 2f out: kpt on fr over 1f out: n.d* **5/1**[1]

4132 8 1 3/4 **Headache**[9] 3734 5-9-6 70 ... (bt) DaneO'Neill 9 65
(B W Duke) *t.k.h: led 1f: chsd ldr to 2f out: wknd fnl f* **7/1**[2]

00 9 1 1/2 **Fernando Torres**[21] 3330 4-9-2 66 ... (p) FrannyNorton 2 57
(Matthew Salaman) *rdn on outer in midfield after 3f: effrt over 2f out: no prog over 1f out: fdd* **16/1**

4222 10 2 1/2 **Gazboolou**[27] 3129 6-9-9 73 ... FergusSweeney 6 60
(David Pinder) *trckd ldrs: shkn up and lost pl 2f out: fdd and eased* **11/1**

40-5 11 1 1/4 **Spiritofthewest (IRE)**[188] 74 4-9-4 68 ... EddieAhern 12 48
(D H Brown) *awkward s and then bmpd: wl in rr: shkn up and no prog over 2f out* **16/1**

3041 **12** *shd* **Hinton Admiral**[41] 2678 6-9-1 **68**........................(t) RussKennemore(3) 14 55
(M S Tuck) *chsd ldrs: wkng whn hmpd wl over 1f out* **12/1**

-306 **13** *2 ½* **Tudor Prince (IRE)**[7] 3777 6-9-6 **70**........................ JamesDoyle 10 43
(A W Carroll) *chsd ldrs on inner tl wknd u.p 2f out* **20/1**

1m 25.36s (-0.64) **Going Correction** 0.0s/f (Stan) **13** Ran SP% **119.2**
Speed ratings (Par 103): **103,102,101,99,99 99,98,96,95,92 90,90,87**
toteswingers:1&2:£4.90, 1&3:£10.80, 2&3:£6.00 CSF £59.19 CT £487.48 TOTE £12.00: £3.60, £3.00, £2.60; EX 44.20.
Owner J A Osborne **Bred** D Johnson **Trained** Upper Lambourn, Berks
■ Stewards' Enquiry : Sophie Doyle caution: used whip with excessive frequency.

FOCUS
A run-of-the-mill handicap in which most could be given some sort of chance. The third is rated close to form and sets the standard.
Spiritofthewest(IRE) Official explanation: trainer said gelding was found to be coughing

4025 PANORAMIC BAR & RESTAURANT H'CAP 7f (P)
9:20 (9:22) (Class 6) (0-65,65) 3-Y-O **£1,637** (£483; £241) **Stalls** High

Form RPR

4604 **1** **Master Mylo (IRE)**[16] 3511 3-9-7 **65**........................ JimCrowley 5 78
(D K Ivory) *t.k.h: hld up wl in rr off str pce: gd prog over 2f out: led over 1f out: r.o wl fnl f* **14/1**

000- **2** *1 ¼* **Hayek**[273] 6781 3-9-7 **65**........................ JoeFanning 10 75+
(W Jarvis) *hld up wl in rr: eased to outer over 2f out and gd prog to go 2nd jst over 1f out: r.o but no imp on wnr last 100yds* **4/1**[2]

6200 **3** *5* **Mack's Sister**[43] 2633 3-9-0 **58**........................ LukeMorris 8 54
(D K Ivory) *trckd ldr 1f: stdd: looking for room 2f out: swtchd lft over 1f out: styd on to take 3rd ins fnl f but no ch* **25/1**

40-2 **4** *4 ½* **Via Aurelia (IRE)**[35] 2876 3-9-1 **59**........................ PatCosgrave 11 43
(J R Fanshawe) *hld up in midfield: prog and swtchd to inner 2f out: sn wl outpcd by ldng pair: lost 3rd fnl f* **11/8**[1]

40-0 **5** *2 ¼* **Rodrigo De Freitas (IRE)**[30] 3039 3-9-2 **60**........................ EddieAhern 1 38
(J R Boyle) *prog on outer to join ldrs over 4f out: upsides over 2f out: sn lft bhd* **33/1**

20 **6** *hd* **Young Simon**[34] 2906 3-9-6 **64**........................(p) DaneO'Neill 9 41
(G G Margarson) *t.k.h: hld up in midfield: rdn and no prog over 2f out: nvr on terms after* **20/1**

0210 **7** *1 ½* **Miss Kitty Grey (IRE)**[18] 3441 3-9-2 **60**........................ NickyMackay 2 33
(J R Boyle) *sn w ldrs: led wl over 2f out to over 1f out: wknd rapidly* **25/1**

4004 **8** *¾* **Giulietta Da Vinci**[17] 3479 3-9-1 **59**........................ GeorgeBaker 13 30
(S Woodman) *nvr beyond midfield: lft wl bhd fr 2f out* **12/1**[3]

0-05 **9** *1 ¼* **Spinning Spirit (IRE)**[45] 2566 3-9-2 **60**........................ PaulMulrennan 4 28
(J G Given) *pressed ldr at str pce after 1f: upsides 3f out: sn wknd* **16/1**

2050 **10** *4* **Mororless**[21] 3325 3-8-11 **58**........................ AndrewHeffernan(3) 6 15
(Miss Z C Davison) *drvn thrght: a bhd* **50/1**

-025 **11** *1 ¼* **Naseby (USA)**[38] 2780 3-9-0 **58**........................ FergusSweeney 7 12
(Miss S L Davison) *chsd ldrs: rdn 1/2-way: wknd over 2f out* **14/1**

050 **12** *5* **Dilys Maud**[27] 3125 3-9-6 **64**........................ SteveDrowne 3 —
(R Ingram) *dwlt: in tch on outer after 3f: wknd 3f out: sn wl bhd* **33/1**

0400 **13** *6* **Marjolly (IRE)**[57] 2215 3-9-7 **65**........................(b¹) TadhgO'Shea 12 —
(J Gallagher) *rdn in rr after 2f: sn bhd: t.o* **20/1**

215 **14** *7* **Bookiesindex Girl (IRE)**[149] 566 3-9-7 **65**........................ RobertWinston 14 —
(J R Jenkins) *free to post: led at v str pce: hdd & wknd wl over 2f out: t.o* **14/1**

1m 25.51s (-0.49) **Going Correction** 0.0s/f (Stan) **14** Ran SP% **120.7**
Speed ratings (Par 98): **102,100,94,89,87 86,85,84,82,78 76,71,64,56**
toteswingers:1&2:£15.50, 1&3:£34.90, 2&3:£44.40 CSF £63.87 CT £1426.19 Place 6 £375.15, Place 5 £115.40..
Owner K Quinn/ C Benham/ I Saunders **Bred** David Eiffe **Trained** Radlett, Herts

FOCUS
A weak finale, with the top-weight rated 65 and little solid recent form to evaluate, but the pace was strong for the grade. The winner is rated as having recorded a slight personal best.
T/Plt: £824.00 to a £1 stake. Pool: £65,753.41. 58.25 winning tickets. T/Qpdt: £289.40 to a £1 stake. Pool: £5,397.63. 13.80 winning tickets. JN

3784 LINGFIELD (L-H)
Wednesday, July 14

OFFICIAL GOING: Turf course - firm (good to firm in places; 9.1); all-weather - standard
Wind: Light, half behind Weather: Overcast, showers

4026 BET BRITISH OPEN GOLF - BETDAQ H'CAP 2m
2:30 (2:31) (Class 5) (0-75,72) 3-Y-0+ **£2,729** (£806; £403) **Stalls** Low

Form RPR

1-23 **1** **Ambrose Princess (IRE)**[24] 3241 5-9-6 **60**........................(p) PatCosgrave 4 72+
(M J Scudamore) *chsd ldrs: pushed along 12f out: hdwy to ld 5f out: pushed clr 3f out and in command fnl 2f: heavily eased ins fnl f* **3/1**[2]

0-10 **2** *2 ½* **Swordsman (GER)**[14] 1849 8-10-0 **68**........................(t) DaneO'Neill 1 70
(C Gordon) *dwlt and sn bustled along: led after 1f tl 5f out: rdn and outpcd over 3f out: plugged on and wnt modest 2nd over 1f out: clsd on eased wnr towards fin* **16/1**

1535 **3** *½* **Free Falling**[6] 3819 4-8-2 **49** oh2........................(v) AdamBeschizza(7) 3 50
(Miss Gay Kelleway) *lw: chsd ldrs: rdn and wl outpcd over 3f out: plugged on u.p to go modest 3rd over 1f out: clsd fnl and pressing for 2nd towards fin: no ch w wnr* **14/1**

5022 **4** *8* **Cloudy City (USA)**[7] 3772 3-8-13 **72**........................ JoeFanning 5 63
(M Johnston) *chsd ldrs: hdwy to trck wnr 4f out: rdn and fnd nil 3f out: no ch w wnr fnl 2f: lost 2 pls fr over 1f out* **8/13**[1]

0-65 **5** *2 ¾* **Yonder**[20] 3352 6-9-8 **62**........................(t) SteveDrowne 2 50
(H Morrison) *taken down early and led to s: led for 1f: styd chsng ldr tl 5f out: rdn and wl outpcd over 3f out: wl bhd fnl 2f* **10/1**[3]

3m 34.8s **Going Correction** +0.075s/f (Good)
WFA 3 from 4yo+ 19lb **5** Ran SP% **108.6**
Speed ratings (Par 103): **103,101,101,97,96**
CSF £37.58 TOTE £3.00: £1.10, £4.00; EX 26.60.
Owner The Yes No Wait Sorries **Bred** Tally-Ho Stud **Trained** Bromsash, Herefordshire

FOCUS
They seemed to go a decent pace in this modest handicap and there was an easy winner. The favourite disappointed and the form is none too solid.

4027 LINGFIELD MARRIOTT HOTEL & COUNTRY CLUB H'CAP 1m 2f
3:00 (3:01) (Class 6) (0-65,65) 3-Y-O **£1,842** (£544; £272) **Stalls** Low

Form RPR

4-01 **1** **Explorator (IRE)**[7] 3788 3-9-9 **65** 6ex........................ TonyCulhane 2 72+
(George Baker) *lw: in tch in midfield: rdn and effrt 3f out: drvn to ld over 1f out: styd on wl fnl f* **4/6**[1]

6334 **2** *½* **Sheila's Bond**[9] 3723 3-9-3 **59**........................ LukeMorris 7 65
(J S Moore) *s.i.s: in rr of main gp: rdn and effrt over 2f out: nt clr run over 1f out: hdwy u.p 1f out: chsd wnr fnl 75yds: kpt on but hld towards fin* **8/1**

-054 **3** *1 ¼* **Shianda**[16] 3513 3-8-10 **52**........................ RyanMoore 3 55
(G L Moore) *t.k.h early: hld up in tch: swtchd lft and rdn ent fnl 2f: ev ch and drvn over 1f out: hung rt and btn ins fnl f* **4/1**[2]

503U **4** *2 ¾* **Little Meadow (IRE)**[7] 3788 3-8-5 **47**........................ CathyGannon 6 45
(Miss J Feilden) *w ldr for 2f: chsd ldr again 4f out: rdn to ld over 2f out: hdd over 1f out: wknd u.p fnl 150yds* **50/1**

4404 **5** *1* **New Code**[19] 3390 3-9-7 **63**........................ MartinDwyer 1 59
(W R Muir) *led at stdy gallop for 2f: chsd ldr tl 4f out: swtchd ins and effrt u.p wl over 2f out: wknd u.p ins fnl f* **11/2**[3]

0005 **6** *12* **Calm And Serene (USA)**[11] 3662 3-8-3 **45**........................(bt) AndreaAtzeni 4 24
(Rae Guest) *plld hrd: hld up in tch into hdwy to ld after 2f: sn clr: rdn and hdd over 2f out: wknd qckly over 1f out: wl btn and eased ins fnl f* **50/1**

500 **7** *29* **Mujdy (IRE)**[14] 3557 3-7-10 **45**........................(p) RichardRowe(7) 5 —
(Miss Z C Davison) *taken down early: v.s.a: sn rdn and a detached in last: lost tch 4f out: t.o* **100/1**

2m 10.24s (-0.26) **Going Correction** +0.075s/f (Good) **7** Ran SP% **111.4**
Speed ratings (Par 98): **104,103,102,100,99 90,66**
toteswingers: 1&2 £1.70, 1&3 £1.10, 2&3 £4.40 CSF £6.54 TOTE £1.50: £1.10, £3.60; EX 7.00.
Owner Kismet Partnership **Bred** Joseph Stewart Investments **Trained** Moreton Morrell, Warwicks

FOCUS
A moderate 3-y-o handicap, run at a sound pace. The time was fair and the winner ran to a similar level to last week's win.
Calm And Serene(USA) Official explanation: jockey said filly ran too free
Mujdy(IRE) Official explanation: jockey said gelding missed the break and never travelled

4028 BET IN RUNNING - BETDAQ MAIDEN STKS 1m 1f
3:30 (3:34) (Class 5) 3-4-Y-O **£2,388** (£705; £352) **Stalls** Low

Form RPR

5 **1** **Jet Away**[13] 3586 3-9-2 0........................ TomQueally 7 88+
(H R A Cecil) *w'like: str: lw: stdd s: hld up in tch: hdwy 4f out: chsd ldng pair 3f out: pushed along hands and heels to chal 1f out: led fnl 100yds: r.o wl: comf* **8/11**[1]

422 **2** *1* **Give Your Verdict (USA)**[23] 3272 3-9-2 80........................ RyanMoore 1 86
(Sir Michael Stoute) *lw: led: rdn wl over 2f out: kpt on wl u.p tl hdd fnl 100yds: one pce after* **13/8**[2]

3 *1 ¼* **Autumn Riches** 3-9-2 0........................ JoeFanning 3 83
(M Johnston) *w'like: chsd ldrs: rdn to chse ldr jst over 2f out tl ins fnl f: one pce fnl 100yds* **12/1**

02 **4** *3 ¼* **Free As A Lark**[43] 2632 3-8-11 0........................ AlanMunro 4 71
(C F Wall) *hld up in tch in midfield: rdn and hdwy 3f out: outpcd by ldng trio over 1f out: styd on same pce fnl f* **7/1**[3]

5 **5** *3 ½* **Beautiful One**[23] 3266 3-8-11 0........................ LukeMorris 6 63?
(T D McCarthy) *w'like: taken down early: t.k.h and racd awkwardly: hld up in tch: rdn and effrt over 2f out: hung lft and wknd over 1f out* **66/1**

5 **6** *5* **Officer Lily (USA)**[15] 3523 3-8-11 0........................ SteveDrowne 5 52?
(J R Best) *leggy: s.i.s: hld up in tch towards rr: rdn over 2f out: wknd 2f out* **50/1**

0 **7** *5* **Queen Ranavola (USA)**[9] 3738 3-8-6 0........................ KierenFox(5) 8 41?
(J R Best) *chsd ldr tl over 3f out: wknd u.p 2f out: sn wl bhd* **50/1**

8 *23* **Shemita's Song (USA)** 3-8-11 0........................ TonyCulhane 2 —
(George Baker) *unf: s.i.s: sn pushed along and detached in last: t.o fnl 2f* **66/1**

1m 58.13s (1.53) **Going Correction** +0.075s/f (Good) **8** Ran SP% **123.1**
Speed ratings (Par 103): **96,95,94,91,88 83,79,58**
toteswingers: 1&2 £1.10, 1&3 £3.60, 2&3 £3.40 CSF £2.40 TOTE £1.80: £1.10, £1.10, £2.60; EX 2.50 Trifecta £9.20 Pool: £939.80 - 75.26 winning units..
Owner K Abdulla **Bred** Juddmonte Farms Ltd **Trained** Newmarket, Suffolk

FOCUS
A good maiden although it was steadily run. The form makes some sense at face value.
Shemita's Song(USA) Official explanation: jockey said filly was slowly away

4029 EUROPEAN BREEDERS' FUND MAIDEN FILLIES' STKS 6f (P)
4:00 (4:03) (Class 5) 2-Y-O **£3,076** (£915; £457; £228) **Stalls** Low

Form RPR

000 **1** **Rafella (IRE)**[32] 2951 2-9-0 0........................ JimCrowley 4 76
(R M Beckett) *chsd ldr: rdn to chal over 1f out: led ins fnl f: kpt on wl u.p* **33/1**

33 **2** *¾* **Freckenham (IRE)**[29] 3053 2-9-0 0........................ HayleyTurner 7 74
(M L W Bell) *sn led and grad crossed to rail: rdn ent fnl 2f: drvn and hdd ins fnl f: styd on same pce fnl 100yds* **8/1**[3]

4 **3** *1* **Apace (IRE)**[13] 3590 2-9-0 0........................ RyanMoore 6 71+
(Sir Michael Stoute) *athletic: hld up in tch: hdwy to chse ldrs 2f out: rdn and unable qck over 1f out: kpt on u.p ins fnl f: nvr gng pce to rch ldng pair* **8/13**[1]

5 **4** *1 ¼* **Spennymoor (IRE)**[19] 3411 2-8-7 0........................ AntiocoMurgia(7) 3 67
(Mahmood Al Zarooni) *leggy: unf: chsd ldrs: rdn and effrt over 1f out: one pce and no imp fnl f* **8/1**[3]

0 **5** *6* **Bouzy**[22] 3295 2-9-0 0........................ FrankieMcDonald 1 49
(P Winkworth) *sn pushed along in midfield: rdn and struggling ent fnl 2f: wl btn fr over 1f out* **50/1**

60 **6** *nk* **Amber Mist**[16] 3509 2-8-9 0........................ KierenFox(5) 2 48
(David Pinder) *leggy: chsd ldrs: rdn and unable qck 2f out: wknd over 1f out* **50/1**

7 *1 ¼* **Red Oleander** 2-9-0 0........................ PaulMulrennan 8 50+
(Sir Mark Prescott) *leggy: bit bkwd: s.i.s: sn bustled along in rr: struggling u.p over 2f out: lost tch wl over 1f out* **20/1**

8 *1 ¼* **Formidable Girl (USA)** 2-9-0 0........................ NeilCallan 5 46+
(K A Ryan) *unf: scope: awkward leaving stalls and s.i.s towards rr: pushed along and sme hdwy whn hmpd over 3f out: rdn and struggling over 2f out: wl btn over 1f out* **4/1**[2]

9 *2 ½* **Century Dancer** 2-9-0 0........................ DaneO'Neill 10 33
(Miss Tor Sturgis) *w'like: bit bkwd: s.i.s: sn rcvrd and in tch: rdn and unable qck over 2f out: wl btn over 1f out* **66/1**

0 **10** *10* **Veuveveuvevoom**[39] 2749 2-8-11 0............. Louis-PhilippeBeuzelin(3) 9 —
(G P Enright) *leggy: a last trio: dropped to last and struggling 1/2-way: lost tch over 2f out: t.o* **100/1**

1m 13.8s (1.90) **Going Correction** +0.125s/f (Slow) **10** Ran SP% **118.2**
Speed ratings (Par 91): **92,91,89,88,80 79,77,76,72,59**
toteswingers: 1&2 £28.70, 1&3 £10.80, 2&3 £3.10 CSF £264.28 TOTE £37.60: £5.50, £1.20, £1.10; EX 116.20 Trifecta £316.30 Pool: £598.59 - 1.40 winning units..
Owner Favourites Racing IX **Bred** Mrs Ellen Lyons **Trained** Whitsbury, Hants

FOCUS
The bare form of this fillies' maiden looks just modest, but the race still ought to produce winners. It paid to race prominently off the steady pace, which limits the form.

NOTEBOOK
Rafella(IRE) had achieved little on her first three starts, recording a top RPR of just 45, but she clearly proved well suited by the return to 6f, as well as the switch to Polytrack. She's expected to switch to nurseries now. (op 25-1)
Freckenham(IRE), who didn't look comfortable at Brighton last time, had her chance from the front on this switch to Polytrack and can have no excuse. (op 5-1)
Apace(IRE) was well backed to improve on a promising debut effort, but she disappointed, finding only the one speed after coming wide into the straight. Perhaps a more galloping track will suit her better, and she gives the impression she's still learning. (op Evens)
Spennymoor(IRE) showed only modest form on debut and, despite travelling kindly, didn't really build on that performance.
Bouzy is probably one for low-grade nursery/handicap company.
Red Oleander, who is out of a useful 7f-1m4f winner, ran green throughout and should come on a bundle for this. (tchd 16-1)
Formidable Girl(USA), a Lowther entrant, took an age to come out of the stalls and generally seemed overawed by this initial experience. (op 9-2)

4030 E B F PAUL KELLEWAY MEMORIAL CLASSIFIED STKS 1m (P)
4:30 (4:32) (Class 3) 3-Y-O+ **£6,476** (£1,927; £963; £481) **Stalls** High

Form				RPR
0022	**1**		**Benandonner (USA)**[13] 3585 7-9-4 87.......................... AndreaAtzeni 7 (Mike Murphy) *chsd ldrs: rdn to ld wl over 1f out: r.o wl u.p ins fnl f* **7/1**[3]	100
30-0	**2**	*3/4*	**Layline (IRE)**[27] 3103 3-8-9 89.......................... JimCrowley 10 (R M Beckett) *stdd s: hld up towards rr: gd hdwy on outer to chse ldrs ent fnl 2f: ev ch and rdn 1f out: no ex u.p fnl 75yds* **6/1**[2]	96
5600	**3**	*7*	**Mr Willis**[11] 3692 4-9-4 88.......................... SteveDrowne 5 (J R Best) *in tch in midfield: pushed along and lost pl 1/2-way: hdwy u.p on outer over 1f out: kpt on to go modest 3rd ins fnl f: no ch w ldng pair* **7/1**[3]	82
3500	**4**	*2 1/4*	**Highly Regal (IRE)**[21] 3334 5-9-4 85..........................(b) LiamKeniry 8 (R A Teal) *in tch in midfield: pushed along and unable qck over 2f out: edgd rt u.p and wknd over 1f out* **33/1**	77
5010	**5**	*1/2*	**Den's Gift (IRE)**[32] 2971 6-8-13 89..........................(b) JohnFahy(5) 9 (C G Cox) *lw: chsd ldr tl led wl over 2f out: rdn and hdd wl over 1f out: wknd over 1f out: no ch w ldrs after: lost 2 pls fnl f* **9/1**	76
0500	**6**	*nse*	**Docofthebay (IRE)**[28] 3069 6-9-4 89..........................(b) ChrisCatlin 4 (J A Glover) *s.i.s: a in rr: no prog u.p over 2f out: nvr trbld ldrs* **6/1**[2]	76
1002	**7**	*1/2*	**Jake The Snake (IRE)**[28] 3083 9-9-4 87.......................... NeilCallan 3 (A W Carroll) *dwlt: hld up in tch in midfield: rdn and effrt ent fnl 2f: wknd over 1f out: wl btn fnl f* **14/1**	75
2-12	**8**	*1 3/4*	**Bintalwaadi**[34] 2898 3-8-6 89.......................... TadhgO'Shea 2 (E A L Dunlop) *lw: t.k.h: chsd ldrs: rdn and unable qck jst over 2f out: wknd qckly over 1f out: wl btn fnl f* **11/8**[1]	66
0U13	**9**	*13*	**Samarinda (USA)**[27] 3107 7-9-4 88.......................... MickyFenton 1 (Mrs P Sly) *led tl wl over 2f out: sn dropped out and bhd: eased fnl f* **25/1**	41

1m 37.31s (-0.89) **Going Correction** +0.125s/f (Slow)
WFA 3 from 4yo+ 9lb **9** Ran SP% **119.1**
Speed ratings (Par 107): **109,108,101,99,98 98,97,96,83**
toteswingers: 1&2 £9.70, 1&3 £8.50, 2&3 £7.80 CSF £50.13 TOTE £6.90: £1.30, £2.80, £2.40; EX 44.80 Trifecta £227.10 Pool: £675.45 - 2.20 winning units..
Owner Phil Woods **Bred** Gainsborough Farm Llc **Trained** Westoning, Beds

FOCUS
A fair handicap which was well run. The first pair came well clear and the form is rated around the winner.

NOTEBOOK
Benandonner(USA), in good form in turf handicaps lately, including when runner-up to Ginger Jack (subsequently broke a track record at Musselburgh) at Haydock latest, gained his first success since landing a 7f claimer around here last December for Richard Fahey. Having been nicely placed throughout by Atzeni, he showed a good attitude to hold off the less-experienced runner-up. He ought to remain competitive. (op 8-1)
Layline(IRE) ◆ ran better than when 15th of 27 in the Britannia on his belated reappearance, but this was only his fifth start and he still looked immature. After making good headway out wide around the turn into the straight, he briefly seemed the likeliest winner, but he didn't knuckle down sufficiently, very much giving the impression the experience was still needed. There ought to be better to come. (op 8-1 tchd 9-1)
Mr Willis ◆ was being niggled along from a fair way out and took too long to get going. He's surely worth another try at around 1m2f seeing as his career-best RPR was achieved on his sole run beyond 1m.
Highly Regal(IRE) is probably a better horse at Kempton, where he has six course wins to his name.
Den's Gift(IRE) had his chance under a positive ride. (op 11-1 tchd 8-1)
Bintalwaadi was disappointing. She had upwards of 3lb in hand at the weights, and had won her maiden over C&D, but she ran flat this time. Tadhg O'Shea duly reported that the filly did not pick up. Official explanation: jockey said filly did not pick up (op 5-4 tchd 6-4)
Samarinda(USA) Official explanation: jockey said gelding was unable to dominate

4031 BET TRI-NATIONS RUGBY - BETDAQ H'CAP 6f (P)
5:00 (5:02) (Class 5) (0-75,76) 3-Y-O **£2,729** (£806; £403) **Stalls** Low

Form				RPR
00-	**1**		**Stefanki (IRE)**[228] 7580 3-9-1 69.......................... TonyCulhane 8 (George Baker) *lw: stdd s: hld up in rr: pushed along and hdwy on outer ent fnl 2f: stl plenty to do over 1f out: qcknd wl under hands and heels to ld fnl 100yds: sn wl clr: v easily* **6/4**[1]	81+
0566	**2**	*3 1/4*	**Valmina**[14] 3561 3-8-13 67..........................(tp) LukeMorris 10 (Andrew Turnell) *in tch: effrt u.p to join ldrs over 1f out: led ent fnl f: hdd and nt pce of wnr fnl 100yds: hld on for 2nd* **25/1**	69
5552	**3**	*nk*	**Faithful Duchess (IRE)**[16] 3515 3-8-5 59.......................... HayleyTurner 2 (E A L Dunlop) *hld up in last trio: swtchd off of rail and rdn 2f out: n.m.r ent fnl f: gap opened and r.o wl fnl 75yds to press for 2nd cl home: no ch w wnr* **8/1**	60+
1205	**4**	*hd*	**Freddie's Girl (USA)**[14] 3561 3-9-6 74.......................... TomQueally 7 (Stef Higgins) *led: rdn and hrd pressed ent fnl 2f: hdd ent fnl f: stl ev ch tl nt pce of wnr fnl 100yds: kpt on* **10/1**	74
0-62	**5**	*nk*	**Caldermud (IRE)**[26] 3154 3-9-7 75.......................... SteveDrowne 11 (J R Best) *lw: pressed ldr: ev ch and rdn ent fnl 2f: stl ev ch tl nt pce of wnr fnl 100yds: kpt on* **11/2**[3]	74
23-0	**6**	*hd*	**Excellent Thought**[26] 3174 3-9-2 70.......................... J-PGuillambert 6 (P Howling) *in tch in midfield: effrt u.p jst over 2f out: ev ch ent fnl f tl nt pce of wnr fnl 100yds: kpt on* **25/1**	68
0004	**7**	*3/4*	**Dream Number (IRE)**[11] 3677 3-8-5 59.......................... MartinDwyer 9 (W R Muir) *stdd s: hld up in last pair: gd hdwy on outer to press ldrs ent fnl 2f: drvn and kpt on same pce fr over 1f out* **12/1**	55
1416	**8**	*3/4*	**Maoi Chinn Tire (IRE)**[28] 3085 3-9-6 74..........................(p) LiamKeniry 4 (J S Moore) *chsd ldrs: rdn and unable qck ent fnl 2f: one pce and btn ins fnl f: eased towards fin* **8/1**	68
1605	**9**	*1*	**Rightcar**[98] 1163 3-8-2 56 oh1.......................... AndreaAtzeni 5 (Peter Grayson) *dwlt and bmpd s: sn in tch in midfield: rdn and struggling 2f out: styd on same pce after* **50/1**	46
3124	**10**	*4*	**Craicattack (IRE)**[50] 2415 3-9-2 70..........................(p) RyanMoore 1 (J S Moore) *swtg: in tch in midfield: rdn and lost pl 3f out: wl btn over 1f out: eased wl ins fnl f* **5/1**[2]	48

1m 12.57s (0.67) **Going Correction** +0.125s/f (Slow) **10** Ran SP% **120.7**
Speed ratings (Par 100): **100,95,95,95,94 94,93,92,91,85**
toteswingers: 1&2 £26.20, 1&3 £3.80, 2&3 £30.10 CSF £51.67 CT £253.34 TOTE £3.00: £1.70, £9.40, £1.60; EX 57.90 Trifecta £444.50 Part won. Pool: £600.75 - 0.92 winning units. Place 6 £43.26, Place 5 £8.10.
Owner S E Sangster **Bred** Ghana Syndicate **Trained** Moreton Morrell, Warwicks

FOCUS
This looked a tight handicap, but the winner was impressive and looks sure to rate higher. The form looks sound with the winner rated up 6lb.
T/Plt: £68.20 to a £1 stake. Pool: £59,005.50. 631.43 winning tickets. T/Qpdt: £11.20 to a £1 stake. Pool: £4,865.55. 320.75 winning tickets. SP

4032 - 4034a (Foreign Racing) - See Raceform Interactive

4012 HAMBURG (R-H)
Wednesday, July 14

OFFICIAL GOING: Turf: good

4035a WENATEX EUROPA-GRUPPERENNEN (GROUP 3) (3YO+ FILLIES & MARES) (TURF) 1m
7:00 (12:00) 3-Y-O+
£28,318 (£9,734; £4,867; £2,654; £1,769; £1,327)

			RPR
1		**Aslana (IRE)**[25] 3236 3-8-11 0.......................... AStarke 5 (P Schiergen, Germany) *settled midfield: mde gd prog arnd fnl turn: qcknd wl in centre of trck to chse ldrs: ct ldr ins fnl f: r.o wl* **92/10**	103
2	*1/2*	**Vanjura (GER)**[52] 2372 3-8-11 0.......................... APietsch 10 (R Dzubasz, Germany) *racd in 4th: gd prog into st: swtchd outside: gd hdwy to ld 1 1/2f out: r.o wl: ct in fnl 50yds* **2/1**[2]	102
3	*3/4*	**Fabiana**[252] 7249 4-9-4 0.......................... JiriPalik 11 (Andreas Lowe, Germany) *in rr fr s: qcknd wl in st: r.o strly fnl f* **171/10**	100
4	*3/4*	**Artica (GER)**[51] 3-8-11 0.......................... EFrank 8 (T Mundry, Germany) *broke slowly: settled towards rr: shkn up fnl turn: qcknd wl in st: r.o wl* **156/10**	99
5	*1/2*	**Masquenada (FR)**[55] 5-9-4 0.......................... DominiqueBoeuf 2 (W Baltromei, Germany) *bkmarker fr s: mde gd prog at end of bk st: qcknd wl in st: no ex fnl 1 1/2f* **153/10**	97
6	*2*	**Mi Rubina (IRE)**[51] 3-8-11 0.......................... EPedroza 4 (A Wohler, Germany) *one of the early ldrs: rdn early in st: no ex* **122/10**	93
7	*3/4*	**Virginia Hall**[11] 3694 3-8-11 0.......................... SebSanders 1 (Sir Mark Prescott) *sent st to ld and in front ent st: rdn and sn btn* **17/10**[1]	91
8	*3 1/2*	**Magic Eye (IRE)**[25] 3236 5-9-6 0.......................... LennartHammer-Hansen 6 (Andreas Lowe, Germany) *racd in 2nd fr s: chal ldr early in st: no ex* **173/10**	85
9	*4*	**Rock My Soul (IRE)**[80] 4-9-6 0.......................... DPorcu 3 (Uwe Ostmann, Germany) *racd in 3rd: flattered briefly in st: sn wknd* **5/1**[3]	76
10	*25*	**Sunmoon Royale (GER)**[43] 3-8-11 0.......................... THellier 7 (Mario Hofer, Germany) *prom fr s: racing freely: sn btn in st* **28/1**	16

1m 37.6s (97.60)
WFA 3 from 4yo+ 9lb **10** Ran SP% **131.0**
Win (incl. 10 euro stake): 102. PLACES: 28, 20, 45. SF: 293.
Owner Stall Nizza **Bred** J Imm **Trained** Germany

NOTEBOOK
Virginia Hall disappointed after her Listed-race win last time.

3703 LONGCHAMP (R-H)
Wednesday, July 14

OFFICIAL GOING: Turf: very soft

4036a PRIX ROLAND DE CHAMBURE (LISTED RACE) (2YO) (TURF) 7f
5:40 (12:00) 2-Y-O **£24,336** (£9,734; £7,300; £4,867; £2,433)

			RPR
1		**Maiguri (IRE)**[29] 2-8-11 0.......................... JohanVictoire 6 (C Baillet, France) *racd 3rd: qcknd wl 2 1/2f out: tk ld 1 1/2f out: qcknd clr: easy* **18/5**[3]	100+
2	*2 1/2*	**Borysthene (FR)** 2-8-11 0.......................... ChristopheSoumillon 4 (J-C Rouget, France) *racd in 4th on rail: rdn 1 1/2f out: short of room: qcknd wl whn in clr: r.o wl fnl f* **3/1**[2]	94
3	*1 1/2*	**Zacynthus (IRE)**[18] 3452 2-8-11 0.......................... FrankieDettori 3 (Mahmood Al Zarooni) *led fr s tl 2f out: rdn and hdd 1 1/2f out: r.o: no ex fnl f* **13/10**[1]	90
4	*1 1/2*	**Beowulf (FR)**[14] 2-8-11 0.......................... ThierryThulliez 5 (P Bary, France) *racd towards rr: qcknd 1 1/2f and r.o wl ins fnl f* **11/2**	86
5	*1*	**Uldiko (FR)**[21] 2-8-11 0.......................... FranckBlondel 7 (Mme C Barande-Barbe, France) *prom fr s: rdn 2 1/2f out: no ex: styd on* **36/1**	84
6	*shd*	**Passei (FR)**[29] 2-8-8 0.......................... MickaelBarzalona 2 (Mlle V Dissaux, France) *racd towards rr: proged 2f out: no ex fnl 1 1/2f: styd on* **21/1**	81

7 *10* **Trille Divine**[34] 2-8-8 0 ... AnthonyCrastus 1 56
(Mme C De La Soudiere-Niault, France) *missed break and racd in rr: rdn early in st and fnd no ex* **21/1**

1m 23.2s (2.50) **7** Ran SP% **117.4**
WIN (incl. 1 euro stake): 4.60. PLACES: 1.20, 1.20, 1.10. DF: 9.70. SF: 18.50.
Owner Ecurie Jarlan **Bred** Ecurie Jarlan **Trained** France

NOTEBOOK
Zacynthus(IRE), winner of a Newmarket maiden on fast ground on his debut, made the running but could not hold on.

4037a PRIX DE THIBERVILLE (LISTED RACE) (3YO FILLIES) (TURF) 1m 4f
6:10 (12:00) 3-Y-O **£24,336** (£9,734; £7,300; £4,867; £2,433)

RPR

1 **Announce**[39] 3-8-11 0 ... MaximeGuyon 5 95
(A Fabre, France) *hld up towards rr: rushed up to be a cl 3rd 5f out: rdn 1 1/2f out and tk time to qckn: styd on fnl f to ld ins fnl 100yds: r.o wl* **9/10**[1]

2 *3/4* **Oekaki (FR)**[17] 3493 3-8-11 0 ... DavyBonilla 3 94
(Y Barberot, France) *racd in first four thrght: wnt 2nd 1f out: kpt on wl* **28/1**

3 *hd* **Ludiana (FR)**[19] 3-8-11 0 ... GeraldMosse 9 94
(A De Royer-Dupre, France) *a.p: rdn to ld 2f out: hdd ins fnl 100yds: kpt on* **4/1**[2]

4 *1* **Toi Et Moi (IRE)**[28] 3-8-11 0 ... FrankieDettori 6 92
(P Bary, France) *chsd ldrs: 5th and rdn st (2 1/2f out): wnt 4th 1 1/2f out: r.o at one pce* **14/1**

5 *1 1/2* **Foundation Filly**[38] 2800 3-8-11 0 ... ThierryThulliez 1 90
(F Doumen, France) *hld up last: plld wd and rdn over 2f out: styd on fnl f: n.d* **68/10**[3]

6 *1/2* **Roche Ambeau (FR)**[26] 3-8-11 0 ... AnthonyCrastus 4 89
(E Lellouche, France) *hld up: last st (2 1/2f out): 6th 1 1/2f fr home: one pce* **19/1**

7 *1* **Pink Symphony**[34] 2889 3-8-11 0 ... JamieSpencer 2 87
(P F I Cole) *hld up in midfield: 5th and rdn 2f out: no ex fnl f* **9/1**

8 *2* **Sinndarina (FR)**[38] 2800 3-8-11 0 ... (p) OlivierPeslier 8 84
(P Demercastel, France) *broke wl: settled in midfield: 6th and rdn 2 1/2f out: no imp* **43/1**

9 *2 1/2* **Narya (IRE)** 3-8-11 0 ... ChristopheSoumillon 7 80
(M Delcher-Sanchez, Spain) *sn set a stdy pce: hdd 2f out: wknd qckly* **17/1**

2m 38.4s (8.00) **9** Ran SP% **118.4**
WIN (incl. 1 euro stake): 1.90; PLACE 1.20, 3.90, 1.40; DF 39.50; SF 65.90.
Owner K Abdulla **Bred** Juddmonte Farms **Trained** Chantilly, France

NOTEBOOK
Pink Symphony, runner-up in a similar contest at Newbury, was stepping up in trip. A combination of that and the softer ground appeared to find her out.

4038a PRIX MAURICE DE NIEUIL (GROUP 2) (4YO+) (TURF) 1m 6f
6:45 (12:00) 4-Y-O+ **£65,575** (£25,309; £12,079; £8,053; £4,026)

RPR

1 **Blek (FR)**[52] 2375 5-8-11 0 ... YohannBourgois 1 112+
(E Lellouche, France) *racd 2nd: rdn 2f out: qcknd wl and grabbed ld 1 1/2f out: sn clr: easily* **9/4**[2]

2 *3* **Los Cristianos (FR)**[52] 2375 4-8-11 0 ... ThomasHuet 2 107
(A Couetil, France) *racd in 4th along rail: moved 3rd 1 1/2f out: r.o wl fnl f: grabbed 2nd ins fnl 50yds* **6/1**

3 *1* **Titurel (GER)**[35] 5-8-11 0 ... MaximeGuyon 7 106
(Manfred Hofer, Germany) *led fr s and stl in front early in st: rdn 2f out: styd on wl: lost 2nd ins fnl 50yds* **15/1**

4 *5* **Aizavoski (IRE)**[28] 3099 4-8-11 0 ... AnthonyCrastus 4 99
(E Lellouche, France) *racd in 3rd: rdn early in st: failed to qckn u.p 2f out: styd on fnl 1 1/2f* **13/10**[1]

5 *2 1/2* **Redesignation (IRE)**[28] 3099 5-8-11 0 ... ThierryJarnet 5 96
(R Pritchard-Gordon, France) *a in rr: no prog in st* **25/1**

6 *10* **Roatan**[38] 2803 5-8-11 0 ... FrankieDettori 6 82
(P Bary, France) *racd in 5th: rdn early in st: briefly proged: no ex fnl 1 1/2f: fdd* **5/1**[3]

3m 3.20s (183.20) **6** Ran SP% **115.3**
WIN (incl. 1 euro stake): 3.60. PLACES: 1.50, 3.30. SF: 18.90.
Owner Alain Maubert **Bred** Alain Maubert **Trained** Lamorlaye, France

NOTEBOOK
Blek(FR) powered clear for an easy victory, giving his jockey his first Group success. Well suited by the rain-affected ground, the horse will be targeted at the Prix du Cadran in the autumn.

4039a JUDDMONTE GRAND PRIX DE PARIS (GROUP 1) (3YO COLTS & FILLIES) (TURF) 1m 4f
7:20 (12:00) 3-Y-O **£303,398** (£121,380; £60,690; £30,318; £15,185)

RPR

1 **Behkabad (FR)**[38] 2802 3-9-2 0 ... GeraldMosse 1 122+
(J-C Rouget, France) *disp 2nd early: settled in 3rd: 2nd and poised to chal 4f out: led st (2 1/2f out): r.o strly and qcknd whn chal appr fnl f: styd on strly* **5/1**

2 *3/4* **Planteur (IRE)**[38] 2802 3-9-2 0 ... AnthonyCrastus 6 121+
(E Lellouche, France) *hld up towards rr: 6th 4f out: clsd to dispute 2nd st: r.o to chal ldr ins fnl 300yds: nt able to qckn again fnl 150yds* **9/4**[1]

3 *5* **Jan Vermeer (IRE)**[17] 3491 3-9-2 0 ... JMurtagh 9 113
(A P O'Brien, Ire) *plld early and restrained towards rr: hdwy 4f out: 4th st: 3rd and ev ch 2f out: unable qck and jst hld on for 3rd* **11/4**[2]

4 *nse* **Goldwaki (GER)**[31] 3014 3-9-2 0 ... OlivierPeslier 5 113
(A Fabre, France) *hld up in last: prog 2 1/2f out: styd on ins fnl f: jst failed to take 3rd but no imp on front two* **4/1**[3]

5 *3* **Lawspeaker**[46] 2557 3-9-2 0 ... MaximeGuyon 2 108
(A Fabre, France) *racd in midfield: disp 2nd st: rdn and no ex fnl 2f* **14/1**

6 *6* **Ivory Land (FR)**[38] 2802 3-9-2 0 ... (p) ChristopheSoumillon 8 98
(A De Royer-Dupre, France) *racd in midfield: 5th st: sn rdn and unable qck: no ex fnl 1 1/2f* **33/1**

7 *8* **Allesson (FR)**[36] 3-9-2 0 ... ThierryThulliez 3 86
(N Clement, France) *disp 2nd early: 3rd 4f out: grad fdd fr fnl bnd* **20/1**

8 *4* **Ice Blue**[38] 2802 3-9-2 0 ... StephanePasquier 4 79
(P Bary, France) *plld hrd early: racd in 4th: 5th 4f out: sn rdn and btn* **8/1**

9 *15* **Vivre Libre**[38] 2802 3-9-2 0 ... (b) SamuelFargeat 7 55
(E Lellouche, France) *led tl hdd st: wknd qckly and eased* **250/1**

2m 33.3s (2.90) **9** Ran SP% **120.0**
WIN (incl. 1 euro stake): 9.80; PLACE 1.70, 1.20, 1.70; DF 8.70; SF 21.30.
Owner H H Aga Khan **Bred** H H The Aga Khan's Studs S C **Trained** Pau, France

FOCUS
Another of the country's Group 1s to have been remastered distance-wise over the years, having started life as very much a stayers' race before a brief flirtation as a 1m2f feature. Back to 1m4f, and with the Prix du Jockey Club reverting to the shorter trip, this could be deemed to be the French Derby if a common distance is the criteria, although it has also been moved from late June to this Batstille Day date. The big disappointment was the lack of British-trained runners, but at least the English and Irish Derby form was represented by Jan Vermeer in a race with a very mixed level of form but one that has had quite a bearing on the Prix de l'Arc de Triomphe back over the course and distance in October, having produced the winner in Rail Link (2006), Bago (2004) and before that Peintre Celebre. This was turned into an unseasonal stamina test after a morning monsoon of 39mm on what was already official good to soft ground. Pacemaker Vivre Libre did his job and they came home at intervals to confirm the testing conditions.

NOTEBOOK
Behkabad(FR), winner of two Group 3s but beaten in Listed company on heavy ground this year, showed he has stamina in abundance to give connections a second win in three years after Montmartre in 2008. He was one of the principals to cover the pace and turned in second to the pacemaker as the others sat well out of their ground. As such he got first run on them and kept on strongly up the straight. He presumably will be Arc-bound, knowing the Aga Khan, with the Niel in the interim. However, the form looks shy of Arc proportions.
Planteur(IRE) sat close when ahead of Bekhabad in the Prix du Jockey Club but out the back here, racing a shade keenly as well. That, as much as the different ground conditions made the difference. He still came with a strong run down the outside to look a big danger into the last two furlongs, but he was held through the final furlong as he wandered under pressure on the ground after producing the best burst of speed in the straight. His April victim Rewilding has upheld the form and back on a sounder surface he should snag a Group 1 win.
Jan Vermeer(IRE), beaten over 11l into fourth (4l behind third home Rewilding) in the Derby and third in the Irish equivalent, looked to again fail for stamina in these conditions - his soft-ground Criterium International win was over 1m - as he made a swift and daring move hard against the inside rail to get into a challenging position into the straight, but he was floundering early in the last two furlongs. Back over 1m2f or even 1m under similar conditions to these, he remains a danger to all at the top level, but confirms the Irish Derby is the poor relation of its equivalents.
Goldwaki(GER) was the most interesting runner having been supplemented, bidding to give trainer Andre Fabre his 11th win in the race. He boasted the race formline, having won the Prix de Lys, as had Fabre's Rail Link in 2006 and the 2008 winner Montmartre. As such he was most disappointing, never threatening to land a blow from last place, where he had been niggled at various stages of the race, suggesting he was not happy on the ground. He plugged on when it was all over but still failed to reel in the gasping Jan Vermeer. He still deserves another chance to atone on better ground.
Lawspeaker was tightened up early against the running rail but seemed to be travelling well enough inside the last four furlongs before failing to pick up, and this Listed winner was purely outclassed.
Ivory Land(FR) was not energised by the cheekpieces and was eased when dropping away halfway up the straight to accentuate his beating.
Allesson(FR), second to 2,000 Guineas winner Makfi last November on soft ground, has a big question mark against him after this.
Ice Blue again got on his toes in the preliminaries, although not boiling over. He did not want to canter to the start when released from the parade, and when put under pressure he was the first beaten. He looks one to avoid.

3721 BATH (L-H)
Thursday, July 15

OFFICIAL GOING: Firm
Wind: Strong across Weather: Overcast

4040 CORNISH COVE NURSERY 5f 11y
5:50 (5:50) (Class 5) 2-Y-O **£2,100** (£2,100; £481; £240) **Stalls** Centre

Form RPR

01 **1** **Tedious**[66] 1978 2-9-7 **72** ... DavidProbert 3 76
(S Kirk) *let: rdn and kpt on wl fnl 2f: jnd on line* **11/2**

440 **1** *dht* **Indian Ballad (IRE)**[13] 3624 2-9-3 **68** ... RobertWinston 2 72
(E S McMahon) *chsd ldrs: checked 3f out and lost position: sn rcvrd: rdn and edgd rt over 1f out: hung lft u.p ins fnl f: got up on line* **6/4**[1]

221 **3** *2* **Stunning In Purple (IRE)**[10] 3721 2-9-3 **68** 6ex ... NeilCallan 5 66
(A B Haynes) *t.k.h: racd in 2nd: rdn 2f out: fading whn hmpd ins fnl f* **3/1**[2]

0425 **4** *3/4* **Darwin Star**[3] 3959 2-9-3 **68** ... JimmyQuinn 1 62
(D K Ivory) *outpcd: pushed along fr 1/2-way: kpt on fnl f but nvr a threat* **9/2**[3]

2050 **5** *2 1/4* **Lovat Lane**[23] 3295 2-8-8 **59** ... LiamKeniry 4 45
(Eve Johnson Houghton) *towards rr but in tch: rdn 1/2-way: wknd ins fnl 2f* **13/2**

62.09 secs (-0.41) **Going Correction** -0.175s/f (Firm) **5** Ran SP% **111.9**
Speed ratings (Par 94): **96,96,92,91,88**
WIN: Tedious £4.20; Indian Ballad £1.40; PL £2.00 (T), £1.90 (IB); EX: £6.00 (T/IB), £9.90 (IB/T), CSF: £7.27 (T/IB), £5.14 (IB/T).
Owner R Hannon **Bred** A S Reid **Trained** Upper Lambourn, Berks
Owner R L Bedding **Bred** J M Beever **Trained** Lichfield, Staffs

FOCUS
The ground remained firm after the track missed most of the rain, and a strong headwind made things tough for the runners all evening. The card began with a disappointingly small turnout for this nursery. The third sets the level and Indian Ballad was perhaps a shade unlucky not to win outright.

NOTEBOOK
Tedious, comfortable winner of a 5f claimer last time, after which she was acquired by current connections for £13,000, was proven at the trip and again showed plenty of speed throughout. She looks better than claiming standard, and her uncomplicated front-running style will come in handy in similar company over this trip. (op 11-4)
Indian Ballad(IRE) had shown promise in three 6f maidens at Haydock and the drop to 5f was not a problem. His handicap mark looks a fair one and, as long as he is not treated harshly for this, he should continue to make his mark at either trip. (op 11-4)
Stunning In Purple(IRE) was having her seventh race, but this was her first venture into nurseries. She ran a sound race under a 6lb penalty but the fact that she could not match the first two suggests she will find it hard if she is raised too far for her win here earlier in the month. (op 15-8)
Darwin Star, in her first handicap, has creditable form in 5f maidens but ran as if a return to 6f might suit her better. (op 5-1 tchd 11-2)
Lovat Lane has not progressed since making a promising debut and appears to have arrived in nurseries on a stiff mark. (op 8-1)

4041 BATHWICK TYRES BRISTOL H'CAP 5f 11y
6:20 (6:20) (Class 5) (0-75,74) 3-Y-O+ **£3,238** (£963; £481; £240) **Stalls** Centre

Form RPR

3212 **1** **Piazza San Pietro**[2] 3980 4-9-9 **72** ... NeilCallan 8 81
(A B Haynes) *hmpd s: sn t.k.h in rr: hdwy: nt clr run and swtchd rt ins fnl 2f: str run on outside over 1f out: hung lft u.p fnl 120yds: led fnl 50yds: readily* **3/1**[1]

2554 **2** ½ **The Name Is Frank**[10] 3722 5-8-7 **59**..................(t) MichaelStainton(3) 10 66
(Mark Gillard) *chsd ldrs: rdn 1/2-way: drvn to chal fr 1f out and upsides fnl 120yds: nt pce of wnr fnl 50yds* **17/2**

1604 **3** *hd* **Little Edward**[20] 3400 12-9-4 **70**.......................... WilliamCarson(3) 4 76
(R J Hodges) *wnt lft s: chsd ldrs: chal fr 1f out: slt ld fnl 120yds: hdd and outpcd fnl 50yds* **16/1**

3023 **4** *1* **Matterofact (IRE)**[10] 3722 7-8-13 **62**............................ RobertWinston 1 65
(M S Saunders) *in tch: drvn to chse ldrs over 1f out whn n.m.r: styng on whn n.m.r and one pce fnl 120yds* **9/2**[2]

3133 **5** ½ **Cape Royal**[7] 3809 10-9-11 **74**..(bt) LiamKeniry 5 75
(J M Bradley) *led tl hdd & wknd fnl 120yds* **7/1**

0202 **6** ¾ **Baby Queen (IRE)**[5] 3908 4-8-10 **59**........................ J-PGuillambert 2 57
(B P J Baugh) *in rr: rdn 1/2-way: sme prog over 1f out: nvr gng pce to trble ldrs* **6/1**[3]

2450 **7** 2¼ **Nepotism**[41] 2689 3-9-2 **70**.. TomMcLaughlin 7 68+
(M S Saunders) *in tch: rdn 1/2-way: styng on to chse ldrs whn hmpd fnl 120yds: nt rcvr* **10/1**

0-0 **8** ¾ **Elhamri**[3] 3958 6-9-10 **73**.. ChrisCatlin 3 65
(S Kirk) *bmpd s: chsd ldrs: rdn 2f out: n.m.r over 1f out: eased whn hld ins fnl f* **20/1**

4565 **9** 3¾ **Green Lagonda (AUS)**[3] 3958 8-9-1 **64**........................ JimmyFortune 9 38
(P D Evans) *outpcd most of way* **13/2**

5-00 **10** *6* **Miskin Nights**[31] 3030 3-8-1 **55**......................................(t) DavidProbert 6 —
(B Palling) *rdn and bhd fr 1/2-way* **33/1**

61.22 secs (-1.28) **Going Correction** -0.175s/f (Firm)
WFA 3 from 4yo+ 5lb **10** Ran SP% **116.5**
Speed ratings (Par 103): **103,102,101,100,99 98,94,93,87,77**
toteswingers:1&2:£6.60, 1&3:£24.40, 2&3:£24.40 CSF £29.22 CT £359.20 TOTE £3.90: £1.90, £2.80, £5.10; EX 37.70.
Owner K Corke **Bred** T E Pocock **Trained** Limpley Stoke, Bath
■ Stewards' Enquiry : Neil Callan one-day ban: careless riding (Jul 29)

FOCUS
A typically competitive Bath sprint but the in-form winner was just too good. Modest form.

4042 BATHWICK TYRES H'CAP 2m 1f 34y
6:50 (6:50) (Class 6) (0-65,65) 4-Y-O+ **£2,590** (£770; £385; £192) **Stalls** Centre

Form RPR
1-00 **1** **Perception (IRE)**[8] 3780 4-9-7 **65**............................... FergusSweeney 5 69
(A King) *chsd ldrs: slt ld fr ins fnl 3f: sn rdn: narrowly hdd apprching fnl f: styd chalng u.p and led again cl home* **9/1**

030- **2** *hd* **The Composer**[72] 6692 8-8-2 **46** oh1................................ JimmyQuinn 1 50
(M Blanshard) *in tch tl awkward at bnd ins fnl 5f and dropped to rr: gd hdwy 3f out and sn chsng ldrs: slt ld u.p towards outside appr fnl f: hdd fnl 120yds but styd chalng tl no ex last strides* **20/1**

50-3 **3** *shd* **Dark Energy**[25] 2811 6-8-9 **53**...(t) HayleyTurner 4 57
(M J Scudamore) *stdd s: t.k.h in rr tl hdwy towards outside over 4f out: str run on ins fr 3f out to chal 1f out: slt ld fnl 120yds: hdd cl home* **7/2**[2]

1306 **4** *4* **Spiritonthemount (USA)**[13] 3639 5-8-4 **48** ow2.............(b) ChrisCatlin 3 47
(P W Hiatt) *rdn after s and led after 1f: hdd over 8f out: rdn over 3f out and styd chsng ldrs tl wknd ins fnl 2f* **5/1**[3]

06-0 **5** 2½ **Casual Garcia**[26] 3195 5-9-2 **63**.........................(bt) MichaelStainton(3) 6 59
(Mark Gillard) *chsd ldrs: rdn 3f out: wknd ins fnl 2f* **7/1**

-510 **6** *9* **Brave Bugsy (IRE)**[38] 2810 7-8-13 **57**......................(b[1]) JimmyFortune 7 50
(A M Balding) *chsd ldrs: hdwy to ld over 8f out: hdd insde fnl 3f: sn btn: eased whn no ch fnl f* **15/8**[1]

50/ **7** *36* **Nation State**[87] 6205 9-9-7 **65**... LiamKeniry 2 7
(M Madgwick) *led 1f: styd chsng ldrs: rdn along 7f out: styd in tch tl wknd fr 3f out: eased whn no ch fnl 2f: t.o* **14/1**

000/ **8** *96* **Basiliko (USA)**[416] 3046 7-9-2 **63**............................. WilliamCarson(3) 8 —
(R J Hodges) *bhd fr 1/2-way: eased whn no ch fr over 3f out: t.o: virtually p.u* **33/1**

3m 48.33s (-3.57) **Going Correction** -0.175s/f (Firm) **8** Ran SP% **110.5**
Speed ratings (Par 101): **101,100,100,98,97 93,76,31**
toteswingers:1&2:£19.30, 1&3:£5.10, 2&3:£19.30 CSF £152.61 CT £714.10 TOTE £12.60: £2.90, £3.90, £1.10; EX 168.50.
Owner Incipe Partnership **Bred** Zanim Ralphy Meahjohn **Trained** Barbury Castle, Wilts
■ Stewards' Enquiry : Jimmy Quinn caution: used whip with excessive frequency.
Fergus Sweeney one-day ban: used whip with excessive frequency (Jul 29)

FOCUS
The pace was modest until Brave Bugsy moved up to force a better tempo at halfway. However, the duel that ensued between him and early leader Spiritonthemount did neither of them any good. Weakish form, rated through the winner. The runner-up casts doubt over the form.

4043 BATHWICK TYRES CHIPPENHAM H'CAP 5f 161y
7:25 (7:25) (Class 4) (0-80,76) 3-Y-O+ **£5,180** (£1,541; £770; £384) **Stalls** Centre

Form RPR
3121 **1** **Comptonspirit**[13] 3637 6-9-1 **64**.................................... J-PGuillambert 4 73
(B P J Baugh) *mde virtually all: rdn over 2f out: styd on strly ins fnl f* **7/2**[2]

101 **2** 1¼ **Desperate Dan**[2] 3994 9-9-6 **76** 6ex.............................(v) MarkPower(7) 6 81
(A B Haynes) *stdd s: towards rr but in tch: hdwy fr 2f out to chse wnr 1f out: no imp fnl f* **6/1**[3]

0051 **3** 1¼ **Vhujon (IRE)**[5] 3908 5-9-8 **74** 6ex.............................. RichardEvans(3) 2 75
(P D Evans) *chsd ldrs: rdn 1/2-way: styd on to take 3rd fnl f but nvr gng pce to trble wnr* **11/4**[1]

6210 **4** ¾ **Riflessione**[10] 3736 4-9-12 **75**..(b) LukeMorris 9 73
(R A Harris) *chsd ldrs: c rt to r alone on stands' side ins fnl 3f: hrd rdn and styd on same pce fnl 2f* **6/1**[3]

0050 **5** 1¾ **Billy Red**[14] 3578 6-9-12 **75**..(b) FergusSweeney 3 68
(J R Jenkins) *pressed wnr over 3f out: sn rdn: wknd fnl f* **15/2**

4-10 **6** 2¾ **Night Affair**[34] 2929 4-9-13 **76**.. NeilCallan 7 63
(D W P Arbuthnot) *s.i.s: sn rcvrd and chsd ldrs 3f out: wknd fnl f* **7/2**[2]

69.34 secs (-1.86) **Going Correction** -0.175s/f (Firm) **6** Ran SP% **111.4**
Speed ratings (Par 105): **105,103,101,100,98 94**
toteswingers:1&2:£5.30, 1&3:£1.90, 2&3:£2.50 CSF £23.58 CT £62.65 TOTE £4.60: £1.10, £3.80; EX 14.80.
Owner G B Hignett **Bred** Mrs F Wilson **Trained** Audley, Staffs

FOCUS
Like the earlier sprint, this went to a runner who has been flying in recent weeks. Straightforward form at face value.
Vhujon(IRE) Official explanation: jockey said gelding hung right-handed
Riflessione Official explanation: jockey said gelding hung right-handed

4044 BATHWICK TYRES NEWPORT H'CAP 1m 5y
7:55 (7:55) (Class 4) (0-80,79) 3-Y-O+ **£5,180** (£1,541; £770; £384) **Stalls** Low

Form RPR
-604 **1** **Spoken**[36] 2863 3-9-3 **77**..(p) JimmyFortune 3 85
(R Charlton) *mde all: hrd rdn ins fnl 2f: styd on wl u.p to go clr fnl 100yds* **11/10**[1]

0101 **2** 1¾ **Jewelled**[22] 3309 4-9-8 **73**..(v) HayleyTurner 1 79
(J W Hills) *chsd ldrs: wnt 2nd 2f out: rdn and ev ch ins fnl f: no ex u.p fnl 100yds* **5/1**[2]

1406 **3** 2¼ **Magroom**[15] 3558 6-9-2 **70**.. WilliamCarson(3) 4 71
(R J Hodges) *chsd ldrs: rdn and one pce over 2f out: styd on again fnl f to take 3rd but nvr any ch w ldng duo* **11/1**

0-00 **4** *nk* **Pelham Crescent (IRE)**[59] 2173 7-9-10 **75**..................... DavidProbert 5 75
(B Palling) *t.k.h in mid-div: rdn over 2f out: kpt on fr over 1f out to take 4th fnl f but nvr a threat* **16/1**

4446 **5** ½ **Bold Cross (IRE)**[5] 3894 7-9-7 **72**............................... PaulFitzsimons 8 71
(E G Bevan) *t.k.h: hld up in rr: hdwy towards outside fr 2f out: styd on u.p fnl f but nvr a danger* **6/1**[3]

001 **6** *1* **Monashee Rock (IRE)**[30] 3054 5-9-0 **65**............................ LiamKeniry 6 62
(Matthew Salaman) *partly walked to s: chsd wnr: rdn over 2f out: sn lost 2nd: wknd ins fnl f* **12/1**

0050 **7** 1¾ **Desert Dreamer (IRE)**[20] 3389 9-10-0 **79**.................... RobertWinston 9 72
(P D Evans) *stdd s: rdn ins fnl 3f: a outpcd* **14/1**

5305 **8** 4½ **Shaded Edge**[24] 3262 6-9-4 **69**... NeilCallan 7 51
(D W P Arbuthnot) *chsd ldrs: rdn ins fnl 3f: wknd fr 2f out* **9/1**

/-06 **9** *nk* **On The Feather**[19] 3464 4-8-9 **60** oh1........................ FergusSweeney 2 42
(B R Millman) *in tch: rdn 3f out: wknd over 2f out* **33/1**

1m 39.8s (-1.00) **Going Correction** -0.175s/f (Firm)
WFA 3 from 4yo+ 9lb **9** Ran SP% **120.1**
Speed ratings (Par 105): **98,96,94,93,93 92,90,85,85**
toteswingers:1&2:£1.90, 1&3:£6.10, 2&3:£8.60 CSF £7.15 CT £42.39 TOTE £1.80: £1.02, £3.20, £4.50; EX 9.00.
Owner Lady Rothschild **Bred** The Rt Hon Lord Rothschild **Trained** Beckhampton, Wilts

FOCUS
The ground was still firm despite a hefty downpour preceding this race. Weakish handicap form and the winner did not need to improve much.

4045 BATHWICK TYRES CARDIFF FILLIES' H'CAP 1m 3f 144y
8:30 (8:30) (Class 5) (0-70,62) 4-Y-O+ **£3,238** (£963; £481; £240) **Stalls** Low

Form RPR
2432 **1** **Where's Susie**[29] 3084 5-9-6 **61**...(p) ChrisCatlin 1 66
(M Madgwick) *chsd ldrs: drvn to ld jst ins fnl 2f: styd on u.p fnl f: rdn out* **5/2**[1]

006- **2** 1¾ **Bessie Lou (IRE)**[273] 6807 4-9-0 **58**................................... SMGorey(3) 5 60
(Michael Joseph Fitzgerald, Ire) *towards rr but in tch: rdn and hdwy fr 2f out: chsd wnr fnl f but no imp u.p* **7/2**[2]

-040 **3** *nk* **Location**[25] 3238 4-9-1 **56**... HayleyTurner 4 58
(Ian Williams) *in rr: pushed along 4f out: str run on outside fr 3f out to press ldrs ins fnl 2f: no ex u.p fnl f* **6/1**[3]

60-0 **4** *5* **Miss Doodle**[21] 3360 4-9-0 **55**.. NeilCallan 6 49
(Eve Johnson Houghton) *chsd ldrs tl stmbld and lost position bnd ins fnl 5f: rdn 4f out: wknd wl over 2f out* **6/1**[3]

0362 **5** ¾ **Party Palace**[15] 3560 6-8-6 **47**.. JimmyQuinn 7 40
(H S Howe) *led tl hdd over 8f out: rdn 3f out: wknd over 2f out* **7/2**[2]

35-6 **6** *2* **Vita Mia**[2] 3984 4-9-4 **62**... RichardEvans(3) 2 52
(P D Evans) *chsd ldrs tl led over 8f out: rdn 3f out: hdd & wknd jst ins fnl 2f* **8/1**

2m 30.39s (-0.21) **Going Correction** -0.175s/f (Firm) **6** Ran SP% **112.7**
Speed ratings (Par 100): **93,91,91,88,87 86**
toteswingers:1&2:£5.20, 1&3:£3.40, 2&3:£8.90 CSF £11.55 TOTE £3.10: £2.60, £2.60; EX 11.50.
Owner Recycled Products Limited **Bred** Mrs L R Burrage **Trained** Denmead, Hants
■ Stewards' Enquiry : S M Gorey two-day ban: used whip with excessive frequency without giving filly time to respond (Jul 29-30)

FOCUS
Thanks to Vita Mia and Party Palace, they went a good gallop but both paid the penalty in the end, filling the last two places. The form is rated around the winner.

4046 BATHWICK TYRES BRIDGEND FILLIES' H'CAP 1m 2f 46y
9:00 (9:00) (Class 5) (0-75,74) 3-Y-O+ **£3,238** (£963; £481; £240) **Stalls** Low

Form RPR
1-52 **1** **Fastback (IRE)**[17] 3513 4-10-0 **74**................................... JimmyFortune 4 84+
(R M Beckett) *mde all: rdn and qcknd over 2f out: styd on strly over 1f out: unchal* **4/7**[1]

-006 **2** *3* **Jasmeno**[17] 3514 3-7-13 **56**..(t) DavidProbert 2 57
(H Morrison) *chsd wnr thrght: rdn and effrt ins wl over 2f out: nvr gng pce to chal: outpcd fr over 1f out* **8/1**

3013 **3** *5* **Dane Cottage**[3] 3954 3-8-6 **63**... JimmyQuinn 5 54
(P D Evans) *a in 3rd: rdn and sme prog ins fnl 3f: nvr on terms: wknd ins fnl 2f* **4/1**[2]

-044 **4** *1* **Affirmable**[16] 3522 3-8-6 **63**... HayleyTurner 1 52
(J W Hills) *rdn 3f out: no imp and a in last pl* **7/1**[3]

2m 14.5s (3.50) **Going Correction** -0.175s/f (Firm)
WFA 3 from 4yo 11lb **4** Ran SP% **107.3**
Speed ratings (Par 100): **79,76,72,71**
CSF £5.45 TOTE £1.50; EX 5.60 Place 6 £78.48, Place 5 £44.06.
Owner Mrs R J Jacobs **Bred** Newsells Park Stud Limited **Trained** Whitsbury, Hants

FOCUS
An uncompetitive race, and the runners were in the same order throughout, with not a great deal ever threatening to happen. The front-running winner was always in control after slowing the tempo 7f from home and then kicking for home entering the straight. The winner may not have had to improve.

T/Plt: £89.40 to a £1 stake. Pool:£42,792.64 - 349.31 winning tickets T/Qpdt: £12.80 to a £1 stake. Pool:£4,149.68 - 238.28 winning tickets ST

3804 DONCASTER (L-H)

Thursday, July 15

OFFICIAL GOING: Good to firm (good in places; 8.5)

Wind: Fresh against Weather: Clody and breezy

4047 AMATEUR JOCKEYS' ASSOCIATION AMATEUR RIDERS' H'CAP — 5f

6:30 (6:30) (Class 6) (0-65,63) 3-Y-O+ — **£2,637** (£811; £405) **Stalls** High

Form — RPR

0464 **1** **Fashion Icon (USA)**[2] 3977 4-9-10 **45** .... MissSBrotherton 8 — 53
(D O'Meara) *cl up: led after 2f: rdn over 1f out: drvn ins fnl f and kpt on gamely* — **4/1**[1]

0003 **2** *shd* **Kyzer Chief**[2] 3976 5-10-2 **56** .... MissVBarr(5) 10 — 64
(R E Barr) *cl up: effrt 2f out: sn rdn and ev ch tl drvn ins fnl f and no ex nr fin* — **9/2**[2]

4235 **3** *nk* **Red River Boy**[7] 3809 5-9-12 **47** .... MrSDobson 5 — 54
(C W Fairhurst) *trckd ldrs: effrt to chal 2f out: rdn and ev ch over 1f out tl drvn ins fnl f and no ex nr fin* — **11/2**[3]

-201 **4** *1 ¼* **Arriva La Diva**[11] 3711 4-10-8 **57** 6ex .... MissJCoward 4 — 59
(J J Quinn) *trckd ldrs: effrt 2f out: sn rdn: drvn over 1f out and kpt on ins fnl f* — **8/1**

-052 **5** *¾* **Bertie Southstreet**[13] 3615 7-10-7 **63** ....(v) MissDLenge(7) 6 — 62
(J O'Reilly) *chsd ldrs: rdn along over wl over 1f out: kpt on ins fnl f* — **14/1**

26-0 **6** *2* **Avertuoso**[65] 1988 6-10-6 **60** .... MrJNewman(5) 15 — 52
(B Smart) *dwlt and towards rr: hdwy over 2f out: sn rdn and kpt on appr fnl f: nrst fin* — **10/1**

-000 **7** *1 ¼* **Thunder Bay**[11] 3711 5-9-10 **50** .... MrJMQuinlan(5) 16 — 38
(R E Barr) *racd towards stands' rail: towards rr: swtchd lft and rdn 2f out: styd on appr fnl f* — **33/1**

0-06 **8** *½* **Andrasta**[14] 3605 5-9-11 **46** .... MissEJJones 14 — 32
(S A Harris) *racd towards stands' rail: towards rr tl rdn and styd on fnl 2f: nvr nr ldrs* — **25/1**

6005 **9** *1 ¾* **Lithaam (IRE)**[10] 3722 6-10-4 **60** ....(p) MissHDavies(7) 12 — 40
(J M Bradley) *nvr bttr than midfield* — **14/1**

340/ **10** *2* **High Window (IRE)**[704] 4898 10-9-5 **45** .... MissJoannaMason(5) 11 — 17
(G P Kelly) *dwlt and in rr tl sme late hdwy* — **40/1**

1632 **11** *nk* **Fromsong (IRE)**[21] 3358 12-10-4 **60** ....(p) MissECrossman(7) 3 — 31
(D K Ivory) *led 2f: cl up tl rdn 2f out and grad wknd* — **14/1**

0000 **12** *nk* **Town House**[5] 3908 8-9-5 **45** .... MissKECooper(5) 17 — 15
(B P J Baugh) *prom on stands' rail: rdn along 1/2-way: grad wknd* — **33/1**

2500 **13** *1* **Macroy**[12] 3685 3-10-1 **60** ....(v[1]) MrPMillman(5) 9 — 27
(B R Millman) *dwlt: a towards rr* — **14/1**

0600 **14** *2 ¾* **Leolene Starlight**[10] 3732 5-9-13 **55** .... MrSMurray(7) 7 — 12
(D O'Meara) *a towards rr* — **33/1**

020- **15** *3 ¼* **Francis Albert**[295] 6220 4-10-0 **52** .... MissMMullineaux(3) 2 — —
(M Mullineaux) *cl up: rdn along 1/2-way: sn wknd* — **25/1**

500/ **16** *3 ¼* **Cark**[1319] 6704 12-9-3 **45** .... MrARawlinson(7) 13 — —
(D C Griffiths) *a bhd* — **80/1**

61.20 secs (0.70) **Going Correction** +0.175s/f (Good)
WFA 3 from 4yo+ 5lb — **16** Ran SP% **120.6**
Speed ratings (Par 101): **101,100,100,98,97 93,91,91,88,85 84,84,82,78,73 67**
toteswingers:1&2:£7.10, 1&3:£4.30, 2&3:£6.70 CSF £19.48 CT £101.88 TOTE £5.10: £1.40, £1.70, £2.50, £1.90; EX 22.90.
Owner Trendy Ladies **Bred** Mr & Mrs Theodore Kuster **Trained** Nawton, N Yorks

■ Stewards' Enquiry : Mr S Dobson two-day ban: used whip with excessive frequency in incorrect place (tbn)
Miss M Mullineaux caution: used whip when out of contention

FOCUS
Just ordinary fare, with a low to middle draw seemingly an advantage as it was those who raced more towards the centre who came to the fore, with the principals all prominent from the outset. The form reads sound.

Macroy Official explanation: jockey said gelding hung right throughout

4048 E B F BRIAN MCQUEEN SMITH MAIDEN FILLIES' STKS — 7f

7:00 (7:04) (Class 4) 2-Y-O — **£4,776** (£1,410; £705) **Stalls** High

Form — RPR

1 **Clinical** 2-9-0 0 .... SebSanders 8 — 77+
(Sir Mark Prescott) *bmpd s: sn swtchd lft and hld up in rr: smooth hdwy wl over 2f out: chsd ldrs wl over 1f out: sn rdn and edgd lft: drvn ins fnl f and styd on wl to ld nr fin* — **7/4**[1]

2 *½* **Dubawi Gulf** 2-9-0 0 .... KierenFallon 6 — 76
(E A L Dunlop) *prom: effrt 2f out: rdn to ld ent fnl f: sn drvn and no ex nr fin* — **17/2**

3 *nse* **Fenella Fudge** 2-9-0 0 .... PaulMulrennan 9 — 77+
(J G Given) *s.i.s and swtchd lft s: in rr tl hdwy 1/2-way: effrt and n.m.r wl over 2f out: swtchd lft and gd hdwy over 1f out: rdn and edgd lft ent fnl f: ev ch tl nt qckn nr fin* — **40/1**

4 *3* **Pandoro De Lago (IRE)** 2-9-0 0 .... PaulHanagan 1 — 68
(R A Fahey) *dwlt sltly: sn cl up on outer: effrt over 2f out: rdn and ev ch over 1f out tl carried sltly lft ent fnl f and one pce after* — **9/2**[3]

6 **5** *½* **Istishaara (USA)**[20] 3411 2-9-0 0 .... RichardHills 5 — 67
(J L Dunlop) *prom: led over 4f out: rdn over 2f out: drvn and hdd ent fnl f: wknd* — **2/1**[2]

0 **6** *1 ½* **Little Book**[23] 3296 2-9-0 0 .... ShaneKelly 2 — 63
(E F Vaughan) *trckd ldrs: pushed along over 3f out: rdn wl over 1f out and sn one pce* — **40/1**

6 **7** *7* **Playful Girl (IRE)**[44] 2623 2-9-0 0 .... DuranFentiman 3 — 46
(T D Easterby) *trckd ldrs: pushed along 3f out: rdn over 2f out and sn wknd* — **28/1**

0 **8** *nk* **Bright Dictator (IRE)**[40] 2740 2-9-0 0 .... LeeVickers 7 — 45
(J G Given) *wnt rt s: chsd ldrs: rdn along bef 1/2-way: sn wknd* — **100/1**

0 **9** *3 ¾* **Be My Spy**[7] 3805 2-8-9 0 .... BillyCray(5) 11 — 35
(P Salmon) *chsd ldrs: rdn along bef 1/2-way and sn wknd* — **100/1**

10 *¾* **Snow Cannon (IRE)** 2-9-0 0 .... FrankieDettori 4 — 34
(P W Chapple-Hyam) *wnt lft s: a towards rr: bhd fnl 2f* — **20/1**

0 **11** *1 ¾* **Pockett Rockett**[12] 3657 2-9-0 0 .... SilvestreDeSousa 10 — 29
(D O'Meara) *racd towards stands' rail: led over 2f: sn rdn along and bhd fnl 3f* — **33/1**

1m 28.14s (1.84) **Going Correction** +0.175s/f (Good) — **11** Ran SP% **116.4**
Speed ratings (Par 93): **96,95,95,91,91 89,81,81,77,76 74**
toteswingers:1&2:£3.00, 1&3:£28.00, 2&3:£50.30 CSF £16.24 TOTE £2.50: £1.10, £3.60, £10.40; EX 20.70.
Owner Cheveley Park Stud **Bred** Cheveley Park Stud Ltd **Trained** Newmarket, Suffolk

FOCUS
Not much previous form to go on so it was no surprise to see newcomers come to the fore, with the front three all making encouraging debuts. The race averages help with the level of the form. On the back of the first race it was no surprise to see the action unfold up the centre.

NOTEBOOK
Clinical, a half-sister to several winners, including the smart Cupid's Glory, hails from a yard enjoying a good season with its juveniles, and she duly justified the confidence behind her, having to knuckle down in the end but impressing with the smoothness with which she got into things. She's sure to improve. (op 13-8 tchd 11-8)

Dubawi Gulf's stable sent out its first juvenile winner of the season at Newmarket last week and this one shouldn't be long in going one better after a pleasing start, always to the fore and responding really well to Fallon's urgings. Her dam won up to 1m4f, and she should have little difficulty getting 1m this term on this evidence. (op 14-1)

Fenella Fudge's yard is yet to hit the target with 2yos this year, but this daughter of Rock Hard Ten should put that right before long judged on this promising start, where she travelled well under restraint and stuck to her task well once it opened up for approaching the final furlong. (op 50-1)

Pandoro De Lago(IRE) couldn't live with the leading trio in the final two furlongs, but this was still a reasonably encouraging start and she should progress, especially given her connections. (tchd 13-2)

Istishaara(USA) was clearly expected to leave her debut form behind judged on her position in the market but barely did so in the end, fading as though the step up to this trip perhaps wasn't in her favour at this early stage. (op 9-4)

Little Book stepped up a little on her debut without being subjected to an unduly hard time and could be the type to progress with racing, with nurseries an option for her after one more run.

4049 ESG NOVICE STKS — 6f

7:35 (7:35) (Class 4) 2-Y-O — **£3,238** (£963; £481; £240) **Stalls** High

Form — RPR

1 **1** **Wootton Bassett**[26] 3199 2-9-5 0 .... PaulHanagan 6 — 99+
(R A Fahey) *qckly away: mde all: shkn up over 1f out: rdn ins fnl f and kpt on strly* — **2/5**[1]

1 **2** *2* **Forjatt (IRE)**[43] 2649 2-9-5 0 .... FrankieDettori 5 — 93+
(M A Jarvis) *sn trcking ldr: hdwy over 2f out: rdn wl over 1f out: no imp ins fnl f* — **9/4**[2]

241 **3** *11* **Last Destination (IRE)**[28] 3106 2-9-2 0 .... SilvestreDeSousa 1 — 57
(N Tinkler) *t.k.h: hld up: effrt over 2f out: sn rdn and kpt on: no ch w ldng pair* — **16/1**[3]

0 **4** *22* **Logans Rose**[12] 3657 2-9-0 0 .... GrahamGibbons 3 — —
(A D Brown) *t.k.h: chsd ldr early: rdn along 1/2-way: sn outpcd and bhd fnl 2f* — **100/1**

1m 13.26s (-0.34) **Going Correction** +0.175s/f (Good) — **4** Ran SP% **109.1**
Speed ratings (Par 96): **109,106,91,62**
CSF £1.59 TOTE £1.10; EX 1.60.
Owner Frank Brady & The Cosmic Cases **Bred** Laundry Cottage Stud Farm **Trained** Musley Bank, N Yorks

FOCUS
Effectively a match, and it was one which the market got spot-on. Not easy to pin down the worth of the form.

NOTEBOOK
Wootton Bassett, heavily backed, was always finding enough to see off Forjatt once Hanagan quickened the tempo in the final two furlongs. He has plenty of size about him and has created a really good impression when winning both his starts, with the strength behind him in the betting here suggesting he figures highly up his yard's juvenile pecking order, and he'll be well worth his place in stronger company, with the Gimcrack or the valuable DBS Sales race two possible targets for him at York's Ebor meeting. (op 8-13 tchd 4-6 in a place)

Forjatt(IRE) could never quite get on terms with the winner once the tempo increased, but time may show he was taking on a smart rival and he remains a useful prospect, though his Gimcrack entry looks beyond him on this evidence. (op 7-4)

Last Destination(IRE) had benefited from the step up to the extended 7f when scoring at Beverley last time so this return to shorter didn't look an obvious move, though he's not in the same class as the leading pair in any case. (tchd 20-1)

4050 ESQUIRES COFFEE WHEATLEY RETAIL PARK CONDITIONS STKS — 1m (S)

8:05 (8:06) (Class 3) 4-Y-O+ — **£6,476** (£1,927; £963; £481) **Stalls** High

Form — RPR

364- **1** **Cesare**[215] 6030 9-8-9 111 .... KierenFallon 5 — 110+
(J R Fanshawe) *hld up in rr: hdwy over 2f out: swtchd rt and effrt over 1f out: rdn and qcknd ins fnl f to ld nr fin* — **11/4**[2]

-260 **2** *nk* **Vesuve (IRE)**[110] 1022 4-8-9 110 .... TedDurcan 1 — 109
(Saeed Bin Suroor) *wnt lft s: sn led and set stdy pce: qcknd wl over 2f out: rdn over 1f out: drvn ins fnl f: hdd and no ex nr fin* — **4/1**[3]

13-2 **3** *2* **Yamal (IRE)**[21] 3354 5-8-9 109 ....(v[1]) FrankieDettori 2 — 104
(Saeed Bin Suroor) *trckd ldr: swtchd lft and smooth hdwy to chal 2f out: rdn over 1f out: hung lft ent fnl f and sn one pce* — **5/6**[1]

3040 **4** *3 ½* **Lucky Dance (BRZ)**[37] 2835 8-8-9 86 .... LNewman 4 — 96?
(A G Foster) *trckd ldng pair: effrt 1/2-way: rdn along wl over 2f out: wknd wl over 1f out* — **16/1**

1m 39.02s (-0.28) **Going Correction** +0.175s/f (Good) — **4** Ran SP% **107.1**
Speed ratings (Par 107): **108,107,105,102**
CSF £12.66 TOTE £3.70; EX 10.20.
Owner Cheveley Park Stud **Bred** Cheveley Park Stud Ltd **Trained** Newmarket, Suffolk

FOCUS
Smart form in this conditions event, the runner-up dictating what was no more than a fair gallop initially and the race not beginning in earnest until the final 3f. The form may prove far from reliable.

NOTEBOOK
Cesare was last seen finishing only a modest third on his hurdling debut here in December but he'd been as good as ever when second to Paco Boy in the Queen Anne on his return last year and showed he still retains a smart level of ability at the age of nine. He was maintaining his excellent record fresh in the process as this was the fourth time he has started his campaign with a win. Given the way his form tailed off last season there have to be slight doubts whether he'll go on from this but he's been an excellent servant to connections whatever happens from now on. (tchd 5-2 and 3-1)

Vesuve(IRE) looked the yard's second string but he's a smart performer in his own right (runner-up off a mark of 108 at Meydan in February) and made a pleasing enough start for Godolphin. A race of this nature should come his way before long. He has winning form over as far as 1m2f. (op 7-2)

Yamal(IRE) was turned over at short odds for the second time in as many starts this season and there have to be doubts about his attitude for the time being. He was visored for the first time here and did noy find much (edged left) when Dettori asked him to set about his stable companion. (op 10-11 tchd 4-5)

Lucky Dance(BRZ) was out of his depth. (op 20-1)

4051 ARTSIGN H'CAP — 1m 2f 60y

8:40 (8:40) (Class 4) (0-85,84) 4-Y-O+ **£3,885** (£1,156; £577; £288) **Stalls Low**

Form — RPR

0112 **1** **Scamperdale**[22] 3329 8-9-3 **80** TomQueally 7 88
(B P J Baugh) *trckd ldrs: hdwy over 3f out: led 2f out: rdn over 1f out: edgd rt ins fnl f: kpt on wl* **12/1**

6610 **2** *1* **Ellemujie**[34] 2934 5-9-7 **84** FrankieDettori 6 90
(D K Ivory) *hld up in rr: swtchd outside and hdwy 2f out: rdn to chse wnr ent fnl f: swtchd lft and kpt on towards fin* **6/1**

1323 **3** *1* **Visions Of Johanna (USA)**[19] 3432 5-8-11 **74** ShaneKelly 3 78
(Ian Williams) *hld up in tch: pushed along and sltly outpcd 3f out: rdn and chsd ldrs 2f out: drvn over 1f out: kpt on ins fnl f* **6/1**

5004 **4** *1* **Jeer (IRE)**[12] 3688 6-8-11 **74** (b) KierenFallon 1 76
(M W Easterby) *led: rdn along 3f out: hdd 2f out and sn drvn: one pce aqpproaching fnl f* **11/1**

4311 **5** *nk* **That'll Do Nicely (IRE)**[20] 3405 7-9-1 **78** PaulHanagan 8 79
(N G Richards) *hld up: hdwy on outer over 3f out: rdn along 2f out and sn one pce* **5/2**[1]

-234 **6** *nk* **Norwegian Dancer (UAE)**[24] 3265 4-9-5 **82** GrahamGibbons 2 83
(E S McMahon) *trckd ldr on inner: effrt 3f out: rdn along 2f out: drvn and one pce appr fnl f* **7/2**[2]

53-3 **7** *shd* **Wild Desert (FR)**[38] 2821 5-9-2 **79** TedDurcan 4 80
(A King) *trckd ldr: effrt 3f out: rdn along 2f out: drvn wl over 1f out: grad wknd* **11/2**[3]

2m 7.19s (-2.21) **Going Correction** -0.275s/f (Firm) 7 Ran SP% **110.8**
Speed ratings (Par 105): **105,104,103,102,102 102,102**
toteswingers:1&2:£13.40, 1&3:£7.10, 2&3:£9.40 CSF £75.40 CT £458.95 TOTE £12.40: £3.60, £2.00; EX 61.90.
Owner Saddle Up Racing **Bred** Mrs J A Prescott **Trained** Audley, Staffs

FOCUS
They went a sound enough pace although the field finished in a bit of a heap. The form is sound enough.

4052 P & A PARTNERSHIP H'CAP — 1m 2f 60y

9:10 (9:10) (Class 5) (0-70,69) 3-Y-O **£2,729** (£806; £403) **Stalls Low**

Form — RPR

0202 **1** **Sharakti (IRE)**[25] 3242 3-8-8 **61** DeclanCannon(5) 2 71
(A J McCabe) *trckd ldrs: hdwy over 3f out: effrt to chal 2f out and sn rdn: drvn to ld jst ins fnl f: edgd lft and kpt on wl towards fin* **4/1**[2]

-165 **2** *1 ¼* **Saint Thomas (IRE)**[13] 3613 3-9-5 **67** GrahamGibbons 9 75
(J Mackie) *trckd ldr: hdwy over 3f out: led wl over 2f out: rdn wl over 1f out: drvn and hdd jst ins fnl f: kpt on same pce* **5/1**[3]

-063 **3** *3* **Venture Girl (IRE)**[12] 3662 3-8-5 **53** DuranFentiman 5 55
(T D Easterby) *hld up: hdwy 3f out: swtchd rt and rdn over 2f out: drvn to chse ldng pair and edgd lft over 1f out: kpt on same pce fnl f* **9/1**

50-2 **4** *3* **The Caped Crusader (IRE)**[35] 2886 3-9-5 **67** PaulHanagan 1 63
(Ollie Pears) *t.k.h: trckd ldng pair on inner: swtchd rt and effrt over 3f out: rdn along over 2f out and sn one pce* **10/11**[1]

050 **5** *nk* **Sinatramania**[32] 2994 3-9-0 **62** AndrewMullen 10 58
(Miss Tracy Waggott) *dwlt: sn in tch: hdwy over 4f out: rdn along to chse ldrs 3f out: drvn 2f out and sn one pce* **28/1**

005- **6** *13* **Groove Master**[290] 6331 3-8-9 **57** TedDurcan 7 28
(A King) *a in rr: outpcd and bhd fnl 3f* **14/1**

-606 **7** *2 ¼* **Irish Eyes**[19] 3451 3-9-2 **64** MickyFenton 4 31
(Jedd O'Keeffe) *led: rdn along over 3f out: hdd wl over 2f out: sn wknd* **25/1**

2m 11.59s (2.19) **Going Correction** -0.275s/f (Firm) 7 Ran SP% **113.0**
Speed ratings (Par 100): **87,86,83,81,80 70,68**
toteswingers:1&2:£2.80, 1&3:£2.10, 2&3:£7.90 CSF £23.49 CT £166.70 TOTE £4.50: £1.70, £1.90; EX 19.40 Place 6 £365.47, Place 5 £297.53.
Owner Mrs D E Sharp **Bred** John Foley **Trained** Averham Park, Notts

FOCUS
A glut of non-runners and doubtful the overall form is anything special, though the leading pair clearly deserve a bit of credit for pulling clear. It was a muddling race and the form is rated around the winner.
T/Plt: £1,080.10 to a £1 stake. Pool:£52,896.72 - 35.75 winning tickets T/Qpdt: £396.60 to a £1 stake. Pool:£4,341.59 - 8.10 winning tickets JR

3810 EPSOM (L-H)
Thursday, July 15

OFFICIAL GOING: Good (good to firm in places)
Wind: Fresh, half against Weather: bright spells, very breezy

4053 BROTHERS PEAR CIDER CLAIMING STKS — 7f

6:10 (6:11) (Class 5) 3-Y-O+ **£3,238** (£963; £481; £240) **Stalls Low**

Form — RPR

301 **1** **Orpenindeed (IRE)**[17] 3518 7-9-1 87 AndrewHeffernan(3) 8 81
(Tim Vaughan) *chsd ldr tl rdn to ld over 2f out: drvn over 1f out: kpt on gamely u.p fnl f: jst hld on* **2/1**[1]

0-62 **2** *shd* **Flying Valentino**[9] 3765 6-8-3 72 JohnFahy(5) 4 71
(Ian Williams) *hld up in tch: rdn and effrt over 1f out: drvn to chse wnr 1f out: styd on wl fnl 100yds: jst failed* **13/2**

0352 **3** *1 ¼* **Blue Noodles**[14] 3580 4-8-7 67 DeanHeslop(5) 5 72
(P D Evans) *chsd ldrs: rdn to chse wnr ent fnl 2f tl 1f out: styd on same pce u.p ins fnl f* **9/2**[2]

0130 **4** *2 ¼* **Lady Kent (IRE)**[24] 3262 4-8-10 70 PatCosgrave 2 64
(J R Boyle) *dwlt: sn rcvrd and chsng ldrs: rdn and effrt on inner over 2f out: wknd ins fnl f* **7/1**

0120 **5** *1 ¼* **Caprio (IRE)**[26] 3226 5-9-8 82 NickyMackay 1 72
(J R Boyle) *racd in last pair: pushed along and hdwy 3f out: one pce and no imp fr over 1f out* **11/2**[3]

5065 **6** *3 ¾* **Feeling Fragile (IRE)**[17] 3510 3-8-4 59 (v[1]) AndreaAtzeni 6 49
(Pat Eddery) *awkward s: in tch in midfield: rdn 2f out: sn hung rt and btn: racing on stands' rail: wl btn 1f out* **12/1**

00 **7** *3 ½* **Fashion Tycoon (IRE)**[33] 2968 3-8-0 0 Louis-PhilippeBeuzelin(3) 7 39
(M F Harris) *a in rr: rdn and lost tch ent fnl 2f* **100/1**

2423 **8** *3 ¾* **Liberty Trail (IRE)**[15] 3557 4-8-13 66 JamesDoyle 3 33
(P D Evans) *sn pushed up to ld: rdn and hdd over 2f out: wknd wl over 1f out: wl bhd fnl f* **17/2**

1m 22.79s (-0.51) **Going Correction** -0.05s/f (Good)
WFA 3 from 4yo+ 8lb 8 Ran SP% **111.9**
Speed ratings (Par 103): **100,99,98,95,94 90,86,81**
toteswingers:1&2:£2.50, 1&3:£2.00, 2&3:£5.20 CSF £14.79 TOTE £3.50: £2.20, £3.70, £1.10; EX 10.00.
Owner Diamond Racing Ltd **Bred** A Pereira **Trained** Aberthin, Vale of Glamorgan
■ Stewards' Enquiry : John Fahy one-day ban: used whip with excessive frequency (Jul 29)

FOCUS
A modest claimer, rated around the second and third. The winner did not need to even match his recent form.
Feeling Fragile(IRE) Official explanation: jockey said gelding hung badly right throughout

4054 BROTHERS STRAWBERRY CIDER EBF MAIDEN STKS — 7f

6:40 (6:42) (Class 4) 2-Y-O **£4,533** (£1,348; £674; £336) **Stalls Low**

Form — RPR

02 **1** **Surrey Star (IRE)**[34] 2932 2-8-12 0 JohnFahy(5) 2 81+
(R A Teal) *t.k.h: chsd ldrs early: stdd and hld up in last trio after 1f: nt clr run and swtchd rt 2f out: rdn to chse clr ldr over 1f out: r.o wl fnl f to ld fnl 50yds* **7/1**[3]

0 **2** *½* **Chain Lightning**[13] 3631 2-9-3 0 PatDobbs 3 80
(R Hannon) *led: pushed clr wl over 1f out: rdn ins fnl f: hdd and no ex fnl 50yds* **11/4**[2]

53 **3** *4 ½* **Zakon (IRE)**[20] 3399 2-9-3 0 EddieAhern 1 69+
(D J Coakley) *dwlt: sn chsng ldrs: rdn and n.m.r 2f out: nt pce of ldng pair and edgd rt over 1f out: styd on same pce fnl f* **12/1**

0 **4** *3 ¼* **Cuban Quality (USA)**[19] 3433 2-9-3 0 RichardKingscote 8 60
(Tom Dascombe) *in tch in midfield: effrt and hung bdly rt over 2f out: no ch w ldrs fr wl over 1f out: kpt edging lft but kpt on ins fnl f to snatch 4th on post* **12/1**

00 **5** *shd* **Mediplomat**[22] 3326 2-9-3 0 DarryllHolland 5 60
(M Botti) *racd in last pair: rdn and no prog over 2f out: no ch w ldrs fnl 2f: sme hdwy ins fnl f* **33/1**

6 *nse* **Book Keeper** 2-9-3 0 AlanMunro 4 60
(Mahmood Al Zarooni) *t.k.h: hld up wl in tch: rdn and chsd ldr briefly wl over 1f: sn outpcd: wknd ent fnl f* **9/1**

3 **7** *¾* **Maher (USA)**[19] 3452 2-9-3 0 WilliamBuick 6 68+
(D M Simcock) *s.i.s: bhd and niggled along early: hdwy 4f out: bdly hmpd and stmbld over 2f out: nt rcvr and no ch after* **7/4**[1]

03 **8** *1 ¾* **Memorabilia**[19] 3433 2-9-3 0 RoystonFfrench 7 56+
(M Johnston) *chsd ldr tl over 1f out: wknd qckly u.p ent fnl f: wl btn and eased ins fnl f* **9/1**

1m 24.28s (0.98) **Going Correction** -0.05s/f (Good) 8 Ran SP% **113.9**
Speed ratings (Par 96): **92,91,86,82,82 82,81,79**
toteswingers:1&2:£5.00, 1&3:£13.10, 2&3:£10.30 CSF £26.37 TOTE £4.40: £1.20, £1.50, £4.90; EX 37.90.
Owner M Vickers **Bred** Anima Negra Gmbh & Co Kg **Trained** Ashtead, Surrey

FOCUS
A fair maiden on paper, but a muddling pace and the favourite finding trouble in the home straight dictate it is form to be treating with a degree of caution.

NOTEBOOK
Surrey Star(IRE), a well-beaten second at Sandown last time, went one better and got off the mark at the third attempt. He attracted support in the betting, but looked likely to play second fiddle two furlongs out. As the leader began to falter, however, he really found his stride from the furlong marker and won a little cosily in the end. He obviously stays well and has a makings of a useful handicapper. (op 9-1)
Chain Lightning was expected to improve on his recent Sandown debut and it wasn't surprising to see him well backed here. He raced a lot more positively, getting pretty much his own way in front, and things looked very good for him a furlong out. However, he started to slow inside the final furlong and was ultimately mugged near the finish. That may have been down to him tiring, but the suspicion is it was still down to greenness and this rates a missed opportunity. (op 7-2 tchd 4-1)
Zakon(IRE) was better than the bare form of his previous Folkestone third and ran a slightly improved race under more positive handling this time. He is now eligible for nurseries. (op 10-1 tchd 14-1 in places)
Cuban Quality(USA), who also met some support, got outpaced at the crucial stage before staying on again inside the final furlong. This was a step in the right direction and he looks one to be more interested in when qualified for nurseries after his next outing. Official explanation: jockey said colt hung right (tchd 9-1 and 14-1)
Mediplomat turned in his most encouraging display to date and can now enter nurseries. (op 28-1 tchd 25-1)
Book Keeper is related to winners on the continent and proved easy to back on his debut. He showed his inexperience through the first half of the race and should be all the sharper for the run. (op 11-1)
Maher(USA) this effort, though he certainly didn't help himself with a sluggish start. He then had to come from behind off an ordinary pace and just as his rider tried to switch him inside around two furlongs out he got badly hampered. His debut effort was full of promise and, while he now has a little to prove, should be given another chance. Official explanation: jockey said colt suffered interference in running (tchd 2-1 and 9-4 in places)
Memorabilia had definite claims on the level of his previous outing at Doncaster, but he proved friendless in the betting and ran no sort of race. (op 11-2)

4055 ALL BETS ARE ON AT TOTESPORT.COM H'CAP — 1m 4f 10y

7:15 (7:18) (Class 4) (0-80,79) 4-Y-O+ **£5,180** (£1,541; £770; £384) **Stalls Centre**

Form — RPR

2355 **1** **Goodwood Starlight (IRE)**[22] 3319 5-9-3 **76** RobertLButler(3) 10 90
(Miss Sheena West) *t.k.h: stdd after s: hld up in last trio: hdwy to trck ldrs 3f out: swtchd rt and jnd ldr 2f out: led on bit over 1f out: sn clr: v easily* **13/2**[3]

1223 **2** *8* **Megalala (IRE)**[14] 3589 9-8-12 **68** NeilChalmers 4 69
(J J Bridger) *led: rdn over 2f out: hdd over 1f out: no ch w wnr after: battled on gamely to hold 2nd* **10/1**

-115 **3** *½* **Hel's Angel (IRE)**[19] 3432 4-9-4 **79** JohnFahy(5) 9 79
(Mrs A Duffield) *hld up in last trio: hdwy over 3f out: rdn to chse ldrs ent fnl 2f: no ch w wnr fr over 1f out: pressing for 2nd and kpt on same pce fnl f* **4/1**[2]

60-3 **4** *¾* **Citizenship**[36] 2857 4-9-7 **77** (t) JimCrowley 1 76
(Ian Williams) *in tch in midfield: rdn and effrt to chse ldng pair over 3f out: no ch w wnr fr over 1f out: styd on same pce u.p after* **11/4**[1]

1-41 **5** *2 ¾* **Silent Applause**[14] 3576 7-8-12 **71** Louis-PhilippeBeuzelin(3) 5 66
(Dr J D Scargill) *hld up in rr: rdn and effrt 3f out: hung lft over 2f out: nvr trbld ldrs* **4/1**[2]

-025 **6** *1 ½* **Herschel (IRE)**[83] 1346 4-9-3 **73** GeorgeBaker 3 65
(G L Moore) *chchsd ldr tl 8f out: wnt 2nd again 4f out tl rdn and fnd nil 2f out: racd awkwardly and fdd tamely over 1f out* **10/1**

300- 7 23 **Atabaas Allure (FR)**[43] 5037 4-9-9 79 DaneO'Neill 7 35
(C Gordon) *chsd ldrs tl wnt 2nd 8f out tl 4f out: sn dropped out: wl bhd fnl 2f: virtually p.u ins fnl f: t.o* **50/1**

251/ 8 2 **Pentathlon (IRE)**[824] 1342 5-9-7 77 RoystonFfrench 2 29
(M Johnston) *in tch in midfield tl wknd qckly over 2f out: wl bhd and virtually p.u ins fnl f: t.o* **13/2**[3]

2m 36.75s (-2.15) **Going Correction** -0.05s/f (Good) 8 Ran SP% **113.5**
Speed ratings (Par 105): **105,99,99,98,97 96,80,79**
toteswingers:1&2:£5.50, 1&3:£8.30, 2&3:£7.80 CSF £67.07 CT £291.79 TOTE £10.00: £2.10, £2.70, £1.40; EX 74.20.
Owner Heart Of The South Racing **Bred** Lynn Lodge Stud **Trained** Falmer, E Sussex

FOCUS
An open handicap, run at an ordinary pace and the winner bolted up. Suspect form and the second and third are rated a few pounds off their recent best.

4056 BET ON LIVE GOLF AT TOTESPORT.COM H'CAP 1m 2f 18y
7:45 (7:47) (Class 4) (0-80,79) 3-Y-O **£6,476** (£1,927; £963; £481) **Stalls Low**

Form RPR

-300 1 **If I Were A Boy (IRE)**[3] 3963 3-8-13 69 JamesDoyle 5 82
(D J S Ffrench Davis) *mde all at stdy gallop: clr fr 6f out: rdn ent fnl 2f: kpt on wl and in n.d after* **20/1**

1-00 2 4 ½ **Solicitor**[22] 3330 3-9-5 75 RoystonFfrench 7 79
(M Johnston) *stmbld s: sn rcvrd and chsd ldr: rdn and no imp over 2f out: edgd lft u.p and kpt on same pce fnl f* **12/1**

5462 3 4 ½ **Raktiman (IRE)**[10] 3723 3-8-8 64 (p) RichardKingscote 10 59
(Tom Dascombe) *s.i.s: hld up in last pair: rdn and effrt over 2f out: kpt hanging lft u.p fr over 2f out: wnt modest 3rd ins fnl f: no ch w wnr* **7/1**

2040 4 1 ½ **Strong Vigilance (IRE)**[21] 3351 3-9-5 75 EddieAhern 9 67
(M L W Bell) *stdd s and dropped in bhd: rdn and no prog over 2f out: nvr a factor* **9/2**[2]

5-02 5 shd **Hierarch (IRE)**[13] 3635 3-9-2 72 PatDobbs 2 64
(R Hannon) *hld up in last trio: rdn and effrt on inner ent fnl 2f: sn drvn and no prog: n.d* **5/1**[3]

4623 6 3 ¾ **Hidden Glory**[12] 3697 3-9-9 79 (p) DarryllHolland 3 63
(Pat Eddery) *chsd ldrs: rdn and prog whn hung lft ent fnl 2f: wl btn after* **7/4**[1]

6002 7 6 **Amends (USA)**[8] 3788 3-8-0 61 ow1 KierenFox(5) 6 33
(J R Best) *plld hrd: hld up off the pce in midfield: c centre and rdn ent fnl 3f: no hdwy and wl btn whn hung lft over 1f out* **6/1**

2m 10.52s (0.82) **Going Correction** -0.05s/f (Good) 7 Ran SP% **110.5**
Speed ratings (Par 102): **94,90,86,85,85 82,77**
toteswingers:1&2:£5.80, 1&3:£7.70, 2&3:£14.50 CSF £209.46 CT £1764.96 TOTE £25.30: £6.50, £5.00; EX 276.20.
Owner R F Haynes **Bred** Kilco Builders **Trained** Lambourn, Berks

FOCUS
This turned into a farce with the winner gifted the race from the front. The form could have been rated higher.
Raktiman(IRE) Official explanation: jockey said colt hung left

4057 BET ON LIVE CRICKET AT TOTESPORT.COM H'CAP 7f
8:20 (8:20) (Class 4) (0-80,82) 3-Y-O+ **£5,180** (£1,541; £770; £384) **Stalls Low**

Form RPR

0-06 1 **Avertis**[77] 1634 5-9-7 73 (tp) PatCosgrave 9 84
(Stef Higgins) *chsd ldr: rdn over 2f out: drvn and hdwy to press ldr ent fnl f: led ins fnl f: r.o wl* **28/1**

5101 2 ¾ **Sailorman (IRE)**[6] 3851 3-9-8 82 6ex RoystonFfrench 7 88
(M Johnston) *led: rdn and fnd ex over 2f out: drvn ent fnl f: hdd ins fnl f: kpt on same pce after* **10/11**[1]

6313 3 3 ¾ **Regeneration (IRE)**[36] 2872 4-9-13 79 JamieSpencer 1 78
(M L W Bell) *t.k.h: chsd ldrs: rdn and unable qck over 2f out: chsd clr ldng pair wl over 1f out: styd on same pce u.p after* **11/4**[2]

0300 4 ¾ **Beaver Patrol (IRE)**[20] 3401 8-10-0 80 JimCrowley 5 77
(Eve Johnson Houghton) *in tch: rdn to chse ldrs over 3f out: drvn and outpcd ent fnl 2f: one pce and no threat to ldrs fr over 1f out* **14/1**

1240 5 hd **Prince Of Thebes (IRE)**[92] 1306 9-8-13 65 JamesDoyle 6 61
(M J Attwater) *sn bustled along: in tch in midfield tl rdn and unable qck 3f out: outpcd and drvn 2f out: no threat to ldrs after* **20/1**

5055 6 hd **Spinning Bailiwick**[15] 3567 4-9-8 74 GeorgeBaker 4 70
(G L Moore) *stdd s: hld up in last trio: rdn and effrt on centre over 2f out: plugged on u.p fnl f: nvr gng pce to threaten ldrs* **33/1**

5614 7 1 ¼ **Another Magic Man (USA)**[5] 3899 3-8-6 71 KierenFox(5) 8 60
(J R Best) *plld hrd: hld up in midfield: hdwy to chse ldrs over 3f out: rdn and outpcd over 2f out: wl btn whn n.m.r jst ins fnl f* **8/1**[3]

1566 8 6 **Buxton**[14] 3579 6-9-4 70 (t) PatDobbs 10 46
(R Ingram) *hld up towards rr: rdn and no prog over 2f out: nvr trbld ldrs: eased wl ins fnl f* **16/1**

4000 9 2 ¼ **Wunder Strike (USA)**[17] 3514 4-8-9 61 (p) NickyMackay 3 31
(J R Boyle) *s.i.s: a bhd: nvr a factor: eased wl ins fnl f* **40/1**

5156 10 5 **Expensive Problem**[16] 3079 7-9-4 73 AndrewHeffernan(3) 2 30
(R J Smith) *hld up in last trio: rdn and struggling wl over 2f out: nvr a factor: eased wl ins fnl f* **40/1**

1m 22.94s (-0.36) **Going Correction** -0.05s/f (Good)
WFA 3 from 4yo+ 8lb 10 Ran SP% **118.7**
Speed ratings (Par 105): **100,99,94,94,93 93,92,85,82,76**
toteswingers:1&2:£5.60, 1&3:£15.20, 2&3:£1.10 CSF £53.53 CT £106.80 TOTE £34.20: £10.50, £1.10, £1.10; EX 107.70.
Owner Mrs Sally Doyle **Bred** Mrs Sally Doyle **Trained** Lambourn, Berks

FOCUS
A fair handicap that was run at a sound enough pace yet still it was a race where it paid to be handy, with the first pair always 1-2. The winner is rated back to his best.

4058 BROTHERS TUTTI FRUTTI CIDER H'CAP 1m 114y
8:50 (8:53) (Class 5) (0-75,81) 3-Y-O **£3,885** (£1,156; £577; £288) **Stalls Low**

Form RPR

-360 1 **Queen Of Wands**[17] 3513 3-8-10 62 JimCrowley 3 69
(H Morrison) *mde all: rdn clr and hung rt ent fnl 2f: styd on strly fnl f: comf* **14/1**

1033 2 3 ¼ **Interakt**[6] 3866 3-9-0 66 CathyGannon 7 66
(M R Channon) *chsd ldrs: rdn and effrt in centre 3f out: chsd clr wnr over 1f out: no imp fnl f* **11/1**

0560 3 2 **Lou Bear (IRE)**[27] 3160 3-8-4 56 oh1 NickyMackay 4 51
(J Akehurst) *chsd ldng pair: rdn and unable qck 3f out: styd on same pce u.p fnl 2f* **16/1**

0343 4 nk **Be A Devil**[13] 3612 3-9-9 75 DaneO'Neill 2 70+
(W R Muir) *hld up in last trio: rdn and effrt on inner ent fnl 2f: swtchd rt over 1f out: kpt on u.p fnl f: no ch w wnr* **6/1**[3]

5-21 5 1 ¼ **Strike A Deal (IRE)**[37] 2837 3-9-5 71 AlanMunro 10 63+
(C F Wall) *stdd and dropped in bhd after s: rdn and effrt on inner 2f out: kpt on fnl f: n.d* **4/1**[2]

0031 6 ¾ **Waveband**[5] 3890 3-9-10 81 6ex AmyRyan(5) 6 71
(M Johnston) *chsd wnr: rdn and unable qck ent fnl 2f: edgd lft and lost 2nd over 1f out: wknd fnl f* **5/2**[1]

4201 7 ¾ **Abhar (USA)**[10] 3739 3-9-0 71 6ex KierenFox(5) 8 59
(J R Best) *t.k.h: hld up in tch: rdn and struggling 3f out: wl hld whn short of room over 1f out* **4/1**[2]

154 8 8 **Fonterutoli (IRE)**[24] 3271 3-9-7 73 (b[1]) WilliamBuick 1 43
(M Botti) *in tch in midfield: rdn and unable qck 3f out: hung rt u.p and btn wl over 1f out: wknd fnl f* **15/2**

1660 9 3 ¼ **Take My Hand**[49] 2460 3-8-8 60 SamHitchcott 5 23
(M R Channon) *stdd and short of room s: a bhd: racd awkwardly downhill over 4f out: lost tch over 3f out* **25/1**

2003 10 9 **Gra Adhmhar (IRE)**[24] 3275 3-9-2 68 EddieAhern 9 10
(D J Coakley) *racd wl off the pce in midfield: lost pl and bhd over 3f out: eased fnl f* **16/1**

1m 45.45s (-0.65) **Going Correction** -0.05s/f (Good) 10 Ran SP% **125.2**
Speed ratings (Par 100): **100,97,95,95,93 93,92,85,82,74**
toteswingers:1&2:£16.30, 1&3:£37.70, 2&3:£22.50 CSF £169.13 CT £2516.61 TOTE £20.40: £4.40, £3.40, £3.50; EX 186.90 Place 6 £4,200.05, Place 5 £2,826.94..
Owner Normandie Stud Ltd **Bred** Normandie Stud Ltd **Trained** East Ilsley, Berks

FOCUS
This was another surprise result on the card as a result of those racing prominently being at a big advantage, and the form is suspect. The favourite was way off her Ascot form and the race is rated around the runner-up.
T/Plt: £8,319.30 to a £1 stake. Pool:£44,445.79 - 3.90 winning tickets T/Qpdt: £1,725.70 to a £1 stake. Pool:£4,197.88 - 1.80 winning tickets SP

3900 HAMILTON (R-H)
Thursday, July 15
OFFICIAL GOING: Good to soft (good in places; 8.6)
Wind: Breezy, across Weather: Overcast, showers

4059 SCOTTISH RACING MAIDEN STKS 6f 5y
2:20 (2:21) (Class 5) 2-Y-O **£3,070** (£906; £453) **Stalls Low**

Form RPR

1 **Satin Love (USA)** 2-9-3 0 JoeFanning 3 89+
(M Johnston) *mde all: shkn up over 1f out: qcknd clr fnl f: eased cl home: promising* **7/4**[1]

43 2 5 **Intrusion**[15] 3550 2-8-12 0 TonyHamilton 4 66
(R A Fahey) *t.k.h early: cl up: rdn 2f out: edgd lft and kpt on fnl f: no ch w wnr* **3/1**[3]

602 3 4 **Captain Loui (IRE)**[39] 2785 2-9-3 0 (p) PhillipMakin 1 59
(K A Ryan) *w wnr: rdn 2f out: wknd appr fnl f* **5/2**[2]

4 1 **Soldiers Point** 2-9-3 0 TomEaves 2 56
(B Smart) *dwlt: trckd ldrs: rdn and rn green 2f out: wknd appr fnl f* **7/2**

1m 13.87s (1.67) **Going Correction** +0.175s/f (Good) 4 Ran SP% **112.2**
Speed ratings (Par 94): **95,88,83,81**
CSF £7.44 TOTE £2.80; EX 4.70.
Owner Crone Stud Farms Ltd **Bred** Sabine Stable **Trained** Middleham Moor, N Yorks

FOCUS
Heavy overnight showers resulted in the ground easing to good to soft, good in places. Just an ordinary maiden, but a likeable performance from a newcomer. The form is rated conservatively around the second and third.

NOTEBOOK
Satin Love(USA) knew his job and powered right away having got to the front over 1f out, being eased close home. It's probable there will be more to come from this promising type on better ground, especially over 7f, and he fully deserves a crack at something a bit better next time. (tchd 13-8 and 2-1 in places)
Intrusion again appeared to run her race without being able to match the smart-looking winner. She can surely a find a race before long. (op 15-8 tchd 10-3)
Captain Loui(IRE), who improved for the fitting of blinkers when second at Southwell latest, didn't prove as effective back on turf tried in the first-time cheekpieces. (op 9-2)
Soldiers Point, the fifth foal of a German middle-distance winner, was too green to do himself justice and should improve. (op 5-1)

4060 HAMILTON-PARK.CO.UK CLAIMING STKS 5f 4y
2:50 (2:51) (Class 6) 3-Y-O+ **£2,266** (£674; £337; £168) **Stalls Centre**

Form RPR

6242 1 **Lesley's Choice**[5] 3902 4-9-6 74 (b) FrankieMcDonald 1 79
(F J Brennan) *trckd ldr: led over 1f out: kpt on wl: jst hld on* **3/1**[2]

5230 2 nk **Bonnie Prince Blue**[22] 3317 7-9-1 75 (b) DaleSwift(7) 5 80
(B Ellison) *sn drvn and outpcd: plenty to do over 2f out: gd hdwy fnl f: jst hld* **11/4**[1]

-000 3 1 ¼ **Galpin Junior (USA)**[15] 3551 4-9-2 75 PaulQuinn 8 70
(D Nicholls) *in tch: outpcd after 2f: hdwy appr fnl f: kpt on fin* **18/1**

3431 4 ½ **Distant Sun (USA)**[16] 3533 6-9-9 72 TomEaves 2 75
(Miss L A Perratt) *trckd ldrs: effrt over 2f out: kpt on same pce fnl f* **12/1**

4363 5 ½ **Mandarin Spirit (IRE)**[3] 3946 10-9-1 64 (b) DavidAllan 9 65
(Miss L A Perratt) *prom: effrt 2f out: no ex ins fnl f* **8/1**

6341 6 1 ¼ **The Bear**[3] 3946 7-9-2 62 TonyHamilton 3 62
(Miss L A Perratt) *led to over 1f out: sn rdn: no ex ins fnl f* **7/2**[3]

6313 7 10 **Artsu**[16] 3529 5-9-3 68 PhillipMakin 6 27
(M Dods) *prom: rdn over 2f out: wknd over 1f out* **8/1**

0060 8 16 **Guest Connections**[7] 3809 7-8-13 58 (v) AdrianNicholls 7 —
(D Nicholls) *dwlt: bhd: lost tch after 2f: t.o* **20/1**

60.18 secs (0.18) **Going Correction** +0.175s/f (Good) 8 Ran SP% **113.8**
Speed ratings (Par 101): **105,104,102,101,100 98,82,57**
toteswingers:1&2:£2.50, 1&3:£12.30, 2&3:£11.40 CSF £11.59 TOTE £3.30: £1.10, £2.00, £7.30; EX 10.80.Lesley's Choice was claimed by Miss L. A. Perratt for £12,000.
Owner B C Allen **Bred** B C Allen **Trained** Lambourn, Berks

FOCUS
An ordinary claimer which looked unevenly run. The form does make a fair bit of sense.
Guest Connections Official explanation: jockey said gelding moved poorly throughout

4061 BILL AND DAVID MCHARG MEMORIAL H'CAP 1m 65y
3:25 (3:25) (Class 6) (0-65,64) 3-Y-O **£2,590** (£770; £385; £192) **Stalls High**

Form RPR

3233 1 **High Resolution**[12] 3668 3-9-0 57 DavidAllan 3 60
(Miss L A Perratt) *t.k.h: hld up: hdwy on outside over 1f out: styd on wl fnl f to ld cl home* **7/1**

0303 **2** ½ **Queen's Scholar (USA)**^{17} [3500] 3-9-7 **64**.......................... JoeFanning 2 66
(M Johnston) *led: qcknd 3l clr over 1f out: hung lft: no ex and hdd cl home* **7/2**^{2}

-600 **3** *nse* **Zambuka (FR)**^{84} [1495] 3-8-2 **45**.......................... FrankieMcDonald 8 47
(F J Brennan) *hld up on ins: n.m.r over 2f out: hdwy over 1f out: styd on fnl f: nrst fin* **22/1**

0600 **4** 1 ½ **Frontline Phantom (IRE)**^{17} [3520] 3-8-12 **55**.................. AndrewElliott 7 53
(J R Weymes) *prom: rdn and outpcd 3f out: rallied 1f out: kpt on fin* **10/1**

0500 **5** ¾ **Key Breeze**^{17} [3515] 3-8-12 **55**..............................(t) TomEaves 6 52
(K A Ryan) *t.k.h: hld up: nt clr run over 2f out: effrt whn clr over 1f out: r.o same pce fnl f* **20/1**

4600 **6** *nk* **Catbells (IRE)**^{30} [3055] 3-9-5 **62**.......................... TonyHamilton 1 58
(A Bailey) *prom: effrt over 2f out: kpt on same pce ins fnl f* **18/1**

0005 **7** *shd* **Acol**^{17} [3501] 3-7-12 **46**.......................... JamesSullivan(5) 9 42
(A G Foster) *cl up: rdn over 2f out: nt qckn fnl f* **33/1**

0-60 **8** 1 ¾ **Wood Fair**^{31} [3023] 3-8-9 **57**.......................... PatrickDonaghy(5) 10 49
(J R Weymes) *dwlt: bhd: rdn over 3f out: nvr able to chal* **50/1**

600 **9** *nk* **Royal Holiday (IRE)**^{55} [2291] 3-8-10 **60**.......................... DaleSwift(7) 4 51
(B Ellison) *hld up on outside: drvn over 2f out: sn no imp* **9/2**^{3}

1342 **10** 6 **Tribal Myth (IRE)**^{12} [3661] 3-9-7 **64**.......................... PhillipMakin 5 41
(K A Ryan) *trckd ldrs: rdn over 2f out: wknd wl over 1f out* **15/8**^{1}

1m 49.9s (1.50) **Going Correction** +0.175s/f (Good) **10** Ran SP% **116.1**
Speed ratings (Par 98): **99,98,98,96,96 95,95,94,93,87**
toteswingers:1&2:£3.60, 1&3:£18.60, 2&3:£20.20 CSF £30.27 CT £531.30 TOTE £8.20: £1.70, £1.10, £7.40; EX 28.30.
Owner Mrs Helen Perratt **Bred** Old Mill Stud Ltd **Trained** East Kilbride, South Lanarks
■ Stewards' Enquiry : Joe Fanning caution: careless riding; caution: used whip without giving filly time to respond.

FOCUS
Just a steady gallop and the form, rated around the front pair, might not be solid.

4062 ALWAYS TRYING OPEN MAIDEN STKS 1m 3f 16y
4:00 (4:04) (Class 5) 3-Y-0+ **£2,590** (£770; £385; £192) **Stalls** High

Form RPR

3-2 **1** **Ashbrittle**^{74} [1735] 3-8-13 0.......................... MartinLane(3) 4 80+
(R M Beckett) *cl up: niggled 1/2-way: drvn over 3f out: no imp tl hdwy appr fnl f: styd on wl to ld towards fin* **1/2**^{1}

3-53 **2** ½ **Wadnaan**^{48} [2497] 3-9-2 72.......................... JoeFanning 6 79
(M Johnston) *cl up: led over 2f out: rdn clr over 1f out: hung lft and hdd nr fin* **10/1**

2-0 **3** 3 **Mighty Mambo**^{89} [1386] 3-9-2 0.......................... AdrianNicholls 2 74
(Jane Chapple-Hyam) *led tl rdn and hdd over 2f out: one pce over 1f out* **25/1**

4-43 **4** 2 ¼ **Dynamic Idol (USA)**^{15} [3563] 3-9-2 80.......................... PhillipMakin 9 70
(M A Magnusson) *in tch: effrt and rdn over 2f out: no ex over 1f out* **5/1**^{2}

4 **5** 10 **Opening Nite (IRE)**^{44} [2627] 3-9-2 0.......................... TonyHamilton 1 52
(R A Fahey) *dwlt: sn prom: pushed along 1/2-way: hung rt and wknd over 2f out* **18/1**

5234 **6** 1 **Forsyth**^{38} [2816] 3-9-2 71.......................... TomEaves 8 50
(G A Swinbank) *hld up in tch: outpcd over 3f out: sn btn* **8/1**^{3}

66 **7** 1 **Farmers Glory**^{27} [3176] 3-9-2 0.......................... AndrewElliott 5 48
(G A Swinbank) *towards rr: struggling 4f out: nvr on termsd* **66/1**

8 1 **Corky Dancer**^{14} 5-9-9 0.......................... JamesSullivan(5) 7 47
(P Monteith) *bhd: struggling over 4f out: sn btn* **20/1**

2m 25.41s (-0.19) **Going Correction** +0.175s/f (Good)
WFA 3 from 4yo+ 12lb **8** Ran SP% **118.9**
Speed ratings (Par 103): **107,106,104,102,95 94,94,93**
toteswingers:1&2:£2.40, 1&3:£7.10, 2&3:£11.30 CSF £7.09 TOTE £1.40: £1.02, £2.70, £6.00; EX 6.80.
Owner J L Rowsell **Bred** Ashbrittle Stud **Trained** Whitsbury, Hants
■ Stewards' Enquiry : Martin Lane one-day ban: used whip with excessive frequency (Jul 29)

FOCUS
An ordinary maiden. The winner made hard work of it and the next two have been credited with improved form.

4063 RACING UK STKS (H'CAP) 6f 5y
4:35 (4:38) (Class 5) (0-75,74) 3-Y-0+ **£4,533** (£1,348; £674; £336) **Stalls** Centre

Form RPR

054 **1** **Imprimis Tagula (IRE)**^{5} [3898] 6-9-7 **74**..................(v) NatashaEaton(7) 4 83
(A Bailey) *cl up: led over 2f out: pushed along and styd on wl fnl f* **9/2**^{2}

1002 **2** 1 ¼ **Skyfire**^{8} [3771] 3-9-7 **73**.......................... JoeFanning 9 77
(M Johnston) *cl up: rdn and ev ch over 2f out: kpt on ins fnl f: nt rch wnr* **7/1**

3543 **3** ½ **Tadalavil**^{5} [3902] 5-9-7 **67**.......................... PhillipMakin 5 70
(Miss L A Perratt) *cl up: effrt and ev ch over 2f out: kpt on same pce fnl f* **4/1**^{1}

4512 **4** 1 ½ **Monte Mayor One**^{5} [3904] 3-8-8 **60** 6ex......................(p) TonyHamilton 1 58
(P Monteith) *hld up in tch: effrt and rdn over 1f out: kpt on same pce fnl f* **9/1**

0200 **5** 1 ¾ **Klynch**^{26} [3200] 4-9-2 **67**..............................(b) JamesSullivan(5) 6 60
(Mrs R A Carr) *in tch: drvn over 2f out: edgd rt and no ex over 1f out* **20/1**

-063 **6** *nk* **Geojimali**^{20} [3409] 8-9-0 **63**..............................(p) GaryBartley(3) 3 55
(J S Goldie) *bhd and outpcd: hdwy and c stands' side over 1f out: nvr able to chal* **14/1**

606 **7** 2 ½ **Bid For Gold**^{38} [2817] 6-8-11 **62**.......................... PatrickDonaghy(5) 8 46
(Jedd O'Keeffe) *in tch: drvn and outpcd over 2f out: n.d after* **11/1**

0222 **8** 4 **Dark Moment**^{12} [3664] 4-9-9 **74**..............................(p) IanBrennan(5) 11 45
(Ollie Pears) *bhd and outpcd: nvr on terms* **7/1**

0-06 **9** *nse* **Monalini (IRE)**^{12} [3668] 3-8-10 **62**.......................... TomEaves 2 32
(B Smart) *prom tl rdn and wknd wl over 1f out* **50/1**

1106 **10** 13 **Top Bid**^{5} [3902] 6-9-8 **68**..............................(b) DavidAllan 10 —
(T D Easterby) *missed break and sn drifted towards stands' side: t.o thrght* **6/1**^{3}

030 **11** 3 ¼ **Excellent Aim**^{46} [2564] 3-9-2 **68**.......................... AdrianNicholls 7 —
(Jane Chapple-Hyam) *led to over 2f out: wknd over 1f out: eased whn no ch fnl f* **10/1**

1m 12.7s (0.50) **Going Correction** +0.175s/f (Good)
WFA 3 from 4yo+ 6lb **11** Ran SP% **118.3**
Speed ratings (Par 103): **103,101,100,98,96 95,92,87,87,69 65**
toteswingers:1&2:£9.00, 1&3:£5.30, 2&3:£5.60 CSF £36.38 CT £140.24 TOTE £6.40: £2.70, £2.00, £1.10; EX 49.50.
Owner Middleham Park Racing XLI & Alan Bailey **Bred** Glashare House Stud **Trained** Newmarket, Suffolk

FOCUS
A competitive sprint handicap and straightforward form.

4064 HAMILTON PARK LADIES NIGHT H'CAP 6f 5y
5:10 (5:10) (Class 6) (0-60,60) 3-Y-0+ **£2,590** (£770; £385; £192) **Stalls** Centre

Form RPR

6612 **1** **Revue Princess (IRE)**^{13} [3637] 5-9-10 **60**..........................(b) DavidAllan 7 71
(T D Easterby) *mde all: rdn clr over 1f out: flashed tail ins fnl f: hld on wl* **9/4**^{1}

0622 **2** *nk* **Botham (USA)**^{5} [3900] 6-9-2 **59**.......................... PaulNorton(7) 2 69
(J S Goldie) *bhd and sn outpcd: hdwy over 1f out: kpt on wl fnl f: hld towards fin* **9/4**^{1}

6036 **3** 4 ½ **Two Turtle Doves (IRE)**^{6} [3854] 4-9-6 **56**.......................... AndrewElliott 5 52
(M Mullineaux) *trckd ldrs: rdn over 2f out: wandered over 1f out: sn outpcd* **9/2**^{2}

0140 **4** 3 ½ **Lake Chini (IRE)**^{13} [3615] 8-9-8 **58**..............................(b) PhillipMakin 12 42
(M W Easterby) *sn bhd and outpcd: hdwy over 1f out: nvr able to chal* **8/1**^{3}

60 **5** 3 ¾ **Future Gem**^{30} [3064] 4-9-5 **55**..............................(p) DanielTudhope 4 27
(N Wilson) *in tch: drvn over 2f out: btn over 1f out* **8/1**^{3}

00-0 **6** *nse* **Frill A Minute**^{36} [2852] 6-8-10 **53** oh1 ow7.......................... DaleSwift(7) 6 25
(Miss L C Siddall) *chsd ldrs: drvn and outpcd over 2f out: n.d after* **66/1**

0-03 **7** 1 **Santiago Atitlan**^{5} [3900] 8-9-5 **55**.......................... TonyHamilton 8 24
(P Monteith) *in tch: outpcd 1/2-way: n.d after* **10/1**

4-00 **8** ½ **Clanachy**^{58} [2213] 4-8-5 **46** oh1.......................... JamesSullivan(5) 10 13
(A G Foster) *chsd ldrs tl rdn and wknd fr 2f out* **33/1**

1m 12.89s (0.69) **Going Correction** +0.175s/f (Good) **8** Ran SP% **115.5**
Speed ratings (Par 101): **102,101,95,90,85 85,84,83**
toteswingers:1&2:£1.60, 1&3:£2.60, 2&3:£3.50 CSF £7.20 CT £20.06 TOTE £2.30: £1.02, £2.20, £1.80; EX 6.50 Place 6 £24.41; Place 5 £8.90.
Owner S A Heley **Bred** Raymond Shanahan **Trained** Great Habton, N Yorks

FOCUS
A low-grade sprint in which the two market leaders drew clear and have been rated back to their best.
T/Plt: £28.20 to a £1 stake. Pool:£41,848.65 - 1,081.15 winning tickets T/Qpdt: £6.20 to a £1 stake. Pool:£3,647.60 - 429.04 winning tickets RY

3677 LEICESTER (R-H)
Thursday, July 15

OFFICIAL GOING: Good (good to soft in places on round course; 7.5)
Wind: Fresh behind Weather: Showers

4065 LADBROKESCASINO.COM H'CAP 7f 9y
2:10 (2:11) (Class 4) (0-80,80) 3-Y-0+ **£4,533** (£1,348; £674; £336) **Stalls** Centre

Form RPR

-201 **1** **Zero Money (IRE)**^{21} [3346] 4-9-13 **80**.......................... SteveDrowne 6 94
(R Charlton) *mde all: hung rt fr over 2f out: pushed clr fnl f* **3/1**^{1}

0666 **2** 2 ¾ **Rio Cobolo (IRE)**^{15} [3553] 4-9-3 **70**..............................(v) JamieSpencer 2 77
(Paul Green) *hld up: hdwy and swtchd rt over 1f out: r.o to go 2nd wl ins fnl f: nt rch wnr* **13/2**

P063 **3** 1 ¼ **Call To Arms (IRE)**^{20} [3394] 3-8-13 **74**.......................... GregFairley 10 75
(M Johnston) *chsd ldrs: jnd wnr 4f out: rdn and hung lft over 1f out: no ex ins fnl f* **8/1**

-000 **4** ½ **Mr Macattack**^{20} [3389] 5-9-11 **78**..........................(vt^{1}) RichardKingscote 7 80
(Tom Dascombe) *a.p: rdn over 2f out: no ex ins fnl f* **5/1**^{3}

1603 **5** 11 **Hobson**^{14} [3604] 5-9-6 **73**.......................... TomQueally 8 46
(Eve Johnson Houghton) *sn pushed along in mid-div: rdn over 2f out: wknd over 1f out* **4/1**^{2}

50-0 **6** 5 **Lordship (IRE)**^{15} [3558] 6-8-11 **71** ow2.......................... DebraEngland(7) 4 30
(A W Carroll) *prom: pushed along 1/2-way: wknd over 2f out* **25/1**

130- **7** *shd* **Mister Tinktastic (IRE)**^{330} [5148] 4-9-11 **78**.......................... PaulHanagan 5 37
(N J Vaughan) *chsd ldrs: rdn and wknd over 2f out* **11/1**

30-0 **8** 3 ¼ **Zebrano**^{34} [2926] 4-9-9 **76**.......................... SebSanders 3 26
(A B Haynes) *hld up: a in rr: bhd fr 1/2-way* **8/1**

1m 23.46s (-2.74) **Going Correction** -0.25s/f (Firm)
WFA 3 from 4yo+ 8lb **8** Ran SP% **109.4**
Speed ratings (Par 105): **105,101,100,99,87 81,81,77**
toteswingers:1&2:£4.20, 1&3:£4.40, 2&3:£6.10 CSF £20.67 CT £127.26 TOTE £3.40: £1.20, £1.80, £2.70; EX 19.60 Trifecta £92.40 Pool: £184.91 - 1.48 winning units..
Owner Ms Gillian Khosla **Bred** Carrigbeg Stud **Trained** Beckhampton, Wilts

FOCUS
A decent handicap but not a strong race for the grade. It has been rated around the runner-up.
Zebrano Official explanation: trainer's rep said gelding was unsuited by the good ground

4066 LADBROKES.COM NURSERY 5f 218y
2:40 (2:40) (Class 4) 2-Y-0 **£3,238** (£963; £481; £240) **Stalls** Centre

Form RPR

440 **1** **Veil Of Night**^{29} [3082] 2-7-12 **60**.......................... AndreaAtzeni 6 67
(D Haydn Jones) *chsd ldrs: rdn to ld over 1f out: r.o* **16/1**

3351 **2** 1 ¼ **Captain Dimitrios**^{6} [3864] 2-8-1 **63** 6ex.......................... CathyGannon 7 66
(P D Evans) *sn led: rdn and hdd over 1f out: styd on same pce insde fnl f* **5/1**^{3}

621 **3** 2 **King Of Aquitaine (IRE)**^{19} [3449] 2-9-7 **83**.......................... PaulHanagan 5 80
(K A Ryan) *chsd ldr: rdn and ev ch over 1f out: no ex ins fnl f* **7/4**^{1}

16 **4** 1 **Tipsy Girl**^{19} [3453] 2-9-6 **82**.......................... RobertWinston 1 76
(D J Coakley) *s.i.s: hld up: hdwy u.p over 1f out: no ex ins fnl f* **4/1**^{2}

045 **5** 1 **Volcanic Dust (IRE)**^{33} [2963] 2-8-4 **66**.......................... JimmyQuinn 2 57
(E A L Dunlop) *hld up in tch: plld hrd: nt clr run over 2f out: rdn over 1f out: no ex fnl f* **6/1**

440 **6** 1 **Diamond Vine (IRE)**^{30} [3053] 2-8-8 **70**.......................... LukeMorris 3 58
(R A Harris) *prom: rdn over 3f out: wknd fnl f* **11/1**

2236 **7** ½ **Silca Conegliano (IRE)**^{26} [3199] 2-8-13 **75**.......................... RyanMoore 4 62
(M R Channon) *prom: rdn over 2f out: wknd fnl f* **7/1**

1m 11.87s (-1.13) **Going Correction** -0.25s/f (Firm) **7** Ran SP% **114.0**
Speed ratings (Par 96): **97,95,92,91,90 88,88**
toteswingers:1&2:£8.90, 1&3:£6.20, 2&3:£1.90 CSF £91.86 TOTE £25.50: £7.30, £2.00; EX 124.20.
Owner Mrs M L Parry **Bred** Mrs M L Parry **Trained** Efail Isaf, Rhondda C Taff

FOCUS
An tight looking nursery if weakly contested but run at a fair pace. The form is rated around the second and third.

NOTEBOOK

Veil Of Night, who looked up against it on her nursery debut after a disappointing showing last time (poor draw on AW debut), came out nicely on top. Always prominent, she stuck to her task well when under pressure to hit the front inside the distance, winning with a little in hand. Connections have always though a bit of her, and she shapes as though a step up to 7f will suit (op 20-1)

Captain Dimitrios landed a valuable seller at Newbury last time so had to overcome a penalty here. He set a fair pace but could not match the winner entering the distance and was basically outstayed, nonetheless, this was another respectable effort. (op 11-2 tchd 7-1 and 9-2)

King Of Aquitaine(IRE), a winner when enterprisingly ridden at Newcastle, holds an entry in the Gimcrack. He travelled well for much of the way in a prominent position but flattened out entering the distance. The ease in the ground might not have been in his favour. (op 2-1)

Tipsy Girl had the winner back in fourth when looking a fair sort on her debut at Bath, but never settled when upped to Listed company last time. This was again a rather flat effort after looking reasonably treated on her nursery debut. She was struggling in last from halfway and, although staying on in the latter stages, she could never get competitive. (op 9-2 tchd 5-1)

Volcanic Dust(IRE) did herself no favours by pulling very hard and will have to learn to settle. (op 9-2)

4067 LADBROKES.COM (S) STKS — 5f 2y

3:15 (3:17) (Class 6) 2-Y-O — £1,942 (£578; £288; £144) Stalls Low

Form				RPR
603	1		**Barista (IRE)**[12] 3678 2-8-11 0 ... RyanMoore 6 (M R Channon) *a.p: chsd ldr over 1f out: rdn to ld ins fnl f: r.o* **11/8**[1]	64
6652	2	1	**Ruby Alexander (IRE)**[8] 3784 2-8-6 0 ...(p) RichardKingscote 2 (R M Beckett) *prom: chsd ldr 1/2-way: sn rdn: outpcd over 1f out: rallied ins fnl f: r.o* **15/8**[2]	55
0542	3	1 ¼	**Liberty Ess (IRE)**[9] 3757 2-8-6 0 ...(p) PaulHanagan 4 (M Wigham) *led: rdn and hung rt over 1f out: hdd and no ex ins fnl f* **4/1**[3]	51
2636	4	3 ½	**Crazy In Love**[9] 3757 2-8-3 0 ow2 ...(b) MatthewDavies(5) 1 (W G M Turner) *chsd ldr 2f: sn rdn: wknd over 1f out* **14/1**	40
	5	13	**Majestic Ridge (IRE)** 2-8-11 0 ... LukeMorris 5 (R A Harris) *difficult to load into stalls: sn drvn along and rn green in rr: lost tch fnl 3f* **12/1**	—

60.49 secs (0.49) **Going Correction** -0.25s/f (Firm) **5** Ran SP% **111.2**

Speed ratings (Par 92): **86,84,82,76,56**

CSF £4.30 TOTE £2.00: £1.10, £1.20; EX 3.60.The winner was bought in for 3,000gns.

Owner Mrs T Burns **Bred** Rathasker Stud **Trained** West Ilsley, Berks

FOCUS

After a prolonged battle Barista finally got the upper hand inside the final furlong to land this weakly contested seller. The form is rated around the placed horses.

NOTEBOOK

Barista(IRE) finally got the upper hand inside the final furlong to land this weakly contested seller. He has shown an improved level of form after being gelded and dropped to this level since switching to present connections. He looks capable of making his presence felt in a low-grade handicap and was retained by connections at the subsequent auction for 3,000gns. (op 7-4 tchd 5-4)

Ruby Alexander(IRE) had been performing respectably in maidens before being touched off in an AW nursery last time in first-time cheekpieces. She had her chance but could only stay on at the same pace eventually collaring the third on the run to the line. She can find a opportunity in a similar affair. (tchd 2-1)

Liberty Ess(IRE), on her first run since joining new connections, ran to a similar level to that of Southwell last time. She cut out a decent pace but drifted right across the course (carrying the winner with her) and could not hold on to her advantage. Official explanation: jockey said filly hung right throughout (tchd 11-2)

Crazy In Love had been beaten at this level in four previous attempts and looks modest. (op 16-1)

Majestic Ridge(IRE) was starting career at this lowly level but ran too green to get involved. (op 9-1 tchd 14-1)

4068 LADBROKES.COM MELTON MOWBRAY CONDITIONS STKS — 1m 1f 218y

3:50 (3:50) (Class 3) 3-Y-O — £6,118 (£1,831; £915; £457; £227) Stalls High

Form				RPR
5140	1		**Myplacelater**[62] 2076 3-9-0 100 ... KierenFallon 3 (D R C Elsworth) *hld up: hdwy over 3f out: rdn to ld and edgd rt ins fnl f: r.o: cosily* **6/1**	103+
15	2	½	**Desert Myth (USA)**[68] 1910 3-9-3 94 ... RyanMoore 7 (Sir Michael Stoute) *led 1f: chsd ldrs: rdn to ld over 1f out: hdd ins fnl f: styd on* **6/4**[1]	105+
33-0	3	4 ½	**Emirates Dream (USA)**[60] 2160 3-9-3 101 ... FrankieDettori 4 (Saeed Bin Suroor) *hld up in tch: rdn and ev ch over 1f out: no ex ins fnl f* **7/2**[2]	96
2-50	4	3 ½	**Tominator**[54] 2323 3-9-3 88 ... GrahamGibbons 1 (R Hollinshead) *racd keenly: trckd ldr after 1f: led 2f out: rdn: edgd lft and hdd sn after: wknd ins fnl f* **11/1**	89
2-20	5	2 ¼	**Prompter**[69] 1858 3-9-3 106 ... HayleyTurner 2 (M L W Bell) *led after 1f: rdn and hdd 2f out: wknd over 1f out* **5/1**[3]	85
6-05	6	1 ¼	**Mingun Bell (USA)**[33] 2979 3-9-3 80 ... TomQueally 5 (H R A Cecil) *hld up: rdn over 3f out: sn lost tch* **12/1**	82

2m 6.47s (-1.43) **Going Correction** -0.025s/f (Good) **6** Ran SP% **109.2**

Speed ratings (Par 104): **104,103,100,97,95 94**

toteswingers:1&2:£2.60, 1&3:£4.10, 2&3:£2.50 CSF £14.66 TOTE £10.40: £6.60, £1.10; EX 16.40.

Owner A J Thompson **Bred** Mrs N A Ward **Trained** Newmarket, Suffolk

FOCUS

A decent enough pace for this middle-distance conditions stakes where all the runners were coming here off the back of disappointing efforts. A good race for the grade, bordering on Listed level. Fairly sound form with the winner rated in line with her Newbury win.

NOTEBOOK

Myplacelater beat Lingfield Derby Trial winner Bullet Train at the same level at Newbury on her turf debut but, after getting no run in the Cheshire Oaks, ran as though something was amiss last time. That performance can be readily ignored as the run was too bad to be true. She bounced back to form here with a vengeance, coming from the rear with a surging run to outstay the runner-up in the closing stages. Connections will now look to add some black type, and she has a tentative entry in the Nassau Stakes at Goodwood but the more likely is the Galtres Stakes at York. (tchd 5-1 and 13-2)

Desert Myth(USA) looked a good prospect when landing Newmarket maiden (form worked out well) but failed to give a true account of himself when favourite for the Lingfield Derby Trial back in May. He had been given plenty of time to recover from his exertions and this was a better effort. He settled well in behind the leading pair and, although, nudged along to hold his place at the 3f marker, he hit the front over a furlong out. He kept on well enough when headed inside the distance and remains a decent prospect. (tchd 11-8 and 7-4)

Emirates Dream(USA) was twice placed at Group level as a juvenile but a rather below-par performance on his return when the yard were not quite firing left him with something to prove. This was a respectable effort after a break of 60 days, and he ought to be capable of now going on from this. (tchd 3-1)

Tominator had been placed in Listed company as a juvenile but had been a shade disappointing on two starts this term. He raced freely, tracking the leader before taking up the running over 2f out. He had no more to give after his early exertions entering the final furlong. (op 12-1 tchd 14-1)

Prompter made a promising reappearance but finished sore when well held in the Dee Stakes last time. He took a keen hold in front and, after being headed over 2f out, could only stay on at the same pace. (op 11-2)

Mingun Bell(USA) was up against it in this company on recent efforts and found himself outpaced at the 3f marker. (op 10-1)

4069 LADBROKES.COM MOUNTSORREL MAIDEN STKS — 1m 1f 218y

4:25 (4:25) (Class 5) 3-4-Y-O — £2,590 (£770; £288; £288) Stalls High

Form				RPR
	1		**Mortbet (IRE)** 3-8-13 0 ... PhilipRobinson 12 (M A Jarvis) *chsd ldrs: rdn to ld over 1f out: styd on* **15/8**[1]	84+
	2	½	**Vibrant Force (USA)** 3-8-13 0 ... FrankieDettori 6 (Mahmood Al Zarooni) *mid-div: hdwy 1/2-way: rdn: carried hd high and ev ch ins fnl f: nt qckn nr fin* **9/1**	83+
6	3	5	**Mutanaker**[18] 3477 3-8-13 0 ... RichardHills 10 (Sir Michael Stoute) *chsd ldrs: rdn over 1f out: styd on same pce* **17/2**	73
32	3	dht	**Bitter Fortune (USA)**[16] 3523 3-8-13 0 ... JamieSpencer 8 (J Noseda) *chsd ldr tl led over 2f out: rdn and hdd over 1f out: wknd wl ins fnl f* **7/2**[2]	73
	5	¾	**Pickwick** 3-8-13 0 ... RyanMoore 14 (Sir Michael Stoute) *trckd ldrs: racd keenly: pushed along and swtchd lft over 1f out: styd on* **13/2**[3]	71+
	6	3	**Politbureau** 3-8-13 0 ... GregFairley 11 (M Johnston) *prom: pushed along 6f out: outpcd fr over 2f out* **25/1**	65+
63	7	3 ½	**Seriy Tzarina**[48] 2487 4-8-12 0 ... AdamBeschizza(7) 1 (Miss Gay Kelleway) *hld up: hdwy on outer over 3f out: hung rt over 2f out: nvr nr to chal* **40/1**	53
60	8	3 ½	**Gracie May**[14] 3586 3-8-8 0 ... GrahamGibbons 7 (R Hollinshead) *led: rdn and hdd over 2f out: wknd over 1f out* **150/1**	46
40	9	12	**Egmarey (IRE)**[19] 3437 3-8-8 0 ... TedDurcan 5 (D R Lanigan) *s.i.s: swtchd rt sn after s: hld up: nvr on terms* **14/1**	22
	10	1 ½	**Chief Storm Eagle (IRE)**[262] 7073 3-8-8 0 ...(t) TobyAtkinson(5) 4 (M Botti) *hld up: racd keenly: hdwy over 3f out: wknd 2f out* **50/1**	24
	11	4	**Mawazin** 4-9-10 0 ... TadhgO'Shea 9 (E A L Dunlop) *hld up: bhd fr 1/2-way* **50/1**	16
0	12	½	**Isobar (GER)**[31] 3038 4-9-10 0 ... KierenFallon 13 (L M Cumani) *mid-div: hdwy over 3f out: wknd wl over 1f out* **25/1**	15
6	13	3 ¾	**Large Scotch**[19] 3428 3-8-8 0 ... VinceSlattery 2 (Paul Green) *hld up: bhd fr 1/2-way* **100/1**	3
0	14	1 ¾	**Dark Shines**[24] 3258 3-8-13 0 ow3 ... JamesMillman(3) 15 (B R Millman) *hld up: rdn over 4f out: sme hdwy over 3f out: sn wknd* **100/1**	7
0	15	17	**Ginger Jalapeno**[17] 3518 4-9-5 0 ... SaleemGolam 16 (E G Bevan) *hld up: plld hrd: wknd over 3f out: t.o* **150/1**	—
0	16	4 ½	**Jinn And Tinick**[31] 3038 4-9-5 0 ... TomQueally 3 (A W Carroll) *hld up: hdwy over 3f out: rdn: hung rt and wknd over 2f out: t.o* **125/1**	—

2m 7.74s (-0.16) **Going Correction** -0.025s/f (Good)

WFA 3 from 4yo 11lb **16** Ran SP% **115.7**

Speed ratings (Par 103): **99,98,94,94,94 91,88,86,76,75 72,71,68,67,53 50**

PL: Bitter Fortune £1.10, Muntanaker £0.80 TC: MB/VF/BF £37.70 MB/VF/MR £44.00. toteswingers:MB&VF:£6.30, VF&BF:£2.80, MB&BF:£1.50, VF&MR:£4.50, MB&MR:£3.30 CSF £17.62 TOTE £3.00: £1.50, £3.40; EX 22.50 Trifecta £37.70 Pool: £319.18 - 3.13 winning units..

Owner Sheikh Ahmed Al Maktoum **Bred** Darley **Trained** Newmarket, Suffolk

FOCUS

Not much previous form to go on, but an interesting maiden with several well-bred newcomers, and run at a fair pace so the form should work out. The front pair are above average.

Isobar(GER) Official explanation: jockey said colt lost its action

4070 LADBROKES.COM H'CAP — 1m 3f 183y

5:00 (5:00) (Class 6) (0-65,63) 4-Y-O+ — £2,266 (£674; £337; £168) Stalls High

Form				RPR
3-42	1		**Astronomical (IRE)**[13] 3617 8-9-6 **60** ...(p) GrahamGibbons 4 (R Hollinshead) *mde all: rdn over 1f out: styd on wl* **4/1**[2]	67
3131	2	1 ½	**Dazzling Begum**[13] 3641 5-8-11 **56** ... SimonPearce(5) 2 (J Pearce) *chsd ldrs: rdn over 1f out: chsd wnr ins fnl f: styd on* **9/1**	61
6012	3	1 ¼	**Outland (IRE)**[28] 3128 4-9-9 **63** ... KierenFallon 5 (J R Jenkins) *prom: chsd wnr over 2f out: sn rdn and ev ch: styd on same pce ins fnl f* **7/4**[1]	66
60-3	4	¾	**Marino Prince (FR)**[21] 3360 5-8-2 **49** ow4 ... JamesRogers(7) 7 (B D Leavy) *hld up: hdwy over 3f out: nt clr run and lost pl sn after: hdwy over 1f out: r.o* **12/1**	51+
5353	5	nk	**Zaif (IRE)**[5] 3917 7-8-10 **55** ... BillyCray(5) 10 (D J S Ffrench Davis) *hld up: hdwy over 2f out: rdn and hung rt over 1f out: styd on same pce fnl f* **7/1**[3]	56
0054	6	nk	**Arashi**[13] 3613 4-9-3 **60** ...(p) RussKennemore(3) 3 (Lucinda Featherstone) *hld up: hdwy over 4f out: rdn over 1f out: styd on same pce* **12/1**	61
0003	7	2	**Desert Fairy**[12] 3684 4-8-5 **45** ... KirstyMilczarek 8 (J W Unett) *chsd wnr tl rdn over 2f out: no ex fnl f* **22/1**	43
	8	2 ½	**Moonwolf (NZ)**[139] 6-8-8 **55** ... DavidKenny(7) 12 (Miss Sheena West) *s.i.s: hld up: hdwy over 4f out: rdn over 2f out: sn outpcd* **28/1**	49
0-00	9	3	**Dr Light (IRE)**[21] 3370 6-8-5 **45** ...(p) SaleemGolam 1 (M A Peill) *s.i.s: hld up: hdwy over 2f out: sn rdn and hung rt: wknd over 1f out* **33/1**	34
3606	10	5	**Carlton Scroop (FR)**[16] 3522 7-9-6 **60** ... MickyFenton 6 (A W Carroll) *broke wl: racd keenly: sn stdd and lost pl: rdn and hung rt over 2f out: n.d after* **20/1**	41
000	11	3 ¾	**Four Quartets (GER)**[28] 3116 4-8-10 **50** ... TomQueally 11 (D Shaw) *prom tl rdn and wknd over 2f out* **33/1**	25
-003	12	10	**Rowan Light**[26] 3214 4-9-1 **55** ... StephenCraine 9 (J R Boyle) *hld up in tch: rdn and wknd over 2f out: t.o* **20/1**	14

2m 36.83s (2.93) **Going Correction** -0.025s/f (Good) **12** Ran SP% **117.5**

Speed ratings (Par 101): **89,88,87,86,86 86,84,83,81,77 75,68**

toteswingers:1&2:£6.40, 1&3:£3.40, 2&3:£4.60 CSF £34.72 CT £83.74 TOTE £3.50: £1.30, £3.00, £1.50; EX 35.70 Trifecta £22.50 Pool: £79.23 - 2.60 winning units..

Owner FWH Partnership **Bred** Pollards Stables **Trained** Upper Longdon, Staffs

FOCUS

A modest handicap and a bit muddling, but won in a decent manner by the in-form Astronomical. He is rated close to his best.

Desert Fairy Official explanation: jockey said filly stumbled leaving stalls

Carlton Scroop(FR) Official explanation: jockey said gelding hung right-handed

4071 LADBROKES.COM APPRENTICE H'CAP 5f 218y
5:30 (5:31) (Class 5) (0-70,70) 3-Y-O+ **£2,590** (£770; £385; £192) **Stalls** Centre

Form RPR
610 **1** **Boldinor**[23] 3292 7-9-2 **58** RyanPowell 6 61
(M R Bosley) *a.p: hmpd 2f out: rdn to ld ins fnl f: r.o* **8/1**
3350 **2** 1/2 **Misterisland (IRE)**[6] 3855 5-8-6 **51** oh5 (p) JosephYoung(3) 8 52
(M Mullineaux) *chsd ldrs: rdn over 1f out: unbalanced u.p ins fnl f: r.o* **12/1**
0/0 **3** *hd* **Call The Law (IRE)**[23] 3287 4-8-4 **51** oh1 ChristyMews(5) 2 51
(Mrs P Sly) *s.i.s: hdwy 1/2-way: hung rt fnl 2f: ev ch over 1f out: styd on* **25/1**
2642 **4** *shd* **Peopleton Brook**[11] 3748 8-8-13 **58** (t) MatthewCosham(3) 7 58
(B G Powell) *hld up: hdwy over 1f out: r.o: nt quite rch ldrs* **10/1**
-050 **5** 3/4 **Charlietoo**[15] 3556 4-8-9 **51** (p) RyanClark 3 49
(E G Bevan) *sn pushed along in rr: hdwy 1/2-way: rdn over 1f out: r.o* **9/2**[3]
0650 **6** *hd* **Athboy Auction**[16] 3526 5-8-9 **51** oh3 RosieJessop 4 48
(H J Collingridge) *hld up: hdwy u.p and edgd lft over 1f out: r.o* **8/1**
0000 **7** *shd* **Commander Wish**[13] 3615 7-8-9 **51** oh6 (v[1]) AdamBeschizza 5 48
(Lucinda Featherstone) *s.i.s: sn prom: led over 1f out: edgd lft: rdn and hdd ins fnl f: styd on same pce* **22/1**
2230 **8** *1* **Tag Team (IRE)**[24] 3280 9-8-9 **51** oh6 (p) DavidKenny 9 44
(John A Harris) *led: rdn and hdd over 1f out: no ex towards fin* **22/1**
-110 **9** *nk* **Feeling Fresh (IRE)**[6] 3855 5-9-9 **70** JordanDodd(5) 10 63
(Paul Green) *s.s: hdwy 1/2-way: rdn over 1f out: no ex wl ins fnl f* **11/4**[1]
1003 **10** *5* **The History Man (IRE)**[9] 3763 7-9-1 **60** (p) JamesRogers(3) 1 37
(B D Leavy) *chsd ldr: rdn over 2f out: wknd over 1f out* **7/2**[2]

1m 11.98s (-1.02) **Going Correction** -0.25s/f (Firm) **10** Ran SP% **118.6**
Speed ratings (Par 103): **96,95,95,94,93 93,93,92,91,85**
toteswingers:1&2:£12.80, 1&3:£14.90, 2&3:£43.80 CSF £97.58 CT £2338.48 TOTE £10.60: £4.10, £7.00, £14.20; EX 118.10 TRIFECTA Not won. Place 6 £25.81; Place 5 £12.62.
Owner Ron Collins **Bred** Ron Collins **Trained** Chalfont St Giles, Bucks

FOCUS
An exposed field for this apprentice sprint handicap that resulted in a tight scrap to the line. Half the field were out of the handicap and the form is rated around the winner, but the form is far from solid.
T/Plt: £32.10 to a £1 stake. Pool:£54,417.92 - 1,236.10 winning tickets T/Qpdt: £2.80 to a £1 stake. Pool:£4,138.01 - 1,059.37 winning tickets CR

4072 - 4076a (Foreign Racing) - See Raceform Interactive

3835 LEOPARDSTOWN (L-H)
Thursday, July 15

OFFICIAL GOING: Good

4077a SILVER FLASH STKS (GROUP 3) (FILLIES) 7f
6:55 (6:58) 2-Y-O **£28,761** (£8,407; £3,982; £1,327)

RPR
1 **Together (IRE)**[35] 2910 2-8-12 JMurtagh 5 106
(A P O'Brien, Ire) *trckd ldr in 2nd: hdwy to ld under 2f out: sn drvn clr: kpt on wl fnl f* **9/10**[1]
2 *1* **Laughing Lashes (USA)**[19] 3465 2-8-12 FMBerry 4 104
(Mrs John Harrington, Ire) *trckd ldrs: 3rd appr st: wnt 2nd under 2f out: sn no imp on wnr: kpt on same pce fnl f* **4/1**[2]
3 1 3/4 **Kissable (IRE)**[14] 3642 2-8-12 CDHayes 6 99+
(Kevin Prendergast, Ire) *in rr of mid-div: 6th appr st: drvn along in 5th and swtchd rt over 1f out: kpt on wl ins fnl f* **7/1**[3]
4 1 3/4 **Highly Composed**[32] 3004 2-8-12 WMLordan 8 95
(T Stack, Ire) *settled towards rr on outer: 5th 3f out: wnt 4th early st: no imp on wnr wl over 1f out: kpt on one pce* **8/1**
5 1 1/4 **Palinode (USA)**[14] 3642 2-8-12 KJManning 7 92
(J S Bolger, Ire) *rdn early to trck ldrs: 4th 1/2-way: pushed along appr st: wnt 3rd 1 1/2f out: sn no imp and kpt on one pce* **10/1**
6 *5* **Looking Lovely (IRE)**[20] 3421 2-8-12 CO'Donoghue 2 79
(A P O'Brien, Ire) *a towards rr: swtchd to outer in st: no imp and kpt on one pce* **16/1**
7 3 1/2 **Gemstone (IRE)**[27] 3184 2-8-12 JAHeffernan 1 70
(A P O'Brien, Ire) *led: strly pressed ent st: hdd under 2f out: sn no ex and wknd* **10/1**
8 *11* **Isis Song (IRE)**[15] 3568 2-8-12 DPMcDonogh 3 43
(Joseph G Murphy, Ire) *mid-div on inner: 7th in tch ent st: sn no ex u.p: wknd* **16/1**

1m 28.65s (-0.05) **Going Correction** +0.05s/f (Good) **8** Ran SP% **126.2**
Speed ratings: **102,100,98,96,95 89,85,73**
CSF £5.54 TOTE £1.70: £1.10, £1.20, £1.30; DF 5.60.
Owner Derrick Smith **Bred** Lynch Bages And Samac **Trained** Ballydoyle, Co Tipperary

NOTEBOOK
Together(IRE) looks a filly with a big future that should be among the leading juvenile fillies at the end of the season. Tracking her pacemaker, she showed a good turn of foot to get to the front over a furlong out which her opponents couldn't match, and she ran on well to the line. She has a very smart turn of foot, will get further and gives every indication that better is to come. The second and third were a shade unlucky but there's no reason to believe they would have beaten the winner whatever happened. (op 11/10)
Laughing Lashes(USA) showed herself to be on the upgrade as well. She settled better here just behind the pace, but when the tempo quickened in the straight she was just caught in a pocket on the inside and couldn't get out immediately. When she did she ran on strongly, although the winner was always going to hold her. She's very talented but might have to answer some niggling questions about her, particularly her tail-swishing under pressure and the possible fact that she may have to be covered up for as long as possible. (op 5/1)
Kissable(IRE) ◆ looks very progressive. She raced close enough to the pace, just caught for tactical speed when the tempo quickened in the straight and ended up having to switch right around the field to find racing room. When she did get room though the way she ran on inside the last was very pleasing. (op 6/1)
Highly Composed stepped up on her two performances so far over this trip and on slightly easier ground. Held up, she came with an effort in the straight but wasn't good enough to make an impression. She kept going at one pace and should pick up a maiden. (op 7/1)
Palinode(USA) was sent up to race prominently and was close enough to the pace when the winner quickened on in the straight. She could find no extra from there but wasn't at all disgraced. (op 16/1)
Isis Song(IRE) was stepping up hugely in class but better might have been expected from her. She was beaten before they turned out of the back straight and came home a remote back-marker. (op 14/1)

4081a CHALLENGE STKS (LISTED RACE) 1m 6f
9:05 (9:05) 3-Y-O+ **£24,446** (£7,146; £3,384; £1,128)

RPR
1 **Profound Beauty (IRE)**[19] 3470 6-9-9 115 PJSmullen 4 109+
(D K Weld, Ire) *settled in mid-div: mod 5th 1/2-way: prog on outer to go 2nd ent st: led over 1f out: sn drew clr: easily* **2/5**[1]
2 5 1/2 **Drumfire (IRE)**[320] 5447 6-9-9 110 JMurtagh 7 94+
(Eoin Griffin, Ire) *towards rr: mod 7th 4f out: clsr ent st: 6th on outer over 1f out: kpt on wl fnl f to go 2nd cl home* **12/1**
3 1/2 **Unity (IRE)**[32] 3007 3-8-7 98 (p) WMLordan 2 92+
(David Wachman, Ire) *mod 4th: clsr in 3rd ent st: rdn and no ch w wnr fr 1f out: kpt on one pce* **11/1**
4 *hd* **Spinning Wings (IRE)**[19] 3471 4-9-6 90 (tp) JAHeffernan 10 90
(T Hogan, Ire) *led: sn clr: 15 l ld 1/2-way: reduced advantage appr st: strly pressed and hdd over 1f out: no ex* **25/1**
5 *3* **Pointilliste (USA)**[284] 6527 7-9-9 111 FMBerry 1 89
(Noel Meade, Ire) *mod 3rd: clsr in 4th appr st: no ex fr 2f out* **8/1**[3]
6 2 1/2 **Shahwardi (FR)**[19] 3454 4-9-12 SteveDrowne 3 88
(J R Gask) *towards rr: mod 6th 1/2-way: clsr ent st: 4th u.p early st: no ex fr over 1f out* **7/1**[2]
7 *20* **Celtic Soprano (IRE)**[81] 1560 5-9-6 89 WJSupple 5 54
(P D Deegan, Ire) *chsd clr ldr in 2nd: drvn along and no ex appr st: wknd* **33/1**

3m 4.82s (3.82) **Going Correction** +0.05s/f (Good)
WFA 3 from 4yo+ 15lb **7** Ran SP% **117.9**
Speed ratings: **91,87,87,87,85 84,72**
CSF £7.41 TOTE £1.30: £1.20, £1.70; DF 7.60.
Owner Moyglare Stud Farm **Bred** Moyglare Stud Farm Ltd **Trained** The Curragh, Co Kildare

NOTEBOOK
Profound Beauty(IRE) completed a hat-trick of victories in this event and shows every sign of being at least as good as ever on ground which probably was as easy as she would like it. Held up off the pace, she cruised through most of the race although she did have to be shaken up for a few strides early in the straight to close on the one-time clear leader. However, once getting into gear she picked that one off readily and drew clear inside the last. A mare of tremendous quality and durability, perhaps this is the season where she can gain a success at better than Group 3 level.
Drumfire(IRE) shaped creditably without really being involved. Held up in rear in a race where they were well strung out for a lot of the way, he did close up to some extent before the straight but it was inside the final furlong and a half where he did his best work as he passed a few horses to get up close home for second. He should go on from this but might be difficult to win with as he has a very high rating. (op 8/1)
Unity(IRE) probably ran her race but just wasn't good enough. Racing in mid-division, she was just about close enough if good enough before the straight but the winner quickened past her and she just kept on at the same pace. (op 8/1)
Spinning Wings(IRE) set a good gallop and had a clear lead for much of the race. Indeed, she was the only one in the race to get the winner off the bridle, albeit very briefly. Once the winner picked her off she ran out of steam but was unlucky to be run out of the first three inside the final half-furlong.
Pointilliste(USA) chased the pace for a lot of the way before fading inside the final quarter mile. (op 7/1)
Shahwardi(FR) was feeling the pinch half a mile out and just kept on at the same pace. (op 8/1)
Celtic Soprano(IRE) chased the winner early on but dropped right away entering the straight and looked out of her depth.
T/Jkpt: @937.50. Pool of @10,000.00 - 8 winning units. T/Plt: @57.80. Pool of @13,147.00 - 170.57 winning units. II

4078 - 4081a (Foreign Racing) - See Raceform Interactive

4059 HAMILTON (R-H)
Friday, July 16

OFFICIAL GOING: Good to soft (8.3)
Wind: Strong, half behind Weather: Cloudy

4082 TOTEPOOL FLEXI BETTING APPRENTICE SERIES H'CAP (ROUND 3) 1m 65y
6:10 (6:10) (Class 6) (0-60,60) 4-Y-O+ **£2,047** (£604; £302) **Stalls** High

Form RPR
0033 **1** **Carlitos Spirit (IRE)**[4] 3948 6-9-5 **60** (v) LeeTopliss 10 75
(I W McInnes) *mde all: rdn and drew clr fr 2 out: styd on strly: eased towards fin* **4/1**[1]
0454 **2** *10* **Coole Dodger (IRE)**[28] 3180 5-8-9 **50** DavidKenny 8 42+
(B Ellison) *dwlt: t.k.h: hld up: hdwy whn nt clr run over 3f out to over 2f out: hdwy to chse (clr) wnr ins fnl f: no imp* **13/2**
0151 **3** 2 1/4 **Glenluji**[18] 3500 5-8-9 **55** PaulNorton(5) 5 42
(J S Goldie) *hld up: hdwy and drifted rt wl over 1f out: sn swtchd lft: kpt on fnl f: no imp* **9/2**[2]
104 **4** 1/2 **Applaude**[13] 3683 5-9-5 **60** (b) CharlesEddery 2 46
(R C Guest) *in tch: hdwy 3f out: chsd (clr) wnr over 1f out to ins fnl f: no ex* **9/1**
6436 **5** *10* **Cold Quest (USA)**[18] 3500 6-8-8 **49** (b[1]) JamesSullivan 1 12
(Miss L A Perratt) *in tch on ins: rdn whn hmpd over 2f out: btn over 1f out* **12/1**
35-5 **6** 1 3/4 **Cils Blancs (IRE)**[59] 2211 4-8-13 **57** AdamCarter(3) 3 16
(B Smart) *chsd ldrs: drvn over 2f out: wknd over 1f out* **4/1**[1]
00-0 **7** *2* **Navajo Joe (IRE)**[40] 2788 5-8-11 **57** ShaneBKelly(5) 4 11
(R Johnson) *plld hrd: in tch: nt clr run over 2f out: wknd over 1f out* **18/1**
400/ **8** *6* **Goodenough Magic**[661] 6191 4-8-0 **46** oh1 NoelGarbutt(5) 7 —
(A G Foster) *chsd wnr tl rdn and wknd over 3f out* **50/1**
-036 **9** *9* **Rain Stops Play (IRE)**[22] 3369 8-8-0 **46** MarzenaJeziorek(5) 6 —
(N G Richards) *t.k.h: in tch: hdwy over 4f out: rdn and wknd over 3f out* **5/1**[3]

1m 49.14s (0.74) **Going Correction** +0.15s/f (Good) **9** Ran SP% **113.1**
Speed ratings (Par 101): **102,92,89,89,79 77,75,69,60**
toteswingers: 1&2 £4.60, 1&3 £3.40, 2&3 £5.20. CSF £29.51 CT £120.46 TOTE £5.70: £2.60, £2.60, £1.70; EX 32.30.
Owner Wold Construction Company **Bred** Tally-Ho Stud **Trained** Catwick, E Yorks
■ Stewards' Enquiry : Lee Topliss one-day ban: used whip when clearly winning (Jul 30)
Shane B Kelly one-day ban: careless riding (Jul 30)
Noel Garbutt two-day ban: careless riding (Jul 30-31)

FOCUS
The ground had changed from the previous night's racing to good to soft after nearly an inch of rain but the general opinion was that it was riding soft.

Coole Dodger(IRE) Official explanation: trainer's rep agreed with stewards that gelding was not a suitable ride for an apprentice, and gave an assurance that it would not be ridden by an apprentrice in future.

4083 JOHN SMITH'S EXTRA SMOOTH MAIDEN AUCTION STKS 5f 4y
6:45 (6:45) (Class 5) 2-Y-O **£2,729** (£806; £403) **Stalls** Low

Form RPR

2 **1** **Ballinargh Girl (IRE)**[27] 3204 2-8-5 0 AndrewElliott 5 73
(R D Wylie) *cl up: effrt over 1f out: led ins fnl f: styd on strly* **15/8**[1]

2 **2** *1 ¾* **Nine Before Ten (IRE)**[10] 3756 2-8-6 0 SilvestreDeSousa 1 68
(Mrs D J Sanderson) *led: rdn over 1f out: hdd ins fnl f: kpt on same pce* **2/1**[2]

63 **3** *1* **Upark Flyer**[8] 3811 2-8-0 0 JamesSullivan(5) 2 63
(Patrick Morris) *dwlt: sn trcking ldrs: effrt over 1f out: kpt on same pce ins fnl f* **25/1**

30U **4** *4* **Chestival (IRE)**[6] 3897 2-7-13 0 BillyCray(5) 6 48
(Patrick Morris) *bhd and pushed along: drvn 1/2-way: hung rt and no imp fnl f* **28/1**

043 **5** *nse* **Sapphire Girl**[23] 3315 2-8-6 0 PaulHanagan 3 50
(R A Fahey) *t.k.h: cl up tl rdn and wknd over 1f out* **10/3**[3]

0 **6** *½* **Paragons Folly (IRE)**[30] 3087 2-8-12 0 TomEaves 4 54
(J J Quinn) *t.k.h: prom: drvn and outpcd over 2f out: sn btn* **7/1**

61.36 secs (1.36) **Going Correction** +0.15s/f (Good) 6 Ran SP% **111.0**
Speed ratings (Par 94): **95,92,90,84,84 83**
toteswingers: 1&2 £1.40, 1&3 £6.90, 2&3 £6.80. CSF £5.80 TOTE £2.50: £1.10, £1.70; EX 6.90.
Owner M R Johnson **Bred** Des Vere Hunt & Jack Ronan **Trained** Westhead, Lancs

FOCUS
Just an ordinary maiden

NOTEBOOK
Ballinargh Girl(IRE) confirmed the promise she showed on her debut by running out a likeable winner. Always up with the pace, she forged ahead inside the distance to win with something in hand. She is progressing and connections will now go down the handicap route, with better ground and a step up in distance expected to bring further improvement. (op 7-4 tchd 13-8)
Nine Before Ten(IRE) made a pleasing start to her career when second on the all-weather at Southwell. Stepping up in trip, she cut out much of the running but was ultimately outstayed. Another pleasing effort. (op 9-4 tchd 5-2)
Upark Flyer showed little on her debut and was last of three at Epsom last time so it was difficult to gauge what she had achieved. She missed the break but stayed on well enough from over a furlong out. (tchd 22-1)
Chestival(IRE) found the pace a little hot early on and as a result could never get involved. (op 40-1)
Sapphire Girl has some respectable efforts to her name but failed to get home after tracking the leaders until over a furlong out. (op 3-1 tchd 9-4)
Paragons Folly(IRE) did not have the best of introductions on his debut last time but raced too freely this time and could never land a blow. (op 9-1 tchd 13-2)

4084 JOHN BANKS CLAIMING STKS 6f 5y
7:15 (7:15) (Class 6) 3-Y-O+ **£2,047** (£604; £302) **Stalls** Low

Form RPR

0-06 **1** **Mister Hardy**[41] 2736 5-9-12 89 PaulHanagan 7 89
(R A Fahey) *prom: hdwy to ld over 1f out: rdn and edgd lft ins fnl f: r.o* **1/1**[1]

1531 **2** *1 ½* **Ace Of Spies (IRE)**[17] 3534 5-9-2 67 SilvestreDeSousa 5 74
(G A Harker) *trckd ldrs: effrt and ev ch wl over 1f out: kpt on fnl f: nt pce of wnr* **11/2**[3]

5103 **3** *1 ¾* **Apache Ridge (IRE)**[13] 3664 4-9-8 73 (b) PJMcDonald 1 75
(K A Ryan) *cl up: led over 2f out to over 1f out: kpt on same pce fnl f* **20/1**

2302 **4** *2* **Bonnie Prince Blue**[1] 4060 7-9-10 75 (b) DavidAllan 8 70
(B Ellison) *prom: rdn and ev ch 2f out: hung rt and sn one pce* **3/1**[2]

2500 **5** *1 ¾* **Dickie Le Davoir**[10] 3753 6-8-12 66 (v) JamesSullivan(5) 6 58
(R C Guest) *sn outpcd and pushed along: effrt over 2f out: no imp fr over 1f out* **18/1**

6142 **6** *3 ½* **Cawdor (IRE)**[43] 2668 4-9-5 73 TomEaves 3 48
(Mrs L Stubbs) *led to over 2f out: rdn and wknd over 1f out* **10/1**

1m 13.02s (0.82) **Going Correction** +0.15s/f (Good) 6 Ran SP% **109.5**
Speed ratings (Par 101): **100,98,95,93,90 86**
toteswingers: 1&2 £2.60, 1&3 £5.40, 2&3 £8.20. CSF £6.60 TOTE £2.40: £1.90, £2.80; EX 7.00.Ace Of Spies was claimed by C R Dore for £6,000. Mister Hardy and Bonnie Prince Blue were subject to friendly claims.
Owner The Cosmic Cases **Bred** Mrs M Bryce **Trained** Musley Bank, N Yorks

FOCUS
A reasonable claimer.

4085 JOHN SMITH'S SCOTTISH STEWARDS' CUP (H'CAP) 6f 5y
7:45 (7:46) (Class 2) (0-105,102) 3-Y-O+
£20,562 (£6,157; £3,078; £1,541; £768; £386) **Stalls** Low

Form RPR

2001 **1** **Lowdown (IRE)**[11] 3731 3-9-0 93 6ex JoeFanning 2 106
(M Johnston) *cl up stands' side: led that gp and overall ldr 1/2-way: styd on strly fnl f: 1st of 10 in gp* **20/1**

1106 **2** *3 ¼* **Damika (IRE)**[14] 3619 7-9-3 94 MichaelStainton(3) 1 98
(R M Whitaker) *midfield stands' side: rdn over 2f out: hdwy over 1f out: chsd wnr fnl f: r.o: 2nd of 10 in gp* **33/1**

2620 **3** *2 ¼* **The Nifty Fox**[21] 3406 6-9-0 88 DavidAllan 4 85
(T D Easterby) *cl up stands' side: rdn and effrt over 2f out: kpt on same pce ins fnl f: 3rd of 10 in gp* **33/1**

10 **4** *2* **Tajneed (IRE)**[33] 2992 7-9-2 95 BillyCray(5) 7 85
(D Nicholls) *led stands' side to 1/2-way: sn rdn: one pce over 1f out: 4th of 10 in gp* **14/1**

0-01 **5** *½* **Baby Strange**[33] 2992 6-9-2 90 AndrewElliott 10 79+
(D Shaw) *towards rr on outside of stands' side gp: hdwy u.p over 1f out: kpt on fnl f: nrst fin: 5th of 10 in gp* **16/1**

0-10 **6** *½* **Irish Heartbeat (IRE)**[90] 1383 5-9-5 93 PaulHanagan 5 80+
(R A Fahey) *in tch stands' side: effrt and rdn over 2f out: one pce fr over 1f out: 6th of 10 in gp* **9/4**[1]

4200 **7** *¾* **Esprit De Midas**[28] 3178 4-8-11 88 AndrewHeffernan(3) 14 73+
(K A Ryan) *hld up in tch far side: rdn and outpcd over 2f out: rallied to ld that gp wl ins fnl f: no ch w stands' side ldrs: 1st of 6 in gp* **50/1**

6-60 **8** *1 ¼* **Captain Ramius (IRE)**[33] 2992 4-9-5 93 (p) SilvestreDeSousa 6 74
(K A Ryan) *chsd stands' side ldrs: drvn over 2f out: sn wknd: 7th of 10 in gp* **33/1**

6200 **9** *hd* **Baldemar**[20] 3446 5-8-10 91 LeeTopliss(7) 15 71
(R A Fahey) *rdr lost iron briefly sn after s: chsd far side ldr: rdn over 2f out: kpt on u.p fnl f: 2nd of 6 in gp* **16/1**

1030 **10** *hd* **Thebes**[20] 3461 5-9-7 95 GregFairley 13 75
(M Johnston) *led far side: rdn over 2f out: hdd in that gp wl ins fnl f: no ex: 3rd of 6 in gp* **20/1**

3033 **11** *3 ¼* **Esoterica (IRE)**[14] 3619 7-8-11 92 (v) PaulNorton(7) 3 61
(J S Goldie) *bhd and sn rdn stands' side: sme late hdwy: nvr on terms: 8th of 10 in gp* **20/1**

5024 **12** *nk* **Enderby Spirit (GR)**[13] 3674 4-9-7 95 (v) TomEaves 8 63
(B Smart) *in tch on outside of stands' side gp: drvn and outpcd over 2f out: sn btn: 9th of 10 in gp* **20/1**

1123 **13** *2* **Hawkeyethenoo (IRE)**[19] 3489 4-9-0 91 GaryBartley(3) 11 53
(J S Goldie) *hld up far side: shortlived effrt over 2f out: nvr able to chal: 4th of 6 in gp* **11/4**[2]

2-03 **14** *7* **Bonnie Charlie**[20] 3445 4-10-0 102 LiamJones 9 41
(W J Haggas) *swtchd to r far side sn after s: hld up: rdn and outpcd over 2f out: n.d after: 5th of 6 in gp* **12/1**[3]

0400 **15** *nk* **Oldjoesaid**[19] 3489 6-9-1 89 PJMcDonald 12 27
(K A Ryan) *taken early to post: upset in stalls: bhd stands' side: drvn 1/2-way: nvr on terms: last of 10 in gp* **16/1**

020 **16** *2 ½* **Redford (IRE)**[27] 3193 5-9-7 100 AmyRyan(5) 16 30
(K A Ryan) *dwlt: sn in tch far side: drvn and outpcd over 2f out: btn over 1f out: last of 6 in gp* **12/1**[3]

1m 12.07s (-0.13) **Going Correction** +0.15s/f (Good)
WFA 3 from 4yo+ 5lb 16 Ran SP% **127.0**
Speed ratings (Par 109): **106,101,98,96,95 94,93,92,91,91 87,86,84,74,74 71**
toteswingers: 1&2 £84.80, 1&3 £101.20, 2&3 £157.80. CSF £546.39 CT £9664.97 TOTE £36.30: £5.90, £8.00, £6.30, £3.20; EX 776.50.
Owner Sheikh Hamdan Bin Mohammed Al Maktoum **Bred** A Stroud And J Hanly **Trained** Middleham Moor, N Yorks

FOCUS
A decent, well-contested renewal of this fascinating sprint with the field splitting into two groups and the nearside rails producing the first six home. It was run at a fair pace with not many hard-luck stories but a few who did under-perform.

NOTEBOOK
Lowdown(IRE), the only three-year-old in the race, soon gained the nearside rail to take the field along at a decent clip. He found plenty entering the distance to score convincingly. He had a penalty to overcome after bouncing back to form at Ripon last time but this was again an improved performance and rates probably his best yet. He holds an engagement for the Stewards' Cup but will struggle to make the cut. (op 25-1)
Damika(IRE) has not won off a mark as high as this but had returned to form with two victories in May. He chased the leaders on the nearside rail and kept on well enough in the closing stages but was no match for the winner. The rain had aided his cause but this was a decent effort and he looks capable of handling this mark, especially in a less competitive heat. (op 40-1)
The Nifty Fox has been in good form and has plenty of winning form on soft but has yet to win at this distance. He was travelling well on the heels of the leaders at the 2f marker and saw out the trip well enough, but could not quite get on terms to lay down a serious challenge. (op 66-1)
Tajneed(IRE) is a useful sprinter on good or softer. He was back up in the weights after winning at Ripon two starts previously but posted another sound effort and remains in good heart. (op 12-1)
Baby Strange beat a subsequent winner last time but remained fairly treated. He soon tacked across to the nearside rails to track the leaders but could only stay on at the same pace. (op 14-1)
Irish Heartbeat(IRE) was a well-supported favourite but found little when push came to shove. (op 4-1)
Esprit De Midas did best of those racing on the unfavourable far side but could never get competitive. (op 66-1)
Thebes led the far-side group before weakening entering the final furlong.
Hawkeyethenoo(IRE) has been progressive this season but was another who could not land a blow on the far side before fading over a furlong out. Official explanation: trainer said gelding became upset in the stalls (op 9-4)
Oldjoesaid Official explanation: jockey said gelding became upset in stalls

4086 JOHN SMITH'S STAYERS H'CAP 1m 5f 9y
8:20 (8:20) (Class 4) (0-85,85) 3-Y-O+ **£5,180** (£1,541; £770; £384) **Stalls** High

Form RPR

6046 **1** **Bollin Felix**[15] 3588 6-9-7 78 (b) DavidAllan 7 88
(T D Easterby) *in tch: swtchd to stands' side over 4f out: effrt and rdn over 2f out: led ins fnl f: styd on wl* **3/1**[2]

6-33 **2** *1 ¼* **Lady Luachmhar (IRE)**[49] 2513 4-9-10 81 PaulHanagan 5 89
(R A Fahey) *t.k.h: hld up: swtchd to stands' side ent st: effrt over 2f out: styd on wl fnl f: tk 2nd cl home* **3/1**[2]

4010 **3** *hd* **Proud Times (USA)**[23] 3319 4-9-3 74 PJMcDonald 8 82
(G A Swinbank) *chsd ldrs: swtchd to stands' side over 3f out: led over 2f out to ins fnl f: kpt on same pce* **12/1**

0041 **4** *1* **Mister Angry (IRE)**[11] 3730 3-8-13 83 6ex JoeFanning 1 89
(M Johnston) *cl up: swtchd to stands' side over 4f out: effrt and ev ch over 2f out: kpt on same pce ins fnl f* **5/2**[1]

-465 **5** *13* **Grey Granite (IRE)**[23] 3329 4-9-4 75 LiamJones 11 62
(W Jarvis) *pressed ldr: led and styd far side over 4f out: hdd over 2f out: wknd wl over 1f out* **9/2**[3]

0060 **6** *3 ¾* **Wind Shuffle (GER)**[15] 3025 7-8-4 66 oh4 JamesSullivan(5) 3 47
(J S Goldie) *led to over 4f out: hung rt over 3f out: sn rdn and outpcd: btn fnl 2f* **25/1**

-055 **7** *nse* **Lochiel**[27] 3198 6-9-7 85 LeeTopliss(7) 6 66
(Mrs L B Normile) *hld up: swtchd to stands' side over 3f out: sn drvn and outpcd: n.d after* **14/1**

2m 53.58s (-0.32) **Going Correction** +0.15s/f (Good)
WFA 3 from 4yo+ 13lb 7 Ran SP% **115.0**
Speed ratings (Par 105): **106,105,105,104,96 94,94**
toteswingers: 1&2 £1.90, 1&3 £6.10, 2&3 £8.20. CSF £12.61 CT £91.95 TOTE £3.50: £1.10, £1.90; EX 15.20.
Owner Sir Neil Westbrook **Bred** Sir Neil & Exors Of Late Lady Westbrook **Trained** Great Habton, N Yorks

FOCUS
A competitive, if ordinary, handicap with the field spanning the width of the course soon after entering the straight but eventually the near side again prevailed.

4087 BULMERS H'CAP 1m 3f 16y
8:50 (8:50) (Class 6) (0-65,65) 3-Y-O **£2,266** (£674; £337; £168) **Stalls** High

Form RPR

656 **1** **Robbie Burnett**[45] 2627 3-9-1 59 PJMcDonald 3 66
(G A Swinbank) *trckd ldrs: effrt over 2f out: led appr fnl f: styd on strly* **9/1**

3542 **2** *3* **Sheiling (IRE)**[18] 3506 3-9-7 65 PaulHanagan 4 67
(R A Fahey) *led: rdn and edgd rt fr 4f out: hdd appr fnl f: kpt on: nt pce of wnr* **7/4**[1]

1324 **3** *nk* **Meetings Man (IRE)**[18] 3506 3-9-5 63 TomEaves 2 64
(Micky Hammond) *cl up: rdn over 2f out: hung rt: ev ch over 1f out: one pce ins fnl f* **7/2**[3]

6321 **4** 1 1/2 **Dubawi King**[17] 3532 3-8-13 **57** .... JoeFanning 5 55
(N Tinkler) *t.k.h: in tch: effrt over 2f out: ev ch over 1f out: no ex ins fnl f* **5/2**[2]

-000 **5** 3 1/4 **Star Of Kalani (IRE)**[17] 3532 3-8-2 **46** oh1 .... AndrewElliott 1 38
(R D Wylie) *t.k.h: in tch: rdn and outpcd over 3f out: rallied wl over 1f out: no imp* **25/1**

-002 **6** 15 **Reel Love**[11] 3728 3-7-11 **46** oh1 .... JamesSullivan(5) 6 11
(Mrs L Stubbs) *in tch: rdn over 3f out: wknd over 2f out* **8/1**

2m 28.0s (2.40) **Going Correction** +0.15s/f (Good) 6 Ran SP% **112.1**
Speed ratings (Par 98): **97,94,94,93,91 80**
toteswingers: 1&2 £4.00, 1&3 £5.50, 2&3 £1.60. CSF £25.24 TOTE £15.20: £6.10, £1.10; EX 27.90.
Owner Mrs Greta Sparks **Bred** The National Stud **Trained** Melsonby, N Yorks

FOCUS
A tight but relatively weak handicap run at a sound enough pace.
Robbie Burnett ◆ Official explanation: trainer's rep said, regarding apparent improvement in form, having missed the break on its previous start, the gelding was better suited by the step up in trip.
Dubawi King Official explanation: jockey said gelding hung badly left in straight

4088 BOOK NOW FOR LADIES NIGHT H'CAP (QUALIFIER FOR THE SCOTTISH TROPHY HANDICAP SERIES FINAL) 1m 1f 36y

9:20 (9:21) (Class 5) (0-70,70) 3-Y-0+ **£2,914** (£867; £433; £216) **Stalls** Low

Form RPR

2331 **1** **High Resolution**[1] 4061 3-8-7 **63** 6ex .... JamesSullivan(5) 1 72+
(Miss L A Perratt) *hld up in last pl: hdwy over 2f out: led over 1f out: kpt on wl fnl f: comf* **6/1**[3]

0502 **2** 1 **River Ardeche**[10] 3750 5-9-7 **70** .... LeeTopliss(7) 2 76
(B M R Haslam) *stdd in tch: effrt and hdwy over 3f out: kpt on u.p fnl f: nt rch wnr* **7/4**[1]

1526 **3** 3/4 **Finsbury**[15] 3582 7-9-8 **67** .... GaryBartley(3) 4 71
(Miss L A Perratt) *hld up: hdwy over 2f out: kpt on fnl f: nrst fin* **12/1**

0 **4** nk **Rare Malt (IRE)**[44] 2644 3-9-5 **70** .... (p) AndrewElliott 8 72
(Miss Amy Weaver) *chsd ldrs: wnt 2nd after 2f: drvn fr 4f out: rallied: kpt on same pce fnl f* **18/1**

0366 **5** 4 1/2 **King Of The Moors (USA)**[3] 3973 7-9-9 **68** ..... (b) AndrewHeffernan(3) 9 61
(R C Guest) *t.k.h: led: rdn over 2f out: hung rt and hdd over 1f out: sn btn* **6/1**[3]

522 **6** 6 **Nisaal (IRE)**[98] 1203 5-9-12 **68** .... (p) TomEaves 5 48
(J J Quinn) *hld up in tch: drvn and outpcd over 2f out: sn btn* **11/2**[2]

0054 **7** 8 **Wovoka (IRE)**[11] 3732 7-9-4 **65** .... (tp) AmyRyan(5) 7 28
(K A Ryan) *hld up in tch: hdwy over 3f out: wknd fr 2f out* **8/1**

0-65 **8** 7 **Silkenveil (IRE)**[49] 2497 3-8-8 **59** .... PaulHanagan 6 5
(R A Fahey) *t.k.h: chsd ldr 2f: cl up: outpcd whn hung rt and n.m.r briefly over 2f out: sn btn* **9/1**

2m 1.19s (1.49) **Going Correction** +0.15s/f (Good)
WFA 3 from 5yo+ 9lb 8 Ran SP% **114.4**
Speed ratings (Par 103): **99,98,97,97,93 87,80,74**
toteswingers: 1&2 £3.40, 1&3 £7.40, 2&3 £2.50. CSF £16.95 CT £121.98 TOTE £6.80: £1.50, £1.80, £3.30; EX 19.70 Place 6 £98.82; Place 5 £54.76.
Owner Mrs Helen Perratt **Bred** Old Mill Stud Ltd **Trained** East Kilbride, South Lanarks

FOCUS
A few with solid claims for this handicap run at good rattle.
Rare Malt(IRE) Official explanation: jockey said filly never travelled
T/Plt: £382.00 to a £1 stake. Pool:£49,249.35 - 94.11 winning tickets T/Qpdt: £86.10 to a £1 stake. Pool:£4,459.43 - 38.30 winning tickets RY

3670 HAYDOCK (L-H)

Friday, July 16

OFFICIAL GOING: 5f and 6f - good (9.2); 7f and 1m - good to soft; 1m 2f and 1m 6f - good to soft (good in places; 8.1)
Wind: moderate 1/2 against Weather: overcast

4089 ENTERPRISE MAIDEN STKS 7f 30y

2:20 (2:22) (Class 5) 2-Y-0 **£2,590** (£770; £385; £192) **Stalls** Low

Form RPR

1 **Silvertrees (IRE)** 2-9-3 0 .... PJMcDonald 2 81+
(G A Swinbank) *mde virtually all: styd on strly: readily* **5/1**[3]

2 1 1/4 **Splash Point (USA)** 2-9-3 0 .... RoystonFfrench 11 78+
(Mahmood Al Zarooni) *trckd ldrs: effrt over 3f out: chsd wnr fnl 2f: no real imp* **11/4**[1]

3 4 1/2 **Adlington** 2-9-3 0 .... TonyHamilton 3 67+
(R A Fahey) *trckd ldrs: t.k.h: styd on same pce fnl 2f* **4/1**[2]

4 9 **Supermarine** 2-9-3 0 .... PaulMulrennan 7 44
(J A Glover) *dwlt: sn trcking ldrs: wknd over 1f out* **16/1**

06 **5** 1/2 **Downtown Boy (IRE)**[27] 3222 2-9-3 0 .... AndrewMullen 9 43
(T P Tate) *w ldr: t.k.h: wknd over 1f out* **14/1**

0 **6** 1 1/2 **Suave Character**[16] 3555 2-9-3 0 .... SteveDrowne 4 39
(M Blanshard) *hld up in rr: hdwy and edgd rt over 2f out: nvr nr ldrs* **14/1**

7 1 **Byron Bear (IRE)** 2-9-3 0 .... PhillipMakin 12 37
(P T Midgley) *s.i.s: drvn over 3f out: kpt on on outside fnl 2f: nvr nr ldrs* **22/1**

00 **8** 1/2 **Indian Giver**[37] 2861 2-8-12 0 .... DavidAllan 13 30
(H A McWilliams) *in rr-div: hdwy on outside over 2f out: nvr nr ldrs* **125/1**

9 4 1/2 **Allegorio (FR)** 2-9-3 0 .... RichardKingscote 1 24
(Tom Dascombe) *dwlt: a towards rr* **10/1**

10 1/2 **Raphaeleyen** 2-9-3 0 .... DuranFentiman 6 23
(T D Walford) *dwlt: a in rr* **40/1**

11 2 1/2 **Climaxfortackle (IRE)** 2-8-9 0 .... MartinLane(3) 14 12
(D Shaw) *mid-div: drvn over 3f out: lost pl 2f out* **25/1**

12 nk **Hobbesian War** 2-9-3 0 .... MickyFenton 10 16
(T P Tate) *dwlt: drvn to sn chse ldrs: lost pl over 2f out* **8/1**

13 1 3/4 **Sandpipers Dream** 2-9-3 0 .... DanielTudhope 5 12
(T D Walford) *dwlt: a in rr* **14/1**

1m 35.98s (3.28) **Going Correction** +0.35s/f (Good) 13 Ran SP% **120.8**
Speed ratings (Par 94): **95,93,88,78,77 75,74,74,69,68 65,65,63**
toteswingers:1&2:£3.00, 1&3:£3.90, 2&3:£2.00 CSF £18.70 TOTE £7.20: £2.40, £1.80, £1.10; EX 18.40.
Owner Mrs I Gibson **Bred** Ben Sangster **Trained** Melsonby, N Yorks

FOCUS
Following 24mm of rain on Wednesday and 3mm of rain overnight, the going was given as good (5f & 6f), good to soft (7f &1m) and good to soft, good in places (1m2f and 1m6f). The three at the head of the betting came clear in this maiden and probably beat little, but the winner did it well.

NOTEBOOK
Silvertrees(IRE) was well backed, had a nice draw and got a good position early next to the rail. He always had things under control and saw his race out strongly. A half-brother to four-time winner Lap Of Honour, he should get another furlong in time. (op 9-1)
Splash Point(USA), who stood out in the paddock beforehand, ran well considering he was drawn out wider and forced to race around the outside of the pack into the straight. A 300,000gns purchase, he can go one better in similarly modest company. (op 3-1 tchd 5-2)
Adlington was also well drawn and, quickly away, tracked the winner on the rail. A half-brother to a couple of maidens, he ran well enough on his debut and might be able to find a little race. (op 7-2 tchd 9-2)
Supermarine, a half-brother to two 3-y-o winners, one over 6f and the other over 1m, showed up well to 2f out and is likely to improve for the run. (op 14-1)
Downtown Boy(IRE) might do better in nurseries. (tchd 16-1)
Suave Character didn't help his cause by once again racing keenly through the early stages. (op 25-1)

4090 ROTHWELL PLUMBING H'CAP 5f

2:55 (2:56) (Class 4) (0-80,80) 3-Y-0+ **£4,533** (£1,348; £674; £336) **Stalls** Centre

Form RPR

-340 **1** **Evelyn May (IRE)**[45] 2626 4-9-1 **69** .... RobertWinston 3 81
(B W Hills) *chsd ldr far side: led 1f out: kpt on wl* **20/1**

3201 **2** 1 1/4 **Brierty (IRE)**[7] 3879 4-9-2 **77** .... NeilFarley(7) 6 84
(D Carroll) *mid-div: gd hdwy 2f out: styd on to take 2nd nr fin* **13/2**

4-0 **3** nk **Avertor**[91] 1349 4-9-12 **80** .... SteveDrowne 4 86
(R Charlton) *dwlt: sn chsng ldrs: styd on ins fnl f* **3/1**[1]

-326 **4** 1 1/2 **Spring Green**[34] 2973 4-9-7 **75** .... JoeFanning 2 76
(H Morrison) *overall ldr far side: hdd 1f out: no ex* **10/1**

00 **5** 2 **Taurus Twins**[41] 2756 4-9-7 **75** .... (b) MickyFenton 14 68
(R J Price) *led gp of 4 on stands' side: kpt on same pce fnl f* **33/1**

2321 **6** nk **Hazelrigg (IRE)**[13] 3675 5-9-5 **73** .... (bt) DavidAllan 12 65
(T D Easterby) *hood removed v late: s.s: hdwy to chse ldrs stands' side over 2f out: kpt on same pce fnl f: 2nd of 4 that gp* **4/1**[2]

4041 **7** 1/2 **Sands Crooner (IRE)**[8] 3809 7-9-2 **70** 6ex .... (vt) PaulMulrennan 9 60
(J G Given) *mid-div: hung lft and sme hdwy over 1f out: nvr nr ldrs* **25/1**

-005 **8** 1/2 **Tyrannosaurus Rex (IRE)**[13] 3675 6-8-12 **69** .... GaryBartley(3) 7 58
(D Shaw) *mid-div: kpt on fnl 2f: nvr a threat* **25/1**

6013 **9** 2 **Make My Dream**[11] 3736 7-9-2 **73** .... MartinLane(3) 13 54
(J Gallagher) *racd stands' side: chsd ldr: edgd lft over 2f out: wknd over 1f out: 3rd of 4 that gp* **16/1**

-160 **10** 1/2 **Igoyougo**[51] 2431 4-9-10 **78** .... SilvestreDeSousa 8 58
(G A Harker) *mid-div: drvn over 2f out: nvr on terms* **6/1**[3]

2603 **11** 1/2 **Sir Geoffrey (IRE)**[17] 3540 4-9-5 **73** .... (b) PhillipMakin 5 51
(J A Glover) *chsd ldrs far side: wknd over 1f out* **20/1**

1205 **12** 1 1/2 **Highland Warrior**[7] 3879 11-8-13 **70** .... PaulPickard(3) 11 42
(P T Midgley) *a in rr* **28/1**

500 **13** 1 1/4 **Northern Dare (IRE)**[15] 3584 6-9-9 **77** .... (b) TonyHamilton 1 45
(R A Fahey) *s.i.s: sn chsng ldrs far side: reminders after 1f: lost pl over 1f out* **12/1**

2355 **14** 1 3/4 **Sulis Minerva (IRE)**[23] 3328 3-8-13 **71** .... (bt[1]) JamieSpencer 15 32
(J R Gask) *racd stands' side: chsd ldr: wknd 2f out: last of 4 that gp* **28/1**

0004 **15** 17 **Red Rosanna**[14] 3637 4-8-9 **63** .... (p) PaulQuinn 10 —
(R Hollinshead) *lost pl over 3f out: sn bhd: virtually p.u fnl f: t.o* **20/1**

61.42 secs (0.42) **Going Correction** +0.225s/f (Good)
WFA 3 from 4yo+ 4lb 15 Ran SP% **127.1**
Speed ratings (Par 105): **105,103,102,100,96 96,95,94,91,90 90,87,85,82,55**
toteswingers:1&2:£16.30, 1&3:£22.30, 2&3:£6.70 CSF £138.43 CT £518.93 TOTE £26.70: £5.90, £3.10, £2.40; EX 195.30.
Owner Mrs B W Hills **Bred** Mrs S Dutfield **Trained** Lambourn, Berks

FOCUS
The field was spread across the track, but those racing middle to far side dominated.
Evelyn May(IRE) Official explanation: trainer's rep said, regarding apparent improvement in form, that the filly was better suited by the good ground
Hazelrigg(IRE) Official explanation: jockey said gelding missed the break

4091 PARRY & COMPANY H'CAP 6f

3:30 (3:31) (Class 4) (0-85,84) 3-Y-0 **£4,533** (£1,348; £674; £336) **Stalls** Centre

Form RPR

3062 **1** **Gramercy (IRE)**[7] 3845 3-9-7 **84** .... JamieSpencer 1 99+
(M L W Bell) *swtchd rt s: pushed along in rr early: sn hld up: smooth hdwy 2f out: shkn up to ld 1f out: hung lft: rdn clr: eased towards fin* **6/4**[1]

1 **2** 3 3/4 **Supreme Spirit (IRE)**[30] 3091 3-8-12 **75** .... FrannyNorton 11 78
(D Nicholls) *t.k.h in rr: hdwy over 2f out: led appr fnl f: sn hdd and carried lft: styd on same pce* **12/1**

0-04 **3** 1 **Dancing Red Devil (IRE)**[7] 3856 3-8-4 **72** .... PatrickDonaghy(5) 5 72
(Paul Green) *swvd rt s: sn drvn along: hdwy over 2f out: kpt on fnl f* **25/1**

-016 **4** hd **Commanche Raider (IRE)**[28] 3151 3-9-1 **78** .... PhillipMakin 8 77
(M Dods) *hmpd s: hld up towards rr: nt clr run and swtchd rt over 1f out: r.o ins fnl f* **14/1**

6-63 **5** 1 1/2 **Walvis Bay (IRE)**[37] 2862 3-9-4 **81** .... MickyFenton 6 76+
(T P Tate) *hmpd s: sn chsng ldr: one pce whn hmpd jst ins fnl f: wknd fnl 75yds* **7/2**[2]

-056 **6** 1 **Tasmeem (IRE)**[13] 3673 3-9-2 **79** .... TonyHamilton 3 70
(R A Fahey) *chsd ldrs: one pce appr fnl f* **16/1**

3132 **7** 2 1/4 **Bonheurs Art (IRE)**[25] 3270 3-8-9 **72** .... RobertWinston 7 56
(B W Hills) *lft short of room s: chsd ldrs: wknd appr fnl f* **7/1**[3]

354 **8** 1/2 **Solstice**[27] 3225 3-9-2 **79** .... PaulMulrennan 10 62
(Julie Camacho) *led: swtchd far side after 1f: hdd & wknd appr fnl f* **14/1**

5100 **9** 7 **Belinsky (IRE)**[20] 3436 3-8-10 **73** .... J-PGuillambert 2 33
(N Tinkler) *prom: wknd over 1f out: eased whn bhd ins fnl f* **33/1**

3331 **10** 3/4 **Kakapuka**[20] 3436 3-9-0 **77** .... SteveDrowne 9 35
(Mrs A L M King) *sn pushed along in rr: rdn 2f out: sn bhd: eased ins fnl f* **8/1**

1m 13.85s (0.35) **Going Correction** +0.225s/f (Good) 10 Ran SP% **119.5**
Speed ratings (Par 102): **106,101,99,99,97 96,93,92,83,82**
toteswingers:1&2:£3.90, 1&3:£12.30, 2&3:£68.40 CSF £22.67 CT £346.07 TOTE £2.50: £1.10, £2.60, £5.00; EX 25.60.
Owner M B Hawtin **Bred** Michael Mullins **Trained** Newmarket, Suffolk

FOCUS
A fairly open handicap on paper, but it was taken apart by the winner. The whole field edged over to race centre to far side.
Bonheurs Art(IRE) Official explanation: trainer's rep said filly was unsuited by the good ground

Kakapuka Official explanation: trainer said colt lost a tooth in the stalls and a front shoe in running

4092 WHYTE & MACKAY H'CAP 1m 6f
4:05 (4:05) (Class 4) (0-85,84) 3-Y-O £4,533 (£1,348; £674; £336) Stalls Low

Form RPR
1132 1 **Comedy Act**[11] 3724 3-8-12 **75** PaulMulrennan 2 90
(Sir Mark Prescott) *mde all: qcknd over 6f out: edgd lft over 1f out: styd on wl* **4/1**[3]
5012 2 1 1/4 **Bowdler's Magic**[13] 3670 3-9-7 **84** JoeFanning 4 97
(M Johnston) *trckd wnr: effrt 4f out: styd on same pce ins fnl f* **10/11**[1]
-412 3 7 **Domination**[23] 3335 3-9-1 **78** RobertWinston 5 81
(H Morrison) *hld up in last: effrt 4f out: sn rdn: hung lft over 2f out: fdd appr fnl f* **2/1**[2]
0-54 4 22 **Straversjoy**[14] 3626 3-8-2 **65** oh17 PaulQuinn 1 37
(R Hollinshead) *dwlt: t.k.h: sn trcking ldrs: drvn 4f out: sn lost pl: bhd whn eased ins fnl f* **33/1**
2405 5 22 **Brooklands Bay (IRE)**[39] 2816 3-8-9 **72** TonyHamilton 6 14
(J R Weymes) *trckd ldrs: rdn 4f out: sn lost pl and bhd: eased fnl f* **25/1**
3m 5.18s (3.98) **Going Correction** +0.35s/f (Good) 5 Ran SP% **112.5**
Speed ratings (Par 102): **102,101,97,84,72**
CSF £8.37 TOTE £3.40: £1.30, £1.10; EX 10.10.
Owner Neil Greig - Osborne House **Bred** Floors Farming & The Duke Of Devonshire **Trained** Newmarket, Suffolk

4093 NEW PADDY POWER SHOP OPEN IN LIVERPOOL H'CAP 1m 30y
4:40 (4:41) (Class 5) (0-75,75) 3-Y-O+ £2,590 (£770; £385; £192) Stalls Low

Form RPR
0251 1 **One Scoop Or Two**[10] 3765 4-8-10 **57** 6ex RichardKingscote 10 66
(R Hollinshead) *hdwy to ld after 1f: rdn over 2f out: hung lft: hld on wl* **10/1**
0602 2 1 1/4 **Chosen Forever**[35] 2937 5-9-12 **73** DarryllHolland 5 79
(G R Oldroyd) *squeezed out s: hld up in rr: drvn and c stands' side over 3f out: wnt 2nd over 1f out: edgd rt and styd on same pce fnl f* **9/2**[3]
-300 3 1/2 **Arabian Spirit**[35] 2937 5-10-0 **75** TonyHamilton 1 80
(R A Fahey) *swvd rt s: sn chsng ldrs: drvn over 3f out: styd on same pce fnl f* **5/1**
0-53 4 4 **Rosko**[21] 3408 6-9-1 **69** DaleSwift(7) 8 65
(B Ellison) *sn chsng ldrs: drvn over 3f out: edgd rt: fdd appr fnl f* **11/4**[1]
554 5 2 1/2 **Roose Blox (IRE)**[27] 3220 3-9-3 **72** MickyFenton 6 60
(R F Fisher) *n.m.r s: hdwy to trck ldrs over 5f out: c wd: wknd over 1f out* **12/1**
4300 6 4 1/2 **Timber Treasure (USA)**[13] 3676 6-8-7 **59** PatrickDonaghy(5) 11 39
(Paul Green) *in rr: hdwy on outer over 3f out: edgd lft and wknd over 1f out* **40/1**
1661 7 3 **Sir Frank Wappat**[13] 3676 3-9-6 **75** JoeFanning 3 46
(M Johnston) *hmpd s: effrt 3f out: lost pl over 1f out* **3/1**[2]
6330 8 3 **Kings Point (IRE)**[17] 3537 9-9-6 **70** MichaelGeran(3) 7 36
(D Nicholls) *led 1f: chsd ldrs: wknd 2f out* **12/1**
0301 9 3 3/4 **Border Owl (IRE)**[11] 3732 5-9-5 **71** 6ex TobyAtkinson(5) 9 28
(P Salmon) *chsd ldrs: chal over 3f out: lost pl over 1f out* **12/1**
1m 47.89s (3.19) **Going Correction** +0.35s/f (Good)
WFA 3 from 4yo+ 8lb 9 Ran SP% **121.1**
Speed ratings (Par 103): **98,96,96,92,89 85,82,79,75**
toteswingers:1&2:£6.40, 1&3:£9.70, 2&3:£5.70 CSF £57.32 CT £261.33 TOTE £8.60: £1.70, £2.00, £2.90; EX 70.40.
Owner Showtime Ice Cream Concessionaire **Bred** S And R Ewart **Trained** Upper Longdon, Staffs
■ Stewards' Enquiry : Darryll Holland caution: used whip with excessive frequency.
FOCUS
An ordinary handicap.

4094 BETDAQ THE BETTING EXCHANGE APPRENTICE TRAINING SERIES H'CAP (RACING EXCELLENCE INITIATIVE) 1m 2f 95y
5:15 (5:15) (Class 5) (0-75,74) 4-Y-O+ £2,590 (£770; £385; £192) Stalls Centre

Form RPR
4110 1 **King Zeal (IRE)**[16] 3559 6-8-10 **63** JamesRogers(3) 1 70
(B D Leavy) *sn led: qcknd over 3f out: drvn along: styd on strly clsng stages* **9/4**[2]
1215 2 2 1/4 **Ghufa (IRE)**[14] 3618 6-9-5 **74** SophieSilvester(5) 4 77
(J Pearce) *hld up in tch: effrt on ins 3f out: chsd wnr over 1f out: kpt on same pce fnl 100yds* **9/4**[2]
2-30 3 2 **Cool Baranca (GER)**[14] 3627 4-9-9 **73** DebraEngland 3 72
(P Monteith) *sn chsng ldr: drvn over 2f out: kpt on same pce* **2/1**[1]
6660 4 11 **Ra Junior (USA)**[35] 2937 4-9-7 **71** JohnCavanagh 6 49
(D Nicholls) *wl away and led early: chsd ldrs: drvn over 3f out: wknd fnl 2f* **13/2**[3]
0060 5 53 **Pitbull**[32] 3025 7-8-2 **55** oh10 (b) MatthewLawson(3) 5 —
(A Berry) *t.k.h in last: rapid hdwy to chse ldrs over 4f out: drvn over 3f out: hung lft and lost pl over 2f out: sn bhd: virtually p.u: t.o* **25/1**
2m 19.43s (3.43) **Going Correction** +0.35s/f (Good) 5 Ran SP% **112.1**
Speed ratings (Par 103): **100,98,96,87,45**
CSF £7.89 TOTE £3.60: £3.80, £1.10; EX 5.20 Place 6 £39.99; Place 5 £27.98.
Owner Deborah Hart & Alan Jackson **Bred** Janus Bloodstock **Trained** Forsbrook, Staffs
FOCUS
A small field for this apprentice riders' handicap.
T/Plt: £24.60 to a £1 stake. Pool:£55,623.67 - 1,646.77 winning tickets T/Qpdt: £10.00 to a £1 stake. Pool:£3,724.28 - 273.60 winning tickets WG

3861 NEWBURY (L-H)
Friday, July 16

OFFICIAL GOING: Good (good to soft in places; 7.2)
Wind: Brisk across Weather: Showers

4095 HIGHCLERE THOROUGHBRED RACING E B F MAIDEN FILLIES' STKS 6f 8y
2:00 (2:02) (Class 4) 2-Y-O £5,180 (£1,541; £770; £384) Stalls Centre

Form RPR
0 1 **Celebrity**[24] 3296 2-9-0 0 RyanMoore 12 84+
(R Hannon) *trckd ldrs: drvn and qcknd to ld ins fnl f: rdn out* **9/2**[2]
2 2 1/2 **Sylvestris (IRE)** 2-9-0 0 JimCrowley 5 76+
(R M Beckett) *chsd ldrs: rdn and kpt on fr 2f out: tk 2nd fnl 120yds and kpt on but no ch w wnr* **12/1**
3 hd **Electra Star** 2-9-0 0 MichaelHills 3 76+
(W J Haggas) *in tch: drvn and styd on fr over 1f out: kpt on ins fnl f to press for 2nd cl home but no ch w wnr* **4/1**[1]
53 4 1 1/4 **Eshoog (IRE)**[15] 3590 2-9-0 0 NeilCallan 4 72
(C E Brittain) *slt ld: pushed along 2f out: rdn over 1f out: hdd ins fnl f: wknd fnl 100yds* **7/1**[3]
5 1/2 **Winter's Night (IRE)** 2-9-0 0 PhilipRobinson 9 71+
(C G Cox) *pushed along and outpcd fr 1/2-way: stl struggling 2f out: rdn and hdwy 1f out: fin wl* **22/1**
6 1/2 **Sadafiya** 2-9-0 0 RichardHills 11 69
(E A L Dunlop) *chsd ldrs: pushed along and green over 2f out: styd wl there tl wknd ins fnl f* **4/1**[1]
7 1/2 **Swift Bird (IRE)** 2-8-11 0 WilliamCarson(3) 6 68
(M G Quinlan) *pressed ldr: rdn over 2f out: wknd ins fnl f* **20/1**
8 1 **Picabo (IRE)** 2-9-0 0 HayleyTurner 2 65+
(Mrs L Wadham) *s.i.s: sn rcvrd and chsd ldrs: rdn 2f out: wknd fnl f* **20/1**
9 3/4 **Kalahaag (IRE)** 2-9-0 0 PatDobbs 13 65+
(R Hannon) *s.i.s: towards rr: pushed along and hdwy over 1f out: n.m.r: swtchd lft and styd on wl fnl 120yds* **28/1**
00 10 1 1/4 **Folly Drove**[24] 3296 2-9-0 0 (t) StephenCraine 1 59
(J G Portman) *chsd ldrs: rdn over 2f out: wknd over 1f out* **50/1**
0 11 1/2 **Red Lite (IRE)**[16] 3562 2-9-0 0 KierenFallon 8 57
(B J Meehan) *chsd ldrs: rdn and wknd ins fnl 2f* **25/1**
00 12 1 1/2 **Slumbering Sioux**[27] 3209 2-9-0 0 DavidProbert 15 53
(H J L Dunlop) *s.i.s: rcvrd into mid-div 1/2-way: sn rdn: no further prog* **50/1**
6 13 shd **Ponte Di Rosa**[24] 3296 2-9-0 0 FergusSweeney 18 52
(B G Powell) *chsd ldrs over 3f* **20/1**
14 shd **Chewdeh (USA)** 2-9-0 0 TadhgO'Shea 7 52
(J L Dunlop) *v.s.a: rcvrd into mid-div 1/2-way: sn wknd* **20/1**
15 1/2 **Queen O'The Desert (IRE)** 2-9-0 0 JimmyFortune 17 50
(A M Balding) *s.i.s: outpcd most of way* **16/1**
0 16 3 1/2 **Run Daisy Run**[10] 3769 2-9-0 0 TedDurcan 16 40
(B J Meehan) *outpcd fr 1/2-way* **66/1**
17 nk **Avon Causeway** 2-8-11 0 JackDean(3) 14 39
(J M Bradley) *outpcd* **100/1**
00 18 2 **Brandy Snap (IRE)**[55] 2330 2-9-0 0 FrankieMcDonald 10 33
(R Hannon) *spd to 1/2-way: lame* **80/1**
1m 15.89s (2.89) **Going Correction** +0.525s/f (Yiel) 18 Ran SP% **122.6**
Speed ratings (Par 93): **101,97,97,95,95 94,93,92,91,89 89,87,86,86,86 81,81,78**
toteswingers:1&2:£24.80, 1&3:£9.80, 2&3:£36.30 CSF £47.28 TOTE £5.20: £2.20, £4.50, £2.10; EX 76.30 TRIFECTA Not won..
Owner Kingwood Racing **Bred** The Kingwood Partnership **Trained** East Everleigh, Wilts
FOCUS
The most notable winner of this maiden in recent years was Silca's Sister, who took the Prix Morny next time and was fourth in the 1,000 Guineas. There is unlikely to have been anything of that calibre in the field this year, but the race should still provide winners. The winner built on her debut effort. The runners spread across the track and the winner ended up nearest the stands' rail, while the next two home raced on the far side of the pack.
NOTEBOOK
Celebrity ran out a fairly comfortable winner in the end, getting well on top after moving over to race against the rail in the final furlong. She had been green on her debut at Goodwood, when finishing two places behind Ponte Di Rosa, but was much more professional this time and the easier ground seemed to suit. Out of a half-sister to crack miler Excellent Art, she was dropping down in trip here but should get the seventh furlong in time. (op 5-1 tchd 6-1)
Sylvestris(IRE) was always towards the fore on the far side of the group and stuck on to shade second. Her yard is doing well with its 2-y-os and this half-sister to useful sprint juvenile Roof Fiddle should be placed to win before long. (op 14-1)
Electra Star, a half-sister to several winners including useful 2-y-o scorer Asia Winds, from the family of Dabaweyaa, was supported in the market. She came under pressure a quarter-mile out but stuck well to her task and just missed out on second. (tchd 7-2 and 9-2)
Eshoog(IRE) was one of the most experienced in the line-up, with two previous outings. She made much of the running, racing towards the outside before edging to her right and being worn down inside the final furlong. She is pacey and might well benefit from a drop back to 5f. (op 11-2 tchd 5-1)
Winter's Night(IRE) ◆, whose dam is a half-sister to the owner's smart sprinter Baron's Pit, shaped well. She was outpaced midway through the race before picking up nicely late on and coming home in good style. (op 20-1)
Sadafiya tracked the winner before coming through to pose a threat, but her lack of race experience then told and she faded out of the picture. The first foal of a Listed 2-y-o winner at this trip, she should know more next time. (op 9-2 tchd 7-2)
Swift Bird(IRE) showed pace for a long way before weakening. (op 25-1)
Picabo(IRE) ◆, a first ever juvenile runner for the yard, travelled strongly before fading and looks one to keep an eye on. (op 22-1 tchd 25-1)
Kalahaag(IRE) ◆, a stablemate of the winner who cost 50,000gns as a yearling, shaped with promise. She kept on very nicely from the rear without being subjected to a hard introduction and looks sure to improve considerably on the bare form. (op 33-1 tchd 25-1)
Folly Drove confirmed that she has ability and is now eligible for nurseries.
Red Lite(IRE) showed more than she had on her debut on sand. (op 28-1)
Chewdeh(USA), in the Hamdan Al Maktoum second colours, should come on for the experience. (op 16-1)
Brandy Snap(IRE) Official explanation: jockey said filly finished lame

4096 HIGHCLERE THOROUGHBRED RACING E B F MAIDEN STKS 7f (S)
2:35 (2:37) (Class 4) 2-Y-O £5,180 (£1,541; £770; £384) Stalls Centre

Form RPR
62 1 **Waiter's Dream**[19] 3472 2-9-3 0 KierenFallon 3 87+
(B J Meehan) *mde all: drvn clr over 1f out: readily* **7/2**[2]
3 2 4 **Tick Tock Lover**[23] 3326 2-9-3 0 FergusSweeney 7 77
(Miss Jo Crowley) *chsd ldrs: chsd wnr ins fnl 2f: kpt on fnl f but a readily hld* **11/1**
3 1/2 **Captain Bertie (IRE)** 2-9-3 0 MichaelHills 8 76+
(B W Hills) *hld up in rr and keen: n.m.r 3f out: hdwy on outside fr 2f out: str run ins fnl f fin fast* **16/1**
4 nk **Profondo Rosso (IRE)** 2-9-3 0 RyanMoore 18 75+
(Sir Michael Stoute) *in tch: pushed along over 2f: kpt on ins fnl f: gng on cl home* **8/1**
5 nse **Life And Times (USA)** 2-9-3 0 FrankieDettori 6 75
(Mahmood Al Zarooni) *s.i.s: sn in tch: pushed along over 2f out: kpt on same pce ins fnl f* **5/2**[1]
6 3/4 **Kingarrick** 2-9-3 0 PatDobbs 2 73
(Eve Johnson Houghton) *press ldrs: rdn 2f out: wknd fnl f* **66/1**
0 7 3 1/4 **Barathea Dancer (IRE)**[22] 3349 2-8-7 0 JohnFahy(5) 15 60
(R A Teal) *in tch: pushed along 3f out: wknd fr 2f out* **33/1**
8 3 3/4 **Moriarty (IRE)** 2-9-3 0 JimmyFortune 17 56
(R Hannon) *chsd ldrs: wnt 2nd and rdn 3f out tl ins fnl 2f: sn wknd* **15/2**[3]

9 1 1/4 **Korngold** 2-9-3 0 .... TedDurcan 1 62+
(J L Dunlop) *s.i.s: bhd: stdy hdwy over 1f out: kpt on ins fnl f but nvr a threat* **16/1**

10 1 1/4 **Young Sahib (USA)** 2-9-3 0 .... TadhgO'Shea 11 49
(B J Meehan) *s.i.s: in rr: swtchd lft to outside over 2f out: sme hdwy fnl f* **66/1**

11 3 1/2 **Invigilator** 2-9-3 0 .... GeorgeBaker 5 41
(H J L Dunlop) *rdn 1/2-way: nvr beyond mid-div* **33/1**

U6 12 1 1/2 **Blackleyf (IRE)**[11] 3721 2-9-3 0 .... RichardSmith 13 37
(Tom Dascombe) *chsd wnr tl ins fnl 3f: sn btn* **50/1**

13 hd **Aciano (IRE)** 2-9-3 0 .... RichardHills 12 36
(B J Meehan) *t.k.h: a towards rr* **12/1**

14 2 1/4 **Anton Dolin (IRE)** 2-9-3 0 .... JimmyQuinn 16 31
(J L Dunlop) *a in rr* **66/1**

15 nk **Luckyreno** 2-9-3 0 .... NeilCallan 4 30
(Sir Michael Stoute) *chsd ldrs: rdn 3f out: sn wknd* **28/1**

16 6 **Tony Hollis** 2-9-3 0 .... LiamKeniry 14 15
(B R Millman) *chsd ldrs 3f* **100/1**

17 26 **Endorser** 2-9-3 0 .... HayleyTurner 9 —
(W R Muir) *sn rdn: bhd fr 1/2-way* **40/1**

1m 29.51s (3.81) **Going Correction** +0.525s/f (Yiel) **17** Ran SP% **120.7**
Speed ratings (Par 96): **99,94,93,93,93 92,88,84,83,81 77,76,75,73,72 66,36**
toteswingers:1&2:£4.40, 1&3:£8.70, 2&3:£54.80 CSF £38.46 TOTE £4.00: £1.60, £2.70, £4.20; EX 29.70 Trifecta £238.30 Pool: £415.50 - 1.29 winning units..
Owner R P Foden **Bred** Ridgecourt Stud **Trained** Manton, Wilts

FOCUS
Plenty of big stables were represented in this maiden, won last year by subsequent Group 3 scorer Emerald Commander. Only four of this year's line-up had previous experience and they included the first two home. The winner did it well and several of those close up in behind showed considerable promise. The runner-up helps with the form.

NOTEBOOK
Waiter's Dream, a close second to a Hannon newcomer on debut at Salisbury, put his experience to full use and ran out a clear-cut winner. He was drawn in stall three, but showed bright pace and Kieren Fallon was able to get his mount over to the stands' rail by the two pole. The colt drew right away and, highly regarded in his yard, he will try his luck in better company next time. (op 10-3 tchd 4-1)
Tick Tock Lover, third on his debut on Kempton's Polytrack, ran another race full of promise despite taking a keen hold through the early stages. He could not prevent the winner from pulling clear but a maiden victory should be a formality. (op 8-1)
Captain Bertie(IRE) ◆, a half-brother to 7f 2-y-o winner Amazing Star, from the family of Sueboog, made a very taking debut, still only eighth passing the furlong pole before running on strongly. He is another who should have no trouble collecting that initial win.
Profondo Rosso(IRE) ◆ is a half-brother to the useful Red Dune from the female line of Islington and Hellenic. After being switched away from the rail for a clear passage, he came home nicely and he will certainly have learned from this. He should get 1m.
Life And Times(USA) is out of a half-sister to some high-class French performers and cost 70,000gns as a yearling. He raced on the far side of the pack and, only fading out of a frame finish late on, showed more than enough to suggest he will be winning races. (op 7-2)
Kingarrick showed up well before fading and it may be significant that his half-brother won a maiden second time out for the yard.
Barathea Dancer(IRE), the only filly in the libe up, had also finished seventh on her debut at Goodwood. She has ability but perhaps holds this form down a little. (op 40-1)
Moriarty(IRE), a 52,000gns newcomer from the Richard Hannon yard, was soon prominent and still showed in third place a furlong or so out before weakening. It would be foolish to write him off. (op 8-1)
Korngold, a half-brother to November Handicap winner Charm School, shaped with a bit of promise. (op 12-1)

4097 ROSE BOWL STKS - SPONSORED BY COMPTON BEAUCHAMP ESTATES LTD (LISTED RACE) 6f 8y
3:10 (3:10) (Class 1) 2-Y-O
£14,192 (£5,380; £2,692; £1,342; £672; £337) **Stalls** Centre

Form RPR

310 1 **Al Aasifh (IRE)**[29] 3100 2-9-0 0 .... FrankieDettori 1 104+
(Saeed Bin Suroor) *in tch towards centre of crse: styd on wl fr over 1f out to chse ldr: qcknd to ld fnl 120yds: comf* **2/1**[1]

113 2 1/2 **Cape To Rio (IRE)**[50] 2468 2-9-0 0 .... RyanMoore 6 103+
(R Hannon) *trckd ldr tl led wl over 1f out: sn rdn: hdd and outpcd fnl 120yds* **5/2**[2]

21 3 6 **Sir Reginald**[34] 2980 2-9-0 0 .... KierenFallon 8 85
(R A Fahey) *led on stands' rail: rdn and hdd wl over 1f out: sn outpcd by ldng duo but kpt on for clr 3rd* **5/1**[3]

11 4 2 1/2 **Bahceli (IRE)**[65] 2032 2-9-0 0 .... PatDobbs 7 77
(R Hannon) *towards rr and pushed along 2f out: styd on same pce* **7/1**

6021 5 2 3/4 **Sonoran Sands (IRE)**[12] 3712 2-9-0 0 .... LiamKeniry 2 69
(J S Moore) *chsd ldrs: rdn and wknd 2f out: no ch whn hung lft ins fnl f* **25/1**

4315 6 3/4 **Emma's Gift (IRE)**[28] 3141 2-8-9 0 .... JimmyQuinn 4 62
(Miss J Feilden) *s.i.s: in tch tl rdn and btn 2f out* **13/2**

3101 7 15 **Black Moth (IRE)**[14] 3611 2-9-0 0 .... (b) JimmyFortune 5 22
(B J Meehan) *stdd s: plld hrd and sn chsng ldr: wknd qckly ins fnl 2f* **12/1**

513 8 3 3/4 **Minch Man**[18] 3504 2-9-0 0 .... JimCrowley 3 10
(J R Weymes) *chsd ldrs over 3f: sn bhd* **33/1**

1m 15.74s (2.74) **Going Correction** +0.525s/f (Yiel) **8** Ran SP% **118.9**
Speed ratings (Par 102): **102,101,93,90,86 85,65,60**
toteswingers:1&2:£1.70, 1&3:£3.20, 2&3:£2.70 CSF £7.54 TOTE £2.90: £1.50, £1.30, £1.70; EX 8.70 Trifecta £27.70 Pool: £873.79 - 23.34 winning units..
Owner Godolphin **Bred** Rockfield Farm **Trained** Newmarket, Suffolk

FOCUS
A good edition of this event, which has not always proved the strongest of Listed races. The whole field tacked towards the stands' rail but the winner raced on the outer of the bunch and rather scotched the theory that the centre of the track was disadvantaged. The first two pulled clear and the form could be rated up to 6lb higher.

NOTEBOOK
Al Aasifh(IRE) found himself rather isolated with 2f or so to run, but he knuckled down well to collar the leader inside the last and win with a bit in hand. After landing his maiden by 7l at Haydock, quicker ground combined with the drop in trip did for him in the Norfolk Stakes at Ascot, but he had his optimum conditions here. He will step up to a Group race now and is in the Gimcrack. (op 3-1 tchd 7-2 and 4-1 in a place)
Cape To Rio(IRE)'s stable had won this event four times in the last six runnings, including with Duplicity a year ago. Stepping up in trip after finishing third in this grade at Sandown, he looked to be moving well when taking it up but he drifted away from the rail inside the final furlong and gave the winner something to run at, eventually being beaten more comfortably than the margin might suggest. It was a good effort to pull so far clear of the rest, though. (tchd 9-4 and 11-4)
Sir Reginald quickly secured the rail and set the pace until the runner-up went by. He finished well held back in third but is a useful colt and this has secured him some black type. (tchd 11-2)
Bahceli(IRE) was unbeaten in two prior starts but had been off the track for two months. After tracking the third near the fence, he was left behind by the principals when the race developed. His effectiveness at this trip remains unproven, in softish ground at any rate. (tchd 6-1)
Sonoran Sands(IRE) landed the odds on firm ground at Brighton and ran only respectably back in this grade under different underfoot conditions. He was one of the first to be brought under pressure but did stay on past toiling rivals and might be ready for 7f now.
Emma's Gift(IRE) was found wanting against the colts and it could be that she was flattered by her improved effort in the Albany Stakes at Ascot, where she was first home on the far side. (tchd 6-1)
Black Moth(IRE), over 4l behind Al Aasifh in the Norfolk, won grittily in blinkers at Beverley but was much too free in the headgear here, pulling his way up to dispute the lead before running out of gas. The ground was not ideal for him either. Official explanation: jockey said colt ran too free (op 11-1)

4098 SMITH & WILLIAMSON FILLIES' H'CAP 1m 2f 6y
3:45 (3:45) (Class 4) (0-80,80) 3-Y-O **£4,857** (£1,445; £722; £360) **Stalls** Low

Form RPR

-034 1 **Madhaaq (IRE)**[42] 2718 3-9-0 73 .... TadhgO'Shea 9 87+
(J L Dunlop) *hld up towards rr: stdy hdwy to ld ins fnl 2f: clr fnl f: easily* **7/1**

-621 2 4 1/2 **Ice Diva**[59] 2219 3-9-4 77 .... TonyCulhane 1 82
(P W D'Arcy) *trckd ldrs: wnt 2nd 3f out: sn rdn: chsd wnr fnl f but nvr any ch* **4/1**[2]

06-1 3 3 3/4 **Love Action (IRE)**[67] 1975 3-9-1 77 .... PatrickHills(3) 8 75
(R Hannon) *in rr: pushed along and hdwy over 2f out: styd on u.p to take wl hld 3rd ins fnl f* **9/1**

-214 4 2 **Centime**[25] 3268 3-8-10 69 .... JimmyFortune 2 63
(B J Meehan) *chsd ldrs: drivem along over 2f out: wknd wl over 1f out* **9/2**[3]

0-53 5 3/4 **Treasure Way**[33] 2998 3-8-11 70 .... LiamKeniry 7 62
(P R Chamings) *led tl hdd ins fnl 2f: no ch w wnr over 1f out: hung lft and wknd ins fnl f* **15/2**

6-21 6 7 **Mazamorra (USA)**[28] 3157 3-9-3 76 .... RyanMoore 4 54
(M Botti) *chsd ldr: rdn 3f out and sn wknd* **9/4**[1]

5000 7 4 **Silver Symphony (IRE)**[7] 3866 3-8-11 70 .... JimCrowley 10 40
(P F I Cole) *hld up in rr: sme hdwy to get into contention 3f out: sn wknd* **33/1**

415 8 13 **Bakongo (IRE)**[50] 2479 3-9-4 77 .... HayleyTurner 6 21
(M L W Bell) *in rr tl hdwy to get into contention 3f out: sn rdn and wknd* **9/1**

2m 11.04s (2.24) **Going Correction** +0.20s/f (Good) **8** Ran SP% **116.2**
Speed ratings (Par 99): **99,95,92,90,90 84,81,71**
toteswingers:1&2:£9.30, 1&3:£13.50, 2&3:£5.50 CSF £35.68 CT £256.84 TOTE £6.60: £1.80, £1.80, £2.10; EX 46.90 Trifecta £149.00 Pool: £463.34 - 2.30 winning units..
Owner Hamdan Al Maktoum **Bred** Shadwell Estate Company Limited **Trained** Arundel, W Sussex

FOCUS
Rail alignments meant races on the round course were run over 25 yards further than usual. This was just a fair fillies' handicap. Despite going only a steady pace they finished strung out, after coming down the centre of the course in the straight. The time was over eight seconds outside the standard.

4099 TKP SURFACING H'CAP 5f 34y
4:20 (4:20) (Class 5) (0-70,70) 3-Y-O+ **£3,238** (£963; £481; £240) **Stalls** Centre

Form RPR

030 1 **Blessed Place**[13] 3687 10-8-1 51 oh5 .... JohnFahy(5) 1 62
(D J S Ffrench Davis) *taken to r alone far side and sn clr: rdn and hld on wl fnl f: unchal* **12/1**

0-32 2 1 1/2 **Volito**[11] 3722 4-9-5 64 .... GeorgeBaker 4 70
(Jonjo O'Neill) *stdd s: in rr tl hdwy on outside fr 2f out on stands' side: led that gp and hung rt fr over 1f out and led that gp but no imp on wnr far side* **10/3**[2]

615 3 1 1/2 **Doctor Hilary**[20] 3463 8-9-7 66 .... (v) JimCrowley 5 67
(M R Hoad) *led stands' side gp but nvr on terms w wnr far side: lost 2nd over 1f out: styd on same pce* **11/1**

4004 4 nk **Silvee**[9] 3786 3-8-6 55 .... NeilChalmers 3 54
(J J Bridger) *chsd ldrs stands' side: nvr on terms w wnr far side: carried rt appr fnl f and sn outpcd* **25/1**

4366 5 3/4 **The Tatling (IRE)**[4] 3958 13-9-7 69 .... JackDean(3) 7 66+
(J M Bradley) *hld up in rr: racd stands' side: nt clr run 2f out: hdwy whn hmpd on stands' side appr fnl f: swtchd lft and kpt on but nvr any ch w wnr on far side* **14/1**

6424 6 3/4 **Peopleton Brook**[1] 4071 8-8-13 58 .... (t) KierenFallon 9 52+
(B G Powell) *in rr: hdwy and hmpd stands' side appr fnl f: swtchd lft and kpt on but no ch w wnr far side* **15/2**[3]

5640 7 1/2 **The Jobber (IRE)**[45] 2622 9-9-11 70 .... FergusSweeney 8 62
(M Blanshard) *chsd ldrs stands' side: rdn over 1f out: wknd ins fnl f* **12/1**

-362 8 3 **Pragmatist**[6] 3914 6-9-3 62 .... RyanMoore 2 44
(B R Millman) *chsd ldrs stands' side: wknd over 1f out: eased whn no ch ins fnl f* **2/1**[1]

00-3 9 3 1/2 **Rebecca Romero**[32] 3030 3-8-2 51 oh4 .... CathyGannon 6 19
(D J Coakley) *chsd ldrs stands' side: u.p whn bdly hmpd and lost pl appr fnl f* **15/2**[3]

64.49 secs (3.09) **Going Correction** +0.525s/f (Yiel)
WFA 3 from 4yo+ 4lb **9** Ran SP% **114.2**
Speed ratings (Par 103): **96,93,91,90,89 88,87,82,77**
toteswingers:1&2:£10.00, 1&3:£16.20, 2&3:£8.40 CSF £51.32 CT £462.80 TOTE £15.40: £3.90, £1.50, £3.60; EX 75.90 Trifecta £593.50 Part won. Pool: £802.15 - 0.10 winning units..
Owner S J Edwards **Bred** Mrs W H Gibson Fleming **Trained** Lambourn, Berks
■ Stewards' Enquiry : George Baker three-day ban: careless riding (Jul 30,Aug 1-2)

FOCUS
A modest handicap in which the winner ploughed a lone furrow while the remainder congregated on the stands' side.
The Tatling(IRE) Official explanation: jockey said gelding was denied a clear run
Pragmatist Official explanation: vet said mare had been struck into left-hind

4100 SHADWELL "STANDING FOR SUCCESS" H'CAP 1m 2f 6y
4:55 (4:55) (Class 3) (0-95,95) 3-Y-O+
£6,231 (£1,866; £933; £467; £233; £117) **Stalls** Low

Form RPR

412 1 **Emerging Artist (FR)**[7] 3877 4-9-5 86 .... FrankieDettori 2 99+
(M Johnston) *chsd ldrs: chal and wnt 2nd 3f out: drvn and qcknd to ld over 1f out: rdn ins fnl f: won gng away* **11/4**[1]

31-1 2 1 3/4 **Con Artist (IRE)**[19] 3481 3-8-6 83 .... TedDurcan 10 93+
(Saeed Bin Suroor) *chsd ldr: led ins fnl 4f: rdn 2f out: hdd over 1f out: no ex u.p ins fnl f* **7/2**[2]

-212 **3** 1 1/4 **Grey Bunting**[23] 3337 3-8-5 **82** .... JimmyQuinn 7 89
(B W Hills) *chsd ldrs: rdn along fr 3f out: styd on u.p for 3rd fnl f but no imp on ldng duo* **6/1**[3]

2635 **4** 3/4 **Changing The Guard**[14] 3627 4-9-1 **82** .... PatDobbs 3 88
(R A Fahey) *t.k.h: towards rr: hdwy and n.m.r over 2f out: styd on fnl f but nvr gng pce to rch ldrs* **12/1**

5515 **5** 1 1/2 **Reve De Nuit (USA)**[13] 3672 4-9-8 **89** .... JamesDoyle 1 92
(A J McCabe) *in tch: chsd ldrs and rdn over 3f out: wknd appr fnl f* **10/1**

6260 **6** 3/4 **Sohcahtoa (IRE)**[44] 2640 4-9-6 **87** .... RyanMoore 8 88
(R Hannon) *in rr: rdn along fr 3f out: sme prog ins fnl f* **16/1**

2204 **7** hd **Safari Sunup (IRE)**[14] 3633 5-9-9 **95** ....(p) AshleyMorgan(5) 4 96
(P Winkworth) *chsd ldrs: rdn 3f out: wknd over 1f out* **16/1**

3212 **8** 5 **Major Phil (IRE)**[23] 3318 4-9-7 **88** .... KierenFallon 5 79
(L M Cumani) *t.k.h and hld up in rr: hdwy fr 2f out: styd on fnl f but nvr a threat* **6/1**[3]

060/ **9** 9 **Strategic Mission (IRE)**[720] 4404 5-9-4 **85** .... JimCrowley 13 58
(P F I Cole) *rdn 3f out: a in rr* **20/1**

1250 **10** 1 **Officer In Command (USA)**[25] 3265 4-8-9 **76** .... LiamKeniry 9 47
(J S Moore) *chsd ldrs: rdn 3f out: wknd qckly 2f out: eased whn no ch* **66/1**

3-00 **11** 1 1/4 **Wing Play (IRE)**[14] 3627 5-9-2 **83** ....(p) HayleyTurner 12 51
(H Morrison) *slowly away: in rr: sme prog on ins 3f out: sn rdn and wknd* **20/1**

101- **12** 1 **Braveheart Move (IRE)**[135] 6138 4-10-0 **95** .... JimmyFortune 6 61
(Jonjo O'Neill) *led tl hdd ins fnl 4f: wknd 3f out* **33/1**

6030 **13** 1 3/4 **Donaldson (GER)**[64] 2044 8-9-4 **85** .... GeorgeBaker 11 48
(Jonjo O'Neill) *in tch to 1/2-way* **66/1**

2m 11.2s (2.40) **Going Correction** +0.20s/f (Good)
WFA 3 from 4yo+ 10lb **13** Ran SP% **121.5**
Speed ratings (Par 107): **98,96,95,95,93 93,93,89,81,81 80,79,77**
toteswingers:1&2:£3.50, 1&3:£6.10, 2&3:£5.50 CSF £11.50 CT £54.42 TOTE £3.80: £1.90, £1.90, £1.90; EX 11.50 Trifecta £56.20 Pool: £966.91 - 12.72 winning units..
Owner Sheikh Hamdan Bin Mohammed Al Maktoum **Bred** Gainsborough Stud Management Ltd **Trained** Middleham Moor, N Yorks

FOCUS
A decent handicap. The pace was fairly steady and not many got involved. They raced closer to the inside rail than the runners in the fillies' handicap had. The first two came clear and are progressive types, and the form looks solid enough despite the lack of a true gallop.

NOTEBOOK
Emerging Artist(FR) only made his debut last month but he is improving all the time, and lost nothing in defeat to La De Two at York latest. The runner-up appeared to be going better than him with a quarter of a mile left, but his stamina then began to kick in and he came away to win in very pleasing style. He will be suited by a return to 1m4f and might well get a bit further still. (op 5-2 tchd 9-4 and 3-1 in places)
Con Artist(IRE), from the stable of La De Two, only went up 3lb for his win at Windsor last time, where he had made all. After tracking the leader he went on half a mile out and was going best with two furlongs left, but the winner stayed on the stronger from that point. He should continue to go the right way. (op 11-2)
Grey Bunting was outpaced by the leading pair in the straight but stayed on for third. This was a respectable effort off a 5lb higher mark against a couple of progressive types. (op 7-1)
Changing The Guard kept on from out of the pack for fourth, but although he is gradually edging down the weights he gives the impression that he remains a shade high in the handicap. (tchd 16-1)
Reve De Nuit(USA) ran his race but is another who may be held by the handicapper. (op 9-1)
Sohcahtoa(IRE) ran a better race with the headgear removed, keeping on from the rear, but is essentially a frustrating individual. (tchd 18-1)
Safari Sunup(IRE) had cheekpieces on for the first time and again ran his race, but he is hard to place successfully. He was third in this a year ago. (op 14-1)
Major Phil(IRE) was expected to relish the step up to 1m2f, but he could never get into the race from off the steady gallop. He is worth another chance to prove himself at this trip. (op 5-1)

4101 BOB MOTTRAM MEMORIAL APPRENTICE H'CAP — 1m 3f 5y
5:30 (5:31) (Class 5) (0-75,74) 4-Y-O+ £2,590 (£770; £385; £192) Stalls Low

Form RPR

-504 **1** **Straight Laced**[37] 2870 4-8-5 **55** oh2........(v) HarryBentley 3 65
(W J Knight) *chsd ldr: rdn and hung lft fr 2f out: led jst ins fnl f: drvn out* **9/2**

41-0 **2** 4 **Laish Ya Hajar (IRE)**[21] 3416 6-9-5 **74** .... MatthewCosham(5) 5 77
(P R Webber) *led: rdn fr 3f out: hdd and no ex fr ins fnl f: sn btn* **10/1**

6625 **3** 6 **Admirable Duque (IRE)**[13] 3688 4-9-4 **73** .... LewisWalsh(5) 4 65
(D J S Ffrench Davis) *towards rr: hdwy on outside fr 3f out to take 3rd ins fnl 2f but nvr any ch w ldng duo* **5/2**[1]

1163 **4** 1 **Mountain Forest (GER)**[30] 3084 4-8-5 **55** .... NathanAlison 1 45
(H Morrison) *chsd ldrs: rdn to take 3rd 3f out: wknd ins fnl 2f* **3/1**[2]

4-16 **5** 3 **Ebiayn (FR)**[18] 3512 4-9-9 **73** .... RichardRowe 6 58
(A King) *chsd ldrs: rdn 4f out: wknd 3f out* **10/1**

6316 **6** 4 **Sgt Schultz (IRE)**[7] 3847 7-9-5 **69** .... HollyHall 2 47
(J S Moore) *in rr: sme prog 3f out: wknd sn after* **7/2**[3]

2m 25.61s (4.41) **Going Correction** +0.20s/f (Good) **6** Ran SP% **112.2**
Speed ratings (Par 103): **91,88,83,83,80 77**
toteswingers:1&2:£5.80, 1&3:£2.80, 2&3:£4.40 CSF £44.68 TOTE £4.60: £1.60, £4.80; EX 22.70 Place 6 £91.34; Place 5 £44.24.
Owner Mrs P A Cooke **Bred** Wrottesley Limited **Trained** Patching, W Sussex
■ Stewards' Enquiry : Matthew Cosham three-day ban: used whip with excessive force above shoulder height (tbn)

FOCUS
A very modest apprentice handicap but the pace was reasonable. It was hard work up the straight and they finished strung out.
T/Jkpt: Not won. T/Plt: £58.00 to a £1 stake. Pool:£67,561.96 - 850.05 winning tickets T/Qpdt: £9.80 to a £1 stake. Pool:£5,294.45 - 397.90 winning tickets ST

3867 NEWMARKET (July Course) (R-H)
Friday, July 16

OFFICIAL GOING: Good to firm
Wind: Strong half-behind Weather: Sunny

4102 TURFTV H'CAP — 1m 2f
5:50 (5:54) (Class 5) (0-70,70) 3-Y-O+ £3,238 (£963; £481; £240) Stalls Centre

Form RPR

2532 **1** **Sunley Spinalonga**[4] 3963 3-8-10 **62** .... PhilipRobinson 11 69
(D R C Elsworth) *chsd ldr: led over 2f out: rdn: edgd lft and hdd wl ins fnl f: rallied to ld post* **11/8**[1]

2000 **2** hd **Laconicos (IRE)**[32] 3028 8-8-8 **57** ....(t) LauraPike(7) 2 64
(W B Stone) *a.p: chsd wnr over 1f out: rdn to ld and edgd rt wl ins fnl f: hdd post* **11/1**

4063 **3** 4 1/2 **Orpen Wide (IRE)**[6] 3912 8-9-2 **61** ....(b) RobertLButler(3) 10 59
(M C Chapman) *led: hdd over 2f out: wknd ins fnl f* **10/1**

4-60 **4** 1 1/2 **Coiled Spring**[38] 2845 4-9-9 **70** ....(p) SimonPearce(5) 1 65
(Mrs A J Perrett) *chsd ldrs: rdn over 1f out: wknd fnl f* **6/1**[3]

0025 **5** 1/2 **Folio (IRE)**[21] 3416 10-9-5 **61** .... TomQueally 9 55
(W J Musson) *hld up: hdwy 2f out: rdn over 1f out: wknd ins fnl f* **9/2**[2]

5114 **6** nk **Sacrilege**[6] 3912 5-9-9 **70** ....(p) MarkCoumbe(5) 7 63
(M C Chapman) *rel to r and sn wl bhd: clsd on to the rr of the field over 7f out: rdn over 2f out: no rspnse* **14/1**

112 **7** 1 1/2 **Iceman George**[15] 3608 6-9-6 **62** ....(v) ShaneKelly 8 52
(G C Bravery) *prom: rdn over 2f out: wknd over 1f out* **6/1**[3]

2m 6.50s (1.00) **Going Correction** +0.15s/f (Good)
WFA 3 from 4yo+ 10lb **7** Ran SP% **112.9**
Speed ratings (Par 103): **102,101,98,97,96 96,95**
toteswingers: 1&2 £7.10, 1&3 £4.00, 2&3 £15.80. CSF £17.54 CT £108.79 TOTE £2.70: £1.70, £6.00; EX 23.10.
Owner Sunley, Heaney & Elsworth **Bred** Sunley Stud **Trained** Newmarket, Suffolk

FOCUS
The whole course was watered in the morning with 5mm applied. The jockeys returned from the first to confirm the ground was riding as per the going description with a couple noting there was a decent covering of grass. There was a strong cross-wind, stemming from the jockeys' right. This was a modest contest run only at a steady pace and there are likely to be few winners coming from it.

4103 TYRRELL AND COMPANY MAIDEN FILLIES' STKS — 7f
6:20 (6:23) (Class 4) 2-Y-O £4,533 (£1,348; £674; £336) Stalls Low

Form RPR

1 **Sunset Avenue (USA)** 2-9-0 0 .... TedDurcan 2 80+
(Mahmood Al Zarooni) *str: lw: prom: nt clr run and lost pl 1/2-way: hdwy over 1f out: r.o to ld wl ins fnl f* **11/2**[3]

2 1 **Azzoom (IRE)** 2-9-0 0 .... NeilCallan 7 78
(C E Brittain) *unf: a.p: led 2f out: sn rdn: hdd and unable qck wl ins fnl f* **11/1**

3 1 3/4 **Native Picture (IRE)** 2-9-0 0 .... RyanMoore 6 73
(R Hannon) *w'like: neat: lw: hld up: hdwy 1/2-way: rdn over 1f out: styng on same pce whn hung rt ins fnl f* **4/1**[2]

0 **4** 2 **Fastada (IRE)**[55] 2338 2-9-0 0 .... JimCrowley 3 68
(J G Portman) *led to 1/2-way: outpcd over 2f out: r.o ins fnl f* **16/1**

5 nse **Renoir's Lady** 2-9-0 0 .... StephenCraine 1 68+
(S Dow) *w'like: scope: w ldr tl outpcd 1/2-way: rallied over 1f out: r.o* **20/1**

6 3 3/4 **Panoptic** 2-9-0 0 .... TomQueally 10 59+
(H R A Cecil) *w'like: hld up in tch: plld hrd: led 1/2-way: hdd 2f out: hung rt and wknd ins fnl f* **11/10**[1]

7 hd **Miss Chicane** 2-9-0 0 .... ShaneKelly 9 58
(W R Swinburn) *w'like: bit bkwd: s.i.s and hmpd s: sn pushed along in rr: hung lft over 1f out: nvr on terms* **14/1**

0 **8** 6 **Bishops Moon**[95] 1256 2-8-11 0 .... WilliamCarson(3) 5 43
(M G Quinlan) *hld up in tch: plld hrd: rdn and wkng whn hung lft over 1f out* **22/1**

9 2 1/2 **Sheedal (IRE)** 2-8-9 0 .... SimonPearce(5) 8 37
(W G Harrison) *unf: scope: bit bkwd: edgd rt s: a bhd* **66/1**

000 **10** 5 **Dallas Legend (IRE)**[9] 3778 2-8-9 0 .... SophieDoyle(5) 4 24
(J Ryan) *w ldrs 3f: wknd over 2f out* **66/1**

1m 29.01s (3.31) **Going Correction** +0.15s/f (Good) **10** Ran SP% **116.0**
Speed ratings (Par 93): **87,85,83,81,81 77,77,70,67,61**
toteswingers: 1&2 £10.40, 1&3 £2.60, 2&3 £9.60. CSF £60.55 TOTE £6.10: £1.60, £2.90, £1.60; EX 61.80.
Owner Godolphin **Bred** Darley **Trained** Newmarket, Suffolk

FOCUS
On paddock inspection, this didn't appear the strongest of maidens for the course and the time was considerably beyond standard.

NOTEBOOK
Sunset Avenue(USA) stood out in the preliminaries as she appeared to possess considerably more scope than most of her rivals. She is not the finished article, which makes her debut effort all the more pleasing, especially when the amount of ground she made up late on is taken into account. With over 2f to run she was under pressure and looked unlikely to trouble the trio ahead of her, but she really got the hang of things late on, sticking her neck out and powering home to score in taking fashion. She is quite well bred and looks sure to get 1m this year. (op 6-1 tchd 13-2)
Azzoom(IRE), a half-sister to the very smart Levera, looked fit enough and appeared to have the race won upon mastering Panoptic. She simply wasn't able to cope with Sunset Avenue's late flourish but there is at least a maiden to be won with her this season. (op 12-1 tchd 9-1)
Native Picture(IRE) hails from a speedy family and is a half-sister to Kingsgate Native. A racey type, she is entitled to improve for her debut and can add to the vast tally of juvenile winners from her yard. (op 7-2 tchd 11-4)
Fastada(IRE) has plenty of stamina on the dam's side and the way she stayed on was encouraging for the long term. (op 20-1)
Panoptic, the short-priced favourite, must have shown plenty at home but did herself no favours by running too free and failed to finish her race. She does need to settle better but it would be unfair to judge her on this debut effort. (and 6-4 in places)

4104 WALKER TRANSPORT H'CAP — 7f
6:55 (6:56) (Class 4) (0-85,85) 3-Y-O £4,857 (£1,445; £722; £360) Stalls Low

Form RPR

1520 **1** **Glen Shiel (USA)**[15] 3579 3-9-6 **82** .... RichardHills 3 91
(M Johnston) *chsd ldrs: led over 2f out: edgd lft fnl f: rdn out* **11/2**

01- **2** 3/4 **Right Grand**[217] 7705 3-9-2 **78** .... NeilCallan 7 85
(W J Haggas) *hld up: hdwy 3f out: rdn and hung lft over 1f out: r.o to go 2nd wl ins fnl f: nt rch wnr* **16/1**

6-14 **3** 2 **Rockabilly Rebel**[27] 3215 3-8-9 **71** .... MichaelHills 4 73
(B W Hills) *led over 4f: rdn and ev ch over 1f out: styd on same pce ins fnl f* **7/2**[2]

05-0 **4** 1 1/2 **Suffolk Punch (IRE)**[29] 3103 3-9-9 **85** .... LiamKeniry 2 83
(A M Balding) *w ldr: rdn and ev ch over 1f out: no ex ins fnl f* **11/1**

2-15 **5** 6 **Illustrious Prince (IRE)**[27] 3215 3-9-6 **82** .... RyanMoore 6 64
(J Noseda) *s.i.s: sn hld up in tch: rdn over 2f out: wknd over 1f out* **2/1**[1]

0341 **6** 4 1/2 **Goolagong (IRE)**[13] 3680 3-8-9 **71** .... JimCrowley 1 41
(R M Beckett) *hld up: hdwy over 2f out: rdn and wknd over 1f out* **9/2**[3]

The Form Book, Raceform Ltd, Compton, RG20 6NL

0462 **7** *23* **Syrian**21 3413 3-9-6 **82** .... KierenFallon 5 —
(M L W Bell) *stdd s: hld up: effrt over 2f out: sn wknd and eased* **8/1**

1m 26.21s (0.51) **Going Correction** +0.15s/f (Good) 7 Ran SP% **114.4**
Speed ratings (Par 102): **103,102,99,98,91 86,59**
toteswingers: 1&2 £21.40, 1&3 £2.10, 2&3 £10.00. CSF £82.05 TOTE £7.40: £3.40, £4.90; EX 79.30.
Owner Sheikh Hamdan Bin Mohammed Al Maktoum **Bred** Marablue Farm Llc **Trained** Middleham Moor, N Yorks

FOCUS
The time was much quicker than the preceding two-year-old race and the first two home should be kept on the right side of.
Rockabilly Rebel Official explanation: jockey said gelding hung left throughout
Syrian Official explanation: jockey said gelding felt wrong behind

4105 HENBRANDT LTD CONDITIONS STKS 5f
7:25 (7:26) (Class 3) 3-Y-O+
£8,723 (£2,612; £1,306; £653; £326; £163) **Stalls** Low

Form RPR
3623 **1** **Elnawin**19 3486 4-8-9 104 .... RyanMoore 1 105
(R Hannon) *w ldr tl led over 3f out: shkn up and qcknd clr fnl f* **2/5**1
0250 **2** *5* **Angus Newz**14 3629 7-8-4 82 .... AndreaAtzeni 2 82
(M Quinn) *led: hdd over 3f out: rdn over 1f out: sn outpcd* **11/1**
50-0 **3** *1 1/2* **Red Avalanche (IRE)**34 2972 3-8-6 95 ow1 .... KierenFallon 4 82
(P F I Cole) *hld up in tch: pushed along 2f out: rdr dropped whip over 1f out: styng on same pce whn edgd lft ins fnl f: wnt 3rd nr fin* **8/1**3
1-06 **4** *nk* **Nota Bene**47 2563 8-9-0 97 .... LiamKeniry 5 86
(D R C Elsworth) *dwlt: hdwy 3f out: rdn and hung lft over 1f out: wknd ins fnl f* **13/2**2
0500 **5** *2* **Bel Cantor**10 3753 7-8-2 78 .... AdamBeschizza(7) 6 73
(W J H Ratcliffe) *chsd ldrs tl wknd over 1f out* **20/1**
000 **6** *19* **Slap And Tickle (IRE)**21 3415 4-8-2 48 ow5 .... CarolineKelly(7) 3 5
(M D Squance) *plld hrd early: trckd ldrs: wknd 1/2-way* **100/1**

58.89 secs (-0.21) **Going Correction** +0.15s/f (Good)
WFA 3 from 4yo+ 4lb 6 Ran SP% **110.0**
Speed ratings (Par 107): **107,99,96,96,92 62**
toteswingers: 1&2 £3.00, 1&3 £1.10, 2&3 £5.90. CSF £5.61 TOTE £1.30: £1.10, £4.60; EX 5.00.
Owner Noodles Racing **Bred** D R Tucker **Trained** East Everleigh, Wilts

FOCUS
On official figures there was only going to be one outcome.

NOTEBOOK
Elnawin stood out on offfical ratings and duly obliged with a confidence-boosting win, his first since his two-year-old days. His third-placed effort in a Group 3 in Ireland last month read well and he outclassed his rivals to deliver an emphatic success. His previous winning had all been done at 6f but this stiff 5f was ideal. This triumph should stand him in good stead for stiffer assignments. (op 4-7)
Angus Newz is no longer the force she was was, but this was a genuine effort, and back in handicap company deserves to be considered off her current mark. (op 12-1 tchd 10-1)
Red Avalanche(IRE) probably ran to a similar level as his seasonal bow at Sandown last month. He may have finished closer if his rider had not dropped his whip over 1f out. (op 11-2)
Nota Bene won this race in the soft a year ago but was then sidelined for ten months. His chance was significantly affected as he dwelt upon the stalls opening, but in his three runs this year has yet to recapture anything like his best form. (op 9-2)
Bel Cantor was always going to find this a difficult task based on his handicap mark and the way the race was framed. (tchd 14-1)

4106 RACING UK H'CAP 1m 2f
7:55 (7:56) (Class 3) (0-95,93) 3-Y-O
£8,723 (£2,612; £1,306; £653; £326; £163) **Stalls** Centre

Form RPR
1005 **1** **Cumulus Nimbus**8 3827 3-9-4 **88** .... RyanMoore 5 96
(R Hannon) *hld up: swtchd lft over 3f out: rdn to chse ldr over 1f out: r.o to ld wl ins fnl f* **10/1**
0-1 **2** *nk* **Sour Mash (IRE)**64 2043 3-9-4 **88** .... KierenFallon 2 95
(L M Cumani) *a.p: led over 1f out: sn rdn: edgd lft and hdd wl ins fnl f: r.o* **7/2**2
3-24 **3** *hd* **Sand Skier**8 3824 3-9-3 **87** .... RoystonFfrench 4 94
(M Johnston) *sn chsng ldr: rdn over 2f out: outpcd over 1f out: r.o wl towards fin* **6/4**1
-401 **4** *3 1/2* **Chain Of Events**28 3176 3-8-4 **74** oh1 .... HayleyTurner 1 74
(N B King) *hld up: hdwy over 2f out: sn rdn: no ex ins fnl f* **25/1**
3-01 **5** *3/4* **Munsarim (IRE)**15 3587 3-9-3 **87** .... TadhgO'Shea 7 86
(J L Dunlop) *hmpd s: sn led: rdn and hdd over 1f out: no ex* **9/1**
31 **6** *nse* **Sharedah (IRE)**43 2674 3-8-9 **79** .... RichardHills 3 77
(Sir Michael Stoute) *hld up in tch: nt clr run and swtchd lft over 1f out: nvr trbld ldrs* **9/2**3
11-0 **7** *3/4* **Fareej (USA)**155 510 3-9-9 **93** .... TedDurcan 6 90
(Saeed Bin Suroor) *wnt rt s: chsd ldrs: nt clr run over 1f out: no imp after* **8/1**

2m 5.77s (0.27) **Going Correction** +0.15s/f (Good) 7 Ran SP% **114.5**
Speed ratings (Par 104): **104,103,103,100,100 100,99**
toteswingers: 1&2 £7.00, 1&3 £3.80, 2&3 £2.50. CSF £44.81 TOTE £9.90: £3.10, £2.00; EX 52.00.
Owner Mrs John Lee **Bred** Chantilly Bloodstock Agency **Trained** East Everleigh, Wilts

FOCUS
An interesting race with four of the seven runners coming into it off the back of last-time-out successes. There was only a modest gallop which didn't favour a couple of them but the race should throw up a number of winners.

NOTEBOOK
Cumulus Nimbus built upon a fair effort in a 1m conditions event at the July Festival eight days earlier. Held up off a modest gallop, he was switched to the outside and got the better of Sour Mash after a lengthy battle. He should continue to pay his way. (op 8-1)
Sour Mash(IRE) ◆ had broken his maiden on the Rowley Mile course last time and ran another good race for one still relatively inexperienced. He'll improve again for this and is sure to be found plenty more opportunities. (op 4-1 tchd 10-3)
Sand Skier had two fair pieces of form to his name this season, not least when going down by only half a length in a hot handicap eight days earlier over C&D. Due to race from a 3lb higher mark in the future, he ran another good race but wasn't suited by the steady tempo. From 2f out he appeared a little outpaced as the race turned into something of a dash for home. However, once he got motoring he finished in impressive style, and it shouldn't be long before he gets his head in front. (op 9-4 tchd 11-8)
Chain Of Events, from 1lb out of the handicap, gave a decent account of himself on his first run for new trainer after going through the sales ring for 18,000gns the previous week. There will be easier tasks for him, and he shaped as if capable of building on his Redcar maiden win last month. (op 20-1)
Munsarim(IRE) wasn't helped at the start by Fareej edging into his ground. Trying this trip for the first time, he was asked to race on the front end but couldn't find any extra when the action warmed up. He remains of interest but the hefty rise in the weights that he received for his Haydock maiden win may have him in check at present. (op 15-2 tchd 11-1)
Sharedah(IRE) was held up towards the rear and didn't get the splits when needed. The experience will have benefited this lightly-raced, well-bred filly and she is open to plenty of improvement. (op 7-2 tchd 5-1)
Fareej(USA) was returning from a 155-day break and, on his last two runs, has yet to live up to the promise he showed at two. (op 10-1 tchd 15-2)

4107 HOME OF RACING MAIDEN STKS 1m
8:30 (8:31) (Class 4) 3-Y-O
£4,533 (£1,348; £674; £336) **Stalls** Low

Form RPR
33 **1** **Linnens Star (IRE)**42 2692 3-9-3 0 .... JimCrowley 2 88
(R M Beckett) *mde all: rdn ins fnl f and r.o wl* **7/2**2
2- **2** *3 1/4* **Forest Runner**309 5785 3-9-3 0 .... TedDurcan 6 81
(Saeed Bin Suroor) *a.p: rdn to chse wnr and edgd rt 2f out: styd on same pce ins fnl f* **7/2**2
-324 **3** *6* **Azimuth (USA)**32 3038 3-9-3 83 .... TomQueally 4 67
(J Noseda) *chsd wnr tl rdn over 2f out: wknd over 1f out* **3/1**1
4 *1 1/2* **Kalk Bay (IRE)** 3-9-3 0 .... MichaelHills 1 64
(W J Haggas) *dwlt: sn prom: rdn and wknd over 1f out* **10/1**
20 **5** *4 1/2* **Warm Memories**15 3587 3-9-3 0 .... RyanMoore 11 53
(Sir Michael Stoute) *racd alone on stands' side: up w the pce tl rdn: hung lft and wknd over 1f out* **7/1**3
30 **6** *nse* **Startle**35 2925 3-9-3 0 .... FergusSweeney 10 53
(R Hannon) *hld up: sme hdwy over 2f out: wknd over 1f out* **14/1**
0 **7** *2* **Namehim**25 3272 3-9-3 0 .... LiamKeniry 3 49
(E F Vaughan) *sn pushed along in rr: bhd fnl 3f* **33/1**
6- **8** *1/2* **Waabel**363 4093 3-9-3 0 .... MarcHalford 8 48
(A Bailey) *hld up: hdwy over 2f out: hung rt and wknd over 1f out* **12/1**
5 **9** *10* **Wallis**27 3220 3-8-12 0 .... KierenFallon 7 20
(L M Cumani) *chsd ldrs: rdn over 2f out: sn wknd* **10/1**
10 *3 3/4* **Minnie McGinn (USA)** 3-8-12 0 .... IvaMilickova 5 11
(Jane Chapple-Hyam) *s.i.s: a in rr: bhd fnl 3f* **22/1**

1m 39.73s (-0.27) **Going Correction** +0.15s/f (Good) 10 Ran SP% **121.8**
Speed ratings (Par 102): **107,103,97,96,91 91,89,89,79,75**
toteswingers: 1&2 £3.90, 1&3 £3.30, 2&3 £3.80. CSF £17.07 TOTE £5.10: £1.80, £1.70, £1.60; EX 16.50.
Owner D & J Newell **Bred** Derek & Judith Newell **Trained** Whitsbury, Hants

FOCUS
The race was over 3secs beyond standard and very few got into it. It didn't appear to be a particularly strong maiden for the track.

4108 NEWMARKETRACECOURSES.CO.UK H'CAP 1m
9:00 (9:03) (Class 5) (0-75,75) 4-Y-O+
£3,238 (£963; £481; £240) **Stalls** Low

Form RPR
0010 **1** **Aviso (GER)**21 3412 6-9-1 **67** .... TomQueally 11 75
(B J Curley) *chsd ldrs: led 2f out: rdn and hdd 1f out: rallied to ld nr fin* **25/1**
6336 **2** *hd* **Perfect Class**34 2956 4-8-7 **64** .... (v) JohnFahy(5) 14 72
(C G Cox) *hld up: hdwy 2f out: led 1f out: rdn and hdd nr fin* **10/1**
00-0 **3** *nk* **Sonny Parkin**21 3416 8-8-10 **62** .... (v) KierenFallon 15 69+
(J Pearce) *sn pushed along in rr: hdwy and nt clr run fr over 1f out: r.o wl* **12/1**
205 **4** *1/2* **Baylini**7 3846 6-9-4 **75** .... SophieDoyle(5) 7 81
(Ms J S Doyle) *hld up: hdwy over 1f out: edgd lft ins fnl f: r.o* **13/2**2
-000 **5** *nse* **Lord Theo**60 2173 6-9-8 **74** .... TedDurcan 3 80
(N P Littmoden) *chsd ldrs: rdn over 1f out: r.o* **12/1**
0333 **6** *1 3/4* **King Columbo (IRE)**21 3412 5-9-1 **67** .... JimmyQuinn 12 69
(Miss J Feilden) *a.p: rdn over 1f out: no ex wl ins fnl f* **8/1**3
0005 **7** *shd* **Aflaam (IRE)**16 3558 5-9-2 **73** .... KierenFox(5) 2 74
(R A Harris) *hld up in tch: swtchd rt over 2f out: nt clr run over 1f out: r.o* **12/1**
0060 **8** *3/4* **Trafalgar Square**28 3160 8-8-4 **56** oh1 .... (v) AndreaAtzeni 1 56
(M J Attwater) *hld up: hdwy over 1f out: sn rdn: styd on: nt rch ldrs* **14/1**
5515 **9** *1/2* **Unlimited**11 3725 8-8-9 **61** .... NeilCallan 9 59
(A W Carroll) *hld up: plld hrd: hdwy over 2f out: styd on* **16/1**
4406 **10** *nk* **Edgeworth (IRE)**39 2823 4-9-6 **72** .... FergusSweeney 8 70
(B G Powell) *chsd ldr tl led over 2f out: sn hdd: wknd ins fnl f* **10/1**
2621 **11** *3/4* **Eastern Gift**6 3911 5-9-1 **74** 6ex .... StephanieBancroft(7) 10 70
(Miss Gay Kelleway) *hld up: r.o ins fnl f: nvr nrr* **12/1**
2205 **12** *1/2* **Yourgolftravel Com**7 3863 5-8-11 **63** .... StephenCraine 6 60+
(M Wigham) *hld up in tch: racd keenly: nt clr run over 1f out: hmpd ins fnl f: nt trble ldrs* **9/1**
33-0 **13** *4* **Hilltop Artistry**44 2643 4-8-11 **63** .... RyanMoore 5 49
(J R Jenkins) *hld up: effrt over 2f out: wknd over 1f out* **16/1**
0031 **14** *1 1/4* **Hustle (IRE)**20 3458 5-9-2 **75** .... AdamBeschizza(7) 13 58
(Miss Gay Kelleway) *hld up: hung rt fr 1/2-way: rdn over 2f out: wknd over 1f out* **7/2**1
330- **15** *21* **The Happy Hammer (IRE)**237 7479 4-8-5 **60** .... WilliamCarson(3) 4 —
(Eugene Stanford) *led over 5f: wknd and eased over 1f out* **25/1**

1m 39.96s (-0.04) **Going Correction** +0.15s/f (Good) 15 Ran SP% **131.7**
Speed ratings (Par 103): **106,105,105,105,104 103,103,102,101,101 100,100,96,95,74**
toteswingers: 1&2 £185.10, 1&3 £38.70, 2&3 £12.10. CSF £278.72 CT £1931.67 TOTE £33.50: £9.50, £3.00, £3.10; EX 230.80 Place 6 £198.46; Place 5 £100.87.
Owner Curley Leisure **Bred** Gestut Schlenderhan **Trained** Newmarket, Suffolk

FOCUS
A competitive race of its type that was fractionally slower than the 3y-o maiden that preceded it. It was run at an acceptable pace for the grade and the form looks reliable. There should be a few winners to come out of it.
Aviso(GER) Official explanation: trainer's rep said, regarding apparent improvement in form, that the gelding is an inconsistent performer.

T/Plt: £122.80 to a £1 stake. Pool:£52,960.16 - 314.78 winning tickets T/Qpdt: £20.90 to a £1 stake. Pool:£5,377.39 - 189.90 winning tickets CR

[3906]NOTTINGHAM (L-H)

Friday, July 16

OFFICIAL GOING: Good to soft (6.6)

Wind: Fresh against Weather: Cloudy - sunny periods - showers

4109 PADDOCKS CONFERENCE CENTRE H'CAP — 6f 15y

2:10 (2:12) (Class 5) (0-70,70) 3-Y-O — £2,266 (£674; £337; £168) Stalls Centre

Form — RPR

0402 **1** **Kings 'n Dreams**[21] 3393 3-9-6 **69**....(b) AdamKirby 1 — 78
(D K Ivory) hld up towards rr: smooth hdwy 1/2-way: effrt to ld wl over 1f out: rdn and edgd rt ins fnl f: rdr dropped reins: kpt on — **11/2**[2]

0013 **2** ½ **Grand Zafeen**[13] 3677 3-9-7 **70**.... AlanMunro 7 — 77+
(M R Channon) hld up towards rr on inner: hdwy 1/2-way: swtchd lft and rdn wl over 1f out: styd on to chse wnr ins fnl f: kpt on — **9/1**

5000 **3** 3½ **Bossy Kitty**[20] 3436 3-9-7 **70**.... KirstyMilczarek 6 — 66+
(N Tinkler) trckd ldrs: swtchd lft and hdwy whn nt clr run and hmpd 1 1/2f out: squeezed through to chse wnr whn hmpd ins fnl f: one pce after — **14/1**

0-20 **4** 2¼ **French Fantasy**[11] 3727 3-8-5 **54**.... ChrisCatlin 2 — 43
(H Morrison) led 1f: cl up tl led again wl over 2f out: sn rdn and hdd over 1f out: drvn: edgd rt and wknd ent fnl f — **6/1**[3]

006 **5** 3¾ **Fair Bunny**[26] 3243 3-8-8 **57**.... EddieAhern 9 — 34
(A D Brown) prom: swtchd lft and hdwy to chal wl over 1f out: sn rdn and ev ch tl wknd over 1f out — **16/1**

-235 **6** 2½ **Suzy Alexander**[40] 2784 3-9-3 **66**.... SebSanders 4 — 35+
(G G Margarson) trckd ldrs: hdwy whn nt clr run and bmpd 1 1/2f out: nt rcvr — **10/1**

231 **7** ¾ **Blackdown Boy**[18] 3511 3-9-2 **68**.... JamesMillman(3) 3 — 34
(B R Millman) prom: effrt to chal wl over 2f out and ev ch: rdn 2f out and sn wknd — **11/8**[1]

0-06 **8** ½ **Little Buddy**[25] 3258 3-8-2 **51** oh6....(t) NickyMackay 5 — 16
(R J Price) a in rr — **66/1**

5500 **9** 2¾ **Cookie Galore**[10] 3763 3-8-2 **51** oh1....(p) JamieMackay 8 — —
(J A Glover) dwlt: swtchd rt and hdwy to ld after 1f: rdn along and hdd wl over 2f out: sn wknd — **16/1**

1m 16.83s (1.93) **Going Correction** +0.15s/f (Good) — **9** Ran SP% **110.8**

Speed ratings (Par 100): **93,92,87,84,79 76,75,74,71**

toteswingers:1&2:£5.20, 1&3:£13.40, 2&3:£11.00 CSF £50.47 CT £628.17 TOTE £3.60: £1.60, £2.40, £4.10; EX 43.70.

Owner PaulBlows, IanRGethin, MrsMelanieDoughty **Bred** P A Blows **Trained** Radlett, Herts

■ Stewards' Enquiry : Kirsty Milczarek four-day ban: careless riding (Jul 30,Aug 1-3)

FOCUS

A moderate sprint handicap. The field were soon racing towards the stands' side and it looked pretty hard work from halfway, on the easing ground and with the wind blowing.

Blackdown Boy Official explanation: trainer's rep had no explanation for the poor form shown

4110 EUROPEAN BREEDERS' FUND MAIDEN STKS — 6f 15y

2:45 (2:47) (Class 5) 2-Y-O — £3,561 (£1,059; £529; £264) Stalls Centre

Form — RPR

1 **Dream Ahead (USA)** 2-9-3 0.... WilliamBuick 7 — 95+
(D M Simcock) towards rr: smooth hdwy on outer to trck ldrs after 2f: cl up 2f out: qcknd to ld over 1f out: hung bdly lft ins fnl f and sn clr: easily — **7/4**[1]

3 **2** 9 **Formal Demand**[15] 3602 2-9-3 0.... EddieAhern 9 — 65
(E F Vaughan) a.p: led 2f out: sn rdn and hdd over 1f out: kpt on: no ch w wnr — **10/1**

6 **3** 1 **Cape Rambler**[23] 3332 2-9-3 0.... DaneO'Neill 3 — 62
(H Candy) prom: effrt and cl up 1/2-way: rdn 2f out: drvn and one pce appr fnl f — **15/2**[3]

4 2½ **Chibchan (IRE)** 2-8-10 0.... AntiocoMurgia(7) 11 — 55
(Mahmood Al Zarooni) in tch: hdwy over 2f out: sn rdn and edgd lft over 1f out: kpt on ins fnl f: nrst fin — **16/1**

63 **5** ½ **Spirit Of Oakdale (IRE)**[20] 3459 2-9-3 0.... AdamKirby 8 — 53
(W R Swinburn) chsd ldrs: pushed along and outpcd 1/2-way: sn rdn and kpt on fnl f — **13/2**[2]

6 ¾ **Busker (USA)** 2-9-3 0.... AlanMunro 14 — 51
(Mahmood Al Zarooni) prom: led after 2f: rdn along and hdd 2f out: grad wknd — **8/1**

0 **7** 4 **High Avon**[20] 3459 2-9-3 0.... PatCosgrave 1 — 39
(D K Ivory) chsd ldrs: rdn along over 2f out: grad wknd — **28/1**

8 4 **Tigerino (IRE)** 2-9-0 0.... BarryMcHugh(3) 12 — 27
(C W Thornton) a towards rr — **28/1**

9 1 **Retreat Content (IRE)** 2-9-3 0.... ChrisCatlin 4 — 24
(J A Osborne) dwlt: a in rr — **20/1**

10 10 **Bodie** 2-9-3 0.... JamieMackay 13 — —
(Mrs P Sly) s.i.s: a bhd — **33/1**

11 3¾ **Coracle** 2-9-3 0.... LeeVickers 5 — —
(J A Glover) led 2f: rdn along 1/2-way: sn edgd lft and wknd qckly 2f out — **40/1**

12 30 **Gulbank (IRE)** 2-9-3 0.... SebSanders 6 — —
(J Noseda) chsd ldrs: rdn along and lost pl 1/2-way: sn bhd and eased fnl 2f — **13/2**[2]

1m 16.7s (1.80) **Going Correction** +0.15s/f (Good) — **12** Ran SP% **117.9**

Speed ratings (Par 94): **94,82,80,77,76 75,70,65,63,50 45,5**

toteswingers:1&2:£6.40, 1&3:£7.10, 2&3:£10.60 CSF £18.69 TOTE £2.70: £1.30, £2.60, £2.30; EX 17.30.

Owner Khalifa Dasmal **Bred** Darley **Trained** Newmarket, Suffolk

FOCUS

These juveniles raced down the middle of the track. The race might not have taken much winning but Dream Ahead proved a class apart.

NOTEBOOK

Dream Ahead(USA) ◆ was very well backed and proved far too good for his rivals. The winner took time to get organised but arrived on the scene cantering near the furlong marker and, despite veering left when in the lead, came right away when asked for maximum effort. The ground was no doubt in his favour as he showed a pronounced knee action. He is bred to be decent, being out of the former smart sprinter Land Of Dreams, and she has already produced a decent 1m4f winner, so staying further should be well within his compass as he matures. His hanging should be put down to greenness at this stage, though his trainer later said he thought this was a quirky colt and regarded him as the best 2-y-o in his care. He's in the Gimcrack and it wouldn't be at all surprising to see him take up that engagement. (op 15-8 tchd 2-1)

Formal Demand, a well-beaten third on debut at Yarmouth, travelled nicely into contention and showed the clear benefit of his debut experience. He ultimately found the winner in a different league, but looked more at home on the easier ground and seems sure to win a race or two this year, probably when switching to nurseries. (tchd 9-1)

Cape Rambler stepped up on the level of his Salisbury debut as expected, but didn't look as suited by the softer ground as the two in front of him. He should be off the mark before long. (op 6-1)

Chibchan(IRE) is a half-brother to the very useful Sabotage, who has won up to 2m for Godolphin. He was unsurprisingly doing his best work towards the finish and looks as though he will appreciate quicker ground, so this was a fair debut effort.

Spirit Of Oakdale(IRE) attracted some support on this switch to easy ground, but got badly outpaced from halfway before staying on again, suggesting a stiffer test is now required. Nurseries are now an option for him. (op 9-1 tchd 6-1)

Busker(USA) attracted some support on this switch to easy ground, but got badly outpaced from halfway before staying on again, suggesting a stiffer test is now required. Nurseries are now an option for him. (tchd 7-1)

4111 FINDARACEHORSE.COM THE WEBSITE FOR BUYING RACEHORSES NURSERY — 6f 15y

3:20 (3:20) (Class 5) 2-Y-O — £2,388 (£705; £352) Stalls Centre

Form — RPR

400 **1** **Reginald Claude**[46] 2594 2-8-12 **66**.... DaneO'Neill 2 — 75
(M D I Usher) hld up in tch: swtchd lft and hdwy 2f out: rdn to chse ldr over 1f out: chal and bmpd ins fnl f: rallied to ld last 75yds — **7/1**

51 **2** hd **Krypton Factor**[43] 2667 2-9-7 **75**.... SebSanders 7 — 83
(Sir Mark Prescott) led: rdn 2f out: drvn and hung bdly lft ins fnl f: hdd last 75yds — **13/8**[1]

445 **3** 8 **Brave Dream**[13] 3658 2-8-12 **66**.... ChrisCatlin 3 — 50
(K A Ryan) prom: effrt over 2f out and ev ch: rdn wl over 1f out and wknd appr fnl f — **5/1**[3]

0020 **4** 1¼ **Gower Rules (IRE)**[10] 3767 2-8-10 **69** ow2.... LeeNewnes(5) 4 — 49
(M D I Usher) in rr and rdn along 1/2-way: swtchd lft over 1f out: kpt on u.p ins fnl f: nvr a factor — **25/1**

4035 **5** 1¼ **Comrade Bond**[24] 3288 2-8-9 **63**.... PatCosgrave 6 — 40
(M H Tompkins) trckd ldr: effrt 2f out and cl up tl rdn and wknd appr fnl f — **9/1**

3322 **6** 11 **Battle Of Britain**[17] 3536 2-8-11 **72**....(v) AntiocoMurgia(7) 1 — 16
(Mahmood Al Zarooni) cl up: rdn along 1/2-way: sn wknd — **9/2**[2]

015 **7** 1¾ **Believe It Or Not (IRE)**[14] 3630 2-9-5 **73**.... AlanMunro 5 — 17
(J S Moore) trckd ldrs: hdwy and cl up 1/2-way: rdn 2f out and sn wknd — **6/1**

1m 16.64s (1.74) **Going Correction** +0.15s/f (Good) — **7** Ran SP% **113.6**

Speed ratings (Par 94): **94,93,83,81,79 65,62**

toteswingers:1&2:£3.90, 1&3:£6.30, 2&3:£3.60 CSF £18.61 TOTE £9.70: £5.20, £2.00; EX 28.10.

Owner High Five Racing **Bred** Whitsbury Manor Stud **Trained** Upper Lambourn, Berks

FOCUS

A moderate nursery. There were two groups early on with three of the runners coming stands' side early on and the rest joining them pretty much from halfway. The first two did well to pull clear, but overall this is not form to get carried away with.

NOTEBOOK

Reginald Claude opened his account at the fourth attempt on this nursery debut. He had shown promise on debut, but not been so good the last twice. However, the easier ground proved to his liking and he did well to score after getting such a bump from the winner nearing the finish. There should be a little more to come. (op 11-1)

Krypton Factor came in for strong late support on this switch to a nursery. Conceding weight all around, he was quick to bag the stands'-side rail and lead. Things looked good for his supporters 1f out, but he failed to sustain his effort as the winner was pulled out to challenge and veered right into that rival under maximum pressure. He again did so near the finish and, remembering he hung markedly right when winning last time, is clearly a quirky customer. He should win a nursery and has entries later this week, but did endure a very hard race here. (op 15-8 tchd 9-4)

Brave Dream, well backed, led them down the centre of the track early on. He came under pressure 2f out, though, and failed to see out the extra furlong well on this ground. (op 4-1)

Gower Rules(IRE) was never really going that well on this return to turf, but this was a little better again. Returning to 7f should only help. (tchd 28-1)

Comrade Bond looked a brief threat on the near side around halfway, but lacked anything like the sort of pace required to mount a challenge. (op 11-1)

Battle Of Britain refused to settle on this nursery debut and now looks one to avoid at all costs. (op 4-1 tchd 7-2)

Believe It Or Not(IRE) was feeling the pinch from halfway and was beaten before the return to this extra furlong became an issue, perhaps on account of the different ground. He nevertheless now has a lot to prove. (tchd 13-2)

4112 DIGIBET.COM H'CAP — 1m 75y

3:55 (3:55) (Class 4) (0-85,82) 3-Y-O+

£6,231 (£1,866; £933; £467; £233; £117) Stalls Centre

Form — RPR

-435 **1** **Christmas Carnival**[27] 3207 3-8-13 **76**....(b[1]) WilliamBuick 4 — 87
(B J Meehan) trckd ldrs: hdwy 4f out: cl up 2f out: sn chal and rdn: styd on to ld jst ins fnl f: drvn out — **12/1**

2414 **2** ½ **Sir George (IRE)**[23] 3318 5-9-7 **79**.... BarryMcHugh(3) 1 — 91
(Ollie Pears) t.k.h early: trckd ldng pair: effrt on inner 3f out: rdn to ld 2f out: drvn over 1f out: hdd jst ins fnl f: rallied and ev ch tl no ex last 50yds — **6/1**

5-10 **3** 1½ **Oriental Scot**[57] 2253 3-9-5 **82**.... AlanMunro 5 — 89
(W Jarvis) trckd ldrs: hdwy 3f out: rdn 2f out: drvn and kpt on same pce fnl f — **9/2**[2]

4040 **4** 1½ **Exit Smiling**[38] 2835 8-9-6 **82**.... AdamBeschizza(7) 6 — 87
(P T Midgley) trckd ldr: hdwy to ld over 3f out: rdn and hdd 2f out: drvn and one pce ent fnl f — **10/1**

0211 **5** 4 **Mejd (IRE)**[6] 3899 3-9-0 **82**.... MatthewDavies(5) 7 — 76
(M R Channon) in rr: hdwy on wd outside over 3f out: rdn along over 2f out: sn no imp — **5/1**[3]

6003 **6** 1¼ **Rainbow Mirage (IRE)**[7] 3863 6-9-5 **74**....(t) SebSanders 8 — 67
(E S McMahon) hld up: hdwy 4f out: rdn to chse ldrs 3f out: drvn and no imp fnl 2f — **2/1**[1]

-200 **7** 15 **Marvo**[33] 2991 6-9-11 **80**.... PatCosgrave 9 — 39
(M H Tompkins) dwlt: hld up in rr: hdwy on inner 4f out: rdn along 3f out and sn wknd — **9/1**

/2-0 **8** 14 **San Antonio**[34] 2959 10-9-5 **74**....(b) AdamKirby 3 — —
(Mrs P Sly) led: rdn along and hdd over 3f out: sn wknd and eased fnl 2f — **40/1**

03-6 **9** 1 **Trailblazing**[39] 2807 3-9-5 **82**.... AdrianNicholls 2 — —
(M Johnston) chsd ldrs: rdn along 1/2-way: sn wknd and bhd whn eased fnl 2f — **25/1**

1m 48.12s (2.52) **Going Correction** +0.45s/f (Yiel)

WFA 3 from 5yo+ 8lb — **9** Ran SP% **115.5**

Speed ratings (Par 105): **105,104,103,101,97 96,81,67,66**

toteswingers:1&2:£9.00, 1&3:£9.10, 2&3:£5.80 CSF £82.03 CT £379.79 TOTE £14.00: £3.70, £1.50, £1.60; EX 68.40.

Owner Jaber Abdullah **Bred** David John Brown **Trained** Manton, Wilts

FOCUS
A modest handicap, run at a solid pace.
Mejd(IRE) Official explanation: trainer had no explanation for the poor form shown
Rainbow Mirage(IRE) Official explanation: trainer had no explanation for the poor form shown
Trailblazing Official explanation: jockey said colt never travelled

4113 NOTTINGHAMRACECOURSE.CO.UK (S) STKS — 1m 2f 50y
4:30 (4:31) (Class 6) 3-Y-O — £1,706 (£503; £252) Stalls Low

Form				RPR
0550	1		**Sternian**[13] 3662 3-8-9 55 (b) JamieMackay 7 (M E Rimmer) *trckd ldrs: hdwy 3f out: rdn to ld over 1f out: clr ins fnl f: kpt on* 5/1[3]	57
-440	2	6	**Optimistic Duke (IRE)**[18] 3521 3-8-9 55 (p) EddieAhern 1 (W R Muir) *trckd ldng pair: pushed along on inner 4f out: rdn wl over 2f out: swtchd rt and drvn wl over 1f out: styd on to take 2nd ins fnl f* 6/4[1]	45
3500	3	1 1/4	**Captain Clint (IRE)**[27] 3213 3-8-9 42 PatCosgrave 5 (M H Tompkins) *trckd ldr: led 3f out: rdn 2f out: drvn and hdd over 1f out: sn one pce* 7/2[2]	43
0060	4	1/2	**Better Be Blue (IRE)**[7] 3852 3-8-1 43 Louis-PhilippeBeuzelin(3) 4 (A W Carroll) *dwlt and in rr: pushed along and bhd 4f out: rdn over 2f out: styd on appr fnl f: n.d* 16/1	37
	5	2 1/4	**Daneside (IRE)** 3-8-9 0 ChrisCatlin 3 (W G Harrison) *s.i.s and in rr: hdwy to chse ldrs over 3f out: rdn over 2f out and sn wknd* 8/1	37
0305	6	11	**Otterton**[13] 3685 3-8-4 45 PaulEddery 6 (R Hollinshead) *in tch: hdwy to chse ldrs over 3f out: rdn wl over 2f out and sn wknd* 10/1	10
05	7	12	**Feed The Goat (IRE)**[13] 3666 3-8-9 0 (bt[1]) DaneO'Neill 2 (Miss Amy Weaver) *led: rdn along and hdd 3f out: sn wknd* 16/1	—

2m 19.68s (7.98) **Going Correction** +0.45s/f (Yiel) **7** Ran SP% **110.9**
Speed ratings (Par 98): **86,81,80,79,78 69,59**
toteswingers:1&2:£2.30, 1&3:£2.70, 2&3:£2.40 CSF £12.13 TOTE £5.80: £2.50, £1.10; EX 13.90.There was no bid for the winner.
Owner Clive Dennett **Bred** Clive Dennett **Trained** Newmarket, Suffolk
FOCUS
A desperate 3-y-o event and not one to dwell on.

4114 HOSPITALITY AT NOTTINGHAM RACECOURSE MAIDEN FILLIES' STKS (DIV I) — 1m 2f 50y
5:05 (5:08) (Class 5) 3-Y-O — £2,266 (£674; £337; £168) Stalls Low

Form				RPR
	1		**Jivry** 3-9-0 0 DaneO'Neill 1 (H Candy) *dwlt: sn chsng ldng pair on inner: hdwy over 2f out: rdn to ld over 1f out: clr ins fnl f: kpt on strly* 12/1	79+
2	2	3 1/4	**Dolphina (USA)**[43] 2674 3-9-0 0 IanMongan 7 (H R A Cecil) *trckd ldr: effrt and cl 3f out: rdn over 2f out: drvn wl over 1f out: kpt on same pce fnl f* 4/6[1]	73
0-0	3	2 3/4	**Cheerfully**[16] 3563 3-9-0 0 NickyMackay 8 (J H M Gosden) *led: rdn along 3f out: drvn 2f out: hdd over 1f out: grad wknd fnl f* 12/1	68
	4	3/4	**Piano** 3-9-0 0 WilliamBuick 9 (J H M Gosden) *towards rr: pushed along and green on outer 3f out: rdn 2f out: hdwy appr fnl f: edgd lft and styd on: nrst fin* 5/2[2]	66+
	5	1 3/4	**Kristalette (IRE)** 3-9-0 0 AdamKirby 6 (W R Swinburn) *hld up: stdy hdwy 1/2-way: trckd ldrs over 3f out: rdn over 2f out and sn btn* 10/1[3]	63
50	6	1 1/2	**Nabari (JPN)**[42] 2697 3-9-0 0 KirstyMilczarek 5 (L M Cumani) *in tch on inner: hdwy over 4f out: rdn along 3f out: sn drvn and btn 2f out* 16/1	60
0	7	3/4	**Topaze Star**[14] 3620 3-9-0 0 IvaMilickova 4 (Jane Chapple-Hyam) *chsd ldrs: rdn along over 3f out: grad wknd* 100/1	59
0	8	10	**Chaqueta**[27] 3220 3-9-0 0 AlanMunro 11 (C F Wall) *in tch: effrt 4f out: rdn along 3f out: sn wknd* 50/1	40
	9	30	**Epernay** 3-9-0 0 EddieAhern 3 (Ian Williams) *s.i.s: sn rdn along and green in rr: bhd and eased fnl 3f* 25/1	—

2m 19.13s (7.43) **Going Correction** +0.45s/f (Yiel) **9** Ran SP% **125.7**
Speed ratings (Par 97): **88,85,83,82,81 80,79,71,47**
toteswingers:1&2:£4.60, 1&3:£11.50, 2&3:£3.70 CSF £22.33 TOTE £16.00: £2.50, £1.10, £2.00; EX 37.50.
Owner Mrs Susan Brimble **Bred** Mrs S L Brimble **Trained** Kingston Warren, Oxon
FOCUS
This wasn't a strong fillies' maiden and few got involved.

4115 HOSPITALITY AT NOTTINGHAM RACECOURSE MAIDEN FILLIES' STKS (DIV II) — 1m 2f 50y
5:40 (5:41) (Class 5) 3-Y-O — £2,266 (£674; £337; £168) Stalls Low

Form				RPR
6	1		**Sea Of Galilee**[20] 3437 3-9-0 0 DaneO'Neill 5 (H Candy) *cl up on inner: led after 3f: rdn clr wl over 1f out: styd on strly* 7/1[3]	89+
3-53	2	3	**Chelsea Morning (USA)**[34] 2981 3-9-0 74 PaulEddery 6 (B W Hills) *hld up in tch: hdwy 3f out: rdn to chse ldng pair 2f out: drvn and kpt on ins fnl f* 10/1	80
	3	8	**Lady Chaparral** 3-9-0 0 IanMongan 4 (M Dods) *hld up in rr: hdwy on outer 4f out: rdn along wl over 2f out: drvn over 1f out: kpt on same pce* 25/1	65
4	4	3/4	**Minikin (IRE)**[30] 3080 3-9-0 0 ChrisCatlin 8 (H Morrison) *trckd ldrs: hdwy 4f out: rdn along 3f out: drvn and plugged on same pce fnl 2f* 7/1[3]	63
4	5	4 1/2	**Belle Boleyn**[36] 2899 3-9-0 0 SebSanders 1 (C F Wall) *towards rr: hdwy over 3f out: rdn over 2f out and nvr nr ldrs* 16/1	55
0-4	6	1/2	**Ertiyaad**[20] 3437 3-8-11 0 Louis-PhilippeBeuzelin(3) 10 (Sir Michael Stoute) *led 3f: cl up: rdn along 3f out: drvn over 2f out and grad wknd* 8/1	54
04	7	17	**Fuzzypeg (IRE)**[26] 3242 3-9-0 0 EddieAhern 9 (J R Fanshawe) *chsd ldrs: lost pl bef 1/2-way: bhd fnl 3f* 40/1	22
2	8	1 3/4	**Cookie Crumbles (IRE)**[77] 1654 3-9-0 0 AlanMunro 2 (C F Wall) *chsd ldrs on inner: rdn along 3f out: drvn over 2f out and sn wknd* 7/2[2]	18
2222	9	8	**Scorn (USA)**[22] 3347 3-9-0 80 WilliamBuick 7 (J H M Gosden) *trckd ldng pair: rdn to chse wnr wl over 2f out: sn drvn and wknd qckly* 15/8[1]	—
	10	30	**Spring Stock** 3-8-11 0 RussKennemore(3) 3 (B G Powell) *t.k.h: a towards rr: rdn along over 4f out: sn bhd and eased* 100/1	—
00	11	17	**Suleimah**[26] 3242 3-8-9 0 DeanHeslop(5) 11 (C J Teague) *s.i.s: a bhd: t.o fnl 4f* 150/1	—

2m 18.53s (6.83) **Going Correction** +0.625s/f (Yiel) **11** Ran SP% **116.0**
Speed ratings (Par 97): **97,94,88,87,84 83,70,68,62,38 24**
toteswingers:1&2:£14.10, 1&3:£23.80, 2&3:£19.80 CSF £72.23 TOTE £9.60: £3.30, £2.30, £10.90; EX 76.50 Place 6 £69.77; Place 5 £15.03.
Owner D J Burke **Bred** Whitley Stud **Trained** Kingston Warren, Oxon
FOCUS
This second division of the fillies' maiden looked the strongest of the pair, but there was a deluge of rain just before it commenced and looking at the way they finished strung out it does seems suspect form.
Fuzzypeg(IRE) Official explanation: jockey said, regarding running and riding, that his orders were to lay close up, keep the filly handy and ride his race from there, he got shuffled back shortly after start, lost position, and found it was struggling to hold its place over a trip he considered to be too short.
T/Plt: £49.80 to a £1 stake. Pool:£42,057.12 - 615.28 winning tickets T/Qpdt: £20.50 to a £1 stake. Pool:£3,724.99 - 133.94 winning tickets JR

3749 PONTEFRACT (L-H)
Friday, July 16

OFFICIAL GOING: Good to firm (8.5)
Wind: Light behind

4116 COUNTRYWIDE FREIGHT MAIDEN AUCTION STKS — 6f
6:35 (6:37) (Class 4) 2-Y-O — £3,885 (£1,156; £577; £288) Stalls Low

Form				RPR
2	1		**Easy Ticket (IRE)**[27] 3199 2-8-13 0 RichardMullen 5 (D H Brown) *trckd ldrs racing keenly: hdwy to ld over 1f out: pushed clr fnl f: comf* 1/2[1]	83+
03	2	3 1/4	**Bajan Bear**[22] 3362 2-8-9 0 SteveDrowne 12 (M Blanshard) *trckd ldrs: rdn 2f out: swtchd rt over 1f out: kpt on wl fnl f* 33/1	67
	3	hd	**Fieldgunner Kirkup (GER)** 2-8-11 0 PhillipMakin 8 (T D Barron) *chsd ldrs: rdn and outpcd over 2f out: kpt on wl over 1f out* 16/1	68+
4	4	1 3/4	**Alensgrove (IRE)**[83] 1510 2-8-5 0 PaulPickard(3) 3 (P T Midgley) *s.i.s: hld up towards inner: rdn over 2f out: kpt on fnl f: nrst fin* 16/1	60
0	5	1/2	**Grazeon Again (IRE)**[16] 3550 2-9-2 0 JamieSpencer 9 (J J Quinn) *midfield: chsd along 1/2-way: rdn over 2f out: swtchd rt 1f out: kpt on fnl f: nvr nrr* 40/1	67
6	6	1/2	**Sleights Boy (IRE)**[17] 3536 2-8-6 0 MartinLane(3) 2 (I W McInnes) *led after 1f: rdn and hdd over 2f out: bmpd over 1f out: wknd fnl f* 50/1	58
	7	2 1/2	**The Mellor Fella** 2-8-9 0 LeeVickers 10 (R A Fahey) *s.i.s: chsd along 1/2-way: nvr threatened* 40/1	51+
	8	nk	**Smart Step** 2-8-4 0 AdrianNicholls 1 (M Johnston) *led 1f: w ldr: led again over 2f out: hdd over 1f out: wknd fnl f* 14/1[3]	45
2	9	8	**El Viento (FR)**[13] 3658 2-8-10 0 BarryMcHugh(3) 6 (R A Fahey) *midfield: rdn and lost pl over 2f out: sn wknd* 7/2[2]	30
	10	2	**Commander Veejay** 2-8-2 0 TimothyAyres(7) 13 (B S Rothwell) *s.i.s: a towards rr* 100/1	20

1m 17.09s (0.19) **Going Correction** -0.175s/f (Firm) **10** Ran SP% **118.1**
Speed ratings (Par 96): **91,86,86,84,83 82,79,79,68,65**
toteswingers:1&2:£2.80, 1&3:£5.90, 2&3:£44.30 CSF £32.96 TOTE £1.60: £1.10, £3.00, £3.20; EX 22.70.
Owner J C Fretwell **Bred** A Butler **Trained** Maltby, S Yorks
FOCUS
There were a couple of showers during the afternoon but the ground remained good to firm all round. A few decent stables were represented in this maiden but the betting suggested it was all about the favourite.
NOTEBOOK
Easy Ticket(IRE), after finishing second to an above-average recruit at Ayr (winner has won since, and holds an entry in the Group 2 Gimcrack Stakes) he clearly came on from that and won with any amount in hand. What the form is worth is questionable, but he is a likeable sort who can keep progressing. (op 4-6 tchd 2-5)
Bajan Bear, despite having had two starts already, still looked a little green from an outside stall. Although no match for the winner, this was an improved effort and he looks an ideal nursery type.
Fieldgunner Kirkup(GER), coming from a respected yard, was the best of the newcomers and has clearly got a future on the evidence of this.
Grazeon Again(IRE) looked very green on this second start, but showed enough to warrant keeping him on side for later in the term. (tchd 50-1)
Sleights Boy(IRE) Official explanation: jockey said gelding hung both ways
El Viento(FR), was the disappointment of the race, having shown clear ability on his debut. He gave problems at the start, and it's probably best to pencil through this run. Official explanation: jockey said colt boiled over prior to start (op 10-3)

4117 TOTEPOOL FILLIES' H'CAP — 1m 4f 8y
7:05 (7:05) (Class 5) (0-75,75) 3-Y-O+ — £2,914 (£867; £433; £216) Stalls Low

Form				RPR
3020	1		**Umverti**[14] 3613 5-9-2 63 DanielTudhope 3 (N Bycroft) *mde all: rdn 2f out: kpt on wl* 6/1	76
/21-	2	2 3/4	**Chilly Filly (IRE)**[454] 1349 4-10-0 75 PaulMulrennan 6 (M Johnston) *hld up: hdwy on inner to trck wnr over 3f out: rdn 2f out: hung rt over 1f out: jinked lft jst ins fnl f: no imp after* 13/2	83
5-63	3	3/4	**Effervesce (IRE)**[25] 3266 3-9-1 74 RichardMullen 2 (Sir Michael Stoute) *trckd ldr: rdn over 2f out: kpt on same pce* 11/4[1]	81
3244	4	5	**Kathlatino**[15] 3601 3-8-10 69 PhillipMakin 4 (Micky Hammond) *in tch: rdn over 3f out: sn no imp* 12/1	68
5062	5	2 1/2	**Bollin Greta**[30] 3090 5-9-10 71 DavidNolan 5 (T D Easterby) *midfield: chsd along over 4f out: wknd over 2f out* 7/2[2]	66
-453	6	3 1/2	**Madamlily (IRE)**[14] 3617 4-9-1 62 (p) JamieSpencer 7 (J J Quinn) *trckd ldr: rdn over 3f out: wknd over 2f out* 7/1	51
-043	7	4	**Fantastic Cuix (FR)**[36] 2893 3-9-2 75 J-PGuillambert 8 (L M Cumani) *hld up: chsd along over 5f out: rdn 3f out: sn btn* 4/1[3]	58

2m 37.73s (-3.07) **Going Correction** -0.175s/f (Firm)
WFA 3 from 4yo+ 12lb **7** Ran SP% **116.7**
Speed ratings (Par 100): **103,101,100,97,95 93,90**
toteswingers:1&2:£13.40, 1&3:£7.00, 2&3:£4.20 CSF £45.19 CT £131.83 TOTE £9.50: £6.80, £4.30; EX 48.50.
Owner Mrs C M Whatley **Bred** N Bycroft **Trained** Brandsby, N Yorks

FOCUS
Just an ordinary gallop for this fillies' handicap.
Fantastic Cuix(FR) Official explanation: trainer's rep had no explanation for the poor form shown

4118 SIMPLY RED H'CAP — 5f
7:35 (7:37) (Class 3) (0-90,90) 3-Y-0+
£9,346 (£2,799; £1,399; £700; £349; £175) **Stalls** Low

Form — RPR

4-00 **1** **Kingdom Of Light**[34] 2978 3-9-11 **90** .... PaulMulrennan 5 — 102
(J Howard Johnson) *midfield: hdwy on inner over 2f out: rdn to ld 1f out: kpt on wl* **12/1**

3015 **2** *1 ¾* **Lucky Numbers (IRE)**[20] 3435 4-9-10 **85** .... JamieSpencer 2 — 92
(Paul Green) *led: rdn 2f out: hdd 1f out: kpt on* **17/2**

0622 **3** *nk* **Green Park (IRE)**[6] 3898 7-9-2 **77** ....(v) DavidNolan 1 — 83
(D Carroll) *trckd ldr: rdn and ev ch over 1f out: kpt on* **6/1**[2]

5031 **4** *nk* **Haajes**[6] 3902 6-9-5 **83** 6ex .... PaulPickard(3) 7 — 88
(P T Midgley) *in rr: outpcd bef 1/2-way: kpt on towards inner fr over 1f out: nrst fin* **8/1**

0453 **5** *nk* **Invincible Lad (IRE)**[8] 3828 6-9-9 **84** .... TonyHamilton 3 — 88
(E J Alston) *chsd ldrs: rdn over 2f out: kpt on* **8/1**

4501 **6** *¾* **Piscean (USA)**[14] 3629 5-9-10 **85** .... AdamKirby 4 — 87
(T Keddy) *slowly away: hld up: hdwy 2f out: kpt on one pce* **14/1**

0004 **7** *3 ¼* **Ishetoo**[21] 3406 6-9-6 **86** ....(bt) IanBrennan(5) 8 — 77
(Ollie Pears) *towards rr: chsd along bef 1/2-way: swtchd rt over 1f out: kpt on fnl f* **7/1**[3]

4011 **8** *½* **Ryan Style (IRE)**[20] 3430 4-9-3 **81** .... BarryMcHugh(3) 9 — 71
(Mrs L Williamson) *midfield: rdn 1/2-way: no imp fr over 1f out* **10/1**

2611 **9** *nk* **Atlantic Beach**[13] 3660 5-9-3 **78** .... RichardMullen 10 — 67
(D O'Meara) *chsd ldrs on outer: wknd over 1f out* **8/1**

-040 **10** *3 ½* **Go Go Green (IRE)**[20] 3435 4-9-8 **83** .... PhillipMakin 11 — 61
(D H Brown) *hld up on outer: nvr threatened* **11/2**[1]

4506 **11** *½* **Rowayton**[20] 3435 4-9-3 **78** ....(b[1]) DarryllHolland 14 — 54
(J D Bethell) *sn prom on outer: rdn over 2f out: wknd over 1f out* **16/1**

0010 **12** *3* **Ghostwing**[37] 2862 3-9-8 **90** ....(v) MartinLane(3) 12 — 55
(J Gallagher) *mid-div towards outer: rdn over 2f out: sn wknd* **20/1**

62.11 secs (-1.19) **Going Correction** -0.175s/f (Firm)
WFA 3 from 4yo+ 4lb — **12** Ran SP% **120.1**
Speed ratings (Par 107): **102,99,98,98,97 96,91,90,90,84 83,78**
toteswingers:1&2:£90.10, 1&3:£99.10, 2&3:£8.60 CSF £111.76 CT £684.36 TOTE £21.90: £5.70, £3.30, £2.30; EX 208.40.
Owner Transcend Bloodstock LLP **Bred** D M I Simcock **Trained** Billy Row, Co Durham
■ Stewards' Enquiry : David Nolan caution: used whip down shoulder in the forehand.

FOCUS
A competitive sprint handicap run at a sound pace. The first three home were all drawn in five and below.

NOTEBOOK
Kingdom Of Light, never far off the pace, this was only his tenth start and the Handicapper had given him a chance, dropping him 10lb in just two starts. He will be set for a rise back up the weights, but if able to reproduce this, can make his presence felt in similar valuable sprints. (op 20-1)
Lucky Numbers(IRE) ran a solid race, but after 27 starts he is rated 5lb higher than he has ever been successful from. (op 11-1 tchd 8-1)
Green Park(IRE), well backed beforehand, got very warm at the start. That said, he still appeared to run his race, but it is nearly two years since his last win on turf. (op 7-1 tchd 4-1)
Haajes, a winner last time out at Hamilton, found himself a long way back before doing some good late work. He remains in good form and should continue to pay his way in the coming weeks. (op 5-1)
Invincible Lad(IRE), running off a career-high mark, ran bang up to form. (op 7-1)
Piscean(USA) again didn't help himself with a slow start. (op 12-1 tchd 10-1)
Ryan Style(IRE) Official explanation: trainer's rep said gelding was unsuited by the track
Atlantic Beach, a hat-trick seeker, could never land a blow from his double-figure draw. (op 10-1)
Go Go Green(IRE), a course specialist, was another who was not helped by his high draw and can be forgiven this. (op 8-1)

4119 COLSTROPE CUP H'CAP — 1m 4y
8:10 (8:12) (Class 5) (0-70,70) 3-Y-0+ — **£2,914** (£867; £433; £216) **Stalls** Low

Form — RPR

-342 **1** **Flying Silks (IRE)**[37] 2864 4-9-12 **68** ....(v[1]) JamieSpencer 4 — 76
(J R Gask) *trckd ldr: rdn over 1f out: kpt on u.str.p fnl f to ld fnl 75yds* **7/2**[2]

0004 **2** *½* **Cheam Forever (USA)**[16] 3558 4-9-13 **69** .... SteveDrowne 1 — 76
(R Charlton) *led: rdn 2f out: hdd fnl 75yds* **10/3**[1]

0-50 **3** *½* **Boy Blue**[29] 3107 5-9-13 **69** .... DarryllHolland 2 — 75+
(P Salmon) *hld up in midfield: hdwy on inner 2f out: rdn and edgd rt 1f out: kpt on* **12/1**

2201 **4** *nk* **Desert Hunter (IRE)**[18] 3508 7-8-12 **59** .... PatrickDonaghy(5) 14 — 64+
(Micky Hammond) *trckd ldrs: rdn and outpcd over 2f out: briefly short of room over 1f out: r.o wl ins fnl f* **16/1**

5040 **5** *3* **French Art**[6] 3911 5-9-13 **69** ....(p) KirstyMilczarek 3 — 67
(N Tinkler) *midfield: hdwy to chse ldrs over 1f out: kpt on same pce* **14/1**

2424 **6** *nse* **Classic Descent**[6] 3911 5-9-4 **60** ....(t) TomMcLaughlin 9 — 58
(Mrs R A Carr) *hld up: swtchd rt over 1f out: r.o wl fnl f: nrst fin* **11/1**

6506 **7** *nk* **Glenmuir (IRE)**[20] 3438 7-9-5 **66** .... IanBrennan(5) 6 — 63
(J J Quinn) *midfield: rdn and wandered lft and rt over 1f out: kpt on fnl f* **16/1**

0053 **8** *hd* **Just Timmy Marcus**[37] 2864 4-9-2 **58** .... AdamKirby 15 — 55+
(B P J Baugh) *stdd s: hld up: kpt on fr over 1f out: nvr rchd ldrs* **14/1**

2460 **9** *¾* **Whipma Whopma Gate (IRE)**[23] 3317 5-9-3 **66** ....(v) NeilFarley(7) 10 — 61
(D Carroll) *trckd ldrs: rdn over 2f out: wknd ins fnl f* **25/1**

01 **10** *nse* **Celtic Step**[40] 2788 6-9-5 **61** .... TonyHamilton 7 — 56
(P D Niven) *prom: rdn over 2f out: wknd fnl f* **14/1**

0603 **11** *½* **Champain Sands (IRE)**[17] 3538 11-8-10 **55** .... PaulPickard(3) 5 — 49
(E J Alston) *s.i.s: hld up: n.d* **20/1**

1220 **12** *nk* **Chief Red Cloud (USA)**[23] 3317 4-10-0 **70** .... PaulMulrennan 13 — 63
(J R Weymes) *midfield on outer: rdn over 2f out: lost pl over 1f out* **14/1**

4061 **13** *6* **Nurai**[18] 3503 3-8-5 **55** .... DuranFentiman 8 — 33
(P W D'Arcy) *hld up in midfield: rdn over 2f out: sn no imp* **8/1**[3]

-143 **14** *1 ¼* **Ours (IRE)**[150] 572 7-9-11 **70** ....(p) BarryMcHugh(3) 12 — 47
(John A Harris) *midfield on outer: brief hdwy over 2f out: sn wknd* **16/1**

0-52 **15** *18* **Betteras Bertie**[18] 3508 7-9-9 **65** .... PhillipMakin 11 — —
(M Brittain) *hld up: a bhd* **20/1**

1m 44.5s (-1.40) **Going Correction** -0.175s/f (Firm)
WFA 3 from 4yo+ 8lb — **15** Ran SP% **130.1**
Speed ratings (Par 103): **100,99,99,98,95 95,95,95,94,94 93,93,87,86,68**
toteswingers:1&2:£5.30, 1&3:£6.50, 2&3:£15.80 CSF £16.36 CT £127.36 TOTE £4.50: £2.00, £2.50, £4.60; EX 20.10.
Owner Coffen Construction **Bred** Ennistown Stud **Trained** Sutton Veny, Wilts

FOCUS
Six course and distance winners in this 51-70 handicap made it competitive and wide open. It was run at a sound pace and the form looks solid enough.
Celtic Step Official explanation: jockey said gelding hung both ways
Nurai Official explanation: jockey said filly never travelled
Betteras Bertie Official explanation: trainer said gelding was unsuited by fast ground

4120 GREYHOUNDS MAKE GREAT PETS MAIDEN H'CAP — 1m 2f 6y
8:40 (8:40) (Class 5) (0-70,70) 3-Y-0+ — **£2,914** (£867; £433; £216) **Stalls** Low

Form — RPR

0223 **1** **Avitus**[16] 3552 4-9-7 **55** .... PhillipMakin 7 — 63
(Micky Hammond) *trckd ldrs: hdwy over 2f out: rdn to ld over 1f out: kpt on* **9/2**[2]

0 **2** *1 ¼* **Descaro (USA)**[14] 3613 4-9-11 **59** .... SteveDrowne 2 — 65
(D O'Meara) *hld up in midfield: rdn and hdwy over 2f out: kpt on to take 2nd ins fnl f* **8/1**

5522 **3** *nk* **Star Addition**[13] 3676 4-9-8 **56** .... DarryllHolland 1 — 61
(E J Alston) *hld up in rr: rdn and hdwy over 3f out: styd on fr over 1f out* **9/2**[2]

0326 **4** *2 ¼* **High Rolling**[18] 3506 3-9-3 **61** .... DuranFentiman 4 — 61
(T D Easterby) *led: rdn 2f out: hdd over 1f out: no ex fnl f* **7/1**

4-03 **5** *7* **Chicane**[28] 3157 3-9-12 **70** .... RichardMullen 10 — 56
(W J Haggas) *trckd ldrs: rdn over 3f out: wknd wl over 1f out* **7/2**[1]

6066 **6** *shd* **Maybeme**[18] 3496 4-9-9 **57** .... DanielTudhope 12 — 43
(N Bycroft) *s.i.s: sn in tch: chsd along over 3f out: sn no imp* **14/1**

45-4 **7** *2 ½* **Gosforth Park**[57] 2259 4-8-12 **53** .... JohnCavanagh(7) 5 — 34
(M Brittain) *s.i.s: racd keenly: hdwy on outer 5f out: rdn over 3f out: sn wknd* **12/1**

5203 **8** *8* **Pedasus (USA)**[14] 3614 4-10-0 **62** ....(p) AdamKirby 8 — 27
(T Keddy) *hld up: rdn 4f out: sn btn* **14/1**

0600 **9** *9* **Fantastic Favour**[18] 3506 3-9-2 **60** .... TonyHamilton 9 — 7
(Jedd O'Keeffe) *prom: rdn over 3f out: sn wknd* **33/1**

4244 **10** *4* **Cat O' Nine Tails**[17] 3532 3-9-7 **65** .... PaulMulrennan 11 — 4
(M Johnston) *pressed ldr: rdn 3f out: sn wknd* **13/2**[3]

2m 12.37s (-1.33) **Going Correction** -0.175s/f (Firm)
WFA 3 from 4yo+ 10lb — **10** Ran SP% **119.5**
Speed ratings (Par 103): **98,97,96,94,89 89,87,80,73,70**
toteswingers:1&2:£25.10, 1&3:£3.00, 2&3:£9.40 CSF £41.54 CT £174.13 TOTE £6.00: £1.20, £2.20, £2.60; EX 42.70.
Owner Paul & Anne Sellars **Bred** Downland Bloodstock **Trained** Middleham Moor, N Yorks

FOCUS
A maiden handicap for those rated 51-70 but the top-weight was 8lb below the ceiling rating. It was run at a sound pace.
Pedasus(USA) Official explanation: jockey said gelding never travelled

4121 JUST-A-BET H'CAP — 6f
9:10 (9:10) (Class 5) (0-75,75) 3-Y-0+ — **£2,914** (£867; £433; £216) **Stalls** Low

Form — RPR

0005 **1** **Orpsie Boy (IRE)**[16] 3551 7-9-5 **74** .... DaleSwift(7) 3 — 89
(Mrs R A Carr) *midfield: rdn and hdwy 2f out: drvn to ld ins fnl f: kpt on* **7/2**[2]

344 **2** *¾* **Fadhb Ar Bith (IRE)**[29] 3107 5-9-7 **69** .... JamieSpencer 10 — 81+
(John A Harris) *stdd s: niggled in rr bef 1/2-way: hdwy on inner over 1f out: swtchd rt 1f out: r.o strly: nrst fin* **3/1**[1]

6323 **3** *2 ½* **Minturno (USA)**[22] 3357 4-8-12 **63** ....(p) BarryMcHugh(3) 1 — 67
(Mrs A Duffield) *trckd ldrs: hdwy over 2f out: rdn to ld over 1f out: hdd ins fnl f* **13/2**

0435 **4** *2 ½* **Mr Wolf**[22] 3356 9-9-0 **67** ....(p) IanBrennan(5) 9 — 63
(J J Quinn) *led: hdd over 1f out: sn wknd* **8/1**

0-50 **5** *1 ½* **Spiritofthewest (IRE)**[2] 4024 4-9-6 **68** .... PhillipMakin 2 — 60
(D H Brown) *hld up: rdn 2f out: kpt on one pce* **14/1**

0000 **6** *1* **Pearly Wey**[15] 3584 7-9-11 **73** .... DanielTudhope 6 — 61
(I W McInnes) *hld up: rdn and brief hdwy 2f out: no imp fr over 1f out* **14/1**

3000 **7** *2* **Northern Bolt**[4] 3970 5-9-8 **73** ....(v) MartinLane(3) 4 — 55
(I W McInnes) *hld up: rdn over 2f out: nvr threatened* **14/1**

40-0 **8** *1 ¼* **Commando Scott (IRE)**[15] 3584 9-8-10 **65** .... NeilFarley(7) 5 — 43
(D Carroll) *midfield: rdn over 2f out: sn one pce* **16/1**

0246 **9** *¾* **Tawzeea (IRE)**[21] 3409 5-9-6 **68** .... DarryllHolland 11 — 44
(J D Bethell) *sn prom: rdn over 2f out: wknd over 1f out* **12/1**

204 **10** *20* **Coolree Star (IRE)**[6] 3904 3-9-8 **75** ....(p) LeeVickers 7 — —
(J A Glover) *chsd ldrs on outer: rdn 1/2-way and sn wknd: eased* **28/1**

0332 **11** *2 ¾* **The Hermitage (IRE)**[9] 3773 3-9-7 **74** .... PaulMulrennan 13 — —
(M Johnston) *sn prom on outer: rdn over 2f out: sn wknd: eased* **6/1**[3]

1m 14.92s (-1.98) **Going Correction** -0.175s/f (Firm)
WFA 3 from 4yo+ 5lb — **11** Ran SP% **123.0**
Speed ratings (Par 103): **106,105,101,98,96 95,92,90,89,63 59**
toteswingers:1&2:£3.10, 1&3:£6.90, 2&3:£5.70 CSF £15.20 CT £68.96 TOTE £3.60: £1.80, £1.90, £1.80; EX 23.70 Place 6 £187.11; Place 5 £127.70.
Owner Miss Vanessa Church **Bred** Minch Bloodstock **Trained** Huby, N Yorks

FOCUS
A sound gallop for this 56-75 handicap.
The Hermitage(IRE) Official explanation: jockey said filly ran flat
T/Plt: £679.20 to a £1 stake. Pool:£57,135.49 - 61.40 winning tickets. T/Qpdt: £38.90 to a £1 stake. Pool:£4,806.14 - 91.20 winning tickets AS

4035 HAMBURG (R-H)
Friday, July 16

OFFICIAL GOING: Turf: good

4122 GROSSER PREIS DER JUNGHEINRICH GABELSTAPLER (HAMBURG FLIEGER-TROPHY) (GROUP 3) (3YO+) (TURF) — 6f
6:45 (12:00) 3-Y-0+
£28,318 (£9,734; £4,867; £2,654; £1,769; £1,327)

Form — RPR

1 **Govinda (USA)**[60] 3-8-8 0 .... EPedroza 2 — 103
(A Wohler, Germany) *broke wl: settled in 5th: mde gd prog to vie for ld early in st: grabbed ld 1 1/2f out: r.o wl: won comf* **109/10**

4-02 **2** *1* **Smooth Operator (GER)**[68] 1955 4-9-2 0 .... THellier 8 — 104
(Mario Hofer, Germany) *racd in 4th: swtchd to outside in st: matched strides w wnr tl 1 1/2f out: r.o wl* **7/5**[1]

-213 **3** 2 ½ **Cadeau For Maggi**[32] 5-9-0 0 GeraldMosse 1 94
(H-A Pantall, France) *settled towards rr: mde gd prog on ins into st: r.o wl* **17/2**

5-05 **4** *shd* **Nareion (GER)**[40] 2805 4-9-0 0 DominiqueBoeuf 4 94
(W Baltromei, Germany) *a.p fr s: gd prog in st once finding clr run: r.o wl* **6/1**[3]

6-00 **5** ½ **Atlantic Sport (USA)**[33] 5-9-2 0 (b) AStarke 5 94
(P Schiergen, Germany) *broke wl: shkn up ent st: flattered briefly: r.o one pce* **32/5**

2 **6** 3 ½ **Alcohuaz (CHI)**[45] 5-9-2 0 (b) LennartHammer-Hansen 7 83
(Lennart Reuterskiold Jr, Sweden) *led fr s for 1 1/2f: then settled in 2nd: began to weaken ent st: fdd* **147/10**

0-13 **7** *nk* **Contat (GER)**[40] 2805 7-9-4 0 RJuracek 9 84
(P Vovcenko, Germany) *broke slowly: mde sme prog ent st: flattered briefly then fdd* **39/10**[2]

8 ½ **Intigra (GER)**[33] 4-8-13 0 NRichter 6 77
(T Mundry, Germany) *a towards rr and nvr figured* **106/10**

9 *1* **Vianello (IRE)**[110] 3-8-10 0 (b) FilipMinarik 3 75
(P Schiergen, Germany) *broke fast: initially racing in 2nd: tk ld after 1 1/2f: hdd early in st: sn btn* **117/10**

1m 10.24s (-2.45)
WFA 3 from 4yo+ 5lb **9** Ran SP% **131.7**
WIN (incl. 10 euro stake): 119. PLACES: 23, 15, 22. SF: 589.
Owner Dr Christoph Berglar **Bred** F N Sahadi **Trained** Germany

NOTEBOOK
Govinda(USA) swept to the front for a surprise victory.

4089 HAYDOCK (L-H)
Saturday, July 17

OFFICIAL GOING: 5f and 6f - good to soft (good in places); 7f and 1m - good to soft; 1m2f and 1m6f - good to soft (good in places)
Wind: Fresh, against Weather: Sunny periods and showers

4123 E B F HATTONS TRAVEL MAIDEN STKS 6f
6:40 (6:41) (Class 5) 2-Y-O **£3,238** (£963; £481; £240) **Stalls** Centre

Form RPR

1 **Shropshire (IRE)** 2-9-3 0 MichaelHills 9 90+
(B W Hills) *dwlt: swtchd lft after s and sn trcking ldrs: swtchd outside and smooth hdwy to chse ldr wl over 1f out: qckn wl to ld ent fnl f and sn clr* **4/1**[2]

233 **2** *4* **Lexi's Hero (IRE)**[21] 3426 2-9-3 0 JamieSpencer 10 81
(K A Ryan) *led: pushed clr 2f out: rdn over 1f out: hdd ent fnl f: sn one pce* **9/2**[3]

2 **3** *5* **Uptown Guy (USA)**[21] 3449 2-9-3 0 TomEaves 8 63
(M Dods) *t.k.h early: in tch: hdwy to trck ldrs 1/2-way: effrt 2f out: sn rdn and one pce* **2/1**[1]

4 2 ½ **Chosen Character (IRE)** 2-9-3 0 RichardKingscote 15 56+
(Tom Dascombe) *towards rr and pushed along after 2f: hdwy 2f out: sn rdn and styd on ins fnl f: nrst fin* **25/1**

4 **5** *1* **Roman Strait**[37] 2895 2-9-3 0 FrannyNorton 5 53
(M Blanshard) *chsd ldrs: rdn along and sltly outpcd 1/2-way: kpt on u.p fnl 2f* **40/1**

6 *nk* **The Nought Man (FR)** 2-9-3 0 TonyHamilton 14 52+
(R A Fahey) *dwlt and bhd: hdwy 2f out: shkn up and styd on wl fnl f: nrst fin* **33/1**

7 1 ¼ **Kingscroft (IRE)** 2-9-3 0 JoeFanning 1 48
(M Johnston) *cl up on outer: rdn along over 2f out: grad wknd* **20/1**

8 *nk* **Silver Tigress** 2-8-12 0 PJMcDonald 13 42+
(C W Thornton) *dwlt and bhd: hdwy and sltly checked 2f out: sn rdn and kpt on ins fnl f* **66/1**

02 **9** *nse* **Shaabek (IRE)**[8] 3842 2-9-3 0 TonyCulhane 3 47
(M R Channon) *chsd ldrs: rdn along over 2f out: drvn wl over 1f out and sn wknd* **16/1**

03 **10** 4 ½ **Peters Spirit (IRE)**[21] 3449 2-8-12 0 PaulHanagan 16 28
(R A Fahey) *in tch on wd outside: hdwy to chse ldrs 1/2-way: rdn over 2f out and sn wknd* **6/1**

0 **11** 2 ¾ **C P Joe (IRE)**[15] 3624 2-9-3 0 PatCosgrave 2 25
(Paul Green) *cl up: rdn along 1/2-way: wknd 2f out* **9/1**

50 **12** ½ **Token Gift**[7] 3915 2-9-0 0 MartinLane(3) 4 24
(P D Evans) *midfield: rdn along bef 1/2-way: sn bhd* **66/1**

6 **13** *dist* **Immacolata (IRE)**[57] 2292 2-8-9 0 ow2 MarkCoumbe(5) 12 —
(A Berry) *chsd ldrs: rdn along and lost pl bef 1/2-way: sn bhd: t.o and eased fnl 2f* **200/1**

1m 15.08s (1.58) **Going Correction** +0.125s/f (Good) **13** Ran SP% **119.2**
Speed ratings (Par 94): **94,88,82,78,77 76,75,74,74,68 65,64,—**
toteswingers: 1&2 £4.70, 1&3 £2.60, 2&3 £3.60 CSF £21.14 TOTE £5.70: £2.00, £2.00, £1.40; EX 27.30.
Owner The Hon Mrs J M Corbett & C Wright **Bred** Tally-Ho Stud **Trained** Lambourn, Berks

FOCUS
A fair maiden, made more interesting by the presence of some well-bred newcomers. The winner impressed. They raced up the centre of the track.

NOTEBOOK
Shropshire(IRE), a 70,000euros newcomer with a Gimcrack entry, made an encouraging debut. He missed the break slightly and was well back in the early stages, but began to make progress 2f out and led inside the last. He should stay farther than this and, although the bare form is not overly exciting, he won with a fair bit in hand and seems sure to improve. (op 9-2 tchd 7-2 and 10-3 in places)
Lexi's Hero(IRE), whose trio of first-three placings suggested he can win a small race of this type, looks the ideal marker for assessing the level achieved by the winner. Smartly away, he was always helping to force the pace and stayed on well, even when overhauled. He just needs a little luck to break his duck. (tchd 11-2)
Uptown Guy(USA), a 215,000gns Gimcrack entry who had finished second on his Newcastle debut three weeks earlier, was rather disappointing. He ran okay, chasing the pace from the outset, but was left behind in the closing stages. This looked a step backwards. (op 9-4 tchd 5-2 and 3-1 in places)
Chosen Character(IRE), a half-brother to last season's decent juvenile Love Lockdown, hinted at better things to come. He was slowly away, but stayed on in good style from the rear and was still plugging away inside the final furlong.
Roman Strait, a dip-backed colt who had finished fourth on his Nottingham debut in June, was another to make some late progress. This run does not in itself indicate he has the talent to win an average maiden, but he might make a mark in nurseries, for which he will be eligible after one more run.
Kingscroft(IRE) showed early speed before fading in the closing stages, as if the run would bring him on. (tchd 25-1)

4124 SAFEVENT WINDOW NURSERY 5f
7:10 (7:11) (Class 5) 2-Y-O **£2,590** (£770; £385; £192) **Stalls** Centre

Form RPR

421 **1** **Electric Waves (IRE)**[33] 3029 2-9-7 **80** RichardMullen 7 89+
(E S McMahon) *dwlt: sn trcking ldrs: smooth hdwy on outer 1/2-way: rdn to ld over 1f out: kpt on* **3/1**[1]

623 **2** 1 ¾ **Royal Liaison**[22] 3392 2-8-7 **69** MartinLane(3) 2 72+
(M L W Bell) *dwlt and towards rr: hdwy 1/2-way: effrt: nt clr run and swtchd lft over 1f out: rdn to chse wnr ins fnl f: sn edgd rt and no imp* **3/1**[1]

2213 **3** *4* **Madam Markievicz (IRE)**[16] 3598 2-8-13 **72** (p) PhillipMakin 3 60
(M Dods) *chsd ldrs: effrt over 2f out: rdn wl over 1f out: kpt on same pce* **8/1**

004 **4** *nk* **Roman Ruler (IRE)**[18] 3528 2-7-12 **57** oh2 PaulQuinn 1 44
(C W Fairhurst) *chsd ldrs: rdn along 2f out: edgd rt and sltly outpcd wl over 1f out: kpt on u.p ins fnl f* **25/1**

6652 **5** *1* **Wild Hysteria (IRE)**[16] 3598 2-8-0 **59** JamieMackay 4 43
(T P Tate) *hld up in rr: swtchd rt and hdwy 2f out: rdn over 1f out: edgd lft and kpt on same pce fnl f* **10/1**

4641 **6** 1 ½ **Johnny Hancocks (IRE)**[10] 3770 2-8-9 **68** JamieSpencer 8 46
(P D Evans) *qckly away and led: rdn and hdd 2f out: sn wknd* **9/2**[2]

5461 **7** ¾ **Coconut Ice**[9] 3817 2-8-8 **72** RossAtkinson(5) 10 48
(Tom Dascombe) *plld hrd: chsd ldr: rdn 2f out and sn wknd* **5/1**[3]

066 **8** *30* **Love Club**[49] 2540 2-8-1 **60** FrannyNorton 6 —
(B P J Baugh) *a in rr: rdn along and outpcd fr 1/2-way* **20/1**

61.80 secs (0.80) **Going Correction** +0.125s/f (Good) **8** Ran SP% **113.7**
Speed ratings (Par 94): **98,95,88,88,86 84,83,35**
toteswingers: 1&2 £1.50, 1&3 £2.90, 2&3 £16.10 CSF £11.69 CT £63.18 TOTE £3.60: £1.30, £1.60, £1.80; EX 6.10.
Owner J C Fretwell **Bred** Ms Michelle Lyons **Trained** Lichfield, Staffs
■ Stewards' Enquiry : Jamie Spencer one-day ban: careless riding (Aug 1)

FOCUS
An interesting nursery, in which they raced up the far rail and the winner continued her progression. The first pair were clear. The 'official' ratings shown next to each horse are estimated and for information purposes only.

NOTEBOOK
Electric Waves(IRE) had been progressing nicely, winning a Warwick maiden on her latest start, and took another step forward here. She quickened smartly approaching the final furlong and won going away. The handicapper will take note of this, but she is improving and may well remain competitive in nurseries even when reassessed. A step up to Listed level, in search of some black type, appears to be connections' alternative plan. (op 5-2)
Royal Liaison, switched to a nursery and dropping in trip after three encouraging runs in 6f maidens, was also relatively slow to stride. She tagged on the back of the pack early on, but was travelling well 2f out and, when eased left between rivals, stayed on encouragingly.
Madam Markievicz(IRE), third in a Redcar nursery at the start of the month, probably ran to much the same level here. Always close up, she stayed on in the closing stages, without exhibiting much of a finishing kick. (op 6-1)
Roman Ruler(IRE), racing from 1lb out of the handicap, performed with credit. In midfield early, he improved his position in the closing stages as others tired. (op 33-1)
Johnny Hancocks(IRE), successful in a Catterick seller ten days earlier, took them along at a good clip but had nothing left in the tank by the final furlong. (op 6-1 tchd 7-1 in places)
Coconut Ice, winner of a weak Folkestone maiden last time out, also showed speed in the first half of the race. She, too, faded late on, though. (op 7-1)

4125 LIVESEY SPOTTISWOOD H'CAP 1m 6f
7:40 (7:40) (Class 4) (0-85,83) 4-Y-O+ **£4,533** (£1,348; £674; £336) **Stalls** Low

Form RPR

-625 **1** **Cotillion**[31] 3090 4-9-0 **76** TomEaves 5 88
(Ian Williams) *hld up in rr: hdwy 3f out: effrt on outer wl over 1f out: rdn to ld appr fnl f: sn clr and styd on strly* **8/1**

-600 **2** *5* **Omokoroa (IRE)**[36] 2941 4-9-2 **78** PatCosgrave 3 83
(M H Tompkins) *trckd ldr: hdwy over 3f out: effrt to chal over 2f out: rdn and slt ld 1 1/2f out: sn drvn and hdd appr fnl f: kpt on same pce* **5/1**[2]

4633 **3** *nk* **Abayaan**[35] 2975 4-9-0 **76** (p) TomMcLaughlin 10 81
(Jane Chapple-Hyam) *led: rdn along over 3f out: jnd over 2f out and sn drvn: hdd 1 1/2f out: kpt on u.p fnl f* **15/2**

4060 **4** *1* **Rangefinder**[17] 3566 6-9-7 **83** (p) JamieSpencer 12 86
(Jane Chapple-Hyam) *hld up and bhd: hdwy 3f out: rdn to chse ldrs wl over 1f out: sn drvn and one pce fnl f* **9/2**[1]

4200 **5** *4* **Highland Legacy**[17] 3566 6-9-2 **81** MartinLane(3) 11 79
(M L W Bell) *trckd ldng pair: effrt 3f out and sn rdn: drvn 2f out and sn wknd* **6/1**[3]

2-03 **6** 3 ¾ **Bollin Judith**[23] 3367 4-8-3 **65** PaulHanagan 9 57
(T D Easterby) *in tch on outer: hdwy to chse ldrs 5f out: rdn along over 3f out: sn wknd* **6/1**[3]

0230 **7** *3* **Red Kestrel (USA)**[11] 3764 5-8-11 **73** TonyHamilton 7 61
(K A Ryan) *chsd ldrs: pushed along and lost pl over 5f out: rdn over 3f out and sn in rr* **20/1**

-526 **8** *13* **Crocus Rose**[15] 3634 4-9-1 **77** RichardMullen 2 47
(H J L Dunlop) *chsd ldrs: rdn along over 3f out: sn drvn and wknd* **8/1**

-056 **9** *16* **Featherweight (IRE)**[17] 3566 4-9-0 **76** MichaelHills 4 24
(B W Hills) *hld up: hdwy on inner to trck ldrs 1/2-way: rdn along over 3f out and sn wknd* **13/2**

3m 8.60s (7.40) **Going Correction** +0.25s/f (Good) **9** Ran SP% **115.5**
Speed ratings (Par 105): **88,85,84,84,82 79,78,70,61**
toteswingers: 1&2 £12.70, 1&3 £7.30, 2&3 £4.60 CSF £47.70 CT £314.70 TOTE £10.20: £3.10, £2.20, £2.70; EX 77.50.
Owner Mr & Mrs G Middlebrook **Bred** Mr & Mrs G Middlebrook **Trained** Portway, Worcs

FOCUS
A fair handicap and an impressive winner.
Bollin Judith Official explanation: trainer's rep said filly had a breathing problem
Crocus Rose Official explanation: jockey said filly had no more to give
Featherweight(IRE) Official explanation: jockey said filly lost its action 3f out

4126 HATTONS SOLICITORS WELSH EMPEROR CONDITIONS STKS 7f 30y
8:10 (8:11) (Class 3) 3-Y-O+ **£8,095** (£2,408; £1,203; £601) **Stalls** Low

Form RPR

0110 **1** **Harrison George (IRE)**[43] 2707 5-9-9 108 PaulHanagan 8 114
(R A Fahey) *trckd ldr: hdwy and cl up 4f out: rdn to ld over 2f out: drvn ent fnl f and kpt on gamely* **11/2**[3]

1036 **2** 1 ¼ **Sirocco Breeze**[34] 2999 5-9-1 105 TedDurcan 5 103
(Saeed Bin Suroor) *trckd ldrs: hdwy on outer 3f out: rdn to chse ldrs wl over 1f out: drvn to chal ent fnl f and ev ch tl no ex last 75yds* **7/2**[2]

0-3 **3** 1 ½ **Suruor (IRE)**[71] 1857 4-9-1 100 .... JamieSpencer 2 99
(D M Simcock) *hld up and bhd: hdwy on inner 3f out: rdn to chal wl over 1f out and ev ch tl drvn: edgd rt and one pce ins fnl f* **10/3**[1]

12-0 **4** ½ **Za Za Zoom (IRE)**[31] 3071 3-8-7 96 ow1 .... MichaelHills 6 93
(B W Hills) *trckd ldrs: hdwy over 3f out: rdn 2f out: drvn and one pce ent fnl f* **8/1**

3205 **5** 2 ½ **Asset (IRE)**[21] 3460 7-9-1 105 .... (b) RichardMullen 4 90
(Saeed Bin Suroor) *dwlt: hld up in rr: hdwy over 2f out: n.m.r and rdn over 1f out: kpt on ins fnl f* **13/2**

0P-5 **6** 6 **Welsh Emperor (IRE)**[70] 1904 11-9-9 104 .... TonyCulhane 3 82
(T P Tate) *led: rdn along over 3f out: hdd over 2f out: sn drvn and wknd appr fnl f* **10/1**

0140 **7** 1 **Kaptain Kirkup (IRE)**[31] 3066 3-8-8 104 .... TomEaves 7 69
(M Dods) *t.k.h early: trckd ldng pair: effrt 3f out: rdn along over 2f out and cl up tl drvn and wknd over 1f out* **11/2**[3]

1m 32.7s **Going Correction** +0.25s/f (Good)
WFA 3 from 4yo+ 7lb **7** Ran SP% **109.6**
Speed ratings (Par 107): **110,108,106,106,103 96,95**
toteswingers: 1&2 £2.50, 1&3 £4.00, 2&3 £2.80 CSF £22.86 TOTE £5.70: £2.80, £2.40; EX 26.50.
Owner P D Smith Holdings Ltd **Bred** R P Ryan **Trained** Musley Bank, N Yorks

FOCUS
A decent and wide-open conditions event.

NOTEBOOK
Harrison George(IRE) was officially top-rated, but he had to give weight to all bar one of his rivals, so this was a creditable effort. He chased the leader from the outset and was driven to take the lead over 2f out. Challenged strongly afterwards, he stayed on bravely and never looked likely to be overtaken. This was markedly better than his last run at Epsom, where the undulations seemed to find him out, and connections are now looking at a Listed race over 1m at Pontefract on July 25. (op 6-1 tchd 13-2)
Sirocco Breeze, twice successful at Meydan early in the year, made his bid closest to the stands' rail. He had been held up in the early stages, but worked his way into contention turning for home and was second 2f out. From there on, though, he could not match the winner's determination. (op 10-3 tchd 3-1)
Suruor(IRE), a close third in a Chester handicap on his latest start, posted a commendable effort considering he was up against it at the weights. He stayed on bravely enough in the closing stages, but his mark of 100 may make him difficult to place. (op 11-4)
Za Za Zoom(IRE), the only filly in the line-up, was always in much the same place. She did not quicken in the closing stages and may benefit from even softer condtions. (op 6-1)
Asset(IRE), three times successful at Listed level but on an extended losing run, never looked likely to regain winning ways. (op 8-1)
Welsh Emperor(IRE), winner of this race, now named after him, in 2008 and 2009, made a bold bid to land the hat-trick by setting a decent gallop from the start. He does not look the force of old at the age of 11, though, and connections will surely be at least half contemplating retirement for this grand servant. (op 16-1 tchd 8-1)

4127 GPW RECRUITMENT H'CAP — 1m 30y
8:40 (8:41) (Class 5) (0-70,68) 3-Y-O — £2,590 (£770; £385; £192) Stalls Low

Form RPR

0020 **1** **Pintura**[22] 3387 3-9-9 68 .... (p) JamieSpencer 17 76
(D M Simcock) *hld up in midfield: hdwy 3f out: swtchd rt and rdn to chse ldrs over 1f out: drvn to chal ent fnl f: styd on to ld last 100yds* **5/1**[1]

0061 **2** nk **Scottish Boogie (IRE)**[5] 3957 3-9-6 65 .... JamesDoyle 5 72
(S Kirk) *a.p: hdwy to chse ldr 4f out: rdn to ld 2f out: drvn and jnd ent fnl f: hdd and no ex last 100yds* **5/1**[1]

0-60 **3** 2 ¾ **North Shadow**[13] 3710 3-8-10 55 .... FrannyNorton 8 56
(A D Brown) *led: rdn along over 3f out: hdd 2f out and sn drvn: kpt on u.p* **25/1**

-005 **4** ½ **Diamondgeezer Luke (IRE)**[5] 3957 3-9-3 62 .... StephenCraine 11 62
(Patrick Morris) *midfield: hdwy on inner to chse ldrs over 2f out and sn rdn: drvn and kpt on same pce fnl f* **14/1**

0024 **5** 1 ¼ **Dazeen**[22] 3387 3-9-6 65 .... TonyCulhane 3 62
(P T Midgley) *trckd ldrs: effrt 3f out: rdn and ch 2f out: sn drvn and kpt on same pce* **7/1**[3]

44-2 **6** shd **Zenarinda**[103] 1132 3-9-9 68 .... PatCosgrave 10 65
(M H Tompkins) *trckd ldrs: effrt 3f out: rdn along over 2f out: no imp fr over 1f out* **7/1**[3]

0500 **7** 1 ½ **Elegant Dancer (IRE)**[14] 3677 3-8-2 50 .... (p) PaulPickard(3) 2 43
(Paul Green) *in tch: hdwy to chse ldrs 1/2-way: rdn 3f out: drvn wl over 1f out and grad wknd* **25/1**

02-0 **8** 1 ½ **Madame Excelerate**[31] 3074 3-9-4 63 .... TomMcLaughlin 4 53
(W M Brisbourne) *dwlt and towards rr: hdwy 3f out: sn rdn along and nvr rchd ldrs* **40/1**

0-U3 **9** 2 ¼ **Koo And The Gang (IRE)**[23] 3371 3-8-13 65 .... DaleSwift(7) 12 50
(B Ellison) *s.i.s: hmpd and carried lft after s: sme hdwy wl over 2f out: sn rdn and nvr a factor* **8/1**

-000 **10** 1 ¾ **Quaker Parrot**[15] 3628 3-9-1 67 .... SoniaEaton(7) 7 48
(Tom Dascombe) *in tch: rdn along 3f out: grad wknd* **40/1**

4006 **11** 1 **Music Maestro (IRE)**[14] 3676 3-9-9 68 .... MichaelHills 16 46
(B W Hills) *s.i.s and swtchd lft s: sme hdwy on inner over 2f out and sn rdn: nvr a factor* **10/1**

0-00 **12** 1 ½ **Silk Runner (IRE)**[56] 2336 3-8-7 55 .... (t) PatrickHills(3) 14 30
(J W Hills) *a in rr* **33/1**

5-40 **13** 1 ½ **Peckforton Castle**[21] 3428 3-8-10 55 .... TomEaves 1 26
(Patrick Morris) *midfield on inner: rdn along 1/2-way: sn wknd* **25/1**

0-00 **14** 2 ½ **Miss Chaumiere**[37] 2900 3-8-7 55 .... MartinLane(3) 9 21
(M L W Bell) *midfield: effrt to chse ldrs over 4f out: rdn along over 3f out and sn wknd* **20/1**

6246 **15** 3 ¼ **Clare Harrier (IRE)**[9] 3808 3-8-8 58 .... MarkCoumbe(5) 6 16
(A Berry) *a in rr* **50/1**

1461 **16** 6 **Ellies Image**[10] 3775 3-9-1 60 .... PaulHanagan 13 4
(B P J Baugh) *midfield: rdn along over 3f out: sn wknd* **6/1**[2]

1m 49.16s (4.46) **Going Correction** +0.25s/f (Good) **16** Ran SP% **125.6**
Speed ratings (Par 100): **87,86,83,83,82 82,80,79,76,75 74,72,71,68,65 59**
toteswingers: 1&2 £5.60, 1&3 £31.30, 2&3 £28.30 TOTE £5.70: £1.40, £1.70, £6.30, £3.20; EX 17.70.
Owner Dr Marwan Koukash **Bred** Dulverton Equine **Trained** Newmarket, Suffolk
■ Stewards' Enquiry : Michael Hills three-day ban: careless riding (Aug 1-3)

FOCUS
A modest event, with the top weight rated just 68. They came stands' side in the home straight.

Silk Runner(IRE) Official explanation: jockey filly never travelled

4128 STRADONE LIMITED MARKETING H'CAP — 1m 2f 95y
9:10 (9:12) (Class 5) (0-75,74) 3-Y-O — £2,590 (£770; £385; £192) Stalls Centre

Form RPR

1-50 **1** **Think Its All Over (USA)**[66] 2033 3-9-9 73 .... JamieSpencer 1 80
(T P Tate) *mde virtually all: rdn along 3f out: jnd 2f out and sn drvn: kpt on gamely ins fnl f* **9/4**[1]

3302 **2** 1 ¼ **Ice Viking (IRE)**[36] 2935 3-9-0 64 .... (b) PaulMulrennan 4 69
(J G Given) *hld up in rr: smooth hdwy 3f out: chal 2f out: rdn to dispute ld and ev ch whn edgd lft jst ins fnl f: kpt on same pce* **10/3**[2]

1455 **3** 2 ¼ **Mighty Clarets (IRE)**[15] 3612 3-9-4 68 .... PaulHanagan 7 69
(R A Fahey) *trckd ldrs: pushed along over 3f out: swtchd lft and rdn over 2f out: chsd ldng pair wl over 1f out: no imp fnl f* **10/3**[2]

0000 **4** 5 **Toga Tiger (IRE)**[28] 3208 3-9-0 64 .... TonyCulhane 6 55
(P T Midgley) *in rr: hdwy wl over 2f out: sn rdn and n.d* **18/1**

0165 **5** 5 **Count Bertoni (IRE)**[14] 3661 3-9-10 74 .... (p) StephenCraine 2 56
(S Gollings) *t.k.h: sn chsng wnr: rdn along 3f out: wknd over 2f out* **16/1**

0062 **6** 19 **Resolute Road**[42] 2753 3-8-11 61 .... MichaelHills 5 7
(B W Hills) *t.k.h: chsd ldng pair: rdn along over 3f out: wknd wl over 2f out* **4/1**[3]

2m 20.57s (4.57) **Going Correction** +0.25s/f (Good) **6** Ran SP% **108.1**
Speed ratings (Par 100): **91,90,88,84,80 65**
toteswingers: 1&2 £2.50, 1&3 £1.50, 2&3 £1.90 CSF £9.16 CT £19.67 TOTE £3.20: £1.80, £1.80; EX 9.80 Place 6 £44.66, Place 5 £35.88.
Owner Mrs Fitri Hay **Bred** B Wayne Hughes **Trained** Tadcaster, N Yorks

FOCUS
A moderate 3-y-o handicap.
T/Plt: £38.70 to a £1 stake. Pool: £75,786.39. 1,426.26 winning tickets. T/Qpdt: £30.90 to a £1 stake. Pool: £5,083.88. 121.67 winning tickets. JR

4026 LINGFIELD (L-H)
Saturday, July 17

OFFICIAL GOING: Turf course - good to firm (8.9); all-weather - standard
Wind: Fairly light, across Weather: Bright spells

4129 CROWHURST NURSERY — 6f
6:20 (6:20) (Class 5) 2-Y-O — £2,388 (£705; £352) Stalls High

Form RPR

065 **1** **Miss Dutee**[33] 3029 2-8-5 61 .... FrankieMcDonald 1 68
(R Hannon) *in tch: effrt and edging out lft 2f out: rdn to ld over 1f out: r.o wl to draw clr fnl 100yds: readily* **8/1**

0044 **2** 1 ½ **Jamaica Grande**[6] 3874 2-8-6 62 .... SamHitchcott 7 64
(P S McEntee) *led: rdn and racd awkwardly u.p wl over 1f out: hdd over 1f out: styd on one pce ins fnl f* **9/2**[2]

01 **3** 1 ¾ **Half Truth (IRE)**[24] 3310 2-8-12 75 .... AntiocoMurgia(7) 4 72
(Mahmood Al Zarooni) *hld up in last pair: hdwy and pushed along ent fnl 2f: rdn and chsd ldng pair over 1f out: edgd rt u.p and no imp fnl f* **7/4**[1]

000 **4** 1 ½ **Salvationist**[43] 2715 2-8-4 60 .... NickyMackay 6 52
(J L Dunlop) *in tch: rdn and effrt ent fnl 2f: unable qck over 1f out: no imp fnl f* **6/1**[3]

2414 **5** ½ **Alfraamsey**[11] 3749 2-9-7 77 .... CathyGannon 2 68
(M R Channon) *stdd s: sn swtchd rt to r on stands' rail: rdn and effrt ent fnl 2f: no prog u.p over 1f out* **9/2**[2]

505 **6** 4 **Ridgeway Hawk**[11] 3757 2-8-1 57 .... DavidProbert 5 36
(M D I Usher) *chsd ldr: rdn 1/2-way: lost pl u.p wl over 1f out: wl hld fnl f* **17/2**

1m 10.95s (-0.25) **Going Correction** -0.225s/f (Firm) **6** Ran SP% **108.7**
Speed ratings (Par 94): **92,90,87,85,85 79**
toteswingers: 1&2 £8.50, 1&3 £3.10, 2&3 £2.40 CSF £39.99 TOTE £13.30: £5.40, £2.10; EX 58.80.
Owner Alan Franklin Neville Poole Stuart Laws **Bred** N Poole And A Franklin **Trained** East Everleigh, Wilts

FOCUS
Probably not a strong nursery and favourite Half Truth proved quite disappointing. The winner was much improved. The 'official' ratings shown next to each horse are estimated and for information purposes only.

NOTEBOOK
Miss Dutee had been sent off at double-figure prices on her three maiden starts, in which she showed only limited ability. However, she took a significant step forward here, making light of her opening handicap mark of 62, showing a nice turn of foot to hit the front and see her race out strongly. There is more than enough in her pedigree to suggest another furlong won't be a problem. Official explanation: trainer's rep said, regarding apparent improvement in form, that the filly had benefitted from its first run under handicap conditions and by the step back up in trip of 6f. (op 15-2)
Jamaica Grande showed up well for a long way on the usually favoured stands' rail but didn't have the gears to cope with the less exposed winner. While this was a perfectly creditable performance, he may do better upped in trip. (tchd 5-1)
Half Truth(IRE) was forced to make her challenge out wide but didn't pick up for pressure and, on this evidence at least, she's going to struggle. (tchd 6-4)
Salvationist shaped encouragingly without screaming certain future winner. (op 8-1)
Alfraamsey just plugged on at the one pace. His form has dropped away since winning at Newcastle last month. (op 10-3)

4130 IN MEMORY OF DOUG COCHRANE H'CAP — 6f
6:50 (6:51) (Class 6) (0-65,64) 3-Y-O+ — £2,047 (£604; £302) Stalls High

Form RPR

5241 **1** **Chinese Democracy (USA)**[9] 3831 3-9-0 57 .... (v[1]) CathyGannon 16 65
(P D Evans) *towards rr: rdn and hdwy ent fnl 2f: chsd ldrs and nt clr run over 1f out: swtchd rt and str run ins fnl f to ld nr fin* **9/1**

0400 **2** ½ **Titus Gent**[17] 3556 5-9-9 61 .... KirstyMilczarek 5 68
(R A Harris) *chsd ldrs: rdn to chse ldng pair over 1f out: drvn ahd ins fnl f: kpt on wl tl hdd and no ex nr fin* **33/1**

1000 **3** ½ **Bateleur**[7] 3914 6-9-7 59 .... ChrisCatlin 3 64
(M R Channon) *hld up in midfield on outer: rdn and hdwy over 1f out: ev ch ins fnl f: no ex fnl 50yds* **33/1**

422 **4** 1 ¼ **Sermons Mount (USA)**[26] 3254 4-9-10 62 .... (v) TomQueally 12 63
(Mouse Hamilton-Fairley) *broke wl: led and crossed to r on stands' rail: rdn and edging lft fr wl over 1f out: hdd ins fnl f: wknd fnl 75yds* **5/2**[1]

004 **5** nk **Ever Cheerful**[11] 3763 9-8-9 47 .... (p) FergusSweeney 6 47
(A B Haynes) *in tch on outer: rdn and effrt wl over 1f out: kpt on same pce u.p ins fnl f* **20/1**

0034 **6** 1 **Stamford Blue**[17] 3556 9-9-0 **57**......(b) KierenFox(5) 11 54
(R A Harris) *chsd ldr: rdn ent fnl 2f: ev ch over 1f out tl wknd jst ins fnl f* **8/1**[3]

4555 **7** 1/2 **Super Frank (IRE)**[13] 3716 7-9-5 **57**......(p) SebSanders 10 53
(J Akehurst) *stdd and swtchd rt after s: bhd and bustled along early: hdwy over 1f out: nt clr run and swtchd lft jst ins fnl f: gng on wl fin: nt rch ldrs* **10/1**

-001 **8** 1/2 **Panpiper**[12] 3726 3-9-7 **64**...... RyanMoore 15 57
(G L Moore) *chsd ldrs: rdn and unable qck over 1f out: styng on same pce u.p and hld whn hmpd ins fnl f* **13/2**[2]

1430 **9** nk **Dvinsky (USA)**[8] 3855 9-9-12 **64**......(b) IanMongan 14 57
(P Howling) *sn bustled along but failed to grab ld: chsd ldrs: rdn and outpcd ent fnl 2f: swtchd lft over 1f out: kpt on ins fnl f* **8/1**[3]

3023 **10** 1 1/2 **Eye For The Girls**[7] 3914 4-9-2 **54**...... SamHitchcott 8 42
(M R Channon) *chsd ldrs: rdn ent fnl 2f: wknd u.p over 1f out* **14/1**

0660 **11** nk **Connor's Choice**[17] 3556 5-8-13 **56**...... SimonPearce(5) 9 43
(Andrew Turnell) *stdd s: hld up towards rr early: hdwy into midfield 1/2-way: rdn and no prog wl over 1f out* **20/1**

0000 **12** 1 1/2 **Bishopbriggs (USA)**[70] 1929 5-8-13 **58**...... LeonnaMayor(7) 4 41
(M G Quinlan) *awkward s and s.i.s: a in rr: hung rt fr over 1f out: n.d* **50/1**

0030 **13** hd **Rio Royale (IRE)**[25] 3292 4-8-13 **58**...... HarryBentley(7) 7 40
(Mrs A J Perrett) *s.i.s: hld up towards rr: rdn and effrt ent fnl 2f: wknd u.p over 1f out* **14/1**

2302 **14** 2 3/4 **Cwmni**[17] 3556 4-9-7 **59**...... DavidProbert 13 32
(B Palling) *taken down early: racd in midfield: rdn and struggling whn hmpd and stmbld over 1f out: no ch after* **8/1**[3]

69.65 secs (-1.55) **Going Correction** -0.225s/f (Firm)
WFA 3 from 4yo+ 5lb **14** Ran SP% **125.0**
Speed ratings (Par 101): **101,100,99,98,97 96,95,94,94,92 92,90,89,86**
toteswingers: 1&2 £89.60, 1&3 £94.00, 2&3 £68.80 CSF £293.93 CT £9278.20 TOTE £17.80: £5.20, £12.30, £14.50; EX 699.30.
Owner Mrs I M Folkes **Bred** Hurstland Farm **Trained** Pandy, Monmouths
■ Stewards' Enquiry : Cathy Gannon two-day ban: careless riding (Aug 1-2)

FOCUS
Low-grade handicap form and hard to learn anything new about these exposed performers.

4131 EUROPEAN BREEDERS' FUND MAIDEN STKS 7f
7:20 (7:21) (Class 5) 2-Y-O £3,076 (£915; £457; £228) **Stalls** High

Form RPR

5 **1** **Major Art**[10] 3794 2-9-3 0...... RyanMoore 13 86+
(R Hannon) *broke wl: mde all and sn crossed to r on stands' rail: pushed clr over 1f out: r.o strly: v easily* **10/11**[1]

4 **2** 5 **Midnight Rider (IRE)**[43] 2701 2-9-3 0...... IanMongan 7 71
(C F Wall) *chsd wnr thrght: rdn and effrt wl over 1f out: wl btn ent fnl f: kpt on for clr 2nd* **5/1**[3]

03 **3** 4 **Silken Thoughts**[43] 2701 2-8-12 0...... CathyGannon 4 56
(John Berry) *chsd ldrs: rdn and outpcd by ldng pair over 1f out: wnt modest 3rd jst ins fnl f* **16/1**

0 **4** 1 **Bright Applause**[23] 3349 2-9-3 0...... DavidProbert 6 58
(G L Moore) *chsd ldrs: rdn and outpcd ldrs over 1f out: plugged on same pce and wl hld fnl f* **25/1**

0 **5** 3/4 **Striking Box**[12] 3735 2-9-0 0...... JamesMillman(3) 16 56+
(B R Millman) *in tch in midfield on stands' rail: rdn and effrt over 2f out: outpcd and no ch w ldrs over 1f out: plugged on fnl f* **66/1**

3 **6** 6 **Hard Bargain (IRE)**[39] 2839 2-9-3 0...... TomQueally 10 41
(D J Coakley) *t.k.h: hld up in midfield: rdn and btn ent fnl 2f: wl btn after* **7/2**[2]

00 **7** 3/4 **King Bling (IRE)**[39] 2839 2-9-3 0...... ChrisCatlin 8 39
(S Kirk) *chsd ldr tl wknd qckly ent fnl 2f: wl bhd over 1f out* **40/1**

8 nk **Christmas Aria (IRE)** 2-9-3 0...... SebSanders 2 39
(S Dow) *s.i.s: swtchd rt after s: racd off the pce in midfield: pushed along and struggling 3f out: no ch fnl 2f* **16/1**

00 **9** 2 3/4 **Cantonese Cat (IRE)**[28] 3219 2-9-0 0...... Louis-PhilippeBeuzelin(3) 3 32
(B J Meehan) *towards rr: rdn and struggling 1/2-way: n.d* **50/1**

10 1/2 **His Grace (IRE)** 2-9-3 0...... FergusSweeney 14 30
(A B Haynes) *hld up towards rr: n.m.r over 2f out: pushed along and rn green 2f out: sn wl btn* **66/1**

11 5 **Tullius (IRE)** 2-9-3 0...... FrankieMcDonald 15 18
(P Winkworth) *sn outpcd and early reminders: a wl bhd* **25/1**

5 **12** 1/2 **Echos Of Motivator**[11] 3769 2-9-3 0...... MarcHalford 11 21
(R A Harris) *in tch in midfield rdn and hung lft ent fnl 2f: sn wl btn: eased ent fnl f* **66/1**

13 5 **Love Nest** 2-9-3 0...... JimmyQuinn 5 4
(J L Dunlop) *stdd s: a bhd: lost tch over 2f out* **20/1**

05 **14** 1/2 **Amore Et Labore**[11] 3767 2-9-3 0...... LiamKeniry 1 —
(S Kirk) *racd in midfield on outer: rdn and btn ent fnl 2f: wl btn and edging rt fr over 1f out: eased fnl f* **80/1**

1m 22.17s (-1.13) **Going Correction** -0.225s/f (Firm) **14** Ran SP% **125.6**
Speed ratings (Par 94): **97,91,86,85,84 77,77,76,73,72 67,66,60,60**
toteswingers: 1&2 £2.40, 1&3 £6.60, 2&3 £12.80 CSF £5.49 TOTE £2.00: £1.40, £1.90, £3.30; EX 8.00.
Owner W P Drew **Bred** Horizon Bloodstock Limited **Trained** East Everleigh, Wilts

FOCUS
A cakewalk for the odds-on favourite. He was the pre-race form choice but improved here.

NOTEBOOK
Major Art didn't have to improve too much on his encouraging Newmarket debut to get off the mark, but the manner of his victory suggests he has progressed. Soon in front on the rail, the Compton Place colt stretched away in the final couple of furlongs to win with any amount in hand. He doesn't have any big-race entries but he looks stakes class. (op 8-11 tchd 11-10 and 6-5 in places)
Midnight Rider(IRE) was no match for the winner, but beat the rest emphatically. He should have no problem winning a maiden. (op 11-2 tchd 6-1 and 9-2)
Silken Thoughts didn't run badly out wide and is now qualified for nurseries. She is bred to appreciate a little further, so could be capable of better in handicaps. (tchd 12-1)
Bright Applause wasn't disgraced and looks a nursery type. (op 33-1)
Striking Box also looks the type for nurseries. (op 80-1)
Hard Bargain(IRE), who shaped promisingly at Salisbury on debut, spoilt his chance by racing too keenly. (op 5-1 tchd 10-3)
Echos Of Motivator Official explanation: jockey said colt hung left

4132 BET BRITISH OPEN GOLF - BETDAQ (S) STKS 1m 2f (P)
7:50 (7:50) (Class 6) 3-Y-O+ £2,047 (£604; £302) **Stalls** Low

Form RPR

5005 **1** **Dream Of Fortune (IRE)**[31] 3079 6-9-5 62......(t) TomQueally 5 66
(P D Evans) *hld up in last trio: rdn and gd hdwy on outer over 2f out: chsd ldr over 1f out: drvn ahd jst ins fnl f: styd on u.p* **5/1**[2]

60/1 **2** 3/4 **Domino Dancer (IRE)**[10] 3787 6-9-11 82......(b) IanMongan 3 71
(Jim Best) *led: rdn jst over 2f out: drvn over 1f out: hdd jst ins fnl f: no ex u.p fnl 75yds* **4/7**[1]

3000 **3** 4 **Kings Topic (USA)**[28] 3214 10-9-5 52......(p) NeilCallan 8 57
(A B Haynes) *dwlt: reminders sn after s: sn in midfield: rdn 3f out: hrd drvn to chse ldrs ent fnl 2f: outpcd by ldng pair ent fnl f: plugged on to go 3rd fnl 75yds* **22/1**

21-0 **4** 1 **Shark Man (IRE)**[53] 2416 3-8-9 70...... PaulFitzsimons 1 55
(Miss J R Tooth) *in tch: hdwy to chse ldr on inner over 2f out tl over 1f out: wknd fnl 150yds* **8/1**

5300 **5** 1 3/4 **Felicia**[28] 3214 5-9-0 46...... SamHitchcott 9 46
(J E Long) *in tch in midfield: rdn and effrt to chse ldng pair 3f out: struggling whn n.m.r over 1f out: sn outpcd* **25/1**

3403 **6** hd **Cupid's Glory**[93] 1318 8-9-11 68......(b) RyanMoore 2 57
(G L Moore) *dwlt: hld up in last trio: rdn and effrt on inner wl over 1f out: fnd nil and wl btn ent fnl f* **6/1**[3]

6000 **7** 1 1/2 **Lilly Royal (IRE)**[5] 3967 4-9-0 52......(p) NeilChalmers 6 43
(B Palling) *chsd ldrs tl wnt 2nd 4f out tl over 2f out: wkng whn n.m.r ent fnl 2f: wl btn over 1f out* **25/1**

0-00 **8** 10 **Jinksy Minx**[34] 3002 3-8-4 43...... FrankieMcDonald 4 23
(Miss Suzy Smith) *dwlt and pushed along: in tch in rr tl lost tch qckly wl over 2f out* **50/1**

00-0 **9** 38 **Michelle (IRE)**[26] 3264 4-8-11 42......(p) RobertLButler(3) 7 —
(P Butler) *t.k.h: chsd ldr tl 4f out: sn lost tch: t.o fr wl over 1f out* **100/1**

2m 8.23s (1.63) **Going Correction** +0.175s/f (Slow)
WFA 3 from 4yo+ 10lb **9** Ran SP% **120.7**
Speed ratings (Par 101): **100,99,96,95,94 93,92,84,54**
toteswingers: 1&2 £2.00, 1&3 £52.20, 2&3 £8.00 CSF £8.37 TOTE £5.10: £1.30, £1.10, £4.00; EX 10.30.There was no bid for the winner. Shark Man was claimed by Mr R. T. Goodes for £6,000.
Owner Mrs I M Folkes **Bred** Newborough Stud **Trained** Pandy, Monmouths

FOCUS
A modest seller.

4133 BET IRISH OAKS - BETDAQ CLAIMING STKS 1m (P)
8:20 (8:21) (Class 6) 3-5-Y-O £2,047 (£604; £302) **Stalls** High

Form RPR

0014 **1** **Calypso Star (IRE)**[8] 3853 3-8-13 75......(b) RyanMoore 2 77
(R Hannon) *in tch: hdwy to trck ldr ent fnl 2f: rdn to ld over 1f out: r.o strly and drew wl clr fnl f: easily* **9/4**[1]

2-06 **2** 4 1/2 **Sabatini (IRE)**[22] 3394 3-8-4 79...... ChrisCatlin 11 58
(J Pearce) *chsd ldrs tl led after 2f: rdn over 2f out: hdd over 1f out: no ch w wnr ins fnl f: hld on for 2nd cl home* **15/2**

3263 **3** nk **I Confess**[22] 3391 5-9-0 69......(b) IanMongan 7 61
(Jim Best) *led for 2f: chsd ldr tl ent fnl 3f: drvn and outpcd by ldrs wl over 1f out: no ch w wnr fnl f: kpt on to press for 2nd cl home* **5/1**[3]

5016 **4** 3/4 **Bell's Ocean (USA)**[7] 3911 3-8-1 55...... Louis-PhilippeBeuzelin(3) 9 55
(J Ryan) *chsd ldr for 1f: styd chsng ldrs tl outpcd u.p ent fnl 2f: wl btn over 1f out: kpt on u.p fnl f* **33/1**

0660 **5** 1 1/4 **Totally Focussed (IRE)**[17] 3565 5-9-1 77...... HayleyTurner 12 57
(S Dow) *v.s.a: hld up in rr: pushed along and hdwy into midfield jst over 2f out: rdn and no rspnse wl over 1f out: nvr trbld ldrs* **10/3**[2]

006- **6** 5 **Easy Target (FR)**[337] 4983 5-9-3 85...... AmirQuinn 6 48
(G L Moore) *t.k.h: hld up in tch towards rr: effrt and hdwy into midfield over 2f out: rdn and struggling ent fnl 2f: wl btn after* **8/1**

4425 **7** 6 **Kenswick**[53] 2414 3-7-12 55......(p) AndreaAtzeni 10 21
(Pat Eddery) *dwlt: in tch in last trio: rdn along and racd awkwardly bnd over 4f out: hdwy on outer 3f out: rn wd and lost pl bnd ent fnl 2f: wl btn after* **12/1**

10 **8** shd **Lord Fidelio (IRE)**[38] 2864 4-8-10 73...... AndrewHeffernan(3) 1 30
(P D Evans) *dwlt: hld up in tch towards rr: hdwy on inner over 2f out: rdn and wl btn ent fnl 2f* **16/1**

6250 **9** 1 3/4 **Stef And Stelio**[26] 3276 3-9-1 70......(t) NickyMackay 8 34
(G A Butler) *hld up in tch in rr: rdn and toiling over 2f out: wl bhd fnl 2f* **33/1**

0-04 **10** 21 **Fidler Bay**[46] 2632 4-9-3 69...... DaneO'Neill 3 —
(H Candy) *dwlt: sn pushed along and in tch after 1f: rdn and lost pl ent fnl 3f: wl bhd fnl 2f: t.o* **16/1**

00 **11** 5 **Gilderoy**[11] 3759 3-8-5 0...... FrankieMcDonald 4 —
(D J S Ffrench Davis) *chsd ldrs tl lost pl qckly 3f out: wl bhd fnl 2f: t.o* **100/1**

1m 38.58s (0.38) **Going Correction** +0.175s/f (Slow)
WFA 3 from 4yo+ 8lb **11** Ran SP% **119.7**
Speed ratings (Par 101): **105,100,100,99,98 93,87,87,85,64 59**
toteswingers: 1&2 £4.50, 1&3 £2.70, 2&3 £10.30 CSF £20.17 TOTE £3.70: £1.70, £3.50, £1.20; EX 21.10.
Owner A C Pickford & N A Woodcock **Bred** Lisieux Stud **Trained** East Everleigh, Wilts

FOCUS
An ordinary claimer.
Kenswick Official explanation: jockey said filly hung right

4134 BET WORLD MATCHPLAY DARTS - BETDAQ FILLIES' H'CAP 1m 2f (P)
8:50 (8:52) (Class 5) (0-75,75) 3-Y-O+ £2,729 (£806; £403) **Stalls** Low

Form RPR

51 **1** **Akhmatova**[20] 3484 3-8-12 **69**...... DaneO'Neill 10 78
(G A Butler) *t.k.h: hld up in tch in midfield: hdwy to chse ldr 2f out: rdn to ld 1f out: r.o strly and clr fnl 100yds* **11/1**

-521 **2** 2 **Baoli**[42] 2753 3-8-3 **60**...... KirstyMilczarek 12 65
(L M Cumani) *hld up in tch towards rr: hdwy on outer jst over 2f out: rdn over 1f out: styd on u.p fnl f to snatch 2nd on post: nt pce to rch wnr* **4/1**[2]

-025 **3** nse **Aquarius Star (IRE)**[37] 2893 3-9-4 **75**...... AndreaAtzeni 3 80
(Pat Eddery) *chsd ldrs: rdn over 2f out: swtchd lft and drvn to chse ldng pair over 1f out: racd awkwardly u.p: chsd wnr fnl 100yds: no imp and lost 2nd on post* **5/1**[3]

0/11 **4** 1 1/4 **Dolcetto (IRE)**[26] 3268 5-10-0 **75**...... RyanMoore 9 77
(A King) *sn bustled up to chse ldr: rdn to ld over 2f out: drvn and hdd ent fnl f: lost 2nd and wknd fnl 100yds* **7/2**[1]

2405 **5** 1/2 **Mavalenta (IRE)**[20] 3477 3-8-13 **70**...... HayleyTurner 5 71
(J W Hills) *hld up in midfield: hdwy jst over 2f out: rdn and nt clr run over 1f out: swtchd lft and hdwy ent fnl f: keeping on but no ch w wnr whn nt clr run towards fin* **25/1**

06-2 **6** 3 **Bessie Lou (IRE)**[2] 4045 4-8-11 **58**...... CathyGannon 11 53
(Michael Joseph Fitzgerald, Ire) *hld up in last trio: rdn and effrt jst over 2f out: switching out rt and unable qck over 1f out: nvr trbld ldrs* **8/1**

300 **7** 1 3/4 **Derecho**[31] 3080 3-8-4 **66**...... JohnFahy(5) 13 58
(C G Cox) *s.i.s: in tch in last trio: hdwy on outer 3f out: rdn and no hdwy wl over 1f out: wl hld fr over 1f out* **20/1**

-202 **8** *hd* **Ellbeedee (IRE)**[21] 3428 3-9-3 **74** NeilCallan 2 66
(M A Jarvis) *chsd ldrs: rdn and struggling ent fnl 2f: wknd u.p ent fnl f* **11/2**

000- **9** *hd* **Ildiko (USA)**[255] 7243 3-8-10 **67** SebSanders 6 58
(Sir Mark Prescott) *restless stalls: chsd ldrs: rdn along 4f out: drvn to press ldrs ent fnl 2f: wkng whn sltly hmpd 1f out: fdd fnl f* **10/1**

0000 **10** *1 1/4* **Asterales**[29] 3171 3-8-1 **58** NickyMackay 8 47
(W J Musson) *hld up in tch in last trio: rdn and no prog jst over 2f out: nvr trbld ldrs* **66/1**

0/45 **11** *3/4* **Al Aqabah (IRE)**[24] 3330 5-9-1 **62** DavidProbert 7 49
(B Gubby) *led: rdn and hdd over 2f out: wknd qckly wl over 1f out: wl btn fnl f* **16/1**

000 **12** *6* **Tymora (USA)**[44] 2674 3-8-7 **64** TomQueally 1 39
(H R A Cecil) *restless stalls: in tch in midfield tl rdn and dropped to rr wl over 2f out: wl bhd fnl 2f* **20/1**

2m 7.47s (0.87) **Going Correction** +0.175s/f (Slow)
WFA 3 from 4yo+ 10lb **12** Ran SP% **123.6**
Speed ratings (Par 100): **103,101,101,100,99 97,96,96,95,94 94,89**
toteswingers: 1&2 £4.90, 1&3 £18.70, 2&3 £6.00 CSF £54.74 CT £258.47 TOTE £12.00: £4.00, £1.80, £3.60; EX 67.90 Place 6 £339.69, Place 5 £84.80.
Owner Trevor C Stewart **Bred** Sunny Days Ltd **Trained** Newmarket, Suffolk

FOCUS
An open fillies' handicap.
T/Plt: £260.70 to a £1 stake. Pool: £63,482.53. 177.70 winning tickets. T/Qpdt: £5.10 to a £1 stake. Pool: £6,657.85. 962.68 winning tickets. SP

4095 NEWBURY (L-H)
Saturday, July 17

OFFICIAL GOING: Good (good to soft in places; 7.4)
Wind: Brisk ahead Weather: Cloudy

4135 HAROLD PACK MEMORIAL CONDITIONS STKS 7f (S)
1:45 (1:47) (Class 3) 2-Y-O **£5,607** (£1,679; £839; £420) **Stalls** Centre

Form RPR

1 **1** **Measuring Time**[7] 3915 2-8-13 0 RyanMoore 4 92+
(R Hannon) *w'like: lengthy: lw: mde all: pushed along 2f out: rdn and hung rt ins fnl f: styd on strly cl home* **1/1**[1]

102 **2** *1/2* **Amwell Pinot**[8] 3872 2-8-13 0 KierenFallon 2 91
(A Bailey) *lw: chsd ldr 3f: pushed along 3f out: wnt 2nd again 2f out: drvn and pressed wnr ins fnl f: no ex cl home* **5/2**[2]

34 **3** *2 1/2* **Galloping Queen (IRE)**[22] 3421 2-8-5 0 TadhgO'Shea 3 77
(M R Channon) *chsd ldrs in 4th: pushed along 3f out: sme prog over 1f out: nvr gng pce to trble ldng duo but styd on u.p cl home to take 3rd* **3/1**[3]

4 *shd* **Hung Parliament (FR)** 2-8-7 0 RichardKingscote 5 79+
(Tom Dascombe) *unf: scope: swtg: racd in 3rd after 3f: pushed along: immature and lost 2nd 2f out: fdd fnl f and lost 3rd cl home: should improve* **16/1**

1m 29.96s (4.26) **Going Correction** +0.40s/f (Good) **4** Ran SP% **109.5**
Speed ratings (Par 98): **91,90,87,87**
CSF £3.84 TOTE £2.20; EX 3.80.
Owner Woodcote Stud Ltd **Bred** Woodcote Stud Ltd **Trained** East Everleigh, Wilts

FOCUS
This was a good conditions race, despite the small field, but the winner dictated a modest gallop. They all raced up the middle of the track for much of the way, before edging slightly towards the stands' rail late on. The winner built on her debut but the third was below par.

NOTEBOOK
Measuring Time, turned out just a week after winning a maiden over this trip on debut at Salisbury, had to work hard, despite being allowed a soft lead and edged right under pressure, but his attitude couldn't be faulted. Everything went his way, but he looked to defeat quite a useful type, and his breeding suggests he'll keep improving with time and distance. Still a bit weak according to the jockey, Richard Hannon said he'll give him a six-week break. (op 11-8 tchd 13-8 in a place and 6-4 in places)
Amwell Pinot, runner-up off an estimated official mark of 85 in a nursery over this distance at the July course last time, was always being held by the winner and probably would have preferred a stronger end-to-end gallop. He can probably rate higher. (op 2-1)
Galloping Queen(IRE), fourth in a 6f Listed race at the Curragh on her previous start, was held up last in a steadily run race and only ran on past a beaten rival near the line. It's hard to know whether or not she stayed. (tchd 11-4)
Hung Parliament(FR), a 48,000euros half-brother to very useful 2-y-o Shamandar (just touched off in last year's Super Sprint), was keen early and looked green in the closing stages. He didn't see his race out, in part due to his inexperience, although time may show his stamina was stretched over this trip. (op 14-1)

4136 SHADWELL STKS (REGISTERED AS THE HACKWOOD STAKES) (GROUP 3) 6f 8y
2:15 (2:15) (Class 1) 3-Y-O+
£34,062 (£12,912; £6,462; £3,222; £1,614; £810) **Stalls** Centre

Form RPR

1-00 **1** **Regal Parade**[28] 3192 6-9-3 117 AdrianNicholls 7 117
(D Nicholls) *lw: n.m.r s and hld up in rr: rapid hdwy on outside to ld ins fnl 2f: drvn clr fnl f* **15/2**

4-10 **2** *3* **High Standing (USA)**[28] 3192 5-9-3 110 RyanMoore 2 107
(W J Haggas) *trckd ldrs: nt clr run and swtchd lft ins fnl 2f: drvn and styd on to chse wnr over 1f out but nvr any ch* **5/2**[2]

6425 **3** *1* **Secret Asset (IRE)**[15] 3629 5-9-3 97 JamieSpencer 8 104
(Jane Chapple-Hyam) *hld up in rr: gd hdwy on stands' rail over 1f out: edgd lft and wnt 2nd fnl f but no imp* **20/1**

3423 **4** *3* **Doncaster Rover (USA)**[21] 3455 4-9-3 110 RobertWinston 3 94
(D H Brown) *chsd ldrs and rdn along over 3f out: no ch w ldrs fnl 2f* **5/1**[3]

5020 **5** *1/2* **Fravashi (AUS)**[28] 3192 5-9-3 115 (b) TedDurcan 1 93
(Saeed Bin Suroor) *chsd ldrs: rdn 2f out: fnd nthing and wknd qckly fnl f* **16/1**

-112 **6** *4 1/2* **Markab**[32] 3047 7-9-7 113 PatCosgrave 4 82
(H Candy) *led tl hdd ins fnl 2f: sn btn* **9/4**[1]

3055 **7** *2* **Edge Closer**[14] 3674 6-9-3 100 JimmyFortune 9 72
(R Hannon) *lw: in tch: rdn 2f out: no imp and wknd wl over 1f out* **25/1**

-143 **8** *shd* **Angel's Pursuit (IRE)**[34] 2999 3-8-12 108 PatDobbs 6 72
(R Hannon) *lw: in tch: rdn: sme prog and edgd lft fr 2f out: sn wknd* **10/1**

5001 **9** *11* **Barney McGrew (IRE)**[21] 3445 7-9-7 108 TomEaves 5 40
(M Dods) *pressed ldrs: rdn over 2f out and sn wknd* **28/1**

1m 14.33s (1.33) **Going Correction** +0.40s/f (Good)
WFA 3 from 4yo+ 5lb **9** Ran SP% **114.8**
Speed ratings (Par 113): **107,103,101,97,97 91,88,88,73**
toteswingers: 1&2 £5.30, 1&3 £23.90, 2&3 £11.50 CSF £25.81 TOTE £9.10: £2.90, £1.40, £3.50; EX 22.00 TRIFECTA Not won..
Owner Dab Hand Racing **Bred** Highclere Stud And Harry Herbert **Trained** Sessay, N Yorks

FOCUS
This looked a decent Group 3, but the leaders went off too fast in the conditions, suiting those held up. Indeed, the first three came from the rear, including third-placed Secret Asset, who was officially rated just 97, and as such the form needs treating with caution. The field gradually edged across towards the stands' side.

NOTEBOOK
Regal Parade had been well below his best in two runs since winning last year's Haydock Sprint Cup, but in fairness the first of those was on Tapeta in Dubai, and the latest was on quick ground on his return to Britain in the Golden Jubilee. Dropped in grade and remarkably penalty free, he had the ground in his favour, as well as the race run to suit, and took full advantage to record a convincing success. Having been held up last of all at one stage, the winner made rapid headway out wide from over 2f from the finish and basically outclassed the other closers. A return to better company no doubt awaits, and he'll surely bid to follow up last year's Haydock success, although it seems a bit of ease in the ground is important to him these days. (op 13-2)
High Standing(USA) who, like the winner could make no impression in the Golden Jubilee, returned to form with the race run to suit, but he couldn't repeat last year's success. (tchd 2-1 and 11-4)
Secret Asset(IRE), rated only 97, seems to limit the form, but he has a smart cruising speed and was well suited by a hold-up ride considering the leaders had gone too fast. Once under pressure after making good headway against the stands' rail, he hung left and never looked likely to make a telling impression. (op 33-1)
Doncaster Rover(USA), third in this last year, fared best of those to chase the pace on this return to sprinting and emerges with credit. (op 13-2)
Fravashi(AUS), down the field in the Golden Jubilee on his British debut, is probably better than he showed this time, as he raced close to the overly strong gallop. (op 12-1)
Markab was nowhere near the form he showed when runner-up in the King's Stand last time, but he's easily excused. His top four RPRs have been achieved over either 5f (last time) or on quick ground over this trip, and he simply went off too fast (pressed by Barney McGrew, who dropped right out) on going softer than ideal. (op 11-4)

4137 BATHWICK TYRES EBF FILLIES' H'CAP 1m (S)
2:45 (2:46) (Class 2) (0-100,99) 3-Y-O+
£9,969 (£2,985; £1,492; £747; £372; £187) **Stalls** Centre

Form RPR

5220 **1** **First City**[42] 2744 4-9-13 **98** HayleyTurner 3 106
(D M Simcock) *hld up towards rr: stdy hdwy fr 3f out to trckd ldrs 2f out: rdn to chal over 1f out: led fnl 120yds: veered rt cl home* **8/1**[2]

1415 **2** *nk* **Gobama**[21] 3457 3-8-3 **87** KierenFox(5) 5 92
(J W Hills) *lw: chsd ldrs: hung lft and rdn along over 3f out: drvn to take slt ld 2f out: strly chal fr over 1f out: hdd fnl 120yds and jst hld whn pushed rt cl home* **8/1**[2]

65-0 **3** *1/2* **What's Up Pussycat (IRE)**[36] 2929 4-9-7 **92** JimmyFortune 10 98
(D M Simcock) *hld up in rr: gd hdwy over 1f out: str run ins fnl f and clsng on ldng duo whn bdly hmpd cl home* **20/1**

0453 **4** *1* **She's In The Money**[32] 3063 4-8-12 **83** PaulHanagan 4 87
(R A Fahey) *lw: in rr tl hdwy 2f out: drvn to chse ldrs fnl f and styng on whn bdly hmpd cl home* **10/1**

54-4 **5** *7* **Baileys Cacao (IRE)**[54] 2387 4-10-0 **99** RyanMoore 9 87
(R Hannon) *lw: in rr: rdn and styd on fr 2f out but nvr anywhere nr ldrs* **12/1**

1-21 **6** *3 1/4* **Forest Crown**[45] 2652 3-8-11 **90** JimCrowley 2 68
(R M Beckett) *lw: t.k.h: led tl hdd & wknd qckly 2f out* **1/1**[1]

6143 **7** *1* **Ela Gorrie Mou**[5] 3962 4-8-9 **80** oh6 RobertWinston 1 58
(P Charalambous) *chsd ldrs: rdn over 2f out: sn btn* **9/1**

1000 **8** *1/2* **Amary (IRE)**[40] 2815 3-8-6 **85** (p) KoseiMiura 6 60
(C E Brittain) *chsd ldr: rdn and wknd appr fnl 2f* **66/1**

-000 **9** *6* **Sarah Park (IRE)**[11] 3752 5-9-5 **90** KierenFallon 8 53
(B J Meehan) *chsd ldrs: rdn ins fnl 3f: wknd over 2f out* **17/2**[3]

1m 41.6s (1.90) **Going Correction** +0.40s/f (Good)
WFA 3 from 4yo+ 8lb **9** Ran SP% **115.8**
Speed ratings (Par 96): **106,105,105,104,97 93,92,92,86**
toteswingers: 1&2 £8.00, 1&3 £20.90, 2&3 £17.70 CSF £70.18 CT £1242.01 TOTE £10.10: £2.30, £2.30, £3.70; EX 81.80 TRIFECTA Not won..
Owner Saeed Misleh **Bred** Darley **Trained** Newmarket, Suffolk

FOCUS
This fillies' handicap was an unsatisfactory contest. First up, the favourite Forest Crown went off much too fast, and then late on there was significant trouble in running concerning the first four.

NOTEBOOK
First City was carried towards the far side in the closing stages, before then herself veering badly right near the line, bumping the second. She was just able to hang on, but would surely have been beaten had the runner-up stayed straight. (op 13-2)
Gobama looked the likeliest winner when staying on from off the pace over 1f out (touched a low of 1.12), but she continually hung left and couldn't shake off First City. She then received a hefty bump from the winner near the line, forcing her to in turn bump the third-placed finisher. Had she stayed straight, she surely would have won. (op 9-1 tchd 10-1)
What's Up Pussycat(IRE), who touched 2.2 in running, finished strongly and would have been slightly closer but for a bad bump near the line, although she had earlier been going slightly left herself. She was trying this trip for the first time, on just her second start since coming over from Ireland, but clearly stayed. (op 16-1)
She's In The Money was held when squeezed for room in the final few yards and looks better suited by a strongly run 7f. (op 9-1 tchd 8-1)
Baileys Cacao(IRE), off the track since being reported to have moved poorly on quick ground at Leicester in May, was never involved. (tchd 10-1)
Forest Crown didn't settle and was soon upwards of 2l clear. She had all of her rivals off the bridle over 2f out (matched at 1.62), but capitulated when she came under pressure. It seems she needs a quick surface, as she showed when successful off a 7lb lower mark at Nottingham last time. Official explanation: jockey said filly ran too free (op 6-4 tchd 10-11)

4138 WEATHERBYS SUPER SPRINT 5f 34y
3:20 (3:21) (Class 2) 2-Y-O
£98,480 (£41,860; £19,700; £11,820; £7,860; £5,900) **Stalls** Centre

Form RPR

1 **1** **Temple Meads**[76] 1728 2-8-6 0 RichardMullen 1 97+
(E S McMahon) *in tch: gd hdwy fr 2f out to chse ldr over 1f out: rdn and kpt on to ld fnl 120yds: styd on strly* **5/1**[2]

0611 **2** *1* **Bold Bidder**[4] 3986 2-7-13 0 Louis-PhilippeBeuzelin 19 86
(K A Ryan) *sn led: rdn 2f out: hdd and outpcd fnl 120yds* **22/1**

010 **3** ½ **Move In Time**[32] 3049 2-8-6 0 TomEaves 16 92
(B Smart) *chsd ldrs: rdn 1/2-way: styd on wl to take 3rd nr fin but no imp on ldng duo* **22/1**

1532 **4** ¾ **Mappin Time (IRE)**[7] 3925 2-8-6 0 (b[1]) FergusSweeney 12 89
(T D Easterby) *chsd ldrs: rdn 1/2-way: disp 3rd ins fnl f but no imp on ldng duo and kpt on same pce* **33/1**

210 **5** 1 **Dress Up (IRE)**[31] 3070 2-7-12 0 DavidProbert 25 77
(S Kirk) *chsd ldrs: rdn and styd on ins fnl f: one pce fnl 50yds* **8/1[3]**

312 **6** nk **Shoshoni Wind**[21] 3453 2-8-1 0 FrannyNorton 3 79
(K A Ryan) *lw: chsd ldrs: wnt 2nd and rdn 2f out: no imp on ldr: lost 2nd over 1f out: wknd fnl 100yds* **9/1**

3201 **7** nk **Remotelinx (IRE)**[21] 3439 2-8-11 0 MichaelHills 11 88
(J W Hills) *in tch: hdwy and hung rt over 1f out: styd on ins fnl f but nt rch ldrs* **33/1**

2021 **8** nk **Fifth Commandment (IRE)**[35] 2951 2-8-3 0 HayleyTurner 10 79
(J A Osborne) *chsd ldrs: rdn and one pce 1/2-way: kpt on again fnl f but nvr a threat* **40/1**

412 **9** ¾ **Silence Is Bliss (IRE)**[35] 2950 2-8-1 0 JimmyQuinn 4 74
(J S Moore) *in tch: rdn 1/2-way: kpt on fnl f but nvr a danger* **50/1**

612 **10** ¾ **Reckless Reward (IRE)**[30] 3100 2-9-0 0 RyanMoore 2 85
(R Hannon) *lw: chsd ldrs: rdn 2f out: wknd fnl f* **7/2[1]**

1430 **11** ½ **Takeaway**[54] 2397 2-8-2 0 FrankieMcDonald 13 71
(R Hannon) *in tch: rdn and styd on same pce fnl f* **66/1**

1613 **12** ¾ **Jamesway (IRE)**[15] 3630 2-9-1 0 TonyHamilton 7 81
(R A Fahey) *lw: in tch: rdn and styd on same pce fnl f* **50/1**

13 **13** ½ **Ballista (IRE)**[20] 3476 2-8-4 0 RichardKingscote 23 68
(Tom Dascombe) *chsd ldrs: rdn 1/2-way: wknd fnl f* **9/1**

0125 **14** 2¼ **Waking Warrior**[6] 3939 2-8-3 0 TadhgO'Shea 9 59
(K A Ryan) *s.i.s: in rr: sn rdn: styd on fnl f but nvr in contention* **40/1**

16 **15** 2 **Nasharra (IRE)**[51] 2468 2-9-0 0 JamieSpencer 5 70
(K A Ryan) *outpcd: sn rdn: sme prog fnl f* **66/1**

1124 **16** 1¼ **Bathwick Bear (IRE)**[49] 2525 2-8-8 0 CathyGannon 21 53
(P D Evans) *rdn and outpcd fr 1/2-way* **66/1**

010 **17** 1¾ **Roche Des Vents**[32] 3051 2-8-6 0 LiamKeniry 15 44
(R Hannon) *sn rdn: outpcd most of way* **40/1**

221 **18** nse **Jaahiz (IRE)**[7] 3923 2-8-6 0 ow1 KierenFallon 17 44
(R Hannon) *lw: chsd ldrs tl wknd fnl f* **8/1[3]**

5215 **19** 2 **Extra Power (IRE)**[9] 3826 2-9-0 0 RobertWinston 6 45
(M R Channon) *chsd ldrs 3f* **100/1**

5110 **20** shd **Boundless Spirit**[32] 3051 2-9-0 0 GregFairley 14 45
(B Smart) *chsd ldrs: wknd 2f out: no ch whn hmpd sn after* **40/1**

U251 **21** hd **Kojak (IRE)**[32] 3053 2-8-10 0 PatDobbs 20 40
(R Hannon) *spd to 1/2-way* **25/1**

3152 **22** 1½ **Golden Shine**[20] 3482 2-8-6 0 SamHitchcott 22 30
(M R Channon) *lw: rdn and bhd fr 1/2-way* **33/1**

5121 **23** 3½ **Bilko Pak (IRE)**[24] 3327 2-8-9 0 JimmyFortune 18 21
(R Hannon) *lw: rdn and bhd fr 1/2-way* **33/1**

323 **24** 2¾ **Button Moon (IRE)**[45] 2638 2-8-9 0 JimCrowley 24 11
(I A Wood) *spd to 1/2-way* **40/1**

63.55 secs (2.15) **Going Correction** +0.40s/f (Good) **24** Ran SP% **127.0**
Speed ratings (Par 100): **98,96,95,94,92 92,91,91,90,88 88,86,86,82,79 77,74,74,71,71 70,68,62,58**
toteswingers:1&2:£38.80, 2&3:£161.50, 1&3:£50.40 CSF £108.37 TOTE £5.00: £2.80, £8.40, £8.30; EX 218.40 Trifecta £6112.40 Pool: £20,652.32 - 2.50 winning units..
Owner J C Fretwell **Bred** Whitsbury Manor Stud **Trained** Lichfield, Staffs
■ Arctic Feeling was withdrawn (10/1, spread plate at s). Deduct 5p in the £ under R4.

FOCUS
This looked a good edition of the Super Sprint. The runners were spread out almost the entire width of the course for much of the way, although the far rail was shunned throughout, and the main action ultimately took place middle to stands' side. As such, this looked a tremendous effort from Temple Meads to win from stall one, with the next four home all drawn in double figures. The form is limited to an extent by the likes of the fifth.

NOTEBOOK
Temple Meads ◆ overcame an unfavourable draw, as well as an interrupted preparation. He had been off for 76 days since winning a red-hot maiden on debut at Newmarket (the third won a Listed race at this meeting a day earlier), missing Royal Ascot (apparently had spots in his throat), and came here as the least experienced of the 24 runners. Racing away from the pace, he was being niggled along before halfway, but he responded impressively to his rider's urgings, coming under more vigorous pressure over 1f out, and was well on top by the time he edged towards the centre of the track late on. Described by owner John Fretwell as "the best horse I've ever had", it's likely he'll be aimed at the Gimcrack, with the sixth furlong likely to suit. In the slightly longer term, it wouldn't surprise to see him end his campaign where it started, back at Newmarket for the Middle Park. (tchd 9-2)
Bold Bidder, the winner of a maiden before following up in a nursery earlier in the week off an estimated mark of 80, had a light weight and showed tremendous speed up the middle of the track, only tiring near the line to be overhauled by a potential Group horse. Her natural pace should see her pick up black type over this trip as a juvenile.
Move In Time, not helped by a wide draw when down the field in the Coventry, couldn't match the runner-up's natural speed on this first run over 5f, but he stayed on towards up the middle of the track, suggesting a return to further will suit. (tchd 20-1)
Mappin Time(IRE), fitted with blinkers for the first time, showed plenty of speed, racing enthusiastically close to the lead, and he kept on well for pressure. It wouldn't surprise to see the headgear retained.
Dress Up(IRE), held in the Queen Mary, ran well, faring best of those who raced towards the stands' side. (op 11-1)
Shoshoni Wind, runner-up in a 6f Listed race latest, didn't run badly (second best of those drawn in single figures) but, considering the early speed she showed on this return to the minimum trip, she could have been expected to finish even closer. She was one-paced after coming off the bride, lacking the finishing pace of some of these and/or being unsuited by the ground (previously raced exclusively on fast). (op 15-2)
Remotelinx(IRE), a maiden winner over this trip on the Lingfield turf last time, was given a patient ride and could make no impression, edging right near the line. The impression was that he's a little better than he showed.
Reckless Reward(IRE) disappointed, yet still fared best of Richard Hannon's sextet. Niggled along before halfway, he found little when under more vigorous pressure and was nowhere near the form he showed when runner-up in the Norfolk. His draw was not ideal, and the ground might not have suited, but whatever, his connections think he now needs further. Official explanation: jockey said colt was unsuited by the good (good to soft places) (op 5-1 tchd 11-2 and 6-1 in a place)
Ballista(IRE) looked smart when winning on debut and was dropping back in trip after being too keen last time, but he offered little.
Jaahiz(IRE), a winner over 6f on quick ground at York last time, was seemingly unsuited by these different conditions. (op 12-1)

4139 SHADWELL BEECH HOUSE STUD STKS (REGISTERED AS THE STEVENTON STAKES) (LISTED RACE) 1m 2f 6y
3:55 (3:55) (Class 1) 3-Y-O+

£21,004 (£7,962; £3,984; £1,986; £995; £499) **Stalls** Low

Form RPR

-420 **1** **Red Badge (IRE)**[9] 3824 3-8-7 98 RichardMullen 8 118
(R Hannon) *in rr: pushed along 7f out: rdn and hdwy fr 3f out to take slt ld ins fnl 2f: edgd lft and drvn out fnl f* **28/1**

1-21 **2** 1 **Distant Memories (IRE)**[35] 2977 4-9-3 109 JamieSpencer 4 116
(T P Tate) *chsd ldrs: drvn to chal fr 2f out: stl upsides over 1f out: styd on but nt pce of wnr ins fnl f* **7/2[2]**

-006 **3** 3¼ **Poet**[15] 3632 5-9-3 107 TomQueally 9 110
(C G Cox) *led: rdn 3f out: hdd ins fnl 2f: wknd fnl f* **20/1**

6504 **4** ½ **Steele Tango (USA)**[15] 3632 5-9-3 104 LiamKeniry 6 109
(R A Teal) *b.hind: in rr: rdn over 3f out: styd on fr 2f out: tk 4th u.p fnl f but nvr any threat to ldng duo* **22/1**

-053 **5** hd **Kingdom Of Fife**[29] 3144 5-9-3 112 (v) RyanMoore 1 108
(Sir Michael Stoute) *swtg: in rr: rdn and hdwy 3f out: chsd ldrs 2f out: sn no imp and one pce* **5/1[3]**

2-42 **6** nk **Prince Siegfried (FR)**[15] 3632 4-9-3 110 TedDurcan 5 108
(Saeed Bin Suroor) *in rr: pushed along and hdwy to cl on ldrs fr 3f out: nvr quite on terms and wknd fnl f* **5/2[1]**

0-10 **7** 8 **Kings Destiny**[43] 2710 4-9-3 104 PhilipRobinson 11 92
(M A Jarvis) *t.k.h: chsd ldr over 3f: styd wl there tl wknd ins fnl 3f* **12/1**

4-64 **8** 6 **Stimulation (IRE)**[31] 3068 5-9-3 117 DarryllHolland 7 80
(H Morrison) *rdn along 3f out: a bhd* **7/2[2]**

1-20 **9** 9 **Peligroso (FR)**[51] 2470 4-9-3 109 TadhgO'Shea 10 62
(Saeed Bin Suroor) *lw: chsd ldrs: wnt 2nd over 6f out: rdn and btn ins fnl 3f* **16/1**

1030 **10** ½ **Srda (USA)**[14] 3694 3-8-2 86 HirokiGoto 3 56
(C E Brittain) *chsd ldrs tl shkn up: hung lft and wknd 3f out* **80/1**

2m 7.10s (-1.70) **Going Correction** +0.125s/f (Good)
WFA 3 from 4yo+ 10lb **10** Ran SP% **117.0**
Speed ratings (Par 111): **111,110,107,107,107 106,100,95,88,88**
toteswingers:1&2:£12.20, 1&3:£31.90, 2&3:£10.90 CSF £120.90 TOTE £29.90: £5.70, £1.70, £4.50; EX 166.40.
Owner Michael Pescod **Bred** Thomas Foy **Trained** East Everleigh, Wilts

FOCUS
This looked a decent, competitive Listed event, but there was a surprise winner in the shape of the 98-rated Red Badge, suggesting the form is limited. The pace seemed reasonable in the conditions, and they all raced up the middle of the track in the straight.

NOTEBOOK
Red Badge(IRE) made little impression in a good 3-y-o handicap off a mark of 100 over this trip on quick ground at the July meeting, but he showed improved form on this easier surface. He was under pressure a fair way out, but kept responding and displayed a tremendous attitude to hold off the runner-up's persistent challenge. It's possible he'll stay even further, but he won't really appeal as worth backing in similar company, or better, until proving he can back up this sort of performance. (op 33-1)
Distant Memories(IRE), successful in a 1m1f handicap off a mark of 104 at York last time, had his chance but simply couldn't get by the winner, with whom he had 11lb in hand on official figures. (op 9-2 tchd 11-2 in a place)
Poet, on his second start for this yard, reversed recent Sandown form with Prince Siegfried and Steele Tango, plugging on dourly for pressure once headed. The cut in the ground suited him, and he'll appreciate even easier conditions. (tchd 22-1)
Steele Tango(USA) is generally holding his form without managing to win this season, and he kept on without threatening. (op 25-1)
Kingdom Of Fife was below the form he showed when third in the Wolferton at Royal Ascot on his previous start and may prefer quicker ground these days. (op 9-2 tchd 4-1)
Prince Siegfried(FR) should have appreciated the ground but he found little after travelling well until over 3f out, failing to run to the form he showed when runner-up in this grade at Sandown latest. (op 11-4 tchd 3-1)
Stimulation(IRE) ran surprisingly well to take fourth in the Prince of Wales's Stakes at Royal Ascot on his first try at this trip, but that was a muddling race and he failed to get anywhere near that level of form this time. Official explanation: jockey said horse ran flat (tchd 11-4)

4140 SHADWELL "NUNNERY STUD" CONDITIONS STKS 7f (S)
4:30 (4:31) (Class 3) 3-Y-O

£6,231 (£1,866; £933; £467; £233; £117) **Stalls** Centre

Form RPR

-510 **1** **Oasis Dancer**[56] 2354 3-8-12 102 JimCrowley 2 108
(R M Beckett) *hld up in rr but in tch: hdwy fr 2f out: rdn and styd on to ld fnl 120yds: drvn out* **4/1[2]**

-142 **2** nk **Dafeef**[16] 3591 3-8-9 102 (p) TedDurcan 4 104
(Saeed Bin Suroor) *trckd ldrs: drvn to take narrow ld 1f out: hd high and hung rt ins fnl f: hdd and fnd little fnl 120yds* **5/1[3]**

4130 **3** 4 **Rodrigo De Torres**[31] 3066 3-9-1 104 TomQueally 1 99
(H R A Cecil) *lw: led tl hdd over 4f out: led again over 2f out: rdn and hdd 1f out: btn whn veered rt fnl 20yds* **5/1[3]**

0-60 **4** 1¾ **Hanson'D (IRE)**[94] 1311 3-8-9 98 RyanMoore 3 89
(K A Ryan) *chsd ldrs tl outpcd and dropped to rr 3f out: pushed along over 2f out: mod prog again ins fnl f* **10/1**

1250 **5** hd **Meezaan (IRE)**[31] 3066 3-8-9 111 TadhgO'Shea 5 88
(J H M Gosden) *in tch: drvn to chse ldrs 2f out: wknd fnl f and no ch whn hmpd and carried rt fnl 120yds* **9/4[1]**

4656 **6** 16 **Jira**[42] 2744 3-8-4 94 (b[1]) HirokiGoto 6 40
(C E Brittain) *slowly away: sn w ldrs and led over 4f out tl hdd & wknd qckly over 2f out* **16/1**

1m 27.73s (2.03) **Going Correction** +0.40s/f (Good) **6** Ran SP% **99.1**
Speed ratings (Par 104): **104,103,99,97,96 78**
toteswingers:1&2:£2.70, 1&3:£2.90, 2&3:£2.70 CSF £18.10 TOTE £4.20: £2.20, £2.10; EX 16.20.
Owner Mrs M E Slade **Bred** Whitsbury Manor Stud And Mrs M E Slade **Trained** Whitsbury, Hants

FOCUS
A decent enough conditions contest.

NOTEBOOK
Oasis Dancer, off the track since doing too much early on in the Irish Guineas, was suited by a hold-up ride (he was last at one point) and the drop in grade, and he took advantage of the runner-up's lack of resolution. His trainer thinks he'll be better suited by quicker ground, and he's apparently now going to be aimed at the totesport Mile at Goodwood, for which he has picked up a 3lb penalty, putting him on a mark of 105. Granted a good draw, he must go there with a chance and 12-1 in the best price on offer. (op 9-2 tchd 5-1)

Dafeef didn't respond in the desired manner to first-time cheekpieces, wandering around under pressure, before hanging right, while also carrying his head awkwardly. He would surely have won had he knuckled down, and clearly has plenty of natural talent, but he can't be trusted. (op 9-2 tchd 7-2)
Rodrigo De Torres had to concede weight all round and was readily left behind by the front pair. (op 4-1 tchd 7-2)
Hanson'D(IRE), although finally running on near the line, had been under pressure and struggling from some way out, and basically offered little encouragement. (op 12-1)
Meezaan(IRE) might have finished fourth but for being hampered late on, but even so, this was a disappointing performance. He had also underperformed in the Jersey Stakes on his previous start and has not built on early season promise. (op 3-1 tchd 100-30)

4141 SHADWELL "DUBAI SUMMER FESTIVAL" H'CAP — 2m

5:05 (5:05) (Class 4) (0-80,79) 4-Y-O+ **£4,209** (£1,252; £625; £312) **Stalls** Low

Form — RPR

5251 **1** **Yemeni Princess (IRE)**[30] 3127 4-8-11 **72**........... RussKennemore(3) 2 — 81
(B G Powell) *lw: in tch: drvn: led 3f out: sn rdn: styd on wl fnl f* **12/1**

-351 **2** *1 1/4* **Strathcal**[39] 2845 4-9-7 **79**........... DarryllHolland 9 — 86
(H Morrison) *hld up towards rr: hdwy on ins fr 4f out: n.m.r 3f out: hrd rdn fr 2f out: styd on same pce ins fnl f* **8/1**

04-3 **3** *3/4* **Sir Freddie**[40] 2810 4-8-11 **69**........... RobertWinston 5 — 75
(Lady Herries) *swtg: chsd ldr: c wd to r along bnd over 4f out: upsides and u.p 3f out: edgd lft and outpcd 2f out: rallied u.p fnl f and kpt on to take 3rd but nt rch ldng duo* **8/1**

6422 **4** *5* **Mykingdomforahorse**[8] 3865 4-9-1 **73**........... (v) RyanMoore 11 — 73
(M R Channon) *hld up in rr tl stdy hdwy to trck ldrs 3f out: rdn to press ldrs 2 out: wknd fnl f* **3/1**[1]

0014 **5** *6* **Uncle Keef (IRE)**[24] 3324 4-8-4 **62**........... (b) TadhgO'Shea 8 — 55
(M P Tregoning) *chsd ldrs: rdn 3f out: hung lft and wknd 2f out* **6/1**[3]

-463 **6** *6* **Alnwick**[10] 3780 6-9-5 **77**........... JimmyFortune 7 — 63
(P D Cundell) *in rr: hdwy 4f out to trck ldrs 3f out: sn rdn and btn* **9/2**[2]

-505 **7** *3 1/4* **Brooklyn Spirit**[8] 3847 4-8-4 **67**........... (v[1]) JohnFahy(5) 1 — 49
(C G Cox) *chsd ldrs: rdn over 3f out: sn wknd* **20/1**

-102 **8** *5* **Swordsman (GER)**[3] 4026 8-8-10 **68**........... (vt[1]) HayleyTurner 4 — 44
(C Gordon) *led tl hdd & wknd 3f out* **16/1**

2331 **9** *10* **Graylyn Ruby (FR)**[24] 3324 5-8-4 **62**........... JimmyQuinn 6 — 26
(R Dickin) *chsd ldrs: rdn 4f out: sn btn* **7/1**

-204 **10** *23* **Twist Again (IRE)**[22] 3398 4-9-3 **75**........... KierenFallon 10 — 11
(P Howling) *a in rr: lost tch fr 4f out* **11/1**

3m 34.03s (2.03) **Going Correction** +0.125s/f (Good) **10** Ran SP% **118.9**
Speed ratings (Par 105): **99,98,98,95,92 89,87,85,80,68**
toteswingers:1&2:£16.40, 1&3:£17.80, 2&3:£13.60 CSF £106.32 CT £826.00 TOTE £14.40: £3.10, £2.40, £2.70; EX 93.00 Place 6 £596.75, Place 5 £292.38.
Owner Miss Juliet E Reed **Bred** P D Savill **Trained** Upper Lambourn, Berks

FOCUS
A fair staying handicap run at a reasonable gallop. All bar Sir Freddie stayed far side for much of the straight, but the main action ended up taking place towards the middle of the track.
Twist Again(IRE) Official explanation: trainer said filly scoped badly after race
T/Jkpt: Not won. T/Plt: £1,358.40 to a £1 stake. Pool: £134,900.50. 72.49 winning tickets. T/Qpdt: £322.10 to a £1 stake. Pool: £7,619.52. 17.50 winning tickets. ST

4102
NEWMARKET (July Course) (R-H)
Saturday, July 17

OFFICIAL GOING: Good to firm (firm in places)
Wind: Fresh behind Weather: Overcast

4142 LETTERGOLD MAIDEN STKS — 6f

1:55 (1:55) (Class 4) 2-Y-O **£4,533** (£1,348; £674; £336) **Stalls** High

Form — RPR

532 **1** **Fight The Chance (IRE)**[15] 3624 2-9-3 0........... ChrisCatlin 3 — 85
(M R Channon) *mde all: rdn and edgd lft ins fnl f: hung rt towards fin: r.o* **4/1**[3]

4 **2** *1 3/4* **Custom House (IRE)**[8] 3844 2-9-3 0........... EddieAhern 7 — 80
(R Hannon) *dwlt: hdwy over 4f out: rdn and hung lft over 1f out: r.o: wnt 2nd post: nt rch wnr* **3/1**[2]

5 **3** *nse* **Marston Moor (USA)**[9] 3823 2-9-3 0........... WilliamBuick 10 — 80
(Mahmood Al Zarooni) *a.p: rdn to chse ldr and hung lft over 1f out: styd on: lost 2nd post* **9/4**[1]

04 **4** *3 3/4* **Right Said Fred (IRE)**[21] 3459 2-9-3 0........... GeorgeBaker 5 — 68
(R M Beckett) *chsd ldr: rdn and hung lft over 2f out: wknd ins fnl f* **14/1**

5 *hd* **Ice Cold Bex** 2-9-3 0........... IanMongan 4 — 68
(P J McBride) *prom: rdn over 1f out: styd on same pce* **33/1**

6 *1 1/2* **Forty Proof (IRE)** 2-9-3 0........... NeilCallan 1 — 63
(W J Knight) *chsd ldrs: rdn over 1f out: wknd fnl f* **10/1**

7 *hd* **Exchange** 2-9-3 0........... RichardHills 6 — 63+
(W J Haggas) *s.i.s: hld up: shkn up over 1f out: nvr nr to chal: should improve* **8/1**

8 *9* **Street Band (IRE)** 2-9-3 0........... DaneO'Neill 2 — 36
(H Candy) *s.s: sn pushed along in rr: bhd fr 1/2-way* **8/1**

1m 12.02s (-0.48) **Going Correction** -0.20s/f (Firm) **8** Ran SP% **116.7**
Speed ratings (Par 96): **95,92,92,87,87 85,85,73**
toteswingers:1&2:£2.80, 1&3:£2.20, 2&3:£1.30 CSF £16.84 TOTE £5.20: £1.70, £2.00, £1.20; EX 12.80.
Owner Jaber Abdullah **Bred** J Cullinan **Trained** West Ilsley, Berks

FOCUS
Racing took place on the nearside track, and the ground was changed to good to firm, firm in places before this first race. This juvenile maiden has fallen to some decent types in recent seasons, the best of them being the subsequent 2000 Guineas winner Cockney Rebel. Half of the field were newcomers but the form has a sound feel.

NOTEBOOK
Fight The Chance(IRE) dictated the pace as those with experience dominated. He has not been beaten far in a couple of 6f maidens on fast ground and was given a good ride by Catlin, who dictated the gallop before kicking on 2f out and getting first run on his rivals. He will be aimed at nurseries now. (op 9-2)
Custom House(IRE) made a promising debut in an Ascot novice event, but was dropping in trip here and being held up might not have been ideal. He went in pursuit of Fight The Chance over a furlong out but could not make much impression. (op 11-4 tchd 5-2 and 100-30 in places)
Marston Moor(USA) cost $375,000 and is by a high-class sprinter in the US. He had finished last of five but was not disgraced on his debut in the Group 2 July Stakes over C&D the previous week, but he still looked green when asked to go in pursuit of the winner, and like the runner-up, could not close the gap. (op 5-2 tchd 3-1)
Right Said Fred(IRE) had improved on his debut when fourth at Windsor last time and helped make the running. He faded gradually as the winner kicked, but now qualifies for a handicap mark and should do better in that sphere. (op 18-1)
Ice Cold Bex, a cheaply bought half-brother to a couple of 5f winners out of a 5f winner, stayed on late on this debut and should benefit from the experience. (op 50-1)
Forty Proof(IRE) ◆, a 70,000gns half-brother to a sprint winner from the family of Abou Zouz, was quite keen on this debut and was not given a hard time once his chance had gone. If he settles better next time, he can be expected to step up on this effort.
Exchange, a 45,000gns half-brother to three winners at 7f-1m, was held up on this debut and only kept on steadily in the closing stages. (op 15-2)

4143 PLANTATION STUD STKS (REGISTERED AS THE APHRODITE STAKES) (LISTED RACE) (F&M) — 1m 4f

2:30 (2:30) (Class 1) 3-Y-O+

£21,004 (£7,962; £3,984; £1,986; £995; £499) **Stalls** Centre

Form — RPR

-040 **1** **Eastern Aria (UAE)**[29] 3144 4-9-2 102........... RichardHills 13 — 105
(M Johnston) *sn led: hdd 5f out: led again 3f out: rdn over 1f out: styd on gamely* **7/1**[3]

0-50 **2** *1* **Snoqualmie Girl (IRE)**[43] 2716 4-9-2 97........... DaneO'Neill 3 — 103
(D R C Elsworth) *hld up in tch: outpcd over 2f out: hdwy over 1f out: r.o* **10/1**

-223 **3** *nk* **Lady Artemisia (IRE)**[33] 3031 4-9-2 95........... WilliamBuick 5 — 103
(M Botti) *chsd wnr 7f: wnt 2nd again 3f out: rdn: hung lft and ev ch fr over 1f out tl unable qck wl ins fnl f* **8/1**

2463 **4** *1/2* **Honimiere (IRE)**[23] 3368 4-9-2 100........... PJMcDonald 8 — 102
(G A Swinbank) *hld up: hdwy u.p and hung lft fr over 1f out: r.o* **8/1**

-421 **5** *3/4* **Cill Rialaig**[28] 3194 5-9-2 95........... GeorgeBaker 1 — 101
(H Morrison) *hld up in tch: rdn and hung rt over 1f out: styd on same pce ins fnl f* **7/4**[1]

6-00 **6** *1 3/4* **Becqu Adoree (FR)**[33] 3031 4-9-2 99........... J-PGuillambert 2 — 98
(L M Cumani) *hld up: hdwy over 2f out: nt clr run over 1f out: sn rdn: styng on whn hmpd ins fnl f: nt rcvr* **10/1**

-030 **7** *7* **Theatrical Award (NOR)**[11] 3752 5-9-2 107........... SaleemGolam 12 — 87
(Michael Taylor, Norway) *prom: racd keenly: rdn over 2f out: wkng whn nt clr run over 1f out* **28/1**

0-05 **8** *hd* **Uvinza**[33] 3031 4-9-2 94........... (v) EddieAhern 7 — 86
(W J Knight) *hld up: hdwy 1/2-way: led 5f out to 3f out: wknd over 1f out* **14/1**

-405 **9** *9* **Three Moons (IRE)**[29] 3144 4-9-2 100........... SebSanders 9 — 72
(H J L Dunlop) *chsd ldrs: rdn over 2f out: hmpd and wknd over 1f out* **6/1**[2]

60-0 **10** *21* **All Annalena (IRE)**[77] 1693 4-9-2 94........... AdamKirby 10 — 38
(Mrs L Wadham) *mid-div: plld hrd: rdn over 3f out: wknd over 2f out* **50/1**

2m 28.08s (-4.82) **Going Correction** -0.20s/f (Firm)
WFA 3 from 4yo+ 12lb **10** Ran SP% **115.6**
Speed ratings (Par 111): **108,107,107,106,106 105,100,100,94,80**
toteswingers:1&2:£8.10, 1&3:£6.20, 2&3:£12.50 CSF £74.12 TOTE £6.90: £2.00, £3.00, £1.90; EX 70.10 Trifecta £428.20 Part won. Pool: £578.76 - 0.75 winning units..
Owner Sheikh Hamdan Bin Mohammed Al Maktoum **Bred** Darley **Trained** Middleham Moor, N Yorks
■ Stewards' Enquiry : George Baker two-day ban: careless riding (Aug 3-4)

FOCUS
The quality of recent winners of this fillies' Listed race has increased in the last couple of years, with two of the last three winners having come here after scoring the Group 2 Lancashire Oaks, and the third, Dar Re Mi, having gone on to score three times at Group 1 level, including the Yorkshire Oaks and Dubai Sheema Classic. This year's line-up promised no performers of that quality, but looked a fairly open contest and produced a good finish.

NOTEBOOK
Eastern Aria(UAE), a Listed winner at this trip in 2009, had struggled a bit this term after seven wins in a busy season last year. However, she dictated the pace and, despite being headed briefly by Uvinza around the halfway mark and by the third over a furlong out, she battled back in a fashion typical of runners from this yard and ran out a game winner. Connections will try to find a race for her at Goodwood later in the month. (op 5-1)
Snoqualmie Girl(IRE) ◆, a winner at this level over the trip and on ground last season but well beaten in four of five starts since, was held up at the rear before making headway on the outside of her field to challenge inside the last. This was a step back in the right direction and, as her wins in the past have been gained in August and September, it is approaching her time of year. (tchd 11-1)
Lady Artemisia(IRE) finished ahead of three of today's rivals in the Warwickshire Oaks last time. Her only win was over 1m4f on fast ground and she had not had either the trip or the ground to suit since. She was never far away and looked to take the lead briefly over a furlong out, but the winner rallied and she could not respond. (op 9-1)
Honimiere(IRE), touched off by Strawberrydaiquiri in a Group 3 in May but held in lesser contests since, was stepping up in trip and was held up at the rear. She came to challenge more towards the stands' side in the straight and could never quite get to the leaders.
Cill Rialaig, the winner of Duke of Edinburgh Handicap at Royal Ascot, was stepping up in grade but had the trip and ground to suit. She looked to be travelling well enough over two furlongs from home but could not produce a change of gear in the closing stages. (op 5-2)
Becqu Adoree(FR), an ex-French filly who was Group 3 placed, had been well beaten on both starts for this yard. Ponied to the start, she was keen in the early stages but ran on under pressure to challenge, only to be short of room late on. She would have finished a little closer without the interference, and it will give connections some encouragement for the future. (op 8-1)
Three Moons(IRE), a 1m2f winner on fast ground who has run well at this level since, was having her second try at the trip and had her chance, but she did not appear to get home. (op 11-2)

4144 RACING UK H'CAP — 1m

3:00 (3:07) (Class 2) (0-100,97) 3-Y-O

£11,215 (£3,358; £1,679; £840; £419; £210) **Stalls** High

Form — RPR

020 **1** **Start Right**[9] 3824 3-8-10 **84**........... J-PGuillambert 4 — 93
(L M Cumani) *chsd ldrs: rdn over 1f out: r.o to ld wl ins fnl f* **13/2**

-201 **2** *1/2* **Rakaan (IRE)**[35] 2970 3-9-9 **97**........... GeorgeBaker 3 — 105
(J A Osborne) *hld up: hdwy 2f out: rdn to ld 1f out: hdd wl ins fnl f* **12/1**

2251 **3** *shd* **King Of Reason**[13] 3713 3-8-9 **83**........... DaneO'Neill 2 — 91
(D M Simcock) *hld up and bhd: stl last over 1f out: rdn and r.o wl ins fnl f: too much to do* **15/8**[1]

5310 **4** *1 1/2* **Hacienda (IRE)**[14] 3692 3-9-8 **96**........... NeilCallan 8 — 100
(M Johnston) *set stdy pce tl hung rt and qcknd over 2f out: rdn and hdd 1f out: no ex ins fiinal f* **5/1**[3]

-130 **5** *2 1/2* **Huygens**[56] 2324 3-9-4 **92**........... SebSanders 9 — 90
(D J Coakley) *hld up in tch: rdn over 1f out: edgd lft and wknd ins fnl f* **9/1**

3-1 **6** *3/4* **Parvaaz (IRE)**[23] 3374 3-8-4 **78**........... ChrisCatlin 5 — 75
(M A Jarvis) *trckd ldr: plld hrd: hmpd 2f out: rdn over 1f out: wknd ins fnl f* **9/2**[2]

The Form Book, Raceform Ltd, Compton, RG20 6NL

1566 7 nse **Bullwhip (IRE)**[35] 2971 3-9-7 **95** .... WilliamBuick 7 92
(J H M Gosden) *chsd ldrs: rdn over 2f out: wknd fnl f* **7/1**

1m 38.82s (-1.18) **Going Correction** -0.20s/f (Firm) **7** Ran SP% **113.2**
Speed ratings (Par 106): **97,96,96,94,92 91,91**
toteswingers:1&2:£18.40, 1&3:£3.00, 2&3:£3.90 CSF £75.06 CT £201.22 TOTE £6.50: £2.60, £6.30; EX 103.00 Trifecta £268.70 Pool: £926.21 - 2.55 winning units..

Owner Leonidas Marinopoulos **Bred** Dukes Stud & Overbury Stallions Ltd **Trained** Newmarket, Suffolk

FOCUS
A decent 3yo handicap despite the four withdrawals. The early pace was steady and it developed into something of a three-furlong sprint. They raced up the centre in the early stages and, although the leaders drifted towards the stands' rail, the first three stayed up the middle.

NOTEBOOK
Start Right, a 1m Polytrack winner and with form over further on fast ground, was dropping in trip. Not for the first time he proved difficult to load, but ran his race, getting cover this time before coming to challenge over a furlong out and holding the favourite's late run. (tchd 6-1 and 7-1)

Rakaan(IRE) was raised 7lb for his win over 7f at Sandown last time, but was a market drifter. He ran well though, having every chance entering the final furlong before just being run out of it near the finish. (op 17-2)

King Of Reason ◆ had won a match at Brighton to get off the mark but had fair form before that over 1m on fast ground. He was held up at the back in a race that was not strongly run early, and did well to make up the ground in the closing stages. He should be up to gaining compensation at a similar level. (op 5-2 tchd 7-4)

Hacienda(IRE) set the pace and tried to wind it up in the last three furlongs. However, he drifted towards the stands' rail under pressure, conceding the advantage and, although keeping on, that effectively lost him his chance. His rider reported that the colt hung right. Official explanation: jockey said colt hung right (op 13-2 tchd 7-1)

Huygens, a 1m winner on Polytrack who has scored on fast ground, finished behind Hacienda at Haydock and was only slightly better off. He was ridden to challenge over a furlong out but his effort petered out in the Dip. (op 7-1)

Parvaaz(IRE) had scored on his seasonal return over 7f at Warwick and was making a handicap debut for his in-form yard. He had his chance but was another to wander under pressure and faded up the hill. (tchd 4-1 and 5-1)

Bullwhip(IRE), a 7f easy ground winner on his debut, had been held in a Group 3 and handicaps since. He raced up with the pace early before fading and his best hope of a revival is a return to softer ground. (op 11-2)

4145 EUROPEAN BREEDERS' FUND FILLIES' H'CAP 6f
3:30 (3:34) (Class 3) (0-95,93) 3-Y-O+
£8,723 (£2,612; £1,306; £653; £326; £163) **Stalls** High

Form RPR

1113 1 **Dever Dream**[23] 3375 3-9-9 **90** .... EddieAhern 10 102+
(W J Haggas) *hld up: hdwy over 1f out: rdn to ld wl ins fnl f* **11/2**

5-13 2 hd **Flambeau**[22] 3415 3-9-12 **93** .... DaneO'Neill 9 104
(H Candy) *trckd ldrs: led over 1f out: sn rdn: edgd lft and hdd wl ins fnl f* **4/1**[3]

3505 3 3 1/4 **Bella Swan**[14] 3694 3-9-12 **93** .... AdamKirby 8 94
(W R Swinburn) *hld up in tch: rdn over 1f out: styd on same pce ins fnl f* **11/1**

-222 4 3/4 **Rule Of Nature**[36] 2928 3-9-1 **82** .... WilliamBuick 6 81
(Sir Michael Stoute) *hld up: hdwy and swtchd lft over 1f out: sn rdn: styd on same pce ins fnl f* **7/2**[2]

6041 5 3/4 **Pretty Bonnie**[19] 3505 5-9-5 **84** .... NataliaGemelova(3) 1 81
(A E Price) *chsd ldr: rdn over 2f out: sn hung rt: no ex fnl f* **20/1**

11 6 1/2 **Moretta Blanche**[34] 3001 3-9-2 **83** .... SebSanders 4 78
(R M Beckett) *trckd ldrs: racd keenly: rdn over 1f out: wknd wl ins fnl f* **3/1**[1]

0125 7 hd **Cape Melody**[8] 3845 4-8-13 **75** .... (v[1]) NickyMackay 3 70
(H Morrison) *awkward leaving stalls: sn rcvrd to ld: rdn and hdd over 1f out: wknd ins fnl f* **16/1**

0522 8 1 **Bahati (IRE)**[23] 3375 3-9-10 **91** .... StephenCraine 11 82
(J G Portman) *hld up: hdwy over 2f out: rdn over 1f out: wknd ins fnl f* **14/1**

0-40 9 1 1/2 **Chaussini**[23] 3375 3-8-12 **79** .... IanMongan 7 65
(J A R Toller) *prom: rdn over 2f out: wknd over 1f out* **22/1**

0140 10 1/2 **Kerrys Requiem (IRE)**[8] 3850 4-9-11 **87** .... ChrisCatlin 5 72
(M R Channon) *prom: rdn and swtchd lft over 1f out: wknd ins fnl f* **28/1**

1m 11.36s (-1.14) **Going Correction** -0.20s/f (Firm)
WFA 3 from 4yo+ 5lb **10** Ran SP% **116.0**
Speed ratings (Par 104): **99,98,94,93,92 91,91,90,88,87**
toteswingers:1&2:£5.70, 1&3:£8.90, 2&3:£17.90 CSF £26.86 CT £200.52 TOTE £5.90: £1.80, £2.00, £3.40; EX 27.20.

Owner Options O Syndicate **Bred** F C T Wilson **Trained** Newmarket, Suffolk

■ Stewards' Enquiry : Natalia Gemelova three-day ban: used whip with excessive frequency down shoulder in the forehand (Aug 1-3)

FOCUS
A competitive fillies' sprint handicap which often falls to an improving type.

NOTEBOOK
Dever Dream, a three-time winner over 6f on fast ground and Polytrack before finishing behind Bahati at Warwick, appreciated the return to this trip and reversed the form in no uncertain terms. The winner came from off the pace to challenge inside the last furlong and got her head in front near the line. She will not go up much for this and could still have more to offer. Connections will look to earn some black type for her now, with the Listed race at Pontefract in the middle of next month the target. (op 5-1 tchd 9-2)

Flambeau, the winner of a maiden over 7f at Newbury and a good third in a conditions stakes over C&D last time, travelled well on this handicap debut and looked sure to win entering the final furlong. However, she could not resist the winner's late surge. She still looks to be progressing. (op 7-2 tchd 3-1)

Bella Swan, a C&D winner here last season and with form at up to 1m2f, was dropping in trip for this handicap debut. She came from off the pace to challenge shortly after halfway but could not pick up again in the latter stages. (op 14-1)

Rule Of Nature, a consistent sort whose win was over 6f on fast ground, had been beaten off lower marks. She was held up early before being switched to deliver her challenge on the wide outside, rather away from the main action, and could never land a blow. (tchd 11-4)

Pretty Bonnie, a 6f winner on fast ground last time when she made all, was unable to lead this time but appeared to run her race, keeping on under pressure. (tchd 16-1)

Moretta Blanche, both of whose wins were over 7f on fast ground, was up in grade and down in trip for this handicap debut and it appeared to find her out, as she was one of the first under pressure. (op 5-1 tchd 13-2)

Cape Melody, a dual 6f winner on fast ground, was 9lb above her last winning mark, and the visor for the first time instead of blinkers did not make an appreciable difference. (op 14-1 tchd 12-1)

4146 BOX CLEVER DISPLAY MAIDEN STKS 7f
4:05 (4:07) (Class 4) 3-Y-O
£4,533 (£1,348; £674; £336) **Stalls** High

Form RPR

2222 1 **Soviet Secret**[35] 2981 3-9-3 79 .... DaneO'Neill 5 80
(P J McBride) *chsd ldr tl led over 2f out: rdn out* **15/8**[1]

2 1/2 **Al Muthanaa** 3-9-3 0 .... RichardHills 2 79
(W J Haggas) *dwlt: sn prom: rdn over 1f out: sn edgd lft: r.o wl to go 2nd towards fin* **5/2**[2]

2-46 3 1/2 **Hooligan Sean**[19] 3511 3-8-10 75 .... AmyScott(7) 6 77
(H Candy) *chsd ldrs: rdn and ev ch fr over 1f out tl no ex and lost 2nd towards fin* **8/1**

223 4 3 **City Ground (USA)**[16] 3586 3-9-3 78 .... NeilCallan 3 69
(M A Jarvis) *chsd ldrs: rdn over 1f out: no ex ins fnl f* **7/2**[3]

0-0 5 11 **Filibuster**[23] 3374 3-9-3 0 .... GeorgeBaker 7 40
(C F Wall) *hood removed late and s.s: hld up: pushed along over 2f out: sn wknd* **20/1**

06 6 1 **Plan A (IRE)**[28] 3220 3-9-3 0 .... AdamKirby 8 37
(M G Quinlan) *hld up: pushed along 1/2-way: wknd over 2f out* **40/1**

7 1 **Marble Arch (USA)**[155] 3-8-10 0 .... (p) LewisWalsh(7) 10 34
(Jane Chapple-Hyam) *hld up: reminders over 4f out: wknd over 2f out* **12/1**

0-0 8 12 **Natalie N G**[20] 3484 3-8-12 0 .... IanMongan 4 —
(J R Jenkins) *led: hdd over 2f out: sn wknd: t.o* **100/1**

9 6 **Only You Maggie (IRE)** 3-8-12 0 .... ChrisCatlin 12 —
(W G Harrison) *s.s: a in rr: lost tch fnl 3f: t.o* **33/1**

1m 24.96s (-0.74) **Going Correction** -0.20s/f (Firm) **9** Ran SP% **115.5**
Speed ratings (Par 102): **96,95,94,91,78 77,76,62,56**
toteswingers:1&2:£1.60, 1&3:£3.80, 2&3:£5.70 CSF £6.49 TOTE £3.10: £1.40, £1.30, £1.60; EX 7.30.

Owner PMRacing **Bred** Miss D Fleming **Trained** Newmarket, Suffolk

FOCUS
Just a fair maiden judged on the form of those with experience.
Filibuster Official explanation: jockey said, regarding running and riding, he was slow to remove blindfold.

4147 ATKINSON BOLTON H'CAP (IN MEMORY OF REG DAY) 1m 6f 175y
4:40 (4:41) (Class 4) (0-85,82) 4-Y-O+
£4,857 (£1,445; £722; £360) **Stalls** Centre

Form RPR

3244 1 **Curacao**[15] 3634 4-9-3 **76** .... NeilCallan 1 83
(Mrs A J Perrett) *chsd ldrs: hung rt over 2f out: rdn to ld over 1f out: hung lft ins fnl f: styd on* **5/2**[1]

-440 2 2 1/4 **Akbabend**[34] 2996 4-9-9 **82** .... RichardHills 3 87
(M Johnston) *racd wd for the first 6f: chsd ldr tl led 12f out: hdd over 8f out: remained w ldr: rdn and hung rt over 2f out: ev ch over 1f out: styd on same pce ins fnl f* **9/2**[3]

-122 3 1/2 **My Mate Max**[22] 3398 5-9-3 **76** .... (p) WilliamBuick 5 80
(R Hollinshead) *led: hdd 12f out: led again over 8f out: rdn and hung rt over 2f out: hdd over 1f out: styd on same pce ins fnl f* **5/2**[1]

6-43 4 3/4 **Rockfella**[29] 3159 4-9-2 **75** .... EddieAhern 2 78
(D J Coakley) *racd wd for the first 6f: prom: rdn over 2f out: sn edgd rt: no ex ins fnl f* **11/4**[2]

-000 5 10 **Judgethemoment (USA)**[40] 2814 5-9-2 **75** .... IvaMilickova 4 66
(Jane Chapple-Hyam) *hld up: a in rr: rdn and wknd over 2f out* **12/1**

3m 6.14s (-5.16) **Going Correction** -0.20s/f (Firm) **5** Ran SP% **109.7**
Speed ratings (Par 105): **105,103,103,103,97**
CSF £13.60 TOTE £3.70: £1.80, £2.30; EX 13.70.

Owner Mrs S Conway, Coombelands Racing Stables **Bred** Granham Farm **Trained** Pulborough, W Sussex

FOCUS
A small field for this stayers' handicap but they looked tightly matched and it was only inside the final furlong that the winner drew away.

4148 DODSON & HORRELL H'CAP 5f
5:15 (5:15) (Class 3) (0-95,91) 3-Y-O+
£7,771 (£2,312; £1,155; £577) **Stalls** High

Form RPR

1202 1 **Five Star Junior (USA)**[9] 3828 4-9-13 **91** .... EddieAhern 1 99
(Mrs L Stubbs) *racd centre: hld up: hdwy over 1f out: rdn to ld overall ins fnl f: r.o* **9/2**[2]

5232 2 hd **Rocket Rob (IRE)**[15] 3629 4-9-10 **88** .... WilliamBuick 5 95
(M Botti) *racd stands' side: hld up in tch: nt clr run over 1f out: rdn and r.o wl ins fnl f* **4/1**[1]

10 3 hd **Bougainvilia (IRE)**[28] 3217 3-8-11 **79** .... DaneO'Neill 11 85
(R Hannon) *racd stands' side: prom: lost pl over 3f out: rdn and r.o wl fnl f* **12/1**

-113 4 nse **Sutton Veny (IRE)**[26] 3261 4-9-4 **82** .... AdamKirby 9 88
(J R Gask) *led stands' side gp: hung lft 1/2-way: hdd that gp wl ins fnl f: r.o* **8/1**

6606 5 nk **Tabaret**[9] 3828 7-9-5 **83** .... (p) NeilCallan 10 88
(R M Whitaker) *racd stands' side: chsd ldrs: rdn and edgd lft over 1f out: r.o* **8/1**

50-1 6 1/2 **Alis Aquilae (IRE)**[14] 3663 4-8-11 **75** .... SaleemGolam 4 79
(T J Etherington) *racd stands' side: trckd ldrs: rdn over 1f out: r.o* **4/1**[1]

5111 7 2 **Brandywell Boy (IRE)**[7] 3892 7-8-7 **76** .... BillyCray(5) 8 72
(D J S Ffrench Davis) *racd stands' side: dwlt: sn pushed along in rr: r.o ins fnl f: nvr nrr* **7/1**[3]

134 8 1/2 **Steelcut**[12] 3736 6-8-12 **76** .... RichardHills 3 71
(Andrew Reid) *racd centre: chsd ldr tl led overall 2f out: rdn over 1f out: hdd and no ex ins fnl f* **10/1**

-123 9 4 1/2 **Osiris Way**[15] 3629 8-9-12 **90** .... GeorgeBaker 7 68
(P R Chamings) *racd stands' side: chsd ldr: rdn and hung lft 1/2-way: wknd ins fnl f* **8/1**

0000 10 6 **Rievaulx World**[56] 2346 4-9-4 **82** .... J-PGuillambert 2 39
(K A Ryan) *racd centre: overall ldr tl hdd 2f out: sn rdn: wknd over 1f out* **16/1**

58.00 secs (-1.10) **Going Correction** -0.20s/f (Firm)
WFA 3 from 4yo+ 4lb **10** Ran SP% **126.7**
Speed ratings (Par 107): **100,99,99,99,98 98,94,94,86,77**
toteswingers:1&2:£4.70, 1&3:£13.60, 2&3:£8.90 CSF £25.15 CT £218.37 TOTE £6.10: £1.80, £2.20, £3.50; EX 18.90 Place 6 £292.55, Place 5 £233.81.

Owner Moyns Park Stud **Bred** Robert W Sanford **Trained** Norton, N Yorks

FOCUS
A competitive sprint handicap and the majority of the field came into this in reasonable form and it produced a blanket finish with the runners spread across the track.

NOTEBOOK

Five Star Junior(USA) came up against a progressive type here last time, but showed he is in good heart with a fine performance under top weight. He tracked the leaders up the centre before hitting the front entering the final furlong, and then held off the late challengers towards the stands' side. (op 11-2)

Rocket Rob(IRE) is a consistent sort but has not had the best of luck of late. That was the case again here, as he did not get the opening straight away when he needed it before finishing best of all, not quite catching the winner. He deserves to pick up one of these. (op 7-2)

Bougainvilia(IRE) got off the mark over 1m on her belated debut but pulled too hard over the trip next time and was taking a big drop in distance. She was held up early before finishing well towards the stands' side, and sprinting looks her game after this effort. (tchd 14-1)

Sutton Veny(IRE) completed a hat-trick on Polytrack over the winter but has won on turf. All her wins have been at 6f, but she ran with plenty of credit and only narrowly missed out on the places. There is more to come. (tchd 10-1)

Tabaret finished behind today's winner here last time and was backed despite being only 1lb better off. He ran pretty well and finished closer this time, and his turn might not be far away with 6f on a flat track ideal. (op 12-1)

Alis Aquilae(IRE) is pretty inexperienced, having won his maiden last time at the third attempt. He showed plenty of pace but was a little exposed on the outside of those racing nearer the stands' side, and he faded up the hill. It was still not a bad effort on his handicap debut. (op 6-1 tchd 13-2)

Brandywell Boy(IRE) came into this bidding for a four-timer but was a stone higher than for the first of those successes, and he effectively lost his chance by dwelling in the stalls. Official explanation: jockey said gelding missed the break (tchd 6-1)

Steelcut did not get the best of runs when held up last time but had made all for his previous success. He got involved in a battle for the lead up the centre here but weakened after being headed over a furlong from home. (op 8-1)

Osiris Way Official explanation: jockey said gelding had no more to give

T/Plt: £193.30 to a £1 stake. Pool: £84,448.97. 318.92 winning tickets. T/Qpdt: £38.40 to a £1 stake. Pool: £5,292.70. 101.90 winnign tickets. CR

3728 RIPON (R-H)

Saturday, July 17

OFFICIAL GOING: Good (8.6)

Wind: Light, half behind Weather: Sunny

4149 E.B.F. STOWE FAMILY LAW LLP MAIDEN FILLIES' STKS — 5f

1:50 (1:50) (Class 4) 2-Y-O **£4,857** (£1,445; £722; £360) **Stalls** Low

Form / RPR

2 **1** **Ishbelle**[14] 3686 2-8-11 0 .... MartinLane(3) 2 — 83+
(R M Beckett) *prom: rdn to ld 2f out: kpt on wl* **10/11**[1]

66 **2** *3 1/2* **Jameela Girl**[10] 3778 2-9-0 0 .... AndrewElliott 8 — 70
(R M H Cowell) *w ldr: rdn over 2f out: kpt on but no match for wnr* **16/1**

0 **3** *3 3/4* **Infectious (IRE)**[28] 3204 2-9-0 0 .... PaulMulrennan 3 — 57
(D H Brown) *hld up: niggled 1/2-way: stl only 7th over 1f out: r.o wl fnl f* **25/1**

54 **4** *nk* **Empress Royal**[17] 3549 2-9-0 0 .... PhillipMakin 6 — 56
(M Dods) *chsd ldrs: rdn over 2f out: one pce* **9/1**[3]

5 *2 3/4* **Abzolutely (IRE)** 2-9-0 0 .... DuranFentiman 5 — 46
(D O'Meara) *led: rdn and hdd 2f out: wknd over 1f out* **16/1**

0 **6** *nk* **Winning Draw (IRE)**[11] 3756 2-9-0 0 .... TonyCulhane 4 — 45
(P T Midgley) *chsd ldrs: rdn over 2f out: edgd lft over 1f out: one pce* **33/1**

7 *1/2* **Saxonette** 2-8-9 0 .... MatthewDavies(5) 7 — 43
(M R Channon) *s.i.s: hld up: chsd along 1/2-way: nvr on terms* **10/1**

34 **8** *hd* **Misscomplacent**[24] 3315 2-8-11 0 ....(p) BarryMcHugh(3) 1 — 42
(Mrs A Duffield) *chsd ldrs: rdn over 2f out: already lost pl whn short of room on rail over 1f out* **13/2**[2]

9 *3* **Madam Mayem** 2-9-0 0 .... RichardSmith 10 — 32+
(Tom Dascombe) *s.i.s: a in rr* **50/1**

10 *9* **Marie Du Plessis** 2-9-0 0 .... JoeFanning 9 — —
(M Johnston) *green: a in rr* **13/2**[2]

59.86 secs (-0.84) **Going Correction** -0.075s/f (Good) **10** Ran SP% **118.7**

Speed ratings (Par 93): **103,97,91,90,86 86,85,84,80,65**

toteswingers: 1&2 £5.60, 1&3 £4.50, 2&3 £50.20 CSF £18.65 TOTE £2.10: £1.10, £4.60, £8.40; EX 18.60 TRIFECTA Not won..

Owner Mrs M E Slade **Bred** Mrs M E Slade **Trained** Whitsbury, Hants

FOCUS

Following 30mm of rain over the previous week, with the last significant rain falling on Thursday night into Friday, the ground was expected to ride just on the slow side of good, and the time of this maiden seemed to back that up. Not a strong race but the winner did it well.

NOTEBOOK

Ishbelle was provided a straightforward opportunity to get off the mark at the second attempt. She'd shown enough on her debut to suggest she could win an ordinary race like this and, having broken well, she was always prominent and only had to be pushed out to score. She still showed signs of greenness, so there could be more to come from her. (op 11-8)

Jameela Girl was also up with the pace throughout, although she was stuck out wider, having been drawn in stall eight. The winner was too strong for her, but this was a solid effort in second on her turf debut and moderate handicaps will offer her better opportunities.

Infectious(IRE) still looked green but she stayed on nicely for third and is slowly getting the hang of things. She's a sister to multiple winner Wovoka and looks the type to keep improving. (op 22-1)

Empress Royal, who raced a bit keenly early, looks all speed and might be best making the running round a bend. (op 8-1)

Abzolutely(IRE), whose stable is in form, showed bright speed on her debut and is entitled to be better for the outing. (op 14-1)

Winning Draw(IRE) looks like she needs further than this. Official explanation: jockey said filly lost its action

4150 WELCOME TO YORKSHIRE THIS IS Y (S) STKS — 6f

2:25 (2:27) (Class 6) 2-Y-O **£2,590** (£770; £385; £192) **Stalls** Low

Form / RPR

446 **1** **Peppercorn Rent (IRE)**[12] 3729 2-8-3 0 ....(e) KellyHarrison(3) 14 — 53
(T D Easterby) *chsd ldrs far side: drvn and hdwy 2f out: led ins fnl f: jst hld on* **16/1**

0604 **2** *nse* **Blind Stag (IRE)**[11] 3757 2-8-11 0 .... TonyCulhane 8 — 58
(P T Midgley) *trckd ldrs far side: drvn and ev ch fr over 1f out: kpt on: jst failed* **25/1**

04 **3** *shd* **Bigalo's Laura B (IRE)**[10] 3770 2-8-1 0 ....(be1) DeclanCannon(5) 11 — 53
(L A Mullaney) *sn prom far side: rdn over 2f out: kpt on wl* **40/1**

4 *1 1/4* **Evening In (IRE)** 2-8-3 0 .... PaulPickard(3) 5 — 49+
(P T Midgley) *chsd ldrs stands' side: rdn and hdwy to ld her side 2f out: sn edgd rt: kpt on* **50/1**

4423 **5** *1* **Crown Ridge (IRE)**[15] 3625 2-8-6 0 .... MatthewDavies(5) 13 — 51
(M R Channon) *chsd ldrs far side: rdn over 2f out: kpt on same pce* **3/1**[2]

1 **6** *1/2* **Sweet Cheeks (IRE)**[36] 2939 2-8-8 0 .... BarryMcHugh(3) 15 — 49
(R A Fahey) *prom far side: rdn to ld 2f out: hdd ins fnl f: wknd* **11/10**[1]

000 **7** *3/4* **Miss Cosette (IRE)**[30] 3106 2-8-1 0 .... PatrickDonaghy(5) 10 — 42
(T D Barron) *slowly away: hld up far side: rdn over 2f out: kpt on fnl f: nvr on terms* **33/1**

003 **8** *1 1/4* **Karafuse (IRE)**[29] 3175 2-8-6 0 ....(b) DuranFentiman 4 — 38+
(T D Easterby) *led stands' side: hdd 2f out: wknd fnl f* **20/1**

4006 **9** *3* **Muse To Use**[10] 3770 2-8-3 0 .... MartinLane(3) 7 — 29
(I W McInnes) *sn led far side: hdd 2f out: sn wknd* **80/1**

4530 **10** *1/2* **King Of Cassis**[36] 2939 2-8-8 0 ....(p) JackDean(3) 6 — 33+
(W G M Turner) *prom stands' side: rdn over 2f out: wknd over 1f out: hung rt and eased fnl f* **7/1**[3]

62 **11** *1 3/4* **Lighthouse Keeper (IRE)**[16] 3603 2-8-6 0 .... IanBrennan(5) 1 — 28+
(Miss Amy Weaver) *racd stands' side: rdn bef 1/2-way: sn btn* **8/1**

055 **12** *3/4* **Dark Times (IRE)**[32] 3058 2-8-6 0 .... AndrewElliott 3 — 20+
(J R Weymes) *sn chsd along in rr stands' side: nvr threatened* **33/1**

360 **13** *1* **Gartsherrie**[19] 3498 2-8-6 0 .... JoeFanning 2 — 17
(P T Midgley) *prom stands' side: wknd fnl 2f* **40/1**

00 **14** *6* **Bonded Spirit**[24] 3315 2-8-11 0 ....(e1) PaulMulrennan 12 — 4
(Mrs K Walton) *chsd ldrs far side: wknd 2f out: eased* **66/1**

15 *4 1/2* **Nippy Nikki** 2-8-1 0 .... JamesSullivan(5) 9 — —
(J R Norton) *slowly away: sn detached in rr far side* **80/1**

1m 14.26s (1.26) **Going Correction** -0.075s/f (Good) **15** Ran SP% **127.4**

Speed ratings (Par 92): **88,87,87,86,84 84,83,81,77,76 74,73,72,64,58**

toteswingers: 1&2 £37.00, 1&3 £117.10, 2&3 £117.10 CSF £368.88 TOTE £24.70: £5.30, £6.60, £7.90; EX 486.30 TRIFECTA Not won..The winner was bought in for 5,500gns. Sweet Cheeks was claimed by Ken McGarrity for £6,000.

Owner Habton Farms **Bred** Canice M Farrell Jnr **Trained** Great Habton, N Yorks

■ Stewards' Enquiry : Kelly Harrison caution: used whip with excessive frequency.

FOCUS

The field split for this seller with the majority heading to the far side. The first three home came from that larger group. Weak form with the favourite well off his debut mark.

NOTEBOOK

Peppercorn Rent(IRE) hadn't achieved a great deal in her previous three starts in maiden company but this drop in class, coupled with a high draw and being able to race closest to the far-side rail, saw her just edge a three-way photo. It might be dangerous to take this form at face value. (op 14-1)

Blind Stag(IRE) finished fourth in similar company on the Fibresand last time, but he ran a better race here, seemingly very much aided by racing close to the far-side rail. (tchd 22-1)

Bigalo's Laura B(IRE) didn't run much of a race in similar grade at Catterick ten days earlier, but the application of an eye-shield for the first time brought about improvement, although she might well have won had she not hung left into the centre of the track under pressure. (op 50-1)

Evening In(IRE) did by far the best of the six who raced on the stands' side despite hanging right towards the centre of the track under pressure. Her effort should be upgraded and she clearly has the ability to win a little race. (op 100-1)

Crown Ridge(IRE) hung left as he weakened and was ultimately disappointing considering he raced in the favoured far-side group. He didn't seem happy on the undulating course. Official explanation: jockey said colt hung left-handed (op 6-1)

Sweet Cheeks(IRE) was also disappointing as she didn't get home after showing plenty of early speed. Official explanation: jockey said filly was unsuited by the track (op 10-11)

King Of Cassis Official explanation: jockey said gelding hung right-handed

4151 MIKE BOON MEMORIAL MAIDEN H'CAP (DIV I) — 6f

2:55 (2:55) (Class 5) (0-70,65) 3-Y-O+ **£2,914** (£867; £433; £216) **Stalls** Low

Form / RPR

0033 **1** **Offspring**[17] 3554 3-9-9 **65** .... DuranFentiman 6 — 73
(T D Easterby) *prom: hdwy to ld over 1f out: sn rdn: kpt on wl* **9/2**[2]

2203 **2** *2 3/4* **Mrs Mogg**[12] 3726 3-9-7 **63** .... RichardSmith 9 — 62
(Tom Dascombe) *chsd ldrs: rdn over 2f out: kpt on but nvr trbld wnr* **5/1**[3]

0620 **3** *2 3/4* **Pelmanism**[10] 3773 3-9-9 **65** ....(b) PaulMulrennan 7 — 55
(K A Ryan) *led: rdn and hdd over 1f out: no ex fnl f* **8/1**

5440 **4** *3/4* **Eeny Mac (IRE)**[68] 1970 3-8-9 **51** .... PaulQuinn 2 — 39
(N Bycroft) *trckd ldrs: rdn over 2f out: kpt on one pce* **9/2**[2]

6-06 **5** *2 3/4* **Gold Crusher (USA)**[56] 2329 3-9-1 **60** ....(p) BarryMcHugh(3) 3 — 39
(Julie Camacho) *hld up: rdn and hdwy over 2f out: kpt on one pce* **12/1**

-000 **6** *1/2* **Twisted**[11] 3761 4-9-7 **63** .... JamesSullivan(5) 5 — 41
(M W Easterby) *hld up: rdn 1/2-way: nvr on terms* **10/1**

6005 **7** *nk* **Hill Of Miller (IRE)**[4] 3993 3-8-13 **58** ....(bt) MartinLane(3) 1 — 34
(Rae Guest) *hld up: drvn over 2f out: sn no imp* **7/2**[1]

0600 **8** *6* **Pavement Games**[38] 2879 3-8-3 **45** .... PaulEddery 8 — 2
(R C Guest) *s.i.s: sn in tch: hdwy to chse ldrs over 2f out: rdn and wknd over 1f out: eased fnl f* **20/1**

0-00 **9** *1 1/2* **Stanley Bridge**[60] 2209 3-8-0 **45** .... PaulPickard(3) 4 — —
(A Berry) *hld up: a towards rr* **40/1**

0-60 **10** *2* **Royal Record**[46] 2628 3-8-4 **53** .... JohnCavanagh(7) 11 — —
(M Brittain) *s.i.s and wnt rt s: hld up: a bhd* **16/1**

1m 12.89s (-0.11) **Going Correction** -0.075s/f (Good)

WFA 3 from 4yo 5lb **10** Ran SP% **116.2**

Speed ratings (Par 103): **97,93,89,88,85 84,83,75,73,71**

toteswingers: 1&2 £2.40, 1&3 £3.80, 2&3 £4.20 CSF £27.23 CT £175.31 TOTE £5.50: £2.00, £1.60, £2.90; EX 18.30 Trifecta £170.20 Pool: £241.50 - 1.05 winning units..

Owner L B Holliday **Bred** Cleaboy Farms Co **Trained** Great Habton, N Yorks

FOCUS

Despite the evidence of the previous race the whole field came stands' side.

Hill Of Miller(IRE) Official explanation: jockey said gelding was slow away and never travelled

Pavement Games Official explanation: jockey said filly finished distressed

Royal Record Official explanation: jockey said filly hung right final 3f

4152 SKY BET SUPPORTING YORKSHIRE RACING SUMMER FESTIVAL H'CAP — 1m 1f 170y

3:25 (3:26) (Class 4) (0-85,89) 3-Y-O+ **£5,677** (£1,699; £849; £424; £211) **Stalls** High

Form / RPR

2162 **1** **Jonny Lesters Hair (IRE)**[15] 3627 5-9-4 **75** .... DavidNolan 7 — 87
(T D Easterby) *w ldr: led 3f out: drvn 2f out: kpt on wl* **7/1**

-014 **2** *1 1/4* **Kindest**[15] 3627 4-9-8 **79** .... TonyCulhane 6 — 88
(C F Wall) *midfield: rdn wl over 3f out: hdwy to chse wnr 2f out: kpt on wl fnl f* **15/2**

5-51 **3** *1 1/4* **Mushreq (USA)**[14] 3689 3-8-11 **81** .... MartinLane(3) 5 — 87
(Sir Michael Stoute) *prom: rdn over 3f out: sn hung rt: kpt on same pce* **7/2**[1]

2322 **4** *hd* **Hawaana (IRE)**[14] 3688 5-9-1 **79** .... AdamBeschizza(7) 8 — 85
(Miss Gay Kelleway) *midfield: rdn over 2f out: hdwy to chse ldrs over 1f out: kpt on* **10/1**

-126 **5** *2 3/4* **Music Of The Moor (IRE)**[15] 3627 3-8-12 **79** .... AndrewElliott 12 — 79
(T P Tate) *hld up in midfield: rdn over 3f out: kpt on fnl f: nvr on terms* **6/1**[3]

10-5 **6** 1 ½ **Knight's Victory (IRE)**[11] 3750 4-8-9 **69**................ MichaelStainton(3) 9 66
(Michael Smith) *s.i.s: sn rcvrd into midfield: hdwy to chse ldrs over 2f out: sn drvn: wknd fnl f* **33/1**

6303 **7** 1 ½ **Persian Peril**[31] 3089 6-9-10 **81**...................... PaulMulrennan 2 75
(G A Swinbank) *hld up: rdn over 3f out: sme late hdwy: nvr rchd ldrs* **9/1**

0550 **8** *nse* **Rosbay (IRE)**[24] 3319 6-9-7 **78**...................... DuranFentiman 1 72
(T D Easterby) *stdd s: hld up: nvr threatened* **16/1**

0324 **9** ½ **Moheebb (IRE)**[14] 3667 6-9-12 **83**..................(b) PhillipMakin 13 76
(Mrs R A Carr) *trckd ldrs: rdn over 3f out: lost pl and sn wknd* **4/1**[2]

1126 **10** *10* **Templetuohy Max (IRE)**[22] 3408 5-9-4 **78**...........(v) BarryMcHugh(3) 10 50
(J D Bethell) *led: rdn and hdd 3f out: sn wknd* **9/1**

10-0 **11** ½ **Nevada Desert (IRE)**[75] 1751 10-9-5 **76**................ DaraghO'Donohoe 3 47
(R M Whitaker) *plld hrd in rr: nvr a factor* **40/1**

2m 3.58s (-1.82) **Going Correction** -0.075s/f (Good)
WFA 3 from 4yo+ 10lb **11** Ran SP% **121.1**
Speed ratings (Par 105): **104,103,102,101,99 98,97,97,96,88 88**
toteswingers: 1&2 £12.20, 1&3 £7.10, 2&3 £4.90 CSF £60.58 CT £219.27 TOTE £7.90: £2.50, £2.00, £2.10; EX 68.10 Trifecta £214.70 Pool: £290.25 - 0.85 winning units..
Owner Reality Partnerships II **Bred** Gary O'Reilly **Trained** Great Habton, N Yorks

FOCUS
There threatened to be a strong pace here with a number of front-runners in the line-up, but clearly their connections had noticed that too and Templetuohy Max was not strongly challenged for the lead. Not too many got into this from off the pace.
Moheebb(IRE) Official explanation: trainer said gelding lost its off-fore shoe
Nevada Desert(IRE) Official explanation: jockey said gelding ran too free

4153 RIPON BELL-RINGER H'CAP 1m 4f 10y
4:00 (4:00) (Class 2) (0-100,92) 3-Y-£12,462 (£3,732; £1,866; £934; £466) **Stalls** High

Form RPR
1011 **1** **Vulcanite (IRE)**[24] 3335 3-8-13 **87**...................... MartinLane(3) 1 102+
(R M Beckett) *hld up: smooth hdwy to chse ldr over 3f out: led 2f out: pushed clr: comf* **7/4**[1]

2141 **2** 4 ½ **Beat The Rush**[30] 3123 3-8-10 **84**...................... BarryMcHugh(3) 6 91
(Julie Camacho) *led: rdn whn hdd 2f out: sn no match wnr* **2/1**[2]

-104 **3** 1 ½ **Shernando**[7] 3889 3-8-12 **83**...................... JoeFanning 5 88
(M Johnston) *hld up: rdn over 4f out: no imp tl kpt on fnl f* **7/2**[3]

313 **4** *7* **Law To Himself (IRE)**[21] 3451 3-8-6 **77**...................... AndrewElliott 4 71
(G A Swinbank) *in tch: rdn and outpcd 4f out: wknd over 2f out* **11/2**

0 **5** *42* **Kingdom Of Munster (IRE)**[72] 1834 3-8-9 **80**............ PaulMulrennan 3 7
(Ian Williams) *trckd ldr: effrt 4f out: sn wknd: eased fnl 2f* **20/1**

2m 34.41s (-2.29) **Going Correction** -0.075s/f (Good) **5** Ran SP% **112.1**
Speed ratings (Par 106): **104,101,100,95,67**
toteswingers: 1&2 £1.80 CSF £5.72 TOTE £2.70: £1.60, £1.60; EX 5.20.
Owner Mrs Barbara Facchino **Bred** Barouche Stud Ireland Ltd **Trained** Whitsbury, Hants

FOCUS
Not as good a race as the conditions would suggest, as in the absence of the top-weight the highest-rated horse in the race had a mark of just 87.

NOTEBOOK
Vulcanite(IRE) cruised through from the back of the field to challenge the leader 2f out and only had to be kept up to his work to score with a nice bit in hand. He looks very progressive, coped with this easier ground really well and looks capable of taking a decent handicap before the season is out. (op 9-4)
Beat The Rush enjoyed the run of things out in front but was powerless to stop the impressive winner coming by inside the last 2f. The handicapper might just have him now after putting him up 5lb for his last success, but equally he might just have bumped into a very well-handicapped rival here. (tchd 15-8 and 9-4)
Shernando promised to be suited by the step up to 1m4f but he could never land a blow from off the pace and is becoming a little disappointing. (op 3-1)
Law To Himself(IRE) was taking a big step up in trip from 1m and was done with early in the straight. (op 6-1 tchd 9-2)

4154 YORKSHIRE RACING SUMMER FESTIVAL H'CAP 1m
4:35 (4:36) (Class 4) (0-85,84) 3-Y-0+ **£5,677** (£1,699; £849; £424; £211) **Stalls** High

Form RPR
-006 **1** **San Cassiano (IRE)**[28] 3226 3-9-0 **78**...................... PhillipMakin 4 89
(Mrs R A Carr) *prom: chal fr over 2f out: led ins fnl f: styd on* **25/1**

0411 **2** *2* **Reel Buddy Star**[18] 3537 5-9-12 **82**...................... DanielTudhope 1 90
(G M Moore) *midfield: hdwy to chal 3f out: drvn to ld narrowly over 2f out: hdd and no ex ins fnl f* **13/2**

3401 **3** 1 ½ **Moody Tunes**[15] 3616 7-9-10 **80**...................... AndrewElliott 14 85
(J R Weymes) *prom: rdn over 3f out: kpt on* **8/1**

0065 **4** ¾ **Medici Pearl**[14] 3667 6-9-13 **83**...................... DuranFentiman 10 86
(T D Easterby) *midfield: hdwy to chse ldrs 3f out: drvn 2f out: kpt on* **11/2**[3]

2204 **5** *hd* **Jordaura**[23] 3366 4-10-0 **84**...................... TonyCulhane 13 86
(J R Holt) *hld up in midfield: n.m.r towards inner fr over 2f out: swtchd lft over 1f out: kpt on wl fnl f: nrst fin* **5/1**[2]

0442 **6** *shd* **Bolodenka (IRE)**[15] 3616 8-8-11 **74**...................... MarzenaJeziorek(7) 8 76
(R A Fahey) *dwlt: hld up: stl plenty to do 3f out: hdwy over 2f out: kpt on fnl f: nvr rchd ldrs* **8/1**

-100 **7** *3* **Steel Stockholder**[8] 3876 4-9-0 **70**...................... PaulMulrennan 2 65
(M Brittain) *chsd ldrs: rdn over 3f out: wknd over 1f out* **33/1**

-000 **8** 1 ½ **Quanah Parker (IRE)**[21] 3448 4-9-9 **82**...................... MichaelStainton(3) 3 74
(R M Whitaker) *trckd ldrs: rdn over 3f out: wknd fnl 2f* **22/1**

0-06 **9** ¾ **City Of The Kings (IRE)**[53] 2423 5-9-8 **83**............ JamesSullivan(5) 11 73
(G A Harker) *s.i.s: hld up: rdn over 3f out: sn no imp* **9/2**[1]

0/0 **10** 3 ¾ **Jackson (BRZ)**[11] 3750 8-9-2 **72**...................... PaulEddery 5 53
(R C Guest) *dwlt: hld up: a towards rr* **40/1**

3- **11** *7* **Zarilan (IRE)**[512] 488 5-8-11 **70**...................... BarryMcHugh(3) 7 35
(Michael Smith) *led: rdn whn hdd over 2f out: sn wknd* **33/1**

2005 **12** 3 ¼ **Magic Omen (USA)**[17] 3553 3-8-8 **72**......................(b¹) JoeFanning 9 28
(M Johnston) *hld up in midfield: rdn 4f out: sn wknd* **7/1**

4100 **13** *12* **Toto Skyllachy**[7] 3920 5-9-3 **78**...................... DeclanCannon(5) 12 8
(J O'Reilly) *hld up: a in rr: eased fnl 2f* **10/1**

1m 40.13s (-1.27) **Going Correction** -0.075s/f (Good)
WFA 3 from 4yo+ 8lb **13** Ran SP% **123.9**
Speed ratings (Par 105): **103,101,99,98,98 98,95,93,93,89 82,79,67**
toteswingers: 1&2 £23.60, 1&3 £38.80, 2&3 £10.10 CSF £178.90 CT £1498.42 TOTE £35.30: £8.00, £3.10, £3.50; EX 271.80 TRIFECTA Not won..
Owner P D Savill **Bred** Peter Savill **Trained** Huby, N Yorks

FOCUS
As is often the case on the round course here, it paid to race handily.
Jordaura Official explanation: jockey said colt was denied a clear run
City Of The Kings(IRE) Official explanation: jockey said gelding was unsuited by the good ground
Toto Skyllachy Official explanation: jockey said gelding moved poorly throughout

4155 MIKE BOON MEMORIAL MAIDEN H'CAP (DIV II) 6f
5:10 (5:11) (Class 5) (0-70,69) 3-Y-0+ **£2,914** (£867; £433; £216) **Stalls** Low

Form RPR
2356 **1** **Chushka**[32] 3061 3-9-6 **63**......................(v) PaulMulrennan 10 74
(B Smart) *cl up: led after 2f: rdn clr fnl 2f* **11/4**[1]

3503 **2** 3 ½ **Could It Be Magic**[32] 3062 3-9-9 **69**......................(b¹) JackDean(3) 7 69
(W G M Turner) *trckd ldrs: wnt 2nd over 3f out: hrd drvn over 2f out: kpt on but nvr trbld wnr* **7/2**[2]

054- **3** 2 ½ **Uddy Mac**[304] 5980 3-9-2 **62**...................... KellyHarrison(3) 5 54
(N Bycroft) *hld up: stl plenty to do over 2f out: rdn over 1f out: kpt on wl fnl f: nrst fin* **14/1**

2354 **4** 1 ¾ **Sea Crest**[45] 2647 4-8-12 **57**...................... JohnCavanagh(7) 3 44
(M Brittain) *hld up: hdwy to chse ldrs over 1f out: kpt on same pce* **5/1**[3]

6303 **5** 1 ¼ **Avonlini**[18] 3526 4-8-10 **48**...................... AndrewElliott 2 31
(B P J Baugh) *led 2f: remained prom: drvn over 2f out: wknd over 1f out* **8/1**

2004 **6** *hd* **Rio Caribe (IRE)**[14] 3685 3-9-8 **65**......................(v¹) DanielTudhope 1 47
(T D Walford) *midfield: rdn over 2f out: sn no imp* **12/1**

-564 **7** *4* **Whitby (IRE)**[11] 3758 3-8-4 **52**......................(t) JamesSullivan(5) 9 21
(M W Easterby) *trckd ldrs: wknd over 1f out* **13/2**

0-05 **8** *10* **Zelos Spirit**[49] 2535 3-7-10 **46**...................... NoelGarbutt(7) 4 —
(Rae Guest) *slowly away: a towards rr* **9/1**

1m 12.02s (-0.98) **Going Correction** -0.075s/f (Good)
WFA 3 from 4yo 5lb **8** Ran SP% **114.4**
Speed ratings (Par 103): **103,98,95,92,91 90,85,72**
toteswingers: 1&2 £3.30, 1&3 £7.50, 2&3 £8.50 CSF £12.01 CT £98.48 TOTE £3.30: £1.10, £1.40, £4.70; EX 13.10 Trifecta £68.70 Pool: £209.15 - 2.25 winning units..
Owner Crossfields Racing **Bred** Highclere Stud & Cheveley Park Stud Ltd **Trained** Hambleton, N Yorks
■ Stewards' Enquiry : John Cavanagh caution: used whip with excessive force

FOCUS
The quicker of the two divisions by 0.87sec.

4156 BET BRITISH WITH TOTEPOOL H'CAP 1m 1f 170y
5:40 (5:42) (Class 6) (0-60,75) 3-Y-0+ **£2,729** (£806; £403) **Stalls** High

Form RPR
-011 **1** **Explorator (IRE)**[3] 4027 3-9-10 **75** 6ex...................... MatthewDavies(5) 8 89
(George Baker) *hld up: rapid hdwy fr 4f out to ld 3f out: sn drvn clr: r.o strly* **5/2**[1]

0613 **2** *7* **Silly Gilly (IRE)**[19] 3503 6-8-13 **56**...................... DaleSwift(7) 10 55
(R E Barr) *midfield: hdwy over 3f out: kpt on wl fnl 2f: no ch w wnr* **15/2**

-350 **3** *nk* **Joinedupwriting**[46] 2625 5-9-9 **59**...................... DaraghO'Donohoe 2 57
(R M Whitaker) *chsd ldrs: hrd rdn to chal 3f out: kpt on same pce* **22/1**

0052 **4** *3* **Green Community (USA)**[11] 3758 3-8-9 **62**........ AdamBeschizza(7) 7 54
(E F Vaughan) *hld up in midfield: rdn and hdwy 3f out: drvn 2f out: kpt on tl no ex ins fnl f* **8/1**

006 **5** *1* **Grey Command (USA)**[82] 1576 5-8-13 **56**............ JohnCavanagh(7) 14 46
(M Brittain) *chsd ldrs: rdn over 3f out: wknd fnl 2f* **16/1**

60-5 **6** 1 ¼ **Tae Kwon Do (USA)**[23] 3370 4-8-8 **47**...................... BarryMcHugh(3) 11 34
(Julie Camacho) *s.i.s: hld up: rdn over 3f out: kpt on: nvr rchd ldrs* **15/2**

000- **7** 1 ½ **Fireflash (IRE)**[285] 6533 3-8-0 **49** ow2...................... KellyHarrison(3) 1 33
(N Tinkler) *stdd s: hld up last: stl plenty to do 3f out: kpt on: nvr rchd ldrs* **50/1**

4345 **8** 4 ½ **Carter**[7] 3894 4-9-9 **59**...................... PaulMulrennan 5 34
(W M Brisbourne) *midfield: rdn over 3f out: wknd ins fnl 2f* **6/1**[2]

6-00 **9** *6* **Royal Applord**[23] 3369 5-8-7 **46** oh1...................... MichaelStainton(3) 13 8
(N Tinkler) *led: hdd 3f out: sn wknd* **33/1**

2-63 **10** 4 ½ **It's Josr**[15] 3641 5-8-9 **50**......................(b) DeclanCannon(5) 3 3
(I A Wood) *w ldr: rdn over 3f out: sn wknd* **7/1**[3]

000 **11** *6* **Motirani**[60] 2220 3-8-7 **53**...................... AndrewElliott 6 —
(M L W Bell) *midfield: chsd along over 3f out: sn no imp: wknd fnl 2f* **12/1**

000- **12** 1 ¼ **Top Jaro (FR)**[516] 567 7-9-1 **56**...................... JamesSullivan(5) 4 —
(Mrs R A Carr) *hld up: a towards rr* **22/1**

0000 **13** *15* **Amber Ridge**[19] 3502 5-8-12 **55** oh1 ow9...................... TWoodley(7) 9 —
(B P J Baugh) *hld up: a bhd* **66/1**

0000 **14** *15* **Peter Tchaikovsky**[15] 3610 4-9-10 **60**..................(p) DuranFentiman 12 —
(B S Rothwell) *prom: rdn over 4f out: sn wknd* **40/1**

2m 4.93s (-0.47) **Going Correction** -0.075s/f (Good)
WFA 3 from 4yo+ 10lb **14** Ran SP% **121.1**
Speed ratings (Par 101): **98,92,92,89,88 87,86,83,78,74 69,68,56,44**
toteswingers: 1&2 £6.00, 1&3 £18.60, 2&3 £31.10 CSF £19.68 CT £348.21 TOTE £3.60: £1.60, £2.50, £5.80; EX 23.10 Trifecta £293.90 Part won. Pool: £397.23 - 0.42 winning units. Place 6 £1,477.13, Place 5 £852.84.
Owner Kismet Partnership **Bred** Joseph Stewart Investments **Trained** Moreton Morrell, Warwicks
■ Stewards' Enquiry : Adam Beschizza two-day ban: careless riding (Aug 1-2)

FOCUS
A moderate handicap.
Fireflash(IRE) Official explanation: jockey said colt was denied a clear run
Carter Official explanation: jockey said gelding ran flat
It's Josr Official explanation: vet said gelding finished lame off-fore
T/Plt: £1,091.40 to a £1 stake. Pool: £62,422.03. 41.75 winning tickets. T/Qpdt: £7.30 to a £1 stake. Pool: £5,418.77. 543.90 winning tickets. AS

4157 - 4159a (Foreign Racing) - See Raceform Interactive

3485 CURRAGH (R-H)
Saturday, July 17

OFFICIAL GOING: Round course - good; straight course - good to yielding

4160a WWW.THETOTE.COM MINSTREL STKS (GROUP 3) 7f
3:40 (3:45) 3-Y-0+ **£34,513** (£10,088; £4,778; £1,592)

RPR
1 **Air Chief Marshal (IRE)**[5] 3998 3-9-0 103...................... JMurtagh 9 112
(A P O'Brien, Ire) *chsd ldr in 2nd: impr to ld 1/2-way: rdn and kpt on wl fr over 1f out* **5/1**[2]

2 1 ¾ **Duff (IRE)**[20] 3489 7-9-12 104......................(b¹) PJSmullen 6 115
(Edward Lynam, Ire) *led: hdd 1/2-way: rdn in 2nd 2f out: no imp on ldr 1f out: kpt on same pce fnl f* **14/1**

3 1 ½ **Dandy Boy (ITY)**[31] 3069 4-9-7 100...................... CO'Donoghue 4 106
(David Marnane, Ire) *chsd ldrs in 4th: rdn into 3rd 2f out: no imp on ldrs: kpt on same pce* **5/1**[2]

4 *shd* **Rayeni (IRE)**[37] 2913 4-9-7 109 FMBerry 5 106
(John M Oxx, Ire) *mid-div: 7th 1/2-way: rdn 2 1/2f out: styd on to go mod 5th 1f out: kpt on same pce* **4/1**[1]
5 *nk* **Croisultan (IRE)**[7] 3928 4-9-7 106 PShanahan 2 105
(Liam McAteer, Ire) *chsd ldrs in 3rd: rdn 2 1/2f out: no ex in 4th 2f out: kpt on same pce* **7/1**[3]
6 *2 1/2* **Arabian Gleam**[273] 6848 6-9-12 (p) WJSupple 3 103
(J Noseda) *chsd ldrs: 5th 1/2-way: rdn in 6th 2f out: no imp over 1f out: kpt on same pce* **4/1**[1]
7 *1* **Free Judgement (USA)**[31] 3066 3-9-5 115 (p) KJManning 8 97
(J S Bolger, Ire) *towards rr for most: nvr a factor* **4/1**[1]
8 *1/2* **Six Of Hearts**[7] 3928 6-9-10 99 DJMoran 7 97
(Cecil Ross, Ire) *mid-div: 6th 1/2-way: rdn in 5th 2f out: no ex in 7th 1f out: kpt on one pce* **33/1**
9 *2 1/2* **Zayaan**[34] 3006 3-9-0 100 DPMcDonogh 1 84
(Kevin Prendergast, Ire) *a towards rr* **16/1**

1m 23.92s (-6.88) **Going Correction** -0.675s/f (Hard)
WFA 3 from 4yo+ 7lb 9 Ran SP% **121.3**
Speed ratings: **112,110,108,108,107 104,103,103,100**
CSF £75.31 TOTE £5.20: £1.60, £3.60, £2.20; DF 69.40.
Owner Mrs John Magnier **Bred** Barronstown Stud **Trained** Ballydoyle, Co Tipperary

NOTEBOOK
Air Chief Marshal(IRE) ◆ bounced back to something like his best with a comfortable win. His form this season had been well below what he showed as a juvenile, but perhaps his confidence was restored somewhat with an easy win on the all-weather and he looked on top of his game. Always close up, he had everything in trouble at the 2f pole and, with the rail as an aid, never gave any impression that he was wilting in the battle. The ease in the ground would have boosted his chance and this is probably his level, though the planned step up to a Group 2 makes sense. (op 11/2)
Duff(IRE) looked a threat briefly about 2f out but made no impression under pressure. It is hard to know if the first-time blinkers made much of a difference but they did no apparent harm. (op 16/1)
Dandy Boy(ITY) was making the apparent step-up from handicap company but he was still entitled to do well. He emerged best of those who came from off the speed. (op 5/1 tchd 9/2)
Rayeni(IRE) has been a disappointing horse, since he kicked off last season by finishing second in the Irish Guineas. With the rain to help his cause, it now seems difficult to conclude that he is much better than what he showed. (op 4/1 tchd 7/2)
Croisultan(IRE) is a reliable performer at this level but had no excuses as he was close enough to the pace. (op 10/1)
Arabian Gleam never got involved on his seasonal bow, having run a bit freely. (op 7/2 tchd 5/1)
Free Judgement(USA) was one of the first beaten.

4161 - 4163a (Foreign Racing) - See Raceform Interactive

4122 HAMBURG (R-H)
Saturday, July 17

OFFICIAL GOING: Turf: good

4164a GROSSER PREIS VON LOTTO HAMBURG (DEUTSCHLAND PREIS/GROSSER HANSA PREIS) (GROUP 1) (3YO+) (TURF) 1m 4f
4:10 (4:18) 3-Y-O+ **£79,646** (£30,973; £15,044; £7,522; £3,982)

RPR
1 **Campanologist (USA)**[34] 3019 5-9-6 0 FrankieDettori 3 118
(Saeed Bin Suroor) *settled in 3rd: gd prog arnd fnl turn: qcknd to join battle w ldr 2f out and grabbed ld 1 1/2f out: r.o wl* **9/2**[2]
2 *3/4* **Wiener Walzer (GER)**[31] 3068 4-9-6 0 ADeVries 5 116
(J Hirschberger, Germany) *wnt st to ld: set gd pce: increased tempo bef st: stl led 2f out whn jnd by wnr: hdd 1 1/2f out: r.o wl* **1/1**[1]
3 *hd* **Quijano (GER)**[34] 3019 8-9-6 0 AStarke 1 116
(P Schiergen, Germany) *bkmaker fr s: proged down bk st and gng wl ent st: r.o wl wout threatening wnr* **7/1**
4 *hd* **Jukebox Jury (IRE)**[28] 3191 4-9-6 0 RoystonFfrench 6 116
(M Johnston) *racd in 5th: looked to be struggling at end of bk st: shkn up and r.o wl: flattered briefly 2f out: styd on wl* **6/1**
5 *hd* **Allied Powers (IRE)**[41] 2803 5-9-6 0 IoritzMendizabal 4 115
(M L W Bell) *racd in 4th: effrt ent st: styd on* **5/1**[3]
6 *9* **Burma Gold (IRE)**[34] 3-8-8 0 FilipMinarik 7 101
(P Schiergen, Germany) *trckd ldr: outpcd bef st: wknd* **50/1**

2m 33.04s (-1.51)
WFA 3 from 4yo+ 12lb 6 Ran SP% **113.6**
WIN (incl. 10 euro stake): 43. PLACES: 17, 12. SF: 89.
Owner Godolphin **Bred** Darley **Trained** Newmarket, Suffolk
■ Saeed Bin Suroor's first Group 1 winner of the season.

FOCUS
They went no gallop early and this developed into a sprint. The form is far from strong.

NOTEBOOK
Campanologist(USA), settled just in behind, was expertly placed to strike when the tempo increased to claim a deserved Group 1 success. Considering he goes on fast ground, one would imagine that connections are looking at the Hong Kong Vase or Cup at the end of the year with him.
Wiener Walzer(GER), a two-time winner at this level during his 3-y-o career, including the German Derby over C&D, set out to make all. His form this season had been decent over distances short of his best, and his trainer was looking to take this race for the third year in a row, but he was undoubtedly undone by the lack of pace, despite battling on well to claim second. If the going is not on the soft side in the Arc, he could be an interesting runner for that contest at a long price.
Quijano(GER) finished behind Campanologist for the fourth time this year, but showed he retains all of his ability with a strong finish. He does, however, find it difficult to get his head in front nowadays.
Jukebox Jury(IRE) gained his biggest success in Germany when on a roll of good form, but apart from a win in a small-field Group 2 at Newmarket in May, his efforts this season have been a shade disappointing. He looked in trouble at one stage even when the gallop was not strong, but his jockey galvanised his mount and the pair were not beaten far in the end.
Allied Powers(IRE), whose win in a Group 2 at Chantilly had already been enhanced by Chinchon in an American Grade 1, was taking another big step in class, but he handled it well on ground that possibly does not play to his strengths. He has to be respected at this level, and has the ability to win a Group 1 judged on this performance.

3944 MAISONS-LAFFITTE (R-H)
Saturday, July 17

OFFICIAL GOING: Turf: good

4165a PRIX DE RIS-ORANGIS (GROUP 3) (3YO+) (TURF) 6f (S)
1:35 (12:00) 3-Y-O+ **£35,398** (£14,159; £10,619; £7,079; £3,539)

RPR
1 **War Artist (AUS)**[28] 3192 7-9-6 0 OlivierPeslier 2 112
(A De Royer-Dupre, France) *broke wl: racd in 2nd tl 1/2-way: rdn and qcknd into ld 2f out: r.o wl: comf hld off all chalrs* **4/5**[1]
2 *1/2* **Tiza (SAF)**[22] 3425 8-9-0 0 (p) GeraldMosse 1 104
(A De Royer-Dupre, France) *racd in rr towards stands' rail: qcknd wl 2f out: r.o strly ins fnl f but no threat to wnr* **15/1**
3 *snk* **Dam D'Augy (FR)**[22] 3425 5-8-10 0 (b) ThierryJarnet 3 100
(Mlle S-V Tarrou, France) *racd in 4th trcking wnr: rdn at 1/2-way: fin wl u.p ins fnl f* **10/1**
4 *hd* **Mariol (FR)**[62] 2153 7-9-4 0 FranckBlondel 5 107
(Robert Collet, France) *racd towards rr on outside: rdn at 1/2-way: r.o wl ins fnl f* **24/1**
5 *1 1/2* **Salut L'Africain (FR)**[14] 3704 5-9-0 0 (p) MaximeGuyon 4 98
(Robert Collet, France) *in rr fr s: mde late prog wl ins fnl f* **17/2**
6 *nse* **Delvita (FR)**[22] 3425 6-8-10 0 GregoryBenoist 7 94
(J-V Toux, France) *led fr s in centre of trck: rdn at 1/2-way: hdd 2f out: no ex: styd on* **7/1**[3]
7 *1 1/2* **Orpen Shadow (IRE)**[22] 3425 3-8-8 0 ChristopheSoumillon 6 90
(J-C Rouget, France) *racd in 3rd: trcking ldr in centre of trck: rdn at 1/2-way: began to weaken 1 1/2f out: fdd and eased fnl f* **4/1**[2]

1m 11.6s (-1.80)
WFA 3 from 5yo+ 5lb 7 Ran SP% **117.9**
WIN (incl. 1 euro stake): 1.80. PLACES: 1.60, 4.80. SF: 21.10.
Owner Rupert Plersch **Bred** S Kirkham **Trained** Chantilly, France

NOTEBOOK
War Artist(AUS), having his second run for the yard, was a comfortable winner. This was a good effort conceding weight all round. He may go for the Prix Maurice de Gheest.
Tiza(SAF), last year's winner, was put in his place by his stablemate.

4166a PRIX MESSIDOR (GROUP 3) (3YO+) (TURF) 1m (S)
2:40 (12:00) 3-Y-O+ **£35,398** (£14,159; £10,619; £7,079; £3,539)

RPR
1 **Fuisse (FR)**[34] 3017 4-9-5 0 StephanePasquier 8 120
(Mme C Head-Maarek, France) *settled bhd ldrs: qcknd 3f out: tk command and led 2f out: wnt clr: easily* **7/10**[1]
2 *4* **Beacon Lodge (IRE)**[68] 1974 5-9-1 0 GeraldMosse 4 107
(C G Cox) *settled bhd ldrs: qcknd wl into 2nd 2f out: styd on wl* **8/1**
3 *1* **Silver Frost (IRE)**[33] 4-9-1 0 ChristopheSoumillon 3 105
(Y De Nicolay, France) *settled towards rr on outer: wnt 3rd 2f out: styd on wl* **53/10**[3]
4 *nk* **Celebrissime (IRE)**[27] 5-9-1 0 OlivierPeslier 1 104
(F Head, France) *w.w towards rr: qcknd wl 1 1/2f out: fin wl wout ever threatening* **35/1**
5 *1* **Shakespearean (IRE)**[31] 3066 3-8-7 0 MaximeGuyon 5 100
(Saeed Bin Suroor) *settled in rr: trcking wnr: rdn 2 1/2f out: no ex fnl 1 1/2f: styd on* **4/1**[2]
6 *8* **The Rectifier (USA)**[21] 3460 3-8-7 0 MickyFenton 6 81
(Stef Higgins) *led: hdd 2f out: outpcd 1 1/2f out: no ex: fdd* **19/1**
7 *4* **Mr Brock (SAF)**[112] 1027 7-9-1 0 JohanVictoire 2 74
(Mme C Head-Maarek, France) *settled midfield: outpcd 2f out: fdd* **38/1**
8 *15* **Rectangulaire (FR)**[34] 3017 4-9-1 0 TonyPiccone 7 39
(Mme C Head-Maarek, France) *pcemaker for wnr but nvr got to front: wknd fr 1/2-way* **42/1**

1m 35.3s (-7.00)
WFA 3 from 4yo+ 8lb 8 Ran SP% **118.5**
WIN (incl. 1 euro stake): 1.50 (Fuisse combined with Celebrissime, Mr Brock & Rectangulaire): PLACES: 1.10, 1.30, 1.20; DF 5.50; SF 5.80.
Owner Haras Du Quesnay **Bred** Alec & Ghislaine Head **Trained** Chantilly, France

NOTEBOOK
Fuisse(FR), well suited by a decent test at this trip, ran out an impressive winner. He will go back up in grade in the Prix Jacques Le Marois at Deauville next month.
Beacon Lodge(IRE), freshened up by a break, was putting in his best work late but was never going to get to the winner. He may go for Goodwood's Celebration Mile.
Silver Frost(IRE) ran a decent race back at a mile.
Shakespearean(IRE)'s last three wins had been from the front and he was ridden differently here.
The Rectifier(USA)'s rider reported that the 3yo's lack of experience at this level let him down.

3595 REDCAR (L-H)
Sunday, July 18

OFFICIAL GOING: Firm (good to firm in places; watered; 9.5)
Wind: fresh behind Weather: cloudy

4167 E B F PETER MITCHELL LOVED RACING AT REDCAR MAIDEN STKS 7f
2:10 (2:10) (Class 5) 2-Y-O **£3,238** (£963; £481; £240) **Stalls** Centre

Form RPR
22 1 **Next Edition (IRE)**[14] 3705 2-9-3 0 PaulMulrennan 4 80
(J Howard Johnson) *mde all: rdn over 2f out: drvn and kpt on wl fnl f* **3/1**[2]
2 *1 1/2* **Ollon (USA)** 2-9-3 0 PaulHanagan 3 76+
(R A Fahey) *slowly away: racd keenly: hld up: rdn and hdwy over 2f out: chsd wnr over 1f out: edgd lft: kpt on fnl f* **15/8**[1]
23 3 *1 1/4* **Residence And Spa (IRE)**[30] 3162 2-9-3 0 DavidAllan 8 73
(T D Easterby) *w ldr: rdn over 2f out: outpcd over 1f out: drvn and kpt on fnl f* **4/1**[3]
4 *hd* **Golden Hinde** 2-9-3 0 JoeFanning 5 72+
(M Johnston) *prom: rdn over 2f out: remained w ev ch tl no ex ins fnl f* **8/1**
00 5 *6* **Buzz Law (IRE)**[37] 2939 2-9-3 0 AndrewElliott 2 57
(J R Weymes) *midfield: bdly outpcd and lost pl wl over 3f out: kpt on fr over 1f out* **100/1**
2 6 *nk* **Piccoluck**[24] 3365 2-9-3 0 TonyHamilton 6 56
(Mrs D J Sanderson) *chsd ldrs: wknd over 1f out* **8/1**

7 17 **Lord Westlake** 2-8-12 0 ... IanBrennan(5) 10 12
(G R Oldroyd) *wnt rt s and s.i.s: a towards rr* **33/1**
8 2 1/2 **Regimental (IRE)** 2-9-0 0 ... BarryMcHugh(3) 9 5
(Mrs A Duffield) *slowly away: a bhd* **22/1**
9 3/4 **Ozzies Storm Cats (USA)** 2-9-3 0 ... LiamJones 7 3
(J J Quinn) *chsd ldrs: wknd 3f out* **66/1**
10 18 **Tom Bowler** 2-9-3 0 ... PhillipMakin 1 —
(Mrs A Duffield) *s.i.s: sn in tch: lost pl over 3f out: sn wknd* **50/1**

1m 22.56s (-1.94) **Going Correction** -0.30s/f (Firm) 10 Ran SP% **113.7**
Speed ratings (Par 94): **99,97,95,95,88 88,69,66,65,44**
toteswingers:1&2:£3.10, 1&3:£1.30, 2&3:£2.50 CSF £8.47 TOTE £3.70: £1.60, £2.10, £1.20; EX 18.20 Trifecta £45.60 Pool: £136.34 - 2.21 winning units..
Owner Transcend Bloodstock LLP **Bred** Manister House Stud **Trained** Billy Row, Co Durham

FOCUS
The first four finished clear and all look to have at least a fair amount of ability. The winner's previous form has been well advertised of late.

NOTEBOOK
Next Edition(IRE) confirmed the promise he showed when runner-up on his first two starts, producing a relentless display of galloping from the front. He should make a useful nursery type and, out of a Galileo mare, he ought to stay further.
Ollon(USA), a well-backed favourite, raced off the pace early following a sluggish start and, although keeping on, he edged slightly left in the closing stages under a hard enough ride for a newcomer. A 75,000gns purchase, he clearly has plenty of ability should find a similar race, provided he goes the right way. (op 13-8 tchd 2-1)
Residence And Spa(IRE) was always prominent and had his chance. He might find a weak maiden, but is probably more of a nursery type. (op 5-1)
Golden Hinde ◆, a 95,000gns half-brother to 7.4f 2-y-o winner Malacara, showed up well for a long way and looked a big threat around 1f out, but he got tired late on. He should come on a good deal for this. (op 15-2)
Buzz Law(IRE), well beaten in a valuable seller last time, made only moderate late progress.

4168 REDCAR CRICKET CLUB H'CAP (DIV I) 1m 1f
2:40 (2:40) (Class 6) (0-60,60) 3-Y-O+ **£1,295** (£385; £192; £96) **Stalls** Low

Form RPR
6014 1 **Prime Circle**[14] 3706 4-9-2 **60** ... (p) DaleSwift(7) 11 69
(A D Brown) *midfield: smooth hdwy to chal 3f out: rdn to ld 2f out: sn drvn: kpt on wl* **17/2**
0020 2 1/2 **Maybe I Wont**[14] 3707 5-9-4 **58** ... RussKennemore(3) 3 66
(Lucinda Featherstone) *trckd ldrs: rdn to chal over 3f out: sn drvn: kpt on wl* **7/1**[3]
-514 3 1 **King's Counsel (IRE)**[30] 3149 4-9-8 **59** ... PaulMulrennan 10 65
(D O'Meara) *led: rdn wl over 3f out: drvn whn hdd 2f out: kpt on tl no ex ins fnl f* **13/8**[1]
-042 4 1 **Miss Ferney**[17] 3601 6-8-10 **50** ... PaulPickard(5) 5 54
(A Kirtley) *hld up in midfield: rdn and hdwy to chse ldrs over 2f out: kpt on same pce fnl 2f* **11/4**[2]
00-0 5 10 **Efidium**[39] 2851 12-8-13 **55** ... DanielleMcCreery(5) 2 37
(N Bycroft) *v.s.a: bhd tl mod late prog* **25/1**
0036 6 hd **Alright Chuck**[15] 3690 6-8-10 **47** ... (b1) PhillipMakin 8 28
(P W Hiatt) *prom: wknd 3f out* **12/1**
0-06 7 3 1/4 **Jobekani (IRE)**[21] 433 4-8-9 **46** oh1 ... (t) PaulHanagan 4 20
(Mrs L Williamson) *hld up: rdn over 4f out: nvr threatened* **10/1**
00-0 8 3/4 **Convitezza**[11] 3776 4-8-4 **46** oh1 ... JamesSullivan(5) 1 18
(M E Sowersby) *trckd ldrs: rdn over 3f out: sn wknd* **66/1**
6/00 9 2 1/4 **Royal Indulgence**[18] 3559 10-8-9 **46** ... LiamJones 6 13
(W M Brisbourne) *s.i.s: a bhd* **28/1**

1m 52.53s (-0.47) **Going Correction** -0.075s/f (Good) 9 Ran SP% **113.4**
Speed ratings (Par 101): **99,98,97,96,87 87,84,84,82**
toteswingers:1&2:£4.00, 1&3:£2.70, 2&3:£1.80 CSF £63.79 CT £145.05 TOTE £11.50: £2.50, £2.00, £1.10; EX 69.30 Trifecta £142.90 Pool: £206.69 - 1.07 winning units..
Owner S Pedersen **Bred** Gainsborough Stud Management Ltd **Trained** Yedingham, N Yorks
■ Stewards' Enquiry : Russ Kennemore two-day ban: used whip with excessive frequency (Aug 1-2)

FOCUS
A moderate contest run in a time 0.46 seconds quicker than the second division, and few were ever seriously involved.

4169 SKY BET SUPPORTING YORKSHIRE SUMMER RACING FESTIVAL H'CAP 5f
3:10 (3:12) (Class 5) (0-70,69) 3-Y-O **£2,266** (£674; £337; £168) **Stalls** Centre

Form RPR
3213 1 **Bronze Beau**[5] 3988 3-8-12 **65** ... (t) JamesSullivan(5) 6 73
(Mrs L Stubbs) *mde all: rdn over 1f out: kpt on wl* **8/1**
0000 2 1 1/2 **On The Piste (IRE)**[15] 3687 3-8-2 **53** ... (p) PaulPickard(3) 4 56
(L A Mullaney) *chsd ldr: rdn over 2f out: wnt 2nd over 1f out: kpt on: nvr rchd ldr* **16/1**
6612 3 1/2 **Patch Patch**[23] 3410 3-9-6 **68** ... PhillipMakin 1 69
(M Dods) *chsd ldrs: rdn and effrt over 2f out: kpt on same pce fnl f* **5/2**[2]
0222 4 4 1/2 **Sharp Eclipse**[15] 3663 3-9-7 **69** ... PaulHanagan 7 54
(K A Ryan) *in tch: rdn and outpcd 3f out: drvn and prog to chse ldrs 2f out: wknd fnl f* **13/8**[1]
0300 5 1 3/4 **Gower Sophia**[61] 2217 3-8-2 **50** ... (v) FrannyNorton 5 28
(M Brittain) *pressed ldr: rdn over 2f out: sn wknd* **20/1**
6020 6 6 **Taborcillo**[30] 3174 3-9-2 **64** ... (v1) TomEaves 3 21
(T D Barron) *sn outpcd and reminders in rr: a bhd* **10/1**
2224 7 47 **Lees Anthem**[23] 3410 3-9-0 **62** ... DavidNolan 2 —
(C J Teague) *sn bdly outpcd in rr: t.o* **13/2**[3]

57.08 secs (-1.52) **Going Correction** -0.30s/f (Firm) 7 Ran SP% **110.8**
Speed ratings (Par 100): **100,97,96,89,86 77,2**
toteswingers:1&2:£16.90, 1&3:£4.50, 2&3:£11.10 CSF £109.86 TOTE £6.10: £1.70, £10.90; EX 113.00.
Owner D Arundale **Bred** Meon Valley Stud **Trained** Norton, N Yorks
■ Stewards' Enquiry : David Nolan three-day ban: struck gelding at start (Aug 1-3)

FOCUS
A tailwind made it hard to make up ground.
Sharp Eclipse Official explanation: jockey said gelding missed the break
Lees Anthem Official explanation: jockey said gelding never travelled

4170 WELCOME TO YORKSHIRE A WHOLE LOT MORE CLAIMING STKS 1m 2f
3:45 (3:45) (Class 6) 3-Y-O+ **£1,706** (£503; £252) **Stalls** Low

Form RPR
0-00 1 **Ballinteni**[37] 2934 8-9-1 80 ... AdamBeschizza(7) 8 63
(Miss Gay Kelleway) *trckd ldrs: hdwy to ld over 2f out: sn rdn: kpt on wl* **5/2**[2]
5460 2 1 **Back To Paris (IRE)**[6] 3967 8-9-1 57 ... (t) AndrewMullen 1 54
(P A Kirby) *led: rdn and hdd over 2f out: rallied to chse wnr ins fnl f: kpt on* **15/2**
1100 3 1/2 **Tropical Bachelor (IRE)**[7] 3319 4-9-1 73 ... JohnFahy(5) 5 58
(T J Pitt) *hld up: outpcd over 2f out: drvn and styd on wl fnl f: tk 3rd nr fin* **3/1**[3]
0200 4 nk **Media Stars**[7] 3496 5-8-7 42 ... LeeTopliss(7) 6 51
(R Johnson) *hld up in midfield: rapid hdwy to chal 3 out: sn rdn: stl ev ch over 1f out: no ex ins fnl f* **50/1**
200- 5 nk **Kashimin (IRE)**[227] 7617 5-9-6 73 ... PJMcDonald 2 56
(G A Swinbank) *s.i.s: hld up: hdwy on outer 3f out: rdn 2f out: styd on same pce* **2/1**[1]
-050 6 1/2 **Melkatant**[17] 3597 4-8-10 42 ... FrannyNorton 9 45
(N Bycroft) *prom: lost pl over 2f out: sn rdn: kpt on same pce* **16/1**
3-60 7 1/2 **Bold Indian (IRE)**[23] 1503 6-9-0 54 ... TomEaves 4 48
(M E Sowersby) *in tch: outpcd and lost pl over 2f out: swtchd rt and kpt on again nr fin* **16/1**

2m 8.14s (1.04) **Going Correction** -0.075s/f (Good) 7 Ran SP% **112.4**
Speed ratings (Par 101): **92,91,90,90,90 89,89**
toteswingers:1&2:£5.00, 1&3:£1.40, 2&3:£4.90 CSF £20.55 TOTE £2.70: £1.10, £7.30; EX 27.80 Trifecta £64.50 Pool: £147.42 - 1.69 winning units..Tropical Bachelor was claimed by Mrs Pippa Bickerton for £10,000.
Owner David Cohen **Bred** Gainsborough Stud Management Ltd **Trained** Exning, Suffolk
■ Stewards' Enquiry : Andrew Mullen two-day ban: used whip with excessive frequency without giving gelding time to respond (Aug 1-2)
Adam Beschizza one-day ban: used whip down the shoulder in the forehand (Aug 3)

FOCUS
They finished in a bit of a bunch behind the winner in this moderate claimer.

4171 YORKSHIRE RADIO H'CAP 6f
4:20 (4:20) (Class 4) (0-85,84) 3-Y-O+ **£3,885** (£1,156; £577; £288) **Stalls** Centre

Form RPR
0-10 1 **Beat Baby (IRE)**[33] 3065 3-9-7 **84** ... PaulMulrennan 7 92
(J Howard Johnson) *trckd wnr: drvn to ld over 1f out: edgd lft and styd on wl fnl f* **11/1**
5050 2 1 **Just Sam (IRE)**[9] 3854 5-8-7 **68** ... BarryMcHugh(3) 8 74
(R E Barr) *hld up: rdn and hdwy towards stands' side over 2f out: ev ch 1f out: styd on* **8/1**
3120 3 nse **Red Cape (FR)**[8] 3919 7-9-6 **83** ... IanBrennan(5) 4 89
(Mrs R A Carr) *chsd ldrs: outpcd 3f out: drvn and hdwy over 1f out: kpt on fnl f* **15/8**[1]
0132 4 3/4 **Sir Nod**[18] 3551 8-9-5 **77** ... PaulHanagan 6 80
(Julie Camacho) *in tch: drvn and sltly short of room over 1f out: styd on ins fnl f* **7/1**
/0-3 5 1 1/2 **Go Nani Go**[22] 3435 4-9-12 **84** ... RichardMullen 5 83
(B Smart) *chsd ldrs: drvn to chal over 1f out: wknd ins fnl f* **7/2**[2]
1062 6 2 1/2 **Peter Island (FR)**[10] 3833 7-9-7 **82** ... (v) MartinLane(3) 3 73
(J Gallagher) *led: drvn whn hdd over 1f out: sn wknd* **5/1**[3]
4004 7 2 1/2 **Baybshambles (IRE)**[11] 3775 6-8-7 **65** oh2 ... PJMcDonald 2 48
(R E Barr) *s.i.s: hld up: a bhd* **11/1**

69.15 secs (-2.65) **Going Correction** -0.30s/f (Firm)
WFA 3 from 4yo+ 5lb 7 Ran SP% **113.9**
Speed ratings (Par 105): **105,103,103,102,100 97,93**
toteswingers:1&2:£7.70, 1&3:£4.80, 2&3:£4.80 CSF £91.61 CT £238.51 TOTE £13.10: £7.60, £9.30; EX 117.80 Trifecta £167.90 Part won. Pool: £226.98 - 0.50 winning units..
Owner J Howard Johnson **Bred** Paget Bloodstock **Trained** Billy Row, Co Durham

FOCUS
A fair sprint handicap, predictably run at a strong pace courtesy of Peter Island. The runners ended up towards the near rail.

4172 HELP FOR HEROES AND YORKSHIRE REGIMENT FILLIES' H'CAP 1m
4:50 (4:50) (Class 5) (0-75,74) 3-Y-O+ **£2,266** (£674; £337; £168) **Stalls** Centre

Form RPR
0145 1 **Very Well Red**[31] 3130 7-9-8 **74** ... BillyCray(5) 2 80
(P W Hiatt) *stmbld s: sn led: drvn over 2f out: chal strly fr over 1f out: kpt on wl* **8/1**
3000 2 hd **Salerosa (IRE)**[9] 3876 5-9-2 **66** ... (v1) BarryMcHugh(3) 3 72
(Mrs A Duffield) *hld up: racd keenly: smooth hdwy to chal 2f out: rdn over 1f out: kpt on: jst hld* **5/1**[3]
0026 3 hd **Wiseman's Diamond (USA)**[10] 3806 5-9-4 **68** ... PaulPickard(3) 5 73
(P T Midgley) *hld up: hdwy over 2f out: chal over 1f out: kpt on wl* **13/2**
4-65 4 3 3/4 **Briary Mac**[8] 3924 3-8-7 **62** ... FrannyNorton 8 56
(N Bycroft) *prom: rdn over 2f out: wknd appr fnl f* **9/1**
3211 5 1 3/4 **Rascal In The Mix (USA)**[9] 3854 4-8-13 **65** ... (p) AmyRyan(5) 7 57
(R M Whitaker) *s.i.s: racd keenly: hdwy to chal 2f out: sn rdn: wknd over 1f out* **2/1**[1]
30-3 6 3 3/4 **Love In The West (IRE)**[87] 1489 4-8-12 **59** ... PJMcDonald 6 43
(G A Swinbank) *in tch: rdn over 2f out: sn wknd* **7/2**[2]
5034 7 3 1/4 **Hettie Hubble**[8] 3900 4-8-3 **55** oh10 ... JamesSullivan(5) 1 31
(D W Thompson) *prom: rdn over 2f out: sn wknd* **25/1**

1m 35.9s (-2.10) **Going Correction** -0.30s/f (Firm)
WFA 3 from 4yo+ 8lb 7 Ran SP% **110.5**
Speed ratings (Par 100): **98,97,97,93,92 88,85**
toteswingers:1&2:£6.80, 1&3:£4.00, 2&3:£6.30 CSF £43.88 CT £261.76 TOTE £9.50: £3.00, £2.10; EX 43.70 TRIFECTA Not won..
Owner Phil Kelly **Bred** Butts Enterprises Limited **Trained** Hook Norton, Oxon

FOCUS
A modest fillies' handicap.

4173 REDCAR CRICKET CLUB H'CAP (DIV II) 1m 1f
5:20 (5:20) (Class 6) (0-60,60) 3-Y-O+ **£1,295** (£385; £192; £96) **Stalls** Low

Form RPR
1044 1 **Applaude**[2] 4082 5-9-2 **60** ... (b) CharlesEddery(7) 10 67
(R C Guest) *midfield: smooth hdwy to trck ldr 3f out: chal 2f out: drvn to ld jst ins fnl f: kpt on* **6/4**[1]
6050 2 1/2 **Indian Violet (IRE)**[20] 3500 4-8-8 **52** ... (p) DuilioDaSilva(7) 6 58
(D W Thompson) *led: rdn over 3f out: drvn and hdd jst ins fnl f: kpt on: hld nr fin* **7/1**[3]
0400 3 2 **Aussie Blue (IRE)**[55] 2382 6-9-5 **59** ... MichaelStainton(3) 8 61
(R M Whitaker) *hld up in midfield: hdwy on outer to chse ldrs 3f out: rdn over 2f out: kpt on fnl f* **11/2**[2]
-000 4 1/2 **Prince Andjo (USA)**[29] 3223 4-8-2 **46** oh1 ... NeilFarley(7) 2 46
(D Carroll) *trckd ldr: drvn over 2f out: sn one pce: no ex and lost 3rd ins fnl f* **10/1**
0506 5 8 **Obara D'Avril (FR)**[17] 3600 8-8-6 **46** oh1 ... PaulPickard(3) 4 29
(S G West) *s.i.s: rdn and brief hdwy on inner over 3f out: sn no imp* **8/1**

-060 **5** *dht* **Musigny (USA)**[46] 2655 4-8-12 **54**.................................... AmyRyan(5) 5 37
(Miss S E Hall) *midfield: racd keenly: rdn over 3f out: sn no imp: wknd over 1f out* **18/1**

-005 **7** *4 1/2* **Marillos Proterras**[14] 3707 4-8-6 **46** oh1.................(b) BarryMcHugh(3) 7 19
(Mrs A Duffield) *in tch: rdn to chse ldrs over 3f out: wknd 2f out* **7/1**[3]

0-00 **8** *5* **Lily Jicaro (IRE)**[13] 3727 4-8-2 **46** oh1..............(t) JosephYoung(7) 9 8
(Mrs L Williamson) *awkward leaving stall: hld up: hrd drvn in rr whn sddle slipped and rdr lost iron over 1f out* **33/1**

00-0 **9** *8* **Boy Racer (IRE)**[47] 2629 5-8-9 **53** ow7......................... AdamCarter(7) 3 —
(C J Teague) *trckd ldrs: rdn over 3f out: sn wknd* **16/1**

1m 52.99s (-0.01) **Going Correction** -0.075s/f (Good) **9** Ran SP% **114.7**
Speed ratings (Par 101): **97,96,94,94,87 87,83,78,71**
toteswingers:1&2:£4.00, 1&3:£4.20, 2&3:£6.90 CSF £12.29 CT £46.11 TOTE £2.40: £1.40, £2.40, £1.90; EX 13.10 Trifecta £21.90 Pool: £74.10 - 2.50 winning units..
Owner Stan Wright **Bred** G Reed **Trained** Stainforth, S Yorks
■ Stewards' Enquiry : Joseph Young three-day ban: used whip when out of contention (Aug 1-3)

FOCUS
A really weak contest run in a time 0.46 seconds slower than the first division.
Lily Jicaro(IRE) Official explanation: jockey said saddle slipped

4174 YORKSHIRE POST COMPETITION WINNER APPRENTICE H'CAP 1m 6f 19y
5:50 (5:50) (Class 5) (0-70,61) 4-Y-0+ **£2,266** (£674; £337; £168) **Stalls** Low

Form RPR

0262 **1** **Drop The Hammer**[18] 3552 4-8-11 **51**............................... JohnFahy(3) 7 60
(D O'Meara) *hld up: hdwy to trck ldrs 4f out: rdn to chal 3f out: led 2f out: styd on wl* **2/1**[1]

2031 **2** *1 1/2* **Amir Pasha (UAE)**[17] 3600 5-9-4 **60**..........................(p) AdamCarter(5) 2 67
(Micky Hammond) *trckd ldr: drvn to ld over 3f out: hdd 2f out: rallied and ev ch tl no ex ins fnl f* **6/1**[3]

045 **3** *4* **Jenny Soba**[34] 3032 7-8-9 **46** ow1............................... RussKennemore 3 47
(Lucinda Featherstone) *trckd ldrs: drvn and outpcd over 3f out: styd on ins fnl 2f: nvr trble ldng pair* **16/1**

3431 **4** *5* **Dovedon Angel**[27] 3267 4-9-0 **54**............................... DeclanCannon(3) 1 48
(Miss Gay Kelleway) *hld up: hdwy to trck ldrs over 3f out: sn rdn: wknd over 1f out* **7/2**[2]

226- **5** *3 1/4* **Carmela Maria**[59] 6097 5-9-3 **57**................................ JamesSullivan(3) 5 47
(M E Sowersby) *hld up: rdn 9f out: drvn over 4f out: bhd tl mod late hdwy* **20/1**

5-32 **6** *2 3/4* **Zefooha (FR)**[17] 3600 6-9-3 **61**....................................(b[1]) LukeStrong(7) 4 47
(T D Walford) *led: hdd over 3f out: sn wknd* **7/2**[2]

026/ **7** *49* **Young Scotton**[846] 988 10-8-12 **54**............................... LeeTopliss(5) 6 —
(C Grant) *trckd ldrs: rdn over 3f out: sn wknd* **12/1**

3m 2.51s (-2.19) **Going Correction** -0.075s/f (Good) **7** Ran SP% **110.4**
Speed ratings (Par 103): **103,102,99,97,95 93,65**
toteswingers:1&2:£3.00, 1&3:£5.70, 2&3:£5.40 CSF £13.45 CT £135.68 TOTE £3.30: £1.80, £3.60; EX 17.10 Trifecta £85.30 Pool: £115.37 - 1.00 winning units. Place 6 £5292.33; Place 5 £4433.82.
Owner A Crowther **Bred** Mrs N J Gidley Wright **Trained** Nawton, N Yorks
■ Stewards' Enquiry : Adam Carter two-day ban: used whip without giving gelding time to respond down shoulder in the forehand (Aug 1-2)
John Fahy two-day ban: used whip with excessive frequency (Aug 1-2)

FOCUS
A modest apprentice handicap in which Zefooha seemed to go off too fast.
T/Jkpt: Not won. T/Plt: £3,102.80 to a £1 stake. Pool: £64,395.08. 15.15 winning tickets T/Qpdt: £653.40 to a £1 stake. Pool: £3,267.04. 3.70 winning tickets AS

4157 CURRAGH (R-H)
Sunday, July 18

OFFICIAL GOING: Round course - good to yielding; straight course - yielding

4175a L BEHAN TARMAC & ASPHALT EUROPEAN BREEDERS FUND (C & G) MAIDEN 7f
2:05 (2:07) 2-Y-O **£9,464** (£2,194; £960; £548)

RPR

1 **Pathfork (USA)** 2-8-11 .... ShaneFoley(3) 7 93+
(Mrs John Harrington, Ire) *trckd ldrs: 2nd 1/2-way: impr to chal 2f out: led 1f out: rdn to assert fnl f: comf* **9/2**[2]

2 *4* **Robin Hood (IRE)**[22] 3469 2-9-0 .... JMurtagh 9 83
(A P O'Brien, Ire) *sn led: rdn and chal 2f out: hdd 1f out: no ex ins fnl f and kpt on same pce* **8/11**[1]

3 *2* **Zabarajad (IRE)**[21] 3485 2-9-0 .... FMBerry 5 78
(John M Oxx, Ire) *chsd ldrs: 4th 1/2-way: hdwy into 3rd 2f out: rdn and no ex 1 1/2f out: kpt on same pce fr over 1f out* **8/1**

4 *shd* **Mawaakef (IRE)** 2-9-0 .... DPMcDonogh 10 78
(Kevin Prendergast, Ire) *chsd ldrs: 6th 1/2-way: rdn 2f out: no imp in 5th 1f out: kpt on same pce* **25/1**

5 *3/4* **King Of The Ring** 2-9-0 .... NGMcCullagh 4 76+
(John M Oxx, Ire) *mid-div: 8th 1/2-way: rdn in 7th 2f out: kpt on same pce fr over 1f out* **50/1**

6 *1* **Free Art**[17] 3645 2-9-0 90.. WJSupple 2 73
(P D Deegan, Ire) *chsd ldrs: 7th 1/2-way: hdwy into 5th 2f out: rdn into 4th and no imp 1 1/2f out: no ex fnl f* **11/2**[3]

7 *2 1/2* **Lechevalier Choisi (IRE)**[11] 3798 2-9-0 .... CDHayes 11 67
(James Bernard McCabe, Ire) *chsd ldrs: 5th 1/2-way: rdn in 8th 2f out: no ex and kpt on one pce* **80/1**

8 *2 1/2* **Honey Of A Kitten (USA)** 2-9-0 .... PJSmullen 8 61
(D K Weld, Ire) *towards rr for most: rdn and no imp 2f out: kpt on one pce fr over 1f out* **33/1**

9 *nk* **Harrison's Cave** 2-9-0 .... JAHeffernan 12 60
(A P O'Brien, Ire) *in rr of mid-div: rdn in 9th 2f out: no imp and kpt on one pce* **14/1**

10 *2* **Late Debate (USA)**[9] 3881 2-9-0 .... KJManning 6 55
(J S Bolger, Ire) *chsd ldr: 3rd 1/2-way: rdn in 4th 2f out: no ex in 6th over 1f out: kpt on one pce* **16/1**

11 *2 1/2* **Bad Cigar (IRE)** 2-8-9 .... SMLevey(5) 1 49
(F Costello, Ire) *s.i.s: in rr of mid-div for most: nvr a factor* **66/1**

12 *1 1/4* **Tower Hill Gate (IRE)**[9] 3881 2-9-0 .... PBBeggy 3 46
(Patrick Martin, Ire) *a towards rr* **100/1**

13 *1 1/4* **Celestial Flyer (IRE)**[31] 3133 2-9-0 .... KLatham 14 43
(G M Lyons, Ire) *mid-div: 9th 1/2-way: rdn and no ex 2f out: wknd* **50/1**

14 *7* **Tropical Spirit (IRE)** 2-8-11 .... BACurtis(3) 13 25
(John M Oxx, Ire) *a towards rr* **33/1**

1m 27.27s (-3.53) **Going Correction** -0.50s/f (Hard) **14** Ran SP% **132.5**
Speed ratings: **100,95,93,93,92 91,88,85,84,82 79,78,76,68**
CSF £8.65 TOTE £6.80: £1.30, £1.10, £1.40; DF 11.90.
Owner Silverton Hill Partnership **Bred** Flaxman Holdings Limited **Trained** Moone, Co Kildare

NOTEBOOK
Pathfork(USA) ◆ has regularly been beating very smart filly Laughing Lashes in his homework as we were informed afterwards. This performance would suggest it'll take a fair horse to get him off the bridle, as on ground that was probably softer than ideal, he quickened up smartly past the favourite a furlong out and maintained that pace to the line. Four lengths just about summed up his superiority on the day and it would be a surprise if he couldn't make the step up to stakes company. He looks a very smart colt indeed that should improve on better ground. (op 4/1 tchd 11/2)
Robin Hood(IRE) showed plenty of ability on his debut at this venue the previous month, and while he did improve he was probably unlucky to come up against a horse as smart as the winner. Attempting to make all, he came under pressure over a furlong out and ran on, but just had no chance with the winner. (op 1/1)
Zabarajad(IRE) was disappointing on his debut here the previous month but put up a much improved effort in this contest, racing just off the pace towards the outside and did come with a semblance of a challenge just over a furlong out before he was found to be one-paced. The softer surface probably suited him and there should be more to come. (op 7/1)
Mawaakef(IRE) showed ability. He was never quite on terms but kept on to good effect inside the final furlong. He would probably be suited by better ground. (op 20/1)
Tropical Spirit(IRE) Official explanation: jockey said colt ducked and collided with rails early on and ran green throughout

4176a JEBEL ALI STABLES & RACECOURSE ANGLESEY STKS (GROUP 3) 6f 63y
2:35 (2:35) 2-Y-O **£31,637** (£9,247; £4,380; £1,460)

RPR

1 **Dunboyne Express (IRE)**[38] 2911 2-9-1 .... DPMcDonogh 3 112+
(Kevin Prendergast, Ire) *chsd ldr: impr to ld 1/2-way: rdn and kpt on wl fr over 1f out: styd on strly to go clr fnl f* **9/2**[3]

2 *8* **Samuel Morse (IRE)**[21] 3488 2-9-1 107.................................. JMurtagh 1 90
(A P O'Brien, Ire) *chsd ldr: 2nd 1/2-way: rdn and no imp on ldr over 1f out: kpt on same pce fnl f* **1/1**[1]

3 *2* **Rudolf Valentino**[11] 3798 2-9-1 .... JAHeffernan 4 84+
(A P O'Brien, Ire) *led: rdn and hdd 1/2-way: no ex in 4th over 2f out: kpt on one pce: 3rd cl home* **12/1**

4 *2 1/2* **Glor Na Mara (IRE)** 2-9-1 .... KJManning 2 77
(J S Bolger, Ire) *hld up in rr: clsr in 3rd over 2f out: rdn 1 1/2f out: no ex over 1f out: wknd fnl f* **2/1**[2]

1m 18.97s (0.37) **Going Correction** +0.15s/f (Good) **4** Ran SP% **109.2**
Speed ratings: **103,92,89,86**
CSF £9.67 TOTE £4.40; DF 9.30.
Owner J Connaughton **Bred** John Connaughton **Trained** Friarstown, Co Kildare

FOCUS
A pretty disappointing turn out, but the winner impressed with the easing ground in his favour. The runner-up was clearly below form and the third is rated 6lb off.

NOTEBOOK
Dunboyne Express(IRE) came right away from his rivals inside the final furlong and was an impressive winner. The easing ground looked much to his liking and there was plenty to like about the way he responded to getting some early reminders to keep his mind on the job. Reverting to 7f should be in his favour again and the Group 1 National Stakes looks the logical next step, which his yard won last year with Kingsfort. (op 9/2 tchd 5/1)
Samuel Morse(IRE) arrived here after his runs in the Coventry Stakes and Railway Stakes and it may have been a case of too many hard races in too short a space of time. He certainly ran very flat here, didn't pick up at all when challenged and in the end only finished a couple of lengths in front of his pacemaker. All in all it was a most disappointing display, but perhaps returning to quicker ground is what he wants. (op 5/4)
Rudolf Valentino was deployed as a pacemarker and did his job. He could still develop into a nice horse over further. (op 8/1)
Glor Na Mara(IRE) arrived at the track with a strong reputation and went off a very short price for a debutant in such a race, despite his yard hitting top form of late. He looked to need the run and was another that probably could have done without the rain. (op 13/8)

4178a DARLEY IRISH OAKS (GROUP 1) (FILLIES) 1m 4f
3:40 (3:48) 3-Y-O
£218,141 (£71,460; £33,849; £11,283; £7,522; £3,761)

RPR

1 **Snow Fairy (IRE)**[44] 2711 3-9-0 .... RyanMoore 9 120+
(E A L Dunlop) *settled mid-div: 9th 1/2-way: hdwy in 7th 3f out: clsd in 3rd 2f out: led over 1 1/2f out: rdn clr fr over 1f out: kpt on strly: impressive* **7/2**[2]

2 *8* **Miss Jean Brodie (USA)**[22] 3437 3-9-0 .... WilliamBuick 14 105+
(Mahmood Al Zarooni) *chsd ldrs: 6th 1/2-way: rdn in 5th 3f out: no imp over 2f out: styd on in 4th 1f out: kpt on to go 2nd cl home* **33/1**

3 *3/4* **Lady Lupus (IRE)**[35] 3007 3-9-0 92..........................(p) JPO'Brien 13 104
(A P O'Brien, Ire) *chsd ldrs: 3rd 1/2-way: rdn to ld and dispute 3f out: strly pressed 2f out: hdd and no ex in 2nd over 1 1/2f out: kpt on same pce: lost 2nd cl home* **66/1**

4 *1/2* **Meeznah (USA)**[44] 2711 3-9-0 .... TedDurcan 3 103
(D R Lanigan) *chsd ldrs: 4th 1/2-way: hdwy into 3rd 3f out: rdn to chal 2f out: no ex in 3rd 1 1/2f out: kpt on same pce* **6/1**[3]

5 *7* **Awe Inspiring (IRE)**[31] 3101 3-9-0 93.......................(p) JAHeffernan 10 92
(A P O'Brien, Ire) *mid-div: 8th 1/2-way: rdn 3f out: no imp in 6th 2f out: kpt on same pce* **33/1**

6 *1 1/4* **Akdarena**[22] 3467 3-9-0 114...(bt) KJManning 4 90
(J S Bolger, Ire) *chsd ldr in 2nd: rdn to dispute 3f out: no ex in 4th under 2f out: kpt on one pce* **9/1**

7 *5 1/2* **Desert Sage**[37] 2921 3-9-0 .... JimCrowley 7 81
(R M Beckett) *chsd ldrs: 5th 1/2-way: rdn in 6th 3f out: no imp in 7th 2f out: kpt on one pce* **12/1**

8 *7* **King's Vintage (IRE)**[5] 4010 3-9-0 80.................................. FMBerry 15 70
(Thomas Mullins, Ire) *hld up towards rr: no imp 3f out: kpt on one pce fr over 2f out* **25/1**

9 *3* **Remember When (IRE)**[22] 3467 3-9-0 110.............................. JMurtagh 6 65
(A P O'Brien, Ire) *hld up towards rr: sme hdwy into mod 9th 2f out: rdn and kpt on one pce* **6/1**[3]

10 *4 1/2* **Crystal Gal (IRE)**[22] 3467 3-9-0 105............................. DPMcDonogh 8 58
(Kevin Prendergast, Ire) *in rr of mid-div thrght: nvr a factor* **16/1**

11 *2 1/2* **Eldalil**[31] 3101 3-9-0 .... RichardHills 2 54
(Sir Michael Stoute) *mid-div: 7th 1/2-way: rdn in 9th 3f out: no ex over 2f out: wknd* **10/1**

12 1 **Ice Empress (IRE)**[5] 4008 3-9-0 80 (p) SMLevey 11 52
(A P O'Brien, Ire) *led: rdn and hdd 3f out: sn no ex and wknd* **50/1**
13 5 1/2 **Brazilian Beauty**[22] 3468 3-9-0 89 CDHayes 5 44
(Kevin Prendergast, Ire) *a towards rr* **66/1**
14 1 1/2 **Dance On By (IRE)**[7] 3942 3-9-0 74 (b[1]) CO'Donoghue 16 41
(A P O'Brien, Ire) *a towards rr* **100/1**
15 2 1/2 **Hibaayeb**[31] 3101 3-9-0 (t) FrankieDettori 12 37
(Saeed Bin Suroor) *in rr of mid-div: 10th 1/2-way: rdn and no ex over 3f out: wknd* **10/3**[1]

2m 34.87s (-4.23) **Going Correction** -0.075s/f (Good) **15** Ran SP% **122.2**
Speed ratings: **111,105,105,104,100 99,95,91,89,86 84,83,80,79,77**
CSF £126.62 TOTE £3.50: £1.30, £7.10, £10.70; DF 103.10.
Owner Anamoine Limited **Bred** Windflower Overseas Holdings Inc **Trained** Newmarket, Suffolk
■ Stewards' Enquiry : J P O'Brien two-day ban: used whip with excessive frequency (Aug 1-2)

FOCUS
Snow Fairy impressed and the form is rated around the fifth.

NOTEBOOK
Snow Fairy(IRE), supplemented for 50,000euros, left her rivals for dead from a furlong and a half down to complete an Oaks double that marks her down as a top-class filly. She has come from humble beginnings, and with the likelihood that she will remain in training at four, it was not surprising to hear her trainer invoke the name of Ouija Board as he looked to the future. The Yorkshire Oaks is an obvious target now, and the manner in which she coped with the ground adds further gloss to a growing reputation. A trip to the Breeders' Cup later on is also at the back of her trainer's mind. (op 4/1)
Miss Jean Brodie(USA), a recent Doncaster maiden winner having only the third start of her career, ran a smashing race for one so inexperienced. She got the trip well at the first attempt, and there is every chance that she will continue to improve. A Group 3 race at this trip should be within her scope.
Lady Lupus(IRE) emerged best of the quintet from Ballydoyle. The ease in the ground was probably the main factor in helping her to retrieve the from that she lost after winning a Listed event over 1m at the venue last October. Her stamina began to run out in the closing stages, but it was still a very pleasing effort, vastly superior to what she had been showing on quicker surfaces.
Meeznah(USA) was easy to back and having run such a bold race at Epsom it was disappointing that she failed to make an equivalent impact here. The ground was probably a major issue. (op 9/2)
Akdarena, who faded after briefly challenging for the lead around three furlongs down, has not progressed in the manner that might have been anticipated early in the season, but is probably best at around 1m2f. (op 10/1)
Desert Sage, off the mark in a Chepstow maiden last time, was out of her depth.
Remember When(IRE) fell short of her Epsom form for the second time in succession and now has it to prove. Official explanation: jockey said filly clipped heels on leaving stalls (op 11/2)
Eldalil proved disappointing, but probably did not like this surface and is too lightly raced to be writing off. (op 8/1)
Hibaayeb was well supported back up in class, but was very disappointing even allowing for the fact the ground may have turned against her. Official explanation: jockey said filly struggled throughout and did not handle the ground (op 4/1 tchd 9/2)

4180a BETTOR.COM ROCKINGHAM H'CAP (PREMIER HANDICAP) 5f
4:45 (4:48) 3-Y-0+

£47,787 (£15,132; £7,168; £2,389; £1,592; £796)

RPR
1 **Bay Knight (IRE)**[3] 4078 4-9-3 93 5ex DPMcDonogh 4 101
(K J Condon, Ire) *hld up towards rr: hdwy 1 1/2f out: rdn into 5th and swtchd 1f out: kpt on wl fnl f to ld cl home* **12/1**
2 hd **Luisant**[32] 3094 7-9-5 102 JPO'Brien[(7)] 12 109
(J A Nash, Ire) *chsd ldrs: 4th 1/2-way: rdn into 3rd 1f out: kpt on to ld and dispute fnl 100yds: drifted lft 50yds out: hdd cl home* **8/1**
3 1/2 **Bajan Tryst (USA)**[27] 3261 4-8-12 88 PJSmullen 9 93
(K A Ryan) *prom: cl 2nd 1/2-way: narrowly led 2f out: rdn and hdd over 1f out: kpt on again to chal fnl 100yds: no ex cl home* **12/1**
4 1/2 **Partner (IRE)**[63] 2145 4-8-5 84 (b) EJMcNamara[(3)] 11 87
(David Marnane, Ire) *chsd ldrs: cl 3rd 1/2-way: chal 2f out: rdn to ld over 1f out: hdd last 100yds: no ex* **12/1**
5 shd **Captain Carey**[27] 3261 4-9-3 93 TomMcLaughlin 5 96
(M S Saunders) *chsd ldrs: 5th 1/2-way: rdn into 4th 1f out: kpt on whn hmpd 50yds out: no ex* **6/1**[3]
6 3/4 **Collingwood (IRE)**[23] 3422 8-8-4 80 oh1 (bt) WMLordan 7 80
(T M Walsh, Ire) *in rr of mid-div: 10th 1/2-way: rdn 2f out: no imp over 1f out: kpt on same pce fnl f* **8/1**
7 3/4 **Masta Plasta (IRE)**[43] 2745 7-9-11 101 CDHayes 8 99
(D Nicholls) *mid-div: 8th 1/2-way: rdn 2f out: no imp over 1f out: kpt on same pce* **9/2**[2]
8 1/2 **Tornadodancer (IRE)**[21] 3489 7-8-9 88 (b) BACurtis[(3)] 10 84
(T G McCourt, Ire) *mid-div: 7th 1/2-way: rdn 2f out: no ex in 6th 1f out: kpt on one pce fnl f* **25/1**
9 shd **Lough Mist (IRE)**[21] 3489 4-8-11 87 PShanahan 6 82
(Tracey Collins, Ire) *j. qckly: sn chsd ldrs: 6th 1/2-way: rdn 2f out: no ex in 7th 1f out: kpt on one pce* **6/1**[3]
10 5 1/2 **Just For Mary**[23] 3422 6-8-7 83 RPCleary 2 59
(Daniel Mark Loughnane, Ire) *a towards rr* **7/1**
11 1 1/2 **Airspace (IRE)**[23] 3422 4-9-1 91 JMurtagh 1 61
(M Halford, Ire) *sn led: rdn and hdd 2f out: wknd over 1f out* **4/1**[1]

62.41 secs (-0.09) **Going Correction** +0.15s/f (Good)
WFA 3 from 4yo+ 4lb **11** Ran SP% **128.4**
Speed ratings: **109,108,107,107,106 105,104,103,103,94 92**
CSF £114.19 CT £1234.08 TOTE £16.50: £4.20, £3.00, £4.30; DF 125.20.
Owner Iona Equine Syndicate **Bred** Pat Roach **Trained** Frairstown Co Kildare
■ Stewards' Enquiry : J P O'Brien two-day ban: careless riding (Aug 4-5)
D P McDonogh severe caution: used whip without giving gelding time to respond

NOTEBOOK
Bay Knight(IRE) followed up his win at Leopardstown a few days previously in a race where all the cards fell perfectly for him. They went off at the predicted blistering pace which this horse couldn't really go, but his rider was happy to sit and wait. He had to slightly manufacture a gap when the front-runners were in the process of coming back to him but when getting proper racing room he kept on strongly inside the last to get his head in front close home. He's likely to try his hand in stakes company over an extra furlong. (op 10/1)
Luisant was back to his best, indeed he has been very consistent all season. Racing close to the pace throughout, he had every chance when coming under pressure a furlong or so from the finish but just hung left for a few strides inside the last and it might just have cost him. (op 7/1)
Bajan Tryst(USA) raced up with the pace the whole way and kept on at the same pace inside the last with the stands' rail to help him. Considering the ground and the pace they went it was a fair performance to stay there as long as he did. (op 10/1)
Captain Carey raced just behind the pacesetters and got plenty of cover but was struggling a bit for racing room inside the last and in the end was squeezed up when the runner-up edged left. He didn't look a likely winner anyway but would have been closer.
Collingwood(IRE) was towards the back as usual and ran on inside the last to be nearest at the finish without being a factor.
Masta Plasta(IRE) seemed to struggle somewhat to go the pace and never got into it. (op 9/2 tchd 5/1)
Airspace(IRE) showed his usual speed but dropped right out of contention in the last couple of furlongs. (op 9/2)

4181 - 4183a (Foreign Racing) - See Raceform Interactive

4164 HAMBURG (R-H)
Sunday, July 18

OFFICIAL GOING: Turf: good

4184a DEUTSCHES DERBY (GROUP 1) (3YO COLTS & FILLIES) (TURF) 1m 4f
4:30 (4:30) 3-Y-0 **£265,486** (£88,495; £53,097; £26,548; £8,849)

RPR
1 **Buzzword**[30] 3142 3-9-2 0 RoystonFfrench 7 108
(Mahmood Al Zarooni) *a.p: travelling strly: mde gd prog through fnl turn: qcknd to take ld 1 1/2f out: r.o strly: wnt clr: comf* **178/10**
2 1 1/4 **Zazou (GER)**[35] 3018 3-9-2 0 OlivierPeslier 1 106
(Mario Hofer, Germany) *broke wl to be prom along rail: mde move early in st: r.o wl on inner and chsd wnr home* **33/10**[2]
3 1/2 **Russian Tango (GER)**[30] 3-9-2 0 JBojko 2 105
(A Wohler, Germany) *racd in 6th: travelling wl: r.o wl u.p: fin wl: fin 4th: plcd 3rd* **131/10**
4 2 **Sir Lando**[30] 3-9-2 0 JimmyFortune 19 102
(Wido Neuroth, Norway) *racd in midfield: qcknd wl in centre of trck in st: r.o wl to fin 3rd: plcd 4th* **71/1**
5 1/2 **Lamool (GER)**[35] 3014 3-9-2 0 ADeVries 3 101
(Mario Hofer, Germany) *led fr s: r.o wl in st but outpcd fnl 2f* **76/1**
6 3/4 **Lindentree**[35] 3018 3-9-2 0 YannLerner 5 100
(W Hickst, Germany) *racd in midfield: mde prog early in st: styd on* **138/10**
7 3/4 **Monterosso**[21] 3491 3-9-2 0 KierenFallon 15 99
(M Johnston) *racd promly bhd ldrs fr s: flattered briefly early in st: rdn: fnd no ex* **3/1**[1]
8 1 1/2 **Lyssio (GER)**[30] 3-9-2 0 JohanVictoire 6 96
(P Schiergen, Germany) *a.p in ldng gp: hit traffic problems arnd fnl turn: fin wl whn clr* **30/1**
9 1/2 **Scalo**[35] 3018 3-9-2 0 EPedroza 8 96
(A Wohler, Germany) *bkmarker fr s: swtchd wd on home turn: r.o wl through btn horses but effrt c too late* **43/10**[3]
10 nk **Neatico (GER)**[14] 3-9-2 0 ChristopheSoumillon 17 95
(P Schiergen, Germany) *a.p: trckd pce in 2nd: flattered briefly early in st: wknd* **28/1**
11 nk **Val Mondo (GER)**[30] 3-9-2 0 IoritzMendizabal 12 95
(Uwe Ostmann, Germany) *towards rr fr s: mde prog early in st: suffered traffic problems: styd on* **28/1**
12 1 1/2 **Nightdance Paolo (GER)**[55] 2406 3-9-2 0 JiriPalik 10 92
(P Schiergen, Germany) *broke fast: racd freely in midfield: produced early in st: r.o but mde no imp* **99/1**
13 3/4 **Seventh Sky (GER)**[22] 3-9-2 0 AStarke 4 91
(P Schiergen, Germany) *racd in midfield: ev ch early in st: no ex: styd on* **26/5**
14 4 **Next Hight (IRE)**[35] 3018 3-9-2 0 FilipMinarik 14 85
(P Schiergen, Germany) *a towards rr: a short of room to make any sort of prog: nvr a threat* **70/1**
15 7 **Supersonic Flight (GER)**[22] 3-9-2 0 DPorcu 20 73
(M Rulec, Germany) *racd promly initially then settled midfield: flattered briefly early in st: sn wknd* **42/1**
16 hd **Keep Cool**[55] 2406 3-9-2 0 THellier 16 73
(Andreas Lowe, Germany) *racd in midfield: nvr proged: wknd qckly in st* **29/1**
17 6 **Baschar**[35] 3018 3-9-2 0 AnthonyCrastus 11 64
(M G Mintchev, Germany) *broke poorly and nvr gng wl* **62/1**
18 nse **Ustilago (GER)**[44] 2735 3-9-2 0 DominiqueBoeuf 18 63
(W Baltromei, Germany) *racd freely in midfield: mde sme prog in bk st: prom early in st: sn wknd* **30/1**
19 nk **Nordfalke (IRE)**[35] 3018 3-9-2 0 AGoritz 9 63
(P Schiergen, Germany) *a towards rr: nvr proged* **75/1**
20 19 **Jammy Shot (GER)**[22] 3-9-2 0 MircoDemuro 13 33
(A Wohler, Germany) *a towards rr: nvr proged* **63/1**

2m 29.51s (-5.04) **20** Ran SP% **131.0**
WIN (incl. 10 euro stake): 188. PLACES: 63, 23, 38. SF: 898.
Owner Godolphin **Bred** Darley **Trained** Newmarket, Suffolk
■ The first overseas winner of the German Derby, which was opened up to foreign competition in 1993.

NOTEBOOK
Buzzword, who was contesting his fourth classic of the season, has been freshened up since finishing third to Monterosso at Royal Ascot. He was supplemented for this at a cost of 50,000euros. Always well placed, he drew alongside a furlong out and stayed on well to give his trainer a first Group 1 win.
Zazou(GER) had won the main trial for this, but his stamina let him down in the latter stages and he is likely to revert to 1m2f.
Russian Tango(GER), who is owned by the race sponsor, was promoted a place by the stewards.
Sir Lando, a Norwegian challenger, lost third in the stewards' room. This was a good run from his wide draw.
Monterosso had Buzzword behind in third when winning the King Edward II Stakes and was a supplementary entry for this. He never really got competitive here and Kieren Fallon though the track was too tight for the colt, who is more of a galloper.

NAPLES (R-H)
Sunday, July 18

OFFICIAL GOING: Turf: good

4185a GRAN PREMIO CITTA' DI NAPOLI (LISTED RACE) (3YO+) (TURF) 5f
9:30 (12:00) 3-Y-0+ **£35,398** (£15,575; £8,495; £4,247)

RPR
1 **Rebecca Rolfe**[91] 1419 4-8-8 0 GMarcelli 8 103
(M Gasparini, Italy) **101/10**

2 2 **Above Limits (IRE)**[36] 2972 3-8-4 0 CathyGannon 6 95
(D M Simcock) **71/20**[3]
3 1/2 **Dagda Mor (ITY)**[92] 3-8-7 0 FabioBranca 2 96
(S Botti, Italy) **101/10**
4 nse **Titus Shadow (IRE)**[19] 6-8-11 0 DVargiu 7 97
(B Grizzetti, Italy) **282/100**[2]
5 2 **El Suacillo (IRE)**[71] 1944 3-8-7 0 GErcegovic 10 89
(D Camuffo, Italy) **60/1**
6 nk **Madda's Force (ITY)**[71] 1944 4-8-8 0 GBietolini 3 86
(R Betti, Italy) **37/1**
7 nk **Grenso (ITY)**[71] 1944 3-8-7 0 UmbertoRispoli 11 87
(S Botti, Italy) **59/10**
8 4 **Thinking Robins (IRE)**[71] 1944 7-8-11 0 (b) SSulas 12 73
(A Turco, Italy) **17/10**[1]
9 nk **Sleek Falcon (IRE)** 3-8-4 0 APolli 4 68
(V di Napoli, Italy) **28/1**
10 3 **Golden Ramon (IRE)**[28] 3-8-4 0 CDemuro 5 57
(B Grizzetti, Italy) **99/10**
11 3 **Xenes**[71] 1944 6-8-11 0 CFiocchi 1 51
(R Menichetti, Italy) **37/1**

WFA 3 from 4yo+ 4lb **11** Ran SP% **137.2**
PARI-MUTUEL (all including 1 euro stakes): WIN 11.12; PLACE 3.73, 2.67, 3.54; DF 33.96.
Owner Aston House Stud **Bred** Cheveley Park Stud **Trained** Italy

NOTEBOOK
Above Limits(IRE), third at this level three times, only succumbed to the winner's late burst.

3945 AYR (L-H)
Monday, July 19

OFFICIAL GOING: Good changing to good to soft after race 1 (2:30) changing to soft after race 2 (3:00).
Rail on back straight out 4m added 6yds to races at 7f and above. Stands' side rail in 3m and far side rail on innermost line.

4187 EUROPEAN BREEDERS' FUND MAIDEN STKS 7f 50y
2:30 (2:30) (Class 4) 2-Y-O **£4,274** (£1,271; £635; £317) **Stalls** High

Form RPR
3 **1** **Goldenveil (IRE)**[15] 3705 2-8-12 0 PaulHanagan 4 80+
(R A Fahey) *prom: smooth hdwy to ld over 2f out: rdn and edgd lft over 1f out: sn clr* **1/1**[1]
5 **2** 7 **Spring Bouquet (IRE)**[12] 3778 2-8-12 0 PaulEddery 11 63
(M R Channon) *cl up: effrt and ev ch over 2f out: sn chsng wnr: kpt on fnl f: no ch w wnr* **20/1**
3 nk **Good Boy Jackson** 2-9-3 0 PJMcDonald 10 67+
(K A Ryan) *dwlt: sn midfield: effrt over 2f out: styd on fnl f: nvr able to chal* **20/1**
4 **4** 1 1/4 **Loukoumi**[24] 3392 2-8-12 0 TomEaves 12 59
(B Smart) *t.k.h: cl up: effrt and ev ch over 2f out: one pce fr over 1f out* **4/1**[2]
0 **5** nk **Denices Moonlight**[38] 2932 2-9-3 0 GregFairley 9 63
(M Johnston) *trckd ldrs: effrt and chal over 2f out: no ex ins fnl f* **12/1**
6 3 1/2 **Oasis Storm** 2-9-3 0 PhillipMakin 7 55
(M Dods) *hld up in tch: pushed along over 2f out: wknd over 1f out* **10/1**[3]
7 2 1/2 **Janet's Pearl (IRE)** 2-8-9 0 BarryMcHugh(3) 3 44
(Mrs A Duffield) *midfield: drvn and outpcd over 2f out: n.d after* **33/1**
8 2 **Face The Future** 2-9-3 0 FrannyNorton 5 44
(M Dods) *dwlt: bhd: rdn 3f out: nvr on terms* **33/1**
0 **9** 3/4 **Whitby Warrior (USA)**[23] 3433 2-9-3 0 TonyHamilton 6 42
(C Grant) *towards rr: rdn on outside 3f out: nvr on terms* **100/1**
10 1/2 **Monel** 2-9-0 0 GaryBartley(3) 13 41+
(J S Goldie) *s.i.s: bhd and pushed along 1/2-way: nvr on terms* **50/1**
45 **11** 8 **Mysterious Bounty (IRE)**[52] 2498 2-8-12 0 PatrickDonaghy(5) 1 21
(M Dods) *dwlt: towards rr: struggling over 3f out: sn btn* **12/1**
0 **12** 1 **Irelandisuperman**[20] 3536 2-9-3 0 AdrianNicholls 2 19
(D Nicholls) *led to over 2f out: sn rdn and wknd qckly* **14/1**

1m 34.78s (1.38) **Going Correction** +0.05s/f (Good) **12** Ran SP% **119.5**
Speed ratings (Par 96): **94,86,85,84,83 79,77,74,73,73 64,63**
toteswingers:1&2:£10.30, 1&3:£6.60, 2&3:£30.40 CSF £31.33 TOTE £2.20: £1.10, £6.70, £3.90; EX 20.40.
Owner Mrs H Steel **Bred** Tom & Geraldine Molan **Trained** Musley Bank, N Yorks

FOCUS
Heavy rain throughout the day meant conditions were very different from the 48-hour entry stage, and although the official description was 'good' prior to the opening contest, it was changed to good to soft after the race and the winning time was over five seconds slower than standard. Not a great deal of depth to this maiden and it paid to be handy. The winner improved for her debut but the level was modest in behind.

NOTEBOOK
Goldenveil(IRE) confirmed the promise she showed over C&D on debut by storming away in the final furlong, despite edging to her left. She had no problems with conditions, indeed it was on the slow side when she ran here first time, and she could be decent, but the likelihood is that she's not beaten a great deal. (op 11-10)
Spring Bouquet(IRE), who caught the eye in the paddock, was blown away by the winner but she saw out the extra furlong well enough and probably stepped forward on her Kempton debut. (op 25-1)
Good Boy Jackson finished his race better than anything. From a family that his trainer knows well, he was the only runner to get involved from off the pace and looks sure to rank highly next time. (op 16-1)
Loukoumi was trapped wide from her high draw and raced a little keenly through the early stages. As a result, she didn't see her race out and may prefer a return to 6f. (tchd 7-2)
Denices Moonlight shaped more encouragingly than on debut. (op 25-1)
Irelandisuperman Official explanation: jockey said gelding ran too free

4188 EL TORO GRANDE DOS H'CAP (DIV I) 1m
3:00 (3:00) (Class 6) (0-65,65) 3-Y-O+ **£1,706** (£503; £252) **Stalls** Low

Form RPR
1513 **1** **Glenluji**[3] 4082 5-9-4 55 PaulHanagan 1 68+
(J S Goldie) *prom gng wl: smooth hdwy to ld 2f out: drvn clr appr fnl f* **4/1**[2]
0401 **2** 5 **Frontline Girl (IRE)**[7] 3948 4-9-12 63 6ex AndrewElliott 2 65
(J R Weymes) *prom: rdn 3f out: rallied to chse wnr over 1f out: no imp ins fnl f* **11/4**[1]
605 **3** 6 **Morocchius (USA)**[40] 2864 5-9-7 58 (p) TomEaves 10 46
(Julie Camacho) *trckd ldrs: effrt and rdn over 2f out: nt qckn fnl f* **5/1**[3]
000- **4** 3/4 **Nolecce**[305] 6009 3-8-1 46 oh1 PaulEddery 6 30
(R C Guest) *stdd s: hld up: hdwy over 2f out: no imp fnl f* **50/1**
0406 **5** 1 1/4 **Regal Emperor (IRE)**[12] 3773 3-8-13 58 FrannyNorton 5 39
(D Nicholls) *led tl rdn and hdd 2f out: wknd 1f out* **33/1**
024- **6** 1/2 **Ella Grace (USA)**[292] 6391 3-8-9 61 MarzenaJeziorek(7) 4 41
(R A Fahey) *hld up: niggled 1/2-way: shortlived effrt over 2f out: no imp over 1f out* **9/1**
6436 **7** 1 **King's Jester (IRE)**[17] 3654 8-9-1 52 (b) AdrianNicholls 8 32
(Lee Smyth, Ire) *bhd and sn pushed along: effrt on ins over 2f out: nvr on terms* **25/1**
0322 **8** 11 **San Silvestro (IRE)**[12] 3775 5-9-11 65 (b) BarryMcHugh(3) 9 19
(Mrs A Duffield) *cl up: gng wl over 2f out: rdn wl over 1f out: wknd qckly* **4/1**[2]
00/- **9** 29 **Billy One Punch**[592] 7548 8-9-11 62 LNewman 3 —
(A G Foster) *trckd ldrs tl wknd qckly 3f out: eased whn no ch over 1f out* **33/1**
4365 **10** 1 1/4 **Cold Quest (USA)**[3] 4082 6-8-12 49 (b) PhillipMakin 7 —
(Miss L A Perratt) *cl up tl wknd qckly over 2f out: sn eased* **7/1**

1m 44.52s (0.72) **Going Correction** +0.125s/f (Good)
WFA 3 from 4yo+ 8lb **10** Ran SP% **117.5**
Speed ratings (Par 101): **101,96,90,89,88 87,86,75,46,45**
toteswingers:1&2:£3.60, 1&3:£6.80, 2&3:£3.30 CSF £15.08 CT £57.18 TOTE £5.70: £1.90, £1.70, £2.30; EX 16.20.
Owner Jim Goldie Racing Club **Bred** Jim Goldie **Trained** Uplawmoor, E Renfrews

FOCUS
The ground was changed to soft after this race. Handicaps are rarely won as easily as this, but it was a weak race and is probably not form to take too literally.
Cold Quest(USA) Official explanation: jockey said gelding stopped very quickly

4189 EL TORO GRANDE DOS H'CAP (DIV II) 1m
3:30 (3:30) (Class 6) (0-65,65) 3-Y-O+ **£1,706** (£503; £252) **Stalls** Low

Form RPR
05-0 **1** **Only A Splash**[7] 3948 6-9-0 50 PJMcDonald 3 60
(Mrs R A Carr) *led tl rdn and hdd over 1f out: styd on wl u.p fnl f: regained ld cl home* **12/1**
6002 **2** hd **Bed Fellow (IRE)**[9] 3905 6-9-4 54 TonyHamilton 2 63
(P Monteith) *t.k.h: trckd ldrs: led gng wl over 1f out: sn rdn and edgd lft: kpt on fnl f: hdd cl home* **7/2**[1]
0055 **3** 7 **Red Dagger (IRE)**[10] 3853 4-8-10 49 (p) AndrewHeffernan(3) 7 42
(R J Price) *hld up in tch: rdn and outpcd over 2f out: edgd lft and rallied over 1f out: rdr dropped whip ins fnl f: no ch w first two* **8/1**[2]
0506 **4** 1 1/2 **Primo Way**[15] 3707 9-8-9 45 (be) FrannyNorton 10 35
(D A Nolan) *prom: drvn and outpcd over 2f out: n.d after* **10/1**
540 **5** 3 1/2 **Amity (IRE)**[9] 3924 3-9-7 65 GregFairley 5 45
(M Johnston) *trckd ldrs: drvn and outpcd over 2f out: btn fnl f* **10/1**
3514 **6** 2 3/4 **Crocodile Bay (IRE)**[10] 3855 7-9-12 62 PaulEddery 8 37
(R C Guest) *in tch: rdn over 2f out: btn over 1f out* **7/2**[1]
3450 **7** 3 1/2 **Transmission (IRE)**[105] 1115 5-9-13 63 TomEaves 1 30
(B Smart) *sn drvn along in rr: nvr on terms* **7/2**[1]
0-66 **8** 4 **Secret Hero**[7] 3948 4-9-2 52 (b) AdrianNicholls 6 10
(Lee Smyth, Ire) *sn pushed along towards rr: struggling fnl 3f: nvr on terms* **9/1**[3]
0530 **9** 19 **Rosbertini**[9] 3905 4-9-9 59 PhillipMakin 9 —
(Miss L A Perratt) *hld up: rdn on outside over 2f out: sn wknd: t.o* **20/1**

1m 44.46s (0.66) **Going Correction** +0.20s/f (Good)
WFA 3 from 4yo+ 8lb **9** Ran SP% **118.4**
Speed ratings (Par 101): **104,103,96,95,91 89,85,81,62**
toteswingers:1&2:£9.80, 1&3:£22.80, 2&3:£7.40 CSF £55.25 CT £368.99 TOTE £13.70: £3.90, £1.50, £3.00; EX 66.10.
Owner Mrs Ruth A Carr **Bred** Mrs M J Hills **Trained** Huby, N Yorks

FOCUS
The weaker of the two divisions and most of these find winning very difficult. The first pair were clear but this is very ordinary form.
Only A Splash Official explanation: trainer said, regarding apparent improvement in form that the gelding was better suited by the softer ground.
Crocodile Bay(IRE) Official explanation: vet said gelding lost a near-fore shoe
Transmission(IRE) Official explanation: jockey said gelding never travelled
Rosbertini Official explanation: jockey said gelding was unsuited by the soft ground

4190 BEST ODDS GUARANTEED AT VICTOR CHANDLER H'CAP 1m 5f 13y
4:00 (4:00) (Class 5) (0-70,70) 4-Y-O+ **£2,729** (£806; £403) **Stalls** Low

Form RPR
3126 **1** **Silent Lucidity (IRE)**[13] 3760 6-8-5 54 (p) PaulHanagan 9 63
(P D Niven) *hld up in tch: hdwy over 4f out: led and drvn over 2f out: hld on gamely u.p fnl f* **5/2**[1]
-213 **2** 1/2 **Forrest Flyer (IRE)**[15] 3709 6-9-7 70 JamieSpencer 1 78
(J S Goldie) *prom: rdn over 4f out: rallied and chsd wnr 2f out: kpt on u.p fnl f but a hld* **3/1**[2]
6233 **3** 1 3/4 **Mohawk Ridge**[40] 2851 4-9-1 64 PhillipMakin 6 69
(M Dods) *hld up in tch: hdwy and disp cl 2nd pl 2f out: sn drvn: one pce ins fnl f* **4/1**[3]
0 **4** 3 1/4 **Amical Risks (FR)**[36] 2995 6-8-3 52 DuranFentiman 7 53
(Joss Saville) *bhd: drvn over 4f out: no imp tl styd on fnl f: nrst fin* **12/1**
00 **5** 1/2 **Kimberley Downs (USA)**[18] 3588 4-8-13 65 BarryMcHugh(3) 8 65
(N Wilson) *led: rdn and hdd over 2f out: wknd over 1f out* **10/1**
6/50 **6** 10 **Tuxsumdoin**[63] 2182 6-7-9 51 oh4 NeilFarley(7) 4 36
(J R Weymes) *in tch: outpcd over 5f out: n.d after* **40/1**
-451 **7** 24 **Balwearie (IRE)**[15] 3709 9-8-8 57 FrannyNorton 2 6
(Miss L A Perratt) *chsd ldrs: wnt 2nd over 5f out to over 2f out: wknd and eased over 1f out* **5/1**
400/ **8** 4 1/2 **Ohana**[632] 5575 7-8-2 51 oh6 AndrewElliott 5 —
(A C Whillans) *chsd ldr to over 5f out: sn lost pl and struggling* **20/1**

2m 59.48s (5.48) **Going Correction** +0.275s/f (Good) **8** Ran SP% **114.2**
Speed ratings (Par 103): **94,93,92,90,90 84,69,66**
toteswingers:1&2:£1.90, 1&3:£3.00, 2&3:£3.50 CSF £10.14 CT £27.87 TOTE £4.30: £1.40, £1.50, £1.40; EX 11.50.
Owner P D Niven **Bred** Mrs Jacqueline Donnelly **Trained** Barton-le-Street, N Yorks
■ Stewards' Enquiry : Jamie Spencer three-day ban: used whip with excessive frequency (Aug 2-4)

FOCUS
A strong gallop and this turned into quite a gruelling test. The winner is rated back to his best old form.

The Form Book, Raceform Ltd, Compton, RG20 6NL

Balwearie(IRE) Official explanation: jockey said gelding was unsuited by the soft ground

4191 BET AT VICTOR CHANDLER ON 08000 78 78 78 H'CAP 5f
4:30 (4:32) (Class 2) 3-Y-O+ £21,370 (£6,359; £3,177; £1,587) Stalls Low

Form RPR
1211 **1** **Favourite Girl (IRE)**[17] 3622 4-8-4 **88**........................(v) DuranFentiman 3 99
(T D Easterby) *cl up: rdn to ld over 1f out: hld on gamely u.p fnl f* 7/1[2]

-060 **2** ¾ **Pavershooz**[65] 2135 5-8-3 **87**.................................. AndrewElliott 2 95
(N Wilson) *led tl rdn and hdd over 1f out: kpt on fnl f: hld towards fin* 12/1

000 **3** ¾ **Cheveton**[17] 3629 6-7-12 **85**.................................. AndrewHeffernan(3) 4 91
(R J Price) *in tch: rdn over 2f out: effrt appr fnl f: kpt on same pce last 75yds* 6/1[1]

1434 **4** ¾ **Duchess Dora (IRE)**[37] 2972 3-8-1 **94**.......................... IanBrennan(5) 6 96
(J J Quinn) *cl up: rdn wl over 1f out: one pce ins fnl f* 10/1

1-53 **5** 2 ¼ **Quest For Success (IRE)**[84] 1573 5-9-0 **101**.......... BarryMcHugh(3) 11 96
(R A Fahey) *midfield: effrt over 2f out: edgd lft over 1f out: no imp fnl f* 9/1

000 **6** 1 ½ **Fullandby (IRE)**[36] 2992 8-8-6 **97** ow5.......................... DaleSwift(7) 7 86
(T J Etherington) *bhd: drvn along 1/2-way: hdwy over 1f out: kpt on: nvr able to chal* 10/1

-005 **7** ¾ **Sonny Red (IRE)**[9] 3891 6-8-11 **95**.............................. FrannyNorton 12 82
(D Nicholls) *bhd: drvn along 1/2-way: sme hdwy over 1f out: nvr rchd ldrs* 10/1

0100 **8** ½ **Rasaman (IRE)**[11] 3828 6-7-13 **86** ow3....................(v) KellyHarrison(3) 5 71
(J S Goldie) *bhd and pushed along 1/2-way: no imp fnl 2f* 20/1

1500 **9** ½ **Look Busy (IRE)**[10] 3875 5-9-0 **98**.............................. TomEaves 8 81
(A Berry) *in tch: drvn 1/2-way: wknd over 1f out* 17/2

1004 **10** nk **Wi Dud**[32] 3108 6-9-2 **100**.. PaulHanagan 14 82
(K A Ryan) *bhd and sn pushed along: nvr on terms* 7/1[2]

0102 **11** 2 **Captain Dunne (IRE)**[9] 3895 5-9-10 **108**.......................... PhillipMakin 9 83
(T D Easterby) *cl up tl rdn and wknd qckly over 1f out* 8/1[3]

-000 **12** 4 ½ **Strike Up The Band**[44] 2745 7-8-10 **94**....................... AdrianNicholls 10 53
(D Nicholls) *w ldrs: outpcd 2f out: sn btn* 14/1

58.40 secs (-1.70) **Going Correction** -0.10s/f (Good)
WFA 3 from 4yo+ 4lb 12 Ran SP% **117.3**
Speed ratings (Par 109): **109,107,106,105,101 99,98,97,96,96 92,85**
toteswingers:1&2:£9.80, 1&3:£7.20, 2&3:£13.70 CSF £87.26 CT £408.39 TOTE £7.30: £2.10, £4.40, £2.20; EX 78.50.

Owner Peter C Bourke **Bred** Limestone And Tara Studs **Trained** Great Habton, N Yorks

■ Stewards' Enquiry : Duran Fentiman caution: used whip with excessive frequency
Ian Brennan one-day ban: failed to ride to draw (Aug 2)

FOCUS
Competitive stuff, unsurprisingly given the money on offer. The action unfolded down the middle of the track and the pace pretty much held up. Interestingly, the first four home were all carrying light weights. Good handicap form, the winner back to something like his best.

NOTEBOOK
Favourite Girl(IRE), a versatile filly, was always well placed and she battled on strongly to land her biggest prize of the season. Her form has taken off since being fitted with a visor and all ground seems to come alike. (op 8-1)

Pavershooz's wind operation has clearly had a positive effect and he bounced back to form on his favourite track. He's a well handicapped horse nowadays. (op 11-1)

Cheveton looks well handicapped, now 6lb lower than when scoring at Haydock in September. He ideally needs some give underfoot and, having got his conditions for the first time this season, finished strongly towards the far side. (op 7-1)

Duchess Dora(IRE) has never raced on ground like this but she ran well, keeping on nicely, and she has proved this year that she is capable of winning a handicap off this mark.

Quest For Success(IRE) faced a tough task off this career-high mark and, while he was far from disgraced, couldn't get into it. (op 10-1)

Fullandby(IRE) is well suited by some juice in the ground but he could never get into it and is probably better suited by 6f nowadays. (op 12-1)

Look Busy(IRE) Official explanation: trainer said mare finished lame right-hind

4192 BET LIVE AT VICTORCHANDLER.COM H'CAP 6f
5:00 (5:01) (Class 4) (0-80,80) 3-Y-O+ £4,533 (£1,011; £1,011; £336) Stalls Low

Form RPR
5433 **1** **Tadalavil**[4] 4063 5-8-9 **66**.. BarryMcHugh(3) 2 74
(Miss L A Perratt) *mde all: edgd rt fr 2f out: hld on wl u.p fnl f* 9/2[1]

204 **2** ½ **Lochan Mor**[35] 3033 4-9-12 **80**.................................. JamieSpencer 11 86
(M L W Bell) *prom: rdn to chse wnr over 1f out: kpt on u.p fnl f* 6/1[2]

50 **2** dht **Ginger Ted (IRE)**[30] 3215 3-9-4 **80**....................(p) AndrewHeffernan(3) 3 85
(R C Guest) *prom: effrt and rdn over 1f out: edgd lft: kpt on u.p fnl f* 11/1

0000 **4** 2 ¼ **River Falcon**[9] 3919 10-9-4 **72**.................................. PaulHanagan 1 71
(J S Goldie) *racd alone far side tl swtchd over to join main gp 1/2-way: in tch: rdn and one pce fr over 1f out* 7/1[3]

6416 **5** ½ **Thrust Control (IRE)**[9] 3886 3-8-13 **79**.......................... DaleSwift(7) 5 75
(B Ellison) *cl up: rdn over 2f out: no ex over 1f out* 9/2[1]

0-00 **6** nse **Commando Scott (IRE)**[3] 4121 9-8-4 **65**.......................... NeilFarley(7) 9 62
(D Carroll) *in tch: effrt over 2f out: no imp over 1f out* 9/1

0636 **7** 1 ¾ **Geojimali**[4] 4063 8-8-4 **63**......................................(v[1]) IanBrennan(5) 13 54
(J S Goldie) *bhd and sn pushed along: hdwy over 1f out: nrst fin* 20/1

0-60 **8** 1 **Turnkey**[34] 3065 8-9-9 **77**.. AdrianNicholls 10 65
(D Nicholls) *sn drvn along towards rr: hdwy u.p over 1f out: nvr able to chal* 6/1[2]

400- **9** nk **Dubai Hills**[322] 5523 4-9-4 **72**.................................. TomEaves 8 59
(B Smart) *cl up tl rdn and wknd wl over 1f out* 33/1

-542 **10** 3 ¼ **Cheyenne Red (IRE)**[46] 2671 4-9-2 **70**.......................... PhillipMakin 4 47
(M Dods) *hld up: rdn over 2f out: nvr able to chal* 7/1[3]

0006 **11** ½ **Bravely (IRE)**[10] 3879 6-8-7 **61**.................................. DuranFentiman 12 36
(T D Easterby) *hld up: drvn over 2f out: btn over 1f out* 25/1

2540 **12** 4 **Rothesay Dancer**[7] 3947 7-9-0 **71**.............................. KellyHarrison(3) 6 33
(J S Goldie) *bhd: pushed along 1/2-way: sn struggling* 20/1

1m 12.68s (-0.92) **Going Correction** -0.02s/f (Good)
WFA 3 from 4yo+ 5lb 12 Ran SP% **124.6**
Speed ratings (Par 105): **105,104,104,101,100 100,98,96,96,92 91,86**
PL: LM £2.20, GT £6.00. CFC: TL> £27.76 , TL&LM £15.59. EX: TL> £33.50 , TL&LM £20.90. TC: TL>&LM £156.95, TL&LM> £147.44. toteswingers:TL&LM:£3.60, LM>:£20.40, TL>:£13.00 TOTE £6.20: £1.90.

Owner Ayrshire Racing **Bred** Theakston Stud **Trained** East Kilbride, South Lanarks

FOCUS
Again it paid to be prominent and not much got into it. The winner was back to his early-season form.

4193 WATCH LIVE RACING AT VICTORCHANDLER.COM H'CAP 6f
5:30 (5:31) (Class 5) (0-70,70) 3-Y-O £2,729 (£806; £403) Stalls Low

Form RPR
2320 **1** **Rasselas (IRE)**[16] 3680 3-9-7 **70**.................................. AdrianNicholls 1 75
(D Nicholls) *prom: effrt and chsd ldr over 1f out: styd on to ld last 50yds: kpt on* 3/1[1]

0463 **2** nk **Reach For The Sky (IRE)**[12] 3773 3-8-3 **52**.................. FrannyNorton 11 56
(A Berry) *cl up: led and hung lft over 1f out: hdd last 50yds: kpt on* 28/1

5124 **3** 1 ¾ **Monte Mayor One**[4] 4063 3-9-0 **63**.............................(p) TonyHamilton 9 61
(P Monteith) *t.k.h: trckd ldrs: effrt over 1f out: kpt on ins fnl f* 9/1

2310 **4** hd **Red Scintilla**[24] 3393 3-9-4 **67**.................................. PhillipMakin 4 64+
(N Tinkler) *hld up: n.m.r over 2f out: sn rdn: hdwy over 1f out: nvr able to chal* 14/1

0000 **5** ½ **The Human League**[9] 3898 3-9-2 **65**.......................... PaulEddery 7 61
(M R Channon) *hld up: rdn over 2f out: hdwy over 1f out: no imp fnl f* 7/2[2]

-612 **6** ¾ **Dies Solis**[15] 3710 3-9-0 **63**.. PaulHanagan 2 56
(D A Nolan) *t.k.h: w ldrs tl rdn and no ex fnl f* 9/2[3]

100 **7** 2 ½ **Steed**[41] 2834 3-9-3 **66**..(b[1]) PJMcDonald 5 51
(K A Ryan) *towards rr: drvn over 2f out: nvr able to chal* 20/1

0603 **8** hd **Weetentherty**[15] 3710 3-7-13 **51**....................(v) AndrewHeffernan(3) 10 36
(J S Goldie) *in tch: rdn and outpcd over 2f out: n.d after* 16/1

1206 **9** ½ **Master Leon**[25] 3371 3-9-7 **70**......................................(v) TomEaves 8 53
(B Smart) *dwlt: bhd: rdn over 2f out: nvr on terms* 10/1

10-0 **10** 2 ½ **Cian Rooney (IRE)**[44] 2768 3-9-4 **70**.......................... BarryMcHugh(3) 6 45
(Mrs A Duffield) *led tl rdn and hdd over 1f out: sn btn* 40/1

-501 **11** 4 ½ **Thinking**[12] 3773 3-8-12 **61**.. DuranFentiman 3 22
(T D Easterby) *cl up tl rdn and wknd qckly fr 2f out* 8/1

1m 13.73s (0.13) **Going Correction** +0.05s/f (Good) 11 Ran SP% **118.8**
Speed ratings (Par 100): **101,100,98,98,97 96,93,92,92,88 82**
toteswingers:1&2:£27.50, 1&3:£10.20, 2&3:£23.40 CSF £95.71 CT £706.02 TOTE £4.70: £1.40, £6.50, £4.00; EX 135.50.

Owner J P Honeyman **Bred** Lynch Bages Ltd **Trained** Sessay, N Yorks

■ Stewards' Enquiry : P J McDonald caution: used whip without giving gelding time to respond.

FOCUS
They were spread right across the track in this modest handicap. The winner is rated back to his maiden best but this is not a race to be with.

Thinking Official explanation: jockey said gelding ran flat

4194 VICTORCHANDLER.COM H'CAP 5f
6:00 (6:01) (Class 6) (0-60,59) 3-Y-O £2,047 (£604; £302) Stalls Low

Form RPR
0316 **1** **Ya Boy Sir (IRE)**[24] 3410 3-8-13 **59**.............................. DeanHeslop(5) 4 63
(N Wilson) *prom: rdn to ld over 1f out: hld on wl fnl f* 4/1[2]

5400 **2** nk **Thewinnatakesitall**[18] 3597 3-8-5 **46**....................(p) AndrewElliott 2 48
(N Tinkler) *w ldrs: rdn and outpcd 2f out: rallied fnl f: jst hld* 8/1

0304 **3** 1 ¼ **Vilnius**[30] 3228 3-9-2 **57**.. PhillipMakin 11 55
(M R Channon) *in tch: effrt and rdn 2f out: kpt on ins fnl f* 6/1

4040 **4** shd **Sharp Shoes**[6] 3979 3-8-9 **53**..............................(b[1]) BarryMcHugh(3) 1 51
(Mrs A Duffield) *led tl hung rt and hdd over 1f out: kpt on u.p ins fnl f* 5/1[3]

00-0 **5** ½ **Areeg (IRE)**[14] 3728 3-8-1 **45**.................................. KellyHarrison(3) 9 41
(A Berry) *dwlt: bhd: hdwy and edgd lft over 1f out: kpt on fnl f: no imp* 50/1

6300 **6** ½ **Classlin**[7] 3946 3-8-8 **49**.. PaulHanagan 8 43
(J S Goldie) *bhd: rdn 1/2-way: kpt on fnl f: nrst fin* 17/2

0023 **7** 2 ½ **Loss Leader (IRE)**[9] 3904 3-8-13 **54**.......................... DuranFentiman 3 39
(T D Easterby) *chsd ldrs: rdn 1/2-way: edgd lft and wknd over 1f out* 10/3[1]

5040 **8** nk **Midget**[47] 2648 3-9-2 **57**.. DavidNolan 6 41
(D Carroll) *trckd ldrs: effrt and ev ch 2f out: wknd ins fnl f* 6/1

0 **9** 1 **Bombay Mist**[28] 3277 3-8-4 **45**..............................(e[1]) PaulEddery 12 25
(R C Guest) *prom: rdn over 2f out: wknd over 1f out* 40/1

6-50 **10** 7 **The Two G'S**[16] 3682 3-8-1 **45**..............................(b) AndrewHeffernan(3) 7 —
(R J Price) *w ldrs tl rdn and wknd wl over 1f out* 18/1

0-60 **11** 13 **Rightcar Marian**[89] 1468 3-8-2 **48** ow3.......................... IanBrennan(5) 10 —
(Peter Grayson) *dwlt: bhd and outpcd: lost tch fr 1/2-way* 80/1

60.82 secs (0.72) **Going Correction** +0.125s/f (Good) 11 Ran SP% **120.9**
Speed ratings (Par 98): **99,98,96,96,95 94,90,90,88,77 56**
toteswingers:1&2:£5.40, 1&3:£6.80, 2&3:£10.90 CSF £37.02 CT £198.19 TOTE £3.70: £1.10, £3.90, £3.00; EX 36.00 Place 6 £27.04; Place 5 £15.68.

Owner David M Roan **Bred** Basil Brindley **Trained** Sandhutton, N Yorks

■ Stewards' Enquiry : Barry McHugh caution: careless riding.
Andrew Elliott caution: used whip with excessive frequency.

FOCUS
A weak sprintnin which the third and fourth set the standard.

Rightcar Marian Official explanation: jockey said filly hung right throughout

T/Jkpt: Not won. T/Plt: £51.80 to a £1 stake. Pool:£81,184.90 - 1,142.20 winning ticket. T/Qpdt: £34.50 to a £1 stake. Pool:£4,905.58 - 105.10 winning tickets. RY

3971 BEVERLEY (R-H)
Monday, July 19

OFFICIAL GOING: Good to firm (9.2)
Rail around the bottom bend moved out to provide fresh ground increasing distances of races of 7f and over by 6yds.
Wind: Moderate across Weather: Cloudy and warm

4195 WELCOME TO YORKSHIRE CHELSEA RHUBARB GARDEN CLAIMING STKS 5f
6:30 (6:30) (Class 5) 2-Y-O £2,388 (£705; £352) Stalls High

Form RPR
4415 **1** **Nellie Ellis (IRE)**[16] 3678 2-8-9 0.................................. PaulMulrennan 5 65
(K A Ryan) *cl up: rdn to ld over 1f out: drvn ins fnl f and kpt on wl* 4/1[2]

2 ½ **Red Gold And Green (IRE)** 2-8-9 0.......................... BillyCray(5) 8 68+
(D Nicholls) *cl up on inner: led wl over 1f out: sn rdn: edgd lft and hdd over 1f out: drvn and edgd lft ins fnl f: kpt on* 14/1

3202 **3** 1 ¼ **Saltergate**[6] 3971 2-9-0 0......................................(p) SilvestreDeSousa 4 64
(N Tinkler) *in tch: pushed along to chse ldrs 1/2-way: rdn 2f out: drvn to chal over 1f out and ev ch tl no ex ins fnl f* 13/8[1]

13 **4** *6* **My Lord**[10] 3864 2-8-9 0 JackDean(3) 7 40
(W G M Turner) *led: rdn along 1/2-way: hdd wl over 1f out: sn drvn and wknd* **4/1**[2]

0020 **5** *3* **Reel Amber**[64] 2139 2-8-7 0 (b) RobertWinston 10 24
(T D Easterby) *in tch on inner: effrt over 2f out: sn rdn and no imp* **16/1**

6463 **6** *3 1/4* **Press Release**[12] 3784 2-8-10 0 (vt) RichardKingscote 3 16
(Tom Dascombe) *s.i.s and bhd: hdwy 3f out: rdn and in tch over 2f out: sn drvn and wknd* **11/2**[3]

03 **7** *6* **Forever Vienna**[12] 3770 2-8-7 0 LeeTopliss(7) 1 —
(J Howard Johnson) *wnt lft s: chsd ldrs on wd outside: rdn along bef 1/2-way and sn wknd* **40/1**

006 **8** *1* **Key To The Motion (IRE)**[16] 3686 2-8-9 0 TonyCulhane 2 —
(P T Midgley) *in tch: rdn along 1/2-way and sn wknd* **20/1**

62.98 secs (-0.52) **Going Correction** -0.125s/f (Firm) 8 Ran SP% **113.2**
Speed ratings (Par 94): **99,98,96,86,81 76,67,65**
toteswingers:1&2:£11.10, 1&3:£1.80, 2&3:£7.60 CSF £55.62 TOTE £6.00: £2.60, £7.60, £1.30; EX 49.40.
Owner Mrs Margaret Forsyth **Bred** Mrs E Thompson **Trained** Hambleton, N Yorks

FOCUS
A run of the mill two-year-old claimer. The form is best viewed through the winner and third.

NOTEBOOK
Nellie Ellis(IRE), who took an identical event here two outings ago, had flopped in a seller at Leicester since. Weak in the market, she raced widest of the first three but knuckled down to see off the challenge of the runner-up. This is her grade. (op 3-1 tchd 9-2)
Red Gold And Green(IRE) ◆ showed bags of toe against the far side rail. His inexperience showed as he hung away from the fence but, to his credit, was coming back for more at the line. He looks sure to go one better in similar company. (op 12-1 tchd 10-1)
Saltergate, who is only small, lives on his nerves. He swerved badly when runner-up in a maiden here a week earlier. This time he moved up looking the likely winner but found little and was on the retreat at the line. He is proving very expensive to follow. (op 2-1 tchd 6-4)
My Lord, winner over 6f in selling company on his debut, had finished third over an extended 6f at Newbury where he ran very freely. After showing plenty of toe he fell in a heap and does not look to be progressing. (op 5-1)
Reel Amber is another seemingly going backwards. (op 10-1 tchd 9-1)
Press Release stood still when the stalls opened then ran far too freely before dropping right away. He is another to have reservations about now. Official explanation: jockey said colt missed the break (op 13-2 tchd 5-1)

4196 YORKSHIRE POST COMPETITION WINNER H'CAP — 1m 1f 207y
7:00 (7:00) (Class 5) (0-75,76) 3-Y-O+ **£3,238** (£963; £481; £240) **Stalls** High

Form RPR

-002 **1** **Solicitor**[4] 4056 3-9-5 **75** JoeFanning 3 91+
(M Johnston) *cl up: led 2f out: rdn clr appr fnl f: comf* **11/4**[2]

2111 **2** *7* **Marjury Daw (IRE)**[7] 3950 4-10-2 **76** 6ex PaulMulrennan 5 78
(J G Given) *led: rdn along and hdd 2f out: sn drvn and one pce fnl f* **5/2**[1]

0552 **3** *nk* **Snowed Under**[17] 3613 9-9-6 **73** LeeTopliss(7) 8 74
(J D Bethell) *trckd ldrs: hdwy over 2f out: rdn wl over 1f out: drvn and kpt on fnl f* **15/2**

064- **4** *1 1/4* **Helieorbea**[164] 6537 4-9-5 **70** LanceBetts(5) 1 69
(T D Easterby) *hld up in rr: hdwy over 2f out: rdn wl over 1f out: kpt on wl fnl f: nrst fin* **20/1**

5344 **5** *nse* **Veiled Applause**[33] 3089 7-10-0 **74** RoystonFfrench 6 72
(J J Quinn) *trckd ldng pair: effrt over 2f out: sn rdn and ch tl drvn and wknd over 1f out* **9/1**

1043 **6** *3/4* **General Tufto**[17] 3613 5-9-9 **74** (b) JamesSullivan(5) 2 71
(C Smith) *hld up in rr: hdwy over 2f out: rdn wl over 1f out: kpt on fnl f: nrst fin* **13/2**

46-4 **7** *1 1/4* **Autumn Harvest**[13] 3750 6-10-0 **74** SilvestreDeSousa 7 68
(G A Harker) *trckd ldrs: hdwy 4f out: rdn along over 2f out: drvn and wknd over 1f out* **5/1**[3]

0240 **8** *12* **Rub Of The Relic (IRE)**[6] 3978 5-8-13 **62** (be) PaulPickard(3) 4 32
(P T Midgley) *a in rr: bhd fnl 3f* **20/1**

2m 3.05s (-3.95) **Going Correction** -0.30s/f (Firm)
WFA 3 from 4yo+ 10lb 8 Ran SP% **116.5**
Speed ratings (Par 103): **103,97,97,96,96 95,94,84**
toteswingers:1&2:£2.30, 1&3:£8.30, 2&3:£2.20 CSF £10.32 CT £43.07 TOTE £4.30: £1.90, £1.10, £2.30; EX 8.20.
Owner Sheikh Hamdan Bin Mohammed Al Maktoum **Bred** Darley **Trained** Middleham Moor, N Yorks

FOCUS
A well contested 62-76 handicap but in the end a runaway, facile winner. They came stands' side in the home straight. The winner is rated in line with his early maiden promise.

4197 SKYBET SUPPORTING THE YORKSHIRE RACING SUMMER FESTIVAL H'CAP — 7f 100y
7:30 (7:31) (Class 5) (0-75,70) 3-Y-O+ **£4,533** (£1,348; £674; £336) **Stalls** High

Form RPR

6060 **1** **Seldom (IRE)**[40] 2850 4-9-2 **58** SilvestreDeSousa 6 68
(M Brittain) *in tch: hdwy 1/2-way to trck ldrs 1/2-way: effrt to ld 2f out: rdn and edgd lft over 1f out: drvn ins fnl f and kpt on gamely* **15/2**

1451 **2** *1 1/4* **Honest Broker (IRE)**[26] 3325 3-9-7 **70** JoeFanning 7 74
(M Johnston) *hld up towards rr: hdwy 1/2-way: effrt 2f out: sn rdn to chal: edgd lft and ev ch over 1f out tl drvn and no ex towards fin* **10/3**[2]

0601 **3** *3 1/2* **Stonehaugh (IRE)**[16] 3659 7-9-7 **70** (t) LeeTopliss(7) 5 68
(J Howard Johnson) *trckd ldng pair: hdwy 3f out: rdn and ch whn n.m.r and swtchd rt over 1f out: kpt on u.p ins fnl f* **6/1**[3]

1113 **4** *1 1/2* **Polish World (USA)**[14] 3732 6-9-11 **70** PaulPickard(3) 1 64
(P T Midgley) *led and set str pce: racd alone far rail in home st and rdn over 2f out: sn hdd and drvn: kpt on same pce* **15/8**[1]

4001 **5** *2 3/4* **Dhhamaan (IRE)**[12] 3774 5-8-11 **58** (b) JamesSullivan(5) 8 46
(Mrs R A Carr) *cl up: c wd to stands' rail in home st: rdn and ev ch 2f out: sn drvn and wknd over 1f out* **6/1**[3]

-402 **6** *2 3/4* **Quite Sparky**[19] 3554 3-9-7 **70** MickyFenton 4 48
(T P Tate) *in tch: hdwy 1/2-way: rdn to chse ldrs over 2f out: sn drvn and wknd wl over 1f out* **9/1**

5446 **7** *30* **Zephyron (IRE)**[88] 1490 3-8-11 **60** NickyMackay 3 —
(J R Holt) *a outpcd in rr: bhd fr 1/2-way* **28/1**

1m 31.06s (-2.74) **Going Correction** -0.30s/f (Firm)
WFA 3 from 4yo+ 7lb 7 Ran SP% **111.6**
Speed ratings (Par 103): **103,101,97,95,92 89,55**
toteswingers:1&2:£6.00, 1&3:£6.90, 2&3:£2.30 CSF £31.03 CT £157.09 TOTE £12.50: £7.50, £3.90; EX 45.10.
Owner Mel Brittain **Bred** Stephen Moloney **Trained** Warthill, N Yorks

FOCUS
A modest 60-70 handicap run at a breakneck pace and all but one runner elected to come to the stands' side in the home straight. The winner is rated back to something like his best.
Seldom(IRE) Official explanation: trainer's rep had no explanation for the apparent improvement in form

4198 CARL SKELTON HAPPY BIRTHDAY H'CAP — 1m 100y
8:00 (8:00) (Class 5) (0-75,77) 3-Y-O+ **£3,238** (£963; £481; £240) **Stalls** High

Form RPR

0331 **1** **Carlitos Spirit (IRE)**[3] 4082 6-8-9 **60** (v) LeeTopliss(7) 3 68
(I W McInnes) *t.k.h early: trckd ldrs: racd alone on far rail st: cl up and rdn 2f out: drvn over 1f out: styd on to ld last 100yds* **2/1**[2]

0651 **2** *1* **Shadowtime**[6] 3973 5-10-5 **77** 6ex AndrewMullen 4 83
(Miss Tracy Waggott) *t.k.h early: trckd ldng pair: hdwy on inner to ld 1/2-way: c wd st: rdn over 2f out: drvn over 1f out: hdd and no ex last 100yds* **15/8**[1]

4616 **3** *hd* **Raleigh Quay (IRE)**[9] 3905 3-9-6 **72** PaulMulrennan 5 75
(Micky Hammond) *hld up: hdwy 3f out: rdn along 2f out: drvn to chal ent fnl f: kpt on* **10/1**

6604 **4** *1 1/4* **Ra Junior (USA)**[3] 4094 4-9-8 **71** BillyCray(5) 2 73
(D Nicholls) *cl up: rdn along and outpcd over 3f out: styd on u.p appr fnl f* **12/1**

0031 **5** *nse* **Baltimore Jack (IRE)**[16] 3690 6-10-0 **72** DanielTudhope 6 74
(T D Walford) *led: to 1/2-way: cl up: rdn over 2f out: drvn over 1f out and ev ch tl same pce ins fnl f* **6/1**

-000 **6** *1* **Muftarres (IRE)**[29] 3239 5-9-12 **70** TonyCulhane 1 70
(P T Midgley) *hld up: hdwy on outer 1/2-way: cl up over 2f out: sn rdn and ch tl drvn and wknd over 1f out* **5/1**[3]

1m 44.76s (-2.84) **Going Correction** -0.30s/f (Firm)
WFA 3 from 4yo+ 8lb 6 Ran SP% **115.9**
Speed ratings (Par 103): **102,101,100,99,99 98**
toteswingers:1&2:£1.40, 1&3:£1.60, 2&3:£4.80 CSF £6.48 TOTE £3.40: £2.30, £2.00; EX 4.20.
Owner Wold Construction Company **Bred** Tally-Ho Stud **Trained** Catwick, E Yorks

FOCUS
A 60-77 handicap and, despite the presence of two front-runners, the pace was not strong. All bar one came to the stands' side in the home straight, the exception being the winner, who did not need to match his Hamilton form.

4199 YORKSHIRE RADIO H'CAP — 5f
8:30 (8:30) (Class 5) (0-75,72) 3-Y-O+ **£3,238** (£963; £481; £240) **Stalls** High

Form RPR

-600 **1** **Caranbola**[52] 2504 4-9-2 **62** SilvestreDeSousa 3 70
(M Brittain) *a.p: swtchd lft and hdwy over 1f out: sn rdn to chal: drvn to ld ins fnl f: jst hld on* **5/1**[3]

1163 **2** *shd* **Ryedane (IRE)**[16] 3664 8-9-3 **68** (b) LanceBetts(5) 5 76
(T D Easterby) *led 1f: cl up: rdn to ld again over 1f out: drvn and hdd ins fnl f: rallied towards fin: jst hld* **5/1**[3]

1214 **3** *1 1/4* **Silvanus (IRE)**[16] 3687 5-9-8 **68** PaulMulrennan 8 71
(P T Midgley) *trckd ldrs: effrt 2f out: sn rdn and ev ch tl drvn and one pce wl ins fnl f* **5/1**[3]

1550 **4** *3 1/4* **Chosen One (IRE)**[26] 3321 5-9-3 **68** JamesSullivan(5) 2 59
(Mrs R A Carr) *cl up: led after 1f: rdn over 2f out: hdd over 1f out: wknd* **4/1**[2]

-003 **5** *nk* **Liberty Ship**[10] 3879 5-9-5 **65** (bt) JoeFanning 1 55
(J D Bethell) *wnt lft s: hld up in rr: hdwy wl over 1f out: sn rdn and btn ent fnl f* **10/3**[1]

01- **6** *3/4* **Mission Impossible**[257] 7241 5-8-9 **55** AndrewMullen 7 43
(Miss Tracy Waggott) *chsd ldrs: rdn along wl over 1f out: sn wknd* **12/1**

2545 **7** *3 1/4* **Select Committee**[16] 3660 5-9-8 **68** (v) RoystonFfrench 6 44
(J J Quinn) *dwlt: in tch: effrt over 2f out: sn rdn and wknd over 1f out* **6/1**

62.40 secs (-1.10) **Going Correction** -0.125s/f (Firm) 7 Ran SP% **115.1**
Speed ratings (Par 103): **103,102,100,95,95 93,88**
toteswingers:1&2:£16.00, 1&3:£8.60, 2&3:£1.10 CSF £30.22 CT £131.14 TOTE £7.20: £2.60, £3.20; EX 47.20.
Owner Mel Brittain **Bred** T E Pocock **Trained** Warthill, N Yorks

FOCUS
A modest 55-68 sprint handicap. They all raced towards the far side at the 2f marker but in the end they were spread right across the track with the winner hard under the stands' side rail. Fairly sound form.
Liberty Ship Official explanation: trainer had no explanation for the poor form shown

4200 BEVERLEY BNI MEETS AT THE RACECOURSE MAIDEN H'CAP — 2m 35y
9:00 (9:01) (Class 6) (0-65,65) 3-Y-O **£2,590** (£770; £385; £192) **Stalls** High

Form RPR

-265 **1** **Escape Artist**[17] 3626 3-8-7 **51** ow1 (t) RobertWinston 8 54
(T D Easterby) *t.k.h: trckd ldrs: hdwy to trck ldr 1/2-way: chal over 2f out: rdn wl over 1f out: drvn to ld and edgd rt ins fnl f: kpt on* **15/8**[2]

66-4 **2** *nk* **Leopard Hills (IRE)**[49] 2606 3-9-7 **65** PaulMulrennan 2 68
(J Howard Johnson) *led: wd st: rdn along and jnd over 2f out: drvn over 1f out: hdd and bmpd ins fnl f: no ex nr fin* **8/1**

055P **3** *4* **Light The City (IRE)**[5] 4015 3-7-11 **46** oh1 JamesSullivan(5) 9 44
(Mrs R A Carr) *plld hrd: in tch: hdwy over 3f out: rdn to chse ldng pair 2f out: drvn and no imp fnl f* **16/1**

-006 **4** *hd* **Lava Lamp (GER)**[5] 4017 3-9-7 **65** (v) PaddyAspell 4 63
(G A Harker) *hld up and bhd: hdwy 3f out: rdn wl over 1f out: kpt on ins fnl f: nrst fin* **22/1**

0-23 **5** *2 3/4* **Consult**[6] 3996 3-8-1 **50** [1] RosieJessop(5) 7 44
(Sir Mark Prescott) *unruly in stalls: hld up towards rr: hdwy on inner 5f out: rdn to chse ldrs over 2f out: sn no imp* **7/4**[1]

0-00 **6** *1/2* **Amylyn**[32] 3116 3-8-2 **46** oh1 NickyMackay 6 40
(J R Holt) *trckd ldrs: rdn along over 3f out: drvn 2f out and kpt on same pce* **50/1**

5003 **7** *15* **Henry Havelock**[21] 3506 3-8-5 **56** LeeTopliss(7) 3 32
(C Grant) *trckd ldrs tl rn wd bnd after 6f: sn in tch on outer tl rdn along 3f out and sn wknd* **6/1**[3]

00-5 **8** *30* **Kwami Biscuit**[27] 3282 3-8-2 **46** oh1 SilvestreDeSousa 1 —
(G A Harker) *plld hrd: chsd ldrs: rdn along over 3f out and sn wknd* **16/1**

000 **9** *4* **Farmer Palmer**[44] 2754 3-8-0 **49** oh1 ow3 BillyCray(5) 5 —
(Louise Best) *a in rr: bhd fnl 3f* **12/1**

3m 42.13s (2.33) **Going Correction** -0.30s/f (Firm) 9 Ran SP% **122.3**
Speed ratings (Par 98): **82,81,79,79,78 78,70,55,53**
toteswingers:1&2:£2.30, 1&3:£10.50, 2&3:£20.30 CSF £19.04 CT £196.53 TOTE £2.80: £1.10, £1.60, £6.00; EX 12.20 Place 6 £63.46; Place 5 £46.81.
Owner Habtons Baggie Rams **Bred** Sarah J Leigh And Robin S Leigh **Trained** Great Habton, N Yorks
■ Stewards' Enquiry : Robert Winston one-day ban: used whip with excessive frequency (Aug 2)

FOCUS
The pace was funereal until the final half-mile and the first two were one-two from soon after the halfway mark. Muddling form which may not prove that solid.
Amylyn Official explanation: jockey said filly failed to handle bottom bend

Kwami Biscuit Official explanation: jockey said gelding ran too free
T/Plt: £94.80 to a £1 stake. Pool:£59,502.72 - 94.80 winning tickets T/Qpdt: £36.10 to a £1 stake. Pool:£4,431.60 - 90.70 winning tickets JR

3958 WINDSOR (R-H)

Monday, July 19

OFFICIAL GOING: Good to firm (watered; 8.1)
Stands' rail dolled out 6yds at 6f and 1yd at winning post. Top bend dolled out 9yds from innermost line, adding 24yds to races of one mile and over.
Wind: Light, across Weather: Fine, very warm

4201 FOOTBALL FURLONG 8TH AUGUST H'CAP — 1m 2f 7y
6:10 (6:11) (Class 5) (0-70,70) 3-Y-0+ £2,593 (£765; £383) Stalls Low

Form RPR
5-23 **1** **Urban Space**[10] 3848 4-9-5 **66** KierenFox(5) 7 79
(J L Flint) *hld up towards rr: gd prog towards outer fr over 2f out: led jst over 1f out: rdn clr* 9/2[2]
3530 **2** 2 ½ **Choral Festival**[10] 3862 4-9-2 **58** (v) NeilChalmers 5 66
(J J Bridger) *hld up in last trio: pushed along and gd prog over 2f out: hanging but styd on to take 2nd ins fnl f* 10/1
2-04 **3** nk **Recalcitrant**[19] 3559 7-8-12 **59** SimonPearce(5) 10 66
(S Dow) *pressed ldr: led after 4f: kicked on 3f out: edgd lft and hdd jst over 1f out: sn btn* 12/1
-052 **4** ¾ **Sweet Secret**[17] 3628 3-8-10 **62** RichardHughes 16 68
(R Hannon) *trckd ldng trio: rdn to dispute 2nd 2f out: nt qckn sn after: kpt on fnl f* 3/1[1]
650 **5** shd **First In The Queue (IRE)**[39] 2888 3-9-1 **67** LiamKeniry 14 72+
(S Kirk) *hld up: 10th over 4f out: stuck bhd rivals over 2f out and dropped to last pair: swtchd lft over 1f out: rdn and r.o fnl f: nvr nr ldrs* 9/1
2000 **6** ¾ **Diamond Twister (USA)**[9] 3911 4-9-4 **60** SteveDrowne 8 64
(J R Best) *wl in tch: rdn and nt qckn on outer over 2f out: one pce after* 14/1
04 **7** 1 **Shooting Party (IRE)**[27] 3294 4-9-6 **65** PatrickHills(3) 3 67
(R Hannon) *hld up in last trio: drvn on wd outside 3f out: kpt on: n.d* 12/1
06-0 **8** hd **Mt Kintyre (IRE)**[10] 3862 4-9-9 **65** SamHitchcott 12 66
(M R Channon) *t.k.h: hld up bhd ldrs: rdn to dispute 2nd 2f out: wknd over 1f out* 33/1
0-44 **9** 3 ¾ **Gwenllian (IRE)**[28] 3275 3-8-12 **64** JimCrowley 13 58
(Ian Williams) *trckd ldrs: 5th 4f out: lost pl and shkn up 3f out: grad fdd* 16/1
2603 **10** 2 ¼ **Full Victory (IRE)**[13] 3765 8-9-7 **63** DaneO'Neill 15 52
(R A Farrant) *hld up in midfield: no prog on inner over 2f out: wknd over 1f out* 10/1
0633 **11** nk **Orpen Wide (IRE)**[3] 4102 8-9-1 **60** (b) RobertLButler(3) 1 49
(M C Chapman) *mde most 4f: chsd ldr tl wknd over 2f out* 16/1
-000 **12** 3 ½ **Transfer**[19] 3559 5-9-2 **58** IanMongan 2 40
(C P Morlock) *towards rr: wd bnd 6f out and dropped to last trio: rdn and struggling over 3f out* 22/1
23-6 **13** 13 **No Mean Trick (USA)**[18] 3586 4-9-9 **70** JohnFahy(5) 9 26
(C G Cox) *chsd ldng pair: wknd rapidly u.p 3f out: t.o* 15/2[3]
1146 **P** **Sacrilege**[3] 4102 5-9-9 **70** (p) MarkCoumbe(5) 11 —
(M C Chapman) *ref to r in any meaningful fashion: t.o tl p.u 1/2-way* 25/1

2m 7.13s (-1.57) **Going Correction** -0.075s/f (Good)
WFA 3 from 4yo+ 10lb **14** Ran SP% **128.1**
Speed ratings (Par 103): **103,101,100,100,100 99,98,98,95,93 93,90,80,—**
toteswingers:1&2:£7.50, 1&3:£5.10, 2&3:£16.90 CSF £51.65 CT £529.84 TOTE £6.00: £2.50, £4.50, £2.90; EX 63.10 Trifecta £561.40 Part won. Pool: £758.74 - 0.65 winning units..
Owner Jason Tucker **Bred** Winterbeck Manor Stud **Trained** Kenfig Hill, Bridgend

FOCUS
Unsurprisingly on what was a warm day, the ground conditions had dried to good to form. A low-grade handicap which was sound run. Straightforward form.

4202 GOLDTEAM.CO.UK (S) STKS — 1m 3f 135y
6:40 (6:40) (Class 6) 3-Y-0+ £1,910 (£564; £282) Stalls Low

Form RPR
1111 **1** **Timocracy**[23] 3442 5-9-12 68 RyanMoore 5 71
(A B Haynes) *mde all: wound it up fr 4f out: drvn over 2f out: pressed 1f out: styd on gamely* 5/4[1]
/030 **2** 1 ¼ **Celtic Dragon**[10] 3865 5-9-7 65 (b) PatDobbs 8 64
(Mrs A J Perrett) *hld up in 7th: stdy prog to go 2nd 2f out: rdn to chal 1f out: nt qckn* 9/2[3]
0/0- **3** ¾ **Talenti (IRE)**[14] 1007 7-9-7 89 (t) DaneO'Neill 7 63
(Mrs Lawney Hill) *s.i.s: rousted along and prog to go 2nd 8f out to 4f out: sn rdn: struggling in 4th 2f out: styd on again fnl f* 5/2[2]
6040 **4** 1 ¼ **Pennfield Pirate**[36] 3002 3-8-9 55 SteveDrowne 2 60
(H Morrison) *chsd wnr to 8f out and fr 4f out to 2f out: one pce u.p* 16/1
5 3 ¾ **Vacario (GER)**[54] 6-9-7 0 (t) EddieAhern 1 54
(Mark Gillard) *s.i.s: settled in 8th: rdn and effrt over 3f out: no imp 2f out: fdd* 16/1
0005 **6** 7 **Brave Ghurka**[12] 3788 3-8-9 50 LiamKeniry 3 42
(S Kirk) *hld up in last: rdn over 3f out: no prog over 2f out* 33/1
4004 **7** 12 **Land Of Plenty (IRE)**[11] 3820 3-7-11 41 RyanPowell(7) 6 17
(Jamie Poulton) *wl in tch: effrt and cl enough over 3f out: wknd rapidly over 2f out: t.o* 50/1
006- **8** 9 **Rockson (IRE)**[212] 7818 4-9-2 44 JimCrowley 4 —
(Ian Williams) *t.k.h: hld up bhd ldrs: clsd looking dangerous 4f out: wknd rapidly 3f out: t.o* 25/1
45-2 **9** 1 ½ **Alrafid (IRE)**[27] 237 11-9-7 60 (b) GeorgeBaker 9 —
(G L Moore) *prom tl wknd 4f out: sn t.o* 16/1

2m 29.88s (0.38) **Going Correction** -0.075s/f (Good)
WFA 3 from 4yo+ 12lb **9** Ran SP% **117.6**
Speed ratings (Par 101): **95,94,93,92,90 85,77,71,70**
toteswingers:1&2:£2.00, 1&3:£1.60, 2&3:£3.50 CSF £7.35 TOTE £2.30: £1.10, £1.80, £1.10; EX 7.30 Trifecta £19.90 Pool: £1,463.42 - 54.36 winning units..The winner was bought in for 5,600gns. Celtic Dragon was claimed by Mr P. D. Evans for £6,000.
Owner Ms C Berry **Bred** Gainsborough Stud Management Ltd **Trained** Limpley Stoke, Bath

FOCUS
Not the most competitive of sellers.

Alrafid(IRE) Official explanation: jockey said gelding had no more to give

4203 E B F SPORTINGBET.COM MAIDEN FILLIES' STKS — 6f
7:10 (7:12) (Class 4) 2-Y-0 £4,533 (£1,348; £674; £336) Stalls High

Form RPR
2522 **1** **Whisper Louise (IRE)**[33] 3087 2-9-0 0 LiamKeniry 9 84+
(Mrs P Sly) *a gng wl: trckd ldrs: led over 1f out: pushed clr* 7/2[2]
22 **2** 5 **Mama Lulu (USA)**[29] 3237 2-9-0 0 HayleyTurner 14 69
(M L W Bell) *dwlt but sn led: hdd and edgd lft over 1f out: no ch w wnr* 2/1[1]
3 **3** ¾ **Golden Tempest (IRE)**[21] 3509 2-9-0 0 ShaneKelly 3 67
(W R Swinburn) *wnt lft s: t.k.h: hld up in tch: prog 1/2-way: cl up over 1f out: outpcd after* 13/2
3 **4** ¾ **Out Of The Storm**[12] 3778 2-9-0 0 TomQueally 8 65
(S Dow) *t.k.h early and hld up in midfield: pushed along 1/2-way: no prog tl styd on fnl f: nrst fin* 16/1
02 **5** hd **Silver Show (IRE)**[11] 3817 2-9-0 0 ChrisCatlin 7 64
(M R Channon) *pressed ldr: rdn 2f out: cl enough over 1f out: outpcd* 33/1
6 hd **Chokurei (IRE)** 2-9-0 0 PhilipRobinson 4 64
(C G Cox) *chsd ldrs on outer: shkn up 2f out: cl enough over 1f out: outpcd after* 33/1
7 2 ½ **Miss Sinatra (IRE)** 2-9-0 0 MartinDwyer 2 56+
(B J Meehan) *dwlt and hmpd s: wl bhd in last pair: prog fr 2f out: styd on: nrst fin* 33/1
8 ½ **Days Of Summer (IRE)** 2-9-0 0 JimCrowley 13 55
(R M Beckett) *pressed ldr: shkn up and upsides 2f out: wknd over 1f out* 11/2[3]
6 **9** 1 ½ **Bilidn**[24] 3392 2-9-0 0 AhmedAjtebi 12 50
(C E Brittain) *chsd ldrs and wl in tch: shkn up over 2f out: hanging and wknd over 1f out* 50/1
0 **10** 2 ½ **Make My Mark (IRE)**[18] 3590 2-8-11 0 MartinLane(3) 16 43
(Pat Eddery) *wl off the pce in last quartet: effrt 2f out: no prog* 66/1
0 **11** 1 ½ **Boogie Down (IRE)**[18] 3590 2-9-0 0 AdamKirby 5 38
(W R Swinburn) *sn off the pce in last quartet: pushed along 2f out: no prog* 33/1
12 hd **Ninfea (IRE)** 2-9-0 0 JamesDoyle 10 37
(S Kirk) *dwlt: wl in rr: rn v green and wandered arnd 2f out: no ch* 66/1
13 9 **Tweenie (IRE)** 2-9-0 0 RyanMoore 11 10
(R Hannon) *dwlt: a wl bhd* 14/1
66 **14** 4 ½ **Cheers**[7] 3959 2-9-0 0 RichardHughes 15 —
(R Hannon) *chsd ldrs and in tch: pushed along over 2f out: wknd and eased over 1f out: t.o* 8/1

1m 12.25s (-0.75) **Going Correction** -0.175s/f (Firm) **14** Ran SP% **124.6**
Speed ratings (Par 93): **98,91,90,89,89 88,85,84,82,79 77,77,65,59**
toteswingers:1&2:£1.40, 1&3:£4.90, 2&3:£2.60 CSF £10.79 TOTE £4.60: £1.80, £1.60, £2.10; EX 11.10 Trifecta £38.00 Pool: £1,488.73 - 29.94 winning units..
Owner G A Libson **Bred** Tom Twomey **Trained** Thorney, Cambs

FOCUS
An ordinary fillies' maiden dominated by those at the head of the market. The winner appeared to improve but there seemed no fluke and she could rate higher. The third helps to underpin the level.

NOTEBOOK
Whisper Louise(IRE), second on three of her four previous starts, including over 5f at Ripon last time, had no trouble with the return to 6f, leading well over 1f out and staying on to draw right away close home. On this evidence she will have no trouble with 7f and there may be more to come. (op 10-3 tchd 4-1and 11-4 in a place)
Mama Lulu(USA) has now finished second on all three starts, being a beaten favourite on each occasion. Her finishing effort wasn't the strongest, considering she has already run over 7f, and it would come as no surprise to see the headgear fitted at some stage. (op 5-2 tchd 3-1 and 11-4 in a place)
Golden Tempest(IRE), third over 5f at the course on her debut, was keen under restraint, but did stay on to reach the places. She may be more of a nursery type. (op 6-1 tchd 7-1)
Out Of The Storm, an eyecatcher on her debut, was again noted doing her best work late, just getting up for fourth. Her dam was a winner up to 1m2f, and there is staying blood in the family, so expect her to be winning races once granted a stiffer test. Official explanation: jockey said filly was denied a clear run
Silver Show(IRE) was soon prominent and ran well. She should so better in nurseries. (op 40-1)
Chokurei(IRE), nothing special on breeding, made a promising enough debut without suggesting she's a winner in waiting.
Miss Sinatra(IRE) got behind having been hampered, but did stay on well late in the day. Official explanation: jockey said filly ran green (op 40-1)
Days Of Summer(IRE), whose dam has produced numerous winners, was nicely backed beforehand and appeared to know her job, but the finishing effort left a bit to be desired. She may improve, but needs to. (op 10-1)
Ninfea(IRE) Official explanation: jockey said filly hung right
Tweenie(IRE) Official explanation: jockey said filly never travelled
Cheers Official explanation: jockey said filly lost its action

4204 SPORTINGBET.COM H'CAP — 6f
7:40 (7:41) (Class 4) (0-85,85) 3-Y-0 £4,857 (£1,445; £722; £360) Stalls High

Form RPR
-321 **1** **Poppy Seed**[30] 3210 3-9-4 **82** RichardHughes 2 93
(R Hannon) *hld up in tch: prog on outer over 2f out: led wl over 1f out: jnd fnl f: drvn and hld on wl* 5/2[1]
5514 **2** hd **R Woody**[17] 3638 3-9-1 **79** TomQueally 4 89
(D K Ivory) *settled in rr: prog fr 1/2-way on outer: drvn 2f out: clsd on ldng pair 1f out: swtchd lft ins fnl f: styd on to take 2nd nr fin: jst failed* 12/1
-121 **3** nk **Addictive Dream (IRE)**[33] 3085 3-9-7 **85** ShaneKelly 1 94
(W R Swinburn) *hld up towards rr: prog on outer over 2f out: drvn to chal and upsides fnl f: jst hld and lost 2nd last strides* 11/4[2]
341- **4** 2 ½ **Pan American**[225] 7655 3-8-13 **77** FergusSweeney 6 78
(P J Makin) *w ldng pair: upsides 2f out: nt qckn over 1f out: one pce* 25/1
-100 **5** hd **Felsham**[12] 3779 3-8-12 **76** DaneO'Neill 3 76
(H Candy) *hld up in last pair: rdn and prog on outer fr 1/2-way: plugged on fr over 1f out: n.d* 12/1
5-12 **6** 1 **Pose (IRE)**[26] 3328 3-8-11 **75** RyanMoore 9 72
(R Hannon) *pushed along in last pair 1/2-way: swtchd to wd outside over 1f out: kpt on: n.d* 8/1[3]
-502 **7** 1 ½ **Planet Red (IRE)**[42] 2807 3-9-7 **85** PatDobbs 11 77
(R Hannon) *trckd ldng trio: shkn up and grad fdd fr 2f out* 11/1
-453 **8** ¾ **Danny's Choice**[30] 3225 3-9-5 **83** JimCrowley 12 73
(R M Beckett) *racd against nr side rail: w ldr to 2f out: wknd* 12/1
6023 **9** nk **Nubar Boy**[9] 3899 3-8-6 **73** (v) MartinLane(3) 5 62
(P D Evans) *stdd s: hld up towards rr: gng wl 1/2-way: shkn up and no rspnse wl over 1f out* 20/1

051 **10** 2 3/4 **Hairspray**[11] 3815 3-9-3 81 ChrisCatlin 7 61
(M R Channon) *mde most to wl over 1f out: wknd* **9/1**

0-00 **11** 1 **Pictures (IRE)**[18] 3592 3-8-6 70 NeilChalmers 10 47
(J J Bridger) *in tch on inner: shkn up and no prog over 2f out: sn btn* **50/1**

0-00 **12** 1 1/4 **Goodwood Maestro**[46] 2682 3-8-10 74 EddieAhern 8 47
(J L Dunlop) *trckd ldrs: jst pushed along over 2f out: lost pl over 1f out: eased* **12/1**

1m 11.52s (-1.48) **Going Correction** -0.175s/f (Firm) 12 Ran SP% **126.0**
Speed ratings (Par 102): **102,101,101,98,97 96,94,93,93,89 88,86**
toteswingers:1&2:£16.10, 1&3:£1.40, 2&3:£7.70 CSF £35.70 CT £93.95 TOTE £3.70: £1.70, £3.90, £1.70; EX 57.80 Trifecta £329.60 Pool: £944.45 - 2.12 winning units..
Owner Lady Whent **Bred** Raffin Bloodstock **Trained** East Everleigh, Wilts

FOCUS
A competitive enough sprint handicap.

4205 THYSSENKRUPP AEROSPACE MAIDEN STKS 1m 2f 7y
8:10 (8:11) (Class 5) 3-4-Y-O **£2,593** (£765; £383) **Stalls** Low

Form RPR

4-3 **1** **Blissful Moment (USA)**[23] 3428 3-9-3 0 RyanMoore 13 92
(Sir Michael Stoute) *pressed ldr: shkn up over 3f out: determined chal fr over 2f out: narrow ld ins fnl f: drvn out* **2/1**[1]

34-0 **2** nk **Lunar Victory (USA)**[96] 1314 3-9-3 83 WilliamBuick 12 91
(J H M Gosden) *led: racd against rail and pressed fr 3f out: hrd rdn over 1f out: narrowly hdd ins fnl f: r.o* **9/2**[3]

4 **3** 8 **Pearl Huntsman (USA)**[50] 2564 3-9-3 0 TomQueally 11 75
(J Noseda) *trckd ldng pair: rdn and cl enough jst over 2f out: hd high and sn lft bhd* **4/1**[2]

6 **4** 5 **Silver Colors (USA)**[38] 2925 3-8-12 0 ShaneKelly 6 60
(J Noseda) *dwlt: rcvrd to chse ldrs in abt 6th: outpcd fr 3f out* **20/1**

3 **5** 2 1/2 **Pedantic**[52] 2496 3-9-3 0 J-PGuillambert 1 60
(L M Cumani) *trckd ldng pair: rdn over 3f out: wl outpcd fr over 2f out* **9/2**[3]

64 **6** 4 1/2 **Byrd In Hand (IRE)**[38] 2925 3-9-3 0 NeilChalmers 7 51
(J J Bridger) *trckd ldrs in abt 5th: pushed along and wl outpcd fr 3f out* **14/1**

0 **7** 2 1/4 **Proud Tuscan**[65] 2121 3-9-0 0 RussKennemore(3) 14 47
(J S Moore) *in tch in midfield: wl outpcd fr 3f out* **80/1**

8 shd **Hoodie (IRE)** 3-9-3 0 TadhgO'Shea 3 46
(Saeed Bin Suroor) *s.s: rcvrd into midfield by 1/2-way: wl outpcd fr 3f out* **15/2**

9 1 3/4 **Crystal Celebre (IRE)** 4-9-13 0 DaneO'Neill 2 43
(H Candy) *dwlt: hld up last: wl bhd fr 4f out: passed a few stragglers fnl f* **33/1**

6 **10** 3/4 **Penshurst Lad (IRE)**[28] 3272 3-9-3 0 JimCrowley 10 41
(R T Phillips) *a in last quartet: wl bhd fr 4f out* **50/1**

11 3 1/2 **Stuff Of Legends** 3-8-12 0 LiamKeniry 9 29
(H J L Dunlop) *s.s: a wl in rr: bhd fnl 4f* **66/1**

00 **12** 15 **Queen Ranavola (USA)**[5] 4028 3-8-12 0 SteveDrowne 5 —
(J R Best) *a in last quartet: wl bhd fr 4f out: t.o* **80/1**

2m 6.74s (-1.96) **Going Correction** -0.075s/f (Good)
WFA 3 from 4yo 10lb 12 Ran SP% **121.8**
Speed ratings (Par 103): **104,103,97,93,91 87,85,85,84,83 81,69**
toteswingers:1&2:£3.20, 1&3:£4.80, 2&3:£3.10 CSF £11.00 TOTE £3.70: £1.50, £1.60, £1.90; EX 10.50 Trifecta £31.30 Pool: £619.27 - 14.60 winning units..
Owner Saeed Suhail **Bred** Greenwood Farm Inc **Trained** Newmarket, Suffolk
■ Stewards' Enquiry : William Buick one-day ban: used whip without giving colt time to respond (Aug 2)

FOCUS
Not the strongest of maidens but the front two pulled 8l clear and are useful. The form is rated around the runner-up and is pretty solid.

4206 RONNIE SCOTT'S 50TH ANNIVERSARY H'CAP 1m 67y
8:40 (8:40) (Class 5) (0-75,75) 3-Y-0+ **£2,729** (£806; £403) **Stalls** High

Form RPR

0130 **1** **Kilburn**[12] 3782 6-9-10 71 (p) SteveDrowne 4 79
(A J Lidderdale) *pushed up to ld: rdn over 2f out: kpt on wl fr over 1f out* **8/1**

50-2 **2** 3/4 **Petomic (IRE)**[22] 3473 5-9-1 62 TadhgO'Shea 1 68
(M Hill) *t.k.h early: chsd wnr: rdn to chal 2f out: nt qckn and hld fnl f* **9/1**

0-22 **3** 1 3/4 **Patavium Prince (IRE)**[15] 3716 7-9-12 73 DaneO'Neill 11 75
(Miss Jo Crowley) *chsd ldng pair: rdn over 2f out: kpt on same pce: no imp fnl f* **16/1**

3532 **4** 1 3/4 **My Best Bet**[7] 3962 4-10-0 75 TomQueally 10 73+
(Stef Higgins) *hld up in last pair: swtchd to inner 3f out and outer 2f out: drvn and styd on: nt rch ldrs* **3/1**[2]

0521 **5** shd **Our Drama Queen (IRE)**[10] 3866 3-9-3 72 RichardHughes 3 70+
(R Hannon) *hld up in 7th: tried to make prog on inner over 2f out: styd on fnl f: nt rch ldrs* **6/4**[1]

2005 **6** 1 **Fawley Green**[17] 3638 3-9-3 72 EddieAhern 6 67
(W R Muir) *chsd ldng trio: rdn 3f out: no imp 2f out: fdd* **28/1**

43-0 **7** 2 1/4 **Serious Drinking (USA)**[45] 2718 4-9-6 67 ShaneKelly 9 57
(W R Swinburn) *hld up in 5th: rdn and no imp over 2f out: fdd* **20/1**

5/00 **8** 2 1/4 **Acheekyone (IRE)**[19] 3558 7-9-4 70 JohnFahy(5) 2 55
(B J Meehan) *hld up in last trio: rdn over 2f out: no prog* **14/1**

1000 **9** shd **Durham Town (IRE)**[5] 4022 3-8-8 63 MartinDwyer 7 48
(D K Ivory) *hld up in 8th: rdn over 3f out: no prog* **22/1**

6400 **10** 1/2 **Straight Face (IRE)**[12] 3774 6-9-1 62 (v) CathyGannon 5 46
(P D Evans) *chsd ldrs in 6th: rdn over 3f out: sn struggling and lost pl* **50/1**

-230 **11** 1 **Saturn Way (GR)**[24] 3412 4-9-11 72 LiamKeniry 8 53
(P R Chamings) *hld up last: nt asked for effrt whn hmpd wl over 2f out: no ch after* **11/2**[3]

1m 44.27s (-0.43) **Going Correction** -0.075s/f (Good)
WFA 3 from 4yo+ 8lb 11 Ran SP% **128.6**
Speed ratings (Par 103): **99,98,96,94,94 93,91,89,89,88 87**
toteswingers:1&2:£19.80, 1&3:£43.70, 2&3:£11.10 CSF £81.49 CT £1172.55 TOTE £10.30: £2.70, £3.20, £5.80; EX 101.90 Trifecta £569.10 Part won. Pool: £769.13 - 0.10 winning units. Place 6 £55.75; Place 5 £13.58.
Owner Royal Windsor Racing Club **Bred** B Walters **Trained** Eastbury, Berks

FOCUS
Just a moderate handicap.
T/Plt: £69.70 to a £1 stake. Pool:£102,251.45 - 1,069.61 winning tickets T/Qpdt: £27.80 to a £1 stake. Pool:£7,606.26 - 202.20 winning tickets JN

3991 YARMOUTH (L-H)
Monday, July 19

OFFICIAL GOING: Good to firm (watered; 7.9)
Wind: light, against Weather: warm and muggy

4207 INJURED JOCKEYS FUND MEDIAN AUCTION MAIDEN STKS 1m 1f
2:15 (2:20) (Class 6) 3-5-Y-O **£2,266** (£674; £337; £168) **Stalls** Low

Form RPR

4-5 **1** **Knotgarden (IRE)**[23] 3437 4-9-7 0 PatCosgrave 2 70
(J R Fanshawe) *chsd ldrs tl hdwy to ld over 3f out: hanging rt u.p fr 2f out: hrd pressed ent fnl f: kpt on u.p: jst hld on* **7/2**[3]

3 **2** shd **My Manikato**[56] 2401 3-9-3 0 KierenFallon 6 74+
(L M Cumani) *dwlt: sn rcvrd and in tch in midfield: pushed and wanting to hang lft fr 4f out: chsd ldng pair over 2f out: one pce and looked wl hld tl styd on fnl 75yds: pressing wnr cl home: jst hld* **2/1**[2]

43 **3** nk **Tariq Too**[38] 2925 3-9-3 0 NeilCallan 7 73
(D M Simcock) *hld up in tch in last pair: hdwy on outer to chse ldr ent fnl 2f: ev ch ent fnl f: hrd rdn and nt qckn ins fnl f: lost 2nd towards fin* **15/8**[1]

4 1 **Personified (GER)** 3-8-12 0 EddieAhern 3 66
(E F Vaughan) *in tch in midfield: effrt over 2f out: chsd ldrs and pushed along over 2f out: hanging lft fr wl over 1f out: kpt on same pce fnl f* **14/1**

5 1 **Herculean** 3-9-3 0 LiamJones 1 69
(W J Haggas) *dwlt: sn wl in tch in last pair: hdwy on inner 3f out: chsng ldrs whn short of room wl over 1f out: styd on same pce fr over 1f out* **10/1**

50- **6** 5 **Sleepy Dove**[249] 7361 5-9-4 0 MichaelStainton(3) 5 53?
(M E Sowersby) *led: rdn and hdd over 3f out: wkng whn bumping match w rival 2f out: sn bhd* **150/1**

0 **7** 8 **Jenny Dawson (IRE)**[22] 3484 4-9-7 0 IvaMilickova 8 35?
(John Berry) *chsd ldr tl ent fnl 4f: sn dropped out: wl bhd fnl 2f* **100/1**

1m 55.22s (-0.58) **Going Correction** -0.225s/f (Firm)
WFA 3 from 4yo+ 9lb 7 Ran SP% **107.7**
Speed ratings (Par 101): **93,92,92,91,90 86,79**
toteswingers:1&2:£1.90, 1&3:£1.40, 2&3:£1.40 CSF £9.60 TOTE £5.80: £3.40, £1.10; EX 10.80 Trifecta £18.00 Pool: £608.07 - 24.93 winning units..
Owner Dr Catherine Wills **Bred** St Clare Hall Stud **Trained** Newmarket, Suffolk
■ Stewards' Enquiry : Kieren Fallon one-day ban: used whip down shoulder in the forehand (Aug 2)

FOCUS
A modest maiden featuring late-maturing horses. They went an ordinary gallop and there was a bunched finish, so the form should be treated with a degree of caution. That said, it makes sense amongst the principals.
Personified(GER) Official explanation: jockey said filly was denied a clear run

4208 PLEASUREWOOD HILLS AMUSEMENT MEDIAN AUCTION MAIDEN STKS 7f 3y
2:45 (2:46) (Class 6) 2-Y-O **£2,266** (£674; £337; £168) **Stalls** High

Form RPR

36 **1** **Highlife Dancer**[11] 3832 2-9-3 0 AlanMunro 9 74
(M R Channon) *in tch: hdwy to trck ldrs ent fnl 2f: rdn to chal ent fnl f: led fnl 100yds: edgd lft after: r.o wl* **6/1**[3]

03 **2** 3/4 **Sixty Roses (IRE)**[44] 2740 2-8-12 0 EddieAhern 6 67
(J L Dunlop) *led tl hdd and pushed along 2f out: stl ev ch ins fnl f: one pce fnl 100yds* **2/1**[1]

3 nse **Timothy T** 2-9-3 0 SebSanders 10 72
(M Botti) *chsd ldr tl pushed into ld 2f out: rdn over 1f out: hdd and no ex fnl 100yds: lost 2nd on post* **15/2**

4 **4** 1/2 **Piccarello**[18] 3602 2-9-3 0 DarryllHolland 7 71
(M H Tompkins) *in tch: pushed along and outpcd ent fnl 2f: hdwy and edging lft ent fnl f: keeping on wl at fin: nt rch ldrs* **22/1**

50 **5** nk **Titus Two (IRE)**[41] 2839 2-9-3 0 RichardMullen 3 70
(P W Chapple-Hyam) *chsd ldrs: rdn and effrt wl over 1f out: keeping on same pce whn n.m.r briefly ins fnl f: no imp after* **7/1**

32 **6** 4 1/2 **A Little Bit Dusty**[24] 3399 2-8-12 0 MatthewDavies(5) 2 59
(W G M Turner) *chsd ldrs: rdn over 2f out: wknd u.p over 1f out* **7/2**[2]

2 **7** 9 **Alantina**[67] 2041 2-9-3 0 DavidProbert 4 36
(J R Jenkins) *t.k.h early: in tch tl rdn and struggling ent fnl 2f: wl btn over 1f out* **33/1**

8 15 **Beating Harmony** 2-9-3 0 PatCosgrave 5 —
(J R Fanshawe) *dwlt: in tch in rr tl rdn and struggling 1/2-way: lost tch over 2f out: t.o over 1f out* **16/1**

9 11 **Coeur (USA)** 2-8-12 0 NeilCallan 8 —
(D W P Arbuthnot) *taken down early and ponied to s: in tch tl hung bdly lft u.p and dropped out rapidly 3f out: t.o fnl 2f: virtually p.u ins fnl f* **16/1**

1m 28.72s (2.12) **Going Correction** +0.025s/f (Good) 9 Ran SP% **113.2**
Speed ratings (Par 92): **88,87,87,86,86 81,70,53,41**
toteswingers:1&2:£4.40, 1&3:£6.10, 2&3:£4.80 CSF £17.98 TOTE £9.70: £1.90, £1.30, £3.50; EX 19.70 Trifecta £197.40 Pool: £392.28 - 1.47 winning units..
Owner The Highlife Racing Club **Bred** Imperial & Mike Channon Bloodstock Ltd **Trained** West Ilsley, Berks
■ Stewards' Enquiry : Alan Munro two-day ban: used whip without giving gelding time to respond (Aug 2-3)

FOCUS
There was a blanket finish between the first five in this juvenile maiden and again the form looks somewhat muddling, but all five look horses with a future nevertheless. It is hard to be too confident over the level of the form but the winner has been rated up 5lb.

NOTEBOOK
Highlife Dancer came out on top under a fine ride from Alan Munro. He ran too free when disappointing second time out, but was much better on that score here and deserves credit for going through with his effort after being a little intimidated once being produced against the stands' rail from the furlong marker. This straight track also played more to his strengths and he looks a useful handicapper in the making. (op 8-1)
Sixty Roses(IRE) was still green when running third on her second start at Doncaster 44 days earlier and that form set the standard here, so she was clearly entitled to go close with a bit of further improvement. She was only just held, but did plenty through the early parts and is evidently still learning her trade. Nurseries are now an option for her.
Timothy T ◆, already gelded, ran a debut race full of promise and is certainly the one to take from the race with the immediate future in mind. He moved well through the race before running around a little when put under pressure and only just lost out for second place. There should be a nice bit of improvement in him for this initial experience and he has the scope to rate higher. (op 9-1 tchd 10-1)
Piccarello, fourth on debut here 18 days earlier, appreciated the step up a furlong and left the clear impression he would come on a bundle again for the outing. He is just the sort his trainer does well with. (op 16-1)

Titus Two(IRE) was having his third outing and got a bit warm beforehand. He didn't get the clearest of runs when making his effort late on, but it made no real difference to the overall result and he looks the type to fare better in nurseries, for which he is now eligible. (op 8-1)
A Little Bit Dusty had been placed on his two previous outings, so this obviously rates a backwards step. He never looked that happy, though, and it may be that something was amiss this time. (op 3-1 tchd 11-4)
Coeur(USA) Official explanation: jockey said bit slipped through filly's mouth

4209 RACING WELFARE H'CAP 6f 3y
3:15 (3:17) (Class 5) (0-75,74) 3-Y-0+ **£2,719** (£809; £404; £202) **Stalls** High

Form RPR
0625 **1** **Rough Rock (IRE)**[6] 3994 5-8-8 **63**.......................... AdamBeschizza(7) 4 70
(C A Dwyer) *trckd ldr: swtchd out lft and rdn to chal 1f out: led fnl 100yds: r.o wl* **5/2**[3]
3630 **2** 1/2 **Whiskey Junction**[37] 2954 6-9-12 **74**.......................... KierenFallon 5 79
(M Quinn) *led: pushed along and qcknd 2f out: rdn over 1f out: hdd fnl 100yds: no ex* **9/4**[2]
6451 **3** 9 **Ask Jenny (IRE)**[14] 3722 8-8-8 **61**.......................... DeclanCannon(5) 2 37
(Patrick Morris) *hld up in last: rdn and effrt over 1f out: wknd ent fnl f* **9/1**
4641 **4** 3 3/4 **Bonnie Brae**[40] 2879 3-9-5 **72**..........................(b) SebSanders 3 35
(G G Margarson) *chsd ldr: rdn and nt qckn 2f out: wknd u.p over 1f out: wl btn fnl f* **13/8**[1]
1m 14.03s (-0.37) **Going Correction** +0.025s/f (Good)
WFA 3 from 4yo+ 5lb **4** Ran SP% **107.4**
Speed ratings (Par 103): **103,102,90,85**
CSF £8.23 TOTE £3.60; EX 9.60.
Owner M M Foulger **Bred** Mrs B Stroomer **Trained** Burrough Green, Cambs

FOCUS
The first pair came right away in this moderate sprint. The form is limited with the favourite disappointing. The action developed towards the stands' rail.
Bonnie Brae Official explanation: trainer had no explanation for the poor form shown

4210 ROYCE BURROWS - A LIFETIME IN RACING AWARD H'CAP 6f 3y
3:45 (3:47) (Class 6) (0-55,55) 3-Y-O **£2,072** (£616; £308; £153) **Stalls** High

Form RPR
5005 **1** **Watch Chain (IRE)**[11] 3818 3-8-9 **49**.......................... DarryllHolland 6 54+
(M H Tompkins) *towards rr: hdwy to chse ldrs 2f out: nt clr run over 1f out: rdn and hdwy 1f out: swtchd rt and qcknd to ld fnl 100yds: sn clr: readily* **13/2**[3]
0000 **2** 2 1/4 **A Pocketful Of Rye (IRE)**[17] 3637 3-8-11 **54**....... MichaelStainton(3) 13 52
(P Howling) *bhd: rdn and hdwy over 1f out: swtchd rt ent fnl f: r.o wl ins fnl f to go 2nd nr fin: no ch w wnr* **12/1**
5000 **3** 1/2 **Black Baccara**[18] 3606 3-9-0 **54**..........................(p) KierenFallon 4 50
(P S McEntee) *prom tl led jst over 2f out: rdn over 1f out: hdd fnl 100yds: no ch w wnr after: fdd and lost 2nd nr fin* **9/2**[1]
-606 **4** 1/2 **Princess Shamal**[152] 581 3-8-10 **50**.......................... DavidProbert 7 45
(J R Jenkins) *chsd ldr: rdn wl over 1f out: kpt on same pce u.p fnl f* **25/1**
3560 **5** 1/2 **Slasl**[25] 3350 3-9-0 **54**.......................... HirokiGoto 9 47
(C E Brittain) *in tch in midfield: rdn and unable qck over 1f out: kpt on same pce ins fnl f* **14/1**
0000 **6** nk **Rileys Crane**[6] 3993 3-8-8 **55**.......................... AdamBeschizza(7) 8 47
(Mrs C A Dunnett) *bhd: rdn and hdwy over 1f out: nt clr run 1f out: swtchd lft jst ins fnl f: flashed tail u.p but styd on fnl 150yds: nt rch ldrs* **33/1**
030- **7** shd **Hellenio**[265] 7097 3-9-1 **55**..........................(b[1]) AndreaAtzeni 12 47
(M G Quinlan) *in tch in midfield: rdn and nt qckn wl over 1f out: edgd lft and one pce ent fnl f* **9/1**
-000 **8** 2 1/2 **Tudor Princess**[22] 3478 3-8-12 **52**..........................(p) RichardMullen 10 36
(W R Muir) *s.i.s: bhd: rdn over 2f out: kpt on past btn horses fnl f: nvr trbld ldrs* **16/1**
0653 **9** nk **Ellen Vannin (IRE)**[21] 3507 3-9-1 **55**..........................(p) NeilCallan 5 38
(Eve Johnson Houghton) *led tl jst over 2f out: sn rdn: wknd u.p jst over 1f out* **7/1**
4503 **10** 2 1/4 **Speedyfix**[21] 3515 3-8-9 **49**..........................(vt) JimmyQuinn 1 25
(Mrs C A Dunnett) *t.k.h: chsd ldrs: rdn and unable qck 2f out: wknd u.p ent fnl f* **5/1**[2]
5604 **11** 1/2 **Patachou**[30] 3210 3-8-4 **49** ow3..........................(v) DeclanCannon(5) 11 23
(R J Smith) *in tch in midfield: rdn and struggling over 2f out: no ch fr over 1f out* **25/1**
660 **12** 1 1/4 **Haafhd Sharp**[39] 2903 3-9-0 **54**..........................(b[1]) JerryO'Dwyer 3 24
(M G Quinlan) *t.k.h: chsd ldrs tl wknd u.p 2f out: no ch over 1f out* **14/1**
0604 **13** 5 **Barastar**[9] 3907 3-8-6 **46** oh1..........................(v) KirstyMilczarek 2 —
(N Tinkler) *s.i.s: a towards rr: rdn and struggling over 2f out: wl bhd over 1f out* **12/1**
1m 14.8s (0.40) **Going Correction** +0.025s/f (Good) **13** Ran SP% **115.9**
Speed ratings (Par 98): **98,95,94,93,93 92,92,89,88,85 85,83,76**
toteswingers:1&2:£16.70, 1&3:£8.00, 2&3:£18.30 CSF £77.78 CT £399.79 TOTE £5.50: £1.60, £4.30, £1.70; EX 97.90 Trifecta £209.90 Part won. Pool: £283.74 - 0.84 winning units..
Owner Miss Clare Hollest **Bred** Miss S Von Schilcher **Trained** Newmarket, Suffolk

FOCUS
A weak if open handicap. There was no great pace on early. The winner may do a bit better.
Hellenio Official explanation: jockey said colt hung right throughout
Barastar Official explanation: trainer's rep said gelding was unsuited by the good to firm ground

4211 GREAT YARMOUTH GREYHOUND STADIUM H'CAP 1m 3f 101y
4:15 (4:15) (Class 6) (0-60,66) 3-Y-0+ **£2,072** (£616; £308; £153) **Stalls** Low

Form RPR
-621 **1** **Allannah Abu**[5] 4017 3-9-13 **66** 6ex.......................... SebSanders 5 77+
(Sir Mark Prescott) *led after 1f: mde rest: pushed clr ent fnl 2f: rdn over 1f out: styd on wl: eased towards fin* **6/5**[1]
-403 **2** 3 1/4 **Mayfair's Future**[6] 3983 5-9-10 **52**.......................... DavidProbert 1 57
(J R Jenkins) *led for 1f: chsd wnr after: rdn and unable qck over 2f out: no ch w wnr fr over 1f out: kpt on to hold 2nd* **13/2**[3]
5333 **3** 1 **Spinning Waters**[19] 3560 4-9-7 **49**..........................(b) NeilCallan 4 52
(Eve Johnson Houghton) *in tch in midfield: hdwy to chse ldng pair over 3f out: drvn and kpt on same pce fr over 2f out* **7/1**
60-1 **4** 3/4 **Pattern Mark**[25] 3369 4-9-12 **54**.......................... KierenFallon 3 56
(Ollie Pears) *racd in last trio: pushed along and hdwy 4f out: rdn and effrt over 2f out: pressing for 2nd but no ch w wnr over 1f out: one pce fnl f* **3/1**[2]
-610 **5** 5 **Al Shababiya (IRE)**[33] 3074 3-9-0 **60**.......................... LauraPike(7) 6 53
(D M Simcock) *hld up in last pair: rdn along and no prog wl over 2f out: wl hld whn hung lft over 1f out* **11/1**
0422 **6** 4 **Rosewood Lad**[17] 3640 3-8-8 **52**.......................... DeclanCannon(5) 8 38
(J S Moore) *chsd ldrs: rdn 4f out: wknd u.p over 2f out: wl bhd over 1f out* **20/1**
0000 **7** 13 **Four Quartets (GER)**[4] 4070 4-9-8 **50**..........................(t) JimmyQuinn 7 14
(D Shaw) *s.i.s: a bhd: lost tch 3f out: eased ins fnl f* **80/1**
0-60 **8** 3 **That's Showbiz**[46] 2684 3-8-9 **55**.......................... HarryBentley(7) 9 14
(W J Knight) *chsd ldrs: rdn and struggling over 3f out: wl bhd fnl 2f: eased ins fnl f* **33/1**
2m 25.87s (-2.83) **Going Correction** -0.225s/f (Firm)
WFA 3 from 4yo+ 11lb **8** Ran SP% **113.6**
Speed ratings (Par 101): **101,98,97,97,93 90,81,79**
toteswingers:1&2:£2.80, 1&3:£2.50, 2&3:£4.80 CSF £9.46 CT £38.18 TOTE £2.30: £1.10, £2.60, £1.60; EX 11.20 Trifecta £78.20 Pool: £333.07 - 3.15 winning units..
Owner Ennistown Stud **Bred** Miss K Rausing And Mrs S Rogers **Trained** Newmarket, Suffolk

FOCUS
A moderate handicap in which it paid to race handily and is rated around the runner-up. The time was good for the grade.

4212 LORD NELSON MUSEUM H'CAP 1m 2f 21y
4:45 (4:45) (Class 6) (0-65,65) 3-Y-O **£2,072** (£616; £308; £153) **Stalls** Low

Form RPR
5051 **1** **Seattle Speight (USA)**[18] 3607 3-8-9 **60**..................(v) HarryBentley(7) 1 74
(W J Knight) *chsd ldrs: effrt on inner and rdn over 2f out: ev ch 2f out: led over 1f out: styd on wl ins fnl f* **11/4**[2]
0-53 **2** 3/4 **Azaday (IRE)**[70] 1970 3-9-0 **58**.......................... AlanMunro 10 70
(C F Wall) *stdd s: hld up in last pair: hdwy to chse ldrs 3f out: led 2f out: rdn and hdd over 1f out: stl ev ch and drvn ins fnl f: no ex and btn fnl 75yds* **5/2**[1]
5003 **3** 8 **Abu Wathab**[18] 3607 3-9-4 **62**.......................... RichardMullen 5 59
(P W Chapple-Hyam) *dwlt: sn pushed along: chsd ldrs: rdn and outpcd ent fnl 2f: no ch w ldrs over 1f out: wnt modest 3rd 1f out* **4/1**[3]
4045 **4** 3 1/2 **New Code**[5] 4027 3-9-5 **63**.......................... DarryllHolland 7 53
(W R Muir) *in tch: hdwy to press ldrs over 2f out: rdn and ev ch 2f out: wknd qckly u.p over 1f out* **6/1**
4-45 **5** 1/2 **Zinjbar (USA)**[25] 3347 3-9-7 **65**.......................... NeilCallan 9 54
(C E Brittain) *hld up in tch in midfield: nt clr run 3f out tl wl over 1f out: sn rdn and no rspnse: wl btn after* **16/1**
0434 **6** 2 1/4 **Miss Whippy**[12] 3788 3-8-8 **52**.......................... JimmyQuinn 4 37
(P Howling) *flashed tail thrght: chsd ldr tl led 3f out: rdn and hdd 2f out: wknd qckly over 1f out* **14/1**
5501 **7** 1 **Sternian**[3] 4113 3-9-3 **61** 6ex..........................(b) JamieMackay 2 44
(M E Rimmer) *led tl rdn and hdd 3f out: wknd qckly 2f out: wl btn over 1f out* **20/1**
0051 **8** 32 **Market Puzzle (IRE)**[14] 3728 3-8-10 **54**.......................... KierenFallon 8 —
(W M Brisbourne) *nvr gng wl and sn pushed along in rr: rdn and btn over 2f out: virtually p.u fnl f: t.o* **12/1**
2m 7.53s (-2.97) **Going Correction** -0.225s/f (Firm) **8** Ran SP% **114.5**
Speed ratings (Par 98): **102,101,95,92,91 90,89,63**
toteswingers:1&2:£2.70, 1&3:£3.30, 2&3:£3.80 CSF £10.10 CT £26.06 TOTE £3.40: £1.40, £1.10, £2.30; EX 13.00 Trifecta £26.70 Pool: £383.06 - 10.58 winning units..
Owner Bluehills Racing Limited **Bred** Blue Mountain Equine **Trained** Patching, W Sussex

FOCUS
There was a sound pace on in this moderate 3-y-o handicap and the first pair dominated from 2f out. A slightly positive view has been taken of the front two but this may not be form to take too literally.
Market Puzzle(IRE) Official explanation: jockey said gelding lost its action

4213 HELP THE HOSPICES APPRENTICE H'CAP 1m 2f 21y
5:15 (5:15) (Class 6) (0-60,58) 4-Y-0+ **£2,072** (£616; £308; £153) **Stalls** Low

Form RPR
4061 **1** **Count Ceprano (IRE)**[10] 3862 6-8-11 **55**................ SophieSilvester(5) 8 63+
(J Pearce) *t.k.h: hld up in last trio: pushed along and hdwy wl over 1f out: chsd ldr over 1f out: led ins fnl f: r.o strly: readily* **85/40**[1]
0-06 **2** 3 **Clearing House**[6] 3982 5-8-6 **48**.......................... NatashaEaton(3) 5 50
(J Ryan) *t.k.h: hld up in tch in midfield: hdwy over 3f out: rdn to ld wl over 1f out: hdd and nt pce of wnr ins fnl f* **9/1**
5340 **3** 3 1/2 **Alfredtheordinary**[12] 3783 5-8-9 **53**.......................... BarryAdams(5) 4 48
(M R Channon) *chsd ldrs: rdn and pressing ldrs whn n.m.r wl over 1f out: sn drvn and outpcd: no ch w ldng pair fnl f* **5/1**[3]
0036 **4** 1/2 **Bookiebasher Babe (IRE)**[13] 3765 5-8-7 **49**............. HarryBentley(3) 3 43
(M Quinn) *led at stdy gallop: hdd and rdn wl over 1f out: sn outpcd: wknd fnl f* **7/2**[2]
0-40 **5** 1/2 **Exopuntia**[29] 3238 4-8-12 **51**..........................(p) AdamBeschizza 1 44
(Miss J Feilden) *stdd s: hld up in rr: pushed along 4f out: drvn and effrt 2f out: no prog tl kpt on u.p ins fnl f: nvr trbld ldrs* **7/1**
055 **6** 1 1/4 **Summers Target (USA)**[28] 3264 4-8-13 **52**..........................(t) RyanClark 6 43
(S C Williams) *t.k.h: sn chsng ldr: jnd ldr 5f out tl ent fnl 2f: wknd qckly over 1f out* **11/2**
00-0 **7** 13 **Hilltop Alchemy**[60] 2263 4-8-1 **45**..........................(b) DannyBrock(5) 7 10
(J R Jenkins) *t.k.h early: hld up in last trio: rdn and short-lived effrt 3f out: wknd qckly over 2f out: wl bhd over 1f out* **28/1**
2m 11.63s (1.13) **Going Correction** -0.225s/f (Firm) **7** Ran SP% **112.2**
Speed ratings (Par 101): **86,83,80,80,80 79,68**
toteswingers:1&2:£3.30, 1&3:£2.00, 2&3:£5.20 CSF £21.24 CT £83.85 TOTE £2.90: £1.80, £6.60; EX 28.70 Trifecta £227.60 Pool: £350.64 - 1.14 winning units. Place 6 £41.69; Place 5 £15.15.
Owner Mrs Louise Marsh **Bred** Pendley Farm **Trained** Newmarket, Suffolk

■ Stewards' Enquiry : Natasha Eaton caution: careless riding

FOCUS
A typically weak handicap for apprentice riders. There was no real pace on early and that caused most to take a keen hold. It is doubtful if the winner had to improve.
Summers Target(USA) Official explanation: jockey said gelding hung right

T/Plt: £39.10 to a £1 stake. Pool:£74,292.09 - 1,383.96 winning tickets T/Qpdt: £14.50 to a £1 stake. Pool:£4,248.65 - 215.60 winning tickets SP

4214 - 4220a (Foreign Racing) - See Raceform Interactive

3952 FFOS LAS (L-H)

Tuesday, July 20

OFFICIAL GOING: Good to soft changing to good to soft (soft in places) after race 1 (2.30) changing to soft after race 2 (3.00)

Wind: Virtually nil Weather: Rain

4221 E.B.F./JANET AND JEFF RACECOURSES COMPLETION MAIDEN STKS 6f

2:30 (2:32) (Class 4) 2-Y-O £2,941 (£2,941; £674; £336) **Stalls** High

Form				RPR
0	1		**Dozy Joe**[27] 3332 2-9-0 0 ... MartinLane(3) 2 *(I A Wood) chsd ldrs: rdn 2f out: led ins fnl f: r.o u.p: jnd on line* **80/1**	77
6342	1	dht	**Royal Opera**[10] 3887 2-9-3 0 ... DavidProbert 10 *(B R Millman) chsd ldrs: rdn 2f out: styd on u.p fnl f: r.o wl to force dead heat on line* **11/2**[3]	77
2334	3	½	**Malpas Missile (IRE)**[11] 3858 2-8-12 0 ... RichardKingscote 9 *(Tom Dascombe) chsd ldr: rdn fr 2f out: styd on wl fnl f but nt pce of ldng duo fnl 50yds* **11/4**[2]	71
502	4	1 ¼	**Kyncraighe (IRE)**[20] 3555 2-9-3 0 ... FergusSweeney 3 *(Eve Johnson Houghton) led: rdn fr 2f out: hdd ins fnl f: wknd nr fin* **10/1**	72
	5	¾	**Earl Of Leitrim (IRE)** 2-9-3 0 ... ShaneKelly 4 *(B J Meehan) s.i.s: in rr and pushed along 1/2-way: hdwy fr 2f out: kpt on fnl f but nvr gng pce to rch ldrs* **50/1**	70+
	6	shd	**Lamasaas (USA)** 2-9-3 0 ... TadhgO'Shea 7 *(B W Hills) s.i.s: in rr: pushed along and green 1/2-way: edge lft and styd on fr over 1f out but nvr a threat* **2/1**[1]	69
6	7	2	**Clever Man**[24] 3459 2-9-3 0 ... ChrisCatlin 8 *(M R Channon) chsd ldrs: rdn over 2f out: wknd appr fnl f* **8/1**	63
	8	½	**Pearl Arch (IRE)** 2-9-3 0 ... MartinDwyer 5 *(B J Meehan) s.i.s and green: drvn along 1/2-way: sme prog fr 2f out* **7/1**	64+
0	9	6	**Better Offer (IRE)**[20] 3550 2-9-0 0 ... GFCarroll(3) 1 *(Miss Amy Weaver) sn rdn: a outpcd* **100/1**	44
4	10	½	**Rowan Ridge**[19] 3577 2-9-3 0 ... RichardHughes 11 *(J R Boyle) rdn and bhd fr 1/2-way* **22/1**	42
	11	5	**Lettering** 2-8-12 0 ... DaneO'Neill 6 *(D Haydn Jones) unruly paddock: s.i.s: a in rr* **66/1**	22

1m 11.39s (1.69) **Going Correction** +0.20s/f (Good) 11 Ran SP% **118.1**

Speed ratings (Par 96): **96,96,95,93,92 92,89,89,81,80 73**

WIN: DJ £34.70, RO £2.40; PL: DJ £12.20, RO £1.80, MM £1.30; EX: DJ-RO £133.20, RO-DJ £257.80; CSF: DJ-RO £238.54, RO-DJ £194.01; toteswingers DJ-RO £25.20, DJ-MM £37.50, RO-MM £3.10.

Owner Paddy Barrett **Bred** J Morton **Trained** Upper Lambourn, Berks

Owner The Links Partnership **Bred** Redmyre Bloodstock & Newhall Farm Estate **Trained** Kentisbeare, Devon

FOCUS

Following 8mm of rain overnight and more in the run up to the meeting, the ground had eased from good to good to soft. Just an ordinary maiden, but a dramatic finish and the judge couldn't separate the front pair in the photo. The form is rated around the front trio.

NOTEBOOK

Dozy Joe, out of a multiple winning sprinter on dirt in the US, was always outpaced on his Salisbury debut, but it was a different story here, as he was always in a handy position. He came off the bridle out in the centre of the track a fair way out and still showed signs of greenness, but kept on going and looked like winning outright until joined right on the line. He looks sure to step up again from this. (op 100-1)

Royal Opera, one of the most experienced in the field and only just beaten in an Ascot nursery last time, was also ridden close to the pace and responded to pressure to share the spoils on the line. He showed here that he is versatile with regards to ground. (op 100-1)

Malpas Missile(IRE), in the frame all four previous starts, including in decent company on her last two outings, had every chance but couldn't make the most of this seemingly easier opportunity, which has to be a worry. (op 9-4 tchd 7-4)

Kyncraighe(IRE), in front of a subsequent winner when runner-up at Chepstow last time, tried to make all the running but didn't quite get home on this easier ground. He may be better off in nurseries. (op 8-1 tchd 12-1)

Earl Of Leitrim(IRE) ◆, a 46,000gns colt out of a winning half-sister to the high-class Ocean Silk, may be the one to take from the race as he ran green off the pace early, but was noted doing some good late work.

Lamasaas(USA), a $230,000 colt out of a sister to the high-class New Story, was all the rage in the betting throughout the day, but he missed the break and then ran green and hung when asked to make his effort. The market suggested he was thought capable of much better than this and perhaps the rain didn't help him. His next effort should tell us more. (tchd 3-1)

4222 REDUCE UTILITY COSTS WITH UES MAIDEN STKS 5f

3:00 (3:02) (Class 5) 3-Y-O £2,590 (£770; £385; £192) **Stalls** High

Form				RPR
45	1		**Mirza**[105] 1137 3-9-3 0 ... RichardHughes 3 *(Rae Guest) chsd ldrs: rdn 1/2-way: led ins fnl 2f: drvn clr ins fnl f: readily* **5/1**[3]	88
5-26	2	1 ½	**Superior Edge**[76] 1825 3-8-7 73 ... DeclanCannon(5) 4 *(B Palling) led: rdn 1/2-way: hdd ins fnl 2f: no ch w wnr and one pce ins fnl f* **2/1**[1]	78
54	3	2	**Rare Tern (IRE)**[17] 3663 3-8-12 0 ... StevieDonohoe 6 *(Sir Mark Prescott) rdn fr stalls and bdly outpcd 1f: rcvrd and in tch 3f out: styd on to go one pce 3rd 1f out* **9/4**[2]	71
5-5	4	6	**Mr Money Maker**[14] 3766 3-9-3 0 ... DavidProbert 2 *(B Palling) chsd ldrs: rdn and hung lft 1/2-way and sn wknd* **5/1**[3]	54
05	5	2 ¼	**Attrition**[40] 2903 3-9-3 0 ... MartinDwyer 5 *(Andrew Reid) chsd ldr 2f: rdn and wknd 2f out* **12/1**	46
0	6	6	**Midnight M**[33] 3125 3-8-5 0 ... NoelGarbutt(7) 1 *(Rae Guest) slowly away: a bdly outpcd* **25/1**	20

58.37 secs (0.97) **Going Correction** +0.20s/f (Good) 6 Ran SP% **109.0**

Speed ratings (Par 100): **100,97,94,84,81 71**

toteswingers: 1&2 £1.60, 1&3 £1.60, 2&3 £1.80 CSF £14.52 TOTE £5.90: £4.90, £1.30; EX 12.30.

Owner C J Mills **Bred** C J Mills **Trained** Newmarket, Suffolk

FOCUS

The rain continued and the ground was changed to good to soft, soft in places before this race. This didn't look a strong maiden and the conditions seemed to take their toll on a few.

4223 INSIDER MEDIA H'CAP 2m (R)

3:30 (3:31) (Class 5) (0-70,68) 3-Y-O+ £2,590 (£770; £385; £192) **Stalls** Low

Form				RPR
-210	1		**Any Given Moment (IRE)**[40] 2907 4-9-0 57 ... (b[1]) MartinLane(3) 8 *(D M Simcock) chsd ldrs: wnt 2nd 7f out: led over 3f out: sn rdn: drvn out fnl f* **2/1**[1]	65+
0-50	2	1 ½	**Miniyamba (IRE)**[40] 2893 3-8-6 63 ... MartinDwyer 7 *(J L Dunlop) led tl hdd 9f out: rdn and lost position over 4f out: rallied fr 3f out to chse wnr fr 2f out: styd on fnl f but no imp on wnr* **7/1**	69
0/54	3	1 ¾	**Mutadarrej (IRE)**[14] 3760 6-8-13 53 ... ShaneKelly 3 *(Ian Williams) towards rr but in tch: rdn and hdwy fr 3f out: wnt 3rd over 1f out: styd on same pce ins fnl f* **7/2**[2]	57
5-06	4	4 ½	**Go Amwell**[98] 1273 7-8-3 50 ... DannyBrock(7) 6 *(J R Jenkins) towards rr but in tch: rdn over 4f out: styd on fnl 2f but nvr gng pce to rch ldng trio* **16/1**	49
1100	5	3	**Aaman (IRE)**[54] 2464 4-9-6 60 ... JoeFanning 5 *(E F Vaughan) chsd ldrs: rdn over 3f out: wknd appr fnl 2f* **6/1**[3]	55
520	6	12	**William's Way**[46] 2723 8-10-0 68 ... RichardHughes 1 *(I A Wood) hld up in rr: sme hdwy fr 5f out: nvr quite on terms: rdn 3f out: wknd over 2f out* **7/1**	49
6-05	7	½	**Casual Garcia**[5] 4042 5-9-9 63 ... (bt) NeilChalmers 2 *(Mark Gillard) in tch: rdn after 6f: wknd ins fnl 5f* **11/1**	43
40-0	8	44	**La Polka**[117] 982 4-9-6 60 ... StevieDonohoe 4 *(Mark Gillard) a bhd: t.o* **25/1**	—
/304	P		**Dancing Sword**[29] 3278 5-9-3 57 ... DavidProbert 9 *(D Burchell) chsd ldrs: led 9f out: hdd over 3f out: wknd sn after: eased fnl 2f: p.u: lame* **11/1**	—

3m 40.53s (10.53) **Going Correction** +0.475s/f (Yiel)

WFA 3 from 4yo+ 17lb 9 Ran SP% **121.2**

Speed ratings (Par 103): **92,91,90,88,86 80,80,58,—**

toteswingers: 1&2 £4.90, 1&3 £2.30, 2&3 £5.20 CSF £17.82 CT £48.70 TOTE £3.30: £1.70, £3.40, £1.60; EX 18.90.

Owner Malcolm Caine **Bred** W Lazy T Ranch **Trained** Newmarket, Suffolk

FOCUS

The ground was changed to soft before this contest, which therefore became a proper test of stamina especially as the pace seemed solid enough for the conditions.

4224 DIRECT NURSING H'CAP 1m (R)

4:00 (4:03) (Class 3) (0-95,94) 3-Y-O+ £6,476 (£1,927; £963; £481) **Stalls** Low

Form				RPR
214	1		**Innocuous**[39] 2933 3-8-3 80 ... MartinLane(3) 1 *(D M Simcock) chsd ldrs: drvn along 4f out: led appr fnl 2f: r.o strly fnl f* **2/1**[1]	93+
1424	2	3	**Secretive**[13] 3796 3-8-12 86 ... (b) JoeFanning 7 *(M Johnston) chsd ldr: rdn 3f out: styd on to chse wnr over 1f out but no imp* **2/1**[1]	92
2600	3	2 ¾	**Swift Chap**[27] 3334 4-8-13 79 ... DavidProbert 8 *(B R Millman) chsd ldrs: rdn over 3f out: styd on same pce u.p to take wl hld 3rd last strides* **14/1**	81
041	4	shd	**Zubova**[14] 3759 3-7-8 75 oh2 ... (t) NoelGarbutt(7) 5 *(Rae Guest) in rr: hdwy on outside to chse ldrs 5 out: rdn 3f out: sn one pce: mod prog u.p ins fnl f* **25/1**	74
1001	5	¾	**Guilded Warrior**[23] 3483 7-9-11 91 ... FergusSweeney 3 *(W S Kittow) led tl rdn and hdd appr fnl 2f: wknd wl over 1f out* **15/2**[3]	91
604	6	9	**Huzzah (IRE)**[38] 2971 5-9-6 86 ... RobertWinston 6 *(B W Hills) s.i.s as hood removed: rdn over 4f out: lost tch over 3f out* **11/4**[2]	65

1m 42.89s (2.39) **Going Correction** +0.475s/f (Yiel)

WFA 3 from 4yo+ 8lb 6 Ran SP% **115.6**

Speed ratings (Par 107): **107,104,101,101,100 91**

toteswingers: 1&2 £1.60, 1&3 £4.00, 2&3 £5.00 CSF £6.54 CT £40.67 TOTE £3.80: £2.40, £1.10; EX 8.80.

Owner Saeed Misleh **Bred** Darley **Trained** Newmarket, Suffolk

FOCUS

A fair handicap despite the two absentees.

NOTEBOOK

Innocuous ◆, who was having only his second start on turf, appreciated the rain-softened conditions. His chances didn't look that good when he had to be niggled along from an early stage and was under serious pressure against the inside rail starting up the home straight, but the further he went the stronger he became and he eventually won this with some authority. Still unexposed, he can go on to better things if kept away from quick ground and he may be an even better horse next year. (op 15-8 tchd 9-4)

Secretive is 12lb higher than for his last success, having run well in red-hot handicaps at Royal Ascot and the Newmarket July meeting in the meantime. He did his best and had every chance, but ran into a progressive rival. He has won on slow Fibresand, but this was his first try on soft turf and he seemed to cope with it well enough. (op 11-4)

Swift Chap, disappointing since finishing runner-up off 6lb lower over C&D in May, made some late progress but never looked like winning and the rain probably didn't help him. (op 9-1)

Zubova, who got off the mark at the 11th attempt in a Fibresand claimer last time, made a sudden move around the outside of the field on the home bend but had little more to offer once into the straight. She doesn't look that well handicapped at present. (op 22-1 tchd 33-1)

Guilded Warrior, up 5lb for his Windsor success, has gained both of his victories this season when left alone in front and that was the case here, but although he handles soft ground his only win over this trip came on a quick surface and he had nothing left once headed by the winner 2f from home. (op 8-1 tchd 10-1)

Huzzah(IRE), without a win in well over two years, is brilliantly handicapped these days and ran much better off this mark at Sandown last time, but he never figured here following a tardy start. (op 7-2 tchd 5-2)

4225 QUANTUM GB GEOTECHNICAL & CIVIL ENGINEERING H'CAP 6f

4:30 (4:33) (Class 4) (0-80,79) 3-Y-O+ £3,885 (£1,156; £577; £288) **Stalls** High

Form				RPR
001	1		**Signore Momento (IRE)**[16] 3706 4-9-2 72 ... (tp) GFCarroll(3) 1 *(Miss Amy Weaver) hld up in rr: swtchd lft and rapid hdwy over 1f out to ld fnl 120yds: easily* **7/2**[2]	85+
12U3	2	2	**Requisite**[8] 3947 5-9-5 75 ... (v) MartinLane(3) 8 *(I A Wood) chsd ldrs: rdn over 2f out: tk slt ld 1f out: hdd and easily outpcd fnl 120yds* **13/2**	82
6201	3	1 ¾	**Westwood**[14] 3761 5-9-2 69 ... DaneO'Neill 7 *(D Haydn Jones) led tl narrowly hdd 1f out: wknd fnl 120yds* **9/4**[1]	70

0656 **4** 1¾ **Memphis Man**[10] 3898 7-9-0 **70**.................................... RichardEvans(3) 6 66
(P D Evans) *chsd ldrs tl rdn and outpcd 3f out: n.m.r ins fnl 2f: sme prog again ins fnl f* **4/1**[3]
6251 **5** ¾ **Ray Of Joy**[78] 1770 4-9-12 **79**.. FergusSweeney 5 72
(J R Jenkins) *in rr: rdn and mod prog whn edgd lft fr 2f out: nvr in contention* **14/1**
0142 **6** 3¾ **Quasi Congaree (GER)**[13] 3779 4-9-11 **78**..............(t) RichardHughes 4 59
(I A Wood) *t.k.h: chsd ldrs tl wknd qckly ins fnl 2f* **11/2**
45-0 **7** 17 **Fiftyfourth Street**[24] 3440 4-9-1 **68**....................................(t) ChrisCatlin 2 —
(P J Makin) *chsd ldrs tl wknd qckly over 2f out* **33/1**
1m 11.66s (1.96) **Going Correction** +0.475s/f (Yiel) 7 Ran SP% **111.3**
Speed ratings (Par 105): **105,102,100,97,96 91,69**
toteswingers: 1&2 £4.80, 1&3 £2.10, 2&3 £2.70 CSF £24.63 TOTE £5.30: £2.50, £1.90; EX 32.30.
Owner White, Bringloe, Warner and Murphy **Bred** P J Moloney **Trained** Newmarket, Suffolk
FOCUS
A fair sprint handicap despite the runners having to splash through the puddles.

4226 WALTERS UK H'CAP 1m 4f (R)
5:00 (5:00) (Class 5) (0-75,75) 4-Y-0+ **£2,590** (£770; £385; £192) **Stalls** Low

Form RPR
0353 **1** **Rowan Tiger**[19] 3576 4-9-5 **73**.. RichardHughes 3 80
(J R Boyle) *mde all: drvn along 3f out: styd on wl whn chal 1f out: asserted fnl 20yds* **15/8**[1]
10-3 **2** nk **Gandalf**[140] 764 8-8-9 **66**.. GFCarroll(3) 7 73
(Miss Amy Weaver) *trckd wnr 5f: disp 2nd tl chsd wnr again over 2f out: chal u.p 1f out: outpcd fnl 120yds* **9/2**
-504 **3** 6 **Norman The Great**[19] 3576 6-9-4 **72**......................(b[1]) FergusSweeney 6 69
(A King) *hld up towards rr but in tch: sme hdwy fr 3f out but sn hung lft and btn: tk mod 3rd over 1f out* **9/4**[2]
1555 **4** 2 **Mr Plod**[70] 2014 5-8-4 **58** ow1.. MartinDwyer 2 52
(Andrew Reid) *wnt 2nd after 5f: rdn 3f out: lost 2nd over 2f out: sn btn and lost 3rd ffr over 1f out* **7/2**[3]
/60 **5** 2 **Gold Ring**[8] 3967 10-8-6 **60**...(t) NeilChalmers 1 51
(Mark Gillard) *awkward stalls and slowly away: sn rcvrd: wknd 3f out* **14/1**
2m 45.84s (9.04) **Going Correction** +0.475s/f (Yiel) 5 Ran SP% **112.6**
Speed ratings (Par 103): **88,87,83,82,81**
toteswingers: 1&2 £7.10 CSF £10.84 TOTE £2.80: £2.80, £3.20; EX 7.80 Place 6 £45.31, Place 5 £13.77.
Owner Rowan Stud Partnership 1 **Bred** Rowan Farm Stud **Trained** Epsom, Surrey
FOCUS
A modest event. They went no pace early.
T/Plt: £23.80 to a £1 stake. Pool: £71,495.90. 2,186.51 winning tickets. T/Qpdt: £7.80 to a £1 stake. Pool: £5,355.10. 504.30 winning tickets. ST

4019 KEMPTON (A.W) (R-H)
Tuesday, July 20

OFFICIAL GOING: Standard
Wind: Light, half behind Weather: Warm and humid

4227 PANORAMIC BAR & RESTAURANT H'CAP 1m 3f (P)
6:50 (6:50) (Class 5) (0-70,69) 3-Y-0+ **£2,320** (£685; £342) **Stalls** High

Form RPR
2260 **1** **Blue Tango (IRE)**[38] 2966 4-9-12 **67**..........................(v[1]) SebSanders 10 77
(Mrs A J Perrett) *trckd ldrs gng wl: led 2f out: rdn out: a holding runner-up* **13/2**[3]
52-0 **2** ¾ **Cast Of Stars (IRE)**[10] 3917 3-9-2 **68**.............................. JimCrowley 7 77
(R M Beckett) *chsd ldr most of way: drvn along over 2f out: styd on to regain 2nd ins fnl f: a hld* **7/2**[1]
0-53 **3** 4 **Josr's Magic (IRE)**[13] 3783 6-8-11 **57**...................... MatthewDavies(5) 1 58
(P R Hedger) *led tl 2f out: hrd rdn: one pce* **11/1**
0664 **4** ½ **Resplendent Ace (IRE)**[8] 3967 6-9-5 **60**....................... JimmyQuinn 12 61
(P Howling) *mid-div: effrt 3f out: styd on u.p fnl 2f* **16/1**
50-1 **5** 1½ **Savaronola (USA)**[25] 1983 5-9-13 **68**................................ TomQueally 4 66
(B J Curley) *hld up in midfield: hdwy on outer over 4f out: hrd rdn over 2f out: styd on same pce* **9/2**[2]
3-40 **6** 1¾ **Aegean King**[28] 3294 4-9-5 **60**.................................. StephenCraine 3 55
(M Wigham) *s.s: bhd: rdn 3f out: styd on fnl f: nvr nrr* **10/1**
4506 **7** 1¼ **Bolanderi (USA)**[11] 3862 5-9-6 **68**............................. AlexEdwards(7) 14 60
(Andrew Turnell) *mid-div: drvn along 3f out: no hdwy* **10/1**
0323 **8** 2½ **Filun**[7] 3984 5-9-3 **58**.. EddieAhern 9 46
(A Middleton) *dwlt: towards rr tl rapid hdwy to chse ldrs 7f out: wknd over 2f out* **10/1**
4004 **9** hd **Illuminative (USA)**[56] 2414 4-9-6 **66**........... GemmaGracey-Davison(5) 6 54
(Miss Z C Davison) *s.s: towards rr: rdn 3f out: nvr trbld ldrs* **20/1**
1260 **10** 4 **Winning Show**[26] 3348 6-9-5 **60**...(t) AdamKirby 5 40
(C Gordon) *reluctant to leave stall and lost 10 l: a bhd* **8/1**
1004 **11** ¾ **Slip**[28] 3282 5-9-7 **62**...(bt) LiamKeniry 2 41
(C R Dore) *sn towards rr: rdn and n.d fnl 3f* **16/1**
6306 **12** 3¼ **Annambo**[8] 3967 10-9-0 **58**..(v) RussKennemore(3) 13 31
(Andrew Reid) *prom tl wknd 3f out* **25/1**
2m 22.21s (0.31) **Going Correction** +0.025s/f (Slow)
WFA 3 from 4yo+ 11lb 12 Ran SP% **120.8**
Speed ratings (Par 103): **99,98,95,95,94 92,91,90,89,87 86,84**
toteswingers: 1&2 £7.30, 1&3 £14.40, 2&3 £13.20 CSF £30.03 CT £254.03 TOTE £9.10: £3.60, £1.90, £4.70; EX 46.40.
Owner The Green Dot Partnership **Bred** Paul Ennis **Trained** Pulborough, W Sussex
FOCUS
Mainly exposed performers in a modest handicap in which the moderate gallop meant those up with the pace were at an advantage. The winner raced against the inside rail in the straight and the first two pulled clear in the closing stages.
Blue Tango(IRE) Official explanation: trainer's rep said, regarding apparent improvement in form, that the colt was better suited by the change of headgear.
Winning Show Official explanation: jockey said gelding was slowly away

4228 MIX BUSINESS WITH PLEASURE AT KEMPTON NOVICE STKS 6f (P)
7:20 (7:28) (Class 5) 2-Y-0 **£2,201** (£655; £327; £163) **Stalls** High

Form RPR
0413 **1** **Eucharist (IRE)**[23] 3482 2-8-11 0.............................. RyanMoore 1 90+
(R Hannon) *trckd ldrs: wnt 2nd 2f out: led over 1f out: rdn clr: comf* **1/1**[1]
4134 **2** 6 **Whoatealthepius (IRE)**[10] 3887 2-8-9 0......................... JimCrowley 7 70
(D K Ivory) *led tl over 1f out: nt pce of wnr* **7/1**[3]
3 5 **King Of The Desert (IRE)** 2-9-0 0.................................. EddieAhern 4 60
(E A L Dunlop) *stdd s: hld up in 5th: rdn and outpcd over 2f out: wnt mod 3rd ins fnl f* **12/1**
66 **4** ¾ **Avalon Bay**[13] 3785 2-9-0 0... SteveDrowne 6 58
(Pat Eddery) *plld hrd early: chsd ldr: pushed along over 3f out: lost 2nd and wknd 2f out* **33/1**
5411 **5** 5 **Belle Bayardo (IRE)**[11] 3849 2-9-7 0........................... PhilipRobinson 3 50+
(R A Harris) *chsd ldrs on outer: nt handle bnd fr 4f out: wnt wd: sn struggling* **6/1**[2]
000 **6** 6 **Shesanindian (IRE)**[29] 3269 2-8-9 0................................ JimmyQuinn 2 20
(A W Carroll) *sn outpcd: no ch fnl 3f* **100/1**
1m 12.96s (-0.14) **Going Correction** +0.025s/f (Slow) 6 Ran SP% **88.4**
Speed ratings (Par 94): **101,93,86,85,78 70**
toteswingers: 1&2 £1.50, 1&3 £1.80, 2&3 £3.50 CSF £4.42 TOTE £1.80: £1.10, £3.10; EX 3.80.
Owner Mrs J Wood **Bred** M Kelly **Trained** East Everleigh, Wilts
FOCUS
Several previous winners but an eventful race even before the stalls opened with in-form Belle Bayardo getting loose on the way to the start and second-favourite Magic Casement (withdrawn) rearing in the stalls (5/2), deduct 25p in the £ under R4. The gallop was an ordinary one and the winner came down the centre in the straight. Decent form, with improvement from the winner.
NOTEBOOK
Eucharist(IRE), having her first run over this trip on her all-weather debut, took advantage of the misfortunes of her main market rivals and probably did not have to improve too much to beat her former stable-companion with plenty in hand to justify the market confidence. Although this race wasn't as competitive as it promised to be, she is a steadily progressive sort who may well be capable of further improvement and she should be able to win more races. (op 13-8 tchd 2-1 in a place)
Whoatealthepius(IRE) was fairly easy to back but had the run of the race and ran creditably on this all-weather debut. She has been a reliable sort so far over this trip, she should be suited by the step into ordinary nursery company and she should continue to give a good account. (op 5-1)
King Of The Desert(IRE), a £22,000 half-brother to winners from 5f-7f, was fairly easy to back but was far from disgraced against more experienced rivals on this racecourse debut. He should be suited by the step up to 7f, should come on a fair bit for this experience and is capable of picking up an ordinary event. (op 16-1)
Avalon Bay had shown only moderate form on two previous starts and had his limitations exposed against a couple of previous winners in this grade. He is now qualified for a nursery mark but really needs to settle better than he did here if he is to progress. (op 20-1)
Belle Bayardo(IRE) looked an interesting runner returned to Polytrack and stepped up to 6f after a couple of wins on turf, but he not surprisingly failed to give his running after getting loose and crashing through a couple of rails before the start and after pulling hard and hanging badly (cocked jaw) in the race itself. While obviously this was not his true running, he would not be one to go in head down for next time after this display. Official explanation: jockey said gelding cocked its jaw and was unrideable (op 4-1 tchd 7-2)

4229 DIGIBET.COM MAIDEN FILLIES' STKS 1m 4f (P)
7:50 (8:19) (Class 5) 3-Y-0+ **£2,320** (£685; £342) **Stalls** Centre

Form RPR
2233 **1** **Sing Sweetly**[13] 3795 3-8-12 82.. HayleyTurner 4 83+
(G A Butler) *trckd ldrs: led on bit over 2f out: sn qcknd wl clr: easily* **11/10**[1]
43 **2** 12 **Affinity**[67] 2092 3-8-12 .... EddieAhern 13 64+
(H R A Cecil) *hld up towards rr: rdn and hdwy 2f out: r.o to take 2nd on line: no ch of catching wnr* **4/1**[2]
50 **3** hd **Royal Dalakhani (IRE)**[20] 3563 3-8-12 .... LiamJones 3 64
(P W D'Arcy) *prom: led 4f out tl over 2f out: kpt on same pce* **33/1**
3-2 **4** 1¾ **Privy Speech (IRE)**[131] 858 3-8-12 .... JimmyQuinn 9 61
(Rae Guest) *mid-div: rdn and hdwy 3f out: wnt 3rd 2f out: one pce* **16/1**
5 3½ **Naughty Naughty**[42] 5-9-10 .... SebSanders 12 55+
(B G Powell) *s.s: bhd: rdn and sme hdwy whn nt clr rn over 2f out: styd on: nt trble ldrs* **40/1**
6 1 **Utern**[37] 6-9-10 .... LiamKeniry 1 54
(Miss Venetia Williams) *in tch in 6th: rdn and no hdwy fnl 3f* **66/1**
5-0 **7** ¾ **Danube (IRE)**[80] 1705 3-8-12 .... TomQueally 8 52
(H R A Cecil) *mid-div: effrt and n.m.r 3f out: no imp* **10/1**
8 nk **Tigress Hill** 3-8-12 .... JimCrowley 2 52
(Mrs A J Perrett) *s.s: bhd: rdn and wd st: nvr rchd ldrs* **20/1**
00 **9** 1¼ **Melinoise**[24] 3443 3-8-9 .... WilliamCarson(3) 6 50?
(Rae Guest) *towards rr: rdn 6f out: wd st: nvr trbld ldrs* **66/1**
0 **10** 8 **In Your Time**[66] 2115 3-8-12 .... RyanMoore 10 37
(Sir Michael Stoute) *awkward s: chsd ldrs tl wknd 3f out* **9/2**[3]
0 **11** 2 **Sunshineofyourlove**[40] 2891 3-8-12 .... SteveDrowne 5 34
(J W Hills) *dwlt: sn in midfield: rdn and no imp whn n.m.r ent st: sn bhd* **66/1**
63 **12** 12 **Thingathong (FR)**[87] 1515 3-8-12 .... RichardKingscote 14 15
(Tom Dascombe) *led tl 4f out: wknd qckly over 2f out* **33/1**
13 1¼ **Quartz D'Anjou (FR)**[382] 6-9-5 .... JemmaMarshall(5) 11 13
(P M Phelan) *w ldrs tl wknd over 3f out* **80/1**
2m 34.15s (-0.35) **Going Correction** +0.025s/f (Slow)
WFA 3 from 5yo+ 12lb 13 Ran SP% **119.6**
Speed ratings (Par 100): **102,94,93,92,90 89,89,89,88,82 81,73,72**
toteswingers: 1&2 £1.70, 1&3 £9.40, 2&3 £26.80 CSF £5.00 TOTE £2.10: £1.20, £1.10, £9.70; EX 6.80.
Owner The Distaff 2 Partnership **Bred** Mrs M Lavell **Trained** Newmarket, Suffolk
FOCUS
A fillies' maiden with very little strength in depth and a substantial delay to proceedings as With Hope was fatally injured in the stalls. The gallop was an ordinary one and the easy winner came down the centre in the straight.

4230 MORE HORSE POWER KIA SPORTAGE H'CAP 2m (P)
8:20 (8:50) (Class 5) (0-75,74) 3-Y-O **£2,320** (£685; £342) **Stalls** High

Form RPR
3623 **1** **Spice Fair**[8] 3963 3-8-13 **66**.. RyanMoore 4 77
(M D I Usher) *hld up in 5th: smooth effrt over 2f out: led wl over 1f out: sn qcknd clr: rdn out* **7/2**[3]
06-2 **2** 6 **Tuscan Gold**[60] 2289 3-9-3 **70**...................................... SebSanders 7 78+
(Sir Mark Prescott) *hld up 2nd last: effrt on ins rail whn bdly hmpd over 2f out: swtchd wd: styd on wl to take 2nd nr fin* **6/5**[1]
0000 **3** 1 **Bethlehem (IRE)**[15] 3723 3-8-2 **55** oh3.......................... NickyMackay 8 58
(H Morrison) *prom: led briefly 2f out: nt pce of wnr* **25/1**
-052 **4** ¾ **High Ransom**[18] 3626 3-9-3 **70**.......................................(p) PhilipRobinson 2 72
(M A Jarvis) *led: 3f out tl 2f out: one pce* **11/4**[2]
214 **5** ¾ **Lauberhorn**[12] 3807 3-9-7 **74**... TomQueally 3 75
(Eve Johnson Houghton) *in tch in 4th: effrt on outer ent st: one pce* **15/2**
00-0 **6** 3 **Lis Pendens**[74] 1880 3-8-3 **56**.. JimmyQuinn 5 54
(W R Muir) *dwlt: hld up in 6th: rdn over 3f out: nt trble ldrs* **28/1**

-050 **7** *9* **Pollan Bay (IRE)**[8] 3960 3-7-11 **55** oh7 SophieDoyle(5) 1 42
(Ms J S Doyle) *in rr: rdn 4f out: n.d after* **66/1**
-505 **8** *28* **Baibars (USA)**[14] 3754 3-9-7 **74** (b) DarryllHolland 6 27
(G A Butler) *led tl 3f out: wknd qckly* **25/1**

3m 30.5s (0.40) **Going Correction** +0.025s/f (Slow) **8** Ran SP% **118.7**
Speed ratings (Par 100): **100,97,96,96,95 94,89,75**
toteswingers: 1&2 £2.10, 1&3 £12.30, 2&3 £13.60 CSF £8.24 CT £89.96 TOTE £3.80: £1.30, £1.50, £8.20; EX 8.60.
Owner Saxon House Racing **Bred** Mrs D Hughes **Trained** Upper Lambourn, Berks

FOCUS
A fair handicap in which nothing had previous form over the distance. The gallop was not surprisingly a modest one and the winner ended up towards the inside rail in the closing stages.
Lis Pendens Official explanation: vet said gelding lost a left-fore shoe

4231 EPSOM TRAINERS OPEN DAY 22ND AUGUST H'CAP 6f (P)
8:50 (9:22) (Class 3) (0-95,91) 3-Y-O
£6,044 (£1,810; £905; £452; £226; £113) **Stalls** High

Form RPR
1224 **1** **Bohemian Melody**[10] 3886 3-9-1 **85** WilliamBuick 6 94+
(M Botti) *trckd ldrs in 3rd: led ins fnl f: drvn out* **13/8**[1]
0100 **2** *3/4* **Ghostwing**[4] 4118 3-9-6 **90** DarryllHolland 3 97
(J Gallagher) *trckd ldr: led 2f out tl ins fnl f: r.o* **8/1**
0500 **3** *5* **Edgewater (IRE)**[19] 3578 3-8-12 **82** (p) HayleyTurner 4 73
(J Akehurst) *in rr: pushed along 4f out: styd on fnl f: wnt 3rd fnl strides* **11/1**
-440 **4** *nk* **Tomintoul Singer (IRE)**[38] 2978 3-9-7 **91** TomQueally 5 81
(H R A Cecil) *hld up 2nd last: effrt 2f out: chsd clr ldng pair 1f out: one pce: lost 3rd fnl strides* **4/1**[3]
0-06 **5** *1* **Swan Wings**[10] 3891 3-8-12 **82** RyanMoore 1 69
(A M Balding) *in tch on outer: outpcd fnl 3f* **16/1**
261 **6** *2 1/2* **Qudwah (IRE)**[12] 3808 3-9-1 **85** TadhgO'Shea 7 64
(M A Jarvis) *led tl 2f out: wknd over 1f out* **9/4**[2]
44-0 **7** *5* **Rahya Cass (IRE)**[17] 3673 3-9-6 **90** (vt[1]) SteveDrowne 2 53
(J R Gask) *chsd ldrs tl wknd 2f out* **33/1**

1m 11.94s (-1.16) **Going Correction** +0.025s/f (Slow) **7** Ran SP% **117.1**
Speed ratings (Par 104): **108,107,100,99,98 95,88**
toteswingers: 1&2 £3.20, 1&3 £5.80, 2&3 £8.60 CSF £16.38 TOTE £1.90: £1.10, £6.60; EX 11.40.
Owner Mrs L Botti **Bred** Ivan W Allan **Trained** Newmarket, Suffolk

FOCUS
A useful handicap featuring a couple of unexposed sorts. The gallop was reasonable and the first two who raced towards the far rail in the straight pulled clear in the closing stages.

NOTEBOOK
Bohemian Melody ◆'s record is one of improvement and he had no problems with the switch back to Polytrack or the drop to this trip when justifying the strong market support. This lightly raced type has quickly made up into a very useful sort, should prove equally effective back over 7f or on turf and he appeals strongly as the type to win a decent handicap. (op 9-4)
Ghostwing isn't very reliable but he ran as well as he ever has done returned to Polytrack against a progressive and very well-backed winner. He pulled clear of the remainder but consistency isn't his strong suit. He'll be up in the weights and it remains to be seen whether this will be reproduced next time. (op 12-1 tchd 14-1)
Edgewater(IRE) hadn't been at his best in cheekpieces on turf on his last couple of starts but ran better to fare the best of those held up. There will be easier opportunities than this one and he has been consistent on Polytrack but is likely to remain vulnerable to an improver or a progressive sort from this mark. (op 12-1)
Tomintoul Singer(IRE) wasn't totally disgraced on this Polytrack debut in a race where the leaders weren't stopping in the straight, but she'll have to improve to win a competitive handicap on Polytrack from her current mark.
Swan Wings has been essentially disappointing since winning her maiden last summer and, although she continues to drop in the weights, she didn't show enough (despite racing on the outside) on this all-weather debut to suggest she is of much immediate interest.
Qudwah(IRE) had substantially more on her plate for this all-weather and handicap debut than when bossing an ordinary field of maidens at Doncaster on her previous start but was the disappointment. As with many of her stable companions she didn't help her cause by taking a good hold but, given her connections and her pedigree it would be unwise to write her off just yet. (op 15-8 tchd 5-2 and 11-4 in a place)

4232 BOOK KEMPTON TICKETS ON 0844 579 3008 H'CAP 7f (P)
9:20 (9:46) (Class 6) (0-60,60) 3-Y-O+ **£1,637** (£483; £241) **Stalls** High

Form RPR
3121 **1** **Eager To Bow (IRE)**[35] 3056 4-9-6 **59** JimCrowley 12 67
(P R Chamings) *trckd ldrs: rdn over 2f out: drvn to ld ins fnl f: jst hld on* **7/4**[1]
5544 **2** *hd* **Pha Mai Blue**[13] 3777 5-9-6 **59** (v) PatCosgrave 8 66
(J R Boyle) *t.k.h towards rr: gd hdwy fnl 2f: clsng fast at fin: jst failed* **5/1**[2]
5-00 **3** *nk* **Downhill Skier (IRE)**[14] 3763 6-8-12 **56** KierenFox(5) 6 63
(W M Brisbourne) *towards rr: gd hdwy over 1f out: r.o wl fnl f* **16/1**
0205 **4** *3/4* **Grey Boy (GER)**[13] 3783 9-8-11 **57** GeorgeDowning(7) 10 62
(A W Carroll) *prom: slt ld over 1f out tl ins fnl f: one pce: 4th and hld whn n.m.r fnl strides* **16/1**
-400 **5** *2 1/4* **Foxtrot Alpha (IRE)**[38] 2967 4-9-2 **55** IanMongan 13 54
(P Winkworth) *led tl over 1f out: no ex fnl f* **9/1**
3605 **6** *1 1/4* **Fly By Nelly**[38] 2967 4-9-2 **55** (p) SteveDrowne 3 50
(H Morrison) *chsd ldrs: rdn over 2f out: one pce* **8/1**[3]
0004 **7** *1/2* **Pipers Piping (IRE)**[29] 3280 4-8-13 **55** MichaelStainton(3) 9 49
(P Howling) *mid-div: effrt over 2f out: styd on same pce* **8/1**[3]
41-5 **8** *1* **Eliza Doolittle**[29] 3280 4-9-6 **59** AdamKirby 1 50
(Matthew Salaman) *bhd: sme hdwy over 1f out: nt rch ldrs* **14/1**
0044 **9** *1/2* **Song Of Praise**[14] 3762 4-9-4 **57** NeilChalmers 4 47
(M Blanshard) *bhd: sme hdwy over 1f out: no imp* **14/1**
0000 **10** *hd* **Woolston Ferry (IRE)**[29] 3279 4-8-11 **57** (p) DavidKenny(7) 2 46
(David Pinder) *rdn leaving stalls: sn in midfield: outpcd fnl 3f* **33/1**
0213 **11** *5* **Goodbye Cash (IRE)**[8] 3968 6-9-4 **60** RichardEvans(3) 11 36
(R J Smith) *dwlt: sn in midfield on rail: rdn 4f out: sn outpcd* **12/1**
010- **12** *18* **Philmack Dot Com**[221] 7719 4-9-6 **59** AndreaAtzeni 14 —
(D Donovan) *dwlt: sn prom: hrd rdn and wknd over 2f out* **25/1**

1m 26.38s (0.38) **Going Correction** +0.025s/f (Slow) **12** Ran SP% **124.8**
Speed ratings (Par 101): **98,97,97,96,94 92,92,90,90,90 84,63**
toteswingers: 1&2 £4.10, 1&3 £10.50, 2&3 £35.70 CSF £10.50 CT £115.73 TOTE £2.60: £1.40, £2.40, £6.80; EX 12.80 Place 6 £9.35, Place 5 £4.28.
Owner Mrs J E L Wright **Bred** Stone Ridge Farm **Trained** Baughurst, Hants
■ Stewards' Enquiry : Jim Crowley caution: careless riding.

FOCUS
A moderate handicap run at just an ordinary gallop. The principals raced in the centre in the straight.
T/Plt: £18.00 to a £1 stake. Pool: £67,306.06. 2,729.05 winning tickets. T/Qpdt: £7.50 to a £1 stake. Pool: £7,015.36. 686.59 winning tickets. LM

[4207] YARMOUTH (L-H)
Tuesday, July 20

OFFICIAL GOING: Good to firm (8.1)
Wind: Light, against Weather: Overcast, warm and muggy

4233 CRABBIES ALCOHOLIC GINGER BEER MAIDEN AUCTION STKS 6f 3y
2:15 (2:16) (Class 5) 2-Y-O **£2,590** (£770; £385; £192) **Stalls** High

Form RPR
303 **1** **Elkmait**[19] 3583 2-8-11 0 SebSanders 2 80+
(C E Brittain) *t.k.h early: w ldr tl led after 1f: mde rest: rdn clr wl over 1f out: r.o strly: easily* **5/2**[1]
2025 **2** *6* **Never Can Stop**[22] 3509 2-8-1 0 ow2 JohnFahy(5) 8 57
(J G Portman) *chsd ldr tl chsd wnr ent fnl 2f: rdn and nt pce of wnr wl over 1f out: kpt on same pce after* **3/1**[2]
3 *1 1/4* **Acclamazing (IRE)** 2-8-11 0 TobyAtkinson(5) 5 63
(M Botti) *hld up in rr: hdwy 1/2-way: rdn to chse ldng pair 2f out: sn outpcd by wnr: kpt on same pce after* **8/1**
0 **4** *1 1/2* **Sabratha (IRE)**[41] 2873 2-8-4 0 DaraghO'Donohoe 4 47
(B J Curley) *plld hrd: led for 1f: chsd wnr after tl ent fnl 2f: sn rdn and btn* **6/1**[3]
6 **5** *1/2* **Nettis**[19] 3602 2-8-12 0 SaleemGolam 1 53
(G Prodromou) *s.i.s: in tch: rdn and outpcd over 2f out: no ch fnl 2f: kpt on same pce ins fnl f* **33/1**
6 *6* **Masonic Lady (IRE)** 2-8-7 0 LiamJones 7 30
(W J Haggas) *towards rr: rdn and struggling 1/2-way: lost tch ent fnl 2f* **6/1**[3]
03 **7** *3/4* **Princess Izzy**[30] 3237 2-8-11 0 KierenFallon 6 32
(M H Tompkins) *chsd ldrs: rdn and wknd qckly ent fnl 2f: wl btn over 1f out: eased ins fnl f* **6/1**[3]
8 *12* **Fajer Al Kuwait** 2-8-2 0 CharlotteKerton(7) 3 —
(G Prodromou) *s.i.s: a bhd: lost tch over 2f out* **66/1**

1m 13.85s (-0.55) **Going Correction** -0.075s/f (Good) **8** Ran SP% **112.0**
Speed ratings (Par 94): **100,92,90,88,87 79,78,62**
toteswingers: 1&2 £2.40, 1&3 £3.00, 2&3 £4.80 CSF £9.67 TOTE £2.60: £1.10, £1.40, £4.10; EX 11.40 Trifecta £55.40 Pool: £487.33 - 6.50 winning units..
Owner Saeed Manana **Bred** Fernhill Stud **Trained** Newmarket, Suffolk

FOCUS
A weak juvenile maiden in which they raced up the middle of the track. The easy winner showed improved form, but how much by is hard to gauge.

NOTEBOOK
Elkmait failed to progress from a promising debut behind Memory on her next two starts, playing up on the stalls on both occasions, but she was calmer this time and totally outclassed her rivals. Now clearly going the right way, she can hold her own in better company. (op 11-4)
Never Can Stop, reported to have been unsuited by fast ground at Windsor last time, carried 2lb overweight and couldn't go with the winner. She might be more of a nursery filly. (op 7-2)
Acclamazing(IRE), a 23,000euros half-brother to 5f-6f winner Tagula Breeze, was under pressure by about halfway and looked in need of the experience, but showed ability. (op 7-1)
Sabratha(IRE), who showed ability over 5f here on debut, was keen early and displayed a bit of a knee action. She has ability and should find her level once handicapped. (op 14-1)
Nettis also showed ability and, being a strong colt with plenty of size, he should come on again. (tchd 40-1)
Masonic Lady(IRE), a 15,000gns purchase, was under pressure soon after the start and needed the experience. (op 4-1)
Princess Izzy rather ran in snatches before dropping right out. Official explanation: trainer said filly was unsuited by the good to firm ground (op 9-2)

4234 SUZUKI AT M R KING AT LOWESTOFT H'CAP 6f 3y
2:45 (2:45) (Class 6) (0-60,60) 3-Y-O+ **£2,072** (£616; £308; £153) **Stalls** High

Form RPR
0401 **1** **Clerical (USA)**[7] 3993 4-9-0 **51** 6ex (p) J-PGuillambert 1 61
(R M H Cowell) *led tl rdn and hdd over 1f out: drvn to ld again ins fnl f: styd on wl to assert fnl 50yds* **7/1**
0040 **2** *2* **Errigal Lad**[12] 3809 5-9-9 **60** (p) AndrewElliott 13 64
(J Balding) *racd alone on stands' rail: in tch: rdn and hung lft 2f out: drvn and chsd ldng pair ins fnl f: kpt on to snatch 2nd last stride* **16/1**
0320 **3** *shd* **Bathwick Xaara**[11] 3866 3-8-11 **58** JohnFahy(5) 2 61
(J G Portman) *w wnr: rdn ent fnl 2f: led over 1f out tl hdd ins fnl f: wknd fnl 50yds: lost 2nd last stride* **7/2**[2]
0040 **4** *nk* **He's A Humbug (IRE)**[35] 3061 6-9-9 **60** TedDurcan 5 63
(J O'Reilly) *in tch: rdn and unable qck 2f out: hdwy u.p ins fnl f: styng on at fin: nvr gng pce to threaten wnr* **14/1**
0006 **5** *1 1/2* **City For Conquest (IRE)**[7] 3976 7-8-6 **46** oh1 (b) KellyHarrison(3) 8 44
(John A Harris) *s.i.s: hld up in rr: stl plenty to do and nt clr run ent fnl 2f: edging lft and hdwy over 1f out: kpt on u.p fnl f: nvr trbld ldrs* **33/1**
2042 **6** *1/2* **Maryolini**[16] 3717 5-9-4 **55** NickyMackay 12 51
(T Keddy) *in tch: hdwy to chse ldng pair over 1f out: rdn ent fnl f: wknd fnl 150yds* **15/2**
6254 **7** *2* **Sirjosh**[7] 3993 4-9-4 **55** AndreaAtzeni 9 45
(D Donovan) *hld up in rr: switching rt and effrt ent fnl 2f: no prog and wl hld ent fnl f* **5/1**[3]
0300 **8** *2 1/2* **Sweet Applause (IRE)**[7] 3993 4-9-1 **52** KirstyMilczarek 10 34
(G Prodromou) *plld hrd: stdd after s: hld up in rr: rdn and short-lived effrt ent fnl 2f: nvr trbld ldrs* **25/1**
00-0 **9** *1/2* **Kings On The Roof**[132] 845 4-8-9 **46** oh1 PaulEddery 11 26
(P Leech) *chsd ldrs tl rdn and wknd ent fnl 2f: wl btn fnl f* **40/1**
60/4 **10** *1* **Emma's Secrets**[95] 1345 5-8-12 **49** NeilCallan 6 26
(D Shaw) *stdd s: t.k.h: hld up in tch in midfield: rdn and effrt ent fnl 2f: sn struggling: wl btn over 1f out* **40/1**
4045 **11** *6* **Nawaaff**[19] 3605 5-8-6 **46** oh1 WilliamCarson(3) 4 4
(M Quinn) *hld up towards rr: rdn and no prog 2f out: wl btn after* **33/1**
3-02 **12** *shd* **Baby Rock**[22] 3510 5-9-4 **55** GeorgeBaker 3 13
(C F Wall) *hld up towards rr: shkn up and no rspnse ent fnl 2f: wl btn over 1f out* **3/1**[1]
650- **13** *32* **Chris's Jem**[293] 6377 4-9-7 **58** LiamJones 7 —
(J R Jenkins) *chsd ldrs tl dropped out qckly over 2f out: virtually p.u fnl f: t.o* **33/1**

1m 13.01s (-1.39) **Going Correction** -0.075s/f (Good)
WFA 3 from 4yo+ 5lb **13** Ran SP% **118.3**
Speed ratings (Par 101): **106,103,103,102,100 100,97,94,93,92 84,84,41**
toteswingers: 1&2 £14.30, 1&3 £5.10, 2&3 £11.70 CSF £102.52 CT £470.63 TOTE £9.60: £3.10, £6.80, £1.70; EX 116.60 Trifecta £637.60 Part won. Pool: £861.71 - 0.60 winning units..
Owner J Sargeant **Bred** Walmac Stud Management Llc **Trained** Six Mile Bottom, Cambs

FOCUS
A moderate sprint handicap. They all raced up the centre of the track, with the exception of Errigal Lad, who was alone towards the stands' rail for much of the way.
Sirjosh Official explanation: jockey said gelding lost a front shoe
Sweet Applause(IRE) Official explanation: jockey said filly was unsuited by the good to firm ground
Baby Rock Official explanation: trainer's rep had no explanation for the poor form shown

4235 GREAT YARMOUTH SEALIFE CENTRE H'CAP 1m 3f 101y
3:15 (3:16) (Class 6) (0-65,65) 3-Y-O £2,007 (£597; £298; £149) Stalls Low

Form RPR
000- 1 **Albacocca**[297] 6284 3-8-7 51 ow1 SebSanders 6 60
(Sir Mark Prescott) *chsd ldr: rdn 4f out: drvn to ld 2f out: hrd drvn ent fnl f: kpt on gamely* **13/2**
04-6 2 *hd* **Little Oz (IRE)**[22] 3513 3-9-1 59 KierenFallon 7 68
(E A L Dunlop) *stdd s: hld up in last pair: pushed along wl over 3f out: rdn and hdwy 3f out: chsd wnr and flashing tail u.p over 1f out: ev ch ins fnl f: nt qckn and hld towards fin* **13/8**[1]
0-60 3 *7* **Polebrook**[70] 1989 3-8-1 50 JohnFahy(5) 2 47
(J R Jenkins) *s.i.s: hld up bhd: hdwy on outer 3f out: rdn 2f out: no ch w ldng pair 1f out: plugged on to go modest 3rd ins fnl f* **33/1**
0422 4 *3 1/4* **Apache Kid (IRE)**[20] 3564 3-9-7 65 NeilCallan 5 57
(D M Simcock) *in tch in midfield: rdn and effrt over 3f out: no prog wl over 1f out: wknd over 1f out* **7/4**[2]
035 5 *1 1/4* **Best Of Broadway (IRE)**[20] 3564 3-8-9 53 (b) TedDurcan 4 42
(D R Lanigan) *led: rdn and hdd 2f out: btn jst over 1f out: wknd fnl f* **6/1**[3]
00-5 6 *4 1/2* **Rock Of Behistun (IRE)**[7] 3996 3-8-2 46 oh1 JamieMackay 3 28
(P L Gilligan) *dwlt: sn bustled up to chse ldrs: struggling u.p wl over 3f out: wl bhd fnl 2f* **66/1**
000- 7 *13* **Sarmad (USA)**[322] 5547 3-8-2 46 oh1 KoseiMiura 8 6
(C E Brittain) *chsd ldrs tl lost pl 5f out: wl bhd fnl 2f: t.o* **20/1**
2m 26.36s (-2.34) **Going Correction** -0.25s/f (Firm) 7 Ran SP% **111.3**
Speed ratings (Par 98): **98,97,92,90,89 86,76**
toteswingers: 1&2 £3.70, 1&3 £12.70, 2&3 £10.40 CSF £16.61 CT £310.46 TOTE £6.30: £4.40, £1.10; EX 15.60 Trifecta £456.90 Pool: £710.14 - 1.15 winning units..
Owner Miss K Rausing **Bred** Miss K Rausing **Trained** Newmarket, Suffolk
■ Stewards' Enquiry : Seb Sanders one-day ban: used whip with excessive frequency (Aug 3)
FOCUS
Just a modest handicap but the front two, who pulled clear, look well handicapped.
Albacocca ◆ Official explanation: trainer's rep said, regarding apparent improvement in form, that the filly appreciated being stepped up in trip and strengthening over the winter, having not run since September.

4236 STANLEY THREADWELL MEMORIAL FILLIES' H'CAP 1m 3y
3:45 (3:48) (Class 5) (0-70,70) 3-Y-O+ £2,201 (£655; £327; £163) Stalls High

Form RPR
1-65 1 **Avon Lady**[29] 3268 3-9-10 69 PatCosgrave 1 78
(J R Fanshawe) *in tch: hdwy to press ldrs ent fnl 2f: rdn to ld over 1f out: hung rt ent fnl f: styd on wl fnl 100yds: rdn out* **10/3**[1]
4024 2 *1* **Russian Rave**[8] 3962 4-9-9 65 JohnFahy(5) 3 74
(J G Portman) *dwlt: t.k.h: chsd ldrs after 2f: rdn and ev ch ent fnl 2f: led wl over 1f out: sn hdd: styd on same pce u.p fnl 100yds* **7/2**[2]
0550 3 *1* **Al Rayanah**[17] 3690 7-8-13 50 (p) SaleemGolam 6 57
(G Prodromou) *stdd s: t.k.h: hld up towards rr: hdwy and hanging rt over 1f out: chsd ldng pair whn nt clr run and swtchd lft ins fnl f: no imp fnl 100yds* **20/1**
5015 4 *1 1/2* **Amber Sunset**[48] 2643 4-9-10 64 WilliamCarson(3) 9 67
(D Morris) *racd alone on stands' rail: prom: chsd overall ldr over 3f out tl 2f out: wknd ent fnl f: btn whn nt clr run ins fnl f* **14/1**
5040 5 *nk* **Astrodonna**[11] 3854 5-9-9 65 AshleyMorgan(5) 4 68
(M H Tompkins) *in tch: hdwy to chse ldrs over 1f out: rdn and unable qck ent fnl f: wknd fnl 100yds* **6/1**
0-26 6 *2 1/4* **Iptkaar (USA)**[111] 1060 3-9-11 70 (b) NeilCallan 2 65
(C E Brittain) *sn bustled up to ld: rdn and hdd wl over 1f out: wknd u.p jst over 1f out* **8/1**
000 7 *4* **Blue Zealot (IRE)**[56] 2425 3-9-4 63 HayleyTurner 7 49
(M L W Bell) *rn green and sn pushed along in last: struggling over 3f out: no hdwy tl plugged on past btn horses fnl f: n.d* **14/1**
4314 8 *nk* **Denton Ryal**[16] 3714 3-8-6 58 AdamBeschizza(7) 8 43
(M E Rimmer) *hld up towards rr: rdn and hdwy over 2f out: drvn and wknd over 1f out* **9/2**[3]
5-40 9 *4* **Chantilly Dancer (IRE)**[29] 3264 4-8-6 46 Louis-PhilippeBeuzelin(3) 5 24
(M Quinn) *chsd ldr tl over 3f out: sn struggling u.p: wl btn over 1f out* **20/1**
0002 10 *3 1/4* **Montego Breeze**[10] 3911 4-9-1 52 (p) DaraghO'Donohoe 10 23
(John A Harris) *t.k.h: hld up in tch: rdn and btn ent fnl 2f: wl bhd over 1f out* **22/1**
1m 39.84s (-0.76) **Going Correction** -0.075s/f (Good)
WFA 3 from 4yo+ 8lb 10 Ran SP% **116.1**
Speed ratings (Par 100): **100,99,98,96,96 93,89,89,85,82**
toteswingers: 1&2 £2.90, 1&3 £11.80, 2&3 £14.30 CSF £14.53 CT £203.53 TOTE £3.50: £1.10, £1.40, £4.70; EX 18.00 Trifecta £211.60 Pool: £560.56 - 1.96 winning units..
Owner Helena Springfield Ltd **Bred** Meon Valley Stud **Trained** Newmarket, Suffolk
FOCUS
A modest fillies' handicap. Amber Sunset raced alone against the stands' rail for much of the way, while the remainder were positioned up the middle, but the principals ended up edging towards the near side.

4237 AVENUE PUBLIC HOUSE H'CAP 7f 3y
4:15 (4:16) (Class 5) (0-70,69) 3-Y-O+ £2,201 (£655; £327; £163) Stalls High

Form RPR
4334 1 **Aleqa**[12] 3816 3-9-8 67 AlanMunro 3 72+
(C F Wall) *trckd ldrs: rdn and qcknd to ld jst over 1f out: r.o strly fnl 100yds* **9/4**[1]
0205 2 *1* **Darcey**[12] 3830 4-9-9 66 IanBrennan(5) 8 71
(Miss Amy Weaver) *in tch: rdn and effrt over 1f out: ev ch jst ins fnl f: nt pce of wnr fnl 100yds* **9/2**[3]
432 3 *shd* **Cardinal**[38] 2965 5-9-3 55 (t) FrankieDettori 10 60
(R M H Cowell) *led at stdy gallop tl over 4f out: trckd ldr after: rdn: qcknd and ev ch ent fnl f: nt pce of wnr fnl 100yds* **3/1**[2]
4-00 4 *1 1/4* **Freedom Pass (USA)**[51] 2564 3-8-13 58 (t) KirstyMilczarek 9 56
(J A R Toller) *stdd after s: t.k.h: hld up in tch in rr: rdn and hdwy over 1f out: nt clr run and swtchd lft 1f out: keeping on but hld whn nt clr run towards fin* **16/1**
-300 5 *3* **Mudhish (IRE)**[70] 2009 5-10-0 66 (b) KoseiMiura 1 59
(C E Brittain) *chsd ldrs tl rdn and unable qck ent fnl 2f: edgd rt and kpt on one pce fr over 1f out* **10/1**
000- 6 *3* **Norcroft**[250] 7348 8-8-4 49 (p) LeonnaMayor(7) 4 34
(Mrs C A Dunnett) *stdd after s: t.k.h: hld up in tch tl hdwy to ld over 4f out: rdn 2f out: hdd jst over 1f out: sn btn* **33/1**
0-00 7 *hd* **This Ones For Eddy**[14] 3761 5-9-6 58 AndrewElliott 2 43
(J Balding) *hld up in tch towards rr: shkn up and no rspnse wl over 1f out: swtchd rt 1f out and then lft jst ins fnl f: nvr trbld ldrs* **9/2**[3]
0-00 8 *24* **Melting Bob (USA)**[139] 768 4-8-12 53 Louis-PhilippeBeuzelin(3) 7 —
(Dr J D Scargill) *stdd s: hld up in tch in rr: struggling over 2f out: sn lost tch: eased fnl f* **33/1**
1m 27.06s (0.46) **Going Correction** -0.075s/f (Good)
WFA 3 from 4yo+ 7lb 8 Ran SP% **113.0**
Speed ratings (Par 103): **94,92,92,91,87 84,84,56**
toteswingers: 1&2 £2.60, 1&3 £1.70, 2&3 £3.20 CSF £12.39 CT £29.27 TOTE £3.10: £1.10, £2.00, £1.90; EX 14.60 Trifecta £35.80 Pool: £476.82 - 9.85 winning units..
Owner Ms Aida Fustoq **Bred** Deerfield Farm **Trained** Newmarket, Suffolk
■ Stewards' Enquiry : Alan Munro two-day ban: used whip without giving filly time to respond (Aug 4-5)
FOCUS
Just a modest handicap, run in a time 1.66 seconds slower than the following maiden, and they raced towards the stands' side.
Melting Bob(USA) Official explanation: jockey said filly jumped the road and lost its action

4238 PEUGEOT AT M R KING LOWESTOFT MAIDEN STKS 7f 3y
4:45 (4:50) (Class 5) 3-4-Y-O £2,460 (£732; £365; £182) Stalls High

Form RPR
3 1 **Wear 'Em Out Wilf**[26] 3374 3-9-3 0 JamieSpencer 11 79
(P W Chapple-Hyam) *in tch: rdn and effrt to chal wl over 1f out: edgd lft u.p and led 1f out: r.o wl u.p fnl f* **13/2**[3]
3- 2 *shd* **Barq (IRE)**[249] 7376 3-9-3 0 (t) FrankieDettori 2 79
(Saeed Bin Suroor) *chsd ldr tl pushed into ld wl over 1f out: hdd 1f out: r.o wl u.p fnl f but a jst hld* **2/1**[2]
3 *6* **Bizarrely (IRE)**[69] 2038 3-8-12 0 SimonPearce(5) 6 63
(J Pearce) *racd keenly: led tl pushed along and hdd wl over 1f out: wl outpcd by ldng pair jst over 1f out: kpt on same pce fnl f* **33/1**
20 4 *2 3/4* **Librettista (AUS)**[34] 3080 4-9-5 0 KierenFallon 10 53
(L M Cumani) *in tch towards rr: pushed and effrt over 2f out: wl outpcd by ldrs 2f out: plugged on to go modest 4th ins fnl f* **9/1**
32-6 5 *1* **Esaar (USA)**[17] 1308 3-9-3 80 RichardHills 7 52
(B W Hills) *bmpd and hmpd s: t.k.h and sn trcking ldrs: rdn and effrt ent fnl 2f: fnd virtually nil and wl btn over 1f out* **1/1**[1]
6-0 6 *1 1/2* **Waabel**[4] 4107 3-9-0 0 RobertLButler(3) 1 48
(Jim Best) *in tch: pushed along and wknd jst over 2f out: wl btn over 1f out* **33/1**
00- 7 *23* **Lily Eva**[202] 7882 4-9-5 0 AndreaAtzeni 8 —
(D Donovan) *sltly hmpd s: a bhd: pushed along 4f out: rdn and lost tch over 3f out: t.o* **66/1**
8 *1/2* **She's Untouchable** 3-8-12 0 MickyFenton 5 —
(P Leech) *in tch tl rn green and dropped out rapidly wl over 2f out: t.o* **100/1**
1m 25.4s (-1.20) **Going Correction** -0.075s/f (Good)
WFA 3 from 4yo 7lb 8 Ran SP% **115.0**
Speed ratings (Par 103): **103,102,96,92,91 90,63,63**
toteswingers: 1&2 £2.50, 1&3 £6.10, 2&3 £9.20 CSF £19.92 TOTE £5.00: £1.40, £1.40, £5.00; EX 19.30 Trifecta £239.10 Pool: £1,008.22 - 3.12 winning units..
Owner The Comic Strip Heroes **Bred** Bumble Bloodstock **Trained** Newmarket, Suffolk
■ Stewards' Enquiry : Robert L Butler ten-day ban: in breach of Rule (B) 59.4 (Aug 3-12)
FOCUS
The time was 1.66 seconds quicker than the earlier Class 5 handicap and the front two pulled clear. The action took place centre-field.
Esaar(USA) Official explanation: trainer's rep had no explanation for the poor form shown
Waabel Official explanation: jockey said, regarding running and riding, that his orders were to bounce out, sit handy, keep hold of the gelding and to finish the race.

4239 VOLVO AT M R KING HALESWORTH H'CAP 5f 43y
5:15 (5:17) (Class 6) (0-60,60) 4-Y-O+ £2,115 (£624; £312) Stalls High

Form RPR
5312 1 **You'relikemefrank**[18] 3623 4-8-10 52 (p) AndrewElliott 7 59
(J Balding) *taken down early: hld up in tch in rr: hdwy 1/2-way: rdn to chse ldrs over 1f out: drvn to ld ins fnl f: r.o wl* **11/4**[2]
3502 2 *1/2* **Pocket's Pick (IRE)**[19] 3605 4-9-4 60 (b) IanMongan 4 65
(Jim Best) *taken down early: led: rdn over 1f out: drvn and hdd ins fnl f: no ex towards fin* **6/1**
6610 3 *1* **Greek Secret**[7] 3976 7-9-4 60 (b) KierenFallon 5 62
(J O'Reilly) *stdd s: hld up in tch: effrt: nt clr run and switching lft ent fnl f: r.o fnl 150yds: nt rch ldrs* **15/2**
6333 4 *1 1/2* **Thoughtsofstardom**[7] 3994 7-9-2 58 (be) FrankieDettori 2 54
(P S McEntee) *trckd ldr: swtchd lft and nt clr run over 1f out tl ins fnl f: styd on same pce after* **5/2**[1]
2432 5 *1/2* **Bookiesindex Boy**[14] 3761 6-8-10 52 (b) JamieSpencer 1 46
(J R Jenkins) *racd along in centre tl c towards stands' side 2f out: chsd ldrs: wnt 2nd 2f out: shkn up and fnd little jst over 1f out: rdn and wknd ins fnl f* **7/2**[3]
0000 6 *8* **Russian Rocket (IRE)**[7] 3994 8-8-8 50 SaleemGolam 3 16
(Mrs C A Dunnett) *a in rr: pushed along 1/2-way: rdn and lost tch wl over 1f out* **14/1**
62.31 secs (-0.39) **Going Correction** -0.075s/f (Good) 6 Ran SP% **110.2**
Speed ratings (Par 101): **96,95,93,91,90 77**
toteswingers: 1&2 £2.40, 1&3 £4.20, 2&3 £4.60 CSF £18.33 TOTE £4.20: £2.10, £3.00; EX 22.10 Place 6 £43.87, Place 5 £25.12.
Owner Kate Barrett, Paul & David Clarkson **Bred** J R Mitchell **Trained** Scrooby, Notts
■ Stewards' Enquiry : Frankie Dettori three-day ban: careless riding (Aug 3-5); one-day ban: failed to ride to draw (Aug 6)
FOCUS
A moderate sprint in which they all ended up towards the near rail.
T/Jkpt: £5,730.10 to a £1 stake. Pool: £100,882.85. 12.50 winning tickets. T/Plt: £46.40 to a £1 stake. Pool: £81,407.17. 1,278.30 winning tickets. T/Qpdt: £10.00 to a £1 stake. Pool: £5,880.02. 431.95 winning tickets. SP

4013 CATTERICK (L-H)

Wednesday, July 21

OFFICIAL GOING: Good to soft (good in places; 7.5)

Wind: Light across Weather: cloudy - sunny periods

4240 EUROPEAN BREEDERS' FUND MAIDEN STKS 5f 212y

2:10 (2:13) (Class 5) 2-Y-O **£3,140** (£934; £467; £233) **Stalls** Low

Form RPR

4 **1** **Talley Close**[27] 3365 2-9-3 0 PaulHanagan 8 76+
(R A Fahey) *trckd ldrs on outer: hdwy 1/2-way: rdn to chal wl over 1f out: kpt on to ld jst ins fnl f: drvn out* **9/4**[1]

3 **2** *1 1/4* **Malgoof (IRE)**[19] 3611 2-9-3 0 TomEaves 11 71
(B Smart) *prom: trckd ldr after 2f: swtchd lft and effrt to chal wl over 1f out: sn rdn and ev ch: drvn ent fnl f: edgd rt and no ex towards fin* **10/3**[2]

64 **3** *shd* **Top Care (USA)**[13] 3805 2-9-3 0 GregFairley 2 71
(M Johnston) *led: c wd to stands' rail home st and sn rdn: jnd wl over 1f out and sn drvn: hdd jst ins fnl f: n.m.r and kpt on* **8/1**

5 **4** *6* **Reason To Believe (IRE)**[34] 3118 2-9-3 0 PhillipMakin 7 53
(B M R Haslam) *chsd ldrs: hdwy over 2f out: sn rdn and one pce fr over 1f out* **13/2**

02 **5** *3 1/4* **Baby Driver**[22] 3528 2-9-3 0 PaulMulrennan 10 43
(J Howard Johnson) *cl up: rdn along 1/2-way: grad wknd* **14/1**

5 **6** *hd* **Hal Of A Lover**[13] 3805 2-9-3 0 TonyHamilton 5 43
(R A Fahey) *midfield: effrt over 2f out: sn rdn and no imp* **18/1**

00 **7** *1/2* **C P Joe (IRE)**[4] 4123 2-9-3 0 FrannyNorton 3 41
(Paul Green) *a towards rr* **5/1**[3]

0 **8** *shd* **Better Self**[21] 3550 2-8-12 0 RoystonFfrench 1 36
(Mrs A Duffield) *s.i.s and in rr tl sme late hdwy* **33/1**

0 **9** *3/4* **Newport Arch**[18] 3657 2-9-3 0 RobertWinston 4 39
(J J Quinn) *dwlt: hdwy and in tch 1/2-way: sn rdn and no further prog* **66/1**

00 **10** *7* **Carver County (IRE)**[15] 3756 2-9-3 0 RichardMullen 9 18
(K A Ryan) *s.i.s: a in rr* **50/1**

1m 15.52s (1.92) **Going Correction** +0.25s/f (Good) **10** Ran SP% **113.3**

Speed ratings (Par 94): **97,95,95,87,82 82,81,81,80,71**

toteswingers:1&2:£2.20, 1&3:£3.80, 2&3:£6.00 CSF £9.16 TOTE £2.80: £1.20, £1.40, £2.00; EX 12.10.

Owner Skeltools Ltd **Bred** A B Phipps **Trained** Musley Bank, N Yorks

FOCUS

It was no surprise to see a change in the going, with 32mm of overnight rain making it good to soft, good in places. The time of the opener was 3.52secs slower than standard, with winning rider Paul Hanagan describing the ground as 'pretty soft'. The runners came stands' side in the straight, as is often the case here when it rains.

NOTEBOOK

Talley Close, who had been comfortably held when favourite at Newcastle on debut, drew clear in the final furlong. He has obviously learned from that initial experience and appeals as the type to go forward again when upped to 7f. (op 2-1 tchd 11-4)

Malgoof(IRE), well held when third of five on debut, seemed suited by the ease in the going and showed much-improved form. (op 7-2 tchd 4-1)

Top Care(USA) stepped up on his first two efforts, leading them across to the stands' side and keeping on right the way to the line. He should make his mark in nurseries. (op 7-1 tchd 6-1)

Reason To Believe(IRE) was under pressure before the straight and could only plug on at the one pace. (op 11-1 tchd 6-1)

Baby Driver didn't get home having been up there early. (op 11-1)

C P Joe(IRE) Official explanation: jockey said colt hung left-handed in straight

4241 ST TERESA'S HOSPICE (S) STKS 7f

2:40 (2:47) (Class 6) 2-Y-O **£1,706** (£503; £252) **Stalls** Low

Form RPR

0021 **1** **Lord Of The Storm**[8] 3992 2-9-0 0 (p) JackDean(3) 9 65
(W G M Turner) *chsd ldrs: hdwy 2f out: rdn to ld ent fnl f: edgd lft and kpt on towards fin* **3/1**[2]

030 **2** *3/4* **Kodibelle (IRE)**[58] 2391 2-8-6 0 (b) DuranFentiman 11 52
(T D Easterby) *qckly away and sn led: jnd and rdn over 2f out: drvn and edgd rt over 1f out: hdd ent fnl f: kpt on* **12/1**

5322 **3** *3 1/4* **Alhoni**[33] 3175 2-8-6 0 PaulHanagan 13 44
(J J Quinn) *chsd ldrs: rdn along over 2f out: kpt on fnl f* **11/4**[1]

0 **4** *2* **Commander Veejay**[5] 4116 2-8-11 0 TomEaves 14 44
(B S Rothwell) *s.i.s and in rr: hdwy wl over 2f out: rdn over 1f out: kpt on ins fnl f: nrst fin* **50/1**

4305 **5** *1 1/4* **Sarandjam**[33] 3175 2-8-11 0 RobertWinston 1 49
(M R Channon) *trckd ldng pair: hdwy 1/2-way: chal over 2f out and sn rdn: stl cl up on inner and drvn whn n.m.r and hmpd appr fnl f: nt rcvr* **7/1**[3]

5566 **6** *1 3/4* **Dispol Snapper (IRE)**[29] 3281 2-8-11 0 PhillipMakin 4 37
(P T Midgley) *towards rr: hdwy wl over 2f out: sn rdn and no imp fnl f* **22/1**

2000 **7** *3/4* **Box Of Frogs (IRE)**[15] 3757 2-8-1 0 (b) DeclanCannon(5) 7 30
(A J McCabe) *chsd ldr: rdn along 3f out: grad wknd* **25/1**

0 **8** *nk* **Thunderway (IRE)**[27] 3365 2-8-1 0 PatrickDonaghy(5) 2 29
(M Dods) *midfield and n.m.r on inner bnd after 2f: pushed along 1/2-way: rdn 2f out: sme late hdwy* **25/1**

006 **9** *4 1/2* **Buon Compleanno (IRE)**[19] 3625 2-8-6 0 FrannyNorton 8 18
(A Berry) *a towards rr* **100/1**

6 **10** *1* **Fol Pickle**[47] 2693 2-8-6 0 BillyCray(5) 5 20
(D Nicholls) *t.k.h: chsd ldrs tl hung bdly rt home turn: sn lost pl and bhd* **11/4**[1]

006 **11** *12* **Bert And Ernie**[18] 3678 2-8-11 0 SamHitchcott 10 —
(M R Channon) *dwlt: sn outpcd and bhd fr 1/2-way* **33/1**

00 **12** *1/2* **Plumsum**[43] 2836 2-8-9 0 ow3 DanielTudhope 6 —
(N Bycroft) *s.i.s: a towards rr* **150/1**

0 **13** *24* **Cono (IRE)**[97] 1331 2-8-11 0 AndrewMullen 3 —
(Miss Tracy Waggott) *midfield: lost pl and bhd fr 1/2-way* **50/1**

1m 31.41s (4.41) **Going Correction** +0.25s/f (Good) **13** Ran SP% **119.1**

Speed ratings (Par 92): **84,83,79,77,75 73,72,72,67,66 52,51,24**

toteswingers:1&2:£11.20, 1&3:£2.60, 2&3:£7.60 CSF £35.27 TOTE £3.40: £1.30, £5.50, £1.80; EX 62.20.The winner was bought in for 8,500gns.

Owner Mrs M S Teversham **Bred** Mrs Monica Teversham **Trained** Sigwells, Somerset

FOCUS

An ordinary seller, but one that should produce winners. The field again headed over to the stands' side on straightening. The winning time was 1.5secs slower than the following nursery.

NOTEBOOK

Lord Of The Storm, narrow winner of a selling nursery at Yarmouth, was experiencing a soft surface for the first time and conceding weight all round, but the first-time cheekpieces seemed to coax further improvement and he kept on well down the straight to get on top inside the final furlong. He was bought in for 8,500gns. (op 7-2 tchd 10-3 in a place)

Kodibelle(IRE) did well to get across and lead. She battled on well inside the final 2f, having been joined, and was far enough clear of the remainder to suggest a similar race can be found. (op 28-1)

Alhoni, runner-up to the winner of the following nursery in a Redcar seller last-time-out, appeared to run her race and is building a consistent profile at this level. (op 5-2 tchd 10-3 and 7-2 in a place)

Commander Veejay, beaten 19 lengths when last of ten on his debut five days earlier, was quickly dropped in grade and that, combined with the extra furlong enabled him to show dramatically improved form. He was finishing better than anything, having got behind with a slow start, and appeals as a likely future winner at this level. (op 66-1)

Sarandjam had finished behind Alhoni last time and would probably have reversed the form had he not been squeezed out against the rail over 1f out. (op 17-2 tchd 13-2)

Fol Pickle was walked part of the way down, but then refused to settle in the race and lost his chance having hung badly right off the home bend. (op 5-2 tchd 3-1)

Plumsum Official explanation: jockey said filly lost its action

4242 BEAUTY AND THE BEAST NURSERY 7f

3:10 (3:11) (Class 5) 2-Y-O **£2,266** (£674; £337; £168) **Stalls** Low

Form RPR

5321 **1** **Mica Mika (IRE)**[33] 3175 2-8-8 **67** PaulHanagan 6 68
(R A Fahey) *chsd ldrs: rdn along 3f out: hdwy 2f out and sn ev ch drvn and kpt on to ld ins fnl f* **7/2**[2]

045 **2** *1/2* **Unknown Rebel (IRE)**[78] 1806 2-8-3 **62** SilvestreDeSousa 4 62+
(K A Ryan) *hld up towards rr: hdwy wl over 1f out: rdn to chal ins fnl f: nt qckn towards fin* **7/1**

463 **3** *1* **Hortensis**[21] 3550 2-8-5 **64** DuranFentiman 8 62
(T D Easterby) *trckd ldrs: hdwy on outer and cl up over 2f out: sn rdn: led over 1f out: drvn and hdd ins fnl f: one pce towards fin* **15/2**

446 **4** *2* **Golden Blaze**[17] 3705 2-8-1 **57** oh2 ow3 FrannyNorton 3 53
(James Moffatt) *hld up in rr: hdwy 2f out: rdn over 1f out: kpt on ins fnl f: nrst fin* **25/1**

312 **5** *shd* **Azzurra Du Caprio (IRE)**[20] 3596 2-9-3 **76** TomEaves 5 68
(B M R Haslam) *chsd ldng pair: rdn along over 2f out: sn drvn and kpt on same pce* **11/4**[1]

433 **6** *1* **Night Singer**[35] 3072 2-7-13 **63** JamesSullivan(5) 1 53
(J Howard Johnson) *in rr: rdn along over 2f out: sme late hdwy* **11/2**

0000 **7** *1 3/4* **Whats For Pudding (IRE)**[28] 3315 2-7-5 **57** oh7 NeilFarley(7) 9 42
(D Carroll) *sn led: rdn along over 2f out: hdd & wknd over 1f out* **100/1**

0423 **8** *15* **Beyaz Villas**[11] 3923 2-8-13 **72** AdrianNicholls 7 20
(D Nicholls) *cl up on inner: rdn along over 2f out: sn wknd and eased over 1f out* **9/2**[3]

1m 29.91s (2.91) **Going Correction** +0.25s/f (Good) **8** Ran SP% **111.6**

Speed ratings (Par 94): **93,92,91,89,88 87,85,68**

toteswingers:1&2:£5.70, 1&3:£3.80, 2&3:£9.00 CSF £26.60 CT £168.74 TOTE £3.30: £1.10, £3.70, £3.40; EX 24.10.

Owner Mrs Una Towell **Bred** Yeomanstown Stud **Trained** Musley Bank, N Yorks

FOCUS

A decent little nursery proved to be a good test at the distance. The time was 1.5 seconds quicker than the earlier seller. Once again the field headed over in the straight.

NOTEBOOK

Mica Mika(IRE), ready winner of a seller at Redcar, when appreciating the step up to 7f, looked certain to have more to come switched to handicaps and he really came strong inside the final 2f, getting to the front under strong pressure and then keeping on well. His dam was a 1m2f winner, so he should have no trouble with 1m, and there might be more to come. (op 9-2)

Unknown Rebel(IRE), gelded since last seen, was up 2f in trip and came in for good support throughout the day. He stayed on well having been outpaced, posting improved form, and could pick up something similar if improving again. (op 6-1)

Hortensis, another nursery debutante, improved a little with each start in maidens and she took another step forward. (op 8-1 tchd 7-1)

Golden Blaze showed improved form on this switch to handicaps, despite racing from 2lb 'wrong'. He will stay 1m on this evidence.

Azzurra Du Caprio(IRE), runner-up at Redcar on his nursery debut (form worked out really well), was tackling ground slower than good for the first time and found herself in trouble before they reached the straight. This clearly wasn't her form. (op 9-4 tchd 3-1)

Night Singer, who had run behind some fair types in maidens, was never going on his nursery debut. (tchd 5-1)

Beyaz Villas was eased once beaten, something having presumably gone amiss. Official explanation: jockey said gelding hung left-handed (op 6-1)

4243 SKY BET SUPPORTING THE YORKSHIRE RACING SUMMER FESTIVAL H'CAP 5f

3:40 (3:41) (Class 4) (0-85,85) 3-Y-O+ **£3,885** (£1,156; £577; £288) **Stalls** Low

Form RPR

0152 **1** **Lucky Numbers (IRE)**[5] 4118 4-9-6 **85** JamesSullivan(5) 8 93
(Paul Green) *towards rr and switched to stands' rails after 1f: hdwy 2f out: rdn over 1f out: str run ins fnl f to ld last 40yds* **7/2**[1]

3116 **2** *3/4* **Mey Blossom**[13] 3809 5-8-9 **72** MichaelStainton(3) 4 77
(R M Whitaker) *towards rr: swtchd rt and hdwy 2f out: sn rdn and edgd rt: styd on to ld ins fnl f: drvn: hdd and nt qckn last 40yds* **7/2**[1]

2210 **3** *1* **Wicked Wilma (IRE)**[22] 3533 6-8-6 **66** oh1 FrannyNorton 5 68
(A Berry) *prom: effrt 2f out: rdn to ld over 1f out: hdd and drvn ins fnl f: one pce towards fin* **22/1**

0000 **4** *nk* **Equuleus Pictor**[16] 3736 6-9-1 **78** JackDean(3) 9 79
(J L Spearing) *swtchd to r towards stands' rails and towards rr: hdwy 1/2-way and sn cl up: rdn over 1f out and ev ch tl drvn and one pce ins fnl f* **13/2**[3]

515 **5** *1/2* **La Capriosa**[11] 3902 4-8-12 **72** RobertWinston 3 71
(J A Glover) *prom: effrt to chal wl over 1f out: sn rdn and ev ch tl wknd ent fnl f* **16/1**

0054 **6** *nk* **Le Toreador**[11] 3891 5-9-11 **85** (tp) PaulHanagan 1 83
(K A Ryan) *led: rdn over 1f out: drvn and hdd appr fnl f: wknd* **7/1**

3503 **7** *1 1/2* **Hypnosis**[19] 3622 7-9-0 **74** TonyHamilton 2 66
(N Wilson) *prom: effrt to chse ldr 2f out: sn rdn and wknd appr fnl f* **14/1**

6623 **8** *3* **Mullglen**[18] 3660 4-9-0 **74** (tp) DavidAllan 6 56
(T D Easterby) *hmpd s: a in rr* **5/1**[2]

0144 **9** *hd* **Nomoreblondes**[13] 3809 6-8-10 **70** (p) PaulMulrennan 10 51
(P T Midgley) *wnt rt s: a in rr* **22/1**

0615 **10** 3 1/2 **Crimea (IRE)**[13] 3828 4-9-11 **85** AdrianNicholls 7 53
(D Nicholls) *chsd ldrs: rdn 2f out: sn wknd* **12/1**

60.15 secs (0.35) **Going Correction** +0.20s/f (Good) **10** Ran SP% **115.9**
Speed ratings (Par 105): **105,103,102,101,100 100,98,93,92,87**
toteswingers: 1&2 £3.00, 1&3 £9.90, 2&3 £24.30 CSF £15.04 CT £225.03 TOTE £3.80: £1.20, £1.10, £8.60; EX 20.00.
Owner Men Behaving Badly Two **Bred** Rory O'Brien **Trained** Lydiate, Merseyside

FOCUS
A decent little sprint handicap. For the first time the majority of runners stayed far side in the straight, and though the winner was one of the two to come stands' side, the result suggested there was little in it.
Mullglen Official explanation: jockey said gelding clipped heels at start and never travelled

4244 YORKSHIRE RADIO H'CAP 5f 212y
4:10 (4:10) (Class 6) (0-60,60) 3-Y-O+ **£1,942** (£578; £288; £144) **Stalls** Low

Form RPR

0-03 **1** **Ursus**[14] 3775 5-9-2 **53** (p) PaddyAspell 6 63
(C R Wilson) *t.k.h: chsd ldrs on inner: hdwy to ld over 2f out: swtchd rt to stands' rails and rdn over 1f out: drvn ins fnl f: kpt on wl* **10/1**

3203 **2** 3/4 **Albero Di Giuda (IRE)**[8] 3979 5-9-2 **53** (bt) LeeVickers 9 61
(F Sheridan) *hld up towards rr: hdwy 2f out: rdn to chse ldrs over 1f out: drvn to chal ent fnl f and ev ch tl no ex towards fin* **10/1**

4-52 **3** 3/4 **Residency (IRE)**[11] 3903 4-9-9 **60** TomEaves 12 65
(B Smart) *in tch on wd outside: hdwy 2f out: swtchd rt and rdn over 1f out: styd on ins fnl f: nrst fin* **8/1**

2215 **4** 1/2 **Bermondsey Bob (IRE)**[16] 3734 4-9-4 **58** JackDean(3) 4 62
(J L Spearing) *in tch on inner: hdwy 2f out: rdn to chse ldrs over 1f out: kpt on same pce* **9/2**[1]

0363 **5** hd **Two Turtle Doves (IRE)**[6] 4064 4-9-5 **56** AndrewElliott 1 59
(M Mullineaux) *hld up: hdwy 1/2-way: rdn to chse ldrs wl over 1f out: drvn and one pce ent fnl f* **6/1**[2]

0660 **6** 1 1/4 **Redwater River**[22] 3538 6-8-11 **48** (b) PJMcDonald 10 47
(Mrs R A Carr) *prom: rdn along 2f out: sn drvn and wknd over 1f out* **8/1**

2650 **7** 1 3/4 **Charles Parnell (IRE)**[15] 3761 7-9-4 **58** MichaelStainton(3) 2 51
(S P Griffiths) *s.i.s and in rr tl styd on appr fnl f* **10/1**

0050 **8** 1 1/4 **Head To Head (IRE)**[15] 3763 6-8-13 **50** (tp) SilvestreDeSousa 3 39
(A D Brown) *towards rr: hdwy 2f out: rdn over 1f out: sn no imp* **25/1**

00-0 **9** 1/2 **Danum Dancer**[42] 2849 6-9-9 **60** (b) DanielTudhope 11 48
(N Bycroft) *stdd s: t.k.h: a in rr* **9/1**

6416 **10** 1 3/4 **Almaty Express**[8] 3979 8-8-11 **51** (b) KellyHarrison(3) 5 33
(J R Weymes) *led: rdn over 2f out and racd alone far side: sn hdd & wknd* **18/1**

50-0 **11** 2 3/4 **Captain Royale (IRE)**[8] 3977 5-9-2 **53** (p) RobertWinston 8 26
(Miss Tracy Waggott) *chsd ldrs: rdn along 2f out: sn wknd* **20/1**

-155 **12** 2 3/4 **Secret City (IRE)**[18] 3664 4-9-2 **60** (b) MatthewLawson(7) 7 25
(R Bastiman) *prom: chsd ldr after 2f: rdn along over 2f out: sn drvn and wknd* **15/2**[3]

1m 15.46s (1.86) **Going Correction** +0.25s/f (Good) **12** Ran SP% **117.6**
Speed ratings (Par 101): **97,96,95,94,94 92,90,88,87,85 81,78**
toteswingers:1&2:£11.10, 1&3:£13.60, 2&3:£7.10 CSF £105.34 CT £856.70 TOTE £17.30: £5.50, £5.10, £3.80; EX 126.00.
Owner David Bartlett **Bred** Mrs Andrea Bartlett **Trained** Manfield, N Yorks

FOCUS
Pretty much all of these held a chance of sorts, in what was a wide-open handicap.
Danum Dancer Official explanation: jockey said gelding hung right-handed on bend

4245 WELCOME TO YORKSHIRE MICHELIN STAR EXPERIENCE CLAIMING STKS 5f
4:40 (4:40) (Class 6) 3-Y-O+ **£1,706** (£503; £252) **Stalls** Low

Form RPR

0003 **1** **Galpin Junior (USA)**[6] 4060 4-9-0 75 AdrianNicholls 8 70
(D Nicholls) *trckd ldrs: hdwy to chse ldr wl over 1f out: drvn to chal ent fnl f: sn led and kpt on wl* **11/4**[2]

3405 **2** 2 **Raccoon (IRE)**[23] 3497 10-8-9 62 PJMcDonald 4 57
(Mrs R A Carr) *led 1 1/2f: cl up: rdn over 1f out: kpt on ins fnl f* **9/1**

-000 **3** hd **Supermassive Muse (IRE)**[41] 2883 5-9-0 63 (p) RobertWinston 1 62
(E S McMahon) *in tch on outer: hdwy 2f out: rdn over 1f out: kpt on ins fnl f* **13/2**

00-5 **4** 1 **Windjammer**[61] 2278 6-8-9 50 (b) KellyHarrison(3) 7 56
(L A Mullaney) *cl up: led after 1 1/2f: rdn over 1f out: drvn and hdd ins fnl f: sn wknd* **20/1**

-100 **5** shd **Efistorm**[24] 3474 9-9-1 79 PaulHanagan 2 59
(C R Dore) *trckd ldrs: effrt 2f out: rdn over 1f out: sn drvn and no imp fnl f* **11/8**[1]

-540 **6** 3 1/2 **Makbullet**[20] 3599 3-8-12 70 PaulMulrennan 5 46
(J Howard Johnson) *chsd ldrs: rdn along 2f out: drvn over 1f out and sn wknd* **11/2**[3]

040 **7** 4 1/2 **Mr Rooney (IRE)**[9] 3946 7-8-4 35 (b) VictorSantos(7) 3 26
(A Berry) *s.i.s: a in rr* **100/1**

60.48 secs (0.68) **Going Correction** +0.20s/f (Good)
WFA 3 from 4yo+ 4lb **7** Ran SP% **113.2**
Speed ratings (Par 101): **102,98,98,96,96 91,83**
toteswingers:1&2:£3.60, 1&3:£3.40, 2&3:£5.90 CSF £26.50 TOTE £4.30: £3.10, £6.00; EX 24.30.
Owner Middleham Park Racing XXVII **Bred** Meadow Oaks Farm Llc **Trained** Sessay, N Yorks
■ Stewards' Enquiry : Victor Santos one-day ban: used whip when out of contention (Aug 4)

FOCUS
A competitive claimer.

4246 RACING AGAIN ON 3RD AUGUST APPRENTICE H'CAP 1m 3f 214y
5:10 (5:10) (Class 6) (60-92,65) 4-Y-O+ **£2,047** (£604; £302) **Stalls** Low

Form RPR

40/ **1** **Daytime Dreamer (IRE)**[10] 7545 6-9-10 **65** LeeTopliss 14 73
(M Todhunter) *trckd ldrs gng wl: smooth hdwy over 3f out: chsd ldr 2f out: rdn over 1f out: styd on ins fnl f: squeezed through on inner to ld nr fin* **25/1**

0614 **2** nk **Maneki Neko (IRE)**[21] 3552 8-9-9 **64** RyanClark 2 71
(E W Tuer) *trckd ldrs gng wl: smooth hdwy on inner 3f out: led over 2f out: rdn and two l up over 1f out: drvn ins fnl f: hdd and no ex nr line* **3/1**[2]

04 **3** 1 3/4 **Amical Risks (FR)**[2] 4190 6-8-4 **52** EleanorMcGowan(7) 10 56
(Joss Saville) *s.i.s and lost many l s: bhd tl hdwy over 4f out: in tch wl over 1f out: swtchd lft and styd on strly ins fnl f: tk 3rd nr fin* **7/1**

0-34 **4** hd **Marino Prince (FR)**[6] 4070 5-8-2 **46** oh1 JamesRogers(3) 1 50
(B D Leavy) *trckd ldrs on inner: hdwy 3f out: rdn 2f out: drvn and kpt on same pce fnl f: lost 3rd nr fin* **13/2**[3]

2621 **5** 2 3/4 **Drop The Hammer**[3] 4174 4-9-2 **57** 6ex CharlesEddery 8 57
(D O'Meara) *in rr: pushed along after 3f and rn in snatches: hdwy to chse ldrs over 4f out: rdn along over 3f out: outpcd over 2f out: kpt on u.p fnl f* **11/4**[1]

0/00 **6** 1/2 **Parchment (IRE)**[7] 4015 8-8-0 **46** oh1 MarzenaJeziorek(5) 3 45
(A J Lockwood) *chsd ldrs: rdn along 3f out: drvn to chse ldng pair wl over 1f out: grad wknd* **33/1**

0565 **7** 2 1/2 **Gulf Coast**[49] 2655 5-8-7 **53** LukeStrong(5) 5 48
(T D Walford) *chsd ldrs: rdn along 3f out: drvn and wknd 2f out* **8/1**

4564 **8** 4 1/2 **Papa's Princess**[17] 3707 6-8-2 **46** oh1 MatthewLawson(3) 6 34
(James Moffatt) *a towards rr* **33/1**

6065 **9** 2 **Classic Contours (USA)**[21] 3552 4-9-3 **63** (b[1]) ShaneBKelly(5) 13 47
(J J Quinn) *chsd ldr: rdn along over 3f out: wknd over 2f out* **10/1**

3334 **10** 1 **Without Equal**[22] 3535 4-8-2 **48** NeilFarley(5) 4 31
(N Wilson) *dwlt: a towards rr* **18/1**

3-06 **11** 3 3/4 **Lady Norlela**[7] 4015 4-7-12 **46** oh1 TimothyAyres(7) 11 23
(B S Rothwell) *led: rdn along over 3f out: hdd over 2f out and sn wknd* **18/1**

0/P **12** 29 **Treason Trial**[68] 2085 9-8-10 **54** ow1 AdamCarter(3) 9 —
(Joss Saville) *a bhd: t.o fnl 3f* **66/1**

2m 41.35s (2.45) **Going Correction** +0.25s/f (Good) **12** Ran SP% **119.4**
Speed ratings (Par 101): **101,100,99,99,97 97,95,92,91,90 88,68**
toteswingers:1&2:£12.20, 1&3:£32.20, 2&3:£6.30 CSF £97.87 CT £609.30 TOTE £44.50: £11.60, £1.20, £1.90; EX 83.50 Place 6 £147.94; Place 5 £100.24.
Owner James Callow **Bred** Genesis Green Stud Ltd **Trained** Orton, Cumbria

FOCUS
A good duel down the straight for this moderate handicap.
Amical Risks(FR) Official explanation: jockey said, regarding running and riding, her orders were to settle in rear and ask the gelding for an effort from 5f out, but it was slowly away and felt that she was unable to rush along too early, adding that having begun to make a move it was denied a clear run 1 1/2f out and then stayed on one pace.
T/Jkpt: £4,733.30 to a £1 stake. Pool:£10,000.00 - 1.50 winning tickets T/Plt: £51.40 to a £1 stake. Pool:£59,654.08 - 846.30 winning tickets T/Qpdt: £22.00 to a £1 stake. Pool:£3,451.35 - 115.80 winning tickets JR

4065 LEICESTER (R-H)
Wednesday, July 21

OFFICIAL GOING: Good to firm (8.6)
Wind: Light behind Weather: Coudy with sunny spells

4247 NORTHCLIFFE MEDIA MAIDEN AUCTION STKS 7f 9y
6:15 (6:16) (Class 5) 2-Y-O **£2,590** (£770; £385; £192) **Stalls** Centre

Form RPR

53 **1** **Sky Falcon (USA)**[13] 3832 2-8-10 0 RoystonFfrench 2 75+
(M Johnston) *led to 1/2-way: rdn to ld over 1f out: edgd rt ins fnl f: styd on gamely* **9/1**[3]

032 **2** nk **Nothing To Hide (IRE)**[14] 3785 2-8-10 0 JamesDoyle 1 74
(D J S Ffrench Davis) *w ldrs: rdn and ev ch fr over 1f out: styd on* **9/2**[2]

0 **3** 3/4 **Menadati (USA)**[19] 3631 2-9-0 0 TedDurcan 9 76
(D R Lanigan) *s.i.s: hdwy over 2f out: rdn and edgd rt ins fnl f: styd on* **11/4**[1]

00 **4** 2 **Talk Talk (IRE)**[53] 2547 2-8-13 0 Louis-PhilippeBeuzelin(3) 3 73+
(B J Meehan) *chsd ldrs: rdn over 2f out: styd on same pce fnl f* **20/1**

052 **5** 1/2 **Danzigs Grandchild (USA)**[13] 3832 2-8-8 0 FergusSweeney 5 64
(J S Moore) *chsd ldrs: led 1/2-way: rdn and hdd over 1f out: no ex ins fnl f* **14/1**

6 2 1/4 **September Draw (USA)** 2-8-10 0 PatDobbs 4 60+
(R Hannon) *chsd ldrs: outpcd over 2f out: styd on ins fnl f* **10/1**

2 **7** shd **U A E Storm (USA)**[28] 3326 2-9-1 0 RichardMullen 10 65
(D M Simcock) *chsd ldrs: rdn over 1f out: wknd ins fnl f* **11/4**[1]

00 **8** 6 **Back For Tea (IRE)**[14] 3785 2-8-11 0 RichardSmith 8 46
(Tom Dascombe) *prom: rdn over 2f out: wknd over 1f out* **100/1**

5 **9** 3 1/4 **Laffraaj (IRE)**[29] 3281 2-8-9 0 AndreaAtzeni 6 36
(Pat Eddery) *prom: rdn over 4f out: wknd 3f out* **22/1**

10 10 **Caledonia Prince** 2-8-9 0 FrankieMcDonald 12 11
(F J Brennan) *s.i.s: outpcd* **100/1**

0 **11** 4 **Henry Bond**[34] 3106 2-8-10 0 SamHitchcott 7 —
(S A Harris) *sn drvn along and a in rr: bhd fr 1/2-way* **200/1**

12 nk **Al Rannan** 2-8-13 0 HayleyTurner 11 —
(M L W Bell) *s.i.s: outpcd* **25/1**

1m 24.29s (-1.91) **Going Correction** -0.40s/f (Firm) **12** Ran SP% **112.7**
Speed ratings (Par 94): **94,93,92,90,89 87,87,80,76,65 60,60**
toteswingers:1&2:£6.40, 1&3:£6.80, 2&3:£3.70 CSF £44.22 TOTE £15.60: £4.50, £1.50, £1.20; EX 48.30.
Owner Jaber Abdullah **Bred** Woodford Thoroughbreds LLC **Trained** Middleham Moor, N Yorks

FOCUS
A race containing largely unexposed maidens, including three debutants.

NOTEBOOK
Sky Falcon(USA), progressive in his three maidens, was good enough to win but the fact that he had looked nothing special in his earlier races suggests that the form is ordinary. However, he battled hard to hold off the runner-up and has the tenacity to make his mark in handicaps. (op 11-2)
Nothing To Hide(IRE), like the winner, had shown ability in previous races without setting the world alight. However, he went down fighting and could yet find a maiden if connections decide to delay the nursery route (op 8-1)
Menadati(USA) did well to finish so close after missing the break, especially as the first two had been prominent throughout. This was a step up on his debut and there should be further improvement to come, so he can be given another chance. (op 7-2 tchd 5-2)
Talk Talk(IRE), down the field in two maidens on good tracks, shaped better this time and now looks capable of winning races. He looks an obvious nursery type and will be worth considering when he makes the switch. (op 10-1)
Danzigs Grandchild(USA) is showing plenty of early speed these days, but she is falling short in maidens and ought to have a better chance in nurseries. (op 12-1 tchd 10-1)
September Draw(USA), by the top-class US dirt performer Southern Image, who peaked in his second and third seasons, made a satisfactory debut from which she should improve a bit. On this evidence she stays 7f well. (op 9-1 tchd 8-1)

U A E Storm(USA), difficult to load, had run better on his debut. That was on Polytrack, and it remains to be seen if that will be his ideal surface. Official explanation: trainer said colt was unsuited by the good to firm ground (tchd 5-2 and 3-1)

4248 JAYNE FERGUSON MEMORIAL H'CAP 5f 218y
6:45 (6:45) (Class 5) (0-70,70) 3-Y-O £2,914 (£867; £433; £216) **Stalls** Centre

Form RPR

6633 1 **Jimmy The Poacher (IRE)**[18] 3680 3-9-6 **67**...............(b) DavidNolan 11 81
(T D Easterby) *s.i.s: sn pushed along in rr: hdwy over 2f out: rdn to ld and hung lft over 1f out: r.o wl* **9/4**[1]

0423 2 3 ¼ **Rosiliant (IRE)**[11] 3907 3-8-7 **54**...............(b) PhilipRobinson 3 58
(C G Cox) *w ldr tl led over 4f out: rdn and hdd over 2f out: hung lft and styd on same pce fnl f: wnt 2nd nr fin* **8/1**

310 3 ½ **Erebus (IRE)**[11] 3914 3-8-13 **67**............... AdamBeschizza(7) 9 69
(S Kirk) *chsd ldrs: led over 2f out: rdn and hdd over 1f out: no ex ins fnl f: lost 2nd nr fin* **10/1**

3656 4 1 ¾ **Blue Again**[25] 3441 3-9-5 **66**............... AdamKirby 1 62
(W R Swinburn) *hld up: hdwy u.p over 2f out: no imp fnl f* **7/1**

560- 5 ½ **George Baker (IRE)**[282] 6721 3-9-4 **65**............... GeorgeBaker 5 60
(George Baker) *chsd ldrs: rdn over 2f out: styd on same pce appr fnl f* **4/1**[2]

2356 6 3 ¼ **Suzy Alexander**[5] 4109 3-9-5 **66**............... SebSanders 6 50
(G G Margarson) *mid-div: outpcd 1/2-way: n.d after* **16/1**

6640 7 ½ **Sophie's Beau (USA)**[8] 3975 3-8-10 **62**............... MarkCoumbe(5) 4 45
(M C Chapman) *prom: rdn over 2f out: sn wknd* **18/1**

0-60 8 1 ½ **Brody's Boy**[40] 2925 3-8-12 **59**............... PatDobbs 8 37
(G L Moore) *sn outpcd: nvr nrr* **25/1**

2362 9 ½ **Danzoe (IRE)**[25] 3463 3-9-9 **70**...............(p) TomMcLaughlin 12 46
(Mrs C A Dunnett) *chsd ldrs: rdn over 1f out: wknd fnl f* **13/2**[3]

100- 10 44 **Gwynedd (IRE)**[345] 4850 3-9-9 **70**............... RichardMullen 10 —
(E S McMahon) *plld hrd: led: hdd over 4f out: wknd over 2f out: t.o* **25/1**

1m 10.59s (-2.41) **Going Correction** -0.40s/f (Firm) 10 Ran SP% **115.6**
Speed ratings (Par 100): **100,95,95,92,92 87,87,85,84,25**
toteswingers:1&2:£2.60, 1&3:£8.30, 2&3:£11.00 CSF £20.73 CT £148.70 TOTE £2.80: £1.10, £1.60, £5.20; EX 13.50.
Owner Stephen Lee & James McDonald **Bred** Jim McDonald **Trained** Great Habton, N Yorks

FOCUS
Contested by some generally exposed second-season horses, and with maidens filling the first two places, this was a moderate event but the winner is interesting.
Gwynedd(IRE) Official explanation: jockey said filly ran too free

4249 RAINBOWS BUILDING FOR FUTURE (S) STKS 1m 60y
7:20 (7:20) (Class 6) 3-Y-O £1,942 (£578; £288; £144) **Stalls** High

Form RPR

5000 1 **Angelena Ballerina (IRE)**[15] 3765 3-8-6 **55**...........(v[1]) KirstyMilczarek 2 55
(Karen George) *chsd ldrs: rdn to ld 1f out: edgd rt: r.o* **20/1**

602F 2 ¾ **Louisiana Gift (IRE)**[26] 3413 3-8-11 **61**...............(p) SebSanders 11 58
(J W Hills) *w ldrs: led over 5f out: rdn and hdd 1f out: styd on* **10/3**[1]

6000 3 ¾ **Transfixed (IRE)**[26] 3387 3-8-6 **64**............... CathyGannon 8 52
(P D Evans) *trckd ldrs: plld hrd: rdn over 1f out: styd on* **15/2**

6542 4 nk **Magenta Strait**[11] 3910 3-8-7 **57**............... TobyAtkinson(5) 7 57
(R Hollinshead) *hld up: hdwy 3f out: rdn over 1f out: edgd rt ins fnl f: r.o* **8/1**

0 5 nk **River Tease**[19] 3635 3-8-11 **0**............... FergusSweeney 14 55
(J S Moore) *hld up: rdn 1/2-way: edgd rt and r.o ins fnl f: nt rch ldrs* **33/1**

6666 6 1 ¼ **Hounds Ditch**[18] 3685 3-8-11 **54**...............(t) JackMitchell 6 52
(Eve Johnson Houghton) *hld up: rdn over 2f out: edgd rt and r.o ins fnl f: nvr nrr* **16/1**

0062 7 1 **Electric City (IRE)**[9] 3951 3-8-6 **52**...............(p) FrankieMcDonald 12 48
(M G Quinlan) *chsd ldrs: hmpd and lost pl over 2f out: nt rcvr* **10/1**

0040 8 1 ½ **Ravens Rose**[12] 3852 3-8-3 **52**............... Louis-PhilippeBeuzelin(3) 13 42
(J G Portman) *prom: racd keenly: rdn over 2f out: no ex fnl f* **5/1**[3]

4250 9 ½ **Kenswick**[4] 4133 3-8-6 **55**...............(b) AndreaAtzeni 10 40
(Pat Eddery) *prom: rdn over 2f out: no ex fnl f* **7/2**[2]

0000 10 9 **Strike Shot**[23] 3515 3-8-11 **50**............... DarryllHolland 4 25
(W R Muir) *led: hdd over 5f out: rdn over 2f out: wknd over 1f out* **25/1**

000 11 8 **Labretella (IRE)**[15] 3759 3-8-6 **44**...............(p) SamHitchcott 5 —
(S A Harris) *mid-div: hdwy 3f out: wknd 2f out* **50/1**

0 12 2 **Wizzacus**[9] 3966 3-8-6 **0**............... SaleemGolam 1 —
(P D Evans) *got loose prior to the s: a in rr: bhd fr 1/2-way* **66/1**

060 13 1 ¾ **Octaviana**[9] 3966 3-8-8 **0** ow2............... TedDurcan 3 —
(E J Alston) *s.s: a in rr: bhd fr 1/2-way* **66/1**

00 14 ½ **Miss Halfordbridge**[19] 3635 3-8-6 **0**............... TadhgO'Shea 9 —
(J Gallagher) *sn pushed along in rr: bhd fr 1/2-way* **50/1**

1m 44.52s (-0.58) **Going Correction** -0.10s/f (Good) 14 Ran SP% **118.3**
Speed ratings (Par 98): **98,97,96,96,95 94,93,92,91,82 74,72,70,70**
toteswingers:1&2:£21.10, 1&3:£14.20, 2&3:£5.00 CSF £81.44 TOTE £29.20: £5.50, £2.70, £3.40; EX 182.30.There was no bid for the winner.
Owner Mrs Isabel Fraser **Bred** Waterford Hall Stud **Trained** Higher Eastington, Devon

FOCUS
A competitive seller run at a respectable tempo.

4250 EUROPEAN BREEDERS' FUND WATERLOO FILLIES' H'CAP 7f 9y
7:50 (7:50) (Class 4) (0-80,80) 3-Y-O £6,308 (£1,888; £944; £472; £235) **Stalls** Centre

Form RPR

6-1 1 **Naddwah**[55] 2473 3-9-0 **73**............... PhilipRobinson 1 81+
(M A Jarvis) *trckd ldr: racd keenly: led over 2f out: rdn over 1f out: hung rt ins fnl f: styd on wl* **15/8**[1]

20-6 2 1 ½ **Falling Angel**[12] 3866 3-9-0 **73**............... TedDurcan 6 77
(P F I Cole) *s.i.s: hld up: hdwy over 2f out: rdn to chse wnr fnl f: no imp* **12/1**

0653 3 ½ **Kurtanella**[20] 3592 3-9-7 **80**............... PatDobbs 3 83
(R Hannon) *hld up in tch: rdn and swtchd rt over 1f out: styd on same pce ins fnl f* **6/1**

4142 4 7 **Angel Of Fashion (IRE)**[19] 3610 3-8-3 **62**............... PaulHanagan 5 46
(P Charalambous) *prom: rdn over 2f out: wknd fnl f* **11/2**[3]

-012 5 1 ¾ **Lenkiewicz**[12] 3866 3-9-1 **77**............... JamesMillman(3) 8 56
(B R Millman) *chsd ldrs: rdn whn hmpd over 1f out: sn wknd* **6/1**

-445 6 1 **Bidruma**[19] 3620 3-8-5 **64**............... AndreaAtzeni 7 41
(Mike Murphy) *chsd ldrs: pushed along 1/2-way: rdn over 2f out: sn wknd* **33/1**

3-02 7 1 ¾ **Queen's Envoy**[33] 3157 3-8-13 **72**............... J-PGuillambert 4 44
(L M Cumani) *led: rdn and hdd over 2f out: wknd over 1f out* **7/2**[2]

1m 23.23s (-2.97) **Going Correction** -0.40s/f (Firm) 7 Ran SP% **111.6**
Speed ratings (Par 99): **100,98,97,89,87 86,84**
toteswingers:1&2:£3.60, 1&3:£3.90, 2&3:£10.80 CSF £24.45 CT £110.30 TOTE £2.80: £3.40, £2.90; EX 31.20.
Owner Sheikh Ahmed Al Maktoum **Bred** Darley **Trained** Newmarket, Suffolk

FOCUS
The quality was reasonable for a fillies' handicap, with the prize going to the least-exposed in the field.

4251 ROTARY CLUB OF LEICESTER DE MONTFORT MAIDEN STKS 5f 218y
8:25 (8:27) (Class 5) 3-Y-O+ £2,590 (£770; £385; £192) **Stalls** Centre

Form RPR

0 1 **Ritual (IRE)**[95] 1381 3-9-3 **0**............... PaulHanagan 11 73+
(J Noseda) *sn prom: led 2f out: rdn and hung lft ins fnl f: r.o* **5/6**[1]

0006 2 1 ¼ **Mata Hari Blue**[9] 3966 4-9-3 **55**............... KirstyMilczarek 15 65
(J R Holt) *a.p: chsd wnr 2f out: rdn and carried lft ins fnl f: no ex nr fin* **25/1**

30-0 3 1 ½ **Aalsmeer**[75] 1870 3-8-12 **90**............... DarryllHolland 10 59
(Karen George) *trckd ldrs: rdn over 1f out: styd on* **5/1**[3]

03 4 ¾ **Mottley Crewe**[53] 2530 3-9-3 **0**............... JamesDoyle 3 62+
(M Dods) *prom: rdn over 1f out: edgd rt and styd on ins fnl f* **20/1**

00 5 2 **Crimson Queen**[19] 3635 3-8-12 **0**............... RoystonFfrench 13 50
(R Brotherton) *mid-div: sn pushed along: styd on fnl 2f: nt trble ldrs* **40/1**

00 6 4 ½ **Best Known Secret (IRE)**[34] 3111 4-9-3 **0**............... AdamKirby 6 37
(C C Bealby) *led: hung lft and hdd 2f out: wknd fnl f* **100/1**

22 7 nse **Oh So Spicy**[13] 3808 3-8-12 **0**............... JackMitchell 2 36
(C F Wall) *chsd ldrs: rdn over 2f out: wknd over 1f out* **9/2**[2]

P 8 1 **Ming Meng (IRE)**[99] 1275 3-8-12 **0**............... HayleyTurner 7 33+
(M L W Bell) *s.i.s: sn pushed along in rr: styd on fr over 1f out: nvr nrr* **28/1**

9 1 **Bouncy Bouncy (IRE)** 3-8-12 **0**............... MickyFenton 14 29+
(M L W Bell) *s.i.s: in rr: hdwy over 1f out: nvr trbld ldrs* **12/1**

00 10 6 **Shamarlane**[13] 3808 3-8-12 **0**............... StephenCraine 12 10
(M Wigham) *mid-div: hmpd and lost pl after 1f: bhd fr 1/2-way* **100/1**

11 2 ¼ **Mistress Shy** 3-8-12 **0**............... SebSanders 8 —
(R Dickin) *s.i.s: hld up: sme hdwy over 2f out: sn wknd* **40/1**

0 12 nk **Salamera (IRE)**[11] 3903 4-9-3 **0**............... FrankieMcDonald 5 —
(F J Brennan) *sn pushed along in mid-div: bhd fr 1/2-way* **125/1**

0/ 13 4 ½ **Our Angel**[712] 4815 4-9-3 **0**............... TedDurcan 9 —
(E J Alston) *hld up in tch: wknd over 2f out* **50/1**

0-0 14 5 **Sue And Sue**[13] 3808 3-8-12 **0**............... TomMcLaughlin 1 —
(G Woodward) *sn outpcd* **100/1**

1m 10.74s (-2.26) **Going Correction** -0.40s/f (Firm)
WFA 3 from 4yo 5lb 14 Ran SP% **119.8**
Speed ratings (Par 103): **99,97,95,94,91 85,85,84,82,74 71,71,65,58**
toteswingers:1&2:£5.20, 1&3:£4.20, 2&3:£33.40 CSF £33.44 TOTE £2.00: £1.10, £7.70, £1.80; EX 30.30.
Owner Highclere Thoroughbred Racing Churchill **Bred** Agricola Del Parco **Trained** Newmarket, Suffolk
■ Stewards' Enquiry : Kirsty Milczarek four-day ban: careless riding (Aug 4-7)

FOCUS
A maiden containing runners of mixed ability, but the late-developing winner is potentially a decent long-term prospect.
Crimson Queen Official explanation: jockey said filly hung right-handed
Mistress Shy Official explanation: jockey said filly lost its action

4252 SANDICLIFFE "THE VAN MAN THAT CAN" H'CAP 1m 3f 183y
9:00 (9:01) (Class 4) (0-80,79) 4-Y-O+ £3,885 (£1,156; £577; £288) **Stalls** High

Form RPR

3053 1 **Incendo**[28] 3329 4-9-3 **75**...............(vt[1]) AdamKirby 3 86+
(J R Fanshawe) *chsd ldrs: wnt 2nd 2f out: led on bit over 1f out: sn clr: easily* **5/2**[2]

3111 2 5 **Aestival**[47] 2690 4-9-7 **79**............... SebSanders 2 80
(Sir Mark Prescott) *led 1f: chsd ldr tl led on bit over 3f out: rdn over 2f out: hdd over 1f out: sn outpcd* **4/7**[1]

5200 3 1 **Trachonitis (IRE)**[14] 3781 6-9-4 **76**............... PaulHanagan 8 75
(J R Jenkins) *hld up: rdn over 2f out: styd on same pce appr fnl f* **14/1**

216/ 4 nk **Daylami Dreams**[721] 4516 6-9-1 **73**............... MickyFenton 1 72?
(John A Harris) *led after 1f and set stdy pce: qcknd 5f out: rdn and hdd over 3f out: styd on same pce fnl 2f* **11/1**[3]

2m 32.61s (-1.29) **Going Correction** -0.10s/f (Good) 4 Ran SP% **107.2**
Speed ratings (Par 105): **100,96,96,95**
CSF £4.33 TOTE £5.00; EX 4.10 Place 6 £58.86; Place 5 £35.14.
Owner Andrew & Julia Turner **Bred** London Thoroughbred Services Ltd **Trained** Newmarket, Suffolk

FOCUS
The four runners dawdled until the pace suddenly increased off the home turn, making this a hard race to assess with any accuracy.
T/Plt: £209.90 to a £1 stake. Pool:£69,520.35 - 241.77 winning tickets T/Qpdt: £67.10 to a £1 stake. Pool:£6,454.06 - 71.14 winning tickets CR

4129 LINGFIELD (L-H)
Wednesday, July 21

OFFICIAL GOING: Standard
Wind: light, half behind Weather: bright, partly cloudy

4253 ASHURST WOOD MEDIAN AUCTION MAIDEN STKS (DIV I) 7f (P)
2:00 (2:01) (Class 6) 2-Y-O £1,706 (£503; £252) **Stalls** Low

Form RPR

23 1 **Introvert (IRE)**[19] 3631 2-9-3 **0**............... FrankieDettori 8 73
(Mahmood Al Zarooni) *mde all: rdn 2f out: drvn and forged ahd ent fnl f: styd on u.p fnl f* **1/4**[1]

0 2 1 ¼ **Tagansky**[53] 2547 2-9-3 **0**............... NeilCallan 9 70+
(S Dow) *in tch: hdwy to join ldrs wl over 2f out: ev ch and rdn ent fnl 2f: unable qck ent fnl f and kpt on same pce after* **25/1**

04 3 2 ¼ **Ya Hafed**[15] 3767 2-9-3 **0**............... KierenFallon 11 64
(E A L Dunlop) *chsd ldrs tl wnt 2nd 4f out tl ent fnl 2f: outpce by ldng pair and drvn wl over 1f out: one pce and no imp fnl f* **10/1**[3]

4 2 ¼ **Safari Team (IRE)** 2-9-3 **0**............... JimCrowley 3 61+
(P Winkworth) *sn chsng wnr tl 4f out: rdn and outpce by ldng trio over 2f out: kpt on but wl hld fnl 2f* **14/1**

0 5 3 ½ **Persian Herald**[27] 3349 2-9-3 **0**............... AndreaAtzeni 6 52+
(Pat Eddery) *chsd ldrs: rdn and struggling ent fnl 3f: sn wl outpcd by ldrs: n.d after* **40/1**

6 2 ¼ **Drawn Free (IRE)** 2-9-3 **0**............... ShaneKelly 7 44
(W J Knight) *in tch towards rr: hdwy to chse ldrs and pushed along wl over 2f out: outpcd by ldrs ent fnl 2f and wl btn after* **14/1**

05 **7** *1* **Dew Reward (IRE)**[20] 3577 2-9-3 0 TonyCulhane 5 42
(Eve Johnson Houghton) *sn pushed along and outpcd in last: lost tch over 3f out: nvr on terms* **33/1**

0 **8** *hd* **Cometh**[26] 3411 2-8-12 0 MickyFenton 4 36
(N P Littmoden) *sn pushed along: dropped to rr 5f out: wl bhd fnl 3f* **40/1**

6 **9** *1 ¾* **So Choosy**[33] 3156 2-8-12 0 RichardHughes 10 32+
(R Hannon) *racd wd: short of room after s: a bhd: lost tch wl over 2f out* **13/2**[2]

1m 27.04s (2.24) **Going Correction** +0.175s/f (Slow) **9** Ran SP% **127.4**
Speed ratings (Par 92): **94,92,90,87,83 80,79,79,77**
toteswingers:1&2:£6.00, 1&3:£1.80, 2&3:£15.40 CSF £17.90 TOTE £1.20: £1.02, £6.50, £2.10; EX 15.60 Trifecta £43.50 Pool: £470.22 - 7.99 winning units..
Owner Godolphin **Bred** Mrs T Marnane **Trained** Newmarket, Suffolk

FOCUS
A weak maiden in which it paid to race prominently. The time was 0.60 seconds slower than the second division, won by another Godolphin runner, Rutterkin.

NOTEBOOK
Introvert(IRE), who raced keenly when third in a better race than this at Sandown on his second start, settled just fine in front on this occasion and ran on well for pressure, despite racing towards the sometimes unfavoured far rail in the straight. He probably didn't beat much. (op 3-10 tchd 2-5 and 4-11 in a place)
Tagansky, who ran better than the bare form suggested when down the field in a decent Newmarket maiden on debut over 6f almost two months earlier, shaped nicely. He's entitled to come on again for this and might be able to win a similar race.
Ya Hafed lacked the pace of the front two. He's probably going to want further, and nurseries are now an option. (tchd 11-1)
Safari Team(IRE), a 36,000euros half-brother to Perfectly Quiet, a fairly useful winner of four races in the US, out of a quite useful multiple winner in the States, came under pressure before the straight and, after making brief headway, soon faded.
Persian Herald, well beaten on debut, offered little and probably needs more time.
So Choosy Official explanation: jockey said filly suffered interference leaving stalls

4254 ASHURST WOOD MEDIAN AUCTION MAIDEN STKS (DIV II) 7f (P)
2:30 (2:30) (Class 6) 2-Y-O **£1,706** (£503; £252) **Stalls** Low

Form RPR

033 **1** **Rutterkin (USA)**[23] 3517 2-9-3 0 FrankieDettori 6 75
(Mahmood Al Zarooni) *mde all: rdn and drew clr wl over 1f out: 3 l clr 1f out: drvn and tiring fnl 100yds: jst hld on: all out* **3/1**[2]

06 **2** *shd* **Jacobs Son**[25] 3452 2-9-3 0 StevieDonohoe 2 75+
(R A Mills) *in tch in midfield: rdn and hdwy to chse ldrs ent fnl 2f: drvn over 1f out: styd on wl ins fnl f: pressing wnr cl home: jst hld* **4/1**[3]

6 **3** *½* **Bearheart (IRE)**[13] 3805 2-9-3 0 RyanMoore 4 74
(E A L Dunlop) *chsd ldrs: pushed along to chse wnr over 2f out: rdn and outpcd wl over 1f out: kpt on ins fnl f* **13/2**

60 **4** *2* **George Woolf**[38] 2990 2-9-3 0 JamesDoyle 11 69
(A J McCabe) *in tch: hdwy on outer to chse ldng pair wl over 2f out: drvn and unable qck 2f out: kpt on same pce ins fnl f* **25/1**

35 **5** *11* **Paco Belle (IRE)**[21] 3562 2-8-12 0 RichardHughes 3 36
(R Hannon) *chsd wnr tl over 2f out: wknd qckly ent fnl 2f: wl btn whn edgd rt fnl f* **9/4**[1]

00 **6** *nk* **Amistress**[29] 3296 2-8-12 0 TomQueally 7 35
(Eve Johnson Houghton) *in tch in midfield tl rdn and wl outpcd 3f out: no ch fnl 2f* **50/1**

044 **7** *2 ¾* **Mystica (IRE)**[14] 3778 2-8-12 0 LiamKeniry 1 28
(D J S Ffrench Davis) *chsd ldrs: rdn and losing pl whn hit rail over 3f out: wl btn fr over 2f out* **16/1**

8 *1 ¾* **Focail Maith** 2-9-3 0 PatCosgrave 5 29
(J Ryan) *s.i.s: rdn along and a struggling in rr: wl bhd fr over 2f out* **33/1**

6 **9** *3* **Jack's Revenge (IRE)**[21] 3555 2-9-3 0 TonyCulhane 9 22
(George Baker) *a towards rr: rdn and struggling ent fnl 3f: wl bhd fr over 2f out* **25/1**

00 **10** *3 ¾* **Arakova (IRE)**[14] 3778 2-8-12 0 MickyFenton 10 7
(Matthew Salaman) *stdd s: a towards rr: lost tch 3f out* **66/1**

11 *15* **Drummer Boy** 2-9-3 0 JimCrowley 8 —
(P Winkworth) *s.i.s: sn rdn along and a wl outpcd in last: t.o over 2f out* **16/1**

1m 26.44s (1.64) **Going Correction** +0.175s/f (Slow) **11** Ran SP% **115.0**
Speed ratings (Par 92): **97,96,96,94,81 81,77,75,72,68 51**
toteswingers:1&2:£3.90, 1&3:£3.80, 2&3:£4.20 CSF £14.25 TOTE £2.40: £1.10, £2.30, £2.10; EX 16.70 Trifecta £78.90 Pool: £447.27 - 4.19 winning units..
Owner Godolphin **Bred** Stonerside Stable **Trained** Newmarket, Suffolk

FOCUS
As in the first division, there was little strength in depth, but the time was 0.60 seconds quicker than the first leg.

NOTEBOOK
Rutterkin(USA), like his winning stablemate in the opener, made all of the running, but having looked set to win decisively, he only just held on, possibly not being helped by sticking towards the far rail. He had recorded an RPR of only 71 on his last two starts and probably didn't have to improve much on that sort of level, but the way he travelled suggests he could do better over 6f. (op 15-8)
Jacobs Son started sluggishly and didn't travel all that well, but he finally responded to strong pressure late on, albeit the visual impression was slightly misleading as the winner was getting tired. He was never really involved on his first two starts, but will have learnt plenty from this, and will also benefit from a longer trip. (op 5-1)
Bearheart(IRE), well beaten over 6f on debut, fared better this time under a positive ride, but he was always being held. (op 8-1)
George Woolf should find his level now that nurseries are an option. (op 33-1)
Paco Belle(IRE) had recorded an RPR in the 60s on her first two starts, but was nowhere near that level this time and it looks questionable whether or not she'll progress. (op 11-4 tchd 3-1 and 2-1 and 10-3 in a place)

4255 GODSTONE H'CAP 6f (P)
3:00 (3:03) (Class 5) (0-70,70) 3-Y-O+ **£2,388** (£705; £352) **Stalls** Low

Form RPR

4300 **1** **Dvinsky (USA)**[4] 4130 9-9-8 68 (b) IanMongan 7 76
(P Howling) *chsd ldrs: drvn and effrt to chse ldr over 1f out: led ins fnl f: kpt on wl u.p: drvn out* **14/1**

0143 **2** *¾* **Dashing Beauty (IRE)**[8] 3980 4-9-5 68 WilliamCarson(3) 8 74
(M G Quinlan) *sn pushed along and outpcd in midfield: rdn and hdwy over 1f out: kpt on u.p fnl f to go 2nd towards fin: nt rch wnr* **10/1**

4461 **3** *1* **Cativo Cavallino**[30] 3262 7-9-0 63 NataliaGemelova(3) 1 65
(J E Long) *sn outpcd and pushed along in rr: hdwy u.p ent fnl f: r.o wl ins fnl f to snatch 3rd on post: nt rch wnr* **13/2**[3]

0025 **4** *nse* **Bobs Dreamflight**[36] 3052 4-9-3 63 ChrisCatlin 10 65
(D K Ivory) *sn pushed along and outpcd in midfield: lost pl bnd 2f out: rallied u.p ins fnl f: r.o wl fnl 100yds to go 4th last strides: nt rch ldrs* **12/1**

0230 **5** *hd* **Not My Choice (IRE)**[37] 3024 5-9-2 62 (t) RichardHughes 4 64
(D C Griffiths) *w ldrs tl led over 2f out: rdn and hdd over 1f out: wknd and lost 3 pls towards fin* **5/1**[2]

2400 **6** *1* **What Katie Did (IRE)**[8] 3993 5-9-2 62 (p) AdamKirby 6 60
(J M Bradley) *chsd ldrs: rdn and unable qck ent fnl 2f: kpt on same pce u.p fnl f* **10/1**

3051 **7** *1 ½* **Athaakeel (IRE)**[15] 3762 4-9-7 67 KierenFallon 11 61
(R A Harris) *s.i.s: sn struggling to go pce and pushed along towards rr: hanging rt and wd fr over 3f out: sme prog over 1f out: no imp ins fnl f: eased towards fin* **4/1**[1]

5-04 **8** *nk* **Speak The Truth (IRE)**[43] 2846 4-9-3 66 (p) MatthewDavies(3) 12 59
(J R Boyle) *fly-jmpd leaving stalls and v.s.a: sn swtchd lft: bhd: hdwy over 1f out: keeping on but stl plenty to do whn swtchd rt jst ins fnl f: nvr trbld ldrs* **12/1**

1110 **9** *1 ½* **Collect Art (IRE)**[33] 3171 3-9-2 67 StevieDonohoe 3 54
(A B Haynes) *s.i.s: sn outpcd in rr: rdn wl over 1f out: n.d* **8/1**

6320 **10** *1 ½* **Fromsong (IRE)**[6] 4047 12-9-6 66 MartinDwyer 5 49
(D K Ivory) *taken down early: w ldrs: ev ch and rdn ent fnl 2f: btn ent fnl f: fdd fnl 150yds* **16/1**

0-00 **11** *9* **Fardyieh**[19] 3612 3-9-5 70 NeilCallan 2 23
(C E Brittain) *led tl over 2f out: wknd qckly 2f out: wl bhd fnl f* **5/1**[2]

1m 12.92s (1.02) **Going Correction** +0.175s/f (Slow)
WFA 3 from 4yo+ 5lb **11** Ran SP% **123.9**
Speed ratings (Par 103): **100,99,97,97,97 96,94,93,91,89 77**
toteswingers: 1&2 £16.50, 1&3 £9.40, 2&3 £17.30 CSF £154.22 CT £1030.68 TOTE £13.30: £4.80, £3.80, £2.70; EX 115.90 TRIFECTA Not won..
Owner Richard Berenson **Bred** Eclipse Bloodstock & Tipperary Bloodstock **Trained** Newmarket, Suffolk

FOCUS
A modest but competitive sprint handicap, and with the lead contested, the pace was strong.
Not My Choice(IRE) Official explanation: jockey said gelding hung right
Speak The Truth(IRE) Official explanation: jockey said gelding fly-leapt on leaving stalls

4256 HINDLEAP WALK H'CAP 5f (P)
3:30 (3:32) (Class 6) (0-65,64) 3-Y-O+ **£2,047** (£604; £302) **Stalls** High

Form RPR

5-03 **1** **Scottish Glen**[23] 3511 4-9-9 62 LiamKeniry 9 69
(P R Chamings) *sn wl outpcd towards rr: rdn and effrt on outer over 1f out: stl modest 7th ent fnl f: str run fnl f to ld last strides* **12/1**

332 **2** *nk* **Green Velvet**[22] 3527 5-9-9 62 RyanMoore 7 68
(P J Makin) *prom in main gp: chsd clr ldng pair wl over 2f out: stl 10 l down ent fnl f: r.o ins fnl f: wnt 2nd last strides* **13/8**[1]

0260 **3** *hd* **Island Legend (IRE)**[8] 3994 4-9-11 64 (p) DaneO'Neill 10 69
(J M Bradley) *w ldr and sn wl clr: rdn to ld but edging lft over 1f out: tiring ins fnl f: hdd last strides* **10/1**

1505 **4** *shd* **Pressed For Time (IRE)**[9] 3966 4-9-0 53 (vt) KierenFallon 4 58
(E J Creighton) *led and sn wl clr w rival: rdn and hdd narrowly over 1f out: n.m.r but stl ev ch: tiring ins fnl f: lost 2 pls last strides* **11/2**[3]

0106 **5** *3* **Figaro Flyer (IRE)**[15] 3761 7-9-10 63 J-PGuillambert 6 57
(P Howling) *prom in main gp: rdn 4f out: no imp tl kpt on ins fnl f: nvr able to chal* **5/1**[2]

-035 **6** *2 ½* **Sorrel Point**[47] 2720 7-9-0 53 (vt) JimmyQuinn 2 38
(H J Collingridge) *stdd after s: sn pushed along in rr: sme hdwy u.p over 1f out: nvr trbld ldrs* **12/1**

-203 **7** *nk* **Nollaig Shona (IRE)**[28] 3313 3-9-6 63 RichardHughes 1 46
(J W Mullins) *chsd clr ldng pair tl wl over 2f out: kpt on ins fnl f: nvr trbld ldrs* **14/1**

0 **8** *1 ¼* **D'Allziance (IRE)**[16] 3727 4-9-1 54 GeorgeBaker 5 34
(Jonjo O'Neill) *taken down early: stdd s: sn pushed along and outpcd in rr: nvr on terms* **25/1**

0004 **9** *2 ¼* **Serious Matters (IRE)**[23] 3515 3-9-1 58 AdamKirby 8 28
(W R Swinburn) *s.i.s: a outpcd in last pair* **14/1**

0641 **10** *3 ¾* **Best One**[8] 3979 6-9-4 57 6ex (b) ChrisCatlin 3 15
(R A Harris) *restless stalls: s.i.s: a last: nvr on terms* **14/1**

59.57 secs (0.77) **Going Correction** +0.175s/f (Slow)
WFA 3 from 4yo+ 4lb **10** Ran SP% **118.5**
Speed ratings (Par 101): **100,99,99,99,94 90,89,87,84,78**
toteswingers: 1&2 £6.60, 1&3 £15.00, 2&3 £6.50 CSF £32.37 CT £205.27 TOTE £19.00: £5.00, £1.30, £2.60; EX 44.80 TRIFECTA Not won..
Owner The Foxford House Partnership **Bred** Mrs Ann Jenkins **Trained** Baughurst, Hants

FOCUS
A modest sprint handicap in which Island Legend and Pressed For Time were around 7l clear by the time they reached the straight, and still held a decent advantage at the furlong pole, but the complexion of the race changed dramatically late on.
Island Legend(IRE) Official explanation: jockey said gelding hung left
Serious Matters(IRE) Official explanation: jockey said gelding was slowly away
Best One Official explanation: jockey said gelding was slowly away

4257 BET TRI-NATIONS RUGBY - BETDAQ MAIDEN STKS (DIV I) 1m 4f (P)
4:00 (4:01) (Class 5) 3-Y-O+ **£2,047** (£604; £302) **Stalls** Low

Form RPR

0-05 **1** **Kansai Spirit (IRE)**[15] 3764 4-9-13 74 NickyMackay 9 94+
(J H M Gosden) *chsd ldrs tl led over 10f out: pushed wl clr over 2f out: in n.d after: eased ins fnl f: v easily* **10/1**

63 **2** *4 ½* **Joseph Lister**[42] 2860 3-9-1 0 SteveDrowne 10 86+
(J H M Gosden) *prom tl chsd wnr over 10f out: rdn over 3f out: nt pce of wnr over 2f out and wl hld after: plugged on for clr 2nd* **9/2**[3]

0 **3** *12* **Sea Change (IRE)**[14] 3795 3-9-1 0 RichardHughes 8 67
(J Noseda) *s.i.s: hld up towards rr: rdn and sme hdwy over 4f out: no ch w wnr over 2f out: wnt modest 3rd and hung lft wl over 1f out: no imp and eased ins fnl f* **10/1**

0-2 **4** *5* **Sir Walter Raleigh**[24] 3477 3-9-1 0 RyanMoore 4 59
(Sir Michael Stoute) *in tch in midfield: niggled along 8f out: rdn over 5f out: outpcd and wl btn 3f out: plugged on fnl f to go poor 4th nr fin* **9/4**[1]

0-02 **5** *1 ¼* **Out Of Eden**[48] 2684 3-9-1 73 TomQueally 2 57
(H R A Cecil) *led tl over 10f out: chsd ldrs after tl rdn and wl outpcd over 2f out: 3rd and wl btn 2f out* **10/3**[2]

60 **6** *8* **Genes Of A Dancer (AUS)**[20] 3593 4-9-9 0 DavidProbert 11 40
(M Appleby) *chsd ldrs: rdn 4f out: wkng and hung rt 3f out: wl btn fnl 2f* **66/1**

7 *1 ¼* **Mutasareb (USA)** 3-9-1 0 FrankieDettori 5 42
(Saeed Bin Suroor) *chsd ldrs: rdn and struggling over 3f out: wknd 3f out: sn wl bhd: eased ins fnl f: t.o* **6/1**

-606 **8** *6* **Red Willow**[32] 3214 4-9-3 44 SophieDoyle(5) 12 27
(J E Long) *racd in midfield: rdn and struggling over 4f out: no ch fnl 3f: eased fr over 1f out: t.o* **100/1**

00 **9** *nk* **Rio Prince**[24] 3477 3-9-1 0 NeilChalmers 1 32
(J J Bridger) *s.i.s: a wl bhd: lost tch 4f out: eased fnl f: t.o* **100/1**

3-00 **10** *1 3/4* **Ultravox (USA)**[14] 3795 3-9-1 76 MartinDwyer 6 29
(B J Meehan) *towards rr: rdn 8f out: nvr gng wl after: lost tch wl over 3f out: eased fnl f: t.o* **25/1**

50 **11** *1 1/2* **Shannon Falls (FR)**[30] 3256 6-9-8 0 IanMongan 3 22
(Miss Jo Crowley) *stdd s: hld up in rr: lost tch over 4f out: t.o* **66/1**

0 **12** *1 1/2* **Voysey (IRE)**[48] 2684 3-9-1 0 NeilCallan 13 24
(Mrs A J Perrett) *s.i.s: sn in midfield: pushed along 7f out: rdn and wknd ent fnl 4f: t.o and eased over 1f out: t.o* **33/1**

0-00 **13** *15* **D'Artagnans Dream**[32] 3214 4-9-13 52 (v) JimmyQuinn 7 —
(G D Blake) *stdd s: hld up towards rr: rdn and struggling bdly over 4f out: t.o fr over 2f: eased fnl f* **66/1**

0 **14** *38* **Grey Gauntlet**[98] 1302 3-9-1 0 LiamKeniry 14 —
(R Ingram) *s.i.s: a in rr: rdn over 8f out: lost tch 6f out: wl t.o and virtually p.u fr over 2f out* **100/1**

2m 32.9s (-0.10) **Going Correction** +0.175s/f (Slow)
WFA 3 from 4yo+ 12lb **14** Ran SP% **118.7**
Speed ratings (Par 103): **107,104,96,92,91 86,85,81,81,80 79,78,68,42**
toteswingers: 1&2 £6.30, 1&3 £20.50, 2&3 £9.00 CSF £52.55 TOTE £15.40: £3.10, £1.30, £3.30; EX 52.10 Trifecta £342.20 Pool: £462.52 - 1.00 winning unit..
Owner R Van Gelder **Bred** Keatly Overseas Ltd **Trained** Newmarket, Suffolk

FOCUS
The time was 0.93 seconds quicker than the second division, but this still looked the weaker of the two races and they came home remarkably strung out.
Red Willow Official explanation: jockey said filly never travelled

4258 BET TRI-NATIONS RUGBY - BETDAQ MAIDEN STKS (DIV II) 1m 4f (P)
4:30 (4:31) (Class 5) 3-Y-O+ **£2,047** (£604; £302) **Stalls** Low

Form RPR

55 **1** **Zigato**[21] 3563 3-9-1 0 FrankieDettori 13 85
(J H M Gosden) *s.i.s: in tch in midfield: rdn to chse ldrs wl over 2f out: edgd lft u.p ent fnl f: styd on fnl 100yds to ld towards fin* **9/2**[3]

-043 **2** *nk* **Plato (JPN)**[23] 3519 3-9-1 80 TomQueally 8 85
(H R A Cecil) *prom tl led 10f out: rdn and hdd ent fnl 2f: ev ch after: unable qck u.p nr fin: wnt 2nd again last strides* **10/3**[2]

2-03 **3** *hd* **Longliner**[77] 1824 3-9-1 86 RyanMoore 6 85
(Sir Michael Stoute) *in tch: hdwy to chse ldr over 3f out: rdn to ld ent fnl 2f: edgd lft u.p over 1f out: kpt on same pce fnl f: hdd and lost 2 pls towards fin* **5/4**[1]

24 **4** *6* **Marching Song (USA)**[21] 3563 4-9-13 0 RichardHughes 5 78
(Andrew Turnell) *t.k.h: hld up in tch: hdwy to trck ldrs over 3f out: rdn and n.m.r over 1f out: btn and eased ins fnl f* **9/1**

5 *32* **Missionary** 3-9-1 0 KierenFallon 9 24
(W J Haggas) *dwlt: sn pushed along and chsd ldrs after 2f: rdn and wknd qckly wl over 3f out: t.o fnl 2f* **16/1**

60 **6** *3/4* **Deejan (IRE)**[21] 3563 5-9-8 0 DavidProbert 3 18
(B Palling) *led tl 10f out: chsd ldr tl wl over 3f out: sn rdn and wknd: t.o fnl 2f* **66/1**

440 **7** *7* **Suhailah**[37] 3038 4-9-3 45 JemmaMarshall(5) 4 6
(M J Attwater) *in tch in midfield tl rdn and lost tch 4f out: t.o fr over 2f out* **100/1**

0 **8** *31* **Ancestral Dream**[44] 2812 3-8-12 0 (v[1]) RussKennemore(3) 11 —
(Andrew Reid) *s.i.s and rdn along early: in tch tl hrd rdn and dropped out rapidly 6f out: wl t.o and virtually p.u fr over 2f out* **66/1**

0 **9** *1* **Kirkum (IRE)**[24] 1705 5-9-13 0 (b[1]) ShaneKelly 10 —
(Miss Diana Weeden) *s.i.s: detached in last and nvr gng: lost tch 6f out: wl t.o and virtually p.u fnl 3f* **66/1**

06 **10** *14* **Sheklaan (USA)**[14] 3795 3-9-1 0 (p) RichardHills 2 —
(M A Jarvis) *chsd ldrs tl rdn and lost pl qckly 9f out: nvr gng after: lost tch over 4f out: wl t.o and virtually p.u fnl 3f* **10/1**

2m 33.83s (0.83) **Going Correction** +0.175s/f (Slow)
WFA 3 from 4yo+ 12lb **10** Ran SP% **116.1**
Speed ratings (Par 103): **104,103,103,99,78 77,73,52,51,42**
toteswingers:1&2:£3.70, 1&3:£2.70, 2&3:£1.50 CSF £19.81 TOTE £6.20: £1.50, £1.10, £2.00; EX 22.50 Trifecta £33.90 Pool: £463.03 - 10.10 winning units..
Owner Lady Bamford & Ms Rachel D S Hood **Bred** Lady Bamford **Trained** Newmarket, Suffolk

FOCUS
A more interesting older-horse maiden than is often the case at this time of year, and the form among the three who came clear looks useful. The time was 0.93 seconds slower than the first division (won by another Gosden runner, Kansai Spirit), suggesting they didn't go that quick.
Sheklaan(USA) Official explanation: jockey said colt never travelled

4259 BET WORLD MATCHPLAY DARTS - BETDAQ H'CAP 1m 4f (P)
5:00 (5:00) (Class 5) (0-75,73) 3-Y-O **£2,729** (£806; £403) **Stalls** Low

Form RPR

03-6 **1** **Mme De Stael**[20] 3606 3-8-7 59 (b[1]) JimmyQuinn 5 68
(Sir Mark Prescott) *taken down early and ponied to s: in tch: pushed along to chse ldng pair over 2f out: rdn to chse ldr wl over 1f out: led ent fnl f: sn clr: comf* **6/1**

0222 **2** *4* **Saggiatore**[33] 3170 3-9-6 72 RyanMoore 1 75+
(E A L Dunlop) *led at stdy gallop tl hdd 8f out: chsd ldng pair after: rdn and effrt ent fnl 2f: keeping on same pce and n.m.r over 1f out: no ch w wnr ins fnl f: kpt on to go 2nd fnl 100yds* **2/1**[1]

4455 **3** *1* **Dr Finley (IRE)**[40] 2924 3-8-9 66 SimonPearce(5) 2 67
(J Pearce) *hld up in tch: rdn and effrt on inner ent fnl 2f: no threat to wnr but pressing for 2nd 1f out: kpt on same pce* **16/1**

2336 **4** *hd* **Gordon Flash**[40] 2924 3-9-0 66 KierenFallon 7 67
(R Hannon) *chsd ldrs tl led and qcknd gallop 8f out: rdn over 2f out: hdd ent fnl f: sn no ch w wnr: lost 2 pls fnl 100yds* **9/2**[3]

6642 **5** *1* **Head Hunted**[41] 2908 3-8-7 62 MartinLane(3) 3 61
(D M Simcock) *bmpd s and bustled along early: in tch in last pair: rdn and hdwy on outer 3f out: no imp and wl hld fr over 1f out* **7/2**[2]

-200 **6** *1* **Fairy Flight (USA)**[19] 3626 3-9-7 73 JimCrowley 6 71
(W J Knight) *chsd ldr tl wl over 1f out: sn edgd rt u.p and unable qck: styd on same pce after* **6/1**

062 **7** *12* **Ancient Greece**[30] 3258 3-9-7 73 DaraghO'Donohoe 4 58
(George Baker) *wnt lft and bmpd s: in tch in last pair: rdn and short-lived effrt 2f out: wl btn ent fnl f: eased fnl 100yds* **10/1**

2m 36.72s (3.72) **Going Correction** +0.175s/f (Slow) **7** Ran SP% **117.3**
Speed ratings (Par 100): **94,91,90,90,89 89,81**
toteswingers:1&2:£3.20, 1&3:£7.90, 2&3:£3.80 CSF £19.24 TOTE £6.80: £2.40, £3.10; EX 24.30.
Owner Miss K Rausing **Bred** Miss K Rausing **Trained** Newmarket, Suffolk

FOCUS
This looked a competitive enough 3-y-o handicap, despite the small field, but Mme De Stael showed herself well treated. The pace was steady, resulting in a time significantly slower than both divisions of the maiden.

4260 BETDAQEXTRA.COM H'CAP 7f (P)
5:30 (5:32) (Class 5) (0-75,75) 3-Y-O+ **£2,729** (£806; £403) **Stalls** Low

Form RPR

2362 **1** **For Life (IRE)**[46] 2750 8-9-10 74 NataliaGemelova(3) 12 82
(J E Long) *taken down early: mde all: rdn wl over 1f out: kpt on gamely fnl f* **12/1**

4332 **2** *nk* **Rondeau (GR)**[45] 2783 5-9-11 72 JimCrowley 8 79
(P R Chamings) *stdd after s: hld up towards rr: hdwy on outer over 2f out: r.o wl u.p ins fnl f: pressed wnr cl home: nt quite rch wnr* **7/1**[3]

6263 **3** *1/2* **Copperwood**[7] 4024 5-9-9 70 NeilCallan 5 76
(M Blanshard) *stdd s: hld up towards rr: hdwy jst over 2f out: swtchd lft ent fnl f: r.o u.p ins fnl f: nt quite rch ldrs* **5/1**[2]

5030 **4** *shd* **Cape Quarter (USA)**[14] 3777 4-9-2 63 (t) RichardHughes 13 68
(W J Haggas) *stdd s: hld up towards rr: hmpd and shuffled further bk bnd 5f out: swtchd rt and hdwy over 1f out: kpt on wl u.p fnl f: nt quite rch ldrs* **4/1**[1]

-414 **5** *1 1/2* **Cuthbert (IRE)**[171] 366 3-9-6 74 KierenFallon 14 72
(W Jarvis) *chsd ldrs: wnt 2nd over 3f out: rdn and unable qck over 1f out: styd on same pce ins fnl f* **12/1**

-004 **6** *3/4* **First Service (IRE)**[7] 4024 4-9-6 67 (p) ShaneKelly 2 66
(M J Attwater) *dwlt: sn in tch in midfield: hdwy 3f out: chsd ldr ent fnl 2f: sn rdn and nt qckn: styd on same pce ins fnl f* **14/1**

1030 **7** *3/4* **Batchworth Blaise**[28] 3323 7-8-7 59 KierenFox(5) 7 56
(E A Wheeler) *stdd s: bhd: niggled along over 4f out: c wd and effrt bnd 2f out: no imp ent fnl f* **12/1**

2500 **8** *1/2* **Kipchak (IRE)**[14] 3777 5-9-6 67 (p) LiamKeniry 11 63
(C R Dore) *taken down early: chsd ldrs: rdn and struggling ent fnl 2f: wknd fnl f* **20/1**

2633 **9** *2* **I Confess**[4] 4133 5-9-5 69 (b) RobertLButler(3) 3 60
(Jim Best) *chsd ldr tl over 3f out: styd prom tl wknd u.p ent fnl f* **10/1**

3310 **10** *11* **Roshina (IRE)**[32] 3212 4-9-6 67 IanMongan 9 28
(Miss Jo Crowley) *in tch in midfield: effrt u.p jst over 2f out: no prog and btn 1f out: eased ins fnl f* **20/1**

000- **11** *1 1/4* **Koraleva Tectona (IRE)**[263] 7189 5-9-10 74 MartinLane(3) 1 31
(Pat Eddery) *in tch in midfield tl n.m.r and hmpd bnd 5f out: rdn and dropped to rr wl over 3f out: sn lost tch* **25/1**

2320 **12** *20* **Lingfield Bound (IRE)**[92] 1448 3-9-4 72 SteveDrowne 4 —
(J R Best) *in tch in midfield: pushed along whn hmpd and lost pl bnd 5f out: bhd and rdn over 3f out: lost tch 3f out* **4/1**[1]

0-46 **13** *hd* **Times Ahead (USA)**[32] 3227 3-9-4 72 ChrisCatlin 10 —
(P W Chapple-Hyam) *sn detached in last and rdn along: t.o over 3f out* **16/1**

1m 26.89s (2.09) **Going Correction** +0.175s/f (Slow)
WFA 3 from 4yo+ 7lb **13** Ran SP% **127.3**
Speed ratings (Par 103): **95,94,94,93,92 91,90,89,87,75 73,50,50**
toteswingers:1&2:£10.70, 1&3:£11.50, 2&3:£3.30 CSF £97.22 CT £506.28 TOTE £24.80: £7.60, £3.00, £1.60; EX 86.70 Trifecta £220.50 Part won. Pool: £298.05 - 0.84 winning units. Place 6 £73.74; Place 5 £59.00..
Owner T H Bambridge **Bred** R N Auld **Trained** Caterham, Surrey

FOCUS
An ordinary handicap.
First Service(IRE) Official explanation: jockey said gelding suffered interference on first bend
Lingfield Bound(IRE) Official explanation: jockey said colt suffered interference on first bend never travelled
T/Plt: £44.00 to a £1 stake. Pool:£59,502.07 - 987.07 winning tickets T/Qpdt: £33.90 to a £1 stake. Pool:£3,996.69 - 87.10 winning tickets SP

3691 SANDOWN (R-H)
Wednesday, July 21

OFFICIAL GOING: Good to firm (firm in places; watered; rnd 8.9, sprint 9.0)
Round course at innermost configuration and distances as advertised. Far rail on sprint course moved in 3yds.
Wind: Moderate, half against Weather: Fine, very warm

4261 THAMES DITTON APPRENTICE H'CAP 1m 2f 7y
6:05 (6:05) (Class 5) (0-75,76) 4-Y-O+ **£2,590** (£770; £385; £192) **Stalls** High

Form RPR

2054 **1** **Baylini**[5] 4108 6-9-5 73 SophieDoyle(3) 3 83
(Ms J S Doyle) *hld up in last pair: prog to go 2nd over 2f out: clsd and shkn up to ld 1f out: a doing enough to hold on* **5/2**[2]

1621 **2** *1/2* **Dream Win**[23] 3520 4-8-11 67 DaleSwift(5) 7 76
(B Ellison) *led 1f: led again 3f out and sn kicked at least 2 l clr: hrd rdn and hdd 1f out: styd on but a hld* **85/40**[1]

1262 **3** *7* **The Hague**[13] 3810 4-9-6 71 AndrewHeffernan 1 66
(P D Evans) *trckd ldng pair: rdn to dispute 2nd briefly over 2f out: sn lft bhd* **4/1**[3]

5235 **4** *2* **Mons Calpe (IRE)**[11] 3917 4-8-11 67 (b) DuilioDaSilva(5) 4 58
(P F I Cole) *hld up in 4th: rdn 3f out: nt clr run on inner 2f out to over 1f out: no prog after* **9/2**

0-32 **5** *7* **Sinchiroka (FR)**[148] 669 4-9-4 72 RichardEvans(3) 6 49
(R J Smith) *rousted along to ld after 1f: rdn and hdd 3f out: sn wknd* **25/1**

3-40 **6** *97* **Piccolo Mondo**[37] 3036 4-9-4 69 (p) WilliamCarson 8 —
(P Winkworth) *t.k.h early: hld up in last pair: wknd rapidly over 3f out: virtually p.u after* **10/1**

2m 6.93s (-3.57) **Going Correction** -0.125s/f (Firm) **6** Ran SP% **111.7**
Speed ratings (Par 103): **109,108,103,101,95 18**
toteswingers:1&2:£1.60, 1&3:£3.10, 2&3:£1.40 CSF £8.16 TOTE £3.90: £1.80, £1.50; EX 9.90.
Owner J P Doyle **Bred** Templeton Stud **Trained**
■ Stewards' Enquiry : Duilio Da Silva two-day ban: used whip above shoulder height (Aug 4-5)

FOCUS
An ordinary handicap was run at a fair pace, with the runner-up prominent throughout and the winner coming from the back of the field.

The Form Book, Raceform Ltd, Compton, RG20 6NL

Piccolo Mondo Official explanation: vet said gelding was suffering from atrial fibrillation

4262 ABSOLUTE RADIO NURSERY 5f 6y
6:35 (6:36) (Class 5) 2-Y-O **£2,590** (£770; £385; £192) **Stalls** High

Form RPR

512 **1** **Krypton Factor**[5] 4111 2-9-1 **76**..............................(b[1]) StevieDonohoe 1 83
(Sir Mark Prescott) *s.i.s: rcvrd to join ldr over 3f out: narrow ld jst over 1f out: drvn and styd on wl* **9/2**[3]

510 **2** *1 ½* **Swiss Dream**[35] 3070 2-9-6 **81**.. RyanMoore 2 83
(D R C Elsworth) *t.k.h early: hld up: effrt 2f out: drvn to go 2nd ins fnl f: no imp on wnr* **5/4**[1]

045 **3** *1* **Golden Taurus (IRE)**[23] 3498 2-8-11 **72**........................ MichaelHills 6 70
(J W Hills) *hld up last: swtchd outside over 1f out: shkn up and styd on to take 3rd nr fin: no ch* **16/1**

231 **4** *nk* **Ahtoug**[18] 3658 2-9-7 **82**.. AhmedAjtebi 4 79
(Mahmood Al Zarooni) *led: jnd over 3f out: edgd rt 2f out: hdd jst over 1f out: fdd fnl f* **11/4**[2]

1350 **5** *½* **Rosina Grey**[11] 3887 2-8-12 **73**..(p) AlanMunro 3 68
(B R Millman) *t.k.h: hld up: rdn and nt qcknd over 1f out: no imp on ldrs after* **18/1**

3341 **6** *3* **Master Macho (IRE)**[11] 3897 2-8-10 **74**.................. MatthewDavies(3) 8 58
(M R Channon) *cl up against rail: hmpd 2f out: wknd over 1f out* **8/1**

61.82 secs (0.22) **Going Correction** -0.125s/f (Firm) **6** Ran SP% **111.5**
Speed ratings (Par 94): **93,90,89,88,87 82**
toteswingers:1&2:£1.10, 1&3:£9.20, 2&3:£5.00 CSF £10.47 CT £76.29 TOTE £4.70: £2.30, £1.10; EX 7.70.
Owner Lady Fairhaven & The Hon C & H Broughton **Bred** Lady Fairhaven **Trained** Newmarket, Suffolk
■ Stewards' Enquiry : Stevie Donohoe two-day ban: careless riding (Aug 4-5)

FOCUS
An ordinary nursery but the form has a sound feel to it.

NOTEBOOK
Krypton Factor was weak in the market beforehand, but he got the job done quite cleverly. He was well in at the weights based on his head defeat at Nottingham five days earlier, but the appearance of blinkers for the first time was off-putting and he didn't make things easy for himself back down in trip by missing the break. He quickly made up the lost ground to dispute the lead, though, and, despite wandering about when first asked to quicken, he finished well on top. There's more to come from him and he can defy a higher mark. (op 5-2 tchd 5-1)
Swiss Dream, who was sent off third-favourite but could only finish in midfield in the Queen Mary last time out, holds a Lowther entry and had to be of interest on this drop in class. A stronger gallop would have helped as she was a bit keen out the back and the winner got first run on her. (op 6-4 tchd 13-8 and 7-4 in places)
Golden Taurus(IRE), whose best effort in three maidens came over this C&D, lost momentum when switched off the rail to come with his challenge out wide. He was running on well at the finish, though. (op 25-1)
Ahtoug didn't look to have been set an easy task off top weight and, having raced prominently for much of the race, was easily seen off inside the last. (op 4-1 tchd 5-2)
Rosina Grey ran too free on her nursery debut at Ascot and again she wanted to go quicker than her rider. The cheekpieces were of no obvious benefit. (op 22-1 tchd 25-1)
Master Macho(IRE), by far the most experienced horse in the field, was up against some less-exposed rivals open to more improvement than him, and that's likely to remain a problem. (tchd 6-1)

4263 DEVINE HOMES EBF MAIDEN STKS 7f 16y
7:10 (7:12) (Class 4) 2-Y-O **£4,533** (£1,348; £674; £336) **Stalls** High

Form RPR

05 **1** **Star Surprise**[19] 3631 2-9-3 0....................................... JamieSpencer 12 78
(M L W Bell) *led: rdn and hdd briefly jst over 1f out: drvn to assert ins fnl f: hld on* **8/1**

2 *nk* **Johnny Castle** 2-9-3 0.. RichardHills 8 80+
(J H M Gosden) *towards rr: shuffled bk to last pair 3f out: gd prog and threaded through fr over 2f out: r.o to take 2nd nr fin and cl on wnr* **12/1**

52 **3** *¾* **Baransky**[14] 3794 2-9-3 0.. AhmedAjtebi 4 75
(Mahmood Al Zarooni) *trckd ldng pair: chsd wnr over 2f out: rdn to ld briefly jst over 1f out: hld ins fnl f and lost 2nd nr fin* **13/8**[1]

4 *¾* **Kinyras (IRE)** 2-9-3 0.. RyanMoore 5 73
(Sir Michael Stoute) *chsd ldng quartet: pushed along 3f out: kpt on fr 2f out: nrst fin* **9/1**

5 *¾* **Bawaab (USA)** 2-9-3 0.. FrankieDettori 6 71+
(Saeed Bin Suroor) *green to post: slowly away and off the pce in last pair: rchd midfield by 1/2-way: shkn up and kpt on fnl 2f: nrst fin* **4/1**[2]

6 *nk* **El Maachi** 2-9-0 0.. AndrewHeffernan(3) 9 71
(P D Evans) *chsd ldng pair: rdn over 2f out: kpt on fr over 1f out: no real imp* **66/1**

7 *3* **Cuban Piece (IRE)** 2-9-3 0.................................... RichardKingscote 2 63
(Tom Dascombe) *green preliminaries: wl in rr: rdn on inner 3f out: plugged on fnl 2f: nvr on terms* **33/1**

06 **8** *nk* **Maratib (USA)**[23] 3517 2-9-3 0.. DaneO'Neill 1 62
(D R Lanigan) *a towards rr: shkn up and no prog over 2f out: n.d fr over 1f out* **100/1**

0 **9** *¾* **Prince Freddie**[32] 3219 2-9-3 0.. PatCosgrave 3 60
(M H Tompkins) *chsd ldng quartet: rdn and no prog whn sltly hmpd over 1f out: fdd* **66/1**

10 *3 ¾* **Enlightening (IRE)** 2-9-3 0...................................... RichardHughes 10 51
(R Hannon) *chsd wnr to over 2f out: wknd qckly over 1f out* **7/1**[3]

11 *2 ½* **Cross Culture (IRE)** 2-9-3 0.. JimmyFortune 7 45
(A M Balding) *slowest away: wl off the pce in last: wd bnd over 4f out: gng wl enough 3f out: wknd 2f out* **14/1**

12 *1 ½* **Mi Sun Donk** 2-8-12 0.. KierenFox(5) 11 41
(B R Johnson) *a towards rr: wknd over 2f out* **33/1**

1m 30.83s (1.33) **Going Correction** -0.125s/f (Firm) **12** Ran SP% **115.9**
Speed ratings (Par 96): **87,86,85,84,84 83,80,79,79,74 71,70**
toteswingers:1&2:£12.10, 1&3:£3.50, 2&3:£5.60 CSF £94.31 TOTE £6.70: £1.60, £3.30, £1.30; EX 65.00.
Owner Dr Ali Ridha **Bred** Rabbah Bloodstock Limited **Trained** Newmarket, Suffolk

FOCUS
They finished in a bit of a heap thus giving the impression that it was not a strong maiden for the track.

NOTEBOOK
Star Surprise is improving with racing and he built on his fifth over the C&D last time with a gritty display, showing far more resolution than the eventual third inside the final furlong. He should get another furlong this year and cannot be hammered for this by the handicapper, with nurseries in mind. (op 9-1 tchd 15-2)
Johnny Castle ◆ is the obvious one to take from the race as from 3f out to 1f out he couldn't get a clear run. Once the gaps came, he stayed on well to take second close home. He looked an unlucky loser and should be capable of winning an ordinary maiden. A mile should suit him too later this year.
Baransky was very much the one to beat on his second in a Newmarket maiden last time out, but having been brought to have every chance, he showed no inclination to go past the battling winner, hanging into him under pressure. He looks one to be wary of. (op 7-4 tchd 15-8)
Kinyras(IRE), who is bred to stay well next year, is likely to want to step up to a mile as soon as possible this term. (op 8-1 tchd 15-2)
Bawaab(USA) ran a promising enough race on his debut while displaying signs of greenness. By Street Cry out of a speedy Canadian-bred mare, he's entitled to improve for this. (op 9-2)
El Maachi, an already gelded son of Librettist, showed up well for a long way and, despite his cheap purchase price, clearly has some ability. (op 50-1)

4264 MAUREEN STURT & THE CHILDREN'S TRUST H'CAP 7f 16y
7:40 (7:41) (Class 3) (0-90,88) 3-Y-O **£6,476** (£1,927; £963; £481) **Stalls** High

Form RPR

-211 **1** **Kakatosi**[18] 3696 3-9-7 **88**... JimmyFortune 9 103
(A M Balding) *mde all: rdn and pressed over 1f out: styd on in gd style fnl f* **11/4**[2]

0331 **2** *1* **Ertikaan**[19] 3621 3-9-1 **82**... RichardHills 1 94
(M A Jarvis) *trckd wnr: shkn up to chal over 1f out: styd on wl fnl f but a hld* **6/1**

-310 **3** *4* **Fleeting Echo**[14] 3790 3-9-6 **87**.. RyanMoore 8 88
(R Hannon) *hld up in 5th: rdn and prog to go 3rd wl over 1f out: no imp on ldng pair and lost grnd on them fnl f* **11/2**[3]

4030 **4** *¾* **Fivefold (USA)**[20] 3579 3-8-10 **77**...................................... AlanMunro 6 76
(J Akehurst) *t.k.h: trckd ldng pair: rdn over 2f out: lost 3rd wl over 1f out: one pce after* **16/1**

0-05 **5** *1 ¾* **Wisecraic**[82] 1663 3-9-1 **82**...................................... RichardKingscote 7 76
(Tom Dascombe) *hld up in 7th: rdn over 2f out: plugged on w limited enthusiasm fr over 1f out* **22/1**

0430 **6** *6* **Ongoodform (IRE)**[34] 3103 3-9-2 **83**................................... NeilCallan 3 61
(P W D'Arcy) *trckd ldng trio: rdn over 2f out: no prog: wknd over 1f out* **14/1**

1012 **7** *½* **Sailorman (IRE)**[6] 4057 3-9-6 **87**................................. FrankieDettori 5 64
(M Johnston) *s.i.s: hld up in 6th: shkn up on outer 2f out: nt qckn and situation sn accepted* **2/1**[1]

6033 **8** *1 ½* **Dubai Set**[11] 3916 3-9-1 **82**.......................................(b) RichardHughes 2 55
(R Hannon) *hld up in detached last: pushed along 3f out: no prog* **12/1**

1m 27.89s (-1.61) **Going Correction** -0.125s/f (Firm) **8** Ran SP% **114.3**
Speed ratings (Par 104): **104,102,98,97,95 88,88,86**
toteswingers:1&2:£1.80, 1&3:£3.10, 2&3:£3.60 CSF £19.64 CT £84.71 TOTE £4.00: £1.50, £1.60, £1.50; EX 16.30.
Owner Robert E Tillett **Bred** T E Pocock **Trained** Kingsclere, Hants

FOCUS
Two of these stood out beforehand as improving types on attractive marks, and they fought out the finish.

NOTEBOOK
Kakatosi was aided by the fact he was allowed an easy lead. Setting a pace to suit, he was always going to be tough to pass in the straight as he has a real will to win. He is coping well with fast ground, but he hits the turf pretty hard and a little ease will suit him ideally. The type to keep finding more, he remains one to keep on side. (op 5-2 tchd 3-1)
Ertikaan looked like he might have been let in lightly on his handicap debut and he proved it, despite not winning. He has plenty of speed and gives the impression that he won't mind dropping back to 6f. (op 4-1)
Fleeting Echo is another who could probably cope with a drop back to 6f, although there wasn't any disgrace in this effort, as the first two are nicely ahead of the handicapper. (op 7-1)
Fivefold(USA), not for the first time, pulled for his head in the early stages. A stronger all-round pace would undoubtedly have suited him better.
Wisecraic was set a difficult task given the way the race was run. There should be some improvement to come given he was returning from an 82-day break. (op 25-1 tchd 20-1)
Ongoodform(IRE) remains vulnerable to improvers off his current mark. (op 16-1)
Sailorman(IRE) was backed into favouritism despite being beaten off a 5lb lower mark at Epsom six days earlier. He was awkward out of the stalls, which meant that any ideas about making the running had to be ditched. Trapped wide and keen in midfield, he made little impression once into the straight. (op 11-4)

4265 DEVINE HOMES 25TH ANNIVERSARY H'CAP 1m 14y
8:15 (8:15) (Class 4) (0-80,80) 3-Y-O+ **£3,885** (£1,156; £577; £288) **Stalls** High

Form RPR

43-2 **1** **Tartan Trip**[92] 1453 3-9-5 **78**... JimmyFortune 4 84
(A M Balding) *trckd ldr: drvn ahd over 1f out: hrd pressed whn edgd rt and hmpd chalr last 100yds* **3/1**[1]

2405 **2** *½* **Prince Of Thebes (IRE)**[6] 4057 9-9-0 **65**......................... NeilCallan 10 73+
(M J Attwater) *trckd ldng pair: sltly hmpd over 2f out: squeezed through ent fnl f: str chal whn bdly hmpd 100yds out: nt rcvr* **16/1**

3541 **3** *nk* **Squall**[16] 3733 3-9-4 **77**... FrankieDettori 3 81
(J Noseda) *hld up in 5th: prog to press wnr jst over 1f out and looked dangerous: nt qckn and lost 2nd jst ins fnl f: kpt on* **3/1**[1]

0050 **4** *2 ¼* **Aflaam (IRE)**[5] 4108 5-9-3 **73**... JohnFahy(5) 7 74
(R A Harris) *hld up in last pair: effrt on wd outside: cl enough over 1f out: nt qckn u.p: one pce after* **10/1**

-130 **5** *2 ¼* **Circus Girl (IRE)**[43] 2843 3-9-7 **80**.................................... JimCrowley 6 76
(R M Beckett) *led: drvn and hdd over 1f out: began to lose pl whn short of room ent fnl f: wknd* **4/1**[2]

6540 **6** *2 ¼* **Halsion Chancer**[28] 3317 6-9-5 **75**.................................. KierenFox(5) 9 66
(J R Best) *hld up in last pair: effrt on outer over 2f out: rdn and cl enough over 1f out: nt qckn: wknd fnl f* **4/1**[2]

-000 **7** *6* **Truly Asia (IRE)**[25] 3438 4-9-10 **75**................................ SteveDrowne 1 52
(R Charlton) *trckd ldng trio: lost pl over 2f out: wknd tamely sn after* **8/1**[3]

1m 42.92s (-0.38) **Going Correction** -0.125s/f (Firm)
WFA 3 from 4yo+ 8lb **7** Ran SP% **116.1**
Speed ratings (Par 105): **96,95,95,92,90 88,82**
toteswingers:1&2:£1.80, 1&3:£3.10, 2&3:£3.60 CSF £51.57 CT £156.57 TOTE £3.90: £2.00, £4.70; EX 47.20.
Owner Kingsclere Racing CLub **Bred** Kingsclere Stud **Trained** Kingsclere, Hants
■ Stewards' Enquiry : Neil Callan two-day ban: careless riding (Aug 4-5)
Jimmy Fortune four-day ban: careless riding (Aug 4-7)

FOCUS
Quite an open-looking handicap, and there was a messy finish, but the first past the post kept the race in the subsequent inquiry.

4266 DON'T LOSE YOUR BOTTLE BROTHERS CIDER H'CAP 1m 6f
8:50 (8:50) (Class 4) (0-80,78) 4-Y-O+ **£3,885** (£1,156; £577; £288) **Stalls** High

Form RPR

3632 **1** **Blazing Desert**[17] 3709 6-8-11 **71**.................................. IanBrennan(5) 4 78+
(J J Quinn) *trckd ldng trio: prog to go 2nd over 2f out and sn chalng: drvn to ld 1f out: in command whn edgd rt nr fin* **7/2**[2]

0123 **2** 1 3/4 **Outland (IRE)**[6] 4070 4-8-8 **63** JimCrowley 1 68
(J R Jenkins) *hld up in last pair: rdn and nt qckn whn pce lifted 3f out: kpt on fr 2f out: nvr able to chal but lft in 2nd pl nr fin* **4/1**[3]

0313 **3** nk **Lastroseofsummer (IRE)**[24] 3475 4-8-8 **63** ChrisCatlin 3 68+
(Rae Guest) *t.k.h: led after 3f and set modest pce: kicked on 3f out: hrd rdn and hdd 1f out: hld whn hmpd nr fin and lost 2nd* **5/1**

5062 **4** 1 **Tilos Gem (IRE)**[8] 3989 4-8-6 **61** JoeFanning 5 64
(M Johnston) *led 3f: trckd ldr to over 2f out: drvn and one pce after* **9/4**[1]

-000 **5** 3 1/4 **Bon Spiel**[12] 3873 6-9-7 **76** (tp) DaneO'Neill 6 74
(C Gordon) *trckd ldng pair: nt qckn wl over 2f out and lost pl: effrt wl over 1f out: sn fdd* **6/1**

-656 **6** 1 1/2 **Dani's Girl (IRE)**[116] 1020 7-9-9 **78** IanMongan 2 74
(P M Phelan) *t.k.h: hld up in last pair: rdn whn pce lifted 3f out: n.m.r briefly over 2f out: nt qckn sn after: fdd over 1f out* **11/1**

3m 5.08s (0.58) **Going Correction** -0.125s/f (Firm) **6** Ran SP% **112.3**
Speed ratings (Par 105): **93,92,91,91,89 88**
toteswingers:1&2:£1.60, 1&3:£4.20, 2&3:£3.70 CSF £17.67 TOTE £4.20: £2.50, £2.60; EX 16.80 Place 6 £45.22; Place 5 £31.43.
Owner Allan Stennett **Bred** Mrs Brenda Howlett-Nye **Trained** Settrington, N Yorks
■ Stewards' Enquiry : Ian Brennan three-day ban: careless riding (Aug 4-6)

FOCUS
An ordinary staying event.
T/Plt: £29.80 to a £1 stake. Pool:£65,370.59 - 1,598.52 winning tickets T/Qpdt: £10.60 to a £1 stake. Pool:£5,915.60 - 412.80 winning tickets JN

4267 - 4268a (Foreign Racing) - See Raceform Interactive

3797 NAAS (L-H)
Wednesday, July 21

OFFICIAL GOING: Good to yielding (yielding in places) changing to yielding after race 1 (6:00)

4269a ITBA & GAIN HORSE FEEDS SUPPORT LOCAL RACETRACKS E B F SWEET MIMOSA STKS (LISTED RACE) (FILLIES) 6f
7:00 (7:03) 3-Y-0+ **£35,951** (£10,508; £4,977; £1,659)

RPR

1 **Bewitched (IRE)**[21] 3571 3-9-1 105 (t) JMurtagh 6 112+
(Charles O'Brien, Ire) *chsd ldrs on nr side: 6th 1 1/2f out: sn rdn to chal: 2nd 1f out: styd on wl to ld ins fnl f* **6/1**[3]

2 3/4 **Swiss Diva**[12] 3875 4-9-3 FMBerry 7 108
(D R C Elsworth) *chsd ldrs: prog to ld and rdn 1 1/2f out: strly pressed 1f out: hdd ins fnl f: kpt on wl* **5/1**[2]

3 3 **Prescription**[74] 1918 5-9-6 DPMcDonogh 1 101+
(Sir Mark Prescott) *s.i.s and pushed along to chse ldrs in centre early: rdn fr 2f out: mod 5th 1 1/2f out: kpt on wout threatening to go 3rd fnl f* **2/1**[1]

4 1 1/2 **Wrong Answer**[44] 2827 3-8-12 99 CDHayes 9 93
(Kevin Prendergast, Ire) *mid-div on nr side: rdn fr 1/2-way: kpt on wout threatening to go mod 4th ins fnl f* **16/1**

5 1 1/4 **Tweedy (IRE)**[28] 3340 3-8-12 89 CO'Donoghue 12 89
(Edward Lynam, Ire) *cl up in 2nd on nr side: rdn fr 2f out: no ex 1 1/2f out* **20/1**

6 nk **Dawn Eclipse (IRE)**[3] 4182 5-9-3 77 BACurtis 11 89
(T G McCourt, Ire) *chsd ldrs in 5th on nr side: rdn and kpt on one pce fr 2f out* **9/1**

7 1 1/4 **Kitty Kiernan**[21] 3571 3-8-12 106 (t) KJManning 3 84
(J S Bolger, Ire) *cl up in 3rd on far side: rdn and wknd fr 2f out* **10/1**

8 1/2 **Miss Gorica (IRE)**[21] 3571 6-9-6 105 WMLordan 13 86
(Ms Joanna Morgan, Ire) *led on nr side: rdn and hdd 1 1/2f out: sn wknd* **9/1**

9 1/2 **Zorija Rose (IRE)**[82] 1676 5-9-3 98 WJLee 8 81
(T Stack, Ire) *chsd ldrs early: mid-div 1/2-way: sn rdn and wknd* **20/1**

10 2 **Queen Of Troy (IRE)**[11] 3928 3-8-12 94 JAHeffernan 5 74
(A P O'Brien, Ire) *a towards rr* **33/1**

11 5 1/2 **Brushed Aside**[24] 3489 3-8-12 90 (b) PJSmullen 4 56
(D K Weld, Ire) *chsd ldrs in 6th on far side: rdn and wknd fr 2f out: eased ins fnl f* **9/1**

12 12 **Lough Mist (IRE)**[3] 4180 4-9-3 87 PShanahan 2 19
(Tracey Collins, Ire) *stmbld leaving stalls: racd along on far rail and sn overall 4th: rdn and wknd fr 1/2-way: eased over 1f out* **28/1**

1m 10.82s (-2.38)
WFA 3 from 4yo+ 5lb **12** Ran SP% **125.2**
CSF £36.44 TOTE £7.20: £2.20, £1.90, £1.50; DF 45.20.
Owner Mrs John Magnier **Bred** Monsieur J C Coude **Trained** Straffan, Co Kildare

FOCUS
The winner and third have been rated close to their marks.

NOTEBOOK
Bewitched(IRE) was dropped out at the start and tracked the stands' side group before working her way forward from 2f out. Switched left inside the final furlong, she hit the front about 100 yards from the finish. The ground was good to soft when she won at Haydock in May but trainer Charles O'Brien does not believe ground is an issue for the filly. He said: "She was very free at Fairyhouse and 7f was probably a step too far. We rode her differently tonight and it paid off. We'll look for a suitable Group 3 now, even if it means having to travel with her." (op 4/1)
Swiss Diva, having her third run of the season, won two handicaps last season and was also placed over this trip at this level on fast ground. She got to the front about 1½f out and kept on only for the winner to take her measure well inside the final furlong. (op 9/2)
Prescription began her effort under 2f out and kept on steadily without posing a serious threat. (op 9/4)
Wrong Answer chased the leaders towards the stands' side and kept on for pressure from 1f out.
Tweedy(IRE) ran fast towards the stands' side and was second 2f out before weakening into the final furlong.
Miss Gorica(IRE) was sthe overall leader before weakening once headed over a furlong out. (op 8/1)
Lough Mist(IRE) Official explanation: jockey said filly stumbled badly leaving stalls

4270 - 4273a (Foreign Racing) - See Raceform Interactive

DIEPPE (R-H)
Wednesday, July 21

OFFICIAL GOING: Turf: good to soft

4274a PRIX SAINTE-MARINE (CONDITIONS) (2YO) (TURF) 5f 110y
12:55 (12:00) 2-Y-0 **£11,061** (£4,424; £3,318; £2,212; £1,106)

RPR

1 **Mi Amor (SWI)** 2-8-9 0 FabriceVeron 1 86
(H-A Pantall, France) **58/10**

2 1 **Matreshka (IRE)**[14] 2-8-13 0 SylvainRuis 2 87
(N Clement, France) **43/10**[3]

3 4 **Veri One (FR)**[26] 2-8-6 0 JohannBensimon 5 67
(J Van Handenhove, France) **7/1**

4 1 1/2 **Mister Segway (IRE)**[14] 2-8-9 0 SebastienMaillot 9 65
(Robert Collet, France) **7/2**[2]

5 3/4 **Allez Les Bleus (FR)**[12] 2-8-9 0 WilliamsSaraiva(4) 8 66
(Mme J Bidgood, Spain) **14/5**[1]

6 1/2 **Sainte Colombe (IRE)**[12] 2-8-3 0 MorganDelalande(3) 3 57
(Y Barberot, France) **14/1**

7 8 **Bloody Sunday (FR)** 2-8-6 0 (p) ThomasHuet 7 31
(M Boutin, France) **28/1**

8 4 **Beach Patrol (IRE)**[66] 2139 2-8-9 0 EddieCreighton 4 21
(E J Creighton) *broke wl and pressed ldr showing gd spd: 2nd whn rdn appr fnl f: sn wknd and dropped away qckly* **13/1**

9 1/2 **Furiosa (IRE)**[12] 3858 2-8-6 0 MickaelBarzalona 6 16
(E J Creighton) *disp 4th tl wknd u.p fnl 300yds* **18/1**

63.18 secs (63.18) **9** Ran SP% **117.1**
PARI-MUTUEL (all including 1 euro stakes): WIN 6.80; PLACE 2.10, 2.00, 2.50; DF 19.60; SF 37.20.
Owner Erich Schmid **Bred** E Schmid **Trained** France

NOTEBOOK
Beach Patrol(IRE), beaten in a seller on his previous start, showed good early pace but paid for it in the closing stages.
Furiosa(IRE), having her third start, may not have handled the easier surface.

VICHY
Wednesday, July 21

OFFICIAL GOING: Turf: good to soft changing to soft after race 3

4275a PRIX DES REVES D'OR - JACQUES BOUCHARA (LISTED RACE) (2YO) (TURF) 5f
6:55 (12:00) 2-Y-0 **£24,336** (£9,734; £7,300; £4,867; £2,433)

RPR

1 **Marlinka**[24] 3482 2-8-10 0 IoritzMendizabal 9 93
(R Charlton) *broke fast: sn established clr ld: rdn 1 1/2f out and styd on wl* **14/5**[2]

2 3/4 **Boccalino (GER)**[24] 2-9-0 0 MaximeGuyon 1 94
(H-A Pantall, France) **63/10**[3]

3 1/2 **Bulliciosa (USA)**[21] 2-8-10 0 FranckBlondel 2 89
(M Pimbonnet, France) **13/1**

4 2 **Chinese Wall (IRE)**[56] 2-8-10 0 ThierryJarnet 5 81
(D Guillemin, France) **6/4**[1]

5 1 **Ulivate (IRE)**[35] 2-8-10 0 DavyBonilla 8 78
(M Pimbonnet, France) **12/1**

6 2 **Pinielde (FR)**[12] 2-8-10 0 StephanePasquier 6 71
(C Boutin, France) **10/1**

7 1/2 **Anawin (FR)**[41] 2-8-10 0 JohanVictoire 7 69
(F Chappet, France) **31/1**

8 5 **Villerville (IRE)**[114] 2-8-10 0 (b1) StephaneRichardot 3 51
(T Larriviere, France) **24/1**

9 6 **Tangamani (FR)**[35] 2-8-10 0 (p) OlivierTrigodet 4 29
(C Baillet, France) **18/1**

59.43 secs (59.43) **9** Ran SP% **116.3**
WIN (incl. 1 euro stake): 3.80. PLACES: 1.80, 2.30, 4.70. DF: 13.40. SF: 18.80.
Owner Elite Racing Club **Bred** Elite Racing Club **Trained** Beckhampton, Wilts

NOTEBOOK
Marlinka is very speedy and, for the third time made all over the minimum trip to score. She handled the easy ground well enough and picked up valuable black type in the process.

4276a GRAND PRIX DE VICHY - AUVERGNE 6EME ETAPE DU DEFI DU GALOP (GROUP 3) (3YO+) (TURF) 1m 2f
8:25 (12:00) 3-Y-0+ **£35,398** (£14,159; £10,619; £7,079; £3,539)

RPR

1 **Agent Secret (IRE)**[31] 3252 4-9-2 0 Francois-XavierBertras 6 106
(F Rohaut, France) *racd in 2nd fr s: qcknd to ld 1 1/2f out: wnt clr: comf* **19/5**[2]

2 8 **Pont Des Arts (FR)**[31] 6-9-2 0 FredericSpanu 4 90
(A Scharer, Germany) *led fr s and stl in front 2f out: rdn and hdd 1 1/2f out: styd on wl: jst hld 2nd* **19/1**

3 nk **Tip Toe (FR)**[45] 2802 3-8-6 0 FranckBlondel 2 89
(F Doumen, France) *racd in 5th: qcknd wl 2f out: r.o wl ins fnl f: narrowly failed to claim 2nd spot* **53/10**

4 1 1/2 **Wysiwyg Lucky (FR)**[31] 3252 7-8-13 0 StephanePasquier 7 83
(J-L Gay, France) *racd in 4th: rdn 2f out: styd on wl ins fnl f* **9/1**

5 4 **Russian Cross (IRE)**[37] 3045 5-9-2 0 MaximeGuyon 1 78
(A Fabre, France) *racd in 3rd: rdn 2f out: no ex: wknd* **4/1**[3]

6 3/4 **Court Canibal**[37] 3045 5-9-2 0 GeraldMosse 3 77
(M Delzangles, France) *racd in rr: swtchd to outer in st: hrd rdn: no ex* **6/4**[1]

7 3/4 **Danehill's Pearl (IRE)**[37] 3031 4-8-13 0 DavyBonilla 5 72
(Tom Dascombe) *settled towards rr: rdn early in st: no ex: wknd* **21/1**

2m 15.12s (6.52)
WFA 3 from 4yo+ 10lb **7** Ran SP% **116.3**
WIN (incl. 1 euro stake): 4.80. PLACES: 2.30, 5.70. SF: 46.80.
Owner Raoul Temam **Bred** J Hutchinson **Trained** Sauvagnon, France

NOTEBOOK
Danehill's Pearl(IRE), who won a Listed race here last year, has not rediscovered here form since returning this season and failed to figure.

4040 BATH (L-H)
Thursday, July 22

OFFICIAL GOING: Firm (9.1)
Wind: Mild breeze across Weather: Cloudy with sunny periods, heavy rain from 4.00pm.

4277 ASSET PROPERTY BROKERS MEDIAN AUCTION MAIDEN STKS 5f 161y
1:50 (1:50) (Class 6) 2-Y-O £1,554 (£462; £231; £115) Stalls Centre

Form				RPR
042	1		**Fantasy Fry**[17] 3721 2-9-3 0 SteveDrowne 1 (H Morrison) *trckd ldr: led 3f out: pushed clr wl over 1f out: comf* **4/5**[1]	70+
	2	2 ¾	**Rigolleto (IRE)** 2-9-3 0 ChrisCatlin 4 (M R Channon) *trckd ldrs: pressed wnr fr 3f out: rdn 2f out: edgd slty rt: no ex fnl f* **9/4**[2]	61+
4406	3	6	**Diamond Vine (IRE)**[7] 4066 2-9-3 0 (p) TomMcLaughlin 5 (R A Harris) *trckd ldrs: rdn 3f out: kpt on same pce fnl 2f* **5/1**[3]	41
00	4	4	**Local Diktator**[17] 3721 2-9-3 0 TadhgO'Shea 6 (R A Harris) *chsd ldrs: rdn 3f out: nt pce to chal: hung lft and wknd ent fnl f* **33/1**	28
00	5	dist	**Minus Tolerance**[28] 3349 2-8-12 0 J-PGuillambert 3 (Miss S L Davison) *broke wl: led tl 3f out: sn btn: eased fnl f* **66/1**	—

1m 11.76s (0.56) **Going Correction** -0.125s/f (Firm) **5** Ran SP% **107.4**
Speed ratings (Par 92): **91,87,79,74,—**
toteswinger: 1&2 £2.70. CSF £2.65 TOTE £1.10: £1.02, £3.10; EX 3.40.
Owner Michael Kerr-Dineen,Bob Tullett&Partners **Bred** Meon Valley Stud **Trained** East Ilsley, Berks

FOCUS
Following a dry night and morning, the ground was officially firm all round. This was an uncompetitive maiden and the market got it completely right. Limited form. The runners tended to race away from the inside rail in the straight, which rather set the trend for the afternoon.

NOTEBOOK
Fantasy Fry had improved in each of his first three starts and was possibly unlucky when runner-up here last time, but he made no mistake on this occasion. He was always going well and once asked to go and win his race, had no problem in romping clear. He may not have beaten much, but he continues to progress and should prove competitive in nurseries. (op 10-11 tchd 8-11and Evens in places)
Rigolleto(IRE), a 28,000gns half-brother to two winners at up to 1m, had every chance but the previous experience of the winner told in the latter stages. He should improve for this and may appreciated less-quick ground. (tchd 5-2)
Diamond Vine(IRE) had cheekpieces on for the first time, but still proved no match for the front pair and he is not confirming early promise. (op 4-1 tchd 11-2)
Local Diktator, beaten a long way in his first two starts and well behind Fantasy Fry here last time, was caught out wide from an early stage and ended up well beaten. He now gets a mark, but will need to improve plenty if he is to win a race.

4278 E B F PARKGARDENCENTRES.CO.UK NOVICE STKS 5f 11y
2:20 (2:20) (Class 4) 2-Y-O £4,274 (£1,271; £635; £317) Stalls Centre

Form				RPR
4115	1		**Belle Bayardo (IRE)**[2] 4228 2-9-7 0 TomMcLaughlin 4 (R A Harris) *trckd ldr: rdn to chal wl over 1f out: led jst ins fnl f: kpt on gamely: rdn out* **15/2**	94
2122	2	½	**The Thrill Is Gone**[20] 3630 2-8-11 0 ChrisCatlin 5 (M R Channon) *broke wl: led: rdn and edgd sltly lft over 1f out: hdd jst ins fnl f: kpt on: hld nr fin* **10/11**[1]	82
164	3	4 ½	**Tipsy Girl**[7] 4066 2-8-11 0 RobertWinston 1 (D J Coakley) *stdd s: sn nudged along in last pair: hdwy 3f out to chse ldrs: rdn 2f out: kpt on same pce fnl f* **7/2**[2]	65
1525	4	3 ¼	**Pick A Little**[40] 2950 2-9-2 0 DaneO'Neill 3 (B W Duke) *trckd ldr: chal over 2f out: sn rdn: wknd ent fnl f* **12/1**	58
1	5	2	**Snow Bear (IRE)**[62] 2272 2-8-11 0 MartinLane(3) 6 (J J Quinn) *awkward and slowly away: sn pushed along in last: hdwy u.p wl over 2f out: wknd over 1f out* **11/2**[3]	48
5100	6	14	**Molly Mylenis**[34] 3163 2-9-0 0 StevieDonohoe 2 (P D Evans) *chsd ldrs: rdn 3f out: nt pce to chal: wknd over 1f out* **66/1**	—

62.12 secs (-0.38) **Going Correction** -0.125s/f (Firm) **6** Ran SP% **110.9**
Speed ratings (Par 96): **98,97,90,84,81 59**
toteswingers: 1&2 £1.20, 1&3 £2.30, 2&3 £1.40. CSF £14.58 TOTE £4.80: £3.00, £1.80; EX 18.00.
Owner William Jones **Bred** L Mulryan **Trained** Earlswood, Monmouths

FOCUS
Not a bad novice event with all six participants previous winners. The winner more than confirmed his Chepstow level and the form could be rated 4lb+ more.

NOTEBOOK
Belle Bayardo(IRE) had little go right when bidding for a hat-trick at Kempton two days earlier, not least getting loose beforehand and crashing through some rails. However, he showed no ill-effects and displayed a fine attitude to pick up the favourite inside the last furlong. This was a decent effort conceding weight all round, but he may not be very easy to place from now on. (op 7-1)
The Thrill Is Gone has been taking on some smart rivals and excelled herself when runner-up to Zebedee in a Sandown Listed event last time. She tried to make all again and seemed to be in control for most of the contest, but having been keen early, she was worn down by the winner in the closing stages. She may have found this ground a bit quicker than ideal. (tchd 11-10)
Tipsy Girl, held in a Listed race and a nursery since making a winning debut over slightly further here last month, travelled well after missing the break but she didn't find a great deal for pressure. She had been shaping as though in need of 7f, so this drop in trip probably wasn't ideal. (op 5-1 tchd 10-3)
Pick A Little has been held, including in claiming company, since winning a Kempton maiden in April and he dropped away after showing early speed on this occasion. (op 14-1 tchd 10-1)
Snow Bear(IRE), not seen since making a winning debut in a weak Catterick maiden in May, could never get into the race after missing the break. (op 4-1)

4279 KINDERTONS ACCIDENT MANAGEMENT H'CAP 1m 5f 22y
2:55 (2:55) (Class 6) (0-65,60) 4-Y-O+ £1,619 (£481; £240; £120) Stalls High

Form				RPR
030-	1		**Abulharith**[29] 6804 4-9-2 55 DaneO'Neill 3 (M J Scudamore) *led for 1f: dropped to cl 5th: shkn up briefly over 4f out: hdwy on inner fr over 3f out to ld wl over 2f out: styd on strly fnl f: rdn out* **6/1**[3]	60
4360	2	1 ¼	**War Of The Roses (IRE)**[20] 3639 7-9-7 60 J-PGuillambert 1 (R Brotherton) *hld up: hdwy on wd outside ent st: rdn and ev ch over 2f out tl 1f out: no ex* **9/2**[2]	63
3205	3	¾	**Prickles**[13] 3848 5-8-8 47 ChrisCatlin 2 (Karen George) *trckd ldrs: racd keenly whn pce stdd after 3f: rdn and ev ch over 2f out: styd on but no ex fnl f* **9/2**[2]	49
434-	4	nk	**Penolva (IRE)**[20] 3655 4-9-3 56 SteveDrowne 4 (Mrs Sarah Dawson, Ire) *squeezed up s: hdwy on outer to trck ldr after 2f: rdn wl over 2f out: styd on ins fnl f* **2/1**[1]	58
-620	5	shd	**Looks The Business (IRE)**[20] 3641 9-9-5 58 FergusSweeney 6 (A B Haynes) *led after 1f: stdd pce after 3f: hdd whn sltly outpcd wl over 2f out: remained in tch: disputing 4th and styng on ins fnl f whn short of room and snatched up nring fin* **9/2**[2]	59
0054	6	nk	**Laura Land**[13] 3848 4-8-6 46 TadhgO'Shea 5 (W M Brisbourne) *racd keenly trcking ldrs: rdn 3f out: styd on fnl f* **12/1**	46

2m 51.35s (-0.65) **Going Correction** -0.125s/f (Firm) **6** Ran SP% **109.9**
Speed ratings (Par 101): **97,96,95,95,95 95**
toteswingers: 1&2 £5.80, 1&3 £5.00, 2&3 £3.50. CSF £30.92 TOTE £14.00: £5.50, £2.70; EX 50.10.
Owner The Yes No Wait Sorries **Bred** Lakin Bloodstock And H And W Thornton **Trained** Bromsash, Herefordshire

FOCUS
A moderate staying event in which the early pace was frantic, but it had slowed down well over 1m from home and the six runners were in a line passing the 3f pole. The first two home were both held up at the back of the field in the early stages. Muddling form with the sixth not beaten far.
Penolva(IRE) Official explanation: jockey said filly was unsuited by the firm ground
Looks The Business(IRE) Official explanation: jockey said he dropped his hands shortly before line to avoid clipping heels of second.

4280 GRANGE JAGUAR SWINDON H'CAP (DIV I) 1m 5y
3:30 (3:30) (Class 6) (0-60,60) 3-Y-O £1,295 (£385; £192; £96) Stalls Low

Form				RPR
0-50	1		**Lady Of Garmoran (USA)**[17] 3738 3-8-8 50 (b[1]) TadhgO'Shea 1 (P F I Cole) *led: rdn 4 l clr 3f out: hung lft and hdd ent fnl f: rallied v gamely to regain ld nr fin: all out* **12/1**	58
6-50	2	nk	**Fever Tree**[39] 3002 3-8-13 55 FergusSweeney 6 (P J Makin) *mid-div: hdwy over 3f out: wnt 2nd wl over 2f out: str chal u.p fr over 1f out: ev ch whn n.m.r ins fnl f: jst hld* **9/4**[2]	62
006-	3	½	**Farmers Dream (IRE)**[260] 7234 3-8-8 53 WilliamCarson(3) 7 (J L Spearing) *hld up towards rr: hdwy on outer over 3f out: chalng whn hung rt 2f out: led ent fnl f: no ex whn hdd nr fin* **16/1**	59
0-66	4	4 ½	**Satin Princess (IRE)**[19] 3682 3-8-4 46 oh1 FrankieMcDonald 4 (A M Hales) *hld up towards rr: stdy prog fr over 3f out: pushed along in cl 4th and abt to mount chal whn bmpd: sn squeezed up: rdn but nt gng pce to get bk on terms* **33/1**	42
00-0	5	4 ½	**Gee Major**[31] 3275 3-8-4 46 oh1 KirstyMilczarek 5 (N J Vaughan) *trckd ldrs: rdn 3f out: wknd ent fnl f* **33/1**	31
6600	6	7	**Take My Hand**[7] 4058 3-9-4 60 ChrisCatlin 8 (M R Channon) *t.k.h early: trckd ldrs: rdn over 3f out: wknd wl over 1f out* **13/2**[3]	29
0520	7	1 ¼	**Flyinflyout**[15] 3788 3-8-11 56 (p) RobertLButler(3) 10 (Miss Sheena West) *trckd ldrs: struggling on outer over 3f out and sn lost pl: nt a threat after: wknd wl over 1f out* **8/1**	22
0-00	8	7	**Krysanthe**[29] 3336 3-8-12 54 SteveDrowne 2 (M Blanshard) *mid-div: rdn over 3f out: hung rt over 2f out: sn wknd* **25/1**	—
6-54	9	6	**Mr Maximas**[31] 3264 3-8-9 51 StevieDonohoe 11 (B Palling) *broke wl: sn drvn to hold prom position: abt to be pushed wd and eased up after 2f: nvr travelling in rr after* **7/4**[1]	—

1m 40.69s (-0.11) **Going Correction** -0.125s/f (Firm) **9** Ran SP% **114.9**
Speed ratings (Par 98): **95,94,94,89,85 78,76,69,63**
toteswingers: 1&2 £6.60, 1&3 £17.00, 2&3 £12.60. CSF £38.53 CT £441.26 TOTE £14.60: £3.30, £1.60, £4.70; EX 51.50 Trifecta £131.70.
Owner Mrs Fitri Hay **Bred** B Wayne Hughes **Trained** Whatcombe, Oxon

■ Stewards' Enquiry : William Carson one-day ban: careless riding (Aug 5); two-day ban: used whip with excessive frequency (Aug 6-7)

FOCUS
A very moderate handicap with only two of these having been successful before. The time was slightly quicker than the first division but the form looks weak.
Lady Of Garmoran(USA) Official explanation: trainer's rep said, regarding apparent improvement in form, that the filly benefited from first-time blinkers and the stable running into form.
Mr Maximas Official explanation: jockey said gelding was unsuited by the firm ground

4281 GRANGE JAGUAR SWINDON H'CAP (DIV II) 1m 5y
4:05 (4:17) (Class 6) (0-60,57) 3-Y-O £1,295 (£385; £192; £96) Stalls Low

Form				RPR
-033	1		**Regal Rave (USA)**[15] 3788 3-9-2 55 RobertWinston 6 (J R Best) *trckd ldrs: rdn over 3f out: edgd rt but led wl over 1f out: styd on: rdn out* **15/8**[1]	63
5-00	2	1 ¾	**Qaraqum (USA)**[47] 2753 3-9-2 55 TadhgO'Shea 4 (D J Coakley) *sn pushed along in rr: rdn and no imp over 3f out: hdwy over 1f out: wnt 2nd ent fnl f: styd on: nt rch wnr* **9/1**	58
6400	3	4 ½	**Force To Spend**[24] 3515 3-8-13 52 StevieDonohoe 2 (N P Littmoden) *restrained s: rdn in last pair over 3f out: swtchd rt and hdwy 2f out: clsng but edging lft whn hmpd jst ins fnl f: styd on: nvr trbld ldrs* **14/1**	45
5045	4	¾	**Pie Poudre**[25] 3479 3-9-1 54 J-PGuillambert 5 (R Brotherton) *pushed along in mid-div: hdwy over 2f out: sn wandered u.p: chalng for 3rd whn veered rt jst ins fnl f: no ex* **4/1**[3]	45
0006	5	1	**Massachusetts**[10] 3960 3-8-6 45 (b) FergusSweeney 10 (B G Powell) *led at gd pce: rdn 3f out: hdd wl over 1f out: no ex fnl f* **15/2**	34
0000	6	shd	**Dancing Poppy**[9] 3978 3-8-12 51 DaneO'Neill 8 (R A Farrant) *chsd ldrs: rdn and ev ch over 2f out: sn one pce: fdd fnl f* **14/1**	39
0053	7	2 ½	**Princess Seren**[10] 3957 3-8-10 49 ChrisCatlin 7 (B R Millman) *s.i.s: sn trcking ldrs: rdn over 3f out: wknd over 1f out* **7/2**[2]	32

1m 41.27s (0.47) **Going Correction** -0.125s/f (Firm) **7** Ran SP% **112.1**
Speed ratings (Par 98): **92,90,85,85,84 83,81**
toteswingers: 1&2 £4.30, 1&3 £4.50, 2&3 £10.10. CSF £18.92 CT £178.53 TOTE £2.50: £1.80, £6.40; EX 22.70 TRIFECTA Not won..
Owner The Lurchers **Bred** John H Cataldo **Trained** Hucking, Kent

FOCUS
The rain started to come down before this contest, which was delayed when the subsequently withdrawn Avon Castle unseated her rider and then got loose twice before the start. This was an even weaker race than the first division with all seven remaining runners maidens coming into this. The first pair finished clear and the winning time was 0.58 seconds slower than division one.

4282 TRENT SERVICES FILLIES' H'CAP — 1m 2f 46y
4:40 (4:41) (Class 5) (0-70,69) 3-Y-O — £2,201 (£655; £327; £163) Stalls Low

Form / RPR

5452 **1** **Sandy Shaw**[27] 3390 3-9-3 **65** .... DaneO'Neill 5 — 72
(J W Hills) *set gd pce: sn 5 l clr: mde all: kpt on gamely: rdn out* **2/1**[1]

004 **2** 1 ¾ **Now What**[26] 3443 3-8-12 **60** .... RobertWinston 7 — 63
(J G Portman) *t.k.h early: in tch: rdn to dispute 2nd over 3f out: clr 2nd ent fnl f: styd on but a being hld by wnr* **6/1**

0-65 **3** 4 **Rose Aurora**[14] 3816 3-8-5 **53** .... KirstyMilczarek 6 — 49
(M P Tregoning) *trckd ldrs: rdn to chse wnr wl over 2f out tl hung lft over 1f out: no ex fnl f* **11/1**

6326 **4** 9 **Pastello**[31] 3268 3-9-1 **66** .... PatrickHills(3) 3 — 45
(R Hannon) *hld up: hdwy 3f out to trck ldrs: rdn and hung lft 2f out: wknd* **5/1**[3]

4603 **5** ¾ **Faith Jicaro (IRE)**[13] 3857 3-9-7 **69** .... FergusSweeney 2 — 47
(N J Vaughan) *trckd wnr tl rdn wl over 2f out: wknd over 1f out* **7/2**[2]

0644 **6** 12 **Tallawalla (IRE)**[61] 2333 3-8-4 **52** .... ChrisCatlin 1 — 7
(M R Channon) *cl up: rdn wl over 2f out: sn wknd* **15/2**

650- **7** dist **Primrose Bankes**[309] 5984 3-9-3 **68** .... WilliamCarson(3) 8 — —
(W G M Turner) *slowly away: sn struggling in rr: wknd 3f out: sn virtually p.u* **25/1**

2m 8.96s (-2.04) **Going Correction** -0.125s/f (Firm) — 7 Ran SP% **110.5**
Speed ratings (Par 97): **103,101,98,91,90 81,—**
toteswingers: 1&2 £2.80, 1&3 £4.70, 2&3 £8.30. CSF £13.39 CT £95.97 TOTE £2.20: £1.10, £4.00; EX 13.00 Trifecta £96.70.
Owner Burton Agnes Bloodstock & Partners **Bred** Burton Agnes Stud Co Ltd **Trained** Upper Lambourn, Berks

FOCUS
The rain didn't seem to have made much difference to the ground conditions. This was a fair fillies' handicap run at a solid pace thanks to the winner. She posted a 5lb personal best.
Primrose Bankes Official explanation: jockey said filly was unsuited by the firm ground

4283 WINNING POST BOOKMAKERS 25TH YEAR RACING H'CAP — 5f 161y
5:10 (5:11) (Class 6) (0-65,61) 3-Y-O+ — £1,619 (£481; £240; £120) Stalls Centre

Form / RPR

5542 **1** **The Name Is Frank**[7] 4041 5-9-10 **58** .... (t) FergusSweeney 2 — 68
(Mark Gillard) *mde all: rdn and hung rt over 2f out: drifted lft ins fnl f: r.o wl* **9/2**[3]

4002 **2** 1 ¾ **Titus Gent**[5] 4130 5-9-13 **61** .... KirstyMilczarek 10 — 65
(R A Harris) *in tch: rdn to chse wnr over 2f out: ch ent fnl f: kpt on: hld towards fin* **6/1**

00-0 **3** nk **Witchry**[63] 2246 8-9-4 **57** .... MarkCoumbe(5) 12 — 60
(A G Newcombe) *towards rr: hdwy 3f out: sn rdn: ch over 1f out: kpt on* **12/1**

0003 **4** 1 ½ **Bateleur**[5] 4130 6-9-11 **59** .... DaneO'Neill 5 — 57
(M R Channon) *s.i.s: towards rr: hdwy over 2f out: rdn over 1f out: kpt on same pce fnl f* **4/1**[2]

0532 **5** nk **Wooden King (IRE)**[9] 3979 5-9-2 **50** .... TomMcLaughlin 11 — 47
(M S Saunders) *mid-div on wd outside: rdn and hdwy to chse ldrs over 2f out: one pce whn edgd lft over 1f out* **7/1**

3001 **6** 1 ½ **Emiratesdotcom**[17] 3727 4-9-4 **52** .... RobertWinston 3 — 44
(J M Bradley) *chsd ldrs: rdn over 3f out: one pce fr over 1f out: edgd lft jst ins fnl f* **7/2**[1]

6111 **7** nk **Mandhooma**[9] 3980 4-9-11 **59** 6ex .... ChrisCatlin 9 — 50
(P W Hiatt) *squeezed out sn after s: towards rr: rdn over 2f out: little imp* **8/1**

0000 **8** 1 ¼ **Dynamo Dave (USA)**[29] 3338 5-8-11 **45** .... (b) RichardThomas 1 — 32
(M D I Usher) *a towards rr* **25/1**

00-0 **9** ½ **Like For Like (IRE)**[29] 3338 4-8-8 **45** .... (p) WilliamCarson(3) 8 — 30
(R J Hodges) *in tch: effrt over 2f out: bmpd jst ins fnl f: fdd* **28/1**

0324 **10** ¾ **Talamahana**[9] 3979 5-9-4 **52** .... (v) StevieDonohoe 6 — 34
(A B Haynes) *mid-div: rdn 3f out: wknd over 1f out* **14/1**

-000 **11** 8 **Blushing Maid**[52] 2589 4-8-12 **46** .... DaraghO'Donohoe 13 — 1
(H S Howe) *chsd ldrs: rdn over 2f out: wknd over 1f out* **33/1**

1m 10.58s (-0.62) **Going Correction** -0.125s/f (Firm) — 11 Ran SP% **122.9**
Speed ratings (Par 101): **99,96,96,94,93 91,91,89,89,88 77**
toteswingers: 1&2 £4.80, 1&3 £7.80, 2&3 £15.40. CSF £32.68 CT £317.63 TOTE £4.20: £1.20, £4.30, £5.00; EX 21.40 Trifecta £119.20.
Owner Don Hazzard **Bred** Fifehead Farms M C Denning **Trained** Holwell, Dorset
■ Stewards' Enquiry : Fergus Sweeney caution: used whip with excessive frequency.
Kirsty Milczarek caution: used whip with excessive frequency.

FOCUS
A competitive if modest sprint handicap in which the runners came more centre-to-stands' side than had been the case in the earlier races. Fairly sound form.
Emiratesdotcom Official explanation: jockey said gelding hung left closing stages

4284 PARKGARDENCENTRES.CO.UK H'CAP — 5f 11y
5:40 (5:42) (Class 5) (0-70,70) 3-Y-O — £2,201 (£655; £327; £163) Stalls Centre

Form / RPR

3301 **1** **Lutine Bell**[15] 3786 3-9-7 **70** .... (b) StevieDonohoe 6 — 80+
(Sir Mark Prescott) *v.s.a: bhd: pushed along and hdwy on wd outside fr over 3f out: rdn 2f out: led ent fnl f: edgd lft: r.o strly: readily* **9/4**[1]

0-30 **2** 2 ¾ **Rebecca Romero**[6] 4099 3-8-2 **51** oh4 .... (v[1]) FrankieMcDonald 8 — 51
(D J Coakley) *towards rr: hdwy over 3f out: rdn to ld 2f out: hung lft and hdd ent fnl f: nt pce of wnr* **14/1**

4500 **3** 1 ¾ **Nepotism**[7] 4041 3-9-7 **70** .... TomMcLaughlin 7 — 64
(M S Saunders) *chsd ldrs: rdn over 2f out: ev ch over 1f out: kpt on same pce* **6/1**

24-0 **4** 1 ¾ **Going French (IRE)**[153] 625 3-9-7 **70** .... SimonWhitworth 1 — 58
(F J Brennan) *s.i.s: towards rr: rdn 3f out: kpt on fnl f: wnt 4th fnl stride: nvr nrr* **20/1**

4620 **5** hd **Leleyf (IRE)**[16] 3751 3-9-7 **70** .... (v) ChrisCatlin 3 — 57
(M R Channon) *prom: led 3f out: rdn and hdd 2f out: no ex fnl f: lost 4th fnl stride* **10/1**

0400 **6** shd **Avongate**[34] 3154 3-9-3 **66** .... (b[1]) TadhgO'Shea 4 — 52
(R A Harris) *mid-div: rdn wl over 2f out: kpt on same pce* **25/1**

0030 **7** 1 ¼ **Flaxen Lake**[38] 3030 3-8-11 **60** .... (p) RobertWinston 2 — 42
(J M Bradley) *led for 2f: sn rdn: wknd over 1f out* **16/1**

3222 **8** 1 ¼ **Pherousa**[19] 3682 3-9-3 **66** .... FergusSweeney 5 — 43
(M Blanshard) *towards rr: checked whn sme hdwy 3f out: immediately lost grnd: sn rdn: no imp after* **7/2**[3]

-460 **9** 1 ½ **Final Turn**[41] 2931 3-9-0 **63** .... DaneO'Neill 9 — 35
(H Candy) *chsd ldrs: rdn 3f out: wknd over 1f out: eased* **3/1**[2]

61.46 secs (-1.04) **Going Correction** -0.125s/f (Firm) — 9 Ran SP% **122.5**
Speed ratings (Par 100): **103,98,95,93,92 92,90,88,86**
toteswinger: 1&2 £7.20, 1&3 £5.10, 2&3 £15.20. CSF £38.83 CT £177.36 TOTE £2.80: £1.02, £6.80, £3.60; EX 61.40 Trifecta £97.70 Place 6: £60.99, Place 5: £59.56..
Owner Tom Wilson/Nicholas Jones **Bred** Coln Valley Stud **Trained** Newmarket, Suffolk

FOCUS
A fair sprint handicap run at a generous pace.
T/Plt: £126.80 to a £1 stake. Pool:£44,664.74 - 257.09 winning tickets T/Qpdt: £50.40 to a £1 stake. Pool:£3,329.50 - 48.80 winning tickets TM

4047 DONCASTER (L-H)
Thursday, July 22

OFFICIAL GOING: Good to firm (8.9)
Wind: Virtually nil Weather: Overcast

4285 MOSS PROPERTIES H'CAP — 6f
6:20 (6:20) (Class 5) (0-70,68) 4-Y-O+ — £2,729 (£806; £403) Stalls High

Form / RPR

2233 **1** **Divertimenti (IRE)**[16] 3762 6-8-5 **52** .... (b) JimmyQuinn 13 — 70
(S R Bowring) *qckly away: racd nr stands' rails and mde all: rdn and qcknd clr appr fnl f: kpt on strly* **9/2**[1]

5005 **2** 4 ½ **Dickie Le Davoir**[6] 4084 6-9-4 **65** .... (b) PaulEddery 2 — 69
(R C Guest) *s.i.s and swtchd rt to stands' rails s: bhd: hdwy 2f out: sn rdn and styd on strly ins fnl f* **12/1**

000 **3** 1 ¼ **Sea Salt**[37] 3062 7-8-11 **63** .... DaleSwift(5) 12 — 63
(R E Barr) *a.p: rdn 2f out and ev ch whn hung bdly lft over 1f out: drvn and one pce ins fnl f* **8/1**

1144 **4** nk **Arjemis**[15] 3774 4-9-3 **64** .... SilvestreDeSousa 9 — 65+
(C R Wilson) *prom: rdn along 2f out: drvn whn hmpd and swtchd rt over 1f out: kpt on same pce fnl f* **9/2**[1]

020 **5** 1 **Double Carpet (IRE)**[16] 3763 7-8-5 **57** ow5 .... RossAtkinson(5) 11 — 52
(G Woodward) *chsd ldrs: rdn along 2f out: drvn over 1f out: kpt on same pce* **28/1**

0000 **6** ½ **Desert Falls**[26] 3435 4-8-12 **62** .... (p) MichaelStainton(3) 8 — 56
(R M Whitaker) *chsd ldrs: rdn 2f out and styng on whn nt clr run and hmpd over 1f out: swtchd rt and kpt on same pce fnl f* **14/1**

3544 **7** nk **Sea Crest**[6] 4155 4-8-10 **57** .... FrannyNorton 7 — 50
(M Brittain) *chsd ldrs: rdn along over 2f out: drvn wl over 1f out and kpt on same pce* **11/2**[2]

1306 **8** nk **Port Ronan (USA)**[9] 3977 4-7-12 **50** .... JamesSullivan(5) 5 — 42
(J S Wainwright) *dwlt: sn in tch on wd outside: hdwy to chse ldrs 1/2-way: rdn along over 2f out and sn wknd* **16/1**

/060 **9** 1 ¼ **Cutting Comments**[10] 3946 4-9-4 **65** .... PhillipMakin 14 — 53
(M Dods) *chsd ldrs: rdn along over 2f out: sn btn* **10/1**

3300 **10** ¾ **Fuzzy Cat**[16] 3761 4-8-12 **59** .... (b) TomEaves 3 — 45
(T D Barron) *prom: cl up wl over 2f out and ev ch tl rdn wl over 1f out and sn wknd* **15/2**[3]

0506 **11** 5 **Cheery Cat (USA)**[48] 2698 6-8-5 **52** .... (p) AndrewElliott 6 — 22
(J Balding) *towards rr: rdn along over 2f out and sn outpcd* **16/1**

40/0 **12** 15 **High Window (IRE)**[7] 4047 10-8-2 **49** oh4 .... AndrewMullen 1 — —
(G P Kelly) *in tch: rdn along 1/2-way: sn wknd* **66/1**

1m 10.9s (-2.70) **Going Correction** -0.375s/f (Firm) — 12 Ran SP% **114.8**
Speed ratings (Par 103): **103,97,95,94,93 92,92,92,90,89 82,62**
toteswingers: 1&2 £11.70, 1&3 £9.20, 2&3 £17.10. CSF £57.32 CT £425.22 TOTE £6.50: £1.90, £4.20, £3.40; EX 43.90.
Owner K Nicholls **Bred** Airlie Stud **Trained** Edwinstowe, Notts
■ Stewards' Enquiry : Dale Swift three-day ban: careless riding (Aug 5-7)

FOCUS
A low grade 49-65 sprint handicap opened proceedings. The winner made all against the rail and is rated in line with his post-2yo turf form.
Arjemis Official explanation: trainer said filly lost a front and hind shoe
High Window(IRE) Official explanation: trainer said gelding lost a rear shoe

4286 WELCOME TO YORKSHIRE ONTO A WINNER MAIDEN AUCTION FILLIES' STKS — 7f
6:50 (6:51) (Class 4) 2-Y-O — £3,238 (£963; £481; £240) Stalls High

Form / RPR

0 **1** **Toms River Tess (IRE)**[22] 3562 2-8-8 0 .... MichaelHills 5 — 81+
(B W Hills) *cl up: effrt 2f out: rdn to ld 1f out: kpt on* **9/2**[3]

0322 **2** 2 **Kissing Clara (IRE)**[20] 3636 2-8-4 0 .... GregFairley 2 — 70
(J S Moore) *prom: led 1/2-way: rdn wl over 1f out: drvn and hdd 1f out: kpt on same pce* **4/1**[2]

03 **3** 1 ¼ **Ransom Request**[9] 3985 2-8-1 0 .... AdamBeschizza(7) 6 — 71
(E F Vaughan) *wnt rt s: in tch: hdwy wl over 2f out: rdn to chse ldrs wl over 1f out: kpt on ins fnl f* **11/2**

05 **4** 1 ¾ **Deva Le Deva (IRE)**[17] 3729 2-8-6 0 .... RichardKingscote 3 — 65
(Tom Dascombe) *in tch: hdwy 1/2-way: chsd ldrs 2f out: sn rdn and ev ch tl drvn: edgd lft and wknd ent fnl f* **9/1**

0 **5** ½ **Levantera (IRE)**[13] 3861 2-8-1 0 .... JohnFahy(5) 13 — 63+
(C G Cox) *chsd ldrs: rdn along and outpcd 3f out: kpt on u.p fnl f* **14/1**

4 **6** 8 **Maggie Mey (IRE)**[17] 3729 2-8-4 0 .... SilvestreDeSousa 12 — 41
(D O'Meara) *chsd ldrs and sn pushed along: rdn and hung rt over 3f out: hung lft wl over 1f out and wknd* **11/4**[1]

0 **7** 1 **Imaginary World (IRE)**[10] 3964 2-8-7 0 .... RichardMullen 7 — 42
(E S McMahon) *s.i.s: green and in rr: sme hdwy 2f out: nvr a factor* **14/1**

8 7 **Detailedassessment** 2-8-7 0 ow1 .... TomEaves 14 — 24
(B Smart) *dwlt: a towards rr: rdn along and outpcd fr over 2f out* **14/1**

0 **9** 5 **Milly Filly**[19] 3657 2-8-5 0 ow1 .... AndrewElliott 4 — 10
(Miss Amy Weaver) *led: rdn along and hdd 1/2-way: sn wknd* **80/1**

0 **10** 1 ½ **Gothic Chick**[19] 3657 2-8-5 0 .... JamieMackay 10 — 6
(Miss Amy Weaver) *a in rr: bhd fnl 3f* **80/1**

1m 25.05s (-1.25) **Going Correction** -0.375s/f (Firm) — 10 Ran SP% **112.7**
Speed ratings (Par 93): **92,89,88,86,85 76,75,67,61,60**
toteswingers: 1&2 £4.70, 1&3 £5.10, 2&3 £4.00. CSF £22.00 TOTE £5.00: £2.10, £1.20, £2.50; EX 30.40.
Owner John C Grant **Bred** Noel O'Callaghan **Trained** Lambourn, Berks

FOCUS
Probably just an ordinary 7f maiden auction fillies' race, but the winner looks progressive and likely to go on better things. The runner-up limits the form.

NOTEBOOK

Toms River Tess(IRE), well beaten on her debut on the all-weather when reportedly she would not face the kickback, did not lack support. After a tardy start she showed a very willing attitude and won going away in the end. She looks ideal nursery material. (op 13-2)

Kissing Clara(IRE), having her sixth start, has a provisional rating of 72. Racing wide, she took overall charge but in the end the winner proved much too strong. Beaten at odds-on on her previous starts, she does nothing wrong but is hardly progressing and will remain vulnerable. (op 5-2)

Ransom Request, having her third start, seemed to improve slightly after not the best of breaks and she will be suited by a stiffer test in nursery company. (op 13-2 tchd 7-1)

Deva Le Deva(IRE), two lengths adrift of Maggie Mey when they were fourth and fifth at Ripon on her third start, seems to be going the right way and is another likely nursery type. (op 11-1 tchd 14-1)

Levantera(IRE), who found herself rather isolated towards the stands' side, had finished last of 14 on her debut at Newbury. She still looked very inexperienced but was putting in some solid work at the finish and there ought to be even better to come. (op 16-1)

Maggie Mey(IRE), fourth first time at Ripon, hung badly left after struggling to keep up at the halfway mark and she may need easier ground. Official explanation: jockey said filly hung left (tchd 10-3)

4287 SKY BET SUPPORTING THE YORKSHIRE RACING SUMMER FESTIVAL FILLIES' H'CAP — 7f

7:25 (7:25) (Class 3) (0-90,90) 3-Y-O+

£6,231 (£1,866; £933; £467; £233; £117) **Stalls** High

Form — RPR

-130 **1** **Whirly Dancer**[28] 3361 3-8-13 **82** ... TomQueally 13 — 89
(H R A Cecil) *hld up: hdwy to trck ldrs 1/2-way: effrt and ev ch 2f out: sn rdn and sltly outpcd: styd on strly ins fnl f to ld nr fin* **5/1**[2]

1513 **2** *hd* **Cheers For Thea (IRE)**[14] 3830 5-8-13 **75** ... (bt) DavidAllan 2 — 84
(T D Easterby) *trckd ldrs on wd outside: smooth hdwy 1/2-way: rdn to ld over 1f out: drvn ins fnl f: hdd and no ex nr fin* **10/3**[1]

04-4 **3** *½* **Perfect Silence**[28] 3346 5-8-11 **78** ... (b) JohnFahy(5) 3 — 86
(C G Cox) *sn prom: led 1/2-way: rdn 2f out: hdd and drvn over 1f out: kpt on u.p fnl f* **5/1**[2]

0004 **4** *¾* **Black Dahlia**[10] 3969 5-9-9 **85** ... PJMcDonald 12 — 91
(J A Glover) *bhd: hdwy over 2f out: sn rdn and styd on wl fnl f: nrst fin* **10/1**

5-00 **5** *nk* **Transvaal Sky**[26] 3457 3-8-13 **82** ... RichardKingscote 5 — 84
(Tom Dascombe) *prom: rdn along over 2f out: drvn over 1f out: kpt on same pce fnl f* **9/1**

0224 **6** *¾* **Breathless Kiss (USA)**[28] 3361 3-8-12 **81** ... NeilCallan 4 — 81
(K A Ryan) *trckd ldrs: hdwy 3f out: rdn 2f out: drvn and n.m.r over 1f out: one pce ins fnl f* **6/1**[3]

-265 **7** *4* **Celtic Lynn (IRE)**[29] 3320 5-8-9 **71** oh1 ... TomEaves 14 — 63
(M Dods) *dwlt and hld up in rr: swtchd lft and hdwy over 2f out: sn rdn and chsd ldrs tl drvn and no imp appr fnl f* **16/1**

4403 **8** *½* **Sakhee's Pearl**[12] 3890 4-9-1 **77** ... MickyFenton 11 — 68
(Miss Gay Kelleway) *hld up: effrt and sme hdwy over 2f out: sn rdn and btn* **8/1**

-300 **9** *1 ¾* **Shaws Diamond (USA)**[85] 1629 4-8-12 **74** ... RichardMullen 10 — 60
(D Shaw) *chsd ldrs: rdn along 3f out: grad wknd fnl 2f* **28/1**

10-0 **10** *7* **Ishe Mac**[82] 1707 4-9-1 **77** ... DanielTudhope 9 — 44
(N Bycroft) *led: rdn along and hdd 1/2-way: sn wknd* **25/1**

1m 23.75s (-2.55) **Going Correction** -0.375s/f (Firm)
WFA 3 from 4yo+ 7lb — **10** Ran SP% **114.1**
Speed ratings (Par 104): **99,98,98,97,97 96,91,91,89,81**
toteswingers: 1&2 £3.60, 1&3 £4.70, 2&3 £4.50. CSF £21.49 CT £88.34 TOTE £4.10: £2.00, £1.50, £2.20; EX 18.00.
Owner Woodcote Stud Ltd **Bred** Woodcote Stud Ltd **Trained** Newmarket, Suffolk

■ Stewards' Enquiry : John Fahy caution: used whip with excessive frequency
David Allan two-day ban: used whip with excessive frequency (Aug 5-6)

FOCUS

A tight-knit 71-85 fillies' handicap and a large horse blanket would have covered the first six at the line. Fair form which reads sound enough.

NOTEBOOK

Whirly Dancer put a poor run at Leicester last time behind her. A good third over a mile at Goodwood on her previous start, she tended to hang under pressure but battled well to force her head in front near the line. She has a progressive profile overall but might not want the ground any quicker than she encountered here. (op 9-2 tchd 6-1 in a place)

Cheers For Thea(IRE), who raced wide and was 3lb higher than her Carlisle success two outings ago, almost made it six wins from her last ten starts. She was only edged out near the line and is a credit to her trainer. She should continue to give a good account of herself at this level. (tchd 7-2)

Perfect Silence, who had to be given some sharp reminders soon after the start, showed ahead overall at the halfway mark racing wide. Having just her second outing this time, in the end she was just found lacking. She has now won five times from just 15 starts. (op 13-2)

Black Dahlia, 10lb higher than her last success in November, stayed on in fine style and looks right back to her best. (op 8-1)

Transvaal Sky, well beaten on her two previous outings this time, is now 7lb lower than when a good fifth in a competitive nursery at Newmarket in October. Connections will have been encouraged by this. (op 14-1 tchd 16-1 in places)

Breathless Kiss(USA), 6lb higher than her last win over 5f on the all-weather at Kempton in February, finds 7f no problem but she is rated to the limit at present. (tchd 5-1)

4288 KEEPMOAT "DELIVERING COMMUNITY REGENERATION" H'CAP — 6f

7:55 (7:56) (Class 4) (0-80,80) 3-Y-O — **£3,885** (£1,156; £577; £288) **Stalls** High

Form — RPR

5535 **1** **Amenable (IRE)**[10] 3949 3-9-1 **74** ... AdrianNicholls 8 — 80
(D Nicholls) *wnt lft s: mde all: rdn 2f out: drvn over 1f out: edgd lft ins fnl f: hld on gamely* **5/1**[3]

01 **2** *nk* **Barren Brook**[22] 3554 3-9-1 **79** ... JamesSullivan(5) 5 — 84+
(M W Easterby) *hld up in tch: smooth hdwy 2f out: swtchd rt and effrt to chal over 1f out: sn rdn and ev ch tl nt qckn towards fin* **9/1**

1060 **3** *½* **Transmit (IRE)**[33] 3208 3-8-11 **70** ... (b[1]) DavidAllan 4 — 73
(T D Easterby) *cl up: rdn over 2f out: drvn and ev ch over 1f out: edgd lft ins fnl f and nt qckn towards fin* **14/1**

5210 **4** *nk* **Sheer Force (IRE)**[34] 3154 3-9-1 **74** ... NeilCallan 2 — 76
(W J Knight) *t.k.h: trckd ldrs: swtchd lft and hdwy 2f out: rdn wl over 1f out and ev ch tl drvn ins fnl f and wknd towards fin* **9/2**[2]

3430 **5** *1* **Night Trade (IRE)**[28] 3373 3-9-3 **76** ... (p) SilvestreDeSousa 9 — 75
(Mrs D J Sanderson) *in tch on wd outside: hdwy over 2f out: sn rdn and hung lft wl over 1f out: drvn and one pce fnl f* **4/1**[1]

0164 **6** *1 ¾* **Commanche Raider (IRE)**[6] 4091 3-9-5 **78** ... PhillipMakin 11 — 72
(M Dods) *dwlt and hld up in rr: swtchd lft and hdwy over 2f out: rdn wl over 1f out: no imp appr fnl f* **5/1**[3]

0053 **7** *7* **Gertmegalush (IRE)**[16] 3753 3-8-11 **75** ... LeeTopliss(5) 6 — 46
(John A Harris) *prom: rdn along over 2f out and wkng whn n.m.r wl over 1f out: sn btn* **7/1**

1-30 **8** *4* **Mark Anthony (IRE)**[58] 2426 3-8-11 **70** ... StephenCraine 7 — 28
(K A Ryan) *hmpd and squeezed out s: in tch: hdwy 1/2-way: in tch whn hmpd wl over 1f out and sn wknd* **8/1**

0600 **9** *4* **Bond Fastrac**[17] 3731 3-9-7 **80** ... TomEaves 3 — 26
(G R Oldroyd) *dwlt hdwy on outer to chse ldrs 1/2-way: rdn over 2f out and sn wknd* **22/1**

1m 10.78s (-2.82) **Going Correction** -0.375s/f (Firm) — **9** Ran SP% **116.1**
Speed ratings (Par 102): **103,102,101,101,100 97,88,83,77**
toteswingers: 1&2 £25.50, 1&3 £20.20, 2&3 £23.60. CSF £49.42 CT £595.40 TOTE £5.90: £1.70, £2.20, £4.50; EX 61.10.
Owner Turton Brown Williams Lindley **Bred** Michael Downey & Roalso Ltd **Trained** Sessay, N Yorks

FOCUS

A highly competitive 70-80 three-year-olds' sprint handicap. The winner rates a small personal best.

4289 ATTEYS SOLICITORS H'CAP — 1m 2f 60y

8:30 (8:30) (Class 5) (0-70,68) 3-Y-O — **£2,590** (£770; £385; £192) **Stalls** Low

Form — RPR

5000 **1** **Epic (IRE)**[16] 3750 3-9-2 **63** ... (b) JoeFanning 5 — 71
(M Johnston) *trckd ldrs: effrt 3f out and sn pushed along: rdn 2f out: styd on to ld ins fnl f: sn clr and kpt on strly* **6/1**[3]

-021 **2** *3 ¾* **Grams And Ounces**[10] 3951 3-9-1 **62** ... JerryO'Dwyer 4 — 63
(Miss Amy Weaver) *led: rdn 2f out: drvn over 1f out: hdd and one pce ins fnl f* **11/8**[1]

5006 **3** *hd* **The Starboard Bow**[39] 2993 3-9-7 **68** ... StephenCraine 6 — 69
(S Kirk) *trckd ldr: effrt 3f out: rdn 2f out: sn drvn and kpt on same pce fnl f* **10/1**

5205 **4** *2 ¼* **Edition**[17] 3739 3-9-4 **65** ... NeilCallan 2 — 61
(J R Gask) *trckd ldng pair on inner: hdwy over 2f out: effrt and n.m.r wl over 1f out: sn rdn to chse ldr: drvn and wknd ins fnl f* **7/2**[2]

000 **5** *2 ¾* **Converre**[16] 3766 3-8-8 **55** ... TomQueally 3 — 46
(G A Butler) *in tch: effrt 3f out: rdn over 2f out and sn one pce* **14/1**

4303 **6** *½* **Saxby (IRE)**[9] 3972 3-9-6 **67** ... SilvestreDeSousa 8 — 57
(G A Harker) *hld up towards rr: hdwy on inner 3f out: rdn wl over 2f out: sn drvn and wknd* **10/1**

00-4 **7** *6* **Carnival Time (IRE)**[21] 3587 3-8-3 **55** ... JohnFahy(5) 9 — 34
(C G Cox) *hld up in tch: effrt over 3f out: rdn over 2f out and n.d* **8/1**

2035 **8** *30* **Mary Helen**[48] 2724 3-8-11 **58** ... EddieAhern 10 — —
(W M Brisbourne) *dwlt: hld up in rr: effrt and sme hdwy 4f out: rdn along 3f out and sn wknd* **16/1**

2m 8.96s (-0.44) **Going Correction** -0.20s/f (Firm) — **8** Ran SP% **120.5**
Speed ratings (Par 100): **100,97,96,95,92 92,87,63**
toteswingers: 1&2 £4.50, 1&3 £16.10, 2&3 £4.50. CSF £15.55 CT £85.71 TOTE £7.80: £1.90, £1.20, £2.20; EX 21.20.
Owner Racegoers Club Owners Group **Bred** P D Savill **Trained** Middleham Moor, N Yorks

FOCUS

A low-grade 55-68 handicap run at a sound pace. The winner produced his best run since his AW efforts early in the year.

Epic(IRE) Official explanation: trainer said, regarding apparent improvement in form, that he considered the race to be lower grade and was not convinced the gelding showed improvement.

Mary Helen Official explanation: jockey said filly was unsuited by the good to firm ground

4290 STRATSTONE LAND ROVER DONCASTER H'CAP — 1m 4f

9:00 (9:00) (Class 5) (0-75,75) 3-Y-O+ — **£2,590** (£770; £385; £192) **Stalls** Low

Form — RPR

21-2 **1** **Chilly Filly (IRE)**[6] 4117 4-10-0 **75** ... JoeFanning 3 — 83+
(M Johnston) *trckd ldr: hdwy on inner to ld over 3f out: rdn over 1f out: styd on* **11/10**[1]

-035 **2** *1 ¼* **Old Hundred (IRE)**[21] 3593 3-9-1 **74** ... PatCosgrave 9 — 78+
(J R Fanshawe) *hld up in tch: hdwy 3f out: chsd wnr over 2f out: rdn wl over 1f out: drvn and kpt on ins fnl f* **11/4**[2]

5-00 **3** *2 ¼* **Best Prospect (IRE)**[41] 2937 8-10-0 **75** ... (t) PhillipMakin 8 — 75
(M Dods) *hld up in tch: hdwy on inner 3f out: trckd wnr 2f out: effrt and n.m.r over 1f out: rdn and one pce ins fnl f* **7/1**

445 **4** *8* **Invitee**[14] 3829 3-8-11 **70** ... EddieAhern 6 — 57
(E A L Dunlop) *trckd ldng pair: hdwy to chse ldr after 4f: rdn along 3f out: drvn 2f out and sn wknd* **9/2**[3]

360- **5** *8* **Inside Knowledge (USA)**[268] 7080 4-8-5 **57** oh9 ... RossAtkinson(5) 4 — 31
(G Woodward) *led: rdn along over 4f out: hdd over 3f out: drvn and wknd over 2f out* **40/1**

2m 33.23s (-1.67) **Going Correction** -0.20s/f (Firm)
WFA 3 from 4yo+ 12lb — **5** Ran SP% **107.4**
Speed ratings (Par 103): **98,97,95,90,85**
toteswinger: 1&2 £2.80. CSF £4.09 TOTE £1.90: £1.30, £1.90; EX 4.50 Place 6: £49.28, Place 5: £18.34..
Owner J Barson **Bred** Moyglare Stud Farm Ltd **Trained** Middleham Moor, N Yorks

FOCUS

A modest 57-75 handicap depleted by four non-runners. The winner did it nicely and the runner-up progressed.

T/Plt: £27.90 to a £1 stake. Pool:£77,676.23 - 2,027.03 winning tickets T/Qpdt: £9.00 to a £1 stake. Pool:£9,682.88 - 788.40 winning tickets JR

4053 EPSOM (L-H)

Thursday, July 22

OFFICIAL GOING: Derby course - good (good to firm in places); 5f course - good to firm (good in places)

Rail dolled out up to 4yds from 1m to winning post increasing distances by about 6yds on round course.

Wind: Light, across Weather: Fine, warm

4291 ALL BETS ARE ON AT TOTESPORT.COM H'CAP — 5f

6:10 (6:10) (Class 4) (0-80,76) 3-Y-O — **£4,533** (£1,348; £674; £336) **Stalls** High

Form — RPR

6111 **1** **Perfect Blossom**[8] 4016 3-9-2 **76** 6ex ... AmyRyan(5) 1 — 90+
(K A Ryan) *led after 1f but nvr racd against rail: drew 2 l clr over 1f out: tended to hang but in command after: pushed out* **5/4**[1]

-002 **2** *¾* **La Fortunata**[22] 3561 3-8-12 **67** ... TonyCulhane 3 — 75
(Mike Murphy) *racd against rail: led 1f: chsd wnr: nt qckn 2f out: styd on to cl gap ins fnl f* **7/1**

4245 **3** ½ **Starwatch**[28] 3350 3-8-2 **57** oh1 NeilChalmers 2 63
(J J Bridger) *chsd ldrs: outpcd 1/2-way and struggling: styd on wl fnl f: nrst fin* **10/1**

0241 **4** 3 **Six Diamonds**[14] 3834 3-9-7 **76** NickyMackay 4 71
(H Morrison) *hld up: rdn to try to keep tabs on ldng pair 2f out: no imp after: wl btn 1f out* **10/3**[2]

5140 **5** 3½ **Lucky Flyer**[12] 3892 3-8-13 **68** RyanMoore 5 50
(S Kirk) *chsd ldrs: struggling to stay in tch 1/2-way: sn btn* **9/2**[3]

56.13 secs (0.43) **Going Correction** +0.075s/f (Good) **5** Ran SP% **107.3**
Speed ratings (Par 102): **99,97,97,92,86**
CSF £9.76 TOTE £2.20: £1.10, £3.30; EX 9.20.

Owner Mrs Ann Morris **Bred** Mrs A Morris **Trained** Hambleton, N Yorks

FOCUS
A dry night but a couple of showers during the day saw the ground ease slightly on the sprint and the Derby courses. The time of the opener confirmed the ground on the sprint track to be on the quick side. The inside rail was dolled out by four yards from the mile to the winning post, adding approximately six yards to races on the Derby course. This fair handicap had a couple of in-form types but took less winning than seemed likely, with the second and third favourites disappointing. The progressive winner was value for 2l+. The gallop was sound.

4292 PLAY BLACKJACK AT TOTESPORT.COM H'CAP 5f
6:40 (6:40) (Class 4) (0-85,83) 4-Y-0+ **£5,828** (£1,734; £866; £432) **Stalls** High

Form RPR

3526 **1** **Brynfa Boy**[12] 3892 4-8-13 **73** (t) TonyCulhane 9 83
(P W D'Arcy) *racd against rail: trckd ldrs: plld out over 1f out: urged along and r.o to ld last 100yds: readily* **5/1**[2]

1335 **2** ¾ **Cape Royal**[7] 4041 10-9-0 **74** (bt) NickyMackay 10 81
(J M Bradley) *racd against rail: pressed ldr: rdn and upsides ent fnl f: outpcd last 100yds* **7/1**[3]

1313 **3** 1 **Lost In Paris (IRE)**[26] 3430 4-9-6 **80** (v) RyanMoore 6 83
(T D Easterby) *sweating: narrow ld but nvr able to r against rail: jnd fnl f: hdd and nt qckn last 100yds* **7/4**[1]

3400 **4** nse **Our Piccadilly (IRE)**[17] 3736 5-9-0 **74** SamHitchcott 4 77+
(W S Kittow) *dwlt and bmpd s: swtchd to r against rail and hld up in last quartet: tried to cl over 1f out: swtchd out ins fnl f: r.o and nrly snatched 3rd* **14/1**

0410 **5** ¾ **Ocean Blaze**[17] 3736 6-9-3 **77** SteveDrowne 7 78
(B R Millman) *trckd ldrs: effrt and cl enough over 1f out: hanging and nt qckn ent fnl f* **12/1**

-000 **6** 2¾ **Safari Mischief**[12] 3892 7-9-4 **83** AshleyMorgan(5) 8 74
(P Winkworth) *settled in last quartet: pushed along 2f out: no prog over 1f out: plugged on* **12/1**

0000 **7** ½ **Step It Up (IRE)**[26] 3440 6-8-8 **68** MartinDwyer 2 57
(J R Boyle) *pressed ldng pair on outer: hanging and wknd 1f out* **18/1**

1304 **8** 2 **Master Lightfoot**[31] 3261 4-9-3 **77** ShaneKelly 5 59
(W R Swinburn) *a in last quartet: struggling fr wl over 1f out: sn no ch* **8/1**

2021 **9** 1¾ **Highland Harvest**[23] 3527 6-8-5 **68** MartinLane(3) 3 43
(Jamie Poulton) *awkward s: a in rr: last and struggling 1/2-way* **14/1**

0052 **10** ½ **Edith's Boy (IRE)**[14] 3818 4-7-13 **64** oh3 SimonPearce(5) 1 38
(S Dow) *racd wdst of all: spd and on terms 3f: wknd rapidly* **14/1**

55.40 secs (-0.30) **Going Correction** +0.075s/f (Good) **10** Ran SP% **117.3**
Speed ratings (Par 105): **105,103,102,102,100 96,95,92,89,88**
toteswingers: 1&2 £7.80, 1&3 £2.50, 2&3 £3.80. CSF £40.20 CT £85.06 TOTE £6.50: £2.00, £2.00, £1.20; EX 51.40.

Owner The Golf Oil Partnership **Bred** David And Mrs Vicki Fleet **Trained** Newmarket, Suffolk

FOCUS
Mainly exposed performers in a reasonable handicap. The pace was sound (0.73 seconds quicker than the opener) and this form should prove reliable, although the rail was favoured. The form is rated through the runner-up.

Master Lightfoot Official explanation: jockey said colt suffered interference at start

Edith's Boy(IRE) Official explanation: jockey said gelding was unsuited by the track

4293 EUROPEAN BREEDERS' FUND MAIDEN STKS 6f
7:15 (7:16) (Class 4) 2-Y-0 **£4,533** (£1,348; £674; £336) **Stalls** High

Form RPR

2 **1** **Regal Approval**[17] 3735 2-9-3 0 SteveDrowne 3 82
(H Morrison) *trckd ldng pair: wnt 2nd wl over 2f out: pushed into ld over 1f out: looked uneasy and nvr established command: drvn and jst hld on* **8/11**[1]

42 **2** hd **Chevise (IRE)**[12] 3913 2-8-12 0 JimCrowley 4 76
(R M Beckett) *led: rdn and hdd over 1f out: styd on wl u.p: jst denied* **5/2**[2]

56 **3** 3 **Star Today**[21] 3590 2-8-12 0 MartinDwyer 2 67+
(B J Meehan) *hld up in 4th: chsd ldng pair over 2f out: sn outpcd: pushed along and kpt on same pce fnl f* **6/1**[3]

00 **4** 17 **Will Barrow**[17] 3735 2-8-10 0 NathanAlison(7) 5 21
(J R Boyle) *mostly last: struggling fr 1/2-way: t.o* **66/1**

06 **5** 5 **Ventose**[13] 3861 2-8-12 0 SamHitchcott 1 1
(M R Channon) *wnt lft s: sn rcvrd to join ldr: wknd rapidly wl over 2f out: t.o* **12/1**

1m 10.57s (1.17) **Going Correction** +0.075s/f (Good) **5** Ran SP% **109.9**
Speed ratings (Par 96): **95,94,90,68,61**
CSF £2.77 TOTE £1.80: £1.20, £1.30; EX 3.00.

Owner Christopher Hammond **Bred** P V And Mrs J P Jackson **Trained** East Ilsley, Berks

FOCUS
Not a strong maiden but the two market leaders, both fair sorts, pulled clear in the closing stages. The gallop was an ordinary one until they quickened around the 2f pole. A step up from the winer with the runner-up matching her recent level.

NOTEBOOK
Regal Approval ◆ confirmed debut promise to justify the market support and, although the margin of victory was narrow, he showed a gritty attitude in the closing stages after taking a good hold early on. He's a big, scopey type who will probably turn out to be a fair bit better than the bare form of this race. Connections are reportedly not averse to dropping him back to 5f and, although Middle Park and Gimcrack entries look optimistic at this stage, he will be one to keep an eye on in handicap company. (op Evens)

Chevise(IRE), a much smaller individual than the winner, had the run of the race and ran to a similar level of her previous start at Salisbury. She showed a willing attitude under pressure and, although likely to remain vulnerable to the better sorts in this grade, she is more than capable of picking up a minor event around this trip. (op 15-8)

Star Today again showed ability at a modest level. She wasn't unduly knocked about, will be suited by a stiffer test of stamina and is capable of winning a race in due course. The step into ordinary nursery company will suit. (op 11-2 tchd 5-1)

Will Barrow was again soundly beaten and is of little immediate interest. (tchd 50-1)

Ventose dropped out in a matter of strides after helping to force just an ordinary gallop and she too will have to show a fair bit more before she is a solid betting proposition. (op 14-1 tchd 16-1)

4294 BROTHERS PEAR CIDER MAIDEN FILLIES' STKS 1m 2f 18y
7:45 (7:48) (Class 5) 3-Y-0+ **£2,590** (£770; £385; £192) **Stalls** Low

Form RPR

33 **1** **Eastern Paramour (IRE)**[25] 3477 5-9-9 0 SteveDrowne 7 80
(B R Millman) *trckd ldr after 3f: led over 2f out: urged along and kpt on wl after: a holding rivals* **6/1**

34 **2** 1 **Mascarene (USA)**[21] 3593 3-8-13 0 RyanMoore 6 78
(Sir Michael Stoute) *hld up in 4th: rdn and effrt over 2f out: wnt 2nd jst over 1f out: nt qckn and a hld* **7/4**[1]

-433 **3** 1¾ **Best Intent**[28] 3347 3-8-13 75 PhilipRobinson 1 75
(M A Jarvis) *t.k.h early: trckd ldr 3f: 3rd st: shkn up to chse wnr jst over 2f out to jst over 1f out: nt qckn* **11/4**[2]

4 **4** 4½ **Pebble Beech (IRE)**[25] 3484 3-8-13 0 KierenFallon 3 66+
(W J Haggas) *hld up in last: pushed along fr 1/2-way: sn strugglng: wnt modest 4th over 1f out: nt handle trck* **7/1**

02- **5** 12 **Thousandkissesdeep (IRE)**[275] 6920 3-8-13 0 (b[1]) NickyMackay 5 48
(J H M Gosden) *racd freely: led to over 2f out: wkng whn tightened up on inner sn after* **9/2**[3]

2m 9.83s (0.13) **Going Correction** +0.075s/f (Good)
WFA 3 from 5yo+ 10lb **5** Ran SP% **108.0**
Speed ratings (Par 100): **102,101,99,96,86**
toteswinger: 1&2 £12.70. CSF £16.32 TOTE £9.10: £3.00, £1.30; EX 38.00.

Owner W A Harrison-Allan **Bred** Masaichiro Abe **Trained** Kentisbeare, Devon

FOCUS
A couple of fair performers in an ordinary fillies' maiden. The gallop was only moderate and this bare form may not be entirely reliable. The winner rates a 4lb personal best.

4295 WEATHERBYS BLOODSTOCK INSURANCE H'CAP 1m 4f 10y
8:20 (8:20) (Class 5) (0-70,70) 3-Y-0+ **£3,238** (£963; £481; £240) **Stalls** Centre

Form RPR

5-32 **1** **Kings Troop**[21] 3589 4-10-0 **70** RyanMoore 3 80
(A King) *hld up: prog and 4th st: rdn to cl fr over 2f out: led jst over 1f out: edgd rt: drvn out* **7/2**[2]

0020 **2** nk **Vinces**[13] 3862 6-9-1 **57** MartinDwyer 4 67
(T D McCarthy) *hld up: 5th st: n.m.r over 2f out: prog and drvn on outer wl over 1f out: pressed wnr fnl f: carried rt and a jst hld* **11/1**

0-03 **3** 3¼ **Super Duplex**[49] 2675 3-7-11 **56** SimonPearce(5) 1 61
(P M Phelan) *trckd ldr: led 3f out: rdn and hdd jst over 1f out: hung rt and nt qckn* **9/4**[1]

2232 **4** 8 **Megalala (IRE)**[7] 4055 9-9-12 **68** NeilChalmers 2 60
(J J Bridger) *led to 3f out: wknd qckly over 1f out* **4/1**[3]

0044 **5** ¾ **Aurora Sky (IRE)**[15] 3781 4-9-4 **60** SamHitchcott 7 51
(J Akehurst) *t.k.h: trckd ldng pair: rdn 3f out: wknd qckly fr 2f out* **7/2**[2]

-005 **6** 1¼ **Red Eddie**[17] 3723 3-7-12 **59** oh3 ow7 NathanAlison(7) 5 48
(S Dow) *hld up in last: losing tch w ldrs st: sn no ch* **14/1**

0040 **7** 8 **Land Of Plenty (IRE)**[3] 4202 3-7-8 **55** oh7 ow3 RyanPowell(7) 6 31
(Jamie Poulton) *hld up: 6th and losing tch w ldrs st: sn bhd* **33/1**

2m 40.69s (1.79) **Going Correction** +0.075s/f (Good)
WFA 3 from 4yo+ 12lb **7** Ran SP% **113.2**
Speed ratings (Par 103): **97,96,94,89,88 87,82**
toteswingers: 1&2 £6.20, 1&3 £1.90, 2&3 £6.90. CSF £39.02 TOTE £3.60: £2.30, £4.00; EX 46.80.

Owner W H Ponsonby **Bred** Wickfield Stud And Hartshill Stud **Trained** Barbury Castle, Wilts

■ Stewards' Enquiry : Ryan Moore two-day ban: careless riding (Aug 5-6)

FOCUS
A modest handicap featuring mainly exposed types. The pace was just an ordinary one and the runner-up looks the best guide.

4296 PLAY ROULETTE AT TOTESPORT.COM H'CAP 7f
8:50 (8:50) (Class 4) (0-85,85) 3-Y-0+ **£4,533** (£1,348; £674; £336) **Stalls** Low

Form RPR

0014 **1** **Seneschal**[13] 3851 9-9-9 **75** NeilChalmers 4 82
(M Appleby) *enterprisingly rdn: led and sn clr: 6 l up st: drvn over 1f out: jst hld on* **16/1**

6602 **2** nse **Woodcote Place**[13] 3851 7-10-0 **80** JimCrowley 3 87
(P R Chamings) *chsd clr wnr: rdn over 2f out: grad clsd fr over 1f out: jst failed* **15/2**

0211 **3** 1½ **Space Station**[21] 3579 4-10-0 **80** (b) ShaneKelly 5 83+
(S Dow) *hld up in 5th: wl off the pce st: prog over 2f out: wnt 3rd over 1f out but stl at least 6 l bhd: styd on and nrst fin: too much to do* **2/1**[2]

6141 **4** ¾ **Brannagh (USA)**[27] 3394 3-9-12 **85** (t) RyanMoore 2 83+
(J Noseda) *dwlt: hld up in 4th and wl off the pce: rdn and hanging lft all the way up the st: styd on fr over 1f out: nrst fin* **15/8**[1]

0100 **5** 3 **Universal Circus**[20] 3628 3-9-0 **73** SamHitchcott 1 63
(M R Channon) *chsd clr wnr tl 3rd st: sn rdn: grad lost pl fr over 2f out* **16/1**

6011 **6** 46 **Admire The View (IRE)**[14] 3806 3-9-12 **85** TedDurcan 6 —
(D R Lanigan) *hld up in last and sn wl off the pce: nudged along and no prog over 2f out: virtually p.u over 1f out* **9/2**[3]

1m 23.62s (0.32) **Going Correction** +0.075s/f (Good)
WFA 3 from 4yo+ 7lb **6** Ran SP% **109.8**
Speed ratings (Par 105): **101,100,99,98,94 42**
toteswingers: 1&2 £2.30, 1&3 £7.00, 2&3 £2.30. CSF £116.66 TOTE £16.90: £4.70, £3.00; EX 66.80 Place 6: £200.90, Place 5: £119.74..

Owner Colin Rogers **Bred** Michael E Broughton **Trained** Compton Verney, Warwicks

FOCUS
A useful handicap on paper with several previous winners and a couple of progressive types but in the end a race that didn't take anything like as much winning as seemed likely with the three market leaders failing to land a blow. The winner was given an enterprising ride and the race is rated around him. It may pay to treat this form with a bit of caution.

T/Plt: £108.40 to a £1 stake. Pool:£44,149.58 - 297.09 winning tickets T/Qpdt: £27.50 to a £1 stake. Pool:£3,749.80 - 100.60 winning tickets JN

3816 FOLKESTONE (R-H)

Thursday, July 22

OFFICIAL GOING: Good to firm (8.5)

Wind: Virtually nil Weather: bright and sunny

4297 RACING SYNDICATE LIMITED TO LADIES LAUNCHES SATURDAY APPRENTICE H'CAP — 6f

6:00 (6:00) (Class 5) (0-70,75) 3-Y-O — **£2,388** (£705; £352) **Stalls** Low

Form — RPR

0132 **1** **Grand Zafeen**[6] 4109 3-9-5 **70** .... AmyScott(5) 1 — 80
(M R Channon) *hld up off the pce in last pair: clsd and in tch ent fnl 2f: nt clr run over 1f out: rdn and hdwy between horses ent fnl f: qcknd u.p to ld ins fnl f: r.o wl* **5/1**[2]

00-1 **2** *hd* **Stefanki (IRE)**[8] 4031 3-9-12 **75** 6ex .... MatthewDavies(3) 3 — 84
(George Baker) *dwlt: wl off the pce in last pair: clsd and in tch 1/2-way: smooth hdwy on outer 2f out: pushed ahd ent fnl f: shkn up ins fnl f: sn hdd and rdn: r.o but a jst hld after* **1/3**[1]

044 **3** *4 ½* **Lady Berta**[12] 3924 3-9-2 **67** .... CharlesEddery(5) 5 — 62
(R Hannon) *t.k.h: trckd ldng pair: rdn to ld over 1f out: sn hdd and drvn: edgd rt and outpcd fnl f* **10/1**[3]

1500 **4** *1 ¾* **Sonny G (IRE)**[29] 3322 3-8-7 **53** .... AndreaAtzeni 7 — 42
(J R Best) *led and crossed to stands' rail after 1f: rdn and hdd over 1f out: sn wknd* **16/1**

4260 **5** *½* **Lockantanks**[28] 3359 3-9-5 **68** .... DeclanCannon(3) 6 — 56
(A B Haynes) *chsd ldr: rdn ent fnl 2f: lost pl and wknd over 1f out* **18/1**

1m 11.95s (-0.75) **Going Correction** -0.125s/f (Firm) — **5** Ran SP% **111.9**

Speed ratings (Par 100): **100,99,93,91,90**

CSF £7.35 TOTE £4.10: £1.60, £1.70; EX 7.50.

Owner Jaber Abdullah **Bred** Rabbah Bloodstock Limited **Trained** West Ilsley, Berks

FOCUS

A modest heat with no depth, but it was well run. The winner is rated back to her 2yo best.

4298 LADBROKESCASINO.COM (S) STKS — 6f

6:30 (6:31) (Class 6) 3-Y-O+ — **£2,047** (£604; £302) **Stalls** Low

Form — RPR

0004 **1** **Daddy's Gift (IRE)**[22] 3557 4-8-9 64 .... RichardHughes 5 — 64
(R Hannon) *w ldr tl rdn to ld over 1f out: clr and edgd lft ent fnl f: kpt on wl: rdn out* **7/2**[2]

4160 **2** *1 ½* **Maoi Chinn Tire (IRE)**[8] 4031 3-9-1 74 ....(p) JamesDoyle 3 — 69
(J S Moore) *sn bustled along to ld: rdn and hdd over 1f out: swtchd rt ent fnl f: styd on same pce u.p fnl f* **11/4**[1]

4163 **3** *shd* **Anjomarba (IRE)**[19] 3685 3-8-7 62 ....(p) JackDean(3) 2 — 64
(W G M Turner) *t.k.h: trckd ldrs: effrt and rdn to chse ldng pair jst over 1f out: styd on same pce ins fnl f* **7/1**

0066 **4** *½* **Fault**[27] 3400 4-9-6 62 ....(t) SebSanders 1 — 68+
(Stef Higgins) *trckd ldrs on stands' rail: pushed along wl over 1f out: nt clr run and shuffled bk over 1f out tl jst ins fnl f: kpt on u.p fnl 100yds: unable to chal* **6/1**

5502 **5** *1 ¾* **Caribbean Coral**[9] 3993 11-8-9 53 .... DeclanCannon(5) 6 — 57
(A B Haynes) *hld up in tch in last trio: effrt and nt clr run 2f out tl jst over 1f out: one pce and no imp ins fnl f* **8/1**

0244 **6** *2 ¾* **Misaro (GER)**[17] 3734 9-9-6 74 ....(b) SaleemGolam 8 — 54
(R A Harris) *chsd ldrs: rdn and unable qck wl over 1f out: wknd ent fnl f* **11/2**[3]

0/0- **7** *7* **Derby Desire (IRE)**[251] 7369 6-8-9 33 .... AndreaAtzeni 9 — 20
(D Donovan) *in tch in last trio: rdn and edgd lft ent fnl 2f: sn wknd* **40/1**

4230 **8** *1 ½* **Bold Ring**[30] 3292 4-8-9 53 ....(b[1]) EddieCreighton 4 — 16
(E J Creighton) *in tch in last trio: effrt and hdwy to chse ldrs over 2f out: rdn 2f out: sn struggling: wknd qckly ent fnl f* **11/1**

1m 11.96s (-0.74) **Going Correction** -0.125s/f (Firm)

WFA 3 from 4yo+ 5lb — **8** Ran SP% **112.9**

Speed ratings (Par 101): **99,97,96,96,93 90,80,78**

Tote Swingers:1&2:£3.40, 2&3:£2.60, 1&3:£10.90 CSF £13.21 TOTE £4.10: £1.70, £2.60, £1.20; EX 18.80.There was no bid for the winner.

Owner Charlee & Hollie Allan **Bred** Vincent Dunne **Trained** East Everleigh, Wilts

FOCUS

A weak race and the form isn't strong, especially given the tame effort of favourite and form choice Misaro. The winner only needed to run to her recent turf form. The principals all raced on or close to the pace.

Caribbean Coral Official explanation: jockey said gelding was denied a clear run

4299 EUROPEAN BREEDERS' FUND MAIDEN FILLIES' STKS — 7f (S)

7:05 (7:08) (Class 5) 2-Y-O — **£3,885** (£1,156; £577; £288) **Stalls** Low

Form — RPR

46 **1** **Our Way Only (IRE)**[13] 3871 2-9-0 0 .... RichardHughes 2 — 80+
(R Hannon) *chsd ldrs: rdn and effrt to chal over 1f out: led 1f out: r.o wl and a holding runner-up fnl f: rdn out* **3/1**[2]

52 **2** *hd* **Bakoura**[27] 3392 2-9-0 0 .... RichardHills 10 — 80+
(J L Dunlop) *in tch: hdwy to chse ldr 5f out: rdn to ld over 1f out: hdd 1f out: r.o wl u.p fnl f but a jst hld* **7/4**[1]

5 **3** *8* **Rosa Midnight (USA)**[13] 3861 2-9-0 0 .... HayleyTurner 6 — 60
(M L W Bell) *s.i.s: in tch towards rr: rdn and effrt jst over 2f out: rn green and wl outpcd over 1f out: kpt on to go modest 3rd wl ins fnl f* **9/2**[3]

0 **4** *2* **Sensational Love (IRE)**[52] 2594 2-9-0 0 .... GeorgeBaker 8 — 55
(R A Mills) *led and crossed to stands' rail: rdn and hdd over 1f out: hung rt and wknd qckly ent fnl f: lost 3rd wl ins fnl f* **6/1**

5 **5** *hd* **Storm Tide**[21] 3590 2-9-0 0 .... SaleemGolam 4 — 54
(G D Blake) *in tch: chsd ldng pair 1/2-way: rdn and edging rt ent fnl 2f: wknd over 1f out* **16/1**

0 **6** *2 ½* **Red Oleander**[8] 4029 2-9-0 0 .... SebSanders 7 — 53+
(Sir Mark Prescott) *in tch in midfield on outer: pushed along and struggling over 2f out: wl btn over 1f out* **8/1**

0 **7** *7* **Erythrina (IRE)**[13] 3861 2-9-0 0 .... JamesDoyle 3 — 30
(B G Powell) *in tch towards rr: rdn and lost tch wl over 2f out* **80/1**

00 **8** *13* **Compton Lass**[29] 3310 2-8-11 0 .... MatthewDavies(3) 1 — —
(B G Powell) *a towards rr: rdn and lost tch 3f out: t.o fnl 2f* **100/1**

0 **9** *6* **Brendan's Gift**[8] 4021 2-8-9 0 .... SophieDoyle(5) 5 — —
(B G Powell) *restless stalls: t.k.h and racd awkwardly: prom tl lost pl rapidly 1/2-way: sn hung rt and t.o* **100/1**

10 *6* **Jacquotte (IRE)** 2-9-0 0 .... EddieCreighton 9 — —
(E J Creighton) *s.i.s: a wl outpcd in last: t.o fr 1/2-way* **100/1**

1m 27.06s (-0.24) **Going Correction** -0.125s/f (Firm) — **10** Ran SP% **115.0**

Speed ratings (Par 91): **96,95,86,84,84 81,73,58,51,44**

Tote Swingers:1&2:£2.20, 2&3:£2.90, 1&3:£3.90 CSF £8.55 TOTE £3.60: £1.50, £1.80, £1.50; EX 6.50.

Owner Noel O'Callaghan **Bred** Fergus Cousins **Trained** East Everleigh, Wilts

FOCUS

This didn't look very strong on paper, so it doesn't say much for those in behind that the front two managed to pull so far clear. The first two have been rated positively.

NOTEBOOK

Our Way Only(IRE) just edged it, staying on strongly with the rail to help. She was prominent in the market for a much better maiden than this at Newmarket's July festival, so the chances are she shows up well in her work, and she transferred that to the racecourse here. It will probably be nurseries next, but everything about her pedigree, and the way she toughed this out, suggest another furlong will suit. (tchd 5-2 and 7-2)

Bakoura set the standard on her latest Doncaster second, but had a wide draw to contend with and was forced to race quite wide for the first couple of furlongs. It's unlikely that has cost her the race, but she was far from disgraced and a similar event shouldn't be long in coming her way. (op 5-4)

Rosa Midnight(USA) made only modest late headway and this relatively pricey purchase hasn't built on her Newbury debut. (op 5-1)

Sensational Love(IRE), well-backed, showed up well for a long way but kept hanging to her right for pressure and weakened away. This was a step in the right direction, though, after such a modest debut. Official explanation: jockey said filly hung right throughout (op 9-1 tchd 10-1)

4300 "UPTOWN GIRLS" H'CAP — 7f (S)

7:35 (7:37) (Class 6) (0-65,65) 3-Y-O — **£2,047** (£604; £302) **Stalls** Low

Form — RPR

4050 **1** **Sheila Toss (IRE)**[31] 3268 3-9-7 **65** ....(b) RichardHughes 5 — 76+
(R Hannon) *chsd ldr tl led wl over 4f out: mde rest: pushed clr over 2f out: wl clr and rdn over 1f out: eased ins fnl f* **6/5**[1]

50-6 **2** *7* **Accountable**[44] 2841 3-9-4 **65** .... RussKennemore(3) 9 — 54
(B G Powell) *wnt lft and bmpd s: sn rcvrd and led: hdd wl over 4f out: rdn and nt pce of wnr over 2f out: and wl btn after: kpt on for 2nd ins fnl f* **25/1**

-004 **3** *¾* **Resuscitator (USA)**[14] 3831 3-9-6 **64** ....(p) GeorgeBaker 3 — 51
(Mrs H S Main) *hld up in last trio: pushed along and hdwy 4f out: chsd ldng pair u.p wl over 2f out: no prog and wl hld after* **7/2**[2]

0440 **4** *1 ¾* **King's Approach (IRE)**[9] 3982 3-9-2 **60** ....(p) SaleemGolam 2 — 42
(R A Harris) *hld up in midfield: rdn and struggling 1/2-way: no ch and hung rt wl over 1f out: n.d* **14/1**

6026 **5** *2 ¼* **Orsett Lad (USA)**[31] 3264 3-8-11 **55** .... HayleyTurner 8 — 31
(J R Best) *hld up in rr: swtchd to inner over 3f out: sn pushed along and no hdwy: nvr on terms* **6/1**[3]

0003 **6** *6* **Thoughtful (IRE)**[10] 3952 3-8-4 **48** .... LiamJones 7 — 8
(J W Hills) *wnt rt and bmpd s: sn chsng ldrs: rdn and struggling 3f out: wl bhd fnl 2f* **14/1**

5300 **7** *3 ¾* **Chandrayaan**[29] 3325 3-8-8 **55** .... NataliaGemelova(3) 10 — 5
(J E Long) *sn rdn along and a struggling in rr: nvr on terms* **8/1**

060- **8** *3 ¾* **Magneto (IRE)**[260] 7235 3-9-0 **58** .... EddieCreighton 1 — —
(E J Creighton) *in tch tl rdn and struggling 1/2-way: bhd fnl 2f* **33/1**

1m 26.26s (-1.04) **Going Correction** -0.125s/f (Firm) — **8** Ran SP% **113.2**

Speed ratings (Par 98): **100,92,91,89,86 79,75,71**

Tote Swingers:1&2:£9.10, 2&3:£12.10, 1&3:£1.30 CSF £36.32 CT £88.03 TOTE £2.10: £1.30, £4.70, £1.20; EX 44.00.

Owner P A Byrne **Bred** P Syndicate **Trained** East Everleigh, Wilts

FOCUS

A weak handicap, a seller in all but name. The well backed winner is rated back to her early maiden form.

Resuscitator(USA) Official explanation: jockey said colt slipped on leaving stalls

Chandrayaan Official explanation: jockey said gelding did not handle the track

4301 LADBROKESPOKER.COM H'CAP — 1m 4f

8:10 (8:10) (Class 6) (0-60,72) 3-Y-O — **£2,047** (£604; £302) **Stalls** Low

Form — RPR

6211 **1** **Allannah Abu**[3] 4211 3-9-11 **72** 12ex .... RosieJessop(5) 7 — 86+
(Sir Mark Prescott) *mde all: pushed along over 2f out: clr and rdn wl over 1f out: kpt on u.p and a holding on fnl f* **8/13**[1]

0-06 **2** *¾* **Albeed**[34] 3155 3-9-0 **56** .... RichardHughes 3 — 65
(J L Dunlop) *stdd s: hld up in last: effrt and swtchd lft ent fnl 2f: drvn to chse clr wnr over 1f out: kpt on wl u.p fnl f: nvr quite getting to wnr* **8/1**[3]

6506 **3** *3* **Green Energy**[26] 3444 3-8-10 **52** .... PatDobbs 8 — 56
(Mrs A J Perrett) *chsd ldng pair: rdn to chse wnr ent fnl 2f: unable qck and edgd lft over 1f out: edgd bk rt u.p and kpt on same pce ins fnl f* **12/1**

3342 **4** *16* **Sheila's Bond**[8] 4027 3-9-2 **58** .... LiamKeniry 2 — 36
(J S Moore) *chsd wnr tl ent fnl 2f: sn drvn and struggling: wl btn 1f out: eased ins fnl f* **7/2**[2]

0140 **5** *40* **Othello (IRE)**[10] 3967 3-9-1 **57** ....(b) HayleyTurner 1 — —
(E F Vaughan) *in tch: effrt on outer over 3f out: drvn and fnd nil ent fnl 2f: sn wl btn and virtually p.u fr over 1f out* **10/1**

2m 40.02s (-0.88) **Going Correction** -0.125s/f (Firm) — **5** Ran SP% **112.0**

Speed ratings (Par 98): **97,96,94,83,57**

CSF £6.52 TOTE £2.00: £1.30, £2.10; EX 8.40.

Owner Ennistown Stud **Bred** Miss K Rausing And Mrs S Rogers **Trained** Newmarket, Suffolk

FOCUS

An ordinary handicap. The winner was well in and did not need to improve much, but was a bit better than the bare form.

Sheila's Bond Official explanation: jockey said the filly was unsuited by the good to firm ground

4302 LADBROKESBINGO.COM H'CAP — 1m 1f 149y

8:40 (8:40) (Class 4) (0-85,85) 3-Y-O — **£4,533** (£1,348; £674) **Stalls** Centre

Form — RPR

61- **1** **Psychic Ability (USA)**[267] 7121 3-9-7 **85** ....(p) FrankieDettori 4 — 91
(Saeed Bin Suroor) *mde all: set stdy gallop tl rdn and qcknd over 2f out: r.o wl and a jst holding runner-up ins fnl f* **6/4**[1]

421 **2** *hd* **Sumerian**[23] 3523 3-8-13 **77** .... SebSanders 2 — 83
(Sir Mark Prescott) *hld up in last: hdwy on outer and qcknd over 2f out: ev ch fr over 1f out: r.o but a jst hld ins fnl f* **9/4**[3]

0511 **3** *7* **Warning Song (USA)**[17] 3725 3-8-12 **76** .... PatDobbs 3 — 67
(Mrs A J Perrett) *chsd wnr: rdn and qcknd over 2f out: ev ch wl over 1f out tl outpcd and btn ent fnl f* **15/8**[2]

2m 12.69s (7.79) **Going Correction** -0.125s/f (Firm) — **3** Ran SP% **105.6**

Speed ratings (Par 102): **63,62,57**

CSF £4.74 TOTE £1.70; EX 2.80 Place 6 £4.17, Place 5: £3.88..

Owner Godolphin **Bred** Flaxman Holdings Ltd **Trained** Newmarket, Suffolk

FOCUS

All three of these are promising types.

T/Plt: £7.20 to a £1 stake. Pool:£41,984.89 - 4,246.96 winning tickets T/Qpdt: £3.80 to a £1 stake. Pool:£3,836.98 - 732.54 winning tickets SP

4261 SANDOWN (R-H)

Thursday, July 22

OFFICIAL GOING: Good to firm (round course 8.9; sprint course 9.0)

Round course at innermost configuration and distances as advertised. Far rail on Sprint course moved in 3yds.

Wind: Virtually nil Weather: Sunny intervals

4303 LUBRICATORS E B F MAIDEN STKS 5f 6y

2:10 (2:12) (Class 4) 2-Y-O £4,533 (£1,348; £674; £336) **Stalls** High

Form / RPR

52 **1** **Cadeaux Pearl**[14] 3805 2-9-3 0 ... RichardHughes 6 90+
(R Hannon) *mde all: c clr fnl 2f: v easily* **1/4**[1]

2 *10* **Oh My Days (IRE)** 2-9-3 0 ... AdamKirby 1 54
(C G Cox) *s.i.s: sn in tch: styd on fr 2f out and kpt on wl fnl f to take 2nd last strides but nvr any ch w v easy wnr* **12/1**

3 *nk* **Ezzles (USA)** 2-9-3 0 ... KierenFallon 3 53
(P F I Cole) *chsd wnr: rdn over 2f out and sn easily outpcd: one pce fnl f and lost 2nd last strides* **8/1**[2]

0 **4** *shd* **Sabot D'Or**[13] 3842 2-9-3 0 ... JackMitchell 5 53+
(R Ingram) *chsd ldrs: rdn and one pce 2f out: styd on ins fnl f to press plcd horses cl home but nvr any ch w wnr* **100/1**

0 **5** *1 ¾* **Partout Le Magasin**[75] 1901 2-9-3 0 ... LiamKeniry 2 51+
(J S Moore) *t.k.h: in tch but stl green: effrt whn nt clr run wl over 1f out: styng on same pce whn nt clr run again fnl 50yds and eased* **11/1**[3]

62.72 secs (1.12) **Going Correction** +0.075s/f (Good) **5** Ran SP% **108.1**

Speed ratings (Par 96): **94,78,77,77,74**

toteswinger: 1&2 £4.00. CSF £4.03 TOTE £1.20: £1.02, £4.50; EX 2.80.

Owner Pearl Bloodstock Ltd **Bred** Catridge Farm Stud Ltd **Trained** East Everleigh, Wilts

FOCUS

An uncompetitive maiden and a very easy winner. It is tricky to pin the merit of this down.

NOTEBOOK

Cadeaux Pearl proved all the rage to hand his top team yet another juvenile winner and he completed the task with a most decisive display. His previous experience was a big advantage and, leading from the offset, he came right away from his rivals when asked to win the race from 2f out. This was a deserved success and another improved effort, but a likely reaction from the handicapper will probably force him markedly up in class. Connections will now reportedly send him to the competitive nursery at Glorious Goodwood next week. (op 3-10 tchd 1-3 in places)

Oh My Days(IRE) is a half-brother to Imperial Guest and Excellent Guest, who were both decent at two for Mick Channon. The market suggested this debut would be needed and he advertised that during the race, but still showed definite ability. Another furlong will be within his compass in due course. (op 8-1)

Ezzles(USA) is out of a half-sister to Elusive City and has scope. He took time to settle just off the winner early on and showed his inexperience, so there should be better to come from this speedy colt. (op 15-2 tchd 9-1)

Sabot D'Or had finished last of seven on debut at Ascot, so this was clearly an improvement and he's a little better than the bare form as he looked somewhat intimidated against the far rail from the two-furlong pole. He will enjoy reverting to another furlong when switching to nurseries when eligible for that sphere after his next assignment and has a future. (op 80-1)

Partout Le Magasin finished out the back on debut at Ascot when last seen in May and his return was delayed due to developing a bout of ringworm. Despite the small field he managed to endure a nightmare passage in the race and is certainly better than he could show. The added experience should see him go forward, though, and he ought to be winning races at the right level later on this season. Official explanation: jockey said colt was denied a clear run (op 14-1 tchd 10-1)

4304 INKERMAN LONDON H'CAP 1m 6f

2:45 (2:47) (Class 3) (0-95,88) 3-Y-O £6,476 (£1,927; £963; £481) **Stalls** High

Form / RPR

0122 **1** **Bowdler's Magic**[6] 4092 3-9-3 **84** ... KierenFallon 2 97+
(M Johnston) *t.k.h: mde all: shkn up and c readily clr over 2f out: eased considerably nr fin: unchal* **5/4**[1]

4-10 **2** *7* **Tactician**[35] 3105 3-9-6 **87** ... HayleyTurner 3 88
(M L W Bell) *wnt 3rd 9f out: rdn and one pce over 3f out: styd on to take 2nd wl over 1f out but nvr any ch w eased down wnr* **10/3**[2]

3-13 **3** *3 ½* **Mecox Bay (IRE)**[19] 3670 3-8-9 **76** ... DavidProbert 5 72
(A M Balding) *chsd wnr: rdn and no imp ins fnl 3f: lost 2nd wl over 1f out: jst hld on for wl hld 3rd cl home* **8/1**

51 **4** *shd* **Nezhenka**[15] 3776 3-9-7 **88** ... SebSanders 1 84
(Sir Mark Prescott) *racd in last pl tl wnt 4th 9f out: rdn and one pce over 3f out: mod prog to press for wl btn 3rd cl home* **6/1**

103 **P** **Ugalla**[20] 3634 3-8-1 **75** ... HarryBentley(7) 4 —
(W J Knight) *racd in 3rd tl sddle slipped 9f out and no ch after: p.u and dismntd over 1f out* **5/1**[3]

3m 9.69s (5.19) **Going Correction** +0.075s/f (Good) **5** Ran SP% **109.6**

Speed ratings (Par 104): **88,84,82,81,—**

CSF £5.56 TOTE £2.00: £1.10, £1.90; EX 4.70.

Owner Paul Dean **Bred** Miss K Rausing **Trained** Middleham Moor, N Yorks

FOCUS

What looked an interesting little staying handicap for 3-y-os was turned into a procession by the winner, who dictated from the front. He more than confirmed last week's Haydock improvement.

NOTEBOOK

Bowdler's Magic ◆ turned this into a procession with a clear-cut success from the front. Mark Johnston has a decent record in this race and his colt had run well on his first try over this trip six days earlier, the form of which made him look well handicapped here. He did endure a hard race that day, but this return to quick ground was much more to his liking and getting out in front clearly suited better. He was allowed to dictate as he pleased, but did take a keen hold early on and is obviously an improving stayer. He has two entries already at Glorious Goodwood next week and should make a bold bid if turning up as expected there, remembering his stable has won with very similar types at the meeting in the past. (op 7-4 tchd 15-8)

Tactician was given time to settle on this step up from 1m4f and stayed on best of the rest in the home straight, but is flattered by his proximity to the winner. He doesn't appear the most straightforward, but deserves a more positive ride over this trip and probably wants genuinely quick ground, so he isn't one to write off yet. (op 7-2 tchd 3-1)

Mecox Bay(IRE) looked a possible improver over this stiffer test, but he was well held prior to his rider losing his whip nearing the two-furlong marker. He doesn't have many miles on the clock and ought to find his level as he matures. (op 6-1)

Nezhenka won well at Catterick 15 days earlier, but the handicapper took no chances with her and she proved easy to back under top weight. She looked likely to appreciate stepping up in trip, but was ridden out the back and this wasn't a truly run race. It wouldn't be surprising to see her ridden more prominently next time. (op 5-1 tchd 15-2)

Ugalla's tack went on the back straight and her chance was soon over as a result. Official explanation: jockey said saddle slipped (op 11-2 tchd 9-2)

4305 WEATHERBYS BLOODSTOCK INSURANCE STAR STKS (LISTED RACE) 7f 16y

3:20 (3:20) (Class 1) 2-Y-O

£14,192 (£5,380; £2,692; £1,342; £672; £337) **Stalls** High

Form / RPR

125 **1** **Lily Again**[15] 3792 2-8-12 0 ... JamieSpencer 5 98
(P F I Cole) *mde all: rdn 2f out: hung lft u.p wl ins fnl f: drvn out* **9/2**[2]

1 **2** *1* **Cochabamba (IRE)**[15] 3785 2-8-12 0 ... JackMitchell 4 96
(R A Teal) *t.k.h early: chsd ldrs: rdn 2f out: chsd wnr ins fnl f: kpt on but no imp* **5/1**[3]

16 **3** *hd* **Crying Lightening (IRE)**[34] 3141 2-8-12 0 ... MartinDwyer 6 95
(P W Chapple-Hyam) *s.i.s: in rr: hdwy and swtchd lft 2f out: wnt rt to far rail and r.o fnl f to press for 2nd cl home but no imp on wnr* **5/2**[1]

1 **4** *2* **Fork Handles**[62] 2286 2-8-12 0 ... AlanMunro 1 90+
(M R Channon) *unruly in stalls and slowly away: stl last and pushed along 2f out: shkn up and styd on strly thrght fnl f to take 4th cl home* **14/1**

10 **5** *nk* **Penny's Pearl (IRE)**[36] 3070 2-8-12 0 ... RyanMoore 2 89
(R Hannon) *chsd ldrs: rdn and edgd rt wl over 1f out: kpt on again ins fnl f: gng on cl home but nvr a threat* **8/1**

1 **6** *nse* **Admirable Spirit**[21] 3590 2-8-12 0 ... RichardHughes 7 89
(R Hannon) *chsd wnr: rdn 2f out: sn no imp: lost 2nd ins fnl f: wknd fnl 100yds* **5/2**[1]

3100 **7** *1* **Singapore Lilly (IRE)**[13] 3872 2-8-12 0 ... TedDurcan 3 87
(M R Channon) *in rr: pushed along and sme hdwy whn nt clr run wl over 1f out: kpt on ins fnl f wout ever looking a threat* **66/1**

1 **8** *6* **Miss Boops (IRE)**[47] 2740 2-8-12 0 ... AdamKirby 8 72
(M G Quinlan) *chsd ldrs: rdn 3f out: wknd over 2f out* **22/1**

1m 31.71s (2.21) **Going Correction** +0.075s/f (Good) **8** Ran SP% **115.6**

Speed ratings (Par 102): **90,88,88,86,86 85,84,77**

toteswingers: 1&2 £5.90, 1&3 £3.00, 2&3 £5.30. CSF £27.54 TOTE £7.10: £2.30, £2.90, £1.30; EX 36.10.

Owner R A Instone **Bred** R A Instone **Trained** Whatcombe, Oxon

FOCUS

A good Listed prize for juvenile fillies, rewarded with four maiden winners in attendance and three dropping down from Group company. It was run at just a routine sort of pace, though, and the form looks average for the class. The winner ran to her Cherry Hinton form, paying a minor compliment to Memory.

NOTEBOOK

Lily Again relished this step up a furlong, as her previous fifth in the Cheery Hinton suggested she might, and readily made all. Obviously she was given the run of the race, and she displayed a slightly awkward head carriage after straightening for home, but there was no faulting her attitude throughout the final 2f. A step back up in class for the Debutante Stakes in Ireland next month is now most likely, and it's possible that she could improve again for the experience, but the suspicion is that this was her big day. Her success was another compliment for her Newmarket conqueror Memory. (op 13-2 tchd 7-1)

Cochabamba(IRE)was a taking debut winner on Lingfield's Polytrack 15 days earlier and promised to enjoy the extra furlong. She ran a big race in defeat in this tougher grade, getting the trip well, and left the impression there is still improvement in her. (op 11-2 tchd 6-1)

Crying Lightening(IRE), sixth behind Memory in the Albany last month, is out of a dam who scored over 1m at two and was well backed. Ridden in midfield, she had to wait for her challenge in the home straight and then took time to get reorganised when in the clear. The manner in which she motored home inside the final furlong dictates she is better than the bare form, but she wasn't unlucky as she was run out of second by the runner-up nearing the line. (op 9-4 tchd 15-8)

Fork Handles ◆ was a decisive winner of a weak Haydock maiden in May. She hampered her cause in this much better company by missing the break and still looked green out the back through the first half. She really caught the eye running on towards the finish, however, relishing the stiffer test, and is well worth persevering with in this class.

Penny's Pearl(IRE) is bred to enjoy this sort of trip. She was restrained after taking a keen hold and found just the same pace for pressure. (op 7-1 tchd 13-2)

Admirable Spirit went into plenty of notebooks when winning on her debut at Newbury earlier this month. She was her powerful stable's first string and got ridden as though the extra furlong wouldn't be an issue. She held every chance, but clearly failed to see it out and this stiff 7f was too much for her at this stage. (op 11-4 tchd 10-3)

Singapore Lilly(IRE) was the only one of these to have previously run over this trip when well beaten in a competitive nursery at Newmarket 13 days previously. She bettered that effort with an honest performance, but her proximity does rather hold down this form somewhat. (op 50-1)

Miss Boops(IRE), a Doncaster maiden winner over 6.5f, was outclassed. (op 25-1 tchd 20-1)

4306 WISECALL CLAIMS ASSISTANCE H'CAP 1m 2f 7y

3:55 (3:55) (Class 3) (0-90,86) 3-Y-O+ £6,476 (£1,927; £963; £481) **Stalls** High

Form / RPR

1542 **1** **Flying Destination**[21] 3581 3-8-12 **80** ... ShaneKelly 9 89+
(W J Knight) *chsd ldrs: rdn to chse ldr ins fnl 2f: led appr fnl f styd on wl u.p* **6/1**[3]

2-00 **2** *1* **Rumble Of Thunder (IRE)**[56] 2467 4-9-8 **80** ... MartinDwyer 12 87+
(D W P Arbuthnot) *chsd ldrs: n.m.r on ins and lost position ins fnl 2f: styd on again and swtchd lft ins fnl f: styd on wl u.p to take 2nd cl home: nt rch wnr* **20/1**

5203 **3** *shd* **Resurge (IRE)**[17] 3737 5-9-8 **80** ... IanMongan 3 87
(W S Kittow) *chsd ldrs: rdn and styng on whn bmpd over 1f out: styd on to chse wnr fnl 120yds but a hld: lost 2nd cl home* **10/1**

0000 **4** *3 ½* **Captain Macarry (IRE)**[15] 3796 5-8-12 **75** ...(v) IanBrennan(5) 11 75
(J J Quinn) *sn led: drvn along fr 3f out: hdd appr fnl f: wknd ins fnl f* **40/1**

3-02 **5** *½* **Ethics Girl (IRE)**[19] 3679 4-9-3 **75** ... IvaMilickova 7 74+
(John Berry) *slowly away: in rr: hdwy over 2f out: swtchd lft to outside and r.o fnl f: fin wl but nvr a threat* **20/1**

3303 **6** *1* **Tinshu (IRE)**[13] 3846 4-9-13 **85** ... DarryllHolland 2 82
(D Haydn Jones) *chsd ldrs tl rdn and outpcd over 3f out: rallied to chse ldrs and chal betwen horses over 1f out: hung rt and wknd ins fnl f* **14/1**

5104 **7** *1 ½* **Dukes Art**[22] 3565 4-9-12 **84** ... GeorgeBaker 5 78+
(J A R Toller) *chsd ldrs: drvn along 3f out: stl wl there whn bmpd over 1f out: btn whn pushed rt ins fnl f* **15/2**

1020 **8** *nk* **Bugaku**[13] 3873 5-10-0 **86** ... RyanMoore 13 79
(Sir Michael Stoute) *in rr: pushed along over 3f out and little rspnse tl styd on fr over 1f out: kpt on cl home* **11/2**[2]

2266 **9** *1 ¾* **Penchesco (IRE)**[17] 3737 5-9-4 **76** ... TedDurcan 10 66
(Mrs A J Perrett) *towards rr tl hdwy on ins fr 4f out: rdn: swtchd lft and styd on same pce fr 2f out* **14/1**

432- **10** *nk* **Harlestone Times (IRE)**[280] 6786 3-8-6 **74** ... DavidProbert 6 63
(J L Dunlop) *in rr: rdn 4f out: styd on fr over 1f out: kpt on cl home wout ever being a danger* **12/1**

-401 **11** ½ **Yorgunnabelucky (USA)**[9] 3995 4-9-12 **84** 6ex..........(p) RichardHills 4 72
(M Johnston) *chsd ldr: rdn over 2f out: lost 2nd and edgd rt ins fnl 2f: sn btn* **5/1**[1]

5342 **12** 1 **Spiritual Art**[13] 3862 4-8-10 **68**........................ RichardHughes 8 54
(L A Dace) *bhd most of the way* **18/1**

/0-2 **13** 7 **All The Winds (GER)**[44] 2845 5-9-5 **77**.................. LiamKeniry 14 49
(S Lycett) *s.i.s: rdn 4f out: hung rt ins fnl 3f: a bhd* **6/1**[3]

2m 9.33s (-1.17) **Going Correction** +0.075s/f (Good)
WFA 3 from 4yo+ 10lb **13** Ran SP% **119.7**
Speed ratings (Par 107): **107,106,106,103,102 102,100,100,99,99 98,97,92**
toteswingers: 1&2 £34.50, 1&3 £12.20, 2&3 £33.30. CSF £123.91 CT £1190.98 TOTE £5.70: £1.70, £8.60, £4.10; EX 102.80.
Owner The Pheasant Rew Partnership **Bred** Biddestone Stud **Trained** Patching, W Sussex
■ Stewards' Enquiry : Ian Mongan one-day ban: used whip down shoulder in the forehand (Aug 5)

FOCUS
An open handicap and a race where racing prominently was a distinct advantage. The winner is progressing nicely and the form seems sound enough.

NOTEBOOK
Flying Destination was well placed throughout and hit top gear nearing the final furlong. He soon had matters sewn up and was likely idling a bit when the placed horses closed late on. This was his second win of the campaign and he promises to find further improvement over a stiffer test. (op 9-1)
Rumble Of Thunder(IRE) showed much-improved form on this return from a 56-day break and should be rated a little better than the bare result as he didn't get the best of runs on the inside at a crucial stage. He can build on this. (op 16-1)
Resurge(IRE) travelled nicely and did best of those coming from off the pace, but is a hard horse to actually win with. Official explanation: jockey said gelding hung right (op 9-1)
Captain Macarry(IRE) attempted to make all and is flattered to have had the run of the race. This was his first attempt over the longer trip, though, and it was a more much encouraging display.
Ethics Girl(IRE) had to come from off the pace as a result of getting behind early on and is better than she showed, so her turn may not be far off again providing she can lie up near the pace once more.
Tinshu(IRE) could've done with more of a test, but still looks held by the handicapper.
Dukes Art, who attracted support, left the impression this stiffer test stretched his stamina.
Bugaku had a hopeless task in getting so far back on this drop in distance and, staying on well when the race was effectively over, this run is best forgiven. (op 7-1)
Yorgunnabelucky(USA) was penalised for winning a lesser race at Yarmouth and ultimately shaped as though the run came too soon. (op 7-1 tchd 9-2)
All The Winds(GER) missed the kick and raced out the back, but his response when asked for an effort would suggest something was amiss. (op 9-2 tchd 13-2)

4307 BETFAIR MAIDEN STKS 1m 14y
4:30 (4:31) (Class 5) 3-4-Y-O **£2,590** (£770; £385; £192) Stalls High

Form RPR

22 **1** **Nationalism**[15] 3795 3-9-2 0.............................. RyanMoore 6 92+
(J H M Gosden) *trckd ldrs: pushed along and ld ins fnl 2f: drvn out fnl f* **8/11**[1]

3024 **2** 1¾ **Mata Keranjang (USA)**[15] 3795 3-9-2 100..............(p) JamieSpencer 4 88+
(P F I Cole) *hld up in tch: drvn and qcknd ins fnl 2f to chse wnr wl over 1f out: sn no ex u.p* **5/2**[2]

3 7 **Waheed** 3-9-2 0...................................... PatDobbs 10 71+
(M P Tregoning) *chsd ldrs: rdn and styd on to take n.d 3rd over 1f out* **33/1**

5 **4** 4½ **Perfect Point (IRE)**[83] 1661 3-9-2 0...................... AdamKirby 5 61
(W R Swinburn) *chsd ldrs: pushed along and lost position over 2f out: kpt on again fnl f to take wl hld 4th fnl f* **14/1**

5 ¾ **Priors Gold** 3-8-9 0................................. KatiaScallan(7) 9 59
(M P Tregoning) *in tch: rdn over 2f out: nvr gng pce to get into contention* **50/1**

6 **6** ½ **Bill's Story**[17] 3738 3-8-11 0.............................. AlanMunro 2 53
(M R Channon) *in rr: pushed along and sme prog on outside fr over 1f out* **50/1**

4045 **7** 2¼ **Ruby Dazzler**[20] 3635 3-8-11 64............................ LiamKeniry 3 48
(S Lycett) *sn pressing ldr: upsides 5f out tl slt ld 2f out: sn hdd: wknd over 1f out* **66/1**

8 1¼ **Warlu Way** 3-9-2 0.................................... TedDurcan 11 50
(J L Dunlop) *slowly away: a towards rr* **20/1**

4 **9** ¾ **Sunset Place**[31] 3272 3-9-2 0.......................... PhilipRobinson 12 48
(C G Cox) *mde most tl hdd 2f out: sn wknd* **25/1**

10 7 **Immovable (USA)** 3-9-2 0............................ GeorgeBaker 1 32
(M A Magnusson) *slowly away: a towards rr* **12/1**[3]

05 **11** 3½ **Medici Brave**[68] 2121 3-9-2 0.......................... ShaneKelly 7 24
(Mrs A J Perrett) *a towards rr* **66/1**

1m 43.65s (0.35) **Going Correction** +0.075s/f (Good) **11** Ran SP% **119.3**
Speed ratings (Par 103): **101,99,92,87,87 86,84,83,82,75 71**
toteswinger: 1&2 £2.00, 1&3 £9.30, 2&3 £10.40. CSF £2.40 TOTE £2.20: £1.10, £1.10, £6.50; EX 3.20.
Owner George Strawbridge **Bred** George Strawbridge **Trained** Newmarket, Suffolk

FOCUS
The two market leaders came a long way clear in this 3-y-o maiden, showing above-average maiden form. The winner is progressive and the second is rated in line with his recent efforts.

4308 AFFINITY 10 YEAR ANNIVERSARY H'CAP 7f 16y
5:00 (5:03) (Class 5) (0-70,70) 3-Y-O+ **£3,238** (£963; £481; £240) Stalls High

Form RPR

0020 **1** **Lady Florence**[18] 3715 5-9-2 **61**.................... RussKennemore(3) 5 70
(A B Coogan) *sn led: rdn over 2f out: narrowly hdd 1f out: rallied gamley to ld again fnl 30yds: all out* **28/1**

6601 **2** ¾ **Annes Rocket (IRE)**[29] 3338 5-9-3 **59**...................... PatDobbs 10 66
(J C Fox) *in rr: swtchd sharply lft to outside and rapid hdwy wl over 1f out: str run fnl f: fin wl to take 2nd last strides but nt rch wnr* **12/1**

5660 **3** shd **Buxton**[7] 4057 6-10-0 **70**.............................(t) JackMitchell 8 77
(R Ingram) *chsd ldrs: drvn to chal 2f out: slt ld 1f out: hdd and no ex fnl 30yds: lost 2nd last strides* **16/1**

1343 **4** ½ **Lastkingofscotland (IRE)**[10] 3970 4-10-0 **70**..........(v[1]) LiamKeniry 15 75
(C R Dore) *in tch: chsd ldrs fr 3f out: styd on u.p fnl f: gng on cl home* **6/1**[2]

0164 **5** 2 **Al Khimiya (IRE)**[26] 3441 3-9-6 **69**...................... JimCrowley 12 66
(S Woodman) *chsd ldrs: rdn and ev ch 2f out: wknd ins fnl f* **12/1**

1214 **6** 1¼ **Sairaam (IRE)**[26] 3434 4-9-5 **66**.................... IanBrennan(5) 6 63
(C Smith) *chsd ldrs: rdn and ev ch 2f out: hung rt wl over 1f out: wknd fnl f* **8/1**

0366 **7** 1¼ **Lodi (IRE)**[8] 4024 5-9-12 **68**.............................(t) AdamKirby 4 61
(J Akehurst) *t.k.h towards rr: hdwy 4f out: rdn along fr 3f out: nvr rchd ldrs and wknd fnl f* **9/1**

6220 **8** ½ **El Libertador (USA)**[16] 3768 4-9-1 **62**.................... KierenFox(5) 2 54
(E A Wheeler) *in rr: stl plenty to do whn rdn 2f out: styd on wl fnl f but nvr a threat* **10/1**

1365 **9** 1½ **Musical Script (USA)**[9] 3982 7-9-4 **60**..............(b) JamieSpencer 13 48
(Mouse Hamilton-Fairley) *in rr: stl plenty to do over 2f out: rdn and hdwy over 1f out: kpt on ins fnl f: eased whn no ch cl home* **13/2**[3]

0000 **10** 3¼ **Ymir**[40] 2965 4-8-9 **51** oh1..............................(tp) DavidProbert 14 30
(M J Attwater) *chsd ldrs: rdn over 3f out: wknd 2f out* **22/1**

-062 **11** 5 **Clearing House**[3] 4213 5-8-9 **51** oh3....................... AlanMunro 9 17
(J Ryan) *in rr: rdn and sme hdwy whn nt clr run on ins 2f out: nvr in contention after* **12/1**

-040 **12** 2 **Twilight Star (IRE)**[14] 3813 6-9-12 **68**.................... TedDurcan 7 28
(R A Teal) *chsd ldrs: rdn and ev ch over 2f out: hmpd and wknd sn after* **9/2**[1]

1402 **13** 3½ **Art Market (CAN)**[37] 3056 7-9-10 **66**..............(p) IanMongan 11 17
(Miss Jo Crowley) *chsd wnr: rdn 3f out: wknd over 2f out* **12/1**

00- **14** 17 **Calabaza**[374] 3917 8-8-4 **51** oh1..................... JemmaMarshall(5) 3 —
(M J Attwater) *a in rr* **100/1**

1m 31.29s (1.79) **Going Correction** +0.075s/f (Good)
WFA 3 from 4yo+ 7lb **14** Ran SP% **121.4**
Speed ratings (Par 103): **92,91,91,90,88 86,85,84,83,79 73,71,67,47**
toteswingers: 1&2 £133.00, 1&2 £48.70, 2&3 £56.10. CSF £333.20 CT £5493.55 TOTE £18.20: £7.00, £2.90, £10.60; EX 239.00 Place 6: £122.35, Place 5: £103.31..
Owner A B Coogan **Bred** The National Stud **Trained** Soham, Cambs

FOCUS
A moderate and wide-open handicap. There were a host of chances, but ultimately this was another race on the card where it paid to race handily.
Musical Script(USA) Official explanation: jockey said gelding ran too free and hung right
T/Jkpt: Not won. T/Plt: £111.20 to a £1 stake. Pool £61,184.00 - 401.39 winning units. T/Qpdt: £27.50 to a £1 stake. Pool £4,960.00 - 133.10 winning units. ST

4309 - (Foreign Racing) - See Raceform Interactive

4075 LEOPARDSTOWN (L-H)
Thursday, July 22

OFFICIAL GOING: Yielding (yielding to soft in places)

4310a KOREAN RACING AUTHORITY TYROS STKS (GROUP 3) 7f
6:25 (6:27) 2-Y-O **£28,761** (£8,407; £3,982; £1,327)

RPR

1 **Zoffany (IRE)**[21] 3645 2-9-1 105............................ JMurtagh 2 108+
(A P O'Brien, Ire) *trckd ldr in 2nd: impr travelling wl to ld 1 1/2f out: shkn up briefly ins fnl f: easily* **1/7**[1]

2 2 **High Ruler (USA)**[17] 3740 2-9-1 .... JAHeffernan 3 98
(A P O'Brien, Ire) *led: rdn and hdd 1 1/2f out: no ex over 1f out and kpt on same pce* **9/1**[2]

3 ½ **Jolie Jioconde (IRE)**[17] 3740 2-8-12 .... CDHayes 4 94
(Edward Lynam, Ire) *settled in rr early: 3rd after 2f: rdn 1 1/2f out: no ex over 1f out: kpt on same pce* **14/1**

4 1½ **Triple Eight (IRE)**[39] 3004 2-9-1 89....................... PJSmullen 1 93
(D K Weld, Ire) *settled 3rd early: in rr after 2f: rdn and no imp 2f out: kpt on one pce* **10/1**[3]

1m 32.61s (3.91) **Going Correction** +0.475s/f (Yiel) **4** Ran SP% **113.2**
Speed ratings: **96,93,93,91**
CSF £2.62 TOTE £1.10; DF 2.20.
Owner Michael Tabor **Bred** Epona Bloodstock Ltd **Trained** Ballydoyle, Co Tipperary

FOCUS
The winner didn't need to run to his mark to win and tougher tasks await him.

NOTEBOOK
Zoffany(IRE) made it four wins from five starts, three of them at this track, with a comfortably achieved victory. The previous four winners of this race - Cape Blanco, Rip Van Winkle, New Approach and Teofilo - all went on to achieve Group 1 success, and it remains to be seen how high up the ladder Zoffany, more exposed than any of that quartet were prior to winning this event, will reach. The winner's only defeat came in the Coventry Stakes in which he raced quite keenly and finished sixth, but he is a smart type and coped with the slowest ground he has raced on without much difficulty. (op 2/9)
High Ruler(USA), a stablemate of the winner, had won a maiden over this trip at Roscommon on his second start. He made the running until headed by the winner and kept on, although was well held in the closing stages. (op 7/1)
Jolie Jioconde(IRE), clear of the rest when three-quarters of a length second to High Ruler at Roscommon, settled better on this occasion and was always in touch. She kept on but never posed much of a threat once the winner had taken control of the race. (op 12/1)
Triple Eight(IRE) was always in touch but, after being ridden along on the final bend, could only keep on at the same pace over the last 1½f. (op 8/1)

4312a JOCKEY CLUB OF TURKEY MELD STKS (GROUP 3) 1m 1f
7:30 (7:32) 3-Y-O+ **£34,513** (£10,088; £4,778; £1,592)

RPR

1 **Famous Name**[74] 1954 5-9-12 117.......................... PJSmullen 3 121
(D K Weld, Ire) *trckd ldr in 2nd: impr to ld under 2f out: rdn and kpt on wl fr over 1f out: comf* **4/6**[1]

2 2½ **Steinbeck (IRE)**[37] 3048 3-8-12 115...................... JMurtagh 6 110
(A P O'Brien, Ire) *chsd ldrs in 3rd: rdn into 2nd 1 1/2f out: no imp on ldr over 1f out: kpt on same pce* **7/4**[2]

3 5 **Bea Remembered**[25] 3490 3-8-9 95........................ WJSupple 2 97
(Francis Ennis, Ire) *settled bhd ldrs in 4th: rdn 2f out: styd on to mod 3rd 1f out: no imp on ldrs: kpt on same pce* **40/1**

4 nk **Finicius (USA)**[25] 3490 6-9-7 100.......................(t) FMBerry 4 100
(Eoin Griffin, Ire) *s.i.s: in rr: rdn 2f out: no imp 1 1/2f out: kpt on same pce fnl f into 4th* **50/1**

5 hd **Vita Venturi (IRE)**[5] 4163 3-8-12 .... KJManning 5 98
(J S Bolger, Ire) *settled bhd ldrs in 5th: pushed along 3f out: rdn and no imp 2f out: kpt on same pce* **9/1**[3]

6 5½ **Lord High Admiral (IRE)**[269] 7072 3-8-12 106............... JAHeffernan 1 87
(A P O'Brien, Ire) *led: rdn and hdd under 2f out: no ex in 3rd 1 1/2f out: wknd fnl f* **28/1**

1m 54.62s (0.52) **Going Correction** +0.25s/f (Good)
WFA 3 from 5yo+ 9lb **6** Ran SP% **114.2**
Speed ratings: **107,104,100,100,99 95**
CSF £2.11 TOTE £1.70: £1.02, £1.30; DF 2.30.
Owner K Abdulla **Bred** Juddmonte Farms Ltd **Trained** The Curragh, Co Kildare

FOCUS
The third helps set the standard here.

NOTEBOOK
Famous Name recorded his fifth Group 3 win and his ninth victory overall with an excellent performance. He had the ease in the ground that he relishes and, after being sent to the front under 2f out in what was a truly run race, he kept on strongly. The Prix Jacques Le Marois and the Arlington Million were among possible options mentioned by trainer Dermot Weld for the winner next month and, wherever he goes, ground will be a factor in the decision made. (op 8/11)
Steinbeck(IRE), racing beyond 1m for the first time and also encountering easy ground for the first time, has yet to deliver on the promise he showed last season but this was a fair effort on his part and he should not be written off as a contender for a major prize down the line on the evidence of his run here. He broke well but was immediately taken back to race in third place. He went in pursuit of the winner over 1½f out and stuck to his task, although never able to trouble the winner.
Bea Remembered had plenty on her plate but this Curragh maiden winner acquitted herself well to earn some black type in a three-way scramble for third place in a race in which only the first two counted over the last 2f. (op 33/1)
Finicius(USA), four of whose five wins have been achieved on the Polytrack at Dundalk, started slowly and kept on in the straight without ever posing a threat. (op 33/1)
Vita Venturi(IRE), winner of a 1m2f maiden here on his debut five days previously, was unable to make much impression when things got serious in the straight, but he kept on. (op 8/1)
Lord High Admiral(IRE), having his first run of the season, made the running. Joined by the winner off the final bend and headed soon afterwards, he was quickly done with.

4313 - 4316a (Foreign Racing) - See Raceform Interactive

3886 ASCOT (R-H)
Friday, July 23

OFFICIAL GOING: Good (stands' side: 7.9 centre: 8.3 far side: 8.1 round: 8.1)
Wind: Virtually nil Weather: Dull

4317 JOHN GUEST MAIDEN FILLIES' STKS 6f
2:10 (2:12) (Class 4) 2-Y-O **£5,828** (£1,734; £866; £432) **Stalls** Centre

Form				RPR
	1		**White Moonstone (USA)** 2-9-0 ... FrankieDettori 5 (Saeed Bin Suroor) *racd wd: c to stands' side 3f out: rdn and r.o strly fnl f: led fnl 120yds: won gng away* 15/2	86+
32	2	1¼	**Florestans Match**[22] 3590 2-9-0 ... JimCrowley 10 (R M Beckett) *chsd ldr: led over 2f out: rdn: edgd lft and styd on wl fnl f: hdd and outpcd fnl 120yds* 9/4[1]	82
4	3	2	**Layla Jamil (IRE)**[14] 3871 2-9-0 ... KierenFallon 1 (M R Channon) *chsd ldr: drvn to dispute 2nd over 1f out: styd on same pce ins fnl f* 15/2	76+
0	4	2	**Saskia's Dream**[37] 3070 2-9-0 ... ShaneKelly 4 (Jane Chapple-Hyam) *pressed ldrs: rdn 2f out: outpcd ins fnl f* 15/2	70
	5	1	**Candys Girl** 2-9-0 ... HayleyTurner 3 (M L W Bell) *chsd ldrs: rdn along 3f out: styd on fnl f but nvr a threat* 7/2[2]	67+
	6	hd	**Queen's Silk** 2-9-0 ... PatDobbs 8 (R Hannon) *s.i.s: bhd: rdn and styd on fnl f: nvr a threat* 66/1	67
5	7	nk	**Sodashy (IRE)**[14] 3871 2-9-0 ... JerryO'Dwyer 6 (Miss Amy Weaver) *outpcd in rr: rdn 3f out: sme hdwy fnl f* 20/1	66
	8	nse	**Jahanara (IRE)** 2-9-0 ... RichardHughes 9 (R Hannon) *led tl hdd over 2f out: wknd fnl f* 11/2[3]	66+
	9	1½	**Speedfit Girl (IRE)** 2-9-0 ... TomQueally 7 (G G Margarson) *chsd ldrs: rdn 3f out: wknd ins fnl 2f* 66/1	61
00	10	3¼	**Ellie In The Pink (IRE)**[14] 3861 2-8-11 ... MartinLane(3) 11 (A P Jarvis) *outpcd most of way* 100/1	51
	11	2	**Tymismoni (IRE)** 2-9-0 ... DavidProbert 2 (R J Smith) *outpcd most of way* 100/1	45

1m 15.72s (1.32) **Going Correction** +0.375s/f (Good) 11 Ran SP% **113.4**
Speed ratings (Par 93): **106,104,101,99,97 97,97,96,94,90 87**
Tote Swingers: 1&2 £4.40, 1&3 £7.80, 2&3 £3.00 CSF £23.39 TOTE £7.30: £2.10, £1.20, £2.20; EX 26.10 Trifecta £87.40 Pool: £867.79 - 7.34 winning units..
Owner Godolphin **Bred** Stonerside Stable **Trained** Newmarket, Suffolk

FOCUS
Traditionally a good maiden. The winner was the only one to race against the stands' rail and looks very useful, possibly Listed class. The second sets the level.

NOTEBOOK
White Moonstone(USA) ◆ hails from the same family as a Breeders' Cup Sprint winner, but is bred to appreciate longer trips as she matures. She wasn't the best away and took time to get organised, but her response when the penny dropped was taking. There is obviously reason to believe she may be flattered in being the only one to exploit the strip on the near rail, and once again her top-class rider emerges with top marks, but she does seem assured to improve a bundle for the initial experience. Her leading connections obviously have a decent prospect on their hands and it will be very interesting to see where she pitches up next, perhaps the Group 3 Sweet Solera over another furlong at Newmarket next month would suit. The stable took that last year with Long Lashes. (op 7-1)
Florestans Match set the standard on the form of her two previous outings and, never far away, looked all over the winner when lengthening to the front. Indeed she was matched for £27,000 at 1.01 on Betfair, but the punters involved were unable to see White Moonstone's effort on the near side until the cameraman finally caught on and panned over. She was a clear second-best and although she has been placed on each of her three outings now, winning a maiden ought to be a formality for her when switching to one of the smaller tracks. (tchd 5-2 in places)
Layla Jamil(IRE) proved easy to back despite her yard's good record in the race and her having run a race full of promise on debut at Newmarket a fortnight earlier. She posted an improved effort, in turn finishing nicely clear in third, and left the clear impression she would come on again for the experience. She won't remain a maiden for long. (op 6-1 tchd 8-1)
Saskia's Dream was far from disgraced when making her debut in the Queen Mary at the Royal meeting here last month. She held every chance, but failed to see out the extra furlong like the principals and switching to a sharper 6f ought to see her winning. (op 14-1)
Candys Girl is entered in the Group 1 Cheveley Park and had reportedly prepped for this when working with the stable's promising filly Margot Did earlier in the week. She hit a flat spot at a crucial stage and ultimately looked in need of the run. (tchd 11-4 and 4-1)
Queen's Silk, half-sister to a juvenile winner over 6f, was friendless in the betting despite coming from a powerful stable. She showed some ability and is sure to come on a bundle for the experience.
Sodashy(IRE) finished just behind the third at Newmarket on debut and was never a player here. She will be eligible for nurseries after her next outing. (op 16-1 tchd 14-1)
Jahanara(IRE), a 110,000gns half-sister to Cavalryman, was the first choice from her leading yard. She showed early pace before fading and was another who shaped as though the outing was needed. (op 6-1 tchd 7-1)

4318 JOHN GUEST EBF MAIDEN STKS 7f
2:45 (2:46) (Class 4) 2-Y-O **£5,828** (£1,734; £866; £432) **Stalls** Centre

Form				RPR
	1		**Titus Mills (IRE)** 2-9-3 ... MartinDwyer 6 (B J Meehan) *in tch: rdn over 2f out: styd on u.p fnl f: r.o wl to ld fnl strides* 16/1[3]	85+
5	2	hd	**Noonenose**[13] 3915 2-9-3 ... JimCrowley 3 (W J Knight) *sn led: rdn 2f out: styd on wl u.p fnl f: ct fnl strides* 33/1	84
4	3	1¼	**Azrael**[27] 3433 2-9-3 ... JamesDoyle 7 (A J McCabe) *chsd ldrs: rdn over 2f out: wnt 2nd over 1f out: no imp and styd on same pce fnl f* 33/1	81
2	4	shd	**Jehanbux (USA)**[21] 3631 2-9-3 ... RichardHughes 4 (R Hannon) *t.k.h: stdd in rr but in tch: rdn and one pce 3f out: n.m.r over 1f out: edgd lft ins fnl f: kpt on cl home* 4/6[1]	81
	5	6	**Dream Achieved** 2-9-3 ... MichaelHills 5 (B W Hills) *t.k.h and chsd ldr: rdn over 2f out: wknd over 1f out* 9/4[2]	66+
	6	4½	**Lemon Drop Red (USA)** 2-9-3 ... KierenFallon 1 (E A L Dunlop) *chsd ldrs: rdn 3f out: wknd 2f out* 16/1[3]	54
	7	12	**Kyllachy Spirit** 2-9-3 ... EddieAhern 2 (B R Johnson) *outpcd* 40/1	24

1m 30.43s (2.43) **Going Correction** +0.375s/f (Good) 7 Ran SP% **110.8**
Speed ratings (Par 96): **101,100,99,99,92 87,73**
Tote Swingers: 1&2 £8.90, 1&3 £13.50, 2&3 £14.20 CSF £342.95 TOTE £13.20: £4.10, £5.80; EX 149.80.
Owner Sangster Family **Bred** Irish National Stud **Trained** Manton, Wilts

FOCUS
A maiden that has been won by some smart colts in the past. It was run at an ordinary pace and they raced up the middle. There was a surprise outcome but the form has been positively rated, with the winner capable of better.

NOTEBOOK
Titus Mills(IRE) got on top nearing the finish and made a perfect start to his career. Brian Meehan's debutants most often improve for their initial outings and this son of Dubawi looked to be carrying condition beforehand. That makes his effort more meritorious and there should be plenty more to come for this experience, indeed he will have learnt an awful lot due to fighting out a tight finish. His pedigree dictates that an extra furlong should be within his compass this year and he is entered in the Group 2 Royal Lodge at this venue later in the season. That will surely now be his main target, remembering connections sent out City Leader to win this race on debut before later taking that Group event in 2007. (op 20-1)
Noonenose, who missed the break when fifth on debut at Salisbury, was a lot more professional here and led for most of the race. He knuckled down gamely when pressed from 2f out and was only narrowly held, so compensation likely awaits in the coming weeks.
Azrael, fourth on debut at Doncaster last month, showed the benefit of that experience and is clearly progressing. He ought to be well up to winning a maiden on one of the smaller tracks. (op 50-1)
Jehanbux(USA) was sent off a very short price on the back of his near miss on debut at Sandown 21 days previously. He took a keen hold due to the lack of early pace, though, and was forced to wait when trying to make a challenge from the 2f marker. This could be deemed as disappointing, but it wouldn't be at all surprising to see him make amends on his next assignment. (tchd 8-13 and 8-11 in places)
Dream Achieved is a half-brother to two 6f juvenile winners, but has plenty of stamina on his dam's side of the pedigree. His stable boasts a decent record in the race and he was the subject of strong support ahead of this racecourse debut. However, he was another that failed to settle and had nothing to give when the race got serious late on. Better was evidently expected and he may just be better off dropping back a furlong in the short term. (op 5-2 tchd 11-4)

4319 WOODCOTE STUD EBF VALIANT STKS (LISTED RACE) 1m (R)
3:20 (3:21) (Class 1) 3-Y-O+
£21,004 (£7,962; £3,984; £1,986; £995; £499) **Stalls** High

Form				RPR
1-21	1		**Field Day (IRE)**[13] 3918 3-8-7 92 ... (t) MartinDwyer 1 (B J Meehan) *in tch: rdn and gd hdwy fr 2f out: led over 1f out: styd on strly* 9/2[2]	109+
5-10	2	3	**Chachamaidee (IRE)**[35] 3143 3-8-11 105 ... TomQueally 5 (H R A Cecil) *slowly away and lost 7 l at s: plld hrd and sn in tch: rdn and hdwy on outside: chsd wnr ins fnl f: no imp but hld on wl for 2nd* 8/1[3]	106
2-14	3	nk	**Alsace Lorraine (IRE)**[37] 3067 5-9-1 105 ... JamieSpencer 6 (J R Fanshawe) *hld up in rr: rdn over 2f out: swtchd lft to outside: r.o to press for 2nd wl ins fnl f but no imp on wnr* 6/4[1]	103
0402	4	1¾	**Please Sing**[17] 3752 4-9-1 98 ... ChrisCatlin 4 (M R Channon) *chsd ldr: rdn over 2f out: one pce over 1f out: wknd ins fnl f* 16/1	99
111	5	½	**I'm A Dreamer (IRE)**[34] 3217 3-8-7 87 ... HayleyTurner 8 (D M Simcock) *hld up in rr: hdwy on ins whn hmpd wl over 1f out: swtchd lft and kpt on fnl f: nt rcvr* 9/2[2]	98+
-414	6	shd	**Flora Trevelyan**[17] 3752 4-9-1 98 ... AdamKirby 2 (W R Swinburn) *led at modest pce: rdn along and qcknd over 2f out: hdd over 1f out: sn btn* 9/2[2]	98
6-20	7	2½	**Blue Angel (IRE)**[76] 1899 3-8-7 100 ... RichardHughes 9 (R Hannon) *chsd ldrs: rdn 3f out: wkng whn edgd rt wl over 1f out* 12/1	90

1m 41.07s (0.37) **Going Correction** +0.225s/f (Good)
WFA 3 from 4yo+ 8lb 7 Ran SP% **119.2**
Speed ratings (Par 111): **107,104,103,101,101 101,98**
Tote Swingers: 1&2 £5.00, 1&3 £2.70, 2&3 £4.00 CSF £41.43 TOTE £6.10: £2.10, £3.50; EX 47.70 Trifecta £248.00 Pool: £828.07 - 2.47 winning units..
Owner Ballymacoll Stud **Bred** Ballymacoll Stud Farm Ltd **Trained** Manton, Wilts

FOCUS
A very interesting Listed event for fillies. It developed into a messy race, with a steady early pace set and the overall form should be treated with caution, but the winner was very impressive. The runner-up is the best guide.

NOTEBOOK
Field Day(IRE) ◆ was an impressive winner, registering her third success from just four career starts. She was well placed to strike as the tempo increased from the home turn, but came right away when asked for her effort in the style of a classy performer. The recent addition of a tongue tie has been a help to her and it's hard to gauge just how good she may be at this stage. It wouldn't be too surprising to see her follow the same path as last year's winner, Strawberrydaiquiri, and head for another race of this class at Sandown next month before then having a crack at Group company. She certainly appeals as a likely scorer in that sphere before the season's end. (op 13-2)
Chachamaidee(IRE), out the back in the Group 1 Coronation Stakes over C&D last month, could hardly have done much more wrong through the first half of the race, and therefore her finishing effort was a taking one under the circumstances. She is obviously not that straightforward, but looks nailed on to score again at this level in due course. (tchd 7-1)
Alsace Lorraine(IRE) was a worthy favourite on the strength of her fourth to Strawberrydaiquiri in the Windsor Forest over the straight mile at the Royal meeting on her previous outing. She wasn't suited by the lack of early pace, but cannot be deemed in anyway unlucky. (op 11-8 tchd 13-8 in places and 7-4 in places)
Please Sing raced just off the early leader and it was no doubt an advantage in doing so. This rates another sound effort from a filly that is tricky to place successfully. (op 20-1 tchd 25-1 in places)
I'm A Dreamer(IRE) ◆, previously unbeaten, was making her debut at this level. She too was undone by a lack of early pace, but after going for a daring run on the inside 2f out she found the door shut firmly in her place and lost any chance she may have held. She wouldn't have beaten the winner with a clear passage, but the way she motored home inside the final furlong dictates she must be given another chance to prove herself in such company. (op 13-2 tchd 7-1)

Flora Trevelyan, just behind Please Sing on her previous outing, was responsible for setting the dawdling early fractions and was made to look paceless when the winner swept past. (tchd 5-1)
Blue Angel(IRE), who ensured I'm A Dreamer had no run on the far rail 2f out, ultimately shaped as though this first outing for 76 days would do her good. A stiffer test may also now help her cause. (tchd 14-1 and 16-1 in places)

4320 JOHN GUEST BROWN JACK STKS (H'CAP) 2m
3:55 (3:55) (Class 2) (0-100,98) 3-Y-0+ £12,952 (£3,854; £1,926; £962) Stalls High

Form				RPR
/001	1		**Colloquial**[21] 3634 9-9-5 89 ....(v) FergusSweeney 3 (H Candy) *chsd ldrs: rdn 3f out: styd on to ld wl over 1f out: drvn out* **8/1**	95
3630	2	¾	**Aaim To Prosper (IRE)**[27] 3447 6-9-3 87 .... MartinDwyer 9 (B J Meehan) *pushed along in rr after 4f: rdn over 4f out: hdwy on outside over 2f out: wnt 2nd ins fnl f: kpt on but a hld* **5/2**[1]	92
0625	3	½	**Hevelius**[14] 3843 5-9-6 90 .... AdamKirby 8 (W R Swinburn) *in tch: hdwy 3f out: drvn to dispute 2nd 1f out: one pce ins fnl f* **6/1**[3]	94
3116	4	1 ½	**Desert Recluse (IRE)**[14] 3843 3-8-0 92 .... KierenFox(5) 7 (Pat Eddery) *towards rr but in tch: rdn 3f out: styd on fr 2f out: one pce ins fnl f* **3/1**[2]	94
3000	5	¾	**Becausewecan (USA)**[27] 3447 4-9-7 91 .... KierenFallon 2 (M Johnston) *led: rdn 3f out: hdd wl over 1f out: wknd ins fnl f* **16/1**	92
2606	6	1 ½	**Sohcahtoa (IRE)**[7] 4100 4-9-3 87 .... RichardHughes 4 (R Hannon) *in rr: rdn fr 3f out: styd on fnl f: nvr nr ldrs* **16/1**	87
-020	7	nk	**Keenes Day (FR)**[14] 3843 5-9-4 88 .... GregFairley 1 (M Johnston) *chsd ldr: rdn 3f out: wknd over 1f out* **10/1**	87
1443	8	1	**Satwa Gold (USA)**[14] 3843 4-8-13 83 .... TomQueally 5 (Stef Higgins) *in rr: rdn wl over 2f out: nvr gng pce to get into contention* **8/1**	81
00-6	9	½	**Centennial (IRE)**[69] 2116 5-10-0 98 ....(b) GeorgeBaker 6 (Jonjo O'Neill) *chsd ldrs: rdn over 2f out sn btn* **28/1**	95

3m 29.53s (0.53) **Going Correction** +0.225s/f (Good)
WFA 3 from 4yo+ 17lb 9 Ran SP% **114.4**
Speed ratings (Par 109): **107,106,106,105,105 104,104,103,103**
Tote Swingers: 1&2:£5.20, 1&3:£9.70, 2&3:£4.40 CSF £28.05 CT £129.96 TOTE £10.40: £3.00, £1.50, £2.30; EX 36.80 TRIFECTA Not won..
Owner Mrs David Blackburn & M Blackburn **Bred** Mrs M J Blackburn **Trained** Kingston Warren, Oxon

FOCUS
A good staying handicap, but there was an uneven pace on. The front three ran pretty much to their marks.

NOTEBOOK
Colloquial followed up his Sandown success earlier this month off a 4lb higher mark under a well-judged ride. He was never that far away and found plenty when asked for everything in the home straight. Another rise will make things tougher, but he should still make a bold bid for the hat-trick while in this sort of mood. (op 15-2 tchd 7-1)
Aaim To Prosper(IRE) had to be niggled at from an early stage and would've no doubt enjoyed more of a test. He ran a solid race all told and richly deserves to win another race. (op 10-3)
Hevelius, fifth over C&D a fortnight earlier, gave his all and probably ran very close to his previous level. His stable is just struggling for winners at present. (op 7-1, tchd 15-2 in a place)
Desert Recluse(IRE) strictly ran up to his previous C&D form with the third, but again left the impression he has more to offer as a stayer. He lost out by being taken back just as the pace steadied and didn't get the best of passages when trying to make up ground from the home turn. (op 7-2)
Becausewecan(USA), whose stable has a decent record in this race, had his own way out in front and ran a fair race, but ideally wants an easier surface.
Sohcahtoa(IRE) was ridden right out the back on this big step up in trip. He finished strongly, albeit too late in the day, and would've likely had much more of a say off a stronger overall pace.
Keenes Day(FR) went without the blinkers this time and performed more respectably, but still looks a little out of sorts. (op 8-1 tchd 12-1)
Satwa Gold(USA) travelled well under restraint, but really needs more of a test. (op 11-2)
Centennial(IRE) was making his handicap debut under a big weight. He wants softer ground and is one to keep an eye on. (tchd 25-1)

4321 NEWSMITH CAPITAL OCTOBER CLUB CHARITY H'CAP 1m 2f
4:30 (4:33) (Class 2) (0-105,96) 3-Y-0£9,221 (£2,761; £1,380; £691; £344) Stalls High

Form				RPR
-210	1		**Hanoverian Baron**[20] 3672 5-9-6 88 .... KierenFallon 4 (A G Newcombe) *trckd ldrs: pushed along 3f out: hung rt 2f out: swtchd lft and gd hdwy over 1f out: drvn to ld fnl 100yds: styd on strly* **3/1**[3]	97
-112	2	nse	**Breakheart (IRE)**[15] 3824 3-8-11 89 .... JimmyFortune 5 (A M Balding) *trckd ldr: rdn 2f out: chal jst ins fnl f: kpt on to press wnr cl home but a jst hld* **15/8**[1]	98
-243	3	1 ¼	**Sand Skier**[7] 4106 3-8-12 90 .... GregFairley 3 (M Johnston) *led: rdn and kpt on fr 2f out: hdd fnl 100yds wknd nr fin* **85/40**[2]	96
-001	4	4	**Greylami (IRE)**[13] 3889 5-10-0 96 .... EddieAhern 2 (R A Mills) *in rr: rdn over 2f out: styd on same pce* **13/2**	94
4135	5	2 ¼	**Vainglory (USA)**[30] 3334 6-9-8 93 .... MartinLane(3) 1 (D M Simcock) *chsd ldrs: rdn 3f out: wknd 2f out* **16/1**	87

2m 6.93s (-0.07) **Going Correction** +0.225s/f (Good)
WFA 3 from 5yo+ 10lb 5 Ran SP% **111.0**
Speed ratings (Par 109): **109,108,107,104,102**
CSF £9.14 TOTE £3.50: £1.40, £1.60; EX 8.90.
Owner Paul Moulton **Bred** S Coughlan **Trained** Yarnscombe, Devon

FOCUS
Despite the small field this was a good handicap and it was run at a fair pace. The first three dominated and the winner produced a personal best.

NOTEBOOK
Hanoverian Baron was struck into when running down the field in the Old Newton Cup at Haydock earlier this month, when well fancied. He showed his true colours here, though, and made amends with a narrow success. He made his move at just the right time off the final turn and was very game in getting up at the business end. It's likely to be the Ebor next for this likeable 5-y-o and, although he has stamina to prove for that, he was impressive when winning over 1m4f at the track two runs back. Winning here should help him get a run in that race next month. (op 11-4 tchd 10-3)
Breakheart(IRE) ◆ took an age to hit top gear off the home turn, but was still only just denied. The best is surely still to come from this lightly raced and scopey 3-y-o. (op 11-4 tchd 3-1 and 10-3 in places)
Sand Skier was 1lb better off with the runner-up than when the pair were closely matched at Newmarket on his penultimate outing. He was soon sent to the front and looked a likely winner when lengthening on 2f out. However, getting so warm beforehand cannot have helped his cause and he eventually paid for his early exertions. (op 2-1 tchd 7-4 and 9-4 in places)
Greylami(IRE) faced a tough task off his 6lb higher mark and is best when coming off a really strong pace. He would surely have been a little closer had he made his move earlier here, though. (tchd 6-1 and 7-1)
Vainglory(USA)'s effort was very short-lived and he is happier over 1m. (op 12-1 tchd 10-1)

4322 SACO SERVICED APARTMENTS H'CAP 1m (S)
5:05 (5:06) (Class 4) (0-85,85) 3-Y-0+ £5,180 (£1,541; £770; £384) Stalls Centre

Form				RPR
4032	1		**Avonrose**[10] 3973 3-8-5 70 .... GregFairley 3 (M Johnston) *mde virtually all: rdn over 2f out: r.o strly fnl f* **9/2**[3]	81
04U1	2	2 ¾	**First Post (IRE)**[14] 3863 3-8-8 73 .... HayleyTurner 9 (D Haydn Jones) *racd alone centre crse: tl hung bdly lft to join main gp over 3 f out: rdn to chal appr fnl f: kpt on same pce* **2/1**[1]	77+
2045	3	½	**Jordaura**[6] 4154 4-9-10 84 .... MartinLane(3) 4 (J R Holt) *plunged s: t.k.h: disp 2nd tl chsd wnr over 2f out: ev ch over 1f out: wknd fnl 120yds* **7/2**[2]	89
-402	4	¾	**Habshan (USA)**[27] 3438 10-9-11 82 .... JackMitchell 2 (C F Wall) *hld up towards rr: stdy hdwy fr 2 out: chsd ldrs over 1f out: no imp fnl f* **12/1**	85
-140	5	1 ¾	**Compton Blue**[14] 3863 4-9-6 77 ....(b) JimmyFortune 1 (R Hannon) *chsd ldr rdn 3f out: nt keen and lost pl 2f out: kpt on again ins fnl f* **14/1**	76
2500	6	¾	**Officer In Command (USA)**[7] 4100 4-9-5 76 .... MartinDwyer 5 (J S Moore) *s.i.s: in tch: rdn over 4f out: styd on fr over 1f out: nvr rchd ldrs* **20/1**	73
0045	7	4 ½	**Nezami (IRE)**[20] 3681 5-9-9 85 .... JohnFahy(5) 8 (J Akehurst) *towards rr: hdwy to chse ldrs over 3f out: rdn over 2f out: wknd wl over 1f out* **15/2**	71
1020	8	5	**Red Somerset (USA)**[9] 4023 7-9-2 80 .... BarryAdams(7) 7 (Mike Murphy) *disp 2nd: rdn 3f out: wknd 2f out* **20/1**	54
43-0	9	1 ¼	**Club Tahiti**[39] 3031 4-10-0 85 .... JamesDoyle 6 (A W Carroll) *s.i.s: rdn over 3f out: a outpcd* **10/1**	56

1m 43.06s (2.46) **Going Correction** +0.375s/f (Good)
WFA 3 from 4yo+ 8lb 9 Ran SP% **118.5**
Speed ratings (Par 105): **102,99,98,98,96 95,91,86,84**
Tote Swingers: 1&2 £3.20, 1&3 £4.70, 2&3 £3.40 CSF £14.31 CT £34.29 TOTE £6.20: £2.10, £1.40, £2.00; EX 14.70 Trifecta £45.70 Pool: £949.17 - 15.34 winning units. Place 6: £805.40 Place 5: £400.23 .
Owner Around The World Partnership **Bred** Mrs Mary Taylor **Trained** Middleham Moor, N Yorks

FOCUS
A tight handicap and another messy race with the majority coming over to the stands' side early on and it being run at just a moderate pace. The winner's best run since early as a 2yo.
Club Tahiti Official explanation: jockey said filly lost its action
T/Plt: £473.20 to a £1 stake. Pool:£97,165.27 - 149.88 winning tickets T/Qpdt: £24.10 to a £1 stake. Pool:£9,127.60 - 279.82 winning tickets ST

3848 CHEPSTOW (L-H)
Friday, July 23

OFFICIAL GOING: Good to soft (soft in places; 6.4)
Wind: mild against Weather: Overcast

4323 CHAIRMAN'S RESERVE FINE RUM MAIDEN AUCTION STKS 6f 16y
6:20 (6:21) (Class 5) 2-Y-0 £2,266 (£674; £337; £168) Stalls Centre

Form				RPR
64	1		**Arctic Mirage**[32] 3269 2-8-8 0 .... WilliamCarson(3) 2 (M Blanshard) *trckd ldrs: led over 1f out: sn rdn: drifted lft fnl f: r.o wl* **5/1**[3]	70
0	2	2	**Summer Jasmine**[14] 3861 2-8-4 0 .... FrannyNorton 1 (H J L Dunlop) *prom: led over 3f out: rdn and hdd over 1f out: kpt on but sn hld by wnr* **16/1**	57
0	3	1 ½	**May's Boy**[11] 3964 2-8-9 0 .... RichardThomas 9 (M D I Usher) *trckd ldrs: jnd ldrs 3f out: sn rdn: kpt on same pce fnl 2f* **40/1**	58
030	4	nk	**May Be Some Time**[50] 2680 2-8-4 0 .... SimonPearce(5) 7 (W S Kittow) *trckd ldrs: outpcd and edgd lft 3f out: kpt on wl ins fnl f* **9/2**[2]	57+
	5	¾	**Miskin Diamond (IRE)** 2-8-8 0 .... DavidProbert 5 (B Palling) *led tl over 3f out: pressed ldr: rdn over 2f out: one pce fr over 1f out* **16/1**	53
65	6	4 ½	**Red Zeus (IRE)**[16] 3785 2-8-11 0 .... LiamKeniry 4 (J S Moore) *prom: rdn over 3f out: one pce fr 2f out tl fdd ins fnl f* **15/2**	43
	7	3 ¾	**Titan Diamond (IRE)** 2-8-9 0 .... RichardKingscote 3 (M D I Usher) *in tch: struggling 3f out: wknd and hung bdly lft fr over 1f out* **33/1**	30
0	8	2 ½	**Ignore The Advice (IRE)**[16] 3785 2-8-9 0 .... PatDobbs 6 (J S Moore) *prom: rdn over 3f out: wknd over 1f out* **25/1**	22
	9	¾	**Sluggsy Morant** 2-8-9 0 .... DaneO'Neill 10 (H Candy) *s.i.s: sn in tch: jnd ldrs 3f out: sn rdn and hung lft: wknd sn after* **5/4**[1]	20
	10	14	**Cool Land (IRE)** 2-8-9 0 .... LukeMorris 8 (R A Harris) *little slowly away: sn outpcd: a in rr* **28/1**	—

1m 15.03s (3.03) **Going Correction** +0.425s/f (Yiel) 10 Ran SP% **115.5**
Speed ratings (Par 94): **96,93,91,90,89 83,78,75,74,55**
Tote Swingers: 1&2 £13.60, 1&3 £24.30 CSF £74.88 TOTE £4.30: £1.40, £5.10, £14.00; EX 94.30.
Owner J Gale, J Oliver & V Ward **Bred** Simon Balding **Trained** Upper Lambourn, Berks

FOCUS
After 20mm of rain overnight the going was changed to good to soft, soft in places. An ordinary maiden auction and the standard is limited in behind the winner.

NOTEBOOK
Arctic Mirage improved on his debut run when 5l fourth in a 6f Windsor maiden behind a decent type who ran respectably off 85 next time. The speedily bred gelding had solid form claims and found a surging run to storm clear on his first try on slow ground, despite edging left. This form probably doesn't amount to much and it is a slight worry that he got a bit worked up beforehand, but he looks a steadily progressive type who is decent value at 11,000gns and it will be interesting to see what mark he receives for nurseries. (op 7-2 tchd 11-2)
Summer Jasmine made a little late headway when 66-1 eighth in a 7f Newbury maiden on debut. The daughter of Kyllachy had plenty to find but put in another encouraging display and has probably found quite a bit of improvement. (tchd 14-1)
May's Boy got a bit restless in the stalls but he kept plugging away and showed signs of ability at a big price on his second start. (tchd 33-1 and 50-1)
May Be Some Time had a decent chance on his third at Salisbury two runs back but he got a bit outpaced and found some trouble at a crucial stage before flashing home when it was all over. (op 5-1)
Miskin Diamond(IRE) showed some natural speed before fading on debut. She should improve for the experience and is a half-sister to nine winners, notably very useful 2-y-os Catch A Glimpse and Crystal Clear. (op 12-1)
Ignore The Advice(IRE) Official explanation: jockey said gelding hung right-handed

Sluggsy Morant, a £3,000 gelded half-brother to 7f winner Rockie, was the subject of a massive gamble on debut but didn't find much and dropped away when things got serious. Official explanation: jockey said gelding stopped quickly (op 5-2)

4324 EUROPEAN BREEDERS' FUND FILLIES' H'CAP 7f 16y
6:50 (6:52) (Class 5) (0-70,70) 3-Y-O+ £3,238 (£963; £481; £240) Stalls Centre

Form RPR

40-0 **1** **Polar Annie**[123] 965 5-9-6 **62** LukeMorris 1 71
(M S Saunders) *trckd ldr: rdn into narrow advantage 2f out: rdr lost whip ent fnl f: hld on gamely: pushed out* **25/1**

-615 **2** *hd* **You've Been Mowed**[14] 3854 4-9-11 **70** WilliamCarson(3) 6 78
(R J Price) *led: rdn whn narrowly hdd 2f out: kpt on gamely: ev ch thrght fnl f: jst hld* **6/1[3]**

/0-0 **3** *4 1/2* **Out Of Nothing**[30] 3329 7-8-13 **60** KierenFox(5) 11 56
(D Burchell) *in tch: rdn over 3f out: outpcd over 2f out: styd on wl fnl f: snatched 3rd nr fin* **16/1**

-000 **4** *1/2* **Fiancee (IRE)**[11] 3968 4-9-2 **58** (v[1]) GeorgeBaker 3 53
(R Brotherton) *s.i.s: bhd: drvn and stdy prog fr 4f out: styd on to go 3rd ent fnl f: lost 3rd cl home* **33/1**

0-24 **5** *nk* **Via Aurelia (IRE)**[9] 4025 3-8-10 **59** (v[1]) DavidProbert 4 50
(J R Fanshawe) *s.i.s: sn mid-div: hdwy to chse ldrs 3f out: sn rdn: lost 3rd ent fnl f: kpt on same pce* **7/2[1]**

34-1 **6** *1* **Leelu**[41] 2967 4-9-1 **57** LiamKeniry 2 48
(D W P Arbuthnot) *trckd ldrs: outpcd and plenty to do in last 4 3f out: styd on wl fnl f* **10/1**

0332 **7** *2* **Interakt**[8] 4058 3-9-5 **68** ChrisCatlin 9 51
(M R Channon) *mid-div: hdwy 3f out: sn rdn to chse ldrs: wknd fnl f* **15/2**

-416 **8** *1* **Sweet Pilgrim**[30] 3336 3-9-4 **67** JimCrowley 8 47
(M D I Usher) *prom: rdn and ev ch over 2f out: wknd over 1f out* **12/1**

2411 **9** *nk* **Chinese Democracy (USA)**[6] 4130 3-9-0 **63** 6ex (v) DaneO'Neill 10 42
(P D Evans) *hld up towards rr: hdwy into midfield 3f out: sn rdn: no further imp* **5/1[2]**

0144 **10** *1 1/4* **Ken's Girl**[22] 3592 6-9-11 **67** IanMongan 14 46
(W S Kittow) *stmbld leaving stalls: nvr bttr than mid-div* **8/1**

-060 **11** *6* **Andrasta**[8] 4047 5-8-4 **51** oh5 SimonPearce(5) 7 14
(S A Harris) *mid-div: rdn 3f out: sn wknd* **33/1**

-426 **12** *2 3/4* **Dancing Welcome**[126] 937 4-9-1 **57** (b) RichardKingscote 12 12
(J M Bradley) *a towards rr* **16/1**

0-50 **13** *3 1/4* **Superstitious Me (IRE)**[20] 3683 4-8-9 **51** oh5 NeilChalmers 13 —
(B Palling) *s.i.s: a towards rr* **20/1**

1m 25.72s (2.52) **Going Correction** +0.425s/f (Yiel)
WFA 3 from 4yo+ 7lb **13** Ran SP% **119.1**
Speed ratings (Par 100): **102,101,96,96,95 94,92,91,90,89 82,79,75**
Tote Swingers: 1&2 £6.00, 1&3 £21.50, 2&3 £12.70 CSF £163.00 CT £2571.27 TOTE £37.90: £9.20, £2.50, £8.00; EX 529.80.
Owner Lockstone Business Services Ltd **Bred** Cobhall Court Stud **Trained** Green Ore, Somerset

FOCUS
A fairly competitive handicap. The field raced mostly down the centre of the track and the first two pulled clear. The form could be underrated.
Leelu Official explanation: jockey said filly never travelled

4325 LINDLEY CATERING H'CAP 7f 16y
7:20 (7:21) (Class 5) (0-75,75) 3-Y-0 £3,561 (£1,059; £529; £264) Stalls Centre

Form RPR

1132 **1** **Kingsdine (IRE)**[11] 3970 3-8-13 **67** TomMcLaughlin 1 83+
(M S Saunders) *outside of chsng gp: moved across to stands' side to ld comf 2f out: clr ent fnl f: v easily* **3/1[2]**

3402 **2** *4 1/2* **Yes Chef**[23] 3558 3-9-4 **72** IanMongan 13 74
(J Gallagher) *wnt lft s: sn prom: led briefly u.p over 2f out: styd on: regained 2nd nr fin: no ch w wnr* **8/1[3]**

2662 **3** *1/2* **Purple Gallery (IRE)**[34] 3212 3-9-5 **73** (p) LukeMorris 12 74
(J S Moore) *wnt rt s: rcvrd to sit promly after 2f: rdn and ev ch 2f out: sn no ch w wnr: lost 2nd nr fin* **10/1**

1200 **4** *2 1/4* **Our Boy Barrington (IRE)**[14] 3863 3-9-7 **75** PatDobbs 3 69
(R Hannon) *chsd ldrs: sltly outpcd 3f out: styd on same pce fnl 2f* **9/1**

400 **5** *5* **Whisper Wind**[32] 3272 3-9-4 **72** GeorgeBaker 4 53
(G L Moore) *in tch: effrt 3f out: no ex ent fnl f* **33/1**

6020 **6** *3/4* **Excellent Day (IRE)**[40] 3001 3-9-7 **75** ChrisCatlin 5 54
(M R Channon) *hld up: hdwy over 3f out: sn rdn: one pce fnl 2f* **20/1**

0230 **7** *1/2* **Nubar Boy**[4] 4204 3-9-2 **73** (b[1]) RichardEvans(3) 15 51
(P D Evans) *hld up towards rr: sme hdwy over 3f out: sn rdn: no further imp fnl 2f* **20/1**

0222 **8** *4 1/2* **Primo De Vida (IRE)**[30] 3325 3-9-6 **74** JimCrowley 9 39
(R M Beckett) *sn prom whn swtchd to stands' side rails: led 4f out: rdn and hdd over 2f out: wknd over 1f out* **8/1[3]**

-642 **9** *3 1/4* **Sir Bruno (FR)**[20] 3680 3-9-2 **70** DavidProbert 7 27
(B Palling) *awkward leaving stalls: towards rr: hdwy to chse ldrs over 3f out: sn rdn: wknd 2f out* **5/2[1]**

1-50 **10** *hd* **Empress Leizu (IRE)**[18] 3739 3-7-13 **58** ow1 KierenFox(5) 14 14
(A W Carroll) *rrd leaving stalls: a towards rr* **33/1**

3204 **11** *3 3/4* **Minortransgression (USA)**[18] 3728 3-8-6 **65** (t) SimonPearce(5) 11 11
(P D Evans) *chsd ldrs tl wknd over 2f out* **28/1**

50-0 **12** *6* **Kyoatee Kilt**[193] 118 3-8-2 **56** oh3 (p) FrannyNorton 2 —
(P F I Cole) *clr ldr tl 4f out: sn wknd* **33/1**

6310 **13** *7* **Wadi Wanderer (IRE)**[51] 2644 3-9-3 **74** WilliamCarson(3) 8 —
(E F Vaughan) *chsd ldrs tl dropped out tamely over 3f out* **20/1**

1m 26.39s (3.19) **Going Correction** +0.425s/f (Yiel) **13** Ran SP% **121.4**
Speed ratings (Par 100): **98,92,92,89,84 83,82,77,73,73 69,62,54**
Tote Swingers: 1&2 £3.60, 1&3 £7.50, 2&3 £12.40 CSF £24.84 CT £220.90 TOTE £5.10: £1.90, £3.70, £3.20; EX 31.30.
Owner M S Saunders **Bred** Deer Forest Stud Ltd **Trained** Green Ore, Somerset
■ Stewards' Enquiry : Luke Morris caution: careless riding.

FOCUS
Most of the runners were fairly exposed in this handicap for 3-y-os but the winner is a likeable type who overcame a poor draw to hammer his rivals. It looked like he improved but the time was modest.
Sir Bruno(FR) Official explanation: jockey said gelding was unsuited by the good to soft (soft in places) ground
Empress Leizu(IRE) Official explanation: jockey said filly fly leapt on leaving stalls

4326 SUNSHINE RADIO H'CAP 5f 16y
7:50 (7:52) (Class 5) (0-70,70) 3-Y-O+ £2,914 (£867; £433; £216) Stalls Centre

Form RPR

0234 **1** **Matterofact (IRE)**[8] 4041 7-9-4 **63** TomMcLaughlin 4 73
(M S Saunders) *trckd ldr: shkn up to ld ent fnl f: r.o strly: comf* **6/1[3]**

0346 **2** *2* **Stamford Blue**[6] 4130 9-8-12 **57** (b) LukeMorris 3 59
(R A Harris) *pushed along in rr over 3f out: nt clr run briefly whn swtchd lft 2f out: hdwy over 1f out: r.o ins fnl f: wnt 2nd towards fin: no ch w wnr* **4/1[1]**

2524 **3** *shd* **Tenancy (IRE)**[41] 2965 6-8-6 **51** oh1 ChrisCatlin 7 53
(S A Harris) *chsd ldr: rdn 3f out: kpt on to chse wnr ins fnl f but no ch: lost 2nd towards fin* **7/1**

6410 **4** *1* **Best One**[2] 4256 6-8-12 **57** 6ex (b) DaneO'Neill 8 55
(R A Harris) *s.i.s: bhd: hdwy over 1f out: styd on to go 4th ins fnl f: nvr any ch w ldrs* **11/1**

-153 **5** *3/4* **The Jailer**[19] 3717 7-8-8 **56** RussKennemore(3) 10 52
(J G M O'Shea) *in tch: rdn 3f out: kpt on same pce ins fnl f* **7/1**

2066 **6** *shd* **Spic 'n Span**[18] 3722 5-8-11 **56** (b) JimCrowley 6 51
(R A Harris) *led: rdn 2f out: hdd ent fnl f: fdd* **9/1**

6043 **7** *3 1/2* **Little Edward**[8] 4041 12-9-8 **70** WilliamCarson(3) 5 53
(R J Hodges) *little slow away: towards rr: swtchd rt 2f out: sn rdn: no imp* **12/1**

0005 **8** *3 1/2* **Abhainn (IRE)**[32] 3254 4-8-8 **53** DavidProbert 9 23
(B Palling) *sn drvn along and dropped to rr* **11/2[2]**

6436 **9** *1/2* **Captain Kallis (IRE)**[31] 3299 4-8-8 **58** (e[1]) BillyCray(5) 1 26
(D J S Ffrench Davis) *mid-div: rdn over 2f out: wknd over 1f out* **9/1**

0050 **10** *1* **Lithaam (IRE)**[8] 4047 6-9-0 **59** (b[1]) LiamKeniry 11 24
(J M Bradley) *in tch: rdn 2f out: sn wknd* **16/1**

61.00 secs (1.70) **Going Correction** +0.425s/f (Yiel) **10** Ran SP% **116.6**
Speed ratings (Par 103): **103,99,99,98,96 96,91,85,84,83**
Tote Swingers: 1&2 £6.00, 1&3 £21.50, 2&3 £12.70 CSF £30.24 CT £173.33 TOTE £8.40: £2.60, £2.00, £2.40.
Owner Prempro Racing **Bred** Tony Gleeson **Trained** Green Ore, Somerset

FOCUS
This sprint handicap was run at a decent pace but the hold-up performers struggled to land a blow. Straightforward form.

4327 WYVERN ICES H'CAP 1m 4f 23y
8:20 (8:20) (Class 6) (0-65,65) 3-Y-O+ £1,942 (£578; £288; £144) Stalls Low

Form RPR

040- **1** **Clare Glen (IRE)**[6] 4158 4-9-12 **61** TomMcLaughlin 9 74
(Mrs Sarah Dawson, Ire) *hld up in last pair: c wd w str run fr 4f out to ld 3f out: sn clr: v easily* **14/1**

-141 **2** *6* **Le Corvee (IRE)**[10] 3984 8-8-10 **50** KierenFox(5) 3 53
(A W Carroll) *mid-div: hdwy 4f out: sn rdn: disp 2nd fr 2f out: wnt clr 2nd ins fnl f but nvr any ch w wnr* **11/2[2]**

50/0 **3** *1/2* **Erdeli (IRE)**[9] 469 6-9-11 **60** (tp) DavidProbert 8 62
(Tim Vaughan) *chsd ldrs early: pushed along in midfield after 2f: towards rr 5f out: rdn and hdwy fr 4f out: disp 2nd and hung lft fr 2f out: styd on same pce* **8/1**

0-40 **4** *1 1/2* **Oriental Girl**[32] 3268 5-9-8 **57** (p) LiamKeniry 17 57
(J S Moore) *mid-div: rdn and hdwy wl over 2f out: disp 2nd sn after: no ex ent fnl f* **16/1**

0150 **5** *9* **Harare**[14] 3860 9-9-8 **60** (v) WilliamCarson(3) 5 45
(R J Price) *rdn over 3f out: a mid-div* **14/1**

0/42 **6** *hd* **Garafena**[14] 3848 7-8-10 **52** (p) NathanAlison(7) 6 37
(R Lee) *in tch: hdwy to ld over 3f out: sn rdn and hdd: no ch w wnr sn after lost 2nd 2f out: wknd* **8/1**

5060 **7** *3/4* **Sirdave**[14] 3848 4-9-10 **59** LukeMorris 2 43
(P W Hiatt) *hld up towards rr: hdwy u.p over 3f out: wknd over 1f out* **25/1**

8 *3 1/2* **Aughcarra (IRE)**[33] 5705 5-9-7 **56** NeilChalmers 16 34
(Harry Chisman) *a towards rr* **50/1**

1460 **9** *nk* **Captain Cool (IRE)**[23] 3564 3-9-0 **61** PatDobbs 10 39
(R Hannon) *hld up towards rr: nt clr run on rails and swtchd rt 3f out: sn rdn: no imp* **9/2[1]**

0600 **10** *9* **Dove Cottage (IRE)**[14] 3860 8-9-13 **62** (b[1]) IanMongan 13 25
(W S Kittow) *racd keenly: led tl over 3f out: sn wknd* **10/1**

230 **11** *6* **Search For The Key (USA)**[40] 2993 3-9-4 **65** ChrisCatlin 12 19
(P F I Cole) *chsd ldrs tl wknd 3f out* **7/1[3]**

6-05 **12** *14* **Gearbox (IRE)**[46] 2812 4-10-0 **63** FrannyNorton 14 —
(H J L Dunlop) *chsd ldrs tl wknd over 3f out* **20/1**

216 **13** *1 3/4* **Duneen Dream (USA)**[23] 3559 5-9-0 **49** DaneO'Neill 11 —
(Mrs N S Evans) *trckd ldrs: rdn over 3f out: wknd over 2f out* **20/1**

6-00 **14** *3/4* **Attainable**[31] 3294 4-9-8 **60** RobertLButler(3) 1 —
(J A B Old) *s.i.s: a bhd* **40/1**

005 **15** *dist* **Kuantan Two (IRE)**[27] 3443 3-9-1 **62** JimCrowley 15 —
(P F I Cole) *in tch tl rdn over 5f out: virtually p.u* **14/1**

2m 40.48s (1.48) **Going Correction** +0.15s/f (Good)
WFA 3 from 4yo+ 12lb **15** Ran SP% **121.0**
Speed ratings (Par 101): **101,97,96,95,89 89,89,86,86,80 76,67,66,65,—**
Tote Swingers: 1&2 £17.80, 1&3 £34.10, 2&3 £7.90 CSF £83.63 CT £676.08 TOTE £17.30: £3.70, £2.20, £3.60; EX 156.20.
Owner Leslie Laverty **Bred** Hadi Al Tajir **Trained** Banbridge, Co. Down

FOCUS
There was a surprise runaway winner in this modest middle-distance handicap. She seemed to show much-improved form.

4328 DIGIBET.COM H'CAP 2m 49y
8:55 (8:55) (Class 6) (0-60,58) 3-Y-O+ £1,942 (£578; £288; £144) Stalls Low

Form RPR

-021 **1** **Vertueux (FR)**[14] 3848 5-9-6 **57** DebraEngland(7) 5 65
(A W Carroll) *chsd clr ldr in clr 2nd: steadily clsd on ldr fr 4f out: rdn 2f out: styd on to narrowly ld fnl 50yds* **11/8[1]**

3064 **2** *hd* **Spiritonthemount (USA)**[8] 4042 5-8-13 **46** (b) WilliamCarson(3) 1 54
(P W Hiatt) *aggressively rdn fr the s: led: sn clr: 15 l clr over 7f out: hrd rdn over 2f out: edgd rt ins fnl f: narrowly hdd fnl 50yds* **8/1[3]**

6330 **3** *4* **Minder**[31] 3294 4-9-9 **53** (p) RichardKingscote 6 56
(J G Portman) *hld up towards rr: stdy prog fr 7f out: wnt 3rd over 3f out: sn rdn: styd on same pce* **8/1[3]**

6500 **4** *3 1/2* **Princess Flame (GER)**[31] 3294 8-9-0 **49** KylieManser(5) 3 48
(B G Powell) *hld up last: hdwy into midfield over 3f out: sn rdn: wnt 4th over 1f out: styd on wout rching ldrs* **22/1**

/0-0 **5** *3* **Olivino (GER)**[50] 2023 9-9-1 **45** DavidProbert 7 40
(B J Llewellyn) *mid-div: stdy prog into 3rd over 7f out: rdn 4f out: sn one pce* **14/1**

2546 **6** *3 3/4* **Street Runner**[11] 3965 4-9-13 **57** JerryO'Dwyer 11 48
(R Hollinshead) *prom in chsng gp: rdn over 4f out: no imp on ldrs* **10/1**

0420 **7** *2* **Sir Sandicliffe (IRE)**[11] 3965 6-9-6 **55** KierenFox(5) 13 44
(W M Brisbourne) *mid-div: rdn 4f out: no real imp* **17/2**

0033 **8** *12* **Il Portico**[15] 3820 3-8-8 **55**.......................... ChrisCatlin 2 29
(M R Channon) *hld up towards rr: rdn and sme prog into midfield over 6f out: nvr threatened: wknd over 1f out* **17/2**

00-6 **9** *1 1/4* **Be Kind**[41] 2952 4-9-1 **45**.......................... JamieMackay 9 18
(Karen George) *led chsng gp tl over 7f out: wknd over 2f out* **22/1**

0/0- **10** *28* **Contrada**[95] 1073 5-9-11 **58**.......................... RobertLButler(3) 8 —
(J A B Old) *mid-div tl wknd over 4f out: virtually p.u* **40/1**

0-40 **11** *7* **Chateauneuf (IRE)**[20] 3669 4-9-3 **47**.......................... TomMcLaughlin 4 —
(W M Brisbourne) *mid-div tl wknd over 5f out: virtually p.u* **7/1**[2]

3m 44.7s (5.80) **Going Correction** +0.15s/f (Good)
WFA 3 from 4yo+ 17lb **11** Ran SP% **124.8**
Speed ratings (Par 101): **91,90,88,87,85 83,82,76,76,62 58**
CSF £13.71 CT £73.08 TOTE £2.20: £1.40, £2.70, £1.40 Place 6: £331.29 Place 5: £72.52 .
Owner John Rutter **Bred** Roger Baudouin **Trained** Cropthorne, Worcs
■ Stewards' Enquiry : William Carson three-day ban: used whip without giving gelding time to respond start and with excessive frequency throughout (Aug 8-10)

FOCUS
A low-grade staying handicap run at a decent pace. The first two filled those positions throughout and a big gamble was landed. The runner-up was clear for a long way and looks the best guide.
T/Plt: £696.00 to a £1 stake. Pool:£68,079 - 71.40 winning tickets T/Qpdt: £13.20 to a £1 stake. Pool:£6,681 - 373.25 winning tickets TM

[4142] NEWMARKET (R-H)
Friday, July 23

OFFICIAL GOING: Good to firm (good in places; watered; 7.7)
Stands' side of July Course utilised.
Wind: Light half-behind Weather: Overcast

4329 SPORTINGBET.COM FILLIES' H'CAP — 1m 2f
5:40 (5:43) (Class 5) (0-70,72) 3-Y-0+ **£3,238** (£963; £481; £240) **Stalls** Centre

Form RPR

-601 **1** **Snoqualmie Star**[9] 4022 3-9-0 **72** 6ex.......................... (b) RyanPowell(7) 8 86
(D R C Elsworth) *mde all: set stdy pce tl qcknd over 3f out: rdn and hung lft fr over 1f out: styd on* **4/1**[3]

2523 **2** *2* **Broughtons Paradis (IRE)**[32] 3268 4-9-6 **61**.......................... TonyCulhane 10 71
(W J Musson) *chsd wnr: rdn and hung lft over 1f out: styd on same pce ins fnl f* **7/4**[1]

12-5 **3** *3/4* **Silent Act (USA)**[60] 2402 4-10-0 **69**.......................... PhilipRobinson 4 77
(Mrs A J Perrett) *hld up: plld hrd: hdwy 4f out: rdn and hung lft over 1f out: no ex ins fnl f* **11/4**[2]

6006 **4** *4* **Catbells (IRE)**[8] 4061 3-8-4 **62**.......................... NatashaEaton(7) 2 62
(A Bailey) *plld hrd: trckd ldrs: rdn 2f out: styd on same pce* **16/1**

-623 **5** *3 1/2* **Quiquillo (USA)**[14] 3853 4-9-7 **67**.......................... (b) DeanHeslop(5) 7 60
(P D Evans) *hld up in tch: rdn over 2f out: wknd over 1f out* **9/1**

555 **6** *37* **Starburst**[20] 3684 5-8-2 **50**.......................... StephanieBancroft(7) 3 —
(Miss Gay Kelleway) *hood removed late: s.s: hld up: hdwy over 6f out: hung rt and wknd over 3f out: t.o* **8/1**

2m 8.98s (3.48) **Going Correction** +0.075s/f (Good)
WFA 3 from 4yo+ 10lb **6** Ran SP% **110.0**
Speed ratings (Par 100): **89,87,86,83,80 51**
toteswingers:1&2:£1.70, 1&3:£2.40, 2&3:£1.80 CSF £10.98 CT £19.51 TOTE £3.70: £1.60, £1.70; EX 6.10.
Owner J C Smith **Bred** Littleton Stud **Trained** Newmarket, Suffolk

FOCUS
The field was reduced to only six after four withdrawals. A weak handicap in which the winner is rated up 8lb.
Starburst Official explanation: jockey said, regarding running and riding, she was slow to remove blindfold.

4330 SPORTINGBET.COM MAIDEN STKS — 1m 4f
6:10 (6:13) (Class 4) 3-Y-0 **£4,533** (£1,348; £674; £336) **Stalls** Centre

Form RPR

3 **1** **Mountain Hiker (IRE)**[39] 3038 3-9-3 0.......................... DarryllHolland 2 89+
(J Noseda) *hld up: hdwy: nt clr run over 2f out: rdn to ld 1f out: r.o wl* **11/4**[1]

02 **2** *3 3/4* **La Concorde (FR)**[40] 2994 3-8-9 0.......................... Louis-PhilippeBeuzelin(3) 7 78+
(Sir Michael Stoute) *chsd ldrs: nt clr run and lost pl over 3f out: rallied and swtchd lft over 1f out: wnt 2nd ins fnl f: no imp* **10/1**[3]

0-32 **3** *2* **Donna Elvira**[42] 2921 3-8-12 **80**.......................... RichardHughes 3 75
(R Hannon) *chsd ldrs: led over 9f out: rdn and hdd 1f out: no ex ins fnl f* **7/2**[2]

5 **4** *1/2* **Short Break**[16] 3795 3-8-12 0.......................... TomQueally 1 74
(H R A Cecil) *s.s: hld up: hdwy on outside over 2f out: rdn and hung lft over 1f out: styd on same pce* **11/4**[1]

0 **5** *shd* **Honest Strike (USA)**[23] 3563 3-9-3 0.......................... PatCosgrave 8 79
(H R A Cecil) *hld up: plld hrd: swtchd lft and hdwy over 1f out: rdn and edgd rt ins fnl f: one pce* **20/1**

52 **6** *2 1/4* **Dance Tempo**[22] 3593 3-9-3 0.......................... SteveDrowne 6 75
(H Morrison) *chsd ldr 2f: wnt 2nd again over 5f out: rdn and ev ch over 1f out: wknd ins fnl f* **7/2**[2]

3 **7** *2 3/4* **Joan D'Arc (IRE)**[47] 2782 3-8-12 0.......................... AndreaAtzeni 4 66
(M G Quinlan) *mid-div: hdwy over 7f out: rdn over 1f out: wknd fnl f* **40/1**

00 **8** *11* **Telescopic**[41] 2974 3-8-12 0.......................... StevieDonohoe 5 48
(W Jarvis) *prom tl rdn and wknd over 2f out* **80/1**

00 **9** *39* **Ancestral Dream**[2] 4258 3-9-3 0.......................... (v) J-PGuillambert 9 —
(Andrew Reid) *rdn to ld sn after s: hdd over 9f out: chsd ldr tl over 5f out: wknd over 2f out* **100/1**

2m 32.19s (-0.71) **Going Correction** +0.075s/f (Good) **9** Ran SP% **116.3**
Speed ratings (Par 102): **105,102,101,100,100 99,97,90,64**
toteswingers:1&2:£5.50, 1&3:£2.20, 2&3:£3.40 CSF £30.82 TOTE £3.90: £1.50, £2.30, £1.60; EX 39.30.
Owner Saeed Suhail **Bred** Manfred Hoffer & Ballygrelihan Farm **Trained** Newmarket, Suffolk

FOCUS
Some well-bred 3yos contested what was probably, despite the fact the time was quite slow, a fair maiden. The first pair both improved to the tune of around 10lb.
Short Break Official explanation: jockey said filly hung left

4331 SPORTINGBET.COM NURSERY — 7f
6:40 (6:41) (Class 4) 2-Y-0 **£4,533** (£1,348; £674; £336) **Stalls** Centre

Form RPR

6641 **1** **Byrony (IRE)**[9] 4020 2-9-4 **78** 6ex.......................... RichardHughes 6 79
(R Hannon) *racd wd for much of the trip: hld up in tch: pushed along over 2f out: rdn over 1f out: r.o u.p to ld and hung lft towards fin* **7/2**[2]

01 **2** *3/4* **Ocean Drift (USA)**[15] 3832 2-9-7 **81**.......................... TadhgO'Shea 4 80
(Mahmood Al Zarooni) *dwlt: hdwy 1/2-way: rdn to ld: carried hd high and hung lft fr over 1f out: hdd towards fin* **7/4**[1]

031 **3** *hd* **Honourable Knight (IRE)**[45] 2839 2-8-11 **71**.......................... SteveDrowne 3 70
(M D I Usher) *prom: rdn and ev ch fr over 1f out: r.o* **7/1**

51 **4** *nse* **Da Ponte**[34] 3209 2-9-1 **75**.......................... AndreaAtzeni 2 73
(Pat Eddery) *chsd ldr: rdn over 2f out: ev ch fr over 1f out: r.o* **5/1**[3]

3512 **5** *3 1/4* **Captain Dimitrios**[8] 4066 2-8-8 **67** ow1.......................... StevieDonohoe 1 58
(P D Evans) *led: rdn and hdd over 1f out: nt clr run sn after: no ex ins fnl f* **11/2**

5013 **6** *8* **Silly Billy (IRE)**[13] 3887 2-8-7 **67**.......................... RichardSmith 5 37
(S Kirk) *racd keenly: prom: rdn over 2f out: wknd over 1f out* **10/1**

1m 26.76s (1.06) **Going Correction** +0.075s/f (Good) **6** Ran SP% **112.2**
Speed ratings (Par 96): **96,95,94,94,91 82**
toteswingers:1&2:£1.30, 1&3:£3.80, 2&3:£4.00 CSF £10.07 TOTE £3.70: £2.40, £1.60; EX 5.70.
Owner Axom XXIII **Bred** Mr & Mrs C Booth **Trained** East Everleigh, Wilts

FOCUS
A small but competitive field for this nursery. The gallop was steady at best and a couple of these were keen early on. The form is limited but sound.

NOTEBOOK
Byrony(IRE) raced alone towards the stands' side and rallied in very determined fashion to land the prize close home. \n\x\x She certainly showed a far more resolute attitude than a couple of her rivals. She has plenty of speed in her pedigree, but a mile is already looking imperative. She shouldn't be too harshly dealt with for this and her game attitude should see her continue to progress. (op 10-3)
Ocean Drift(USA)'s Warwick maiden win had been franked since. However, he once again showed a very awkward head carriage and gave his jockey very little assistance in the three-horse battle he was engaged in entering the final furlong. A try in some kind of head-gear could be worth a try. He wasn't beaten here for lack of stamina and ought to get a mile. (op 11-4)
Honourable Knight(IRE) improved on his win in a big field last time. He only gave best near home and certainly handled the extra furlong. He will remain competitive in nurseries. (op 11-2 tchd 5-1)
Da Ponte's response when asked for his effort was disappointing, consiging how well he travelled. He may have needed a better gallop to get a bit of cover during the race. His win came on the less testing turf track at Lingfield and he may have found the uphill final furlong against him. (op 9-2 tchd 11-2)
Captain Dimitrios made the running at a medium gallop. He has performed creditably in his two starts since taking a Newbury seller but will keep finding things tough against less exposed rivals. (op 13-2 tchd 5-1)
Silly Billy(IRE) had posted a better effort in nursery, having got off the mark in a seller previously. He dropped away quickly here and found this company too hot. (op 13-2)

4332 SPORTINGBET.COM E B F CONDITIONS STKS — 6f
7:10 (7:10) (Class 3) 2-Y-0 **£7,771** (£2,312; £1,155; £577) **Stalls** Centre

Form RPR

41 **1** **Excelebration (IRE)**[49] 2701 2-9-3 0.......................... DarryllHolland 3 90+
(M Botti) *hld up in tch: shkn up and n.m.r 2f out: led 1f out: r.o wl: eased nr fin* **5/6**[1]

03 **2** *2* **Point Du Jour (FR)**[11] 3945 2-8-13 0.......................... (t) TomQueally 5 78
(I A Wood) *hmpd s: hld up: swtchd rt and hdwy over 2f out: rdn over 1f out: styd on* **17/2**

4331 **3** *nk* **Local Singer (IRE)**[23] 3550 2-9-3 0.......................... TedDurcan 7 81
(M R Channon) *prom: led over 1f out: sn rdn and hdd: styd on same pce ins fnl f* **13/2**[3]

1 **4** *4 1/2* **Alaskan Spirit (IRE)**[20] 3665 2-9-0 0.......................... BarryMcHugh(3) 6 68
(Mrs A Duffield) *racd keenly: trckd ldrs: pushed along over 2f out: wknd fnl f* **9/2**[2]

1262 **5** *nk* **Inagh River**[14] 3849 2-8-12 0.......................... RichardHughes 1 62
(R Hannon) *chsd ldr: rdn and edgd rt over 1f out: wknd ins fnl f* **7/1**

0442 **6** *6* **Jamaica Grande**[6] 4129 2-8-13 0.......................... PatCosgrave 4 45
(P S McEntee) *wnt rt s: led: rdn: edgd rt and hdd over 1f out: hung lft and wknd fnl f* **50/1**

7 *4 1/2* **Millies Dancer (IRE)** 2-8-2 0.......................... Louis-PhilippeBeuzelin(3) 2 23
(M G Quinlan) *a in rr: pushed along 1/2-way: wknd wl over 1f out* **25/1**

1m 12.45s (-0.05) **Going Correction** +0.075s/f (Good) **7** Ran SP% **114.9**
Speed ratings (Par 98): **103,100,99,93,93 85,79**
toteswingers:1&2:£2.70, 1&3:£1.90, 2&3:£6.50 CSF £9.20 TOTE £1.80: £1.30, £4.20; EX 9.70.
Owner Giuliano Manfredini **Bred** Owenstown Stud **Trained** Newmarket, Suffolk
■ Stewards' Enquiry : Darryll Holland caution: careless riding.

FOCUS
Again a small field containing two interesting recent winners and a decent gallop was set. Pretty solid form, and the winner is potentially smart.

NOTEBOOK
Excelebration(IRE) was well backed and scored impressively drawing away on the climb to the line. He couldn't overcome a tardy start on his debut, but has moved on markedly since and showed a good turn of foot here. Half-brother to a fair handicapper at 1m, he can stay at least another final and looks well able to handle another upgrade. He is likely to take in a Listed race at York's Ebor meeting next month (op 5-4)
Point Du Jour(FR) posted much his best effort here, sticking on in real determined fashion in the final furlong to grab second close home. He is likely to be rated in the low 80s after this, taking a line through the third, and will need to maintain the improvement to score off that mark. He should have no problem in getting further, though, and 1m should be within his scope. (op 9-1 tchd 10-1)
Local Singer(IRE) improved on his Catterick win. He came well clear of the rest of the field in the final furlong, without being any match for the winner. He has been a model of consistency and can remain competitive in a nurseries despite a fairly stiff mark. (op 5-1)
Alaskan Spirit(IRE), an impressive winner of a Carlisle auction race on debut, found this a step too far, continually wanting to hang when coming under pressure. Ground conditions were similar here to when he won, so it was disappointing he was not involved in the finish. (op 11-2)
Inagh River dropped away quickly over a furlong out, and this was her third slightly disappointing run in a row. She needs to bounce back, and a mark of 77 looks too stiff at the moment. (op 5-1)
Millies Dancer(IRE) was outclassed, but is well-related so she can improve on this effort. (op 14-1 tchd 12-1)

4333 SPORTINGBET.COM H'CAP — 6f
7:40 (7:42) (Class 3) (0-90,89) 3-Y-0+ **£7,771** (£2,312; £1,155; £577) **Stalls** Centre

Form RPR

6025 **1** **Lujeanie**[28] 3401 4-9-3 **78**.......................... (p) PhilipRobinson 1 88
(D K Ivory) *a.p: rdn to ld 1f out: r.o* **9/1**

3210 **2** *nk* **Deacon Blues**[16] 3791 3-9-9 **89**.......................... KierenFallon 5 97
(J R Fanshawe) *s.i.s: hld up: hdwy over 1f out: sn rdn and hung lft: hung rt and r.o wl towards fin* **6/4**[1]

0063 **3** *3* **Viking Spirit**[13] 3898 8-9-4 **79**.......................... AdamKirby 4 78
(W R Swinburn) *hld up: racd keenly: rdn over 1f out: r.o to go 3rd nr fin: nt rch ldrs* **15/2**

-000 **4** *1 1/4* **Seamus Shindig**[40] 2992 8-9-1 **83**.......................... AmyScott(7) 7 78
(H Candy) *chsd ldrs: rdn and edgd lft over 1f out: styd on same pce ins fnl f: lost 3rd nr fin* **8/1**

-644 **5** *1* **Spanish Bounty**[14] 3850 5-9-12 **87**.................................... TomQueally 2 79
(J G Portman) *set stdy pce tl qcknd over 2f out: rdn and hdd 1f out: sn edgd rt and no ex* **11/4**[2]

1-44 **6** *shd* **Fantasy Gladiator**[14] 3845 4-8-12 **73**.............................. PatCosgrave 9 65
(R M H Cowell) *dwlt: hdwy over 4f out: rdn and ev ch whn hung lft fr over 1f out: wknd ins fnl f* **6/1**[3]

3406 **7** *3 ¼* **Southandwest (IRE)**[25] 3518 6-8-12 **73**........................ DarryllHolland 8 55
(A M Hales) *w ldr: rdn over 1f out: btn whn hmpd ins fnl f* **25/1**

-005 **8** *3 ¼* **Footstepsofspring (FR)**[32] 3270 3-8-12 **78**.................. TonyCulhane 6 48
(W J Musson) *chsd ldrs tl rdn over 2f out: sn hung lft and wknd* **50/1**

1m 12.06s (-0.44) **Going Correction** +0.075s/f (Good)
WFA 3 from 4yo+ 5lb **8** Ran SP% **119.6**
Speed ratings (Par 107): **105,104,100,98,97 97,93,88**
toteswingers:1&2:£5.20, 1&3:£14.20, 2&3:£1.50 CSF £24.13 CT £113.31 TOTE £12.70: £3.10, £1.10, £1.90; EX 39.80.
Owner K T Ivory **Bred** K T Ivory **Trained** Radlett, Herts
■ Stewards' Enquiry : Philip Robinson two-day ban: careless riding (Aug 6-7)

FOCUS
As one would expect a quicker time in this decent sprint handicap, than the previous two-year-old contest. Ordinary form for the grade.

NOTEBOOK
Lujeanie needs strong handling and had that here in the exprienced Philip Robinson here. His only win on turf came off a 6lb lower mark last August, and he hasn't always enjoyed the best of luck in these ultra-competitive sprint handicaps. He enjoys a fast surface and the handicapper shouldn't be too harsh on him for this, but these races are tough to win. (op 14-1 tchd 8-1)
Deacon Blues started a short-priced favourite here on the back of a good win at Yarmouth on his penultimate start before not enjoying the clearest of passages in a big field of three-year-olds at the July meeting. He could have done with a slightly stronger gallop here, and delivered his challenge when looking to be intimidated by the winner edging towards him inside the final furlong. He couldn't quite reel in Lujeanie after that, but it was a decent effort from a young sprinter still going in the right direction, especially as this ground would have been plenty quick enough for him. (op 11-10 tchd Evens)
Viking Spirit ran one of his better races. He continues to drop in the weights, but it is over two years since he last scored. (op 7-1)
Seamus Shindig gave much his best run of the season. He is now 2lb lower than when winning here last year. He can take a similar race now he's showing more like his old form. (op 15-2 tchd 9-1)
Spanish Bounty was well backed to gain his first win since scoring here at the July meeting three years ago. He had to make his own running here and was swept aside in the final furlong. He gets little respite from the handicapper and will continue to find things tough in these contests. (op 6-1)
Fantasy Gladiator's wins have come on the all-weather. He doesn't always impress with his head carriage and he may have found this ground a bit too quick for him. (tchd 11-2 and 13-2)

4334 SPORTINGBET H'CAP 1m 4f
8:10 (8:13) (Class 3) (0-90,89) 3-Y-O+ **£7,771** (£2,312; £1,155; £577) **Stalls** Centre

Form RPR

2000 **1** **Spirit Is Needed (IRE)**[20] 3672 4-10-0 **89**.....................(b[1]) GregFairley 3 97
(M Johnston) *a.p: chsd ldr 8f out: led over 2f out: sn rdn: styd on* **5/1**[3]

-532 **2** *1* **Sierra Alpha**[44] 2869 3-8-7 **80**.. PhilipRobinson 1 86
(Mrs A J Perrett) *a.p: chsd wnr over 2f out: rdn and edgd rt over 1f out: styd on: saddle slipped* **9/4**[1]

1251 **3** *nk* **Granny McPhee**[13] 3894 4-9-5 **80**...................................... AdamKirby 4 86
(A Bailey) *hld up: hdwy over 2f out: rdn over 1f out: styd on* **12/1**

0-04 **4** *1 ½* **Strategic Mount**[14] 3873 7-9-13 **88**............................ KierenFallon 10 92
(P F I Cole) *stdd s: hld up: hdwy u.p over 1f out: nt rch ldrs* **13/2**

0-60 **5** *¾* **Magicalmysterytour (IRE)**[14] 3873 7-9-9 **84**............. StevieDonohoe 6 86
(W J Musson) *hld up: hdwy over 1f out: nt rch ldrs* **16/1**

1203 **6** *1* **Aurorian (IRE)**[21] 3633 4-9-11 **86**................................. RichardHughes 5 87
(R Hannon) *chsd ldrs: rdn and hung lft over 2f out: no ex fnl f* **5/1**[3]

1111 **7** *6* **Captain John Nixon**[23] 3564 3-8-12 **85**........................ AndreaAtzeni 7 76
(Pat Eddery) *chsd ldr 4f: remained handy: rdn over 1f out: wknd fnl f* **4/1**[2]

231- **8** *3 ¼* **Clear Reef**[206] 7867 6-9-3 **85**.......................................(p) LewisWalsh(7) 2 71
(Jane Chapple-Hyam) *hld up: sme hdwy 2f out: wknd over 1f out* **20/1**

2-62 **9** *9* **Eton Fable (IRE)**[56] 2513 5-9-4 **79**.................................(p) TravisBlock 9 51
(W J H Ratcliffe) *led and sn clr: rdn and hdd over 2f out: wknd over 1f out* **25/1**

2m 31.48s (-1.42) **Going Correction** +0.075s/f (Good)
WFA 3 from 4yo+ 12lb **9** Ran SP% **119.6**
Speed ratings (Par 107): **107,106,106,105,104 103,99,97,91**
toteswingers:1&2:£4.00, 1&3:£17.80, 2&3:£3.90 CSF £17.32 CT £131.60 TOTE £7.90: £2.10, £1.30, £2.70; EX 30.60 Trifecta £235.90 Pool: £414.50 - 1.30 winning units..
Owner Mrs Joan Keaney **Bred** Mrs Joan Keaney **Trained** Middleham Moor, N Yorks

FOCUS
Another race run at muddling gallop, as Eton Fable was allowed a long lead before being reeled in. The winner got back to his early-season form.

NOTEBOOK
Spirit Is Needed(IRE) ground out the win by staying on dourly in his first-time blinkers. He defied a big weight in the process and deserves plenty of credit for this. This was such a vastly different effort in the headgear that one can only attribute the improvement to them. He will go up into the low 90s again now and the blinkers will most likely need to work the oracle again. Official explanation: trainer said, regarding apparent improvement in form, that the gelding appeared to have benefited from the first-time blinkers. (op 8-1)
Sierra Alpha came here as the least experienced of the field, but also on the back of a good run on the all-weather at Kempton. Despite his saddle reportedly slipping, he ran his best race on turf here and looks sure to go one better in the near future. He has form on a slower surface. Official explanation: jockey said saddle slipped (op 11-4 tchd 3-1)
Granny McPhee failed to beat the rise in the weights. She ran another solid race and remains a filly on the upgrade. (op 8-1)
Strategic Mount was the subject of a market move to take advantage of a falling mark. He ran a perfectly respectable race and is knocking on the door. He is 6lb lower than his last winning mark in 2008. (op 7-1 tchd 6-1)
Magicalmysterytour(IRE) is another whose handicap mark is dropping, but he looks to need a little more help from the assessor. (op 14-1)
Aurorian(IRE) was another who attracted market support. He couldn't get competitive and must have disappointed his supporters. (tchd 9-2 and 11-2)
Captain John Nixon has gone up 39lb since his winning run began. He dropped away quickly here and failed to give his running, reportedly losing his action. Official explanation: jockey said colt lost its action (tchd 9-2)
Eton Fable(IRE) was allowed a long lead before being reeled in at the three-furlong marker and ultimately finish well beaten. (op 16-1)

4335 WIN AT SPORTINGBET H'CAP 1m
8:45 (8:46) (Class 5) (0-75,74) 3-Y-O **£3,238** (£963; £481; £240) **Stalls** Centre

Form RPR

-355 **1** **Beaumont's Party (IRE)**[20] 3680 3-9-3 **68**........................ PatCosgrave 9 77
(R Hannon) *hld up: hdwy over 1f out: sn chsng ldr: r.o u.p to ld nr fin* **6/1**

4033 **2** *½* **Gifted Apakay (USA)**[15] 3806 3-9-6 **71**............................ EddieAhern 11 79
(E A L Dunlop) *hld up: hdwy 2f out: rdn to ld over 1f out: edgd lft: hdd nr fin* **12/1**

5004 **3** *1 ¾* **Ishtar Gate (USA)**[31] 3297 3-9-1 **66**............................... DarryllHolland 12 70+
(P F I Cole) *stdd s: hld up: pushed along over 2f out: r.o u.p ins fnl f: nt rch ldrs* **16/1**

0515 **4** *¾* **Yabtree (IRE)**[20] 3676 3-9-6 **71**...................................... SteveDrowne 4 73
(R Charlton) *chsd ldrs: rdn and ev ch over 1f out: styd on same pce ins fnl f* **5/1**[3]

3032 **5** *½* **Queen's Scholar (USA)**[8] 4061 3-8-13 **64**...................(b[1]) GregFairley 1 65
(M Johnston) *led over 6f out: rdn: edgd rt and hdd over 1f out: no ex ins fnl f* **11/4**[1]

5-56 **6** *hd* **Before The War (USA)**[22] 3607 3-9-1 **66**........................ KierenFallon 3 67+
(L M Cumani) *sn pushed along in rr: rdn over 2f out: r.o ins fnl f: nrst fin* **14/1**

-025 **7** *1 ¼* **Hierarch (IRE)**[8] 4056 3-9-7 **72**.................................... RichardHughes 6 70
(R Hannon) *led: hdd over 6f out: chsd ldrs: reminders 1/2-way: no ex fnl f* **7/2**[2]

6422 **8** *½* **Marosh (FR)**[35] 3171 3-9-9 **74**...(p) TomQueally 5 71
(R M H Cowell) *hld up: rdn over 1f out: hung lft ins fnl f: nvr trbld ldrs* **15/2**

6035 **9** *1 ¼* **Charpoy Cobra**[22] 3606 3-8-1 **55** oh2............ Louis-PhilippeBeuzelin(3) 7 49
(J A R Toller) *chsd ldrs: rdn over 2f out: wknd over 1f out* **25/1**

0405 **10** *3* **Prince Of Sorrento**[15] 3831 3-9-1 **66**............................ J-PGuillambert 2 53
(J Akehurst) *prom: rdn over 1f out: wknd ins fnl f* **16/1**

0610 **11** *1* **Nurai**[7] 4119 3-8-4 **55**...(p) AndreaAtzeni 8 40
(P W D'Arcy) *chsd ldrs tl rdn and wknd over 1f out* **25/1**

1m 40.81s (0.81) **Going Correction** +0.075s/f (Good) **11** Ran SP% **125.4**
Speed ratings (Par 100): **98,97,95,95,94 94,93,92,91,88 87**
toteswingers:1&2:£18.50, 1&3:£28.50, 2&3:£24.60 CSF £81.19 CT £783.61 TOTE £8.30: £2.30, £3.40, £5.90; EX 105.60 TRIFECTA Not won. Place 6: £11.31 Place 5: £6.80 .
Owner Thurloe Thoroughbreds XXV **Bred** Mrs Joan Murphy **Trained** East Everleigh, Wilts

FOCUS
Another race run at only a medium gallop. the first two both raced on the outer of the group and the form is ordinary.
Nurai Official explanation: jockey said filly ran too free
T/Plt: £7.80 to a £1 stake. Pool:£53,632.61 - 4,957.63 winning tickets. T/Qpdt: £4.30 to a £1 stake. Pool:£3,555.00 - 604.10 winning tickets. CR

3535 THIRSK (L-H)
Friday, July 23

OFFICIAL GOING: Good (good to firm in places; 9.7)
Wind: Breezy half against Weather: Fine and dry

4336 BRAWBY PARKS MEDIAN AUCTION MAIDEN STKS 5f
1:30 (1:31) (Class 5) 2-Y-O **£3,691** (£1,098; £548; £274) **Stalls** High

Form RPR

32 **1** **Cathedral Spires**[23] 3550 2-9-3 0... TomEaves 4 74
(J Howard Johnson) *led to over 1f out: sn drvn: edgd lft ins fnl f: styd on wl to regain ld cl home* **1/1**[1]

425 **2** *hd* **Ice Trooper**[45] 2832 2-8-12 0....................................... JamesSullivan(5) 1 73
(Mrs L Stubbs) *cl up: rdn to ld over 1f out: kpt on fnl f: hdd cl home* **11/4**[2]

3 *½* **Indieslad** 2-9-3 0... SebSanders 10 71+
(Mrs A Duffield) *prom: effrt and chal on outside over 1f out: sn drvn and rn green: kpt on fnl f: hld nr fin* **6/1**[3]

4 *1 ¾* **Look Who's Kool** 2-9-3 0.. AdrianNicholls 13 65+
(E S McMahon) *in tch: effrt and rdn over 1f out: edgd lft: kpt on same pce ins fnl f* **12/1**

0 **5** *1* **Pineapple Pete (IRE)**[11] 3959 2-9-3 0............................... PaulHanagan 5 61
(P F I Cole) *t.k.h: in tch: effrt 2f out: no ex ins fnl f* **12/1**

53 **6** *7* **Countrywide Flame**[24] 3528 2-9-3 0.............................. PaulMulrennan 11 36
(K A Ryan) *trckd ldrs tl rdn and wknd wl over 1f out* **20/1**

0 **7** *6* **Black Annis Bower**[32] 3274 2-8-12 0................................. DavidAllan 8 10
(M W Easterby) *s.i.s: sn drvn in rr: no ch fr 1/2-way* **125/1**

8 *2* **Littlepromisedland (IRE)** 2-8-12 0............................... PaulEddery 6 —
(R C Guest) *bhd and sn outpcd: nvr on terms* **100/1**

9 *5* **Mrs G** 2-8-12 0.. SilvestreDeSousa 3 —
(R C Guest) *s.i.s: rn green in rr: nvr on terms* **50/1**

59.27 secs (-0.33) **Going Correction** -0.25s/f (Firm) **9** Ran SP% **114.8**
Speed ratings (Par 94): **92,91,90,88,86 75,65,62,54**
Tote swingers:1&2:£1.10, 1&3:£4.90, 2&3:£3.20 CSF £3.68 TOTE £2.00: £1.10, £1.30, £1.90; EX 4.50.
Owner Transcend Bloodstock LLP **Bred** D Curran **Trained** Billy Row, Co Durham

FOCUS
Little depth to this maiden and doubtful the form is anything out of the ordinary, the winner probably not having to improve on previous efforts, though there was promise on debut from the third and fourth.

NOTEBOOK
Cathedral Spires had been placed on his two previous starts, both over 6f, and probably didn't have to step up to get off the mark, rallying after being headed by the runner-up over 1f out. Sprint nurseries will presumably be next up, but he's not an obvious sort to improve much further. (op 6-4)
Ice Trooper matched the form he showed when runner-up at Beverley a couple of starts back, the drop back to the minimum trip as expected suiting this speedy sort, and he should pick up an ordinary maiden somewhere down the line. (op 3-1 tchd 9-4)
Indieslad took the eye as much as any beforehand, being a strong, lengthy individual, and should build on this encouraging first effort. Inexperience is probably all that cost him victory, edging left off the bridle after getting upsides over 1f out. (op 5-1 tchd 13-2)
Look Who's Kool is a half-brother to several winners, including the smart Now Look Here, and made a promising debut, travelling well to halfway and keeping on after running green when first off the bridle. He will improve. (op 9-1)
Pineapple Pete(IRE) stepped up on his debut effort and he could be the type to progress with racing, though he's unlikely to be of real interest until eligible for nurseries. (op 11-1 tchd 14-1)
Black Annis Bower Official explanation: jockey said filly reared as stalls opened

4337 HABTON (S) H'CAP 1m
2:00 (2:02) (Class 6) (0-65,65) 3-Y-O **£2,460** (£732; £365; £182) **Stalls** Low

Form RPR

3000 **1** **Emeralds Spirit (IRE)**[18] 3728 3-7-13 **46** oh1............ KellyHarrison(3) 4 51
(J R Weymes) *t.k.h: cl up: rdn to ld over 1f out: edgd lft: styd on strly fnl f* **50/1**

0000 **2** *2 ½* **Silver Symphony (IRE)**[7] 4098 3-9-7 **65**.............(p) SilvestreDeSousa 9 64
(P F I Cole) *prom: effrt and rdn over 2f out: chsd wnr ins fnl f: r.o* **15/2**[3]

620 **3** *½* **Hail Bold Chief (USA)**[19] 3708 3-9-5 **63**...................... PJMcDonald 13 61
(G A Swinbank) *hld up in tch: hdwy 2f out: styd on fnl f: nrst fin* **12/1**

-400 **4** *shd* **No Quarter (IRE)**[56] [2503] 3-8-10 **54**.......... PhillipMakin 17 52
(M Dods) *midfield: effrt and hdwy wl over 1f out: kpt on fnl f: nvr able to chal* **10/1**

0242 **5** *1 ¼* **Miami Gator (IRE)**[20] [3666] 3-9-6 **64**..........(v) AndrewElliott 15 59+
(J R Weymes) *in tch on outside: rdn and outpcd over 2f out: rallied over 1f out: nvr rchd ldrs* **5/1**[1]

1550 **6** *½* **Hathaway (IRE)**[14] [3852] 3-8-11 **55**.......... PaulMulrennan 5 49
(W M Brisbourne) *midfield: effrt on ins over 2f out: no imp fr over 1f out* **17/2**

3436 **7** *1 ½* **On The Cusp (IRE)**[20] [3680] 3-9-4 **65**..........(p) RobertLButler(3) 12 55+
(P Butler) *hld up on outside: rdn over 2f out: hdwy over 1f out: no imp* **10/1**

0000 **8** *1 ½* **Marsh's Gift**[9] [4017] 3-8-9 **53**.......... PatrickMathers 10 40
(R E Barr) *s.i.s: bhd: rdn over 2f out: sme late hdwy: nvr on terms* **66/1**

-000 **9** *2 ½* **Hot Rod Mamma (IRE)**[19] [3710] 3-7-13 **46** oh1.......... PaulPickard(3) 2 27
(Mrs Dianne Sayer) *led: rdn over 2f out: hdd over 1f out: wknd ent fnl f* **50/1**

0465 **10** *hd* **Scooby Dee**[22] [3597] 3-8-2 **46** oh1..........(p) PaulQuinn 3 26
(R M Whitaker) *trckd ldrs: rdn over 3f out: wknd wl over 1f out* **20/1**

0164 **11** *¾* **Bell's Ocean (USA)**[6] [4133] 3-8-11 **55**.......... PaulHanagan 8 34
(J Ryan) *towards rr: drvn 3f out: nvr on terms* **11/2**[2]

0520 **12** *2 ½* **Rescent**[10] [3975] 3-8-3 **47**..........(p) DuranFentiman 11 20
(Mrs R A Carr) *in tch: rdn over 3f out: wknd fnl 2f* **20/1**

-060 **13** *5* **Forshour**[17] [3758] 3-8-6 **50**..........(b1) AdrianNicholls 6 12
(E S McMahon) *s.i.s: bhd: pushed along over 3f out: nvr on terms* **15/2**[3]

0500 **14** *2 ¼* **Always Dixie (IRE)**[52] [2620] 3-8-4 **48**.......... JoeFanning 16 4
(M Johnston) *bhd on outside: struggling fr 3f out* **22/1**

-144 **15** *4* **Step To It (IRE)**[128] [909] 3-9-2 **60**..........(p) TonyHamilton 18 7
(K A Ryan) *hld up on outside: drvn over 2f out: sn btn* **25/1**

0-36 **16** *6* **Alfalevva**[22] [3597] 3-9-1 **59**.......... SamHitchcott 7 —
(M R Channon) *midfield on ins: rdn over 3f out: btn fnl 2f* **16/1**

5104 **17** *4* **Petrocelli**[39] [2617] 3-8-13 **62**..........(b) JamesSullivan(5) 14 —
(W Storey) *bhd on ins: rdn 1/2-way: btn over 2f out* **40/1**

1m 38.49s (-1.61) **Going Correction** -0.25s/f (Firm) **17** Ran SP% **123.4**
Speed ratings (Par 98): **98,95,95,94,93 93,91,90,87,87 86,84,79,76,72 66,62**
Tote Swingers: 1&2 £69.40, 2&3 £97.90 CSF £372.02 CT £4969.08 TOTE £71.30: £11.00, £1.70, £4.40, £3.10; EX 890.50.There was no bid for the winner.
Owner T A Scothern **Bred** Epona Bloodstock Ltd **Trained** Middleham Moor, N Yorks

FOCUS
Low-grade fare and, typical of many races round here, it paid to race handily, the leaders not coming back despite the gallop being a solid one.
Bell's Ocean(USA) Official explanation: trainer said filly had been struck into
Petrocelli Official explanation: jockey said gelding hung left-handed throughout

4338 E B F DEEPDALE SOLUTIONS MAIDEN FILLIES' STKS 7f
2:35 (2:36) (Class 4) 2-Y-O **£5,666** (£1,686; £842; £420) **Stalls** Low

Form RPR

1 **Bridle Belle** 2-9-0 0.......... PaulHanagan 1 81+
(R A Fahey) *prom: jinked rt after 3f: effrt whn n.m.r over 2f out: plld out over 1f out: led wl ins fnl f: comf* **4/1**[2]

03 **2** *2* **Regal Kiss**[10] [3991] 2-9-0 0.......... JoeFanning 3 74
(M Johnston) *led 1f: pressed ldr: rdn and regained ld 1f out: hdd and no ex wl ins fnl f* **9/1**

243 **3** *2* **Jetfire**[23] [3562] 2-9-0 0.......... SilvestreDeSousa 5 69
(P F I Cole) *led after 1f: rdn over 2f out: hdd 1f out: no ex* **6/4**[1]

5 **4** *2 ¾* **Soie De Chine**[9] [4021] 2-9-0 0.......... SebSanders 7 65+
(Sir Mark Prescott) *dwlt: hld up: shkn up over 2f out: styd on fnl f: nvr nr ldrs* **5/1**[3]

0 **5** *½* **Kalleidoscope**[65] [2223] 2-9-0 0.......... SamHitchcott 8 61
(M R Channon) *trckd ldrs: rdn 3f out: wknd over 1f out* **12/1**

0 **6** *1* **Indian Wish (USA)**[37] [3082] 2-9-0 0.......... PhillipMakin 10 58
(M L W Bell) *hld up: effrt on outside 3f out: hung lft and wknd over 1f out* **5/1**[3]

00 **7** *4 ½* **Run Daisy Run**[7] [4095] 2-8-9 0.......... JamesSullivan(5) 4 48
(B J Meehan) *t.k.h: hld up: checked after 3f: sn rdn: wknd fnl 2f* **66/1**

8 *6* **Sokolka** 2-9-0 0.......... DavidAllan 9 32
(T D Easterby) *s.i.s: bhd and outpcd: no ch fr 1/2-way* **33/1**

04 **9** *1* **Cool In The Shade**[33] [3237] 2-9-0 0.......... MickyFenton 2 30
(P T Midgley) *trckd ldrs: rdn and hung lft over 2f out: wknd wl over 1f out* **66/1**

10 *62* **Cootehill Lass (IRE)** 2-9-0 0.......... PaddyAspell 6 —
(G A Harker) *s.i.s: bhd and outpcd: nvr on terms* **100/1**

1m 25.75s (-1.45) **Going Correction** -0.25s/f (Firm) **10** Ran SP% **117.9**
Speed ratings (Par 93): **98,95,93,90,89 88,83,76,75,4**
Tote Swingers: 1&2 £6.50, 1&3 £1.30, 2&3 £2.90 CSF £39.48 TOTE £4.50: £1.90, £2.40, £1.10; EX 35.30.
Owner Mrs H Steel **Bred** Mrs C R Philipson & Mrs H G Lascelles **Trained** Musley Bank, N Yorks

FOCUS
A fair maiden.

NOTEBOOK
Bridle Belle achieved quite a pretty useful level at the first time of asking. A close-coupled daughter of Dansili, she showed signs of greenness through the race, but picked up well to win going away in the end and is sure to improve and win more races. (op 13-2 tchd 7-2)
Regal Kiss won't always run into one of the winner's potential in ordinary maidens and is likely to go one better before long. She's improved with each start so far and, in excellent hands, there's a good chance there'll be more to come. (op 6-1 tchd 11-2)
Jetfire has made the frame in all four starts, this her first on turf, but is starting to look exposed already and is always likely to be vulnerable to improvers in maidens, while it's hard to see her being good enough in nurseries off a mark of 82. (op 9-4)
Soie De Chine wasn't subjected to an unduly hard time as she kept on from off the pace and has shown promise in both her starts. There's certainly more to come from her. (op 13-2 tchd 7-1)
Kalleidoscope faded in the end, but has plenty of size about her and looks the sort who'll progress with racing. Nurseries will be an option for her after another run. (op 11-1 tchd 9-1)
Indian Wish(USA) failed to build on her debut switched to turf, but it's clearly still early days. (op 7-2)
Run Daisy Run has yet to achieve much in three starts, but being quite badly hampered before halfway clearly didn't help and she can't get much of a mark for nurseries. (op 100-1)
Sokolka was too green to do herself justice at the first time of asking and looks more of a long-term project. (op 28-1)
Cootehill Lass(IRE) Official explanation: jockey said he was unable to ride the filly as he suffered an ankle during the race

4339 SKY BET SUPPORTING THEYORKSHIRE SUMMER RACING FESTIVAL MAIDEN STKS (DIV I) 7f
3:10 (3:10) (Class 5) 3-Y-O+ **£3,367** (£1,002; £500; £250) **Stalls** Low

Form RPR

5-22 **1** **Touch Tone**[60] [2393] 3-8-12 72.......... RobertWinston 10 83
(B W Hills) *trckd ldrs: hdwy to chse ldr 3f out: chal 2f out: rdn to ld appr fnl f: drvn and edgd rt last 100yds: hld on wl* **11/4**[1]

06 **2** *hd* **Fork Lightning (USA)**[48] [2755] 3-8-12 0.......... SebSanders 11 82+
(Sir Mark Prescott) *in tch: hdwy 3f out: rdn to chse ldng pair over 1f out: drvn and styd on wl fnl f: jst hld* **14/1**

3253 **3** *½* **Nimue (USA)**[21] [3620] 3-8-12 73.......... SilvestreDeSousa 5 81
(P F I Cole) *led: pushed clr 3f out: rdn 2f out: drvn and hdd over 1f out: kpt on wl u.p fnl f* **13/2**[3]

2332 **4** *5* **Raqeeb (USA)**[21] [3612] 3-8-12 79..........(v) JamesSullivan(5) 13 73
(Mrs R A Carr) *in tch: hdwy to chse ldrs 1/2-way: rdn along over 2f out: sn drvn and kpt on same pce* **7/2**[2]

23- **5** *5* **Barreq (USA)**[217] [7800] 3-9-3 0.......... RoystonFfrench 7 59
(B Smart) *dwlt and towards rr: pushed along and hdwy 3f out: rdn over 2f out: kpt on fnl f* **11/1**

3 **6** *hd* **Swiftly Done (IRE)**[22] [3587] 3-9-3 0.......... DavidNolan 2 59
(D Carroll) *s.i.s and bhd: hdwy 3f out: rdn 2f out: styd on ins fnl f* **40/1**

7 *shd* **Ardent** 3-8-12 0.......... NickyMackay 3 53
(J H M Gosden) *trckd ldrs: hdwy to chse ldr 1/2-way: rdn along wl over 2f out: sn edgd rt and wknd* **11/4**[1]

8 *2 ¾* **Barton Bounty** 3-9-3 0.......... TonyHamilton 4 51
(P D Niven) *a towards rr* **100/1**

9 *4* **The Chester Giant** 3-8-12 0.......... StephenCraine 9 35
(Patrick Morris) *s.i.s: a in rr* **100/1**

0-6 **10** *1 ½* **Stargazing (IRE)**[35] [3157] 4-9-5 0.......... PaulHanagan 6 31
(B J Meehan) *prom: rdn along wl over 2f out: sn wknd* **22/1**

11 *6* **Premier Contender (IRE)** 3-9-3 0.......... AdrianNicholls 8 20
(D Nicholls) *towards rr: hdwy and in tch 1/2-way: rdn wl over 2f out and sn wknd* **25/1**

12 *6* **Grey Crystal** 4-8-12 0.......... JohnCavanagh(7) 1 —
(M Brittain) *s.i.s: a bhd* **100/1**

1m 24.64s (-2.56) **Going Correction** -0.25s/f (Firm)
WFA 3 from 4yo 7lb **12** Ran SP% **117.5**
Speed ratings (Par 103): **104,103,103,97,91 91,91,88,83,82 75,68**
Tote Swingers: 1&2 £9.10, 1&3 £5.00, 2&3 £17.80 CSF £41.13 TOTE £4.20: £1.60, £3.80, £2.00; EX 56.80.
Owner K Abdulla **Bred** Juddmonte Farms Ltd **Trained** Lambourn, Berks

FOCUS
A fair level of form in this maiden, the first and third both rated in the low 70s coming into it.

4340 SKY BET SUPPORTING THEYORKSHIRE SUMMER RACING FESTIVAL MAIDEN STKS (DIV II) 7f
3:45 (3:49) (Class 5) 3-Y-O+ **£3,367** (£1,002; £500; £250) **Stalls** Low

Form RPR

235- **1** **Ghost (IRE)**[302] [6231] 3-9-3 82.......... RobertWinston 13 81
(B W Hills) *taken early to post: t.k.h: mde all: clr 2f out: hld on wl fnl f* **3/1**[2]

2 *1* **Calipatria** 3-8-12 0.......... NickyMackay 4 73+
(J H M Gosden) *bhd and rn green: plenty to do over 2f out: gd hdwy over 1f out: chsd wnr ins fnl f: kpt on: nt pce to chal* **5/2**[1]

3 **3** *4* **Shethoughtshewas (IRE)**[28] [3407] 3-8-12 0.......... PJMcDonald 5 63
(G A Swinbank) *in tch: hdwy to chse wnr over 1f out to ins fnl f: sn outpcd* **4/1**[3]

4 *¾* **Crimson Empire (USA)** 3-8-12 0.......... RichardMullen 10 60+
(B Smart) *s.i.s: bhd and pushed along 1/2-way: hdwy over 1f out: nvr able to chal* **14/1**

44 **5** *2 ½* **Spread Boy (IRE)**[9] [4018] 3-8-12 0.......... MarkCoumbe(5) 1 59
(A Berry) *prom: rdn and edgd lft 2f out: sn outpcd* **28/1**

5- **6** *6* **Billionaire Boy (IRE)**[296] [6381] 3-9-3 0.......... StephenCraine 12 43
(Patrick Morris) *dwlt: sn prom: rdn and wknd fr 2f out* **50/1**

7 *2* **Spanish Island (USA)** 3-9-3 0.......... PaulHanagan 3 37+
(M A Magnusson) *t.k.h: sn prom: hmpd and lost pl after 3f: sn struggling: styd on fnl f: nvr on terms* **9/2**

00 **8** *3* **Gower Diva**[83] [1685] 3-8-12 0.......... AdrianNicholls 11 24
(D Nicholls) *chsd wnr: rdn over 2f out: wknd over 1f out* **10/1**

0- **9** *3 ¾* **Champagne All Day**[280] [6823] 4-9-7 0.......... MichaelStainton(3) 2 19
(S P Griffiths) *bhd on ins: struggling over 3f out: nvr on terms* **125/1**

0 **10** *27* **The Nifty Belle**[18] [3733] 4-9-5 0.......... PatrickMathers 8 —
(N Wilson) *trckd ldrs tl wknd qckly 1/2-way: t.o* **200/1**

000 **11** *28* **Hannah Hawk**[34] [3207] 3-8-9 37.......... AshleyHamblett(3) 7 —
(Lucinda Featherstone) *bhd: struggling fr 1/2-way: t.o* **125/1**

1m 26.64s (-0.56) **Going Correction** -0.25s/f (Firm)
WFA 3 from 4yo 7lb **11** Ran SP% **115.0**
Speed ratings (Par 103): **93,91,87,86,83 76,74,71,66,35 3**
Tote Swingers: 1&2 £2.60, 1&3 £1.40, 2&3 £3.80 CSF £10.56 TOTE £3.80: £1.40, £1.50, £2.10; EX 11.30.
Owner The Mystic Mogg Partnership **Bred** Mountarmstrong Stud **Trained** Lambourn, Berks
■ Stewards' Enquiry : Robert Winston two-day ban: careless riding (Aug 6-7)
Paul Mulrennan two-day ban: improper riding, jabbed filly in mouth at start (Aug 6-7)

FOCUS
Very little depth to this maiden.
Spanish Island(USA) Official explanation: jockey said colt failed to handle the bend
The Nifty Belle Official explanation: jockey said filly lost its action

4341 STANLAND H'CAP 1m 4f
4:20 (4:21) (Class 4) (0-80,79) 3-Y-O **£4,766** (£1,418; £708; £354) **Stalls** Low

Form RPR

2432 **1** **Baltimore Clipper (USA)**[15] [3820] 3-9-3 **75**.......... TomEaves 5 84
(P F I Cole) *hld up: rdn over 3f out: hdwy over 2f out: led ent fnl f: styd on wl* **7/1**

22-5 **2** *¾* **Nave (USA)**[106] [1189] 3-9-0 **72**.......... JoeFanning 3 80
(M Johnston) *prom: effrt over 2f out: sn rdn: chsd wnr ins fnl f: r.o* **10/1**

24-3 **3** *¾* **Giants Play (USA)**[71] [2050] 3-9-5 **77**.......... RichardMullen 6 84
(Sir Michael Stoute) *trckd ldrs: rdn to ld 2f out: hdd ent fnl f: kpt on same pce* **6/4**[1]

5520 **4** *6* **Hail Tiberius**[46] [2816] 3-9-6 **77**.......... PaulHanagan 1 74
(T D Walford) *t.k.h: hld up: rdn and effrt over 2f out: kpt on fnl f: no ch w first three* **14/1**

3304 **5** *¾* **Wild Rose**[36] [3123] 3-9-6 **78**.......... PhillipMakin 2 74
(M L W Bell) *disp ld to 2f out: sn rdn and wknd* **6/1**[3]

01-5 **6** *2 ½* **Tamanaco (IRE)**[100] 1297 3-9-5 **77** .... DuranFentiman 9 69
(T D Walford) *disp ld to 2f out: sn struggling* **33/1**

5323 **7** *2 ½* **Tut (IRE)**[20] 3679 3-9-7 **79** .... AndrewElliott 4 67
(J R Weymes) *hld up in tch: struggling over 3f out: sn btn* **15/2**

044 **8** *12* **Rio Tinto**[26] 3477 3-9-1 **73** .... AhmedAjtebi 8 42
(Mahmood Al Zarooni) *t.k.h: trckd ldrs: faltered over 4f out: sn rdn: wknd fr over 3f out* **5/1**[2]

2m 33.78s (-2.42) **Going Correction** -0.25s/f (Firm) 8 Ran SP% **113.9**
Speed ratings (Par 102): **98,97,97,93,92 90,89,81**
Tote Swingers: 1&2 £7.70, 1&3 £3.50, 2&3 £4.00 CSF £72.58 CT £158.67 TOTE £7.30: £1.40, £2.70, £1.50; EX 60.00.
Owner Meyrick & Dunnington-Jefferson **Bred** Timothy Byrnes & Leah Byrnes **Trained** Whatcombe, Oxon

FOCUS
Fairly useful efforts from the first three who deserve some credit for pulling clear of the rest, particularly as the gallop was no more than a modest one for the most part.
Rio Tinto Official explanation: jockey said colt stumbled on bend leaving back straight

4342 WELCOME TO YORKSHIRE HOLE IN ONE FILLIES' H'CAP 6f
4:55 (4:55) (Class 5) (0-70,70) 3-Y-0+ **£3,691** (£1,098; £548; £274) **Stalls High**

Form RPR

3554 **1** **Flouncing (IRE)**[17] 3751 3-9-10 **67** .... PaulHanagan 15 77
(W J Haggas) *trckd ldrs: hdwy on inner over 2f out: rdn to ld wl over 1f out: kpt on* **7/2**[2]

2032 **2** *1* **Albero Di Giuda (IRE)**[2] 4244 5-9-1 **53** ....(bt) LeeVickers 14 61
(F Sheridan) *t.k.h: trckd ldrs: effrt 2f out and sn edgd lft: n.m.r wl over 1f out: rdn and styd on to chse wnr ins fnl f* **7/2**[2]

6604 **3** *3 ¾* **Clumber Place**[14] 3854 4-9-1 **53** .... PaulEddery 2 49
(R C Guest) *a.p on wd outside: rdn over 2f out: drvn wl over 1f out: kpt on same pce fnl f* **8/1**

-235 **4** *nk* **Shaluca**[14] 3866 3-9-10 **67** .... AdrianNicholls 5 61+
(E S McMahon) *hld up towards rr: hdwy over 2f out: sn rdn and kpt on ins fnl f* **5/1**[3]

2250 **5** *1 ¼* **Darcy's Pride (IRE)**[10] 3976 6-9-2 **54** .... TonyHamilton 11 45
(P T Midgley) *dwlt and in rr: rdn along 1/2-way: kpt on fnl 2f: nt rch ldrs* **25/1**

52-0 **6** *2 ¾* **Alacity (IRE)**[14] 3879 4-9-5 **57** .... DanielTudhope 10 39
(N Bycroft) *dwlt and in rr: hdwy 1/2-way: swtchd lft to outer 2f out and sn chsng ldrs: rdn and one pce fr over 1f out* **50/1**

6121 **7** *½* **Revue Princess (IRE)**[8] 4064 5-10-0 **66** 6ex ....(b) DavidAllan 12 46
(T D Easterby) *prom: hdwy and cl up 1/2-way: rdn to ld briefly 2f out: sn hdd and drvn: wknd appr fnl f* **3/1**[1]

50-0 **8** *3 ½* **Kookie**[74] 1966 3-8-5 **48** .... PatrickMathers 9 16
(R E Barr) *s.i.s: a in rr* **66/1**

0-00 **9** *1* **Ensign's Trick**[41] 2965 6-8-4 **45** .... PaulPickard(3) 16 11
(W M Brisbourne) *led: rdn along 1/2-way: edgd lft and hdd 2f out: sn wknd* **25/1**

-555 **10** *nk* **Real Diamond**[49] 2699 4-9-11 **63** .... TomEaves 4 28
(Ollie Pears) *cl up: rdn along over 2f out: wkng whn n.m.r wl over 1f out* **22/1**

3305 **11** *2 ½* **Pure Nostalgia (IRE)**[20] 3668 3-9-6 **63** .... PaulMulrennan 8 19
(J Howard Johnson) *cl up: rdn along 1/2-way: drvn over 2f out and sn wknd* **25/1**

1m 11.1s (-1.60) **Going Correction** -0.25s/f (Firm)
WFA 3 from 4yo+ 5lb 11 Ran SP% **116.6**
Speed ratings (Par 100): **100,98,93,93,91 87,87,82,81,80 77**
Tote Swingers: 1&2 £4.20, 1&3 £7.10, 2&3 £6.00 CSF £14.67 CT £92.38 TOTE £5.70: £1.70, £2.20, £3.10; EX 22.10.
Owner Goddard, Hamer & Hawkes **Bred** Mrs Noelle Walsh **Trained** Newmarket, Suffolk

FOCUS
They finished quite well strung out here for a sprint handicap, the first two pulling clear. The field remained in one group towards the near rail and a high draw was an advantage.

4343 YORKSHIRE POST COMPETITION WINNER "HANDS AND HEELS" APPRENTICE SERIES H'CAP 5f
5:30 (5:31) (Class 5) (0-75,72) 3-Y-0+ **£3,691** (£1,098; £548; £274) **Stalls High**

Form RPR

6146 **1** **Poppy's Rose**[21] 3622 6-9-5 **69** .... IanBurns(5) 7 78
(T J Etherington) *bhd: gd hdwy over 1f out: led ins fnl f: comf* **4/1**[2]

1346 **2** *1 ¾* **Simple Rhythm**[13] 3908 4-9-1 **65** .... JoshCrane(5) 5 68+
(J Ryan) *chsd ldrs: rdn whn bmpd over 1f out: styd on to go 2nd wl ins fnl f: nt rchd wnr* **20/1**

0063 **3** *1 ½* **King Of Swords (IRE)**[13] 3908 6-8-7 **55** ....(p) NoraLooby(3) 6 52
(N Tinkler) *bhd: effrt whn nt clr run and swtchd rt wl over 1f out: r.o fnl f: nrst fin* **9/2**[3]

0100 **4** *nk* **Bosun Breese**[13] 3902 5-9-10 **72** .... AnthonyBetts(3) 4 68
(T D Barron) *prom: effrt on outside 2f out: kpt on same pce fnl f* **20/1**

6252 **5** *shd* **Speedy Senorita (IRE)**[11] 3946 5-9-1 **63** .... ShaneBKelly(3) 9 59
(J J Quinn) *w ldrs: led 1/2-way to ins fnl f: one pce* **7/1**

0301 **6** *½* **Blessed Place**[7] 4099 10-8-5 **52** 6ex .... LucyBarry(3) 2 47
(D J S Ffrench Davis) *led to 1/2-way: ev ch tl no ex ins fnl f* **17/2**

3133 **7** *2* **Jigajig**[15] 3834 3-9-8 **71** ....(p) JulieBurke 10 58+
(K A Ryan) *w ldrs: rdn whn hung lft, faltered and nrly uns rdr over 1f out: nt rcvr* **5/2**[1]

0065 **8** *1 ¾* **Lord Of The Reins (IRE)**[13] 3908 6-9-2 **64** .... SophieSilvester(3) 3 45
(J G Given) *dwlt: sn wl bhd: sme late hdwy: nvr on terms* **16/1**

58.34 secs (-1.26) **Going Correction** -0.25s/f (Firm)
WFA 3 from 4yo+ 4lb 8 Ran SP% **105.2**
Speed ratings (Par 103): **100,97,94,94,94 93,90,87**
Tote Swingers: 1&2 £12.20, 1&3 £3.10, 2&3 £10.50 CSF £63.55 CT £269.71 TOTE £4.30: £1.70, £6.10, £1.70; EX 73.80 Place 6: £21.16 Place 5: £18.77 .
Owner Mrs Ann Morris **Bred** Mrs A Morris **Trained** Norton, N Yorks
■ Angelo Poliziano (7/1) was withdrawn after breaking out of the stalls. Deduct 10p in the £ under R4.

FOCUS
A run-of-the-mill hands and heels apprentice event. They shunned the rail, the action unfolding more towards the centre.
Jigajig Official explanation: jockey said gelding lost its action
T/Plt: £27.30 to a £1 stake. Pool:£46,731.90 - 1,247.25 winning tickets T/Qpdt: £2.40 to a £1 stake. Pool:£3,515.27 - 1,068.53 winning tickets RY

3919 YORK (L-H)
Friday, July 23

OFFICIAL GOING: Good (7.6)
Rail realignment added about 8yds to races of one mile and over.
Wind: Light across Weather: Fine and dry

4344 FUTURE CLEANING SERVICES APPRENTICE STKS (H'CAP) 1m
6:00 (6:01) (Class 5) (0-70,70) 3-Y-0 **£4,533** (£1,348; £674; £336) **Stalls Low**

Form RPR

6003 **1** **Zambuka (FR)**[8] 4061 3-8-5 **54** oh6 ow3 .... RossAtkinson(3) 14 68
(F J Brennan) *in tch: hdwy over 3f out: led 2f out: rdn clr over 1f out: kpt on* **33/1**

2051 **2** *3* **Luv U Noo**[10] 3975 3-8-10 **61** 6ex .... DaleSwift(5) 11 68
(B Ellison) *hld up towards rr: hdwy on outer 3f out: rdn to chse ldrs 2f out: drvn and kpt on ins fnl f* **6/1**[3]

0030 **3** *¾* **Wild Rockette**[20] 3680 3-9-8 **68** ....(b) AshleyHamblett 12 73
(B J Meehan) *hld up towards rr: hdwy on outer 3f out: rdn to chse ldrs over 1f out: drvn and kpt on ins fnl f* **14/1**

3-00 **4** *4 ½* **Kenyan Cat**[20] 3677 3-9-2 **65** .... MatthewDavies(3) 2 65+
(George Baker) *midfield: hdwy and in tch 1/2-way: effrt and nt clr run 2f out and over 1f out: swtchd rt ent fnl f and styd on wl towards fin* **20/1**

3354 **5** *3 ¾* **Mason Hindmarsh**[13] 3905 3-9-1 **64** ....(p) JamesSullivan(3) 9 50
(Karen McLintock) *led: rdn along over 3f out: drvn and hdd 2f out: grad wknd* **10/1**

-563 **6** *nse* **Sadler's Mark**[17] 3750 3-8-13 **64** .... CharlesEddery(5) 15 50
(T P Tate) *prom on outer: rdn along over 3f out: drvn 2f out and grad wknd* **9/1**

2001 **7** *½* **Choc'A'Moca (IRE)**[25] 3501 3-7-13 **52** ....(v) NeilFarley(7) 6 37
(D Carroll) *t.k.h: chsd ldrs on inner: rdn along 3f out: drvn 2f out and grad wknd* **12/1**

055 **8** *1* **Hairy Maclary**[18] 3733 3-8-8 **57** .... LanceBetts(3) 10 40
(T D Easterby) *trckd ldr: effrt and cl up 1/2-way: rdn to chal 3f out: drvn 2f out: grad wknd* **28/1**

00-2 **9** *¾* **Hayek**[9] 4025 3-9-0 **65** .... AdamBeschizza(5) 1 46
(W Jarvis) *in rr: pushed along and sme hdwy on inner 3f out: rdn 2f out and n.d* **3/1**[1]

-405 **10** *2 ½* **Banana Republic (IRE)**[28] 3414 3-9-4 **69** .... DuilioDaSilva(5) 8 44
(P F I Cole) *chsd ldrs: rdn along over 3f out: sn wknd* **18/1**

6544 **11** *5* **Battle Study (IRE)**[10] 3975 3-8-10 **59** ....(b) DeclanCannon(3) 5 23
(A J McCabe) *a in rr* **25/1**

0-40 **12** *1 ¾* **Baraconti (IRE)**[43] 2886 3-9-1 **66** .... LeeTopliss(5) 7 26
(R A Fahey) *a in rr* **9/1**

5266 **13** *¾* **Osgood**[14] 3863 3-9-7 **70** .... AshleyMorgan(3) 3 28
(M R Channon) *a in rr* **5/1**[2]

0033 **14** *¾* **Monsieur Pontaven**[25] 3501 3-8-0 **51** oh3 .... MatthewLawson(5) 13 7
(R Bastiman) *s.i.s and in rr: hdwy on wd outside 3f out: rdn and in tch over 2f out: sn wknd* **20/1**

1m 39.3s (0.50) **Going Correction** +0.075s/f (Good) 14 Ran SP% **124.4**
Speed ratings (Par 100): **100,97,96,91,88 87,87,86,85,83 78,76,75,74**
Tote Swingers: 1&2 £84.60, 1&3 £93.20, 2&3 £22.00 CSF £216.38 CT £1911.57 TOTE £42.30: £9.50, £2.50, £4.30; EX 436.70.
Owner Ms M J Hughes **Bred** Pierre Talvard & Patrick Barbe **Trained** Lambourn, Berks

FOCUS
Some unexposed types for this 51-70 apprentice handicap which was run at a very sound pace and the first three pulled well clear. None of the first four home had anything to do with the early gallop. The well in favourite disappointed abd there was a surprise winner, but it looked no fluke.
Hayek Official explanation: jockey said gelding ran flat

4345 SEDDON PROPERTY SERVICES STKS (H'CAP) 6f
6:30 (6:31) (Class 4) (0-80,80) 4-Y-0+ **£5,180** (£1,541; £770; £384) **Stalls Low**

Form RPR

4160 **1** **La Zamora**[15] 3830 4-9-4 **77** .... RyanMoore 3 89
(T D Barron) *prom: effrt and cl up 2f out: rdn to ld ent fnl f: sn edgd rt: drvn out* **16/1**

3323 **2** *1 ½* **Tyfos**[15] 3815 5-9-4 **77** .... JoeFanning 5 84
(B P J Baugh) *led: rdn along 2f out: drvn and hdd ent fnl f: kpt on* **4/1**[2]

4111 **3** *hd* **King Of Eden (IRE)**[22] 3584 4-9-4 **77** .... MickyFenton 1 84
(E J Alston) *chsd ldrs on outer: hdwy 2f out: rdn over 1f out: drvn and kpt on ins fnl f* **9/4**[1]

3560 **4** *½* **Floor Show**[41] 2982 4-9-5 **78** .... PaulMulrennan 10 83
(N Wilson) *dwlt: towards rr whn sltly hmpd after 1f and sn swtchd lft: hdwy 2f out: rdn wl over 1f out: styd on ins fnl f* **7/1**[3]

2012 **5** *½* **Brierty (IRE)**[7] 4090 4-9-0 **80** .... NeilFarley(7) 8 83
(D Carroll) *in tch: hdwy wl over 1f out: rdn to chse ldrs whn nt much froom ins fnl f: kpt on* **8/1**

6223 **6** *nk* **Green Park (IRE)**[7] 4118 7-9-5 **78** ....(be) DavidNolan 11 80
(D Carroll) *in tch: hdwy to chse ldrs 2f out: rdn over 1f out: kpt on same pce ins fnl f* **14/1**

-600 **7** *1* **Turnkey**[4] 4192 8-9-4 **77** .... AdrianNicholls 12 76
(D Nicholls) *towards rr and reminders after 1f: hdwy on wd outside to chse ldrs over 2f out: sn rdn and wknd over 1f out* **11/1**

20-0 **8** *2 ¼* **Sea Rover (IRE)**[46] 2817 6-8-5 **64** .... RichardMullen 2 56
(M Brittain) *prom: rdn along over 2f out: grad wknd* **25/1**

4026 **9** *nk* **Mandalay King (IRE)**[14] 3876 5-8-4 **68** .... IanBrennan(5) 9 59
(Mrs Marjorie Fife) *s.i.s and bhd: rdn along 1/2-way: sme late hdwy* **15/2**

1060 **10** *¾* **Top Bid**[8] 4063 6-8-6 **68** .... KellyHarrison(3) 14 57
(T D Easterby) *v.s.a and lost many l s: a bhd* **33/1**

0014 **11** *3 ¾* **Lucy Brown**[13] 3914 4-8-13 **72** .... PhillipMakin 13 49
(M W Easterby) *a towards rr: pushed along 1/2-way: rdn and hung lft wl over 1f out* **20/1**

0536 **12** *3 ½* **Coleorton Choice**[22] 3584 4-9-6 **79** ....(p) RobertWinston 6 44
(R Hollinshead) *cl up: rdn along over 2f out: sn wknd* **16/1**

1m 11.32s (-0.58) **Going Correction** -0.025s/f (Good) 12 Ran SP% **124.5**
Speed ratings (Par 105): **102,100,99,99,98 98,96,93,93,92 87,82**
Tote Swingers: 1&2 £19.20, 1&3 £15.90, 2&3 £3.70 CSF £81.32 CT £201.76 TOTE £20.50: £4.90, £2.10, £1.70; EX 214.00.
Owner J G Brown **Bred** Miss S J Smith **Trained** Maunby, N Yorks

FOCUS
A competitive 61-80 handicap run at a sound pace and it proved hard to make ground from off the pace. A small personal best from the winner.
La Zamora Official explanation: trainer said, regarding apparent improvement in form, that the filly was unreliable who has come good recently.

Top Bid Official explanation: jockey said gelding missed the break

4346 CO-OPERATIVE GOOD WITH FOOD MEDIAN AUCTION MAIDEN STKS 7f

7:00 (7:02) (Class 4) 2-Y-O £5,180 (£1,541; £770; £384) **Stalls** Low

Form RPR

1 **Samurai Sword** 2-9-3 0 AhmedAjtebi 5 79+
(Mahmood Al Zarooni) *t.k.h: prom: hdwy to ld 3f out: rdn and edgd rt over 1f out: drvn ins fnl f: kpt on wl towards fin* **13/2**[3]

54 2 ½ **Diamond Penny (IRE)**[15] 3832 2-9-3 0 FrankieDettori 12 78
(P F I Cole) *cl up on wd outside: effrt to chal 2f out: rdn and edgd lft over 1f out: ev ch tl drvn ins fnl f and nt qckn last 50yds* **10/1**

32 3 ¾ **King Of The Celts (IRE)**[14] 3874 2-9-3 0 DavidAllan 7 76
(T D Easterby) *hld up towards rr: hdwy 1/2-way: rdn to chse ldng pair over 1f out: kpt on wl fnl f* **7/2**[2]

60 4 1 ½ **Early Applause**[55] 2547 2-9-3 0 RobertWinston 3 72
(B W Hills) *dwlt: sn in tch: hdwy 2f out: rdn over 1f out: kpt on u.p fnl f* **16/1**

4 5 2 ¾ **Swift Alhaarth (IRE)**[35] 3162 2-9-3 0 JoeFanning 10 65
(M Johnston) *dwlt: sn chsng ldrs: pushed along 3f out: rdn: green and edgd lft 2f out: kpt on same pce* **12/1**

3 6 5 **Muzdahi (USA)**[35] 3169 2-9-3 0 RichardHills 8 53
(J L Dunlop) *prom: effrt and cl up over 2f out: rdn whn n.m.r over 1f out: sn wknd* **5/2**[1]

62 7 3 ¾ **Cotton Spirit**[30] 3316 2-9-3 0 PaulHanagan 6 44
(R A Fahey) *chsd ldrs: pushed along 1/2-way: sn rdn and wknd* **7/1**

0 8 ½ **Mayan Flight (IRE)**[27] 3449 2-9-0 0 MichaelStainton(3) 1 42
(R M Whitaker) *led: rdn along 4f out: hdd 3f out: sn drvn and wknd* **50/1**

4 9 ½ **Ice Magic**[52] 2621 2-9-3 0 RyanMoore 9 41
(M H Tompkins) *towards rr: rdn along bef 1/2-way: sn outpcd and bhd fnl 2f* **15/2**

05 10 ¾ **My Mate Jake (IRE)**[21] 3624 2-9-3 0 PaulMulrennan 4 39
(J G Given) *cl up: rdn along 1/2-way: sn drvn and wknd* **12/1**

11 *hd* **Tapis Libre** 2-8-12 0 JamesSullivan(5) 11 39
(M W Easterby) *sn outpcd and a bhd* **100/1**

00 12 6 **Kings Arms**[14] 3874 2-8-10 0 DavidSimmonson(7) 2 24
(M W Easterby) *a in rr: rdn along bef 1/2-way: sn outpcd and bhd* **100/1**

1m 25.98s (0.68) **Going Correction** -0.025s/f (Good) 12 Ran SP% **122.7**
Speed ratings (Par 96): **95,94,93,91,88 83,78,78,77,76 76,69**
Tote Swingers: 1&2 £7.00, 1&3 £2.90, 2&3 £7.10 CSF £72.48 TOTE £8.50: £2.40, £3.20, £1.30; EX 85.50.
Owner Godolphin **Bred** Darley **Trained** Newmarket, Suffolk

FOCUS
An interesting maiden with plenty of top stables represented. It was run at an even pace. A nice start from the winner and the third helps with the level.

NOTEBOOK
Samurai Sword made a very pleasing debut. Always racing up with the pace, he can go on from this and should stay further in due course. (op 8-1)
Diamond Penny(IRE), having his third start, appears to be going the right way and should have little trouble going one better in similar company shortly; he can also go down the nursery route. (op 8-1)
King Of The Celts(IRE) has shown a similar level of ability on all three starts. He can lose his maiden tag this term, but should make up into a better three-year-old, if looks are to be believed. (op 9-2)
Early Applause has a good pedigree and can make his mark in due course for a yard going well. (op 12-1)
Swift Alhaarth(IRE) put up a better effort and appears to be going the right way. (op 16-1)
Muzdahi(USA) was disappointing and failed to confirm the promise of his Newmarket debut over this extra furlong. (op 11-4 tchd 3-1)
Cotton Spirit, withdrawn last time out after getting restless in the stalls, was ridden at halfway and never threatened to land a blow. Whether he found the ground on the fast side, only time will tell. (tchd 13-2)

4347 EUROPEAN BREEDERS' FUND LYRIC STKS (LISTED RACE) (F&M) 1m 2f 88y

7:30 (7:30) (Class 1) 3-Y-O+

£22,708 (£8,608; £4,308; £2,148; £1,076; £540) **Stalls** Low

Form RPR

4-31 1 **Nouriya**[43] 2890 3-8-8 95 RyanMoore 1 105+
(Sir Michael Stoute) *sn trcking ldrs on inner: smooth hdwy and cl up 3f out: sn led: rdn over 1f out: kpt on wl fnl f* **7/4**[1]

-540 2 1 ¾ **Mudaaraah**[37] 3071 3-8-8 96 RichardHills 4 102
(J L Dunlop) *dwlt: hld up in rr: hdwy over 3f out: effrt 2f out: rdn to chse wnr over 1f out: drvn ins fnl f and kpt on same pce* **11/2**

-104 3 1 **Totally Ours**[20] 3694 3-8-8 89 RichardMullen 8 100
(W R Muir) *hld up in tch: hdwy over 2f out: rdn wl over 1f out: kpt on ins fnl f: nrst fin* **25/1**

3241 4 3 **Off Chance**[17] 3752 4-9-7 100 DuranFentiman 7 97
(T D Easterby) *dwlt: hld up in rr: hdwy over 3f out: effrt 2f out and sn chsng ldrs: rdn over 1f out: sn no imp* **8/1**

023- 5 1 **Copperbeech (IRE)**[258] 7291 4-9-4 99 FrankieDettori 3 93
(Saeed Bin Suroor) *trckd ldr: effrt and cl up 3f out: sn rdn: edgd rt over 2f out and sn btn* **10/3**[2]

4500 6 ¾ **Bikini Babe (IRE)**[36] 3101 3-8-8 97 JoeFanning 2 91
(M Johnston) *led: rdn along and jnd 3f out: sn hdd and drvn: wknd wl over 1f out* **9/2**[3]

-210 7 17 **Acquainted**[36] 3101 3-8-8 101 RobertWinston 5 71
(B W Hills) *trckd ldng pair: effrt and cl up over 3f out: sn rdn and wknd wl over 2f out: sn eased* **14/1**

2m 11.94s (-0.56) **Going Correction** +0.075s/f (Good)
WFA 3 from 4yo+ 10lb 7 Ran SP% **114.6**
Speed ratings (Par 111): **105,103,102,100,99 99,85**
Tote Swingers: 1&2 £3.30, 1&3 £27.70, 2&3 £10.30 CSF £12.00 TOTE £2.60: £1.40, £3.20; EX 10.40.
Owner Saleh Al Homaizi & Imad Al Sagar **Bred** Saleh Al Homaizi **Trained** Newmarket, Suffolk

FOCUS
Last year this Listed event was won by a three-year-old in High Heeled and this time around the first three home were all three-year-olds. It was run at just an ordinary gallop and the form is not entirely solid, but the winner looks sure to do a good bit better.

NOTEBOOK
Nouriya, rated 95 and having only her fourth start, showed a good attitude. She can clearly go on from this and it will be interesting to see where her respected trainer sends her next time out. (op 2-1 tchd 9-4)
Mudaaraah, rated 96 and having her ninth start, ran well and puts the form in some context. She can continue to pay her way in similar company. (op 7-1)
Totally Ours put up a career-best effort. Rated 89, this was only her third start on turf and she should remain of interest, although the handicapper will have his say. (op 16-1)
Off Chance, rated 100, ran with credit and had a tough task giving the weight to the younger, more progressive fillies. She might prove hard to place now. (op 7-1 tchd 13-2)
Copperbeech(IRE) was well held, but might well have found the ground on the fast side (both career wins have come with ease in the ground). (op 3-1)
Bikini Babe(IRE), who appeared to get the run of the race, weakened quickly and can only be watched after this below par effort. (op 6-1 tchd 4-1)
Acquainted Official explanation: jockey said filly was unsuited by the good ground

4348 SKY BET SUPPORTING THE YORKSHIRE RACING SUMMER FESTIVAL CLAIMING STKS 1m 4f

8:00 (8:01) (Class 4) 3-Y-O+ £5,180 (£1,541; £770; £384) **Stalls** Centre

Form RPR

0030 1 **Porgy**[13] 3921 5-9-12 90 TonyHamilton 9 95
(R A Fahey) *led 3f: cl up tl led again over 5f out: rdn: put hd in air and hdd 2f out: led again over 1f out: drvn and kpt on fnl f* **4/1**[3]

4466 2 2 ¾ **Paktolos (FR)**[55] 2549 7-9-2 77 (p) RobertWinston 7 81
(John A Harris) *hld up in rr: hdwy 3f out: rdn 2f out: chsd wnr ins fnl f: sn no imp* **10/1**

0512 3 *hd* **Kames Park (IRE)**[15] 3807 8-9-2 75 PaulEddery 1 80
(R C Guest) *dwlt: hld up in rr: hdwy 3f out: rdn to chse wnr over 1f out: sn drvn and no imp* **7/1**

30 4 5 **Managua**[44] 2857 4-9-7 80 RyanMoore 4 77
(M R Channon) *trckd ldng pair: smooth hdwy 3f out: led 2f out: sn rdn and hdd over 1f out: sn wknd* **11/4**[1]

1625 5 5 **Trip The Light**[14] 3877 5-9-5 87 (v) MarzenaJeziorek(7) 8 74
(R A Fahey) *t.k.h: chsd ldrs: sddle slipped after 3f: rdn wl over 2f out and grad wknd* **6/1**

6 24 **King Of The Titans (IRE)**[54] 7-9-3 0 AshleyHamblett(3) 6 30
(P L Gilligan) *in tch: hdwy to chse ldrs over 3f out: sn rdn and wknd wl over 2f out* **25/1**

0-00 7 28 **Nevada Desert (IRE)**[6] 4152 10-9-2 76 DaraghO'Donohoe 2 —
(R M Whitaker) *plld hrd: in tch tl rapid hdwy to ld after 3f: hdd over 5f out: rdn along 4f out and sn wknd* **20/1**

45 8 11 **Captain Cornelius (IRE)**[70] 2083 3-8-10 0 DuranFentiman 5 —
(Joss Saville) *hld up towards rr: hdwy and in tch over 3f out: sn rdn and wknd* **40/1**

-620 9 4 **High Ambition**[30] 3319 7-9-5 78 PaulHanagan 3 —
(R A Fahey) *hld up: hdwy to chse ldrs 4f out: rdn along 3f out: sn btn and eased* **7/2**[2]

2m 35.61s (2.41) **Going Correction** +0.075s/f (Good)
WFA 3 from 4yo+ 12lb 9 Ran SP% **115.8**
Speed ratings (Par 105): **94,92,92,88,85 69,50,43,40**
Tote Swingers: 1&2 £13.50, 1&3 £6.00, 2&3 £3.70 CSF £42.03 TOTE £4.80: £1.80, £3.70, £2.40.
Owner Dr Marwan Koukash **Bred** Juddmonte Farms Ltd **Trained** Musley Bank, N Yorks

■ Stewards' Enquiry : Robert Winston two-day ban: used whip with excessive frequency (Aug 8-9)

FOCUS
With High Ambition running below-par and the saddle slipping on Trip The Light, this claimer probably didn't take as much winning as first thought. Only the first three showed their form. The early pace was just steady.

Trip The Light Official explanation: jockey said saddle slipped
High Ambition Official explanation: jockey said gelding finished lame

4349 WELCOME TO YORKSHIRE BACKING A WINNER STKS (H'CAP) 5f 89y

8:30 (8:31) (Class 4) (0-80,80) 3-Y-O £5,180 (£1,541; £770; £384) **Stalls** Low

Form RPR

5245 1 *nse* **Mon Brav**[16] 3779 3-9-2 **75** (v) DavidNolan 2 81
(D Carroll) *in tch: hdwy to chse ldrs 2f out: rdn to ld over 1f out: drvn and hdd ins fnl f: rallying and ev ch whn bmpd nr fin: fin 2nd: plcd 1st* **9/2**[2]

2262 2 **Diman Waters (IRE)**[14] 3856 3-9-7 **80** DavidAllan 9 86
(E J Alston) *prom on wd outside: effrt 2f out and sn ev ch: rdn to ld ins fnl f and sn hung lft: drvn and hung bdly lft nr fin: jst hld on: Finished 1st: disqualified and plcd 2nd* **9/2**[2]

0003 3 1 ¼ **Bossy Kitty**[7] 4109 3-8-11 **70** SilvestreDeSousa 1 72
(N Tinkler) *sn rdn along and outpcd in rr: hdwy 2f out: drvn to chse ldng pair and ch ent fnl f: sn drvn and one pce towards fin* **9/2**[2]

0601 4 2 ¼ **Boragh Jamal (IRE)**[23] 3561 3-8-4 **68** (b) JamesSullivan(5) 5 62
(B J Meehan) *in tch: hdwy to chse ldrs wl over 1f out: sn rdn and kpt on same pce fnl f* **14/1**

0100 5 1 ½ **Ventura Cove (IRE)**[41] 2982 3-9-5 **78** PaulHanagan 8 67
(R A Fahey) *sn rdn along: outpcd and in rr 1/2-way: sme late hdwy* **13/2**[3]

-401 6 *shd* **Melody In The Mist (FR)**[20] 3682 3-9-1 **74** RyanMoore 6 63
(T D Barron) *cl up: rdn along 2f out: sn wknd* **3/1**[1]

0032 7 1 ½ **Tillys Tale**[9] 4016 3-9-1 **74** MickyFenton 4 58
(P T Midgley) *led: rdn along 2f out: hdd over 1f out and sn wknd* **8/1**

4440 8 12 **Trade Secret**[48] 2768 3-9-0 **73** TomEaves 7 16
(M Brittain) *chsd ldrs: rdn 2f out: sn wknd* **12/1**

63.85 secs (-0.45) **Going Correction** -0.025s/f (Good) 8 Ran SP% **118.3**
Speed ratings (Par 102): **101,102,99,96,93 93,91,72**
Tote Swingers: 1&2 £4.20, 1&3 £5.10, 2&3 £5.60 CSF £26.02 CT £98.22 TOTE £5.00: £1.50, £1.60, £1.70; EX 19.50 Place 6: £168.43 Place 5: £37.13 .
Owner D Wallis **Bred** J D Graham **Trained** Sledmere, E Yorks

■ Stewards' Enquiry : David Nolan caution: used whip with excessive frequency.
David Allan two-day ban: careless riding (Aug 6-7); caution: used whip with excessive frequency.

FOCUS
Plenty of exposed handicappers for this sprint, and a controversial finish, with the first two home having their placing reversed in the stewards' room afterwards with Diman Waters drifting left and interfering with Mon Brav. The form is sound enough.

T/Jkpt: Not won. T/Plt: £178.90 to a £1 stake. Pool:£73,632.74 - 300.35 winning tickets T/Qpdt: £15.90 to a £1 stake. Pool:£5,834.08 - 270.80 winning tickets JR

4350 - 4353a (Foreign Racing) - See Raceform Interactive

4317 ASCOT (R-H)

Saturday, July 24

OFFICIAL GOING: Good changing to good (good to firm in places) after race 3 (2:40)

An Arab race was run at 5.00.

Wind: very light, across Weather: mainly sunny, light clouds

4354 LONGINES H'CAP (LADIES RACE) 7f

1:30 (1:32) (Class 3) (0-90,86) 3-Y-O+ **£6,058** (£1,878; £938; £469) **Stalls** Centre

Form				RPR
-534	**1**		**Rosko**[8] 4093 6-9-3 **68**....................(b[1]) MissSBrotherton 9 (B Ellison) *racd stands' side: s.i.s: t.k.h and sn handy: hdwy to ld wl over 1f out: pushed along ent fnl f: r.o wl* **9/1**	78
3100	**2**	*1*	**Methaaly (IRE)**[14] 3902 7-9-1 **69**....................(be) MissMMullineaux(3) 7 (M Mullineaux) *racd stands' side: wnt rt and stdd s: hld up in rr: rdn and hdwy wl over 1f out: edging lft and chsd ldrs 1f out: styd on wl to go 2nd nr fin: nt rch wnr: 2nd of 12 in gp* **50/1**	76
031	**3**	*nk*	**Dabbers Ridge (IRE)**[12] 3968 8-9-8 **73**.................... MrsCBartley 12 (I W McInnes) *racd stands' side: hld up towards rr: rdn and gd hdwy to chse wnr over 1f out: kpt on but no imp fnl f: lost 2nd nr fin: 3rd of 12 in gp* **16/1**	79
0405	**4**	*1 1/4*	**French Art**[8] 4119 5-8-11 **67**....................(p) MissJoannaMason(5) 16 (N Tinkler) *racd far side: chsd that gp ldr and in midfield overall: rdn and effrt 2f out: kpt on u.p fnl f: 1st of 5 in gp* **20/1**	70
1502	**5**	*1/2*	**Summer Dancer (IRE)**[21] 3659 6-9-12 **82**.................... MissWGibson(5) 17 (P T Midgley) *taken down early: racd far side: chsd far side ldrs and midfield overall: rdn and effrt 2f out: swtchd lft over 1f out: kpt on u.p fnl f: nt rch ldrs: 2nd of 5 in gp* **25/1**	84
3-22	**6**	*3/4*	**Fishforcompliments**[15] 3876 6-9-8 **78**.................... MrsVFahey(5) 10 (R A Fahey) *racd stands' side: in rr: pushed along and hdwy 2f out: kpt on steadily fnl f but nvr gng pce to rch ldrs: 4th of 12 in gp* **5/1**[1]	78
3023	**7**	*nk*	**Flowing Cape (IRE)**[12] 3969 5-9-12 **82**.................... MissRKneller(5) 14 (R Hollinshead) *racd stands' side: stdd s: hld up in rr: rdn and effrt wl over 1f out: kpt on ins fnl f: nt rch ldrs: 5th of 12 in gp* **12/1**	81
3222	**8**	*nk*	**Ocean Legend (IRE)**[40] 3033 5-10-2 **86**.................... MissJennyCarr(5) 15 (A W Carroll) *racd far side: led that gp and handy overall: rdn wl over 1f out: unable qck over 1f out: kpt on same pce fnl f: 3rd of 5 in gp* **14/1**	84
0000	**9**	*nk*	**Arachnophobia (IRE)**[38] 3083 4-9-9 **79**.................... MissRachelKing(5) 4 (Pat Eddery) *racd stands' side: w ldrs: rdn and unable qck ent fnl 2f: one pce and btn ent fnl f: 6th of 12 in gp* **16/1**	76
0403	**10**	*4 1/2*	**Piquante**[15] 3854 4-9-2 **67** oh2....................(p) MissADeniel 11 (N Tinkler) *racd stands' side: hld up in midfield: rdn and effrt to chse ldrs 2f out: btn over 1f out: wknd ins fnl f: 7th in gp* **25/1**	52
2-01	**11**	*1 3/4*	**King's Colour**[16] 3813 5-10-7 **86**.................... MissEJJones 6 (B R Johnson) *racd stands' side: in tch tl rdn and unable qck ent fnl 2f: wknd over 1f out: 8th of 12 in gp* **8/1**[3]	66
1113	**12**	*1 1/2*	**Abbondanza (IRE)**[23] 3595 7-10-2 **81**.................... MissNCarberry 5 (D Nicholls) *racd stands' side: w ldrs tl rdn and wknd over 2f out: wl btn over 1f out: 9th of 12 in gp* **8/1**[3]	57
-040	**13**	*nse*	**Rock Anthem (IRE)**[15] 3863 6-9-8 **73**.................... MissGAndrews 2 (Mike Murphy) *racd stands' side: s.i.s: sn in tch: lost pl and dropped towards rr 1/2-way: swtchd rt and drvn ent fnl 2f: no prog and wl btn over 1f out: 10th of 12 in gp* **16/1**	49
0020	**14**	*2 1/2*	**Jake The Snake (IRE)**[10] 4030 9-9-8 **76**.................... MissLAllan(3) 13 (A W Carroll) *racd far side: stdd s: t.k.h early: hld up towards rr: rdn and no prog ent fnl 2f: wl bhd and eased ins fnl f: 4th of 5 in gp* **16/1**	46
2060	**15**	*3/4*	**Pegasus Again (USA)**[63] 2322 5-10-3 **82**.................... MsKWalsh 1 (R A Mills) *racd stands' side: overall ldr tl rdn and hdd wl over 1f out: wknd qckly over 1f out: 11th of 12 in gp* **13/2**[2]	49
0500	**16**	*1 1/4*	**Desert Dreamer (IRE)**[9] 4044 9-9-12 **77**.......... MissIsabelTompsett 18 (P D Evans) *taken down early: racd far side: hld up in rr: rdn and no prog ent fnl 2f: wl bhd and eased ins fnl f: 5th of 5 in gp* **33/1**	41
0260	**17**	*27*	**Bomber Command (USA)**[24] 3565 7-8-11 **67**..(v) MissPhillipaTutty(5) 8 (J W Hills) *racd stands' side: sn prom: rdn and wknd qckly over 2f out: t.o and eased fnl f: 12th of 12 in gp* **25/1**	—

1m 30.23s (2.23) **Going Correction** +0.175s/f (Good) **17 Ran SP% 123.1**

Speed ratings (Par 107): **94,92,92,91,90 89,89,88,88,83 81,79,79,76,76 74,43**

toteswingers:1&2:£67.90, 1&3:£22.20, 2&3:£128.50 CSF £424.98 CT £6929.64 TOTE £10.40: £2.50, £12.90, £3.20, £6.60; EX 561.40 TRIFECTA Not won..

Owner Racing Management & Training Ltd **Bred** Normandie Stud Ltd **Trained** Norton, N Yorks

■ Stewards' Enquiry : Miss E J Jones two-day ban: used whip when out of contention (tbn)

FOCUS

This was a typically competitive contest, but the form is only ordinary judged around the principals. The second and third are rated to this year's form.

NOTEBOOK

Rosko, having only his second start over a trip this short, had blinkers on for the first time and had the assistance of one of the more experienced riders. While the headgear may have had a positive effect, it's just as likely that the strong pace brought his stamina into play and once he had taken over in front on the nearside over two furlongs from home, he was never going to stop. (op 17-2)

Methaaly(IRE), 1lb higher than when successful under today's rider at Leicester last month, was held up in the nearside group and ran on well from over a furlong out, but the winner had gone beyond recall. He is better known as a sprinter, though he has won over this sort of trip on Polytrack.

Dabbers Ridge(IRE), winner of three of his last five starts, likes to come late off a strong pace so the race was run to suit, and he duly posted a decent effort. He moved into contention in the nearside group inside the last quarter-mile and had every chance, but couldn't go with Rosko. (op 14-1)

French Art ◆, back down to the same mark as when winning at Pontefract in April, had never previously run over a trip this short, so the decent tempo was in his favour but he may have found himself racing on the wrong side. He stayed on well to hit the front on the far side half a furlong out, but the main action was unfolding on the opposite flank. He is worth keeping an eye on. (op 33-1)

Summer Dancer(IRE), now 6lb higher than when winning at Beverley in May, is yet another that likes to come from off a strong pace and he ran on well late, but he also may have been at a disadvantage over on the far side.

Fishforcompliments, representing last year's winning trainer/jockey combination, made only limited progress in the nearside group and a record of 2-39 isn't great for a horse of his ability. (op 6-1 tchd 9-2)

Flowing Cape(IRE), 2lb higher than when last on turf and 7lb higher than when scoring at Leicester last month, made some late headway on the outside of the nearside group, but it was never enough. (op 11-1 tchd 10-1)

Ocean Legend(IRE), creeping up the handicap despite being narrowly beaten in his last four starts, led the quintet on the far side but was swallowed up by two of his rivals on that flank well inside the last furlong. (op 11-1)

Arachnophobia(IRE), making a rare appearance on turf, had run poorly since winning off 2lb higher at Wolverhampton in March, but even though he ended up well beaten here, he didn't run that badly as he disputed the advantage on the nearside until over a furlong out. (op 25-1)

4355 JAGUAR XK WINKFIELD STKS (LISTED RACE) 7f

2:05 (2:06) (Class 1) 2-Y-O

£14,192 (£5,380; £2,692; £1,342; £672; £337) **Stalls** Centre

Form				RPR
U1	**1**		**Toolain (IRE)**[26] 3517 2-9-2 0.................... PhilipRobinson 5 (M A Jarvis) *in tch: pushed along 3f out: rdn and hdwy to ld jst over 1f out: sn hung lft: hld on wl fnl f* **11/4**[1]	102
4110	**2**	*3/4*	**Galtymore Lad**[39] 3049 2-9-2 100.................... TonyCulhane 4 (M R Channon) *stdd s: hld up in tch in last pair: gd hdwy between horses to chal wnr ent fnl f: sn hung lft: unable qck and hld fnl 100yds* **9/1**	100
2131	**3**	*2*	**Premier Clarets (IRE)**[26] 3504 2-9-2 93.................... RyanMoore 3 (R A Fahey) *t.k.h: chsd ldr for 1f: hld up wl in tch after: rdn and effrt 2f out: chsd ldrs and swtchd rt ins fnl f: kpt on same pce u.p after* **4/1**[3]	95
1	**4**	*1/2*	**Auld Burns**[27] 3472 2-9-2 0.................... RichardHughes 1 (R Hannon) *in tch: pushed along wl over 2f out: rdn to chse ldrs over 1f out: no ex u.p 1f out: kpt on same pce after* **3/1**[2]	94
1	**5**	*3/4*	**Deep South**[31] 3326 2-9-2 0.................... RoystonFfrench 7 (Mahmood Al Zarooni) *chsd ldrs: wnt 2nd over 2f out: ev ch and rdn 2f out: carried hd awkwardly and unable qck u.p over 1f out: btn whn hung lft ins fnl f* **9/2**	92
0215	**6**	*1 1/2*	**Sonoran Sands (IRE)**[8] 4097 2-9-2 86.................... LiamKeniry 6 (J S Moore) *stdd and stmbld s: hld up in tch in rr: effrt on outer over 2f out: rdn and btn ent fnl f* **33/1**	88
112	**7**	*nk*	**Drawing Board**[26] 3504 2-9-2 94.................... RichardMullen 8 (K A Ryan) *led: rdn 2f out: hdd jst over 1f out: wknd qckly ins fnl f* **10/1**	87
0105	**8**	*11*	**Planet Waves (IRE)**[26] 3504 2-9-2 81.................... RichardHills 2 (C E Brittain) *chsd ldr after 1f tl over 2f out: wknd 2f out: wl bhd fnl f* **28/1**	60+

1m 29.72s (1.72) **Going Correction** +0.175s/f (Good) **8 Ran SP% 115.3**

Speed ratings (Par 102): **97,96,93,93,92 90,90,77**

toteswingers:1&2:£5.50, 1&3:£3.90, 2&3:£4.60 CSF £28.37 TOTE £3.60: £1.40, £2.40, £1.40; EX 37.30 Trifecta £302.10 Pool: £1,229.15 - 3.01 winning units..

Owner Sheikh Ahmed Al Maktoum **Bred** Darley **Trained** Newmarket, Suffolk

FOCUS

A really interesting Listed contest, won in 2007 by subsequent Breeders' Cup Classic winner Raven's Pass, and the field elected to head centre-field, though with the front two both edging left under pressure they ended up more towards the stands' side. Solid enough form, rated around the second, third and sixth.

NOTEBOOK

Toolain(IRE), who swerved left and unseated his rider with the race apparently in safe keeping at Sandown on debut (eventual winner runner-up in Group 2 Superlative Stakes next time), readily got the job done at Wolverhampton last month when looking much more straightforward. He coped fine with this rise in grade, picking up well to lead over a furlong out, but did edge considerably left under pressure, in the end being all out to score. A fine, big horse, it's possible the winner will need a slower surface to produce his best, and maybe that's why he didn't run straight under pressure, but he will need to progress again, and in a major way, if he is to challenge for Group honours later in the season. The Champagne Stakes was mentioned as a possible aim. (tchd 5-2 and 3-1 in places)

Galtymore Lad shaped as though this trip would suit when a keeping-on seventh in the Coventry and he made good headway to challenge a furlong out, but started to hang left and was always just coming off second best. This represented a further step forward and he can pick up another prize at some stage. (op 10-1 tchd 12-1)

Premier Clarets(IRE), third in the Listed Woodcote Stakes prior to winning at Pontefract, was up in trip and didn't settle overly well, but he kept on right the way to the line and can win more races just below this level. He was later reported to have lost a shoe. Official explanation: jockey said colt lost a left-fore shoe (op 5-1)

Auld Burns, who won despite fast ground on his debut, could have done with some rain and he stayed on best he could without suggesting he was entirely comfortable. It's likely there's more to come from him, especially over 1m, and he may do better in the autumn. (op 5-2 tchd 10-3 in places)

Deep South raced keenly on this rise in grade and then looked very awkward under pressure, carrying his head high and then hanging. (op 6-1)

Sonoran Sands(IRE), well held in a 6f Listed contest at Newbury latest time, ran as well as could have been expected without suggesting he's up to Pattern level. Official explanation: jockey said colt was slowly away

Drawing Board, narrowly beaten by Premier Clarets at Pontefract, stopped quickly having been headed over a furlong out. (op 12-1)

Planet Waves(IRE) was completely outclassed and will find life easier in nurseries. (op 22-1)

4356 PRINCESS MARGARET ABU DHABI STKS (GROUP 3) (FILLIES) 6f

2:40 (2:40) (Class 1) 2-Y-O

£22,708 (£8,608; £4,308; £2,148; £1,076; £540) **Stalls** Centre

Form				RPR
12	**1**		**Soraaya (IRE)**[17] 3792 2-8-12 0.................... RyanMoore 2 (M R Channon) *racd stands' side: hld up in rr: hdwy over 2f out: rdn and ev ch fr wl over 1f out: r.o wl u.p to ld towards fin* **3/1**[2]	106
112	**2**	*1/2*	**Margot Did (IRE)**[36] 3141 2-8-12 105.................... HayleyTurner 12 (M L W Bell) *racd in centre: hdwy to trck ldrs whn gps merged over 2f out: jnd ldrs 2f out: rdn to ld over 1f out: hrd drvn and edgd lft ins fnl f: hdd and no ex towards fin* **2/1**[1]	105+
1	**3**	*2*	**Perfect Tribute**[31] 3331 2-8-12 0.................... LukeMorris 6 (C G Cox) *racd on stands' side: t.k.h: sn chsng ldrs: ev ch over 2f out: rdn wl over 1f out: stl ev ch tl wknd fnl 75yds* **14/1**	98
2413	**4**	*nk*	**Imperialistic Diva (IRE)**[28] 3453 2-8-12 93.................... OlivierPeslier 7 (T D Easterby) *racd in centre: in tch in midfield: nt clr run ent fnl 2f: swtchd rt and hdwy u.p over 1f out: kpt on steadily u.p ins fnl f: nt pce to rch ldrs* **16/1**	97+
21	**5**	*hd*	**Sweet Cecily (IRE)**[29] 3411 2-8-12 0.................... RichardHughes 9 (R Hannon) *racd in centre: in tch: effrt 2f out: rdn to press ldrs 2f out: unable qck u.p jst over 1f out: kpt on one pce ins fnl f* **6/1**[3]	97
0	**6**	*2*	**Queen Of Spain (IRE)**[17] 3797 2-8-12 0.................... CO'Donoghue 3 (A P O'Brien, Ire) *racd stands' side: chsd ldrs tl overall ldr over 2f out: drvn and hdd over 1f out: wknd ins fnl f* **6/1**[3]	91
1	**7**	*2 1/2*	**Al Madina (IRE)**[31] 3316 2-8-12 0.................... RoystonFfrench 5 (B Smart) *racd stands' side: in tch in midfield: rdn 1/2-way: struggling 2f out: wl btn whn edgd rt over 1f out* **33/1**	83
3126	**8**	*7*	**Shoshoni Wind**[7] 4138 2-8-12 94.................... RichardMullen 10 (K A Ryan) *racd in centre: s.i.s: hld up in rr: rdn and effrt to chse ldrs on outer 2f out: wknd over 1f out: wl btn and eased ins fnl f* **25/1**	68
4146	**9**	*3 1/4*	**Serena's Pride**[17] 3792 2-8-12 95.................... MatthewDavies 8 (A P Jarvis) *racd in centre: overall ldr: carried lft and hdd over 2f out: wknd qckly over 1f out: wl bhd fnl f* **33/1**	52

1 **10** *5* **Catfish (IRE)**[15] 3871 2-8-12 0 DavidProbert 11 40
(Miss Gay Kelleway) *racd in centre: w ldr: rdn and hung lft fr over 2f out: dropped out rapidly wl over 1f out: wl bhd and eased ins fnl f* **14/1**

2354 **11** *9* **Catalinas Diamond (IRE)**[14] 3906 2-8-12 86 RobertWinston 1 10
(B W Duke) *racd stands' side: chsd ldrs tl wknd qckly u.p ent fnl 2f: wl bhd and eased fnl f: t.o* **40/1**

1m 14.86s (0.46) **Going Correction** +0.175s/f (Good) **11** Ran SP% **118.3**
Speed ratings (Par 101): **103,102,99,99,99 96,93,83,79,72 60**
toteswingers:1&2:£1.70, 1&3:£10.50, 2&3:£9.10 CSF £9.10 TOTE £4.30: £1.60, £1.30, £5.70; EX 9.20 Trifecta £169.40 Pool: £11,077.06 - 48.37 winning units..
Owner Sheikh Ahmed Al Maktoum **Bred** Keogh Family **Trained** West Ilsley, Berks
■ Stewards' Enquiry : David Probert caution: used whip when out of contention.

FOCUS
A decent turnout this year with ten off the 11 fillies previous winners, though none had been successful in Listed or Group company. The field initially split into two with five coming up the stands' rail and six racing up the centre, though the two groups had merged over two furlongs from home. Straightforward form, although the winner was unlucky.

NOTEBOOK
Soraaya(IRE), second to Memory in the Cherry Hinton, was held up in the nearside group and came off the bridle a long time before the runner-up, but her rival gave her something to aim at and she responded well to the pressure to get up in the dying strides. Her rider was of the opinion that she would appreciate another furlong and her trainer mentioned the Moyglare as a possible target, where she would again take on Memory. The alternative is the Lowther followed by the Cheveley Park. She was immediately a top-priced 33-1 for next year's 1,000 Guineas, while the bookies also took the chance to cut Memory to a general 6-1. (op 4-1)
Margot Did(IRE) finished closer to Memory in the Albany Stakes over course and distance last month than Soraaya did in the Cherry Hinton, and she may have been a bit unlucky here. Having been held up in the centre group, she was still on the bridle when leading over a furlong from home, but her rider had little option than to go for it when she did as the two groups were merging and she wouldn't have got the gap had she waited. However, once in front she started to hang about under pressure and was just worried out of it. Connections thought that the stiff 6f may also have just found her out and she will now head for the Lowther. (op 9-4 tchd 5-2)
Perfect Tribute, the form of whose successful Salisbury debut hasn't really worked out, ran a blinder given her inexperience. Always up there, she was travelling as well as anything passing the two-furlong pole and stayed on really well once off the bridle. Connections felt that she might have seen too much daylight and she is now likely to join the runner-up in the Lowther. (op 16-1)
Imperialistic Diva(IRE), just behind Soshoni Wind at Newmarket last month, raced in the centre group and ran on again after seeming to get outpaced passing the two-furlong pole. She will find easier opportunities than this. (tchd 12-1)
Sweet Cecily(IRE) bolted up in a Newmarket maiden on her second start and that race has already produced a couple of winners. She travelled well behind the leaders in the centre group, but could only find one pace when finally coming under pressure. She is worth another chance. (op 5-1)
Queen Of Spain(IRE) had every chance passing the two-furlong pole, but could then only stay on at the one pace. She had finished well behind Margot Did in the Albany and probably ran close to that form. (op 15-2 tchd 8-1)
Al Madina(IRE), impressive when beating the boys on her Carlisle debut, was off the bridle at halfway, but she kept on plugging away and pulled well clear of the others. There are more nice races to be won with her.
Shoshoni Wind, back up to 6f after finishing sixth in the Weatherbys Super Sprint, found herself rather isolated out in the centre of the track passing the two-furlong pole before fading, but this is probably as good as she is. (tchd 22-1)
Serena's Pride, from a stable that has won this race twice since 2003, had a bit to find with Soraaya on Cherry Hinton form and faded over two furlongs out.
Catfish(IRE) faded tamely at the same stage, but is worth another chance to prove that her shock 40-1 debut victory at Newmarket was no fluke. (op 10-1)
Catalinas Diamond(IRE), the only maiden in the field and turned over at odds-on in a Nottingham maiden after her cracking effort in the Queen Mary, dropped right out and seems to be going the wrong way. (op 33-1)

4357 DUBAI DUTY FREE H'CAP — 1m (S)
3:15 (3:18) (Class 2) 3-Y-O

£20,250 (£6,064; £3,032; £1,517; £757; £380) **Stalls** Centre

Form — RPR

2611 **1** **Don't Call Me (IRE)**[12] 3949 3-8-6 84 (t) RichardMullen 2 96
(B Smart) *bhd: pushed along over 4f out: swtchd lft over 1f out: hdwy u.p to chse ldng trio 1f out: str run ins fnl f to ld fnl 50yds* **9/1**

-214 **2** *3/4* **King Of Windsor (IRE)**[15] 3867 3-8-7 85 RichardKingscote 5 95
(R M Beckett) *hld up in rr: rdn and gd hdwy over 1f out: chsd ldng pair ent fnl f: ev ch ins fnl f: kpt on u.p tl nt pce of wnr fnl 50yds: wnt 2nd last strides* **9/1**

4651 **3** *nk* **Side Glance**[14] 3886 3-9-3 95 DavidProbert 12 104
(A M Balding) *hld up in midfield: hdwy to trck ldrs over 2f out: pushed along to chse ldr and carried rt wl over 1f out: ev ch u.p fr over 1f out: edgd rt and no ex fnl 50yds* **4/1**[1]

11-2 **4** *3/4* **Mass Rally (IRE)**[21] 3696 3-9-2 94 RyanMoore 7 102+
(J H M Gosden) *hld up towards rr: pushed along and gd hdwy over 4f out: drvn to ld over 1f out: edgd lft u.p ent fnl f: hdd fnl 50yds: no ex and lost 2 pls towards fin* **9/2**[2]

-460 **5** *4 1/2* **Musaafer (IRE)**[15] 3867 3-9-1 93 TadhgO'Shea 6 90
(M A Jarvis) *t.k.h: hld up wl in tch: hdwy to ld jst over 2f out: rdn and hung rt wl over 1f out: hdd over 1f out: wknd qckly 1f out* **25/1**

-215 **6** *nk* **Highland Knight (IRE)**[15] 3867 3-8-9 87 (t) LiamKeniry 8 84
(A M Balding) *chsd ldr tl led over 4f out: hdd and rdn jst over 2f out: wknd jst over 1f out: plugged on same pce fnl f* **12/1**

1123 **7** *5* **Haatheq (USA)**[14] 3886 3-8-9 87 RichardHills 3 72
(J L Dunlop) *hld up wl in tch: rdn and nt qckn 2f out: wknd qckly over 1f out: wl btn ins fnl f* **6/1**[3]

2324 **8** *6* **Spa's Dancer (IRE)**[15] 3863 3-8-2 80 HayleyTurner 4 51
(J W Hills) *stdd and swtchd lft s: hld up in rr: effrt on stands' rail 3f out: no prog and wl btn over 1f out* **14/1**

6611 **9** *4* **Ginger Jack**[11] 3987 3-9-0 92 JoeFanning 9 54
(M Johnston) *chsd ldrs: rdn over 2f out: wknd wl over 1f out: wl btn fnl f* **9/2**[2]

421 **10** *13* **Zakiy**[42] 2981 3-8-3 81 (t) LiamJones 11 13
(W J Haggas) *chsd ldrs tl wnt 2nd over 4f out tl ent fnl 2f: wknd rapidly: wl bhd and eased ins fnl f: t.o* **14/1**

2-00 **11** *42* **Kalypso King (USA)**[41] 2999 3-9-7 99 RichardHughes 1 —
(S Kirk) *led tl over 4f out: sn hanging bdly rt and eased bk: last whn swtchd to far side and virtually p.u fr over 2f out: t.o* **33/1**

1m 41.04s (0.44) **Going Correction** +0.175s/f (Good) **11** Ran SP% **118.5**
Speed ratings (Par 106): **104,103,102,102,97 97,92,86,82,69 27**
toteswingers:1&2:£13.30, 1&3:£8.10, 2&3:£8.10 CSF £88.11 CT £386.42 TOTE £11.10: £2.70, £3.30, £1.70; EX 103.60 Trifecta £1883.60 Part won. Pool: £2,545.43 - 0.92 winning units..
Owner H E Sheikh Rashid Bin Mohammed **Bred** Darley **Trained** Hambleton, N Yorks

FOCUS
A good-quality 3yo handicap that was certainly competitive and the pace was a good one. The field raced stands' side, though the action took place more towards the centre in the final 2f. Progress from the first two and the first four were clear.

NOTEBOOK
Don't Call Me(IRE) got up in the final strides to complete a hat-trick. Although raised 5lb for his latest Ayr success, the son of Haafhd continues to progress and he again displayed a likeable attitude in really knuckling down to it in the final 100 yards. A good test at 1m suits him best and he can continue to progress. (op 11-1)
King Of Windsor(IRE), beaten 1l in a decent Newmarket handicap last time, was up 2lb, but he looks to have improved again and just managed to get up for second. It's possible he will stay further down the line. (op 10-1 tchd 8-1)
Side Glance, a good winner off 5lb lower over 7f at the course last time, looked worth a shot at this trip and he saw it out well, but just not as strongly as some. He wasn't helped by being carried right two furlongs out and should continue to give a bold show in valuable handicaps. (op 11-2 tchd 7-2)
Mass Rally(IRE) reappeared with a fine effort behind subsequent scorer Kakatosi at Sandown and looked set to defy the 5lb rise when racing to the lead inside the final two furlongs, but he had looked a non-stayer on one previous try at this distance, and that again seemed the case. (op 4-1 tchd 5-1 in places)
Musaafer(IRE), his owner's second-string, took over approaching the final two furlongs, but he soon started to hang right and was quickly brushed aside. He needs further assistance from the handicapper. (op 16-1)
Highland Knight(IRE) came across to lead against the stands' rail, but he wasn't up to it. (op 11-1)
Haatheq(USA)'s progression had looked to be levelling out and this run suggests he may be done winning for the time being. (op 5-1)
Spa's Dancer(IRE) wasn't the best away and ended up well having tried to make headway past halfway. (tchd 16-1)
Ginger Jack was up 5lb and found this much more competitive than the races he has been winning. (op 11-2 tchd 4-1 and 6-1 in places)
Zakiy was too keen and didn't last on this handicap debut. (tchd 16-1)
Kalypso King(USA) was hanging badly and virtually pulled up. Official explanation: jockey said, regarding running, that the colt hung badly right and was unsteerable and he was concerned about clipping heels of other runners. (op 28-1)

4358 VICTORIA RACING CLUB INTERNATIONAL STKS (HERITAGE H'CAP) — 7f
3:50 (3:52) (Class 2) 3-Y-O+

£46,732 (£13,995; £6,997; £3,502; £1,747; £877) **Stalls** Centre

Form — RPR

1003 **1** **Castles In The Air**[21] 3674 5-9-0 100 RichardHughes 12 109
(R A Fahey) *racd stands' side: hld up in midfield: rdn and hdwy over 1f out: drvn and ev ch ent fnl f: led ins fnl f: kpt on wl* **14/1**

3460 **2** *1/2* **Noble Citizen (USA)**[15] 3869 5-8-6 92 (be) TadhgO'Shea 7 99
(D M Simcock) *racd stands' side: hld up towards rr: switching rt over 1f out: switching bk lft and hdwy ent fnl f: r.o wl ins fnl f: wnt 2nd last strides: nt quite rch wnr: 2nd of 16 in gp* **16/1**

0222 **3** *hd* **Himalya (IRE)**[28] 3445 4-9-7 107 RyanMoore 10 114
(J Noseda) *taken down early and ponied to s: racd stands' side: hld up towards rr: hdwy wl over 1f out: drvn and ev ch 1f out tl no ex towards fin: lost 2nd last strides: 3rd of 16 in gp* **7/1**[1]

-121 **4** *1* **Yaa Wayl (IRE)**[23] 3591 3-8-10 103 3ex PhilipRobinson 5 104
(M A Jarvis) *racd stands' side: t.k.h: in tch: rdn and hdwy to ld over 1f out: hrd drvn and hdd ins fnl f: no ex fnl 75yds: 4th of 16 in gp* **12/1**

0-33 **5** *hd* **Suruor (IRE)**[7] 4126 4-9-0 100 RichardMullen 11 103+
(D M Simcock) *racd stands' side: hld up in rr: rdn and hdwy ent fnl 2f: chsd ldrs ent fnl f: kpt on u.p but nt quite pce to rch ldrs: 5th of 16 in gp* **16/1**

6500 **6** *3/4* **Gallagher**[15] 3869 4-8-12 103 JamesSullivan(5) 14 104
(B J Meehan) *racd stands' side: in tch: pushed along over 2f out: rdn and pressed ldrs wl over 1f out: styd on one pce ins fnl f: 6th of 16 in gp* **25/1**

1030 **7** *1/2* **Imperial Guest**[15] 3869 4-8-8 93 ow1 SebSanders 22 94
(G G Margarson) *racd far side: midfield overall: rdn and effrt ent fnl 2f: kpt on u.p fnl f: led far side ins fnl f but nvr quite on terms w stands' side: 1st of 5 in gp* **33/1**

4000 **8** *3/4* **Al Muheer (IRE)**[21] 3692 5-9-1 101 AdrianNicholls 6 99
(D Nicholls) *racd stands' side: stdd s and hld up in rr: hdwy over 1f out: kpt on ins fnl f: nvr rchd ldrs: 7th of 16 in gp* **28/1**

00-6 **9** *hd* **Glen Molly (IRE)**[98] 1397 4-8-1 87 HayleyTurner 20 85
(B W Hills) *racd far side: t.k.h: chsd far side ldr and in tch overall: rdn ent fnl 2f: led far side gp over 1f out tl ins fnl f but no imp on ldrs: 2nd of 5 in gp* **33/1**

-6 **10** *1* **Decent Fella (IRE)**[57] 2508 4-8-1 87 DavidProbert 3 82
(A M Balding) *racd stands' side: dwlt: sn rcvrd and in tch: rdn and unable qck 2f out: wkng whn n.m.r ent fnl f: 8th of 16 in gp* **7/1**[1]

0300 **11** *nse* **Advanced**[15] 3869 7-8-8 99 AmyRyan(5) 13 94
(K A Ryan) *racd stands' side: chsd ldrs: rdn to press ldrs 2f out tl jst over 1f out: wknd ins fnl f: 9th of 16 in gp* **25/1**

-152 **12** *1/2* **Poet's Place (USA)**[28] 3446 5-8-1 87 LukeMorris 4 80
(T D Barron) *racd stands' side: in tch: rdn and effrt ent fnl 2f: drvn and one pce fr over 1f out: 10th of 16 in gp* **10/1**[3]

-206 **13** *shd* **Swift Gift**[36] 3146 5-8-12 98 MartinDwyer 15 91
(B J Meehan) *racd stands' side: swtchd lft s: hld up towards rr: rdn and hdwy 2f out: no imp and one pce ent fnl f: 11th of 16 in gp* **10/1**[3]

0400 **14** *1* **Hajoum (IRE)**[21] 3681 4-8-7 93 RoystonFfrench 2 83
(M Johnston) *racd stands' side: overall ldr tl 1/2-way: pressed ldr after: ev ch and rdn ent 2f out: wknd qckly ent fnl f: 12th of 16 in gp* **25/1**

0301 **15** *1 1/2* **Something (IRE)**[23] 3578 8-8-9 95 3ex DaraghO'Donohoe 8 81
(D Nicholls) *racd stands' side: stdd and short of room s: hld up in rr: swtchd rt and hdwy in centre wl over 1f out: btn 1f out: hung rt ins fnl f: 13th of 16 in gp* **25/1**

0314 **16** *1/2* **Crown Choice**[15] 3869 5-8-7 93 EddieAhern 18 78
(W R Swinburn) *racd stands' side: swtchd sharply lft s: hld up in rr: swtchd rt and effrt u.p 2f out: no hdwy and btn 1f out: 14th of 16 in gp* **14/1**

3200 **17** *nk* **Al Farahidi (USA)**[37] 3103 3-7-13 92 (b) KoseiMiura 9 73
(M Johnston) *take down early: racd stands' side: w overall ldr tl led 1/2-way: rdn and hdd over 1f out: sn wknd: 15th of 16 in gp* **40/1**

3210 **18** *1 1/4* **Mac's Power (IRE)**[14] 3920 4-8-1 87 (t) JimmyQuinn 21 68
(J R Fanshawe) *racd far side: hld up towards rr overall: rdn and hdwy 2f out: wknd and wl btn ent fnl f: 3rd of 5 in gp* **12/1**

-554 **19** *3 3/4* **Big Noise**[21] 3681 6-8-1 90 Louis-PhilippeBeuzelin(3) 19 61
(Dr J D Scargill) *racd far side: hld up in rr: rdn and no hdwy ent fnl 2f wl bhd fr over 1f out: 4th of 5 in gp* **25/1**

3104 **20** 2 ¾ **Hacienda (IRE)**[7] 4144 3-8-3 **96** .... JoeFanning 16 56
(M Johnston) *racd far side: led far side gp and chsd ldrs overall tl over 1f out: sn wknd: wl bhd and eased ins fnl f: 5th of 5 in gp* **20/1**

2111 **21** 3 ½ **Tagseed (IRE)**[35] 3224 4-8-4 **90** .... RichardHills 1 44
(W J Haggas) *racd stands' side: in tch tl rdn and btn wl over 1f out: wl bhd and eased ins fnl f: 16th of 16 in gp* **9/1**[2]

1m 26.85s (-1.15) **Going Correction** +0.175s/f (Good)
WFA 3 from 4yo+ 7lb **21** Ran SP% **129.4**
Speed ratings (Par 109): **113,112,112,111,110 109,109,108,108,107 107,106,106,105,103 103,102,101,96,93 89**
toteswingers:1&2:£51.80, 1&3:£25.80, 2&3:£49.60 CSF £200.76 CT £1731.52 TOTE £16.20: £3.20, £5.30, £2.10, £2.80; EX 433.20 Trifecta £2546.80 Pool: £31,982.44 - 9.29 winning units..
Owner Jim McGrath **Bred** Newgate Stud Company **Trained** Musley Bank, N Yorks

FOCUS
A fiercely competitive renewal of this valuable handicap. Previous course and distance form was well represented with six of these having run in this year's Buckingham Palace and five in the Victoria Cup. The field soon split into two groups, with five racing centre to far side. The front four were all close to the rail. Sound form, rated around the runner-up.

NOTEBOOK
Castles In The Air was 18lb higher than when easily winning the ladies' event on this card last year, but only 6lb higher than when making a winning reappearance at Pontefract in April. Tucked away in the nearside group, he came under pressure passing the two-furlong pole but responded well and forged his way to the front well inside the last furlong. This was probably an even better performance than it looked from the winner as his rider thought the ground was faster than ideal for him. He is still in next Saturday's Stewards' Cup and the drop back to 6f wouldn't bother him, but it remains to be seen if he turns out again at Goodwood. (tchd 12-1)

Noble Citizen(USA) ◆, who had excuses for his two defeats since finishing a close fourth in the Victoria Cup, gave himself plenty to do in the nearside group, but he eventually flew home to snatch second and looks to have a big handicap in him judged on this effort.

Himalya(IRE) 'won' the race on his side in the Buckingham Palace last month and was 4lb higher here, having been a beaten favourite in a 6f Group 3 since. He was produced with his effort at just the right time and may even have hit the front for a few strides inside the last furlong, but once again he was worried out of it. He keeps on finding ways to get himself beaten and is still without a win since his racecourse debut. (op 9-1)

Yaa Wayl(IRE) ◆ was 15lb higher than when scraping home at Chester in May having performed well in a Listed race and a conditions event in the meantime. Still officially 3lb well in here despite his 3lb penalty, he emerges with plenty of credit against his elders as he did much the best of those that were handy from the start and he never stopped trying. He looks well worth a return to Pattern company. (op 11-1)

Suruor(IRE) looked a hard ride as he was having to be ridden along from a long way out, but he stayed on willingly over the last couple of furlongs to finish where he did. He is on a career-high mark now, but is by no means a lost cause. (tchd 18-1 and 20-1 in places)

Gallagher ◆, unplaced in two similarly hot handicaps since returning from Dubai, ran on from the middle of the nearside group and could be interesting now as he is already due to drop another 2lb.

Imperial Guest ◆, very disappointing at Newmarket last time after finishing a cracking third in the Buckingham Palace, ran on to emerge best of those that raced towards the far side, and he is worth bearing in mind.

Al Muheer(IRE) ◆, 2lb higher than when winning this race last year at 40-1 for Clive Brittain, was making his debut for his new yard and was noted doing all his best work late. It will be a surprise if his talented trainer doesn't find the right opportunity for him in the coming months. (op 25-1)

Glen Molly(IRE), still 6lb above her last winning mark, was returning from another short absence as connections were waiting for the ground to ease. She travelled well behind the leader on the far side, but didn't find quite as much off the bridle as had looked likely, and she may not have been helped by racing away from the main action. She might also just have needed it, but she is currently in foal so it remains to be seen whether she will be given another opportunity. (op 25-1)

Decent Fella(IRE), one of the least exposed in the field, was an eyecatcher on his debut for the yard at Newmarket in May, but he could never land a blow in the nearside group here. He is still open to improvement, however.

Poet's Place(USA), having just his fifth start and only his third on turf, was trying beyond 6f for the first time, and this may have been too stiff a task in view of his inexperience. He shouldn't be written off. (op 9-1)

Hajoum(IRE) Official explanation: jockey said colt hung right-handed throughout

Something(IRE), 3lb higher than when just getting up to win over 6f at Epsom last time, has plenty of winning form over this trip, but he was very awkward leaving the stalls and then hung right while coming under maximum pressure. It may be best to forgive him this. (op 28-1)

Tagseed(IRE), much less exposed than most and bidding for a four-timer off a 4lb higher mark, came off the bridle over two furlongs out and dropped right away as though something were amiss. Official explanation: trainer had no explanation for the poor form shown (tchd 8-1)

4359 KING GEORGE VI AND QUEEN ELIZABETH STKS SPONSORED BY BETFAIR (GROUP 1) 1m 4f

4:25 (4:26) (Class 1) 3-Y-O+

£567,700 (£215,200; £107,700; £53,700; £26,900; £13,500) **Stalls** High

Form RPR

-111 **1** **Harbinger**[35] 3191 4-9-7 123 .... OlivierPeslier 6 135
(Sir Michael Stoute) *hld up in midfield: gng wl and swtchd lft ent fnl 2f: pushed into ld over 1f out: sn wl clr: r.o strly: impressive* **4/1**[2]

-101 **2** 11 **Cape Blanco (IRE)**[27] 3491 3-8-9 119 .... CO'Donoghue 7 118
(A P O'Brien, Ire) *chsd ldr: rdn over 3f out: drvn to ld wl over 1f out: sn hdd and nt pce of wnr: wl btn and edgd rt u.p 1f out: kpt on for clr 2nd* **9/2**[3]

-042 **3** 3 ¼ **Youmzain (IRE)**[27] 3494 7-9-7 117 .... RichardHughes 5 112
(M R Channon) *stdd s: hld up in last pair: pushed along ent 2f out: swtchd lft and rdn 1f out: no ch w wnr after: wnt modest 3rd and hung rt ins fnl f* **12/1**

1-33 **4** nk **Daryakana (FR)**[27] 3494 4-9-4 116 .... GeraldMosse 4 109
(A De Royer-Dupre, France) *hld up in last pair: pushed along over 2f out: rdn and effrt on outer 2f out: sn wl outpcd by wnr: wnt modest 4th ins fnl f* **14/1**

1-21 **5** 2 ¼ **Workforce**[49] 2746 3-8-9 128 .... RyanMoore 3 108
(Sir Michael Stoute) *t.k.h: chsd ldrs: disp 2nd fr 8f out tl rdn and wanting to hang lft bnd over 2f out: drvn and btn wl over 1f out: wknd over 1f out* **8/11**[1]

-060 **6** 6 **Confront**[22] 3632 5-9-7 111 .... RichardMullen 1 99
(Sir Michael Stoute) *sn led and set gd gallop: pushed along over 4f out: rdn and hdd wl over 1f out: sn wknd: wl bhd fnl f* **100/1**

2m 26.78s (-5.72) **Going Correction** +0.025s/f (Good)
WFA 3 from 4yo+ 12lb **6** Ran SP% **111.4**
Speed ratings (Par 117): **120,112,110,110,108 104**
toteswingers:1&2:£2.30, 1&3:£4.70, 2&3:£3.70 CSF £21.54 TOTE £4.70: £2.00, £2.80; EX 20.40.
Owner Highclere Thoroughbred Racing (Adm. Rous) **Bred** Mrs A K H Ooi **Trained** Newmarket, Suffolk

FOCUS
Arguably the most eagerly anticipated race of the season so far, with the participation of the Epsom Derby hero for the first time since Kris Kin in 2003 the focal point. Confront ensured they went a decent gallop, nothing more through the early stages, but it slowly increased and the race was set up for something to stamp its class in the straight, and it did. This was an outstanding performance from Harbinger at face value and he is rated up 6lb. On RPRs he is the best horse in the world now and the leading older horse since 2001 Arc winner Sakhee. It is hard to pin down exactly what he achieved, with Workforce below form, but the runner-up appeared to give his running.

NOTEBOOK
Harbinger put in a devastating performance that will live long in the memory, winning by a remarkable 11l and taking 0.46secs off the previous course record. Making his debut at Group 1 level, following an impressive victory in last month's Hardwicke over C&D (race worked out exceptionally well), Olivier Peslier was aboard the winner for the first time, with Moore predictably staying loyal to Workforce, and things could not have gone more smoothly. Always travelling with consummate ease on the tail of his stablemate, Harbinger was absolutely running away as they began to turn for home, with the cracks having already well and truly opened up on his five other rivals, and the response was electrifying when he was finally asked to assert, sprinting clear in the final furlong for one of the easiest ever victories in this historic race. The Arc is the obvious long-term aim, for which he is now a general 7-4 shot, although as short as evens with some bookmakers. That seems skinny enough at this stage, with Stoute having never won the race and the possibility of there being testing conditions at that time of year, which could blunt his speed. Harry Herbert mooted that he may be kept fresh for Longchamp, but if he does run before then, it would come as no surprise to see him drop back n trip for either the Irish Champion Stakes or Juddmonte International. Wherever he does go next, it's hoped he can back this performance up and confirm the impression created here that he's a superstar. (op 7-2 tchd 9-2)

Cape Blanco(IRE) had only met with defeat once prior to today, when tenth on unsuitably soft ground in the French Derby, but he showed his true worth in the Irish equivalent and had been the only horse to beat the favourite in the Dante at York earlier in the season. He comprehensively confirmed form with a below-par Workforce, but was made to look pedestrian by that one's older stablemate, though still kept on grimly for strong pressure, finishing a clear second best. He lacks the brilliance to be a truly top-class performer, but is a thoroughly likeable horse capable of winning more races at Group 1 level, this season and next if kept in training. Aidan O'Brien said afterwards that he wouldn't be frightened to drop back in distance, with a return to York for the Juddmonte International looking a distinct possibility. (op 11-2)

Youmzain(IRE), although twice a winner in Group 1 company, has earned himself title of perennial bridesmaid having now been second or third at the top level on 13 other occasions. Hitting the frame for the third time in this event, there is no reason to believe he didn't run his race, being held up as ever and keeping on down the straight without being able to reach the runner-up. Already second three times in the Arc, he will struggle to reach a position as high this time round, but the 7yo should continue to give a good account at this level. (op 14-1)

Daryakana(FR) hasn't quite matched her 3yo form in two starts this year, though she's still been performing to a high level. That said, realistically she was playing for third or fourth, and she kept on down the straight to claim the latter spot. The return to a right-handed track was expected to suit, but it made little difference to her performance and perhaps she deserves a break by going back against her own sex for her next start.

Workforce won the Derby so impressively, breaking Lammtarra's track record in the process. That must have taken a fair bit out of him, as he missed the Irish Derby and headed straight here. There were many hoping, and indeed some expecting, a Harbinger-like performance from the 3yo, as only last month it was he who looked the superstar. However, there were slight concerns about him going this way round, considering what happened with the bit slipping through his mouth in the Dante, and the Epsom form could have worked out better, with Buzzword in the German Derby being the only subsequent victor from the beaten horses. The ground was also a potential concern, and when it became clear that he hadn't settled as well as Ryan Moore would have liked in tracking the pacesetter, it was always doubtful we were going to see a repeat of his Epsom heroics. He had issues with the home bend, not looking at all comfortable turning right, and he just never picked up once asked to stretch, being beaten over 2f out and slowly fading. This was a shadow of the horse we saw early in June and it's hoped Stoute can give him the necessary care to get him back to his best. Official explanation: jockey said colt was unsuited by the track and failed to switch off (tchd 4-5 in places and 5-6 in places and 10-11 in places and evens places)

Confront was in the race to ensure it wasn't a dawdle and he did just that. He was by no means disgraced, only being a length or so off the favourite when eased right down in the final 100 yards.

4360 CANISBAY BLOODSTOCK H'CAP 1m 4f

5:35 (5:35) (Class 4) (0-85,82) 3-Y-O **£6,476** (£1,927; £963; £481) **Stalls** High

Form RPR

3121 **1** **Yashrid (USA)**[26] 3519 3-9-7 **82** .... PhilipRobinson 6 90
(M A Jarvis) *jostled and n.m.r sn after s: hld up in last trio: hdwy on outer over 2f out: rdn to chse ldrs over 1f out: led fnl 75yds: r.o strly* **9/2**[2]

-142 **2** 1 **Valiant Knight (FR)**[27] 3481 3-9-0 **78** .... PatrickHills(3) 9 85
(R Hannon) *hld up in midfield: rdn and hdwy ent fnl 2f: chal over 1f out: drvn to ld 1f out tl hdd and nt pce of wnr fnl 75yds* **15/2**

331 **3** ½ **Heart Of Hearts**[23] 3593 3-9-3 **78** .... EddieAhern 7 84
(H R A Cecil) *hld up in tch in midfield: switching lft and effrt over 2f out: drvn and ev ch jst ins fnl f: styd on same pce fnl 100yds* **13/2**

50 **4** ½ **Missionaire (USA)**[45] 2869 3-9-2 **77** .... SebSanders 3 82
(W J Knight) *led: rdn over 2f out: drvn and hdd 1f out: stl ev ch tl one pce and btn fnl 75yds* **10/1**

5013 **5** ¾ **Kerchak (USA)**[23] 3581 3-8-12 **73** .... JoeFanning 1 77
(W Jarvis) *stdd and dropped in bhd after s: t.k.h: hld up towards rr: rdn over 2f out: hdwy to chse ldrs jst over 1f out: kpt on same pce and no real imp after* **11/1**

1-42 **6** 4 **Valid Reason**[23] 3594 3-9-6 **81** .... RyanMoore 8 78
(Mrs A J Perrett) *racd in last trio: rdn and unable qck ent fnl 2f: keeping on but n.d whn swtchd lft 1f out: styd on steadily fnl f but nvr gng pce to threaten ldrs* **11/4**[1]

100 **7** 1 **Beat Route**[45] 2869 3-8-2 **68** .... JemmaMarshall(5) 4 64
(M J Attwater) *t.k.h: chsd ldrs: rdn over 2f out: wknd u.p over 1f out* **50/1**

1 **8** nk **Balletlou (IRE)**[27] 3477 3-8-13 **79** .... KierenFox(5) 10 74
(J R Best) *stdd s: hld up in rr: rdn and unable qck ent fnl 2f: kpt on same pce after: nvr trbld ldrs* **5/1**[3]

4-10 **9** 1 ¼ **Countess Comet (IRE)**[23] 3594 3-9-7 **82** .... JackMitchell 2 75
(R M Beckett) *plld hrd: chsd ldrs tl wnt 2nd over 8f out tl over 1f out: sn wknd* **20/1**

6-32 **10** 14 **Blitzed**[28] 3443 3-8-11 **72** .... RichardMullen 5 43
(G L Moore) *t.k.h: chsd ldrs tl rdn and wknd ent fnl 2f: wl bhd and eased ins fnl f* **16/1**

2m 32.19s (-0.31) **Going Correction** +0.025s/f (Good) **10** Ran SP% **116.6**
Speed ratings (Par 102): **102,101,101,100,100 97,96,96,95,86**
toteswingers:1&2:£5.30, 1&3:£5.00, 2&3:£5.40 CSF £38.27 CT £219.81 TOTE £4.90: £1.80, £2.20, £2.00; EX 40.80 Trifecta £109.40 Pool: £2,014.98 - 13.62 winning units. Place 6 £250.81; Place 5 £37.66.
Owner Sheikh Ahmed Al Maktoum **Bred** Darley **Trained** Newmarket, Suffolk

FOCUS
The prize money for this race was only one per cent of the King George purse, but it was still a competitive little 3yo handicap in its own right. The early pace looked ordinary, however, causing a few to pull hard, and the winning time was 5.41 seconds slower than the King George. The form is rated around the fourth and fifth.
Blitzed Official explanation: jockey said gelding ran too free
T/Plt: £627.80 to a £1 stake. Pool:£210,913.34 - 245.21 winning tickets T/Qpdt: £33.60 to a £1 stake. Pool:£13,110.99 - 287.91 winning tickets SP

4253 LINGFIELD (L-H)
Saturday, July 24

OFFICIAL GOING: Firm
Wind: Light, half behind Weather: Fine, warm

4361 VINES REDHILL MINI H'CAP — 1m 2f
5:45 (5:45) (Class 6) (0-65,64) 3-Y-0+ — £2,047 (£604; £302) Stalls Low

Form RPR
240 1 **Lady Lam**[15] 3862 4-9-6 56 ....(t) LiamKeniry 6 66+
(S Kirk) *hld up in 4th: trckd ldng pair 1/2-way: gng bttr than rest and wnt 2nd over 2f out: led over 1f out: drvn out* 7/2[3]
0006 2 1 ¼ **Diamond Twister (USA)**[5] 4201 4-9-10 60 .... LiamJones 10 67
(J R Best) *led: rdn over 2f out: hdd over 1f out: kpt on but a hold* 9/4[2]
0426 3 2 ½ **Farncombe (IRE)**[11] 3983 4-9-3 53 .... EddieCreighton 11 55
(M J Scudamore) *t.k.h: trckd ldng pair to 1/2-way: rdn and nt qckn over 2f out: kpt on to take 3rd over 1f out: one pce* 7/1
0/00 4 2 ½ **Dora Explora**[29] 3403 6-8-11 50 ....(p) RobertLButler(3) 12 47
(Mrs L C Jewell) *hld up in last pair: effrt on outer and wl in tch over 2f out: sn nt qckn and btn* 25/1
4115 5 1 **Under Fire (IRE)**[11] 3983 7-9-1 56 .... JohnFahy(5) 1 51
(A W Carroll) *v s.i.s: plld hrd early: hld up in last pair: rdn on inner over 2f out: no prog: wknd fnl f* 2/1[1]
5500 6 hd **Supercast (IRE)**[40] 3025 7-10-0 64 .... LukeMorris 8 59
(N J Vaughan) *t.k.h: chsd ldr to over 2f out: wknd wl over 1f out* 9/1
2m 11.93s (1.43) **Going Correction** -0.35s/f (Firm)
WFA 3 from 4yo+ 10lb — **6** Ran SP% **112.7**
Speed ratings (Par 101): **80,79,77,75,74 74**
Tote Swingers: 1&2 £2.50, 2&3 £3.20 CSF £11.91 CT £49.74 TOTE £4.50: £2.60, £2.30; EX 12.10 Trifecta £49.74.
Owner J B J Richards **Bred** J B J Richards **Trained** Upper Lambourn, Berks

FOCUS
Officially firm ground and six withdrawals decimated the opener. It was run at a steady pace and the race didn't begin in earnest until the straight. Weak and muddling form, but improvement from the winner.
Under Fire(IRE) Official explanation: jockey said gelding was slowly away

4362 VINESOFREDHILLBMW.CO.UK H'CAP — 2m
6:15 (6:16) (Class 5) (0-70,68) 3-Y-0+ — £2,388 (£705; £352) Stalls Low

Form RPR
1221 1 **Corr Point (IRE)**[22] 3639 3-9-0 68 ....(t) FergusSweeney 5 74+
(J A Osborne) *hld up in 4th: pushed along and prog on outer to ld 2f out: edgd lft over 1f out: hmpd runner-up ins fnl f: styd on* 8/11[1]
4042 2 ½ **Tower**[11] 3996 3-8-5 59 .... SaleemGolam 6 64+
(G Prodromou) *trckd ldng pair: wnt 2nd 7f out: rdn to chal 2f out: chsd wnr after: half a l down and trying whn bdly hmpd against rail ins fnl f: styd on nr fin* 10/1
0-62 3 ¾ **Haldibari (IRE)**[10] 3804 6-9-1 52 .... LiamKeniry 7 54
(S Lycett) *led: tried to kick on over 3f out: hdd and nt qckn 2f out: rallied fnl f: clsng at fin* 3/1[2]
2443 4 2 ¼ **Brad's Luck (IRE)**[16] 3819 4-8-11 48 ....(b) LukeMorris 2 47
(M Blanshard) *trckd ldr to 7f out: drvn 4f out: nt qckn over 2f out: kpt on* 8/1[3]
2500 5 16 **Honorable Endeavor**[10] 2907 4-8-7 47 ....(b) WilliamCarson(3) 3 27
(E F Vaughan) *hld up in last: rdn 5f out: lost tch 4f out: no ch after* 12/1
3m 35.74s (0.94) **Going Correction** -0.35s/f (Firm)
WFA 3 from 4yo+ 17lb — **5** Ran SP% **110.8**
Speed ratings (Par 103): **83,82,82,81,73**
CSF £8.99 TOTE £1.50: £1.10, £4.00; EX 6.90.
Owner J Duddy & R A Pegum **Bred** T J Pabst And Newtown Stud **Trained** Upper Lambourn, Berks
■ Stewards' Enquiry : Fergus Sweeney four-day ban: careless riding (Aug 7-10)

FOCUS
Only five runners and just a modest affair, but it was run at a fair pace considering the size of the field and resulted in a controversial finish with the winner looking fortunate to keep the race after badly hampering the runner-up. The first two are both a bit better than the bare form.

4363 VINES REDHILL BMW MAIDEN AUCTION STKS — 5f
6:45 (6:46) (Class 6) 2-Y-0 — £2,047 (£604; £302) Stalls High

Form RPR
33 1 **Best Be Careful (IRE)**[21] 3686 2-8-6 0 .... LiamKeniry 8 64+
(M D I Usher) *trckd ldr: led over 1f out: drvn out and hld on* 2/1[1]
633 2 ½ **Upark Flyer**[8] 4083 2-8-0 66 .... JohnFahy(5) 4 63
(Patrick Morris) *trckd ldrs against rail: nt clr run and swtchd lft jst over 1f out: rdn to chse wnr ins fnl f: styd on but a jst hld* 6/1[2]
30 3 1 ¼ **My Love Fajer (IRE)**[18] 3756 2-9-0 0 .... KirstyMilczarek 1 66
(G Prodromou) *fast away fr low draw: led and crossed to rail: rdn and hdd over 1f out: one pce* 28/1
4 ¾ **Prince Titus (IRE)** 2-8-6 0 .... JamesSullivan(5) 3 60
(Mrs L Stubbs) *racd alone towards centre: chsd ldrs: rdn 2f out: kpt on but unable to chal* 2/1[1]
5 ½ **Onlyfoalsandhorses (IRE)** 2-8-5 0 .... LukeMorris 9 52
(J S Moore) *pushed along in last pair and outpcd: effrt 2f out and swtchd off rail: rdn and styd on: nvr able to chal* 14/1
6 2 ½ **Smart Performance** 2-8-7 0 .... MatthewDavies(3) 6 48
(A P Jarvis) *hld up in rr on outer: drifted to rail 2f out: shkn up briefly over 1f out: plugged on* 12/1
3400 7 2 ¼ **Kodiac Star (IRE)**[15] 3864 2-8-1 62 .... SophieDoyle(5) 5 36
(J A Osborne) *chsd ldrs tl wknd over 1f out* 8/1[3]
05 8 3 ¼ **One Fat Cat (IRE)**[54] 2591 2-8-5 0 .... NeilChalmers 2 23
(P M Phelan) *chsd ldrs 3f: wknd* 20/1
9 9 **Warbond** 2-8-6 0 .... WilliamCarson(3) 7 —
(M Madgwick) *s.s: rn green in last and a detached: hanging fr over 1f out* 33/1
57.63 secs (-0.57) **Going Correction** -0.35s/f (Firm) — **9** Ran SP% **117.6**
Speed ratings (Par 92): **90,89,87,86,85 81,77,72,58**
Tote Swingers: 1&2 £1.50, 1&3 £8.40, 2&3 £19.80 CSF £14.86 TOTE £3.30: £1.10, £3.20, £11.50; EX 12.80.
Owner Mrs Jill Pellett **Bred** M Phelan **Trained** Upper Lambourn, Berks
■ Stewards' Enquiry : Liam Keniry caution: careless riding.

FOCUS
A modest maiden in which experience came to the fore and, as usual on the straight course here this season, the stands rail was once again the place to be. Solid but limited form.

NOTEBOOK
Best Be Careful(IRE) had some of the best form on offer and made the most of a decent opportunity under a no-nonsense ride, soon well placed on the rail. She looks quite speedy and will probably be best kept to this trip in nurseries. (op 5-2)
Upark Flyer is steadily getting the hang of things and might just have edged out the winner had she got a run on the rail instead of having to switch wide. She's unlikely to find another maiden as winnable as this, however, and might have better prospects in nurseries. (op 4-1)
My Love Fajer(IRE) was given every chance taken straight across to the stand rail from her outside draw. She'll probably stay 6f without necessarily finding any improvement for it. (op 25-1)
Prince Titus(IRE) ◆, from a stable in cracking form and reportedly working well with recent winners, was too inexperienced to do himself justice and found himself isolated in the middle of the track, only for the penny to drop late in the day. A brother to the fair miler Miami Gator, he was well backed beforehand and looks the sort that can leave this form well behind next time. (op 7-2 tchd 15-8)
Onlyfoalsandhorses(IRE), a late foal, took some time to realise what was required but shaped promisingly in the second half of the race. (op 10-1)
Smart Performance looked all at sea in the middle part of the race before staying on nicely at the finish. He's bred to need much further than this, and might not come into his own this season until getting 7f or 1m. (op 10-1 tchd 14-1)

4364 VINES GATWICK MINI MEDIAN AUCTION MAIDEN STKS — 7f
7:20 (7:21) (Class 6) 3-5-Y-0 — £2,047 (£604; £302) Stalls High

Form RPR
0022 1 **Rolling Hills (IRE)**[16] 3816 3-9-3 70 .... FergusSweeney 7 68
(H Candy) *mde virtually all and sn stretched field against rail: hung lft fr 2f out: hrd rdn and jnd fnl f: hld on* 1/1[1]
2 shd **Norman Orpen (IRE)** 3-9-3 0 .... LukeMorris 12 68
(N P Littmoden) *chsd ldng quartet: effrt against rail 2f out: hrd rdn to chal fnl f: jst failed* 14/1
-364 3 shd **Lathaat**[33] 3258 3-8-12 72 .... TadhgO'Shea 10 63
(J L Dunlop) *chsd ldng pair: reminder 4f out and off the bridle after: wnt 2nd over 2f out: chal between rivals fnl f: jst hld* 11/4[2]
00 4 2 ¼ **Into The Wind**[19] 3738 3-8-9 0 .... WilliamCarson(3) 2 57
(B R Millman) *chsd ldrs in 6th and in tch: pushed along and outpcd 2f out: one reminder 1f out: styd on steadily* 33/1
60 5 2 ½ **Tt's Dream**[16] 3827 3-8-12 0 .... SophieDoyle(5) 5 55
(A J Lidderdale) *chsd ldng trio: shkn up and outpcd 2f out: kpt on same pce fnl f* 15/2[3]
6 8 **Mackenzie Spiers** 3-8-12 0 .... IanMongan 4 28
(B R Millman) *dwlt: wl off the pce in 9th: rn green and hanging over 2f out: sme late prog* 25/1
00 7 3 ¾ **Namehim**[8] 4107 3-9-3 0 .... LiamKeniry 8 23
(E F Vaughan) *racd in 8th and wl off the pce: no ch fr 3f out* 16/1
000- 8 hd **Dancing Again**[261] 7254 4-9-0 39 .... KierenFox(5) 6 21
(E A Wheeler) *racd freely: chsd wnr to over 2f out: wknd rapidly* 66/1
00 9 1 ¾ **Final Try**[33] 3272 3-9-0 0 .... RobertLButler(3) 9 18
(P Butler) *dwlt: racd in 7th and wl off the pce: hanging and wknd 2f out* 66/1
10 7 **Sea Tobougie** 3-8-12 0 .... TravisBlock 3 —
(M D I Usher) *dwlt: wl bhd in 10th: nvr a factor* 33/1
0 11 48 **Mushy Peas (IRE)**[26] 3511 3-9-3 0 .... StevieDonohoe 11 —
(P D Evans) *stmbld s: a last and t.o by 1/2-way* 28/1
1m 21.48s (-1.82) **Going Correction** -0.35s/f (Firm)
WFA 3 from 4yo 7lb — **11** Ran SP% **117.1**
Speed ratings (Par 101): **96,95,95,93,90 81,76,76,74,66 11**
Tote Swingers: 1&2 £6.40, 1&3 £1.10, 2&3 £7.90 CSF £16.43 TOTE £2.00: £1.20, £4.60, £1.10; EX 17.60.
Owner Six Too Many **Bred** D Eiffe **Trained** Kingston Warren, Oxon

FOCUS
With two hitherto frustrating sorts heading the betting and a bunch finish, this isn't form to view too positively. The action took place on the stand rail and the field were soon well strung out. The form is rated around the winner and third.
Mackenzie Spiers Official explanation: jockey said filly ran green

4365 VINESOFGATWICKBMW.CO.UK H'CAP — 7f
7:55 (7:55) (Class 5) (0-70,70) 3-Y-0 — £2,388 (£705; £352) Stalls High

Form RPR
4013 1 **Merchant Of Medici**[17] 3771 3-9-5 68 .... EddieAhern 11 75
(W R Muir) *trckd ldrs: wnt 2nd 2f out: shkn up to ld 1f out: rdn out whn pressed last 100yds* 9/4[1]
-350 2 ½ **Tap Dance Way (IRE)**[28] 3464 3-9-1 64 .... LiamKeniry 12 70
(P R Chamings) *dwlt: hld up last: rdn 3f out: prog 2f out: chse wnr jst ins fnl f: styd on but a hld* 10/3[3]
4110 3 2 ¾ **Chinese Democracy (USA)**[1] 4324 3-8-12 61 ....(v) StevieDonohoe 10 60
(P D Evans) *trckd ldrs: shkn up over 2f out: prog to go 3rd ins fnl f: no imp* 11/4[2]
00-0 4 2 **Royal Blade (IRE)**[115] 1058 3-9-2 68 .... MatthewDavies(3) 2 61
(A P Jarvis) *led and crossed to rail: edgd off it fr 3f out: hdd & wknd 1f out* 25/1
-150 5 ½ **Mount Juliet (IRE)**[55] 2565 3-9-1 69 .... TobyAtkinson(5) 5 61+
(M Botti) *hld up in last pair: taken to outer and sme prog 2f out: no imp u.p over 1f out: fdd* 8/1
0-00 6 2 ¾ **Pycian**[29] 3394 3-9-2 70 .... JamesSullivan(5) 13 54
(Mrs L Stubbs) *sn towards rr against rail: rdn wl over 2f out: dropped to last wl over 1f out: plugged on* 16/1
5004 7 2 ½ **Sonny G (IRE)**[2] 4297 3-7-13 53 .... KierenFox(5) 4 31
(J R Best) *pressed ldrs: rdn 1/2-way: wknd 2f out* 9/1
50-5 8 2 ½ **Kate Skate**[14] 3907 3-8-1 57 .... AdamBeschizza(7) 1 28
(Miss Gay Kelleway) *t.k.h: racd on outer: chsd ldr to 2f out: wknd* 14/1
1m 21.01s (-2.29) **Going Correction** -0.35s/f (Firm) — **8** Ran SP% **118.0**
Speed ratings (Par 100): **99,98,95,93,92 89,86,83**
Tote Swingers: 1&2 £2.40, 1&3 £1.10, 2&3 £3.70 CSF £10.42 CT £21.23 TOTE £3.00: £1.30, £1.40, £1.40; EX 11.40.
Owner S Jones & R Haim **Bred** Cheveley Park Stud Ltd **Trained** Lambourn, Berks

FOCUS
A fair handicap run at a reasonable pace in which the action again took place towards the stand rail. The winner is rated in line with his Catterick run.

Pycian Official explanation: jockey said gelding became unbalanced 3f out

4366 VINES GATWICK BMW H'CAP 7f 140y
8:25 (8:28) (Class 6) (0-65,65) 3-Y-0+ £2,047 (£604; £302) **Stalls** Centre

Form RPR

5000 **1** **Kipchak (IRE)**[3] 4260 5-9-7 **59**.........................(p) LiamKeniry 15 69
(C R Dore) *taken down early: one of only two that racd nr side thrght: led: hanging lft: drvn and hdd jst over 1f out: rallied to ld last 50yds* **7/2**[1]

-060 **2** 3/4 **Cavendish Road (IRE)**[40] 3022 4-9-12 **64**................(t) KirstyMilczarek 6 72+
(N J Vaughan) *racd centre: hld up in tch: prog over 2f out: rdn to ld jst over 1f out: hdd and nt qckn last 50yds* **14/1**

0344 **3** 3/4 **Dichoh**[31] 3338 7-9-8 **60**.........................(v) EddieAhern 11 66
(M Madgwick) *swtchd to r nr side after 2f: wl off the pce: pushed along 3f out: no prog tl styd on strly fr over 1f out: nrst fin* **7/1**

5 **4** 1 3/4 **Miss Bounty**[26] 3514 5-9-7 **62**......................... MatthewDavies(3) 2 64+
(George Baker) *racd centre: hld up last of gp: prog fr 2f out: rdn and styd on fnl f: nvr able to chal* **10/1**

0-54 **5** 1/2 **Safari Guide**[42] 2964 4-9-6 **58**......................... LukeMorris 14 59
(P Winkworth) *one of only two to r nr side thrght: plld hrd: pressed ldr: nt qckn 2f out: fdd over 1f out* **5/1**[2]

016 **6** 3 1/4 **Monashee Rock (IRE)**[9] 4044 5-9-6 **65**................. AdamBeschizza(7) 4 58
(Matthew Salaman) *taken down early: blindfold off sltly late and dwlt: racd in centre: u.p in midfield over 3f out: nvr on terms* **10/1**

1350 **7** 3/4 **Know No Fear**[170] 404 5-9-1 **58**......................... RosieJessop(5) 10 49
(A J Lidderdale) *t.k.h: led centre gp to 2f out: wknd and eased* **20/1**

0035 **8** 1 3/4 **Top Flight Splash**[11] 3979 4-8-8 **46**.........................(v) StevieDonohoe 5 33
(P D Evans) *blindfold off sltly late and dwlt: racd centre: pushed along to stay in tch 3f out: wknd over 1f out* **16/1**

2054 **9** nk **Grey Boy (GER)**[4] 4232 9-8-7 **52**......................... GeorgeDowning(7) 8 38
(A W Carroll) *swtchd to r nr side after 2f: t.k.h and hld up off the pce: pushed along wl over 2f out: nvr on terms* **7/2**[1]

-002 **10** nk **Storm Hawk (IRE)**[26] 3514 3-9-3 **63**.........................(v) AndreaAtzeni 9 47
(Pat Eddery) *chsd ldrs in centre: rdn wl over 2f out: wknd wl over 1f out* **6/1**[3]

0-05 **11** 3 1/2 **Bewdley**[24] 3557 5-8-3 **46**......................... JamesSullivan(5) 7 23
(R E Peacock) *racd centre: chsd ldrs tl wknd 2f out* **33/1**

1040 **12** 5 **Stargazy**[19] 3727 6-8-8 **53**.........................(p) HollyHall(7) 16 18
(A J Lidderdale) *s.s: a last: wl bhd fnl 2f* **25/1**

1m 29.11s (-3.19) **Going Correction** -0.35s/f (Firm)
WFA 3 from 4yo+ 8lb **12** Ran SP% **130.2**
Speed ratings (Par 101): **101,100,99,97,97 94,93,91,91,90 87,82**
Tote Swingers: 1&2 £2.40, 1&3 £1.10, 2&3 £3.70 CSF £61.04 CT £352.22 TOTE £5.30: £1.70, £6.40, £3.50; EX 77.30 Place 6: £13.93 Place 5: £5.18.
Owner Liam Breslin **Bred** Miss Mary Davidson & Mrs Steffi Von Schilcher **Trained** Cowbit, Lincs

FOCUS
A modest handicap in which two of the first three raced against the rail throughout yet despite all the recent evidence here, a large number of riders were content to make their way down the middle. The winner is rated to this year's turf best.
Safari Guide Official explanation: jockey said gelding hung badly right
T/Plt: £16.50 to a £1 stake. Pool:£56,009 - 2,477.88 winning tickets T/Qpdt: £4.50 to a £1 stake. Pool:£6,205 - 1,019.24 winning tickets JN

3445 NEWCASTLE (L-H)
Saturday, July 24

OFFICIAL GOING: Good to soft (6.2)
All races on straight course due to drainage work and dolling out 2yds off stands' rail up to winning post.
Wind: Breezy, half behind Weather: Cloudy

4367 TYNE TEES MODELS SUPPORTS MISS NEWCASTLE NURSERY 6f
2:25 (2:25) (Class 5) 2-Y-0 £2,331 (£693; £346; £173) **Stalls** Centre

Form RPR

120 **1** **Chiswick Bey (IRE)**[39] 3049 2-9-7 **85**......................... TonyHamilton 3 89+
(R A Fahey) *cl up: rdn to ld over 1f out: edgd rt ins fnl f: r.o wl* **5/4**[1]

4024 **2** 2 1/4 **Boundaries**[11] 3985 2-8-7 **71**......................... DavidAllan 4 68
(T D Easterby) *t.k.h: led to over 1f out: kpt on same pce fnl f* **11/2**[3]

15 **3** nk **Tro Nesa (IRE)**[22] 3611 2-8-7 **74**......................... BarryMcHugh(3) 5 70
(Mrs A Duffield) *t.k.h: stdd in tch: effrt 2f out: kpt on u.p fnl f* **16/1**

2214 **4** 3 **Defence Council (IRE)**[26] 3504 2-9-4 **82**................... PaulMulrennan 2 69
(J Howard Johnson) *in tch: effrt and rdn 2f out: outpcd fnl f* **3/1**[2]

0044 **5** 11 **Roman Ruler (IRE)**[7] 4124 2-7-5 **62** oh9......................... NeilFarley(7) 6 16
(C W Fairhurst) *trckd ldrs tl rdn and wknd fr 2f out* **10/1**

6042 **6** 5 **Blind Stag (IRE)**[7] 4150 2-7-13 **66** ow3......................... KellyHarrison(3) 1 5
(P T Midgley) *t.k.h: cl up on outside tl wknd over 2f out* **7/1**

1m 16.33s (1.73) **Going Correction** +0.025s/f (Good) **6** Ran SP% **112.3**
Speed ratings (Par 94): **89,86,85,81,66 60**
Tote Swingers: 1&2 £2.40, 1&3 £4.60, 2&3 £37.60 CSF £8.67 TOTE £2.10: £1.60, £2.40.
Owner Mrs H Steel **Bred** Mrs Kay Egan **Trained** Musley Bank, N Yorks

FOCUS
No real depth to this nursery. The winner did it well and the form is rated through the third.

NOTEBOOK
Chiswick Bey(IRE)got his career back on track after finishing down the field in the Coventry Stakes at Royal Ascot. He'd shown his ability to handle an easy surface in the Brocklesby and was always moving like the winner. Things will be harder from now on, a rise to a mark in the low 90s is likely, but he's clearly still going the right way. (op Evens tchd 10-11)
Boundaries is proving consistent, but was no match for the winner after racing freely at the head of affairs and is starting to look exposed even at this early stage. (op 6-1)
Tro Nesa(IRE) put a poor effort at Beverley behind her, getting back to the level she showed when making a winning debut at Carlisle. Although this form is nothing out of the ordinary, improvement will be needed for her to win a nursery off this mark. (tchd 18-1)
Defence Council(IRE)'s mark didn't necessarily look beyond him and this was slightly disappointing. Perhaps the easier ground was against him (raced only on good or firmer previously). (op 9-2)
Blind Stag(IRE), runner-up in a Ripon seller a week ago, had more on in this company but might have been expected to do better. (op 8-1)

4368 NEWCASTLE FLOORING MAIDEN AUCTION STKS 7f
2:55 (2:56) (Class 4) 2-Y-0 £3,238 (£963; £481; £240) **Stalls** Centre

Form RPR

0 **1** **Chin'n Tonic (IRE)**[31] 3316 2-8-10 0......................... PJMcDonald 10 76+
(G A Swinbank) *hld up in tch: hdwy to ld appr fnl f: pushed clr fnl f: readily* **18/1**

66 **2** 4 1/2 **Damascus Symphony**[47] 2813 2-8-8 0......................... AndrewElliott 8 63
(J D Bethell) *w ldr: rdn and ev ch over 1f out: kpt on fnl f: nt pce of wnr* **33/1**

0 **3** 1 3/4 **Beer Flush (IRE)**[21] 3665 2-8-11 0......................... TonyHamilton 9 61
(Jedd O'Keeffe) *trckd ldrs: drvn and outpcd wl over 1f out: kpt on fnl f: nt rch first two* **22/1**

0 **4** 1 **Millies Folly**[34] 3237 2-7-12 0......................... NeilFarley(7) 11 53
(D Carroll) *led tl rdn and hdd appr fnl f: sn no ex* **40/1**

43 **5** 1 1/2 **Eland Ally**[30] 3365 2-8-11 0......................... MickyFenton 12 55
(T P Tate) *prom: effrt over 2f out: sn cl up: wknd ins fnl f* **5/2**[2]

43 **6** 3/4 **Not So Bright (USA)**[18] 3769 2-8-11 0......................... PaulMulrennan 6 58+
(J G Given) *dwlt: bhd: pushed along over 2f out: kpt on fnl f: nvr rchd ldrs* **13/2**[3]

7 1 1/2 **Fairlie Dinkum** 2-8-7 0 ow2......................... TomEaves 5 46+
(B Smart) *hld up: pushed along over 2f out: hdwy over 1f out: nvr able to chal* **11/1**

0 **8** nse **Regimental (IRE)**[6] 4167 2-8-7 0......................... BarryMcHugh(3) 7 48
(Mrs A Duffield) *in tch: rdn and outpcd over 2f out: n.d after* **33/1**

0 **9** 4 1/2 **Twennyshortkid**[30] 3365 2-8-5 0......................... IanBrennan(5) 2 37
(P T Midgley) *prom: drvn and lost pl 1/2-way: n.d after* **33/1**

5 **10** 4 **Another Citizen (IRE)**[14] 3923 2-8-12 0......................... DavidAllan 13 29
(T D Easterby) *midfield: effrt and rdn over 2f out: sn wknd* **6/4**[1]

56 **11** 1 1/2 **Domino Effect (IRE)**[21] 3657 2-9-0 0......................... LeeVickers 4 27
(J Howard Johnson) *prom tl rdn and wknd over 2f out* **20/1**

12 5 **Arashone** 2-8-2 0......................... KellyHarrison(3) 14 6
(J R Weymes) *hld up: rdn over 2f out: sn wknd* **33/1**

00 **13** 5 **Land Bank**[21] 3657 2-8-6 0......................... LanceBetts(5) 3 —
(T D Easterby) *s.i.s: sn drvn in rr: struggling fr 1/2-way* **80/1**

0 **14** 51 **Santorino**[69] 2138 2-8-11 0 ow1......................... LNewman 1 —
(P T Midgley) *bhd: struggling after 3f: sn btn: virtually p.u last 2f* **50/1**

1m 28.66s (-0.04) **Going Correction** +0.025s/f (Good) **14** Ran SP% **122.0**
Speed ratings (Par 96): **101,95,93,92,91 90,88,88,83,78 76,71,65,7**
CSF £510.16 TOTE £19.40: £4.40, £9.10, £4.50; EX 659.00.
Owner Chris Tremewan **Bred** Tally-Ho Stud **Trained** Melsonby, N Yorks

FOCUS
The market leaders were disappointing and it's doubtful this is anything better than an ordinary maiden, though that shouldn't detract too much from the winner who impressed.

NOTEBOOK
Chin'n Tonic(IRE) improved out of all recognition from his debut at Carlisle a month ago, travelling well and pulling right away in the end. Given his closest pursuers hadn't shown much previously the handicapper can't really go overboard with him and he's one to look out for in nurseries. (op 16-1)
Damascus Symphony hadn't achieved much in her two previous starts, but has clearly improved in the seven weeks since last seen, seeing out the longer trip well for all she was no match for the winner in the end. (op 28-1)
Beer Flush(IRE) had been very green on his debut and duly offered more this time, though the form is only modest and it's doubtful he will be up to winning in similar company next time. (op 16-1)
Millies Folly also ran better than on her debut, but may not have achieved much. (op 50-1)
Eland Ally had made the frame over 6f here in his two previous starts and might have been expected to do a lot better, particularly as he'd shaped as if this trip wouldn't be a problem. Perhaps the easier ground was against him. (op 3-1 tchd 9-4)
Not So Bright(USA)'s Wolverhampton third doesn't amount to a great deal and he never looked like getting in a serious blow, though he is at least now eligible for nurseries. (op 15-2 tchd 8-1)
Fairlie Dinkum, a daughter of Tobougg, seemed green and can be expected to do better with this behind her, certainly hinting at ability by the finish. (op 13-2)
Another Citizen(IRE) was sent off a well-backed favourite after a promising debut at York a fortnight ago, but soon went to nothing when push came to shove. He can't have been right and probably deserves another chance. Official explanation: jockey said colt never travelled and hung left final 4f (op 2-1)

4369 MATALAN H'CAP 6f
3:30 (3:30) (Class 3) (0-90,90) 3-Y-0
£6,231 (£1,866; £933; £467; £233; £117) **Stalls** Centre

Form RPR

-000 **1** **Golden Shaheen (IRE)**[15] 3876 3-8-11 **80**.................(b) AndrewElliott 8 99
(M Johnston) *dwlt: hld up: hdwy over 1f out: led ins fnl f: pushed out* **10/1**

4000 **2** 1 3/4 **Colonel Mak**[14] 3886 3-9-2 **85**......................... ShaneKelly 10 98
(T D Barron) *hld up: hdwy to ld over 1f out: hdd ins fnl f: nt pce of wnr* **13/2**[3]

-635 **3** 5 **Walvis Bay (IRE)**[8] 4091 3-8-11 **80**......................... MickyFenton 5 77
(T P Tate) *cl up: led after 2f to over 1f out: no ch w first two* **6/1**[2]

2-20 **4** 1 **Coolminx (IRE)**[42] 2978 3-9-4 **90**......................... BarryMcHugh(3) 6 84
(R A Fahey) *prom: rdn over 2f out: no ex fr over 1f out* **13/2**[3]

-135 **5** 1 1/4 **Little Scotland**[19] 3731 3-9-2 **85**......................... TonyHamilton 4 75
(R A Fahey) *in tch: drvn and outpcd over 2f out: rallied ins fnl f: no imp* **15/2**

1155 **6** 1 **Timeless Elegance (IRE)**[12] 3947 3-8-7 **76**.............. PaulMulrennan 12 63
(J Howard Johnson) *prom: effrt and ev ch over 2f out: wknd fnl f* **20/1**

1246 **7** 9 **Flaneur**[19] 3731 3-8-10 **79**.........................(b) DavidAllan 9 37
(T D Easterby) *chsd ldrs: rdn over 2f out: wknd over 1f out* **11/2**[1]

5221 **8** 1 1/4 **Vito Volterra (IRE)**[18] 3755 3-8-3 **72**......................... PaulEddery 3 26
(Michael Smith) *led 2f: cl up tl rdn and wknd 2f out* **8/1**

1-50 **9** 1 **My One Weakness (IRE)**[14] 3898 3-7-10 **72**......................... IanBurns(7) 7 23
(B Ellison) *fly-jmpd s: cl up tl rdn and wknd over 2f out* **8/1**

2201 **10** 21 **Besty**[14] 3904 3-8-8 **77**......................... TomEaves 2 —
(B Smart) *chsd ldrs: outpcd after 2f: sn drvn and struggling: t.o* **6/1**[2]

1m 13.14s (-1.46) **Going Correction** +0.025s/f (Good) **10** Ran SP% **118.5**
Speed ratings (Par 104): **110,107,101,99,98 96,84,83,81,53**
Tote Swingers: 1&2 £3.80, 1&3 £15.10, 2&3 £7.20 CSF £74.74 CT £441.10 TOTE £13.40: £4.50, £2.70, £2.80; EX 109.90.
Owner Sheikh Hamdan Bin Mohammed Al Maktoum **Bred** Peter Gibbons And Dermot Forde **Trained** Middleham Moor, N Yorks

FOCUS
They went a good pace here and it was set up for something coming from behind, although the leading pair still deserve plenty of credit for pulling so far clear. Decent form, rated around the runner-up.

NOTEBOOK
Golden Shaheen(IRE)'s three previous outings this season had hardly suggested this performance was in the offing, but a return to easier ground (second on soft on debut) and being ridden with more restraint did the trick. He'll go up a fair bit in the weights for this but it is dangerous to rule out anything from this yard once they get on a roll. Official explanation: trainer's rep had no explanation for the apparent improvement in form. (op 9-1 tchd 11-1)
Colonel Mak had some good form on softish ground as a juvenile and ran his best race since joining David Barron. The drop back to sprinting helped, although he may have missed the boat, as he'll be hit with a fairly hefty rise for pulling so far clear of the rest. (op 6-1 tchd 7-1)

Walvis Bay(IRE) was a bit better than the bare result, simply getting tired after showing good speed. This isn't the first time he's shaped as if worth a try over 5f. (op 7-1 tchd 15-2)

Coolminx(IRE) put a below-par effort in a competitive event at York behind her, but this run confirmed she has nothing in hand off a mark of 90. (op 17-2 tchd 9-1)

Little Scotland wasn't discredited but had no excuses. (op 8-1 tchd 7-1)

Timeless Elegance(IRE) has found life tough after going up a lot in the ratings for his two early-season wins. (op 11-1)

Flaneur was most reliable earlier in the season, but has now run two below-par races in a row. Official explanation: jockey said gelding ran flat (op 6-1)

Vito Volterra(IRE) was always going to find this much tougher than when dominating in a less-competitive affair over further at Pontefract last time. (op 9-1)

Besty was beaten after 2f and something must have been amiss. Official explanation: jockey said gelding ran flat (op 13-2 tchd 7-1 and 5-1)

4370 PIMMS BEESWING H'CAP (DIV I) 7f

4:05 (4:05) (Class 3) (0-95,91) 3-Y-O+

£5,919 (£1,772; £886; £443; £221; £111) **Stalls** Centre

Form				RPR
2515	**1**		**Silver Rime (FR)**[11] 3987 5-9-6 **83** LNewman 1	92
			(Miss L A Perratt) *in tch: swtchd rt and hdwy to ld appr fnl f: edgd lft ins fnl f: rdn out* **25/1**	
3500	**2**	1	**Game Lad**[15] 3876 8-9-3 **80** (tp) DavidAllan 2	87
			(T D Easterby) *cl up: effrt and chal over 1f out: sn rdn: kpt on ins fnl f* **11/1**	
2000	**3**	½	**Esprit De Midas**[8] 4085 4-9-10 **87** ShaneKelly 5	92
			(K A Ryan) *hld up in tch: drvn and hdwy over 1f out: kpt on fnl f: nrst fin* **16/1**	
4221	**4**	½	**Ancient Cross**[22] 3619 6-9-8 **85** (t) PaulMulrennan 6	89
			(M W Easterby) *missed break: sn in tch: hdwy and ev ch appr fnl f: edgd lft u.p and no ex wl ins fnl f* **8/1**[3]	
0-02	**5**	3 ¼	**Horatio Carter**[28] 3448 5-9-8 **90** (p) DaleSwift[(5)] 3	85
			(K A Ryan) *cl up: led over 2f out to appr fnl f: sn no ex* **4/1**[2]	
-012	**6**	5	**Mr Rainbow**[12] 3969 4-10-0 **91** PJMcDonald 7	73
			(G A Swinbank) *t.k.h: led to over 2f out: rdn and wknd over 1f out* **4/1**[2]	
3300	**7**	1 ¼	**Beckermet (IRE)**[49] 2736 8-9-4 **84** BarryMcHugh[(3)] 11	62
			(Mrs R A Carr) *prom: drvn and outpcd over 2f out: btn over 1f out* **12/1**	
0566	**8**	3	**Tasmeem (IRE)**[8] 4091 3-8-7 **77** ow1 TonyHamilton 10	44
			(R A Fahey) *trckd ldrs: drvn over 3f out: wknd over 2f out* **16/1**	
-002	**9**	3 ¼	**The Osteopath (IRE)**[71] 2086 7-9-13 **90** TomEaves 4	51
			(M Dods) *in tch: rdn over 2f out: wknd wl over 1f out* **9/1**	
31-1	**10**	*hd*	**Primaeval**[87] 1625 4-9-8 **85** J-PGuillambert 8	46
			(J R Fanshawe) *hld up: sn niggled along: drvn 3f out: shortlived effrt wl over 1f out: sn btn* **2/1**[1]	

1m 28.28s (-0.42) **Going Correction** +0.025s/f (Good)
WFA 3 from 4yo+ 7lb **10** Ran SP% **126.1**
Speed ratings (Par 107): **103,101,101,100,97 91,89,86,82,82**
Tote Swingers: 1&2 £80.60, 1&3 £90.30, 2&3 £37.90 CSF £294.81 CT £4531.76 TOTE £34.80: £6.80, £2.90, £6.20; EX 195.40.
Owner Ken McGarrity **Bred** Jean-Philippe Dubois **Trained** East Kilbride, South Lanarks
■ The first winner in eight years for Lee Newman, who returned to the saddle earlier this season.

FOCUS
A fairly useful handicap, although arguably not as strong as it looked beforehand with a few performing below expectations. It was a bit quicker than division two and the form looks sound.

NOTEBOOK
Silver Rime(FR) has got back to his best this year and put a poor run at Musselburgh last time firmly behind him to make it two wins from his last three starts. He's versatile regards ground and can continue to hold his own in 7f-1m handicaps. (op 20-1)

Game Lad had lost his way recently but has always gone well with give in the ground. He showed he's still in form, sticking to his task after being ridden more prominently than usual. (op 10-1tchd 14-1 in a place)

Esprit De Midas ◆ has now shaped well on his last two starts. He was given too much to do after being ridden with more restraint than usual back up in trip. He finished best of all and is one to keep in mind. (tchd 18-1)

Ancient Cross is in excellent heart at present. He travelled smoothly to challenge over 1f out, but his tendency to hang left cost him again. He's worth another try back over 6f. (op 15-2 tchd 7-1)

Horatio Carter couldn't continue his good record over this course and distance, fading late on. (op 6-1)

Mr Rainbow had a progressive profile but this was clearly a step in the wrong direction. He'd shown his form on soft in the past, so the ground can't be an excuse. (op 5-1 tchd 11-2)

The Osteopath(IRE) usually goes well here but clearly wasn't at his best. (op 8-1)

Primaeval had looked on the up when winning a Kempton handicap in April and deserves another chance. The confidence behind him in the market suggests he's thought capable of better. Official explanation: trainer's rep had no explanation for the poor form shown (op 9-4 tchd 5-2 in places)

4371 PIMMS BEESWING H'CAP (DIV II) 7f

4:40 (4:41) (Class 3) (0-95,91) 3-Y-O+

£5,919 (£1,772; £886; £443; £221; £111) **Stalls** Centre

Form				RPR
0022	**1**		**Skyfire**[9] 4063 3-8-4 **74** AndrewElliott 5	85
			(M Johnston) *cl up: led over 2f out: rdn and hrd pressed over 1f out: edgd lft and styd on wl fnl f* **5/1**[2]	
0404	**2**	1 ¼	**Lucky Dance (BRZ)**[9] 4050 8-9-9 **86** LNewman 3	96
			(A G Foster) *in tch: effrt over 2f out: ev ch fr over 2f out: kpt on: hld towards fin* **16/1**	
10-	**3**	3 ½	**Spying**[317] 5795 3-9-4 **91** BarryMcHugh[(3)] 1	89
			(Mrs A Duffield) *hld up: hdwy on outside over 2f out: ev ch over 1f out: no ex ins fnl f* **16/1**	
-300	**4**	*nk*	**Deadly Secret (USA)**[30] 3366 4-9-2 **79** TonyHamilton 4	79
			(R A Fahey) *hld up in tch: hdwy 3f out: sn rdn: no imp fnl 2f* **20/1**	
-000	**5**	3 ¾	**Roker Park (IRE)**[13] 3937 5-9-8 **85** (p) PJMcDonald 9	75
			(K A Ryan) *midfield: effrt over 2f out: wknd over 1f out* **13/2**[3]	
2640	**6**	1 ¾	**Wigram's Turn (USA)**[36] 3146 5-9-12 **89** DavidAllan 10	74
			(M W Easterby) *hld up: effrt and pushed along 2f out: nvr able to chal* **8/1**	
520	**7**	½	**Nightjar (USA)**[67] 2205 5-9-1 **83** DaleSwift[(5)] 2	67
			(K A Ryan) *prom: rdn over 2f out: wknd over 1f out* **12/1**	
31-4	**8**	14	**Eton Rifles (IRE)**[52] 2657 5-10-0 **91** PaulMulrennan 11	37
			(J Howard Johnson) *prom tl rdn and wknd fr 2f out* **15/8**[1]	
0023	**9**	3	**Espero (IRE)**[11] 3987 4-9-0 **77** TomEaves 6	15
			(Miss L A Perratt) *stdd s: hld up: rdn over 2f out: sn btn* **7/1**	
2010	**10**	10	**Celtic Sultan (IRE)**[22] 3619 6-9-13 **90** (b) MickyFenton 7	1
			(T P Tate) *led: moved over to stands' side 1/2-way: hdd over 2f out: sn wknd* **14/1**	

1m 28.46s (-0.24) **Going Correction** +0.025s/f (Good)
WFA 3 from 4yo+ 7lb **10** Ran SP% **119.3**
Speed ratings (Par 107): **102,100,96,96,91 89,89,73,69,58**
Tote Swingers: 1&2 £12.60, 1&3 £8.50, 2&3 £14.90 CSF £83.27 CT £1203.10 TOTE £6.40: £2.40, £3.60, £5.40; EX 106.30.
Owner Sheikh Hamdan Bin Mohammed Al Maktoum **Bred** Darley **Trained** Middleham Moor, N Yorks

FOCUS
The second division of this fairly useful handicap and it was run in a similar time to the first, the front two pulling clear. Similar sort of form to the first division, with a clear personal best from the winner.

NOTEBOOK
Skyfire had been second off similar marks on his last two starts and went one better, again looking a bit awkward under pressure but always just holding the runner-up. He's in excellent hands and lightly-raced enough to suggest we may not have seen the best of him. (tchd 9-2 and 11-2)

Lucky Dance(BRZ) hadn't been beaten far by some smart types in a conditions race last time and this confirms he's back in much better form now. He was placed off a higher mark last year, so a small rise won't necessarily leave him out of things. (op 11-1)

Spying ◆ was successful on two of his three starts as a juvenile. He ran as though a mark in the low-90s may not prove beyond him, quickening to get upsides the leading pair before his absence told late on. He's one to keep on side.

Deadly Secret(USA) fared better than of late without suggesting his turn is near. (op 14-1)

Roker Park(IRE) has yet to hit top form this season, although this trip stretches him. (op 6-1 tchd 7-1)

Wigram's Turn(USA) wasn't knocked about on his first start since leaving Andrew Balding and is almost certainly in better form than the bare result might imply. (op 9-1 tchd 10-1)

Nightjar(USA) usually goes well when the ground was on the soft side, so this was disappointing. (op 10-1)

Eton Rifles(IRE), runner-up in this race 12 months ago, was backed as if expected to go one better this time round. However, the writing was on the wall a long way out and he'll clearly have a bit to prove next time. Official explanation: trainer had no explanation for the poor form shown (op 3-1)

4372 MATALAN.CO.UK H'CAP 5f

5:15 (5:15) (Class 4) (0-85,85) 3-Y-O+ **£3,784** (£1,132; £566; £283; £141) **Stalls** Centre

Form				RPR
0-00	**1**		**Captain Scooby**[54] 2578 4-8-7 **67** PaulMulrennan 4	75
			(R M Whitaker) *hld up: hdwy on outside over 1f out: led and hrd pressed ins fnl f: jst hld on* **12/1**	
3216	**2**	*nse*	**Hazelrigg (IRE)**[8] 4090 5-8-13 **73** (bt) DavidAllan 10	81
			(T D Easterby) *hld up: smooth hdwy over 1f out: rdn to chal whn carried hd high and edgd lft last 75yds: nt go past* **11/4**[2]	
0314	**3**	*shd*	**Haajes**[8] 4118 6-9-11 **85** MickyFenton 7	92+
			(P T Midgley) *chsd ldrs: led over 1f out to ins fnl f: kpt on: hld cl home* **15/2**	
0500	**4**	4 ½	**Lakeman (IRE)**[50] 2705 4-8-6 **66** oh1 PJMcDonald 5	57
			(B Ellison) *bhd and sn pushed along: hdwy appr fnl f: kpt on: nvr nr ldrs* **20/1**	
2421	**5**	¾	**Lesley's Choice**[9] 4060 4-8-10 **73** (b) BarryMcHugh[(3)] 2	62
			(Miss L A Perratt) *cl up: led over 2f to 1f out: wknd ins fnl f* **9/4**[1]	
65/0	**6**	2 ¼	**Marvellous Value (IRE)**[14] 3919 5-9-11 **85** TomEaves 1	65
			(M Dods) *in tch: hdwy over 2f out: rdn and wknd appr fnl f* **8/1**	
0-12	**7**	¾	**Foxy Music**[21] 3675 6-9-9 **83** ShaneKelly 11	64
			(E J Alston) *led to over 2f out: rdn and wknd over 1f out* **9/2**[3]	
-000	**8**	*hd*	**Van Bossed (CAN)**[78] 1888 5-8-9 **72** MichaelGeran[(3)] 8	49
			(D Nicholls) *prom tl rdn and wknd fr 2f out* **9/1**	

62.25 secs (1.15) **Going Correction** +0.025s/f (Good) **8** Ran SP% **120.9**
Speed ratings (Par 105): **91,90,90,83,82 78,77,77**
Tote Swingers: 1&2 £11.50, 1&3 £7.00, 2&3 £4.50 CSF £47.87 CT £278.43 TOTE £11.00: £2.40, £1.30, £2.70; EX 51.60.
Owner Paul Davies (H'gte) **Bred** Hellwood Stud Farm & Paul Davies (h'Gate) **Trained** Scarcroft, W Yorks
■ Stewards' Enquiry : David Allan caution: used whip without giving gelding time to respond.

FOCUS
Just a run-of-the-mill sprint handicap, although it did provide a thrilling finish. The winner is rated back to his best.

Captain Scooby Official explanation: trainer said, regarding apparent improvement in form, that the gelding was better suited by the softer ground.

Foxy Music Official explanation: jockey said gelding lost its action

4373 AONE+ AND COLAS SAFE ROADWORKS H'CAP 5f

5:50 (5:50) (Class 6) (0-60,65) 3-Y-O+ **£1,813** (£539; £269; £134) **Stalls** Centre

Form				RPR
0061	**1**		**Cross Of Lorraine (IRE)**[10] 4014 7-8-13 **56** (b) LanceBetts[(5)] 9	72
			(C Grant) *chsd ldrs: rdn to ld over 1f out: styd on strly to go clr fnl f* **14/1**	
031	**2**	4	**Ursus**[3] 4244 5-9-4 **59** 6ex (p) BarryMcHugh[(3)] 10	61
			(C R Wilson) *in tch: effrt 2f out: chsd wnr appr fnl f: kpt on: no imp* **4/1**[1]	
0055	**3**	2 ¼	**Divine Spirit**[11] 3977 9-8-10 **53** PatrickDonaghy[(5)] 14	47+
			(M Dods) *bhd tl hdwy over 1f out: kpt on fnl f: no ch w first two* **16/1**	
0235	**4**	*shd*	**Sandwith**[12] 3946 7-9-5 **57** LNewman 7	51
			(A G Foster) *dwlt: bhd: hdwy and prom over 1f out: kpt on same pce ins fnl f* **20/1**	
0051	**5**	2 ½	**Red China Blues (USA)**[40] 3027 4-9-3 **55** PJMcDonald 3	40
			(Mrs R A Carr) *in tch: outpcd after 2f: rallied appr fnl f: no imp* **12/1**	
3532	**6**	*nse*	**First Swallow**[11] 3977 5-9-5 **62** (t) IanBrennan[(5)] 16	46
			(D H Brown) *midfield: drvn and outpcd 1/2-way: rallied appr fnl f: nvr able to chal* **6/1**[2]	
6-06	**7**	1	**Avertuoso**[9] 4047 6-9-0 **59** AdamCarter[(7)] 11	40
			(B Smart) *dwlt: bhd and rdn tl sme late hdwy: nvr on terms* **12/1**	
0654	**8**	½	**Dancing Wave**[50] 2698 4-8-8 **51** MarkCoumbe[(5)] 6	30
			(M C Chapman) *in tch tl rdn and wknd over 1f out* **25/1**	
0041	**9**	2 ¼	**Hitches Dubai (BRZ)**[11] 3977 5-9-13 **65** TonyHamilton 5	36
			(G A Harker) *midfield: rdn and edgd lft over 2f out: wknd over 1f out* **7/1**[3]	
-010	**10**	1	**Pinball (IRE)**[19] 3722 4-9-2 **54** (v) TomEaves 4	21
			(Mrs L Williamson) *pressed ldr: led and maintained str pce 1/2-way: drifted rt and hdd over 1f out: sn btn* **16/1**	
000-	**11**	*nk*	**Sleepy Blue Ocean**[249] 7418 4-9-5 **57** AndrewElliott 1	23
			(J Balding) *midfield: outpcd after 2f: n.d after* **25/1**	
5401	**12**	¾	**Miss Daawe**[11] 3976 6-9-5 **62** DaleSwift[(5)] 13	25
			(B Ellison) *bhd and sn drvn along: nvr on terms* **7/1**[3]	
550	**13**	1	**Embra (IRE)**[29] 3409 5-9-4 **56** (b[1]) PaulMulrennan 12	16
			(T J Etherington) *midfield: rdn over 2f out: wknd wl over 1f out* **16/1**	
2353	**14**	3 ¼	**Red River Boy**[9] 4047 5-8-10 **51** KellyHarrison[(3)] 15	—
			(C W Fairhurst) *bhd and sn rdn along: nvr on terms* **7/1**[3]	

-505 15 *16* **Cayman Fox**[25] 3533 5-9-4 **56**......(v[1]) MickyFenton 2 —
(James Moffatt) *set str pce to 1/2-way: rdn and wknd fr 2f out* **14/1**
61.10 secs **Going Correction** +0.025s/f (Good) **15** Ran SP% **130.6**
Speed ratings (Par 101): **101,94,91,90,86 86,85,84,80,79 78,77,75,70,45**
Tote Swingers: 1&2 £16.90, 2&3 £30.10 CSF £72.78 CT £949.56 TOTE £18.80: £5.00, £2.30, £5.00; EX 133.30.
Owner John Wade **Bred** Kildaragh Stud **Trained** Newton Bewley, Co Durham

FOCUS
A sprint which very few ever got into. The main action unfolded up the centre, but those towards the stands side' were at a bit of a disadvantage. It was faster than the previous higher-grade handicap, but this is possibly not form to take too literally.
First Swallow Official explanation: jockey said saddle slipped
Hitches Dubai(BRZ) Official explanation: jockey said gelding never travelled
Pinball(IRE) Official explanation: jockey said filly hung right-handed
Miss Daawe Official explanation: jockey said mare banged its head in stalls and never travelled
Red River Boy Official explanation: jockey said gelding was unsuited by the good to soft ground
Cayman Fox Official explanation: jockey said mare had no more to give

4374 PIMMS APPRENTICE H'CAP — 1m 3y(S)
6:20 (6:20) (Class 6) (0-60,60) 3-Y-0+ **£1,683** (£501; £250; £125) **Stalls** Centre

Form RPR
0553 **1** **Red Dagger (IRE)**[5] 4189 4-9-1 **49**...... JamesRogers 5 58
(R J Price) *in tch: hdwy to ld over 2f out: edgd rt ins fnl f: kpt on wl* **10/1**
340 **2** *1 1/4* **Blue Moon**[38] 3091 3-9-0 **56**...... JulieBurke 8 60
(K A Ryan) *hld up: hdwy over 2f out: sn chsng wnr: kpt on u.p fnl f* **8/1**[3]
-600 **3** *2* **Wood Fair**[9] 4061 3-8-8 **52**...... NeilFarley[(2)] 7 51+
(J R Weymes) *s.i.s: bhd tl hdwy appr fnl f: nrst fin* **25/1**
-000 **4** *1 3/4* **Charity Fair**[12] 3948 3-7-12 **46** oh1...... VictorSantos[(6)] 6 41
(A Berry) *bhd and sn pushed along: effrt on outside 2f out: no imp fnl f* **33/1**
0022 **5** *hd* **Bed Fellow (IRE)**[5] 4189 6-9-4 **54**......(v) PaulNorton[(2)] 4 51
(P Monteith) *trckd ldrs: smooth hdwy and ev ch over 2f out: sn rdn: fnd little* **6/4**[1]
506- **6** *1 3/4* **Bourse (IRE)**[313] 5947 5-8-12 **46**...... NathanAlison 10 39
(A G Foster) *bhd: rdn and hdwy over 2f out: no further imp fnl f* **10/1**
000 **7** *1/2* **Royal Holiday (IRE)**[9] 4061 3-8-7 **55**...... IanBurns[(6)] 3 45
(B Ellison) *bhd and outpcd: hdwy over 1f out: nvr able to chal* **14/1**
6330 **8** *3* **Orpen Wide (IRE)**[5] 4201 8-9-8 **60**......(b) LucyBarry[(4)] 2 45
(M C Chapman) *cl up tl rdn and wknd over 2f out* **8/1**[3]
2-20 **9** *30* **Jozafeen**[22] 3628 3-9-4 **60**...... MatthewLawson 9 —
(R Bastiman) *t.k.h: cl up tl wknd 2f out: eased whn no ch* **15/2**[2]
0502 **10** *1 1/4* **Indian Violet (IRE)**[6] 4173 4-9-4 **52**......(p) AdamCarter 1 —
(D W Thompson) *led to over 2f out: sn rdn and wknd: eased whn no ch over 1f out* **15/2**[2]
1m 44.42s (1.02) **Going Correction** +0.025s/f (Good)
WFA 3 from 4yo+ 8lb **10** Ran SP% **117.4**
Speed ratings (Par 101): **95,93,91,90,89 88,87,84,54,53**
Tote Swingers:1&2:£15.80, 2&3:£61.00, 1&3:£31.60 CSF £88.00 CT £1948.11 TOTE £14.40: £3.60, £2.20, £7.70; EX 99.40 Place 6 £23,060.00; Place 5 £14,428.16.
Owner Karl and Patricia Reece **Bred** Glending Bloodstock **Trained** Ullingswick, H'fords
■ Stewards' Enquiry : Adam Carter two-day ban: careless riding (Aug 7-8)
Julie Burke two-day ban: used whip with excessive frequency (Aug 7-8)

FOCUS
Low-grade fare and unlikely to be a race which throws up many winners. The winner got back to his flattering Warwick form.
T/Plt: Part won. £47,792.60 to a £1 stake. Pool: £65,469.44 - 0.45 winning tickets. T/Qpdt: £387.60 to a £1 stake. Pool:£6,129.64 - 287.91 winning tickets. RY

4329 NEWMARKET (R-H)
Saturday, July 24

OFFICIAL GOING: Good to firm (good in places; 8.3)
Stands' side of July Course utilised.
Wind: Light half-behind Weather: Cloudy with sunny spells

4375 BALLYGALLON STUD, IRELAND E B F MAIDEN STKS — 7f
1:45 (1:45) (Class 4) 2-Y-0 **£4,533** (£1,348; £674; £336) **Stalls** Low

Form RPR
1 **Farhh** 2-9-3 0...... TedDurcan 3 92+
(Saeed Bin Suroor) *chsd ldrs: led 2f out: rdn clr and hung lft fnl f: eased towards fin* **13/8**[1]
0 **2** *6* **Flodden (USA)**[17] 3794 2-9-3 0...... JamieSpencer 2 75
(P F I Cole) *led: rdn and hdd 2f out: hung lft and outpcd fnl f* **9/2**[2]
35 **3** *6* **Ocean Bay**[15] 3868 2-9-3 0...... AdamKirby 4 60
(J Ryan) *chsd ldrs: rdn over 2f out: sn hung rt: wknd over 1f out: hung lft ins fnl f* **13/8**[1]
4 *nk* **Olynthos (IRE)** 2-9-3 0...... AndreaAtzeni 6 59
(Jane Chapple-Hyam) *prom: rdn and hung lft over 1f out: sn wknd* **33/1**
5 *1 3/4* **Corsican Boy** 2-9-3 0...... SteveDrowne 5 55+
(R Charlton) *s.s: hdwy 2f out: wknd over 1f out* **14/1**[3]
50 **6** *5* **Mabsam**[23] 3590 2-8-12 0...... JimCrowley 7 37
(E A L Dunlop) *racd alone tl jnd main gp over 5f out: prom tl rdn and wknd over 1f out* **33/1**
7 *15* **Handel's Messiah (IRE)** 2-9-3 0...... PatDobbs 1 5
(M L W Bell) *hld up: rdn and wknd over 2f out* **22/1**
1m 25.88s (0.18) **Going Correction** -0.10s/f (Good) **7** Ran SP% **111.3**
Speed ratings (Par 96): **94,87,80,79,77 72,55**
toteswingers:1&2:£2.50, 1&3:£1.10, 2&3:£1.40 CSF £8.99 TOTE £2.50: £1.70, £2.60; EX 9.80.
Owner Godolphin **Bred** Darley **Trained** Newmarket, Suffolk

FOCUS
Drying conditions saw the ground described as good to firm all round. Jockeys agreed with that assessment after the first, but added that the ground was safe. A decent maiden, despite the small field, and the runners raced down the centre of the track. They finished well spread out behind the impressive winner. The favourite was very disappointing.

NOTEBOOK
Farhh is the first foal of a dual German 1m4f Group 1 winner who was acquired by Godolphin but never ran for them. Looking fit for this debut, he travelled strongly before coming right away for a most emphatic win. A rise in grade will tell us more but he looks a smart prospect. (op 6-4 tchd 7-4)
Flodden(USA) had been noticeably green on his debut in a warm maiden at the July festival here. Building on that experience and making the running, he stuck on in honest fashion when headed but the winner was much too good. (op 5-1 tchd 4-1)
Ocean Bay had been beaten less than 3l into fifth behind King Torus in the Group 2 Superlative Stakes over C&D last time. That form looked comfortably good enough to win a maiden, and his trainer expected him to strip fitter here, but the colt lacked a change of gear when the race hotted up and wandered when the pressure was on. While he may have been slightly flattered last time, this was not his running. (op 5-2 tchd 6-4)
Olynthos(IRE), a half-brother to a juvenile winner over 7f, showed signs of greenness but stuck on after hanging over to the far rail. (op 14-1)
Corsican Boy, a 27,000gns half-brother to several winners, looked in need of the run. He stood still as the gates opened but showed promise mid-race and will be more streetwise next time. (op 9-1 tchd 16-1)
Mabsam, the only filly in the field, was drawn against the stands' rail and raced there at first until her rider realised the others had gone down the centre and gradually tacked his mount over. She was soon toiling when the race developed but is now eligible for nurseries. (op 25-1)
Handel's Messiah(IRE), a half-brother to three winners out of an unraced sister to Grade 1 scorer Urgent Request, was a little green on this debut and found himself left behind in the last quarter-mile. Official explanation: jockey said colt pulled up lame (op 16-1)

4376 SPORTINGBET.COM H'CAP — 1m 2f
2:15 (2:16) (Class 3) (0-95,94) 3-Y-0+
£8,723 (£2,612; £1,306; £653; £326; £163) **Stalls** Centre

Form RPR
5022 **1** **Classic Punch (IRE)**[28] 3456 7-10-0 **94**...... JamieSpencer 2 107+
(D R C Elsworth) *mde all: sn clr: shkn up and r.o strly fr over 1f out: eased nr fin* **5/2**[2]
611 **2** *9* **Abergavenny**[19] 3737 3-8-6 **82**...... GregFairley 3 77
(M Johnston) *chsd wnr: rdn to cl over 2f out: outpcd fr over 1f out* **9/4**[1]
2516 **3** *6* **Arizona John (IRE)**[14] 3889 5-9-3 **83**...... PatCosgrave 5 66
(J Mackie) *chsd ldrs: rdn over 2f out: wknd over 1f out* **7/1**
5044 **4** *2 1/4* **Sequillo**[19] 3737 4-8-13 **79**...... PatDobbs 7 58
(R Hannon) *hld up: a in rr: rdn over 2f out: wknd over 1f out* **12/1**
5233 **5** *4 1/2* **Follow The Flag (IRE)**[17] 3796 6-9-9 **89**......(p) JamesDoyle 4 59
(A J McCabe) *prom: rdn over 3f out: wknd over 1f out* **9/2**[3]
60/0 **6** *1* **Strategic Mission (IRE)**[8] 4100 5-9-0 **80**...... JimCrowley 6 48
(P F I Cole) *hld up in tch: rdn over 3f out: wknd over 2f out* **12/1**
0-20 **7** *nk* **Cwm Rhondda (USA)**[51] 2685 5-8-10 **76**...... JackMitchell 8 43
(P W Chapple-Hyam) *hld up: a in rr: rdn over 2f out: sn wknd* **12/1**
2m 1.64s (-3.86) **Going Correction** -0.10s/f (Good)
WFA 3 from 4yo+ 10lb **7** Ran SP% **113.1**
Speed ratings (Par 107): **111,103,99,97,93 92,92**
toteswingers:1&2:£1.10, 2&3:£4.40, 1&3:£4.60 CSF £8.37 CT £32.33 TOTE £3.40: £2.00, £2.00; EX 6.50 Trifecta £52.80 Pool: £569.41 - 7.98 winning units..
Owner The Classic Bunch **Bred** Granham Farm **Trained** Newmarket, Suffolk

FOCUS
The order changed little in this fair handicap, in which Classic Punch made every yard in a fast time. He is rated in line with his best form of the past year.

NOTEBOOK
Classic Punch(IRE) made all to slam his field. He was eased down close home with the race in the bag and was value for an even more emphatic margin of victory. This was only his second win since he took back-to-back races on this course in the summer of 2007, though he had found just one too good for him when down at this trip on his latest two starts. Long something of a 'twilight' horse, he will go back up to a three-figure mark for this. He may run in a Shergar Cup race at Ascot next month. (op 4-1)
Abergavenny, a progressive 3yo, was 7lb higher than when a gutsy scorer at Windsor. Chasing the winner all the way and the last of the pursuers to come off the bridle, he kept on for a well-beaten second and showed enough to suggest he remains in good heart. (op 2-1 tchd 7-4)
Arizona John(IRE), who held third throughout but was beaten 15l, was below par. (op 6-1)
Sequillo stayed on from the rear past toiling opponents but finished further behind Abergavenny than he had at Windsor. (op 8-1 tchd 14-1)
Follow The Flag(IRE) is on a career-high mark and was never within striking distance. (op 11-2)
Strategic Mission(IRE) was never in the hunt on his second run back after a two-year absence. (op 14-1 tchd 16-1)
Cwm Rhondda(USA) broke fine from the stalls this time but was in the last pair all the way. (op 9-1 tchd 14-1)

4377 SPORTINGBET H'CAP — 1m
2:45 (2:45) (Class 3) (0-90,90) 3-Y-0
£8,723 (£2,612; £1,306; £653; £326; £163) **Stalls** Low

Form RPR
0061 **1** **San Cassiano (IRE)**[7] 4154 3-9-3 **84**...... JimCrowley 6 93
(Mrs R A Carr) *a.p: chsd ldr 1/2-way: rdn to ld wl over 1f out: sn hdd: rallied to ld ins fnl f: edgd lft: drvn out* **15/2**
2332 **2** *1 1/4* **First Cat**[15] 3867 3-9-2 **83**...... FrankieMcDonald 4 89
(R Hannon) *hld up: plld hrd: hdwy over 2f out: led over 1f out: carried hd to one side: rdn: hung lft and hdd ins fnl f: nt run on* **7/2**[2]
0030 **3** *2 1/2* **Kona Coast**[37] 3103 3-9-4 **85**......(b) SaleemGolam 3 85
(J H M Gosden) *chsd ldrs: rdn over 2f out: no ex ins fnl f* **9/2**[3]
2412 **4** *1 1/2* **Rule Maker**[14] 3916 3-9-9 **90**...... JamieSpencer 2 87
(J Noseda) *s.i.s: rcvrd to chse ldr to 1/2-way: remained handy: rdn over 1f out: wknd ins fnl f* **5/4**[1]
2140 **5** *2 1/4* **Rule Breaker (IRE)**[14] 3886 3-9-3 **84**...... GregFairley 1 76
(M Johnston) *led: rdn and hdd wl over 1f out: wknd ins fnl f* **15/2**
1-04 **6** *20* **Jibrrya**[27] 3481 3-8-9 **76**...... ChrisCatlin 5 22
(M R Channon) *hld up: plld hrd: wknd over 2f out* **25/1**
1m 38.23s (-1.77) **Going Correction** -0.10s/f (Good) **6** Ran SP% **112.2**
Speed ratings (Par 104): **104,102,100,98,96 76**
toteswingers:1&2:£4.90, 1&3:£6.10, 2&3:£3.90 CSF £33.42 TOTE £9.00: £2.50, £1.80; EX 28.10.
Owner P D Savill **Bred** Peter Savill **Trained** Huby, N Yorks

FOCUS
A decent handicap. The runners made for the far side when the stalls opened, with the third home racing on the rail and the other five a few horse widths off it. The form is best judgeda round the runner-up, with the winner up 4lb.

NOTEBOOK
San Cassiano(IRE), who raced widest, responded well to pressure to win a shade comfortably in the end. Following up his Redcar success (when 6lb lower) and now unbeaten in two since being transferred to Ruth Carr, he looks the type to find further improvement for his new yard. (op 9-2 tchd 8-1)
First Cat got away on terms this time and had every chance, but had to settle for his fifth placing in as many starts. Missing his right eye, he holds his head very awkwardly as a result and is probably at a disadvantage when it comes down to a battle. (tchd 3-1)
Kona Coast's connections won this a year ago with Invisible Man, who won this season's Royal Hunt Cup for Godolphin. Bagging the far rail and racing keenly in the reapplied blinkers, the colt only gave best inside the last. (op 5-1)
Rule Maker, raised 6lb for his second at Salisbury, was unable to lead this time and did not sustain his effort for long when the pressure was on. All his runs have been on fast ground and he may be worth trying on a slightly easier surface. (tchd 2-1 in a place)

The Form Book, Raceform Ltd, Compton, RG20 6NL

Rule Breaker(IRE) made the running again before fading back over this longer trip and has something to prove now. (op 8-1 tchd 9-1)
Jibrrya failed to settle even with this drop back in trip and has now been beaten an awfully long way on all three of his starts this season. (op 20-1)

4378 SPORTINGBET.COM E B F FILLIES' H'CAP 7f
3:20 (3:20) (Class 2) (0-100,93) 3-Y-O+ **£16,190** (£4,817; £2,407; £1,202) **Stalls** Low

Form RPR
-100 **1** **Miss Zooter (IRE)**[17] 3790 3-9-2 **88** .... JimCrowley 5 102+
(R M Beckett) *hld up: hdwy and hung lft fr over 1f out: rdn to ld ins fnl f: r.o* **3/1**[2]
0316 **2** *2* **Waveband**[9] 4058 3-8-12 **84** .... GregFairley 8 92
(M Johnston) *led: rdn and hung lft fr over 1f out: hdd ins fnl f: styd on same pce* **13/2**[3]
0101 **3** *1 3/4* **Folly Bridge**[17] 3790 3-9-6 **92** .... SteveDrowne 10 96
(R Charlton) *chsd ldrs: rdn over 2f out: hung lft over 1f out: styd on same pce fnl f: wnt 3rd post* **11/4**[1]
4651 **4** *hd* **Poppet's Lovein**[16] 3830 4-9-0 **79** .... StevieDonohoe 6 85
(A B Haynes) *hld up: pushed along over 2f out: r.o ins fnl f: nrst fin* **12/1**
-021 **5** *nse* **Arabian Mirage**[21] 3681 4-9-11 **90** .... PatCosgrave 3 96
(B J Meehan) *trckd ldr: racd keenly: rdn over 1f out: no ex ins fnl f* **7/1**
-005 **6** *3 3/4* **Good Again**[18] 3752 4-9-11 **93** .... MartinLane(3) 9 89
(G A Butler) *chsd ldrs: rdn over 2f out: wknd over 1f out* **13/2**[3]
4562 **7** *3/4* **Absa Lutte (IRE)**[42] 2954 7-9-1 **80** .... JamieSpencer 4 74
(Dr R D P Newland) *dwlt: hld up: racd keenly: hdwy over 2f out: rdn over 1f out: wknd fnl f* **9/1**
2060 **8** *1/2* **Tarita (IRE)**[23] 3592 3-8-2 **74** oh2 .... FrankieMcDonald 2 63
(R Hannon) *hld up in tch: rdn over 2f out: wknd over 1f out* **50/1**
3165 **9** *1 3/4* **Fly Silca Fly (IRE)**[17] 3790 3-8-10 **82** .... ChrisCatlin 7 67
(M R Channon) *chsd ldrs: rdn over 2f out: wknd over 1f out* **18/1**

1m 24.48s (-1.22) **Going Correction** -0.10s/f (Good)
WFA 3 from 4yo+ 7lb **9** Ran SP% **115.7**
Speed ratings (Par 96): **102,99,97,97,97 93,92,91,89**
toteswingers:1&2:£8.20, 1&3:£1.80, 2&3:£3.60 CSF £23.01 CT £59.32 TOTE £4.00: £1.30, £2.40, £1.80; EX 28.30 Trifecta £82.90 Pool: £280.29 - 2.50 winning units..
Owner Pearl Bloodstock Ltd **Bred** Rathyork Stud **Trained** Whitsbury, Hants

FOCUS
A valuable fillies' handicap, and the form should prove solid. It has been taken at face value. This time the runners came centre to stands' side before fanning out approaching the two pole.

NOTEBOOK
Miss Zooter(IRE) was unlucky not to finish closer in Folly Bridge's race over C&D at the big meeting earlier in the month and she turned the tables with a decent performance. She came with a sustained run to lead, edging to her left all the while, and was well on top at the end. There may be further improvement in her, and it is likely that connections will search out some black type. (tchd 11-4)
Waveband didn't get home over an extended 1m last time but she ran well back down in trip, if unable to fend off the winner, who carried her to the left in the latter stages. This effort suggests that perhaps she was not flattered after all by her Ascot win two starts ago when she had raced alone under the stands' rail. (op 15-2 tchd 8-1)
Folly Bridge was 5lb worse off with Miss Zooter than when winning at the July festival here last time. She ran her race but lacked a finishing kick after racing a little keenly and might be ready to go up in trip now. (op 7-2 tchd 5-2)
Poppet's Lovein ran with credit off a 4lb higher mark than when winning at Warwick, staying on nearest the stands' fence. (op 11-1)
Arabian Mirage took time to settle but still knuckled down well when required and did not miss out on third by far. This was a sound run off a 5lb higher mark than when winning at Leicester. (op 13-2 tchd 15-2)
Good Again was a shade disappointing after her Listed fifth, with the drop back in trip not looking ideal. (tchd 11-2 and 7-1)
Absa Lutte(IRE), having her first run for Richard Newland, was without her regular tongue tie. Keen to post and not away the best, she was never really in the hunt and faded late on over a trip she had not tackled since her Irish days. (op 10-1)

4379 LLOYDS TSB COMMERCIAL MEDIAN AUCTION MAIDEN STKS 6f
3:55 (3:57) (Class 4) 2-Y-O **£3,238** (£963; £481; £240) **Stalls** Low

Form RPR
3 **1** **Hammer Home (USA)**[16] 3805 2-9-3 0 .... JamieSpencer 6 77+
(B J Meehan) *led 2f: w ldr tl edgd lft and led again 2f out: hrd rdn and edgd rt ins fnl f: all out* **8/11**[1]
2 **2** *shd* **Enthusing (IRE)**[40] 3034 2-9-3 0 .... TedDurcan 2 77
(D R C Elsworth) *trckd ldrs: rdn to chal fnl f: edgd rt: r.o* **2/1**[2]
0 **3** *1 1/2* **Kingscroft (IRE)**[7] 4123 2-9-3 0 .... GregFairley 4 73
(M Johnston) *chsd ldr tl led 4f out: hdd 2f out: sn rdn: styd on same pce ins fnl f* **16/1**
54 **4** *2 3/4* **St Oswald**[31] 3332 2-9-3 0 .... SteveDrowne 8 65+
(R Charlton) *prom: rdn over 1f out: hung lft and no ex ins fnl f* **10/1**[3]
5 *2 1/4* **Great Acclaim** 2-9-3 0 .... PatCosgrave 5 58
(J R Fanshawe) *chsd ldrs: rdn over 2f out: wknd over 1f out* **16/1**
6 *shd* **Ivan Vasilevich (IRE)** 2-9-3 0 .... TomMcLaughlin 1 57+
(Jane Chapple-Hyam) *hld up: rdn over 2f out: wknd over 1f out* **33/1**
7 *6* **Flight Lieutenant** 2-8-10 0 .... LewisWalsh(7) 7 39
(Jane Chapple-Hyam) *dwlt: sn pushed along in rr: wkng whn hung lft wl over 1f out* **33/1**
8 *4 1/2* **Unex Monet** 2-9-3 0 .... PatDobbs 3 26
(M L W Bell) *sn pushed along in rr: bhd fr 1/2-way* **20/1**

1m 13.18s (0.68) **Going Correction** -0.10s/f (Good) **8** Ran SP% **122.7**
Speed ratings (Par 96): **91,90,88,85,82 82,74,68**
toteswingers:1&2:£1.60, 1&3:£3.30, 2&3:£3.60 CSF £2.56 TOTE £2.00: £1.30, £1.10, £2.60; EX 2.40.
Owner Roldvale Limited **Bred** W G Lyster III Et Al **Trained** Manton, Wilts

FOCUS
Won last year by the smart filly Blue Maiden, this was an ordinary maiden for the track, dominated by those with previous racecourse experience. There was a fine finish with Hammer Home, who stepped up on his debut form, just pipping Enthusing who ran to his pre-race mark.

NOTEBOOK
Hammer Home(USA) edged out Enthusing on the nod. Third at Doncaster on his debut, form since boosted by the runner-up, he was heavily backed here, but after travelling best he really had to work to get the verdict. He is still in the Gimcrack but that would appear an unrealistic target now. (op 10-11)
Enthusing(IRE), second at Windsor on his debut, was upped in trip for this second start. After challenging out widest, he changed his legs inside the last and just came out worse in a driving finish. He should soon go one better, perhaps on a slightly easier surface. (op 9-4 tchd 5-2)
Kingscroft(IRE) improved on what he had shown in softish ground on his debut but could not quicken with the front pair in the latter stages. (op 20-1)
St Oswald ◆ was not given too hard a time when his measure had been taken by the principals. He is now qualified for nurseries and should do well in that sphere. (tchd 11-1)
Great Acclaim did best of the debutants. A gelded brother to useful sprinter Berbice, who was third in the Mill Reef Stakes, he showed signs of greenness and a bit of improvement can be expected. (op 14-1)
Ivan Vasilevich(IRE), a half-brother to smart sprinter Al Qasi, was getting the hang of things late on and improvement should be forthcoming. Softer conditions might be in his favour. (tchd 28-1)
Flight Lieutenant, whose dam won at 1m-1m2f in france, appeared green on this debut. (tchd 25-1)
Unex Monet, a half-brother to the useful Akhenaten, missed the kick and was always trailing. (tchd 25-1)

4380 NSPCC H'CAP 1m 5f
4:30 (4:31) (Class 4) (0-80,80) 3-Y-O **£4,533** (£1,348; £674; £336) **Stalls** Centre

Form RPR
-141 **1** **Trovare (USA)**[29] 3414 3-9-6 **77** .... PatDobbs 4 87+
(Mrs A J Perrett) *led: hdd over 3f out: rallied to ld over 1f out: styd on gamely* **11/4**[2]
5241 **2** *1* **Reality Show (IRE)**[18] 3764 3-9-9 **80** .... AhmedAjtebi 5 88
(Mahmood Al Zarooni) *chsd wnr over 4f: remained handy: rdn over 2f out: wnt 2nd again ins fnl f: styd on* **5/1**
6644 **3** *4 1/2* **Pullyourfingerout (IRE)**[12] 3954 3-8-8 **65** .... JamieSpencer 3 68
(B G Powell) *hld up: plld hrd: hdwy to trck wnr over 8f out: led over 3f out: rdn and hdd over 1f out: no ex ins fnl f* **12/1**
6111 **4** *7* **Home Advantage**[19] 3724 3-9-8 **79** .... SteveDrowne 1 70
(R Charlton) *chsd ldrs: rdn over 3f out: wknd over 1f out* **13/8**[1]
1212 **5** *6* **Leader Of The Land (IRE)**[33] 3273 3-9-6 **77** ....(p) TedDurcan 2 59
(D R Lanigan) *hld up: rdn over 3f out: wknd over 2f out* **7/2**[3]

2m 46.32s (2.32) **Going Correction** -0.10s/f (Good) **5** Ran SP% **111.3**
Speed ratings (Par 102): **88,87,84,80,76**
CSF £16.26 TOTE £3.60: £1.90, £3.00; EX 16.50.
Owner John Connolly **Bred** James Heyward **Trained** Pulborough, W Sussex

FOCUS
An interesting handicap featuring some progressive 3yos, this was run at just a steady pace. The runners raced a little way off the stands rail up the long straight. The form is rated around the third.
Home Advantage Official explanation: jockey said colt had no more to give
Leader Of The Land(IRE) Official explanation: jockey said colt had no more to give

4381 NSPCC APPRENTICE H'CAP 1m 2f
5:05 (5:06) (Class 5) (0-75,85) 3-Y-O **£3,238** (£963; £481; £240) **Stalls** Centre

Form RPR
-655 **1** **Fame Is The Spur**[12] 3954 3-8-12 **68** .... HollyHall(5) 2 77
(J W Hills) *hld up: hdwy over 2f out: led ins fnl f: rdn out* **8/1**
-000 **2** *nk* **Dashing Doc (IRE)**[12] 3963 3-8-13 **69** .... RyanPowell(5) 1 77
(D R C Elsworth) *led: rdn and edgd rt over 1f out: hdd ins fnl f: r.o* **8/1**
0111 **3** *2* **Explorator (IRE)**[7] 4156 3-10-1 **85** .... AdamBeschizza(5) 3 89
(George Baker) *hld up: pushed along over 4f out: hdwy over 2f out: rdn and ev ch over 1f out: no ex ins fnl f* **5/6**[1]
-051 **4** *3 3/4* **Ajool (USA)**[32] 3285 3-9-7 **72** .... AndreaAtzeni 5 69
(P W D'Arcy) *chsd ldr 4f: wnt 2nd again 3f out: rdn over 1f out: wknd fnl f* **4/1**[2]
-215 **5** *5* **Strike A Deal (IRE)**[9] 4058 3-8-13 **71** .... RoryHanley(7) 4 58
(C F Wall) *prom: chsd ldr 6f out to 3f out: rdn and wknd over 1f out* **13/2**[3]

2m 5.90s (0.40) **Going Correction** -0.10s/f (Good) **5** Ran SP% **110.1**
Speed ratings: **94,93,92,89,85**
CSF £60.64 TOTE £8.60: £3.00, £3.60; EX 65.40 Place 6 £28.78; Place 5 £16.46.
Owner John M Cole **Bred** W S Farish **Trained** Upper Lambourn, Berks

FOCUS
An ordinary apprentice handicap and, with the first three in the market proving disappointing, the form has a muddling look to it. The pace was steady early on but had picked up by the time they reached the straight, where they raced down the centre.
Fame Is The Spur Official explanation: trainer's rep said, regarding apparent improvement in form, that the filly is improving and has been working well at home.
T/Plt: £24.60 to a £1 stake. Pool:£67,872.39 - 2,010.46 winning tickets T/Qpdt: £10.20 to a £1 stake. Pool:£3,494.31 - 251.14 winning tickets CR

3913 SALISBURY (R-H)
Saturday, July 24

OFFICIAL GOING: Good (good to firm in places; 8.0)
Temporary rail up to 16ft off permanent far side rail between 6.5f and 1f.
Wind: mild against Weather: overcast but muggy

4382 CHIPMUNK EQUINE DUST EXTRACTED HORSE BEDDING "CARNARVON" H'CAP (GENTLEMEN AMATEUR RIDERS) 1m
6:00 (6:00) (Class 5) (0-75,74) 3-Y-O+ **£3,123** (£968; £484; £242) **Stalls** High

Form RPR
2553 **1** **Advertise**[24] 3558 4-10-6 **66** .... MrARawlinson(7) 4 78
(A M Balding) *travelled wl: hld up towards rr: hdwy on bit but hung rt over 2f out: sn led: in command after: comf* **4/1**[2]
3054 **2** *2 1/4* **Sula Two**[15] 3852 3-9-8 **60** .... MrPPrince(5) 13 64
(R J Hodges) *mid-div on rails: hdwy to chse wnr whn nt clr run and swtchd lft over 1f out: kpt on same pce* **14/1**
0660 **3** *1 1/4* **Gallego**[31] 3323 8-10-5 **61** .... MrMPrice(3) 14 65+
(R J Price) *s.i.s: hld up: hdwy 3f out: swtchd lft 2f out: sn rdn: styd on same pce* **10/3**[1]
0540 **4** *3 1/2* **Apex**[38] 3079 9-10-1 **61** .... MrMHerbert(7) 8 57
(M Hill) *s.i.s: hld up: hdwy in centre over 2f out: sn rdn: styd on wout threatening* **20/1**
4325 **5** *1 3/4* **Leitzu (IRE)**[15] 3852 3-9-9 **63** .... MrCBishop(7) 1 52
(M R Channon) *awkward leaving stalls: sn in tch: rdn whn hmpd over 2f out: kpt on same pce* **15/2**
0066 **6** *3 1/4* **Mr Udagawa**[15] 3853 4-10-1 **61** .... MrRJWilliams(7) 12 45
(B J Llewellyn) *in tch: rdn over 2f out: wknd over 1f out* **20/1**
3336 **7** *3/4* **King Columbo (IRE)**[8] 4108 5-10-10 **66** .... MrRBirkett(3) 11 48
(Miss J Feilden) *led for 1f: prom: led 3f out: rdn and sn hdd: sltly hmpd over 1f out: wknd fnl f* **9/2**[3]
5650 **8** *4* **Mountain Pass (USA)**[43] 2920 8-9-13 **55** oh1 ....(t) MrDGPrichard(3) 7 28
(B J Llewellyn) *s.i.s: a towards rr* **40/1**
4465 **9** *1 3/4* **Bold Cross (IRE)**[9] 4044 7-10-12 **70** .... MrJFlook(5) 3 39
(E G Bevan) *trckd ldrs: rdn over 3f out: hmpd over 2f out: wknd over 1f out* **10/1**
-000 **10** *9* **Magic Warrior**[63] 2337 10-9-9 **55** oh10 .... MrOGarner(7) 2 3
(J C Fox) *trckd ldrs tl rdn 4f out: sn btn* **66/1**
14-0 **11** *1 1/2* **Classically (IRE)**[10] 4023 4-10-12 **70** .... MrRPooles(5) 5 15
(H Morrison) *trckd ldrs: rdn over 3f out: sn wknd* **11/2**

00-0 **12** 1 1/4 **Sir Tom**196 98 5-10-0 58 oh9 ow3 MrJackSalmon(5) 10 —
(J J Bridger) *prom: rdn and ev ch 3f out: sn wknd* **66/1**
5000 **13** 1 1/4 **Macroy**9 4047 3-9-5 57 MrPMillman(5) 9 —
(B R Millman) *t.k.h: led after 1f: hdd 3f out: sn wknd* **40/1**
1m 43.79s (0.29) **Going Correction** -0.025s/f (Good)
WFA 3 from 4yo+ 8lb 13 Ran SP% **121.6**
Speed ratings (Par 103): **97,94,93,90,88 85,84,80,78,69 68,66,65**
Tote Swingers: 1&2 £7.40, 1&3 £6.30, 2&3 £9.30 CSF £55.24 CT £215.99 TOTE £4.30: £1.40, £3.10, £2.40; EX 65.90.
Owner Kingsclere Racing CLub **Bred** Kingsclere Stud **Trained** Kingsclere, Hants
■ Ali Rawlinson's first winner.
■ Stewards' Enquiry : Mr A Rawlinson three-day ban: careless riding (tbn)
FOCUS
There had been no rain in the past 48 hours, after 15mm on Thursday. Racing began with a run-of-the-mill amateur riders' event, the top weight rated 74. Ordinary form, with the winner rated up 3lb.

4383 DEREK BURRIDGE TROPHIES 50TH ANNIVERSARY CLAIMING STKS 1m
6:30 (6:31) (Class 5) 3-4-Y-O **£3,238** (£963; £481; £240) **Stalls** High

Form RPR
-145 **1** **Mercoliano**75 1969 3-8-2 76 AntiocoMurgia(7) 2 72
(M Botti) *led for 1f: prom: led jst over 3f out: kpt on wl and a in command after: pushed out* **4/1**2
0141 **2** 1/2 **Calypso Star (IRE)**7 4133 3-8-10 66 (b) RichardHughes 6 72
(R Hannon) *hld up in last pair but cl up: hdwy whn swtchd rt 2f out: sn rdn: kpt on but nvr gng pce to chal: edgd lft towards fin* **1/2**1
3541 **3** 4 1/2 **Frank Street**14 3910 4-8-13 58 (t) DaneO'Neill 8 59
(Eve Johnson Houghton) *trckd ldrs: effrt 3f out: kpt on same pce fnl 2f* **7/1**3
0003 **4** 2 **Marafong**14 3910 3-8-5 56 JimmyQuinn 1 52
(Miss J Feilden) *trckd ldrs: reminders over 3f out: rdn over 2f out: sn one pce* **28/1**
-304 **5** 13 **Decree Absolute (USA)**18 3768 3-8-11 62 (b) PaulFitzsimons 4 28
(Miss J R Tooth) *slowly away and bmpd sn after s: in last pair but cl up: rdn 3f out: wknd 2f out* **16/1**
00 **6** 21 **Proud Tuscan**5 4205 3-8-7 0 MartinDwyer 7 —
(J S Moore) *t.k.h: led after 1f: rdn and hdd over 3f out: sn wknd* **28/1**
1m 42.98s (-0.52) **Going Correction** -0.025s/f (Good)
WFA 3 from 4yo 8lb 6 Ran SP% **111.9**
Speed ratings (Par 103): **101,100,96,94,81 60**
Tote Swingers: 1&2 £1.20, 1&3 £1.80, 2&3 £1.30 CSF £6.36 TOTE £4.40: £1.80, £1.20.
Owner Giuliano Manfredini **Bred** Mystic Meg Limited **Trained** Newmarket, Suffolk
FOCUS
Little depth to this ordinary claimer. The winner did not need to match his AW win.

4384 PICADOR CHEVROLET MAIDEN STKS 6f
7:05 (7:05) (Class 4) 2-Y-O **£3,885** (£1,156; £577; £288) **Stalls** High

Form RPR
2 **1** **Ardour (IRE)**12 3961 2-9-3 0 RichardHughes 2 85
(R Hannon) *prom: led 3f out: shkn up ent fnl f: a holding on: readily* **4/9**1
2 1/2 **Codemaster** 2-9-3 0 DaneO'Neill 4 84+
(H Candy) *in tch: swtchd lft and hdwy to chse wnr over 2f out: sn rn green and wandered u.p: kpt on wl but a being hld fnl f* **7/1**3
3 3 3/4 **Lowawatha** 2-9-3 0 JimCrowley 5 72+
(R M Beckett) *cl up: nt clr run and swtchd rt 2f out: sn rdn: kpt on but nt pce of ldrs* **16/1**
4 1 1/4 **Chief Of Men** 2-9-3 0 RobertWinston 6 69
(D J Coakley) *trckd ldrs: rdn 3f out: kpt on same pce fnl 2f* **6/1**2
45 **5** 3 **Painters Easel (IRE)**22 3625 2-9-3 0 HayleyTurner 7 60
(J S Moore) *trckd ldrs: rdn wl over 2f out: wknd ent fnl f* **50/1**
6 4 1/2 **Madame Solitaire** 2-8-12 0 MartinDwyer 3 41
(R Hannon) *s.i.s: a outpcd* **12/1**
0 **7** 1 1/4 **Invigilator**8 4096 2-9-3 0 DavidProbert 1 42
(H J L Dunlop) *led tl rdn 3f out: wknd over 1f out* **40/1**
1m 15.51s (0.71) **Going Correction** -0.025s/f (Good) 7 Ran SP% **114.0**
Speed ratings (Par 96): **94,93,88,86,82 76,75**
Tote Swingers: 1&2 £1.70, 1&3 £2.20, 2&3 £3.90 CSF £4.27 TOTE £1.40: £1.10, £3.70; EX 3.90.
Owner Miss Yvonne Jacques **Bred** Old Carhue Stud **Trained** East Everleigh, Wilts
FOCUS
An ordinary maiden made more interesting by a clutch of nicely-bred newcomers. The fifth helps with the standard and the winner only ran to his debut form on the face of things.
NOTEBOOK
Ardour(IRE), a 100,000gns purchase who had finished second on his Windsor debut, got off the mark with a workmanlike display. Always close up, he took the lead approaching 2f out and stayed on dourly, despite drifting slightly left in the closing stages. He looked very fit for this, so, even though he may stay a little farther, is not guaranteed to improve that much and looks a nursery type. (op 4-7 tchd 8-13 in places)
Codemaster, a first-time-out half-brother to several smart performers, did enough to suggest he can find a suitable opening at this level. Held up in touch early on, he went third just after halfway and threw down a solid challenge inside the final furlong. He wandered a little under pressure, probably through greenness, and ought to improve for the run.
Lowawatha, a 20,000gns newcomer from a decent family, also made an encouraging start to his career, though he will need to do better in order to take an average maiden. He plugged on gamely enough, though, and should be fitter next time.
Chief Of Men cost 90,000gns as a yearling and looked a nice type beforehand, so his run was slightly disappointing. He was second approaching 2f out, but failed to quicken when asked, climbing a little and fading late on. (op 11-2)
Painters Easel(IRE), unable to make the first three in sellers on his two previous starts, finished close enough to indicate this form should not be over-rated. Keen in the early stages, he lost touch on the leaders only late on.
Madame Solitaire, a debutante half-sister to the useful Skilling Spirit, was slow to start and outpaced in last place in the first half of the race. She gained just one position in the closing stages and does not look a potential superstar.

4385 COLD SERVICE LTD MAIDEN STKS 6f
7:35 (7:36) (Class 5) 3-Y-O+ **£3,885** (£1,156; £577; £288) **Stalls** High

Form RPR
22 **1** **Valencha**17 3786 3-8-12 0 SteveDrowne 1 75
(H Morrison) *quite keen early: trckd ldrs: rdn to chal wl over 1f out: tk v narrow advantage ent fnl f: kpt on: hld on to advantage on nod: all out* **9/4**2
-022 **2** shd **Advertisement (USA)**45 2852 3-9-3 77 RichardHughes 5 80
(J Noseda) *a.p: led over 2f out: rdn whn chal over 1f out: v narrowly hdd ent fnl f: kpt on: jst hld on nod* **2/1**1
-352 **3** 4 1/2 **Lay Claim (USA)**20 3713 3-9-3 75 (v) RichardMullen 6 66+
(Sir Michael Stoute) *in last pair but cl up: nt clr run on rails 2f out: swtchd lft and sn rdn: r.o fnl f* **7/2**3
0-4 **4** 1/2 **Millden**22 3635 3-8-10 0 AmyScott(7) 7 64
(H Candy) *trckd ldrs: effrt over 2f out: one pce fnl f* **17/2**
5 hd **Brewers Boy** 3-9-0 0 JamesMillman(3) 2 63
(B R Millman) *s.i.s: in last pair but cl up: nvr gng pce to chal but kpt on fnl f* **28/1**
0- **6** 4 1/2 **Ahwahnee**275 6971 3-8-12 0 JimCrowley 4 44
(R M Beckett) *little awkward leaving stalls: trckd ldrs: rdn 3f out: fdd ins fnl f* **9/1**
0 **7** 3 **Kargarann (IRE)**22 3635 3-9-3 0 AdamKirby 8 39
(Stef Higgins) *led tl over 2f out: sn rdn: wknd over 1f out* **25/1**
1m 15.41s (0.61) **Going Correction** -0.025s/f (Good) 7 Ran SP% **114.1**
Speed ratings (Par 103): **94,93,87,87,86 80,76**
Tote Swingers: 1&2 £2.40, 1&3 £2.10, 2&3 £1.30 CSF £7.15 TOTE £3.20: £1.30, £2.20; EX 6.70.
Owner Pangfield Partners **Bred** T J Billington **Trained** East Ilsley, Berks
■ Stewards' Enquiry : Amy Scott three-day ban: careless riding (Aug 7-9)
FOCUS
Not much depth to this modest maden. The winner was up 8lb on her debut form, with the second rated to his best.

4386 OLIVER GRUBB 16TH BIRTHDAY H'CAP 1m 6f 21y
8:10 (8:10) (Class 5) (0-75,73) 3-Y-O+ **£3,238** (£963; £481; £240)

Form RPR
3043 **1** **Hawridge King**37 3127 8-9-10 72 JamesMillman(3) 4 80
(W S Kittow) *trckd ldrs: led over 2f out: styd on: rdn out* **5/2**1
4133 **2** 2 **Seventh Hill**15 3865 5-9-7 66 JimmyQuinn 1 71
(M Blanshard) *cl up: hdwy 3f out: sn rdn: wnt 2nd ent fnl f: styd on* **3/1**2
3535 **3** 1/2 **Zaif (IRE)**9 4070 7-8-12 57 JamesDoyle 7 62
(D J S Ffrench Davis) *hld up last: hdwy over 3f out: rdn to chse wnr 2f out tl ent fnl f: no ex* **7/1**
0-33 **4** 1 3/4 **Dark Energy**9 4042 6-8-12 57 oh2 (t) HayleyTurner 3 59
(M J Scudamore) *trckd ldrs: wnt 2nd 4f out tl rdn 2f out: styd on same pce* **4/1**3
1064 **5** 4 **Cote D'Argent**14 3917 7-9-9 68 (t) DaneO'Neill 5 64
(C J Down) *led tl over 2f out: fdd fnl f* **14/1**
6 3 1/4 **Moment Present (FR)**29 5-10-0 73 (b1) SteveDrowne 6 65
(C J Mann) *trckd ldr tl rdn 4f out: wknd over 1f out* **20/1**
-604 **7** hd **Coiled Spring**8 4102 4-9-7 66 (p) RichardHughes 2 58
(Mrs A J Perrett) *cl up: rdn 3f out: no imp: wknd over 1f out* **11/2**
3m 5.86s (-1.54) **Going Correction** -0.025s/f (Good) 7 Ran SP% **112.9**
Speed ratings (Par 103): **103,101,101,100,98 96,96**
Tote Swingers: 1&2 £1.80, 1&3 £3.50, 2&3 £2.90 CSF £9.93 TOTE £3.50: £1.80, £2.10; EX 11.40.
Owner Eric Gadsden **Bred** Old Mill Stud **Trained** Blackborough, Devon
FOCUS
A modest handicap, but the pace was sound, given the grade. Straightforward form, the winner only needing to match this season's best.

4387 FAMOUS GROUSE H'CAP 6f 212y
8:40 (8:40) (Class 4) (0-85,85) 3-Y-O **£4,209** (£1,252; £625; £312) **Stalls** Centre

Form RPR
33-1 **1** **The Confessor**83 1731 3-8-13 77 DaneO'Neill 2 86
(H Candy) *led: rdn and narrowly hdd wl over 1f out: kpt on wl ins fnl f: regained ld towards fin* **4/1**2
0-43 **2** hd **Oil Strike**21 3696 3-9-7 85 JimCrowley 1 93
(P Winkworth) *a.p: led wl over 1f out: sn rdn: no ex whn hdd towards fin* **2/1**1
-510 **3** 1 1/2 **Starclass**15 3863 3-9-0 78 AdamKirby 3 82
(W R Swinburn) *trckd ldrs: swtchd lft over 2f out: sn rdn: kpt on ins fnl f wout threatening* **5/1**
1352 **4** 1 1/2 **Red Gulch**14 3899 3-8-10 77 AshleyHamblett(3) 7 77+
(E A L Dunlop) *hld up bt wl in tch: rdn whn nt best of runs over 1f out: kpt on ins fnl f* **8/1**
6533 **5** 2 3/4 **Kurtanella**3 4250 3-9-2 80 RichardHughes 5 72
(R Hannon) *hld up but wl in tch: rdn 2f out: no imp* **9/2**3
-066 **6** 2 3/4 **Haadeeth**21 3696 3-9-7 85 PatDobbs 4 70
(M P Tregoning) *trckd ldrs: rdn 2f out: wknd ent fnl f* **13/2**
2133 **7** 7 **Vanilla Rum**16 3833 3-9-0 78 FrankieMcDonald 6 44
(H Candy) *trckd ldrs: rdn over 3f out: wknd over 1f out* **16/1**
1m 28.55s (-0.45) **Going Correction** -0.025s/f (Good) 7 Ran SP% **118.5**
Speed ratings (Par 102): **101,100,99,97,94 91,83**
Tote Swingers: 1&2 £2.40, 1&3 £5.50, 2&3 £4.70 CSF £13.16 TOTE £4.60: £2.20, £1.10; EX 14.90 Place 6: £3.26 Place 5: £1.90 .
Owner Six Too Many **Bred** Mrs C R D Wilson **Trained** Kingston Warren, Oxon
FOCUS
A competitive-looking handicap, with the whole field covered by just 8lb, but the first two dominated throughout. Fair form for the grade, with the winner up 7lb.
T/Plt: £6.90 to a £1 stake. Pool:£55,377 - 5,822.79 winning tickets T/Qpdt: £4.10 to a £1 stake. Pool:£6,614 - 814.46 winning tickets TM

4344YORK (L-H)
Saturday, July 24

OFFICIAL GOING: Good to firm (good in places; 7.9)
Rail realignment added about 8yds to races of one mile and over.
Wind: light 1/2 against Weather: fine

4388 SKYPOKER.COM STKS (NURSERY) 5f
2:00 (2:00) (Class 3) 2-Y-O **£6,799** (£2,023; £1,011; £505) **Stalls** Low

Form RPR
41 **1** **Face The Problem (IRE)**12 3961 2-9-4 82 FrankieDettori 5 91+
(B W Hills) *sn trcking ldrs: led over 2f out: edgd lft over 1f out: styd on strly* **7/4**1
4453 **2** 1 1/4 **Brave Dream**8 4111 2-8-2 66 FrannyNorton 1 70
(K A Ryan) *chsd ldrs far side: outpcd over 2f out: hdwy over 1f out: edgd rt and styd on to take 2nd clsng stages* **25/1**
411 **3** 3/4 **Dingle View (IRE)**83 1733 2-9-6 84 CathyGannon 2 85
(P D Evans) *chsd ldrs: styng on same pce whn crowded ins fnl f* **7/1**
4531 **4** 1 1/2 **Lady Royale**14 3925 2-9-5 83 (b) SilvestreDeSousa 3 79
(G R Oldroyd) *sn drvn and outpcd: hdwy and edgd rt over 1f out: kpt on same pce* **13/2**3

001 **5** ½ **Lizzie (IRE)**[25] 3536 2-8-8 **72**......(b) GrahamGibbons 4 66
(T D Easterby) *led tl over 2f out: wkng whn n.m.r ins fnl f* **10/1**

51 **6** 1½ **Blaze Of Thunder (IRE)**[22] 3624 2-9-7 **85**...... PaulHanagan 9 74
(R A Fahey) *in rr: hmpd over 1f out: nvr a factor* **4/1**[2]

355 **7** 1¾ **Barkston Ash**[14] 3897 2-8-4 **68** ow2......(b[1]) WJSupple 7 50
(E J Alston) *wnt lft s: hld up in rr: hdwy and carried lft over 2f out: edgd lft over 1f out: sn wknd* **25/1**

641 **8** ½ **Dubai Celebration**[35] 3204 2-9-0 **83**...... PatrickDonaghy(5) 6 64
(Jedd O'Keeffe) *chsd ldrs: wknd over 1f out* **8/1**

5162 **9** 1½ **Lady Brookie**[11] 3986 2-8-7 **71**...... KierenFallon 8 46
(Peter Grayson) *in rr centre: sme hdwy 2f out: sn wknd* **16/1**

58.49 secs (-0.81) **Going Correction** -0.10s/f (Good) **9** Ran SP% **116.0**
Speed ratings (Par 98): **102,100,98,96,95 93,90,89,87**
toteswingers:1&2:£15.20, 1&3:£2.90, 2&3:£57.50 CSF £53.02 CT £249.75 TOTE £2.70: £1.20, £7.70, £1.90; EX 69.60 Trifecta £327.00 Part won. Pool: £441.92 - 0.42 winning units..
Owner Sir A Ferguson,Cavendish InvLtd,J Hanson **Bred** J Joyce **Trained** Lambourn, Berks

FOCUS
A competitive nursery, run at a frantic early pace. Improved efforts from the first two.

NOTEBOOK
Face The Problem(IRE) looked to have got in lightly for this nursery debut and so it proved, as he won readily to justify strong support. The winner was off the mark at Windsor 12 days earlier and, despite again showing errant traits here, was comfortably too good for his rivals over this sharper test. He still has some way to go before looking quite up to his Gimcrack entry, but this very speedy colt should only improve as he gains further experience. Connections later hinted they were leaning more towards the Group 2 Flying Childers at Doncaster in September for him, now he has shown so much dash, instead of going back up a furlong in the short term. (op 2-1 tchd 9-4)
Brave Dream ◆ proved a lot more effective on this return to a quicker surface, but really found this drop to a sharp 5f happening too quickly for him. He should not be long in winning when reverting to a stiffer test. (op 20-1)
Dingle View(IRE) was returning from an 83-day break. She was another that found this drop back a furlong too sharp, but it was still a good effort and the best of her has probably still to be seen.
Lady Royale came in for solid support. She was taken off her feet as the leaders scorched off early on and lacked the pace to land a significant blow. (op 15-2 tchd 8-1)
Lizzie(IRE) showed real early speed on this switch to a nursery, in contrast to when winning at Thirsk over 6f last time, and paid the price for her early exertions at the furlong marker. (op 9-1 tchd 11-1)
Blaze Of Thunder(IRE) simply could not go the pace on this drop back a furlong and shouldn't be judged too harshly on this effort. (tchd 7-2 and 9-2 in a place)

4389 SKYBET.COM E B F FILLIES' H'CAP 1m 2f 88y
2:30 (2:31) (Class 3) (0-90,85) 3-Y-O+ **£9,714** (£2,890; £1,444; £721) **Stalls** Low

Form RPR

3132 **1** **Destinys Dream (IRE)**[28] 3432 5-9-12 **81**...... AndrewMullen 3 89
(Miss Tracy Waggott) *hld up towards rr: stdy hdwy over 2f out: swtchd rt over 1f out: edgd lft and r.o to ld towards fin* **8/1**

511 **2** ½ **Akhmatova**[7] 4134 3-8-10 **75**...... NickyMackay 8 82
(G A Butler) *trckd ldrs: chal over 2f out: led jst ins fnl f: hung lft: hdd and no ex towards fin* **5/1**[2]

6416 **3** ½ **Aphrodisia**[87] 1629 6-9-11 **80**...... GrahamGibbons 2 86
(Ian Williams) *mid-div: hdwy over 2f out: chsd ldrs ins fnl f: no ex towards fin* **20/1**

31 **4** 1 **Viewing**[28] 3443 3-8-12 **77**...... WilliamBuick 7 81
(J H M Gosden) *s.i.s: hdwy to ld after 2f: hdd 3f out: remained upsides: nt qckn last 150yds* **6/1**[3]

1425 **5** ½ **Antigua Sunrise (IRE)**[42] 2976 4-9-9 **78**...... PaulHanagan 4 81
(R A Fahey) *mid-div: hdwy 3f out: sn drvn and outpcd: kpt on fnl f* **4/1**[1]

41 **6** 1¼ **Christmas Light**[14] 3924 3-9-1 **80**...... SilvestreDeSousa 10 81+
(D O'Meara) *chsd ldrs: led and wnt lft over 2f out: hdd jst ins fnl f: hung lft and fdd* **17/2**

51-0 **7** 1¼ **Tipperary Boutique (IRE)**[99] 1354 3-9-6 **85**...... MichaelHills 14 83
(B W Hills) *swtchd lft after s: hdwy on inner over 3f out: keeping on whn hmpd ins fnl f* **12/1**

3051 **8** 1¼ **Law Of The Range**[22] 3628 3-8-11 **76**...... NeilCallan 12 72
(M Botti) *led early: trckd ldrs: led 3f out: sn hdd: wkng whn hmpd ins fnl f* **11/1**

0241 **9** 2¾ **Bollin Dolly**[21] 3679 7-10-0 **83**...... DavidNolan 11 74
(T D Easterby) *sn led: hdd after 2f: chsd ldrs: wknd over 1f out* **14/1**

5-66 **10** 1 **Amanda Carter**[22] 3618 6-9-12 **81**...... KierenFallon 1 70
(R A Fahey) *in rr: nvr a factor* **20/1**

0412 **11** 3½ **Snow Dancer (IRE)**[14] 3894 6-9-8 **77**...... DuranFentiman 9 59
(H A McWilliams) *in rr: hdwy on outer 4f out: lost pl over 2f out* **20/1**

6035 **12** ¾ **Starla Dancer (GER)**[35] 3202 4-8-13 **73**...... LeeTopliss(5) 5 54
(R A Fahey) *hld up in rr-div: hdwy 6f out: lost pl over 2f out* **16/1**

315 **13** 13 **Magic Echo**[45] 2865 6-9-13 **82**...... PhillipMakin 6 38
(M Dods) *in rr: drvn over 3f out: bhd fnl 2f* **25/1**

2m 11.8s (-0.70) **Going Correction** +0.05s/f (Good)
WFA 3 from 4yo+ 10lb **13** Ran SP% **119.3**
Speed ratings (Par 104): **104,103,103,102,102 101,100,99,96,96 93,92,82**
toteswingers:1&2:£6.00, 1&3:£5.30, 2&3:£3.20 CSF £44.75 CT £786.23 TOTE £8.20: £2.40, £2.30, £7.50; EX 55.90 TRIFECTA Not won..
Owner H Conlon **Bred** Sean Burke **Trained** Spennymoor, Co Durham
■ Stewards' Enquiry : Silvestre De Sousa caution: careless riding.

FOCUS
With the top weight being rated 7lb below the race ceiling this may not have been the strongest of fillies' handicaps for the class, but it was certainly competitive. There was something of an uneven pace on and a host of chances at the furlong marker, but eventually the first pair fought it out. The form seems pretty solid.

NOTEBOOK
Destinys Dream(IRE) resumed winning ways with a game display on this drop in trip. She travelled strongly into the home straight and knuckled down in gutsy fashion when hitting the front to hold off the runner-up. She doesn't know how to run a bad race and this was a deserved third success of the season. (tchd 7-1)
Akhmatova ◆ ran a big race in this quest for the hat-trick, but found the more-experienced winner too tough at the business end. This rates another personal-best in defeat off her 6lb higher mark and she can be found another opening before that long, despite going up again for this.
Aphrodisia came from a similar position as the winner and also moved well through the race. This was her first outing for 87 days and it was much more like it again, so this is a performance she can build on. (op 16-1)
Viewing, off the mark at the second attempt on Lingfield's Polytrack last month, eventually got to the front and slowed things up turning for home. She kept battling away once headed and is well up to winning in this grade, but may just prefer slightly easier ground. (op 13-2 tchd 9-2)
Antigua Sunrise(IRE) ran better on this return from a 42-day break, but lacked an extra gear when it mattered and could be more effective back at 1m4f. (op 9-2 tchd 5-1)
Christmas Light won her maiden at this track a fortnight earlier and was backed for this step up in trip. She was given a confident ride, but edged left shortly after being asked for everything and may prefer reverting to 1m. (op 16-1)
Tipperary Boutique(IRE), having her first outing since April, was immediately dropped in from her outside stall. She lacked the pace to get seriously involved, but should improve for the run and looks well worth a try over further. (tchd 14-1)
Law Of The Range, 2lb higher, saw plenty of daylight through the first half of the race and found such company too demanding at this stage of her career. (op 12-1)

4390 SKY BET YORK STKS (GROUP 2) 1m 2f 88y
3:05 (3:06) (Class 1) 3-Y-O+
£56,770 (£21,520; £10,770; £5,370; £2,690; £1,350) **Stalls** Low

Form RPR

6302 **1** **Summit Surge (IRE)**[55] 2576 6-9-2 **112**......(t) KierenFallon 6 117
(L M Cumani) *t.k.h in last: effrt on outside 3f out: edgd lft and r.o to ld last 75yds* **8/1**

3-11 **2** 1¼ **Bushman**[50] 2707 6-9-2 **110**...... NeilCallan 1 115
(D M Simcock) *sn trcking ldrs: led over 1f out: hdd and no ex last 75yds* **5/1**

1430 **3** 1½ **Allybar (IRE)**[38] 3068 4-9-2 **109**...... FrankieDettori 7 112
(Mahmood Al Zarooni) *hld up in rr-div: hdwy 7f out: drvn on outer 4f out: edgd lft and styd on same pce fnl f* **4/1**[3]

0010 **4** hd **Debussy (IRE)**[38] 3068 4-9-2 **115**...... WilliamBuick 5 112
(J H M Gosden) *trckd ldrs: slt ld 2f out: sn hdd and rdr dropped whip: carried lft and styd on same pce ins fnl f* **3/1**[1]

2526 **5** ½ **Nanton (USA)**[16] 3825 8-9-2 **106**...... PhillipMakin 2 111
(J S Goldie) *sn chsng ldrs: drvn over 3f out: kpt on same pce and carried lft wl ins fnl f* **22/1**

030 **6** 3¼ **Dream Lodge (IRE)**[14] 3921 6-9-2 **104**...... PaulHanagan 3 104
(R A Fahey) *mid-div: effrt over 3f out: sn rdn and no imp* **10/1**

513- **7** 3 **Monitor Closely (IRE)**[315] 5861 4-9-2 **116**...... JimmyFortune 4 99
(M L W Bell) *led: hdd 2f out: wknd over 1f out* **7/2**[2]

105- **8** hd **Balius (IRE)**[258] 7313 7-9-2 **115**......(b) AlanMunro 8 98
(Saeed Bin Suroor) *hld up in rr: hdwy over 3f out: sn drvn: lost pl over 1f out* **16/1**

2m 8.82s (-3.68) **Going Correction** +0.05s/f (Good) **8** Ran SP% **114.3**
Speed ratings (Par 115): **116,115,113,113,113 110,108,108**
toteswingers:1&2:£6.00, 1&3:£5.30, 2&3:£3.20 CSF £47.47 TOTE £8.80: £2.60, £1.70, £1.70; EX 40.80 Trifecta £52.60 Pool: £1,030.38 - 14.47 winning units..
Owner W Bellew **Bred** Norelands Bloodstock **Trained** Newmarket, Suffolk

FOCUS
An open-looking Group 2 and not the strongest race for the class. It was run at a sound pace and there were plenty of chances from 2f out. The winner is credited with a length personal best but the fifth rather limits the form.

NOTEBOOK
Summit Surge(IRE) opened his account for current connections on this first run beyond 1m. He was ridden to get the trip, taking a keen early hold, and found the gap coming at the right time when produced with his challenge in the home straight. There was plenty to like about his attitude late on and his ability to handle quick ground was no doubt a big advantage in this field. It could be he has more to offer over the distance when getting his ground. (op 7-1 tchd 13-2)
Bushman was up in trip and could've done without the ground drying out. The quicker surface probably helped him see out the longer trip, but he edged right late in the day and that suggests his stamina was stretched to the limit. He helps to set the standard and is a very likeable 6-y-o (op 9-2 tchd 4-1)
Allybar(IRE) was bitterly disappointing in the Prince Of Wales's Stakes on his British debut last month. He showed that run to be all wrong and travelled into contention like the best horse in the race, but his response when put under pressure was very limited. He did keep on to bag third and it may be this ground was quicker than he cares for, but he has a little to prove with his attitude now. (tchd 7-2)
Debussy(IRE) ran well in the Prince Of Wales's Stakes and previously scored in this class. He got a little warm beforehand and wasn't able to lead, which appeared his early intention. He still held every chance, but is another that really needs an easier surface and ran some way below his recent level. (tchd 11-4 and 10-3 in places)
Nanton(USA) posted a bold effort, but is a little short of this level. (op 20-1)
Monitor Closely(IRE) was making his belated return and debut for Michael Bell, having been kept off the track with knee problems. He was solid in the market and was ridden from the front over this sharper test. The way he folded from the furlong marker would indicate the run was needed and he should enjoy getting back over 1m4f in due course. Official explanation: jockey said colt had no more to give (op 5-1)

4391 SKY BET DASH (H'CAP) 6f
3:40 (3:46) (Class 2) (0-105,104) 3-Y-O+**£32,380** (£9,635; £4,815; £2,405) **Stalls** Low

Form RPR

1230 **1** **Hawkeyethenoo (IRE)**[8] 4085 4-9-0 **91**...... KierenFallon 18 102
(J S Goldie) *in rr: gd hdwy over 1f out: sddle slipped: r.o wl to ld fnl strides* **7/1**[2]

-130 **2** hd **Kaldoun Kingdom (IRE)**[35] 3193 5-9-5 **101**...... LeeTopliss(5) 9 111
(R A Fahey) *dwlt: hld up in mid-div: hdwy 2f out: led last 75yds: hdd nr fin* **16/1**

0151 **3** ¾ **Parisian Pyramid (IRE)**[28] 3461 4-9-5 **96**...... StephenCraine 7 104
(K A Ryan) *led: hdd and no ex last 75yds* **16/1**

4130 **4** nk **Tiddliwinks**[14] 3919 4-9-1 **92**...... DarryllHolland 14 99
(K A Ryan) *in rr: gd hdwy stands' side over 1f out: r.o wl* **20/1**

4-14 **5** 1¼ **Novellen Lad (IRE)**[27] 3489 5-9-2 **93**...... WJSupple 10 96
(E J Alston) *chsd ldrs: kpt on same pce fnl f* **10/1**

4200 **6** nse **Damien (IRE)**[35] 3193 4-9-10 **101**...... WilliamBuick 20 104
(B W Hills) *hld up stands' side: hdwy over 2f out: edgd lft and styd on same pce fnl f* **25/1**

35-0 **7** ½ **Hitchens (IRE)**[27] 3489 5-9-7 **98**...... JimmyFortune 4 99
(T D Barron) *racd far side: hdwy 2f out: kpt on same pce fnl f* **20/1**

2000 **8** nk **Baldemar**[8] 4085 5-8-13 **90**...... FrannyNorton 6 90
(R A Fahey) *chsd ldrs: kpt on same pce appr fnl f* **16/1**

-331 **9** nse **Sunraider (IRE)**[45] 2862 3-9-0 **96**...... MichaelHills 8 95
(B W Hills) *in rr: hdwy 2f out: kpt on wl ins fnl f* **7/1**[2]

0430 **10** hd **Singeur (IRE)**[17] 3791 3-9-4 **100**...... NeilCallan 1 99
(R Bastiman) *chsd ldrs far side: kpt on same pce fnl f* **25/1**

104 **11** hd **Tajneed (IRE)**[8] 4085 7-8-12 **94**...... BillyCray(5) 13 93+
(D Nicholls) *hood removed late and swvd violently rt s: detached in last: styd on wl fnl f: nvr on terms* **25/1**

504U **12** ½ **Sea Of Leaves (USA)**[49] 2759 4-9-1 **92**...... PhillipMakin 16 89
(J S Goldie) *hld up in mid-div: effrt 2f out: nvr nr ldrs* **33/1**

0050 **13** nk **Sonny Red (IRE)**[5] 4191 6-9-4 **95**...... PaulQuinn 19 91
(D Nicholls) *in tch: effrt over 2f out: wknd over 1f out* **40/1**

1062 **14** 2¼ **Damika (IRE)**[8] 4085 7-9-1 **95**...... MichaelStainton(3) 15 84
(R M Whitaker) *mid-div: effrt over 2f out: nvr a threat* **33/1**

0056 **15** nk **Star Rover (IRE)**[14] 3895 3-8-13 **95**...... CathyGannon 12 82
(P D Evans) *chsd ldrs: wknd 1f out* **66/1**

5265 **16** ¾ **Iver Bridge Lad**[17] 3791 3-9-8 **104**...... AlanMunro 2 89
(J Ryan) *racd far side: hdwy over 2f out: wknd over 1f out* **10/1**

-130 **17** *nk* **Ingleby Lady**[35] 3193 4-9-6 97 GrahamGibbons 17 82
(T D Barron) *mid-div: hdwy over 2f out: wknd appr fnl f* **8/1**[3]

0-05 **18** *2 1/4* **Tombi (USA)**[56] 2526 6-9-7 98 SilvestreDeSousa 5 76
(J Howard Johnson) *a towards rr* **20/1**

-500 **19** *shd* **Valery Borzov (IRE)**[35] 3193 6-9-3 94 (v) PaulHanagan 11 71
(R A Fahey) *chsd ldrs: lost pl over 1f out* **9/1**

0011 **20** *1* **Lowdown (IRE)**[8] 4085 3-9-6 102 FrankieDettori 3 75
(M Johnston) *in tch towards far side: drvn over 2f out: sn lost pl* **6/1**[1]

69.88 secs (-2.02) **Going Correction** -0.10s/f (Good)
WFA 3 from 4yo+ 5lb **20** Ran SP% **131.9**
Speed ratings (Par 109): **109,108,107,107,105 105,104,104,104,104 103,103,102,99,99 98,98,95,94,93**
toteswingers:1&2:£18.90, 1&3:£23.90, 2&3:£79.30 CSF £105.63 CT £1817.38 TOTE £6.80: £1.80, £5.60, £4.60, £4.10; EX 211.10 Trifecta £2601.40 Part won. Pool: £3,515.46 - 0.20 winning units..
Owner Johnnie Delta Racing **Bred** S Leigh & R Leigh & Islandmore Stud **Trained** Uplawmoor, E Renfrews

FOCUS
This was seriously competitive and unsurprisingly there was no hanging about. The field raced mainly down the middle to far side, with the stands' rail being shunned. Solid form, with improved efforts from the first two.

NOTEBOOK
Hawkeyethenoo(IRE), who lost his race in the stalls last time, showed his true colours again and got up late in the day under a classic ride by Kieren Fallon. He got behind early on and almost needed to be kidded into the race from halfway. His electric turn of foot was deployed passing the furlong marker and he was always going to emerge on top where it mattered. His trainer has excelled already in training him to improve so rapidly in the last year, but better things could still await this 4-y-o and his versatility as regards underfoot conditions is a big plus. He now gets a penalty for the Stewards' Cup at Glorious Goodwood next weekend and that will obviously help his chances of getting a run, with most bookmakers immediately slashing his odds in the ante-post market for that. Connections will aim to run him next Saturday providing he emerges from this sufficiently, but later said his big target was the Ayr Gold Cup in September. (tchd 8-1 in a place)
Kaldoun Kingdom(IRE) turned in a blinder under top weight and was only mugged by the winner near the finish. This pretty much confirms him best on a flat track and he will no doubt continue to pay his way in such races, but his season is probably geared around the Ayr Gold Cup (won Silver Cup last term).
Parisian Pyramid(IRE) had plenty go his way when winning off 5lb lower at Windsor last month, but his front-running style often affords him such luxuries. He ran a very pleasing race and only tired out of things late in the day, so clearly remains in top form. (tchd 20-1)
Tiddliwinks ◆ showed the clear benefit of her return over C&D a fortnight previously and posted a solid effort under a waiting ride. She is rated 10lb higher on the AW as a result of not yet winning on turf, but on this showing she may be about to correct that. (op 16-1)
Novellen Lad(IRE) ran close to his last-time-out form in Ireland with the winner, but did well to finish so close considering he sweated up badly beforehand. (op 8-1)
Damien(IRE) returned to form with a decent effort, but he remains one to avoid for win-only betting. (tchd 22-1)
Hitchens(IRE) was doing his best work late on and finished a deal closer to the winner than was the case on his seasonal debut behind the winner at the Curragh last time. He should come on again for the run. (op 16-1)
Baldemar ran one of his better races and can find less competitive races. (tchd 18-1)
Sunraider(IRE), well fancied, narrowly fared best of the 3-y-os and ran a solid race on ground quicker than he cares for. (op 13-2 tchd 6-1)
Tajneed(IRE) Official explanation: jockey said, regarding slow removal of the blind, that the gelding dipped its head and veered to the right.
Lowdown(IRE) was the obvious disappointment. He went up 9lb for his clear-cut Musselburgh success eight days earlier. He got very warm beforehand, however, and took time to load into the stalls, so clearly wasn't on a going day. (tchd 5-1)

4392 SKYVEGAS.COM MEDIAN AUCTION MAIDEN STKS 6f
4:10 (4:18) (Class 4) 2-Y-O **£6,022** (£1,792; £895; £447) **Stalls** Low

Form RPR

1 **Common Touch (IRE)** 2-9-3 0 PaulHanagan 1 81+
(R A Fahey) *stmbld sn after s: sn chsng ldrs: effrt 2f out: sn rdn: edgd rt ins fnl f: r.o to ld last 50yds* **15/8**[1]

30 **2** *1/2* **Squires Gate (IRE)**[22] 3624 2-9-3 0 MichaelHills 3 79
(B W Hills) *led: edgd lft 1f out: hdd and no ex nr fin* **7/2**[2]

0 **3** *3 1/2* **Set Me Free (IRE)**[14] 3923 2-9-3 0 KierenFallon 8 69+
(L M Cumani) *mid-div: effrt and hung lft over 2f out: kpt on same pce fnl f* **7/2**[2]

663 **4** *1/2* **Mother Jones**[19] 3729 2-8-12 74 PhillipMakin 2 62
(D H Brown) *w ldr: hmpd and swtchd rt jst ins fnl f: fdd* **6/1**[3]

0 **5** *5* **Assertion**[43] 2936 2-9-3 0 AlanMunro 6 52
(M Brittain) *t.k.h: trckd ldrs: wnt lft over 1f out: sn wknd* **50/1**

6 *13* **Ryedale Dancer (IRE)** 2-8-12 0 DuranFentiman 5 8
(T D Easterby) *chsd ldrs: outpcd over 2f out: lost pl over 1f out* **33/1**

6 **7** *6* **Pitkin**[14] 3923 2-9-3 0 GrahamGibbons 11 —
(M W Easterby) *sn outpcd and bhd* **11/1**

8 *3/4* **Rudegirl (IRE)** 2-8-12 0 SilvestreDeSousa 9 —
(N Tinkler) *s.i.s: a outpcd and bhd* **20/1**

1m 11.99s (0.09) **Going Correction** -0.10s/f (Good) **8** Ran SP% **111.5**
Speed ratings (Par 96): **95,94,89,89,82 65,57,56**
toteswingers:1&2:£2.00, 1&3:£2.50, 2&3:£2.10 CSF £7.99 TOTE £3.10: £1.40, £1.30, £1.50; EX 9.20.
Owner Nicholas Wrigley & Kevin Hart **Bred** Overbury Stallions Ltd And D Boocock **Trained** Musley Bank, N Yorks

FOCUS
The first pair dominated this average juvenile maiden. A good start from the winner and the runner-up built slightly on his early form.

NOTEBOOK
Common Touch(IRE) arrived for this racecourse debut with a good reputation and justified strong support, under a very strong ride. He is bred to get a good bit further as he matures and there was a great deal to like about his ground-gaining attitude to master the runner-up inside the final furlong. He could be very useful as he ought to improve a deal for the experience. (tchd 7-4 and 2-1)
Squires Gate(IRE) was always on the front end and went down fighting near the finish. This was better from him again and he should have little trouble winning an ordinary maiden, but he does now have the option of nurseries. This ground would've been quick enough for him too. (op 4-1)
Set Me Free(IRE) ◆, eighth over C&D on debut a fortnight earlier, was well backed to improve and did so but was still too green to do himself full justice. He now also looks to be crying out for a stiffer test and should be winning before long. (op 5-1 tchd 3-1)
Mother Jones helped force the pace and gave her all, but was beaten off from the furlong marker. She will appreciate a switch to nurseries. (op 9-2)
Assertion was again distinctly green, but this was a step in the right direction and his pronounced knee action suggests easier ground will suit.

Pitkin Official explanation: jockey said gelding was unsuited by the good (good to firm places) ground

4393 SKY BET SUPPORTING THE YORKSHIRE RACING SUMMER FESTIVAL STKS (H'CAP) 2m 88y
4:45 (4:47) (Class 3) (0-90,90) 4-Y-O+ **£9,066** (£2,697; £1,348; £673) **Stalls** Low

Form RPR

223 **1** **Wicked Daze (IRE)**[23] 3588 7-8-10 79 PhillipMakin 3 87
(Miss L A Perratt) *mde all: hld on gamely* **12/1**

0-10 **2** *3/4* **Dazinski**[15] 3843 4-9-3 86 DarrylHolland 5 93
(M H Tompkins) *hld up in rr: drvn over 5f out: chsng ldrs over 3f out: edgd rt over 1f out: styd on same pce fnl 75yds* **4/1**[1]

5143 **3** *nk* **Dayia (IRE)**[24] 3566 6-9-2 90 SimonPearce(5) 9 97
(J Pearce) *hld up in mid-div: wnt prom 10f out: drvn over 5f out: rallied over 2f out: kpt on same pce ins fnl f: tk 3rd towards fin* **6/1**[2]

/026 **4** *1/2* **La Vecchia Scuola (IRE)**[28] 3447 6-9-4 87 PaulHanagan 4 93
(J S Goldie) *trckd ldrs: t.k.h: effrt over 3f out: chal over 1f out: kpt on same pce ins fnl f* **8/1**[3]

6343 **5** *3/4* **Palomar (USA)**[11] 3974 8-8-9 78 NeilCallan 7 83
(B Ellison) *stdd s: t.k.h in rr: effrt on outside over 2f out: kpt on fnl f* **6/1**[2]

0054 **6** *2 1/2* **Ocean's Minstrel**[15] 3843 4-9-5 88 AlanMunro 6 90
(J Ryan) *hld up: hdwy over 3f out: chsng ldrs 2f out: fdd ins fnl f* **6/1**[2]

6040 **7** *9* **Blue Nymph**[42] 2975 4-8-4 73 SilvestreDeSousa 12 64
(J J Quinn) *sn chsng ldrs: drvn over 4f out: wkng whn n.m.r 1f out: sn eased* **16/1**

1660 **8** *8* **Dazzling Light (UAE)**[15] 3873 5-8-10 79 KierenFallon 8 61
(J S Goldie) *t.k.h: trckd ldrs: jnd ldr 10f out: wknd over 1f out: eased ins fnl f* **9/1**

3303 **9** *1 1/4* **Crackentorp**[15] 3877 5-9-7 90 GrahamGibbons 11 70
(T D Easterby) *hld up: hdwy to trck ldrs after 4f: drvn over 3f out: lost pl 2f out: eased ins fnl f* **4/1**[1]

3m 33.68s (-0.82) **Going Correction** +0.05s/f (Good) **9** Ran SP% **117.5**
Speed ratings (Par 107): **104,103,103,103,102 101,97,93,92**
toteswingers:1&2:£11.40, 1&3:£8.40, 2&3:£5.80 CSF £60.66 CT £324.65 TOTE £10.70: £2.40, £1.90, £2.20; EX 65.70.
Owner Ken McGarrity **Bred** Bloomsbury Stud **Trained** East Kilbride, South Lanarks

FOCUS
This open staying handicap was run at an uneven pace and those racing under restraint were no doubt at a disadvantage. The winner had a fairly easy lead and is rated to his turf best. The form seems sound enough.

NOTEBOOK
Wicked Daze(IRE) was given a freebie out in front and made all to deservedly resume to winning ways. His rider got the fractions spot on and he was still going strongly at the 2f pole. He dug very deep to repel challengers thereafter and is very consistent, but he has to rate as somewhat flattered. His profile also suggests he is one to be taking on next time out. (op 10-1)
Dazinski ◆ got going late in the day and left behind his disappointing effort at Ascot earlier this month. He would have enjoyed more of a test and continues on an upwards curve. (op 9-2)
Dayia(IRE) is another that would have benefited from a more truly run race and this was another creditable effort on ground plenty quick enough for her. (op 5-1)
La Vecchia Scuola(IRE), easy to back, would have likely been better off racing more prominently yet still posted a pleasing effort in the circumstances. (op 7-1)
Palomar(USA) ◆ was ridden a lot more patiently this time and was the chief sufferer due to the uneven pace on. He could be about to end his losing run. (op 8-1)
Dazzling Light(UAE) proved free due to the way the race was run and dropped out in the home straight. Her stamina for this sort of test remains a question mark. Official explanation: jockey said mare ran too free (op 8-1)
Crackentorp was very disappointing, even allowing for the fact he was held up off the stop-start pace. He is another who still has to prove truly he needs this far. Official explanation: trainer had no explanation for the poor form shown (op 9-2 tchd 7-2)

4394 SKYBINGO.COM STKS (H'CAP) 7f
5:20 (5:22) (Class 4) (0-80,80) 3-Y-O+ **£6,540** (£1,946; £972; £485) **Stalls** Low

Form RPR

0033 **1** **Smarty Socks (IRE)**[15] 3876 6-10-0 80 SilvestreDeSousa 9 92
(D O'Meara) *stmbld s: bhd: hdwy on ins over 2f out: styd on wl to ld jst ins fnl f: edgd rt: drvn out* **4/1**[1]

0064 **2** *1 1/4* **Zomerlust**[15] 3876 8-10-0 80 (v) JimmyFortune 3 89+
(J J Quinn) *in rr: hdwy and swtchd rt 2f out: styd on to take 2nd nr fin* **7/1**[2]

2-15 **3** *hd* **Bawaardi (IRE)**[192] 151 4-9-12 78 PaulHanagan 4 86+
(R A Fahey) *in rr: hdwy and edgd rt over 1f out: keeping on same pce whn nt clr run towards fin* **7/1**[2]

2120 **4** *1/2* **Imperial Djay (IRE)**[29] 3396 5-9-8 74 FrannyNorton 19 81
(Mrs R A Carr) *mid-div: effrt 3f out: styng on same pce whn n.m.r whn swtchd lft last 100yds* **14/1**

4251 **5** *4 1/2* **Nufoudh (IRE)**[24] 3553 6-9-5 71 AndrewMullen 11 66
(Miss Tracy Waggott) *wnt rt s: led: hdd over 1f out: wknd fnl 150yds* **20/1**

0000 **6** *nk* **Violent Velocity (IRE)**[21] 3659 7-8-8 67 ShaneBKelly(7) 12 61
(J J Quinn) *bmpd s: chsd ldrs: led over 1f out: hdd jst ins fnl f: sn wknd* **25/1**

541 **7** *3/4* **Imprimis Tagula (IRE)**[9] 4063 6-9-5 78 (v) NatashaEaton(7) 17 70
(A Bailey) *w ldrs: wknd fnl f* **12/1**

0006 **8** *nse* **Pearly Wey**[8] 4121 7-9-4 70 PatrickMathers 2 62
(I W McInnes) *in rr: hdwy over 2f out: nt clr run and swtchd lft 1f out: kpt on* **33/1**

1000 **9** *nse* **Steel Stockholder**[7] 4154 4-9-2 68 AlanMunro 1 60
(M Brittain) *chsd ldrs on inner: one pce fnl 2f* **22/1**

5064 **10** *nk* **Antoniola (IRE)**[28] 3451 3-9-3 76 (t) GrahamGibbons 20 67
(T D Easterby) *in rr-div: drvn over 3f out: nvr nr ldrs* **12/1**

1006 **11** *1* **Deadly Encounter (IRE)**[28] 3448 4-9-9 80 (p) LeeTopliss(5) 7 68
(R A Fahey) *in rr: drvn over 3f out: sme hdwy on outside 2f out: no ex* **16/1**

5425 **12** *1/2* **Bold Marc (IRE)**[14] 3905 8-8-10 65 (p) GaryBartley(3) 5 52
(J R Weymes) *mid-div: effrt over 2f out: nvr a factor* **20/1**

5551 **13** *1* **Step In Time (IRE)**[11] 3990 3-9-2 75 FrankieDettori 13 59
(M Johnston) *chsd ldrs: drvn over 3f out: lost pl over 1f out* **4/1**[1]

-505 **14** *2 1/2* **Spiritofthewest (IRE)**[8] 4121 4-8-10 65 MichaelStainton(3) 6 42
(D H Brown) *chsd ldrs: wkng whn hmpd and swtchd lft 1f out* **25/1**

2530 **15** *4 1/2* **William Morgan (IRE)**[15] 3876 3-9-2 75 KierenFallon 18 40
(R A Fahey) *a in rr* **8/1**[3]

-650 **16** *5* **Diamond Daisy (IRE)**[15] 3876 4-9-1 67 WJSupple 10 19
(Mrs A Duffield) *hld up in rr: bhd fnl 2f* **25/1**

1m 23.65s (-1.65) **Going Correction** -0.10s/f (Good)
WFA 3 from 4yo+ 7lb **16** Ran SP% **132.4**
Speed ratings (Par 105): **105,103,103,102,97 97,96,96,96,95 94,94,93,90,85 79**
toteswingers:1&2:£6.30, 1&3:£9.00, 2&3:£9.20 CSF £30.58 CT £204.79 TOTE £5.20: £1.70, £1.90, £2.80, £3.20; EX 34.50 Place 6 £154.89; Place 5 £76.56.
Owner R G Fell **Bred** Mick McGinn **Trained** Nawton, N Yorks

The Form Book, Raceform Ltd, Compton, RG20 6NL

■ Stewards' Enquiry : Silvestre De Sousa three-day ban: careless riding (Aug 7-9)

FOCUS

A competitive handicap for the class, run at a solid pace. The first four came clear and the form looks solid amongst them.

Pearly Wey Official explanation: jockey said gelding was denied a clear run

T/Jkpt: Not won. T/Plt: £141.40 to a £1 stake. Pool:£147,285.05 - 759.90 winning tickets T/Qpdt: £23.70 to a £1 stake. Pool:£6,658.56 207.12 winning tickets WG

4354 ASCOT (R-H)

Sunday, July 25

OFFICIAL GOING: Good to firm (straight course: centre 9.5 far side: 9.0 stands' side: 8.8 round course: 9.3)

Wind: virtually nil Weather: sunny, light cloud

4396 E B F GL EVENTS OWEN BROWN CROCKER BULTEEL MAIDEN STKS 6f

2:15 (2:16) (Class 4) 2-Y-O **£6,476** (£1,927; £963; £481) **Stalls** Centre

Form RPR

1 **Malthouse (GER)** 2-9-0 0 RichardHills 8 83+
(M Johnston) *w'like: scope: in tch: hdwy and carried sltly rt over 2f out: led wl over 1f out: clr ent fnl f: edgd lft ins fnl f: r.o wl: comf* **7/2**[2]

2 2 ¾ **Escholido (IRE)** 2-9-0 0 MichaelHills 7 75+
(B W Hills) *w'like: athletic: chsd ldrs: effrt and carried rt jst over 2f out: ev ch and rdn wl over 1f out: sn outpcd by wnr: styd on same pce fnl f* **11/2**

3 ½ **Apollo D'Negro (IRE)** 2-9-0 0 PhilipRobinson 4 73+
(C G Cox) *unf: in tch: rdn to chse ldng pair and edgd rt over 1f out: sn outpcd by wnr: kpt on same pce fnl f* **3/1**[1]

4 6 **Plenty Power** 2-9-0 0 ChrisCatlin 3 55
(M R Channon) *unf: s.i.s: in tch in rr: hdwy and nt clr run ent fnl 2f tl over 1f out: no prog and wl hld whn edging rt ins fnl f* **4/1**[3]

5 2 **Gekko (IRE)** 2-9-0 0 StephenCraine 1 49
(Patrick Morris) *unf: led: rdn and hung rt over 2f out: hdd and edgd lft wl over 1f out: wkng whn shied at rivals whip over 1f out: wl btn fnl f* **12/1**

6 4 **Go** 2-9-0 0 JimmyFortune 2 37
(R Hannon) *w'like: s.i.s: in tch in rr: pushed along 1/2-way: rdn and btn 2f out: wl bhd over 1f out* **4/1**[3]

7 11 **Abadejo** 2-9-0 0 FergusSweeney 6 4+
(J R Jenkins) *w'like: s.i.s: rn green thrght: bhd: hdwy to chse ldrs 1/2-way: wknd qckly wl over 1f out: wl bhd and eased ins fnl f* **33/1**

1m 16.43s (2.03) **Going Correction** +0.175s/f (Good) **7** Ran SP% **113.2**

Speed ratings (Par 96): **93,89,88,80,78 72,58**

Tote Swingers: 1&2 £3.30, 1&3 £2.70, 2&3 £5.40 CSF £22.38 TOTE £4.70: £2.80, £2.50; EX 16.50 Trifecta £58.60 Pool: £611.03 - 7.70 winning units..

Owner Sheikh Hamdan Bin Mohammed Al Maktoum **Bred** Dr Chr Berglar **Trained** Middleham Moor, N Yorks

FOCUS

Drying conditions, and the going description was altered to good to firm all round. The GoingStick read 9.5 in the centre of the track, faster than on either flank, and the runners in the first came down the middle. The winning rider described the ground as on the firm side of good to firm. This event for unraced juveniles has not produced many stars in the past decade, but there was a better edition in 2007 with Prix du Moulin winner Aqlaam finishing third to Atlantic Sport. The pace was ordinary and the time was just under three seconds outside the Racing Post standard.

NOTEBOOK

Malthouse(GER), a 100,000euros buy, is closely related to Group 2-winning miler Martillo (by Anabaa). Coltish in the preliminaries, and not the most robust-looking, he travelled strongly in the race, showing a fluent, long-striding action, and came away in nice style despite edging to his left. He will have no problem with a seventh furlong and looks potentially a useful colt. (op 3-1)

Escholido(IRE), a 50,000gns yearling, is a half-brother to a couple of winners in France at 1m-1m4f. A strong colt, he was alongside the winner at the two pole but could not quicken from there. This was a pleasing start to his career. (op 5-1 tchd 6-1)

Apollo D'Negro(IRE) came in for support, but he could not quicken at the business end. A speedily bred half-brother to Molecomb winner Inya Lake, herself dam of Ayr Gold Cup winner Jimmy Styles, he should find an ordinary maiden. (op 4-1 tchd 9-2 in a place)

Plenty Power, a half-brother to the smart sprinter Bould Mover, is not the biggest. Slow to break, and slightly squeezed up when trying to improve, he should leave this bare form behind. He holds an entry in the Middle Park Stakes. (op 11-2)

Gekko(IRE), a 40,000euros foal, is a half-brother to a couple of useful winners in He's A Humbug and Mister Dee Bee. He broke well and made the running until fading. (op 28-1)

Go, out of a multiple winner at 6-7f, lacks a bit of size and may not have been as forward first time as a lot of the Hannon juveniles. He raced on the stands-side flank of the bunch and was no threat to the principals from halfway. (op 10-3)

Abadejo, whose dam won over 1m4f in France, will probably need further in time. One of the fittest in the field but keen in the preliminaries, he raced widest out on the track and was one of the first beaten. The experience will have done him good.

4397 TURFTV MAIDEN FILLIES' STKS 1m (S)

2:50 (2:50) (Class 4) 3-Y-O **£3,885** (£1,156; £577; £288) **Stalls** Centre

Form RPR

03 **1** **Ishraaqat**[51] 2718 3-9-0 0 RichardHills 6 79
(M P Tregoning) *lw: bmpd s: sn rcvrd and chsng ldrs: jnd ldr wl over 2f out: rdn and clr w ldr over 1f out: edgd lft u.p but sustained effrt to ld ins fnl f: r.o wl* **2/1**[1]

4 **2** ¾ **Sennockian Storm (USA)**[106] 1222 3-9-0 0 JoeFanning 8 77
(M Johnston) *w'like: scope: bmpd and awkward leaving stalls: sn rcvrd and led: jnd wl over 2f out: rdn and clr w wnr over 1f out: carried lft fnl f: hdd fnl 150yds: no ex* **11/2**[3]

3 3 **Shamardal Phantom (IRE)** 3-9-0 0 ShaneKelly 9 70
(D M Simcock) *w'like: stdd and dropped in bhd s: t.k.h: hld up towards rr: hdwy 1/2-way: n.m.r over 2f out: rdn and outpcd by ldng pair over 1f out: flashed tail u.p and one pce fnl f* **7/1**

4 hd **Dazzle The Crowd (IRE)** 3-9-0 0 SaleemGolam 11 70
(J H M Gosden) *w'like: stdd and dropped in bhd s: hld up in rr: swtchd rt and effrt over 2f out: outpcd by ldng pair over 1f out: kpt on same pce fnl f* **14/1**

00- **5** shd **Child Of Our Time (IRE)**[278] 6921 3-9-0 0 AlanMunro 1 70
(P W Chapple-Hyam) *hld up towards rr: hdwy over 2f out: kpt wanting to hang rt u.p fr wl over 1f out: kpt on same pce fnl f* **25/1**

3 **6** 1 ¾ **Snow Magic (IRE)**[20] 3738 3-9-0 0 PatCosgrave 5 66
(J R Fanshawe) *leggy: wnt rt s: in tch: rdn to chse ldng pair and edgd rt ent fnl 2f: outpcd over 1f out: wknd ins fnl f: n.m.r and hmpd and eased nr fin* **11/4**[2]

5 **7** 5 **Mexican Deb**[20] 3738 3-9-0 0 MartinDwyer 3 54
(W R Muir) *w'like: str: t.k.h: in tch: rdn over 2f out: wknd u.p wl over 1f out* **9/1**

66 **8** 3 ¾ **Youm Al Mizayin**[15] 3924 3-9-0 0 ChrisCatlin 2 46
(M R Channon) *fly-jmpd leaving stalls: t.k.h: hld up in rr: pushed along and effrt ent fnl 2f: sn struggling: wl btn over 1f out* **33/1**

0 **9** ½ **Queenie's Star (IRE)**[43] 2968 3-9-0 0 AdamKirby 4 44
(M J Attwater) *chsd ldr tl wl over 2f out: wknd u.p over 2f out: bhd whn sltly hmpd 2f out* **50/1**

1m 42.27s (1.67) **Going Correction** +0.175s/f (Good) **9** Ran SP% **113.3**

Speed ratings (Par 99): **98,97,94,94,93 92,87,83,82**

Tote Swingers: 1&2 £2.10, 1&3 £4.90, 2&3 £10.10 CSF £12.89 TOTE £2.80: £1.30, £1.40, £2.40; EX 12.80 Trifecta £36.10 Pool: £638.98 - 13.07 winning units..

Owner Hamdan Al Maktoum **Bred** Shadwell Estate Company Limited **Trained** Lambourn, Berks

FOCUS

A very modest event for the track and not form to treat too positively. They came down the middle again, although a little closer to the stands' side than the runners in the first. Marcus Tregoning has now won half of the last ten runnings, including last year's edition.

4398 TURFTV H'CAP 6f

3:25 (3:25) (Class 4) (0-85,81) 3-Y-O **£3,885** (£1,156; £577; £288) **Stalls** Centre

Form RPR

0016 **1** **Slip Sliding Away (IRE)**[23] 3638 3-8-2 **67** JohnFahy(5) 3 85
(P R Hedger) *stdd s: hld up in tch in last trio: swtchd rt and hdwy wl over 1f out: rdn to chse ldng pair over 1f out: str chal ent fnl f: led fnl 100yds: r.o wl* **8/1**

-513 **2** ½ **Dungannon**[46] 2868 3-9-1 **75** JimmyFortune 4 91
(A M Balding) *stdd s: t.k.h: hld up in tch: hdwy to chse ldr wl over 1f out: rdn to ld ent fnl f: hdd fnl 100yds: no ex towards fin* **4/1**[2]

103 **3** 2 ¼ **Erebus (IRE)**[4] 4248 3-8-7 **67** ChrisCatlin 8 76
(S Kirk) *chsd ldr: led 3f out: hdd and rdn over 1f out: stl ev ch tl wknd fnl 150yds* **11/1**

1342 **4** ½ **Kanaf (IRE)**[29] 3436 3-9-7 **81** RichardHills 5 88
(E A L Dunlop) *lw: hld up in last pair: nt clr run ent fnl 2f: hdwy and edging rt wl over 1f out: kpt edging rt but styd on ins fnl f: nvr able to chal* **10/3**[1]

4021 **5** 2 **Kings 'n Dreams**[9] 4109 3-9-0 **74** (b) AdamKirby 10 75
(D K Ivory) *wnt bdly rt s: hld up in last pair: hdwy and rdn wl over 1f out: edgd rt and btn ent fnl f* **5/1**[3]

-035 **6** 4 **Perfect Ch'l (IRE)**[15] 3899 3-8-11 **71** RichardMullen 7 59
(I A Wood) *led tl 3f out: wknd u.p over 1f out: wl btn fnl f* **6/1**

4321 **7** 4 **Alkhataaf (USA)**[30] 3397 3-9-4 **78** TadhgO'Shea 1 53
(J L Dunlop) *trckd ldrs: rdn and fnd nil 2f out: sn wl btn* **5/1**[3]

3156 **8** 4 ½ **Avow (USA)**[25] 3567 3-8-1 **66** (b) DeclanCannon(5) 9 27
(J J Bridger) *in tch: rdn over 2f out: wknd qckly 2f out: wl bhd over 1f out* **33/1**

1m 14.65s (0.25) **Going Correction** +0.175s/f (Good) **8** Ran SP% **113.1**

Speed ratings (Par 102): **105,104,101,100,98 92,87,81**

Tote Swingers: 1&2 £10.50, 1&3 £9.90, 2&3 £10.40 CSF £39.05 CT £355.87 TOTE £8.20: £2.20, £1.70, £3.20; EX 39.70 Trifecta £506.70 Part won. Pool: £684.82 - 0.31 winning units..

Owner Bernard Keay & Partners **Bred** S Holt & A C Beggan & R J Beggan **Trained** Dogmersfield, Hampshire

FOCUS

An ordinary sprint handicap and once more they remained in the centre of the track.

4399 SODEXO PRESTIGE H'CAP 1m 2f

4:00 (4:01) (Class 3) (0-90,89) 3-Y-O+

£6,044 (£1,810; £905; £452; £226; £113) **Stalls** High

Form RPR

221 **1** **Pendragon (USA)**[23] 3613 7-9-1 **81** JohnFahy(5) 4 91
(B Ellison) *chsd ldrs: swtchd rt over 2f out: rdn to chal ent fnl f: qckned to ld ins fnl f: sn in command: rdn out* **7/2**[2]

5-06 **2** 1 ½ **Seeking The Buck (USA)**[34] 3265 6-9-12 **87** (b) JimCrowley 6 94
(R M Beckett) *lw: chsd ldr: rdn and ev ch ent fnl 2f: led over 1f out tl hdd ins fnl f: one pce fnl 100yds* **5/1**[3]

0004 **3** nk **The Which Doctor**[28] 3483 5-9-8 **83** JamieSpencer 5 89+
(J Noseda) *s.i.s: hld up in last trio: rdn and effrt ent fnl 2f: kpt hanging rt u.p: r.o to go 3rd wl ins fnl f: nvr threatened wnr* **15/8**[1]

1223 **4** 1 ¼ **King's Masque**[15] 3894 4-9-3 **78** JimmyFortune 9 82
(B J Llewellyn) *wnt lft s: led: jnd and rdn ent fnl 2f: hdd over 1f out: stl ev ch tl wknd fnl 150yds* **8/1**

2205 **5** 2 ¾ **Mabuya (UAE)**[15] 3889 4-9-7 **82** SebSanders 3 80
(P J Makin) *hld up in last trio: rdn 3f out: drvn and no prog 2f out: nvr trbld ldrs* **11/2**

3-00 **6** ½ **Credit Swap**[80] 1837 5-9-11 **89** WilliamCarson(3) 8 86
(M Wigham) *lw: bmpd s: t.k.h: hld up in last trio: rdn and effrt ent fnl 2f: no prog and nvr trbld ldrs* **10/1**

14-3 **7** 3 ¾ **Dishdasha (IRE)**[14] 2411 8-8-10 **71** (t) ShaneKelly 1 61
(Mrs A M Thorpe) *t.k.h: chsd ldrs tl rdn and wknd 2f out: bhd fnl f* **22/1**

2m 8.06s (1.06) **Going Correction** +0.025s/f (Good) **7** Ran SP% **113.6**

Speed ratings (Par 107): **96,94,94,93,91 90,87**

Tote Swingers: 1&2 £3.20, 1&3 £3.20, 2&3 £3.70 CSF £20.91 CT £41.06 TOTE £4.40: £2.40, £1.70; EX 21.40 Trifecta £50.80 Pool: £792.67 - 11.53 winning units..

Owner Dan Gilbert & Kristian Strangeway **Bred** Flaxman Holdings Ltd **Trained** Norton, N Yorks

FOCUS

This fair handicap was run at just a modest pace and is was hard to make up ground from the rear. The form may not prove to be the most solid.

NOTEBOOK

Pendragon(USA) was soon well placed behind the two leaders and he quickened nicely under his good apprentice to make it five wins for the year. He was up another 6lb but may not have reached the limit of his improvement. The return to 1m4f should pose him no problems. (tchd 3-1, 4-1 in places and 9-2 in a place)

Seeking The Buck(USA) has descended to his last winning mark and had the blinkers on for the first time since 2007. He ran a decent race but his time in the lead proved all too brief. (tchd 9-2 and 11-2)

The Which Doctor was not best suited by the steadily run nature of this race and his finishing effort was always coming too late. He has dropped to an attractive mark and is worth keeping to this trip for the time being. (op 2-1 tchd 7-4 in places)

King's Masque kicked on turning in but could not get away from his field. He continues to perform with credit but is 10lb higher than when winning at Chepstow two months ago. (tchd 9-1)

Mabuya(UAE), a frustrating type, reverted to hold-up tactics, which did not pay off in a falsely run race. (op 8-1)

Credit Swap, a winner at this fixture 12 months ago, was in action for the first time since the Chester May meeting. This regular hold-up performer was always in rear and his effectiveness at this trip remains unproven. (tchd 9-1 and 11-1)

Dishdasha(IRE) has been in action over hurdles and fences since his last run on the Flat, when behind King's Masque. He was upsides the winner turning into the straight but was quickly in trouble from there. (op 16-1)

4400 RENDEZVOUS CASINO STKS (H'CAP) 1m 4f

4:35 (4:35) (Class 2) (0-105,98) 3-Y-O+

£20,250 (£6,064; £3,032; £1,517; £757; £380) Stalls High

Form RPR

1412 **1** **Bay Willow (IRE)**[16] 3873 3-9-0 **98** JoeFanning 11 107
(M Johnston) *mde all: rdn and fnd ex wl over 1f out: edgd lft u.p fnl f: hld on gamely* **4/1**[1]

-241 **2** ¾ **Opera Gal (IRE)**[17] 3829 3-8-0 **84** oh2 ow2 FrannyNorton 10 92
(A M Balding) *tk keen: chsd wnr: rdn ent fnl 2f: sltly outpcd wl over 1f out: lost 2nd kpt on wl u.p ins fnl f: carried lft fnl 150yds: n.m.r towards fin: regained 2nd on post* **9/2**[2]

3105 **3** nse **Sandor**[15] 3921 4-9-6 **92** SteveDrowne 5 100
(P J Makin) *hld up in tch in midfield: n.m.r over 2f out: swtchd out lft and rdn 2f out: drvn to chse ldng pair jst over 1f out: chsd wnr ins fnl f: no imp fnl 75yds: lost 2nd on post* **8/1**

0-51 **4** 1 ¾ **Times Up**[16] 3873 4-9-9 **95** JamieSpencer 8 100
(J L Dunlop) *in tch: rdn and effrt to chse ldrs wl over 1f out: edgd lft u.p ent fnl f: kpt on same pce after* **6/1**[3]

1641 **5** 1 **High Office**[36] 3203 4-8-5 **77** MartinDwyer 2 80
(R A Fahey) *hld up in midfield: n.m.r and shuffled bk ent fnl 3f: hdwy u.p over 1f out: no imp ins fnl f* **20/1**

0313 **6** 1 **Ouster (GER)**[16] 3873 4-8-9 **86** DeclanCannon(5) 9 88
(D R C Elsworth) *trckd ldrs: rdn and hung rt ent fnl 2f: unable qck and no prog fr over 1f out* **12/1**

0503 **7** shd **Record Breaker (IRE)**[29] 3462 6-9-1 **87** (v) RichardHills 4 89
(M Johnston) *s.i.s: hld up in last pair: c wd and effrt ent fnl 2f: kpt on but nvr gng pce to rch ldrs* **4/1**[1]

1260 **8** ¾ **Quinsman**[32] 3329 4-8-4 **76** JimmyQuinn 7 76
(J S Moore) *stdd s: t.k.h: hld up towards rr: bhd and rdn over 2f out: nvr trbld ldrs* **40/1**

-060 **9** 2 ¾ **Red Merlin (IRE)**[22] 3672 5-9-10 **96** (v) PhilipRobinson 6 92
(C G Cox) *lw: s.i.s: hld up in last pair: hdwy on outer to chse ldrs 3f out: rdn and fnd little ent fnl 2f: sn btn* **12/1**

3134 **10** 3 ¾ **Jawaab (IRE)**[16] 3847 6-8-7 **79** RichardMullen 1 69
(Mark Buckley) *lw: hld up towards rr: rdn and unable qck over 2f out: no ch fr wl over 1f out* **40/1**

1444 **11** 11 **Stanstill (IRE)**[29] 3447 4-9-8 **94** RobertWinston 3 66
(G A Swinbank) *lw: plld hrd: chsd ldrs: rdn 3f out: wknd qckly ent fnl 2f: wl bhd and eased ins fnl f* **10/1**

2m 30.03s (-2.47) **Going Correction** +0.025s/f (Good)
WFA 3 from 4yo+ 12lb **11** Ran SP% **117.7**
Speed ratings (Par 109): **109,108,108,107,106 105,105,105,103,101 93**
Tote Swingers: 1&2 £4.60, 1&3 £7.00, 2&3 £9.10 CSF £21.42 CT £136.73 TOTE £5.40: £1.60, £2.10, £3.00; EX 23.80 Trifecta £158.30 Pool: £1,560.57 - 7.29 winning units..
Owner Sheikh Hamdan Bin Mohammed Al Maktoum **Bred** Philip Brady **Trained** Middleham Moor, N Yorks

■ Stewards' Enquiry : Joe Fanning two-day ban: careless riding (Aug 8-9)

FOCUS

A valuable handicap and sound enough form with the first pair both progressive 3yos. The pace was not not strong though, and the first two, drawn in the two highest stalls, were up there throughout.

NOTEBOOK

Bay Willow(IRE) is an admirably progressive 3yo and he shrugged off another 5lb rise to notch his third win from his last five starts. After winning an early skirmish for the lead with the runner-up, he went for home in the straight and ran on most willingly. He turned around Newmarket form with Times Up, having set an insufficiently quick gallop there, and is a typically tough galloper from the Johnston yard. He holds an entry in the Ebor but is unlikely to run. (op 9-2 tchd 7-2)
Opera Gal(IRE) landed her maiden last time after a fine fourth behind Harris Tweed at Musselburgh on her handicap debut. The plan looked to be for her to make the running again, but with Bay Willow also intent on that role, her rider sensibly anchored her in second. She could not quite get to her rival up the straight and was relegated to third for a few strides late on before rallying. She was 2lb out of the handicap and her rider put up 2lb overweight too. This was a fine effort and she should continue to thrive. (op 11-2 tchd 6-1)
Sandor did best of those who came from off the pace and might have held second had he not been carried a little to his left late on. This was only his second try over this far and he got it well. (op 7-1)
Times Up went up 6lb for his win over Bay Willow and Ouster at Newmarket. He probably ran his race again but was unable to quicken up when required to. (op 5-1 tchd 13-2 in places)
High Office travelled well into the straight but did not get the clearest of passages and was then another unable to make much headway off the ordinary gallop. He remains in good order and is worth trying at this trip again. (op 25-1 tchd 28-1)
Ouster(GER) was nicely positioned on the rail turning in but hung when asked for an effort and could not find a turn of foot. (op 10-1 tchd 14-1)
Record Breaker(IRE), the winner's stablemate, has a good record at Ascot and a fruitless season has seen him drop to a mark no less than 9lb lower than when winning here last September. Held up this time and last into the straight, he ran on late but was never going to trouble the leaders. He is set to go to Goodwood. (op 11-2 tchd 7-2)
Quinsman was not disgraced on this rare run on turf but was never a factor. (op 50-1 tchd 33-1)
Red Merlin(IRE) is not really firing this year. (tchd 14-1 in places)
Stanstill(IRE), fourth last time in the Northumberland Plate, dropped away in the straight to finish last. He had pulled far too hard in the early stages on this drop back in trip and was unable to slot in from his wide draw. (op 8-1)

4401 JAPAN RACING ASSOCIATION SPRINT STKS (H'CAP) 5f

5:10 (5:11) (Class 2) 3-Y-O+

£20,250 (£6,064; £3,032; £1,517; £757; £380) Stalls Centre

Form RPR

1404 **1** **Masamah (IRE)**[15] 3895 4-9-1 **96** JamieSpencer 4 107
(K A Ryan) *lw: racd stands' side: mde all: rdn over 1f out: kpt on wl fnl f* **13/2**[2]

6003 **2** 1 **Matsunosuke**[48] 2808 8-8-6 **87** ChrisCatlin 2 94
(R A Harris) *racd stands' side: hld up towards rr overall: hdwy 2f out: rdn ent fnl f: r.o to 2nd overall towards fin: nt rch wnr: 2nd of 4 in gp* **33/1**

3436 **3** ¾ **Secret Millionaire (IRE)**[16] 3856 3-7-12 **86** oh1 ow3 Louis-PhilippeBeuzelin(3) 11 90
(Patrick Morris) *racd in centre: in tch: rdn and hdwy wl over 1f out: kpt on u.p fnl f: nt pce to rch wnr:1st of 15 in gp* **20/1**

4023 **4** nk **Prohibit**[15] 3891 5-8-13 **99** (p) JohnFahy(5) 21 103
(R M H Cowell) *racd in centre: stdd s: hld up towards rr: gd hdwy 2f out: rdn and pressing gp ldrs 1f out: chsd wnr ins fnl f: no imp: edgd lft and lost 2 pls towards fin: 2nd of 15 in gp* **13/2**[2]

-100 **5** ¾ **Drawnfromthepast (IRE)**[16] 3845 5-8-0 **86** SophieDoyle(5) 15 87+
(J A Osborne) *racd in centre: s.i.s: bhd: hdwy 3f out: chsng ldrs and nt clr run wl over 1f out tl hmpd ent fnl f: r.o u.p and swtchd rt ins fnl f: gng on fin: 3rd of 15 in gp* **33/1**

1134 **6** nse **Hamish McGonagall**[22] 3691 5-9-10 **105** DavidAllan 14 106
(T D Easterby) *lw: racd in centre: led that gp and chsd wnr: rdn wl over 1f out: no ex ins fnl f: btn whn carried lft fnl 75yds: 4th of 15 in gp* **8/1**[3]

0222 **7** hd **Solemn**[20] 3736 5-8-0 **81** (b) NickyMackay 12 81
(J M Bradley) *racd in centre: w gp ldrs and chsd wnr: rdn wl over 1f out: no ex and one pce ins fnl f: 5th of 15 in gp* **10/1**

0050 **8** 1 ¼ **Tony The Tap**[23] 3629 9-7-13 **80** JimmyQuinn 5 76
(W R Muir) *racd stands' side: bhd: rdn wl over 2f out: styd on u.p fnl f: nvr trbld ldrs: 3rd of 4 in gp* **20/1**

1512 **9** shd **Monsieur Joe (IRE)**[15] 3891 3-8-13 **98** EddieAhern 13 92
(W R Swinburn) *racd in centre: towards rr: hdwy 3f out: rdn and chsd ldrs over 1f out: no ex and btn ins fnl f: 6th of 15 in gp* **6/1**[1]

5000 **10** hd **Sohraab**[17] 3828 6-8-9 **90** SteveDrowne 9 84+
(H Morrison) *racd in centre: rdn and sn outpcd in rr: hdwy u.p ent fnl f: styng on but no ch w ldrs: whn nt clr run and eased fnl 50yds:7th of 15 in gp* **16/1**

5401 **11** hd **Rowe Park**[15] 3891 7-9-6 **101** AlanMunro 7 95
(Mrs L C Jewell) *racd in centre: bmpd s: sn in midfield: rdn and no prog ent fnl 2f: kpt on same pce fr over 1f out: 8th of 15 in gp* **12/1**

-200 **12** 1 ½ **Golden Destiny (IRE)**[16] 3875 4-9-3 **98** (p) SebSanders 16 86
(P J Makin) *racd in centre: chsd ldrs: rdn over 2f out: wknd ent fnl f: 9th of 15 in gp* **20/1**

2060 **13** nse **Abraham Lincoln (IRE)**[16] 3850 6-8-7 **88** (p) JoeFanning 10 76
(R A Harris) *racd in centre: stdd s: a towards rr: rdn and no real prog over 1f out: nvr trbld ldrs: 10th of 15 in gp* **20/1**

2600 **14** 1 ¼ **Even Bolder**[15] 3892 7-7-5 **79** oh6 HarryBentley(7) 18 63
(E A Wheeler) *racd in centre: prom: rdn ent fnl 2f: btn over 1f out: wknd fnl frlong: 11th of 15 in gp* **66/1**

0000 **15** nse **Hoh Hoh Hoh**[29] 3430 8-7-13 **83** ow1 AndrewHeffernan(3) 19 66
(R J Price) *racd in centre: in tch: rdn and effrt to press gp ldrs 2f out: btn over 1f out: eased whn no ch ins fnl f: 12th of 15 in gp* **33/1**

5460 **16** ½ **Judge 'n Jury**[28] 3486 6-9-4 **99** (t) TadhgO'Shea 20 81
(R A Harris) *racd in centre: chsd ldrs tl hung rt and wknd over 1f out: wl btn and eased ins fnl f: 13th of 15 in gp* **16/1**

2643 **17** ½ **Rapid Water**[15] 3892 4-7-8 **80** (v[1]) SimonPearce(5) 6 60
(A M Balding) *restless in stalls: racd in centre: wnt rt s and s.i.s: a bhd: n.d: 14th of 15 in gp* **8/1**[3]

0125 **18** nse **Fol Hollow (IRE)**[30] 3406 5-9-3 **98** AdrianNicholls 22 78
(D Nicholls) *racd in centre: chsd ldrs: rdn wl over 2f out: wknd over 1f out: 15th of 15 in gp* **12/1**

6655 **19** hd **Canadian Danehill (IRE)**[158] 578 8-8-4 **85** (p) MartinDwyer 3 64
(R M H Cowell) *racd stands' side: midfield overall: rdn and hung rt ent fnl 2f: wl bhd over 1f out: 4th of 4 in gp* **40/1**

60.14 secs (-0.36) **Going Correction** +0.175s/f (Good)
WFA 3 from 4yo+ 4lb **19** Ran SP% **131.2**
Speed ratings (Par 109): **109,107,106,105,104 104,104,102,101,101 101,98,98,96,96 95,95,95,94**
Tote Swingers: 1&2 £55.00, 1&3 £127.00, 2&3 £165.10 CSF £223.61 CT £4212.15 TOTE £7.70: £2.60, £7.70, £5.30, £1.90; EX 209.00 TRIFECTA Not won. Place 6: £220.06 Place 5: £75.93..
Owner Dr Marwan Koukash **Bred** Stanley Estate & Stud Co & Mount Coote Stud **Trained** Hambleton, N Yorks

■ Stewards' Enquiry : John Fahy one-day ban: careless riding (Aug 8)

FOCUS

A typically open and competitive renewal of this valuable sprint. They split into two groups from the stalls with the majority going down the centre and four racing stands" side, and the first two home both came from the quartet who took the near-side route.

NOTEBOOK

Masamah(IRE) had the tongue tie left off and showed none of the reluctance that had been in evidence at Chester. Well suited by having a rail to race against, he made all on his side. He is a smart sprinter when on song and appeared to like racing away from the main body of the field. (op 17-2)

Matsunosuke, claimed from the Scobie Coogan yard for £12,000, was having his first run for Ron Harris, who had landed the last two runnings of this. The 8yo remains without a win on turf since 2007 but ran a good race for his new connections, albeit from what turned out to be the optimum part of the track.

Secret Millionaire(IRE) came out best of the large centre-course group, and it is perhaps worth noting that he raced on the stands-side flank of that group. He was one of only two 3yos in the field and this was a solid effort from 4lb wrong at the weights. (op 33-1)

Prohibit turned around recent C&D form with Rowe Park and Monsieur Joe, but while he remains in good form he is the type who does not find a great deal when let down and needs things to drop right. (op 7-1)

Drawnfromthepast(IRE) did not enjoy the breaks but was running on solidly for pressure late on and holds entries at Goodwood this week. Official explanation: jockey said gelding was denied a clear run

Hamish McGonagall was runner-up in this last year and ran a thoroughly creditable race off his hefty mark. (tchd 10-1)

Solemn is consistent and he ran his race again. (op 11-1 tchd 12-1)

Tony The Tap, third of four on his side, has now run well in this race three times.

Monsieur Joe(IRE) showed up well for a long way before faltering inside the last. He should be kept on the right side. (op 7-1 tchd 11-2)

Sohraab ◆ ran on strongly from the back of the field late on until his jockey had to ease him near the finish. This hinted at a return to form. Official explanation: jockey said gelding was denied a clear run (tchd 25-1 in a place)

Rowe Park, sixth off 3lb higher a year ago, could not confirm recent course superiority over Monsieur Joe and Prohibit.

Judge 'n Jury, stablemate of the runner-up, won this last year. He showed plenty of pace from his high draw before dropping away. Official explanation: jockey said gelding hung right-handed (tchd 22-1 in a place)

Rapid Water, visored for the first time, came in for support. His rider opted to go with the main pack down the centre when he could have gone stands' side, and the gelding was never seen with a chance. (tchd 9-1 in a place)

T/Jkpt: Not won. T/Plt: £381.90 to a £1 stake. Pool:£223,592.18 - 427.32 winning tickets T/Qpdt: £89.50 to a £1 stake. Pool:£10,612.94 - 87.70 winning tickets SP

3664 **CARLISLE** (R-H)

Sunday, July 25

OFFICIAL GOING: Good (good to firm in places final 3f; 7.5)

Wind: Fresh, across Weather: Overcast

4402 JEDWARD LIVE AFTER RACING TODAY MAIDEN AUCTION STKS 5f
1:50 (1:50) (Class 5) 2-Y-O £2,266 (£674; £337; £168) Stalls High

Form RPR

22 **1** **Earl Wild (IRE)**[15] 3897 2-9-1 0 PaulMulrennan 5 79+
(J Howard Johnson) *mde all: shkn up over 1f out: clr whn drifted lft ins fnl f: readily* 1/5[1]

2 3 1/4 **Riverdale (IRE)** 2-8-6 0 BarryMcHugh(3) 2 61+
(Mrs A Duffield) *cl up: effrt and chsd wnr 1/2-way: kpt on same pce fnl f: bttr for r* 8/1[2]

05 **3** 2 1/2 **Lexi's Boy (IRE)**[27] 3517 2-9-1 0 TonyHamilton 9 58+
(K A Ryan) *in tch: drvn 1/2-way: styd on steadily fnl f: nt rch first two* 11/1[3]

4 11 **Kinlochrannoch** 2-8-4 0 AndrewElliott 3 7
(B M R Haslam) *cl up: drvn 1/2-way: wknd over 1f out* 25/1

00 **5** 7 **Willow's Wish**[20] 3729 2-8-4 0 DuranFentiman 1 —
(G M Moore) *s.i.s: a outpcd and bhd* 80/1

0 **6** hd **Tom Bowler**[7] 4167 2-8-9 0 RoystonFfrench 7 —
(Mrs A Duffield) *in tch: drvn 1/2-way: wknd over 1f out* 50/1

6 **7** 2 1/4 **Holy Arrangement (IRE)**[25] 3549 2-8-10 0 TomEaves 8 —
(Patrick Morris) *chsd ldrs: rdn 1/2-way: hung rt and wknd 2f out* 40/1

61.75 secs (0.95) **Going Correction** +0.125s/f (Good) 7 Ran SP% **112.3**

Speed ratings (Par 94): **97,91,87,70,59 58,55**

Tote Swingers: 1&2 £1.10, 1&3 £1.10, 2&3 £3.90 CSF £2.20 TOTE £1.10: £1.02, £2.30.

Owner W M G Black & J Howard Johnson **Bred** Tally-Ho Stud **Trained** Billy Row, Co Durham

FOCUS

A weak maiden won in clear-cut fashion by the red-hot favourite.

NOTEBOOK

Earl Wild(IRE) was quickly away and made every yard of the running. He was entitled to win well on form and could do better still in nurseries. (op 2-9)

Riverdale(IRE), a half-brother to several winners, shaped nicely in second and should improve considerably for the outing. (op 6-1 tchd 9-1)

Lexi's Boy(IRE) should do better now qualified for nurseries, with the step back up in trip also likely to help. (op 12-1)

Kinlochrannoch is bred to need 1m, and maybe more, so should leave this form behind in time. (op 28-1)

4403 PENRITH BUILDING SUPPLIES CLAIMING STKS 7f 200y
2:25 (2:27) (Class 6) 3-Y-O+ £2,047 (£604; £302) Stalls High

Form RPR

5053 **1** **Sunnyside Tom (IRE)**[22] 3667 6-9-12 82 TonyHamilton 5 85
(R A Fahey) *cl up: led and rdn over 2f out: hld on gamely fnl f* 11/8[1]

4013 **2** hd **Moody Tunes**[8] 4154 7-9-10 80 AndrewElliott 14 83
(J R Weymes) *led to over 2f out: rdn and outpcd over 1f out: rallied ins fnl f but a hld* 3/1[2]

5443 **3** 1/2 **Observatory Star (IRE)**[12] 3973 7-9-7 73 (p) PaulMulrennan 7 78
(T D Easterby) *s.i.s: sn rcvrd and in tch: effrt and rdn 2f out: kpt on same pce fnl f* 5/1[3]

00-5 **4** 3/4 **Kashimin (IRE)**[7] 4170 5-9-5 73 (p) PJMcDonald 10 74
(G A Swinbank) *prom: effrt whn hung rt over 1f out and ins fnl f: nt run on* 11/1

5240 **5** 1 1/4 **King's Sabre**[12] 3973 4-9-1 62 (e) PaulEddery 3 67
(R C Guest) *hld up: hdwy and swtchd to far side wl over 1f out: kpt on fnl f: nrst fin* 28/1

2033 **6** 2 **Plush**[23] 3616 7-9-2 71 RossAtkinson(5) 6 68
(Tom Dascombe) *dwlt: bhd: effrt and edgd rt fr 2f out: no imp fnl f* 20/1

0 **7** 1 **Binglybonglyboo**[24] 3595 4-9-0 0 (p) BarryMcHugh(3) 8 62
(L A Mullaney) *t.k.h in midfield: rdn and outpcd over 2f out: n.d after* 100/1

3160 **8** 2 1/4 **Just Five (IRE)**[38] 3107 4-9-4 79 PatrickDonaghy(5) 2 62
(M Dods) *hld up: rdn and hung rt over 2f out: sn n.d* 10/1

0006 **9** 11 **Officer Mor (USA)**[11] 4014 4-9-1 43 DuranFentiman 11 27
(Mrs Dianne Sayer) *bhd: drvn 1/2-way: nvr on terms* 150/1

-000 **10** 1/2 **Ten To The Dozen**[24] 3595 7-8-8 47 (p) DuilioDaSilva(7) 4 25
(D W Thompson) *chsd ldrs: rdn 1/2-way: wknd fr 3f out* 150/1

6465 **11** 18 **Guertino (IRE)**[41] 3022 5-9-7 54 PatrickMathers 9 —
(C J Teague) *s.i.s: bhd and sn pushed along: no ch fr 1/2-way* 80/1

1m 40.78s (0.78) **Going Correction** +0.125s/f (Good)

WFA 3 from 4yo+ 8lb 11 Ran SP% **113.0**

Speed ratings (Par 101): **101,100,100,99,98 96,95,93,82,81 63**

Tote Swingers: 1&2 £1.60, 1&3 £1.90, 2&3 £2.80 CSF £4.92 TOTE £2.80: £1.50, £1.40, £1.10; EX 6.40.

Owner The Sunnyside Racing Partnership **Bred** S W D McIlveen **Trained** Musley Bank, N Yorks

FOCUS

A tight finish to this claimer.

4404 PES-SECURITY.COM H'CAP 6f 192y
3:00 (3:00) (Class 5) (0-75,73) 3-Y-O+ £2,914 (£867; £433; £216) Stalls High

Form RPR

42 **1** **Fadhb Ar Bith (IRE)**[9] 4121 5-9-11 73 BarryMcHugh(3) 13 86
(John A Harris) *chsd ldr: rdn to ld over 1f out: edgd rt ins fnl f: drvn out* 3/1[1]

2103 **2** 3/4 **Amethyst Dawn (IRE)**[22] 3659 4-9-10 69 DuranFentiman 15 80
(T D Easterby) *led: rdn over 2f out: hdd over 1f out: rallied u.p ins fnl f: hld nr fin* 9/2[2]

3232 **3** 2 1/4 **Call Of Duty (IRE)**[18] 3774 5-9-0 59 RoystonFfrench 3 64
(Mrs Dianne Sayer) *trckd ldrs: drvn 3f out: kpt on u.p fnl f: nt rch first two* 13/2[3]

163- **4** nk **Scrapper Smith (IRE)**[267] 7172 4-9-6 65 AndrewElliott 12 69+
(A C Whillans) *bhd on ins: drvn over 3f out: hdwy over 1f out: nvr rchd ldrs* 33/1

604- **5** shd **Midwestern (USA)**[278] 6922 3-9-5 71 TomEaves 9 72
(B Smart) *prom: effrt and rdn over 2f out: kpt on same pce fnl f* 22/1

6360 **6** 3/4 **Geojimali**[6] 4192 8-8-10 62 (p) PaulNorton(7) 6 64
(J S Goldie) *hld up: rdn over 2f out: hdwy over 1f out: nrst fin* 16/1

0/1- **7** 1 **More Than Many (USA)**[466] 1281 4-9-13 72 TonyHamilton 7 71
(R A Fahey) *in tch: rdn over 2f out: kpt on same pce fr over 1f out: bttr for r* 8/1

0052 **8** 2 **Dickie Le Davoir**[3] 4285 6-8-13 63 MarkCoumbe(5) 2 57
(R C Guest) *dwlt: bhd tl rdn and hdwy over 1f out: nt pce to chal* 12/1

6662 **9** 1/2 **Rio Cobolo (IRE)**[10] 4065 4-9-11 70 (v) SilvestreDeSousa 8 62
(Paul Green) *towards rr: drvn and wandered 2f out: nvr able to chal* 7/1

050- **10** 1 **Hartshead**[305] 6218 11-8-12 62 DeanHeslop(5) 11 52
(Miss Tracy Waggott) *towards rr: drvn over 3f out: btn fnl 2f* 28/1

023 **11** 7 **Bold Diktator**[29] 3438 8-9-0 64 (v) AmyRyan(5) 14 35
(R M Whitaker) *dwlt: bhd: drvn over 3f out: nvr on terms* 14/1

0-05 **12** shd **Olympic Dream**[30] 3408 4-9-9 68 PaulMulrennan 4 38
(M Herrington) *hld up in tch: rdn over 2f out: hung rt and wknd wl over 1f out* 25/1

6000 **13** 9 **Rising Kheleyf (IRE)**[50] 2764 4-9-5 64 PJMcDonald 10 10
(G A Swinbank) *midfield: rdn over 3f out: no imp fnl 2f* 25/1

1m 27.38s (0.28) **Going Correction** +0.125s/f (Good)

WFA 3 from 4yo+ 7lb 13 Ran SP% **118.8**

Speed ratings (Par 103): **103,102,99,99,99 98,97,94,94,93 85,85,74**

Tote Swingers: 1&2 £4.10, 1&3 £4.90, 2&3 £6.50 CSF £14.32 CT £85.38 TOTE £3.30: £1.10, £2.40, £1.90; EX 21.00.

Owner Mrs A E Harris **Bred** Glending Bloodstock **Trained** Eastwell, Leics

FOCUS

A modest handicap.

Rio Cobolo(IRE) Official explanation: jockey said gelding hung right-handed throughout

4405 STOBART LADIES NORTHERN DERBY BOWL H'CAP (FOR LADY AMATEUR RIDERS) 1m 3f 107y
3:35 (3:36) (Class 3) (0-90,87) 4-Y-O+ £9,369 (£2,905; £1,452; £726) Stalls Low

Form RPR

5012 **1** **Film Festival (USA)**[11] 4015 7-8-11 68 oh1 MissNVorster(5) 14 81
(B Ellison) *mde all at decent gallop: pushed along over 2f out: styd on strly to go clr fnl f* 14/1

4341 **2** 4 **Graceful Descent (FR)**[15] 3901 5-8-11 68 oh1 MissRKneller(5) 1 74
(J S Goldie) *pressed wnr and clr of rest: effrt over 2f out: kpt on fnl f: nt pce of wnr* 20/1

134 **3** 1 1/2 **Quarante Deux (USA)**[19] 3764 4-9-10 76 MissIsabelTompsett 8 80
(G A Butler) *hld up in tch: effrt over 2f out: no imp tl styd on wl fnl f: nt rch first two* 12/1

1023 **4** nk **Royal Straight**[15] 3905 5-9-4 70 MissADeniel 2 73
(Miss L A Perratt) *prom: effrt over 2f out: kpt on same pce fnl f* 28/1

1412 **5** nk **Inspirina (IRE)**[16] 3860 6-9-9 78 MissPernillaHermansson(3) 11 81
(R Ford) *hld up in tch: hdwy over 1f out: nrst fin* 25/1

00-6 **6** 3/4 **Overrule (USA)**[16] 3873 6-10-6 86 MissSBrotherton 9 88+
(B Ellison) *bhd: drvn over 3f out: styd on fnl 2f: nrst fin* 4/1[2]

-605 **7** 1 1/4 **Edas**[27] 3502 8-8-11 68 oh2 MissHCuthbert(5) 15 68
(T A K Cuthbert) *bhd: rdn and styd far side ent st: styd on fnl 2f: nrst fin* 100/1

-212 **8** 1 1/4 **The Last Alzao (IRE)**[44] 2938 4-9-9 80 MrsVFahey(5) 13 78
(R A Fahey) *prom: shkn up over 2f out: sn outpcd: n.d after* 3/1[1]

0353 **9** shd **Bavarian Nordic (USA)**[19] 3764 5-9-1 72 (v) MissCharlotteHolmes(5) 12 69
(Mrs A Duffield) *hld up on ins: rdn over 3f out: no imp fnl 2f* 18/1

1413 **10** 8 **Haljaferia (UAE)**[11] 4019 4-9-9 78 MissLAllan(3) 6 62
(D R C Elsworth) *t.k.h in midfield: rdn and outpcd over 2f out: sn btn* 10/1[3]

200- **11** 2 1/4 **Yossi (IRE)**[92] 5802 6-9-5 76 MissWGibson(5) 10 56
(R C Guest) *bhd: pushed along over 3f out: nvr able to chal* 100/1

-103 **12** 3 3/4 **Oneofapear (IRE)**[38] 3121 4-10-7 87 MissNCarberry 5 61
(G A Swinbank) *prom: effrt and rdn over 2f out: sn wknd* 3/1[1]

-410 **13** 2 **Callisto Moon**[40] 3050 6-10-0 87 (p) MissCBoxall(7) 3 58
(F J Brennan) *prom tl wknd over 2f out* 25/1

6142 **14** 47 **Brouhaha**[16] 3847 6-10-3 83 MsKWalsh 4 —
(Tom Dascombe) *hld up in midfield on outside: struggling over 2f out: sn lost tch* 18/1

5563 **15** 10 **King's Head (IRE)**[15] 3901 7-8-11 68 oh2 MissPhillipaTutty(5) 7 —
(Miss L A Perratt) *prom tl wknd qckly over 4f out: lost tch fr 3f out* 50/1

2m 24.97s (1.87) **Going Correction** +0.125s/f (Good) 15 Ran SP% **123.8**

Speed ratings (Par 107): **98,95,94,93,93 93,92,91,91,85 83,80,79,45,38**

Tote Swingers: 1&2 £46.40, 1&3 £2.50, 2&3 £31.00 CSF £274.73 CT £3449.58 TOTE £19.20: £6.30, £3.60, £5.70; EX 268.40.

Owner Koo's Racing Club **Bred** Jim Ryan And Geraldine Ryan **Trained** Norton, N Yorks

FOCUS

A really competitive handicap, run at a decent gallop.

NOTEBOOK

Film Festival(USA) set a decent gallop but didn't wilt under pressure, anything but in fact. A winner two starts back before finishing second in a claimer last time, he kept galloping away when challenged, and actually pulled further away from them inside the final furlong. The fact he was 1lb out of the handicap made no difference, and he is clearly in cracking form. (op 12-1 tchd 16-1)

Graceful Descent(FR) was soon prominent and stayed on right the way to the line for second. This trip seems to suit her best these days. (op 22-1)

Quarante Deux(USA) again performed well considering his inexperience. He's going to stay further and will probably make a hurdler at some stage. (op 11-1)

Royal Straight has been running well off this mark and again ran his race. (op 20-1)

Inspirina(IRE), another in good form, was going on at the end of the race and may have benefited from a more positive. (op 16-1)

Overrule(USA), sixth in a decent handicap at Newmarket, could never get into it having been held up. (op 9-2)

Edas, who stayed far side in the straight, ran creditably considering his 100-1 odds.

The Last Alzao(IRE), up 3lb, was particularly disappointing, although he was dropping back 4f in trip, which may go some way to explaining his below-par effort. (op 4-1)

Oneofapear(IRE) could have been expected to fare an awful lot better, although this was the furthest he had raced, and his stamina simply looked to fail him. Official explanation: trainer said gelding failed to stay the trip on the stiff course (op 7-2 tchd 5-2)

King's Head(IRE) Official explanation: trainer said gelding bled from the nose

4406 CFM CASH FOR KIDS H'CAP 5f
4:10 (4:10) (Class 5) (0-70,70) 3-Y-O £2,266 (£674; £337; £168) Stalls High

Form RPR

1-32 **1** **Jack Luey**[19] 3751 3-8-13 65 BarryMcHugh(3) 9 70
(L A Mullaney) *cl up: drvn to ld over 1f out: hld on wl fnl f* 9/4[1]

6066 **2** hd **Dancing Freddy (IRE)**[29] 3436 3-9-7 70 (b[1]) PaulMulrennan 10 74
(J G Given) *cl up: drvn and ev ch over 1f out: kpt on wl fnl f: jst hld* 6/1[3]

0400 **3** nse **Midget**[6] 4194 3-8-1 57 NeilFarley(7) 4 61
(D Carroll) *t.k.h: in tch: rdn over 2f out: styd on wl fnl f: jst hld* 20/1

4-00 **4** 1 1/4 **Kalahari Desert (IRE)**[47] 2834 3-8-4 58 AmyRyan(5) 6 58
(R M Whitaker) *midfield: lost pl 1/2-way: hdwy over 1f out: kpt on fin* 7/1

3660 **5** hd **Duke Of Rainford**[13] 3966 3-8-2 51 oh2 (v[1]) DuranFentiman 7 50
(M Herrington) *dwlt: bhd and rdn along: hdwy on outside over 1f out: nrst fin* 33/1

00 **6** ½ **Bombay Mist**[6] 4194 3-8-2 51 oh6....(e) PaulEddery 12 48
(R C Guest) *led tl drvn and hdd over 1f out: rallied: no ex wl ins fnl f* **66/1**

0065 **7** nse **Fair Bunny**[9] 4109 3-8-5 54....(b¹) SilvestreDeSousa 5 51
(A D Brown) *bhd: drvn along 1/2-way: hdwy appr fnl f: nvr able to chal* **14/1**

6123 **8** 1½ **Patch Patch**[7] 4169 3-9-5 68.... TomEaves 11 60
(M Dods) *hld up in midfield: effrt and rdn 1/2-way: btn fnl f* **5/1**[2]

0546 **9** 3¼ **Kirkby's Gem**[15] 3903 3-8-2 51 oh6.... PatrickMathers 8 31
(A Berry) *in tch: drvn and outpcd 1/2-way: n.d after* **100/1**

4632 **10** nk **Reach For The Sky (IRE)**[6] 4193 3-8-4 53 ow1.... RoystonFfrench 3 32
(A Berry) *bhd and drvn along 1/2-way: nvr on terms* **9/1**

51 **11** 1¾ **Tabiet**[50] 2741 3-9-0 63.... LeeVickers 2 35
(James Moffatt) *t.k.h: prom tl hung rt and wknd fr 2f out* **10/1**

6026 **12** 7 **Captain Bluebird (IRE)**[94] 1491 3-8-11 60.... AndreaAtzeni 1 7
(D Donovan) *in tch: drvn 1/2-way: sn struggling* **16/1**

62.29 secs (1.49) **Going Correction** +0.125s/f (Good) 12 Ran SP% **116.0**
Speed ratings (Par 100): **93,92,92,90,90 89,89,87,81,81 78,67**
Tote Swingers: 1&2 £3.90, 1&3 £14.90, 2&3 £25.40 CSF £14.54 CT £217.06 TOTE £2.70: £1.10, £4.00, £7.60; EX 18.90.
Owner The Jack Partnership & S Rimmer **Bred** Miss D A Johnson **Trained** Great Habton, N Yorks
■ Stewards' Enquiry : Andrea Atzeni one-day ban: used whip without giving gelding time to respond (Aug 8)

FOCUS
A desperately tight finish to this sprint handicap.

4407 OLLY MURS LIVE AFTER RACING TODAY MAIDEN STKS 1m 1f 61y
4:45 (4:45) (Class 5) 3-Y-0+ **£2,266** (£674; £337; £168) **Stalls** High

Form RPR

02-2 **1** **Fourth Generation (IRE)**[19] 3766 3-9-3 78.... PJMcDonald 8 79+
(G A Swinbank) *trckd ldrs: hdwy to ld over 2f out: edgd lft and drew clr over 1f out* **10/11**[1]

45 **2** 5 **Opening Nite (IRE)**[10] 4062 3-9-3 0.... TonyHamilton 7 69
(R A Fahey) *in tch: hdwy to chse wnr over 2f out: kpt on fnl f: no imp* **6/1**[3]

4 **3** 4 **La Bacouetteuse (FR)**[15] 3901 5-9-12 0.... PaulMulrennan 3 61
(A G Foster) *hld up: shkn up and stdy hdwy over 1f out: kpt on fnl f: nvr nr ldrs* **20/1**

0 **4** ½ **Corky Dancer**[10] 4062 5-9-12 0.... AndrewElliott 6 60+
(P Monteith) *hld up and bhd: stdy hdwy on outside 2f out: nvr nr to chal* **12/1**

0 **5** ¾ **Tobernea (IRE)**[37] 3176 3-9-3 0.... RoystonFfrench 12 57
(M Johnston) *in tch: drvn and effrt over 3f out: no imp fnl 2f* **5/1**[2]

3- **6** 5 **Mexican Jay (USA)**[423] 2403 4-9-7 0.... TomEaves 11 43
(B Smart) *midfield: drvn over 3f out: outpcd fr 2f out* **12/1**

60 **7** nk **Barra Raider**[71] 2131 3-9-0 0.... BarryMcHugh(3) 14 46
(R F Fisher) *hld up: rdn over 3f out: swtchd rt over 1f out: nvr able to chal* **100/1**

0-00 **8** 1¾ **Chardonnay Star (IRE)**[49] 2792 3-8-7 32....(p) DeanHeslop(5) 15 38
(C J Teague) *towards rr: drvn over 4f out: no imp fr 2f out* **200/1**

60 **9** nk **Large Scotch**[10] 4069 3-8-9 0.... RobertLButler(3) 1 37
(Paul Green) *bhd: struggling over 4f out: sme late hdwy: nvr on terms* **150/1**

0 **10** 1½ **Red Storm Rising**[50] 2755 3-9-3 0.... AndreaAtzeni 2 39
(K A Morgan) *prom tl rdn and wknd fr 2f out* **66/1**

00-0 **11** 2 **Real Desire**[13] 3950 4-9-12 46.... DuranFentiman 5 36
(P Monteith) *led: rdn and hdd over 2f out: edgd rt and wknd over 1f out* **66/1**

4-50 **12** 1 **Barbarian**[19] 3758 4-9-12 57.... SilvestreDeSousa 9 34
(A D Brown) *bhd: pushed along over 4f out: nvr on terms* **28/1**

0 **13** hd **Secret Sortie (IRE)**[29] 3437 5-9-7 0.... LeeVickers 16 28
(T J Etherington) *s.i.s: bhd and pushed along 1/2-way: nvr on terms* **66/1**

000- **14** 11 **Mister Fantastic**[323] 5672 4-9-7 64.... PatrickDonaghy(5) 4 —
(N J Vaughan) *t.k.h: pressed ldr tl hung rt and wknd over 2f out* **40/1**

04 **15** 23 **Sposalizio (IRE)**[58] 2499 3-9-3 0.... PatrickMathers 10 —
(E J Cooper) *hld up: rdn and outpcd over 4f out: sn struggling: t.o* **66/1**

1m 57.65s (0.05) **Going Correction** +0.125s/f (Good)
WFA 3 from 4yo+ 9lb 15 Ran SP% **117.5**
Speed ratings (Par 103): **104,99,96,95,94 90,90,88,88,87 85,84,84,74,53**
Tote Swingers: 1&2 £2.90, 1&3 £7.90, 2&3 £18.30 CSF £5.76 TOTE £1.90: £1.30, £1.70, £4.40; EX 8.10.
Owner J V Layton **Bred** Mrs Christine Kelly **Trained** Melsonby, N Yorks

FOCUS
A weak maiden.

4408 JAMIE ARCHER & LUCIE JONES LIVE H'CAP 1m 1f 61y
5:20 (5:20) (Class 5) (0-70,64) 3-Y-O **£2,590** (£770; £385; £192) **Stalls** High

Form RPR

6004 **1** **Frontline Phantom (IRE)**[10] 4061 3-8-11 54.... AndrewElliott 1 65
(J R Weymes) *prom: effrt and rdn over 2f out: chal fnl f: styd on to ld cl home* **6/1**[3]

6561 **2** hd **Robbie Burnett**[9] 4087 3-9-7 64.... PJMcDonald 9 75
(G A Swinbank) *led: rdn and edgd lft 2f out: hrd pressed fnl f: kpt on wl: hdd cl home* **1/1**[1]

0555 **3** 2¾ **Leaving Alone (USA)**[27] 3513 3-9-3 60.... TonyHamilton 2 65
(E W Tuer) *hld up: rdn 3f out: hdwy and edgd rt over 1f out: kpt on fnl f: nt rch first two* **13/2**

0-00 **4** 5 **Footsie (IRE)**[22] 3662 3-9-4 61.... PaulMulrennan 6 56
(J G Given) *hld up in tch: drvn and outpcd over 2f out: plugged on fnl f: no imp* **14/1**

005- **5** ¾ **Franki J**[206] 7887 3-8-8 51.... AndreaAtzeni 4 44
(D Donovan) *hld up: rdn 3f out: hdwy on outside and edgd rt wl over 1f out: nvr rchd ldrs* **20/1**

0054 **6** 6 **Diamondgeezer Luke (IRE)**[8] 4127 3-9-2 62.... BarryMcHugh(3) 3 43
(Patrick Morris) *prom tl drvn and wknd over 2f out* **5/1**[2]

0000 **7** nk **Hot Rod Mamma (IRE)**[2] 4337 3-8-2 45.... DuranFentiman 8 25
(Mrs Dianne Sayer) *t.k.h: chsd ldrs tl rdn and wknd over 1f out* **20/1**

0000 **8** 4 **Hotgrove Boy**[37] 3148 3-8-4 47 ow1....(p) RoystonFfrench 10 19
(A G Foster) *cl up tl rdn and wknd over 2f out* **33/1**

000- **9** shd **Princess Neenee (IRE)**[303] 6245 3-8-2 45.... SilvestreDeSousa 5 17
(Paul Green) *in tch: rdn and struggling over 2f out: sn btn* **25/1**

1m 57.61s (0.01) **Going Correction** +0.125s/f (Good) 9 Ran SP% **117.3**
Speed ratings (Par 100): **104,103,101,96,96 90,90,87,87**
Tote Swingers: 1&2 £1.40, 1&3 £4.00, 2&3 £2.90 CSF £12.03 CT £41.65 TOTE £7.80: £1.70, £1.10, £1.50; EX 15.10 Place 6: £24.93 Place 5: £22.90.
Owner Frontline Bathrooms **Bred** Joe Rogers **Trained** Middleham Moor, N Yorks

FOCUS
A moderate handicap.

T/Plt: £46.80 to a £1 stake. Pool:£55.53.58 - 864.90 winning tickets T/Qpdt: £56.20 to a £1 stake. Pool:£3,669.62 - 48.30 winning tickets RY

4116 PONTEFRACT (L-H)
Sunday, July 25

OFFICIAL GOING: Good to firm (8.1)

4409 WELCOME TO YORKSHIRE ACTION PACKED OUTDOORS MAIDEN STKS 5f
2:05 (2:07) (Class 4) 2-Y-0 **£3,885** (£1,156; £577; £288) **Stalls** Low

Form RPR

1 **New Planet (IRE)** 2-8-12 0.... IanBrennan(5) 3 86+
(J J Quinn) *dwlt: sn chsng ldrs: effrt 2f out: r.o wl to ld last 100yds* **7/2**[3]

2 **2** 2½ **Major Muscari (IRE)**[13] 3964 2-9-3 0.... JamesDoyle 9 77
(A J McCabe) *w ldrs: led appr fnl f: hdd ins fnl f: kpt on same pce* **2/1**[1]

45U **3** 2¼ **So Is She (IRE)**[43] 2951 2-8-5 0.... NatashaEaton(7) 2 64
(A Bailey) *w ldrs: kpt on ins fnl f* **17/2**

4 hd **Flash City (ITY)** 2-9-3 0.... PaulHanagan 1 68
(B Smart) *charged gate: led: hdd appr fnl f: wknd clsng stages* **3/1**[2]

00 **5** 4 **Piceno (IRE)**[20] 3735 2-9-3 0.... KierenFallon 4 55
(L M Cumani) *chsd ldrs: outpcd over 2f out: no threat after* **6/1**

6 11 **Watts Up Son** 2-9-3 0....(t) DavidNolan 5 14
(D Carroll) *s.s: a bhd* **28/1**

5500 **7** hd **Ever Roses**[18] 3770 2-8-12 0.... MickyFenton 8 8
(P T Midgley) *chsd ldrs: led over 2f out tl appr fnl f* **100/1**

04 **8** 17 **Capall Dorcha**[85] 1704 2-9-3 0.... GrahamGibbons 10 —
(J R Holt) *chsd ldrs: lost pl over 2f out: bhd whn eased ins fnl f* **66/1**

9 ½ **Mr Mo Jo** 2-8-10 0.... MatthewLawson(7) 6 —
(R Bastiman) *hung bdly rt and lost pl after 1f: virtually p.u fnl 2f* **50/1**

62.98 secs (-0.32) **Going Correction** -0.125s/f (Firm) 9 Ran SP% **113.3**
Speed ratings (Par 96): **97,93,89,89,82 65,64,37,36**
Tote Swingers: 1&2 £2.40, 1&3 £5.10, 2&3 £4.10 CSF £10.55 TOTE £5.00: £1.80, £1.10, £2.50; EX 12.80.
Owner Ross Harmon **Bred** Mrs Diane Williams **Trained** Settrington, N Yorks
■ Stewards' Enquiry : David Nolan two-day ban: used whip when out of contention (Aug 8-9)

FOCUS
A modest juvenile maiden. It was run at a fair tempo and few got involved from off the pace.

NOTEBOOK
New Planet(IRE) got his career off to a perfect start and won going away. He wasn't the best away, but was soon racing in a nice rhythm on the inside just off the early leaders. He picked up strongly once pulled out for his challenge nearing the furlong marker and it was clear soon after he wasn't going to have to be fully extended to win. Another furlong will suit down the line, but he clearly has the speed to win more prizes at this distance and he looks a useful prospect. It will be interesting to see how the handicapper rates this. (op 11-2)
Major Muscari(IRE) set the standard on his debut second over 5f at Wolverhampton 13 days earlier. He was forced to race on the outer of the two early pacesetters from his wide draw, but still took it up going well off the home turn and simply met a speedier horse in the winner. There ought to be a small maiden within his compass, but he is obviously more of a nursery type. (tchd 5-2)
So Is She(IRE) was having her fourth outing and showed plenty of early dash. She lacked a gear change from the top of the home straight, but kept on gamely and this was her most encouraging effort yet. (op 8-1 tchd 9-1)
Flash City(ITY) dam has produced winners over further, but his sire is a speed influence and he was another that showed real early zip on his racecourse debut. He couldn't sustain his effort off the home bend, but is entitled to be sharper for the experience and has a future. (tchd 11-4 and 10-3 in a place)
Piceno(IRE) ◆ was having his third outing and, lacking the early pace to get seriously involved, wasn't given that hard a time over a trip clearly too sharp. He is now eligible for nurseries and is no doubt capable of better back over further in that sphere. (op 9-2)
Mr Mo Jo Official explanation: jockey said colt hung badly right

4410 YORKSHIRE SOCIETY H'CAP 1m 4f 8y
2:40 (2:40) (Class 5) (0-70,85) 3-Y-0+ **£3,238** (£963; £481; £240) **Stalls** Low

Form RPR

5650 **1** **Gulf Coast**[4] 4246 5-8-11 53....(p) GrahamGibbons 6 62
(T D Walford) *trckd ldrs: wnt 2nd over 2f out: styd on to ld last 50yds* **12/1**

0201 **2** ½ **Umverti**[9] 4117 5-9-12 68.... DanielTudhope 1 76
(N Bycroft) *led: qcknd over 2f out: hdd and no ex last 50yds* **7/2**[2]

-025 **3** 2½ **Master Nimbus**[55] 2610 10-9-1 62....(t) IanBrennan(5) 5 66+
(J J Quinn) *t.k.h in mid-div: effrt and n.m.r over 2f out: hung lft and kpt on to take 3rd 1f out* **9/1**

00-2 **4** ¾ **Winged Farasi**[27] 3502 6-8-7 52 oh2.... KellyHarrison(3) 7 55+
(Miss J E Foster) *in rr: styd on fnl 2f: nrst fin* **40/1**

3332 **5** ½ **Danceintothelight**[11] 4017 3-8-1 60.... BillyCray(5) 4 62
(Micky Hammond) *t.k.h towards rr: effrt over 2f out: styd on fnl f* **6/1**

4321 **6** 1¼ **Dean Iarracht (IRE)**[23] 3614 4-9-1 57.... AndrewMullen 2 57
(Miss Tracy Waggott) *trckd ldrs: drvn over 1f out: wknd fnl f* **11/2**[3]

0054 **7** 2 **Regal Lyric (IRE)**[27] 3502 4-9-0 56.... MickyFenton 10 53
(T P Tate) *swtchd lft after s: hld up in rr: hdwy on wd outside over 4f out: chsng ldrs over 2f out: wknd over 1f out* **9/1**

3-52 **8** 9 **Golden Future**[38] 3122 7-8-10 52.... PaulHanagan 8 35
(P D Niven) *chsd ldrs: pushed along 6f out: hung rt and lost pl over 2f out: sn bhd* **11/4**[1]

2034 **9** 37 **Dispol Diva**[11] 4015 4-8-10 52 oh2....(v) PhillipMakin 9 —
(P T Midgley) *drvn to chse ldrs: lost pl over 2f out: sn bhd: eased ins fnl f: t.o* **20/1**

2m 38.29s (-2.51) **Going Correction** -0.125s/f (Firm)
WFA 3 from 4yo+ 12lb 9 Ran SP% **113.5**
Speed ratings (Par 103): **103,102,101,100,100 99,98,92,67**
Tote Swingers: 1&2 £6.70, 1&3 £16.40, 2&3 £6.00 CSF £52.88 CT £400.95 TOTE £11.30: £2.40, £1.80, £3.10; EX 78.00.
Owner Mrs Mary & David Longstaff **Bred** R J Turner **Trained** Sheriff Hutton, N Yorks

FOCUS
A moderate handicap, run at an uneven gallop and it proved hard to sufficiently make up ground from off the pace.
Golden Future Official explanation: jockey said gelding hung right-handed throughout

4411 GRAHAM ROCK MEMORIAL H'CAP 1m 2f 6y
3:15 (3:16) (Class 5) (0-70,67) 3-Y-0+ **£3,238** (£963; £481; £240) **Stalls** Low

Form RPR

002 **1** **Northside Prince (IRE)**[66] 2259 4-10-0 67.... KierenFallon 3 80
(G A Swinbank) *hld up in midfield: smooth hdwy and nt clr run over 2f out: styd on fnl f: drvn to ld nr fin* **9/2**[2]

404 **2** ½ **Holiday Cocktail**[13] 3950 8-9-4 **57**................................(p) PaulHanagan 2 69
(J J Quinn) *chsd ldrs: wnt 2nd over 2f out: led jst ins fnl f: hdd and no ex clsng stages* **7/2**[1]
00-0 **3** 6 **Scarab (IRE)**[71] 2109 5-9-12 **65**................................ GrahamGibbons 1 65
(T D Walford) *led after 2f: hdd jst ins fnl f: one pce* **14/1**
0-50 **4** 1 ¾ **Roman History (IRE)**[31] 3370 7-8-9 **48** oh3.............(p) AndrewMullen 11 45
(Miss Tracy Waggott) *swtchd lft s s: in rr: pushed along 4f out: hdwy on ins over 2f out: one pce* **66/1**
0042 **5** 6 **Sea Land (FR)**[30] 3405 6-8-8 **52**................................ DaleSwift(5) 6 37
(B Ellison) *hld up in midfield: effrt over 2f out: kpt on: no imp* **6/1**[3]
3503 **6** 4 **Joinedupwriting**[8] 4156 5-9-5 **58**.......................... DaraghO'Donohoe 5 35
(R M Whitaker) *in rr: effrt over 2f out: nvr a factor* **12/1**
0605 **7** ½ **Pitbull**[9] 4094 7-8-4 **48** oh3................................(b) BillyCray(5) 4 24
(A Berry) *s.s: t.k.h detached in last: sme hdwy over 2f out: nvr a factor* **50/1**
0424 **8** ¾ **Miss Ferney**[7] 4168 6-8-8 **50**................................ PaulPickard(3) 7 24
(A Kirtley) *in rr: hdwy on wd outside over 2f out: nvr a factor* **8/1**
000 **9** 11 **Stephie**[24] 3595 4-8-2 **48** oh2................................ RyanPowell(7) 12 —
(M W Easterby) *swvd rt s: led 2f: w ldrs: wknd 2f out: sn bhd* **50/1**
2231 **10** 9 **Avitus**[9] 4120 4-9-4 **57**................................ PhillipMakin 9 —
(Micky Hammond) *chsd ldrs: lost pl 2f out: bhd whn eased ins fnl f* **9/2**[2]
114 **11** ¾ **Bajan Pride**[12] 3973 6-10-0 **67**................................ MickyFenton 8 —
(P T Midgley) *chsd ldrs: rdn over 2f out: sn lost pl: bhd whn eased towards fin* **14/1**

2m 11.6s (-2.10) **Going Correction** -0.125s/f (Firm) 11 Ran SP% **110.4**
Speed ratings (Par 103): **103,102,97,96,91 88,88,87,78,71 70**
Tote Swingers: 1&2 £3.30, 1&3 £12.10, 2&3 £10.00 CSF £19.05 CT £188.34 TOTE £5.10: £1.70, £1.80, £5.00; EX 17.40.
Owner S S Anderson **Bred** F Dunne **Trained** Melsonby, N Yorks

FOCUS
An open handicap, run at a fair enough pace. The first two dominated.
Miss Ferney Official explanation: jockey said mare was in season
Avitus Official explanation: trainer had no explanation for the poor form shown

4412 SKY BET SUPPORTING THE YORKSHIRE RACING FESTIVAL POMFRET STKS (LISTED RACE) 1m 4y
3:50 (3:50) (Class 1) 3-Y-O+

£15,658 (£15,658; £4,308; £2,148; £1,076; £540) **Stalls** Low

Form RPR
5-01 **1** **Rio De La Plata (USA)**[53] 2651 5-9-1 114.............. DaraghO'Donohoe 5 116
(Saeed Bin Suroor) *w ldr: effrt over 2f out: led jst ins fnl f: jnd post* **5/2**[2]
1230 **1** *dht* **Mabait**[29] 3455 4-9-1 108................................ KierenFallon 3 116+
(L M Cumani) *trckd ldrs: t.k.h: effrt over 2f out: styd on fnl f to dead-heat on post* **5/1**
1101 **3** 1 ¼ **Harrison George (IRE)**[8] 4126 5-9-1 114.................. PaulHanagan 1 113
(R A Fahey) *led: qckd 3f out: hdd last 150yds: keeping on same pce whn n.m.r nr fin* **4/1**[3]
110- **4** 3 ¼ **Sirvino**[295] 6480 5-9-1 101................................ PhillipMakin 2 105+
(T D Barron) *hld up in rr: effrt over 2f out: kpt on fnl f: tk n.d 4th line* **14/1**
-045 **5** *nse* **Zacinto**[22] 3693 4-9-1 116................................ RyanMoore 4 105
(Sir Michael Stoute) *trckd ldrs: t.k.h: effrt over 2f out: hung lft over 1f out: unable to chal* **15/8**[1]
3603 **6** 5 **Light From Mars**[16] 3869 5-9-1 98.......................... JamesMillman 6 93
(B R Millman) *hld up in rr: drvn over 1f out: lost pl over 1f out* **14/1**

1m 43.25s (-2.65) **Going Correction** -0.125s/f (Firm) 6 Ran SP% **113.4**
Speed ratings (Par 111): **108,108,106,103,103 98**
WIN: Mabait £3.30 Rio De La Plata £1.50 PLACE: M £2.90 RDLP £1.60 EX: M-RDLP £6.40 RDLP-M £7.70 CSF: M-RDLP £9.10 RDLP-M £7.74. Tote Swingers: M&RDLP £2.50, M&3 £2.70, RDLP&3 £2.00..
Owner Godolphin **Bred** Jose De Camargo, Robert N Clay Et Al **Trained** Newmarket, Suffolk
Owner Sheikh Mohammed Obaid Al Maktoum **Bred** L A C Ashby Newhall Estate Farm **Trained** Newmarket, Suffolk
■ Stewards' Enquiry : Daragh O'Donohoe two-day ban: careless riding (Aug 8-9); one-day ban: used whip with excessive frequency (Aug 10)

FOCUS
There was a cracking finish to this decent Listed race and the first three dominated.

NOTEBOOK
Rio De La Plata(USA) was having his first run since resuming winning ways in a conditions race at Nottingham 53 days earlier and this confirms he is now back in decent heart. He deserves extra credit as he had to fight to master the third and then the extra challenge of Mabait, but still his Group 1 entries later on look too ambitious. His rider said later that the ground was plenty quick enough for him. (op 3-1 tchd 7-2)
Mabait left his lifeless effort at Newmarket 29 days earlier firmly behind and got a typically strong ride from Kieren Fallon. Not for the first time he took time to settle, but hit top gear at the furlong marker and looked as though he had done enough nearing the line, but Rio De La Plata found that little bit extra and joined him on the line for a share of the spoils. Luca Cumani's 4-y-o has shown greatly improved form since resuming this year and leaves the impression there is still more to come from him when he is faced with an end-to-end gallop in Pattern company. (op 3-1 tchd 7-2)
Harrison George(IRE) set out to make all and went off at a fair pace. He gave everything when asked for maximum effort, but ultimately got outstayed by the first pair. He finished an awful lot closer to Mabait than was the case when failing to handle Epsom in June and is a very likeable performer who deserves to find one of these. (tchd 9-2)
Sirvino remarkably improved 36lb on official figures last year and his winning sequence culminated with success in the John Smith's Cup at York. This was a belated seasonal return and, although he never figured seriously, he still showed the engine remains. He has it to prove in this sort of company, but wasn't given a hard time and should improve a bundle for the run. (op 16-1)
Zacinto bombed out again in the Eclipse on his previous outing. His last five races had been Group 1s and, while he was only 2lb clear of his nearest rivals on BHB ratings, his best form would have seen him winning this. He does shape as though he wants a stiffer test now, but it was still a puzzling effort from a horse that once looked so promising. Perhaps connections will now reach for some form of headgear. Official explanation: trainer had no explanation for the poor form shown (op 7-4 tchd 6-4 and 2-1 in places)
Light From Mars faced a very tough task at the weights and was the first beaten. (op 20-1 tchd 25-1)

4413 FAMILY DAY ON 15TH AUGUST H'CAP 6f
4:25 (4:25) (Class 3) (0-90,86) 3-Y-O+

£6,231 (£1,866; £933; £467; £233; £117) **Stalls** Low

Form RPR
-006 **1** **Stevie Gee (IRE)**[22] 3667 6-8-6 **71**..............................(v[1]) IanBrennan(5) 1 82
(Ian Williams) *chsd ldrs: slt ld over 1f out: sn hdd: styd on to ld towards fin* **17/2**
6122 **2** ½ **Misplaced Fortune**[27] 3505 5-9-4 **85**.................... AdamBeschizza(7) 2 94
(N Tinkler) *s.i.s: sn mid-div: n.m.r over 2f out: styd on to ld 1f out: hdd and no ex wl ins fnl f* **5/1**[2]
5201 **3** 3 ½ **Glen Shiel (USA)**[9] 4104 3-9-7 **86**.............................. KierenFallon 10 83+
(M Johnston) *chsd ldrs: drvn on outer and lost pl over 4f out: hdwy on ins 2f out: kpt on to take 3rd jst ins fnl f* **7/1**[3]
0062 **4** 1 ¼ **Discanti (IRE)**[15] 3919 5-9-10 **84**..........................(t) GrahamGibbons 7 78
(T D Easterby) *trckd ldrs: t.k.h: kpt on same pce fnl f* **8/1**
0051 **5** 1 ½ **Orpsie Boy (IRE)**[9] 4121 7-9-1 **80**.............................. DaleSwift(5) 4 69+
(Mrs R A Carr) *in rr: drvn over 3f out: swtchd lft 1f out: kpt on* **3/1**[1]
0165 **6** 2 ½ **Indian Skipper (IRE)**[19] 3753 5-9-7 **84**..............(be) MichaelStainton(3) 9 65
(R C Guest) *s.i.s: hld up: effrt on outer 2f out: nvr nr to chal* **16/1**
5005 **7** 2 **Bel Cantor**[9] 4105 7-8-12 **75**.............................. KellyHarrison(3) 5 50
(W J H Ratcliffe) *w ldr: led over 2f out: hdd over 1f out: fdd* **33/1**
6040 **8** *nse* **Sunrise Safari (IRE)**[29] 3446 7-9-10 **84**..................(v) PaulHanagan 3 58
(R A Fahey) *mid-div: hdwy on outside over 2f out: wknd over 1f out* **8/1**
1116 **9** 7 **Cornus**[15] 3919 8-9-12 **86**..............................(be) JamesDoyle 6 38
(A J McCabe) *prom: effrt on outer over 2f out: lost pl over 1f out: eased towards fin* **11/1**
1000 **10** *nk* **Atlantic Story (USA)**[15] 3919 8-9-9 **83**....................(t) PhillipMakin 8 34
(M W Easterby) *led: hdd over 2f out: wknd fnl f: eased towards fin* **22/1**
2322 **11** 1 **Noodles Blue Boy**[22] 3660 4-9-8 **82**.............................. RyanMoore 11 30
(Ollie Pears) *in rr: effrt over 2f out: nvr a factor: eased nr fin* **9/1**

1m 14.82s (-2.08) **Going Correction** -0.125s/f (Firm)
WFA 3 from 4yo+ 5lb 11 Ran SP% **118.4**
Speed ratings (Par 107): **108,107,102,101,99 95,93,92,83,83 81**
Tote Swingers: 1&2 £9.60, 1&3 £16.40, 2&3 £6.80 CSF £51.05 CT £324.40 TOTE £11.50: £3.20, £2.10, £1.50; EX 82.20.
Owner Steve Gray **Bred** Irish National Stud **Trained** Portway, Worcs

FOCUS
A very competitive sprint handicap and it was another race where the majority of those held up struggled to make a serious impact.

NOTEBOOK
Stevie Gee(IRE) attracted support in a first-time visor and completed the task in ready fashion. He was soon on the front end despite this being a drop in trip and found plenty down the centre of the track when asked to win the race. His rider didn't have to get all that serious with him to fend off the runner-up and he will still look nicely treated after a rise in the handicap, but his future hopes probably rest on the headgear holding the same effect in the future. (op 8-1)
Misplaced Fortune has now finished second on three outings since winning off an 8lb lower mark in May. She travelled sweetly into contention, but ultimately found her concession of weight to the winner beyond her. She was a clear second-best and rates a solid benchmark. (op 8-1)
Glen Shiel(USA) ◆ had been upped 4lb for winning over 7f at Newmarket nine days previously. He was found out by this sharper test through the first half, but stayed on strongly when straightening for home and looks well up to winning again when reverting to another furlong. (op 4-1)
Discanti(IRE) proved free early on and that didn't help his finishing effort, but he still posted a fair effort in defeat. The handicapper probably has his measure. (op 9-1 tchd 7-1)
Orpsie Boy(IRE) was still very well handicapped on his previous best efforts despite being 6lb higher than when finally ending his losing run over C&D nine days earlier. He stayed on all too late, but it looked as though he got further back early on than his rider wanted and he shouldn't be judged too harshly for this. (op 7-2 tchd 4-1)
Atlantic Story(USA) Official explanation: jockey said gelding stopped quickly

4414 KEEPMOAT DELIVERING COMMUNITY REGENERATION MAIDEN STKS 1m 4y
5:00 (5:01) (Class 5) 3-4-Y-O **£2,914** (£867; £433; £216) **Stalls** Low

Form RPR
3 **1** **Autumn Riches**[11] 4028 3-9-3 0.............................. PaulHanagan 3 88+
(M Johnston) *mde all: qcknd over 2f out: rdn over 1f out: jst hld on* **5/4**[2]
2 **2** *nk* **Entitled**[20] 3738 3-8-12 0.............................. RyanMoore 1 82+
(Sir Michael Stoute) *trckd ldrs: chsd wnr over 2f out: rdn and edgd rt 1f out: styd on towards fin: jst hld* **10/11**[1]
00 **3** 12 **Isobar (GER)**[10] 4069 4-9-11 0.............................. KirstyMilczarek 9 61
(L M Cumani) *trckd ldrs: wnt 3rd 2f out: one pce* **25/1**
6 **4** 7 **Wolf Rock**[94] 1485 3-9-3 0.............................. PhillipMakin 8 43
(T D Barron) *hld up: effrt over 2f out: wnt modest 4th over 1f out: nvr a factor* **14/1**[3]
04 **5** 4 **Roydmore**[33] 3285 3-9-3 0.............................. MickyFenton 4 34
(R A Fahey) *dwlt: drvn over 3f out: lost pl over 2f out* **66/1**
0/0- **6** 44 **Bluebaru**[464] 1335 4-9-11 35.............................. J-PGuillambert 5 —
(P Salmon) *trckd ldrs: drvn over 3f out: wknd 2f out: virtually p.u: t.o* **100/1**

1m 44.16s (-1.74) **Going Correction** -0.125s/f (Firm)
WFA 3 from 4yo 8lb 6 Ran SP% **109.8**
Speed ratings (Par 103): **103,102,90,83,79 35**
Tote Swingers: 1&2 £1.10, 1&3 £3.00, 2&3 £3.20 CSF £2.53 TOTE £2.30: £1.10, £1.30; EX 2.70.
Owner Sheikh Hamdan Bin Mohammed Al Maktoum **Bred** Darley **Trained** Middleham Moor, N Yorks

FOCUS
This maiden was a match between the two clear marker leaders and so it played out as they came right away from the rest.

4415 LADIES DAY ON WEDNESDAY 4TH AUGUST H'CAP 5f
5:30 (5:32) (Class 5) (0-70,69) 3-Y-O+ **£2,914** (£867; £433; £216) **Stalls** Low

Form RPR
4354 **1** **Mr Wolf**[9] 4121 9-9-7 **65**.............................. PaulHanagan 1 80
(J J Quinn) *mde all: hld on towards fin* **5/2**[1]
0633 **2** ½ **King Of Swords (IRE)**[2] 4343 6-8-11 **55**..................(p) KirstyMilczarek 2 68
(N Tinkler) *prom: effrt on inner 2f out: chsd wnr fnl 100yds: jst hld* **10/3**[2]
1211 **3** 2 ¼ **Comptonspirit**[10] 4043 6-9-10 **68**.............................. J-PGuillambert 3 73
(B P J Baugh) *chsd wnr: kpt on same pce fnl f* **9/2**[3]
2505 **4** *nk* **Darcy's Pride (IRE)**[2] 4342 6-8-5 **52**.............................. PaulPickard(3) 4 56+
(P T Midgley) *in rr: hdwy on ins 2f out: kpt on wl fnl f* **12/1**
1524 **5** 4 **Verinco**[51] 2695 4-9-1 **66**..............................(v) AdamCarter(7) 5 55
(B Smart) *chsd ldrs: hmpd over 3f out: fdd appr fnl f* **8/1**
565 **6** 1 **Colorus (IRE)**[28] 3474 7-9-1 **66**..........................(p) AdamBeschizza(7) 10 52+
(W J H Ratcliffe) *chsd ldrs: edgd lft over 3f out: wknd over 1f out* **25/1**
2305 **7** 2 ¼ **Not My Choice (IRE)**[4] 4255 5-9-4 **62**..........................(t) MickyFenton 9 40
(D C Griffiths) *chsd ldrs: hmpd over 3f out: wknd over 1f out* **14/1**
-300 **8** ¾ **Grand Stitch (USA)**[68] 2206 4-9-11 **69**.............................. DavidNolan 7 44
(D Carroll) *mid-div: hmpd over 3f out: nvr nr ldrs* **33/1**
400- **9** ¾ **Silent Treatment (IRE)**[366] 4279 4-8-8 **55**.............. MichaelStainton(3) 6 27
(R C Guest) *in rr: effrt over 2f out: nvr on terms* **66/1**
3060 **10** ¾ **Port Ronan (USA)**[3] 4285 4-8-2 **51** oh1 ow1................. IanBrennan(5) 8 21
(J S Wainwright) *dwlt: a in rr* **33/1**
6502 **11** ½ **Namir (IRE)**[12] 3976 8-9-4 **62**..............................(vt) GrahamGibbons 11 30
(H J Evans) *in rr: sme hdwy on outer over 1f out: nvr a factor* **10/1**

4044 **12** 2 ¾ **Rio Sands**[23] [3623] 5-8-8 **52**.. DaraghO'Donohoe 12 10
(R M Whitaker) *chsd ldrs on outer: lost pl over 1f out* **33/1**

62.33 secs (-0.97) **Going Correction** -0.125s/f (Firm) **12** Ran SP% **118.6**
Speed ratings (Par 103): **102,101,97,97,90 89,85,84,83,81 81,76**
Tote Swingers: 1&2 £2.90, 1&3 £3.80, 2&3 £5.00 CSF £10.03 CT £35.73 TOTE £3.60: £1.40, £1.60, £1.70; EX 10.80 Place 6: £24.93 Place 5: £22.90.
Owner Andrew Turton & David Barker **Bred** P Asquith **Trained** Settrington, N Yorks

FOCUS
A strongly run sprint handicap and solid form for the class.
T/Plt: £71.50 to a £1 stake. Pool:£77,360.56 - 788.86 winning tickets T/Qpdt: £14.90 to a £1 stake. Pool:£4,901.52 - 242.30 winning tickets WG

DEL MAR (L-H)
Sunday, July 25

OFFICIAL GOING: Turf: firm

4417a EDDIE READ H'CAP (GRADE 1) (3YO+) (TURF) 1m 1f (T)
1:30 (1:57) 3-Y-0+ **£111,111** (£37,037; £22,222; £11,111; £3,703)

RPR

1 **The Usual Q. T. (USA)**[28] 4-8-11 **0**.. VEspinoza 3 119
(James Cassidy, U.S.A) *broke wl and settled in 3rd: chal ldrs 2f out and led appr fnl f: r.o wl u.p* **7/5**[1]

2 2 **Victor's Cry (USA)**[54] 5-8-11 **0**.. CNakatani 2 115
(Eoin Harty, U.S.A) *hld up towards rr: hdwy 2f out: r.o to take 2nd fnl f: no ch w wnr* **54/10**

3 1 ¼ **Enriched (USA)**[64] 5-8-7 **0**..(b) JRosario 6 108
(Doug O'Neill, U.S.A) *chsd ldr tl lost 2nd appr fnl f: unable qck and jst hld on for 3rd* **48/10**[3]

4 nse **Crowded House**[17] [3825] 4-8-7 **0**..(b) MESmith 1 108
(B J Meehan) *hld up in last: hdwy ins fnl 2f: r.o wl and jst missed 3rd* **133/10**

5 ¾ **Hyades (USA)**[20] 4-8-7 **0**.. MGarcia 7 107
(B Cecil, U.S.A) *chsd ldrs: one pce fnl 2f* **139/10**

6 1 ¼ **Acclamation (USA)**[22] 4-8-11 **0**.. CSantiagoReyes 4 108
(Donald Warren, U.S.A) *sn led: hdd appr fnl f: wknd* **77/10**

7 ½ **Loup Breton (IRE)**[49] 6-8-9 **0**.. RBejarano 5 105
(Julio C Canani, U.S.A) *racd in 4th: ev ch st: unable qck* **4/1**[2]

1m 47.28s (0.19) **7** Ran SP% **119.7**
PARI-MUTUEL (all including $2 stake): WIN 4.80; PLACE (1-2) 3.20, 5.00; SHOW (1-2-3) 2.60, 3.60, 3.40; DF 12.00; SF 22.40.
Owner Don Van Racing Inc, M Nentwig Et Al **Bred** Carlee Van Kempen **Trained** USA

NOTEBOOK
Crowded House, dropping in trip for this first start in the USA, ran with credit looking as if a slightly longer trip will be in his favour. He will remain in the US now, and will be trained by Ben Cecil.

2406 MUNICH (L-H)
Sunday, July 25

OFFICIAL GOING: Turf: soft

4418a GROSSER DALLMAYR-PREIS BAYERISCHES ZUCHTRENNEN (GROUP 1) (3YO+) (TURF) 1m 2f
4:05 (12:00) 3-Y-0+ **£80,530** (£31,858; £15,929; £8,849)

RPR

1 **Lady Jane Digby**[22] [3671] 5-9-3 0.. GregFairley 2 112
(M Johnston) *broke wl and led for 100yds bef hdd: trckd ldr: dropped to 3rd ins fnl 4f: rdn 2f out to ld 1 1/2f out: styd on strly u.p* **12/1**

2 1 **Night Magic (GER)**[49] [2806] 4-9-3 0.. KKerekes 4 110
(W Figge, Germany) *racd in 6th: clsd up on home turn 2 1/2f out: rdn and r.o fnl 1 1/2f to take 2nd w 100yds to run: a hld by wnr* **3/1**[3]

3 1 ½ **Alexandros**[51] [2707] 5-9-6 0.. FrankieDettori 1 110
(Saeed Bin Suroor) *settled on heels of ldrs: racd in 4th: tk clsr order to have ev ch 2f out: sn rdn and kpt on at one pce fnl f* **5/2**[1]

4 ½ **Liang Kay (GER)**[49] [2806] 5-9-6 0.. YannLerner 6 109
(Uwe Ostmann, Germany) *racd towards rr: mde sme hdwy 2f out to go 5th: unable qck fnl f* **14/1**

5 ¾ **Scolari**[35] [3251] 5-9-6 0.. THellier 3 108
(T Mundry, Germany) *racd in midfield: hdwy on outside in st: ev ch fnl 2f: effrt short-lived: plugged on at one pce* **12/1**

6 ½ **White Lightning (GER)**[49] [2806] 8-9-6 0.. APietsch 7 107
(U Stech, Germany) *drvn along to ld after 100yds: chal in st 2 1/2f out: hdd ins fnl 2f: no ex: wknd* **33/1**

7 3 **Norderney (GER)**[35] [3251] 4-9-3 0.. AStarke 9 98
(P Schiergen, Germany) *a bhd* **11/1**

8 2 **Noble Alpha (IRE)**[15] [3934] 3-8-10 0.. TedDurcan 5 97
(Mario Hofer, Germany) *nvr plcd to chal* **14/1**

9 1 **Querari (GER)**[70] [2152] 4-9-6 0.. EPedroza 8 95
(A Wohler, Germany) *racd in 3rd: pushed up to take 2nd ins fnl 4f: rdn and chal ldr in st 2 1/2f out: led briefly ins fnl 2f: hdd 1 1/2f: wknd qckly* **11/4**[2]

2m 9.70s (0.73)
WFA 3 from 4yo+ 10lb **9** Ran SP% **120.2**
WIN (incl. 10 euro stake): 121. PLACES: 33, 16, 18. SF: 477.
Owner Miss K Rausing **Bred** Miss K Rausing **Trained** Middleham Moor, N Yorks

NOTEBOOK
Lady Jane Digby, a multiple Listed winning in Britain, had gained her previous Group victory at Bremen last summer. She caused a bit of a surprise on this step up to the highest class, but it was thoroughly deserved, and she will be off to North America now, with the Arlington Million next followed by the E P Taylor Stakes.
Alexandros was sent off favourite on this slight step up in trip, but could only produce the one speed late on and might have been unsuited by the soft ground, although he has handled it in a lower grade in the past.

4165 MAISONS-LAFFITTE (R-H)
Sunday, July 25

OFFICIAL GOING: Turf: good to soft

4419a PRIX ROBERT PAPIN (GROUP 2) (2YO COLTS & FILLIES) (TURF) 5f 110y
1:35 (12:00) 2-Y-0 **£65,575** (£25,309; £12,079; £8,053; £4,026)

RPR

1 **Irish Field (IRE)**[21] [3718] 2-9-2 0.. ChristopheSoumillon 3 113+
(M Delcher-Sanchez, Spain) *trckd ldr in centre of trck: rdn at 1/2-way: qcknd wl: grabbed ld 2f out: r.o wl: wnt clr: styd on wl: comf* **9/2**[3]

2 1 ½ **Broox (IRE)**[33] 2-9-2 0.. OlivierPeslier 5 108
(E J O'Neill, France) *smartly away to ld in centre of trck: stl led at 1/2-way: chal and hdd 2f out: styd on wl: jst hld 2nd* **4/1**[2]

3 shd **Approve (IRE)**[17] [3823] 2-9-2 0.. RichardHughes 4 108
(W J Haggas) *broke wl: swtchd to stands' side: racd in 3rd: r.o wl fr 1 1/2f out: jst missed 2nd* **4/1**[2]

4 nk **Wizz Kid (IRE)**[24] [3609] 2-8-13 0.. GregoryBenoist 2 104
(Robert Collet, France) *in rr fr s in centre of trck: rdn 2f out: r.o wl wout threatening ldrs in fnl f* **3/1**[1]

5 1 ½ **Tin Horse (IRE)**[53] 2-9-2 0.. ThierryJarnet 6 102
(D Guillemin, France) *broke wl on outside: racd bhd ldrs: rdn 2f out: no ex fnl 1 1/2f* **4/1**[2]

6 shd **Split Trois (FR)**[33] [3307] 2-8-13 0.. StephanePasquier 1 99
(Y De Nicolay, France) *in rr fr s towards stands' rail: rdn 2f out: styd on u.p* **7/1**

65.90 secs (-1.40) **Going Correction** -0.075s/f (Good) **6** Ran SP% **115.7**
Speed ratings: **106,104,103,103,101 101**
WIN (incl. 1 euro stake): 7.40. PLACES: 3.00, 2.10. SF: 21.80.
Owner Sunday Horses Club S.L. **Bred** Denis McDonnell **Trained** Spain

NOTEBOOK
Irish Field(IRE), twice a winner in his home country, had narrowly missed out in the Prix du Bois last time. He improved on that to win this comfortably but will not be returning for the Prix Morny as he has been sold to race in Hong Kong.
Broox(IRE), a dual winner at Chantilly, made the running and did not drop away once the winner went by and just held on for second. He might take his chance in the Prix Morny.
Approve(IRE), the Norfolk Stakes winner, had failed to fire last time but ran better on this occasion, finishing well. He will now be aimed at the Gimcrack over slightly further.

4420a PRIX EUGENE ADAM (GRAND PRIX DE MAISONS-LAFFITTE) (GROUP 2) (3YO) (TURF) 1m 2f (S)
2:40 (12:00) 3-Y-0 **£201,769** (£77,876; £37,168; £24,778; £12,389)

RPR

1 **Shimraan (FR)**[63] 3-9-2 0.. GeraldMosse 2 117
(A De Royer-Dupre, France) *racd in rr tl 2f out whn mde swift prog on stands' side: qcknd to ld 1f out: r.o strly* **9/2**[3]

2 nk **Shamalgan (FR)**[49] [2802] 3-9-2 0.. IoritzMendizabal 7 116
(A Savujev, Czech Republic) *racd in rr fr s: qcknd wl 2f out on wd outside: r.o wl fnl f* **20/1**

3 3 **Hollywood Kiss (GER)**[56] 3-9-2 0.. MaximeGuyon 9 110
(A Wohler, Germany) *racd towards rr: tk clsr order 2f out: qcknd wl 1 1/2f out: r.o wl* **22/1**

4 nk **Xtension (IRE)**[21] [3719] 3-9-2 0.. ChristopheSoumillon 3 109
(C G Cox) *racd bhd ldrs fr s: qcknd wl 2f out: styd on wl: lost 3rd cl home* **4/1**[2]

5 ½ **Black Spirit (USA)**[22] [3692] 3-9-2 0.. LukeMorris 4 108
(C G Cox) *cl up bhd ldrs fr s: ev ch 2f out: failed to qckn: styd on* **16/1**

6 shd **Lumineux**[25] [3575] 3-9-2 0.. OlivierPeslier 6 108
(A Fabre, France) *one of the early ldrs: in front 2f out: rdn and failed to qckn fnl f: fdd* **3/1**[1]

7 hd **Emerald Commander (IRE)**[22] [3703] 3-9-2 0.. MickaelBarzalona 10 108
(Saeed Bin Suroor) *one of the early ldrs: settled jst off pce: failed to qckn 2f out: styd on one pce* **11/2**

8 1 ½ **Quadrille**[38] [3104] 3-9-2 0.. RichardHughes 1 105
(R Hannon) *racd promly fr s: rdn 2f out: no ex: fdd* **6/1**

9 ¾ **Azmeel**[50] [2746] 3-9-2 0.. WilliamBuick 8 103
(J H M Gosden) *racd promly fr s: failed to qckn 2f out: no ex fr 1 1/2f out: fdd* **7/1**

10 15 **Badguy (IRE)**[28] 3-9-2 0.. FabienLefebvre 5 73
(O Valachovic, Slovakia) *racd bhd ldrs: wknd whn pce qcknd 2f out* **100/1**

2m 6.20s (3.80) **10** Ran SP% **121.3**
WIN (incl. 1 euro stake): 4.70. PLACES: 1.90, 4.90, 4.30. DF: 58.10. SF: 69.70.
Owner H H Aga Khan **Bred** H H Aga Khan **Trained** Chantilly, France

NOTEBOOK
Shimraan(FR), dropping back in trip, found a change of gear up the rail to score more cosily than the official distance indicates. He will be aimed at the Arc but the Champion Stakes is also under consideration.
Shamalgan(FR), who finished third in the Poulains, ran another fine race over this longer trip after being well beaten in the Prix du Jockey-Club. The better ground may have helped and he will nopw be aimed at the Prix du Moulin.
Hollywood Kiss(GER), a Listed winner in Germany, looks on the upgrade as he finished well to take third.
Xtension(IRE), stepping up in trip, ran reasonably well but this distance might not be his optimum. He is likely to return to a mile for his next start.
Black Spirit(USA), the surprise winner of a valuable handicap last time, came here instead of going to Goodwood. He ran a creditable race and handicaps are likely to be out of the question now.
Emerald Commander(IRE), who has been campaigned exclusively in France since joining Godolphin, failed to build on his Prix Daphnis success without an obvious excuse.
Quadrille, touched off in the Hampton Court Stakes at Royal Ascot last time, proved less effective on this softer surface.
Azmeel dropped away in the closing stages and connections reported that he hated the ground.

[4201] WINDSOR (R-H)

Monday, July 26

OFFICIAL GOING: Good to firm

Stands' rail dolled out 12yds at 6f and 7yds at winning post. Top bend dolled out 9yds from innermost line adding 27yds to races of one mile or over.

Wind: Light, across Weather: Overcast, heavy shower race 2

4421 E B F FRANCESSCA TIZZARD 21ST BIRTHDAY TODAY MAIDEN STKS — 6f

6:10 (6:12) (Class 4) 2-Y-O — **£4,209** (£1,252; £625; £312) **Stalls** High

Form				RPR
6	**1**		**Majestic Dream (IRE)**[21] 3735 2-9-3 0 ... AdamKirby 3 (W R Swinburn) *dwlt: settled in last trio: pushed along bef 1/2-way: prog on outer over 2f out: edgd rt but led 1f out: rdn out* **2/1**[2]	74
0	**2**	*1 ½*	**Putin (IRE)**[21] 3735 2-9-3 0 ... AndreaAtzeni 7 (D Haydn Jones) *mde most: edgd lft and hdd 1f out: nt qckn* **50/1**	70
	3	*½*	**City Legend** 2-9-3 0 ...(v[1]) JamesDoyle 9 (A J McCabe) *reminders gng to post: pressed ldr and racd against rail: upsides over 1f out: one pce* **33/1**	68
05	**4**	*2 ¾*	**Empress Charlotte**[16] 3906 2-8-12 0 ... MickyFenton 8 (M L W Bell) *trckd ldrs: lost pl 1/2-way: stl in tch wl over 1f out: nudged along and lft bhd after: do bttr* **12/1**	57+
	5	*¾*	**Tijori (IRE)** 2-9-3 0 ... RichardHughes 4 (R Hannon) *pressed ldrs: shkn up over 2f out: nt qckn and hld over 1f out: edgd lft fnl f* **11/8**[1]	58
	6	*nse*	**Brandy Alexander** 2-9-3 0 ... PatDobbs 2 (R Hannon) *towards rr on outer: shkn up over 2f out: no prog over 1f out: plugged on* **15/2**[3]	58
	7	*3*	**Luv U Too** 2-8-12 0 ... SimonWhitworth 5 (F J Brennan) *mostly last: taken wd and effrt 2f out: nvr on terms* **66/1**	44
0	**8**	*1*	**Watered Silk**[81] 1845 2-9-3 0 ... MartinDwyer 1 (M P Tregoning) *prog on outer to join ldrs after 2f: shkn up over 2f out: wknd over 1f out* **9/1**	46
	9	*1 ¾*	**Silver Angel (IRE)** 2-8-12 0 ... ChrisCatlin 6 (M R Channon) *trckd ldrs against rail: cl enough over 1f out: wknd rapidly* **20/1**	35

1m 13.68s (0.68) **Going Correction** -0.15s/f (Firm) **9 Ran SP% 116.1**

Speed ratings (Par 96): **89,87,86,82,81 81,77,76,73**

toteswingers: 1&2 £7.70, 1&3 £13.70, 2&3 £11.90. CSF £105.78 TOTE £3.70: £1.60, £3.10, £9.20; EX 72.90 Trifecta £1258.20 Pool: £4,420.76 - 2.60 winning units..

Owner Mark Goodall **Bred** Thomas Hassett **Trained** Aldbury, Herts

FOCUS

The stands rail was dolled out 12yds at 6f, and the top bed was moved out 9yds from the inner most line. The rail movements added 27yds to race distances of 1m+. The going was good to firm on a watered track. A pretty weak maiden for the track and the pace was not particularly strong.

NOTEBOOK

Majestic Dream(IRE) made late headway when 33-1 sixth of 15 in a C&D maiden on debut this month. He was again a bit slowly away, but found a sustained run to get off the mark in decent style. The 25,000gns colt is closely related to a 7f winner and out of a sister to high-class multiple 7f-1m2f winner Handsome Ridge. He did not run particularly straight here and still has a bit to learn, but looks a fair type open to further improvement. (op 3-1 tchd 15-8 and 7-2 in places)

Putin(IRE) did not show much at 80-1 on debut, but he gave it a decent try, ridden more positively this time. His dam's first three foals have all been winners for the same yard, and he should be able to continue that trend. (op 66-1)

City Legend showed some natural speed and ability with a visor applied on this debut. He is bred to make a sprinting 2-y-o and should improve for the experience.

Empress Charlotte, fifth in a fair 6f Nottingham maiden last time, took a while to pick up before staying on steadily. She is going the right way and should appreciate a slightly stiffer test. (op 9-1 tchd 14-1)

Tijori(IRE) was strongly supported in the morning, but was a drifter on course and was never quite travelling well enough to pose a big threat on this debut. Official explanation: jockey said colt ran green (op Evens tchd 13-8)

Brandy Alexander, looked the Richard Hannon second-string on jockey bookings and ran green before doing some late work down the middle of the track. (op 11-1)

4422 SEVENTH-HEAVEN-EVENTS.CO.UK H'CAP — 1m 2f 7y

6:40 (6:40) (Class 5) (0-75,75) 3-Y-O+ — **£2,729** (£806; £403) **Stalls** Low

Form				RPR
5302	**1**		**Choral Festival**[7] 4201 4-9-2 **58** ...(v) NeilChalmers 1 (J J Bridger) *hld up in 7th: smooth prog fr 3f out: led jst over 1f out and looked likely to score comf: idled fnl f: jst hld on* **8/1**	66
3001	**2**	*shd*	**If I Were A Boy (IRE)**[11] 4056 3-9-9 **75** ... JamesDoyle 3 (D J S Ffrench Davis) *mde most: rdn and hdd over 1f out: rallied fnl f: jst failed* **7/2**[1]	83
0523	**3**	*¾*	**Beauchamp Xiara**[18] 3821 4-9-6 **69** ... AmyScott[(7)] 7 (H Candy) *stdd s: hld up last: stl there over 2f out: prog on outer after: wnt 3rd fnl f: styd on but unable to chal* **6/1**[3]	75
4036	**4**	*3 ¾*	**Singbella**[44] 2961 4-8-12 **59** ...(p) JohnFahy[(5)] 6 (C G Cox) *trckd ldng pair: cl enough and gng strly 3f out: shkn up and nt qckn 2f out: fdd* **9/2**[2]	58
0003	**5**	*6*	**Smart Endeavour (USA)**[21] 3725 4-10-0 **70** ... AdamKirby 4 (W R Swinburn) *chsd ldr: urged along 1/2-way: drvn 3f out: lost 2nd wl over 1f out: wknd fnl f* **7/1**	57
313	**6**	*1 ½*	**Welsh Anthem**[19] 3789 4-9-13 **69** ...(p) MartinDwyer 5 (W R Muir) *chsd ldng trio: pushed along over 3f out: lost pl 2f out: sn wknd* **7/2**[1]	53
-563	**7**	*½*	**Mountrath**[59] 2510 3-9-2 **73** ... DaleSwift[(5)] 8 (B R Johnson) *t.k.h: hld up in 5th: rdn and no prog 3f out: wl btn over 1f out* **9/1**	56
0-06	**8**	*13*	**Kinian (USA)**[76] 2003 3-8-5 **62** ... KierenFox[(5)] 2 (J R Best) *settled in 6th: pushed along 4f out: wknd over 2f out: t.o* **40/1**	19

2m 8.88s (0.18) **Going Correction** +0.10s/f (Good)

WFA 3 from 4yo 10lb **8 Ran SP% 113.0**

Speed ratings (Par 103): **103,102,102,99,94 93,92,82**

toteswingers: 1&2 £3.40, 1&3 £14.40, 2&3 £1.10. CSF £35.24 CT £180.08 TOTE £12.40: £4.30, £1.30, £1.10; EX 36.70 Trifecta £255.70 Pool: £2,858.47 - 8.27 winning units..

Owner Mrs Liz Gardner **Bred** Cheveley Park Stud Ltd **Trained** Liphook, Hants

FOCUS

A tight-looking handicap, involving a last-time-out winner and five others who were placed on their previous run. The pace was not very strong, but the first three pulled clear of the rest, and the form is rated around the winner and third.

Welsh Anthem Official explanation: trainer said filly lost an off-fore shoe

4423 SPORTINGBET.COM MAIDEN AUCTION STKS — 5f 10y

7:10 (7:10) (Class 4) 2-Y-O — **£3,561** (£1,059; £529; £264) **Stalls** High

Form				RPR
246	**1**		**Millyluvstobougie**[34] 3295 2-8-4 67 ... LukeMorris 5 (C G Cox) *chsd ldr: rdn 2f out: drvn to chal fnl f: led last 100yds: hld on* **11/8**[1]	66
0	**2**	*nk*	**Barking (IRE)**[92] 1541 2-8-13 0 ... RichardHughes 6 (R Hannon) *cl up: looking for gap against rail over 1f out: rdn to chal fnl f: edgd lft and tail whirling: jst hld* **2/1**[2]	74
6	**3**	*1 ½*	**Veeb (IRE)**[76] 1999 2-8-8 0 ... ChrisCatlin 4 (M R Channon) *led: rdn and pressed 1f out: hdd & wknd last 100yds* **3/1**[3]	64
0	**4**	*3 ½*	**King Cobra (IRE)**[14] 3964 2-8-9 0 ... SimonWhitworth 3 (J W Hills) *sn detached in last: pushed along to take 4th wl over 1f out: no imp* **11/1**	52
004	**5**	*19*	**Fairy Tales**[30] 3439 2-8-4 43 ... NeilChalmers 2 (J J Bridger) *chsd ldr to over 2f out: wknd rapidly wl over 1f out: t.o* **33/1**	—

60.30 secs **Going Correction** -0.15s/f (Firm) **5 Ran SP% 111.7**

Speed ratings (Par 96): **94,93,91,85,55**

toteswinger: 1&2 £1.40. CSF £4.52 TOTE £3.10: £1.40, £1.40; EX 6.40.

Owner Ken Lock Racing **Bred** Ken Lock Racing **Trained** Lambourn, Berks

FOCUS

A modest maiden auction. The pace was decent and there was a tight three-way battle between the market leaders in the final furlong. The winner sets the level.

NOTEBOOK

Millyluvstobougie set a clear standard on her near-miss in a good-ground fillies' maiden over C&D on debut, but had run well below that form in both runs since. There were a few questions to answer, but the return to 5f was a potential positive and she put in a brave display to justify favouritism and get back on track. There is a slight doubt whether she will build on this next time given her profile, but an opening mark of 67 looks realistic for nurseries. (op 13-8 tchd 15-8)

Barking(IRE) flopped when favourite for a Bath maiden in April. He had a bit to prove conceding weight all round on return from three-months off, but bounced back with a dynamic staying-on effort against the stands' rail. He has plenty of winning speedsters on the dam's side of his pedigree and should be able to win races. (op 7-4 tchd 9-4 in a place)

Veeb(IRE) gave it a good shot under a forcing ride and has improved on her debut sixth at Warwick in May. She is a half-sister to 5f/6f winners in France by Hawk Wing and should have more to offer as a sprinting 2-y-o. (op 7-2 tchd 5-2)

King Cobra(IRE) found things happening too quickly early on, but did some encouraging late work on his second start. He is a half-brother to quite useful 5.5f/7f 2yo winners and should continue to do better with time and distance. (op 12-1)

Fairy Tales has an official rating of just 43 and was left well behind. (op 28-1)

4424 SPORTINGBET.COM FILLIES' H'CAP — 6f

7:40 (7:40) (Class 4) (0-80,80) 3-Y-O+ — **£4,533** (£1,348; £674; £336) **Stalls** High

Form				RPR
001	**1**		**Caledonia Princess**[14] 3958 4-9-0 **66** ... RossAtkinson[(5)] 3 (F J Brennan) *sweating: t.k.h: trckd ldrs: smooth prog to go 2nd jst over 2f out: rdn to ld 1f out: styd on wl* **12/1**	81
103	**2**	*1 ½*	**Bougainvilia (IRE)**[9] 4148 3-10-0 **80** ... RichardHughes 7 (R Hannon) *led against rail: drvn 2f out: hdd and outpcd 1f out: styd on* **7/4**[1]	90
0562	**3**	*2 ¾*	**Key Light (IRE)**[14] 3958 3-9-3 **74** ... KierenFox[(5)] 5 (J W Hills) *hld up in 7th: prog on outer over 2f out: drvn wl over 1f out: kpt on same pce* **4/1**[2]	75
-006	**4**	*2 ¼*	**Sweet Gale (IRE)**[16] 3914 6-9-1 **62** ... AndreaAtzeni 4 (Mike Murphy) *settled in 6th: rdn and prog 2f out: chsd ldrs 1f out: fdd* **6/1**[3]	57
2U32	**5**	*hd*	**Requisite**[6] 4225 5-9-9 **75** ...(v) JohnFahy[(5)] 9 (I A Wood) *blindfold off late and dwlt: hld up in last pair: taken to wd outside and smooth prog over 2f out: rdn and fnd nil over 1f out* **4/1**[2]	69
6202	**6**	*3*	**Farmers Wish (IRE)**[24] 3638 3-9-4 **73** ... JackDean[(3)] 8 (J L Spearing) *t.k.h: trckd ldr to jst over 2f out: wknd quite qckly* **12/1**	56
2054	**7**	*nse*	**Freddie's Girl (USA)**[12] 4031 3-9-7 **73** ... AdamKirby 6 (Stef Higgins) *trckd ldng trio: lost pl and shkn up 2f out: sn wknd* **16/1**	56
0420	**8**	*10*	**Lucky Leigh**[46] 2904 4-9-6 **67** ... ChrisCatlin 2 (M R Channon) *t.k.h: hld up in last pair: shuffled along 2f out: sn wknd* **20/1**	19
6525	**9**	*22*	**Yurituni**[18] 3834 3-9-8 **74** ... MartinDwyer 1 (Eve Johnson Houghton) *chsd ldr to jst over 2f out: wknd rapidly: eased and t.o* **20/1**	—

1m 11.79s (-1.21) **Going Correction** -0.15s/f (Firm)

WFA 3 from 4yo+ 5lb **9 Ran SP% 121.4**

Speed ratings (Par 102): **102,100,96,93,93 89,89,75,46**

toteswingers: 1&2 £3.70, 1&3 £7.10, 2&3 £1.30. CSF £35.20 CT £104.50 TOTE £19.30: £4.50, £2.00, £1.10; EX 48.30 Trifecta £105.70 Pool: £663.37 - 4.64 winning units..

Owner Isla & Colin Cage **Bred** Mrs I M Cage And C J Cage **Trained** Lambourn, Berks

FOCUS

It had become gloomy and was raining before this competitive sprint handicap. They finished quite well strung out and the form could work out. The winner is rated better than ever.

Requisite Official explanation: jockey said mare was slowly away

Freddie's Girl(USA) Official explanation: jockey said filly's stride shortened closing stages

Yurituni Official explanation: jockey said filly stopped quickly

4425 PIERS BRADFORD HI DUDE MAIDEN STKS — 1m 67y

8:10 (8:13) (Class 5) 3-4-Y-O — **£2,593** (£765; £383) **Stalls** High

Form				RPR
4-	**1**		**Julienas (IRE)**[278] 6943 3-9-3 0 ... AdamKirby 9 (W R Swinburn) *trckd ldng trio: prog to ld over 2f out: rdn clr over 1f out: readily* **2/1**[1]	83+
035-	**2**	*3*	**Sasheen**[222] 7763 3-8-12 70 ... StephenCraine 7 (J R Boyle) *led 2f: trckd ldr: led 3f out to over 2f out: styd on but no match for wnr* **12/1**[3]	71
	3	*4 ½*	**Bianca De Medici** 3-8-12 0 ... SteveDrowne 2 (H Morrison) *dwlt: hld up in 10th: taken v wd and prog fr 3f out: kpt on to take 3rd ins fnl f* **16/1**	61+
0-53	**4**	*1 ¼*	**Pebblesonthebeach**[12] 4022 3-9-3 69 ... RichardHughes 6 (J W Hills) *dwlt: hld up in 11th: plenty to do whn prog over 2f out: sn rdn: chsd clr ldng pair over 1f out: pushed along and lost 3rd ins fnl f* **2/1**[1]	63
054-	**5**	*1*	**Seaside Sizzler**[299] 6393 3-9-3 75 ... RichardKingscote 10 (R M Beckett) *hld up in 9th: pushed along over 3f out: no real prog tl styd on quite wl fr over 1f out: nrst fin* **7/2**[2]	65+
0	**6**	*1 ¾*	**Hotfoot**[21] 3738 3-8-12 0 ... IvaMilickova 12 (John Berry) *chsd ldrs in 6th: rdn over 3f out: outpcd wl over 2f out* **66/1**	51

7 shd **Boom And Bust (IRE)** 3-9-3 0 .... PatDobbs 3 56
(M P Tregoning) *dwlt: hld up in last pair: sme prog over 2f out: rdn over 1f out: kpt on: n.d* **14/1**

00 8 ½ **Mandate**[30] 3443 3-9-3 0 .... KirstyMilczarek 8 55
(J A R Toller) *hld up in 8th: rn wd bnd over 5f out: rdn 3f out: sn outpcd* **33/1**

-00 9 ½ **Trecase**[44] 2974 3-9-3 0 .... AndreaAtzeni 11 54
(A W Carroll) *chsd ldrs in 7th: rdn over 3f out: outpcd wl over 2f out* **40/1**

0-0 10 1¼ **Satwa Excel**[25] 3586 3-8-12 0 .... TomMcLaughlin 4 46
(E A L Dunlop) *plld hrd: chsd ldng pair to over 3f out: sn wknd* **14/1**

00 11 3¼ **Jovial (IRE)**[24] 3635 3-9-3 0 .... CathyGannon 13 44
(D J Coakley) *dwlt: hld up in last pair: brief effrt on outer over 2f out: sn no prog* **28/1**

6 12 17 **Trendy Way (IRE)**[29] 3484 3-8-12 0 .... LiamKeniry 1 —
(P R Chamings) *led after 2f to 3f out: wknd rapidly: t.o* **33/1**

13 18 **Silverini**[27] 4-9-6 0 .... (t) SamHitchcott 5 —
(M F Harris) *chsd ldrs to over 3f out: wknd rapidly: wl t.o* **100/1**

1m 45.28s (0.58) **Going Correction** +0.10s/f (Good)
WFA 3 from 4yo 8lb **13** Ran SP% **130.0**
Speed ratings (Par 103): **101,98,93,92,91 89,89,88,88,87 83,66,48**
toteswingers: 1&2 £10.00, 1&3 £14.20, 2&3 £49.00. CSF £32.10 TOTE £3.20: £1.30, £4.50, £5.50; EX 47.10 TRIFECTA Not won..
Owner P W Harris **Bred** Pendley Farm **Trained** Aldbury, Herts

FOCUS
An ordinary maiden but they finished well strung out and it was won in striking style by a strong form contender who could go on to better things. The race is rated around the runner-up to juvenile form and looks sound enough initially.
Bianca De Medici Official explanation: jockey said filly ran green
Pebblesonthebeach Official explanation: jockey said gelding was slowly away
Seaside Sizzler Official explanation: jockey said gelding was slowly away and denied a clear run
Mandate Official explanation: jockey said gelding slipped on bend
Trendy Way(IRE) Official explanation: jockey said filly ran too free

4426 MACDONALD WINDSOR HOTEL AND CALEYS LOUNGE H'CAP 1m 3f 135y
8:40 (8:41) (Class 5) (0-70,72) 3-Y-O+ **£2,593** (£765; £383) **Stalls** Low

Form RPR

-125 1 **On Khee**[48] 2843 3-8-13 **66** .... SteveDrowne 10 82+
(H Morrison) *trckd ldng trio: prog to ld 3f out: pushed clr and in n.d fr 2f out: eased nr fin* **9/4**[1]

-231 2 4 **Urban Space**[7] 4201 4-9-12 **72** 6ex .... KierenFox(5) 3 79
(J L Flint) *hld up in last pair: prog over 4f out: rdn to chse wnr wl over 2f out: sn no imp and btn: kpt on* **11/4**[2]

3023 3 2¾ **Maslak (IRE)**[17] 3860 6-9-13 **68** .... ChrisCatlin 8 70
(P W Hiatt) *trckd ldng pair: outpcd 3f out: drvn to take modest 3rd again over 1f out: no imp* **6/1**

6-00 4 ½ **Weliketobouggie**[30] 3444 3-7-13 **52** .... CathyGannon 9 53
(A M Hales) *chsd ldrs in 5th: wl outpcd fr 3f out: plugged on to press for 3rd nr fin* **40/1**

26-0 5 3¼ **Into The Light**[189] 220 5-9-11 **66** .... GrahamGibbons 1 62
(E S McMahon) *led 1f: trckd ldr: upsides 3f out: wknd fnl 2f* **16/1**

40 6 3¾ **Shooting Party (IRE)**[7] 4201 4-9-3 **65** .... CharlesEddery(7) 5 55
(R Hannon) *hld up in midfield: dropped to rr 6f out: last over 3f out: sme late prog: nvr a factor* **14/1**

2500 7 2¾ **Act Three**[20] 3760 6-8-10 **51** oh2 .... (t) AndreaAtzeni 7 36
(Mouse Hamilton-Fairley) *rdn to ld after 1f: hdd & wknd 3f out* **40/1**

0010 8 7 **Beaubrav**[17] 3862 4-9-9 **64** .... (t) LiamKeniry 2 37
(M Madgwick) *t.k.h: hld up in last pair: rdn 4f out: lft bhd fr 3f out* **8/1**

0104 9 10 **Cereal Killer (IRE)**[21] 3739 3-9-1 **68** .... RichardHughes 4 24
(R Hannon) *settled midfield: pushed along 1/2-way: struggling u.p 3f out: wknd and eased* **5/1**[3]

2m 29.67s (0.17) **Going Correction** +0.10s/f (Good)
WFA 3 from 4yo+ 12lb **9** Ran SP% **116.9**
Speed ratings (Par 103): **103,100,98,98,96 93,91,87,80**
toteswingers: 1&2 £2.30, 1&3 £2.30, 2&3 £1.30. CSF £8.65 CT £31.09 TOTE £3.20: £1.10, £1.70, £1.70; EX 11.20 Trifecta £17.50 Pool: £593.81 - 25.01 winning units. Place 6: £30.19, Place 5: £7.50..
Owner Mr & Mrs R Sweet & G Balding **Bred** Miss B Swire **Trained** East Ilsley, Berks

FOCUS
A minor handicap but the winner hammered her rivals and looks one to follow. The form looks solid enough.
Act Three Official explanation: jockey said mare had no more to give
T/Plt: £29.60 to a £1 stake. Pool:£75,714.71 - 1,863.44 winning tickets. T/Qpdt: £3.40 to a £1 stake. Pool:£7,151.46 - 1,542.50 winning tickets. JN

3964 WOLVERHAMPTON (A.W) (L-H)
Monday, July 26
OFFICIAL GOING: Standard changing to standard to fast after race 4 (4.00).
Wind: Light across Weather: Overcast with the odd spot of rain

4427 BET GALWAY FESTIVAL - BETDAQ H'CAP (DIV I) 7f 32y(P)
2:30 (2:30) (Class 6) (0-65,65) 3-Y-O+ **£1,364** (£403; £201) **Stalls** High

Form RPR

313 1 **Whispering Spirit (IRE)**[28] 3520 4-9-10 **64** .... (v) BarryMcHugh(3) 5 76
(Mrs A Duffield) *mid-div: hdwy over 2f out: rdn over 1f out: hung lft and styd on u.p to ld wl ins fnl f* **9/2**[3]

-000 2 ½ **First Blade**[52] 2698 4-9-11 **62** .... (b) GrahamGibbons 8 73
(S R Bowring) *chsd ldrs: rdn over 2f out: led over 1f out: hdd wl ins fnl f* **40/1**

2512 3 3 **The City Kid (IRE)**[28] 3521 7-9-11 **62** .... SaleemGolam 1 65+
(G D Blake) *prom: hmpd and lost pl over 6f out: rdn over 2f out: hdwy over 1f out: styd on ins fnl f: nt rch ldrs* **3/1**[1]

232 4 2 **Towy Boy (IRE)**[20] 3762 5-8-9 **51** .... (bt) JohnFahy(5) 7 49
(I A Wood) *pushed along early to go prom: racd keenly and led over 5f out: rdn and hdd over 1f out: wknd ins fnl f* **4/1**[2]

1-50 5 2 **Eliza Doolittle**[6] 4232 4-9-8 **59** .... J-PGuillambert 10 51
(N P Littmoden) *prom: sn pushed along: rdn over 2f out: wknd fnl f* **11/1**

0-00 6 shd **Lilly Blue (IRE)**[44] 2955 4-8-13 **50** .... (p) PatCosgrave 4 42
(R Brotherton) *s.i.s: sn pushed along in rr: styd on fr over 1f out: nvr nrr* **16/1**

03U 7 1½ **Landucci**[28] 3518 9-9-7 **65** .... (p) AnthonyFreeman(7) 9 53
(S Curran) *prom: rdn over 2f out: wknd over 1f out* **20/1**

-130 8 ¾ **Ambrogina**[20] 3761 3-9-1 **64** .... TobyAtkinson(5) 2 47
(M Botti) *hld up: nvr on terms* **18/1**

6040 9 shd **Majestatic**[12] 4022 3-9-5 **63** .... (t) SamHitchcott 3 45
(S W James) *sn pushed along and a in rr* **14/1**

4041 10 5 **Bob Stock (IRE)**[19] 3783 4-9-9 **60** .... TonyCulhane 11 32
(W J Musson) *hld up: rdn over 2f out: a in rr* **9/1**

0110 11 5 **Ride A White Swan**[85] 1719 5-9-10 **64** .... (p) GaryBartley(3) 12 22
(D Shaw) *s.s: a bhd* **12/1**

000/ 12 49 **Doctor's Cave**[752] 3691 8-9-7 **58** .... (b) FergusSweeney 6 —
(K O Cunningham-Brown) *led: hdd over 5f out: rdn and wknd over 2f out: t.o* **80/1**

1m 29.12s (-0.48) **Going Correction** -0.125s/f (Stan)
WFA 3 from 4yo+ 7lb **12** Ran SP% **115.5**
Speed ratings (Par 101): **97,96,93,90,88 88,86,85,85,79 74,18**
toteswingers: 1&2 £28.50, 1&3 £2.70, 2&3 £19.40. CSF £174.62 CT £631.90 TOTE £4.50: £1.40, £14.20, £1.20; EX 235.50.
Owner Middleham Park Racing XLII **Bred** David Barry **Trained** Constable Burton, N Yorks

FOCUS
A modest handicap run at a good gallop, although the time was 0.29 seconds slower than the second division. The form looks sound despite the presence of the outsider in second.

4428 BET GALWAY FESTIVAL - BETDAQ H'CAP (DIV II) 7f 32y(P)
3:00 (3:01) (Class 6) (0-65,64) 3-Y-O+ **£1,364** (£403; £201) **Stalls** High

Form RPR

0503 1 **Glenridding**[17] 3855 6-10-0 **64** .... (p) PaulMulrennan 8 77+
(J G Given) *mde all: clr 3f out: rdn and edgd rt fr over 1f out: styd on* **7/2**[1]

6001 2 2¾ **Provost**[28] 3521 6-9-10 **60** .... (b) GrahamGibbons 1 66
(M W Easterby) *dwlt: sn pushed along in rr: hdwy over 1f out: r.o: nt rch wnr* **7/1**[3]

5-42 3 ½ **Cottonfields (USA)**[14] 3968 4-9-11 **61** .... (p) EddieAhern 3 65
(Mrs H S Main) *prom: outpcd over 2f out: rallied over 1f out: r.o* **9/2**[2]

5505 4 2 **Lucas Pitt**[20] 3762 3-8-13 **56** .... PatCosgrave 6 52
(M J Scudamore) *s.i.s: hld up: nt clr run over 1f out: r.o ins fnl f: nrst fin* **12/1**

6016 5 ½ **Bold Diva**[20] 3768 5-9-3 **58** .... (v) BillyCray(5) 2 55
(A W Carroll) *s.i.s: hld up: hdwy and nt clr run over 1f out: nt trble ldrs* **9/1**

4260 6 nk **Dancing Welcome**[3] 4324 4-9-7 **57** .... (b) PaulHanagan 5 54
(J M Bradley) *mid-div: rdn over 2f out: nvr trble ldrs* **14/1**

6213 7 2½ **Chjimes (IRE)**[28] 3516 6-10-0 **64** .... LiamKeniry 9 54
(C R Dore) *prom: rdn over 2f out: wknd over 1f out* **14/1**

5146 8 ½ **Crocodile Bay (IRE)**[7] 4189 7-9-12 **62** .... PaulEddery 12 55+
(R C Guest) *prom: rdn over 2f out: wkng whn nt clr run over 1f out* **20/1**

3400 9 1 **Trade Centre**[20] 3765 5-9-12 **62** .... (b) LukeMorris 4 48
(R A Harris) *prom: chsd wnr 1/2-way: rdn over 2f out: wknd fnl f* **8/1**

/063 10 7 **Ganache (IRE)**[44] 2965 8-9-0 **50** .... JimCrowley 10 17
(P R Chamings) *chsd ldr to 1/2-way: rdn and wknd over 1f out* **12/1**

0642 11 3½ **Guildenstern (IRE)**[20] 3768 8-9-5 **55** .... J-PGuillambert 7 13
(P Howling) *hld up: a in rr: eased whn btn fnl f* **12/1**

1m 28.83s (-0.77) **Going Correction** -0.125s/f (Stan)
WFA 3 from 4yo+ 7lb **11** Ran SP% **115.2**
Speed ratings (Par 101): **99,95,95,93,92 92,89,88,87,79 75**
toteswingers: 1&2 £5.30, 1&3 £3.50, 2&3 £4.20. CSF £27.14 CT £113.32 TOTE £3.30: £1.10, £3.30, £1.10; EX 28.90.
Owner Tremousser Partnership **Bred** Bolton Grange **Trained** Willoughton, Lincs

FOCUS
The time was 0.29 seconds quicker than the first division, and the form looks sound rated through the winner to this year's turf best.
Dancing Welcome Official explanation: vet said filly had been struck into
Guildenstern(IRE) Official explanation: jockey said gelding never travelled; vet said gelding was sore behind

4429 JLT PERSONAL INSURANCE PROVIDERS NURSERY 7f 32y(P)
3:30 (3:32) (Class 5) 2-Y-O **£2,388** (£705; £352) **Stalls** High

Form RPR

000 1 **Water Ice**[34] 3295 2-8-6 **68** .... RichardKingscote 8 76+
(Tom Dascombe) *chsd ldr tl led wl over 1f out: rdn clr fnl f: comf* **9/2**[3]

4604 2 3¼ **Prophet In A Dream**[12] 4020 2-8-3 **65** .... LukeMorris 12 63
(M R Channon) *hld up: hdwy over 1f out: rdn and hung lft ins fnl f: no imp* **13/2**

010 3 ½ **Liberty Cap (USA)**[17] 3872 2-9-7 **83** .... (p) WilliamBuick 5 80
(J H M Gosden) *hld up in tch: rdn over 1f out: hung lft ins fnl f: styd on same pce* **3/1**[2]

3115 4 5 **Bachelor Knight (IRE)**[16] 3925 2-8-9 **71** .... PaulHanagan 2 56
(R A Fahey) *s.i.s and hmpd s: hdwy into mid-div after 1f: pushed along 1/2-way: rdn over 2f out: wknd fnl f* **5/2**[1]

050 5 nse **Bathwick Freeze**[67] 2245 2-7-12 **60** oh3 .... SilvestreDeSousa 10 44
(P D Evans) *chsd ldrs: rdn 1/2-way: wknd over 1f out* **20/1**

0300 6 1¼ **He's The Star (IRE)**[45] 2939 2-7-12 **60** .... CathyGannon 1 41
(P D Evans) *chsd ldrs: rdn over 2f out: wknd fnl f* **10/1**

0046 7 3¼ **Bendigedig**[17] 3864 2-7-12 **60** oh3 .... JamieMackay 9 33
(S Kirk) *s.i.s: hld up: rdn over 2f out: n.d* **33/1**

0000 8 ¾ **Whats For Pudding (IRE)**[5] 4242 2-7-5 **60** oh7 .... (v[1]) NeilFarley(7) 3 32
(D Carroll) *s.i.s and edgd lft s: a in rr* **40/1**

3100 9 2½ **Yarooh (USA)**[12] 4020 2-8-13 **75** .... HirokiGoto 6 40
(C E Brittain) *led: hdd wl over 1f out: wknd fnl f* **12/1**

1m 29.35s (-0.25) **Going Correction** -0.125s/f (Stan) **9** Ran SP% **112.0**
Speed ratings (Par 94): **96,92,91,86,85 84,80,79,77**
toteswingers: 1&2 £5.00, 1&3 £4.20, 2&3 £4.70. CSF £31.78 CT £100.09 TOTE £6.70: £2.80, £3.00, £2.40; EX 31.10.
Owner De La Warr Racing **Bred** Darley **Trained** Malpas, Cheshire

FOCUS
An ordinary nursery but a decent effort from the winner.

NOTEBOOK
Water Ice, upped in trip and trying Polytrack for the first time on her nursery debut, showed improved form to win nicely. She looks capable of winning again in this sort of company. Official explanation: trainer said, regarding apparent improvement in form, that the filly may have benefited from the drop in class and the all-weather surface. (op 5-1 tchd 11-2)
Prophet In A Dream, dropped in from the widest stall, did well to get second as he was well off the pace around the final bend and had to make his move widest. (op 8-1)
Liberty Cap(USA), well held in a Class 2 nursery last time, found this easier but still wasn't good enough. He's not progressing. (tchd 7-2)
Bachelor Knight(IRE), stepped up in trip, was short of room at the start but that was no real excuse. He was a bit disappointing. (tchd 15-8 and 11-4)

The Form Book, Raceform Ltd, Compton, RG20 6NL

Bathwick Freeze, up 2f in trip on her handicap debut, looked well but was comfortably held from 3lb out of the weights. (op 16-1)

4430 ROOFTOP HOUSING GROUP CLAIMING STKS 5f 216y(P)
4:00 (4:01) (Class 6) 3-Y-O+ £1,706 (£503; £252) Stalls Low

Form RPR

0410 **1** **Hinton Admiral**[12] 4024 6-9-0 68 StevieDonohoe 10 77
(M S Tuck) *a.p: chsd ldr 1/2-way: led over 1f out: rdn out* **10/1**

2604 **2** *4* **Interchoice Star**[16] 3908 5-8-10 60 (p) JerryO'Dwyer 2 60
(R Hollinshead) *chsd ldrs: rdn over 2f out: swtchd rt over 1f out: styd on same pce: wnt 2nd nr fin* **16/1**

011 **3** *½* **Orpenindeed (IRE)**[11] 4053 7-9-9 87 AndrewHeffernan(3) 4 75
(Tim Vaughan) *chsd ldrs: rdn over 1f out: edgd lft and no ex ins fnl f: lost 2nd nr fin* **6/4**[1]

0212 **4** *1 ½* **Romantic Queen**[14] 3966 4-8-7 67 ow1 (t) TonyCulhane 8 51
(George Baker) *hld up: hdwy over 1f out: hung lft and r.o ins fnl f: nvr nrr* **4/1**[2]

1034 **5** *nk* **Faited To Pretend (IRE)**[46] 2904 3-8-7 70 TobyAtkinson(5) 9 59
(M Botti) *led 1f: chsd ldr to 1/2-way: rdn over 1f out: wknd ins fnl f* **14/1**

6000 **6** *nk* **Hellbender (IRE)**[19] 3779 4-9-4 69 LiamKeniry 5 60
(S Kirk) *hld up: hdwy over 2f out: rdn over 1f out: styd on same pce* **25/1**

2446 **7** *½* **Misaro (GER)**[4] 4298 9-9-2 74 (b) PaulHanagan 11 56
(R A Harris) *led 5f out: rdn and hdd over 1f out: hung lft and wknd ins fnl f* **7/1**[3]

6540 **8** *½* **Kinigi (IRE)**[20] 3763 4-8-3 49 (p) LukeMorris 3 42
(R A Harris) *s.i.s: hld up: hung lft over 1f out: nvr nrr* **28/1**

5110 **9** *¾* **Timeteam (IRE)**[16] 3914 4-9-0 77 CathyGannon 6 50
(P D Evans) *s.s: bhd tl styd on ins fnl f: nvr nrr* **18/1**

6406 **10** *½* **Equinity**[20] 3762 4-8-5 54 (t) SaleemGolam 7 40
(J Pearce) *hld up: hdwy over 2f out: rdn and wknd over 1f out* **40/1**

350 **11** *½* **Belle Park**[39] 3129 3-8-0 55 JamieMackay 13 37
(Karen George) *hld up: rdn over 2f out: nvr on terms* **40/1**

000- **12** *10* **Avon Rock**[277] 6962 3-8-11 54 GregFairley 1 16
(A J Lidderdale) *prom: lost pl over 4f out: n.d after* **100/1**

326- **13** *6* **Braddock (IRE)**[106] 1248 7-9-4 61 (b) FergusSweeney 12 —
(K O Cunningham-Brown) *mid-div: wknd over 2f out* **66/1**

1m 13.42s (-1.58) **Going Correction** -0.125s/f (Stan)
WFA 3 from 4yo+ 5lb 13 Ran SP% **114.1**
Speed ratings (Par 101): **105,99,99,97,96 96,95,94,93,93 92,79,71**
toteswingers: 1&2 £23.30, 1&3 £6.10, 2&3 £8.00. CSF £141.66 TOTE £17.90: £3.80, £5.20, £1.10; EX 207.70.Hinton Admiral was claimed by Paul Howling for £6,000.
Owner M Bell **Bred** Gainsborough Stud Management Ltd **Trained** Oldbury on the Hill, Gloucs

FOCUS
The going was changed from standard to standard to fast following this contest. This was a fair claimer and could be rated higher, but assessed through the winner to recent best for now.

4431 WILLMOTT DIXON HOUSING H'CAP 5f 216y(P)
4:30 (4:30) (Class 5) (0-75,72) 3-Y-O+ £2,388 (£705; £352) Stalls Low

Form RPR

3030 **1** **Dancing Maite**[17] 3876 5-9-12 72 GrahamGibbons 6 83+
(S R Bowring) *chsd ldrs: led 1f out: rdn and hung rt ins fnl f: r.o* **13/8**[1]

205 **2** *½* **Loyal Royal (IRE)**[21] 3727 7-8-11 57 (bt) PatCosgrave 7 66
(J M Bradley) *s.i.s: hld up: racd keenly: hdwy over 1f out: chsd wnr and carried rt ins fnl f: r.o: bmpd nr fin* **16/1**

1504 **3** *2 ¼* **Perlachy**[23] 3660 6-9-7 70 (v) KellyHarrison(3) 5 72
(D Shaw) *broke wl: sn steaded and lost pl: hdwy over 1f out: hung rt ins fnl f: styd on* **14/1**

1222 **4** *1 ¼* **Cavitie**[20] 3763 4-8-8 57 ow1 RussKennemore(3) 10 55
(Andrew Reid) *trckd ldrs: racd keenly: rdn over 1f out: styd on same pce* **8/1**

5312 **5** *1 ¼* **Ace Of Spies (IRE)**[10] 4084 5-9-10 70 LiamKeniry 1 64
(C R Dore) *s.i.s: sn prom: rdn over 1f out: wknd ins fnl f* **7/1**

4605 **6** *1 ½* **Welcome Approach**[13] 3976 7-9-0 60 PaulHanagan 9 49
(J R Weymes) *chsd ldrs: led over 4f out: hdd over 2f out: wknd ins fnl f* **6/1**[3]

4006 **7** *½* **What Katie Did (IRE)**[5] 4255 5-9-1 61 (p) RichardKingscote 8 48
(J M Bradley) *hld up in tch: racd keenly: rdn over 1f out: wkng whn hung lft fnl f* **12/1**

-000 **8** *½* **Yungaburra (IRE)**[28] 3516 6-9-5 68 (t) AndrewHeffernan(3) 4 54
(D C Griffiths) *sn led: hdd over 4f out: chsd ldr tl led again over 2f out: rdn and hdd 1f out: sn wknd* **40/1**

0000 **9** *5* **Brunelleschi**[72] 2123 7-8-12 65 (b) SophieSilvester(7) 3 35
(P L Gilligan) *s.i.s: sn pushed along and a in rr* **33/1**

0510 **10** *8* **Athaakeel (IRE)**[5] 4255 4-9-7 67 CathyGannon 2 11
(R A Harris) *s.s: a wl bhd* **11/2**[2]

1m 14.04s (-0.96) **Going Correction** -0.125s/f (Stan) 10 Ran SP% **117.0**
Speed ratings (Par 103): **101,100,97,95,94 92,91,90,84,73**
toteswingers: 1&2 £9.10, 1&3 £7.00, 2&3 £17.40. CSF £32.03 CT £281.48 TOTE £3.00: £1.40, £3.20, £6.20; EX 40.00.
Owner Stuart Burgan **Bred** S R Bowring **Trained** Edwinstowe, Notts

■ Stewards' Enquiry : Graham Gibbons 18-day ban (takes into account earlier offences; four days deferred): careless riding: Aug 13,16-28

FOCUS
An ordinary sprint handicap. It was run at a solid pace and the two horses who travelled best through the race came clear. That pair set the standard.

4432 E B F EXTRACARE CHARITABLE TRUST MAIDEN STKS 5f 20y(P)
5:00 (5:00) (Class 5) 2-Y-O £3,412 (£1,007; £504) Stalls Low

Form RPR

402 **1** **Overwhelm**[19] 3778 2-8-9 71 RussKennemore(3) 1 71+
(Andrew Reid) *mde all: rdn clr and hung rt over 1f out: r.o wl* **5/2**[2]

3 **2** *3 ¾* **Golden Creek (USA)**[17] 3842 2-9-3 0 JimCrowley 9 61
(R M Beckett) *chsd ldrs: rdn over 1f out: wnt 2nd and edgd rt ins fnl f: no imp* **2/1**[1]

0 **3** *shd* **Cruise Tothelimit (IRE)**[117] 1066 2-9-3 0 StephenCraine 5 60
(Patrick Morris) *prom: outpcd 2f out: swtchd lft over 1f out: r.o ins fnl f: hung rt towards fin* **22/1**

00 **4** *1 ¼* **Till Dawn (IRE)**[12] 4021 2-8-12 0 EddieAhern 3 51
(A W Carroll) *chsd wnr: rdn and hung rt fr over 1f out: no ex ins fnl f* **25/1**

04 **5** *1 ¾* **Magic Cross**[18] 3817 2-8-12 0 PatCosgrave 8 44
(P J McBride) *s.i.s: outpcd: hdwy u.p over 1f out: nrst fin* **28/1**

0 **6** *nk* **Quadra Hop (IRE)**[49] 2819 2-9-3 0 TonyCulhane 2 48
(B Palling) *prom: rdn over 1f out: wknd ins fnl f* **9/1**

65 **7** *1 ¾* **Imperial Look**[20] 3756 2-9-3 0 GrahamGibbons 7 42
(E S McMahon) *hld up: hdwy 1/2-way: wknd over 1f out* **9/1**

8 *½* **Good Timin'** 2-9-3 0 PaulHanagan 4 40
(D H Brown) *dwlt: outpcd* **5/1**[3]

0660 **9** *13* **Love Club**[9] 4124 2-9-3 55 SilvestreDeSousa 10 —
(B P J Baugh) *prom tl wknd 1/2-way* **50/1**

61.73 secs (-0.57) **Going Correction** -0.125s/f (Stan) 9 Ran SP% **112.2**
Speed ratings (Par 94): **99,93,92,90,88 87,84,83,63**
toteswingers: 1&2 £1.90, 1&3 £9.90, 2&3 £7.20. CSF £7.25 TOTE £2.70: £1.02, £1.70, £6.40; EX 6.70.
Owner A S Reid **Bred** A S Reid **Trained** Mill Hill, London NW7

FOCUS
A non-bonus maiden and the form looks weak.

NOTEBOOK
Overwhelm, runner-up over 6f at Kempton last time, proved suited by the drop in trip, showing good speed throughout, although the switch to a left-handed track didn't help her as she hung badly right in the straight, all the way over to the stands' rail. She did well to win so convincingly and could be quite useful over this distance when she has a right-handed rail to race against. (tchd 2-1)
Golden Creek(USA) showed only moderate form on debut over 6f and this looked little better. He was an expensive purchase but is so far not living up to expectations. (op 7-4)
Cruise Tothelimit(IRE) showed nothing on debut on Fibresand in March, but this was better after four months off. (op 50-1 tchd 20-1)
Till Dawn(IRE) hadn't shown much on her first two starts, but this was an improvement. Nurseries are now an option and she should find her level. (op 22-1)
Good Timin', a half-brother to Moorhouse Lad, started slowly and was outpaced for most of the way, looking badly in need of the experience. (op 6-1)

4433 BETDAQ ON 0870 178 1221 H'CAP 1m 4f 50y(P)
5:30 (5:34) (Class 6) (0-65,65) 3-Y-O+ £1,706 (£503; £252) Stalls Low

Form RPR

2362 **1** **Hypnotic Gaze (IRE)**[12] 994 4-10-0 65 SilvestreDeSousa 3 80
(J Mackie) *chsd ldr tl led over 2f out: rdn clr and hung rt fr over 1f out: styd on wl* **20/1**

/000 **2** *7* **Pertemps Networks**[14] 3965 6-9-8 59 GrahamGibbons 2 63
(M W Easterby) *led: rdn and hdd over 2f out: styd on same pce appr fnl f* **33/1**

225- **3** *1* **Eagle Nebula**[229] 7695 6-9-9 60 LiamKeniry 1 62
(B R Johnson) *chsd ldrs: rdn over 2f out: styd on same pce appr fnl f* **12/1**

3300 **4** *hd* **Ancient Times (USA)**[28] 3508 3-9-2 65 PaulHanagan 4 67
(Joss Saville) *hld up in tch: rdn over 3f out: styd on same pce appr fnl f* **50/1**

4500 **5** *4 ½* **Love In The Park**[28] 3513 5-9-8 59 TomEaves 8 54
(R Brotherton) *chsd ldrs: rdn over 4f out: wknd over 1f out* **33/1**

0-00 **6** *½* **St Savarin (FR)**[84] 1755 9-9-5 56 StevieDonohoe 9 50
(M S Tuck) *hld up: rdn over 3f out: hung lft over 1f out: nvr on terms* **66/1**

0004 **7** *2 ½* **Formidable Guest**[12] 4019 6-9-13 64 SaleemGolam 7 54
(J Pearce) *hld up: hdwy 5f out: wknd over 1f out* **14/1**

2026 **8** *1 ½* **Dan Buoy (FR)**[36] 3241 7-9-0 56 (p) MarkCoumbe(5) 11 43
(R C Guest) *hld up in tch: rdn and lost pl over 5f out: n.d after* **10/1**[3]

3-61 **9** *1 ½* **Mme De Stael**[5] 4259 3-9-2 65 6ex (b) SebSanders 10 50
(Sir Mark Prescott) *ponied to the s and wnt down early: chsd ldrs: rdn over 2f out: wknd over 1f out* **4/6**[1]

630- **10** *7* **Dubburg (USA)**[264] 7248 5-9-9 60 TonyCulhane 5 34
(W J Musson) *hld up: a in rr: pushed along 7f out: bhd fnl 4f* **3/1**[2]

500 **11** *18* **National Theatre (USA)**[20] 3754 4-9-6 57 (b[1]) JerryO'Dwyer 6 2
(Miss Olivia Maylam) *hld up: rdn and wknd over 3f out: t.o* **100/1**

2m 39.01s (-2.09) **Going Correction** -0.125s/f (Stan)
WFA 3 from 4yo+ 12lb 11 Ran SP% **123.5**
Speed ratings (Par 101): **101,96,95,95,92 92,90,89,88,83 71**
toteswingers: 1&2 £25.30, 1&3 £7.30, 2&3 £24.60. CSF £524.62 CT £8005.54 TOTE £16.00: £3.50, £7.80, £1.70; EX 216.50.
Owner W I Bloomfield **Bred** Tally-Ho Stud **Trained** Church Broughton , Derbys

FOCUS
The favourite disappointed, and so too did the gamble of the race, so this was a weak contest. The pace seemed to increase down the back straight and the time was reasonable, but the form does not look the strongest.
St Savarin(FR) Official explanation: jockey said gelding hung left throughout
Mme De Stael Official explanation: vet said filly finished distressed
Dubburg(USA) Official explanation: jockey said gelding never travelled

4434 BET GLORIOUS GOODWOOD - BETDAQ APPRENTICE H'CAP 1m 141y(P)
6:00 (6:00) (Class 6) (0-55,56) 3-Y-O+ £1,706 (£503; £252) Stalls Low

Form RPR

0-15 **1** **Cyril The Squirrel**[33] 3314 6-8-12 51 LewisWalsh(5) 1 60
(Karen George) *chsd ldrs: led over 1f out: edgd lft: rdn out* **11/2**[2]

3220 **2** *2* **Join Up**[129] 939 4-9-1 52 AlexEdwards(3) 6 56
(W M Brisbourne) *a.p: rdn to chse wnr over 1f out: edgd lft: styd on same pce* **15/2**

6051 **3** *1* **Corrib (IRE)**[26] 3559 7-8-9 50 (p) ThomasBrown(7) 10 52+
(B Palling) *hld up: hdwy over 2f out: hung lft ins fnl f: styd on* **8/1**

550 **4** *¾* **Royal Acclamation (IRE)**[50] 2779 5-8-11 50 LucyBarry(5) 2 50
(H J Evans) *a.p: rdn over 1f out: styd on same pce fnl f* **8/1**

006 **5** *2 ¼* **Pab Special (IRE)**[19] 3783 7-9-0 55 IanBurns(7) 11 50
(B R Johnson) *prom: rdn over 1f out: hung lft and wknd fnl f* **7/2**[1]

0040 **6** *nse* **Pipers Piping (IRE)**[6] 4232 4-9-0 55 LeonnaMayor(7) 9 50+
(P Howling) *hld up: r.o ins fnl f: nvr nrr* **20/1**

0004 **7** *1 ½* **Prince Andjo (USA)**[8] 4173 4-8-13 50 NeilFarley(3) 7 42
(D Carroll) *chsd ldr tl led 3f out: rdn and hdd over 1f out: wknd ins fnl f* **14/1**

0045 **8** *hd* **Holyfield Warrior (IRE)**[14] 3967 6-9-4 52 RichardRowe 4 43
(R J Smith) *hld up: hdwy over 2f out: nt trble ldrs* **6/1**[3]

0500 **9** *1 ¼* **Flighty Fellow (IRE)**[19] 3783 10-9-5 56 ow1 (v) MJMurphy(3) 5 44
(Miss Olivia Maylam) *hld up: rdn over 2f out: n.d* **22/1**

00-0 **10** *½* **Warren Bank**[39] 3127 5-9-4 52 SoniaEaton 3 39
(Mrs Mary Hambro) *led: hdd 3f out: sn rdn: wknd fnl f* **12/1**

0060 **11** *nk* **Queen Of Thebes (IRE)**[20] 3762 4-8-13 50 SophieSilvester(3) 12 36
(S Kirk) *s.i.s: hld up: a in rr* **33/1**

0400 **12** *½* **Stargazy**[2] 4366 6-9-5 53 HollyHall 8 38
(A J Lidderdale) *s.s: a bhd* **25/1**

46-0 **13** *5* **Autumn Morning (IRE)**[13] 3983 4-8-11 50 MatthewCosham(5) 13 24
(P D Evans) *hld up: a in rr: bhd fnl 3f* **25/1**

1m 50.38s (-0.12) **Going Correction** -0.125s/f (Stan) 13 Ran SP% **120.0**
Speed ratings (Par 101): **95,93,92,91,89 89,88,88,87,86 86,85,81**
toteswingers: 1&2 £6.10, 1&3 £4.70, 2&3 £5.80. totesuper7: Win: Not won. Place: £508.50. CSF £42.94 CT £345.01 TOTE £6.90: £2.70, £1.30, £3.80; EX 38.60 Place 6: £16.52, Place 5: £8.22..

Owner R E Baskerville **Bred** R E Baskerville **Trained** Higher Eastington, Devon

FOCUS
A moderate apprentice handicap with the runner-up rated close to their winter form.
T/Plt: £31.70 to a £1 stake. Pool:£73,326.15 - 1,686.72 winning tickets. T/Qpdt: £13.10 to a £1 stake. Pool:£4,363.32 - 246.10 winning tickets. CR

4233 YARMOUTH (L-H)
Monday, July 26

OFFICIAL GOING: Good to firm (7.9)
Wind: Fresh, behind Weather: Bright and breezy

4435 CAISTER LIFEBOAT H'CAP — 5f 43y
2:15 (2:15) (Class 6) (0-65,63) 3-Y-0+ **£1,554** (£462; £231; £115) **Stalls** High

Form				RPR
0525	1		**Bertie Southstreet**[11] 4047 7-9-6 **63**........................(v) JamesO'Reilly(5) 8	69
			(J O'Reilly) *chsd ldrs: rdn and effrt wl over 1f out: drvn to ld fnl 75yds: r.o wl* **6/1**	
6600	2	1 1/4	**Socceroo**[16] 3895 5-8-12 **50**........................(e) DaneO'Neill 6	52
			(D C Griffiths) *led: rdn over 1f out: kpt on wl tl hdd and nt pce of wnr fnl 75yds* **14/1**	
0003	3	hd	**Black Baccara**[7] 4210 3-8-12 **54**........................(p) JamieSpencer 7	54
			(P S McEntee) *stdd s: hld up in last trio: hdwy 1/2-way: rdn and ev ch jst over 1f out tl nt pce of wnr fnl 75yds* **5/1**[3]	
533	4	3	**Punching**[41] 3064 6-9-9 **61**........................ HayleyTurner 1	51
			(C R Dore) *racd off the pce in midfield: effrt u.p 2f out: chsd ldrs ent fnl f: no imp after* **10/3**[1]	
0306	5	1/2	**Bahama Baileys**[13] 3993 5-8-7 **45**........................ JimmyQuinn 4	33
			(C A Dwyer) *sn outpcd in last pair: hdwy u.p over 1f out: kpt on fnl f: nvr trbld ldrs* **9/1**	
5022	6	2 3/4	**Pocket's Pick (IRE)**[6] 4239 4-9-8 **60**........................(b) IanMongan 2	39
			(Jim Best) *w ldrs: ev ch and rdn ent fnl 2f: wknd jst over 1f out: fdd ins fnl f* **7/2**[2]	
1060	7	10	**Waterloo Dock**[35] 3262 5-9-11 **63**........................(v) ShaneKelly 3	6
			(M Quinn) *sn wl outpcd and rdn in last pair: lost tch 1/2-way* **14/1**	
3334	8	2	**Thoughtsofstardom**[6] 4239 7-9-8 **60**........................ AlanMunro 9	—
			(P S McEntee) *in tch tl eased fr jst over 2f out: wl bhd 1f out: dismntd after fin* **9/1**	
0166	9	4 1/2	**Gleaming Spirit (IRE)**[131] 899 6-8-8 **46**........................(v) KirstyMilczarek 5	—
			(Peter Grayson) *chsd ldr tl 1/2-way: sn dropped out: wl bhd fnl f* **40/1**	

61.18 secs (-1.52) **Going Correction** -0.475s/f (Firm)
WFA 3 from 4yo+ 4lb **9** Ran SP% **112.0**
Speed ratings (Par 101): **89,87,86,81,81 76,60,57,50**
toteswingers: 1&2 £17.90, 1&3 £4.70, 2&3 £16.20. CSF £81.72 CT £446.11 TOTE £8.20: £2.60, £5.00, £1.20; EX 32.00 Trifecta £269.70 Part won. Pool: £364.48 - 0.42 winning units..
Owner J D Walker **Bred** B Whitehouse **Trained** Doncaster, S Yorks

FOCUS
A moderate sprint handicap and the winner did not have to improve to score, so is rated to his recent best.
Waterloo Dock Official explanation: jockey said gelding lost its action
Thoughtsofstardom Official explanation: jockey said, regarding running and riding, that his orders were to track the leaders, obtain a clear run and win if he could, adding that the gelding faltered and lost its position at halfway when asked to quicken, and felt uneven in its action, therefore, he felt it prudent to ride sympathetically after.

4436 NORFOLK BROADS (S) STKS — 6f 3y
2:45 (2:46) (Class 6) 2-Y-0 **£1,554** (£462; £231; £115) **Stalls** High

Form				RPR
6023	1		**Captain Loui (IRE)**[11] 4059 2-8-11 65........................(b) JamieSpencer 6	59
			(K A Ryan) *led tl over 4f out: chsd ldrs after tl rdn to ld ent fnl f: drvn ins fnl f: hld on cl home: all out* **5/2**[1]	
134	2	hd	**My Lord**[7] 4195 2-8-13 60........................ JackDean(3) 3	63
			(W G M Turner) *hld up in tch in midfield: rdn and hdwy wl over 1f out: chsd wnr fnl 100yds: r.o wl: nt quite get up* **11/2**[2]	
0	3	1 3/4	**One Cool Bex**[58] 2547 2-8-11 0........................(e[1]) JackMitchell 8	53
			(P J McBride) *hld up towards rr: hdwy over 2f out: rdn to chse ldrs over 1f out: kpt on same pce ins fnl f* **13/2**[3]	
510	4	nk	**Mini Bon Bon**[25] 3598 2-8-4 60........................ NatashaEaton(7) 2	52
			(A Bailey) *dwlt and short of room at s: hdwy to ld over 4f out: rdn and hdd ent fnl f: kpt pressing wnr tl wknd fnl 75yds* **8/1**	
3203	5	nk	**Ivan's A Star (IRE)**[66] 2300 2-8-11 62........................ DaneO'Neill 12	51
			(J S Moore) *chsd ldrs: rdn ent fnl 2f: styd on same pce u.p fnl f* **7/1**	
00	6	5	**Bishops Moon**[10] 4103 2-8-6 0........................(b[1]) LiamJones 7	31
			(M G Quinlan) *chsd ldrs: rdn and struggling ent fnl 2f: wknd over 1f out: wl btn fnl f* **33/1**	
000	7	2 1/2	**Bathwick Nero**[67] 2245 2-8-1 52........................ SophieDoyle(5) 9	24
			(P D Evans) *in tch: rdn along over 2f out: sn struggling: wl btn over 1f out* **25/1**	
500	8	10	**Token Gift**[9] 4123 2-8-11 59........................ NeilCallan 1	—
			(P D Evans) *in tch: rdn and lost pl wl over 2f out: wl btn fnl 2f* **9/1**	
000	9	shd	**Time For Applause**[16] 3906 2-8-6 50........................ JoeFanning 11	—
			(E A L Dunlop) *hld up bhd: rdn and effrt over 2f out: sn hung lft and wl btn fnl 2f* **12/1**	
0	10	3 1/2	**Newstarmcgrath**[41] 3053 2-8-4 0........................ AdamBeschizza(7) 4	—
			(Miss Gay Kelleway) *a outpcd in rr and sn rdn along: wl bhd fr 1/2-way* **40/1**	
	11	1 1/4	**Renn** 2-8-6 0........................ KirstyMilczarek 5	—
			(Peter Grayson) *s.i.s: a outpcd in rr: lost tch over 3f out* **80/1**	
0	12	9	**Endorser**[10] 4096 2-8-11 0........................(b[1]) RichardMullen 10	—
			(W R Muir) *a outpcd towards rr: rdn and lost tch over 3f out: eased ins fnl f: t.o* **28/1**	

1m 12.52s (-1.88) **Going Correction** -0.475s/f (Firm) **12** Ran SP% **112.5**
Speed ratings (Par 92): **93,92,90,90,89 82,79,66,66,61 59,47**
toteswingers: 1&2 £3.00, 1&3 £4.20, 2&3 £7.80. CSF £13.78 TOTE £2.50: £1.10, £2.00, £2.50; EX 13.50 Trifecta £61.10 Pool: £597.71 - 7.23 winning units..There was no bid for the winner.
Owner Dr Marwan Koukash **Bred** Denis McDonnell **Trained** Hambleton, N Yorks

FOCUS
A competitive but routine little seller. The form makes sense.

NOTEBOOK
Captain Loui(IRE) ◆, well held in a Hamilton maiden latest, looked a big player on this drop in grade and, though it proved to be very hard work, he was just able to hold on. He's probably capable of making his mark in nurseries. (op 9-4 tchd 11-4 in places)
My Lord, who won a C&D seller on debut, was comfortably held in a claimer latest, but this was more his true form, staying on well and just failing to get up. (op 5-1 tchd 9-2)
One Cool Bex beat only one home on her debut at Newmarket, but the drop in grade and first-time eyeshield brought about a much-improved display. (op 9-1)
Mini Bon Bon, another previous course winner in this grade, wasn't the best away but did get to the lead. She didn't see it out in the end, though. (op 7-1)
Ivan's A Star(IRE) again ran creditably, but is finding winning hard. (op 13-2 tchd 6-1)
Token Gift Official explanation: jockey said colt hung right; trainer's rep said colt was unsuited by the good to firm ground and had also been struck into

4437 GREAT YARMOUTH ADVERTISER MAIDEN AUCTION STKS — 7f 3y
3:15 (3:15) (Class 6) 2-Y-0 **£1,942** (£578; £288; £144) **Stalls** High

Form				RPR
0	1		**Bloodsweatandtears**[19] 3794 2-9-1 0........................ ShaneKelly 14	77
			(W J Knight) *stdd s: hld up towards rr: gd hdwy 1/2-way: chsd ldr wl over 1f out: rdn to chal and hld hd awkwardly ent fnl f: carried lft ins fnl f: pushed ahd towards fin* **11/10**[1]	
505	2	hd	**Titus Two (IRE)**[7] 4208 2-8-12 0........................ JackMitchell 10	74
			(P W Chapple-Hyam) *chsd ldrs: pushed along 4f out: rdn to ld ent fnl 2f: hrd pressed fr over 1f out: edgd lft u.p but kpt on wl tl hdd towards fin* **14/1**	
4	3	3 3/4	**Zamina (IRE)**[34] 3295 2-8-7 0........................ RichardMullen 15	61+
			(S Kirk) *towards rr: rdn over 2f out: hdwy and edging lft 2f out: kpt on wl to go 3rd ins fnl f: no threat to ldng pair* **8/1**	
04	4	2	**Bright Applause**[9] 4131 2-8-8 0........................ HarryBentley(7) 2	62
			(G L Moore) *chsd ldrs: rdn to chse ldng pair wl over 1f out: outpcd by ldng pair jst over 1f out: lost 3rd ins fnl f* **33/1**	
6235	5	3/4	**No Poppy (IRE)**[26] 3550 2-8-4 71........................ DuranFentiman 1	49
			(T D Easterby) *in tch: rdn and effrt over 2f out: no ch w ldng pair ent fnl f: plugged on same pce after* **7/1**[3]	
644	6	shd	**Dazzling Valentine**[12] 4021 2-7-11 73........................ NatashaEaton(7) 5	49
			(A Bailey) *hld up in midfield: pushed along and hdwy ent fnl 2f: rdn and no prog over 1f out: wl hld and edgd lft ins fnl f* **11/2**[2]	
44	7	5	**Piccarello**[7] 4208 2-8-12 0........................ DarryllHolland 7	45
			(M H Tompkins) *in tch: rdn 1/2-way: wknd wl over 1f out: wl btn and hung rt ent fnl f* **7/1**[3]	
50	8	7	**Bonniebridge**[20] 3769 2-8-4 0........................ JimmyQuinn 13	22
			(Miss J Feilden) *a towards rr: rdn and struggling 1/2-way: wl bhd fnl 2f: eased ins fnl f* **100/1**	
54	9	5	**Algurayn (IRE)**[13] 3991 2-9-1 0........................ KirstyMilczarek 4	21
			(G Prodromou) *a towards rr: rdn and struggling ent fnl 2f: wl btn after: eased ins fnl f* **33/1**	
0	10	4 1/2	**Only Ten Per Cent (IRE)**[14] 3961 2-8-2 0........................ RyanPowell(7) 16	—
			(J S Moore) *led tl rdn and hdd ent fnl 2f: sn dropped out: wl bhd over 1f out: eased ins fnl f* **100/1**	
	11	5	**Lough Corrib (USA)** 2-8-12 0........................ NeilCallan 8	—
			(K A Ryan) *a towards rr: rdn and struggling wl over 3f out: wl bhd and eased ins fnl f: t.o* **40/1**	
	12	1 1/4	**Patricia's Hope** 2-8-4 0........................ LiamJones 11	—
			(P W D'Arcy) *w ldr tl ent fnl 3f: sn lost pl: wl bhd fnl 2f: eased ins fnl f: t.o* **50/1**	
6	13	3 1/2	**Miss Toldyaso (IRE)**[20] 3767 2-8-7 0........................ AlanMunro 12	—
			(M G Quinlan) *a bhd: rdn and struggling bdly over 3f out: wl bhd fnl 2f: eased ins fnl f: t.o* **50/1**	

1m 24.86s (-1.74) **Going Correction** -0.475s/f (Firm) **13** Ran SP% **120.0**
Speed ratings (Par 92): **90,89,85,83,82 82,76,68,62,57 51,50,46**
toteswingers: 1&2 £6.20, 1&3 £3.90, 2&3 £13.30. CSF £18.97 TOTE £2.20: £1.30, £3.80, £2.80; EX 25.70 Trifecta £135.40 Pool: £342.21 - 1.87 winning units..
Owner Four Men & A Dream Partnership **Bred** Oakhill Stud **Trained** Patching, W Sussex

FOCUS
The front two came clear in this modest maiden and the form is rated around them.

NOTEBOOK
Bloodsweatandtears shaped better than the bare result implied in a good-looking maiden on his debut at Newmarket and, although making harder work of it than expected, he managed to get his head in front. He's holds Group 2 entries in both the Champagne Stakes and Royal Lodge and ought to progress, but will need to improve markedly if he's to take his place in either of those. Connections feel a slower surface will suit. (op 11-8 after early 6-4, 13-8 and 7-4 in places)
Titus Two(IRE) improved again on last week's course effort, making the winner fight all the way to the line, and he looks capable of winning a modest maiden before going handicapping. (op 16-1)
Zamina(IRE) has now shaped with promise on both starts, again getting going too late, and she has the option of reverting to mares-only company. (op 6-1)
Bright Applause seems to have got better with each run and he will make more appeal once contesting nurseries.
No Poppy(IRE) again her had chance without being good enough. (op 15-2)
Dazzling Valentine failed to reproduce the form shown on either of her last two starts. Official explanation: jockey said filly clipped heels in running
Algurayn(IRE) Official explanation: jockey said colt was coltish

4438 SHIRLEY GILL MEMORIAL H'CAP — 7f 3y
3:45 (3:45) (Class 4) (0-80,79) 3-Y-0+ **£3,784** (£1,132; £566; £283; £141) **Stalls** High

Form				RPR
13-1	1		**Wake Up Call**[66] 2298 4-9-12 **76**........................ JackMitchell 5	90+
			(C F Wall) *t.k.h: hld up in tch in last pair: swtchd rt and hdwy ent fnl 2f: rdn to chal 1f out: led fnl 100yds: kpt on wl towards fin* **11/10**[1]	
2221	2	hd	**Soviet Secret**[9] 4146 3-9-8 **79**........................ DaneO'Neill 6	89
			(P J McBride) *chsd ldr: rdn and ev ch wl over 1f out: drvn to ld 1f out: hdd fnl 100yds: kpt on wl but a jst hld after* **9/4**[2]	
0043	3	2	**Malcheek (IRE)**[26] 3553 8-10-0 **78**........................ DavidAllan 3	86
			(T D Easterby) *led: rdn ent fnl 2f: drvn and hdd 1f out: kpt on u.p tl no ex and btn fnl 100yds* **16/1**	
5003	4	1 3/4	**Always Dazzling**[13] 3993 3-8-3 **60**........................ JoeFanning 4	60
			(M Johnston) *chsd ldrs: rdn and unable qck ent fnl 2f: styd on same pce u.p fr over 1f out* **10/1**	
3005	5	nk	**Mudhish (IRE)**[6] 4237 5-9-2 **66**........................(b) KoseiMiura 1	69
			(C E Brittain) *chsd ldrs: rdn and effrt ent fnl 2f: unable qck over 1f out: styd on same pce fnl f* **33/1**	
0310	6	10	**Hustle (IRE)**[10] 4108 5-9-1 **72**........................ AdamBeschizza(7) 2	48
			(Miss Gay Kelleway) *dwlt: nvr gng wl and sn niggled along in last: rdn over 3f out: hung rt and wknd 2f out: wl bhd fnl f* **6/1**[3]	

1m 23.47s (-3.13) **Going Correction** -0.475s/f (Firm)
WFA 3 from 4yo+ 7lb **6** Ran SP% **110.6**
Speed ratings (Par 105): **98,97,95,93,93 81**
toteswingers: 1&2 £1.10, 1&3 £3.50, 2&3 £4.50. CSF £3.61 TOTE £2.10: £1.30, £1.50; EX 4.10.
Owner J G Lambton **Bred** Whatton Manor Stud **Trained** Newmarket, Suffolk

FOCUS
An ordinary handicap that saw the front two in the market dominate. The placed horses are rated to their recent best.

4439 BETTERBET AT NORWICH CITY CENTRE H'CAP 1m 3y
4:15 (4:16) (Class 6) (0-65,64) 3-Y-O+ **£1,554** (£462; £231; £115) **Stalls** High

Form RPR
1522 **1** **Mr Harmoosh (IRE)**[46] 2906 3-8-13 **62**.................. AdamBeschizza(7) 3 73
(E F Vaughan) *hld up in tch in midfield: hdwy to chse ldrs gng wl over 2f out: rdn to ld wl over 1f out: r.o wl and drew clr ins fnl f: rdn out* **5/2**[1]
2506 **2** 2 ½ **Caracal**[16] 3899 3-9-6 **62**.. JoeFanning 6 67
(M Johnston) *chsd ldrs: wnt 2nd over 2f out: rdn to ld ent fnl 2f: hdd wl over 1f out: drvn ent fnl f: wknd ins fnl f* **7/2**[2]
6630 **3** 1 ¾ **Easy Wonder (GER)**[13] 3982 5-8-11 **45**...................... RichardMullen 5 48
(I A Wood) *hld up in tch in midfield: rdn and effrt over 2f out: chsd ldrs and drvn over 1f out: one pce and no imp fnl f* **20/1**
2050 **4** ¾ **Yourgolftravel Com**[10] 4108 5-10-0 **62**...................... NickyMackay 11 64
(M Wigham) *stdd s: hld up in midfield: effrt over 2f out: chsd ldrs and drvn over 1f out: no prog and one pce after* **9/2**[3]
1506 **5** ¾ **Cool Kitten (IRE)**[19] 3788 3-8-12 **54**........................ ShaneKelly 10 52
(W J Knight) *towards rr: rdn 4f out: hdwy u.p over 1f out: styd on ins fnl f: nvr trbld ldrs* **14/1**
0050 **6** 1 ¼ **Barataria**[28] 3500 8-9-8 **56**.. HayleyTurner 7 53
(R Bastiman) *stdd s: hld up bhd: effrt and n.m.r ent fnl 2f: plugged on ins fnl f: nvr trbld ldrs* **20/1**
5600 **7** 1 ¾ **Bubbly Braveheart (IRE)**[12] 4022 3-9-1 **64**.........(v[1]) NatashaEaton(7) 1 55
(A Bailey) *led: clr after 1f: rdn 3f out: hdd ent fnl 2f: wknd qckly over 1f out: wl btn fnl f* **16/1**
4-00 **8** 3 ¼ **Big Sur**[66] 2299 4-9-8 **56**.. DaneO'Neill 9 41
(T Keddy) *sn bustled along to chse ldr: lost pl over 2f out: wl bhd fr wl over 1f out* **11/1**
30-0 **9** ½ **Pont De Nuit**[14] 3948 3-9-7 **63**.. NeilCallan 2 45
(A B Haynes) *a towards rr: struggling u.p 3f out: wl btn fnl 2f* **33/1**
0-06 **10** 1 ¼ **Singing Scott (IRE)**[21] 3733 3-8-3 **45**.......................... JimmyQuinn 4 24
(R Bastiman) *in tch in midfield: rdn and no rspnse over 2f out: sn bhd* **66/1**
2605 **11** 11 **Man In The Mirror (IRE)**[20] 3765 3-8-6 **51**..........(p) AshleyHamblett(3) 8 5
(P L Gilligan) *racd keenly: chsd ldrs: rdn over 3f out: wknd ent fnl 2f: wl bhd and virtually p.u ins fnl f* **15/2**

1m 37.17s (-3.43) **Going Correction** -0.475s/f (Firm)
WFA 3 from 4yo+ 8lb **11** Ran SP% **115.6**
Speed ratings (Par 101): **98,95,93,93,92 91,89,86,85,84 73**
toteswingers: 1&2 £2.50, 1&3 £10.80, 2&3 £13.30. CSF £10.21 CT £139.51 TOTE £2.60: £1.10, £2.20, £7.70; EX 10.70 Trifecta £240.10 Pool: £499.68 - 1.54 winning units..
Owner Salem Rashid **Bred** Thomas G Cooke **Trained** Newmarket, Suffolk

FOCUS
A modest enough handicap that was soundly run and the form looks sound enough.
Man In The Mirror(IRE) Official explanation: jockey said gelding lost its action

4440 MARTIN FOULGER MEMORIAL H'CAP 6f 3y
4:45 (4:45) (Class 4) (0-85,85) 3-Y-O+ **£3,784** (£1,132; £566; £283; £141) **Stalls** High

Form RPR
2121 **1** **Piazza San Pietro**[11] 4041 4-9-3 **76**................................ JoeFanning 4 86
(A B Haynes) *t.k.h: hld up in tch: shkn up and hdwy over 1f out: pushed along hands and heels to ld fnl 100yds: r.o wl* **5/1**
4514 **2** ½ **Arabian Pearl (IRE)**[44] 2959 4-9-2 **75**.....................(b) JackMitchell 3 83
(P W Chapple-Hyam) *chsd ldrs: rdn to chse ldr over 1f out: drvn to ld ent fnl f: hdd fnl f: styd on same pce towards fin* **7/1**
4430 **3** ½ **Fathsta (IRE)**[31] 3389 5-9-12 **85**.................................... JamieSpencer 6 92
(D M Simcock) *taken down early: stdd s: hld up in last: swtchd lft and pushed along over 1f out: drvn and gd hdwy ins fnl f: chsd ldrs fnl 100yds: hung rt but r.o: nt rch ldrs* **9/2**[3]
6251 **4** ¾ **Rough Rock (IRE)**[7] 4209 5-8-3 **69** 6ex.................. AdamBeschizza(7) 8 73
(C A Dwyer) *in tch in last pair: swtchd lft and effrt u.p over 1f out: hdwy to chse ldrs ins fnl f: kpt on same pce fnl 100yds* **14/1**
2502 **5** 1 ¼ **Angus Newz**[10] 4105 7-9-9 **82**.. ShaneKelly 7 82
(M Quinn) *chsd ldrs: rdn and unable qck wl over 1f out: kpt on same pce ins fnl f* **20/1**
5410 **6** 1 **Imprimis Tagula (IRE)**[2] 4394 6-8-12 **78**.................. NatashaEaton(7) 1 75
(A Bailey) *chsd ldr tl wl over 1f out: wknd u.p 1f out* **4/1**[2]
0000 **7** ¾ **Green Manalishi**[20] 3753 9-9-12 **85**..............................(p) NeilCallan 5 80
(K A Ryan) *led: rdn ent fnl 2f: hdd ent fnl f: wknd fnl 100yds* **22/1**
2200 **8** hd **Excellent Guest**[19] 3791 3-9-4 **82**................................ DaneO'Neill 2 75
(G G Margarson) *hld up in tch: rdn and unable qck wl over 1f out: one pce and no imp fnl f* **2/1**[1]

1m 10.79s (-3.61) **Going Correction** -0.475s/f (Firm)
WFA 3 from 4yo+ 5lb **8** Ran SP% **116.5**
Speed ratings (Par 105): **105,104,103,102,101 99,98,98**
toteswingers: 1&2 £5.90, 1&3 £3.80, 2&3 £5.20. CSF £40.29 CT £169.46 TOTE £2.90: £1.10, £2.30, £1.70; EX 31.10 Trifecta £104.40 Pool: £599.71 - 4.25 winning units..
Owner K Corke **Bred** T E Pocock **Trained** Limpley Stoke, Bath

FOCUS
A fair enough sprint handicap with the runner-up close to his best.
Fathsta(IRE) Official explanation: jockey said gelding hung right
Excellent Guest Official explanation: jockey said gelding lost its action

4441 EASTERN DAILY PRESS H'CAP 2m
5:15 (5:15) (Class 6) (0-65,62) 4-Y-O+ **£1,554** (£462; £231; £115) **Stalls** High

Form RPR
532 **1** **Stage Acclaim (IRE)**[9] 3324 5-9-0 **55**.......................(p) JamieSpencer 2 62+
(Dr R D P Newland) *mde all: rdn and qcknd 5f out: c centre over 4f out: hung lft u.p over 2f out: styd on fnl f* **1/1**[1]
3452 **2** 1 ¾ **Purely By Chance**[18] 3819 5-8-6 **52**..........................(v) SimonPearce(5) 3 57
(J Pearce) *chsd wnr: rdn along over 3f out: swtchd rt over 2f out: styd on same pce fnl f* **7/2**[2]
0464 **3** 1 ½ **Snowberry Hill (USA)**[14] 3965 7-8-4 **45**........................ JimmyQuinn 1 48
(Lucinda Featherstone) *chsd ldrs: effrt to dispute 2nd over 3f out: short of room and hmpd over 2f out: 3rd and kpt on same pce after* **7/1**[3]
3-60 **4** ½ **Extremely So**[109] 1194 4-8-13 **54**................................ JackMitchell 6 56
(P J McBride) *in tch: rdn and effrt over 2f out: one pce and no imp fr over 1f out* **15/2**
2660 **5** 9 **Leyte Gulf (USA)**[20] 3764 7-9-7 **62**................................ DaneO'Neill 5 54
(C C Bealby) *stdd s: hld up in last: rdn and effrt wl over 1f out: no prog and btn ent fnl f: eased ins fnl f* **20/1**
0060 **6** 8 **Dovedon Earl**[37] 3221 4-8-9 **50**.. NickyMackay 4 32
(T Keddy) *a in last pair: rdn and struggling 4f out: wl bhd fnl 2f: eased ins fnl f* **12/1**

3m 33.84s (-0.76) **Going Correction** -0.475s/f (Firm) **6** Ran SP% **108.9**
Speed ratings (Par 101): **82,81,80,80,75 71**
toteswingers: 1&2 £1.20, 1&3 £1.80, 2&3 £2.20. CSF £4.31 TOTE £1.90: £1.20, £2.30; EX 3.30 Place 6: £30.26, Place 5: £6.59..
Owner G Carstairs **Bred** Oaks Stud **Trained** Claines, Worcs
■ Stewards' Enquiry : Jamie Spencer caution: careless riding.

FOCUS
A weak staying handicap rated around the placed horses.
T/Jkpt: £2,422.00 to a £1 stake. Pool: £49,464.80 - 14.50 winning tickets. T/Plt: £17.30 to a £1 stake. Pool:£79,600.70 - 3,351.61winning tickets. T/Qpdt: £4.20 to a £1 stake. Pool:£5,783.94 - 1,006.90 winning tickets SP

4442 - 4446a (Foreign Racing) - See Raceform Interactive

4195 BEVERLEY (R-H)
Tuesday, July 27

OFFICIAL GOING: Good to firm (9.1)
Rail around bottom bend moved out adding 6yds to races of 7f and over.
Wind: Light against Weather: Overcast

4447 EBF HOLDERNESS PONY CLUB MAIDEN STKS 7f 100y
2:00 (2:02) (Class 5) 2-Y-O **£3,885** (£1,156; £577; £288) **Stalls** High

Form RPR
1 **Mutual Force (USA)** 2-8-10 0.................................. AntiocoMurgia(7) 1 75+
(Mahmood Al Zarooni) *stdd s and swtchd rt to ins rail: hld up in last pl: hdwy on inner over 2f out: rdn over 1f out: styd on wl to ld last 75yds* **12/1**
0 **2** ½ **Janet's Pearl (IRE)**[8] 4187 2-8-9 0.......................... BarryMcHugh(3) 14 69
(Mrs A Duffield) *in tch: hdwy on inner wl over 2f out: rdn over 1f out: drvn to ld and hung lft ins fnl f: hdd and no ex last 75yds* **33/1**
3 **3** 1 ½ **Adlington**[11] 4089 2-9-3 0.. TonyHamilton 6 70
(R A Fahey) *trckd ldrs: hdwy 3f out: led over 2f out: rdn and edgd rt over 1f out: drvn and hdd ins fnl f* **5/1**[3]
63 **4** ¾ **Il Battista**[40] 3112 2-9-3 0.. JamesDoyle 7 69
(A J McCabe) *midfield: hdwy over 2f out: rdn to chse ldrs wl over 1f out: drvn and one pce fnl f* **9/1**
03 **5** nse **Dubai Glory**[24] 3657 2-8-12 0.. SebSanders 13 63
(E A L Dunlop) *hld up towards rr: hdwy wl over 2f out: rdn wl over 1f out: kpt on ins fnl f* **4/1**[2]
05 **6** 1 ½ **Kalkan Bay**[24] 3657 2-9-3 0.. PJMcDonald 4 65
(Jedd O'Keeffe) *hld up towards rr: hdwy on outer over 2f out: rdn to chse ldrs over 1f out: sn drvn and no imp fnl f* **50/1**
7 2 **Layali Al Arab (IRE)** 2-9-3 0.. TedDurcan 12 60+
(Saeed Bin Suroor) *prom: effrt and nt clr run 2f out and again over 1f out: kpt on same pce* **11/10**[1]
00 **8** 7 **Green Pastures (IRE)**[24] 3665 2-9-3 0............................ PhillipMakin 3 44
(J Howard Johnson) *cl up: led 3f out: sn rdn: hdd 2f out: sn drvn and wknd* **66/1**
05 **9** 2 **Grazeon Again (IRE)**[11] 4116 2-9-3 0.............................. TomEaves 10 39
(J J Quinn) *chsd ldrs: rdn along wl over 2f out: drvn wl over 1f out: sn wknd* **12/1**
00 **10** nk **Be My Spy**[12] 4048 2-8-12 0.. GregFairley 8 33
(P Salmon) *t.k.h: a towards rr* **100/1**
04 **11** nk **Logans Rose**[12] 4049 2-9-3 0...................................... GrahamGibbons 11 38
(A D Brown) *sn led: rdn along and hdd 3f out: drvn over 2f out and sn wknd* **100/1**
00 **12** 2 **Adzing (IRE)**[40] 3106 2-9-3 0.. LukeMorris 9 33
(R A Harris) *midfield: rdn along 3f out: sn wknd* **100/1**
00 **13** 2 ¼ **Pockett Rockett**[12] 4048 2-8-12 0.................................. DuranFentiman 2 23
(D O'Meara) *a in rr* **100/1**

1m 33.61s (-0.19) **Going Correction** -0.30s/f (Firm) **13** Ran SP% **120.0**
Speed ratings (Par 94): **89,88,86,85,85 84,81,73,71,71 70,68,65**
toteswingers:1&2:£35.70, 1&3:£6.70, 2&3:£26.10 CSF £343.23 TOTE £21.50: £4.90, £8.50, £2.00; EX 522.10.
Owner Godolphin **Bred** Claiborne Farm **Trained** Newmarket, Suffolk
■ Stewards' Enquiry : Barry McHugh one-day ban; careless riding (10th Aug)

FOCUS
An interesting extended 7f maiden race run at a sound pace. They spread out coming off the final turn but the winner stuck to the formerly favoured far rail. Straightforward form.

NOTEBOOK
Mutual Force(USA) ◆, supposedly the Godolphin second string, was just about the pick of the paddock. Worst drawn, he was settled in the rear after being switched right after the start before improving against the far rail once in line for home. He stuck on really well despite a marked tendency to drift left in the closing stages, and he looks sure to go on from here. (tchd 14-1)
Janet's Pearl(IRE), considered a backward type, had shown little on her debut a week earlier. She was in the thick of things from the off and went down fighting despite hanging towards the centre of the track. She will improve again and can go one better. (op 40-1 tchd 50-1)
Adlington, who made his effort away from the far rail, raced quite keenly. After having every chance he had little more to give when given a nudge by the runner-up near the line. An easier 7f might suit him better. (op 9-2)
Il Battista, on his third start, stayed on from midfield after meeting traffic problems and he is now qualified for a nursery mark. (op 11-1)
Dubai Glory, happy to sit off the pace, stayed on when it was all over after a poor run and is another now qualified for nurseries. (op 9-2)
Kalkan Bay, a 100-1 shot when fifth here on his second start, showed that was no fluke, staying on widest of all. He too can now try the nursery route.
Layali Al Arab(IRE), supposedly the Godolphin number one, is a half-brother to the Sussex Stakes winner Court Masterpiece. He travelled strongly but after being messed about didn't see it out. He ought to be capable of a fair bit better. (op 5-4)

4448 NATIONAL FESTIVAL CIRCUS (S) H'CAP 1m 4f 16y
2:30 (2:30) (Class 6) (0-65,56) 3-Y-O **£2,266** (£674; £337; £168) **Stalls** High

Form RPR
0-14 **1** **Valantino Oyster (IRE)**[15] 3951 3-8-12 **52**...................... IanBrennan(5) 2 56+
(J Howard Johnson) *trckd ldrs: pushed wd and hmpd bnd over 3f out and sn lost pl: hdwy 2f out: swtchd lft and rdn to chse ldrs whn sltly hmpd ent fnl f: drvn and styd on wl to ld nr fin* **7/2**[1]
55P3 **2** nk **Light The City (IRE)**[8] 4200 3-8-5 **45**.......................... JamesSullivan(5) 1 49
(Mrs R A Carr) *hld up towards rr: hdwy on outer 5f out: chsd ldrs over 2f out: rdn to chal over 1f out: drvn and edgd lft ent fnl f: sn led: hdd and no ex nr fin* **5/1**[2]
0665 **3** ½ **Miereveld**[15] 3951 3-9-1 **50**..(v[1]) SebSanders 7 53
(Sir Mark Prescott) *led: rdn along 3f out: drvn and hdd wl over 1f out: rallied u.p and ev ch ent fnl f: no ex towards fin* **9/1**

5000 **4** 1 **Always Dixie (IRE)**[4] 4337 3-8-13 **48** .... SilvestreDeSousa 6 49
(M Johnston) *trckd ldr: hdwy and cl up 4f out: rdn to ld wl over 1f out: drvn ent fnl f: sn hdd and one pce* **14/1**

-600 **5** ½ **Lily Rio (IRE)**[20] 3788 3-9-6 **55** .... PhillipMakin 8 55
(W R Muir) *trckd ldrs on inner: hdwy over 3f out: rdn 2f out: drvn and ch over 1f out: kpt on same pce* **20/1**

0305 **6** 2 **Tom Wade (IRE)**[28] 3522 3-9-4 **56** ....(p) GaryBartley(3) 5 53
(John A Harris) *hld up in tch: hdwy on inner over 2f out: rdn over 1f out: sn drvn and kpt on same pce* **7/1**

4226 **7** 1¼ **Rosewood Lad**[8] 4211 3-9-3 **52** .... LukeMorris 10 47
(J S Moore) *chsd ldng pair: effrt and edgd lft over 3f out: rdn 2f out and grad wknd* **7/2**[1]

4402 **8** 1¾ **Optimistic Duke (IRE)**[11] 4113 3-9-5 **54** ....(p) DarryllHolland 9 46
(W R Muir) *hld up: a towards rr* **11/2**[3]

-000 **9** 3¼ **Patricks Lodge**[22] 3728 3-8-10 **45** .... PJMcDonald 4 32
(Mrs R A Carr) *a in rr* **50/1**

0026 **10** 11 **Reel Love**[11] 4087 3-8-12 **50** .... BarryMcHugh(3) 3 20
(Mrs L Stubbs) *hld up towards rr: hdwy on outer 4f out: rdn to chse ldrs 3f out: wknd 2f out* **16/1**

2m 40.39s (0.59) **Going Correction** -0.30s/f (Firm) **10** Ran SP% **118.3**
Speed ratings (Par 98): **89,88,88,87,87 86,85,84,81,74**
toteswingers:1&2:£4.50, 1&3:£9.00, 2&3:£8.70 CSF £21.22 CT £147.09 TOTE £5.20: £1.50, £1.70, £3.40; EX 25.60.The winner was sold to Ben Haslam for 7,000gns. Miereveld was claimed by Brian Ellison for £6,000.
Owner J Howard Johnson **Bred** Des Vere Hunt Farm Co And Jack Ronan **Trained** Billy Row, Co Durham
■ Stewards' Enquiry : Seb Sanders caution; excessive use of whip

FOCUS
A 45-56 selling handicap and five were in line inside the final furlong. The form is not solid with the fourth the best guide.
Rosewood Lad Official explanation: jockey said gelding hung left throughout

4449 JOURNAL LADIES DAY NEXT 11 AUGUST H'CAP — 1m 4f 16y
3:05 (3:05) (Class 5) (0-75,75) 3-Y-O+ **£2,914** (£867; £433; £216) **Stalls** High

Form RPR

-532 **1** **Wadnaan**[12] 4062 3-9-7 **75** .... GregFairley 5 90+
(M Johnston) *mde all: rdn clr wl over 1f out: styd on strly: eased towards fin* **6/4**[1]

4331 **2** 10 **Park's Prodigy**[29] 3499 6-9-6 **62** .... SilvestreDeSousa 1 61
(G A Harker) *trckd wnr: cl up 1/2-way: rdn along wl over 2f out: drvn over 1f out: kpt on same pce* **9/4**[2]

1631 **3** nk **Patavium (IRE)**[19] 3807 7-10-0 **70** .... TonyHamilton 3 69
(E W Tuer) *trckd ldng pair: hdwy on inner 3f out: effrt 2f out: chsd wnr wl over 1f out and sn rdn: drvn and one pce ent fnl f: lost 2nd nr fin* **9/2**[3]

0666 **4** ¾ **Maybeme**[11] 4120 4-8-13 **55** .... DanielTudhope 4 52
(N Bycroft) *in tch: pushed along and hdwy 3f out: rdn over 2f out: n.d* **12/1**

3114 **5** 5 **Dunaskin (IRE)**[10] 2897 10-9-4 **67** ....(b) CharlesEddery(7) 2 56
(R C Guest) *s.i.s and in rr: t.k.h and hdwy to chse ldrs 1/2-way: rdn along over 3f out: wknd over 2f out* **7/1**

2m 36.31s (-3.49) **Going Correction** -0.30s/f (Firm)
WFA 3 from 4yo+ 12lb **5** Ran SP% **109.1**
Speed ratings (Par 103): **103,96,96,95,92**
CSF £5.02 TOTE £2.00: £1.10, £3.10; EX 4.50.
Owner Sheikh Hamdan Bin Mohammed Al Maktoum **Bred** New England Stud And M R P Barrett **Trained** Middleham Moor, N Yorks

FOCUS
A modest 55-70 handicap turned into a procession by the unexposed winner. Not easy to rate with the winner an improver and the placed horses 6lb below their best.

4450 WILFORD WATTS MEMORIAL H'CAP — 1m 100y
3:40 (3:41) (Class 4) (0-85,85) 3-Y-O+ **£5,180** (£1,541; £770; £384) **Stalls** High

Form RPR

6512 **1** **Shadowtime**[8] 4198 5-9-6 **77** .... AndrewMullen 4 88
(Miss Tracy Waggott) *in tch: hdwy to chse ldrs 3f out: swtchd lft and effrt wl over 1f out: sn rdn: styd on strly to ld ins fnl f* **5/2**[1]

5123 **2** 2 **Celtic Change (IRE)**[49] 2835 6-10-0 **85** ....(bt) PhillipMakin 3 91
(M Dods) *led: rdn along wl over 1f out: drvn ent fnl f: sn hdd and kpt on same pce* **6/1**[3]

0411 **3** 2¾ **Ailsa Craig (IRE)**[34] 3317 4-9-4 **75** .... TonyHamilton 6 75
(E W Tuer) *trckd ldrs: hdwy to chse ldr over 2f out: rdn along wl over 1f out: drvn and one pce appr fnl f* **4/1**[2]

45-4 **4** ¾ **Faithful Ruler (USA)**[207] 6 6-9-8 **84** .... LeeTopliss(5) 7 82
(R A Fahey) *dwlt and in rr: hdwy over 3f out: rdn over 2f out: styd on appr fnl f: nrst fin* **22/1**

231- **5** ¾ **Cherry Bee**[337] 5320 3-8-6 **71** .... SilvestreDeSousa 9 65
(M Johnston) *chsd ldr: rdn along over 3f out: drvn 2f out: grad wknd* **7/1**

6520 **6** ½ **Bullet Man (USA)**[48] 2865 5-9-7 **81** .... BarryMcHugh(3) 5 76
(R A Fahey) *dwlt and in rr: hdwy wl over 2f out: rdn along wl over 1f out: kpt on appr fnl f: n.d* **7/1**

6210 **7** ½ **Danehillsundance (IRE)**[17] 3889 6-9-13 **84** ....(t) RobertWinston 8 78
(D H Brown) *midfield: hdwy over 3f out: rdn over 2f out: drvn over 1f out: n.d* **8/1**

5400 **8** 30 **Carnivore**[24] 3659 8-9-1 **72** .... GrahamGibbons 2 —
(T D Barron) *chsd ldr: rdn along 3f out: sn wknd* **40/1**

-503 **9** 2¼ **Boy Blue**[11] 4119 5-9-0 **71** .... DarryllHolland 1 —
(P Salmon) *dwlt: a in rr: bhd fr 1/2-way* **8/1**

1m 44.05s (-3.55) **Going Correction** -0.30s/f (Firm)
WFA 3 from 4yo+ 8lb **9** Ran SP% **116.9**
Speed ratings (Par 105): **105,103,100,99,98 98,97,67,65**
toteswingers:1&2:£2.80, 1&3:£2.80, 2&3:£3.20 CSF £18.09 CT £58.60 TOTE £3.80: £1.70, £1.50, £2.20; EX 16.80.
Owner H Conlon **Bred** Darley **Trained** Spennymoor, Co Durham

FOCUS
A 71-85 handicap run at a furious pace. The form looks sound.
Boy Blue Official explanation: trainer said gelding was unsuited by good to firm ground

4451 BEVERLEY ANNUAL BADGEHOLDERS MAIDEN AUCTION FILLIES' STKS — 5f
4:15 (4:15) (Class 5) 2-Y-O **£2,590** (£770; £385; £192) **Stalls** High

Form RPR

1 **Tallahasse (IRE)** 2-8-7 0 .... PJMcDonald 8 76+
(G A Swinbank) *s.i.s and in rr: hdwy 2f out: effrt to chse ldrs whn hmpd over 1f out: rdn and kpt on wl to ld ins fnl f: sn clr* **6/1**[3]

5 **2** 2¾ **Abzolutely (IRE)**[10] 4149 2-8-4 0 .... SilvestreDeSousa 13 61
(D O'Meara) *led: rdn and edgd lft 1 1/2f out: drvn and hung lft to stands' rail ent fnl f: sn hdd and one pce* **4/1**[1]

53 **3** nk **Scommettitrice (IRE)**[22] 3721 2-8-4 0 .... LukeMorris 11 60
(R A Harris) *trckd ldrs: hdwy 2f out: rdn to chal wl over 1f out: ev ch whn hung bdly lft appr fnl f: sn drvn and one pce* **5/1**[2]

0 **4** ¾ **Madam Mayem**[10] 4149 2-8-4 0 .... RichardKingscote 12 57
(Tom Dascombe) *dwlt: sn in tch: hdwy to chse ldrs 2f out: effrt and ch whn n.m.r and hmpd over 1f out: sn swtchd rt and rdn: kpt on same pce fnl f* **25/1**

5 1¾ **Norwegian Liberty (IRE)** 2-8-7 0 .... AndrewElliott 10 54
(B M R Haslam) *s.i.s and in rr: hdwy wl over 1f out: swtchd rt and rdn over 1f out: kpt on ins fnl f: nrst fin* **4/1**[1]

6 1½ **Granny Anne (IRE)** 2-8-7 0 .... GrahamGibbons 7 49
(A Bailey) *sn outpcd and bhd: hdwy wl over 1f out: kpt on ins fnl f: nrst fin* **12/1**

356 **7** 1¾ **Dotty Darroch**[24] 3665 2-8-1 **61** .... KellyHarrison(3) 9 39
(R Bastiman) *chsd ldrs: rdn along 2f out: hld whn sltly hmpd over 1f out: wknd* **14/1**

0 **8** 2 **None Sweeter**[14] 3971 2-8-7 0 .... DavidAllan 6 40+
(T D Easterby) *in tch: hdwy over 2f out: rdn wl over 1f out: sn wknd* **25/1**

04 **9** shd **Venus Empress**[24] 3686 2-8-7 0 .... RichardMullen 5 42+
(E S McMahon) *chsd ldr: rdn along 2f out: drvn and hld whn hmpd over 1f out: sn eased* **4/1**[1]

0423 **10** 1¼ **Chester Deelyte (IRE)**[14] 3986 2-7-13 **55** .... JamesSullivan(5) 1 27
(Mrs L Williamson) *chsd ldrs on outer: rdn along over 2f out: sn wknd* **20/1**

11 1¼ **Avoncharm** 2-8-7 0 .... TomEaves 4 26
(M Brittain) *sn outpcd in rr* **33/1**

06 **12** shd **Bonne Millie**[14] 3971 2-8-7 0 .... TonyHamilton 2 25
(R A Fahey) *chsd ldrs: rdn along over 2f out: sn wknd* **25/1**

64.28 secs (0.78) **Going Correction** +0.05s/f (Good) **12** Ran SP% **124.6**
Speed ratings (Par 91): **95,90,90,88,86 83,80,77,77,75 73,73**
toteswingers:1&2:£6.60 ,1&3:£9.20, 2&3:£4.80 CSF £29.69 TOTE £10.90: £6.00, £1.20, £1.10; EX 40.00.
Owner Mrs J Porter **Bred** John P Jones **Trained** Melsonby, N Yorks

FOCUS
An ordinary maiden auction fillies' race with the likes of the third helping with the form. They set off racing in one group towards the far side but the leader hung violently left and took them towards the stands' side.

NOTEBOOK
Tallahasse(IRE) ◆, who looks to have a fair bit of improvement in her, was not well away then met serious traffic problems when improving soon after the halfway mark. She came clear in the end and looks a fair prospect. (op 8-1)
Abzolutely(IRE), who made the running when fifth first time at Ripon a week earlier, again led the charge racing towards the far side rail. Under pressure she hung violently left coming to the final furlong and ended up under the stands' side rail. She clearly has the ability to go one better if she can be taught to keep straight. (op 5-1)
Scommettitrice(IRE), having her third run, had no excuse and this may be as good as she is. (op 7-2)
Madam Mayem improved a good deal on her debut effort behind Abzolutely at Ripon and will be suited by a step up to six. Official explanation: jockey said filly suffered interference in running (op 22-1)
Norwegian Liberty(IRE) did not go without support on her debut and showed a fair level of ability. She should improve for the outing. (op 7-1)
Granny Anne(IRE), last away, stayed on nicely and will be wiser next time. (op 14-1)
Venus Empress, fourth at Nottingham in a race that has worked out well, was disappointing fading badly late on. (op 5-1)

4452 I DO WEDDING FAIR HERE 8 AUGUST H'CAP — 5f
4:50 (4:50) (Class 5) (0-75,75) 3-Y-O+ **£3,238** (£963; £481; £240) **Stalls** High

Form RPR

5462 **1** **Frognal (IRE)**[19] 3809 4-9-7 **75** ....(b) JamesSullivan(5) 12 83
(Mrs R A Carr) *stdd s: hld up in rr: hdwy wl over 1f out: swtchd lft and effrt ins fnl f: sn rdn and kpt on to ld nr line* **7/1**

0440 **2** shd **Rio Sands**[2] 4415 5-8-2 **56** oh4 .... AmyRyan(5) 8 64
(R M Whitaker) *in tch: hdwy to chse ldrs 2f out: effrt and n.m.r over 1f out: squeezed through and rdn to chal ins fnl f: drvn and led briefly towards fin: hdd nr line* **40/1**

5020 **3** nse **Ingleby Star (IRE)**[39] 3165 5-9-8 **74** ....(p) GaryBartley(3) 2 81
(N Wilson) *slt ld: rdn wl over 1f out: drvn ent fnl f: hdd and nt qckn towards fin* **25/1**

5060 **4** 1 **Rowayton**[11] 4118 4-9-12 **75** .... PhillipMakin 3 79
(J D Bethell) *hld up in rr: hdwy wl over 1f out: rdn and styd on strly ins fnl f: nrst fin* **12/1**

6332 **5** 1¼ **King Of Swords (IRE)**[2] 4415 6-8-7 **56** oh1 ....(p) KirstyMilczarek 7 55
(N Tinkler) *in tch: swtchd lft to outer and hdwy to chse ldrs wl over 1f out: sn rdn: sn hung bdly lft to stands' rail appr fnl f: sn drvn and one pce* **7/2**[1]

2104 **6** ½ **Riflessione**[12] 4043 4-9-11 **74** ....(b) LukeMorris 1 72
(R A Harris) *cl up: rdn along wl over 1f out and ev ch: drvn appr fnl f and kpt on same pce* **16/1**

0-51 **7** hd **Bahamian Ballet**[24] 3687 8-9-10 **73** .... GrahamGibbons 11 70
(E S McMahon) *trckd ldrs on inner: swtchd lft and hdwy over 1f out: rdn ent fnl f and kpt on same pce* **10/1**

0410 **8** nk **Hitches Dubai (BRZ)**[3] 4373 5-9-2 **65** .... SilvestreDeSousa 6 61
(G A Harker) *chsd ldrs: rdn along 2f out: drvn whn n.m.r over 1f out: wknd* **5/1**[3]

1632 **9** nk **Ryedane (IRE)**[8] 4199 8-9-5 **68** ....(b) DavidAllan 5 63
(T D Easterby) *chsd ldrs: rdn along wl over 1f out: sn carried lft to stands' rail: n.m.r and swtchd rt ins fnl f: no hdwy* **11/2**

1004 **10** nse **Bosun Breese**[4] 4343 5-9-4 **72** .... DeanHeslop(5) 4 67
(T D Barron) *chsd ldrs on outer: rdn along 2f out: drvn whn carried lft to stands' rail ent fnl f and grad wknd* **28/1**

0032 **11** ½ **Kyzer Chief**[12] 4047 5-8-7 **59** ....(v) BarryMcHugh(3) 10 52
(R E Barr) *cl up: ev ch 2f out: sn rdn and wknd over 1f out* **9/2**[2]

63.34 secs (-0.16) **Going Correction** +0.05s/f (Good) **11** Ran SP% **117.4**
Speed ratings (Par 103): **103,102,102,101,99 98,98,97,97,97 96**
toteswingers::1&2:£4.90, 1&3:£10.90, 2&3:£9.50 CSF £260.44 CT £6583.39 TOTE £8.20: £2.30, £11.20, £7.70; EX 265.50.
Owner Reach For The Moon **Bred** Bryan Ryan **Trained** Huby, N Yorks

FOCUS
A tight 56-75 sprint handicap. They raced in one group towards the far side with plenty of traffic problems. Three came towards the stands' side in the end, headed home by King Of Swords. The form is rated around the first two.

4453 DOROTHY LAIRD MEMORIAL TROPHY (LADIES RACE) (H'CAP) (DIV I) 1m 1f 207y
5:25 (5:26) (Class 6) (0-65,65) 3-Y-O+ **£2,388** (£705; £352) **Stalls** High

Form				RPR
5025	1		**Hurricane Thomas (IRE)**[14] 3978 6-9-6 **55**.......... MissPhillipaTutty(5) 3	64
			(R A Fahey) *chsd ldrs: hdwy over 2f out: rdn on inner over 1f out: led jst ins fnl f and kpt on wl* **5/1**[3]	
132	2	2 ¼	**Silly Gilly (IRE)**[10] 4156 6-9-6 **55**.......... MissVBarr(5) 5	60
			(R E Barr) *chsd clr ldr: rdn 2f out: led over 1f out: drvn and hdd jst ins fnl f: kpt on same pce* **13/2**	
0064	3	2 ¼	**Catbells (IRE)**[4] 4329 3-9-6 **60**.......... NatashaEaton 10	62+
			(A Bailey) *hld up towards rr: hdwy on inner 2f out: nt clr run and swtchd lft over 1f out: sn rdn and kpt on ins fnl f* **9/1**	
/006	4	1	**Parchment (IRE)**[6] 4246 8-8-11 **46** oh1..........(b) MarzenaJeziorek(5) 1	44
			(A J Lockwood) *chsd ldrs: hdwy over 3f out: rdn along 2f out: drvn and one pce over 1f out* **16/1**	
0036	5	shd	**Tres Froide (FR)**[24] 3684 5-9-5 **49**..........(p) KirstyMilczarek 8	47
			(N Tinkler) *chsd ldrs: hdwy over 2f out: rdn wl over 1f out: sn one pce* **12/1**	
02	6	1 ¼	**Descaro (USA)**[11] 4120 4-10-1 **59**.......... KellyHarrison 9	54
			(D O'Meara) *chsd ldrs: hdwy 3f out: rdn along 2f out: drvn and no imp appr fnl f* **85/40**[1]	
5043	7	½	**Country Road (IRE)**[14] 3978 4-10-2 **65**..........(e) MissJoannaMason(5) 4	59
			(M W Easterby) *hld up towards rr: hdwy on inner over 2f out: nt clr run and swtchd lft ent fnl f: n.d* **7/2**[2]	
6505	8	1	**Mojeerr**[29] 3521 4-8-11 **46** oh1..........(v) MissAWallace(5) 6	38
			(A J McCabe) *towards rr: hdwy on outer 4f out: rdn along to chse ldrs over 2f out: sn btn* **28/1**	
0024	9	8	**Mississippian (IRE)**[28] 3538 6-9-1 **50**.......... MissDLenge(5) 7	26
			(Mrs D J Sanderson) *led and sn wl clr: rdn 2f out: hung lft and hdd over 1f out: wknd qckly* **16/1**	
0000	10	25	**Sacco D'Oro**[55] 2653 4-9-2 **46** oh1.......... MissMMullineaux 2	—
			(M Mullineaux) *dwlt: a outpcd and bhd fr 1/2-way* **50/1**	

2m 5.55s (-1.45) **Going Correction** -0.30s/f (Firm)
WFA 3 from 4yo+ 10lb **10** Ran SP% **119.1**
Speed ratings (Par 101): **93,91,89,88,88 87,87,86,79,59**
toteswingers:1&2:£4.90, 1&3:£10.90, 2&3:£9.50 CSF £38.43 CT £289.19 TOTE £8.60: £2.80, £1.20, £4.00; EX 24.80.

Owner N D Tutty **Bred** P D Savill **Trained** Musley Bank, N Yorks

■ Stewards' Enquiry : Miss D Lenge one-day ban; careless riding (tbd)

FOCUS
A low-grade 46-65 lady riders' handicap and the leader set a suicidal pace. The runner-up is rated to this year's form.

4454 DOROTHY LAIRD MEMORIAL TROPHY (LADIES RACE) (H'CAP) (DIV II) 1m 1f 207y
6:00 (6:01) (Class 6) (0-65,61) 3-Y-O+ **£2,388** (£705; £352) **Stalls** High

Form				RPR
6252	1		**Royal Composer (IRE)**[14] 3978 7-9-3 **48**.......... MissRKneller(5) 8	55
			(T D Easterby) *trckd ldrs: hdwy 2f out: cl up over 1f out: rdn to chal ent fnl f: styd on to ld last 100yds* **9/4**[2]	
2000	2	1 ½	**Fitzwarren**[33] 3369 9-9-0 **45**..........(tp) MissNVorster(5) 7	49
			(A D Brown) *dwlt: hdwy to ld after 1f and set stdy pce: qcknd 3f out: rdn wl over 1f out: drvn ent fnl f: hdd and no ex last 100yds* **20/1**	
0440	3	½	**Tivers Song (USA)**[21] 3754 6-9-10 **50**..........(b) SoniaEaton 5	53
			(John A Harris) *t.k.h: trckd ldrs: hdwy and cl up over 3f out: rdn 2f out: kpt on u.p fnl f* **12/1**	
341	4	nk	**Kyle Of Bute**[14] 3978 4-10-7 **61**.......... MissSBrotherton 6	63
			(B P J Baugh) *plld hrd: trckd ldrs: effrt 2f out: sn rdn: drvn and ch appr fnl f: kpt on same pce* **6/4**[1]	
-060	5	2 ¼	**Emperor's Well**[14] 3978 11-9-0 **45**.......... MissJoannaMason(5) 3	43
			(M W Easterby) *hld up in tch: hdwy on inner 2f out: rdn to chse ldrs over 1f out: drvn and hung lft fnl f: no imp* **7/1**[3]	
-000	6	½	**Masterofceremonies**[14] 3978 7-9-12 **57**..........(v) MissALMurphy(5) 1	54
			(W M Brisbourne) *hld up: hdwy on outer 4f out: rdn over 2f out: sn wandered and wknd* **20/1**	
0060	7	½	**Pacific Bay (IRE)**[40] 3131 4-9-10 **50**.......... MissPernillaHermansson 9	46
			(R Ford) *plld hrd: led 1f: trckd ldr: cl up 3f out: rdn and ev ch 2f out: edgd lft over 1f out and grad wknd* **33/1**	
0-60	8	nk	**Grethel (IRE)**[12] 3352 6-9-0 **45**.......... MissWGibson(5) 10	40
			(A Berry) *dwlt: towards rr: hdwy over 2f out: rdn wl over 1f out: sn no imp* **16/1**	
5000	9	nk	**Sitwell**[14] 3978 4-9-10 **55**..........(p) MissCBell(5) 4	50
			(I W McInnes) *t.k.h: hld up: effrt over 2f out: sn rdn and nvr a factor* **40/1**	
100	10	4 ½	**Chicamia**[29] 3502 6-9-11 **51**.......... MissMMullineaux 2	37
			(M Mullineaux) *a in rr* **25/1**	

2m 11.34s (4.34) **Going Correction** -0.30s/f (Firm) **10** Ran SP% **115.6**
Speed ratings (Par 101): **70,68,68,68,66 65,65,65,65,61**
toteswingers:1&2:£8.50, 2&3:£36.40, 1&3:£4.40; totesuper7: Win: Not won. Place: Not won. CSF £51.56 CT £450.22 TOTE £2.90: £1.40, £5.40, £3.10; EX 43.50 Place 6 £243.42, Place 5 £41.20..

Owner Mrs B Oughtred **Bred** Paul Hearson Bloodstock **Trained** Great Habton, N Yorks

■ Stewards' Enquiry : Miss A L Murphy one-day ban; not giving mount time to respond (tbd)

FOCUS
Part two was a 45-61 handicap and in marked contrast the pace this time was positively funereal. The winner's time was nearly 6secs slower than division one and the form looks messy.

T/Plt: £204.20 to a £1 stake. Pool:£46,049.19 - 164.58 winning tickets T/Qpdt: £21.40 to £1 stake. Pool:£5,222.05 - 180.43 winning tickets JR

3346 GOODWOOD (R-H)
Tuesday, July 27

OFFICIAL GOING: Straight course - good; round course - good to firm (good in places; 8.1)
Rail from 6f to winning post on lower bend dolled out approx 6yd, top bend out 3yds increasing distances on round course by circa 15yds.
Wind: Almost nil Weather: Cloudy, humid

4455 BETFAIR APP FOR IPHONE STKS (H'CAP) 1m 1f 192y
2:10 (2:10) (Class 2) 4-Y-O+
£31,155 (£9,330; £4,665; £2,335; £1,165; £585) **Stalls** High

Form				RPR
2460	1		**Indian Days**[17] 3921 5-9-1 **102**.......... DaleSwift(5) 2	113
			(J G Given) *hld up in midfield: 8th 1/2-way: rdn and gd prog on outer fr 3f out: narrow ld over 1f out: drvn to assert last 75yds* **12/1**	
6354	2	½	**Changing The Guard**[11] 4100 4-7-13 **81**.......... PaulHanagan 4	91
			(R A Fahey) *hld up in midfield: 7th 1/2-way: gd prog on outer w eventual wnr fr 3f out: chal and upsides over 1f out: nt qckn last 75yds* **16/1**	
-132	3	2 ¼	**Satwa Moon (USA)**[48] 2865 4-8-0 **82**.......... JimmyQuinn 5	88+
			(E A L Dunlop) *hld up in last trio: last over 3f out and great deal to do: sn rdn: gd prog fr 2f out: styd on strly to take 3rd last 50yds* **20/1**	
-254	4	1 ¼	**Almiqdaad**[24] 3672 4-9-3 **99**..........(b) RichardHills 3	102
			(M A Jarvis) *trckd ldr after 2f: clsng whn first pair home swept past 2f out: kpt on same pce after* **11/2**[2]	
-042	5	1	**Australia Day (IRE)**[10] 3633 7-8-13 **95**.......... MartinDwyer 15	97
			(P R Webber) *taken down early: led: drvn and qcknd clr 1/2-way: hdd and no ex over 1f out* **9/2**[1]	
6015	6	½	**Tartan Gunna**[25] 3633 4-8-10 **92**..........(b) JoeFanning 12	93
			(M Johnston) *s.i.s: hld up in last trio: stdy prog against rail fr 3f out: sltly checked over 1f out: nvr gng pce to rch ldrs* **14/1**	
1100	7	nk	**Submariner (USA)**[24] 3672 4-8-9 **91**.......... RoystonFfrench 13	91
			(M Johnston) *chsd ldr 2f: racd in 3rd after: rdn whn pce lifted 1/2-way: nt pce to rch ldrs fr over 2f out: kpt on* **8/1**	
3560	8	nk	**December Draw (IRE)**[41] 3069 4-9-1 **97**.......... ShaneKelly 7	96
			(W J Knight) *settled in rr: 12th 1/2-way: rdn and no prog 3f out: kpt on fr 2f out: n.d* **20/1**	
5112	9	¾	**Jo'Burg (USA)**[17] 3889 6-8-3 **88**.......... MartinLane(3) 10	86+
			(Lady Herries) *s.s and lost 3 l: hld up in last trio: rdn on outer 3f out: kpt on fr 2f out: nt pce to threaten* **16/1**	
1-30	10	hd	**Roman Republic (FR)**[144] 821 4-9-3 **99**.......... AlanMunro 8	97
			(Saeed Bin Suroor) *t.k.h: prom: trckd ldng trio 6f out: rdn and no imp over 2f out: wknd over 1f out* **15/2**[3]	
4106	11	3 ¼	**Moynahan (USA)**[24] 3692 5-8-8 **90**.......... TomQueally 11	81+
			(P F I Cole) *taken down early: towards rr: 10th 1/2-way: rdn over 3f out: limited prog whn hmpd 2f out: no ch after* **12/1**	
1100	12	5	**Tartan Gigha (IRE)**[24] 3692 5-9-7 **103**.......... KierenFallon 9	85
			(M Johnston) *t.k.h: hld up in midfield: 9th 1/2-way: lost pl and struggling 3f out: brief effrt 2f out: sn wknd* **16/1**	
0423	13	3	**Ramona Chase**[31] 3456 5-7-13 **81**..........(t) NickyMackay 6	57
			(M J Attwater) *taken down early: s.i.s: a in rr and nvr gng wl: 11th 1/2-way: no prog 3f out* **25/1**	
3-23	14	1	**Yamal (IRE)**[12] 4050 5-9-10 **106**..........(v) FrankieDettori 16	80
			(Saeed Bin Suroor) *chsd ldrs: 6th 1/2-way: no prog 3f out: wknd 2f out* **16/1**	
1543	15	6	**Gaily Noble (IRE)**[34] 3334 4-8-9 **91**.......... JimCrowley 14	54
			(A B Haynes) *trckd ldng trio to 6f out: u.p and wknd 3f out: t.o* **33/1**	

2m 5.55s (-2.45) **Going Correction** +0.025s/f (Good) **15** Ran SP% **118.3**
Speed ratings (Par 109): **110,109,107,106,106 105,105,105,104,104 101,97,95,94,89**
toteswingers:1&2:£39.40, 1&3:£58.20, 2&3:£29.50 CSF £176.76 CT £3769.13 TOTE £12.20: £4.50, £5.50, £5.30; EX 250.00 TRIFECTA Not won..

Owner D J Fish **Bred** Mrs C Regalado-Gonzalez **Trained** Willoughton, Lincs

■ Stewards' Enquiry : Dale Swift caution; careless riding

FOCUS
They went a decent pace thanks to established front-runner Australia Day and the field were well strung out at halfway. The form looks pretty solid.

NOTEBOOK
Indian Days was still 11lb higher than for his last win over C&D two years ago, but had been campaigned mainly at Pattern level in the meantime and had run several good races in that company. He was ridden a little more patiently than he has been of late, and was happy to sit in the middle of the field on the wide outside. The change of tactics worked a treat, and it's probably significant that he was ridden in a similar way when winning here in 2008. It did look as though the runner-up might get the better of him inside the last furlong after he had hit the front, but he pulled out a bit more with his young rider giving him only one crack with the whip. His jockey looked very tidy, and very strong. (op 14-1)
Changing The Guard, running well this season but without a win in over a year, likes to come late off a strong pace so the race was run to suit. He made his move down the outside of the field over 2f from home and looked likely to win inside the last, but was just held in the dying strides. He deserves to get his head back in front.
Satwa Moon(USA) ◆, 5lb higher than when narrowly beaten on his turf debut at Haydock last month, was still last with 3f left to run but he then weaved his way through the field and was still going forward at the line. He is still comparatively unexposed and is one to note. (op 16-1)
Almiqdaad, back down to probably his best trip, got a nice tow from Australia Day and was happy to sit in his slipstream starting up the straight. However, once pulled out for his effort he didn't find much and was making no impression when getting a little short of room. (op 6-1)
Australia Day(IRE), back on the Flat after running away with a valuable handicap hurdle at Market Rasen, was much better drawn than when well beaten in this race last year and tried to make every yard as he usually does. He quickened around 5f out and soon established a clear advantage, but he didn't get home and was swamped before reaching the furlong pole. (op 5-1 tchd 11-2)
Tartan Gunna, from the stable that had won this three times in the previous ten years, was successful in his only previous visit here. He can be given extra credit as he was trying for a daring run up the inside rail when getting into a barging match with Gaily Noble inside the last 2f, who in turn bumped the ridden-along Moynahan, and was never going to land a blow after that. He is worth keeping an eye on, though he has never won over as far as this. (op 12-1 tchd 16-1 in a place)
Submariner(USA) ◆ had twice finished unplaced over further since winning a couple of times at around this trip. He came off the bridle a long way out, but plugged on again and this still comparatively lightly raced colt shapes as though 1m4f will turn out to be his best trip. (tchd 9-1 in a place)
December Draw(IRE) had twice finished unplaced on turf since a successful spell on Polytrack over the winter, but he ran well in the Royal Hunt Cup last time and the return to this longer trip should have been in his favour, but despite the strong pace he didn't find his stride until it was far too late.

Jo'Burg(USA), up another 2lb after being thwarted in his hat-trick bid at Ascot last time, is a renowned slow starter and missed the break again. He gave himself plenty to do in such a strongly run race and his late rush down the wide outside was never going to get him into the money.
Moynahan(USA) Official explanation: jockey said gelding suffered interference in running
Tartan Gigha(IRE) was reported to have been moving poorly in the closing stages. Official explanation: jockey said gelding moved poorly in closing stages (op 12-1 tchd 11-1)

4456 BETFAIR GORDON STKS (GROUP 3) 1m 4f
2:45 (2:45) (Class 1) 3-Y-O

£39,739 (£15,064; £7,539; £3,759; £1,883; £945) **Stalls** Low

Form RPR

101 **1** **Rebel Soldier (IRE)**[45] 2979 3-9-0 102 .... RyanMoore 3 116
(J Noseda) *trckd clr ldng trio: rdn to cl on outer fr 3f out: led wl over 1f out: drvn 2 l clr fnl f: jst hld on* **4/1**[1]

1111 **2** *hd* **Dandino**[40] 3105 3-9-0 100 .... PaulMulrennan 7 116
(J G Given) *hld up in 6th: rdn on outer wl over 2f out: struggling to cl on ldrs wl over 1f out: r.o wl to take 2nd ins fnl f: clsd on wnr: jst failed* **9/2**[2]

1312 **3** *1 1/4* **Arctic Cosmos (USA)**[39] 3142 3-9-0 113 .... WilliamBuick 4 114+
(J H M Gosden) *hld up last: plenty to do whn rdn over 3f out: sme prog over 2f out: stl only 7th over 1f out and hanging: r.o wl to take 3rd last 75yds: nrst fin* **5/1**[3]

-006 **4** *1 3/4* **Fencing Master**[6] 4271 3-9-0 113 ....(v[1]) CO'Donoghue 8 111
(A P O'Brien, Ire) *trckd ldng pair and clr of rest after 5f: clsd fr 3f out: rdn to chal and upsides 2f out: nt qckn* **10/1**

1341 **5** *1/2* **Corsica (IRE)**[19] 3822 3-9-3 105 .... JoeFanning 2 113
(M Johnston) *led: stretched field after 4f: drvn and hdd wl over 1f out: sn outpcd: kpt on* **8/1**

-412 **6** *3 3/4* **Theology**[39] 3145 3-9-0 110 .... PaulHanagan 1 104
(J Noseda) *hld up in 9th: shkn up and prog 3f out: disp 5th on inner over 1f out: fdd* **8/1**

-315 **7** *4 1/2* **Very Good Day (FR)**[19] 3822 3-9-0 100 .... RichardHughes 6 97
(M R Channon) *hld up in 8th: rdn and struggling over 3f out: sn btn* **33/1**

-351 **8** *1 3/4* **Circumvent**[19] 3824 3-9-0 108 .... TomQueally 10 94
(P F I Cole) *trckd ldr: clsd to chal and upsides over 2f out: wknd rapidly over 1f out* **14/1**

-420 **9** *3 3/4* **Dubawi Phantom**[30] 3491 3-9-0 103 ....(b) RoystonFfrench 9 88
(D M Simcock) *settled in 7th: rdn over 3f out: sn struggling: wknd 2f out* **40/1**

14 **F** **Film Score (USA)**[40] 3104 3-9-0 106 .... FrankieDettori 11 —
(Mahmood Al Zarooni) *hld up in 6th: rdn over 3f out: wkng and last whn fatally injured and fell 2f out* **6/1**

2m 35.04s (-3.36) **Going Correction** +0.025s/f (Good) **10** Ran SP% **112.5**
Speed ratings (Par 110): **112,111,111,109,109 107,104,102,100,—**
toteswingers:1&2:£4.40, 1&3:£5.50, 2&3:£5.70 CSF £20.95 TOTE £4.30: £1.70, £1.80, £1.70; EX 14.30 Trifecta £113.70 Pool £2,643.67 - 17.19 winning units..
Owner The Honorable Earle I Mack **Bred** En Garde Syndicate **Trained** Newmarket, Suffolk
■ Stewards' Enquiry : Paul Mulrennan two day ban; excessive use of whip (10th-11th Aug)

FOCUS
Since 2000, three winners of this race - Millenary, Sixties Icon and Conduit - followed up in the St Leger, while Harbinger won last season's renewal. This year's contest was competitive, with a case to be made for most of the field, and the form seems solid for the level. The pace was quick courtesy of Corsica and the form is up to the normal race level.

NOTEBOOK
Rebel Soldier(IRE), a wide-margin handicap winner off a mark of 88 over 1m21/2f at York on his previous outing, justified his connections' decision to bypass the John Smith's Cup and instead wait for a Pattern race. He was always beautifully placed by Ryan Moore, far enough off the strong gallop, but this looked the absolute limit of his stamina and he only just held off the runner-up's strong challenge. Jeremy Noseda feels the winner is probably not a St Leger horse, but is likely to point him towards the Great Voltigeur. His connections may learn more at York, but it's interesting to note that the aforementioned trio who won this before taking the St Leger all went straight to the big one. Whatever, this lightly raced colt looks likely to go on improving. (tchd 9-2 and 7-2)
Dandino, a rapidly progressive handicapper whose latest win came off 91 in the King George V Stakes at Royal Ascot, showed himself up to pattern company and ran a fine St Leger trial. Having raced further back than the winner, he compromised his chance by going right when his rider pulled his whip through to his left hand inside the final furlong, although he was quickly corrected, and just failed. His pedigree offers hope that he'll stay further (a half-brother was placed over hurdles), and that's certainly the visual impression. However, before Doncaster he could be off to York for the Great Voltigeur, and another hard race there (jockey picked up a whip ban this time) would temper enthusiasm. (op 4-1 tchd 5-1)
Arctic Cosmos(USA) ◆ was having his first start since finishing runner-up in the King Edward VII Stakes at Royal Ascot. He was soon last after not applying himself through the early stages, needing to be niggled along on occasions, and was at least 3l behind the winner entering the straight, at which point he began to hang right. He continued to do so for the duration of the closing stages, patently not handling the track, and it's to his credit he was able to finish so close. It's possible he'll now go to York for the Great Voltigeur, but while that would mean the St Leger being his seventh start of the year, John Gosden's Lucarno won the race on his eighth run of 2007, and this one's dam took her racing particularly well. He looks likely to relish the 1m61/2f trip, while easier ground should suit, and all things considered, prices of around 14-1 for the final Classic of the season are probably fair. He is likely to head straight for Doncaster. (op 6-1)
Fencing Master, turned over at 1-3 over 1m six days earlier, had a visor replacing cheekpieces, and was upped significantly in trip, but he still didn't travel that fluently. He plugged on to post a respectable effort, but is still struggling to fulfil the potential he showed when runner-up in last year's Dewhurst. (op 11-1)
Corsica(IRE), who was burdened with a 3lb penalty for his success in the Group 3 Bahrain Trophy, was much too free to post and had little hope of sustaining his gallop when strongly challenged in the straight. All things considered, this was a commendable effort, and it would be no surprise to see him in the Voltigeur, where he won't be penalised. (tchd 15-2)
Theology, a stable companion of the winner, was beaten a nose in the Queen's Vase latest but could make no impression on this drop in trip. He won his maiden over C&D, but didn't look comfortable on the track this time, hanging right on to the far rail in the straight. (op 12-1)
Very Good Day(FR) hasn't progressed since chasing home Rewilding in a Listed event here earlier in the year. (tchd 40-1 in a place)
Circumvent found this tougher than the 1m2f July course handicap he won off a mark of 103 last time and failed to prove his stamina. (op 12-1 tchd 16-1)
Film Score(USA), who had looked promising and was having only his third start, sadly suffered a fatal injury early in the straight.

4457 BETFAIR CUP (REGISTERED AS THE LENNOX STKS) (GROUP 2) 7f
3:25 (3:26) (Class 1) 3-Y-O+

£87,993 (£33,356; £16,693; £8,323; £4,169; £2,092) **Stalls** High

Form RPR

3401 **1** **Lord Shanakill (USA)**[17] 3893 4-9-2 113 .... TomQueally 7 117
(H R A Cecil) *trckd ldng quartet: prog on outer to chse ldr over 1f out: drvn and r.o wl fnl f to ld last 50yds: hld on wl* **13/2**[2]

1040 **2** *hd* **Cat Junior (USA)**[42] 3046 5-9-2 112 ....(vt[1]) JamieSpencer 3 116
(B J Meehan) *stdd s: hld up in last pair: plld out wdst of all 2f out: rapid prog over 1f out: chal u.str.p last 100yds: nt qckn nr fin* **33/1**

1-15 **3** *1/2* **Dalghar (FR)**[42] 3046 4-9-2 0 .... GeraldMosse 4 115+
(A De Royer-Dupre, France) *t.k.h: trckd ldr: cruised into the ld jst over 2f out: drew more than 2 l clr over 1f out: hanging and hdd last 50yds* **7/2**[1]

-310 **4** *1/2* **Main Aim**[38] 3192 5-9-2 115 .... RyanMoore 10 113
(Sir Michael Stoute) *hld up disputing 6th: effrt over 2f out: drvn on inner and styd on fnl f: nvr quite able to chal* **9/1**

5-00 **5** *1* **Balthazaar's Gift (IRE)**[18] 3870 7-9-2 113 .... PhilipRobinson 12 111+
(C G Cox) *hld up in 9th: prog against rail fr 2f out: styd on but nvr gng pce of ldrs on outer* **8/1**

0-32 **6** *1/2* **Riggins (IRE)**[41] 3069 6-9-2 105 .... JimmyFortune 6 109
(A M Balding) *stdd s: hld up in 10th: drvn on outer over 2f out: styd on fr over 1f out: nt pce to threaten: nrst fin* **7/1**[3]

10-0 **7** *1 1/2* **Finjaan**[122] 1021 4-9-2 117 .... RichardHills 8 105
(M P Tregoning) *hld up disputing 6th: effrt on outer over 2f out: nt qckn over 1f out: fdd ins fnl f* **8/1**

0222 **8** *nse* **Red Jazz (USA)**[31] 3455 3-8-9 113 .... MichaelHills 1 102
(B W Hills) *chsd ldng pair: rdn over 2f out: steadily wknd over 1f out* **7/1**[3]

1603 **9** *1 1/2* **Lovelace**[24] 3704 6-9-2 106 .... AdrianNicholls 11 101
(D Nicholls) *hld up in last pair: rdn over 2f out: no prog over 1f out and btn after* **16/1**

1302 **10** *3/4* **Dunelight (IRE)**[17] 3893 7-9-2 106 ....(v) AdamKirby 5 99
(C G Cox) *led: hdd jst over 2f out: hanging and wknd over 1f out* **33/1**

-001 **11** *6* **Air Chief Marshal (IRE)**[10] 4160 3-8-9 110 .... CO'Donoghue 9 80
(A P O'Brien, Ire) *trckd ldng trio: pushed along 3f out: lost pl and btn 2f out: wknd* **16/1**

0505 **12** *4 1/2* **Forgotten Voice (IRE)**[17] 3888 5-9-2 111 ....(v) RichardHughes 2 71
(J Noseda) *stdd s: dropped in fr wd draw and hld up: t.k.h and 8th 1/2-way: wknd 2f out: eased* **14/1**

1m 25.52s (-1.38) **Going Correction** +0.025s/f (Good)
WFA 3 from 4yo+ 7lb **12** Ran SP% **117.1**
Speed ratings (Par 115): **108,107,107,106,105 104,103,103,101,100 93,88**
toteswingers:1&2:£40.40, 1&3:£4.30, 2&3:£26.00 CSF £196.35 TOTE £7.30: £2.70, £9.30, £1.90; EX 242.90 Trifecta £2672.50 Pool £4,333.86 - 1.20 winning units..
Owner Mogeely Stud & Mark T Gittins **Bred** Vimal Khosla, Gillian Khosla Et Al **Trained** Newmarket, Suffolk
■ Stewards' Enquiry : Jamie Spencer one-day ban; used whip with excessive frequency (10th Aug)

FOCUS
Amongst those successful in the previous ten runnings are the subsequent Group 1 winners Observatory, Court Masterpiece and Paco Boy. The pace was decent with Dunelight establishing his usual position out in front until getting swallowed up over 2f from home. The solid tempo would have been a help to the winner but the form looks sound enough overall.

NOTEBOOK
Lord Shanakill(USA) was back up in grade following a victory over Dunelight in a Chester Listed event, and he wouldn't be the first horse from the yard to bounce back to top form after a confidence-boosting success. He was always within striking distance of the leaders and, with his proven stamina coming into play, he responded to the pressure, and to the presence of the runner-up, to hit the front around 50 yards from the line. There are no firm plans for him at present. (op 7-1 tchd 6-1)
Cat Junior(USA), who has been running over 1m since finishing fourth over this trip in the Prix de la Foret last October, had a visor on for the first time (instead of the blinkers) alongside the usual tongue tie. He was ridden much more patiently than he has been, racing in last pace well off the pace. He eventually finished very strongly down the wide outside and looked like getting up inside the last furlong, but the winner just outstayed him. All the big races over 7f are options for him in the coming months, such as the Hungerford and Park Stakes.
Dalghar(FR) had pulled his chance away when fifth behind Goldikova in the Queen Anne last time so the return to 7f promised to suit, but he still took a grip again. Sent to the front over 2f from home, he was soon clear and looked sure to win, but he was treading water inside the last furlong and was run out of it in the last 50 yards. If his jockey could ride the race again, he would surely have held on to him for longer and he may head for the Park Stakes next. (op 4-1 tchd 100-30 and 5-1 in places)
Main Aim, last of eight when favourite for this race last year, tends to blow hot and cold and followed his success in a Haydock Group 3 with a poor effort in the Golden Jubilee last time. He was under pressure 2f from home, but battled on well up the inside rail to go down by a little over a length. It's hard to know how he will perform next time, however. (tchd 17-2)
Balthazaar's Gift(IRE), runner-up to Finjaan in this last year, had been far from disgraced behind Starspangledbanner in both the Golden Jubilee and July Cup and had shaped as though this return to 7f would suit him on each occasion. However, he got very warm beforehand and, although he made late progress tight against the inside rail, he never looked like getting there.
Riggins(IRE) was taking on Pattern company for the first time over a trip shorter than ideal so it was no surprise that he was doing his best work late, but this was still a fair effort at this level. He looks well up to winning a Listed race on this evidence. (op 11-1 tchd 12-1 in a place)
Finjaan, previously 2-2 here including this race last year, has been seen only once since last September, when well beaten over 6f at Meydan in March. He made a short-lived effort over a furlong from home, but it amounted to little and perhaps he just needed it. He was reported to have hung left. Official explanation: jockey said gelding hung left (op 7-1)
Red Jazz(USA), one of the two 3-y-os, had been beaten less than a length in his last three starts but although he had his chance over 2f from home, he was soon fighting a losing battle. (op 15-2)
Lovelace, a C&D winner in September 2007 when beating Dunelight, had a bit to find at this level but he would have finished a length or two closer had he not met some traffic problems over a furlong from home. (tchd 20-1)
Dunelight(IRE) soon established his usual position out in front until getting swallowed up over 2f from home.
Air Chief Marshal(IRE) seemed to have bounced back to his best with a couple of recent successes in lesser company, but he folded tamely over 2f from home and needs softer ground than this. (op 12-1)
Forgotten Voice(IRE), without a win since taking the Royal Hunt Cup last year, was racing over a trip this short for the first time since his racecourse debut, but he never got into the race at any stage. (tchd 16-1)

4458 BETFAIR MOLECOMB STKS (GROUP 3) 5f
4:00 (4:03) (Class 1) 2-Y-O

£34,062 (£12,912; £6,462; £3,222; £1,614; £810) **Stalls** Low

Form RPR

1151 **1** **Zebedee**[25] 3630 2-9-0 104 .... RichardHughes 9 103+
(R Hannon) *racd centre: hld up in tch: prog over 1f out: rdn and r.o to ld last 75yds: cleverly* **2/1**[1]

244 **2** *nk* **Stone Of Folca**[40] 3100 2-9-0 101 .... JimmyQuinn 10 102
(J R Best) *taken down early: t.k.h: trckd ldrs in centre: stl gng easily over 1f out: prog to chal fnl f: upsides last 100yds: nt qckn* **4/1**[2]

0315 **3** *hd* **Choose Wisely (IRE)**[47] 2917 2-9-0 95 .... NeilCallan 12 101
(K A Ryan) *racd centre: chsd ldr: led over 1f out: hrd pressed fnl f: hdd last 75yds: styd on* **33/1**

21 **4** 2 **Mayson**[28] 3528 2-9-0 0 .... PaulHanagan 3 94
(R A Fahey) *racd towards nr side: chsd ldrs: rdn over 1f out: styd on: nvr able to chal* **11/2**

3121 **5** ½ **Avonmore Star**[17] 3913 2-9-0 91 .... RyanMoore 11 92
(R Hannon) *racd centre: led to over 1f out: fdd fnl f* **5/1**[3]

2112 **6** *hd* **Leiba Leiba**[18] 3858 2-9-0 89 .... WilliamBuick 1 91+
(M Botti) *racd against nr side rail: hld up bhd rivals: effrt 2f out: styd on: nvr on terms* **16/1**

12 **7** *shd* **Lord Of The Stars (USA)**[19] 3826 2-9-0 0 .... JimCrowley 4 91+
(R M Beckett) *awkward s and dwlt: chsd ldrs in centre: outpcd u.p wl over 1f out: kpt on fnl f* **9/1**

1460 **8** 1 ¾ **Serena's Pride**[3] 4356 2-8-11 95 .... (v[1]) KierenFallon 2 82
(A P Jarvis) *racd nr side: prom in that gp: fdd over 1f out* **33/1**

3104 **9** 1 **Primo Lady**[31] 3453 2-8-11 89 .... (v) JimmyFortune 5 78
(Miss Gay Kelleway) *awkward s but lost no grnd: prom towards nr side: wknd over 1f out* **25/1**

1546 **10** ½ **Style And Panache (IRE)**[42] 3051 2-8-11 77 .... CathyGannon 7 76
(P D Evans) *racd towards centre: wl on terms w ldrs: edgd rt and wknd over 1f out* **100/1**

6112 **11** 1 ½ **Bold Bidder**[10] 4138 2-8-11 88 .... RoystonFfrench 8 71
(K A Ryan) *racd centre: chsd ldrs: wknd 2f out* **18/1**

1441 **12** 6 **Scarlet Rocks (IRE)**[18] 3858 2-8-11 85 .... TomQueally 6 49
(P D Evans) *nvr gng the pce: a struggling* **50/1**

58.49 secs (0.09) **Going Correction** +0.125s/f (Good) **12** Ran SP% **119.2**
Speed ratings (Par 104): **104,103,103,100,99 98,98,95,94,93 91,81**
toteswingers:1&2:£3.00, 1&3:£13.80, 2&3:£29.50 CSF £9.32 TOTE £2.60: £1.20, £1.70, £7.80; EX 9.70 Trifecta £459.70 Pool £3,305.20 - 5.32 winning units..
Owner Mrs J Wood **Bred** Hascombe & Valiant Studs **Trained** East Everleigh, Wilts

FOCUS
Straightforward but limited form, based around the principals and race averages. The front three look a little better than the bare form. The main action took place up the middle of the track and a high draw seemed an advantage.

NOTEBOOK
Zebedee ◆ reversed Norfolk Stakes form with Stone Of Folca, benefiting from more patient tactics than when meeting that rival at Royal Ascot. He was given a terrific ride by Richard Hughes, who tracked his old rival until just over 1f out, and he picked up smartly when switched widest of all to ultimately win a shade cosily. It's a shame he's not in the Nunthorpe, but he can be supplemented for £20,000 and his connections will surely be tempted, especially as his trainer won the race with a juvenile in 1992. He is entered in three sales races, although two of them are over 7f, and the other is over 6f. (op 9-4 tchd 5-2 and 13-5 in a place)
Stone Of Folca ◆ faded into fourth after being committed too soon in the Norfolk last time, so a patient ride was an absolute must this time, but he didn't help himself by resenting such tactics early, pulling hard. He soon managed to get a lead off Avonmore Star, and travelled powerfully, but the impression was that he would have preferred more cover, off an even stronger pace, and after being committed over 1f out, he was picked off near the line by a rival who had raced in his slipstream. He was on trial for the Nunthorpe, a race Kingsgate Native won for John Best and Jimmy Quinn as a juvenile in 2007, following a second placing in this race, and this colt showed more than enough to be of interest for that Group 1 contest. (tchd 7-2 and 9-2)
Choose Wisely(IRE), well drawn, showed good speed up the middle of the track and was only picked off by a couple of smart closers. This was an improvement of the form he showed in a French Listed race last time, with the quicker ground clearly suiting better. His owner is apparently keen to run him in the Nunthorpe, but the trainer favours going for the Gimcrack. (tchd 40-1)
Mayson ◆, a Hamilton maiden winner, fared best of those drawn low and this was a decent effort. This Middle Park entry looks likely to be suited by 6f and can do better. (op 13-2 tchd 7-1)
Avonmore Star, dropped back to 5f for the first time since his debut, showed loads of speed up the middle of the track from his favourable draw and had his chance. (op 8-1 tchd 9-1)
Leiba Leiba wasn't helped his draw, racing closest to the stands' rail in the closing stages, and can be given another chance. (op 14-1 tchd 20-1)
Lord Of The Stars(USA), trying 5f for the first time, was sensibly switched to middle of the track soon after exiting his unfavourable stall, and he showed early speed, but he was in trouble 2f out. A return to further should suit. (op 17-2 tchd 8-1)
Primo Lady leapt forward leaving the stalls, but while that didn't seem to stop her quickly building up momentum, she raced more towards the near side than ideal. (op 20-1)
Bold Bidder did nothing for the form of the Super Sprint. (op 12-1 tchd 20-1)
Scarlet Rocks(IRE) was reported to have lost her action. Official explanation: jockey said filly lost her action

4459 TATLER SUMMER SEASON STKS (H'CAP) 1m
4:35 (4:39) (Class 3) (0-90,90) 3-Y-O+ **£12,952** (£3,854; £1,926; £962) **Stalls** High

Form RPR

201 **1** **Start Right**[10] 4144 3-9-4 88 .... KierenFallon 13 103+
(L M Cumani) *dwlt: hld up wl in rr on inner: stdy prog over 2f out: looking for room over 1f out: squeezed through and plld out ent fnl f: r.o to ld last 100yds: sn clr* **7/2**[1]

6105 **2** 2 ¼ **Satwa Laird**[20] 3796 4-9-9 85 .... GeraldMosse 19 93
(E A L Dunlop) *hld up bhd ldrs in abt 9th: rdn and prog fr 2f out to ld 1f out: hdd and outpcd last 100yds* **12/1**

-533 **3** 1 **Truism**[33] 3346 4-9-9 85 .... RyanMoore 20 93+
(Mrs A J Perrett) *trckd ldng trio on inner: looking for gap fr 2f out: styd on same pce whn in the clr fnl f* **5/1**[2]

0221 **4** *nk* **Benandonner (USA)**[13] 4030 7-9-9 90 .... JohnFahy(5) 11 95+
(Mike Murphy) *hld up wl in rr: plenty to do whn effrt on outer over 2f out: styd on wl after: nrst fin* **20/1**

6122 **5** ½ **Mambo Spirit (IRE)**[13] 4024 6-9-2 78 .... TomQueally 17 82
(Stef Higgins) *hld up in midfield: plld out wd 3f out and prog: tried to cl on ldrs over 1f out: one pce* **33/1**

5040 **6** *nse* **Kavachi (IRE)**[17] 3889 7-9-2 78 .... FergusSweeney 4 82+
(G L Moore) *hld up wl in rr: prog towards inner over 2f out: short of room over 1f out and lost pl: styd on again fnl f* **33/1**

3536 **7** *nk* **My Gacho (IRE)**[19] 3813 8-9-9 85 .... (v) J-PGuillambert 2 88
(M Johnston) *led and crossed fr v wd draw: 3 l clr 1/2-way: hdd and fdd 1f out* **33/1**

3140 **8** *nk* **Cape Rock**[20] 3796 5-9-10 86 .... JimCrowley 7 88
(W J Knight) *hld up wl in rr and racd wd: rdn and prog fr 3f out: hanging rt fr 2f out: kpt on but nvr gng pce to threaten* **20/1**

-200 **9** 2 ¼ **Hail Promenader (IRE)**[54] 2683 4-9-6 82 .... FrankieDettori 15 79
(B W Hills) *hld up in midfield on inner: effrt over 2f out: short of room over 1f out: tried to cl ent fnl f: wknd last 100yds* **20/1**

2415 **10** 2 ¾ **My Kingdom (IRE)**[26] 3579 4-9-8 84 .... (t) RichardHughes 8 75
(H Morrison) *hld up off the pce: abt 12th 1/2-way: effrt but nt much prog whn hmpd over 1f out: no ch after* **15/2**[3]

046 **11** ½ **Huzzah (IRE)**[7] 4224 5-9-10 86 .... MichaelHills 6 76
(B W Hills) *dwlt: hld up in last trio and racd wd: no prog 3f out and wl btn sn after: modest late hdwy* **14/1**

-156 **12** 1 ¼ **Justonefortheroad**[17] 3920 4-9-3 79 .... PaulHanagan 18 66
(R A Fahey) *chsd clr ldr to over 1f out: wknd rapidly* **8/1**

-530 **13** 1 ¾ **Bencoolen (IRE)**[45] 2977 5-9-11 90 .... MichaelGeran(3) 10 73+
(D Nicholls) *trckd ldng pair: rdn over 2f out: sing to lose pl whn bdly hmpd over 1f out* **33/1**

0003 **14** ¾ **Mujood**[26] 3591 7-10-0 90 .... (v) WilliamBuick 12 71
(Eve Johnson Houghton) *nvr bttr than midfield: 10th 1/2-way: rdn and no prog wl over 2f out* **25/1**

6005 **15** 2 ¼ **Cyflymder (IRE)**[30] 3483 4-9-8 87 .... PatrickHills(3) 3 63
(R Hannon) *dwlt: dropped in fr wd draw and detached in last early: effrt against rail 3f out: no ch* **50/1**

401 **16** 2 **L'Hirondelle (IRE)**[13] 4023 6-9-3 79 .... NeilCallan 16 50+
(M J Attwater) *chsd ldng quartet: rdn and losing pl whn hmpd over 1f out: wknd* **25/1**

0531 **17** 4 **Kay Gee Be (IRE)**[18] 3846 6-9-11 87 .... AlanMunro 14 49
(W Jarvis) *a wl in rr: rdn and struggling 3f out* **10/1**

5004 **18** 14 **Highly Regal (IRE)**[13] 4030 5-9-4 80 .... (bt) LiamKeniry 9 10
(R A Teal) *prom to 1/2-way: wknd rapidly: t.o* **50/1**

3602 **19** 4 ½ **Keys Of Cyprus**[14] 3987 8-9-7 83 .... AdrianNicholls 5 3
(D Nicholls) *chsd ldrs on outer to 1/2-way: wknd rapidly: t.o* **25/1**

1m 38.6s (-1.30) **Going Correction** +0.025s/f (Good)
WFA 3 from 4yo+ 8lb **19** Ran SP% **126.7**
Speed ratings (Par 107): **107,104,103,103,102 102,102,102,100,97 96,95,93,93,90 88,84,70,66**
toteswingers:1&2:£10.80, 1&3:£4.00, 2&3:£12.40 CSF £38.42 CT £224.36 TOTE £4.10: £1.40, £3.00, £1.80, £4.40; EX 46.80 Trifecta £214.30 Pool £3,229.82 - 11.15 winning units..
Owner Leonidas Marinopoulos **Bred** Dukes Stud & Overbury Stallions Ltd **Trained** Newmarket, Suffolk

■ Stewards' Enquiry : Kieren Fallon one-day ban: careless riding (Aug 10)

FOCUS
A fiercely competitive handicap run at a strong pace. Five of the past seven winners of this race had been drawn 13 or higher and that trend continued, with the first five horses home all drawn in double figures. The placed horses set the standard.

NOTEBOOK
Start Right ◆, raised 4lb for his recent narrow Newmarket success, would have been an unlucky loser here as he was travelling well amongst horses all the way up the home straight, but with no daylight. Fortunately a gap appeared entering the last furlong and he made no mistake. He seems to have come to himself now, and it wouldn't be a surprise to see him win something even better. (tchd 4-1 and 9-2 in a place)
Satwa Laird ◆ was well drawn here and travelled well in the middle of the field. He seemed likely to win when leading inside the last furlong, but the winner's turn of foot proved too much for him. He is 2lb higher than when just getting up to win at Chepstow in May and will go up again for this, but he still looks to have a decent handicap in him. (tchd 14-1)
Truism, still relatively lightly raced, has been shaping as though this return to 1m would suit. He was always close to the pace from the best draw, but didn't see much daylight from the 2f pole to just over a furlong out and by the time he got through, it was too late. It would be pushing things to say that he would have troubled the winner with a clear run, however. (op 11-2 tchd 13-2)
Benandonner(USA) has been running well of late and was put up 3lb for his recent Polytrack success. He was given plenty to do, but finished with a real rattle down the wide outside and still looks capable of winning races off this sort of mark on either turf or sand. (op 16-1)
Mambo Spirit(IRE), up another 3lb following a narrow defeat on Polytrack last time, was trying this trip for the first time. Having made headway down the outside 2f from home, his effort flattened out inside the last furlong but it would be harsh to say that he didn't see the trip out in a race as competitive as this. He is well worth another try.
Kavachi(IRE) ◆ has been under-performing despite a slipping mark, but this was much better, especially as he did best of those drawn in single figures. He is now superbly handicapped if this signals a general return to form.
My Gacho(IRE) found himself drawn on the wide outside so did very well to get over to the rail in front early. He set a strong gallop and had established a clear lead by halfway, but it was always going to be hard for him to see his race out and he was swamped entering the last furlong.
Cape Rock, another drawn in single figures, hadn't shone in two previous tries over 1m but he ran on well down the wide outside, and it wasn't the trip that beat him here. (op 25-1)
Hail Promenader(IRE), beaten ten times in handicaps since winning a Redcar maiden in October 2008 (albeit beaten less than a length into second on four occasions), was in with a chance of a place when getting short of room on the inside over a furlong from home. He was reported to have been struck into on his right hind. Official explanation: vet said colt had been struck into right hind (op 25-1)
My Kingdom(IRE), an unlucky fifth off this mark at Epsom last time, was beaten less than a length in his only previous try over this trip, but that was in a steadily run race on Polytrack. He did not get the clearest of runs, but never managed to get into the race at any stage. (op 8-1 tchd 7-1)
Justonefortheroad, twice unplaced since making all on his Ayr reappearance and still 4lb higher, showed up for a long way but didn't get home. (op 10-1)
Bencoolen(IRE) was another to race prominently from the start, but was already beaten when getting into barging match with the weakening L'Hirondelle over a furlong from home. (op 25-1)
Keys Of Cyprus was reported to have hung right. Official explanation: jockey said gelding hung right handed

4460 E.B.F DALLAGLIO FOUNDATION MAIDEN STKS (C&G) (IN SUPPORT OF TICKETS FOR TROOPS) 6f
5:05 (5:09) (Class 2) 2-Y-O **£9,714** (£2,890; £1,444; £721) **Stalls** Low

Form RPR

5 **1** **Pabusar**[62] 2440 2-9-0 0 .... JimCrowley 3 87+
(R M Beckett) *mde virtually all: stretched at least 2 l clr fnl f: jst pushed out and nvr gng to be ct* **10/1**

2 ½ **Big Issue (IRE)** 2-9-0 0 .... RichardHughes 11 87+
(R Hannon) *hld up bhd ldrs: effrt 2f out: wnt 2nd 1f out: r.o and clsd on wnr qckly nr fin* **5/2**[2]

3402 **3** 3 **Straight Line (IRE)**[18] 3844 2-9-0 89 .... KierenFallon 1 77
(A P Jarvis) *wl in tch: effrt over 1f out: tk 3rd fnl f but wl outpcd by ldng pair* **11/2**[3]

4 **4** 1 **Golden Hinde**[9] 4167 2-9-0 0 .... FrankieDettori 9 74
(M Johnston) *w ldrs: shkn up 2f out: outpcd fr over 1f out* **9/4**[1]

5 ¾ **Barney Rebel (IRE)** 2-9-0 0 .... MichaelHills 4 74+
(B W Hills) *mostly last: pushed along over 1f out: styd on takingly fnl f: nrst fin* **16/1**

6 **6** 1 ½ **Kingarrick**[11] 4096 2-9-0 0 .... PatDobbs 10 67
(Eve Johnson Houghton) *wl on terms w ldrs tl fdd over 1f out* **16/1**

7 1 ½ **Macho's Magic (IRE)** 2-9-0 0 .... AdrianNicholls 5 62+
(D Nicholls) *hld up in tch: effrt over 2f out and n.m.r: rn green and wknd over 1f out* **20/1**

8 ¾ **Fists And Stones** 2-9-0 0 .... AlanMunro 6 60
(M R Channon) *wl in tch tl wknd over 1f out* **40/1**

40 **9** ½ **Welsh Dancer**[47] 2887 2-9-0 0 .... RyanMoore 7 59
(R Hannon) *w ldrs 4f: wknd qckly over 1f out* **8/1**

10 6 **Kingfisher Blue (IRE)** 2-9-0 0 .... FergusSweeney 2 41
(J A Osborne) *in tch in rr 4f: wknd* **66/1**

1m 12.81s (0.61) **Going Correction** +0.125s/f (Good) **10** Ran SP% **115.4**
Speed ratings (Par 100): **100,99,95,94,93 91,89,88,87,79**
toteswingers:1&2:£8.50, 1&3:£9.30, 2&3:£2.80 CSF £34.42 TOTE £12.00: £3.20, £1.50, £1.90; EX 50.20 Trifecta £183.90 Pool £1,874.95 - 7.54 winning units..
Owner Mr & Mrs Kevan Watts **Bred** Mr & Mrs Kevan Watts **Trained** Whitsbury, Hants

FOCUS
This looked a strong maiden, as you'd expect for the meeting, and the race should produce some nice winners. Just as in the only other race on the straight track on this card, the Molecomb, the middle of the track was the place to be.

NOTEBOOK
Pabusar ◆ got upset in the stalls before missing the break badly when beaten at Ffos Las (went off 15-8) on his debut in May, and was then withdrawn from an intended engagement at Windsor the following month after again getting worked up in the gates. However, he was gelded the very next day and showed what he is capable of on this return to action. Always travelling well, he picked up in good style to draw clear of some decent rivals and this looked a very useful performance. His connections expect him to have the speed for 5f - that was the visual impression - although the Mill Reef is said to be his main target. (op 11-1 tchd 9-1)
Big Issue(IRE) ◆ was described by his trainer as a "lovely colt" beforehand and this first foal of a 6f winner (also Listed placed at 7f) shaped pleasingly behind a potentially smart sort. His sales price increased from £25,000 as a yearling to £140,000 this year, and he should be extremely tough to beat in similar company next time, before stepping up in grade. (tchd 3-1 and 9-4 in places)
Straight Line(IRE), dropped in trip, was a little keen and proved no match for the front pair, but he plugged on to post a respectable effort. He can find easier opportunities. (op 9-2)
Golden Hinde didn't see his race out over 7f on debut, but he lacked the finishing speed of some of these on this drop in trip. A return to further should suit. (op 5-2 tchd 3-1 in places)
Barney Rebel(IRE) ◆, described by his rider as "a lovely horse", was a major eyecatcher. A 40,000gns purchase who is closely related to 1m2f winner Street Entertainer, he raced out the back for most of the way and was not given anything like a hard time, but he finished in taking fashion. (op 12-1 tchd 11-1)
Kingarrick showed ability when sixth on debut at Newbury over 7f, but this was another tough ask and he was well held. (op 20-1)
Macho's Magic(IRE) showed up well to a point and should be better for the experience. (tchd 22-1)

4461 ROA SUMMER STKS (H'CAP) 1m 6f
5:40 (5:40) (Class 2) (0-105,102) 3-Y-O+

£12,462 (£3,732; £1,866; £934; £466; £234) **Stalls** Low

Form				RPR
0131	**1**		**Martyr**[18] 3843 5-9-8 **96** .... RichardHughes 3 (R Hannon) *trckd clr ldr and in ldng trio wl ahd of rest: clsd to ld on bit over 2f out: stl cruising over 1f out: shkn up and readily drew clr fnl f* **7/1**[3]	109+
-414	**2**	3	**Jedi**[48] 2857 4-9-0 **88** .... RyanMoore 2 (Sir Michael Stoute) *prom in chsng gp but wl off the pce: rdn to cl fr over 3f out: styd on wl fr over 1f out to take 2nd ins fnl f: no ch w wnr* **8/1**	94
00/6	**3**	¾	**Sentry Duty (FR)**[38] 3195 8-9-11 **99** .... EddieAhern 8 (N J Henderson) *hld up in midfield and wl off the pce: rdn over 3f out: prog to cl fr over 2f out: styd on to take 3rd last 100yds* **11/1**	104
-401	**4**	2	**Woolfall Treasure**[39] 3159 5-9-6 **94** ....(v[1]) PatDobbs 10 (G L Moore) *prom in chsng gp but wl off the pce: rdn and lost pl 4f out: sn toiling in rr: r.o again over 1f out: tk 4th nr fin* **16/1**	96
4121	**5**	½	**Emerging Artist (FR)**[11] 4100 4-9-7 **95** .... JoeFanning 4 (M Johnston) *trckd ldng pair and clr of rest: chal over 3f out: pressed ldr on suffernce 1f out brushed aside fnl f: wknd last 100yds* **3/1**[1]	97+
0005	**6**	1 ½	**Becausewecan (USA)**[4] 4320 4-9-3 **91** .... RichardHills 11 (M Johnston) *led: clr after 3f: hdd over 2f out: battled on tl wknd fnl f* **16/1**	90
4620	**7**	2 ½	**Classic Vintage (USA)**[38] 3194 4-9-8 **96** .... JimCrowley 6 (Mrs A J Perrett) *wl off the pce in midfield: rdn over 3f out: clsd u.p over 2f out: no imp over 1f out: wknd* **12/1**	92
2450	**8**	shd	**Montaff**[40] 3102 4-10-0 **102** .... AlanMunro 14 (M R Channon) *hld up in rr and wl off the pce: rdn 4f out: no prog 3f out: plugged on fnl 2f* **33/1**	98
-510	**9**	shd	**Perfect Shot (IRE)**[42] 3050 4-9-4 **92** .... MartinDwyer 1 (J L Dunlop) *hld up in rr and wl off the pce: rdn and struggling over 3f out: plugged on fnl 2f* **16/1**	88
2-51	**10**	1 ¾	**Anhar (USA)**[24] 3670 3-8-12 **100** ....(v[1]) FrankieDettori 5 (Saeed Bin Suroor) *s.s: hld up last and wl off the pce: shkn up and no prog over 3f out: btn after* **9/2**[2]	93
201-	**11**	3 ¼	**Precision Break (USA)**[318] 5865 5-9-10 **98** .... JamieSpencer 12 (P F I Cole) *prom in chsng gp but off the pce: tried to cl over 3f out: hanging and no imp 2f out: wknd* **16/1**	87
0202	**12**	1	**Bow To No One (IRE)**[18] 3843 4-9-1 **89** .... NeilCallan 13 (A P Jarvis) *hld up in rr and wl off the pce: effrt on outer over 3f out: no prog over 2f out: wknd* **20/1**	76
2236	**13**	7	**Chink Of Light**[39] 3145 3-8-11 **99** ....(v) JimmyFortune 9 (A M Balding) *nvr on the pce: dropped to last and btn 4f out: t.o* **16/1**	76

3m 1.81s (-1.79) **Going Correction** +0.025s/f (Good)
WFA 3 from 4yo+ 14lb **13** Ran SP% **119.9**
Speed ratings (Par 109): **106,104,103,102,102 101,100,100,100,99 97,96,92**
toteswingers:1&2:£6.40, 1&3:£17.40, 2&3:£20.00 CSF £62.35 CT £619.89 TOTE £6.90: £2.00, £2.80, £4.30; EX 70.60 Trifecta £311.50 Place 6 £152.72, Place 5 £13.02.
Owner Highclere Thoroughbred Racing (Delilah) **Bred** D Maroun **Trained** East Everleigh, Wilts

FOCUS
This race has produced the Ebor winner twice in recent years; Mephisto won both in 2004, and Sergeant Cecil was third here before going in at York in 2005. Like last year, the prize money was disappointing for such a decent handicap. The pace seemed good, courtesy of Becausewecan, who raced around 5l clear for much of the way. However, only two runners kept tabs on him including the winner. The horses in the frame behind the winner set the standard and the form looks sound.

NOTEBOOK
Martyr was arguably flattered by the manner of his success considering how the race unfolded, not coming off the bridle until 1f out, although he's clearly on the upgrade. He had proved suited by a step up from 1m4f when successful (cosily off a 3lb lower mark) over 2m last time, so it was no surprise to see him given a positive ride on this slight drop in distance, and he's obviously improved for staying trips. The Ebor is the obvious target, and he'll look well treated under just a 4lb penalty, but single-figure odds make no appeal considering the doubt about the true worth of this performance. (op 15-2)
Jedi ◆, trying his furthest trip to date after 48 days off, lost ground on the winner when not appearing to handle the downhill run into the straight on this quick surface (well beaten only previous start at this track) and soon had about 7l to find with that rival, but he stuck on well for pressure. He can do better, especially back on easy ground, and looks sure to stay 2m.
Sentry Duty(FR) plugged on to post a respectable effort, but he couldn't muster the required speed. (op 12-1)
Woolfall Treasure, with a visor replacing blinkers, found this tougher than the C&D handicap he won in June and couldn't defy a 6lb higher mark. (tchd 20-1 in a place)
Emerging Artist(FR) could yet make a mockery of the theory that the winner is flattered, if proving he does stay this trip, but his latest success (off 9lb lower) came over 1m2f and his stamina gave out in the final furlong on this occasion. (op 7-2 tchd 4-1 in places and 5-1 in a place)
Becausewecan(USA) raced around 5l clear for much of the way and plugged on even after getting headed, but his exertions eventually took their toll. (tchd 20-1)
Anhar(USA) curiously went without the tongue-tie he had fitted when winning over 1m4f off a 4lb lower mark last time, yet had headgear on for the first time. He started sluggishly and was basically never going. (op 4-1 tchd 5-1 in places)
T/Jkpt: Not won. T/Plt: £124.80 to a £1 stake. Pool:£287,973.84 - 1,683.23 winning tickets
T/Qpdt: £9.50 to a £1 stake. Pool:£18,237.66 - 1,413.75 winning tickets JN

4462 - (Foreign Racing) - See Raceform Interactive

4442 GALWAY (R-H)
Tuesday, July 27

OFFICIAL GOING: Good

4463a TOPAZ MILE EUROPEAN BREEDERS FUND H'CAP (PREMUIER HANDICAP) 1m 100y
7:00 (7:02) 3-Y-O+

£63,716 (£20,176; £9,557; £3,185; £2,123; £1,061)

			RPR
1		**Ask Jack (USA)**[27] 3572 6-8-11 90 ....(p) CDHayes 17 (Joseph G Murphy, Ire) *sn led: rdn clr of remainder w 2nd bef st: forged clr u.p ins fnl f: styd on wl* **9/1**	97
2	2 ½	**Mid Mon Lady (IRE)**[12] 4080 5-8-8 94 ....(b) DCByrne[(7)] 12 (H Rogers, Ire) *chsd ldrs: 7th 1/2-way: rdn into mod 4th bef st: 2nd and kpt on wout troubling wnr fnl f* **25/1**	95
3	2 ½	**Worldly Wise**[17] 3932 7-9-7 100 ....(p) DMGrant 16 (Patrick J Flynn, Ire) *mid-div: 9th 1/2-way: prog to chse ldrs but no imp fr bef st: kpt on wl wout threatening* **14/1**	96
4	shd	**If Per Chance (IRE)**[14] 4009 5-8-13 92 .... FMBerry 9 (M Halford, Ire) *a.p: clr of remainder w wnr bef st: sn no imp u.p and kpt on same pce* **9/1**	87
5	2	**Drombeg Dawn (IRE)**[31] 3468 4-8-10 89 .... WJLee 4 (A J McNamara, Ire) *dwlt: sn mid-div: 10th 1/2-way: briefly short of room bef st: sn mod 7th and no imp: kpt on* **12/1**	80
6	2 ½	**Royal Astronomer (IRE)**[30] 3487 5-8-11 90 .... JAHeffernan 14 (Donal Kinsella, Ire) *towards rr: 11th 1/2-way: prog to chse ldrs fr bef st: kpt on same pce fr 1f out* **8/1**[3]	75
7	hd	**Final Flashback (IRE)**[18] 3883 5-8-3 85 .... BACurtis[(3)] 2 (Patrick J Flynn, Ire) *trckd ldrs: 5th 1/2-way: no imp and kpt on same pce appr st* **14/1**	70
8	½	**Sixteen Forty Two (IRE)**[25] 3652 5-8-7 91 .... MACleere[(5)] 10 (Eoin Doyle, Ire) *towards rr: nvr a factor: kpt on wout threatening fr over 2f out* **25/1**	75
9	1	**Kaitlins Joy (IRE)**[7] 3883 5-7-13 85 .... KarenKenny[(7)] 8 (Patrick Martin, Ire) *towards rr: n.d and kpt on fr over 2f out* **33/1**	67
10	hd	**Big Robert**[18] 3883 6-8-8 92 ....(p) KTO'Neill[(5)] 15 (P D Deegan, Ire) *s.i.s: towards rr and nvr a factor: kpt on fr over 2f out* **16/1**	73
11	¾	**Maundy Money**[30] 3487 7-9-2 95 ....(t) CO'Donoghue 13 (David Marnane, Ire) *trckd ldrs: dropped to mod 3rd u.p bef st: sn no ex* **13/2**[2]	75
12	3	**Mujaazef**[40] 3134 3-8-10 97 .... DPMcDonogh 18 (Kevin Prendergast, Ire) *short of room on inner early: sn chsd ldrs: 6th 1/2-way: rdn in mod 5th and no imp fr bef st: sn no ex* **4/1**[1]	70
13	nk	**Castle Bar Sling (USA)**[12] 4080 5-8-7 86 ....(p) WJSupple 11 (T J O'Mara, Ire) *towards rr for most: nvr a factor* **16/1**	58
14	nk	**Kargali (IRE)**[73] 2118 5-9-10 108 ....(t) MHarley[(5)] 3 (Luke Comer, Ire) *prom: dropped to 4th appr st: sn no ex u.p* **20/1**	80
15	5	**Few Are Chosen (IRE)**[103] 1341 4-8-7 87 .... PShanahan 5 (Tracey Collins, Ire) *a towards rr* **25/1**	48
16	4 ½	**Extraterrestrial**[17] 3921 6-9-2 95 .... MCHussey 7 (R A Fahey) *a towards rr* **11/1**	46
17	3	**Atasari (IRE)**[47] 2912 3-9-1 102 .... KJManning 6 (J S Bolger, Ire) *mid-div best: 12th 1/2-way: wknd appr st* **12/1**	46
18	dist	**Rock And Roll Kid (IRE)**[30] 3487 5-9-8 104 .... DEMullins[(3)] 1 (Anthony Mullins, Ire) *chsd ldrs: 8th 1/2-way: no ex appr st: sn eased: t.o* **12/1**	—

1m 46.82s (-3.38)
WFA 3 from 4yo+ 8lb **18** Ran SP% **140.2**
CSF £242.28 CT £3201.57 TOTE £10.00: £2.10, £7.40, £3.30, £2.80; DF 424.00.
Owner T D Howley Jnr **Bred** John F Dorrian **Trained** Fethard, Co Tipperary

FOCUS
A high draw is usually a big help in this race, and that aspect certainly seemed to be significant this time. The front-running winner has been rated back to his best.

NOTEBOOK
Ask Jack(USA) broke well and made every yard for an emphatic win, the sixth of a 30-race career. Joe Murphy had decided to target this race after Ask Jack had finished second in a valuable 7f event at last year's meeting, and he could reappear again later in the week if none the worse. (op 11/1)
Mid Mon Lady(IRE) initially made her name with three wins on the Polytrack at Dundalk, but has proved a versatile type by winning three races on turf, two of them during a fine spell of form towards the end of last season. She is having a very busy campaign this year, and was right up to her best here with a staying-on effort under her capable 7lb claimer.
Worldly Wise was able to capitalise on a good draw, and was back to form after a below-par display at Fairyhouse. (op 14/1 tchd 16/1)
If Per Chance(IRE) faded after trying to throw down a challenge to the winner before the straight. It seems fair to assume that the 12lb rise in the ratings that he received for his Killarney win took its toll.
Drombeg Dawn(IRE) deserves to pick up another race. She suffered from a slow start from her poor draw and then met trouble in running before the turn in. (op 14/1)
Final Flashback(IRE), a stablemate of the third, was another who ran respectably from a draw that was no help.
Maundy Money blotted his good record at the track by dropping away tamely. (op 13/2 tchd 7/1)
Mujaazef saw his chance was harmed by interference in the early stages. (op 5/1)
Few Are Chosen(IRE)'s rider reported that his mount was short of room on the final bend. Official explanation: jockey said filly was short of room turning for home
Rock And Roll Kid(IRE) struggled badly and was virtually pulled up. (op 12/1 tchd 11/1)

4455 GOODWOOD (R-H)

Wednesday, July 28

OFFICIAL GOING: Straight course - good; round course - good to firm (good in places; 8.3)

Rail from 6f to winning post on lower bend dolled out approx 6yd, top bend out 3yds increasing distances on round course by circa 15yds.

Wind: Moderate, against Weather: Fine

4467 SPORTINGBET.COM GOODWOOD STKS (H'CAP) 2m 5f

2:10 (2:10) (Class 2) (0-95,93) 3-Y-0+

£31,155 (£9,330; £4,665; £2,335; £1,165; £585)

Form				RPR
04-4	**1**		**Ghimaar**[21] 3050 5-9-7 **90** ... EddieAhern 9	98+
			(N J Henderson) *wl plcd bhd ldrs: 6th 5f out: prog against rail to ld wl over 2f out: drvn 2l clr jst over 1f out: styd on* **6/1**[1]	
31/1	**2**	1 ½	**Junior**[43] 3050 7-9-10 **93** ...(b) SebSanders 2	100
			(D E Pipe) *trckd ldr: rdn over 4f out: upsides 3f out: chsd wnr sn after and stl chalng 2f out: nt qckn over 1f out: styd on* **13/2**[2]	
-642	**3**	nk	**Relative Strength (IRE)**[37] 3267 5-8-3 **72** ...(v) DavidProbert 6	79
			(A M Balding) *lw: settled in midfield: 9th 5f out: prog against rail 3f out: drvn to dispute 2nd fr over 1f out: kpt on* **20/1**	
3111	**4**	1 ½	**Lady Eclair (IRE)**[16] 3955 4-9-10 **93** ... JoeFanning 12	98+
			(M Johnston) *wl in tch: 8th 5f out: rdn and effrt wl over 2f out: styd on same pce to take 4th ins fnl f* **13/2**[2]	
-231	**5**	2 ¼	**Ambrose Princess (IRE)**[14] 4026 5-8-3 **72** ow2...(p) HayleyTurner 19	75
			(M J Scudamore) *mostly trckd ldng trio: cl up and rdn over 2f out: no ex fnl 2f* **18/1**	
0-10	**6**	3 ½	**Hollins**[39] 3195 6-9-2 **85** ... FrankieDettori 14	85
			(Micky Hammond) *mostly trckd ldng pair: rdn 3f out: steadily wknd fnl 2f* **12/1**	
2-00	**7**	1 ¼	**Mith Hill**[38] 3241 9-8-8 **77** ... ChrisCatlin 8	76
			(Ian Williams) *trckd ldng quartet: cl enough 3f out: gradually wknd fnl 2f* **50/1**	
0-50	**8**	nse	**Baddam**[39] 3195 8-8-11 **80** ... PaulHanagan 17	79
			(Ian Williams) *rousted along to s: hld up in last: rdn on wd outside over 3f out: plugged on but n.d* **12/1**	
110	**9**	1	**On Terms (USA)**[19] 3843 4-8-10 **79** ... TomQueally 13	77
			(S Dow) *mde most to wl over 2f out: steadily wknd* **22/1**	
-641	**10**	2	**Theola (IRE)**[18] 3896 4-8-12 **81** ... PatCosgrave 1	77
			(M H Tompkins) *lw: nvr gng wl: reminder after 2f in rr: rchd 14th 5f out: effrt u.p on outer 3f out: sn no hdwy* **12/1**	
401/	**11**	1	**Dream Champion**[24] 5421 7-8-10 **79** ... KierenFallon 18	74
			(A J Martin, Ire) *a in midfield: 11th 5f out: sme prog on outer 3f out u.p: fdd over 1f out* **11/1**	
0-11	**12**	¾	**Markington**[15] 3974 7-8-11 **80** ...(b) JimCrowley 7	75
			(P Bowen) *a in midfield: u.p in 12th 5f out: effrt on outer 3f out: no prog* **17/2**[3]	
2441	**13**	6	**Curacao**[11] 4147 4-8-11 **80** ... NeilCallan 3	69
			(Mrs A J Perrett) *lw: settled in midfield: 10th 5f out: rdn over 3f out: no prog over 2f out: wknd over 1f out* **33/1**	
354-	**14**	hd	**Mission Control (IRE)**[43] 7515 5-8-3 **72** ... NickyMackay 5	61
			(Tim Vaughan) *settled towards rr: 13th 5f out: rdn and no prog 3f out: wl btn after* **16/1**	
500-	**15**	4	**Gee Dee Nen**[36] 5235 7-9-2 **85** ...(p) RyanMoore 20	71
			(G L Moore) *wl plcd bhd ldrs: 7th 5f out: hrd rdn over 3f out: sn wknd* **18/1**	
003/	**16**	8	**Hearthstead Dream**[10] 4179 9-8-6 **75** ... LiamKeniry 15	53
			(Gordon Elliott, Ire) *swtg: a wl in rr: rdn and no prog over 3f out: bhd fnl 2f* **66/1**	
60-0	**17**	1 ½	**Enjoy The Moment**[43] 3050 7-9-2 **85** ... FergusSweeney 16	62
			(J A Osborne) *swtg: hld up wl in rr: stl there but seemed to be gng strly over 4f out: rdn and no rspnse 3f out: sn bhd* **33/1**	
41-2	**18**	7	**Excelsior Academy**[16] 3955 4-8-13 **82** ... MartinDwyer 10	53
			(B J Meehan) *hld up wl in rr: rdn and no prog over 3f out: no ch and eased 2f out* **20/1**	
	19	9	**Acambo (GER)**[11] 9-8-11 **80** ... JimmyFortune 4	43
			(D E Pipe) *hld up in last quartet: shkn up and no prog over 3f out: wknd and eased 2f out: t.o* **50/1**	
00/0	**20**	2 ½	**Backbord (GER)**[47] 2938 8-8-10 **79** ...(p) WilliamBuick 11	39
			(Mrs L Wadham) *sn pushed along in rr and nvr gng wl: wknd over 3f out: eased: t.o* **33/1**	

4m 28.83s (-2.17) **Going Correction** +0.025s/f (Good) **20** Ran SP% **127.4**

Speed ratings (Par 109): **105,104,104,103,102 101,101,101,100,99 99,99,96,96,95 92,91,89,85,84**

toteswingers: 1&2 £8.40, 1&3 £37.10, 2&3 £30.80. CSF £39.23 CT £763.90 TOTE £7.10: £2.30, £2.40, £5.10, £2.00; EX 35.90 Trifecta £963.60 Pool: £2,717.38 - 2.08 winning units..

Owner Martin George **Bred** Hunscote House Farm Stud **Trained** Upper Lambourn, Berks

FOCUS

This is always a strong marathon handicap. The early pace wasn't as strong as can often be the case, though, and not for the first time those ridden out the back found it hard to make a significant impact. Most of the riders afterwards described the ground as "perfect" and slightly quicker than the opening day. Sound form, and both the first two improved on their Ascot running.

NOTEBOOK

Ghimaar shaped a little better than the bare form when fourth in the Ascot Stakes on his last outing on the level (subsequently won over hurdles) and was able to race off the same mark. He got an absolute peach of a ride from Ahern, who bided his time in a prominent position and was ideally placed nearing the 3f marker. He was travelling so well Ahern was able to delay asking him for everything and got a dream run on the inside at the crucial stage. His response when sent to the front was most positive and he was in no real danger throughout the final furlong. Surely the Cesarewitch will now come under strong consideration (stable also has Sentry Duty pencilled in for the race), but a likely rise means he will need to improve a good bit to win that. It's debateable whether he had to improve that much to land this as he was 8lb better off with his Ascot conqueror Junior, so obviously the pair ran very close to that form. It's also well worth noting that in the past decade only the 2002 winner of this event Hugs Dancer followed up next time. Officially rated 135 as a hurdler, however, connections are sure to have plenty of fun with him back over jumps in due course. (op 15-2)

Junior made all on debut for current connections at Royal Ascot 43 days previously and was a solid chance to go in again. He wasn't asked to lead this time and proved a little free as a result. No doubt racing near the front was an advantage here, but he still posted another brave effort under joint top weight and rates a rock-solid benchmark. There should still be other days for him and his connections are really looking forward to getting him back over jumps in due course. (op 6-1)

Relative Strength(IRE), back to form when second at Lingfield last time, was 3lb higher and had looked a non-stayer when eighth in this race last season. This wasn't so much of a test this time around, though, and he turned in a dour effort without ever really looking likely to hit the front. He can find lesser assignments despite going up for this and deserves another winning turn. His trainer believes he will make a nice jumper for someone down the line.

Lady Eclair(IRE) was having her first outing beyond 2m off a career-high mark, and was saddled with joint top weight. She was ridden a little more patiently than has often been the case, somewhat understandably in this race, but looking at the way she kept on from 3f out a more positive ride may well have suited better. The Ebor still looks a realistic assignment. (op 7-1 tchd 6-1)

Ambrose Princess(IRE), an easy winner at Lingfield a fortnight earlier, was suited by racing close to the pace and did have bottom weight. She was 10lb higher for this, however, and it must rate another improved effort, so she helps to give the form a good look. (op 20-1)

Hollins, ninth in the Queen Alexandra at Royal Ascot last month, was faced with a more realistic assignment again and ran a fair race in defeat. The Handicapper now looks in charge. (op 20-1 tchd 10-1)

Mith Hill posted one of his better efforts. (op 40-1)

Theola(IRE), 2lb higher for her Chester win, came under pressure nearing the home turn having been held up and wasn't on a going day. (tchd 11-1)

Dream Champion caught the eye with the way he went though the race and, on this showing, failed to get the marathon trip. With that in mind he will be one to consider when reverting to a sharper test. (op 10-1 tchd 12-1)

Markington tends to switch off before running on strongly in his races and this test didn't suit. (op 9-1)

4468 VEUVE CLICQUOT VINTAGE STKS (GROUP 2) 7f

2:45 (2:45) (Class 1) 2-Y-O

£45,416 (£17,216; £8,616; £4,296; £2,152; £1,080) **Stalls** High

Form				RPR
141	**1**		**King Torus (IRE)**[19] 3868 2-9-3 **104** ... RichardHughes 6	114+
			(R Hannon) *lw: trckd ldr: led 2f out: shkn up and drew rt away: impressive* **11/4**[2]	
512	**2**	6	**Stentorian (IRE)**[27] 3645 2-9-0 **0** ... FrankieDettori 3	95
			(M Johnston) *w'like: scope: sn led at decent pce: hdd 2f out: sn outpcd: styd on again to take 2nd ins fnl f* **8/1**	
51	**3**	shd	**Major Art**[11] 4131 2-9-0 **0** ... RyanMoore 5	94
			(R Hannon) *lw: t.k.h: trckd ldng pair: lost pl jst over 2f out: hanging and struggling over 1f out: styd on again fnl f: nrly snatched 2nd* **5/1**[3]	
1254	**4**	1	**Chilworth Lad**[31] 3488 2-9-0 **101** ... JimmyFortune 1	93
			(M R Channon) *hld up in 5th: wnt 3rd jst over 2f out: lost pl and sltly short of room wl over 1f out: kpt on same pce after* **12/1**	
11	**5**	nk	**Waltz Darling (IRE)**[34] 3364 2-9-0 **90** ... PaulHanagan 7	91
			(R A Fahey) *athletic: awkward s: hld up in 4th: outpcd on inner fr 2f out: kpt on again last 100yds* **11/1**	
11	**6**	1	**Crown Prosecutor (IRE)**[31] 3476 2-9-0 **0** ...(t) KierenFallon 4	89+
			(B J Meehan) *str: t.k.h: hld up in last pair: short of room on inner 5f out: stmbld sn after: prog on outer to chse wnr wl over 1f out: sn lft bhd: wknd ins fnl f* **6/4**[1]	
021	**7**	hd	**Surrey Star (IRE)**[13] 4054 2-9-0 **80** ... JohnFahy 2	88
			(R A Teal) *t.k.h: hld up in last pair: shkn up and effrt on outer 3f out: one pce fnl 2f* **33/1**	

1m 27.13s (0.23) **Going Correction** +0.025s/f (Good) **7** Ran SP% **113.4**

Speed ratings (Par 106): **99,92,92,90,90 89,89**

toteswingers: 1&2 £2.40, 1&3 £2.10, 2&3 £4.00. CSF £24.15 TOTE £3.70: £1.80, £3.30; EX 22.60.

Owner Sir Robert Ogden **Bred** Whisperview Trading Ltd **Trained** East Everleigh, Wilts

FOCUS

This didn't look the strongest of line-ups for a Group 2 prize, especially with the favourite performing below expectations.

NOTEBOOK

King Torus(IRE) possibly didn't beat a great deal in following up his Superlative Stakes success. That said, he defied a 3lb penalty for his Newmarket win and came right away to win by a wide margin, so he still comes out of the race with his reputation enhanced. He enjoyed the run of the race in a tactical affair on the July Course, but was denied the lead here by Stentorian, who ended up going off far too fast in front. Quickening to the front inside the final 2f, he immediately crossed over to the rail and soon left his rivals toiling. A mile should be within his compass, but there's no real need to go any further than 7f this season and, given that his tendency to hang right means a right-handed rail is always going to be of benefit to him, all roads will surely now lead to the Prix Jean-Luc Lagardere, where the track will suit him down to the ground. His trainer seemed more interested in going to the Dewhurst or Racing Post Trophy, but the French race looks far more suitable. His Guineas odds were cut to a general 20-1. (tchd 5-2 and 3-1 in places)

Stentorian(IRE), whose trainer often runs one of his better 2-y-os in this race, was proven over the trip and looked an interesting contender, even allowing for the fact that this required a step up on his effort in an Irish Listed race last time out. Determined to make the running, he had to work to get the lead off King Torus and then proceeded to set a strong gallop. When headed inside the final 2f he looked sure to drop right away, but his stamina saw him plug on to retain second. A step up to 1m should suit him, and his trainer mentioned the Royal Lodge as a potential target, which makes sense.

Major Art didn't help his cause by racing keenly early but he's a half-brother to a couple of horses who have won over 1m6f-plus, and he was keeping on well at the finish. There should be further improvement to come from him, and a Listed race at Deauville could be next on his agenda. (op 6-1 tchd 13-2 and 7-1 in places)

Chilworth Lad, the most experienced horse in the race, didn't improve for the step up in trip and is short of this class. (op 10-1)

Waltz Darling(IRE), 2-2 in the north, got a bit outpaced before running on again at the finish. This was a big step up in class for him and he could yet make his mark at Listed level. (tchd 12-1 and 14-1 in places)

Crown Prosecutor(IRE) is evidently highly regarded, but his pedigree is pretty much all about speed, so it was slightly surprising to see him turn up here. Wearing a tongue-tie for the first time, he was a little keen early, hampered next to the inside rail heading into the first turn, and again on the bend, but still came there to have his chance 2f out. Second inside the last, he emptied quickly soon after (vet later reported he'd finished distressed). His trainer blamed the early interference for the disappointing run, but it would be surprising if that was the only reason, and a drop back to 6f looks in order. (op 7-4 tchd 2-1 in places)

Surrey Star(IRE) faced a stiff task on this step up in class from an Epsom maiden, but he wasn't at all disgraced, and nurseries over this trip or 1m will present him with easier opportunities. (op 40-1)

4469 SUSSEX STKS (GROUP 1) 1m

3:25 (3:27) (Class 1) 3-Y-0+

£179,677 (£68,110; £34,087; £16,996; £8,513; £4,272) **Stalls** High

Form				RPR
2311	**1**		**Canford Cliffs (IRE)**[43] 3048 3-8-13 122 .... RichardHughes 1	130+
			(R Hannon) *lw: stdd s: hld up in last trio: plld out and prog 2f out: wnt 2nd jst over 1f out: pushed along firmly and qckned to make up 2 l on ldr: led last 50yds: immediately eased* **4/6**[1]	
10-6	**2**	*nk*	**Rip Van Winkle (IRE)**[43] 3046 4-9-7 129 .... RyanMoore 7	129
			(A P O'Brien, Ire) *lw:trckd clr ldr: clsd to ld wl over 1f out and sn kicked 2 l clr: r.o fnl f: hdd last 50yds* **9/4**[2]	
5011	**3**	*3 ¼*	**Premio Loco (USA)**[18] 3888 6-9-7 119 .... GeorgeBaker 6	122
			(C F Wall) *trckd ldng trio: pushed along over 2f out: outpcd over 1f out: styd on to take 3rd ins fnl f* **17/2**[3]	
16-6	**4**	*¾*	**Beethoven (IRE)**[43] 3048 3-8-13 117 ....(v) JPO'Brien 2	118
			(A P O'Brien, Ire) *lw: trckd ldng pair: wnt 2nd briefly over 1f out: hanging and sn outpcd: lost 3rd ins fnl f* **25/1**	
-333	**5**	*¾*	**Dream Eater (IRE)**[18] 3888 5-9-7 117 ....(t) JimmyFortune 4	118
			(A M Balding) *hld up in last trio: shkn up and effrt 2f out: easily outpcd fr over 1f out: kpt on* **20/1**	
151-	**6**	*8*	**Mac Love**[319] 5875 9-9-7 116 .... MickyFenton 5	100
			(Stef Higgins) *hld up in last: shkn up on outer 2f out: sn lft wl bhd* **50/1**	
500	**7**	*24*	**Encompassing (IRE)**[43] 3048 3-8-13 100 .... CO'Donoghue 3	42
			(A P O'Brien, Ire) *swtg: clr ldr tl hdd & wknd rapidly wl over 1f out: t.o* **200/1**	

1m 37.44s (-2.46) **Going Correction** +0.025s/f (Good)
WFA 3 from 4yo+ 8lb **7** Ran SP% **112.3**
Speed ratings (Par 117): **113,112,109,108,107 99,75**
toteswingers: 1&2 £1.20, 1&3 £1.80, 2&3 £2.10. CSF £2.20 TOTE £1.90: £1.10, £2.10; EX 2.70 Trifecta £8.10 Pool: £20,245.17 - 1,848.49 winning units..

Owner Heffer Syndicate, Mrs Roy & Mrs Instance **Bred** S And S Hubbard Rodwell **Trained** East Everleigh, Wilts

FOCUS

This was an exciting Sussex Stakes despite looking on all known form to be a match race, with a clash of the generations thanks to this season's top 3-y-o miler taking on last year's winner. The Ballydoyle pacemaker Encompassing went off quick, but the remainder of the field, headed by Rip Van Winkle, rather ignored him and it wasn't a searching test. Nevertheless, the form looks rock solid. Canford Cliffs now rates the leading 3yo, but Rip Van Winkle was a little off last year's best.

NOTEBOOK

Canford Cliffs(IRE) handed the Classic generation another win in the race, getting on top of Rip Van Winkle nearing the business end. He had looked set to relish this test after his impressive success in the St James's Palace Stakes and has gone from strength to strength since consenting to settle in his races. He went down to post nicely, but was unusually reluctant to load into the stalls and he made a very tardy start after eventually going in. Hughes soon had him racing in a nice rhythm due to the pace not being overly strong, though, and he again travelled beautifully into contention. Rip Van Winkle quickened things right up when going to the front after the 2f pole, and Hughes momentarily had to get serious with him, but the response was most positive. It was clear nearing the finish he was going to get up and he ultimately won cosily. His jockey's claim before the race that he had improved since Royal Ascot was proved right here, and it has to rate another personal-best effort, taking on his elders for the first time. Indeed Hughes said after the race he felt Canford Cliffs didn't handle the track too well, so there is likely still more to come and the logical next step would be the Queen Elizabeth II Stakes back at Ascot in September. He could meet Rip Van Winkle again, but with his liking for the course already advertised it would only be the possibility of soft ground that would be of some concern there. The Prix du Moulin at Longchamp is his other option. Much depends on connections securing a deal at stud, but they did later hint he may not be doing too much more this year with a view to racing as a 4-y-o, now that he has won three Group 1s. (op 8-11 tchd 4-5 in places)

Rip Van Winkle(IRE) performed miles below his best when reappearing in the Queen Anne, but his preparation for this was reported to have gone smoothly, in contrast to last year when his trainer wasn't even 100% he would be taking part on his way down to the start. Unsurprisingly he was the one who kept closest tabs on his pacemaker, as he did when winning last season, but this time his challenge was delayed as he took up the running later than last year. Some may say that regular rider Johnny Murtagh might have sent him on sooner, and Rip Van Winkle is much more of a grinder than Canford Cliffs, but Ryan Moore still gave him every chance. This was obviously a lot more like it and there is a strong chance he will improve again for the run, as his trainer firmly believes. While no immediate plans were put forward it may well be that he re-opposes the winner in a defence of the Queen Elizabeth II Stakes, but he also holds an entry in the Group 2 Celebration Mile back over C&D next month, where he would be hard to stop, even under a penalty. He could also revert to 1m2f, however, and would have better claims of seeing out that distance this year as an older horse. Therefore the Juddmonte International at York's Ebor meeting could be next, and his trainer only has Irish Derby hero Cape Blanco as a possible strong contender for that at this stage. There is also the Irish Champion Stakes to consider for him in early September. (tchd 5-2 in places)

Premio Loco(USA) was supplemented for this after landing the Group 2 Summer Mile at Ascot 18 days earlier. He was the logical each-way choice and ran his race, so it's disappointing on that front there were only the seven runners. He was done for speed by the first pair, but deserves credit as it later transpired he suffered a cut to his off-hind. That was not thought to be too bad and he could now be off a summer break, though his trainer didn't rule out the possibility of coming back here for the Celebration Mile. Official explanation: vet said gelding had been struck into (tchd 8-1)

Beethoven(IRE) ran close to his official mark when sixth on his belated return behind Canford Cliffs at Royal Ascot. His inclusion here was justified, being a Group 1 winner himself, and he ran an improved race without ever seriously threatening. He has plenty of future entries, but dropping in class looks most likely. (op 28-1 tchd 22-1 and 33-1 in a place)

Dream Eater(IRE) ran close enough to his last-time-out form with Premio Loco. He has yet to win in Group company, but surely can be found an opening down in class before the season is out. (tchd 22-1)

Mac Love was last seen winning over 1m2f in Group 3 company last September. He got taken off his feet early on, but should come on a bundle for the run and left the impression he now wants a stiffer test. (tchd 66-1)

4470 RACING UK H'CAP 1m 4f

4:00 (4:01) (Class 2) (0-105,98) 3-Y-O

£31,155 (£9,330; £4,665; £2,335; £1,165; £585) **Stalls** Low

Form				RPR
1031	**1**		**Verdant**[26] 3633 3-9-7 98 .... RyanMoore 3	109+
			(Sir Michael Stoute) *hld up towards rr: taken to outer and stdy prog fr wl over 2f out: rdn to ld jst over 1f out: jnd nr fin: jst hld on* **5/1**[2]	
-215	**2**	*shd*	**Mataaleb**[35] 3335 3-8-11 88 .... JimmyFortune 1	99
			(J Pearce) *hld up in rr: taken towards outer and stdy prog fr over 2f out following wnr through: hrd rdn to chal fnl f: upsides nr fin: btn on the nod* **40/1**	
4306	**3**	*1 ¾*	**Contract Caterer (IRE)**[20] 3824 3-9-0 91 .... RichardHughes 11	99
			(Pat Eddery) *swtg: hld up in midfield: stdy prog fr over 3f out: rdn to chal and upsides over 1f out: outpcd by ldng pair fnl f* **13/2**	
1320	**4**	*hd*	**Life And Soul (IRE)**[41] 3105 3-8-5 82 .... LukeMorris 9	90
			(Mrs A J Perrett) *hld up in midfield on inner: looking for room fr 3f out: hanging rt over 2f out: drvn and styd on fr over 1f out: nvr able to chal* **20/1**	
3411	**5**	*2*	**Mount Athos (IRE)**[20] 3820 3-8-8 85 .... SebSanders 17	90
			(J W Hills) *lw: rousted along early to rch gd pl on inner: trckd ldrs after: stl cl up 2f out: hanging and nt qckn over 1f out: wknd ins fnl f* **12/1**	
2133	**6**	*hd*	**Boston Blue**[18] 3909 3-8-6 83 .... MartinDwyer 18	87+
			(W J Knight) *sluggish early and drvn in rr: rapid prog to trck ldrs 1/2-way: lost pl bdly on inner over 2f out: styd on again fnl f* **22/1**	
1-00	**7**	*2 ¾*	**Fareej (USA)**[12] 4106 3-8-13 90 .... TedDurcan 5	90
			(Saeed Bin Suroor) *hld up and mostly last: stl there 3f out and shkn up: sme prog jst over 2f out: kpt on but nvr nr ldrs* **33/1**	
6311	**8**	*nse*	**Jutland**[27] 3581 3-9-0 91 .... RoystonFfrench 14	91
			(M Johnston) *mostly trckd ldr: led 3f out: hrd rdn and jnd over 2f out: edgd rt over 1f out: sn hdd & wknd* **14/1**	
1154	**9**	*nk*	**Berling (IRE)**[25] 3670 3-9-0 91 .... EddieAhern 2	90
			(J L Dunlop) *hld up in last trio: taken to outer 3f out: sme prog over 2f out: no hdwy and btn over 1f out* **9/2**[1]	
1221	**10**	*3 ¾*	**Bowdler's Magic**[6] 4304 3-9-2 93 6ex .... JoeFanning 10	86
			(M Johnston) *hld up in midfield: prog on outer fr 1/2-way: trckd ldrs over 4f out and 2nd wl over 2f out: upsides after tl wknd rapidly over 1f out* **14/1**	
0414	**11**	*1 ¾*	**Mister Angry (IRE)**[12] 4086 3-8-8 85 .... RichardHills 7	75
			(M Johnston) *hld up in rr: brief effrt on outer 3f out: no prog and wl btn 2f out: eased* **22/1**	
-263	**12**	*6*	**Issabella Gem (IRE)**[48] 2890 3-8-3 80 .... PaulHanagan 15	61
			(C G Cox) *settled towards rr on inner: shkn up 3f out: no prog: wknd 2f out* **20/1**	
2123	**13**	*4*	**Grey Bunting**[12] 4100 3-8-6 83 .... WilliamBuick 12	57+
			(B W Hills) *trckd ldrs: 4th 5f out: cl up over 2f out: swtchd ins to chal whn nowhere to go and hmpd over 1f out: nt rcvr and eased* **20/1**	
0-12	**14**	*1 ¾*	**Sour Mash (IRE)**[12] 4106 3-9-1 92 .... KierenFallon 4	64
			(L M Cumani) *lw: t.k.h: mostly trckd ldng pair: lost pl 3f out: wknd 2f out* **6/1**[3]	
3-03	**15**	*35*	**Emirates Dream (USA)**[13] 4068 3-9-7 98 .... FrankieDettori 16	14
			(Saeed Bin Suroor) *swtg: mde most to 3f out: wknd rapidly: t.o* **25/1**	
-111	**16**	*8*	**Sea Of Heartbreak (IRE)**[36] 3298 3-9-1 92 .... SteveDrowne 6	—
			(R Charlton) *racd wd in midfield: nt gng wl fr 1/2-way: wknd rapidly 3f out and eased: t.o* **13/2**	

2m 35.54s (-2.86) **Going Correction** +0.025s/f (Good) **16** Ran SP% **129.0**
Speed ratings (Par 106): **110,109,108,108,107 107,105,105,105,102 101,97,94,93,70 64**
toteswingers: 1&2 £28.40, 1&3 £9.00, 2&3 £89.00. CSF £208.59 CT £1359.80 TOTE £5.10: £1.70, £10.90, £2.10, £5.30; EX 546.00 Trifecta £2900.50 Part won. Pool: £3,919.65 - 0.10 winning units..

Owner K Abdulla **Bred** Juddmonte Farms Ltd **Trained** Newmarket, Suffolk

FOCUS

This looked a cracking middle-distance 3-y-o handicap, but there was just an ordinary early pace set, which resulted in a host of chances nearing the furlong marker. The first two eventually came clear and the form looks solid.

NOTEBOOK

Verdant, 8lb higher, just did enough to register a fourth win from six career starts with a very gutsy effort under joint top weight. He was a Dante entry at the start of the campaign but, despite winning on his seasonal return, has taken time to mature. Considering that more of a test would've probably suited, despite this being a step back up in trip, there was plenty to like about the way he went about his business. He is certainly open to further improvement over this distance, indeed he may well get further and it's interesting to note that his trainer's last winner of this event, Regal Flush, went on to follow up over 1m6f in the Old Borough Cup at Haydock. (tchd 9-2, 11-2 in places)

Mataaleb, drawn on the outside, so nearly made a winning debut for new connections. He left the impression he was held by the Handicapper when off this mark in the Bibury Cup on his last outing for Michael Jarvis, but is well bred and lightly raced. The change of scenery has also had a positive effect and it will be fascinating to see whether he can build on this after a likely rise. He should be given the chance to do so.

Contract Caterer(IRE) had run right up to his mark the last twice and was back up in trip here. There can be no coincidence that having Hughes on top made him travel so sweetly into contention, but the steady early pace probably wasn't ideal for him and he is well worth another chance. (op 8-1)

Life And Soul(IRE) looks one to take from the race with a view to stepping up in trip. He didn't get the best of runs around 3f out and didn't look to handle this track that well. He ran on well in the circumstances and is a relentless galloper, so could prove well handicapped over a stiffer test. (op 22-1 tchd 25-1 in places)

Mount Athos(IRE) was fully 15lb higher than when going in again at Folkestone earlier this month. He looked lazy early on, but still had his chance and it appeared to be the track that found him out late on. (op 11-1)

Boston Blue, dropping back in trip, ran a funny race. He had to be ridden from the gates, but was in a handy position nearing the turn for home. He then got chopped up on the inside near the 2f marker, which ended any winning chance, but kept on well inside the final furlong. On this showing he remains on a workable mark and perhaps he now needs further, but he evidently isn't straightforward. (op 33-1)

Fareej(USA) has failed to beat a rival in two previous outings as a 3-y-o so this was clearly a lot better again from him. He was ridden in last early on and finished with promise, so can be ridden more positively in the future. (op 50-1)

Jutland was 7lb higher in his quest for the hat-trick. Given a positive ride over these extra 2f, he ultimately rates a non-stayer. (tchd 16-1, 20-1 in a place)

Berling(IRE) looked a possible back in this bigger field and was again well backed. His effort proved short-lived and, while returning to a more conventional track may help, his progression does appear to have levelled out. (op 5-1 tchd 11-2 in places)

Bowdler's Magic was a clear-cut winner from the front over 1m6f at Sandown last week so it was surprising he wasn't asked to get near the front on this return to a sharper test. Ultimately the run looked to come that bit too soon for him, however. (op 12-1)

Grey Bunting was done no favours whatsoever on the inside around 2f out and his run is best forgiven.

Sour Mash(IRE) may not have enjoyed this course as he ran too badly to be true. (tchd 13-2 in places)

Sea Of Heartbreak(IRE) weakened quickly and presumably something was amiss. Official explanation: jockey said filly stopped quickly (op 8-1)

4471 MARKEL INTERNATIONAL MAIDEN FILLIES' STKS 6f
4:35 (4:35) (Class 2) 2-Y-O **£12,952** (£3,854; £1,926; £962) **Stalls** Low

Form				RPR
44	1		**Mortitia**19 3861 2-9-0 0 PaulHanagan 5 (B J Meehan) *lw: t.k.h: hld up bhd ldrs: squeezed through 1f out and sn chsd ldr: drvn and r.o to ld post* **10/1**	74+
6	2	shd	**Qenaa**47 2930 2-9-0 0 RichardHills 6 (M Johnston) *lw: pressed ldr: led wl over 1f out: rdn and styd on fnl f: hdd post* **5/1**2	74+
	3	1	**Sharnberry** 2-9-0 0 KierenFallon 10 (E A L Dunlop) *str: scope: lw: hld up bhd ldrs: looking for room over 1f out: swtchd rt ent fnl f: styd on to take 3rd: unable to chal* **9/4**1	71+
	4	½	**Brevity (USA)** 2-9-0 0 MartinDwyer 9 (B J Meehan) *w'like: dwlt: sn cl up: pressed ldrs on outer fr 1/2-way: shkn up and nt qckn jst over 1f out: kpt on* **11/1**	69+
	5	½	**Yashila (IRE)** 2-9-0 0 RichardHughes 4 (R Hannon) *neat: wl on terms w ldrs: shkn up over 1f out: one pce fnl f* **5/1**2	68+
	6	nk	**Attracted To You (IRE)** 2-9-0 0 JimmyFortune 7 (R Hannon) *w'like: athletic: scope: plld hrd early: hld up in last pair: swtchd to nr side 2f out: shkn up and kpt on: nvr able to chal* **14/1**	67+
	7	½	**Bint Mazyouna** 2-9-0 0 RyanMoore 2 (M R Channon) *lengthy: athletic: wl in tch towards nr side: hanging fr 1/2-way: effrt 2f out: drvn and one pce fnl f* **8/1**3	65+
	8	2¼	**Indiracer (IRE)** 2-9-0 0 LiamKeniry 8 (A Bailey) *leggy: hld up in last: taken to outer and effrt 2f out: no prog over 1f out: wknd* **50/1**	59
2	9	nk	**Royalorien**18 3906 2-9-0 0 ShaneKelly 3 (W J Knight) *lengthy: lw: mde most at mod pce to wl over 1f out: wandered and wknd* **5/1**2	58

1m 14.79s (2.59) **Going Correction** +0.125s/f (Good) **9** Ran SP% **117.9**
Speed ratings (Par 97): **87,86,85,84,84 83,83,80,79**
toteswingers: 1&2 £9.10, 1&3 £4.70, 2&3 £3.80. CSF £60.59 TOTE £10.40: £2.50, £2.10, £1.70; EX 61.50 Trifecta £211.20 Pool: £1,187.28 - 4.16 winning units..
Owner T G & Mrs M E Holdcroft **Bred** Bearstone Stud **Trained** Manton, Wilts

FOCUS
An interesting fillies' maiden featuring four Cheveley Park entries, and although the early pace was steady and they finished in a bit of a heap, it was that quartet who came to the fore. Not form to trust.

NOTEBOOK
Mortitia, one of her trainer's three entries in the Cheveley Park, had run a promising race on her debut but failed to build on that behind Date With Destiny second time out. This drop back to 6f looked sure to suit, though, and despite being keen in behind the pace and having to make room for herself a furlong out, she picked up well to run down the leader once out in the clear. A stronger pace will suit her better and she can rate higher.
Qenaa was prominent throughout and got first run on the winner, but it wasn't enough and she was caught right on the line. Too green to do herself justice on debut, she'd clearly come on plenty for that, but she did enjoy the run of things the way the race panned out. (op 6-1 tchd 9-2)
Sharnberry, who cost 120,000gns and is a half-sister to a 2-y-o winner over this trip, was popular in the market on her debut and ran a race of promise. As with most from her stable, she can be expected to improve for the outing, and is evidently held in some regard. (op 3-1 tchd 10-3 in places and 7-2 in a place)
Brevity(USA) ◆ could be the one to take from the race as her stable's juveniles rarely win first time up and this daughter of Street Cry, who didn't get much cover on the outside, shaped well for a long way. She can win a similar race in the coming weeks. (op 9-1 tchd 14-1)
Yashila(IRE) ◆ is a sister to 7f Group 3 winning 2-y-o Ashram and looks sure to benefit from this. (tchd 9-2)
Attracted To You(IRE) ◆, who pulled much too hard mid-race, is closely related to a dual Listed winner in Italy and is bred to improve for a longer trip. (op 12-1 tchd 16-1 in a place)
Bint Mazyouna, a half-sister to 5f winner Nosedive, raced nearest the stands' rail for most of the race, which may not have been an advantage. (tchd 9-1)
Royalorien ran with promise on her debut at Nottingham, but she was weak in the betting here and led under sufferance. She was far too keen and dropped right out inside the last. Official explanation: jockey said filly hung right-handed (op 9-2 tchd 11-2 in places)

4472 EUROPEAN BREEDERS' FUND FILLIES' AND MARES' STKS (H'CAP) 1m 1f
5:10 (5:10) (Class 2) (0-100,93) 3-Y-O+
£12,462 (£3,732; £1,866; £934; £466; £234) **Stalls** High

Form				RPR
2113	1		**Dance East**19 3867 3-9-12 **91** RyanMoore 2 (J Noseda) *trckd ldng pair: shkn up 3f out: rdn and prog to ld over 1f out: immediately jnd: gd battle after: jst prevailed* **7/4**1	99
0422	2	shd	**Seradim**20 3806 4-9-13 **83** TomQueally 4 (P F I Cole) *t.k.h: hld up in last trio: rdn and prog on outer over 2f out: chal over 1f out: w wnr all the way after: jst denied* **8/1**	92
5650	3	3	**Kinky Afro (IRE)**32 3467 3-10-0 **93** LiamKeniry 5 (J S Moore) *hld up in last trio: pushed along 3f out: no great prog tl over 1f out: wnt 3rd last 100yds: styd on wl* **11/1**	94
5-11	4	3	**Seasonal Cross**32 3457 5-9-6 **76** HayleyTurner 3 (S Dow) *hld up in detached last: urged along fr 3f out: prog 2f out: kpt on same pce fnl f to take modest 4th nr fin* **11/2**3	72
5-30	5	1	**Flapper (IRE)**21 3782 4-8-8 **71** AmyScott(7) 6 (J W Hills) *pressed ldr: led narrowly wl over 2f out: hdd over 1f out: wknd fnl f* **20/1**	65
13-1	6	1¾	**Agony And Ecstasy**86 1761 3-9-7 **86** (p) JimCrowley 8 (R M Beckett) *lw: racd freely: led to wl over 2f out: pressed ldr to over 1f out: wknd* **10/3**2	75
4534	7	½	**She's In The Money**11 4137 4-9-13 **83** PaulHanagan 1 (R A Fahey) *t.k.h: trckd ldng trio: shkn up and nt qckn over 2f out: sn lost pl and btn* **8/1**	72
-150	8	22	**Water Gipsy**25 3696 3-9-0 **79** RichardHughes 7 (G L Moore) *trckd ldng trio: wknd over 2f out: eased: t.o* **20/1**	18

1m 55.35s (-0.95) **Going Correction** +0.025s/f (Good)
WFA 3 from 4yo+ 9lb **8** Ran SP% **114.9**
Speed ratings (Par 96): **105,104,102,99,98 97,96,77**
toteswingers: 1&2 £2.40, 1&3 £6.10, 2&3 £13.00. CSF £16.85 CT £115.52 TOTE £2.60: £1.50, £2.50, £3.50; EX 18.00 Trifecta £406.80 Pool: £1,511.85 - 2.75 winning units..
Owner Cheveley Park Stud **Bred** Cheveley Park Stud Ltd **Trained** Newmarket, Suffolk

FOCUS
There was a danger of lack of pace here, with Agony And Ecstasy looking to be the only front-runner in the line-up, but in the event she was kept up to her work by Flapper and they went a decent enough gallop. Not a strong race for the grade.

NOTEBOOK
Dance East, back in fillies-only company, enjoyed the perfect trip in behind the leaders but, once brought to challenge a furlong out, was soon joined by Seradim and the pair settled down to battle it out inside the last. There was little to separate the two at the line but the winner showed good battling qualities to maintain a narrow advantage and clearly had no trouble with the extra furlong, despite previous racecourse evidence suggesting otherwise. There could be more to come from her as she seems to be steadily progressive, and can probably keep one step ahead of the Handicapper. (op 15-8 tchd 9-4)
Seradim was another stepping up a furlong in distance, but she too got the trip without any problem. She's been running really well of late, being slightly unlucky to bump into improving 3-y-os on her last two starts now. (tchd 6-1)
Kinky Afro(IRE), who was taking a drop in class having run down the field in the Group 1 Pretty Polly Stakes last time, ran on late to take second but was never a threat to the first two. She probably still needs to drop a pound or two before she wins one of these. (op 16-1)
Seasonal Cross, winner of four of her previous five races, moved poorly to post and was weak in the betting. Held up in a detached last early on, she simply failed to get close enough to land a blow. (op 6-1 tchd 9-2)
Flapper(IRE), whose two wins last year were gained when making the running, was denied the lead by Agony And Ecstasy, but still pressed that rival and the pair of them ended up going off a bit too quick. (tchd 25-1)
Agony And Ecstasy, who is by Captain Rio, had only once run on ground this quick before, recording her lowest RPR to date in the process. She should do better back on an easier surface. (op 3-1 tchd 7-2 in places and 4-1 in a place)
She's In The Money will be happier back over 7f. (op 15-2)

4473 SPORTINGBET.COM EBF CLASSIFIED STKS 7f
5:45 (5:45) (Class 2) 3-Y-O+
£9,346 (£2,799; £1,399; £700; £349; £175) **Stalls** High

Form				RPR
5402	1		**Rulesn'regulations**46 2971 4-9-4 93 GeorgeBaker 9 (Matthew Salaman) *trckd ldrs on inner: plld out 2f out: drvn and prog on outer over 1f out: swept into ld last 150yds: sn clr* **9/1**	102
4300	2	2¾	**Al Khaleej (IRE)**25 3692 6-9-4 95 MartinLane 6 (D M Simcock) *s.i.s: hld up in rr: prog on inner over 2f out: hanging over 1f out: plld out ins fnl f: styd on wl to take 2nd last strides* **14/1**	95
3024	3	½	**Oratory (IRE)**25 3692 4-9-4 94 RichardHughes 8 (R Hannon) *lw: trckd ldr to over 4f out: looking for room on inner over 2f out: plld out over 1f out: styd on to chse wnr last 75yds but no ch: nudged along and lost 2nd fnl strides* **2/1**1	93
0004	4	½	**Manassas (IRE)**16 3956 5-9-4 94 (b1) MartinDwyer 7 (B J Meehan) *lw: led: hrd pressed over 1f out: hdd and fdd last 150yds* **15/2**	92
0300	5	1½	**Thebes**12 4085 5-9-4 94 JoeFanning 3 (M Johnston) *chsd ldr over 4f out: drvn to chal over 1f out: nt qckn and hld ent fnl f: fdd* **6/1**3	88
40-5	6	4½	**Mistic Magic (IRE)**102 1384 3-8-8 95 TomQueally 4 (P F I Cole) *hld up towards rr: rdn wl over 2f out: no prog and sn btn* **16/1**	73
/150	7	2	**Coasting**25 3692 5-9-4 95 NeilCallan 2 (Mrs A J Perrett) *hld up in tch: effrt on outer over 2f out: no prog over 1f out: sn wknd* **6/1**3	70
0-02	8	3¾	**Layline (IRE)**14 4030 3-8-11 93 (p) JimCrowley 5 (R M Beckett) *hld up in last: rdn and no prog over 2f out* **9/2**2	60
226-	9	30	**Silaah**152 6-9-4 85 AdrianNicholls 1 (D Nicholls) *lw: racd wd: hld up: prog 4f out: wknd rapidly 3f out: t.o* **28/1**	—

1m 25.47s (-1.43) **Going Correction** +0.025s/f (Good)
WFA 3 from 4yo+ 7lb **9** Ran SP% **117.8**
Speed ratings (Par 109): **109,105,105,104,103 97,95,91,57**
toteswingers: 1&2 £20.20, 1&3 £3.70, 2&3 £7.90. CSF £127.61 TOTE £11.60: £2.80, £3.90, £1.40; EX 157.00 Trifecta £440.00 Pool: £1,855.27 - 3.12 winning units. Place 6: £68.28, Place 5: £31.02..
Owner M Salaman & J H Widdows **Bred** Marshalla Salaman **Trained** Upper Lambourn, Berks

FOCUS
A competitive race in which all bar Silaah could be given a chance at the weights. Not form to rate too positively.

NOTEBOOK
Rulesn'regulations only went down narrowly at Sandown last time and, although he was a big price that day, he showed it to be no fluke by going one better here. He came home really strongly once switched off the rail and is clearly right at the top of his game at present. Ground this quick was a new experience for him, but he coped with it well. (tchd 10-1)
Al Khaleej(IRE) ◆, who finished down the field on his last two starts for Ed Dunlop, made an encouraging start to his new career with David Simcock, running on well for second despite hanging. He's on a good mark and is one to keep an eye on. (op 16-1)
Oratory(IRE), dropping back in trip, had his chance if good enough but lacked the pace to live with the winner in the closing stages. His rider was easy on him in the closing stages and got done for second, but the stewards accepted his defence that the gelding's stride shortened and he was hanging right in the closing stages. (op 9-4 tchd 5-2 in places)
Manassas(IRE), who lost a shoe when a beaten favourite in a four-runner affair last time, had blinkers on for the first time and was given a positive ride. He seemed to run his race and had no excuses. (op 9-1 tchd 10-1)
Thebes was another who came there to have his chance but again found a few too good. In common with a number of these, he's a difficult horse to place off his current mark. (op 5-1)
Mistic Magic(IRE), not seen since finishing fifth in the Fred Darling when she was apparently struck into, didn't look happy on the track. (op 14-1)
Coasting had the race run to suit but just didn't pick up in the straight and he simply hasn't built on his winning return from a lengthy layoff back in May. (tchd 13-2)
Layline(IRE) didn't go through with his effort on Polytrack last time and connections reached for the cheekpieces here. He looked a possible improver back in distance, but he carried his head high under pressure in the straight and looks one to avoid. (op 5-1)
T/Jkpt: £7,538.60 to a £1 stake. Pool £26,544.40 - 2.50 winning tickets. T/Plt: £65.80 to a £1 stake. Pool £266,822.31 - 2,960.04 winning tickets. T/Qpdt: £13.80 to a £1 stake. Pool £11,736.68 - 626.05 winning tickets. JN

4247 LEICESTER (R-H)
Wednesday, July 28

OFFICIAL GOING: Good to firm (good in places; 8.1)
Wind: Light, half-behind. Weather: Overcast

4474 EBF SWITHLAND MEDIAN AUCTION MAIDEN FILLIES' STKS 5f 218y
6:10 (6:14) (Class 5) 2-Y-O **£3,238** (£963; £481; £240) **Stalls** Low

Form				RPR
	1		**Princess Severus (IRE)** 2-9-0 0 JackMitchell 6 (R M Beckett) *s.i.s: hdwy 1/2-way: chsd ldr over 1f out: edgd lft: rdn to ld ins fnl f: r.o wl* **8/1**	78+

04 **2** *2* **Wolf Slayer**[27] 3583 2-9-0 0 RichardKingscote 13 72
(Tom Dascombe) *led: rdn over 1f out: hdd and unable qck ins fnl f* **13/2**[3]

3 *3 ¾* **Biaraafa (IRE)** 2-9-0 0 JamieSpencer 3 61
(M L W Bell) *difficult to load: prom: rdn over 1f out: styd on same pce: wnt 3rd post* **7/1**

402 **4** *hd* **Grandmas Dream**[16] 3959 2-9-0 85 AlanMunro 7 60
(G C Bravery) *chsd ldr: rdn over 2f out: no ex ins fnl f: lost 3rd post* **13/8**[1]

5 *1 ¾* **High Class Lady** 2-9-0 0 AdamKirby 12 55
(W R Swinburn) *prom: rdn over 1f out: no ex ins fnl f* **16/1**

5 **6** *1* **Sugar Beet**[41] 3126 2-9-0 0 DavidProbert 9 52+
(R Charlton) *s.i.s: hdwy over 4f out: hmpd over 3f out: rdn over 1f out: nt rch ldrs* **11/2**[2]

0 **7** *hd* **Saxonette**[11] 4149 2-9-0 0 ChrisCatlin 5 51
(M R Channon) *hld up in tch: rdn over 2f out: sn swtchd rt: styd on same pce appr fnl f* **40/1**

0 **8** *1 ¼* **Mini's Destination**[23] 3729 2-9-0 0 JerryO'Dwyer 4 48
(J R Holt) *difficult to load: chsd ldrs: rdn over 2f out: wknd over 1f out* **150/1**

9 *½* **Secret Gold (IRE)** 2-9-0 0 TadhgO'Shea 10 51+
(B J Meehan) *mid-div: rdn 1/2-way: wknd over 1f out* **12/1**

0 **10** *3 ¼* **Lettering**[8] 4221 2-9-0 0 DaneO'Neill 11 36
(D Haydn Jones) *chsd ldrs: rdn over 2f out: sn wknd* **100/1**

11 *1 ¼* **Eyes On** 2-9-0 0 FergusSweeney 2 33
(P J McBride) *s.i.s: outpcd* **33/1**

12 *5* **Excellence (IRE)** 2-9-0 0 JamieMackay 8 18
(Karen George) *mid-div: rdn 1/2-way: wknd over 2f out* **100/1**

13 *9* **Royal Classy Cleo** 2-9-0 0 CathyGannon 1 —
(P D Evans) *s.i.s: outpcd* **66/1**

1m 13.43s (0.43) **Going Correction** -0.15s/f (Firm) **13** Ran SP% **113.5**
Speed ratings (Par 91): **91,88,83,83,80 79,79,77,76,72 70,64,52**
Tote Swingers: 1&2 £6.60, 1&3 £5.70, 2&3 £8.40 CSF £55.13 TOTE £9.00: £2.70, £2.50, £2.20; EX 54.30.
Owner Mogeely Stud & Mrs Maura Gittins **Bred** Rathbarry Stud **Trained** Whitsbury, Hants

FOCUS
After the opening race the jockeys reported the ground to be good after some showers in the build-up to racing. The race averages and the runner-up help with the level.

NOTEBOOK
Princess Severus(IRE) cost £20,000 as a yearling and made a winning debut for connections that do well at this venue in 2-y-o races. Her breeding suggests she will be better suited by a longer trip and she was doing all her best work at the end and looks a nice type and should progress. (op 15-2)
Wolf Slayer was making her third start and gave a bold show from the front. She is clearly improving and was possibly benefited by this easier ground. Her connections have not has as much success as expected but she now has handicaps as an option. (op 8-1 tchd 6-1)
Biaraafa(IRE) is out of a Group 1-winning mare Bianca Nera and had reportedly been pleasing in her home work . She unshipped her rider before the start and had to be blindfolded to enter the stalls, but she travelled well enough to suggest she can win a small maiden before long. (op 11-2 tchd 15-2)
Grandmas Dream finished tenth in the Albany Stakes at Royal Ascot and was second at Windsor over 5f last time. This easier ground may not have suited her, and she showed enough speed to suggest a drop in trip would not inconvenience her too much. (op 6-4 tchd 11-8 and 7-4)
High Class Lady, a half-sister to an Irish Guineas second Dimenticar, shaped as if the run would bring her on, which is in common with most from this yard.
Sugar Beet, as on her debut, was slowly away and looked to lack the pace over this trip. She is likely to be of interest in handicaps over a longer trip, as her breeding suggests. (op 6-1)
Secret Gold(IRE) was sent off a big price and this half-sister to Nadeen (who won over 5f) should improve plenty for the run, as most from this yard do. However, her Cheveley Park entry does look a little fanciful at this early stage. (tchd 16-1)

4475 SHANGTON (S) STKS — 7f 9y
6:40 (6:41) (Class 6) 3-Y-O — **£1,942** (£578; £288; £144) **Stalls** Low

Form RPR

0206 **1** **Excellent Day (IRE)**[5] 4325 3-8-7 75 ChrisCatlin 9 64
(M R Channon) *hld up: hdwy 3f out: led over 1f out: edgd rt ins fnl f: drvn out* **15/8**[1]

3540 **2** *1 ¼* **Eywa**[15] 3982 3-8-7 55 AlanMunro 11 60
(W Jarvis) *hld up: hdwy over 2f out: rdn to chse wnr over 1f out: styd on* **15/2**

0002 **3** *3 ¼* **Silver Symphony (IRE)**[5] 4337 3-8-8 65 ow1 (b[1]) JamieSpencer 8 53
(P F I Cole) *chsd ldrs: led over 2f out: rdn and hdd over 1f out: no ex ins fnl f* **9/4**[2]

0000 **4** *3 ¼* **Tudor Princess**[9] 4210 3-8-7 52 TadhgO'Shea 10 43
(W R Muir) *sn pushed along in rr: hdwy u.p over 1f out: nrst fin* **40/1**

1100 **5** *1 ¾* **Collect Art (IRE)**[7] 4255 3-9-3 67 (v) StevieDonohoe 14 48
(A B Haynes) *chsd ldrs: rdn over 2f out: wknd over 1f out* **7/1**[3]

0000 **6** *8* **Strike Shot**[7] 4249 3-8-12 50 DarryllHolland 13 21
(W R Muir) *in rr: sme hdwy over 1f out: nvr on terms* **66/1**

0003 **7** *4* **Transfixed (IRE)**[7] 4249 3-8-7 64 CathyGannon 3 6
(P D Evans) *led: hdd over 4f out: chsd ldrs: rdn 1/2-way: wknd 2f out* **12/1**

-000 **8** *6* **Miskin Nights**[13] 4041 3-8-7 49 (t) DavidProbert 4 —
(B Palling) *chsd ldr tl led over 4f out: rdn and hdd over 2f out: edgd lft and wknd over 1f out* **66/1**

0 **9** *hd* **Home Sweet Home (GER)**[22] 3768 3-8-0 62 LauraPike(7) 2 —
(D M Simcock) *s.i.s: hdwy over 4f out: wknd over 2f out* **20/1**

6-00 **10** *3* **Taeping (IRE)**[15] 3972 3-8-12 45 JackMitchell 5 —
(R Hollinshead) *s.i.s: hdwy over 4f out: sn rdn: wknd over 2f out* **100/1**

0520 **11** *19* **Set To Go**[50] 2844 3-9-3 60 (b) KirstyMilczarek 7 —
(H J L Dunlop) *in rr: hdwy over 4f out: wknd 3f out: eased: t.o* **25/1**

0L- **R** **Jonny No Eyebrows**[226] 7749 3-8-7 0 MarkCoumbe(5) 1 —
(P Leech) *ref to r* **100/1**

1m 24.78s (-1.42) **Going Correction** -0.15s/f (Firm) **12** Ran SP% **113.5**
Speed ratings (Par 98): **102,100,96,93,91 82,77,70,70,66 45,—**
Tote Swingers: 1&2 £4.50, 1&3 £1.50, 2&3 £4.20 CSF £15.00 TOTE £3.00: £1.50, £2.10, £1.60; EX 17.00.The winner was bought in for £6,500.
Owner Billy Parish **Bred** Richard Hall **Trained** West Ilsley, Berks

FOCUS
An ordinary seller where the leading trio were well clear. The level of the form is a bit fluid.
Set To Go Official explanation: jockey said gelding never travelled

4476 KIRSTINE SMITH BIRTHDAY H'CAP — 1m 1f 218y
7:15 (7:15) (Class 4) (0-80,78) 3-Y-O+ — **£3,885** (£1,156; £577; £288) **Stalls** High

Form RPR

0435 **1** **Wiggy Smith**[21] 3781 11-10-0 77 DaneO'Neill 4 84
(H Candy) *hld up: hdwy over 2f out: led over 1f out: rdn and edgd rt ins fnl f: jst hld on* **7/1**[3]

-010 **2** *nse* **Sagredo (USA)**[21] 3781 6-9-11 74 RichardKingscote 2 81
(Jonjo O'Neill) *hld up: hdwy 2f out: rdn and ev ch ins fnl f: r.o* **7/2**[2]

3-11 **3** *½* **Aktia (IRE)**[27] 3606 3-9-5 78 J-PGuillambert 5 84+
(L M Cumani) *racd keenly: trckd ldr to 1/2-way: remained handy: pushed along whn nt clr run and swtchd rt over 1f out: r.o: hmpd nr fin* **1/1**[1]

-004 **4** *1 ¾* **Pelham Crescent (IRE)**[13] 4044 7-9-11 74 DavidProbert 3 76
(B Palling) *prom: chsd ldr 6f out: led over 2f out: rdn and hdd over 1f out: no ex ins fnl f* **16/1**

4266 **5** *8* **Omaruru (IRE)**[37] 3259 3-8-9 68 GregFairley 1 54
(M Johnston) *led at stdy pce tl qcknd over 3f out: rdn and hdd over 2f out: wknd over 1f out* **7/2**[2]

2m 9.07s (1.17) **Going Correction** 0.0s/f (Good)
WFA 3 from 6yo+ 10lb **5** Ran SP% **112.8**
Speed ratings (Par 105): **95,94,94,93,86**
CSF £31.24 TOTE £4.60: £1.80, £2.50; EX 44.90.
Owner Mrs George Tricks **Bred** Mrs V M Tricks **Trained** Kingston Warren, Oxon

FOCUS
A low turnout for this handicap, which was run at a moderate pace and did not suit the market leader. Muddling form which is best rated around the winner.

4477 EBF LUTTERWORTH MAIDEN STKS — 5f 218y
7:45 (7:46) (Class 4) 2-Y-O — **£4,533** (£1,348; £674; £336) **Stalls** Low

Form RPR

1 **None Shall Sleep (IRE)** 2-9-3 0 AlanMunro 8 80+
(P F I Cole) *s.i.s: hdwy 4f out: rdn to ld ins fnl f: r.o* **8/1**

50 **2** *1 ¾* **West Leake Bridge (IRE)**[69] 2238 2-9-3 0 DarryllHolland 5 75
(B W Hills) *led 5f out: rdn and edgd rt over 1f out: hdd and unable qck ins fnl f* **4/1**[3]

0 **3** *1 ¾* **King Kurt (IRE)**[26] 3624 2-9-3 0 PhillipMakin 9 70
(K A Ryan) *led 2f: chsd ldrs: rdn over 2f out: sn outpcd: styd on ins fnl f* **10/3**[2]

5 **4** *2* **Lord Of Persia (USA)**[23] 3735 2-9-3 0 JackMitchell 3 64
(R M Beckett) *prom: pushed along 1/2-way: sn swtchd rt: rdn over 1f out: no ex ins fnl f* **9/4**[1]

4 **5** *1 ¼* **Chibchan (IRE)**[12] 4110 2-9-3 0 TedDurcan 6 60
(Mahmood Al Zarooni) *chsd ldrs: rdn over 1f out: no ex fnl f* **8/1**

6 *¾* **Alajmal (USA)** 2-9-3 0 TadhgO'Shea 4 58+
(M Johnston) *broke wl: sn stdd and lost pl: outpcd over 3f out: styd on fr over 1f out: will improve* **17/2**

5 **7** *1 ½* **Rylee Mooch**[34] 3362 2-9-3 0 PaulEddery 7 53
(R C Guest) *hld up: pushed along 1/2-way: nvr on terms* **66/1**

8 *1* **Royal Reverie** 2-9-3 0 AdamKirby 1 50+
(W R Swinburn) *s.i.s: rn green and a in rr* **20/1**

9 *1 ¼* **Coedmor Boy** 2-9-3 0 DavidProbert 2 47
(B Palling) *s.i.s: sn prom: rdn and wknd over 1f out* **66/1**

1m 13.82s (0.82) **Going Correction** -0.15s/f (Firm) **9** Ran SP% **114.3**
Speed ratings (Par 96): **88,85,83,80,79 78,76,74,73**
Tote Swingers:1&2:£3.70, 2&3:£3.00, 1&3:£5.00 CSF £39.11 TOTE £15.70: £6.70, £1.50, £1.70; EX 47.20.
Owner Mrs Fitri Hay **Bred** Mrs Mary Rose Hayes **Trained** Whatcombe, Oxon

FOCUS
A good-looking maiden on paper that could feature some nice sorts for the future. the second to fourth set the level.

NOTEBOOK
None Shall Sleep(IRE), a market drifter who is a half-brother to the useful Exhibition, made a taking winning debut. The son of Invincible Spirit ran green in the closing stages and dumped his rider after the race. He ought to improve for this experience. (op 6-1)
West Leake Bridge(IRE) showed good form on his debut but then had run poorly next time when sent off a short-priced favourite. He held every chance here but it should not be too long before he is winning a similar race. (op 7-2 tchd 3-1)
King Kurt(IRE) found things happening too quickly for him on his debut and he took a while to hit full stride here. He is sure to improve and will be one to keep a serious eye on when stepped up in trip. (op 8-1)
Lord Of Persia(USA) had run well on his debut but was too green to score that day in a race that has worked out well. He was well backed here but looked as if the experience would bring him on again. However, this does have to go down as a disappointing run. (op 15-8 tchd 5-2)
Chibchan(IRE) shaped as if he wants a longer trip, as suggested by his breeding. (op 9-1 tchd 7-1)
Alajmal(USA) ◆ is a well-related sort and looked the type to improve throughout the season both mentally and physically. (op 8-1)
Royal Reverie is a half-brother to Jordaura and Mellifera, who are best at around 1m. He was withdrawn ahead of his intended debut at Windsor earlier this month and gave trouble before the start here prior to looking less than straightforward in the race. He is clearly a tricky sort who could prove difficult to win with, having already displayed a fair amount of temperament. Official explanation: jockey said colt ran green (tchd 22-1)

4478 QUORN H'CAP — 5f 218y
8:20 (8:21) (Class 5) (0-70,68) 3-Y-O+ — **£2,914** (£867; £433; £216) **Stalls** Low

Form RPR

5255 **1** **Rainy Night**[19] 3855 4-9-5 61 (p) JackMitchell 8 71
(R Hollinshead) *chsd ldrs: rdn to ld ins fnl f: r.o* **11/4**[1]

0520 **2** *1* **Dickie Le Davoir**[3] 4404 6-9-2 63 (b) MarkCoumbe(5) 5 70
(R C Guest) *s.i.s: outpcd: hdwy over 1f out: r.o wl: wnt 2nd nr fin: nt rch wnr* **10/1**

0062 **3** *¾* **Mata Hari Blue**[7] 4251 4-8-11 53 KirstyMilczarek 13 58
(J R Holt) *chsd ldrs: led over 1f out: rdn and hdd ins fnl f: styd on same pce* **4/1**[2]

3635 **4** *1 ¼* **Two Turtle Doves (IRE)**[7] 4244 4-8-13 55 (p) AlanMunro 11 56
(M Mullineaux) *chsd ldrs: led over 3f out: rdn and hdd over 1f out: styd on same pce* **5/1**[3]

3020 **5** *nk* **Cwmni**[11] 4130 4-9-3 59 DavidProbert 7 59
(B Palling) *mid-div: drvn along 1/2-way: hdwy over 2f out: styd on* **14/1**

0005 **6** *2 ¾* **The Human League**[9] 4193 3-9-4 65 (v[1]) PaulEddery 3 56
(M R Channon) *mid-div: sn pushed along: no imp fr over 1f out* **14/1**

0065 **7** *hd* **City For Conquest (IRE)**[8] 4234 7-8-4 49 oh4 (b) KellyHarrison(3) 9 39
(John A Harris) *s.i.s: r.o fnl f: nvr nrr* **50/1**

0340 **8** *½* **Eviction (IRE)**[16] 3970 3-9-6 67 AdamKirby 4 56
(Miss M E Rowland) *hld up in tch: racd keenly: rdn and hung rt over 1f out: no ex* **20/1**

0000 **9** *1 ¾* **Commander Wish**[13] 4071 7-8-4 49 oh3 (v) AndrewHeffernan(3) 12 32
(Lucinda Featherstone) *hld up: rdn 1/2-way: n.d* **33/1**

30-0 **10** *1* **Outshine**[20] 3833 3-9-6 67 DarryllHolland 1 47
(Karen George) *hld up: rdn over 2f out: nvr trbld ldrs* **33/1**

101 **11** *3 ¼* **Boldinor**[13] 4071 7-8-10 59 RyanPowell(7) 10 28
(M R Bosley) *prom: rdn 1/2-way: wknd over 2f out* **8/1**

0013 **12** 2 3/4 **Blue Aura (IRE)**[28] 3556 7-9-1 **62**.................................. DeanHeslop(5) 2 23
(B G Powell) *mid-div: rdn and hung rt over 2f out: sn wknd* **10/1**

2300 **13** 11 **Tag Team (IRE)**[13] 4071 9-8-7 **49** oh4..................(p) DaraghO'Donohoe 6 —
(John A Harris) *led: hdd over 3f out: sn rdn: wknd wl over 1f out* **50/1**

0-06 **14** 2 3/4 **Lordship (IRE)**[13] 4065 6-9-12 **68**.............................. MattieBatchelor 14 —
(A W Carroll) *s.i.s: hdwy over 4f out: wknd over 3f out* **50/1**

1m 11.55s (-1.45) **Going Correction** -0.15s/f (Firm)
WFA 3 from 4yo+ 5lb **14** Ran SP% **122.5**
Speed ratings (Par 103): **103,101,100,99,98 94,94,94,91,90 86,82,67,64**
Tote Swingers: 1&2 £8.10, 1&3 £3.50, 2&3 £7.90 CSF £30.18 CT £114.46 TOTE £3.00: £1.20, £4.80, £1.10; EX 35.00.
Owner N Chapman **Bred** Broughton Bloodstock **Trained** Upper Longdon, Staffs

FOCUS
A lively betting heat that featured numerous gambles and was run at a strong pace. The winner is rated back to his best.

4479 BOOTLEG BEATLES HERE ON 24 AUGUST H'CAP 1m 60y
8:50 (8:51) (Class 5) (0-70,70) 3-Y-O **£2,914** (£867; £433; £216) **Stalls** High

Form RPR

-435 **1** **Jubail (IRE)**[16] 3963 3-9-5 **68**....................................... FergusSweeney 7 80
(A King) *mde virtually all: rdn over 1f out: styd on wl* **5/2**[1]

6420 **2** 2 1/4 **Sir Bruno (FR)**[5] 4325 3-9-7 **70**.. DavidProbert 1 77
(B Palling) *trckd wnr: racd keenly: rdn over 2f out: styd on same pce ins fnl f* **7/2**[3]

0410 **3** 3/4 **Mellifera**[23] 3739 3-9-5 **68**...(p) AdamKirby 4 73
(W R Swinburn) *a.p: rdn over 3f out: swtchd rt over 2f out: styd on same pce ins fnl f* **7/1**

2412 **4** 1 1/4 **Dutiful**[22] 3755 3-9-6 **69**.. TedDurcan 8 71
(M R Channon) *hld up: hdwy over 2f out: rdn over 1f out: no ex ins fnl f* **3/1**[2]

3060 **5** 2 3/4 **Tilsworth Glenboy**[48] 2906 3-8-8 **60**.................... AndrewHeffernan(3) 6 56
(J R Jenkins) *hld up: hdwy and nt clr run over 2f out: rdn over 1f out: hung lft and no ex ins fnl f* **20/1**

0000 **6** 9 **Adoyen Spice**[31] 3478 3-8-2 **51** oh1.............................. AndreaAtzeni 10 26
(Mike Murphy) *chsd ldrs: rdn over 3f out: wknd over 1f out* **50/1**

1000 **7** 2 1/2 **Steed**[9] 4193 3-9-3 **66**..(b) DarryllHolland 11 36
(K A Ryan) *hld up and a bhd* **8/1**

-266 **8** 1/2 **Iptkaar (USA)**[8] 4236 3-9-7 **70**.. ChrisCatlin 3 38
(C E Brittain) *chsd ldrs: pushed along over 5f out: rdn over 3f out: wknd over 2f out* **11/1**

1m 44.92s (-0.18) **Going Correction** 0.0s/f (Good) **8** Ran SP% **114.5**
Speed ratings (Par 100): **100,97,97,95,93 84,81,81**
Tote Swingers:1&2:£3.30, 2&3:£6.20, 1&3:£4.20 CSF £11.51 CT £53.02 TOTE £3.20: £1.10, £3.00, £3.90; EX 13.00 Place 6 £60.34, Place 5 £20.05..
Owner David Mason **Bred** A F O'Callaghan **Trained** Barbury Castle, Wilts

FOCUS
A moderate handicap with little strength but an impressive winner. The front pair were always 1-2 and the form is rated around the second.
Adoyen Spice Official explanation: jockey said filly ran green
Steed Official explanation: jockey said gelding never travelled
T/Plt: £190.60 to a £1 stake. Pool £55,218.90. 211.45 winning tickets. T/Qpdt: £29.00 to a £1 stake. Pool £6,752.23. 172.08 winning tickets. CR

4167 REDCAR (L-H)
Wednesday, July 28

OFFICIAL GOING: Firm (good to firm in places; 9.3)
Wind: Fresh 1/2 against Weather: Overcast with showers

4480 EUROPEAN BREEDERS' FUND MAIDEN STKS 6f
2:00 (2:00) (Class 5) 2-Y-O **£3,412** (£1,007; £504) **Stalls** Centre

Form RPR

40 **1** **Ingleby Exceed (IRE)**[43] 3059 2-8-12 0..................... GrahamGibbons 6 62+
(T D Barron) *trckd ldrs: effrt over 2f out: carried rt jst ins fnl f: hrd rdn and r.o to ld towards fin* **7/4**[1]

4633 **2** hd **Hortensis**[7] 4242 2-8-12 67.. DavidAllan 2 61+
(T D Easterby) *w ldr: drvn over 2f out: led over 1f out: edgd rt jst ins fnl f: hdd and no ex nr fin* **7/4**[1]

06 **3** 3/4 **Paragons Folly (IRE)**[12] 4083 2-8-12 0........................... IanBrennan(5) 5 64+
(J J Quinn) *trckd ldrs: effrt over 2f out: slty hmpd jst ins fnl f: kpt on wl towards fin* **7/1**[2]

0 **4** 1 1/2 **Solo Whisper (IRE)**[71] 2202 2-9-3 0............................... TonyHamilton 3 59+
(J Howard Johnson) *dwlt: in rr: effrt over 2f out: edgd lft and kpt on fnl f* **10/1**

0 **5** 3 1/2 **Sandy Lonnen**[35] 3316 2-9-3 0.. TomEaves 4 49
(J Howard Johnson) *t.k.h: led tl over 1f out: wkng whn sltly hmpd jst ins fnl f* **8/1**[3]

6 3 **Icy Blue** 2-9-0 0.. MichaelStainton(3) 1 39
(R M Whitaker) *s.s: hdwy to chse ldrs after 2f: lost pl over 1f out* **22/1**

1m 13.11s (1.31) **Going Correction** -0.125s/f (Firm) **6** Ran SP% **109.8**
Speed ratings (Par 94): **86,85,84,82,78 74**
toteswingers: 1&2 £1.10, 1&3 £2.40, 2&3 £2.70. CSF £4.53 TOTE £3.00: £2.00, £1.10; EX 3.60.
Owner Dave Scott **Bred** Dave Scott **Trained** Maunby, N Yorks

FOCUS
A moderate maiden and this ground would have been plenty quick enough for these youngsters.

NOTEBOOK
Ingleby Exceed(IRE) was outclassed in a field full of previous winners in a Thirsk novice event last time, but this was easier and she is bred to have appreciated this extra furlong. She missed the break, but was soon in touch and although she looked held for much of the last furlong, she kept trying and got up close to the line. She is still not yet the finished article, so may not do much more this season and will probably make a better 3-y-o. (op 13-8)
Hortensis, the most experienced in the field and already placed in maiden and nursery company, travelled well in touch and looked likely to win when leading over a furlong out, but she seemed to think about it and was run out of it close home. She has the ability to win a small race, but is now looking exposed. (tchd 13-8 and 15-8 in a place)
Paragons Folly(IRE) was well beaten in his first two starts, but he ran on well late here despite seeming to hang on the ground. This half-brother to six winners, including the dual Ayr Gold Cup victor Funfair Wane, could be another type for nurseries now that he gets a mark. (op 8-1)
Solo Whisper(IRE) hadn't been seen since finishing a well-beaten second favourite on his debut at Carlisle in May and never offered a threat here either. (op 12-1)
Sandy Lonnen was keen enough in front, but was already on the retreat when hanging about inside the last furlong. (tchd 9-1)
Icy Blue, a 14,000gns colt out of a winning juvenile sprinter, and the only newcomer in the race, missed the break and ended up well beaten. He needs more time. (op 20-1 tchd 25-1)

4481 IAN HIRD CELEBRATION AT REDCAR RACECOURSE H'CAP 1m 2f
2:35 (2:37) (Class 5) (0-70,70) 3-Y-O+ **£2,266** (£674; £337; £168) **Stalls** Low

Form RPR

0611 **1** **Count Ceprano (IRE)**[9] 4213 6-8-6 **55**.................... SophieSilvester(7) 1 69
(J Pearce) *hld up in mid-div: rdr briefly lost iron bnd over 5f out: stdy hdwy over 2f out: led appr fnl f: pushed clr: v readily* **5/2**[1]

0-56 **2** 6 **Knight's Victory (IRE)**[11] 4152 4-9-7 **66**................ MichaelStainton(3) 2 68
(Michael Smith) *s.i.s: sn chsng ldrs: drvn over 3f out: styd on to take 2nd ins fnl f: no ch w wnr* **13/2**

2015 **3** 2 1/2 **Smirfy's Silver**[33] 3405 6-9-13 **69**.............................. SilvestreDeSousa 7 66
(Mrs D J Sanderson) *hdwy to ld after 1f: hdd appr fnl f: wknd fnl 150yds* **7/2**[2]

4602 **4** 1 **Back To Paris (IRE)**[10] 4170 8-8-11 **53**......................(p) AndrewMullen 4 48
(P A Kirby) *s.i.s: drvn to sn chse ldrs: chsd ldr 3f out: hung lft and carried hd high: one pce* **11/1**

64-4 **5** 8 **Helieorbea**[9] 4196 4-9-9 **70**... LanceBetts(5) 6 49
(T D Easterby) *detached in last: hdwy over 4f out: lost pl over 1f out* **9/2**[3]

0240 **6** 1 1/2 **The Dial House**[14] 4015 4-9-0 **59**............................(t) BarryMcHugh(3) 5 35
(D W Thompson) *trckd ldrs: effrt over 3f out: wknd over 1f out* **20/1**

0-05 **7** nk **Turf Trivia**[23] 3732 3-8-3 **55**... DuranFentiman 8 30
(G M Moore) *in rr: sn pushed along: nvr a factor* **33/1**

0046 **8** 25 **Nayessence**[15] 3978 4-8-10 **52**..................................(t) GrahamGibbons 9 —
(M W Easterby) *led 1f: chsd ldrs: lost pl over 2f out: sn bhd: virtually p.u: t.o: b.b.v* **9/2**[3]

2m 4.66s (-2.44) **Going Correction** -0.125s/f (Firm)
WFA 3 from 4yo+ 10lb **8** Ran SP% **116.5**
Speed ratings (Par 103): **104,99,97,96,90 88,88,68**
toteswingers: 1&2 £3.60, 1&3 £3.00, 2&3 £4.20. CSF £19.88 CT £57.09 TOTE £2.50: £1.10, £3.90, £1.10; EX 24.00.
Owner Mrs Louise Marsh **Bred** Pendley Farm **Trained** Newmarket, Suffolk

FOCUS
An ordinary handicap and there was no great pace on early.
Nayessence Official explanation: vet said gelding bled from the nose

4482 CARIBBEAN CARNIVAL DAY - 7TH AUGUST RATING RELATED MAIDEN STKS 7f
3:10 (3:11) (Class 5) 3-Y-O+ **£2,266** (£674; £337; £168) **Stalls** Centre

Form RPR

5405 **1** **Amity (IRE)**[9] 4189 3-8-12 65.. GregFairley 4 64
(M Johnston) *mde all: rdn over 2f out: wandered: hld on wl towards fin* **9/1**

0032 **2** 3/4 **Piddie's Power**[15] 3975 3-8-12 70.................................. GrahamGibbons 8 62
(E S McMahon) *hmpd s: sn trcking ldrs: drvn to chal 2f out: rdn 1f out: hung rt: kpt on towards fin* **8/13**[1]

54-3 **3** 2 **Uddy Mac**[11] 4155 3-8-12 60... DanielTudhope 2 57
(N Bycroft) *in rr: effrt over 3f out: styd on same pce* **8/1**[3]

-320 **4** 3 1/4 **Bideeya (USA)**[23] 3739 3-8-12 64...............................(p) PhilipRobinson 5 48
(C E Brittain) *chsd ldrs: drvn 3f out: one pce* **7/2**[2]

0-00 **5** 1/2 **One Cat Diesel (IRE)**[95] 1528 3-9-1 35.......................... PatrickMathers 7 50?
(H A McWilliams) *wnt rt s: t.k.h: sn trcking ldrs: drvn over 3f out: hung lft and one pce over 1f out* **100/1**

230- **6** 9 **Precious Coral (IRE)**[285] 6819 3-8-7 68....................... JamesSullivan(5) 6 23
(Mrs R A Carr) *swvd rt s: sn w ldrs: lost pl over 1f out* **14/1**

4-60 **7** 5 **Olympic Ceremony**[34] 3371 3-9-1 67...........................(p) AndrewMullen 1 12
(Miss Tracy Waggott) *chsd ldrs on outside: lost pl 2f out: sn bhd* **20/1**

0-00 **8** 48 **Boy Racer (IRE)**[10] 4173 5-9-3 46.................................(p) DeanHeslop(5) 3 —
(C J Teague) *chsd ldrs: lost pl 3f out: sn bhd and eased: virtually p.u: t.o* **66/1**

1m 24.23s (-0.27) **Going Correction** -0.125s/f (Firm)
WFA 3 from 5yo 7lb **8** Ran SP% **119.2**
Speed ratings (Par 103): **96,95,92,89,88 78,72,17**
toteswingers: 1&2 £2.70, 1&3 £4.70, 2&3 £2.20. CSF £15.66 TOTE £10.70: £3.10, £1.10, £1.20; EX 21.80.
Owner Sheikh Hamdan Bin Mohammed Al Maktoum **Bred** Kevin & Meta Cullen **Trained** Middleham Moor, N Yorks

FOCUS
Not a contest to set the pulse racing.
Precious Coral(IRE) Official explanation: jockey said filly had a breathing problem

4483 JOHN SMITH'S REDCAR STRAIGHT-MILE CHAMPIONSHIP STKS (QUALIFIER) (H'CAP) 1m
3:45 (3:45) (Class 4) (0-85,80) 3-Y-O **£3,885** (£1,156; £577; £288) **Stalls** Centre

Form RPR

3201 **1** **Rasselas (IRE)**[9] 4193 3-8-12 **76** 6ex................................... BillyCray(5) 1 88
(D Nicholls) *in rr: drvn over 3f out: edgd lft and styd on to ld 1f out: drvn clr* **12/1**

0-26 **2** 2 1/4 **Dylanesque**[21] 3790 3-9-7 **80**.. PhilipRobinson 5 87
(M A Jarvis) *hmpd s: trckd ldrs: edgd rt over 2f out: hung lft and styd on to take 2nd last 100yds: no imp* **10/3**[2]

1041 **3** 1 3/4 **On Her Way**[16] 3963 3-9-2 **75**.. IanMongan 3 78
(H R A Cecil) *prom: hdwy to ld over 1f out: edgd rt and hdd 1f out: kpt on same pce* **5/2**[1]

0310 **4** nk **Whispered Times (USA)**[26] 3612 3-9-0 **73**..............(p) RobertWinston 2 75
(Miss Tracy Waggott) *sn trcking ldrs: sltly hmpd and hung lft over 2f out: kpt on one pce appr fnl f* **9/1**

0012 **5** 1 1/4 **Cono Zur (FR)**[15] 3972 3-8-9 **73**................................. JamesSullivan(5) 7 72
(Mrs R A Carr) *trckd ldrs: led over 2f out: hung lft and hdd over 1f out: sn hmpd and swtchd lft: wknd last 100yds* **8/1**

4616 **6** 1 1/2 **I'm Super Too (IRE)**[25] 3661 3-9-2 **75**............................ PJMcDonald 8 71
(G A Swinbank) *led 2f: drvn over 3f out: one pce* **10/1**

302 **7** 3/4 **Bursary (CAN)**[23] 3733 3-9-3 **76**.. GregFairley 4 70
(M Johnston) *wnt rt s: t.k.h: led after 2f: hdd over 2f out: lost pl over 1f out* **4/1**[3]

-106 **8** 6 **Maison Brillet (IRE)**[27] 3595 3-8-13 **72**............................(p) TomEaves 6 52
(J Howard Johnson) *hmpd s: sn trcking ldrs: lost pl over 2f out* **33/1**

1m 35.81s (-2.19) **Going Correction** -0.125s/f (Firm) **8** Ran SP% **112.5**
Speed ratings (Par 102): **105,102,101,100,99 97,97,91**
toteswingers: 1&2 £6.00, 1&3 £6.20, 2&3 £2.50. CSF £50.19 CT £134.84 TOTE £21.40: £4.80, £1.10, £2.20; EX 59.70.
Owner J P Honeyman **Bred** Lynch Bages Ltd **Trained** Sessay, N Yorks
■ Stewards' Enquiry : Philip Robinson one-day ban: careless riding (Aug 11)

FOCUS
A fair handicap run at a decent pace with three sharing the advantage until halfway, but several of these hung about on the ground and it suited those who came from off the pace.

4484 BUY YOUR TICKETS ON-LINE @ REDCARRACING.CO.UK CLAIMING STKS 1m 2f
4:20 (4:20) (Class 6) 3-Y-O+ £1,706 (£503; £252) Stalls Low

Form RPR

-231 1 **Eijaaz (IRE)**[14] 4015 9-9-5 62 (p) SilvestreDeSousa 7 60
(G A Harker) *hld up in rr: stdy hdwy on outside over 3f out: styd on to ld towards fin* 13/8[1]

4400 2 ½ **Fujin Dancer (FR)**[25] 3667 5-9-13 76 (p) TomEaves 9 67
(K A Ryan) *hld up in rr: hdwy on outer over 4f out: nt clr run and swtchd ins over 2f out: nt clr run over 1f out: burst through to ld last 75yds: sn hdd and no ex* 7/4[2]

-504 3 1½ **Roman History (IRE)**[3] 4411 7-9-1 44 (p) AndrewMullen 1 52
(Miss Tracy Waggott) *trckd ldrs: led jst ins fnl f: sn hdd: styd on same pce* 14/1

0506 4 1 **Melkatant**[10] 4170 4-8-11 42 DanielTudhope 5 46
(N Bycroft) *led: qcknd over 3f out: edgd rt and hdd jst ins fnl f: kpt on same pce* 25/1

0260 5 1¾ **Castlebury (IRE)**[14] 4015 5-9-4 58 (v[1]) PJMcDonald 8 50
(G A Swinbank) *trckd ldrs on outside: one pce fnl 2f* 11/2[3]

-226 6 ½ **Night Knight (IRE)**[30] 3502 4-9-6 61 (p) TonyHamilton 6 51
(C Grant) *trckd ldrs: wnt 2nd over 2f out: one pce whn hmpd ins fnl f* 7/1

0/0 7 shd **Power Desert (IRE)**[14] 4015 5-9-2 0 (v[1]) DavidAllan 4 46
(G A Harker) *s.s: sn trcking ldrs: rn in snatches: hung lft over 2f out: wknd fnl 100yds* 33/1

050 8 28 **Arkas**[21] 3776 4-8-7 0 BarryMcHugh(3) 3 —
(C R Wilson) *hld up in mid-div: lost pl over 3f out: sn bhd: t.o* 100/1

2m 7.68s (0.58) **Going Correction** -0.125s/f (Firm) 8 Ran SP% 116.8
Speed ratings (Par 101): **92,91,90,89,88 87,87,65**
toteswingers: 1&2 £1.40, 1&3 £4.40, 2&3 £4.60. CSF £4.81 TOTE £3.10: £1.20, £1.10, £4.20; EX 5.10.
Owner A S Ward **Bred** Shadwell Estate Company Limited **Trained** Thirkleby, N Yorks

FOCUS
A moderate claimer and the winning time was over three seconds slower than the earlier handicap. Despite no pace early, the first two home came from the back of the field, although they were the best two horses in the race anyway.

4485 FOLLOW REDCAR RACING ON FACEBOOK H'CAP 1m
4:55 (4:55) (Class 6) (0-65,65) 3-Y-O+ £1,619 (£481; £240; £120) Stalls Centre

Form RPR

0035 1 **Mr Chocolate Drop (IRE)**[37] 3279 6-8-8 46 oh1 (t) SilvestreDeSousa 5 58
(Miss M E Rowland) *hld up in rr: hdwy over 2f out: swtchd lft over 1f out: styd on to ld last 75yds: hld on nr fin* 14/1

0352 2 nk **Many Welcomes**[19] 3854 5-8-12 55 JemmaMarshall(5) 6 66
(B P J Baugh) *trckd ldrs: led jst ins fnl f: sn hdd: kpt on towards fin* 13/2[3]

-040 3 4 **Lujano**[18] 3911 5-9-10 65 BarryMcHugh(3) 1 67
(Ollie Pears) *t.k.h: led after 2f: hdd jst ins fnl f: no ex* 5/1[2]

3140 4 1 **Abu Dubai (IRE)**[15] 3978 4-9-4 56 (p) PJMcDonald 4 56
(J A Glover) *chsd ldrs: chal over 1f out: kpt on one pce* 15/2

3345 5 ¾ **Northern Flyer (GER)**[30] 3500 4-9-0 57 IanBrennan(5) 7 55
(J J Quinn) *chsd ldrs: hung lft over 1f out: one pce* 3/1[1]

4003 6 1¼ **Aussie Blue (IRE)**[10] 4173 6-9-2 59 (p) AmyRyan(5) 3 54
(R M Whitaker) *mid-div: hdwy on outer over 2f out: hung rt over 1f out: one pce* 7/1

0505 7 5 **Sinatramania**[13] 4052 3-8-13 59 AndrewMullen 13 40
(Miss Tracy Waggott) *hld up in rr: hdwy 3f out: hung lft and wknd over 1f out* 16/1

606 8 3¾ **Ingleby King (USA)**[49] 2852 4-9-10 62 GrahamGibbons 9 37
(T D Barron) *mid-div: drvn over 3f out: lost pl 2f out* 7/1

U0-0 9 ¾ **Princess Aliuska**[49] 2874 5-9-0 55 PaulPickard(3) 2 28
(C Smith) *hld up in rr: effrt on outer over 3f out: hung rt and lost pl over 1f out* 33/1

000 10 ½ **Isle Of Ellis (IRE)**[73] 2143 3-8-2 48 oh1 ow2 PatrickMathers 14 18
(R E Barr) *in rr: drvn over 3f out: nvr a factor* 66/1

5610 11 3 **Piccolo Express**[19] 3855 4-9-2 54 RobertWinston 8 19
(B P J Baugh) *mid-div: hdwy over 2f out: wknd qckly over 1f out* 14/1

00-0 12 1½ **Top Jaro (FR)**[11] 4156 7-8-11 54 (b) JamesSullivan(5) 10 16
(Mrs R A Carr) *in rr: drvn over 3f out: sn bhd* 28/1

004 13 6 **Happy The Man (IRE)**[33] 3397 3-8-0 46 oh1 DuranFentiman 12 —
(T D Easterby) *hld up in midfield: effrt over 3f out: sn lost pl and bhd* 50/1

-000 14 17 **Lily Jicaro (IRE)**[10] 4173 4-8-8 46 oh1 (t) TomEaves 11 —
(Mrs L Williamson) *t.k.h: led 2f: lost pl over 2f out: sn bhd and eased* 66/1

1m 37.46s (-0.54) **Going Correction** -0.125s/f (Firm)
WFA 3 from 4yo+ 8lb 14 Ran SP% 122.3
Speed ratings (Par 101): **97,96,92,91,90 89,84,80,80,79 76,75,69,52**
toteswingers: 1&2 £7.80, 1&3 £10.60, 2&3 £6.80. CSF £101.36 CT £531.00 TOTE £13.20: £6.10, £1.20, £3.40; EX 123.50.
Owner Miss M E Rowland **Bred** P J Munnelly **Trained** Lower Blidworth, Notts

FOCUS
Not as competitive a handicap as the numbers would suggest and the pace was ordinary. The front pair pulled clear and there was also a big gap between the first six and the rest.
Piccolo Express Official explanation: jockey said gelding was unsuited by the firm (good to firm places) ground

4486 RACING UK ON CHANNEL 432 H'CAP (DIV I) 6f
5:30 (5:31) (Class 6) (0-65,65) 3-Y-O+ £1,295 (£385; £192; £96) Stalls Centre

Form RPR

020/ 1 **San Jose City (IRE)**[69] 2267 5-9-7 60 (p) RobertWinston 9 71
(Muredach Kelly, Ire) *chsd ldrs: led 2f out: drvn rt out* 5/1[2]

3233 2 1½ **Minturno (USA)**[12] 4121 4-9-6 62 (p) BarryMcHugh(3) 1 68
(Mrs A Duffield) *hood removed v late: hld up towards rr: hdwy over 2f out: hung lft and styd on to take 2nd nr fin* 7/4[1]

0600 3 ½ **Carnival Dream**[33] 3409 5-8-11 50 PatrickMathers 8 54
(H A McWilliams) *w ldrs: led over 2f out: sn hdd: kpt on same pce fnl f* 50/1

000- 4 1¼ **Parisian Dream**[278] 6998 6-9-2 55 (t) LeeVickers 10 55
(T J Pitt) *hld up in rr: hdwy over 2f out: kpt on fnl f* 33/1

003 5 nse **Sea Salt**[6] 4285 7-9-10 63 SilvestreDeSousa 7 63
(R E Barr) *trckd ldrs: t.k.h: hung bdly lft over 1f out: kpt on same pce* 5/1[2]

-400 6 1½ **Karate Queen**[29] 3538 5-8-7 46 oh1 (v[1]) DuranFentiman 6 41
(R E Barr) *s.i.s: hdwy 3f out: nvr nr ldrs* 33/1

2005 6 dht **Klynch**[13] 4063 4-9-7 65 (b) JamesSullivan(5) 3 60
(Mrs R A Carr) *w ldrs: hung lft and bmpd over 1f out: sn wknd* 9/1

5320 8 3½ **Piste**[35] 3322 4-9-6 59 DavidAllan 4 43
(Miss T Jackson) *in rr-div: hdwy over 2f out: chsng ldrs whn n.m.r over 1f out: sn wknd* 6/1[3]

3035 9 ¾ **Avonlini**[11] 4155 4-8-9 48 AndrewElliott 2 30
(B P J Baugh) *w ldrs: lost pl over 1f out* 16/1

1000 10 3 **Green Poppy**[15] 3977 4-9-2 55 (v[1]) TomEaves 5 27
(B Smart) *t.k.h: led: hdd over 2f out: hung rt: hmpd and lost pl over 1f out: eased whn bhd* 12/1

00/0 11 4½ **Goodenough Magic**[12] 4082 4-8-2 46 oh1 IanBrennan(5) 12 4
(A G Foster) *trckd ldrs: reminders 3f out: sn lost pl and bhd* 50/1

1m 11.44s (-0.36) **Going Correction** -0.125s/f (Firm) 11 Ran SP% 117.4
Speed ratings (Par 101): **97,95,94,92,92 90,90,85,84,80 74**
toteswingers: 1&2 £4.00, 1&3 £34.60, 2&3 £18.50. CSF £13.76 CT £394.99 TOTE £6.40: £2.20, £1.40, £8.40; EX 18.30.
Owner San Jose City Syndicate **Bred** Bryan Ryan **Trained** Ballinasloe, Co. Galway

FOCUS
A poor handicap.

4487 RACING UK ON CHANNEL 432 H'CAP (DIV II) 6f
6:05 (6:06) (Class 6) (0-65,65) 3-Y-O+ £1,295 (£385; £192; £96) Stalls Centre

Form RPR

4011 1 **Clerical (USA)**[8] 4234 4-9-0 53 6ex (p) GrahamGibbons 11 61
(R M H Cowell) *chsd ldrs: led over 1f out: edgd lft: hld on towards fin* 5/4[1]

0034 2 nk **Micky Mac (IRE)**[16] 3946 6-9-4 62 DaleSwift(5) 2 69
(C J Teague) *w ldrs: edgd rt and sltly hmpd 1f out: kpt on wl: no ex towards fin* 7/1[2]

0040 3 2 **Forzarzi (IRE)**[16] 3948 6-8-7 46 PatrickMathers 9 47
(H A McWilliams) *dwlt: in rr: hdwy over 2f out: kpt on fnl f* 16/1

6103 4 ¾ **Greek Secret**[8] 4239 7-9-2 60 JamesO'Reilly(5) 7 58
(J O'Reilly) *hld up in rr: stmbld over 4f out: hdwy 2f out: styd on ins fnl f* 9/1

3-0 5 ¾ **Zarilan (IRE)**[11] 4154 5-9-9 65 MichaelStainton(3) 3 61
(Michael Smith) *chsd ldrs: one pce fnl 2f* 11/1

1605 6 shd **Soto**[14] 4014 7-9-2 60 (b) JamesSullivan(5) 6 56
(M W Easterby) *led tl over 1f out: hung lft: sltyly hmpd and wknd 1f out* 8/1[3]

0000 7 3¼ **Dream Express (IRE)**[21] 3775 5-8-11 50 (p) DavidAllan 10 35
(D W Thompson) *mid-div: rdn and hung lft 2f out: sn wknd* 20/1

5400 8 hd **Avoncreek**[28] 3556 6-8-2 46 oh1 JemmaMarshall(5) 1 30
(B P J Baugh) *chsd ldrs: wknd over 1f out* 10/1

40- 9 6 **San Diego Prince**[61] 2520 6-8-5 49 (p) IanBrennan(5) 5 14
(Muredach Kelly, Ire) *in rr-div: rdn and hung lft over 2f out: sn bhd* 14/1

0-00 10 hd **Neva A Mull Moment (IRE)**[14] 4014 4-8-13 55 BarryMcHugh(3) 8 20
(R E Barr) *towards rr: rdn over 2f out: sn bhd* 40/1

1m 11.57s (-0.23) **Going Correction** -0.125s/f (Firm)
WFA 3 from 4yo+ 5lb 10 Ran SP% 115.2
Speed ratings (Par 101): **96,95,92,91,90 90,86,86,78,77**
toteswingers: 1&2 £3.30, 1&3 £7.20, 2&3 £17.70. totesuper7: Win: Not won. Place: £252.60. CSF £9.98 CT £97.17 TOTE £2.40: £2.20, £1.10, £8.00; EX 9.00 Place 6: £8.69, Place 5: £7.50..
Owner J Sargeant **Bred** Walmac Stud Management Llc **Trained** Six Mile Bottom, Cambs

FOCUS
The winning time was 0.13 seconds slower than the first division.
T/Plt: £6.60 to a £1 stake. Pool £41,693.64 - 4,604.60 winning tickets. T/Qpdt: £4.90 to a £1 stake. Pool £2,296.10 - 343.10 winning tickets. WG

4303 SANDOWN (R-H)
Wednesday, July 28

OFFICIAL GOING: Good to firm (8.8)
Bend at mid-configuration and home straight dolled out 4yds increasing distances on round course by about 5yds.
Wind: Moderate, against. Weather: mainly overcast

4488 AIR CHARTER SERVICE APPRENTICE H'CAP 1m 14y
5:50 (5:50) (Class 5) (0-70,70) 4-Y-O+ £2,590 (£770; £385; £192) Stalls High

Form RPR

6200 1 **Black N Brew (USA)**[35] 3317 4-9-10 70 KierenFox 4 78
(J R Best) *in tch on outer: pushed along 3f out: rdn and hdwy to chse ldr over 1f out: led ins fnl f: styd on wl* 10/1

0600 2 ½ **Trafalgar Square**[12] 4108 8-8-9 55 (v) MatthewDavies 6 62
(M J Attwater) *stdd s: hld up in last trio: hdwy over 2f out: chsd wnr u.p ins fnl f: kpt on but a hld fnl 50yds* 8/1

2220 3 2½ **Gazboolou**[14] 4024 6-9-7 67 SimonPearce 8 68
(David Pinder) *t.k.h: chsd ldrs tl wnt 2nd over 3f out: rdn to ld ent fnl 2f: hdd ins fnl f: wknd fnl 100yds* 10/1

5130 4 ½ **Croeso Cusan**[18] 3905 5-8-13 59 SophieDoyle 2 59
(J L Spearing) *taken down early: stdd s: t.k.h: hld up in rr: hdwy on outer and rdn wl over 1f out: styd on same pce and no imp ins fnl f* 8/1

4-06 5 1¼ **Northern Genes (AUS)**[28] 3556 4-8-0 51 oh5 LucyBarry(5) 11 48
(M Appleby) *taken down early: led: hdd and rdn ent fnl 2f: kpt chsng ldrs tl wknd jst ins fnl f* 25/1

6022 6 1 **Kiss A Prince**[21] 3782 4-9-5 65 (b) AshleyMorgan 7 60
(D K Ivory) *t.k.h: hld up in tch in midfield: shuffled bk and towards rr ent fnl 2f: rallied and kpt on fnl f: no threat to ldrs* 3/1[1]

0040 7 nk **Hilbre Court (USA)**[18] 3911 5-8-8 54 (p) DeclanCannon 3 48
(B P J Baugh) *chsd ldr tl over 3f out: sn rdn: kpt chsng ldrs tl wknd ent fnl f* 16/1

0036 8 nk **War And Peace (IRE)**[19] 3855 6-9-2 67 MatthewCosham(5) 10 61
(P D Evans) *hld up wl in tch in midfield: nt clr run and shuffled bk ent fnl 2f: kpt on same pce and n.d after* 12/1

6012 9 shd **Annes Rocket (IRE)**[6] 4308 5-8-13 59 RossAtkinson 1 52+
(J C Fox) *stdd s: hld up in rr: looking for run on inner and nt clr run fr 2f out tl jst ins fnl f: nvr able to chal* 13/2[2]

0364 10 1½ **Having A Ball**[19] 3862 6-8-2 51 oh1 CharlesEddery(3) 5 41
(P D Cundell) *in tch in midfield: n.m.r and shuffled bk towards rr jst over 2f out: n.d after* 10/1

2200 **11** 3¾ **El Libertador (USA)**[6] 4308 4-9-2 **62**.......... JohnFahy 9 43
(E A Wheeler) *trckd ldrs on inner: rdn and unable qck over 2f out: wknd over 1f out and bhd fnl f* **7/1**[3]

1m 43.5s (0.20) **Going Correction** +0.10s/f (Good) **11** Ran SP% **117.7**
Speed ratings (Par 103): **103,102,100,99,98 97,96,96,96,95 91**
Tote Swingers:1&2:£16.30, 2&3:£12.30, 1&3:£16.50 CSF £87.76 CT £829.46 TOTE £11.90: £3.80, £3.00, £4.60; EX 85.70.
Owner Martin Long **Bred** Ponder Hill Inc **Trained** Hucking, Kent

FOCUS
A modest handicap contested largely by horses that have been finding winning difficult. The pace wasn't strong, there was some bunching in the straight and it paid to race handily. The winner came up the centre.

4489 HAWKER CLAIMING STKS 1m 14y
6:20 (6:21) (Class 5) 4-Y-O+ **£2,590** (£770; £385; £192) **Stalls** High

Form RPR

3050 **1** **Dingaan (IRE)**[18] 3888 7-9-0 77.......... WilliamBuick 3 86
(A M Balding) *stdd s: hld up wl bhd: plld out lft over 2f out: rdn and gd hdwy over 1f out: led 1f out: clr and edgd lft fnl 100yds: r.o strly: rdn out* **5/1**[2]

0360 **2** 3 **Carcinetto (IRE)**[18] 3894 8-8-9 75.......... TomMcLaughlin 1 74
(P D Evans) *wl bhd in last pair: niggled along 5f out: clsng but stl last whn swtchd lft ent fnl f: styd on u.p to snatch 2nd on post: no ch w wnr* **9/1**

0202 **3** shd **Orchard Supreme**[50] 2840 7-9-0 75.......... PatDobbs 2 79
(R Hannon) *racd wl off the pce in midfield: rdn and chsd ldng pair over 2f out: clsd and pressed ldrs 1f out: nt pce of wnr fnl 150yds: lost 2nd on post* **7/1**[3]

004- **4** 1 **Grande Caiman (IRE)**[451] 1709 6-8-8 90.......... CharlesEddery[(7)] 9 78
(R Hannon) *chsd ldng trio: rdn and clsd 2f out: pressing for placings fnl f: kpt on but no ch w wnr* **17/2**

5111 **5** 2 **Lang Shining (IRE)**[20] 3814 6-9-2 87.......... SophieDoyle[(5)] 6 79
(J A Osborne) *stdd and short of room s: hld up off the pce: rdn and effrt whn n.m.r ent fnl 2f tl over 1f out: kpt on same pce fnl f: nvr able to chal* **1/1**[1]

3-60 **6** 4½ **No Mean Trick (USA)**[9] 4201 4-8-9 70..........(p) JohnFahy[(5)] 5 62
(C G Cox) *chsd ldr for 2f: chsd ldng pair after tl wknd u.p over 1f out: fdd fnl f* **25/1**

06-6 **7** 2 **Easy Target (FR)**[11] 4133 5-8-13 80.......... AmirQuinn 8 56
(G L Moore) *taken down early: led at fast gallop: rdn over 2f out: hdd 1f out: sn fdd* **14/1**

004 **8** shd **Leverage (IRE)**[16] 3970 4-9-3 75.......... StephenCraine 7 60
(M Wigham) *chsd ldng pair: wnt 2nd after 2f: upsides ldr 3f out: sn pushed along but hld hd high and wanting to hang lft: wknd qckly over 1f out: fdd fnl f* **20/1**

1m 42.8s (-0.50) **Going Correction** +0.10s/f (Good) **8** Ran SP% **115.0**
Speed ratings (Par 103): **106,103,102,101,99 95,93,93**
Tote Swingers: 1&2 £4.60, 1&3 £4.40, 2&3 £5.50 CSF £48.87 TOTE £7.50: £2.20, £2.90, £2.60; EX 35.20.No Mean Trick was claimed by Declan Carroll for £11,000.
Owner Lady C S Cadbury **Bred** Mrs Gill Wilson **Trained** Kingsclere, Hants

FOCUS
An above-average claimer despite the withdrawal of Desert Dreamer who bolted before the start. It was run at a decent pace and the field were well strung out by the turn, the winner again coming up the centre.
Lang Shining(IRE) Official explanation: jockey said gelding never travelled

4490 PEGASUS EBF MAIDEN STKS 7f 16y
6:55 (6:57) (Class 4) 2-Y-O **£4,533** (£1,348; £674; £336) **Stalls** High

Form RPR

1 **Borug (USA)** 2-9-3 0.......... FrankieDettori 2 77+
(Saeed Bin Suroor) *mde all: set stdy gallop tl rdn and qcknd over 1f out: drvn ent fnl f: r.o wl* **7/2**[3]

2 ¾ **Edmaaj (IRE)** 2-9-3 0.......... RichardHills 6 77+
(B W Hills) *stdd s: hld up in tch in rr: nt clr run 2f out tl swtchd lft ent fnl f: hanging rt but r.o wl to snatch 2nd on post* **3/1**[2]

0 **3** shd **Mr Perceptive (IRE)**[37] 3269 2-9-3 0.......... PatDobbs 4 75+
(R Hannon) *dwlt: sn rcvrd to chse wnr: rdn and ev ch ent fnl 2f: nt quite pce of wnr over 1f out: kpt on but a hld fnl f: lost 2nd on post* **6/1**

0 **4** ½ **Aciano (IRE)**[12] 4096 2-9-3 0.......... ShaneKelly 9 74+
(B J Meehan) *trckd ldrs: n.m.r on inner 2f out: rdn and kpt on fnl f: unable to chal* **33/1**

5 ½ **Ocean War** 2-9-3 0.......... AhmedAjtebi 7 73+
(Mahmood Al Zarooni) *chsd ldrs: rdn and effrt to chse ldng pair ent fnl 2f: n.m.r and styd on at one pce ins fnl f* **15/2**

6 1¼ **Star Of Dance (IRE)** 2-9-3 0.......... RyanMoore 1 69
(Sir Michael Stoute) *dwlt: in tch in last pair: pushed along 3f out: rdn and no prog wl over 1f out: hdwy 1f out: kpt on: nt pce to threaten ldrs* **2/1**[1]

7 hd **Rocky Rebel** 2-9-3 0.......... PatCosgrave 3 70+
(R M Beckett) *s.i.s: sn pushed along and rn green in last pair: effrt on inner and nt clr run 2f out tl swtchd lft over 1f out: styd on same pce after* **25/1**

8 3¼ **Buxfizz (USA)** 2-9-3 0.......... EddieAhern 8 61
(R A Mills) *wl in tch in midfield: n.m.r and shuffled bk jst over 2f out: outpcd wl over 1f out: n.d after* **14/1**

9 ¾ **Frederick William** 2-9-3 0.......... SebSanders 5 59
(P J Makin) *stdd s: t.k.h: hld up in tch: rdn and unable qck wl over 1f out: outpcd over 1f out: wl hld fnl f* **50/1**

1m 33.2s (3.70) **Going Correction** +0.10s/f (Good) **9** Ran SP% **122.0**
Speed ratings (Par 96): **82,81,81,80,79 78,78,74,73**
Tote Swingers:1&2:£2.90, 2&3:£3.70, 1&3:£5.40 CSF £15.20 TOTE £4.80: £2.30, £1.60, £1.90; EX 18.60.
Owner Godolphin **Bred** Rabbah Bloodstock Llc **Trained** Newmarket, Suffolk

FOCUS
With several of the field holding entries in Group races, this was almost certainly a useful maiden despite the bunched finish. The pace was steady and the race didn't really begin in earnest until 2f out.

NOTEBOOK
Borug(USA), a $550,000 half-brother to several winners, notably the Arc winner Marienbard, made an encouraging debut, though his performance perhaps lacked the promise of some of those behind in that he was able to dictate his own gallop and got first run when asked to go and win his race. That said, he looked green off the bridle and is sure to improve, with the experience behind him, not least when stepping up to 1m. (op 10-3 tchd 11-4 and 4-1 in a place)
Edmaaj(IRE) ◆, a half-brother to the fairly useful 6f/1m winner Raiding Party out of a 1m4f winner, looked very unlucky not to make a winning debut. Trapped travelling strongly in a pocket for much of the straight, he had all of four lengths to make up on the winner when finally getting clear and all but managed it despite his rider not being hard on him. He looks a sure-fire winner next time. (op 9-2)
Mr Perceptive(IRE) had been too green in a fair maiden at Windsor on his debut but looked more professional here, only losing second right on the line. He may not have as much improvement in him as some of those behind, but looks more than good enough to win a run-of-mill maiden with a stiffer test also promising to suit better. (op 10-1)
Aciano(IRE) hails from a yard whose juveniles generally improve for a run and he left his Newbury debut behind with a more encouraging effort, albeit better placed than most as the race developed.
Ocean War, a 320,000 gns purchase who is a half-brother to the useful 1m2f winner Seaway, shaped well enough from a handy position while looking to have inherited more stamina from his sire (Dalakhani) than speed from his dam (2yo 6f winner). (op 8-1)
Star Of Dance(IRE) ◆, a 370,000 gns half-brother to a couple of winners and holding an entry in the Champagne Stakes, was an uneasy favourite and ran as if the experience was very much needed, taking an age to grasp what was required and poorly positioned when the sprint began before staying on takingly under a hand ride. He looked to be carrying a bit of condition beforehand and is likely to be a different proposition next time. (op 6-4 tchd 7-4)
Rocky Rebel is a late foal and one that might some time judged on this debut but he wasn't given a hard time and is another potential improver.
Buxfizz(USA) ◆, a half-brother to the useful 6f winner Bernasconi and with a Royal Lodge entry, showed his inexperience when caught flat footed as the tempo lifted, and then had to be snatched up, but he stayed on strongly near the line and he might improve enough to win an ordinary maiden next time. (op 16-1)
Frederick William is from a yard that don't have their juveniles wound up first time as a rule and the fact he was started off here suggests he is held in high regard. He faded late, but would have to be of interest in ordinary company next time.

4491 SOPWITH H'CAP 1m 14y
7:30 (7:30) (Class 4) (0-80,80) 3-Y-O **£5,180** (£1,541; £770; £384) **Stalls** High

Form RPR

6401 **1** **Sooraah**[19] 3852 3-8-13 **75**.......... JohnFahy[(5)] 1 85+
(W J Haggas) *stdd and dropped in bhd after s: hld up in last: smooth hdwy on outer over 2f out: led over 1f out: pushed out fnl f: comf* **15/8**[1]

2213 **2** 1¼ **Cabal**[25] 3661 3-9-8 **79**.......... RyanMoore 7 83
(Sir Michael Stoute) *in tch in midfield: rdn and effrt ent fnl 2f: hdwy between horses to dispute 2nd 1f out: kpt on u.p but no ch w wnr* **4/1**[3]

1231 **3** nk **The Shuffler**[37] 3259 3-9-0 **71**.......... SamHitchcott 3 74
(G L Moore) *stdd s: t.k.h: hld up in last pair: rdn and hdwy on outer wl over 1f out: disp 2nd 1f out: kpt on u.p but no ch w wnr* **14/1**

2010 **4** 2¼ **Abhar (USA)**[13] 4058 3-8-7 **69**.......... KierenFox[(5)] 6 67
(J R Best) *chsd ldrs: rdn over 2f out: plugged on same pce u.p fr over 1f out* **20/1**

5-46 **5** 3½ **William Van Gogh**[76] 2043 3-9-9 **80**.......... WilliamBuick 4 70
(J H M Gosden) *jostled s and s.i.s: sn in tch in midfield: effrt and unable qck 2f out: wknd over 1f out: wl hld fnl f* **11/4**[2]

236- **6** nk **Poor Prince**[288] 6754 3-9-8 **79**.......... EddieAhern 2 68
(C G Cox) *chsd ldr: rdn and hld hd high ent fnl 2f: wkng and towards rr whn hmpd ent fnl 1f: wl btn after* **12/1**

1464 **7** ¾ **Bin Shamardal (IRE)**[24] 3708 3-9-4 **75**..........(b[1]) RichardHills 5 62
(B W Hills) *racd freely: led tl rdn and hdd over 1f out: wknd and edgd lft 1f out: sn bhd* **5/1**

1m 43.98s (0.68) **Going Correction** +0.10s/f (Good) **7** Ran SP% **117.2**
Speed ratings (Par 102): **100,98,98,96,92 92,91**
Tote Swingers:1&2:£1.50, 2&3:£4.50, 1&3:£6.00 CSF £10.24 TOTE £3.50: £1.90, £1.10; EX 12.30.
Owner Mohammed Jaber **Bred** C R Mason **Trained** Newmarket, Suffolk

FOCUS
A fairly useful contest run at a steady pace and won stylishly by an improving filly who made her run up the centre.

4492 DONOHUE FILLIES' H'CAP 1m 1f
8:05 (8:05) (Class 5) (0-75,75) 3-Y-O+ **£3,238** (£963; £481; £240) **Stalls** High

Form RPR

5321 **1** **Sunley Spinalonga**[12] 4102 3-8-10 **66**.......... RyanMoore 6 74+
(D R C Elsworth) *hld up wl in tch: rdn 2f out: swtchd ins and hdwy ent fnl f: rdn to ld ins fnl f: r.o wl: rdn out* **6/4**[1]

0526 **2** ¾ **Steel Free (IRE)**[27] 3592 4-9-6 **67**.......... GeorgeBaker 3 74
(M Madgwick) *in tch: rdn to chse ldr wl over 1f out: ev ch ent fnl f: kpt on same pce fnl 100yds* **12/1**

-003 **3** 1 **Ashkalara**[26] 3628 3-8-1 **57**.......... JimmyQuinn 8 61+
(H S Howe) *s.i.s: hld up in last: nt clr run 2f out: swtchd lft and hdwy over 1f out: chsd ldrs ent fnl f: kpt on: wnt 3rd nr fin* **7/1**

1112 **4** ½ **Marjury Daw (IRE)**[9] 4196 4-10-0 **75**.......... PaulMulrennan 2 79
(J G Given) *trckd ldrs tl hdwy to ld 3f out: rdn and qcknd ent fnl 2f: drvn and hdd ins fnl f: wknd towards fin* **7/2**[2]

6134 **5** 4 **Tamtara**[16] 3963 3-9-5 **75**.......... PatCosgrave 5 69
(Mrs A J Perrett) *trckd ldr tl 3f out: stl handy and rdn 2f out: keeping on same pce whn hmpd ent fnl f: n.d after* **9/1**

-535 **6** 1 **Treasure Way**[12] 4098 3-8-13 **69**.......... LiamKeniry 1 61
(P R Chamings) *t.k.h: hld up in tch in last pair: rdn and effrt on outer 2f out: wknd ent fnl f* **5/1**[3]

40-0 **7** 5 **Lady Slippers (IRE)**[50] 2844 3-8-7 **63** ow2.......... EddieAhern 4 44
(H J L Dunlop) *sn led: hdd 3f out: rdn 2f out: struggling and losing pl whn hmpd ent fnl f: wl hld after* **20/1**

1m 59.75s (4.05) **Going Correction** +0.10s/f (Good)
WFA 3 from 4yo 9lb **7** Ran SP% **113.8**
Speed ratings (Par 100): **86,85,84,84,80 79,75**
Tote Swingers:1&2:£5.30, 2&3:£10.80, 1&3:£3.80 CSF £21.10 CT £97.97 TOTE £2.70: £2.00, £8.80; EX 23.60.
Owner Sunley, Heaney & Elsworth **Bred** Sunley Stud **Trained** Newmarket, Suffolk

FOCUS
A modest handicap that was run at a very steady pace. The winner made her effort up the rail.

4493 HERCULES H'CAP 1m 6f
8:35 (8:36) (Class 4) (0-80,74) 3-Y-O **£3,885** (£1,156; £577; £288) **Stalls** High

Form RPR

6-22 **1** **Tuscan Gold**[8] 4230 3-9-5 **70**.......... SebSanders 3 80+
(Sir Mark Prescott) *stdd s: hld up in rr: hdwy 5f out: chsd ldr over 2f out: rdn to ld over 1f out: edgd lft but styd on wl fnl f: rdn out* **10/11**[1]

-232 **2** 1¼ **Astral Flower**[21] 3789 3-9-4 **69**.......... RyanMoore 5 77
(Sir Michael Stoute) *in tch: n.m.r and shuffled bk towards rr ent fnl 2f: rdn and hdwy jst over 1f out: chsd wnr fnl 100yds: r.o but no imp* **7/2**[2]

2533 **3** 1½ **First Fandango**[16] 3953 3-9-9 **74**.......... GeorgeBaker 6 80
(J W Hills) *stdd after s: hld up in last pair: rdn and hdwy on outer 2f out: chsd wnr 1f out: no imp and swtchd rt ins fnl f: lost 2nd fnl 100yds* **14/1**

2216 **4** 2½ **Dream Spinner**[18] 3909 3-9-8 **73**.......... EddieAhern 1 75
(J L Dunlop) *led: rdn wl over 2f out: hdd over 1f out: wknd jst ins fnl f* **10/1**

5444 **5** *1 ½* **Stadium Of Light (IRE)**[56] 2650 3-9-2 **67**......................(t) SteveDrowne 4 67
(H Morrison) *in tch in midfield: effrt on inner and rdn 2f out: n.m.r and no prog ent fnl f: wl hld and eased towards fin* **9/2**[3]
3132 **6** *7* **Blinka Me**[56] 2650 3-8-11 **62**.. JimmyQuinn 2 53
(A M Hales) *chsd ldr tl wl over 2f out: wknd u.p over 1f out: bhd fnl f* **12/1**
3m 8.61s (4.11) **Going Correction** +0.10s/f (Good) **6** Ran SP% **116.2**
Speed ratings (Par 102): **92,91,90,89,88 84**
Tote Swingers:1&2:£1.02, 2&3:£8.20, 1&3:£6.40 CSF £4.66 TOTE £2.20: £1.80, £1.10; EX 4.40 Place 6 £96.82,Place 5 £18.10..
Owner The Green Door Partnership **Bred** Mrs James Wigan & London TB Services Ltd **Trained** Newmarket, Suffolk
FOCUS
Just a fair handicap despite the rating band but it was run at a reasonable pace considering the small field and the result looks the right one.
T/Plt: £195.70 to a £1 stake. Pool £55,433.82. 206.73 winning tickets. T/Qpdt: £7.60 to a £1 stake. Pool £7,001.20. 678.48 winning tickets. SP

4494 - 4495a (Foreign Racing) - See Raceform Interactive

4462 GALWAY (R-H)
Wednesday, July 28

OFFICIAL GOING: Hurdle/flat course - good to firm (good in places); chase course - good (good to firm in places)

4496a WWW.TOTEGORACINGCLUB.COM H'CAP 1m 100y
6:35 (6:35) (60-95,89) 3-Y-O **£10,991** (£2,548; £1,115; £637)

RPR
1 **New Magic (IRE)**[10] 4177 3-9-12 **89**.................................... KJManning 3 93
(Mrs John Harrington, Ire) *hld up: prog into 2nd and rdn bef st: led under 1f out: jnd ins fnl f: styd on best to edge ahd nr fin* **4/1**[2]
2 *hd* **Flameoftheforest (IRE)**[67] 2356 3-9-6 **83**............................... WJLee 10 87+
(C F Swan, Ire) *wl off pce towards rr: gd prog on inner appr st: sn cl up: briefly short of room and sn got room to chal under 1f out: on terms and ev ch ins fnl f: no ex and hdd nr fin* **7/1**
3 *4* **Snap Alam (IRE)**[36] 3302 3-9-1 **78**...................................(p) PJSmullen 4 73
(Ms Joanna Morgan, Ire) *sn trckd ldrs: impr to ld bef st: hdd under 1f out: sn hmpd and dropped to 3rd: no ex* **6/1**[3]
4 *¾* **The Lock Master (IRE)**[69] 2269 3-8-11 **77**................(b) ShaneFoley(3) 6 71+
(M Halford, Ire) *dwlt: wl off pce towards rr: 8th and prog appr st: sn rdn to chse ldrs and no imp: kpt on wout threatening* **7/1**
5 *1 ½* **Elmfield Giant (USA)**[32] 3451 3-8-13 **76**............................ MCHussey 8 66
(R A Fahey) *chsd ldrs: 6th appr st: sn 5th and no imp u.p: kpt on same pce* **8/1**
6 *4 ½* **Rare Symphony (IRE)**[21] 3803 3-9-3 **80**...........................(p) WJSupple 1 60
(P D Deegan, Ire) *sn led: hdd bef st: sn no imp* **11/1**
7 *1 ¾* **Prince Jock (USA)**[18] 3929 3-9-6 **83**.................................. PShanahan 11 60
(Tracey Collins, Ire) *prom: lost pl appr st: sn no imp* **8/1**
8 *15* **Luddenmore (IRE)**[14] 4034 3-8-2 **68**............................... BACurtis(3) 5 12
(Edward P Mitchell, Ire) *trckd ldrs: rdn fr 1/2-way: 3rd appr st: sn lost pl and wknd: eased fnl f* **25/1**
9 *1 ½* **Yes Missus (IRE)**[9] 4217 3-8-12 **75**...................................... DMGrant 7 15
(Patrick J Flynn, Ire) *prom: on terms bef 1/2-way: rdn and wknd appr st: eased fnl f* **5/2**[1]
10 *3 ½* **Schull Harbour (IRE)**[16] 3999 3-7-11 **67** oh5.................. SHJames(7) 9 —
(H Rogers, Ire) *s.i.s and wl off pce towards rr: nvr a factor: eased st* **50/1**
1m 48.87s (-1.33) **10** Ran SP% **124.2**
CSF £34.66 CT £177.84 TOTE £5.00: £1.50, £2.50, £1.60; DF 41.90.
Owner Patrick Reilly **Bred** Michael Hurley **Trained** Moone, Co Kildare
FOCUS
The third, fourth, fifth and sixth are all in top form and have been rated just off their best, with the winner and runner-up rated as recording personal bests.
NOTEBOOK
New Magic(IRE) carried top weight to victory here in a moderate contest for this grade. Held up just off the pace in a truly run race, she was brought through to challenge and lead a furlong out and, to her credit, pulled out plenty to repel the runner-up. It was a very likeable performance from a filly that will be stepping up in grade after this. (op 11/2)
Flameoftheforest(IRE) had looked a good, progressive juvenile when winning a heavy ground maiden at Tipperary last September, and on this much quicker surface he gave the impression that he could win again soon. Travelling well just off the pace, he was denied a clear run in the straight. Having manufactured a gap, he came there with every chance inside the last but the winner just pulled out that bit extra. (op 10/1)
Snap Alam(IRE) couldn't really find any cover and consequently raced quite keenly. It seemed to cost her in the end as she ran out of steam inside the last after being hampered a little by the runner-up. (op 13/2)
The Lock Master(IRE) actually ran on well quite late having been slowly into his stride.
Elmfield Giant(USA) raced just off the pace and could never get in a blow. (op 7/1)
Yes Missus(IRE) raced in the front two but didn't look happy just beyond halfway and didn't have the pace to keep her position on the climb to the straight. She ended up being squeezed right out but a clear passage would only have delayed the inevitable. Official explanation: jockey said filly changed her legs running into the dip and never travelled thereafter (op 2/1 tchd 15/8)

4497 - (Foreign Racing) - See Raceform Interactive

4291 EPSOM (L-H)
Thursday, July 29

OFFICIAL GOING: Good (good to firm in places; home straight 8.4; stands' side 8.6; far side 8.3)
Rail at inner configuration except 8f to 7f which is dolled out up to 5yds increasing races of 1m and over by about 5yds.
Wind: medium, against Weather: sunny spells, light cloud

4498 OFFICE DEPOT APPRENTICE H'CAP 1m 2f 18y
6:00 (6:02) (Class 5) (0-70,70) 4-Y-O+ **£2,590** (£770; £385; £192) **Stalls** Low

Form RPR
0202 **1** **Maybe I Wont**[11] 4168 5-8-12 **58**................................ RussKennemore 4 70
(Lucinda Featherstone) *chsd ldrs: wnt 3rd 5f out: swtchd ins and effrt 3f out: led ent fnl 2f: clr over 1f out: r.o wl: rdn out: easily* **6/1**
3204 **2** *5* **Markhesa**[21] 3821 4-8-10 **63**...................................... JamesRogers(7) 8 65
(J R Boyle) *chsd ldng pair tl 5f out: outpcd by ldng trio over 3f out: hdwy on inner 2f out: rdn to chse clr wnr over 1f out: no imp fnl f* **9/2**[2]
0242 **3** *2 ½* **Rosy Dawn**[16] 3983 5-8-0 **51** oh6.................................. RyanClark(5) 3 48
(J J Bridger) *led: jnd over 4f out: rdn ent fnl 3f: hdd ent fnl 2f: sn outpcd by wnr: 3rd and wl hld fnl f* **5/1**[3]
0620 **4** *1 ¼* **Clearing House**[7] 4308 5-7-12 **51** oh6.......................... NatashaEaton(7) 5 46
(J Ryan) *hld up off the pce in midfield: outpcd 4f out: sme hdwy and swtchd rt over 1f out: kpt on fnl f: nvr trbld ldrs* **10/1**
4060 **5** *½* **Edgeworth (IRE)**[13] 4108 4-9-5 **70**.......................... AnthonyFreeman(5) 7 64
(B G Powell) *taken down early: chsd ldr: jnd ldr over 4f out: rdn over 2f out: nt pce of wnr wl over 1f out: wknd ent fnl f: wl btn and edgd lft fnl 150yds* **11/4**[1]
0044 **6** *¾* **Lunar River (FR)**[17] 3968 7-8-3 **54**..................................(t) AmyScott(5) 2 46
(David Pinder) *stdd and v.s.a: t.k.h: hld up wl in rr: rdn and sme hdwy over 1f out: nvr on terms* **8/1**
6454 **7** *1 ½* **Quince (IRE)**[28] 3608 7-8-3 **52**..................................(v) SimonPearce(3) 1 41
(J Pearce) *nvr travelling wl: pushed along at times in midfield: dropped to rr and struggling 4f out: no ch after* **12/1**
0040 **8** *nk* **Illuminative (USA)**[9] 4227 4-9-1 **66**..........(p) GemmaGracey-Davison(5) 6 54
(Miss Z C Davison) *stdd s: sn in tch in midfield: struggling on downhill run over 4f out: bhd fnl 2f* **20/1**
556 **9** *7* **Summers Target (USA)**[10] 4213 4-8-3 **52**............(t[1]) AshleyMorgan(3) 9 26
(S C Williams) *taken down early: stdd and dropped in bhd after s: hld up in last pair: losing tch 4f out: n.d* **16/1**
2m 9.59s (-0.11) **Going Correction** +0.075s/f (Good) **9** Ran SP% **114.3**
Speed ratings (Par 103): **103,99,97,96,95 95,93,93,87**
toteswingers:1&2:£3.50, 1&3:£3.40, 2&3:£4.00 CSF £32.79 CT £144.67 TOTE £5.30: £2.20, £1.10, £1.10; EX 15.90.
Owner J Roundtree **Bred** Wheelersland Stud **Trained** Atlow, Derbyshire
■ Stewards' Enquiry : Simon Pearce two-day ban: used whip when out of contention (Aug 12-13)
FOCUS
An ordinary handicap. Very few got involved from off the pace. The winner is rated back to his best.
Quince(IRE) Official explanation: jockey said gelding was unsuited by the track

4499 WEATHERBYS BANK MAIDEN STKS 7f
6:30 (6:30) (Class 4) 2-Y-O **£3,885** (£1,156; £577; £288) **Stalls** Low

Form RPR
6 **1** **Screenprint**[16] 3991 2-9-3 0... HayleyTurner 1 66
(M L W Bell) *chsd ldr tl led over 3f out: mde rest: rdn wl over 1f out: kpt on gamely fnl f: jst lasted* **11/1**
65 **2** *nse* **Pigeon Hollow**[25] 3712 2-9-3 0... SamHitchcott 2 66+
(M R Channon) *sn rdn along in last pair: prog u.p on inner over 1f out: running on wl whn nt clr run and swtchd rt ins fnl f: r.o wl to press wnr cl home: jst failed* **50/1**
6 **3** *½* **Book Keeper**[14] 4054 2-9-3 0.. AhmedAjtebi 4 67
(Mahmood Al Zarooni) *towards rr: hdwy 4f out: effrt on inner to chse wnr over 2f out: n.m.r and swtchd in bhd wnr over 1f out: swtchd lft and effrt again 1f out: short of room and swtchd rt fnl 100yds: r.o cl home* **11/4**[2]
45 **4** *1 ½* **Degly Bo (IRE)**[21] 3832 2-9-3 0... TomQueally 7 61
(P W Chapple-Hyam) *in tch in midfield: rdn and effrt 3f out: kpt on same pce u.p fr over 1f out* **4/1**[3]
0 **5** *hd* **Key West (IRE)**[61] 2547 2-9-3 0.................................(b) WilliamBuick 6 60+
(J H M Gosden) *bhd: pushed along and no prog over 2f out: rdn and hdwy ins fnl f: styd on fnl 100yds: nvr trbld ldrs* **16/1**
0 **6** *2* **Exchange**[12] 4142 2-9-3 0.. FrankieDettori 8 56
(W J Haggas) *t.k.h: chsd ldrs: racd awkwardly on downhill run 4f out: chsd ldng pair ent fnl 2f: hung lft 1f out: wkng whn n.m.r wl ins fnl f* **7/4**[1]
04 **7** *1 ¾* **Dr Darcey**[20] 3842 2-9-3 0.. RichardHughes 3 51
(R Hannon) *reminders sn after s: chsd ldrs: rdn over 3f out: wknd over 1f out* **6/1**
0400 **8** *18* **Blade Pirate**[38] 3269 2-9-3 **50**... DaneO'Neill 5 6
(J Ryan) *sn bustled up to ld: hdd over 3f out: wknd qckly u.p ent fnl 2f: wl bhd fnl f* **50/1**
1m 25.92s (2.62) **Going Correction** +0.075s/f (Good) **8** Ran SP% **115.5**
Speed ratings (Par 96): **88,87,87,85,85 83,81,60**
toteswingers:1&2:£19.50, 1&3:£5.50, 2&3:£45.70 CSF £377.71 TOTE £15.90: £3.80, £6.00, £1.20; EX 310.10.
Owner Sheikh Marwan Al Maktoum **Bred** Darley **Trained** Newmarket, Suffolk
■ Stewards' Enquiry : Hayley Turner caution: careless riding.
FOCUS
This looked a pretty modest maiden on paper and the race itself proved somewhat messy. It is hard to be positive about the form.
NOTEBOOK
Screenprint was keen on his debut but settled much better this time under a front-running ride. He handled the downhill bend better than the rest and his rider kept a bit in reserve to hold off the closers in the final stages. He very much had the run of things but is entitled to come on again for this second outing and, with nurseries in mind, the handicapper can't give him too high a rating on the back of this narrow success (op 16-1)
Pigeon Hollow, tailed off on his debut and beaten a long way last second time out, improved dramatically on this third start. He struggled to go the early pace and only had one behind him at the top of the straight, but he kept on well next to the rail, where the path ahead was far from clear, and once in the clear well inside the last he flew home, only narrowly failing to get up on the line. A stiffer track and/or a mile is going to suit him. (tchd 40-1)
Book Keeper looked the unlucky horse in the race. The gap would not come for him next to the rail from 3f out, with the winner holding his position, so he was angled out to switch around him 1f out, but at that point the winner edged off the rail and jockey Ahmed Ajtebi made the mistake of going back to the rail, where the door was once again shut. With a clear run he would surely have won. (op 4-1)
Degly Bo(IRE) did not handle the downhill run particularly well and did not look that happy in the straight either. He should be more effective on a more galloping track. (op 7-2 tchd 11-4)
Key West(IRE), who has been gelded since his debut two months ago, was last through the early stages but ran on late in the day to post a more encouraging effort. (op 10-1 tchd 9-1)
Exchange only beat one home on his debut but showed ability. He failed to build on that here, though, racing keenly through the early stages and then struggling to handle the camber in the straight. He can do better back on a more conventional track. Official explanation: jockey said colt did not handle the track (op 2-1 tchd 9-4)
Dr Darcey does not appear to be progressing, although a bad run here can always be forgiven. (op 5-1 tchd 9-2)

4500 VIKING DIRECT CONDITIONS STKS 1m 2f 18y
7:05 (7:05) (Class 3) 3-Y-O+ **£6,231** (£1,866; £933; £467) **Stalls** Low

Form RPR
6340 **1** **Pompeyano (IRE)**[124] 1026 5-9-0 **110**............................. FrankieDettori 2 109+
(Saeed Bin Suroor) *trckd ldrs: outpcd downhill 4f out: hdwy over 2f out: rdn to ld wl over 1f out: r.o wl: rdn out* **10/11**[1]
10-0 **2** *½* **Chock A Block (IRE)**[59] 2593 4-9-0 **102**............................ TedDurcan 1 108
(Saeed Bin Suroor) *chsd ldr tl jnd ldr 5f out: rdn and ev ch over 2f out: chsd wnr and wandered u.p 1f out: kpt on but a hld after* **9/2**[3]

3634 **3** *8* **Heliodor (USA)**[75] 2116 4-9-0 **105**.................................. RichardHughes 4 92
(R Hannon) *led: jnd 5f out: rdn and hdd wl over 1f out: sn btn and no ch fnl f* **2/1**[2]

0300 **4** *½* **Dubai Miracle (USA)**[21] 3824 3-8-4 **91**...........................(b) HayleyTurner 3 91
(D M Simcock) *taken down early: hld up in last: rdn and no rspnse over 2f out: wl hld whn hung lft over 1f out* **10/1**

2m 6.91s (-2.79) **Going Correction** +0.075s/f (Good)
WFA 3 from 4yo+ 10lb **4** Ran SP% **113.0**
Speed ratings (Par 107): **114,113,107,106**
CSF £5.68 TOTE £1.90; EX 5.80.
Owner Godolphin **Bred** Loughtown Stud **Trained** Newmarket, Suffolk

FOCUS
An interesting little event dominated by the two Godolphin runners. The winner showed his Dubai form didn't flatter and the second looks the best guide to the form.

NOTEBOOK
Pompeyano(IRE), who has won fresh in the past, was running for the first time since competing in the Dubai Sheema Classic in March. This trip is probably on the short side for him, but having been niggled along coming down the hill and not looked to be enjoying the track, he really found his stride in the straight and stayed on strongly. He was comfortably on top at the finish, but he was entitled to win this on the ratings and he will need to step up if he is to make his mark in Listed company. A return to 1m4f plus will help, though. (op 13-8)
Chock A Block(IRE) is rated 8lb inferior to his stablemate, but had run more recently. He did a good job of denying Heliodor a soft lead and ran a sound race in defeat.
Heliodor(USA) ran below form. He could have done without being taken on for the lead but, even so, he should have finished closer to the first two on the ratings. The track was possibly not to his liking. Official explanation: jockey said colt hung right (op 6-4)
Dubai Miracle(USA) faced a stiff task at the weights and has not been at his best in recent starts. He looks a difficult horse to place off his current rating. (op 8-1)

4501 BROTHERS PEAR CIDER H'CAP 1m 114y
7:35 (7:37) (Class 4) (0-80,80) 3-Y-0+ **£4,533** (£1,348; £674; £336) **Stalls** Low

Form RPR

6156 **1** **Roman Glory (IRE)**[26] 3659 4-9-10 **78**.............................. MartinDwyer 1 85
(B J Meehan) *chsd ldrs: clsd and in tch 5f out: rdn to chse ldng pair over 1f out: hrd drvn ent fnl f: r.o to ld ins fnl f: all out* **7/1**[2]

5003 **2** *nk* **Licence To Till (USA)**[15] 4023 3-9-0 **77**............................ JoeFanning 7 82+
(M Johnston) *chsd ldr: rdn and ev ch over 2f out: led over 1f out: hung lft u.p 1f out: hdd ins fnl f: kpt on u.p but a jst hld* **7/2**[1]

1130 **3** *1 ¼* **Ostentation**[99] 1476 3-8-4 **70**....................................... MatthewDavies(3) 2 72
(R A Teal) *racd off the pce in midfield: clsd and in tch 5f out: outpcd and rdn wl over 2f out: rallied and hdwy on inner over 1f out: rdr dropped reins 1f out: swtchd rt and r.o wl fnl 100yds: nt rch ldrs* **12/1**[3]

2102 **4** *2* **Mishrif (USA)**[15] 4023 4-9-12 **80**................................(b) RichardHughes 6 78+
(J R Jenkins) *led: jnd and rdn over 2f out: hdd over 1f out: stl pressing ldr whn pushed against rail and hmpd ins fnl f: nt rcvr and btn after* **7/2**[1]

200 **5** *4* **Salient**[28] 3579 6-9-7 **77**... KirstyMilczarek 4 66
(M J Attwater) *chsd ldng pair: rdn wl over 2f out: wknd u.p wl over 1f out* **20/1**

4255 **6** *¾* **Effigy**[24] 3737 6-9-10 **78**.. DaneO'Neill 3 65
(H Candy) *racd off the pce in midfield: clsd and in tch 5f out: rdn and unable qck over 2f out: btn whn hung lft over 1f out* **7/2**[1]

224 **7** *1 ½* **Hazzard County (USA)**[45] 3036 6-9-5 **73**.................(p) WilliamBuick 8 57
(D M Simcock) *stdd s: hld up in last pair: rdn and effrt on outer ent fnl 2f: hld hd high and no prog wl over 1f out: nvr trbld ldrs* **7/2**[1]

0545 **8** *16* **Defector (IRE)**[17] 3970 4-8-13 **67**.................................... HayleyTurner 5 14
(W R Muir) *awkward leaving stalls and s.i.s: bhd: clsd 5f out: lost tch u.p wl over 2f out* **14/1**

1m 45.48s (-0.62) **Going Correction** +0.075s/f (Good)
WFA 3 from 4yo+ 9lb **8** Ran SP% **120.5**
Speed ratings (Par 105): **105,104,103,101,98 97,96,82**
toteswingers:1&2:£7.70, 1&3:£8.30, 2&3:£8.20 CSF £33.55 CT £299.38 TOTE £9.10: £2.50, £2.20, £2.20; EX 48.20.
Owner Martin Doran **Bred** G Callanan **Trained** Manton, Wilts

FOCUS
A fair handicap, run at an uneven pace and a bit of a messy race. The winner is rated up a length on his Lingfield win.
Salient Official explanation: vet said gelding lost a shoe
Hazzard County(USA) Official explanation: jockey said gelding did not handle the track

4502 PLAY BINGO AT TOTESPORT.COM FILLIES' H'CAP 7f
8:10 (8:11) (Class 5) (0-75,72) 3-Y-0+ **£3,238** (£722; £722; £240) **Stalls** Low

Form RPR

0154 **1** **Amber Sunset**[9] 4236 4-9-4 **64**.. LukeMorris 4 72
(D Morris) *chsd ldr: rdn to chse clr ldr ent fnl 2f: hrd drvn and kpt on wl to ld wl ins fnl f: edgd rt fnl 50yds: drvn out* **6/1**

0201 **2** *1 ¾* **Lady Florence**[7] 4308 5-9-4 **67** 6ex............................ RussKennemore(3) 9 70
(A B Coogan) *chsd ldr tl led over 3f out: rdn and clr 2f out: drvn ent fnl f: hdd wl ins fnl f: wknd towards fin* **7/1**

-006 **2** *dht* **Leadenhall Lass (IRE)**[21] 3815 4-9-8 **68**.........................(v) IanMongan 8 71
(P M Phelan) *taken down early: hld up in rr: hdwy on outer over 2f out: chsd ldrs but hanging lft u.p fr over 1f out: no imp on wnr fnl 50yds* **6/1**

3416 **4** *3 ¼* **Goolagong (IRE)**[13] 4104 3-9-3 **70**.. JimCrowley 7 61
(R M Beckett) *hld up in last pair: hdwy towards outer over 2f out: chsng ldrs but edging lft fr over 1f out: no prog and btn fnl 100yds: eased nr fin* **3/1**[2]

0500 **5** *1 ¾* **Merorless**[15] 4025 3-8-1 **54**...(p) KirstyMilczarek 2 41
(Miss Z C Davison) *awkward and stmbld leaving stalls: in tch in midfield: rdn and unable qck over 2f out: one pce and no ch fr over 1f out* **25/1**

1110 **6** *2 ¾* **Mandhooma**[7] 4283 4-9-0 **60**.. TomQueally 1 42
(P W Hiatt) *chsd ldrs: rdn and unable qck wl over 2f out: wknd over 1f out* **10/1**

0556 **7** *2 ¼* **Spinning Bailiwick**[14] 4057 4-9-12 **72**................................ GeorgeBaker 5 48
(G L Moore) *s.i.s: towards rr: rdn and effrt ent fnl 2f: wknd and wl btn fnl f* **11/2**[3]

6453 **8** *19* **Mausin (IRE)**[20] 3852 3-9-0 **67**... WilliamBuick 3 —
(H Morrison) *led tl over 3f out: rdn and lost pl qckly jst over 2f out: sn bhd: virtually p.u fnl f* **11/4**[1]

1m 24.11s (0.81) **Going Correction** +0.075s/f (Good)
WFA 3 from 4yo+ 7lb **8** Ran SP% **121.1**
Speed ratings (Par 100): **98,96,96,92,90 87,84,62**
PL: Lady Florence £2.40, Leadenhall Lady £3.00 EX: AS/LF £30.10 AS/LL £26.50 CSF: AS/LL £22.07 AS/LF £25.00. T/C: AS&LL&LF £132.74, AS&LF&LL £135.30. toteswingers:AS&LL:£8.70, AS&LF:£11.40, LL&LF:£6.80 TOTE £9.50: £3.10.
Owner David J Orchard **Bred** Southill Stud **Trained** Baxter's Green, Suffolk

FOCUS
A moderate fillies' handicap, run at a good gallop. The market leaders disappointed and this is pretty ordinary form.
Goolagong(IRE) Official explanation: jockey said filly was unsuited by the track
Mausin(IRE) Official explanation: trainer said filly was unsuited by the track

4503 OFFICEDEPOT.CO.UK H'CAP 6f
8:40 (8:41) (Class 4) (0-80,79) 3-Y-0 **£4,533** (£1,348; £674; £336) **Stalls** High

Form RPR

2453 **1** **Starwatch**[7] 4291 3-8-2 **60** oh4.. NeilChalmers 2 66
(J J Bridger) *mde virtually all: rdn 2f out: r.o gamely u.p fnl f* **20/1**

5541 **2** *¾* **Flouncing (IRE)**[6] 4342 3-9-1 **73** 6ex.............................. RichardHughes 6 77
(W J Haggas) *w ldr: rdn to challege ent fnl f: no ex and btn fnl 75yds* **4/1**[3]

5142 **3** *4 ½* **R Woody**[10] 4204 3-9-6 **78**.. TomQueally 3 68+
(D K Ivory) *trckd ldrs: effrt to press ldrs 2f out: rdn and fnd little over 1f out: wknd fnl f* **2/1**[1]

41 **4** *4* **Pin Cushion**[17] 3952 3-9-7 **79**.. MartinDwyer 1 56
(B J Meehan) *taken down early and ponied to s: stdd s: hld up in last pair: hdwy over 3f out: rdn to chse ldrs 2f out: wknd over 1f out: wl btn fnl f* **9/4**[2]

0021 **5** *10* **Thalia Grace**[26] 3677 3-8-2 **60**.. KirstyMilczarek 4 5
(L Montague Hall) *racd in midfield: rdn and struggling over 2f out: wl btn fnl 2f* **13/2**

4325 **6** *¾* **Super Yellow**[23] 3761 3-8-12 **70**.. WilliamBuick 5 12
(J A Osborne) *a outpcd in rr: lost tch 3f out* **15/2**

1m 10.01s (0.61) **Going Correction** +0.075s/f (Good) **6** Ran SP% **114.0**
Speed ratings (Par 102): **98,97,91,85,72 71**
toteswingers:1&2:£5.40, 1&3:£6.60, 2&3:£2.20 CSF £97.82 TOTE £15.90: £4.30, £1.80; EX 131.70 Place 6 £677.88; Place 5 £348.05.
Owner J J Bridger **Bred** Mrs J A Chapman **Trained** Liphook, Hants

FOCUS
An interesting little handicap but once again very few seemed to handle the track. Dubious form, rated around the runner-up.
R Woody Official explanation: jockey said gelding was unsuited by the track
T/Plt: £1,112.00 to a £1stake. Pool:£58,572.40 - 38.45 winning tickets T/Qpdt: £118.10 to a £1 stake. Pool:£5,734.00 - 35.90 winning tickets SP

4467 GOODWOOD (R-H)
Thursday, July 29

OFFICIAL GOING: Straight course - good (good to firm in places); round course - good to firm (stands' side 8.2, centre 8.2, far side 8.5, round 8.7)
Rail from 6f on lower bend to 3f marker on home straight dolled out 6yds, top bend dolled out 3yd increasing distances on round course by about 15yds.
Wind: Moderate, half against Weather: Fine but cloudy

4504 TURFTV SUMMER VASE STKS (H'CAP) 1m 1f 192y
2:10 (2:10) (Class 2) 3-Y-0
£24,924 (£7,464; £3,732; £1,868; £932; £468) **Stalls** High

Form RPR

1311 **1** **Beachfire**[26] 3697 3-8-9 **91**.. WilliamBuick 13 102
(J H M Gosden) *dwlt: rdn in last pair early: stl there 3f out: prog on wd outside after: r.o u.p fnl f: led last stride* **9/1**

2600 **2** *hd* **Right Step**[42] 3105 3-7-11 **86**.. HarryBentley(7) 4 97
(A P Jarvis) *hld up in 12th: rdn and prog on outer over 3f out: urged along and r.o to ld ins fnl f: hdd last stride* **40/1**

2223 **3** *¾* **Invincible Soul (IRE)**[21] 3827 3-8-12 **94**..................... RichardHughes 1 103
(R Hannon) *swtg: hld up in 8th: stdy prog to trck ldrs over 2f out: effrt over 1f out: rdn to ld for a few strides ins fnl f: outpcd* **16/1**

0051 **4** *2* **Cumulus Nimbus**[13] 4106 3-8-11 **93**.................................... PatDobbs 8 98
(R Hannon) *s.s: hld up last: stl there but gng strly 3f out: prog over 2f out: chsd ldrs and cl enough 1f out: styd on same pce* **22/1**

4211 **5** *½* **Aattash (IRE)**[35] 3351 3-8-4 **86**..................................... SamHitchcott 7 90+
(M R Channon) *pushed up and sn led: clr 1/2-way: gng bttr than most 3f out: rdn over 2f out: hdd & wknd ins fnl f* **14/1**

6112 **6** *¾* **Abergavenny**[5] 4376 3-8-0 **82**.. NickyMackay 5 85+
(M Johnston) *settled in 10th: rdn 3f out: styd on fnl 2f: nrst fin but n.d* **20/1**

3206 **7** *1 ½* **Paintball (IRE)**[48] 2927 3-7-12 **80** oh3............................... DavidProbert 2 80
(W R Muir) *dwlt: hld up in 13th: rdn and prog against rail fr 3f out: kpt on fr over 1f out but nvr gng pce to threaten* **66/1**

1-22 **8** *2* **Rigidity**[78] 2033 3-8-7 **89**... TomQueally 9 85+
(H R A Cecil) *hld up in 9th: effrt 3f out: no imp whn hanging and nt qckn wl over 1f out* **5/1**[2]

1211 **9** *shd* **Capponi (IRE)**[19] 3920 3-9-4 **100**...................................... GregFairley 11 95+
(M Johnston) *lw: trckd ldng trio: rdn and prog to chse ldr over 2f out to over 1f out: wknd* **5/1**[2]

1-12 **10** *hd* **London Stripe (IRE)**[42] 3105 3-8-13 **95**............................ RyanMoore 12 90
(Sir Michael Stoute) *lw: hld up in 7th: prog to dispute 2nd 3f out: rdn and nt qckn over 2f out: wknd over 1f out* **11/4**[1]

-300 **11** *7* **Ingleby Spirit**[54] 2758 3-8-0 **82**....................................... PaulHanagan 16 63
(R A Fahey) *trckd ldng quartet: lost pl wl over 2f out: sn wknd* **25/1**

10-0 **12** *5* **Markazzi**[105] 1327 3-8-10 **92**.. RichardHills 6 63
(Sir Michael Stoute) *hld up in 11th: looking for room 3f out: nt clr run 2f out: sn wknd* **16/1**

41-6 **13** *1* **Big Audio (IRE)**[63] 2471 3-9-7 **103**.............................(vt) FrankieDettori 3 72
(Saeed Bin Suroor) *chsd ldr 4f: wnt 2nd again 3f out to over 2f out: wknd: eased* **20/1**

2101 **14** *1 ¼* **Cultivar**[20] 3857 3-8-4 **86**.. JimmyQuinn 15 52
(B W Hills) *trckd ldrs in 6th: lost pl over 2f out: nt clr run sn after: wknd* **33/1**

0021 **15** *14* **Solicitor**[10] 4196 3-7-13 **81** 6ex.. JoeFanning 17 19
(M Johnston) *lw: prom: chsd ldr after 4f to 3f out: wknd rapidly: t.o: lame* **8/1**[3]

2m 4.20s (-3.80) **Going Correction** -0.125s/f (Firm) **15** Ran SP% **124.1**
Speed ratings (Par 106): **110,109,109,107,107 106,105,103,103,103 98,94,93,92,81**
toteswingers:1&2:£127.20, 1&3:£26.70, 2&3:£101.10 CSF £341.47 CT £5595.62 TOTE £11.90: £3.00, £14.50, £3.70; EX 603.00 TRIFECTA Not won..
Owner H R H Princess Haya Of Jordan **Bred** Bridgewater Equine Ltd **Trained** Newmarket, Suffolk

FOCUS
The course was watered on Wednesday evening and William Buick described it as 'lovely ground', although it did appear to be riding a shade faster than the previous day. They were racing on fresh ground in the last 3f. The rail from the 6f marker on the lower bend to the 3f marker in the straight was dolled out by six yards. This event has had numerous guises since its days as the 'Extel' but it remains one of the most hotly contested 3yo handicaps in the calendar. This year's edition was no exception, featuring any number of progressive types. They went a very strong gallop and the first two, as well as the fourth, both came from the rear. Most of those who had chased the pace paid the price late on, and it may be worth treating the form with a little bit of caution, although it rates sound. The time was just inside the standard.

NOTEBOOK
Beachfire ◆'s trainer won this event in 2003 and in 2007, on the latter occasion with subsequent Cambridgeshire winner Pipedreamer, and had the runner-up 12 months ago. Making it four wins from five career starts, the chestnut has his own ideas and once again required some vigorous early stoking up, but the hot pace was right up his street and he stayed on down the outside to snatch the race on the post. He is a trier despite his quirks and is not the type to win by far, so there is surely further improvement to come. A step up to 1m4f is likely.
Right Step looked more exposed than most, but was well handicapped on his second to John Smith's Cup winner Wigmore Hall at Newmarket in April and the drop back in trip appeared in his favour. Another who came from off the pace, he showed in front under his apprentice rider as the leaders fell away but was just denied. He will be back up in the weights for this. (tchd 50-1 in places and 100-1 in a place)
Invincible Soul(IRE), the choice of Richard Hughes, was ridden closer to the action than the other principals but just lacked another change of gear. Tackling 1m2f for the first time, he got it well and this was another solid effort, but he still has just a single win to his name. He was 8lb higher than when runner-up in Ascot's Britannia Handicap two runs back. (op 14-1)
Cumulus Nimbus, the other Hannon runner, was 5lb higher than when winning at Newmarket last time. He was slowly away and still last turning into the straight, but he stayed on past weary rivals for fourth. He finished a bit closer to Invincible Soul than he had on the July course two runs back. (op 20-1 tchd 25-1)
Aattash(IRE) was responsible for the blistering gallop and he emerges with credit for lasting out for so long. Front-running tactics had brought him back-to-back wins in June, the second in a handicap over 1m1f here off 6lb lower. (tchd 16-1)
Abergavenny, whose trainer has a fine record in this race, was making a quick reappearance after finishing second at Newmarket on Saturday. He plugged away and may be worth a try over 1m4f. (op 22-1)
Paintball(IRE), who was 3lb out of the handicap, was another who raced in the rear quartet before passing struggling rivals in the straight. (op 80-1 tchd 100-1 in a place)
Rigidity was nabbed on the line at York in May and to rub salt in the wound was put up 10lb for that. Put by for this since, he looked one of the more likely contenders, but could never get close enough. He was hanging for pressure and may not be entirely straightforward. (op 13-2)
Capponi(IRE), another of the Mark Johnston trio, shared the winner's profile in that he had won three of his four previous starts, all of which had been this season. He went up 8lb for his recent York win over 1m but failed to see out this longer trip after chasing the searching gallop. (op 11-2 tchd 6-1 in places)
London Stripe(IRE) was runner-up to this week's Gordon Stakes second Dandino in the King George V Handicap at Royal Ascot six weeks ago. Now 7lb higher and back down in trip, he was a shade keen early on even in this strongly run race and, although he reached a challenging position, his exertions told in the latter stages. (op 7-2 tchd 4-1 in a place)
Ingleby Spirit was another who weakened after chasing the pace and probably needs help from the handicapper. (tchd 22-1 and 28--1 in a place)
Markazzi, absent since beating one home in the Craven Stakes and looking unexposed ahead of this handicap debut, was never in with a shout although the gaps weren't there when he wanted them. His stamina for this trip remains in question. (tchd 20-1)
Big Audio(IRE) had a tongue tie added to the visor for this handicap debut. He dropped away after showing prominently on this first attempt over 1m2f and may be worth another chance. (op 25-1)
Cultivar, raised 3lb for winning at Chester, was already retreating when he was short of room at the two pole.
Solicitor was 4lb well in even with the penalty he acquired at Beverley. He had the best draw, and Joe Fanning had got himself down to 7st 13lb, but it was to no avail as the colt weakened alarmingly quickly after chasing the leader. He was reported by the vet to be lame on his left hind. Official explanation: vet said colt was lame left-hind (op 13-2)

4505 AUDI KING GEORGE STKS (GROUP 2) 5f
2:45 (2:47) (Class 1) 3-Y-O+

£56,770 (£21,520; £10,770; £5,370; £2,690; £1,350) **Stalls** Low

Form | | | | RPR
2333 **1** **Borderlescott**[19] 3895 8-9-0 112 KierenFallon 10 115
(R Bastiman) *hld up bhd ldrs in centre: plld out 2f out: prog over 1f out: decisive burst to ld last 100yds: readily* **9/2**[1]
0-12 **2** ½ **Group Therapy**[26] 3691 5-9-0 108 RyanMoore 1 113+
(J Noseda) *racd nr side: towards rr: rdn and effrt over 1f out: r.o wl fnl f to take 2nd nr fin* **8/1**
0261 **3** *hd* **Astrophysical Jet**[21] 3828 3-8-7 101 GrahamGibbons 12 109+
(E S McMahon) *trckd ldrs in centre: repeatedly swtchd lft fr 2f out: ended up nrly against nr side rail fnl f: r.o wl: nrst fin* **7/1**
3F00 **4** *hd* **Mister Hughie (IRE)**[22] 3791 3-8-10 98 AlanMunro 14 111
(M R Channon) *swtg: sn outpcd in last but rdr remained unflustered: swtchd to outer and rapid prog ent fnl f: r.o wl nr fin* **66/1**
0405 **5** ½ **Spin Cycle (IRE)**[32] 3486 4-9-0 110 (v) RichardMullen 16 110
(B Smart) *swtg: racd centre: w ldrs: disp ld 1f out to last 100yds: outpcd* **14/1**
-312 **6** *hd* **Tropical Treat**[20] 3875 3-8-7 102 JimCrowley 9 105+
(R M Beckett) *lw: dwlt: hld up in rr in centre: nt clr run 2f out to over 1f out: prog to press ldrs ins fnl f: one pce last 100yds* **7/1**
1020 **7** *nk* **Captain Dunne (IRE)**[10] 4191 5-9-0 108 (p) DavidAllan 13 108
(T D Easterby) *lw: racd centre: mde most to 1f out: no ex last 100yds* **20/1**
1036 **8** *nse* **Moorhouse Lad**[26] 3691 7-9-0 100 TomEaves 17 108
(B Smart) *swtg: pressed ldr in centre: upsides 1f out: wknd last 100yds* **66/1**
2113 **9** 1 ½ **Gilt Edge Girl**[20] 3875 4-8-11 103 LukeMorris 2 100
(C G Cox) *racd nr side: in tch: swtchd rt jst over 2f out: rdn and styd on same pce: nvr able to chal* **28/1**
10 ¾ **Starfish Bay (USA)**[46] 4-8-11 104 FrankieDettori 7 97
(Todd Pletcher, U.S.A) *str: lw: pressed ldrs in centre: rdn 2f out: no prog whn n.m.r briefly 1f out: fdd* **11/2**[2]
4010 **11** 1 ¾ **Rowe Park**[4] 4401 7-9-0 101 (p) TedDurcan 15 94
(Mrs L C Jewell) *swtg: racd centre: a struggling to stay on terms: btn over 1f out: b.b.v* **50/1**
5-00 **12** ½ **Amour Propre**[44] 3047 4-9-0 110 DaneO'Neill 5 92
(H Candy) *lw: racd towards nr side: wl on terms: effrt 2f out: wknd fnl f* **12/1**
1030 **13** 2 ¾ **Mister Manannan (IRE)**[44] 3047 3-8-10 106 AdrianNicholls 8 81
(D Nicholls) *racd towards centre: wl in tch: rdn 2f out: steadily fdd* **25/1**
0410 **14** 3 **Glamorous Spirit (IRE)**[19] 3895 4-8-11 103 TomMcLaughlin 6 68
(R A Harris) *racd nr side: led that gp to 2f out: wknd rapidly over 1f out* **50/1**
-101 **U** **Triple Aspect (IRE)**[26] 3691 4-9-0 110 LiamJones 3 —
(W J Haggas) *racd nr side: wl in rr: rdn but nt far bhd eventual runner-up whn sddle slipped over 1f out: uns rdr 75yds out* **13/2**[3]

57.22 secs (-1.18) **Going Correction** +0.025s/f (Good)
WFA 3 from 4yo+ 4lb **15** Ran **SP% 116.3**
Speed ratings (Par 115): **110,109,108,108,107 107,106,106,104,103 100,99,95,90,—**
toteswingers:1&2:£5.90, 1&3:£7.50, 2&3:£11.10 CSF £34.34 TOTE £4.90: £1.60, £2.40, £3.00; EX 32.40 Trifecta £156.70 Pool: £4,185.68 - 19.76 winning units..
Owner James Edgar & William Donaldson **Bred** J W P Clark **Trained** Cowthorpe, N Yorks
■ Elnawin was withdrawn (14/1, ref to ent stalls). R4 applies, deduct 5p in the £.
■ Stewards' Enquiry : Graham Gibbons two-day ban: careless riding (Aug 14-15)

FOCUS
The first running of this race as a Group 2, and it was rewarded with a good-quality line-up, including an American raider from a top stable. The pace was quick from the outset, so much so that the winner was being pushed along in the early stages. Not much separated the first eight home and the time was not great. The form makes sense amongsth the first three but the fourth and eighth anchor it.

NOTEBOOK
Borderlescott, who always seems to run well at this course, is a firm favourite among racing fans and clinched another success in an illustrious and consistent career. He has gone well for a change of jockey in the past, and this time got the assistance of Kieren Fallon, but only because Neil Callan was serving a one-day ban. The horse showed all his usual courage under pressure to get on top in the final half-a-furlong, winning a shade comfortably. Sadly, it was reported later in the day that he had suffered an injury to his near hind and he will be out for the rest of the season, ruling out an attempt to win a third Nunthorpe Stakes. (op 11-2 tchd 6-1 in places)
Group Therapy, ponied to the start again, took a good grip under his jockey in the early stages before finding a route to the stands'-side rail. It wasn't immediately obvious that he was going to get involved, but all of a sudden he picked up in the latter stages and finished strongly. The winner came down a different part of the track, so both Group Therapy and the third may have been a bit closer had they come down the middle. (op 15-2)
Astrophysical Jet ◆ was taking a stiff rise in class after running in a couple of handicaps, the last of which she won, considering the calibre of rival she faced here. Travelling strongly just off the pace, she was just over a length in front of the winner at one point, arguably going better, but took a different route to him as the race took shape, edging closer to the stands' side after being towards the far side in the early stages. Once alongside Group Therapy, the pair appeared to run on well but one got the clear impression that the right horse was successful on the day. That said, she is open to plenty of improvement now it seems established that she is a sprinter (connections tried her over further earlier in her career), and this daughter of Dubawi should have a decent future. (op 6-1 tchd 15-2 in places)
Mister Hughie(IRE), dropping in trip, couldn't go the searing gallop set in the early stages but engaged top gear with just over a furlong to go and flew home down the outside of the pack.
Spin Cycle(IRE), with a visor back on, easily reversed placings with Glamorous Spirit on their meeting at the Curragh and is a good sort when at his best. (op 16-1)
Tropical Treat ◆ travelled strongly in behind but got a little short of room 2f out before running on again. Still completely unexposed, there should be plenty more to come from her. (op 9-1)
Captain Dunne(IRE) was something of a surprise leader considering some of the rivals he took on for front-running duties, possibly the fitting of cheekpieces made him come alive. He kept on surprisingly well despite wandering under pressure. (tchd 18-1)
Moorhouse Lad, said to be fresh and well for this after running flat at Sandown, won this race back in 2007 but didn't quite get home as well as some of his rivals after looking a bit free early on towards the head of affairs. (tchd 50-1)
Gilt Edge Girl appeared to run up to her best. (op 33-1 tchd 40-1 in a place)
Starfish Bay(USA), who holds two course records at Monmouth Park in USA, and winner of three of her four previous starts this season at 5f, was ponied to the start. A strong-looking sort, she seemed to get a little upset in the stalls and certainly didn't ping out of them as some may have expected. She soon tacked herself onto the group chasing the leaders but hit a flat spot at about halfway and found only the one pace. Her rider was not hard on her in the final stages and reported afterwards that she did not handle going downhill too well. She was the first runner in Europe for her trainer. (op 6-1 tchd 5-1)
Rowe Park found everything happening too quickly. Official explanation: vet said gelding had bled from the nose (op 40-1)
Amour Propre could not find an extra gear when his jockey came with a promising bid inside the 2f marker. (op 16-1)
Triple Aspect(IRE)'s saddle slipped and he deposited Liam Jones on the floor. The combination were not that far behind the runner-up when the tack came loose, so may well have gone close to placing had everything stayed in intact. Official explanation: jockey said saddle slipped (op 8-1)

4506 ARTEMIS GOODWOOD CUP (GROUP 2) 2m
3:25 (3:25) (Class 1) 3-Y-O+

£56,770 (£21,520; £10,770; £5,370; £2,690; £1,350) **Stalls** Low

Form | | | | RPR
3142 **1** **Illustrious Blue**[26] 3695 7-9-7 110 JimCrowley 10 117
(W J Knight) *lw: hld up in last pair: stdy prog on outer to chse ldr over 2f out: rdn and clsd fr over 1f out: led last 150yds: styd on stoutly* **8/1**
10-3 **2** 1 ¼ **Electrolyser (IRE)**[92] 1615 5-9-7 105 PhilipRobinson 9 115
(C G Cox) *led 1f: chsd ldr: lft in ld 4f out: at least 2 l clr over 2f out: kpt on dourly: worn down last 150yds* **33/1**
023 **3** 2 ¾ **Purple Moon (IRE)**[42] 3102 7-9-7 111 KierenFallon 8 112+
(L M Cumani) *hld up in rr: rdn and effrt on inner over 3f out: swtchd lft over 2f out: styd on to take 3rd over 1f out: no real imp* **13/2**[3]
4-41 **4** 8 **Free Agent**[19] 3922 4-9-7 103 RichardHughes 1 102
(R Hannon) *hld up in tch: outpcd 3f out: hmpd between rivals over 2f out: plugged on fr over 1f out to take 4th nr fin* **20/1**
1-30 **5** ½ **Wajir (FR)**[40] 3191 4-9-7 114 FrankieDettori 6 102
(Saeed Bin Suroor) *lw: prom: chsd ldr over 3f out to over 2f out: steadily wknd* **33/1**
20 **6** 2 ¼ **Kid Charlemagne (IRE)**[40] 3195 7-9-7 0 TomQueally 4 99?
(W J Greatrex) *hld up: prog 5f out: disp 2nd briefly over 3f out: sn wl outpcd* **80/1**
015- **7** 4 ½ **The Betchworth Kid**[132] 6306 5-9-7 103 HayleyTurner 2 93
(A King) *hld up in last pair: urged along over 4f out: lft bhd fr 3f out: no ch after* **50/1**
4-04 **8** 14 **Caracciola (GER)**[40] 3195 13-9-7 101 EddieAhern 11 77
(N J Henderson) *prom: lft 2nd briefly 4f out: wknd 3f out: t.o* **66/1**
-211 **9** 7 **Tactic**[33] 3470 4-9-7 118 RichardHills 5 68
(J L Dunlop) *swtg: t.k.h in midfield after 4f: rdn wl over 4f out: dropped away over 3f out: t.o: lame* **5/1**[2]
-222 **P** **Age Of Aquarius (IRE)**[42] 3102 4-9-7 117 JMurtagh 7 —
(A P O'Brien, Ire) *led after 1f tl broke down 4f out: p.u* **4/6**[1]

3m 22.35s (-6.65) **Going Correction** -0.125s/f (Firm) **10** Ran **SP% 116.4**
Speed ratings (Par 115): **111,110,109,105,104 103,101,94,90,—**
toteswingers:1&2:£18.60, 1&3:£19.30 CSF £225.26 TOTE £11.10: £3.10, £9.00, £2.30; EX 142.10 Trifecta £948.00 Pool: £9,223.78 - 7.20 winning units..
Owner Mr & Mrs I H Bendelow **Bred** B J And Mrs Crangle **Trained** Patching, W Sussex

■ Stewards' Enquiry : Frankie Dettori caution: careless riding.

FOCUS

This looked a decent Goodwood Cup on paper, although it was weakened by the absence of Kite Wood. However, with Age Of Aquarius breaking down and Tactic not giving his running the form may not prove that strong, and it has been rated a slightly below-par renewal. Age Of Aquarius set a solid pace and not many got into it. The first three finished clear and the winner recorded a small personal best.

NOTEBOOK

Illustrious Blue has been reinvented as a stayer this season and has now been successful in half of his 14 appearances at Goodwood. He took the Group 3 Glorious Stakes at this fixture last year and landed a 1m handicap at the meeting four years ago. Held up going well before improving to pursue the leader in the straight, he got well on top in the last half-furlong. Connections will consider going for the Melbourne Cup with him, and in the meantime he has options like the Lonsdale Cup at York and the Doncaster Cup. (op 9-1 tchd 10-1 in places)

Electrolyser(IRE) had been off the track for three months since his third to Illustrious Blue in the Sagaro Stakes at Ascot, reportedly having scoped badly. Left in front when Age Of Aquarius pulled up, he immediately kicked for home, and battled on well but could not fend off the winner. He has more to offer and may be taken to France in pursuit of a first Group win. (tchd 40-1 in a place)

Purple Moon(IRE) was a place and 6l behind Age Of Aquarius in the Gold Cup, when the final quarter-mile of the 2m4f trip found him out. He was slightly inconvenienced here when the favourite broke down then lacked the pace to get to the first two. He has run plenty of good races since taking the 2007 Ebor but that remains his most recent win. (op 6-1)

Free Agent was taking a rise back up in grade after landing a Listed handicap at York. Already with plenty to do when he was hampered going to the two pole, he stayed on late and is worth trying at 2m again. (op 18-1 tchd 16-1)

Wajir(FR), following the defection of Kite Wood, became the sole representative for Godolphin, who won this a year ago with Schiaparelli. He won over 1m7f last September when with Elie Lellouche but faded as if not seeing out the 2m here. Frankie Dettori reported that the colt was unsuited by the ground. Official explanation: jockey said colt was unsuited by the good to firm ground

Kid Charlemagne(IRE) was running on the Flat proper for only the third time. Briefly finding himself in second pace before finishing a respectable sixth, he is now eligible for handicaps but may not be easy to place in this sphere. (op 100-1 tchd 66-1 and 150-1 in a place)

The Betchworth Kid, third in this a year ago for Michael Bell and not seen since the Cheltenham festival, probably needed this and was always towards the back.

Caracciola(GER), the oldest horse ever to win a Listed race and the oldest Royal Ascot winner, entered well deserved retirement after the race.

Tactic came here in fine heart after a wide-margin win in a York Listed event and a Group 3 victory at the Curragh, but his stable's current form was a concern. Edgy beforehand, when he was attended by two handlers, he lost his pitch before the straight and came home well adrift. He returned lame. Official explanation: jockey said gelding was lame (op 7-2)

Age Of Aquarius(IRE) played a full part in a memorable Gold Cup and this looked a fine opportunity for him, but sadly, after going well in front, he broke down on the downhill run to the straight. He reportedly ruptured tore ligaments on his fetlock joint, and although his racing career is over he has been saved for stud. (op 10-11 tchd evens in places)

4507 MOET HENNESSY FILLIES' STKS (REGISTERED AS THE LILLIE LANGTRY STAKES) (GROUP 3) (F&M) 1m 6f

4:00 (4:00) (Class 1) 3-Y-0+

£39,739 (£15,064; £7,539; £3,759; £1,883; £945) **Stalls** Low

Form RPR

0401 **1** **Eastern Aria (UAE)**[12] 4143 4-9-6 104 .... RichardHills 2 114
(M Johnston) *trckd ldrs in 5th: clsd over 4f out: prog to ld wl over 2f out: galloped on strly and in command over 1f out* **16/1**

-422 **2** *2 ¾* **Polly's Mark (IRE)**[26] 3671 4-9-6 106 .... RichardHughes 7 110
(C G Cox) *trckd ldng trio: gng easily 4f out: rdn to chse wnr over 2f out: styd on but no imp* **7/2**[2]

2111 **3** *2 ½* **Motrice**[20] 3878 3-8-7 86 ow1 .... SebSanders 5 108
(Sir Mark Prescott) *lw: hld up in last trio: rdn on wd outside 4f out: prog u.p over 2f out: styd on to take 3rd last 100yds* **10/1**

2-30 **4** *1 ¼* **Rosika**[26] 3671 4-9-6 97 .... JMurtagh 6 105
(Sir Michael Stoute) *hld up in midfield: rdn and effrt 3f out: kpt on fnl 2f and disp 3rd ins fnl f: nvr gng pce to threaten* **12/1**

6-32 **5** *2* **Flying Cloud (IRE)**[33] 3467 4-9-6 114 .... (t) FrankieDettori 12 102
(Saeed Bin Suroor) *hld up in midfield: clsd on ldrs 4f out: effrt on inner 3f out: chsd ldng pair 2f out tl wknd fnl f* **6/4**[1]

5-31 **6** *¾* **Ship's Biscuit**[35] 3347 3-8-7 90 ow1 .... RyanMoore 4 102
(Sir Michael Stoute) *lw: hld up in rr: rdn over 4f out: nudged by rival wl over 3f out: sme prog on outer over 2f out: nvr a threat: fdd fnl f* **8/1**[3]

-355 **7** *4 ½* **Starfala**[40] 3195 5-9-6 102 .... EddieAhern 8 95
(P F I Cole) *s.s and rousted along early: wl in rr: rdn over 4f out and struggling: modest late prog* **14/1**

1106 **8** *4* **Just Lille (IRE)**[23] 3752 7-9-6 94 .... (v) BarryMcHugh 3 89
(Mrs A Duffield) *swtg: led and sn clr: c bk to field 5f out: hdd wl over 2f out: wknd and eased* **50/1**

2130 **9** *¾* **Tinaar (USA)**[26] 3671 4-9-6 97 .... (p) PaulHanagan 9 88
(G A Butler) *chsd clr ldr to 3f out: wknd and eased* **33/1**

-050 **10** *2* **Uvinza**[12] 4143 4-9-6 92 .... JimCrowley 11 85
(W J Knight) *chsd ldrs in 6th: rdn 4f out: wknd 3f out: sn bhd* **100/1**

05-5 **11** *4 ½* **Flame Of Gibraltar (IRE)**[61] 2538 4-9-6 92 .... TomQueally 13 79
(H R A Cecil) *lw: hld up in last trio: plld out gng strly wl over 3f out: rdn wl over 2f out and no rspnse: wknd rapidly wl over 1f out* **25/1**

1401 **12** *8* **Myplacelater**[14] 4068 3-8-7 100 ow1 .... KierenFallon 10 69
(D R C Elsworth) *hld up in last trio: rdn and no prog 4f out: sn wl bhd* **14/1**

-026 **13** *23* **Cassique Lady (IRE)**[26] 3671 5-9-6 101 .... WilliamBuick 1 35
(Mrs L Wadham) *trckd ldng pair to over 4f out: losing pl whn bdly hmpd against rail over 2f out: virtually p.u after* **40/1**

2m 58.05s (-5.55) **Going Correction** -0.125s/f (Firm) course record
WFA 3 from 4yo+ 14lb **13** Ran SP% **121.5**
Speed ratings (Par 110): **110,108,107,106,105 104,102,99,99,98 95,91,78**
toteswingers:1&2:£9.80, 1&3:£13.80, 2&3:£5.30 CSF £70.66 TOTE £18.40: £4.30, £1.60, £2.80; EX 58.90 Trifecta £1029.40 Pool: £2,364.90 - 1.70 winning units..

Owner Sheikh Hamdan Bin Mohammed Al Maktoum **Bred** Darley **Trained** Middleham Moor, N Yorks

■ Stewards' Enquiry : Tom Queally one-day ban: caereless riding (Aug 12)
Seb Sanders caution: used whip with excessive frequency.

FOCUS

Not an easy race to assess accurately, as most of these were unproven at this sort of distance or not obviously bred to stay 1m6f. Quite a few of the runners had clashed before over varying trips, but even though there were a variety of doubts, the winner's time broke the course record. The runner-up is the best guide to the form, which looks good for the grade.

NOTEBOOK

Eastern Aria(UAE) ◆, defending an unbeaten two from two record at this course, including a victory at this meeting last season, was trying 1m6f for the first time and came home a clear winner after receiving a good, positive ride. Fourth in the Group 1 E P Taylor Stakes last year, her trainer had been disappointed with her progress earlier in the year and connections reportedly even contemplated retiring her to the paddocks at one point, but she has returned to her best and won comfortably. The Park Hill Stakes seems the logical next race, but her end of season target is the Canadian International, which is over 2f further than the race she was fourth in at Woodbine in 2009. (op 14-1 tchd 12-1)

Polly's Mark(IRE) has been running well for quite some time and was narrowly beaten in a Group 2 on her previous start after looking a little shy of that level. She was close up here in the chasing bunch and ran a solid race without any obvious excuses. Her performance gives the form some stability due to her consistency at a decent level. (tchd 4-1 in places)

Motrice is a typical improver from this stable and had no worries about the trip, but this was a rise in grade for her. Restrained in rear, she stayed on well once in the clear but the winner had gained a big advantage on her, one that was never going to be eroded. (op 12-1 tchd 8-1)

Rosika was behind the runner-up at Haydock last time and gave the impression that she did not get home after holding every chance. (op 16-1)

Flying Cloud(IRE), who has been running in Group 1s and 2s, was the class filly on show but the trip was the obvious concern. Settled in midfield, she was produced to have every chance despite being bumped by early front-runner Just Lille who knocked her into the weakening Cassique Lady. She gave the impression that she did not get home. (op 15-8 tchd 2-1 in places)

Ship's Biscuit ◆, who won a maiden on her previous outing, and is a half-sister to Hi Calypso, the winner of this race in 2007, ran really nicely and lack of experience more than stamina appeared to find her out in the final furlong. She remains one to follow. (tchd 15-2)

Myplacelater, who has an entry for the St Leger, was always in rear and never threatened to get involved, but Kieren Fallon reported afterwards that she had lost her action. Official explanation: jockey said filly lost its action (op 11-1)

Cassique Lady(IRE) Official explanation: jockey said mare suffered interference in running

4508 EUROPEAN BREEDERS' FUND NEW HAM MAIDEN FILLIES' STKS 7f

4:35 (4:35) (Class 2) 2-Y-0 **£12,952** (£3,854; £1,926; £962) **Stalls** High

Form RPR

0 **1** **Kalahaag (IRE)**[13] 4095 2-9-0 0 .... RichardHughes 9 81+
(R Hannon) *str: athletic: hld up bhd ldrs: prog on inner over 2f out: rdn and r.o to ld ins fnl f: readily* **9/2**[2]

2 **2** *¾* **Dubawi Gulf**[14] 4048 2-9-0 0 .... KierenFallon 7 79
(E A L Dunlop) *leggy: trckd ldng pair: prog to ld narrowly 2f out: edgd lft fr over 1f out: hdd and one pce ins fnl f* **6/1**

3 **3** *shd* **Fenella Fudge**[14] 4048 2-9-0 0 .... PaulMulrennan 10 79
(J G Given) *w'like: led: narrowly hdd 2f out: upsides ldr and edgd lft fr over 1f out: one pce last 100yds* **13/2**

03 **4** *1 ¾* **Opera Dancer**[20] 3861 2-9-0 0 .... PaulHanagan 6 77
(S Kirk) *w'like: str: trckd ldrs: effrt on outer over 2f out: rdn and cl up whn checked jst ins fnl f: no ex* **9/1**

5 *shd* **Regal Heiress** 2-9-0 0 .... RyanMoore 11 74+
(Sir Michael Stoute) *w'like: scope: lengthy: trckd ldng trio: effrt 2f out: cl up and swtchd rt 1f out: fdd last 100yds* **5/1**[3]

6 *¾* **Bonita Star** 2-9-0 0 .... AlanMunro 8 73+
(M R Channon) *w'like: str: lw: hld up towards rr: shkn up over 2f out: outpcd wl over 1f out: styd on quite steadily fnl f* **40/1**

3 **7** *¾* **Electra Star**[13] 4095 2-9-0 0 .... MichaelHills 3 71
(W J Haggas) *str: scope: prog on outer fr last pair 4f out: shkn up over 2f out: nt qckn over 1f out: one pce after* **11/4**[1]

8 *2* **Star Concert (USA)** 2-9-0 0 .... EddieAhern 4 69+
(Mrs A J Perrett) *w'like: scope: tall: hld up in rr: stl there 2f out: nudged along and kpt on fnl f* **66/1**

9 *1* **Magical Flower** 2-9-0 0 .... JimCrowley 5 63+
(W J Knight) *leggy: sn last and nt gng wl: nvr a factor: kpt on fnl f* **33/1**

0 **10** *nk* **Smart Step**[3] 4116 2-9-0 0 .... RoystonFfrench 2 62
(M Johnston) *w'like: leggy: chsd ldr to 3f out: wknd over 1f out* **16/1**

0 **11** *1 ½* **Formidable Girl (USA)**[15] 4029 2-9-0 0 .... JoeFanning 1 59+
(K A Ryan) *leggy: unf: dwlt: hld up in last trio: gng wl enough over 2f out: shkn up and no prog wl over 1f out: wknd* **14/1**

1m 28.36s (1.46) **Going Correction** -0.125s/f (Firm) **11** Ran SP% **118.6**
Speed ratings (Par 97): **86,85,85,83,82 82,81,78,77,77 75**
toteswingers:1&2:£7.00, 1&3:£7.50, 2&3:£5.80 CSF £31.69 TOTE £6.10: £2.00, £2.30, £2.40; EX 33.20 Trifecta £103.60 Pool: £1,941.30 - 13.86 winning units..

Owner Benny Andersson **Bred** Mrs Clodagh McStay **Trained** East Everleigh, Wilts

FOCUS

An interesting fillies' maiden, run at an ordinary pace, and winners should come out of it. The form looks sound with the second and third virtually reproducing their debut running. It was a valuable race of its type, with the Racing Post Yearling Bonus boosting the first prize to just shy of £23,000.

NOTEBOOK

Kalahaag(IRE) very much caught the eye on her Newbury debut behind stablemate Celebrity nearly two weeks ago, and she repaid the kindness of that introduction. Upped in trip, she had work to do with 2f left to cover but came with a strong run once switched to the inside, making up a deal of ground to win comfortably. Potentially a very useful filly, she is eligible for five richly endowed Tattersalls sales races at Newmarket later in the season, the first of them on the July Course in a month's time. (op 6-1)

Dubawi Gulf ◆, third in a Doncaster maiden on her debut, ran another taking race but could not repel the winner inside the last. Bred to make a nice middle-distance filly next year, she can get off the mark before long. Official explanation: jockey said filly hung left-handed (op 5-1)

Fenella Fudge, a short head behind Dubawi Gulf at Doncaster after missing the break, seemed to enjoy bowling along in front and only gave best going to the final furlong. She holds a Fillies' Mile entry and an ordinary maiden should soon come her way. (op 7-1 tchd 15-2)

Opera Dancer was third to the winner's stablemate Date With Destiny last time at Newbury. The only member of this field with two previous outings behind her, she ran a solid race and would have finished closer to the third had she not needed to be pulled off heels inside the final furlong. (op 8-1 tchd 10-1)

Regal Heiress is a daughter of Cheveley Park heroine Regal Rose who has produced six previous winners. Fitted with a sheepskin noseband for this debut, she showed obvious ability but looked to be hanging when the pressure was on, perhaps not handling the track too well. (op 8-1 tchd 9-2)

Bonita Star, a half-sister to several winners both in this country and in the USA, stayed on steadily on the inside and will have benefited from this introduction both physically and mentally. (op 33-1)

Electra Star finished six places and over four lengths ahead of Kalahaag when they made their respective debuts at Newbury. Keeping on from the rear without reaching a challenging position, she was unable to build on what she showed first time, whereas the winner found considerable improvement. (op 5-2 tchd 3-1 in places and 9-4 in a place)

Star Concert(USA) ◆ was given quite a a considerate introduction and should improve considerably on the bare form.

Magical Flower ran green in rear but did show signs of getting it together when it was all over.

Smart Step, up a furlong from her debut, weakened after chasing the pace. (op 14-1)

Formidable Girl(USA) still looked green on this turf debut but is well regarded and may improve. (tchd 16-1)

4509 VINTAGE AT GOODWOOD STKS (H'CAP) 7f

5:10 (5:11) (Class 2) (0-105,102) 3-Y-O

£21,808 (£6,531; £3,265; £1,634; £815; £409) **Stalls** High

Form RPR

3-34 **1** **Citrus Star (USA)**55 2713 3-9-4 **99** ... GeorgeBaker 2 107
(C F Wall) *hld up in 8th: looking for room 3f out: prog fr 2f out: rdn and r.o wl fnl f to ld last 50yds* **8/1**

2012 **2** *nk* **Rakaan (IRE)**12 4144 3-9-4 **99** ... RyanMoore 11 106
(J A Osborne) *s.s: in last pair tl swtchd out wd and drvn 2f out: styd on strly fr over 1f out: tk 2nd last stride* **13/2**2

2513 **3** *nse* **Gene Autry (USA)**22 3791 3-9-0 **95** ... PatDobbs 6 102
(R Hannon) *lw: trckd ldrs: swtchd lft and prog over 2f out: rdn to ld over 1f out: hdd and one pce last 50yds* **7/1**3

2013 **4** *1* **Glen Shiel (USA)**4 4413 3-8-5 **86** ... RoystonFfrench 14 90+
(M Johnston) *pressed ldrs: hrd rdn 2f out: nt qckn over 1f out: styd on fnl f* **11/1**

-264 **5** *1 1/2* **Gunner Lindley (IRE)**49 2898 3-8-6 **87** ... EddieAhern 12 87
(B W Hills) *trckd ldng quartet: rdn 3f out: edgd rt but hld pl over 1f out: outpcd but kpt on fnl f* **14/1**

0440 **6** *3/4* **Freeforaday (USA)**20 3869 3-9-7 **102** ... KierenFallon 5 100+
(J R Best) *hld up in last quartet: shkn up over 2f out: limited prog and n.d whn short of room 1f out: plugged on after* **22/1**

0-00 **7** *3/4* **She's A Character**61 2542 3-8-2 **83** ... PaulHanagan 1 79
(R A Fahey) *hld up in last quartet: rdn and no prog 3f out: kpt on fnl f* **50/1**

6212 **8** *nk* **Venutius**22 3796 3-8-11 **92** ... GrahamGibbons 10 87
(E S McMahon) *lw: led: drvn and pressed over 2f out: hdd & wknd over 1f out* **9/2**1

12 **9** *nk* **Stefanki (IRE)**7 4297 3-7-12 **79** oh1 ... JimmyQuinn 7 73+
(George Baker) *rel to r and lft 10 l: latched on to bk of gp 3f out: shkn up over 2f out: swtchd ins fnl f: kpt on but no ch* **7/1**3

3162 **10** *nk* **Waveband**5 4378 3-8-3 **84** ... GregFairley 9 78
(M Johnston) *lw: chsd ldr: chal over 2f out: upsides over 1f out: sn wknd* **16/1**

2101 **11** *1* **Fireback**22 3791 3-8-10 **91** ... DavidProbert 4 82
(A M Balding) *prom on outer: rdn over 2f out: edgd rt and wknd over 1f out* **7/1**3

-112 **12** *nk* **Cansili Star**33 3429 3-8-12 **93** ... PhilipRobinson 8 83
(M A Jarvis) *trckd ldrs: rdn 3f out: no prog over 2f out: wknd over 1f out* **7/1**3

1m 24.96s (-1.94) **Going Correction** -0.125s/f (Firm) **12** Ran SP% **119.8**
Speed ratings (Par 106): **106,105,105,104,102 101,101,100,100,100 98,98**
toteswingers:1&2:£9.20, 1&3:£10.20, 2&3:£10.00 CSF £59.93 CT £394.80 TOTE £9.90: £3.10, £2.70, £2.30; EX 61.70 Trifecta £473.80 Pool: £2,305.04 - 3.60 winning units..

Owner Induna Racing Partners Two **Bred** Stephen McDonald **Trained** Newmarket, Suffolk

FOCUS

In the last ten renewals of this race, only twice has the winner not been drawn in a double-digit stall. Indeed, in most other cases it was crucial to be drawn as a high as possible. However, possibly due to a fairly small field, that statistic was blown out of the water, as horses drawn 2 and 6 were involved in a tight finish. There wasn't a great deal of distance between first and last, but the pace was strong and the form makes sense.

NOTEBOOK

Citrus Star(USA) looked fairly unexposed in contrast to many in the field but had an awkward-looking to draw to emerge from. He had failed to go into the stalls on his last run, but didn't appear to show those sorts of problems this time, although he was reported to have been a 'little bit naughty'. Settled towards the rear, he was given time to get into the race and only hit the front in the final stages, winning by a small margin. If the handicapper doesn't punish him too much, the trainer feels Citrus Star has another handicap in him, but he also thinks that his horse can make it at Listed level in due course. (op 13-2, tchd 6-1 in places)

Rakaan(IRE), whose trainer won this in 2007 with smart handicapper Docofthebay, chased home the impressive winner at this course on Tuesday, Start Right, on his previous outing and was thought good enough to run in the Group 2 Richmond Stakes at this meeting last year. Another to be ridden with restraint, he took a while to get going but came home strongly once pulled towards the middle of the course after sitting in the pack. He may be given a rest now. (op 15-2, tchd 8-1 in places)

Gene Autry(USA), better off at the weights with Fireback on their clash at Newmarket (6f) earlier this month, travelled nicely towards the inside rail and was produced to have every chance a furlong out. He didn't do a lot once in front without appearing to stop, so possibly 7f in this class stretches his stamina. (tchd 13-2)

Glen Shiel(USA), who ran only four days previously, seemed to have the best of the draw but didn't get away from the stalls as quickly as others. He ran well despite wandering a little under pressure. (tchd 12-1)

Gunner Lindley(IRE), given a break since his last outing, was keeping on at the one pace when his jockey lost his whip just over a furlong from home. That looked to make no difference to his position, but it is worth noting that he was hampered by the fourth when making a challenge over 2f out, and needed to be switched to get a clearer passage. (op 16-1)

Freeforaday(USA), well beaten in the race formerly known as the Bunbury Cup last time, enjoyed a good juvenile campaign and had shown a couple of time this year, including at this course, that he is still capable of running to a good level. Unproven at the trip, he was being ridden along turning into the home straight and met some traffic problems before staying on strongly - he was about tenth with a furlong to go. (op 20-1)

She's A Character, without a win since her racecourse debut, has come down the weights considerably since acquiring an official mark as a juvenile, and shaped a bit better here than she had done on recent starts, albeit without threatening. (op 40-1)

Venutius has done virtually all of his racing over 1m, so this was a drop in trip for him. Now 5lb higher than last time, when narrowly beaten into second, he was quickly into stride and got to the front without too much fuss. He ensured the pace was sound but weakened once joined just over 1f out. (op 8-1)

Stefanki(IRE) ◆, beaten at 1/3 last time in an apprentice handicap, blew away his rivals on the Polytrack in mid-July (handicap debut) and was back up to 7f for the first time since running over it as a 2-y-o. Racing from 1lb out of the handicap, he lost all chance here with a very slow start, but showed enough in defeat to suggest he'll be winning again before too long. Official explanation: jockey said gelding was slowly away (op 8-1)

Fireback, whose trainer won this in 2008 with Blue Sky Basin, had a progressive record but was running in this off a 7lb higher mark than when winning at Newmarket (6f) on his previous outing and only found the one pace when asked for maximum effort. (op 6-1 tchd 11-2)

Cansili Star has been running well this season and beat subsequent Royal Ascot winner Treadwell at Epsom at the start of June (winner here Citrus Star back in fourth that day). However, he seemed a bit keen early on and made no impression in the final stages.

4510 RUK LEADING JOCKEY AWARD STKS (H'CAP) 5f

5:45 (5:46) (Class 3) (0-90,89) 4-Y-O+ **£9,714** (£2,890; £1,444; £721) **Stalls** Low

Form RPR

0040 **1** **Hamoody (USA)**34 3401 6-8-11 **82** ... MichaelGeran(3) 10 92
(D Nicholls) *swtg: awkward s: hld up in centre: effrt 2f out: drvn and r.o fnl f: led nr fin* **14/1**

0023 **2** *hd* **Bajan Tryst (USA)**11 4180 4-9-5 **87** ... EddieAhern 11 96
(K A Ryan) *racd centre: a on terms w ldrs: str chal fnl f: upsides nr fin: jst hld* **10/1**

6150 **3** *nk* **Crimea (IRE)**8 4243 4-9-3 **85** ... AdrianNicholls 14 93
(D Nicholls) *pressed ldrs in centre: effrt over 1f out: drvn ahd ins fnl f towards far side: hdd nr fin* **16/1**

5016 **4** *hd* **Piscean (USA)**13 4118 5-9-3 **85** ... JimmyQuinn 15 92
(T Keddy) *hld up in centre: trckd ldrs 2f out: plld out and drvn towards far side jst over 1f out: str run 150yds out: no ex nr fin* **7/1**2

5000 **5** *3/4* **Indian Trail**21 3828 10-8-13 **81** ...(v) KierenFallon 8 85
(D Nicholls) *hld up in centre: plenty to do in rr 2f out: r.o wl fnl f: nrst fin* **8/1**3

0144 **6** *1/2* **Medici Time**21 3828 5-9-2 **84** ...(v) GrahamGibbons 4 87
(T D Easterby) *racd towards nr side: prom: drvn 2f out: styd on fnl f: nvr quite on terms* **12/1**

3133 **7** *hd* **Lost In Paris (IRE)**7 4292 4-8-12 **80** ...(p) RyanMoore 12 82
(T D Easterby) *w ldrs in centre: stl upsides ent fnl f: fdd* **4/1**1

3004 **8** *1/2* **Courageous (IRE)**19 3919 4-9-4 **86** ...(v) RichardMullen 13 86
(B Smart) *swtg: mde most in centre: hung rt to far side fr over 1f out: hdd & wknd ins fnl f* **7/1**2

0032 **9** *3/4* **Matsunosuke**4 4401 8-9-5 **87** ... LukeMorris 1 84
(R A Harris) *hld up towards nr side: gng strly 1/2-way: rdn 2f out: kpt on fnl f: nvr able to chal* **14/1**

155 **10** *2 1/4* **La Capriosa**8 4243 4-8-4 **72** ... RoystonFfrench 6 61
(J A Glover) *lw: prom towards nr side: wknd over 1f out* **50/1**

0000 **11** *nse* **Mythical Blue (IRE)**21 3809 4-8-2 **70** ... DavidProbert 17 59
(J M Bradley) *pressed ldrs on wd outside: wknd 2f out* **20/1**

200- **12** *3/4* **Titus Andronicus (IRE)**343 5203 4-9-2 **84** ... PaulHanagan 7 70
(R A Fahey) *lw: taken down early: prom in centre 3f: steadily wknd* **12/1**

0005 **13** *1* **Rocker**21 3815 6-8-0 **75** ... HarryBentley(7) 18 58
(G L Moore) *racd centre: dropped to last of gp bef 1/2-way: wl btn after* **16/1**

3544 **14** *3/4* **Feelin Foxy**17 3947 6-8-11 **79** ... PaulMulrennan 3 59
(J G Given) *taken down early: racd nr side: struggling in rr fr 1/2-way* **16/1**

5044 **15** *nse* **Berbice (IRE)**19 3892 5-8-5 **73** ... GregFairley 16 53
(S Kirk) *taken down early: hld up in centre: effrt and cl enough 2f out: sn wknd rapidly* **16/1**

0210 **16** *2 1/2* **Highland Harvest**7 4292 6-8-2 **70** oh2 ... NickyMackay 2 41
(Jamie Poulton) *racd nr side: a struggling* **66/1**

1230 **17** *1 1/2* **Osiris Way**12 4148 8-9-7 **89** ... JimCrowley 5 54
(P R Chamings) *lw: stdd s: hld up in centre: wknd 2f out* **20/1**

57.37 secs (-1.03) **Going Correction** +0.025s/f (Good) **17** Ran SP% **130.4**
Speed ratings (Par 107): **109,108,108,107,106 105,105,104,103,99 99,98,97,95,95 91,89**
toteswingers:1&2:£35.90, 1&3:£71.40, 2&3:£56.90. totesuper7: Win: Not won. Place: £888.30 CSF £151.40 CT £2310.65 TOTE £21.30: £5.60, £2.20, £5.10, £2.90; EX 407.70 Trifecta £2099.10 Part won. Pool: £2,836.74 - 0.10 winning units. Place 6 £1,795.40; Place 5 £197.04.

Owner Hart Inn I **Bred** Ragged Mountain Farm **Trained** Sessay, N Yorks

FOCUS

Plenty of familiar names in this competitive sprint handicap, and typical form for the type of race. It worked out only 4lb slower than the earlier King George. The field raced down the centre of the track initially before fanning out towards the inside rail, and middle-to-high draws were seemingly favoured.

NOTEBOOK

Hamoody(USA) chased the pace before lunging late, posting his first win since he took the Richmond Stakes at the meeting four years ago when trained by Peter Chapple-Hyam. Dropped 6lb for his new handler this season, he was running over 5f for only the second time. He was the sixth winner of this race in a dozen runnings for David Nicholls, who also sent out the third and fifth here, and who won this four times in a row with Zuhair. Hamoody will take his chance under a penalty in the Stewards' Sprint, and Zuhair won both races in 1999. (op 20-1)

Bajan Tryst(USA) had every chance down the centre but was denied by the winner's late thrust. He is currently in fine form but is due to race off a 2lb higher mark now. (tchd 12-1 in places and 8-1 in places)

Crimea(IRE), who raced nearer to the inside rail than the first two, is likely to join his stablemate in the Stewards' Sprint. He is pencilled in for a drop of 3lb after that. (op 14-1)

Piscean(USA), a triple course winner, broke much better than is often the case and was running on well towards the far side, only missing out by around half a length. (op 8-1)

Indian Trail, the third of the Nicholls runners, finished as well as anything and remains well capable of popping up at some stage. Fourth in this race last year, he is now a pound lower than his most recent win, in last season's Investec "Dash" at Epsom. (op 15-2)

Medici Time ran a solid race if finding this a shade sharp.

Lost In Paris(IRE) showed his customary fine pace in this change of headgear. (op 9-2, tchd 5-1 in places)

Courageous(IRE), down at 5f for the first time, showed bags of pace with the visor retained but drifted over to the far rail when the pressure was on. Official explanation: jockey said gelding hung badly right-handed under pressure (op 8-1)

Matsunosuke, runner-up at Ascot four days earlier on his debut for the yard, ran respectably from what turned out to be an unfavourable low draw. (op 11-1)

T/Jkpt: Not won. T/Plt: £672.30 to a £1 stake. Pool:£287,660.09 - 312.34 winning tickets T/Qpdt: £40.30 to a £1 stake. Pool:£14,857.52 - 272.25 winning tickets JN

3985 MUSSELBURGH (R-H)

Thursday, July 29

OFFICIAL GOING: Good (lightly watered; 6.5)

Wind: Slight, half behind Weather: Cloudy

4511 WILKINSON AND ASSOCIATES AMATEUR RIDERS' H'CAP 1m 5f

6:20 (6:22) (Class 6) (0-65,65) 4-Y-O+ **£1,873** (£581; £290; £145) **Stalls** High

Form RPR

0355 **1** **Ballade De La Mer**19 3901 4-9-2 **46** oh1 ...(p) MrGJCockburn(7) 8 51
(A G Foster) *chsd ldrs: led over 4f out: rdn 2f out: hld on wl fnl f* **50/1**

0251 **2** *1 1/2* **Hurricane Thomas (IRE)**2 4453 6-10-5 **61** 6ex... MissPhillipaTutty(5) 2 64
(R A Fahey) *led 2f: cl up: rdn and effrt over 2f out: ev ch 1f out: edgd rt and kpt on same pce ins fnl f* **11/4**2

0064 **3** 1 **Dechiper (IRE)**[35] 3370 8-9-7 **51** ow4......................(t) MissCWalton[(7)] 12 53
(R Johnson) *hld up in midfield: hdwy to trck ldrs 2f out: kpt on ins fnl f* **25/1**

0064 **4** ¾ **Dimashq**[16] 3978 8-9-5 **47**.. MissWGibson[(5)] 6 47
(P T Midgley) *t.k.h: hld up: effrt and prom over 2f out: one pce fnl f* **20/1**

40/1 **5** ¾ **Daytime Dreamer (IRE)**[8] 4246 6-11-0 **65**...................... MrSWalker 10 64
(M Todhunter) *trckd ldrs: effrt and wnt 2nd over 3f out: rdn and one pce fr 2f out* **2/1**[1]

4120 **6** shd **Chocolate Caramel (USA)**[15] 4015 8-10-7 **63**............ MrsVFahey[(5)] 7 62
(R A Fahey) *in tch: shkn up over 2f out: no imp fnl f* **6/1**[3]

-621 **7** 3 ¼ **Regent's Secret (USA)**[35] 3352 10-10-9 **60**............... MrsCBartley 11 54
(J S Goldie) *hld up: pushed along over 2f out: nvr able to chal* **6/1**[3]

42-0 **8** 4 ½ **Night Orbit**[36] 3324 6-10-6 **60**.......................................(v) MrRBirkett[(3)] 3 47
(Miss J Feilden) *led after 2f to over 4f out: wknd fnl 2f* **9/1**

2004 **9** 7 **Media Stars**[11] 4170 5-9-8 **52** oh1 ow6.......................(t) MissEYoung[(7)] 9 29
(R Johnson) *hld up: struggling 4f out: sn btn* **100/1**

0-04 **10** nk **Piermarini**[21] 3804 5-9-3 **47**... MissHDukes[(7)] 5 24
(P T Midgley) *hld up on outside: struggling over 4f out: sn btn* **33/1**

504/ **11** 3 **Follow On**[18] 3718 8-9-4 **46** oh1.........................(t) MissAngelaBarnes[(5)] 1 18
(M A Barnes) *in tch on outside tl wknd fr 3f out* **25/1**

2m 52.21s (0.21) **Going Correction** -0.10s/f (Good) 11 Ran SP% **116.9**
Speed ratings (Par 101): **95,94,93,93,92 92,90,87,83,83 81**
toteswingers:1&2:£31.70, 1&3:£43.30, 2&3:£7.30 CSF £175.92 CT £3635.33 TOTE £51.30: £6.80, £1.70, £5.40; EX 446.40.
Owner Highland Racing 6 **Bred** Southill Stud **Trained** Haddington, East Lothian
■ The first winner under rules for Grant Cockburn, a promising point-to-point rider.

FOCUS
A weak handicap, confined to amateur riders. A surprise winner and the form is dubious.
Regent's Secret(USA) Official explanation: jockey said gelding was unsuited by the slowly run race

4512 EUROPEAN BREEDERS' FUND MAIDEN STKS 5f
6:50 (6:50) (Class 5) 2-Y-O **£3,238** (£963; £481; £240) **Stalls** Low

Form RPR

252 **1** **Ice Trooper**[6] 4336 2-8-12 78.. JamesSullivan[(5)] 1 72
(Mrs L Stubbs) *mde all: rdn clr whn edgd rt ins fnl f: kpt on strly* **2/7**[1]

4230 **2** 2 ¼ **Beyaz Villas**[8] 4242 2-9-3 71.. FrannyNorton 2 64
(D Nicholls) *pressed wnr: rdn and edgd rt over 1f out: sn one pce* **4/1**[2]

40 **3** 2 ½ **Eilean Mor**[31] 3498 2-9-0 0... GaryBartley[(3)] 4 55
(J S Goldie) *prom: pushed along after 2f: effrt over 1f out: sn outpcd* **25/1**

4 9 **Isontonic (IRE)** 2-8-12 0.. MickyFenton 3 18
(P T Midgley) *trckd ldrs: pushed along after 2f: hung rt and wknd over 1f out* **16/1**[3]

60.54 secs (0.14) **Going Correction** -0.10s/f (Good) 4 Ran SP% **107.5**
Speed ratings (Par 94): **94,90,86,72**
CSF £1.72 TOTE £1.40; EX 1.60.
Owner J P Hames **Bred** Low Ground Stud **Trained** Norton, N Yorks

FOCUS
A poor turnout for this juvenile maiden and the form is straightforward but limited, with the runner-up and third having both been beaten in selling company.

NOTEBOOK
Ice Trooper outclassed three inferior rivals. He should be competitive in nurseries.
Beyaz Villas, dropped in trip, had 7lb to find with the winner on official figures and basically was not good enough. (op 9-2)
Eilean Mor, outpaced for most of the way, now has the option of nurseries, although he started off in a seller.
Isontonic(IRE), who has an appealing enough pedigree, needed this experience. After hanging right about 2f out, she was not given a hard time. (op 14-1)

4513 BLACKROCK H'CAP 5f
7:25 (7:25) (Class 4) (0-80,78) 3-Y-O+ **£5,180** (£1,541; £770; £384) **Stalls** Low

Form RPR

3416 **1** **The Bear**[14] 4060 7-9-3 **69**.. TonyHamilton 6 76
(Miss L A Perratt) *mde all: rdn over 1f out: styd on strly fnl f* **7/1**[3]

2050 **2** ¾ **Highland Warrior**[13] 4090 11-8-12 **67**........................... PaulPickard[(3)] 5 71
(P T Midgley) *s.i.s: bhd and pushed along: hdwy over 1f out: chsd wnr ins fnl f: r.o* **12/1**

314 **3** 1 ¾ **Distant Sun (USA)**[14] 4060 6-9-6 **72**.................................. PhillipMakin 1 70
(Miss L A Perratt) *trckd ldrs: rdn over 1f out: rallied and edgd lft ins fnl f: kpt on fin* **15/2**

2240 **4** nk **Lees Anthem**[11] 4169 3-8-6 **62**.. PatrickMathers 4 58
(C J Teague) *hld up in tch: drvn along 1/2-way: kpt on u.p fnl f* **22/1**

0-15 **5** 1 ¼ **Argentine (IRE)**[196] 172 6-9-7 **78**...............................(b) LeeTopliss[(5)] 7 70
(J A McShane) *rn in blinkers instead of declared hood: trckd ldrs: drvn 2f out: kpt on same pce fnl f* **10/1**

2143 **6** nk **Silvanus (IRE)**[10] 4199 5-9-2 **68**.. MickyFenton 2 59
(P T Midgley) *in tch: effrt over 1f out: no imp whn n.m.r ins fnl f* **7/2**[2]

3322 **7** 2 ¼ **Ridley Didley (IRE)**[20] 3879 5-8-11 **68**.............................. DeanHeslop[(5)] 3 51
(N Wilson) *dwlt: sn trcking wnr: rdn over 1f out: wknd ins fnl f* **5/4**[1]

59.25 secs (-1.15) **Going Correction** -0.10s/f (Good)
WFA 3 from 5yo+ 4lb 7 Ran SP% **112.1**
Speed ratings (Par 105): **105,103,101,100,98 98,94**
toteswingers:1&2:£6.50, 1&3:£3.10, 2&3:£9.80 CSF £79.04 TOTE £7.20: £4.70, £7.30; EX 42.30.
Owner Cincinnati Club **Bred** P G Airey And R R Whitton **Trained** East Kilbride, South Lanarks

FOCUS
Most of these sprinters looked badly handicapped. The winner is rated to his post 2yo best.
Silvanus(IRE) Official explanation: jockey said gelding was denied a clear run

4514 MCQUAY HIGH EFFICIENCY CLASSIC (S) STKS 1m 1f
7:55 (7:55) (Class 6) 4-Y-O+ **£1,942** (£578; £288; £144) **Stalls** High

Form RPR

0441 **1** **Applaude**[11] 4173 5-9-3 60..(b) PaulEddery 8 69
(R C Guest) *hld up on ins: hdwy to ld appr fnl f: drvn out* **7/2**[2]

1140 **2** ¾ **Bajan Pride**[4] 4411 6-9-3 67.. MickyFenton 7 67
(P T Midgley) *hld up: hdwy 2f out: kpt on fnl f: nt rch wnr* **8/1**

5300 **3** shd **Rosbertini**[10] 4189 4-8-12 59.. LNewman 10 62
(Miss L A Perratt) *prom: effrt and swtchd lft 2f out: kpt on fnl f: hld towards fin* **50/1**

3300 **4** 2 **Kings Point (IRE)**[13] 4093 9-8-7 68.................................... BillyCray[(5)] 5 57
(D Nicholls) *cl up: ev ch 2f out to over 1f out: one pce fnl f* **9/2**[3]

3220 **5** shd **San Silvestro (IRE)**[10] 4188 5-8-7 65..........................(b) IanBrennan[(5)] 1 57
(Mrs A Duffield) *t.k.h: cl up: led over 2f out to appr fnl f: kpt on same pce* **3/1**[1]

5263 **6** 1 ¾ **Finsbury**[13] 4088 7-9-3 67.. PhillipMakin 4 58
(Miss L A Perratt) *unruly in preliminaries: dwlt: hld up: hdwy over 2f out: hrd rdn and no imp whn nt clr run last 100yds* **11/2**

401 **7** 1 **Red Skipper (IRE)**[25] 3707 5-9-3 54................................ TonyHamilton 6 56
(N Wilson) *led to over 2f out: no ex fr over 1f out* **6/1**

0030 **8** 7 **Desert Fairy**[14] 4070 4-8-4 44.. KellyHarrison[(3)] 2 31
(J W Unett) *sn drvn along towards rr: shortlived effrt over 2f out: sn wknd* **28/1**

00-0 **9** 20 **Wilmington**[19] 3901 6-8-12 43.. AndrewMullen 3 —
(Mrs J C McGregor) *trckd ldrs: drvn and outpcd 3f out: sn struggling: t.o* **100/1**

1m 52.61s (-1.29) **Going Correction** -0.10s/f (Good) 9 Ran SP% **112.6**
Speed ratings (Par 101): **105,104,104,102,102 100,99,93,75**
toteswingers:1&2:£2.20, 1&3:£33.20, 2&3:£69.70 CSF £30.18 TOTE £4.60: £2.30, £1.10, £7.60; EX 23.90.There was no bid for the winner.
Owner Stan Wright **Bred** G Reed **Trained** Stainforth, S Yorks

FOCUS
They went a decent gallop here. Ordinary selling form, the winner only needing to run to his Redcar latest.

4515 EASTERN ELECTRIC SCOTLAND LTD H'CAP 7f 30y
8:30 (8:31) (Class 5) (0-70,70) 3-Y-O+ **£3,238** (£963; £481; £240) **Stalls** High

Form RPR

1134 **1** **Polish World (USA)**[10] 4197 6-9-12 **70**.............................. MickyFenton 13 82
(P T Midgley) *mde all: rdn 2f out: hld on wl fnl f* **5/1**[3]

6-00 **2** ½ **Star Links (USA)**[27] 3652 4-9-8 **66**......................................(tp) LNewman 9 76
(S Donohoe, Ire) *prom: effrt and hung lft over 1f out: edgd rt u.p ins fnl f: kpt on* **4/1**[1]

3341 **3** 1 ¼ **Gemma's Delight (IRE)**[20] 3855 3-8-4 **58**.............(p) KellyHarrison[(3)] 10 62
(J W Unett) *midfield: effrt over 2f out: kpt on fnl f: nrst fin* **14/1**

-044 **4** hd **Zabeel Tower**[16] 3990 7-8-13 **57**.. TonyHamilton 12 63
(R Allan) *trckd ldrs: effrt over 1f out: kpt on same pce fnl f* **20/1**

-002 **5** 1 ½ **Shunkawakhan (IRE)**[16] 3990 7-8-3 **52**..................... JamesSullivan[(5)] 4 54
(Miss L A Perratt) *in tch: effrt on outside 2f out: kpt on same pce fnl f* **22/1**

0-00 **6** 1 ¼ **Cara's Request (AUS)**[63] 2451 5-9-10 **68**................... AndrewMullen 14 67
(D Nicholls) *cl up tl rdn and nt qckn over 1f out* **20/1**

1042 **7** ½ **Elijah Pepper (USA)**[20] 3855 5-9-5 **63**................................ PhillipMakin 7 61
(T D Barron) *hld up: rdn over 2f out: kpt on: nvr able to chal* **9/2**[2]

4512 **8** nk **Honest Broker (IRE)**[10] 4197 3-9-5 **70**............................ PJMcDonald 5 64+
(M Johnston) *bhd: drvn over 2f out: sme late hdwy: nvr able to chal* **5/1**[3]

6222 **9** 1 ¼ **Botham (USA)**[14] 4064 6-8-11 **62**................................ PaulNorton[(7)] 11 56
(J S Goldie) *bhd: drvn over 2f out: nvr rchd ldrs* **12/1**

6043 **10** nk **Clumber Place**[6] 4342 4-8-9 **53**.. PaulEddery 3 46
(R C Guest) *trckd ldrs tl rdn and no ex fr 2f out* **18/1**

0060 **11** 2 **Sendreni (FR)**[19] 3900 6-8-7 **51** oh1.............................(p) FrannyNorton 1 38
(Mrs J C McGregor) *towards rr: drvn over 2f out: sn no imp* **100/1**

-060 **12** nk **Burns Night**[50] 2850 4-9-10 **68**................................ SilvestreDeSousa 8 54
(G A Harker) *s.v.s: nvr on terms* **7/1**

0225 **13** 1 ¼ **Hosanna**[16] 3990 4-8-8 **52**.. PatrickMathers 2 35
(J Barclay) *hld up on outside: drvn over 2f out: sn wknd* **50/1**

0-20 **14** 14 **Ocean Rosie (IRE)**[38] 3272 3-9-0 **70**.............................. IanBrennan[(5)] 6 12
(Miss J Feilden) *midfield: lost pl over 4f out: struggling fnl 3f* **50/1**

1m 27.93s (-1.07) **Going Correction** -0.10s/f (Good)
WFA 3 from 4yo+ 7lb 14 Ran SP% **122.4**
Speed ratings (Par 103): **102,101,100,99,98 96,96,95,94,93 91,91,89,73**
toteswingers:1&2:£5.90, 1&3:£13.60, 2&3:£20.70 CSF £23.88 CT £272.01 TOTE £6.20: £1.90, £2.20, £5.40; EX 46.00.
Owner C R Green **Bred** Racehorse Management, Llc **Trained** Westow, N Yorks

FOCUS
A fair handicap for the grade in which it paid to be handy. The time was decent and the form is rated on the positive side, with a clear personal best from the winner.
Burns Night Official explanation: jockey said gelding was slowly away

4516 WILKINSON AND ASSOCIATES H'CAP 5f
9:00 (9:03) (Class 6) (0-65,64) 3-Y-O+ **£1,942** (£578; £288; £144) **Stalls** Low

Form RPR

-055 **1** **Rio's Girl**[21] 3808 3-8-3 **45**.. PaulQuinn 6 53
(R M Whitaker) *cl up: effrt over 1f out: styd on to ld last 50yds* **33/1**

3635 **2** nk **Mandarin Spirit (IRE)**[14] 4060 10-9-12 **64**.................(b) TonyHamilton 1 72
(Miss L A Perratt) *prom: effrt over 1f out: styd on strly fnl f* **9/2**[3]

2014 **3** nse **Arriva La Diva**[14] 4047 4-8-13 **56**.................................. IanBrennan[(5)] 8 64
(J J Quinn) *cl up: hdwy to ld over 1f out: sn rdn: hdd ins fnl f: kpt on* **10/3**[1]

2354 **4** 1 **Sandwith**[5] 4373 7-9-5 **57**...(v[1]) LNewman 2 61
(A G Foster) *prom: rdn 2f out: kpt on same pce fnl f* **4/1**[2]

6056 **5** nk **Welcome Approach**[3] 4431 7-8-7 **48**............................ KellyHarrison[(3)] 4 51+
(J R Weymes) *bhd tl gd hdwy ins fnl f: nrst fin* **13/2**

006 **6** ½ **Bombay Mist**[4] 4406 3-8-3 **45**..(e) PaulEddery 13 45
(R C Guest) *led to over 1f out: no ex ins fnl f* **16/1**

4160 **7** 1 ¾ **Almaty Express**[8] 4244 8-8-6 **51**.................................(b) NeilFarley[(7)] 9 46
(J R Weymes) *towards rr on outside: hdwy and edgd rt over 1f out: nvr able to chal* **14/1**

-000 **8** 3 ¼ **Clanachy**[14] 4064 4-8-2 **45**...(p) JamesSullivan[(5)] 5 28
(A G Foster) *bhd: drvn 1/2-way: nvr rchd ldrs* **50/1**

0050 **9** 2 ¼ **Spirit Of Coniston**[25] 3711 7-9-3 **55**................................ MickyFenton 12 30
(P T Midgley) *prom tl hung lft and wknd fr 2f out* **25/1**

0404 **10** 3 ½ **Sharp Shoes**[10] 4194 3-8-10 **52**............................(b) SilvestreDeSousa 11 14
(Mrs A Duffield) *cl up tl hung rt and wknd over 1f out* **10/1**

0-03 **11** hd **Angelofthenorth**[43] 3075 8-8-9 **47**.................................. PatrickMathers 10 9
(C J Teague) *bhd on outside: struggling 1/2-way: sn btn* **33/1**

2-5 **12** nk **Grace And Virtue (IRE)**[26] 3700 3-8-11 **53**.....................(tp) PhillipMakin 7 13
(S Donohoe, Ire) *prom: n.m.r briefly 1/2-way: sn rdn: wknd wl over 1f out* **12/1**

60.34 secs (-0.06) **Going Correction** -0.10s/f (Good)
WFA 3 from 4yo+ 4lb 12 Ran SP% **115.6**
Speed ratings (Par 101): **96,95,95,93,93 92,89,84,80,75 75,74**
toteswingers:1&2:£41.30, 1&3:£31.70, 2&3:£3.40 CSF £160.40 CT £572.86 TOTE £43.40: £11.90, £1.10, £1.70; EX 379.00 Place 6 £447.34; Place 5 £124.15.
Owner Tracey Gaunt & David Gibbons **Bred** Hellwood Stud Farm **Trained** Scarcroft, W Yorks
■ Stewards' Enquiry : Paul Quinn caution: careless riding.

FOCUS
A moderate but competitive sprint handicap run in a time 1.09 seconds slower than the earlier Class 4 contest. The winner is improving.
Rio's Girl Official explanation: trainer's rep said, regarding apparent improvement in form, that the filly had been suited by a drop back to 5f in a lower grade.
Spirit Of Coniston Official explanation: jockey said gelding hung left-handed throughout
Sharp Shoes Official explanation: jockey said gelding hung right throughout

T/Plt: £997.80 to a £1 stake. Pool:£54,306.01 - 39.73 winning tickets T/Qpdt: £196.20 to a £1 stake. Pool:£6,339.38 - 23.90 winning tickets RY

4109 NOTTINGHAM (L-H)

Thursday, July 29

OFFICIAL GOING: Good to firm (watered; 7.1)

All races on outer track. Rail out 5m from 2nd dog leg to 4.5f out and then 2m up to 1m2f start increasing distances on round course by about 24yds.

Wind: Light half-behind Weather: Overcast

4517 EUROPEAN BREEDERS' FUND MAIDEN FILLIES' STKS 6f 15y

2:00 (2:01) (Class 5) 2-Y-O £3,561 (£1,059; £529; £264) Stalls Centre

Form RPR

1 **Warm Breeze** 2-9-0 0 JackMitchell 8 88+
(M A Jarvis) *a.p: chsd ldr over 2f out: sn drifted lft: led over 1f out: r.o wl: eased towards fin* 5/6[1]

6 2 5 **Scantily Clad (IRE)**[19] 3906 2-9-0 0 RobertWinston 2 71+
(E S McMahon) *led: rdn and hdd over 1f out: no ex fnl f* 6/1[3]

3 8 **Poplin** 2-9-0 0 J-PGuillambert 9 47+
(L M Cumani) *s.i.s and sn pushed along: wnt mod 3rd wl ins fnl f: nvr nrr* 4/1[2]

00 4 1½ **Bright Dictator (IRE)**[14] 4048 2-9-0 0 LeeVickers 7 42
(J G Given) *chsd ldrs tl rdn and wknd over 2f out: lost 3rd wl ins fnl f* 100/1

5 4½ **Illmindu (IRE)** 2-8-11 0 JamesMillman(3) 1 29
(B R Millman) *wnt lft s and s.i.s: hdwy 4f out: wknd wl over 2f out* 20/1

6 1½ **Duquesa (IRE)** 2-9-0 0 CathyGannon 6 24
(P D Evans) *chsd ldrs: rdn and hung lft 1/2-way: wknd over 2f out* 33/1

7 1¼ **Here To Eternity (USA)** 2-9-0 0 PatCosgrave 4 20
(P W Chapple-Hyam) *chsd ldr tl rdn and wknd over 2f out* 8/1

8 7 **Lindo Erro** 2-9-0 0 StephenCraine 5 —
(J Mackie) *s.s: a in rr: bhd fr 1/2-way* 50/1

1m 15.95s (1.05) **Going Correction** +0.075s/f (Good) 8 Ran SP% **110.6**

Speed ratings (Par 91): **96,89,78,76,70 68,67,57**

toteswingers:1&2:£1.90, 1&3:£1.70, 2&3:£2.80 CSF £5.67 TOTE £2.20: £1.20, £1.10, £1.10; EX 6.80.

Owner Saif Ali & Saeed H Altayer **Bred** Dr J Ahmadzadeh **Trained** Newmarket, Suffolk

FOCUS

All races were run on the outer course. The rail had been moved out five metres from the second dogleg to 4.5f out and then two metres as far as the 1m2f start, increasing race distances by about 24 yards. The runners raced centre to far side and some fascinating newcomers lined up for this fillies' maiden. The winner impressed and the bare figure might underestimate her.

NOTEBOOK

Warm Breeze ◆, an 80,000gns filly out of a winning half-sister to Banjo Patterson, hails from a yard that could hardly be in better form with its juveniles. She certainly knew her job as she travelled beautifully on the outside of the field early and, although she drifted over towards the far rail in the final couple of furlongs, she cruised into the lead and then came right away. She is entered in the Cheveley Park, plus numerous valuable sales races later in the year, and looks sure to go on to better things. (op 11-10)

Scantily Clad(IRE) looked in need of the experience when unplaced in a C&D maiden earlier this month that hasn't as yet worked out, but she was more organised here and took them along against the far rail until outclassed by the favourite inside the last 2f. She won't always come up against such a smart rival. (op 9-2)

Poplin, a half-sister to a 1m2f winner out of the Lancashire Oaks winner Pongee, unlike the winner looked as green as grass. She took an age to realise what was required, but ran on to take a remote third and this Fillies' Mile entry is likely to improve plenty both for the experience and for a step up in trip. (tchd 3-1)

Bright Dictator(IRE), well beaten in her first two starts over further, ran better here but probably needs a drop in class or a switch to nurseries.

Here To Eternity(USA), first foal of a 1m Listed winner, took a grip early and found little once off the bridle. (op 7-1 tchd 9-1)

4518 IT'S CIRCUS DAY TODAY H'CAP 5f 13y

2:35 (2:37) (Class 5) (0-75,74) 3-Y-O+ £2,266 (£674; £337; £168) Stalls Centre

Form RPR

0523 1 **Triple Dream**[17] 3958 5-9-8 72 (p) LiamKeniry 1 81
(J M Bradley) *led: rdn and hdd over 1f out: rallied to ld and hung rt ins fnl f: r.o* 9/2[3]

5656 2 1¼ **Colorus (IRE)**[4] 4415 7-8-9 66 (p) AdamBeschizza(7) 7 71
(W J H Ratcliffe) *chsd ldr: rdn over 1f out: hung lft ins fnl f: styd on* 13/2

-322 3 hd **Volito**[13] 4099 4-9-3 67 RichardKingscote 5 71
(Jonjo O'Neill) *hld up: hdwy over 1f out: hmpd ins fnl f: r.o to go 3rd towards fin: nvr able to chal* 4/1[2]

0-41 4 ½ **Luminous Gold**[21] 3818 5-9-10 74 JackMitchell 2 76
(C F Wall) *chsd ldrs: rdn to ld over 1f out: hdd and unable qck ins fnl f* 85/40[1]

3665 5 ¾ **The Tatling (IRE)**[13] 4099 13-9-0 67 JackDean(3) 6 67
(J M Bradley) *s.i.s: hld up: rdn over 1f out: r.o: nt pce to chal* 14/1

6400 6 1¼ **The Jobber (IRE)**[13] 4099 9-9-3 67 SteveDrowne 3 62
(M Blanshard) *prom: rdn over 1f out: no ex ins fnl f* 11/1

-00 7 ½ **Elhamri**[14] 4041 6-9-4 68 JamesDoyle 8 61
(S Kirk) *chsd ldrs: rdn over 1f out: no ex fnl f* 25/1

0410 8 1¼ **Sands Crooner (IRE)**[13] 4090 7-9-4 68 (vt) PatCosgrave 4 57
(J G Given) *s.i.s: hld up: rdn over 1f out: nvr on terms* 9/1

60.89 secs (-0.11) **Going Correction** +0.075s/f (Good) 8 Ran SP% **112.4**

Speed ratings (Par 103): **103,101,100,99,98 96,95,93**

toteswingers:1&2:£7.00, 1&3:£2.20, 2&3:£7.50 CSF £32.36 CT £125.35 TOTE £5.90: £1.90, £3.50, £1.40; EX 39.20.

Owner J M Bradley **Bred** Hesmonds Stud Ltd **Trained** Sedbury, Gloucs

FOCUS

A modest sprint handicap and this time the runners raced against the stands' rail. Sound enough form with the second and third close to their recent best.

4519 FIND US ON FACEBOOK H'CAP 2m 9y

3:10 (3:11) (Class 6) (0-65,56) 3-Y-O £1,706 (£503; £252) Stalls Low

Form RPR

3146 1 **Dubara Reef (IRE)**[27] 3626 3-9-7 55 SteveDrowne 3 66
(Paul Green) *chsd ldrs: led over 2f out: sn rdn: hung lft over 1f out: styd on wl* 13/2[3]

3214 2 7 **Dubawi King**[13] 4087 3-9-7 55 J-PGuillambert 8 58
(N Tinkler) *hld up: hdwy over 3f out: chsd wnr over 2f out: sn rdn: no ex and eased ins fnl f* 5/1[2]

-060 3 1¾ **Torran Sound**[12] 2412 3-8-12 46 CathyGannon 7 46
(J M P Eustace) *led: rdn and hdd 5f out: wknd over 1f out* 11/1

00-1 4 ½ **Albacocca**[9] 4235 3-9-8 56 6ex PatCosgrave 4 55
(Sir Mark Prescott) *s.i.s and sn pushed along: hdwy to chse ldr after 2f: led 5f out: rdn: hdd and wandered over 2f out: wknd over 1f out* 4/6[1]

-044 5 23 **Chichina (USA)**[15] 4017 3-8-13 47 AndrewElliott 5 19
(M Johnston) *prom: pushed along 10f out: wknd over 4f out: t.o* 8/1

05-6 6 32 **Groove Master**[14] 4052 3-9-6 54 LiamKeniry 6 —
(A King) *hld up: rdn and wknd over 5f out: t.o* 33/1

060 7 106 **Silver Astralis**[54] 2754 3-8-4 45 AdamBeschizza(7) 2 —
(Mrs C A Dunnett) *prom tl rdn and wknd over 6f out: t.o: btn 106 l* 100/1

0530 8 2¼ **Royal Torbo (ISR)**[17] 3967 3-9-4 55 MatthewDavies(3) 9 —
(George Baker) *trckd ldrs: pushed along 7f out: wknd over 5f out: t.o* 33/1

3m 35.12s (4.82) **Going Correction** +0.275s/f (Good) 8 Ran SP% **116.3**

Speed ratings (Par 98): **98,94,93,93,81 65,—,—**

toteswingers:1&2:£2.80, 1&3:£5.70, 2&3:£4.00 CSF £38.92 CT £354.30 TOTE £4.90: £1.30, £1.80, £1.40; EX 19.60.

Owner The Four Aces **Bred** M Duffy **Trained** Lydiate, Merseyside

FOCUS

This trip was a new experience for all of these (on the Flat at least) and it proved too much for a few as they finished spread out all over Nottingham. The race provided a 1-2 for gelded sons of Dubawi. The favourite disappointed but the first two both improved. The form is rated around the third.

4520 ROSELAND GROUP LTD H'CAP 1m 2f 50y

3:45 (3:46) (Class 4) (0-85,85) 3-Y-O+ £6,476 (£1,927; £963; £481) Stalls Low

Form RPR

6041 1 **Spoken**[14] 4044 3-9-1 82 (p) SteveDrowne 1 95+
(R Charlton) *mde all: shkn up over 2f out: sn clr: readily* 9/4[1]

0644 2 1¾ **Bahamian Music (IRE)**[21] 3806 3-8-6 73 DuranFentiman 11 79+
(R A Fahey) *hld up: hdwy over 3f out: rdn over 2f out: styd on to go 2nd wl ins fnl f: no ch w wnr* 22/1

2346 3 1¼ **Norwegian Dancer (UAE)**[14] 4051 4-9-10 81 RobertWinston 10 85
(E S McMahon) *chsd wnr: rdn over 2f out: styd on same pce fr over 1f out: lost 2nd wl ins fnl f* 13/2

1121 4 1¼ **Scamperdale**[14] 4051 8-10-0 85 TonyCulhane 7 87
(B P J Baugh) *a.p: rdn over 2f out: no imp fr over 1f out* 13/2

221/ 5 1 **Top Mark**[393] 7413 8-9-4 75 LiamKeniry 3 75
(A King) *chsd ldrs: rdn over 2f out: no ex fnl f* 16/1

3233 6 1¾ **Visions Of Johanna (USA)**[14] 4051 5-9-3 74 ShaneKelly 13 70
(Ian Williams) *hld up: hdwy over 3f out: rdn over 2f out: btn whn swtchd rt ins fnl f* 9/2[2]

0001 7 ½ **Epic (IRE)**[7] 4289 3-8-2 69 6ex (b) AndrewElliott 9 64
(M Johnston) *hld up: rdn over 2f out: nvr nrr* 5/1[3]

340- 8 nk **Summer Winds**[325] 5725 5-9-4 82 AdamBeschizza(7) 12 77
(R A Mills) *hld up: last 1/2-way: nvr nrr* 20/1

0300 9 hd **Donaldson (GER)**[13] 4100 8-9-9 80 RichardKingscote 4 75
(Jonjo O'Neill) *hld up: rdn over 2f out: nvr on terms* 50/1

0020 10 1¾ **Dragon Slayer (IRE)**[19] 3894 8-9-1 72 DaraghO'Donohoe 5 63
(John A Harris) *s.s: bhd and plld hrd: hdwy over 7f out: wknd over 2f out* 33/1

2352 11 1½ **Wind Star**[11] 1960 7-9-10 81 FrankieMcDonald 8 69
(M F Harris) *prom tl rdn and wknd over 2f out* 28/1

2m 15.23s (3.53) **Going Correction** +0.275s/f (Good)

WFA 3 from 4yo+ 10lb 11 Ran SP% **115.6**

Speed ratings (Par 105): **96,94,93,92,91 90,90,89,89,88 87**

toteswingers:1&2:£14.90, 1&3:£4.30, 2&3:£32.90 CSF £61.58 CT £286.20 TOTE £2.90: £1.70, £8.40, £2.30; EX 63.50.

Owner Lady Rothschild **Bred** The Rt Hon Lord Rothschild **Trained** Beckhampton, Wilts

FOCUS

A fair handicap, but it paid to be handy with four of the first five horses home prominent from the off. The winner was value for further with the third a fair guide to the form.

Dragon Slayer(IRE) Official explanation: jockey said gelding ran too free

4521 NOTTINGHAMRACECOURSE.CO.UK MEDIAN AUCTION MAIDEN STKS 1m 75y

4:20 (4:21) (Class 5) 3-4-Y-O £2,729 (£806; £403) Stalls Centre

Form RPR

4222 1 **Give Your Verdict (USA)**[15] 4028 3-9-0 80.. Louis-PhilippeBeuzelin(3) 6 79+
(Sir Michael Stoute) *w ldr tl led 6f out: shkn up over 2f out: clr fnl f: comf* 8/13[1]

0-26 2 2¼ **Battle Honour**[23] 3766 3-9-3 84 FrankieMcDonald 7 74
(H Candy) *led 2f: chsd wnr: rdn over 2f out: sn hung lft: styd on same pce fnl f* 7/2[2]

3 3 ½ **Forever Hope**[19] 3924 3-8-12 0 DanielTudhope 3 68
(T D Walford) *trckd ldrs: racd keenly: rdn over 2f out: styd on same pce fnl f* 16/1

20 4 1½ **Cookie Crumbles (IRE)**[13] 4115 3-8-12 0 JackMitchell 1 64
(C F Wall) *hld up: hdwy over 2f out: rdn and hung lft over 1f out: no ex fnl f* 6/1[3]

00- 5 1¾ **Chichi (IRE)**[210] 7885 3-8-12 0 RichardKingscote 10 60
(Tom Dascombe) *hld up: styd on fr over 1f out: nvr nrr* 125/1

0 6 hd **Dirakh Shan**[60] 2564 3-9-3 0 J-PGuillambert 9 65+
(L M Cumani) *hld up: shkn up over 1f out: r.o ins fnl f: nvr nr to chal* 40/1

46 7 3¾ **Eastern Magic**[38] 3275 3-9-3 0 LiamKeniry 8 56
(R Hollinshead) *chsd ldrs: rdn over 3f out: wknd over 2f out* 33/1

0 8 1¾ **Norville (IRE)**[28] 3586 3-9-3 0 CathyGannon 5 51?
(P D Evans) *prom: racd keenly: rdn over 3f out: wknd over 2f out* 125/1

0 9 3½ **Hedonist (IRE)**[114] 1137 3-9-3 0 SteveDrowne 2 43?
(J R Gask) *hld up: rdn over 3f out: sn wknd* 125/1

1m 50.16s (4.56) **Going Correction** +0.275s/f (Good)

WFA 3 from 4yo 8lb 9 Ran SP% **112.1**

Speed ratings (Par 103): **88,85,85,83,82 81,78,76,72**

toteswingers:1&2:£1.60, 1&3:£3.80, 2&3:£3.70 CSF £2.76 TOTE £1.90: £1.10, £1.10, £2.90; EX 3.30.

Owner Saeed Suhail **Bred** Hot Pepper Farm **Trained** Newmarket, Suffolk

FOCUS

An uncompetitive maiden and the two market leaders dominated from the off. The time was slow and the form is rated around the front pair.

4522 RAT PACK NIGHT 10TH AUGUST H'CAP 1m 75y

4:55 (4:55) (Class 5) (0-75,74) 3-Y-O+ £2,266 (£674; £337; £168) Stalls Centre

Form RPR

1100 1 **West End Lad**[47] 2961 7-9-13 73 (b) RobertWinston 4 82
(S R Bowring) *a.p: chsd ldr over 2f out: led over 1f out: rdn out* 9/1

4426 **2** *2 1/2* **Bolodenka (IRE)**[12] 4154 8-10-0 **74** .... LeeVickers 2 77
(R A Fahey) *hld up: hdwy over 2f out: chsd wnr over 1f out: styd on same pce ins fnl f* **12/1**

3434 **3** *1/2* **Lastkingofscotland (IRE)**[7] 4308 4-9-10 **70** ....(v) LiamKeniry 11 72
(C R Dore) *hld up: hdwy u.p 2f out: edgd lft: styd on: nt rch ldrs* **5/1**[2]

00-2 **4** *2 1/4* **High Five Society**[171] 469 6-8-11 **60** ....(b) AshleyHamblett(3) 10 57
(S R Bowring) *hld up: hdwy and nt clr run over 1f out: no imp ins fnl f* **12/1**

5440 **5** *3 1/4* **Battle Study (IRE)**[6] 4344 3-7-11 **58** .... NoraLooby(7) 8 48+
(A J McCabe) *hld up: hdwy 2f out: nt clr run and lost pl over 1f out: swtchd rt ins fnl f: nvr able to chal* **20/1**

33-4 **6** *shd* **Bonded (IRE)**[100] 1448 3-9-0 **71** ....(b[1]) Louis-PhilippeBeuzelin(3) 5 58
(B J Meehan) *hld up: hdwy 3f out: rdn over 1f out: wknd fnl f* **5/1**[2]

0315 **7** *3 1/2* **Baltimore Jack (IRE)**[10] 4198 6-9-12 **72** .... DuranFentiman 6 53
(T D Walford) *chsd ldr tl rdn over 2f out: wknd over 1f out* **11/2**[3]

3421 **8** *3 1/4* **Flying Silks (IRE)**[13] 4119 4-9-13 **73** ....(v) SteveDrowne 1 46
(J R Gask) *chsd ldrs: rdn over 2f out: wknd over 1f out* **5/2**[1]

3064 **9** *1* **Kingaroo (IRE)**[53] 2788 4-8-4 **55** oh8 .... RossAtkinson(5) 3 26
(G Woodward) *chsd ldrs: rdn over 3f out: sn wknd* **50/1**

0020 **10** *1* **Montego Breeze**[9] 4236 4-8-9 **55** oh3 ....(p) DaraghO'Donohoe 7 24
(John A Harris) *hld up: nvr on terms* **50/1**

600 **11** *6* **Gracie May**[14] 4069 3-7-12 **55** oh4 .... AndrewHeffernan(3) 9 —
(R Hollinshead) *racd keenly: led: hung rt fr over 4f out: hdd over 2f out: wknd over 1f out* **40/1**

1m 47.17s (1.57) **Going Correction** +0.275s/f (Good)
WFA 3 from 4yo+ 8lb **11** Ran SP% **113.8**
Speed ratings (Par 103): **103,100,100,97,94 94,90,87,86,85 79**
toteswingers:1&2:£11.50, 1&3:£8.00, 2&3:£6.20 CSF £103.67 CT £607.86 TOTE £12.70: £3.10, £3.30, £2.30; EX 85.90 Place 6 £48.64; Place 5 £43.85.
Owner K Nicholls **Bred** Keith Nicholls **Trained** Edwinstowe, Notts

FOCUS
An ordinary handicap, but they went a serious pace thanks to Gracie May until she folded 2f from home. The winning time was nearly 3secs faster than the preceding maiden. Unconvincing form, rated around the runner-up.
Flying Silks(IRE) Official explanation: jockey said gelding hung right-handed
T/Plt: £62.90 to a £1 stake. Pool:£43,648.74 - 505.87 winning tickets T/Qpdt: £16.80 to a £1 stake. Pool:£2,876.66 - 126.50 winning tickets CR

4494 GALWAY (R-H)
Thursday, July 29

OFFICIAL GOING: Good to firm

4524a ARTHUR GUINNESS EUROPEAN BREEDERS FUND FILLIES H'CAP 7f
3:35 (3:43) 3-Y-O+ **£20,707** (£6,053; £2,867; £955)

RPR

1 **Smart Striking (USA)**[21] 3835 3-8-6 84 ....(b) BACurtis(3) 16 85
(John M Oxx, Ire) *chsd ldrs: 4th 1/2-way: rdn 2f out: styd on in 2nd 1f out: chal ins fnl f and led cl home* **5/2**[1]

2 *hd* **Anam Chara (IRE)**[8] 4273 4-8-8 83 .... JPO'Brien(7) 15 86
(Andrew Oliver, Ire) *attempted to make all: rdn ent st: chal ins fnl f: hdd cl home* **10/1**

3 *3* **Kardyls Hope (IRE)**[55] 2733 4-8-9 77 .... JAHeffernan 7 72
(Jarlath P Fahey, Ire) *chsd ldrs early: 8th 1/2-way: rdn into 5th 2f out: 4th 1f out: kpt on same pce into 3rd fnl f: no imp on ldrs* **16/1**

4 *shd* **Miss Eze**[2] 4465 4-8-13 84 5ex .... DEMullins(3) 2 79+
(Paul Cashman, Ire) *hld up towards rr: rdn into 9th ent st: 6th 1f out: kpt on same pce fnl f* **7/1**[3]

5 *1 1/4* **Hallie's Comet (IRE)**[8] 4271 4-9-10 92 ....(b[1]) PJSmullen 13 83
(D K Weld, Ire) *mid-div: rdn into 7th 2f out: 5th 1f out: kpt on same pce fnl f* **6/1**[2]

6 *nk* **July Days (IRE)**[24] 3742 4-8-13 81 .... CO'Donoghue 1 71
(David Marnane, Ire) *hld up towards rr: late hdwy into 8th 1f out: kpt on same pce fnl f* **16/1**

7 *nk* **Tellelle (IRE)**[11] 4182 4-8-9 82 .... MHarley(5) 12 72
(Liam McAteer, Ire) *chsd ldrs: 3rd 1/2-way: rdn into 2nd 2f out: 3rd and no ex over 1f out: kpt on same pce* **9/1**

8 *1* **The Silver Crown (IRE)**[10] 4219 3-8-5 80 .... CDHayes 11 64
(Michael Mulvany, Ire) *dwlt: towards rr: rdn and no imp over 2f out: kpt on one pce st* **16/1**

9 *1 3/4* **Camira (IRE)**[14] 4080 5-9-0 82 ....(p) DJMoran 6 64
(Edward P Harty, Ire) *mid-div: 10th 1/2-way: rdn and no ex over 2f out: kpt on one pce* **12/1**

10 *2 1/2* **Jeannie Galloway (IRE)**[17] 3947 3-8-8 83 .... MCHussey 10 55
(R A Fahey) *chsd ldrs: 5th 1/2-way: rdn in 8th 2f out: no ex ent st: kpt on one pce* **8/1**

11 *shd* **Mean Lae (IRE)**[29] 3570 4-9-2 84 .... KJManning 14 59
(J S Bolger, Ire) *chsd ldr: 2nd 1/2-way: rdn in 3rd 2f out: no ex in 5th ent st: wknd 1f out* **20/1**

12 *1 1/2* **Intapeace (IRE)**[24] 3742 3-8-10 92 ....(p) LFRoche(7) 5 60
(Francis Ennis, Ire) *mid-div early: 6th 1/2-way: rdn in 8th ent st: no ex* **16/1**

13 *nk* **Dametime (IRE)**[55] 2696 4-8-10 78 .... WMLordan 9 48
(Daniel Mark Loughnane, Ire) *mid-div best: rdn and no ex 3f out* **25/1**

14 *1* **Miranda's Girl (IRE)**[12] 4159 5-9-3 85 ....(p) RPCleary 8 53
(Thomas Cleary, Ire) *chsd ldrs: 7th 1/2-way: rdn and no ex over 2f out: wknd* **10/1**

15 *10* **Blaze Brightly (IRE)**[22] 3800 3-8-7 85 .... ShaneFoley(3) 3 23
(Mrs John Harrington, Ire) *mid-div: 9th 1/2-way: rdn and wknd over 2f out* **14/1**

1m 27.91s (-3.69)
WFA 3 from 4yo+ 7lb **15** Ran SP% **141.1**
CSF £33.84 CT £388.30 TOTE £3.60: £1.50, £5.10, £18.70; DF 57.10.
Owner J P Dunne **Bred** Rathbarry Stud **Trained** Curragh, Co Kildare

FOCUS
The winner and second were always well placed from good draws, but they are both lightly raced and a chance is taken that they recorded personal bests, with the third rated to her previous run.

NOTEBOOK
Smart Striking(USA) ◆, whose ability to handle this track was unknown, was running in her first handicap and this was a very good performance. Ben Curtis made good use of her good draw, tracking the pace, and despite her just getting outpaced for a stride or two, she was soon on an even keel. She just got slightly unbalanced entering the straight but once Curtis straightened her up she really came home strongly and always looked as though she was going to get up. She's improving, should get a mile and this experience will stand her in very good stead. (op 9/2)
Anam Chara(IRE) responded well in the straight when challenged but was just worn down by a better filly. Conditions were in her favour on this day and it almost paid off. (op 12/1)
Kardyls Hope(IRE) was never that far from the pace and did keep on pretty well although she wasn't quite good enough to make an impression on the first two.
Miss Eze was very slowly away and was poorly drawn anyway, so had a double handicap to contend with. She couldn't get into the race due to that but was very much doing her best work at the finish.
Hallie's Comet(IRE) closed up from mid-division entering the straight and had a chance if good enough but her effort flattened out up the hill. (op 13/2)
July Days(IRE) was saddled with the worst possible draw and in the circumstances did well to stay on from off the pace to be never nearer. (op 16/1 tchd 14/1)
Tellelle(IRE) was bang there most of the way but just ran out of steam inside the last. (op 8/1)
Jeannie Galloway(IRE) would have found this ground plenty quick enough and was ultimately well below par. (op 7/1)

4525 - (Foreign Racing) - See Raceform Interactive

2195 OVREVOLL (R-H)
Thursday, July 29

OFFICIAL GOING: Turf: heavy

4526a POLAR CUP (GROUP 3) (3YO+) (TURF) 6f 187y
7:20 (12:00) 3-Y-O+ **£32,085** (£10,695; £5,347; £3,208; £2,139)

RPR

1 **Alyshakeys (DEN)**[109] 1250 3-8-7 0 .... ManuelSantos 5 —
(Wido Neuroth, Norway) *broke wl: chsd ldr: rdn 2 1/2f out and qckned wl and sn in command: won easing down* **73/10**

2 *1/2* **Heureux (USA)**[21] 7-9-4 0 .... CarlosLopez 2 —
(Jens Erik Lindstol, Norway) *racd in 3rd: wnt 2nd 2 1/2f out: r.o wl: no ch w wnr* **58/10**[2]

3 *1/2* **Indomito (GER)**[26] 3704 4-9-4 0 .... AStarke 10 —
(P Vovcenko, Germany) *hld up in rr: hdwy 2f out: fin wl to take 3rd cl home* **125/10**

4 *nk* **Hansinger (IRE)**[42] 5-9-4 0 .... LennartHammer-Hansen 13 —
(Cathrine Erichsen, Norway) *chsd ldrs: no ex fnl f* **81/10**

5 *2 1/2* **Steve's Champ (CHI)**[42] 10-9-4 0 ....(b) EspenSki 3 —
(Rune Haugen, Norway) *led til hdd 2 1/2f out: wknd fnl f* **7/1**

6 *hd* **Emil (DEN)**[42] 6-9-4 0 .... KimAndersen 9 —
(Ole Larsen, Sweden) *racd in midfield: unable qck fnl 2f* **96/10**

7 *3 1/2* **Fair Flair (IRE)**[42] 6-9-0 0 ....(b) ShaneKarlsson 8 —
(Pal Jorgen Nordbye, Norway) *n.d* **215/10**

8 *1/2* **Chicken Momo**[42] 4-9-8 0 .... PascolinaPinto 7 —
(Arnfinn Lund, Norway) *chsd ldrs: wknd fnl 2f* **16/5**[1]

9 *1/2* **Exhibition (IRE)**[58] 5-9-4 0 .... RafaelSchistl 6 —
(Francisco Castro, Sweden) *nvr in contention* **7/1**

10 *5* **Smokey Storm**[17] 4-9-4 0 ....(b) JacobJohansen 11 —
(Bent Olsen, Denmark) *a bhd* **222/10**

11 *24* **Cadeau For Maggi**[13] 4122 5-9-4 0 .... FabriceVeron 12 —
(H-A Pantall, France) *nvr out of last three: seemed ill at ease on trck: eased* **32/5**[3]

1m 24.4s (84.40)
WFA 3 from 4yo+ 7lb **11** Ran SP% **125.7**
PARI-MUTUEL (all including 1 krone stakes): WIN 8.34; PLACE 2.84, 3.50, 5.29; DF 76.34.
Owner Stall Trick Or Treat **Bred** I D & H Seerup **Trained** Norway

4277 BATH (L-H)
Friday, July 30

OFFICIAL GOING: Firm
Wind: Moderate across Weather: low cloud but warm

4528 BLACKTHORN MAIDEN AUCTION STKS 5f 161y
5:30 (5:36) (Class 5) 2-Y-O **£3,238** (£963; £481; £240) **Stalls** Centre

Form RPR

1 **Try The Chance** 2-8-13 0 .... SaleemGolam 4 69+
(M R Channon) *s.i.s: sn trcking ldrs: wnt 2nd fnl f: edgd rt: drvn and narrow ld fnl 50yds: rdn and hung rt last strides* **11/4**[2]

00 **2** *shd* **Indian Shuffle (IRE)**[24] 3767 2-8-11 0 .... TonyCulhane 2 67
(J G Portman) *led tl narrowly hdd 3f out: styd chalng and led again over 2f out: kpt slt advantage tl narrowly hdd u.p fnl 50yds and pushed rt: hld whn carried rt last strides* **7/1**[3]

00 **3** *4* **Ignore The Advice (IRE)**[7] 4323 2-8-9 0 .... JamesDoyle 6 52
(J S Moore) *unruly stalls: sn chsng ldrs: chal over 2f out tl wknd into 3rd fnl f* **14/1**

02 **4** *2* **Summer Jasmine**[7] 4323 2-8-6 0 .... FrankieMcDonald 1 42
(H J L Dunlop) *w ldr tl slt advantage 3f out tl hdd over 2f out: sn rdn: wknd qckly fnl f* **9/4**[1]

5 **5** *4 1/2* **Onlyfoalsandhorses (IRE)**[6] 4363 2-7-11 0 .... RyanPowell(7) 3 25
(J S Moore) *s.i.s: sn rcvrd and chsd ldrs on ins 3f out: wknd ins fnl 2f* **9/4**[1]

1m 11.53s (0.33) **Going Correction** -0.275s/f (Firm) **5** Ran SP% **107.4**
Speed ratings (Par 94): **86,85,80,77,71**
CSF £19.36 TOTE £3.20: £1.10, £3.80; EX 13.80.
Owner Jaber Abdullah **Bred** Ms Jon Horley & C A Vanner **Trained** West Ilsley, Berks

FOCUS
Firm ground and small fields (barring the last) were the theme for the evening. This was a weak race but the winner can improve on the bare form.

NOTEBOOK
Try The Chance, despite being very slowly away from the stalls and looking very green through the first half of the race, proved good enough to make a winning debut. The first foal of an unraced dam related to plenty of winners (most over slightly further), Mick Channon's colt really got the hang of things once switched to the inside, and he picked up strongly to overhaul Indian Shuffle and just hold on. The form isn't strong but Try The Chance is entitled to come on plenty for this, he looks sure to improve for a step up in trip, and the handicapper can hardly go overboard given the margin of victory, so he's got to be of interest in nurseries. (op 5-2 tchd 3-1)
Indian Shuffle(IRE), who showed good speed from the gate and kept battling away, proved suited by the drop back to this trip. He's qualified for nurseries now where he can make his mark. (op 8-1 tchd 9-1)
Ignore The Advice(IRE), also having his third start, showed speed before being left behind by the front two. He looks an out and out sprinter but is clearly only modest. (op 16-1)
Summer Jasmine was disappointing but she was dropping back in trip on the fastest ground she had encountered, so looks to have found these conditions too quick. A step back up in trip beckons. (op 2-1 tchd 15-8)

Onlyfoalsandhorses(IRE) was left behind at the business end and was very disappointing. (op 5-2)

4529 GRANGE JAGUAR SWINDON H'CAP — 5f 161y
6:05 (6:06) (Class 5) (0-75,73) 3-Y-O — **£3,238** (£963; £481; £240) **Stalls** Centre

Form — RPR

0010 **1** **Panpiper**[13] 4130 3-8-12 **64** .... TomMcLaughlin 2 — 73
(G L Moore) *mde all: hrd drvn fr over 1f out: hld on wl u.p* **9/2**[3]

1321 **2** *1 ¼* **Grand Zafeen**[8] 4297 3-9-0 **73** .... AmyScott(7) 8 — 78
(M R Channon) *s.i.s and lost 5 l s: sn in tch hdwy and swtchd rt wl over 1f out: swtchd lft and chsd wnr appr fnl f: shkn up and kpt on but a hld* **7/4**[1]

2000 **3** *5* **Candyfloss Girl**[22] 3830 3-9-4 **70** .... ShaneKelly 5 — 58
(H J L Dunlop) *sn chsng wnr: rdn 2f out: lost 2nd appr fnl f and sn wknd* **14/1**

3203 **4** *¾* **Bathwick Xaara**[10] 4234 3-8-6 **58** .... SaleemGolam 4 — 44
(J G Portman) *in tch: drvn and sme prog whn nt clr run wl over 1f out: nvr any ch after* **3/1**[2]

0320 **5** *nk* **Poppy Golightly**[21] 3866 3-9-3 **69** .... TravisBlock 3 — 54
(R J Hodges) *chsd ldrs tl wknd over 1f out* **10/1**

4-04 **6** *13* **Going French (IRE)**[8] 4284 3-9-4 **70** .... SimonWhitworth 6 — 12
(F J Brennan) *in tch: rdn on outside to chse ldrs over 2f out: sn wknd* **8/1**

5300 **7** *3 ½* **Great Intrigue (IRE)**[22] 3816 3-9-0 **66** ....(b[1]) JamesDoyle 1 — —
(J S Moore) *chsd ldrs tl wknd qckly over 2f out* **16/1**

1m 10.59s (-0.61) **Going Correction** -0.275s/f (Firm) — **7** Ran SP% **112.3**
Speed ratings (Par 100): **93,91,84,83,83 65,61**
toteswingers:1&2:£2.00, 1&3:£2.90, 2&3:£14.00 CSF £12.34 CT £97.76 TOTE £3.70: £1.20, £2.30; EX 9.70.
Owner Pillar To Post Racing (IV) **Bred** Pillar To Post Racing **Trained** Lower Beeding, W Sussex

FOCUS
A run-of-the-mill sprint handicap and the two horses with a confirmed liking for quick ground dominated, coming clear. Ordinary form.

4530 GAYMERS ORIGINAL H'CAP — 2m 1f 34y
6:35 (6:35) (Class 5) (0-75,75) 4-Y-O+ — **£3,238** (£963; £481; £240) **Stalls** Centre

Form — RPR

/543 **1** **Mutadarrej (IRE)**[10] 4223 6-7-9 **56** oh3 .... RyanPowell(7) 3 — 66
(Ian Williams) *in rr but wl in tch: hdwy on ins to dispute 2nd 6f out: drvn to ld over 2f out: sn hung rt then veered bdly rt whn clr fr over 1f out: rdn ins fnl f but in n.d* **2/1**[2]

-001 **2** *6* **Perception (IRE)**[15] 4042 4-9-0 **68** .... SebSanders 5 — 71
(A King) *chsd ldr after 7f: disp 2nd fr 6f out tl rdn to ld 3f out: hdd over 2f out: sn no ch w wnr wl over 1f out but styd on for 2nd ins fnl f* **15/8**[1]

231- **3** *1* **Count Of Tuscany (USA)**[282] 6941 4-9-7 **75** .... ShaneKelly 2 — 77
(C R Egerton) *led tl hdd 3f out: no ch w wnr sn after but kpt on to try and press for 2nd ins fnl f* **4/1**[3]

4306 **4** *8* **Wightgold**[36] 3348 4-8-2 **56** oh2 .... FrankieMcDonald 4 — 50
(H J L Dunlop) *in rr but in tch: hdwy and wd bnd ins fnl 5f: wknd over 2f out* **5/1**

0556 **5** *26* **Robbmaa (FR)**[10] 3848 5-7-11 **56** oh11 ....(b) SophieDoyle(5) 1 — —
(A W Carroll) *t.k.h: chsd ldrs tl wknd qckly over 3f out* **16/1**

3m 44.74s (-7.16) **Going Correction** -0.275s/f (Firm) — **5** Ran SP% **110.7**
Speed ratings (Par 103): **105,102,101,97,85**
CSF £6.20 TOTE £3.20: £3.00, £2.20; EX 7.40.
Owner Jarlath McDonagh **Bred** Shadwell Estate Company Limited **Trained** Portway, Worcs

FOCUS
The market suggested a bold showing from the winner, who is rated to last year's Irish best. Weak form.
Wightgold Official explanation: jockey said filly ran too free; vet said filly returned lame
Robbmaa(FR) Official explanation: jockey said gelding was unsuited by the firm ground

4531 PARKGARDENCENTRES.CO.UK H'CAP — 5f 11y
7:10 (7:10) (Class 5) (0-75,76) 3-Y-O — **£3,238** (£963; £481; £240) **Stalls** Centre

Form — RPR

2422 **1** **Admirable Duchess**[18] 3952 3-8-13 **67** .... JamesDoyle 5 — 76
(D J S Ffrench Davis) *mde all: jnd and rdn over 1f out: styd on gamely u.p ins fnl f* **8/1**[3]

01-3 **2** *½* **Hot Pursuits**[96] 1546 3-9-5 **73** .... SteveDrowne 2 — 80
(H Morrison) *trckd ldrs: wnt 2nd 3f out: drvn to chal fr over 1f out: no ex u.p thrght fnl f* **4/1**[2]

3011 **3** *1 ¾* **Lutine Bell**[8] 4284 3-9-8 **76** 6ex ....(b) SebSanders 4 — 77
(Sir Mark Prescott) *s.i.s as blindfold removed: drvn and qcknd over 2f out to chal over 1f out: no ex ins fnl f and wknd fnl 100yds* **2/5**[1]

1-00 **4** *6* **Chat De La Burg (USA)**[23] 3779 3-9-0 **75** .... RyanPowell(7) 1 — 54
(J R Best) *chsd wnr to 3f out: sn rdn: wknd ins fnl 2f* **14/1**

61.03 secs (-1.47) **Going Correction** -0.275s/f (Firm) — **4** Ran SP% **109.2**
Speed ratings (Par 100): **100,99,96,86**
CSF £34.95 TOTE £7.50; EX 21.30.
Owner Brian W Taylor **Bred** Whitsbury Manor Stud & Pigeon House Stud **Trained** Lambourn, Berks

FOCUS
There was a bit of a turn-up here. Weakish form, rated around the front pair.

4532 IPS PARTNERSHIP H'CAP — 1m 2f 46y
7:40 (7:40) (Class 4) (0-80,77) 3-Y-O — **£5,180** (£1,541; £770; £384) **Stalls** Low

Form — RPR

2-52 **1** **Nave (USA)**[7] 4341 3-9-2 **72** .... GregFairley 1 — 85
(M Johnston) *chsd ldrs tl lost position 6f out: awkward bnd ins fnl 5f: rdn over 3f out and styd on to press ldrs over 2f out: led appr fnl f: styd on gamely* **10/3**[2]

-123 **2** *1* **Park View**[21] 3878 3-9-6 **76** .... SteveDrowne 3 — 87
(B W Hills) *led tl hdd 7f out: styd w ldr and awkward bnd ins fnl 5f: chal ins fnl 3f: narrow advantage ins fnl 2f: hdd appr fnl f: one pce u.p* **7/2**[3]

4212 **3** *3* **Sumerian**[8] 4302 3-9-7 **77** .... SebSanders 5 — 82
(Sir Mark Prescott) *stdd in rr: clsd on ldrs 6f out: awkward bnd ins fnl 5f: rdn to press ldrs over 2f out: wknd fnl f* **11/10**[1]

0612 **4** *hd* **Scottish Boogie (IRE)**[13] 4127 3-8-8 **71** .... AdamBeschizza(7) 2 — 76
(S Kirk) *t.k.h: chsd ldr tl led 7f out: awkward bnd ins fnl 5f: rdn and narrowly hdd ins fnl 2f: wknd fnl f* **9/1**

5353 **5** *9* **Whiepa Snappa (IRE)**[26] 3714 3-7-13 **62** .... RyanPowell(7) 4 — 49
(P M Phelan) *in rr tl hdwy and awkward bnd ins fnl 5f: rdn 3f out: wknd qckly 2f out* **8/1**

2m 7.81s (-3.19) **Going Correction** -0.275s/f (Firm) — **5** Ran SP% **114.0**
Speed ratings (Par 102): **101,100,97,97,90**
CSF £15.58 TOTE £5.00: £3.70, £1.10; EX 10.90.
Owner Anthony Hogarth **Bred** Mineola Farm II Llc Et Al **Trained** Middleham Moor, N Yorks

FOCUS
They went hard early on, but the pace collapsed mid-race and the field suddenly found themselves on top of one another. The overall pace was good. The winner improved by a length on his Thirsk form.
Scottish Boogie(IRE) Official explanation: jockey said colt was unsuited by the firm ground

4533 GAYMERS PEAR FILLIES' H'CAP — 1m 5y
8:15 (8:15) (Class 4) (0-80,78) 3-Y-O+ — **£5,180** (£1,541; £770; £384) **Stalls** Low

Form — RPR

1262 **1** **Night Lily (IRE)**[22] 3830 4-9-13 **78** .... TonyCulhane 3 — 85
(P W D'Arcy) *trckd ldr: slt ld ins fnl 2f: sn jnd: rdn appr fnl f: styd on strly and asserted fnl 100yds: readily* **13/8**[1]

6114 **2** *1* **Dr Wintringham (IRE)**[22] 3830 4-9-11 **76** .... JerryO'Dwyer 2 — 81
(Karen George) *trckd ldrs in 3rd: hdwy to press ldrs 2f out and jnd wnr sn after but u.p: styd on terms tl no ex ins fnl f: outpcd fnl 100yds* **6/1**

1012 **3** *3 ¼* **Jewelled**[15] 4044 4-9-9 **74** ....(v) SebSanders 4 — 71
(J W Hills) *hld up in 3rd: rdn and hdwy to chse ldrs 2f out: no imp over 1f out: wknd ins fnl f* **15/8**[2]

0-12 **4** *2 ½* **Cotswold Village (AUS)**[21] 3853 4-9-7 **72** .... NeilChalmers 5 — 63
(M Appleby) *led: t.k.h: rdn and hdd ins fnl 2f: wknd over 1f out* **4/1**[3]

1m 39.32s (-1.48) **Going Correction** -0.275s/f (Firm)
WFA 3 from 4yo 8lb — **4** Ran SP% **107.2**
Speed ratings (Par 102): **96,95,91,89**
CSF £10.39 TOTE £2.60; EX 11.90.
Owner K Snell **Bred** Keith Wills **Trained** Newmarket, Suffolk

FOCUS
Only four runners but all of them came into this in good form and the pace was a decent one. The front pair are rated close to their best.

4534 PARK GARDEN CENTRES ALMONDSBURY H'CAP — 1m 5y
8:45 (8:51) (Class 6) (0-60,61) 3-Y-O — **£2,590** (£770; £385; £192) **Stalls** Low

Form — RPR

0-05 **1** **Gee Major**[8] 4280 3-8-5 **45** .... NeilChalmers 8 — 47
(N J Vaughan) *trckd ldr: rdn to chal fr over 2f out: upsides thrght fnl f: led last stride* **33/1**

-501 **2** *shd* **Lady Of Garmoran (USA)**[8] 4280 3-9-2 **56** 6ex ....(b) SebSanders 6 — 57
(P F I Cole) *led: rdn and jnd fr over 2f out: kpt on slt advantage ins fnl f tl hdd last stride* **9/2**[3]

6006 **3** *½* **Take My Hand**[8] 4280 3-9-4 **58** .... TonyCulhane 2 — 58
(M R Channon) *in tch: rdn and one pce 3f out: styd on strly fnl f: gaining on ldng duo cl home to take 3rd* **9/1**

0331 **4** *hd* **Regal Rave (USA)**[8] 4281 3-9-7 **61** 6ex .... RobertWinston 9 — 61
(J R Best) *chsd ldrs in 3rd fr 6f out: rdn 3f out and one pce: styd on ins fnl f and gng on cl home but jst lost 3rd last strides* **7/2**[1]

-664 **5** *¾* **Satin Princess (IRE)**[8] 4280 3-8-5 **45** .... FrankieMcDonald 7 — 43+
(A M Hales) *stdd s: plld hrd in rr: pushed along and hdwy over 2f out: swtchd rt to outside and r.o fr over 1f out: gng on cl home* **16/1**

0001 **6** *½* **Angelena Ballerina (IRE)**[9] 4249 3-9-0 **61** 6ex...(v) AdamBeschizza(7) 3 — 58
(Karen George) *mid-div: rdn and hdwy over 2f out: styd on same pce ins fnl f* **9/1**

4404 **7** *2 ¾* **King's Approach (IRE)**[8] 4300 3-9-4 **58** ....(p) TomMcLaughlin 10 — 49
(R A Harris) *chsd ldrs: awkward bnd ins fnl 5f: rdn over 2f out: wknd ins fnl f* **14/1**

4032 **8** *3 ¼* **Motty's Gift**[17] 3982 3-9-3 **57** ....(v) ShaneKelly 11 — 40
(W R Swinburn) *chsd ldrs: rdn 3f out: wknd 2f out* **4/1**[2]

06-3 **9** *1 ½* **Farmers Dream (IRE)**[8] 4280 3-8-10 **53** .... JackDean(3) 5 — 33
(J L Spearing) *in rr: awkward bnd ins fnl 5f: rdn 3f out and no imp on ldrs* **7/2**[1]

00-0 **10** *8* **Khazara**[47] 2998 3-8-5 **45** .... SaleemGolam 12 — 6
(P D Evans) *broke wl: plld hrd and stdd in rr: rdn 3f out and nvr in contention* **40/1**

-000 **11** *1 ¼* **Silk Runner (IRE)**[13] 4127 3-8-10 **50** ....(tp) SteveDrowne 4 — 8
(J W Hills) *in rr: awkward bnd ins fnl 5f: nvr in contention* **25/1**

1m 41.52s (0.72) **Going Correction** -0.275s/f (Firm) — **11** Ran SP% **124.4**
Speed ratings (Par 98): **85,84,84,84,83 82,80,76,75,67 66**
toteswingers:1&2:Not won, 1&3:£23.40, 2&3:£7.20 CSF £183.91 CT £1526.99 TOTE £61.60: £12.00, £1.90, £4.00; EX 358.60 Place 6 £389.29, Place 5 £114.23.
Owner David Sykes **Bred** D Sykes **Trained** Helshaw Grange, Shropshire

FOCUS
The pace held up well here as the first two, who didn't hang about out in front, were still ahead at the finish, albeit with a diminishing lead. Weak form, the winer reversing recent course form with the runner-up.
Gee Major Official explanation: trainer said, regarding apparent improvement in form, it was the gelding's third run for the stable, having been immature and the penny finally dropped.
T/Plt: £407.70 to a £1 stake. Pool:£39,183.99 - 70.15 winning tickets T/Qpdt: £47.10 to a £1 stake. Pool:£5,433.77 - 85.32 winning tickets ST

4504 GOODWOOD (R-H)
Friday, July 30

OFFICIAL GOING: Straight: good (good to firm in places); round course: good to firm (stands' side 7.9, centre 7.9, far side 8.1, round 9.0)
Fresh ground on lower bend and top bend dolled out 3yds.
Wind: medium, half against Weather: mainly overcast, brighter patches

4535 COUTTS GLORIOUS STKS (GROUP 3) — 1m 4f
2:10 (2:10) (Class 1) 4-Y-O+
£39,739 (£15,064; £7,539; £3,759; £1,883; £945) **Stalls** Low

Form — RPR

2052 **1** **Redwood**[22] 3825 4-9-0 **113** .... MichaelHills 1 — 117
(B W Hills) *stdd s: hld up in last trio: hdwy on outer over 2f out: shkn up and hung rt wl over 1f out: kpt edging rt but rdn to chal 1f out: led ins fnl f: r.o wl: rdn out* **7/1**[3]

-102 **2** *1 ½* **Sri Putra**[27] 3693 4-9-3 **117** .... PhilipRobinson 3 — 118
(M A Jarvis) *lw: hld up in midfield: rdn and effrt on outer ent fnl 2f: led over 1f out: hrd pressed 1f out: edgd rt u.p and hdd ins fnl f: nt pce of wnr fnl 100yds: kpt on* **5/1**[2]

4503 **3** *1 ¾* **Traffic Guard (USA)**[28] 3632 6-9-0 **105** .... TomQueally 10 — 112+
(P F I Cole) *stdd s: hld up in rr: clsd and wl in tch and gng wl whn nt clr run jst over 2f out: hmpd and swtchd lft wl over 1f out: r.o u.p to go 3rd ins fnl f: no threat to ldng pair* **16/1**

3-22 **4** 2 ¼ **Duncan**[41] 3191 5-9-0 116 .... WilliamBuick 5 111+
(J H M Gosden) *t.k.h: hld up in tch: hdwy to press ldrs over 2f out: rdn and nt qckning whn squeezed out and bdly hmpd wl over 1f out: no threat to ldrs after: plugged on fnl f* **5/4**[1]

3-25 **5** nk **Manighar (FR)**[27] 3695 4-9-0 114 .... KierenFallon 7 108
(L M Cumani) *in tch in midfield: hdwy ent fnl 3f: rdn to ld 2f out: sn hdd: fdd tamely u.p ent fnl f* **15/2**

0535 **6** 3 ¼ **Kingdom Of Fife**[13] 4139 5-9-0 112 .... (v) RyanMoore 2 103
(Sir Michael Stoute) *racd keenly: chsd ldr: rdn and ev ch ent fnl 2f: drvn and btn jst over 1f out: wknd fnl f* **9/1**

-142 **7** 1 ¼ **Whispering Gallery**[34] 3454 4-9-0 107 .... FrankieDettori 8 101
(Saeed Bin Suroor) *lw: led: stdd gallop after 2f: rdn and qcknd ent fnl 3f: hdd 2f out: wknd qckly over 1f out: wl btn fnl f* **12/1**

-030 **8** 2 **Golden Sword**[125] 1026 4-9-0 111 .... ShaneKelly 6 98
(Jane Chapple-Hyam) *swtg: chsd ldrs: rdn and unable qck ent fnl 3f: lost pl and bhd whn n.m.r ent fnl 2f: sn wknd: wl bhd fnl f* **33/1**

2m 33.86s (-4.54) **Going Correction** -0.05s/f (Good) **8** Ran SP% **111.9**
Speed ratings (Par 113): **113,112,110,109,109 106,106,104**
toteswingers:1&2:£5.80, 1&3:£15.00, 2&3:£9.20 CSF £39.88 TOTE £8.30: £1.70, £1.90, £5.60; EX 40.60 Trifecta £873.30 Pool: £9,583.10 - 8.12 winning units..
Owner K Abdulla **Bred** Juddmonte Farms Ltd **Trained** Lambourn, Berks

FOCUS
There was 8mm of water applied to the straight track overnight and the going remained good, good to firm. The Goingstick readings suggested the far side was marginally quicker (8.1), compared with the stands' side and centre (7.9). There was also fresh ground on the far side from the 6f to the 3f marker. It was slightly quicker on the round course, though, being good to firm all over with a Goingstick reading of 9.0. Two significant non-runners here in the shape of Cavalryman and La De Two, but it still looked a decent enough race for the grade. The pace was just a steady one, but despite this the time was good. The winner recorded a slight personal best with the runner-up rated to his Eclipse mark.

NOTEBOOK
Redwood, along with the favourite, was bidding to enhance the Hardwicke form further, but as a surprise to many it was the latter who came out on top. His latest second in the Group 2 Princess Of Wales's Stakes at Newmarket arguably represented a career-best and, despite being last and niggled racing past the 3f marker here, he picked up strongly in the final quarter mile, challenging widest of all. He has always looked a horse of quality and is now beginning to fulfil his potential, with connections mulling races such as the Bosphorus Cup in Turkey and Canadian International as possible long-term aims. (op 8-1)
Sri Putra, for all that he ran a blinder when second at 33-1 in the Eclipse, looked vulnerable under a 3lb penalty, but he ran a pleasing race. Stepping up 2f, he took over approaching the final furlong but soon became a sitting duck for the winner and he couldn't stay on quite as well. He appeared to get the trip, for all that this wasn't a thorough test, but the penalty will continue to make things tricky at this level. The Grand Prix de Deauville was nominated as a possible aim. (tchd 11-2 in places)
Traffic Guard(USA) is an honest sort who runs his race more often than not. He was unlucky not to finish a length or two closer as, having travelled strongly, he was twice impeded by the winner inside the final 2f, in the end running on well once the race was over. He deserves to win again. (op 22-1)
Duncan, the Hardwicke runner-up, was particularly disappointing. He looked the standout pick on his Ascot effort, having put distance between himself and the remainder, who included Redwood, but he was a little keen and probably came through to challenge too soon, just starting to look in trouble when being squeezed out inside the final 2f. He did stay on for fourth, but doesn't win as often as his ability entitles him to, and as he's already twice shown this season, isn't one to be taking a short price about. (op 6-5, tchd 11-8 in places)
Manighar(FR), an odds-on flop over 2m at Sandown latest, was stoked up a fair way from home and came through to lead over 2f out, so to see him fade so meekly was rather disappointing, considering he has proven stamina over further. The ground may still have been lively enough for him, though. (op 7-1)
Kingdom Of Fife probably doesn't warrant his rating of 112, and he was comfortably held on this return to 1m4f. (tchd 8-1 and 10-1 in a place)
Whispering Gallery should have put up more of a fight considering he had the run of things. (op 16-1)
Golden Sword, last year's Derby runner-up, ran a stinker when last seen in Dubai, and he offered little promise for the future on this first start for a new yard. (op 28-1)

4536 ROLF GROUP STEWARDS' SPRINT (H'CAP) 6f
2:45 (2:46) (Class 2) 3-Y-O+

£18,693 (£5,598; £2,799; £1,401; £699; £351) **Stalls** Low

Form RPR

3435 **1** **Joseph Henry**[34] 3446 8-9-1 **84** .... DavidProbert 14 94
(D Nicholls) *racd in centre: led that gp and chsd ldrs overall: rdn over 1f out: drvn and kpt on wl fnl f: led fnl 75yds: hld on wl* **28/1**

6-11 **2** hd **Victoire De Lyphar (IRE)**[48] 2978 3-9-9 **97** .... AdrianNicholls 18 105
(D Nicholls) *taken down early: racd on far side: chsd ldrs and prom overall: rdn wl over 1f out: ev ch ins fnl f: kpt on wl: jst hld cl home: 1st of 13 in gp* **13/2**[1]

2300 **3** 1 ¼ **Wildcat Wizard (USA)**[21] 3850 4-9-10 **93** .... RichardHughes 20 98+
(P F I Cole) *racd on far side: s.i.s: hld up wl bhd: hdwy over 1f out: stl plenty to do whn nt clr run and swtchd lft jst ins fnl f: r.o strly to snatch 3rd on post: nt rch ldrs: 2nd of 13 in gp* **25/1**

1304 **4** nse **Tiddliwinks**[6] 4391 4-9-10 **93** .... NeilCallan 1 98+
(K A Ryan) *lw: racd in stands' side pair: dwlt: towards rr overall: swtchd rt to join centre gp but stl only midfield 1/2-way: hdwy and rdn 2f out: drvn and chsng ldrs 1f out: styd on u.p: 2nd of 13 in gp* **10/1**[3]

1503 **5** nk **Crimea (IRE)**[1] 4510 4-9-0 **83** 3ex .... AlanMunro 22 87
(D Nicholls) *racd on far side: overall ldr: rdn over 1f out: drvn ins fnl f: hdd fnl 75yds: wknd towards fin: 3rd of 13 in gp* **33/1**

2021 **6** hd **Five Star Junior (USA)**[13] 4148 4-9-11 **94** 3ex .... TomEaves 17 97
(Mrs L Stubbs) *swtg: racd on far side: hld up in rr: nt clr run wl over 1f out tl swtchd lft 1f out: r.o wl u.p fnl f: nt rch ldrs: 4th of 13 in gp* **33/1**

-202 **7** ½ **Bagamoyo**[23] 3791 3-9-8 **96** .... EddieAhern 16 97
(J R Fanshawe) *racd on far side: in tch: rdn and effrt 2f out: drvn and kpt on same pce ent fnl f: 5th of 13 in gp* **13/2**[1]

3001 **8** 1 **Olynard (IRE)**[21] 3850 4-9-9 **92** 3ex .... JimCrowley 7 91
(R M Beckett) *racd in centre: s.i.s: bhd: rdn and hdwy but edging rt over 1f out: swtchd lft ins fnl f: styd on wl fnl 100yds: nvr threatened ldrs: 3rd of 13 in gp* **20/1**

04U0 **9** ½ **Sea Of Leaves (USA)**[6] 4391 4-9-9 **92** .... KierenFallon 9 89
(J S Goldie) *racd in centre: off the pce in midfield: rdn and effrt wl over 1f out: hdwy u.p ins fnl f: kpt on but nvr quite gng pce to rch ldrs: 4th of 13 in gp* **25/1**

5033 **10** hd **King's Wonder**[21] 3845 5-9-0 **86** .... MichaelGeran(3) 23 82
(D Nicholls) *b: taken down early: racd far side: in tch and gng wl: n.m.r ent fnl 2f: rdn and unable qck over 1f out: one pce ins fnl f: 6th of 13 in gp* **14/1**

0-04 **11** shd **Aye Aye Digby (IRE)**[29] 3578 5-9-7 **90** .... PatCosgrave 27 86
(J R Boyle) *racd on far side: chsd ldrs: rdn and effrt 2f out: drvn and no ex ent fnl f: wknd fnl 100yds: 7th of 13 in gp* **20/1**

1002 **12** ¾ **Ghostwing**[10] 4231 3-9-2 **90** .... HayleyTurner 25 83
(J Gallagher) *racd on far side: hld up in tch in midfield: switching rt and effrt wl over 1f out: styd on same pce ins fnl f: 8th of 13 in gp* **28/1**

0401 **13** ½ **Hamoody (USA)**[1] 4510 6-9-2 **85** 3ex .... NeilChalmers 26 77
(D Nicholls) *lw: racd on far side: chsd ldrs: rdn ent fnl 2f: wknd u.p ins fnl f: 9th of 13 in gp* **20/1**

1400 **14** shd **Kerrys Requiem (IRE)**[13] 4145 4-9-5 **88** .... RyanMoore 3 80
(M R Channon) *racd in centre: s.i.s: wl bhd: rdn and looking for run wl over 1f out: styd on ins fnl f: nvr trbld ldrs: 5th of 13 in gp* **33/1**

0400 **15** hd **Sunrise Safari (IRE)**[5] 4413 7-9-1 **84** .... (v) RoystonFfrench 13 75
(R A Fahey) *taken down early: racd in centre: towards rr: rdn and effrt 2f out: sn hung rt and barging match w rival wl over 1f out: kpt on but nvr trbld ldrs: 6th of 13 in gp* **50/1**

1203 **16** ½ **Red Cape (FR)**[12] 4171 7-8-13 **82** .... PaulHanagan 10 71
(Mrs R A Carr) *racd in centre: chsd ldrs: rdn jst over 2f out: wknd u.p ent fnl f: 7th of 13 in gp* **20/1**

0006 **17** nse **Mac Gille Eoin**[21] 3850 6-9-5 **91** .... MartinLane(3) 15 80
(J Gallagher) *racd in centre: w gp ldrs and prom overall tl ent fnl 2f: wknd u.p over 1f out: 8th of 13 in gp* **33/1**

1110 **18** nse **Kellys Eye (IRE)**[23] 3791 3-9-8 **96** .... RobertWinston 24 84+
(D H Brown) *racd on far side: in tch: rdn and effrt 2f out: keeping on same pce and threat to ldrs whn nt short of room and hmpd ins fnl f: 10th of 13 in gp* **12/1**

0110 **19** ½ **Lowdown (IRE)**[6] 4391 3-9-5 **93** 6ex .... JoeFanning 12 80
(M Johnston) *racd in centre: chsd gp ldrs and in tch overall: rdn and struggling ent fnl f: wl hld fnl f: 9th of 13 in gp* **8/1**[2]

110 **20** 1 **Averoo**[41] 3216 5-8-9 **78** .... (p) PhilipRobinson 28 62
(M D Squance) *racd on far side: a outpcd in rr: u.p and no hdwy 1/2-way: n.d: 11th of 13 in gp* **25/1**

2040 **21** ¾ **Pastoral Player**[23] 3791 3-9-8 **96** .... SteveDrowne 5 77
(H Morrison) *racd in centre: a towards rr: rdn and no real prog wl over 1f out: n.d: 10th of 13 in gp* **10/1**[3]

4000 **22** hd **Oldjoesaid**[14] 4085 6-9-8 **91** .... FergusSweeney 8 72
(K A Ryan) *racd in centre: towards rr: hdwy 1/2-way: struggling u.p wl over 1f out: wl btn fnl f: 11th of 13 in gp* **33/1**

1302 **23** nk **Secret Witness**[34] 3435 4-9-2 **85** .... (b) TomMcLaughlin 6 65
(R A Harris) *b.hind: racd in centre: a towards rr: rdn and effrt 1/2-way: no prog and no ch fnl f: 12th of 13 in gp* **50/1**

1005 **24** 2 **Drawnfromthepast (IRE)**[5] 4401 5-8-13 **87** .... SophieDoyle(5) 21 61
(J A Osborne) *racd on far side: in tch in midfield: rdn ent fnl 2f: wknd qckly wl over 1f out: bhd fnl f: 12th of 13 in gp* **28/1**

1000 **25** ½ **Rasaman (IRE)**[11] 4191 6-9-1 **84** .... TomQueally 19 56
(J S Goldie) *racd on far side: bhd: rdn 3f out: no real prog whn barging match w rival wl over 1f out: n.d: 13th of 13 in gp* **66/1**

0550 **26** 5 **Saucy Brown (IRE)**[20] 3919 4-9-6 **89** .... DaraghO'Donohoe 11 45
(D Nicholls) *racd in centre: chsd gp ldrs but midfield overall: wkng u.p and dropping out whn hmpd over 1f out: wl bhd and eased ins fnl f: 13th of 13 in gp* **50/1**

0422 **27** 9 **We Have A Dream**[21] 3850 5-9-5 **88** .... MartinDwyer 2 16
(W R Muir) *led stands' side pair tl lft solo fr 1/2-way: rdn and hung rt ent fnl 2f: sn bhd: eased ins fnl f* **16/1**

1m 10.79s (-1.41) **Going Correction** 0.0s/f (Good)
WFA 3 from 4yo+ 5lb **27** Ran SP% **139.2**
Speed ratings (Par 109): **109,108,107,107,106 106,105,104,103,103 103,102,101,101,101 100,100,100,99,98 97,97,96,94,93**
toteswingers:1&2:£58.30, 1&3:£506.40, 2&3:£41.90 CSF £176.14 CT £4714.54 TOTE £44.50: £8.90, £2.30, £8.20, £2.50; EX 295.00 Trifecta £3771.20 Part won. Pool: £5,096.34 - 0.01 winning units..
Owner Billy Hughes **Bred** John Brown & Megan Dennis **Trained** Sessay, N Yorks

FOCUS
This consolation race for tomorrow's Stewards' Cup was dominated by David Nicholls in the early years of this century with four winners in five years, including the three-time winner Flak Jacket. As is often the case he had multiple entries and it paid off with a one-two, although not in the order the market anticipated. The form looks straightforward rated around the third to sixth.

NOTEBOOK
Joseph Henry, runner-up to Pearly Wey in 2007 and third to the same horse in this race the following year, had not won since April 2009 but had been running creditably and deserved a change of luck. He made most in the group racing up the centre and did enough to just deny his stable companion.
Victoire De Lyphar(IRE), raised 7lb for winning hot 3-y-o handicap at York in June, was one of the first under pressure but again found plenty and was only just held. He probably needs a stiffer test at this trip and could well be given another try at 7f before long. (tchd 7-1)
Wildcat Wizard(USA) ◆ had not won since his second start back in 2008 but ran well in a couple of decent races this spring before finishing last on his two most recent starts. He looked unlucky as he had to be switched round a wall of horses over a furlong out before finishing strongest of all. If he can repeat this there is a decent sprint in him.
Tiddliwinks ◆ is a multiple winner on Polytrack but ran well in a hot sprint at York last time. He raced on the near rail early - which was not the place to be - but then switched to come more towards the centre and would have gone close had he been in that group from the start. His turn is not far away and the Portland is on the agenda. (op 12-1 tchd 9-1)
Crimea(IRE), third behind Hamoody here the previous day, is best at 5f on fast ground and that was confirmed, as he had every chance over a furlong out before fading late on. He is clearly in good heart and will be of interest back at the minimum trip.
Five Star Junior(USA) is developing into a very useful sprinter and ran with credit under top weight. He seems equally effective at five and 6f. (tchd 40-1 in place)
Bagamoyo is consistent and lightly raced and was another to run his race. His only success was on his only try on soft ground, so he is one to bear in mind for when the rains come. (op 8-1)
Olynard(IRE) was a promising sprinter last summer and bounced back in a handicap at Chepstow recently, where today's third finished last. He was another to stay on late having not got the clearest of runs and can be expected to build on this. (op 22-1)
Sea Of Leaves(USA), for whom Fallon was a significant booking, could be coming to herself now and is one to bear in mind if going to Newmarket, a course where she has run well before. (tchd 28-1)
King's Wonder, both of whose wins were at 7f, likes this track and could be of interest if returning here and stepped up in distance. (op 16-1)
Aye Aye Digby(IRE), a C&D winner last season, was 7lb higher and, after showing early pace, faded in the closing stages. (op 18-1)
Hamoody(USA) won the Richmond Stakes at this meeting in 2006 and scored narrowly here the previous day. However, on this occasion he probably saw too much daylight on the outside of his field and faded late on. (op 25-1)
Sunrise Safari(IRE) Official explanation: jockey said gelding never travelled

Kellys Eye(IRE) ◆, a three-time winner over 6f at Ripon earlier this year, was 9lb higher but was unlucky in running, being short of room when making ground in the final furlong. He is clearly still in form and looks an interesting contender for the Great St Wilfrid at the Yorkshire track in just over a fortnight. (op 16-1)
Lowdown(IRE), another C&D winner, had gone up 9lb for his last two wins but was able to race off his last winning mark as this was an early closing race. In the circumstances a better effort could have been expected. (op 11-1)
Pastoral Player was 6lb better off for 2 1/2l with today's runner-up compared with York running and he appeared to have his chance before fading. (op 11-1 tchd 12-1)
Saucy Brown(IRE) Official explanation: trainer said gelding had a breathing problem
We Have A Dream had been running well of late but he tried to race up the stands' rail from his low draw and was struggling to keep up from halfway, eventually being eased when beaten.

4537 TOTESPORT MILE (HERITAGE H'CAP) 1m
3:25 (3:25) (Class 2) 3-Y-0+

£93,465 (£27,990; £13,995; £7,005; £3,495; £1,755) **Stalls** High

Form RPR
1011 **1** **Sea Lord (IRE)**[21] 3867 3-9-3 **106** 3ex........................ RoystonFfrench 16 116
(M Johnston) *lw: mde all: kpt on extremely gamely whn pressed jst ins fnl f: drvn out* **6/1**[2]

-441 **2** 3/4 **Invisible Man**[44] 3069 4-9-6 **101**..................................(b) FrankieDettori 17 111
(Saeed Bin Suroor) *lw: mid-div: smooth hdwy on rails fr over 2f out: swtchd lft ent fnl f to chal: sn rdn: kpt on but a being hld* **8/1**[3]

0454 **3** 3 1/2 **Webbow (IRE)**[20] 3920 8-8-7 **91**...............(p) Louis-PhilippeBeuzelin(3) 21 93
(N Tinkler) *in tch: nt clr run 3f out tl ent fnl 2f: sn rdn: styd on wout rching ldng pair* **12/1**

0055 **4** 1/2 **Proponent (IRE)**[44] 3069 6-9-2 **97**.................................... WilliamBuick 9 98+
(R Charlton) *b.hind: mid-div: nt best of runs whn swtchd lft over 2f out: sn rdn: hdwy over 1f out: drifted rt: styd on* **20/1**

2326 **5** nk **Vitznau (IRE)**[56] 2708 6-9-5 **100**...................................... RichardHughes 7 100
(R Hannon) *hld up towards rr: sme hdwy into midfield over 5f out: nt clr run and lost pl whn swtchd lft over 2f out: swtchd rt and kpt on against rails fr over 1f out* **33/1**

0000 **6** 1 1/4 **Al Muheer (IRE)**[6] 4358 5-9-3 **98**................................. AdrianNicholls 20 95+
(D Nicholls) *hld up towards rr: looking for room and nt clr run fr over 2f out: kpt on whn clr run ent fnl f: nrst fin* **20/1**

2304 **7** 3/4 **Marajaa (IRE)**[21] 3869 8-9-0 **95**...................................... JamieMackay 15 91+
(W J Musson) *towards rr of midfield: nt best of runs whn swtchd rt over 2f out: kpt on ins fnl f* **14/1**

0462 **8** 3/4 **Aspectus (IRE)**[18] 3956 7-9-5 **100**............................... FergusSweeney 22 94
(J A Osborne) *lw: trckd ldrs: rdn over 2f out: kpt on same pce* **33/1**

1210 **9** 1/2 **Ransom Note**[22] 3824 3-8-11 **100**....................................... MichaelHills 5 91
(B W Hills) *mid-div: rdn 3f out: little imp* **8/1**[3]

0246 **10** 1 3/4 **Signor Peltro**[21] 3869 7-9-5 **100**... DaneO'Neill 6 89
(H Candy) *mid-div: nt clr run over 2f out: rdn whn gap appeared over 1f out: kpt on same pce* **20/1**

0156 **11** hd **Tartan Gunna**[3] 4455 4-8-11 **92**......................................(v[1]) JoeFanning 14 80
(M Johnston) *s.i.s: towards rr: rdn over 2f out: sme late prog: nvr a factor* **14/1**

0-50 **12** nk **Royal Destination (IRE)**[20] 3921 5-9-1 **96**...................... RyanMoore 10 83
(J Noseda) *rough passage whn u.p fr over 2f out: nvr bttr than mid-div* **14/1**

5101 **13** 3/4 **Oasis Dancer**[13] 4140 3-9-2 **105** 3ex................................ JimCrowley 19 89
(R M Beckett) *racd keenly: in tch: effrt 2f out: wknd ent fnl f* **5/1**[1]

-402 **14** 2 **Acrostic**[27] 3692 5-9-10 **105**... KierenFallon 11 86
(L M Cumani) *lw: s.i.s: hld up towards rr: swtchd lft then rt whn nt clr run over 2f out: sme late prog: nvr able to get on terms* **11/1**

-106 **15** 4 1/2 **Irish Heartbeat (IRE)**[14] 4085 5-8-12 **93**...................... PaulHanagan 4 64+
(R A Fahey) *in tch: nt clr run twice over fr wl over 1f out: squeezed bdly out jst over 1f out: no ch after* **33/1**

1505 **16** 4 **Beauchamp Xerxes**[34] 3455 4-9-7 **102**............................. TomQueally 2 64
(G A Butler) *mid-div: effrt on wd outside over 2f out: wknd over 1f out* **40/1**

2103 **17** 3 1/4 **Charlie Cool**[20] 3920 7-9-0 **95**...................................(b) RobertWinston 12 49
(Mrs R A Carr) *lw: trckd ldrs: rdn 3f out: wknd wl over 1f out* **25/1**

-000 **18** 2 **Spectait**[18] 3969 8-8-11 **92**...(p) SebSanders 3 42
(Jonjo O'Neill) *racd wd: mid-div: effrt over 2f out: wknd over 1f out* **33/1**

0012 **19** 6 **Mahadee (IRE)**[28] 3619 5-8-11 **95**..............................(b) MartinLane(3) 13 31
(R M Beckett) *trckd wnr: rdn over 2f out: wknd over 1f out* **25/1**

1m 37.33s (-2.57) **Going Correction** -0.05s/f (Good)
WFA 3 from 4yo+ 8lb **19** Ran SP% **125.4**
Speed ratings (Par 109): **110,109,105,105,104 103,102,102,101,99 99,99,98,96,92 88,84,82,76**
toteswingers:1&2:£4.30, 1&3:£35.30, 2&3:£24.30 CSF £46.28 CT £412.52 TOTE £7.80: £2.00, £2.10, £3.80, £4.90; EX 43.00 Trifecta £1361.60 Pool: £5,640.80 - 3.06 winning units..
Owner Sheikh Hamdan Bin Mohammed Al Maktoum **Bred** Darley **Trained** Middleham Moor, N Yorks

FOCUS
A race in which the result is traditionally affected by the draw, with the high-berthed runners often enjoying a significant advantage. That wasn't the case last year, however, with Laa Rayb (stall 8), being the first horse of the century to win from a single-figure stall. Prior to that every winner since 2000 had been drawn 16 or higher, and the common trend was upheld. The winner is worth trying in Group company and the runner-up is rated as having improved 4lb on his Hunt Cup form.

NOTEBOOK
Sea Lord(IRE) has really got it together this season, winning four of his last five prior to this, including valuable handicaps at the Curragh and Newmarket the last twice. The penalty left him well in, albeit just by 1lb, and Ffrench soon had him in front against the rail. Things didn't look so good when the runner-up was cruising in behind racing into the final 2f, but as is well documented, Mark Johnston's horses keep finding, and this one was always maintaining a comfy advantage on the run to the line. Rated 107, he will be forced into pattern-company now (holds Group 2 entries later in year) and it's not hard to see him continuing his progression. (tchd 7-1)
Invisible Man, the Hunt Cup winner, was up 6lb and again sporting the blinkers, but got a dream run round against the inner and Dettori seemed full of confidence, but the response wasn't immediate when he was asked for his effort, and in the end he couldn't stay on as well as the winner. Clear of the third, there was nothing wrong with his attitude, but he's going to be bumped up a few pounds for this, and may soon be forced into Pattern-company. (op 15-2 tchd 7-1)
Webbow(IRE) looked interesting in the cheekpieces and was drawn one away from the rail. Perfectly positioned, his rider was slow to take a gap against the rail 2f out, which ended up going to Invisible Man, but then in fairness was unable to quicken once in the open anyway. He continues to give a good account without winning. (op 14-1)
Proponent(IRE) was the first home of those with a single-figure draw, and wasn't far off Hunt Cup form with the runner-up. He was forced to challenge very wide and finished well, as was to be expected for a horse who needs an end-to-end gallop at the trip.
Vitznau(IRE) travelled well off the pace and challenged against the rail, but he never got close to the front pair and could only plug on at the one pace inside the final furlong. A mark of 100 makes life very tough indeed in handicaps.
Al Muheer(IRE) ◆ travelled strongly but had nowhere to go before switching out off the rail late on. He was running on nicely as they hit the line and will be of definite interest for similarly competitive handicaps, having slipped back to a good mark. (op 16-1)
Marajaa(IRE), a C&D winner off 11lb lower last summer, is a horse who needs luck and he never really got the breaks, making modest late gains having got well behind. His rider reported that the gelding did not get a clear run. Official explanation: jockey said gelding was denied a clear run (op 12-1)
Aspectus(IRE) had the highest draw of all and ran really well for a long way, only backing out of it from 1f out. He was a multiple Group winner in Germany, so has a high rating as a result, but connections may be able to pick up a conditions race with him. (tchd 50-1 in a place)
Ransom Note, a progressive 3-y-o, had a tough draw to overcome and never got involved. He deserves another chance.
Signor Peltro was beginning to close when murdered 2f out. He did run on afterwards, but his chance had gone.
Tartan Gunna made modest late gains having got too far back following a slow start. (op 16-1)
Royal Destination(IRE) didn't get the best of trips buried in the middle of the pack. (op 16-1)
Oasis Dancer was the major disappointment of the race. Outclassed in the Irish 2000 Guineas in May, he had earlier won impressively at Newmarket and he returned to winning ways in a 7f conditions race at Newbury latest. He was just 1lb well-in under a penalty, but had an ideal draw in 19, so to see him drop away so tamely was disconcerting, for all that he did race a touch keenly. (op 11-2 tchd 9-2)
Acrostic wasn't the best away and got behind before meeting trouble when trying to stay on down the straight. He can be rated a good deal better than the bare form.
Irish Heartbeat(IRE) twice had the door shut in his face when looking for a run inside the final 2f and is another who is better than the bare result suggests.
Mahadee(IRE) reportedly moved badly down the hill. Official explanation: jockey said gelding moved poorly down the hill (op 22-1)

4538 TANQUERAY RICHMOND STKS (GROUP 2) (C&G) 6f
4:00 (4:00) (Class 1) 2-Y-0

£45,416 (£17,216; £8,616; £4,296; £2,152; £1,080) **Stalls** Low

Form RPR
11 **1** **Libranno**[22] 3823 2-9-3 0.. RichardHughes 1 111+
(R Hannon) *mde all: gng best wl over 1f out: rdn and edging rt ent fnl f: r.o wl: eased nr fin: comf* **5/4**[1]

21 **2** 1 1/4 **The Paddyman (IRE)**[29] 3602 2-9-0 0.............................. PhilipRobinson 6 104
(W J Haggas) *a chsng wnr: rdn and edgd sltly rt wl over 1f out: kpt on u.p fnl f but a hld* **4/1**[2]

5133 **3** 1 1/4 **Roayh (USA)**[22] 3826 2-9-0 106.. FrankieDettori 3 101
(Saeed Bin Suroor) *awkward leaving stalls and s.i.s: racd in last pair: rdn and effrt 2f out: hdwy u.p 1f out: wnt 3rd fnl 100yds: kpt on but nt pce to trble ldrs* **9/1**

31 **4** 1 3/4 **The Long Game**[21] 3842 2-9-0 0...................................... MartinDwyer 4 95
(B J Meehan) *sn niggled along in last: rdn over 2f out: hdwy to chse ldng pair 1f out: sn no imp: lost 3rd and wknd fnl 100yds* **20/1**

1 **5** 1/2 **Satin Love (USA)**[15] 4059 2-9-0 0.................................... JoeFanning 5 94
(M Johnston) *str: in tch: rdn along after 2f out: drvn and unable qck whn sltly hmpd wl over 1f out: wknd ent fnl f* **7/1**

11 **6** 1/2 **Marine Commando**[45] 3051 2-9-0 0................................ PaulHanagan 2 92
(R A Fahey) *t.k.h: trckd ldng pair: shkn up and unable qck wl over 1f out: rdn over 1f out: wknd ins fnl f* **9/2**[3]

1m 11.48s (-0.72) **Going Correction** 0.0s/f (Good) **6** Ran SP% **109.9**
Speed ratings (Par 106): **104,102,100,98,97 97**
toteswingers:1&2:£1.90, 1&3:£2.90, 2&3:£3.60 CSF £6.14 TOTE £1.90: £1.30, £3.10; EX 7.90.
Owner Mcdowell Racing **Bred** O McDowell **Trained** East Everleigh, Wilts

FOCUS
This juvenile Group 2 was first run in 1877 but has not proved to be much of a guide to the following year's Classics. That said, last year's winner was Dick Turpin, who finished runner-up in this season's 2,000 Guineas and Poule D'Essai des Poulains before scoring at Group 1 level. This was not the strongest field for the grade and Libranno only had to improve a fraction on his July Stakes win. The runner-up is one of the keys to the level of the form.

NOTEBOOK
Libranno, from a yard whose juveniles have been particularly dominant this season, overcame a 3lb penalty for his July Stakes win to give them another major prize. As in both his previous starts, he made all the running and, asked for his effort entering the final furlong, he never looked like being caught. He was a little unsettled at the start beforehand but soon calmed down and won in a professional manner, in a time just 0.69secs slower than the earlier sprint handicap. His rider believes he will step up to Group 1 company now, with the Prix Morny and Middle Park the likely targets. He is not convinced he will stay the Guineas mile as he will need to settle better, but his pedigree suggests he should, as his sire was a miler and his dam, who won at 7f, is by Singspiel out of an Ela-Mana-Mou mare. Most bookmakers left him at 20/1 for the first Classic. (op 6-5, tchd 11-8 in places)
The Paddyman(IRE) built on his promising debut by running away with a Yarmouth maiden last time and improved again. He was never far off the winner and made him fight, so looks more than capable of making his mark at this level. He has an entry in the Champagne Stakes but the Mill Reef the following week might be the better option at this stage. (op 11-2)
Roayh(USA) finished a good third to the winner's stable companion Strong Suit in the Coventry Stakes but had subsequently failed to build on that in a decent conditions race at Newmarket, behind yet another useful Hannon colt. He was held up here before staying on and looks worth a try over another furlong now. (op 10-1)
The Long Game is a sibling to several decent sprinters but was pushed along from an early stage on this step up in grade. He made some progress at halfway but could not mount a challenge. He might not be quite up to this level yet. (op 16-1, tchd 25-1 in a place)
Satin Love(USA) was a clear-cut winner of a small race at Hamilton on his debut and this was a big jump in grade. He ran reasonably, despite still looking a bit green, and is likely to appreciate a step up in distance before long. The experience should not be lost on him. (op 9-1 tchd 10-1)
Marine Commando came into this unbeaten, having taken the Windsor Castle on his second start. However, he was too keen early on this step up in trip and gradually faded on the run to the line. This was disappointing but perhaps he is better suited by a stiff 5f. He has several big-race entries but possibly the Roses Stakes at York or the Flying Childers at Doncaster might be more up his street. (op 10-3)

4539 RSA NURSERY 7f
4:35 (4:35) (Class 2) 2-Y-0 **£12,952** (£3,854; £1,926; £962) **Stalls** High

Form RPR
221 **1** **Royal Exchange**[37] 3332 2-9-5 **89**................................ RichardHughes 6 97+
(R Hannon) *lw: hld up wl in tch: swtchd lft ent fnl 2f: hdwy to chse ldr over 1f out: chal fnl 150yds: pushed ahd fnl 75yds: cleverly* **3/1**[1]

2401 **2** 1/2 **Diamond Geezah (IRE)**[26] 3705 2-9-0 **84**........................ MichaelHills 3 91
(B W Hills) *lw: pushed lft s: sn rcvrd and chsng ldrs: wnt 2nd 3f out: rdn to ld 2f out: drvn ent fnl f: hdd and no ex fnl 75yds* **5/1**[2]

1000 **3** 2 1/4 **Singapore Lilly (IRE)**[8] 4305 2-8-4 **74**................................ HirokiGoto 8 78+
(M R Channon) *in tch tl hmpd and lost pl 5f out: swtchd lft and hdwy over 2f out: chsd ldrs u.p over 1f out: kpt on to go 3rd ins fnl f: no ch w ldrs* **16/1**

0231 **4** 2 **Sir Lunchalott**[90] 1704 2-8-5 **75** MartinDwyer 5 71
(J S Moore) *racd keenly: sn led: hdd and rdn 2f out: wknd fnl 150yds* **33/1**

2126 **5** 1 **Falkland Flyer (IRE)**[21] 3844 2-8-9 **79** AlanMunro 4 73
(M R Channon) *wnt lft s: t.k.h early: hld up towards rr: swtchd lft and effrt on outer over 2f out: hdwy and edging rt 1f out: kpt on fnl f but nvr gng pce to threaten ldrs* **33/1**

4145 **6** 1 **Alfraamsey**[13] 4129 2-8-3 **73** DavidProbert 10 64
(M R Channon) *swtg: chsd ldr: sltly hmpd 5f out: lost 2nd and rdn 3f out: wknd u.p wl over 1f out: no ch fnl f* **20/1**

1240 **7** nk **Bathwick Bear (IRE)**[13] 4138 2-9-6 **90** JimmyFortune 12 82+
(P D Evans) *in tch: hmpd and lost pl 5f out: nt clr run on inner and switching out lft ent fnl 2f: kpt on same pce and wl hld fr over 1f out* **20/1**

033 **8** 1 3/4 **Silken Thoughts**[13] 4131 2-8-0 **70** AndreaAtzeni 2 56
(John Berry) *dwlt: sn in tch: shkn up and unable qck wl over 2f out: rdn and btn wl over 1f out* **25/1**

4141 **9** 3/4 **Memen (IRE)**[21] 3872 2-9-7 **91** TomQueally 9 77+
(P F I Cole) *dwlt and short of room sn after s: hld up in rr: hmpd 5f out: swtchd lft and hdwy u.p over 2f out: no hdwy over 1f out: wknd fnl f* **3/1**[1]

4120 **10** 2 1/2 **Silence Is Bliss (IRE)**[13] 4138 2-9-0 **84** RyanMoore 7 67
(J S Moore) *a bhd: rdn and no prog over 3f out: n.d* **8/1**[3]

5411 **11** 3/4 **Major Conquest (IRE)**[20] 3887 2-9-1 **85** RichardHills 1 61
(J W Hills) *stdd and dropped in bhd after s: hld up in last trio: hampererd 5f out: n.d* **8/1**[3]

304 **12** 1/2 **Philharmonic Hall**[27] 3665 2-7-12 **68** oh2 PaulHanagan 11 43
(R A Fahey) *w'like: leggy: wnt lft s: t.k.h: hld up in midfield: sltly hmpd 5f out: c wd and rdn over 2f out: racd awkwardly and sn no hdwy: wl btn over 1f out* **16/1**

1m 27.2s (0.30) **Going Correction** -0.05s/f (Good) **12** Ran SP% **119.9**
Speed ratings (Par 100): **96,95,92,90,89 88,87,85,85,82 81,80**
toteswingers:1&2:£4.30, 1&3:£11.20, 2&3:£13.50 CSF £16.54 CT £209.31 TOTE £3.70: £1.60, £2.30, £3.40; EX 18.90 Trifecta £154.80 Pool: £3,328.90 - 15.90 winning units..
Owner The Queen **Bred** The Queen **Trained** East Everleigh, Wilts

FOCUS
Typically a very competitive nursery and this year's running looked no different. The form is strong and should work out. There was a bit of trouble after 2f, Sir Lunchalott squeezing up Alfraamsey which caused a knock on effect, resulting in joint-favourite Memen getting hampered.

NOTEBOOK
Royal Exchange, whose rider avoided the trouble, relished the step up to 7f on this handicap debut, getting up late on to score with a bit in hand. On this evidence he will get 1m (dam stayed it well), and there may be more to come in these sort of races. (op 7-2, tchd 4-1 in place)
Diamond Geezah(IRE) left his earlier efforts behind when upped to this trip for the first time at Ayr, and a mark of 85 looked reasonable enough for this handicap debut. He looked the winner when going on, but was soon challenged by Royal Exchange and eventually outstayed. (op 6-1)
Singapore Lilly(IRE) posted a good effort considering she was affected by the early interference. She has twice struggled in Listed events since winning her maiden, but there was a bit of promise in her latest effort, and she is of obvious interest for similar races despite her mark being reassessed. (op 14-1 tchd 12-1)
Sir Lunchalott, up 2f in trip for this nursery debut, caused trouble in getting across to lead, but actually ran quite well, holding on for fourth despite having been slightly checked when headed. (op 25-1)
Falkland Flyer(IRE) stayed on well from over 1f out, leaving behind a dismal effort at Ascot latest.
Alfraamsey was done no favours early, but looked a non-stayer on this first try at 7f.
Bathwick Bear(IRE), who was denied a clear run, was another who did not appear to get home. (op 28-1)
Silken Thoughts will find easier opportunities down in grade.
Memen(IRE), who won readily off 10lb lower on his nursery debut, wasn't the best away and was then hampered. His effort in the final 3f was disappointing, but he probably deserves another chance. (op 11-4, tchd 7-2 and 5-2 in places)

4540 OAK TREE STKS (GROUP 3) (F&M) 7f
5:15 (5:15) (Class 1) 3-Y-O+

£34,062 (£12,912; £6,462; £3,222; £1,614; £810) **Stalls** High

Form RPR

-613 **1** **Tropical Paradise (IRE)**[24] 3752 4-9-2 102 IanMongan 9 108
(P Winkworth) *trckd ldng pair: swtchd lft and rdn 2f out: sn chsng ldr: drvn to ld 1f out: kpt on gamely fnl f: drvn out* **16/1**

-625 **2** 3/4 **Golden Stream (IRE)**[44] 3067 4-9-2 103 RyanMoore 4 106
(Sir Michael Stoute) *swtg: hld up in last pair: rdn and effrt ent fnl 2f: hdwy u.p on outer ent fnl f: r.o wl to go 2nd fnl 50yds: nvr gng to rch wnr* **9/2**[3]

1-10 **3** nk **Pyrrha**[44] 3067 4-9-5 105 AlanMunro 10 108
(C F Wall) *dwlt: sn rcvrd and led after 1f: rdn ent fnl 2f: hdd 1f out: kpt on same pce u.p but lost 2nd fnl 50yds* **8/1**

-200 **4** 1/2 **Blue Angel (IRE)**[7] 4319 3-8-10 100 ow1 RichardHughes 3 104+
(R Hannon) *stdd after s: hld up in rr: looking for run on inner 2f out: nt clr run and swtchd lft over 1f out: hdwy ent fnl f: running on and swtchd rt fnl 100yds: gng on wl at fin: unable to rch ldrs* **25/1**

-013 **5** 1/2 **Jacqueline Quest (IRE)**[42] 3143 3-8-9 111 TomQueally 1 99
(H R A Cecil) *hld up in midfield: hdwy on outer over 2f out: rdn to chal wl over 1f out: edgd rt and drvn ent fnl f: no ex and wknd fnl 150yds* **15/8**[1]

2-10 **6** 2 3/4 **Puff (IRE)**[42] 3143 3-8-12 108 JimCrowley 8 95
(R M Beckett) *lw: bmpd s: t.k.h: hld up wl in tch: nt clr run and shuffled bk towards rr over 2f out: rdn and styd on same pce fr wl over 1f out* **4/1**[2]

310- **7** nk **Summer Fete (IRE)**[327] 5710 4-9-2 104 TomEaves 5 94
(B Smart) *t.k.h: hld up wl in tch: nt clr run on inner ent fnl 2f: unable qck u.p wl over 1f out: styd on same pce and no imp after* **20/1**

13-0 **8** 8 **Tabassum (IRE)**[42] 3143 3-8-9 108 RichardHills 6 70
(Sir Michael Stoute) *taken down early: t.k.h: led: sn hdd: stdd to chse ldrs: rdn and wknd ent fnl 2f: wl bhd fnl f* **7/1**

2122 **9** nk **Strictly Dancing (IRE)**[23] 3790 3-8-9 91 JimmyFortune 7 69
(A M Balding) *stmbld leaving stalls: t.k.h and rcvrd to chse ldr over 5f out: rdn and unable qck whn hmpd 2f out: sn wknd: wl bhd fnl f* **14/1**

1m 25.6s (-1.30) **Going Correction** -0.05s/f (Good)
WFA 3 from 4yo 7lb **9** Ran SP% **117.7**
Speed ratings (Par 113): **105,104,103,103,102 99,99,90,89**
toteswingers:1&2:£13.30, 1&3:£18.10, 2&3:£8.30 CSF £88.20 TOTE £21.60: £4.10, £2.10, £2.90; EX 116.30 Trifecta £754.30 Pool: £2,871.32 - 2.81 winning units..
Owner S Lovelace & R Muddle **Bred** George E McMahon **Trained** Chiddingfold, Surrey
■ Stewards' Enquiry : Ian Mongan two-day ban: careless riding (Aug 13-14)

FOCUS
This Group 3 has been run under its present title since 1982. Plenty of good fillies have won this race without there being any stars. The race was dominated by the older fillies, and the time was 1.6secs faster than the preceding nursery, but there was something of a surprise result and the form looks ordinary for the grade.

NOTEBOOK
Tropical Paradise(IRE) probably found the combination of the fast ground and longer trip on a stiff track too much for her last time, and the return to a C&D over which she won her previous start proved to her liking. She got a good lead from the third and, although she had to wait for a gap before mounting her challenge, picked up well when in the clear and was always holding the late effort of the runner-up. She has no major entries but can win again, particularly if there is a little ease in the ground, and might go abroad in search of it. (op 20-1)
Golden Stream(IRE), who finished runner-up to today's third earlier in the season, was 3lb better off and the pair ran pretty much to that form. Held up off the pace, she picked up well down the outside, but could not produce an extra gear to reel in the winner. Connections reported that she did not handle the track. (op 6-1, tchd 13-2 in a place)
Pyrrha bounced back from her Ascot disappointment and ran close to previous form with the runner-up. She made the running as usual and kept going under pressure when headed. This was a creditable effort under her penalty. (op 12-1)
Blue Angel(IRE) was held up out the back and then had to switch to get a run over a furlong out. She responded really well to pressure to make the frame, and this track clearly suits, as she finished fourth in a Group 3 here last year, just behind the subsequent dual Oaks winner Snow Fairy. (op 20-1)
Jacqueline Quest(IRE) had an outstanding chance on paper, and came to win her race over a furlong out. However, her effort petered out in the latter stages and she failed to make the frame. Her trainer was disappointed as he said the filly had been working well, and she has to bounce back after this. (op 6-4, tchd 2-1 in places)
Puff(IRE) had a penalty for beating Habaayib earlier in the season but her chance was not helped by getting involved in some scrimmaging in the early stages. She was quite keen as a result and can be given another chance on a more conventional track. (op 5-1, tchd 6-1 in places)
Summer Fete(IRE), last year's winner, was having her first start of the season. Although she appeared fit enough she never got involved having been held up. (op 25-1)
Tabassum(IRE) was another to be quite keen in the early stages, and like her dam has not gone on from a promising juvenile season. (op 8-1 tchd 13-2)
Strictly Dancing(IRE), stepping up in grade, stumbled slightly leaving the gate but was soon racing prominently. However, she could not get to the front with Pyrrha in the line-up, and paid for racing freely in the closing stages; her rider reported that the filly hung right. She might be better returned to 6f if connections are going to continue in search of black type. Official explanation: jockey said filly hung right (op 10-1)

4541 TURF CLUB STKS (H'CAP) 5f
5:45 (5:47) (Class 3) (0-95,95) 3-Y-O

£9,346 (£2,799; £1,399; £700; £349; £175) **Stalls** Low

Form RPR

1111 **1** **Perfect Blossom**[8] 4291 3-8-5 **84** 6ex AmyRyan(5) 6 96
(K A Ryan) *b.hind: lw: chsd ldr tl led over 2f out: rdn clr over 1f out: kpt on wl fnl f: rdn out* **15/2**[3]

1335 **2** 1 3/4 **Confessional**[27] 3673 3-8-13 **87** (e[1]) AdrianNicholls 4 93
(T D Easterby) *hld up off the pce towards rr: rdn and effrt ent fnl 2f: kpt on wl u.p fnl f to go 2nd towards fin: no ch w wnr* **16/1**

0560 **3** 1/2 **Star Rover (IRE)**[6] 4391 3-9-4 **95** MartinLane(3) 10 99
(P D Evans) *chsd ldng pair: rdn and outpcd ent fnl 2f: chsd clr wnr jst over 1f out: no imp fnl f: lost 2nd towards fin* **16/1**

4-10 **4** 3/4 **Archers Road (IRE)**[20] 3891 3-9-7 **95** DaneO'Neill 7 97
(T D Barron) *t.k.h: hld up towards rr: hdwy over 2f out: rdn and kpt on steadily fr over 1f out: no threat to wnr* **16/1**

-053 **5** 1/2 **Tawaabb**[21] 3856 3-9-7 **95** (v) AlanMunro 15 95
(M R Channon) *in tch on far side of field: rdn and pressing for placings over 1f out: keeping on same pce and no threat to wnr whn rdr dropped whip ins fnl f* **9/1**

0-30 **6** hd **Skylla**[23] 3791 3-9-4 **92** PaulHanagan 5 91
(R A Fahey) *hld up off the pce towards rr: rdn and hdwy ent fnl 2f: drvn and kpt on ins fnl f: nvr trbld ldrs* **6/1**[2]

4122 **7** 3/4 **Little Garcon (USA)**[27] 3673 3-9-0 **88** MartinDwyer 16 84+
(M Botti) *s.i.s: bhd: hdwy 1/2-way: swtchd rt and effrt over 1f out: no imp ins fnl f: nvr trbld ldrs* **7/2**[1]

4231 **8** hd **Ignatieff (IRE)**[41] 3225 3-8-10 **84** DuranFentiman 1 80
(Mrs L Stubbs) *led: hung rt thrght: hdd over 2f out: outpcd by wnr wl over 1f out: lost 2nd jst over 1f out: wknd ins fnl f* **20/1**

2224 **9** 3/4 **Rule Of Nature**[13] 4145 3-8-8 **82** RyanMoore 2 75
(Sir Michael Stoute) *s.i.s: sn outpcd and niggled along in rr: modest hdwy ins fnl f: n.d* **7/2**[1]

1040 **10** 1/2 **Magical Macey (USA)**[21] 3856 3-8-7 **86** (b) DeanHeslop(5) 8 77
(T D Barron) *swtg: hmpd s and s.i.s: hdwy and chsng ldrs after 2f: rdn and struggling wl over 1f out: wknd fnl f* **25/1**

4641 **11** nk **Diamond Johnny G (USA)**[21] 3856 3-8-5 **79** ow1 ...(t) EddieCreighton 3 69
(E J Creighton) *s.i.s: a outpcd in rr: sme hdwy ins fnl f: n.d* **16/1**

-000 **12** 1 **Goodwood Maestro**[11] 4204 3-7-13 **76** oh2. Louis-PhilippeBeuzelin(3) 9 62
(J L Dunlop) *pushed rt s and s.i.s: a outpcd in rr: n.d* **25/1**

3624 **13** 1 **Living It Large (FR)**[27] 3673 3-9-1 **89** TomEaves 11 72
(R F Fisher) *chsd ldrs: rdn 1/2-way: sn struggling: wl btn fnl f* **16/1**

58.04 secs (-0.36) **Going Correction** 0.0s/f (Good) **13** Ran SP% **122.4**
Speed ratings (Par 104): **102,99,98,97,96 96,94,94,93,92 92,90,88**
toteswingers:1&2:£21.10, 1&3:£31.50, 2&3:£50.80. totesuper7: Win: Not won. Place: Not won. CSF £121.13 CT £1920.86 TOTE £6.70: £2.30, £4.30, £6.60; EX 113.90 Trifecta £2170.40 Part won. Pool: £2,933.08 - 0.62 winning units. Place 6 £223.09; Place 5 £74.58.
Owner Mrs Ann Morris **Bred** Mrs A Morris **Trained** Hambleton, N Yorks

FOCUS
This had appeared to be a wide-open 3-y-o sprint handicap, but few got into it. The third and fourth set the standard with the first two improvers.

NOTEBOOK
Perfect Blossom defied her penalty and kept up the searching pace throughout to record her fifth straight win, and sixth in all this season. Despite having been taken on for the lead, she showed serious speed to skip clear inside the final 2f, and it surely won't be long before she's trying her luck at Pattern level. She will reportedly head for a 5f 3-y-o handicap at York's Ebor meeting next. (op 5-1)
Confessional has been running consistently well all season in blinkers and cheekpieces, and the application of a first-time eyeshield coaxed an apparently improved display from the son of Dubawi, running on well late for second. (op 12-1)
Star Rover(IRE) produced a cracking effort. He has been running well off lofty marks in handicaps, but is slowly edging the right way and this effort suggests he remains capable of smart handicap form. (tchd 18-1)
Archers Road(IRE) was on the same mark as when winning at Chester on his reappearance, and he bounced back from a below-par effort at Ascot last time.
Tawaabb again ran well without necessarily suggesting he's up to winning off this mark. (op 11-1, tchd 12-1 in places)
Skylla never got into it having been held up off the pace, running on late. (op 15-2)
Little Garcon(USA) was found wanting for pace on this drop to 5f. (op 9-2)
Ignatieff(IRE) showed blistering early speed, but he was readily dropped by the winner and ended up well held. (tchd 22-1)
Rule Of Nature was unable to recover from a slow start on this drop to the minimum. (op 9-2)

Magical Macey(USA) was hampered early and then got lit up, so probably deserves another chance.
T/Jkpt: Not won. T/Plt: £467.10 to a £1 stake. Pool:£278,158.19 - 434.70 winning tickets T/Qpdt: £42.30 to a £1 stake. Pool:£16,938.11 - 295.62 winning tickets SP

[4123]HAYDOCK (L-H)

Friday, July 30

OFFICIAL GOING: Good to soft (soft in places in home straight for races over 1m+) changing to soft (heavy in places in home straight for races over 1m+) after race 2 (6.45)

Inner Sprint track used. Other races on new inner bend and outer home straight reducing distances on round course by about 25yds.
Wind: Virtually nil Weather: Overcast and rain

4542 BETDAQ THE BETTING EXCHANGE APPRENTICE TRAINING SERIES H'CAP (PART OF RACING EXCELLENCE INITIATIVE) 5f

6:10 (6:12) (Class 4) (0-80,77) 4-Y-O+ **£4,533** (£1,348; £674; £336) **Stalls** Centre

Form RPR
5504 **1** **Chosen One (IRE)**[11] 4199 5-8-10 **68** SophieSilvester(5) 3 76
(Mrs R A Carr) *led 1f: cl up tl led again 1/2-way: pushed clr wl over 1f out: rdn and edgd lft ins fnl f: kpt on* **8/1**

0344 **2** *1 1/4* **Lucky Dan (IRE)**[34] 3430 4-9-10 **77** DebraEngland 7 81
(Paul Green) *stdd s: hld up towards rr: hdwy 2f out: n.m.r and swtchd lft over 1f out: rdn and kpt on ins fnl f: chsd wnr towards fin* **7/2[3]**

2162 **3** *nk* **Hazelrigg (IRE)**[6] 4372 5-9-6 **73** (bt) AntiocoMurgia 4 75
(T D Easterby) *trckd ldrs: hdwy 1/2-way: chsd wnr and sltly hmpd over 1f out: sn rdn and one pce ins fnl f* **15/8[1]**

1461 **4** *6* **Poppy's Rose**[7] 4343 6-9-8 **75** 6ex DaleSwift 1 56
(T J Etherington) *towards rr: hdwy on wd outside over 2f out: sn rdn and chsd ldrs over 1f out: drvn and no imp ent fnl f* **5/2[2]**

6564 **5** *1 3/4* **Memphis Man**[10] 4225 7-8-10 **70** KevinLundie(7) 2 45
(P D Evans) *sn rdn along and outpcd in rr: sme late hdwy: nvr a factor* **12/1**

5563 **6** *3/4* **Desert Strike**[18] 3966 4-8-5 **58** oh3 (p) DuilioDaSilva 5 30
(P F I Cole) *cl up: led after 1f: hdd 1/2-way: sn rdn along and wknd* **14/1**

0050 **7** *5* **Miacarla**[18] 3946 7-7-13 **59** oh13 ow1 DanielleMooney(7) 6 13
(H A McWilliams) *chsd ldng pair: rdn along bef 1/2-way: sn wknd* **100/1**

61.35 secs (0.35) **Going Correction** +0.20s/f (Good) **7** Ran SP% **112.0**
Speed ratings (Par 105): **105,103,102,92,90 88,80**
toteswingers:1&2:£2.60, 1&3:£3.30, 2&3:£2.10 CSF £34.50 TOTE £10.50: £4.50, £1.40; EX 45.60.
Owner David W Chapman **Bred** Carl Holt **Trained** Huby, N Yorks

FOCUS
Not a strong sprint handicap by any means, with a smaller field than usually contests races of this nature and a couple racing from out of the weights. The main action unfolded up the centre of the track. The winner is rated back to his summer best.

4543 CHESHIRE OAKS DESIGNER OUTLET MAIDEN AUCTION STKS 6f

6:45 (6:45) (Class 5) 2-Y-O **£2,590** (£770; £385; £192) **Stalls** Centre

Form RPR
1 **Rhythm Of Light** 2-8-4 0 RichardKingscote 7 70+
(Tom Dascombe) *trckd ldrs: hdwy over 2f out: chsd ldr over 1f out: rdn to chal ent fnl f: styd on to ld last 100yds: readily* **20/1**

2332 **2** *1* **Lexi's Hero (IRE)**[13] 4123 2-9-1 83 TadhgO'Shea 5 78
(K A Ryan) *led: pushed along over 1f out: rdn ent fnl f: hdd and no ex last 100yds* **4/6[1]**

3 *2 3/4* **Glen's Diamond** 2-9-1 0 TonyHamilton 1 70+
(R A Fahey) *t.k.h early: hld up towards rr: hdwy 2f out: styd on ins fnl f: nrst fin* **8/1[3]**

4 *nk* **Easy Over (IRE)** 2-8-11 0 GrahamGibbons 6 65
(E S McMahon) *dwlt and towards rr: hdwy over 2f out: rdn to chse ldng pair over 1f out: kpt on same pce: lost 3rd nr line* **11/2[2]**

U60 **5** *1 1/2* **Blackleyf (IRE)**[14] 4096 2-8-6 0 (p) RossAtkinson(5) 8 60
(Tom Dascombe) *towards rr: hdwy over 2f out: rdn and n.m.r wl over 1f out: kpt on same pce appr fnl f* **25/1**

6 *1* **Secret Tycoon (IRE)** 2-8-13 0 CathyGannon 2 59
(Patrick Morris) *chsd ldrs on outer: pushed along over 2f out: rdn wl over 1f out and grad wknd* **40/1**

0 **7** *8* **Snow Legend (IRE)**[36] 3362 2-8-4 0 RichardSmith 3 26
(Tom Dascombe) *t.k.h: chsd ldrs: rdn along to chse ldr 2f out: sn rdn and grad wknd appr fnl f* **40/1**

06 **8** *1/2* **Suave Character**[14] 4089 2-8-9 0 FrannyNorton 9 30
(M Blanshard) *t.k.h: chsd ldrs: rdn along over 2f out and sn wknd* **25/1**

9 *2 1/2* **Tsarina Louise** 2-8-10 0 PaulMulrennan 10 23
(J G Given) *hld up towards rr: hdwy on outer and in tch 1/2-way: rdn over 2f out and sn wknd* **12/1**

0 **10** *1 1/2* **Alhoralhora (IRE)**[27] 3686 2-8-6 0 PJMcDonald 4 15
(J G Given) *sn prom: cl up after 2f: rdn along wl over 2f out and sn wknd* **28/1**

1m 16.33s (2.83) **Going Correction** +0.35s/f (Good) **10** Ran SP% **115.0**
Speed ratings (Par 94): **95,93,90,89,87 86,75,74,71,69**
toteswingers::1&2:£7.20, 1&3:£20.70, 2&3:£2.00 CSF £32.02 TOTE £28.10: £4.70, £1.10, £2.00; EX 45.90.
Owner Lowe Silver Deal **Bred** Hermes Services Ltd **Trained** Malpas, Cheshire
■ Stewards' Enquiry : Tony Hamilton one-day ban: careless riding (Aug 13)

FOCUS
A fair maiden with the runner-up very much the marker to the form, which is sound. The field came up the centre, the pace understandably steady through the early stages on the rain-softened ground.

NOTEBOOK
Rhythm Of Light can be expected to go from here, as her pedigree suggesting she's sure to benefit from longer trips. Whatever happens from now on she's certainly been a bargain buy at just 500gns.
Lexi's Hero(IRE) has now finished runner-up on three occasions and will be vulnerable to more progressive types in these events. (op 4-5 tchd 5-6 and evens in a place)
Glen's Diamond ◆ still had the majority in front of him over 1f out. He finished to really good effect once getting the hang of things and is sure to improve, particularly over further (half-brother to a 1m6f winner). (op 13-2)
Easy Over(IRE) ◆ is a half-brother to a couple of useful sorts and looks to have a future himself judged on this first effort, green initially (started slowly) but keeping on as he grasped what was required. (tchd 5-1)
Blackleyf(IRE), a stablemate of the winner, was staying on at the death in first-time cheekpieces but is likely to have a more realistic chance in nurseries. (op 28-1)
Secret Tycoon(IRE) was another newcomer who was green, though he did show clear ability by the finish and this gelded son of Aussie Rules should do better with this behind him.
Tsarina Louise boasts a smart pedigree and will do better as she wasn't subjected to a hard time at any stage on this debut. (op 11-1)

4544 SUPPLY UK HIRE SHOPS NURSERY 6f

7:20 (7:21) (Class 4) 2-Y-O **£4,533** (£1,348; £674; £336) **Stalls** Centre

Form RPR
221 **1** **Madany (IRE)**[29] 3583 2-9-3 **81** TadhgO'Shea 6 90+
(B W Hills) *hmpd s: hld up in rr: gd hdwy over 2f out: rdn to chal ent fnl f: kpt on to ld last 100yds* **9/4[1]**

6102 **2** *1/2* **Belle Royale (IRE)**[21] 3859 2-8-4 **68** FrannyNorton 3 76
(W M Brisbourne) *a.p: cl up 1/2-way: chal 2f out: rdn to ld 1f out: drvn ins fnl f: hdd and no ex last 100yds* **14/1**

010 **3** *3 1/2* **Las Verglas Star (IRE)**[29] 3598 2-8-11 **75** TonyHamilton 2 72
(R A Fahey) *chsd ldrs on outer: effrt over 2f out: rdn wl over 1f out: drvn and kpt on same pce fnl f* **12/1**

041 **4** *nk* **Bussa**[50] 2895 2-9-7 **85** SilvestreDeSousa 4 81
(P D Evans) *led 2f: cl up tl rdn and led again 2f out: drvn and hdd over 1f out: kpt on same pce* **10/1**

0534 **5** *1* **Lady Platinum Club**[29] 3596 2-8-1 **70** ow1 (p) IanBrennan(5) 1 63
(G R Oldroyd) *chsd ldrs: rdn along over 2f out: drvn over 1f out and sn one pce* **9/1[3]**

0452 **6** *nk* **Unknown Rebel (IRE)**[9] 4242 2-7-6 **63** ow1 (p) JulieBurke(7) 7 55+
(K A Ryan) *t.k.h: cl up: led after 2f: rdn along and hdd 2f out: edgd lft and wknd over 1f out* **10/1**

132 **7** *12* **On The High Tops (IRE)**[36] 3364 2-9-7 **85** MickyFenton 8 41
(T P Tate) *t.k.h: trckd ldrs: hdwy 1/2-way: rdn over 2f out and sn wknd* **15/2[2]**

4001 **8** *11* **Reginald Claude**[14] 4111 2-8-11 **75** GrahamGibbons 5 —
(M D I Usher) *hmpd s: in tch: hdwy to trck ldrs over 2f out: rdn and wkng whn squeezed out and stmbld bdly over 1f out: eased after* **9/4[1]**

1m 16.43s (2.93) **Going Correction** +0.35s/f (Good) **8** Ran SP% **115.8**
Speed ratings (Par 96): **94,93,88,88,86 86,70,55**
toteswingers:1&2:£7.70, 1&3:£7.10, 2&3:£10.20 CSF £38.18 CT £317.64 TOTE £3.50: £1.50, £3.00, £2.40; EX 28.20.
Owner Hamdan Al Maktoum **Bred** Mesnil Investments Ltd **Trained** Lambourn, Berks
■ Stewards' Enquiry : Julie Burke four-day ban: careless riding (Aug 13-16)

FOCUS
It's hard to know what the overall strength of this form is worth with a few presumably failing to cope with conditions, but the leading pair deserve credit for pulling clear. Pretty solid form despite the ground.

NOTEBOOK
Madany(IRE) landed her second course-and-distance win of the month in good style, coming from off the pace to always just shade the runner-up inside the last. Clearly versatile regards ground, she'll continue to progress. (op 5-2)
Belle Royale(IRE) has now run well to finish second on both nursery starts, this a further improvement in making a progressive rival pull out all the stops, seeing off the rest comfortably. She'll look fairly treated if taking up her entry at Chester on Sunday.
Las Verglas Star(IRE) should stay further still if his pedigree is any guide. (op 20-1)
Bussa beat a subsequent winner at Nottingham and wasn't discredited on his nursery bow, though he doesn't have anything in hand of his opening mark on this evidence. (op 9-1)
Lady Platinum Club looks pretty exposed but was better than the bare result, still going well enough when a bit short of room just as things were starting to take shape. (op 10-1)
Unknown Rebel(IRE) had shown improved form on softish ground at Catterick last week but didn't come close to reproducing it with cheekpieces fitted this time. (tchd 12-1)
On The High Tops(IRE) is probably on a stiff enough mark but this was disappointing, and he presumably failed to cope with more testing conditions. Official explanation: jockey said gelding ran too free early stages (op 6-1)
Reginald Claude was eased after being hampered when switched to deliver his challenge over 1f out and shouldn't be judged on this. Official explanation: jockey said colt suffered interference in running (op 5-2)

4545 COMPLETE CONSTRUCTION FACILITIES H'CAP 1m 6f

7:50 (7:55) (Class 5) (0-70,70) 3-Y-O **£2,590** (£770; £385; £192) **Stalls** Low

Form RPR
5P32 **1** **Light The City (IRE)**[3] 4448 3-7-11 **51** oh6 JamesSullivan(5) 1 62
(Mrs R A Carr) *hld up in tch: hdwy 6f out: c wd st towards stands' rail: led over 2f out: rdn over 1f out: kpt on wl u.p fnl f* **8/1**

6425 **2** *2 1/4* **Head Hunted**[9] 4259 3-9-1 **64** NickyMackay 4 72
(D M Simcock) *hld up towards rr: hdwy over 4f out: rdn to chse wnr over 1f out: drvn ins fnl f and no imp towards fin* **7/1[3]**

4553 **3** *2 3/4* **Dr Finley (IRE)**[9] 4259 3-8-12 **66** SimonPearce(5) 6 70
(J Pearce) *hld up towards rr: stdy hdwy on inner 1/2-way: trckd ldrs and wd st: effrt to chse wnr 2f out and sn rdn: drvn over 1f out and sn one pce* **8/1**

5-30 **4** *3/4* **Fine Lace (IRE)**[34] 3444 3-8-9 **58** FrannyNorton 13 61
(D J S Ffrench Davis) *chsd ldrs: hdwy 4f out: rdn along 3f out: drvn and kpt on same pce fnl 2f* **16/1**

4533 **5** *3/4* **Pena Dorada (IRE)**[28] 3626 3-9-4 **67** (p) AndrewElliott 11 69
(J R Weymes) *led and sn clr: rdn along and styd far side to r alone in home st: hdd over 3f out: sn drvn and grad wknd fnl 2f* **5/1[1]**

544 **6** *3 1/4* **Straversjoy**[14] 4092 3-7-13 **51** oh4 PaulPickard(3) 12 49
(R Hollinshead) *hld up and bhd: hdwy 3f out: rdn over 2f out: styd on appr fnl f: n.d* **6/1[2]**

0030 **7** *4 1/2* **Henry Havelock**[11] 4200 3-8-7 **56** TonyHamilton 3 47
(C Grant) *chsd clr ldr: hdwy to take clsr order 6f out: rdn along over 3f out: sn drvn and grad wknd* **33/1**

5 **8** *1/2* **Kingdom Of Munster (IRE)**[13] 4153 3-9-7 **70** (v[1]) PaulMulrennan 9 61
(Ian Williams) *prom: hdwy 5f out: c wd st to stands' rail: rdn to ld over 3f out: drvn and hdd over 2f out: grad wknd* **12/1**

06-4 **9** *10* **Astromoon**[94] 1607 3-8-8 **62** AshleyMorgan(5) 10 39
(M H Tompkins) *a towards rr* **14/1**

4103 **10** *7* **Firehawk**[25] 3730 3-8-7 **56** CathyGannon 7 23
(P D Evans) *a towards rr: bhd fnl 3f* **12/1**

660 **11** *4 1/2* **Farmers Glory**[15] 4062 3-8-8 **57** PJMcDonald 2 17
(G A Swinbank) *midfield: rdn along over 5f out: sn wknd and bhd fnl 3f* **11/1**

3240 **12** *3 3/4* **Musical Mark**[32] 3519 3-9-2 **70** TobyAtkinson(5) 5 25
(M Botti) *a in rr: bhd fnl 3f* **33/1**

3m 10.22s (9.02) **Going Correction** +0.35s/f (Good) **12** Ran SP% **107.8**
Speed ratings (Par 100): **88,86,85,84,84 82,79,79,73,69 67,65**
toteswingers:1&2:£13.60, 1&3:£9.00, 2&3:£7.70 CSF £49.53 CT £292.71 TOTE £9.20: £3.20, £2.60, £1.10; EX 53.90.
Owner David W Chapman **Bred** Rabbah Bloodstock Limited **Trained** Huby, N Yorks

FOCUS
Conditions meant this was a test of stamina for these and the field was well strung out despite the gallop appearing on the steady side for much of the way. The majority came centre to stand's side in the straight. A clear personal best from the winner but the form may not mean much.

4546 ST HELENS H'CAP — 1m 2f 95y
8:20 (8:20) (Class 5) (0-75,75) 3-Y-O+ £2,590 (£770; £385; £192) Stalls High

Form / RPR

0-63 **1** **Denton (NZ)**[23] [3781] 7-9-9 **73**....(t) SimonPearce(5) 2 — 88
(J R Gask) *wnt rt s: trckd ldrs on inner: hdwy 3f out: rdn to chal 2f out: drvn to ld over 1f out: kpt on strly* **4/1**[2]

0000 **2** 3 1/2 **Amazing Blue Sky**[83] [1925] 4-9-6 **70**.... JamesSullivan(5) 12 — 78
(Mrs R A Carr) *trckd ldr: hdwy and wd st to stands' rails: led 4f out: rdn along over 2f out: sn jnd and drvn: hdd over 1f out: no ex ins fnl f* **20/1**

0201 **3** 1 **Pintura**[13] [4127] 3-9-6 **75**....(p) CathyGannon 1 — 81
(D M Simcock) *hld up in rr: hdwy over 4f out: rdn to chse ldrs over 2f out: drvn over 1f out: kpt on same pce fnl f* **7/2**[1]

-535 **4** 1 1/4 **Chantilly Pearl (USA)**[18] [3950] 4-9-2 **61**.... PaulMulrennan 10 — 65
(J G Given) *hld up in rr: gd hdwy 1/2-way: wd st to stands' rail and sn chsng ldrs: effrt and ev ch over 2f out: sn rdn and wknd over 1f out* **8/1**

5223 **5** 5 **Star Addition**[14] [4120] 4-8-11 **56**.... DavidAllan 7 — 51
(E J Alston) *trckd ldrs: effrt 4f out: rdn along 3f out: drvn over 2f out and sn wknd* **8/1**

500- **6** 4 **Nouailhas**[288] [6788] 4-8-9 **54** oh9.... GrahamGibbons 4 — 41
(R Hollinshead) *stlty hmpd s: sn trcking ldrs: hdwy 4f out: rdn along 3f out: sn drvn and grad wknd fnl 2f* **66/1**

4065 **7** 7 **French Applause (IRE)**[28] [3617] 4-9-5 **64**.... MickyFenton 9 — 38
(T P Tate) *led: rdn along and hdd 4f out: sn wknd* **16/1**

3-13 **8** 6 **Eltheeb**[56] [2717] 3-9-5 **74**.... TadhgO'Shea 3 — 36
(J L Dunlop) *hmpd s: a in rr* **5/1**[3]

0-50 **9** 3/4 **Dream Of Olwyn (IRE)**[18] [3950] 5-9-3 **67**.... DaleSwift(5) 8 — 28
(J G Given) *hld up towards rr: hdwy on outer and in tch 1/2-way: rdn along over 3f out and sn wknd* **9/1**

4016 **10** 2 3/4 **Smarty Sam (USA)**[31] [3532] 3-8-9 **64**.... PJMcDonald 5 — 20
(G A Swinbank) *a towards rr: bhd fnl 3f* **8/1**

030 **11** 24 **Miss Flash Dancer**[24] [3766] 4-8-13 **58**.... TonyHamilton 11 — —
(C C Bealby) *in tch: rdn along over 4f out: sn wknd: bhd and eased fnl 2f* **40/1**

2m 17.27s (1.27) **Going Correction** +0.35s/f (Good)
WFA 3 from 4yo+ 10lb — 11 Ran SP% **116.8**
Speed ratings (Par 103): **108,105,104,103,99 96,90,85,85,83 63**
toteswingers:1&2:£4.90, 1&3:£3.60, 2&3:£5.30 CSF £82.56 CT £308.24 TOTE £6.20: £2.00, £4.20, £1.10; EX 104.90.

Owner Horses First Racing Limited **Bred** Windsor Park Stud Ltd **Trained** Sutton Veny, Wilts

FOCUS
A one-sided contest in the end, the winner clearly well ahead of his mark and posting a personal best. As in the previous race they came towards the near side in the straight.

Eltheeb Official explanation: jockey said colt never travelled

4547 IDEAL RECRUIT H'CAP — 1m 30y
8:55 (8:56) (Class 5) (0-70,69) 3-Y-O+ £2,590 (£770; £385; £192) Stalls Low

Form / RPR

2511 **1** **One Scoop Or Two**[14] [4093] 4-9-9 **61**.... GrahamGibbons 4 — 73+
(R Hollinshead) *mde all: c wd to stands' rail st: rdn along 3f out: drvn wl over 1f out: edgd lft and kpt on wl fnl f* **5/2**[1]

000 **2** 2 **Wavertree Bounty**[29] [3606] 3-8-2 **48**.... SilvestreDeSousa 10 — 53
(J Ryan) *hld up in rr: stdy hdwy over 4f out: rdn to chse wnr 2f out: drvn and ev ch over 1f out: one pce fnl f* **16/1**

1635 **3** 2 1/4 **Tanforan**[20] [3911] 8-9-10 **62**.... CathyGannon 11 — 64
(B P J Baugh) *hld up in tch: hdwy 3f out: rdn to chse ldng pair wl over 1f out: drvn and no imp ins fnl f* **8/1**

5-01 **4** 1 **Only A Splash**[11] [4189] 6-9-2 **54** 6ex.... PJMcDonald 7 — 54
(Mrs R A Carr) *chsd wnr: rdn along 3f out: drvn over 2f out and sn one pce* **8/1**

-006 **5** 4 1/2 **Commando Scott (IRE)**[11] [4192] 9-9-3 **62**.... NeilFarley(7) 12 — 51
(D Carroll) *t.k.h: trckd ldrs on outer: hdwy 3f out: rdn over 2f out: drvn and one pce fr over 1f out* **5/1**[2]

/030 **6** nk **Cheddar George**[29] [3586] 4-9-12 **64**.... TadhgO'Shea 5 — 52
(B J Meehan) *chsd ldrs: rdn along over 3f out: drvn over 2f out and grad wknd* **10/1**

1005 **7** 12 **Feet Of Fury**[18] [3968] 4-9-1 **53**....(p) LiamJones 8 — 14
(W M Brisbourne) *hld up in rr: hdwy 3f out: rdn to chse ldrs 2f out: sn drvn and wknd* **28/1**

22-2 **8** 4 1/2 **Midnight Strider (IRE)**[196] [189] 4-9-13 **65**....(t) RichardKingscote 3 — 16
(Tom Dascombe) *chsd ldrs: rdn along 3f out: drvn over 2f out and sn wknd* **9/1**

2033 **9** 6 **Law Of Attraction (IRE)**[24] [3759] 3-9-4 **69**.... SimonPearce(5) 2 — —
(J R Gask) *t.k.h: chsd ldrs on inner: rdn along over 3f out and sn wknd* **7/1**[3]

4500 **10** shd **Flores Sea (USA)**[24] [3765] 6-9-7 **64**....(b) JamesSullivan(5) 1 — —
(Mrs R A Carr) *a towards rr* **14/1**

6010 **11** 24 **Lord Of The Dance (IRE)**[60] [2596] 4-9-11 **63**.... PaulMulrennan 6 — —
(W M Brisbourne) *hld up: a bhd* **14/1**

1m 46.87s (2.17) **Going Correction** +0.35s/f (Good)
WFA 3 from 4yo+ 8lb — 11 Ran SP% **121.7**
Speed ratings (Par 103): **103,101,98,97,93 92,80,76,70,70 46**
toteswingers:1&2:£13.30, 1&3:£7.40, 2&3:£43.90 CSF £49.07 CT £297.90 TOTE £3.40: £1.30, £5.70, £3.10; EX 96.00 Place 6 £166.14, Place 5 £23.40..

Owner Showtime Ice Cream Concessionaire **Bred** S And R Ewart **Trained** Upper Longdon, Staffs

■ Stewards' Enquiry : Neil Farley three-day ban: careless riding (Aug 13-15)

FOCUS
An ordinary contest. The winner is progressing and the form is taken at face value.

T/Plt: £121.20 to a £1 stake. Pool £52,701.52 - 317.38 winning tickets T/Qpdt: £30.40 to a £1 stake. Pool £6,091.09 - 148.10 winning tickets JR

4375 NEWMARKET (R-H)
Friday, July 30

OFFICIAL GOING: Good to firm
Far side of July Course utilised.
Wind: Light half-behind Weather: Coudy with sunny spells

4548 PRODUCE GLOBAL SOLUTIONS "EAT MORE MUSHROOMS" H'CAP — 1m
5:55 (5:56) (Class 4) (0-80,80) 3-Y-O+ £4,533 (£1,348; £674; £336) Stalls Low

Form / RPR

0-03 **1** **Sonny Parkin**[14] [4108] 8-8-13 **63**....(v) KierenFallon 7 — 75+
(J Pearce) *racd centre and sn pushed along in rr: wnt far side 3f out: hdwy and nt clr run over 1f out: swtchd rt: r.o wl to ld towards fin: comf* **9/2**[2]

3110 **2** 1/2 **Right Rave (IRE)**[34] [3457] 3-9-4 **76**.... RichardMullen 2 — 83
(P J McBride) *racd centre: hld up: wnt far side 3f out: swtchd lft and hdwy over 1f out: rdn to ld 1f out: hdd towards fin* **11/2**[3]

0504 **3** 1 3/4 **Aflaam (IRE)**[9] [4265] 5-9-5 **72**.... AndrewHeffernan(3) 9 — 77
(R A Harris) *sn led centre tl wnt far side 3f out: chsd ldr: rdn and ev ch fr over 1f out tl styd on same pce ins fnl f* **9/1**

6152 **4** 1 3/4 **You've Been Mowed**[7] [4324] 4-9-6 **70**.... WilliamCarson 4 — 71
(R J Price) *racd alone far side 5f: overall ldr tl rdn and hdd 2f out: no ex ins fnl f* **9/2**[2]

4321 **5** 3 1/4 **Belgique (IRE)**[25] [3738] 3-9-6 **78**.... DarryllHolland 1 — 71
(R Hannon) *racd far side tl swtchd to centre 7f out: hld up in tch: wnt far side 3f out: led 2f out: rdn and hdd 1f out: wknd ins fnl f* **8/1**

26 **6** 1 1/4 **Sweet Child O'Mine**[23] [3796] 3-9-7 **79**.... TedDurcan 6 — 68
(R C Guest) *racd centre: prom: wnt far side 3f out: rdn: edgd lft and wknd over 1f out* **5/2**[1]

2350 **7** 21 **Jay's Treaty (USA)**[18] [3970] 3-8-12 **70**.... FrankieDettori 5 — —
(M Johnston) *racd centre: chsd ldrs: wnt far side 3f out: rdn whn hmpd over 2f out: sn wknd and eased over 1f out* **6/1**

1m 39.17s (-0.83) **Going Correction** +0.025s/f (Good)
WFA 3 from 4yo+ 8lb — 7 Ran SP% **115.7**
Speed ratings (Par 105): **105,104,102,101,97 96,75**
toteswingers:1&2:£8.10, 1&3:£11.10, 2&3:£9.80 CSF £29.78 CT £213.76 TOTE £5.30: £2.80, £2.40; EX 27.70.

Owner S & M Supplies (Aylsham) Ltd **Bred** Blenheim Bloodstock **Trained** Newmarket, Suffolk

FOCUS
A dry night and warm day combined with a strong wind prompted a ground change to good to firm and the riders confirmed conditions to be on the quick side. The far side course, that hadn't been raced on since the July Festival, was used. A fair handicap in which all bar You've Been Mowed shunned the far rail in the first half of the race. The gallop was a reasonable one. Modest form, with the favourite disappointing.

4549 EUROPEAN BREEDERS' FUND MAIDEN STKS — 6f
6:25 (6:26) (Class 4) 2-Y-O £4,533 (£1,348; £674; £336) Stalls Low

Form / RPR

1 **Janood (IRE)** 2-9-3 0.... FrankieDettori 3 — 81+
(Saeed Bin Suroor) *trckd ldrs: rdn over 1f out: r.o to ld nr fin* **5/4**[1]

6 **2** nk **Busker (USA)**[14] [4110] 2-9-3 0.... AhmedAjtebi 7 — 80
(Mahmood Al Zarooni) *chsd ldr: led over 2f out: rdn over 1f out: hdd nr fin* **14/1**

3 3/4 **Red Riverman** 2-9-3 0.... KoseiMiura 10 — 78+
(W J Haggas) *hld up: pushed along over 2f out: r.o wl ins fnl f: edgd lft towards fin: nt rch ldrs* **16/1**

5 **4** 2 **Proper Charlie**[17] [3991] 2-9-3 0.... NeilCallan 4 — 72
(W J Knight) *a.p: rdn over 1f out: styd on same pce ins fnl f* **9/1**

5 **5** nk **Ice Cold Bex**[13] [4142] 2-9-3 0.... KierenFallon 11 — 71
(P J McBride) *hld up in tch: rdn over 2f out: hung lft over 1f out: no ex ins fnl f* **7/1**[3]

6 1 1/2 **Labarinto** 2-9-3 0.... RichardMullen 8 — 67+
(Sir Michael Stoute) *hld up: pushed along over 2f out: outpcd over 1f out: styd on ins fnl f* **12/1**

0 **7** 1/2 **Focail Maith**[9] [4254] 2-9-3 0.... StevieDonohoe 6 — 65
(J Ryan) *led over 3f: rdn and wknd over 1f out* **100/1**

6 **8** 1 3/4 **Hero From Zero (IRE)**[18] [3961] 2-9-3 0.... DarryllHolland 5 — 60
(B J Meehan) *hld up in tch: rdn and wknd over 1f out* **5/1**[2]

6 **9** 1 1/4 **Granny Anne (IRE)**[3] [4451] 2-8-12 0.... AdamKirby 2 — 51
(A Bailey) *prom: rdn over 2f out: wknd over 1f out* **28/1**

10 12 **Owain (USA)** 2-9-3 0.... WilliamCarson 1 — 20+
(C A Dwyer) *rn green and a in rr: bhd fr 1/2-way* **80/1**

11 1 1/4 **Flinty** 2-9-3 0.... PatCosgrave 9 — 16
(R Hannon) *s.s and sn hung rt: rn green and a wl bhd* **16/1**

1m 14.12s (1.62) **Going Correction** +0.025s/f (Good) — 11 Ran SP% **115.4**
Speed ratings (Par 96): **90,89,88,85,85 83,82,80,78,62 61**
toteswingers:1&2:£9.60, 1&3:£40.60, 2&3:£69.40 CSF £20.81 TOTE £2.30: £1.50, £3.40, £5.50; EX 16.20.

Owner Godolphin **Bred** Lodge Park Stud **Trained** Newmarket, Suffolk

FOCUS
Several smart sorts on the roll of honour for this race since 2000, the best of them being 2003 scorer Haafhd, who went on to take the 2000 Guineas and the Champion Stakes the following year. Although the runner-up, fourth and fifth had previously shown no more than modest form in this latest renewal, this year's winner looks a promising type and should be able to hold his own in stronger company, with improvment to come. The gallop was a moderate one and the whole field raced away from the far rail.

NOTEBOOK
Janood(IRE) ◆, out of a debut winner who was subsequently placed in Listed company over 6f, justified the market support he had attracted throughout the day and created a favourable impression on this racecourse debut. He took some time to get on top of his stable-companion but won a shade snugly in the end and, although this bare form couldn't be rated too highly given the proximity of the placed horses, this Mill Reef entry and good-looking sort should be able to leave these bare facts a long way behind in due course. He should prove equally effective over 7f. (op 11-8 tchd 6-5)

Busker(USA), in the same ownership as the winner and easy to back, had the run of the race and turned in a much-improved effort on this first outing on a sound surface, despite edging off a true line in the closing stages. Things went his way here but he is more than capable of picking up a run-of-the-mill race in this grade. (op 12-1)

Red Riverman ◆ was backed at big odds and very much caught the eye on this racecourse debut. This gelded son of a 1m2f winner made up a fair amount of ground in the closing stages without his rider resorting to the whip, he will be very suited by the step up to 7f+ and appeals strongly as the sort to win races. (op 33-1 tchd 14-1)

Proper Charlie, who finished in front of a subsequent winner when showing ability at a modest level on his debut, was easy to back and probably ran to a similar level, despite the drop in distance not looking to be entirely in his favour. He will be seen to better effect over further when qualified for a nursery mark. (op 8-1 tchd 12-1)

Ice Cold Bex again showed ability at an ordinary level. He should do better in due course and ordinary nurseries over a bit further could offer his best chance of success. (op 11-2 tchd 5-1)

Labarinto has a long way to go before an entry in the Champagne Stakes at Doncaster can be considered a realistic target on the evidence of this debut performance but runners from this yard invariably come on a good deal from their debut runs.

Owain(USA) Official explanation: jockey said gelding was slowly away and ran green

4550 RUSSIAN STANDARD NOVICE STKS 7f

7:00 (7:00) (Class 4) 2-Y-O **£6,476** (£1,927; £963; £481) **Stalls** Low

Form RPR

1 **Peter Martins (USA)** 2-9-0 0 FrankieDettori 3 98+
(J Noseda) *trckd ldrs and a gng wl: shkn up to ld over 1f out: qcknd clr ins fnl f: impressive* **2/1**[1]

2561 2 *5* **Colorado Gold**[36] 3362 2-9-2 87 KierenFallon 1 85
(P F I Cole) *led: rdn and hdd over 1f out: no ex ins fnl f* **8/1**

1022 3 *¾* **Amwell Pinot**[13] 4135 2-9-5 89 AdamKirby 8 86
(A Bailey) *hld up: hdwy 1/2-way: rdn and hung lft over 1f out: styd on same pce* **11/4**[2]

4 *4* **Dux Scholar** 2-9-0 0 RichardMullen 9 73+
(Sir Michael Stoute) *s.i.s: hld up: hdwy over 2f out: edgd lft and lost pl over 1f out: nt clr run sn after: kpt on again towards fin* **20/1**

5 *1 ¾* **Claret'N'Blue (USA)** 2-9-0 0 NeilCallan 2 66
(B J Meehan) *hld up: pushed along 1/2-way: wknd over 1f out* **10/1**

6 *hd* **Cadore (IRE)** 2-9-0 0 JackMitchell 6 66
(P W Chapple-Hyam) *s.i.s: sn prom: nt clr run over 2f out: wknd over 1f out* **20/1**

123 7 *1* **My Son Max**[63] 2514 2-9-5 90 RichardHughes 7 68
(R Hannon) *prom: chsd ldr 4f out tl rdn and edgd rt over 1f out: wknd fnl f* **4/1**[3]

8 *42* **Chieftan** 2-9-0 0 WilliamBuick 4 —
(Sir Michael Stoute) *in rr: bhd fnl 4f: t.o* **20/1**

0 9 *3 ½* **Millies Dancer (IRE)**[7] 4332 2-8-9 0 WilliamCarson 5 —
(M G Quinlan) *chsd ldr 3f: wknd over 2f out: t.o* **100/1**

1m 25.31s (-0.39) **Going Correction** +0.025s/f (Good) 9 Ran SP% **115.5**
Speed ratings (Par 96): **103,97,96,91,89 89,88,40,36**
toteswingers:1&2:£5.60, 1&3:£2.60, 2&3:£5.50 CSF £17.78 TOTE £3.10: £1.60, £2.60, £1.10; EX 19.00.

Owner The Honorable Earle I Mack **Bred** Jim Wells & Cheyenne Stables **Trained** Newmarket, Suffolk

FOCUS

The two previous runnings of this race have thrown up good-quality performers in Awinnersgame in 2008 and Poet's Voice last year and this year's renewal has unearthed another potentially smart sort, who pulled clear with the minimum of fuss to beat two previous winners (both rated in high 80's), who in turn finished clear. The second and third set the level. The gallop was just an ordinary one.

NOTEBOOK

Peter Martins(USA) ◆, who cost $145,000 and is the second foal of a multiple 6f-1m1f winner in the US, justified the market support and created a lasting impression when striding clear of two much more experienced rivals and previous winners on this racecourse debut. This highly regarded sort holds several entries in Group races, including the Middle Park, is open to a good deal of improvement, should have no problems with 1m and he appeals strongly as one to keep on the right side. He may now head for the Acomb Stakes at York. (op 7-4 tchd 9-4)

Colorado Gold had shown fair form when beating a subsequent winner at Leicester on his previous start and, after enjoying the run of the race against the far rail, looked to better that effort in this stronger grade upped to this trip for the first time. However he's always likely to remain vulnerable to the better types in this grade and his current mark of 87 may leave him with little or no margin for error when he goes into nurseries.

Amwell Pinot had shown useful sort up to this trip but, although anything but disgraced after conceding weight nearly all round, had his limitations exposed against a potentially smart performer. However he pulled clear of the remainder, should have no problems with 1m and should continue to give a good account away from the better types. (op 3-1)

Dux Scholar ◆, the first foal of the 2005 Cheshire Oaks winner, was noticeably easy in the market before this racecourse debut but showed a fair level of ability, despite his apparent greenness. He should come on a good deal for this, especially granted a stiffer test of stamina and is more than capable of picking up an ordinary maiden in due course. (tchd 25-1)

Claret'N'Blue(USA), who cost $135,000 at the breeze-ups and is a half-brother to winners in the US, attracted support and was far from disgraced in this decent-quality event on this racecourse debut. Runners from this yard usually come on for a run and it will be interesting to see if this can be built on next time. (op 14-1 tchd 9-1)

Cadore(IRE), the first foal of a half-sister to a couple of useful sorts up to 1m3f, was easy to back and wasn't totally disgraced on this racecourse debut. This Derby and Royal Lodge entry should improve for this experience. (tchd 22-1 in a place)

My Son Max hadn't been at his best on his previous start and was again soundly beaten on this first start over 7f and this first run for two months. His yard continues in blistering form but this one has something to prove at present. (tchd 100-30)

Chieftan Official explanation: jockey said colt ran green

4551 GL EVENTS H'CAP 6f

7:30 (7:30) (Class 3) (0-90,90) 3-Y-0+ **£7,771** (£2,312; £1,155; £577) **Stalls** Low

Form RPR

0550 1 **Nosedive**[48] 2978 3-9-7 90 KierenFallon 2 95
(R C Guest) *hld up: hdwy and swtchd rt over 1f out: rdn to ld wl ins fnl f: r.o* **7/1**[3]

0221 2 *¾* **Skyfire**[6] 4371 3-8-11 80 6ex FrankieDettori 3 83
(M Johnston) *chsd ldr tl led 2f out: rdn and hdd ins fnl f: r.o* **5/1**[2]

1426 3 *nk* **Quasi Congaree (GER)**[10] 4225 4-9-0 78 (t) PatCosgrave 10 81
(I A Wood) *hld up: rdn and edgd lft over 1f out: swtchd rt and r.o wl ins fnl f: nt rch ldrs* **20/1**

3111 4 *nk* **Joe Packet**[21] 3845 3-9-2 90 JohnFahy[(5)] 7 91
(J G Portman) *trckd ldrs: racd keenly: rdn to ld briefly ins fnl f: unable qck nr fin* **9/4**[1]

3150 5 *hd* **Yer Woman (IRE)**[23] 3790 3-9-7 90 RichardHughes 9 90
(R Hannon) *hld up: rdn over 1f out: r.o wl towards fin: nt rch ldrs* **16/1**

0500 6 *½* **Desert Icon (IRE)**[21] 3845 4-8-8 72 ow1 (v[1]) WilliamBuick 5 72
(W J Knight) *wnt rt s: led: hdd 2f out: styd on u.p* **14/1**

1160 7 *nk* **Cornus**[5] 4413 8-9-3 86 (be) DeclanCannon[(5)] 8 85
(A J McCabe) *hld up: rdn over 2f out: r.o ins fnl f: nrest at fin* **16/1**

2405 8 *shd* **Shifting Star (IRE)**[21] 3850 5-9-12 90 (p) AdamKirby 1 92+
(W R Swinburn) *trckd ldrs: nt clr run fr over 1f out: nvr able to chal* **15/2**

U325 9 *4 ½* **Requisite**[4] 4424 5-8-11 75 (v) RichardMullen 11 59
(I A Wood) *s.s: n.d* **16/1**

1134 10 *1* **Tubby Isaacs**[34] 3435 6-8-13 77 NeilCallan 6 58
(D K Ivory) *hmpd s: prom: rdn over 2f out: wknd fnl f* **5/1**[2]

1m 12.55s (0.05) **Going Correction** +0.025s/f (Good)
WFA 3 from 4yo+ 5lb 10 Ran SP% **117.4**
Speed ratings (Par 107): **100,99,98,98,97 97,96,96,90,89**
toteswingers:1&2:£2.70, 1&3:£61.50, 2&3:£49.60 CSF £42.26 CT £695.62 TOTE £8.80: £2.40, £1.90, £8.00; EX 24.20.

Owner EERC **Bred** Brook Stud Bloodstock Ltd **Trained** Stainforth, S Yorks

FOCUS

A useful handicap in which the gallop was sound. All the runners raced towards the far side and the first eight finished in a bit of a heap. Very ordinary form for the grade.

NOTEBOOK

Nosedive, who cost current connections 17,000gns at Tattersalls earlier in the month, got an instant return on their investment when he showed a good turn of foot after being ridden closer to the pace than is often the case to notch his first victory since his debut last summer. Several finished in a heap but it will be interesting to see if this victory can be built on for this yard. (op 8-1)

Skyfire is the lightly raced and progressive sort his yard does so well with and he ran right up to his best dropped in trip and returned to a sound surface under a penalty for his Newcastle victory. The return to further should be in his favour and he appeals as the type to win more races. (op 4-1)

Quasi Congaree(GER) had floundered in soft ground on his previous start but fared a good deal better back on this much quicker ground. He is arguably better on Polytrack and should be able to win again on either surface when things go his way. (op 22-1 tchd 33-1)

Joe Packet came into this race at the very top of his game but, while he seemed to give it his best shot, the 9lb rise for his Ascot win may well have just found him out. However he travelled so strongly that he may be well worth a first try over the minimum distance and he may not be finished winning just yet. (op 2-1)

Yer Woman(IRE) has shown very useful form on Polytrack and ran as well as she ever has done on turf under a usual hold-up ride. She will need everything to drop perfectly into place if she is to win a similar event on turf from her current mark. (op 14-1 tchd 12-1)

Desert Icon(IRE) hasn't won since landing his maiden just over two years ago but he has slipped a fair way in the weights and fared a good deal better with the visor fitted for the first time. He is undoubtedly well treated and it will be interesting to see if the headgear works as well next time. (op 16-1)

Shifting Star(IRE) was repeatedly denied room in the last quarter mile in the first-time cheekpieces and is better than this bare form. He is high enough in the weights, though, and a losing run of two years means he would not be one to go in head down for next time. Official explanation: jockey said gelding was denied a clear run (op 11-1 tchd 7-1)

Requisite Official explanation: jockey said mare was slowly away

Tubby Isaacs Official explanation: jockey said gelding ran too free

4552 PETA PARKHOUSE BIRTHDAY H'CAP 1m 4f

8:05 (8:07) (Class 5) (0-70,76) 3-Y-O **£3,238** (£963; £481; £240) **Stalls** Centre

Form RPR

3243 1 **Meetings Man (IRE)**[14] 4087 3-9-1 62 KierenFallon 1 76
(Micky Hammond) *hld up: racd keenly: hdwy over 5f out: edgd rt and led over 2f out: rdn ins fnl f: styd on wl* **6/1**[3]

-532 2 *1 ½* **Azaday (IRE)**[11] 4212 3-8-11 58 TedDurcan 7 70
(C F Wall) *s.i.s: hld up: hdwy to chse wnr over 2f out: rdn over 1f out: styd on same pce ins fnl f* **10/11**[1]

-263 3 *10* **Red Barcelona (IRE)**[50] 2908 3-8-10 57 DarryllHolland 4 53
(M H Tompkins) *chsd ldrs: rdn over 1f out: wknd fnl f* **9/2**[2]

-603 4 *4* **Polebrook**[10] 4235 3-8-4 51 oh1 JimmyQuinn 3 41
(J R Jenkins) *s.i.s: rdn over 3f out: wknd over 1f out* **33/1**

0666 5 *6* **Highland Cadett**[25] 3723 3-8-5 52 (v) WilliamCarson 8 32
(B R Millman) *led 2f: chsd ldrs: rdn over 3f out: nt clr run over 2f out: sn wknd* **16/1**

4360 6 *2* **On The Cusp (IRE)**[7] 4337 3-9-1 65 RobertLButler[(3)] 6 42
(P Butler) *chsd ldrs: rdn over 3f out: hmpd over 2f out: wknd over 1f out* **25/1**

0-03 7 *17* **Cheerfully**[14] 4114 3-9-9 70 WilliamBuick 5 20
(J H M Gosden) *led 10f out: rdn over 3f out: hdd over 2f out: wknd and eased over 1f out* **13/2**

2m 32.27s (-0.63) **Going Correction** +0.025s/f (Good) 7 Ran SP% **110.9**
Speed ratings (Par 100): **103,102,95,92,88 87,76**
toteswingers:1&2:£1.50, 1&3:£4.30, 2&3:£1.50 CSF £11.15 CT £24.74 TOTE £4.50: £1.90, £1.50; EX 9.20.

Owner Paul R Snook **Bred** Hakan Keles **Trained** Middleham Moor, N Yorks

FOCUS

A modest handicap in which the gallop was just an ordinary one. The first two pulled clear in the last furlong and a half and the form, which is tricky to pin down, has been rated around them.

Highland Cadett Official explanation: jockey said gelding was denied a clear run

4553 NGK SPARK PLUGS H'CAP 6f

8:35 (8:35) (Class 5) (0-70,70) 3-Y-O **£3,238** (£963; £481; £240) **Stalls** Low

Form RPR

3123 1 **Pirate's Song**[28] 3638 3-9-8 69 (t) RichardHughes 3 74+
(J A R Toller) *trckd ldrs: rdn to ld over 1f out: r.o: jst hld on* **5/4**[1]

2440 2 *nk* **Mrs Boss**[27] 3677 3-9-0 64 JamesMillman[(3)] 1 68
(B R Millman) *hld up: hdwy over 1f out: r.o wl: nt quite get up* **7/1**

0051 3 *hd* **Watch Chain (IRE)**[11] 4210 3-8-8 55 6ex DarryllHolland 4 58+
(M H Tompkins) *hld up: r.o wl ins fnl f: nrst fin* **10/3**[2]

2-30 4 *hd* **Praesepe**[27] 3663 3-8-11 58 KoseiMiura 5 61
(W J Haggas) *hld up: r.o ins fnl f: nrst fin* **6/1**[3]

3-06 5 *nse* **Excellent Thought**[16] 4031 3-9-7 68 J-PGuillambert 6 71?
(P Howling) *s.i.s: plld hrd and led after 1f: edgd rt and hdd over 1f out: styd on u.p* **10/1**

3620 6 *5* **Danzoe (IRE)**[9] 4248 3-9-9 70 (p) StevieDonohoe 2 57
(Mrs C A Dunnett) *led 1f: chsd ldr: rdn over 1f out: wknd fnl f* **12/1**

1m 13.89s (1.39) **Going Correction** +0.025s/f (Good) 6 Ran SP% **111.1**
Speed ratings (Par 100): **91,90,90,90,90 83**
toteswingers:1&2:£3.00, 1&3:£1.40, 2&3:£2.40 CSF £10.41 CT £22.26 TOTE £2.00: £1.40, £2.50; EX 11.80 Place 6 £55.18, Place 5 £12.17..

Owner Saeed Manana **Bred** Genesis Green Stud Ltd And Thurso Ltd **Trained** Newmarket, Suffolk

FOCUS

Another modest handicap. The gallop was only fair and the first five finished in a heap. The runner-up makes the best guide to the form.

Watch Chain(IRE) Official explanation: jockey said colt was denied a clear run

T/Plt: £103.80 to a £1 stake. Pool £50,962.96 - 358.08 winning tickets. T/Qpdt: £11.80 to a £1 stake. Pool £4,964.66 - 308.79 winning tickets CR

[4336]THIRSK (L-H)

Friday, July 30

OFFICIAL GOING: Good to firm (good in places; watered; 10.4)

Top bend rail moved out 5yds.

Wind: light 1/2 behind Weather: overcast, light rain

4554 PICKERING CASTLE CLAIMING STKS 7f

2:25 (2:28) (Class 4) 2-Y-O £3,691 (£1,098; £548; £274) Stalls Low

Form RPR

3006 1 **He's The Star (IRE)**[4] 4429 2-8-9 60 CathyGannon 3 62
(P D Evans) *chsd ldrs: swtchd rt 2f out: led 1f out: kpt on* 9/1

0630 2 1/2 **Chilworth Lass (IRE)**[21] 3864 2-8-5 53 (v[1]) LiamJones 13 56
(M R Channon) *gave problems in stalls: chsd ldrs: led 2f out: hdd 1f out: no ex clsng stages* 22/1

3223 3 2 1/2 **Alhoni**[9] 4241 2-8-4 56 (v[1]) JimmyQuinn 7 49
(J J Quinn) *s.i.s: hmpd after 1f: hdwy over 3f out: kpt on fnl 2f: tk n.d 3rd last 100yds* 7/2[1]

4 1 **El Torbellino (IRE)** 2-8-7 0 SilvestreDeSousa 8 50
(D O'Meara) *in rr and green: hdwy over 2f out: hung lft over 1f out: kpt on same pce* 14/1

030 5 2 **Karafuse (IRE)**[13] 4150 2-8-7 56 (b) DavidAllan 12 45
(T D Easterby) *led over 1f: led over 2f out: sn hdd: wknd ins fnl f* 10/1

065 6 1 3/4 **Ventose**[8] 4293 2-8-5 0 SamHitchcott 4 38
(M R Channon) *towards rr: effrt on outside over 2f out: nvr nr ldrs* 8/1

5666 7 1 3/4 **Dispol Snapper (IRE)**[9] 4241 2-8-10 52 PhillipMakin 2 39
(P T Midgley) *rrd s: bhd tl styd on fnl 2f* 28/1

000 8 1/2 **Jealousy Defined (IRE)**[49] 2939 2-8-7 48 AndrewElliott 10 35
(N Tinkler) *unruly s: in rr: effrt 3f out: hung lft: nvr a factor* 40/1

4 9 hd **Evening In (IRE)**[13] 4150 2-8-3 0 PaulPickard(3) 6 33
(P T Midgley) *prom: effrt over 2f out: sn wknd* 5/1[3]

4 10 1 3/4 **Roi Du Boeuf (IRE)**[33] 3472 2-8-13 0 PatrickHills(3) 14 39
(R Hannon) *chsd ldrs on outside: effrt 3f out: hung lft and lost pl over 1f out* 7/1

00 11 2 1/2 **Romano (IRE)**[27] 3657 2-8-12 0 TonyHamilton 9 28
(P T Midgley) *lost pl and in rr over 4f out: drvn over 2f out: sn wknd* 80/1

0302 12 3 **Kodibelle (IRE)**[9] 4241 2-8-2 54 (b) KellyHarrison(3) 1 14
(T D Easterby) *dwlt: drvn to ld over 5f out: hdd over 2f out: lost pl over 1f out* 9/2[2]

0000 13 2 3/4 **Dallas Legend (IRE)**[14] 4103 2-8-1 42 (v[1]) NickyMackay 5 3
(J Ryan) *s.i.s: a in rr: bhd fnl 3f* 66/1

1m 28.19s (0.99) **Going Correction** +0.025s/f (Good) 13 Ran SP% 119.4

Speed ratings (Par 96): **95,94,91,90,88 86,84,83,83,81 78,75,71**

toteswingers:1&2:£85.40, 1&3:£9.80, 2&3:£23.20 CSF £198.09 TOTE £12.90: £3.60, £8.00, £1.10; EX 226.60.

Owner Bathwick Gold Partnership **Bred** Hong Kong Breeders Club **Trained** Pandy, Monmouths

FOCUS

This was a very modest claimer and it hardly looked a rich source of future winners, but at least the pace was sound. Not form to dwell on. There was a bit of a delay to proceedings as a couple became upset beforehand, which wouldn't have helped those already in the stalls.

NOTEBOOK

He's The Star(IRE), held in a nursery at Wolverhampton four days earlier, had done little since finishing third at Bath on his second run and has been beaten in a seller. He needed a strong ride to assert and does not make much appeal to follow this up. (op 10-1)

Chilworth Lass(IRE) is another who has been beaten in selling company. She ran better in the first-time visor and rallied late on after wandering when in front. (op 16-1)

Alhoni has now been placed on her last five starts. She ran respectably in the first-time headgear and has the basic ability to win a similar event, but the conclusion has to be that she is not one to trust. (op 5-1 tchd 10-3)

El Torbellino(IRE) ◆ ran decidedly green in rear but was keeping on nicely at the end and looks the one to take from the race. She can be expected to step up on this next time. Official explanation: jockey said filly hung left in straight (op 10-1)

Karafuse(IRE), who faded after racing up with the pace, was a nose behind Alhoni at Redcar two runs back and was 3lb worse off on these terms. (op 12-1)

Ventose was the pick on adjusted official figures. Down in grade after contesting three maidens, she briefly threatened to take a hand in the finish before fading. (op 10-1)

Dispol Snapper(IRE) Official explanation: jockey said colt missed the break

Evening In(IRE) finished ahead of Karafuse when fourth on her debut, but she ran as if this extra furlong was against her. (op 7-2)

Roi Du Boeuf(IRE), Richard Hannon's first runner at Thirsk for more than five years, offered little and is clearly one of his yard's least talented juveniles. (op 8-1 tchd 6-1)

4555 BYLAND ABBEY H'CAP 7f

3:00 (3:00) (Class 5) (0-70,74) 3-Y-O+ £3,691 (£1,098; £548; £274) Stalls Low

Form RPR

5031 1 **Glenridding**[4] 4428 6-9-11 74 6ex (p) DaleSwift(5) 8 85
(J G Given) *drvn early to ld: mde all: over 2 l clr 1f out: styd on gamely: hld on towards fin* 11/4[2]

3233 2 3/4 **Kilt Rock (IRE)**[22] 3831 3-9-0 70 IanBrennan(5) 1 76
(R C Guest) *in tch: styd on to chse wnr over 1f out: kpt on ins fnl f* 15/2[3]

530- 3 nse **Diggeratt (USA)**[303] 6370 4-9-0 65 MarzenaJeziorek(7) 13 74+
(R A Fahey) *swtchd lft after s: in rr: effrt and nt clr run several time fr over 2f out: swtchd rt over 1f out: fin wl* 14/1

0550 4 2 **Nacho Libre**[21] 3855 5-9-9 67 (b) PaulMulrennan 11 70
(M W Easterby) *stdd s: towards rr: hdwy on outside over 2f out: kpt on same pce fnl f* 12/1

0501 5 2 **Sheila Toss (IRE)**[8] 4300 3-9-3 71 6ex (b) PatrickHills(3) 9 66
(R Hannon) *chsd ldrs: drvn over 2f out: one pce appr fnl f* 9/4[1]

0601 6 nk **Seldom (IRE)**[11] 4197 4-9-6 64 6ex SilvestreDeSousa 10 61
(M Brittain) *in rr: drvn over 3f out: hdwy over 2f out: nt clr run: swtchd rt over 1f out: styd on ins fnl f* 8/1

0-02 7 2 1/4 **Musca (IRE)**[16] 4014 6-9-2 60 TonyHamilton 3 51
(C Grant) *prom: drvn 3f out: wknd appr fnl f* 25/1

0040 8 1/2 **Baybshambles (IRE)**[12] 4171 6-9-5 63 PJMcDonald 6 53
(R E Barr) *chsd ldrs: wknd fnl f* 16/1

04-0 9 1/2 **Ubenkor (IRE)**[83] 1926 5-9-9 67 DavidAllan 2 55
(M Herrington) *s.i.s: in rr: sme hdwy on inner over 2f out: hung lft: nvr a factor* 18/1

1204 10 4 1/2 **Spin Again (IRE)**[31] 3539 5-9-3 66 BillyCray(5) 12 42
(D Nicholls) *chsd ldrs on outer: lost pl over 1f out: eased towards fin* 14/1

1m 26.74s (-0.46) **Going Correction** +0.025s/f (Good)

WFA 3 from 4yo+ 7lb 10 Ran SP% 116.3

Speed ratings (Par 103): **103,102,102,99,97 97,94,94,93,88**

toteswingers:1&2:£5.40, 1&3:£7.80, 2&3:£14.00 CSF £23.87 CT £254.97 TOTE £3.90: £1.60, £1.20, £5.10; EX 25.60.

Owner Tremousser Partnership **Bred** Bolton Grange **Trained** Willoughton, Lincs

FOCUS

A modest handicap. The winner is the best guide to the form.

4556 ROE HEAD MAIDEN STKS 1m

3:35 (3:36) (Class 4) 3-Y-O+ £4,792 (£1,425; £712; £355) Stalls Low

Form RPR

0242 1 **Mata Keranjang (USA)**[8] 4307 3-9-3 100 (b[1]) SilvestreDeSousa 11 78+
(P F I Cole) *t.k.h on outside in midfield: hdwy 3f out: sn drvn: led over 1f out: forged 4 l clr: eased wl ins fnl f* 1/4[1]

2 2 **Tarooq (USA)** 4-9-11 0 TonyHamilton 8 70+
(R A Fahey) *s.s: swtchd lft after s: hdwy over 2f out: styd on to take 2nd ins fnl f: no ch w wnr* 20/1[3]

03 3 3/4 **Forks**[92] 1648 3-9-3 0 PaulMulrennan 6 66
(B Smart) *led: hung bdly lft over 2f out: hdd over 1f out: kpt on same pce* 10/1[2]

0 4 1 1/2 **March Forth**[25] 3733 3-9-3 0 JimmyQuinn 12 62
(Tom Dascombe) *chsd ldrs: hmpd and swtchd lft 2f out: kpt on same pce* 50/1

0 5 nk **Nephele (IRE)**[42] 3176 3-8-12 0 DavidAllan 4 57
(T D Easterby) *chsd ldrs: one pce fnl 2f* 25/1

6 6 1/2 **Hades (IRE)**[67] 2393 3-9-3 0 DavidNolan 5 60
(T D Easterby) *chsd ldrs: chal 3f out: hmpd and swtchd lft 2f out: one pce* 10/1[2]

- 7 3 **Prince James** 3-8-10 0 DavidSimmonson(7) 2 53
(M W Easterby) *dwlt: in rr: hdwy on wd outside over 2f out: nvr nr ldrs* 66/1

8 3/4 **Denison Flyer** 3-9-0 0 BarryMcHugh(3) 13 51
(L A Mullaney) *in rr: sme late hdwy* 80/1

0-0 9 4 **Up At Last**[37] 3333 3-8-12 0 LiamJones 10 37
(W J Haggas) *trckd ldrs: t.k.h: wknd over 1f out* 22/1

0 10 2 1/4 **Barton Bounty**[7] 4339 3-9-3 0 PhillipMakin 3 36
(P D Niven) *a towards rr* 66/1

0 11 1/2 **Shamo Hill Theatre**[16] 4018 3-9-3 0 PatrickMathers 1 35
(C J Teague) *a in rr* 100/1

5 12 3 3/4 **Majic Mojo**[38] 3285 3-8-9 0 MichaelStainton(3) 7 21
(R M Whitaker) *t.k.h in midfield: awkward bnd 4f out: wknd over 2f out* 66/1

0 13 9 **Sandgate Story**[25] 3733 4-9-3 0 GaryBartley(3) 9 —
(N Wilson) *in tch: lost pl 3f out* 100/1

1m 40.38s (0.28) **Going Correction** +0.025s/f (Good)

WFA 3 from 4yo 8lb 13 Ran SP% 120.8

Speed ratings (Par 105): **99,97,96,94,94 93,90,90,86,83 83,79,70**

toteswingers:1&2:£2.60, 1&3:£2.00, 2&3:£3.70 CSF £11.30 TOTE £1.20: £1.02, £3.60, £1.80; EX 7.90.

Owner Mrs Fitri Hay **Bred** Dan Dixon **Trained** Whatcombe, Oxon

FOCUS

The winner apart this was a very moderate maiden, lacking strength in depth. The pace was just ordinary. The form is rated around the third and sixth with the winner well below his best.

Forks Official explanation: jockey said gelding hung right throughout

4557 THIRSK CASTLE FILLIES' H'CAP 1m 4f

4:10 (4:11) (Class 5) (0-70,70) 3-Y-O £3,691 (£1,098; £548; £274) Stalls Low

Form RPR

2440 1 **Cat O' Nine Tails**[14] 4120 3-9-0 63 AndrewElliott 11 71
(M Johnston) *led: qcknd over 3f out: drvn rt out: nvr threatened* 12/1

-023 2 3/4 **Yankee Bright (USA)**[40] 3242 3-9-5 68 LeeVickers 4 75
(J G Given) *chsd wnr: kpt on fnl f: no real imp* 20/1

4-62 3 1 **Little Oz (IRE)**[10] 4235 3-8-10 59 JimmyQuinn 9 64
(E A L Dunlop) *swtchd lft after s: sn chsng ldrs: effrt over 2f out: hrd rdn and styd on same pce fnl f* 9/4[1]

-035 4 2 1/4 **Chicane**[14] 4120 3-9-4 67 LiamJones 3 69+
(W J Haggas) *s.i.s: in rr: pushed along 5f out: hung lft over 2f out: kpt on fnl f* 9/1

3013 5 1 1/2 **Magic Millie (IRE)**[16] 4017 3-8-7 56 SilvestreDeSousa 6 55
(D O'Meara) *mid-div: effrt over 3f out: one pce fnl 2f* 5/1[3]

5422 6 1 **Sheiling (IRE)**[14] 4087 3-8-12 64 BarryMcHugh(3) 2 62
(R A Fahey) *mid-div: drvn over 2f out: nvr a threat* 3/1[2]

0406 7 1 **Juwireya**[29] 3593 3-9-7 70 PhillipMakin 8 66
(P W Hiatt) *in rr: drvn 4f out: outpcd over 2f out: kpt on ins fnl f* 20/1

4-03 8 nse **Lovely Eyes (IRE)**[48] 2953 3-9-2 65 NickyMackay 7 61
(D M Simcock) *chsd ldrs: hung lft and wknd 2f out* 6/1

00-4 9 2 1/2 **Astrovenus**[88] 1777 3-8-3 57 AshleyMorgan(5) 1 49
(M H Tompkins) *dwlt: hld up in rr: effrt over 2f out: nvr on terms* 20/1

2m 34.92s (-1.28) **Going Correction** +0.025s/f (Good) 9 Ran SP% 118.7

Speed ratings (Par 97): **105,104,103,102,101 100,100,99,98**

toteswingers:1&2:£21.10, 1&3:£7.40, 2&3:£10.80 CSF £225.99 CT £732.58 TOTE £17.90: £4.90, £6.30, £1.10; EX 166.70.

Owner S And D Richards, N Browne And M Broke **Bred** The Duke Of Devonshire & Floors Farming **Trained** Middleham Moor, N Yorks

FOCUS

A modest handicap for fillies. The winner dictated the pace and a lot of these failed to get into it. The form makes some sense and has been rated around the first three, but there are one or two doubts.

Cat O' Nine Tails Official explanation: trainer's rep had no explanation for the apparent improvement in form

4558 PETER BELL MEMORIAL H'CAP 6f

4:45 (4:46) (Class 4) (0-85,85) 3-Y-O+ £4,792 (£1,425; £712; £355) Stalls High

Form RPR

1025 1 **Bahamian Lad**[20] 3898 5-8-10 72 (p) KellyHarrison(3) 10 82
(R Hollinshead) *chsd ldrs stands' side: hung lft and styd on fnl f: led nr fin* 7/1[3]

6065 2 hd **Tabaret**[13] 4148 7-9-7 83 (p) MichaelStainton(3) 9 92
(R M Whitaker) *trckd ldrs: hung lft and led 1f out: hdd and no ex nr fin* 9/2[2]

410- 3 1 1/4 **Electioneer (USA)**[349] 5033 3-8-12 76 DavidAllan 12 80
(M W Easterby) *s.i.s: hdwy over 2f out: edgd lft and kpt on fnl f: will improve* 25/1

1230 4 1 1/4 **Legal Eagle (IRE)**[20] 3898 5-8-11 77 (p) JordanDodd(7) 6 78
(Paul Green) *led on outer: edgd lft over 1f out: sn hdd and fdd* 10/1

0502 5 2 1/4 **Just Sam (IRE)**[12] 4171 5-8-6 68 BarryMcHugh(3) 4 62
(R E Barr) *chsd ldrs: wknd over 1f out* 10/1

001 6 2 1/2 **Caranbola**[11] 4199 4-8-9 68 6ex JimmyQuinn 2 54
(M Brittain) *s.i.s: sme hdwy over 1f out: nvr nr ldrs* 20/1

0040 **7** ½ **Ishetoo**[14] 4118 6-9-11 **84**....(bt) PhillipMakin 11 68
(Ollie Pears) *chsd ldrs stands' side: rdn and outpcd over 2f out: kpt on fnl f* **11/4**[1]

0220 **8** 2½ **Silver Wind**[29] 3584 5-9-2 **75**....(v) SilvestreDeSousa 3 51
(P D Evans) *mid-div on outside: reminders over 3f out: nvr a factor* **10/1**

30-0 **9** ½ **Mister Tinktastic (IRE)**[15] 4065 4-8-12 **76**.... PatrickDonaghy(5) 5 51
(N J Vaughan) *s.v.s: sme late hdwy* **25/1**

3320 **10** hd **The Hermitage (IRE)**[14] 4121 3-8-13 **77**.... AndrewElliott 7 50
(M Johnston) *chsd ldr: wknd over 1f out* **10/1**

0000 **11** ½ **Green Manalishi**[4] 4440 9-9-12 **85**....(p) StephenCraine 8 57
(K A Ryan) *chsd ldrs: hung lft and lost pl over 1f out* **16/1**

1002 **12** ½ **Methaaly (IRE)**[6] 4354 7-8-10 **69**....(be) LiamJones 1 40
(M Mullineaux) *s.v.s: nvr on terms* **9/1**

1m 10.2s (-2.50) **Going Correction** -0.275s/f (Firm)
WFA 3 from 4yo+ 5lb 12 Ran SP% **122.0**
Speed ratings (Par 105): **105,104,103,101,98 95,94,91,90,90 89,88**
toteswingers:1&2:£8.00, 1&3:£36.60, 2&3:£39.60 CSF £38.71 CT £574.29 TOTE £7.50: £2.50, £2.30, £9.90; EX 38.70.
Owner Graham Brothers Racing Partnership **Bred** J D Graham **Trained** Upper Longdon, Staffs

FOCUS
A fair sprint handicap, run in a time inside standard. As is often the case here a high draw was advantageous, with the main action taking place towards the stands' side. A turf personal best from the winner.
Electioneer(USA) ◆ Official explanation: jockey said gelding missed the break
Green Manalishi Official explanation: vet said gelding finished distressed
Methaaly(IRE) Official explanation: jockey said blindfold became entangled on eye shield and gelding was slowly away

4559 HELMSLEY APPRENTICE H'CAP 6f
5:20 (5:21) (Class 5) (0-70,68) 3-Y-0+ **£3,691** (£1,098; £548; £274) **Stalls** High

Form RPR

3006 **1** **Timber Treasure (USA)**[14] 4093 6-8-7 **55**....(b) JordanDodd(8) 8 63
(Paul Green) *s.i.s: hdwy on wd outside over 2f out: led jst ins fnl f: kpt on wl* **12/1**

6320 **2** ¾ **Ryedane (IRE)**[3] 4452 8-10-0 **68**....(b) NeilFarley 7 74
(T D Easterby) *hld up: hdwy over 2f out: edgd lft and styd on wl fnl f: snatched 2nd nr fin: sddle slipped* **9/2**[2]

-303 **3** ¾ **Needy McCredie**[23] 3774 4-8-10 **50**.... IanBurns 12 54
(J R Turner) *s.i.s: hdwy stands' side over 1f out: led and hung violently lft over 1f out: hdd jst ins fnl f: kpt on same pce* **13/2**

0322 **4** 2¾ **Albero Di Giuda (IRE)**[7] 4342 5-9-0 **54**....(bt) AlexEdwards 9 49
(F Sheridan) *w ldrs: one pce fnl f* **10/3**[1]

1600 **5** 1¼ **Almaty Express**[1] 4516 8-8-6 **51**....(b) EleanorMcGowan(5) 1 42
(J R Weymes) *chsd ldrs on outer: kpt on fnl f* **28/1**

0/03 **6** ½ **Call The Law (IRE)**[15] 4071 4-8-2 **50**.... ChristyMews(8) 13 39
(Mrs P Sly) *led tl over 1f out: fdd* **7/1**

605 **7** 3 **Future Gem**[15] 4064 4-8-12 **52**....(p) MarzenaJeziorek 11 32
(N Wilson) *mid-div: hdwy towards stands' side over 2f out: wknd over 1f out* **28/1**

5 **8** nk **Boy The Bell**[27] 3682 3-9-0 **62**.... JosephYoung(3) 5 40
(M Mullineaux) *w ldrs on outer: wknd over 1f out* **16/1**

5000 **9** ½ **Royal Crest**[143] 838 4-8-4 **49** oh4....(b1) ThomasBrown(5) 3 26
(A Crook) *chsd ldrs on outer: outpcd fnl 2f* **33/1**

0-00 **10** ½ **Sea Rover (IRE)**[7] 4345 6-9-10 **64**.... FrancisHayes 14 39
(M Brittain) *w ldrs stands' side: wknd over 1f out* **11/2**[3]

-160 **11** 1 **Helping Hand (IRE)**[17] 3977 5-8-7 **50**.... NicolaJackson(3) 2 22
(R Hollinshead) *chsd ldrs on outer: wknd appr fnl f* **18/1**

3462 **12** shd **Simple Rhythm**[7] 4343 4-9-3 **65**.... JoshCrane(8) 4 37
(J Ryan) *chsd ldrs on outer: lost pl appr fnl f* **12/1**

1m 11.41s (-1.29) **Going Correction** -0.275s/f (Firm)
WFA 3 from 4yo+ 5lb 12 Ran SP% **118.8**
Speed ratings (Par 103): **97,96,95,91,89 89,85,84,83,83 81,81**
toteswingers:1&2:£10.50, 1&3:£15.80, 2&3:£5.40 CSF £64.32 CT £391.74 TOTE £16.50: £3.00, £1.20, £3.20; EX 105.50 Place 6 £131.95; Place 5 £49.45.
Owner Gary Williams **Bred** London Thoroughbred Services & Derry Mee **Trained** Lydiate, Merseyside
■ Jordan Dodd's first winner.
■ Stewards' Enquiry : Ian Burns caution: careless riding

FOCUS
A very modest apprentice handicap, run acce and in a time 1.21 seconds slower than the earlier 66-85 handicap. There were plenty with chances approaching the final furlong and in contrast to the previous race the principals came up the centre. They came from the rear too. The winner is rated to this year's form.
T/Plt: £418.00 to a £1 stake. Pool:£44,793.73 - 78.22 winning tickets T/Qpdt: £39.10 to a £1 stake. Pool:£3,400.50 - 64.30 winning tickets WG

4523 GALWAY (R-H)
Friday, July 30

OFFICIAL GOING: Good to firm

4563a ARTHUR GUINNESS H'CAP 1m 100y
7:55 (7:56) (50-70,68) 3-Y-0 **£7,632** (£1,769; £774; £442)

RPR

1 **Days Ahead (IRE)**[16] 4034 3-9-6 64....(p) JAHeffernan 10 71+
(Eoin Doyle, Ire) *chsd ldrs: 7th 1/2-way: rdn into 4th 2f out: 2nd 1f out: styd on to ld last 100yds: kpt on wl* **8/1**

2 3 **Elusive Art (IRE)**[16] 4034 3-9-2 60....(p) CO'Donoghue 9 60
(David Marnane, Ire) *chsd ldrs: 4th 1/2-way: rdn into 2nd 2f out: 3rd 1f out: swished tail: kpt on to take 2nd on line* **7/1**[3]

3 shd **Push Me (IRE)**[22] 3839 3-9-6 64.... PTownend 8 64
(John A Quinn, Ire) *disp early: led after 2f: rdn 2f out: kpt on ent st: hdd fnl 100yds and no ex: lost 2nd on line* **20/1**

4 2½ **Ebony Cat (IRE)**[25] 3745 3-9-2 60....(p) KLatham 4 55
(B P Galvin, Ire) *mid-div: 8th 1/2-way: rdn into 5th 2f out: 4th 1f out: kpt on same pce fnl f* **25/1**

5 ½ **Red Fighter (IRE)**[4] 4444 3-9-2 67.... JPO'Brien(7) 15 60
(Daniel Mark Loughnane, Ire) *mid-div: 9th 1/2-way: rdn 2f out: styd on into 7th 1f out: kpt on same pce fnl f* **12/1**

6 hd **Al Khawarezmi**[20] 3929 3-9-6 64.... FMBerry 2 57
(Cecil Ross, Ire) *hld up towards rr: rdn and hdwy under 2f out: 7th ent st: 5th 1f out: kpt on same pce fnl f* **16/1**

7 shd **Almadaa**[23] 3801 3-8-8 55.... ShaneFoley(3) 5 48
(David Marnane, Ire) *hld up towards rr early: 11th 1/2-way: hdwy into 7th 2f out: rdn in 6th 1f out: no ex ins fnl f and kpt on same pce* **12/1**

8 hd **Walter De La Mare (IRE)**[7] 4352 3-9-3 64.... GFCarroll(3) 16 56
(John Joseph Murphy, Ire) *mid-div: rdn in 10th 2f out: 8th 1f out: kpt on same pce fnl f* **5/1**[2]

9 ¾ **Cognomen (IRE)**[11] 4219 3-9-3 64.... EJMcNamara(3) 7 55
(V T O'Brien, Ire) *mid-div: 13th 1/2-way: rdn into 9th 2f out: no ex over 1f out: kpt on same pce* **20/1**

10 nk **Lily's Star (IRE)**[18] 3998 3-8-8 59.... DCByrne(7) 13 49
(H Rogers, Ire) *towards rr: rdn and no imp over 2f out: 14th ent st: kpt on one pce st* **25/1**

11 1¼ **First In The Queue (IRE)**[11] 4201 3-9-9 67.... LiamKeniry 11 54
(S Kirk) *mid-div best: 12th 1/2-way: rdn and no imp over 2f out: kpt on one pce st* **3/1**[1]

12 3½ **New Atalanta (IRE)**[9] 4272 3-8-13 57.... MCHussey 6 37
(Ms Maria Kelly, Ire) *in rr of mid-div: rdn and no imp over 2f out: kpt on one pce* **33/1**

13 1¾ **Sughera (IRE)**[11] 4217 3-8-13 57.... KJManning 3 33
(A J Martin, Ire) *towards rr for most: nvr a factor* **16/1**

14 7 **Breezed Well (IRE)**[28] 3654 3-8-11 58....(bt) BACurtis(3) 12 18
(James McAuley, Ire) *disp early: 2nd after 2f: rdn in 3rd 2f out: no ex in 5th ent st: wknd* **16/1**

15 1¾ **Non Tiscordardime**[64] 2453 3-8-9 60....(p) LFRoche(7) 17 16
(Niall Moran, Ire) *mid-div: 10th 1/2-way: rdn and no ex over 2f out* **25/1**

16 1 **Goldarover (IRE)**[23] 3802 3-9-3 68.... TCCarroll(7) 18 22
(Noel Meade, Ire) *chsd ldrs: 6th 1/2-way: rdn 2f out: no ex and wknd bef st* **9/1**

17 1¼ **Lady L (IRE)**[16] 4034 3-9-5 68....(b1) MACleere(5) 1 19
(David Wachman, Ire) *chsd ldrs: 3rd 1/2-way: rdn in 8th 2f out: no ex and wknd* **14/1**

18 15 **Rockin N Reelin (USA)**[18] 4006 3-9-5 63....(p) CDHayes 14 —
(J T Gorman, Ire) *chsd ldrs: 5th 1/2-way: rdn and no ex 3f out: sn wknd and eased ent st* **12/1**

1m 50.09s (-0.11) 18 Ran SP% **146.7**
CSF £69.18 CT £1164.42 TOTE £7.30: £1.70, £1.70, £5.80, £10.00; DF 50.70.
Owner M F Mason **Bred** Leo Hayes **Trained** Mooncoin, Co. Kilkenny

FOCUS
A competitive handicap rated around the third.

NOTEBOOK
Days Ahead(IRE) went close to causing a bit of an upset at Killarney early this month and went one better here. Held up just behind the early pace, he made good headway to pursue the leader into the straight and sustained his effort to lead inside the last and win going away. He's only an ordinary handicapper but probably progressive in this sort of grade and there are reasons why he shouldn't get too harsh a penalty for this success. (op 7/1)
Elusive Art(IRE) doesn't exactly look like a filly to trust with one's life. Racing close enough to the pace, she didn't have a change of pace to cope with the eventual third when that one kicked on. When coming under pressure in the straight though she cocked her jaw, ducked in behind a horse in front of her and swished her tail, a most unholy trinity of bad attributes. For all that, she still got up to be second. Official explanation: jockey said filly hung right throughout (op 8/1)
Push Me(IRE) was certainly given a positive ride in the manner of a filly whose stamina didn't seem to be in doubt. Kicking on turning into the straight, she got about three lengths but was unable to respond when the winner challenged.
Ebony Cat(IRE) ran without a shoe having lost one while being unruly in the parade ring. It may well have had an effect. She was closing under pressure on the outside on the downhill run to the straight but her effort flattened out inside the last. Under the circumstances it was a good effort.
Red Fighter(IRE) stayed on past beaten horses late in the race but was never really a factor. (op 20/1)
Al Khawarezmi was slowly into stride but made some good headway to be on the heels of the leaders coming down the hill until his effort flattened out.
First In The Queue(IRE) was never a factor. Official explanation: trainer and colt made a respratorey noise in running; vet said gelding was found to have an upper respiratory tract infection following a post-race endoscopic examination (op 3/1 tchd 7/2)

4564 - (Foreign Racing) - See Raceform Interactive

3933 DEAUVILLE (R-H)
Friday, July 30

OFFICIAL GOING: Turf - good; fibresand - standard

4565a PRIX D'ETREHAM (CONDITIONS) (2YO COLTS & GELDINGS) (FIBRESAND) 7f 110y
12:30 (12:00) 2-Y-0 **£15,044** (£6,017; £4,513; £3,008; £1,504)

RPR

1 **Nashi (FR)**[30] 2-8-10 0.... JulienAuge 5 80
(E J O'Neill, France) **133/10**

2 snk **Hung Parliament (FR)**[13] 4135 2-8-10 0.... DavyBonilla 7 80
(Tom Dascombe) *broke slowly: settled in rr on rail: swtchd to outside ent st: rdn and qcknd wl 2f out: wnt 2nd ent fnl f: r.o wl: jst failed* **9/2**[3]

3 ¾ **Halowin**[38] 2-8-10 0.... ChristopheSoumillon 4 78
(J-V Toux, France) **6/1**

4 3 **Ocean Gold (FR)** 2-8-10 0.... GregoryBenoist 6 71
(S Loeuillet, France) **14/1**

5 shd **Afrikanos (FR)**[24] 2-8-10 0.... JohanVictoire 1 71
(F-X De Chevigny, France) **5/1**

6 4 **Bungur (FR)**[35] 2-9-0 0.... StephanePasquier 3 65
(R Gibson, France) **4/1**[2]

7 2 **Trevieres (FR)**[14] 2-8-10 0.... OlivierPeslier 2 57
(C Laffon-Parias, France) **2/1**[1]

1m 33.7s (93.70) 7 Ran SP% **116.1**
WIN (incl. 1 euro stake): 14.30. PLACES: 4.90, 3.10. SF: 66.00.
Owner David Barlow **Bred** Serge Becerra **Trained** France

NOTEBOOK
Hung Parliament(FR), last of four in a conditions race at Newbury on his debut, went close to getting off the mark on his debut on sand. He shouldn't have a great deal of trouble winning a maiden.

4566a PRIX DU CARROUSEL (LISTED) (4YO+) (TURF) 1m 7f
2:35 (12:00) 4-Y-0+ **£23,008** (£9,203; £6,902; £4,601; £2,300)

RPR

1 **Americain (USA)**[22] 5-8-11 0.... GeraldMosse 5 100
(A De Royer-Dupre, France) **13/10**[1]

2 3 **La Tournesol (GER)**[108] 1291 5-8-8 0.... FlavienPrat 7 93
(R Rohne, Germany) **60/1**

3 *hd* **Sybelio (FR)**22 6-8-11 0 ChristopheSoumillon 10 96
(J Rossi, France) **11/1**
4 *nk* **Shawnee Saga (FR)**22 5-8-11 0 DominiqueBoeuf 4 95
(W Baltromei, Germany) **13/1**
5 *1* **Green Tango (FR)**44 3099 7-9-1 0 RonanThomas 8 98
(P Van De Poele, France) **11/2**2
6 *3/4* **Tarkheena Prince (USA)**17 4012 5-9-1 0 StephanePasquier 2 97
(C Von Der Recke, Germany) **31/1**
7 *snk* **Watar (IRE)**642 7008 5-8-11 0 DavyBonilla 6 93
(F Head, France) **8/1**3
8 *2* **Irish Queen (FR)**38 4-8-8 0 MaximeGuyon 1 88
(H-A Pantall, France) **33/1**
9 *nk* **Diamond Boy (FR)**40 3252 4-8-11 0 FranckBlondel 9 90
(F Doumen, France) **17/2**
10 *nk* **Winter Dream (IRE)**52 6-8-11 0 GregoryBenoist 3 90
(Robert Collet, France) **21/1**
11 *snk* **Swingkeel (IRE)**41 3195 5-8-11 0 (p) OlivierPeslier 11 90
(J L Dunlop) *racd in 3rd in early stages: moved into 2nd briefly at 1/2-way: 3rd ent st: rdn 2f out: no ex: wknd* **83/10**

3m 11.9s (-7.20) **11** Ran SP% **119.0**
WIN (incl. 1 euro stake): 2.30. PLACES: 1.30, 8.40, 3.00. DF: 70.50. SF: 124.40.
Owner Gerard Thomas Ryan **Bred** Wertheimer Et Frere **Trained** Chantilly, France

4285 DONCASTER (L-H)
Saturday, July 31

OFFICIAL GOING: Good to firm changing to good (good to firm in places) after race 1 (2:05)
Wind: light 1/2 against Weather: overcast

4567 UNISON "YOUR FRIEND AT WORK" H'CAP 5f
2:05 (2:06) (Class 5) (0-70,70) 3-Y-O **£2,590** (£770; £385; £192) **Stalls** High

Form RPR
0022 1 **La Fortunata**9 4291 3-9-5 **68** TonyCulhane 2 82
(Mike Murphy) *w ldrs racing wd: styd on wl to ld last 100yds* **13/2**3
2131 2 *1 1/2* **Bronze Beau**13 4169 3-9-2 **70** (t) JamesSullivan(5) 9 79
(Mrs L Stubbs) *led: hdd and no ex ins fnl f* **7/2**1
2224 3 *1 3/4* **Sharp Eclipse**13 4169 3-8-13 **69** (p) JulieBurke(7) 5 72+
(K A Ryan) *rrd s: bhd: hdwy on wd outside over 2f out: kpt on wl fnl f* **13/2**3
0662 4 *3 1/4* **Dancing Freddy (IRE)**6 4406 3-9-2 **70** (v1) IanBrennan(5) 3 61
(J G Given) *chsd ldrs: rdn and hung lft 1f out: sn wknd* **9/2**2
0033 5 *1 1/4* **Bossy Kitty**8 4349 3-9-6 **69** KirstyMilczarek 1 56
(N Tinkler) *s.i.s: sme hdwy over 1f out: nvr nr ldrs* **13/2**3
0624 6 *2 3/4* **Morgans Choice**18 3994 3-8-13 **62** (b) AdamKirby 8 39
(J L Spearing) *w ldr: hung lft thrght: wknd over 1f out* **15/2**
0002 7 *nk* **On The Piste (IRE)**13 4169 3-8-1 **53** (p) PaulPickard(3) 4 29
(L A Mullaney) *chsd ldrs: outpcd over 2f out: nt clr run and swtchd lft 1f out* **11/1**
0-20 8 *5* **Saucy Girl (IRE)**42 3228 3-8-7 **56** DuranFentiman 6 14
(T D Easterby) *chsd ldrs: rdn and outpcd over 2f out: sn lost pl* **25/1**
3161 9 *8* **Ya Boy Sir (IRE)**12 4194 3-8-9 **63** DeanHeslop(5) 7 —
(N Wilson) *s.i.s: drvn along and a in rr: bhd fnl 2f* **10/1**

59.87 secs (-0.63) **Going Correction** -0.10s/f (Good) **9** Ran SP% **113.4**
Speed ratings (Par 100): **101,98,95,90,88 84,83,75,62**
toteswingers:1&2:£3.30, 1&3:£5.80, 2&3:£43.70 CSF £28.95 CT £153.95 TOTE £7.60: £2.30, £2.20, £1.80; EX 33.10 Trifecta £158.10 Part won. Pool £213.78 - 0.50 winning units..
Owner James Patton **Bred** James Patton **Trained** Westoning, Beds

FOCUS
The ground was changed after this race was run to good, good to firm in place from the good to firm given before the off. Ordinary form with most of these pretty exposed.
Bossy Kitty ◆ Official explanation: jockey said filly never travelled
Ya Boy Sir(IRE) Official explanation: jockey said colt never travelled

4568 UNISON AND LV= FRIZZELL "CAR INSURANCE" MAIDEN AUCTION STKS 7f
2:40 (2:42) (Class 4) 2-Y-O **£3,238** (£963; £481; £240) **Stalls** High

Form RPR
0 1 **Indigo Way**78 2078 2-8-11 0 WilliamBuick 3 73
(B J Meehan) *hld up: hdwy 3f out: styd on strly fnl f: led last stride* **5/2**2
42 2 *nse* **Midnight Rider (IRE)**14 4131 2-8-13 0 JackMitchell 8 75+
(C F Wall) *trckd ldrs: t.k.h: nt clr run over 2f out: styd on to ld last 150yds: hdd post* **5/4**1
02 3 *1/2* **Fabiello**25 3767 2-8-4 0 RossAtkinson(5) 4 70
(Tom Dascombe) *wnt rt s: led: edgd lft over 1f out: hdd jst ins fnl f: no ex* **11/1**
4 *3/4* **Pintrada** 2-8-13 0 DarryllHolland 5 72
(J D Bethell) *sltly hmpd s: in rr: swtchd to wd outside over 2f out: styd on to chse ldrs 1f out: kpt on same pce* **14/1**
5 *hd* **Abjer (FR)** 2-8-13 0 HirokiGoto 6 71
(C E Brittain) *s.i.s: hdwy to chse ldrs after 2f: chal over 1f out: styd on same pce last 150yds: eased slighly and lost 4th nr line* **14/1**
6 6 *1/2* **Masonic Lady (IRE)**11 4233 2-8-6 0 LiamJones 2 63
(W J Haggas) *trckd ldrs: drvn and outpcd over 2f out: styd on ins fnl f* **28/1**
7 *23* **History Repeating** 2-8-8 0 RichardMullen 1 8
(M L W Bell) *s.s: reminders after 1f: swtchd outside: chsng ldrs over 3f out: sn lost pl and bhd: t.o* **13/2**3

1m 29.81s (3.51) **Going Correction** -0.10s/f (Good) **7** Ran SP% **111.5**
Speed ratings (Par 96): **75,74,74,73,73 72,46**
toteswingers:1&2:£1.10, 1&3:£7.10, 2&3:£1.40 CSF £5.65 TOTE £2.50: £1.20, £1.80; EX 3.70 Trifecta £17.30 Pool £383.28 - 16.35 winning units..
Owner N Attenborough,Mrs L Mann,Mrs L Way **Bred** Mrs Johnny Eddis **Trained** Manton, Wilts
■ Stewards' Enquiry : Hiroki Goto four-day ban: failed to ride out for 4th (Aug 14-16,18)

FOCUS
A fair-looking contest but they finished rather compressed. Not the most solid form.

NOTEBOOK
Indigo Way, whose trainer reported beforehand that the reason for the horse's absence since a good effort in Strong Suit's maiden was due to a minor setback, won by only a small margin but seems sure to progress from this start. he has a sales-race entry later in the year, and one would imagine that's where he will ultimately be aimed. (op 9-2)
Midnight Rider(IRE) finished runner-up to the subsequent Group 2 third Major Art last time, and travelled strongly here in behind a wall of horses. He did appear to get out in plenty of time to win but was beaten on the nod by a workmanlike winner. (op 11-10 tchd 11-8)
Fabiello went close at Wolverhampton on his previous outing, and appeared to run right up to that form with a solid display in this from the front. (op 9-1)
Pintrada, a 25,000gns purchase and out of a dual winner over 1m4f+ in France, was a little awkward on loading but kept on after racing greenly to suggest he has ability. (tchd 16-1)
Abjer(FR), who cost 28,000gns at the sales, and is a brother to three winners from 1m-1m4f, showed plenty of ability on debut and only faded a little inside the final furlong. The jockey was banned for four days for failing to ride out for fourth, which did seem a bit harsh. (op 12-1)
Masonic Lady(IRE) looked green on debut but ran a lot better here with that experienced under her belt. (op 20-1)
History Repeating, who cost 30,000gns, holds a host of entries in some of the valuable sales races at Newmarket later in the season, but appeared far too inexperienced to do herself justice on debut. (op 6-1)

4569 UNISON THE TRADE UNION AND THOMPSONS SOLICITORS CONDITIONS STKS 6f
3:15 (3:16) (Class 3) 3-Y-O+ **£7,788** (£2,332; £1,166; £583; £291) **Stalls** High

Form RPR
132- 1 **Vitoria (IRE)**288 6814 4-8-8 96 RichardMullen 1 95
(B Smart) *rrd s: sn chsng ldrs: effrt over 2f out: led over 1f out: hld on wl* **4/1**2
5-20 2 *nk* **Lui Rei (ITY)**32 4-9-2 99 TobyAtkinson(5) 2 107
(M Botti) *hld up: effrt over 2f out: swtchd outside over 1f out: chsd wnr last 150yds: no ex* **10/1**
-030 3 *3/4* **Bonnie Charlie**15 4085 4-8-13 99 LiamJones 3 97
(W J Haggas) *w ldr: chal over 1f out: kpt on same pce* **5/1**3
440- 4 *nk* **Capercaillie (USA)**294 6677 3-8-3 95 RoystonFfrench 4 90
(M Johnston) *led: qcknd over 2f out: hdd over 1f out: kpt on same pce* **7/1**
11-3 5 *1 1/2* **Arcano (IRE)**105 1385 3-9-2 118 TadhgO'Shea 5 99
(B J Meehan) *t.k.h: trckd ldrs: nt clr run 2f out: no imp whn edgd lft ins fnl f* **10/11**1

1m 12.7s (-0.90) **Going Correction** -0.10s/f (Good)
WFA 3 from 4yo 5lb **5** Ran SP% **110.6**
Speed ratings (Par 107): **102,101,100,100,98**
CSF £36.96 TOTE £4.80: £2.40, £3.80; EX 51.10.
Owner H E Sheikh Rashid Bin Mohammed **Bred** Tom Deane **Trained** Hambleton, N Yorks

FOCUS
An interesting conditions event but muddling form with Arcano way off his best. The race has not been rated too positively.

NOTEBOOK
Vitoria(IRE), not seen since finishing runner-up in the Listed Boadicea Stakes as a 3-y-o, appeared to rear/fly-jump leaving the stalls, losing her ground, but kept on well inside the final furlong to gain success. A mucky lung was responsible for her absence, so this big filly can be expected to have more to come. Connections will try and find a Listed or Group 3 contest for her. (tchd 9-2)
Lui Rei(ITY) was having his first outing for this stable, and emerges with lots of credit giving weight away to all bar the favourite. A Group 2 and 3 winner when trained in Italy, he looks a good sort capable of winning soon.
Bonnie Charlie, disappointing in the Scottish Stewards' Cup in mid-July, but only one place behind recent winner Hawkeyethenoo there, sat prominent and kept going all the way to the line. (op 11-2 tchd 6-1)
Capercaillie(USA) was well regarded as a juvenile and didn't run too badly in a couple of Group 2s before a disappointing effort back down at Listed level in the Rockingham Stakes. She showed good pace here but ran like a horse that may have just needed it. (op 15-2 tchd 13-2)
Arcano(IRE), absent since finishing third in the Greenham Stakes back in April behind Dick Turpin and Canford Cliffs, tucked in just behind the leading pair, and took a very strong hold under his rider, failing to settle for much of the contest. It wasn't too much of a surprise that he found little off the bridle in the latter stages. It would have been interesting to see what would have happened had Tadhg O'Shea got an immediate gap when he was looking to quicken, and although it's disappointing that a former Group 1 winner finished last here, there were plenty of positives in this run to suggest he is not one to discount too readily next time if given a stronger gallop to chase.
Official explanation: trainer said, regarding running, that the colt's run was not disappointing having been absent from the racecourse for 105 days (tchd 4-5 and Evens)

4570 UNISON "A MILLION VOICES FOR PUBLIC SERVICES" H'CAP 1m 2f 60y
3:50 (3:51) (Class 2) (0-100,92) 3-Y-O+
£12,462 (£3,732; £1,866; £934; £466; £234) **Stalls** Low

Form RPR
-412 1 **Tepmokea (IRE)**35 3450 4-9-4 **82** WilliamBuick 7 91
(R A Fahey) *chsd ldrs: drvn 3f out: styd on to ld 1f out: hung rt: hld on wl* **13/2**
3402 2 *3/4* **Bonfire Knight**49 2979 3-8-2 **81** IanBrennan(5) 2 89
(J J Quinn) *led early: chsd ldrs: hdwy over 1f out: edgd lft ins fnl f: no ex* **4/1**3
6103 3 *1* **Arlequin**23 3824 3-9-4 **92** DarryllHolland 1 98
(J D Bethell) *hld up: hdwy over 3f out: styd on same pce fnl f* **5/2**1
2433 4 *1* **Sand Skier**8 4321 3-9-2 **90** (b1) RoystonFfrench 6 94
(M Johnston) *led after 100yds: r keenly: hdd 1f out: kpt on same pce* **3/1**2
2335 5 *1* **Follow The Flag (IRE)**7 4376 6-9-3 **88** (p) ConorQuish(7) 4 90
(A J McCabe) *chsd ldr: drvn 3f out: one pce whn hmpd 100yds out* **14/1**
6031 6 *3/4* **The Galloping Shoe**35 3450 5-9-4 **82** AdamKirby 3 83
(A C Whillans) *hld up: hdwy over 3f out: edgd rt and kpt on same pce fnl f* **10/1**
0105 7 *2 1/4* **Kiwi Bay**21 3920 5-10-0 **92** RichardMullen 8 89
(M Dods) *dwlt: hld up in rr: effrt 3f out: no imp whn hmpd over 1f out: nvr a factor* **20/1**
0300 8 *32* **Fastnet Storm (IRE)**24 3796 4-9-9 **87** MickyFenton 5 23
(T P Tate) *hit hd on stalls and dwlt: hld up in rr: effrt 4f out: hung lft and lost pl over 2f out: virtually p.u: t.o* **25/1**

2m 7.90s (-1.50) **Going Correction** -0.10s/f (Good)
WFA 3 from 4yo+ 10lb **8** Ran SP% **111.3**
Speed ratings (Par 109): **109,108,107,106,106 105,103,78**
toteswingers:1&2:£6.10, 1&3:£7.10, 2&3:£4.80 CSF £30.83 CT £79.33 TOTE £7.00: £2.00, £1.50, £1.50; EX 38.40 Trifecta £102.70 Pool £382.00 - 2.75 winning units..
Owner Keep Racing **Bred** J H A Baggen **Trained** Musley Bank, N Yorks
■ Stewards' Enquiry : Adam Kirby two-day ban: careless riding (Aug 14-15)
Ian Brennan two-day ban: careless riding (Aug 14-15)

FOCUS
The pace set by the leader seemed sound, so this form ought to prove to be reliable. It has been rated at face value.

NOTEBOOK
Tepmokea(IRE), runner-up to a rival he met here again last time, usually runs his race and proved too good under a strong ride, despite hanging right. This victory came off a career-high mark, but he is not over-raced and may have some more to come for his age. (op 11-2)
Bonfire Knight was thrashed into second place by this week's Gordon Stakes's winner Rebel Soldier last time, so upheld that form to some extent with a fair effort here.

Arlequin ran a blinder at Newmarket last time in a race that has thrown up some winners already, but shaped like a horse in the handicappers grip here, despite a valiant third place. (op 10-3 tchd 7-2)

Sand Skier has been a model of consistency but connections reached for the blinkers for the first time to bring about a bit more improvement. He set off in front and looked a little free at the mid-race point (his jockey reported afterwards that he felt his mount was too keen), and did not get home. Official explanation: jockey said colt ran too free (tchd 11-4)

Follow The Flag(IRE), beaten over 20 lengths last time, and with an inexperienced jockey on this time, didn't run too badly and the interference he met inside the furlong marker did not make any difference to his final position. (op 18-1)

The Galloping Shoe, 7lb higher than when beating Tepmokea last time over a similar trip at Newcastle, hit a flat spot before running on. (op 15-2 tchd 7-1)

Fastnet Storm(IRE) reportedly hit his head on the stalls. Official explanation: jockey said gelding hit its head in the stalls (op 20-1)

4571 UNISON AND UIA HOME INSURANCE H'CAP — 1m 4f

4:25 (4:26) (Class 4) (0-85,83) 3-Y-O — £5,180 (£1,541; £770; £384) Stalls Low

Form				RPR
1310	1		**Zuider Zee (GER)**[56] 2758 3-9-6 **82** WilliamBuick 7 (J H M Gosden) *trckd ldrs: effrt 4f out: nt clr run and swtchd rt over 2f out: styd on strly to ld last 50yds: readily* 5/2[1]	94+
2301	2	1 1/2	**Woodford Belle (USA)**[19] 3953 3-8-13 **75** (b) LiamJones 3 (B J Meehan) *chsd ldrs: pushed along 7f out: led on inner over 1f out: hdd and no ex wl ins fnl f* 22/1	82
06-3	3	2 1/4	**Argaum (IRE)**[114] 1189 3-8-11 **73** AdamKirby 6 (W R Swinburn) *led: hung rt and hdd over 1f out: kpt on same pce* 12/1	76
2412	4	hd	**Reality Show (IRE)**[7] 4380 3-9-0 **83** AntiocoMurgia(7) 2 (Mahmood Al Zarooni) *hld up: effrt: nt clr run and swtchd rt 3f out: chal over 1f out: kpt on same pce* 4/1[2]	86
1225	5	6	**Buffett**[28] 3697 3-9-4 **80** J-PGuillambert 8 (L M Cumani) *hld up in rr: drvn over 4f out: wknd 2f out* 8/1	73
-160	6	1/2	**Rawnaq (IRE)**[44] 3105 3-9-1 **77** TadhgO'Shea 4 (M Johnston) *swtchd rt and drvn after s: hdwy to chse ldrs over 4f out: hmpd over 2f out: hung lft and sn wknd* 5/1	69
6212	7	1 3/4	**Ice Diva**[15] 4098 3-9-1 **77** TonyCulhane 5 (P W D'Arcy) *trckd ldrs: effrt 3f out: wknd over 1f out* 9/2[3]	66
0404	8	3/4	**Strong Vigilance (IRE)**[16] 4056 3-8-11 **73** RichardMullen 1 (M L W Bell) *stdd s: hld up in rr: effrt on ins whn n.m.r 3f out: wknd fnl 2f* 16/1	61

2m 32.11s (-2.79) **Going Correction** -0.10s/f (Good) **8** Ran SP% **112.5**
Speed ratings (Par 102): **105,104,102,102,98 98,96,96**
toteswingers:1&2:£9.00, 1&3:£9.20, 2&3:£39.00 CSF £57.70 CT £551.01 TOTE £2.90: £1.50, £3.80, £2.70; EX 37.10 Trifecta £239.10 Part won. Pool £323.14 - 0.42 winning units..

Owner H R H Princess Haya Of Jordan **Bred** Graf U Grafin V Stauffenberg **Trained** Newmarket, Suffolk

FOCUS

The gallop set in this was only ordinary, which meant virtually all of these had a chance with about 3f to go. The form seems solid and the winner was value for more.

4572 UNISON "BEYOND BARRIERS" MAIDEN STKS — 1m 2f 60y

4:55 (5:01) (Class 5) 3-4-Y-O — £2,590 (£770; £385; £192) Stalls Low

Form				RPR
6-	1		**Willing Foe (USA)**[259] 7400 3-9-0 0 DaraghO'Donohoe 3 (Saeed Bin Suroor) *trckd ldrs: drvn over 4f out: led 2f out: clr ins fnl f: r.o* 7/2[2]	85+
	2	1 1/4	**Sagamore** 3-9-0 0 WilliamBuick 5 (J H M Gosden) *chsd ldrs: drvn and outpcd over 3f out: hdwy over 1f out: styd on wl to take 4 l 2nd 100yds out: nt rch wnr* 6/1	82+
63	3	2	**Mutanaker**[16] 4069 3-9-0 0 TadhgO'Shea 1 (Sir Michael Stoute) *led 1f: led over 6f out: hdd 2f out: kpt on same pce* 5/2[1]	78
5	4	5	**Missionary**[10] 4258 3-9-0 0 LiamJones 6 (W J Haggas) *led after 1f: hdd over 6f out: hung lft and one pce fnl 2f* 22/1	69
	5	3 1/2	**Toymaker** 3-9-0 0 J-PGuillambert 7 (L M Cumani) *in rr: hdwy on ins over 4f out: chsng ldrs over 2f out: fdd: will improve* 14/1	62+
30	6	1 3/4	**Joan D'Arc (IRE)**[8] 4330 3-8-9 0 WilliamCarson 9 (M G Quinlan) *in rr: hdwy on outside over 2f out: nvr nr ldrs* 33/1	54
0/	7	2 1/2	**Four Star General (IRE)**[650] 6844 4-9-10 0 DarryllHolland 2 (H R A Cecil) *uns rdr after leaving paddock: led rdrless to post: trckd ldrs: effrt over 2f out: wknd over 1f out* 6/1	54
	8	1 1/2	**Herostatus** 3-9-0 0 RoystonFfrench 8 (M Johnston) *dwlt: mid-div: drvn 7f out: lost pl over 2f out* 4/1[3]	51
0-0	9	18	**Smirfys Copper (IRE)**[45] 3080 3-8-10 0 ow1 MickyFenton 4 (Mrs D J Sanderson) *stdd s: hld up in rr: drvn over 3f out: sn wknd: eased* 66/1	13

2m 9.83s (0.43) **Going Correction** -0.10s/f (Good)
WFA 3 from 4yo 10lb **9** Ran SP% **114.8**
Speed ratings (Par 103): **101,100,98,94,91 90,88,87,72**
toteswingers:1&2:£9.00, 1&3:£1.20, 2&3:£2.70 CSF £24.17 TOTE £4.80: £1.60, £2.50, £1.30; EX 26.60 Trifecta £47.10 Pool £280.56 - 4.40 winning units. Place 6 £31.69; Place 5 £18.08.

Owner Godolphin **Bred** Stoneside Stable **Trained** Newmarket, Suffolk

FOCUS

An ordinary-looking maiden but won in impressive style by a well-bred sort, and the form could be underrated. He and the second can both rate higher. The winning time was poor in comparison to the 81-100 handicap earlier on the card.

Four Star General(IRE) Official explanation: jockey said, regarding running and riding, that his orders were to jump the colt off handy and win if he could but it ran free early and was suffering from a breathing problem throughout, adding that it had had an operation and was fitted with a cross-noseband, having travelled well into the home straight he asked for an effort to go forward at which point it became very tired and pushed out with hands and heels to the line

T/Plt: £77.20 to a £1 stake. Pool:£68,999.35 - 652.05 winning tickets T/Qpdt: £40.40 to a £1 stake. Pool:£4,306.71 - 78.80 winning tickets WG

4535 GOODWOOD (R-H)

Saturday, July 31

OFFICIAL GOING: Straight course - good; round course - good to firm (good in places) (goingstick: stands' side 7.5, centre 7.5, far side 7.7, round 8.5)
Fresh ground on top bend and all distances as advertised.
Wind: Moderate, half against Weather: Fine but cloudy

4573 PLAY BRITAIN'S GOT TALENT BINGO AT MECCABINGO.COM STKS (H'CAP) — 1m 3f

1:55 (1:55) (Class 3) (0-90,90) 3-Y-O

£12,462 (£3,732; £1,866; £934; £466; £234) Stalls Low

Form				RPR
-213	1		**Roxy Flyer (IRE)**[39] 3298 3-8-11 **80** JimmyQuinn 10 (Mrs A J Perrett) *hld up towards rr: rdn and prog on inner wl over 2f out: clsd on ldrs and squeezed through rivals 1f out: led last 100yds: styd on wl* 16/1	93
-212	2	1	**Shimmering Moment (USA)**[61] 2607 3-9-0 **83** TomQueally 7 (H R A Cecil) *hld up in rr: prog on wd outside over 3f out: clsd on ldrs 2f out: drvn ahd ent fnl f: hdd and one pce last 100yds* 12/1	94
2042	3	1 3/4	**Dromore (IRE)**[24] 3781 3-8-6 **75** DavidProbert 9 (A M Balding) *drvn in rr sn after s: prog u.p over 2f out: hanging rt but styd on to take 3rd ins fnl f: one pce last 100yds* 12/1	83
-320	4	1 1/2	**Averroes (IRE)**[73] 2226 3-9-2 **90** JohnFahy(5) 8 (C G Cox) *hld up in rr: disputing last jst over 3f out: taken to outer and prog over 2f out: styd on to take 4th nr fin: no ch* 8/1[3]	95+
5321	5	3/4	**Wadnaan**[4] 4449 3-8-12 **81** 6ex FrankieDettori 6 (M Johnston) *drvn in rr sn after s: sn in midfield: prog and prom over 4f out: rdn to go 2nd jst over 2f out: led over 1f out: hdd & wknd ent fnl f* 9/2[2]	85
0025	6	1 1/4	**Meglio Ancora**[30] 3594 3-8-6 **75** AlanMunro 11 (J G Portman) *hld up in last trio: prog on wd outside over 2f out: kpt on fr over 1f out: no ch* 50/1	76+
11	7	hd	**Rock N Roll Ransom**[21] 3916 3-9-5 **88** KierenFallon 3 (L M Cumani) *racd wd: hld up in rr: prog over 4f out: rdn to chse ldrs over 2f out: hld whn n.m.r over 1f out: fdd* 4/1[1]	89+
1065	8	3 1/2	**Street Entertainer (IRE)**[38] 3337 3-8-1 **73** MartinLane(3) 2 (Mrs A J Perrett) *dwlt: hld up wl in rr: effrt on wd outside 3f out: no prog and btn 2f out* 25/1	68
1422	9	3 1/4	**Valiant Knight (FR)**[7] 4360 3-8-11 **80** RichardHughes 4 (R Hannon) *trckd ldrs: lost pl after 4f: lost further grnd bhd wkng rival 5f out: shkn up and effrt over 2f out: no imp over 1f out* 8/1[3]	69+
0012	10	2	**If I Were A Boy (IRE)**[5] 4422 3-8-6 **75** JamesDoyle 16 (D J S Ffrench Davis) *led: clr 4f out: hdd & wknd over 1f out: eased* 14/1	60
3146	11	nk	**Finest Reserve (IRE)**[22] 3867 3-8-12 **81** RyanMoore 15 (M R Channon) *hld up in last trio: rdn on inner over 2f out: no prog wl over 1f out: wknd* 8/1[3]	66
-110	12	3/4	**Lovers Causeway (USA)**[28] 3697 3-8-6 **75** GregFairley 5 (M Johnston) *chsd ldr 2f: prom tl wknd over 2f out* 33/1	58
2361	13	1	**Ebony Boom (IRE)**[55] 2782 3-8-8 **77** EddieAhern 13 (G L Moore) *trckd ldng trio on inner: shkn up 3f out: sn wknd and eased* 33/1	59
361	14	1 1/2	**Kensei (IRE)**[58] 2684 3-8-10 **79** RichardKingscote 1 (R M Beckett) *racd wd: chsd ldr after 2f to jst over 2f out: wknd* 16/1	58
2201	15	6	**Monkton Vale (IRE)**[25] 3750 3-8-7 **76** PaulHanagan 14 (R A Fahey) *nvr bttr than midfield: lost pl and struggling in rr 3f out* 25/1	44
016	16	23	**City Vaults Girl (IRE)**[29] 3613 3-8-4 **73** AndreaAtzeni 12 (R A Fahey) *drvn in midfield 1/2-way: sn lost pl: wknd over 3f out: t.o and eased* 66/1	—

2m 24.97s (-1.53) **Going Correction** +0.025s/f (Good) **16** Ran SP% **122.4**
Speed ratings (Par 104): **106,105,104,102,102 101,101,98,96,94 94,94,93,92,88 71**
toteswingers:1&2:£34.00, 1&3:£37.10, 2&3:£16.50 CSF £185.38 CT £2401.95 TOTE £21.20: £3.30, £2.50, £3.40, £2.50; EX 184.20 Trifecta £1109.80 Part won. Pool £1,499.84 - 0.70 winning units..

Owner Mr & Mrs F Cotton Mrs S Conway **Bred** Narvick International **Trained** Pulborough, W Sussex

FOCUS

This looked a decent, competitive handicap containing some progressive types. It was run at a solid gallop and should throw up a few winners. A clear personal best from the winner but she may be a little flattered.

NOTEBOOK

Roxy Flyer(IRE), who showed her liking for this track when successful in a classified event two starts back, was briefly chopped for room 1f out, but showed admirable determination to squeeze between rivals inside the last and then quicken up nicely to score. Her connections suggested that they will now look for a fillies' Listed event for her, in the hope of picking up some black type. (op 20-1)

Shimmering Moment(USA) beat Roxy Flyer in a maiden at Salisbury two starts back, but over this extra furlong and 3lb worse off at the weights she wasn't quite able to confirm the form. She'd been off the track for a couple of months though, and was also forced quite wide into the straight, so she deserves plenty of credit, and there's probably more to come from her.

Dromore(IRE) had finished down the field in his last three starts on turf, which left a bit of a question mark, despite the fact that he looked well handicapped on his recent Polytrack efforts. He did win his maiden on turf, though, and clearly handles the surface, although on this evidence he's a little better on the AW. (op 9-1)

Averroes(IRE) hasn't had things go his way since his promising reappearance behind Verdant at Sandown, as he didn't get the best of runs at Chester and bled last time when down the field in a Listed race here. Nicely backed beforehand, he returned to form with a staying-on effort, and hopefully he can now get his season back on track. (op 12-1)

Wadnaan, making a quick reappearance following his runaway win in an ordinary affair at Beverley, looked well in at the weights under his penalty. Having chased the pace, he went for home plenty soon enough and, in the end, was run down by rivals that had been ridden more patiently. (op 4-1 tchd 5-1 in places)

Meglio Ancora, half a length second to Roxy Flyer over this C&D off levels two starts back, could be given a chance of reversing that form on 5lb better terms, but he had run poorly since and, while running a solid race here, especially considering he came widest round the final bend, he's clearly not as progressive as the Perrett filly. (tchd 66-1 in a place)

Rock N Roll Ransom, winner of his first two starts, was stepping up 3f in distance and, considering his dam is a half-sister to Kayf Tara, it was reasonable to expect further improvement. He got bumped about a bit early in the straight, though, and weakened inside the final 2f. This was a tough race for such an inexperienced horse, and he's not one to give up on. (op 9-2 tchd 5-1 in places)

Street Entertainer(IRE), another who came wide off the bend into the straight, struggled to land a blow from off the pace. Official explanation: jockey said colt never travelled (tchd 28-1)

If I Were A Boy(IRE), who is at her best when making the running, set a solid tempo in front but could not sustain it from well over 1f out. (op 16-1 tchd 12-1)
Finest Reserve(IRE) looked a possible improver for the step up in trip as he always tends to finish his races off well but, having tried his luck up the inside rail, he was making no impression inside the final 2f. (op 9-1)
City Vaults Girl(IRE) Official explanation: jockey said filly never travelled

4574 BLUESQ.COM "FOR 5 PLACES IN STEWARDS' CUP" STKS (REGISTERED AS THOROUGHBRED STAKES) (LISTED RACE) 1m

2:30 (2:30) (Class 1) 3-Y-O

£28,385 (£10,760; £5,385; £2,685; £1,345; £675) **Stalls** High

Form				RPR
3051	1		**Critical Moment (USA)**[23] 3827 3-9-0 105 ... MichaelHills 9	110
			(B W Hills) *led after 2f: mde rest: hrd pressed fnl f: r.o wl: jst hld on* **7/2**[2]	
152	2	*hd*	**Desert Myth (USA)**[16] 4068 3-9-0 100 ... RyanMoore 8	110
			(Sir Michael Stoute) *hld up in 6th: prog on inner over 2f out: chsd wnr over 1f out: hrd rdn and clsd fnl f: jst failed* **3/1**[1]	
-515	3	*3 ¼*	**Field Of Dream**[45] 3066 3-9-4 110 ... KierenFallon 10	106
			(L M Cumani) *chsd ldng trio: pushed along over 3f out: outpcd u.p 2f out: styd on wl fnl f to take 3rd post* **7/1**	
140-	4	*shd*	**Long Lashes (USA)**[308] 6269 3-8-9 105 ... FrankieDettori 11	97
			(Saeed Bin Suroor) *trckd ldng quartet: smooth prog to chse wnr wl over 2f out: nt qckn and lost 2nd over 1f out: wknd and lost 3rd on post* **9/2**[3]	
4406	5	*nk*	**Freeforaday (USA)**[2] 4509 3-9-0 102 ... SteveDrowne 7	101+
			(J R Best) *stdd s: hld up in last trio: gng strly but plenty to do whn nt clr run wl over 1f out: styd on wl fnl f: nrst fin* **16/1**	
0611	6	*4 ½*	**San Cassiano (IRE)**[7] 4377 3-9-0 90 ... SebSanders 3	91
			(Mrs R A Carr) *trckd ldng pair: rdn over 2f out: hanging rt and wknd fr over 1f out* **16/1**	
-006	7	*1*	**Mont Agel**[21] 3933 3-9-0 98 ... TomQueally 1	88
			(M L W Bell) *wnt lft s: hld up in 7th: pushed along 3f out: no prog u.p 2f out: fdd* **20/1**	
3221	8	*¾*	**Treadwell (IRE)**[43] 3146 3-9-0 105 ... FergusSweeney 5	87
			(J A Osborne) *t.k.h: hld up in last trio: effrt on outer over 2f out: sn no prog and btn* **6/1**	
3-00	9	*7*	**Quarrel (USA)**[45] 3066 3-9-0 105 ... PaulHanagan 2	71
			(W J Haggas) *led 2f: chsd wnr to wl over 2f out: wknd* **33/1**	
311-	10	*1*	**Rum King (USA)**[274] 7150 3-9-0 96 ... RichardHughes 6	68
			(R Hannon) *s.s: hld up in last: shkn up and no prog over 2f out: wknd* **14/1**	

1m 38.16s (-1.74) **Going Correction** +0.025s/f (Good) **10** Ran SP% **118.3**
Speed ratings (Par 108): **109,108,105,105,105 100,99,98,91,90**
toteswingers:1&2:£3.40, 1&3:£5.30, 2&3:£5.10 CSF £14.69 TOTE £4.60: £1.80, £1.70, £2.40; EX 13.80 Trifecta £68.00 Pool £2,126.38 - 23.12 winning units.
Owner K Abdulla **Bred** Juddmonte Farms Inc **Trained** Lambourn, Berks

FOCUS
An ordinary Listed event run at no more than a fair gallop. Sound form for the grade, rated around the fourth and fifth.

NOTEBOOK
Critical Moment(USA) made most of the running, despite having sweated up and been free to post. He looked likely to be passed when strongly challenged by the runner-up inside the final furlong, but proved tremendously game. Likely to be kept at this trip, he could be aimed at the Group 3 Strensall Stakes at York on August 20 (op 4-1 tchd 9-2 in places)
Desert Myth(USA), trying this trip for the first time after being beaten in a 1m2f conditions contest on his previous start, was matched at 1.01 in running when produced with his chance, but he didn't do enough to get by the winner. There didn't appear to be anything wrong with his attitude, and he was nicely clear of the remainder. (op 9-2)
Field Of Dream, beaten 8l in the Jersey Stakes on his previous start, ran respectably without really improving for the return to 1m. He doesn't seem to be progressing. (op 8-1)
Long Lashes(USA) ◆, off the track since disappointing when favourite for last year's Fillies' Mile, travelled well enough but found little for pressure. She is likely to come on plenty for this. (op 5-1 tchd 4-1)
Freeforaday(USA), who ran respectably in a handicap at this meeting two days earlier, looked to be going better than most early in the straight, but he didn't have a great deal of room and was in the clear too late. He might have been third had he enjoyed a better trip. Official explanation: jockey said colt was denied a clear run
San Cassiano(IRE) came into this off the back of two handicap wins (off 78 and then 84), but still had plenty to find, being the worst off at the weights, and was well held. (op 14-1)
Treadwell(IRE), upped to 1m for the first time, was nowhere near the form he showed when winning the Buckingham Palace at Royal Ascot, finding little after racing keenly. (op 4-1)
Rum King(USA) Official explanation: jockey said colt was upset in stalls

4575 BLUE SQUARE NASSAU STKS (GROUP 1) (F&M) 1m 1f 192y

3:05 (3:08) (Class 1) 3-Y-O+

£122,169 (£46,311; £23,177; £11,556; £5,788; £2,905) **Stalls** High

Form				RPR
31-2	1		**Midday**[79] 2055 4-9-6 120 ... TomQueally 2	123+
			(H R A Cecil) *trckd ldrs: qcknd to ld jst over 2f out and sn 2 l clr: idled 1f out: hung lft and hdd ins fnl f: continued to hang lft but sn picked up to ld again: gng away fin* **15/8**[1]	
0-41	2	*1 ¼*	**Stacelita (FR)**[47] 3045 4-9-6 122 ... ChristopheSoumillon 7	119
			(J-C Rouget, France) *trckd ldr: led briefly over 2f out: chsd wnr after: clsd to ld ins fnl f: sn hdd: wl hld whn sltly hmpd nr fin* **9/2**[3]	
1-13	3	*1*	**Antara (GER)**[45] 3067 4-9-6 114 ... FrankieDettori 6	117
			(Saeed Bin Suroor) *trckd ldrs: rdn and nt qckn 2f out: styd on and ch ins fnl f: one pce* **8/1**	
-114	4	*¾*	**Strawberrydaiquiri**[24] 3793 4-9-6 114 ... RyanMoore 3	116
			(Sir Michael Stoute) *hld up in 5th: nt qckn and outpcd 2f out: styd on fr over 1f out: nvr able to chal* **9/2**[3]	
-111	5	*2 ¼*	**Contredanse (IRE)**[62] 2575 3-8-10 109 ... KierenFallon 4	111
			(L M Cumani) *hld up in last pair: outpcd over 2f out: plugged on one pce after* **20/1**	
1431	6	*¾*	**Barshiba (IRE)**[28] 3671 6-9-6 108 ... HayleyTurner 1	110
			(D R C Elsworth) *led at mod pce: increased tempo fr 4f out: hdd over 2f out: fdd* **25/1**	
-352	7	*3*	**Rosanara (FR)**[48] 3015 3-8-10 117 ... GeraldMosse 5	104
			(A De Royer-Dupre, France) *stdd s: hld up in last pair: lft bhd fr over 2f out and no ch after* **4/1**[2]	

2m 7.25s (-0.75) **Going Correction** +0.025s/f (Good)
WFA 3 from 4yo+ 10lb **7** Ran SP% **110.9**
Speed ratings (Par 117): **104,103,102,101,99 99,96**
toteswingers:1&2:£2.30, 1&3:£3.20, 2&3:£6.10 CSF £9.84 TOTE £3.10: £1.70, £2.20; EX 8.60.
Owner K Abdulla **Bred** Juddmonte Farms Ltd **Trained** Newmarket, Suffolk
■ Stewards' Enquiry : Tom Queally two-day ban: careless riding (Aug 14-15)

FOCUS
The smallest field since Ouija Board beat six rivals in 2006, but three previous Group 1 winners lined up, including last year's heroine Midday, and it looked an up-to-scratch renewal. The early pace was steady before gradually increasing, and it paid to race handily. The winner is rated better than ever, and the runner-up was close to form.

NOTEBOOK
Midday ◆ was always well placed considering how the race unfolded and looked set to follow up last season's success in style when quickening over a length clear of main danger Stacelita inside the final 2f, but she soon idled quite noticeably, pricking her ears and then hanging left into the whip. That allowed the runner-up to get upsides, seemingly with more momentum, but Henry Cecil's filly asserted again late on, and crossed the line looking value for more than the winning margin. She had to survive a stewards' inquiry, having briefly inconvenienced the second filly late on, but the result was never in doubt. Midday apparently got jarred up when beaten into second by Sariska in the Middleton Stakes in May on her only previous start this season, so Cecil wants to avoid running her on firm ground from now on. However, her connections will surely be keen to see her defend her Breeders' Cup Filly & Mare Turf title (or maybe they'll even consider taking on the males in the Turf this year), and the going could well be quick at Churchill Downs in November. Before then, her main target is said to be the Yorkshire Oaks, ground permitting. (tchd 7-4 and 2-1 and 9-4 in a place)
Stacelita(FR), a triple French Group 1 winner who was having her first start outside her homeland, played up beforehand, but she ran her race. She was readily outpaced by Midday when that one went by her in the straight, and although she was allowed a second chance when the winner idled, briefly looking like she might take advantage, she was ultimately flattered to finish so close. Still, this was a highly creditable performance in defeat, and there should be more wins to come when she returns to her favoured soft ground. She may now go to Deauville for the Prix Jean Romanet, and the Prix de l'Opera is also on her agenda, although the Breeders' Cup Filly & Mare Turf is said to be her main objective. (op 4-1 tchd 5-1 in places)
Antara(GER), who won a German Group 3 by 8l on her only previous try at this trip, reversed Windsor Forest placings with Strawberrydaiquiri. She couldn't go with the front two when they committed, but stuck on well for third, giving the impression she would have preferred a stronger-run race. (op 12-1)
Strawberrydaiquiri, trying this trip for the first time following her fourth in the Falmouth, was in trouble before stamina became an issue and basically didn't seem quite good enough. (op 11-2 tchd 6-1)
Contredanse(IRE) has made tremendous progress since joining Luca Cumani this year, bagging a couple of handicaps before landing the Group 2 Italian Oaks, but she's not up to this level yet. This was a creditable effort nonetheless and she looks the type to keep improving. (op 14-1)
Barshiba(IRE), last year's fourth who came into this off the back of a second Lancashire Oaks success, was allowed her own way in front, but was gradually left behind in the straight. (op 18-1)
Rosanara(FR), who failed to make the Irish Oaks after getting upset when boarding the plane in France, travelled over by train this time. She lacks pace, so the steady gallop was no use, but even so, this was a disappointing performance. (tchd 9-2 in places and 7-2 in places)

4576 BLUESQ.COM STEWARDS' CUP (HERITAGE H'CAP) 6f

3:40 (3:41) (Class 2) 3-Y-O+

£62,310 (£18,660; £9,330; £4,670; £2,330; £1,170) **Stalls** Low

Form				RPR
4000	1		**Evens And Odds (IRE)**[22] 3869 6-8-10 **98** ... BillyCray(5) 18	110
			(D Nicholls) *pressed ldng pair in centre: led gp 2f out: drvn and styd on wl fnl f to ld nr fin* **20/1**	
0221	2	*nk*	**Jonny Mudball**[35] 3446 4-9-2 **99** ... (t) SebSanders 19	110+
			(Tom Dascombe) *led far side gp and wl on terms: clr of rest fr 1/2-way and overall ldr: kpt on wl fnl f: hdd nr fin* **14/1**	
0234	3	*1 ¼*	**Prohibit**[6] 4401 5-9-1 **98** ... (p) EddieAhern 12	105
			(R M H Cowell) *trckd ldng trio in centre: poised to chal gng easily 2f out: rdn and nt qckn over 1f out: styd on* **33/1**	
3002	4	*nk*	**Rileyskeepingfaith**[28] 3674 4-9-4 **101** ... (v) RichardHughes 15	107
			(M R Channon) *hld up last of gp of 10 in centre: rdn and gd prog over 1f out: r.o fnl f: nrst fin* **12/1**	
4310	5	*½*	**Noverre To Go (IRE)**[42] 3193 4-9-0 **97** ... (t) RichardKingscote 24	101+
			(Tom Dascombe) *chsd far side ldr: clr of rest over 2f out: kpt on same pce fnl f* **12/1**	
4253	6	*1 ¾*	**Secret Asset (IRE)**[14] 4136 5-8-7 **97** ... LewisWalsh(7) 10	96
			(Jane Chapple-Hyam) *pressed ldr in centre: on terms 2f out: fdd fnl f* **25/1**	
2105	7	*½*	**Sir Gerry (USA)**[35] 3445 5-9-6 **106** ... GFCarroll(3) 16	103
			(C A Dwyer) *hld up in 8th in centre gp: prog and plld out 2f out: kpt on fnl f: no imp* **33/1**	
3000	8	*½*	**Advanced**[7] 4358 7-8-11 **99** ... AmyRyan(5) 14	95
			(K A Ryan) *chsd ldng quartet in centre: cl enough 2f out: grad fdd fnl f* **50/1**	
2650	9	*nse*	**Iver Bridge Lad**[7] 4391 3-9-2 **104** ... (b) AlanMunro 17	99
			(J Ryan) *chsd ldrs in centre in 6th: effrt and wl on terms 2f out: hrd rdn over 1f out: fdd* **50/1**	
-040	10	*hd*	**Jimmy Styles**[42] 3193 6-9-2 **104** ... (b[1]) JohnFahy(5) 6	99
			(C G Cox) *chsd nr side ldrs: jnd centre gp 1/2-way: wl in tch 2f out: fdd fnl f* **33/1**	
0031	11	*nk*	**Castles In The Air**[7] 4358 5-9-6 **103** 3ex ... PaulHanagan 2	97
			(R A Fahey) *trckd ldng pair nr side: chal for ld 2f out: nt on terms w other gps after* **16/1**	
4300	12	*1 ¼*	**Singeur (IRE)**[7] 4391 3-8-12 **100** ... (b[1]) TomQueally 21	89
			(R Bastiman) *swtchd to r centre and 9th in gp: plld out and effrt over 2f out: nvr goin pce to threaten* **40/1**	
-100	13	*nk*	**Johannes (IRE)**[42] 3193 7-8-13 **99** ... MartinLane(3) 3	88
			(R A Fahey) *chsd ldr nr side: chal for ld 2f out: nt on terms w other gps after* **25/1**	
5-00	14	*hd*	**Hitchens (IRE)**[7] 4391 5-9-2 **99** ... ChristopheSoumillon 28	87
			(T D Barron) *one of trio who racd against far rail: nt on terms fr 1/2-way: styd on fnl f* **20/1**	
0550	15	*½*	**Edge Closer**[14] 4136 6-9-2 **102** ... PatrickHills(3) 11	89
			(R Hannon) *racd in 7th in centre gp: no prog after gps merged over 2f out: n.d over 1f out* **66/1**	
0500	16	*½*	**Sonny Red (IRE)**[7] 4391 6-9-0 **97** ... JimmyQuinn 7	82
			(D Nicholls) *racd nr side: wl in rr: kpt on fnl 2f: no ch* **33/1**	
6360	16	*dht*	**Run For The Hills**[43] 3146 4-9-1 **98** ... HayleyTurner 22	83
			(R Charlton) *dwlt: swtchd to r against far rail and last of trio there: no ch whn swtchd sharply lft 2f out: kpt on* **25/1**	
-044	18	*½*	**Knot In Wood (IRE)**[35] 3445 8-9-7 **107** ... BarryMcHugh(3) 9	91
			(R A Fahey) *stmbld s: hld up in nr side gp: jnd centre 1/2-way: in rr of gp 2f out: fdd* **25/1**	
2001	19	*shd*	**Prime Exhibit**[19] 3969 5-8-9 **97** 3ex ... DaleSwift(5) 13	80
			(R A Fahey) *led centre gp to 2f out: wknd* **28/1**	
1513	20	*1 ½*	**Parisian Pyramid (IRE)**[7] 4391 4-8-13 **96** ... StephenCraine 1	74
			(K A Ryan) *led nr side gp: nt on terms fr 1/2-way: wknd over 1f out* **22/1**	
0000	21	*1 ¾*	**Everymanforhimself (IRE)**[22] 3869 6-9-1 **98** ... (v) MichaelHills 8	71
			(K A Ryan) *sn wl bhd on nr side: nvr a factor* **100/1**	

1302 **22** *1* **Kaldoun Kingdom (IRE)**[7] 4391 5-8-13 **101**.................. LeeTopliss(5) 4 71
(R A Fahey) *dwlt and n.m.r s: chsd nr side ldrs: no prog 2f out: wknd* **20/1**

-461 **23** *shd* **Genki (IRE)**[28] 3674 6-9-9 **106** 3ex............................(v1) SteveDrowne 25 75
(R Charlton) *chsd ldrs far side: nt on terms fr 1/2-way: no ch fnl 2f* **8/1**[3]

23-2 **24** *1* **Enact**[90] 1727 4-9-1 **98**.. RyanMoore 27 64
(Sir Michael Stoute) *blindfold off late and dwlt: racd far side: nvr on terms w ldrs: bhd fnl 2f* **6/1**[1]

1300 **25** *½* **Ingleby Lady**[7] 4391 4-9-0 **97**.................................... GrahamGibbons 26 61
(T D Barron) *led trio that racd against far rail: nowhere nr ldrs fr 1/2-way: wknd 2f out* **50/1**

2422 **26** *2 ¼* **Striking Spirit**[42] 3193 5-9-2 **99**...................................... AdrianNicholls 5 56
(D Nicholls) *dwlt and n.m.r s: chsd ldng pair nr side: wknd 2f out* **14/1**

-532 **27** *7* **Palace Moon**[22] 3869 5-9-8 **105**.....................................(t) KierenFallon 20 40
(W J Knight) *racd far side: a in rr: wknd 2f out: eased* **7/1**[2]

00-0 **28** *½* **Ancien Regime (IRE)**[62] 2563 5-9-1 **98**..................(bt1) FrankieDettori 23 31
(Saeed Bin Suroor) *racd far side: nvr on terms w ldrs: wknd 2f out: heavily eased* **33/1**

1m 11.55s (-0.65) **Going Correction** +0.20s/f (Good)
WFA 3 from 4yo+ 5lb **28** Ran SP% **135.5**
Speed ratings (Par 109): **112,111,109,109,108 106,105,105,105,104 104,102,102,102,101 100,100,100,100,98 95,94,94,92,92**
toteswingers:1&2:£42.50, 1&3:£578.80, 2&3:£993.70 CSF £234.00 CT £9003.81 TOTE £24.70: £4.90, £3.30, £14.00, £3.10; EX 221.90 Trifecta £13933.60 Pool £112,034.36 - 5.95 winning units.

Owner Dab Hand Racing **Bred** Old Carhue Stud **Trained** Sessay, N Yorks

FOCUS
As usual a fiercely competitive handicap. They initially split into four groups before merging to form a far-side and a stands' side group, although in the closing stages they fanned out again and were spread right across the track. Apart from those racing nearest the stands' side, the draw didn't seem to greatly inconvenience any of the rest of the field. Sound form amongst the principals with the winner up 2lb on last year's second in this.

NOTEBOOK
Evens And Odds(IRE) hadn't been in the best of form since running well behind Equiano in a Listed race in the spring, but as a result he'd slipped in the handicap to the mark he ran off in this race last year. On that occasion he was second, doing best on his side, so from a handicapping point of view he had to be of interest here, especially with the ground more in his favour than last season. His stable, which had the first two in the consolation race the previous day and took the 5f handicap on Thursday, has been in terrific form at the meeting, and with a strong staying-on performance, reminiscent of last year, he eventually overhauled long-time leader Jonny Mudball well inside the last. He was fourth in the Ayr Gold Cup after this race last year and one would imagine that race will be his target again this time.

Jonny Mudball ◆ looked to have been flattered by the bare form of his success at Newcastle last time but still had the look of a progressive sprinter, and it looked significant that he'd been kept for this race rather than taking up a Group-race entry at Sandown earlier in the month. He ran a blinder in defeat, making the running in the far-side group and holding off his stablemate to 'win' comfortably on his side. It is easy to see him developing into a Pattern-class sprinter.

Prohibit, who had run quite well on his last two starts over 5f, is more effective over this trip. He travelled strongly but, although he stayed on well while carrying his head a little high, the winner was always holding him.

Rileyskeepingfaith finished his race off strongly, having been held up in the centre of the track, and is another for whom the Ayr Gold Cup looks a suitable target. That race often suits a horse who stays 7f, and he handles easier ground, too. (op 14-1)

Noverre To Go(IRE) came out second-best on the far side, running a fine race considering the morning rain and watering over the previous days would not have been in his favour. There's still a decent handicap to be won with him when he gets his favoured fast ground. (op 14-1)

Secret Asset(IRE), who was 3lb well in at the weights, was prominent throughout and kept plugging away. He's been very consistent for his current stable this season since returning from a lengthy absence.

Sir Gerry(USA) was having his first start for Chris Dwyer and dropping in class, having contested Pattern races. He put up a good effort and, while his current mark makes things difficult in handicaps, he has shown this term that he can be competitive in Listed company.

Advanced ran better than in his two previous attempts in this race. He ran well in the Great St Wilfrid off this mark last year, and Ripon's highlight looks the way to go with him again. (tchd 80-1 in a place)

Iver Bridge Lad, who had the blinkers back on, was one of only two three-year-olds in the race, and it takes a special horse to win this competitive handicap at that tender age. (tchd 66-1 in a place)

Jimmy Styles ran poorly in the Wokingham last time out and connections reached for the blinkers here. Although first home from a single-figure draw, he still probably needs to drop a few pounds to be in with a shot in a race like this.

Castles In The Air was another compromised by a low draw. He was officially 2lb well in under his penalty, but a stiffer track suits him best over this trip. (tchd 18-1 in a place)

Singeur(IRE), the other 3-y-o in the field, was wearing blinkers for the first time, but is handicapped up to his best and couldn't get seriously involved. (tchd 66-1 in a place)

Johannes(IRE), along with the others who raced close to the stands' side, can have his effort upgraded slightly, due to him racing on what looked the slowest part of the track.

Hitchens(IRE) didn't get a clear run next to the far-side rail and, once in the open, wasn't knocked about in a lost cause. He shaped better than his finishing position suggests and is one to keep in mind as he's on a fair mark based on his best form from last year.

Knot In Wood(IRE) had run well in this race in each of the previous three years, but couldn't match his high standards this time around. Perhaps the ground didn't suit him. (op 20-1)

Kaldoun Kingdom(IRE) was 4lb well in at the weights but failed to show it.

Genki(IRE), successful in this race last year off 96, had to race off a 10lb higher mark this time around. He proved disappointing in the first-time visor. Official explanation: trainer said gelding was unsuited by the loose ground on the crossing (op 17-2)

Enact hadn't been seen since running a good second at York back in May, but she looked on a good mark and was popular in the market. She has run well on most surfaces in the past, but never threatened to get into this, and it probably says a lot that she was later reported to have been unsuited by the good ground. Official explanation: jockey said filly was unsuited by the good ground (op 13-2 tchd 7-1 in places)

Striking Spirit loves hearing his hooves rattle, but the days of having genuine fast ground at this meeting are perhaps over. He simply didn't run up to his Wokingham form on this loose surface. (op 16-1)

Palace Moon looked to hold strong claims as he was coming here on the back of two placed efforts in competitive handicaps and was 5lb well in at the weights. He's another who enjoys genuine fast ground, though, and this surface probably didn't suit him. He was another reported to have been unsuited by the good ground. Official explanation: trainer said gelding was unsuited by the good ground (op 9-1)

4577 MOBILE BETTING AT IPHONE.BLUESQ.COM EBF MAIDEN STKS (C&G) 7f

4:15 (4:15) (Class 2) 2-Y-O **£12,952** (£3,854; £1,926; £962) **Stalls** High

Form RPR

1 **Pausanias** 2-9-0 0.. RichardHughes 4 85+
(R Hannon) *trckd ldng pair: disp ld 2f out: shkn up over 1f out: pushed out to assert last 100yds* **3/1**[2]

3 **2** *nk* **Captain Bertie (IRE)**[15] 4096 2-9-0 0................................ MichaelHills 2 84+
(B W Hills) *trckd ldr: disp ld 2f out: shkn up over 1f out: upsides tl no ex last 100yds* **2/1**[1]

3 *2 ¼* **Aerial Acclaim (IRE)** 2-9-0 0.. TomQueally 1 78+
(C G Cox) *s.s: sn wl in tch in 5th: effrt on outer over 2f out: shkn up to chal over 1f out: fdd last 150yds* **15/2**

4 *2 ½* **The Mongoose** 2-9-0 0.. RyanMoore 8 72+
(Sir Michael Stoute) *dwlt: trckd ldng trio: cl enough 2f out: pushed along and fdd fnl f* **9/2**[3]

5 *2 ¼* **Sagramor** 2-9-0 0... SteveDrowne 7 67+
(H Morrison) *stdd s: t.k.h: hld up towards rr: outpcd over 2f out: pushed along and kpt on steadily* **22/1**

6 *hd* **Fine Art Dealer (IRE)** 2-9-0 0... EddieAhern 9 66+
(G L Moore) *hld up in rr: outpcd fr 3f out: pushed along and kpt on steadily fr over 1f out* **10/1**

2 **7** *4* **Sinadinou**[66] 2427 2-9-0 0.. AdrianNicholls 6 56
(D Nicholls) *led to 2f out: losing pl whn short of room over 1f out* **9/1**

8 *7* **Hurricane Spear** 2-9-0 0... FergusSweeney 5 39
(G L Moore) *s.s: a in rr: wknd over 2f out* **20/1**

9 *15* **Hawridge Knight** 2-9-0 0... JamesMillman 3 —
(B R Millman) *a in rr: pushed along 1/2-way: sn wknd: t.o* **40/1**

1m 28.71s (1.81) **Going Correction** +0.025s/f (Good) **9** Ran SP% **118.9**
Speed ratings (Par 100): **90,89,87,84,81 81,76,68,51**
toteswingers:1&2:£1.70, 1&3:£5.40, 2&3:£5.60 CSF £9.51 TOTE £3.80: £1.50, £1.40, £2.40; EX 7.00 Trifecta £41.30 Pool £1,305.22 - 23.36 winning units.

Owner Sir Alex Ferguson & Sotirios Hassiakos **Bred** Granham Farm And P Hearson Bloodstock **Trained** East Everleigh, Wilts

FOCUS
Recent winners of this maiden include Archduke Ferdinand, Opera Cape and Jukebox Jury, and this year's race looked a decent contest. Winners should certainly come from it.

NOTEBOOK
Pausanias ◆, according to Richard Hannon, did a nice piece of work in between Zebedee (Molecomb winner) and Casual Glimpse (won Newmarket conditions contest latest) ten days prior to this, and this sizeable colt confirmed himself a useful prospect with a winning debut. Richard Hughes seemed keen to avoid giving him a hard race, and although the jockey ultimately had to get relatively serious, the colt showed a willing attitude. This 29,000gns purchase has the scope to progress into a smart type. (op 5-2 tchd 7-2)

Captain Bertie(IRE) confirmed the promise he showed on his debut at Newbury, finishing nicely clear of all bar the potentially decent winner. He's clearly well up to taking a similar race. (op 9-4 tchd 15-8 and 7-4 in places and 5-2 in places)

Aerial Acclaim(IRE) ◆, described beforehand by Clive Cox as a "very nice horse", has been entered in the Champagne Stakes and the Royal Lodge. A £55,000 purchase, he showed a deal of ability on this debut and should come on plenty for the run. (op 8-1 tchd 9-1)

The Mongoose, a Champagne Stakes, Royal Lodge and Derby entrant, wasn't given a hard time. This first foal of a dual Grade 1 winner in the US should be suited by further and can do better. (op 5-1 tchd 11-2)

Sagramor, whose pedigree is a mix of speed and stamina, cost just £500 but ran well on his debut, looking as though he'll be better for the experience. (op 25-1 tchd 20-1)

Fine Art Dealer(IRE), a 220,000 euros purchase, showed a pronounced action when off the bridle, really grabbing at the ground, and ran green. (op 14-1)

Sinadinou didn't build on the form he showed when runner-up over 6f on his debut.

4578 PLAY POKER AT GCASINO.COM NURSERY STKS (H'CAP) 6f

4:50 (4:51) (Class 2) 2-Y-O **£9,714** (£2,890; £1,444; £721) **Stalls** Low

Form RPR

4131 **1** **Eucharist (IRE)**[11] 4228 2-9-0 **83**................................ RichardHughes 11 90+
(R Hannon) *hld up in last pair in centre: effrt whn hmpd wl over 1f out: hdwy ent fnl f: drvn and r.o gamely to ld last 50yds* **10/3**[1]

1411 **2** *nk* **Majestic Myles (IRE)**[25] 3749 2-9-4 **90**..................... BarryMcHugh(3) 3 95
(R A Fahey) *dwlt: trckd ldrs in centre: prog to ld wl over 1f out: drvn and styd on fnl f: hdd last 50yds* **8/1**

31 **3** *¾* **Rossetti**[31] 3555 2-8-7 **76**... HayleyTurner 14 80+
(R Hannon) *hld up in rr of centre gp: last 2f out but gng easily: prog jst over 1f out: rdn and r.o wl nr fin: too much to do* **9/1**

31 **4** *hd* **Bahamian Sunset**[19] 3945 2-8-8 **77**................................ PaulHanagan 5 79
(R A Fahey) *trckd ldrs in centre: rdn and effrt 2f out: styd on fnl f: nvr quite able to chal* **5/1**[2]

4151 **5** *½* **Puddle Duck**[22] 3859 2-8-7 **76**..................................... FergusSweeney 6 77
(K A Ryan) *dwlt: trckd ldrs in centre: effrt to chal over 1f out: no ex ins fnl f* **12/1**

0525 **6** *1 ¾* **Danzigs Grandchild (USA)**[10] 4247 2-8-1 **70**................. JimmyQuinn 7 66
(J S Moore) *wl in rr in centre: rdn 2f out: styd on u.p fr over 1f out: nvr able to chal* **40/1**

6031 **7** *¾* **Barista (IRE)**[16] 4067 2-7-12 **67** oh1................................ AndreaAtzeni 2 60+
(M R Channon) *dwlt: hld up last of nr side trio: led gp against rail 2f out: drvn and kpt on: nvr quite on terms* **33/1**

060 **8** *¾* **Saucy Buck (IRE)**[21] 3887 2-8-1 **75**............................... KierenFox(5) 15 66
(M R Channon) *wl in rr in centre gp: rdn and effrt 2f out: no imp 1f out: fdd* **25/1**

0453 **9** *7* **Golden Taurus (IRE)**[10] 4262 2-8-2 **71**.......................... DavidProbert 9 41
(J W Hills) *pressed ldr in centre: led over 2f out to wl over 1f out: wknd rapidly* **12/1**

3223 **10** *1 ¼* **With Hindsight (IRE)**[22] 3859 2-8-3 **77**............................ JohnFahy(5) 1 43+
(C G Cox) *racd in nr side trio: nt on terms w main gp fr over 2f out* **22/1**

5460 **11** *1 ¾* **Style And Panache (IRE)**[4] 4458 2-8-8 **77**...................... KierenFallon 4 38+
(P D Evans) *led nr side trio to 2f out: wknd* **16/1**

213 **12** *nk* **Goodwood Treasure**[21] 3913 2-8-7 **76**............................ EddieAhern 12 36
(J L Dunlop) *chsd ldrs in centre: wknd 2f out: sn bhd* **15/2**[3]

5024 **13** *6* **Kyncraighe (IRE)**[11] 4221 2-8-0 **72**............................ MartinLane(3) 10 14
(Eve Johnson Houghton) *trckd ldng pair in centre to over 2f out: wknd rapidly* **22/1**

2101 **14** 3 ¼ **Dolly Parton (IRE)**[29] 3625 2-8-6 **75** AdrianNicholls 8 7
(D Nicholls) *led centre gp to over 2f out: edgd lft and wknd rapidly* **10/1**

1m 13.36s (1.16) **Going Correction** +0.20s/f (Good) **14** Ran SP% **120.9**
Speed ratings (Par 100): **100,99,98,98,97 95,94,93,84,82 80,79,71,67**
toteswingers:1&2:£4.90, 1&3:£6.60, 2&3:£15.50 CSF £27.69 CT £231.47 TOTE £3.70: £2.10, £2.30, £3.40; EX 25.20 Trifecta £162.20 Pool £2,603.46 - 11.87 winning units.
Owner Mrs J Wood **Bred** M Kelly **Trained** East Everleigh, Wilts
■ A ninth winner of the meeting for Richard Hannon and Richard Hughes, a record for both trainer and jockey.

FOCUS
A good, competitive nursery, and solid form. The majority raced up the middle and three who were positioned towards the stands' rail - Barista, With Hindsight and Style And Panache - were well beaten.

NOTEBOOK
Eucharist(IRE) overcome a slightly troubled trip to get on top in the final few strides and record her third victory from her last four starts. She looks the type who can keep progressing and stay ahead of the handicapper. (op 11-4 tchd 5-2 in places)
Majestic Myles(IRE), beaten only once in his first four starts, was chasing a nursery hat-trick off a mark 6lb higher than last time, and he ran a tremendous race in defeat. He's very useful.
Rossetti ◆ improved a fair bit on the form he showed when winning a Chepstow maiden and looked a bit unlucky as he was set a lot to do and didn't seem to have a great deal of room when staying on, for all that he was never blocked off. (op 11-1)
Bahamian Sunset, the winner of a fair maiden at Ayr last time, ran a creditable race on her nursery debut. There's plenty of speed in her pedigree, but she shapes as though she will stay 7f. (op 13-2)
Puddle Duck, 5lb higher than when winning at Chester, just came up short. (op 11-1)
Danzigs Grandchild(USA) proved unsuited by the drop in trip, although she shaped encouragingly, running on well.
Goodwood Treasure seemed to get a bit upset in the stalls and failed to run her race. Official explanation: jockey said filly hung right (op 8-1)

4579 BLUESQ.COM SUPPORTING MARIE CURIE APPRENTICE STKS (H'CAP) 1m 1f

5:25 (5:25) (Class 3) (0-90,90) 4-Y-0+ **£9,714** (£2,890; £1,444; £721) **Stalls** High

Form RPR
2240 **1** **Elliptical (USA)**[49] 2977 4-9-4 **87** JohnFahy(3) 4 100
(G A Butler) *s.i.s: hld up wl in rr: stdy prog fr over 3f out: trckd ldrs 2f out: rdn to ld 1f out: styd on wl* **7/1**[3]
5333 **2** 2 ¾ **Truism**[4] 4459 4-9-5 **85** MartinLane 13 92
(Mrs A J Perrett) *trckd ldrs: rdn to ld 2f out: hdd and one pce 1f out* **7/2**[1]
0030 **3** 2 ½ **Mujood**[4] 4459 7-9-10 **90** (v) PatrickHills 16 92
(Eve Johnson Houghton) *trckd ldrs: drvn to chal and upsides 2f out: pressed ldr after: one pce fnl f* **20/1**
1134 **4** 1 ¾ **Touch Of Style (IRE)**[30] 3589 6-8-5 **71** oh14 AshleyHamblett 3 69
(Matthew Salaman) *hld up wl in rr: rdn and prog on outer fr 3f out: kpt on fnl 2f: nvr threatened ldrs* **33/1**
5300 **5** shd **Bencoolen (IRE)**[4] 4459 5-9-10 **90** MichaelGeran 17 88
(D Nicholls) *s.s: pushed up into midfield: rdn and cl up bhd ldrs 2f out: sn outpcd: kpt on* **11/1**
3052 **6** 1 **Addwaitya**[17] 4019 5-8-7 **80** CharlotteJenner(7) 6 76
(Mrs L J Mongan) *s.s: detached in last pair: looked like being t.o 4f out: decided to r 3f out and prog on outer: effrt flattened out fnl f* **16/1**
1301 **7** ¾ **Kilburn**[12] 4206 6-8-5 **76** (p) RosieJessop(5) 12 70
(A J Lidderdale) *racd freely: disp ld at str pce 2f: led 3f out to 2f out: wknd* **14/1**
0541 **8** 1 ¾ **Baylini**[10] 4261 6-8-11 **77** JamesMillman 8 68
(Ms J S Doyle) *hld up in rr: nudged along and sme prog 3f out: drvn 2f out: kpt on same pce after: nvr a threat* **8/1**
1115 **9** 1 **Lang Shining (IRE)**[3] 4489 6-9-4 **87** SophieDoyle(3) 5 76
(J A Osborne) *sn wl off the pce in last trio: urged along and no prog 3f out: modest late hdwy* **14/1**
2-23 **10** 3 ½ **Peponi**[70] 2328 4-8-11 **77** GFCarroll 15 58
(P J Makin) *t.k.h: hld up in midfield: gng easily 3f out: rdn 2f out: wknd rapidly over 1f out* **5/1**[2]
3311 **11** 4 ½ **Carlitos Spirit (IRE)**[12] 4198 6-8-4 **75** ow1 (v) LeeTopliss(5) 9 47
(I W McInnes) *led after 2f and maintained str pce: hdd & wknd 3f out* **12/1**
0040 **12** 3 ½ **Euston Square**[22] 3876 4-8-9 **78** BillyCray(3) 14 43
(D Nicholls) *rel to r and lft at least 10 l: managed to latch on to gp over 3f out: sn wknd* **12/1**
5130 **13** 3 ½ **Buddy Holly**[58] 2685 5-9-0 **80** AndreaAtzeni 10 37
(Pat Eddery) *hld up: prog to trck ldrs 4f out: rdn 3f out: wknd over 2f out* **14/1**
0450 **14** 2 ½ **Ivory Lace**[23] 3821 9-8-2 **71** oh4 KierenFox(3) 7 23
(S Woodman) *hld up wl in rr: rdn on outer over 3f out: no prog and sn btn* **33/1**
42-6 **15** 14 **Merrymadcap (IRE)**[34] 3473 8-8-2 **71** oh3 (t) DeclanCannon(3) 1 —
(Miss Tor Sturgis) *racd freely: disp ld 2f: prom tl wknd rapidly 3f out: t.o* **50/1**

1m 54.82s (-1.48) **Going Correction** +0.025s/f (Good) **15** Ran SP% **124.7**
Speed ratings (Par 107): **107,104,102,100,100 99,99,97,96,93 89,86,83,81,68**
toteswingers:1&2:£3.70, 1&3:£27.90, 2&3:£19.60. totesuper7: Win: Not won. Place: £1,726.50. CSF £31.39 CT £499.20 TOTE £7.60: £2.90, £1.90, £7.00; EX 25.90 Trifecta £728.20 Pool £2,339.30 - 2.37 winning units. Place 6 £115.92; Place 5 £25.77.
Owner Keen As Mustard **Bred** Lavin Bloodstock **Trained** Newmarket, Suffolk

FOCUS
They went a solid gallop in this apprentices' race. The fourth is a doubt but the form looks sound overall, with the winner up 4lb.

NOTEBOOK
Elliptical(USA) settled much better under a patient ride and found plenty in the straight to run out a comfortable winner. He was fully entitled to win this on the form he showed when second at Newbury and Newmarket in the spring, and is probably capable of further improvement given similar tactics and a decent gallop. (op 13-2 tchd 6-1)
Truism, third to Start Right in the 1m handicap at this meeting four days earlier, looked to hold solid claims in this weaker contest in the light of that effort, but his lack of a change of pace was once again for all to see, and he simply kept galloping, despite having another furlong to cover. (op 3-1)
Mujood loves it here, having notched up five wins at the track in the past. This trip stretches his stamina a touch, though, and he couldn't quite live with the first two in the closing stages.
Touch Of Style(IRE) deserves plenty of credit for finishing fourth from a stone out of the handicap. His best recent effort did come over this C&D, though, and once again a liking for this track proved very valuable. (op 40-1)
Bencoolen(IRE), who won this race last year after a down-the-field effort at the meeting four days earlier, was trying to repeat the trick. Only 1lb higher this year, he ran a sound staying-on race. (op 12-1)
Addwaitya, as is often the case, was slowly away and detached for much of the race. He had been successful in his previous two starts at this track, though and, despite appearing to be going nowhere at the top of the straight, he really found his stride inside the final 2f and was never nearer than at the finish. Official explanation: jockey said gelding was slowly away (op 28-1 tchd 33-1)
Kilburn, successful in two of his previous three starts at this track, was racing beyond his optimum trip and didn't see out his race after racing freely.
Baylini, a tricky ride whose challenge needs to be timed just right, didn't enjoy the clearest of runs but genuinely quick ground probably suits her best on turf. (op 14-1)
Peponi was disappointing, failing to get home after racing keenly. (op 11-2)
Euston Square didn't help his cause by losing considerable ground at the start. Official explanation: jockey said gelding stopped quickly (op 11-1 tchd 10-1)
Buddy Holly Official explanation: jockey said gelding stopped quickly
T/Jkpt: Not won. T/Plt: £115.20 to a £1 stake. Pool:£278,710.31 - 1,766.10 winning tickets
T/Qpdt: £14.50 to a £1 stake. Pool:£13,952.16 - 711.44 winning tickets JN

4082 HAMILTON (R-H)
Saturday, July 31

OFFICIAL GOING: Good (8.9)
Wind: Light, half behind. Weather: Sunny

4580 CHAMPAGNE COCKTAILS AT HAMILTON PARK NURSERY 6f 5y

6:40 (6:41) (Class 5) 2-Y-0 **£3,238** (£963; £481; £240) **Stalls** Low

Form RPR
160 **1** **Nasharra (IRE)**[14] 4138 2-9-7 **76** TomEaves 5 82+
(K A Ryan) *cl up: rdn to ld over 1f out: drvn and styd on wl fnl f* **11/4**[1]
432 **2** 1 ¼ **Intrusion**[16] 4059 2-8-12 **67** TonyHamilton 6 69
(R A Fahey) *prom: effrt and rdn 2f out: styd on u.p ins fnl f: nt rch wnr* **9/2**
646 **3** ½ **Fast Shot**[25] 3756 2-8-1 **59** KellyHarrison(3) 4 60
(T D Easterby) *chsd ldng gp: sn drvn along: hdwy on outside over 2f out: effrt and ev ch ins fnl f: no ex towards fin* **8/1**
144 **4** 6 **Novabridge**[38] 3327 2-9-4 **73** PhillipMakin 7 56
(A B Haynes) *cl up: led over 2f out to over 1f out: wknd ent fnl f* **14/1**
5223 **5** 3 ½ **Crimson Knot (IRE)**[21] 3897 2-8-12 **67** FrannyNorton 1 39
(A Berry) *led 2f: cl up: rdn 1/2-way: wknd over 1f out* **10/3**[3]
030 **6** 2 ¼ **Memorabilia**[16] 4054 2-9-4 **73** AndrewMullen 3 39
(M Johnston) *led after 2f to over 2f out: sn rdn: wknd over 1f out* **3/1**[2]

1m 13.14s (0.94) **Going Correction** +0.15s/f (Good) **6** Ran SP% **110.7**
Speed ratings (Par 94): **99,97,96,88,84 81**
Tote Swingers:1&2:£1.50, 2&3:£4.40, 1&3:£4.50 CSF £14.88 TOTE £4.20: £2.70, £1.10; EX 13.00.
Owner Mr & Mrs Julian And Rosie Richer **Bred** P McCutcheon **Trained** Hambleton, N Yorks

FOCUS
This nursery was run at a sound pace. The form is solid, with the first three clear.

NOTEBOOK
Nasharra(IRE) had no trouble adding to his debut success, which came over 5f. Travelling well throughout, the step up in trip posed no problem and he can win again. (tchd 5-2)
Intrusion, coming from a yard who continue in fine form, was a little keen early but ran on well and can lose her maiden tag shortly. She should improve for a step up to 7f. (op 10-3 tchd 11-4)
Fast Shot, having his third start on turf, didn't appear to come down the hill very well but ran on strongly when getting the hang of things. He looks the type to continue to improve. (op 11-1 tchd 14-1)
Novabridge didn't appear to have any excuses. (op 11-1)
Crimson Knot(IRE) didn't last home over this trip. (op 9-2)
Memorabilia, coming from a yard going very well, ran below par and will need to bounce back. (op 7-2 tchd 9-2)

4581 AVIA SIGNS CLASSIFIED CLAIMING STKS 1m 65y

7:10 (7:11) (Class 6) 3-4-Y-0 **£2,047** (£604; £302) **Stalls** High

Form RPR
2425 **1** **Miami Gator (IRE)**[8] 4337 3-8-13 63 (v) AndrewElliott 2 62
(J R Weymes) *mde all: rdn over 2f out: sn edgd rt: styd on wl fnl f* **11/4**[2]
3500 **2** ¾ **Island Chief**[73] 1995 4-9-5 65 (p) TonyHamilton 3 60
(K A Ryan) *trckd ldrs: swtchd lft and effrt over 1f out: edgd lft and kpt on ins fnl f* **6/1**
3202 **3** 1 ¼ **North Central (USA)**[32] 3529 3-8-12 64 PaulNorton(7) 7 63
(J S Goldie) *hld up: hdwy 2f out: kpt on u.p ins fnl f* **9/2**[3]
2405 **4** 1 **King's Sabre**[6] 4403 4-9-1 62 (e) PaulEddery 9 51
(R C Guest) *t.k.h: hld up: hdwy 2f out: kpt on fin* **9/4**[1]
0-00 **5** nse **Strevelyn**[16] 3669 4-8-11 35 ow2 PhillipMakin 10 47?
(Mrs A Duffield) *towards rr: hdwy over 2f out: rdn and edgd rt over 1f out: one pce fnl f* **50/1**
5045 **6** 2 ¾ **Lord's Seat**[32] 3530 3-8-5 45 FrannyNorton 6 41
(A Berry) *chsd ldrs: rdn 3f out: n.m.r over 1f out: sn n.d* **25/1**
4004 **7** 2 **No Quarter (IRE)**[8] 4337 3-8-7 54 TomEaves 5 38
(M Dods) *hld up in tch: hdwy over 2f out: wknd fnl f* **10/1**
0340 **8** 16 **Hettie Hubble**[13] 4172 4-8-6 45 (p) KellyHarrison(3) 1 —
(D W Thompson) *chsd ldrs tl rdn and wknd over 2f out* **28/1**
005- **9** nk **Old Firm**[253] 7459 4-9-6 53 GarryWhillans(7) 8 15
(J A McShane) *bhd: struggling over 4f out: nvr on terms* **25/1**

1m 48.82s (0.42) **Going Correction** -0.05s/f (Good)
WFA 3 from 4yo 8lb **9** Ran SP% **112.1**
Speed ratings (Par 101): **95,94,93,92,91 89,87,71,70**
Tote Swingers:1&2:£4.20, 2&3:£3.50, 1&3:£2.80 CSF £17.96 TOTE £3.60: £2.10, £2.90, £1.20; EX 20.10.
Owner Mrs Elaine M Burke **Bred** Newlands House Stud **Trained** Middleham Moor, N Yorks
■ Stewards' Enquiry : Andrew Elliott One-day ban: careless riding (Aug 14)

FOCUS
A modest claimer run at a sound gallop, and it proved hard to make ground off the pace. The winner did not need to match his recent best.
Hettie Hubble Official explanation: jockey said filly had no more to give

4582 MACGREGOR FLOORING H'CAP 1m 3f 16y

7:40 (7:41) (Class 6) (0-60,60) 3-Y-0+ **£2,266** (£674; £337; £168) **Stalls** High

Form RPR
0-05 **1** **Short Supply (USA)**[64] 2499 4-9-0 **46** DanielTudhope 8 58+
(T D Walford) *in tch: hdwy to ld over 2f out: hld on wl fnl f* **33/1**
043 **2** 1 ½ **Amical Risks (FR)**[10] 4246 6-9-3 **56** EleanorMcGowan(7) 13 65
(Joss Saville) *dwlt: bhd: hdwy over 3f out: chsd wnr ins fnl f: kpt on* **7/1**
1233 **3** 2 ¾ **Sharp Sovereign (USA)**[37] 3369 4-9-7 **53** PhillipMakin 12 57
(T D Barron) *cl up: led over 3f out to over 2f out: kpt on same pce fr over 1f out* **3/1**[1]
6210 **4** hd **Regent's Secret (USA)**[2] 4511 10-9-7 **60** PaulNorton(7) 15 64
(J S Goldie) *hld up and bhd: hdwy over 2f out: kpt on fnl f: nrest at fin* **4/1**[2]

3216 **5** *7* **Dean Iarracht (IRE)**[6] 4410 4-9-11 **57**......................(p) AndrewMullen 10 48
(Miss Tracy Waggott) *bhd tl hdwy 2f out: nvr able to chal* **9/2**[3]

6525 **6** *1 3/4* **New England**[52] 2870 8-8-12 **51**...................... NeilFarley(7) 14 39
(N J Vaughan) *midfield: hdwy and ev ch over 3f out: wknd wl over 1f out* **9/1**

00-2 **7** *hd* **Orpen Bid (IRE)**[21] 3901 5-8-11 **46** oh1...................... KellyHarrison(3) 7 34
(M Mullineaux) *midfield: hdwy to chse ldrs over 3f out: edgd rt and wknd wl over 1f out* **20/1**

0000 **8** *4* **Suburbia (USA)**[18] 3989 4-9-0 **46** oh1...................... PatrickMathers 9 26
(J Barclay) *in tch tl rdn and wknd over 3f out* **100/1**

0-54 **9** *2 1/4* **Goodison Park**[43] 3153 3-8-10 **53**...................... LNewman 6 29
(A G Foster) *prom: rdn whn n.m.r briefly over 3f out: sn rdn and wknd* **11/1**

0-00 **10** *1 1/4* **Real Desire**[6] 4407 4-9-0 **46**...................... TonyHamilton 3 20
(P Monteith) *midfield: hdwy and ev ch over 3f out: wknd 2f out* **33/1**

05 **11** *1/2* **Tifoso (FR)**[27] 1828 5-9-2 **48**......................(v[1]) PaulEddery 5 21
(R C Guest) *cl up: led over 4f out to over 3f out: sn wknd* **33/1**

000/ **12** *3/4* **Bollin Ruth**[49] 1990 8-8-11 **50**...................... GarryWhillans(7) 1 22
(D W Whillans) *towards rr: drvn over 4f out: nvr on terms* **20/1**

0-00 **13** *3/4* **Funky Munky**[21] 3905 5-9-10 **56**...................... TomEaves 2 26
(A C Whillans) *towards rr: struggling over 3f out: sn wknd* **16/1**

0 **14** *9* **Hawk Junior (IRE)**[59] 2653 4-9-0 **46** oh1...................... AndrewElliott 4 —
(Patrick Morris) *hld up: struggling 4f out: sn btn* **66/1**

35-0 **15** *32* **Noble Attitude**[186] 298 4-9-5 **54**...................... MichaelStainton(3) 11 —
(N Tinkler) *mde most to over 4f out: sn wknd: t.o* **50/1**

2m 25.2s (-0.40) **Going Correction** -0.05s/f (Good)
WFA 3 from 4yo+ 11lb **15** Ran SP% **122.7**
Speed ratings (Par 101): **99,97,95,95,90 89,89,86,84,83 83,82,82,75,52**
Tote Swingers:1&2:£19.60, 2&3:£3.80, 1&3:£22.00 CSF £241.05 CT £924.74 TOTE £69.60: £15.80, £1.50, £2.30; EX 437.30.
Owner Mrs G B Walford **Bred** Juddmonte Farms Inc **Trained** Sheriff Hutton, N Yorks

FOCUS
A wide open 46-60 handicap run at a generous pace. The winner showed his first form and the runner-up was the best guide.
Short Supply(USA) Official explanation: trainer's rep said, regarding apparent improvement in form, that the yard was under a cloud but the filly had been in good form
Amical Risks(FR) Official explanation: jockey said gelding suffered interference at start and she lost an iron

4583 EUROPEAN BREEDERS' FUND FILLIES' H'CAP 5f 4y
8:10 (8:12) (Class 4) (0-85,82) 3-Y-0+ **£6,476** (£1,927; £963; £481) **Stalls** Centre

Form RPR
1162 **1** **Mey Blossom**[10] 4243 5-9-2 **74**...................... MichaelStainton(3) 5 84
(R M Whitaker) *hld up: sn pushed along: hdwy stands' side wl over 1f out: led ins fnl f: styd on strly* **7/2**[3]

0125 **2** *hd* **Brierty (IRE)**[8] 4345 4-9-3 **79**...................... NeilFarley(7) 2 88
(D Carroll) *in tch: hdwy towards stands' side over 1f out: ev ch whn rdr dropped whip ins fnl f: kpt on u.p* **5/2**[1]

2103 **3** *2* **Wicked Wilma (IRE)**[10] 4243 6-8-11 **66**...................... FrannyNorton 8 68
(A Berry) *t.k.h: led to ins fnl f: kpt on same pce* **8/1**

1513 **4** *1/2* **Gap Princess (IRE)**[21] 3919 6-9-13 **82**...................... SilvestreDeSousa 7 82
(G A Harker) *prom: rdn and sltly outpcd wl over 1f out: kpt on ins fnl f: no imp* **3/1**[2]

-510 **5** *1 1/2* **Basle**[38] 3328 3-9-3 **76**......................(t) PhillipMakin 6 71
(Miss Gay Kelleway) *in tch: effrt over 2f out: sn rdn: kpt on same pce fnl f* **15/2**

04-3 **6** *3 3/4* **Eternal Instinct**[65] 2450 3-9-1 **77**...................... GaryBartley(3) 9 58
(J S Goldie) *t.k.h: trckd ldrs on outside: rdn: edgd rt and wknd over 1f out* **14/1**

2525 **7** *hd* **Speedy Senorita (IRE)**[8] 4343 5-8-8 **63** oh1......................(p) TonyHamilton 1 43
(J J Quinn) *w ldr: rdn over 2f out: wknd over 1f out* **10/1**

60.09 secs (0.09) **Going Correction** +0.15s/f (Good)
WFA 3 from 4yo+ 4lb **7** Ran SP% **114.4**
Speed ratings (Par 102): **105,104,101,100,98 92,91**
Tote Swingers:1&2:£3.10, 2&3:£5.40, 1&3:£3.10 CSF £12.72 CT £63.51 TOTE £5.70: £2.60, £1.70; EX 18.70.
Owner Waz Developments Ltd **Bred** Hellwood Stud Farm **Trained** Scarcroft, W Yorks
■ Stewards' Enquiry : Neil Farley caution: careless riding

FOCUS
A 66-85 fillies handicap in which the top weight was 3lb below the ceiling rating. The winner's best run since she was a 3yo.
Basle Official explanation: jockey said filly hung left final furlong

4584 KANE GANG MAIDEN STKS 6f 5y
8:40 (8:43) (Class 5) 3-Y-0+ **£2,590** (£770; £385; £192) **Stalls** Centre

Form RPR
3 **1** **Henry Morgan**[36] 3397 3-9-3 0...................... TomEaves 5 63
(B Smart) *tubed: mde all: rdn over 2f out: kpt on wl fnl f* **15/8**[2]

-60 **2** *1/2* **Red Roar (IRE)**[44] 3111 3-8-12 0...................... FrannyNorton 8 56
(A Berry) *in tch: swtchd lft after 2f: effrt wl over 1f out: chsd wnr wl ins fnl f: r.o* **10/1**

532 **3** *2 1/2* **Kristen Jane (USA)**[18] 3988 3-8-12 47...................... PhillipMakin 3 48
(Miss L A Perratt) *trckd ldrs: effrt and ev ch over 1f out: no ex ins fnl f* **8/1**[3]

5-6 **4** *hd* **Billionaire Boy (IRE)**[8] 4340 3-9-3 0...................... DanielTudhope 6 52
(Patrick Morris) *t.k.h: prom: effrt over 1f out: one pce fnl f* **20/1**

22 **5** *3/4* **Jemima Nicholas**[36] 3407 3-8-12 0...................... PaulMulrennan 1 45
(W J Haggas) *racd nr stands' rail and jst away fr main gp: prom: effrt over 2f out: edgd rt and no imp over 1f out* **1/1**[1]

0/0 **6** *24* **Our Angel**[10] 4251 4-9-0 0...................... KellyHarrison(3) 2 —
(E J Alston) *t.k.h: cl up tl wknd fr 2f out: t.o* **33/1**

00- **7** *31* **Mark Carmers**[327] 5728 3-8-10 0...................... NeilFarley(7) 4 —
(D A Nolan) *bhd and sn struggling: hung rt and lost tch over 3f out* **100/1**

1m 13.03s (0.83) **Going Correction** +0.15s/f (Good)
WFA 3 from 4yo 5lb **7** Ran SP% **113.7**
Speed ratings (Par 103): **100,99,96,95,94 62,21**
Tote Swingers:1&2:£1.60, 2&3:£4.90, 1&3:£2.30 CSF £19.71 TOTE £2.70: £1.50, £4.20; EX 16.70.
Owner Mrs F Denniff **Bred** A S Denniff **Trained** Hambleton, N Yorks

FOCUS
A weak maiden and the favourite was below form. The third looks the key.
Jemima Nicholas Official explanation: jockey said filly never travelled

4585 DALUCIANO RESTAURANT & BAR H'CAP (FINAL QUALIFIER FOR THE SCOTTISH TROPHY HANDICAP SERIES) 1m 1f 36y
9:10 (9:11) (Class 5) (0-75,74) 3-Y-0+ **£2,590** (£770; £385; £192) **Stalls** High

Form RPR
3311 **1** **High Resolution**[15] 4088 3-8-12 **67**...................... SilvestreDeSousa 5 80+
(Miss L A Perratt) *hld up: nt clr run over 2f out: swtchd to outside over 1f out: qcknd to ld ins fnl f: readily* **4/1**[1]

1-56 **2** *2 1/2* **Starry Mount**[19] 3949 3-9-2 **71**...................... PhillipMakin 1 76
(A B Haynes) *trckd ldrs: effrt over 2f out: led and hung lft over 1f out: hdd ins fnl f: no ch w wnr* **16/1**

2440 **3** *1 1/4* **Veroon (IRE)**[21] 3894 4-10-0 **74**......................(p) PaulMulrennan 2 77
(J G Given) *hld up: hdwy on outside over 1f out: rdn and kpt on fnl f: nrst fin* **15/2**

5062 **4** *3/4* **Caracal**[5] 4439 3-8-7 **62**...................... AndrewElliott 4 62
(M Johnston) *hld up on outside: gd hdwy to ld over 2f out: hdd over 1f out: kpt on same pce* **6/1**[3]

3552 **5** *2* **Talk Of Saafend (IRE)**[19] 3950 5-9-2 **62**...................... TonyHamilton 11 59
(P Monteith) *hld up: hdwy and prom over 1f out: rdn and sn one pce* **14/1**

0234 **6** *2 3/4* **Royal Straight**[6] 4405 5-9-10 **70**...................... TomEaves 14 61
(Miss L A Perratt) *hld up in tch on ins: hdwy whn n.m.r briefly over 2f out: wknd fnl f* **9/2**[2]

0031 **7** *nk* **Zambuka (FR)**[8] 4344 3-8-2 **62**...................... RossAtkinson(5) 7 51
(F J Brennan) *in tch: effrt whn n.m.r briefly over 2f out: sn rdn: wknd fnl f* **9/2**[2]

-303 **8** *1 1/4* **Cool Baranca (GER)**[15] 4094 4-9-6 **71**...................... JamesSullivan(5) 10 58
(P Monteith) *hld up: effrt over 2f out: nvr able to chal* **7/1**

2431 **9** *4* **Stellite**[21] 3905 10-9-5 **68**...................... GaryBartley(3) 13 47
(J S Goldie) *midfield: rdn over 2f out: wknd over 1f out* **12/1**

5064 **10** *4 1/2* **Primo Way**[12] 4189 9-8-9 **55** oh10......................(be) FrannyNorton 8 24
(D A Nolan) *cl up: rdn over 2f out: wknd over 1f out* **66/1**

0-00 **11** *27* **Defi (IRE)**[27] 3706 8-8-2 **55** oh10......................(t) NeilFarley(7) 6 —
(D A Nolan) *led to over 4f out: wknd fr 3f out: t.o* **100/1**

0/-0 **12** *12* **Billy One Punch**[12] 4188 8-9-0 **60**...................... LNewman 9 —
(A G Foster) *in tch: led over 4f out to over 2f out: sn struggling* **50/1**

1m 58.51s (-1.19) **Going Correction** -0.05s/f (Good)
WFA 3 from 4yo+ 9lb **12** Ran SP% **119.6**
Speed ratings (Par 103): **103,100,99,99,97 94,94,93,89,85 61,51**
Tote Swingers:1&2:£17.40, 2&3:£21.80, 1&3:£7.60 CSF £70.27 CT £470.56 TOTE £4.20: £2.30, £6.10, £2.60; EX 109.50 Place 6 £97.77, Place 5 £48.54..
Owner Mrs Helen Perratt **Bred** Old Mill Stud Ltd **Trained** East Kilbride, South Lanarks

FOCUS
An open 56-75 handicap run at a sound pace. The progressive winner looks better than the bare form, which is rated around the third.
T/Plt: £92.50 to a £1 stake. Pool:£57,915.61 - 456.74 winning tickets T/Qpdt: £37.90 to a £1 stake. Pool:£5,777.10 - 112.70 winning tickets RY

4361 LINGFIELD (L-H)
Saturday, July 31

OFFICIAL GOING: Turf course - good to firm (9.4); awt - standard
Wind: Fresh, across. Weather: overcast, breezy

4586 BET ON LIVE GOLF AT TOTESPORT.COM APPRENTICE H'CAP 7f 140y
5:55 (5:56) (Class 6) (0-65,63) 3-Y-0+ **£2,047** (£604; £302) **Stalls** Centre

Form RPR
0001 **1** **Kipchak (IRE)**[7] 4366 5-9-10 **63**......................(p) FrancisHayes(4) 8 72
(C R Dore) *mde all: crossed to r on stands' rail and sn clr: pushed along over 1f out: kpt on: unchal* **13/8**[1]

5300 **2** *3 1/4* **Crystallize**[25] 3762 4-9-7 **60**...................... MarkPower(4) 7 61
(A B Haynes) *chsd clr wnr thrght: rdn ent fnl 2f: kpt on same pce and no imp after* **11/2**[3]

0020 **3** *1 3/4* **Amends (USA)**[16] 4056 3-9-1 **62**...................... IanBurns(4) 12 57
(J R Best) *chsd ldng pair: rdn over 2f out: plugged on same pce fnl 2f: swtchd lft ins fnl f: nvr trbld wnr* **7/2**[2]

0040 **4** *1 1/4* **Sonny G (IRE)**[7] 4365 3-8-2 **49**...................... MatthewCosham(4) 6 41
(J R Best) *chsd ldng trio but nvr on terms w wnr: rdn and plugged on same pce fr wl over 1f out* **9/1**

0000 **5** *2 1/2* **Wunder Strike (USA)**[16] 4057 4-9-4 **57**...................... LucyBarry(4) 9 45
(J R Boyle) *stdd s: hld up wl off the pce in rr: sme hdwy into midfield over 2f out: pushed along and styd on same pce fr over 1f out: nvr on terms* **8/1**

00-6 **6** *7* **Norcroft**[11] 4237 8-8-12 **47**......................(tp) SoniaEaton 11 18
(Mrs C A Dunnett) *v.s.a: bhd: rdn over 2f out: nvr on terms* **20/1**

505/ **7** *1 3/4* **Raise Again (IRE)**[32] 1053 7-8-8 **45**...................... AlexEdwards(2) 2 12
(Mrs P N Dutfield) *stdd s: hld up wl off the pce in rr: rdn over 2f out: lost tch wl over 1f out* **12/1**

/000 **8** *13* **Turtle Dove**[26] 3727 5-8-9 **48**...................... NoelGarbutt(4) 5 —
(Mark Gillard) *s.i.s: a wl bhd: lost tch over 2f out: t.o* **33/1**

0-00 **9** *25* **Swirl Tango**[31] 3556 4-8-6 **45**......................(t) ThomasBrown(4) 4 —
(F Jordan) *midfield tl 1/2-way: sn struggling: lost tch over 2f out: wl t.o fr over 1f out* **100/1**

1m 30.74s (-1.56) **Going Correction** -0.15s/f (Firm)
WFA 3 from 4yo+ 8lb **9** Ran SP% **113.2**
Speed ratings (Par 101): **101,97,96,94,92 85,83,70,45**
Tote Swingers:1&2:£2.70, 2&3:£4.00, 1&3:£1.80. CSF £10.39 CT £27.13 TOTE £2.20: £1.30, £2.00, £1.20; EX 10.30.
Owner Liam Breslin **Bred** Miss Mary Davidson & Mrs Steffi Von Schilcher **Trained** Cowbit, Lincs

FOCUS
Drying conditions in the afternoon countered the effect of a little earlier drizzle, and racing took place on an overcast, muggy evening. All four winners on the straight course raced against the stands' rail, and Kipchak enjoyed an easy lead. The next pair raced on the rail too. The form potentially flatters the winner.

4587 BET ON LIVE CRICKET AT TOTESPORT.COM MEDIAN AUCTION MAIDEN STKS 7f 140y
6:25 (6:26) (Class 6) 2-Y-O **£2,047** (£604; £302) **Stalls** Centre

Form RPR
3 **1** **Timothy T**[12] 4208 2-9-3 0...................... SebSanders 11 81+
(M Botti) *mde all: rdn clr wl over 1f out: in n.d after: pushed out: easily* **5/4**[1]

0 **2** 2½ **Fly By White (IRE)**[17] 4021 2-8-12 0 .... AlanMunro 7 70+
(R Hannon) *awkward leaving stalls and s.i.s: bhd and rn green on outer: pushed along and hdwy 1/2-way: chsd clr wnr ent fnl f: kpt on but no ch w wnr* **2/1**[2]

0 **3** 6 **Educated Son**[23] 3832 2-9-3 0 .... GeorgeBaker 3 61
(W R Muir) *chsd ldrs: rdn and outpcd wl over 1f out: 3rd and wl btn whn hung lft ent fnl f* **13/2**[3]

00 **4** 2¾ **Captain Sharpe**[23] 3832 2-9-3 0 .... (b[1]) TomQueally 6 55
(H J L Dunlop) *chsd ldrs: rdn and outpcd wl over 1f out: no ch w wnr whn nt clr run and swtchd lft 1f out: wl btn fnl f* **33/1**

0 **5** 1¼ **Dances With Words (IRE)**[19] 3961 2-9-3 0 .... LiamKeniry 4 52
(R A Farrant) *hld up in rr: outpcd 2f out: rdn and sme hdwy whn swtchd lft ent fnl f: plugged on: nvr trbld ldrs* **50/1**

00 **6** nse **Wanchai Minx**[45] 3082 2-8-12 0 .... KirstyMilczarek 10 47
(A P Jarvis) *chsd wnr: rdn and wl outpcd wl over 1f out: lost 2nd and edgd rt ent fnl f: wknd* **16/1**

7 2½ **Endaxi Mana Mou** 2-8-12 0 .... JerryO'Dwyer 9 41
(M G Quinlan) *s.i.s: a bhd: rdn ent fnl 2f: wknd and lost tch wl over 1f out* **25/1**

060 **8** ½ **Robber Stone**[26] 3735 2-9-3 56 .... ChrisCatlin 8 44+
(M R Channon) *stdd s: t.k.h: hld up in rr: rdn and btn ent fnl 2f: wl bhd fnl f* **16/1**

00 **9** ½ **Bernie's Tune**[23] 3832 2-9-0 0 .... JackDean(3) 1 43
(J L Spearing) *wnt lft s and s.i.s: sn pushed along in midfield: hung lft and lost tch wl over 1f out* **80/1**

5 **10** 23 **Miss Nimbus**[18] 3981 2-8-9 0 .... MatthewDavies(3) 5 —
(George Baker) *chsd ldrs tl lost pl qckly 1/2-way: hung lft and lost tch wl over 2f out: eased fnl f: t.o* **66/1**

1m 31.12s (-1.18) **Going Correction** -0.15s/f (Firm) **10** Ran SP% **114.4**
Speed ratings (Par 92): **99,96,90,87,86 86,83,83,82,59**
Tote Swingers:1&2:£1.10, 2&3:£2.80, 1&3:£2.40 CSF £3.55 TOTE £3.00: £1.60, £1.30, £1.20.
Owner Op - Center **Bred** Mrs Susan Cole & Miss Lesley McGrath **Trained** Newmarket, Suffolk

FOCUS
It was 16-1 bar three in a maiden lacking much strength in depth, and the market eventually got it right despite some late volatility. The winning time was 0.38 seconds slower than in the preceding 0-65 handicap. Timothy T set his own pace on the rail for an easy win. The form is limited in behind.

NOTEBOOK
Timothy T, 10-11 in places in the morning, drifted to 13-8 before regaining favouritism just before the off. By far the smartest away of the two main protagonists, he didn't need to be asked many questions to assert and confirmed the promise of his Yarmouth debut with an authoritative display. Future plans are to be confirmed, but he could make into a decent recruit for a yard returning a very respectable strike-rate with its small number of juveniles this term. (op 11-10 tchd 13-8)
Fly By White(IRE) was keen to post and awkward out of the stalls. He can be judged better than the bare result, as he also had to run down the centre of the course. He still has a little to learn, but may have a routine maiden in him. (tchd 6-4 and 9-4)
Educated Son is regarded as a long-term prospect by connections. His improved performance here owed much to him consenting to settle better than on debut, although more would be needed to land a maiden next time. (op 15-2)
Captain Sharpe showed up for longer in first-time blinkers and now has the option of handicaps. (op 25-1)
Wanchai Minx Official explanation: jockey said filly made a noise
Miss Nimbus Official explanation: jockey said filly hung badly left

4588 PLAY BINGO AT TOTESPORT.COM H'CAP 7f
6:55 (6:56) (Class 5) (0-75,70) 3-Y-O **£2,729** (£806; £403) **Stalls** High

Form RPR

0220 **1** **Red Yarn**[19] 3962 3-9-7 70 .... (b) GeorgeBaker 6 78
(G L Moore) *reminders sn after s: led: rdn and jnd wl over 1f out: hdd ent fnl f: kpt on wl u.p to ld again fnl 75yds: drvn out* **4/1**[2]

0056 **2** ½ **Fawley Green**[12] 4206 3-9-7 70 .... RichardHughes 5 77
(W R Muir) *t.k.h early: trckd wnr on stands' rail: swtchd lft and jnd wnr on bit wl over 1f out: rdn ins fnl f: nt qckn u.p and hdd fnl 75yds* **4/1**[2]

3001 **3** 4 **Batgirl**[21] 3907 3-8-11 60 .... KirstyMilczarek 2 56
(John Berry) *racd keenly: chsd ldr: rdn wl over 1f out: hung lft and btn ent fnl f* **5/1**[3]

3341 **4** 2¼ **Aleqa**[11] 4237 3-9-7 70 .... AlanMunro 4 60
(C F Wall) *trckd ldrs: swtchd lft and effrt ent fnl 2f: edgd lft u.p and wknd over 1f out: wl hld fnl f* **11/8**[1]

001- **5** ½ **Skyflight**[304] 6386 3-9-5 68 .... TomQueally 3 56
(Eve Johnson Houghton) *n.m.r and dropped to last sn after s: in tch: rdn and unable qck ent fnl 2f: wl btn over 1f out* **14/1**

336 **6** nk **Fazza**[40] 3270 3-9-7 70 .... DavidProbert 1 58
(D W P Arbuthnot) *in tch in last pair on outer: rdn and unable qck 2f out: drvn and wknd wl over 1f out: wl btn fnl f* **12/1**

1m 22.88s (-0.42) **Going Correction** -0.15s/f (Firm) **6** Ran SP% **113.1**
Speed ratings (Par 100): **96,95,90,88,87 87**
Tote Swingers:1&2:£3.50, 2&3:£2.50, 1&3:£2.70 CSF £20.38 TOTE £3.80: £2.60, £2.70; EX 18.30.
Owner Heart Of The South Racing **Bred** John And Caroline Penny **Trained** Lower Beeding, W Sussex

FOCUS
A tight handicap, which featured some trouble in running despite the small field. The front pair raced on the favoured rail and the form is weakish.
Batgirl Official explanation: jockey said filly was unsuited by the track

4589 PLAY BLACKJACK AT TOTESPORT.COM H'CAP 6f
7:25 (7:25) (Class 6) (0-65,65) 3-Y-O+ **£2,047** (£604; £302) **Stalls** High

Form RPR

0022 **1** **Titus Gent**[9] 4283 5-9-13 63 .... KirstyMilczarek 16 70
(R A Harris) *mde all: rdn clr ent fnl f: idling fnl 100yds: kpt on and a doing enough* **4/1**[1]

240 **2** nk **Talamahana**[9] 4283 5-9-2 52 .... (v) ChrisCatlin 15 58
(A B Haynes) *racd in midfield: pushed along 1/2-way: drvn and hdwy jst over 1f out: nt clr run 1f out: r.o to chse wnr ins fnl f: clsng at fin: nvr quite gng pce to rch wnr* **25/1**

6316 **3** 1 **Decency (IRE)**[28] 3677 3-9-10 65 .... RichardHughes 13 69+
(H J L Dunlop) *stdd s and dropped in bhd: stl plenty to do wl over 1f out: hdwy and looking for run over 1f out: swtchd bk to rail and r.o to go 3rd ins fnl f: gng on at fin* **9/2**[2]

2300 **4** 2 **Nativity**[18] 3993 4-8-13 52 .... JackDean(3) 12 48+
(J L Spearing) *in tch: rdn and effrt wl over 1f out: nt clr run ent fnl f: kpt on u.p but nvr gng pce to rch ldrs* **11/2**

5030 **5** nse **Mr Skipiton (IRE)**[25] 3762 5-9-8 58 .... SebSanders 14 54
(B J McMath) *pressed wnr: rdn ent fnl 2f: nt pce of wnr over 1f out: styd on same pce fnl f* **5/1**[3]

0540 **6** ¾ **Commandingpresence (USA)**[18] 3979 4-8-11 47 .... NeilChalmers 10 41+
(J J Bridger) *chsd ldrs: outpcd and edging lft wl over 2f out: rallied u.p ent fnl f: styd on same pce fnl 150yds* **33/1**

5550 **7** 1 **Super Frank (IRE)**[14] 4130 7-9-5 55 .... (p) TomQueally 8 46
(J Akehurst) *chsd ldrs: rdn wl over 1f out: wknd jst ins fnl f* **8/1**

0034 **8** hd **Bateleur**[9] 4283 6-9-7 60 .... MatthewDavies(3) 5 50+
(M R Channon) *hld up wl bhd: pushed along 2f out: hdwy over 1f out: swtchd lft ins fnl f: kpt on: nvr trbld ldrs* **16/1**

4360 **9** ¾ **Captain Kallis (IRE)**[8] 4326 4-9-2 57 .... JohnFahy(5) 2 45
(D J S Ffrench Davis) *chsd ldrs tl wknd u.p over 1f out* **20/1**

2130 **10** 1¾ **Goodbye Cash (IRE)**[11] 4232 6-9-6 59 .... AndrewHeffernan(3) 6 41
(R J Smith) *hld up towards rr: rdn and struggling ent fnl 2f: n.d fr over 1f out* **20/1**

-046 **11** 1¼ **Imperial Warrior**[53] 2844 3-9-4 59 .... (p) SteveDrowne 3 36
(H Morrison) *racd out wd: racd off the pce in midfield: rdn and no prog 1/2-way: no ch fnl 2f* **8/1**

000 **12** 3¼ **Lilli Palmer (IRE)**[24] 3786 3-8-13 54 .... PaulFitzsimons 7 21
(Miss J R Tooth) *a towards rr: rdn and struggling 1/2-way: no ch fnl 2f* **80/1**

10-0 **13** 1 **Philmack Dot Com**[11] 4232 4-9-8 58 .... (b[1]) LiamKeniry 4 22
(D Donovan) *a in rr: struggling u.p over 2f out: bhd fr wl over 1f out* **40/1**

00-0 **14** 17 **Mogok Ruby**[209] 26 6-9-10 60 .... AlanMunro 11 —
(L Montague Hall) *a bhd: lost tch 1/2-way: t.o fr wl over 1f out* **16/1**

1m 10.42s (-0.78) **Going Correction** -0.15s/f (Firm)
WFA 3 from 4yo+ 5lb **14** Ran SP% **124.2**
Speed ratings (Par 101): **99,98,97,94,94 93,92,91,90,88 86,82,81,58**
Tote Swingers:1&2:£31.90, 2&3:£35.50, 1&3:£1.80 CSF £116.26 CT £398.54 TOTE £3.20: £1.10, £13.10, £2.80; EX 77.40.
Owner Alan & Adam Darlow, A Darlow Productions **Bred** Heather Raw **Trained** Earlswood, Monmouths

FOCUS
A weak contest in which those drawn high dominated, and a third win in five renewals for Ron Harris. With the rail playing a big part it is important not to rate the form too positively.
Nativity Official explanation: jockey said filly was denied a clear run
Goodbye Cash(IRE) Official explanation: jockey said mare hung badly left

4590 PLAY ROULETTE AT TOTESPORT.COM EBF MAIDEN STKS 5f (P)
7:55 (7:55) (Class 5) 2-Y-O **£3,076** (£915; £457; £228) **Stalls** High

Form RPR

3256 **1** **Foghorn Leghorn**[56] 2743 2-9-3 87 .... JimmyFortune 6 79
(P W Chapple-Hyam) *led for 1f: chsd ldr after: rdn and qcknd to chal 1f out: led ins fnl f: sn in command: pushed out* **1/1**[1]

2360 **2** 1¼ **Silca Conegliano (IRE)**[16] 4066 2-8-12 71 .... ChrisCatlin 3 67
(M R Channon) *hld up in tch in last: rdn and hdwy ent fnl f: r.o to go 2nd towards fin: no threat to wnr* **10/1**

05 **3** ½ **Dubai Affair**[48] 3000 2-8-12 0 .... SteveDrowne 2 65
(H Morrison) *dwlt: sn rcvrd and led after 1f: rdn over 1f out: hdd ins fnl f: no ex and lost 2nd towards fin* **15/8**[2]

05 **4** 1½ **Partout Le Magasin**[9] 4303 2-9-3 0 .... RichardHughes 1 67
(J S Moore) *stdd sn after s: chsd ldrs: rdn and effrt on inner over 1f out: hung rt u.p ent fnl f: wknd fnl 150yds* **6/1**[3]

5 1¼ **Hackett (IRE)** 2-9-3 0 .... SebSanders 5 60
(M Quinn) *chsd ldrs: rdn and unable qck 2f out: hung lft and btn ent fnl f* **25/1**

60.86 secs (2.06) **Going Correction** +0.225s/f (Slow) **5** Ran SP% **112.0**
Speed ratings (Par 94): **92,90,89,86,84**
CSF £11.88 TOTE £1.80: £1.70, £4.60; EX 8.20.
Owner The Comic Strip Heroes **Bred** Cheveley Park Stud Ltd **Trained** Newmarket, Suffolk

FOCUS
Not a particularly competitive maiden. The winner was just off his best efforts, with the runner-up the best guide.

NOTEBOOK
Foghorn Leghorn, sixth in the Woodcote Stakes at Epsom when last seen, appreciated the drop in class to record a first win at the fifth time of asking. Quickly reined in after finding himself in the lead early on, he required little more than pushing out to oblige. This will have done plenty for his confidence, although he has it to prove at a higher level. (op 5-6 tchd 11-10)
Silca Conegliano(IRE) has three placed finishes to her name, all recorded in 6f turf maidens, and showed a lack of extra gears on this Polytrack bow. Although staying on, she never looked like mastering the winner and is likely to need 6f or more in this discipline. (tchd 8-1)
Dubai Affair, a Polytrack debutante, dwelt for the second race in three, and the energy expended in wresting the lead after that poor start dulled her finishing effort. She has ability, but still has a little to learn. She qualifies for a handicap mark. (op 5-2)
Partout Le Magasin, although he has had three career starts now, still hasn't quite worked out what the job of racing entails, proving green on the way to post and under the whip late on. He remains capable of better when developing mentally. Official explanation: jockey said colt hung right (op 9-1)

4591 TRYST - EAST GRINSTEAD'S ULTIMATE NIGHT CLUB H'CAP 1m 2f (P)
8:25 (8:25) (Class 6) (0-55,55) 3-Y-O+ **£2,047** (£604; £302) **Stalls** Low

Form RPR

030 **1** **Fitzolini**[37] 3370 4-9-4 54 .... (p) JimmyQuinn 12 61
(A D Brown) *dwlt: t.k.h: sn chsng ldrs: hdwy to ld over 7f out: mde rest: rdn wl over 1f out: drvn and edgd rt ent fnl f: edgd rt ins fnl f: hld on cl home: all out* **10/1**

-441 **2** hd **Ubiquitous**[23] 3821 5-8-12 53 .... (t) SimonPearce(5) 4 60
(S Dow) *hld up in tch in midfield: hdwy on inner over 2f out: swtchd rt and rdn ent fnl f: ev ch fnl 100yds: r.o but jst hld cl home* **6/1**[3]

0001 **3** ¾ **Litenup (IRE)**[52] 2870 4-9-4 54 .... (t) DavidProbert 14 59
(A J Lidderdale) *led after 1f tl over 7f out: chsd ldr tl 4f out: rdn and sltly outpcd ent fnl 2f: rallied u.p jst over 1f out: chsd ldng pair ins fnl f: carried rt and one pce towards fin* **11/2**[2]

-006 **4** 2¾ **Burnbrake**[40] 3263 5-9-2 52 .... AlanMunro 7 52
(L Montague Hall) *bhd: hdwy into midfield wl over 2f out: rdn over 1f out: styd on steadily ins fnl f: nt pce to rch ldrs* **9/1**

0000 **5** ¾ **Chadwell Spring (IRE)**[28] 3683 4-9-5 55 .... SebSanders 11 53
(Miss J Feilden) *t.k.h: chsd ldrs: wnt 2nd 4f out: rdn ent fnl 2f: hrd drvn and unable qck over 1f out: wknd ins fnl f* **16/1**

0030 **6** 1 **Rowan Light**[16] 4070 4-9-5 55 .... PatCosgrave 9 51
(J R Boyle) *led for 1f: chsd ldrs after: jostled over 2f out: drvn and unable qck ent fnl 2f: one pce and btn 1f out* **12/1**

0-04 **7** 2½ **Straight And Level (CAN)**[95] 1591 5-9-5 55 .... IanMongan 8 46
(Miss Jo Crowley) *hld up in midfield on outer: rdn and effrt ent fnl 2f: wknd jst over 1f out: wl hld fnl f* **7/2**[1]

1013 **8** 1¾ **Inquisitress**[18] 3982 6-9-4 54 .... NeilChalmers 2 42
(J J Bridger) *hld up in midfield: hdwy to trck ldrs over 2f out: rdn and btn wl over 1f out: wknd fnl f* **8/1**

0 **9** 1/2 **Moonwolf (NZ)**[16] 4070 6-9-0 **53** .... RobertLButler(3) 3 40
(Miss Sheena West) *in tch on outer: hdwy and jostling match w rival over 2f out: lost pl qckly bnd 2f out: wl btn after* **33/1**

065 **10** 1 1/4 **Pab Special (IRE)**[5] 4434 7-9-0 **55** .... DaleSwift(5) 5 39
(B R Johnson) *hld up in rr: rdn and effrt on inner jst over 2f out: wknd u.p wl over 1f out: no ch fnl f* **7/1**

100- **11** 22 **Manchestermaverick (USA)**[215] 7861 5-9-5 **55** ...... RichardThomas 10 —
(Dr J R J Naylor) *in tch tl pushed along and losing pl over 4f out: wl bhd fr over 2f out: eased fnl f: t.o* **50/1**

-003 **12** 19 **Bold Hawk**[33] 3518 4-8-13 **54** ....(tp) KierenFox(5) 6 —
(Mrs C A Dunnett) *nvr gng wl and a bhd: lost tch over 3f out: wl t.o fnl 2f* **20/1**

500/ **13** 24 **Real Dandy**[640] 7079 4-9-1 **54** ....(p) AndrewHeffernan(3) 1 —
(Lucinda Featherstone) *towards rr: rdn and dropped to last over 4f out: sn lost tch: wl t.o fr over 2f out: virtually p.u fnl f* **40/1**

2m 8.29s (1.69) **Going Correction** +0.225s/f (Slow) **13** Ran SP% **120.3**
Speed ratings (Par 101): **102,101,101,99,98 97,95,94,93,92 75,60,40**
Tote Swingers:1&2:£14.80, 2&3:£6.60, 1&3:£20.00 CSF £67.21 CT £372.18 TOTE £14.10: £4.50, £1.50, £3.30; EX 108.00 Place 6 £26.30, Place 5 £21.41..
Owner Mrs Susan Johnson **Bred** Mrs S Johnson **Trained** Yedingham, N Yorks

FOCUS
A tight handicap on paper, with only 3lb separating the entire field. There was a brisk early pace which soon subsided. The winner is rated back to his winter form.
Ubiquitous Official explanation: jockey said mare hung right
T/Plt: £29.20 to a £1 stake. Pool:£58,114.67 - 1,452.60 winning tickets T/Qpdt: £25.40 to a £1 stake. Pool:£5,115.36 - 149.00 winning tickets SP

4548 NEWMARKET (R-H)
Saturday, July 31

OFFICIAL GOING: Good (6.8)
Far side of July Course utilised.
Wind: Light, half-behind. Weather: Cloudy with sunny spells

4592 ADNAMS BITTER FILLIES' NURSERY 6f
2:10 (2:10) (Class 2) 2-Y-O **£12,952** (£3,854; £1,926; £962) **Stalls** High

Form RPR

0210 **1** **Fifth Commandment (IRE)**[14] 4138 2-8-5 **84** .... SophieDoyle(5) 7 89
(J A Osborne) *mde virtually all: rdn over 1f out: edgd rt ins fnl f: jst hld on* **10/1**

10 **2** hd **Masaya**[45] 3070 2-7-12 **72** oh4 .... KoseiMiura 9 76
(C E Brittain) *a.p: rdn over 1f out: r.o to go 2nd nr fin: nt quite rch wnr* **10/1**

2603 **3** 1 **Magic Stella**[21] 3906 2-7-10 **77** .... HarryBentley(7) 5 78
(A P Jarvis) *w wnr: rdn and ev ch over 1f out: styd on same pce wl ins fnl f: lost 2nd nr fin* **14/1**

3156 **4** 1 **Emma's Gift (IRE)**[15] 4097 2-9-2 **97** .... AdamBeschizza(7) 12 96+
(Miss J Feilden) *hld up: nt clr run over 1f out: r.o wl ins fnl f: nt rch ldrs* **12/1**

21 **5** 3/4 **Ballinargh Girl (IRE)**[15] 4083 2-7-11 **74** .... AndrewHeffernan(3) 6 70
(R D Wylie) *trckd ldrs: plld hrd: rdn over 1f out: no ex ins fnl f* **4/1**[2]

5102 **6** 1 3/4 **Swiss Dream**[10] 4262 2-8-9 **83** .... JimmyFortune 11 74+
(D R C Elsworth) *hld up: plld hrd: r.o ins fnl f: nvr trbld ldrs* **7/2**[1]

6440 **7** shd **On Wings Of Love (IRE)**[42] 3190 2-7-7 **72** oh3.......... RosieJessop(5) 1 62
(A Bailey) *hld up: hdwy and hung lft over 2f out: rdn over 1f out: styd on same pce fnl f* **33/1**

332 **8** shd **Freckenham (IRE)**[17] 4029 2-7-5 **72** oh3.................... IanBurns(7) 15 62
(M L W Bell) *chsd ldrs: rdn over 1f out: no ex ins fnl f* **15/2**[3]

3215 **9** nse **Two Feet Of Snow (IRE)**[35] 3453 2-8-5 **79** .... MartinDwyer 10 69
(R Hannon) *hld up: hdwy 1/2-way: rdn over 1f out: no ex ins fnl f* **10/1**

2625 **10** nse **Inagh River**[8] 4332 2-8-1 **75** .... FrankieMcDonald 2 65
(R Hannon) *sn pushed along in rr: rdn over 1f out: styd on: nt trble ldrs* **25/1**

1520 **11** 4 **Golden Shine**[14] 4138 2-8-8 **82** .... ChrisCatlin 8 60
(M R Channon) *hld up: rdn over 2f out: n.d* **25/1**

610 **12** 1 **Danube Dancer (IRE)**[68] 2397 2-7-5 **72** oh1.............. RyanPowell(7) 14 47
(J S Moore) *in rr and sn pushed along: nvr on terms* **50/1**

301 **13** 1 **Miss Moneypenni**[18] 3981 2-7-12 **75** oh2 ow3
Louis-PhilippeBeuzelin(3) 3 47
(N P Littmoden) *w wnr to over 3f out: rdn and wknd over 1f out* **28/1**

614 **14** 1 **Instructress**[21] 3925 2-8-0 **74** .... JamieMackay 13 43
(R M H Cowell) *hld up in tch: rdn over 2f out: wknd over 1f out* **25/1**

3101 **15** 4 **Bay Of Fires (IRE)**[17] 4013 2-8-7 **81** .... TedDurcan 4 38
(D O'Meara) *hld up: hdwy over 2f out: wknd over 1f out* **12/1**

1m 13.02s (0.52) **Going Correction** +0.075s/f (Good) **15** Ran SP% **123.2**
Speed ratings (Par 97): **99,98,97,96,95 92,92,92,92,92 87,85,84,83,77**
Tote Swingers:1&2:£46.30, 2&3:£58.60, 1&3:£31.40 CSF £99.87 CT £1422.95 TOTE £13.60: £3.70, £3.80, £4.90; EX 132.50 Trifecta £400.70 Part won. Pool £487.38 - 0.10 winning units..
Owner Durkan, Hearn, Pennick **Bred** Keatly Overseas Ltd **Trained** Upper Lambourn, Berks

FOCUS
A very competitive race on paper but in reality very few got into it. It favoured those who raced close to the speed and the time was 2.72 seconds beyond standard. The winner was a surprise improver and the fourth helps with the level.

NOTEBOOK
Fifth Commandment(IRE) had plenty to commend her based on a solid effort in the Super Sprint at Newbury a fortnight earlier. She broke well and was never headed, holding on well as Masaya delivered a concerted late effort. She is not the biggest, but what she lacks in size she makes up for in heart. (op 12-1)
Masaya, a Windsor maiden winner, did nothing wrong in defeat and benefited from having her sights lowered. She was well beaten in the Queen Mary Stakes last time, but certainly appreciated being stepped up in trip and there should be further progress to come. (op 9-1 tchd 11-1)
Magic Stella appears to be improving, although she has yet to win in five races. Rated 77, she can be placed to score in maiden company, if connections choose to return to that route. (tchd 12-1)
Emma's Gift(IRE) fared best of those held up at the rear. She finished off her race in eyecatching fashion, despite being momentarily short of space over 1f out. She may be difficult to place off her current mark, but certainly has enough ability to add to her sole career win. (op 11-1 tchd 10-1)
Ballinargh Girl(IRE) was a little keen early on and paid the price. (op 5-1 tchd 11-2 and 6-1 in places)
Swiss Dream certainly wanted to over-race and wasn't able to get competitive. Official explanation: jockey said filly ran too keen early (op 9-2)

Two Feet Of Snow(IRE) Official explanation: jockey said filly hung left

4593 ADNAMS BROADSIDE H'CAP 7f
2:45 (2:46) (Class 3) (0-90,86) 3-Y-O **£9,066** (£2,697; £1,348; £673) **Stalls** High

Form RPR

6244 **1** **Hot Spark**[26] 3731 3-9-0 **77** ....(t) DaneO'Neill 9 88
(J Akehurst) *chsd ldrs: rdn to ld ins fnl f: r.o* **33/1**

2123 **2** 2 **Tesslam**[28] 3681 3-9-9 **86** .... PhilipRobinson 10 92
(M A Jarvis) *chsd ldrs: rdn to ld and hung rt fr over 1f out: hdd and unable qck ins fnl f* **8/1**

-016 **3** 3 **Tres Coronas (IRE)**[42] 3196 3-9-5 **82** ....(b) ChrisCatlin 1 80
(T D Barron) *led: hdd over 2f out: rdn and ev ch over 1f out: no ex ins fnl f* **20/1**

4 **4** 1 1/4 **Aghadoe (IRE)**[70] 2356 3-9-8 **85** ....[1] JimmyFortune 8 80
(A M Balding) *hld up: hdwy u.p over 1f out: nt rch ldrs* **5/1**[3]

043 **5** 1 1/4 **Alice Alleyne (IRE)**[24] 3790 3-9-5 **82** .... PatDobbs 5 73
(Sir Michael Stoute) *chsd ldrs: rdn over 2f out: wknd over 1f out* **7/1**

0303 **6** 1 1/2 **Kona Coast**[7] 4377 3-9-7 **84** ....(b) SaleemGolam 12 71
(J H M Gosden) *dwlt: racd alone stands' side: sn up w the pce: led over 2f out: rdn and hdd over 1f out: wknd fnl f* **10/1**

62-3 **7** 3 3/4 **Walcot Square (IRE)**[101] 1480 3-8-13 **76** .... TedDurcan 4 53
(R Charlton) *hld up: rdn over 2f out: n.d* **10/1**

1544 **8** 12 **Sweet Clementine (IRE)**[24] 3790 3-9-5 **82** .... ShaneKelly 3 27
(W J Knight) *hld up in tch: rdn over 2f out: sn wknd* **4/1**[2]

2212 **9** 2 1/2 **Soviet Secret**[5] 4438 3-9-1 **78** .... MartinDwyer 2 16
(P J McBride) *mid-div: rdn over 2f out: wknd and eased over 1f out* **10/3**[1]

4235 **10** 2 1/4 **Tell Halaf**[30] 3604 3-8-10 **73** .... StevieDonohoe 7 5
(M G Quinlan) *sn pushed along in rr: bhd fr 1/2-way* **22/1**

1620 **11** 7 **Battlemaiden (IRE)**[23] 3830 3-9-3 **80** ....(b[1]) NeilCallan 11 —
(M Johnston) *prom: rdn over 2f out: sn wknd and eased* **20/1**

1m 25.08s (-0.62) **Going Correction** +0.075s/f (Good) **11** Ran SP% **118.4**
Speed ratings (Par 104): **106,103,100,98,97 95,91,77,74,72 64**
Tote Swingers:1&2:£34.70, 2&3:£24.10, 1&3:£53.00 CSF £267.69 CT £5468.26 TOTE £36.00: £7.10, £2.30, £7.00; EX 337.00 Trifecta £652.10 Part won. Pool £881.22 - 0.40 winning units..
Owner Green Pastures Partnership **Bred** Bearstone Stud **Trained** Epsom, Surrey

FOCUS
An open handicap and another race where it was a must to race handily - pace was dominant through the card. A personal best from the winner, the form rated around the first two.

NOTEBOOK
Hot Spark was the outsider of the field but an examination of his previous form revealed a useful effort at Haydock on similar ground in early June. His two subsequent efforts were respectable and he slipped in under the radar for this on his switch to a new yard, but this victory was far from lucky. He was never far away and came to lead over 2f out and closed the deal in determined fashion. His immediate future is likely to depend on what sort of reassessment figure the handicapper comes up with. (op 28-1)
Tesslam, another to race prominently, continues to run well but looks held on his current mark. (op 7-1)
Tres Coronas(IRE) has form over further and so set out to make this a proper test but wasn't quite able to maintain his brisk tempo in the closing exchanges. The rain-softened ground was probably in his favour, based on his two previous successes. (op 14-1)
Aghadoe(IRE) ran best of those who were held up, making up considerable ground on his first start for the yard. Hooded for the first time, he has winning form over 1m and it would be no surprise to see him returned to that trip after the way he did his best work late on. (op 15-2)
Alice Alleyne(IRE) was raised for 3lb for finishing third over course and distance and doesn't give the impression of being a well-handicapped horse. (op 13-2 tchd 6-1)
Kona Coast raced alone on the stands' rail. He was back in trip but became tired in the easier ground - his sole win came on a firm surface. (op 9-1)
Sweet Clementine(IRE) failed to fire after finishing a relatively close-up fourth in a better class of race over course and distance at the July Festival and may need quicker ground. (op 11-2)
Soviet Secret had never finished outside the first two before but it may be that he is suited by quicker ground as he ran well below his usual standard. Official explanation: jockey said colt ran flat (op 9-2)

4594 ADNAMS EXPLORER H'CAP 1m 2f
3:20 (3:23) (Class 3) (0-90,90) 3-Y-O+ **£9,066** (£2,697; £1,348; £673) **Stalls** Centre

Form RPR

5-61 **1** **Critical Path (IRE)**[50] 2922 4-9-1 **77** .... JimmyFortune 8 86
(A M Balding) *a.p: chsd ldr over 2f out: rdn to ld ins fnl f: styd on wl* **9/2**[2]

4014 **2** 1 **Chain Of Events**[15] 4106 3-7-10 **73** .... SimonPearce(5) 9 80
(N B King) *chsd ldrs: led over 1f out: rdn: edgd rt and hdd ins fnl f: styd on same pce* **10/1**

0005 **3** 2 **Lord Theo**[15] 4108 6-8-12 **74** .... TedDurcan 3 77
(N P Littmoden) *chsd ldrs: rdn over 1f out: no ex wl ins fnl f* **13/2**

0031 **4** 2 **Shabak Hom (IRE)**[19] 3954 3-7-7 **72** .... HarryBentley(7) 5 71+
(D M Simcock) *hld up: hdwy over 2f out: rdn over 1f out: no ex fnl f* **11/4**[1]

3015 **5** 2 1/4 **Archie Rice (USA)**[17] 4019 4-9-0 **76** .... DaneO'Neill 7 71
(T Keddy) *led: rdn and hdd over 1f out: wknd ins fnl f* **20/1**

234 **6** 1 3/4 **Sedgwick**[23] 3813 8-9-0 **76** .... StevieDonohoe 2 67
(S A Harris) *hld up: hdwy over 2f out: sn rdn: wknd fnl f* **12/1**

6102 **7** 1 **Ellemujie**[16] 4051 5-9-10 **86** .... PhilipRobinson 6 75
(D K Ivory) *hld up: hdwy over 2f out: rdn over 1f out: wknd fnl f* **5/1**[3]

4234 **8** 1 1/2 **Dance The Star (USA)**[126] 1020 5-10-0 **90** .... GeorgeBaker 10 76
(E A L Dunlop) *s.i.s: hld up: a in rr* **12/1**

6036 **9** 1 1/2 **Prince Of Johanne (IRE)**[22] 3877 4-9-4 **80** ....(p) ChrisCatlin 4 63
(T P Tate) *hld up: effrt over 2f out: wknd over 1f out* **14/1**

51/0 **10** 13 **Pentathlon (IRE)**[16] 4055 5-8-11 **73** .... NeilCallan 1 30
(M Johnston) *chsd ldr tl rdn over 2f out: wknd qckly* **14/1**

2m 6.43s (0.93) **Going Correction** +0.075s/f (Good)
WFA 3 from 4yo+ 10lb **10** Ran SP% **117.4**
Speed ratings (Par 107): **99,98,96,95,93 91,91,89,88,78**
Tote Swingers:1&2:£9.30, 2&3:£21.40, 1&3:£3.00 CSF £49.32 CT £294.08 TOTE £5.50: £1.80, £3.30, £1.90; EX 82.80 Trifecta £540.90 Part won. Pool £731.07 - 0.64 winning units..
Owner Trebles Holford Thoroughbreds **Bred** Trebles Holford Farm Thoroughbreds **Trained** Kingsclere, Hants

FOCUS
A modest handicap in which the first pair came clear and again it paid to race prominently. The form is rated around the second and third.

NOTEBOOK
Critical Path(IRE) defied a 5lb rise in the weights for her Chepstow win over this trip 50 days earlier. The time was 3.43 sec outside standard and confirmed the impression that the overnight rain had made the conditions a little more testing. She was one of the first off the bridle but responded well to pressure with her jockey Jimmy Fortune getting her into a nice rhythm that she was able to sustain all the way to the line. She left the impression that she would stay further and her winning for the season is probably not at an end yet. (op 11-2)

Chain Of Events ◆, fourth over course and distance two weeks earlier, again ran well but probably bumped into one on the upgrade. He pulled a couple of lengths clear of the third and is entitled to still be progressing at this point in his career, so should find the winner's enclosure again in the not-too distant future. (op 12-1 tchd 9-1)
Lord Theo ◆ is returning to his best form. His last victory came over course and distance last summer off a 5lb higher mark and he has now run two encouraging races in the past fortnight. He is potentially well treated and should be kept on the right side of. (op 5-1 tchd 7-1 in places)
Shabak Hom(IRE) got his head in front for the first time at Ffos Las almost three weeks earlier and was 4lb higher for that success. But he became very warm beforehand and never threatened to take a hand in the finish. It may also have been that the overnight rain was against him. (op 7-2 tchd 9-4)
Archie Rice(USA) set a sensible pace but wasn't able to quite able to sustain it late on in ground that was probably not quite firm enough for him. (op 16-1)
Ellemujie's form this year has an in-and-out look about it and, on the face of it, this was a disappointing effort. Official explanation: jockey said gelding was unsuited by the good ground (op 7-1)
Dance The Star(USA), having his first run for a new yard and back in action after 126 days off, is entitled to be sharper for this and he, too, would appear favoured by quicker ground. Official explanation: jockey said horse was unsuited by the good ground (op 11-1)

4595 TALLY HO TIPSTER EBF MAIDEN FILLIES' STKS 7f
3:55 (3:56) (Class 4) 2-Y-O **£4,533** (£1,348; £674; £336) **Stalls** High

Form				RPR
0	**1**		**Theyskens' Theory (USA)**[22] 3871 2-9-0 0 MartinDwyer 3	95+
			(B J Meehan) *mde all: shkn up and c clr fr over 1f out: easily* **3/1**[2]	
	2	*5*	**Blue Bunting (USA)** 2-9-0 0 AhmedAjtebi 7	83+
			(Mahmood Al Zarooni) *chsd ldrs: rdn to go 2nd ins fnl f: no ch w wnr* **8/1**	
2	**3**	*3*	**Sylvestris (IRE)**[15] 4095 2-9-0 0 JimCrowley 4	75
			(R M Beckett) *chsd wnr: rdn over 1f out: wknd ins fnl f* **7/4**[1]	
	4	*2*	**Baraaya (IRE)** 2-9-0 0 KoseiMiura 8	70+
			(W J Haggas) *s.i.s: rdn 1/2-way: hdwy over 2f out: wknd over 1f out* **33/1**	
	5	*1*	**Masaraat (FR)** 2-9-0 0 ShaneKelly 2	68
			(J L Dunlop) *s.i.s: pushed along and hdwy over 2f out: wknd over 1f out* **25/1**	
	6	*1*	**Focal** 2-9-0 0 JimmyFortune 5	65
			(Sir Michael Stoute) *hld up in tch: rdn over 2f out: hung lft and wknd over 1f out* **9/1**	
65	**7**	*¾*	**Jolah**[45] 3082 2-9-0 0 NeilCallan 11	63
			(C E Brittain) *racd wd and plld hrd: up w the pce: hung lft fr over 2f out: wknd fnl f* **20/1**	
	8	*3 ¾*	**Dolcezza (IRE)** 2-8-11 0 Louis-PhilippeBeuzelin(3) 9	54
			(B J Meehan) *s.i.s: sn pushed along and a in rr* **50/1**	
	9	*4 ½*	**Ayaarah (IRE)** 2-9-0 0 PhilipRobinson 6	43
			(M A Jarvis) *dwlt: sn prom: wknd 2f out* **6/1**[3]	
	10	*¾*	**Hello Tomorrow (USA)** 2-9-0 0 TedDurcan 12	41
			(D R Lanigan) *s.i.s: hld up: wknd over 2f out* **25/1**	
	11	*1 ¾*	**Ajla (IRE)** 2-9-0 0 PatDobbs 1	36
			(R Hannon) *trckd ldrs: plld hrd: wknd over 1f out* **16/1**	
0	**12**	*23*	**Jam Maker**[85] 1879 2-8-7 0 DannyBrock(7) 10	—
			(J R Jenkins) *sn pushed along in rr: lost tch over 2f out: t.o* **100/1**	

1m 25.03s (-0.67) **Going Correction** +0.075s/f (Good) **12** Ran SP% **121.0**
Speed ratings (Par 93): **106,100,96,94,93 92,91,87,82,81 79,52**
Tote Swingers:1&2:£5.70, 2&3:£4.80, 1&3:£2.50 CSF £25.69 TOTE £4.30: £1.70, £2.50, £1.10; EX 37.60.
Owner Andrew Rosen **Bred** Ar Enterprises Llc **Trained** Manton, Wilts

FOCUS
An average-looking maiden that threw up a most impressive winner. She looks well up to Pattern company.

NOTEBOOK
Theyskens' Theory(USA) ◆ won as she pleased in a time that was marginally quicker than the three-year-old handicap run over the same distance earlier in the card. She'd clearly learned plenty from her racecourse debut here earlier in the month, jumping out well to make every yard and she could have been called the winner a long way from home. A sizeable filly with a powerful, long stride, she finished her race strongly to indicate that she would get further this year. It's possible that she could go straight to the Fillies' Mile but the May Hill at Doncaster would be another option worth considering. She'll need to improve again to make her mark in such company but certainly looks worth a try on this evidence. (op 4-1 tchd 11-4 and 9-2 in places)
Blue Bunting(USA), a $200,000 newcomer from a powerful yard, gave an encouraging debut display. On breeding, the likelihood is she'll need further in time. She will have tightened up for this and should be very competitive in a maiden next time. (tchd 9-1)
Sylvestris(IRE), second in a 6f maiden on her debut, may have been found out by the extra furlong as she weakened when meeting the rising ground late on. By Arch, she may prefer a quicker surface. (op 5-2)
Baraaya(IRE), who is light-framed, is related to plenty of winners and can improve for this experience. (op 28-1)
Masaraat(FR) ran an acceptable race for one whose pedigree indicates she'll need a trip in time. (op 20-1)
Jolah is now qualified for nurseries but doesn't look the easiest of rides. She was notable for a high head carriage and doing too much too early, which is why she weakened away late on. (op 16-1 tchd 14-1)

4596 ADNAMS DISTILLERY EBF CONDITIONS STKS 1m
4:35 (4:35) (Class 2) 4-Y-O+ **£9,969** (£2,985; £1,492; £747; £372) **Stalls** High

Form				RPR
2602	**1**		**Vesuve (IRE)**[16] 4050 4-8-9 110 TedDurcan 4	107+
			(Saeed Bin Suroor) *chsd ldrs: rdn to ld over 1f out: edgd rt ins fnl f: r.o wl* **1/2**[1]	
5-40	**2**	*4 ½*	**Smokey Oakey (IRE)**[45] 3069 6-8-9 94 PatCosgrave 5	97
			(M H Tompkins) *chsd clr ldr: rdn: edgd rt and ev ch over 1f out: no ex ins fnl f* **9/2**[3]	
/11-	**3**	*1 ¼*	**Harald Bluetooth (IRE)**[556] 232 5-8-9 94 NeilCallan 1	94+
			(D M Simcock) *hld up: hdwy over 2f out: edgd rt over 1f out: styd on same pce fnl f* **7/2**[2]	
460-	**4**	*14*	**Richo**[9] 7246 4-8-9 64 StevieDonohoe 3	62?
			(S A Harris) *s.s: a in rr: lost tch over 2f out* **66/1**	
006	**5**	*11*	**Slap And Tickle (IRE)**[15] 4105 4-8-4 48 SimonPearce 2	32
			(M D Squance) *set suicidal pce and sn wl clr: wknd over 2f out: hdd over 1f out: t.o* **100/1**	

1m 38.79s (-1.21) **Going Correction** +0.075s/f (Good) **5** Ran SP% **109.6**
Speed ratings (Par 109): **109,104,103,89,78**
CSF £3.20 TOTE £1.50: £1.10, £1.70; EX 2.90.
Owner Godolphin **Bred** Dayton Investments Ltd **Trained** Newmarket, Suffolk

FOCUS
An uncompetitive conditions event. Slightly muddling form, but it reads sound among the front pair.

NOTEBOOK
Vesuve(IRE) won this as he was entitled to, based on official figures. Rated 110, he was taking on the second and third on equal terms, despite being markedly superior to both on official figures. This will have been a nice confidence booster for him as he asserted over 1f out before winning as he pleased. It was his second British start after finishing second to Cesare at Doncaster and it will be interesting to see where he is placed next, but it is likely that he won't get an opportunity as straightforward as that in a hurry. (op 4-9 tchd 4-7)
Smokey Oakey(IRE)'s best form is with ease in the ground. It had probably been too quick for him in the Royal Hunt Cup in which he was beaten 25 lengths last time out. (op 11-2)
Harald Bluetooth(IRE) made an encouraging comeback after a 556-day absence. He'd finished lame after his victory over this trip at Kempton early in 2009. He is a lightly raced five-year-old who is entitled to strip fitter next time and remains one to keep tabs on. (tchd 11-4)

4597 MAY DAY H'CAP 1m 4f
5:05 (5:08) (Class 4) (0-85,83) 4-Y-O+ **£4,533** (£1,348; £674; £336) **Stalls** Centre

Form				RPR
6550	**1**		**Topolski (IRE)**[22] 3843 4-9-8 **82** (p) JimmyFortune 2	90
			(A M Balding) *chsd ldrs: rdn to ld ins fnl f: styd on* **15/8**[1]	
4301	**2**	*¾*	**North Cape (USA)**[23] 3810 4-8-9 **76** AmyScott(7) 3	83
			(H Candy) *led: clr 8f out: rdn and edgd rt over 1f out: hdd ins fnl f: styd on* **13/2**	
4131	**3**	*1*	**Peintre D'Argent (IRE)**[22] 3847 4-8-3 **70** HarryBentley(7) 8	75
			(W J Knight) *chsd ldrs: rdn and ev ch ins fnl f: no ex towards fin* **7/2**[2]	
2152	**4**	*6*	**Ghufa (IRE)**[15] 4094 6-8-9 **74** SimonPearce(5) 6	70
			(J Pearce) *prom: rdn over 2f out: wknd fnl f* **8/1**	
0036	**5**	*½*	**Monte Cavallo (SAF)**[21] 3896 5-9-3 **77** ShaneKelly 1	72
			(M Wigham) *hld up: sme hdwy over 1f out: sn rdn: wknd fnl f* **9/2**[3]	
31-0	**6**	*2 ¼*	**Clear Reef**[8] 4334 6-9-9 **83** (p) NeilCallan 7	74
			(Jane Chapple-Hyam) *hld up: rdn and wknd over 1f out* **25/1**	
061-	**7**	*2 ¾*	**Spensley (IRE)**[291] 6760 4-8-11 **71** PatCosgrave 5	58
			(J R Fanshawe) *prom: rdn over 2f out: wknd over 1f out* **14/1**	
0100	**8**	*hd*	**Brett Vale (IRE)**[22] 3843 4-9-6 **80** DaneO'Neill 4	66
			(P R Hedger) *hld up: a in rr: rdn over 2f out: hung lft and wknd over 1f out* **20/1**	

2m 32.12s (-0.78) **Going Correction** +0.075s/f (Good) **8** Ran SP% **114.9**
Speed ratings (Par 105): **105,104,103,99,99 98,96,96**
Tote Swingers:1&2:£3.20, 2&3:£4.60, 1&3:£2.00 CSF £14.84 CT £39.32 TOTE £2.30: £1.10, £2.50, £1.30; EX 17.90.
Owner Kennet Valley Thoroughbreds V **Bred** C H Wacker Iii **Trained** Kingsclere, Hants

FOCUS
A fair handicap and again the first three were always up there. The winner is the best guide.

4598 ROBERT PALMER MEMORIAL H'CAP 7f
5:40 (5:40) (Class 4) (0-85,82) 4-Y-O+ **£4,533** (£1,348; £674; £336) **Stalls** High

Form				RPR
-414	**1**		**Watch Amigo (IRE)**[56] 2736 4-9-7 **80** ShaneKelly 1	87+
			(W R Swinburn) *trckd ldr: rdn to ld ins fnl f: r.o* **2/1**[1]	
1200	**2**	*½*	**New Leyf (IRE)**[48] 2992 4-9-5 **78** MartinDwyer 5	84
			(J R Gask) *trckd ldrs: racd keenly: rdn and ev ch ins fnl f* **8/1**	
5501	**3**	*shd*	**Last Sovereign**[21] 3898 6-9-8 **81** PatCosgrave 6	87
			(Jane Chapple-Hyam) *led: rdn over 1f out: hdd ins fnl f: r.o* **5/1**[3]	
0000	**4**	*½*	**Arachnophobia (IRE)**[7] 4354 4-9-4 **77** NeilCallan 8	81
			(Pat Eddery) *chsd ldrs: rdn over 1f out: r.o* **9/1**	
6522	**5**	*1 ¼*	**Wilfred Pickles (IRE)**[26] 3725 4-9-4 **77** DaneO'Neill 7	78
			(Miss Jo Crowley) *hld up: rdn over 1f out: nvr able to chal* **4/1**[2]	
1204	**6**	*½*	**Imperial Djay (IRE)**[7] 4394 5-9-2 **75** TedDurcan 3	75
			(Mrs R A Carr) *s.i.s: sn prom: rdn over 1f out: styd on* **13/2**	
5025	**7**	*1*	**Summer Dancer (IRE)**[7] 4354 6-9-9 **82** JimCrowley 4	79
			(P T Midgley) *stdd s and hld up: rdn over 1f out: nvr able to chal* **12/1**	

1m 26.45s (0.75) **Going Correction** +0.075s/f (Good) **7** Ran SP% **112.1**
Speed ratings (Par 105): **98,97,97,96,95 94,93**
Tote Swingers:1&2:£3.10, 2&3:£8.80, 1&3:£3.20 CSF £17.97 CT £68.71 TOTE £2.70: £1.50, £4.00; EX 19.30 Place 6 £292.00; Place 5 £50.19.
Owner Ian Harris & Tim Halpin **Bred** Thurso Limited **Trained** Aldbury, Herts

FOCUS
A competitive handicap, but run at a slow pace and the form is muddling. It is doubtful if the winner had to match his Doncaster win.
T/Plt: £219.60 to a £1 stake. Pool £86,360.86 - 287.03 winning tickets T/Qpdt: £8.70 to a £1 stake. Pool £5,542.18 - 467.56 winning tickets CR

4554 THIRSK (L-H)
Saturday, July 31

OFFICIAL GOING: Good to firm (good in places; 10.0)
Top bend rail moved out 5yds.
Wind: Virtually nil. Weather: Showers with sunny periods

4599 EUROPEAN BREEDERS' FUND MAIDEN STKS 5f
1:45 (1:47) (Class 4) 2-Y-O **£5,504** (£1,637; £818; £408) **Stalls** High

Form				RPR
3	**1**		**Normandy Maid**[31] 3549 2-8-12 0 TonyHamilton 9	68+
			(R A Fahey) *trckd ldrs on inner: swtchd lft and hdwy 2f out: rdn to ld over 1f out and sn hung lft: kpt on u.p ins fnl f* **9/2**[2]	
0242	**2**	*1*	**Boundaries**[7] 4367 2-9-3 72 DavidAllan 10	69
			(T D Easterby) *in tch: hdwy over 2f out: rdn over 1f out: chsd wnr ins fnl f: kpt on* **7/2**[1]	
6	**3**	*½*	**Gottcher**[42] 3204 2-9-3 0 PhillipMakin 8	67
			(T D Barron) *sn led: rdn 2f out: hdd over 1f out: drvn and kpt on same pce fnl f* **6/1**	
6	**4**	*½*	**Watts Up Son**[6] 4409 2-9-3 0 (t) DavidNolan 6	65
			(D Carroll) *prom: effrt and cl up 2f out: sn rdn and ch whn sltly hmpd 1f out: kpt on same pce* **40/1**	
	5	*hd*	**Shesastar** 2-8-12 0 SamHitchcott 13	60+
			(T D Barron) *dwlt and sn bustled along in midfield: rdn 1/2-way: hdwy wl over 1f out: kpt on ins fnl f: nrst fin* **16/1**	
54	**6**	*3 ¼*	**Reason To Believe (IRE)**[10] 4240 2-9-3 0 PJMcDonald 5	53
			(B M R Haslam) *chsd ldrs: rdn along 2f out: drvn and one pce appr fnl f* **12/1**	
	7	*2 ¼*	**Vetvey (IRE)** 2-9-3 0 PaulMulrennan 4	45
			(M Johnston) *sn prom on outer: pushed along 1/2-way: rdn and hung lft 2f out: rn green and wkng whn edgd rt over 1f out* **5/1**[3]	
3	**8**	*1 ¼*	**Ezzles (USA)**[9] 4303 2-9-3 0 SilvestreDeSousa 14	40+
			(P F I Cole) *towards rr whn n.m.r and swtchd lft after 1f: rdn along 1/2-way: nvr a factor* **9/2**[2]	

0 9 1 ½ **Urban Kode (IRE)**[19] 3959 2-9-3 0 .... AndrewMullen 11 35
(P D Evans) *sn pushed along to chse ldrs: rdn 1/2-way and sn wknd* **33/1**
0 10 ½ **Iwantobreakfree**[19] 3961 2-9-3 0 .... CathyGannon 3 33
(P D Evans) *s.i.s: a in rr* **100/1**
11 ½ **Je Suis Unrockstar** 2-9-3 0 .... LeeVickers 2 31
(J A Glover) *s.i.s: a in rr* **50/1**
6 12 *hd* **Brave Tiger (IRE)**[51] 2895 2-9-3 0 ....(t) WilliamCarson 1 31
(S C Williams) *in tch: hdwy to chse ldrs 1/2-way: rdn 2f out and sn wknd* **16/1**
0 13 1 ¼ **Ozzies Storm Cats (USA)**[13] 4167 2-9-3 0 .... TomEaves 12 26
(J J Quinn) *sn rdn along and a in rr* **33/1**

58.91 secs (-0.69) **Going Correction** -0.30s/f (Firm) 13 Ran SP% **120.3**
Speed ratings (Par 96): **93,91,90,89,89 84,80,78,76,75 74,74,72**
Tote Swingers:1&2:£2.10, 2&3:£53.20, 1&3:£87.30 CSF £20.14 TOTE £5.80: £2.30, £1.40, £2.70; EX 15.90.
Owner Mrs Sheila Oakes **Bred** Mrs Sheila Oakes **Trained** Musley Bank, N Yorks

FOCUS
Fayr Jag was the best recent winner of this maiden and all the previous ten winners had experience and had made the frame. That trend continued in what was quite an open race; the whole field raced near the stands' rail. Routine form, best viewed through the second.

NOTEBOOK
Normandy Maid, from the family of smart sprinters Corrybrough and Artie, built on her promising debut at Catterick, getting a good lead before hitting the front over a furlong out. Despite tending to edge left, she kept running and in the end won cosily. She can go on from this.
Boundaries was the most experienced in the field but was racing over the minimum trip for the first time since his debut. He chased the leaders throughout but could not find an extra gear in the closing stages.
Gottcher got to the rails and made the running. He stuck on well when headed and looks capable of picking up a similar contest. (op 9-1)
Watts Up Son built on his debut effort when he was slowly away. He was always up with the pace and was another to keep on under pressure. (op 66-1)
Shesastar, a half-sister to three winners over further, showed promise on this debut and can be expected to improve for the outing, possibly over an extra furlong. (op 20-1)
Reason To Believe(IRE), dropping in trip for this third start, again hinted at ability and now qualifies for handicaps. (op 11-1)
Vetvey(IRE), a brother to the Norfolk Stakes winner Russian Valour, showed good early speed on this debut before fading, and can last longer with this under his belt. (op 9-2 tchd 11-2)
Urban Kode(IRE) Official explanation: jockey said colt hung left from halfway

4600 MARTINDALE NURSERY 5f
2:20 (2:20) (Class 3) 2-Y-O **£6,929** (£2,061; £1,030; £514) **Stalls** High

Form RPR
411 1 **Face The Problem (IRE)**[7] 4388 2-9-4 **89** .... AshleyMorgan(5) 8 105+
(B W Hills) *trckd ldrs: hdwy on inner to ld over 3f out: rdn and qcknd clr over 1f out: edgd lft ins fnl f: readily* **4/6**[1]
3416 2 6 **Master Macho (IRE)**[10] 4262 2-8-8 **74** .... SamHitchcott 3 68
(M R Channon) *chsd ldrs: rdn along 2f out: styd on to chse wnr and hung rt jst ins fnl f: sn no imp* **12/1**
0213 3 *nk* **Orchid Street (USA)**[21] 3925 2-8-11 **77** .... PaulMulrennan 1 74+
(Mrs A Duffield) *swtchd rt sn after s to stands' rail: in tch: smooth hdwy to trck ldrs 1/2-way: effrt and nt clr run wl over 1f out: swtchd lft and nt clr run ent fnl f: swtchd lft again and kpt on towards fin* **7/1**[2]
3103 4 1 ½ **First Class Favour (IRE)**[43] 3163 2-8-7 **73** .... DavidAllan 6 61
(T D Easterby) *cl up: led briefly after 1f tl hdd over 3f out: rdn along 2f out: drvn over 1f out and sn one pce* **12/1**
201 5 1 ¼ **Melodize**[44] 3126 2-8-2 **68** .... SilvestreDeSousa 7 51
(W R Muir) *led 1f: prom on inner: rdn along 2f out: sn drvn and wknd over 1f out* **8/1**[3]
563 6 *nk* **Star Today**[9] 4293 2-8-1 **67** ....(b[1]) NickyMackay 2 49
(B J Meehan) *dwlt and sn pushed along in rr: rdn 1/2-way: n.d* **10/1**
4426 7 2 **Jamaica Grande**[8] 4332 2-7-6 **65** ow1 .... LeonnaMayor(7) 4 40
(P S McEntee) *s.i.s: a in rr* **40/1**
6416 8 2 ¼ **Johnny Hancocks (IRE)**[14] 4124 2-7-13 **65** .... CathyGannon 5 32
(P D Evans) *cl up on outer: rdn along over 2f out: sn wknd* **25/1**

57.99 secs (-1.61) **Going Correction** -0.30s/f (Firm) 8 Ran SP% **114.4**
Speed ratings (Par 98): **100,90,89,87,85 85,81,78**
Tote Swingers:1&2:£4.10, 2&3:£13.40, 1&3:£1.30 CSF £10.23 CT £33.85 TOTE £1.70: £1.02, £2.60, £2.50; EX 10.70.
Owner Sir A Ferguson,Cavendish InvLtd,J Hanson **Bred** J Joyce **Trained** Lambourn, Berks

FOCUS
This decent nursery has produced some useful sprinters, including Proud Boast, Sierra Vista and Look Busy. The time was 0.92secs faster than the preceding maiden. This was a one-horse race and Face The Problem is progressing fast. he could be rated 5-8lb higher.

NOTEBOOK
Face The Problem(IRE) ◆ was odds-on to complete the hat-trick despite giving 12lb and more to his rivals. He resisted the attempt of Melodize to get the rail and, once in front around halfway, was always going to win and drew right away in the closing stages. He looks sure to be stepped up in grade now and, although he has Gimcrack and Mill Reef entries, with his speed he could well go for the Roses Stakes at York and then the Flying Childers, both over the minimum trip, and it might even be worth supplementing him for the Nunthorpe. (op 8-11 tchd 4-5 in places)
Master Macho(IRE) has had plenty of racing but ran his race and looks a good guide to the form. (op 16-1)
Orchid Street(USA) looked the unlucky one. Held up and switched inside from her outside stall, she had nowhere to go from the quarter-mile pole until switched to the outer again entering the final furlong. She stayed on without her rider getting serious and can be rated as finishing closer, although she would not have won. Official explanation: jockey said filly was denied a clear run (op 15-2 tchd 13-2)
First Class Favour(IRE) raced up with the pace and ran well again, confirming previous form with Melodize on worse terms.
Melodize led early but could not get the rail and gradually faded from halfway. (op 17-2 tchd 9-1)

4601 GLENRIDDING MAIDEN FILLIES' STKS 7f
2:50 (2:52) (Class 4) 3-Y-O+ **£4,792** (£1,425; £712; £355) **Stalls** Low

Form RPR
2533 1 **Nimue (USA)**[8] 4339 3-9-0 72 .... SilvestreDeSousa 5 78+
(P F I Cole) *mde all: qcknd clr 2f out: easily* **7/4**[2]
3 2 8 **Broadway Dancer**[26] 3733 3-9-0 0 .... TonyHamilton 2 56
(R A Fahey) *chsd ldng pair: rdn along wl over 2f out: drvn and edgd lft wl over 1f out: kpt on to take 2nd ins fnl f: no ch w wnr* **9/2**[3]
42 3 ½ **Sennockian Storm (USA)**[6] 4397 3-9-0 0 .... PaulMulrennan 7 55
(M Johnston) *trckd wnr: effrt 3f out and sn pushed along: rdn 2f out: drvn wl over 1f out: sn outpcd and lost 2nd ins fnl f* **6/5**[1]
0 4 1 ¼ **Only You Maggie (IRE)**[14] 4146 3-8-7 0 .... JosephineBruning(7) 1 52
(W G Harrison) *in tch: hdwy on inner 3f out and sn rdn: drvn over 1f out: kpt on same pce fnl f* **80/1**
33 5 *nk* **Shethoughtshewas (IRE)**[8] 4340 3-9-0 0 .... RobertWinston 6 51
(G A Swinbank) *chsd ldrs: rdn along 3f out: drvn wl over 1f out: kpt on same pce* **12/1**
5 6 ¾ **Tasza (USA)**[30] 3587 3-9-0 0 .... AndrewMullen 8 49
(A J McCabe) *in tch: hdwy 3f out: rdn over 2f out: drvn and one pce fr wl over 1f out* **33/1**
0- 7 14 **Destiny Rules**[299] 6542 3-9-0 0 .... IvaMilickova 9 11
(John Berry) *unruly in stalls: s.i.s and a bhd* **50/1**
8 *shd* **Rukhsana** 3-9-0 0 .... PatrickMathers 3 11
(C J Teague) *s.i.s: a bhd* **80/1**

1m 26.5s (-0.70) **Going Correction** -0.15s/f (Firm) 8 Ran SP% **115.1**
Speed ratings (Par 102): **98,88,88,86,86 85,69,69**
Tote Swingers:1&2:£1.40, 2&3:£1.70, 1&3:£1.10 CSF £10.05 TOTE £3.00: £1.10, £1.30, £1.10; EX 9.70.
Owner Mrs Fitri Hay **Bred** William A Carl **Trained** Whatcombe, Oxon

FOCUS
A modest and uncompetitive maiden for 3yo fillies, and very few had much experience. Nimue was finally off the mark but she is not one to be positive about and this form isn't easy to pin down.
Sennockian Storm(USA) Official explanation: jockey said filly hung left in straight

4602 SHIRLEY ANNE FAILL MEMORIAL H'CAP 1m
3:25 (3:25) (Class 5) (0-75,74) 3-Y-O+ **£3,691** (£823; £823; £274) **Stalls** Low

Form RPR
3143 1 **Daring Dream (GER)**[27] 3708 5-9-5 **67** .... GaryBartley(3) 7 76+
(J S Goldie) *towards rr: pushed along 3f out: rdn 2f out: drvn and hdwy over 1f out: styd on u.p ins fnl f to ld nr line* **5/1**[2]
3264 2 *nk* **High Rolling**[15] 4120 3-8-7 **60** .... SamHitchcott 9 66
(T D Easterby) *a.p: hdwy and cl up 3f out: rdn over 1f out: drvn to ld ent fnl f: hdd and no ex nr line* **10/1**
0633 2 *dht* **Call To Arms (IRE)**[16] 4065 3-9-7 **74** .... PaulMulrennan 11 80
(M Johnston) *trckd ldrs: hdwy 3f out: rdn along wl over 1f out: drvn to chal ins fnl f: nt qckn towards fin* **5/1**[2]
2200 4 1 ½ **Chief Red Cloud (USA)**[15] 4119 4-9-9 **68** .... AndrewElliott 3 73
(J R Weymes) *trckd ldrs: effrt and n.m.r wl over 1f out: swtchd rt and rdn whn n.m.r ins fnl f: kpt on towards fin* **5/1**[2]
0141 5 *hd* **Prime Circle**[13] 4168 4-9-5 **64** ....(p) SilvestreDeSousa 1 68
(A D Brown) *in tch: hdwy on outer over 2f out: rdn to chse ldrs over 1f out: drvn and kpt on ins fnl f* **8/1**
3315 6 1 ¼ **Smalljohn**[28] 3659 4-9-6 **72** ....(v) AdamCarter(7) 4 74
(B Smart) *led: rdn over 2f out: drvn over 1f out: hdd ent fnl f: grad wknd* **15/2**[3]
6030 7 ¾ **Champain Sands (IRE)**[15] 4119 11-8-6 **54** .... KellyHarrison(3) 6 54
(E J Alston) *hld up towards rr: hdwy over 2f out: rdn to chse ldrs over 1f out: drvn and no imp fnl f* **10/1**
3440 8 ¾ **Ninth House (USA)**[18] 3973 8-9-4 **63** ....(t) PJMcDonald 2 61
(Mrs R A Carr) *awkward s and towards rr: hdwy over 2f out: styng on to chse ldrs whn hmpd over 1f out: nt rcvr* **9/2**[1]
2220 9 *nk* **Dark Moment**[16] 4063 4-10-0 **73** .... DavidAllan 8 70
(Ollie Pears) *bhd: hdwy on inner over 2f out: in tch and rdn wl over 1f out: sn btn* **16/1**
1460 10 ½ **Crocodile Bay (IRE)**[5] 4428 7-8-12 **62** .... MarkCoumbe(5) 10 58
(R C Guest) *prom: chsd ldr after 2f: rdn along 3f out: drvn over 2f out: grad wknd* **33/1**
-520 11 9 **Betteras Bertie**[15] 4119 7-9-5 **64** .... RobertWinston 5 40
(M Brittain) *s.i.s: a bhd* **33/1**

1m 40.11s (0.01) **Going Correction** -0.15s/f (Firm)
WFA 3 from 4yo+ 8lb 11 Ran SP% **121.0**
Speed ratings (Par 103): **93,92,92,91,91 89,89,88,87,87 78**Place: Call To Arms £2.50, High Rolling £4.50. Exacta: DD/CTA £22.30, DD/HR £35.90; CSF: DD/CTA £15.62, DD/HR £28.04; Tricast: DD/CTA/HR £121.93, DD/HR/CTA £132.82. Tote Swingers:1&2 (CTA):£4.50, DH2&DH2:£23.70, 1&2(HR):£44.10 TOTE £5.50: £2.20 27 Trifecta £Owner George Barclay & Graeme McGinlay Bred.

FOCUS
A modest handicap. The pace did not appear that strong early and it resulted in a blanket finish. The form may not be entirely sound.
Ninth House(USA) Official explanation: jockey said horse was denied a clear run

4603 EKOSGEN H'CAP 1m
4:05 (4:05) (Class 3) (0-90,87) 3-Y-O+ **£6,929** (£2,061; £1,030; £514) **Stalls** Low

Form RPR
1002 1 **Signor Verdi**[22] 3863 3-8-13 **80** .... SilvestreDeSousa 9 94
(B J Meehan) *hld up: hdwy 3f out: chsd ldrs 2f out: rdn to ld appr fnl f: kpt on wl* **9/2**[1]
5132 2 2 **Cheers For Thea (IRE)**[9] 4287 5-9-4 **77** ....(bt) DavidAllan 15 88
(T D Easterby) *hld up in rr: hdwy on outer wl over 2f out: rdn over 1f out: styd on strly ins fnl f* **17/2**
0321 3 *hd* **Avonrose**[8] 4322 3-8-9 **76** .... PaulMulrennan 11 85+
(M Johnston) *stdd and swtchd lft s: hld up in rr: hdwy on inner over 2f out: rdn over 1f out: styd on wl fnl f: nrst fin* **13/2**[2]
4142 4 1 ¼ **Sir George (IRE)**[15] 4112 5-9-4 **82** .... JamesSullivan(5) 8 90
(Ollie Pears) *t.k.h early: trckd ldrs: hdwy over 2f out: swtchd lft and rdn over 1f out: ev ch tl drvn and one pce ins fnl f* **7/1**[3]
4000 5 ½ **Billy Dane (IRE)**[21] 3920 6-9-7 **80** ....(p) RobertWinston 13 87
(F P Murtagh) *led: rdn along and jnd 2f out: drvn wl over 1f out: hdd appr fnl f and grad wknd* **12/1**
4422 6 1 **Standpoint**[22] 3846 4-9-5 **81** .... RussKennemore(3) 1 86
(R Hollinshead) *prom: trckd ldr after 2f: effrt over 3f out: rdn to chal 2f out: drvn wl over 1f out and ev ch tl wknd ins fnl f* **8/1**
2120 7 *hd* **Harriet's Girl**[28] 3667 4-9-2 **75** .... AndrewElliott 10 79
(J R Weymes) *hld up in rr: hdwy wl over 2f out: rdn over 1f out: kpt on* **16/1**
5500 8 ½ **Rosbay (IRE)**[14] 4152 6-8-12 **76** .... LanceBetts(5) 14 79
(T D Easterby) *in rr: hdwy on inner 2f out: sn rdn and kpt on: nrst fin* **20/1**
4112 9 ¾ **Reel Buddy Star**[14] 4154 5-9-11 **84** .... PJMcDonald 3 85
(G M Moore) *prom: rdn along wl over 2f out: sn edgd lft and wknd wl over 1f out* **7/1**[3]
0300 10 1 **Aquarian Spirit**[23] 3824 3-8-13 **80** .... LeeVickers 5 77
(R A Fahey) *hld up towards rr: effrt and sme hdwy 3f out: rdn over 2f out and sn btn* **7/1**[3]
1426 11 3 ½ **Turn Me On (IRE)**[32] 3537 7-9-3 **83** .... LukeStrong(7) 4 74
(T D Walford) *trckd ldrs: rdn along wl over 2f out: sn drvn and wknd wl over 1f out* **25/1**
115 12 *hd* **Mejd (IRE)**[15] 4112 3-9-6 **87** .... SamHitchcott 6 75
(M R Channon) *in tch: effrt 3f out: rdn along over 2f out and sn btn* **14/1**
6406 13 4 **Wigram's Turn (USA)**[7] 4371 5-10-0 **87** .... DavidNolan 7 68
(M W Easterby) *prom: rdn along 3f out: wknd over 2f out* **20/1**

050- 14 14 **Alpen Glen**[232] 7720 4-9-11 **84** IvaMilickova 2 33
(John Berry) *in tch on inner whn hmpd and lost pl after 3f: sn bhd* **50/1**

1m 39.25s (-0.85) **Going Correction** -0.15s/f (Firm)
WFA 3 from 4yo+ 8lb **14** Ran SP% **126.2**
Speed ratings (Par 107): **98,96,95,94,94 93,92,92,91,90 87,86,82,68**
Tote Swingers:1&2:£9.10, 2&3:£4.20, 1&3:£6.90 CSF £42.56 CT £258.86 TOTE £5.50: £2.20, £2.80, £2.90; EX 46.50.
Owner Mrs Sheila Tucker **Bred** Newsells Park Stud Limited **Trained** Manton, Wilts

FOCUS
A decent, competitive handicap but something of a rough race and the first three came from the back off a good pace. The winner built on his better recent effort.

NOTEBOOK
Signor Verdi was well backed and built on his best previous effort. He was not the quickest away but his rider made good ground by sticking to the rail on the home turn, and had a clear run as the majority of the field raced towards the centre of the track. He picked up well for pressure and scored decisively, so could be of interest even off his revised mark. he might even step up in trip. (op 13-2)
Cheers For Thea(IRE) ran well and stayed on for a place. She could win again soon, possible in a fillies-only handicap. (op 8-1)
Avonrose was another to stick to the inside and came from last place in the straight. She never looked likely to catch the winner but this was a fair effort off a 6lb higher mark. Official explanation: jockey said filly missed the break (tchd 5-1)
Sir George(IRE) has progressed really well for new connections and again ran his race. He is however, 6lb above his last winning mark and might be in the handicapper's grip.
Billy Dane(IRE), whose best recent run was on this track, put up another solid effort from the front. He is now 1lb below his last winning mark so his winning turn might not be far away.
Standpoint has been knocking at the door of late and was another to run with credit. He only faded late on and a turning 7f or mile seems to suit him ideally. (tchd 9-1)
Reel Buddy Star is now 11lb higher than for the first of his two successes in June, and is another that the assessor seems to have caught up with. (op 6-1)
Aquarian Spirit was backed on this drop back in trip and appeared to have his chance before fading. (op 11-1)

4604 BUCK INN MAUNBY H'CAP 2m
4:40 (4:41) (Class 5) (0-75,70) 4-Y-O+ £3,691 (£1,098; £548; £274) Stalls Low

Form RPR
1313 1 **Simple Jim (FR)**[30] 3600 6-8-13 **62** SilvestreDeSousa 4 70+
(D O'Meara) *hld up towards rr: smooth hdwy on wd outside 2f out: chsd ldrs over 1f out: rdn ent fnl f and str run to ld last 50yds* **11/4**[2]
30/1 2 ½ **Dan's Heir**[63] 2533 8-8-2 **56** ow2 (p) DeanHeslop(5) 6 63
(W Storey) *hld up towards rr: hdwy over 5f out: chsd ldrs 3f out: rdn over 2f out: drvn to ld briefly ins fnl f: hdd and no ex last 50yds* **25/1**
-425 3 1 ¼ **French Hollow**[106] 1357 5-9-2 **65** PaulMulrennan 14 71
(T J Fitzgerald) *trckd ldrs: hdwy 4f out: effrt over 2f out: rdn to ld over 1f out: drvn and hdd ins fnl f: no ex* **14/1**
0625 4 ¾ **Bollin Greta**[15] 4117 5-9-7 **70** (t) DavidAllan 5 75
(T D Easterby) *hld up in midfield: stdy hdwy 4f out: trckd ldrs 3f out: effrt 2f out: rdn over 1f out and ev ch tl drvn and one pce fnl f* **6/1**
3112 5 1 ¼ **Tillietudlem (FR)**[18] 3974 4-8-13 **69** DebraEngland(7) 3 73
(J S Goldie) *led 1f: trckd ldr tl led again 3f out: rdn 2f out: drvn and hdd over 1f out: kpt on same pce* **5/2**[1]
4602 6 ½ **Bandanaman (IRE)**[28] 3669 4-8-13 **62** PJMcDonald 7 65
(G A Swinbank) *trckd ldrs: hdwy 3f out: rdn 2f out and ev ch tl drvn and one pce appr fnl f* **9/2**[3]
0-24 7 1 ½ **Winged Farasi**[6] 4410 6-8-2 **51** oh1 CathyGannon 12 52
(Miss J E Foster) *hld up in rr: hdwy over 3f out: rdn over 2f out: styd on appr fnl f: nt rch ldrs* **18/1**
4200 8 ¾ **Sir Sandicliffe (IRE)**[8] 4328 6-8-3 **52** DuranFentiman 1 52
(W M Brisbourne) *chsd ldrs on inner: rdn along over 3f out: drvn 2f out and grad wknd* **25/1**
0022 9 8 **Hi Dancer**[32] 3535 7-9-0 **66** PaulPickard(3) 13 57
(B M R Haslam) *hld up: a in rr* **10/1**
126- 10 ½ **Rosewin (IRE)**[298] 6560 4-9-0 **68** JamesSullivan(5) 11 58
(Ollie Pears) *a in rr* **25/1**
006 11 12 **Finellas Fortune**[25] 3754 5-8-8 **62** PatrickDonaghy(5) 8 38
(G M Moore) *trckd ldng pair: rdn along over 3f out: wknd over 2f out* **66/1**
20/0 12 6 **Motarid (USA)**[84] 1916 5-9-4 **67** (b) DavidNolan 10 35
(T D Walford) *prom: led after 1f: rdn along and hdd 3f out: sn wknd* **33/1**

3m 29.1s (-3.70) **Going Correction** -0.15s/f (Firm) **12** Ran SP% **124.7**
Speed ratings (Par 103): **103,102,102,101,101 100,100,99,95,95 89,86**
Tote Swingers:1&2:£17.70, 2&3:£66.20, 1&3:£7.40 CSF £81.28 CT £865.12 TOTE £3.20: £1.60, £4.70, £4.20; EX 70.30.
Owner R G Fell **Bred** Snc Haras Des Peltrais, Laurent Thibault **Trained** Nawton, N Yorks
■ Stewards' Enquiry : Patrick Donaghy caution: used whip down the shoulder in the forehand.
Debra England four-day ban: failed to ride out for 4th (Aug 14-16,18)

FOCUS
A modest staying handicap, but it was well run and the form looks solid. A personal best from the winner.
Rosewin(IRE) Official explanation: jockey said filly hung left throughout

4605 HOWTOWN H'CAP (FOR LADY AMATEUR RIDERS) (DIV I) 6f
5:15 (5:16) (Class 6) (0-55,55) 3-Y-O+ £2,061 (£639; £319; £159) Stalls High

Form RPR
6354 1 **Two Turtle Doves (IRE)**[3] 4478 4-10-4 **55** MissMMullineaux(3) 4 66
(M Mullineaux) *trckd ldrs: hdwy 1/2-way: led 2f out: rdn and edgd rt ins fnl f: styd on* **5/1**[3]
0000 2 2 ½ **Dream Express (IRE)**[3] 4487 5-10-2 **50** MissLHorner 9 53
(D W Thompson) *prom: led 1/2-way and hdd 2f out: drvn over 1f out: kpt on same pce fnl f* **14/1**
5041 3 1 **Angaric (IRE)**[21] 3900 7-10-0 **55** MissKBannon(7) 12 55
(B Smart) *prom: effrt 2f out: sn rdn and ch tl one pce ins fnl f* **7/2**[1]
4400 4 hd **Braille**[24] 3774 5-9-13 **52** MissJoannaMason(5) 7 51
(T D Walford) *chsd ldrs: rdn 2f out: n.m.r ins fnl f: kpt on same pce* **7/1**
4006 5 1 ¼ **Karate Queen**[3] 4486 5-9-7 **46** oh1 MissVBarr(5) 11 41
(R E Barr) *in tch: rdn along 2f out: styd on u.p fnl f* **10/1**
6000 6 2 **Leolene Starlight**[16] 4047 5-9-12 **51** MissPhillipaTutty(5) 6 40
(D O'Meara) *midfield: hdwy and in tch 1/2-way: rdn 2f out and sn no imp* **28/1**
0003 7 nse **Barraland**[18] 3990 5-10-5 **53** MrsCBartley 10 42
(J S Goldie) *prom towards stands' rail: rdn over 2f out: drvn and edgd lft wl over 1f out: sn wknd* **9/2**[2]
/006 8 nk **Prigsnov Dancer (IRE)**[24] 3774 5-9-6 **47** MissFrancesHarper(7) 3 35
(O Brennan) *nvr nr ldrs* **25/1**
0230 9 1 ¾ **Loss Leader (IRE)**[12] 4194 3-9-8 **54** MissSMStaveley(7) 1 36
(T D Easterby) *stall opened early and led to 1/2-way: sn rdn along and wknd fnl 2f* **12/1**
00-0 10 ½ **Le Reve Royal**[195] 211 4-9-10 **51** MissMKeegan(7) 2 31
(G R Oldroyd) *sn outpcd and a bhd* **28/1**
400 11 1 ½ **Mr Rooney (IRE)**[10] 4245 7-9-7 **46** oh1 MissWGibson(5) 5 22
(A Berry) *a in rr* **40/1**
0350 12 ¾ **Top Flight Splash**[7] 4366 4-9-12 **46** MissIsabelTompsett 8 19
(P D Evans) *a towards rr: rdn along 2f out: sn hung bdly lft* **9/2**[2]

1m 12.01s (-0.69) **Going Correction** -0.30s/f (Firm)
WFA 3 from 4yo+ 5lb **12** Ran SP% **124.4**
Speed ratings (Par 101): **92,88,87,87,85 82,82,82,79,79 77,76**
Tote Swingers:1&2:£9.40, 2&3:£23.60, 1&3:£3.50 CSF £73.47 CT £288.07 TOTE £4.60: £1.60, £4.40, £1.10; EX 73.90.
Owner J P Turner **Bred** M Sharkey **Trained** Alpraham, Cheshire

FOCUS
The first division of this very moderate amateur riders' sprint. It was dominated by prominent runers and the winner is rated to her best.
Dream Express(IRE) Official explanation: jockey said gelding hung right

4606 HOWTOWN H'CAP (FOR LADY AMATEUR RIDERS) (DIV II) 6f
5:45 (5:47) (Class 6) (0-55,55) 3-Y-O+ £2,061 (£639; £319; £159) Stalls High

Form RPR
0000 1 **Yungaburra (IRE)**[5] 4431 6-10-0 **53** (t) MissJoannaMason(5) 9 63
(D C Griffiths) *outpcd and bhd early: hdwy 1/2-way: swtchd lft and rdn wl over 1f out: styd on ent fnl f to ld last 100yds* **12/1**
-536 2 ¾ **Forever's Girl**[117] 1112 4-9-10 **51** MissMKeegan(7) 11 59
(G R Oldroyd) *sn led nr stands' rail: rdn along and hdd over 2f out: drvn and edgd lft over 1f out: ev ch tl no ex last 100yds* **5/1**[3]
2622 3 ½ **Foreign Rhythm (IRE)**[27] 3711 5-10-1 **54** MissVBarr(5) 1 60
(R E Barr) *racd wd: cl up: led over 2f out: rdn over 1f out: edgd rt ent fnl f: hdd and no ex last 100yds* **6/1**
3042 4 1 ¼ **Bentley**[38] 3322 6-10-1 **49** (p) MissSBrotherton 3 51
(B P J Baugh) *chsd ldrs: rdn along 1/2-way: drvn over 1f out: kpt on same pce* **11/4**[1]
2300 5 ½ **All You Need (IRE)**[169] 530 6-9-10 **49** MissRKneller(5) 2 50
(R Hollinshead) *chsd ldrs on outer: rdn along 2f out: drvn and kpt on ins fnl f* **20/1**
3502 6 6 **Misterisland (IRE)**[16] 4071 5-9-13 **50** (p) MissMMullineaux(3) 4 32
(M Mullineaux) *in tch on outer: rdn to chse ldrs 2f out: sn one pce* **8/1**
0060 7 nk **Officer Mor (USA)**[6] 4403 4-9-7 **46** oh1 MissECSayer(5) 12 27
(Mrs Dianne Sayer) *racd nr stands' rail: a towards rr* **16/1**
0000 8 2 ¼ **Thunder Bay**[16] 4047 5-9-13 **47** MrsCBartley 5 20
(R E Barr) *cl up: rdn along over 2f out: sn wknd* **16/1**
000- 9 2 ½ **Second Reef**[288] 6817 8-9-7 **46** oh1 MissHCuthbert(5) 10 11
(T A K Cuthbert) *chsd ldrs: rdn along over 2f out: sn drvn: edgd lft and wknd* **50/1**
0425 10 ½ **Sea Land (FR)**[6] 4411 6-9-13 **52** MissNVorster(5) 7 16
(B Ellison) *chsd ldrs: rdn along over 2f out: hld whn hmpd wl over 1f out and sn in rr* **7/2**[2]
-000 11 nk **Ensign's Trick**[8] 4342 6-9-5 **46** oh1 MissALMurphy(7) 8 9
(W M Brisbourne) *chsd ldrs: rdn along over 2f out: wkng whn hmpd wl over 1f out and sn bhd* **33/1**
00-0 12 ½ **Silent Treatment (IRE)**[6] 4415 4-10-2 **55** MissWGibson(5) 6 16
(R C Guest) *in tch: pushed along and hdwy 1/2-way: rdn 2f out: hmpd wl over 1f out and sn wknd* **22/1**

1m 11.46s (-1.24) **Going Correction** -0.30s/f (Firm) **12** Ran SP% **124.4**
Speed ratings (Par 101): **96,95,94,92,92 84,83,80,77,76 76,75**
Tote Swingers:1&2:£47.20, 2&3:£12.10, 1&3:£16.80 CSF £71.87 CT £416.13 TOTE £19.60: £5.30, £2.40, £2.50; EX 121.10 Place 6 £37.22; Place 5 £20.79.
Owner P Sutherland **Bred** Newlands House Stud **Trained** Bawtry, S Yorks
■ Stewards' Enquiry : Miss Joanna Mason three-day ban: careless riding (tbn)

FOCUS
The time of this second division was 0.55secs faster than the first leg. The form is possibly a bit sounder overall.
Yungaburra(IRE) Official explanation: trainer said, regarding apparent improvement in form, that the gelding was having its second run for the yard and was better suited by being dropped in off a strong pace.
T/Plt: £19.10 to a £1 stake. Pool:£50,996.76 - 1,946.30 winning tickets T/Qpdt: £12.50 to a £1 stake. Pool:£2,654.00 - 156.20 winning tickets JR

4565 DEAUVILLE (R-H)
Saturday, July 31

OFFICIAL GOING: Turf: good; fibresand: standard

4611a PRIX SIX PERFECTIONS (LISTED RACE) (2YO FILLIES) (TURF) 7f
4:00 (12:00) 2-Y-O £24,336 (£9,734; £7,300; £4,867; £2,433)

RPR
1 **Helleborine**[36] 2-9-0 0 StephanePasquier 2 97
(Mme C Head-Maarek, France) **7/5**[1]
2 2 ½ **Zabeel Park (USA)**[41] 3237 2-9-0 0 OlivierPeslier 7 91
(Saeed Bin Suroor) *broke wl: led after 1f: stl in front ent fnl f: hdd 100yds out: r.o wl to jst hold 2nd pl* **48/10**[3]
3 shd **Militante (IRE)**[26] 2-9-0 0 Pierre-CharlesBoudot 6 91
(Y De Nicolay, France) **9/1**
4 nk **Fanny May**[42] 3190 2-9-0 0 RichardHills 5 90
(D J Coakley) *towards rr tl 1/2-way whn rdn to go 3rd bef st: hrd rdn and qcknd wl ent fnl f: styd on wl* **73/10**
5 2 **Sabratah** 2-9-0 0 MaximeGuyon 4 85
(H-A Pantall, France) **11/1**
6 2 ½ **Peace Of Oasis (FR)** 2-9-0 0 IoritzMendizabal 1 79
(J-C Rouget, France) **3/1**[2]
7 6 **Irish Chope (FR)**[4] 2-9-0 0 TonyPiccone 3 64
(C Boutin, France) **26/1**

1m 27.6s (-0.70) **7** Ran SP% **118.0**
WIN (incl. 1 euro stake): 2.40. PLACES: 1.50, 2.80. SF: 10.10.
Owner K Abdulla **Bred** Juddmonte Farms Ltd **Trained** Chantilly, France

NOTEBOOK

Zabeel Park(USA), winner of a Pontefract maiden last time out, ran a decent race on this step up in class and got the longer trip perfectly well.

4612a PRIX DE PSYCHE (GROUP 3) (3YO FILLIES) (TURF) 1m 2f

5:10 (12:00) 3-Y-O £35,398 (£14,159; £10,619; £7,079; £3,539)

RPR

1 **Zagora (FR)**[48] 3015 3-9-2 0 IoritzMendizabal 1 108
(J-C Rouget, France) *settled in midfield on rail: travelling easily ent st: short of room 1 1/2f out: swtchd to centre of trck causing interference: chal between horses 100yds out and fin strly to grab ld fnl 50yds: comf* **1/1**[1]

2 1/2 **Bikini Babe (IRE)**[8] 4347 3-8-11 0 DominiqueBoeuf 3 102
(M Johnston) *racd in rr fr s: swtchd to wd outside ent st: disp ld and qckned wl 1 1/2f out: led briefly 100yds out: ct by wnr 50yds out: styd on wl* **23/1**

3 3/4 **Rumoush (USA)**[57] 2711 3-8-11 0 RichardHills 6 100
(M P Tregoning) *racd in midfield: rdn ent st: wnt 2nd ent fnl f: styd on wl* **9/5**[2]

4 2 **Silver Grey (IRE)**[170] 514 3-8-11 0 (p) OlivierPeslier 4 96
(R Ingram) *racd in 2nd: rdn to ld briefly 1 1/2f out: no ex ins fnl f* **15/1**

5 hd **Marie De Medici (USA)**[28] 3694 3-8-11 0 JoeFanning 2 96
(M Johnston) *broke wl to ld fr s: rdn early in st: stl in front 1 1/2f out: hdd and no ex fnl f* **19/1**

6 1 **Pearl Away (FR)**[34] 3493 3-8-11 0 StephanePasquier 5 94
(Y De Nicolay, France) *racd towards rr: rdn early in st: making prog whn hmpd by eventual wnr 1 1/2f out: eased* **53/10**[3]

2m 5.00s (-5.20) **6 Ran SP% 117.0**

WIN (incl. 1 euro stake); 2.00. PLACES: 1.40, 4.70. SF: 23.20.

Owner Martin S Schwartz **Bred** E Puerari & Oceanic Bloodstock **Trained** Pau, France

NOTEBOOK

Zagora(FR), fifth in the Prix de Diane last time out and the only runner carrying a 3lb penalty, overcame trouble in running but still had to survive a stewards' enquiry to get back on the winning trail. She showed a good turn of foot to score and looks well worth another go at a higher level now.

Bikini Babe(IRE) ran on well from the back of the field but didn't quite have the speed of the winner, who won a shade cosily.

Rumoush(USA) ran a solid race but lacked the acceleration of the winner. She should be suited by a return to a longer trip.

Silver Grey(IRE) looked to face a stiff task in this class and was far from disgraced on her first start since February.

Marie De Medici(USA) made most of the running but the others quickened by her in the closing stages. She has become rather disappointing this summer.

Pearl Away(FR), dropping 2f in trip, was making some progress when nudged sideways by the winner. She was not given a hard time after that.

SARATOGA (R-H)

Saturday, July 31

OFFICIAL GOING: Turf: firm; dirt: fast

4613a JIM DANDY STKS (GRADE 2) (3YO) (DIRT) 1m 1f (D)

10:48 (10:50) 3-Y-O

£185,185 (£61,728; £30,864; £15,432; £9,259; £2,058)

RPR

1 **A Little Warm (USA)**[126] 3-8-3 0 JRVelazquez 5 110
(Anthony Dutrow, U.S.A) *broke wl: settled in 2nd chsng ldr: a nk down 4f out: rdn st and initially lost grnd on ldr: wore down ldr to go on jst ins fnl f: styd on wl u.p* **41/10**[3]

2 1 3/4 **Miner's Reserve (USA)**[98] 3-8-6 0 ow3 CHBorel 6 109
(Nicholas Zito, U.S.A) *broke wl on outside and drvn up to ld: qcknd st: hdd jst ins fnl f: no ex* **158/10**

3 3/4 **Afleet Express (USA)**[42] 3-8-7 0 JJCastellano 2 109
(James Jerkens, U.S.A) *bmpd s: racd in 5th: sixth st: rdn and swtchd appr fnl f: styd on wl to take 3rd fnl 50yds* **51/20**[2]

4 1/2 **Friend Or Foe (USA)**[41] 3-8-3 0 RMaragh 7 104
(John C Kimmel, U.S.A) *racd in 4th early but wnt 3rd after 2f: 3rd and rdn 2f out: brushed w afleet express a f out: unable qck fnl 100yds* **9/1**

5 1 1/2 **Fly Down (USA)**[56] 2776 3-8-9 0 JLezcano 8 107
(Nicholas Zito, U.S.A) *hld up in last (12l off the ldr): hdwy 2 1/2f out: 5th st: 3rd on rail 1f out: btn whn tightened on rail and snatched up fnl 50yds* **39/20**[1]

6 4 3/4 **Steinbeck (IRE)**[9] 4312 3-8-3 0 GKGomez 1 92
(A P O'Brien, Ire) *bmpd s: racd in seventh (10l off the ldr): sixth and rdn st: no imp: nvr in contention* **102/10**

7 3/4 **Aikenite (USA)**[77] 2137 3-8-5 0 ow2 DCohen 4 93
(Todd Pletcher, U.S.A) *hld up towards rr: seventh st: n.d* **155/10**

8 8 1/4 **Stormy's Majesty (USA)** 3-8-3 0 EPrado 3 75
(Dominic G Galluscio, U.S.A) *broke wl and racd in 3rd: demoted to 4th after 2f: steadily fdd fr 2f out* **126/10**

1m 47.98s (107.98) **8 Ran SP% 120.0**

PARI-MUTUEL (all including $2 stake): WIN 10.20; PLACE (1-2) 5.50, 13.60; SHOW (1-2-3) 3.80, 7.90, 3.50; SF 96.00.

Owner Edward P Evans **Bred** Edward P Evans **Trained** USA

NOTEBOOK

Steinbeck(IRE) was left with no chance after missing the break and it's difficult to judge whether or not he handled the dirt.

3893 CHESTER (L-H)

Sunday, August 1

OFFICIAL GOING: Good to soft (good in places; 7.4)

Wind: Almost nil Weather: Overcast

4614 M&S MONEY EBF MAIDEN STKS 7f 2y

2:25 (2:26) (Class 4) 2-Y-O £5,180 (£1,541; £770; £384) Stalls Low

Form RPR

2 1 **Rigolleto (IRE)**[10] 4277 2-9-3 0 SamHitchcott 2 83
(M R Channon) *mde all: rdn over 1f out: strly pressed wl ins fnl f: hld on wl* **17/2**[3]

4 2 nk **Profondo Rosso (IRE)**[16] 4096 2-9-3 0 RyanMoore 6 83+
(Sir Michael Stoute) *racd keenly: sn dropped to midfield: pushed along and hdwy 2f out: wnt 2nd 1f out: str chal and r.o towards fin* **5/6**[1]

0 3 2 1/4 **Power Punch (IRE)**[25] 3794 2-9-3 0 SebSanders 7 76+
(B W Hills) *swtchd lft s: bhd: nt clr run 2f out and over 1f out: gd prog ins fnl f: gng on at fin* **25/1**

0 4 1/2 **Sole Danser (IRE)**[25] 3794 2-9-3 0 RobertWinston 4 75+
(B W Hills) *in tch: effrt to chse ldrs 2f out: kpt on u.p: no ex towards fin* **4/1**[2]

5 1 1/4 **Ibsaar** 2-9-3 0 TadhgO'Shea 5 72+
(W J Haggas) *pressed wnr tl u.p and nt qckn jst over 1f out: no ex ins fnl f* **14/1**

6446 6 shd **Dazzling Valentine**[6] 4437 2-8-12 71 FrannyNorton 3 67
(A Bailey) *hld up: pushed along over 2f out: styd on ins fnl f: nt pce to trble ldrs* **9/1**

04 7 10 **Cuban Quality (USA)**[17] 4054 2-9-3 0 RichardSmith 1 47
(Tom Dascombe) *chsd ldrs: pushed along 3f out: wknd wl over 1f out* **14/1**

000 8 10 **Bonjour Bongee**[69] 2384 2-8-12 60 DeclanCannon(5) 8 22
(A J McCabe) *racd on outer and chsd ldrs: rdn over 2f out: sn wknd* **66/1**

00 9 14 **Princess Gail**[27] 3729 2-8-12 0 ShaneKelly 9 —
(W M Brisbourne) *a bhd: wl outpcd fnl 2f* **80/1**

1m 27.66s (1.16) **Going Correction** +0.10s/f (Good) **9 Ran SP% 115.0**

Speed ratings (Par 96): **97,96,94,93,92 91,80,69,53**

Tote Swingers: 1&2 £3.60, 1&3 £16.20, 2&3 £5.80 CSF £15.85 TOTE £9.90: £2.20, £1.10, £4.00; EX 18.60 Trifecta £303.80 Pool: £853.99 - 2.08 winning units..

Owner Box 41 **Bred** Michael O'Mahony **Trained** West Ilsley, Berks

FOCUS

An average juvenile maiden, run at a fair enough pace. The runners were faced with a headwind in the home straight. The winner improved from his debut but had the run of things.

NOTEBOOK

Rigolleto(IRE) finished second on debut at Bath ten days earlier and went one better with a very game effort from the front. He had the run of things out in front, but relished the longer trip and showed a very willing attitude to fend off challengers from the home turn. His rider believes he will improve again off this now. (op 8-1 tchd 9-1)

Profondo Rosso(IRE) set the standard on his debut fourth at Newbury 16 days earlier and looked sure to improve for that experience. He was uneasy in the betting and got outpaced during the race, still showing his inexperience. His stamina began to kick in off the final bend and he held every chance inside the final furlong, but ultimately found the winner too resolute. There ought to be a race in him soon as this experience will no doubt bring him forward again, and he should appreciate another furlong before long. (op Evens, tchd 5-4 in places)

Power Punch(IRE) ◆, again his stable's second string, took time to get organised around this vastly different track and didn't get the best of runs from 2f out. He stayed on very nicely once straightening for home and should improve a deal for this added experience, so can soon be found an opening. (op 20-1 tchd 28-1)

Sole Danser(IRE) finished last on debut at Newmarket, when one place behind stablemate Power Punch, but had been expected to fare a lot better that day and is well regarded as his Group 1 entry implies. He settled a lot better getting cover here and looked a likely winner turning into the home straight. He was still too green when asked for his effort to get to the front, however, but would've surely finished in third had his rider not taken things too easy near the finish. Anyone who backed him each-way has genuine reason to feel aggrieved. (op 7-2)

Ibsaar is a half-brother to most notably Mosqueras Romance, a useful miler at three. He was easy to back for his racecourse debut, but knew his job and left the impression he would come on nicely for the outing. (op 16-1)

4615 M&S MONEY NURSERY 6f 18y

2:55 (2:56) (Class 4) (0-85,80) 2-Y-O £4,857 (£1,445; £722; £360) Stalls Low

Form RPR

1022 1 **Belle Royale (IRE)**[2] 4544 2-8-4 68 KierenFox(5) 5 78
(W M Brisbourne) *midfield: hdwy on outer wl over 2f out: rdn over 1f out: r.o to ld ins fnl f: pushed out and in command towards fin* **9/2**[2]

5125 2 1 **Captain Dimitrios**[9] 4331 2-8-8 67 SilvestreDeSousa 6 74
(P D Evans) *trckd ldrs: rdn to ld over 1f out: hdd ins fnl f: nt qckn and hld fnl 75yds* **11/2**[3]

6634 3 6 **Mother Jones**[8] 4392 2-9-0 73 PhillipMakin 2 62
(D H Brown) *led: rdn and hdd over 1f out: outpcd by front pair fnl f* **11/2**[3]

153 4 1 1/4 **Tro Nesa (IRE)**[8] 4367 2-8-12 74 BarryMcHugh(3) 1 59
(Mrs A Duffield) *hld up: rdn wl over 1f out: one pce and no imp on ldrs fnl f* **7/1**

324 5 1 1/2 **Loki's Revenge**[26] 3756 2-8-10 69 SteveDrowne 4 50
(W Jarvis) *w ldr tl rdn over 1f out: wknd fnl f* **7/2**[1]

2150 6 1 3/4 **Extra Power (IRE)**[15] 4138 2-9-7 80 RyanMoore 7 56
(M R Channon) *towards rr: rdn over 1f out: nvr able to get on terms* **6/1**

104 7 3 1/4 **Mini Bon Bon**[6] 4436 2-8-1 60 FrannyNorton 8 26
(A Bailey) *bhd: nt clr run over 2f out: nvr on terms* **25/1**

2426 8 6 **Bajan Bullet**[70] 2358 2-8-9 68 PaulHanagan 3 16
(P D Evans) *w ldrs to 4f out: rdn and wknd over 2f out* **8/1**

1m 14.98s (1.18) **Going Correction** +0.10s/f (Good) **8 Ran SP% 112.9**

Speed ratings (Par 96): **96,94,86,85,83 80,76,68**

Tote Swingers: 1&2 £4.30, 1&3 £2.80, 2&3 £6.00 CSF £28.56 CT £138.34 TOTE £5.30: £2.10, £2.00, £1.70; EX 34.70 Trifecta £83.50 Pool: £492.41 - 4.36 winning units..

Owner Peter Mort **Bred** Dxb Ltd **Trained** Great Ness, Shropshire

FOCUS

This moderate nursery was run at a sound pace and it saw the first pair come clear from the furlong marker. The winner more than confirmed her recent improvement.

NOTEBOOK

Belle Royale(IRE), second again at Haydock two days earlier, ran out a much-deserved winner under strong handling from her claiming rider. She was asked for an effort at the halfway stage and had to come very wide off the home turn. That didn't stop her from mastering the runner-up with something to spare, though, and she has developed into a likeable performer this term. (tchd 4-1 and 5-1)

Captain Dimitrios did well to get across to the inside early on from his modest drawn and was given every chance. He just found the winner that bit too speedy back over this sharper test and deserves to find another opening. (op 6-1 tchd 13-2)

Mother Jones, making her nursery debut, had to be vigorously ridden to get to the front end early on. She couldn't sustain her effort shortly after turning for home and probably needs a little further respite from the handicapper, but there is also a chance this ground was easier than she cares for. (op 5-1, tchd 6-1 in places)

Tro Nesa(IRE) was given a patient ride and was always staying on too late in the day.

Loki's Revenge failed to see out the extra furlong on this return to turf. (tchd 4-1)

The Form Book, Raceform Ltd, Compton, RG20 6NL

Extra Power(IRE) was well backed on this drop in class and switch to a nursery, despite conceding upwards of 6lb all round. He was never a serious player back over the extra furlong and now has something to prove. (op 8-1)

4616 FREEBETS.CO.UK QUEENSFERRY STKS (LISTED RACE) 6f 18y
3:30 (3:30) (Class 1) 3-Y-O+

£21,004 (£7,962; £3,984; £1,986; £995; £499) **Stalls** Low

Form RPR

4041 **1** **Masamah (IRE)**[7] 4401 4-9-0 96 PaulHanagan 4 103
(K A Ryan) *mde all: qcknd over 1f out: r.o wl and in command fnl f* **9/2**[2]

-535 **2** 1 ½ **Quest For Success (IRE)**[13] 4191 5-9-0 100 TonyHamilton 1 98
(R A Fahey) *a.p: n.m.r briefly 2f out: nt qckn over 1f out: styd on u.p ins fnl f: tk 2nd cl home: n.d to wnr* **9/1**

5603 **3** shd **Star Rover (IRE)**[2] 4541 3-8-10 92 SilvestreDeSousa 7 98
(P D Evans) *a.p: rdn and outpcd by wnr over 1f out: styd on u.p after: lost 2nd cl home* **33/1**

5414 **4** 2 **Bounty Box**[23] 3875 4-8-9 93 JackMitchell 3 87
(C F Wall) *midfield: nt clr run briefly 2f out: swtchd rt and hdwy over 1f out: carried hd to one side whn chsd ldrs ins fnl f: nt pce to mount serious chal* **9/2**[2]

0040 **5** 1 ½ **Wi Dud**[13] 4191 6-9-0 97 (b) RyanMoore 9 87
(K A Ryan) *chsd ldrs: rdn and no imp over 1f out: one pce ins fnl f* **22/1**

4234 **6** 1 **Doncaster Rover (USA)**[15] 4136 4-9-0 109 PhillipMakin 8 84+
(D H Brown) *hld up: nt clr run 2f out: sn pushed along: kpt on ins fnl f: nvr able to trble ldrs* **11/4**[1]

11-6 **7** 2 ½ **Our Jonathan**[95] 1616 3-8-10 111 NeilCallan 6 76
(K A Ryan) *awkward s: hld up: pushed along over 1f out: nvr a threat* **6/1**[3]

5000 **8** 3 ¾ **Look Busy (IRE)**[13] 4191 5-8-9 97 FrannyNorton 10 59
(A Berry) *midfield: sddle slipped early: dropped away fr over 1f out* **20/1**

1160 **9** 3 **Global City (IRE)**[29] 3674 4-9-0 105 (t) DaraghO'Donohoe 2 54
(Saeed Bin Suroor) *a bhd: wl outpcd over 1f out* **12/1**

1-04 **10** 2 ½ **Queen's Grace**[85] 1908 3-8-6 98 ow1 SteveDrowne 5 42
(H Morrison) *midfield: pushed along 2f out: rdn and wknd over 1f out* **11/1**

1m 13.15s (-0.65) **Going Correction** +0.10s/f (Good)
WFA 3 from 4yo+ 4lb **10** Ran SP% **115.4**
Speed ratings (Par 111): **108,106,105,103,101 99,96,91,87,84**
Tote Swingers: 1&2 £8.50, 1&3 £21.20, 2&3 £39.50 CSF £42.72 TOTE £5.10: £1.60, £3.00, £8.40; EX 36.80 TRIFECTA Not won..
Owner Dr Marwan Koukash **Bred** Stanley Estate & Stud Co & Mount Coote Stud **Trained** Hambleton, N Yorks

FOCUS

This was a competitive Listed sprint. The bottom two stalls had been responsible for half of the winners in the past decade and the draw was once more of real importance. The first three were always to the fore and the form looks just average for the grade, rated around the third.

NOTEBOOK

Masamah(IRE) comfortably made all to follow up his Ascot success a week earlier. He wasn't at his best here on his previous outing in this company over 5f two runs back, but is proven at the track and getting an uncontested lead again here was right up his street. He never looked in any real danger in the home straight and is clearly thriving. His connections later commented that if he was going to get 6f anywhere it was going to be around here. (op 5-1 tchd 11-2)

Quest For Success(IRE) got a lovely trip through the race from his inside draw, until being done few favours by the third on the home turn. He is therefore a little better than the bare form and ideally needs a stiffer test over this trip, so is worth persevering with in this grade. (tchd 8-1 and 11-1 in places)

Star Rover(IRE), third at Glorious Goodwood two days previously, was back up in trip and class. He took the Lily Agnes here at two, so the track suits him, but this was still a decent effort considering he was drawn in stall seven and he looks to be coming back into top form. (op 25-1)

Bounty Box, who headed the chasing pack, left the impression this sharp, turning track was not for her. (op 6-1)

Wi Dud, with the blinkers back on, proved somewhat free early on and could get no cover on the outside from his poor draw. This was a little more encouraging in the circumstances, but he has yet to win beyond 5f and is not simple to place. (op 20-1 tchd 25-1)

Doncaster Rover(USA) overcame a troubled passage when winning this from stall one last season. Drawn in eight this year, he again got dropped in and was never a serious player. Official explanation: jockey said gelding never travelled (op 10-3 tchd 7-2)

Our Jonathan, returning from a 95-day absence, not for the first time blighted his chance with a shocking start. He was running on too late in the home straight and probably does need a more galloping track, but still has to fully proved he has trained on this year. (op 9-2)

Look Busy(IRE) was never in the hunt from the outside stall after her saddle slipped. Official explanation: jockey said saddle slipped

Global City(IRE) lacked anything like the early pace required to take advantage of his decent draw. That one really needs quicker ground. (op 9-1)

Queen's Grace, back from an 85-day break, was having her first outing over the trip since winning in this class on her final outing as a juvenile. She got taken off her feet, though, and it's a case of back to the drawing board for her connections. (tchd 10-1)

4617 HALLIWELL JONES BMW MILE (H'CAP) 7f 122y
4:05 (4:05) (Class 3) (0-95,95) 3-Y-O+ **£9,390** (£2,794; £1,396; £697) **Stalls** Low

Form RPR

0035 **1** **Kyllachy Star**[31] 3585 4-9-7 88 TonyHamilton 10 96
(R A Fahey) *hld up: hdwy over 1f out: str run ins fnl f to ld post* **20/1**

4100 **2** nse **Brae Hill (IRE)**[23] 3869 4-10-0 95 PaulHanagan 11 103
(R A Fahey) *in tch: rdn to ld 1f out: styd on gamly ins fnl f: hdd post* **8/1**

3103 **3** 1 **Opus Maximus (IRE)**[20] 3956 5-9-7 88 JoeFanning 2 94+
(M Johnston) *trckd ldrs: rdn to chal ins fnl f: nt qckn cl home* **9/2**[1]

0605 **4** 1 **Internationaldebut (IRE)**[22] 3919 5-9-4 85 TonyCulhane 8 88
(P T Midgley) *missed break: hld up: nt clr run over 1f out: prog ins fnl f: gng on at fin* **15/2**

1122 **5** ½ **Academy Blues (USA)**[86] 1857 5-9-8 89 AdrianNicholls 9 91+
(D Nicholls) *midfield: effrt over 1f out: no real imp on ldrs: kpt on same pce u.p ins fnl f* **6/1**[2]

6110 **6** ¾ **Maid In Heaven (IRE)**[25] 3790 3-9-4 92 ShaneKelly 6 91
(W R Swinburn) *midfield: effrt over 1f out: no real imp on ldrs: one pce u.p ins fnl f* **13/2**[3]

0232 **7** hd **Ithinkbest**[29] 3667 4-9-7 88 RyanMoore 14 87
(Sir Michael Stoute) *led for 1f: remained prom: rdn and str chal ent fnl f: fdd fnl 75yds* **7/1**

4154 **8** nk **Snow Bay**[78] 2133 4-9-3 84 TomEaves 4 83
(B Smart) *led after 1f: rdn and hdd 1f out: no ex fnl 100yds* **14/1**

00 **9** nk **Jeninsky (USA)**[50] 2971 5-9-4 90 KierenFox(5) 15 88
(Rae Guest) *hld up: pushed along and nt clr run 2f out: kpt on one pce u.p ins fnl f: nt gng pce to chal* **25/1**

4106 **10** 3 ¾ **Imprimis Tagula (IRE)**[6] 4440 6-8-4 78 (v) NatashaEaton(7) 1 67
(A Bailey) *in tch: rdn over 1f out: sn btn* **16/1**

000 **11** 5 **Shotley Mac**[39] 3318 6-8-11 78 (b) SteveDrowne 13 54
(N Bycroft) *trckd ldrs: lost pl on outer over 2f out: bhd over 1f out* **40/1**

0-60 **12** 3 ¼ **Glen Molly (IRE)**[8] 4358 4-9-6 87 RobertWinston 12 55
(B W Hills) *hld up: pushed along over 2f out: nvr on terms w ldrs* **15/2**

1m 34.13s (0.33) **Going Correction** +0.10s/f (Good)
WFA 3 from 4yo+ 7lb **12** Ran SP% **116.5**
Speed ratings (Par 107): **102,101,100,99,99 98,98,98,97,94 89,85**
Tote Swingers: 1&2 £28.90, 1&3 £26.50, 2&3 £9.40 CSF £166.38 CT £870.48 TOTE £28.90: £7.20, £2.90, £2.10; EX 130.20 TRIFECTA Not won..
Owner Dr Marwan Koukash **Bred** John James **Trained** Musley Bank, N Yorks

FOCUS

A fair handicap, run at a sound pace. Due to the three non-runners those drawn wide were not at so much of a disadvantage and stalls ten and eleven filled the first two places. A 1-2 for Richard Fahey and sound form amongst the principals.

NOTEBOOK

Kyllachy Star just did enough to get up on the line and score from his better-fancied stablemate. Held up from his wide stall, he was being ridden a fair way out and still had plenty to do turning into the home straight. The generous early pace suited, though, and he dug really deep to come between horses late on and prevail. It was his first success since winning on Polytrack last year, which also came off this mark. (tchd 25-1)

Brae Hill(IRE) is something of a track specialist and had registered his last two wins at the course. He so nearly went in again, doing really well from his wide draw under top weight, but ultimately the extra half furlong just found him out where it mattered most. He richly deserves to go on again after this. (tchd 9-1)

Opus Maximus(IRE) won over C&D on his last visit to the track and never runs a bad race here. He had every chance from his advantageous draw and rates a solid benchmark. (tchd 5-1 and 11-2 in places)

Internationaldebut(IRE) ◆, back up in trip, has to rate a little unlucky. He came from out the back after making a tardy start and found nowhere to go at the top of the home straight. He was motoring inside the closing stages and an end to his losing run is surely not that far off. (op 12-1)

Academy Blues(USA) ran better than the bare form as he didn't get the breaks in the home straight, having travelled strongly through the race. He is evidently still capable of further progression and is entitled to come on for the run. (op 5-1 tchd 9-2)

Maid In Heaven(IRE) ran a sound enough race taking on her elders for the first time (op 7-1)

Ithinkbest unsurprisingly paid late on for his early exertions from the outside draw. (op 6-1)

4618 M&S TRAVEL MONEY H'CAP 1m 2f 75y
4:40 (4:41) (Class 5) (0-75,74) 3-Y-O **£4,094** (£1,209; £604) **Stalls** High

Form RPR

362 **1** **Lord Raglan (IRE)**[20] 3949 3-9-3 70 AndrewElliott 2 79
(J R Weymes) *mde all: rdn over 1f out: r.o gamely and kpt finding more ins fnl f* **11/2**[3]

-633 **2** 1 ¼ **Effervesce (IRE)**[16] 4117 3-9-7 74 RyanMoore 1 80
(Sir Michael Stoute) *a.p: chsd wnr wl over 1f out: nt qckn and no imp fnl 50yds* **9/4**[1]

3022 **3** 1 ½ **Ice Viking (IRE)**[15] 4128 3-8-12 65 (b) PaulMulrennan 6 68
(J G Given) *hld up: hdwy over 1f out: chsd ldrs and styd on u.p ins fnl f: nt pce to get to front 2* **9/2**[2]

6035 **4** ¾ **Faith Jicaro (IRE)**[10] 4282 3-8-10 68 DeanHeslop(5) 3 70
(N J Vaughan) *midfield: hdwy to chse ldrs over 1f out: kpt on and hung rt ins fnl f: no further imp fnl 75yds* **18/1**

4055 **5** 2 ½ **Brooklands Bay (IRE)**[16] 4092 3-9-3 70 TomEaves 4 67
(J R Weymes) *hld up: rdn and hdwy over 1f out: hung rt ins fnl f: nt pce to trble front quartet* **25/1**

2314 **6** hd **Layla's Lexi**[23] 3857 3-9-5 72 PaulHanagan 5 68
(Ian Williams) *racd keenly: hld up: pushed along over 1f out: nvr able to rch ldrs* **6/1**

4623 **7** 3 ½ **Raktiman (IRE)**[17] 4056 3-8-6 64 (p) RossAtkinson(5) 9 53
(Tom Dascombe) *hld up in midfield: n.m.r and lost pl 3f out: toiling over 1f out* **14/1**

0133 **8** 2 ¼ **Dane Cottage**[17] 4046 3-8-8 61 SilvestreDeSousa 10 46
(P D Evans) *midfield: hdwy to trck ldrs after 2f: wnt 2nd 6f out: rdn and lost 2nd wl over 1f out: wknd ins fnl f* **14/1**

-603 **9** 6 **North Shadow**[15] 4127 3-8-3 56 FrannyNorton 8 29
(A D Brown) *racd keenly: prom: pushed along and wknd over 2f out* **14/1**

0002 **10** 2 ½ **Takajan (IRE)**[26] 3759 3-8-12 65 SebSanders 7 33
(W M Brisbourne) *racd keenly on outer in midfield: hdwy 3f out: effrt to chse ldrs over 2f out: wknd over 1f out* **20/1**

2m 14.37s (2.17) **Going Correction** +0.10s/f (Good) **10** Ran SP% **112.5**
Speed ratings (Par 100): **95,94,92,92,90 90,87,85,80,78**
Tote Swingers: 1&2 £3.90, 1&3 £4.40, 2&3 £3.20 CSF £17.51 CT £59.14 TOTE £6.70: £2.40, £1.30, £1.40; EX 18.10 Trifecta £32.90 Pool: £639.27 - 14.35 winning units..
Owner John A Duffy **Bred** Skymarc Farm **Trained** Middleham Moor, N Yorks

FOCUS

This moderate 3-y-o handicap was run at an average pace and it paid to race handily. The form makes sense but may not prove entirely solid.

Layla's Lexi Official explanation: jockey said filly stumbled leaving stalls

4619 M&S MONEY 25TH ANNIVERSARY H'CAP 1m 4f 66y
5:10 (5:12) (Class 4) (0-85,85) 3-Y-O+ **£5,180** (£1,541; £770; £384) **Stalls** Low

Form RPR

3 **1** **Dubai Bounty**[19] 3995 3-8-9 77 (p) RyanMoore 1 87
(G A Butler) *trckd ldrs: styd on 2nd 2f out: led jst over 1f out: edgd rt and r.o ins fnl f: hld on gamely cl home* **9/2**[1]

0604 **2** hd **Rangefinder**[15] 4125 6-9-11 82 ShaneKelly 5 91
(Jane Chapple-Hyam) *trckd ldrs: nt clr run and swtchd rt over 1f out: wnt 2nd ins fnl f: str chal towards fin: r.o: jst hld* **10/1**

-343 **3** 1 ¼ **Layla's Dancer**[20] 3949 3-8-8 76 PaulHanagan 11 83
(R A Fahey) *midfield: rdn and hdwy whn carried rt over 1f out: sn swtchd ins: styd on: nt pce to chal front pair* **11/2**[3]

-004 **4** 1 ½ **Cosmic Sun**[23] 3877 4-9-9 85 LeeTopliss(5) 3 90
(R A Fahey) *led after 1f: rdn over 2f out: hdd jst over 1f out: no ex fnl 75yds* **12/1**

210 **5** 2 ¼ **Veloso (FR)**[53] 2857 8-9-9 83 BarryMcHugh(3) 12 84
(J A Glover) *dropped to midfield after 2f: rdn 2f out: hdwy over 1f out: kpt on ins fnl f: nt pce to rch ldrs* **20/1**

3412 **6** ½ **Graceful Descent (FR)**[7] 4405 5-8-10 67 GregFairley 9 68
(J S Goldie) *prom: rdn over 1f out: no rspnse: one pce fnl f* **9/1**

2513 **7** 7 **Granny McPhee**[9] 4334 4-9-10 81 FrannyNorton 8 70+
(A Bailey) *dwlt: hld up: hmpd whn nt clr run over 2f out: nvr able to rch ldrs* **5/1**[2]

20-6 **8** ½ **Sanctuary**[53] 2865 4-9-8 79 TomEaves 14 68
(B Smart) *midfield: outpcd fnl 2f: n.d after* **16/1**

34 **9** 1 ¾ **Citizenship**[17] 4055 4-9-3 74 (t) TonyHamilton 13 60
(Ian Williams) *racd freely: led for 1f: trckd ldrs after: nt qckn and outpcd 2f out: dropped away fnl f* **14/1**

0-43 **10** *9* **Union Island (IRE)**[30] 3618 4-9-8 **79**.................... NeilCallan 6 50
(A King) *midfield: rdn over 2f out: eased whn no imp ins fnl f* **8/1**
3520 **11** *½* **Wind Star**[3] 4520 7-9-5 **81**.................... MarkCoumbe(5) 7 52
(M F Harris) *hld up: rdn over 1f out: nvr on terms* **28/1**
4662 **12** *hd* **Paktolos (FR)**[9] 4348 7-9-5 **76**....................(p) RobertWinston 2 46
(John A Harris) *a bhd: struggling over 1f out: eased whn btn ins fnl f* **12/1**
4600 **13** *16* **Mujaadel (USA)**[22] 3920 5-9-2 **73**....................(p) PaulMulrennan 15 18
(D Nicholls) *a bhd: struggling over 1f out: eased whn btn ins fnl f* **33/1**

2m 39.54s (-0.36) **Going Correction** +0.10s/f (Good)
WFA 3 from 4yo+ 11lb **13** Ran SP% **119.5**
Speed ratings (Par 105): **105,104,104,103,101 101,96,96,95,89 88,88,77**
Tote Swingers: 1&2 £10.30, 1&3 £3.90, 2&3 £8.80. totesuper7: Win: Not won. Place: Not won. CSF £48.32 CT £257.09 TOTE £4.80: £1.90, £3.20, £2.40; EX 54.90 Trifecta £206.70 Pool: £715.39 - 2.56 winning units. Place 6: £65.10 Place 5: £48.86 .
Owner The Distaff 2 Partnership **Bred** A S Denniff **Trained** Newmarket, Suffolk

FOCUS
Perhaps unsurprisingly after the way the earlier races on the card had panned out this open-looking handicap was run at a strong early pace as runners jostled for an early position. It no doubt slowed up around halfway, though, and again it proved hard to get seriously involved from off the pace. Sound form among the prominent runners.
Granny McPhee Official explanation: jockey said filly suffered interference
T/Jkpt: Not won. T/Plt: £109.50 to a £1 stake. Pool:£112,505.85 - 749.50 winning tickets T/Qpdt: £37.40 to a £1 stake. Pool:£6,531.49 - 129.20 winning tickets DO

4135 NEWBURY (L-H)
Sunday, August 1

OFFICIAL GOING: Good to firm (7.9)
Rail out between 7f and 5f on round course increasing distances on that course by about 30yds.
Wind: Moderate ahead Weather: Bright periods

4620 BATHWICK TYRES AMATEUR RIDERS' H'CAP (DIV I) 1m 2f 6y
2:10 (2:10) (Class 5) (0-70,67) 3-Y-O+ £2,186 (£677; £338; £169) Stalls Low

Form RPR
0021 **1** **Alternative Choice (USA)**[20] 3967 4-10-5 **51**... MrsEmmaLittmoden 10 59
(N P Littmoden) *hld up in tch: hdwy over 2f out: rdn to chse ldr ins fnl f: led fnl 50yds: styd on wl* **7/1**
6603 **2** *hd* **Gallego**[8] 4382 8-10-12 **61**.................... MrMPrice(3) 3 69+
(R J Price) *hld up in rr tl stdy hdwy on ins to ld 3f out: shkn up w jnd over 1f out: rdn ins fnl f: hdd and no ex fnl 50yds* **3/1**[1]
0006 **3** *2½* **Muftarres (IRE)**[13] 4198 5-11-2 **67**.................... MissWGibson(5) 9 70
(P T Midgley) *chsd ldrs: drvn to chal 2f out: stl wl there over 1f out: lost 2nd and outpcd ins fnl f* **6/1**[3]
0006 **4** *1½* **Masterofceremonies**[5] 4454 7-10-4 **57**....................(v) MissALMurphy(7) 1 57
(W M Brisbourne) *chsd ldr: pushed along and ev ch 2f out: drvn and one pce whn rdr dropped whip wl over 1f out: no ch after* **17/2**
206 **5** *1* **William's Way**[12] 4223 8-10-12 **63**....................(t) MrCMartin(5) 4 61
(I A Wood) *s.i.s: in rr: pushed along 3f out: styd on towards outside over 1f out: kpt on fnl f but nvr a threat* **4/1**[2]
0666 **6** *2½* **Mr Udagawa**[8] 4382 4-10-6 **59**.................... MrRJWilliams(7) 11 52
(B J Llewellyn) *s.i.s: in rr: rdn 2f out: mod prog fr over 1f out* **12/1**
5404 **7** *1¼* **Apex**[8] 4382 9-10-7 **60**.................... MrMHerbert(7) 2 51
(M Hill) *chsd ldrs: rdn 3f out: wknd wl over 1f out* **8/1**
060- **8** *¾* **Itsy Bitsy**[353] 4927 8-9-9 **48** oh3.................... MissLaurenShea(7) 7 37
(W J Musson) *sn led: hdd 3f out: wknd ins fnl 2f* **33/1**
642- **9** *shd* **Captain Oats (IRE)**[328] 5720 7-10-7 **53**.................... MrSWalker 6 42
(Mrs P Ford) *t.k.h: in tch: rdn 3f out: wknd 2f out* **10/1**

2m 12.3s (3.50) **Going Correction** 0.0s/f (Good)
WFA 3 from 4yo+ 9lb **9** Ran SP% **113.1**
Speed ratings (Par 103): **86,85,83,82,81 79,78,78,78**
Tote Swingers: 1&2 £3.50, 1&3 £5.20, 2&3 £2.30 CSF £27.69 CT £133.16 TOTE £9.20: £2.40, £1.60, £2.00; EX 21.80.
Owner A A Goodman **Bred** Gainesway Thoroughbreds Ltd **Trained** Newmarket, Suffolk

FOCUS
This appeared to be the weaker division of the amateur riders' handicap, with the time being almost 2secs slower. Muddling form, rated around the third.

4621 BATHWICK TYRES AMATEUR RIDERS' H'CAP (DIV II) 1m 2f 6y
2:45 (2:45) (Class 5) (0-70,70) 3-Y-O+ £2,186 (£677; £338; £169) Stalls Low

Form RPR
0542 **1** **Sula Two**[8] 4382 3-10-2 **60**.................... MrPPrince(5) 9 72
(R J Hodges) *in rr tl stdy hdwy on ins fr 3f out: drvn to chal ins fnl f: led fnl 120yds: edgd rt cl home* **9/2**[2]
0002 **2** *½* **Dashing Doc (IRE)**[8] 4381 3-11-0 **70**.................... MissLAllan(3) 2 81
(D R C Elsworth) *chsd ldrs: wnt 2nd over 3f out: pushed along over 2f out and kpt on to chal ins fnl f: chsd wnr fnl 100yds but no imp* **9/4**[1]
0-02 **3** *1¾* **Rockweiller**[20] 3960 3-10-1 **54**.................... MrsEEvans 10 62
(P D Evans) *c lft fr stalls and led at str pce after 2f: rdn along over 2f out: jnd ins fnl f: hdd fnl 120yds: hld whn n.m.r and wknd cl home* **8/1**
0002 **4** *nk* **Laconicos (IRE)**[16] 4102 8-10-9 **60**....................(t) MissCScott(7) 1 67
(W B Stone) *take down early: led 2f: styd chsng ldrs: styd on and swtchd rt wl over 1f out: styd on same pce ins fnl f* **13/2**[3]
0063 **5** *9* **The Starboard Bow**[10] 4289 3-10-12 **68**.................... MrMWall(3) 4 57
(S Kirk) *chsd ldrs: rdn 4f out: wknd 2f out* **7/1**
5000 **6** *½* **Sleep Over**[23] 3865 5-10-6 **55**.................... MrBMMorris(5) 8 43
(D Morris) *s.i.s: in rr: sme hdwy 3f out: rdn: hung lft and wknd 2f out* **16/1**
1030 **7** *3¼* **Binnion Bay (IRE)**[25] 3783 9-10-2 **51**....................(b) MrJackSalmon(5) 5 32
(J J Bridger) *s.i.s: a towards rr* **20/1**
0/0- **8** *nse* **Mister Benedictine**[15] 3734 7-11-0 **65**....................(t) MrTGarner(7) 3 46
(B W Duke) *in tch: rdn 3f out: wknd over 2f out* **14/1**
40-0 **9** *12* **Ermyntrude**[25] 3788 3-9-3 **49**.................... MissLWilliams(7) 6 6
(P M Phelan) *n.m.r after s: tch: wd bnd 7f out: nvr in contention after* **33/1**
6-00 **10** *1¼* **Mt Kintyre (IRE)**[13] 4201 4-10-11 **62**.................... MrCBishop(7) 7 17
(M R Channon) *chsd ldr after 3f tl wknd ins fnl 3f* **8/1**

2m 10.38s (1.58) **Going Correction** 0.0s/f (Good)
WFA 3 from 4yo+ 9lb **10** Ran SP% **117.3**
Speed ratings (Par 103): **93,92,91,90,83 83,80,80,71,70**
Tote Swingers: 1&2 £3.50, 2&3 £6.30 CSF £15.10 CT £79.17 TOTE £5.40: £2.00, £1.70, £2.10.
Owner Richard Prince **Bred** D R Tucker **Trained** Charlton Mackrell, Somerset

FOCUS
This second division was dominated by the 3-y-os. The winning time was almost 2secs quicker than the opener and the form looks pretty solid.

4622 WEDGEWOOD ESTATES EBF MAIDEN STKS 6f 8y
3:20 (3:20) (Class 4) 2-Y-O £4,533 (£1,348; £674; £336) Stalls Centre

Form RPR
1 **Murbeh (IRE)** 2-9-3 0.................... RichardHills 1 80+
(B J Meehan) *trckd ldrs: led ins fnl f and reminder to keep narrow advantage: styng on wl whn pushed lft then veered rt cl home* **6/1**
0 **2** *shd* **Moriarty (IRE)**[16] 4096 2-9-3 0.................... JimmyFortune 11 80
(R Hannon) *towards rr: hdwy 2f out: rdn to chse ldrs and hung lft thrght fnl f: str chal cl home whn pushed rt* **7/2**[1]
3 *1* **Buckland (IRE)** 2-9-3 0.................... WilliamBuick 2 77+
(B J Meehan) *in tch: pushed along and hdwy over 1f out: nt clr run and swtchd lft ins fnl f: styd on strly and avoided multiple interference to take 3rd cl home: should improve* **20/1**
4 *½* **Gentle Lord** 2-9-3 0.................... RichardKingscote 10 77+
(Tom Dascombe) *led: rdn and edgd lft whn hdd ins fnl f: stl chalng u.p whn bdly hmpd and dropped to 4th cl home* **5/1**[2]
0 **5** *hd* **Buddy Miracle**[58] 2687 2-8-12 0.................... DavidProbert 4 72
(A M Balding) *pressed ldrs: rdn over 1f out: stl pressing ldrs whn bdly hmpd and lost 2 pls cl home* **16/1**
6 *1½* **Cruiser** 2-9-3 0.................... DaneO'Neill 7 70
(W R Muir) *chsd ldrs: ev ch 2f out: rdn and wknd insde fnl f* **9/1**
6 **7** *1* **Forty Proof (IRE)**[15] 4142 2-9-3 0.................... JimCrowley 8 67
(W J Knight) *chsd ldrs: rdn 2f out: wknd 1f out* **11/2**[3]
8 *nk* **Cai Shen (IRE)** 2-9-3 0.................... PatDobbs 6 66
(R Hannon) *in rr but in tch: rdn and sme prog 2f out: nvr in contention and sn outpcd* **5/1**[2]
9 *2* **Papas Fritas** 2-9-0 0.................... Louis-PhilippeBeuzelin(3) 5 60
(B J Meehan) *rdn 1/2-way: a outpcd* **33/1**
06 **10** *2¼* **Aramid (IRE)**[69] 2384 2-9-3 0.................... DarryllHolland 3 53
(B W Hills) *stdd in rr: plld hrd early: a bhd* **14/1**
0 **11** *3¾* **Titan Diamond (IRE)**[9] 4323 2-8-12 0.................... LeeNewnes(5) 9 42
(M D I Usher) *pressed ldrs tl wknd ins fnl 2f* **66/1**

1m 14.32s (1.32) **Going Correction** +0.10s/f (Good) **11** Ran SP% **117.0**
Speed ratings (Par 96): **95,94,93,92,92 90,89,88,86,83 78**
Tote Swingers: 1&2 £4.60, 1&3 £15.50, 2&3 £16.40 CSF £26.65 TOTE £6.30: £2.30, £1.70, £4.50; EX 18.30.
Owner Hamdan Al Maktoum **Bred** Ann & Joe Hallinan **Trained** Manton, Wilts

FOCUS
Probably a fair juvenile maiden.

NOTEBOOK
Murbeh(IRE), entered in the Group 2 Mill Reef Stakes, was always going nicely on the outside of the field and found plenty when asked for more of an effort, keeping on well and just holding on despite edging right close home. He's clearly thought to be above average, but will need to take a big step forward if he is to make an impact at Group level. He seems likely to return here now and take up his engagement in the Group 2 contest. (tchd 9-2)
Moriarty(IRE), well held on his debut over 7f, moved up smoothly to challenge, but veered left inside the final furlong, tightening up both the fourth of fifth. He was then hanging quite badly as they crossed the line, losing out by just a short head, and he would almost certainly have won had he held a straight line under pressure. (tchd 4-1)
Buckland(IRE) ◆ was green early and became outpaced when the tempo quickened, but did stay on well close home and, although slightly fortunate to get third, he showed more than enough to suggest he will win an ordinary maiden. This was a very promising start. (op 16-1)
Gentle Lord, a brother to multiple sprint winner Gentle Guru, knew his job and was right there 1f out, but he had already started to edge left when the runner-up veered left and he ended up getting squeezed out close home. (op 4-1)
Buddy Miracle was right there scrapping for third when tightened up close home, causing her rider to sit up on her. This was a step up on her debut effort. Official explanation: jockey said filly hung badly left
Cruiser, a Mill Reef entrant, is bred for speed and should do better at 6f. (op 12-1)
Forty Proof(IRE) failed to improve on his initial effort. (op 15-2)
Cai Shen(IRE) shaped with just a little promise on this racecourse debut. (op 9-2 tchd 6-1)

4623 GRUNDON RECYCLE NURSERY 7f (S)
3:50 (3:53) (Class 4) (0-85,76) 2-Y-O £3,561 (£1,059; £529; £264) Stalls Centre

Form RPR
5246 **1** **Arabian Star (IRE)**[36] 3449 2-9-0 **69**.................... AlanMunro 2 75
(M R Channon) *hld up in rr: hdwy 2f out: rdn to ld ins fnl f: styd on strly nr fin* **11/2**[2]
0322 **2** *¾* **Nothing To Hide (IRE)**[11] 4247 2-9-5 **74**.................... JamesDoyle 1 78
(D J S Ffrench Davis) *chsd ldrs: rdn fr 2f out: styd on u.p fnl f to chse wnr fnl 120yds but a hld* **13/2**
3421 **3** *¾* **Royal Opera**[12] 4221 2-9-7 **76**.................... DavidProbert 3 78
(B R Millman) *disp ld: rdn 2f out slt advantage over 1f out: hdd ins fnl f: outpcd into 3rd fnl 120yds* **7/1**
1453 **4** *nk* **Orientalist**[26] 3749 2-9-6 **75**.................... TomQueally 5 77
(Eve Johnson Houghton) *disp ld tl narrwly hdd appr fnl f: styd on same pce fnl 120yds* **10/1**
652 **5** *2* **Presto Volante (IRE)**[31] 3577 2-8-13 **68**.................... JimmyQuinn 7 65
(Mrs A J Perrett) *s.i.s: sn rcvrd and in tch: rdn over 2f out: styd on same pce fr over 1f out* **6/1**[3]
12 **6** *¾* **Shewalksinbeauty (IRE)**[91] 1733 2-9-4 **73**.................... PatDobbs 6 68
(R Hannon) *in rr but in tch: rdn over 2f out: kpt on fnl f but nvr a threat* **7/1**
021 **7** *1½* **Whodathought (IRE)**[31] 3577 2-9-2 **71**.................... JimmyFortune 11 62
(R Hannon) *chsd ldrs: rdn fr 2f out: wknd fnl f* **9/2**[1]
163 **8** *3¼* **Malice Or Mischief (IRE)**[30] 3636 2-9-7 **76**.................... JimCrowley 10 61
(R M Beckett) *towards rr but in tch: rdn and mod prog whn hmpd ins fnl 2f: nvr in contention after* **14/1**
3222 **9** *3* **Kissing Clara (IRE)**[10] 4286 2-9-3 **72**.................... LiamKeniry 12 47
(J S Moore) *towards rr but in tch: rdn and sme prog whn carried rt ins fnl 2f: nvr in contention after* **25/1**
2035 **10** *1¼* **Ivan's A Star (IRE)**[6] 4436 2-8-7 **62**.................... HayleyTurner 13 34
(J S Moore) *chsd ldrs: rdn and wknd qckly 2f out* **40/1**
0043 **11** *¾* **Stacey**[26] 3767 2-8-3 **58**.................... NeilChalmers 4 28
(M Blanshard) *in tch: rdn 3f out: wknd over 2f out* **33/1**
054 **12** *2¾* **Blaze On By**[30] 3625 2-8-3 **58**.................... FrankieMcDonald 8 21
(R Hannon) *chsd ldrs: wknd qckly 3f out* **40/1**
4401 **13** *5* **Veil Of Night**[17] 4066 2-8-13 **68**.................... AndreaAtzeni 9 23
(D Haydn Jones) *chsd ldrs: rdn and wkng whn edgd rt ins fnl 2f: eased whn no ch fnl f* **28/1**

1m 26.81s (1.11) **Going Correction** +0.10s/f (Good) **13** Ran SP% **117.1**
Speed ratings (Par 96): **97,96,95,94,92 91,90,86,82,81 80,77,71**
Tote Swingers: 1&2 £11.80, 1&3 £9.00, 2&3 £8.40 CSF £38.04 CT £207.23 TOTE £7.60: £2.80, £2.60, £1.60; EX 48.10.

Owner Jackie & George Smith **Bred** G A E And J Smith Bloodstock Ltd **Trained** West Ilsley, Berks
■ Stewards' Enquiry : Alan Munro one-day ban: used whip without giving colt time to respond (Aug 15)
David Probert one-day ban: used whip with excessive frequency (Aug 15)

FOCUS
A competitive nursery. The form seems sound enough.

NOTEBOOK
Arabian Star(IRE), below par at Newcastle latest, was up in trip for this nursery debut and came with a strong run inside the final furlong to get well on top. His dam was a 1m4f winner, so there's every chance he will progress again up to 1m. (op 6-1 tchd 5-1)
Nothing To Hide(IRE) has now finished runner-up on each of his last three starts. He looked sure to be competitive on this nursery debut and didn't give in without a fight, but was always just being held. (op 11-1)
Royal Opera, a dead-heater at Ffos Las latest, was up 1f in trip for this return to handicaps and he ran really well. It's probable 6f is his trip, though. (op 8-1)
Orientalist was soon up there and held every chance, just lacking a change of pace. (op 11-1 tchd 12-1)
Presto Volante(IRE), making his nursery debut, was up 1f in trip but still wasn't quick enough. He will be of interest over 1m. (op 9-2)
Shewalksinbeauty(IRE), up 2f in trip and returning from a break on this nursery debut, travelled well before being unable to quicken and should do better next time. (op 15-2 tchd 6-1)
Whodathought(IRE) had beaten Presto Volante last time, but was unable to confirm the form over this longer trip.
Malice Or Mischief(IRE) didn't get the best of runs. (op 11-1)

4624 EUROPEAN BREEDERS' FUND CHALICE STKS (LISTED RACE) (F&M) 1m 4f 5y
4:30 (4:30) (Class 1) 3-Y-0+
£21,004 (£7,962; £3,984; £1,986; £995; £499) **Stalls** Low

Form				RPR
3031	**1**		**Pachattack (USA)**[38] 3368 4-9-5 104 (p) TomQueally 10 (G A Butler) *s.i.s: sn trcking ldr: led ins fnl 2f: hrd drvn and responded wl whn strly chal thrght fnl f: hld on all out* **9/2**[2]	108
2-13	**2**	*shd*	**Shimmering Surf (IRE)**[52] 2889 3-8-5 100 FrankieMcDonald 4 (P Winkworth) *in rr: hdwy: hmpd and lost pl ins fnl 3f: swtchd rt and gd hdwy over 1f out: str run fnl f: fin wl to take 2nd cl home: jst failed to catch wnr: unlucky* **7/1**	106+
4-40	**3**	*½*	**Saphira's Fire (IRE)**[36] 3467 5-9-2 100 HayleyTurner 9 (W R Muir) *hld up in rr: stdy hdwy on ins fr 3f out: rdn to chal fr over 1f out and stl upsides fnl 120yds: no ex and lost 2nd cl home* **14/1**	104
-006	**4**	*2 ¼*	**Becqu Adoree (FR)**[15] 4143 4-9-2 99 J-PGuillambert 3 (L M Cumani) *in tch: edgd rt ins fnl 3f: styd on to chse ldrs ins fnl 2f: kpt on same pce fnl f* **10/1**	100
653	**5**	*1 ¼*	**Gallic Star (IRE)**[45] 3101 3-8-5 110 ChrisCatlin 6 (M R Channon) *in rr tl hdwy on outside fr 3f out: drvn and no imp on ldrs fnl 2f* **7/2**[1]	98
2233	**6**	*½*	**Lady Artemisia (IRE)**[15] 4143 4-9-2 101 WilliamBuick 1 (M Botti) *trckd ldrs: swtchd rt off rails ins fnl 4f: hmpd ins fnl 3f: wknd u.p and btn whn carried rt over 1f out: no ch whn hung lft wl ins fnl f* **13/2**	98
4-0	**7**	*6*	**Wedding March (IRE)**[74] 2224 3-8-5 107 TedDurcan 7 (Saeed Bin Suroor) *s.i.s: sn led: hdd & wknd ins fnl 2f* **6/1**[3]	88
-502	**8**	*10*	**Snoqualmie Girl (IRE)**[15] 4143 4-9-2 101 DaneO'Neill 8 (D R C Elsworth) *chsd ldrs: rdn and wkng on outside whn bmpd 3f out* **6/1**[3]	72
3322	**9**	*22*	**Mildoura (FR)**[36] 3462 5-9-2 88 IanMongan 2 (Mrs L J Mongan) *chsd ldrs: rdn and wkng whn bmpd 3f out* **20/1**	37

2m 32.69s (-2.81) **Going Correction** 0.0s/f (Good)
WFA 3 from 4yo+ 11lb **9** Ran SP% **115.3**
Speed ratings (Par 111): **109,108,108,107,106 105,101,95,80**
Tote Swingers: 1&2 £6.70, 1&3 £9.30, 2&3 £15.60 CSF £35.89 TOTE £5.90: £1.90, £2.70, £4.20; EX 42.30.
Owner M V Deegan **Bred** Dapple Broodmares 2004 **Trained** Newmarket, Suffolk
■ Stewards' Enquiry : J-P Guillambert two-day ban: careless riding (Aug 15-16)

FOCUS
An ordinary fillies' Listed race that was run in a decent time. The form looks pretty solid.

NOTEBOOK
Pachattack(USA) may have been a bit fortunate, but she stuck out a willing head under pressure over a distance at which she was previously unproven, so it was hard to begrudge her victory. The form of her latest win had received a significant boost with the subsequent exploits of runner-up Lady Jane Digby, who won a Group 1 in Germany, and it was no mean feat here conceding 14lb to the younger generation. She will presumably chance her arm back in Group company now, with connections talking of a potential trip to America for the Beverly D Stakes. (op 5-1)
Shimmering Surf(IRE) looked likely to be suited by this trip when third in a 3-y-o Listed event at the course in June and she was beginning to stay on when hampered and losing her position inside the final 3f. It took her a while to pick up afterwards and, although rattling home, the line arrived a stride too soon. She was most unlucky and may not find many better opportunities to gain winning black type. (op 6-1)
Saphira's Fire(IRE), outclassed in Group 1 company in Ireland latest, was more at home back at this level and ran really well, just backing out of it close home. (op 16-1)
Becqu Adoree(FR) again wasn't beaten that far, but she remains some way short of her best French form. (op 9-1)
Gallic Star(IRE) was unable to repeat her Riddlesdale form, even dropped to Listed company, just plodding on late at the one pace. (op 4-1)
Lady Artemisia(IRE) failed to go on having been hampered and was below her best (op 6-1 tchd 11-2)
Wedding March(IRE) had been given a break since disappointing on her return, but she fared no better, dropping out tamely once headed. (op 7-1 tchd 15-2)
Snoqualmie Girl(IRE) had finished ahead of Lady Artemisia last time and failed to reproduce her form. (op 11-2)

4625 FRANK TAIT MEMORIAL H'CAP 5f 34y
5:00 (5:00) (Class 4) (0-85,81) 3-Y-0+ **£4,209** (£1,252; £625; £312) **Stalls** Centre

Form				RPR
2220	**1**		**Solemn**[7] 4401 5-9-10 81 (b) LiamKeniry 10 (J M Bradley) *s.i.s: in rr tl gd hdwy appr fnl f: str run u.p to ld on line* **11/2**[2]	91
22-1	**2**	*nse*	**Desert Poppy (IRE)**[27] 3736 3-9-5 79 AdamKirby 9 (W R Swinburn) *chsd ldrs: wnt 2nd appr fnl f: hrd rdn and chal fnl 120yds: led fnl 20yds: ct on line* **3/1**[1]	89
3352	**3**	*¾*	**Cape Royal**[10] 4292 10-9-3 74 (bt) PatCosgrave 1 (J M Bradley) *led and racd wd for 3f: jnd main gp and stl travelling wl fr 2f out: rdn and kpt on whn strly chal fnl 120yds: hdd & wknd fnl 20yds* **10/1**	81
1005	**4**	*1 ½*	**Efistorm**[11] 4245 9-9-6 77 HayleyTurner 5 (C R Dore) *in rr tl hdwy fr 2f out: chsd ldrs fnl f: styd on same pce* **16/1**	79
1110	**5**	*½*	**Brandywell Boy (IRE)**[15] 4148 7-9-0 76 BillyCray[(5)] 8 (D J S Ffrench Davis) *chsd ldrs: rdn and effrt over 1f out: one pce ins fnl f* **13/2**[3]	76
4105	**6**	*2 ½*	**Ocean Blaze**[10] 4292 6-9-4 75 DarryllHolland 3 (B R Millman) *chsd ldrs: rdn and hung rt and wknd fnl f* **10/1**	66
0004	**7**	*2*	**Equuleus Pictor**[11] 4243 6-9-4 78 JackDean[(3)] 2 (J L Spearing) *chsd ldr: rdn 2f out: wknd fnl f* **12/1**	62
5421	**8**	*2 ¾*	**The Name Is Frank**[10] 4283 5-8-8 65 (t) FergusSweeney 7 (Mark Gillard) *outpcd* **12/1**	39
-105	**9**	*2 ¼*	**Clifton Bridge**[22] 3892 3-9-7 81 (b[1]) JimCrowley 6 (R M Beckett) *outpcd* **7/1**	47
5	**10**	*38*	**Taurus Twins**[16] 4090 4-9-3 74 (b) TomQueally 4 (R J Price) *s.i.s: sn in tch: wknd 2f out: eased: t.o* **8/1**	—

61.17 secs (-0.23) **Going Correction** +0.10s/f (Good)
WFA 3 from 4yo+ 3lb **10** Ran SP% **116.8**
Speed ratings (Par 105): **105,104,103,101,100 96,93,88,85,24**
Tote Swingers: 1&2 £5.00, 1&3 £10.50, 2&3 £4.10 CSF £22.39 CT £165.73 TOTE £7.70: £2.40, £1.80, £3.70; EX 28.80.
Owner E A Hayward **Bred** Cheveley Park Stud Ltd **Trained** Sedbury, Gloucs
■ Stewards' Enquiry : Adam Kirby one-day ban: used whip with excessive frequency (Aug 16)

FOCUS
This was always likely to be fast and furious, with so many potential front-runners, so it was no surprise to see the winner come from behind. Sound form.
Taurus Twins Official explanation: trainer said gelding finished distressed

4626 AJC PREMIER FILLIES' H'CAP 1m 2f 6y
5:30 (5:30) (Class 5) (0-75,75) 3-Y-0 **£2,590** (£770; £385; £192) **Stalls** Low

Form				RPR
5326	**1**		**Granite Girl**[24] 3821 3-9-2 70 PatCosgrave 4 (P J McBride) *hld up in rr: hdwy on ins fr over 3f out: drvn to ld jst ins fnl f: c readily clr last 100yds* **7/1**[3]	81
0042	**2**	*2 ¾*	**Now What**[10] 4282 3-8-7 61 RichardKingscote 2 (J G Portman) *led 1f: styd chsng ldrs: rdn and hung lft fr over 2f out: styd on to chse wnr ins fnl f: sn no ch but kpt on wl whn hrd pressed for 2nd* **4/1**[2]	67
003-	**3**	*nse*	**Red Intrigue (IRE)**[291] 6772 3-9-4 72 JimCrowley 5 (Mrs A J Perrett) *chsd ldrs: drvn and hung lft fr 3f out: styd on to press for 2nd ins fnl f but nvr any ch w wnr* **7/1**[3]	78
0053	**4**	*1 ¾*	**Sunarise (IRE)**[22] 3918 3-9-7 75 PatDobbs 1 (R Hannon) *in tch: hdwy whn nt clr run over 3f out: styd on fnl 2f to take one pce 4th last strides* **4/1**[2]	78
2144	**5**	*shd*	**Centime**[16] 4098 3-9-0 68 WilliamBuick 8 (B J Meehan) *t.k.h: led after 1f: rdn and qcknd over 2f out: hdd jst ins fnl f: sn wknd* **9/4**[1]	70
4-45	**6**	*2*	**Santa Margherita**[24] 3821 3-8-10 64 TomQueally 7 (H J L Dunlop) *in tch: rdn and continually hung lft fr over 3f out: no ch after* **12/1**	62
4-0	**7**	*shd*	**Ermyn Express**[97] 1582 3-8-6 60 NeilChalmers 11 (P M Phelan) *in rr: rdn 3f out: sme prog fnl 2f: nvr any threat* **33/1**	58
-560	**8**	*3 ¼*	**Tammela**[46] 3080 3-7-12 59 HarryBentley[(7)] 6 (A P Jarvis) *s.i.s: in rr: racd on outside fr over 4f out: rdn: hun lft and no rspnse fr ins fnl 3f* **25/1**	50
00-1	**9**	*5*	**Nom De La Rosa (IRE)**[152] 760 3-8-8 62 (p) FergusSweeney 3 (Miss Sheena West) *chsd ldrs: rdn 3f out: wknd qckly 2f out* **12/1**	43

2m 9.54s (0.74) **Going Correction** 0.0s/f (Good) **9** Ran SP% **117.9**
Speed ratings (Par 97): **97,94,94,93,93 91,91,89,85**
Tote Swingers: 1&2 £5.10, 1&3 £8.50, 2&3 £9.50 CSF £35.94 CT £207.09 TOTE £7.30: £2.20, £1.90, £2.30; EX 33.40 Place 6: £84.32 Place 5: £48.24.
Owner P J McBride **Bred** Wood Farm Stud (Waresley) **Trained** Newmarket, Suffolk

FOCUS
Just an ordinary fillies' handicap but probably fair form for the grade. The winner is generally progressive.
T/Plt: £135.80 to a £1 stake. Pool:£60,249.78 - 323.75 winning tickets T/Qpdt: £55.50 to a £1 stake. Pool:£4,528.77 - 60.30 winning tickets ST

4627 - 4629a (Foreign Racing) - See Raceform Interactive

3003 CORK (R-H)
Sunday, August 1

OFFICIAL GOING: Good changing to good to yielding after race 4 (3.40)

4630a PLATINUM STKS (LISTED RACE) 1m
3:40 (3:41) 3-Y-0+ **£24,446** (£7,146; £3,384; £1,128)

			RPR
1		**Hen Night (IRE)**[84] 1952 3-8-12 99 WMLordan 13 (David Wachman, Ire) *trckd ldrs in 4th: 3rd st: sn rdn: chal under 2f out: led 1f out: styd on wl* **10/1**	100
2	*2 ½*	**Maybe Grace (IRE)**[11] 4273 4-9-5 94 (p) KLatham 11 (Mrs John Harrington, Ire) *trckd ldrs: 5th 1/2-way: 4th st: styd on wl fr over 1f out* **11/1**	95
3	*½*	**Famous (IRE)**[14] 4177 3-8-12 103 (p) JMurtagh 14 (A P O'Brien, Ire) *attempted to make all: rdn and strly pressed st: hdd 1f out: sn no ex: kpt on same pce* **6/1**[2]	93
4	*1*	**Scarlet O'Hara (IRE)**[14] 4177 5-9-5 90 (b) PJSmullen 7 (D K Weld, Ire) *mid-div: 6th appr st: 5th 2f out: kpt on fr over 1f out* **16/1**	92
5	*hd*	**St Moritz (IRE)**[23] 3869 4-9-8 WJSupple 4 (M Johnston) *cl up in 2nd: rdn to chal early st: 3rd and no ex over 1f out: one pce* **1/1**[1]	94
6	*1 ¾*	**Fourpenny Lane**[133] 957 5-9-8 99 DJMoran 1 (Ms Joanna Morgan, Ire) *hld up: 7th and hdwy appr st: 6th and kpt on same pce fr 1 1/2f out* **33/1**	90
7	*2*	**Always Be True (IRE)**[35] 3490 4-9-5 94 (p) MACleere 9 (David Wachman, Ire) *towards rr: sme prog st: mod 7th and kpt on fnl f* **20/1**	82
8	*8*	**Rose Hip (IRE)**[36] 3467 6-9-8 101 CDHayes 5 (Joseph G Murphy, Ire) *hld up: racd wd st: no imp fr 2f out* **12/1**	67
9	*3 ½*	**Gan Amhras (IRE)**[105] 1413 4-9-8 110 (p) KJManning 6 (J S Bolger, Ire) *a towards rr* **13/2**[3]	59
10	*nk*	**School Holidays (USA)**[39] 3343 3-8-12 79 DPMcDonogh 2 (David Wachman, Ire) *settled in 3rd: 4th u.p 1/2-way: wknd appr st* **25/1**	54
11	*1 ¾*	**Aznavour (IRE)**[55] 2829 3-9-1 92 (p) FMBerry 3 (John M Oxx, Ire) *mid-div: 7th 1/2-way: wknd early st* **12/1**	53
12	*hd*	**Rain Rush (IRE)**[618] 7409 7-9-8 93 EJMcNamara 10 (David Marnane, Ire) *a towards rr* **33/1**	54

13 *28* **Lord High Admiral (IRE)**[10] 4312 3-9-1 105 .... JAHeffernan 8 —
(A P O'Brien, Ire) *chsd ldrs to 1/2-way: sn wknd: trailing whn eased 2f out: t.o* **14/1**

1m 38.98s (-5.92)
WFA 3 from 4yo+ 7lb **13** Ran SP% **137.5**
CSF £127.76 TOTE £7.20: £2.10, £3.00, £2.40; DF 116.20.

Owner Gigginstown House Stud **Bred** Gigginstown House Stud **Trained** Goolds Cross, Co Tipperary

FOCUS
The fourth is the best guide to the level.

NOTEBOOK
Hen Night(IRE) showed her undoubted progression by landing this decent Listed race. After a busy spring campaign, she was returning from a break and looked the pick of the three runners from this yard. She took over at the furlong pole and stuck to her task well on this ground, described as on the slow side of good by the riders and changed afterwards officially to good to yielding from good. Her trainer will look at a possible assault on the likes of the Garden City at Belmont or the Queen Elizabeth II in Keeneland later in the season with the progressive daughter of Danehill Dancer. (op 10/1 tchd 12/1)

Maybe Grace(IRE) got some valuable black type with a career-best effort. She was seeking a hat-trick after handicap wins at Fairyhouse and Naas and took this step forward in admirable fashion. She is clearly a filly going the right way on this evidence. (op 8/1 tchd 12/1)

Famous(IRE) had competed in a couple of Group 1 events without success and was dropped back to a mile after trailing home last at the Curragh last time. She set a decent clip up front but began to weaken approaching the furlong pole and soon gave way. (op 8/1)

Scarlet O'Hara(IRE) showed more on her second start of the year. (op 12/1)

St Moritz(IRE) was backed into a very short price. He had every chance when they straightened for home but was found wanting when asked for more on this easier surface, which was probably against him. (op 11/10 tchd 9/10)

Fourpenny Lane ◆ shaped well considering this was her first start since last March. In foal to Verglas, she might have needed this.

Gan Amhras(IRE) has not progressed as expected and, although this was his first run since he ran fourth to Famous Name at Leopardstown in April, this was a below-par display. (op 6/1)

4631a GIVE THANKS STKS (GROUP 3) (F&M) 1m 4f
4:10 (4:12) 3-Y-O+ **£46,017** (£13,451; £6,371; £2,123)

RPR

1 **She's Our Mark**[14] 4177 6-9-7 106 .... DMGrant 7 106+
(Patrick J Flynn, Ire) *hld up in rr: hdwy on outer early st: 6th 2f out: chal 1f out: led 100yds out: styd on wl* **4/1**[2]

2 *1 ½* **Leo Gali (IRE)**[27] 3744 3-8-10 93 .... WMLordan 3 102
(David Wachman, Ire) *chsd ldrs in 3rd: drvn along 4f out: 4th st: impr to chal 2f out: led 1 1/2f out: strly pressed fnl f: swvd lft whn hdd 100yds out: kpt on u.p* **14/1**

3 *shd* **Zarebiya (IRE)**[52] 2916 3-8-10 .... FMBerry 9 102+
(John M Oxx, Ire) *hld up in tch: smooth prog into 5th 4f out: rdn early st: hdwy 1 1/2f out: 2nd and chal 1f out: kpt on same pce* **6/4**[1]

4 *3* **Sense Of Purpose (IRE)**[27] 3744 3-8-10 95 .... PJSmullen 5 97
(D K Weld, Ire) *trckd ldrs in 5th: prog into 3rd ent st: sn rdn: 4th under 2f out: kpt on same pce fr over 1f out* **13/2**[3]

5 *4 ½* **Karasiyra (IRE)**[27] 3744 3-8-10 98 .... NGMcCullagh 2 90
(John M Oxx, Ire) *settled in 2nd: chal ent st: led over 2f out: hdd 1 1/2f out: sn no ex* **7/1**

6 *1 ¾* **Awe Inspiring (IRE)**[14] 4178 3-8-10 95 ....(p) JMurtagh 1 87
(A P O'Brien, Ire) *sn led: strly pressed st: hdd over 2f out: no ex fr 1 1/2f out* **10/1**

7 *¾* **Indiana Gal (IRE)**[27] 3744 5-9-7 99 ....(p) CDHayes 10 86
(Patrick Martin, Ire) *hld up towards rr: kpt on one pce st* **16/1**

8 *2 ½* **Cilium (IRE)**[18] 4033 4-9-7 89 .... KJManning 8 82
(Andrew Oliver, Ire) *towards rr: rdn and no imp st* **25/1**

9 *5 ½* **Unity (IRE)**[17] 4081 3-8-10 97 ....(p) MACleere 4 73
(David Wachman, Ire) *chsd ldrs in 6th: no ex ent st* **16/1**

10 *3* **Catchafallingstar**[22] 3932 3-8-10 .... JAHeffernan 11 68
(A P O'Brien, Ire) *hld up in tch: 7th 1/2-way: 6th bef st: sn no ex and wknd* **25/1**

11 *20* **Alaia (IRE)**[73] 2270 3-8-10 .... KLatham 6 36
(John M Oxx, Ire) *trckd ldrs in 4th: dropped to 7th bef st: sn wknd: trailing whn eased 2f out* **12/1**

2m 36.04s (-11.86)
WFA 3 from 4yo+ 11lb **11** Ran SP% **128.7**
CSF £65.28 TOTE £4.10: £1.30, £2.40, £1.30; DF 188.60.

Owner B & M Syndicate **Bred** M Barrett And Redmyre Bloodstock **Trained** Carrick-On-Suir, Co Waterford

FOCUS
The winner was the clear form choice, and the runner-up has been rated to her best, with the third improving from her maiden win.

NOTEBOOK
She's Our Mark came from last to first for her eighth career win. Pat Flynn's 6yo cost just 12,500 gns and what a bargain she is proving for connections. Her trainer intends keeping her on the go and the ease in the ground certainly played to her strengths. They went a good clip and, under a hard at work Danny Grant, she got to the front inside the final furlong on the nearside to land the spoils. (op 10/3 tchd 9/2)

Leo Gali(IRE) showed more progression with this display. She took over 1½f down but veered left under pressure. (op 10/1)

Zarebiya(IRE) ◆ travelled well and began to close in the straight on the outer but she couldn't quicken again to make her presence felt, although this was still a decent effort from the 3-y-o daughter of Galileo. The Leopardstown 1m4f maiden winner looks sure to be winning again before long. (op 9/4)

Sense Of Purpose(IRE) was supplemented for this race but the distress signals went up before the straight. To her credit, she kept on under pressure in the straight but never looked likely to pose a threat when the race unfolded. (op 6/1 tchd 7/1)

Karasiyra(IRE), stablemate of the third, raced in second for a long way but the ease in the ground was against her when asked for more into the straight. (op 6/1)

Awe Inspiring(IRE) led the way from the outset until she dropped away in the straight. (op 7/1)

4632 - 4636a (Foreign Racing) - See Raceform Interactive

[4611] DEAUVILLE (R-H)
Sunday, August 1

OFFICIAL GOING: Turf: good to soft; fibresand: standard

4637a PRIX DE CABOURG - JOCKEY CLUB DE TURQUIE (GROUP 3) (2YO) (TURF) 6f
1:05 (12:00) 2-Y-O **£35,398** (£14,159; £10,619; £7,079; £3,539)

RPR

1 **Pontenuovo (FR)**[37] 2-8-8 0 .... StephanePasquier 4 107
(Y De Nicolay, France) *racd in 4th: qcknd wl 2 1/2f out: led 1 1/2f out: wnt clr: comf* **8/1**

2 *2* **Captain Chop (FR)**[28] 3718 2-8-11 0 .... FlavienPrat 5 104
(D Guillemin, France) *led: rdn 2f out: hdd 1 1/2f out: styd on wl* **13/2**[3]

3 *½* **Khawatim**[25] 2-8-11 0 .... ChristopheSoumillon 3 103
(J-C Rouget, France) *settled in 3rd: rdn 2f out: no ex: styd on one pce* **8/13**[1]

4 *2 ½* **Living Art (USA)**[16] 2-8-8 0 .... GregoryBenoist 1 92
(X Nakkachdji, France) *racd in 2nd: rdn 2f out: no ex* **11/1**

5 *4* **Katerini (FR)**[31] 3609 2-8-8 0 .... DavyBonilla 2 80
(F Head, France) *a in rr: rdn 2f out: no ex* **9/2**[2]

1m 14.1s (3.10) **5** Ran SP% **112.9**
WIN (incl. 1 euro stake): 6.10. PLACES: 3.20, 5.60. SF: 43.20.
Owner Mme Erika Hilger **Bred** P Hilger **Trained** France

NOTEBOOK
Pontenuovo(FR), who is well regarded by her trainer, quickened up well to win with authority and could well now head for a Group 1 contest. The Morny is possible, as is the Cheveley Park and Prix Marcel Boussac.

4639a PRIX ROTHSCHILD (EX PRIX D'ASTARTE) (GROUP 1) (3YO+ FILLIES & MARES) (TURF) 1m (R)
2:40 (12:00) 3-Y-O+ **£151,699** (£60,690; £30,345; £15,159; £7,592)

RPR

1 **Goldikova (IRE)**[47] 3046 5-9-0 0 .... OlivierPeslier 8 124+
(F Head, France) *settled midfield: cruised to ld 2f out: wnt clr: easily* **1/3**[1]

2 *3* **Music Show (IRE)**[25] 3793 3-8-7 0 .... RichardHughes 5 112
(M R Channon) *racd in 2nd: rdn 2 1/2f out to ld briefly: hdd 2f out: r.o wl: no ch w wnr* **4/1**[2]

3 *1* **Elusive Wave (IRE)**[49] 3017 4-9-0 0 .... IoritzMendizabal 1 111
(J-C Rouget, France) *racd in 5th: hrd rdn 2 1/2f out: styd on wl* **14/1**

4 *hd* **Fabiana**[18] 4035 4-9-0 0 .... MaximeGuyon 6 110
(Andreas Lowe, Germany) *racd towards rr: hrd rdn 2 1/2f out: styd on wl* **66/1**

5 *¾* **Rainfall (IRE)**[25] 3793 3-8-7 0 .... KierenFallon 7 108
(M Johnston) *racd midfield on outside: rdn 2 1/2f out: wnt 3rd 1f out: wknd ins fnl f* **12/1**[3]

6 *shd* **Evaporation (FR)**[21] 3944 3-8-7 0 .... MickaelBarzalona 4 107
(C Laffon-Parias, France) *racd in rr fr s: late hdwy ins fnl f* **33/1**

7 *15* **Only Green (IRE)**[57] 2778 4-9-0 0 .... DavyBonilla 3 74
(F Head, France) *led fr s: eased fr 2 1/2f out* **100/1**

1m 37.5s (-3.30) **Going Correction** -0.05s/f (Good)
WFA 3 from 4yo+ 7lb **7** Ran SP% **114.8**
Speed ratings: **114,111,110,109,109 108,93**
WIN (incl. 1 euro stake): 1.30 (Goldikova combined with Evaporation & Only Green). PLACES: 1.10, 1.10, 1.10 DF: 2.30. SF: 2.00.
Owner Wertheimer & Frere **Bred** Wertheimer Et Frere **Trained** France

NOTEBOOK
Goldikova(IRE) recorded her tenth Group 1 succcess with the minimum of fuss, in the process emulating Miesque as the only European-trained horse to have won ten times at the highest level since the introduction of the Pattern in the 1970s. Tracking Music Show, who in turn tracked the pacemaker, she quickened to the front with effortless ease and only had to be pushed out to record a three-length victory. Another Jacques le Marois and a third Breeders' Cup Mile look very much at her mercy. (op 4-11)
Music Show(IRE), the Falmouth Stakes winner, confirmed herself as the leading 3-y-o filly over a mile but was still comprehensively outclassed by the winner. Quicker ground would have suited her ideally, and the Matron Stakes and Sun Chariot were mentioned as possible targets later this season.
Rainfall(IRE), third in the Falmouth, got a bit closer to Music Show this time, but she was another who could have done with the ground riding quicker.

[3236] DUSSELDORF (R-H)
Sunday, August 1

OFFICIAL GOING: Turf: soft

4640a HENKEL PREIS DER DIANA - DEUTSCHES STUTEN-DERBY (GROUP 1) (3YO FILLIES) (TURF) 1m 3f
4:10 (12:00) 3-Y-O **£203,539** (£79,646; £39,823; £22,123; £8,849)

RPR

1 **Enora (GER)**[32] 3-9-2 0 .... THellier 9 106
(T Mundry, Germany) *bkmarker fr s: mde gd prog down bkstretch and into fnl turn: qcknd smartly early in st on wd outside to chal for ld ent fnl f: grabbed ld 50yds out: comf* **20/1**

2 *½* **Elle Shadow (IRE)**[21] 3943 3-9-2 0 .... AStarke 10 105
(P Schiergen, Germany) *racd in midfeld: travelng smoothly: rnded horses ent st: qcknd wl to take ld 1f out: hdd 50yds out* **4/1**[2]

3 *1 ¼* **Nicea (GER)**[28] 3-9-2 0 .... MartinDwyer 6 103
(P Schiergen, Germany) *setled in midfield: qcknd wl early in st: r.o wl u.p to get 3rd* **25/1**

4 *1 ¼* **Lagalp (GER)**[28] 3-9-2 0 .... AGoritz 7 101
(P Schiergen, Germany) *racd towards rr: proged arnd fnl turn: qcknd wl in st: r.o wl* **25/1**

5 *nk* **Tech Exceed (GER)**[35] 3495 3-9-2 0 .... EPedroza 1 100
(A Wohler, Germany) *broke wl to r in 5th: bmpd ent st but picked up again and fin wl* **15/2**

6 *½* **Semina (GER)** 3-9-2 0 .... KKerekes 11 99
(S Smrczek, Germany) *sent st to ld fr s: set gd pce: stl in front 1 1/2f out: hdd 1f out: styd on wl* **33/1**

7 hd **Hibaayeb**^{14} 4178 3-9-2 0 .... FrankieDettori 16 99
(Saeed Bin Suroor) *broke fast: racd keenly in 6th: swtchd to outside on home turn: r.o wl: wknd ins fnl f* **2/1**^{1}
8 1 **Waldjagd**^{21} 3943 3-9-2 0 .... APietsch 8 97
(A Wohler, Germany) *settled in 4th: racing freely: wl plcd early in st: r.o: wknd ins fnl f* **10/1**
9 1/2 **Warsaw Ballet (CAN)** 3-9-2 0 .... JBojko 3 96
(A Wohler, Germany) *broke fast: racing feely: settled in 3rd bhd ldr: threatened briefly in st: wknd* **12/1**
10 nk **Saldennahe (GER)**^{28} 3-9-2 0 .... FilipMinarik 2 96
(P Schiergen, Germany) *settled in midfield: bmpd on first turn: mde prog early in st: r.o but wknd in clsng stages* **25/1**
11 3 **Nianga (GER)**^{21} 3943 3-9-2 0 .... JiriPalik 14 90
(P Schiergen, Germany) *settled in rr fr s: r.o past btn horses in st* **33/1**
12 hd **Amare**^{28} 3-9-2 0 .... EFrank 15 90
(T Mundry, Germany) *broke wl but bmpd a few times in early stages: settled midfield: hit traffic problems early in st: wknd* **7/1**^{3}
13 1 1/2 **Glady Romana (GER)**^{21} 3943 3-9-2 0 .... DominiqueBoeuf 13 87
(W Baltromei, Germany) *broke wl to r midfield: styd on in st but no threat* **50/1**
14 3/4 **Isantha (GER)**^{63} 2575 3-9-2 0 .... YannLerner 12 86
(T Mundry, Germany) *a.p: trckd ldr in 2nd: wknd qckly arnd fnl turn* **25/1**
15 hd **Mountain Rose (GER)**^{28} 3-9-2 0 .... ADeVries 4 86
(J Hirschberger, Germany) *racd in midfield: nvr threatened* **33/1**
16 3 **Amoya (GER)**^{28} 3-9-2 0 .... AHelfenbein 5 80
(P Schiergen, Germany) *sed towards rr: nvr figured* **66/1**

2m 14.68s (134.68) **16** Ran SP% **126.8**
WIN (incl. 10 euro stake): 162; PLACES: 41, 18, 68. SF: 631.
Owner Gestut Roettgen **Bred** Gestut Rottgen **Trained** Germany

NOTEBOOK
Enora(GER), reportedly the trainer's third string due to a lack of experience, and a half-sister to dual Group 2 winner/Group 1 placed Egerton (who was ridden by Torsten Mundry), finished strongly in the straight to get up close home. The Prix Vermeille was mentioned as a possible autumn target.
Elle Shadow(IRE) picked up well to come with what looked a winning run, only to find the Enora, who had been ridden patiently out the back, finishing even stronger down the outside.
Lagalp(GER) had started a short-priced favourite on her previous two outings (behind some she faced here) but ran poorly on her most recent run. She took a while to get going up the straight but nothing was finishing faster than her in the latter stages and is surely capable of winning a decent race.
Semina(GER) led well into the final stages and ran respectably.
Hibaayeb, drawn widest of all, had a lot of use made of her early to try and get a prominent position, but she couldn't get over to the rail and ended up racing wider than ideal throughout. She still looked to have some sort of a chance at the top of the straight but, along with the other early leaders, weakened right out in the closing stages. After the race her connections suggested she might have been coming into season, but in any case, she doesn't want the ground this soft.
Amare beat a lot of the rivals she met here on her previous start, but failed to confirm that form here.

KLAMPENBORG
Sunday, August 1
OFFICIAL GOING: Turf: good

4641a SCANDINAVIAN OPEN CHAMPIONSHIP (GROUP 3) (TURF) 1m 4f
3:30 (12:00) 3-Y-0+ **£35,799** (£11,933; £5,966; £3,579; £2,386)

RPR
1 **Django (SWE)**^{322} 5933 7-9-2 0 .... LennartHammer-Hansen 8 96
(Jessica Long, Sweden) **127/20**^{3}
2 1/2 **Peas And Carrots (DEN)**^{61} 2637 7-9-4 0 .... EddieAhern 2 97
(Lennart Reuterskiold Jr, Sweden) **4/5**^{1}
3 1 **Master Kid (DEN)**^{721} 4918 5-9-2 0 .... JacobJohansen 10 94
(Bent Olsen, Denmark) **17/2**
4 1/2 **Volo Cat (FR)**^{24} 6-9-2 0 .... JerryO'Dwyer 5 93
(Bent Olsen, Denmark) **40/1**
5 1 **Alnitak (USA)**^{24} 9-9-2 0 .... (b) EspenSki 9 91
(Bent Olsen, Denmark) **42/1**
6 1 **Condor (DEN)**^{24} 5-9-2 0 .... KimAndersen 6 90
(Soren Jensen, Denmark) **124/10**
7 1 **Classical World (USA)**^{24} 5-9-2 0 .... NikolajStott 3 88
(Torben Christensen, Denmark) **32/1**
8 shd **Fricoteiro (ARG)**^{24} 7-9-2 0 .... Per-AndersGraberg 4 88
(Niels Petersen, Norway) **27/1**
9 4 **Boxing Day**^{336} 5485 3-8-5 0 .... ShaneKarlsson 7 81
(Bent Olsen, Denmark) **14/1**
10 5 1/2 **Alpacco (IRE)**^{24} 8-9-2 0 .... RafaelSchistl 11 73
(Sandie Kjaer Nortoft, Denmark) **4/1**^{2}
11 hd **El Miracle (SWE)** 4-9-2 0 .... (b) ElioneChaves 1 72
(Ole Larsen, Sweden) **53/1**

2m 25.6s (145.60)
WFA 3 from 4yo+ 11lb **11** Ran SP% **127.0**
PARI-MUTUEL (all including 1 dkk stakes): WIN 7.34; PLACE 1.53, 1.32, 1.99; DF 22.66.
Owner Chess Racing AB & Mona Norklit **Bred** Chess Racing Ab **Trained** Sweden

MONMOUTH PARK (L-H)
Sunday, August 1
OFFICIAL GOING: Dirt: fast; turf: firm

4642a JERSEY DERBY (TURF CHUTE) 1m 110y
7:57 (8:00) 3-Y-0
£50,925 (£18,518; £9,259; £4,629; £1,543; £1,543)

RPR
1 **Hudson Steele (USA)**^{31} 3-8-5 .... JLezcano 8 —
(Todd Pletcher, U.S.A) **78/10**
2 2 1/4 **Audacity Of Hope**^{45} 3103 3-8-5 .... (b) RADominguez 6 —
(J Noseda) **49/10**^{3}
3 1/2 **They Call Me Giant (USA)**^{27} 3-8-5 .... (b) JBravo 4 —
(Kelly Breen, U.S.A) **74/10**
4 1 1/2 **Two Notch Road (USA)**^{15} 3-8-9 .... RMaragh 1 —
(Glenn R Thompson, U.S.A) **13/5**^{2}
5 1/2 **Houngun (USA)**^{27} 3-8-5 .... PLopez 3 —
(Dennis J Manning, U.S.A) **38/1**
6 1 1/2 **The Cognac Kid (USA)** 3-8-5 .... FMaysonett 2 —
(Amy Tarrant, U.S.A) **69/10**
7 nk **Fantastico Roberto (IRE)**^{27} 3-8-9 .... (b) AGarcia 5 —
(Todd Pletcher, U.S.A) **11/5**^{1}
8 2 1/4 **Sun Dance Moon (USA)** 3-8-5 .... MGarcia 7 —
(Richard Dutrow Jr, U.S.A) **129/10**

1m 41.07s (101.07) **8** Ran SP% **121.7**
Owner Roger J Weiss **Bred** Jay W Bligh **Trained** USA

4643a IZOD HASKELL INVITATIONAL STKS (GRADE 1) (3YO) (DIRT) 1m 1f
10:43 (10:44) 3-Y-0
£370,370 (£123,456; £61,728; £37,037; £18,518; £6,172)

RPR
1 **Lookin At Lucky (USA)**^{78} 2137 3-8-10 0 .... MGarcia 1 129+
(Bob Baffert, U.S.A) **6/5**^{1}
2 4 **Trappe Shot (USA)**^{22} 3-8-6 0 .... AGarcia 7 116
(Kiaran McLaughlin, U.S.A) **14/5**^{2}
3 3/4 **First Dude (USA)**^{57} 2776 3-8-6 0 .... RADominguez 4 115
(Dale Romans, U.S.A) **26/5**^{3}
4 nse **Super Saver (USA)**^{78} 2137 3-8-10 0 .... CHBorel 6 119
(Todd Pletcher, U.S.A) **63/10**
5 1 1/2 **Afleet Again (USA)**^{43} 3-8-6 0 .... (b) JBravo 2 112
(Robert E Reid Jr, U.S.A) **198/10**
6 1 **Ice Box (USA)**^{57} 2776 3-8-8 0 .... JLezcano 3 112
(Nicholas Zito, U.S.A) **77/10**
7 2 **Our Dark Knight (USA)**^{43} 3-8-6 0 .... ElvisTrujillo 5 106
(Nicholas Zito, U.S.A) **28/1**

1m 49.83s (109.83) **7** Ran SP% **121.3**
PARI-MUTUEL (all including $2 stake): WIN 4.40; PLACE (1-2) 3.00, 3.40; SHOW (1-2-3) 2.40, 2.60, 3.00; SF 17.20.
Owner Karl Watson, Michael E Pegram & Paul Weitman **Bred** Gulf Coast Farms LLC **Trained** USA

FOCUS
The best 3-y-o race of the year so far in the US.

NOTEBOOK
Lookin At Lucky(USA), the Preakness winner, comprehensively proved himself the best 3-y-o male in the states with an impressive success. The Travers Stakes, a 1m2f Grade 1 contest at Saratoga that would allow him to stay against his own age group, could be next on his agenda, and later in the year the Breeders' Cup Classic will surely also be considered.
Trappe Shot(USA), 4-4 this year but trying Graded company for the first time, came up short but still ran well. He's entitled to still be improving.
First Dude(USA) couldn't reverse Preakness form with Lookin At Lucky, despite being 4lb better off, although he may well have been a clear second had his rider kicked on sooner, rather than allowing his main rivals to build up momentum around the bend into the straight.
Super Saver(USA) seems badly flattered by his Kentucky Derby success, although he might not be done with yet. This year the Breeders' Cup is staged at Churchill Downs, where this colt excels, and a sloppy track for the Classic would bring him into the equation.
Afleet Again(USA) needed a stronger pace to chase.
Ice Box(USA) is flattered by his staying-on second in a muddling Kentucky Derby.
Our Dark Knight(USA) wasn't up to this level.

4402 CARLISLE (R-H)
Monday, August 2
OFFICIAL GOING: Good to firm changing to good to firm (good in places) after race 3 (7.25)
Wind: Light, half-against. Weather: Overcast, dry

4644 LLOYD MINI LADY AMATEUR RIDERS' H'CAP 7f 200y
6:25 (6:26) (Class 5) (0-70,68) 3-Y-0+ **£2,186** (£677; £338; £169) **Stalls** High

Form RPR
2323 1 **Call Of Duty (IRE)**^{8} 4404 5-9-7 **59** .... MissECSayer$^{(5)}$ 2 69
(Mrs Dianne Sayer) *mde all: pushed along and drifted rt over 1f out: styd on strly* **9/2**^{2}
322 2 1 1/2 **Silly Gilly (IRE)**^{6} 4453 6-9-3 **55** .... MissVBarr$^{(5)}$ 11 61
(R E Barr) *chsd wnr thrght: rdn over 2f out: kpt on fnl f* **5/1**^{3}
0605 3 1 1/2 **Emperor's Well**^{6} 4454 11-8-11 **49** oh4 .... MissJoannaMason$^{(5)}$ 10 52
(M W Easterby) *prom: effrt over 2f out: kpt on fnl f* **11/1**
0530 4 2 1/4 **Just Timmy Marcus**^{17} 4119 4-9-9 **56** .... MissSBrotherton 6 53
(B P J Baugh) *midfield: effrt whn n.m.r briefly over 2f out: hdwy over 1f out: no imp fnl f* **7/2**^{1}
0002 5 1 **Salerosa (IRE)**^{15} 4172 5-9-12 **66** .... (v) MissKMargarson$^{(7)}$ 12 61
(Mrs A Duffield) *midfield: effrt and hdwy on outside wl over 1f out: no imp fnl f* **14/1**
0263 6 1/2 **Wiseman's Diamond (USA)**^{15} 4172 5-10-2 **68** .... MissWGibson$^{(5)}$ 13 62+
(P T Midgley) *bhd tl hdwy over 1f out: nvr rchd ldrs* **12/1**
2014 7 hd **Ivestar (IRE)**^{46} 3124 5-9-11 **63** .... (bt^{1}) MissCharlotteHolmes$^{(5)}$ 8 56
(B M R Haslam) *dwlt: bhd: effrt whn nt clr run and swtchd rt over 2f out: kpt on fnl f: nvr able to chal* **16/1**
0240 8 4 1/2 **Mississippian (IRE)**^{6} 4453 6-8-10 **50** .... MissDLenge$^{(7)}$ 9 33
(Mrs D J Sanderson) *midfield: pushed along 2f out: sn outpcd* **16/1**
00-0 9 hd **Second Reef**^{2} 4606 8-8-11 **49** oh4 .... MissHCuthbert$^{(5)}$ 5 31
(T A K Cuthbert) *hld up in midfield: pushed along on ins over 2f out: n.d* **100/1**
0360 10 3 1/4 **Rain Stops Play (IRE)**^{17} 4082 8-8-11 **49** oh4 ... (t) MissJRRichards$^{(5)}$ 14 23
(N G Richards) *trckd ldrs tl wknd over 1f out* **28/1**
0611 11 1 **Cross Of Lorraine (IRE)**^{9} 4373 7-9-11 **65** .... (b) MissCJones$^{(7)}$ 3 37
(C Grant) *hld up on outside: c wd bnd ent st: nvr on terms* **12/1**
6304 12 1 **Fortunate Bid (IRE)**^{32} 3597 4-9-4 **56** .... MissSLWatson$^{(5)}$ 15 25
(Mrs L Stubbs) *bhd: struggling 1/2-way: nvr on terms* **10/1**
-360 13 1 **Al Wasef (USA)**^{45} 3164 5-9-12 **59** .... MrsCBartley 1 26
(J S Goldie) *t.k.h: hld up on outside: rdn over 2f out: sn btn* **40/1**
2400 14 9 **Anthemion (IRE)**^{34} 3531 13-9-6 **60** oh2 ow11 .... MissAMcGregor$^{(7)}$ 4 5
(Mrs J C McGregor) *cl up tl rdn and wknd over 2f out* **66/1**

1m 41.42s (1.42) **Going Correction** +0.20s/f (Good) **14** Ran SP% **116.7**
Speed ratings (Par 103): **100,98,97,94,93 93,93,88,88,85 84,83,82,73**
Tote Swingers:1&2:£4.80, 2&3:£59.30, 1&3:£17.00 CSF £25.82 CT £240.80 TOTE £5.10: £1.80, £1.40, £3.60; EX 26.80.
Owner T W Rebanks **Bred** Gainsborough Stud Management Ltd **Trained** Hackthorpe, Cumbria
■ Stewards' Enquiry : Miss V Barr two-day ban: careless riding (tbn)

FOCUS
On a dry evening the ground was described as good to firm all around. A good gallop for this lady riders' contest and it proved hard to make ground off the pace. The front pair were always 1-2 and the second is a fair guide.

4645 CARLISLE LIVING MAIDEN AUCTION STKS 5f 193y
6:55 (6:56) (Class 5) 2-Y-O £2,590 (£770; £385; £192) Stalls High

Form RPR
04 1 **Thirteen Shivers**[20] 3971 2-8-9 0 GrahamGibbons 13 74
(M W Easterby) *cl up: led over 1f out: pushed out fnl f* **8/1**[3]
000 2 1 ¾ **Indian Giver**[17] 4089 2-8-4 0 PatrickMathers 8 63
(H A McWilliams) *bhd and sn pushed along: hdwy on outside over 2f out: edgd lft and chsd wnr ins fnl f: no imp* **150/1**
5 3 1 ½ **Norwegian Liberty (IRE)**[6] 4451 2-8-6 0 AndrewElliott 12 60
(B M R Haslam) *prom: drvn over 2f out: rallied over 1f out: kpt on ins fnl f* **11/1**
33 4 1 **Heartbreak**[21] 3964 2-8-12 0 PaulHanagan 6 63
(R A Fahey) *plld hrd early: w ldr: led over 2f out to over 1f out: drvn and kpt on same pce* **13/8**[1]
03 5 shd **Kingscroft (IRE)**[9] 4379 2-8-10 0 RoystonFfrench 4 61
(M Johnston) *led to over 2f out: rallied: kpt on same pce u.p fnl f* **9/4**[2]
0 6 ¾ **Rothesay Chancer**[40] 3315 2-8-8 0 GaryBartley(3) 10 59
(J S Goldie) *midfield: effrt and rdn over 2f out: no imp fr over 1f out* **66/1**
7 2 **Chilledtothebone** 2-8-10 0 (b[1]) TomEaves 3 55+
(Mrs L Stubbs) *s.i.s: bhd tl hdwy 2f out: nvr able to chal* **50/1**
35 8 3 ½ **Ajaafa**[30] 3665 2-8-10 0 PaulMulrennan 2 41
(J G Given) *prom: effrt over 2f out: wknd over 1f out* **8/1**[3]
43 9 3 **Glenns Princess**[100] 1527 2-7-11 0 MarzenaJeziorek(7) 9 25
(R A Fahey) *in tch: pushed along over 2f out: wknd over 1f out* **10/1**
5 10 ¾ **Microlight**[21] 3964 2-8-10 0 (b[1]) DavidAllan 7 29
(T D Easterby) *hld up: drvn along 1/2-way: wknd fr 2f out* **25/1**
0 11 hd **Arashone**[9] 4368 2-8-1 0 KellyHarrison(3) 5 22
(J R Weymes) *bhd: struggling 1/2-way: nvr on terms* **66/1**
06 12 11 **Tom Bowler**[8] 4402 2-8-8 0 (b[1]) BarryMcHugh(3) 11 —
(Mrs A Duffield) *in tch tl rdn and wknd fr over 2f out* **100/1**
1m 15.23s (1.53) **Going Correction** +0.20s/f (Good) 12 Ran SP% **119.0**
Speed ratings (Par 94): **97,94,92,91,91 90,87,82,78,77 77,62**
Tote Swingers:1&2:£21.20, 2&3:£42.60, 1&3:£9.70 CSF £876.54 TOTE £12.30: £3.60, £19.40, £3.50; EX 347.50.
Owner K Wreglesworth **Bred** Cheveley Park Stud Ltd **Trained** Sheriff Hutton, N Yorks

FOCUS
Probably just an ordinary maiden which was run at a sound pace and the race developed under the stands' side rail. The winner improved by a stone on his latest form with the runner-up the key.

NOTEBOOK
Thirteen Shivers, sent off favourite last time out, appears to be going the right way and should be able to make his mark in nursery company as well. (tchd 10-1)
Indian Giver put up a career-best effort here after failing to trouble the judge in her first three starts. Nurseries will also be the way forward for her. (op 100-1)
Norwegian Liberty(IRE), who only made her debut six days ago, again showed she has got some ability and might be up to winning a fillies' event. (op 12-1 tchd 8-1)
Heartbreak didn't help his chance by racing keenly and might prove better back at 5f. (op 2-1)
Kingscroft(IRE) couldn't build on his Newmarket third. (op 5-2 tchd 11-4)
Rothesay Chancer, whose half-sister Rothesay Dancer has been a grand servant to this yard, can make his mark in due course.
Ajaafa hasn't progressed from his debut run, while the rest of the field offered little short-term hope. (op 7-1)

4646 BEADLE & HILL CLAIMING STKS 7f 200y
7:25 (7:25) (Class 6) 3-Y-O £2,047 (£604; £302) Stalls High

Form RPR
4251 1 **Miami Gator (IRE)**[2] 4581 3-8-11 63 (v) AndrewElliott 6 75
(J R Weymes) *mde all: qcknd over 2f out: drew wl clr fr over 1f out* **9/4**[2]
0001 2 6 **Jupiter Fidius**[20] 3972 3-8-9 70 (p) JamesSullivan(3) 5 62
(Mrs K Walton) *prom: effrt over 2f out: styd on fnl f to take 2nd nr fin: no ch w wnr* **7/2**[3]
201 3 nk **George Benjamin**[19] 4018 3-9-2 74 AdrianNicholls 4 65
(D Nicholls) *chsd wnr: rdn over 2f out: plugged on same pce fnl f: lost 2nd cl home* **5/1**
4165 4 8 **Thrust Control (IRE)**[14] 4192 3-8-12 78 DaleSwift(5) 1 47
(B Ellison) *plld hrd early: hld up in tch: rn wd bnd over 4f out: effrt 3f out: wknd fr 2f out* **13/8**[1]
5 6 **Deferto Delphi** 3-8-9 0 BarryMcHugh(3) 3 27
(F P Murtagh) *hld up in tch: rdn over 3f out: wknd over 2f out* **40/1**
1m 41.29s (1.29) **Going Correction** +0.20s/f (Good) 5 Ran SP% **110.2**
Speed ratings (Par 98): **101,95,94,86,80**
CSF £10.37 TOTE £4.30: £2.70, £2.80; EX 10.60.
Owner Mrs Elaine M Burke **Bred** Newlands House Stud **Trained** Middleham Moor, N Yorks

FOCUS
Only five runners in this claimer but it was run at a very sound pace. The jockeys decided to stay over on the far side in this race. Tricky form to pin down with the winner runing a clear personal best at face value, but this doesn't look form to be too positive about.
Thrust Control(IRE) Official explanation: jockey said gelding hung badly left on bend

4647 EDINBURGH WOOLLEN MILL H'CAP 6f 192y
7:55 (7:55) (Class 4) (0-85,80) 3-Y-O £4,857 (£1,445; £722; £360) Stalls High

Form RPR
3-16 1 **Parvaaz (IRE)**[16] 4144 3-9-3 76 PhilipRobinson 5 84
(M A Jarvis) *cl up: rdn to ld over 1f out: kpt on wl fnl f* **5/2**[1]
0640 2 1 ¼ **Antoniola (IRE)**[9] 4394 3-9-1 74 (t) GrahamGibbons 7 78+
(T D Easterby) *dwlt: hld up on ins: hdwy over 1f out: chsd wnr ins fnl f: r.o* **7/2**[2]
2212 3 ¾ **Skyfire**[3] 4551 3-9-7 80 RoystonFfrench 1 82
(M Johnston) *prom: effrt 2f out: kpt on u.p ins fnl f* **7/2**[2]
0603 4 shd **Transmit (IRE)**[11] 4288 3-8-12 71 (b) DavidAllan 6 73
(T D Easterby) *led: rdn over 2f out: hdd over 1f out: rallied: one pce ins fnl f* **16/1**
101- 5 hd **Lord Aeryn (IRE)**[303] 6471 3-8-12 71 PaulHanagan 8 72
(R A Fahey) *t.k.h: trckd ldrs: effrt and drvn over 1f out: edgd lft over 1f out: kpt on same pce* **11/2**[3]
0245 6 1 ¾ **Dazeen**[16] 4127 3-8-6 65 FrannyNorton 3 62
(P T Midgley) *t.k.h: hld up in tch: n.m.r briefly over 2f out: effrt over 1f out: nt qckn* **14/1**
2246 7 7 **Breathless Kiss (USA)**[11] 4287 3-9-2 80 AmyRyan(5) 4 58
(K A Ryan) *t.k.h: trckd ldrs: outpcd over 2f out: btn over 1f out* **17/2**
2551 8 4 ½ **Kielder (IRE)**[35] 3507 3-8-13 72 (t) PhillipMakin 2 38
(T D Barron) *dwlt: hld up in tch: rn wd bnd over 4f out: effrt on outside over 2f out: sn wknd* **28/1**
1m 28.03s (0.93) **Going Correction** +0.20s/f (Good) 8 Ran SP% **114.9**
Speed ratings (Par 102): **102,100,99,99,99 97,89,84**
Tote Swingers:1&2:£1.50, 2&3:£9.20, 1&3:£1.40 CSF £11.42 CT £30.00 TOTE £3.90: £1.80, £2.00, £2.20; EX 15.70.
Owner Sheikh Ahmed Al Maktoum **Bred** Darley **Trained** Newmarket, Suffolk

FOCUS
A tight 66-85 handicap, in which the top weight was 5lb below the ceiling rating. It was run at a sound pace and the form should prove reliable with the fourth probably the key. The winner improved by 9l on his maiden form.

4648 CHAMPAGNE LANSON H'CAP 1m 3f 107y
8:25 (8:26) (Class 6) (0-60,60) 3-Y-O+ £1,706 (£503; £252) Stalls Low

Form RPR
-250 1 **Emerald Glade (IRE)**[38] 3390 3-8-12 54 DavidAllan 9 63
(T D Easterby) *trckd ldrs: led and wandered u.p fr over 1f out: hld on wl fnl f* **9/2**[2]
5422 2 nk **Destiny's Dancer**[22] 3073 3-8-7 54 PatrickDonaghy(5) 14 62+
(B M R Haslam) *hld up towards rr: effrt over 2f out: chsd wnr ins fnl f: r.o wl towards fin* **5/1**[3]
-500 3 2 **Barbarian**[8] 4407 4-9-11 57 SilvestreDeSousa 1 62
(A D Brown) *led: hung lft and hdd over 1f out: kpt on same pce fnl f* **33/1**
6501 4 ½ **Gulf Coast**[8] 4410 5-9-11 57 6ex (p) GrahamGibbons 15 61
(T D Walford) *trckd ldrs: effrt over 2f out: kpt on same pce fnl f* **7/2**[1]
4240 5 1 ½ **Miss Ferney**[8] 4411 6-9-1 50 PaulPickard(3) 10 52+
(A Kirtley) *hld up: hdwy on ins over 2f out: rdn and no imp appr fnl f* **22/1**
-403 6 1 ½ **Perez (IRE)**[22] 3352 8-8-11 46 oh1 (vt) JamesSullivan(3) 16 45
(W Storey) *prom: rdn and outpcd over 2f out: one pce fr over 1f out* **14/1**
4-03 7 ½ **San Deng**[27] 2500 8-9-2 48 PaulHanagan 3 46
(Micky Hammond) *hld up on outside: rdn over 2f out: no imp over 1f out* **8/1**
0-33 8 nse **Annibale Caro**[5] 3166 8-9-5 58 PaulNorton(7) 8 56
(J S Goldie) *hld up: hdwy and squeezed between horses 2f out: rdn and sn no imp* **10/1**
1326 9 1 ¼ **They All Laughed**[20] 3974 7-9-9 55 (p) PhillipMakin 11 51
(Mrs Marjorie Fife) *hld up: effrt whn n.m.r briefly over 2f out: no imp over 1f out* **9/1**
126- 10 11 **King's Chorister**[22] 4397 4-9-7 58 (t) DaleSwift(5) 7 35
(F P Murtagh) *bhd: drvn over 3f out: nvr on terms* **33/1**
0/6- 11 nse **Clueless**[13] 923 8-9-11 57 (b) TomEaves 2 34
(B Storey) *dwlt: sn cl up: rdn and hung rt wl over 1f out: sn btn* **40/1**
046 12 7 **Sumner (IRE)**[53] 2881 6-10-0 60 PJMcDonald 5 25
(F Sheridan) *hld up in tch: effrt over 2f out: wknd wl over 1f out* **22/1**
4626 13 14 **Tia Juana (IRE)**[32] 3601 3-9-1 60 KellyHarrison(3) 4 2
(B M R Haslam) *t.k.h: in midfield on outside: struggling over 3f out: btn fnl 2f* **28/1**
0000 14 9 **Stephie**[8] 4411 4-9-0 46 PaulMulrennan 12 —
(M W Easterby) *hld up: pushed along over 3f out: btn fnl 2f* **100/1**
3340 15 15 **Without Equal**[12] 4246 4-9-0 46 oh1 DanielTudhope 6 —
(N Wilson) *bhd on outside: struggling over 3f out: sn btn* **25/1**
2m 27.37s (4.27) **Going Correction** +0.20s/f (Good)
WFA 3 from 4yo+ 10lb 15 Ran SP% **119.2**
Speed ratings (Par 101): **92,91,90,89,88 87,87,87,86,78 78,73,63,56,45**
Tote Swingers:1&2:£14.80, 2&3:£60.90, 1&3:Not won. CSF £24.02 CT £671.17 TOTE £5.70: £2.30, £2.50, £8.30; EX 29.70.
Owner D A West **Bred** J T And Mrs Thomas **Trained** Great Habton, N Yorks
■ Stewards' Enquiry : David Allan caution: used whip with excessive frequency.

FOCUS
The going was changed to good to firm, good in places before this wide-open 46-60 handicap. It was run at a sound pace. Clear personal bests from the first two.

4649 DEBENHAMS H'CAP 5f 193y
8:55 (8:56) (Class 6) (0-60,60) 3-Y-O £1,706 (£503; £252) Stalls High

Form RPR
4020 1 **Amoureuse**[49] 3030 3-7-11 46 oh1 NeilFarley(7) 8 51
(D Carroll) *mde all: rdn 2f out: hld on wl fnl f* **8/1**
5-60 2 ½ **Major Monty (IRE)**[30] 3676 3-8-8 55 (p) RossAtkinson(5) 4 58
(Tom Dascombe) *chsd wnr thrght: effrt over 1f out: kpt on ins fnl f* **5/1**[3]
0000 3 4 **Lieu Day Louie (IRE)**[47] 3086 3-8-2 49 DeanHeslop(5) 5 40
(N Wilson) *hld up: effrt on outside 2f out: no further imp fnl f* **8/1**
6030 4 2 **Weetentherty**[14] 4193 3-8-6 48 (v) PaulHanagan 9 32
(J S Goldie) *trckd ldrs: effrt over 2f out: wknd ins fnl f* **7/2**[2]
2644 5 3 **Coolella (IRE)**[35] 3501 3-8-8 53 KellyHarrison(3) 7 28
(J R Weymes) *in tch: effrt over 2f out: btn fnl f* **10/3**[1]
-065 6 5 **Gold Crusher (USA)**[16] 4151 3-8-13 55 (p) TomEaves 2 14
(Julie Camacho) *hld up on outside: rdn over 2f out: sn btn* **12/1**
0055 7 2 ½ **Colamandis**[19] 4018 3-8-13 55 PatrickMathers 3 6
(H A McWilliams) *trckd ldrs tl rdn and wknd wl over 1f out* **25/1**
5400 8 6 **Autocracy**[44] 3205 3-9-4 60 (t) DavidAllan 1 —
(E J Alston) *hld up in tch: rdn over 2f out: sn wknd* **5/1**[3]
0- 9 11 **Somewhere Else**[307] 6355 3-7-11 46 oh1 VictorSantos(7) 6 —
(A Berry) *s.s: wl bhd: hung lft bnd ent st: nvr on terms* **66/1**
1m 15.06s (1.36) **Going Correction** +0.20s/f (Good) 9 Ran SP% **113.9**
Speed ratings (Par 98): **98,97,92,89,85 78,75,67,52**
Tote Swingers:1&2:£8.10, 2&3:£14.70, 1&3:£8.40. totesuper7: Win: Not won. Place: £237.50. CSF £47.00 CT £332.78 TOTE £8.20: £2.10, £2.30, £3.90; EX 27.60 Place 6 £208.74, Place 5 £101.75..
Owner Mrs Ann Milburn **Bred** R F And S D Knipe **Trained** Sledmere, E Yorks
■ Stewards' Enquiry : Ross Atkinson one-day ban: used whip with excessive frequency (Aug 16)

FOCUS
All nine runners were maidens going into the race and some will hold that status for a while on the evidence of this. Yet again it proved to be an advantage to race up with the pace. Not form to be positive about.
Amoureuse Official explanation: trainer said, regarding apparent improvement in form, that the filly benefitted from a 49-day break.
Somewhere Else Official explanation: jockey said filly missed the break
T/Plt: £872.20 to a £1 stake. Pool:£60,875.42 - 50.95 winning tickets T/Qpdt: £47.50 to a £1 stake. Pool:£6,237.23 - 97.10 winning tickets RY

4149 RIPON (R-H)

Monday, August 2

OFFICIAL GOING: Good to firm (watered; 8.8)

Rail on bend from back to home straight moved out 4m adding circa 9yds to advertised distance on round course.

Wind: almost nil Weather: fine, sharp shower race 4

4650 E B F CHILDREN'S DAY MAIDEN STKS 6f
2:15 (2:17) (Class 5) 2-Y-O £3,561 (£1,059; £529; £264) Stalls Low

Form				RPR
56	1		**My Single Malt (IRE)**[37] 3433 2-9-3 0 MickyFenton 9 (T P Tate) *chsd ldrs: effrt over 2f out: led ins fnl f: hld on wl towards fin* 10/1[3]	71+
44	2	¾	**Alensgrove (IRE)**[17] 4116 2-8-12 0 TonyCulhane 3 (P T Midgley) *s.i.s: sn wl outpcd and drvn along: hdwy over 2f out: styd on to chse ldrs jst ins fnl f: tk 2nd towards fin* 25/1	62
340	3	nk	**Misscomplacent**[16] 4149 2-8-9 67 (v[1]) BarryMcHugh(3) 6 (Mrs A Duffield) *w ldr: racd keenly: led 2f out: hung rt: hdd ins fnl f: kpt on same pce* 28/1	61
5	4	3 ½	**Myjestic Melody (IRE)**[44] 3199 2-8-12 0 PaulMulrennan 7 (N Wilson) *chsd ldrs: effrt over 2f out: wknd fnl 150yds* 50/1	49
302	5	6	**Squires Gate (IRE)**[9] 4392 2-9-3 83 PaulHanagan 5 (B W Hills) *led: shkn up over 2f out: sn hdd: rdn and wknd over 1f out* 1/4[1]	35
	6	8	**Chagal (IRE)** 2-9-3 0 NeilCallan 1 (K A Ryan) *s.i.s: sn wl outpcd and hung lft* 15/2[2]	10
	7	19	**Auburn Lady** 2-8-12 0 SilvestreDeSousa 8 (A D Brown) *v.s.a: a t.o last* 80/1	—

1m 14.06s (1.06) **Going Correction** -0.10s/f (Good) 7 Ran SP% 111.3

Speed ratings (Par 94): **88,87,86,81,73 63,37**

toteswingers:1&2:£5.10, 1&3:£8.50, 2&3:£9.40 CSF £160.52 TOTE £10.80: £2.70, £5.00; EX 66.40 Trifecta £560.40 Part won. Pool £757.34 - 0.42 winning units..

Owner Mrs Fitri Hay **Bred** Ballylinch Stud **Trained** Tadcaster, N Yorks

FOCUS

The course had seen no rain since last Tuesday night, and the official going description was good to firm (GoingStick 8.8), although Micky Fenton described the ground as "good". The rail on the bend from the back straight to the home straight was moved out four metres, adding nine yards to races on the round course. This was just a modest maiden and the form is pretty weak with the favourite blowing out.

NOTEBOOK

My Single Malt(IRE) proved suited by the return to 6f and took advantage of the favourite's disappointing performance. This is weak form, but he has the size to progress. (op 9-1)

Alensgrove(IRE) was outpaced for most of the way, detached from the front quartet, but she ran on reasonably well for second. Nurseries are now an option and she might get further.

Misscomplacent, upped in trip and visored for the first time, showed speed but was a bit keen and didn't see her race out. It's debatable whether or not she ran up to her official mark of 67. (op 33-1)

Myjestic Melody(IRE), reported to have been unsuited by ground on the quick side on debut, fared a little better this time. (tchd 66-1)

Squires Gate(IRE), officially rated 83, would surely have won this had he run to form, but he was a major disappointment. He seemed to be a bit free through the early stages, but was off the bridle and in trouble over 2f out. Official explanation: trainer's rep had no explanation for the poor form shown (op 1-3 tchd 4-11 in a place)

Chagal(IRE) was extremely green. (op 13-2 tchd 8-1)

Auburn Lady Official explanation: jockey said filly was slowly away

4651 MICHAEL MOORHEAD MEMORIAL (S) H'CAP 5f
2:45 (2:45) (Class 6) (0-65,59) 3-Y-O £2,590 (£770; £385; £192) Stalls Low

Form				RPR
2565	1		**Drumpellier (IRE)**[29] 3710 3-9-2 57 PaulPickard(3) 8 (P T Midgley) *chsd ldr: led over 1f out: jst hld on* 12/1	62
3005	2	nse	**Gower Sophia**[15] 4169 3-8-10 48 SilvestreDeSousa 7 (M Brittain) *chsd ldrs: swtchd rt jst ins fnl f: r.o: jst failed* 16/1	53
6605	3	1 ¼	**Duke Of Rainford**[8] 4406 3-8-11 49 TonyHamilton 3 (M Herrington) *dwlt: hdwy and swtchd rt over 1f out: styd on same pce fnl f* 16/1	50
4666	4	shd	**Turf Time**[41] 3286 3-8-12 50 MickyFenton 4 (J A Glover) *chsd ldrs: hmpd after 100yds: hdwy over 1f out: nt clr run and eased fnl 50yds: nt rcvr* 33/1	52
-021	5	shd	**Oondiri (IRE)**[20] 3988 3-9-5 57 PaulHanagan 5 (T D Easterby) *led: swtchd stands' side rail after 100yds: hdd over 1f out: kpt on same pce ins fnl f* 6/4[1]	57
6504	6	½	**Itsthursdayalready**[21] 3966 3-9-6 58 (b) PaulMulrennan 9 (J G Given) *in rr: hdwy over 2f out: hung rt and kpt on same pce fnl f* 8/1[3]	56
0-50	7	nk	**Kate Skate**[9] 4365 3-9-2 54 (t) NeilCallan 1 (Miss Gay Kelleway) *hmpd after 100yds: swtchd rt and chsd ldrs 3f out: kpt on same pce fnl f* 9/2[2]	51
4650	8	1 ¾	**Scooby Dee**[10] 4337 3-8-2 45 (v[1]) AmyRyan(5) 10 (R M Whitaker) *mid-div and sn drvn along: kpt on fnl 2f: nvr a factor* 14/1	36
4002	9	¾	**Thewinnatakesitall**[14] 4194 3-8-11 49 AndrewElliott 11 (N Tinkler) *swtchd lft after 100yds and taken to r alone far side: edgd lft over 1f out: nvr a threat* 8/1[3]	37
0560	10	4	**Sandy Toes**[41] 3287 3-8-7 45 JamieMackay 6 (J A Glover) *drvn along and sn outpcd: a in rr* 40/1	19
0-05	11	1 ¾	**Areeg (IRE)**[14] 4194 3-8-7 45 PatrickMathers 12 (A Berry) *hmpd after 100yds: a towards rr* 50/1	12
6400	12	nk	**Sophie's Beau (USA)**[12] 4248 3-9-2 59 MarkCoumbe(5) 2 (M C Chapman) *s.i.s: a in rr* 16/1	25

60.09 secs (-0.61) **Going Correction** -0.10s/f (Good) 12 Ran SP% 119.8

Speed ratings (Par 98): **100,99,97,97,97 96,96,93,92,85 83,82**

toteswingers:1&2:£28.60, 1&3:£26.40, 2&3:£21.70 CSF £188.55 CT £3118.76 TOTE £8.10: £2.80, £5.20, £2.60; EX 215.00 TRIFECTA Not won..There was no bid for winner.

Owner R Wardlaw & Peter Mee **Bred** Hong Kong Breeders Club **Trained** Westow, N Yorks

FOCUS

A very moderate contest but straightforward form. The main action took place stands' side.

Drumpellier(IRE) Official explanation: trainer said, regarding apparent improvment in form, that the filly was suited by the drop back into selling company.

Turf Time Official explanation: jockey said gelding was denied a clear run

Kate Skate Official explanation: jockey said filly got checked at start

Areeg(IRE) Official explanation: jockey said filly was unsuited by the track

4652 DESTINATION HARROGATE H'CAP 1m 1f 170y
3:15 (3:16) (Class 4) (0-85,84) 3-Y-O+ £4,100 (£1,227; £613; £306; £152) Stalls High

Form				RPR
-060	1		**City Of The Kings (IRE)**[16] 4154 5-9-12 80 (p) SilvestreDeSousa 6 (G A Harker) *hld up in midfield: drvn over 3f out: styd on to ld over 1f out: styd on wl: eased nr fin* 11/1[3]	93
3445	2	1 ¼	**Veiled Applause**[14] 4196 7-9-4 72 PaulHanagan 9 (J J Quinn) *hld up in midfield: effrt over 3f out: edgd lft and styd on fnl f: tk 2nd nr fin* 16/1	82
3-13	3	½	**Sarrsar**[39] 3351 3-9-7 84 PhilipRobinson 7 (M A Jarvis) *led after 1f: hdd after 2f: led over 2f out: hdd over 1f out: styd on same pce* 4/5[1]	93
1621	4	nk	**Jonny Lesters Hair (IRE)**[16] 4152 5-9-12 80 DavidAllan 1 (T D Easterby) *racd wd: t.k.h: led after 2f and sn clr: hdd over 2f out: kpt on same pce fnl f* 4/1[2]	88
1265	5	4 ½	**Music Of The Moor (IRE)**[16] 4152 3-9-1 78 MickyFenton 4 (T P Tate) *stdd s: hld up in last: hdwy on outside over 3f out: kpt on wl fnl f* 20/1	77+
146	6	2	**Ahlawy (IRE)**[41] 3283 7-9-8 76 (t) LeeVickers 5 (F Sheridan) *s.i.s: sn chsng ldrs: chal over 1f out: wknd jst ins fnl f* 50/1	71
3653	7	2 ¼	**Come And Go (UAE)**[34] 3537 4-9-11 79 PJMcDonald 8 (G A Swinbank) *led 1f: chsd ldrs: edgd rt over 1f out: wknd jst ins fnl f* 14/1	69
421-	8	1 ¾	**Burma Rock (IRE)**[280] 7048 4-9-11 79 J-PGuillambert 10 (L M Cumani) *t.k.h towards rr: effrt over 3f out: lost pl 2f out* 14/1	66
503-	9	nk	**Anthology**[426] 2571 4-9-10 78 RichardMullen 2 (B Smart) *s.i.s: drvn 4f out: nvr on terms* 16/1	64

2m 2.93s (-2.47) **Going Correction** -0.10s/f (Good)

WFA 3 from 4yo+ 9lb 9 Ran SP% 115.7

Speed ratings (Par 105): **105,104,103,103,99 98,96,94,94**

toteswingers:1&2:£13.60, 1&3:£4.30, 2&3:£4.90 CSF £169.42 CT £298.69 TOTE £16.20: £3.10, £3.40, £1.20; EX 126.70 Trifecta £467.70 Part won. Pool £632.03 - 0.60 winning units..

Owner John J Maguire **Bred** Tom McDonald **Trained** Thirkleby, N Yorks

FOCUS

A fair handicap run at a strong pace. The winner was still 10lb off his best form of last year and the race is rated around the fourth.

4653 ARMSTRONG MEMORIAL H'CAP 6f
3:45 (3:46) (Class 3) (0-95,95) 3-Y-O+

£7,477 (£2,239; £1,119; £560; £279; £140) Stalls Low

Form				RPR
5134	1		**Gap Princess (IRE)**[2] 4583 6-9-1 82 SilvestreDeSousa 11 (G A Harker) *s.i.s: swtchd lft sn after s: hdwy over 2f out: r.o to ld ins fnl f: hld on wl* 8/1	91
160-	2	¾	**Sioux Rising (IRE)**[352] 5032 4-9-1 82 TonyHamilton 5 (R A Fahey) *w ldrs: led over 1f out: hdd: edgd lft and no ex ins fnl f* 28/1	89
0000	3	hd	**Baldemar**[9] 4391 5-9-7 88 PaulHanagan 7 (R A Fahey) *chsd ldrs: upsides jst ins fnl f: no ex* 3/1[1]	94
0034	4	¾	**Excusez Moi (USA)**[31] 3619 8-9-5 86 PJMcDonald 12 (Mrs R A Carr) *reluctant to post: gave problems in stalls: s.i.s: nt clr run over 1f out: swtchd rt and styd on wl last 75yds* 12/1	90+
2030	5	nk	**Red Cape (FR)**[3] 4536 7-8-13 83 JamesSullivan(3) 1 (Mrs R A Carr) *led 100yds: trckd ldrs: n.m.r over 1f out: nt clr run and swtchd rt ins fnl f: styd on towards fin* 4/1[3]	86+
0000	6	nse	**Rievaulx World**[16] 4148 4-8-12 79 (p) NeilCallan 4 (K A Ryan) *sn led: hdd over 1f out: kpt on same pce* 66/1	81
-220	7	½	**Midnight Martini**[51] 2978 3-9-9 94 (t) DavidAllan 3 (T D Easterby) *w ldrs: kpt on same pce fnl f* 8/1	95
1100	8	nk	**Kellys Eye (IRE)**[3] 4536 3-9-10 95 GrahamGibbons 9 (D H Brown) *chsd ldrs: n.m.r appr fnl f: kpt on same pce* 7/2[2]	95
0-35	9	nk	**Go Nani Go**[15] 4171 4-9-2 83 RichardMullen 8 (B Smart) *in rr: hdwy and n.m.r over 1f out: nvr rchd ldrs* 16/1	82
040-	10	1 ½	**Mastership (IRE)**[296] 6675 6-9-6 87 TomEaves 2 (J J Quinn) *hld up towards rr on ins: nvr a factor* 22/1	81
0550	11	8	**Jarrow (IRE)**[26] 3791 3-9-1 86 JoeFanning 10 (M Johnston) *in rr: hdwy on outside over 2f out: sn chsng ldrs: lost pl over 1f out: eased towards fin* 20/1	55

1m 11.73s (-1.27) **Going Correction** -0.10s/f (Good)

WFA 3 from 4yo+ 4lb 11 Ran SP% 117.1

Speed ratings (Par 107): **104,103,102,101,101 101,100,100,99,97 87**

toteswingers:1&2:£15.50, 1&3:£6.90, 2&3:£21.70 CSF £215.10 CT £839.53 TOTE £5.80: £1.50, £6.90, £1.80; EX 142.90 Trifecta £666.70 Part won. Pool £901.06 - 0.30 winning units..

Owner Northumbria Leisure Ltd C H McGhie **Bred** D Veitch And Musagd Abo Salim **Trained** Thirkleby, N Yorks

■ Stewards' Enquiry : Tony Hamilton two-day ban: careless riding (Aug 16,18)

FOCUS

A good, competitive sprint handicap in which they all raced towards the stands' side. Pretty straightforward form for the grade.

NOTEBOOK

Gap Princess(IRE) ◆ proved suited by the return to 6f, having found 5f inadequate two days earlier, and stayed on strongest of all out wide under her in-form jockey. She's now 4-10 since joining this yard and gives the impression that there's more to come. (op 7-1)

Sioux Rising(IRE), seemingly the lesser fancied of Richard Fahey's two runners, had been off for the best part of a year (apparently had a stress fracture behind) and this was a terrific effort on her return. She should go on from this, provided she doesn't bounce next time. (op 40-1)

Baldemar looked well beforehand and was only 1lb higher than when last winning. He didn't get much of a run and is better than he showed. (op 11-2)

Excusez Moi(USA) played up beforehand, proving reluctant to go to the start and being restless in the stalls, but he still ran well. His run style means he needs luck in running, which he didn't get this time, and he could have been closer. (op 9-1)

Red Cape(FR), 2lb higher than when winning this last year, was another denied a clear run and looked unlucky not to finish closer. (tchd 7-2)

Rievaulx World, racing beyond the minimum trip for the first time, with cheekpieces re-fitted, offered some encouragement.

Kellys Eye(IRE) was 3-3 over C&D coming into this, but he wasn't at his best this time. He was a bit short of room on occasions, but didn't look unlucky. (op 4-1 tchd 9-2)

Go Nani Go didn't get much of a run and is better than he showed. (op 14-1)

4654 AT THE RACES SKY 415 H'CAP 5f
4:15 (4:15) (Class 4) (0-85,83) 3-Y-O £4,209 (£1,252; £625; £312) Stalls Low

Form				RPR
6353	1		**Walvis Bay (IRE)**[9] 4369 3-9-2 78 MickyFenton 4 (T P Tate) *led after 1f: shkn up 1f out: styd on wl* 15/8[1]	91

4363 **2** *2* **Secret Millionaire (IRE)**[8] 4401 3-9-6 **82** .... StephenCraine 3 88
(Patrick Morris) *trckd ldrs: effrt over 1f out: kpt on to take 2nd nr fin* **3/1**[2]
1330 **3** *½* **Jigajig**[10] 4343 3-8-9 **71** .... PaulHanagan 1 75
(K A Ryan) *led 1f: chsd wnr: kpt on same pce fnl f* **7/1**
13 **4** *3½* **High Spice (USA)**[19] 4016 3-9-7 **83** ....(p) GrahamGibbons 2 75
(R M H Cowell) *trckd ldrs: effrt over 2f out: wknd fnl 150yds* **9/1**
10-3 **5** *2¾* **Electioneer (USA)**[3] 4558 3-8-11 **76** .... JamesSullivan(3) 7 58
(M W Easterby) *s.i.s: outpcd and detached in last: kpt on fnl f: nvr on terms* **9/2**[3]
0320 **6** *hd* **Tillys Tale**[10] 4349 3-8-8 **73** .... PaulPickard(3) 5 54
(P T Midgley) *chsd ldrs: wknd over 1f out* **9/1**
0-00 **7** *11* **Cian Rooney (IRE)**[14] 4193 3-8-5 **67** .... JoeFanning 6 8
(Mrs A Duffield) *chsd ldrs: lost pl over 1f out: eased fnl 100yds* **40/1**

59.00 secs (-1.70) **Going Correction** -0.10s/f (Good) 7 Ran SP% **112.9**
Speed ratings (Par 102): **109,105,105,99,95 94,77**
toteswingers:1&2:£2.30, 1&3:£3.00, 2&3:£4.00 CSF £7.42 TOTE £3.30: £1.60, £1.90; EX 8.10.
Owner Mrs Sylvia Clegg **Bred** Swordlestown Stud **Trained** Tadcaster, N Yorks

FOCUS
A fair 3-y-o sprint handicap. The winner posted a length personal best.
Electioneer(USA) Official explanation: jockey said gelding never travelled
Cian Rooney(IRE) Official explanation: jockey said gelding finished distressed

4655 TOTEEXACTA MAIDEN STKS 1m 4f 10y
4:45 (4:46) (Class 5) 3-Y-O+ **£2,914** (£867; £433; £216) **Stalls** High

Form RPR
-532 **1** **Chelsea Morning (USA)**[17] 4115 3-8-12 72 .... EddieAhern 6 81+
(B W Hills) *trckd ldr: led 2f out: pushed clr appr fnl f: eased clsng stages* **Evs**[2]
342 **2** *9* **Ceoil An Aith (IRE)**[26] 3776 4-9-9 78 .... JoeFanning 1 74
(M Johnston) *led: shkn up 4f out: edgd lft over 2f out: sn hdd and outpcd: eased towards fin* **10/11**[1]
5 **3** *21* **Fantastic Storm**[47] 3077 3-8-10 0 .... MatthewLawson(7) 3 45?
(R Bastiman) *trckd ldng pair: t.k.h: drvn and wl outpcd over 3f out* **66/1**[3]
00 **4** *7* **Sandgate Story**[3] 4556 4-9-9 0 .... TonyHamilton 2 29?
(N Wilson) *hld up in last: drvn over 4f out: nvr on terns: eased nr fin* **100/1**

2m 36.73s (0.03) **Going Correction** -0.10s/f (Good)
WFA 3 from 4yo 11lb 4 Ran SP% **104.9**
Speed ratings (Par 103): **95,89,75,70**
CSF £2.04 TOTE £1.90; EX 1.70.
Owner Mr & Mrs Christopher Wright **Bred** Joseph Allen **Trained** Lambourn, Berks

FOCUS
There was absolutely no strength in depth to this maiden, which was essentially a match. The winner is rated value for 9l as both the first two were eased.

4656 SIS LIVE H'CAP 1m 4f 10y
5:15 (5:15) (Class 5) (0-70,69) 3-Y-O+ **£2,914** (£867; £433; £216) **Stalls** High

Form RPR
23 **1** **George Adamson (IRE)**[38] 3405 4-10-0 **69** .... PJMcDonald 2 80+
(G A Swinbank) *hld up in midfield: hdwy 3f out: rdn to ld over 1f out: kpt on wl towards fin* **5/2**[1]
6604 **2** *1* **Hurlingham**[48] 3060 6-9-9 **64** ....(b) NeilCallan 6 73
(M W Easterby) *led 1f: chsd ldr: led over 4f out tl over 1f out: kpt on same pce last 150yds* **13/2**[3]
-103 **3** *3* **Capable Guest (IRE)**[29] 2694 8-9-8 **63** .... EddieAhern 1 67
(G M Moore) *in rr: effrt 4f out: kpt on same pce fnl 2f* **16/1**
-036 **4** *nk* **Bollin Judith**[16] 4125 4-9-9 **64** ....(t) TonyHamilton 5 68
(T D Easterby) *chsd ldrs: wnt 2nd over 3f out: one pce fnl 2f* **15/2**
3325 **5** *1¼* **Danceintothelight**[8] 4410 3-8-8 **60** .... JoeFanning 9 63
(Micky Hammond) *hld up in rr: effrt over 4f out: nt clr run over 3f out tl swtchd rt over 1f out: swtchd lft and styd on ins fnl f* **9/2**[2]
0-65 **6** *1* **Buckie Boy (IRE)**[25] 3807 4-9-12 **67** .... LNewman 3 67
(J S Goldie) *in rr: drvn over 3f out: hung rt and kpt on fnl 2f: nvr nr ldrs* **8/1**
065 **7** *2¾* **Grey Command (USA)**[16] 4156 5-8-13 **54** .... RichardMullen 7 50
(M Brittain) *in rr: drvn over 4f out: nvr a factor* **12/1**
4522 **8** *1¾* **Rowan Lodge (IRE)**[31] 3614 8-9-6 **64** ....(b) MatthewDavies(3) 4 57
(Ollie Pears) *trckd ldrs: t.k.h: wknd over 1f out* **12/1**
0340 **9** *3* **Dispol Diva**[8] 4410 4-8-10 **51** ow1 ....(v) TonyCulhane 10 39
(P T Midgley) *chsd ldrs: lost pl over 3f out* **22/1**
2-30 **10** *1¼* **Molon Labe (IRE)**[61] 2650 3-9-3 **69** .... MickyFenton 8 55
(T P Tate) *drvn to ld after 1f: hdd over 4f out: lost pl over 2f out* **14/1**

2m 34.59s (-2.11) **Going Correction** -0.10s/f (Good)
WFA 3 from 4yo+ 11lb 10 Ran SP% **115.2**
Speed ratings (Par 103): **103,102,100,100,99 98,96,95,93,92**
toteswingers:1&2:£4.90, 1&3:£9.80, 2&3:£11.40 CSF £18.48 CT £213.43 TOTE £2.40: £1.02, £2.80, £4.70; EX 19.50 TRIFECTA Not won. Place 6 £1,615.99; Place 5 £81.91.
Owner Mrs S Sanbrook **Bred** Miss O O'Connor & Stephanie Von Schilcher **Trained** Melsonby, N Yorks

FOCUS
An ordinary handicap run at a fair gallop. The form is rated slightly positively with a clear personal best from the winner.
Danceintothelight Official explanation: jockey said gelding was denied a clear run
T/Plt: £2,215.40 to a £1 stake. Pool:£69,648.81 - 22.95 winning tickets T/Qpdt: £13.50 to a £1 stake. Pool:£7,466.85 - 407.72 winning tickets WG

4421 WINDSOR (R-H)
Monday, August 2

OFFICIAL GOING: Good to firm (good in places; 7.8)
Stands' rail dolled out 12yds at 6f and 7yds at winning post. Top bend dolled out 9yds from innermost line, adding 27yds to races of 1m and over.
Wind: Light, behind. Weather: Cloudy

4657 BERKSHIRE LIFE AMATEUR RIDERS' H'CAP 1m 3f 135y
5:40 (5:41) (Class 5) (0-75,75) 3-Y-O+ **£2,505** (£770; £385) **Stalls** Low

Form RPR
0233 **1** **Maslak (IRE)**[7] 4426 6-10-4 **68** .... MrPCollington(3) 1 75
(P W Hiatt) *chsd ldr: rdn to ld jst over 2f out: drvn out* **4/1**[1]
5412 **2** *½* **Bavarica**[23] 3912 8-10-9 **73** .... MrRBirkett(3) 3 79
(Miss J Feilden) *trckd ldng pair: rdn over 2f out: wnt 2nd over 1f out: styd on: a jst hld* **13/2**
6253 **3** *1½* **Admirable Duque (IRE)**[17] 4101 4-10-5 **71** ....(p) MrCMartin(5) 9 74
(D J S Ffrench Davis) *hld up in 7th: rdn 3f out: prog towards outer 2f out: styd on fnl f to take 3rd nr fin* **15/2**
2324 **4** *½* **Megalala (IRE)**[11] 4295 9-10-0 **66** ow1 .... MrJackSalmon(5) 4 69
(J J Bridger) *led to jst over 2f out: one pce* **10/1**
/0-3 **5** *1¾* **Talenti (IRE)**[14] 4202 7-11-0 **75** ....(t) MissGAndrews 10 75
(Mrs Lawney Hill) *chsd ldng pair: rdn 3f out: stl on terms 2f out: grad fdd* **6/1**[3]
0230 **6** *hd* **James Pollard (IRE)**[21] 3954 5-9-2 **56** oh9 ....(t) MrRJWilliams(7) 7 55?
(B J Llewellyn) *v awkward s: in last pair tl prog 4f out: drvn along furiously and chsd ldrs 2f out: one pce fnl f* **40/1**
-165 **7** *2* **Ebiayn (FR)**[17] 4101 4-10-4 **70** ....(v[1]) MrJBanks(5) 8 66
(A King) *chsd ldrs in 6th: lost pl and struggling in rr 3f out: n.d after* **20/1**
-010 **8** *½* **Marju King (IRE)**[44] 3221 4-10-9 **70** .... MrSWalker 2 65
(W S Kittow) *hld up in 7th: rdn 3f out: no prog 2f out: wl btn whn hanging lft 1f out* **9/2**[2]
600- **9** *3¾* **Isabella Romee (IRE)**[352] 5031 4-9-2 **56** oh2 ...... MissAZetterholm(7) 11 45
(Jane Chapple-Hyam) *trckd ldrs in 5th: pushed along 3f out: steadily wknd* **25/1**
3104 **10** *10* **Soundbyte**[91] 1768 5-10-2 **68** .... MrKApark(5) 6 40
(J Gallagher) *sn last: lost tch 1/2-way: t.o* **14/1**
0302 **11** *17* **Celtic Dragon**[14] 4202 5-10-2 **63** .... MrsEEvans 5 6
(P D Evans) *a in rr: wknd 4f out: t.o* **9/1**

2m 31.31s (1.81) **Going Correction** +0.025s/f (Good) 11 Ran SP% **114.4**
Speed ratings (Par 103): **94,93,92,92,91 91,89,89,86,80 68**
Tote Swingers:1&2:£6.40, 2&3:£16.30, 1&3:£14.30 CSF £28.26 CT £186.24 TOTE £4.00: £1.50, £4.00, £2.80; EX 37.30 Trifecta £294.90 Pool £2,806.19 - 7.04 winning units..
Owner Alan Swinburne **Bred** Shadwell Estate Company Limited **Trained** Hook Norton, Oxon

FOCUS
The rails were dolled out from the stands' side so that the fields raced more towards the far side in the straight. An ordinary amateur riders' handicap featuring several familiar faces in this grade. The front pair are the best guides to the form.

4658 EUROPEAN BREEDERS' FUND MAIDEN FILLIES' STKS 6f
6:10 (6:11) (Class 4) 2-Y-O **£4,306** (£1,281; £640; £319) **Stalls** High

Form RPR
3 **1** **Native Picture (IRE)**[17] 4103 2-9-0 0 .... RichardHughes 15 73+
(R Hannon) *t.k.h: mde virtually all against nr side rail: shkn up over 1f out: pushed out fnl f* **6/5**[1]
2 *1¾* **Latin Lashes (USA)** 2-9-0 0 .... PatDobbs 9 67+
(R Hannon) *s.s: hld up in rr gng wl: prog on outer fr 2f out: pushed along and styd on wl fnl f to take 2nd nr fin: sddle slipped* **10/1**
00 **3** *hd* **Red Lite (IRE)**[17] 4095 2-9-0 0 .... MartinDwyer 2 66
(B J Meehan) *prom: chsd wnr 2f out: readily hld fnl f: lost 2nd nr fin* **10/1**
4 *¾* **My Little Star (IRE)** 2-9-0 0 .... TadhgO'Shea 1 64+
(B W Hills) *s.s: hld up in last trio: no prog tl 2f out: pushed along and r.o wl fnl f: nrest at fin* **8/1**[3]
5 *1½* **Jonelha** 2-9-0 0 .... LiamJones 3 59
(P W D'Arcy) *prom on outer: shkn up to dispute 2nd 2f out to 1f out: wknd* **50/1**
6 *1* **Queen Of Cash (IRE)** 2-9-0 0 .... RyanMoore 13 56+
(H Morrison) *s.s: off the pce towards rr: pushed along bef 1/2-way: no prog and wl btn 2f out: styd on fnl f* **5/2**[2]
00 **7** *1* **Make My Mark (IRE)**[14] 4203 2-9-0 0 .... AndreaAtzeni 8 53
(Pat Eddery) *t.k.h: mostly chsd wnr to 2f out: grad wknd* **66/1**
0 **8** *1½* **Complicate**[35] 3517 2-9-0 0 .... SebSanders 14 48
(Andrew Reid) *chsd ldrs against nr side rail: shkn up over 2f out: sn outpcd: one pce after* **100/1**
9 *2¼* **Cloud Illusions (USA)** 2-9-0 0 .... ChrisCatlin 6 41
(Mrs H S Main) *dwlt and squeezed out s: detached in last: taken to wd outside over 2f out: pushed along and kpt on* **80/1**
10 *1* **Talkative Guest (IRE)** 2-9-0 0 .... TomQueally 12 38
(G G Margarson) *in tch in midfield to 2f out: grad wknd* **33/1**
11 *2¼* **Barbieri (IRE)** 2-9-0 0 .... SteveDrowne 4 30
(J R Gask) *t.k.h: chsd ldrs and wl in tch tl wknd 2f out* **33/1**
00 **12** *2½* **Thank You Joy**[26] 3778 2-9-0 0 .... GregFairley 5 22
(J R Jenkins) *sn rdn in last trio: nvr a factor* **100/1**
13 *½* **Dorothy's Dancing (IRE)** 2-9-0 0 .... FergusSweeney 10 21
(G L Moore) *chsd ldrs and wl in tch tl pushed along and wknd 2f out: eased* **40/1**
00 **14** *5* **Veuveveuvevoom**[19] 4029 2-8-11 0 .... Louis-PhilippeBeuzelin(3) 11 5
(G P Enright) *pressed ldrs to over 2f out: wknd rapidly: sddle slipped* **150/1**

1m 13.86s (0.86) **Going Correction** +0.025s/f (Good) 14 Ran SP% **119.0**
Speed ratings (Par 93): **95,92,92,91,89 88,86,84,81,80 77,74,73,66**
Tote Swingers: 1&2 £1.30, 1&3 £5.10, 2&3 £23.20 CSF £14.36 TOTE £1.90: £1.10, £1.50, £2.80; EX 7.70 Trifecta £52.80 Pool £3,036.95 - 42.56 winning units..
Owner Malih L Al Basti **Bred** P McCutcheon **Trained** East Everleigh, Wilts
■ Stewards' Enquiry : Martin Dwyer one-day ban: careless riding (Aug 16)

FOCUS
A big field for this juvenile maiden with a number of interesting runners, including two from the pre-eminent Hannon yard. The market was only about five but heavy support for the newcomer Queen Of Cash resulted in the Hannon-trained favourite going off at odds against. The winner is rated a length up on her debut form.

NOTEBOOK
Native Picture(IRE), a half-sister to Kingsgate Native, had made a nice debut over a furlong further and made no mistake from the rail draw here. Always in the leading trio, she went on 2f out and eventually scored comfortably. She should be capable of winning a nursery after this. (op 8-11 tchd 5-4 and 4-6 in places)
Latin Lashes(USA) ◆, a stable companion of the winner, is out of a half-sister to a Breeders' Cup Mile winner. She came from off the pace to take second place inside the last furlong without being knocked about, and should come on a good deal for the experience. The rider reported the saddle slipped in the last few strides. Official explanation: jockey said saddle slipped (op 9-1 tchd 8-1)
Red Lite(IRE), whose trainer won this twice early this century with similar types, ran her best race so far and now qualifies for a handicap mark. (op 12-1 tchd 9-1)
My Little Star(IRE) ◆ was another to catch the eye on her debut. Related to winners at various trips, she missed the break from the outside stall but really picked up once getting the hang of things in the final quarter-mile, and finished on the heels of the placed horses. She should come on a lot for the outing. (op 9-1 tchd 15-2)
Jonelha, a speedily bred filly whose half-brother won over C&D on his debut, looked like emulating her sibling when coming to challenge 2f out, before fading in the closing stages. She has clearly inherited some ability and should build on this. She might appreciate a drop to the minimum trip in the short-term.
Queen Of Cash(IRE), the plunge horse, blew her chance by missing the break and going left at the start. She was behind and looked to be going nowhere over 2f out but ran on late under hands and heels riding, and her shrewd yard can expect to recover losses sooner rather than later. (op 11-2 tchd 6-1)

Veuveveuvevoom's rider reported that the saddle slipped. Official explanation: jockey said saddle slipped

4659 SPORTINGBET.COM H'CAP 5f 10y
6:40 (6:40) (Class 5) (0-70,69) 3-Y-0+ £2,456 (£725; £362) Stalls High

Form RPR
46-0 1 **Imaginary Diva**[20] 3994 4-8-9 52 ... TomQueally 2 60
(G G Margarson) *chsd ldrs: hrd rdn on outer of gp to chal fnl f: styd on to ld nr fin* 12/1
153 2 hd **Doctor Hilary**[17] 4099 8-9-8 65 ... ChrisCatlin 10 72
(M R Hoad) *chsd ldrs: hrd rdn over 1f out: hung lft but styd on wl fnl f: tk 2nd post* 8/1
3134 3 hd **Wanchai Whisper**[25] 3834 3-9-1 64 ...(p) AndrewHeffernan(3) 9 69
(P R Hedger) *dwlt: hld up in tch: hmpd after 2f: drvn and prog to ld narrowly over 1f out: hung lft fnl f: hdd nr fin* 13/2
0-60 4 1/2 **Six Wives**[38] 3410 3-9-2 62 ... IanMongan 7 65
(J A Glover) *pressed ldr: upsides over 1f out: edgd lft and nt qckn ins fnl f* 40/1
2242 5 nk **Wreningham**[20] 3994 5-8-10 60 ... RyanClark(7) 6 63
(S C Williams) *swtchd to r alone on far side: nt on terms over 1f out: styd on ins fnl f: gaining at fin* 7/2[2]
6562 6 1 **Colorus (IRE)**[4] 4518 7-9-9 66 ...(p) RichardHughes 1 67
(W J R Ratcliffe) *trckd ldrs: hrd rdn to chal over 1f out: nt qckn ins fnl f: eased whn hld last 75yds* 3/1[1]
6655 7 1/2 **The Tatling (IRE)**[4] 4518 13-9-7 67 ... JackDean(3) 4 65
(J M Bradley) *dwlt: a struggling to get on terms w ldrs: no prog over 1f out: kpt on* 8/1
016 8 hd **Blessed Place**[10] 4343 10-8-9 55 ... MartinLane(3) 8 52
(D J S Ffrench Davis) *led to over 1f out: sn btn* 16/1
6205 9 2 1/4 **Leleyf (IRE)**[11] 4284 3-9-9 69 ... RyanMoore 3 57
(M R Channon) *a in rr: hrd rdn and no prog over 1f out* 11/2[3]

60.04 secs (-0.26) **Going Correction** +0.025s/f (Good)
WFA 3 from 4yo+ 3lb 9 Ran SP% 114.2
Speed ratings (Par 103): **103,102,102,101,101 99,98,98,94**
Tote Swingers: 1&2 £70.60, 1&3 £13.60, 2&3 £8.30 CSF £102.52 CT £685.53 TOTE £10.50: £3.70, £4.50, £2.20; EX 141.20 Trifecta £647.70 Pool £2,275.88 - 2.60 winning units..
Owner Graham Lodge Partnership **Bred** Norcroft Park Stud **Trained** Newmarket, Suffolk
■ Stewards' Enquiry : Andrew Heffernan three-day ban: careless riding (Aug 16, 18,21)

FOCUS
A modest sprint handicap with a couple of three-year-olds taking on a number of old-stagers. The pace was good but not a race to be too positive about, with the third the best guide.
Colorus(IRE) Official explanation: jockey said gelding was denied a clear run at finish

4660 FOOTBALL FURLONG 8TH AUGUST H'CAP 1m 67y
7:10 (7:10) (Class 4) (0-85,85) 3-Y-0+ £4,533 (£1,348; £674; £336) Stalls High

Form RPR
002 1 **Be Invincible (IRE)**[53] 2888 3-8-13 77 ... RyanMoore 1 92
(B W Hills) *chsd ldng pair: drvn and no imp over 2f out: r.o to ld jst over 1f out: styd on strly* 11/10[1]
2004 2 5 **Our Boy Barrington (IRE)**[10] 4325 3-8-9 73 ... RichardHughes 6 77
(R Hannon) *trckd ldr: led 2f out: drvn over 1f out: sn hdd and lft bhd* 7/2[2]
0060 3 1 1/2 **Majuro (IRE)**[26] 3796 6-10-0 85 ... TedDurcan 7 86
(C F Wall) *rousted along to ld and then plld hrd in front: hdd 2f out: lft bhd fnl f* 5/1[3]
323 4 8 **Bitter Fortune (USA)**[18] 4069 3-8-12 76 ...(p) SebSanders 4 58
(J Noseda) *hld up in tch: rdn and no rspnse over 2f out: wknd over 1f out* 6/1
000- 5 1 1/2 **Voortrekker**[287] 6908 4-8-10 67 ... TadhgO'Shea 5 46
(D J Coakley) *hld up in last: rdn and fnd nil over 2f out: racd awkwardly after* 25/1
64-0 6 7 **Magnus Thrax (USA)**[121] 1086 3-9-0 78 ... PatDobbs 8 40
(R Hannon) *in tch: reminders 1/2-way: wknd over 2f out: sn wl bhd* 11/1

1m 44.22s (-0.48) **Going Correction** +0.025s/f (Good)
WFA 3 from 4yo+ 7lb 6 Ran SP% 113.0
Speed ratings (Par 105): **103,98,96,88,87 80**
Tote Swingers:1&2:£1.02, 2&3:£5.40, 1&3:£2.60 CSF £5.27 CT £12.52 TOTE £2.30: £1.80, £2.50; EX 7.50 Trifecta £18.20 Pool £5,206.93 - 210.59 winning units..
Owner A L R Morton & John C Grant **Bred** Jaykayenn Syndicate **Trained** Lambourn, Berks

FOCUS
A couple of withdrawals reduced the field to six and they finished well strung out. The winner was impressive but the form behind is on the weak side.

4661 SPORTINGBET.COM MAIDEN STKS 1m 2f 7y
7:40 (7:44) (Class 5) 3-4-Y-0 £2,456 (£725; £362) Stalls Low

Form RPR
1 **Fox Hunt (IRE)** 3-9-3 0 ... GregFairley 6 90+
(M Johnston) *a ldng trio: shkn up to ld wl over 1f out: drew rt away fr one pce rivals* 12/1[3]
2 8 **Flower Fairy (USA)** 3-8-12 0 ... NickyMackay 13 69+
(J H M Gosden) *dwlt: hld up wl in rr: prog on wd outside fr 4f out: shkn up 2f out: styd on to take 2nd fnl f* 7/1[1]
44 3 1 1/4 **Minikin (IRE)**[17] 4115 3-8-12 0 ... SteveDrowne 15 66+
(H Morrison) *hld up in midfield: pushed along 3f out: kpt on steadily fnl 2f to take 3rd nr fin* 15/2[2]
0 4 1/2 **Warlu Way**[11] 4307 3-9-3 0 ... TedDurcan 11 70+
(J L Dunlop) *hld up in midfield: gng wl enough 3f out: pushed along and one pce fnl 2f* 18/1
0 5 1/2 **Tattler**[53] 2900 3-9-3 0 ... RichardHughes 2 69
(M Johnston) *mde most to wl over 1f out: grad fdd fnl f* 22/1
04 6 nse **Aldo**[27] 3766 3-9-3 0 ...(t) TomQueally 14 69
(A J Lidderdale) *hld up in midfield: taken to wd outside over 2f out: hanging lft after: one pce* 14/1
0 7 1 1/2 **Epernay**[17] 4114 3-8-12 0 ... ShaneKelly 1 61
(Ian Williams) *trckd ldrs: cl enough over 2f out: wknd over 1f out* 100/1
0 8 3 **Immovable (USA)**[11] 4307 3-9-3 0 ... FergusSweeney 8 60
(M A Magnusson) *trckd ldrs: rdn over 2f out: wknd wl over 1f out* 25/1
9 1 1/4 **Present Story** 3-8-8 0w1 ... MarkCoumbe(5) 4 53
(P Leech) *t.k.h: hld up in rr: reminders 2f out: swtchd lft over 1f out: nvr a factor* 100/1
10 3 1/4 **Zawadi** 3-8-12 0 ... JimCrowley 12 46
(R M Beckett) *slowest away: hld up in last pair: pushed along 3f out: nvr on terms* 20/1
44 11 nk **Pebble Beech (IRE)**[11] 4294 3-8-12 0 ... LiamJones 7 45
(W J Haggas) *mostly chsd ldr to over 2f out: wknd rapidly over 1f out* 20/1
12 2 **Fashion Lady (IRE)** 3-8-12 0 ... SebSanders 16 41
(C F Wall) *hld up in rr: pushed along and no prog over 2f out* 28/1
0-6 13 13 **Clifton Encore (USA)**[25] 3816 3-8-12 0 ... RichardKingscote 5 15
(Tom Dascombe) *plld hrd early: in tch tl wknd over 3f out: t.o* 80/1
0- 14 7 **Bravo Bravo**[325] 5831 3-9-3 0 ... ChrisCatlin 10 6
(M R Channon) *a in last pair and nvr gng wl: t.o* 66/1

2m 8.97s (0.27) **Going Correction** +0.025s/f (Good) 14 Ran SP% 69.8
Speed ratings (Par 103): **99,92,91,91,90 90,89,87,86,83 83,81,71,65**
Tote Swingers:1&2:£2.50, 2&3:£5.70, 1&3:£5.10 CSF £24.72 TOTE £7.60: £2.10, £1.80, £1.70; EX 33.30 Trifecta £64.20 Part won. Pool £86.86 - 0.33 winning units..
Owner Sheikh Hamdan Bin Mohammed Al Maktoum **Bred** Ballylinch Stud **Trained** Middleham Moor, N Yorks
■ Pickwick (Evens) and Pre Raphaelite (100-1) were withdrawn. Rules 4 applies, deduction 45p in the £ to all bets.

FOCUS
Another big field of inexperienced horses for this three-year-old maiden, which in its short history has invariably fallen to a major stable. Once again several big yards were represented but the market suggested it was an uncompetitive race with the market going 16/1 bar four. However, the betting was thrown into disarray when the hot favourite Pickwick was one of two withdrawn at the start, having played up in the stalls, and there was a massive deduction. The winner was impressive and the form is taken at face value rated around the third and sixth.
Aldo Official explanation: jockey said colt hung badly left in straight

4662 A C BECK H'CAP 6f
8:10 (8:11) (Class 5) (0-75,75) 3-Y-0+ £2,593 (£765; £383) Stalls High

Form RPR
203- 1 **Boogie Diva**[300] 6567 3-9-7 75 ... IvaMilickova 2 85
(Jane Chapple-Hyam) *hld up in last pair: taken to wd outside fr 1/2-way: gd prog fr 2f out: led 1f out: ended up against far rail: styd on* 16/1
3036 2 1 **Bold Tie**[26] 3779 4-9-10 74 ... RichardHughes 9 82
(R Hannon) *trckd ldng pair: rdn to ld 2f out against rail: hdd 1f out: one pce* 10/3[1]
6120 3 2 **Alfresco**[38] 3401 6-9-9 73 ...(b) TedDurcan 3 75
(J R Best) *trckd ldng pair: rdn 2f out: cl enough over 1f out: hung lft and one pce fnl f* 8/1
531 4 hd **Gwilym (GER)**[49] 3037 7-9-8 72 ... JimCrowley 11 73+
(D Haydn Jones) *t.k.h: hld up in midfield against rail: looking for room over 2f out: rdn and kpt on fr over 1f out: nvr nr to chal* 9/2[2]
1100 5 1 1/2 **Timeteam (IRE)**[7] 4430 4-9-6 73 ... RichardEvans(3) 7 69+
(P D Evans) *s.v.s: hld up wl in rr: effrt against rail whn hmpd 1f out: running on at fin* 28/1
1030 6 nk **Charles Darwin (IRE)**[32] 3584 7-9-1 65 ... SteveDrowne 6 60
(M Blanshard) *trckd ldng pair: rdn wl over 1f out: grad wknd* 14/1
2200 7 1 1/4 **Silver Wind**[3] 4558 5-9-8 75 ...(v) MartinLane(3) 4 66+
(P D Evans) *blindfold removed late and missed break completely: drvn thrght: rchd midfield 1/2-way: wknd over 1f out* 15/2
6302 8 1 1/4 **Whiskey Junction**[14] 4209 6-9-11 75 ... SebSanders 8 62
(M Quinn) *led 2f: led again briefly over 2f out: wknd over 1f out* 7/1[3]
2040 9 3/4 **Coolree Star (IRE)**[17] 4121 3-9-2 70 ... ChrisCatlin 10 54
(J A Glover) *in tch in midfield: rdn over 2f out: wknd wl over 1f out* 20/1
0021 10 2 3/4 **Army Of Stars (IRE)**[19] 4024 4-9-4 73 ...(p) SophieDoyle(5) 5 49
(J A Osborne) *led after 2f to over 2f out: wknd rapidly* 8/1
5-60 11 1/2 **C'Mon You Irons (IRE)**[49] 3037 5-9-7 71 ... IanMongan 1 45
(M R Hoad) *hld up in tch: shkn up over 2f out: sn wknd* 12/1

1m 12.65s (-0.35) **Going Correction** +0.025s/f (Good)
WFA 3 from 4yo+ 4lb 11 Ran SP% 116.2
Speed ratings (Par 103): **103,101,99,98,96 96,94,93,92,88 87**
Tote Swingers:1&2:£60.80, 2&3:£18.80, 1&3:£62.00 CSF £68.04 CT £478.83 TOTE £14.30: £3.30, £1.90, £2.00; EX 55.50 Trifecta £481.30 Part won. Pool £650.47 - 0.50 winning units. Place 6 £53.81, Place 5 £24.98..
Owner Norcroft Park Stud **Bred** Norcroft Park Stud **Trained** Dalham, Suffolk
■ The first winner in Britain for Czech rider Iva Milickova.
■ Stewards' Enquiry : Jim Crowley two-day ban: careless riding (Aug 16,18)

FOCUS
In the history of this sprint low numbers had the better record, with only one of the six runnings falling to a double-figure stall. The trend continued with the winner coming from stall two. The runner-up is rated to recent form and sets the standard.
Silver Wind Official explanation: jockey said he was slow to remove blindfold
T/Jkpt: Not won. T/Plt: £26.00 to a £1 stake. Pool:£83,219.61 - 2,335.31 winning tickets T/Qpdt: £8.30 to a £1 stake. Pool:£7,808.94 - 696.07 winning tickets JN

4663 - 4667a (Foreign Racing) - See Raceform Interactive

4240 CATTERICK (L-H)
Tuesday, August 3

OFFICIAL GOING: Good to firm (good in places; 8.4)
Wind: Light 1/2 behind Weather: fine

4668 EUROPEAN BREEDERS' FUND MAIDEN STKS 7f
2:00 (2:01) (Class 5) 2-Y-0 £2,784 (£828; £414; £206) Stalls Low

Form RPR
1 **Campos (IRE)**[12] 4309 2-9-3 0 ... ShaneKelly 6 76
(T Stack, Ire) *chsd ldrs: wnt 2nd over 3f out: rdn to ld jst ins fnl f: edgd lft: drvn out* 1/1[1]
02 2 1 3/4 **Janet's Pearl (IRE)**[7] 4447 2-8-9 0 ... BarryMcHugh(3) 5 66
(Mrs A Duffield) *led: hdd jst ins fnl f: no ex* 11/4[2]
00 3 3/4 **Better Self**[13] 4240 2-8-12 0 ... SilvestreDeSousa 4 64+
(Mrs A Duffield) *drvn to chse ldrs: wnt 3rd 2f out: styd on ins fnl f* 25/1
4 3 **Phoenix Flame** 2-8-12 0 ... AndrewMullen 1 56
(A J McCabe) *s.s: hdwy 3f out: hung rt and kpt on fnl f* 80/1
00 5 4 1/2 **Regimental (IRE)**[10] 4368 2-9-3 0 ... PhillipMakin 10 49
(Mrs A Duffield) *in rr: hdwy over 2f out: kpt on fnl f* 80/1
0 6 3/4 **Marie Du Plessis**[17] 4149 2-8-12 0 ... JoeFanning 8 42
(M Johnston) *s.i.s: sn chsng ldrs: hung lft over 1f out: sn wknd* 14/1
0 7 3/4 **Hartforth**[24] 3923 2-9-3 0 ... GrahamGibbons 9 45
(J D Bethell) *chsd ldrs: drvn 4f out: wknd fnl 2f* 40/1
06 8 8 **Red Oleander**[12] 4299 2-8-12 0 ... PaulMulrennan 11 18
(Sir Mark Prescott) *s.i.s: in rr: bhd fnl 2f* 16/1
9 nk **White Fusion** 2-9-3 0 ... TomEaves 2 22
(J Howard Johnson) *mid-div: t.k.h: drvn over 3f out: sn lost pl* 9/1[3]
60 10 1 3/4 **Playful Girl (IRE)**[19] 4048 2-8-12 0 ... DavidAllan 3 13
(T D Easterby) *a in rr: bhd fnl 2f* 40/1
00 11 2 **Salagadoola**[40] 3365 2-8-12 0 ... DuranFentiman 7 7
(T D Easterby) *s.i.s: a bhd* 150/1

1m 27.49s (0.49) **Going Correction** 0.0s/f (Good) 11 Ran SP% 111.1
Speed ratings (Par 94): **97,95,94,90,85 84,83,74,74,72 70**
toteswingers:1&2:£2.10, 1&3:£6.70, 2&3:£8.70 CSF £3.16 TOTE £2.10: £1.20, £1.20, £4.40; EX 4.10.
Owner J A Stack **Bred** James Stack & J P Spencer Ltd **Trained** Golden, Co Tipperary

FOCUS
This was a modest maiden, but seven of these now qualify for nurseries so may improve for the switch to that company. The form is rated around the runner-up.

NOTEBOOK
Campos(IRE) had already run well in a couple of Irish maidens that have already produced winners and probably didn't need to step up much on that form in order to take this. He did flash his tail a couple of times after taking it up a furlong from home, which suggests that he is still not yet the finished article, so he may still have more to offer in nurseries if connections decide on that route. (op 5-4, tchd 11-8 in places)

Janet's Pearl(IRE), narrowly beaten at 33-1 in a Beverley maiden on her second outing seven days earlier, was given a positive ride and though taken on by Hartforth in the early part of the contest, she kept on gamely to the line if no match for the winner. She is another that now qualifies for nurseries. (op 5-2)

Better Self, who had been well beaten in two 6f maidens here, ran much better this time especially as she had to be rousted along to take a handy position early and tended to hang out into the centre of the track inside the last 2f. She is yet another interesting prospect for nurseries. (op 28-1)

Phoenix Flame, out of a 1m4f winner and one of two newcomers in the race, did some pleasing late work after missing the break. From a stable not renowned for winning juvenile debutants, she will appreciate a stiffer test in due course. (op 66-1)

Regimental(IRE), a stable companion of both the second and third and well beaten in his first two starts, made some late progress up the inside rail and this was an improvement.

White Fusion pulled hard early and then looked awkward taking the home bend. A 68,000gns half-brother to three winners at up to 7f, he needs more time. (tchd 10-1)

4669 YORKSHIRE4X4.COM ADVENTURE ACTIVITIES (S) STKS — 1m 7f 177y
2:30 (2:31) (Class 6) 3-5-Y-O — £1,706 (£503; £252) Stalls Low

Form — RPR

0064 **1** **Lava Lamp (GER)**[15] 4200 3-8-7 61 (v) SilvestreDeSousa 2 — 69
(G A Harker) *dwlt: hld up: hdwy to chse ldrs 4f out: wnt 2nd over 1f out: styd on to ld jst ins fnl f: eased towards fin* **13/8**[2]

01-0 **2** 2 1/4 **Shannersburg (IRE)**[37] 280 5-9-8 63 (t) PaulHanagan 1 — 66
(Ian Williams) *trckd ldrs: wnt 2nd 4f out: led over 2f out: edgd lft: hdd jst ins fnl f: no ex* **7/2**[3]

4623 **3** 4 1/2 **Strikemaster (IRE)**[59] 2765 4-9-3 64 (b) DaleSwift(5) 4 — 61
(B Ellison) *trckd ldrs: wnt 2nd after 6f: led over 6f out: drvn over 4f out: hdd over 2f out: one pce* **11/8**[1]

-060 **4** 10 **Lady Norlela**[13] 4246 4-9-3 44 TomEaves 6 — 44
(B S Rothwell) *hld up in last: effrt over 3f out: hung lft over 1f out: sn wknd* **33/1**

0-00 **5** 17 **Napoletano (ITY)**[40] 3369 4-9-3 39 (t) LeeTopliss(5) 3 — 29
(R Johnson) *led 1f: trckd ldrs: lost pl over 3f out: sn bhd* **100/1**

60-0 **6** 32 **Magneto (IRE)**[12] 4300 3-8-7 55 (t) JoeFanning 5 — —
(E J Creighton) *led after 1f: hdd over 6f out: lost pl over 3f out: sn bhd: t.o* **40/1**

3m 33.81s (1.81) **Going Correction** 0.0s/f (Good)
WFA 3 from 4yo+ 15lb — 6 Ran SP% **108.8**
Speed ratings (Par 101): **95,93,91,86,78 62**
toteswingers:1&2:£1.50, 1&3:£1.20, 2&3:£1.50 CSF £7.10 TOTE £2.10: £1.10, £1.60; EX 8.10.There was no bid for the winner.
Owner An Englishman, Irishman & Scotsman **Bred** Graf And Grafin Von Stauffenberg **Trained** Thirkleby, N Yorks

■ Stewards' Enquiry : Paul Hanagan caution: careless riding.

FOCUS
A weak seller and they went no pace until the tempo quickened after halfway. Hard form to pin down, and it has been rated a bit negatively.

4670 13TH AUGUST IS LADIES EVENING H'CAP — 5f 212y
3:00 (3:01) (Class 5) (0-75,75) 3-Y-O+ — £2,072 (£616; £308; £153) Stalls Low

Form — RPR

4305 **1** **Night Trade (IRE)**[12] 4288 3-9-5 75 (p) JamesO'Reilly(5) 8 — 85
(Mrs D J Sanderson) *trckd ldrs: t.k.h: stmbld over 3f out: led over 1f out: styd on wl* **9/2**[2]

0260 **2** 1 **Mandalay King (IRE)**[11] 4345 5-9-7 68 PJMcDonald 7 — 76
(Mrs Marjorie Fife) *in rr: hdwy 2f out: styd on wl to take 2nd clsng stages* **9/2**[2]

6640 **3** 3/4 **Slikback Jack (IRE)**[39] 3409 3-9-7 72 PaulMulrennan 1 — 76
(J A Glover) *mid-div: hdwy over 2f out: n.m.r on inner over 1f out: kpt on wl* **11/1**

0056 **4** 1 **Klynch**[6] 4486 4-9-1 65 (b) JamesSullivan(3) 9 — 67
(Mrs R A Carr) *mid-div: effrt over 2f out: kpt on fnl f* **14/1**

-043 **5** 1 1/4 **Dancing Red Devil (IRE)**[18] 4091 3-9-8 73 SilvestreDeSousa 5 — 70
(Paul Green) *in rr: drvn 4f out: hmpd on ins over 1f out: kpt on fnl f* **5/1**[3]

2332 **6** 1/2 **Minturno (USA)**[6] 4486 4-8-12 62 BarryMcHugh(3) 2 — 59+
(Mrs A Duffield) *s.i.s: hld up in last: hdwy 2f out: swtchd ins and n.m.r over 1f out: nvr rchd ldrs* **7/2**[1]

2010 **7** hd **Chambers (IRE)**[25] 3855 4-8-8 58 PaulPickard(3) 6 — 54
(E J Alston) *w ldrs: chal over 2f out: fdd fnl f* **14/1**

1000 **8** 2 3/4 **Wyatt Earp (IRE)**[24] 3898 9-9-8 74 (p) TobyAtkinson(5) 4 — 61
(P Salmon) *led: hdd over 1f out: sn wknd* **8/1**

3000 **9** 1/2 **Grand Stitch (USA)**[9] 4415 4-9-1 69 NeilFarley(7) 3 — 55
(D Carroll) *w ldrs: lost pl over 1f out* **33/1**

1m 13.12s (-0.48) **Going Correction** 0.0s/f (Good)
WFA 3 from 4yo+ 4lb — 9 Ran SP% **111.0**
Speed ratings (Par 103): **103,101,100,99,97 97,96,93,92**
toteswingers:1&2:£4.50, 1&3:£10.70, 2&3:£11.80 CSF £23.54 CT £199.53 TOTE £6.40: £2.60, £1.10, £4.90; EX 22.30.
Owner R J Budge **Bred** John Foley **Trained** Wiseton, Notts

■ Stewards' Enquiry : Barry McHugh two-day ban: careless riding (Aug 18,21)

FOCUS
A modest handicap and quite a rough race. The early pace was quick, but the leaders may have gone off too fast as the front three at halfway were the last three home. The form looks sound.

4671 RACINGUK.COM H'CAP — 1m 5f 175y
3:30 (3:31) (Class 4) (0-85,82) 3-Y-O+ — £3,691 (£1,098; £548; £274) Stalls Low

Form — RPR

-261 **1** **Bergonzi (IRE)**[27] 3772 6-9-11 79 PaulMulrennan 4 — 85
(J Howard Johnson) *led after 2f: qcknd 4f out: hld on wl towards fin* **7/4**[1]

-010 **2** 3/4 **Sir Royal (USA)**[41] 3319 5-9-9 77 TomEaves 1 — 82
(G A Swinbank) *trckd ldrs: effrt over 3f out: sn outpcd: rallied over 2f out: edgd lft and styd on to take 2nd nr fin* **7/2**[3]

4402 **3** 3/4 **Akbabend**[17] 4147 4-10-0 82 JoeFanning 2 — 86
(M Johnston) *led 2f: chsd wnr: pushed along 4f out: styng on same pce whn n.m.r and eased nr fin* **2/1**[2]

6-40 **4** 9 **Autumn Harvest**[15] 4196 6-9-4 72 SilvestreDeSousa 5 — 63
(G A Harker) *led to s: stdd s: effrt over 3f out: nvr a threat: eased fnl 100yds* **5/1**

3m 4.45s (0.85) **Going Correction** 0.0s/f (Good)
WFA 3 from 4yo+ 13lb — 4 Ran SP% **108.6**
Speed ratings (Par 105): **97,96,96,91**
CSF £7.89 TOTE £2.40; EX 6.20.
Owner Transcend Bloodstock LLP **Bred** Deer Forest Stud **Trained** Billy Row, Co Durham

FOCUS
A fair handicap despite the small field, run at an even pace. The form seems sound.
Autumn Harvest Official explanation: trainer said gelding had a breathing problem

4672 GORACING.CO.UK H'CAP — 5f
4:00 (4:00) (Class 6) (0-60,60) 3-Y-O+ — £2,047 (£604; £302) Stalls Low

Form — RPR

2-06 **1** **Alacity (IRE)**[11] 4342 4-9-2 55 FrannyNorton 7 — 64
(N Bycroft) *in tch: outpcd 3f out: hdwy over 1f out: crowded: styd on to ld nr fin* **16/1**

4052 **2** 3/4 **Raccoon (IRE)**[13] 4245 10-9-7 60 PJMcDonald 11 — 66
(Mrs R A Carr) *hld up on outer: hdwy over 2f out: chsng ldrs whn hung lft 1f out: upsides whn hung rt clsng stages* **8/1**

/66- **3** nk **Ballarina**[432] 2394 4-8-7 46 DuranFentiman 6 — 51
(E J Alston) *led: edgd lft over 1f out: hdd towards fin* **20/1**

4641 **4** 1 **Fashion Icon (USA)**[19] 4047 4-8-10 49 SilvestreDeSousa 2 — 50
(D O'Meara) *chsd ldrs: kpt on same pce appr fnl f* **3/1**[1]

0320 **5** 1 **Kyzer Chief**[7] 4452 5-9-1 59 DaleSwift(5) 4 — 60+
(R E Barr) *prom: hdwy and n.m.r over 1f out: styd on same pce fnl f* **11/2**[3]

5054 **6** nk **Pressed For Time (IRE)**[13] 4256 4-8-9 48 (vt) KierenFallon 5 — 45
(E J Creighton) *chsd ldrs: 2nd over 1f out: wknd fnl 75yds* **11/2**[3]

2300 **7** hd **Loss Leader (IRE)**[3] 4605 3-8-12 54 (p) PaulHanagan 8 — 49
(T D Easterby) *sn outpcd and in rr: kpt on fnl f: nvr a factor* **12/1**

455- **8** 1/2 **Maragna (IRE)**[243] 7619 3-8-1 46 oh1 JamesSullivan(3) 10 — 39
(Paul Green) *in rr: kpt on wl fnl f* **18/1**

0500 **9** 1 1/4 **Spirit Of Coniston**[5] 4516 7-9-2 55 PhillipMakin 14 — 45+
(P T Midgley) *in rr on outside: hdwy and hung lft over 1f out: keeping on whn nt clr run and swtchd rt nr fin: no ex* **28/1**

2026 **10** hd **Baby Queen (IRE)**[19] 4041 4-9-3 56 J-PGuillambert 1 — 45
(B P J Baugh) *chsd ldrs: outpcd 1/2-way: rallied over 1f out: wknd ins fnl f* **4/1**[2]

-20U **11** shd **Azygous**[21] 3977 7-8-6 52 (b) DavidSimmonson(7) 9 — 41
(G P Kelly) *chsd ldrs: wkng whn hmpd jst ins fnl f* **40/1**

60.12 secs (0.32) **Going Correction** 0.0s/f (Good)
WFA 3 from 4yo+ 3lb — 11 Ran SP% **116.4**
Speed ratings (Par 101): **97,95,95,93,92 91,91,90,88,88 88**
toteswingers:1&2:£14.00, 1&3:£42.80, 2&3:£22.50 CSF £133.90 CT £2610.52 TOTE £26.70: £5.80, £1.80, £8.20; EX 128.10.
Owner Mrs J Dickinson **Bred** Camogue Stud Ltd **Trained** Brandsby, N Yorks

FOCUS
A modest sprint handicap run at a true pace. The four non-runners included those that would have started from stalls 12, 13 and 15. The form has a sound look to it.
Alacity(IRE) Official explanation: trainer said, regarding apparent improvement in form, that the filly broke better from the stalls.
Spirit Of Coniston Official explanation: jockey said gelding hung badly throughout
Baby Queen(IRE) Official explanation: jockey said filly never travelled

4673 TELEPHONE 01748 810165 TO BOOK HOSPITALITY CLAIMING STKS — 1m 3f 214y
4:30 (4:31) (Class 6) 3-Y-O+ — £1,706 (£503; £252) Stalls Low

Form — RPR

2311 **1** **Eijaaz (IRE)**[6] 4484 9-9-3 62 (p) SilvestreDeSousa 5 — 62
(G A Harker) *trckd ldrs: effrt over 2f out: led 1f out: drvn rt out* **1/2**[1]

0453 **2** hd **Jenny Soba**[16] 4174 7-8-13 43 RussKennemore(3) 7 — 61
(Lucinda Featherstone) *trckd ldr: chal over 4f out: led 3f out: hdd 1f out: rallied ins fnl f: jst hld* **11/1**

2045 **3** 2 1/4 **Lucayan Dancer**[20] 4015 10-8-10 65 DanielleMcCreery(5) 4 — 56
(N Bycroft) *hld up in tch: hdwy to trck ldrs 6f out: effrt 2f out: sn chsng 1st 2: kpt on same pce* **7/1**[3]

1565 **4** 13 **Sudden Impulse**[46] 3166 9-8-9 60 PaulHanagan 1 — 30
(A D Brown) *led tl 3f out: wknd fnl f* **7/2**[2]

0 **5** 57 **Dark Gem**[29] 3728 3-8-0 0 (p) PaulPickard(3) 2 — —
(S G West) *trckd ldrs: t.k.h: drvn and lost pl over 7f out: sn bhd: t.o 4f out: eased over 1f out* **66/1**

/0-6 **6** 11 **Bluebaru**[9] 4414 4-9-7 35 TobyAtkinson(5) 8 — —
(P Salmon) *dwlt: drvn and sme hdwy over 6f out: sn reminders: bhd 4f out: t.o whn eased over 1f out: virtually p.u towards fin* **150/1**

2m 39.22s (0.32) **Going Correction** 0.0s/f (Good)
WFA 3 from 4yo+ 11lb — 6 Ran SP% **111.9**
Speed ratings (Par 101): **98,97,96,87,49 42**
toteswingers:1&2:£2.00, 1&3:£1.80, 2&3:£2.60 CSF £7.49 TOTE £2.10: £1.60, £5.40; EX 6.40.
Owner A S Ward **Bred** Shadwell Estate Company Limited **Trained** Thirkleby, N Yorks

■ Stewards' Enquiry : Russ Kennemore one-day ban: used whip with excessive frequency (Aug 18)

FOCUS
Only four mattered in this weak and uncompetitive claimer. The form has been cautiously rated.

4674 BOOK NOW FOR SATURDAY 18TH SEPTEMBER H'CAP — 7f
5:00 (5:00) (Class 6) (0-65,64) 3-Y-O — £2,047 (£604; £302) Stalls Low

Form — RPR

4610 **1** **Ellies Image**[17] 4127 3-9-3 60 PaulHanagan 12 — 66
(B P J Baugh) *mid-div: hdwy 3f out: chal over 1f out: kpt on to ld nr fin* **3/1**[1]

6060 **2** hd **Sweet Mirasol (IRE)**[52] 2962 3-8-6 49 (t) JoeFanning 3 — 54
(Miss M E Rowland) *s.i.s: sn chsng ldrs: led appr fnl f: hdd towards fin* **14/1**

3244 **3** 1 1/2 **Powerful Pierre**[20] 4014 3-9-2 64 PatrickDonaghy(5) 9 — 65+
(Jedd O'Keeffe) *in rr: hdwy over 2f out: styd on fnl f* **6/1**

4065 **4** 1 3/4 **Regal Emperor (IRE)**[15] 4188 3-8-7 55 BillyCray(5) 14 — 51
(D Nicholls) *led: hdd appr fnl f: wknd towards fin* **9/1**

5460 **5** 3 **Kirkby's Gem**[9] 4406 3-8-2 45 PatrickMathers 1 — 33
(A Berry) *mid-div: effrt on ins over 2f out: nvr nr ldrs* **66/1**

0010 **6** nk **Choc'A'Moca (IRE)**[11] 4344 3-8-2 52 (v) NeilFarley(7) 11 — 39
(D Carroll) *mid-div: rdr lost rt-hand iron sn after s tl over 3f out: hdwy on outside 2f out: kpt on: nvr trbld ldrs* **9/2**[2]

5010 **7** hd **Thinking**[15] 4193 3-9-4 61 DuranFentiman 4 — 48
(T D Easterby) *trckd ldrs: fdd fnl 2f* **5/1**[3]

0640 **8** *1* **Dispol Kabira**[28] 3759 3-8-4 **47** ow1 AndrewElliott 6 31
(D W Thompson) *towards rr: sme hdwy 2f out: nvr a factor* **20/1**
005 **9** *5* **Royal Cheer**[24] 3900 3-8-5 **51** ow2 BarryMcHugh(3) 7 22
(Mrs A Duffield) *in rr: sme hdwy on ins over 2f out: sn wknd* **25/1**
5000 **10** *½* **Cookie Galore**[18] 4109 3-8-4 **47** AndrewMullen 2 16
(J A Glover) *rrd and s.v.s: a bhd* **22/1**
5200 **11** *1½* **Rescent**[11] 4337 3-8-0 **46** (b1) JamesSullivan(3) 8 11
(Mrs R A Carr) *chsd ldrs: lost pl over 3f out* **10/1**
1m 27.74s (0.74) **Going Correction** 0.0s/f (Good) **11** Ran SP% **114.3**
Speed ratings (Par 98): **95,94,93,91,87 87,87,85,80,79 77**
toteswingers:1&2:£11.00, 1&3:£4.50, 2&3:£15.50 CSF £43.59 CT £240.57 TOTE £3.70: £2.10, £3.50, £1.30; EX 52.90 Place 6 £140.03, Place 5 £114.16..
Owner F Gillespie **Bred** Miss S M Potts **Trained** Audley, Staffs

FOCUS
A weak handicap. The progressive winner produced a personal best.
Choc'A'Moca(IRE) Official explanation: jockey said he lost an iron shortly after leaving stalls
Cookie Galore Official explanation: jockey said filly reared as stalls opened
T/Plt: £232.60 to a £1 stake. Pool:£50,295.48 - 157.81 winning tickets T/Qpdt: £77.30 to a £1 stake. Pool:£3,552.30 - 34.00 winning tickets WG

4323 CHEPSTOW (L-H)
Tuesday, August 3

OFFICIAL GOING: Good (good to firm in places) changing to good (good to soft in places) after race 2 (2.45)
Wind: Virtually nil Weather: bright/showers

4675 RHOMCO CONSULTING LTD MEDIAN AUCTION MAIDEN FILLIES' STKS 5f 16y
2:15 (2:15) (Class 5) 2-Y-O **£2,460** (£732; £365; £182) **Stalls** Centre

Form RPR
533 **1** **Scommettitrice (IRE)**[7] 4451 2-9-0 0 TomMcLaughlin 1 72+
(R A Harris) *racd far side: chsd ldrs: swtchd rt ins fnl 2f: led jst ins fnl f: readily* **7/1**
2 *3* **Kilk** 2-9-0 0 FergusSweeney 4 61
(A G Newcombe) *chsd ldrs towards centre crse: rdn and styd on fr 2f out: kpt on fnl f: tk 2nd last strides: no ch w wnr* **50/1**
6332 **3** *nk* **Upark Flyer**[10] 4363 2-9-0 66 StephenCraine 3 60
(Patrick Morris) *racd far side: led overall appr fnl 2f: rdn and hdd jst ins fnl f: sn no ch w wnr: lost 2nd last strides* **8/1**
4 *¾* **Pearl Opera** 2-9-0 0 JimCrowley 7 57+
(R M Beckett) *s.i.s: in rr: pushed along centre crse and hdwy fr 2f out: styd on fnl f but nvr a threat* **11/4**[1]
04 **5** *1¼* **Madam Mayem**[7] 4451 2-9-0 0 RichardKingscote 9 53
(Tom Dascombe) *chsd ldrs centre crse: rdn over 2f out: ev ch over 1f out: wknd fnl f* **7/2**[3]
63 **6** *1¼* **Veeb (IRE)**[8] 4423 2-9-0 0 ChrisCatlin 8 48
(M R Channon) *racd centre crse: rdn 1/2-way: wknd fnl f* **3/1**[2]
U03 **7** *2¼* **Manasha**[26] 3817 2-9-0 0 IanMongan 5 40
(J L Dunlop) *a outpcd* **25/1**
0 **8** *14* **Princess Eliza**[43] 3274 2-9-0 0 VinceSlattery 6 —
(Miss Joanne Priest) *chsd ldrs in centre crse 3f: wknd qckly* **150/1**
000 **9** *11* **Magical Star**[43] 3269 2-9-0 41 RichardHughes 2 —
(R Hannon) *led overall on far side rail: hdd appr fnl 2f: wknd and eased fnl f* **10/1**
62.52 secs (3.22) **Going Correction** +0.20s/f (Good) **9** Ran SP% **113.1**
Speed ratings (Par 91): **82,77,76,75,73 71,67,45,27**
toteswingers:1&2:£19.90, 1&3:£4.00, 2&3:£22.40 CSF £282.29 TOTE £10.10: £2.50, £9.20, £2.20; EX 585.90 TRIFECTA Not won..
Owner Paul Moulton **Bred** L Mulryan **Trained** Earlswood, Monmouths

FOCUS
A heavy shower around lunchtime meant conditions weren't anything like as quick as predicted. Given the way the race panned out it's hard to be dogmatic that there was any discernible track advantage. Probably not form to be too positive about, but the winner is rated up 10lb.

NOTEBOOK
Scommettitrice(IRE) was initially in the small group that went far side but she gradually edged towards the middle of the track once asked to make her effort, before coming nicely clear to get off the mark at the fourth time of asking. She hadn't looked straightforward in her last two starts but she behaved impeccably here, travelling nicely and picking up smartly to win with authority. This wasn't a strong heat though and her future is now in the hands of the assessor, as nurseries beckon. (tchd 13-2)
Kilk, given her stable are not known for juvenile winners, especially on debut, ran a blinder to finish second on her first start. Sprint bred, she is entitled to come on a good deal and deserves plenty of respect next time.
Upark Flyer is proving most consistent, albeit a little exposed now, but she's always going to be vulnerable in this company with a rating of 66 and could fare better in handicaps. (op 6-1)
Pearl Opera, a nicely bred debutante, shaped encouragingly and looks a sure-fire improver next time. (op 3-1)
Madam Mayem broke better this time but could not sustain her effort. (op 11-2)
Veeb(IRE) failed to maintain her challenge down the middle of the track and was a little disappointing, unable to repeat the level of her recent Windsor third. (op 5-2)
Magical Star's rider made a bee-line for the far rail, suggesting he felt it might be a bit quicker on that part of the track. The filly ended up well beaten after setting the pace. Official explanation: jockey said filly lost its action (op 11-1 tchd 14-1)

4676 BREWIN DOLPHIN H'CAP 1m 4f 23y
2:45 (2:48) (Class 6) (0-60,60) 3-Y-O+ **£1,942** (£578; £288; £144) **Stalls** Low

Form RPR
10-0 **1** **Bute Street**[53] 2923 5-8-11 **46** RichardKingscote 16 61
(R J Hodges) *trckd ldrs: led over 2f out: pushed along fr 2f out: styd on wl thrght fnl f* **12/1**
060- **2** *1¼* **Dancing Storm**[171] 6968 7-9-4 **53** IanMongan 8 66
(W S Kittow) *trckd ldrs: chal over 2f out: pressed wnr sn after tl no ex u.p ins fnl f* **15/2**
0 **3** *6* **Suor Angelica (IRE)**[35] 3538 5-8-8 **46** oh1 MatthewDavies(3) 12 49
(George Baker) *in rr tl hdwy on outside over 3f out: styd on fr over 1f out but no ch w ldng duo* **20/1**
5004 **4** *hd* **Princess Flame (GER)**[11] 4328 8-8-10 **50** ow3 KylieManser(5) 7 53
(B G Powell) *stdd in rr: hdwy 3f out: styd on fr over 1f out but nvr in contention* **7/1**[3]
/426 **5** *1½* **Garafena**[11] 4327 7-8-10 **52** (p) NathanAlison(7) 14 53
(R Lee) *t.k.h in mid-div: sme hdwy fr 3f out: nvr in contention* **11/2**[2]
1505 **6** *1¼* **Harare**[11] 4327 9-9-8 **57** (p) WilliamCarson 15 56
(R J Price) *towards rr tl sme hdwy 3f out: nvr in contention* **8/1**
0062 **7** *1½* **Jasmeno**[19] 4046 3-8-7 **53** (t) ChrisCatlin 9 49
(H Morrison) *chsd ldr: rdn 4f out: wknd 2f out* **10/3**[1]
/40- **8** *13* **Bonnie Bea**[295] 6741 4-9-1 **50** TravisBlock 11 25
(B I Case) *chsd ldrs: led appr 3f out: hdd appr fnl 2f: sn btn* **40/1**
/0-0 **9** *5* **Contrada**[11] 4328 5-9-5 **54** (b) RichardHughes 6 21
(J A B Old) *led tl hdd appr fnl 3f: wknd qckly u.p 2f out* **25/1**
0-00 **10** *7* **Steely Bird**[38] 3444 3-8-10 **56** SamHitchcott 1 12
(Miss Jo Crowley) *in rr: sme prog into mid-div over 3f out: sn wknd* **8/1**
540 **11** *9* **Mr Maximas**[12] 4280 3-8-5 **51** NeilChalmers 4 —
(B Palling) *chsd ldrs 9f* **12/1**
000- **12** *2* **Monaadi (IRE)**[348] 3594 5-9-3 **52** FergusSweeney 3 —
(B G Powell) *chsd ldrs tl wknd 3f out* **16/1**
-000 **13** *10* **Aston Boy**[52] 2955 5-8-6 **46** oh1 KierenFox(5) 2 —
(M Blanshard) *bhd fr 1/2-way* **33/1**
2m 41.05s (2.05) **Going Correction** +0.20s/f (Good)
WFA 3 from 4yo+ 11lb **13** Ran SP% **120.2**
Speed ratings (Par 101): **101,100,96,96,95 94,93,84,81,76 70,69,62**
toteswingers:1&2:£15.10, 1&3:£52.30, 2&3:£36.10 CSF £95.85 CT £1804.66 TOTE £15.70: £5.30, £1.20, £6.50; EX 145.50 TRIFECTA Not won..
Owner J W Mursell **Bred** J W Mursell **Trained** Charlton Mackrell, Somerset
■ Starstruck Peter (10/1) was withdrawn after getting loose at the start. Deduct 10p in the £ under R4. New market formed.

FOCUS
A low-grade handicap but run at a decent pace and the first two came nicely clear. Not form to be positive about though.
Bute Street Official explanation: trainer said, regarding apparent improvement in form, that the gelding was better suited by the trip and easier ground.

4677 GDS INTERNATIONAL NURSERY 6f 16y
3:15 (3:17) (Class 5) 2-Y-O **£2,460** (£732; £365; £182) **Stalls** Centre

Form RPR
3505 **1** **Rosina Grey**[13] 4262 2-9-0 **71** JamesMillman(3) 2 78
(B R Millman) *in rr: stdy hdwy fr 2f out to ld over 1f out: gng clr whn hung bdly rt to stands' rail ins fnl f: comf* **6/1**[3]
460 **2** *3¾* **Maggie's Treasure (IRE)**[29] 3721 2-9-1 **69** TadhgO'Shea 1 64
(J Gallagher) *chsd ldrs: rdn and faltered whn sltly hmpd 1f out: chsd wnr sn after but nvr any ch* **7/1**
0310 **3** *½* **Barista (IRE)**[3] 4578 2-8-12 **66** ChrisCatlin 5 63+
(M R Channon) *in tch: hdwy whn hmpd appr fnl f: swtchd rt and styd on ins fnl f to cl on 2nd cl home but nvr any ch w wnr* **5/2**[2]
3032 **4** *1* **Just For Leo (IRE)**[69] 2440 2-9-3 **71** CathyGannon 8 61
(P D Evans) *t.k.h: chsd ldrs: ev ch fr 2f out tl wknd u.p 1f out* **13/2**
0440 **5** *1¾* **Mystica (IRE)**[13] 4254 2-8-11 **65** JamesDoyle 7 50
(D J S Ffrench Davis) *led 2f: styd pressing ldr: rdn 2f out and edgd rt 1f out: wknd sn after* **25/1**
0651 **6** *4* **Miss Dutee**[17] 4129 2-8-13 **67** RichardHughes 3 39
(R Hannon) *w ldr tl led after 2f: hdd over 1f out: wknd fnl f* **2/1**[1]
5254 **7** *shd* **Pick A Little**[12] 4278 2-9-7 **75** IanMongan 4 46
(B W Duke) *struggling to go pce most of way* **16/1**
0004 **8** *1¼* **Salvationist**[17] 4129 2-8-0 **57** MartinLane(3) 6 24
(J L Dunlop) *s.i.s: sn drvn along and a outpcd* **10/1**
1m 13.74s (1.74) **Going Correction** +0.20s/f (Good) **8** Ran SP% **120.8**
Speed ratings (Par 94): **96,91,90,89,86 81,81,79**
toteswingers:1&2:£8.10, 1&3:£4.20, 2&3:£4.60 CSF £49.90 CT £135.44 TOTE £10.30: £3.70, £3.90, £1.10; EX 50.90 Trifecta £312.10 Pool £632.66 - 1.50 winning units..
Owner P Gibbins M Daly **Bred** The Three Point Partnership **Trained** Kentisbeare, Devon

FOCUS
An interesting little nursery run at a decent gallop. A 6l personal best from the winner.

NOTEBOOK
Rosina Grey fairly bolted up despite edging all the way over to the stands' rail in the final half furlong. She had disappointed on her only previous try at 6f, but she put to bed any fears about stamina by sweeping to the front down the outside at the furlong pole and quickly skipping clear of her rivals in impressive style. On this evidence she'd be well up to defying a penalty if connections can find a suitable contest before she is reassessed. (op 11-1)
Maggie's Treasure(IRE), stepping up in trip for this nursery debut, ran very well, keeping on nicely having raced close to the pace throughout, and he's definitely got races in him. (op 8-1 tchd 9-1)
Barista(IRE) can be marked up because he appeared full of running when stuck behind a wall of horses approaching the final furlong, and the winner had flown by the time he saw daylight. He may not have won, but would certainly have finished a lot closer with a clear run. (op 11-4 tchd 9-4)
Just For Leo(IRE), who has been gelded since last seen, kept on but lacked a change of gear. (tchd 5-1)
Miss Duteedropped away having raced front rank. It may be she didn't appreciate the ease in the ground. (op 7-4 tchd 5-2)
Pick A Little Official explanation: jockey said colt was unsuited by the good (good to soft places) ground

4678 YOLK RECRUITMENT (S) STKS 6f 16y
3:45 (3:47) (Class 6) 2-Y-O **£1,942** (£578; £288; £144) **Stalls** Centre

Form RPR
4063 **1** **Diamond Vine (IRE)**[12] 4277 2-8-11 64 (p) TomMcLaughlin 6 68
(R A Harris) *t.k.h: w ldr tl led after 2f: rdn: hung lft 1f out: styd on wl fnl f: drvn out* **4/1**[1]
455 **2** *2¼* **Painters Easel (IRE)**[10] 4384 2-8-11 60 JamesDoyle 9 61
(J S Moore) *chsd ldrs: wnt 2nd 2f out: chsng ldr but one pce whn carried lft 1f out: swtchd rt: kpt on but nvr any ch* **9/2**[2]
4235 **3** *3¾* **Crown Ridge (IRE)**[17] 4150 2-8-11 ChrisCatlin 13 49
(M R Channon) *in rr: rdn along and hdwy over 2f out: styd on for one-pced 3rd fnl f* **4/1**[1]
4 *½* **Silver Age (IRE)** 2-8-4 0 RyanPowell(7) 8 47+
(J S Moore) *hld up in rr: stdy hdwy fnl 2f: gng on cl home* **25/1**
0306 **5** *1* **The Best Mode (IRE)**[55] 2873 2-8-11 65 CathyGannon 3 44
(P D Evans) *chsd ldrs: rdn over 2f out: wknd fnl f* **13/2**[3]
3055 **6** *1¾* **Sarandjam**[13] 4241 2-8-11 57 SamHitchcott 4 38
(M R Channon) *towards rr: drvn and hdwy fr over 2f out: nvr gng pce to get into contention* **9/1**
5 **7** *3* **Majestic Ridge (IRE)**[19] 4067 2-8-8 0 AndrewHeffernan(3) 5 29
(R A Harris) *plld hrd: led 2f: styd upsides tl over 2f out: sn btn* **40/1**
045 **8** *8* **River Blade**[33] 3603 2-8-11 55 LiamJones 10 3
(W M Brisbourne) *chsd ldrs 1/2-way: wknd fr 2f out* **20/1**
040 **9** *3½* **Capall Dorcha**[9] 4409 2-8-8 0 (v1) MartinLane(3) 12 —
(J R Holt) *s.i.s: sn rcvrd to chse ldrs: rdn and wknd over 2f out* **66/1**
00 **10** *1½* **Snapshott (IRE)**[55] 2867 2-8-11 0 SaleemGolam 11 —
(R A Harris) *chsd ldrs to 1/2-way* **66/1**
0 **11** *¾* **Avon Causeway**[18] 4095 2-8-6 0 NeilChalmers 2 —
(J M Bradley) *wnt lft s: spd to 1/2-way* **16/1**

006 **12** *2¾* **Ad Vitam (IRE)**[28] 3769 2-8-11 50................................ RichardHughes 7 —
(S Kirk) *sn outpcd* **15/2**

1m 14.61s (2.61) **Going Correction** +0.20s/f (Good) **12** Ran SP% **113.2**
Speed ratings (Par 92): **90,87,82,81,80 77,73,63,58,56 55,51**
toteswingers:1&2:£5.40, 1&3:£4.40, 2&3:£4.60 CSF £19.61 TOTE £4.30: £1.70, £3.10, £1.10; EX 24.00 Trifecta £73.40 Pool £737.23 - 7.43 winning units..There was no bid for the winner.
Owner Ridge House Stables Ltd **Bred** Michael O'Mahony **Trained** Earlswood, Monmouths

FOCUS
Little depth to this seller and the time was slow compared with the previous nursery. The form is rated around the winner.

NOTEBOOK
Diamond Vine(IRE) had some of the best form on offer and, despite edging out to the middle of the track in the final furlong, he fairly bolted up and looks sure to win more races at this level. (tchd 7-2)
Painters Easel(IRE) was the only one to get within striking distance of the winner at the business end and can win a similar race. (op 8-1)
Crown Ridge(IRE) has been running creditably in this company and looks the horse around whom the form can be rated. (op 11-4)
Silver Age(IRE) ◆, a newcomer, was the big eye-catcher of the race. Having been slowly away and almost detached at the back, he picked up through beaten horses as the race progressed, despite not really coming under serious pressure, and very nearly caught Crown Ridge for third. His jockey was clearly at pains not to be too hard on him but this already-gelded juvenile clearly has the potential to come on a good deal from this, which would make him a major player in similar company. (op 22-1)

4679 ABSOLUTE RECRUITMENT MAIDEN STKS 7f 16y
4:15 (4:18) (Class 5) 3-Y-O+ £2,460 (£732; £365; £182) Stalls Centre

Form RPR

4 **1** **Kalk Bay (IRE)**[18] 4107 3-9-3 0.. LiamJones 10 84+
(W J Haggas) *in tch: hdwy 3f out: chsd ldr fr 2f out: drvn and styd on wl to ld fnl 100yds* **3/1**[2]

6-06 **2** *nk* **Waabel**[14] 4238 3-9-3 0.. RichardThomas 4 78
(Jim Best) *led: 3 l clr over 2f out: shkn up fnl f: hdd and no ex fnl 100yds but stl wl clr of 3rd* **40/1**

3 *7* **Astound**[37] 3-8-12 0.. CathyGannon 2 54
(P D Evans) *s.i.s: sn chsng ldrs: rdn along 4f out: styd on for mod 3rd fr over 1f out* **33/1**

0222 **4** *4½* **Advertisement (USA)**[10] 4385 3-9-3 77.................. RichardHughes 3 47
(J Noseda) *t.k.h: chsd ldr and sn c rt to r on stands' rail: rdn over 2f out: hung lft and wknd over 1f out* **4/6**[1]

5 **5** *3¾* **Naughty Naughty**[14] 4229 5-9-4 0.......................... FergusSweeney 6 32
(B G Powell) *chsd ldrs: rdn 3f out: wknd 2f out* **14/1**

00 **6** *2½* **Mushy Peas (IRE)**[10] 4364 3-9-0 0........................... RichardEvans(3) 12 30
(P D Evans) *chsd ldrs: rdn 3f out: hung lft and wknd ins fnl 2f* **80/1**

0500 **7** *shd* **Tigers Charm**[21] 3993 3-9-3 45................................(t) RichardKingscote 14 30
(J M Bradley) *in rr: rdn and sme prog fr 1/2-way but nvr anywhere nr ldrs* **66/1**

0 **8** *shd* **Spanish Island (USA)**[11] 4340 3-9-3 0........................... ChrisCatlin 11 30
(M A Magnusson) *chsd ldrs: rdn 3f out: wknd qckly 2f out* **8/1**[3]

9 *½* **Swingle** 3-8-9 0.. MartinLane(3) 13 23
(D Haydn Jones) *in rr tl pushed along and styd on through btn horses fnl 2f* **25/1**

10 *1¾* **Katmai River (IRE)** 3-9-3 0.. TravisBlock 7 23
(M D I Usher) *v.s.a: rdn and sme hdwy into midfield 1/2-way: sn wknd* **66/1**

0-05 **11** *½* **Filibuster**[17] 4146 3-9-3 0.. IanMongan 9 22
(C F Wall) *s.i.s: in rr: pushed along 3f out: a towards rr* **50/1**

-060 **12** *4* **Little Buddy**[18] 4109 3-9-0 30..............................(t) AndrewHeffernan(3) 5 11
(R J Price) *v.s.a: sn in tch: wknd qckly 1/2-way* **100/1**

0 **13** *5* **Mistress Shy**[13] 4251 3-8-12 0... VinceSlattery 8 —
(R Dickin) *a in rr* **80/1**

14 *1* **Tiscaline (FR)** 3-8-12 0... NeilChalmers 1 —
(B Palling) *a in rr* **66/1**

1m 24.89s (1.69) **Going Correction** +0.20s/f (Good)
WFA 3 from 5yo 6lb **14** Ran SP% **121.9**
Speed ratings (Par 103): **98,97,89,84,80 77,77,77,76,74 74,69,63,62**
toteswingers:1&2:£14.50, 1&3:£14.80, 2&3:£41.60 CSF £124.91 TOTE £3.30: £1.10, £7.80, £7.10; EX 154.80 TRIFECTA Not won..
Owner Bernard Kantor **Bred** Wentworth Racing **Trained** Newmarket, Suffolk

FOCUS
A pretty weak maiden. Very few got into it and positives are hard to find for those out of the frame. The form is rated around the race averages with little solid form to go on.
Tigers Charm Official explanation: jockey said gelding was unsuited by the good (good to soft places) ground
Filibuster Official explanation: jockey said gelding was unsuited by the good (good to soft places) ground

4680 DIGIBET.COM FILLIES' H'CAP 1m 14y
4:45 (4:46) (Class 5) (0-75,75) 3-Y-O+ £2,460 (£732; £365; £182) Stalls Centre

Form RPR

1304 **1** **Croeso Cusan**[6] 4488 5-9-0 59...................................... SophieDoyle(5) 1 75
(J L Spearing) *hld up in rr but in tch: stdy hdwy fr 3f out to trck ldr ins fnl 2f: qcknd to ld jst ins fnl f: easily* **3/1**[2]

1440 **2** *3½* **Ken's Girl**[11] 4324 6-9-12 66.. IanMongan 3 74
(W S Kittow) *led: rdn 2f out: hdd jst ins fnl f and sn outpcd by wnr but clr 2nd best* **5/1**

5215 **3** *8* **Our Drama Queen (IRE)**[15] 4206 3-9-11 72............. RichardHughes 6 61
(R Hannon) *stdd s: in rr and off pce: hdwy fr 3f out: swtchd lft over 2f out and styd on to take 3rd sn after but nvr any ch w ldng duo* **6/4**[1]

0005 **4** *5* **Dubai Gem**[22] 3962 4-8-11 51... LiamJones 5 29
(Jamie Poulton) *disp 2nd: rdn 4f out: wknd qckly ins fnl 2f* **9/2**[3]

-500 **5** *1* **Future Regime (IRE)**[130] 998 3-7-12 50.................. SimonPearce(5) 4 25
(Patrick Morris) *chsd ldrs: rdn 4f out: wknd wl over 2f out* **66/1**

21-0 **6** *13* **Vegas Palace (IRE)**[22] 3962 3-9-9 75....................... RossAtkinson(5) 2 20
(Tom Dascombe) *disp 2nd: rdn and wknd over 2f out* **9/1**

1m 36.45s (0.25) **Going Correction** +0.20s/f (Good)
WFA 3 from 4yo+ 7lb **6** Ran SP% **111.3**
Speed ratings (Par 100): **106,102,94,89,88 75**
toteswingers:1&2:£2.90, 1&3:£1.90, 2&3:£2.20 CSF £17.71 TOTE £2.50: £1.10, £4.30; EX 16.90.
Owner Oxstalls Farm Stud **Bred** Richard Evans Bloodstock **Trained** Kinnersley, Worcs

FOCUS
They finished well strung out here and a few of these didn't handle the rain-eased ground. The form is rated around the runner-up.

4681 LINDLEY CATERING H'CAP (FOR LADY AMATEUR RIDERS) 1m 14y
5:15 (5:16) (Class 5) (0-70,68) 3-Y-O+ £2,373 (£736; £367; £183) Stalls Centre

Form RPR

000- **1** **Poca A Poca (IRE)**[48] 5179 6-9-4 49 oh4................... MissSBrotherton 3 58
(D Burchell) *chsd ldrs: led appr fnl 2f: drvn and styd on wl thrght fnl f* **33/1**

4151 **2** *1½* **Bidable**[25] 3853 6-10-5 64.. MissEJJones 5 70
(B Palling) *chsd ldrs: rdn to chal over 1f out: no ex u.p ins fnl f* **4/1**[2]

0345 **3** *3¼* **Alqaahir (USA)**[27] 3782 8-10-3 67................................ MissMBryant(5) 12 66+
(P Butler) *in rr tl gd hdwy fr 3f out: styd on fr over 1f out but no imp on ldng duo* **7/1**[3]

-060 **4** *1¾* **Lordship (IRE)**[6] 4478 6-10-4 68.............................. MissJennyCarr(5) 6 63
(A W Carroll) *led tl hdd appr fnl 2f: wknd appr fnl f* **25/1**

6060 **5** *1* **Carlton Scroop (FR)**[19] 4070 7-9-5 57.............. MissJessicaLodge(7) 7 49
(A W Carroll) *hmpd s and s.i.s: hdwy fr 3f out: chsd ldrs and rdn 2f out: no imp and wknd ins fnl f* **12/1**

4000 **6** *nk* **Ermine Grey**[27] 3783 9-9-9 57.. MissLAllan(3) 1 49
(A W Carroll) *in tch: rdn to chse ldrs 3f out: wknd over 1f out* **4/1**[2]

0350 **7** *¾* **Bere Davis (FR)**[42] 3291 5-9-9 54.......................... MissIsabelTompsett 14 44
(P D Evans) *racd wd 3f: chsd ldrs tl wknd fr 2f out* **7/2**[1]

0300 **8** *½* **Batchworth Blaise**[13] 4260 7-9-3 55..................... MissCNosworthy(7) 4 44
(E A Wheeler) *towards rr: sme prog 3f out: nvr in contention* **11/1**

-066 **9** *3½* **Just Jimmy (IRE)**[183] 373 5-9-7 59.............................. MissCBoxall(7) 8 40
(K Bishop) *in tch: rdn 3f out: wknd 2f out* **20/1**

4000 **10** *shd* **Straight Face (IRE)**[15] 4206 6-10-0 59.........................(b) MrsEEvans 13 39
(P D Evans) *racd alone stands' side: a struggling to go pce of main gp* **14/1**

66-0 **11** *1* **Croeso Ynol**[55] 2874 4-8-13 49 oh4....................... MissRachelKing(5) 2 27
(H J Evans) *in tch tl wknd over 2f out* **25/1**

60- **12** *9* **Hill Of Clare (IRE)**[296] 6692 8-9-1 49 oh4.............. MissMMullineaux(3) 9 6
(G H Jones) *in rr: sme hdwy 1/2-way: sn wknd* **50/1**

030/ **13** *9* **Wrecking Crew (IRE)**[689] 5915 6-9-11 63............... MissDO'Brien(7) 10 —
(B R Millman) *chsd ldrs 5f* **14/1**

0-00 **14** *19* **Michelle (IRE)**[17] 4132 4-9-1 49 oh4......................... MissZoeLilly(3) 11 —
(P Butler) *chsd ldrs to 1/2-way* **100/1**

1m 38.44s (2.24) **Going Correction** +0.20s/f (Good) **14** Ran SP% **122.4**
Speed ratings (Par 103): **96,94,91,89,88 88,87,86,83,83 82,73,64,45**
toteswingers:1&2:£19.30, 1&3:£43.20, 2&3:£5.10 CSF £156.71 CT £1096.48 TOTE £38.80: £10.50, £2.20, £3.80; EX 138.50 Trifecta £397.80 Pool £537.60 - 1 winning unit. Place 6 £838.85, Place 5 £147.56.
Owner J Parfitt **Bred** Bryan Ryan **Trained** Briery Hill, Blaenau Gwent

FOCUS
A modest event. The winner showed her first real form despite being 9lb wrong, but the race is rated at face value around the runner-up.
Poca A Poca(IRE) Official explanation: trainer said, regarding apparent improvement in form, that this was the mare's first run for him having been hurdling and, in his opinion, was better suited by a mile.
Michelle(IRE) Official explanation: jockey said filly ran too free
T/Plt: £3,176.50 to a £1 stake. Pool: £65,097.88 - 14.96 winning tickets. T/Qpdt: £31.00 to a £1 stake. Pool: £7,227.82 - 172.00 winning tickets ST

[3756]SOUTHWELL (L-H)
Tuesday, August 3

OFFICIAL GOING: Standard
Wind: Virtually nil Weather: Sunny periods and warm

4682 EUROPEAN BREEDERS' FUND MAIDEN STKS 1m (F)
5:55 (5:55) (Class 5) 2-Y-O £3,302 (£982; £491; £245) Stalls Low

Form RPR

0 **1** **Pisco Sour (USA)**[27] 3794 2-9-3 0.............................. RobertWinston 1 76+
(H Morrison) *trckd ldrs: pushed along and green 1/2-way: hdwy on inner 3f out: rdn wl over 2f out: styd on to chal over 1f out: led ins fnl f and sn edgd rt: styng on whn hung rt nr fin* **5/2**[1]

062 **2** *¾* **Jacobs Son**[13] 4254 2-9-3 74... EddieAhern 10 74
(R A Mills) *trckd ldrs: hdwy on outer over 3f out: chal over 2f out: rdn to ld wl over 1f out and sn edgd lft: jnd and drvn over 1f out: hdd ins fnl f: hld whn sltly hmpd nr fin* **11/4**[2]

04 **3** *6* **Eduardo**[28] 3769 2-9-3 0... JackMitchell 8 60
(Jedd O'Keeffe) *towards rr: hdwy 3f out: swtchd wd and rdn over 2f out: styd on appr fnl f: nrst fin* **33/1**

00 **4** *2½* **Endorser**[8] 4436 2-9-3 0...(b) DavidProbert 7 54
(W R Muir) *sn led: rdn along 1/2-way: hdd 3f out: cl up and drvn 2f out: grad wknd* **66/1**

05 **5** *4½* **Denices Moonlight**[15] 4187 2-9-3 0.......................... RoystonFfrench 9 44
(M Johnston) *cl up: led 3f out: rdn over 2f out: drvn and hdd wl over 1f out: grad wknd* **11/1**

54 **6** *5* **Soie De Chine**[11] 4338 2-8-12 0................................... StevieDonohoe 2 35+
(Sir Mark Prescott) *chsd ldrs: rdn along 3f out: sn wknd* **9/2**[3]

3 **7** *5* **Good Boy Jackson**[15] 4187 2-9-3 0.................................... NeilCallan 5 23
(K A Ryan) *cl up on outer: rdn along 3f out: drvn over 2f out and sn wknd* **9/2**[3]

06 **8** *10* **Little Book**[19] 4048 2-8-12 0... ShaneKelly 3 —
(E F Vaughan) *a towards rr: rdn along and outpcd fnl 3f* **16/1**

060 **9** *22* **Silver Writer**[24] 3923 2-8-13 53 ow1...................... MichaelO'Connell(5) 11 —
(M W Easterby) *sn outpcd and a in rr: bhd fnl 3f* **80/1**

10 *1* **Bollin Hugo** 2-9-3 0.. DavidAllan 6 —
(T D Easterby) *dwlt: hdwy and in tch after 2f: rdn along 1/2-way: sn wknd and bhd fnl 3f* **33/1**

1m 45.79s (2.09) **Going Correction** +0.125s/f (Slow) **10** Ran SP% **114.4**
Speed ratings (Par 94): **94,93,87,84,80 75,70,60,38,37**
toteswingers:1&2:£1.50, 1&3:£18.00, 2&3:£16.10 CSF £9.16 TOTE £4.80: £1.90, £1.10, £6.50; EX 12.10.
Owner Michael Kerr-Dineen **Bred** Hascombe Stud **Trained** East Ilsley, Berks

FOCUS
The going remained standard for this mile maiden that was run at a fair pace with the front pair drawing clear of the remainder. Ordinary form rated around the first two.

NOTEBOOK
Pisco Sour(USA) ran better than his finishing position suggested when running green on debut but looked capable of building on that with the step up to a mile. He again ran green after missing the break and he was soon being nudged along, but he looked good for a bit more than the winning margin would suggest. He is clearly progressing with experience and can only go on from this. (op 11-4 tchd 100-30)

Jacobs Son stepped up on his first two runs on turf when narrowly touched off at Lingfield on his all-weather debut. This was another encouraging effort and had his chance when taking over in the straight. He drifted left before getting leaned on towards the finish by the winner but was being held. He saw out the step up in trip well and with his willing attitude his turn will come. (tchd 5-2)
Eduardo never threatened the leaders but stepped up on a previous turf effort on all-weather his debut last time and this was of a similar standard. The step up to a mile did appear to suit. (op 40-1)
Endorser has shown little in two outings, beaten in a seller last time. He showed a little more promise with more forceful tactics but probably could do with dropping back in trip.
Denices Moonlight had shown some promise in two runs to date but appeared not to get home after sharing the early pace. (op 12-1 tchd 10-1)
Soie De Chine was close enough turning in but tired over a furlong out and is now qualified for a mark. (op 5-1)

4683 2ND BEST PLAYER H'CAP — 1m 6f (F)
6:25 (6:27) (Class 6) (0-65,65) 3-Y-O+ £2,047 (£604; £302) Stalls Low

Form — RPR

30-5 **1** **Budva**[58] 2792 3-8-7 **57** ... RobertWinston 6 — 67+
(H Morrison) *cl up: led after 5f: rdn clr over 2f out: styd on strly* **6/1**[3]

-110 **2** *6* **Mediterranean Sea (IRE)**[54] 2907 4-9-6 **57** ... StephenCraine 4 — 58+
(J R Jenkins) *trckd ldrs: n.m.r and lost pl over 3f out: swtchd rt and hdwy over 2f out: sn rdn and styd on: tk 2nd ins fnl f: no ch w wnr* **20/1**

0546 **3** *½* **Laura Land**[12] 4279 4-8-11 **48** oh3 ... EddieAhern 3 — 46
(W M Brisbourne) *trckd ldrs on inner: n.m.r bnd after 6f: hdwy 4f out: chsd wnr over 3f out: rdn over 2f out: drvn wl over 1f out: kpt on same pce: lost 2nd ins fnl f* **28/1**

000 **4** *2¾* **Pound Lane (IRE)**[26] 3829 4-8-8 **48** oh3 ... JackDean(3) 13 — 42
(Miss T Spearing) *reminders early and t.k.h in rr: hdwy 4f out: rdn along 3f out: styd on u.p fnl 2f: nrst fin* **100/1**

0-06 **5** *3¾* **Lis Pendens**[14] 4230 3-8-2 **52** ... FrannyNorton 2 — 41
(W R Muir) *in tch: hdwy to chse ldrs over 4f out: rdn along over 3f out: grad wknd fnl 2f* **14/1**

00/0 **6** *19* **Red Lancer**[27] 3780 9-10-0 **65** ... PatCosgrave 12 — 27
(J A T De Giles) *chsd ldng pair: cl up 1/2-way: rdn along over 3f out: sn wknd* **25/1**

1402 **7** *1* **Three Boars**[28] 3760 8-9-7 **58** ...(b) DavidProbert 5 — 19
(S Gollings) *hld up and bhd: hdwy on outer 7f out: chsd ldrs over 4f out: rdn along over 3f out and sn wknd* **5/2**[1]

-405 **8** *1¼* **Swords**[153] 777 8-9-1 **52** ... JimmyQuinn 7 — 11
(R E Peacock) *hld up towards rr: hdwy and in tch 1/2-way: rdn along 5f out and sn wknd* **8/1**

000/ **9** *9* **Flower Haven**[12] 443 8-8-13 **50** ... StevieDonohoe 8 — —
(V R A Dartnall) *rn in snatches: midfield: rdn along and lost pl after 3f: hdwy 1/2-way: chsd ldrs on outer over 5f out: rdn along over 4f out and sn wknd* **7/2**[2]

000 **10** *3½* **Melinoise**[14] 4229 3-8-4 **54** ... WilliamCarson 10 — —
(Rae Guest) *in tch: rdn along to chse ldrs 4f out: drvn over 3f out and sn wknd* **50/1**

0 **11** *8* **Ferney Boy**[59] 2765 4-9-7 **58** ... PJMcDonald 1 — —
(G A Swinbank) *in tch: rdn along over 4f out: sn wknd* **22/1**

0624 **12** *½* **Tilos Gem (IRE)**[13] 4266 4-9-12 **63** ... RoystonFfrench 14 — —
(M Johnston) *dwlt: sn in tch: rdn along 5f out: sn wknd* **6/1**[3]

00-0 **13** *12* **Transfered (IRE)**[69] 874 4-8-11 **48** oh2 ... FrankieMcDonald 11 — —
(Lucinda Featherstone) *a towards rr: rdn along over 4f out and sn bhd* **100/1**

60-5 **14** *nk* **Inside Knowledge (USA)**[12] 4290 4-8-11 **48** oh3 ... AndreaAtzeni 9 — —
(G Woodward) *led 5f: cl up tl rdn along and wknd 5f out: sn bhd* **66/1**

3m 12.03s (3.73) **Going Correction** +0.125s/f (Slow)
WFA 3 from 4yo+ 13lb — **14** Ran SP% **119.0**
Speed ratings (Par 101): **94,90,90,88,86 75,75,74,69,67 62,62,55,55**
toteswingers:1&2:£19.60, 1&3:£33.00, 2&3:£41.30 CSF £123.57 CT £3095.55 TOTE £10.90: £3.60, £4.40, £7.60; EX 113.90.
Owner C M Budgett **Bred** Kirtlington Stud Ltd And C M Budgett **Trained** East Ilsley, Berks

FOCUS
A modest looking staying handicap with only a few that could be seriously given chances to. It was run at just an ordinary pace with the field finishing well strung out. The winner produced a clear personal best.

4684 SUPPORT MARIE CURIE CANCER CARE H'CAP — 6f (F)
6:55 (6:57) (Class 4) (0-85,83) 3-Y-O+ £4,533 (£1,348; £674; £336) Stalls Low

Form — RPR

5351 **1** **Amenable (IRE)**[12] 4288 3-9-1 **77** ... AdrianNicholls 8 — 96+
(D Nicholls) *cl up: led wl over 2f out: rdn wl over 1f out: drvn and edgd rt ins fnl f: kpt on strly* **5/1**[2]

2013 **2** *2¼* **Westwood**[14] 4225 5-8-13 **71** ... AndreaAtzeni 12 — 84
(D Haydn Jones) *sn led: hdd wl over 2f out and sn rdn: drvn and ev ch ent fnl f: kpt on same pce* **7/1**

-446 **3** *2* **Fantasy Gladiator**[11] 4333 4-8-13 **71** ... JimmyQuinn 2 — 78+
(R M H Cowell) *s.i.s and bhd: hdwy on inner 1/2-way: rdn and hung rt 2f out: styd on u.p to take 3rd ins fnl f: nrst fin* **4/1**[1]

334 **4** *¾* **Punching**[8] 4435 6-9-2 **74** ... LiamKeniry 10 — 78
(C R Dore) *trckd ldrs: hdwy to chse ldng pair over 2f out: swtchd lft and rdn wl over 1f out: swtchd rt: drvn and one pce ent fnl f* **12/1**

5503 **5** *2¼* **Elusive Warrior (USA)**[28] 3761 7-8-4 **67** ...(p) DeclanCannon(5) 6 — 64
(A J McCabe) *chsd ldng pair on inner: rdn along wl over 2f out: drvn and wknd wl over 1f out* **14/1**

0050 **6** *6* **Bel Cantor**[9] 4413 7-9-0 **75** ... KellyHarrison(3) 14 — 53
(W J H Ratcliffe) *chsd ldrs: rdn along wl over 2f out: sn drvn and no hdwy* **25/1**

6315 **7** *hd* **Neduardo**[117] 1191 3-9-1 **77** ... JackMitchell 1 — 53
(P W Chapple-Hyam) *chsd ldrs on inner: rdn along wl over 2f out: sn wknd* **16/1**

1000 **8** *1* **Bond City (IRE)**[22] 3969 8-9-5 **82** ... DaleSwift(5) 9 — 56
(G R Oldroyd) *towards rr: wd st and rdn 2f out: nvr a factor* **12/1**

0000 **9** *½* **Elusive Fame (USA)**[22] 3969 4-9-4 **83** ...(b) CharlesPerkins(7) 11 — 55
(M Johnston) *swtchd lft s: a towards rr* **33/1**

331- **10** *1¼* **Great Charm (IRE)**[252] 7506 5-9-6 **78** ... ShaneKelly 5 — 46
(E J Alston) *midfield: wd st and rdn over 2f out: sn drvn and wknd* **6/1**[3]

5-30 **11** *6* **Cape Kimberley**[62] 2656 3-8-11 **73** ... PaulMulrennan 4 — 21
(J G Given) *a towards rr* **14/1**

5620 **12** *7* **Absa Lutte (IRE)**[10] 4378 7-9-8 **80** ...(t) HayleyTurner 13 — —
(Dr R D P Newland) *hld up: a bhd* **10/1**

254/ **13** *14* **Crimson King (IRE)**[835] 1500 9-9-3 **75** ... JamieMackay 3 — —
(T T Clement) *s.i.s: a bhd* **16/1**

1m 15.62s (-0.88) **Going Correction** +0.125s/f (Slow)
WFA 3 from 4yo+ 4lb — **13** Ran SP% **119.8**
Speed ratings (Par 105): **110,107,104,103,100 92,92,90,90,88 80,71,52**
toteswingers:1&2:£6.50, 1&3:£4.90, 2&3:£8.30 CSF £40.13 CT £161.34 TOTE £8.00: £2.90, £3.50, £2.00; EX 47.50.
Owner Turton Brown Williams Lindley **Bred** Michael Downey & Roalso Ltd **Trained** Sessay, N Yorks

FOCUS
A strong pace assured with so many trailblazers in the field, so not many got into this sprint handicap. The winner is rated better than ever.

4685 CORAL.CO.UK H'CAP — 5f (F)
7:30 (7:30) (Class 3) (0-95,93) 3-Y-O+ £7,123 (£2,119; £1,059; £529) Stalls High

Form — RPR

010 **1** **Luscivious**[53] 2940 6-9-4 **86** ...(b) PaulMulrennan 4 — 99
(J A Glover) *qckly away: mde all: clr 2f out: styd on strly fnl f: eased nr fin* **16/1**

3352 **2** *4* **Confessional**[4] 4541 3-9-2 **87** ...(e) DavidAllan 11 — 85
(T D Easterby) *trckd ldrs: hdwy 2f out: rdn to chse wnr over 1f out: drvn and no imp ins fnl f* **5/1**[3]

3024 **3** *¾* **Bonnie Prince Blue**[18] 4084 7-8-1 **74** ...(be) JohnFahy(5) 7 — 70+
(B Ellison) *chsd ldrs: rdn along: outpcd and lost pl after 1f: bhd 1/2-way: drvn wl over 1f out and sn edgd rt to stands' rail: styd on strly ins fnl f* **16/1**

1615 **4** *hd* **Captain Carey**[16] 4180 4-9-11 **93** ... TomMcLaughlin 8 — 88
(M S Saunders) *in tch: rdn along and sltly outpcd 2f out: drvn and styd on fr over 1f out* **4/1**[2]

4535 **5** *hd* **Invincible Lad (IRE)**[18] 4118 6-9-8 **90** ... PatCosgrave 2 — 84
(E J Alston) *prom on outer: hdwy to chse wnr wl over 1f out and sn rdn: drvn ent fnl f: sn one pce* **7/4**[1]

015 **6** *½* **Baby Strange**[18] 4085 6-9-3 **85** ... FrannyNorton 6 — 78
(D Shaw) *chsd ldrs: rdn and outpcd over 2f out: swtchd lft and rdn wl over 1f out: styd on ins fnl f: nrst fin* **14/1**

1521 **7** *½* **Lucky Numbers (IRE)**[13] 4243 4-9-4 **89** ... JamesSullivan(3) 3 — 80
(Paul Green) *sn chsng wnr: rdn along 1/2-way: drvn 2f out and sn wknd* **14/1**

2452 **8** *3¾* **Mon Brav**[11] 4349 3-8-7 **78** ...(v) JimmyQuinn 5 — 54
(D Carroll) *sn rdn along and outpcd: swtchd lft to wd outside after 1f: a in rr* **7/1**

1060 **9** *5* **Imprimis Tagula (IRE)**[2] 4617 6-9-11 **93** ...(v) DavidProbert 9 — 52
(A Bailey) *dwlt: sn in tch: rdn along bef 1/2-way and sn wknd* **12/1**

-050 **10** *½* **Doric Lady**[26] 3828 5-8-12 **80** ... HayleyTurner 10 — 38
(J A R Toller) *sn outpcd and a in rr* **33/1**

58.44 secs (-1.26) **Going Correction** -0.075s/f (Stan)
WFA 3 from 4yo+ 3lb — **10** Ran SP% **121.3**
Speed ratings (Par 107): **107,100,99,99,98 97,97,91,83,82**
toteswingers:1&2:£20.90, 1&3:£39.40, 2&3:£18.60 CSF £97.90 CT £1357.87 TOTE £27.10: £6.50, £1.40, £4.90; EX 148.30.
Owner Paul J Dixon & Brian Morton **Bred** R J Turner **Trained** Babworth, Notts

FOCUS
On paper a competitive field for this 5f handicap, but it was turned into a procession by the winner. He seemed to run a clear personal best.

NOTEBOOK
Luscivious travelled very comfortably setting a decent gallop. He only had to be nudged clear and won this with plenty in hand. He is a better horse on this surface compared to that of his performances on the turf, albeit scoring at Musselburgh in May. He will be of plenty of interest if he comes out of this well and connections decide to take on his engagement at Musselburgh on Friday night. (op 20-1)
Confessional has a consistent profile and was again racing in an eye-shield that saw him to good effect when runner up at Goodwood last week. He kept on well enough in the closing stages and remains in good heart. (op 11-2 tchd 6-1)
Bonnie Prince Blue had been beaten in a claimer over 6f last time and was doing all his best work late on after getting outpaced here but, nonetheless, this was a fair effort over the minimum distance. (op 14-1 tchd 18-1)
Captain Carey was another to feel the pinch when the tempo increased at the 2f pole, but stayed on again inside the distance. He remains of interest after a progressive and rewarding season. (op 5-1)
Invincible Lad(IRE) was strongly supported to remain unbeaten after his two previous efforts over C&D but he could not get to the winner after tracking him for much of the way, ultimately losing two places inside the distance. (op 2-1)

4686 CORAL TV H'CAP — 2m (F)
8:05 (8:05) (Class 4) (0-80,79) 4-Y-O+ £4,533 (£1,348; £674; £336) Stalls Low

Form — RPR

4230 **1** **Calculating (IRE)**[57] 2814 6-8-9 **72** ... LeeNewnes(5) 7 — 83
(M D I Usher) *hld up towards rr: hdwy to trck ldrs after 5f: pushed along over 3f out: hdwy to chse ldr wl over 1f out: drvn ent fnl f: styd on to ld nr line* **15/2**

4033 **2** *hd* **Act Of Kalanisi (IRE)**[27] 3772 4-9-2 **74** ... RoystonFfrench 2 — 85
(M Johnston) *a.p: trckd ldr 1/2-way: led wl over 2f out: rdn wl over 1f out: drvn ins fnl f: hdd and no ex nr line* **9/1**

4522 **3** *10* **Simonside**[24] 3896 7-8-8 **71** ... DaleSwift(5) 4 — 70
(B Ellison) *led: rdn along 4f out: drvn 3f out: sn hdd and kpt on same pce* **7/2**[1]

1150 **4** *1¼* **Bivouac (UAE)**[28] 3764 6-9-1 **73** ... PJMcDonald 10 — 70
(G A Swinbank) *t.k.h: trckd ldrs tl stdd and dropped to rr after 3f: smooth hdwy on outer 5f out: chsd ldng pair over 3f out: rdn over 2f out and sn btn* **7/1**

2005 **5** *8* **Highland Legacy**[17] 4125 6-9-7 **79** ...(v) HayleyTurner 8 — 67
(M L W Bell) *trckd ldr: pushed along over 5f out: rdn and wknd 3f out* **9/2**[3]

343 **6** *17* **Quarante Deux (USA)**[9] 4405 4-9-4 **76** ... TomEaves 1 — 43
(G A Butler) *stmbld s and in rr tl hdwy on inner to trck ldrs after 4f: rdn along over 4f out and sn wknd* **4/1**[2]

/032 **7** *3½* **Kentmere (IRE)**[76] 554 9-8-7 **65** ... EddieAhern 5 — 28
(P R Webber) *hld up towards rr: sme hdwy on inner 1/2-way: rdn along 4f out: sn wknd* **12/1**

61/0 **8** *15* **Hareem (IRE)**[28] 3760 6-8-4 **62** ...(b) FrannyNorton 3 — 7
(W R Muir) *chsd ldrs: rdn along after 5f: sn lost pl and bhd fnl 4f* **25/1**

2060 **9** *30* **Heathyards Junior**[75] 2259 4-8-4 **67** ... DeclanCannon(5) 6 — —
(A J McCabe) *hld up: a towards rr: outpcd and bhd fnl 4f* **12/1**

3m 45.14s (-0.36) **Going Correction** +0.125s/f (Slow) — **9** Ran SP% **113.9**
Speed ratings (Par 105): **105,104,99,99,95 86,85,77,62**
toteswingers:1&2:£13.00, 1&3:£6.50, 2&3:£10.50 CSF £71.53 CT £277.18 TOTE £14.80: £3.00, £3.60, £2.00; EX 58.80.
Owner Brian Rogan **Bred** Darley **Trained** Upper Lambourn, Berks

FOCUS
An ordinary handicap that was run at a similar pace with the front two pulling well clear in the straight. Probably not form to take literally.

4687 SOUTHWELL LADIES DAY AUGUST 15TH H'CAP — 1m (F)
8:40 (8:40) (Class 6) (0-60,60) 3-Y-O — £2,047 (£604; £302) Stalls Low

Form — RPR

1640 **1** **Bell's Ocean (USA)**[11] 4337 3-8-13 **55** .... StevieDonohoe 9 — 61
(J Ryan) *in tch: hdwy to chse ldrs over 3f out: rdn to chal 2f out: led 1 1/2f out: drvn ins fnl f and kpt on wl* — **9/1**

00-2 **2** *nk* **Master Of Song**[24] 3907 3-8-4 **46** oh1 .... (p) JimmyQuinn 14 — 51
(S R Bowring) *trckd ldrs: smooth hdwy 3f out: chal 2f out: sn rdn and ev ch tl drvn and no ex wl ins fnl f* — **9/2**[2]

-000 **3** *6* **Miss Chaumiere**[17] 4127 3-8-9 **51** .... (v[1]) HayleyTurner 13 — 43
(M L W Bell) *a.p: trckd ldr after 2f: effrt to chal 3f out: sn rdn and ev ch tl drvn and one pce fr over 1f out* — **14/1**

0400 **4** *nk* **Ravens Rose**[13] 4249 3-8-8 **50** .... EddieAhern 7 — 41+
(J G Portman) *s.i.s and in rr: hdwy on wd outside to chse ldrs after 3f: effrt to chal over 2f out: sn rdn and one pce fr over 1f out* — **16/1**

-050 **5** *nk* **Zelos Spirit**[17] 4155 3-8-4 **46** oh1 .... WilliamCarson 6 — 36
(Rae Guest) *in tch: hdwy 3f out: rdn along to chse ldrs 2f out: drvn and one pce appr fnl f* — **33/1**

002 **6** *1 1/2* **Wavertree Bounty**[4] 4547 3-8-3 **48** .... Louis-PhilippeBeuzelin(3) 5 — 35+
(J Ryan) *dwlt and towards rr: hdwy 3f out: rdn wl over 2f out: styd on appr fnl f: nrst fin* — **4/1**[1]

0620 **7** *1/2* **Electric City (IRE)**[13] 4249 3-8-4 **51** .... (p) JohnFahy(5) 12 — 37
(M G Quinlan) *pushed along to ld after 1f: rdn wl over 2f out: drvn and hdd 1 1/2f out: grad wknd* — **9/1**

0250 **8** *9* **Naseby (USA)**[20] 4025 3-9-1 **57** .... DavidProbert 8 — 22
(Miss S L Davison) *led 1f: chsd ldrs: rdn over 3f out and sn wknd* — **10/1**

1440 **9** *3 3/4* **Step To It (IRE)**[11] 4337 3-8-13 **55** .... (p) FrannyNorton 1 — 11
(K A Ryan) *a in rr* — **10/1**

05-6 **10** *1* **Inshaallah**[85] 1970 3-8-8 **50** .... PaulMulrennan 11 — 4
(J G Given) *chsd ldrs: rdn along 3f out and sn wknd* — **5/1**[3]

0605 **11** *12* **Tilsworth Glenboy**[6] 4479 3-9-4 **60** .... StephenCraine 10 — —
(J R Jenkins) *a towards rr* — **12/1**

-006 **12** *3 1/2* **Jemimaville (IRE)**[54] 2906 3-9-4 **60** .... (v[1]) TravisBlock 4 — —
(G C Bravery) *s.i.s: a bhd* — **28/1**

-660 **13** *30* **Mr Prize Fighter**[55] 2879 3-8-4 **46** oh1 .... RoystonFfrench 2 — —
(I W McInnes) *t.k.h: chsd ldrs on inner: lost pl 1/2-way and bhd whn eased 2f out* — **50/1**

1m 44.94s (1.24) **Going Correction** +0.125s/f (Slow) — 13 Ran SP% **121.6**
Speed ratings (Par 98): **98,97,91,91,91 89,89,80,76,75 63,59,29**
toteswingers:1&2:£12.50, 1&3:£38.20, 2&3:£19.60 CSF £49.45 CT £580.25 TOTE £9.80: £3.20, £2.50, £5.10; EX 60.10 Place 6 £536.40, Place 5 £303.13..
Owner Ocean Trailers Ltd **Bred** Brereton C Jones **Trained** Newmarket, Suffolk

FOCUS
A modest mile handicap but run at good pace with a good battle between the principals. The first two came clear and the form is weak, rated around the winner.
T/Jkpt: Not won. T/Plt: £851.30 to a £1 stake. Pool: £84,088.67 - 72.10 winning tickets T/Qpdt: £47.80 to a £1 stake. Pool:£7,674.43 - 118.70 winning tickets JR

3979 BRIGHTON (L-H)
Wednesday, August 4

OFFICIAL GOING: Good to firm (watered; 8.3)
Rail moved out 3yds from 6f to 2f increasing distances by about 15yds.
Wind: blustery Weather: showery and overcast

4688 CORRINGHAM SOCIAL CLUB NURSERY — 5f 59y
2:30 (2:30) (Class 5) (0-75,74) 2-Y-O — £2,331 (£693; £346; £173) Stalls Low

Form — RPR

0455 **1** **Volcanic Dust (IRE)**[20] 4066 2-8-10 **63** .... RyanMoore 6 — 66
(E A L Dunlop) *plld hrd: hld up: hrd drvn and effrt over 1f out: led fnl 100yds: edgd clr* — **9/2**[3]

4160 **2** *1 1/2* **Johnny Hancocks (IRE)**[4] 4600 2-8-12 **65** .... CathyGannon 5 — 63
(P D Evans) *led: rdn 2f out: hdd 100yds out: nt qckn* — **16/1**

4162 **3** *1/2* **Master Macho (IRE)**[4] 4600 2-9-4 **74** .... MatthewDavies(3) 4 — 70
(M R Channon) *prom: rdn over 2f out: jnd ldr 1f out: no ex whn wnr went past fnl 100yds* — **5/2**[1]

331 **4** *1 1/4* **Best Be Careful (IRE)**[11] 4363 2-9-0 **67** .... LiamKeniry 1 — 59
(M D I Usher) *awkward leaving stalls: hld up chsng ldrs: rdn over 2f out: no imp fnl f* — **10/3**[2]

4055 **5** *1 1/2* **Frankish Dynasty (GER)**[30] 3721 2-8-12 **65** .... TomQueally 3 — 52
(P F I Cole) *pushed along and outpcd in last: btn over 1f out: hanging bdly lft after* — **9/2**[3]

2015 **6** *3* **Melodize**[4] 4600 2-9-1 **68** .... KierenFallon 7 — 44
(W R Muir) *plld hrd: pressed ldr over 4f out: wknd over 1f out: eased clsng stages* — **11/2**

64.29 secs (1.99) **Going Correction** +0.15s/f (Good) — 6 Ran SP% **109.3**
Speed ratings (Par 94): **90,87,86,84,82 77**
toteswingers:1&2:£10.40, 1&3:£2.90, 2&3:£8.00 CSF £60.09 TOTE £5.30: £4.00, £7.30; EX 44.90.
Owner Byculla Thoroughbreds **Bred** Top Of The Form Syndicate **Trained** Newmarket, Suffolk

FOCUS
A modest nursery that was relatively slowly run and the form is muddling. The runner-up is rated to his previous seller winning mark.

NOTEBOOK
Volcanic Dust(IRE) pulled too hard at Leicester last time and, although again keen through the early stages, the decent gallop back in trip suited her and she was able to keep enough energy in reserve to produce a finish inside the last. The quicker they go in future the better it will be for her. (op 7-2)
Johnny Hancocks(IRE) couldn't get to the front at Thirsk last time but had no problem securing the lead here, and he returned to his best as a result. (op 14-1)
Master Macho(IRE), well in front of Johnny Hancocks at Thirsk, hit the front a furlong out but couldn't put the race to bed. He's pretty exposed now but is a fairly reliable guide to the level. (op 7-2)
Best Be Careful(IRE), a little awkward away, had her chance but couldn't land a blow while challenging nearest the far-side rail. (op 7-2 tchd 3-1)
Frankish Dynasty(GER) hung left towards the far rail from 1½f out and then found his path blocked somewhat. This might not be his ideal course. (tchd 4-1)
Melodize was another who didn't look entirely at home on the track. He was reported to have hung right. Official explanation: jockey said filly hung right-handed (op 5-1 tchd 4-1)

4689 DRINK IN BRIGHTON (S) H'CAP — 1m 3f 196y
3:00 (3:00) (Class 6) (0-55,56) 3-Y-O+ — £1,554 (£462; £231; £115) Stalls High

Form — RPR

044 **1** **Noah Jameel**[22] 3983 8-8-13 **48** .... FergusSweeney 10 — 56
(A G Newcombe) *in rr div: effrt 3f out: rdn and stl fair bit to do in 6th over 1f out: str run to ld fnl 100yds: edgd lft but hld on wl* — **12/1**

4540 **2** *3/4* **Quince (IRE)**[6] 4498 7-8-12 **52** .... (v) SimonPearce(5) 11 — 59
(J Pearce) *bhd: shkn up after 4f: lot to do 2f out: stl poor 7th 1f out: rdn and styd on to go 2nd fnl 75yds: declined to overtake: set himself a hopeless task* — **12/1**

3333 **3** *3 3/4* **Spinning Waters**[16] 4211 4-8-12 **47** .... (b) LiamKeniry 12 — 48
(Eve Johnson Houghton) *chsd ldrs: effrt 4f out: tried to chal 2f out: fnd v little after and plugged on* — **4/1**[1]

3500 **4** *1 3/4* **Special Cuvee**[88] 1922 4-9-6 **55** .... WilliamBuick 13 — 53
(Mrs A M Thorpe) *bhd: brought v wd 4f out: hanging lft and v reluctant whn chsng ldrs 2f out: no imp fnl f* — **20/1**

5254 **5** *shd* **Bussell Along (IRE)**[54] 2923 4-9-3 **52** .... (tp) TomQueally 8 — 50
(Stef Higgins) *s.i.s: hdwy 4f out: drvn and tried to chal 1f out: sn wknd* **8/1**

2000 **6** *1/2* **Oak Leaves**[23] 3960 3-8-1 **52** ow2 .... JohnFahy(5) 1 — 49
(J G Portman) *prom: led over 1f out: hdd & wknd fnl 100yds* — **17/2**

0404 **7** *2* **Pennfield Pirate**[16] 4202 3-8-9 **55** .... (v) SteveDrowne 9 — 49
(H Morrison) *prom: drvn and w ldr over 1f out: wknd ins fnl f* — **13/2**[2]

0450 **8** *2 3/4* **Holyfield Warrior (IRE)**[9] 4434 6-8-6 **46** oh1 .... (p) KierenFox(5) 7 — 36
(R J Smith) *pressed ldr: lft in front 5f out: rdn and hdd over 1f out: fdd ins fnl f* — **14/1**

4645 **9** *16* **Little Sark (IRE)**[22] 3984 5-9-2 **51** .... CathyGannon 14 — 15
(P D Evans) *towards rr and sn pushed along: u.p 1/2-way: no rspnse: t.o fnl 2f* — **13/2**[2]

0650 **10** *40* **Federal Reserve**[23] 3960 3-8-1 **47** oh1 ow1 .... (t) FrankieMcDonald 5 — —
(M Madgwick) *chsd ldrs but sn pushed along and racing awkwardly: lost pl 4f out: virtually p.u over 1f out* — **66/1**

0600 **11** *32* **Queen Of Thebes (IRE)**[9] 4434 4-9-1 **50** .... (t) DavidProbert 4 — —
(S Kirk) *v.s.a: drvn 1/2-way: t.o and virtually p.u over 1f out* — **25/1**

-000 **12** *9* **High Holborn (IRE)**[18] 3564 3-8-10 **56** ow1 .... (v) SebSanders 3 — —
(D E Pipe) *sn led: hdd 5f out and immediately drvn and tried to pull himself up: hopelessly t.o and virtually up 2f out* — **25/1**

2054 **13** *3 1/2* **Turner's Touch**[22] 3984 8-8-11 **46** oh1 .... (b) RyanMoore 6 — —
(G L Moore) *chsd ldrs to 1/2-way: nt run on: t.o and virtually p.u 2f out* — **15/2**[3]

2m 34.85s (2.15) **Going Correction** +0.15s/f (Good)
WFA 3 from 4yo+ 11lb — 13 Ran SP% **116.1**
Speed ratings (Par 101): **98,97,95,93,93 93,92,90,79,52 31,25,23**
toteswingers:1&2:£32.00, 1&3:£12.10, 2&3:£3.00 CSF £137.72 CT £682.53 TOTE £13.40: £3.10, £4.30, £2.20; EX 204.90 Trifecta £156.30 Part won. Pool £211.25 - 0.20 winning units..There was no bid for the winner.
Owner A G Newcombe **Bred** Michael Ng **Trained** Yarnscombe, Devon

FOCUS
They went a fair gallop in this seller and the first three came from off the pace. The form is limited though and not a race to be with.
Turner's Touch Official explanation: jockey said gelding had no more to give

4690 JOHN SMITH'S BRIGHTON MILE CHALLENGE TROPHY (H'CAP) — 7f 214y
3:30 (3:30) (Class 4) (0-80,80) 3-Y-O+
£5,231 (£5,231; £1,207; £601; £301; £152) Stalls Low

Form — RPR

4343 **1** **Lastkingofscotland (IRE)**[6] 4522 4-9-1 **71** .... (v) HayleyTurner 14 — 81
(C R Dore) *midfield: brought to stands' rails and led 2f out: drvn and r.o gamely: jnd on line* — **8/1**

0032 **1** *dht* **Licence To Till (USA)**[6] 4501 3-9-0 **77** .... KierenFallon 12 — 86
(M Johnston) *chsd ldrs: effrt stands' side to press wnr fnl 2f: r.o gamely u.p to force a dead-heat* — **3/1**[1]

3650 **3** *3* **Musical Script (USA)**[13] 4308 7-8-2 **58** .... (b) AndreaAtzeni 8 — 61
(Mouse Hamilton-Fairley) *slowly away and sn drvn along: towards rr tl gd prog over 1f out: fin strly to snatch 3rd: nt rch ldrs* — **22/1**

1333 **4** *nk* **Ocean Countess (IRE)**[31] 3716 4-9-0 **70** .... CathyGannon 6 — 72
(Miss J Feilden) *hld up and bhd: rdn and stdy prog 2f out: r.o gamely to try to chal last 100yds: no imp after: lost 3rd nr fin* — **7/1**[3]

0011 **5** *1 3/4* **Kipchak (IRE)**[4] 4586 5-8-7 **63** .... (p) LiamKeniry 13 — 61
(C R Dore) *taken down early: plld hrd: led 4f: lost pl qckly: rdn and kpt on again ins fnl f* — **13/2**[2]

6210 **6** *1 3/4* **Eastern Gift**[19] 4108 5-8-11 **72** .... DeclanCannon(5) 9 — 66
(Miss Gay Kelleway) *chsd ldrs: rdn and effrt over 1f out: sn hanging bdly lft: nt rcvr* — **20/1**

0042 **7** *3/4* **Cheam Forever (USA)**[19] 4119 4-9-2 **72** .... SteveDrowne 3 — 65
(R Charlton) *cl up: drvn 2f out: btn over 1f out* — **7/1**[3]

0600 **8** *1* **Pegasus Again (USA)**[11] 4354 5-9-10 **80** .... (p) TomQueally 2 — 70
(R A Mills) *prom briefly: towards rr and drvn 1/2-way: sn btn* — **12/1**

0130 **9** *2 1/2* **Inquisitress**[4] 4591 6-8-2 **58** ow4 .... NeilChalmers 1 — 43
(J J Bridger) *effrt far side 1/2-way: tried gamely to chal over 1f out: sn wknd* — **20/1**

0062 **10** *1 1/2* **Leadenhall Lass (IRE)**[6] 4502 4-8-12 **68** .... (v) IanMongan 5 — 49
(P M Phelan) *taken down early: a bhd: no ch fnl 2f: lost action* — **14/1**

0400 **11** *nk* **Twilight Star (IRE)**[13] 4308 6-8-6 **67** .... (p) JohnFahy(5) 4 — 47
(R A Teal) *plld hrd: pressed ldrs over 4f: sn lost pl* — **12/1**

1451 **12** *2 1/4* **Very Well Red**[17] 4172 7-9-5 **75** .... ShaneKelly 10 — 50
(P W Hiatt) *pressed ldr 4f: lost pl qckly* — **16/1**

1m 36.83s (0.83) **Going Correction** +0.15s/f (Good)
WFA 3 from 4yo+ 7lb — 12 Ran SP% **116.2**
Speed ratings (Par 105): **101,101,98,97,95 94,93,92,89,88 88,85**WIN: Lastkingofscotland £4.30 Licence to Till £1.60 PL: LKS £2.30, LT £1.90 EX: LKS/LT £13.50 LT/LKS £17.10 CSF: LKS/LT £15.24, LT/LKS £12.49. T/C: LKS<&MS £260.73, LT&LKS&MS £226.35. toteswingers: LKS& LT £6.20, LKS&MS £39.60, LT&MS £30.80. TOTE £260.73 & £226.35
Owner Mrs Jennifer Marsh **Bred** Baronrath Stud **Trained** Cowbit, Lincs.
Owner The Vine Accord **Bred** John Hettinger **Trained** Middleham Moor, N Yorks

FOCUS
A competitive handicap in which the whole field headed over to the stands' rail. As a result a high draw proved an advantage and the form is rated around the dead-heaters.

Leadenhall Lass(IRE) Official explanation: jockey said filly lost its action inside final 2f

4691 E.B.F./ JACK SANDHU MAIDEN STKS 6f 209y

4:00 (4:01) (Class 5) 2-Y-O **£3,154** (£944; £472; £236; £117) **Stalls** Centre

Form RPR

042 **1** **Ahlaain (USA)**[22] 3991 2-9-3 79 .... WilliamBuick 5 84+
(D M Simcock) *sn pressing ldr: brought to stands' rails to ld wl over 2f out: sn rdn clr: unchal* **5/6**[1]

2 *4* **Muntasib (USA)** 2-9-3 0 .... TadhgO'Shea 4 73+
(M P Tregoning) *chsd ldrs: rdn 1/2-way: tk 2nd fnl 2f: rn green and wl hld by wnr after* **7/2**[2]

34 **3** *5* **Out Of The Storm**[16] 4203 2-8-12 0 .... SebSanders 3 55
(S Dow) *stdd s and plld v hrd: bhd: outpcd 1/2-way: wnt poor 3rd ins fnl f: carried hd v high* **4/1**[3]

05 **4** *4 ½* **Pineapple Pete (IRE)**[12] 4336 2-9-3 0 .... TomQueally 2 48
(P F I Cole) *chsd ldrs: wnt 2nd briefly over 2f out: sn struggling* **16/1**

0 **5** *nk* **Aquilifer (IRE)**[39] 3459 2-9-3 0 .... ShaneKelly 7 47
(W Jarvis) *s.s: sn in tch: pushed along 1/2-way: fdd over 2f out* **33/1**

06 **6** *17* **Van Doesburg (IRE)**[25] 3915 2-8-12 0 .... JohnFahy(5) 1 1
(J G Portman) *led tl wl over 2f out: racd alone centre crse and sn struggling: bdly t.o* **40/1**

1m 23.76s (0.66) **Going Correction** +0.15s/f (Good) **6 Ran SP% 108.0**
Speed ratings (Par 94): **102,97,91,86,86 66**
toteswingers:1&2:£1.30, 1&3:£1.60, 2&3:£2.50 CSF £3.62 TOTE £1.50: £1.10, £3.10; EX 4.00 TRIFECTA Not won..
Owner Sultan Ali **Bred** Kilboy Estate Inc **Trained** Newmarket, Suffolk

FOCUS
An ordinary maiden but another improved run from the winner.

NOTEBOOK
Ahlaain(USA) had shown more than enough on his latest start at Yarmouth to suggest that a race of this nature was within his ability and, with his main market rival a newcomer, he put his previous experience to good use, being ridden positively, grabbing the stands' side rail and drawing clear for an easy win. He might not have had to improve to win this, but he's still progressing nicely and will be interesting in nurseries. (op 4-5 tchd 8-11 and 10-11 in a place)
Muntasib(USA), an expensive purchase who holds Group 1 entries, hails from a stable that rarely strikes first time with its juveniles. He showed his inexperience in running green and was perhaps not totally at home on the track, but he showed more than enough to suggest that he'll do a lot better in time. A son of Mr Greeley, it's no surprise he's thought to want quick ground. (op 3-1)
Out Of The Storm, who tracked the winner through next to the stands' side rail, made little progress in the closing stages, but was hardly knocked about. Nurseries are now open to her and should offer better opportunities. (op 5-1)
Pineapple Pete(IRE) wasn't sure to appreciate the step up to 7f, but he needed this for a mark and can do better in handicaps. (op 14-1 tchd 12-1)
Aquilifer(IRE) has been gelded and shaped better than on his debut. (tchd 28-1)
Van Doesburg(IRE) is bred to stay all day and will be of more interest once handicapping over further. (op 66-1)

4692 JOHN MCDONNELL PUBS AND BOOKMAKERS H'CAP 5f 213y

4:30 (4:31) (Class 6) (0-55,55) 3-Y-O **£1,683** (£501; £250; £125) **Stalls** Low

Form RPR

6530 **1** **Ellen Vannin (IRE)**[16] 4210 3-8-9 53 ....(p) PatrickHills(3) 4 58
(Eve Johnson Houghton) *cl up: led 2f out: rdn and gng best fnl f: styd on stoutly* **7/1**

000 **2** *1* **Gilderoy**[18] 4133 3-8-5 48 ow1 .... AshleyHamblett(3) 3 51
(D J S Ffrench Davis) *chsd ldrs: rdn 2f out: styd on and wnt 2nd wl ins fnl f: nt rch wnr* **16/1**

4232 **3** *½* **Rosiliant (IRE)**[14] 4248 3-8-8 54 ....(b) JohnFahy(5) 9 54
(C G Cox) *prom: drvn and chsng wnr 2f out: nt qckn and lost 2nd wl ins fnl f* **2/1**[1]

4000 **4** *2 ½* **Marjolly (IRE)**[21] 4025 3-9-0 55 .... TadhgO'Shea 6 47
(J Gallagher) *bhd: drvn 1/2-way: wnt mod 4th 1f out: no ch w ldrs* **16/1**

5605 **5** *nse* **Slasi**[16] 4210 3-8-12 53 ....(b[1]) SebSanders 1 45
(C E Brittain) *led: crossed to stands' side 1/2-way: drvn and hdd 2f out: sn lost pl* **7/2**[2]

4-00 **6** *1 ¾* **Old Devil Moon (IRE)**[157] 745 3-8-7 48 .... JamesDoyle 7 34
(R A Mills) *drvn vigorously thrght: w ldr 2f out but nvr gng wl: wknd wl over 1f out* **5/1**[3]

6040 **7** *3 ¼* **Patachou**[16] 4210 3-8-0 46 oh1 ....(v) KierenFox(5) 5 22
(R J Smith) *drvn and struggling fr 1/2-way* **22/1**

-046 **8** *3 ¾* **Lady Hetherington**[17] 998 3-8-5 53 ....(v[1]) LucyBarry(7) 8 17
(G Brown) *rdn and struggling bdly fr 1/2-way* **20/1**

9 *44* **Silent Annie**[341] 5414 3-8-9 50 .... LiamKeniry 10 —
(Matthew Salaman) *sddle slipped leaving stalls: eased bef 1/2-way: hacked on t.o* **9/1**

1m 11.31s (1.11) **Going Correction** +0.15s/f (Good) **9 Ran SP% 115.6**
Speed ratings (Par 98): **98,96,96,92,92 90,85,80,22**
toteswingers:1&2:£15.80, 1&3:£3.40, 2&3:£7.50 CSF £110.26 CT £307.01 TOTE £10.50: £2.90, £7.30, £1.10; EX 187.50.
Owner Mrs J E O'Halloran **Bred** Mrs J O'Halloran **Trained** Blewbury, Oxon

FOCUS
An ordinary sprint handicap, no better than a seller. The third is rated just below her recent best but the form is not solid.
Silent Annie Official explanation: jockey said saddle slipped leaving stalls

4693 ALICE RYAN MEMORIAL H'CAP 5f 59y

5:00 (5:00) (Class 5) (0-75,74) 4-Y-O+ **£2,201** (£655; £327; £163) **Stalls** Low

Form RPR

0505 **1** **Billy Red**[20] 4043 6-9-5 72 ....(b) FergusSweeney 6 81
(J R Jenkins) *sn led: towed bunch to stands' side 1/2-way: hd cocked to one side but a holding rivals fnl f* **9/2**

0513 **2** *1 ¾* **Vhujon (IRE)**[20] 4043 5-9-4 74 .... RichardEvans(3) 5 77
(P D Evans) *hld up: rdn and effrt over 1f out: chsd wnr fnl f: wl hld* **11/2**

6-03 **3** *¾* **Comadoir (IRE)**[22] 3980 4-9-6 73 .... IanMongan 2 73
(Miss Jo Crowley) *chsd ldr: rdn wl over 1f out: lost 2nd 1f out: plugged on same pce* **4/1**[3]

0130 **4** *½* **Make My Dream**[19] 4090 7-9-5 72 .... TadhgO'Shea 1 71
(J Gallagher) *chsd ldrs: drvn fr 1/2-way: no ex 1f out* **10/3**[1]

3450 **5** *3* **Magical Speedfit (IRE)**[23] 3958 5-8-12 65 .... TomQueally 3 53
(G G Margarson) *last away: bhd: effrt 2f out: rdn and carried hd high: flattered briefly: fdd 1f out* **7/2**[2]

2123 **6** *1 ½* **Multahab**[36] 3527 11-8-13 66 ....(t) MarcHalford 4 49
(M Wigham) *chsd ldrs: rdn 1/2-way: btn over 1f out: eased ins fnl f* **13/2**

61.91 secs (-0.39) **Going Correction** +0.15s/f (Good) **6 Ran SP% 112.2**
Speed ratings (Par 103): **109,106,105,104,99 97**
toteswingers:1&2:£3.70, 1&3:£3.50, 2&3:£3.60 CSF £28.43 CT £104.94 TOTE £5.30: £3.50, £3.90; EX 26.20 Trifecta £79.70 Pool £483.06 - 4.48 winning units. Place 6 £413.22; Place 5 £50.87..
Owner Mrs Irene Hampson **Bred** D R Tucker **Trained** Royston, Herts

FOCUS
The betting suggested this was a very tight handicap and indeed there were five in line with a furlong to run. The placed horses are rated close to recent form.
T/Plt: £181.70 to a £1 stake. Pool:£57,944.89 - 232.72 winning tickets T/Qpdt: £12.50 to a £1 stake. Pool:£5,716.10 - 338.30 winning tickets IM

4227 KEMPTON (A.W) (R-H)

Wednesday, August 4

OFFICIAL GOING: Standard
Wind: Moderate, against Weather: Overcast, heavy rain before racing.

4694 KEMPTON.CO.UK APPRENTICE H'CAP 1m 3f (P)

6:05 (6:06) (Class 4) (0-85,85) 4-Y-O+ **£3,885** (£1,156; £577; £288) **Stalls** High

Form RPR

1331 **1** **Resentful Angel**[28] 3781 5-9-1 81 .... JamesRogers(5) 5 91
(Pat Eddery) *trckd ldr: pushed into ld 2f out: sn jnd: rdn and styd on wl fr over 1f out* **3/1**[2]

1125 **2** *1 ¼* **Speed Dating**[26] 3873 4-9-7 85 ....(b) RosieJessop(3) 3 93
(Sir Mark Prescott) *hld up in 5th: smooth prog to chal 2f out: w wnr over 1f out: nt qckn* **2/1**[1]

2601 **3** *2 ½* **Blue Tango (IRE)**[15] 4227 4-8-12 73 ....(v) SimonPearce 1 76
(Mrs A J Perrett) *trckd ldng pair: lost pl sltly 3f out: effrt to chse ldng pair over 1f out: kpt on but no imp* **15/2**

254- **4** *4 ½* **Panto Princess**[281] 7101 4-8-7 71 .... AmyScott(3) 6 66
(H Candy) *led: kicked on 4f out: hdd and fdd 2f out* **8/1**

1650 **5** *6* **Ebiayn (FR)**[2] 4657 4-8-9 70 ....(v) RossAtkinson 4 54
(A King) *chsd ldng pair: rdn 3f out: wknd qckly 2f out* **10/1**

2-01 **6** *1* **Sircozy (IRE)**[40] 3416 4-8-7 73 .... HarryBentley(5) 2 56
(G L Moore) *hld up in last: lost tch whn pce lifted 4f out: nvr on terms after* **7/2**[3]

2m 20.29s (-1.61) **Going Correction** -0.025s/f (Stan) **6 Ran SP% 112.5**
Speed ratings (Par 105): **104,103,101,98,93 92**
toteswingers:1&2:£1.60, 1&3:£4.20, 2&3:£3.60 CSF £9.49 TOTE £5.20: £3.30, £1.10; EX 9.70.
Owner P J J Eddery **Bred** Patrick Eddery Ltd **Trained** Nether Winchendon, Bucks

FOCUS
Only six runners but a very tight apprentice handicap. The form isd a bit muddling with the third the best guide, but the winner is progresive.
Sircozy(IRE) Official explanation: jockey said gelding ran flat

4695 HOROHOE CONSTRUCTION MEDIAN AUCTION MAIDEN STKS 7f (P)

6:35 (6:35) (Class 5) 2-Y-O **£2,320** (£685; £342) **Stalls** High

Form RPR

53 **1** **Marston Moor (USA)**[18] 4142 2-9-3 0 .... AhmedAjtebi 1 76+
(Mahmood Al Zarooni) *pressed ldr: led narrowly 2f out: hrd pressed and rdn over 1f out: styd on wl fnl f* **11/4**[1]

2 *1* **Amhran (IRE)** 2-9-3 0 .... MartinDwyer 8 73+
(B J Meehan) *trckd ldng pair: pushed up to chal over 1f out and nrly upsides: shkn up and nt qckn fnl f* **12/1**

4 **3** *nk* **Safari Team (IRE)**[14] 4253 2-9-3 0 .... JimCrowley 13 72
(P Winkworth) *mde most: rdn and narrowly hdd 2f out: styd on same pce fnl f* **8/1**

4 *3 ¼* **Night Carnation** 2-8-12 0 .... DavidProbert 9 59+
(A M Balding) *dwlt: hld up towards rr: prog on inner over 2f out: styd on same pce to take 4th fnl f* **20/1**

5 *1 ¾* **Mark Harbour (IRE)** 2-9-3 0 .... RichardHughes 3 59+
(R Hannon) *trckd ldng trio: shkn up and no imp over 2f out: one pce and pushed along after* **6/1**

6 *1* **Iron Green (FR)** 2-9-3 0 .... EddieAhern 14 56
(Mrs H S Main) *hld up in midfield: outpcd by ldrs over 2f out: kpt on same pce after* **66/1**

7 *¾* **Kalgoolie** 2-8-12 0 .... ChrisCatlin 2 49
(Rae Guest) *rn green in midfield: outpcd by ldrs over 2f out: no prog after* **66/1**

8 *1 ½* **Rain Mac** 2-9-3 0 .... WilliamBuick 6 50+
(J H M Gosden) *dwlt: wl in rr and rn green: hanging lft bnd 4f out: bhd and rdn over 2f out: styd on wl fnl f* **7/2**[2]

9 *4 ½* **Dells Breezer** 2-8-12 0 .... JemmaMarshall(5) 10 38
(P M Phelan) *chsd ldng trio: rdn over 2f out: wknd qckly over 1f out* **100/1**

10 *shd* **Memory Lane** 2-8-12 0 .... SebSanders 11 33
(Sir Mark Prescott) *nvr bttr than midfield: wl off the pce over 2f out: bhd after* **11/1**

11 *2* **Droxford (USA)** 2-8-12 0 .... SophieDoyle(5) 5 32
(J A Osborne) *a wl in rr: rdn in last pair bef 1/2-way: bhd after* **100/1**

0 **12** *4 ½* **Blue Cossack (IRE)**[55] 2887 2-8-12 0 .... LeeNewnes(5) 4 20
(M D I Usher) *a wl in rr: rdn in last pair bef 1/2-way: bhd after* **66/1**

13 *6* **Govenor General (IRE)** 2-9-3 0 .... RyanMoore 12 4
(J Noseda) *s.v.s: mostly in last trio: brief effrt 3f out: sn wknd and wl bhd* **11/2**[3]

1m 27.21s (1.21) **Going Correction** -0.025s/f (Stan) **13 Ran SP% 116.9**
Speed ratings (Par 94): **92,90,90,86,84 83,82,81,75,75 73,68,61**
toteswingers:1&2:£5.80, 1&3:£6.00, 2&3:£12.00 CSF £35.58 TOTE £3.70: £1.40, £4.10, £2.50; EX 43.40.
Owner Godolphin **Bred** Giles Tucker **Trained** Newmarket, Suffolk

FOCUS
Little public form with which to measure this maiden auction. The winner did not need to run to his previous form to score.

NOTEBOOK
Marston Moor(USA) had finished last on his debut in a Group 2 then third in a 6f Newmarket maiden that doesn't look much at present. However, he had the experience to overcome a moderate draw to get on the pace and the extra furlong here really helped him. It's hard to say how much improvement there is in him. (op 3-1 tchd 7-2)
Amhran(IRE) was another of Brian Meehan's recent juvenile runners to show real promise and while his Mill Reef entry might be asking too much in the immediate future he will be very hard to beat next time given the improvement his stable's horses make from their debut. He seems to have the pace to cope with 6f. (op 9-1)
Safari Team(IRE) lasted considerably longer than on his debut over this trip at Lingfield 14 days earlier and should win a race of this type without much bother. (tchd 10-1 in a place)
Night Carnation was extremely immature on her debut and did well to overcome greeness after the start to get into the race. This was a big ask for a filly and against her own sex next time she'll be a handful. (op 25-1)
Mark Harbour(IRE) overcame a moderate draw but just ran out of steam as his prolific stable's debutants can sometimes do. He'll be a different proposition next time. (op 5-1 tchd 9-2)

Iron Green(FR) represented a yard that has yet to have a winner, but he will come on for this debut and has several decent winners in his pedigree. He'll win a race on this providing he is played at a smaller venue over this trip.
Kalgoolie showed pace but will be better against her own sex.
Rain Mac is bred to want considerably further than this and immaturity plus a moderate draw didn't help him, indeed he was still showing signs of greeness before buckling down well in the closing stages. A mile and a more galloping track would seem more suitable. Official explanation: jockey ssid, regarding running and riding, that his orders were to give the colt a good race and look after it on it first run, adding that it shied away from other horses and ran too freely in the home straight. (op 4-1)
Blue Cossack(IRE) Official explanation: jockey said colt hung left-handed
Govenor General(IRE) Official explanation: jockey said colt missed the break

4696 DIGIBET NURSERY — 6f (P)
7:05 (7:06) (Class 4) (0-85,83) 2-Y-O — £3,238 (£963; £481; £240) Stalls High

Form — RPR
01 **1** **Dozy Joe**[15] 4221 2-9-0 **76** ...... RyanMoore 4 — 79+
(I A Wood) *wl in tch on outer: tapped for spd over 2f out and dropped to last briefly: drvn and r.o fr over 1f out: led fnl 150yds: sn clr* **13/2**
664 **2** *1* **Avalon Bay**[15] 4228 2-8-0 **62** ...... AndreaAtzeni 1 — 62
(Pat Eddery) *stdd s: t.k.h: hld up in last pair: rdn 2f out: styd on wl fnl f to take 2nd nr fin* **12/1**
461 **3** *nk* **Our Way Only (IRE)**[13] 4299 2-8-11 **73** ...... RichardHughes 5 — 72
(R Hannon) *trckd ldr: edgd lft whn rdn over 2f out: effrt to dispute ld briefly jst ins fnl f: nt qckn* **7/2**[3]
024 **4** *hd* **Hortensia (IRE)**[26] 3859 2-9-4 **80** ...... ChrisCatlin 8 — 78
(M R Channon) *trckd ldng pair: rdn to chse ldr 2f out: disp ld briefly jst ins fnl f: outpcd* **12/1**
441 **5** *2* **Miss Clairton**[44] 3260 2-9-3 **79** ...... SebSanders 6 — 71
(Sir Mark Prescott) *led at mod pce: kicked on over 2f out and styd on inner: hdd & wknd jst ins fnl f* **11/4**[1]
012 **6** *1* **Ocean Drift (USA)**[12] 4331 2-9-7 **83** ...... (p) AhmedAjtebi 7 — 72
(Mahmood Al Zarooni) *awkward s: t.k.h: hld up in tch: rdn over 2f out: fnd nil and btn over 1f out* **10/3**[2]
4526 **7** *1 ¾* **Good Morning Dubai (IRE)**[32] 3658 2-9-1 **77** ...... MartinDwyer 3 — 60
(B J Meehan) *hld up in last pair: rdn over 2f out: no prog over 1f out: wknd* **8/1**

1m 13.61s (0.51) **Going Correction** -0.025s/f (Stan) — **7** Ran SP% **111.8**
Speed ratings (Par 96): **95,93,93,93,90 89,86**
toteswingers:1&2:£3.50, 1&3:£3.70, 2&3:£2.80 CSF £73.31 CT £311.69 TOTE £8.20: £6.20, £8.30; EX 124.70.
Owner Paddy Barrett **Bred** J Morton **Trained** Upper Lambourn, Berks

FOCUS
Five of the seven runners were making their nursery debuts. The form is a bit muddling with the placed horses the best guides.

NOTEBOOK
Dozy Joe continued his upward profile having dead-heated at Ffos Las 15 days earlier after showing little on debut, but showed a good attitude and turn of pace here. It remains to be seen how far he will be moved off a mark of 76 but he stays this trip well and might be able to win another of these if he improves at the same rate. (op 6-1 tchd 7-1)
Avalon Bay was another nursery debutant having made his previous three appearances on this surface and off 62 produced much his best effort, and coming from slightly off the pace seemed to suit him. (tchd 16-1)
Our Way Only(IRE) won over 7f on turf last time and ran with credit. It's possible moving back to his winning trip might be beneficial. (op 5-2)
Hortensia(IRE) had gone up 2lb for finishing a readily held fourth last time but this looked a better effort and he could be knocking on the door next time. (tchd 14-1)
Miss Clairton, another nursery debutant, had done her running and winning over 5f and, running from the front, seemed to be caught out by this sixth furlong. (op 10-3 tchd 5-2)
Ocean Drift(USA) already doesn't look a nice ride, pulling hard then carrying his head high. Cheekpieces didn't help and neither did a 2lb weight rise and a drop back to 6f. Certainly not one to trust. (op 4-1)

4697 DIGIBET.COM MAIDEN STKS — 1m (P)
7:35 (7:39) (Class 5) 3-Y-O+ — £2,320 (£685; £342) Stalls High

Form — RPR
64 **1** **Conciliatory**[40] 3407 3-8-12 0 ...... MartinDwyer 14 — 78
(Rae Guest) *hld up in 6th on inner: prog 2f out: rdn to chal fnl f: styd on wl to ld nr fin* **12/1**
3- **2** *nk* **Hamloola**[270] 7288 3-8-12 0 ...... RichardHills 3 — 77
(W J Haggas) *trckd ldng pair: gng easily over 2f out: shkn up to ld jst over 1f out: hdd and nt qckn nr fin* **9/4**[1]
2 **3** *1 ½* **Calipatria**[12] 4340 3-8-12 0 ...... WilliamBuick 10 — 74
(J H M Gosden) *chsd ldng quartet: shkn up over 2f out and no prog: r.o wl fnl f to take 3rd nr fin* **3/1**[2]
20 **4** *¾* **Captivator**[34] 3586 3-8-12 0 ...... HayleyTurner 1 — 72+
(J R Fanshawe) *v s.i.s and green: wl in rr: pushed along and gd prog 2f out: chsd ldng trio over 1f out: shkn up and styd on same pce* **14/1**
5 *¾* **Alioonagh (USA)** 3-8-12 0 ...... RyanMoore 12 — 70
(N P Littmoden) *led 1f: restrained bhd ldng pair: shkn up to ld 2f out: hdd jst over 1f out: fdd* **15/2**
6 *6* **Equine Science** 3-8-12 0 ...... SophieDoyle(5) 8 — 61?
(G D Blake) *in tch in midfield: rdn and outpcd fr 2f out: styd on again fnl f* **100/1**
7 *2 ½* **Hear Hear** 3-8-12 0 ...... ChrisCatlin 2 — 51
(D R Lanigan) *s.i.s and rn green in rr: shkn up and sme prog fr 2f out: wl outpcd over 1f out* **50/1**
8 *1 ¼* **Saint Pierre (USA)** 3-9-3 0 ...... KierenFallon 13 — 53
(L M Cumani) *t.k.h: pressed ldr after 1f to over 2f out: wknd rapidly over 1f out* **13/2**[3]
35 **9** *2 ¼* **Mount Acclaim (IRE)**[23] 3952 4-9-5 0 ...... FergusSweeney 4 — 44
(J A Osborne) *led after 1f to 2f out: wknd rapidly over 1f out* **100/1**
10 *4 ½* **Mouchez** 3-9-3 0 ...... SamHitchcott 11 — 37
(D K Ivory) *a in rr: in tch to 2f out: wknd rapidly* **100/1**
20 **11** *2 ¼* **Storming Redd**[85] 2011 3-9-3 0 ...... SebSanders 7 — 32
(J M P Eustace) *in tch: rdn and wknd over 2f out* **50/1**
12 *3 ¼* **Tristar Way (GR)** 3-9-3 0 ...... JimCrowley 6 — 25
(P R Chamings) *s.i.s: racd wd and a in rr: brought to nr side rail 2f out: bhd after* **50/1**
13 *1 ¼* **Chateau Galliard (IRE)** 4-9-10 0 ...... DaneO'Neill 5 — 23
(T T Clement) *s.s: a in last pair: carried lft to nr side rail 2f out: bhd after* **100/1**

1m 40.06s (0.26) **Going Correction** -0.025s/f (Stan)
WFA 3 from 4yo 7lb — **13** Ran SP% **105.1**
Speed ratings (Par 103): **97,96,95,94,93 87,85,83,81,77 74,71,70**
toteswingers:1&2:£6.70, 1&3:£9.30, 2&3:£1.50 CSF £31.19 TOTE £11.80: £2.50, £1.30, £1.30; EX 52.20.
Owner Miss K Rausing **Bred** Miss K Rausing **Trained** Newmarket, Suffolk

FOCUS
Not a strong early pace and four were having their third run to get a rating. The form is rated around those in the frame behind the winner.
Tristar Way(GR) Official explanation: jockey said colt hung left-handed throughout

4698 DIGIBET CASINO H'CAP — 1m 3f (P)
8:05 (8:08) (Class 5) (0-75,75) 3-Y-O — £2,320 (£685; £342) Stalls High

Form — RPR
3045 **1** **Wild Rose**[12] 4341 3-9-7 **75** ...... (t) HayleyTurner 1 — 90
(M L W Bell) *trckd ldr: gng easily 3f out: pushed into ld 2f out and sn clr: in n.d after* **15/2**
2500 **2** *3* **Iron Condor**[41] 3376 3-8-12 **66** ...... SebSanders 6 — 76
(J M P Eustace) *hld up in last pair early: stdy prog fr 4f out: hrd rdn to go 2nd over 1f out: styd on but no ch w wnr* **20/1**
000 **3** *4 ½* **Beat Route**[11] 4360 3-8-7 **66** ...... JemmaMarshall(5) 5 — 68
(M J Attwater) *trckd ldrs: shkn up over 2f out: sn outpcd: disp 2nd over 1f out: one pce* **16/1**
0146 **4** *2* **Onyx Of Arabia (IRE)**[23] 3963 3-9-6 **74** ...... (b) MartinDwyer 10 — 72
(B J Meehan) *wl in rr: last and pushed along 1/2-way: stl there and hrd rdn 3f out: styd on fr over 2f out to take modest 4th fnl f* **13/2**[3]
605- **5** *1 ½* **Viviani (IRE)**[286] 6965 3-8-11 **65** ...... (t) PatDobbs 11 — 60
(Mrs A J Perrett) *trckd ldng pair: rdn over 2f out: wknd over 1f out* **10/1**
065 **6** *hd* **Balatoma (IRE)**[53] 2974 3-9-1 **69** ...... WilliamBuick 7 — 64
(M P Tregoning) *hld up last early: rdn wl over 2f out: plugged on: n.d* **14/1**
320 **7** *hd* **Norse Dame**[28] 3795 3-9-4 **72** ...... DaneO'Neill 8 — 66
(D R C Elsworth) *hld up in 7th: shkn up and outpcd over 2f out: nvr on terms w ldrs after* **16/1**
02-5 **8** *1 ¼* **Flipping**[26] 3857 3-9-2 **70** ...... FergusSweeney 2 — 62
(W S Kittow) *led: drvn and hdd 2f out: wknd* **20/1**
3-43 **9** *10* **Elvira Madigan**[25] 3889 3-9-3 **71** ...... DavidProbert 12 — 45
(A M Balding) *chsd ldrs: rdn 3f out: wknd 2f out: sn bhd* **9/2**[2]
1- **10** *8* **Too Putra (IRE)**[251] 7538 3-9-5 **73** ...... SteveDrowne 3 — 33
(R Charlton) *chsd ldrs: pushed along on outer 4f out: sn lost pl and struggling: t.o* **3/1**[1]

2m 19.71s (-2.19) **Going Correction** -0.025s/f (Stan) — **10** Ran SP% **105.3**
Speed ratings (Par 100): **106,103,100,99,98 97,97,96,89,83**
toteswingers:1&2:£19.40, 1&3:£33.00, 2&3:£56.00 CSF £118.07 CT £1668.71 TOTE £8.80: £2.60, £6.60, £4.40; EX 116.70.
Owner Saif Ali & Saeed H Altayer **Bred** Biddestone Stud **Trained** Newmarket, Suffolk

FOCUS
A modest class 5 handicap with some exposed performers. The time was decent and the form is rated at face value.
Too Putra(IRE) Official explanation: jockey said colt never travelled

4699 PREMIER LEAGUE H'CAP (LONDON MILE QUALIFIER) — 1m (P)
8:35 (8:36) (Class 4) (0-85,84) 3-Y-O — £3,885 (£1,156; £577; £288) Stalls High

Form — RPR
3415 **1** **Shamir**[21] 4023 3-9-6 **83** ...... IanMongan 8 — 90
(Miss Jo Crowley) *chsd ldrs: rdn and prog to go 3rd 2f out: drvn to ld ins fnl f: hld on wl* **10/1**
3-21 **2** *nk* **Tartan Trip**[14] 4265 3-9-4 **81** ...... DavidProbert 6 — 87
(A M Balding) *hld up in last trio: prog on outer fr 2f out: r.o to press wnr last 100yds: a jst hld* **5/1**
5113 **3** *nk* **Warning Song (USA)**[13] 4302 3-8-13 **76** ...... PatDobbs 7 — 82+
(Mrs A J Perrett) *hld up in last trio: prog on outer over 1f out: r.o wl fnl f to take 3rd nr fin* **25/1**
4531 **4** *nk* **State Gathering**[28] 3782 3-9-6 **83** ...... DaneO'Neill 2 — 88
(H Candy) *pressed ldr after 2f: led jst over 2f out: hdd and one pce ins fnl f* **4/1**[3]
6-11 **5** *3 ¾* **Naddwah**[14] 4250 3-9-2 **79** ...... PhilipRobinson 10 — 75
(M A Jarvis) *t.k.h early: trckd ldr 2f: cl up 2f out: sn rdn and nt qckn: fdd* **7/2**[2]
0345 **6** *½* **Burghley**[25] 3886 3-9-6 **83** ...... HayleyTurner 5 — 78
(M L W Bell) *led at decent pce: hdd jst over 2f out: btn whn faltered briefly over 1f out: wknd* **12/1**
06-2 **7** *1 ¾* **Aultcharn (FR)**[106] 1450 3-9-4 **81** ...... MartinDwyer 9 — 72
(B J Meehan) *t.k.h: lost pl after 2f: rdn on inner over 2f out: sme prog over 1f out: wknd fnl f* **12/1**
1-2 **8** *11* **Gracious Melange**[119] 1159 3-9-3 **80** ...... KierenFallon 4 — 46
(M Botti) *t.k.h: hld up: trckd ldrs 1/2-way: wknd rapidly 2f out: t.o* **3/1**[1]
1500 **9** *1* **Admiral Cochrane (IRE)**[112] 1315 3-9-7 **84** ...... JimCrowley 1 — 48
(W Jarvis) *settled in last fr wd draw: rdn and wknd over 2f out: t.o* **40/1**

1m 38.61s (-1.19) **Going Correction** -0.025s/f (Stan) — **9** Ran SP% **114.6**
Speed ratings (Par 102): **104,103,103,103,99 98,97,86,85**
toteswingers:1&2:£17.10, 1&3:£24.10, 2&3:£25.40 CSF £58.86 CT £1218.63 TOTE £16.60: £3.80, £2.70, £6.80; EX 66.50.
Owner Kilstone Limited **Bred** Plantation Stud **Trained** Whitcombe, Dorset

FOCUS
A tricky handicap with not a particularly strong early pace which saw several of these pulling too hard. However, the time was reasonable and the winner is progressive.

4700 EPSOM TRAINERS OPEN DAY 22ND AUGUST H'CAP — 1m (P)
9:05 (9:05) (Class 6) (0-65,65) 3-Y-O+ — £1,637 (£483; £241) Stalls High

Form — RPR
5200 **1** **Sovereignty (JPN)**[37] 3510 8-8-11 **53** ...... SophieDoyle(5) 1 — 64
(D K Ivory) *t.k.h: racd wd: w ldrs: led over 2f out and sn at least 2l clr: rdn and pressed fnl f: styd on wl* **20/1**
-545 **2** *¾* **Safari Guide**[11] 4366 4-9-6 **57** ...... JimCrowley 8 — 66
(P Winkworth) *t.k.h: hld up in last trio: prog on outer over 2f out: chsd wnr over 1f out: clsd to chal fnl f: nt qckn last 100yds* **17/2**
0223 **3** *4* **Harting Hill**[28] 3777 5-9-12 **63** ...... PatDobbs 9 — 63+
(M P Tregoning) *trckd ldrs: prog on inner over 2f out: kpt on same pce fr over 1f out* **3/1**[1]
250- **4** *hd* **Lend A Grand (IRE)**[436] 2330 6-9-9 **60** ...... IanMongan 4 — 59
(Miss Jo Crowley) *s.i.s: t.k.h: hld up in last trio: prog on outer over 1f out: styd on: nrly tk 3rd* **14/1**
0540 **5** *1 ½* **Grey Boy (GER)**[11] 4366 9-8-13 **57** ...... GeorgeDowning(7) 10 — 53
(A W Carroll) *hld up in tch: effrt and chsd ldrs wl over 1f out: one pce after* **14/1**
4426 **6** *1 ¾* **Fire Raiser**[23] 3954 3-9-3 **61** ...... DavidProbert 12 — 52+
(A M Balding) *hld up on inner: looking for room over 2f out: kpt on same pce fr over 1f out: no ch* **7/2**[2]

050 **7** *1* **Medici Brave**[13] 4307 3-9-1 **59** MartinDwyer 6 48
(Mrs A J Perrett) *pressed ldr: disp ld briefly wl over 2f out: wknd over 1f out* **14/1**

-100 **8** *1* **Munich (IRE)**[8] 3683 6-9-11 **62** (v[1]) DaneO'Neill 3 49
(R Curtis) *hld up towards rr: rdn 3f out: sn struggling: n.d after* **14/1**

0005 **9** *1 ¼* **Kilmanseck**[28] 3771 3-9-4 **62** (p) AndreaAtzeni 5 45
(Eve Johnson Houghton) *pressed ldng pair: upsides over 2f out: wknd over 1f out* **20/1**

-423 **10** *1 ¼* **Cottonfields (USA)**[9] 4428 4-9-10 **61** (p) EddieAhern 2 43
(Mrs H S Main) *trckd ldrs: pushed along and nt qckn 2f out: steadily wknd* **11/2**[3]

3066 **11** *3 ¾* **Blue Charm**[48] 3124 6-9-11 **62** (b[1]) LiamKeniry 11 35
(I W McInnes) *v awkward leaving stalls and lost abt 8 l: in tch at bk of field after 4f to over 2f out: wknd* **11/1**

3045 **12** *¾* **Decree Absolute (USA)**[11] 4383 3-9-2 **60** (e[1]) PaulFitzsimons 14 30
(Miss J R Tooth) *led to wl over 2f out: wknd rapidly* **33/1**

1m 38.99s (-0.81) **Going Correction** -0.025s/f (Stan)
WFA 3 from 4yo+ 7lb **12** Ran SP% **120.6**
Speed ratings (Par 101): **103,102,98,98,96 94,93,92,91,90 86,85**
toteswingers:1&2:£22.10, 1&3:£10.80, 2&3:£8.40 CSF £180.17 CT £677.20 TOTE £33.10: £8.20, £2.00, £1.70; EX 345.90 Place 6 £1,341.11; Place 5 £1,031.90.
Owner Radlett Racing **Bred** Darley Stud Management, L L C **Trained** Radlett, Herts

FOCUS
A moderate contest but the pace was good and the winner is rated back to last year's form.
Blue Charm Official explanation: jockey said gelding anticipated stalls opening
T/Plt: £486.50 to a £1 stake. Pool:£53,684.62 - 80.55 winning tickets T/Qpdt: £217.10 to a £1 stake. Pool:£5,664.06 - 19.30 winning tickets JN

4367 NEWCASTLE (L-H)
Wednesday, August 4

OFFICIAL GOING: Good to firm (good in places; watered; stands' side to centre 7.5; far side to centre 7.6)
Rail dolled out 2yds from 4.5f to winning post on stands' rail.
Wind: Slight, half against Weather: Overcast, dry

4701 ODDSCHECKER.COM WEDNESDAYS NURSERY 7f
2:20 (2:20) (Class 4) (0-85,75) 2-Y-O **£3,238** (£963; £481; £240) **Stalls** Centre

Form RPR

531 **1** **Sky Falcon (USA)**[14] 4247 2-9-7 **75** RoystonFfrench 11 78+
(M Johnston) *cl up: effrt over 2f out: led ins fnl f: drvn out* **2/1**[1]

344 **2** *¾* **Nicola's Dream**[25] 3923 2-8-13 **67** PaulHanagan 6 68
(R A Fahey) *prom: effrt and rdn over 2f out: chsd wnr wl ins fnl f: r.o* **7/2**[2]

435 **3** *nk* **Eland Ally**[11] 4368 2-8-13 **67** AndrewMullen 5 67
(T P Tate) *led: hung to far rail over 2f out: hdd ins fnl f: kpt on same pce* **7/1**

4464 **4** *hd* **Golden Blaze**[14] 4242 2-8-0 **57** JamesSullivan[(3)] 9 57
(James Moffatt) *hld up: rdn and hdwy over 2f out: kpt on fin* **20/1**

0001 **5** *1* **Water Ice**[9] 4429 2-9-6 **74** 6ex RichardKingscote 7 71
(Tom Dascombe) *uns rdr leaving paddock: trckd ldrs: rdn over 2f out: rallied: no ex wl ins fnl f* **9/2**[3]

4526 **6** *2* **Unknown Rebel (IRE)**[5] 4544 2-8-11 **65** (p) SilvestreDeSousa 10 57
(K A Ryan) *t.k.h: trckd ldrs: rdn over 2f out: nt qckn appr fnl f* **9/1**

0003 **7** *½* **Market Maker (IRE)**[48] 3106 2-8-13 **67** (b[1]) DavidAllan 4 57
(T D Easterby) *bhd: rdn 1/2-way: hdwy u.p over 1f out: nvr able to chal* **12/1**

4461 **8** *6* **Peppercorn Rent (IRE)**[18] 4150 2-8-5 **59** (e) DuranFentiman 2 33
(T D Easterby) *trckd ldrs tl rdn and wknd over 2f out* **25/1**

560 **9** *2 ½* **Louis Girl**[32] 3665 2-8-2 **56** AndrewElliott 1 23
(R A Fahey) *prom: lost pl 1/2-way: n.d after* **50/1**

630 **10** *3 ¾* **Imperial Waltzer**[92] 1806 2-8-7 **61** TomEaves 8 18
(G M Moore) *hld up bhd ldng gp: struggling over 2f out: sn btn* **50/1**

1m 28.87s (0.17) **Going Correction** -0.30s/f (Firm) **10** Ran SP% **116.5**
Speed ratings (Par 96): **87,86,85,85,84 82,81,74,71,67**
toteswingers:1&2:£2.30, 1&3:£5.30, 2&3:£4.60 CSF £8.50 CT £40.52 TOTE £2.00: £1.02, £3.00, £3.00; EX 8.20.
Owner Jaber Abdullah **Bred** Woodford Thoroughbreds LLC **Trained** Middleham Moor, N Yorks

FOCUS
A modest nursery rated around the placed horses. The runners came down the middle, with the exception of the third, and were faced with a headwind.

NOTEBOOK
Sky Falcon(USA) was a typically game winner for one from his stable when narrowly off the mark at Leicester a fortnight earlier and was popular for this nursery debut. He followed up with another brave effort under top weight and is clearly progressive. He will enjoy another furlong and remains one to follow, as he shouldn't be put up too much for this. (op 9-4)
Nicola's Dream was solid in the betting for this switch to a nursery and she ran well, enjoying the longer trip as expected. Indeed she left the impression a stronger overall pace would've been more up her street and can soon go one better. (op 3-1 tchd 11-4)
Eland Ally improved for the return to quicker ground, but would've likely gone closer still had he kept a true line and is evidently still learning his trade. (op 8-1 tchd 9-1)
Golden Blaze was doing his best work late in the day and reversed last-time-out form with Unknown Rebel on 2lb better terms. (op 25-1)
Water Ice showed her true colours when off the mark at the first attempt in this sphere nine days earlier and she ran a fair race under her penalty, but was unable to land a serious blow back on turf. (op 4-1)

4702 ENVIRONMENTAL ENGINEERING MEDIAN AUCTION MAIDEN STKS 6f
2:50 (2:51) (Class 6) 2-Y-O **£1,942** (£578; £288; £144) **Stalls** Centre

Form RPR

32 **1** **Malgoof (IRE)**[14] 4240 2-9-3 0 TomEaves 2 83
(B Smart) *mde all: rdn over 1f out: styd on strly to go clr last 100yds* **11/4**[1]

2 *3 ¾* **Celtic Sixpence (IRE)** 2-8-12 0 WilliamCarson 11 68+
(M G Quinlan) *t.k.h: prom: effrt and chsd wnr over 2f out: plld clr of rest fnl f but no ch w wnr last 100yds* **6/1**

3 *3 ¾* **Inside** 2-8-12 0 PaulHanagan 1 54
(R A Fahey) *trckd ldrs: effrt and rdn over 2f out: outpcd by first two fnl f* **11/1**

4 **4** *nk* **Chosen Character (IRE)**[18] 4123 2-9-3 0 RichardKingscote 5 58
(Tom Dascombe) *hld up bhd ldng gp: pushed along 1/2-way: rallied over 1f out: kpt on fnl f: nvr able to chal* **4/1**[2]

0 **5** *1 ¼* **Say A Prayer**[33] 3624 2-8-12 0 (b[1]) DavidAllan 10 49
(T D Easterby) *dwlt: sn in tch: effrt 2f out: no imp fnl f* **33/1**

6 *½* **Elusive Love (IRE)** 2-9-3 0 RoystonFfrench 9 52
(M Johnston) *hld up bhd ldng gp: pushed along over 2f out: no imp fnl f* **8/1**

26 **7** *3 ½* **Piccoluck**[17] 4167 2-9-3 0 SilvestreDeSousa 3 41
(Mrs D J Sanderson) *trckd ldrs tl rdn and wknd appr fnl f* **11/2**[3]

4 **8** *½* **Purkab**[46] 3199 2-9-3 0 LNewman 7 40
(J S Goldie) *cl up tl rdn and outpcd over 2f out: sn btn* **11/1**

9 *4* **Cottam Donny** 2-8-10 0 JohnCavanagh[(7)] 8 27
(M Brittain) *uns rdr setting off for s: s.i.s: bhd and outpcd: hung lft and struggling fr 1/2-way* **100/1**

10 *1 ¾* **I Got You Babe (IRE)** 2-8-12 0 PaulEddery 6 16
(R C Guest) *hld up: drvn over 3f out: wknd over 2f out* **33/1**

11 *hd* **Ted's Brother (IRE)** 2-8-12 0 MarkCoumbe[(5)] 4 21
(R C Guest) *s.i.s: bhd: rdn and hung lft 3f out: sn struggling* **66/1**

1m 13.51s (-1.09) **Going Correction** -0.30s/f (Firm) **11** Ran SP% **112.5**
Speed ratings (Par 92): **95,90,85,84,82 82,77,76,71,69 69**
toteswingers:1&2:£5.00, 1&3:£4.30, 2&3:£11.90 CSF £18.03 TOTE £2.80: £1.60, £2.30, £2.40; EX 15.90.
Owner Fawzi Nass & Mahran Jamsheer **Bred** Holborn Trust Co **Trained** Hambleton, N Yorks
■ Stewards' Enquiry : William Carson one-day ban: failed to ride to draw (Aug 18)

FOCUS
An average juvenile maiden in which the runners elected to come down the centre. The winning time would suggest the ground was riding near good. The fourth is the best guide to the level.

NOTEBOOK
Malgoof(IRE) made it third time lucky with a ready effort from the front. He put the pressure on 2f out and was well on top at the finish, looking happier on this return to a sounder surface. He should be more than capable of making his mark in nurseries as connections believe there is plenty more to come from him as he matures physically. (tchd 9-4)
Celtic Sixpence(IRE) is a half-sister to two older winners and such moves for ones from her stable are always to be respected. She posted a solid debut effort, just losing out to a more-experienced rival, and this outing will not be lost on her. (op 9-2)
Inside ◆, bred to want further in due course, was easy to back for this initial outing and did more than enough to suggest she has a future. One could see her going very close next time out if faced with another furlong. (op 17-2)
Chosen Character(IRE), well backed late on, raced more professionally than had been the case on debut 18 days earlier, yet still left the impression this experience would help bring him on. (op 7-1)
Say A Prayer was equipped with first-time blinkers for this second outing and, making her effort more towards the nearside, turned in a much-improved effort. She looks more of a nursery sort and is entitled to come on again, providing the headgear continues to have a positive effect.
Elusive Love(IRE), whose stable had won this twice in the past decade from three runners, proved easy enough to back and ultimately needed this debut experience. He will know more next time.

4703 SENDRIG CONSTRUCTION H'CAP 5f
3:20 (3:20) (Class 5) (0-75,70) 3-Y-O **£2,331** (£693; £346; £173) **Stalls** Centre

Form RPR

2243 **1** **Sharp Eclipse**[4] 4567 3-9-6 **69** (p) PaulHanagan 5 80
(K A Ryan) *trckd ldr: rdn 2f out: led ins fnl f: drvn out* **5/2**[1]

1312 **2** *1* **Bronze Beau**[4] 4567 3-9-4 **70** (t) JamesSullivan[(3)] 3 77
(Mrs L Stubbs) *led: rdn and hdd ins fnl f: kpt on towards fin* **5/2**[1]

-004 **3** *2 ¼* **Kalahari Desert (IRE)**[10] 4406 3-8-4 **58** AmyRyan[(5)] 1 57
(R M Whitaker) *hld up in tch: effrt and cl up over 1f out: rdn and kpt on same pce fnl f* **12/1**

0001 **4** *2 ½* **Arch Walker (IRE)**[46] 3228 3-8-13 **65** MichaelStainton[(3)] 4 55
(Jedd O'Keeffe) *trckd ldrs: rdn and outpcd 2f out: no imp fnl f* **13/2**[3]

1230 **5** *½* **Patch Patch**[10] 4406 3-9-5 **68** PhillipMakin 2 56
(M Dods) *dwlt: t.k.h and sn prom: rdn and outpcd 2f out: n.d after* **7/1**

0335 **6** *½* **Bossy Kitty**[4] 4567 3-9-6 **69** (v[1]) SilvestreDeSousa 6 55
(N Tinkler) *hld up in tch: rdn over 2f out: sn no imp* **9/2**[2]

59.54 secs (-1.56) **Going Correction** -0.30s/f (Firm) **6** Ran SP% **108.9**
Speed ratings (Par 100): **100,98,94,90,90 89**
toteswingers:1&2:£1.80, 1&3:£4.90, 2&3:£5.40 CSF £8.17 TOTE £2.70: £1.10, £2.40; EX 8.90.
Owner Hambleton Racing Ltd XI **Bred** Bumble Bs, C Liesack & Mrs S Nicholls **Trained** Hambleton, N Yorks
■ Stewards' Enquiry : Paul Hanagan one-day ban: used whip with excessive frequency (Aug 18)

FOCUS
A moderate sprint, run at a decent pace. The form is straightforward but not a trace to rate too positively.

4704 REGISTER @ SPORTPOOL.CO.UK H'CAP 7f
3:50 (3:50) (Class 5) (0-75,80) 3-Y-O+ **£2,331** (£693; £346; £173) **Stalls** Centre

Form RPR

5600 **1** **Tukitinyasok (IRE)**[37] 3519 3-9-3 **70** (p) TomEaves 10 76
(R F Fisher) *prom: rdn over 2f out: styd on wl fnl f: led nr fin* **40/1**

5341 **2** *½* **Rosko**[11] 4354 6-9-7 **73** (b) DaleSwift[(5)] 4 80
(B Ellison) *t.k.h: cl up: rdn and led over 1f out: kpt on fnl f: hdd nr fin* **4/1**[2]

2011 **3** *nk* **Rasselas (IRE)**[7] 4483 3-9-8 **80** 6ex BillyCray[(5)] 11 84+
(D Nicholls) *hld up in midfield: pushed along after 2f: drvn over 2f out: edgd lft: styd on wl fnl f: nrst fin* **10/3**[1]

3104 **4** *½* **Whispered Times (USA)**[7] 4483 3-9-6 **73** (p) AndrewMullen 1 76
(Miss Tracy Waggott) *chsd overall ldr far side: rdn and effrt 2f out: kpt on same pce fnl f* **14/1**

0310 **5** *½* **Verluga (IRE)**[22] 3975 3-8-9 **62** (b[1]) DavidAllan 8 63
(T D Easterby) *t.k.h: sn in tch: effrt and drvn over 2f out: kpt on same pce fnl f* **16/1**

100/ **6** *nk* **Casela Park (IRE)**[13] 4311 5-9-13 **74** JJBehan 12 77+
(Eamon Tyrrell, Ire) *swtchd to centre after 2f: hld up and bhd: stdy hdwy gng wl whn swtchd repeatedly fr over 1f out: nudged along and kpt on strly last 100yds: nvr nr to chal* **17/2**

0015 **7** *½* **Dhhamaan (IRE)**[16] 4197 5-8-8 **58** (b) JamesSullivan[(3)] 2 59
(Mrs R A Carr) *led and overall ldr far side to over 1f out: rdn and kpt on same pce* **14/1**

0400 **8** *hd* **Baybshambles (IRE)**[5] 4555 6-8-12 **62** MichaelStainton[(3)] 9 63
(R E Barr) *hld up: effrt and drvn 2f out: kpt on same pce fnl f* **16/1**

3606 **9** *½* **Geojimali**[10] 4404 8-8-6 **60** (p) PaulNorton[(7)] 7 59
(J S Goldie) *bhd and sn pushed along: plenty to do over 2f out: gd hdwy fnl f: fin wl* **12/1**

6016 **10** *hd* **Seldom (IRE)**[5] 4555 4-9-3 **64** SilvestreDeSousa 3 63
(M Brittain) *in tch: rdn over 2f out: wknd over 1f out* **8/1**[3]

3045 **11** *3 ¼* **Istiqdaam**[26] 3876 5-9-12 **73** (b) PhillipMakin 6 63
(M W Easterby) *hld up: rdn over 2f out: sme hdwy over 1f out: nvr on terms* **10/1**

1432 **12** *8* **Dashing Beauty (IRE)**[14] 4255 4-9-9 **70**........................ WilliamCarson 5 39
(M G Quinlan) *in tch tl rdn and wknd fr over 2f out* **10/1**

1m 26.82s (-1.88) **Going Correction** -0.30s/f (Firm)
WFA 3 from 4yo+ 6lb 12 Ran SP% **118.1**
Speed ratings (Par 103): **98,97,97,96,95 95,95,94,94,94 90,81**
toteswingers:1&2:£32.90, 1&3:£23.00, 2&3:£3.50 CSF £194.40 CT £711.62 TOTE £54.10: £12.40, £1.80, £1.90; EX 348.10.
Owner Des Johnston **Bred** Newlands House Stud **Trained** Ulverston, Cumbria
■ Stewards' Enquiry : J J Behan three-year ban: breach of rule (B)59.2 (Oct 6 2010 - Oct 5 2013)

FOCUS
A moderate handicap and a messy race with the runners spread out across the track early before they merged middle to far side from 2f out. The pace was also muddling as they went quick early before the leaders rather slowed things up around halfway. There was a very tight finish and the form should be treated with a bit of caution.
Casela Park(IRE) Official explanation: forty-two day ban: non-trier rule (Oct 6-Nov 16)

4705 SUPPORT GOOD CAUSES @ SPORTPOOL.CO.UK RATING RELATED MAIDEN STKS 1m 3y(S)
4:20 (4:21) (Class 5) 3-Y-0+ **£2,331** (£693; £346; £173) **Stalls** Centre

Form RPR
46-6 **1** **Mufti (IRE)**[53] 2968 3-9-1 70........................ PaulHanagan 3 79
(J Noseda) *cl up: hdwy to ld over 2f out: rdn and kpt on strly fnl f* **3/1**[2]
400 **2** *3 ¾* **Egmarey (IRE)**[20] 4069 3-8-12 68........................ PhillipMakin 5 67
(D R Lanigan) *loaded w blanket and edgy in stalls: dwlt: bhd: smooth hdwy over 2f out: sn chsng wnr: rdn and kpt on same pce fnl f* **10/1**
550 **3** *5* **Red Skies (IRE)**[57] 2837 3-8-9 69........................ JamesSullivan(3) 7 56
(Mrs L Stubbs) *hld up in tch: rdn and outpcd 3f out: rallied over 1f out: no imp* **16/1**
5042 **4** *6* **Khajaaly (IRE)**[32] 3683 3-8-8 68........................ AdamBeschizza(7) 4 45
(Miss J Feilden) *in tch: hdwy and cl up over 2f out: sn rdn and edgd lft: wknd over 1f out* **11/4**[1]
5545 **5** *4* **Roose Blox (IRE)**[19] 4093 3-9-1 69........................ TomEaves 2 36
(R F Fisher) *chsd ldrs tl rdn and wknd over 2f out* **4/1**[3]
0203 **6** *1 ½* **Peaceful Rule (USA)**[27] 3810 4-9-8 65........................(v[1]) AndrewMullen 6 32
(D Nicholls) *led to over 2f out: sn rdn and wknd* **17/2**
-500 **7** *31* **Romancea (USA)**[34] 3592 3-8-9 69........................ MartinLane(3) 1 —
(E F Vaughan) *chsd ldrs tl wknd over 2f out: lost tch and eased over 1f out* **11/2**

1m 39.55s (-3.85) **Going Correction** -0.30s/f (Firm)
WFA 3 from 4yo 7lb 7 Ran SP% **112.6**
Speed ratings (Par 103): **107,103,98,92,88 86,55**
toteswingers:1&2:£4.50, 1&3:£9.40, 2&3:£17.70 CSF £30.91 TOTE £3.60: £2.30, £2.20; EX 21.40.
Owner Saleh Al Homaizi & Imad Al Sagar **Bred** Ken Lynch **Trained** Newmarket, Suffolk

FOCUS
A weak maiden rated around the first two.
Romancea(USA) Official explanation: jockey said filly hung right-handed from halfway

4706 WIN £10,000 FOR £2 @ SPORTPOOL.CO.UK H'CAP 6f
4:50 (4:50) (Class 6) (0-65,65) 3-Y-0+ **£1,942** (£578; £288; £144) **Stalls** Centre

Form RPR
-060 **1** **Who's Shirl**[60] 2764 4-9-10 **64**........................ RoystonFfrench 8 79
(C W Fairhurst) *towards rr and sn rdn along: hdwy over 1f out: led wl ins fnl f: r.o wl* **11/1**
1404 **2** *1 ½* **Lake Chini (IRE)**[20] 4064 8-9-3 **57**........................(b) PaulHanagan 9 67
(M W Easterby) *led: rdn over 2f out: hdd wl ins fnl f: one pce* **12/1**
0266 **3** *1 ½* **Hansomis (IRE)**[51] 3022 6-9-1 **60**........................ DaleSwift(5) 3 65
(B Mactaggart) *t.k.h: trckd ldrs: rdn 2f out: kpt on same pce fnl f* **9/1**
0035 **4** *2 ¼* **Sea Salt**[7] 4486 7-9-8 **62**........................ SilvestreDeSousa 7 60
(R E Barr) *hld up in midfield: effrt over 2f out: kpt on u.p fnl f: nvr able to chal* **10/1**
2460 **5** *nse* **Tawzeea (IRE)**[19] 4121 5-9-11 **65**........................ PhillipMakin 16 63+
(M Dods) *hld up: stdy hdwy over 2f out: rdn over 1f out: no imp fnl f* **5/1**[1]
0006 **6** *nk* **Desert Falls**[13] 4285 4-9-2 **59**........................(v[1]) MichaelStainton(3) 1 56
(R M Whitaker) *racd alone far side: cl up: rdn over 2f out: one pce fnl f* **14/1**
6050 **7** *1 ¼* **Future Gem**[5] 4559 4-8-12 **52**........................(p) DanielTudhope 15 45
(N Wilson) *prom: effrt over 2f out: outpcd fnl f* **25/1**
0060 **8** *¾* **Bravely (IRE)**[16] 4192 6-9-4 **58**........................(e[1]) DavidAllan 10 49
(T D Easterby) *midfield: rdn over 2f out: btn fnl f* **8/1**[3]
00-0 **9** *½* **Sleepy Blue Ocean**[11] 4373 4-8-9 **54**........................ BillyCray(5) 2 43
(J Balding) *cl up: rdn over 2f out: wknd appr fnl f* **25/1**
464/ **10** *2* **Bella's Story**[706] 5414 4-8-12 **52**........................ LNewman 14 35
(J S Goldie) *dwlt: towards rr: outpcd over 2f out: n.d after* **20/1**
0402 **11** *½* **Errigal Lad**[15] 4234 5-9-6 **60**........................(p) AndrewElliott 12 41
(J Balding) *prom: rdn along 1/2-way: wknd 2f out* **8/1**[3]
0-00 **12** *½* **Captain Royale (IRE)**[14] 4244 5-8-11 **51**........................(p) AndrewMullen 6 30
(Miss Tracy Waggott) *in tch: drvn over 2f out: wknd over 1f out* **33/1**
0515 **13** *½* **Red China Blues (USA)**[11] 4373 4-9-0 **54**........................ PatrickMathers 5 32
(Mrs R A Carr) *cl up tl rdn and wknd appr fnl f* **12/1**
312 **14** *1 ¾* **Ursus**[11] 4373 5-9-1 **60**........................(p) LeeTopliss(5) 4 32
(C R Wilson) *dwlt: sn in tch: rdn and edgd lft over 2f out: wknd over 1f out* **13/2**[2]
0010 **15** *1* **Crianza**[39] 3434 4-8-11 **58**........................ NoraLooby(7) 11 27
(N Tinkler) *dwlt: bhd: outpcd and swtchd stands' side 1/2-way: nvr on terms* **28/1**
0050 **16** *¾* **Fulford**[76] 2263 5-8-13 **53**........................ TomEaves 13 20
(M Brittain) *bhd: drvn along over 2f out: sn wknd* **18/1**

1m 13.21s (-1.39) **Going Correction** -0.30s/f (Firm) 16 Ran SP% **125.8**
Speed ratings (Par 101): **97,95,93,90,89 89,87,86,86,83 82,82,81,79,77 76**
toteswingers:1&2:£37.80, 1&3:£23.40, 2&3:£19.30 CSF £131.72 CT £1263.10 TOTE £12.00: £2.20, £2.10, £3.60, £2.10; EX 151.90.
Owner Mrs Shirley France **Bred** Mrs S France **Trained** Middleham Moor, N Yorks

FOCUS
A wide-open and very ordinary sprint, run at a sound pace and the winner is rated to last year's form. The main action was again down the middle.

4707 FUNDRAISING @ SPORTPOOL.CO.UK APPRENTICE H'CAP 1m 3y(S)
5:20 (5:20) (Class 6) (0-60,60) 3-Y-0+ **£1,683** (£501; £250; £125) **Stalls** Centre

Form RPR
0-00 **1** **Gadobout Dancer**[46] 3226 3-8-0 **46** oh1........................ NeilFarley(5) 1 57
(D Carroll) *t.k.h: mde all: rdn and styd on strly to go clr fnl f* **16/1**
0-00 **2** *4 ½* **Navajo Joe (IRE)**[19] 4082 5-9-3 **51**........................(t) LeeTopliss 7 53
(R Johnson) *awkward s: hld up: hdwy over 2f out: chsd wnr over 1f out: no imp fnl f* **7/1**[3]
432/ **3** *2* **Vigano (IRE)**[12] 4351 5-9-10 **58**........................(b[1]) KTO'Neill 4 57
(Eamon Tyrrell, Ire) *t.k.h: sn prom: effrt and drifted to far rail fr over 2f out: one pce whn sddle slipped and rdr rode wout irons last 50yds* **8/1**
0-00 **4** *1 ¾* **Carragold**[100] 1575 4-9-4 **52**........................ JohnCavanagh 2 45
(M Brittain) *chsd ldrs: drvn and outpcd over 2f out: no imp fr over 1f out* **5/1**[2]
6-45 **5** *3 ½* **Nicholas Pocock (IRE)**[40] 3397 4-9-12 **60**........................ DaleSwift 8 45
(B Ellison) *in tch: effrt over 3f out: wknd fr 2f out* **5/4**[1]
000 **6** *3 ¾* **Labretella (IRE)**[14] 4249 3-8-0 **46** oh1........................ NoelGarbutt(5) 3 22
(S A Harris) *cl up: rdn 3f out: wknd over 1f out* **33/1**
6020 **7** *2 ½* **Catcher Of Dreams (IRE)**[29] 3758 4-9-2 **50**........................(t) CharlesEddery 5 21
(A G Foster) *cl up tl rdn and wknd over 2f out* **8/1**
0-00 **8** *20* **Rainbow Zest**[41] 3370 7-8-7 **46** oh1........................ NoraLooby(5) 6 —
(W Storey) *rdr slow to remove blindfold: dwlt: hld up: struggling 3f out: sn lost tch* **12/1**

1m 40.89s (-2.51) **Going Correction** -0.30s/f (Firm)
WFA 3 from 4yo+ 7lb 8 Ran SP% **112.3**
Speed ratings (Par 101): **100,95,93,91,88 84,82,62**
toteswingers:1&2:£12.80, 1&3:£15.60, 2&3:£7.60. totesuper7: Win: Not won. Place: £231.70. CSF £117.67 CT £973.42 TOTE £17.40: £4.40, £1.30, £2.60; EX 161.60 Place 6 £63.29; Place 5 £49.43.
Owner White Rose & Thistle **Bred** P Cutler **Trained** Sledmere, E Yorks

FOCUS
A very weak handicap, confined to apprentice riders. The winner is rated to last year's course form.
Rainbow Zest Official explanation: jockey said gelding had lost its action 3f out
T/Jkpt: Not won. T/Plt: £35.50 to a £1 stake. Pool:£87,045.97 - 1,789.12 winning tickets T/Qpdt: £18.00 to a £1 stake. Pool:£3,328.12 - 136.30 winning tickets RY

4409 PONTEFRACT (L-H)
Wednesday, August 4

OFFICIAL GOING: Good (good to firm in places; watered; 7.9)
Wind: Virtually nil Weather: Overcast & showers

4708 PONTEFRACT H'CAP (FOR GENTLEMAN AMATEUR RIDERS) 1m 2f 6y
2:10 (2:10) (Class 5) (0-75,73) 3-Y-0+ **£2,810** (£871; £435; £217) **Stalls** Low

Form RPR
2012 **1** **Umverti**[10] 4410 5-10-12 **68**........................ MrSebSpencer(5) 7 81
(N Bycroft) *mde all: rdn clr wl over 1f out: kpt on strly* **15/2**
2310 **2** *7* **Avitus**[10] 4411 4-10-1 **57**........................ HenryBrooke(5) 3 56
(Micky Hammond) *trckd ldrs: hdwy over 4f out: chsd wnr over 2f out: sn rdn and no imp* **11/2**[3]
14-0 **3** *hd* **Bateau Bleu**[22] 3978 3-9-9 **62**........................(v) MrCBishop(7) 8 61
(B M R Haslam) *hld up towards rr: hdwy on inner to trck ldrs 1/2-way: rdn along over 2f out: kpt on same pce* **14/1**
6500 **4** *7* **Mountain Pass (USA)**[11] 4382 8-9-9 **53**........................(t) MrRJWilliams(7) 2 38
(B J Llewellyn) *rrd and lost many l s: bhd: hdwy over 3f out: rdn 2f out: nvr rch ldrs* **50/1**
-315 **5** *2 ¼* **Prince Golan (IRE)**[55] 2894 6-10-7 **61**........................ MrMPrice(3) 6 41
(R J Price) *a towards rr* **9/1**
36-0 **6** *¾* **Farleigh**[192] 284 4-10-12 **70**........................ MrMMitchell(7) 4 49
(George Baker) *chsd ldrs: niggled along bef 1/2-way: sn outpcd and bhd fnl 3f* **28/1**
042 **7** *3 ¼* **Holiday Cocktail**[10] 4411 8-10-6 **57**........................(p) MrSWalker 9 29
(J J Quinn) *trckd ldrs: rdn along 3f out: drvn over 2f out and sn wknd* **15/8**[1]
0121 **8** *6* **Film Festival (USA)**[10] 4405 7-11-1 **73** 6ex........................ MrJohnWilley(7) 5 33
(B Ellison) *trckd wnr: rdn along over 3f out: wknd qckly over 2f out* **11/4**[2]

2m 14.65s (0.95) **Going Correction** +0.10s/f (Good)
WFA 3 from 4yo+ 9lb 8 Ran SP% **110.7**
Speed ratings (Par 103): **100,94,94,88,86 86,83,78**
toteswingers:1&2:£4.80, 1&3:£10.90, 2&3:£8.00 CSF £44.99 CT £538.22 TOTE £7.40: £2.00, £1.90, £2.50; EX 50.20.
Owner Mrs C M Whatley **Bred** N Bycroft **Trained** Brandsby, N Yorks

FOCUS
Overnight rain eased the ground a little to Good, Good to firm in places, with a GoingStick reading of 7.9. An ordinary handicap for amateur riders, this was run in a time 3.35 seconds outside the standard. Three of the runners were officially 4lb ahead of the handicapper, but two of them ran badly which raises doubts about value of the form.
Mountain Pass(USA) Official explanation: jockey said gelding reared as stalls opened
Film Festival(USA) Official explanation: jockey said gelding had been unable to dominate

4709 EBF HATFIELDS JAGUAR MAIDEN STKS 6f
2:40 (2:41) (Class 4) 2-Y-O **£4,533** (£1,348; £674; £336) **Stalls** Low

Form RPR
0 **1** **The Mellor Fella**[19] 4116 2-9-3 0........................ TonyHamilton 1 81
(R A Fahey) *trckd ldrs on inner: hdwy and cl up 1/2-way: led over 2f out: rdn clr wl over 1f out: kpt on strly* **20/1**[3]
6 **2** *5* **Lamasaas (USA)**[15] 4221 2-9-3 0........................ RichardHills 7 68+
(B W Hills) *s.i.s: t.k.h and sn in tch: hdwy on outer whn carried rt home turn: sn rdn to chse wnr and hung lft over 1f out: no imp* **4/7**[1]
3 *2 ¼* **Like A Charm (IRE)** 2-8-12 0........................ PaulMulrennan 2 53
(J Howard Johnson) *trckd ldrs: hdwy 1/2-way: chsd wnr 2f out: sn rdn and one pce* **28/1**
45 **4** *1* **Roman Strait**[18] 4123 2-9-3 0........................ FrannyNorton 6 55
(M Blanshard) *trckd ldrs: effrt over 2f out: sn rdn and kpt on same pce* **28/1**
00 **5** *5* **Dance For Livvy (IRE)**[32] 3665 2-8-12 0........................ PJMcDonald 3 34
(B M R Haslam) *cl up: rdn along 1/2-way: wknd over 2f out* **66/1**
03 **6** *nk* **King Kurt (IRE)**[7] 4477 2-9-3 0........................ TedDurcan 4 38
(K A Ryan) *led: rdn along and hdd whn hung rt home turn 2f out: sn drvn and wknd* **2/1**[2]

1m 18.72s (1.82) **Going Correction** +0.10s/f (Good) 6 Ran SP% **110.1**
Speed ratings (Par 96): **91,84,81,80,73 72**
toteswingers:1&2:£2.30, 1&3:£4.50, 2&3:£3.40 CSF £31.90 TOTE £15.70: £4.10, £1.10; EX 44.50.
Owner Mr & Mrs G Calder **Bred** Mr & Mrs G Calder **Trained** Musley Bank, N Yorks

FOCUS
The rain was falling quite heavily by this stage and looked to be getting into the ground a bit. The time was over 3secs outside the standard. This modest maiden looked for all the world like a two-horse race, but neither market leader was on song. The form is loosely rated around the runner-up and fourth.

NOTEBOOK

The Mellor Fella ran out a clear-cut winner. A shade slowly away again but soon close up on the inside, he railed well in front and never looked in much danger of being caught. This was a considerable improvement on his debut effort here, but there are doubts over what he beat with the two market leaders below par. (op 16-1)

Lamasaas(USA) still looked green and took a hold keen early on after missing the break. He was forced a little wider than was desirable turning in and although he came through into second, the winner was firmly in command by then. He is not going to live up to his big-race entries, but he should be afforded one more chance. (op 4-6 tchd 8-11)

Like A Charm(IRE), whose dam was placed over 5f, ran with credit on this debut and looked the main threat to the winner on straightening up. She lost second at the furlong pole and might be worth dropping to the minimum. (op 25-1 tchd 33-1)

Roman Strait, now qualified for nurseries, who has yet to get the chance to tackle a sound surface, shaped as if he will get another furlong. (tchd 25-1)

King Kurt(IRE) failed to match the promise of his Leicester run and had already lost his lead when he came wide into the home straight. Nurseries over 7f look the way forward with him, but he has something to prove now. Official explanation: jockey said colt was unsuited by the good (good to firm places) ground (tchd 15-8 and 9-4)

4710 HEAVEN LAP DANCING BAR PONTEFRACT H'CAP — 1m 4y

3:10 (3:10) (Class 5) (0-75,75) 3-Y-O — **£2,914** (£867; £433; £216) **Stalls** Low

Form				RPR
04-5	1		**Midwestern (USA)**[10] 4404 3-9-3 **71** ... RichardMullen 2 (B Smart) *hld up in tch: hdwy over 2f out: rdn to chse clr ldr over 1f out: drvn ins fnl f: styd on to ld last stride* **10/3**[2]	74+
2210	2	*shd*	**Vito Volterra (IRE)**[11] 4369 3-9-1 **72** ... BarryMcHugh(3) 6 (Michael Smith) *led: rdn and qcknd clr wl over 1f out: drvn and edgd rt ins fnl f: hdd last stride* **11/2**	75
6610	3	*9*	**Sir Frank Wappat**[19] 4093 3-9-7 **75** ... JoeFanning 1 (M Johnston) *trckd ldng pair: effrt to chse ldr 2f out and sn rdn: drvn over 1f out and kpt on same pce* **4/1**	57
6163	4	*8*	**Raleigh Quay (IRE)**[16] 4198 3-9-4 **72** ... PaulMulrennan 3 (Micky Hammond) *hld up in tch: hdwy to trck ldrs 1/2-way: rdn along 3f out and sn outpcd* **7/2**[3]	36
0450	5	*14*	**Ruby Dazzler**[13] 4307 3-8-8 **62** ... TonyCulhane 4 (S Lycett) *dwlt and in rr: sme hdwy 3f out: sn rdn along and nvr a factor* **28/1**	—
1533	6	*20*	**Flag Of Glory**[30] 3739 3-9-2 **70** ... TedDurcan 5 (C F Wall) *trckd ldr: pushed along 3f out: rdn over 2f out and wknd qckly* **3/1**[1]	—

1m 46.91s (1.01) **Going Correction** +0.10s/f (Good) **6** Ran SP% **109.1**
Speed ratings (Par 100): **98,97,88,80,66 46**
toteswingers:1&2:£4.20, 1&3:£3.00, 2&3:£3.00 CSF £20.15 TOTE £3.60: £1.80, £2.50; EX 26.40.
Owner H E Sheikh Rashid Bin Mohammed **Bred** Michael L Cooper & Pamela C Ziebarth **Trained** Hambleton, N Yorks

FOCUS

The market suggested this was an open handicap. There was a tight finish but they were strung out behind the first two, and the conclusion must be that only the front pair gave their running. The runner-up is rated to his previous best.

Flag Of Glory Official explanation: jockey said gelding was unsuited by the good (good to firm places) ground

4711 BIG FELLAS & SILKS NIGHTCLUB PONTEFRACT H'CAP — 1m 4f 8y

3:40 (3:41) (Class 2) (0-100,99) 3-Y-O+
£9,346 (£2,799; £1,399; £700; £349; £175) **Stalls** Low

Form				RPR
4010	1		**Yorgunnabelucky (USA)**[13] 4306 4-8-13 **84** ...(p) AdrianNicholls 3 (M Johnston) *set stdy pce: qcknd 1/2-way: rdn and qcknd again 2f out: drvn ins fnl f and hld on gamely* **9/1**	92
1-21	2	*½*	**Chilly Filly (IRE)**[13] 4290 4-8-9 **80** ... JoeFanning 5 (M Johnston) *hld up in tch: hdwy over 3f out: rdn and nt clr run over 1f out: hmpd and squeezed through ins fnl f: drvn and styd on wl towards fin* **3/1**[2]	88+
0001	3	*1 ½*	**Spirit Is Needed (IRE)**[12] 4334 4-9-8 **93** ...(b) PaulMulrennan 1 (M Johnston) *trckd ldng pair: hdwy to chse wnr over 2f out: rdn to chal and edgd rt 1f out: drvn and edgd lft ins fnl f: no ex last 100yds* **9/2**[3]	98
-010	4	*5*	**Red Cadeaux**[91] 1821 4-9-9 **94** ... RichardMullen 7 (E A L Dunlop) *trckd ldrs: effrt and hdwy 3f out: rdn along over 2f out: sn drvn and wknd* **5/2**[1]	91
-105	5	*6*	**Highland Glen**[39] 3454 4-10-0 **99** ...(t) TedDurcan 6 (Saeed Bin Suroor) *hld up in rr: hdwy over 2f out: sn rdn and no imp* **7/1**	86
01-0	6	*nk*	**Precision Break (USA)**[8] 4461 5-9-13 **98** ... JimmyQuinn 2 (P F I Cole) *sn chsng wnr: rdn along 3f out: drvn 2f out and sn wknd* **11/2**	85

2m 42.16s (1.36) **Going Correction** +0.10s/f (Good) **6** Ran SP% **109.6**
Speed ratings (Par 109): **99,98,97,94,90 90**
toteswingers:1&2:£3.70, 1&3:£6.40, 2&3:£2.00 CSF £34.21 TOTE £11.60: £4.70, £1.90; EX 33.30.
Owner Mrs S J Brookhouse **Bred** March Thoroughbreds **Trained** Middleham Moor, N Yorks

FOCUS

A decent handicap which was run at a modest early pace before picking up past halfway. It proved a triumph for Mark Johnston and the Kingsley House team with their three representatives filling the first three places. It paid to race up with the pace on this card and the form looks muddling.

NOTEBOOK

Yorgunnabelucky(USA) was another to make all on the day. His poor run on his previous start might have been due to the race coming too soon for him and he bounced back on this first try at 1m4f, holding off his stablemates in gritty style. He will bid for a quick follow-up over this trip in a Shergar Cup race at Ascot. (op 8-1)

Chilly Filly(IRE), raised 5lb after her Doncaster win, travelled well covered up and went after the other Johnston pair off the home turn. Hampered by the third when squeezing through between horses, she was always just being held from that point. She is a progressive filly, but not entirely straightforward. (op 9-2)

Spirit Is Needed(IRE) had every chance but the winner already had his measure when he rolled across the runner-up inside the last. This was a solid effort from a 4lb higher mark than when winning at Newmarket last time and he is set to reoppose the winner at Ascot. (op 7-2)

Red Cadeaux was the first of the six runners to come under pressure and could only plug on for a well-beaten fourth on this first start since the Chester Cup in early May. A return to further may suit. (op 2-1)

Highland Glen found little when asked to improve and has not shown much in three starts now since returning from Dubai. (op 9-1)

Precision Break(USA), who made a belated seasonal reappearance at Goodwood last week, faded from the turn in. He is set for a 2lb drop in the weights now.

4712 CHAPLINS CLUB H'CAP — 5f

4:10 (4:12) (Class 5) (0-75,75) 3-Y-O+ — **£3,238** (£963; £481; £240) **Stalls** Low

Form				RPR
3325	1		**King Of Swords (IRE)**[8] 4452 6-8-5 **55** ...(p) RichardMullen 1 (N Tinkler) *trckd ldrs on inner: hdwy 2f out: swtchd rt and effrt to chal over 1f out: rdn to ld jst ins fnl f: kpt on* **10/3**[1]	69
3541	2	*2 ¼*	**Mr Wolf**[10] 4415 9-9-7 **71** 6ex ... TonyHamilton 7 (J J Quinn) *led: rdn along wl over 1f out: drvn and hdd jst ins fnl f: kpt on same pce towards fin* **17/2**	77
5041	3	*¾*	**Chosen One (IRE)**[5] 4542 5-9-3 **67** ... PJMcDonald 6 (Mrs R A Carr) *cl up: rdn to chal 2f out: ev ch whn bmpd jst over 1f out: drvn and one pce ins fnl f* **4/1**[2]	70
0203	4	*½*	**Ingleby Star (IRE)**[8] 4452 5-9-7 **74** ...(p) BarryMcHugh(3) 3 (N Wilson) *in tch: hdwy on inner 2f out: sn rdn and kpt on ins fnl f: nrst fin* **7/1**	75
5450	5	*¾*	**Select Committee**[16] 4199 5-8-8 **65** ... ShaneBKelly(7) 13 (J J Quinn) *racd wd: midfield: rdn along 2f out: edgd lft and kpt on ins fnl f: nrst fin* **22/1**	64+
0031	6	*nk*	**Galpin Junior (USA)**[14] 4245 4-9-8 **72** ... AdrianNicholls 2 (D Nicholls) *s.i.s and in rr: hdwy over 2f out: rdn over 1f out: kpt on ins fnl f: nrst fin* **5/1**[3]	70
1556	7	*½*	**Timeless Elegance (IRE)**[11] 4369 3-9-8 **75** ... PaulMulrennan 8 (J Howard Johnson) *in tch: effrt to chse ldrs over 2f out: rdn wl over 1f out: wknd ins fnl f* **16/1**	70
0050	8	*2*	**Tyrannosaurus Rex (IRE)**[19] 4090 6-8-13 **66** ... GaryBartley(3) 4 (D Shaw) *in rr: rdn and sme hdwy on inner wl over 1f out: no imp ins fnl f* **16/1**	55
016	9	*5*	**Caranbola**[5] 4558 4-9-1 **65** ... FrannyNorton 11 (M Brittain) *prom: rdn along over 2f out and sn wknd* **20/1**	36
0003	10	*2 ¾*	**Supermassive Muse (IRE)**[14] 4245 5-8-13 **63** ...(p) GrahamGibbons 9 (E S McMahon) *prom: rdn along 1/2-way: sn wknd* **16/1**	24
3050	11	*2 ¾*	**Not My Choice (IRE)**[10] 4415 5-8-11 **61** ...(t) RobertWinston 10 (D C Griffiths) *a in rr* **33/1**	12

63.61 secs (0.31) **Going Correction** +0.10s/f (Good)
WFA 3 from 4yo+ 3lb **11** Ran SP% **112.5**
Speed ratings (Par 103): **101,97,96,95,94 93,92,89,81,77 72**
toteswingers:1&2:£3.70, 1&3:£6.40, 2&3:£2.00 CSF £28.33 CT £103.24 TOTE £4.20: £1.70, £2.40, £2.00; EX 14.60.
Owner J Raybould, C Spalding, P Alderson **Bred** Maurice G McAuley **Trained** Langton, N Yorks

FOCUS

An ordinary sprint handicap, but the form amongst the principals has a solid look to it, with the first two setting the level.

Not My Choice(IRE) Official explanation: jockey said gelding had a breathing problem

4713 MATTY BOWN VETERANS H'CAP — 1m 4y

4:40 (4:40) (Class 4) (0-80,80) 6-Y-O+ — **£3,885** (£1,156; £577; £288) **Stalls** Low

Form				RPR
313	1		**Dabbers Ridge (IRE)**[11] 4354 8-9-1 **75** ... GaryBartley(3) 4 (I W McInnes) *hld up in rr: hdwy on inner 2f out: rdn over 1f out: styd on to ld ins fnl f: drvn out* **5/1**[2]	83
6060	2	*½*	**Ilie Nastase (FR)**[21] 4024 6-9-2 **73** ... JimmyQuinn 5 (C R Dore) *trckd ldrs on inner: hdwy 2f out: swtchd rt and rdn over 1f out: drvn ins fnl f: kpt on wl towards fin* **6/1**[3]	80
-001	3	*nk*	**Ballinteni**[17] 4170 8-9-4 **75** ... RobertWinston 1 (Miss Gay Kelleway) *trckd ldrs on inner: swtchd rt and hdwy over 2f out: rdn to ld over 1f out: drvn and hdd ins fnl f: kpt on* **7/1**	81
1430	4	*8*	**Ours (IRE)**[19] 4119 7-8-7 **67** ...(p) BarryMcHugh(3) 12 (John A Harris) *hld up in tch: effrt on outer 3f out: rdn and outpcd 2f out: kpt on ins fnl f* **11/1**	55
1134	5	*2 ½*	**Royal Dignitary (USA)**[34] 3580 10-9-8 **79** ... AdrianNicholls 2 (D Nicholls) *led: rdn along 2f out: drvn and hdd over 1f out: wknd fnl f* **13/2**	61
4400	6	*2*	**Ninth House (USA)**[4] 4602 8-8-6 **63** ...(t) JoeFanning 8 (Mrs R A Carr) *dwlt and in rr: hdwy and in tch 1/2-way: rdn along over 2f out and sn btn* **5/1**[2]	40
0036	7	*½*	**Rainbow Mirage (IRE)**[19] 4112 6-9-3 **74** ... GrahamGibbons 6 (E S McMahon) *prom: effrt and cl up 3f out: rdn over 2f out and sn wknd* **7/2**[1]	50
030-	8	*2 ¼*	**Motafarred (IRE)**[299] 6648 8-9-4 **75** ... PaulMulrennan 7 (Miss T Jackson) *chsd ldr: rdn along over 2f out and sn wknd* **9/1**	46

1m 45.51s (-0.39) **Going Correction** +0.10s/f (Good) **8** Ran SP% **114.0**
Speed ratings: **105,104,104,96,93 91,91,88**
toteswingers:1&2:£8.30, 1&3:£5.60, 2&3:£8.90 CSF £34.61 CT £208.84 TOTE £4.10: £1.90, £2.10, £2.90; EX 41.90.
Owner G Parkinson **Bred** Franco Castelfranci **Trained** Catwick, E Yorks

FOCUS

There were four non-runners in this old-timers' handicap. The first three home finished nicely clear but not form to rate too positively.

4714 KEITH HAMMILL MEMORIAL H'CAP — 6f

5:10 (5:11) (Class 5) (0-75,75) 3-Y-O — **£2,914** (£867; £433; £216) **Stalls** Low

Form				RPR
-300	1		**Mark Anthony (IRE)**[13] 4288 3-8-13 **67** ... FrannyNorton 7 (K A Ryan) *qckly away: mde all: rdn clr over 1f out: styd on strly* **12/1**	79
3104	2	*4*	**Red Scintilla**[16] 4193 3-8-12 **66** ... PaulMulrennan 3 (N Tinkler) *t.k.h: trckd ldrs: hdwy to chse wnr 2f out and sn rdn: drvn over 1f out: no imp fnl f* **8/1**	65
6331	3	*5*	**Jimmy The Poacher (IRE)**[14] 4248 3-9-7 **75** ...(b) TedDurcan 4 (T D Easterby) *dwlt: rdn along in rr 1/2-way: hdwy on wd outside 2f out: styd on ins fnl f* **2/1**[1]	58+
4-33	4	*¾*	**Uddy Mac**[7] 4482 3-8-6 **60** ...(b) PaulQuinn 1 (N Bycroft) *hld up towards rr: hdwy on inner over 2f out: rdn to chse ldrs over 1f out: sn no imp* **12/1**	41
0530	5	*1*	**Gertmegalush (IRE)**[13] 4288 3-9-3 **74** ... BarryMcHugh(3) 2 (John A Harris) *hld up in rr: hdwy on inner wl over 1f out: swtchd rt and rdn ins fnl f: no imp* **15/2**	52
-625	6	*4*	**Caldermud (IRE)**[21] 4031 3-9-6 **74** ... JoeFanning 8 (J R Best) *chsd wnr: rdn along over 2f out: drvn wl over 1f out and sn wknd* **8/1**	39
1320	7	*2*	**Bonheurs Art (IRE)**[19] 4091 3-9-4 **72** ... RobertWinston 9 (B W Hills) *prom: rdn along over 2f out: grad wknd* **13/2**[3]	30

4260 **8** 2 3/4 **We'll Deal Again**[22] 3975 3-8-10 **64**........................(b[1]) GrahamGibbons 6 14
(M W Easterby) *t.k.h: chsd ldrs on outer: rdn along over 2f out: sn wknd* **11/2**[2]

5024 **9** 2 3/4 **Bahamian Jazz (IRE)**[27] 3808 3-9-7 **75**........................ RichardMullen 5 16
(R Bastiman) *chsd ldrs: rdn along 1/2-way: wknd over 2f out* **20/1**

1m 16.66s (-0.24) **Going Correction** +0.10s/f (Good) **9** Ran SP% **116.2**
Speed ratings (Par 100): **105,99,93,92,90 85,82,79,75**
toteswingers:1&2:£20.10, 1&3:£8.20, 2&3:£7.10 CSF £104.29 CT £276.60 TOTE £17.90: £5.10, £3.20, £1.80; EX 150.40 Place 6 £187.72; Place 5 £49.44.
Owner J Nattrass **Bred** J F Tuthill **Trained** Hambleton, N Yorks

FOCUS
An ordinary 3-y-o handicap. Once more the inside rail proved the place to be and the runner-up is rated to her latest mark.
T/Plt: £427.00 to a £1 stake. Pool:£48,823.69 - 83.45 winning tickets T/Qpdt: £69.20 to a £1 stake. Pool:£4,227.81 - 45.20 winning tickets JR

4435 YARMOUTH (L-H)

Wednesday, August 4

OFFICIAL GOING: Good (good to soft in places; 6.8)
Back straight bend dolled out 3m, increasing distances of 9, 10, 11f, by about 10yds and 14f by 15yds.
Wind: modest, across Weather: overcast, chilly

4715 GEORGE DARLING MEMORIAL APPRENTICE H'CAP 7f 3y
5:50 (5:50) (Class 5) (0-70,69) 4-Y-O+ **£2,590** (£770; £385; £192) **Stalls** High

Form RPR

40/0 **1** **Colinca's Lad (IRE)**[47] 3168 8-8-1 **53**........................ LeonnaMayor(7) 2 64
(P Charalambous) *stdd s: hld up in tch in midfield: hdwy and swtchd rt over 2f out: sn chsng ldng pair: rdn to ld 1f out: pushed along and drew clr fnl 100yds* **10/1**

4620 **2** 2 1/4 **Simple Rhythm**[5] 4559 4-8-13 **65**........................ JoshCrane(7) 3 70
(J Ryan) *broke wl: sn stdd and trcking ldrs gng wl: chsd ldr over 2f out tl led over 1f out: rdn and hdd 1f out: wknd fnl 100yds* **12/1**

0-50 **3** 1 **Oh So Saucy**[53] 2959 6-9-3 **69**........................ RoryHanley(7) 5 71+
(C F Wall) *stdd s: hld up in last trio: pushed along and effrt 2f out: hdwy over 1f out: chsd ldng trio jst ins fnl f: r.o wl to go 3rd towards fin: nvr gng to rch ldrs* **8/1**

323 **4** 1 **Cardinal**[15] 4237 5-8-5 **55**........................(t) MatthewCosham(5) 9 55
(R M H Cowell) *awkward leaving stalls and s.i.s: sn rcvrd and in tch: led ent fnl 3f: rdn and hdd over 1f out: wknd fnl f* **9/2**[1]

0406 **5** 1 1/4 **Pipers Piping (IRE)**[9] 4434 4-8-0 **50** oh2........................ MarzenaJeziorek(5) 12 46
(P Howling) *chsd ldrs: pushed along and unable qck ent fnl 2f: edgd lft and plugged on same pce fnl f* **15/2**[3]

-030 **6** 7 **Orangeleg**[44] 3279 4-8-10 **60**........................(t) LewisWalsh(5) 11 37
(S C Williams) *led tl ent 3f out: sn rdn: wknd wl over 1f out: wl btn fnl f* **12/1**

2146 **7** 1 1/4 **Sairaam (IRE)**[13] 4308 4-9-5 **64**........................ SoniaEaton 10 38
(C Smith) *chsd ldrs tl lost pl and rdn over 2f out: sn wl btn: no ch fr over 1f out* **11/2**[2]

3002 **8** 3/4 **Crystallize**[4] 4586 4-8-8 **60**........................ MarkPower(7) 8 32
(A B Haynes) *racd in midfield: rdn and struggling wl over 2f out: wl btn fnl 2f* **9/2**[1]

00-6 **9** 1/2 **Renege The Joker**[34] 3608 7-8-0 **50** oh5........................ IanBurns(5) 1 21
(S Regan) *in tch tl rdn and struggling ent fnl 3f: wl btn fnl 2f* **100/1**

0500 **10** 1 1/2 **Whotsit (IRE)**[47] 3168 4-8-6 **51**........................ RichardRowe 4 18
(Miss Amy Weaver) *racd in midfield: rdn and dropped to rr ent fnl 3f: wl btn over 2f out* **12/1**

6506 **11** 3/4 **Athboy Auction**[20] 4071 5-8-5 **50** oh2........................ NatashaEaton 7 15
(H J Collingridge) *stdd s: hld up in last trio: rdn and toiling 3f out: sn bhd* **22/1**

161- **12** 3/4 **Takaamul**[364] 4665 7-8-12 **57**........................ SophieSilvester 6 19
(K A Morgan) *hld up in rr: edgd lft and lost tch over 2f out* **14/1**

1m 25.68s (-0.92) **Going Correction** -0.05s/f (Good) **12** Ran SP% **118.8**
Speed ratings (Par 103): **103,100,99,98,96 88,87,86,85,84 83,82**
toteswingers:1&2:£28.40, 1&3:£23.10, 2&3:£8.70 CSF £124.57 CT £1015.89 TOTE £12.00: £4.10, £5.30, £2.20; EX 167.10.
Owner P Charalambous **Bred** Peter Charles **Trained** Newmarket, Suffolk

FOCUS
The going was good, good to soft in places. A modest apprentice handicap rated through the runner-up to this season's form. The field raced down the centre of the track and the first five finished a long way clear of the rest.

4716 GREAT YARMOUTH GREYHOUND HOMEFINDERS MAIDEN AUCTION STKS 7f 3y
6:20 (6:20) (Class 6) 2-Y-O **£2,460** (£732; £365; £182) **Stalls** High

Form RPR

5052 **1** **Titus Two (IRE)**[9] 4437 2-8-11 74........................ JackMitchell 1 74
(P W Chapple-Hyam) *mde all: rdn and clr w runner-up whn veered lft u.p over 1f out: wnt rt and lft u.p ins fnl f: r.o wl and drew clr fnl 150yds* **11/8**[1]

5 **2** 2 3/4 **Park Ballet (IRE)**[43] 3295 2-8-3 0........................ Louis-PhilippeBeuzelin(3) 5 61
(J G Portman) *t.k.h: trckd ldrs: rdn and chsd wnr 2f out: carried lft ins fnl f: btn fnl 100yds: wknd towards fin* **5/2**[2]

0 **3** 1 3/4 **Ninfea (IRE)**[16] 4203 2-8-5 0........................ JamieMackay 11 56+
(S Kirk) *rn green thrght: towards rr: swtchd rt and bmpd rival 2f out: no ch w ldng pair over 1f out: edgd lft but styd on to go 3rd ins fnl f: no threat to ldng pair* **50/1**

043 **4** 1/2 **Ya Hafed**[14] 4253 2-8-10 68........................ TomMcLaughlin 8 59
(E A L Dunlop) *chsd ldrs: drvn and unable qck ent fnl 2f: no ch w ldng pair over 1f out: plugged on u.p ins fnl f* **10/1**[3]

5 2 **Rural Pursuits** 2-8-4 0........................ NickyMackay 7 48
(Mrs C A Dunnett) *in tch tl rdn and outpcd 2f out: kpt on again u.p ins fnl f: no threat to ldrs* **100/1**

04 **6** 3/4 **Sabratha (IRE)**[15] 4233 2-8-4 0........................ DaraghO'Donohoe 6 46+
(B J Curley) *t.k.h: hld up towards rr: wnt rt over 5f out: hdwy into midfield and bmpd 2f out: hanging lft and kpt on same pce fnl f* **16/1**

4000 **7** nk **Blade Pirate**[6] 4499 2-8-10 50........................(be[1]) PatCosgrave 4 51
(J Ryan) *t.k.h: chsd ldr tl 2f out: sn outpcd and drvn: wl btn 1f out: wknd fnl f* **100/1**

8 nk **Boogie Star** 2-8-10 0........................ MickyFenton 3 50+
(J S Moore) *v s.i.s: pushed along and rn green in rr: sme hdwy over 1f out: styd on ins fnl f: n.m.r fnl 50yds: nvr trbld ldrs* **40/1**

9 3/4 **Bouggatti** 2-8-12 0........................ J-PGuillambert 12 54+
(W Jarvis) *s.i.s: rn green in rr: wl bhd tl styd on ins fnl f: nvr trbld ldrs* **25/1**

6 **10** hd **Izzet**[47] 3169 2-8-10 0........................ DarryllHolland 2 51+
(M H Tompkins) *hld up towards rr: rdn and struggling over 2f out: no ch but styd on ins fnl f: nt clr run and eased fnl 50yds: nvr trbld* **14/1**

4423 **11** 8 **Lady Morganna (IRE)**[21] 4020 2-8-5 63........................ LiamJones 13 21
(Miss Gay Kelleway) *chsd ldrs tl wknd qckly u.p ent fnl 2f: wl btn and eased ins fnl f* **12/1**

12 3 3/4 **Chasing Pirates** 2-8-5 0........................ SaleemGolam 9 11
(Rae Guest) *s.i.s: hld up in rr: hmpd over 5f out: lost tch over 2f out* **33/1**

1m 27.54s (0.94) **Going Correction** -0.05s/f (Good) **12** Ran SP% **113.2**
Speed ratings (Par 92): **92,88,86,86,84 83,82,82,81,81 72,67**
toteswingers:1&2:£1.60, 1&3:£45.30, 2&3:£33.60 CSF £4.07 TOTE £2.50: £1.10, £1.20, £13.20; EX 5.30.
Owner Hintlesham Thoroughbreds **Bred** Noel Fagan **Trained** Newmarket, Suffolk

FOCUS
There did not seem to be much strength in depth in this maiden auction but the two market leaders dominated and the form looks solid enough rated around the winner and seventh.

NOTEBOOK
Titus Two(IRE) registered a personal best on his fourth run when giving a hot favourite a real battle over course and distance last time. The 74-rated colt had solid form claims and ran out a fairly comfortable winner under a forcing ride, despite veering both ways in the closing stages. A generally progressive son of Titus Livius, he seems versatile regarding ground and may be able to make an impact in nurseries. (op 2-1)
Park Ballet(IRE) ran into repeated traffic problems when a promising 20-1 fifth in a 6f Newbury fillies' maiden on debut in June. She was closely matched with the winner on form and gave it a decent try switched to slower ground. (op 3-1tchd 7-2 in a place)
Ninfea(IRE) looked very inexperienced when well held at 66-1 at Windsor on debut. The half-sister to fair 1m2f winner If I Were A Boy seemed to know a bit more this time and did some good late work. She could be a quick learner and should be capable of further progress. (tchd 66-1)
Ya Hafed, rated 68, ran respectably behind some rivals with stronger form credentials. There are bumper winners in his family and he could find a stronger competitive edge in nurseries over further, if he learns to settle a bit better. (op 9-1 tchd 13-2)
Rural Pursuits ran green but showed a bit of ability at a big price on debut.
Sabratha(IRE) showed a glimmer of promise on her third run. The daughter of Hawk Wing is in very shrewd hands and could find a burst of improvement switched to nurseries over a stiffer test. (op 9-1)
Boogie Star Official explanation: jockey said colt was denied a clear run

4717 THISTLES & THORNS FLORIST CAISTER H'CAP 6f 3y
6:50 (6:50) (Class 5) (0-70,69) 3-Y-O+ **£2,978** (£886; £442; £221) **Stalls** High

Form RPR

050- **1** **Elusive Hawk (IRE)**[232] 7758 6-9-11 **68**........................ MickyFenton 4 78
(B J Curley) *chsd ldr tl rdn to ld over 1f out: r.o wl and in command fnl 75yds: rdn out* **7/2**[1]

5251 **2** 2 **Bertie Southstreet**[9] 4435 7-9-7 **69** 6ex........................(v) JamesO'Reilly(5) 3 73
(J O'Reilly) *t.k.h: chsd ldrs: effrt to chse wnr over 1f out: wandered u.p 1f out: nt pce of wnr ins fnl f: kpt on to hold 2nd* **4/1**[2]

1424 **3** 1/2 **Angel Of Fashion (IRE)**[14] 4250 3-8-9 **61**........................ TobyAtkinson(5) 2 62
(P Charalambous) *chsd ldrs: rdn and effrt over 1f out: styd on same pce u.p ins fnl f* **4/1**[2]

6453 **4** hd **Fantasy Fighter (IRE)**[33] 3615 5-8-6 **49** oh2........................ LiamJones 6 50
(J J Quinn) *t.k.h: hld up in tch in last trio: effrt and rdn jst over 1f out: flashed tail u.p and styd on same pce ins fnl f* **9/1**

5043 **5** nse **Perlachy**[9] 4431 6-9-5 **65**........................(v) KellyHarrison(3) 7 66
(D Shaw) *stdd s: hld up in tch in last pair: rdn and effrt jst over 1f out: kpt on same pce fnl 150yds* **15/2**[3]

2514 **6** nk **Rough Rock (IRE)**[9] 4440 5-9-4 **66**........................ AshleyMorgan(5) 8 66
(C A Dwyer) *in tch in last: rdn and hdwy ent fnl f: kpt on same pce ins fnl f* **7/2**[1]

-106 **7** 11 **Silver Prelude**[152] 806 9-9-6 **63**........................(t) JackMitchell 1 28
(S C Williams) *led tl hdd and rdn over 1f out: wknd qckly jst over 1f out: eased wl ins fnl f* **16/1**

1m 13.89s (-0.51) **Going Correction** -0.05s/f (Good)
WFA 3 from 5yo+ 4lb **7** Ran SP% **112.1**
Speed ratings (Par 103): **101,98,97,97,97 96,82**
toteswingers:1&2:£3.50, 1&3:£3.70, 2&3:£2.80 CSF £16.94 CT £56.21 TOTE £2.70: £1.10, £3.60; EX 21.30.
Owner Curley Leisure **Bred** J Fike **Trained** Newmarket, Suffolk

FOCUS
A minor sprint handicap. It was run at a steady gallop and time was over 2secs slower than standard but the form makes sense rated around the placed horses.

4718 YARMOUTH GREYHOUND STADIUM CLAIMING STKS 1m 2f 21y
7:20 (7:20) (Class 6) 3-Y-O **£2,201** (£655; £327; £163) **Stalls** Low

Form RPR

0620 **1** **Ancient Greece**[14] 4259 3-8-13 73........................(t) MatthewDavies(3) 5 77
(George Baker) *dwlt: sn rcvrd and led: mde rest: rdn over 2f out: clr over 1f out: styd on wl* **6/1**[2]

1451 **2** 3 1/2 **Mercoliano**[11] 4383 3-8-11 75........................ TobyAtkinson(5) 6 70
(M Botti) *chsd wnr after 2f: jnd ldr 3f out: shkn up and nt qckn ent fnl 2f: sn rdn: hld hd high and hung lft in bhd wnr: btn 1f out: wknd fnl f* **8/11**[1]

5010 **3** 4 1/2 **Sternian**[16] 4212 3-8-4 55........................(b) JamieMackay 4 49
(M E Rimmer) *t.k.h early: chsd ldrs: rdn and outpcd by ldng pair wl over 2f out: n.d fnl 2f: plugged on* **8/1**

05 **4** 1 3/4 **River Tease**[14] 4249 3-8-11 0........................ PatCosgrave 3 53
(J S Moore) *chsd wnr for 2f: lost pl and rdn 6f out: struggling u.p wl over 3f out: no ch w ldrs fnl 2f: plugged on u.p* **10/1**

5 **5** shd **Daneside (IRE)**[19] 4113 3-8-12 0 ow1........................ AdamKirby 2 53
(W G Harrison) *hld up in tch: hdwy 4f out: chsd ldng pair and edgd lft u.p over 2f out: sn outpcd: no ch w ldrs fr over 1f out* **50/1**

0010 **6** 17 **Fasette**[48] 3113 3-8-0 58........................ AshleyMorgan(5) 1 12
(M H Tompkins) *hld up in last: rdn and no rspnse over 3f out: wl bhd fnl 2f: eased fnl f* **13/2**[3]

2m 11.43s (0.93) **Going Correction** +0.05s/f (Good) **6** Ran SP% **107.7**
Speed ratings (Par 98): **98,95,91,90,90 76**
toteswingers:1&2:£1.10, 1&3:£3.90, 2&3:£2.20 CSF £9.98 TOTE £6.60: £3.20, £1.70; EX 10.00.
Owner Inkin, Inkin, Byng, Baker & Partners **Bred** Darley **Trained** Moreton Morrell, Warwicks

FOCUS
They finished well strung out in this fair three-year-old claimer and nothing really got into it from behind. The form is rated around the first two.

4719 BANHAM POULTRY H'CAP 1m 6f 17y
7:50 (7:50) (Class 5) (0-75,75) 3-Y-O+ **£3,108** (£924; £462; £230) **Stalls** Low

Form RPR

4341 **1** **Broughtons Point**[22] 3996 4-8-12 **59**........................ JamieMackay 6 73+
(W J Musson) *hld up wl off the pce in last pair: smooth hdwy on inner 4f out: led on bit over 1f out: pushed clr 1f out: eased towards fin* **13/2**

2222 **2** *1 ¼* **Saggiatore**[14] 4259 3-8-12 **72**........................ TomMcLaughlin 4 81
(E A L Dunlop) *hld up wl off the pce in last trio: rdn and clsng whn swtchd rt wl over 3f out: ev ch 2f out: nt pce of wnr over 1f out and wl hld fnl f: clsd on eased wnr towards fin* **3/1**[2]

3133 **3** *6* **Lastroseofsummer (IRE)**[14] 4266 4-9-3 **64**.................. SaleemGolam 2 65
(Rae Guest) *led for 1f: allowed ldr to go wl clr: clsd and rdn to ld wl over 3f out: drvn and hdd over 1f out: sn outpcd and wl btn 1f out* **8/1**

3621 **4** *9* **Hypnotic Gaze (IRE)**[9] 4433 4-9-10 **71** 6ex............ DaraghO'Donohoe 1 59
(J Mackie) *prom in main gp: clsd on clr ldr over 4f out: pressed ldrs and rdn 3f out: struggling whn short of room and lost pl jst over 2f out: wl btn fr over 1f out* **5/1**[3]

-243 **5** *1 ¼* **Big Wave Bay (IRE)**[51] 3039 3-8-3 **66**...................... MatthewDavies(3) 7 52
(A P Jarvis) *racd wl off the pce towards rr: rdn and clsng whn sltly hmpd over 3f out: drvn and wknd wl over 1f out: wl btn fnl f* **7/1**

1232 **6** *nk* **Outland (IRE)**[14] 4266 4-9-2 **63**.. DarrylHolland 3 49
(J R Jenkins) *stdd s: t.k.h: hld up wl off the pce in midfield: clsd and chsng ldrs over 3f out: lost pl u.p over 2f out: wl hld fnl 2f* **11/4**[1]

000- **7** *48* **Allanit (GER)**[348] 5227 6-10-0 **75**...................................... MickyFenton 5 —
(B J Curley) *taken down early: awkward leaving stalls and s.i.s: racd freely and led after 1f: sn wl clr: stopped rapidly and hdd wl over 3f out: sn c to stands' rail and lost tch: t.o fnl 3f* **12/1**

3m 7.12s (-0.48) **Going Correction** +0.05s/f (Good)
WFA 3 from 4yo+ 13lb 7 Ran SP% **113.0**
Speed ratings (Par 103): **103,102,98,93,93 92,65**
toteswingers:1&2:£2.80, 1&3:£6.80, 2&3:£5.90 CSF £25.63 TOTE £5.40: £3.40, £2.80; EX 30.00.
Owner Broughton Thermal Insulation **Bred** Broughton Bloodstock **Trained** Newmarket, Suffolk

FOCUS
A competitive contest won in great style by a progressive sort. The first two finished a long way clear of the rest and the winner is value for more than the official margin.
Allanit(GER) Official explanation: jockey said gelding had run too freely and hung right-handed

4720 J&H SIGNS H'CAP 5f 43y
8:20 (8:21) (Class 6) (0-60,60) 3-Y-O **£2,201** (£655; £327; £163) **Stalls** High

Form RPR

00-3 **1** **Star Twilight**[63] 2648 3-9-4 **60**.. AdamKirby 8 67
(D Shaw) *chsd ldr: rdn and hung lft u.p fr over 1f out: drvn to ld ins fnl f: in command and eased nr finsh* **9/4**[1]

-302 **2** *1 ½* **Rebecca Romero**[13] 4284 3-8-8 **50**.............................(v) CathyGannon 1 52
(D J Coakley) *sltly hmpd s: t.k.h: hld up towards rr: hdwy and rdn ent fnl 2f: hung lft u.p ent fnl f: kpt on to go 2nd wl ins fnl f* **9/2**[2]

3345 **3** *1* **Annia Galeria (IRE)**[33] 3637 3-7-12 **47**..............(b) MatthewCosham(7) 2 45
(C A Dwyer) *wnt lft s: sn led but hung lft thrght: rdn wl over 1f out: continued to hang and racing on far rail whn hdd ins fnl f: fdd towards fin* **6/1**[3]

0033 **4** *3 ¼* **Black Baccara**[9] 4435 3-8-12 **54**....................................(b[1]) JerryO'Dwyer 4 40
(P S McEntee) *stdd after s: t.k.h: hld up in last pair: hdwy ent fnl 2f: rdn and no prog over 1f out: nvr quite ev ch: nvr trbld ldrs* **9/4**[1]

0060 **5** *1 ¼* **Gessabelle**[27] 3827 3-7-11 **46** oh1..............................(t) LeonnaMayor(7) 7 28
(P S McEntee) *dwlt: sn in tch in midfield: rdn and btn wl over 1f out: no ch fnl f* **33/1**

00-6 **6** *1 ¼* **Rosetta Hill**[25] 3907 3-8-6 **48**.. LiamJones 3 25
(J R Jenkins) *broke wl: sn stdd but plld hrd: chsd ldrs tl rdn and wknd qckly wl over 1f out: wl btn fnl f* **7/1**

0-00 **7** *8* **Natalie N G**[18] 4146 3-7-11 **46** oh1.................................. DannyBrock(7) 5 —
(J R Jenkins) *chsd ldrs tl lost pl rapidly 1/2-way: sn wl bhd* **28/1**

63.53 secs (0.83) **Going Correction** -0.05s/f (Good) 7 Ran SP% **112.9**
Speed ratings (Par 98): **87,84,83,77,75 73,61**
toteswingers:1&2:£2.20, 1&3:£2.90, 2&3:£3.40 CSF £12.48 CT £51.55 TOTE £3.50: £2.00, £2.60; EX 8.70 Place 6 £62.06; Place 5 £8.83.
Owner Houghton Bloodstock **Bred** Rabbah Bloodstock Limited **Trained** Sproxton, Leics

FOCUS
A low-grade handicap. The field had managed just two wins between them in a total of 55 starts. Two of the first three were prominent throughout and most of the hold-up runners struggled to get involved. The placed horses set the level.
Annia Galeria(IRE) Official explanation: jockey said filly hung left-handed
T/Plt: £187.90 to a £1 stake. Pool:£56,076.91 - 217.79 winning tickets T/Qpdt: £8.50 to a £1 stake. Pool:£6,741.30 - 581.20 winning tickets SP

4721 - 4727a (Foreign Racing) - See Raceform Interactive

4528 BATH (L-H)
Thursday, August 5

OFFICIAL GOING: Firm
Wind: quite strong breeze against Weather: overcast with sunny periods

4728 BATHWICK TYRES APPRENTICE H'CAP 1m 3f 144y
5:20 (5:20) (Class 5) (0-75,68) 3-Y-O **£2,072** (£616; £308; £153) **Stalls** Low

Form RPR

6230 **1** **Raktiman (IRE)**[4] 4618 3-9-3 **64**..................................(p) SoniaEaton(3) 1 74
(Tom Dascombe) *led for 3f: trckd clr ldr: rdn to ld wl over 1f out: sn hrd pressed: hld on gamely: all out* **6/4**[1]

0635 **2** *nk* **The Starboard Bow**[4] 4621 3-9-5 **68**...................... MatthewCosham(5) 4 77
(S Kirk) *trckd ldrs: rdn 3f out: upsides wnr 2f out: ev ch thrght fnl f: edgd rt and no ex nr fin* **5/2**[2]

0444 **3** *7* **Affirmable**[21] 4046 3-8-13 **60**.. HollyHall(3) 2 57
(J W Hills) *trckd ldrs: rdn over 2f out: kpt on same pce* **4/1**

1330 **4** *54* **Dane Cottage**[4] 4618 3-8-10 **61**.. KevinLundie(7) 3 —
(P D Evans) *s.i.s: sddle slipped bdly sn after: hdwy to ld after 3f: sn wl clr: rdn over 2f out: hdd wl over 1f out: sn eased: nvr rcvrd* **7/2**[3]

2m 31.56s (0.96) **Going Correction** -0.025s/f (Good) 4 Ran SP% **110.8**
Speed ratings (Par 100): **95,94,90,54**
CSF £5.64 TOTE £2.10; EX 5.30.
Owner Daniel Perchard **Bred** Kilbride Stud Ltd **Trained** Malpas, Cheshire

FOCUS
The going was officially described as firm. A modest apprentice handicap. The early pace was very steady and then there was a breakaway leader who had equipment problems, so not a race to be positive about although the first two are the best guides.
Dane Cottage Official explanation: jockey said saddle slipped

4729 BATHWICK TYRES BRISTOL MAIDEN AUCTION FILLIES' STKS 5f 161y
5:50 (5:51) (Class 6) 2-Y-O **£1,942** (£578; £288; £144) **Stalls** Centre

Form RPR

0 **1** **Miss Sinatra (IRE)**[17] 4203 2-8-10 **0**.................................... MartinDwyer 2 76+
(B J Meehan) *mde all: pushed ahd 2f out: in command after: eased towards fin* **4/5**[1]

620 **2** *2 ½* **Delira (IRE)**[44] 3295 2-8-3 **64**...................................... AndrewHeffernan(3) 6 63
(J G Portman) *trckd ldrs: rdn 3f out: wnt 2nd over 1f out: no ch w wnr* **7/1**[3]

33 **3** *2* **Golden Tempest (IRE)**[17] 4203 2-8-10 **0**............................ ShaneKelly 5 60
(W R Swinburn) *w wnr tl rdn 2f out: hung lft and lost 2nd over 1f out: no ex* **9/4**[2]

6 **4** *2 ¾* **Libertia**[43] 3331 2-8-1 **0**.. SimonPearce(5) 1 47
(A G Newcombe) *sn outpcd: sme late prog into 4th fnl f: nvr any danger* **40/1**

5 *5* **Hi Note** 2-8-8 **0**.. ChrisCatlin 3 33
(M R Channon) *s.i.s: sn outpcd: nvr on terms* **16/1**

6 *1* **Shutupandrive** 2-8-1 **0**.. KierenFox(5) 4 28
(M D I Usher) *trckd ldrs: rdn 3f out: wknd over 1f out* **40/1**

1m 12.65s (1.45) **Going Correction** -0.025s/f (Good) 6 Ran SP% **109.6**
Speed ratings (Par 89): **89,85,83,79,72 71**
Tote Swingers: 1&2 £1.80, 2&3 £1.50 CSF £6.89 TOTE £2.00: £1.10, £1.40; EX 7.80.
Owner Mrs Johnny McKeever **Bred** J F Tuthill & Mrs A W F Whitehead **Trained** Manton, Wilts

FOCUS
An ordinary fillies' maiden auction won in impressive style by a much improved performer who landed a big gamble. The runner-up sets the level of the form.

NOTEBOOK
Miss Sinatra(IRE) stayed on into seventh after a slow start when 33-1 for a Windsor fillies' maiden on debut. She had a bit to do to reverse the form with Golden Tempest but was the subject of sustained support throughout the day, and put in a smooth front-running display to get off the mark in good style. The form does not amount to much but she is out of a half-sister to high-class 5f-7f performer Indian Ridge, and could go on to better things. (op Evens tchd 11-10 in a place)
Delira(IRE) showed determination to keep battling away but could never get close enough to give the winner a scare. This was a solid enough effort by a 64-rated filly who was disappointing when 4-1 for a Newbury fillies' maiden in June on her third start. (op 5-1)
Golden Tempest(IRE) had decent claims on her third-placed efforts in a pair of 5f/6f Windsor fillies' maidens but she was under pressure some way out and could only plug on. The 12,000gns half-sister to 6f-1m winners by Titus Livius has not really progressed so far but she could do better in nurseries over a bit further. (tchd 2-1, 5-2 in places)
Libertia stayed on steadily from a long way back and probably found a bit of improvement on her debut sixth of eight at Salisbury. She is out of a half-sister to German 2,000 Guineas winner Irian and is bred to want a stiffer test. (op 33-1)
Hi Note was never involved after a very slow start on debut. (tchd 12-1)

4730 EUROPEAN BREEDERS' FUND & BATHWICK TYRES CHIPPENHAM FILLIES' H'CAP 5f 11y
6:20 (6:20) (Class 5) (0-75,75) 3-Y-O+ **£2,719** (£809; £404; £202) **Stalls** Centre

Form RPR

-106 **1** **Night Affair**[21] 4043 4-9-10 **75**.. MartinDwyer 5 82
(D W P Arbuthnot) *trckd ldrs: rdn to ld jst over 1f out: kpt on wl* **5/1**

4004 **2** *½* **Our Piccadilly (IRE)**[14] 4292 5-9-9 **74**............................ ChrisCatlin 3 79
(W S Kittow) *sn covered up on heels of ldrs: swtchd rt jst over 1f out: sn rdn: nvr quite ev ch: kpt on: hld towards fin* **2/1**[2]

1056 **3** *hd* **Ocean Blaze**[4] 4625 6-9-7 **75**..............................(b[1]) JamesMillman(3) 1 79
(B R Millman) *prom: rdn and ev ch jst over 1f out: kpt on: hld towards fin* **13/8**[1]

2034 **4** *5* **Bathwick Xaara**[6] 4529 3-8-1 **58**........................(p) AndrewHeffernan(3) 2 44
(J G Portman) *led: rdn and hdd jst over 1f out: no ex* **7/2**[3]

62.29 secs (-0.21) **Going Correction** -0.025s/f (Good)
WFA 3 from 4yo+ 3lb 4 Ran SP% **110.3**
Speed ratings (Par 100): **100,99,98,90**
CSF £15.23 TOTE £8.00; EX 16.50.
Owner Godfrey Wilson **Bred** Mrs C R D Wilson **Trained** Compton, Berks

FOCUS
A small-field fillies' sprint handicap. The pace was decent and there was a slight hard-luck story but the form looks relatively weak for the grade.

4731 BATHWICK TYRES CARDIFF H'CAP 2m 1f 34y
6:55 (6:56) (Class 6) (0-60,60) 4-Y-O+ **£1,554** (£462; £231; £115) **Stalls** Centre

Form RPR

5431 **1** **Mutadarrej (IRE)**[6] 4530 6-8-10 **59** 6ex.......................... RyanPowell(7) 1 63
(Ian Williams) *hld up in last pair: tk clsr order 8f out: led over 3f out: rdn and narrowly hdd ent fnl f: sn regained ld: styd on strly to assert fnl 75yds* **5/6**[1]

30-2 **2** *2* **The Composer**[21] 4042 8-8-6 **48**...................................... MartinDwyer 6 50
(M Blanshard) *hld up in last pair: hdwy into 2nd over 4f out: ev ch over 3f out: sn rdn: kpt pressing ldrs: styd on but hld fnl f* **4/1**[3]

1412 **3** *1* **Le Corvee (IRE)**[7] 4327 8-8-5 **52**.................................. KierenFox(5) 5 53
(A W Carroll) *trckd ldng pair tl dropped to last but wl in tch over 7f out: hdwy to ld briefly over 3f out: sn rdn: tk narrow advatage ent fnl f: sn hdd: fdd fnl 75yds* **9/4**[2]

50/0 **4** *23* **Nation State**[21] 4042 9-9-4 **60**.. ChrisCatlin 4 33
(M Madgwick) *trckd ldr: nudged along over 7f out: rdn whn lost 2nd over 4f out: sn one pce: wknd over 1f out* **22/1**

0-00 **5** *¾* **Iron Man Of Mersey (FR)**[7] 1172 4-8-1 **46** oh1(b) AndrewHeffernan(3) 3 18
(A W Carroll) *racd keenly: led: rdn and hdd over 3f out: sn hld: wknd over 1f out* **33/1**

3m 48.2s (-3.70) **Going Correction** -0.025s/f (Good) 5 Ran SP% **112.6**
Speed ratings (Par 101): **107,106,105,94,94**
CSF £4.84 TOTE £2.10: £1.20, £2.00; EX 4.10.
Owner Jarlath McDonagh **Bred** Shadwell Estate Company Limited **Trained** Portway, Worcs

FOCUS
Not many runners but this was a fairly competitive marathon handicap. The pace was decent and the three market leaders pulled a long way clear of the rest. The time was good but the form is pretty weak.

4732 BATHWICK TYRES NEWPORT H'CAP 1m 5y
7:30 (7:31) (Class 5) (0-75,73) 3-Y-O **£2,201** (£655; £327; £163) **Stalls** Low

Form RPR

6623 **1** **Purple Gallery (IRE)**[13] 4325 3-9-0 **73**......................(p) RyanPowell(7) 5 80
(J S Moore) *trckd ldr: chal over 3f out: rdn 2f out: led jst over 1f out: kpt on wl* **7/2**[3]

6045 **2** *2* **Southern Cape (IRE)**[77] 2250 3-9-0 **66**............................ ShaneKelly 2 68+
(D J Coakley) *trckd ldrs tl outpcd over 3f out: styd on fr jst over 1f out: wnt 2nd nr fin: no ch w wnr* **6/1**

4202 **3** *1* **Sir Bruno (FR)**[8] 4479 3-8-12 **69**................................ DeclanCannon(5) 1 69
(B Palling) *led: rdn over 2f out: hdd jst over 1f out: no ex: lost 2nd towards fin* **9/4**[1]

2660 **4** *½* **Osgood**[13] 4344 3-9-2 **68**..(v[1]) ChrisCatlin 4 67
(M R Channon) *hld up in cl 5th: hdwy over 3f out to chse ldng pair: nvr gng pce to chal: kpt on: no ex whn lost 3rd towards fin* **9/2**

0603 5 2 1/4 **Michael's Nook**[39] 3479 3-8-4 **56**.................................... FrannyNorton 3 50
(W S Kittow) *trckd ldrs: rdn 3f out: kpt on same pce fnl 2f* **10/3**[2]
1m 40.42s (-0.38) **Going Correction** -0.025s/f (Good) 5 Ran SP% **108.5**
Speed ratings (Par 100): **100,98,97,96,94**
CSF £22.20 TOTE £4.60: £1.70, £6.10; EX 12.10.
Owner The Chicken On A Chain Partnership **Bred** Fergus Cousins **Trained** Upper Lambourn, Berks
FOCUS
An ordinary handicap run at a solid tempo and the form is rated around the first two.

4733 BATHWICK TYRES SWINDON H'CAP 1m 5y
8:05 (8:06) (Class 6) (0-55,55) 3-Y-O **£1,554** (£462; £231; £115) **Stalls** Low

Form RPR
-051 1 **Gee Major**[6] 4534 3-8-12 **51** 6ex.................................... ShaneKelly 3 60
(N J Vaughan) *mde all: rdn whn hrd pressed fr over 2f out: hld on gamely fnl f: drvn out* **7/2**[2]
3500 2 1/2 **Belle Park**[10] 4430 3-8-9 **53**.................................... KierenFox(5) 2 61
(Karen George) *trckd ldrs: rdn to chal over 2f out: kpt on but a being jst hld fnl f* **10/1**
6056 3 4 1/2 **Cuckoo Rock (IRE)**[31] 3739 3-9-2 **55**.................................... MartinDwyer 8 52
(J G Portman) *trckd ldrs: rdn and drifted rt over 2f out: kpt on same pce fnl f* **4/1**[3]
0000 4 1 1/2 **Ayam Zainah**[29] 3788 3-9-2 **55**.................................... ChrisCatlin 7 49
(M R Channon) *w wnr tl rdn over 2f out: kpt on same pce* **10/1**
-005 5 hd **Securitisation (IRE)**[19] 2418 3-8-9 **48**.................................... MickyFenton 5 41
(B J Curley) *pushed along whn squeezed out sn after s: in tch: pushed along and hdwy on inner 4f out: sn rdn to chse ldrs: one pce fnl 2f* **10/3**[1]
0004 6 3 **Tudor Princess**[8] 4475 3-8-10 **49**.................................... FrannyNorton 6 35
(W R Muir) *a towards rr: nvr gng pce to get on terms* **7/1**
0454 7 2 1/4 **Pie Poudre**[14] 4281 3-8-13 **52**.................................... StephenCraine 1 33
(R Brotherton) *in tch whn short of room and snatched up after 1f: rdn and clsng whn squeezed out on rails 3f out: no ch after: wknd fnl f* **7/1**
0460 8 2 1/4 **Lady Hetherington**[1] 4692 3-8-7 **53**.................................... LeonnaMayor(7) 4 29
(G Brown) *trckd ldrs: rdn on outer 4f out: wknd over 1f out* **25/1**
3400 9 3/4 **Dolly Will Do**[31] 3727 3-8-4 **46** oh1.................................... AndrewHeffernan(3) 9 20
(N P Mulholland) *awkward leaving stalls: a towards rr* **25/1**
1m 40.99s (0.19) **Going Correction** -0.025s/f (Good) 9 Ran SP% **116.2**
Speed ratings (Par 98): **98,97,93,91,91 88,86,83,83**
CSF £38.51 CT £143.97 TOTE £6.20: £2.10, £6.80, £2.20; EX 39.60.
Owner David Sykes **Bred** D Sykes **Trained** Helshaw Grange, Shropshire
■ Stewards' Enquiry : Micky Fenton one-day ban: careless riding (Aug 21)
FOCUS
A modest handicap. It was run at a good pace and the first two pulled clear. The runner-up is rated to her best AW mark.

4734 BATHWICK TYRES BRIDGEND FILLIES' H'CAP 1m 5f 22y
8:35 (8:35) (Class 5) (0-70,66) 4-Y-O+ **£2,201** (£655; £327; £163) **Stalls** High

Form RPR
4321 1 **Where's Susie**[21] 4045 5-9-6 **65**....................................(p) ChrisCatlin 4 71
(M Madgwick) *trckd ldr: chal over 2f out: rdn to ld jst over 1f out: kpt on: rdn out* **6/4**[1]
4026 2 1/2 **Chincoteague (IRE)**[26] 3917 4-9-7 **66**.................................... MartinDwyer 3 71
(B J Meehan) *led: hung rt on bnd after 1f: rdn whn pressed over 2f out: hdd jst over 1f out: kpt on* **6/4**[1]
4314 3 9 **Dovedon Angel**[18] 4174 4-8-2 **52**.................................... DeclanCannon(5) 1 44
(Miss Gay Kelleway) *trckd ldrs: rdn wl over 2f out: kpt on same pce tl fdd fnl 100yds* **3/1**[2]
0050 4 10 **Behest**[54] 2952 5-8-0 **48** oh2 ow1.................................... AndrewHeffernan(3) 2 25
(D G Bridgwater) *s.i.s: sn trcking ldrs: wnt 2nd over 4f out tl rdn over 3f out: sn btn* **25/1**[3]
2m 53.14s (1.14) **Going Correction** -0.025s/f (Good) 4 Ran SP% **108.8**
Speed ratings (Par 100): **95,94,89,83**
CSF £4.06 TOTE £2.30; EX 2.80 Place 6 £370.02, Place 5 £161.83.
Owner Recycled Products Limited **Bred** Mrs L R Burrage **Trained** Denmead, Hants
FOCUS
There was an exciting and sustained battle between the two market leaders in this steadily run fillies' handicap and the form is modest.
T/Plt: £283.30 to a £1 stake. Pool:£33,851.19 - 87.20 winning tickets T/Qpdt: £43.20 to a £1 stake. Pool:£3,698.23 - 63.31 winning tickets TM

4688 BRIGHTON (L-H)
Thursday, August 5
OFFICIAL GOING: Good to firm (8.3)
Rail moved out 3yds from 6f to 2f increasing distances by about 15yds.
Wind: moderate across Weather: cloudy and breezy but very warm

4735 E.B.F./TOTEPLACEPOT FILLIES' H'CAP 6f 209y
2:30 (2:30) (Class 5) (0-70,70) 3-Y-O+ **£3,532** (£1,057; £528; £264; £131) **Stalls** Centre

Form RPR
2012 1 **Lady Florence**[7] 4502 5-9-5 **65**.................................... RussKennemore(3) 4 72
(A B Coogan) *mde all: rdn to go clr 2f out: changed legs and wobbled briefly 1f out: looked vulnerable ins fnl f but hld on v gamely* **10/3**[2]
4205 2 1/2 **Perfect Friend**[26] 3890 4-9-13 **70**.................................... RichardHughes 2 76
(S Kirk) *pressed ldng pair: rdn to chse wnr wl over 1f out: kpt on cl home but a jst hld* **11/2**
-565 3 1 1/4 **Al Jaadi**[45] 3259 3-9-6 **69**.................................... SebSanders 5 69
(W Jarvis) *t.k.h in rr: effrt 2f out: sn rdn: no real imp fnl 100yds* **11/1**
1404 4 1 3/4 **Rosedale**[27] 3866 3-8-13 **62**.................................... SteveDrowne 6 58
(J A R Toller) *t.k.h: chsd ldrs: rdn and outpcd 2f out: edgd lft ins fnl f: kpt on wout threatening* **3/1**[1]
1106 5 hd **Mandhooma**[7] 4502 4-9-3 **60**.................................... LiamJones 3 57
(P W Hiatt) *sn pushed along in last: outpcd tl sme prog ins fnl f* **20/1**
0030 6 1 1/4 **Transfixed (IRE)**[8] 4475 3-8-11 **60**....................................(b[1]) SamHitchcott 1 52
(P D Evans) *plld hrd early: bhd: hrd drvn and btn over 2f out* **33/1**
2402 7 2 1/2 **Talamahana**[5] 4589 5-9-6 **52**....................................(v) FergusSweeney 8 39
(A B Haynes) *pressed wnr tl rdn and fdd wl over 1f out* **8/1**
3320 8 3 **Interakt**[13] 4324 3-9-4 **67**.................................... CathyGannon 7 44
(M R Channon) *t.k.h: chsd ldrs 5f: drvn and sn wknd: eased cl home* **4/1**[3]
1m 23.62s (0.52) **Going Correction** +0.15s/f (Good)
WFA 3 from 4yo+ 6lb 8 Ran SP% **110.6**
Speed ratings (Par 100): **103,102,101,99,98 97,94,91**
Tote Swingers: 1&2 £4.40, 1&3 £6.00, 2&3 £16.20 CSF £20.45 CT £167.96 TOTE £3.30: £1.60, £1.70, £2.10; EX 20.90 Trifecta £101.30 Pool: £432.79 - 3.16 winning units..
Owner A B Coogan **Bred** The National Stud **Trained** Soham, Cambs

FOCUS
A modest fillies' handicap, run at an average pace, and the runners stayed on the inside after the false rail ended 2f out. The form looks sound enough, rated around the first three.
Rosedale Official explanation: jockey said filly hung left and did not pick up when asked
Talamahana Official explanation: vet said mare lost her left hind shoe
Interakt Official explanation: jockey said filly hung right

4736 TOTESWINGER FLEXI BETTING MAIDEN AUCTION STKS 7f 214y
3:00 (3:00) (Class 5) 2-Y-O **£2,201** (£655; £327; £163) **Stalls** Low

Form RPR
1 **Zain Al Boldan** 2-8-8 0.................................... SamHitchcott 4 72+
(M R Channon) *dropped out last: shkn up 1/2-way: drvn 2f out: led and sltly isolated on far rails 1f out: r.o wl* **17/2**
2220 2 1 1/2 **Kissing Clara (IRE)**[4] 4623 2-8-5 72....................................(p) CathyGannon 6 66
(J S Moore) *set stdy pce: rdn 2f out: hdd 1f out: nt qckn after* **3/1**[2]
6 3 2 1/4 **September Draw (USA)**[15] 4247 2-8-11 0.................................... RichardHughes 2 67
(R Hannon) *t.k.h in 3rd: hrd drvn over 2f out: no ex over 1f out: asserted for 3rd cl home* **10/11**[1]
044 4 1/2 **Bright Applause**[10] 4437 2-8-12 0.................................... SebSanders 1 67
(G L Moore) *pressed ldr: rdn over 2f out: lost pl over 1f out: trying to edge lft after* **7/1**[3]
5 9 **Les Landes (IRE)** 2-9-1 0.................................... FergusSweeney 5 49
(J A Osborne) *chsd ldrs: rdn and fdd tamely 2f out: wl bhd and hanging lft whn eased ins fnl f* **12/1**
1m 38.12s (2.12) **Going Correction** +0.15s/f (Good) 5 Ran SP% **108.1**
Speed ratings (Par 94): **95,93,91,90,81**
CSF £32.10 TOTE £10.00: £3.70, £1.60; EX 38.60.
Owner Jaber Abdullah **Bred** Tweenhills & R & L Warner Bloodstock **Trained** West Ilsley, Berks
FOCUS
An ordinary maiden in which the early pace was modest. As in the opener, the winner was the one who stuck closest to the far rail after the cutaway. The races is rated through the runner-up.
NOTEBOOK
Zain Al Boldan, who cost 19,000euros as a 2-y-o, was well ridden to make a winning debut. Settled out the back, she travelled well and quickened up nicely towards the inside after the false rail ended to hit the front with over a furlong left. Connections expect her to come on plenty for this initial experience and, a half-sister to three winners at up to 1m2f in France, she should eventually get further. (op 8-1 tchd 10-1)
Kissing Clara(IRE), placed in four of her seven previous starts and officially rated 72, had cheekpieces on for this step up in trip and tried to make her experience count under a positive ride, but again she found one to beat her. She now looks exposed and her stable is struggling for winners at present. (op 11-4 tchd 5-2)
September Draw(USA) finished a staying-on sixth of 12 in a 7f Leicester maiden on debut last month (winner followed up in a nursery at Newcastle the previous day) so this extra furlong ought to have suited, but she didn't find as much off the bridle as had seemed likely. Any horse can be forgiven a modest effort at this track. (op Evens tchd 11-10)
Bright Applause was stepping up a furlong for this fourth outing and had every chance, but he tended to carry his head to one side over the last 2f and didn't look happy on the track. Rated 69, he may be better off in nurseries. (op 13-2 tchd 6-1)
Les Landes(IRE), a 25,000euros half-brother to five winners, didn't offer much promise for the future on this debut. (op 11-1 tchd 14-1)

4737 TOTEQUADPOT CHALLENGE CUP H'CAP 1m 3f 196y
3:30 (3:31) (Class 4) (0-80,79) 3-Y-O+
£8,049 (£2,412; £1,207; £601; £301; £152) **Stalls** High

Form RPR
3224 1 **Hawaana (IRE)**[19] 4152 5-9-5 **79**.................................... DeclanCannon(5) 2 90
(Miss Gay Kelleway) *bhd: effrt and swtchd rt over 1f out: rdn and qcknd to ld ins fnl f: sn clr* **13/2**[3]
-400 2 3 1/2 **Resplendent Light**[40] 3462 5-9-10 **79**.................................... DavidProbert 1 84
(W R Muir) *prom: rdn 2f out: ev ch ins fnl f: sn no match for wnr* **10/1**
4063 3 1 3/4 **Potentiale (IRE)**[28] 3814 6-9-6 **75**....................................(p) JimCrowley 7 77
(J W Hills) *towards rr: rdn and n.m.r over 2f out: kpt on ins fnl f but no threat* **8/1**
-025 4 1/2 **Ethics Girl (IRE)**[14] 4306 4-9-5 **74**.................................... GeorgeBaker 3 75
(John Berry) *bhd: rdn over 2f out: kpt on ins fnl f: nvr able to chal* **9/2**[2]
1112 5 1/2 **Aestival**[15] 4252 4-9-10 **79**.................................... SebSanders 8 80
(Sir Mark Prescott) *prom: led over 2f out: sn drvn and racd awkwardly: hdd ins fnl f: lost pl qckly fnl 75yds and nt hrd pushed* **9/4**[1]
2354 6 3/4 **Mons Calpe (IRE)**[15] 4261 4-8-10 **65**....................................(v[1]) LiamJones 5 64
(P F I Cole) *wnt rt s: t.k.h and chsd ldrs: rdn and styng on one pce whn hmpd over 1f out* **14/1**
-620 7 shd **Eton Fable (IRE)**[13] 4334 5-9-9 **78**....................................(p) TravisBlock 4 77
(W J H Ratcliffe) *led: drvn wl over 3f out: hdd over 2f out: plodded on and grad lost pl* **16/1**
2165 8 19 **Penang Cinta**[35] 3576 7-9-1 **70**.................................... CathyGannon 9 39
(P D Evans) *climbing in stalls jst bef the off: pressed ldrs: rdn over 3f out: wknd bdly 2f out: eased ins fnl f: t.o* **10/1**
0211 P **Vertueux (FR)**[13] 4328 5-8-2 **64** ow1.................................... AmyScott(7) 6 —
(A W Carroll) *hmpd s: bhd tl stmbld on mat crossing Wilson Avenue 5f out: rdr lost irons and sddle slipped: sn p.u* **15/2**
2m 34.03s (1.33) **Going Correction** +0.15s/f (Good) 9 Ran SP% **115.9**
Speed ratings (Par 105): **101,98,97,97,96 96,96,83,—**
Tote Swingers: 1&2 £10.20, 1&3 £16.30, 2&3 £20.30 CSF £69.32 CT £528.78 TOTE £8.60: £2.40, £2.70, £2.70; EX 88.60 Trifecta £313.50 Part won. Pool: £432.72 - 0.41 winning units..
Owner T Jagger & P Kerridge **Bred** Norelands Bloodstock, J Hanly & H Lascelles **Trained** Exning, Suffolk
■ Stewards' Enquiry : Declan Cannon one-day ban: careless riding (Aug 21)
FOCUS
The most valuable race of the day, but they only went a modest pace so this wasn't the test of stamina that it might have been. The third and fourth are rated close to recent efforts.
Mons Calpe(IRE) Official explanation: jockey said gelding hung left
Penang Cinta Official explanation: jockey said gelding was upset in the stalls and stopped quickly in the race
Vertueux(FR) Official explanation: jockey said saddle slipped

4738 TOTESUPER7 H'CAP 7f 214y
4:00 (4:00) (Class 6) (0-60,60) 3-Y-O+ **£1,683** (£501; £250; £125) **Stalls** Low

Form RPR
6221 1 **Fire King**[23] 3982 4-9-5 **56**....................................(p) SteveDrowne 4 64
(A B Haynes) *hld up in 5th: looked to be gng best although bit to do over 2f out: sn shkn up: sustained run after: grad wore down ldr to poke his hd in front nr fin: sddle slipped bk* **8/13**[1]
0544 2 1/2 **Prince Valentine**[23] 3982 9-8-9 **46** oh1....................................(p) FergusSweeney 3 53
(G L Moore) *cl up: rdn over 2f out: led over 1f out: drvn and r.o: jst ct* **8/1**

00-5 **3** *2* **Phluke**[51] 3056 9-9-2 **60** AmyScott(7) 1 62
(Eve Johnson Houghton) *led: rdn over 2f out: hdd over 1f out: kpt on same pce* **7/1**[3]

2040 **4** *1* **Minortransgression (USA)**[13] 4325 3-9-2 **60** (t) GeorgeBaker 6 59
(P D Evans) *t.k.h and chsd ldrs: drvn over 2f out: one pce and finding little fnl f* **6/1**[2]

4000 **5** *8* **Stargazy**[10] 4434 6-9-2 **53** DavidProbert 7 34
(A J Lidderdale) *last mostly: rdn over 3f out: struggling over 1f out: retired* **12/1**

0006 **6** *½* **Miss Jabba (IRE)**[44] 3290 4-8-9 **46** oh1 (p) CathyGannon 5 26
(Miss J Feilden) *dwlt: jnd ldr after 300yds: drvn over 2f out: wknd and wl bhd fnl f* **25/1**

1m 37.5s (1.50) **Going Correction** +0.15s/f (Good)
WFA 3 from 4yo+ 7lb **6** Ran SP% **111.4**
Speed ratings (Par 101): **98,97,95,94,86 86**
Tote Swingers: 1&2 £1.70, 1&3 £1.70, 2&3 £2.50 CSF £6.19 TOTE £1.70: £1.20, £2.70; EX 4.60.
Owner Dr J M Leigh, T Suttle & S Wicks **Bred** Dr J M Leigh **Trained** Limpley Stoke, Bath

FOCUS
A moderate handicap run at an ordinary pace, but quite a dramatic race. The form is rated around the first two.

4739 TOTEEXACTA FLEXI BETTING H'CAP 5f 213y
4:30 (4:30) (Class 5) (0-75,71) 3-Y-O **£2,331** (£693; £346; £173) **Stalls** Low

Form RPR

-414 **1** **Spanish Acclaim**[28] 3833 3-9-7 **71** NeilChalmers 5 76
(A M Balding) *mde all: rdn over 2f out: a holding chalrs through fnl f* **13/8**[1]

3154 **2** *¾* **Rathbawn Girl (IRE)**[33] 3682 3-8-6 **56** LiamJones 4 58
(Miss J Feilden) *t.k.h: towards rr tl rdn and effrt to go 2nd over 1f out: kpt trying but nvr quite able to rch wnr* **17/2**

0044 **3** *shd* **Silvee**[20] 4099 3-8-4 **54** DavidProbert 2 56
(J J Bridger) *t.k.h pressing ldng pair: rdn over 1f out: kpt on w ev ch of 2nd but one pce ins fnl f* **13/2**

0056 **4** *5* **The Human League**[8] 4478 3-9-0 **64** (v) PaulEddery 1 50
(M R Channon) *outpcd in last and sn rdn along: kpt hanging lft and nvr looked like taking a hand* **4/1**[3]

1103 **5** *3½* **Chinese Democracy (USA)**[12] 4365 3-8-11 **61** (v) CathyGannon 3 36
(P D Evans) *chsd ldr over 3f: drvn and carried hd high and nt run on: wl bhd fnl f* **5/2**[2]

1m 11.07s (0.87) **Going Correction** +0.15s/f (Good) **5** Ran SP% **110.5**
Speed ratings (Par 100): **100,99,98,92,87**
CSF £15.27 TOTE £2.90: £1.40, £3.80; EX 10.40.
Owner The Farleigh Court Racing Partnership **Bred** Farleigh Court Racing Partnership **Trained** Kingsclere, Hants

FOCUS
Another ordinary handicap, but at least the pace was fair and the winner scored with a bit in hand. The placed horses set the level but the pair are not the most solid.
The Human League Official explanation: jockey said gelding hung badly left

4740 TOTETRIFECTA FLEXI BETTING LADY AMATEUR RIDERS' H'CAP 1m 1f 209y
5:00 (5:00) (Class 5) (0-70,70) 3-Y-O+ **£2,123** (£658; £329; £164) **Stalls** High

Form RPR

0022 **1** **Dashing Doc (IRE)**[4] 4621 3-10-7 **70** MissLAllan(3) 9 83+
(D R C Elsworth) *trckd ldrs gng wl: led and clr of rest 2f out: sn hung lft to far rails and in command: urged along after: rdr peeped rnd five times whn wl in command ins fnl f* **13/8**[1]

2423 **2** *4½* **Rosy Dawn**[7] 4498 5-9-8 **45** MissGAndrews 7 48
(J J Bridger) *2nd tl led 1/2-way: rdn and hdd 2f out: one pce and no match for wnr* **5/1**[2]

-345 **3** *1¼* **Strike Force**[76] 2303 6-9-10 **52** (t) MissALHutchinson(5) 5 53
(Miss Olivia Maylam) *chsd ldrs: rdn and completely outpcd by ldng pair over 2f out but kpt battling on* **13/2**[3]

0403 **4** *10* **Location**[21] 4045 4-10-5 **56** MissSBrotherton 6 37
(Ian Williams) *towards rr: rdn wl over 2f out: nvr nr ldrs after: wnt poor 4th ins fnl f* **5/1**[2]

3224 **5** *nse* **Wavertree Warrior (IRE)**[157] 757 8-10-1 **52**(b) MrsEmmaLittmoden 10 32
(N P Littmoden) *towards rr: rdn and btn wl over 2f out* **15/2**

0064 **6** *3¼* **Masterofceremonies**[4] 4620 7-9-13 **57** (v) MissALMurphy(7) 2 31
(W M Brisbourne) *chsd ldrs: flapped along and fdd over 2f out: lost two pls ins fnl f: t.o* **14/1**

-000 **7** *8* **Coral Shores**[179] 457 5-10-4 **55** (v) MissEJJones 1 13
(P W Hiatt) *chsd ldrs: pushed along 1/2-way: fdd bdly over 2f out: t.o* **14/1**

00-0 **8** *34* **Western Roots**[206] 124 9-9-11 **53** ow3 (p) MissMBryant(5) 8 —
(P Butler) *led tl 1/2-way: sn lost pl: t.o over 2f out* **40/1**

2m 6.22s (2.62) **Going Correction** +0.15s/f (Good)
WFA 3 from 4yo+ 9lb **8** Ran SP% **112.3**
Speed ratings (Par 103): **95,91,90,82,82 79,73,46**
Tote Swingers: 1&2 £3.00, 1&3 £3.00, 2&3 £4.50 CSF £9.44 CT £39.99 TOTE £3.00: £1.50, £2.20, £1.30; EX 12.60 Trifecta £48.60 Pool: £48.60 - 6.02 winning units. Place 6: £92.01 Place 5: £38.22. .
Owner J C Smith **Bred** Littleton Stud **Trained** Newmarket, Suffolk

FOCUS
A routine lady amateur riders' event in which the early pace was solid with the freely sweating Western Roots virtually bolting out in front. Not many ever got into it but the form looks reliable for the grade rated through the placed horses.
T/Plt: £143.30 to a £1 stake. Pool:£52,674.05 - 268.23 winning tickets T/Qpdt: £19.70 to a £1 stake. Pool:£4,162.16 - 155.90 winning tickets IM

4297 FOLKESTONE (R-H)
Thursday, August 5

OFFICIAL GOING: Good to firm (8.3)
Wind: Moderate, behind Weather: Fine

4741 LADBROKESBINGO.COM MEDIAN AUCTION MAIDEN STKS 7f (S)
5:30 (5:31) (Class 6) 2-Y-O **£2,047** (£604; £302) **Stalls** Low

Form RPR

1 **Fluvial (IRE)** 2-8-5 0 AntiocoMurgia(7) 5 77+
(Mahmood Al Zarooni) *racd against rail: hld up in 5th: plld out and prog 2f out: rdn to ld jst ins fnl f: styd on wl* **9/2**[3]

00 **2** *1¾* **One Lucky Lady**[22] 4021 2-8-12 0 PatDobbs 2 69
(B W Hills) *w ldr: reminders 1/2-way: rdn to ld over 1f out: hdd and one pce jst ins fnl f* **13/2**

652 **3** *3* **Pigeon Hollow**[7] 4499 2-9-3 0 SamHitchcott 7 66
(M R Channon) *dwlt: sn chsd ldng trio: rdn fr 1/2-way: stl cl up over 1f out: outpcd* **4/1**[2]

0 **4** *½* **Soviet Spring (IRE)**[47] 3209 2-9-3 0 LiamKeniry 3 67+
(A M Balding) *racd against rail: trckd ldng pair: gng wl 2f out: nt clr run after: rdn and one pce fnl f* **7/1**

54 **5** *4* **Spennymoor (IRE)**[22] 4029 2-8-12 0 RoystonFfrench 1 49
(Mahmood Al Zarooni) *racd against rail: led to over 1f out: wknd qckly* **11/4**[1]

6 *4* **Avid Kale** 2-8-12 0 TobyAtkinson(5) 6 43
(M Botti) *struggling in last pair bef 1/2-way: nvr a factor* **8/1**

00 **7** *3¾* **Boogie Down (IRE)**[17] 4203 2-8-12 0 AdamKirby 9 28
(W R Swinburn) *settled in 6th: rdn 3f out: wknd 2f out* **14/1**

8 *1¾* **Drumadoon (IRE)** 2-9-3 0 TomMcLaughlin 4 28
(J L Dunlop) *s.s: a in last pair: bhd fnl 3f* **10/1**

1m 26.4s (-0.90) **Going Correction** -0.15s/f (Firm) **8** Ran SP% **117.6**
Speed ratings (Par 92): **99,97,93,93,88 83,79,77**
toteswingers:1&2:£5.60, 1&3:£3.70, 2&3:£1.30 CSF £34.64 TOTE £4.10: £1.10, £2.10, £1.40; EX 59.30.
Owner Godolphin **Bred** Timothy Gleeson And Miss Ashley O'Leary **Trained** Newmarket, Suffolk

FOCUS
A modest maiden, in which those having form were not obvious highfliers. The winner can go on to better things and the third is rated to her latest mark.

NOTEBOOK
Fluvial(IRE), who cost 105,000 euros as a foal, was well backed beforehand and landed a decent touch. Quickly away, she was soon tucked in behind the leaders, going nicely. She was eased out to her right with 2f left and, after hitting the front inside the last, scored with a fair but in hand. This event did not take a great deal of winning, but she should progress and collect again at some stage. (op 15-2)
One Lucky Lady, making her turf debut after two ordinary runs at Kempton, stepped up on what she had shown before. She chased the pace from the start and led two out, but could not compete with the winner's late thrust. (op 6-1)
Pigeon Hollow, beaten just a nose over this trip at Epsom last time out, probably ran close to that level again. He was never far off the pace, racing in fourth for much of the contest, but could not quicken in the closing stages. (tchd 10-3)
Soviet Spring(IRE) had shown a glimpse of ability on his debut and took a step forward here. He will need to improve further to land an ordinary maiden, but seems to have enough ability to make a mark in nurseries. (op 15-2)
Spennymoor(IRE), a solid fourth over 6f on Lingfield's Polytrack three weeks previously, was disappointing. She broke fast and grabbed the lead, taking a position close to the rails, but folded tamely once overhauled. A step back in trip may be called for. Official explanation: jockey said filly hung right (op 3-1)

4742 RONNIE AND DOLLY 60TH ANNIVERSARY H'CAP 7f (S)
6:00 (6:01) (Class 5) (0-75,75) 3-Y-O **£2,729** (£806; £403) **Stalls** Low

Form RPR

5132 **1** **Dungannon**[11] 4398 3-9-7 **75** LiamKeniry 2 91
(A M Balding) *racd against rail: trckd ldng pair: eased out and smooth effrt to ld over 1f out: hrd rdn fnl f: hld on* **11/10**[1]

543 **2** *hd* **Rare Tern (IRE)**[16] 4222 3-8-12 **66** SebSanders 6 81
(Sir Mark Prescott) *fast away fr wd draw and crossed to rail: led: drvn and hdd over 1f out: styd on wl fnl f: jst hld* **5/2**[2]

0265 **3** *6* **Orsett Lad (USA)**[14] 4300 3-7-9 **56** oh2 IanBurns(7) 5 55
(J R Best) *pressed ldr to wl over 1f out: wknd qckly u.p fnl f* **16/1**

5620 **4** *¾* **White Dart**[39] 3479 3-9-2 **70** SamHitchcott 4 67
(M R Channon) *t.k.h: hld up in 4th: shkn up 2f out: sn lft bhd* **4/1**[3]

1655 **5** *4* **Count Bertoni (IRE)**[19] 4128 3-9-5 **73** (b) AdamKirby 1 59
(S Gollings) *early reminders: a last: rdn over 2f out: sn btn* **17/2**

1m 26.15s (-1.15) **Going Correction** -0.15s/f (Firm) **5** Ran SP% **112.6**
Speed ratings (Par 100): **100,99,92,92,87**
toteswingers:1&2:£5.60, 1&3:£3.70, 2&3:£1.30 CSF £4.25 TOTE £2.30: £1.50, £1.50; EX 4.50.
Owner I G Burbidge **Bred** J A E Hobby **Trained** Kingsclere, Hants

FOCUS
A run-of-the-mill handicap, with the top weight rated 75, but an exciting finish and the form is rated at face value around the principals.

4743 EBF COMMUNICAR MAIDEN STKS 6f
6:35 (6:35) (Class 5) 2-Y-O **£3,140** (£934; £467; £233) **Stalls** Low

Form RPR

433 **1** **Diamond Charlie (IRE)**[43] 3310 2-9-3 77 SebSanders 4 77+
(S Dow) *stdd and awkward s: t.k.h: hld up last: gd prog over 1f out: led last 150yds: sn clr: rdr nvr used whip* **7/4**[2]

02 **2** *1½* **Barking (IRE)**[10] 4423 2-9-3 0 PatDobbs 1 72
(R Hannon) *led against rail: rdn jst over 1f out: hdd and outpcd last 150yds* **6/4**[1]

6 **3** *2* **Ivan Vasilevich (IRE)**[12] 4379 2-9-3 0 TomMcLaughlin 3 66
(Jane Chapple-Hyam) *pressed ldr: upsides over 1f out: fdd fnl f* **8/1**

60 **4** *nk* **Clever Man**[16] 4221 2-9-3 0 SamHitchcott 5 65
(M R Channon) *hld up in 4th on outer: shkn up 2f out: outpcd fnl f* **7/1**

50 **5** *½* **Sodashy (IRE)**[13] 4317 2-8-12 0 JerryO'Dwyer 2 58
(Miss Amy Weaver) *stdd s: racd against rail: trckd ldng pair: losing pl whn n.m.r briefly over 1f out: no ch after* **7/2**[3]

1m 13.04s (0.34) **Going Correction** -0.15s/f (Firm) **5** Ran SP% **122.2**
Speed ratings (Par 94): **91,89,86,85,85**
CSF £5.50 TOTE £2.30: £1.10, £1.40; EX 4.40.
Owner David & Stanley Adams **Bred** John Malone **Trained** Epsom, Surrey

FOCUS
An ordinary maiden, won with authority by the best-backed runner who probably did not need to improve to score.

NOTEBOOK
Diamond Charlie(IRE), third in a better contest at Sandown in June and again at Bath last time out, was found some cover this time, despite the small field, and finally broke his duck with a comfortable success. Held up in rear early on, he was asked to go through a gap between rivals approaching the final furlong and quickened decisively. He won going away and seems likely to handle an extra furlong. Already rated 77, he could well go up for this and, if so, may find life tougher in nurseries. (op 2-1)
Barking(IRE), second in a weak event at Windsor ten days earlier, set out to make all. He was never going an especially strong gallop, however, and, when the winner quickened, looked one-paced. A longer trip may help, given his pedigree, but he appears to have only limited ability. (op 11-8 tchd 2-1)
Ivan Vasilevich(IRE) had been well beaten on his Newmarket debut, but he is big, scopey sort and took a step forward here. He raced in second for much of the race and held off the others gamely when the winner swept past. (op 16-1)
Clever Man, not beaten far when seventh at Ffos Las 16 days previously, probably ran to much the same level again. His form does not suggest he will find it easy to win a maiden, but he now qualifies for nurseries. (op 8-1 tchd 13-2)

Sodashy(IRE), seventh at Ascot behind a potentially smart rival last time out, did not match that performance. Never closer than third, she could not quicken at the business end and was disappointing. She was reported to be in season. Official explanation: jockey said filly was in season (op 11-2)

4744 CONGRATULATIONS TO GEORGE DIGWEED, WORLD CHAMPION, FILLIES' H'CAP — 6f

7:10 (7:11) (Class 5) (0-70,70) 3-Y-O+ — **£2,729** (£806; £403) **Stalls** Low

Form	Pos	Dist	Horse / Trainer / Comment	RPR
0664	1		**Dualagi**[37] 3526 6-8-7 **52** oh1 ow1 .... LiamKeniry 4 (M R Bosley) *racd against rail: trckd ldr over 3f out: gng easily over 1f out: clsd fnl f: rdn to ld last 100yds: sn in command* **5/1**[3]	61
24	2	1 ¾	**Miss Firefly**[45] 3254 5-9-1 **60** ....(p) SebSanders 1 (R J Hodges) *led but racd off the rail: drvn over 1f out: hdd & wknd last 100yds* **2/1**[1]	63
0040	3	nk	**Dream Number (IRE)**[22] 4031 3-8-13 **62** .... RoystonFfrench 3 (W R Muir) *stdd s: hld up against rail: rdn and effrt over 1f out: r.o fnl f: nrly snatched 2nd* **9/2**[2]	64
3163	4	1 ¼	**Decency (IRE)**[5] 4589 3-9-2 **65** .... PatDobbs 5 (H J L Dunlop) *stdd s: in tch: drvn over 1f out: one pce and no imp after* **2/1**[1]	63
4200	5	14	**Lucky Leigh**[10] 4424 4-9-8 **67** ....(v) SamHitchcott 7 (M R Channon) *racd on outer: in tch: rdn 2f out: wknd rapidly over 1f out* **9/1**	20
/0-0	6	22	**Sienna Lake (IRE)**[43] 3323 4-7-13 **51** .... RyanClark(7) 6 (T D McCarthy) *chsd ldr over 2f: wknd rapidly: t.o* **33/1**	—

1m 12.11s (-0.59) **Going Correction** -0.15s/f (Firm)
WFA 3 from 4yo+ 4lb — **6** Ran SP% **114.5**
Speed ratings (Par 100): **97,94,94,92,73 44**
toteswingers:1&2:£5.60, 1&3:£3.70, 2&3:£1.30 CSF £15.91 TOTE £11.90: £3.40, £1.80; EX 27.70.
Owner Inca Financial Services **Bred** B Burrough **Trained** Chalfont St Giles, Bucks

FOCUS
Not the greatest of handicaps, the top-weight being rated just 70, but it looked competitive on paper and the form looks sound rated around the first three.
Miss Firefly Official explanation: jockey said mare hung right throughout
Dream Number(IRE) Official explanation: jockey said filly lost a left fore shoe

4745 LADBROKESPOKER.COM H'CAP — 1m 7f 92y

7:45 (7:48) (Class 5) (0-70,70) 3-Y-O+ — **£2,729** (£806; £403) **Stalls** Low

Form	Pos	Dist	Horse / Trainer / Comment	RPR
-501	1		**Saborido (USA)**[29] 3780 4-10-0 **70** .... PatDobbs 7 (Mrs A J Perrett) *cl up: rdn to chse ldr wl over 3f out: clsd over 1f out: drvn ahd ins fnl f: did jst enough* **10/11**[1]	73
1020	2	nk	**Swordsman (GER)**[19] 4141 8-9-12 **68** ....(vt) LiamKeniry 3 (C Gordon) *cl up: quick move to join ldr 7f out: led over 4f out: gng bttr than rest over 2f out: drvn over 1f out: hdd ins fnl f: kpt on* **11/4**[2]	71
0330	3	nse	**Il Portico**[13] 4328 3-7-12 **54** oh2........ CathyGannon 6 (M R Channon) *hld up in last pair: rdn to chse ldng pair on outer over 3f out: drvn and clsd to chal 1f out: nt qckn* **5/1**[3]	57
5005	4	1 ½	**Honorable Endeavor**[12] 4362 4-8-12 **54** oh9........(v) FrankieMcDonald 4 (E F Vaughan) *hld up in last pair: reminders over 5f out: rdn to chse ldng trio 3f out: kpt on but nvr looked like chalng* **16/1**	55
6	5	53	**Moment Present (FR)**[12] 4386 5-10-0 **70** ....(b) SebSanders 2 (C J Mann) *led after 3f: hdd over 4f out: sn wknd: t.o* **15/2**	2
000/	6	17	**Native American**[67] 309 8-8-12 **54** oh5........ LiamJones 1 (T D McCarthy) *led 3f: wknd rapidly over 6f out: t.o* **40/1**	—

3m 28.33s (-1.37) **Going Correction** 0.0s/f (Good)
WFA 3 from 4yo+ 14lb — **6** Ran SP% **115.8**
Speed ratings (Par 103): **103,102,102,102,73 64**
toteswingers:1&2:£1.10, 1&3:£1.50, 2&3:£1.80 CSF £3.85 TOTE £2.40: £1.70, £1.80; EX 5.50.
Owner Tracey, Cotton, James, Slade **Bred** R D Hubbard And R Masterson **Trained** Pulborough, W Sussex
■ Stewards' Enquiry : Cathy Gannon two-day ban: used whip with excessive frequency (Aug 21-23)

FOCUS
A modest stayers' handicap, but run at a decent pace and producing a tight finish. The form is muddling and not solid, being limited by the proximity of the third and fourth.

4746 LADBROKESCASINO.COM FILLIES' H'CAP — 1m 1f 149y

8:15 (8:16) (Class 5) (0-70,65) 3-Y-O+ — **£2,729** (£806; £403) **Stalls** Centre

Form	Pos	Dist	Horse / Trainer / Comment	RPR
000-	1		**Dhan Dhana (IRE)**[278] 7183 3-9-0 **55** .... LiamJones 6 (W J Haggas) *pushed up to ld but set stdy pce: shkn up and drew clr 3f out: unchal* **3/1**[2]	72+
-653	2	7	**Rose Aurora**[14] 4282 3-8-10 **51** .... PatDobbs 7 (M P Tregoning) *hld up in tch: rdn to chse wnr 3f out: kpt on but no imp fnl 2f* **7/2**[3]	53
2401	3	4 ½	**Lady Lam**[12] 4361 4-10-0 **60** .... LiamKeniry 5 (S Kirk) *cl up: wl outpcd over 3f out and no ch: kpt on to take modest 3rd over 1f out* **4/1**	53
0-10	4	7	**Nom De La Rosa (IRE)**[4] 4626 3-9-7 **62** ....(p) SamHitchcott 2 (Miss Sheena West) *chsd wnr to 4f out: sn wknd u.p* **10/1**	40
1-60	5	¾	**Why Nee Amy**[24] 3968 4-9-4 **55** .... KylieManser(5) 4 (Miss Olivia Maylam) *t.k.h: hld up in last pair: easily outpcd over 3f out: wl adrift after* **14/1**	31
000-	6	27	**Mater Mater**[244] 7624 3-9-7 **65** .... RussKennemore(3) 1 (Andrew Reid) *t.k.h: hld up in last pair: wknd over 3f out: t.o* **20/1**	—
0122	7	11	**Eye Of Eternity**[28] 3821 3-8-13 **54** .... SebSanders 3 (Rae Guest) *cl up: chsd wnr briefly over 3f out: wknd rapidly over 2f out: sn virtually p.u* **85/40**[1]	—

2m 5.48s (0.58) **Going Correction** 0.0s/f (Good)
WFA 3 from 4yo 9lb — **7** Ran SP% **119.7**
Speed ratings (Par 100): **97,91,87,82,81 60,51**
toteswingers:1&2:£1.80, 1&3:£15.20, 2&3:£2.80 CSF £14.95 TOTE £4.80: £3.80, £3.80; EX 24.50 Place 6 £13.13; Place 5 £4.65.
Owner Mohammed Jaber **Bred** Swordlestown Stud **Trained** Newmarket, Suffolk

FOCUS
A weak finale, with the top-weight rated 60. The runner-up looks the best guide to the form.
Dhan Dhana(IRE) Official explanation: trainer's rep said, regarding the apparent improvemnt in form shown, filly had taken a long time to mature
Mater Mater Official explanation: jockey said filly hung left
Eye Of Eternity Official explanation: trainer said filly lost its action
T/Plt: £25.20 to a £1 stake. Pool:£40,142.86 - 1,158.47 winning tickets T/Qpdt: £10.80 to a £1 stake. Pool:£3,679.20 - 251.08 winning tickets JN

[4542]HAYDOCK (L-H)

Thursday, August 5

OFFICIAL GOING: 6f - good to soft (7.2); 1m & further - soft (heavy in places; 6.2)
Sprints on inner track but strong headwind impacted on race times. Other races on old outer bend out of back straight distances increased by about 10yds.
Wind: Fresh, against Weather: Overcast, brightening up throughout the day

4747 DAVE TATLOCK MAIDEN AUCTION STKS — 1m 30y

2:10 (2:12) (Class 5) 2-Y-O — **£2,590** (£770; £385; £192) **Stalls** Low

Form	Pos	Dist	Horse / Trainer / Comment	RPR
023	1		**Fabiello**[5] 4568 2-8-9 0........ RichardKingscote 6 (Tom Dascombe) *a.p: rdn to ld under 2f out: styd on wl and in command ins fnl f* **11/2**[3]	77
233	2	3	**Residence And Spa (IRE)**[18] 4167 2-8-11 74........ PaulHanagan 1 (T D Easterby) *a 7th prom: rdn 3f out: nt qckn 2f out: edgd rt over 1f out: styd on to take 2nd towards fin: no imp on wnr* **11/10**[1]	72
04	3	1 ½	**Millies Folly**[12] 4368 2-7-11 0........ NeilFarley(7) 5 (D Carroll) *racd keenly: led: rdn and hdd under 2f out: no ex ins fnl f: lost 2nd towards fin* **9/1**	62
	4	1 ¼	**Geblah (IRE)** 2-8-11 0........ JoeFanning 2 (D M Simcock) *trckd ldrs: rdn and outpcd 3f out: edgd lft over 1f out: kpt on u.p fnl f: nt pce to chal* **9/1**	66+
0	5	2 ¾	**Al Rannan**[15] 4247 2-8-13 0........ JamieSpencer 8 (M L W Bell) *in rr: u.p over 2f out: nvr able to chal* **16/1**	61
04	6	10	**Commander Veejay**[15] 4241 2-8-9 0........ PaulMulrennan 3 (B S Rothwell) *in tch: rdn 3f out: wknd 2f out* **50/1**	34
	7	7	**Generous Genella** 2-8-6 0........ JimmyQuinn 7 (Miss J Feilden) *s.i.s: hld up: pushed along 2f out: sn btn* **5/1**[2]	15
00	8	6	**Whitby Warrior (USA)**[17] 4187 2-8-13 0........ TonyHamilton 4 (C Grant) *hld up: rdn over 2f out: sn btn* **66/1**	8

1m 49.99s (5.29) **Going Correction** +0.375s/f (Good) — **8** Ran SP% **109.0**
Speed ratings (Par 94): **88,85,83,82,79 69,62,56**
Tote Swingers: 1&2 £2.10, 1&3 £3.50, 2&3 £2.90 CSF £10.78 TOTE £5.90: £2.10, £1.20, £3.10; EX 12.90.
Owner Sport Relief Partnership **Bred** Ambersham Stud **Trained** Malpas, Cheshire

FOCUS
An ordinary maiden with the winner rated a 5lb improver and the second slightly off his latest mark.

NOTEBOOK
Fabiello, on his toes beforehand, was up 1f in trip after running respectably the previous Saturday. He settled quite nicely towards the head of affairs and kept finding under pressure, despite dossing once in front. He needs gelding according to his trainer, but he's likely to be kept on the go whilst he is running well. (op 4-1)
Residence And Spa(IRE) had been running well in some ordinary maidens at up to 7f and was made a short-priced favourite. Always prominent, he kept plugging away to stay on for second in the latter stages. (op 6-4 tchd 13-8 in places)
Millies Folly got to the front going strongly in the early stages, and lasted surprisingly well in the going. She appears to be progressing and can make her mark in nurseries. (op 8-1 tchd 15-2)
Geblah(IRE) ◆, a Green Desert half-sister to the Group 3 middle-distance winner this year Corsica, was fitted with a blanket for stalls entry. She showed plenty of promise on ground that may not play to her strengths when considering her sire, and is one for the notebooks. (op 11-1)
Al Rannan, a half-brother to the smart Godolphin sprinter Hatta Fort, was last of 12 on debut at Leicester and only did a little better here after racing in rear early. (op 14-1 tchd 20-1)
Generous Genella doesn't have any illustrious relations but was seemingly quietly fancied for this. She didn't show a great deal in this but may be capable of better. (op 4-1)

4748 E B F AARON MOON NOVICE FILLIES' STKS — 6f

2:40 (2:40) (Class 4) 2-Y-O — **£4,533** (£1,348; £674; £336) **Stalls** High

Form	Pos	Dist	Horse / Trainer / Comment	RPR
1	1		**Tallahasse (IRE)**[9] 4451 2-9-0 0........ PJMcDonald 1 (G A Swinbank) *mde all: rdn whn pressed ins fnl f: r.o gamely and kpt finding more towards fin* **3/1**[3]	84+
01	2	nk	**Sweetie Time**[57] 2861 2-9-3 0........ JamieSpencer 4 (M L W Bell) *hld up: hdwy over 3f out: str chal fr over 2f out: rdn over 1f out: r.o u.p: hld fnl strides* **6/5**[1]	86+
100	3	7	**Turn The Tide**[48] 3141 2-9-3 83........ RobertWinston 3 (A Bailey) *racd keenly: hld up: pushed along over 2f out whn chsng ldrs: no imp and no ch w front pair fnl f* **9/4**[2]	64
0	4	½	**Climaxfortackle (IRE)**[20] 4089 2-8-12 0........ DaneO'Neill 6 (D Shaw) *trckd ldrs: lost pl 3f out: swtchd lft over 2f out: kpt on u.p to chal for 3rd over 1f out: no imp on front pair* **66/1**	57
	5	2	**Thatstheone** 2-8-7 0........ BillyCray(5) 2 (C W Moore) *prom: pushed along over 2f out: wknd over 1f out* **66/1**	51
0	6	2 ¾	**Silver Tigress**[19] 4123 2-8-12 0........ PaulMulrennan 7 (C W Thornton) *prom: lost pl over 2f out: bhd over 1f out* **14/1**	42

1m 17.49s (3.99) **Going Correction** +0.475s/f (Yiel) — **6** Ran SP% **110.9**
Speed ratings (Par 93): **92,91,82,81,78 75**
Tote Swingers: 1&2 £1.02, 1&3 £3.20, 2&3 £3.00 CSF £6.82 TOTE £3.80: £1.60, £1.50; EX 6.30.
Owner Mrs J Porter **Bred** John P Jones **Trained** Melsonby, N Yorks
■ Stewards' Enquiry : Jamie Spencer caution: careless riding
Billy Cray one-day ban: used whip with excessive frequency (Aug 21)

FOCUS
Not many could be seriously fancied but only two performed up to their best, and that pair drew well clear some way from home. The level is fluid and the runner-up looks the best guide to the level.

NOTEBOOK
Tallahasse(IRE), who made an eyecatching winning debut at Beverley over 5f, remained unbeaten after clearing away from the stalls quickly and getting over to the stands' rail. She showed plenty of resolution to keep holding the runner-up and possibly won with a little bit in hand. It's possible to make an excuse for Sweetie Time, but that shouldn't detract from the winner's performance, as she looks well up to at least Listed level. One would imagine that connections will see what handicap mark she gets before making too many plans. (op 5-2 tchd 9-4)
Sweetie Time, given a break since winning over C&D in June, a race that included subsequent Listed winner Khor Sheed, missed the break a little and gave away a bit of an advantage. Jamie Spencer came around the field to be more or less alongside the winner over 2f out but, despite coming under strong pressure, could not force his mount to the front. (op Evens tchd 6-4)
Turn The Tide, off since a fair effort in the Albany Stakes at Royal Ascot, pulled far too hard, which would not have been beneficial in this ground. (op 4-1)

Silver Tigress caught the eye. She seems sure to get further and can make up in a fair sort, probably next season. (op 25-1)

4749 YELP FOR HEROES H'CAP — 6f
3:10 (3:15) (Class 5) (0-70,70) 3-Y-O — **£2,590** (£770; £385; £192) **Stalls** High

Form — RPR

-050 **1** **Spinning Spirit (IRE)**[22] 4025 3-8-9 **58** .... SilvestreDeSousa 5 — 67
(J G Given) *chsd ldrs: rdn to ld over 1f out: r.o gamely whn pressed ins fnl f: on top at fin* **9/2**[2]

034 **2** 1 **Mottley Crewe**[15] 4251 3-8-10 **59** .... PhillipMakin 4 — 65+
(M Dods) *hld up: hdwy over 2f out: wnt 2nd over 1f out: ev ch and str chal ins fnl f: nt qckn and hld cl home* **13/2**

50 **3** 2 1/4 **Schoolboy Champ**[30] 3761 3-9-2 **65** .... JamieSpencer 8 — 64
(Patrick Morris) *hld up: nt clr run briefly whn effrt 2f out: chsd ldrs over 1f out: kpt on to take 3rd fnl 75yds: nt pce of front pair* **7/1**

0331 **4** 3/4 **Offspring**[19] 4151 3-9-7 **70** .... DuranFentiman 1 — 66
(T D Easterby) *in tch: rdn to chal over 1f out: nt qckn ent fnl f: no ex fnl 75yds* **5/1**[3]

1420 **5** 3 **Newbury Street**[23] 3972 3-9-4 **67** .... AndrewElliott 6 — 54
(P F Holmes) *chsd ldr tl wl over 2f out: pushed along to go pce whn n.m.r over 1f out: sn swtchd lft: no imp fnl f* **12/1**

0046 **6** 3/4 **Tartufo Dolce (IRE)**[26] 3904 3-8-10 **59** .... PaulMulrennan 3 — 43
(J G Given) *led: rdn and hdd over 1f out: sn wknd* **16/1**

-130 **7** 1 1/4 **Sir Louis**[49] 3119 3-8-13 **62** .... PaulHanagan 9 — 42+
(R A Fahey) *in tch: effrt to chse ldrs wl over 2f out: sn n.m.r and lost pl: no imp after* **5/2**[1]

6320 **8** 1 **Reach For The Sky (IRE)**[11] 4406 3-8-6 **55** .... FrannyNorton 7 — 32
(A Berry) *dismntd and led 2f to post: a bhd: nigged along after 2f: nvr on terms* **12/1**

1m 16.31s (2.81) **Going Correction** +0.475s/f (Yiel) — **8** Ran SP% **110.5**
Speed ratings (Par 100): **100,98,95,94,90 89,88,86**
Tote Swingers: 1&2 £7.50, 1&3 £6.20, 2&3 £4.80 CSF £31.24 CT £190.70 TOTE £4.40: £1.10, £2.60, £3.10; EX 38.50.
Owner R Jones & Patrick B Doyle Construction **Bred** T Pabst **Trained** Willoughton, Lincs

FOCUS
Modest form with the winner getting back to his juvenile best.
Sir Louis Official explanation: jockey said gelding was never travelling

4750 BETFRED H'CAP — 1m 30y
3:40 (3:40) (Class 3) (0-95,95) 3-Y-O — **£8,095** (£2,408; £1,203; £601) **Stalls** Low

Form — RPR

0-1 **1** **Uphold**[56] 2900 3-8-13 **87** .... RobertWinston 3 — 96
(B W Hills) *trckd ldrs: rdn to chal fr over 2f out: r.o gamely ins fnl f: led fnl stride* **10/1**

2312 **2** *shd* **Dolphin Rock**[27] 3857 3-8-6 **80** .... GrahamGibbons 9 — 89
(T D Barron) *w ldr: led over 3f out: rdn 2f out: a pressed: hdd narrowly fnl stride* **5/1**[2]

2156 **3** 1 **Highland Knight (IRE)**[12] 4357 3-8-12 **86** ....(t) FrannyNorton 13 — 92
(A M Balding) *a.p: rdn over 2f out: hung lft whn chsng ldrs ins fnl f: nt quite pce to get to front pair* **11/2**[3]

4660 **4** 2 **Layla's Hero (IRE)**[40] 3429 3-9-7 **95** .... JamieSpencer 8 — 96
(D M Simcock) *hld up: hdwy whn swtchd lft 2f out: chsng ldrs whn n.m.r and swtchd rt over 1f out: no imp on ldrs ins fnl f* **16/1**

416 **5** *hd* **Christmas Light**[12] 4389 3-8-4 **78** .... SilvestreDeSousa 12 — 79+
(D O'Meara) *midfield: lost pl after 2f: hdwy u.p on outer over 2f out: chsd ldrs over 1f out: hung lft ins fnl f: one pce fnl 100yds* **7/1**

5660 **6** 7 **Bullwhip (IRE)**[19] 4144 3-9-4 **92** .... NickyMackay 11 — 77
(J H M Gosden) *racd in tch on wd outer: pushed along and sltly outpcd over 4f out: rallied to chse ldrs over 3f out: u.p over 2f out: wknd 1f out* **7/1**

1- **7** 6 **Beauchamp Yorker**[320] 6108 3-9-4 **92** .... DaneO'Neill 2 — 63
(H Candy) *towards rr: u.p 2f out: nvr a danger* **12/1**

4242 **8** 21 **Secretive**[16] 4224 3-8-12 **86** ....(b) JoeFanning 1 — 9
(M Johnston) *led: hdd over 3f out: rdn over 2f out: wknd over 1f out: eased whn wl btn fnl f* **6/1**

320 **9** 1 1/2 **Fifty Moore**[57] 2852 3-8-11 **85** .... AndrewElliott 5 — 4
(Jedd O'Keeffe) *trckd ldrs: n.m.r over 3f out: sn lost pl: u.p and dropped away after* **40/1**

01-2 **10** 3/4 **Right Grand**[20] 4104 3-8-6 **80** .... PaulHanagan 10 — —
(W J Haggas) *towards rr: niggled along 5f out: toiling fnl 2f* **9/2**[1]

1m 47.67s (2.97) **Going Correction** +0.375s/f (Good) — **10** Ran SP% **114.6**
Speed ratings (Par 104): **100,99,98,96,96 89,83,62,61,60**
Tote Swingers: 1&2 £5.50, 1&3 £8.40, 2&3 £9.70 CSF £58.37 CT £312.89 TOTE £10.20: £3.40, £1.30, £2.80; EX 40.00.
Owner K Abdulla **Bred** Juddmonte Farms Ltd **Trained** Lambourn, Berks
■ Stewards' Enquiry : Robert Winston three-day ban: used whip with excessiev frequency (Aug 21-23)

FOCUS
Three runners came out during the morning due to the going, but that did not stop this looking a fiercely competitive handicap. It paid to race handily and the third and fourth are rated close to form.

NOTEBOOK
Uphold got his career going on his 3-y-o return at Nottingham, and maintained that progression with another good performance. He could be spotted going well just behind the lead and produced plenty when asked, gaining a narrow success from a consistent and useful yardstick. He doesn't hold any entries but one would imagine that he can land a classy handicap later on in the year. The winning rider got a three-day ban for excessive use of the whip. (op 17-2)
Dolphin Rock, beaten a head over 1m2f at Chester on his previous outing, raced prominently and kept on all the way to the line. He rarely puts up a bad performance. (op 7-1)
Highland Knight(IRE) had looked a little high in the weights since his victory at Lingfield in June but seemed a little unlucky here, as he was hampered over 2f out when in with every chance. He then tended to hang under pressure, but still stayed on. (op 8-1)
Layla's Hero(IRE), dropped 3lb since his previous start, enjoyed a great campaign as a juvenile but had unsurprisingly been held in handicap company this year. Trying 1m for the first time, he was always going to struggle to get involved in this ground after being held up, so this probably wasn't a bad performance. (op 14-1)
Christmas Light, down 2f in trip, made an effort over 3f out and ran respectably after being towards the rear on turning in. (op 10-1)
Bullwhip(IRE)'s last race could not have been working out much better, but he lost ground at the start here and never made much impact once back on terms. (op 6-1)
Beauchamp Yorker won a maiden at Newbury as a 2-y-o on his only previous start, a race that had produced lots of decent winners, including The Rectifier and Fireback. He didn't seem that fancied for his return judged on his starting price (he missed a recent engagement after rearing in the stalls), and was fully entitled to need this. (op 14-1)
Secretive has been consistent throughout the season over this sort of distance, but dropped away tamely after leading. (op 4-1)
Fifty Moore, trying this trip for the first time, appeared to pull too hard under restraint. (op 66-1)
Right Grand looked an obvious candidate on form but was another who was too far off the leaders in these conditions to get involved at the end. He was squeezed for room at one stage down the home straight when coming up the inside rail, but that made little difference. (tchd 4-1 and 5-1 in places)

4751 FIVESTARSAPPEAL.CO.UK H'CAP — 1m 3f 200y
4:10 (4:11) (Class 4) (0-80,79) 3-Y-O — **£4,533** (£1,348; £674; £336) **Stalls** High

Form — RPR

632 **1** **Joseph Lister**[15] 4257 3-9-5 **77** .... NickyMackay 4 — 87
(J H M Gosden) *racd keenly: dropped to midfield after 1f: hdwy over 3f out: edgd lft and led 2f out: hrd pressed after: kpt on wl towards fin* **8/1**

-140 **2** 1/2 **Hayzoom**[49] 3105 3-9-7 **79** .... PaulMulrennan 2 — 88
(P W Chapple-Hyam) *hld up: hdwy 3f out: chsd ldrs over 1f out: edgd lft whn chalng and ev ch ins fnl f: jst hld cl home* **9/1**

3433 **3** 1 **Layla's Dancer**[4] 4619 3-9-4 **76** .... PaulHanagan 3 — 83
(R A Fahey) *trckd ldrs: str chal fr 2f out: hld whn n.m.r fnl strides* **5/2**[1]

461 **4** 3/4 **Line Of Duty (IRE)**[50] 3077 3-9-6 **78** .... PJMcDonald 6 — 84
(G A Swinbank) *led for 2f: remained prom: rdn 2f out: nt qckn: kpt on ins fnl f but nt quite pce of ldrs* **14/1**

-123 **5** 2 3/4 **Activate**[57] 2869 3-9-7 **79** .... HayleyTurner 1 — 81
(M L W Bell) *in rr: niggled along 5f out: hdwy over 3f out: chsd ldrs over 1f out: kpt on but no imp on ldrs ins fnl f* **4/1**[2]

503 **6** 5 **Royal Dalakhani (IRE)**[16] 4229 3-8-7 **65** .... TonyCulhane 5 — 59
(P W D'Arcy) *hld up: rdn over 3f out: nvr able to chal* **16/1**

-501 **7** 3 1/2 **Think Its All Over (USA)**[19] 4128 3-9-5 **77** .... JamieSpencer 10 — 65
(T P Tate) *prom: led after 2f: hdd 2f out: wknd over 1f out* **9/2**[3]

-000 **8** 6 **Ultravox (USA)**[15] 4257 3-9-1 **73** ....(b[1]) SilvestreDeSousa 7 — 52
(B J Meehan) *midfield: hdwy to go handy 6f out: rdn and wknd over 3f out* **16/1**

62-1 **9** 2 **Cornish Beau (IRE)**[108] 1422 3-9-1 **73** .... PhillipMakin 9 — 48
(M H Tompkins) *prom: chal 3f out: rdn over 2f out: wknd over 1f out* **11/1**

2m 37.85s (3.85) **Going Correction** +0.375s/f (Good) — **9** Ran SP% **114.6**
Speed ratings (Par 102): **102,101,101,100,98 95,93,89,87**
Tote Swingers: 1&2 £10.20, 1&3 £4.40, 2&3 £5.20 CSF £76.63 CT £231.90 TOTE £10.70: £2.90, £3.00, £1.70; EX 53.70.
Owner W J Gredley **Bred** Middle Park Stud Ltd **Trained** Newmarket, Suffolk
■ Stewards' Enquiry : Nicky Mackay two-day ban: careless riding (Aug 21-22)

FOCUS
A few unexposed sorts lined up for this dour test, so those who fought out the finish should be capable of finding more improvement. However, the result may not be that reliable in the coming weeks, unless the ground remains on the easy side. The form looks sound and the winner is unexposed.

4752 M.E.N. MEDIA H'CAP — 1m 2f 95y
4:40 (4:40) (Class 5) (0-70,70) 3-Y-O+ — **£2,590** (£770; £385; £192) **Stalls** High

Form — RPR

-40 **1** **Starkat**[30] 3764 4-10-0 **70** .... JamieSpencer 1 — 81
(Jane Chapple-Hyam) *hld up: hdwy over 2f out: rdn to ld over 1f out: hdd briefly fnl 120yds: r.o gamely and plld out more towards fin* **7/1**[3]

1101 **2** 1/2 **King Zeal (IRE)**[20] 4094 6-9-4 **67** .... JamesRogers[(7)] 8 — 77
(B D Leavy) *dwlt: hld up: hdwy over 2f out: swtchd rt whn nt clr run over 1f out: r.o to ld briefly fnl 120yds: nt quiken cl home* **4/1**[2]

4 **3** 1 **Rare Malt (IRE)**[20] 4088 3-9-4 **69** ....(v[1]) AndrewElliott 2 — 77
(Miss Amy Weaver) *dwlt: hld up: rdn over 3f out: plld to outer and hdwy over 1f out: styd on ins fnl f: nt rch ldrs* **10/1**

550 **4** *nk* **Casino Night**[32] 3707 5-9-1 **57** .... SilvestreDeSousa 9 — 65
(G A Harker) *racd keenly in tch: rdn 2f out: effrt to chse ldrs and hung lft over 1f out: one pce fnl 50yds* **3/1**[1]

0613 **5** 9 **Highland Love**[49] 3110 5-9-1 **57** .... TonyHamilton 7 — 47
(Jedd O'Keeffe) *prom: rdn to ld 2f out: hdd over 1f out: wknd ins fnl f* **10/1**

0-03 **6** 1 1/4 **Scarab (IRE)**[11] 4411 5-9-9 **65** .... GrahamGibbons 3 — 53
(T D Walford) *in tch: rdn 2f out: no imp on ldrs: wl btn ins fnl f:* **8/1**

0052 **7** 3 3/4 **Laverre (IRE)**[31] 3730 3-9-2 **67** .... PaulHanagan 5 — 48
(T D Easterby) *led: rdn and hdd 2f out: wknd over 1f out* **8/1**

00-6 **8** *nk* **Theonebox (USA)**[49] 3130 5-9-13 **69** .... PJMcDonald 6 — 49
(Ian Williams) *midfield: hdwy 3f out: chsd ldrs 2f out: wknd over 1f out* **16/1**

3450 **9** 3 1/4 **Carter**[19] 4156 4-9-3 **59** .... PaulMulrennan 4 — 33
(W M Brisbourne) *prom: rdn 2f out: wknd 1f out* **11/1**

6050 **10** 15 **Pitbull**[11] 4411 7-8-9 **51** oh6 ....(b) PatrickMathers 10 — —
(A Berry) *missed break: hld up: rdn over 3f out: toiling after* **40/1**

2m 18.94s (2.94) **Going Correction** +0.375s/f (Good)
WFA 3 from 4yo+ 9lb — **10** Ran SP% **114.6**
Speed ratings (Par 103): **103,102,101,101,94 93,90,90,87,75**
Tote Swingers: 1&2 £5.70, 1&3 £14.80, 2&3 £10.90 CSF £34.48 CT £280.50 TOTE £6.00: £2.00, £1.80, £2.40; EX 43.50 Place 6: £56.08 Place 5: £41.10..
Owner Norcroft Park Stud **Bred** Norcroft Park Stud **Trained** Dalham, Suffolk

FOCUS
A modest handicap with the runner-up recording another personal best and the third getting back to her juvenile form.
T/Jkpt: £113,054.10 to a £1 stake. Pool:£2,308,851.83 - 14.50 winning tickets T/Plt: £76.00 to a £1 stake. Pool:£123,234.23 - 1,182.32 winning tickets T/Qpdt: £18.30 to a £1 stake. Pool:£4,580.85 - 184.45 winning tickets DO

4488 SANDOWN (R-H)
Thursday, August 5

OFFICIAL GOING: Good to firm
Bend at mid-configuration and home straight dolled out 4yds, increasing distances on round course by about 5yds.
Wind: Moderate ahead Weather: Bright early

4753 CLARE MORUM MEMORIAL E B F MAIDEN FILLIES' STKS — 5f 6y
5:40 (5:41) (Class 5) 2-Y-O — **£3,238** (£963; £481; £240) **Stalls** High

Form — RPR

35 **1** **Take Flight (IRE)**[64] 2641 2-9-0 0 .... WilliamBuick 3 — 84+
(J Noseda) *broke wl: mde all: rdn clr ins fnl f: drvn out: unchal* **5/4**[1]

2 4 1/2 **Choose The Moment** 2-9-0 0 .... JimCrowley 5 — 68+
(Eve Johnson Houghton) *chsd ldrs: rdn 1/2-way: drvn and hdwy 2f out: green: hung lft and chsd wnr appr fnl f: nvr any ch but kpt on* **10/1**

3 1 1/4 **Yasmeena (USA)** 2-9-0 0 .... TadhgO'Shea 4 — 63+
(B W Hills) *s.i.s: t.k.h: sn in tch: hdwy 2f out: green but tk wl hld 3rd 1f out: styd on same pce* **2/1**[2]

0 **4** *5* **Dualite (IRE)**[27] 3871 2-9-0 0 TedDurcan 1 45
(J L Dunlop) *wnt lft s: sn chsng wnr but no ch fr 1/2-way: wkng whn n.m.r and wknd appr fnl f* **20/1**

5 *1 3/4* **Piece Of Mind** 2-9-0 0 RichardHughes 2 39
(R Hannon) *wnt bdly lft s: racd wd: shkn up and green 1/2-way: a outpcd* **9/2**[3]

63.29 secs (1.69) **Going Correction** +0.15s/f (Good) **5** Ran SP% **109.8**
Speed ratings (Par 91): **92,84,82,74,72**
CSF £13.76 TOTE £2.20: £1.10, £2.90; EX 10.00.
Owner The Honorable Earle I Mack **Bred** J Joyce **Trained** Newmarket, Suffolk

FOCUS
Not much pace or strength in depth in this opening maiden, which went the way of one of the two pattern entries.

NOTEBOOK
Take Flight(IRE) reportedly failed to handle the kickback on AW last time but set a good standard on her third to the subsequent Queen Mary winner Maqaasid here on her debut and put her experience to good use to win easily, able to grab the rail and dictate and then settling matters quickly with a turn of foot 2f out. Her debut form means a high mark will be coming her way in nurseries, but she doesn't look a filly with much scope and whether she proves up to her Moyglare Stud entry remains to be seen. (op 6-5 tchd 11-8)
Choose The Moment, by Choisir out of a mare who has produced winners at various distances, was just a cheapish yearling purchase but she looks to have a bit about her and saw her race out well after looking inexperienced for much of the way. She'll improve, particularly when tried at 6f.
Yasmeena(USA), blanketed for stalls entry, looked an interesting newcomer being the first foal of the top-class sprinter La Cucuracha from a speedy family and with a Cheveley Park entry to boot, but she never looked like justifying good market support, restrained in midfield then fading inside the last after drifting right with her rider seemingly at pains not to knock her about. He reported ahead of the race that she would improve for the run, and that's how it looked. (op 3-1)
Dualite(IRE) showed up while the pace was still modest but was quickly left behind when it increased (op 16-1)
Piece Of Mind, by Mind Games and the first foal of an unraced mare related to winners, looked very green for the first half of the race racing wide and was allowed to coast home once it was clear she wasn't going to be involved. She's entitled to improve, for all her pedigree is just a modest one. Official explanation: jockey said filly ran green (op 7-2)

4754 BETTOR.COM H'CAP 5f 6y
6:10 (6:11) (Class 4) (0-80,76) 3-Y-O **£4,533** (£1,348; £674; £336) **Stalls** High

Form RPR
-413 **1** **Drift And Dream**[40] 3436 3-9-9 **76** TedDurcan 8 86+
(C F Wall) *hld up in tch: gd hdwy on ins 2f out: drvn to ld ins fnl f: r.o strly u.p: edgd lft cl home* **5/2**[1]

033 **2** *1 1/2* **Erebus (IRE)**[11] 4398 3-8-13 **66** JamesDoyle 5 71+
(S Kirk) *in rr: rdn and hdwy fr over 1f out: styd on wl fnl f to take 2nd nr fin but no imp on wnr* **13/2**

6014 **3** *1/2* **Boragh Jamal (IRE)**[13] 4349 3-9-0 **67** (b) WilliamBuick 7 70
(B J Meehan) *trckd ldrs: n.m.r and rdn 2f out: edgd rt and styd on ins fnl f: tk 3rd cl home but no imp on wnr* **9/1**

2414 **4** *1/2* **Six Diamonds**[14] 4291 3-9-2 **76** AmyScott(7) 4 77
(H Morrison) *led: pushed along and hdd ins fnl f: sn outpcd by wnr: wknd into 4th nr fin* **13/2**

1005 **5** *1* **Felsham**[17] 4204 3-9-8 **75** FergusSweeney 2 73
(H Candy) *wnt lft s: chsd ldrs: rdn and one pce fnl f: readily hld whn n.m.r cl home* **9/2**[2]

1-05 **6** *1 1/2* **Adventure Story**[48] 3154 3-9-5 **72** RichardHughes 1 64+
(R Hannon) *v.s.a and detached early: swtchd lft to outside and sme prog fr 1/2-way: swtchd rt and hdwy over 1f out: styd on ins fnl f but nt rcvr: eased whn no ch w ldrs clsng stages* **6/1**[3]

2220 **7** *2 3/4* **Pherousa**[14] 4284 3-8-12 **65** SteveDrowne 3 48
(M Blanshard) *chsd ldrs: rdn 1/2-way: wknd over 1f out* **10/1**

0-04 **8** *4 1/2* **Royal Blade (IRE)**[12] 4365 3-8-9 **65** MatthewDavies(3) 6 31
(A P Jarvis) *chsd ldr: rdn over 2f out: n.m.r and wknd qckly over 1f out* **16/1**

62.06 secs (0.46) **Going Correction** +0.15s/f (Good) **8** Ran SP% **112.7**
Speed ratings (Par 102): **102,99,98,98,96 94,89,82**
Tote Swingers: 1&2 £4.20, 1&3 £5.80, 2&3 £12.70 CSF £18.47 CT £123.02 TOTE £3.30: £2.00, £2.60, £3.40; EX 23.60.
Owner Lady Juliet Tadgell **Bred** Lady Juliet Tadgell **Trained** Newmarket, Suffolk

FOCUS
An ordinary sprint handicap in which arguably the two best-treated runners occupied the first two places at the end of a well-run race. The runner-up is a fair guide with the third to his AW form.
Adventure Story Official explanation: jockey said filly missed the break

4755 BROTHERS PEAR CIDER E B F MAIDEN STKS 1m 14y
6:45 (6:47) (Class 5) 2-Y-O **£3,238** (£963; £481; £240) **Stalls** High

Form RPR
24 **1** **Jehanbux (USA)**[13] 4318 2-9-3 0 RichardHughes 7 83+
(R Hannon) *disp ld tl hdd appr fnl 3f: hmpd sn after and lost position: rdn and rallied over 1f out: styd on u.p and sn chsng ldr: led fnl 70yds: kpt on wl* **2/1**[2]

2 **2** *nk* **Johnny Castle**[15] 4263 2-9-3 0 WilliamBuick 9 80+
(J H M Gosden) *trckd ldrs: qcknd to ld and edgd rt appr fnl 3f: rdn over 1f out: edgd rt and hdd fnl 70yds: kpt on same pce* **13/8**[1]

0 **3** *3 1/2* **Miss Chicane**[20] 4103 2-8-12 0 TedDurcan 8 67
(W R Swinburn) *in rr: pushed along and flashed tail over 3f out: hdwy fr 2f out: stl green but styd on to take 3rd fnl f: no ch w ldng duo* **25/1**

0 **4** *shd* **Kyllachy Spirit**[13] 4318 2-9-3 0 GeorgeBaker 5 72
(B R Johnson) *disp ld tl hdd over 3f out and hmpd and lost pl sn after: rallied fr over 1f out but stl green: kpt on to dispute 3rd ins fnl f but no ch w ldng duo* **50/1**

23 **5** *4* **Bowermaster (USA)**[29] 3794 2-9-3 0 AhmedAjtebi 2 63
(Mahmood Al Zarooni) *chsd ldrs: rdn and effrt to press ldr 3f out: hung rt and wknd ins fnl 2f* **3/1**[3]

4 **6** *1 1/2* **Coachlight**[26] 3915 2-9-3 0 EddieAhern 1 59
(J L Dunlop) *in rr: pushed along and in tch over 2f out but nvr gng pce to get into contention* **10/1**

7 *hd* **Illustrious Forest** 2-9-3 0 DavidProbert 6 59
(J Mackie) *in rr: sme hdwy whn sltly hmpd 3f out: sme prog over 2f out: wknd sn after* **28/1**

5 **8** *hd* **Oetzi**[27] 3842 2-9-0 0 MatthewDavies(3) 3 58
(A P Jarvis) *chsd ldrs on outside: rdn ins fnl 3f: no ch w ldrs fnl 2f* **50/1**

1m 46.25s (2.95) **Going Correction** +0.25s/f (Good) **8** Ran SP% **116.7**
Speed ratings (Par 94): **95,94,91,91,87 85,85,85**
Tote Swingers: 1&2 £1.30, 1&3 £12.00, 2&3 £5.90 CSF £5.63 TOTE £3.10: £1.10, £1.40, £3.30; EX 5.90.
Owner K N Dhunjibhoy, V B Shirke, B M Desai **Bred** Brereton C Jones **Trained** East Everleigh, Wilts
■ Stewards' Enquiry : William Buick two-day ban: careless riding (Aug 21, 23)

FOCUS
An interesting maiden with all three market leaders having shown form just about good enough to have won this in previous years, but the pace was just steady to halfway and the field didn't really sort themselves out until 2f out, the result is potentially muddling as a consequence.

NOTEBOOK
Jehanbux(USA) had been disappointing at Ascot following his promising 7f debut here but he bounced back to get off the mark in gutsy fashion after losing two lengths or so when bumped just as the runner-up moved to the front, getting there a shade readily in the end. He'll have learnt plenty from this and appeals as the sort that would fare better in something like the Listed Stonehenge Stakes at Salisbury later this month rather than dropping back in trip for the Acomb at York. (op 11-4)
Johnny Castle had been unlucky on his debut at 7f here but was unable to provide his stable with a second successive win in this race despite getting first run on the eventual winner. He's not always going to meet one so useful, and would take plenty of beating in a similar event at one of the lesser tracks. His rider was banned for three days for causing interference. (op 6-4 tchd 15-8 and 2-1 in places)
Miss Chicane had shown some promise on her debut at Newmarket and did so again, relishing the extra yardage as her breeding suggested. Blanketed for stalls entry, she possibly isn't totally straightforward, flashing her tail wildly early in the straight, but her finishing effort was hard to fault. (op 20-1)
Kyllachy Spirit, out of a mare still looking for first winner on Flat, isn't bred to relish 1m as a two-year-old but he left his debut Ascot form behind with a decent effort and may have edged third had he not also been involved in the incident that affected the winner. Official explanation: jockey said colt ran green (tchd 66-1)
Bowermaster(USA) was a disappointment in view of his first two efforts at Newmarket, but he wasn't asked to lead on this occasion and perhaps resented it, carrying his head awkwardly when hanging and asked to improve then fading as if the trip was too far. He's a bit to prove after this. (op 5-2 tchd 2-1)
Coachlight was quickly stepped up in trip following a promising debut but speed clearly isn't his foremost asset given how he laboured once the pace increased. (op 12-1)
Illustrious Forest, a brother to the stable's middle-distance winner Fantino from a yard not known for debut winners, took the eye beforehand and ought to improve having not been knocked about. (op 25-1 tchd 33-1)

4756 BCL BURTON COPELAND H'CAP 1m 14y
7:20 (7:20) (Class 5) (0-75,75) 3-Y-O+ **£3,238** (£963; £481; £240) **Stalls** High

Form RPR
4000 **1** **Hip Hip Hooray**[52] 3040 4-8-10 **57** FergusSweeney 2 64
(L A Dace) *towards rr: rdn and hdwy over 2f out: chsd ldr 1f out: styd on u.p to ld fnl 50yds: drvn out* **10/1**

002- **2** *nk* **Three Ducks**[399] 3551 4-9-6 **70** PatrickHills(3) 3 76
(R Hannon) *disp ld: t.k.h: narrow ld 3f out: drvn and kpt on fr 2f out: hdd and outpcd fnl 50yds* **10/1**

4522 **3** *3/4* **Catchanova (IRE)**[24] 3957 3-8-5 **59** DavidProbert 8 62
(Eve Johnson Houghton) *chsd ldrs: rdn and outpcd 2f out: rallied and styd on wl fnl f: gng on cl home* **4/1**[2]

0665 **4** *1 1/4* **Meydan Dubai (IRE)**[167] 613 5-9-9 **70** SteveDrowne 5 71
(J R Best) *t.k.h: in tch: rdn: outpcd and lost position over 2f out: styd on again u.p fnl f: nt rch ldrs* **25/1**

4055 **5** *1/2* **Mavalenta (IRE)**[19] 4134 3-8-11 **65** MichaelHills 4 64
(J W Hills) *chsd ldrs: rdn to go 2nd over 2f out: sn rdn: wknd ins fnl f* **11/2**[3]

4052 **6** *1/2* **Prince Of Thebes (IRE)**[15] 4265 9-9-6 **67** JimCrowley 10 66
(M J Attwater) *t.k.h: wl there tl rdn and outpcd over 3f out: styd on again fnl f but nvr a threat* **4/1**[2]

0200 **7** *2 3/4* **Red Somerset (USA)**[13] 4322 7-10-0 **75** AndreaAtzeni 9 68
(Mike Murphy) *towards rr: rdn fr 3f out on ins: sme prog fnl 2f but nvr any threat* **10/1**

-000 **8** *1/2* **Pictures (IRE)**[17] 4204 3-8-11 **65** NeilChalmers 1 56
(J J Bridger) *stdd in rr: pushed along fr 3f out: mod prog fr over 1f out* **33/1**

3065 **9** *9* **Goose Green (IRE)**[41] 3404 6-8-13 **60** TravisBlock 6 31
(R J Hodges) *a towards rr* **16/1**

4-40 **10** *22* **Lean Machine**[63] 2682 3-9-6 **74** RichardHughes 7 —
(R Hannon) *disp ld tl rdn and narrowly hdd 3f out: rung bdly rt u.p and wknd qckly: eased* **7/2**[1]

1m 45.08s (1.78) **Going Correction** +0.25s/f (Good)
WFA 3 from 4yo+ 7lb **10** Ran SP% **117.5**
Speed ratings (Par 103): **101,100,99,98,98 97,94,94,85,63**
Tote Swingers: 1&2 £21.20, 1&3 £9.00, 2&3 £5.70 CSF £106.32 CT £479.40 TOTE £13.00: £3.50, £2.30, £2.00; EX 99.70.
Owner M C S D Racing Partnership **Bred** Mrs R S Evans **Trained** Five Oaks, W Sussex
■ Stewards' Enquiry : Fergus Sweeney two-day ban: used whip with excessive frequency (Aug 21-22)

FOCUS
Not a strong handicap for the grade with several runners hard to fancy and it was steadily run to boot, leading to something of a sprint finish. Modest and probably misleading form although the winner is rated to this year's form and the third is rated to his best.
Lean Machine Official explanation: jockey said colt was unsuited by the track

4757 GUY SALMON H'CAP 1m 2f 7y
7:55 (7:57) (Class 3) (0-90,90) 3-Y-O **£7,123** (£2,119; £1,059; £529) **Stalls** High

Form RPR
51 **1** **Jet Away**[22] 4028 3-9-3 **86** TomQueally 1 101+
(H R A Cecil) *t.k.h: hld up in rr: stdy hdwy on outside fr 3f out to chse ldr jst ins fnl 2f: drvn and styd on strly fnl f to ld cl home: readily* **2/1**[1]

1-12 **2** *nk* **Con Artist (IRE)**[20] 4100 3-9-3 **86** TedDurcan 2 100
(Saeed Bin Suroor) *led: pushed along and styd on wl fr 2f out: hdd cl home* **3/1**[2]

0-10 **3** *1 1/4* **Senate**[104] 1502 3-9-2 **85** WilliamBuick 6 97
(J H M Gosden) *chsd ldrs: rdn and outpcd fr 2f out: styd on again fnl f and kpt on cl home but no ch w ldng duo* **9/1**

-524 **4** *2 3/4* **Sharaayeen**[92] 1823 3-8-8 **77** TadhgO'Shea 7 83
(B W Hills) *chsd ldrs: pushed along: nt clr run and lost position over 2f out: sn shkn up but no ch after* **10/1**

0065 **5** *3 1/2* **Whistleinthewind (IRE)**[42] 3351 3-8-5 **74** (b[1]) DavidProbert 4 73
(G L Moore) *disp 2nd: rdn 3f out: lost disp 2nd jst ins fnl 2f: wknd over 1f out* **18/1**

6002 **6** *1 3/4* **Right Step**[7] 4504 3-9-3 **86** RichardHughes 3 82
(A P Jarvis) *disp 2nd: rdn 3f out: lost disp 2nd ins fnl 2f: wknd over 1f out* **9/2**[3]

1 **7** *9* **Mortbet (IRE)**[21] 4069 3-9-7 **90** PhilipRobinson 5 68
(M A Jarvis) *t.k.h in rr: rdn and hung lft fr 2f out: a bhd* **5/1**

2m 9.59s (-0.91) **Going Correction** +0.25s/f (Good) **7** Ran SP% **117.5**
Speed ratings (Par 104): **113,112,111,109,106 105,98**
Tote Swingers: 1&2 £2.00, 1&3 £7.50, 2&3 £6.80 CSF £8.59 TOTE £3.00: £2.00, £2.10; EX 6.80.

Owner K Abdulla **Bred** Juddmonte Farms Ltd **Trained** Newmarket, Suffolk

FOCUS

A cracking handicap that featured several horses probably well ahead of their marks as well as a couple that had looked promising in the spring coming back from breaks. The winner looks potentially Listed class and this is sound and form to view positively.

NOTEBOOK

Jet Away ◆ had looked a very smart prospect when winning a maiden at Lingfield last time from two subsequent winners and he more than confirmed that impression with a hard-earned success, produced from further off the pace than the other two placed horses and knuckling down really well as the first two came clear over 1f out. This trip clearly suits better than shorter and being out of a Kahyasi mare, he ought to have few problems with 1m4f. A 6lb or 7lb rise in his mark is unlikely to stop him winning again before stepping up in class. (op 7-4 tchd 13-8)

Con Artist(IRE) had looked ahead of his mark last time when second in a decent Newbury handicap and filled the same position again under a sensible ride from the front, setting a tempo to suit himself (bit free down the back straight) and giving it the best he could. Time will show he bumped into a useful one here and he still appeals as the sort to win a decent handicap. (op 7-2 tchd 4-1 in places)

Senate ◆ hadn't been seen since April having made a very taking reappearance in March but he's clearly over whatever ailed him last time and left the impression the best has still to be seen of him, staying on strongly having been caught flat footed when the tempo lifted in the straight. Longer trips and easier ground will suit him, and he may well develop into a November Handicap contender before the season is out. (op 8-1)

Sharaayeen had been absent since failing to settle at 1m4f at Chester in May but he made an encouraging comeback without being at all knocked about and he would make some appeal with this behind him back in something less competitive. (op 14-1 tchd 16-1)

Whistleinthewind(IRE) had been disappointing in handicaps since switched to turf from AW but showed a bit more in first-time blinkers, albeit handily positioned as the race developed. (op 16-1)

Right Step had come back to form when runner-up at Goodwood last time but, for all he isn't the most consistent, he'd had quite a tough race then and might have found this coming too quickly. (op 5-1 tchd 11-2)

Mortbet(IRE) had looked promising when winning a maiden at Leicester on his debut but he ran in snatches and never threatened after once again being hooded and blanketed for stalls entry (also a handful in preliminaries). On a stiff enough mark anyway, he has plenty of growing up to do.

Official explanation: jockey said gelding hung left (op 6-1 tchd 13-2)

4758 GENEPOOL PERSONNEL H'CAP — 1m 2f 7y

8:25 (8:25) (Class 4) (0-80,80) 3-Y-O+ — **£4,533** (£1,348; £674; £336) **Stalls High**

Form — RPR

22-3 **1** **Absinthe (IRE)**[120] 1156 4-9-13 **79** AdamKirby 4 — 87
(W R Swinburn) *led 1f: styd trcking ldrs: drvn to chal 2f out: led sn after: pushed out ins fnl f* **6/1**[3]

2130 **2** ½ **Blues Music (IRE)**[42] 3351 3-9-3 **78** MichaelHills 1 — 85
(B W Hills) *chsd ldrs: drvn to chal fr over 2f out: chsd wnr fnl f but a hld* **6/1**[3]

6236 **3** 1¼ **Hidden Glory**[21] 4056 3-9-4 **79** AndreaAtzeni 9 — 84
(Pat Eddery) *led after 1f: kpt slt ld tl narrowly hdd ins fnl 3f: n.m.r on inner and lost position ins fnl 2f: kpt on again fnl f* **11/2**[2]

0204 **4** *nk* **Essexbridge**[33] 3697 3-9-1 **76** RichardHughes 2 — 80
(R Hannon) *chsd ldr after 2f: chal 4f out: narrow ld jst ins fnl 3f: edgd rt and hdd jst ins fnl 2f: wknd ins fnl f* **7/2**[1]

-000 **5** 1½ **Wing Play (IRE)**[20] 4100 5-10-0 **80** (p) EddieAhern 7 — 81+
(H Morrison) *in rr: rdn and styd on fnl 2f: kpt on but nt rch ldrs* **14/1**

1344 **6** *nk* **Touch Of Style (IRE)**[5] 4579 6-8-6 **61** oh4 AshleyHamblett(3) 8 — 61+
(Matthew Salaman) *in tch: rdn and styd on same pce fnl 2f* **7/1**

2311 **7** 1 **Rosco Flyer (IRE)**[22] 4019 4-9-7 **76** MatthewDavies(3) 5 — 74
(R A Teal) *chsd ldrs: rdn over 2f out: sn btn* **7/1**

8 1¼ **Pool Of Knowledge (FR)**[13] 4-9-10 **76** WilliamBuick 3 — 72
(Miss Venetia Williams) *n.m.r 2f out but a towards rr* **25/1**

/30- **9** 4½ **Green Wadi**[239] 7684 5-9-8 **74** GeorgeBaker 10 — 61
(G L Moore) *bhd most of way* **20/1**

6354 **10** *shd* **Uncle Fred**[22] 4023 5-9-11 **77** JimCrowley 6 — 64
(P R Chamings) *in rr: hdwy over 3f out: sn wknd* **8/1**

2m 11.67s (1.17) **Going Correction** +0.25s/f (Good)
WFA 3 from 4yo+ 9lb — **10** Ran SP% **117.6**
Speed ratings (Par 105): **105,104,103,103,102 101,101,100,96,96**
Tote Swingers: 1&2 £17.40, 1&3 £8.00, 2&3 £7.10 CSF £42.27 CT £211.63 TOTE £7.30: £2.50, £2.30, £2.20; EX 58.00 Place 6 £42.10; Place 5 £22.14.
Owner P W Harris **Bred** Moyglare Stud Farm Ltd **Trained** Aldbury, Herts

FOCUS

A fair handicap and another race on the card run at steady pace. The first four held those places turning in and nothing got into the race from the rear. The placed horses are rated close to their earlier Goodwood form.

T/Plt: £44.20 to a £1 stake. Pool:£45,046.25 - 743.18 winning tickets T/Qpdt: £15.90 to a £1 stake. Pool:£5,472.82 - 254.05 winning tickets ST

4715 YARMOUTH (L-H)

Thursday, August 5

OFFICIAL GOING: Good

Back straight bend dolled out 3m, increasing distances of 9, 10, 11f, by about 10yds and 14f by 15yds.

Wind: fresh, across Weather: bright, sunny spells

4759 E B F NORFOLK RACING CLUB MAIDEN STKS — 6f 3y

2:20 (2:21) (Class 5) 2-Y-O — **£2,901** (£868; £434; £217; £108) **Stalls High**

Form — RPR

1 **Darej (USA)** 2-9-3 0 RichardHills 7 — 80+
(W J Haggas) *trckd ldng pair: rdn to chal over 1f out: led ins fnl f: r.o wl and asserted fnl 50yds* **1/2**[1]

0 **2** 1¼ **His Grace (IRE)**[19] 4131 2-9-3 0 EddieAhern 6 — 72
(A B Haynes) *racd keenly: led: rdn over 1f out: hdd ins fnl f: no ex fnl 75yds* **40/1**

00 **3** 2 **Better Offer (IRE)**[16] 4221 2-8-12 0 JohnFahy(5) 4 — 66
(Miss Amy Weaver) *chsd ldr tl over 1f out: styd on same pce u.p ins fnl f* **80/1**

0 **4** *nk* **Eyes On**[8] 4474 2-8-12 0 RichardMullen 5 — 60
(P J McBride) *hld up in tch in last trio: rdn and unable qck over 2f out: styd on again ins fnl f: nvr gng pce to trble ldrs* **50/1**

05 **5** *nk* **Key West (IRE)**[7] 4499 2-9-3 0 (b) SaleemGolam 1 — 64
(J H M Gosden) *stdd s: hld up in tch in last trio: rdn and effrt 2f out: kpt on same pce fnl f* **15/2**[3]

6 *hd* **Cat Island** 2-8-12 0 PatCosgrave 8 — 58
(M H Tompkins) *in tch: rdn and unable qck 2f out: kpt on same pce fr over 1f out* **33/1**

5 **7** ½ **Toparichi**[53] 2990 2-9-3 0 DarryllHolland 3 — 64+
(M H Tompkins) *dwlt: sn in tch in midfield: rdn and unable qck ent fnl 2f: keeping on same pce and wl hld whn nt clr run ins fnl f* **4/1**[2]

8 9 **Burnem Green** 2-8-12 0 KierenFallon 2 — 28
(A Bailey) *s.i.s: rn green and sn pushed along in last: lost tch wl over 1f out: eased ins fnl f* **9/1**

1m 14.42s (0.02) **Going Correction** -0.20s/f (Firm) — **8** Ran SP% **117.0**
Speed ratings (Par 94): **91,89,86,86,85 85,84,72**
Tote Swingers: 1&2 £6.70, 1&3 £7.00, 2&3 £14.60 CSF £35.97 TOTE £1.60: £1.10, £5.20, £10.00; EX 28.30.
Owner Hamdan Al Maktoum **Bred** Extern Developments **Trained** Newmarket, Suffolk

FOCUS

This was an ordinary juvenile maiden and the form looks pretty weak.

NOTEBOOK

Darej(USA), a nicely bred son of Speightstown from a top yard who is well entered up, was backed beforehand to the exclusion of his rivals, so had clearly been pleasing in his home work and was on his best behaviour in the preliminaries. He got the job done, but had to work harder than many expected and this form is a far cry from justifying a trip for any of his Group-race entries. However, it was no doubt down to greenness and he was comfortably on top nearing the finish, so it wouldn't be surprising if he turned out to be very useful down the line. (op 4-7, tchd 8-13 in a place)

His Grace(IRE), well beaten at odds of 66-1 on debut 19 days earlier, had run distinctly green that day and looked set for a similar outcome as he played up in the preliminaries. He ran a big race from the front, though, and is evidently improving. His stable also had the dam, who was a very useful miler on her day, and he is entitled to progress again from this experience. Another furlong should also be to his liking before long. (tchd 33-1)

Better Offer(IRE) had finished ninth on his two previous outings. He was never far away and, although readily outpaced when it mattered by the first two, this obviously rates a big step in the right direction. He may be a little flattered, but now has the option of nurseries and should find a small race this term. (op 66-1)

Eyes On was one of the first off the bridle and lacked the pace to get seriously involved, but there was a fair bit to like about the way she finished her race. This was a marked improvement from her debut eight days earlier and, although related to winners over this trip, another furlong ought to prove right up her street. (op 66-1)

Key West(IRE) is clearly one of his connections' lesser lights but again hinted that he may come good when faced with another furlong in nurseries, for which he now qualifies. (op 6-1 tchd 8-1)

Cat Island is from a decent family her trainer knows all about. She moved nicely on debut before her lack of experience told and this rates an encouraging introduction. (op 22-1)

Toparichi, who showed definite promise on his Doncaster debut, was returning from a 53-day break and ultimately shaped as though the run was again needed. He is yet another that probably wants another furlong already. (op 9-2 tchd 7-2)

4760 NORFOLK RACING CLUB / RED HERRING RESTAURANT MAIDEN H'CAP — 6f 3y

2:50 (2:51) (Class 6) (0-65,63) 3-Y-O+ — **£2,072** (£616; £308; £153) **Stalls High**

Form — RPR

6500 **1** **Gracie's Games**[183] 389 4-8-4 **45** (v1) HarryBentley(7) 11 — 60
(R J Price) *chsd ldrs: wnt 2nd 3f out: led over 2f out: clr and rdn over 1f out: pushed out ins fnl f* **33/1**

005 **2** 1½ **Picansort**[38] 3511 3-9-10 **62** EddieAhern 9 — 71+
(B R Johnson) *s.i.s: bhd: rdn 1/2-way: hdwy u.p wl over 1f out: edgd lft but kpt on to chse wnr fnl 100yds: kpt on but nvr gng to rch wnr* **9/2**[3]

0605 **3** 2½ **Gessabelle**[1] 4720 3-8-2 **45** (t) JohnFahy(5) 6 — 46
(P S McEntee) *chsd ldr tl led over 4f out: rdn and hdd over 2f out: sn outpcd by wnr: kpt on same u.p fr over 1f out: lost 2nd fnl 100yds* **33/1**

220 **4** 2½ **Oh So Spicy**[15] 4251 3-9-11 **63** JackMitchell 5 — 56
(C F Wall) *restless in stalls: chsd ldrs: rdn and unable qck ent fnl 2f: one pce and no ch w wnr fr over 1f out* **7/2**[2]

0020 **5** ½ **Thewinnatakesitall**[3] 4651 3-8-11 **49** KierenFallon 2 — 41
(N Tinkler) *chsd ldrs: rdn and unable qck ent fnl 2f: drvn and styd on same pce fr over 1f out* **11/4**[1]

0002 **6** 1 **A Pocketful Of Rye (IRE)**[17] 4210 3-8-10 **55** LauraSimpson(7) 8 — 43
(P Howling) *s.i.s: bhd: hdwy and hung lft 1/2-way: no prog fr wl over 1f out: nvr trbld ldrs* **10/1**

650U **7** *hd* **Music Lover**[26] 3907 3-9-9 **61** SaleemGolam 7 — 49
(R A Harris) *t.k.h: chsd ldrs tl struggling u.p ent fnl 2f: wknd wl over 1f out* **11/1**

560 **8** 2 **Summers Target (USA)**[7] 4498 4-9-2 **50** J-PGuillambert 3 — 32
(S C Williams) *taken down early: dwlt: a towards rr: rdn and short-lived effrt over 2f out: wl btn fnl 2f: n.d* **5/1**

0000 **9** 2 **Northumberland**[64] 2647 4-8-11 **50** MarkCoumbe(5) 10 — 26
(M C Chapman) *taken down early: led tl over 4f out: wknd u.p ent fnl 2f: bhd fr wl over 1f out* **33/1**

0066 **10** 1½ **Riggs (IRE)**[24] 3946 4-8-12 **46** ow1 PatCosgrave 4 — 17
(Peter Grayson) *bhd: sme prog into midfield u.p 2f out: wknd wl over 1f out* **50/1**

0-05 **11** 10 **Harley Fern**[38] 3507 4-8-4 **45** (p) AdamBeschizza(7) 1 — —
(T T Clement) *dwlt: sn in tch in midfield: struggling u.p over 2f out: wl bhd over 1f out: eased ins fnl f* **22/1**

1m 13.04s (-1.36) **Going Correction** -0.20s/f (Firm)
WFA 3 from 4yo+ 4lb — **11** Ran SP% **116.3**
Speed ratings (Par 101): **101,99,95,92,91 90,90,87,84,82 69**
Tote Swingers: 1&2 £33.30, 1&3 £65.30, 2&3 £18.50 CSF £168.45 CT £5044.41 TOTE £44.80: £8.40, £3.50, £9.90; EX 196.70.
Owner David Prosser & Keith Warrington **Bred** David Prosser & Keith Warrington **Trained** Ullingswick, H'fords

FOCUS

A 0-65 maiden handicap, so obviously moderate form. The runner-up is rated in line with his best maiden form.

4761 NORFOLKRACINGCLUB.CO.UK / EAST ANGLIAN AIR AMBULANCE (S) STKS — 1m 3y

3:20 (3:21) (Class 6) 3-Y-O — **£1,683** (£501; £250; £125) **Stalls High**

Form — RPR

3140 **1** **Denton Ryal**[16] 4236 3-8-5 57 (b1) AdamBeschizza(7) 6 — 55
(M E Rimmer) *chsd ldrs: rdn to go 2nd 2f out: rdn to ld ent fnl f: r.o strly u.p and clr fnl 150yds: eased towards fin* **15/8**[1]

604 **2** 3½ **Baby Judge (IRE)**[23] 3972 3-8-12 47 MarkCoumbe(5) 7 — 52
(M C Chapman) *led: hdd and rdn ent fnl 2f: outpcd u.p jst over 1f out: no ch w wnr fnl f but kpt on to go 2nd towards fin* **20/1**

6051 **3** ½ **Avonvalley**[24] 3966 3-9-0 65 MatthewDavies(3) 5 — 51
(George Baker) *rrd s and s.i.s: hld up in tch: rdn and hdwy to ld ent fnl 2f: sn drvn: hdd ent fnl f: wknd fnl f: lost 2nd towards fin* **2/1**[2]

0034 **4** 4 **Marafong**[12] 4383 3-9-3 53 SaleemGolam 1 — 41
(Miss J Feilden) *stdd s: t.k.h: hld up in last pair: rdn and no prog ent fnl 2f: no ch fr wl over 1f out* **4/1**[3]

5003 **5** 3 ¼ **Captain Clint (IRE)**[20] 4113 3-9-3 42 DarrylHolland 4 33
(M H Tompkins) *chsd ldr tl jst over 2f out: sn struggling u.p: wl bhd fnl f* **11/2**

1m 40.87s (0.27) **Going Correction** -0.20s/f (Firm) **5** Ran SP% **108.3**
Speed ratings (Par 98): **90,86,86,82,78**
CSF £29.66 TOTE £2.70: £1.10, £5.90; EX 29.40.Winner bought by Sheena West for 4,800gns.
Owner Clive Dennett **Bred** Clive Dennett **Trained** Newmarket, Suffolk

FOCUS
A typically weak 3-y-o seller, run at an average pace and the winner did not need to improve on her best form to score.

4762 NORFOLKRACINGCLUB.CO.UK / PREMIER RACING "FREE BET TODAY" FILLIES' H'CAP 1m 3y
3:50 (3:51) (Class 5) (0-75,81) 3-Y-O £2,590 (£770; £385; £192) Stalls High

Form RPR

0303 **1** **Wild Rockette**[13] 4344 3-8-11 68 (b) Louis-PhilippeBeuzelin(3) 5 78
(B J Meehan) *stdd s: hld up in tch in last trio: hdwy to trck ldr over 1f out: swtchd lft and rdn jst ins fnl f: qckng to ld fnl 50yds: r.o strly* **5/1**[2]

4011 **2** 1 **Sooraah**[8] 4491 3-9-8 81 6ex JohnFahy(5) 1 89+
(W J Haggas) *t.k.h: chsd ldrs: cruised upsides ldr over 2f out: led over 1f out: rdn and flashed tail jst ins fnl f: hdd fnl 50yds: sn btn* **4/6**[1]

010 **3** 2 **Shesells Seashells**[45] 3268 3-9-2 70 KierenFallon 7 73
(M L W Bell) *stdd s: t.k.h: hld up wl in tch: rdn and effrt to chse ldrs over 1f out: drvn 1f out: no ex and btn fnl 100yds* **8/1**[3]

4-26 **4** nk **Zenarinda**[19] 4127 3-8-13 67 DarrylHolland 4 69
(M H Tompkins) *t.k.h: led at stdy gallop: jnd over 2f out: rdn and qcknd 2f out: hdd over 1f out: sn drvn: no ex ins fnl f* **12/1**

-004 **5** 7 **Kenyan Cat**[13] 4344 3-8-6 63 MatthewDavies(3) 6 49
(George Baker) *stdd s: t.k.h: hld up in tch in last trio: shkn up and effrt over 2f out: wknd u.p and edgd lft over 1f out* **12/1**

-400 **6** 1 ¾ **Half Sister (IRE)**[84] 2042 3-9-1 69 JamieMackay 2 51
(M E Rimmer) *in tch: rdn and unable qck over 2f out: wknd over 1f out* **66/1**

0060 **7** nse **Jemimaville (IRE)**[2] 4687 3-8-6 60 (v[1]) RichardMullen 8 42
(G C Bravery) *t.k.h: chsd ldr tl over 2f out: wknd u.p wl over 1f out* **40/1**

024 **8** 3 ¼ **Free As A Lark**[22] 4028 3-9-1 69 JackMitchell 3 44
(C F Wall) *hld up in tch in last trio: rdn and struggling over 2f out: bhd fr wl over 1f out* **11/1**

1m 39.13s (-1.47) **Going Correction** -0.20s/f (Firm) **8** Ran SP% **115.4**
Speed ratings (Par 97): **99,98,96,95,88 86,86,83**
Tote Swingers: 1&2 £2.20, 1&3 £3.10, 2&3 £2.90 CSF £8.77 CT £26.07 TOTE £3.40: £1.02, £2.00, £2.70; EX 11.90.
Owner Mrs M D Stewart **Bred** Wellsummers Partnership One **Trained** Manton, Wilts

FOCUS
They didn't go that quick in this fillies' handicap and racing near the front appeared an advantage. The first four came clear and the third and fourth are rated to their maiden form.
Free As A Lark Official explanation: jockey said filly hung left

4763 NORFOLK RACING CLUB / ZIMZALABIM.CO.UK HOWLING DANDY H'CAP 1m 1f
4:20 (4:20) (Class 6) (0-65,68) 3-Y-0+ £2,072 (£616; £308; £153) Stalls Low

Form RPR

5000 **1D** **Negotiation (IRE)**[35] 3604 4-9-13 63 PatCosgrave 2 75
(M Quinn) *mde all: rdn over 2f out: hrd pressed fr wl over 1f out: battled on u.p fnl f: forged ahd towards fin: fin 1st, ½l, disq: (prohibited substance)* **22/1**

5221 **1** **Mr Harmoosh (IRE)**[10] 4439 3-9-3 68 6ex AdamBeschizza(7) 5 78
(E F Vaughan) *hld up wl in tch: n.m.r ent fnl 3f: rdn and hdwy to chse wnr 2f out: ev ch over 1f out: hrd drvn fnl f: unable qckn: fin 2nd, ½l: awrdd r* **3/1**[1]

6650 **2** 2 **Akamon**[22] 4022 3-8-11 55 RichardMullen 3 61
(E A L Dunlop) *dwlt: racd in last pair: hdwy on inner and nt clr run over 2f out: swtchd rt and rdn wl over 1f out: kpt on to go 3rd ins fnl f: nt rch ldng pair: fin 3rd, nk & 2l; plcd 2nd* **5/1**[3]

026 **3** 3 ¼ **Wavertree Bounty**[2] 4687 3-8-1 48 Louis-PhilippeBeuzelin(3) 9 47
(J Ryan) *hld up wl in tch: hdwy on outer to chse ldrs 2f out: drvn wl over 1f out: btn ent fnl f: wknd ins fnl f: fin 4th, plcd 3rd* **5/1**[3]

3 **4** 3 ½ **Bizarrely (IRE)**[16] 4238 3-9-7 65 KierenFallon 6 56
(J Pearce) *taken down early: t.k.h: hld up in rr: hdwy on outer wl over 2f out: hung lft fr over 1f out: no imp after: fin 5th, plcd 4th* **9/2**[2]

0050 **5** 1 **Gheed (IRE)**[105] 1489 5-9-0 55 (t) JohnFahy(5) 4 44
(K A Morgan) *chsd wnr tl 2f out: sn wknd u.p: wl hld: fin 6th, plcd 5th* **18/1**

-405 **6** ½ **Exopuntia**[17] 4213 4-8-10 49 MichaelStainton(3) 1 37
(Miss J Feilden) *chsd ldng pair: rdn 3f out: wknd over 1f out: plcd 6th* **28/1**

6303 **7** 2 ¾ **Easy Wonder (GER)**[10] 4439 5-8-6 45 MartinLane(3) 8 27
(I A Wood) *hld up in tch midfield: rdn and lost pl over 2f out: n.d fnl 2f fin 8th, plcd 7th* **20/1**

0405 **8** 2 **Astrodonna**[16] 4236 5-10-0 64 DarrylHolland 7 41
(M H Tompkins) *hld up towards rr: hmpd after 1f: rdn and no prog over 2f out: n.d: fin 9th, plcd 8th* **7/1**

3-00 **9** nk **Hilltop Artistry**[20] 4108 4-9-10 60 J-PGuillambert 12 37
(J R Jenkins) *t.k.h: hld up towards rr: rdn and no real prog ent fnl 2f: wl btn whn hmpd over 1f out: fin 10th, plcd 9th* **14/1**

0-60 **10** shd **Sancho Panza**[56] 2909 3-8-5 49 ow1 SaleemGolam 11 26
(Miss J Feilden) *in tch: rdn ent fnl 4f: bhd fnl 2f: fin 11th, plcd 10th* **33/1**

1m 55.1s (-0.70) **Going Correction** -0.10s/f (Good)
WFA 3 from 4yo+ 8lb **11** Ran SP% **116.4**
Speed ratings (Par 101): **99,98,96,93,90 89,89,87,85,84 84**
Tote Swingers: 1&2 £17.70, 1&3 £35.40, 2&3 £6.90 CSF £83.41 CT £396.91 TOTE £35.90: £7.10, £1.60, £2.60; EX 123.00 Trifecta £396.91.
Owner A G MacLennan **Bred** Loughbrown Stud **Trained** Newmarket, Suffolk
■ Stewards' Enquiry : Adam Beschizza four-day ban: careless riding (Aug 21-24)

FOCUS
A weak handicap, run at a fair enough pace. The third is the best guide to the level.
Wavertree Bounty Official explanation: trainer said filly was in season
Bizarrely(IRE) Official explanation: jockey said gelding hung left and right
Hilltop Artistry Official explanation: jockey said colt hung left under pressure

4764 NORFOLK RACING CLUB / THIRD CROSSING RESTAURANT H'CAP 1m 3f 101y
4:50 (4:52) (Class 6) (0-65,64) 3-Y-O £2,072 (£616; £308; £153) Stalls Low

Form RPR

004- **1** **Jinto**[272] 7266 3-8-10 60 AdamBeschizza(7) 11 70
(R M H Cowell) *stdd s: hld up in last pair tl dashed up to chse ldr after 2f: rdn to ld wl over 2f out: hdd over 1f out: led again 1f out: styd on wl u.p fnl f* **20/1**

006 **2** nk **Budding Daffodil**[40] 3443 3-8-12 62 HarryBentley(7) 12 71
(W J Knight) *hld up in tch in midfield: hdwy to chse wnr 2f out: rdn to ld over 1f out tl hdd 1f out: edgd rt ins fnl f: no ex nr fin* **16/1**

-050 **3** 6 **Top Tigress**[38] 3513 3-9-3 60 RichardMullen 2 59
(Sir Michael Stoute) *hmpd sn after s: hld up towards rr: swtchd rt and rdn 3f out: chsd clr ldng pair over 1f out: no imp* **11/1**

4224 **4** hd **Apache Kid (IRE)**[16] 4235 3-9-3 63 MartinLane(3) 7 61
(D M Simcock) *in tch in midfield: rdn 4f out: kpt on to press for placings fr over 1f out: kpt plugging on u.p but nvr gng pce to trble ldrs* **9/2**[1]

5610 **5** 4 **Broughtons Swinger**[56] 2909 3-9-6 63 JamieMackay 6 55
(W J Musson) *broke wl: led at stdy gallop for 2f: trckd ldrs after tl rdn and fnd nil 2f out: wl btn over 1f out* **10/1**[3]

002 **6** 4 ½ **Jewellery (IRE)**[28] 3829 3-9-7 64 PatCosgrave 3 48
(J R Fanshawe) *hld up in last trio: hdwy towards inner over 2f out: no prog and wl btn over 1f out: wknd fnl f* **9/2**[1]

00-5 **7** 7 **Forethought**[69] 2501 3-9-3 60 J-PGuillambert 10 32
(P Howling) *chsd ldrs: rdn and wknd qckly over 2f out: wl bhd fr over 1f out* **40/1**

0000 **8** 2 **Tymora (USA)**[19] 4134 3-9-4 61 DarrylHolland 5 30
(H R A Cecil) *hld up towards rr: hdwy on inner whn nt clr run and swtchd rt ent fnl 2f: sn rdn and dropped out: wl bhd fr wl over 1f out* **16/1**

0005 **9** 1 ¼ **Converre**[14] 4289 3-8-5 53 JohnFahy(5) 4 20
(G A Butler) *stdd s: hld up in rr: rdn and no prog wl over 2f out: wl bhd fnl 2f* **7/1**[2]

5050 **10** 3 ½ **Quick Deal (USA)**[22] 4022 3-9-5 62 SaleemGolam 9 23
(J H M Gosden) *in tch in midfield: rdn and no rspnse 4f out: wknd qckly over 2f out and sn wl bhd* **14/1**

0-06 **11** 2 **Annelko**[73] 2390 3-8-12 55 DaraghO'Donohoe 8 12
(A B Haynes) *stdd s: hld up in last pair tl dashed up to ld after 2f: hdd wl over 2f out: sn wknd: wl bhd fr wl over 1f out* **40/1**

2m 31.0s (2.30) **Going Correction** -0.10s/f (Good) **11** Ran SP% **94.4**
Speed ratings (Par 98): **87,86,82,82,79 76,71,69,68,66 64**
Tote Swingers: 1&2 £30.40, 1&3 £17.70, 2&3 £11.30 CSF £183.86 CT £1594.48 TOTE £23.60: £5.90, £4.00, £3.30; EX 156.70.
Owner Khalifa Dasmal **Bred** Darley **Trained** Six Mile Bottom, Cambs

FOCUS
Despite the favourite being withdrawn down at the start in this low-grade 3-y-o handicap, there were potential improvers in attendance with six making their debuts in this sphere, and two of them pulled well clear in a tight finish. The first two are rated big improvers on their maiden form with the next two home a few pounds off.
Annelko Official explanation: jockey said colt hung badly right

4765 NORFOLKRACINGCLUB.CO.UK / KEITH LOADS-NORFOLK'S FAVOURITE COMEDIAN H'CAP 1m 6f 17y
5:25 (5:26) (Class 6) (0-58,57) 3-Y-0+ £2,072 (£616; £308; £153) Stalls Low

Form RPR

040 **1** **Fuzzypeg (IRE)**[20] 4115 3-8-0 48 ow3 MartinLane(3) 3 56
(J R Fanshawe) *in tch: rdn and effrt 3f out: chsd ldr over 2f out: drvn to ld 2f out: kpt on gamely u.p fnl f: all out* **8/1**

3040 **2** nk **Mymateeric**[162] 584 4-9-1 47 RichardMullen 14 54
(J Pearce) *in tch in midfield: rdn and effrt over 3f out: drvn and hdwy to chal ent fnl f: ev ch after tl unable qck fnl 75yds* **11/1**

3500 **3** 2 ¼ **Jennerous Blue**[51] 3055 3-8-2 47 (p) PaulQuinn 13 51
(D K Ivory) *t.k.h early: hld up in midfield: hmpd after 1f: rdn wl over 3f out: hdwy u.p 2f out: pressed ldrs ent fnl f tl wknd fnl 100yds* **25/1**

-604 **4** 4 **Extremely So**[10] 4441 4-9-3 54 JohnFahy(5) 4 52
(P J McBride) *stdd s: hld up in rr: hdwy on outer 3f out: chsng ldrs but hanging lft and racing awkwardly wl over 1f out: no prog and btn 1f out: no ch whn stmbld bdly nr fin* **7/1**[3]

-420 **5** 2 ¾ **Astroleo**[56] 2907 4-9-2 48 DarrylHolland 1 43
(M H Tompkins) *chsd ldrs: rdn to chse ldr over 4f out: led over 2f out tl hdd 2f out: kpt pressing ldrs tl wknd qckly ent fnl f* **13/2**[2]

6060 **6** 1 ½ **Court Wing (IRE)**[54] 2955 4-8-6 45 HarryBentley(7) 5 37
(R J Price) *hld up off the pce in midfield: hdwy on inner 4f out: chsng ldrs and rdn wl over 1f out: wknd qckly ent fnl f* **40/1**

6006 **7** 3 ½ **Sparkaway**[94] 1756 4-9-8 54 JamieMackay 12 42
(W J Musson) *s.i.s: hld up in rr: hdwy towards inner 4f out: no prog 2f out and wl btn after* **9/1**

1005 **8** 1 **Aaman (IRE)**[16] 4223 4-9-4 57 AdamBeschizza(7) 8 43
(E F Vaughan) *chsd ldrs tl led 10f out: clr 8f out tl rdn and hdd over 2f out: wknd u.p wl over 1f out: wl btn fnl f* **17/2**

6- **9** 2 **River Danube**[243] 7635 7-8-10 45 (b[1]) Louis-PhilippeBeuzelin(3) 2 28
(T J Fitzgerald) *racd off the pce in midfield: rdn and no rspnse over 3f out: wl btn fnl 2f* **20/1**

4032 **10** 2 **Mayfair's Future**[17] 4211 5-9-6 52 J-PGuillambert 7 33
(J R Jenkins) *chsd ldr tl over 10f out: styd chsng ldrs tl wknd u.p over 2f out: wl btn over 1f out* **13/2**[2]

0-04 **11** ½ **Miss Doodle**[21] 4045 4-9-4 50 JackMitchell 6 30
(Eve Johnson Houghton) *towards rr whn hmpd after 1f: rdn and no prog 3f out: n.d* **16/1**

0606 **12** 10 **Dovedon Earl**[10] 4441 4-9-4 50 DaraghO'Donohoe 16 16
(T Keddy) *racd in midfield: rdn btn wl over 3f out: wl bhd and eased ins fnl f* **33/1**

-006 **13** 4 ½ **Amylyn**[17] 4200 3-8-2 47 ow2 RichardThomas 10 7
(J R Holt) *towards rr whn hmpd after 1f: a bhd after: lost tch 4f out: eased ins fnl f* **33/1**

3320 **14** 3 ¼ **Hassadin**[14] 3324 4-9-0 46 PatCosgrave 9 1
(A B Haynes) *led tl 10f out: chsd ldr after tl over 4f out: sn dropped out: wl bhd fnl 2f: eased ins fnl f: t.o* **6/1**[1]

0405 **15** 2 ¼ **Cragganmore Creek**[60] 2786 7-8-13 45 (t) SaleemGolam 15 —
(D Morris) *a in rr: rdn and lost tch 4f out: wl bhd over 2f out: eased ins fnl f: t.o* **50/1**

3m 5.67s (-1.93) **Going Correction** -0.10s/f (Good)
WFA 3 from 4yo+ 13lb **15** Ran SP% **118.2**
Speed ratings (Par 101): **101,100,99,97,95 94,92,92,91,89 89,83,81,79,78**
Tote Swingers: 1&2 £25.80, 1&3 £41.00, 2&3 £59.80. totesuper7: Win: Not won. Place: Not won. CSF £83.67 CT £2104.29 TOTE £10.50: £3.50, £4.40, £7.60; EX 148.60 Place 6: £242.70 Place 5: £153.78..
Owner Lord Halifax **Bred** Lord Halifax **Trained** Newmarket, Suffolk

FOCUS
A weak staying handicap, run at a sound pace and the first four all held every chance. The form looks sound rated around the placed horses.
Jennerous Blue Official explanation: vet said filly sustained a cut on her off foreleg
River Danube Official explanation: trainer's rep said gelding was unsuited by the Good to soft ground
T/Plt: £571.30 to a £1 stake. Pool:£53,224.99 - 68 winning tickets T/Qpdt: £71.40 to a £1 stake. Pool:£4,277.49 - 44.30 winning tickets SP

The Form Book, Raceform Ltd, Compton, RG20 6NL

4766 - 4768a (Foreign Racing) - See Raceform Interactive

4309 LEOPARDSTOWN (L-H)

Thursday, August 5

OFFICIAL GOING: Good to firm

4769a ITM/SPRINGPAARDEN FONDS BALLYROAN STKS (GROUP 3) 1m 4f

7:05 (7:06) 3-Y-O+ £34,513 (£10,088; £4,778; £1,592)

RPR

1 **Profound Beauty (IRE)**[21] 4081 6-9-9 115 PJSmullen 5 108+
(D K Weld, Ire) *mde all: drvn out and r.o wl fr under 2f out: clr fnl f: eased cl home* 4/11[1]

2 3 **Akzar (IRE)**[26] 3932 3-8-12 (p) FMBerry 4 101
(John M Oxx, Ire) *settled 3rd: prog into 2nd ent st: sn rdn and no imp: kpt on same pce* 10/3[2]

3 5 1/2 **Indiana Gal (IRE)**[4] 4631 5-9-6 99 (p) CDHayes 3 90
(Patrick Martin, Ire) *dwlt sltly: hld up in rr: rdn under 3f out: mod 3rd and no imp fr 1 1/2f out* 33/1

4 17 **Snow Blizzard (IRE)**[109] 1416 3-8-12 95 JMurtagh 1 73+
(A P O'Brien, Ire) *chsd ldr in 2nd: pushed along 1/2-way: rdn fr 4f out: 3rd into st: sn no ex and eased* 8/1[3]

2m 30.7s (-4.60) **Going Correction** -0.275s/f (Firm)
WFA 3 from 5yo+ 11lb 4 Ran SP% **110.4**
Speed ratings: **104,102,98,87**
CSF £1.99 TOTE £1.20; DF 1.60.
Owner Moyglare Stud Farm **Bred** Moyglare Stud Farm Ltd **Trained** The Curragh, Co Kildare

NOTEBOOK
Profound Beauty(IRE), winner of this race a year ago, brought her career tally to nine wins by making most for a comfortable victory. It was her third win at Group 3 level to go with four Listed race wins and she was winning for the sixth time at Leopardstown. Sent to the front soon after the start, she dictated the pace and was never in much danger over the last 2f. The Yorkshire Oaks is now a possible target although she could wait instead for the Irish Field St Leger. She remains a 16-1 shot with Boylesports for the Melbourne Cup but trainer Dermot Weld is looking no further than her next race. (op 2/7)
Akzar(IRE), having only his third race and stepping up in trip after a maiden win over 1m2f and a conditions race second over that same trip, has a Melbourne Cup entry, kept in touch and went second into the straight. He kept on under pressure but never looked like troubling the winner. It was a creditable effort considering his lack of experience. (op 4/1)
Indiana Gal(IRE), placed at Listed level over just short of this trip, has done most of her winning over shorter distances. She had plenty on at the weights with the winner and after trailing her three rivals, she kept on in the straight without ever being in serious condition.
Snow Blizzard(IRE) tracked the winner but he was being driven along leaving the back straight and was done with turning for home. He was eased down when all hope had gone. (op 10/1 tchd 11/1)

4770 - 4772a (Foreign Racing) - See Raceform Interactive

4637 DEAUVILLE (R-H)

Thursday, August 5

OFFICIAL GOING: Turf: good to soft; fibresand: standard

4773a PRIX DU CERCLE (LISTED RACE) (3YO+) (TURF) 5f

2:45 (12:00) 3-Y-O+ £23,008 (£9,203; £6,902; £4,601; £2,300)

RPR

1 **Swiss Diva**[15] 4269 4-8-11 0 IoritzMendizabal 3 102
(D R C Elsworth) *broke wl: racd bhd ldr on stands' side: short of room 2 1/2f out: briefly swtchd away fr rail 1f out: swtchd bk to rail and qcknd powerfully 100yds out whn gap opened: fin strly to grab ld fnl strides* 97/10

2 1/2 **Poppet's Treasure**[44] 3-8-8 0 StephanePasquier 10 99
(R Pritchard-Gordon, France) 9/1

3 nk **Tax Free (IRE)**[73] 2400 8-9-1 0 AdrianNicholls 11 103
(D Nicholls) *broke wl on outside: sn prom: grabbed ld 1 1/2f out: hdd 100yds out: r.o wl* 83/10

4 1 1/2 **Tiza (SAF)**[19] 4165 8-9-5 0 (p) GeraldMosse 9 102
(A De Royer-Dupre, France) 11/2[3]

5 1/2 **Salut L'Africain (FR)**[19] 4165 5-9-5 0 (p) MaximeGuyon 4 100
(Robert Collet, France) 13/1

6 nk **Mood Music**[41] 3425 6-9-1 0 (b) DominiqueBoeuf 12 95
(Mario Hofer, Germany) 19/1

7 1 **Lipocco**[29] 6-9-1 0 OlivierPeslier 8 91
(A De Royer-Dupre, France) 5/1[2]

8 2 1/2 **Sorciere (IRE)**[81] 2157 3-8-8 0 GregoryBenoist 2 77
(C Lerner, France) 15/2

9 3/4 **Kolokol (IRE)**[41] 3425 3-9-2 0 FranckBlondel 6 82
(D Prod'Homme, France) 37/1

10 snk **Bluster (FR)**[81] 2157 4-9-5 0 ChristopheSoumillon 5 83
(Robert Collet, France) 43/10[1]

0 **Blagueuse (IRE)**[25] 3944 3-8-8 0 (p) AnthonyCrastus 13 —
(E Lellouche, France) 11/1

0 **Livandar (FR)**[35] 4-9-1 0 (b[1]) JohanVictoire 7 —
(Mlle M Henry, France) 49/1

58.80 secs (1.30)
WFA 3 from 4yo+ 3lb 12 Ran SP% **117.9**
WIN (incl. 1 euro stake): 10.70. PLACES: 3.40, 3.40, 3.50. DF: 46.50. SF: 99.30..
Owner Lordship Stud **Bred** Lordship Stud **Trained** Newmarket, Suffolk

NOTEBOOK
Swiss Diva travelled strongly next to the stands' side and overcame a troubled passage to finish like a train and hit the front close home. It was an impressive performance on her first try over 5f, and she looks well capable of winning in Group company over this trip.
Tax Free(IRE) ran a solid race on his first outing for two and a half months. He will have one more race before being aimed at the Abbaye.

4735 BRIGHTON (L-H)

Friday, August 6

OFFICIAL GOING: Good to firm (8.5)
Rail moved out 6yds from 6f to 2f increasing distances by about 25yds.
Wind: modest, against Weather: overcast, chilly

4774 TOM ALDRIDGE IS NEVER 70 H'CAP 1m 1f 209y

2:30 (2:30) (Class 6) (0-60,60) 3-Y-O £1,554 (£462; £231; £115) Stalls High

Form RPR

0543 1 **Shianda**[23] 4027 3-8-10 52 (b[1]) NeilCallan 3 60
(G L Moore) *t.k.h: hld up in last pair: hdwy to chse ldr ent fnl 2f: drvn and ev ch over 1f out: led jst ins fnl f: kpt on wl* 2/1[1]

5012 2 3/4 **Lady Of Garmoran (USA)**[7] 4534 3-8-12 54 JamieSpencer 7 61
(P F I Cole) *t.k.h early: trckd ldrs tl rdn and qcknd to ld over 2f out: drvn and edgd rt ent fnl f: hdd jst ins fnl f: kpt on same pce fnl 100yds* 2/1[1]

0000 3 9 **Blue Zealot (IRE)**[17] 4236 3-9-4 60 DavidProbert 1 49
(M L W Bell) *t.k.h early: trckd ldrs: rdn and outpcd by ldng pair ent fnl 2f: no ch wl over 1f out: wnt modest 3rd jst over 1f out* 5/1[2]

4346 4 4 **Miss Whippy**[18] 4212 3-8-9 51 RichardThomas 2 32
(P Howling) *flashed tail thrght: led and set stdy gallop: hdd and rdn over 2f out: sn outpcd 2f out: wl btn over 1f out* 13/2[3]

-646 5 1/2 **Vadition (IRE)**[33] 3714 3-8-4 46 oh1 NeilChalmers 6 26
(J J Bridger) *in tch in last: rdn and struggling ent fnl 2f: wl btn over 1f out* 18/1

005 6 16 **Barberhoney**[40] 3484 3-8-13 55 JimCrowley 5 —
(J R Jenkins) *stdd s: plld hrd: hld up in last pair tl hdwy to chse ldr after 1f tl over 2f out: sn wknd: wl bhd and eased ins fnl f: t.o* 14/1

2m 6.04s (2.44) **Going Correction** +0.175s/f (Good) 6 Ran SP% **108.6**
Speed ratings (Par 98): **97,96,89,86,85 72**
toteswingers:1&2:£1.10, 1&3:£3.00, 2&3:£1.70 CSF £5.50 TOTE £2.70: £1.60, £1.50; EX 4.90.
Owner Baraka 2 Partnership **Bred** Lakin Bloodstock And H And W Thornton **Trained** Lower Beeding, W Sussex

FOCUS
A moderate handicap and the field raced into a breeze once again in the straight. The first two came more towards the stands' side in the straight and finished clear of the rest. They set the level of the form.
Vadition(IRE) Official explanation: trainer said that the filly lost a right fore shoe.

4775 GRACE OF BRIGHTON MAIDEN H'CAP 6f 209y

3:00 (3:01) (Class 6) (0-65,65) 3-Y-O+ £1,554 (£462; £231; £115) Stalls Centre

Form RPR

0523 1 **Sunrise Lyric (IRE)**[24] 3975 3-9-2 57 TadhgO'Shea 3 68
(P F I Cole) *stdd s: t.k.h: hld up in rr: hdwy on stands' rail and nt clr run 2f out tl 1f out: qcknd to chal but hld hd high and hung into rival ins fnl f: led fnl 75yds: sn clr: easily* 13/2

224 2 3 **Sermons Mount (USA)**[20] 4130 4-9-13 62 (v) NeilCallan 2 67
(Mouse Hamilton-Fairley) *racd keenly: led: c to stands' rail over 2f out: rdn clr over 1f out: drvn ent fnl f: hdd fnl 75yds: sn btn: fdd and jst hld 2nd* 11/4[1]

0036 3 nk **Thoughtful (IRE)**[15] 4300 3-8-5 46 HayleyTurner 9 48
(J W Hills) *in tch: nt clr run wl over 1f out tl swtchd lft and rdn ent fnl f: kpt on u.p to press for 2nd nr fin: no ch w wnr* 28/1

-056 4 1 **Lutine Charlie (IRE)**[56] 2919 3-9-10 65 JimCrowley 7 64
(P Winkworth) *in tch in midfield: effrt u.p ent fnl 2f: chsd clr ldr over 1f out tl jst ins fnl f: plugged on same pce after* 5/1[3]

-000 5 1 1/2 **Herecomethegirls**[46] 3263 4-8-6 46 (p) RossAtkinson[(5)] 6 43
(W G M Turner) *sn rdn along in rr: styd on u.p fnl f: nvr trbld ldrs* 14/1

6303 6 1 1/4 **Nadinska**[76] 2329 3-9-10 65 JimmyQuinn 8 57
(M R Channon) *t.k.h: chsd ldr after 1f: nt clr run and swtchd lft wl over 1f out: wknd u.p jst over 1f out* 8/1

05-5 7 1 3/4 **Franki J**[12] 4408 3-8-10 51 DavidProbert 1 38
(D Donovan) *in tch: rdn and unable qck 2f out: wknd wl over 1f out: wl btn fnl f* 14/1

5006 8 1 1/4 **Alice Cullen**[28] 3852 3-9-6 61 (b[1]) AdamKirby 4 45
(W R Swinburn) *chsd ldrs for 1f: styd handy tl wknd u.p over 1f out: fdd fnl f* 4/1[2]

0050 9 21 **Kilmanseck**[2] 4700 3-9-0 62 (p) AmyScott[(7)] 5 —
(Eve Johnson Houghton) *nvr gng wl: a bhd: lost tch and eased fr over 1f out: t.o* 17/2

1m 24.04s (0.94) **Going Correction** +0.175s/f (Good)
WFA 3 from 4yo 6lb 9 Ran SP% **115.1**
Speed ratings (Par 101): **101,97,97,96,94 92,90,89,65**
toteswingers:1&2:£2.90, 1&3:£10.00, 2&3:£14.50 CSF £24.63 CT £472.38 TOTE £7.50: £1.70, £1.50, £6.80; EX 19.20 Trifecta £187.60 Part won. Pool: £253.63 - 0.41 winning units..
Owner P F I Cole Ltd **Bred** M Morrissey **Trained** Whatcombe, Oxon

FOCUS
The previous five runnings of this maiden handicap had all been won by 3-y-os and the trend continued. The field all came stands' side in the straight and the first two set the level.

4776 TARPAN VODKA (S) STKS 5f 213y

3:30 (3:30) (Class 6) 3-Y-O+ £1,457 (£433; £216; £108) Stalls Low

Form RPR

012 1 **Desperate Dan**[22] 4043 9-9-7 77 (v) NeilCallan 7 74
(A B Haynes) *taken down early: hld up towards rr: hdwy to chse ldrs over 1f out: pushed along hands and heels to chal ins fnl f: led fnl 75yds: pushed out and a jst doing enough* 1/1[1]

1005 2 nk **Timeteam (IRE)**[4] 4662 4-9-4 73 RichardEvans[(3)] 2 73
(P D Evans) *taken down early: s.i.s: in tch in rr: hdwy to trck ldrs over 2f out: rdn and ev ch over 1f out: drvn to ld ins fnl f: hdd and no ex fnl 75yds* 7/2[2]

4230 3 2 3/4 **Liberty Trail (IRE)**[22] 4053 4-8-13 64 AndrewHeffernan[(3)] 3 59
(P D Evans) *led: rdn and edgd lft u.p over 1f out: hdd jst ins fnl f: wknd fnl 100yds* 9/2[3]

26-0 4 1/2 **Louphole**[101] 1596 8-9-2 61 JimCrowley 8 58
(J R Jenkins) *stdd s: hld up in rr: pushed along and hdwy over 1f out: rdn and styd on same pce fnl f* 7/1

0-00 5 3 3/4 **Like For Like (IRE)**[15] 4283 4-8-11 41 DavidProbert 4 41
(R J Hodges) *chsd ldr tl over 1f out: wknd qckly u.p jst over 1f out: no ch fnl f* 25/1

0000 6 1 3/4 **Dynamo Dave (USA)**[15] 4283 5-8-11 41 LeeNewnes[(5)] 6 40
(M D I Usher) *in tch in midfield: rdn ent fnl 2f: wknd u.p over 1f out: wl btn fnl f* 16/1

0000 **7** *6* **Kalligal**[99] 1633 5-8-11 43 .... RichardThomas 1 16
(R Ingram) *taken down early: chsd ldrs: styd on far side over 2f out: drifted bk towards stands' side u.p and wl btn over 1f out* **50/1**

000- **8** *16* **Countrywide City (IRE)**[404] 3428 4-8-13 60 .... RussKennemore(3) 5 —
(A B Coogan) *dwlt: sn rcvrd and in tch in midfield: wknd qckly wl over 1f out: wl btn 1f out: eased ins fnl f: t.o* **16/1**

1m 10.95s (0.75) **Going Correction** +0.175s/f (Good) 8 Ran SP% **120.5**
Speed ratings (Par 101): **102,101,97,97,92 89,81,60**
toteswingers:1&2:£1.60, 1&3:£1.70, 2&3:£3.30 CSF £5.08 TOTE £2.00: £1.10, £1.50, £1.70; EX 5.50 Trifecta £13.50 Pool: £430.20 - 23.45 winning units..There was no bid for the winner. Timeteam was claimed by G. L. Moore for £6,000.
Owner Joe McCarthy **Bred** Sheikh Amin Dahlawi **Trained** Limpley Stoke, Bath

FOCUS
A mixed bunch based on official ratings in this seller and the form is limited by the proximity of the fifth and sixth, with the runner-up the best guide.

4777 BRIGHTON & HOVE CITY CABS BRIGHTON ROCKET H'CAP (FOR THE HARRY BLOOM MEMORIAL TROPHY) 5f 213y
4:00 (4:00) (Class 4) (0-80,82) 3-Y-0+
£3,738 (£1,119; £559; £280; £139; £70) **Stalls** Low

Form RPR
1211 **1** **Piazza San Pietro**[11] 4440 4-10-3 **82** 6ex .... NeilCallan 7 91
(A B Haynes) *hld up in tch: hdwy and swtchd lft jst over 1f out: rdn to chal jst ins fnl f: r.o wl u.p to ld towards fin* **7/2**[2]

3001 **2** *hd* **Dvinsky (USA)**[16] 4255 9-8-12 **63** ....(b) JimmyQuinn 6 71
(P Howling) *w ldrs: c stands' side and led over 2f out: rdn over 1f out: drvn and hrd pressed ins fnl f: kpt on tl hdd and no ex towards fin* **8/1**

4531 **3** *3* **Starwatch**[8] 4503 3-8-7 **62** 6ex .... NeilChalmers 2 59+
(J J Bridger) *w ldrs tl led over 4f out: styd in centre of crse and hdd over 2f out: styd chsng ldrs tl outpcd by ldng pair fnl 150yds: kpt on same pce after* **9/2**

6503 **4** *1* **Musical Script (USA)**[2] 4690 7-8-7 **58** ....(b) DavidProbert 1 53
(Mouse Hamilton-Fairley) *hld up in tch in last pair: hdwy ent fnl 2f: drvn to chse ldrs over 1f out: nt pce of ldrs jst ins fnl f: plugged on* **4/1**[3]

5-54 **5** *nk* **Hand Painted**[29] 3815 4-9-9 **74** .... JimCrowley 4 68
(P J Makin) *restless in stalls: dwlt: in tch: effrt to chse ldrs and drvn wl over 1f out: no ex and btn jst ins fnl f* **9/4**[1]

2100 **6** *3* **Highland Harvest**[8] 4510 6-9-2 **67** .... IanMongan 5 52
(Jamie Poulton) *broke wl: led tl over 4f out: styd prom: rdn wl over 2f out: btn whn sltly hmpd jst over 1f out: wknd fnl f* **11/1**

1m 10.76s (0.56) **Going Correction** +0.175s/f (Good)
WFA 3 from 4yo+ 4lb 6 Ran SP% **110.6**
Speed ratings (Par 105): **103,102,98,97,97 93**
toteswingers:1&2:£2.80, 1&3:£2.20, 2&3:£3.70 CSF £28.95 TOTE £3.70: £1.90, £5.00; EX 18.50.
Owner K Corke **Bred** T E Pocock **Trained** Limpley Stoke, Bath

FOCUS
The feature race and a fair contest with half of the field last-time-out winners. The time was 0.19secs faster than the preceding seller and the runner-up is rated to form.

4778 CRABBIES ALCOHOLIC GINGER BEER H'CAP 5f 59y
4:30 (4:30) (Class 6) (0-60,57) 3-Y-0+ **£2,266** (£674; £337; £168) **Stalls** Low

Form RPR
0426 **1** **Maryolini**[17] 4234 5-9-6 **55** .... JimmyQuinn 8 63
(T Keddy) *stdd after s: hld up in last pair: hdwy to trck ldrs on stands' rail over 1f out: swtchd lft ent fnl f: rdn to chal between horses ins fnl f: r.o wl to ld fnl 75yds: sn in command* **3/1**[1]

1535 **2** *1* **The Jailer**[14] 4326 7-9-4 **56** ....(p) RussKennemore(3) 5 61
(J G M O'Shea) *led: clr and c to stands' rail 3f out: rdn over 1f out: drvn 1f out: hdd and no ex fnl 75yds* **3/1**[1]

4104 **3** *nk* **Best One**[14] 4326 6-9-5 **54** ....(b) IanMongan 6 57
(R A Harris) *chsd ldrs: wnt 2nd wl over 2f out: rdn: awkward hd carriage and wanting to hang lft over 1f out: drvn and ev ch ins fnl f: one pce fnl 75yds* **3/1**[1]

3043 **4** *4 ½* **Vilnius**[18] 4194 3-9-5 **57** .... JimCrowley 4 44+
(M R Channon) *hld up in last pair: hdwy towards centre of crse over 1f out: drvn and no prog 1f out: wknd ins fnl f* **7/1**[2]

0450 **5** *4* **Nawaaff**[17] 4234 5-8-10 **45** .... DavidProbert 2 19
(M Quinn) *sn bustled along to chse ldr tl wl over 2f out: sn rdn: wknd and edgd rt jst over 1f out* **12/1**

0000 **6** *1 ¾* **Joss Stick**[24] 3979 5-8-7 **45** ....(b) AndrewHeffernan(3) 3 13
(R A Harris) *t.k.h early: chsd ldrs: rdn and nt qckn 2f out: wkng whn sltly hmpd jst over 1f out: fdd fnl f* **9/1**[3]

0-00 **7** *4* **Kyoatee Kilt**[14] 4325 3-8-5 **50** ....(b) DuilioDaSilva(7) 1 3
(P F I Cole) *dwlt: sn in tch in midfield: rdn over 2f out: wknd qckly over 1f out: wl bhd fnl f* **14/1**

63.00 secs (0.70) **Going Correction** +0.175s/f (Good)
WFA 3 from 4yo+ 3lb 7 Ran SP% **111.9**
Speed ratings (Par 101): **101,99,98,91,85 82,76**
toteswingers:1&2:£3.30, 1&3:£2.90, 2&3:£2.50 CSF £11.19 CT £27.38 TOTE £3.80: £2.60, £2.70; EX 13.50 Trifecta £19.10 Pool: £324.51 - 12.57 winning units..
Owner Keith Warth **Bred** Mrs Mary Rowlands **Trained** Newmarket, Suffolk

FOCUS
A moderate sprint but an open betting race and the three co-favourites fought out a good finish. The placed horses set the level.
Best One Official explanation: jockey said that the gelding hung left

4779 GRACE OF BRIGHTON H'CAP 7f 214y
5:00 (5:01) (Class 5) (0-70,70) 3-Y-0 **£2,331** (£693; £346; £173) **Stalls** Low

Form RPR
4124 **1** **Dutiful**[9] 4479 3-9-6 **69** .... HayleyTurner 5 74
(M R Channon) *stdd s: hld up in last: lft 4th 5f out: rdn and effrt over 2f out: drvn to chal ins fnl f: led fnl 75yds: r.o wl* **5/2**[2]

-352 **2** *½* **Plutocraft**[29] 3831 3-9-7 **70** .... PatCosgrave 1 74
(J R Fanshawe) *stdd s: hld up in tch: lft trcking ldng pair 5f out: wnt 2nd over 2f out: rdn to ld wl over 1f out: hrd pressed and hung lft ins fnl f: hdd and no ex fnl 75yds* **6/4**[1]

03U4 **3** *4 ½* **Little Meadow (IRE)**[23] 4027 3-8-2 **51** oh4 .... JimmyQuinn 3 45
(Miss J Feilden) *chsd ldng pair tl lft 2nd 5f out tl over 2f out: sn rdn: keeping on same pce and stl pressing ldrs whn n.m.r over 1f out: wknd ins fnl f* **8/1**

02F2 **4** *1 ½* **Louisiana Gift (IRE)**[16] 4249 3-8-12 **61** ....(p) JimCrowley 2 51
(J W Hills) *chsd ldr tl lft in ld 5f out: rdn and hdd wl over 1f out: wknd u.p ent fnl f* **10/3**[3]

0306 **5** *dist* **Transfixed (IRE)**[1] 4735 3-8-6 **60** .... DeclanCannon(5) 4 —
(P D Evans) *sddle slipped sn after s: led tl plld to outer and hdd 5f out: virtually p.u fr 3f out: btn 137l* **8/1**

1m 37.34s (1.34) **Going Correction** +0.175s/f (Good) 5 Ran SP% **113.9**
Speed ratings (Par 100): **100,99,95,93,—**
CSF £6.97 TOTE £3.10: £1.90, £1.10; EX 7.20.
Owner Wood Street Syndicate II **Bred** J Repard **Trained** West Ilsley, Berks

FOCUS
A small field for this modest 3-y-o handicap. The third is rated to her latest mark.
Transfixed(IRE) Official explanation: jockey said that the saddle slipped

4780 TARPAN VODKA H'CAP 1m 3f 196y
5:30 (5:30) (Class 6) (0-65,65) 3-Y-0+ **£1,683** (£501; £250; £125) **Stalls** High

Form RPR
5063 **1** **Green Energy**[15] 4301 3-8-3 **51** ....(p) JimmyQuinn 7 60
(Mrs A J Perrett) *prom in main gp: clsd on ldr over 3f out: rdn to ld over 2f out: drvn and hdd 1f out: kpt on u.p to ld again last strides* **11/4**[1]

-000 **2** *shd* **Lombok**[50] 3127 4-10-0 **65** .... HayleyTurner 3 74+
(M L W Bell) *hld up wl off the pce towards rr: clsd on ldr over 3f out: rdn to chal over 1f out: led narrowly 1f out: sn drvn: hdd last strides* **13/2**

0100 **3** *9* **Beaubrav**[11] 4426 4-9-13 **64** ....(t) ChrisCatlin 2 58
(M Madgwick) *racd off the pce in midfield: clsd over 3f out: nt clr run and hmpd 3f out: drvn to chse ldng pair over 1f out: wknd qckly ins fnl f* **8/1**

630 **4** *3 ¾* **Seriy Tzarina**[22] 4069 4-9-1 **57** .... DeclanCannon(5) 4 45
(Miss Gay Kelleway) *hld up wl off the pce in rr: clsd and rdn over 3f out: sme hdwy u.p wl over 1f out: btn jst over 1f out: wknd fnl f* **14/1**

1312 **5** *2 ½* **Dazzling Begum**[22] 4070 5-9-7 **58** .... IanMongan 8 42
(J Pearce) *stdd after s: hld up wl off the pce in last pair: clsd and in tch 3f out: rdn wl over 1f out: struggling whn n.m.r over 1f out: sn fdd: wl btn fnl f* **9/2**[2]

5353 **6** *6* **Free Falling**[23] 4026 4-8-10 **47** ....(v) DavidProbert 6 22
(Miss Gay Kelleway) *led and sn clr: c bk to field over 3f out: rdn and hdd over 2f out: wknd qckly wl over 1f out: wl btn and eased ins fnl f* **5/1**[3]

5-66 **7** *4* **Vita Mia**[22] 4045 4-9-6 **57** .... PatCosgrave 1 25
(P D Evans) *chsd clr ldr: clsd over 3f out: ev ch and rdn over 2f out: wknd qckly over 1f out: wl btn and eased ins fnl f* **9/1**

3532 **8** *2* **Foxtrot Bravo (IRE)**[24] 3984 4-8-2 **46** ....(b) RichardRowe(7) 5 11
(Miss S L Davison) *a bhd: lost tch and virtually t.o over 4f out: nvr on terms* **15/2**

2m 33.79s (1.09) **Going Correction** +0.175s/f (Good)
WFA 3 from 4yo+ 11lb 8 Ran SP% **114.4**
Speed ratings (Par 101): **103,102,96,94,92 88,86,84**
toteswingers:1&2:£2.00, 1&3:£5.00, 2&3:£8.10 CSF £20.99 CT £126.19 TOTE £4.20: £1.70, £3.10, £4.70; EX 25.90 Trifecta £232.00 Pool: £391.94 - 1.25 winning units. Place 6 £16.97; Place 5 £12.88.
Owner The Green Dot Partnership **Bred** Newsells Park Stud Limited **Trained** Pulborough, W Sussex

FOCUS
A high draw proved essential in the previous two runnings of this race and the trend continued. The first two were clear and the form is rated slightly positively.
Vita Mia Official explanation: jockey said that the filly moved poorly in the last 2f.
Foxtrot Bravo(IRE) Official explanation: jockey said reported that the gelding was never travelling
T/Plt: £18.20 to a £1 stake. Pool:£58,562.57 - 2,339.90 winning tickets T/Qpdt: £12.10 to a £1 stake. Pool:£3,945.01 - 241.10 winning tickets SP

4747 HAYDOCK (L-H)
Friday, August 6

OFFICIAL GOING: 6f - good (good to soft in places) changing to good to soft after race 2 (6.20); 1m & further - soft (good to soft in places)
Sprints on inner track. Other races on old outer bend out of back straight distances increased by about 10yds.
Wind: Light, half-against Weather: Overcast

4781 BETDAQ THE BETTING EXCHANGE APPRENTICE TRAINING SERIES H'CAP 1m 3f 200y
5:50 (5:50) (Class 5) (0-75,72) 4-Y-0+ **£2,590** (£770; £385; £192) **Stalls** High

Form RPR
0312 **1** **Amir Pasha (UAE)**[19] 4174 5-8-11 **62** ....(p) AdamCarter(3) 1 71
(Micky Hammond) *chsd ldr: rdn to ld over 1f out: kpt on wl thrght fnl f* **5/1**[2]

0002 **2** *¾* **Amazing Blue Sky**[7] 4546 4-9-5 **70** .... SophieSilvester(3) 5 78
(Mrs R A Carr) *led: hdd over 1f out: stl chalng ins fnl f: rdn and nt qckn fnl 110yds: kpt on but hld after* **6/1**[3]

432 **3** *shd* **Amical Risks (FR)**[6] 4582 6-8-1 **56** .... EleanorMcGowan(7) 6 64+
(Joss Saville) *bdly missed break: hld up in rr of field after 2f: hdwy 2f out: chsd ldrs over 1f out: chalng ins fnl f: nt qckn towards fin* **5/1**[2]

3500 **4** *10* **Brockfield**[56] 2941 4-9-1 **63** .... JohnCavanagh 7 55
(M Brittain) *racd keenly: chsd ldrs: rdn and lost pl over 2f out: no imp after* **12/1**

2300 **5** *½* **Red Kestrel (USA)**[20] 4125 5-9-5 **70** .... JulieBurke(3) 4 61
(K A Ryan) *hld up: nt clr run and swtchd lft jst over 3f out: rdn over 2f out: swtchd lft over 1f out and moderte hdwy: n.d to ldrs fnl f* **12/1**

3530 **6** *3 ¼* **Bavarian Nordic (USA)**[12] 4405 5-9-10 **72** ....(v) LeeTopliss 2 58
(Mrs A Duffield) *bdly missed break: racd keenly: w field but towards rr after 2f: hdwy to chse ldrs 7f out: rdn 2f out: wkng whn rdr lost iron briefly over 1f out: wl btn fnl f* **5/1**[2]

0/03 **7** *2* **Black Coffee**[45] 3294 5-9-5 **67** ....(p) RyanClark 3 50
(W M Brisbourne) *midfield: rdn over 2f out: sn wknd* **7/1**

024 **8** *1 ¼* **Hunters Belt (IRE)**[33] 3709 6-9-2 **67** .... NeilFarley(3) 8 48
(N Wilson) *midfield: rdn and outpcd 3f out: bhd over 1f out* **9/2**[1]

2m 40.22s (6.22) **Going Correction** +0.625s/f (Yiel) 8 Ran SP% **110.4**
Speed ratings (Par 103): **104,103,103,96,96 94,92,92**
toteswingers:1&2:£6.00, 1&3:£3.90, 2&3:£5.40 CSF £32.31 CT £147.17 TOTE £6.60: £2.00, £1.40, £2.10; EX 22.80.
Owner J McAllister **Bred** Darley **Trained** Middleham Moor, N Yorks
■ Stewards' Enquiry : Ryan Clark seven-day ban: used whip in the forehand (tbn)

FOCUS
The front three drew clear in this apprentice handicap, with the field coming stands' side in the straight. The winner recorded a personal high with the runner-up to his best and the third to his latest mark.
Bavarian Nordic(USA) Official explanation: jockey said that the gelding missed the break

Hunters Belt(IRE) Official explanation: jockey said the gelding had no more to give

4782 E B F SPORTSBOOK WIRRAL'S LEADING INDEPENDENT BOOKMAKERS MAIDEN STKS 6f
6:20 (6:20) (Class 5) 2-Y-O **£3,238** (£963; £481; £240) **Stalls** Low

Form RPR
03 **1** **Cruise Tothelimit (IRE)**[11] 4432 2-9-3 0 StephenCraine 9 76
(Patrick Morris) *mde all: edgd lft to far rail over 4f out: rdn and stretched clr ins fnl f: r.o wl* **8/1**
502 **2** 4 **West Leake Bridge (IRE)**[9] 4477 2-9-3 0 DarryllHolland 2 63
(B W Hills) *racd keenly: handy: wnt rt over 4f out: sn chsd wnr: rdn over 1f out: no imp fnl f* **11/8**[1]
0 **3** 2 1/4 **Good Timin'**[11] 4432 2-9-3 0 RoystonFfrench 5 56
(D H Brown) *chsd ldrs: forced wd over 4f out: rdn over 2f out: one pce fr over 1f out: bit slipped through mouth* **6/1**[3]
0 **4** nk **Yachtmaster (IRE)**[34] 3658 2-9-3 0 FrannyNorton 1 55
(J J Quinn) *in tch: rdn 1/2-way: outpcd over 2f out: kpt on same pce fnl f: nt pce to chal* **20/1**
5 8 **Cape Of Dance (IRE)** 2-8-12 0 JoeFanning 6 24
(M Johnston) *s.i.s: rn green: towards rr: forced wd over 4f out: effrt to chse ldrs 1/2-way: rdn and outpcd over 2f out: sn dropped away* **4/1**[2]
0 **6** 5 **Lord Cornwall (IRE)**[71] 2474 2-9-3 0 SteveDrowne 3 13
(J R Gask) *hld up: effrt to chse ldrs but no real imp over 2f out: wknd over 1f out* **11/1**
60 **7** 8 **Newzflash**[54] 2990 2-8-12 0 DeanHeslop[(5)] 7 —
(T D Barron) *prom: rdn 1/2-way: wknd over 2f out* **14/1**
0 **8** 1 1/4 **Tigerino (IRE)**[21] 4110 2-9-0 0 BarryMcHugh[(3)] 8 —
(C W Thornton) *in rr: forced wd and hmpd over 4f out: wl outpcd over 2f out* **33/1**

1m 15.88s (2.38) **Going Correction** +0.625s/f (Yiel) 8 Ran SP% **110.2**
Speed ratings (Par 94): **92,86,83,83,72 65,55,53**
toteswingers:1&2:£1.80, 1&3:£4.30, 2&3:£2.30 CSF £18.02 TOTE £8.50: £2.50, £1.02, £3.10; EX 24.00.
Owner Odysian Ltd T/A Cruise Nightspot **Bred** D And Mrs D Veitch **Trained** Tarporley, Cheshire

FOCUS
This wasn't the most competitive juvenile maiden and the form is a bit fluid with the time ordinary.

NOTEBOOK
Cruise Tothelimit(IRE) proved a different proposition upped to 6f for the first time and making his debut on turf, always travelling strongly and galloping right away to win comfortably. The slower surface was reportedly to his liking and he'll probably only have another run or two this season. (op 13-2)
West Leake Bridge(IRE) looked the one to beat, but had never experienced slow ground before and couldn't match the winner. He has shown enough to win a small race. (op 5-4)
Good Timin' improved on his debut effort despite the bit having slipped through his mouth. It's possible there'll be more to come on quicker ground. Official explanation: jockey said that the colt's bit slipped through its mouth (op 8-1)
Yachtmaster(IRE) again shaped with a bit of promise and he'll be of interest once handicapping. (op 16-1)
Cape Of Dance(IRE) showed a bit of promise, despite ending up well beaten, and should improve for the step up to 7f on faster ground. (tchd 7-2)

4783 COUNTRYWIDE FREIGHT NURSERY 6f
6:55 (6:57) (Class 4) (0-80,76) 2-Y-O **£4,533** (£1,348; £674; £336) **Stalls** Low

Form RPR
0221 **1** **Belle Royale (IRE)**[5] 4615 2-9-5 74 6ex FrannyNorton 7 82
(W M Brisbourne) *hld up: hdwy 2f out: led over 1f out: r.o wl and in command fnl 100yds* **7/4**[1]
2355 **2** 2 1/4 **No Poppy (IRE)**[11] 4437 2-9-2 71 (b) DuranFentiman 1 72
(T D Easterby) *led: rdn and hdd over 1f out: nt pce of wnr fnl 100yds* **16/1**
5345 **3** 1/2 **Lady Platinum Club**[7] 4544 2-8-11 69 (p) BarryMcHugh[(3)] 4 68+
(G R Oldroyd) *in tch: effrt over 2f out: nt clr run over 1f out: prog ins fnl f: styd on and gng on towards fin* **7/1**[3]
0421 **4** 3 1/2 **Fantasy Fry**[15] 4277 2-9-1 70 DarryllHolland 3 58+
(H Morrison) *bhd: hdwy over 1f out: chsd ldrs ins fnl f: eased whn no imp fnl 100yds* **10/3**[2]
641 **5** 1 1/4 **Arctic Mirage**[14] 4323 2-9-7 76 SteveDrowne 2 60
(M Blanshard) *in tch: outpcd 1/2-way: kpt on u.p fnl f: nt pce to chal* **15/2**
000 **6** shd **C P Joe (IRE)**[16] 4240 2-8-13 68 (v[1]) TomQueally 5 52
(Paul Green) *w ldr: rdn 2f out: wknd over 1f out* **9/1**
030 **7** 2 1/4 **Peters Spirit (IRE)**[20] 4123 2-8-4 64 LeeTopliss[(5)] 6 41
(R A Fahey) *prom: rdn 2f out: wknd over 1f out* **15/2**

1m 15.23s (1.73) **Going Correction** +0.625s/f (Yiel) 7 Ran SP% **111.4**
Speed ratings (Par 96): **96,93,92,87,86 85,82**
toteswingers:1&2:£9.00, 1&3:£1.90, 2&3:£11.60 CSF £29.57 TOTE £2.40: £1.10, £7.40; EX 28.80.
Owner Peter Mort **Bred** Dxb Ltd **Trained** Great Ness, Shropshire

FOCUS
The going on the sprint track was changed to good to soft all over before this contest. Several of the runners appeared to run below expectations, so probably not form to get carried away with. The winner made another step up with the third rated a few pounds off his best.

NOTEBOOK
Belle Royale(IRE) had little trouble defying the penalty she picked up for winning at Chester just five days earlier, staying on strongly for pressure and getting well on top inside the final furlong. These are her ideal conditions and she's likely to be out again soon, though things will obviously be tougher. (op 9-4)
No Poppy(IRE) is now 0-7, but this was a much better effort with the blinkers back on, soon leading and keeping on well for second. (op 14-1)
Lady Platinum Club got a bit closer to the winner than she had done at the course last month, keeping on late. (op 15-2)
Fantasy Fry has been showing progressive form on quick ground and never looked happy on this slower surface, trying to make a mid-race move out wide before tiring. He was reported to have lost his action and can be given another chance back on a quicker surface. Official explanation: jockey said that the colt lost its action (tchd 3-1 and 7-2)
Arctic Mirage looks to have started handicap life on a stiff mark. (op 11-2)
C P Joe(IRE) finished weakly in the first-time visor. (op 12-1)
Peters Spirit(IRE) dropped away tamely on this handicap debut. (op 13-2)

4784 CHRIS FAYLE MEMORIAL H'CAP 1m 30y
7:25 (7:28) (Class 4) (0-80,80) 3-Y-O **£4,533** (£1,348; £674; £336) **Stalls** Low

Form RPR
4351 **1** **Christmas Carnival**[21] 4112 3-9-7 80 (b) SteveDrowne 4 87+
(B J Meehan) *mde all: pressed fr 3f out: rdn over 2f out: styd on gamely and plld out more towards fin* **7/2**[1]
0600 **2** 1/2 **Mark Twain (IRE)**[46] 3265 3-9-3 76 ShaneKelly 3 82
(D M Simcock) *racd in cl 2nd thrght: upsides and str chal fr 3f out: no ex fnl strides* **7/2**[1]
4-41 **3** 1 **Miss Antonia (IRE)**[31] 3766 3-9-2 75 TomQueally 5 79
(H R A Cecil) *racd keenly: hld up: rdn over 2f out: hdwy to chse ldrs over 1f out: styd on ins fnl f: gng on at fin* **7/2**[1]
3324 **4** 1 3/4 **Raqeeb (USA)**[14] 4339 3-9-6 79 (b[1]) PJMcDonald 1 79
(Mrs R A Carr) *trckd ldrs: rdn over 2f out: no imp on ldrs over 1f out: styd on same pce fnl f* **9/1**
524 **5** 3/4 **Tamarillo Grove (IRE)**[49] 3176 3-9-2 75 RoystonFfrench 2 73
(B Smart) *racd keenly: trckd ldrs: outpcd 3f out: struggling 2f out: styd on fnl 100yds: nt gng pce to rch ldrs* **11/2**[2]
1440 **6** 3/4 **Dream On Buddy (IRE)**[65] 2652 3-8-8 72 AshleyMorgan[(5)] 7 68
(B W Hills) *hld up in rr: hdwy over 2f out: rdn whn chsng ldrs over 1f out but no imp: no ex fnl 100yds* **7/1**[3]
-440 **7** 3 3/4 **Sunnandaeg**[28] 3876 3-9-4 80 MartinLane[(3)] 6 68
(D A Nolan) *hld up: rdn over 3f out: nvr able to get on terms w ldrs* **12/1**

1m 49.13s (4.43) **Going Correction** +0.625s/f (Yiel) 7 Ran SP% **112.2**
Speed ratings (Par 102): **102,101,100,98,98 97,93**
toteswingers:1&2:£2.10, 1&3:£2.10, 2&3:£2.60 CSF £15.04 CT £44.14 TOTE £3.50: £1.70, £2.80; EX 13.90.
Owner Jaber Abdullah **Bred** David John Brown **Trained** Manton, Wilts

FOCUS
A fair handicap but another improvement from the winner, backed up by the third.

4785 J20 WHITE BLEND H'CAP 1m 6f
8:00 (8:01) (Class 4) (0-80,76) 4-Y-O+ **£5,504** (£1,637; £818; £408) **Stalls** Low

Form RPR
36-1 **1** **Beat The Shower**[24] 3989 4-8-6 61 FrannyNorton 6 73
(P D Niven) *hld up: hdwy 4f out: rdn to chse ldr over 1f out: styd on to ld cl home* **9/2**[3]
3204 **2** nk **Royal Trooper (IRE)**[24] 3974 4-9-1 70 TomQueally 8 81
(J G Given) *led after 1f: hdd after 2f: chsd ldr tl led over 2f out: rdn over 1f out: worn down cl home* **3/1**[1]
3-63 **3** 6 **Puy D'Arnac (FR)**[65] 1916 7-9-3 72 PJMcDonald 2 75
(G A Swinbank) *hld up: rdn over 2f out: stdy hdwy to chse front pair jst over 1f out: no imp fnl f* **6/1**
-0 **4** 5 **Red Fama**[56] 2941 6-8-13 68 DanielTudhope 7 64
(N Bycroft) *hld up: effrt and swtchd lft 2f out: no imp on ldrs: wl btn ins fnl f* **14/1**
/641 **5** 5 **Ubi Ace**[51] 3090 4-9-6 75 GrahamGibbons 5 64
(T D Walford) *racd keenly: chsd ldrs: rdn over 3f out: wknd over 1f out* **7/1**
6333 **6** 5 **Abayaan**[20] 4125 4-9-7 76 (b[1]) ShaneKelly 4 58
(Jane Chapple-Hyam) *led after 2f: rdn and hdd over 2f out: wknd over 1f out* **7/2**[2]
0400 **7** 13 **Blue Nymph**[13] 4393 4-9-1 70 JoeFanning 3 34
(J J Quinn) *led for 1f: remained prom: rdn over 3f out: sn wknd: eased whn btn fnl f* **13/2**

3m 8.12s (6.92) **Going Correction** +0.625s/f (Yiel) 7 Ran SP% **112.2**
Speed ratings (Par 105): **105,104,101,98,95 92,85**
toteswingers:1&2:£3.10, 1&3:£5.00, 2&3:£1.50 CSF £17.66 CT £79.36 TOTE £4.30: £1.20, £2.30; EX 19.90.
Owner Mrs Kate Young **Bred** C P E Brooks **Trained** Barton-le-Street, N Yorks

FOCUS
Just an ordinary staying handicap but the first two finished clear, the winner improved again and the runner-up looks the best guide.

4786 CHESHIRE OAKS DESIGNER OUTLET H'CAP 1m 2f 95y
8:30 (8:31) (Class 5) (0-75,75) 3-Y-O **£2,590** (£770; £385; £192) **Stalls** High

Form RPR
1-56 **1** **Tamanaco (IRE)**[14] 4341 3-9-9 75 GrahamGibbons 6 81
(T D Walford) *in tch: effrt whn nt clr run briefly over 2f out: prog and edgd lft ent fnl f: led 110yds out: styd on* **15/2**[3]
0223 **2** 1 1/2 **Ice Viking (IRE)**[5] 4618 3-8-13 65 PJMcDonald 4 68
(J G Given) *hld up: hdwy over 3f out: effrt to chal ins fnl f: kpt on to take 2nd fnl stride* **5/2**[1]
2013 **3** hd **Pintura**[7] 4546 3-9-9 75 (p) ShaneKelly 3 78
(D M Simcock) *a.p: led over 2f out: hdd fnl 110yds: hld cl home* **5/2**[1]
446 **4** 3/4 **Straversjoy**[7] 4545 3-8-4 56 oh9 PaulEddery 2 57
(R Hollinshead) *in tch: effrt 3f out: rdn to chal over 1f out: no ex fnl 75yds* **10/1**
-025 **5** 7 **Out Of Eden**[16] 4257 3-9-6 72 TomQueally 5 60
(H R A Cecil) *led: rdn and hdd over 2f out: wknd over 1f out* **7/2**[2]
3-36 **6** 9 **Hill Tribe**[63] 2717 3-9-8 74 SteveDrowne 7 45
(J R Gask) *prom: struggling to hold pl whn n.m.r and hmpd over 3f out: lost grnd: bhd over 2f out* **8/1**
0000 **7** 3 1/2 **Patricks Lodge**[10] 4448 3-8-4 56 oh11 DuranFentiman 1 20
(Mrs R A Carr) *hld up in rr: struggling over 2f out: nvr on terms* **40/1**

2m 22.62s (6.62) **Going Correction** +0.625s/f (Yiel) 7 Ran SP% **113.8**
Speed ratings (Par 100): **98,96,96,96,90 83,80**
toteswingers:1&2:£3.10, 1&3:£5.00, 2&3:£1.50. totesuper7: Win: Not won. Place: £209.00. CSF £26.34 TOTE £11.80: £6.90, £1.10; EX 39.90 Place 6 £31.20; Place 5 £11.18.
Owner Pedro Rosas **Bred** Tom Kelly **Trained** Sheriff Hutton, N Yorks

FOCUS
A modest handicap and the form is slightly muddling due to the proximity of the runner-up, while the placed horses set the level.
T/Plt: £38.50 to a £1 stake. Pool:£49,887.23 - 943.68 winning tickets T/Qpdt: £19.60 to a £1 stake. Pool:£4,686.63 - 176.22 winning tickets DO

4586 LINGFIELD (L-H)
Friday, August 6

OFFICIAL GOING: Turf course - good to firm (firm in places; watered; 9.0); all-weather - standard
Wind: Strong, behind Weather: Overcast

4787 EAST GRINSTEAD COURIER & OBSERVER NOVICE STKS 5f (P)
2:10 (2:10) (Class 5) 2-Y-O **£3,238** (£963; £481; £240) **Stalls** High

Form RPR
6120 **1** **Reckless Reward (IRE)**[20] 4138 2-9-2 103 RichardHughes 3 90+
(R Hannon) *trckd ldng pair: narrow ld on outer over 1f out: pushed out firmly tl eased last strides* **1/6**[1]
1010 **2** 1/2 **Black Moth (IRE)**[21] 4097 2-9-5 97 JohnFahy[(5)] 2 96
(B J Meehan) *dwlt: hld up last: prog on inner to chal over 1f out: pressed wnr after but readily hld* **9/2**[2]
540 **3** 7 **Sirens**[39] 3509 2-8-2 61 (t) LeonnaMayor[(7)] 4 56
(P S McEntee) *led to jst over 2f out: wknd* **125/1**

054 **4** *4* **Partout Le Magasin**[6] 4590 2-9-0 0 ....(p) LiamKeniry 1 46
(J S Moore) *trckd ldr: led jst over 2f out to over 1f out: wknd rapidly* **33/1**[3]

59.03 secs (0.23) **Going Correction** +0.20s/f (Slow) **4** Ran SP% **107.6**
Speed ratings (Par 94): **106,105,94,87**
CSF £1.27 TOTE £1.20; EX 1.20.
Owner W P Drew **Bred** Ken Carroll **Trained** East Everleigh, Wilts

FOCUS
This only concerned two of the four runners, but they're both very useful types. The winner did not need to be at his best to score.

NOTEBOOK
Reckless Reward(IRE), reported to have been unsuited by ground on the soft side when beaten favourite in the Super Sprint, should have appreciated the return to Polytrack (won his maiden over C&D), but he didn't seem to run up to his best, even in victory. It's true he didn't require pressure from the whip, and the winning jockey always seemed confident, but a more authoritative display could have been expected considering this Norfolk Stakes runner-up had 14lb in hand over the runner-up at the weights. Richard Hughes feels the colt is now in need of 6f. (op 1-5 tchd 2-9 in places)
Black Moth(IRE) missed the break, but he soon recovered and had every chance after nipping through towards the inside in the straight, albeit against the far rail is not always the best place to be at Lingfield. This was a good performance at the weights.
Sirens, reported to have been unsuited by fast ground last time, was the worst off at the weights but didn't run at all badly. (tchd 100-1)
Partout Le Magasin, reported to have hung right over C&D on his previous start, seemed to run some way below his official mark of 69. (tchd 40-1)

4788 FRANCES GAUNT 21 YEARS AT LINGFIELD PARK FILLIES' (S) STKS — 6f (P)
2:40 (2:41) (Class 6) 2-Y-O — **£2,047** (£604; £302) **Stalls** Low

Form — RPR

6302 **1** **Chilworth Lass (IRE)**[7] 4554 2-8-12 53 ....(v) SamHitchcott 3 57
(M R Channon) *trckd ldng trio: wnt 2nd over 2f out: rdn to ld jst ins fnl f: edgd rt and looked less than keen: drvn out* **11/8**[1]

2 *1* **Rather Cool** 2-8-12 0 .... J-PGuillambert 4 54
(R J Hodges) *pushed along in 6th: prog on outer 2f out: wnt 3rd over 1f out: drvn and styd on wl fnl f: tk 2nd post* **9/1**

0460 **3** *shd* **Bendigedig**[11] 4429 2-8-12 57 .... LiamKeniry 2 53
(S Kirk) *trckd ldr: led over 2f out: drvn and hdd jst ins fnl f: kpt on but lost 2nd last stride* **10/3**[2]

4000 **4** *5* **Kodiac Star (IRE)**[13] 4363 2-8-7 60 ....(p) SophieDoyle(5) 1 37
(J A Osborne) *trckd ldng pair to over 2f out: grad wknd* **5/1**[3]

005 **5** *2* **Minus Tolerance**[15] 4277 2-8-7 0 .... KierenFox(5) 5 31
(Miss S L Davison) *sn rdn to stay in tch: effrt u.p over 2f out: wknd wl over 1f out* **20/1**

6546 **6** *1* **Dancing With Fire**[24] 3992 2-8-7 39 .... BillyCray(5) 7 28
(D Donovan) *s.i.s: sn pushed along in detached 7th: nvr on terms* **12/1**

0050 **7** *10* **Bold Deceiver**[24] 3992 2-8-5 40 ....(t) LeonnaMayor(7) 6 —
(P S McEntee) *led to over 2f out: wknd rapidly* **40/1**

50 **8** *30* **Molly Piccles**[30] 3778 2-8-9 0 ....(b[1]) JackDean(3) 8 —
(W G M Turner) *ref to r tl rest had gone 100yds: a t.o* **12/1**

1m 14.48s (2.58) **Going Correction** +0.20s/f (Slow) **8** Ran SP% **114.4**
Speed ratings (Par 89): **90,88,88,81,79 77,64,24**
toteswingers:1&2:£3.40, 1&3:£2.00, 2&3:£4.70 CSF £15.15 TOTE £2.40: £1.30, £2.70, £1.10; EX 16.00.There was no bid for the winner. Rather Cool was claimed by A. B. Haynes for £6,000.
Owner 7Rus **Bred** Norman Court Stud **Trained** West Ilsley, Berks

FOCUS
A really moderate race, even by selling standards with the winner the best guide to the level.

NOTEBOOK
Chilworth Lass(IRE) coped with the drop down from 7f and was persuaded to go through with her effort to record her first success at the sixth attempt. She will probably struggle to follow up. (op 6-4 tchd 13-8 in places)
Rather Cool, who cost only £1,800, needed to be niggled along for much of the way but she gradually responded, getting up for second on the line. With normal improvement she might win a seller. (op 7-1 tchd 13-2 and 10-1)
Bendigedig travelled better than most but was one paced under pressure. She had 4lb in hand over the winner at the weights, so has to be considered disappointing. (op 5-1 tchd 3-1 in places)
Kodiac Star(IRE) was squeezed for room against the inside rail around the turn into the straight and could make no impression thereafter. She didn't run to her official mark of 60. (op 7-2)

4789 CROYDON ADVERTISER H'CAP (DIV I) — 6f (P)
3:10 (3:12) (Class 6) (0-60,60) 3-Y-O+ — **£1,706** (£503; £252) **Stalls** Low

Form — RPR

2324 **1** **Towy Boy (IRE)**[11] 4427 5-8-13 51 ....(bt) TomMcLaughlin 5 62
(I A Wood) *dwlt: sn trckd ldrs: prog over 1f out: wnt 2nd ins fnl f: urged along and styd on to ld nr fin* **11/2**[3]

5523 **2** *hd* **Faithful Duchess (IRE)**[23] 4031 3-9-3 59 .... RichardHughes 11 68
(E A L Dunlop) *trckd ldng pair: wnt 2nd over 2f out: drvn to ld ins fnl f: hdd nr fin* **7/2**[2]

4534 **3** *nse* **Fantasy Fighter (IRE)**[2] 4717 5-9-7 59 .... DaneO'Neill 4 72+
(J J Quinn) *hld up towards rr: smooth prog fr 2f out: trckd ldrs and nt clr run fnl f tl last 75yds: r.o nr fin: nt rcvr* **10/3**[1]

4000 **4** *1 ½* **Briannsta (IRE)**[38] 3526 8-8-3 46 oh1 .... SophieDoyle(5) 8 51
(J E Long) *wl in rr: rdn on outer over 2f out: styd on fnl f: nrst fin* **16/1**

5400 **5** *½* **Kinigi (IRE)**[11] 4430 4-8-6 49 ....(b[1]) BillyCray(5) 9 53
(R A Harris) *led: 2 l clr over 2f out: hdd & wknd ins fnl f* **9/1**

5030 **6** *¾* **Speedyfix**[18] 4210 3-8-7 49 ....(vt) SamHitchcott 7 49
(Mrs C A Dunnett) *wl in rr: pushed along on wd outside 1/2-way: kpt on u.p fnl 2f: nvr a threat* **20/1**

0000 **7** *hd* **Bishopbriggs (USA)**[20] 4130 5-8-13 58 .... LeonnaMayor(7) 6 59
(M G Quinlan) *hld up in last trio: effrt over 1f out: nt clr run ent fnl f: styd on nr fin* **33/1**

0060 **8** *¾* **What Katie Did (IRE)**[11] 4431 5-9-8 60 ....(p) LiamKeniry 2 58
(J M Bradley) *trckd ldng trio: stuck bhd wkng rival fr 1/2-way and lost pl bdly: wl in rr 1f out: plugged on* **8/1**

6000 **9** *1* **Norse Warrior (USA)**[55] 2964 4-8-10 48 ....(b[1]) FergusSweeney 10 43
(Peter Grayson) *prom: chsd ldng pair over 2f out: hrd rdn over 1f out: sn wknd* **33/1**

-003 **10** *nk* **Downhill Skier (IRE)**[17] 4232 6-9-0 57 .... KierenFox(5) 1 51
(W M Brisbourne) *dwlt: hld up in last trio on inner: nt clr run 2f out: no ch after: keeping on at fin* **11/2**[3]

0060 **11** *18* **Lunaticus**[107] 1477 4-8-3 46 oh1 .... JemmaMarshall(5) 3 —
(M J Attwater) *chsd ldr to 1/2-way: wknd rapidly: t.o* **66/1**

1m 13.09s (1.19) **Going Correction** +0.20s/f (Slow)
WFA 3 from 4yo+ 4lb **11** Ran SP% **115.2**
Speed ratings (Par 101): **100,99,99,97,97 96,95,94,93,93 69**
toteswingers:1&2:£3.60, 1&3:£5.70, 2&3:£2.60 CSF £23.64 CT £75.12 TOTE £7.20: £2.20, £1.10, £1.60; EX 25.00.
Owner C R Lambourne **Bred** R W K Lewis **Trained** Upper Lambourn, Berks

FOCUS
A moderate sprint handicap and the time was almost identical to the second division. The winner is rated to his winter best with the unlucky third as rated the length winner.
Fantasy Fighter(IRE) Official explanation: jockey said gelding was denied a clear run
What Katie Did(IRE) Official explanation: jockey said gelding was denied a clear run
Downhill Skier(IRE) Official explanation: jockey said gelding was denied a clear run

4790 CROYDON ADVERTISER H'CAP (DIV II) — 6f (P)
3:40 (3:40) (Class 6) (0-60,59) 3-Y-O+ — **£1,706** (£503; £252) **Stalls** Low

Form — RPR

052 **1** **Loyal Royal (IRE)**[11] 4431 7-9-6 57 ....(bt) LiamKeniry 4 68
(J M Bradley) *dwlt: sn trckd ldrs: gng much bttr than rest fr 2f out: clsd to ld last 150yds: sn clr* **9/4**[1]

0000 **2** *2 ½* **Hart Of Gold**[38] 3526 6-8-11 48 ....(b) TomMcLaughlin 5 51
(R A Harris) *led: drvn 2f out: hdd and outpcd last 150yds* **6/1**[3]

-040 **3** *¾* **Novastasia (IRE)**[38] 3526 4-8-10 47 .... FergusSweeney 2 48
(D K Ivory) *cl up on inner: rdn over 2f out: kpt on same pce fr over 1f out* **16/1**

45 **4** *hd* **Ever Cheerful**[20] 4130 9-8-11 55 ....(p) MarkPower(7) 9 55+
(A B Haynes) *wl in rr on outer: urged along 2f out: styd on fnl f: nrst fin* **13/2**

2530 **5** *¾* **Lord Deevert**[181] 444 5-9-4 58 .... JackDean(3) 10 56
(W G M Turner) *racd wd: prom: chsd ldr over 2f out: drvn to chal over 1f out: wknd ins fnl f* **5/1**[2]

4060 **6** *1 ½* **Equinity**[11] 4430 4-9-3 54 ....(t) SaleemGolam 8 47
(J Pearce) *chsd ldrs: rdn and cl enough 2f out: sn outpcd: plugged on* **8/1**

000 **7** *nk* **Boundless Applause**[25] 3948 4-8-3 45 .... BillyCray(5) 7 37
(I A Wood) *pushed along early: mostly last: rdn and styd on fnl f: n.d* **16/1**

-440 **8** *3 ¼* **Mind The Monarch**[170] 581 3-8-10 54 .... MatthewDavies(3) 1 34
(R A Teal) *wl in rr: rdn 2f out: no prog over 1f out: fdd* **16/1**

0-0 **9** *1* **Calabaza**[15] 4308 8-8-3 45 .... JemmaMarshall(5) 3 23
(M J Attwater) *a in rr: rdn and no prog 2f out* **33/1**

-030 **10** *6* **Agnes Love**[175] 525 4-9-8 59 .... J-PGuillambert 6 18
(J Akehurst) *chsd ldr to over 2f out: wknd rapidly:* **8/1**

1m 13.06s (1.16) **Going Correction** +0.20s/f (Slow)
WFA 3 from 4yo+ 4lb **10** Ran SP% **117.9**
Speed ratings (Par 101): **100,96,95,95,94 92,92,87,86,78**
toteswingers:1&2:£5.20, 1&3:£7.40, 2&3:£16.60 CSF £15.89 CT £176.44 TOTE £2.80: £1.40, £2.10, £3.10; EX 19.00.
Owner JMB Racing.co.uk **Bred** J F Tuthill **Trained** Sedbury, Gloucs

FOCUS
Like the first division, a moderate sprint handicap and the form looks straightforward with the winner back to his best.

4791 MSS H'CAP — 7f (P)
4:10 (4:10) (Class 6) (0-60,60) 3-Y-O — **£2,047** (£604; £302) **Stalls** Low

Form — RPR

2003 **1** **Mack's Sister**[23] 4025 3-9-2 58 .... RichardHughes 9 62
(D K Ivory) *trckd ldrs: gng strly over 2f out: prog over 1f out: drvn to ld last 100yds: fnd enough* **9/2**[1]

4040 **2** *½* **King's Approach (IRE)**[7] 4534 3-9-1 57 ....(p) TomMcLaughlin 3 60
(R A Harris) *chsd ldr: rdn 2f out: clsd to chal fnl f: kpt on same pce* **10/1**

-000 **3** *hd* **Rigid**[41] 3463 3-8-3 50 .... KierenFox(5) 5 52
(A W Carroll) *led: gng strly 2f out: drvn and hdd last 100yds: kpt on* **10/1**

-502 **4** *nk* **Fever Tree**[15] 4280 3-9-2 58 .... FergusSweeney 10 60
(P J Makin) *chsd ldrs: rdn in 6th 2f out: hanging lft over 1f out: styd on fnl f: nrst fin* **9/2**[1]

0-05 **5** *2* **Rodrigo De Freitas (IRE)**[23] 4025 3-9-2 58 .... EddieAhern 7 54+
(J R Boyle) *hld up wl in rr: stl there over 1f out: shkn up and styd on: nvr nr ldrs* **9/2**[1]

0063 **6** *hd* **Take My Hand**[7] 4534 3-9-2 58 .... SamHitchcott 11 54
(M R Channon) *nvr bttr than midfield: u.p over 2f out: kpt on fnl f: n.d* **15/2**[2]

0-00 **7** *½* **James Barrymore**[38] 3525 3-8-13 60 .... BillyCray(5) 2 54
(Miss J R Tooth) *t.k.h and sn restrained to rr: modest prog on inner fr over 1f out: nvr involved* **20/1**

2100 **8** *1 ½* **Miss Kitty Grey (IRE)**[23] 4025 3-8-12 57 .... MatthewDavies(3) 6 47
(J R Boyle) *nvr bttr than midfield: u.p over 2f out: no prog over 1f out* **8/1**[3]

3000 **9** *hd* **Chandrayaan**[15] 4300 3-8-5 52 ....(v) SophieDoyle(5) 14 42
(J E Long) *wl in rr: pushed along on wd outside 3f out: modest late prog: n.d* **16/1**

000 **10** *1* **Fashion Tycoon (IRE)**[22] 4053 3-8-13 55 .... LiamKeniry 4 42
(M F Harris) *chsd ldng trio: rdn over 2f out: wknd over 1f out* **14/1**

0-00 **11** *3* **Singin' The Blues**[106] 1490 3-9-2 58 ....(v[1]) MickyFenton 8 37
(J M P Eustace) *dwlt: nvr bttr than midfield: u.p over 2f out: no ch over 1f out* **25/1**

0000 **12** *9* **Many A Slip**[27] 3907 3-9-4 60 .... DaneO'Neill 12 15
(J L Dunlop) *hld up in last pair: shkn up and no prog 2f out: sn eased: t.o* **25/1**

6050 **13** *nk* **Rightcar**[23] 4031 3-8-12 54 .... AndreaAtzeni 13 8
(Peter Grayson) *chsd ldr to wl over 1f out: wknd rapidly and eased: t.o* **20/1**

0500 **14** *29* **Hope She Does (USA)**[40] 3479 3-9-0 56 ....(p) J-PGuillambert 1 —
(Mrs L C Jewell) *dwlt: a last: lost tch 3f out: wl t.o* **100/1**

1m 26.4s (1.60) **Going Correction** +0.20s/f (Slow) **14** Ran SP% **126.4**
Speed ratings (Par 98): **98,97,97,96,94 94,93,92,91,90 87,76,76,43**
toteswingers:1&2:£8.80, 1&3:£11.00, 2&3:£17.00 CSF £50.33 CT £458.28 TOTE £4.80: £1.30, £3.70, £4.20; EX 56.90.
Owner Recycled Products Limited **Bred** Mrs L R Burrage **Trained** Radlett, Herts
■ Stewards' Enquiry : Tom McLaughlin caution: used whip with excessive frequency.

FOCUS
A moderate contest rated around those in the frame behind the winner.
Hope She Does(USA) Official explanation: jockey said filly was never travelling

4792 THISISSURREYTODAY.CO.UK MAIDEN STKS — 1m 6f
4:40 (4:42) (Class 5) 3-Y-O+ — **£2,388** (£705; £352) **Stalls** High

Form — RPR

0232 **1** **Never Can Tell (IRE)**[46] 3256 3-8-4 75 .... SophieDoyle(5) 4 75+
(J A Osborne) *mde all: pushed clr over 1f out: easily* **1/1**[1]

-035 **2** *7* **Istidlaal**[27] 3909 3-9-0 77 ....(v[1]) RichardHughes 7 70
(Sir Michael Stoute) *chsd wnr: reminders over 5f out: hrd rdn to chal 2f out: sn brushed aside* **5/2**[2]

55 **3** *3* **Naughty Naughty**[3] 4679 5-9-8 0 .... FergusSweeney 5 61
(B G Powell) *hld up: 6th and nt on terms 5f out: rdn and kpt on fr 3f out to take 3rd fnl f* **14/1**

0 **4** *1* **Tigress Hill**[17] 4229 3-8-9 0 EddieAhern 9 60
(Mrs A J Perrett) *wl in tch: rdn over 3f out: chsd ldng pair wl over 2f out: no imp: lost 3rd fnl f* **12/1**

054 **5** *3 1/2* **Stoical (IRE)**[31] 3754 3-9-0 75 DaneO'Neill 1 60
(W Jarvis) *chsd ldng pair: pushed along 4f out: no imp 3f out: sn lost 3rd: wknd over 1f out* **13/2**[3]

6 **6** *20* **Utern**[17] 4229 6-9-8 0 LiamKeniry 2 27
(Miss Venetia Williams) *chsd ldrs: rdn over 3f out: wknd over 2f out: t.o* **20/1**

7 *20* **Tiger Cat** 3-8-6 0 PatrickHills(3) 3 —
(H Morrison) *reluctant to enter stalls: s.s: in tch in rr after 4f: wknd 5f out: t.o* **14/1**

00 **8** *dist* **Juniper Prince**[121] 1157 4-9-13 0 JamieMoore 8 —
(G P Enright) *in tch to 1/2-way: wknd rapidly: barely rchd top of hill 5f out: btn 2f* **100/1**

00-0 **P** **Another Character (USA)**[36] 3593 3-9-0 29 TravisBlock 10 —
(M D I Usher) *nvr gng wl: lost tch 6f out: t.o whn p.u 3f out: dismntd* **100/1**

3m 7.37s (-2.63) **Going Correction** -0.025s/f (Good)
WFA 3 from 4yo+ 13lb 9 Ran SP% **119.7**
Speed ratings (Par 103): **106,102,100,99,97 86,74,—,—**
toteswingers:1&2:£1.70, 1&3:£5.00, 2&3:£5.70 CSF £3.71 TOTE £2.10: £1.40, £1.40, £1.30; EX 4.60.
Owner T Hyde **Bred** Shaanara Syndicate **Trained** Upper Lambourn, Berks

FOCUS
This was a weak maiden, but the pace was fair. The third is the best guide.
Tiger Cat Official explanation: jockey said filly was never travelling
Another Character(USA) Official explanation: vet said colt pulled up lame.

4793 JOHN MARCHANT 70TH BIRTHDAY CELEBRATION H'CAP 1m 2f
5:10 (5:11) (Class 6) (0-65,64) 3-Y-O+ **£2,047** (£604; £302) **Stalls** Low

Form RPR

0062 **1** **Diamond Twister (USA)**[13] 4361 4-9-5 **60** KierenFox(5) 3 70
(J R Best) *trckd ldng pair: quick move on inner to ld over 3f out and kicked on: drvn over 1f out: jst hld on* **11/2**[2]

3-60 **2** *hd* **Brigadoon**[88] 1973 3-9-3 **62** RichardHughes 1 72+
(W Jarvis) *hld up in rr: prog on inner over 3f out: rdn over 2f out: chsd wnr over 1f out: clsd u.p fin: jst failed* **13/8**[1]

0202 **3** *2 1/4* **Vinces**[15] 4295 6-9-6 **61** TobyAtkinson(5) 8 67
(T D McCarthy) *wl plcd: chsd wnr 3f out: drvn and no imp 2f out: lost 2nd over 1f out: one pce* **15/2**[3]

0450 **4** *3 1/2* **Thundering Home**[7] 3581 3-9-4 **63** FergusSweeney 11 62+
(M J Attwater) *dwlt: hld up in rr: in tch over 3f out: effrt jst over 2f out whn ldrs already gone: wnt 4th fnl f: no ch* **20/1**

5603 **5** *5* **Lou Bear (IRE)**[22] 4058 3-8-10 **55** J-PGuillambert 13 44
(J Akehurst) *t.k.h: hld up in tch: effrt to go 4th on outer over 2f out: sn outpcd: fdd* **10/1**

5413 **6** *shd* **Frank Street**[13] 4383 4-9-8 **58** (t) LiamKeniry 10 46
(Eve Johnson Houghton) *trckd ldrs: shkn up and nt qckn wl over 2f out: grad wknd* **8/1**

0040 **7** *2 1/4* **Slip**[17] 4227 5-9-6 **59** (p) MatthewDavies(3) 5 43
(C R Dore) *pushed along in last and nt gng wl early: stl in last pair 3f out: shkn up and sme late prog* **12/1**

1155 **8** *1 3/4* **Under Fire (IRE)**[13] 4361 7-9-5 **55** TomMcLaughlin 7 35
(A W Carroll) *chsd ldrs: lost pl and pushed along over 5f out: effrt 3f out: sn no prog* **16/1**

0-00 **9** *11* **Whitley Bay (USA)**[167] 634 3-8-5 **50** AndreaAtzeni 9 8
(J R Best) *nvr beyond midfield: struggling wl over 2f out* **33/1**

00-0 **10** *3* **Lily Eva**[17] 4238 4-8-2 **45** JamesRogers(7) 6 —
(D Donovan) *a in rr: rdn and no prog 3f out: sn bhd* **66/1**

4050 **11** *3 1/2* **Banana Republic (IRE)**[14] 4344 3-9-5 **64** DaneO'Neill 2 9
(P F I Cole) *led to over 3f out: wknd qckly* **11/1**

5006 **12** *60* **Supercast (IRE)**[13] 4361 7-9-6 **61** SophieDoyle(5) 12 —
(N J Vaughan) *chsd ldr to over 3f out: wknd v rapidly: sn wl t.o* **25/1**

2m 9.90s (-0.60) **Going Correction** -0.025s/f (Good)
WFA 3 from 4yo+ 9lb 12 Ran SP% **120.4**
Speed ratings (Par 101): **101,100,99,96,92 92,90,88,80,77 74,26**
toteswingers:1&2:£3.20, 1&3:£5.20, 2&3:£6.40 CSF £14.44 CT £70.29 TOTE £7.30: £2.80, £1.10, £2.90; EX 19.50.
Owner John Best **Bred** Annabel Murphy & William F Murphy **Trained** Hucking, Kent

FOCUS
A weak handicap with the winner rated in line with his winter form backed up by the third to his latest mark.
Lily Eva Official explanation: trainer said filly was unsuited by the good to firm (firm in places) ground

4794 SURREY MIRROR H'CAP 1m 3f 106y
5:45 (5:45) (Class 5) (0-70,68) 3-Y-O+ **£2,388** (£705; £352) **Stalls** High

Form RPR

2-53 **1** **Silent Act (USA)**[14] 4329 4-10-0 **68** RichardHughes 3 79+
(Mrs A J Perrett) *trckd ldng pair: led wl over 2f out and kicked on: clr over 1f out: 5 l up ins fnl f: eased nr fin* **13/8**[1]

-044 **2** *3 1/4* **Barliffey (IRE)**[42] 3404 5-10-0 **68** EddieAhern 5 71
(D J Coakley) *dwlt: hld up last: stl there gng strly 3f out: pushed along and prog 2f out: wnt 2nd last 100yds: far too much to do* **3/1**[2]

3230 **3** *1 1/2* **Filun**[17] 4227 5-8-9 **49** oh1 SamHitchcott 6 50
(A Middleton) *trckd ldng pair: rdn to chse wnr jst over 2f out: no imp: lost 2nd and tired last 100yds* **9/2**[3]

6000 **4** *1/2* **Dove Cottage (IRE)**[14] 4327 8-9-5 **59** FergusSweeney 4 59
(W S Kittow) *led: rdn and hdd wl over 2f out: sn outpcd: plugged on* **5/1**

2-60 **5** *9* **Merrymadcap (IRE)**[6] 4579 8-10-0 **68** (t) LiamKeniry 2 53
(Miss Tor Sturgis) *hld up in 5th: rdn wl over 2f out: sn wknd* **11/1**

0- **6** *4 1/2* **Gamedor (FR)**[137] 6704 5-9-11 **65** DaneO'Neill 1 42
(G L Moore) *hld up in 4th: rdn and wknd 3f out* **9/1**

2m 30.91s (-0.59) **Going Correction** -0.025s/f (Good) 6 Ran SP% **116.3**
Speed ratings (Par 103): **101,98,97,97,90 87**
toteswingers:1&2:£1.40, 1&3:£2.20, 2&3:£2.90 CSF £7.10 TOTE £2.00: £1.10, £3.40; EX 5.00 Place 6 £7.61; Place 5 £6.24.
Owner Mr & Mrs R Scott **Bred** Allen E Paulson Living Trust **Trained** Pulborough, W Sussex

FOCUS
An uncompetitive handicap and the form is a bit muddling rated around the principals.
T/Plt: £7.50 to a £1 stake. Pool:£44,848.20 - 4,348.51 winning tickets T/Qpdt: £4.90 to a £1 stake. Pool:£3,884.23 - 578.30 winning tickets JN

4511 MUSSELBURGH (R-H)
Friday, August 6

OFFICIAL GOING: Straight course - good (good to firm in places); round course - good to firm (good in places) (6.8)
Wind: Virtually nil Weather: Overcast

4795 SCOTTISH RACING (S) STKS 7f 30y
6:00 (6:00) (Class 6) 3-Y-O+ **£2,590** (£770; £385; £192) **Stalls** High

Form RPR

4002 **1** **Fujin Dancer (FR)**[9] 4484 5-9-3 76 (p) PaulHanagan 5 73
(K A Ryan) *hld up towards rr: hdwy on wd outside over 2f out: chal and hung rt wl over 1f out: sn led and rdn: drvn ins fnl f: jst hld on* **5/2**[2]

5120 **2** *shd* **Honest Broker (IRE)**[8] 4515 3-8-11 74 AndrewElliott 4 72+
(M Johnston) *trckd ldrs: swtchd lft and hdwy over 2f out: cl up whn hmpd and lost pl wl over 1f out: swtchd lft and rdn ent fnl f: statyed on strly towards fin: jst failed* **4/1**[3]

2040 **3** *1 1/4* **Spin Again (IRE)**[7] 4555 5-9-3 66 AndrewMullen 6 69
(D Nicholls) *trckd ldr: hdwy on inner to chal 3f out: rdn over 2f out and ev ch tl drvn and one pce ins fnl f* **12/1**

3000 **4** *2 1/4* **Beckermet (IRE)**[13] 4370 8-8-9 82 JamesSullivan(3) 1 58
(Mrs R A Carr) *trckd ldng pair: effrt over 2f out and sn rdn: drvn wl over 1f out: edgd rt and one pce* **15/8**[1]

6013 **5** *1* **Stonehaugh (IRE)**[18] 4197 7-9-3 70 (t) TomEaves 3 60
(J Howard Johnson) *sn led: jnd 3f out and sn rdn along: drvn and cl up whn hmpd wl over 1f out and wknd after* **13/2**

4600 **6** *4* **Crocodile Bay (IRE)**[6] 4602 7-8-12 62 (b) MarkCoumbe(5) 2 49
(R C Guest) *hld up towards rr: hdwy on outer 3f out: rdn to chal over 2f out: sn bmpd and wknd wl over 1f out* **18/1**

000/ **7** *12* **Mujahope**[587] 7799 5-8-9 47 KellyHarrison(3) 7 12
(C J Teague) *s.i.s: a bhd* **100/1**

1m 28.62s (-0.38) **Going Correction** 0.0s/f (Good)
WFA 3 from 5yo+ 6lb 7 Ran SP% **110.6**
Speed ratings (Par 101): **102,101,100,97,96 92,78**
toteswingers:1&2:£1.40, 1&3:£5.60, 2&3:£8.10 CSF £12.04 TOTE £1.90: £1.02, £6.10; EX 7.80.There was no bid for the winner.
Owner John Duddy **Bred** Loughtown Stud Ltd **Trained** Hambleton, N Yorks

FOCUS
After a dry day the ground had quickened a fraction especially in the back straight and it was described as on the firm side. Ironically, the rain arrived and this opening selling race was run in a blustery shower. The pace was sound and the third looks the best guide.

4796 RACING UK H'CAP 1m
6:30 (6:30) (Class 5) (0-75,74) 3-Y-O+ **£3,885** (£1,156; £577; £288) **Stalls** High

Form RPR

0600 **1** **Burns Night**[8] 4515 4-9-6 **68** SilvestreDeSousa 6 77
(G A Harker) *hld up towards rr: swtchd lft and hdwy over 2f out: sn rdn to chal: led and hung bdly rt ent fnl f: drvn out* **7/2**[3]

3545 **2** *1* **Mason Hindmarsh**[14] 4344 3-8-4 **62** JamesSullivan(3) 5 68
(Karen McLintock) *led: rdn along 2f out: drvn over 1f out: hdd ent fnl f: no ex towards fin* **8/1**

30-3 **3** *nk* **Diggeratt (USA)**[7] 4555 4-9-3 **65** PaulHanagan 8 71+
(R A Fahey) *trckd ldrs: hdwy wl over 2f out: rdn to chal and ev ch over 1f out: hmpd ent fnl f: kpt on u.p* **11/4**[1]

00/6 **4** *shd* **Casela Park (IRE)**[2] 4704 5-9-12 **74** PatrickMathers 1 80
(Eamon Tyrrell, Ire) *stdd and swtchd rt s: hld up in rr and sn keen: hdwy over 2f out: rdn wl over 1f out: carried hd high but styd on wl on wd outside ins fnl f: nrst fin* **3/1**[2]

5131 **5** *3/4* **Glenluji**[18] 4188 5-8-10 **65** PaulNorton(7) 3 69
(J S Goldie) *hld up towards rr: hdwy over 2f out: swtchd ins and rdn to chse ldrs wl over 1f out: nt clr run and swtchd lft ent fnl f: kpt on: nrst fin* **7/1**

0200 **6** *2 3/4* **Ansells Pride (IRE)**[45] 3284 7-9-5 **67** TomEaves 2 65
(B Smart) *cl up: rdn over 2f out and ev ch tl drvn and wknd appr fnl f* **10/1**

1-00 **7** *5* **Number One Guy**[66] 2618 3-9-1 **70** AndrewMullen 7 55
(P A Kirby) *hld up: effrt 2f out and sn rdn: drvn and wknd appr fnl f* **33/1**

0444 **8** *7* **Zabeel Tower**[8] 4515 7-8-9 **57** (v) TonyHamilton 4 27
(R Allan) *trckd ldng pair: rdn along over 2f out: sn drvn and wknd* **12/1**

1m 40.48s (-0.72) **Going Correction** 0.0s/f (Good)
WFA 3 from 4yo+ 7lb 8 Ran SP% **117.2**
Speed ratings (Par 103): **103,102,101,101,100 98,93,86**
toteswingers:1&2:£7.60, 1&3:£3.00, 2&3:£10.80 CSF £32.27 CT £88.06 TOTE £4.70: £1.90, £2.50, £1.10; EX 38.70.
Owner An Englishman, Irishman & Scotsman **Bred** Highclere Stud And Floors Farming **Trained** Thirkleby, N Yorks
■ Stewards' Enquiry : Silvestre De Sousa two-day ban: careless riding (Aug 21-22)

FOCUS
A modest 62-74 handicap with all eyes on Irish-trained Casela Park after his controversial fifth at Newcastle two days earlier. The race was soundly run and the form looks straightforward.

4797 INVESTEC INVESTMENT BANKING CONDITIONS STKS 5f
7:05 (7:05) (Class 3) 2-Y-O **£8,095** (£2,408; £1,203; £601) **Stalls** Low

Form RPR

1202 **1** **Arctic Feeling (IRE)**[35] 3611 2-9-1 96 PaulHanagan 3 93+
(R A Fahey) *cl up: rdn to ld wl over 1f out: kpt on strly ins fnl f* **11/10**[1]

2235 **2** *2* **Crimson Knot (IRE)**[6] 4580 2-8-7 67 PatrickMathers 1 76
(A Berry) *trckd ldng pair: hdwy over 2f out: sn rdn and chsd wnr ins fnl f: no imp* **40/1**

221 **3** *1 3/4* **Earl Wild (IRE)**[12] 4402 2-8-12 0 TomEaves 2 75
(J Howard Johnson) *led: rdn along 1/2-way: hdd and drvn wl over 1f out: wknd ent fnl f* **2/1**[2]

5314 **4** *shd* **Lady Royale**[13] 4388 2-8-7 83 (b) SilvestreDeSousa 4 70
(G R Oldroyd) *in tch: hdwy to chse ldrs 2f out: drvn over 1f out: kpt on same pce* **3/1**[3]

59.73 secs (-0.67) **Going Correction** 0.0s/f (Good) 4 Ran SP% **108.4**
Speed ratings (Par 98): **105,101,99,98**
CSF £22.84 TOTE £1.80; EX 28.10.
Owner Percy/Green Racing 2 **Bred** John McEnery **Trained** Musley Bank, N Yorks

FOCUS
There were three winners and an unconsidered maiden in this conditions event. The winner's task was made easy with the third and fourth below par.

NOTEBOOK

Arctic Feeling(IRE), eighth in the Norfolk Stakes at Royal Ascot, made it two wins from five starts. He was happy to accept a lead and put the race to bed in a matter of strides when called on for an effort. Rated 96 he will need careful placing from now on with the valuable sales races no doubt under consideration. (tchd 8-11 in places)

Crimson Knot(IRE), rated just 67, had a mountain to climb. She stuck on in willing fashion to chase home the winner and it remains to be seen if his rating shoots up, even though he managed only fifth in a nursery on his previous start. (op 33-1)

Earl Wild(IRE), who won a Carlisle maiden easily, had 12lb to find with the winner and was allowed to give him a lead. He was brushed aside in a matter of strides and, considering the lowly-rated runner-up finished ahead of him, this must go down as a disappointing effort. (op 11-4)

Lady Royale, who took a nursery at York in first-time blinkers two outings ago from a mark of 74, was clear second-best on official ratings. She was having her ninth career start and is not progressing at all. (op 7-2)

4798 INVESTEC INVESTMENT BANKING H'CAP — 5f
7:35 (7:36) (Class 4) (0-85,86) 3-Y-O+ **£6,152** (£1,830; £914; £456) **Stalls** Low

Form | | | | RPR
0000 **1** | | **Rasaman (IRE)**[7] 4536 6-9-4 **82** ....(v) GaryBartley[(3)] 5 | 93
(J S Goldie) *sn outpcd and rdn along in rr: hdwy wl over 1f out: nt clr run 1f out and again ins fnl f: squeezed through and fin strly to ld last 30yds* **7/1**

2236 **2** *1* **Green Park (IRE)**[14] 4345 7-9-2 **77** ....(v) DavidNolan 8 | 84
(D Carroll) *midfield: hdwy wl over 1f out: swtchd rt and rdn ent fnl f: kpt on to ld last 75yds: hdd and nt qckn towards fin* **7/1**

1033 **3** *1 ½* **Wicked Wilma (IRE)**[6] 4583 6-8-5 **66** .... PatrickMathers 9 | 68
(A Berry) *chsd ldrs: hdwy 2f out: rdn to ld over 1f out: drvn ins fnl f: hdd and one pce last 75yds* **20/1**

2036 **4** *½* **Doctor Parkes**[31] 3753 4-9-10 **85** .... PaulHanagan 6 | 85
(E J Alston) *chsd ldrs: rdn wl over 1f out: one pce ent fnl f* **4/1**[2]

4161 **5** *2 ½* **The Bear**[8] 4513 7-9-0 **75** 6ex .... TonyHamilton 10 | 66
(Miss L A Perratt) *led: rdn along and hdd over 1f out: grad wknd* **11/1**

-155 **6** *¾* **Argentine (IRE)**[8] 4513 6-9-3 **78** ....(b) LNewman 11 | 66
(J A McShane) *chsd ldrs on outer: rdn wl over 1f out: wknd appr fnl f* **20/1**

2311 **7** *nk* **Nickel Silver**[181] 446 5-9-7 **82** ....(v) TomEaves 4 | 69
(B Smart) *cl up: rdn along wl over 1f out: drvn and wknd appr fnl f* **11/2**[3]

0460 **8** *1 ½* **Mandurah (IRE)**[48] 3205 6-8-8 **72** .... JamesSullivan[(3)] 7 | 54
(Mrs R A Carr) *dwlt: a in rr* **9/1**

1330 **9** *½* **Lost In Paris (IRE)**[8] 4510 4-9-5 **80** ....(p) PhillipMakin 1 | 60
(T D Easterby) *chsd ldrs on inner: rdn along 2f out: sn wknd* **11/4**[1]

59.82 secs (-0.58) **Going Correction** 0.0s/f (Good) 9 Ran SP% **114.9**
Speed ratings (Par 105): **104,102,100,99,95 94,93,91,90**
toteswingers:1&2:£4.70, 1&3:£8.90, 2&3:£20.70 CSF £54.77 CT £929.91 TOTE £12.40: £6.20, £2.70, £6.20; EX 38.80.
Owner Paul Moulton **Bred** Rasana Partnership **Trained** Uplawmoor, E Renfrews

■ Stewards' Enquiry : Gary Bartley one-day ban: careless riding (Aug 21)

FOCUS
A tight-knit 66-85 sprint handicap and the pace was fast and furious with several keen to lead. The first two came from off the pace.

Mandurah(IRE) Official explanation: jockey said the gelding missed the break

Lost In Paris(IRE) Official explanation: jockey said that the gelding ran flat

4799 SCOTTISH RACING YOUR BETTER BET H'CAP — 5f
8:10 (8:13) (Class 6) (0-65,63) 3-Y-O+ **£2,590** (£770; £385; £192) **Stalls** Low

Form | | | | RPR
0143 **1** **Arriva La Diva**[8] 4516 4-9-5 **56** .... PaulHanagan 4 | 68
(J J Quinn) *trckd ldrs: swtchd rt and hdwy over 1f out: rdn to ld ent fnl f: kpt on strly* **11/4**[2]

6352 **2** *1 ¾* **Mandarin Spirit (IRE)**[8] 4516 10-9-12 **63** ....(b) TonyHamilton 5 | 69
(Miss L A Perratt) *cl up: rdn along 2f out and sltly outpcd: styd on to chse wnr ins fnl f: no imp towards fin* **9/2**[3]

5362 **3** *1 ¼* **Forever's Girl**[6] 4606 4-9-0 **51** .... SilvestreDeSousa 2 | 53
(G R Oldroyd) *towards rr: rdn along 1/2-way: hdwy to chse ldrs over 1f out: kpt on u.p fnl f* **15/8**[1]

66-3 **4** *½* **Ballarina**[3] 4672 4-8-9 **46** .... TomEaves 8 | 46
(E J Alston) *led: rdn along wl over 1f out: hdd ent fnl f and wknd* **13/2**

0565 **5** *½* **Welcome Approach**[8] 4516 7-8-8 **48** .... KellyHarrison[(3)] 3 | 46
(J R Weymes) *in tch: hdwy to chse ldrs wl over 1f out: sn rdn and wknd ent fnl f* **10/1**

5210 **6** *8* **Tournedos (IRE)**[24] 3976 8-9-6 **60** ....(b) JamesSullivan[(3)] 7 | 29
(Mrs R A Carr) *chsd ldrs on outer: rdn along 2f out: drvn and wknd over 1f out* **15/2**

60.24 secs (-0.16) **Going Correction** 0.0s/f (Good)
WFA 3 from 4yo+ 3lb 6 Ran SP% **113.8**
Speed ratings (Par 101): **101,98,96,95,94 81**
toteswingers:1&2:£1.10, 1&3:£3.70, 2&3:£4.50 CSF £15.70 CT £27.51 TOTE £3.30: £1.20, £1.80; EX 14.80.
Owner Allan Stennett **Bred** Mickley Stud, Stennett, Hillside Racing **Trained** Settrington, N Yorks

FOCUS
A low grade 46-63 sprint handicap and again the pace was strong. The winner recorded a slight personal best with the runner-up close to his best mark.

4800 BEST RACECOURSES LIVE H'CAP — 1m 4f 100y
8:40 (8:40) (Class 6) (0-65,65) 3-Y-O+ **£2,590** (£770; £385; £192) **Stalls** High

Form | | | | RPR
-520 **1** **Golden Future**[12] 4410 7-9-4 **52** .... PaulHanagan 2 | 58
(P D Niven) *led: rdn along over 2f out: drvn over 1f out: hdd ent fnl f: rallied to ld again last 100yds* **7/2**[3]

3312 **2** *¾* **Park's Prodigy**[10] 4449 6-10-0 **62** .... SilvestreDeSousa 6 | 67
(G A Harker) *hld up in tch: gd hdwy on outer wl over 2f out: rdn to ld over 1f out: drvn and edgd rt ins fnl f: hdd and no ex last 100yds* **6/4**[1]

6343 **3** *1 ¾* **Maid Of Meft**[30] 3776 3-9-6 **65** .... LNewman 5 | 67
(Miss L A Perratt) *hld up in rr: hdwy on inner over 2f out: rdn to chse ldrs over 1f out: kpt on ins fnl f* **16/1**

P321 **4** *½* **Light The City (IRE)**[7] 4545 3-8-3 **51** 6ex .... JamesSullivan[(3)] 4 | 52
(Mrs R A Carr) *trckd ldng pair: hdwy 3f out: rdn 2f out: drvn and one pce fr over 1f out* **5/2**[2]

0004 **5** *1 ¾* **Always Dixie (IRE)**[10] 4448 3-8-1 **46** .... AndrewElliott 1 | 45
(M Johnston) *trckd wnr: effrt and cl up 3f out: rdn and ev ch 2f out: sn drvn and grad wknd* **15/2**

005 **6** *12* **Quitao (GER)**[47] 3242 3-8-0 **48** ow3 .... KellyHarrison[(3)] 3 | 27
(P Monteith) *a in rr: rdn along and outpcd fnl 3f* **40/1**

2m 43.85s (1.85) **Going Correction** 0.0s/f (Good)
WFA 3 from 6yo+ 11lb 6 Ran SP% **110.9**
Speed ratings (Par 101): **93,92,91,91,89 81**
toteswingers:1&2:£3.10, 1&3:£5.00, 2&3:£1.50 CSF £8.96 TOTE £4.10: £1.80, £1.10; EX 10.00 Place 6 £107.20; Place 5 £48.14.
Owner The Little Ice Club **Bred** Larksborough Stud Limited **Trained** Barton-le-Street, N Yorks

FOCUS
A low-grade handicap and the pace was not strong until the final half-mile. The form is a bit muddling, with the third in line with his best maiden form.
T/Plt: £56.20 to a £1 stake. Pool:£47,637.64 - 618.37 winning tickets T/Qpdt: £21.00 to a £1 stake. Pool:£4,166.66 - 146.50 winning tickets JR

4592 NEWMARKET (July Course) (R-H)
Friday, August 6

OFFICIAL GOING: Good (7.4)
Stands' side section of July Course utilised.
Wind: Fresh across Weather: Overcast

4801 HOME OF RACING NURSERY — 7f
5:40 (5:40) (Class 4) (0-85,82) 2-Y-O **£4,533** (£1,348; £674; £168; £168) **Stalls** Low

Form | | | | RPR
005 **1** **Buzz Law (IRE)**[19] 4167 2-7-12 **64** ow3 .... SimonPearce[(5)] 3 | 68
(J R Weymes) *hld up in tch: rdn over 1f out: r.o to ld towards fin* **10/1**

4300 **2** *shd* **Takeaway**[20] 4138 2-9-7 **82** .... PatDobbs 9 | 86
(R Hannon) *hld up: hdwy 4f out: rdn to ld ins fnl f: hung lft: hdd towards fin* **13/2**

016 **3** *½* **Mayhab**[70] 2514 2-9-0 **75** .... TedDurcan 8 | 78
(C E Brittain) *hld up: hdwy over 2f out: rdn to ld 1f out: sn hdd: styd on* **16/1**

6042 **4** *2* **Prophet In A Dream**[11] 4429 2-8-4 **65** .... CathyGannon 5 | 62
(M R Channon) *trckd ldrs: racd keenly: rdn and edgd lft fr over 1f out: styd on same pce ins fnl f* **10/1**

5213 **4** *dht* **Spartic**[23] 4013 2-8-9 **70** .... JamesDoyle 6 | 67
(A J McCabe) *led: rdn and hdd 1f out: styd on same pce* **16/1**

01 **6** *3 ¾* **Toms River Tess (IRE)**[15] 4286 2-9-7 **82** .... MichaelHills 4 | 69
(B W Hills) *chsd ldr: rdn and ev ch over 1f out: wknd ins fnl f* **9/2**[3]

051 **7** *1 ¼* **Star Surprise**[16] 4263 2-9-6 **81** .... GeorgeBaker 2 | 65
(M L W Bell) *chsd ldrs: rdn over 1f out: sn wknd* **11/4**[2]

313 **8** *36* **Honourable Knight (IRE)**[14] 4331 2-8-10 **71** .... KierenFallon 1 | —
(M D I Usher) *s.i.s: sn pushed along and a in rr: lost tch over 2f out* **5/2**[1]

1m 28.3s (2.60) **Going Correction** +0.10s/f (Good) 8 Ran SP% **116.7**
Speed ratings (Par 96): **89,88,88,86,86 81,80,39**
toteswingers:1&2:£12.80, 1&3:£10.50, 2&3:£10.20 CSF £74.23 CT £1047.75 TOTE £11.40: £3.30, £2.20, £4.80; EX 92.80.
Owner Cyril Wall **Bred** C J Wall **Trained** Middleham Moor, N Yorks

FOCUS
This appeared to be run at just a steady pace and the time was slow. The form looks ordinary rated around the placed horses.

NOTEBOOK

Buzz Law(IRE), making his handicap bow off a mark of 61 after failing to find the frame in three previous starts, had to carry 3lb overweight after a jockey change. That makes his winning effort even more admirable as he ran on in a style that suggests he'll get a little further, which can only open up further options. The slight ease in the ground may have helped him after he was soundly beaten on a firm surface at Redcar last time. Official explanation: trainer's rep said, regarding apparent improvement in form, that the colt was a late foal who is strengthening and showing improvement. (op 14-1)

Takeaway had only raced over 5f before this, but the step up in trip proved well within his range. Having been held up towards the rear, he made up plenty of ground in determined fashion, only to get run out of it towards the finish. On this evidence, he should remain competitive in similar races and it could be that there is some more progression to come over this trip. (op 11-2 tchd 5-1)

Mayhab, off for over two months after finishing well beaten in a better race at Pontefract, was another who found a rise in distance to his liking. He, too, was held up for a late challenge and smoothly passed rivals before just being worn down late on. Having been sidelined, he is entitled to come on for this and can add to his maiden win. Official explanation: jockey said colt hung right (op 18-1 tchd 20-1)

Prophet In A Dream was second, beaten over three lengths off this mark on the AW at Wolverhampton towards the end of last month, and has a more exposed look than those who finished ahead of him. (tchd 20-1)

Spartic soon led and set a sensible tempo but just lacked gears late on. This was a creditable effort and a further winning opportunity can be found for this consistent type. (tchd 20-1)

Toms River Tess(IRE) was making her nursery bow on the back of a maiden success 15 days earlier at Doncaster over this trip. On the face of it, this was a disappointing effort as she folded quite quickly at the business end of the race. However, it is far too early to write her off and it may be that she prefers a sounder surface, her maiden win having come on good to firm ground. (op 4-1 tchd 7-2)

Star Surprise had a real battle when winning his maiden at Sandown 16 days earlier and maybe that left an impression, and he should be given another chance. (op 5-2)

Honourable Knight(IRE), beaten less than a length into third over C&D two weeks earlier, never travelled with any fluency here. Official explanation: jockey said the colt lost it's action (op 4-1)

4802 FIRESTONE BUILDING PRODUCTS (S) STKS — 7f
6:10 (6:15) (Class 5) 2-Y-O **£3,238** (£963; £481; £240) **Stalls** Low

Form | | | | RPR
4552 **1** **Painters Easel (IRE)**[3] 4678 2-8-13 60 .... JamesDoyle 17 | 62
(J S Moore) *hld up: hdwy over 2f out: rdn to ld 1f out: hung rt towards fin: jst hld on* **6/1**[2]

00 **2** *shd* **Cometh**[16] 4253 2-8-8 0 .... TedDurcan 5 | 57
(N P Littmoden) *led: rdn and hung rt over 1f out: sn hdd: styd on* **50/1**

0 **3** *1 ½* **Loch Ordie**[24] 3991 2-8-13 0 .... JerryO'Dwyer 18 | 58
(M G Quinlan) *hld up: hdwy and hung lft fr 2f out: styd on u.p* **33/1**

40 **4** *¾* **Roi Du Boeuf (IRE)**[7] 4554 2-8-13 0 .... PatDobbs 12 | 56+
(R Hannon) *hld up: hdwy over 2f out: hdwy and hung lft over 1f out: r.o: nrst fin* **20/1**

2320 **5** *1* **Jambo Bibi (IRE)**[25] 3959 2-8-8 70 .... FrankieMcDonald 15 | 48
(R Hannon) *hld up: hdwy over 2f out: hung lft over 1f out: r.o: nt rch ldrs* **7/1**[3]

0200 **6** *4 ½* **Dancing Tara**[42] 3386 2-8-8 60 .... CathyGannon 13 | 36
(P D Evans) *hld up in tch: rdn and hung lft over 1f out: no ex* **40/1**

60 **7** *¾* **Miss Toldyaso (IRE)**[11] 4437 2-8-1 0 .... AdamBeschizza[(7)] 6 | 34
(M G Quinlan) *chsd ldrs: rdn over 2f out: wknd ins fnl f* **66/1**

The Form Book, Raceform Ltd, Compton, RG20 6NL

8 1 1/2 **Munro's Dragon** 2-8-13 0 LiamJones 7 35
(M H Tompkins) *mid-div: hmpd and lost pl over 4f out: rdn and swtchd rt over 2f out: styd on ins fnl f* **66/1**

0542 9 2 1/2 **Majestic Style (IRE)**[24] 3992 2-8-8 57 AhmedAjtebi 1 23
(A P Jarvis) *w ldr tl rdn over 2f out: wknd ins fnl f* **14/1**

0 10 1 **Petronilla**[53] 3035 2-8-8 0 JamieMackay 9 20
(W J Musson) *s.i.s: sn mid-div: rdn and wknd over 2f out: in rr whn hung lft ins fnl f* **100/1**

050 11 1/2 **Dew Reward (IRE)**[16] 4253 2-8-13 56 (b1) RichardMullen 8 24
(Eve Johnson Houghton) *prom: sn drvn along: wknd wl over 2f out* **40/1**

030 12 2 **Knox Overstreet**[29] 3832 2-8-13 64 TonyCulhane 11 19
(Tom Dascombe) *hung lft thrght: mid-div: sn rdn along: wkng whn swtchd rt wl over 1f out* **8/11**[1]

0 13 3/4 **Royal Classy Cleo**[9] 4474 2-8-3 0 SimonPearce(5) 14 12
(P D Evans) *a in rr* **100/1**

05 14 1 1/4 **Striking Love**[28] 3864 2-8-3 0 JohnFahy(5) 2 8
(R Charlton) *dwlt: sn prom: rdn and wknd over 1f out* **9/1**

15 4 **Senor Sassi (USA)** 2-8-6 0 DannyBrock(7) 10 —
(J S Moore) *s.s: outpcd* **50/1**

00 16 6 **Newstarmcgrath**[11] 4436 2-8-13 0 (bt1) MartinDwyer 3 —
(Miss Gay Kelleway) *prom: rdn over 4f out: wknd over 2f out* **100/1**

1m 28.6s (2.90) **Going Correction** +0.10s/f (Good) **16 Ran SP% 123.8**
Speed ratings (Par 94): **87,86,85,84,83 78,77,75,72,71 70,68,67,66,61 54**
toteswingers:1&2:£33.00, 1&3:£24.40, 2&3:£272.60 CSF £287.24 TOTE £7.30: £1.70, £14.70, £10.10; EX 727.80.The winner sold to by Claus Bjorling for 13,000gns. Roi du Boeuf was claimed by D. M. Simcock for £10,000.
Owner The Moore The Merrier **Bred** Kilboy Estate **Trained** Upper Lambourn, Berks
■ Stewards' Enquiry : James Doyle three-day ban: used whip with excessive frequency down the shoulder in the forehand (Aug 21-23)

FOCUS
A rare seller for the course. Once again the time was slow, 0.3sec beyond the preceding nursery over the same distance, but there will probably be a couple of winners come from it, albeit in similar company. Three of the first four home were held up off the pace. The winner is rated to his latest mark.

NOTEBOOK
Painters Easel(IRE) had shown that he is capable of mixing it at this level when second in a 6f seller at Chepstow last time. Stepped up in trip here, he kept finding extra for pressure after travelling into his race with more fluency than most. Kept to this class, there is no reason why he shouldn't remain competitive. (op 7-1)
Cometh ◆ is of particular interest. She raced on the front end throughout and was the only one of those who were handy to see it out. This effort came after being soundly beaten in his two previous starts, and offers encouragement for the future.
Loch Ordie, seventh in a Yarmouth maiden last month on his debut, was entitled to strip fitter for this and also know more. If he can find a little further progression, a race like this should fall his way.
Roi Du Boeuf(IRE) was another interesting runner, running on at the end after being held up. He made up significant late ground and, being by Hurricane Run, could find further improvement as he is gradually stepped up in trip. The way he closed out his race suggests he'll get 1m this season without a problem. (op 25-1 tchd 33-1)
Jambo Bibi(IRE) finished in the frame on both of her first two starts but the form of those races does not look strong. Trying this trip for the first time, she also made some good late progress and that opens up options for her. (op 6-1)
Knox Overstreet, who had been the subject of significant market support, was the big disappointment of the race. He was one of the first to be ridden and hung badly left. He is best watched next time. (op Evens tchd 4-6)

4803 TALK NIGHT CLUB MAIDEN STKS 7f
6:45 (6:47) (Class 4) 2-Y-0 **£4,533** (£1,348; £674; £336) **Stalls** Low

Form RPR

1 **Biondetti (USA)** 2-9-3 0 AhmedAjtebi 2 87+
(Mahmood Al Zarooni) *chsd ldr: led 2f out: rdn out* **10/1**

2 1 **Buthelezi (USA)** 2-9-3 0 WilliamBuick 1 85+
(J H M Gosden) *a.p: rdn over 2f out: r.o* **9/1**

3 nk **Madawi** 2-9-3 0 TedDurcan 15 84+
(C E Brittain) *chsd ldrs: rdn and ev ch 2f out: styd on* **20/1**

4 1 3/4 **Happy Today (USA)** 2-9-3 0 MartinDwyer 6 79+
(B J Meehan) *hld up in tch: racd keenly: hmpd and lost pl wl over 4f out: hdwy 3f out: no ex wl ins fnl f* **11/2**[2]

5 1/2 **Arc Light (IRE)** 2-8-10 0 AntiocoMurgia(7) 14 78+
(Mahmood Al Zarooni) *s.i.s and hmpd s: hdwy over 4f out: rdn over 1f out: styd on same pce* **5/1**[1]

6 2 1/2 **Blue Destination** 2-9-3 0 JamesDoyle 7 71
(P J McBride) *mid-div: hdwy and edgd lft 2f out: hung lft and no ex ins fnl f* **25/1**

7 3/4 **Ektibaas** 2-9-3 0 MichaelHills 5 71+
(B W Hills) *s.i.s: hld up: rdn over 2f out: styd on fnl f: nt trble ldrs* **12/1**

8 1/2 **A Boy Named Suzi** 2-9-3 0 JackMitchell 13 68+
(T T Clement) *prom: rdn 1/2-way: edgd lft and wknd over 1f out* **66/1**

9 1 1/2 **Sisindu (IRE)** 2-9-0 0 Louis-PhilippeBeuzelin(3) 16 64+
(B J Meehan) *hld up: rdn over 2f out: nvr trbld ldrs* **25/1**

10 2 1/2 **Muhandis (IRE)** 2-8-12 0 JohnFahy(5) 12 57
(E A L Dunlop) *led: racd keenly: rdn and hdd 2f out: wknd fnl f* **20/1**

11 1 1/4 **Audacious** 2-9-3 0 RichardMullen 11 53
(Sir Michael Stoute) *hld up in tch: rdn: hung lft and wknd 2f out* **12/1**

12 1 **Ebony Song (USA)** 2-9-3 0 GeorgeBaker 9 51
(J Noseda) *wnt rt s: sn chsng ldrs: rdn and wknd over 1f out* **8/1**[3]

13 2 **Barwick** 2-9-3 0 LiamJones 17 45
(M H Tompkins) *sn pushed along in rr: hmpd 3f out: nvr on terms* **66/1**

14 3/4 **Fine Style (IRE)** 2-9-3 0 JamieSpencer 3 43
(M L W Bell) *rn green and sn outpcd* **16/1**

15 1/2 **Lejaam** 2-9-3 0 RichardHills 8 42
(J L Dunlop) *s.i.s: in rr whn swtchd rt 3f out: n.d* **9/1**

16 3 1/4 **Touch Of Red (USA)** 2-9-3 0 PatDobbs 10 33
(R Hannon) *hmpd s: sn chsng ldrs: rdn and wknd over 2f out* **14/1**

17 11 **Franciscan** 2-9-3 0 KierenFallon 4 4
(L M Cumani) *prom: pushed along and lost pl over 4f out: wknd over 2f out* **12/1**

1m 27.26s (1.56) **Going Correction** +0.10s/f (Good) **17 Ran SP% 128.1**
Speed ratings (Par 96): **95,93,93,91,90 88,87,86,84,82 80,79,77,76,75 72,59**
toteswingers:1&2:£13.40, 1&3:£88.90, 2&3:£138.40 CSF £93.90 TOTE £13.50: £6.40, £3.70, £9.00; EX 71.50.
Owner Godolphin **Bred** Palides Investments N V Inc **Trained** Newmarket, Suffolk

FOCUS
This was run at a decent pace and the time was over a second quicker than the earlier nursery over the same trip. There are sure to be plenty of winners coming from the race. Traditionally a strong maiden, the indications are that this was another good renewal with plenty impressing on paddock inspection. The form is rated around the averages and should work out.

NOTEBOOK
Biondetti(USA), who cost $350,000 and is related to plenty of winners, appeared more forward than many of his rivals, impressing as a strong type, and he did himself justice on his debut. Always towards the fore, he saw it out well in a manner that hinted he'll stay further. He looks capable of making up into a Pattern performer, although he doesn't have the smart entries that some of these possess. (op 8-1)
Buthelezi(USA), who also cost $350,000, is in the Group 2 Royal Lodge Stakes and that doesn't look beyond him judged on this highly promising debut. He raced wide on the far side but impressed as being very organised and a good mover. He'd already impressed in the preliminaries as a tall horse with plenty of scope, and it is indicative that his powerful yard opted to start him off in a hot contest like this. A similar race is his for the taking next time and he looks sure to go on to bigger and better things. (tchd 8-1 and 10-1)
Madawi was another to run an eyecatching race. Bought for 150,000gns, he is a half-brother to several that won at two, and looks poised to add to the family's reputation in the near future.
Happy Today(USA), closely related to top-class miler Zafeen and also a half-brother to classy pair Ya Hajar and Atlantic Sport, shaped with distinct promise on his racecourse bow. He was tightened up for space to lose a little ground early on before making good progress, only to become tired upon hitting the rising ground. There was plenty to like about this effort and he shouldn't be too long in breaking his maiden. (op 8-1)
Arc Light(IRE), half-brother to Group/Grade 3 winners in France and US among other successful siblings, looked as if he'd tighten up physically for this. A May foal, he possesses a lot scope and is likely to take the beating on his next start and will only improve as he matures. (op 7-1)
Blue Destination, a half-brother to Blue Maiden, who was Group 3 placed over this trip at two, showed up well and would have to be of interest next time. (op 22-1)
Ektibaas, whose brother won over this trip as did his dam, is a May foal and is another for whom time will bring about physical development. This was a more than satisfactory debut. (op 14-1 tchd 11-1)
Audacious, a half-brother to a couple of winners and with plenty of class in the extended family, is another good looker and looks more of a long-term project than some of these. (op 9-1)
Ebony Song(USA), a $150,000 purchase out of a dam who has produced plenty of winners, will doubtless improve for this first run after weakening in the closing exchanges. (op 13-2)

4804 HONEYTRAP AT TALK NIGHT CLUB H'CAP 1m 2f
7:15 (7:18) (Class 5) (0-75,79) 3-Y-0+ **£3,238** (£963; £481; £240) **Stalls** Centre

Form RPR

-631 1 **Denton (NZ)**[7] 4546 7-9-13 79 6ex (t) SimonPearce(5) 12 91
(J R Gask) *mde all: rdn over 1f out: hung rt ins fnl f: r.o* **7/2**[1]

0024 2 1 3/4 **Laconicos (IRE)**[5] 4621 8-8-6 60 (t) LauraPike(7) 6 68
(W B Stone) *chsd wnr: rdn over 1f out: styd on* **14/1**

5232 3 1/2 **Broughtons Paradis (IRE)**[14] 4329 4-9-0 61 TonyCulhane 9 68+
(W J Musson) *hld up: hdwy over 2f out: rdn over 1f out: styd on* **4/1**[2]

0053 4 4 1/2 **Lord Theo**[6] 4594 6-9-13 74 TedDurcan 13 72
(N P Littmoden) *chsd ldrs: rdn over 1f out: wknd ins fnl f* **9/2**[3]

-110 5 5 **Agapanthus (GER)**[44] 3319 5-10-0 75 JerryO'Dwyer 10 63
(B J Curley) *prom: rdn over 2f out: wknd fnl f* **9/1**

0120 6 1/2 **Calahonda**[37] 3565 4-9-9 70 LiamJones 2 57
(P W D'Arcy) *hld up: rdn over 2f out: rdn over 1f out: wknd fnl f* **14/1**

6040 7 7 **Coiled Spring**[13] 4386 4-9-2 63 (v1) PatDobbs 4 36
(Mrs A J Perrett) *hld up in tch: rdn 3f out: hung lft and wknd over 1f out* **14/1**

0036 8 5 **Aussie Blue (IRE)**[9] 4485 6-8-11 58 MichaelHills 3 21
(R M Whitaker) *hld up: rdn over 2f out: sn wknd* **25/1**

0414 9 5 **Zubova**[17] 4224 3-8-10 73 (t) AdamBeschizza(7) 8 26
(Rae Guest) *prom: rdn over 2f out: wknd over 1f out* **14/1**

-405 10 3/4 **Sir Haydn**[135] 970 10-8-2 56 oh11 DannyBrock(7) 1 8
(J R Jenkins) *s.i.s: a in rr: wknd over 2f out* **80/1**

1345 11 6 **Saviour Sand (IRE)**[28] 3862 6-9-0 66 (t) KylieManser(5) 5 6
(Miss Olivia Maylam) *s.s and a bhd* **33/1**

4-51 12 1 **Knotgarden (IRE)**[18] 4207 4-9-10 71 KierenFallon 14 9
(J R Fanshawe) *chsd ldrs tl rdn and wknd over 2f out* **15/2**

2m 4.73s (-0.77) **Going Correction** +0.10s/f (Good)
WFA 3 from 4yo+ 9lb **12 Ran SP% 116.9**
Speed ratings (Par 103): **107,105,105,101,97 97,91,87,83,83 78,77**
toteswingers:1&2:£20.60, 1&3:£3.80, 2&3:£15.40 CSF £47.86 CT £158.75 TOTE £4.50: £1.80, £5.10, £2.10; EX 100.00.
Owner Horses First Racing Limited **Bred** Windsor Park Stud Ltd **Trained** Sutton Veny, Wilts

FOCUS
The first two home raced in that order throughout, and the form looks fair rated through the third.
Saviour Sand(IRE) Official explanation: jockey said colt was slowly away
Dynamic Idol(USA) Official explanation: jockey said that the colt was slowly away

4805 NEWMARKET NIGHTS CONDITIONS STKS 1m 2f
7:50 (7:51) (Class 3) 3-Y-0
£8,723 (£2,612; £1,306; £653; £326; £163) **Stalls** Centre

Form RPR

2231 1 **Wigmore Hall (IRE)**[27] 3921 3-9-0 108 JamieSpencer 5 111+
(M L W Bell) *hld up: hdwy over 2f out: led over 1f out: readily* **7/4**[2]

0-14 2 1 1/2 **Chabal (IRE)**[85] 2056 3-9-0 115 (t) TedDurcan 1 103
(Saeed Bin Suroor) *chsd ldrs: led 2f out: hdd over 1f out: styd on same pce* **10/11**[1]

604 3 4 1/2 **Hanson'D (IRE)**[20] 4140 3-9-0 95 KierenFallon 2 94
(K A Ryan) *chsd ldr tl led over 3f out: rdn and hdd 2f out: no ex fnl f* **20/1**

4 8 **Ela Gonda Mou** 3-8-6 0 EddieCreighton 6 70
(P Charalambous) *s.i.s: hld up: hdwy u.p over 2f out: wknd over 1f out* **100/1**

01 5 2 **Cotton Mill**[30] 3795 3-9-0 96 AlanMunro 3 74
(W Jarvis) *chsd ldrs: rdn over 3f out: wknd over 2f out* **11/1**

21-0 6 27 **Champagne Style (USA)**[50] 3104 3-9-0 103 (b1) WilliamBuick 4 20
(B J Meehan) *led: hung lft over 8f out: rdn and hdd over 3f out: wknd over 2f out: eased: t.o* **9/1**[3]

2m 5.36s (-0.14) **Going Correction** +0.10s/f (Good) **6 Ran SP% 112.8**
Speed ratings (Par 104): **104,102,99,92,91 69**
toteswingers:1&2:£1.10, 1&3:£3.70, 2&3:£4.50 CSF £3.70 TOTE £2.50: £1.40, £1.20; EX 3.70.
Owner M B Hawtin **Bred** K And Mrs Cullen **Trained** Newmarket, Suffolk

FOCUS
This revolved around the first two in the betting. The time was over half a second slower than the preceding handicap but Champagne Style ensured the race was run at a true gallop and that favoured the winner, who is rated to form.

NOTEBOOK
Wigmore Hall(IRE) travelled ominously well out the back before being delivered with his challenge on the bridle. His jockey could even afford to take two or three backward glances inside the final furlong, as this served as the perfect preparation to the colt's Group 1 Secretariat Stakes bid in Chicago on August 21. That represents a significant step up in class but the way this horse is going forward he may well be able to take it in his stride. (op 2-1 tchd 13-8)

Chabal(IRE), rated some 7lb better than Wigmore Hall, looked fit on paddock inspection. He was back in action 85 days after failing to fire in the Dante Stakes. Connections indicated that he needed good ground and he looked more at ease in today's conditions. He travelled well but could not match the turn of foot of the winner. He remains an interesting prospect and this was a relatively encouraging performance after his layoff. (tchd 5-6 and 11-10 in places)
Hanson'D(IRE) had been highly tried before this and was tackling 1m2f for the first time. He appeared to stay the trip and ran a good race but was well beaten by two stakes horses. (op 16-1)
Ela Gonda Mou faced a tough task and fared creditably. She is related to winners and is likely to find life much easier when her sights are lowered.
Cotton Mill, rated 96 for his C&D win at the July festival, looks a difficult horse to place off that mark. He still showed signs of inexperience here. (op 10-1 tchd 9-1)
Champagne Style(USA) was a smart two-year-old but both of his efforts this season have been disappointing. He didn't do himself any favours on this latest assignment by racing too freely. (op 8-1 tchd 10-1)

4806 NEWMARKETRACECOURSES.CO.UK H'CAP — 6f

8:20 (8:21) (Class 4) (0-85,83) 3-Y-O+ — **£4,533** (£1,348; £674; £336) **Stalls** Low

Form — RPR
3232 **1** **Tyfos**[14] 4345 5-9-6 **78** .... TomMcLaughlin 12 — 88
(B P J Baugh) *mde all: rdn over 1f out: edgd rt ins fnl f: r.o* — **6/1**[3]
2 *1* **Miss Faustina (IRE)**[36] 3644 3-9-5 **81** .... RichardMullen 9 — 87
(P J McBride) *a.p: rdn and ev ch fr over 1f out: no ex towards fin* — **8/1**
042 **3** *1 1/4* **Lochan Mor**[18] 4192 4-9-8 **80** .... JamieSpencer 11 — 83
(M L W Bell) *chsd ldrs: rdn over 1f out: styd on* — **7/2**[1]
451 **4** *shd* **Mirza**[17] 4222 3-8-13 **82** .... AdamBeschizza(7) 8 — 83+
(Rae Guest) *hld up: hdwy 2f out: rdn and hung lft fr over 1f out: styd on same pce wl ins fnl f* — **25/1**
0251 **5** *1/2* **Lujeanie**[14] 4333 4-9-10 **82** .... (p) AdamKirby 1 — 83
(D K Ivory) *s.i.s: hld up: hdwy over 2f out: rdn and edgd rt over 1f out: styd on* — **7/1**
502 **6** *2 3/4* **Ginger Ted (IRE)**[18] 4192 3-9-4 **80** .... (p) J-PGuillambert 4 — 71
(R C Guest) *chsd ldrs: rdn over 3f out: no ex fnl f* — **8/1**
0004 **7** *3/4* **Seamus Shindig**[14] 4333 8-9-2 **81** .... AmyScott(7) 6 — 71
(H Candy) *chsd ldrs: rdn over 2f out: styd on same pce appr fnl f* — **7/1**
0652 **8** *2 1/4* **Tabaret**[7] 4558 7-9-11 **83** .... (p) MichaelHills 5 — 65+
(R M Whitaker) *hld up: effrt and nt clr run wl over 1f out: nvr trbld ldrs* — **4/1**[2]
5530 **9** *2 1/4* **Midnight Fantasy**[30] 3779 4-9-0 **72** .... KierenFallon 10 — 47
(Rae Guest) *dwlt: hld up: hdwy 2f out: rdn and wknd over 1f out* — **17/2**
0050 **10** *4 1/2* **Footstepsofspring (FR)**[14] 4333 3-8-8 **70** .... TonyCulhane 2 — 30
(W J Musson) *prom tl rdn and wknd over 2f out* — **33/1**
0000 **11** *2* **Brunelleschi**[11] 4431 7-8-3 **68** .... (b) JosephineBruning(7) 3 — 22
(P L Gilligan) *s.i.s: swtchd rt 5f out: a bhd* — **33/1**

1m 12.23s (-0.27) **Going Correction** +0.10s/f (Good)
WFA 3 from 4yo+ 4lb — **11 Ran SP% 124.0**
Speed ratings (Par 105): **105,103,102,101,101 97,96,93,90,84 81**
toteswingers:1&2:£6.80, 1&3:£3.70, 2&3:£8.10 CSF £55.44 CT £174.95 TOTE £8.30: £2.20, £2.90, £1.50; EX 82.10 Place 6 £723.86; Place 5 £111.76.
Owner J Tomlinson/G Williams **Bred** J Tomlinson And G Williams **Trained** Audley, Staffs

FOCUS
decent handicap and the time was respectable for the conditions, being 1.93sec outside standard. The winner is rated a slight improver.
Midnight Fantasy Official explanation: jockey said that the filly was lost her action
T/Jkpt: Not won. T/Plt: £1,274.50 to a £1 stake. Pool:£64,074.30 - 36.70 winning tickets T/Qpdt: £14.50 to a £1 stake. Pool:£6,991.62 - 355.90 winning tickets CR

4807 - 4813a (Foreign Racing) - See Raceform Interactive

4396 ASCOT (R-H)

Saturday, August 7

OFFICIAL GOING: Good to firm changing to good after race 1 (2.10)
Round course rail positioned 3yds in from 10f start to home straight adding 12yds to 12f and 2m races and 3yds to Old Mile.
Wind: Virtually nil Weather: Showers

4814 BARCLAYS SHERGAR CUP DASH (H'CAP) — 5f

2:10 (2:11) (Class 2) (0-105,102) 3-Y-O+ — **£14,769** (£5,172; £2,364; £1,845; £1,626; £1,182) **Stalls** Low

Form — RPR
2343 **1** **Prohibit**[7] 4576 5-9-12 **100** .... (p) ChristopheSoumillon 2 — 110+
(R M H Cowell) *wnt rt and bmpd rival s: hld up in tch: hdwy to trck ldr gng wl over 1f out: shkn up to ld ins fnl f: pushed out: comf* — **5/2**[1]
2000 **2** *1* **Golden Destiny (IRE)**[13] 4401 4-9-8 **96** .... (b[1]) RichardHughes 3 — 102
(P J Makin) *bmpd s: sn rcvrd and chsd ldr: led wl over 1f out: sn rdn and edgd lft to rail: hdd ins fnl f: nt pce of wnr fnl 100yds: kpt on* — **14/1**
2536 **3** *3/4* **Secret Asset (IRE)**[7] 4576 5-9-9 **97** .... PJSmullen 5 — 101
(Jane Chapple-Hyam) *bmpd s: t.k.h: hld up towards rr: hdwy over 2f out: kpt on u.p fnl f: wnt 3rd nr fin: nt rch ldng pair* — **3/1**[2]
6154 **4** *nk* **Captain Carey**[4] 4685 4-9-5 **93** .... OlivierPeslier 11 — 96+
(M S Saunders) *chsd ldrs: rdn wl over 1f out: styd on one pce u.p fnl f: lost 3rd nr fin* — **5/1**[3]
5120 **5** *1* **Monsieur Joe (IRE)**[13] 4401 3-9-7 **98** .... HayleyTurner 1 — 96
(W R Swinburn) *stmbld as stalls opened and slowly away: sn bustled in rr: hdwy u.p and swtchd rt over 1f out: no imp fnl 150yds* — **13/2**
/00- **6** *1 1/2* **Soap Wars**[55] 3006 5-9-5 **93** .... UmbertoRispoli 7 — 87
(J A Osborne) *racd keenly: chsd ldrs: rdn over 1f out: wknd jst ins fnl f* — **40/1**
-100 **7** *2 3/4* **Fathom Five (IRE)**[36] 3629 6-9-5 **93** .... FMBerry 10 — 77
(C F Wall) *awkward leaving stalls: plld hrd: hld up in tch in midfield: rdn and effrt ent fnl 2f: wkng whn n.m.r ent fnl f* — **16/1**
1250 **8** *nk* **Fol Hollow (IRE)**[13] 4401 5-9-9 **97** .... JimCrowley 6 — 80
(D Nicholls) *led: rdn 1/2-way: hdd wl over 1f out: wknd qckly jst over 1f out* — **12/1**
4600 **9** *2* **Judge 'n Jury**[13] 4401 6-9-10 **98** .... (t) AntonMarcus 9 — 73
(R A Harris) *chsd ldrs on outer tl wknd u.p over 1f out* — **14/1**
4220 **10** *17* **We Have A Dream**[8] 4536 5-9-2 **90** .... LukeNolen 12 — —
(W R Muir) *in tch tl 1/2-way: rdn and lost tch 2f out: eased fnl f* — **16/1**

61.11 secs (0.61) **Going Correction** +0.225s/f (Good)
WFA 3 from 4yo+ 3lb — **10 Ran SP% 118.8**
Speed ratings (Par 109): **104,102,101,100,99 96,92,91,88,61**
toteswingers: 1&2 £9.60, 1&3 £2.40, 2&3 £11.30 CSF £40.36 CT £112.15 TOTE £3.10: £1.30, £3.00, £2.00; EX 36.90 Trifecta £128.50 Pool: £1,002.62 - 5.77 winning units..
Owner Dasmal,Rix,Barr,Morley,Penney **Bred** Juddmonte Farms Ltd **Trained** Six Mile Bottom, Cambs

FOCUS
A decent sprint handicap to kick things off and the action took place towards the stands' rail. The form is rated around the third and fourth.

NOTEBOOK
Prohibit travelled strongly on this return to 5f and coming through to win well under Soumillon, doing little in front and looking value for a bit more than the official winning margin. Third in the Stewards' Cup off 2lb lower a week ago, this was a well-deserved first turf win of the season for the 5-y-o, who will surely try his luck back in Pattern company before long. (op 7-2)
Golden Destiny(IRE) came back to life in the first-time blinkers, recovering from an early bump by the winner and getting to the front over 1f out, but in the end not being quite good enough. (op 12-1)
Secret Asset(IRE) didn't get the best of starts and was a bit lit-up under restraint. He tried to challenge inside the final 2f, but couldn't muster the necessary speed, just getting up for third late on. (op 7-2 tchd 4-1)
Captain Carey, fourth at Southwell just four days earlier, showed good speed more towards the centre of the track and boxed on well, just losing out on third. (tchd 11-2)
Monsieur Joe(IRE) ◆ is probably the one to take from the race. A generally progressive 3-y-o, he didn't get the best of starts and was under pressure before halfway. He ran on well inside the final furlong, though, and can be rated better than the bare form. (op 6-1)
Soap Wars ran creditably on this debut for a new yard. He will be of interest once dropped a few pounds.
Fathom Five(IRE) wasn't that well away and refused to settle under restraint.
Fol Hollow(IRE) teed it up for others. (op 9-1)

4815 TITANIC QUARTER SHERGAR CUP CLASSIC (H'CAP) — 1m 4f

2:45 (2:45) (Class 3) (0-95,93) 3-Y-O — **£14,769** (£5,172; £2,364; £1,845; £1,626; £1,182) **Stalls** High

Form — RPR
4140 **1** **Mister Angry (IRE)**[10] 4470 3-9-5 **84** .... AlanMunro 6 — 94
(M Johnston) *hld up in tch: rdn and effrt ent fnl 2f: drvn to ld 1f out: edgd lft u.p wl ins fnl f: jst lasted* — **16/1**
3204 **2** *shd* **Life And Soul (IRE)**[10] 4470 3-9-3 **82** .... YasunariIwata 5 — 92+
(Mrs A J Perrett) *hld up towards rr: hdwy on inner ent fnl 2f: swtchd lft over 1f out: gd hdwy u.p 1f out: chsd wnr fnl 100yds: str chal fnl 50yds: jst failed* — **11/2**[3]
2412 **3** *4* **Opera Gal (IRE)**[13] 4400 3-9-6 **85** .... UmbertoRispoli 12 — 89
(A M Balding) *led: rdn ent fnl 2f: hdd 1f out: wknd fnl 100yds* — **6/1**
-000 **4** *3/4* **Fareej (USA)**[10] 4470 3-9-8 **87** .... OlivierPeslier 2 — 89
(Saeed Bin Suroor) *chsd ldr: rdn and unable qck ent fnl 2f: outpcd u.p fnl f* — **7/1**
2210 **5** *hd* **Bowdler's Magic**[10] 4470 3-10-0 **93** .... PJSmullen 10 — 95
(M Johnston) *chsd ldrs: effrt u.p ent fnl 2f: outpcd ent fnl f: plugged on same pce fnl f* — **14/1**
2331 **6** *1/2* **Sing Sweetly**[18] 4229 3-9-6 **85** .... ChristopheSoumillon 11 — 86
(G A Butler) *hld up towards rr: hdwy wl over 2f out: chsd ldrs u.p wl over 1f out: outpcd ent fnl f: plugged on same pce after* — **6/1**
0161 **7** *3 1/2* **Christopher Wren (USA)**[37] 3594 3-9-8 **87** .... RichardHughes 4 — 83+
(J R Best) *t.k.h early: hld up in last trio: hdwy on outer 3f out: rdn and btn over 1f out: eased wl ins fnl f* — **5/1**[2]
1132 **8** *3 1/4* **Atlantic Tiger (IRE)**[29] 3878 3-9-8 **87** .... JimCrowley 1 — 77
(M Johnston) *dwlt: reminders sn after s and sn chsng ldrs tl wknd u.p ent fnl 2f* — **8/1**
1606 **9** *13* **Exceedthewildman**[72] 2479 3-9-0 **79** .... (p) LukeNolen 8 — 49
(J S Moore) *hld up in last trio: rdn and btn over 2f out: wl bhd fnl f* — **40/1**
1211 **10** *36* **Yashrid (USA)**[14] 4360 3-9-7 **86** .... HayleyTurner 7 — —
(M A Jarvis) *s.i.s: nvr gng wl in last: lost tch over 2f out: sn eased and virtually p.u fnl f: t.o* — **4/1**[1]

2m 33.81s (1.31) **Going Correction** +0.225s/f (Good) — **10 Ran SP% 119.2**
Speed ratings (Par 104): **104,103,101,100,100 100,97,95,87,63**
toteswingers: 1&2 £21.20, 1&3 £21.50, 2&3 £6.20 CSF £103.86 CT £602.64 TOTE £17.80: £4.00, £2.00, £2.20; EX 174.50 Trifecta £772.80 Pool: £1,357/65 - 1.30 winning units..
Owner The Originals **Bred** Darley **Trained** Middleham Moor, N Yorks
■ Stewards' Enquiry : Alan Munro caution: careless riding; two-day ban: used whip with excessive frequency without giving colt time to respond (Aug 21-22)

FOCUS
A good 3-y-o middle-distance handicap, made up of several progressive types. The form looks solid with the third to sixth close to their marks.

NOTEBOOK
Mister Angry(IRE) took over a furlong out, getting first run on the second, and just held on. Well held in a race contested by several of these at Goodwood last week, he was still 7lb higher than when winning at Ripon in July, but found a fair bit of improvement to take this. It remains to be seen how he will get on off a higher mark, although it's impossible to rule out further progress of one from this yard. Official explanation: trainer had no explanation regarding the apparent improvement in form (op 14-1)
Life And Soul(IRE) has run many good races in top three-year-old handicaps this term and he would have been a deserved winner. On the same mark as when fourth at Goodwood last week, he had to angle out to challenge, meantime the winner was going for home, and he couldn't peg him back. He shapes as though he may stay 1m6f, but a good test at 1m4f is probably ideal. (op 9-2)
Opera Gal(IRE) has been in good form and it was no surprise to see her put up another bold effort, keeping on once headed without being able to race on with the front pair. (op 5-1 tchd 7-1 in a place)
Fareej(USA), another from the Goodwood race, when a promising seventh, was backed beforehand and took a further step forward, keeping on well for fourth. He should soon be winning. (op 12-1)
Bowdler's Magic needs a stiffer test than this, therefore it was surprising he didn't try and get the lead. He travelled well into the straight but simply couldn't quicken when asked and it's possible the handicapper has him as present.
Sing Sweetly was backed beforehand, but her trainer expressed concerns over the ease in the going and she could never get into it, keeping on late without posing a serious threat. (op 9-1 tchd 10-1)
Christopher Wren(USA) managed to win despite the bit having slipped through his mouth at Newbury last time, so a 6lb rise seemed fair enough for this imposing sort. He was a bit disappointing all things considering, not settling as his rider would have liked and then failing to pick up in the straight. (tchd 11-2)
Atlantic Tiger(IRE) was never going like a winner, in the end dropping right out. (op 9-1)
Yashrid(USA), a C&D winner off 4lb lower latest, wasn't the best away and never went a yard. Something was presumably amiss. (op 9-2)

4816 LES AMBASSADEURS CLUB SHERGAR CUP MILE (H'CAP) — 1m (R)

3:20 (3:20) (Class 2) (0-100,100) 4-Y-O+ — **£14,769** (£5,172; £2,364; £1,845; £1,626; £1,182) **Stalls** High

Form — RPR
0-20 **1** **Set The Trend**[35] 3692 4-9-7 **94** .... LukeNolen 9 — 104+
(A M Balding) *chsd ldr tl rdn to ld over 1f out: styd on wl fnl f* — **9/2**[2]

Form	Pos	Dist	Horse / Comment	Jockey	RPR
1355	2	1 ½	**Vainglory (USA)**[15] 4321 6-9-5 **92** (D M Simcock) *chsd ldrs: effrt in inner and chsd wnr over 1f out: kpt on same pce u.p ins fnl f* **9/1**	FMBerry 12	99
2214	3	1 ½	**Benandonner (USA)**[11] 4459 7-9-3 **90** (Mike Murphy) *chsd ldrs: rdn and effrt ent fnl 2f: chsd clr ldng pair jst over 1f out: kpt on but nvr gng pce to threaten ldrs* **11/2**[3]	PJSmullen 7	94
0056	4	hd	**Good Again**[14] 4378 4-9-4 **91** (G A Butler) *hld up off the pce in midfield: rdn and hdwy on outer 2f out: drvn over 1f out: kpt on to press for 3rd ins fnl f: no threat to ldng pair* **9/1**	UmbertoRispoli 5	94+
3265	5	3 ½	**Vitznau (IRE)**[8] 4537 6-9-13 **100** (R Hannon) *hld up towards rr: rdn and hdwy on inner ent fnl 2f: no prog and btn ent fnl f: wknd fnl 150yds* **7/1**	OlivierPeslier 10	95
1560	6	1	**Tartan Gunna**[8] 4537 4-9-3 **90** (v) (M Johnston) *v.s.a: wl behnd: pushed lft and rdn jst over 2f out: kpt on fnl f: nvr trbld ldrs* **9/1**	Yasunarilwata 3	83
3040	7	½	**Marajaa (IRE)**[8] 4537 8-9-7 **94** (W J Musson) *stdd and dropped in bhd after s: hld up wl bhd in last pair: rdn 3f out: swtchd lft and hdwy 2f out: kpt on but nvr trbld ldrs* **10/1**	AlanMunro 4	86
033	8	nk	**Dunn'o (IRE)**[35] 3692 5-9-8 **95** (C G Cox) *led and styd wd tl crossed to ins rail after 3f: rdn and hdd over 1f out: wknd qckly ent fnl f* **7/2**[1]	JimCrowley 2	86
1060	9	1 ½	**Dubai Dynamo**[29] 3869 5-9-9 **96** (Mrs R A Carr) *in tch in midfield: rdn and unable qck ent fnl 2f: wknd over 1f out* **20/1**	AntonMarcus 11	83
4620	10	8	**Aspectus (IRE)**[8] 4537 7-9-12 **99** (J A Osborne) *chsd ldrs tl lost pl qckly jst over 2f out: wl bhd and eased ins fnl f* **16/1**	HayleyTurner 6	68

1m 42.01s (1.31) **Going Correction** +0.225s/f (Good) **10** Ran SP% **118.0**
Speed ratings (Par 109): **102,100,99,98,95 94,93,93,92,84**
toteswingers: 1&2 £11.20, 1&3 £4.30, 2&3 £13.20 CSF £45.30 CT £230.02 TOTE £5.00: £2.00, £3.90, £2.20; EX 46.40 Trifecta £145.50 Pool: £1,258.65 - 6.40 winning units..
Owner Corbett Stud **Bred** Old Suffolk Stud **Trained** Kingsclere, Hants

FOCUS
Not many got into this decent 1m handicap but the winner is progressive and the placed horses are rated to their turf best.

NOTEBOOK
Set The Trend tracked the leader and ran on well for pressure having taken over a furlong out. He was better than the bare form at Sandown last time and the bit of ease in the ground seemed to suit him well, so it would be no surprise to see him do well for the remainder of the campaign, with all the top handicaps at around 1m likely to come under consideration, including the Cambridgeshire. (op 4-1 tchd 5-1)
Vainglory(USA) ran right up to Epsom form from earlier in the season with the winner, challenging against the rail and keeping on without having the speed to win. He was below par over 1m2f last time and a soundly run 1m seems to suit best. (op 14-1)
Benandonner(USA), winner of this back in 2007, has been in good form and finished a fine fourth off this mark at Goodwood last week. It was no surprise to see him run well, keeping on for third, and he should remain competitive. (tchd 9-2 and 6-1 in a place)
Good Again is back on her last winning mark and she appreciated the return to 1m, keeping on to challenge for the places inside the final furlong. (op 10-1 tchd 8-1)
Vitznau(IRE) should have finished closer in a better race than this at Goodwood last week, so has to go down as slightly disappointing, considering he was off the same mark. (op 5-1)
Tartan Gunna lost all chance with a very slow start and his rider only asked him for an effort once they straightened for home, so all in all he didn't run too badly. (op 11-1 tchd 12-1)
Marajaa(IRE) never got into it. (op 15-2)
Dunn'o(IRE) stopped very quickly once headed and was obviously disappointing, considering he had run right up to form at Sandown latest. (op 5-1)

4817 ST HALLETT SHERGAR CUP STAYERS (H'CAP) 2m

3:55 (3:55) (Class 2) (0-100,93) 4-Y-O+

£14,769 (£5,172; £2,364; £1,845; £1,626; £1,182) **Stalls** High

Form	Pos	Dist	Horse / Comment	Jockey	RPR
1-00	1		**Bernie The Bolt (IRE)**[42] 3447 4-9-13 **92** (A M Balding) *stdd s: hld up in rr: hdwy 3f out: led and edgd rt over 1f out: clr fnl f: styd on wl: comf* **3/1**[1]	FMBerry 9	102+
4014	2	3 ¼	**Woolfall Treasure**[11] 4461 5-10-0 **93** (v) (G L Moore) *in tch in midfield: rdn and effrt over 2f out: chsd clr wnr 1f out: kpt on but no imp on wnr* **9/1**	ChristopheSoumillon 11	99
0011	3	2 ¾	**Colloquial**[15] 4320 9-9-13 **92** (v) (H Candy) *in tch: rdn to chse ldng pair ent fnl 2f: keeping on same pce whn edgd rt and n.m.r wl over 1f out: one pce and no ch w wnr fnl f* **8/1**	UmbertoRispoli 4	95
1114	4	hd	**Lady Eclair (IRE)**[10] 4467 4-10-0 **93** (M Johnston) *sn pushed up to chse ldr: rdn 3f out: chsd wnr and unable qck over 1f out: lost 2nd and btn 1f out: plugged on same pce and wl hld fnl f* **7/2**[2]	AntonMarcus 7	95
0056	5	3	**Becausewecan (USA)**[11] 4461 4-9-9 **88** (M Johnston) *led: clr 12f out tl over 5f out: rdn ent fnl 2f: hdd over 1f out: sn wknd* **9/1**	HayleyTurner 3	87
2020	6	nk	**Bow To No One (IRE)**[11] 4461 4-9-8 **87** (A P Jarvis) *hld up towards rr: rdn and effrt jst over 2f out: btn jst over 1f out: wknd fnl f* **11/2**[3]	RichardHughes 6	86
5646	7	14	**Benedict Spirit (IRE)**[41] 1798 5-9-1 **80** (p) (J L Flint) *chsd ldrs tl wknd qckly jst over 2f out: wl bhd fnl f* **33/1**	Yasunarilwata 10	62
6253	8	1 ½	**Hevelius**[15] 4320 5-9-11 **90** (W R Swinburn) *a in rr and nvr gng wl: rdn and lost tch wl over 2f out: eased ins fnl f* **11/2**[3]	AlanMunro 5	70
300/	9	11	**Secret Tune**[21] 4803 6-9-11 **90** (T R George) *chsd ldrs tl rdn and lost pl over 3f out: wl bhd and eased fr over 1f out: t.o* **25/1**	PJSmullen 1	57
300-	10	5	**Heron Bay**[21] 7018 6-9-13 **92** (p) (P Bowen) *a bhd: lost tch wl over 2f out: wl bhd and eased fnl f: t.o* **18/1**	LukeNolen 8	53

3m 30.86s (1.86) **Going Correction** +0.225s/f (Good) **10** Ran SP% **121.2**
Speed ratings (Par 109): **104,102,101,100,99 99,92,91,86,83**
toteswingers: 1&2 £10.10, 1&3 £7.30, 2&3 £11.60 CSF £32.34 CT £203.02 TOTE £4.30: £1.70, £3.20, £2.30; EX 38.10 Trifecta £784.40 Part won. Pool: £1,060.05 - 0.62 winning units..
Owner B P McGuire **Bred** John Munnelly **Trained** Kingsclere, Hants

FOCUS
This staying handicap was run at decent gallop and it was no surprise to see the winner come from off the pace. The form is rated around the placed horses.

NOTEBOOK
Bernie The Bolt(IRE) really motored inside the final 2f and coming right away having got to the front over a furlong out. He had been well held on both previous starts this season, albeit in very competitive races, and this represented a drop in grade, but there's no doubt he will return to the better races at some stage this season, with the Cesarewitch looking the likely long-term aim. (op 9-2)
Woolfall Treasure has been in good form, finishing fourth off 1lb higher at Goodwood, and he ran another solid race in defeat, staying on for a clear second-best. (op 8-1)
Colloquial has been brought right back to his best this season, winning the last twice, including over C&D, and it was no surprise to see him run well again off 3lb higher, just getting up for third. (op 13-2 tchd 6-1)
Lady Eclair(IRE), fourth over 2m5f at Goodwood, has been progressing all season, but she was made to look paceless on this drop in trip. She's clearly all about stamina and the Cesarewitch will presumably be the long-term aim. (tchd 10-3)
Becausewecan(USA) ensured they went a good tempo, but he has never won beyond 1m4f and again blatantly failed to stay. He's not on a bad mark now and a drop in trip is surely in order.
Bow To No One(IRE) again failed to reproduce the form that saw her finish second to Martyr over C&D two starts back. (op 6-1 tchd 13-2)
Hevelius was never travelling and possibly found the ground too slow. (op 7-1 tchd 15-2)

4818 MICHAEL PAGE INTERNATIONAL SHERGAR CUP CHALLENGE (H'CAP) 1m 4f

4:30 (4:30) (Class 3) (0-95,95) 4-Y-O+

£14,769 (£5,172; £2,364; £1,845; £1,626; £1,182) **Stalls** High

Form	Pos	Dist	Horse / Comment	Jockey	RPR
0101	1		**Yorgunnabelucky (USA)**[3] 4711 4-9-3 **87** 3ex (p) (M Johnston) *chsd ldr tl led after 2f: rdn and qcknd jst over 2f out: clr over 1f out: styd on wl: rdn out: comf* **9/1**	HayleyTurner 6	97
1215	2	2 ¼	**Emerging Artist (FR)**[11] 4461 4-9-10 **94** (M Johnston) *led for 2f: styd chsng ldrs: rdn to chse clr wnr 2f out: no imp after but kpt on for clr 2nd* **2/1**[1]	RichardHughes 8	100
1000	3	3	**Submariner (USA)**[11] 4455 4-9-5 **89** (M Johnston) *hld up towards rr: hdwy to chse ldr 4f out: drvn and chsd clr ldng pair over 1f out: no imp* **5/1**[2]	JimCrowley 12	90
2040	4	3 ¾	**Safari Sunup (IRE)**[22] 4100 5-9-8 **92** (P Winkworth) *t.k.h early: hld up in tch: effrt and barging match w rival wl over 2f out: swtchd rt and hdwy ent fnl f: styd on: nvr trbld ldrs* **16/1**	Yasunarilwata 2	87+
-044	5	¾	**Strategic Mount**[15] 4334 7-9-4 **88** (t) (P F I Cole) *stdd after s: hld up in rr: swtchd lft and effrt jst over 2f out: kpt on same pce after: n.d* **12/1**	AntonMarcus 9	82
5-54	6	shd	**Hatton Flight**[48] 3240 6-9-11 **95** (v[1]) (A M Balding) *t.k.h early: hld up in rr: stl towards rr and bhd a wall of horses over 2f out: swtchd lft and sme hdwy ent fnl f: n.d* **16/1**	FMBerry 11	89+
-231	7	1 ½	**Granston (IRE)**[78] 2276 9-9-4 **88** (J D Bethell) *t.k.h early: chsd ldrs: wnt 2nd 7f out tl over 3f out: wknd qckly ent fnl 2f* **16/1**	AlanMunro 1	79
0013	8	1	**Spirit Is Needed (IRE)**[3] 4711 4-9-9 **93** (b) (M Johnston) *hld up in midfield: gd hdwy on inner to chse wnr over 3f out tl over 1f out: sn btn: fdd fnl f* **12/1**	UmbertoRispoli 10	83
0300	9	1 ¾	**Macarthur**[42] 3447 6-9-10 **94** (Jane Chapple-Hyam) *t.k.h early: hld up in tch in midfield: rdn whn barging match w rival wl over 2f out: no ch after* **13/2**[3]	OlivierPeslier 4	81
-062	10	4 ½	**Seeking The Buck (USA)**[13] 4399 6-9-3 **87** (b) (R M Beckett) *hld up in last trio: rdn and effrt whn nt clr run over 2f out: sn wl bhd* **13/2**[3]	ChristopheSoumillon 3	67

2m 35.71s (3.21) **Going Correction** +0.225s/f (Good) **10** Ran SP% **119.7**
Speed ratings (Par 107): **98,96,94,92,91 91,90,89,88,85**
toteswingers: 1&2 £5.30, 1&3 £10.70, 2&3 £2.70 CSF £28.08 CT £105.21 TOTE £11.80: £2.90, £1.80, £1.70; EX 36.60 Trifecta £89.00 Pool: £1,223.48 - 10.17 winning units..
Owner Mrs S J Brookhouse **Bred** March Thoroughbreds **Trained** Middleham Moor, N Yorks
■ Stewards' Enquiry : Anton Marcus two-day ban: careless riding (Aug 21-22)

FOCUS
The outcome of this was dominated by the Mark Johnston-trained runners, with Yorgunnabelucky leading home a 1-2-3 for the yard. The form is a bit muddling, although more solid than the winner's previous success.

NOTEBOOK
Yorgunnabelucky(USA) led home a 1-2-3 for the Johnston-yard for the second successive time. Shouldering a 3lb penalty having recorded a career-best when upped to this distance for the first time at Pontefract just three days earlier, he got to the lead after a couple of furlongs and put the race to bed with a change of pace to extend his lead coming to the final 2f. He's clearly progressing at a rate of knots. (op 10-1)
Emerging Artist(FR) appeared not to stay 1m6f at Goodwood last time, but he was beaten by a quicker horse on this drop back in trip. It's possible a front-running ride would counter that, though, and he remains on the up (op 11-4 tchd 3-1 in places)
Submariner(USA) was suited by the step back up in trip, but still lacked a telling turn of pace. Like the runner-up he's still in his first season, so it's hard to rule out further progress. (op 6-1 tchd 9-2)
Safari Sunup(IRE) is on a decent mark, but he runs well without winning all too often, that again being the case here. (tchd 14-1 and 18-1 in a place)
Strategic Mount, winner of this in 2007 and 2008, has slowly been finding his form, but could never get into the race having been held up. (op 8-1)
Hatton Flight is really well weighted on old form but he didn't do enough in the first-time visor to suggest he's about to capitalise on it. (tchd 18-1)
Spirit Is Needed(IRE), the fourth and final Johnston runner, had finished second to the winner at Pontefract, but couldn't reproduce the form. (op 10-1)
Macarthur is dangerously well weighted, but he got into a barging match and failed to pick up. (op 7-1)
Seeking The Buck(USA) faded having briefly been denied a clear run. (tchd 7-1)

4819 DUBAI DUTY FREE SHERGAR CUP SPRINT (H'CAP) 6f

5:05 (5:06) (Class 2) (0-100,97) 3-Y-O

£14,769 (£5,172; £2,364; £1,845; £1,626; £1,182) **Stalls** Low

Form	Pos	Dist	Horse / Comment	Jockey	RPR
0621	1		**Gramercy (IRE)**[22] 4091 3-9-6 **92** (M L W Bell) *chsd ldng pair tl rdn to ld over 1f out: clr 1f out: r.o wl* **4/1**[2]	OlivierPeslier 6	105
5133	2	1 ¼	**Gene Autry (USA)**[9] 4509 3-9-11 **97** (R Hannon) *stdd s: hld up in last pair: hdwy ent fnl 2f: chsd wnr jst over 1f out: r.o wl but a hld by wnr* **9/4**[1]	FMBerry 1	106
40-4	3	3 ¾	**Capercaillie (USA)**[7] 4569 3-9-6 **92** (M Johnston) *chsd ldr tl over 1f out: edgd lft u.p and wl outpcd by ldng pair 1f out* **16/1**	AntonMarcus 10	89+
6033	4	3	**Star Rover (IRE)**[6] 4616 3-9-9 **95** (P D Evans) *in tch in midfield: rdn 1/2-way: outpcd and no ch w ldrs fr over 1f out* **16/1**	PJSmullen 4	82
5053	5	nk	**Bella Swan**[21] 4145 3-9-6 **92** (v[1]) (W R Swinburn) *hld up in last pair: switching rt and rdn over 1f out: no prog fnl f: nvr trbld ldrs* **15/2**	RichardHughes 2	78
1010	6	¾	**Fireback**[9] 4509 3-9-5 **91** (A M Balding) *dwlt: in tch in midfield: rdn and struggling ent fnl 2f: wl btn over 1f out* **5/1**[3]	AlanMunro 3	75
1114	7	4 ½	**Joe Packet**[8] 4551 3-9-4 **90** (J G Portman) *t.k.h: hld up in tch towards rr: hdwy 1/2-way: wknd qckly over 1f out* **10/1**	Yasunarilwata 12	60

5501 **8** ½ **Nosedive**[8] 4551 3-9-8 **94** .... LukeNolen 9 62
(R C Guest) *hld up in tch towards rr: rdn and struggling ent fnl 2f: wl bhd over 1f out* **14/1**

0410 **9** *nk* **Below Zero (IRE)**[31] 3791 3-9-10 **96** .... ChristopheSoumillon 5 63
(M Johnston) *led tl over 1f out: edgd rt u.p and wknd jst over 1f out: eased whn no ch ins fnl f* **14/1**

11-0 **10** *15* **Rum King (USA)**[7] 4574 3-9-10 **96** .... JimCrowley 8 15
(R Hannon) *in tch towards rr: rdn and dropped out qckly ent fnl 2f: eased fnl f: t.o* **16/1**

1m 14.31s (-0.09) **Going Correction** +0.225s/f (Good) **10** Ran SP% **119.3**
Speed ratings (Par 106): **109,107,102,98,97 96,90,90,89,69**
toteswingers: 1&2 £2.80, 1&3 £9.20, 2&3 £7.50 CSF £13.74 CT £135.00 TOTE £4.10: £1.70, £1.40, £4.40; EX 9.90 Trifecta £137.80 Pool: £1,692.38 - 9.08 winning units. Place 6 £59.60, Place 5 £42.17.
Owner M B Hawtin **Bred** Michael Mullins **Trained** Newmarket, Suffolk

FOCUS
It's likely this is strong form, with two progressive sorts putting distance between themselves and the remainder. The third is rated to form if taken at face value.

NOTEBOOK
Gramercy(IRE) has really got it together of late, winning impressively off 8lb lower at Haydock last time, and he took this in the style of a very useful sprinter. On this evidence he will be contesting a better class of race before long, and it would be no surprise to see him contest something like the Ayr Gold Cup next month. (op 7-2 tchd 9-2 in places)
Gene Autry(USA) is a model of consistency and ran another cracker at Goodwood the previous week. He had no trouble with the drop back to 6f, racing clear with the winner but not quite having his speed. (op 10-3 tchd 7-2 in places)
Capercaillie(USA) reappeared with a fair effort at Doncaster last week and she ran well off a mark of 92 on this handicap debut, showing plenty of speed and keeping on for third. (op 14-1)
Star Rover(IRE) has found his form again and this was another creditable effort in defeat. (op 14-1)
Bella Swan, sporting a first-time visor on this drop in trip, ran creditably without getting close enough to challenge. (op 8-1)
Fireback wasn't the best away and then lacked the pace to challenge. (op 11-2 tchd 6-1)
Joe Packet dropped right out in the end and looks in the grip of the handicapper now. (op 9-1)
T/Plt: £50.10 to a £1 stake. Pool: £115,018.91. 1,675.04 winning tickets. T/Qpdt: £9.40 to a £1 stake. Pool: £6,313.54. 491.90 winning tickets. SP

4187 AYR (L-H)
Saturday, August 7

OFFICIAL GOING: Good (good to firm in places; 9.1)
Rail on back straight moved out 4yds, home bend out 4m inside rail out 6m adding about 12m to distances on round course. Stands' side rail moved in 5m.
Wind: Light, half against Weather: Fine and sunny

4820 CHAMPAGNE G.H. MUMM CORDON ROUGE APPRENTICE H'CAP 6f
5:40 (5:41) (Class 5) (0-70,70) 3-Y-0+ **£2,590** (£770; £385; £192) **Stalls** Centre

Form RPR

0004 **1** **River Falcon**[19] 4192 10-9-9 **70** .... PaulNorton(5) 3 80
(J S Goldie) *sn outpcd and in rr: gd hdwy over 1f out: styd on strly to win last 75yds: won gng rt away* **2/1**[1]

0342 **2** 2¾ **Micky Mac (IRE)**[10] 4487 6-9-7 **66** .... NeilFarley(3) 2 67
(C J Teague) *chsd ldr: kpt on to take 2nd ins fnl f: no ch w wnr* **9/2**

3522 **3** 1¼ **Mandarin Spirit (IRE)**[1] 4799 10-9-6 **65** ....(b) MatthewLawson(3) 7 62
(Miss L A Perratt) *awkward to load: led and sn clr: edgd rt and hdd ins fnl f: fdd* **4/1**[3]

1243 **4** *7* **Monte Mayor One**[19] 4193 3-8-11 **62** .... ShaneBKelly(5) 5 36
(P Monteith) *gave problems in stalls: chsd ldrs: wknd 1f out* **11/4**[2]

0-00 **5** *1* **Broughtons Silk**[26] 3948 5-8-9 **51** oh6 .... GarryWhillans 4 22
(A C Whillans) *outpcd after 2f: in rr whn hung lft over 1f out* **7/1**

1m 12.58s (-1.02) **Going Correction** -0.15s/f (Firm)
WFA 3 from 5yo+ 4lb **5** Ran SP% **110.7**
Speed ratings (Par 103): **100,96,94,85,84**
toteswingers: 1&2 £4.60 CSF £11.23 TOTE £2.50: £1.20, £2.60; EX 12.40.
Owner F Brady & E Bruce **Bred** Manor Farm Packers Ltd **Trained** Uplawmoor, E Renfrews

FOCUS
A disappointing turnout for this 61-70 handicap but it was run at a strong pace. Not a race to be too positive about.

4821 E.B.F./CHAMPAGNE G.H. MUMM DE CRAMANT MAIDEN STKS 7f 50y
6:10 (6:12) (Class 5) 2-Y-0 **£3,238** (£963; £481; £240) **Stalls** High

Form RPR

1 **Dominator** 2-9-3 0 .... PJMcDonald 1 74+
(G A Swinbank) *dwlt: sn w ldr: styd on to ld jst ins fnl f: hld on wl* **9/4**[2]

6 **2** *nk* **Lady Amakhala**[66] 2654 2-8-7 0 .... PatrickDonaghy(5) 5 68
(G M Moore) *dwlt: in rr: hdwy on ins over 2f out: styd on wl fnl f: snatched 2nd nr line* **33/1**

032 **3** *hd* **Regal Kiss**[15] 4338 2-8-12 76 .... RoystonFfrench 3 68
(M Johnston) *led: hdd jst ins fnl f: kpt on same pce* **11/8**[1]

4 ½ **Spes Nostra** 2-8-12 0 .... DeanHeslop(5) 6 71
(T D Barron) *hld up towards rr: hdwy over 1f out: rn green and hung lft over 1f out: carried hd high and kpt on wl fnl 100yds* **25/1**

33 **5** *9* **Adlington**[11] 4447 2-9-3 0 .... TonyHamilton 2 47
(R A Fahey) *chsd ldrs: drvn over 2f out: lost pl over 1f out* **3/1**[3]

0 **6** *6* **Monel**[19] 4187 2-9-3 0 .... LNewman 4 31
(J S Goldie) *t.k.h: trckd ldrs: wknd 2f out* **33/1**

1m 32.75s (-0.65) **Going Correction** -0.15s/f (Firm) **6** Ran SP% **107.6**
Speed ratings (Par 94): **97,96,96,95,85 78**
toteswingers: 1&2 £8.80, 1&3 £1.40, 2&3 £3.30 CSF £55.06 TOTE £3.90: £2.80, £12.40; EX 62.40.
Owner S Rudolf **Bred** W S Farish **Trained** Melsonby, N Yorks

FOCUS
Probably just an ordinary maiden, run at a sound pace. The form looks somewhat fluid at this stage.

NOTEBOOK
Dominator still showed signs of greenness and there should be more to come. He looks the type to make up into a smart 3-y-o, although there should be races to be won with him before then. (tchd 13-8 and 5-2)
Lady Amakhala, who showed ability over 6f on her debut, stayed on strongly and a fillies' maiden over this trip, or even further, should be hers for the taking. She looks the type to continue to improve.
Regal Kiss, having her fourth start and from a yard going very well, appeared to have no excuses. A small maiden might come his way but a mark of 76 would appear to flatter slightly. (tchd 6-5 and 6-4)
Spes Nostra made a pleasing start to his career by doing some good late work. (op 16-1)
Adlington had shown ability on two starts before this but he disappointed. (tchd 7-2)

4822 CHAMPAGNE G.H. MUMM ROSE CLAIMING STKS 7f 50y
6:40 (6:54) (Class 5) 3-Y-0+ **£2,590** (£770; £385; £192) **Stalls** High

Form RPR

5002 **1** **Island Chief**[7] 4581 4-8-9 62 ....(p) AmyRyan(5) 1 61
(K A Ryan) *chsd ldr: chal over 2f out: led over 1f out: rdn and hung lft: hld on towards fin* **4/1**[3]

0-54 **2** ¾ **Kashimin (IRE)**[13] 4403 5-8-13 69 ....(p) PJMcDonald 6 58
(G A Swinbank) *led: qcknd over 3f out: hdd over 1f out: swtchd rt jst ins fnl f: rallied fnl 75yds: a hld* **13/8**[1]

0030 **3** *2* **Barraland**[7] 4605 5-8-9 51 .... JamesSullivan(3) 2 52
(J S Goldie) *trckd ldrs: t.k.h: effrt over 2f out: kpt on same pce appr fnl f* **8/1**

4310 **4** *nk* **Stellite**[7] 4585 10-8-8 68 .... GaryBartley(3) 5 50
(J S Goldie) *hld up: effrt 3f out: sn outpcd: kpt on fnl f: nvr a real threat* **7/4**[2]

0004 **5** 3¾ **Charity Fair**[14] 4374 3-7-10 44 .... VictorSantos(7) 4 38
(A Berry) *stdd s and racd in last: drvn 3f out: nvr on terms* **33/1**

1m 31.86s (-1.54) **Going Correction** -0.15s/f (Firm)
WFA 3 from 4yo+ 6lb **5** Ran SP% **108.5**
Speed ratings (Par 103): **102,101,98,98,94**
toteswingers: 1&2 £5.80 CSF £10.64 TOTE £5.70: £4.70, £1.10; EX 7.70.
Owner Mrs J Ryan **Bred** The C H F Partnership **Trained** Hambleton, N Yorks

FOCUS
A moderate claimer with is limited by the proximity of the third and fifth.

4823 T. FRENCH & SON H'CAP 1m 2f
7:10 (7:17) (Class 5) (0-75,73) 3-Y-0+ **£2,590** (£770; £385; £192) **Stalls** Low

Form RPR

021 **1** **Northside Prince (IRE)**[13] 4411 4-10-0 **73** .... PJMcDonald 11 82
(G A Swinbank) *led early: hld up in midfield on outer: effrt 3f out: r.o to ld over 1f out: styd on wl* **9/2**[2]

4606 **2** *2* **Shy Glance (USA)**[28] 3901 8-8-12 **62** ....(p) DeanHeslop(5) 2 67
(P Monteith) *trckd ldr: led 2f out: sn hdd: styd on same pce* **12/1**

-000 **3** ¾ **Real Desire**[7] 4582 4-8-4 **54** oh9 .... PatrickDonaghy(5) 12 57
(P Monteith) *hld up in rr: hdwy on outside over 2f out: styd on fnl f* **40/1**

2426 **4** *1* **Grand Diamond (IRE)**[26] 3950 6-9-1 **67** .... PaulNorton(7) 5 70+
(J S Goldie) *hld up in midfield: hdwy and swtchd ins 2f out: nt clr run and swtchd rt jst ins fnl f: fin wl* **13/2**[3]

5525 **5** ¾ **Talk Of Saafend (IRE)**[7] 4585 5-8-9 **61** .... ShaneBKelly(7) 9 61
(P Monteith) *mid-div: hdwy 3f out: edgd lft 1f out: one pce* **14/1**

2004 **6** *shd* **Jewelled Dagger (IRE)**[11] 3987 6-9-8 **70** .... GaryBartley(3) 10 69
(J S Goldie) *w ldrs: led 3f out: hdd over 1f out: one pce* **9/1**

31-5 **7** 1¾ **Cherry Bee**[11] 4450 3-9-2 **70** .... RoystonFfrench 6 66
(M Johnston) *sn led: hdd 3f out: wknd fnl f* **5/2**[1]

3030 **8** *nk* **Cool Baranca (GER)**[7] 4585 4-9-6 **70** .... LanceBetts(5) 1 65
(P Monteith) *chsd ldrs: one pce fnl 2f* **11/1**

0000 **9** *3* **Suburbia (USA)**[7] 4582 4-8-6 **54** oh9 ....(bt[1]) KellyHarrison(3) 7 43
(J Barclay) *in rr: nvr a factor* **100/1**

4246 **10** *1* **Classic Descent**[22] 4119 5-8-12 **60** ....(t) JamesSullivan(3) 3 47
(Mrs R A Carr) *s.i.s: a in rr* **8/1**

-540 **11** 3¾ **Goodison Park**[7] 4582 3-7-7 **54** oh5 ....(p) NeilFarley(7) 4 34
(A G Foster) *s.i.s: a in rr: bhd fnl 2f* **25/1**

3003 **12** *5* **Rosbertini**[9] 4514 4-8-13 **58** .... LNewman 8 28
(Miss L A Perratt) *chsd ldrs: wknd 2f out* **22/1**

2m 9.73s (-2.27) **Going Correction** -0.15s/f (Firm)
WFA 3 from 4yo+ 9lb **12** Ran SP% **115.5**
Speed ratings (Par 103): **103,101,100,100,99 99,97,97,95,94 91,87**
toteswingers: 1&2 £11.80, 1&3 £46.90, 2&3 £97.90 CSF £53.75 CT £1900.91 TOTE £3.80: £1.10, £5.30, £23.40; EX 62.10.
Owner S S Anderson **Bred** F Dunne **Trained** Melsonby, N Yorks

FOCUS
A competitive 56-75 handicap run at a sound pace and the form makes sense despite the proximity of the third.

4824 ALLURE BOUTIQUE IRVINE H'CAP 1m
7:40 (7:44) (Class 6) (0-65,65) 3-Y-0+ **£2,047** (£604; £302) **Stalls** Low

Form RPR

0225 **1** **Bed Fellow (IRE)**[14] 4374 6-9-3 **59** .... PatrickDonaghy(5) 11 66
(P Monteith) *mid-div: effrt whn nt clr run and swtchd outside over 2f out: edgd lft and led last 75yds: drvn rt out* **12/1**

010 **2** ½ **Red Skipper (IRE)**[9] 4514 5-9-0 **54** .... GaryBartley(3) 6 60
(N Wilson) *led: hdd wl ins fnl f: no ex* **6/1**[3]

4600 **3** 1½ **Whipma Whopma Gate (IRE)**[22] 4119 5-9-5 **63** ....(v) NeilFarley(7) 5 66
(D Carroll) *hld up in mid-div: effrt on ins 3f out: n.m.r over 1f out: styd on same pce ins fnl f* **9/2**[1]

06-6 **4** ¾ **Bourse (IRE)**[14] 4374 5-8-2 **46** oh1 .... NathanAlison(7) 14 47
(A G Foster) *s.i.s: in rr: hdwy on outer over 2f out: kpt on wl fnl f* **16/1**

6060 **5** 1¼ **Geojimali**[3] 4704 8-9-6 **60** .... JamesSullivan(3) 1 58
(J S Goldie) *hld up in rr: effrt 3f out: swtchd outside over 1f out: styd on wl ins fnl f* **9/2**[1]

0025 **6** *nse* **Shunkawakhan (IRE)**[9] 4515 7-9-1 **52** .... LNewman 8 50
(Miss L A Perratt) *trckd ldrs: effrt over 2f out: one pce whn n.m.r wl ins fnl f* **7/1**

2115 **7** ½ **Rascal In The Mix (USA)**[20] 4172 4-9-9 **65** ....(p) AmyRyan(5) 12 62
(R M Whitaker) *swtchd lft after s: hdwy over 3f out: chal over 1f out: edgd lft: wkng whn hmpd last 50yds* **5/1**[2]

4000 **8** 2½ **Anthemion (IRE)**[5] 4644 13-8-7 **47** .... KellyHarrison(3) 4 38
(Mrs J C McGregor) *chsd ldrs: wknd over 1f out* **40/1**

2250 **9** ½ **Hosanna**[9] 4515 4-9-0 **51** .... RoystonFfrench 2 41
(J Barclay) *chsd ldrs: wknd appr fnl f* **25/1**

3600 **10** 1¼ **Al Wasef (USA)**[5] 4644 5-9-1 **59** .... PaulNorton(7) 10 46
(J S Goldie) *s.i.s: a in rr* **16/1**

-014 **11** *49* **Only A Splash**[8] 4547 6-9-5 **56** .... PJMcDonald 13 —
(Mrs R A Carr) *chsd ldrs: lost pl over 2f out: bhd whn heavily eased over 1f out: tailed rt off* **9/1**

1m 40.84s (-2.96) **Going Correction** -0.15s/f (Firm)
WFA 3 from 4yo+ 7lb **11** Ran SP% **115.6**
Speed ratings (Par 101): **108,107,106,105,104 103,103,100,100,99 50**
toteswingers: 1&2 £10.30, 1&3 £13.70, 2&3 £5.50 CSF £80.92 CT £377.79 TOTE £12.60: £4.20, £3.20, £2.90; EX 111.60.
Owner The Cattlemen **Bred** Rathasker Stud **Trained** Rosewell, Midlothian
■ Stewards' Enquiry : Patrick Donaghy two-day ban: careless riding (Aug 21-22)

FOCUS
A run-of-the-mill 46-65 handicap which was run at an even pace. The form is limited with the runner-up the best guide.

4825 MJD & SONS SCAFFOLDING LTD H'CAP — 1m 7f
8:10 (8:10) (Class 6) (0-65,62) 4-Y-0+ — £2,047 (£604; £302) Stalls Low

Form				RPR
3551	1		**Ballade De La Mer**[9] 4511 4-8-7 48 (p) LNewman 9	55
			(A G Foster) *chsd ldrs: led over 1f out: hld on towards fin* 14/1	
-003	2	nk	**Harcas (IRE)**[25] 3989 8-8-7 48 (b) PJMcDonald 10	55
			(M Todhunter) *sn chsng ldrs: led 2f out: hdd over 1f out: kpt on wl: no ex towards fin* 12/1	
3321	3	½	**Petella**[35] 3669 4-8-6 50 KellyHarrison(3) 1	56+
			(C W Thornton) *racd in last: pushed along 7f out: hdwy on ins 3f out: edgd rt over 1f out: styd on wl* 4/1²	
1261	4	1¾	**Silent Lucidity (IRE)**[19] 4190 6-9-2 57 (p) RoystonFfrench 4	61
			(P D Niven) *chsd ldrs: dropped bk 7f out: hdwy to chse ldrs over 3f out: one pce fnl 2f* 5/2¹	
1206	5	shd	**Chocolate Caramel (USA)**[9] 4511 8-9-1 61 AmyRyan(5) 3	65
			(R A Fahey) *hld up in rr: effrt over 4f out: styd on fnl 2f: hmpd nr fin* 11/2³	
5330	6	3½	**Knock Three Times (IRE)**[25] 3989 4-8-1 45 JamesSullivan(3) 5	44
			(W Storey) *in tch: effrt 3f out: fdd fnl f* 14/1	
2456	7	1¼	**Planetarium**[10] 3989 5-9-1 61 (p) PatrickDonaghy(5) 7	58
			(P Monteith) *hld up in rr: hdwy 7f out: drvn 3f out: nvr a factor* 12/1	
005	8	3¼	**Kimberley Downs (USA)**[19] 4190 4-9-4 62 (p) GaryBartley(3) 2	55
			(N Wilson) *led: hdd 3f out: wknd over 1f out* 6/1	
0045	9	2	**Kyber**[10] 3989 9-7-11 45 NeilFarley(7) 6	36
			(J S Goldie) *mid-div: hdwy 10f out: rdn over 3f out: lost pl over 1f out* 16/1	

3m 22.31s (1.91) **Going Correction** -0.15s/f (Firm) — 9 Ran SP% 112.8
Speed ratings (Par 101): **88,87,87,86,86 84,84,82,81**
toteswingers: 1&2 £12.00, 1&3 £8.20, 2&3 £12.00 CSF £164.17 CT £798.15 TOTE £11.40: £3.30, £4.10, £1.20; EX 139.20.
Owner Highland Racing 6 **Bred** Southill Stud **Trained** Haddington, East Lothian

FOCUS
A wide-open 46-65 staying handicap in which the early pace was just steady. The form is muddling with the third the best guide.

4826 COACH HOUSE INN H'CAP — 5f
8:40 (8:41) (Class 6) (0-65,63) 3-Y-O — £2,047 (£604; £302) Stalls Centre

Form				RPR
0551	1		**Rio's Girl**[9] 4516 3-8-5 47 PaulQuinn 7	60
			(R M Whitaker) *mde all: shkn up over 1f out: edgd lft and rt: styd on strly to forge clr: readily* 11/4¹	
4003	2	3	**Midget**[13] 4406 3-8-10 59 NeilFarley(7) 5	61
			(D Carroll) *w ldrs: styd on same pce fnl f* 5/1²	
0304	3	1¼	**Weetentherty**[5] 4649 3-8-6 48 RoystonFfrench 8	46
			(J S Goldie) *prom: outpcd over 2f out: hdwy over 1f out: kpt on fnl f* 10/1	
5000	4	shd	**Hold On Tiger (IRE)**[37] 3599 3-9-3 59 PJMcDonald 2	56
			(N G Richards) *outpcd after 1f: hdwy 2f out: kpt on same pce fnl f* 13/2³	
1610	5	¾	**Ya Boy Sir (IRE)**[7] 4567 3-9-3 62 GaryBartley(3) 4	57
			(N Wilson) *chsd ldrs: kpt on same pce fnl f* 5/1²	
3006	6	hd	**Classlin**[19] 4194 3-8-3 48 KellyHarrison(3) 1	42
			(J S Goldie) *t.k.h far side: effrt 2f out: kpt on fnl f* 15/2	
-050	7	¾	**Areeg (IRE)**[5] 4651 3-7-10 45 VictorSantos(7) 9	36
			(A Berry) *s.i.s: t.k.h: hdwy over 2f out: nvr trbld ldrs* 33/1	
-626	8	nk	**Melundy**[35] 3663 3-9-4 63 JamesSullivan(3) 10	53
			(Mrs L Stubbs) *towards rr: hdwy stands' side over 2f out: hung lft: nvr trbld ldrs* 11/1	
0206	9	nse	**Taborcillo**[20] 4169 3-9-1 62 DeanHeslop(5) 6	52
			(T D Barron) *chsd ldrs: wkng whn n.m.r jst ins fnl f* 11/1	

59.23 secs (-0.87) **Going Correction** -0.15s/f (Firm) — 9 Ran SP% 113.8
Speed ratings (Par 98): **100,95,93,93,91 91,90,89,89**
toteswingers: 1&2 £3.20, 1&3 £6.30, 2&3 £5.00 CSF £15.98 CT £117.30 TOTE £3.40: £1.10, £2.90, £4.70; EX 13.30 Place 6 £264.95, Place 5 £149.22.
Owner Tracey Gaunt & David Gibbons **Bred** Hellwood Stud Farm **Trained** Scarcroft, W Yorks

FOCUS
A run-of-the-mill 46-65 handicap rated through the second to her latest mark.
T/Plt: £358.50 to a £1 stake. Pool: £47,002.72. 95.69 winning tickets. T/Qpdt: £40.20 to a £1 stake. Pool: £5,367.37. 98.75 winning tickets. WG

4781 HAYDOCK (L-H)
Saturday, August 7

OFFICIAL GOING: 5f & 6f - good to soft; 1m+ - soft (good to soft in places; sprint 7.7; round 6.2)
Inner sprint track used. Other races on old outer bend out of back straight and rail realignment increased distances by about 10yds.
Wind: Light, half-against Weather: Cloudy, light shower in afternoon

4827 RACING UK H'CAP — 1m 6f
1:50 (1:50) (Class 3) (0-95,86) 3-Y-O — £8,095 (£2,408; £1,203; £601) Stalls Low

Form				RPR
551	1		**Zigato**[17] 4258 3-9-3 82 WilliamBuick 1	92+
			(J H M Gosden) *hld up: pushed along over 4f out: prog u.p to take 2nd 2f out: styd on dourly to move upsides wl ins fnl f: led towards fin* 5/1³	
1321	2	½	**Comedy Act**[22] 4092 3-9-3 82 PhillipMakin 5	91+
			(Sir Mark Prescott) *led: kicked abt 4 l clr 3f out: rdn 2f out: jnd whn u.p wl ins fnl f: hdd towards fin* 7/4²	
1	3	5	**Shubaat**[55] 2994 3-9-7 86 NeilCallan 3	88
			(M A Jarvis) *chsd ldr: pushed along over 4f out: hrd at work whn lost 2nd 2f out: edgd rt whn one pce ins fnl f* 5/4¹	
6224	4	shd	**Bombadero (IRE)**[47] 3256 3-9-1 80 TedDurcan 2	82
			(J L Dunlop) *hld up bhd ldrs: pushed along over 3f out: outpcd over 2f out: kpt on same pce and no imp fr over 1f out* 11/1	
	5	45	**Time Square (FR)**[70] 3-9-3 82 AdamKirby 4	21
			(A W Carroll) *ref to settle: chsd ldrs: dropped to rr after 6f: niggled along 5f out: lost tch over 3f out: eased whn t.o over 1f out* 28/1	

3m 9.17s (7.97) **Going Correction** +0.525s/f (Yiel) — 5 Ran SP% 109.3
Speed ratings (Par 104): **98,97,94,94,69**
CSF £14.00 TOTE £5.90: £2.60, £1.40; EX 11.60.
Owner Lady Bamford & Ms Rachel D S Hood **Bred** Lady Bamford **Trained** Newmarket, Suffolk

FOCUS
The ground was described as good to soft on the inner sprint track and soft, good to soft in places on the round course. But jockeys returning after the first described the ground as gluey, sticky, and very hard work. A 3yo handicap flattered by its billing as a class 3 contest, with the top weight rated just 86, 9lb below the race ceiling. That said, it featured some unexposed horses on the up and the fourth sets the level.

NOTEBOOK
Zigato had run his first three races on Polytrack, but he's a half-brother to Sariska and Gull Wing, who have both appreciated give on turf, and that, coupled with the step up in trip – his pedigree is certainly not light on stamina – saw him improve for this different test. He kept galloping on strongly in the closing stages and eventually got on top inside the last. Still babyish according to connections, there's plenty more to come, and while the Melrose will likely come too soon, the Mallard Handicap at Doncaster should suit him well, and that apparently is his likely target. (tchd 9-2 and 11-2)
Comedy Act had the advantage of being proven over this trip and was given a positive ride. Too positive in fact, for despite turning into the straight apparently going well and with the field well strung out, in this holding ground he began to tire inside the final 2f and was in the end reeled in by Zigato. (op 2-1 tchd 9-4)
Shubaat, easy winner of a 1m4f maiden at Doncaster on his debut, was burdened with top weight on his handicap debut. He might have finished a bit closer had he been ridden more conservatively, like the winner, and he remains unexposed and open to improvement. (op 6-5 tchd 11-10)
Bombadero(IRE) did not improve for the combination of an extra 2f on softer ground. He's beginning to look exposed, but surely a modest maiden can be found for him somewhere. (op 10-1 tchd 12-1)
Time Square(FR), formerly trained in France, where he won twice in the provinces, was stepping up 4f in distance on his debut for his new stable. He's certainly bred to stay well, but gave himself no chance of seeing out this contest by racing keenly through the early part of the race. Official explanation: jockey said colt ran too freely (tchd 33-1)

4828 WKD H'CAP — 1m 30y
2:20 (2:26) (Class 2) (0-100,98) 3-Y-O+ — £11,333 (£3,372; £1,685; £841) Stalls Low

Form				RPR
-240	1		**Our Joe Mac (IRE)**[63] 2742 3-9-0 91 TonyHamilton 10	99
			(R A Fahey) *midfield: hdwy over 3f out: led under 2f out: a hrd pressed: styd on dourly towards fin* 5/1¹	
5151	2	nk	**Silver Rime (FR)**[14] 4370 5-9-2 86 LNewman 4	94
			(Miss L A Perratt) *trckd ldrs: chal fr under 2f out: upsides wnr over 1f out: hld fnl stride* 28/1	
5-03	3	¾	**What's Up Pussycat (IRE)**[21] 4137 4-9-9 93 JamieSpencer 3	99+
			(D M Simcock) *hld up: rdn and hdwy over 2f out: styd on ins fnl f: gng on at fin* 11/1	
-010	4	nk	**Tiger Reigns**[52] 3069 4-10-0 98 PhillipMakin 14	103
			(M Dods) *led for 1f: remained prom and racd keenly: rdn to chal 2f out: stl ev ch ins fnl f: nt qckn and hld towards fin* 20/1	
-065	5	nk	**Desert Creek (IRE)**[35] 3692 4-9-5 89 RyanMoore 13	94
			(Sir Michael Stoute) *led after 1f: hdd under 2f out: kpt on u.p and stl chalng ins fnl f: no ex fnl strides* 5/1¹	
0453	6	shd	**Jordaura**[15] 4322 4-9-0 84 NeilCallan 8	88
			(J R Holt) *midfield: hdwy u.p 2f out: chsd ldrs and edgd rt ins fnl f: styd on: nt quite get to ldrs* 25/1	
31	7	2¼	**Autumn Riches**[13] 4414 3-8-6 83 RoystonFfrench 1	81
			(M Johnston) *sn w ldr: rdn 2f out: nt qckn wl over 1f out: styd on same pce after* 14/1	
2000	8	1	**Marvo**[22] 4112 6-8-9 79 oh2 DarryllHolland 7	76
			(M H Tompkins) *trckd ldrs: nt qckn u.p over 2f out: one pce fr over 1f out* 40/1	
402	9	¾	**Smokey Oakey (IRE)**[7] 4596 6-9-5 94 AshleyMorgan(5) 6	89
			(M H Tompkins) *midfield: rdn over 2f out: kpt on same pce and no imp on ldrs fr over 1f out* 14/1	
6620	10	shd	**Collateral Damage (IRE)**[35] 3692 7-9-7 91 (t) GrahamGibbons 16	86
			(T D Easterby) *hld up: rdn and hdwy over 2f out: kpt on u.p ins fnl f: nt trble ldrs* 14/1	
0132	11	1¾	**Moody Tunes**[13] 4403 7-8-9 79 AndrewElliott 9	70
			(J R Weymes) *chsd ldrs: lost pl 4f out: u.p and n.d after* 40/1	
-153	12	7	**Bawaardi (IRE)**[14] 4394 4-8-5 80 LeeTopliss(5) 12	55
			(R A Fahey) *midfield: hdwy to chse ldrs 3f out: wknd over 1f out* 18/1	
3240	13	¾	**Moheebb (IRE)**[21] 4152 6-8-12 82 (b) PJMcDonald 2	55
			(Mrs R A Carr) *towards rr: pushed along over 3f out: nvr on terms* 8/1²	
-600	14	2¾	**Pleasant Day (IRE)**[30] 3824 3-9-5 96 (b) WilliamBuick 15	62
			(B J Meehan) *hld up: u.p 3f out: hung lft whn no imp over 1f out: eased whn btn ins fnl f* 9/1³	
4060	15	14	**Wigram's Turn (USA)**[7] 4603 5-8-11 84 JamesSullivan(3) 17	19
			(M W Easterby) *chsd ldrs tl rdn and wknd qckly over 2f out* 50/1	
0-00	16	¾	**Makaamen**[91] 1900 4-9-6 90 TadhgO'Shea 11	23
			(B W Hills) *hld up: rdn and hung lft fr over 3f out: effrt over 2f out: no imp on ldrs: wknd over 1f out* 12/1	
0060	17	5	**Karaka Jack**[29] 3867 3-8-6 83 FrannyNorton 5	—
			(M Johnston) *squeezed out jst after s: sn struggling in rr: nvr on terms* 14/1	

1m 49.95s (5.25) **Going Correction** +0.525s/f (Yiel)
WFA 3 from 4yo+ 7lb — 17 Ran SP% 121.3
Speed ratings (Par 109): **94,93,92,92,92 92,90,89,88,88 86,79,78,75,61 61,56**
toteswingers:1&2:£18.60, 1&3:£6.30, 2&3:£20.50 CSF £160.16 CT £1539.59 TOTE £5.30: £1.50, £6.20, £2.80, £6.80; EX 185.20 Trifecta £1298.60 Part won. Pool: £1,754.94 - 0.90 winning units..
Owner A Long **Bred** Castlefarm Stud **Trained** Musley Bank, N Yorks

FOCUS
A competitive handicap in which they came centre to stands' side in the straight. The form looks solid and it was won by one of the less-exposed runners in the line-up with the second and fourth setting the level.

NOTEBOOK
Our Joe Mac(IRE) ◆, one of only four 3yos in the field, had been off the track for a couple of months waiting for easier ground, and back to 1m, he proved himself a well-handicapped gelding. He'd run a blinder from the worst draw at the Chester May meeting but found the ground too quick and trip too far the last twice, and these conditions proved far more to his liking. The winner gives the impression that there's more to come from him, and while the ground remains like this, he's one to keep on-side. He could go to York for a 1m handicap, providing the ground is suitable. (tchd 11-2)
Silver Rime(FR) came here on the top of his game following a career-best effort according to RPRs at Newcastle last time. He loves to get his toe in and got the trip well. (op 20-1)
What's Up Pussycat(IRE), who has plenty of form in testing ground in Ireland to her name, came through from the back of the field to be nearest at the finish. She's another who gives the form a good look, as she too recorded a career-high RPR last time out. (op 10-1 tchd 12-1)
Tiger Reigns, drawn on the wrong side in the Hunt Cup last time out, returned to form on his favoured surface. He needs to find some further improvement to defy his current mark, though. (op 18-1 tchd 16-1 and 25-1 in places)

Desert Creek(IRE) ◆, given a prominent ride, settled better than in recent starts, but he quickened things up plenty soon enough in these testing conditions and didn't quite get home. He handled the ground well and remains on a mark he can win off. (op 6-1 tchd 13-2)

Jordaura seems to go on any ground and rarely runs a bad race. As a result, the handicapper seems to know where he is with him. (op 16-1)

Autumn Riches, the least exposed horse in the race, was racing on very different ground to that which he'd encountered in his previous two starts, but he is by Pivotal so there was reason to believe he'd handle it. However, having been towards the front end for a long way, he began to struggle with 2f to run. (op 11-1)

4829 TOTESPORT.COM ROSE OF LANCASTER STKS (GROUP 3) 1m 2f 95y

2:50 (2:52) (Class 1) 3-Y-0+

£32,358 (£12,266; £6,138; £3,060; £1,533; £769) **Stalls** High

Form				RPR
0063	**1**		**Poet**[21] 4139 5-9-3 105 ... AdamKirby 4 (C G Cox) *a.p: led over 3f out: rdn under 2f out: r.o gamely and on top fnl 100yds* **7/1**	118
-001	**2**	*1 ¾*	**Class Is Class (IRE)**[68] 2593 4-9-3 111 ...(v) RyanMoore 6 (Sir Michael Stoute) *in tch: effrt over 2f out: sn chsd wnr: ev ch u.p over 1f out: no ex fnl 100yds* **6/1³**	115
212	**3**	*6*	**Distant Memories (IRE)**[21] 4139 4-9-3 109 ... JamieSpencer 2 (T P Tate) *trckd ldrs: rdn over 2f out: no further imp and no ch w front pair fr over 1f out* **4/1¹**	103
-115	**4**	*3 ¼*	**Fallen Idol**[55] 3016 3-8-8 106 ... WilliamBuick 8 (J H M Gosden) *hld up in rr: pushed along and sme hdwy over 2f out: nvr able to chal: n.d over 1f out* **6/1³**	97
-214	**5**	*6*	**Les Fazzani (IRE)**[35] 3671 6-9-0 108 ... TonyHamilton 7 (K A Ryan) *led: hdd over 3f out: rdn over 2f out: wknd over 1f out* **9/2²**	83
6240	**6**	*4 ½*	**Icon Dream (IRE)**[50] 3145 3-8-8 104 ... DarryllHolland 9 (David Wachman, Ire) *hld up: pushed along 3f out: nvr on terms w ldrs* **14/1**	77
-011	**7**	*38*	**Rio De La Plata (USA)**[13] 4412 5-9-3 114 ... TedDurcan 1 (Saeed Bin Suroor) *hld up: rdn over 2f out: no imp: wl btn over 1f out: sn eased: t.o* **7/1**	5
1115	**8**	*4 ½*	**Green Moon (IRE)**[50] 3142 3-8-8 106 ... NeilCallan 5 (H J L Dunlop) *towards rr: niggled along 5f out: lft bhd over 3f out: eased over 1f out: t.o* **6/1³**	—

2m 17.31s (1.31) **Going Correction** +0.525s/f (Yiel)
WFA 3 from 4yo+ 9lb **8 Ran SP% 112.7**
Speed ratings (Par 113): **115,113,108,106,101 97,67,63**
toteswingers:1&2:£9.90, 1&3:£3.00, 2&3:£4.60 CSF £46.81 TOTE £7.30: £2.40, £2.20, £1.40; EX 54.00 Trifecta £200.20 Pool: £1,437.25 - 5.31 winning units..
Owner H E Sheikh Sultan Bin Khalifa Al Nahyan **Bred** Meon Valley Stud **Trained** Lambourn, Berks

FOCUS
Only 10lb separated the runners on adjusted ratings, but they finished well strung out as a result of going a really good gallop in very testing conditions, which few handled. The form is rated around the first two.

NOTEBOOK
Poet, who raced in second for most of the race, showed how much he relishes these testing conditions by holding off the more patiently ridden Class Is Class to record his second win at this level. He'd hinted at a return to form at Newbury last time when the ground was good, and in these far more suitable conditions he returned to something like his best form, comprehensively reversing form with Distant Memories in the process. The winner holds an entry for another 1m2f Group 3 at Leopardstown next month, and that would make more appeal than taking on the big guns in the Irish Champion. (op 9-1)

Class Is Class(IRE), off the track since winning a Listed race at Goodwood in May, looked to be given the right ride as the pace was pretty hot up front, but having been brought with his chance a furlong out, the winner found that bit extra. He clearly acts perfectly well in these conditions, but Poet revels in them. (tchd 11-2 and 13-2)

Distant Memories(IRE), whose record is that of steady progression, has a good record with give, but he didn't improve for the switch from good ground at Newbury, where he finished in front of today's winner. There's a Listed race to be won with him this season. (op 9-2)

Fallen Idol looked as though he might be suited by a step up to this sort of trip when running on late over 1m in France last time but, having been given a patient ride, he couldn't make any headway in the final 2f. (op 7-1)

Les Fazzani(IRE) made it a real test in the ground, setting a strong gallop in front, but the pace she went wasn't unsustainable as her nearest pursuer was the winner. She'll be more effective back against her own sex. (op 4-1)

Icon Dream(IRE) looked an interesting contender back on soft ground, but he failed to get into the race at all having been held up. He probably needs further. (tchd 16-1)

Rio De La Plata(USA) stumbled on the turn out of the back straight, but the combination of a step up in trip in really testing ground is what got him beaten. Official explanation: trainer's rep said horse was unsuited by the soft (good to soft places) ground (op 15-2 tchd 8-1)

Green Moon(IRE), hampered on the turn out of the back straight, was beaten with half a mile to run, and this soft ground didn't seem to suit him at all. (op 11-2 tchd 13-2)

4830 TOTESCOOP6 STKS (HERITAGE H'CAP) 1m 2f 95y

3:25 (3:26) (Class 2) (0-105,103) 3-Y-0+

£40,501 (£12,129; £6,064; £3,035; £1,514; £760) **Stalls** High

Form				RPR
3305	**1**		**Hot Prospect**[30] 3824 3-9-1 103 ... NeilCallan 10 (M A Jarvis) *midfield: smooth hdwy over 3f out: led gng wl jst over 1f out: shkn up to go clr ins fnl f: comf* **5/1²**	116+
0302	**2**	*1 ¾*	**Magaling (IRE)**[28] 3920 4-8-9 88 ... GrahamGibbons 6 (M W Easterby) *trckd ldrs: rdn to ld 2f out: hdd and edgd rt u.p jst over 1f out: styd on but no ch w wnr after* **10/1³**	93
0316	**3**	*shd*	**The Galloping Shoe**[7] 4570 5-8-4 83 ow1 ...(t) RoystonFfrench 1 (A C Whillans) *midfield: hdwy over 3f out: rdn to chse ldrs over 1f out: styd on u.p to chal for 2nd pl ins fnl f: no ch w wnr* **22/1**	88
0301	**4**	*4 ½*	**Porgy**[15] 4348 5-8-11 90 ... TonyHamilton 7 (R A Fahey) *sn led: rdn and hdd 2f out: styd on same pce u.p after* **10/1³**	86
500-	**5**	*nk*	**Pires**[253] 7567 6-8-10 89 ... WilliamBuick 15 (A J Martin, Ire) *rrd and missed break: in rr: stdy hdwy fr over 2f out: styd on u.p to chse ldrs over 1f out: one pce and no further imp fnl 110yds* **11/1**	85
2411	**6**	*2*	**Brushing**[45] 3319 4-8-7 86 ... DarryllHolland 17 (M H Tompkins) *in tch: racd wd on bk st: effrt and hdwy 3f out: sn chsd ldrs: one pce fr over 1f out* **10/1³**	78
1122	**7**	*2 ½*	**Breakheart (IRE)**[15] 4321 3-8-3 91 ... FrannyNorton 16 (A M Balding) *broke wl: trckd ldrs: rdn and chalng 2f out: wknd ins fnl f* **9/2¹**	78
0-60	**8**	*2*	**Plaisterer**[63] 2747 5-8-13 92 ... JackMitchell 4 (C F Wall) *racd keenly: towards rr: pushed along 5f out: kpt on steadily fnl f: nvr on terms to threaten* **10/1³**	76
1030	**9**	*1 ½*	**Charlie Cool**[8] 4537 7-8-13 95 ...(p) JamesSullivan(3) 3 (Mrs R A Carr) *hld up in midfield: rdn over 2f out: no imp on ldrs over 1f out* **16/1**	76
0306	**10**	*2 ½*	**Dream Lodge (IRE)**[14] 4390 6-9-5 103 ... LeeTopliss(5) 5 (R A Fahey) *towards rr: niggled along 5f out: u.p and gng nowhere over 3f out: nvr on terms* **20/1**	79
0000	**11**	*2 ¼*	**Spectait**[8] 4537 8-8-8 87 ... RichardKingscote 9 (Jonjo O'Neill) *late removal of blindfold and missed break: in rr: rdn over 3f out: no imp on ldrs and no bttr than midfield wl over 1f out: wl btn ins fnl f* **33/1**	59
030	**12**	*9*	**Persian Peril**[21] 4152 6-8-1 80 ... AndrewElliott 2 (G A Swinbank) *s.i.s: racd keenly: hdwy to go prom after 1f: rdn over 2f out: sn wknd* **12/1**	35
3110	**13**	*1 ½*	**Desert Kiss**[28] 3921 5-8-10 94 ... JohnFahy(5) 14 (W R Swinburn) *prom: rdn over 2f out: sn wknd* **16/1**	46
1-53	**14**	*3 ½*	**Take It To The Max**[85] 2070 3-8-4 92 ... PJMcDonald 12 (G M Moore) *in tch tl wknd over 3f out* **14/1**	37
0	**15**	*hd*	**Prince Apollo**[132] 1031 5-8-13 92 ... JamieSpencer 8 (Ian Williams) *prom: racd wd on bk st: wknd qckly over 3f out* **33/1**	37

2m 19.61s (3.61) **Going Correction** +0.525s/f (Yiel)
WFA 3 from 4yo+ 9lb **15 Ran SP% 120.7**
Speed ratings (Par 109): **106,104,104,100,100 99,97,95,94,92 90,83,82,79,79**
toteswingers:1&2:£38.10, 1&3:£81.00, 2&3:£101.20 CSF £51.50 CT £1013.44 TOTE £5.90: £2.40, £3.50, £9.30; EX 56.10 Trifecta £1863.40 Pool: £33,491.10 - 13.30 winning units..
Owner A D Spence **Bred** Highclere Stud & Hmh Management **Trained** Newmarket, Suffolk
■ Stewards' Enquiry : Lee Topliss three-day ban: used whip when out of contention and gelding showed no response (Aug 21-23)

FOCUS
Three of the previous six winners of this heritage handicap had been 3-y-os, and two of the Classic generation's three representatives this time headed the betting. The winner impressed on the ground and the placed horses set the level.

NOTEBOOK
Hot Prospect, a Derby also-ran earlier in the year, travelled strongly throughout, cruised through to lead a furlong out and, shaken up, quickened clear to win with plenty in hand. It was a great effort off a mark of 103 and clearly the softer ground made all the difference. He deserves to return to Pattern company now, but one would imagine that connections will be careful to ensure that he gets his ground in future. (op 9-2, tchd 11-2 in places)

Magaling(IRE) was trying a new trip having finished well over 1m at York last time. He got it well and, together with the third, finished clear of the rest. He was simply unlucky to bump into a very well-handicapped 3-y-o, and connections will be hoping the handicapper doesn't react too harshly. (op 11-1)

The Galloping Shoe perhaps had a breathing problem last time as the tongue-tie made an appearance here, and he ran a career-best in defeat. Another rise in the weights isn't going to help him either. (op 20-1)

Porgy, who made much of the running, only won a claimer last time, but he likes this sort of ground and kept galloping away. His mark doesn't make things easy, though. (op 12-1)

Pires ran well considering he'd been off the track since November. He has prospects off his current mark, but the market is the best guide with horses from his trainer's yard. Official explanation: jockey said gelding reared at start (op 8-1)

Brushing, who along with Prince Apollo, raced wide through the early stages, challenged up the stands' rail in the straight. She weakened inside the final furlong, though, and may have just found the ground a bit too testing over this trip. (op 14-1)

Breakheart(IRE) was expected to appreciate this ground, but he didn't get home. Perhaps the trip in these conditions was too much, or perhaps he actually wants it faster after all. (tchd 5-1 in places)

Plaisterer, returning from a two-month break, likes a bit of give in the ground but perhaps not this tacky or holding. (op 12-1)

Spectait ran a better race than the bare form suggests, as the blindfold came off very late and he missed the break badly. Official explanation: jockey said gelding missed the break

4831 ABACUS SECURITIES NURSERY 5f

4:00 (4:01) (Class 2) 2-Y-O

£8,095 (£2,408; £1,203; £601) **Stalls** Centre

Form				RPR
113	**1**		**Dingle View (IRE)**[14] 4388 2-8-10 85 ... CathyGannon 8 (P D Evans) *chsd ldrs: rdn to ld wl over 1f out: r.o wl: pushed out towards fin* **9/2³**	90
2422	**2**	*1 ¼*	**Boundaries**[7] 4599 2-7-11 75 oh1 ow2 ... JamesSullivan(3) 6 (T D Easterby) *in tch: rdn over 1f out: styd on u.p ins fnl f: wnt 2nd fnl 100yds: nt pce to rch wnr* **15/2**	76
6001	**3**	*1 ½*	**Roman Dancer (IRE)**[26] 3959 2-8-3 78 ow1 ... TadhgO'Shea 1 (J Gallagher) *hld up: hdwy over 2f out: rdn to chal over 1f out: kpt on same pce fnl 100yds* **7/1**	73
6130	**4**	*hd*	**Jamesway (IRE)**[21] 4138 2-9-3 92 ... TonyHamilton 4 (R A Fahey) *plld hrd in rr: rdn and hdwy over 1f out: styd on fnl 100yds: nt pce to chal* **3/1²**	88+
215	**5**	*hd*	**Ballinargh Girl (IRE)**[7] 4592 2-8-1 76 ow2 ... AndrewElliott 2 (R D Wylie) *led: hdd wl over 1f out: sn rdn: stl ch ent fnl f: fdd fnl 75yds* **11/4¹**	70
6140	**6**	*5*	**Sacrosanctus**[37] 3596 2-8-3 78 ... FrannyNorton 3 (J A Glover) *in tch: rdn and wknd over 1f out* **20/1**	54
1620	**7**	*8*	**Lady Brookie**[14] 4388 2-7-12 73 oh2 ... JamieMackay 9 (Peter Grayson) *missed break: in rr: rdn over 2f out: hung lft whn no imp over 1f out: nvr on terms* **33/1**	20
1100	**8**	*5*	**Boundless Spirit**[21] 4138 2-8-11 86 ... RoystonFfrench 7 (B Smart) *racd keenly: prom: rdn and wknd over 1f out* **8/1**	15

63.07 secs (2.07) **Going Correction** +0.425s/f (Yiel) **8 Ran SP% 112.9**
Speed ratings (Par 100): **100,98,95,95,94 86,74,66**
toteswingers:1&2:£7.80, 1&3:£4.70, 2&3:£9.30 CSF £36.78 CT £232.56 TOTE £5.00: £1.50, £2.20, £2.00; EX 34.60.
Owner Mrs I M Folkes **Bred** Robert Berns **Trained** Pandy, Monmouths

FOCUS
They went a decent pace up front here.

NOTEBOOK
Dingle View(IRE) finished third in a York nursery last time out and that effort looked all the better when the winner bolted up by six lengths off a 7lb higher mark next time. That particular piece of form got another boost here as she quickened up nicely in the closing stages, clearly handled the ground well, and could now go for a sales race at the Curragh next month, although it wouldn't be a surprise to see her turn out at York in the meantime. (op 7-2, tchd 10-3 in places)

Boundaries, whose sire Indesatchel had a winner here two days earlier, stayed on well from off the pace, as befits a colt who stays 6f. He had looked to be a touch exposed and was running from out of the handicap here, but he might be able to find further improvement in this sort of ground. (op 8-1 tchd 9-1)

Roman Dancer(IRE), a winner on fast ground at Windsor last time, had very different conditions to deal with here. He showed good pace, but in the end was just outstayed. (op 13-2 tchd 6-1)

Jamesway(IRE) ran a better race than at first glance as he pulled hard and his challenge was delayed as he was switched around horses. He could well win one of these when the leaders go mad up front. (op 10-3, tchd 7-2 in places)

Ballinargh Girl(IRE), back over the minimum trip having pulled too hard over 6f last time, had plenty of use made of her and didn't see it out. (op 7-2)
Boundless Spirit had never run on ground softer than good before and gave himself absolutely no chance of getting home by pulling very hard through the early stages. (op 15-2)

4832 HALLIWELL JONES BMW "JOY" H'CAP 6f
4:35 (4:36) (Class 3) (0-95,94) 3-Y-O+ £8,095 (£2,408; £1,203; £601) Stalls Centre

Form RPR

1520 1 **Poet's Place (USA)**[14] 4358 5-9-3 **86**.......... PhillipMakin 16 109
(T D Barron) *w ldr: led wl over 2f out: a in full control: r.o wl fnl f: comf* 7/2[1]

1/3- 2 3 ¾ **Harry Patch**[463] 1639 4-9-3 **86**.......... NeilCallan 2 97
(M A Jarvis) *chsd ldrs: wnt 2nd 2f out: sn rdn: nt pce of wnr fnl f* 8/1[3]

0620 3 1 **Damika (IRE)**[14] 4391 7-9-8 **94**.......... MichaelStainton(3) 17 102
(R M Whitaker) *in tch: rdn over 2f out: nt qckn: styd on same pce fnl f* 20/1

006 4 nk **Fullandby (IRE)**[19] 4191 8-9-9 **92**.......... WilliamBuick 11 99
(T J Etherington) *chsd ldrs: rdn over 2f out: nt qckn: kpt on u.p ins fnl f: nt quite pce of ldrs* 16/1

5000 5 shd **Valery Borzov (IRE)**[14] 4391 6-9-2 **90**..........(v) LeeTopliss(5) 3 97
(R A Fahey) *led: hdd wl over 2f out: rdn and nt qckn over 1f out: kpt on same pce ins fnl f* 9/2[2]

156 6 nk **Baby Strange**[4] 4685 6-9-7 **90**.......... FrannyNorton 8 96
(D Shaw) *towards rr: hdwy 2f out: styd on u.p ins fnl f: nt quite pce to rch ldrs* 17/2

-145 7 ½ **Novellen Lad (IRE)**[14] 4391 5-9-9 **92**.......... DarryllHolland 4 96
(E J Alston) *trckd ldrs: rdn over 1f out: kpt on u.p: one pce fnl 75yds* 14/1

0-10 8 1 ¼ **Spitfire**[77] 2316 5-9-6 **89**.......... AdamKirby 7 89
(J R Jenkins) *hld up: effrt and hdwy over 2f out: no imp on ldrs: one pce fnl 100yds* 20/1

4303 9 ½ **Fathsta (IRE)**[12] 4440 5-9-2 **85**.......... JamieSpencer 14 83
(D M Simcock) *in tch: rdn over 2f out: wknd over 1f out* 17/2

6203 10 3 ¼ **The Nifty Fox**[22] 4085 6-9-4 **87**.......... GrahamGibbons 13 75
(T D Easterby) *towards rr: hdwy into midfield over 2f out: rdn over 1f out: no imp fnl 100yds* 12/1

316- 11 1 ¼ **Capone (IRE)**[222] 7862 5-9-0 **88**.......... RossAtkinson(5) 15 72
(F J Brennan) *hld up: rdn over 2f out: outpcd over 1f out* 40/1

4503 12 1 **Ishiadancer**[28] 3893 5-9-3 **86**.......... TedDurcan 6 67
(E J Alston) *prom: rdn over 2f out: wknd over 1f out* 40/1

1600 13 2 ¼ **Cornus**[8] 4551 8-8-11 **85**..........(be) TobyAtkinson(5) 10 59
(A J McCabe) *a towards rr* 66/1

0-10 14 hd **Definightly**[55] 2992 4-9-6 **89**.......... SteveDrowne 9 62
(R Charlton) *in rr: outpcd 1/2-way: nvr on terms* 12/1

6-00 15 6 **Icelandic**[84] 2119 8-9-11 **94**..........(t) LeeVickers 1 48
(F Sheridan) *hld up: rdn and outpcd over 1f out: nvr a threat* 25/1

6445 16 3 ¼ **Spanish Bounty**[15] 4333 5-9-2 **85**.......... StephenCraine 5 28
(J G Portman) *chsd ldrs tl lost pl over 3f out: n.d after* 28/1

1m 14.63s (1.13) **Going Correction** +0.425s/f (Yiel) **16** Ran SP% **123.7**
Speed ratings (Par 107): **109,104,102,102,102 101,101,99,98,94 92,91,88,88,80 75**
toteswingers:1&2:£5.80, 1&3:£18.60, 2&3:£14.50 CSF £28.94 CT £527.29 TOTE £4.40: £1.40, £1.80, £4.20, £4.10; EX 33.60.
Owner Mrs Elaine Russell **Bred** Burning Daylight Farms **Trained** Maunby, N Yorks

FOCUS
The handicapper has a pretty good idea where he stands with most of these, so it was no great surprise that the race was dominated by the least exposed duo in the field. The winner was impressive and the third sets the standard.

NOTEBOOK
Poet's Place(USA) was backed in from as big as 13-2 in the morning and won this in the manner of a sprinter very much going places. A dual winner on Fibresand earlier in his career, he hadn't quite built on that promise in three subsequent starts on turf, but this was the first time he'd been given a chance to run on ground with give in it and he improved markedly. (op 4-1 tchd 10-3 and 9-2 in places)
Harry Patch ◆ had been off the track for 15 months but is obviously well regarded and has a liking for soft ground. He couldn't live with the very well-handicapped winner, but is clearly on a mark he can win off, especially if improving for this outing, which he should do. (op 6-1 tchd 11-2)
Damika(IRE) is a versatile sort when it comes to ground conditions, and he ran a solid race off top weight. However, he's never won off a mark this high, and the handicapper isn't going to be easing him after this. (op 25-1 tchd 16-1)
Fullandby(IRE) loves to get his toe in and looks to be running into form. He's the type to pop up when the leaders go off too fast.
Valery Borzov(IRE), winner of this race two years ago, had his ground for the first time this campaign, but he did a bit too much in front and didn't get home. This will have set him up nicely for York, though, where the track suits those up with the pace. (op 11-2 tchd 7-1 and 15-2 in places)
Baby Strange, who finished in midfield on the Fibresand just four days earlier, was well backed but failed to reproduce the form that saw him beat Stewards' Cup runner-up Jonny Mudball at Doncaster three starts back. (op 14-1)
Novellen Lad(IRE) has done all his winning on good to firm and presumably found these conditions more testing than ideal. Official explanation: trainer said gelding was unsuited by the good to soft ground (op 12-1)
Spitfire likes a bit of ease, but he has a history of going well fresh, so he won't necessarily improve on this promising effort following an 11-week break. (op 16-1 tchd 14-1)

4833 DUKE OF LANCASTER'S OWN YEOMANRY H'CAP (DIV I) 6f
5:10 (5:10) (Class 5) (0-70,70) 3-Y-O+ £3,561 (£1,059; £529; £264) Stalls Centre

Form RPR

1100 1 **Feeling Fresh (IRE)**[23] 4071 5-9-10 **69**.......... JamieSpencer 8 78
(Paul Green) *hld up: rdn and hdwy over 2f out: led ins fnl f: r.o gamely: a doing enough towards fin* 4/1[1]

0000 2 nk **Northern Bolt**[22] 4121 5-9-11 **70**..........(v) PatrickMathers 6 78
(I W McInnes) *midfield: pushed along after 1f: hdwy over 3f out: led over 1f out: hdd ins fnl f: r.o u.p but hld cl home* 11/1

1024 3 5 **Caramelita**[65] 2679 3-9-5 **68**.......... WilliamBuick 4 59
(J R Jenkins) *led: rdn and hdd over 1f out: nt pce of front pair fnl f* 10/1

40U0 4 1 **Toby Tyler**[43] 3396 4-9-5 **64**.......... AdamKirby 12 53
(P T Midgley) *in rr: pushed along and hdwy over 3f out: hung lft whn chsng ldrs fr over 1f out: kpt on same pce ins fnl f* 9/1

0-5 5 ½ **Bouggie Daize**[57] 2919 4-9-4 **68**.......... JohnFahy(5) 1 55
(C G Cox) *hld up: rdn and hdwy over 1f out: styd on ins fnl f: one pce fnl 50yds* 6/1[3]

10-0 6 2 ¾ **Sands Of Dee (USA)**[32] 3768 3-8-11 **60**..........(bt[1]) TedDurcan 9 37
(J A Glover) *in tch: rdn and nt qckn whn edgd lft over 1f out: no imp fnl f* 20/1

0-00 7 nk **Danum Dancer**[17] 4244 6-9-0 **59**..........(b) LeeVickers 3 36
(N Bycroft) *w ldr tl rdn over 2f out: wknd ins fnl f* 14/1

3223 8 1 ½ **Volito**[9] 4518 4-9-8 **67**.......... RichardKingscote 11 40
(Jonjo O'Neill) *hld up: hdwy 1/2-way: rdn whn chsng ldrs over 2f out: wknd over 1f out* 11/2[2]

0600 9 nse **Top Bid**[15] 4345 6-9-9 **68**.......... GrahamGibbons 7 40
(T D Easterby) *chsd ldrs: rdn over 2f out: wknd fnl f* 10/1

0030 10 8 **The History Man (IRE)**[23] 4071 7-8-13 **58**..........(p) CathyGannon 5 5
(B D Leavy) *chsd ldrs: rdn over 3f out: sn wknd* 12/1

5004 11 1 ½ **Lakeman (IRE)**[14] 4372 4-9-6 **65**.......... NeilCallan 10 7
(B Ellison) *midfield: rdn and outpcd over 3f out: n.d after* 8/1

-0 12 3 ½ **Nimmy's Special**[204] 193 4-8-6 **51** oh1..........(b) FrannyNorton 2 —
(M Mullineaux) *s.i.s: a bhd* 33/1

1m 16.69s (3.19) **Going Correction** +0.425s/f (Yiel)
WFA 3 from 4yo+ 4lb **12** Ran SP% **119.4**
Speed ratings (Par 103): **95,94,87,86,85 82,81,79,79,69 67,62**
toteswingers:1&2:£10.30, 1&3:£7.60, 2&3:£27.40 CSF £49.22 CT £418.27 TOTE £3.80: £1.60, £4.50, £2.70; EX 57.40.
Owner Paul Green (Oaklea) **Bred** J Mahon **Trained** Lydiate, Merseyside

FOCUS
A modest handicap and the slower of the two divisions. The first two, both held up, came clear and the runner-up sets the level rated to last year's form.
Toby Tyler Official explanation: jockey said gelding hung left-handed from 3f out
Volito Official explanation: trainer had no explanation for the poor form shown

4834 TURFTV.CO.UK H'CAP (DIV II) 6f
5:45 (5:45) (Class 5) (0-70,70) 3-Y-O+ £3,561 (£1,059; £529; £264) Stalls Centre

Form RPR

6620 1 **Rio Cobolo (IRE)**[13] 4404 4-9-11 **70**..........(v) JamieSpencer 6 79
(Paul Green) *in rr: hdwy over 1f out: sn rdn to ld: r.o wl: in command fnl 100yds* 9/2[1]

00-0 2 2 ¼ **Dubai Hills**[19] 4192 4-9-9 **68**.......... GrahamGibbons 9 70
(B Smart) *chsd ldrs: rdn to ld briefly jst over 1f out: nt pce of wnr fnl 100yds* 12/1

5420 3 1 ¾ **Cheyenne Red (IRE)**[19] 4192 4-9-10 **69**.......... PhillipMakin 11 65+
(M Dods) *racd keenly: hld up: rdn and hdwy over 1f out: kpt on ins fnl f: tk 3rd fnl 50yds: nt pce to rch front pair* 8/1

0640 4 nk **Peter's Gift (IRE)**[53] 3061 4-8-13 **58**.......... NeilCallan 8 53
(K A Ryan) *midfield: hdwy 1/2-way: rdn to chal over 1f out: kpt on same pce ins fnl f* 18/1

5243 5 ½ **Tenancy (IRE)**[15] 4326 6-8-1 **51** oh1.......... JohnFahy(5) 7 45
(S A Harris) *led: rdn and hdd jst over 1f out: no ex fnl 75yds* 10/1

6042 6 1 ¾ **Interchoice Star**[12] 4430 5-8-12 **57**.......... JerryO'Dwyer 10 45
(R Hollinshead) *in tch: hdwy 1/2-way: chsd ldrs over 2f out: rdn over 1f out: wknd ins fnl f* 16/1

5645 7 hd **Memphis Man**[8] 4542 7-9-5 **67**.......... RichardEvans(3) 12 55
(P D Evans) *hld up: hdwy 1/2-way: sn chsd ldrs and rdn: edgd lft and btn over 1f out* 12/1

001 8 ½ **Captain Scooby**[14] 4372 4-9-6 **68**.......... MichaelStainton(3) 4 54
(R M Whitaker) *chsd ldrs: rdn 2f out: wknd jst ins fnl f* 15/2

0400 9 ¾ **Coolree Star (IRE)**[5] 4662 3-9-7 **70**.......... LeeVickers 5 54
(J A Glover) *hld up: rdn and outpcd over 2f out: nvr a threat* 33/1

63-4 10 1 ¾ **Scrapper Smith (IRE)**[13] 4404 4-9-6 **65**.......... CathyGannon 1 43
(A C Whillans) *in tch: rdn 1/2-way: lost pl 2f out: n.d and u.p after* 13/2[3]

3541 11 8 **Two Turtle Doves (IRE)**[7] 4605 4-9-3 **62**.......... FrannyNorton 2 14
(M Mullineaux) *prom: rdn 2f out: wknd over 1f out: eased whn btn ins fnl f* 5/1[2]

1210 12 ¾ **Revue Princess (IRE)**[15] 4342 5-9-5 **64**..........(b) TedDurcan 3 14
(T D Easterby) *in tch: lost pl over 2f out: sn u.p: eased whn btn ins fnl f* 8/1

1m 15.88s (2.38) **Going Correction** +0.425s/f (Yiel)
WFA 3 from 4yo+ 4lb **12** Ran SP% **120.7**
Speed ratings (Par 103): **101,98,95,95,94 92,92,91,90,88 77,76**
toteswingers:1&2:£12.00, 1&3:£6.50, 2&3:£27.10 CSF £60.11 CT £434.06 TOTE £6.20: £2.00, £4.50, £2.50; EX 59.40 Place 6 £290.20; Place 5 £140.42.
Owner The Keely Gang **Bred** Yvonne & Gerard Kennedy **Trained** Lydiate, Merseyside

FOCUS
The quicker of the two divisions by 0.81sec. The race is rated slightly positively with the runner-up to 3-y-o form.
Scrapper Smith(IRE) Official explanation: jockey said gelding never travelled
Two Turtle Doves(IRE) Official explanation: trainer had no explanation for the poor form shown
Revue Princess(IRE) Official explanation: jockey said mare had no more to give
T/Plt: £199.30 to a £1 stake. Pool:£109,596.42 - 401.34 winning tickets T/Qpdt: £31.80 to a £1 stake. Pool:£6,441.17 - 149.80 winning tickets DO

4787 LINGFIELD (L-H)
Saturday, August 7

OFFICIAL GOING: Turf course - good to firm (8.7); all-weather - standard
Wind: Light, half behind Weather: Fine but cloudy

4835 CROWHURST MAIDEN STKS 6f
5:50 (5:53) (Class 5) 3-Y-O+ £2,388 (£705; £352) Stalls High

Form RPR

5202 1 **Dubai Media (CAN)**[28] 3924 3-8-12 80.......... TomMcLaughlin 1 83+
(E A L Dunlop) *hld up and racd wd: prog 1/2-way: led 2f out and sn crossed to rail: pushed wl clr* 2/5[1]

0-44 2 8 **Millden**[14] 4385 3-9-3 69.......... DaneO'Neill 7 62
(H Candy) *led against rail: hdd and hanging lft 2f out: no ch w wnr after* 4/1[2]

0 3 1 ¾ **Toms Return**[35] 3663 3-8-12 0.......... KierenFox(5) 6 57
(J R Best) *t.k.h: trckd ldrs: cl up over 2f out: wl btn 3rd fr over 1f out* 14/1[3]

00- 4 4 ½ **Yanbu (USA)**[389] 3951 5-9-2 0.......... EddieCreighton 8 38
(T T Clement) *trckd ldrs: lost pl 1/2-way: racd awkwardly after and n.d* 50/1

00-0 5 ¾ **Dancing Again**[14] 4364 4-8-11 35.......... LeeNewnes(5) 4 36
(E A Wheeler) *prom: pressed ldr over 3f out to over 2f out: wknd* 66/1

60 6 ¾ **Trendy Way (IRE)**[12] 4425 3-8-12 0.......... LiamKeniry 3 33
(P R Chamings) *hld up in rr: hung lft fr over 2f out: nvr on terms* 33/1

06 7 ¾ **Midnight M**[18] 4222 3-8-12 0.......... SaleemGolam 9 30
(Rae Guest) *a in rr: struggling fr 1/2-way* 20/1

00- 8 9 **Chill Out Charley**[406] 3403 3-9-3 0.......... NeilChalmers 5 6
(J J Bridger) *pressed ldr to over 3f out: wknd rapidly: t.o* 66/1

69.83 secs (-1.37) **Going Correction** -0.25s/f (Firm)
WFA 3 from 4yo+ 4lb **8** Ran SP% **110.7**
Speed ratings (Par 103): **99,88,86,80,79 78,77,65**
toteswingers: 1&2 £1.10, 1&3 £2.80, 2&3 £3.00 CSF £1.87 TOTE £1.50: £1.02, £1.10, £3.70; EX 1.30.

Owner Ahmad Al Shaikh **Bred** Kinghaven Farms Limited **Trained** Newmarket, Suffolk

FOCUS

An uncompetitive maiden that looked at the mercy of the favourite so long as she wasn't hindered by the first-time drop to 6f, which she wasn't. The form is very weak behind the winner with the runner-up's previous form shaky.

Trendy Way(IRE) Official explanation: jockey said filly hung badly left-handed

4836 BLACKBERRY LANE H'CAP — 6f

6:20 (6:20) (Class 5) (0-75,75) 3-Y-0+ — **£2,729** (£806; £403) **Stalls** High

Form — RPR

2652 **1** **Another Try (IRE)**[30] 3815 5-9-0 **67** .... MatthewDavies(3) 10 — 79
(A P Jarvis) *dwlt: grabbed rail and led after 1f: rdn 2f out: all out fnl f* **2/1**[1]

-004 **2** *nk* **Chat De La Burg (USA)**[8] 4531 3-8-11 **70** .... KierenFox(5) 9 — 80
(J R Best) *walked to post: led 1f: pressed wnr after: rdn 1/2-way: persistent chal fnl f: jst hld* **25/1**

3660 **3** *1 ¼* **Lodi (IRE)**[16] 4308 5-9-1 **65** ....(tp) GeorgeBaker 8 — 72
(J Akehurst) *racd against rail: trckd ldng pair: plld out over 1f out to chal: rdn and nt qckn* **3/1**[2]

1250 **4** *2 ¼* **Cape Melody**[21] 4145 4-9-10 **74** ....(v) TravisBlock 5 — 74
(H Morrison) *s.s: reminders in last after 2f: plugged on u.p fr over 1f out* **9/1**

1046 **5** *1* **Riflessione**[11] 4452 4-9-9 **73** ....(b) TomMcLaughlin 4 — 70
(R A Harris) *t.k.h: hld up in rr against rail: rdn and no rspnse 2f out* **10/1**

4101 **6** *nse* **Hinton Admiral**[12] 4430 6-9-10 **74** .... J-PGuillambert 7 — 70
(P Howling) *trckd ldng pair: rdn over 2f out: wknd jst over 1f out* **9/2**[3]

5231 **7** *2 ¾* **Triple Dream**[9] 4518 5-9-11 **75** ....(p) LiamKeniry 2 — 63
(J M Bradley) *settled in rr: rdn and no prog 2f out: wknd fnl f* **6/1**

69.70 secs (-1.50) **Going Correction** -0.25s/f (Firm)
WFA 3 from 4yo+ 4lb — 7 Ran SP% **113.7**
Speed ratings (Par 103): **100,99,97,94,93 93,89**
toteswingers: 1&2 £18.00, 1&3 £1.10, 2&3 £11.80 CSF £50.59 CT £148.41 TOTE £1.90: £1.10, £7.60; EX 53.40.

Owner The Twyford Partnership **Bred** Jarvis Associates **Trained** Twyford, Bucks

FOCUS

A fair handicap that turned tactical with the winner able to grab the rail and dictate a steadyish pace to halfway. Probably not form to take at face value with the result having a muddling look to it, although the winner is the best guide.

Riflessione Official explanation: jockey said gelding hung badly right-handed

4837 ASHURSTWOOD H'CAP — 6f

6:50 (6:50) (Class 4) (0-85,83) 3-Y-0 — **£4,209** (£1,252; £625; £312) **Stalls** High

Form — RPR

0221 **1** **La Fortunata**[7] 4567 3-8-13 **75** .... TonyCulhane 3 — 84
(Mike Murphy) *mde all and racd against rail: rdn over 1f out: styd on wl* **10/3**[3]

1032 **2** *1 ¼* **Bougainvilia (IRE)**[12] 4424 3-9-4 **83** .... PatrickHills(3) 2 — 88+
(R Hannon) *trckd wnr: pushed up to chal 2f out: wanting to hang lft over 1f out: already btn whn rdn ins fnl f* **11/4**[2]

0440 **3** *4 ½* **Di Stefano**[33] 3731 3-9-1 **77** .... SamHitchcott 6 — 68
(M R Channon) *stdd s: chsd ldng pair: pushed along 1/2-way: outpcd and btn 2f out* **7/1**

41-4 **4** *½* **Pan American**[19] 4204 3-9-0 **76** .... PatDobbs 5 — 65
(P J Makin) *s.s: racd wd in last pair: outpcd and rdn over 1f out* **2/1**[1]

69.29 secs (-1.91) **Going Correction** -0.25s/f (Firm) — 4 Ran SP% **95.6**
Speed ratings (Par 102): **102,100,94,93**
toteswingers: 1&2 £6.10 CSF £9.46 TOTE £3.80; EX 5.30.

Owner James Patton **Bred** James Patton **Trained** Westoning, Beds
■ Excellent Guest (5/1) withdrawn; Rule 4 applies deduction 15p in the £ from all bets.

FOCUS

An interesting handicap, even after the late withdrawal of one of the intended runners at the start, but it was one that followed the usual pattern here in recent weeks with the winner making all on the stands' rail. The runner-up is rated close toi her best.

Pan American Official explanation: jockey said gelding missed the break

4838 MOORE LANE MAIDEN STKS — 1m (P)

7:20 (7:22) (Class 5) 2-Y-0 — **£2,388** (£705; £352) **Stalls** High

Form — RPR

1 **Questioning (IRE)** 2-9-3 0 .... NickyMackay 4 — 80+
(J H M Gosden) *s.i.s: hld up in last trio: prog on wd outside 2f out: rdn to chal fnl f: r.o to ld last strides* **3/1**[1]

2 *shd* **Tiger Webb** 2-9-3 0 .... TomQueally 8 — 79+
(H R A Cecil) *trckd ldng pair: shkn up to ld on outer wl over 1f out: r.o whn jnd fnl f: hdd last strides* **7/2**[2]

0 **3** *2 ½* **Dubarshi**[58] 2887 2-9-3 0 .... DaneO'Neill 1 — 71
(Miss Jo Crowley) *t.k.h: trckd ldng pair: shkn up to chal on inner wl over 1f out: outpcd fnl f* **25/1**

5 **4** *shd* **Abjer (FR)**[7] 4568 2-9-3 0 .... AhmedAjtebi 9 — 71
(C E Brittain) *prog on outer to trck ldrs 1/2-way: rdn and effrt 2f out: outpcd over 1f out: kpt on* **13/2**

02 **5** *2 ¾* **Tagansky**[17] 4253 2-9-3 0 .... TonyCulhane 3 — 65
(S Dow) *disp ld at mod pce to wl over 1f out: wknd* **11/2**[3]

0 **6** *2* **Buxfizz (USA)**[10] 4490 2-9-3 0 .... AlanMunro 7 — 60
(R A Mills) *t.k.h: hld up in midfield: cl enough 2f out: outpcd over 1f out: no hdwy after* **7/2**[2]

02 **7** *4 ½* **Pahente**[29] 3864 2-9-3 0 .... LiamKeniry 5 — 50
(J S Moore) *a towards rr: pushed along in last trio 2f out: no prog* **12/1**

0 **8** *2* **Jacquotte (IRE)**[16] 4299 2-8-12 0 .... EddieCreighton 12 — 40
(E J Creighton) *disp ld at mod pce to wl over 1f out: wknd rapidly* **100/1**

9 *¾* **Wet Your Whistle** 2-9-3 0 .... MartinDwyer 11 — 43
(B J Meehan) *hld up last: pushed along and no prog 2f out* **14/1**

0 **10** *hd* **Dreams Of Glory**[38] 3555 2-9-3 0 .... SamHitchcott 2 — 43
(R J Hodges) *t.k.h: hld up in tch: lost pl over 3f out and pushed along: wknd 2f out* **100/1**

1m 41.32s (3.12) **Going Correction** +0.25s/f (Slow) — 10 Ran SP% **118.3**
Speed ratings (Par 94): **94,93,91,91,88 86,82,80,79,79**
toteswingers: 1&2 £4.60, 1&3 £15.50, 2&3 £16.50 CSF £13.77 TOTE £4.40: £1.80, £1.80, £4.20; EX 17.60.

Owner H R H Princess Haya Of Jordan **Bred** Fortbarrington Stud **Trained** Newmarket, Suffolk

FOCUS

Probably just fair form but an interesting maiden dominated by two newcomers from powerful yards. The pace was uneven and only the winner got into things from behind. The fourth and sixth are rated to their debut marks.

NOTEBOOK

Questioning(IRE) ◆, who cost 160,000gns as a yearling and has an entry in the Royal Lodge, hails from a yard with a decent strike-rate with juveniles here during the last five years. Slow to break, he was given plenty of time to find his stride but began to make good progress approaching the final turn and did well to get up under hands and heels riding after giving the eventual runner-up first run. Arguably the best long-term prospect in the field, he seems sure to improve plenty for this and rates potentially useful. (op 7-2 tchd 9-2)

Tiger Webb, a 65,000gns yearling by Hurricane Run out of a modest mare, holds no fancy entries but showed enough to suggest he can win a run-of-the-mill maiden without too much fuss. (op 3-1 tchd 11-4)

Dubarshi had been well held at a big price on his debut at Newbury but his performance was another advert for his excellent stable, as he briefly threatened early in the straight before finding the first two too speedy. This looks to be about his trip for now.

Abjer(FR)'s debut form had already been franked and he ran well, clearly suited by the step up in trip while leaving the impression he'd have fared better had his stamina been tested even more. He could be interesting in long-distance nurseries in the autumn. (op 15-2 tchd 8-1 and 6-1)

Tagansky came into this going the right way and with a good course run to his name and ran creditably for all he had the run of the race, not unduly pressed hard in front. He'll have to try his luck in nurseries now. (op 5-1 tchd 9-2)

Buxfizz(USA) had shaped very well on debut at Sandown and looked interesting given his US pedigree switched to the all-weather, but he seemed totally unsuited by being restrained in the pack and was made to look very one-paced when the tempo lifted. Connections should have learned plenty about his limitations from this and he's not one to give up on just yet. Official explanation: jockey said colt suffered interference in running (op 9-2)

Pahente predictably found this harder after finishing second in a seller at Newbury at start of last month (tchd 11-1)

Wet Your Whistle, a half-brother to 1m2f winner Baoli, is from a yard where some of the juveniles have been winning first time out but he was far too green himself. (op 12-1)

4839 HOLLOW LANE H'CAP — 7f (P)

7:50 (7:50) (Class 5) (0-70,70) 3-Y-0+ — **£2,388** (£705; £352) **Stalls** Low

Form — RPR

0226 **1** **Kiss A Prince**[10] 4488 4-9-12 **70** ....(b) TomQueally 9 — 78+
(D K Ivory) *hld up in 7th: looking for a gap whn gng strly over 1f out: rdn and r.o wl fnl f to ld last 50yds* **3/1**[1]

0006 **2** *½* **Hellbender (IRE)**[12] 4430 4-9-9 **67** ....(t) PatDobbs 4 — 74
(S Kirk) *trckd ldng trio: rdn over 1f out: chal fnl f: styd on but outpcd by wnr* **10/1**

4-16 **3** *hd* **Leelu**[15] 4324 4-9-2 **60** .... LiamKeniry 12 — 66
(D W P Arbuthnot) *trckd ldr: rdn to ld wl over 1f out: hdd and outpcd last 50yds* **8/1**[3]

5446 **4** *nk* **Billberry**[51] 3129 5-9-12 **70** ....(vt[1]) GeorgeBaker 10 — 76
(S C Williams) *hld up in last trio: effrt on outer 2f out: r.o u.p fnl f: nrst fin* **8/1**[3]

1505 **5** *1* **Mount Juliet (IRE)**[14] 4365 3-9-3 **67** .... MartinDwyer 7 — 68
(M Botti) *t.k.h: trckd ldrs in 5th: rdn and cl enough over 1f out: nt qckn* **10/1**

0046 **6** *1 ½* **First Service (IRE)**[17] 4260 4-9-6 **64** ....(p) NickyMackay 13 — 63
(M J Attwater) *hld up in last trio: effrt on wd outside 2f out: styd on fnl f: n.d* **8/1**[3]

5662 **7** *2 ¼* **Valmina**[24] 4031 3-9-3 **67** ....(tp) DaneO'Neill 8 — 58
(Andrew Turnell) *hld up in 8th: effrt on outer over 2f out: no prog over 1f out: fdd* **8/1**[3]

0602 **8** *½* **Cavendish Road (IRE)**[14] 4366 4-9-8 **66** ....(t) NeilChalmers 3 — 57
(N J Vaughan) *trckd ldrs in 6th: rdn on inner over 1f out: fdd* **4/1**[2]

1065 **9** *1 ½* **Figaro Flyer (IRE)**[17] 4256 7-9-4 **62** .... J-PGuillambert 5 — 49
(P Howling) *led: 2 l clr 1/2-way: hdd & wknd wl over 1f out* **28/1**

4065 **10** *3 ½* **Prince Namid**[74] 2415 8-9-6 **64** .... SaleemGolam 2 — 42
(J A T De Giles) *chsd ldng pair to over 2f out: wknd over 1f out* **20/1**

6300 **11** *11* **Imperial House**[26] 3966 4-9-5 **63** ....(b) TomMcLaughlin 14 — 11
(R A Harris) *hld up in last: pushed along 1/2-way: no prog: wknd and eased over 1f out: t.o* **25/1**

1m 25.77s (0.97) **Going Correction** +0.25s/f (Slow)
WFA 3 from 4yo+ 6lb — 11 Ran SP% **119.7**
Speed ratings (Par 103): **104,103,103,102,101 100,97,96,95,91 78**
toteswingers: 1&2 £8.20, 1&3 £7.30, 2&3 £8.20 CSF £33.75 CT £228.30 TOTE £2.90: £1.10, £3.90, £2.60; EX 39.70.

Owner A Pryer **Bred** Baroness, Magnusson, Myriade, Redmyre **Trained** Radlett, Herts

FOCUS

Several C&D regulars on show in a modest handicap. The pace was a good one after 2f or so and the complexion changed very late on. The form looks sound rated around those in the frame behind the winner.

4840 TRYST-EAST GRINSTEAD'S ULTIMATE NIGHT CLUB MEDIAN AUCTION MAIDEN STKS — 1m 2f (P)

8:20 (8:20) (Class 6) 3-4-Y-0 — **£2,047** (£604; £302) **Stalls** Low

Form — RPR

2 **1** **Dhaamer (IRE)**[49] 3220 3-9-3 0 .... TadhgO'Shea 4 — 71+
(J H M Gosden) *hld up: prog on wd outside 3f out: led over 2f out: sn pushed wl clr: easily* **8/15**[1]

2 *4 ½* **Bull Five** 3-9-3 0 .... J-PGuillambert 1 — 62
(N P Littmoden) *chsd ldrs: rdn in 5th 3f out: styd on fr over 1f out to take 2nd last 75yds* **6/1**[3]

04 **3** *¾* **Chasse Coeur**[33] 3738 3-8-12 0 .... DavidProbert 6 — 55
(A M Balding) *pressed ldr: led 3f out to over 2f out: sn outpcd: lost 2nd last 75yds* **11/4**[2]

0P-6 **4** *1 ½* **Roar Talent (USA)**[166] 655 3-8-12 0 .... KierenFox(5) 2 — 57
(J R Best) *led to 3f out: outpcd fr 2f out* **12/1**

0- **5** *3 ¾* **Dongola (IRE)**[467] 1569 3-8-12 0 .... FrankieMcDonald 10 — 45
(P Winkworth) *dwlt: pushed along in last after 2f: struggling fr 1/2-way: stl last 2f out: kpt on fr over 1f out* **16/1**

00- **6** *¾* **Bonamassa**[234] 7763 3-9-3 0 .... NickyMackay 8 — 48
(M J Attwater) *hld up in 6th: rdn and outpcd fr 3f out: n.d after: hung rt nr fin* **33/1**

00 **7** *4* **Jenny Dawson (IRE)**[19] 4207 4-9-7 0 .... IvaMilickova 9 — 35
(John Berry) *chsd ldng pair to 3f out: wknd rapidly 2f out* **33/1**

8 *2 ½* **My Last Duchess** 3-8-12 0 .... NeilChalmers 5 — 30
(M Blanshard) *dwlt: rn green: a in last pair: struggling fr 4f out* **28/1**

2m 10.32s (3.72) **Going Correction** +0.25s/f (Slow)
WFA 3 from 4yo 9lb — 8 Ran SP% **129.1**
Speed ratings (Par 101): **95,91,90,89,86 86,82,80**
toteswingers: 1&2 £6.00, 1&3 £1.02, 2&3 £4.60 CSF £5.69 TOTE £1.70: £1.02, £2.50, £1.10; EX 7.30 Place 6 £32.99, Place 5 £31.80.

Owner Hamdan Al Maktoum **Bred** Shadwell Estate Company Limited **Trained** Newmarket, Suffolk

FOCUS

Little strength in depth to a one-sided maiden. The pace was steady and it developed into something of a sprint from the home turn but the winner was totally superior.

T/Plt: £30.70 to a £1 stake.Pool: £50,769.69. 1,206.71 winning tickets. T/Qpdt: £14.60 to a £1 stake. Pool: £4,926.20. 249.40 winning tickets. JN

4801 NEWMARKET (July Course) (R-H)

Saturday, August 7

OFFICIAL GOING: Good to soft

Stands' side section of July Course utilised.

Wind: Light, half-behind Weather: Showers

4841 BBAG-SALES.DE H'CAP 1m 2f

2:05 (2:06) (Class 2) (0-100,91) 3-Y-O+ **£10,361** (£3,083; £1,540; £769) **Stalls** High

Form			Horse	RPR
-010	1		**Spanish Duke (IRE)**[63] 2758 3-9-5 **88** ... EddieAhern 5 (J L Dunlop) *hld up: hdwy over 3f out: led over 1f out: pushed out* **4/1**[2]	103+
61-1	2	3 ¾	**Psychic Ability (USA)**[16] 4302 3-9-8 **91** ... (p) FrankieDettori 7 (Saeed Bin Suroor) *chsd ldrs: led over 2f out: rdn: hung rt and hdd over 1f out: no ex fnl f* **4/1**[2]	98
4230	3	3 ¾	**Ramona Chase**[11] 4455 5-9-5 **79** ... (t) KierenFallon 4 (M J Attwater) *s.i.s: hld up: hdwy over 2f out: rdn over 1f out: wknd fnl f* **14/1**	79
0-00	4	4 ½	**All Annalena (IRE)**[21] 4143 4-9-6 **87** ... AdamBeschizza(7) 8 (Mrs L Wadham) *trckd ldrs: racd keenly: rdn over 2f out: wknd over 1f out* **50/1**	78
0142	5	1 ¼	**Kindest**[21] 4152 4-9-7 **81** ... GeorgeBaker 10 (C F Wall) *hld up: hdwy over 2f out: rdn and wknd over 1f out* **9/2**[3]	69
2410	6	7	**Bollin Dolly**[14] 4389 7-9-8 **82** ... DavidNolan 11 (T D Easterby) *led: rdn and hdd over 2f out: wknd over 1f out* **20/1**	56
-002	7	2	**Rumble Of Thunder (IRE)**[16] 4306 4-9-7 **81** ... MartinDwyer 2 (D W P Arbuthnot) *trckd ldrs: racd keenly: rdn over 2f out: wknd wl over 1f out* **7/1**	51
1126	8	1 ¼	**Abergavenny**[9] 4504 3-8-12 **81** ... RichardHills 9 (M Johnston) *sn chsng ldrs: rdn over 3f out: wknd 2f out* **7/2**[1]	49
610	9	4	**Putra One (IRE)**[59] 2865 4-9-7 **81** ... (b[1]) TomQueally 3 (M A Jarvis) *hld up: rdn and wknd over 2f out* **10/1**	41

2m 5.81s (0.31) **Going Correction** +0.125s/f (Good)

WFA 3 from 4yo+ 9lb **9 Ran SP% 115.4**

Speed ratings (Par 109): **103,100,97,93,92 86,85,84,81**

toteswingers: 1&2 £3.40, 1&3 £9.90, 2&3 £10.30 CSF £20.40 CT £202.39 TOTE £5.00: £1.80, £1.80, £4.20; EX 20.20 Trifecta £262.10 Pool: £665.93 - 1.88 winning units..

Owner Windflower Overseas Holdings Inc **Bred** Windflower Overseas Holdings Inc **Trained** Arundel, W Sussex

FOCUS

The pace was strong considering the conditions, with Bollin Dolly, Rumble Of Thunder and Abergavenny taking each other on up front early in the straight. They all raced up the middle of the track. The first two look ahead of their marks at present.

NOTEBOOK

Spanish Duke(IRE) appreciated the return to easy ground and readily defied a 5lb higher mark than when winning under similar conditions at Salisbury two starts back. This galloping track clearly suited him more than Musselburgh when last seen two months previously (reported to have not handled the bend) and the drop back from 1m4f also helped. He travelled like a smart horse and can progress further when conditions are in his favour. (op 7-1)

Psychic Ability(USA) got warm beforehand and couldn't defy a 6lb rise for his success in a three-runner event at Folkestone on his reappearance. Still, he was clear of the remainder and this was a solid effort on ground that may have been easier than ideal. (op 3-1 tchd 11-4)

Ramona Chase responded to pressure to a point, but was ultimately well held by the front two and remains winless since 2007. (op 12-1)

All Annalena(IRE), well beaten in a couple of Listed races since coming over from Germany, fared better on this drop into handicap company, although she never threatened, having been a bit keen early. (op 66-1)

Kindest has winning form on soft ground, but she was being niggled along from a fair way out and made no impression. Better could have been expected.

Rumble Of Thunder(IRE) Official explanation: jockey said gelding ran too freely

Abergavenny went off fast enough and unsurprisingly had little left when the race got serious. The ground probably didn't help matters either. (op 5-1)

4842 GERMAN-THOROUGHBRED.COM SWEET SOLERA STKS (GROUP 3) (FILLIES) 7f

2:35 (2:38) (Class 1) 2-Y-O

£22,708 (£8,608; £4,308; £2,148; £1,076; £540) **Stalls** High

Form			Horse	RPR
1	1		**White Moonstone (USA)**[15] 4317 2-8-12 0 ... FrankieDettori 6 (Saeed Bin Suroor) *dwlt: hld up: hdwy to ld and hung lft fr over 1f out: r.o: comf* **11/4**[1]	105+
163	2	1 ¼	**Crying Lightening (IRE)**[16] 4305 2-8-12 96 ... MartinDwyer 2 (P W Chapple-Hyam) *led 1f: w ldr tl led again over 2f out: rdn and hdd over 1f out: hung lft: styd on same pce ins fnl f* **7/1**[3]	102+
21	3	3 ½	**Khor Sheed**[42] 3453 2-8-12 0 ... KierenFallon 9 (L M Cumani) *chsd ldrs: rdn over 2f out: hung lft over 1f out: no ex fnl f* **11/4**[1]	93+
10	4	nk	**Al Madina (IRE)**[14] 4356 2-8-12 88 ... TomEaves 4 (B Smart) *hld up: racd keenly: n.m.r after 1f: rdn over 1f out: hung rt and styd on u.p ins fnl f: nt trble ldrs* **33/1**	92
1	5	1	**Musharakaat (IRE)**[24] 4021 2-8-12 0 ... RichardHills 1 (E A L Dunlop) *racd keenly: trckd ldrs: rdn over 1f out: wknd ins fnl f* **15/2**	89
1	6	1 ½	**Clinical**[23] 4048 2-8-12 0 ... SebSanders 3 (Sir Mark Prescott) *prom: rdn over 2f out: wknd over 1f out* **9/2**[2]	85
14	7	1	**Fork Handles**[16] 4305 2-8-12 0 ... TomQueally 8 (M R Channon) *s.i.s: hld up: rdn over 2f out: wknd over 1f out* **12/1**	82
3031	8	1 ¼	**Elkmait**[18] 4233 2-8-12 83 ... AhmedAjtebi 7 (C E Brittain) *racd keenly: led 6f out to over 2f out: rdn and wknd over 1f out* **25/1**	79
1564	9	1 ¼	**Emma's Gift (IRE)**[7] 4592 2-8-12 95 ... JimmyQuinn 5 (Miss J Feilden) *chsd ldrs tl rdn and wknd over 1f out* **14/1**	76

1m 27.02s (1.32) **Going Correction** +0.125s/f (Good) **9 Ran SP% 116.9**

Speed ratings (Par 101): **97,95,91,91,90 88,87,85,84**

toteswingers: 1&2 £3.80, 1&3 £2.00, 2&3 £5.50 CSF £23.20 TOTE £3.80: £1.50, £2.20, £1.60; EX 20.70 Trifecta £59.30 Pool: £906.98 - 11.31 winning units..

Owner Godolphin **Bred** Stoneside Stable **Trained** Newmarket, Suffolk

FOCUS

Some high-class fillies have won this Group 3, with Soviet Song, Maids Causeway and Rainbow View the most notable in recent years. This season's race looked a good contest, but the early pace was steady. They raced up the middle of the track through the opening stages, but gradually edged towards the far rail. The winner is a big improver but not an easy race to rate.

NOTEBOOK

White Moonstone(USA) ◆, whose trainer won this last year with Long Lashes, followed up her Ascot maiden success, probably with more in hand than the margin suggests. She looked set to win impressively when quickening to the front off a slow pace around 1f out, but she then didn't help herself by continually edging left, resulting in a more workmanlike display. The overall impression, though, was that she's a filly with serious ability, and there will surely be more to come provided she goes the right way, especially as her breeding suggests she'll be suited by further in due course. Unsurprisingly the Fillies' Mile is said to be her main target this year, although she'll need to be supplemented, and she could have one run beforehand, which would presumably be in the May Hill at Doncaster. There's only a couple of weeks between the two, but Rainbow View, by the same sire as this one, won both races in 2008. (op 3-1 tchd 5-2)

Crying Lightening(IRE) probably improved on the form she showed when third in a Sandown Listed race over this trip on quick ground last time, although she looks a little flattered to finish so close to the winner. The ease in the ground didn't inconvenience her and she should remain competitive at this sort of level. (op 6-1)

Khor Sheed shaped as though she'd appreciate this trip when winning a 6f Listed contest on quick ground here last time, but she was too keen, especially considering the ground. She did well to hold on for third and can improve if settling better, with a stronger-run race likely to help. (tchd 3-1)

Al Madina(IRE), well held in the Princess Margaret following her debut win, was plenty keen enough on this step up in trip and never threatened. Still, she posted a solid effort and might do better off a stronger gallop.

Musharakaat(IRE) won nicely on her debut over this trip on Polytrack, but she struggled in this better company. Perhaps she wants a better surface. (op 10-1)

Clinical won a reasonable-looking maiden over this trip on quick ground first time up, but she disappointed under these completely different conditions. (op 6-1)

Fork Handles, only 2l behind Crying Lightning when the pair met on quick ground last time, was well beaten and presumably didn't appreciate the soft ground. (op 11-1)

4843 BADEN-RACING.COM H'CAP 7f

3:10 (3:10) (Class 2) (0-105,101) 3-Y-O+

£18,693 (£5,598; £2,799; £1,401; £699; £351) **Stalls** High

Form			Horse	RPR
3002	1		**Al Khaleej (IRE)**[10] 4473 6-9-1 **95** ... MartinLane(3) 18 (D M Simcock) *hld up: hdwy and hmpd over 1f out: rdn to ld ins fnl f: r.o wl* **11/1**	108+
0044	2	2	**Manassas (IRE)**[10] 4473 5-9-2 **93** ... (b) MartinDwyer 1 (B J Meehan) *led: rdn and hung rt fr over 1f out: hdd and unable qck ins fnl f* **16/1**	101
0300	3	2	**Imperial Guest**[14] 4358 4-9-2 **93** ... SebSanders 12 (G G Margarson) *hld up in tch: rdn and hmpd over 1f out: styd on same pce ins fnl f* **16/1**	95
0243	4	¾	**Oratory (IRE)**[10] 4473 4-9-3 **94** ... (v[1]) PatDobbs 3 (R Hannon) *chsd ldrs: rdn over 1f out: edgd rt and no ex ins fnl f* **11/1**	94+
1100	5	2	**Day Of The Eagle (IRE)**[28] 3920 4-8-13 **90** ... KierenFallon 17 (L M Cumani) *sn pushed along in rr: styd on u.p ins fnl f: nrst fin* **8/1**[2]	85
0134	6	shd	**Glen Shiel (USA)**[9] 4509 3-8-3 **86** ... DavidProbert 11 (M Johnston) *chsd ldrs: rdn over 1f out: wknd ins fnl f* **9/1**[3]	79
0460	7	½	**Viva Vettori**[28] 3921 6-8-6 **88** ... DeclanCannon(5) 7 (D R C Elsworth) *prom: outpcd over 2f out: styd on u.p ins fnl f* **25/1**	81
4000	8	½	**Hajoum (IRE)**[14] 4358 4-8-13 **90** ... RichardHills 15 (M Johnston) *chsd ldrs: rdn: nt clr run and edgd rt over 1f out: wknd ins fnl f* **20/1**	82
200	9	nk	**Redford (IRE)**[22] 4085 5-9-7 **98** ... FrankieDettori 10 (D Nicholls) *hld up: swtchd lft and hdwy over 2f out: wknd ins fnl f* **12/1**	89
1-10	10	2 ½	**Primaeval**[14] 4370 4-8-7 **84** ... EddieAhern 16 (J R Fanshawe) *hld up: rdn and wknd over 1f out* **20/1**	68
1000	11	nk	**Spirit Of Sharjah (IRE)**[29] 3869 5-9-1 **99** ... AdamBeschizza(7) 6 (Miss J Feilden) *chsd ldrs: rdn over 2f out: wknd over 1f out* **16/1**	82
5006	12	3 ¾	**Gallagher**[14] 4358 4-9-10 **101** ... CO'Donoghue 2 (B J Meehan) *hld up: hdwy over 2f out: wknd over 1f out* **11/1**	74
1-40	13	2 ½	**Eton Rifles (IRE)**[14] 4371 5-8-12 **89** ... TomEaves 5 (J Howard Johnson) *chsd ldrs: rdn over 2f out: wknd over 1f out* **12/1**	56
3310	14	1 ¾	**Sunraider (IRE)**[14] 4391 3-8-12 **95** ... MichaelHills 8 (B W Hills) *chsd ldrs: rdn over 2f out: wknd over 1f out* **5/2**[1]	55
0005	15	nk	**Titan Triumph**[44] 3346 6-7-7 **77** ... (t) HarryBentley(7) 13 (W J Knight) *hld up in tch: rdn and wknd over 2f out* **40/1**	38

1m 24.85s (-0.85) **Going Correction** +0.125s/f (Good)

WFA 3 from 4yo+ 6lb **15 Ran SP% 123.5**

Speed ratings (Par 109): **109,106,104,103,101 101,100,100,99,96 96,92,89,87,87**

toteswingers: 1&2 £71.60, 1&3 £29.90, 2&3 £22.60 CSF £170.50 CT £2885.08 TOTE £15.60: £4.30, £6.20, £6.40; EX 219.50 TRIFECTA Not won..

Owner C J Murfitt **Bred** A Stroud And J Hanly **Trained** Newmarket, Suffolk

FOCUS

It was raining steadily prior to the off. This was a decent handicap, although three of the first four finishers had been beaten in a Goodwood classified event just ten days earlier, albeit that they had performed creditably. They went a good, even gallop, and all raced up the middle of the track for most of the way, but the front two ended up towards the near rail. The winner is back to his best with the runner-up close to last season's level.

NOTEBOOK

Al Khaleej(IRE) confirmed Goodwood form with the two who had finished behind him, and probably stepped up a little to do so. He was 7lb lower than when a well-beaten 5-1 shot in this race last year, with a decent claimer taking off another 3lb, and won tidily on only his second outing for David Simcock, despite being bumped over 1f out and then carried slightly right by the runner-up. The easy ground suited and there could be another decent handicap in him under similar conditions. (op 9-1)

Manassas(IRE) couldn't reverse recent Goodwood placings with Al Khaleej, but he still looked to step up a notch on that form. He was given a positive ride and stuck on well, although he didn't help himself by hanging right under pressure. Official explanation: jockey said gelding hung right-handed (op 14-1 tchd 20-1)

Imperial Guest travelled well to a point, but he was squeezed for room soon after coming under pressure and couldn't get to the front two. He has run some decent races in defeat in good company since winning at Brighton in April. (op 14-1)

Oratory(IRE), third in the aforementioned Goodwood classified contest, didn't seem to mind the ground and ran respectably in a first-time visor, but he doesn't seem to have much in hand off his current mark. (op 10-1)

Day Of The Eagle(IRE) ran a mulish race. Having started sluggishly, he was simply never going that well and, not for the first time, wandered around when under serious pressure. He finally ran on in the closing stages and the impression is that he has more ability than his finishing position suggests. Headgear has got to be worth a try. Official explanation: jockey said gelding hung right and left-handed (op 9-1 tchd 10-1)

Glen Shiel(USA) ◆ probably didn't appreciate the soft ground but didn't run badly. He's one to keep in mind for when he's returned to a quick surface. (op 10-1)

Viva Vettori ran a respectable race on his first try over a trip this short. (op 22-1)

Redford(IRE) was well held, but his new yard have not had him for long and he could yet rediscover his form. (op 10-1 tchd 9-1)

Spirit Of Sharjah(IRE) can be given another chance back on quick ground.

Sunraider(IRE) had the ground to suit and was really well backed, but he proved totally unsuited by the step up in trip. He looks a sprinter. Official explanation: jockey said colt had no more to give (op 7-2)

4844 HOME OF RACING MAIDEN FILLIES' STKS — 7f

3:45 (3:46) (Class 4) 2-Y-O — £4,533 (£1,348; £674; £336) Stalls High

Form	Pos	Dist	Horse / details	Jockey	RPR
	1		**Morning Charm (USA)** 2-9-0 0 (J H M Gosden) *hld up: pushed along 1/2-way: hdwy over 1f out: led ins fnl f: r.o* 5/1[3]	NickyMackay 10	80+
	2	hd	**Abtasaamah (USA)** 2-9-0 0 (Saeed Bin Suroor) *a.p: led over 1f out: rdn and hdd ins fnl f: r.o* 7/2[1]	FrankieDettori 8	80+
	3	1 1/2	**Quiet Oasis (IRE)** 2-9-0 0 (B J Meehan) *hld up: hdwy over 1f out: r.o* 20/1	CO'Donoghue 15	75+
	4	1 1/4	**Set To Music (IRE)** 2-9-0 0 (M L W Bell) *w ldrs: rdn over 1f out: styd on same pce ins fnl f* 4/1[2]	EddieAhern 11	72+
	5	1/2	**New River (IRE)** 2-9-0 0 (R Hannon) *hld up: hdwy over 1f out: styd on: nt rch ldrs* 14/1	PatDobbs 16	71+
	6	1	**Tameen** 2-9-0 0 (J L Dunlop) *racd keenly: w ldrs: rdn and hung lft fr over 2f out: wknd ins fnl f* 6/1	RichardHills 2	68+
	7	3/4	**Grecian Goddess (IRE)** 2-9-0 0 (J Ryan) *led 4f: rdn over 1f out: no ex ins fnl f* 66/1	MarcHalford 12	66
	8	3/4	**Spade** 2-8-9 0 (D R C Elsworth) *chsd ldrs: led 3f out: rdn and hdd over 1f out: wknd ins fnl f* 25/1	DeclanCannon(5) 5	64
	9	1 3/4	**Malacca Straits** 2-9-0 0 (B W Hills) *s.s: hdwy over 4f out: wknd ins fnl f* 8/1	MichaelHills 1	59+
	10	3/4	**Baqaat (USA)** 2-9-0 0 (E A L Dunlop) *trckd ldrs: racd keenly: hmpd and wknd over 2f out* 28/1	DaraghO'Donohoe 13	57
	11	1 1/4	**Battery Power** 2-9-0 0 (M H Tompkins) *s.i.s: sn pushed along in rr: nvr on terms* 66/1	PatCosgrave 14	54
	12	5	**Super Smile (IRE)** 2-9-0 0 (R Hannon) *hld up: a in rr: wknd over 2f out*	SebSanders 17	40
	13	8	**Ihavenotime (IRE)** 2-9-0 0 (M R Channon) *a in rr: bhd whn hung lft over 2f out* 25/1	TomQueally 4	19

1m 29.22s (3.52) **Going Correction** +0.125s/f (Good) 13 Ran SP% 115.7
Speed ratings (Par 93): **84,83,82,80,80 78,78,77,75,74 72,67,58**
toteswingers: 1&2 £3.20, 1&3 £28.00, 2&3 £29.60 CSF £20.26 TOTE £7.00: £2.30, £1.70, £5.60; EX 30.50.
Owner George Strawbridge **Bred** George Strawbridge Jr **Trained** Newmarket, Suffolk
■ Stewards' Enquiry : Nicky Mackay three-day ban: careless riding (Aug 23-25)

FOCUS
This maiden for unraced fillies' is often a decent contest - subsequent Group 1 scorer Passage Of Time won the 2006 renewal and this season's Ribblesdale winner Hibaayeb was third last year. The time was 2.20sec slower than the Sweet Solera, although there had been more rain since that race was run, but it still looked a decent contest. They raced middle to near side.

NOTEBOOK
Morning Charm(USA) ◆, a half-sister to the same owner and trainer's St Leger winner Lucarno, showed a deal of ability to make a winning debut. This Fillies' Mile entrant seems sure to relish a step up in trip and is potentially smart - maybe she'll even be an Oaks candidate next season. (tchd 11-2)
Abtasaamah(USA) ◆, a half-sister to Breeders' Cup Juvenile winner Midshipman, failed only narrowly on her debut. She's entitled to come on for this and, like the winner, looks a smart prospect. (op 11-4)
Quiet Oasis(IRE) ◆, a sister to Young Pretender, a dual 6f-7f winner at two, was weak in the market but shaped well, keeping on nicely towards the near side. Brian Meehan's newcomers often improve a good deal next time. (op 33-1)
Set To Music(IRE) ◆, a half-sister to a couple of middle-distance winners, seemed to overrace slightly, without cover through the early stages, and she didn't finish her race particularly strongly. She was described by Eddie Ahern beforehand as "definitely above average" and can do better. (tchd 11-2)
New River(IRE), a 50,000gns purchase, shaped as though in need of the run but finished nicely. (op 12-1)
Tameen, who is out of a high-class 1m2f winner, has been given a Fillies' Mile entry. She faded late on and is likely to want further. (tchd 5-1 and 13-2 in a place)
Grecian Goddess(IRE) cost only 800gns, but she showed ability and may do even better over further next year.
Spade was prominent for much of the way and was another who shaped encouragingly. (op 40-1)
Malacca Straits was green on leaving the stalls and was then too keen. She can do better. (tchd 7-1)
Baqaat(USA) ◆ was bumped at a crucial stage but still plugged on. (op 50-1)

4845 JULY COURSE MAIDEN STKS — 1m 4f

4:20 (4:20) (Class 4) 3-Y-O+ — £4,533 (£1,348; £674; £336) Stalls Centre

Form	Pos	Dist	Horse / details	Jockey	RPR
0432	1		**Plato (JPN)**[17] 4258 3-9-1 77 (H R A Cecil) *led 1f: chsd ldrs: rdn to ld over 1f out: styd on wl* 7/2[2]	TomQueally 6	91
5-2	2	5	**Western Pearl**[26] 3953 3-8-10 0 (W J Knight) *led after 1f: rdn: hung lft and hdd over 1f out: no ex ins fnl f* 8/1	MartinDwyer 4	78
32	3	3	**Royal Riviera**[38] 3563 4-9-7 0 (J R Gask) *hld up: hdwy over 5f out: rdn over 1f out: sn hung lft and wknd* 8/1	SimonPearce(5) 8	78
2	4	3/4	**Music City (IRE)**[67] 2627 3-9-1 0 (M Johnston) *hld up in tch: rdn over 2f out: wknd fnl f* 6/1	MichaelHills 2	77
03	5	1 1/2	**Sea Change (IRE)**[17] 4257 3-9-1 0 (J Noseda) *hld up: hdwy over 5f out: rdn and wknd over 1f out* 20/1	SebSanders 7	75
2	6	20	**Vibrant Force (USA)**[23] 4069 3-9-1 0 (Mahmood Al Zarooni) *hld up: rdn over 3f out: hung lft and wknd over 1f out: t.o* 9/4[1]	FrankieDettori 10	43+
32	7	2 3/4	**Pink Palace (USA)**[47] 3266 3-8-10 0 (Sir Michael Stoute) *prom: chsd ldr 7f out tl rdn over 3f out: wknd over 2f out: t.o* 5/1[3]	KierenFallon 1	33
0	8	8	**Mawazin**[23] 4069 4-9-12 0 (E A L Dunlop) *hld up: rdn over 3f out: hung lft and wknd over 2f out: t.o* 66/1	RichardHills 3	25
56	9	71	**Blast Furnace (IRE)**[58] 2890 3-8-10 0 (P W Chapple-Hyam) *chsd ldrs tl wknd over 3f out: eased: t.o* 33/1	PatCosgrave 11	—

2m 34.17s (1.27) **Going Correction** +0.125s/f (Good)
WFA 3 from 4yo 11lb 9 Ran SP% 115.4
Speed ratings (Par 105): **100,96,94,94,93 79,78,72,25**
toteswingers: 1&2 £6.50, 1&3 £4.90, 2&3 £9.70 CSF £30.76 TOTE £4.30: £1.30, £3.10, £2.30; EX 35.50.
Owner Niarchos Family **Bred** Flaxman Holdings Ltd **Trained** Newmarket, Suffolk

FOCUS
This looked a decent older-horse maiden for the time of year. They raced up the middle of the track and the winner is probably the best guide, while the third and fifth were close to earlier efforts.
Royal Riviera Official explanation: jockey said gelding had run too freely

4846 RACING UK SKY 432 H'CAP — 2m 24y

4:55 (4:58) (Class 3) (0-90,90) 3-Y-O+ — £7,123 (£2,119; £1,059; £529) Stalls Centre

Form	Pos	Dist	Horse / details	Jockey	RPR
1225	1		**My Arch**[25] 3974 8-9-9 85 (Ollie Pears) *hld up in tch: wnt 3rd 1/2-way: rdn over 2f out: sn outpcd: rallied 1f out: r.o to ld wl ins fnl f* 5/1[3]	KierenFallon 4	93+
6002	2	nk	**Omokoroa (IRE)**[21] 4125 4-9-2 78 (M H Tompkins) *hld up: hdwy over 2f out: rdn to ld 1f out: hung rt and hdd wl ins fnl f* 9/1	PatCosgrave 7	86
-242	3	1	**Plymouth Rock (IRE)**[37] 3588 4-9-12 88 (v) (J Noseda) *mid-div: hdwy over 6f out: rdn to ld and hung lft wl over 1f out: no ex towards fin* 7/2[1]	TomQueally 6	95
6251	4	hd	**Cotillion**[21] 4125 4-9-9 85 (Ian Williams) *a.p: chsd ldr over 12f out to 1/2-way: rdn: hung lft and ev ch over 1f out: styd on same pce ins fnl f* 9/2[2]	FrankieDettori 12	92
0461	5	1 1/2	**Bollin Felix**[22] 4086 6-9-9 85 (b) (T D Easterby) *hld up: rdn over 3f out: hdwy and swtchd rt over 1f out: styd on: nt rch ldrs* 8/1	DavidNolan 13	90
0332	6	3/4	**Act Of Kalanisi (IRE)**[4] 4686 4-8-12 74 (M Johnston) *a.p: chsd ldr 10f out: rdn to ld 2f out: sn hdd: no ex ins fnl f* 8/1	RichardHills 10	78
114-	7	11	**Veiled**[234] 6258 4-9-5 86 (J Pearce) *hld up: hdwy over 5f out: rdn and wknd over 1f out* 25/1	SimonPearce(5) 5	77
-012	8	1 3/4	**Outrageous Request**[36] 3634 4-9-6 82 (Pat Eddery) *led: rdn and hdd 2f out: wkng whn nt clr run over 1f out* 8/1	AndreaAtzeni 11	71
360-	9	13	**Wells Lyrical (IRE)**[294] 6851 5-10-0 90 (B Smart) *plld hrd: trckd ldr over 3f: remained handy: rdn 5f out: wknd over 2f out* 11/1	TomEaves 14	63
4430	10	2	**Satwa Gold (USA)**[15] 4320 4-9-5 81 (Stef Higgins) *hld up: hdwy over 3f out: wkng whn hung lft over 1f out* 25/1	SebSanders 1	52
-000	11	3/4	**Liszt (IRE)**[77] 2317 4-9-12 88 (Ian Williams) *s.s: sn prom: wknd over 3f out* 25/1	EddieAhern 9	58

3m 32.41s (5.41) **Going Correction** +0.125s/f (Good) 11 Ran SP% 120.3
Speed ratings (Par 107): **91,90,90,90,89 89,83,82,76,75 74**
toteswingers: 1&2 £10.80, 1&3 £5.20, 2&3 £9.30 CSF £49.45 CT £175.45 TOTE £5.60: £1.70, £3.00, £1.90; EX 53.40.
Owner J D Spensley & Mrs M A Spensley **Bred** J And A Spensley **Trained** Norton, N Yorks

FOCUS
A decent staying handicap, although the early pace seemed just modest and the form looks a bit muddling, with the fifth possibly the best guide. They raced middle to far side in the straight.

NOTEBOOK
My Arch looked set to be well held when losing his position over 2f out, but he's a strong stayer and was galvanised by Fallon. The ease in the ground suited him and this must rate a career-best. He's apparently being aimed at the Cesarewitch and he'll relish the step up in trip. (op 6-1)
Omokoroa(IRE), trying 2m for the first time, reversed recent 1m6f Haydock placings with Cotillion and was just denied the victory. In this form he can surely find a similar race. (op 12-1)
Plymouth Rock(IRE), 5lb higher than when second over 1m6f at Haydock on quick ground last time, showed an action that suggests these easier conditions wouldn't have inconvenienced him, but he didn't quite see out the longer trip, having initially travelled as well as anything. (op 9-2)
Cotillion, 9lb higher than when winning over 1m6f at Haydock (Omokoroa runner-up) on his previous start, sweated up badly this time and in the circumstances did well to finish so close. (op 3-1 tchd 5-1 in a place)
Bollin Felix, off the same mark as when third in this race in 2008, having been raised 7lb for a recent Hamilton success, probably would have preferred a stronger gallop. (op 15-2 tchd 9-1)
Act Of Kalanisi(IRE) ran an honest race, but this may have come a bit too soon following his second placing on Fibresand only four days earlier. (tchd 10-1)
Wells Lyrical(IRE) was much too keen on his return from a 294-day absence. (op 16-1)

4847 EBF RUTH WATSON HITS 80 THIS YEAR FILLIES' H'CAP (FOR CHRIS WOTTON CUP) — 1m

5:25 (5:29) (Class 4) (0-80,80) 3-Y-O+ — £5,180 (£1,541; £770; £384) Stalls High

Form	Pos	Dist	Horse / details	Jockey	RPR
01	1		**Titbit**[72] 2478 3-9-2 75 (H R A Cecil) *racd centre tl gps merged over 3f out: chsd ldrs: rdn to ld over 1f out: edgd lft: r.o wl* 4/1[2]	EddieAhern 9	90+
00-0	2	4	**Qalahari (IRE)**[112] 1383 4-10-0 80 (D J Coakley) *racd centre tl gps merged over 3f out: hld up: hdwy u.p and hung lft over 1f out: r.o to go 2nd post: no ch w wnr* 18/1	JimmyQuinn 6	87
-651	3	nse	**Avon Lady**[18] 4236 3-8-13 72 (J R Fanshawe) *racd towards far side tl gps merged over 3f out: prom: rdn over 1f out: chsd wnr fnl f: styd on same pce: lost 2nd post* 11/2[3]	PatCosgrave 4	78
1032	4	1 3/4	**Amethyst Dawn (IRE)**[13] 4404 4-9-7 73 (T D Easterby) *racd towards far side tl gps merged over 3f out: overall ldr: rdn and hdd over 1f out: no ex ins fnl f* 8/1	TomEaves 1	76
31-1	5	nk	**Cloud's End**[42] 3441 3-9-7 80 (W J Haggas) *racd towards far side tl gps merged over 3f out: prom: hung lft over 2f out: sn rdn: no ex ins fnl f* 7/2[1]	MichaelHills 2	81
-305	6	4 1/2	**Flapper (IRE)**[10] 4472 4-9-4 70 (J W Hills) *racd towards centre and led that bunch tl gps merged over 3f out: rdn: hung lft and ev ch over 1f out: wknd fnl f* 4/1[2]	RichardHills 7	62
5324	7	1 3/4	**My Best Bet**[19] 4206 4-9-9 75 (Stef Higgins) *racd towards far side tl gps merged over 3f out: hld up: hdwy u.p over 1f out: wknd fnl f* 12/1	SebSanders 11	63
1-43	8	12	**Blue Lyric**[188] 366 3-9-3 76 (L M Cumani) *racd centre and chsd ldr of that bunch tl gps merged over 3f out: rdn over 2f out: wknd over 1f out* 11/1	KierenFallon 5	35
3000	9	2 1/4	**Shaws Diamond (USA)**[16] 4287 4-9-6 72 (D Shaw) *racd centre tl gps merged over 3f out: hld up: a in rr: wknd over 2f out* 50/1	DavidProbert 10	27
0-00	10	10	**Nizhoni Dancer**[65] 2685 4-9-6 72 (C F Wall) *racd towards far side tl gps merged over 3f out: dwlt: drvn along to chse ldr 7f out: rdn over 3f out: wknd over 2f out* 25/1	IanMongan 3	4

1m 40.6s (0.60) **Going Correction** +0.125s/f (Good)
WFA 3 from 4yo 7lb 10 Ran SP% 115.8
Speed ratings (Par 102): **102,98,97,96,95 91,89,77,75,65**
toteswingers: 1&2 £14.40, 1&3 £4.50, 2&3 £13.40 CSF £72.41 CT £398.83 TOTE £4.30: £1.80, £6.00, £2.20; EX 128.40 Place 6 £210.63, Place 5 £100.23.
Owner Mrs Bruce Bossom **Bred** Penelope Bossom & Bloomsbury Stud **Trained** Newmarket, Suffolk

The Form Book, Raceform Ltd, Compton, RG20 6NL

FOCUS
A fair fillies' handicap run at an honest pace and the form looks sound with the third and fifth close to recent marks. The main action was up the middle of the track.
T/Jkpt: Not won. T/Plt: £371.20 to a £1 stake. Pool £102,170.65. 200.88 winning tickets. T/Qpdt: £62.20 to a £1 stake. Pool: £4,766.51. 56.70 winning tickets. CR

4480 REDCAR (L-H)

Saturday, August 7

OFFICIAL GOING: Good to firm (8.9)
Wind: Virtually nil Weather: Sunny periods and showers

4848 SAINT FABIAN (S) STKS — 6f

1:55 (1:56) (Class 6) 2-Y-O — **£1,706** (£503; £252) **Stalls** Centre

Form — RPR
46 **1** **Maggie Mey (IRE)**[16] 4286 2-8-6 0 .... JoeFanning 1 63
(D O'Meara) *cl up: led over 2f out: rdn over 1f out: kpt on* **85/40**[1]
00 **2** 3/4 **Saxonette**[10] 4474 2-8-6 0 .... ChrisCatlin 7 61
(M R Channon) *in tch: hdwy 1/2-way: cl up 2f out: sn rdn and ev ch tl drvn and one pce wl ins fnl f* **9/2**[3]
00 **3** hd **None Sweeter**[11] 4451 2-8-6 0 .... RichardMullen 8 60
(T D Easterby) *towards rr: hdwy 2f out: sn rdn and styd on wl fnl f* **16/1**
00 **4** 4 1/2 **Irelandisuperman**[19] 4187 2-8-11 0 .... PaulQuinn 4 51
(D Nicholls) *led: rdn along and hdd over 2f out: drvn over 1f out and sn wknd* **9/1**
0000 **5** nse **Jealousy Defined (IRE)**[8] 4554 2-8-5 44 ow2......(p) BarryMcHugh(3) 11 47
(N Tinkler) *dwlt and in rr: pushed along and edgd lft over 2f out: rdn wl over 1f out: kpt on fnl f: nrst fin* **28/1**
0000 **6** 4 **Whats For Pudding (IRE)**[12] 4429 2-8-6 53 .... AndrewMullen 5 33
(D Carroll) *cl up: rdn along 1/2-way: grad wknd fnl 2f* **33/1**
40 **7** 2 1/2 **Evening In (IRE)**[8] 4554 2-8-3 0 .... PaulPickard(3) 9 25
(P T Midgley) *prom on outer: rdn along wl over 2f out: grad wknd* **11/1**
3020 **8** 11 **Kodibelle (IRE)**[8] 4554 2-8-6 58 ....(b) DuranFentiman 3 —
(T D Easterby) *prom: rdn along after 1 1/2f: sn lost pl and bhd fr 1/2-way* **14/1**
055 **9** 3 **Mr Shifter**[44] 3353 2-8-11 55 .... StevieDonohoe 2 —
(Mrs L Stubbs) *chsd ldrs: rdn along 1/2-way and sn wknd* **12/1**
0231 **10** 7 **Captain Loui (IRE)**[12] 4436 2-9-3 63 ....(b) ShaneKelly 6 —
(K A Ryan) *dwlt: rdn along 1/2-way: a in rr* **7/2**[2]

1m 12.68s (0.88) **Going Correction** +0.10s/f (Good) **10** Ran SP% **117.4**
Speed ratings (Par 92): **98,97,96,90,90 85,82,67,63,54**
toteswingers:1&2:£4.00, 1&3:£8.30, 2&3:£16.20 CSF £11.72 TOTE £3.10: £1.30, £1.70, £6.50; EX 13.50.The winner was bought in 3,200 gns.
Owner The Ten Commandments **Bred** Roger O'Callaghan **Trained** Nawton, N Yorks

FOCUS
Run-of-the-mill selling fare, with the front three pulling clear. The winner is rated to her debut form.

NOTEBOOK
Maggie Mey(IRE) was quickly dropped in class after disappointing as favourite for a Doncaster maiden last time, and a return to her debut form was enough to see her get off the mark. The winner left the impression she was doing only what was required after hitting the front soon after halfway, and she will continue to be a force at this level. (op 11-4 tchd 3-1 in a place)
Saxonette made more of an impact dropped in class and should have a race in her in this grade on this evidence. (op 5-1)
None Sweeter, who was well suited by the step up to 6f, stayed on in the manner of one who'll benefit from even further still. (op 18-1)
Irelandisuperman showed speed before fading late on, and he looks well worth a try at 5f. He's one to bear in mind for a low-grade nursery as he can't get much of a mark on what he's achieved to date. (tchd 11-1)
Jealousy Defined(IRE) fared a bit better in first-time cheekpieces, staying on late. A selling nursery would give her a more realistic chance of success. (op 40-1)
Evening In(IRE) has now been disappointing on both starts since a reasonably promising debut fourth at this level. (op 12-1)
Captain Loui(IRE) looked to have a bit more than most going for him having won in similar company at Yarmouth last time, but he ran no sort of race. (op 11-4)

4849 JOHN SMITH'S REDCAR STRAIGHT-MILE CHAMPIONSHIP H'CAP (QUALIFIER) — 1m

2:30 (2:31) (Class 3) (0-90,87) 3-Y-O+ — **£5,828** (£1,734; £866; £432) **Stalls** Centre

Form — RPR
1322 **1** **Cheers For Thea (IRE)**[7] 4603 5-9-3 78 ....(bt) DuranFentiman 6 89
(T D Easterby) *hld up in rr: swtchd rt and gd hdwy over 2f out: rdn to ld over 1f out: kpt on* **11/4**[2]
0601 **2** 1 3/4 **City Of The Kings (IRE)**[5] 4652 5-9-6 86 6ex...(p) MichaelO'Connell(5) 1 93
(G A Harker) *trckd ldrs: edgd lft fr 1/2-way: effrt to chal 2f out: sn rdn: chsd wnr ins fnl f: sn hung rt and no imp towards fin* **9/2**
4262 **3** 1 1/4 **Bolodenka (IRE)**[9] 4522 8-9-0 75 .... JoeFanning 2 79
(R A Fahey) *set stdy pce: qcknd over 3f out: rdn 2f out: drvn and hdd over 1f out: kpt on same pce fnl f* **7/1**
50-0 **4** 1/2 **Iasia (GR)**[28] 3890 4-9-12 87 .... StevieDonohoe 4 90
(Jane Chapple-Hyam) *trckd ldrs: effrt over 2f out: swtchd rt and rdn over 1f out: kpt on same pce* **20/1**
1414 **5** 1 1/2 **Brannagh (USA)**[16] 4296 3-9-3 85 ....(t) ShaneKelly 7 84
(J Noseda) *cl up: effrt over 2f out and ev ch tl rdn and hld whn n.m.r ent fnl f: wknd* **5/2**[1]
6022 **6** 1 **Chosen Forever**[22] 4093 5-8-10 74 .... BarryMcHugh(3) 3 71
(G R Oldroyd) *trckd ldrs: rdn along over 2f out: wknd wl over 1f out* **4/1**[3]

1m 37.27s (-0.73) **Going Correction** +0.10s/f (Good)
WFA 3 from 4yo+ 7lb **6** Ran SP% **110.7**
Speed ratings (Par 107): **107,105,104,103,102 101**
toteswingers:1&2:£2.10, 1&3:£2.10, 2&3:£6.30 CSF £14.86 TOTE £3.70: £1.10, £3.70; EX 13.20.
Owner Ron George **Bred** Crone Stud Farms Ltd **Trained** Great Habton, N Yorks
■ Stewards' Enquiry : Michael O'Connell caution: careless riding; caution: used whip with excessive force.

FOCUS
Not competitive in terms of numbers, but most did at least come into this in form. The winner recorded a personal best with the third to this year's best form.

NOTEBOOK
Cheers For Thea(IRE) has absolutely thrived this year and a fourth success of the campaign rarely looked in doubt. She'll go up to a mark in the low-80s on the back of this, but it won't stop her being of interest the way her career's gone of late. (op 3-1 tchd 10-3)
City Of The Kings(IRE) had a 6lb penalty for his Ripon success earlier in the week and probably ran to a similar level without having any excuses, wandering about a bit under pressure in the cheekpieces. (op 7-2 tchd 10-3 and 5-1 in a place)
Bolodenka(IRE) matched his recent form, but his lengthy losing run is almost certainly no coincidence and, having had the run of things from the front, he couldn't respond once the winner had quickened past him. (op 8-1)
Iasia(GR) at least performed a lot better than her reappearance, but her mark went up on the back of her not being beaten far in a couple of Listed events last autumn, and it's unlikely she'll be the easiest to place near to hand. (op 33-1)
Brannagh(USA) is still relatively lightly raced, but his last couple of efforts suggest the handicapper may have him for the time being, having no excuses back on a more conventional track on this occasion. (op 11-4)
Chosen Forever came into this on the back of two good efforts, with his Haydock second last month having been boosted a couple of times since. But he was just about the first beaten here, clearly not quite himself. (tchd 7-2)

4850 BETFAIR MOBILE TOMORROW H'CAP — 7f

3:05 (3:06) (Class 4) (0-80,79) 3-Y-O+ — **£3,626** (£1,079; £539; £269) **Stalls** Centre

Form — RPR
0433 **1** **Malcheek (IRE)**[12] 4438 8-9-12 78 .... DuranFentiman 1 86
(T D Easterby) *mde all: rdn along 2f out: jnd and drvn jst over 1f out: edgd lft ins fnl f: hld on gamely* **9/1**
6514 **2** hd **Poppet's Lovein**[14] 4378 4-9-13 79 .... StevieDonohoe 6 86
(A B Haynes) *dwlt and towards rr: smooth hdwy 1/2-way: effrt 2f out: rdn to chal over 1f out: ev ch tl drvn: edgd lft and no ex towards fin* **5/1**[2]
2046 **3** 1 3/4 **Imperial Djay (IRE)**[7] 4598 5-9-6 75 .... PaulPickard(3) 5 78
(Mrs R A Carr) *s.i.s and bhd: hdwy over 2f out: rdn wl over 1f out: kpt on ins fnl f: nrst fin* **7/1**
5510 **4** 1/2 **Step In Time (IRE)**[14] 4394 3-9-2 74 .... JoeFanning 2 73
(M Johnston) *trckd wnr: cl up 1/2-way: rdn to chal 2f out and ev ch tl drvn and one pce ent fnl f* **6/1**[3]
2210 **5** nse **Copper Penny**[44] 3361 3-9-6 78 .... ChrisCatlin 8 77
(D R Lanigan) *towards rr and rdn along 1/2-way: hdwy over 2f out: rdn to chse ldrs whn hung lft ent fnl f: sn one pce* **10/1**
0034 **6** 3 **Always Dazzling**[12] 4438 3-8-2 60 .... AndrewMullen 9 51
(M Johnston) *chsd ldrs: rdn along over 2f out: grad wknd* **16/1**
0456 **7** 3/4 **Legal Legacy**[43] 3396 4-9-7 73 .... ShaneKelly 10 64
(M Dods) *s.i.s and bhd: hdwy and in tch 1/2-way: rdn to chse ldrs over 2f out: sn drvn and btn* **6/1**[3]
00-4 **8** 1 1/2 **White Deer (USA)**[49] 3226 6-9-7 78 ....(v) MichaelO'Connell(5) 4 65
(G A Harker) *rdn along in rr 1/2-way: nvr a factor* **11/1**
0-00 **9** 1 **Ishe Mac**[16] 4287 4-9-9 75 .... DanielTudhope 7 59
(N Bycroft) *chsd ldrs: rdn along over 3f out: grad wknd* **22/1**
5604 **10** 1/2 **Floor Show**[15] 4345 4-9-12 78 .... RichardMullen 3 61
(N Wilson) *trckd ldrs: effrt 2f out and sn rdn: edgd lft and wknd qckly appr fnl f: sn eased* **9/2**[1]

1m 24.51s (0.01) **Going Correction** +0.10s/f (Good)
WFA 3 from 4yo+ 6lb **10** Ran SP% **113.6**
Speed ratings (Par 105): **103,102,100,100,100 96,95,94,93,92**
toteswingers:1&2:£5.30, 1&3:£15.30, 2&3:£27.20 CSF £52.14 CT £343.08 TOTE £10.80: £3.60, £1.20, £2.50; EX 52.90.
Owner Habton Farms **Bred** Carrigbeg Stud **Trained** Great Habton, N Yorks
■ Stewards' Enquiry : Stevie Donohoe two-day ban: used whip with excessive frequency in incorrect place (Aug 21-22)

FOCUS
No obviously progressive types in this, and it is doubtful the form is anything out of the ordinary for the grade, though it was at least soundly run. The form looks pretty straightforward with the winner close to his turf best.

4851 NORTHGATE VEHICLE HIRE NURSERY — 6f

3:40 (3:41) (Class 3) (0-95,83) 2-Y-O — **£5,180** (£1,541; £770; £384) **Stalls** Centre

Form — RPR
41 **1** **Talley Close**[17] 4240 2-8-11 78 .... IanBrennan(5) 3 86
(R A Fahey) *trckd ldrs: hdwy over 2f out: rdn to ld and hung bdly rt over 1f out: clr ins fnl f: drvn out* **10/1**
21 **2** 1 3/4 **Easy Ticket (IRE)**[22] 4116 2-9-5 81 .... RichardMullen 7 83+
(D H Brown) *hld up in rr: swtchd lft and hdwy 2f out: sn rdn and hung lft over 1f out: styd on to chse wnr ins fnl f: no imp towards fin* **11/10**[1]
1515 **3** 3/4 **Puddle Duck**[7] 4578 2-9-0 76 .... ShaneKelly 8 76
(K A Ryan) *s.i.s and in rr: gd hdwy 2f out: rdn over 1f out: styd on ins fnl f: nrst fin* **7/1**[3]
214 **4** 1/2 **Lady Del Sol**[44] 3364 2-8-12 77 .... BarryMcHugh(3) 4 75
(G R Oldroyd) *trckd ldr: hdwy to ld over 2f out: rdn: hdd and sltly hmpd over 1f out: sn swtchd lft and drvn: edgd lft and one pce ins fnl f* **14/1**
0015 **5** 3 1/4 **Lizzie (IRE)**[14] 4388 2-8-6 68 ....(b) DuranFentiman 6 56
(T D Easterby) *t.k.h early: hld up: sme hdwy over 2f out: sn rdn and hmpd over 1f out: n.d* **16/1**
1265 **6** shd **Falkland Flyer (IRE)**[8] 4539 2-9-0 76 .... ChrisCatlin 1 64
(M R Channon) *chsd ldrs: rdn along over 2f out: grad wknd* **11/1**
643 **7** 3 1/2 **Top Care (USA)**[17] 4240 2-8-13 75 .... JoeFanning 2 51
(M Johnston) *led: hdd 1/2-way: cl up tl rdn and wknd over 2f out* **9/1**
5121 **8** 2 **Krypton Factor**[17] 4262 2-9-7 83 ....(b) StevieDonohoe 9 53
(Sir Mark Prescott) *trckd ldrs: effrt over 2f out: sn rdn and btn* **13/2**[2]
4260 **9** 6 **Jamaica Grande**[7] 4600 2-7-9 64 .... LeonnaMayor(7) 5 15
(P S McEntee) *chsd ldrs: led briefly 1/2-way: sn hdd & wknd fnl 2f* **66/1**

1m 12.62s (0.82) **Going Correction** +0.10s/f (Good) **9** Ran SP% **114.9**
Speed ratings (Par 98): **98,95,94,94,89 89,84,82,74**
toteswingers:1&2:£4.10, 1&3:£3.70, 2&3:£3.50 CSF £21.31 CT £86.56 TOTE £14.90: £3.50, £1.10, £2.60; EX 23.00 Trifecta £158.40 Pool: £325.46 - 1.52 winning units..
Owner Skeltools Ltd **Bred** A B Phipps **Trained** Musley Bank, N Yorks
■ Stewards' Enquiry : Richard Mullen one-day ban: careless riding (Aug 21)
Ian Brennan caution: careless riding.

FOCUS
A couple of last-time-out maiden winners came to the fore here and this looks form to view positively, with the third and fourth both good yardsticks. The form is rated positively with the runner-up the best guide.

NOTEBOOK
Talley Close's Catterick form had been boosted by the runner-up Malgoof going in earlier in the week, and he showed himself a progressive and useful colt here, getting first run on the favourite to some extent but well on top in the end in any case. He'll stay 7f and there's further improvement in this son of Danbird. (op 17-2 tchd 11-1)
Easy Ticket(IRE) has some Pattern entries and is clearly held in some regard judged on the strength behind him in the market. He couldn't justify that confidence in the end, but certainly travelled for a long way like one ahead of his mark, and his inexperience off the bridle (edged left) is perfectly understandable given this was about the first time he's been asked a serious question (won easily at Pontefract last time). He's one to keep on-side. (op 6-4 tchd 7-4 in places)
Puddle Duck wasn't beaten far in a competitive event at Goodwood a week earlier and ran well again, ridden with more restraint on this occasion after missing the start and finishing well. He should continue to give a good account. (op 6-1 tchd 11-2)

Lady Del Sol's maiden success here a couple of months ago has worked out pretty well, and she ran well on her first outing for six weeks without giving the impression she has much in hand of her mark. (tchd 16-1)
Lizzie(IRE) had been dropped 4lb since her nursery bow, but she never threatened to land a serious blow, and perhaps the effect of the headgear is beginning to wear off. (op 14-1)
Falkland Flyer(IRE) didn't have the pace to land a serious blow back at this shorter trip. (op 14-1 tchd 9-1)
Top Care(USA) hadn't been far behind Talley Close at Catterick and might have been expected to do better on his nursery bow. (op 17-2 tchd 8-1)
Krypton Factor's blinkers didn't have such a positive effect at the second time of asking, with the gelding dropping out tamely. (op 5-1 tchd 9-2)

4852 MARKET CROSS JEWELLERS CLAIMING STKS — 1m 1f
4:10 (4:10) (Class 6) 4-Y-0+ — **£1,706** (£503; £252) **Stalls** Low

Form — RPR
0531 **1** — **Sunnyside Tom (IRE)**[13] 4403 6-9-9 82 ..... BarryMcHugh(3) 3 — 87
(R A Fahey) *mde all: rdn along and jnd over 2f out: drvn over 1f out: styd on wl* **6/5**[1]
0063 **2** 1 ½ **Muftarres (IRE)**[6] 4620 5-9-1 67 ..... JoeFanning 5 — 73
(P T Midgley) *trckd wnr: tk clsr order over 3f out: chal over 2f out: sn rdn and ev ch tl drvn and edgd lft ent fnl f: one pce* **6/1**
4411 **3** 1 ¾ **Applaude**[9] 4514 5-8-9 65 ..... (b) PaulEddery 4 — 63
(R C Guest) *chsd ldng pair: hdwy wl over 2f out: rdn wl over 1f out and sn one pce* **7/2**[3]
0200 **4** nse **Dragon Slayer (IRE)**[9] 4520 8-8-9 71 ..... StevieDonohoe 2 — 63
(John A Harris) *s.i.s: hld up in rr: rdn along and sltly outpcd over 2f out: drvn and styd on ins fnl f* **11/4**[2]

1m 54.97s (1.97) **Going Correction** +0.10s/f (Good) — 4 Ran SP% **108.6**
Speed ratings (Par 101): **95,93,92,92**
CSF £8.31 TOTE £1.70; EX 6.40.
Owner The Sunnyside Racing Partnership **Bred** S W D McIlveen **Trained** Musley Bank, N Yorks

FOCUS
A small field and a predictably steady pace for this claimer, with the order not changing throughout. The winner is rated as having run to this year's form.

4853 WIN A VIP DAY OUT @ REDCARRACING.CO.UK MEDIAN AUCTION MAIDEN STKS — 7f
4:45 (4:46) (Class 5) 3-4-Y-0 — **£2,266** (£674; £337; £168) **Stalls** Centre

Form — RPR
0022 **1** — **Viking Warrior (IRE)**[24] 4018 3-9-3 72 ..... ShaneKelly 5 — 63
(M Dods) *mde all: rdn 2f out: drvn over 1f out: hrd pressed ins fnl f: kpt on towards fin* **7/4**[1]
00 **2** ½ **Tombellini (IRE)**[30] 3808 3-9-3 0 ..... JoeFanning 2 — 62
(D Nicholls) *in tch: hdwy to chse ldrs over 2f out: rdn to challenge over 1f out: sn drvn and ev ch tl no ex towards fin* **33/1**
06- **3** nk **Hambleton**[312] 6356 3-9-0 0 ..... BarryMcHugh(3) 7 — 61
(B Smart) *hld up in tch: hdwy and cl up 3f out: rdn to chal over 1f out: sn rdn and ev ch tl drvn: edgd lft and no ex wl ins fnl f* **12/1**
66 **4** 6 **Hades (IRE)**[8] 4556 3-9-3 0 ..... RichardMullen 1 — 45
(T D Easterby) *dwlt and in rr: pushed along 3f out: rdn over 2f out: sme late hdwy* **7/2**[3]
05 **5** 4 **Nephele (IRE)**[8] 4556 3-8-12 0 ..... DuranFentiman 6 — 29
(T D Easterby) *chsd ldrs: rdn along wl over 2f out: sn wknd* **10/1**
0-0 **6** 1 **Champagne All Day**[15] 4340 4-9-9 0 ..... AndrewMullen 3 — 31
(S P Griffiths) *prom: rdn along 1/2-way: sn wknd* **50/1**
33 **7** 3 **Forever Hope**[9] 4521 3-8-12 0 ..... DanielTudhope 4 — 18
(T D Walford) *trckd ldrs: rdn along wl over 2f out and sn wknd* **85/40**[2]

1m 27.59s (3.09) **Going Correction** +0.10s/f (Good)
WFA 3 from 4yo 6lb — 7 Ran SP% **112.3**
Speed ratings (Par 103): **86,85,85,78,73 72,69**
toteswingers:1&2:£19.60, 1&3:£5.30, 2&3:£21.80 CSF £53.35 TOTE £2.20: £1.30, £24.90; EX 98.70 Place 6 £60.06; Place 5 £39.54.
Owner Transpennine Partnership **Bred** Darley **Trained** Denton, Co Durham

FOCUS
Hard to escape the conclusion that this was a weak maiden, especially with the time so slow.
Forever Hope Official explanation: jockey said filly ran flat

4854 BUY YOUR TICKETS ON-LINE @ REDCARRACING.CO.UK H'CAP — 1m 6f 19y
5:20 (5:21) (Class 6) (0-60,56) 3-Y-0+ — **£1,619** (£481; £240; £120) **Stalls** Low

Form — RPR
112 **1** — **Andorn (GER)**[40] 3496 6-9-7 55 ..... RussKennemore(3) 2 — 65+
(P A Kirby) *trckd ldng pair: pushed along and nt much room wl over 2f out: rdn over 3f out: hdwy on outer over 2f out: sltly outpcd over 2f out: sn swtchd rt and rdn to chse ldr ent fnl f: styd on to ld last 100yds* **9/2**[2]
2405 **2** 1 **Miss Ferney**[5] 4648 6-9-1 49 ..... PaulPickard(3) 14 — 55
(A Kirtley) *hld up towards rr: gd hdwy on outer over 2f out: rdn to ld wl over 1f out: drvn ins fnl f: hdd and no ex last 100yds* **8/1**
0-50 **3** 1 ½ **Heart Of Dubai (USA)**[32] 1922 5-9-1 46 ..... PaulEddery 10 — 50
(Micky Hammond) *hld up in rr: hdwy on inner 2f out: rdn over 1f out: kpt on ins fnl f: nrst fin* **14/1**
0345 **4** ¾ **What A Day**[37] 3600 4-8-12 48 ..... IanBrennan(5) 13 — 51
(J J Quinn) *in tch: hdwy to chse ldrs 3f out: sn rdn and sltly outpcd 2f out: styd on ins fnl f* **6/1**[3]
4036 **5** ½ **Perez (IRE)**[5] 4648 8-9-0 45 ..... (vt) StevieDonohoe 5 — 47
(W Storey) *trckd ldrs: swtchd lft and hdwy 3f out: led briefly 2f out: sn rdn and hdd wl over 1f out: drvn and one pce ent fnl f* **16/1**
04/0 **6** hd **Word Of Warning**[10] 3669 6-9-8 56 ..... BarryMcHugh(3) 1 — 58
(M Todhunter) *hld up in rr: hdwy over 2f out: rdn over 1f out: kpt on ins fnl f: nrst fin* **6/1**[3]
0064 **7** 2 ¼ **Parchment (IRE)**[11] 4453 8-9-0 45 ..... (b) DanielTudhope 9 — 44
(A J Lockwood) *in tch: rdn along and outpcd over 2f out: kpt on ins fnl f* **12/1**
6215 **7** dht **Drop The Hammer**[17] 4246 4-9-11 56 ..... (p) JoeFanning 7 — 55
(D O'Meara) *dispiuted ld: led 1/2-way: rdn along 3f out: hdd 2f out: sn drvn and grad wknd* **4/1**[1]
0/00 **9** 1 ¼ **Power Desert (IRE)**[10] 4484 5-9-1 46 ..... (v) AndrewMullen 12 — 43
(G A Harker) *chsd ldrs: rdn along 3f out: wknd over 2f out* **20/1**
-400 **10** ¾ **Chateauneuf (IRE)**[15] 4328 4-9-0 45 ..... ChrisCatlin 8 — 41
(W M Brisbourne) *midfield: effrt 3f out: sn rdn along and n.d* **20/1**
-040 **11** 1 ¼ **Piermarini**[9] 4511 5-9-0 45 ..... DuranFentiman 11 — 39
(P T Midgley) *a in rr* **40/1**
0-00 **12** 1 ½ **Transfered (IRE)**[4] 4683 4-8-12 46 ..... AndrewHeffernan(3) 3 — 38
(Lucinda Featherstone) *chsd ldrs: hdwy on inner whn hmpd 3f out: nt rcvr* **50/1**
0300 **13** 7 **Henry Havelock**[8] 4545 3-8-9 53 ..... ShaneKelly 4 — 35
(C Grant) *disp ld to 1/2-way: cl up tl rdn along and wknd over 3f out: eased over 1f out* **10/1**

3m 9.39s (4.69) **Going Correction** +0.10s/f (Good)
WFA 3 from 4yo+ 13lb — 13 Ran SP% **121.1**
Speed ratings (Par 101): **90,89,88,88,87 87,86,86,85,85 84,83,79**
toteswingers:1&2:£9.80, 1&3:£30.60, 2&3:£16.10 CSF £39.31 CT £477.45 TOTE £4.30: £1.20, £5.00, £1.70; EX 32.10 Place 6 £60.06, Place 5 £39.54.
Owner Preesall Garage **Bred** Gestut Schlenderhan **Trained** Castleton, N Yorks
■ Stewards' Enquiry : Stevie Donohoe seven-day ban: purposely rode left-handed to cause interference (Aug 23-29); eight-day ban: violent and improper behaviour (tbn)
Andrew Heffernan Fine: £750, attempted to mislead stewards.

FOCUS
Low-grade fare, and it developed into a bit of a sprint in the final 4f with the pace having been steady to that point. The form is not that solid and best rated around the third to seventh.
Henry Havelock Official explanation: jockey said colt hung right-handed
T/Plt: £39.80 to a £1 stake. Pool:£42,301.86 - 775.39 winning tickets T/Qpdt: £10.70 to a £1 stake. Pool:£3,041.10 - 209.70 winning tickets JR

4613 SARATOGA (R-H)
Saturday, August 7

OFFICIAL GOING: Dirt: fast

4855a WHITNEY H'CAP (GRADE 1) (3YO+) (DIRT) — 1m 1f (D)
10:48 (12:00) 3-Y-0+
£277,777 (£92,592; £46,296; £23,148; £13,888; £9,259)

RPR
1 — **Blame (USA)**[56] 4-8-9 0 ..... GKGomez 2 — 125
(Albert M Stall Jr, U.S.A) **17/5**[2]
2 hd **Quality Road (USA)**[68] 4-9-0 0 ..... JRVelazquez 3 — 130
(Todd Pletcher, U.S.A) **1/2**[1]
3 1 ¾ **Musket Man (USA)**[68] 4-8-5 0 ..... RMaragh 6 — 118
(Derek S Ryan, U.S.A) **71/10**[3]
4 9 ½ **Haynesfield (USA)**[35] 4-8-4 0 ..... RADominguez 4 — 99
(Steven Asmussen, U.S.A) **12/1**
5 1 ¼ **Mine That Bird (USA)**[34] 4-8-6 0 ..... CHBorel 1 — 98
(D Wayne Lukas, U.S.A) **97/10**
6 7 ½ **Jardim (BRZ)**[156] 796 4-8-1 0 ..... (b) JRLeparoux 5 — 79
(Eduardo Caramori, U.S.A) **43/1**

1m 48.88s (108.88) — 6 Ran SP% **121.1**
PARI-MUTUEL (all including $2 stake): WIN 8.80; PLACE (1-2) 3.00, 2.40; SHOW (1-2-3) 2.20, 2.10, 2.50; SF 18.20.
Owner Adele B Dilschneider & Claiborne Farm **Bred** Claiborne Farm & Adele B Dilschneider **Trained** USA

NOTEBOOK
Blame(USA) is now 8-11, and this was his second Grade 1 success. He was getting 5lb from Quality Road, but this was still a huge effort to run down that rival in the stretch, considering the favourite had been allowed to dictate a modest pace. A major player for the Breeders' Cup Classic, he's likely to have his prep run in the Jockey Club Gold Cup at Belmont on October 2.
Quality Road(USA) was allowed to set modest fractions on a quick track and it was disappointing he couldn't hold on, albeit his rider didn't help matters by continually looking around, rather than concentrating on securing the win. Strictly on the figures this was another big performance - he was conceding weight and for the third race in succession has been awarded an RPR of 130 - but his finishing kick suggests this trip stretched him.

4474 LEICESTER (R-H)
Sunday, August 8

OFFICIAL GOING: Good to firm (good in places; 8.0)
Wind: Light, behind Weather: Fine and sunny

4856 E B F BAGWORTH MAIDEN STKS — 7f 9y
2:20 (2:21) (Class 4) 2-Y-0 — **£4,533** (£1,348; £674; £336) **Stalls** Low

Form — RPR
43 **1** — **Azrael**[16] 4318 2-9-3 0 ..... JamesDoyle 2 — 85
(A J McCabe) *chsd ldr: led 1/2-way: rdn out* **7/1**
2 ¾ **Man Of The Match (IRE)** 2-9-3 0 ..... AdamKirby 3 — 83+
(A Bailey) *hld up in tch: chsd wnr 2f out: sn rdn: styd on* **13/8**[1]
0 **3** 2 ½ **Enabling (IRE)**[32] 3794 2-9-3 0 ..... PatDobbs 11 — 76
(R Hannon) *a.p: rdn over 1f out: styd on same pce ins fnl f* **7/2**[3]
23 **4** 3 **Harry Luck (IRE)**[27] 3961 2-9-3 0 ..... DaneO'Neill 10 — 68
(H Candy) *chsd ldrs: pushed along 4f out: rdn over 2f out: styd on same pce appr fnl f* **11/4**[2]
244 **5** 4 **Restless Bay (IRE)**[27] 3964 2-9-3 74 ..... DavidProbert 12 — 57
(R Hollinshead) *led to 1/2-way: rdn and wknd over 1f out* **10/1**
0 **6** 1 **Anton Dolin (IRE)**[23] 4096 2-9-3 0 ..... IanMongan 7 — 55
(J L Dunlop) *chsd ldrs: pushed along 1/2-way: wknd 2f out* **66/1**
7 ¾ **Number Theory** 2-9-3 0 ..... JerryO'Dwyer 4 — 53
(J R Holt) *sn pushed along in rr: nvr nrr* **100/1**
0 **8** ½ **Bodie**[23] 4110 2-9-3 0 ..... JamieMackay 9 — 51
(Mrs P Sly) *s.s: hld up: a in rr* **100/1**
0 **9** 14 **Love Nest**[22] 4131 2-9-3 0 ..... SteveDrowne 8 — 13
(J L Dunlop) *hld up: wknd 1/2-way* **50/1**
60 **10** 8 **Brave Tiger (IRE)**[8] 4599 2-9-3 0 ..... (t) NeilCallan 1 — —
(S C Williams) *prom: rdn over 2f out: sn hung lft and wknd* **66/1**

1m 24.9s (-1.30) **Going Correction** -0.25s/f (Firm) — 10 Ran SP% **115.5**
Speed ratings (Par 96): **97,96,93,89,85 84,83,82,66,57**
toteswingers: 1&2 £2.90, 1&3 £3.90, 2&3 £4.70 CSF £18.72 TOTE £6.30: £1.70, £1.40, £1.50; EX 28.90.
Owner The Cor Blimey Partnership **Bred** Ian Neville Marks **Trained** Averham Park, Notts

FOCUS
An interesting maiden, featuring a clutch of runners with sound form and a heavily backed newcomer. The form looks decent rated around the third and fourth.

NOTEBOOK
Azrael, with two previous outings under his belt and a decent third over this trip at Ascot 16 days earlier, put that experience to good use. Never far off the pace, he grabbed the lead around halfway and was never subsequently headed. The form horse here, he now qualifies for nurseries and his future in those will depend on the handicapper's assessment. (op 5-1)
Man Of The Match(IRE), a first-time-out 135,000gns breeze-up purchase, was strongly supported beforehand and, although he could not land the gamble, ran well enough to suggest the cash can soon be recouped. A repeat of this effort should ensure a maiden success. (op 11-4)

Enabling(IRE) had shown promise in a decent Newmarket maiden on his debut and, as is the case with so many from his stable, he stepped up considerably second time out. Although not the fastest away, he stayed on nicely and can find a small race this season. (tchd 4-1)
Harry Luck(IRE), who stayed on well when third over 6f at Windsor last time out, ran below that level here and may at this stage prefer the shorter trip. He was close up early on, but one-paced in the closing stages. (op 9-4 tchd 3-1)
Restless Bay(IRE), a fair second on his debut but below that level in two starts since, seems to be regressing. He led in the initial stages, but was left well behind when the principals quickened up. (op 9-1 tchd 11-1)
Anton Dolin(IRE), well beaten in a Newbury maiden on his only previous outing, showed a little more this time. His pedigree suggests he can progress again when stepped up in distance.

4857 RUTLAND (S) STKS — 7f 9y
2:50 (2:50) (Class 6) 3-4-Y-O — £1,942 (£578; £288; £144) Stalls Low

Form — RPR
0664 **1** **Fault**[17] 4298 4-9-7 65 ....(t) SebSanders 3 — 73
(Stef Higgins) *hld up: hdwy over 2f out: led over 1f out: rdn out* — **8/1**
0041 **2** 3 1/2 **Daddy's Gift (IRE)**[17] 4298 4-9-2 64 .... PatDobbs 6 — 59
(R Hannon) *hld up: hdwy 2f out: rdn over 1f out: styd on* — **13/2[3]**
0505 **3** 1 3/4 **Charlietoo**[24] 4071 4-8-9 50 ....(p) RyanClark[(7)] 9 — 54
(E G Bevan) *prom: rdn over 2f out: styd on same pce fr over 1f out: wnt 3rd towards fin* — **25/1**
1033 **4** 1/2 **Apache Ridge (IRE)**[23] 4084 4-9-7 72 ....(b) NeilCallan 7 — 57
(K A Ryan) *chsd ldrs: led 2f out: rdn and hdd over 1f out: no ex ins fnl f* — **7/4[1]**
3523 **5** 3/4 **Blue Noodles**[24] 4053 4-8-13 67 .... AndrewHeffernan[(3)] 4 — 50
(P D Evans) *chsd ldrs: rdn over 2f out: no ex fnl f* — **2/1[2]**
5050 **6** 1 **Mojeerr**[12] 4453 4-9-2 42 ....(v) JamesDoyle 10 — 48
(A J McCabe) *hld up: rdn over 2f out: nvr trbld ldrs* — **16/1**
6000 **7** 3/4 **Gracie May**[10] 4522 3-8-5 49 .... DavidProbert 11 — 41
(R Hollinshead) *led: rdn and hdd 2f out: wknd fnl f* — **33/1**
0500 **8** 18 **Penderyn**[93] 1887 3-8-5 44 .... JamieMackay 2 — —
(C Smith) *prom: rdn 1/2-way: wknd over 2f out* — **66/1**
06-0 **9** 3 1/2 **Rockson (IRE)**[20] 4202 4-8-4 42 ....(b[1]) RyanPowell[(7)] 5 — —
(Ian Williams) *rrd s: bhd: hdwy over 4f out: wknd 3f out* — **33/1**
0006 **10** 8 **Strike Shot**[11] 4475 3-8-10 45 ....(p) MartinDwyer 8 — —
(W R Muir) *prom: pushed along 1/2-way: wknd over 2f out* — **50/1**

1m 24.7s (-1.50) **Going Correction** -0.25s/f (Firm)
WFA 3 from 4yo 6lb — **10** Ran SP% **113.2**
Speed ratings (Par 101): **98,94,92,91,90 89,88,68,64,54**
toteswingers: 1&2 £5.00, 1&3 £15.30, 2&3 £26.70 CSF £54.12 TOTE £11.90: £1.40, £3.40, £5.70; EX 34.30.There was no bid for the winner.
Owner David Gilbert **Bred** Mrs A M Vestey **Trained** Lambourn, Berks

FOCUS
Not much depth to this run-of-the-mill seller with the winner rated to this year's best.

4858 LEICESTER MERCURY FAMILY FUN DAY H'CAP — 5f 218y
3:20 (3:20) (Class 3) (0-90,87) 3-Y-O
£7,477 (£2,239; £1,119; £560; £279; £140) Stalls Low

Form — RPR
1620 **1** **Waveband**[10] 4509 3-9-6 86 .... KierenFallon 1 — 97+
(M Johnston) *mde all: shkn up over 1f out: r.o wl: eased nr fin* — **9/2[3]**
1213 **2** 1 1/2 **Addictive Dream (IRE)**[20] 4204 3-9-7 87 .... AdamKirby 7 — 91
(W R Swinburn) *hld up: hdwy 2f out: chsd wnr over 1f out: rdn and hung lft ins fnl f: styd on same pce* — **2/1[2]**
3312 **3** nk **Ertikaan**[18] 4264 3-9-6 86 .... RichardHills 4 — 89
(M A Jarvis) *s.i.s: sn prom: chsd wnr 2f out tl rdn over 1f out: styd on same pce ins fnl f* — **11/8[1]**
0435 **4** 2 **Dancing Red Devil (IRE)**[5] 4670 3-8-7 73 .... SteveDrowne 6 — 70
(Paul Green) *chsd ldrs: pushed along and hung rt fr 1/2-way: styd on same pce appr fnl f* — **12/1**
6206 **5** 5 **Danzoe (IRE)**[9] 4553 3-8-2 68 ....(v) DavidProbert 3 — 49
(Mrs C A Dunnett) *chsd wnr tl rdn over 2f out: wknd over 1f out* — **33/1**
5305 **6** 3/4 **Gertmegalush (IRE)**[4] 4714 3-8-5 74 .... BarryMcHugh[(3)] 5 — 52
(John A Harris) *s.i.s: hld up: rdn over 2f out: sn lost tch* — **16/1**

1m 11.4s (-1.60) **Going Correction** -0.25s/f (Firm) — **6** Ran SP% **110.1**
Speed ratings (Par 104): **100,98,97,94,88 87**
toteswingers: 1&2 £2.50, 1&3 £1.90, 2&3 £1.10 CSF £13.40 CT £16.56 TOTE £6.00: £2.30, £1.10; EX 11.50.
Owner Sheikh Hamdan Bin Mohammed Al Maktoum **Bred** Stratford Place Stud **Trained** Middleham Moor, N Yorks
■ Stewards' Enquiry : Adam Kirby caution: use of whip

FOCUS
A decent handicap, but weakened markedly by a clutch of defections. The form is best rated through the fourth to her latest mark.

NOTEBOOK
Waveband was taking a drop in trip after a below-par run over 7f at Goodwood and it suited her down to the ground. Quickly away, she was able to hold her starting position close to the rail and led throughout. The third came at her at the 2f pole, but she showed great resolution to shrug off his challenge and was going away at the finish, underlining her preference for dominating from the front. She is sure to go up for this, so connections may try to find an opportunity under a penalty.
Addictive Dream(IRE), up just 1lb since his narrowly beaten third at Windsor three weeks previously, looks a feasible marker for the form. Held up in touch in the early stages, he made his challenge wide of the winner and third, battling on well in the closing stages. (op 5-2 tchd 11-4 in places)
Ertikaan had been raised 4lb since finishing second to a progressive rival over 7f at Sandown last time out and the rise proved beyond him. He chased the pace from the start and was almost upsides the winner approaching the final furlong, but his effort petered out late on. The drop in distance may not have been entirely to his liking, but his way of racing, and the noseband he wore, suggest also that he is not completely straightforward. (tchd 6-4 and 7-4 in places)
Dancing Red Devil(IRE), hampered when fifth at Catterick the previous Tuesday, had no such traffic problems here and was simply not good enough at the weights. She was prominent early on, but could not maintain the necessary momentum at the business end. Official explanation: jockey said filly had lost a shoe (op 10-1 tchd 9-1)
Danzoe(IRE) was tried in a visor after a couple of modest efforts in cheekpieces, but the changed headgear made no obvious difference. (op 28-1)
Gertmegalush(IRE), third off a 2lb higher mark at Pontefract the previous month, never looked likely to take advantage of his lower mark and finished well beaten. (tchd 14-1)

4859 THURMASTON H'CAP — 1m 1f 218y
3:50 (3:51) (Class 4) (0-85,85) 4-Y-O+ — £3,885 (£1,156; £577; £288) Stalls High

Form — RPR
2234 **1** **King's Masque**[14] 4399 4-9-0 78 .... JimmyFortune 1 — 85
(B J Llewellyn) *a.p: chsd ldr over 3f out: rdn over 1f out: r.o u.p to ld post* — **7/2[1]**
1153 **2** shd **Hel's Angel (IRE)**[24] 4055 4-8-10 77 .... BarryMcHugh[(3)] 5 — 84
(Mrs A Duffield) *led: rdn over 1f out: edgd lft nr fin: hdd post* — **15/2**
61-0 **3** 3/4 **Spensley (IRE)**[8] 4597 4-8-6 70 .... KierenFallon 4 — 75+
(J R Fanshawe) *s.i.s: sn hld up in tch: rdn over 1f out: r.o* — **15/2**
0526 **4** shd **Addwaitya**[8] 4579 5-9-1 79 .... IanMongan 7 — 84
(Mrs L J Mongan) *drvn along in rr early: chsd ldr 8f out tl hmpd by loose horse 4f out: sn rdn: r.o u.p* — **15/2**
3136 **5** nk **Welsh Anthem**[13] 4422 4-8-5 69 ....(p) HayleyTurner 6 — 74
(W R Muir) *chsd ldr 2f: remained handy: rdn over 1f out: r.o* — **11/1**
5006 **6** 1 **Docofthebay (IRE)**[25] 4030 6-9-7 85 .... NeilCallan 9 — 88
(J A Glover) *s.i.s: hld up: plld hrd: hdwy over 2f out: hung rt fr over 1f out: r.o: nvr rchd ldrs* — **5/1[3]**
1214 **7** 5 **Scamperdale**[10] 4520 8-9-6 84 .... SebSanders 8 — 77
(B P J Baugh) *hld up: hmpd and dropped to rr 6f out: hdwy 2f out: sn rdn: hung rt and wknd fnl f* — **4/1[2]**
4650 **8** 1 **Bold Cross (IRE)**[15] 4382 7-8-1 68 .... AndrewHeffernan[(3)] 2 — 59
(E G Bevan) *hld up: plld hrd: rdn over 2f out: wknd over 1f out* — **12/1**
0000 **S** **Truly Asia (IRE)**[18] 4265 4-8-6 70 .... SteveDrowne 10 — —
(R Charlton) *hld up: slipped up and uns rdr bnd leaving bk st* — **16/1**

2m 7.60s (-0.30) **Going Correction** -0.05s/f (Good) — **9** Ran SP% **116.1**
Speed ratings (Par 105): **99,98,98,98,98 97,93,92,—**
toteswingers: 1&2 £5.00, 1&3 £3.40, 2&3 £6.70 CSF £30.26 CT £185.80 TOTE £5.10: £1.20, £1.40, £2.70; EX 37.40.
Owner B J Llewellyn **Bred** Deerfield Farm **Trained** Fochriw, Caerphilly

FOCUS
A competitive handicap in which few, if any, could be confidently discounted. The form is muddling despite the first two being rated to form.

4860 LEICESTERSHIRE LIFE H'CAP — 1m 60y
4:20 (4:21) (Class 5) (0-75,76) 3-Y-O+ — £2,590 (£770; £385; £192) Stalls High

Form — RPR
-524 **1** **Gojeri (IRE)**[53] 3085 3-9-5 75 .... NeilCallan 1 — 88+
(M A Jarvis) *s.i.s: sn prom: chsd ldr 6f out: led over 2f out: drvn out* — **3/1[2]**
4304 **2** 1 1/2 **Ours (IRE)**[4] 4713 7-9-1 67 ....(p) BarryMcHugh[(3)] 4 — 77
(John A Harris) *hld up: hdwy u.p over 1f out: chsd wnr fnl f: no imp towards fin* — **6/1**
-103 **3** 6 **Dancing Jest (IRE)**[30] 3862 6-9-2 65 .... MartinDwyer 6 — 61
(Rae Guest) *chsd ldr 2f: remained handy: rdn over 3f out: styd on same pce fr over 1f out: eased whn btn wl ins fnl f* — **9/4[1]**
2104 **4** 1 1/4 **Golden Rock (IRE)**[34] 3725 4-9-7 70 .... SteveDrowne 5 — 63
(R Charlton) *led: rdn and hdd over 2f out: wknd ins fnl f* — **4/1[3]**
3602 **5** shd **Carcinetto (IRE)**[11] 4489 8-9-6 72 .... RichardEvans[(3)] 2 — 65
(P D Evans) *prom: rdn over 3f out: hung rt and wknd over 1f out* — **4/1[3]**

1m 44.1s (-1.00) **Going Correction** -0.05s/f (Good)
WFA 3 from 4yo+ 7lb — **5** Ran SP% **110.1**
Speed ratings (Par 103): **103,101,95,94,94**
toteswingers: 1&2 £8.10 CSF £19.79 TOTE £2.60: £1.10, £2.80; EX 16.90.
Owner G Moss, J Sims & R Marchant **Bred** Miss Joan Murphy **Trained** Newmarket, Suffolk

FOCUS
A modest handicap in which, following the withdrawal of the likely favourite, the top weight was rated 72. The winner is rated as an improver over the longer trip.
Dancing Jest(IRE) Official explanation: vet said mare was lame

4861 ROTHERBY H'CAP — 5f 218y
4:50 (4:50) (Class 5) (0-70,68) 3-Y-O — £2,590 (£770; £385; £192) Stalls Low

Form — RPR
5-64 **1** **Galatian**[45] 3350 3-9-4 68 .... JamesMillman[(3)] 9 — 81
(B R Millman) *mde all: rdn over 1f out: edgd lft: r.o* — **9/2[3]**
0403 **2** 1 3/4 **Dream Number (IRE)**[3] 4744 3-9-1 62 .... MartinDwyer 6 — 69
(W R Muir) *hld up in tch: trckd wnr over 2f out: rdn over 1f out: r.o* — **3/1[1]**
0-04 **3** 4 1/2 **Swansea Jack**[44] 3393 3-8-4 51 ....(t) NickyMackay 2 — 44
(S C Williams) *chsd ldrs: pushed along and hung rt 1/2-way: rdn over 1f out: no ex fnl f* — **9/2[3]**
0513 **4** 3 **Watch Chain (IRE)**[9] 4553 3-8-9 56 .... LiamJones 1 — 39
(M H Tompkins) *hld up: rdn over 2f out: styd on to go 4th ins fnl f: nvr on terms* — **7/2[2]**
0334 **5** 1/2 **Black Baccara**[4] 4720 3-8-1 55 ....(p) LeonnaMayor[(7)] 4 — 36
(P S McEntee) *hld up: hdwy over 2f out: wknd fnl f* — **14/1**
00-0 **6** 5 **Avon Rock**[13] 4430 3-7-12 52 ....(t) KatiaScallan[(7)] 11 — 17
(A J Lidderdale) *chsd ldrs: rdn over 2f out: wknd over 1f out* — **20/1**
55-0 **7** shd **Maragna (IRE)**[5] 4672 3-7-9 49 oh4 .... RyanPowell[(7)] 3 — 14
(Paul Green) *s.s: hld up: rdn over 2f out: n.d* — **14/1**
-000 **8** 1 1/2 **Taeping (IRE)**[11] 4475 3-8-2 49 oh4 ....(b[1]) DavidProbert 10 — 9
(R Hollinshead) *s.i.s: hdwy over 4f out: rdn and wknd over 1f out* — **50/1**
0000 **9** 17 **Aim'Ees Star**[36] 3685 3-8-0 50 oh4 ow1 ....(p) AndrewHeffernan[(3)] 8 — —
(John A Harris) *chsd ldrs: rdn over 3f out: wknd over 2f out* — **66/1**
0 **U** **Boy The Bell**[9] 4559 3-8-8 62 ow3 ....(p) JosephYoung[(7)] 7 — —
(M Mullineaux) *prom: racd keenly: rdn and wkng whn sddle slipped over 1f out: uns rdr sn after* — **7/1**

1m 11.4s (-1.60) **Going Correction** -0.25s/f (Firm) — **10** Ran SP% **117.6**
Speed ratings (Par 100): **100,97,91,87,87 80,80,78,55,—**
toteswingers: 1&2 £3.60, 1&3 £6.80, 2&3 £4.40 CSF £18.34 CT £66.48 TOTE £6.30: £2.40, £1.40, £2.00; EX 22.90 Place 6 £117.95, Place 5 £81.04.
Owner Tarka Racing **Bred** Mrs B A Matthews **Trained** Kentisbeare, Devon

FOCUS
A weak finale in which they finished well strung out. The runner-up sets the standard to this year's form.
Maragna(IRE) Official explanation: jockey said the gelding stumbled leaving the stalls
Boy The Bell Official explanation: jockey said saddle slipped
T/Plt: £191.80 to a £1 stake. Pool: £63,985.69. 243.52 winning tickets. T/Qpdt: £29.70 to a £1 stake. Pool: £5,743.72. 142.70 winning tickets. CR

4848 REDCAR (L-H)
Sunday, August 8

OFFICIAL GOING: Good to firm (8.6)
Wind: Light, half against Weather: Fine

4862 E B F LEONARD CHESHIRE DISABILITY MARSKE HALL MAIDEN FILLIES' STKS — 7f
2:10 (2:12) (Class 5) 2-Y-O — £3,238 (£963; £481; £240) Stalls Centre

Form — RPR
2 **1** **Najoum (USA)**[39] 3562 2-9-0 0 .... TedDurcan 1 — 81
(Saeed Bin Suroor) *dived lft s: sn trcking ldrs: led over 2f out: edgd rt 1f out: styd on wl towards fin* — **8/13[1]**

4 **2** *1* **Pandoro De Lago (IRE)**[24] 4048 2-9-0 0 TomEaves 8 79
(R A Fahey) *trckd ldrs: chal over 1f out: styd on same pce ins fnl f* **5/1**[3]
343 **3** *3/4* **Galloping Queen (IRE)**[22] 4135 2-9-0 0 ChrisCatlin 7 77
(M R Channon) *chsd ldrs: styd on same pce fnl f* **7/2**[2]
05 **4** *3/4* **Royal Hush**[39] 3549 2-9-0 0 FrannyNorton 4 75
(K A Ryan) *fly j. strt after s: sn chsng ldrs: drvn 3f out: sn outpcd: hdwy over 1f out: styd on same pce* **18/1**
04 **5** *5* **Bernisdale**[40] 3536 2-9-0 0 PJMcDonald 3 61
(G M Moore) *led tl over 2f out: lost pl over 1f out* **50/1**
6 *2 3/4* **Syncopated Lady (IRE)** 2-9-0 0 DuranFentiman 5 54
(D O'Meara) *dwlt: sn chsng ldrs: drvn 3f out: lost pl over 1f out* **66/1**
0 **7** *15* **Lady Of The Knight (IRE)**[37] 3624 2-9-0 0 PatrickMathers 2 13
(H A McWilliams) *s.i.s: in rr: drvn over 3f out: sn bhd* **150/1**

1m 25.25s (0.75) **Going Correction** -0.175s/f (Firm) **7** Ran SP% **110.2**
Speed ratings (Par 91): **88,86,86,85,79 76,59**
toteswingers: 1&2 £2.00, 1&3 £1.20, 2&3 £1.60 CSF £3.81 TOTE £1.80: £1.80, £3.40; EX 3.70.
Owner Godolphin **Bred** Stonerside Stable **Trained** Newmarket, Suffolk

FOCUS
This looked a decent fillies' maiden best rated through the third.

NOTEBOOK
Najoum(USA), whose trainer won this with subsequent UAE 1000 Guineas winner Siyaadah 12 months ago, confirmed the promise she showed when runner-up on Polytrack first time up, but she required a hard enough ride. She didn't look to be concentrating fully in the closing stages, and also displayed a knee action, suggesting the ground was quicker than ideal. Still, this was a useful effort and she could do better. (op 5-6, tchd 10-11 in a place)
Pandoro De Lago(IRE) stepped up on the form she showed when fourth on debut in a fair Doncaster maiden. She looks likely to come on again and ought to go close next time. (op 9-2 tchd 4-1)
Galloping Queen(IRE) ran okay, but she's yet to convince she really stays this trip and may turn out to be a sprinter. (op 11-4, tchd 9-2 in a place)
Royal Hush showed only moderate form in a couple of 5f maidens, but she's quite well regarded and shaped much more encouragingly on this step up in trip. She shaped as though she'll improve again, and can now be handicapped. (op 20-1 tchd 25-1)
Bernisdale ran creditably under a positive ride and could find her level now that handicaps are an option. (op 66-1)
Syncopated Lady(IRE) flashed her tail when starting slowly, but she showed some ability on debut. (op 100-1)

4863 GOODSWENS SOLICITORS REDCAR (S) STKS — 1m 2f
2:40 (2:41) (Class 6) 3-5-Y-O — **£1,706** (£503; £252) **Stalls** Low

Form — RPR
0040 **1** **Media Stars**[10] 4511 5-9-1 46 (t) LeeTopliss(5) 9 55
(R Johnson) *s.i.s: hld up in rr: hdwy and nt clr run over 2f out: styd on wl fnl f: led last strides* **20/1**
2605 **2** *hd* **Castlebury (IRE)**[11] 4484 5-9-6 55 (b) PJMcDonald 2 55
(G A Swinbank) *dwlt: sn chsng ldrs: rdn over 3f out: wnt 2nd jst ins fnl f: led nr fin: hdd post* **11/4**[2]
1164 **3** *1/2* **Guga (IRE)**[21] 3910 4-9-7 65 (b) DaleSwift(5) 3 60
(Dr R D P Newland) *led: t.k.h: 3 l clr 1f out: rdn and wknd fnl 75yds: hdd nr fin* **5/4**[1]
00-0 **4** *5* **Phantom Serenade (IRE)**[104] 1574 5-9-6 57 TomEaves 11 44
(M Dods) *swtchd lft after s: hld up in rr: hdwy over 3f out: chsng ldrs 2f out: wknd appr fnl f* **8/1**[3]
0260 **5** *1 1/4* **Reel Love**[12] 4448 3-8-8 48 JamesSullivan(3) 1 41
(Mrs L Stubbs) *chsd ldrs: wnt 2nd 4f out: wknd fnl f* **16/1**
0-6 **6** *5* **Pobs Trophy**[22] 3728 3-8-7 0 ow1 MarkCoumbe(5) 6 32
(R C Guest) *in rr: pushed along over 5f out: lost pl 3f out* **50/1**
7 *2 1/4* **Don't Hurry Love (IRE)**[16] 4352 3-8-6 0 FrannyNorton 4 22
(T J Pitt) *chsd ldrs: drvn and lost pl over 4f out* **9/1**
5064 **8** *3* **Melkatant**[11] 4484 4-9-1 43 (p) DanielTudhope 10 16
(N Bycroft) *chsd ldrs: drvn over 3f out: wknd 2f out: lame* **12/1**

2m 7.68s (0.58) **Going Correction** -0.175s/f (Firm)
WFA 3 from 4yo+ 9lb **8** Ran SP% **112.5**
Speed ratings (Par 101): **90,89,89,85,84 80,78,76**
toteswingers: 1&2 £6.70, 1&3 £5.50, 2&3 £1.90 CSF £72.44 TOTE £30.40: £5.30, £1.10, £1.10; EX 128.80.There was no bid for the winner. Guga was claimed by G. A. Harker for £6,000.
Owner Robert C Whitelock **Bred** Newsells Park Stud Limited **Trained** Newburn, Tyne & Wear
■ Stewards' Enquiry : P J McDonald caution: use of whip

FOCUS
A moderate seller and not form to dwell on. The time was 1.21 seconds slower than the later Class 5 maiden handicap and the winner is rated to last year's turf best.
Melkatant Official explanation: jockey said that the filly finished lame near fore

4864 LEEDS BUILDING SOCIETY H'CAP — 1m
3:10 (3:11) (Class 6) (0-60,60) 3-Y-O — **£1,706** (£503; £252) **Stalls** Centre

Form — RPR
2-00 **1** **Madame Excelerate**[22] 4127 3-9-3 **59** GrahamGibbons 2 68
(W M Brisbourne) *chsd ldr: led and hung rt 2f out: drvn rt out* **15/2**
0000 **2** *1* **Bring Sweets (IRE)**[22] 2838 3-8-4 **46** oh1 ChrisCatlin 4 53
(B Ellison) *hld up in rr: pushed along and hdwy over 3f out: chsd wnr appr fnl f: kpt on same pce last 100yds* **11/2**[2]
5425 **3** *4* **Green For Luck (IRE)**[26] 3975 3-8-13 **60** IanBrennan(5) 6 58
(S Gollings) *gave problems in stalls: wnt rt s: in rr: hdwy over 2f out: kpt on to take modest 3rd nr fin* **5/2**[1]
6655 **4** *3/4* **Military Call**[27] 3948 3-9-4 **60** LNewman 9 56
(A C Whillans) *trckd ldrs: effrt 2f out: kpt on same pce* **17/2**
0001 **5** *shd* **Emeralds Spirit (IRE)**[16] 4337 3-8-6 **51** KellyHarrison(3) 11 47
(J R Weymes) *sn chsng ldrs: drvn 3f out: carried rt over 1f out: hung lft and one pce* **15/2**
2000 **6** *3* **Rescent**[5] 4674 3-8-1 **46** (b) JamesSullivan(3) 1 35
(Mrs R A Carr) *led: hdd 2f out: hung lft and wknd appr fnl f* **22/1**
-654 **7** *1 1/4* **Briary Mac**[21] 4172 3-9-4 **60** DanielTudhope 3 46
(N Bycroft) *chsd ldrs: rdn over 2f out: sn btn* **6/1**[3]
6400 **8** *5* **Dispol Kabira**[5] 4674 3-8-4 **46** PatrickMathers 10 20
(D W Thompson) *mid-div: drvn over 3f out: wknd over 1f out* **40/1**
0-00 **9** *2* **Kookie**[16] 4342 3-7-11 **46** oh1 SoniaEaton(7) 7 16
(R E Barr) *hmpd s: a in rr* **40/1**
005 **10** *nk* **Tipperary Tickle**[29] 3910 3-8-4 **46** oh1 (v[1]) AndrewElliott 5 15
(J R Weymes) *mid-div: rdn over 3f out: sn lost pl* **14/1**
000- **11** *17* **Bojangles Andrews**[286] 7056 3-8-4 **46** oh1 FrannyNorton 8 —
(T J Pitt) *in rr: drvn over 4f: sn lost pl: wl bhd fnl 2f* **16/1**

1m 37.68s (-0.32) **Going Correction** -0.175s/f (Firm) **11** Ran SP% **114.1**
Speed ratings (Par 98): **94,93,89,88,88 85,83,78,76,76 59**
toteswingers: 1&2 £8.40, 1&3 £5.40, 2&3 £4.20 CSF £46.08 CT £131.06 TOTE £9.80: £3.40, £1.80, £1.10; EX 50.00.
Owner Equiform Nutrition Limited **Bred** Brown Moss Stud **Trained** Great Ness, Shropshire
■ Stewards' Enquiry : Graham Gibbons caution: careless riding

FOCUS
A moderate handicap in which the winner is rated close to her Aw best with the third a solid marker.
Emeralds Spirit(IRE) Official explanation: jockey said that the filly was unsuited by the good to firm ground

4865 ALESSIS ITALIAN RESTAURANT AT SALTBURN H'CAP — 6f
3:40 (3:41) (Class 4) (0-85,81) 3-Y-O — **£3,626** (£1,079; £539; £269) **Stalls** Centre

Form — RPR
012 **1** **Barren Brook**[17] 4288 3-9-4 **81** JamesSullivan(3) 1 85+
(M W Easterby) *trckd ldr: t.k.h: led jst ins fnl f: edgd rt: hld on wl* **2/1**[1]
3-10 **2** *1/2* **Prince Of Vasa (IRE)**[92] 1913 3-9-2 **79** MichaelStainton(3) 5 81
(Michael Smith) *led: hdd jst ins fnl f: no ex* **22/1**
1324 **3** *nk* **Pepper Lane**[30] 3879 3-8-5 **70** IanBrennan(5) 7 71
(D O'Meara) *trckd ldrs: upsides and rdn over 1f out: styd on same pce fnl 100yds* **4/1**[2]
5660 **4** *shd* **Tasmeem (IRE)**[15] 4370 3-9-0 **74** (b[1]) TomEaves 4 75
(R A Fahey) *trckd ldrs: effrt over 1f out: chsng ldrs and swtchd lft ins fnl f: kpt on same pce* **11/2**[3]
050 **5** *1 1/2* **Coin From Heaven (IRE)**[34] 3731 3-8-12 **77** LeeTopliss(5) 2 73
(R A Fahey) *prom: chsd ldrs over 1f out: kpt on one pce* **8/1**
1650 **6** *1* **Fly Silca Fly (IRE)**[15] 4378 3-9-7 **81** ChrisCatlin 3 74
(M R Channon) *chsd ldrs: effrt 2f out: one pce* **8/1**
1000 **7** *6* **Belinsky (IRE)**[23] 4091 3-8-12 **72** J-PGuillambert 8 45
(N Tinkler) *hld up in rr: drvn 3f out: no imp: eased ins fnl f* **22/1**
3310 **8** *1 1/4* **Kakapuka**[23] 4091 3-9-0 **77** RussKennemore(3) 6 46
(Mrs A L M King) *trckd ldrs: t.k.h: drvn over 2f out: lost pl over 1f out: eased ins fnl f* **13/2**

1m 11.08s (-0.72) **Going Correction** -0.175s/f (Firm) **8** Ran SP% **113.0**
Speed ratings (Par 102): **97,96,95,95,93 92,84,82**
toteswingers: 1&2 £9.20, 1&3 £2.60, 2&3 £12.00 CSF £48.68 CT £161.65 TOTE £3.30: £1.40, £5.30, £1.10; EX 68.90.
Owner D Scott, Mrs E Wright & J Clark **Bred** David Allan **Trained** Sheriff Hutton, N Yorks

FOCUS
The early pace looked just steady for a sprint, but this was a fair enough 3-y-o handicap, with a couple of lightly raced sorts coming to the fore. The form appears muddling and the third looks the best guide.

4866 MARSKE VETS CLAIMING STKS — 1m
4:10 (4:10) (Class 6) 3-4-Y-O — **£1,706** (£503; £252) **Stalls** Centre

Form — RPR
0000 **1** **Rising Kheleyf (IRE)**[14] 4404 4-8-13 60 GaryBartley(3) 6 69
(John A Harris) *hld up: effrt over 2f out: styd on fnl f: led towards fin* **28/1**
0125 **2** *1/2* **Cono Zur (FR)**[11] 4483 3-8-11 72 (p) JamesSullivan(3) 2 72
(Mrs R A Carr) *hld up: hdwy to trck ldrs over 3f out: led over 1f out: hdd and no ex nr fin* **6/5**[1]
2511 **3** *3/4* **Miami Gator (IRE)**[6] 4646 3-8-13 63 (v) AndrewElliott 7 69
(J R Weymes) *led 2f: rdn to ld over 2f out: hdd over 1f out: kpt on same pce last 150yds* **7/4**[2]
4054 **4** *1 1/4* **King's Sabre**[8] 4581 4-9-3 62 (e) PaulEddery 10 64
(R C Guest) *hld up in rr: effrt over 2f out: styd on same pce fnl f* **15/2**[3]
00 **5** *7* **Binglybonglyboo**[14] 4403 4-9-1 0 MichaelStainton(3) 5 49
(L A Mullaney) *trckd ldrs: t.k.h: drvn 3f out: hung lft and lost pl over 1f out* **25/1**
3036 **6** *4* **Saxby (IRE)**[17] 4289 3-8-12 63 (b[1]) ChrisCatlin 3 40
(G A Harker) *dwlt: sn trcking ldrs: rdn and hung rt 2f out: sn wknd* **11/1**
2406 **7** *9* **The Dial House**[11] 4481 4-9-4 57 PaulMulrennan 1 19
(D W Thompson) *chsd ldr: led after 2f: hdd over 2f out: sn lost pl* **25/1**
0-00 **8** *9* **Convitezza**[21] 4168 4-8-13 31 (b[1]) TomEaves 4 —
(M E Sowersby) *chsd ldrs: lost pl over 2f out: sn bhd: eased* **100/1**

1m 36.3s (-1.70) **Going Correction** -0.175s/f (Firm)
WFA 3 from 4yo 7lb **8** Ran SP% **114.0**
Speed ratings (Par 101): **101,100,99,98,91 87,78,69**
toteswingers: 1&2 £13.20, 1&3 £11.30, 2&3 £1.70 CSF £61.32 TOTE £39.50: £5.10, £1.02, £1.40; EX 124.30.
Owner N Morgan **Bred** J K Thoroughbreds And M Buckley **Trained** Eastwell, Leics

FOCUS
A modest claimer with the fourth the best guide to the level.

4867 COOPERS CHEMIST PRESCRIPTIONS DELIVERY MAIDEN H'CAP — 1m 2f
4:40 (4:40) (Class 5) (0-75,75) 3-Y-O+ — **£2,266** (£674; £337; £168) **Stalls** Low

Form — RPR
6203 **1** **Hail Bold Chief (USA)**[16] 4337 3-9-2 **63** PJMcDonald 4 69
(G A Swinbank) *w ldr: led after 2f: drvn 3 l clr 1f out: hld on towards fin* **8/1**
5553 **2** *3/4* **Leaving Alone (USA)**[14] 4408 3-8-7 **59** IanBrennan(5) 10 64
(E W Tuer) *hld up in rr: effrt over 3f out: chsd wnr jst ins fnl f: r.o: jst hld* **7/1**
5636 **3** *nk* **Sadler's Mark**[16] 4344 3-9-3 **64** ow2 PhillipMakin 9 68+
(T P Tate) *bhd and swtchd lft after s: effrt and n.m.r over 3f out: swtchd outside over 1f out: styd on wl* **4/1**[1]
2523 **4** *3 1/4* **Plus Ultra (IRE)**[40] 3523 3-9-8 **72** RussKennemore(3) 3 69
(P A Kirby) *chsd ldrs: one pce fnl 2f* **5/1**[3]
24-6 **5** *5* **Ella Grace (USA)**[20] 4188 3-8-9 **61** LeeTopliss(5) 8 48
(R A Fahey) *swtchd lft after s: hdwy over 3f out: chsng ldrs and hung bdly lft fr over 2f out: wknd over 1f out* **12/1**
5050 **6** *1 1/2* **Sinatramania**[11] 4485 3-8-9 **56** AndrewMullen 6 42
(Miss Tracy Waggott) *hld up in rr: hdwy over 3f out: one pce whn bdly hmpd over 1f out* **40/1**
2444 **7** *1 1/2* **Kathlatino**[23] 4117 3-9-7 **68** TomEaves 7 49
(Micky Hammond) *chsd ldrs: wknd over 1f out* **16/1**
5204 **8** *1* **Hail Tiberius**[16] 4341 3-10-0 **75** PaulMulrennan 5 54
(T D Walford) *chsd ldrs: wkng whn hmpd over 1f out* **9/1**
2235 **9** *11* **Star Addition**[9] 4546 4-9-4 **56** TedDurcan 11 13
(E J Alston) *trckd ldrs: lost pl over 3f out: sn bhd* **15/2**
-566 **10** *7* **Before The War (USA)**[16] 4335 3-9-4 **65** J-PGuillambert 1 8
(L M Cumani) *trckd ldrs: awkward and lost pl bnd over 4f out: sme hdwy 3f out: sn lost pl* **9/2**[2]
50-6 **11** *1* **Sleepy Dove**[20] 4207 5-8-9 **50** JamesSullivan(3) 2 —
(M E Sowersby) *t.k.h: led 2f: lost pl over 3f out: sn bhd* **66/1**

2m 6.47s (-0.63) **Going Correction** -0.175s/f (Firm)
WFA 3 from 4yo+ 9lb **11** Ran SP% **117.7**
Speed ratings (Par 103): **95,94,94,91,87 86,85,84,75,69 69**
toteswingers: 1&2 £10.00, 1&3 £10.60, 2&3 £7.10 CSF £63.12 CT £260.39 TOTE £11.60: £3.50, £3.00, £1.50; EX 79.90.
Owner Solway Stayers **Bred** Tracy Farmer **Trained** Melsonby, N Yorks
■ Stewards' Enquiry : Lee Topliss three-day ban: careless riding (Aug 24-26)

The Form Book, Raceform Ltd, Compton, RG20 6NL

FOCUS
A modest handicap for maidens rated around the placed horses. The pace did not look that strong, yet the time was 1.21 seconds quicker than the earlier seller.

4868 GUISBOROUGH AND DISTRICT ROUND TABLE H'CAP (DIV I) 6f
5:10 (5:12) (Class 6) (0-60,60) 3-Y-O+ £1,364 (£403; £201) Stalls Centre

Form RPR
4004 1 **Braille**[8] 4605 5-9-0 52 GrahamGibbons 1 59
(T D Walford) *mde all: hld on gamely* 9/2[1]

6003 2 *hd* **Carnival Dream**[11] 4486 5-8-12 50 (p) PatrickMathers 4 56
(H A McWilliams) *chsd ldrs: wnt 2nd over 1f out: kpt on wl: jst hld* 16/1

3530 3 *1* **Red River Boy**[15] 4373 5-8-9 50 KellyHarrison(3) 11 53
(C W Fairhurst) *hld up in midfield: effrt over 2f out: carried rt over 1f out: styd on same pce* 15/2[3]

4020 4 *1* **Errigal Lad**[4] 4706 5-9-8 60 (p) AndrewElliott 3 60
(J Balding) *chsd wnr: edgd rt over 1f out: kpt on same pce* 8/1

5150 5 *¾* **Red China Blues (USA)**[4] 4706 4-8-13 54 (b[1]) JamesSullivan(3) 12 52
(Mrs R A Carr) *a chsng ldrs: styd on same pce fnl f* 9/1

0-00 6 *hd* **Le Reve Royal**[8] 4605 4-8-11 49 PaulMulrennan 10 46
(G R Oldroyd) *sn outpcd and in rr: hdwy 2f out: hung lft and styd on wl fnl f* 50/1

0404 7 *1* **He's A Humbug (IRE)**[19] 4234 6-9-2 59 JamesO'Reilly(5) 7 53
(J O'Reilly) *chsd ldrs: rdn over 2f out: kpt on ins fnl f* 11/2[2]

3200 8 *nse* **Piste**[11] 4486 4-9-6 58 PhillipMakin 9 52
(Miss T Jackson) *hld up in rr: hdwy and edgd lft over 2f out: kpt on fnl f* 16/1

-020 9 *½* **Musca (IRE)**[9] 4555 6-9-3 60 LeeTopliss(5) 5 52
(C Grant) *s.i.s: in rr: reminders and snatched up 4f out: hdwy over 2f out: edgd rt and kpt on fnl f* 14/1

1550 10 *1¼* **Wotatomboy**[37] 3615 4-8-4 47 AmyRyan(5) 6 35
(R M Whitaker) *mid-div: hdwy to chse ldrs over 2f out: wknd over 1f out* 14/1

0065 11 *4½* **Karate Queen**[8] 4605 5-8-9 47 oh1 ow1 TomEaves 14 21
(R E Barr) *a in rr* 14/1

00-4 12 *½* **Parisian Dream**[11] 4486 6-9-3 55 (t) LeeVickers 13 27
(T J Pitt) *in rr: rdn 3f out: nvr on terms: eased towards fin* 9/2[1]

5550 13 *2½* **Stonecrabstomorrow (IRE)**[143] 914 7-9-2 59 (b) MarkCoumbe(5) 2 23
(John A Harris) *a towards rr* 18/1

0000 14 *6* **Ten To The Dozen**[14] 4403 7-8-5 50 oh1 ow4 (p) DuilioDaSilva(7) 8 —
(D W Thompson) *s.v.s: a detached in last* 66/1

1m 11.53s (-0.27) **Going Correction** -0.175s/f (Firm) 14 Ran SP% 125.1
Speed ratings (Par 101): **94,93,92,91,90 89,88,88,87,86 80,79,76,68**
toteswingers: 1&2 £16.80, 1&3 £7.30, 2&3 £18.80 CSF £82.53 CT £559.97 TOTE £6.60: £2.20, £4.00, £1.90; EX 97.10.
Owner A Quirke & C Backhouse **Bred** Beechgrove Stud Farm Ltd **Trained** Sheriff Hutton, N Yorks

FOCUS
A sprint full of hard-to-win-with types and it paid to race prominently. The time was a full second slower than the second division and the first two look the best guides.
Parisian Dream Official explanation: jockey said gelding was never travelling

4869 GUISBOROUGH AND DISTRICT ROUND TABLE H'CAP (DIV II) 6f
5:40 (5:42) (Class 6) (0-60,60) 3-Y-O+ £1,364 (£403; £201) Stalls Centre

Form RPR
6223 1 **Foreign Rhythm (IRE)**[8] 4606 5-8-11 54 DaleSwift(5) 7 66
(R E Barr) *dwlt: sn chsng ldrs: led over 1f out: styd on strly* 13/2[3]

1550 2 *2¾* **Secret City (IRE)**[18] 4244 4-9-7 59 (b) PhillipMakin 8 62
(R Bastiman) *chsd ldrs: styd on to take 2nd towards fin* 14/1

0001 3 *½* **Yungaburra (IRE)**[8] 4606 6-9-0 57 (t) AmyRyan(5) 12 59
(D C Griffiths) *in rr: gd hdwy 2f out: chsd wnr appr fnl f: kpt on same pce* 8/1

3033 4 *1¼* **Needy McCredie**[9] 4559 4-8-9 50 JamesSullivan(3) 1 48
(J R Turner) *hood removed v late: s.i.s: hdwy over 2f out: edgd lft and chsng ldrs on wd outside over 1f out: kpt on same pce* 7/2[2]

2331 5 *½* **Divertimenti (IRE)**[17] 4285 6-9-5 60 (b) RussKennemore(3) 10 56
(S R Bowring) *led: edgd rt 2f out: hdd over 1f out: kpt on same pce* 11/4[1]

0403 6 *½* **Forzarzi (IRE)**[11] 4487 6-8-8 46 PatrickMathers 9 40
(H A McWilliams) *mid-div: sn drvn along: hdwy over 2f out: chsng ldrs and hung lft over 1f out: one pce* 20/1

5054 7 *½* **Darcy's Pride (IRE)**[14] 4415 6-8-10 51 (p) PaulPickard(3) 2 44
(P T Midgley) *chsd ldrs: outpcd and lost pl over 2f out: kpt on appr fnl f* 12/1

0650 8 *1¾* **City For Conquest (IRE)**[11] 4478 7-8-8 46 oh1 (b) FrannyNorton 3 33
(John A Harris) *chsd ldrs: one pce fnl 2f* 22/1

6056 9 *½* **Soto**[11] 4487 7-9-6 58 PaulMulrennan 5 44
(M W Easterby) *w ldrs: wknd over 1f out* 12/1

1034 10 *hd* **Greek Secret**[11] 4487 7-9-2 59 JamesO'Reilly(5) 4 44
(J O'Reilly) *a in rr and sn drvn along* 12/1

0002 11 *1¾* **Dream Express (IRE)**[8] 4605 5-8-5 50 DuilioDaSilva(7) 6 29
(D W Thompson) *mid-div: drvn over 2f out: sn outpcd* 28/1

0100 12 *½* **Pinball (IRE)**[15] 4373 4-9-1 53 (v) TomEaves 11 31
(Mrs L Williamson) *chsd ldr: wknd over 1f out* 33/1

0020 13 *¾* **On The Piste (IRE)**[8] 4567 3-8-10 55 ow3 (p) GaryBartley(3) 13 30
(L A Mullaney) *sn outpcd and bhd* 20/1

1m 10.53s (-1.27) **Going Correction** -0.175s/f (Firm)
WFA 3 from 4yo+ 4lb 13 Ran SP% 123.3
Speed ratings (Par 101): **101,97,96,95,94 93,93,90,90,89 87,86,85**
toteswingers: 1&2 £20.10, 1&3 £14.00, 2&3 £20.00 CSF £88.96 CT £753.98 TOTE £7.80: £2.40, £5.90, £3.30; EX 121.10 Place 6 £6.05, Place 5 £4.59.
Owner P Cartmell **Bred** Yeomanstown Stud **Trained** Seamer, N Yorks

FOCUS
The time was fully a second quicker than the first division and the placed horses are rated close to this season's form.
Forzarzi(IRE) Official explanation: jockey said the gelding was never travelling
T/Plt: £9.60 to a £1 stake. Pool: £57,126.04. 4,329.15 winning tickets. T/Qpdt: £4.90 to a £1 stake. Pool: £3,208.10. 481.80 winning tickets. WG

4657 WINDSOR (R-H)
Sunday, August 8

OFFICIAL GOING: Good (7.5)
Stands' rail dolled out 18yds at 6f and 7yds at winning post. Top bend dolled out 4yds from innermost line, adding 16yds to races of 1m and over.
Wind: Almost nil Weather: Fine

4870 GIVEMEFOOTBALL.COM H'CAP 1m 67y
2:30 (2:30) (Class 6) (0-65,68) 3-Y-O+ £2,388 (£705; £352) Stalls High

Form RPR
2212 1 **Mr Harmoosh (IRE)**[3] 4763 3-9-8 68 PatCosgrave 3 76
(E F Vaughan) *hld up: prog over 2f out: drvn wl over 1f out: narrow ld ins fnl f: jst hld on* 9/4[1]

000- 2 *shd* **Meer Und Wind (GER)**[310] 6441 3-9-2 62 EddieAhern 4 70
(P R Webber) *chsd clr ldng pair: reminder 1/2-way: drvn and effrt over 2f out: chal and upsides fnl f: jst failed* 66/1

3264 3 *nk* **Pastello**[17] 4282 3-9-4 64 RyanMoore 12 71
(R Hannon) *prom in chsng gp: clsd to ld wl over 1f out: hdd ins fnl f: kpt on* 5/1[3]

3443 4 *¾* **Dichoh**[15] 4366 7-9-7 60 (v) GeorgeBaker 7 65
(M Madgwick) *hld up wl in rr: rdn 3f out: styd on u.p fr over 1f out: nvr quite able to chal* 11/1

0-53 5 *1* **Phluke**[3] 4738 9-9-7 60 (p) LiamKeniry 2 63
(Eve Johnson Houghton) *prom in chsng gp: rdn 3f out: nt qckn over 1f out: kpt on same pce after* 16/1

6002 6 *¾* **Trafalgar Square**[11] 4488 8-9-5 58 (v) JimCrowley 8 59
(M J Attwater) *dwlt: hld up last: stl there 2f out and u.p: swtchd out wd and styd on fnl f* 15/2

0120 7 *1¾* **Annes Rocket (IRE)**[11] 4488 5-9-3 61 SophieDoyle(5) 5 58
(J C Fox) *dwlt: hld up in rr: rdn 3f out: effrt on outer over 2f out: nt qckn over 1f out: fdd fnl f* 11/1

0020 8 *3* **Storm Hawk (IRE)**[15] 4366 3-9-0 63 MartinLane(3) 1 53
(Pat Eddery) *hld up in rr: rdn and no prog over 2f out: btn after* 16/1

0-22 9 *4* **Petomic (IRE)**[20] 4206 5-9-12 65 TadhgO'Shea 6 46
(M Hill) *led at str pce and sn clr w one rival: hdd & wknd rapidly wl over 1f out* 10/3[2]

-000 10 *hd* **Mt Kintyre (IRE)**[7] 4621 4-9-9 62 SamHitchcott 10 43
(M R Channon) *drvn to chse ldr and sn clr of rest: wkng whn hmpd wl over 1f out* 25/1

1m 44.24s (-0.46) **Going Correction** 0.0s/f (Good)
WFA 3 from 4yo+ 7lb 10 Ran SP% 116.0
Speed ratings (Par 101): **102,101,101,100,99 99,97,94,90,90**
toteswingers: 1&2 £72.30, 1&3 £2.40, 2&3 £59.30 CSF £155.91 CT £709.16 TOTE £3.70: £1.10, £19.40, £1.30; EX 152.80 TRIFECTA Not won..
Owner Salem Rashid **Bred** Thomas G Cooke **Trained** Newmarket, Suffolk

FOCUS
The track was at minimum width, with the rail out as far as it can go in the straight. All races on the round course were run over 16 yards longer than advertised. This was a low-grade handicap but the form looks sound despite the proximity of the runner-up., who was making her handicap debut.

4871 JUDICARE MAIDEN AUCTION STKS 6f
3:00 (3:01) (Class 5) 2-Y-O £3,070 (£906; £453) Stalls High

Form RPR
0 1 **Speedfit Girl (IRE)**[16] 4317 2-8-9 0 PhilipRobinson 1 67
(G G Margarson) *fast away fr low draw: mde all and swtchd to inner: rdn over 1f out: hld on wl* 3/1[2]

2 *½* **Bahri Sheen (IRE)** 2-8-6 0 KierenFox(5) 9 67+
(J R Best) *chsd ldrs: shkn up over 2f out: no prog tl styd on strly ins fnl f: tk 2nd last strides* 16/1

5 3 *½* **Green Pearl (IRE)**[42] 3472 2-9-1 0 JimCrowley 10 70
(R M Beckett) *prom: rdn 2f out: chsd wnr fnl f: nt qckn and a jst hld: lost 2nd last strides* 10/1

35 4 *1* **Hawk Moth (IRE)**[26] 3971 2-8-10 0 SamHitchcott 11 62
(J L Spearing) *in tch: shkn up on inner over 2f out: styd on fnl f: nrst fin* 16/1

3 5 *hd* **King Of The Desert (IRE)**[19] 4228 2-8-13 0 EddieAhern 3 64
(E A L Dunlop) *chsd ldrs: effrt towards outer 2f out: cl enough 1f out: no ex* 9/2[3]

0 6 *nk* **Dells Breezer**[4] 4695 2-8-5 0 JemmaMarshall(5) 8 60
(P M Phelan) *t.k.h: mostly chsd wnr tl wknd fnl f* 66/1

6 7 *1¾* **Polar Auroras**[27] 3964 2-8-2 0 MartinLane(3) 7 49
(Pat Eddery) *wnt lft s: effrt on outer fr last trio 1/2-way: cl enough over 1f out: fdd* 8/1

8 *¾* **Homeboy (IRE)** 2-8-12 0 TadhgO'Shea 5 54
(M P Tregoning) *s.s: mostly detached in last: kpt on fnl f* 14/1

9 *nk* **Ceffyl Gwell** 2-8-12 0 RyanMoore 2 53
(R Hannon) *dwlt: racd on outer in midfield: wdst of all and struggling 2f out: fdd* 5/2[1]

10 *1¼* **Sleeping Brave** 2-8-11 0 PatCosgrave 4 48
(J R Boyle) *dwlt: a in last trio: rdn and no prog 2f out* 33/1

1m 14.61s (1.61) **Going Correction** 0.0s/f (Good) 10 Ran SP% 114.8
Speed ratings (Par 94): **89,88,87,86,86 85,83,82,81,80**
toteswingers: 1&2 £27.80, 1&3 £4.80, 2&3 £30.50 CSF £49.37 TOTE £5.80: £2.40, £9.40, £4.80; EX 76.60 Trifecta £180.00 Part won. Pool: £243.34 - 0.42 winning units..
Owner Exors of the Late John Guest **Bred** John Cullinan **Trained** Newmarket, Suffolk

FOCUS
A modest fillies' juvenile maiden with the fifth looking the best guide to the level.

NOTEBOOK
Speedfit Girl(IRE) showed some promise before fading in a much better race than this at Ascot on debut and she was always in control here, having pinged out of the gates and bagged the lead. She had to work still, but always looked to be doing enough and her trainer will now look for either a conditions race or nursery, depending on what sort of mark she gets. Whichever way she goes, she won't be given a hard time of it this season. (op 6-1)
Bahri Sheen(IRE), half-brother to a fair 6f winner, seemed to know his job well enough and tried to close on the winner late on, but was never quite getting up. This was a promising debut. (op 12-1)
Green Pearl(IRE) improved markedly on his debut effort, throwing down a challenge in the straight but not being able to see it out as well as the front pair. (op 9-1 tchd 11-1)
Hawk Moth(IRE) is now qualified for handicaps and should fare better in that sphere. (op 11-1)
King Of The Desert(IRE) has shown ability on both starts, but is more of a handicap prospect. (op 7-2)

Ceffyl Gwell is related to plenty of winners, but she failed to meet with market expectation on this racecourse debut, being beaten after halfway and slowly fading. (op 10-3 tchd 7-2 in a place)

4872 OSSIE & HUTCH MEMORIAL FILLIES' AUCTION NURSERY — 6f

3:30 (3:31) (Class 5) 2-Y-O — **£3,070** (£906; £453) **Stalls** High

Form — RPR

21 **1** **Ishbelle**[22] 4149 2-9-0 **78** ... JimCrowley 7 — 85+
(R M Beckett) *s.v.s: hld up in last trio: gd prog through rivals fr 2f out: led ent fnl f: shkn up and sn in command: readily* **9/4**[1]

5221 **2** *1* **Whisper Louise (IRE)**[20] 4203 2-9-5 **83** ... MickyFenton 8 — 86
(Mrs P Sly) *trckd ldrs: looking for room over 2f out: prog on inner to ld over 1f out: hdd ent fnl f: styd on* **3/1**[2]

0252 **3** *1* **Never Can Stop**[19] 4233 2-7-8 **65** ... HarryBentley(7) 3 — 65
(J G Portman) *hld up on outer: prog fr 1/2-way: rdn to chal over 1f out: kpt on same pce fnl f* **20/1**

4514 **4** *1 1/4* **Wotsthehurry**[30] 3864 2-8-6 **70** ... SamHitchcott 10 — 66
(M R Channon) *dwlt: hld up in last trio: pushed along 2f out: kpt on fr over 1f out: nt pce to threaten* **33/1**

1342 **5** *shd* **Whoatealltheplus (IRE)**[19] 4228 2-8-12 **76** ... PhilipRobinson 2 — 71
(D K Ivory) *t.k.h: pressed ldr to 2f out: nt qckn over 1f out: one pce* **8/1**

4410 **6** *2 3/4* **Scarlet Rocks (IRE)**[12] 4458 2-9-0 **85** ... AdamBeschizza(7) 6 — 71
(P D Evans) *mde most to over 1f out: sn wknd* **16/1**

2150 **7** *nk* **Two Feet Of Snow (IRE)**[8] 4592 2-9-0 **78** ... WilliamBuick 4 — 64
(R Hannon) *trckd ldrs on outer: pushed along and lost pl 2f out: sn btn* **9/1**

1610 **8** *7* **The Sydney Arms (IRE)**[53] 3070 2-9-7 **85** ... RyanMoore 5 — 57
(R Hannon) *trckd ldrs: shkn up 2f out: wknd over 1f out: eased* **10/3**[3]

063 **9** *11* **Atia**[57] 2951 2-8-4 **68** ... SaleemGolam 9 — —
(J G Portman) *hld up in last trio on inner: pushed along whn hmpd over 1f out: nt rcvr and eased: t.o* **25/1**

1m 14.42s (1.42) **Going Correction** 0.0s/f (Good) — **9** Ran SP% **117.4**
Speed ratings (Par 91): **90,88,87,85,85 81,81,72,57**
toteswingers: 1&2 £2.60, 1&3 £8.80, 2&3 £10.00 CSF £9.02 CT £106.60 TOTE £3.20: £1.80, £1.10, £7.20; EX 10.90 Trifecta £418.10 Pool: £565.03 - 1.00 winning units..
Owner Mrs M E Slade **Bred** Mrs M E Slade **Trained** Whitsbury, Hants

FOCUS
A fair nursery and a useful winner with the runner-up rated to previous course form.

NOTEBOOK
Ishbelle ◆, who despite a very slow start, readily made her ground to challenge and then picked up well to make light of her 78-rating. She can be expected to progress again and deserves a crack at a valuable nursery now. (op 11-4 tchd 3-1)
Whisper Louise(IRE) had won really well over C&D the time before and this was a perfectly good effort from a mark of 83 on this nursery debut, just finding the winner too classy. (op 7-2)
Never Can Stop was wide most of the way, but still held every chance and ran an improved race. There's a similar race in her off this sort of mark. (tchd 22-1)
Wotsthehurry ◆, trying 6f for the first time, had finished fourth in a seller latest, so this has to go down as an improved effort. She definitely shaped as though a return to 7f would suit. (op 25-1)
Whoatealltheplus(IRE) had her chance, but was a little keen early and didn't see it out. (op 7-1)
The Sydney Arms(IRE), down in grade having contested the Queen Mary last time, was keen early on this rise in trip and then didn't get the best of runs, already being held when eased. (op 7-2 tchd 3-1 and 4-1 in places)
Atia Official explanation: jockey said filly suffered interference in running

4873 CASE SECURITY H'CAP — 1m 2f 7y

4:00 (4:00) (Class 5) (0-75,74) 3-Y-O+ — **£3,070** (£906; £453) **Stalls** Centre

Form — RPR

2312 **1** **Urban Space**[13] 4426 4-9-8 **73** ... KierenFox(5) 4 — 81
(J L Flint) *trckd ldng pair: wnt 2nd over 3f out: rdn to ld wl over 1f out: wl on top fnl f* **11/4**[2]

-313 **2** *1 1/2* **Peace Corps**[31] 3812 4-10-0 **74** ...(vt) PatCosgrave 9 — 79
(J R Boyle) *trckd ldr to over 3f out: rdn to chal over 2f out: fnd little u.p: readily hld fnl f* **14/1**

0511 **3** *1* **Seattle Speight (USA)**[20] 4212 3-8-5 **67** ...(v) HarryBentley(7) 6 — 70
(W J Knight) *dwlt: wl in tch: effrt against rail over 2f out: chsd ldng pair and edgd lft fnl f: nvr able to chal* **5/2**[1]

0255 **4** *2* **Folio (IRE)**[23] 4102 10-9-0 **60** ... StevieDonohoe 7 — 59
(W J Musson) *hld up in last pair: effrt over 2f out: nt qckn u.p over 1f out: no imp after* **10/1**

3021 **5** *2 1/4* **Choral Festival**[13] 4422 4-9-2 **62** ...(v) NeilChalmers 8 — 57
(J J Bridger) *wl in tch: effrt and cl enough on outer 2f out: wknd over 1f out* **4/1**[3]

03 **6** *hd* **Peaceful Means (IRE)**[28] 3312 7-9-10 **70** ... MickyFenton 5 — 64
(A W Carroll) *hld up in last pair: effrt on wd outside 3f out: wknd over 1f out* **20/1**

1-02 **7** *nk* **Laish Ya Hajar (IRE)**[23] 4101 6-10-0 **74** ... EddieAhern 3 — 68
(P R Webber) *led and sn clr: c bk to field 4f out: hdd & wknd wl over 1f out* **11/2**

2m 7.92s (-0.78) **Going Correction** 0.0s/f (Good)
WFA 3 from 4yo+ 9lb — **7** Ran SP% **111.1**
Speed ratings (Par 103): **103,101,101,99,97 97,97**
toteswingers: 1&2 £4.60, 1&3 £1.50, 2&3 £6.30 CSF £36.51 CT £102.34 TOTE £2.70: £1.10, £4.30; EX 44.20 Trifecta £105.10 Pool: £511.71 - 3.60 winning units..
Owner Jason Tucker **Bred** Winterbeck Manor Stud **Trained** Kenfig Hill, Bridgend

FOCUS
A run-of-the-mill handicap but sound form with the first two setting the level.

4874 VIRGIN ATLANTIC MAIDEN FILLIES' STKS — 1m 2f 7y

4:30 (4:34) (Class 5) 3-Y-O+ — **£3,070** (£906; £453) **Stalls** Centre

Form — RPR

2020 **1** **Ellbeedee (IRE)**[22] 4134 3-8-11 73 ... PhilipRobinson 5 — 75+
(M A Jarvis) *trckd ldr: led wl over 2f out: drvn and styd on wl fr over 1f out* **4/1**[2]

22 **2** *1* **Entitled**[14] 4414 3-8-11 0 ... RyanMoore 7 — 73+
(Sir Michael Stoute) *banged hd in stalls: trckd ldrs: rdn over 2f out: wnt 2nd and chal 1f out: nt qckn* **4/7**[1]

36 **3** *2* **Madonna Dell'Orto**[56] 2998 3-8-11 0 ... ShaneKelly 1 — 69+
(W R Swinburn) *hld up in tch: chsd wnr over 2f out to 1f out: kpt on same pce* **9/2**[3]

26 **4** *4 1/2* **Widow Bird (IRE)**[89] 1993 3-8-11 0 ... JimmyQuinn 11 — 60+
(H Morrison) *s.v.s: hld up in last: pushed along and sme prog over 2f out: wnt modest 4th over 1f out: kpt on* **25/1**

45 **5** *3* **Belle Boleyn**[23] 4115 3-8-11 0 ... JackMitchell 6 — 54
(C F Wall) *hld up in rr: outpcd fr over 2f out: pushed along and no ch after* **16/1**

0 **6** *1/2* **Bedouin Princess (IRE)**[33] 3766 3-8-4 0 ... AdamBeschizza(7) 4 — 53
(Lucinda Featherstone) *s.v.s: hld up in rr: shkn up and wknd over 2f out* **66/1**

0- **7** *nk* **Danvilla**[303] 6628 3-8-11 0 ... EddieAhern 8 — 52
(P R Webber) *in tch in midfield: wknd over 2f out* **50/1**

0-00 **8** *1* **Lily Eva**[2] 4793 4-9-1 36 ... SophieDoyle(5) 9 — 50?
(D Donovan) *led to wl over 2f out: wknd* **66/1**

55 **P** **Beautiful One**[25] 4028 3-8-6 0 ... KierenFox(5) 10 — —
(T D McCarthy) *plld hrd: prom: wkng whn p.u over 2f out: fatally injured* **33/1**

2m 7.79s (-0.91) **Going Correction** 0.0s/f (Good)
WFA 3 from 4yo+ 9lb — **9** Ran SP% **119.5**
Speed ratings (Par 100): **103,102,100,97,94 94,93,93,—**
toteswingers: 1&2 £2.00, 1&3 £2.00, 2&3 £1.90 CSF £6.78 TOTE £4.80: £1.50, £1.02, £1.70; EX 8.80 Trifecta £17.20 Pool: £548.98 - 23.58 winning units..
Owner Stephen Dartnell **Bred** John And Sarah Kelly **Trained** Newmarket, Suffolk

FOCUS
An uncompetitive maiden dominated by the market leaders, while the third sets the level for the form.
Widow Bird(IRE) Official explanation: jockey said filly was slowly away

4875 KICK IT OUT H'CAP — 6f

5:00 (5:03) (Class 6) (0-65,69) 3-Y-O+ — **£2,388** (£705; £352) **Stalls** High

Form — RPR

0254 **1** **Bobs Dreamflight**[18] 4255 4-9-4 **62** ... JimCrowley 1 — 72
(D K Ivory) *awkward s: hld up in rr and racd wd thrght: prog over 2f out: rdn to ld ins fnl f: sn clr* **9/2**[2]

0101 **2** *1 3/4* **Panpiper**[9] 4529 3-9-7 **69** ... RyanMoore 2 — 72
(G L Moore) *led and crossed to nr side rail: drvn 2f out: hdd and outpcd ins fnl f* **9/2**[2]

4505 **3** *3/4* **Magical Speedfit (IRE)**[4] 4693 5-9-2 **65** ... SimonPearce(5) 8 — 67
(G G Margarson) *hld up in rr: looking for room 2f out: limited prog over 1f out: r.o wl fnl f: tk 3rd nr fin* **7/1**[3]

0340 **4** *1* **Bateleur**[8] 4589 6-9-2 **60** ... CathyGannon 4 — 59
(M R Channon) *dwlt: hld up in rr: prog on outer over 2f out: sn drvn: cl enough over 1f out: one pce* **17/2**

6-04 **5** *1/2* **Loupho le**[2] 4776 8-8-10 **61** ... DannyBrock(7) 10 — 58
(J R Jenkins) *dwlt: hld up and racd against rail: cl enough over 1f out: nt qckn after: kpt on* **12/1**

0306 **6** *1/2* **Charles Darwin (IRE)**[6] 4662 7-9-7 **65** ... GeorgeBaker 7 — 61
(M Blanshard) *cl up: chsd ldr 2f out: drvn and nt qckn over 1f out: fdd* **8/1**

0130 **7** *6* **Blue Aura (IRE)**[11] 4478 7-8-12 **61** ... DeanHeslop(5) 3 — 37
(B G Powell) *chsd ldrs: rdn over 2f out: wknd over 1f out* **12/1**

0606 **8** *2 1/4* **White Shift (IRE)**[37] 3637 4-9-7 **65** ... JimmyQuinn 5 — 34
(P Howling) *a towards rr: rdn over 2f out: no prog over 1f out: wknd* **16/1**

0000 **9** *2 1/2* **Ghost Dancer**[48] 3254 6-9-2 **60** ...(p) PatCosgrave 6 — 21
(J M Bradley) *hld up in rr: rdn over 2f out and no prog: wknd over 1f out* **33/1**

0164 **10** *1 1/4* **Learo Dochais (USA)**[43] 3458 4-9-7 **65** ...(b) PhilipRobinson 12 — 22
(M A Jarvis) *chsd ldr to 2f out: wknd* **7/2**[1]

1m 12.67s (-0.33) **Going Correction** 0.0s/f (Good)
WFA 3 from 4yo+ 4lb — **10** Ran SP% **116.9**
Speed ratings (Par 101): **102,99,98,97,96 96,88,85,81,80**
toteswingers: 1&2 £2.90, 1&3 £7.10, 2&3 £8.30 CSF £25.19 CT £143.21 TOTE £4.80: £1.80, £1.90, £2.90; EX 16.40 Trifecta £237.50 Pool: £597.20 - 1.86 winning units. Place 6 £47.53, Place 5 £25.30.
Owner Rahul Bajaj & Dean Ivory **Bred** C J Mills **Trained** Radlett, Herts

FOCUS
A moderate handicap but the form looks sound.
Learo Dochais(USA) Official explanation: jockey said gelding moved poorly in the final furlong
T/Jkpt: Not won. T/Plt: £89.10 to a £1 stake. Pool: £75,316.05. 616.72 winning tickets. T/Qpdt: £6.60 to a £1 stake. Pool: £6,262.69. 695.90 winning tickets. JN

4876 - (Foreign Racing) - See Raceform Interactive

4175 CURRAGH (R-H)

Sunday, August 8

OFFICIAL GOING: Straight course - yielding; round course - good

4877a KEENELAND ROYAL WHIP STKS (GROUP 2) — 1m 2f

2:45 (2:47) 3-Y-O+ — **£53,097** (£16,814; £7,964; £2,654; £1,769)

RPR

1 **Fame And Glory**[65] 2709 4-9-12 128 ... JMurtagh 4 — 114+
(A P O'Brien, Ire) *racd in mod 3rd: niggled along to cl st: gd prog in 2nd 1 1/2f out: led under 1f out: styd on wl to draw clr: comf* **1/12**[1]

2 *3 1/2* **Dixie Music (IRE)**[65] 2709 4-9-9 101 ... JAHeffernan 2 — 101
(A P O'Brien, Ire) *led and clr: reduced ld over 1f out: sn hdd and kpt on same pce* **66/1**

3 *1 1/4* **Grand Admiral (USA)**[34] 3744 4-9-9 97 ...(b) CO'Donoghue 3 — 97
(A P O'Brien, Ire) *chsd ldr: no imp u.p fr 2 1/2f out: sn dropped to 3rd and kpt on same pce* **40/1**

4 *nk* **Choose Me (IRE)**[21] 4177 4-9-6 102 ... DPMcDonogh 5 — 93
(Kevin Prendergast, Ire) *racd wl off pce in rr: no imp u.p fr 2 1/2f out: kpt on same pce in 4th fr 1f out* **16/1**[3]

5 *17* **Precious Gem (IRE)**[43] 3466 4-9-6 103 ... PJSmullen 1 — 59
(D K Weld, Ire) *racd towards rr in mod 4th: no imp u.p fr 2 1/2f out: dropped to last and eased fr under 1f out* **8/1**[2]

2m 6.62s (-5.98) **Going Correction** -0.20s/f (Firm) — **5** Ran SP% **113.3**
Speed ratings: **115,112,111,110,97**
CSF £14.56 TOTE £1.10: £1.02, £7.30; DF 11.00.
Owner Derrick Smith **Bred** Ptarmigan Bloodstock And Miss K Rausing **Trained** Ballydoyle, Co Tipperary

FOCUS
Since this race was promoted to Group 2 status in 1998, it has produced notable winners such as High Chaparral and Casual Conquest.

NOTEBOOK
Fame And Glory justified his prohibitive odds, winning in a canter. With three of the quintet hailing from Ballydoyle, it was no surprise to see the race run for the ante-post Arc favourite. (op 1/10)
Dixie Music(IRE), backed at fancy prices to fill the runner-up berth behind the Coronation Cup winner, was pushed along when the gate opened to make the pace.However, he stuck to his task once the favourite took over to hold on from Grand Admiral.
Grand Admiral(USA) was fighting a losing battle when they straightened for home. (op 33/1 tchd 50/1)
Choose Me(IRE) plugged on under pressure after racing well off the pace approaching the straight.

The Form Book, Raceform Ltd, Compton, RG20 6NL

Precious Gem(IRE)'s rider accepted the situation early in the straight and let his mount come home in her own time. Official explanation: jockey said filly never travelled and ran flat; trainer later said filly was lame post-race (op 9/1)

4879a KEENELAND DEBUTANTE STKS (GROUP 2) (FILLIES) 7f

3:45 (3:46) 2-Y-O **£57,522** (£16,814; £7,964; £2,654)

			RPR
1		**Laughing Lashes (USA)**[24] 4077 2-8-12 ... FMBerry 9 (Mrs John Harrington, Ire) *trckd ldrs in 3rd: chal and on terms fr 2f out: led and styd on best u.p ins fnl f* **5/1**[3]	110+
2	1	**Misty For Me (IRE)**[22] 4157 2-8-12 ... JAHeffernan 2 (A P O'Brien, Ire) *trckd ldr: rdn 1/2-way: led over 2f out: sn jnd: hdd and kpt on wout matching wnr ins fnl f* **8/1**	107
3	3	**Together (IRE)**[24] 4077 2-8-12 106 ... JMurtagh 8 (A P O'Brien, Ire) *trckd ldrs: struggling in 3rd and drifted lft fr over 1f out: kpt on same pce* **6/4**[1]	99+
4	2 ½	**Lily Again**[17] 4305 2-8-12 ... JamieSpencer 3 (P F I Cole) *trckd ldrs: 4th 2f out: no imp u.p and kpt on same pce fr over 1f out* **8/1**	92
5	hd	**Seeharn (IRE)**[44] 3421 2-8-12 ... DPMcDonogh 5 (Kevin Prendergast, Ire) *towards rr: 6th 1/2-way: rdn over 2f out: sn 5th: briefly 4th and no imp fr over 1f out: kpt on same pce* **11/4**[2]	92
6	4 ½	**Gatamalata (IRE)**[17] 4309 2-8-12 98 ... PJSmullen 4 (Joseph G Murphy, Ire) *mid-div: rdn over 2f out: sn no imp and kpt on same pce* **11/1**	80
7	2	**Inca Princess (IRE)**[29] 3926 2-8-12 ... CO'Donoghue 1 (A P O'Brien, Ire) *towards rr: no imp u.p fr over 2f out* **33/1**	74
8	13	**Gemstone (IRE)**[24] 4077 2-8-12 ... SMLevey 7 (A P O'Brien, Ire) *sn led: hdd & wknd fr over 2f out* **66/1**	39
9	10	**Hasty Katie (IRE)**[8] 4609 2-8-12 80 ...(p) KJManning 6 (J S Bolger, Ire) *towards rr: dropped bhd and eased fr 2f out* **20/1**	12

1m 24.49s (-6.31) **Going Correction** -0.825s/f (Hard) **9** Ran SP% **123.1**
Speed ratings: **103,101,98,95,95 90,87,73,61**
CSF £46.51 TOTE £5.50: £1.30, £3.10, £1.10; DF 102.10.
Owner McElroy Syndicate **Bred** Runnymede Farm Inc & Robert P Levy **Trained** Moone, Co Kildare

NOTEBOOK

Laughing Lashes(USA) ◆, one of only two maidens in the line-up, did not lack support here having finished second to Together, the favourite for this race, in a Group 3 event over the same trip at Leopardstown on her second start. The decision to run here paid off handsomely as the Jessica Harrington-trained filly, who raced close up throughout, joined for the lead 2f out before edging ahead just under 1f out. Shaken up to assert, she kept on well. She is likely to have one more run this season, although where that will be is uncertain.

Misty For Me(IRE) ◆, a maiden winner over 6f here last month, emerged with her reputation enhanced. Soon second, she went to the front over 2f out and found for pressure until the winner took her measure inside the final furlong. (op 12/1)

Together(IRE) was on a hat-trick and had beaten Laughing Lashes by a length at Leopardstown last time. She tracked the leaders and was switched left to begin her challenge in third place over 1f out. However, she hung badly across the track and finished close to the stands' side rail, losing any chance she had of getting seriously involved. (op 11/8 tchd 13/8)

Lily Again, twice a winner and successful in a Listed event over the trip at Sandown last month, tracked the leaders and was being niggled along at halfway. She was unable to get in a blow at the leaders but kept plugging away. (op 9/1)

Seeharn(IRE), unbeaten in two previous starts, was held up and was sixth at halfway. She improved one place over 2f out but failed to make any further impression. (op 10/3)

4880a KEENELAND PHOENIX STKS (GROUP 1) (ENTIRE COLTS & FILLIES) 6f

4:15 (4:16) 2-Y-O
£102,654 (£33,628; £15,929; £5,309; £3,539; £1,769)

			RPR
1		**Zoffany (IRE)**[17] 4310 2-9-1 108 ... JMurtagh 2 (A P O'Brien, Ire) *sn settled towards rr on stand's rail: got into clr and chsd ldrs in 4th over 1f out: sn 3rd: r.o wl between to ld nr fin* **3/1**[2]	115+
2	½	**Glor Na Mara (IRE)**[21] 4176 2-9-1 ... KJManning 5 (J S Bolger, Ire) *trckd ldrs: chal in cl 2nd and ev ch fr over 1f out: kpt on same pce nr fin* **12/1**[3]	113
3	shd	**Strong Suit (USA)**[54] 3049 2-9-1 ... RichardHughes 6 (R Hannon) *prom: on terms 2 1/2f out: narrowly in front fr over 1f out: no ex and hdd nr fin* **4/9**[1]	113
4	5	**Emperor Hadrian (IRE)**[30] 3868 2-9-1 99 ...(b[1]) CO'Donoghue 3 (A P O'Brien, Ire) *trckd ldrs: 5th 2 1/2f out: no imp and kpt on same pce fr over 1f out* **33/1**	97
5	1 ¾	**Samuel Morse (IRE)**[21] 4176 2-9-1 107 ... JAHeffernan 9 (A P O'Brien, Ire) *trckd ldrs: rdn into 3rd over 1f out: sn no imp and kpt on same pce* **12/1**[3]	91
6	3	**Foolproof (IRE)**[7] 4628 2-9-1 82 ... DMGrant 4 (John Joseph Murphy, Ire) *chsd ldrs: last 2 1/2f out: sn no imp and kpt on same pce* **100/1**	82
7	5	**Snow Mountain (IRE)**[22] 4161 2-9-1 87 ... SMLevey 1 (A P O'Brien, Ire) *sn led: jnd 2 1/2f out: sn hdd & wknd fr over 1f out* **66/1**	66

1m 11.29s (-3.71) **Going Correction** -0.375s/f (Firm) **7** Ran SP% **115.1**
Speed ratings: **109,108,108,101,99 95,88**
CSF £35.74 TOTE £3.40: £1.80, £3.10; DF 24.00.
Owner Michael Tabor **Bred** Epona Bloodstock Ltd **Trained** Ballydoyle, Co Tipperary

FOCUS

The result, although somewhat unexpected, confirmed two significant trenda; this has not been a good race for Coventry Stakes winners and it is a virtual benefit for Aidan O'Brien, who has now won it 11 times since 1998.

NOTEBOOK

Zoffany(IRE) reversed Royal Ascot form with Strong Suit in comprehensive fashion. Once ridden for a split between Strong Suit and the eventual runner-up, he picked up strongly and there was no argument about his supremacy (op 11/4 tchd 3/1)

Glor Na Mara(IRE) ◆ had finished last of four behind the impressive Dunboyne Express (one of the absentees here) when set a tough task on his debut in the Anglesey Stakes, but has been talked of as smart since an early stage of the season. It's easy to see why now, since he ran a terrific race for one so inexperienced. He should win a decent prize later in the campaign and has the makings of a lovely 3-y-o. (op 12/1 tchd 14/1)

Strong Suit(USA) for whom perhaps the race was not run to suit him (he was in front plenty early enough), and he could still take prime ranking in the stable's squad for next year's 2000 Guineas.

Emperor Hadrian(IRE) Official explanation: jockey said colt hung left in the final 2f

Samuel Morse(IRE) has failed to go forward since finishing fourth in the Coventry.

4882a PATRICK P O'LEARY MEMORIAL PHOENIX SPRINT STKS (GROUP 3) 6f

5:15 (5:18) 3-Y-O+ **£37,389** (£10,929; £5,176; £1,725)

			RPR
1		**Snaefell (IRE)**[29] 3928 6-9-7 108 ...(b) ShaneFoley 6 (M Halford, Ire) *towards rr: prog into 3rd over 1f out: led and styd on wl ins fnl f* **9/1**	113
2	¾	**Luisant**[2] 4808 7-9-4 104 ... FMBerry 5 (J A Nash, Ire) *trckd ldrs: chal u.p in 2nd over 1f out: sn on terms and ev ch: hdd and kpt on same pce ins fnl f* **7/2**[2]	108
3	hd	**Bewitched (IRE)**[18] 4269 3-8-11 105 ...(t) JMurtagh 3 (Charles O'Brien, Ire) *towards rr: prog into 5th over 1f out: kpt on u.p ins fnl f wout getting to 1st 2* **5/2**[1]	104
4	2	**Miss Gorica (IRE)**[18] 4269 6-9-1 104 ...(p) WMLordan 4 (Ms Joanna Morgan, Ire) *led: strly pressed and jnd 1 1/2f out: hdd and dropped to 4th over 1f out: sn no imp and kpt on same pce* **16/1**	98
5	shd	**Rain Delayed (IRE)**[2] 4808 4-9-4 108 ... KLatham 2 (G M Lyons, Ire) *prom: rdn to chal and on terms 1 1/2f out: led over 1f out: hdd and no ex ins fnl f* **8/1**	100
6	4 ½	**Duff (IRE)**[22] 4160 7-9-9 110 ...(b) PJSmullen 1 (Edward Lynam, Ire) *trckd ldrs: 3rd 1/2-way: dropped to 6th and no imp fr over 1f out* **7/1**	91
7	1	**Wrong Answer**[18] 4269 3-8-11 98 ... CDHayes 7 (Kevin Prendergast, Ire) *a towards rr: no imp u.p fr 1 1/2f out* **20/1**	80
8	nk	**Croisultan (IRE)**[22] 4160 4-9-4 106 ... PShanahan 9 (Liam McAteer, Ire) *chsd ldrs: 5th 1/2-way: dropped to 7th and no imp fr over 1f out* **14/1**	82
9	3	**Prescription**[18] 4269 5-9-1 ... DPMcDonogh 10 (Sir Mark Prescott) *sn towards rr: niggled along fr bef 1/2-way: no imp fr 2f out* **4/1**[3]	69

1m 10.8s (-4.20) **Going Correction** -0.375s/f (Firm)
WFA 3 from 4yo+ 4lb **9** Ran SP% **121.7**
Speed ratings: **113,112,111,109,108 102,101,101,97**
CSF £42.89 TOTE £10.10: £2.40, £1.80, £1.70; DF 58.90.
Owner Lady Clague **Bred** Newberry Stud Farm **Trained** Doneany, Co Kildare

NOTEBOOK

Snaefell(IRE), winner of this race two years ago at Leopardstown, had blinkers back on for the first time this season and got off the mark for the year by posting his eighth win – his third at Group 3 level. Seventh and pushed along at halfway, he began to close from 2f out and went to the front well inside the final furlong, keeping on well in the closing stages.

Luisant was making a quick reappearance after finishing third in a 5f Listed event on quicker ground at Tipperary on Friday night. The extra furlong and the slightly slower ground were expected to favour him here and, while he again performed well, he had to settle for minor money. Fourth at halfway, he began his effort under 2f out and came there with every chance only for the winner to prove the stronger in the run to the line. (op 6/1)

Bewitched(IRE), a dual Listed winner, was again held up. Sixth at halfway, she worked her way into a challenging position over 1f out and kept on without finding as much as might have been anticipated. (op 9/4)

Miss Gorica(IRE), who is in-foal and coming to the end of her career, bounced out and made the running. Joined one and a half furlongs out and headed soon afterwards, she could raise no extra inside the final furlong.

Rain Delayed(IRE), fourth in the 5f Listed event in which Luisant ran third at Tipperary on Friday, raced prominently and got to the front over 1f out before finding no extra under pressure when tackled and headed inside the final furlong. (op 6/1)

Prescription Official explanation: jockey said mare hung throughout this race

4881 - 4883a (Foreign Racing) - See Raceform Interactive

4773 DEAUVILLE (R-H)

Sunday, August 8

OFFICIAL GOING: Turf: good to soft; fibresand: standard

4884a PRIX BEACHCOMBER HOTELS LE PARADIS ***** LUXE (PRIX TANIT) (CONDITIONS) (2YO FILLIES) (TURF) 7f 110y

12:35 (12:00) 2-Y-O **£15,044** (£6,017; £4,513; £3,008; £1,504)

			RPR
1		**Espirita (FR)**[23] 2-8-10 0 ... AnthonyCrastus 1 (E Lellouche, France) **13/5**[2]	90
2	2	**Riqa** 2-8-10 0 ... DavyBonilla 6 (F Head, France) **1/1**[1]	85
3	1 ½	**Hoppy's Flyer (FR)**[44] 3386 2-8-10 0 ... MaximeGuyon 3 (Tom Dascombe) *broke smartly to ld: stl in front 2 1/2f out: rdn: r.o: hdd 1 1/2f out: r.o wl* **11/1**	82
4	2	**Action Chope (FR)**[28] 2-9-0 0 ... ThierryJarnet 5 (D Guillemin, France) **11/2**[3]	81
5	1 ½	**Come Back To Me (FR)** 2-8-8 0 ow1 ... ChristopheSoumillon 2 (J-Y Artu, France) **18/1**	72
6	¾	**Yosha (IRE)** 2-8-10 0 ... IoritzMendizabal 4 (P Demercastel, France) **11/1**	72
7	2 ½	**Dream Peace (IRE)** 2-8-11 0 ow1 ... OlivierPeslier 7 (Robert Collet, France) **32/1**	67

1m 33.4s (5.00) **7** Ran SP% **118.1**
WIN (incl. 1 euro stake): 3.60. PLACES: 1.50, 1.30. SF: 7.70.
Owner Bruno Mettoudi **Bred** S C A La Perrigne & Elevage De Courteilles **Trained** Lamorlaye, France

NOTEBOOK

Hoppy's Flyer(FR), a 70-rated maiden, made much of the running and wasn't disgraced on this rise in class on easier ground.

4885a PRIX MAURICE DE GHEEST (GROUP 1) (3YO+) (TURF) 6f 110y(S)

2:40 (12:00) 3-Y-O+ **£126,415** (£50,575; £25,287; £12,632; £6,327)

			RPR
1		**Regal Parade**[22] 4136 6-9-2 0 ... AdrianNicholls 14 (D Nicholls) *hld up in midfield on outside: tk clsr order to chse ldrs gng wl 3f out: rdn and chal 2f out: led 300yds fr home: r.o strly u.p* **5/1**[2]	121
2	nk	**Joanna (IRE)**[36] 3704 3-8-8 0 ... ChristopheSoumillon 13 (J-C Rouget, France) *broke wl and racd promly on outside: disp 4th at 1/2-way: 2nd and gng wl appr 2f out: chal wnr 1f out tl no ex fnl 50yds* **5/1**[2]	116

3 4 **High Standing (USA)**[22] 4136 5-9-2 0 IoritzMendizabal 6 109
(W J Haggas) *hld up towards rr: nowhere to go 2 1/2f out: blocked again 1 1/2f out: had to sit and suffer tl opening appeared 1f out: r.o wl fnl f: tk 3rd on line* **14/1**

4 *shd* **Smooth Operator (GER)**[23] 4122 4-9-2 0 YannLerner 11 108
(Mario Hofer, Germany) *racd in 6th: bmpd 3f out: rdn 2 1/2f out: r.o u.p fr 1 1/2f out but wout pce of first two: lost 3rd on line* **40/1**

5 ½ **Prime Defender**[30] 3870 6-9-2 0 RobertWinston 2 107
(B W Hills) *broke wl and chsd ldrs on rail: 3rd appr 1/2-way: outpcd on rail 2f out: rdn and styd on fnl f* **33/1**

6 *hd* **Mariol (FR)**[22] 4165 7-9-2 0 FranckBlondel 3 106
(Robert Collet, France) *racd towards rr: rdn whn short of room ins fnl 2f: r.o fnl f: nvr nrr* **33/1**

7 *hd* **Alverta (AUS)**[30] 3870 7-8-13 0 (b) TyeAngland 10 103
(Paul Messara, Australia) *broke wl and crossed fr middle of trck to join main gp: racd in 4th: 6th and rdn 2f out: drifted rt u.p ins fnl 300yds and hmpd rival (Amico Fritz): kpt on at one pce* **6/1**

8 *hd* **Indomito (GER)**[10] 4526 4-9-2 0 DavyBonilla 9 105
(P Vovcenko, Germany) *racd in fnl 3rd: plld to outside 2f out: rdn and disp 3rd over 1f out: nt qckn u.p* **66/1**

9 2 **Flash Dance (IRE)**[36] 3704 4-8-13 0 (p) JohanVictoire 5 96
(H-A Pantall, France) *flat-footed as stalls opened and lost four l: sn mde up grnd but hmpd on rail after 1f: last 3f out: rdn and sme late hdwy: nvr a factor* **33/1**

10 *shd* **Planet Five (USA)**[63] 2804 4-9-2 0 StephanePasquier 8 99
(P Bary, France) *hld up towards rr: plld wd 3f out: rdn and r.o appr fnl 300yds: 5th 1f out: wknd ins fnl f* **12/1**

11 *snk* **Chopouest (FR)**[59] 3-8-11 0 FredericSpanu 12 98
(A Spanu, France) *trckd ldr fr far side to stands' rail: racd in 2nd tl chal and led 2 1/2f out: hdd 1 1/2f out: wknd qckly ins fnl f* **25/1**

12 *snk* **Arabian Gleam**[22] 4160 6-9-2 0 (p) DarryllHolland 1 98
(J Noseda) *broke wl on rail: settled and chsd ldrs: squeezed for room and shuffled bk appr 1/2-way: rdn 2f out but no imp* **14/1**

13 ½ **Varenar (FR)**[30] 3870 4-9-2 0 GeraldMosse 15 97
(A De Royer-Dupre, France) *qckly away to ld in centre of trck: sn moved to stands' side: hdd 2 1/2f out: sn fdd* **4/1**[1]

14 1½ **War Artist (AUS)**[22] 4165 7-9-2 0 OlivierPeslier 4 92
(A De Royer-Dupre, France) *broke wl and rn freely on heels of ldrs: rdn 2f out: no imp and wknd* **11/2**[3]

15 10 **Amico Fritz (GER)**[50] 3192 4-9-2 0 MaximeGuyon 7 63
(H-A Pantall, France) *hld up in midfield: rdn 2f out: running on whn hmpd by rival (Alverta) ins fnl 300yds: snatched up and eased* **12/1**

1m 16.8s (-0.40) **Going Correction** +0.375s/f (Good)
WFA 3 from 4yo+ 4lb **15** Ran SP% **128.3**
Speed ratings: **117,116,112,111,111 111,110,110,108,108 108,107,107,105,94**
WIN (incl. 1 euro stake): 9.20. PLACES: 3.60, 1.90, 6.40. DF: 20.10. SF: 61.50.
Owner Dab Hand Racing **Bred** Highclere Stud And Harry Herbert **Trained** Sessay, N Yorks

FOCUS
Perhaps not the strongest of Group 1 sprints, with only bit part players from the Golden Jubilee and July Cup in attendance, but the line-up did include four previous Group 1 winners, and it was one of that quartet who came out on top in what proved to be a two-horse race from a furlong and a half out. The field split into two initially before those drawn high and racing up the middle crossed over to race with the stands' side bunch.

NOTEBOOK
Regal Parade was representing a stable in fantastic form and, while last year's Haydock Sprint Cup winner didn't travel anywhere near as strongly as his main rival Joanna through the race, once it came down to a battle he showed the greater determination. He didn't run well in the Golden Jubilee, but bounced back to form on more suitable ground at Newbury last time and it's now clear he needs a bit of give to be seen at his best. He's now been successful in four of his five starts over shorter than 7f on good ground or softer, and two of those wins have come in Group 1 company. The obvious next race for him is a defence of his Sprint Cup crown, while the Prix de la Foret over 7f the following month will surely also come into consideration.

Joanna(IRE), who wasn't beaten far in the French Guineas earlier in the season, was dropping back slightly in trip after winning a Group 3 race over 7f. She travelled strongly and, when asked to quicken, picked up well, but unfortunately for her she bumped into a rival unwilling to lie down. The way she carried her head to one side suggested she was quite happy for him to lead her home.

High Standing(USA) finished two and a half lengths behind Regal Parade when third in the Haydock Sprint Cup last year and was three lengths behind him at Newbury in a Group 3 last time out. He was beaten even further by his old rival this time, although in fairness he didn't enjoy much luck in running, for while the winner was battling it out in front he was still looking for a gap to appear back in the pack.

Smooth Operator(GER) had run well in defeat in his previous two starts in German Group 3 company, but this was a big step up. His stamina for 7f - he gave weight and a beating to Varenar over that trip at Longchamp last summer - came into play late on.

Prime Defender ran about as well as could be expected as he's a notch or two below the level required in this grade. His form figures in Group 1 company now read 0007859905.

Mariol(FR), who finished second to King's Apostle in this race last year, was stuck behind horses when the front two quickened away, but he stayed on well once in the clear.

Alverta(AUS), an excellent third in the July Cup last time out, got a little outpaced and was hampered, before keeping on again. The plan beforehand was to keep her on the go for the Foret and Park Stakes, and the step up to 7f should suit her - she's a Grade 1 winner over an extended 7f in Australia.

Indomito(GER) was up against it in this class.

Flash Dance(IRE) ran creditably considering she lost several lengths at the start and was then hampered early on in the race. However, giving away ground at the start does seem to be a recurring problem for her.

Planet Five(USA), winner of the Group 2 Prix Gros-Chene over 5f last time out, was ridden patiently to get the trip. He challenged widest of all and was in third briefly before tiring in the closing stages. He clearly didn't stay, but can find further success back over the minimum.

Arabian Gleam shaped better than his finishing position suggests as he didn't get much of a clear run, but whether he has the speed to live with these top sprinters is open to question.

Varenar(FR) looked to hold solid claims beforehand as he was fourth in this race last year before winning the Foret, and had run respectably in both the Golden Jubilee and July Cup this season. The slightly longer trip and easier ground were both expected to suit him but, instead of being held up as he normally is, he attempted to make all, and at a pretty decent gallop. The change in tactics failed and presumably he'll revert to being held up when he tries to repeat in the Foret in October.

War Artist(AUS) never looked like getting a clear run towards the stands' rail and his rider wasn't hard on him in a lost cause.

Amico Fritz(GER) got involved in some scrimmaging mid-race and was badly hampered 1½f out as well. This run is best ignored.

4886 - (Foreign Racing) - See Raceform Interactive

4417 DEL MAR (L-H)
Sunday, August 8

OFFICIAL GOING: Polytrack: fast

4887a CLEMENT L HIRSCH STKS (GRADE 1) (3YO+ FILLIES & MARES) (POLYTRACK) 1m 110y
2:00 (12:00) 3-Y-O+ **£111,111** (£37,037; £22,222; £11,111; £3,703)

RPR

1 **Zenyatta (USA)**[55] 3044 6-8-11 0 MESmith 5 113
(John Shirreffs, U.S.A) *settled towards rr: tk clsr order 2 1/2f out: pressed ldr 1 1/2f out: rdn and led fnl f: hld on wl* **1/10**[1]

2 *nk* **Rinterval (IRE)**[35] 5-8-7 0 RBejarano 6 108
(Eric R Reed, U.S.A) *broke wl fr outside draw and sn led: pressed for much of the way: hdd fnl f: rallied gamely* **106/10**[2]

3 2¼ **Princess Taylor**[42] 6-8-7 0 VEspinoza 1 103
(Patrick Gallagher, U.S.A) *chsd ldng pair: chal between horses 1 1/2f out: kpt on at one pce fnl f* **233/10**

4 3¾ **Spring Style (IRE)**[36] 5-8-8 0 ow1 PValenzuela 3 96
(B Cecil, U.S.A) *hld up in last: sme prog ins fnl 2f: no ex fnl f* **221/10**

5 ½ **Dance To My Tune (CAN)**[83] 6-8-7 0 DFlores 4 94
(Jerry Hollendorfer, U.S.A) *pressed ldr: c wd st: wknd* **125/10**[3]

6 1½ **Made For Magic (USA)**[22] 5-8-9 0 (b) OBerrio 2 92
(A C Avila, U.S.A) *racd in 4th: grad fdd fnl 2f* **14/1**

1m 45.03s (105.03) **6** Ran SP% **122.0**
PARI-MUTUEL (all including $2 stake): WIN 2.20; PLACE (1-2) 2.10, 3.80; DF 6.00; SF 9.20.
Owner Mr & Mrs Jerome S Moss **Bred** Maverick Production Limited **Trained** USA
■ Zenyatta owns the modern-day record for consecutive victories in races not restricted to state-bred horses.

FOCUS
The pace was very steady.

NOTEBOOK
Zenyatta(USA) made it 18-18 with her third successive Clement L Hirsch and her 12th Grade 1 success in total, and she looked to have much more in hand than the official margin suggests. She was set an awful lot to do when getting up literally on the line in this race last year, but on this occasion she was in front sooner than usual after coming wide into the straight, and idled once there, pricking her ears. She had to be given a few light taps with the whip late on, but was always doing just enough. Her main aim is to defend her Breeders' Cup Classic crown, and with that race back on dirt this season, she may have her prep in New York (Beldame Stakes at Belmont Park on October 2 a possible), rather than stick to synthetics.

HANOVER (L-H)
Sunday, August 8

OFFICIAL GOING: Turf: good

4888a GROSSER PREIS DER MEHL-MULHENS STIFTUNG (GROUP 2) (3YO+) (TURF) 1m
4:15 (12:00) 3-Y-O+
£35,398 (£13,716; £5,752; £3,539; £2,212; £1,327)

RPR

1 **Sehrezad (IRE)**[29] 3934 5-9-6 0 JiriPalik 5 110
(Andreas Lowe, Germany) *racd in 5th fr s: pulling freely: qcknd wl on turn into st: short of room at first but whn gap opened qcknd wl and r.o strly in fnl f to catch ldr in fnl strides* **3/1**[1]

2 ¾ **Abbashiva (GER)**[29] 3934 5-9-6 0 EFrank 9 108
(T Mundry, Germany) *settled in midfield: mde gd prog bef fnl turn: qcknd wl early in st to take command 1 1/2f out: r.o wl but ct in fnl strides* **9/1**[3]

3 1¾ **Alianthus (GER)**[29] 3934 5-9-6 0 ADeVries 3 104
(J Hirschberger, Germany) *broke wl and racd in 3rd and hld that position ent st: styd on wl but no match for first two* **25/1**

4 *hd* **Win For Sure (GER)**[29] 3934 5-9-6 0 EPedroza 4 104
(A Wohler, Germany) *settled in midfield: r.o wl ent st but failed to qckn: styd on* **3/1**[1]

5 *nk* **Freminius (GER)**[56] 3017 6-9-6 0 DominiqueBoeuf 10 103
(W Baltromei, Germany) *racd in midfield: mde move at end of bk st: threatened briefly ent st: no ex* **10/1**

6 *hd* **Le Big (GER)**[14] 6-9-6 0 AStarke 8 102
(U Stoltefuss, Germany) *bkmaker fr s: mde gd prog bef end of bk st: r.o through btn horses in st* **33/1**

7 2 **Contat (GER)**[23] 4122 7-9-6 0 RJuracek 11 98
(P Vovcenko, Germany) *broke fast and led: set gd pce: led into st: r.o briefly but then fdd* **25/1**

8 *nk* **Frozen Power (IRE)**[35] 3719 3-9-0 0 RoystonFfrench 1 98
(Mahmood Al Zarooni) *broke wl to r in 4th: mde prog ent st but then fdd rapidly* **3/1**[1]

9 ¾ **Kite Hunter (IRE)**[29] 3934 3-9-0 0 THellier 7 96
(Mario Hofer, Germany) *broke wl and racd freely in early stages: prom: flattered briefly early in st: no ex: wknd qckly* **8/1**[2]

10 *nk* **Konig Concorde (GER)**[57] 5-9-6 0 WPanov 2 95
(C Sprengel, Germany) *settled in midfield: already in trble ent st: nvr a threat* **50/1**

11 3 **Sanjii Danon (GER)**[29] 3934 4-9-6 0 APietsch 6 88
(W Hickst, Germany) *racd towards rr: mde gd prog down bk st: threatened briefly ent st: sn btn* **12/1**

1m 36.88s (96.88)
WFA 3 from 4yo+ 7lb **11** Ran SP% **125.5**
WIN (incl. 10 euro stake): 56. PLACES: 20, 29, 31. SF: 491.
Owner Stall Phillip **Bred** Acorn Stud **Trained** Germany

[4682] SOUTHWELL (L-H)
Monday, August 9

OFFICIAL GOING: Standard
Wind: Light across Weather: Fine and dry

4890 PAULHOWLINGRACING.CO.UK MEDIAN AUCTION MAIDEN STKS 5f (F)
2:30 (2:31) (Class 4) 2-Y-O £3,885 (£1,156; £577; £288) Stalls High

Form RPR
06 1 **Winning Draw (IRE)**[23] 4149 2-8-12 0 TonyCulhane 4 62
(P T Midgley) *chsd ldrs on outer: hdwy 2f out: swtchd rt and rdn over 1f out: drvn and styd on ins fnl f to ld nr fin* 5/1[2]
0 2 nk **Poetically**[56] 3034 2-9-3 0 NeilCallan 11 66+
(J G Portman) *cl up: led over 3f out: rdn 2f out and sn hung bdly lft to far rail: drvn ins fnl f: faltered momentarily ins fnl 30yds: hdd nr fin* 8/1
0 3 1 1/4 **Je Suis Unrockstar**[9] 4599 2-9-3 0 PJMcDonald 10 62
(J A Glover) *cl up: rdn over 2f out: swtchd rt and drvn ent fnl f: kpt on* 18/1
0 4 3/4 **Silent Blessing**[64] 2785 2-9-3 0 TomEaves 7 59+
(R M H Cowell) *reminders s and sn rdn along: in rr tl styd on appr fnl f: nrst fin* 3/1[1]
5 nk **Scoglio** 2-9-3 0 LeeVickers 8 58+
(F Sheridan) *s.i.s and in rr: hdwy wl over 1f out: sn rdn and kpt on ins fnl f: nrst fin* 22/1
000 6 4 **Back For Tea (IRE)**[19] 4247 2-9-3 57 SebSanders 1 44
(Tom Dascombe) *cl up: rdn along 1/2-way: sn wknd* 3/1[1]
4 7 6 **Isontonic (IRE)**[11] 4512 2-8-12 0 MickyFenton 6 17
(P T Midgley) *led 1 1/2f sn rdn along and wknd fr 1/2-way* 28/1
8 1 1/2 **False Promises** 2-9-3 0 DaneO'Neill 9 17
(D Shaw) *s.i.s and a in rr* 12/1
403 9 1/2 **Sirens**[3] 4787 2-8-5 61 (t) LeonnaMayor(7) 5 10
(P S McEntee) *a towards rr* 6/1[3]
56 10 13 **Renesmee (IRE)**[76] 2413 2-8-12 0 PatCosgrave 3 —
(Peter Grayson) *sn outpcd and a in rr* 33/1

61.88 secs (2.18) **Going Correction** +0.275s/f (Slow) 10 Ran SP% 115.8
Speed ratings (Par 96): **93,92,90,89,88 82,72,70,69,48**
toteswingers:1&2:£7.50, 1&3:£22.30, 2&3:£15.40 CSF £43.16 TOTE £5.10: £1.70, £3.90, £5.00; EX 45.10 TRIFECTA Not won..
Owner Peedeetee Syndicate 2 **Bred** Henry O'Callaghan **Trained** Westow, N Yorks

FOCUS
The withdrawal of certain favourite Boundaries gave this maiden a weak look to it, the form almost certainly no better than modest.

NOTEBOOK
Winning Draw(IRE) probably didn't have to improve that much on her previous efforts to get off the mark. However, she can't get too high a mark for nurseries and is one to bear in mind as it'll be a surprise if there isn't more to come when tried at 6f-plus, seeing as she needed all of this trip. (op 13-2 tchd 9-2)
Poetically hadn't shown much on debut in June, but was a different proposition eight weeks on. He travelled like the best horse in the race, but his hanging all the way across to the far rail definitely cost him victory, and his jockey momentarily appearing to ride with less vigour near the finish didn't help matters either. He looks all speed at this stage and should go on again. (op 17-2 tchd 9-1)
Je Suis Unrockstar, clearly sharpened up by his recent debut at Thirsk, was prominent from the off this time and could be the type to progress with racing. (op 25-1)
Silent Blessing has been quite short in the betting on both starts, suggesting he's thought capable of a good bit better, though he still seemed too green to do himself full justice and was off the bridle from an early stage, but he was keeping on at the finish. He's open to further improvement. (op 7-2)
Scoglio, a Monsieur Bond gelding, was a very cheap purchase but showed ability and can surely only improve as he was palpably green early on, keeping on as he got the hang of things. (op 20-1 tchd 25-1)
Back For Tea(IRE) was prominent in the betting but he's had a few chances now. (op 9-2)
Isontonic(IRE) Official explanation: jockey said filly hung right
Sirens ran nowhere near the form she showed on Polytrack last time. (op 7-2)

4891 GOT THE FEELING? GET TO LADBROKES H'CAP 1m 4f (F)
3:00 (3:00) (Class 3) (0-90,86) 3-Y-O+ £6,476 (£1,927; £963; £481) Stalls Low

Form RPR
0103 1 **Proud Times (USA)**[24] 4086 4-9-6 78 PJMcDonald 7 92+
(G A Swinbank) *trckd ldrs: hdwy to chse ldr 4f out: led 3f out: rdn along wl over 1f out: drvn ent fnl f and styd on wl* 13/2
1252 2 4 **Speed Dating**[5] 4694 4-9-13 85 (b) SebSanders 10 93+
(Sir Mark Prescott) *hld up in rr: smooth hdwy to trck ldrs 5f out: trckd wnr on bridle over 2f out: effrt and ev ch over 1f out: sn rdn and edgd lft jst ins fnl f: one pce* 6/4[1]
2-30 3 13 **Miss Glitters (IRE)**[26] 4023 5-9-9 81 TravisBlock 5 68
(H Morrison) *led: rdn along 4f out: hdd 3f out: sn drvn and plugged on same pce* 28/1
105 4 1 3/4 **Veloso (FR)**[8] 4619 8-9-9 86 DaleSwift(5) 9 70
(J A Glover) *sn chsng ldr: pushed along over 5f out: rdn over 4f out and sn outpcd: plugged on u.p fnl 2f* 11/2[3]
3652 5 shd **Profit's Reality (IRE)**[32] 3812 8-9-8 80 NeilCallan 8 64
(M J Attwater) *chsd ldrs: rdn along over 3f out: drvn wl over 2f out and plugegd on same pce* 16/1
-521 6 shd **Nave (USA)**[10] 4532 3-8-8 77 GregFairley 6 61
(M Johnston) *stmbld bdly s and bhd: hdwy over 3f out: sn rdn along: styd on appr fnl f: nvr a factor* 7/2[2]
1145 7 4 1/2 **Dunaskin (IRE)**[13] 4449 10-8-9 67 oh2 (b) PaulEddery 4 43
(R C Guest) *dwlt and towards rr: hdwy and in tch after 4f: rdn along over 4f out and sn wknd* 33/1
5306 8 20 **Bavarian Nordic (USA)**[3] 4781 5-9-3 75 (p) JimmyQuinn 1 19
(Mrs A Duffield) *hld up towards rr: hdwy on inner and in tch 1/2-way: rdn along 4f out and sn wknd* 14/1
-660 9 18 **Amanda Carter**[16] 4389 6-9-6 78 PaulHanagan 3 —
(R A Fahey) *chsd ldrs: rdn along 5f out: sn wknd and bhd fnl 3f* 20/1
55/ 10 30 **Rock Soleil**[595] 7770 6-9-11 83 IvaMilickova 2 —
(Jane Chapple-Hyam) *chsd ldrs: rdn along 5f out: sn lost pl and bhd* 22/1

2m 39.29s (-1.71) **Going Correction** +0.075s/f (Slow)
WFA 3 from 4yo+ 11lb 10 Ran SP% 119.0
Speed ratings (Par 107): **108,105,96,95,95 95,92,79,67,47**
toteswingers:1&2:£4.30, 1&3:£14.70, 2&3:£5.90 CSF £16.26 CT £266.19 TOTE £8.20: £2.40, £1.30, £5.00; EX 22.00 TRIFECTA Not won..
Owner J Townson **Bred** Timothy Thornton & Meg & Mike Buckley **Trained** Melsonby, N Yorks

FOCUS
Not many came close to giving their running in this but the front two are both going the right way and it's best to view their efforts in a positive light.

NOTEBOOK
Proud Times(USA) had just edged out Speed Dating when conceding weight to that rival at Wolverhampton two months ago, so it wasn't that big a surprise to see him confirm placings on these terms. That said, the runner-up has improved since then, and this represents a career-best from Alan Swinbank's gelding, making it 2-2 on the AW. He could be in for a hefty rise given the gap back to the third, but he remains relatively unexposed at 1m4f-plus. (op 5-1 tchd 7-1)
Speed Dating didn't find that much under pressure and this is not the first time he hasn't delivered as much as looked likely, but there's also a chance he's just not that strong a stayer at the trip, a view backed up by his pedigree. He definitely went through the race like one ahead of his mark and will clearly be of interest if turned out before he's reassessed. (op 9-4)
Miss Glitters(IRE) was tackling a 4f longer trip than previously and patently failed to stay, weakening in the straight. She remains in form though. (op 16-1)
Veloso(FR) did really well at this track over the winter, which makes this effort all the more disappointing, and he's run well on turf at Chester recently. (tchd 13-2)
Profit's Reality(IRE) is another who came here with an excellent record at the track, but was some way off his best on this occasion. (tchd 20-1)
Nave(USA) stumbled leaving the stalls and never really looked comfortable on his first try on the surface. He'd been progressing steadily prior to this and deserves another chance. (op 9-2)
Dunaskin(IRE) wasn't on a going day. (op 22-1)
Amanda Carter was another well below form on her first try on this surface. (op 14-1)

4892 BET IN-PLAY AT LADBROKES.COM FILLIES' H'CAP 5f (F)
3:30 (3:31) (Class 4) (0-80,80) 3-Y-O+ £4,209 (£1,252; £625; £312) Stalls High

Form RPR
1133 1 **Boogie Waltzer**[40] 3561 3-8-3 69 (t) RyanClark(7) 5 79
(S C Williams) *trckd ldng pair: hdwy 1/2-way: rdn to ld and edgd lft wl over 1f out: kpt on* 11/4[2]
550 2 2 **La Capriosa**[11] 4510 4-9-0 70 PJMcDonald 1 74
(J A Glover) *dwlt and carried sltly lft s: sn chsng ldr: led after 2f: rdn and hdd wl over 1f out: drvn and one pce ins fnl f* 15/8[1]
5105 3 4 **Basle**[9] 4583 3-8-11 75 (bt[1]) JohnFahy(5) 3 64
(Miss Gay Kelleway) *wnt lft s: in tch: hdwy on outer 1/2-way: rdn to chse ldng pair over 1f out: sn no imp* 9/1
5025 4 1 3/4 **Angus Newz**[14] 4440 7-9-10 80 PatCosgrave 6 63
(M Quinn) *in tch: rdn along 1/2-way: sn outpcd* 15/2
0-31 5 3/4 **Star Twilight**[5] 4720 3-8-2 66 6ex BillyCray(5) 4 46
(D Shaw) *in tch: rdn along and hung bdly rt 2f out: sn wknd* 5/1[3]
6002 6 2 1/2 **Socceroo**[14] 4435 5-8-5 61 oh10 (e) AdrianNicholls 2 33
(D C Griffiths) *carried sltly lft s: sn led: hdd after 2f and cl up tl rdn 2f out and sn wknd* 9/1

60.15 secs (0.45) **Going Correction** +0.275s/f (Slow)
WFA 3 from 4yo+ 3lb 6 Ran SP% 109.9
Speed ratings (Par 102): **107,103,97,94,93 89**
toteswingers:1&2:£2.20, 1&3:£4.30, 2&3:£2.20 CSF £7.95 TOTE £2.90: £1.10, £3.50; EX 9.60.
Owner Michael Edwards and John Parsons **Bred** Michael Edwards And John Parsons **Trained** Newmarket, Suffolk
■ Stewards' Enquiry : Billy Cray caution: careless riding.

FOCUS
Not much depth to this handicap, but the runner-up is always a good yardstick on this surface and the winner is still going the right way.
Basle Official explanation: jockey said filly hung left throughout

4893 LADBROKESCASINO.COM MAIDEN STKS 1m 3f (F)
4:00 (4:01) (Class 5) 3-Y-O+ £3,885 (£1,156; £577; £288) Stalls Low

Form RPR
5 1 **Herculean**[21] 4207 3-8-9 0 NeilCallan 6 86
(W J Haggas) *midfield: hdwy to trck ldrs 1/2-way: chsd ldr over 2f out: rdn to chal wl over 1f out and sn edgd rt: drvn to ld and edgd lft ins fnl f: kpt on* 5/1
22 2 2 1/4 **Dolphina (USA)**[24] 4114 3-8-4 0 JimmyQuinn 9 77
(H R A Cecil) *trckd ldrs: hdwy to ld 1/2-way: rdn along 3f out: jnd wl over 1f out and sn drvn: hdd ins fnl f and kpt on same pce* 5/2[2]
-262 3 3 1/4 **Wulfrida (IRE)**[34] 3764 3-8-1 79 MartinLane(3) 11 71
(J R Fanshawe) *hld up towards rr: hdwy and in tch 1/2-way: chsd ldrs 4f out: rdn along 2f out: drvn 1f out and sn no imp* 9/4[1]
4 4 1 3/4 **My Galway Man (IRE)**[32] 3829 3-8-9 0 GregFairley 8 73
(M Johnston) *chsd ldrs: rdn along over 3f out: drvn and one pce fnl 2f* 9/2[3]
5/2- 5 6 **Repealed**[475] 1440 4-9-5 0 TravisBlock 4 62
(H Morrison) *prom: rdn along 4f out: drvn and one pce fnl 2f* 12/1
6 7 **Diamond MM (IRE)**[62] 4-9-0 0 PJMcDonald 2 45
(G A Swinbank) *a towards rr* 14/1
0 7 nk **Crystal Celebre (IRE)**[21] 4205 4-9-5 0 DaneO'Neill 1 55
(H Candy) *led to 1/2-way: rdn along on inner 4f out: drvn and grad wknd fr over 2f out* 50/1
0000 8 26 **Account Closed**[51] 3207 3-8-1 38 (b[1]) JamesSullivan(3) 5 —
(M W Easterby) *t.k.h in midfield: pushed along over 4f out and sn rdn: lost pl and bhd fnl 3f* 100/1
0- 9 3 1/4 **Princeofthedesert**[373] 4519 4-9-5 0 PatCosgrave 10 —
(G Woodward) *prom: rdn along over 4f out: sn wknd and bhd whn eased fnl 2f* 100/1
10 10 **Bury The Hatchet (IRE)**[8] 4-9-5 0 TomEaves 7 —
(G A Swinbank) *a in rr: wl bhd fnl 4f* 50/1
00 11 5 **Kirkum (IRE)**[19] 4258 5-9-5 0 MickyFenton 3 —
(Miss Diana Weeden) *a in rr: wl bhd fnl 4f* 150/1

2m 28.48s (0.48) **Going Correction** +0.075s/f (Slow)
WFA 3 from 4yo+ 10lb 11 Ran SP% 115.1
Speed ratings (Par 103): **101,99,97,95,91 86,86,67,64,57 53**
toteswingers:1&2:£4.90, 1&3:£4.00, 2&3:£1.60 CSF £17.49 TOTE £7.80: £2.40, £1.40, £1.10; EX 22.10 Trifecta £55.10 Pool: £766.54 - 10.28 winning units..
Owner Highclere Thoroughbred Racing Tudor Min **Bred** Meon Valley Stud **Trained** Newmarket, Suffolk

FOCUS
An above-average maiden for the track, particularly at this time of year, with the second and third both having shown a fairly useful level of ability previously.

4894 BEST ODDS GUARANTEED AT LADBROKES.COM H'CAP 7f (F)
4:30 (4:31) (Class 3) (0-90,90) 3-Y-O+ £6,476 (£1,927; £963; £481) Stalls Low

Form RPR
3-11 1 **The Confessor**[16] 4387 3-8-12 81 DaneO'Neill 1 96
(H Candy) *mde all: rdn clr wl over 1f out: styd on strly* 8/1[3]

0000 **2** *4 ½* **Elusive Fame (USA)**[6] 4684 4-9-6 **83**..............................(b) GregFairley 8 88
(M Johnston) *trckd ldrs: hdwy on inner to chse wnr over 2f out: rdn wl over 1f out: drvn appr fnl f: kpt on but no ch w wnr* **18/1**

4463 **3** *1 ¼* **Fantasy Gladiator**[6] 4684 4-8-8 **71**.............................. JimmyQuinn 11 73
(R M H Cowell) *trckd ldrs: hdwy over 2f out: rdn to chse ldng pair wl over 1f out: no imp fnl f* **5/1**[2]

10-1 **4** *6* **Realt Na Mara (IRE)**[93] 1914 7-8-12 **75**......................(p) SebSanders 10 60
(H Morrison) *chsd ldrs on outer: rdn along over 2f out: sn drvn and wknd wl over 1f out* **12/1**

1225 **5** *1 ¼* **Academy Blues (USA)**[8] 4617 5-9-12 **89**...................... AdrianNicholls 9 71
(D Nicholls) *hld up towards rr: hdwy over 2f out: rdn wl over 1f out: kpt on appr fnl f: nt rch ldrs* **9/2**[1]

0003 **6** *3 ¾* **Esprit De Midas**[16] 4370 4-9-5 **82**.. NeilCallan 12 54
(K A Ryan) *chsd ldrs on outer: rdn along over 2f out: sn drvn and wknd* **9/2**[1]

301- **7** *3 ½* **Leviathan**[289] 7013 3-9-5 **88**.. MickyFenton 5 48
(T P Tate) *s.i.s and in rr: wd st: nvr a factor* **18/1**

0506 **8** *shd* **Bel Cantor**[6] 4684 7-8-6 **72**...(p) KellyHarrison(3) 3 34
(W J H Ratcliffe) *cl up: rdn along 1/2-way: sn wknd* **28/1**

1016 **9** *2 ¾* **Trans Sonic**[81] 2241 7-9-6 **88**... IanBrennan(5) 6 43
(D O'Meara) *towards rr: wd st: sn rdn and nvr a factor* **5/1**[2]

1-06 **10** *2* **Vegas Palace (IRE)**[6] 4680 3-8-2 **78**................................. SoniaEaton(7) 2 25
(Tom Dascombe) *in tch: rdn along 1/2-way: sn wknd* **33/1**

2133 **11** *nk* **Seek The Fair Land**[121] 1219 4-9-12 **89**.........................(p) PatCosgrave 7 38
(J R Boyle) *prom: rdn along over 3f out: wknd over 2f out* **14/1**

3004 **12** *22* **Deadly Secret (USA)**[16] 4371 4-9-0 **77**................................ TomEaves 4 —
(R A Fahey) *s.i.s: a in rr: t.o fnl 3f* **33/1**

110 **13** *6* **Harlech Castle**[30] 3919 5-9-13 **90**...............................(b) StephenCraine 13 —
(J R Boyle) *sn outpcd and bhd: t.o fnl 3f* **25/1**

1m 29.15s (-1.15) **Going Correction** +0.075s/f (Slow)
WFA 3 from 4yo+ 6lb **13** Ran SP% **118.9**
Speed ratings (Par 107): **109,103,102,95,94 89,85,85,82,80 79,54,47**
toteswingers:1&2:£33.20, 1&3:£6.40, 2&3:£36.80 CSF £136.10 CT £819.62 TOTE £12.00: £3.80, £8.80, £2.70; EX 132.70 TRIFECTA Not won..
Owner Six Too Many **Bred** Mrs C R D Wilson **Trained** Kingston Warren, Oxon

FOCUS
This looked really a competitive handicap, making this a most taking performance from The Confessor.

NOTEBOOK
The Confessor ◆ did well to win so convincingly seeing as he raced up with what appeared a fierce gallop from the outset. He made it 3-3 for the season in the manner of a smart performer in the making, clearly taking really well to this surface. A hefty rise is inevitable but this son of Piccolo is clearly still very much heading in the right direction. (op 13-2)
Elusive Fame(USA) has plenty of good efforts to his name here and put a handful of poor runs behind him, though never any match for the winner. (op 33-1)
Fantasy Gladiator had looked worth a try at this trip and ran creditably without improving for it, not appearing to have any obvious excuses, though he's still relatively lightly raced on the surface. (op 11-2)
Realt Na Mara(IRE) has never been the most consistent and wasn't at his best three months on from his win at Lingfield, fading from prominence in the final 2f. (op 10-1)
Academy Blues(USA) had been placed on the surface twice previously but wasn't at his best on this occasion. He'd progressed steadily since joining the yard prior to this and perhaps deserves another chance. Official explanation: jockey said gelding hung badly right (op 5-1 tchd 4-1)
Esprit De Midas had been successful on his three previous attempts over C&D, so this was a little disappointing, particularly as he'd shaped well when third off a 5lb higher mark on turf at Newcastle last time. (tchd 4-1)
Leviathan was largely progressive as a juvenile, winning a competitive Doncaster nursery when last seen in October, and may come on for this, while it's also possible this surface didn't see him in his best light either. (tchd 20-1)
Trans Sonic had won his four previous outings at this track, but seemed rusty after a break. (op 7-1)
Seek The Fair Land is usually reliable on AW surfaces and it's reasonable to assume he needed this first outing in four months. (tchd 12-1)
Harlech Castle, another course specialist, was never going the gallop. (op 14-1)

4895 JOAN ROBINSON'S BIRTHDAY H'CAP 6f (F)
5:00 (5:05) (Class 5) (0-70,69) 3-Y-O+ **£3,238** (£963; £481; £240) **Stalls** Low

Form RPR

3125 **1** **Ace Of Spies (IRE)**[14] 4431 5-9-10 **68**................................ ShaneKelly 3 78
(C R Dore) *cl up on inner: led 1/2-way: rdn wl over 1f out: drvn ins fnl f and hld on wl* **7/1**

4325 **2** *½* **Bookiesindex Boy**[20] 4239 6-9-11 **69**........................(b) StephenCraine 4 77
(J R Jenkins) *trckd ldrs: hdwy on bit to trck wnr 2f out: effrt and clsd up ent fnl f: sn rdn and ev ch tl nt qckn towards fin* **20/1**

4221 **3** *6* **Gracie's Gift (IRE)**[64] 2791 8-9-8 **66**................................ DaneO'Neill 9 55
(R C Guest) *prom: effrt to chse ldng pair wl over 1f out: sn rdn and one pce* **11/4**[1]

1100 **4** *2 ½* **Scruffy Skip (IRE)**[65] 2750 5-9-10 **68**............................(p) MarcHalford 1 49
(Mrs C A Dunnett) *chsd ldrs towards inner: rdn along and sltly outpcd over 2f out: styd on u.p fnl f* **11/2**[3]

5450 **5** *½* **Calmdownmate (IRE)**[34] 3763 5-8-12 **56**........................ PJMcDonald 6 36
(Mrs R A Carr) *hld up in rr: hdwy 2f out: sn rdn and kpt on appr fnl f: n.d* **10/1**

5035 **6** *½* **Elusive Warrior (USA)**[6] 4684 7-9-9 **67**.......................(p) SebSanders 10 45
(A J McCabe) *chsd ldrs on outer: rdn over 2f out: grad wknd* **11/2**[3]

3224 **7** *5* **Albero Di Giuda (IRE)**[10] 4559 5-9-0 **58**.......................(bt) LeeVickers 2 20
(F Sheridan) *hld up: a in rr* **17/2**

5550 **8** *½* **Real Diamond**[17] 4342 4-9-2 **60**.. TomEaves 5 20
(Ollie Pears) *a towards rr* **50/1**

2435 **9** *1 ¼* **Tenancy (IRE)**[2] 4834 6-8-1 **50**.. BillyCray(5) 8 6
(S A Harris) *led: rdn along and hdd 1/2-way: sn wknd* **5/1**[2]

0000 **10** *½* **Van Bossed (CAN)**[16] 4372 5-9-11 **69**.......................... AdrianNicholls 7 24
(D Nicholls) *towards rr: hdwy on outer to chse ldrs 2f out: sn rdn and wknd ent fnl f* **20/1**

1m 17.19s (0.69) **Going Correction** +0.075s/f (Slow) **10** Ran SP% **117.7**
Speed ratings (Par 103): **98,97,89,86,85 84,78,77,75,75**
toteswingers:1&2:£14.40, 1&3:£3.90, 2&3:£11.20 CSF £137.98 CT £488.30 TOTE £3.70: £1.10, £6.40, £1.80; EX 60.20 Trifecta £256.20 Part won. Pool: £346.27 - 0.42 winning units.Place 6 £72.72; Place 5 £15.92.
Owner Mrs Louise Marsh **Bred** Gainsborough Stud Management Ltd **Trained** Cowbit, Lincs

FOCUS
Run-of-the-mill sprint fare, the leading pair pulling well clear in a race in which very few ever got competitive.
Van Bossed(CAN) Official explanation: jockey said gelding had no more to give
T/Plt: £167.90 to a £1 stake. Pool:£72,737.26 - 316.21 winning tickets T/Qpdt: £8.30 to a £1 stake. Pool:£5,680.83 - 502.83 winning tickets JR

4599 THIRSK (L-H)
Monday, August 9

OFFICIAL GOING: Good to firm (good in places; watered; 9.9)
Wind: light 1/2 behind Weather: fine

4896 EUROPEAN BREEDERS' FUND MAIDEN STKS 5f
6:00 (6:02) (Class 4) 2-Y-O **£4,274** (£1,271; £635; £317) **Stalls** High

Form RPR

22 **1** **Major Muscari (IRE)**[15] 4409 2-9-3 0.............................. JamesDoyle 13 80+
(A J McCabe) *w ldrs stands' side: hung bdly lft and led over 1f out: drvn out* **15/8**[1]

3 **2** *¾* **Indieslad**[17] 4336 2-9-0 0.. BarryMcHugh(3) 8 77+
(Mrs A Duffield) *s.i.s: hdwy 2f out: styd on to take 2nd ins fnl f: kpt on wl* **3/1**[2]

52 **3** *2 ¼* **Abzolutely (IRE)**[13] 4451 2-8-12 0.............................. JamieSpencer 2 64
(D O'Meara) *led tl over 1f out: kpt on same pce: rdr lost whip ins fnl f* **7/1**[3]

40 **4** *1 ¼* **Princess Dayna**[44] 3449 2-8-12 0.............................. RichardSmith 1 60
(Tom Dascombe) *swvd lft s: mid-div: kpt on fnl f: nt rch ldrs* **100/1**

0 **5** *½* **Mr Mo Jo**[15] 4409 2-9-0 0.................................. AndrewHeffernan(3) 3 63
(R Bastiman) *chsd ldrs: wknd fnl f* **100/1**

532 **6** *3* **Lady Kildare (IRE)**[40] 3549 2-8-7 72..................... PatrickDonaghy(5) 11 47
(Jedd O'Keeffe) *swvd lft s: chsd ldrs: wknd fnl f* **9/1**

6 **7** *¾* **The Nought Man (FR)**[23] 4123 2-8-12 0.......................... LeeTopliss(5) 4 49
(R A Fahey) *sn outpcd and bhd: kpt on fnl 2f: nvr on terms* **40/1**

8 *¾* **Breezolini** 2-8-10 0 ow1... MichaelStainton(3) 7 43
(R M Whitaker) *dwlt: in rr: sme hdwy 2f out: nvr nr ldrs* **100/1**

9 *nk* **Crimson Cloud** 2-8-12 0.. PaulHanagan 6 41
(R A Fahey) *chsd ldrs: lost pl over 1f out* **15/2**

63 **10** *1 ¾* **Gottcher**[9] 4599 2-9-3 0.. PhillipMakin 5 39
(T D Barron) *chsd ldrs: outpcd over 2f out: hung lft and lost pl over 1f out: eased* **14/1**

4 **11** *5* **Look Who's Kool**[17] 4336 2-9-3 0.................................. GrahamGibbons 12 21
(E S McMahon) *chsd ldrs: wknd over 1f out* **10/1**

12 *½* **Bertiewhittle** 2-8-12 0.. DeanHeslop(5) 10 20
(T D Barron) *v.s.a: a bhd* **50/1**

59.32 secs (-0.28) **Going Correction** -0.20s/f (Firm) **12** Ran SP% **117.2**
Speed ratings (Par 96): **94,92,89,87,86 81,80,79,78,75 67,67**
toteswingers:1&2:£1.80, 1&3:£4.60, 2&3:£4.50 CSF £7.09 TOTE £3.50: £1.60, £1.80, £1.10; EX 7.80.
Owner South Yorkshire Racing **Bred** Simon Holt David Thorpe & R J Beggan **Trained** Averham Park, Notts

FOCUS
A dry night and largely dry day (only a short shower just before racing) saw no change to the ground, which most jockeys described as being on the quick side. Group 1 Golden Jubilee winner Fayr Jag took this in 2001, but the winners since have been no more than useful and it's unlikely this race - which represents only fair form - had any stars on show. The gallop was a reasonable one and the winner hung from stands' side into the centre in the last quarter-mile.

NOTEBOOK
Major Muscari(IRE) had the best form and the best draw and, after attracting support, probably did not have to improve too much to get off the mark, despite hanging markedly left. However, he looks a reliable sort who stays 6f and acts on Polytrack, and who may well have a bit more to offer. (op 9-4 tchd 13-8 and 5-2 in places)
Indieslad ◆ had shaped well on his debut at this track and fully confirmed that form, though he left the strong impression that he is ready for the step up to 6f. He has plenty of physical scope, is open to further improvement and is capable of picking up an ordinary race in this grade. (op 4-1)
Abzolutely(IRE) ran well to divide subsequent winners at Beverley last time and reproduced that effort at this sharper course from her low draw. She kept much straighter than on that occasion, even though her rider dropped her whip (held at the time) in the closing stages, and run-of-the-mill nurseries should provide her with her best chance of success. (op 8-1)
Princess Dayna reportedly lost her action on her previous start but fared a good deal better, despite being unable to go the early gallop from her low draw. Her stable is among the winners and she may be capable of a little better.
Mr Mo Jo had hung badly when tailed-off on his debut, but he left that form a long way behind here. He clearly has ability but is likely to remain vulnerable in this type of event. (op 150-1)
Lady Kildare(IRE), who was easy to back, had her limitations exposed on this first run against the boys. (op 8-1 tchd 10-1)
The Nought Man(FR), who hinted at ability on his debut, was noticeably easy to back but again shaped with a modicum of promise. He'll be one to take into ordinary handicap company over longer trips in due course. (op 33-1 tchd 50-1)
Crimson Cloud, a sister to smart sprinter Corrybrough, showed up for a long way and is entitled to come on for the experience. (op 7-1 tchd 9-1)
Gottcher Official explanation: jockey said colt hung left throughout
Look Who's Kool finished just behind Indieslad on his debut but failed by a long chalk to reproduce that run, despite a favourable draw. (op 9-1 tchd 8-1)
Bertiewhittle Official explanation: jockey said gelding was slow away

4897 ADMIRALS COURT (S) H'CAP 1m
6:30 (6:31) (Class 6) (0-65,68) 3-Y-O+ **£2,214** (£659; £329; £164) **Stalls** Low

Form RPR

0021 **1** **Island Chief**[2] 4822 4-10-4 **68** 6ex..............................(p) JamieSpencer 7 78
(K A Ryan) *charged gate: stmbld s: bhd: gd hdwy over 2f out: led 1f out: hung bdly lft: drvn clr* **5/1**[2]

1404 **2** *3 ¼* **Abu Dubai (IRE)**[12] 4485 4-9-0 **55**..............................(p) DaleSwift(5) 16 58
(J A Glover) *chsd ldrs: chal and hung lft over 1f out: kpt on same pce* **8/1**

3500 **3** *¾* **Bere Davis (FR)**[6] 4681 5-9-4 **54**.................................(b) PaulHanagan 12 55
(P D Evans) *chsd ldrs: led 3f out: hdd 1f out: kpt on same pce* **6/1**[3]

2400 **4** *nk* **Mississippian (IRE)**[7] 4644 6-9-0 **50**............................ DuranFentiman 5 50
(Mrs D J Sanderson) *in rr-div: hdwy on outside over 2f out: styd on fnl f* **13/2**

2205 **5** *2* **San Silvestro (IRE)**[11] 4514 5-9-11 **64**..................(p) BarryMcHugh(3) 10 60
(Mrs A Duffield) *mid-div: styd on fnl 2f: nt rch ldrs* **9/2**[1]

3040 **6** *½* **Fortunate Bid (IRE)**[7] 4644 4-9-6 **56**..................(p) RoystonFfrench 1 50
(Mrs L Stubbs) *mid-div: kpt on fnl 2f: nt clr run on ins and swtchd rt 1f out: nt rch ldrs* **18/1**

0060 **7** *1* **Prigsnov Dancer (IRE)**[9] 4605 5-8-9 **45**..........................(v) DavidAllan 8 37
(O Brennan) *dwlt: sn chsng ldrs: fdd appr fnl f* **40/1**

4306 **8** *2 ½* **Kladester (USA)**[28] 3968 4-8-7 **48**.................................... LeeTopliss(5) 14 34
(M Herrington) *mid-div: hdwy 3f out: one pce* **12/1**

0012 **9** *nk* **Provost**[14] 4428 6-9-11 **61**..(b) PhillipMakin 9 47
(M W Easterby) *s.i.s: bhd tl sme hdwy fnl 2f* **10/1**

0505 **10** *nse* **Kheskianto (IRE)**[38] 3610 4-8-9 **50**.............................. MarkCoumbe(5) 3 36
(M C Chapman) *mid-div: kpt on fnl 2f: nvr a factor* **20/1**

4430 **11** 1 1/2 **Vogarth**[8] 3226 6-8-6 **45**........ AndrewHeffernan(3) 13 27
(M C Chapman) *in rr: nvr on terms* **40/1**
0515 **12** hd **Nuit Sombre (IRE)**[33] 3775 10-9-5 **60**........(p) MichaelO'Connell(5) 11 42
(G A Harker) *led tl 3f out: wknd qckly last 150yds* **12/1**
0-50 **13** 1 1/4 **Kwami Biscuit**[21] 4200 3-8-3 **46** ow1........ AndrewElliott 6 25
(G A Harker) *a in rr* **33/1**
0-05 **14** 1 1/4 **Efidium**[22] 4168 12-8-11 **52**........ DanielleMcCreery(5) 4 28
(N Bycroft) *s.i.s: a bhd* **50/1**
0-00 **15** 2 **Top Jaro (FR)**[12] 4485 7-8-11 **50**........(p) JamesSullivan(3) 2 21
(Mrs R A Carr) *chsd ldrs: reminders over 3f out: wknd 2f out* **50/1**
-660 **16** 8 **Secret Hero**[21] 4189 4-8-12 **48**........(p) GrahamGibbons 15 —
(Lee Smyth, Ire) *mid-div: sn drvn along: lost pl 3f out* **20/1**
1m 41.37s (1.27) **Going Correction** +0.125s/f (Good)
WFA 3 from 4yo+ 7lb **16** Ran SP% **124.6**
Speed ratings (Par 101): **98,94,94,93,91 91,90,87,87,87 85,85,84,83,81 73**
toteswingers:1&2:£4.90, 1&3:£6.10, 2&3:£22.00 CSF £42.62 CT £263.05 TOTE £7.60: £2.30, £1.80, £2.10, £1.70; EX 38.70.The winner was sold to M W Easterby for 8,000gns.
Owner Mrs J Ryan **Bred** The C H F Partnership **Trained** Hambleton, N Yorks

FOCUS
Mainly exposed and disappointing performers in an ordinary selling handicap. The pace was sound throughout.

4898 CALVERTS CARPETS H'CAP 1m
7:00 (7:01) (Class 5) (0-75,71) 3-Y-O **£4,209** (£1,252; £625; £312) **Stalls** Low

Form RPR
0-46 **1** **State Fair**[32] 3831 3-9-1 **68**........ BarryMcHugh(3) 9 75
(Julie Camacho) *hld up towards rr: hdwy over 2f out: styd on wl to ld nr fin* **16/1**
0015 **2** nk **Emeralds Spirit (IRE)**[1] 4864 3-7-13 **52** oh1........ KellyHarrison(3) 1 58
(J R Weymes) *s.i.s: sn chsng ldrs: upsides and hung lft over 1f out: led last 50yds: hdd nr fin* **20/1**
2642 **3** 3/4 **High Rolling**[9] 4602 3-8-11 **61**........ GrahamGibbons 10 65
(T D Easterby) *w ldrs: led over 2f out: hdd last 50yds: no ex* **9/2**[2]
3-46 **4** 1 1/4 **Bonded (IRE)**[11] 4522 3-9-7 **71**........(b) WilliamBuick 4 72
(B J Meehan) *mid-div: drvn over 3f out: hdwy on outside 2f out: edgd rt: kpt on: nt rch ldrs* **6/1**[3]
3420 **5** 1/2 **Tribal Myth (IRE)**[25] 4061 3-9-0 **64**........ JamieSpencer 7 64
(K A Ryan) *led 1f: led 3f out: hdd 2f out: wknd wl ins fnl f* **15/2**
-U30 **6** 6 **Koo And The Gang (IRE)**[23] 4127 3-8-9 **64**........ DaleSwift(5) 12 50
(B Ellison) *sn detached in last: sme hdwy 2f out: edgd rt and kpt on ins fnl f: nvr on terms* **22/1**
452 **7** hd **Opening Nite (IRE)**[15] 4407 3-9-4 **68**........ PaulHanagan 5 54
(R A Fahey) *s.i.s: in rr: sme hdwy 2f out: nvr a factor* **3/1**[1]
2332 **8** 2 **Kilt Rock (IRE)**[10] 4555 3-9-6 **70**........ RoystonFfrench 2 51
(R C Guest) *chsd ldrs: wknd over 1f out* **6/1**[3]
4404 **9** 1 **Eeny Mac (IRE)**[23] 4151 3-8-2 **52** oh3........ PaulQuinn 8 31
(N Bycroft) *t.k.h in rr: hdwy on ins 3f out: wknd over 1f out* **33/1**
4253 **10** 1 **Green For Luck (IRE)**[1] 4864 3-8-10 **60**........ PhillipMakin 3 37
(S Gollings) *hdwy to ld after 1f: hdd 3f out: wknd appr fnl f* **8/1**
4101 **11** 17 **Just The Tonic**[33] 3771 3-8-11 **66**........ IanBrennan(5) 6 4
(Mrs Marjorie Fife) *chsd ldrs: drvn over 3f out: lost pl over 1f out: heavily eased fnl 100yds* **12/1**
1m 41.18s (1.08) **Going Correction** +0.125s/f (Good) **11** Ran SP% **120.3**
Speed ratings (Par 100): **99,98,97,96,96 90,90,88,87,86 69**
toteswingers:1&2:£35.70, 1&3:£10.90, 2&3:£21.20 CSF £303.20 CT £1722.00 TOTE £22.10: £5.50, £8.80, £3.20; EX 358.00.
Owner Elite Racing Club **Bred** Elite Racing Club **Trained** Norton, N Yorks
■ Stewards' Enquiry : Kelly Harrison caution: used whip with excessive frequency.

FOCUS
An ordinary handicap in which a fair gallop picked up turning for home. The first five finished clear of the remainder.
Kilt Rock(IRE) Official explanation: jockey said gelding lost its action 1f out
Just The Tonic Official explanation: trainer said filly had a breathing problem

4899 BROWN CROFTS MAIDEN AUCTION STKS 7f
7:30 (7:31) (Class 5) 2-Y-O **£3,322** (£988; £494; £246) **Stalls** Low

Form RPR
2 **1** **Askaud (IRE)**[42] 3517 2-8-7 0........ PJMcDonald 1 76
(J A Glover) *t.k.h: trckd ldrs: rdn and hung rt over 1f out: styd on to ld last 100yds* **11/4**[1]
043 **2** 1 1/2 **Millies Folly**[4] 4747 2-7-11 0........ NeilFarley(7) 8 69
(D Carroll) *t.k.h: led after 2f: edgd rt over 1f out: hdd and no ex ins fnl f* **7/1**
6 **3** 2 **El Maachi**[19] 4263 2-8-6 0........ AndrewHeffernan(3) 11 69
(P D Evans) *chsd ldrs: styd on same pce fnl f* **9/2**[3]
4 **4** shd **El Torbellino (IRE)**[10] 4554 2-8-4 0........ PaulHanagan 5 63
(D O'Meara) *led 2f: chsd ldrs: kpt on same pce appr fnl f* **11/1**
5 7 **Shadow Catcher** 2-9-1 0........ PhillipMakin 10 55+
(M Dods) *s.i.s: hdwy on ins over 3f out: hung rt and wknd over 1f out* **40/1**
0 **6** 4 **Young Sahib (USA)**[24] 4096 2-9-1 0........ WilliamBuick 3 45
(B J Meehan) *s.i.s: hung rt bnd over 4f out: hdwy on outside over 3f out: wknd over 1f out* **4/1**[2]
502 **7** 1 1/2 **Bradbury (IRE)**[26] 4013 2-8-12 73........ GrahamGibbons 9 38
(J D Bethell) *in rr: hmpd bnd over 4f out: sme hdwy over 2f out: nvr on terms* **12/1**
000 **8** 3 **Aprication (IRE)**[54] 3087 2-8-9 50........ TomEaves 4 26
(J R Weymes) *towards rr: hmpd bnd over 4f out: nvr a factor* **100/1**
66 **9** nk **Masonic Lady (IRE)**[9] 4568 2-8-7 0........ LiamJones 12 24
(W J Haggas) *in rr: hung bdly rt and rn wd bnd over 4f out: no ch after* **16/1**
10 9 **Al Raqi** 2-9-1 0........ RoystonFfrench 6 7
(B Smart) *dwlt: toward rr whn hmpd bnd over 4f out: bhd fnl 2f* **13/2**
1m 29.37s (2.17) **Going Correction** +0.125s/f (Good) **10** Ran SP% **116.0**
Speed ratings (Par 94): **92,90,88,87,79 75,73,70,69,59**
toteswingers:1&2:£7.30,, 1&3:£1.70 2&3:£9.70 CSF £22.45 TOTE £2.40: £1.10, £3.00, £3.10; EX 28.30.
Owner Paul J Dixon **Bred** John P Jones **Trained** Babworth, Notts

FOCUS
Several very useful types have taken this before going on to show a higher level of form, with Listed Polytrack scorer Suits Me the best of those to have won this since 2000. However this year's renewal - run at just a moderate gallop - looked no more than fair form, though the winner remains capable of a little better.

NOTEBOOK
Askaud(IRE), who showed ability at a modest level on her debut on Polytrack, fully confirmed that promise on this turf debut and, despite taking a good hold, showed a willing attitude in the closing stages. She should prove equally effective over 1m and may do better in ordinary handicaps. (op 5-2 tchd 3-1 in places)
Millies Folly has improved with every start and turned in her best effort back in trip and back on a sound surface. She had the rub of things to a large degree and, although she is capable of picking up a minor event, is likely to remain vulnerable to the better types in this grade. (op 15-2 tchd 8-1)
El Maachi had shown a fair level of form in a stronger maiden than this on his debut and, although he failed to build on that, was far from disgraced. The step up to 1m and the switch to ordinary handicap company should suit in due course. (op 6-1)
El Torbellino(IRE) showed ability on her debut and duly bettered that effort after racing closer to the pace this time. This wasn't much of a race, but there is a small event to be won with her somewhere down the line. (op 17-2)
Shadow Catcher, who has several winners from 6f-1m in his pedigree, wasn't totally disgraced on this racecourse debut for a yard recently back among the winners. Ordinary handicaps will be his forte in due course. (tchd 50-1)
Young Sahib(USA), who hinted at ability in a better race than this, was backed throughout the day but proved disappointing. It is too soon to be writing him off, but he is probably one to watch rather than to bet on next time. (op 11-2 tchd 6-1)
Masonic Lady(IRE) looked ill at ease on the track and proved disappointing, but she is in good hands and may do better in ordinary handicaps back over a straight 7f or even when upped to 1m.

Al Raqi Official explanation: jockey said colt finished distressed

4900 TURFTV H'CAP 2m
8:00 (8:01) (Class 6) (0-65,60) 4-Y-O+ **£2,214** (£659; £329; £164) **Stalls** Low

Form RPR
0/15 **1** **Jeu De Roseau (IRE)**[51] 3223 6-9-0 **53**........ JamieSpencer 6 66+
(C Grant) *trckd ldrs: drvn to ld 3f out: edgd rt: rdn clr over 1f out: styd on strly* **3/1**[1]
-326 **2** 5 **Zefooha (FR)**[22] 4174 6-9-7 **60**........(p) GrahamGibbons 3 65
(T D Walford) *chsd ldr: led briefly over 3f out: styd on same pce over 1f out* **7/2**[2]
3260 **3** hd **They All Laughed**[7] 4648 7-9-2 **55**........(p) PhillipMakin 2 60
(Mrs Marjorie Fife) *chsd ldrs: kpt on same pce fnl 2f* **7/1**
0365 **4** 1/2 **Perez (IRE)**[2] 4854 8-8-3 **45**........(vt) JamesSullivan(3) 10 49
(W Storey) *hld up in rr: hdwy over 3f out: one pce fnl 2f* **11/1**
0643 **5** 1 1/2 **Dechiper (IRE)**[11] 4511 8-8-5 **49**........(t) LeeTopliss(5) 4 51
(R Johnson) *hld up in rr: effrt over 3f out: kpt on fnl 2f: nvr a factor* **16/1**
0/12 **6** nse **Dan's Heir**[9] 4604 8-8-13 **57**........(p) DeanHeslop(5) 7 59
(W Storey) *chsd ldrs: one pce fnl 3f* **5/1**[3]
10-4 **7** 4 **Terenzium (IRE)**[59] 1891 8-9-0 **53**........(p) TomEaves 8 50
(Micky Hammond) *hld up in rr: hdwy 7f out: wknd over 1f out* **25/1**
3540 **8** nk **Smugglers Bay (IRE)**[27] 3974 6-9-5 **58**........(b) PJMcDonald 1 55
(T D Easterby) *hld up in last: nvr on terms* **7/1**
9 8 **Ardesia (IRE)**[8] 3808 6-8-6 **45**........ DuranFentiman 9 32
(Miss T Jackson) *led tl over 3f out: lost pl over 1f out: bhd whn eased towards fin* **10/1**
3m 34.4s (1.60) **Going Correction** +0.125s/f (Good) **9** Ran SP% **116.0**
Speed ratings (Par 101): **101,98,98,98,97 97,95,95,91**
toteswingers:1&2:£2.10, 1&3:£5.90, 2&3:£6.20 CSF £13.59 CT £66.99 TOTE £5.40: £2.40, £1.10, £1.60; EX 17.40.
Owner W Raw **Bred** P Connolly **Trained** Newton Bewley, Co Durham

FOCUS
A low-grade handicap in which the gallop was a moderate one and those held up could never land a blow. The winner came down the centre in the straight.

4901 DOWNLANDS H'CAP 5f
8:30 (8:30) (Class 4) (0-85,84) 3-Y-O **£4,313** (£1,283; £641; £320) **Stalls** High

Form RPR
4520 **1** **Mon Brav**[6] 4685 3-9-1 **78**........(v) JamieSpencer 5 82
(D Carroll) *chsd ldrs: sn drvn along: swtchd lft over 1f out: hrd rdn and styd on to ld last 75yds: all out* **11/8**[1]
0400 **2** nk **Magical Macey (USA)**[10] 4541 3-9-7 **84**........(b) PhillipMakin 3 87
(T D Barron) *bmpd s: chsd ldr: led appr fnl f: hdd and kpt on wl* **9/2**[3]
2310 **3** 1 3/4 **Ignatieff (IRE)**[10] 4541 3-9-5 **82**........ DuranFentiman 1 79
(Mrs L Stubbs) *led: swtchd rt to r stands' side after 1f: hung lft and hdd appr fnl f: kpt on same pce* **3/1**[2]
34 **4** 1 3/4 **High Spice (USA)**[7] 4654 3-9-6 **83**........(p) TomEaves 4 73
(R M H Cowell) *wnt rt s: chsd ldrs: hrd drvn over 2f out: swtchd lft jst ins fnl f: one pce* **10/1**
-500 **5** 3/4 **My One Weakness (IRE)**[16] 4369 3-8-2 **68**...(be[1]) AndrewHeffernan(3) 6 56
(B Ellison) *s.i.s: hdwy on outside over 2f out: nvr able to chal* **6/1**
58.29 secs (-1.31) **Going Correction** -0.20s/f (Firm) **5** Ran SP% **108.7**
Speed ratings (Par 102): **102,101,98,95,94**
CSF £7.62 TOTE £1.70: £1.10, £5.10; EX 7.10 Place 6 £38.15; Place 5 £30.86.
Owner D Wallis **Bred** J D Graham **Trained** Sledmere, E Yorks

FOCUS
A couple of useful sprinters but a race was weakened by the late defection of likely market leader Walvis Bay. The gallop was sound throughout.
T/Plt: £32.90 to a £1 stake. Pool:£59,612.19 - 1,319.94 winning tickets T/Qpdt: £18.30 to a £1 stake. Pool:£5,008.15 - 202.10 winning tickets WG

4870 WINDSOR (R-H)
Monday, August 9

OFFICIAL GOING: Good to firm (good in places; 8.6)
Stands' rail dolled out 18yds at 6f and 7yds at winning post. Top bend dolled out 4yds from innermost line, adding 16yds to races of one mile and over.
Wind: Light, half behind Weather: Cloudy

4902 E B F SPORTINGBET.COM MAIDEN STKS 6f
5:40 (5:45) (Class 4) 2-Y-O **£4,112** (£1,223; £611; £305) **Stalls** High

Form RPR
2 **1** **Gold Pearl (USA)**[68] 2649 2-9-3 0........ RyanMoore 9 85
(S C Williams) *racd wd: pressed ldrs: rdn to ld narrowly over 1f out: drvn out* **5/2**[2]
2 nk **Invincible Ridge (IRE)** 2-9-3 0........ RichardHughes 14 84
(R Hannon) *cl up: rdn to chal over 1f out: w wnr fnl f: r.o but jst hld nr fin* **3/1**[3]
2 **3** 2 3/4 **Escholido (IRE)**[15] 4396 2-9-3 0........ MichaelHills 16 75
(B W Hills) *led against nr side rail: hdd and outpcd over 1f out* **2/1**[1]

4 **4** *hd* **Plenty Power**[15] 4396 2-9-3 0 ChrisCatlin 4 75
(M R Channon) *chsd ldrs in 7th: effrt over 2f out: styd on fr over 1f out: nvr able to chal* **12/1**

5 *4 ½* **Thomas Tompion (IRE)** 2-9-3 0 JimmyFortune 1 60+
(G L Moore) *towards rr on outer: sme prog 2f out but nt on terms w ldrs: kpt on* **50/1**

0 **6** *2 ¼* **Papas Fritas**[8] 4622 2-9-0 0 Louis-PhilippeBeuzelin(3) 3 53
(B J Meehan) *sn pushed along in midfield: reminder 1/2-way: sn wl outpcd: styd on fr over 1f out: nrst fin* **66/1**

00 **7** *nse* **Futurism**[47] 3326 2-9-0 0 PatrickHills(3) 6 53
(R Hannon) *hld up in last quartet: pushed along and sme prog 2f out: nvr on terms but styd on fnl f* **80/1**

8 *1 ¼* **Morermaloke** 2-9-3 0 MartinDwyer 11 49
(B J Meehan) *rn green but gd spd to chse ldr to over 2f out: wandered and wknd rapidly fnl f* **40/1**

9 *3* **Tiberius Claudius (IRE)** 2-9-3 0 TomQueally 2 39
(G G Margarson) *dwlt: wl off the pce in last quartet bef 1/2-way: no ch after* **40/1**

04 **10** *1 ½* **Sabot D'Or**[18] 4303 2-9-3 0 LiamKeniry 13 34
(R Ingram) *chsd ldrs in 6th: outpcd 2f out: wknd fnl f* **100/1**

11 *nk* **Sabys Gem (IRE)** 2-9-3 0 JamieMackay 7 33+
(M Wigham) *nvr bttr than midfield: nudged along and lost tch sn after 1/2-way* **100/1**

02 **12** *5* **Putin (IRE)**[14] 4421 2-9-3 0 AndreaAtzeni 12 17
(D Haydn Jones) *chsd ldrs in 5th to 2f out: wknd qckly* **16/1**

00 **13** *2 ¼* **Watered Silk**[14] 4421 2-9-3 0 PatDobbs 8 10
(M P Tregoning) *dwlt: a wl in rr: no ch over 2f out* **100/1**

00 **14** *2* **Sea The Flames (IRE)**[28] 3961 2-9-3 0 TadhgO'Shea 15 4
(M P Tregoning) *wl bhd in last after 2f: nvr a factor* **66/1**

1m 12.17s (-0.83) **Going Correction** -0.225s/f (Firm) **14** Ran SP% **114.5**
Speed ratings (Par 96): **96,95,91,91,85 82,82,80,76,74 74,67,64,62**
toteswingers:1&2:£2.20, 1&3:£1.60, 2&3:£2.10 CSF £9.51 TOTE £4.70: £2.60, £1.70, £1.70; EX 14.50 Trifecta £39.00 Pool: £2,889.04 - 54.76 winning units..
Owner Pearl Bloodstock Ltd **Bred** Copper Cap Farm Inc **Trained** Newmarket, Suffolk

FOCUS
The first four dominated here and it proved hard to get into the race from off the pace.

NOTEBOOK
Gold Pearl(USA) attracted strong support on this first run since a promising debut at Nottingham in June when finishing a well-backed second, and he went one better with a determined effort. He had to race without cover through the race and had to dig deep to repel the runner-up, but there was a lot to like about his attitude when it mattered. His yard is known more for longer-term handicap projects, but connections obviously have a sharp sort on their hands and he is expected to step up again from this outing. An entry in the Gimcrack is an indication of how highly regarded he is and, while that may be aiming a bit high at this stage, he could very well be the sort to land a decent pot down the line. (tchd 11-4)
Invincible Ridge(IRE) ◆, bred for speed, was solid in the betting for this racecourse debut and it looked nearing the furlong marker as if he would hand the stable yet another juvenile winner. He just found the winner that bit more streetwise nearing the business end, but finished a clear second-best and ought to prove very hard to beat next time out. (tchd 11-4)
Escholido(IRE), second on debut at Ascot 15 days earlier, was soon racing in the lead from his inside draw and set a sound pace. He was done with coming to the furlong marker, though, and interestingly his rider soon after came off the stands' rail which suggests it was probably not the place to be. He still ran close enough to his debut form and may now prefer another furlong, as his pedigree suggests. (tchd 7-4, tchd 9-4 in a place)
Plenty Power finished a lot closer to Escholido than was the case on debut last time and so this clearly rates an improved effort. He was free to post and through the early parts of the race, so there is every chance he will come on again for the extra experience, but on the evidence to date his Group 1 entry is aiming far too high. (op 14-1)
Thomas Tompion(IRE) is a half-brother to dual Group 3 winner Lady Springbank and caught the eye staying on from a fair way back from his outside draw. (tchd 66-1)
Putin(IRE) Official explanation: jockey said colt never travelled

4903 SPORTINGBET.COM CONDITIONS STKS 6f
6:10 (6:10) (Class 3) 2-Y-O **£5,828** (£1,734; £866; £432) **Stalls** High

Form RPR

2101 **1** **Fifth Commandment (IRE)**[9] 4592 2-8-0 88 SophieDoyle(5) 5 87
(J A Osborne) *fast away: mde all: racd against rail: clr over 1f out: pushed along fnl f: hld on* **7/2**[3]

1215 **2** *nk* **Avonmore Star**[13] 4458 2-8-12 93 RichardHughes 4 93
(R Hannon) *t.k.h early: hld up last: taken to wd outside and rdn over 2f out: prog to go 2nd jst over 1f out: styd on: jst hld* **15/8**[1]

2156 **3** *1 ½* **Sonoran Sands (IRE)**[16] 4355 2-8-10 89 LiamKeniry 3 86
(J S Moore) *trckd ldng pair: rdn to dispute 2nd briefly over 1f out: kpt on same pce* **22/1**

5321 **4** *nse* **Fight The Chance (IRE)**[23] 4142 2-8-12 87 ChrisCatlin 1 88
(M R Channon) *trckd ldng pair: rdn to chse wnr briefly over 1f out: kpt on same pce* **6/1**

1120 **5** *4 ½* **Drawing Board**[16] 4355 2-8-12 94 RyanMoore 6 74
(K A Ryan) *dropped to last and pushed along 1/2-way: sn rdn: nvr on terms after* **5/2**[2]

1151 **6** *1 ¼* **Belle Bayardo (IRE)**[18] 4278 2-9-0 99 TomMcLaughlin 2 72
(R A Harris) *pressed wnr to 1/2-way: wknd rapidly and lost 2nd over 1f out* **12/1**

1m 11.46s (-1.54) **Going Correction** -0.225s/f (Firm) **6** Ran SP% **111.9**
Speed ratings (Par 98): **101,100,98,98,92 90**
toteswingers:1&2:£1.50, 1&3:£10.90, 2&3:£6.10 CSF £10.44 TOTE £4.40: £1.80, £1.10; EX 14.10.
Owner Durkan, Hearn, Pennick **Bred** Keatly Overseas Ltd **Trained** Upper Lambourn, Berks

FOCUS
A good conditions event, run at a solid enough pace.

NOTEBOOK
Fifth Commandment(IRE) made all against the stands' rail and registered a third success from four runs since getting off the mark at Bath in June. Her only defeat in between came when not disgraced in the Super Sprint at Newbury on ground softer than ideal and she is obviously progressing very well. She isn't the biggest and connections would do well to make hay while the sun shines this year. (tchd 3-1)
Avonmore Star was stepping back up a furlong after coming fifth to his classy stablemate Zebedee in the Molecomb last month. He tended to run somewhat in snatches through the early parts, but responded to his rider's urgings from 2f out and, racing down the centre, was eating into the winner's advantage all the way to the line. He was giving that improving rival 7lb and this was a solid run, but the suspicion is he was not quite at his best. Perhaps a return to more positive tactics will see him back to winning ways. (op 11-8 tchd 2-1)
Sonoran Sands(IRE), dropped back down in trip and class, hit a bit of a flat spot before running on again towards the finish and grabbed third on the line. He looks ready for another crack at 7f. (op 20-1 tchd 25-1)
Fight The Chance(IRE), well backed, couldn't dominate in this classier company and proved free early on as a result. He had every chance, but left the impression the track was sharp enough and a switch to nurseries now looks on the cards. (op 8-1)
Drawing Board got markedly outpaced 3f out and didn't look to be helping his rider that much thereafter. He was one place behind Sonoran Sands in Listed company over 7f last time, but was beaten a lot further here despite the drop back in trip looking sure to suit beforehand, and now has something to prove. (op 7-2)
Belle Bayardo(IRE) was conceding weight to all of his rivals, but he failed to run his race after doing too much through the early stages. His official rating of 99 needs reassessing. (op 14-1)

4904 RIPPLEFFECT.COM H'CAP 6f
6:40 (6:40) (Class 3) (0-95,93) 3-Y-O+ **£7,123** (£2,119; £1,059; £529) **Stalls** High

Form RPR

011 **1** **Caledonia Princess**[14] 4424 4-8-2 75 oh1 ow1 RossAtkinson(5) 10 83
(F J Brennan) *t.k.h: a in ldng trio: shkn up to ld wl over 1f out: hrd pressed fnl f: hld on gamely* **13/2**

3020 **2** *nk* **Secret Witness**[10] 4536 4-9-3 85 (b) TomMcLaughlin 8 92
(R A Harris) *t.k.h: chsd ldng trio: rdn over 2f out: styd on to press wnr fnl f: nt qckn last 50yds* **16/1**

2322 **3** *¾* **Rocket Rob (IRE)**[23] 4148 4-9-8 90 RyanMoore 6 95+
(M Botti) *settled in rr: rdn and prog over 2f out: clsd on ldrs against far rail fnl f: a hld: slipped up after fin* **4/1**[2]

0010 **4** *1* **Olynard (IRE)**[10] 4536 4-9-10 92 JimCrowley 9 93+
(R M Beckett) *chsd ldrs: rdn over 2f out: kpt on fr over 1f out: nvr able to chal* **7/2**[1]

0020 **5** *hd* **Ghostwing**[10] 4536 3-9-6 92 TadhgO'Shea 7 93
(J Gallagher) *t.k.h: pressed ldr: led over 2f out to wl over 1f out: wknd ins fnl f* **16/1**

5006 **6** *½* **Getcarter**[46] 3346 4-9-1 83 JimmyFortune 2 82+
(R Hannon) *s.v.s: last tl effrt u.p over 2f out: kpt on but racd awkwardly: nvr able to chal* **11/2**[3]

03 **7** *2 ¼* **Cheveton**[21] 4191 6-9-0 87 JohnFahy(5) 5 79
(R J Price) *s.s: sn in tch in rr: effrt and rdn over 2f out: no prog over 1f out: wknd* **15/2**

2200 **8** *2 ½* **We Have A Dream**[2] 4814 5-9-8 90 RichardHughes 3 74
(W R Muir) *sn led: hdd over 2f out: wknd over 1f out* **14/1**

0000 **9** *2* **Sohraab**[15] 4401 6-9-7 89 SteveDrowne 4 67
(H Morrison) *settled in last trio: shkn up 1/2-way: no prog: eased fnl f* **17/2**

0-02 **10** *12* **Perfect Flight**[59] 2929 5-9-1 83 MartinDwyer 11 22
(M Blanshard) *chsd ldrs: rdn 1/2-way: wknd 2f out: t.o and eased* **20/1**

1m 10.98s (-2.02) **Going Correction** -0.225s/f (Firm)
WFA 3 from 4yo+ 4lb **10** Ran SP% **116.4**
Speed ratings (Par 107): **104,103,102,101,101 100,97,94,91,75**
toteswingers:1&2:£39.60, 1&3:£4.70, 2&3:£21.90 CSF £104.09 CT £470.47 TOTE £10.50: £3.00, £6.20, £1.20; EX 213.10 Trifecta £1643.30 Part won. Pool: £2,220.70 - 0.42 winning units..
Owner Isla & Colin Cage **Bred** Mrs I M Cage And C J Cage **Trained** Lambourn, Berks

FOCUS
An open-looking sprint handicap. It wasn't run at the strongest pace early on and therefore it wasn't surprising that it paid to race handily. The field shunned the near side this time and the action was more towards the far rail late on.

NOTEBOOK
Caledonia Princess was 1lb out of the handicap and her claiming rider put up 1lb overweight, plus she was again awash with sweat. That was not enough to stop her landing a course hat-trick, however, and she once again ran out a ready winner. She also failed to really settle once more, which makes this success more meritorious, and has improved no end since joining her current trainer. The handicapper will again do his best and she clearly loves this venue, but she has won at two other tracks so it's a good bet she will go very close to bagging a four-timer while in such form. (op 5-1)
Secret Witness, out the back in the Stewards' Cup last time, was another that ran somewhat freely early on but was well positioned when the tempo became serious. This was a lot more like it again, but he is probably a touch flattered and has become an in-and-out performer of late.
Rocket Rob(IRE) fared best of those that were given waiting rides and deserves credit on this step up a furlong. He sets the level and certainly deserves a change of fortune. (op 7-2 tchd 9-2)
Olynard(IRE) ◆ ran better than the bare form in the Stewards' Cup on his previous outing and would've very likely confirmed that form with the runner-up granted a more truly run race. He isn't one to abandon. (op 4-1 tchd 3-1)
Ghostwing, around two lengths behind Olynard at Goodwood last time out, was always on the front end and ran a sound race. He probably paid late on for running freely, though. (tchd 20-1)
Getcarter missed the kick and was immediately dropped in, which wasn't an advantage as the race turned out. He was motoring near the finish and should come on for the run, so will hold good claims next time. (op 8-1)
Cheveton showed his true colours again on his previous outing at Ayr, but that was on suitably easier ground and he was unable to shine on this quicker surface. He is one to look out for when getting his underfoot conditions again, as he remains fairly handicapped. (op 9-1)

4905 "ROYAL BERKSHIRE" ODDFELLOWS BI-CENTENARY H'CAP 1m 67y
7:10 (7:10) (Class 4) (0-85,81) 3-Y-O+ **£4,533** (£1,348; £674; £336) **Stalls** High

Form RPR

-001 **1** **Lost In The Moment (IRE)**[60] 2888 3-9-6 80 JimmyFortune 5 95+
(J Noseda) *sltly s.i.s: hld up in 6th: prog over 3f out: shkn up over 2f out: led over 1f out: wl in command fnl f* **4/6**[1]

1405 **2** *1 ¾* **Rule Breaker (IRE)**[16] 4377 3-9-7 81 FrankieDettori 2 92
(M Johnston) *trckd ldng trio: prog to go 2nd over 2f out: upsides wl over 1f out: chsd wnr after: r.o but readily hld* **8/1**[3]

10 **3** *3 ¾* **Chica Whopa (IRE)**[33] 3790 3-9-6 80 RichardHughes 8 82
(R Hannon) *hld up in 7th and off the pce: prog over 3f out: shkn up to chse clr ldng trio over 1f out: pushed along and kpt on to take 3rd ins fnl f* **12/1**

1225 **4** *¾* **Mambo Spirit (IRE)**[13] 4459 6-9-11 78 TomQueally 7 80
(Stef Higgins) *led after 1f at decent pce: hdd & wknd over 1f out* **11/2**[2]

4024 **5** *½* **Habshan (USA)**[17] 4322 10-10-0 81 AlanMunro 4 81
(C F Wall) *dwlt: hld up last and wl off the pce: stl last over 2f out: taken wd: shkn up and kpt on to take 5th over 1f out: no hdwy after* **11/1**

3004 **6** *8* **Beaver Patrol (IRE)**[25] 4057 8-9-11 78 JimCrowley 9 60
(Eve Johnson Houghton) *chsd ldng quartet: rdn over 3f out: wknd over 2f out: eased fnl f* **20/1**

1524 **7** *¾* **You've Been Mowed**[10] 4548 4-9-2 74 JohnFahy(5) 1 54
(R J Price) *led 1f: chsd ldng pair after tl wknd over 2f out* **16/1**

646 **8** *7* **Byrd In Hand (IRE)**[21] 4205 3-8-7 67 NeilChalmers 6 30
(J J Bridger) *chsd ldr to over 2f out: wknd rapidly: t.o* **25/1**

1m 40.74s (-3.96) **Going Correction** -0.35s/f (Firm)
WFA 3 from 4yo+ 7lb **8** Ran SP% **117.0**
Speed ratings (Par 105): **105,103,99,98,98 90,89,82**
toteswingers:1&2:£1.30, 1&3:£2.70, 2&3:£9.30 CSF £7.12 CT £37.80 TOTE £2.00: £1.10, £1.10, £2.90; EX 6.40 Trifecta £23.00 Pool: £3,607.89 - 115.98 winning units..

The Form Book, Raceform Ltd, Compton, RG20 6NL

Owner M Tabor & Mrs Susan Roy **Bred** Rockhart Trading Ltd **Trained** Newmarket, Suffolk

FOCUS

Not a bad handicap. It was run at something of an uneven pace, but the form should work out.

4906 "ROYAL BERKSHIRE" ODDFELLOWS BI-CENTENARY MAIDEN STKS — 1m 67y

7:40 (7:41) (Class 5) 3-Y-0+ — £2,456 (£725; £362) Stalls High

Form				RPR
0	1		**Boom And Bust (IRE)**[14] 4425 3-9-3 0 ... MartinDwyer 7 (M P Tregoning) *mde virtually all: hrd pressed fr 3f out: jst hld on* **12/1**	74
0-	2	hd	**Gift Of Love (IRE)**[388] 4055 3-8-12 0 ... AlanMunro 14 (D R C Elsworth) *hld up in 7th: shkn up and prog 2f out: clsd on ldrs 1f out: r.o nr fin: jst failed* **10/1**	68+
3	3	½	**Bianca De Medici**[14] 4425 3-8-12 0 ... SteveDrowne 3 (H Morrison) *chsd ldng pair: rdn wl over 2f out: chal over 1f out: jst hld ins fnl f: lost 2nd last strides* **9/2**[3]	67
04	4	1	**Only You Maggie (IRE)**[9] 4601 3-8-5 0 ... JosephineBruning(7) 6 (W G Harrison) *w wnr: chalng fr 3f out to 1f out: nt qckn* **40/1**	65
	5	1¾	**Miss Kingwood** 3-8-12 0 ... PatDobbs 12 (M P Tregoning) *hld up in last trio: pushed along over 2f out: prog over 1f out: styd on: nrst fin* **33/1**	61+
40	6	¾	**Sunset Place**[18] 4307 3-9-3 0 ... AdamKirby 11 (C G Cox) *chsd ldrs disputing 5th: rdn and nt qckn over 2f out: kpt on same pce* **10/1**	64
00	7	nk	**Immovable (USA)**[7] 4661 3-9-3 0 ... TomQueally 13 (M A Magnusson) *trckd ldng pair: chal and upsides 3f out: lost pl 2f out: fdd* **16/1**	64
	8	1¼	**Shallow Bay** 3-9-3 0 ... TedDurcan 8 (W R Swinburn) *hld up in last trio: pushed along over 3f out: kpt on fnl 2f: nrst fin but n.d* **4/1**[2]	61+
	9	5	**Wild Geese (IRE)** 3-9-3 0 ... FrankieDettori 4 (M Johnston) *coltish preliminaries: chsd ldrs disputing 5th: rdn 1/2-way: wknd over 2f out* **3/1**[1]	49
5	10	6	**Fear Factor (IRE)**[38] 3621 3-9-3 0 ... RichardHughes 5 (G A Butler) *hld up towards rr: pushed along and in tch 3f out: wknd 2f out* **20/1**	35
6	11	½	**Sir Sandford (IRE)**[86] 2128 3-9-3 0 ... LiamKeniry 10 (D M Simcock) *s.i.s: a last: bhd fnl 2f* **13/2**	34

1m 43.02s (-1.68) **Going Correction** -0.35s/f (Firm) — 11 Ran SP% 118.4

Speed ratings (Par 103): **94,93,93,92,90 89,89,88,83,77 76**

toteswingers:1&2:£30.10, 1&3:£16.10, 2&3:£13.90 CSF £124.39 TOTE £14.90: £4.10, £2.20, £2.10; EX 124.20 TRIFECTA Not won..

Owner Jas Singh **Bred** Duncan A McGregor **Trained** Lambourn, Berks

FOCUS

A modest maiden and another race where it proved hard to get involved from off the pace. Again the main action developed away from the stands' side.

4907 TRINITY MIRROR SOUTHERN H'CAP — 1m 3f 135y

8:10 (8:10) (Class 5) (0-75,75) 3-Y-0+ — £2,593 (£765; £383) Stalls Centre

Form				RPR
-033	1		**Super Duplex**[18] 4295 3-7-12 56 ... CathyGannon 6 (P M Phelan) *t.k.h: hld up in 5th: slt stumble 5f out: prog over 2f out: rdn to ld over 1f out: hung lft but r.o wl* **5/1**[3]	65+
3211	2	2	**Sunley Spinalonga**[12] 4492 3-8-12 70 ... AlanMunro 4 (D R C Elsworth) *trckd ldng trio: rdn wl over 2f out: chsd wnr over 1f out: one pce fnl f* **3/1**[2]	76
6231	3	shd	**Spice Fair**[20] 4230 3-8-13 71 ... RichardHughes 3 (M D I Usher) *t.k.h: hld up last: prog fr 3f out: chsd ldrs over 1f out: wnt 3rd fnl f: styd on* **5/2**[1]	77+
00-0	4	3½	**Yossi (IRE)**[15] 4405 6-9-10 71 ... (p) FrankieDettori 5 (R C Guest) *dwlt: sn trckd ldr: led 3f out: drvn and hdd over 1f out: wknd* **12/1**	71
0155	5	1	**Archie Rice (USA)**[9] 4594 4-10-0 75 ... SteveDrowne 8 (T Keddy) *racd freely: led: hdd 3f out: nt qckn and sn lost pl: fdd* **8/1**	73
1524	6	2	**Ghufa (IRE)**[9] 4597 6-9-8 74 ... SimonPearce(5) 2 (J Pearce) *hld up in last pair: shkn up 3f out: no prog and wl btn 2f out* **8/1**	69
0/06	7	2	**Strategic Mission (IRE)**[16] 4376 5-10-0 75 ... (bt[1]) JimCrowley 7 (P F I Cole) *trckd ldng pair: rdn 3f out: sn lost pl and btn* **10/1**	66
1040	8	3½	**Soundbyte**[7] 4657 5-9-7 68 ... ChrisCatlin 1 (J Gallagher) *hld up in 6th: shkn up and no prog 3f out: sn wknd* **25/1**	53

2m 28.55s (-0.95) **Going Correction** -0.35s/f (Firm)

WFA 3 from 4yo+ 11lb — 8 Ran SP% 113.1

Speed ratings (Par 103): **89,87,87,85,84 83,81,79**

toteswingers:1&2:£3.20, 1&3:£4.10, 2&3:£1.10 CSF £19.92 CT £45.23 TOTE £6.20: £2.60, £1.10, £1.50; EX 24.90 Trifecta £48.40 Pool: £517.11 - 7.90 winning units. Place 6 £26.19; Place 5 £23.93.

Owner Special Piping Materials Ltd **Bred** Ermyn Lodge Stud Limited **Trained** Epsom, Surrey

FOCUS

A moderate, but competitive enough handicap. It was run at a steady early pace.

T/Jkpt: Not won. T/Plt: £9.50 to a £1 stake. Pool:£88,410.41 - 6,769.57 winning tickets T/Qpdt: £5.40 to a £1 stake. Pool:£6,603.71 - 900.38 winning tickets JN

4427 WOLVERHAMPTON (A.W) (L-H)

Monday, August 9

OFFICIAL GOING: Standard

Wind: Fresh behind Weather: Cloudy with sunny spells

4908 LADBROKES.COM MAIDEN STKS — 5f 20y(P)

2:15 (2:15) (Class 5) 3-Y-0 — £2,388 (£705; £352) Stalls Low

Form				RPR
-0	1		**Prince James**[10] 4556 3-8-10 0 ... DavidSimmonson(7) 4 (M W Easterby) *a.p: chsd ldr over 3f out: pushed along and nt clr run over 1f out: swtchd lft: led ins fnl f: r.o* **12/1**	64
3336	2	¾	**Fear Nothing**[32] 3834 3-9-3 74 ... (b) RichardMullen 2 (E S McMahon) *chsd ldrs: rdn and ev ch fr over 1f out: no ex towards fin* **1/3**[1]	62
2460	3	¾	**Papageno**[43] 3480 3-9-3 61 ... EddieAhern 6 (J R Jenkins) *led: rdn and edgd rt over 1f out: hung lft and hdd ins fnl f: styd on same pce* **11/2**[2]	59
000	4	nk	**Shamarlane**[19] 4251 3-8-12 0 ... NickyMackay 5 (M Wigham) *hld up: shkn up over 1f out: hung lft and r.o ins fnl f: nt rch ldrs* **25/1**	53
	5	4	**Sonia Girl (IRE)** 3-8-12 0 ... DanielTudhope 8 (Patrick Morris) *s.s: swished tail almost thrght: bhd tl styd on ins fnl f: nvr nrr* **12/1**	39
-000	6	4½	**Gibraltar Lass (USA)**[37] 3677 3-8-12 47 ... (v[1]) DarryllHolland 3 (H J Collingridge) *chsd ldrs: rdn 1/2-way: wkng whn hmpd over 1f out* **25/1**	22
4	7	1	**Prince Of Nama (IRE)**[123] 1190 3-9-0 0 ... (t) AshleyHamblett(3) 7 (P L Gilligan) *hld up in tch: rdn: hung lft and wknd over 1f out* **13/2**[3]	24
000	8	3	**Whispering Ridge**[60] 2903 3-9-3 28 ... (v[1]) AdamKirby 1 (M Wellings) *plld hrd and prom: wknd over 1f out* **66/1**	13

63.29 secs (0.99) **Going Correction** +0.15s/f (Slow) — 8 Ran SP% 128.3

Speed ratings (Par 100): **98,96,95,95,88 81,79,75**

toteswingers:1&2:£2.10, 1&3:£4.40, 2&3:£2.90 CSF £18.56 TOTE £14.70: £3.10, £1.02, £1.90; EX 28.60.

Owner A Saha **Bred** A C M Spalding **Trained** Sheriff Hutton, N Yorks

FOCUS

A weak maiden in which the clear form pick was turned over at odds-on.

Prince Of Nama(IRE) Official explanation: vet said colt finished distressed

4909 EUROPEAN BREEDERS' FUND MAIDEN STKS — 5f 216y(P)

2:45 (2:48) (Class 5) 2-Y-0 — £3,238 (£963; £481; £240) Stalls Low

Form				RPR
6	1		**Sadafiya**[24] 4095 2-8-12 0 ... RichardHills 8 (E A L Dunlop) *chsd ldr over 4f out: led over 1f out: rdn out* **13/8**[2]	79+
62	2	½	**Busker (USA)**[10] 4549 2-9-3 0 ... AhmedAjtebi 2 (Mahmood Al Zarooni) *a.p: rdn to chse wnr and edgd lft ins fnl f: r.o* **1/1**[1]	79+
0	3	2¼	**Owain (USA)**[10] 4549 2-8-10 0 ... AdamBeschizza(7) 1 (C A Dwyer) *prom: n.m.r and lost pl 5f out: swtchd lft and hdwy over 1f out: r.o* **50/1**	72
042	4	3¾	**Wolf Slayer**[12] 4474 2-8-12 77 ... RichardKingscote 5 (Tom Dascombe) *led: rdn and hdd over 1f out: wknd ins fnl f* **9/2**[3]	55
	5	nk	**Zalano** 2-9-3 0 ... FrankieMcDonald 3 (D Haydn Jones) *rn green in rr: shkn up and r.o ins fnl f: nrst fin* **40/1**	59+
0	6	4	**Coedmor Boy**[12] 4477 2-9-3 0 ... DavidProbert 6 (B Palling) *prom: rdn over 2f out: edgd lft and wknd over 1f out* **50/1**	46
	7	½	**Callie's Angel** 2-9-3 0 ... NeilChalmers 4 (B Palling) *s.s: outpcd: mod late prog* **50/1**	44
00	8	hd	**Imaginary World (IRE)**[18] 4286 2-8-12 0 ... RichardMullen 7 (E S McMahon) *mid-div: rdn over 2f out: wknd over 1f out* **25/1**	39
	9	1¾	**Volcanic Lady (IRE)** 2-8-12 0 ... NickyMackay 10 (D M Simcock) *sn pushed along and a in rr* **20/1**	33
	10	8	**Primo Muscovado** 2-9-3 0 ... SamHitchcott 11 (M Mullineaux) *prom: rdn over 2f out: wknd wl over 1f out* **50/1**	13

1m 17.51s (2.51) **Going Correction** +0.15s/f (Slow) — 10 Ran SP% 125.2

Speed ratings (Par 94): **89,88,85,80,79 74,73,73,71,60**

toteswingers:1&2:£1.50, 1&3:£28.90, 2&3:£21.40 CSF £3.72 TOTE £3.20: £1.50, £1.02, £13.20; EX 4.10.

Owner Hamdan Al Maktoum **Bred** Shadwell Estate Company Limited **Trained** Newmarket, Suffolk

FOCUS

A fair maiden for 2-y-os. The two market leaders fought out the finish and they were quite well strung out behind.

NOTEBOOK

Sadafiya was in the firing line for a long way before fading into sixth when 4-1 for a decent 6f Newbury fillies' maiden on debut. Well backed in the morning, she was always near the pace and did the job in professional style on her second start. A first foal of a Listed 6f 2-y-o winner, she looks a nice type who should be a force in nurseries. (op 7-4 tchd 15-8)

Busker(USA) took a big step forward on his second start when just caught by a hot favourite/fellow Godolphin representative in a fast-ground Newmarket maiden last month. He had strong form claims but couldn't quite get to the winner, who got first run at a crucial stage. This half-brother to two useful 2-y-o 6f-1m winners should be able to gain compensation for this close call. (op 5-4 tchd 11-8)

Owain(USA) stayed on strongly from some way back and has managed to get almost 17l closer to the runner-up than he did on debut. His sales price plummeted each time he passed through the ring, but this was a promising second effort by a horse whose US pedigree suggests he should make a 2-y-o at this trip.

Wolf Slayer faded after dictating a decent pace on her first try on Polytrack. This was a bit disappointing from the 77-rated filly, who had fair form claims. Official explanation: jockey said filly had no more to give (op 10-3)

Zalano, a £4,000 gelded half-brother to minor 5f-6f winner Monte Mayor One, ran very green before doing a bit of late work on debut.

Coedmor Boy Official explanation: vet said gelding lost right-fore shoe

Callie's Angel Official explanation: jockey said colt was slowly away

4910 GOT THE FEELING? GET TO LADBROKES H'CAP — 7f 32y(P)

3:15 (3:16) (Class 5) (0-70,75) 3-Y-0+ — £2,388 (£705; £352) Stalls High

Form				RPR
131	1		**Whispering Spirit (IRE)**[14] 4427 4-9-2 69 ... (v) AmyRyan(5) 7 (Mrs A Duffield) *chsd ldrs: led 2f out: sn rdn clr: jst hld on* **5/2**[1]	78+
0062	2	shd	**Hellbender (IRE)**[2] 4839 4-8-12 67 ... AdamBeschizza(7) 8 (S Kirk) *hld up: hdwy over 2f out: rdn to chse wnr over 1f out: edgd lft ins fnl f: r.o: jst failed* **10/3**[2]	76
2300	3	¾	**Forward Feline (IRE)**[140] 965 4-8-11 64 ... DeclanCannon(5) 4 (B Palling) *mid-div: hdwy over 2f out: rdn over 1f out: r.o* **20/1**	71
0060	4	1½	**Music Maestro (IRE)**[23] 4127 3-9-2 70 ... DarryllHolland 1 (B W Hills) *sn pushed along to ld: hdd over 5f out: remained handy: rdn over 1f out: r.o* **15/2**	71
4-00	5	1¾	**Classically (IRE)**[16] 4382 4-9-5 67 ... EddieAhern 3 (H Morrison) *prom: nt clr run and lost pl 2f out: r.o ins fnl f* **10/1**	65+
1100	6	2½	**Ride A White Swan**[14] 4427 5-8-13 64 ... (p) GaryBartley(3) 9 (D Shaw) *hld up: hdwy over 1f out: styd on same pce ins fnl f* **20/1**	55
4003	7	2½	**Bahamian Kid**[118] 1276 5-9-7 69 ... (v) AdamKirby 11 (R Hollinshead) *hld up: rdn over 1f out: nvr trbld ldrs* **10/1**	54
1001	8	¾	**Feeling Fresh (IRE)**[2] 4833 5-9-13 75 6ex ... PaulMulrennan 12 (Paul Green) *stdd s: hld up: nvr on terms* **5/1**[3]	58
3604	9	shd	**Kensington (IRE)**[108] 1509 9-9-1 68 ... (p) TobyAtkinson(5) 5 (A J McCabe) *prom: chsd ldr over 4f out: led over 2f out: sn hdd: wknd fnl f* **20/1**	50
2605	10	12	**Lockantanks**[18] 4297 3-9-2 70 ... (v[1]) StevieDonohoe 10 (A B Haynes) *w ldr tl led over 5f out: hdd over 2f out: wknd over 1f out* **33/1**	18
02-0	11	7	**Bull Market (IRE)**[187] 383 7-9-4 69 ... RussKennemore(3) 6 (M S Tuck) *hld up: a in rr: pushed along over 3f out: sn wknd* **16/1**	—

1m 30.26s (0.66) **Going Correction** +0.15s/f (Slow)

WFA 3 from 4yo+ 6lb — 11 Ran SP% 121.4

Speed ratings (Par 103): **102,101,101,99,97 94,91,90,90,76 68**

toteswingers:1&2:£2.90, 1&3:£15.30, 2&3:£18.50 CSF £10.35 CT £139.83 TOTE £2.10: £1.02, £2.30, £5.20; EX 11.50.

Owner Middleham Park Racing XLII **Bred** David Barry **Trained** Constable Burton, N Yorks

FOCUS

A fairly competitive handicap. The pace was not particularly strong but the market leaders filled the first two positions and the form looks solid.

Feeling Fresh(IRE) Official explanation: jockey said horse moved poorly

4911 BET IN-PLAY AT LADBROKES.COM NURSERY 7f 32y(P)

3:45 (3:45) (Class 4) (0-85,81) 2-Y-O £3,885 (£1,156; £577; £288) Stalls High

Form RPR

4415 1 **Miss Clairton**[5] 4696 2-9-5 79 StevieDonohoe 3 92+
(Sir Mark Prescott) *a.p: chsd ldr over 2f out: led over 1f out: sn clr: eased wl ins fnl f* 6/1

033 2 7 **Ransom Request**[18] 4286 2-8-6 73 AdamBeschizza(7) 5 67
(E F Vaughan) *chsd ldrs: rdn over 2f out: styng on same pce whn hung lft and wnt 2nd ins fnl f: no ch w wnr* 5/1[3]

0231 3 2 **Fabiello**[4] 4747 2-9-3 77 6ex RichardKingscote 7 66+
(Tom Dascombe) *s.s: sn rdn along: hdwy over 5f out: hrd drvn over 2f out: styd on same pce appr fnl f* 7/2[2]

020 4 1 **Shaabek (IRE)**[23] 4123 2-8-8 68 SamHitchcott 1 54
(M R Channon) *s.i.s: hld up: hdwy u.p and swtchd rt over 1f out: nvr trbld ldrs* 14/1

0136 5 1 1/2 **Silly Billy (IRE)**[17] 4331 2-8-7 67 DavidProbert 2 49
(S Kirk) *chsd ldrs: lost pl over 5f out: n.d after* 14/1

5222 6 nk **Greek Islands (IRE)**[26] 4020 2-9-0 81 AntiocoMurgia(7) 8 62
(Mahmood Al Zarooni) *chsd ldr tl led 1/2-way: rdn and hdd over 1f out: wknd ins fnl f* 5/2[1]

61 7 74 **Screenprint**[11] 4499 2-8-11 71 HayleyTurner 4 —
(M L W Bell) *led to 1/2-way: sn rdn: wknd and eased over 2f out: t.o* 5/2[1]

1m 30.13s (0.53) **Going Correction** +0.15s/f (Slow) 7 Ran SP% 123.7

Speed ratings (Par 96): **102,94,91,90,88 88,3**

toteswingers:1&2:£5.30, 1&3:£4.90, 2&3:£4.80 CSF £39.12 CT £125.26 TOTE £11.20: £4.50, £3.30; EX 44.60.

Owner Mrs June Rooney **Bred** Grove Farm Stud **Trained** Newmarket, Suffolk

FOCUS

This looked a competitive nursery but there was a runaway winner.

NOTEBOOK

Miss Clairton was brushed aside on her 6f nursery debut at Kempton last time following a gutsy front-running 5f AW maiden win at Lingfield. She had stamina to prove taking another step up in trip, but was ridden with more restraint and romped clear for an impressive success. She will get hit hard for this win, but the sister to smart prolific 5f-7f winner Prince Aaron could find further improvement and she would take some stopping if turned out quickly under a penalty. (op 9-2)

Ransom Request shaped with a bit of promise on her nursery/AW debut. Her mark looks on the high side on what she achieved in maidens, but her style and elements of her pedigree suggest she could improve for a step up to 1m. (op 15-2)

Fabiello, a clear-cut winner over a 74-rated favourite in a soft-ground 1m Haydock maiden last Thursday, was slowly away and looked one paced when things got serious under a penalty on nursery debut. He has a pronounced action and should appreciate a return to a stiffer test on slow turf. (tchd 10-3 and 4-1)

Shaabek(IRE) was one of the first under pressure and was never involved. (op 12-1)

Greek Islands(IRE) looked a possible winner when hitting the front around the final bend, but he went out very quickly and had no excuses regarding trip and surface. He has shown plenty of promise before this, but is proving expensive and a bit frustrating to follow. (tchd 9-4 and 11-4)

Screenprint did the job well when 11-1 for a 7f Epsom maiden on his second start. He was an interesting contender off a fair-looking mark on nursery debut, but got warm beforehand and dropped away very quickly. Official explanation: trainer's rep had no explanation for the poor form shown (op 11-4)

4912 GREAT OFFERS AT WOLVERHAMPTON-RACECOURSE.CO.UK (S) STKS 1m 4f 50y(P)

4:15 (4:16) (Class 6) 3-Y-O+ £1,706 (£503; £252) Stalls Low

Form RPR

1-02 1 **Shannersburg (IRE)**[6] 4669 5-9-7 63 (t) EddieAhern 11 64+
(Ian Williams) *hld up in tch: chsd ldr over 2f out: rdn to ld and edgd lft ins fnl f: r.o: eased nr fin* 7/4[1]

006- 2 1 **Sir Boss (IRE)**[12] 6473 5-9-7 74 (t) DarryllHolland 12 62
(D E Cantillon) *sn chsng ldr: led over 5f out: rdn over 1f out: hdd and unable qck ins fnl f* 5/1[3]

6644 3 2 **Resplendent Ace (IRE)**[20] 4227 6-9-12 58 IanMongan 2 64
(P Howling) *hld up: hdwy over 2f out: rdn over 1f out: styd on* 8/1

-344 4 4 1/2 **Marino Prince (FR)**[19] 4246 5-9-7 48 (p) CathyGannon 5 52
(B D Leavy) *hld up: hdwy over 4f out: rdn over 2f out: styd on same pce appr fnl f* 11/1

5256 5 1 **New England**[9] 4582 8-9-7 50 NeilChalmers 4 50
(N J Vaughan) *s.i.s: hld up: hdwy over 2f out: rdn over 1f out: nt trble ldrs* 12/1

0-30 6 9 **Generous Lad (IRE)**[90] 2012 7-9-7 50 (p) StevieDonohoe 6 36
(A B Haynes) *s.s: hld up: sme hdwy over 2f out: sn wknd* 16/1

0 7 11 **Beck's Bolero (IRE)**[44] 3442 4-9-7 0 PaulMulrennan 10 18
(J A Osborne) *trckd ldrs: racd keenly: rdn 3f out: wknd over 1f out* 66/1

4043 8 9 **Motarjm (USA)**[111] 1439 6-9-7 61 (t) HayleyTurner 7 4
(J Pearce) *chsd ldrs tl wknd over 2f out: t.o* 5/2[2]

9 4 **Commanche Luke**[13] 7-9-7 0 DavidProbert 9 —
(C Roberts) *hld up: rdn over 5f out: wknd 4f out: t.o* 100/1

10 nk **Final Frame** 3-8-9 0 ow2 RussKennemore(3) 8 —
(Lucinda Featherstone) *s.s: hld up: pushed along 7f out: bhd fnl 4f: t.o* 50/1

0004 11 49 **Duke Of Normandy (IRE)**[22] 3960 4-9-7 53 (p) JackMitchell 3 —
(B P J Baugh) *led: hdd over 5f out: wknd over 4f out: t.o* 20/1

000/ 12 57 **High Dee Jay (IRE)**[50] 4334 5-9-2 50 (p) KierenFox(5) 1 —
(D Burchell) *chsd ldrs tl wknd over 5f out: t.o* 66/1

2m 41.84s (0.74) **Going Correction** +0.15s/f (Slow)

WFA 3 from 4yo+ 11lb 12 Ran SP% 125.3

Speed ratings (Par 101): **103,102,101,98,97 91,84,78,75,75 42,4**

toteswingers:1&2:£3.20, 1&3:£4.30, 2&3:£6.10 CSF £11.48 TOTE £3.00: £1.60, £2.20, £1.80; EX 15.10.There was no bid for the winner. Marino Prince was claimed by J. J. Best for £6,000. Sir Boss was claimed by I. S. Ross for £6,000.

Owner R S Brookhouse **Bred** Dermot Cantillon And Fiona Craig **Trained** Portway, Worcs

FOCUS

They went a decent pace in this seller and a big gamble was landed.

4913 BEST ODDS GUARANTEED AT LADBROKES.COM H'CAP (DIV I) 1m 1f 103y(P)

4:45 (4:46) (Class 6) (0-60,60) 4-Y-O+ £1,364 (£403; £201) Stalls Low

Form RPR

/003 1 **Beat Up**[47] 3323 4-9-3 59 SaleemGolam 8 67
(G D Blake) *chsd ldrs: rdn to ld ins fnl f: r.o* 10/1

0005 2 1 3/4 **Herecomethegirls**[3] 4775 4-8-1 48 ow2 (p) KierenFox(5) 12 52
(W G M Turner) *hld up: hdwy over 5f out: led over 3f out: rdn: hung lft and hdd ins fnl f: styd on same pce* 16/1

0446 3 1 **Lunar River (FR)**[11] 4498 7-8-13 55 (t) EddieAhern 7 57
(David Pinder) *dwlt: hld up: hdwy over 1f out: r.o: nt rch ldrs* 10/1

-500 4 nk **Superstitious Me (IRE)**[17] 4324 4-8-4 46 oh1 DavidProbert 10 48
(B Palling) *hld up: hdwy over 4f out: rdn and hung lft over 1f out: styd on* 33/1

4013 5 1 3/4 **Lady Lam**[4] 4746 4-8-11 60 (t) AdamBeschizza(7) 6 58
(S Kirk) *hld up in tch: outpcd over 3f out: nt clr run over 2f out: hdwy u.p over 1f out: no ex ins fnl f* 5/1[3]

301 6 1 1/2 **Fitzolini**[9] 4591 4-9-1 57 (p) DarryllHolland 11 52
(A D Brown) *chsd ldr tl led over 6f out: hdd over 3f out: rdn over 1f out: wknd ins fnl f* 7/2[2]

5354 7 1 1/4 **Chantilly Pearl (USA)**[10] 4546 4-9-4 60 PaulMulrennan 1 52
(J G Given) *chsd ldrs: rdn over 1f out: wknd ins fnl f* 3/1[1]

4561 8 2 1/2 **Ocean Of Peace (FR)**[51] 3214 7-8-0 49 RyanPowell(7) 4 36
(M R Bosley) *hld up: hdwy over 3f out: rdn and wknd wl over 1f out* 8/1

3300 9 1/2 **Turkish Sultan (IRE)**[67] 1503 7-8-5 47 (b) FrankieMcDonald 2 33
(J M Bradley) *s.i.s: hld up: rdn over 1f out: a in rr* 16/1

251 10 4 1/2 **Jezza**[98] 1755 4-9-0 56 SimonWhitworth 9 32
(V R A Dartnall) *hld up: a in rr: bhd fnl 4f* 6/1

-000 11 2 1/2 **Lily Wood**[45] 3391 4-8-7 49 (v) KirstyMilczarek 13 20
(J W Unett) *plld hrd and prom: rdn over 2f out: wknd over 1f out* 28/1

00- 12 49 **Nanny Doe (IRE)**[37] 3700 4-8-4 46 oh1 (p) CathyGannon 5 —
(Lee Smyth, Ire) *led: hdd over 6f out: wknd over 5f out: t.o* 100/1

2m 2.70s (1.00) **Going Correction** +0.15s/f (Slow) 12 Ran SP% 126.6

Speed ratings (Par 101): **101,99,98,98,96 95,94,92,91,87 85,41**

toteswingers:1&2:£25.10, 1&3:£13.20, 2&3:£22.90 CSF £167.51 CT £1669.10 TOTE £14.10: £3.50, £6.80, £4.20; EX 256.90.

Owner R Lyon, P Hayton & G Blake **Bred** Rolyon Stud **Trained** Wendover, Bucks

FOCUS

An ordinary handicap. The pace was steady and the lead changed hands a number of times in the early stages.

Lily Wood Official explanation: jockey said filly ran too free

Nanny Doe(IRE) Official explanation: jockey said filly stopped very quickly

4914 BEST ODDS GUARANTEED AT LADBROKES.COM H'CAP (DIV II) 1m 1f 103y(P)

5:15 (5:20) (Class 6) (0-60,60) 4-Y-O+ £1,364 (£403; £201) Stalls Low

Form RPR

-040 1 **Rebellious Spirit**[49] 3278 7-9-4 60 PaulMulrennan 5 69
(S Curran) *chsd ldrs: rdn and hung lft over 1f out: hung rt and r.o to ld wl ins fnl f* 20/1

0-03 2 3/4 **Out Of Nothing**[17] 4324 7-8-4 51 KierenFox(5) 13 59
(D Burchell) *led: rdn over 1f out: edgd rt: hdd wl ins fnl f* 11/2[3]

0365 3 2 3/4 **Tres Froide (FR)**[13] 4453 5-8-5 47 (p) KirstyMilczarek 2 49
(N Tinkler) *prom: lost pl over 3f out: hdwy 2f out: r.o to go 3rd nr fin: nt rch ldrs* 10/1

0250 4 nk **Hector Spectre (IRE)**[47] 3314 4-8-13 55 (p) DavidProbert 6 56
(Mrs N S Evans) *hld up: hdwy 1/2-way: rdn over 1f out: styd on same pce ins fnl f: lost 3rd nr fin* 12/1

5140 5 1 1/2 **Magnitude**[31] 3860 5-9-3 59 JackMitchell 10 57
(B P J Baugh) *hld up: hdwy 4f out: rdn over 2f out: hung lft and styd on same pce fnl f* 9/1

0-00 6 shd **Lough Beg (IRE)**[159] 771 7-8-0 49 (t) RyanPowell(7) 7 47
(Miss Tor Sturgis) *prom: chsd ldr over 6f out tl rdn over 1f out: no ex fnl f* 20/1

0251 7 2 3/4 **Tomintoul Star**[34] 3758 4-9-3 59 HayleyTurner 8 51
(Mrs R A Carr) *s.i.s: hld up: hdwy over 2f out: rdn and wknd over 1f out* 4/1[2]

0000 8 1 1/4 **Portrush Storm**[31] 3853 5-7-13 48 HarryBentley(7) 3 38
(R E Peacock) *s.i.s: hld up: rdn over 1f out: nvr on terms* 16/1

-151 9 2 1/2 **Cyril The Squirrel**[14] 4434 6-9-0 56 DarryllHolland 4 40
(Karen George) *plld hrd: trckd ldr to over 6f out: remained handy tl rdn and wknd over 1f out* 9/4[1]

000- 10 1 **Incy Wincy**[241] 7719 4-8-4 46 oh1 (b) FrankieMcDonald 9 28
(J M Bradley) *hld up: rdn over 2f out: n.d* 66/1

0- 11 2 1/2 **Lugato (GER)**[38] 3653 8-8-4 46 oh1 (p) CathyGannon 1 23
(Lee Smyth, Ire) *hld up: a in rr: bhd fnl 3f* 40/1

6360 12 1 **Quadrifolio**[37] 3669 4-8-4 46 oh1 NickyMackay 11 21
(Paul Green) *prom: rdn over 3f out: wknd over 1f out* 7/1

2m 2.73s (1.03) **Going Correction** +0.15s/f (Slow) 12 Ran SP% 124.8

Speed ratings (Par 101): **101,100,97,97,96 96,93,92,90,89 87,86**

toteswingers:1&2:£17.00, 1&3:£28.80, 2&3:£7.50 CSF £129.18 CT £1204.05 TOTE £25.00: £7.90, £2.40, £3.70; EX 188.60.

Owner Mrs Donna Hill **Bred** Car Colston Hall Stud **Trained** Hatford, Oxon

■ Stewards' Enquiry : Kieren Fox two-day ban: used whip with excessive frequency (Aug 24-25)

FOCUS

The second division of a modest handicap. It was run at a reasonable pace and there was a surprise winner.

Tomintoul Star Official explanation: trainer said that on returning home filly was found to be heavily in season

4915 STAY AT THE WOLVERHAMPTON HOLIDAY INN APPRENTICE H'CAP 2m 119y(P)

5:45 (5:46) (Class 6) (0-65,64) 4-Y-O+ £1,706 (£503; £252) Stalls Low

Form RPR

0/03 1 **Erdeli (IRE)**[17] 4327 6-8-13 60 (tp) ThomasBrown(7) 9 71
(Tim Vaughan) *hld up in tch: led over 3f out: pushed clr fr over 2f out: eased wl ins fnl f* 8/1

-452 2 5 **Saute**[28] 3965 4-9-5 64 LewisWalsh(5) 8 68
(W R Swinburn) *prom: chsd ldr after 2f tl led over 4f out: hdd over 3f out: sn rdn: styd on same pce fnl 2f* 9/4[1]

3061 3 3 1/2 **Moscow Oznick**[28] 3965 5-9-10 64 (v) JamesRogers 3 64
(D Donovan) *chsd ldr 2f: racd in 3rd pl fr there on: rdn over 2f out: wknd over 1f out* 7/1[3]

1/00 4 2 1/4 **Hareem (IRE)**[6] 4686 6-9-8 62 (v) HarryBentley 5 59
(W R Muir) *hld up: hdwy over 4f out: wknd over 2f out* 33/1

006 5 shd **Anis Etoile**[57] 2994 5-9-1 55 SophieSilvester 4 52
(John Berry) *hld up: hdwy over 4f out: rdn and wknd over 2f out* 5/1[2]

2000 6 nk **Sir Sandicliffe (IRE)**[9] 4604 6-8-6 49 AlexEdwards(3) 7 46
(W M Brisbourne) *hld up: rdn over 3f out: nvr on terms* 7/1[3]

565 7 21 **Rock Tech**[60] 2907 5-8-3 48 DannyBrock(5) 2 19
(J R Jenkins) *prom: pushed along 1/2-way: wknd 4f out: t.o* 16/1

6605 8 12 **Leyte Gulf (USA)**[14] 4441 7-9-1 60 FrancisHayes(5) 6 17
(C C Bealby) *s.s: a bhd: t.o* 12/1

-433 9 6 **Rare Coincidence**[25] 1459 9-8-11 **51**....(p) AdamCarter 1 1
(R F Fisher) *led: hdd over 4f out: wknd 3f out: t.o* **9/4**[1]

3m 43.52s (1.72) **Going Correction** +0.15s/f (Slow) 9 Ran SP% **130.8**
Speed ratings (Par 101): **101,98,97,95,95 95,85,80,77**
toteswingers:1&2:£3.90, 1&3:£8.70, 2&3:£3.90. totesuper7: Win: Not won. Place: Not won. CSF £30.11 CT £145.50 TOTE £16.20: £2.50, £1.50, £3.40; EX 38.70 Place 6 £191.96; Place 5 £159.97.
Owner Select Racing Syndicates II **Bred** His Highness The Aga Khan's Studs S C **Trained** Aberthin, Vale of Glamorgan
■ Stewards' Enquiry : Francis Hayes two-day ban: careless riding (Aug 23-24); one-day ban: used whip when out of contention (Aug 25)

FOCUS
There was a clear-cut winner in this minor staying handicap.
Rare Coincidence Official explanation: jockey said gelding ran flat
T/Plt: £186.50 to a £1 stake. Pool:£64,532.61 - 252.50 winning tickets T/Qpdt: £162.20 to a £1 stake. Pool:£4,057.31 - 18.50 winning tickets CR

4221 FFOS LAS (L-H)
Tuesday, August 10

OFFICIAL GOING: Good (7.9)
Wind: Light, against Weather: Sunny

4920 FINANCIALS AT BET365.COM H'CAP 5f
6:05 (6:06) (Class 6) (0-65,65) 3-Y-O **£1,748** (£520; £260; £129) **Stalls** High

Form RPR
503 1 **Schoolboy Champ**[5] 4749 3-9-7 **65**.... RichardHughes 2 71
(Patrick Morris) *racd towards centre of trck: chsd ldrs: pushed along 3f out: rdn to chal and edgd rt fr over 1f out: r.o gamely ins fnl f to ld fnl strides* **15/8**[1]
0434 2 hd **Vilnius**[4] 4778 3-8-12 **56**.... ChrisCatlin 3 61
(M R Channon) *racd towards centre of trck: hld up: swtchd rt 3f out: effrt 2f out: impr to ld over 1f out: r.o u.p whn pressed ins fnl f: hdd fnl strides* **3/1**[3]
-204 3 3 ½ **French Fantasy**[25] 4109 3-8-9 **53**.... SteveDrowne 1 45
(H Morrison) *racd towards centre of trck: chsd ldr: pushed along over 2f out: rdn to ld briefly wl over 1f out: nt qckn ins fnl f: one pce fnl 110yds* **4/1**
6246 4 16 **Morgans Choice**[10] 4567 3-9-3 **61**....(b) JimCrowley 4 —
(J L Spearing) *racd on stand's rail: led: rdn and hdd wl over 1f out: sn wknd: eased whn wl btn ins fnl f* **11/4**[2]

58.36 secs (0.96) **Going Correction** +0.175s/f (Good) 4 Ran SP% **106.4**
Speed ratings (Par 98): **99,98,93,67**
CSF £7.36 TOTE £2.50; EX 7.20.
Owner Chester Racing Club Ltd **Bred** Stephen Hillen And Hatta Bloodstock **Trained** Tarporley, Cheshire

FOCUS
Steady rain changed the forecast going from good to firm to good.

4921 E.B.F./BET365 MAIDEN FILLIES' STKS 6f
6:35 (6:38) (Class 4) 2-Y-O **£4,015** (£1,194; £597; £298) **Stalls** High

Form RPR
4 1 **Brevity (USA)**[13] 4471 2-9-0 0.... MartinDwyer 7 88+
(B J Meehan) *hld up: hdwy to join ldr 4f out: led narrowly wl over 2f out: hung lft fr 1f out: r.o and in command fnl 75yds* **11/10**[2]
322 2 1 ½ **Florestans Match**[18] 4317 2-9-0 81.... JimCrowley 4 83+
(R M Beckett) *led: tail flashed early: jnd by wnr 4f out: hdd narrowly wl over 2f out: rdn over 1f out whn stl chalng: sn hung lft: nt qckn and hld fnl 75yds* **10/11**[1]
56 3 8 **Sugar Beet**[13] 4474 2-9-0 0.... SteveDrowne 3 57+
(R Charlton) *restless in stalls: dwlt: racd keenly: hld up in tch: effrt to chse ldrs over 2f out: outpcd by front pair over 1f out: n.d after* **20/1**[3]
5 4 6 **Miskin Diamond (IRE)**[18] 4323 2-9-0 0.... DavidProbert 6 38
(B Palling) *chsd ldrs: rdn and hung lft over 2f out: wknd wl over 1f out* **25/1**
00 5 4 ½ **Lettering**[13] 4474 2-9-0 0.... FrankieMcDonald 1 24
(D Haydn Jones) *racd keenly: prom: pushed along and struggling 1/2-way: wknd 2f out* **66/1**
6 2 ¼ **Imperial Pirouette** 2-9-0 0.... ChrisCatlin 5 17
(M R Channon) *prom tl rdn and wknd 2f out* **33/1**
4 7 3 ¾ **Minety Lass**[31] 3913 2-9-0 0.... NeilChalmers 2 5
(M Appleby) *dwlt: hld up in rr: rdn 2f out: no imp: wl btn over 1f out* **50/1**

1m 10.59s (0.89) **Going Correction** +0.175s/f (Good) 7 Ran SP% **115.0**
Speed ratings (Par 93): **101,99,88,80,74 71,66**
toteswingers: 1&2 £1.02, 1&3 £21.00, 2&3 £18.80 CSF £2.34 TOTE £2.40: £1.20, £1.10; EX 2.90.
Owner Mrs Lucinda Freedman **Bred** Cliveden Stud Ltd **Trained** Manton, Wilts

FOCUS
A match in the betting which transferred to the race although it was the marginally less favoured who won.

NOTEBOOK
Brevity(USA) held sway despite a tendency to edge left when asked to lengthen. As is the case with the majority of her stable's juveniles, she had improved considerably for her encouraging debut in a class 2 event won by a more experienced stablemate at Goodwood 13 days earlier. She will improve again for this and while her Cheveley Park entry would be tricky to justify on this, she is more than capable of following up and it will be interesting to see if connections wait to see what kind of nursery mark she gets as the runner up was 81. She wasn't stopping, so another furlong might not be out of the equation. (op 11-8 tchd 6-4 in places)
Florestans Match was just favoured in the betting and despite several flashes of the tail she again went down with credit, although like the winner had a tendency to go left when driven. Her form had been given a boost by the subsequent Group 3 success of White Moonstone, who beat her a length and a quarter at Ascot 18 days previously, but that is probably flattering. She was unfortunate to come up against another useful filly and will certainly be winning soon. (op 4-5 tchd Evens)
Sugar Beet wasn't given anything like a hard time once the first two had gone and stayed on well enough in her own time. She is learning, but needs at least another furlong and will be seen to much greater effect now she qualifies for a nursery mark. (op 25-1)
Miskin Diamond(IRE) is related to nine winners, but needs more experience and a handicap mark before she will be joining them. (op 33-1)
Imperial Pirouette comes from a stable whose first-time-out runners flourish for a run but got tired after being on the pace early.

4922 POKER AT BET365.COM H'CAP 6f
7:05 (7:07) (Class 5) (0-75,75) 3-Y-O **£2,266** (£674; £337; £168) **Stalls** High

Form RPR
1005 1 **Universal Circus**[19] 4296 3-9-4 **72**.... ChrisCatlin 3 76
(M R Channon) *prom: rdn 1/2-way: sn outpcd: rallied u.p 1f out: r.o ins fnl f to ld towards fin* **12/1**
-262 2 ½ **Superior Edge**[21] 4222 3-9-3 **71**.... DavidProbert 4 73
(B Palling) *led: rdn and pressed fr 2f out: hdd towards fin* **9/2**[3]
2104 3 1 **Sheer Force (IRE)**[19] 4288 3-9-6 **74**.... ShaneKelly 2 73
(W J Knight) *racd keenly: wnt lft s: hld up: hdwy and swtchd rt to chse ldrs wl over 1f out: styd on towards fin: nt quite pce to get to front 2* **2/1**[1]
0333 4 1 ¼ **Dimaire**[50] 3279 3-8-5 **59**....(b) JoeFanning 5 54
(D Haydn Jones) *dwlt: hld up: hdwy 1/2-way: chalng fr 2f out: rdn over 1f out: stl ev ch ins fnl f: no ex fnl 50yds* **3/1**[2]
1035 5 2 **Chinese Democracy (USA)**[5] 4739 3-8-7 **61**....(v) CathyGannon 6 50
(P D Evans) *hld up: effrt over 2f out: no real imp on ldrs: hung lft whn btn ins fnl f* **12/1**
2026 6 1 ¼ **Farmers Wish (IRE)**[15] 4424 3-9-2 **73**.... AndrewHeffernan(3) 7 58
(J L Spearing) *prom: carried rt by loose horse over 2f out: rdn and wkng whn hung lft over 1f out* **8/1**
1536 U **Liberty Lady (IRE)**[45] 3440 3-9-2 **75**.... BillyCray(5) 1 —
(D Donovan) *hmpd and uns rdr leaving stalls* **8/1**

1m 10.92s (1.22) **Going Correction** +0.175s/f (Good) 7 Ran SP% **114.1**
Speed ratings (Par 100): **98,97,96,94,91 90,—**
toteswingers: 1&2 £9.70, 1&3 £6.20, 2&3 £2.40 CSF £64.16 TOTE £27.40: £11.50, £2.00; EX 61.10.
Owner Anne & Steve Fisher **Bred** Wansdyke Farms Limited **Trained** West Ilsley, Berks
■ Stewards' Enquiry : David Probert two-day ban: used whip with excessive frequency (Aug 24-25)

FOCUS
A tricky race on paper that was open to several different interpretations.

4923 BET365.COM H'CAP 1m 4f (R)
7:35 (7:35) (Class 4) (0-80,78) 3-Y-O+ **£3,691** (£1,098; £548; £274) **Stalls** Low

Form RPR
2055 1 **Mabuya (UAE)**[16] 4399 4-10-0 **78**.... RichardHughes 7 86+
(P J Makin) *chsd ldr: swtchd rt ins fnl f: sn rdn to chal: styd on to ld fnl 50yds* **9/2**[2]
-020 2 ¾ **Interdiamonds**[95] 1863 4-9-10 **74**.... JoeFanning 3 81
(M Johnston) *led: rdn over 1f out: worn down fnl 50yds* **11/2**[3]
0044 3 ¾ **Pelham Crescent (IRE)**[13] 4476 7-9-8 **72**.... DavidProbert 2 78
(B Palling) *in tch: rdn over 2f out and nt qckn: styd on to cl on front pair ins fnl f: kpt on same pce cl home* **8/1**
0314 4 4 ½ **Shabak Hom (IRE)**[10] 4594 3-8-8 **72**.... MartinLane(3) 6 71+
(D M Simcock) *hld up in midfield: hdwy to chse ldrs 3f out: rdn and lugged lft 2f out: no imp on ldrs over 1f out: no ex ins fnl f* **11/4**[1]
0-16 5 6 **Lucky Breeze (IRE)**[63] 2843 3-9-3 **78**.... ShaneKelly 9 67
(W J Knight) *racd keenly: hld up: rdn 3f out and no rspnse: edgd lft whn n.d over 1f out* **10/1**
522- 6 8 **Grand Art (IRE)**[11] 5943 6-9-8 **75**.... AndrewHeffernan(3) 4 51
(Tim Vaughan) *hld up: rdn 3f out: nvr able to get on terms: lost tch over 1f out* **11/4**[1]
0000 7 12 **Track Record**[64] 2821 5-9-9 **73**.... RichardKingscote 8 30
(Jonjo O'Neill) *chsd ldrs: rdn over 3f out: wknd over 2f out: lost tch over 1f out* **14/1**

2m 37.37s (0.57) **Going Correction** +0.175s/f (Good)
WFA 3 from 4yo+ 11lb 7 Ran SP% **113.8**
Speed ratings (Par 105): **105,104,104,101,97 91,83**
toteswingers: 1&2 £4.80, 1&3 £7.00, 2&3 £9.90 CSF £28.74 CT £190.45 TOTE £5.10: £2.50, £8.40; EX 24.10.
Owner R A Henley **Bred** Darley **Trained** Ogbourne Maisey, Wilts

FOCUS
This was always going to be tactical.
Grand Art(IRE) Official explanation: jockey said gelding was unsuited by the good ground

4924 CASINO AT BET365.COM H'CAP 1m (R)
8:05 (8:05) (Class 3) (0-95,95) 3-Y-O+ **£5,828** (£1,734; £866; £432) **Stalls** Low

Form RPR
2513 1 **King Of Reason**[24] 4144 3-8-10 **85**.... ShaneKelly 7 99+
(D M Simcock) *hld up in tch: a gng wl: led 1f out: sn qcknd clr: comf* **10/11**[1]
314- 2 2 ¾ **Pallantes Cross**[324] 6151 3-9-6 **95**.... JoeFanning 1 100
(M Johnston) *chsd ldrs: effrt over 1f out: styd on u.p to take 2nd wl ins fnl f: nt pce to trble wnr* **8/1**[3]
4-60 3 nk **Arrivederla (IRE)**[61] 2885 4-8-13 **81**.... JamesDoyle 6 86
(H J L Dunlop) *chsd ldr: led 2f out: rdn and hdd 1f out: sn outpcd by wnr: lost 2nd wl ins fnl fklw* **33/1**
5430 4 1 **Gaily Noble (IRE)**[14] 4455 4-9-3 **90**.... JohnFahy(5) 4 93
(A B Haynes) *in tch: swtchd lft wl over 2f out: nt clr run over 1f out: sn rdn and nt qckn: styd on towards fin: nt rch ldrs* **8/1**[3]
2011 5 3 **Zero Money (IRE)**[26] 4065 4-9-4 **86**.... SteveDrowne 5 82
(R Charlton) *led: hdd 2f out: sn rdn: no ex ins fnl f* **3/1**[2]
02-0 6 nk **The Cayterers**[192] 360 8-9-6 **91**.... MichaelGeran(3) 2 86
(A W Carroll) *hld up: n.m.r and sltly hmpd wl over 2f out: rdn over 1f out: nvr able to chal* **20/1**
305 7 11 **Aeroplane**[191] 365 7-9-12 **94**....(p) RichardHughes 8 64
(P D Evans) *hld up in rr: rdn over 1f out: nvr on terms w ldrs: eased whn wl btn ins fnl f* **12/1**

1m 42.84s (2.34) **Going Correction** +0.175s/f (Good)
WFA 3 from 4yo+ 7lb 7 Ran SP% **115.0**
Speed ratings (Par 107): **95,92,91,90,87 87,76**
toteswingers: 1&2 £2.20, 1&3 £10.00, 2&3 £26.70 CSF £9.47 CT £142.42 TOTE £1.50: £1.10, £2.20; EX 11.30.
Owner Saeed Manana **Bred** Darley **Trained** Newmarket, Suffolk

FOCUS
A decent handicap.

NOTEBOOK
King Of Reason confirmed the good impression he made when still a maiden and running fifth off 83 in the Britannia Handicap at Royal Ascot. He wasn't moved for winning a match at Brighton next time and was raised 2lb for finishing third in a class 2 1m handicap at Newmarket 24 days ago when he arrived too late. He hasn't stopped improving and is one to be with in a much better class of handicap next time. Looking further ahead, given no extreme of ground, he could well make up into a serious Cambridgeshire contender. (tchd Evens)

Pallantes Cross was having his first run for 324 days and performed with credit. His stable's runners seldom lack fitness on their reappearance, but time will show this was an impossible task trying to concede 10lb to the fast-improving winner. (op 17-2 tchd 15-2)
Arrivederla(IRE) ran by far her best race in three so far this season. She is still 5lb above her last winning mark but can win again in this frame of mind. (op 40-1)
Gaily Noble(IRE) didn't get much luck looking for a rails run a couple of times and stayed on well enough without looking any threat. He's gradually coming down, but remains 5lb higher than when winning an apprentice handicap, his highest winning mark in four wins. Official explanation: jockey said colt was denied a clear run (op 9-1)
Zero Money(IRE) was always up against it on this hat-trick attempt and a 6lb rise for his latest win 26 days earlier plus an extra furlong proved beyond him. (op 11-4)
The Cayterers Official explanation: jockey said gelding was denied a clear run
Aeroplane Official explanation: jockey said horse had no more to give

4925 BET365 H'CAP — 1m 2f (R)

8:35 (8:36) (Class 6) (0-65,65) 3-Y-O — £1,748 (£520; £260; £129) Stalls Low

Form				RPR
-023	1		**Rockweiller**[9] 4621 3-8-10 **54** (v[1]) CathyGannon 5 (P D Evans) *led after 1f: mde rest: rdn over 3f out: wl clr over 1f out: styd on wl* **11/8**[1]	66+
0626	2	15	**Resolute Road**[24] 4128 3-9-0 **58** JimCrowley 2 (B W Hills) *chsd ldrs: wnt 2nd 4f out: rdn and no imp on wnr fnl 2f* **4/1**[3]	50
50	3	5	**Kingdom Of Munster (IRE)**[11] 4545 3-9-5 **63** (v) JoeFanning 4 (Ian Williams) *led for 1f: chsd wnr tl rdn 4f out: struggling and n.d fnl 3f* **15/8**[2]	35
0-00	4	1 1/4	**Lady Christie**[98] 1796 3-8-2 **46** oh1 NeilChalmers 8 (M Blanshard) *hld up in rr: rdn over 3f out: nvr able to get on terms* **22/1**	16
00-5	5	6	**Chichi (IRE)**[12] 4521 3-9-5 **63** RichardKingscote 3 (Tom Dascombe) *rdn along towards rr over 6f out: u.p after: dropped to last over 4f out: hung rt whn n.d and wl bhd 3f out* **7/1**	21

2m 12.91s (4.51) **Going Correction** +0.175s/f (Good) — 5 Ran SP% **113.7**
Speed ratings (Par 98): **88,76,72,71,66**
toteswingers: 1&2 £4.40 CSF £7.63 TOTE £1.80: £1.10, £2.40; EX 5.50 Place 6 £167.66, Place 5 £60.79.
Owner W Clifford **Bred** Exors Of The Late Mrs E A Hankinson **Trained** Pandy, Monmouths

FOCUS
Some disappointing performers in this small field which was routed by the rejuvenated winner.
T/Plt: £179.00 to a £1 stake. Pool: £57,743.45. 235.38 winning tickets. T/Qpdt: £47.70 to a £1 stake. Pool: £6,443.34. 99.90 winning tickets. DO

4835 LINGFIELD (L-H)

Tuesday, August 10

OFFICIAL GOING: Standard
Wind: Medium, across Weather: Overcast

4926 HOLLOW LANE MEDIAN AUCTION MAIDEN STKS — 1m 4f (P)

2:30 (2:31) (Class 6) 3-5-Y-O — £2,047 (£604; £302) Stalls Low

Form				RPR
2	1		**Sagamore**[10] 4572 3-9-0 0 WilliamBuick 5 (J H M Gosden) *trckd ldrs: led over 2f out: rdn and qcknd wl clr over 1f out: r.o strly: easily* **8/13**[1]	92+
54	2	6	**Short Break**[18] 4330 3-8-9 0 TomQueally 4 (H R A Cecil) *t.k.h: hld up in tch: hdwy to trck wnr over 2f out: rdn 2f out: sn nt pce of wnr and wl btn fnl f* **5/1**[3]	77+
53	3	4	**Pilote Celebre**[81] 2281 3-9-0 0 JimmyFortune 3 (A M Balding) *t.k.h: trckd ldrs: rdn and effrt on inner 3f out: unable qck and hmpd over 2f out: no ch w ldrs after: wnt modest 3rd 1f out* **5/2**[2]	80+
0	4	5	**Present Story**[8] 4661 3-8-2 0 JosephineBruning(7) 6 (P Leech) *sn w ldr: led over 4f out: rdn and hdd over 2f out: wknd qckly u.p over 1f out* **66/1**	63?
	5	40	**Fluter Phil** 3-9-0 0 SamHitchcott 1 (R Ingram) *led tl over 4f out: lost pl rapidly over 3f out: wl t.o fnl 2f* **100/1**	—
	6	12	**Transinski (IRE)**[66] 4-9-4 0 AmyScott(7) 2 (A J Lidderdale) *s.i.s: rdn along thrght and a detached in last: lost tch 5f out: wl t.o fnl 3f* **100/1**	—

2m 33.32s (0.32) **Going Correction** +0.075s/f (Slow)
WFA 3 from 4yo 11lb — 6 Ran SP% **110.6**
Speed ratings (Par 101): **101,97,94,91,64 56**
toteswingers: 1&2 £1.60, 1&3 £1.10, 2&3 £1.10 CSF £4.20 TOTE £1.40: £1.10, £2.70; EX 4.00.
Owner Denford Stud **Bred** Belgrave Bloodstock **Trained** Newmarket, Suffolk
■ Stewards' Enquiry : William Buick one-day ban: careless riding (Aug 26)

FOCUS
Only three mattered in this modest older-horse maiden according to the market. The early pace was generous enough with the outsiders Present Story and Fluter Phil disputing the advantage until past halfway.

4927 OXTED NURSERY — 5f (P)

3:00 (3:00) (Class 5) (0-75,72) 2-Y-O — £2,590 (£770; £385; £192) Stalls High

Form				RPR
2461	1		**Millyluvstobouggie**[15] 4423 2-9-2 **67** AdamKirby 4 (C G Cox) *chsd ldr tl led 2f out: rdn wl over 1f out: r.o wl fnl f* **7/2**[1]	77
4401	2	1 3/4	**Indian Ballad (IRE)**[26] 4040 2-9-6 **71** SebSanders 6 (E S McMahon) *chsd ldrs: rdn and effrt ent fnl 2f: drvn to chse wnr 1f out: kpt on same pce after* **4/1**[2]	75
3245	3	hd	**Loki's Revenge**[9] 4615 2-9-2 **67** JimmyFortune 1 (W Jarvis) *chsd ldrs: rdn and hdwy to dispute 2nd 1f out: one pce and no imp after* **13/2**[3]	70
0020	4	3 1/2	**Welsh Inlet (IRE)**[31] 3897 2-9-7 **72** FrankieDettori 3 (S C Williams) *led tl 2f out: sn rdn: lost 2nd 1f out: wknd fnl f* **8/1**	62
600	5	hd	**Saucy Buck (IRE)**[10] 4578 2-9-7 **72** SamHitchcott 5 (M R Channon) *a in last pair and sn pushed along: rdn and no prog ent fnl 2f: nvr trbld ldrs* **7/2**[1]	62
3602	6	3/4	**Silca Conegliano (IRE)**[10] 4590 2-8-13 **71** AmyScott(7) 2 (M R Channon) *stdd s: hld up in last pair: rdn and no prog over 1f out: nvr trbld ldrs* **7/2**[1]	58

59.51 secs (0.71) **Going Correction** +0.075s/f (Slow) — 6 Ran SP% **111.1**
Speed ratings (Par 94): **97,94,93,88,87 86**
toteswingers: 1&2 £1.70, 1&3 £4.40, 2&3 £3.80 CSF £17.21 TOTE £3.00: £1.10, £3.80; EX 12.00.
Owner Ken Lock Racing **Bred** Ken Lock Racing **Trained** Lambourn, Berks

FOCUS
A fair nursery, run at a solid pace.

NOTEBOOK
Millyluvstobouggie was making her nursery debut after winning a modest five-runner maiden auction at Windsor last time. Always on the shoulder of the leader, she took over in front on the home turn and stayed on well for a comfortable win despite looking around on occasions in the home straight. She looks to still have more to offer and connections would be more than happy to try her back over 6f again. (op 3-1)
Indian Ballad(IRE), 2lb higher than when dead-heating at Bath last time, looked a big threat on the turn for home but he just seemed to hang fire after turning in and took too long in finding top stride. A return to a more galloping track may help him. (op 7-2 tchd 3-1)
Loki's Revenge put in an effort coming to the last furlong and managed to move into second place, but that was as close as he got and he was run out of that position near the line. He hasn't built on the promise of his first two starts, but should find a small race in due course. (op 6-1 tchd 7-1)
Welsh Inlet(IRE), weak in the market, was soon taking them along but gradually faded after the winner headed her passing the 2f pole. She was reported to have hung right and she didn't look happy at Chester last time either, so perhaps she needs a straight track. Official explanation: jockey said filly hung right (op 6-1)
Saucy Buck(IRE), well held in much better company since landing odds of 1-9 in a Hamilton maiden back in May, attracted market support but he came off the bridle at the back of the field after halfway and found little. (op 6-1)
Silca Conegliano(IRE), placed in six of her first eight starts including when runner-up to an 87-rated rival in a C&D maiden last time, gave plenty of trouble in the paddock beforehand and barely got out of last place. She now looks exposed. (op 4-1)

4928 EUROPEAN BREEDERS' FUND NOVICE STKS — 7f (P)

3:30 (3:30) (Class 5) 2-Y-O — £3,238 (£963; £481; £240) Stalls Low

Form				RPR
1563	1		**Sonoran Sands (IRE)**[1] 4903 2-9-2 89 HayleyTurner 2 (J S Moore) *wnt rt s: mde all: rdn ent fnl 2f: kpt on gamely u.p fnl f* **5/1**	90
105	2	nk	**Penny's Pearl (IRE)**[19] 4305 2-9-0 92 JimmyFortune 5 (R Hannon) *t.k.h: hld up in tch: nt clr run and swtchd ins wl over 1f out: drvn and hdwy ent fnl f: ev ch fnl 100yds: no ex and hld last strides* **4/1**[3]	87+
15	3	3/4	**Deep South**[17] 4355 2-9-5 0 FrankieDettori 1 (Mahmood Al Zarooni) *wnt lft s: collided w rail and slowly away: in tch in last: hdwy on outer ent fnl 2f: ev ch and drvn ent fnl f: nt qckn and btn fnl 75yds* **6/4**[1]	92
13	4	1	**Cafe Elektric**[60] 2918 2-9-5 88 SebSanders 4 (Sir Mark Prescott) *short of room s: sn chsng wnr: upsides wnr whn rdn and hung rt bnd ent fnl 2f: ev ch tl wknd ins fnl f* **5/2**[2]	87
1200	5	13	**Silence Is Bliss (IRE)**[11] 4539 2-8-9 81 RyanPowell(7) 3 (J S Moore) *chsd ldrs tl dropped to last and rdn over 2f out: lost tch 2f out* **25/1**	49

1m 26.4s (1.60) **Going Correction** +0.075s/f (Slow) — 5 Ran SP% **109.1**
Speed ratings (Par 94): **93,92,91,90,75**
CSF £23.71 TOTE £6.20: £3.30, £3.30; EX 30.00.
Owner Ernest H Moore **Bred** Lynn Lodge Stud **Trained** Upper Lambourn, Berks

FOCUS
A decent little novice event, but there was early drama when the favourite Deep South swerved left after exiting the stalls, colliding with the inside rail and soon finding himself in last place. Meanwhile, the eventual winner Sonoran Sands swerved right, hampering Silence Is Bliss who in turn collided with Cafe Elektric.

NOTEBOOK
Sonoran Sands(IRE) had been highly tried since bolting up in a weak five-runner Brighton maiden early last month and was making a quick reappearance after finishing third of six in a good conditions event at Windsor the previous evening. It has to be said that he enjoyed the run of the race here whilst his rivals didn't, but he battled back well after being briefly headed and relished the return to 7f. He is likely to be stepped up to 1m now and connections believe that he is at his best when able to lead. (op 8-1)
Penny's Pearl(IRE), twice held in Pattern company since winning a decent Newmarket maiden on debut back in April, was keen enough early but still looked a real danger soon after turning in. However, she made her effort up the inside of the winner rather than on the outside and was never quite able to overhaul the colt. Official explanation: jockey said filly ran too keen early stages (tchd 7-2)
Deep South's rider did his very best after his early shenanigans and allowed the colt to creep into the race gradually. He had every chance down the wide outside passing the furlong pole, but his effort soon flattened out. He is probably best forgiven this and the evidence is that he is better suited to Polytrack than to turf. Official explanation: jockey said colt jumped left into the rails and was slowly away (op 13-8)
Cafe Elektric was probably unlucky not to come into this unbeaten. Returning from a short break, nothing went right for him here. Quite apart from his problems at the start, he failed to handle either bend, especially the final one when still in with every chance. A return to a more galloping track should see him in a much better light. (op 2-1 tchd 11-4)
Silence Is Bliss(IRE), beaten a long way when stepped up to this trip at Goodwood last time, is a half-brother to a dual Polytrack winner but he was beaten before the 2f pole and seems to have gone right off the boil. (op 20-1)

4929 ASHURST WOOD H'CAP — 7f (P)

4:00 (4:00) (Class 4) (0-80,80) 3-Y-O+ — £4,857 (£1,445; £722; £360) Stalls Low

Form				RPR
005	1		**Salient**[12] 4501 6-9-3 **75** KierenFox(5) 7 (M J Attwater) *racd off the pce in main gp: wnt 3rd 3f out: rdn and clsd on ldr 2f out: wnt 2nd 1f out: kpt on wl u.p to ld fnl 50yds* **14/1**	85
5360	2	1/2	**My Gacho (IRE)**[14] 4459 8-9-13 **80** (v) J-PGuillambert 8 (M Johnston) *chsd ldr and clr of field: rdn to ld wl over 1f out: drvn ins fnl f: kpt on wl tl hdd and no ex fnl 50yds* **7/2**[1]	89
0511	3	hd	**Yankee Storm**[29] 3970 5-9-5 **72** (v) JimmyQuinn 2 (H J Collingridge) *stdd s: hld up in rr: rdn and effrt ent fnl 2f: drvn to press ldrs jst ins fnl f: ev ch fnl 100yds: no ex nr fin* **9/2**[3]	80+
3524	4	1 1/2	**Red Gulch**[17] 4387 3-9-4 **77** FrankieDettori 1 (E A L Dunlop) *stdd after s: hld up in rr: swtchd ins and effrt wl over 1f out: hdwy to chse ldrs jst ins fnl f: wknd fnl 50yds* **4/1**[2]	79
4613	5	3 3/4	**Cativo Cavallino**[20] 4255 7-8-7 **63** NataliaGemelova(3) 4 (J E Long) *chsd clr ldng pair tl 3f out: sn rdn along: stl in tch tl wknd ent fnl f* **12/1**	57
1024	6	1/2	**Mishrif (USA)**[12] 4501 4-9-13 **80** (b) WilliamBuick 9 (J R Jenkins) *led: rdn and hdd wl over 1f out: lost 2nd 1f out: wknd fnl f* **15/2**	73
-155	7	shd	**Illustrious Prince (IRE)**[25] 4104 3-9-7 **80** (b[1]) JimmyFortune 5 (J Noseda) *stdd after s: hld up towards rr: hdwy on outer jst over 2f out: drvn and btn over 1f out: eased wl ins fnl f* **4/1**[2]	70
4050	8	7	**Prince Of Sorrento**[18] 4335 3-8-13 **72** AdamKirby 3 (J Akehurst) *dwlt: a in rr: rdn and no rspnse ent fnl 2f: n.d* **20/1**	43

1m 25.18s (0.38) **Going Correction** +0.075s/f (Slow)
WFA 3 from 4yo+ 6lb — 8 Ran SP% **111.3**
Speed ratings (Par 105): **100,99,99,97,93 92,92,84**
toteswingers: 1&2 £9.50, 1&3 £7.60, 2&3 £4.80 CSF £59.27 CT £255.30 TOTE £20.90: £5.60, £2.60, £1.20; EX 56.80 Trifecta £485.80 Part won. Pool: £656.58 - 0.70 winning units..
Owner Canisbay Bloodstock **Bred** Hesmonds Stud Ltd **Trained** Epsom, Surrey

The Form Book, Raceform Ltd, Compton, RG20 6NL

FOCUS
A decent handicap and a solid pace with Mishrif and My Gacho soon skipping clear of the main group.

Prince Of Sorrento Official explanation: jockey said colt missed the break and never travelled

4930 TANDRIDGE H'CAP 6f (P)
4:30 (4:31) (Class 4) (0-85,85) 3-Y-O+ £4,857 (£1,445; £722; £360) Stalls Low

Form RPR

3424 **1** **Kanaf (IRE)**[16] 4398 3-9-3 **81** TadhgO'Shea 9 88
(E A L Dunlop) *taken down early: stdd after s: hld up in last pair: rdn and wd bnd 2f out: stl plenty to do and drvn jst over 1f out: str run ins fnl f to ld nr fin* **9/2**[1]

0540 **2** ½ **Freddie's Girl (USA)**[15] 4424 3-8-10 **74** ow1 SebSanders 6 79
(Stef Higgins) *in tch in midfield: hdwy to chse ldng pair over 2f out: drvn and ev ch ins fnl f: led fnl 75yds tl hdd and no ex nr fin* **16/1**

5003 **3** *hd* **Edgewater (IRE)**[21] 4231 3-9-2 **80** J-PGuillambert 4 84
(J Akehurst) *in tch in midfield: shuffled bk towards rr 2f out: hdwy u.p ins fnl f: r.o wl fnl 100yds: gng on fin* **9/2**[1]

3250 **4** ¾ **Requisite**[11] 4551 5-9-1 **75** (v) GeorgeBaker 5 80+
(I A Wood) *v.s.a: detached in last tl clsd and in tch 3f out: hdwy and rdn over 1f out: in tch whn n.m.r 1f out tl hmpd ins fnl f: r.o fnl 75yds: nt rch ldrs* **12/1**

3200 **5** *nse* **The Hermitage (IRE)**[11] 4558 3-8-11 **75** FrankieDettori 10 77
(M Johnston) *led and grad crossed to rail: hrd pressed and rdn ent fnl 2f: kpt on gamely tl hdd fnl 100yds: no ex and lost 3 pls towards fin* **9/1**

3621 **6** *nk* **For Life (IRE)**[20] 4260 8-8-13 **76** NataliaGemelova(3) 8 78
(J E Long) *taken down early: chsd ldrs: wnt 2nd over 3f out: ev ch over 2f out: drvn and wl over 1f out: led fnl 100yds: sn hdd: wknd towards fin* **7/1**

4000 **7** *nk* **Kerrys Requiem (IRE)**[11] 4536 4-9-11 **85** SamHitchcott 3 86
(M R Channon) *in tch in midfield: shuffled bk towards rr and nt clr run on inner over 2f out: swtchd rt ent fnl f: styd on wl fnl 100yds: nt rch ldrs* **16/1**

0666 **8** ½ **Haadeeth**[17] 4387 3-9-5 **83** JimmyFortune 7 81
(M P Tregoning) *in tch in midfield: effrt and rdn wl over 1f out: chsng ldrs but keeping on same pce whn hmpd ins fnl f: no imp after* **13/2**[3]

062- **9** ½ **Al Gillani (IRE)**[364] 4870 5-9-11 **85** PatCosgrave 2 83
(J R Boyle) *t.k.h: trckd ldrs: rdn and unable qck over 1f out: wknd jst ins fnl f* **5/1**[2]

-040 **10** *nk* **Speak The Truth (IRE)**[20] 4255 4-8-6 **66** oh1 (p) HayleyTurner 1 63
(J R Boyle) *chsd ldr tl over 3f out: rdn over 2f out: drvn and unable qck over 1f out: hld whn n.m.r ins fnl f* **16/1**

2515 **11** *12* **Ray Of Joy**[21] 4225 4-9-8 **82** WilliamBuick 11 40
(J R Jenkins) *in tch in midfield on outer: rdn over 2f out: struggling whn short of room wl over 1f out: eased whn wl btn ins fnl f* **16/1**

1m 12.02s (0.12) **Going Correction** +0.075s/f (Slow)
WFA 3 from 4yo+ 4lb **11** Ran SP% **120.1**
Speed ratings (Par 105): **102,101,101,100,100 99,99,98,97,97 81**
toteswingers: 1&2 £17.00, 1&3 £3.20, 2&3 £20.70 CSF £78.98 CT £353.87 TOTE £5.70: £1.90, £6.60, £1.20; EX 89.60 Trifecta £339.50 Part won. Pool: £458.79 - 0.80 winning units..
Owner Hamdan Al Maktoum **Bred** Catcher Equine Ltd **Trained** Newmarket, Suffolk

■ Stewards' Enquiry : J-P Guillambert three-day ban: careless riding (Aug 24-26)

FOCUS
A typically competitive Lingfield handicap, with only a couple of lengths covering ten of the 11 runners well inside the last furlong. The two horses that were battling for the lead half a furlong out didn't even finish in the first four.

Requisite Official explanation: jockey said mare suffered interference in running

Haadeeth Official explanation: jockey said gelding suffered interference in running

4931 HOLTYE H'CAP 1m (P)
5:00 (5:02) (Class 5) (0-70,70) 3-Y-O £3,238 (£963; £481; £240) Stalls High

Form RPR

0040 **1** **Nelson's Bounty**[40] 3606 3-9-4 **67** TonyCulhane 4 86
(P W D'Arcy) *hld up in tch: hdwy to trck ldrs over 2f out: shkn up to chal over 1f out: led ins fnl f: pushed out: comf* **7/4**[1]

5432 **2** 1 ¾ **Rare Tern (IRE)**[5] 4742 3-9-3 **66** SebSanders 7 81
(Sir Mark Prescott) *chsd ldrs: hdwy to join ldrs over 3f out: led over 2f out: rdn to ld wl over 1f out: hdd ins fnl f: nvr gng pce of wnr but kpt on for clr 2nd* **9/4**[2]

210 **3** *5* **D'Urberville**[56] 3055 3-8-12 **61** AdamKirby 6 65
(J R Jenkins) *chsd ldrs: nt clr run ent fnl 2f tl wl over 1f out: sn rdn and outpcd by ldng pair: plugged on to go 3rd wl ins fnl f* **8/1**

4-06 **4** *2* **Verity Lane (USA)**[43] 3503 3-9-2 **65** J-PGuillambert 8 64
(R M H Cowell) *awkward leaving stalls: sn chsng ldr: ev ch over 2f out: wknd u.p jst over 1f out: fdd fnl f* **25/1**

4051 **5** *4* **Amity (IRE)**[13] 4482 3-9-3 **66** FrankieDettori 5 56
(M Johnston) *led: rdn and hdd wl over 1f out: wknd qckly jst over 1f out: wl btn fnl f* **7/1**

000 **6** *1* **Saigon Kitty (IRE)**[87] 2122 3-8-9 **63** KierenFox(5) 3 50
(J R Best) *in tch tl dropped to rr and rdn wl over 3f out: lost tch over 2f out* **50/1**

605 **7** *5* **Tt's Dream**[17] 4364 3-8-4 **60** AmyScott(7) 2 36
(A J Lidderdale) *v.s.a: a bhd: lost tch over 2f out* **33/1**

0-20 **8** 1 ¼ **Hayek**[18] 4344 3-9-7 **70** JimmyFortune 1 51
(W Jarvis) *in tch tl rdn and lost pl over 2f out: wl bhd and eased fnl f* **11/2**[3]

1m 38.3s (0.10) **Going Correction** +0.075s/f (Slow) **8** Ran SP% **114.9**
Speed ratings (Par 100): **102,100,95,93,89 88,83,82**
toteswingers: 1&2 £2.40, 1&3 £6.50, 2&3 £3.80 CSF £5.79 CT £22.85 TOTE £3.90: £2.70, £1.02, £1.70; EX 7.10 Trifecta £71.00 Pool: £692.10 - 7.21 winning units. Place 6 £61.74, Place 5 £43.96.
Owner The Newmarket Pirates **Bred** Slatch Farm Stud **Trained** Newmarket, Suffolk

FOCUS
A modest 3-y-o handicap which totally revolved around the gamble on the winner.

Nelson's Bounty Official explanation: trainer said, regarding apparent improvement in form, that the gelding was better suited by the Polytrack.

Hayek Official explanation: jockey said gelding ran flat

T/Plt: £43.50 to a £1 stake. Pool: £70,206.83. 1,175.80 winning tickets. T/Qpdt: £23.00 to a £1 stake. Pool: £4,429.53. 142.10 winning tickets. SP

[4517]NOTTINGHAM (L-H)
Tuesday, August 10

OFFICIAL GOING: Good to firm (good in places; 7.4)
All races on outer course. Rail moved out 5m from 2nd dog leg 4.5f out and then 2m as far as 10f start, increasing distances on round course by 24yds.
Wind: Light, across Weather: Fine and dry

4932 SIMPLY CARTONS APPRENTICE H'CAP 1m 2f 50y
5:20 (5:20) (Class 6) (0-65,64) 4-Y-O+ £1,489 (£443; £221; £110) Stalls Low

Form RPR

0-24 **1** **High Five Society**[12] 4522 6-9-6 **60** (b) RyanClark 3 73
(S R Bowring) *hld up in rr: hdwy on wd outside 4f out: cl up over 2f out: rdn to ld and hung lft wl over 1f out: sn clr* **7/1**

2202 **2** 4 ½ **Join Up**[15] 4434 4-8-10 **53** HarryBentley(3) 2 58
(W M Brisbourne) *trckd ldrs on inner: hdwy over 3f out: cl up over 2f out: rdn to chal and ev ch whn sltly hmpd wl over 1f out: sn drvn and edgd lft: kpt on but no ch w wnr* **5/1**[3]

0-14 **3** *2* **Pattern Mark**[22] 4211 4-9-0 **54** (p) LeeTopliss 7 55
(Ollie Pears) *trckd ldr: cl up 4f out: led over 3f out: rdn over 2f out: sn drvn and hdd: kpt on same pce* **2/1**[1]

1415 **4** 3 ¾ **Prime Circle**[10] 4602 4-9-10 **64** (p) DaleSwift 1 58
(A D Brown) *hld up: hdwy over 4f out: effrt 3f out and sn rdn: drvn 2f out and sn no imp* **4/1**[2]

6-00 **5** *4* **Action Girl**[62] 2874 5-8-10 **50** (p) AdamBeschizza 6 36
(R M H Cowell) *chsd ldrs: rdn along over 4f out: drvn 3f out and sn outpcd* **12/1**

00-6 **6** *4* **Nouailhas**[11] 4546 4-8-0 **45** NicolaJackson(5) 8 24
(R Hollinshead) *led: rdn along 4f out: sn hdd & wknd* **14/1**

6260 **7** *3* **Boo**[19] 2864 8-8-8 **53** AlexEdwards(5) 9 26
(J W Unett) *midfield: rdn along 1/2-way: sn wknd* **9/1**

0000 **8** ¾ **Sacco D'Oro**[14] 4453 4-8-2 **45** (p) SoniaEaton(3) 10 17
(M Mullineaux) *t.k.h: chsd ldng pair: rdn along 4f out: sn wknd* **80/1**

0-40 **9** ½ **Ruwain**[53] 3168 6-8-5 **45** AntiocoMurgia 5 16
(P J McBride) *dwlt: hdwy into midfield after 3f: rdn along 4f out and sn wknd* **20/1**

2m 13.72s (2.02) **Going Correction** +0.05s/f (Good) **9** Ran SP% **112.9**
Speed ratings (Par 101): **93,89,87,84,81 78,76,75,75**
toteswingers: 1&2 £5.20, 1&3 £4.90, 2&3 £3.10 CSF £40.81 CT £94.93 TOTE £7.20: £1.90, £1.20, £1.50; EX 27.40.
Owner S R Bowring **Bred** A C M Spalding **Trained** Edwinstowe, Notts

FOCUS
A moderate apprentice handicap run at a fair pace.

4933 J20 WHITE BLEND SUMMER SERIES H'CAP 1m 6f 15y
5:50 (5:50) (Class 3) (0-90,88) 3-Y-O+ £5,828 (£1,734; £866; £432) Stalls Low

Form RPR

-212 **1** **Chilly Filly (IRE)**[6] 4711 4-9-7 **80** GregFairley 3 93+
(M Johnston) *trckd ldrs: smooth hdwy on inner to ld over 3f out: rdn clr wl over 1f out: comf* **9/4**[2]

2036 **2** 3 ¼ **Aurorian (IRE)**[18] 4334 4-9-8 **84** PatrickHills(3) 7 91
(R Hannon) *hld up in rr: hdwy on inner 3f out: rdn 2f out: chsd wnr over 1f out: sn no imp* **12/1**

-054 **3** *3* **Dakiyah (IRE)**[48] 3329 6-9-8 **81** (p) IanMongan 9 84
(Mrs L J Mongan) *hld up towards rr: hdwy over 3f out: rdn 2f out: sn drvn and kpt on same pce* **25/1**

5322 **4** *9* **Sierra Alpha**[18] 4334 3-8-10 **82** PhilipRobinson 6 72
(Mrs A J Perrett) *trckd ldng pair: hdwy on outer to chal 4f out and ev ch tl rdn 3f out and sn btn* **7/4**[1]

16/4 **5** *hd* **Daylami Dreams**[20] 4252 6-8-12 **71** MickyFenton 8 61
(John A Harris) *led: rdn along over 4f out: hdd over 3f out and grad wknd* **33/1**

1223 **6** *19* **My Mate Max**[24] 4147 5-9-3 **76** (p) GrahamGibbons 5 39
(R Hollinshead) *sn hustled along to chse ldr: rdn along over 4f out and sn wknd* **13/2**

0-1 **7** *30* **Lajidaal (USA)**[35] 3754 3-9-2 **88** RichardHills 4 9
(M P Tregoning) *hld up in rr: pushed along after 4f: sme hdwy 6f out: rdn and btn over 3f out: sn bhd and eased* **6/1**[3]

3m 5.43s (-1.87) **Going Correction** +0.05s/f (Good)
WFA 3 from 4yo+ 13lb **7** Ran SP% **109.2**
Speed ratings (Par 107): **107,105,103,98,98 87,70**
toteswingers: 1&2 £5.90, 1&3 £8.40, 2&3 £15.90 CSF £25.73 CT £473.48 TOTE £2.30: £1.10, £15.20; EX 30.50.
Owner J Barson **Bred** Moyglare Stud Farm Ltd **Trained** Middleham Moor, N Yorks

FOCUS
A couple of the fancied runners disappointed and this probably wasn't a strong race for the grade.

NOTEBOOK
Chilly Filly(IRE) ◆, trying this trip for the first time, travelled easily just in behind the leaders and, once getting a gap towards the inside in the straight, picked up in good style, ultimately winning eased down and looking value for at least 5l. She looks capable of progressing into a very useful type now that she's proven her stamina, and she may get further. (tchd 5-2)
Aurorian(IRE) proved suited by this step up in trip, but he was no match at all for the winner. He should benefit from even further. (tchd 14-1 in a place)
Dakiyah(IRE), trying her furthest trip on the Flat to date, offered some encouragement, but she remains high enough in the weights. (op 22-1)
Sierra Alpha was produced with every chance, but his finishing effort was tame and he looked a non-stayer. (op 5-2)
Daylami Dreams was beaten a long way, but this was only his second run back following a lengthy absence.
My Mate Max was not keen through the early stages, needing to be driven along to take up a prominent position, and he finished well beaten. He looks best avoided for now. (tchd 7-1)
Lajidaal(USA), off the mark in a 1m4f maiden on his reappearance, proved most disappointing. He got warm beforehand and was never really going, needing to be niggled along a fair way out. Official explanation: jockey said colt never travelled (op 4-1)

4934 E B F THINK TAXI THINK DG CARS NOVICE STKS 6f 15y
6:20 (6:23) (Class 5) 2-Y-O £3,561 (£1,059; £529; £264) Stalls High

Form RPR

12 **1** **Forjatt (IRE)**[26] 4049 2-9-5 0 PhilipRobinson 1 100+
(M A Jarvis) *unruly in preliminaries: trckd ldrs on outer: smooth hdwy and cl up 1/2-way: led wl over 1f out: sn rdn and edgd rt: clr ent fnl f and kpt on strly* **9/4**[1]

1 **2** *5* **Katell (IRE)**[28] 3971 2-9-2 0 TomEaves 8 81
(Mrs L Stubbs) *hld up in tch: hdwy and n.m.r wl over 1f out: sn rdn and styd on ins fnl f: no ch w wnr* **11/1**

1 **3** *nk* **None Shall Sleep (IRE)**[13] 4477 2-9-5 0 AlanMunro 4 83+
(P F I Cole) *dwlt: t.k.h and in tch: swtchd lft to outer and rdn wl over 1f out: kpt on ins fnl f* **9/1**[3]

1 **4** *2 1/4* **Nordic Spruce (USA)**[31] 3906 2-9-0 0 TomQueally 9 71
(H R A Cecil) *led: rdn along over 2f out: sn hdd: swtchd lft and drvn over 1f out: kpt on same pce* **9/4**[1]

1 **5** *1/2* **Berberana (IRE)**[35] 3756 2-9-0 0 DavidAllan 2 69
(T D Easterby) *t.k.h: chsd ldrs: cl up 1/2-way: rdn over 2f out: drvn and wknd over 1f out* **7/2**[2]

2510 **6** *hd* **Kojak (IRE)**[24] 4138 2-9-5 81 PatDobbs 7 74
(R Hannon) *cl up: rdn along over 2f out: drvn wl over 1f out and grad wknd* **16/1**

7 *1 1/2* **Firstknight** 2-9-0 0 PhillipMakin 6 64
(Tom Dascombe) *in tch: hdwy wl over 2f out: effrt: n.m.r and rn green 2f out: sn wknd* **40/1**

8 *6* **West Leake Melody** 2-9-0 0 MichaelHills 3 45
(B W Hills) *s.i.s: a in rr* **28/1**

043 **9** *11* **Bigalo's Laura B (IRE)**[24] 4150 2-8-9 58 (e) DuranFentiman 5 4
(L A Mullaney) *prom: rdn along bef 1/2-way: sn wknd and bhd* **200/1**

1m 14.52s (-0.38) **Going Correction** -0.05s/f (Good) 9 Ran SP% **114.4**
Speed ratings (Par 94): **100,93,92,89,89 89,87,79,64**
toteswingers: 1&2 £10.70, 1&3 £7.00, 2&3 £7.60 CSF £28.64 TOTE £2.00: £1.02, £9.60, £6.30; EX 32.40.

Owner Sheikh Ahmed Al Maktoum **Bred** Michael Downey & Roalso Ltd **Trained** Newmarket, Suffolk

FOCUS
An interesting novice contest, and there was a potential Pattern-class winner in the shape of Forjatt, who overcame a few negatives to win impressively, in the process recording a time 0.91 seconds quicker than Rock Ace (carried 2lb more) managed in the following nursery.

NOTEBOOK
Forjatt(IRE) ◆ was green in the preliminaries, flashing his tail, and got really warm. Then in the race itself, he was caught out wider than ideal (near rail looked an advantage in the other races on straight track), having started from the outside stall, and travelled enthusiastically without cover. However, despite all of that, he fairly bounded clear of a decent field in the closing stages. This performance obviously paid a big compliment to Wootton Bassett, who Forjatt chased home last time, but he's clearly a smart type in his own right. He may stay further and looks up to contesting Group races (entered in the Mill Reef); it's just hoped he goes the right way mentally. (op 2-1)
Katell(IRE) never threatened the smart-looking winner, but ran on quite nicely for second. He looked a decent type when successful on his debut at Beverley and has the physical scope to keep improving. (op 10-1 tchd 12-1)
None Shall Sleep(IRE), who got rid of his rider soon after making a winning debut at Leicester, unshipped the jockey before the off when behind the stalls this time. In the race itself he compromised his chance by rearing as the stalls opened, and it's to his credit he recovered to finish so close. He seems quite highly strung and needs to mature, but he evidently has plenty of ability. (op 17-2 tchd 8-1)
Nordic Spruce(USA), successful in a fillies' maiden over C&D on her debut, showed good speed against the near rail and briefly looked the winner when responding well when first coming under pressure (touched 1.31 in running), but she was in trouble soon enough. She ultimately struggled against the males on these terms and might be more of a nursery type for now. (tchd 2-1 and 11-4)
Berberana(IRE), off the mark on her debut over 5f on Fibresand, was too free on this step up in trip and switch to turf. Official explanation: jockey said filly ran too free (op 6-1)
Firstknight ◆, weak in the market, ran green but showed ability and can be expected to improve a good deal.
West Leake Melody, who holds a Middle Park entry, had a cross noseband fitted. He badly needed this experience. (op 20-1 tchd 33-1)

4935 SIMPLY CARTONS NURSERY 6f 15y
6:50 (6:51) (Class 5) (0-75,75) 2-Y-O **£2,590** (£770; £385; £192) **Stalls** High

Form RPR

41 **1** **Rock Ace (IRE)**[36] 3729 2-9-7 **75** SilvestreDeSousa 9 79
(Mrs D J Sanderson) *mde all: rdn along 2f out: drvn and edgd lft jst ins fnl f: kpt on wl towards fin* **15/8**[1]

045 **2** *1/2* **Magic Cross**[15] 4432 2-7-12 **52** oh4 NickyMackay 7 55
(P J McBride) *trckd ldrs on inner: hdwy over 2f out: swtchd lft and chal over 1f out: sn rdn and ev ch tl drvn and nt qckn towards fin* **10/1**

436 **3** *1 1/2* **Not So Bright (USA)**[17] 4368 2-8-7 **61** PaulHanagan 8 59+
(J G Given) *dwlt: sn pushed along and outpcd in rr: rdn and hdwy over 1f out: styd on strly ins fnl f: nrst fin* **7/2**[2]

0010 **4** *1/2* **Reginald Claude**[11] 4544 2-9-7 **75** DaneO'Neill 2 71
(M D I Usher) *hld up in rr: hdwy whn sltly hmpd over 2f out: rdn wl over 1f out: styd on ins fnl f* **6/1**

6463 **5** *1* **Fast Shot**[10] 4580 2-8-5 **59** DuranFentiman 4 52
(T D Easterby) *trckd ldrs: swtchd lft and effrt over 2f out: rdn wl over 1f out: kpt on same pce appr fnl f* **4/1**[3]

0235 **6** *1/2* **Fred Willetts (IRE)**[45] 3426 2-9-1 **69** TomEaves 5 61
(P D Evans) *cl up: rdn along wl over 2f out and grad wknd* **18/1**

040 **7** *8* **Logans Rose**[14] 4447 2-7-5 **52** oh2 HarryBentley(7) 3 18
(A D Brown) *chsd ldrs on outer: rdn along 1/2-way: sn wknd* **50/1**

500 **8** *9* **Chadford**[63] 2832 2-8-5 **59** GrahamGibbons 1 —
(T D Walford) *dwlt: sn cl up: rdn along 1/2-way: drvn 2f out and sn wknd* **20/1**

050 **9** *2 1/4* **Bankroller**[34] 3785 2-8-6 **60** ow1 AlanMunro 6 —
(J G Portman) *in tch: effrt and n.m.r over 2f out: sn wknd* **25/1**

1m 15.43s (0.53) **Going Correction** -0.05s/f (Good) 9 Ran SP% **116.2**
Speed ratings (Par 94): **94,93,91,90,89 88,78,66,63**
toteswingers: 1&2 £7.40, 1&3 £2.80, 2&3 £5.90 CSF £21.99 CT £62.06 TOTE £2.50: £1.10, £7.70, £1.10; EX 33.40.

Owner R J Budge **Bred** Jerry O'Sullivan **Trained** Wiseton, Notts

FOCUS
An ordinary-looking nursery, although the time was a respectable 0.91 seconds slower than the potential Group horse Forjatt managed in the earlier novice event. The first three finishers raced close to the near rail for much of the way.

NOTEBOOK
Rock Ace(IRE) showed a good attitude to follow up her Ripon maiden success and is evidently improving. She will be forced up in class once reassessed, but still shouldn't go up much and can remain competitive. It's possible she'll now be aimed at a decent nursery at Doncaster. (op 2-1 tchd 7-4)
Magic Cross proved suited by the return to 6f on her nursery debut and was just held from 4lb out of the handicap. She looks up to taking advantage of a low weight in similar company. (op 12-1 tchd 16-1)
Not So Bright(USA), dropped in trip on this switch to nursery company, didn't apply himself through the early stages - he needed reminders over 4f out - and got going much too late. He shaped as though he'll learn from this, and perhaps a return to 7f may suit, but it's also possible he needs headgear to help him concentrate.
Reginald Claude looks held off this sort of mark. (op 4-1)
Fast Shot didn't build on his recent third at Hamilton. (op 11-2 tchd 6-1)

4936 NOTTINGHAM RACECOURSE H'CAP 6f 15y
7:20 (7:20) (Class 6) (0-60,60) 3-Y-O+ **£1,489** (£443; £221; £110) **Stalls** High

Form RPR

3315 **1** **Divertimenti (IRE)**[2] 4869 6-9-5 **60** (b) RussKennemore(3) 8 78
(S R Bowring) *sn led: rdn and qcknd clr wl over 1f out: comf* **9/2**[1]

4040 **2** *2 3/4* **He's A Humbug (IRE)**[2] 4868 6-9-2 **59** (p) JamesO'Reilly(5) 15 68
(J O'Reilly) *trckd ldrs on inner: hdwy 2f out: swtchd lft and rdn over 1f out: chsd wnr ins fnl f: no imp* **7/1**[3]

0030 **3** *1 1/4* **Downhill Skier (IRE)**[4] 4789 6-9-5 **57** TedDurcan 17 62
(W M Brisbourne) *hld up towards rr: hdwy 2f out: sn swtchd lft and rdn to chse ldrs: styd on fnl f: nrst fin* **6/1**[2]

2154 **4** *3/4* **Bermondsey Bob (IRE)**[20] 4244 4-9-2 **57** JackDean(3) 9 60
(J L Spearing) *cl up: rdn along 2f out: drvn over 1f out and wknd ent fnl f* **9/2**[1]

0426 **5** *4* **Interchoice Star**[3] 4834 5-9-5 **57** (p) JerryO'Dwyer 16 47
(R Hollinshead) *dwlt and hmpd s: in rr tl hdwy over 2f out: sn nt clr run and hmpd: rdn and kpt on ins fnl f: nrst fin* **7/1**[3]

-006 **6** *3/4* **Bold Argument (IRE)**[36] 3734 7-9-1 **58** SophieDoyle(5) 7 45+
(Mrs P N Dutfield) *midfield: hdwy over 2f out: swtchd lft and rdn to chse ldrs wl over 1f out: sn drvn and one pce* **16/1**

5500 **7** *2 1/2* **Stonecrabstomorrow (IRE)**[2] 4868 7-9-2 **59** (b) MarkCoumbe(5) 6 38
(John A Harris) *dwlt and in rr: swtchd rt and rdn 2f out: sme late hdwy* **40/1**

0000 **8** *1* **Resplendent Alpha**[52] 3216 6-9-2 **54** TomQueally 10 30
(P Howling) *in tch: rdn along over 2f out: sn btn* **16/1**

0000 **9** *2* **Ghost Dancer**[2] 4875 6-9-8 **60** (p) LiamKeniry 13 30
(J M Bradley) *chsd ldrs: rdn and edgd lft 2f out: sn wknd* **28/1**

6600 **10** *5* **Connor's Choice**[24] 4130 5-8-10 **53** (b) SimonPearce(5) 2 7
(Andrew Turnell) *wnt lft s: racd wd and chsd ldrs: rdn along over 2f out: sn drvn and wknd* **25/1**

3005 **11** *3/4* **All You Need (IRE)**[10] 4606 6-8-3 **48** AdamBeschizza(7) 4 —
(R Hollinshead) *in tch: rdn along 1/2-way: sn wknd* **11/1**

1065 **12** *1 1/4* **Mandhooma**[5] 4735 4-9-7 **59** PhillipMakin 5 6
(P W Hiatt) *chsd ldrs: rdn along wl over 2f out and sn wknd* **16/1**

5300 **13** *1/2* **Charlie Delta**[172] 614 7-9-6 **58** (b) TomMcLaughlin 3 —
(R A Harris) *chsd ldrs: rdn along 1/2-way: sn wknd* **28/1**

1m 14.34s (-0.56) **Going Correction** -0.05s/f (Good)
WFA 3 from 4yo+ 4lb 13 Ran SP% **114.8**
Speed ratings (Par 101): **101,97,95,94,89 88,85,83,81,74 73,71,71**
toteswingers: 1&2 £6.20, 1&3 £6.30, 2&3 £8.90 CSF £32.30 CT £196.93 TOTE £4.30: £1.60, £2.90, £4.50; EX 33.00.

Owner K Nicholls **Bred** Airlie Stud **Trained** Edwinstowe, Notts

■ Stewards' Enquiry : Jack Dean one-day ban: failed to ride to draw (Aug 24)

FOCUS
Plenty of runners, but this was surprisingly uncompetitive.
Ghost Dancer Official explanation: jockey said gelding lost its action

4937 SIMPLY CARTONS CONDITIONS STKS 5f 13y
7:50 (7:52) (Class 3) 3-Y-O+ **£5,828** (£1,734; £866; £432) **Stalls** High

Form RPR

3250 **1** **Masta Plasta (IRE)**[23] 4180 7-8-11 101 AdrianNicholls 3 108
(D Nicholls) *mde all: rdn and qcknd clr over 1f out: readily* **4/1**[2]

0216 **2** *3 3/4* **Five Star Junior (USA)**[11] 4536 4-8-11 94 EddieAhern 7 95
(Mrs L Stubbs) *dwlt: trcking ldrs whn n.m.r and squeezed out over 3f out: rdn and hdwy to chse ldrs 2f out: drvn to chse wnr ins fnl f: no imp* **4/1**[2]

42-6 **3** *1 1/2* **Noble Storm (USA)**[125] 1174 4-8-11 105 GrahamGibbons 8 89
(E S McMahon) *trckd wnr: n.m.r on inner and swtchd lft 3f out: rdn 2f out: drvn and one pce ent fnl f* **9/4**[1]

0334 **4** *nk* **Star Rover (IRE)**[3] 4819 3-8-11 95 SilvestreDeSousa 6 90
(P D Evans) *prom: rdn along 2f out: drvn and one pce appr fnl f* **4/1**[2]

4404 **5** *1 1/4* **Tomintoul Singer (IRE)**[21] 4231 3-8-3 88 JimmyQuinn 5 78
(H R A Cecil) *dwlt: in tch: rdn along 2f out: kpt on u.p fnl f: nt rch ldrs* **11/1**[3]

0405 **6** *3* **Wi Dud**[9] 4616 6-9-6 97 (b) PaulHanagan 1 82
(K A Ryan) *chsd ldrs on outer: rdn along 2f out and sn wknd* **11/1**[3]

0320 **7** *5* **Matsunosuke**[12] 4510 8-8-11 90 TomMcLaughlin 2 55
(R A Harris) *chsd ldrs: rdn 2f out and sn wknd* **28/1**

000/ **8** *9* **Les Arcs (USA)**[766] 3722 10-8-11 100 LiamKeniry 4 22
(J S Moore) *in tch: rdn along bef 1/2-way: sn outpcd and bhd* **40/1**

59.45 secs (-1.55) **Going Correction** -0.05s/f (Good)
WFA 3 from 4yo+ 3lb 8 Ran SP% **113.3**
Speed ratings (Par 107): **110,104,101,101,99 94,86,71**
toteswingers: 1&2 £3.40, 1&3 £3.30, 2&3 £3.90 CSF £19.99 TOTE £8.50: £2.90, £1.90, £1.02; EX 21.50.

Owner Lady O'Reilly **Bred** Shane Doyle **Trained** Sessay, N Yorks

FOCUS
A decent conditions contest.

NOTEBOOK
Masta Plasta(IRE), just like two other winners on the straight track on this card, made most of the running against the possibly favoured near-side rail. He was beaten in this race last year, and in 2007, but everything went right this time and he gained a potentially confidence-boosting success, his first for almost two years. In this form he's worth his place back in Listed company. (op 10-3 tchd 3-1)
Five Star Junior(USA) lost valuable momentum when short of room around 3f out, but it's hard to argue that cost him the race. He would have been 7lb better off with the winner in a handicap. (tchd 3-1 and 9-2)
Noble Storm(USA) improved on the form he showed when disappointing in a similar event over C&D on his only previous start this year, but better could still have been expected considering he had upwards of 4lb in hand at the weights. He didn't help himself by racing keenly. (op 11-4 tchd 10-3)
Star Rover(IRE), dropped back in trip, ran respectably but wasn't quite good enough. (op 11-2)
Tomintoul Singer(IRE) is proving tricky to place. (op 10-1 tchd 12-1)
Wi Dud, runner-up in this last year, faced a stiff task conceding weight all round. (op 9-1)

Les Arcs(USA) had front bandages fitted on his debut for this yard and showed little after an absence of 766 days. (op 33-1)

4938 SIMPLY CARTONS H'CAP 5f 13y
8:20 (8:21) (Class 5) (0-70,68) 3-Y-0+ £2,007 (£597; £298; £149) Stalls High

Form RPR

2512 1 **Bertie Southstreet**[6] 4717 7-9-5 **68**........(v) JamesO'Reilly[(5)] 10 76
(J O'Reilly) *trckd ldrs: swtchd lft and rdn wl over 1f out: drvn and hung bdly lft ins fnl f: led on line* **11/4**[1]

0004 2 *shd* **Secret Venue**[42] 3540 4-9-7 **65**........ TomEaves 7 73
(Jedd O'Keeffe) *led: rdn over 1f out: drvn ins fnl f: hdd on line* **6/1**[3]

3-14 3 *1 1/4* **Mansii**[40] 3605 5-8-11 **55**........(t) DaneO'Neill 6 58+
(P J McBride) *towards rr: swtchd lft to outer 2f out and sn rdn: styd on ins fnl f: nrst fin* **10/1**

0/40 4 *1 1/4* **Emma's Secrets**[21] 4234 5-8-5 **49** oh4........ JimmyQuinn 11 48
(D Shaw) *towards rr: hdwy 2f out: sn rdn and kpt on fnl f: nrst fin* **33/1**

301 5 *hd* **Tamarind Hill (IRE)**[51] 3243 3-8-9 **63**........(b) NoraLooby[(7)] 9 60
(A J McCabe) *towards rr: hdwy wl over 1f out: rdn and kpt on ins fnl f* **10/1**

6300 6 *1* **Cocktail Party (IRE)**[165] 726 4-8-5 **49** oh2........(v) KirstyMilczarek 8 43
(J W Unett) *chsd ldrs: rdn wl over 1f out: wknd appr fnl f* **33/1**

5626 7 *1/2* **Colorus (IRE)**[8] 4659 7-9-1 **66**........(p) AdamBeschizza[(7)] 4 59
(W J H Ratcliffe) *chsd ldrs: rdn wl over 1f out: grad wknd* **11/2**[2]

0500 8 *1* **Tyrannosaurus Rex (IRE)**[6] 4712 6-9-5 **66**........ GaryBartley[(3)] 5 55
(D Shaw) *rdn along sn after s and towards rr: sme hdwy wl over 1f out: sn btn* **11/2**[2]

4100 9 *1/2* **Sands Crooner (IRE)**[12] 4518 7-9-9 **67**........(vt) TomQueally 3 54
(J G Given) *s.i.s: a in rr* **10/1**

20-0 10 *1 1/2* **Francis Albert**[26] 4047 4-8-5 **49** oh1........(be[1]) AdrianNicholls 1 31
(M Mullineaux) *prom: rdn along 2f out: sn wandered and wknd* **40/1**

0000 11 *3* **Mythical Blue (IRE)**[12] 4510 4-9-10 **68**........ LiamKeniry 2 39
(J M Bradley) *cl up: rdn along 1/2-way: sn wknd* **15/2**

61.06 secs (0.06) **Going Correction** -0.05s/f (Good)
WFA 3 from 4yo+ 3lb **11** Ran SP% **119.1**
Speed ratings (Par 103): **97,96,94,92,92 90,90,88,87,85 80**
toteswingers: 1&2 £4.00, 1&3 £6.00, 2&3 £7.10 CSF £19.03 CT £146.95 TOTE £3.30: £1.20, £1.60, £3.10; EX 27.00 Place 6 £23.19, Place 5 £15.01.
Owner J D Walker **Bred** B Whitehouse **Trained** Doncaster, S Yorks

FOCUS
A modest sprint.
Cocktail Party(IRE) Official explanation: jockey said filly was denied a clear run
Tyrannosaurus Rex(IRE) Official explanation: jockey said gelding was denied a clear run
Francis Albert Official explanation: jockey said gelding hung right
T/Jkpt: £3,692.20 to a £1 stake. Pool: £127,407.46. 24.50 winning tickets. T/Plt: £20.00 to a £1 stake. Pool: £61,283.47. 2,229.62 winning tickets. T/Qpdt: £5.80 to a £1 stake. Pool: £6,814.74. 859.10 winning tickets. JR

4447 BEVERLEY (R-H)
Wednesday, August 11

OFFICIAL GOING: Good to firm (9.0)
Rail moved out around bottom bend increasing distances by about 6yards on round course.
Wind: blustery 1/2 against Weather: fine but breezy

4939 JOURNAL CLAIMING STKS 7f 100y
2:10 (2:10) (Class 5) 3-Y-0+ £2,104 (£626; £312; £156) Stalls High

Form RPR

0021 1 **Fujin Dancer (FR)**[5] 4795 5-9-12 72........(p) DarryllHolland 7 73+
(K A Ryan) *hld up in rr: effrt on ins and nt clr run over 2f out: nt clr run over 1f out: swtchd lft jst ins fnl f: fin wl to ld nr fin* **9/4**[1]

166 2 *3/4* **Monashee Rock (IRE)**[18] 4366 5-8-11 64........(p) RobertWinston 2 56
(Matthew Salaman) *in rr: wd bnd 4f out: hdwy on outside over 2f out: styd on ins fnl f: tk 2nd nr fin* **11/1**

0345 3 *1/2* **Fathey (IRE)**[35] 3774 4-9-4 54........ JoeFanning 4 62
(C Smith) *w ldr: led over 2f out: hdd nr fin* **12/1**

3110 4 *nk* **Carlitos Spirit (IRE)**[11] 4579 6-9-7 74........(v) LeeTopliss[(5)] 6 69
(I W McInnes) *t.k.h in midfield: hdwy over 2f out: styd on same pce last 150yds* **5/1**[3]

4542 5 *nk* **Coole Dodger (IRE)**[26] 4082 5-8-10 50........ LeeVickers 3 52
(B Ellison) *in rr-div: effrt on outer over 2f out: swtchd ins and kpt on same pce fnl 100yds* **18/1**

2443 6 *3/4* **Powerful Pierre**[8] 4674 3-8-5 64........(vt) PatrickDonaghy[(3)] 1 52
(Jedd O'Keeffe) *t.k.h in mid-div: hdwy on outside over 1f out: kpt on same pce fnl f* **10/1**

5050 7 *3/4* **Kheskianto (IRE)**[2] 4897 4-8-10 50 ow4........ MarkCoumbe[(5)] 9 53
(M C Chapman) *chsd ldrs: chal over 1f out: wknd fnl 75yds* **40/1**

8 *2 1/4* **Lady Excel (IRE)**[43] 3544 4-8-11 66........ MickyFenton 14 44
(B S Rothwell) *chsd ldrs: wknd fnl f* **14/1**

-000 9 *1/2* **Union Jack Jackson (IRE)**[40] 3610 8-8-7 48........(b) KellyHarrison[(3)] 13 41
(John A Harris) *chsd ldrs: wkng whn nt clr run ins fnl f* **20/1**

0660 10 *1 1/2* **Blue Charm**[7] 4700 6-9-8 62........(b) PatrickMathers 8 50+
(I W McInnes) *s.i.s: effrt whn nt clr run over 2f out: nvr a factor* **40/1**

0-40 11 *shd* **White Deer (USA)**[4] 4850 6-9-8 78........(p) SilvestreDeSousa 10 49+
(G A Harker) *t.k.h in mid-div: effrt on ins over 2f out: n.m.r over 1f out: nvr rchd ldrs* **7/2**[2]

-200 12 *3/4* **Saucy Girl (IRE)**[11] 4567 3-8-11 51........ DuranFentiman 12 41
(T D Easterby) *chsd ldrs: drvn over 2f out: wknd over 1f out* **33/1**

0 13 *8* **Denison Flyer**[12] 4556 3-9-1 0........ IanBrennan[(5)] 5 30
(L A Mullaney) *in rr: bhd fnl 3f* **66/1**

6540 14 *8* **Dancing Wave**[18] 4373 4-8-9 49 ow1........ RussKennemore[(3)] 11 —
(M C Chapman) *led tl over 2f out: wkng whn nt clr run over 1f out: sn bhd* **66/1**

1m 32.88s (-0.92) **Going Correction** -0.125s/f (Firm)
WFA 3 from 4yo+ 6lb **14** Ran SP% **122.3**
Speed ratings (Par 103): **100,99,98,98,97 97,96,93,93,91 91,90,81,72**
toteswingers:1&2:£6.60, 1&3:£6.60, 2&3:£13.20 CSF £27.72 TOTE £3.60: £1.70, £3.60, £3.60; EX 37.00.
Owner John Duddy **Bred** Loughtown Stud Ltd **Trained** Hambleton, N Yorks
■ Stewards' Enquiry : Lee Vickers two-day ban: careless riding (Aug 25-26)

FOCUS
The field finished pretty well bunched in this claimer.

4940 E B F MOTORS.CO.UK MAIDEN STKS 7f 100y
2:40 (2:41) (Class 4) 2-Y-0 £4,047 (£1,204; £601; £300) Stalls High

Form RPR

03 1 **Menadati (USA)**[21] 4247 2-9-3 0........ TedDurcan 1 71+
(D R Lanigan) *crossed over to rail after 1f: mde all: qcknd 3f out: shkn up and 4 l clr appr fnl f: idled: pushed out* **11/10**[1]

2 *3/4* **Grand Duchy** 2-9-3 0........ AhmedAjtebi 4 69+
(Mahmood Al Zarooni) *trckd ldrs: chsd wnr over 2f out: hung rt and rallied fnl 75yds: a hld* **11/4**[2]

0 3 *3 1/4* **Freehand (USA)**[53] 3219 2-8-10 0........ AntiocoMurgia[(7)] 3 61+
(Mahmood Al Zarooni) *chsd wnr: drvn over 2f out: sn outpcd: hung rt and styd on to take modest 3rd ins fnl f* **16/1**[3]

060 4 *2 1/2* **Livinadream**[33] 3874 2-8-12 42........ PhillipMakin 5 50
(N Tinkler) *chsd ldrs: drvn 3f out: wknd fnl f* **50/1**

0 5 *1/2* **Tapis Libre**[19] 4346 2-9-0 0........ JamesSullivan[(3)] 6 54
(M W Easterby) *t.k.h in last: outpcd over 2f out: kpt on ins fnl f* **33/1**

0 6 *hd* **Auburn Lady**[9] 4650 2-8-12 0........ SilvestreDeSousa 2 48
(A D Brown) *s.s and wnt lft s: hdwy to chse ldrs 6f out: drvn 3f out: wknd fnl f* **50/1**

1m 37.19s (3.39) **Going Correction** -0.125s/f (Firm) **6** Ran SP% **87.0**
Speed ratings (Par 96): **75,74,70,67,67 66**
toteswingers:1&2:£1.10, 1&3:£1.80, 2&3:£2.50 CSF £2.15 TOTE £1.40: £1.02, £2.60; EX 2.80.
Owner Saif Ali **Bred** Stonestreet Thoroughbred Holdings LLC **Trained** Newmarket, Suffolk

FOCUS
Not the most competitive of maidens.

NOTEBOOK
Menadati(USA) made all for a ready success, looking value for more than the official margin of victory as he idled quite badly in front. There was plenty to like about this performance, and he can be expected to improve again, as he still looked green. It will be interesting to see what handicap mark he gets. (tchd 6-4)
Grand Duchy was flattered to get so close to the winner, but still showed enough to suggest he will be up to winning an ordinary race. (op 9-4)
Freehand(USA) was tailed off on his debut at Newmarket, but he had clearly learnt from that initial experience, staying on again inside the final furlong. (op 20-1 tchd 14-1)
Livinadream appeared to run an improved race, although arguably holds the form down. (op 40-1 tchd 33-1)
Tapis Libre may be one for low-grade handicaps. (op 50-1)

4941 HULL DAILY MAIL MAIDEN AUCTION STKS 5f
3:15 (3:16) (Class 5) 2-Y-0 £2,590 (£770; £385; £192) Stalls High

Form RPR

2 1 **Riverdale (IRE)**[17] 4402 2-8-13 0........ PhillipMakin 15 79+
(Mrs A Duffield) *mid-div: drvn on inner over 2f out: hdwy and swtchd lft over 1f out: styd on strly to ld last 150yds: won gng away* **9/2**[2]

0 2 *2 1/4* **Moral Issue**[29] 3971 2-9-0 0........ PatrickDonaghy[(3)] 12 74
(Jedd O'Keeffe) *chsd ldrs: styd on to take 2nd last 100yds: no imp* **33/1**

64 3 *2 1/2* **Watts Up Son**[11] 4599 2-8-11 0........(t) DavidNolan 6 59
(D Carroll) *w ldrs: kpt on same pce fnl f* **7/1**

4306 4 *1* **Surely This Time (IRE)**[32] 3925 2-9-3 67........(v[1]) DarryllHolland 14 61
(K A Ryan) *led: 4 l clr over 2f out: wknd and hdd ins fnl f* **14/1**

00 5 *1/2* **Running Water**[49] 3315 2-8-4 0........ PatrickMathers 16 47
(H A McWilliams) *mid-div: hdwy 2f out: kpt on ins fnl f* **100/1**

6 *3/4* **Crucis Abbey (IRE)** 2-9-3 0........ GrahamGibbons 7 57
(J W Unett) *chsd ldrs: outpcd over 2f out: kpt on fnl f* **66/1**

334 7 *nk* **Heartbreak**[9] 4645 2-9-1 0........ JoeFanning 3 54
(R A Fahey) *chsd ldrs on outer: kpt on same pce appr fnl f* **9/2**[2]

063 8 *3/4* **Paragons Folly (IRE)**[14] 4480 2-8-10 69........ IanBrennan[(5)] 10 51
(J J Quinn) *in tch: outpcd over 2f out: keeping on whn nt clr run ins fnl f* **14/1**

9 *1 1/4* **Gunalt Joy** 2-8-3 0........ JamesSullivan[(3)] 9 38
(M W Easterby) *s.i.s: sme hdwy on far side 2f out: kpt on ins fnl f* **66/1**

03 10 *1/2* **One Cool Bex**[16] 4436 2-8-11 0........(e) JackMitchell 5 41
(P J McBride) *mid-div: reminders after 2f: nvr a factor* **25/1**

2 11 *1 1/2* **Red Gold And Green (IRE)**[23] 4195 2-8-9 0........ AdrianNicholls 1 33
(D Nicholls) *chsd ldrs on outside: drvn over 2f out: grad wknd* **10/3**[1]

12 *hd* **Geronimo Chief (IRE)** 2-8-10 0........ KellyHarrison[(3)] 11 37
(B M R Haslam) *s.i.s: nvr on terms* **66/1**

2023 13 *2* **Saltergate**[23] 4195 2-8-9 69........(p) SilvestreDeSousa 4 25
(N Tinkler) *towards rr on outside: nvr on terms* **11/2**[3]

66 14 *shd* **Sleights Boy (IRE)**[26] 4116 2-8-13 0........ LiamJones 8 29
(I W McInnes) *a towards rr* **33/1**

15 *1 3/4* **Cheeky Wee Red** 2-8-3 0........ LeeTopliss[(5)] 13 18
(R A Fahey) *dwlt: sme hdwy on far side 2f out: sn wknd* **20/1**

05 16 *1 1/4* **Assertion**[18] 4392 2-9-1 0........ RobertWinston 2 20
(M Brittain) *mid-div: lost pl 2f out* **50/1**

64.16 secs (0.66) **Going Correction** +0.125s/f (Good) **16** Ran SP% **122.6**
Speed ratings (Par 94): **99,95,91,89,89 87,87,86,84,83 80,80,77,77,74 72**
toteswingers:1&2:£46.20, 1&3:£6.80, 2&3:£67.50 CSF £158.47 TOTE £5.90: £1.90, £12.30, £2.60; EX 235.10.
Owner James Warrender & Mrs Elaine Culf **Bred** Mark & Pippa Hackett **Trained** Constable Burton, N Yorks

FOCUS
This had the look of an open maiden.

NOTEBOOK
Riverdale(IRE), second to a 1-5 shot on debut, needed to have improved and he did, staying on strongly to get well on top inside the final furlong. This was a likable performance from a horse expected to stay further and he's probably one to keep onside for nurseries.
Moral Issue shaped with promise at the course on debut and should have gained the benefit of that inexperience, just lacking the winner's acceleration. He's a good-looking sort with more to come. (op 28-1)
Watts Up Son again ran well for a long way and has shown enough to suggest he can win a minor race. (op 15-2 tchd 13-2)
Surely This Time(IRE) went blazing off, but was always going to struggle to last and he eventually faded out of the places. (op 12-1)
Running Water left her previous form behind and should improve again upped to 6f. Official explanation: jockey said, regarding running and riding, that the filly ran green and tended to hang to the left.
Crucis Abbey(IRE) made a pleasing debut considering his yard isn't associated with juveniles. (op 50-1)
Heartbreak, expected to prove suited by the drop in trip, couldn't muster the speed to challenge. (tchd 5-1)
Paragons Folly(IRE) should have been closer and will stand more of a chance in nurseries. (op 12-1 tchd 16-1)
Gunalt Joy shaped well considering she was slowly away.

Red Gold And Green(IRE) failed to build on a promising debut effort, struggling from his wide draw. (op 7-2 tchd 3-1)
Saltergate could never get into it. (op 6-1)

4942 RAWFIELD AND PARAGON DATA H'CAP — 5f
3:45 (3:48) (Class 4) (0-85,84) 3-Y-0+ **£5,180** (£1,541; £770; £384) **Stalls** High

Form — RPR

1621 **1** **Mey Blossom**[11] 4583 5-9-1 **76** ... MichaelStainton(3) 11 — 85
(R M Whitaker) *chsd ldrs: led 1f out: hld on towards fin* **5/2**[1]

0624 **2** *nk* **Discanti (IRE)**[17] 4413 5-9-12 **84** ...(t) DuranFentiman 9 — 92+
(T D Easterby) *mid-div on ins: nt clr run over 1f out: burst through to chse wnr last 75yds: jst hld* **8/1**[3]

0054 **3** *¾* **Efistorm**[10] 4625 9-9-0 **77** ... IanBrennan(5) 7 — 82
(C R Dore) *chsd ldrs: nt clr run and edgd lft appr fnl f: kpt on same pce last 75yds* **16/1**

0000 **4** *1 ¼* **Green Manalishi**[12] 4558 9-9-10 **82** ...(tp) DarryllHolland 12 — 83+
(K A Ryan) *mid-div: effrt and nt clr run over 1f out: styd on ins fnl f* **11/1**

0604 **5** *nk* **Rowayton**[15] 4452 4-9-3 **75** ... PhillipMakin 8 — 75+
(J D Bethell) *rrd s: t.k.h in midfield: nt clr run over 1f out: kpt on ins fnl f* **6/1**[2]

0400 **6** *¾* **Ishetoo**[12] 4558 6-9-10 **82** ...(t) SilvestreDeSousa 3 — 79
(Ollie Pears) *mid-div: hdwy on outside over 1f out: hung rt: kpt on same pce* **9/1**

0-35 **7** *1* **Electioneer (USA)**[9] 4654 3-9-1 **76** ... LeeVickers 2 — 68+
(M W Easterby) *in rr on outer: kpt on fnl f: nvr threatened* **33/1**

0400 **8** *hd* **Go Go Green (IRE)**[26] 4118 4-9-9 **81** ... GrahamGibbons 10 — 74
(D H Brown) *chsd ldrs: wknd jst ins fnl f* **8/1**[3]

00-0 **9** *nk* **Titus Andronicus (IRE)**[13] 4510 4-9-5 **82** ... LeeTopliss(5) 13 — 74
(R A Fahey) *led: hdd 1f out: fdd last 150yds* **8/1**[3]

2100 **10** *1* **Espy**[160] 789 5-8-7 **65** oh1 ... PatrickMathers 5 — 53
(I W McInnes) *in rr: sme hdwy over 1f out: nvr a factor* **80/1**

4621 **11** *¾* **Frognal (IRE)**[15] 4452 4-9-2 **77** ...(b) JamesSullivan(3) 1 — 62
(Mrs R A Carr) *towards rr on outer: effrt 2f out: nvr nr ldrs* **16/1**

2362 **12** *1 ½* **Green Park (IRE)**[5] 4798 7-9-5 **77** ...(v) DavidNolan 6 — 57
(D Carroll) *chsd ldrs: wkng whn hmpd appr fnl f* **6/1**[2]

20U0 **13** *3* **Azygous**[8] 4672 7-8-2 **65** oh13 ... DeclanCannon(5) 4 — 34
(G P Kelly) *chsd ldrs: lost pl over 1f out* **100/1**

63.44 secs (-0.06) **Going Correction** +0.125s/f (Good)
WFA 3 from 4yo+ 3lb **13** Ran SP% **125.7**
Speed ratings (Par 105): **105,104,103,101,100 99,98,97,97,95 94,92,87**
toteswingers:1&2:£3.60, 1&3:£12.00, 2&3:£17.20 CSF £24.12 CT £282.90 TOTE £3.90: £1.70, £2.80, £5.20; EX 26.30.
Owner Waz Developments Ltd **Bred** Hellwood Stud Farm **Trained** Scarcroft, W Yorks
■ Stewards' Enquiry : Ian Brennan two-day ban: careless riding (Aug 25-26)

FOCUS
A good, competitive sprint handicap.
Green Manalishi Official explanation: jockey said gelding was denied a clear run
Rowayton Official explanation: jockey said filly was denied a clear run
Ishetoo Official explanation: jockey said gelding hung right
Green Park(IRE) Official explanation: jockey said gelding never travelled

4943 WOLD CONSTRUCTION COMPANY H'CAP — 1m 1f 207y
4:20 (4:20) (Class 3) (0-90,90) 3-Y-0+ **£4,201** (£4,201; £963; £481) **Stalls** High

Form — RPR

3005 **1** **Bencoolen (IRE)**[11] 4579 5-9-7 **88** ... MichaelO'Connell(5) 14 — 95
(D Nicholls) *chsd ldrs: nt clr run 1f out: swtchd lft: styd on strly towards fin: dead-heated on line* **16/1**

6214 **1** *dht* **Jonny Lesters Hair (IRE)**[9] 4652 5-9-4 **80** ... DavidNolan 2 — 87
(T D Easterby) *w ldr: led last 75yds: bmpd: jnd on line* **7/1**[3]

3231 **3** *nk* **Gritstone**[43] 3531 3-8-9 **80** ... JoeFanning 5 — 86+
(R A Fahey) *trckd ldrs: t.k.h: nt clr run on ins fr over 2f out: squeezed through wl ins fnl f: r.o wl: nt quite get there* **13/8**[1]

3000 **4** *¾* **Fastnet Storm (IRE)**[11] 4570 4-9-11 **87** ... MickyFenton 6 — 92
(T P Tate) *led: rdn 2f out: hdd last 75yds: no ex* **33/1**

4120 **5** *½* **Snow Dancer (IRE)**[18] 4389 6-9-1 **77** ... PatrickMathers 7 — 81
(H A McWilliams) *in rr: hdwy over 2f out: hung rt over 1f out: kpt on wl last 100yds* **33/1**

3463 **6** *¾* **Norwegian Dancer (UAE)**[13] 4520 4-9-4 **80** ... GrahamGibbons 1 — 82
(E S McMahon) *chsd ldrs: n.m.r 2f out: kpt on same pce fnl f* **11/2**[2]

3355 **7** *½* **Follow The Flag (IRE)**[11] 4570 6-9-6 **87** ...(p) DeclanCannon(5) 15 — 88
(A J McCabe) *mid-div: hdwy 3f out: edgd rt over 1f out: kpt on same pce fnl f* **14/1**

-000 **8** *nse* **Mirrored**[40] 3619 4-10-0 **90** ... TedDurcan 8 — 91+
(T D Easterby) *hld up in rr: nt clr run over 2f out: swtchd lft over 1f out: nt clr run jst ins fnl f: fin wl* **50/1**

5163 **9** *1 ½* **Arizona John (IRE)**[18] 4376 5-9-6 **82** ... StephenCraine 13 — 80
(J Mackie) *mid-div: effrt over 2f out: nvr trbld ldrs* **14/1**

1330 **10** *¾* **King Fingal (IRE)**[60] 2976 5-8-13 **80** ... IanBrennan(5) 11 — 77
(J J Quinn) *in rr: drvn on outer over 2f out: nvr a factor* **8/1**

5523 **11** *1 ½* **Snowed Under**[23] 4196 9-8-11 **73** ... SilvestreDeSousa 4 — 67
(J D Bethell) *prom: effrt over 2f out: wknd over 1f out* **14/1**

-006 **12** *2 ½* **Credit Swap**[17] 4399 5-9-10 **86** ... DarryllHolland 10 — 75
(M Wigham) *s.s: a in rr* **12/1**

526- **13** *3 ½* **Grazeon Gold Blend**[286] 6645 7-9-0 **76** ... FrannyNorton 9 — 58
(J J Quinn) *t.k.h in rr: hdwy on ins over 2f out: bdly hmpd over 1f out: eased ins fnl f* **33/1**

2m 3.90s (-3.10) **Going Correction** -0.125s/f (Firm)
WFA 3 from 4yo+ 9lb **13** Ran SP% **121.4**
Speed ratings (Par 107): **107,107,106,106,105 105,104,104,103,102 101,99,96**toteswingers:1&1:£23.30,1&3:£9.90 (B),1&3:£3.90 (J); WIN £11.80 (Bencoolen), £2.70 (Jonny Lesters Hair); PL: £5.00 (B), £1.30 (JLH), £1.70; Ex: £80.90 (B/JLH), £102.00 (JLH/B), CSF: £61.48 (B/JLH), £55.94 (JLH/B); TC: £144.01 (B/JLH/G), £135.77 (JLH/B/G) CSF £27 CT £Owner TOTE £Eamon Maher: £Bred, £Darley, £Trained, £Sessay, N Yorks .
Owner Reality Partnerships II **Bred** Gary O'Reilly **Trained** Great Habton, N Yorks
■ Stewards' Enquiry : Declan Cannon two-day ban: careless riding (Aug 25-26)

FOCUS
A good-quality handicap that produced a tight finish, the front two proving inseparable as they crossed the line.

NOTEBOOK
Bencoolen(IRE) had been shaping as though a return to winning form was not far off, and he would have scored outright in another stride, finishing strongly having been denied a run and forced to switch. He's a very useful handicapper on his day and will presumably go back up in grade now. (op 15-2 tchd 8-1)
Jonny Lesters Hair(IRE) appeared to find this career-high mark beyond him at Ripon last time, but he boxed on dourly under a positive ride and managed to hold on for a share of the prize. (op 15-2 tchd 8-1)
Gritstone ◆ would almost certainly have won had he got a clear run under Joe Fanning. He was twice denied a clear run and, despite forcing his way through a gap late on, the line came too soon. He's a good-looking sort with more to offer. (op 9-4)
Fastnet Storm(IRE) has returned to a fair mark and he ran a bold race off the front, only backing out of it in the final half-furlong.
Snow Dancer(IRE) finished well having attempted to come from quite a way back.
Norwegian Dancer(UAE) could only muster the one pace having briefly been short of room. (op 6-1 tchd 7-1)
Mirrored ◆, making his debut for Tim Easterby, shaped with plenty of promise considering he was denied a clear run on more than one occasion. He was another finishing well and will warrant obvious interest in future. (op 40-1)
Credit Swap Official explanation: trainer said gelding was unsuited by the good to firm ground
Grazeon Gold Blend was murdered on the inner and quickly eased. (op 25-1)

4944 EAST RIDING MAIL H'CAP — 1m 1f 207y
4:50 (4:52) (Class 5) (0-70,69) 3-Y-0 **£2,914** (£867; £433; £216) **Stalls** High

Form — RPR

1652 **1** **Saint Thomas (IRE)**[27] 4052 3-9-6 **68** ... GrahamGibbons 5 — 77
(J Mackie) *trckd ldr: led over 2f out: edgd lft ins fnl f: hld on wl* **11/2**[2]

2431 **2** *2 ¼* **Meetings Man (IRE)**[12] 4552 3-9-7 **69** ... PhillipMakin 2 — 73
(Micky Hammond) *hld up in rr: stdy hdwy 3f out: drvn and hung rt over 1f out: kpt on to take 2nd towards fin* **13/2**

0135 **3** *¾* **Magic Millie (IRE)**[12] 4557 3-8-8 **56** ... SilvestreDeSousa 4 — 59
(D O'Meara) *chsd ldrs: chal over 2f out: swtchd rt and kpt on same pce ins fnl f* **6/1**[3]

2021 **4** *2* **Sharakti (IRE)**[27] 4052 3-8-11 **64** ... DeclanCannon(5) 6 — 63
(A J McCabe) *in rr: effrt over 3f out: edgd rt 2f out: styd on same pce appr fnl f* **7/1**

00 **5** *20* **Both Ends Burning (IRE)**[29] 3972 3-7-13 **50** oh5.... JamesSullivan(3) 3 — 9
(J S Wainwright) *swtchd rt after s: in rr: drvn over 5f out: nvr on terms* **80/1**

00-1 **6** *1 ¾* **Dhan Dhana (IRE)**[6] 4746 3-8-13 **61** 6ex ... LiamJones 1 — 16
(W J Haggas) *sn trcking ldr: wd bnd over 3f out: lost pl 2f out: sn bhd* **5/6**[1]

6030 **7** *6* **North Shadow**[10] 4618 3-8-7 **55** ... FrannyNorton 8 — —
(A D Brown) *led: hdd over 2f out: wkng whn sn hmpd: sn bhd* **33/1**

6060 **8** *43* **Irish Eyes**[27] 4052 3-8-7 **58** ... PatrickDonaghy(3) 7 — —
(Jedd O'Keeffe) *stmbld s: chsd ldrs: lost pl over 2f out: bhd whn heavily eased ins fnl f: t.o* **40/1**

2m 4.37s (-2.63) **Going Correction** -0.125s/f (Firm) **8** Ran SP% **116.7**
Speed ratings (Par 100): **105,103,102,101,85 83,78,44**
toteswingers:1&2:£4.50, 1&3:£3.40, 2&3:£4.50 CSF £40.82 CT £223.14 TOTE £7.60: £2.70, £1.10, £1.30; EX 36.60.
Owner P Riley **Bred** S Coughlan **Trained** Church Broughton , Derbys
■ Stewards' Enquiry : Declan Cannon one-day ban: careless riding (Aug 27)

FOCUS
They went a decent gallop in this 3-y-o handicap.
Meetings Man(IRE) Official explanation: jockey said gelding hung right
Dhan Dhana(IRE) Official explanation: trainer said filly was unsuited by the track

4945 FINDAPROPERTY H'CAP (DIV I) — 1m 4f 16y
5:25 (5:25) (Class 6) (0-65,65) 3-Y-0+ **£1,780** (£529; £264; £132) **Stalls** High

Form — RPR

0253 **1** **Master Nimbus**[17] 4410 10-9-6 **62** ...(t) IanBrennan(5) 5 — 70
(J J Quinn) *trckd ldrs: led over 1f out: jst hld on* **11/2**[2]

0546 **2** *hd* **Arashi**[27] 4070 4-9-5 **59** ...(v[1]) RussKennemore(3) 9 — 67
(Lucinda Featherstone) *hld up towards rr: hdwy on ins 3f out: chsng ldrs whn hmpd over 1f out: styd on wl last 75yds: jst failed* **17/2**

3121 **3** *½* **Amir Pasha (UAE)**[5] 4781 5-9-11 **62** ...(p) PhillipMakin 4 — 69
(Micky Hammond) *chsd ldr: led over 2f out: hung rt and hdd over 1f out: no ex last 50yds* **2/1**[1]

0430 **4** *1* **Country Road (IRE)**[15] 4453 4-9-11 **65** ...(be[1]) JamesSullivan(3) 7 — 71
(M W Easterby) *t.k.h: trckd ldrs: nt clr run over 1f out: styd on same pce* **10/1**

106- **5** *1 ¾* **Sphere (IRE)**[36] 7357 5-8-12 **54** ...(p) DeclanCannon(5) 8 — 57
(J Mackie) *chsd ldrs: effrt 3f out: one pce* **20/1**

0355 **6** *1 ¾* **The Mighty Mod (USA)**[28] 4017 3-8-0 **48** ...(b[1]) JoeFanning 3 — 48
(M Johnston) *s.i.s: pushed along over 3f out: kpt on fnl 2f: nvr a factor* **7/1**[3]

650 **7** *1 ½* **Grey Command (USA)**[9] 4656 5-9-3 **54** ... RobertWinston 2 — 52
(M Brittain) *mid-div: effrt 3f out: kpt on: nvr able to chal* **14/1**

4-03 **8** *3 ¾* **Bateau Bleu**[7] 4708 3-8-11 **62** ... KellyHarrison(3) 1 — 54
(B M R Haslam) *s.i.s: swtchd rt after s: hld up in rr: swtchd lft over 2f out: hung rt: nvr on terms* **8/1**

5003 **9** *2* **Barbarian**[9] 4648 4-9-2 **53** ...(p) SilvestreDeSousa 6 — 41
(A D Brown) *led tl over 2f out: wkng whn hmpd over 1f out* **7/1**[3]

0604 **10** *2 ¼* **Lady Norlela**[8] 4669 4-8-10 **47** oh1 ow1 ... MickyFenton 11 — 32
(B S Rothwell) *chsd ldrs: lost pl over 1f out* **40/1**

006- **11** *7* **Shanavaz**[257] 7557 4-8-12 **49** ...(p) PatrickMathers 10 — 23
(C J Teague) *hld up in rr: effrt over 3f out: lost pl 2f out* **66/1**

2m 37.8s (-2.00) **Going Correction** -0.125s/f (Firm)
WFA 3 from 4yo+ 11lb **11** Ran SP% **119.8**
Speed ratings (Par 101): **105,104,104,103,102 101,100,98,96,95 90**
toteswingers:1&2:£10.20, 1&3:£3.00, 2&3:£9.10 CSF £51.85 CT £126.49 TOTE £5.90: £2.10, £3.20, £1.10; EX 58.40.
Owner J H Hewitt **Bred** A H Bennett **Trained** Settrington, N Yorks

FOCUS
The first division of a moderate handicap.
Amir Pasha(UAE) Official explanation: jockey said gelding hung right throughout
Barbarian Official explanation: jockey said gelding ran flat

4946 FINDAPROPERTY H'CAP (DIV II) — 1m 4f 16y
5:55 (5:56) (Class 6) (0-65,63) 3-Y-0+ **£1,780** (£529; £264; £132) **Stalls** High

Form — RPR

5-40 **1** **Gosforth Park**[26] 4120 4-9-3 **52** ... RobertWinston 7 — 58
(M Brittain) *sn trcking ldrs: t.k.h: led jst ins fnl f: hld on towards fin* **15/2**

6-05 **2** *¾* **Into The Light**[16] 4426 5-10-0 **63** ... GrahamGibbons 5 — 68
(E S McMahon) *led: hung lft and hdd jst ins fnl f: hung lft: no ex* **11/2**[2]

3122 **3** *shd* **Park's Prodigy**[5] 4800 6-9-13 **62** ... SilvestreDeSousa 10 — 67+
(G A Harker) *t.k.h in rr: nt clr run over 2f out tl over 1f out: swtchd lft: styd on last 75yds* **5/4**[1]

01/0 **4** *1 ¼* **Banquet (IRE)**[41] 3600 5-9-5 **54** ...(b) DuranFentiman 4 — 57
(T D Walford) *t.k.h: trckd ldr: chal over 3f out: hung rt: keeping on same pce whn hmpd last 100yds* **20/1**

6664 **5** *nk* **Maybeme**[15] 4449 4-9-5 **54** DanielTudhope 8 58+
(N Bycroft) *trckd ldrs: nt clr run fr over 2f out: nt rcvr: eased towards fin* **7/1**
230- **6** *2* **Follow The Sun (IRE)**[21] 7798 6-9-0 **54** IanBrennan(5) 9 53
(Ronald O'Leary, Ire) *hld up in rr: effrt on ins over 2f out: n.m.r ins fnl f: kpt on: nvr trbld ldrs* **18/1**
045 **7** *1 1/2* **Roydmore**[17] 4414 3-8-2 **48** JoeFanning 6 45
(R A Fahey) *mid-div: effrt over 2f out: nvr trbld ldrs* **20/1**
0-56 **8** *nk* **Tae Kwon Do (USA)**[25] 4156 4-8-7 **45** PatrickDonaghy(3) 3 41
(Julie Camacho) *t.k.h and overshot s: t.k.h towards rr: effrt on outside over 2f out: nvr nr ldrs* **6/1**[3]
0-00 **9** *6* **Princess Aliuska**[14] 4485 5-8-12 **50** PaulPickard(3) 1 36
(C Smith) *sn chsng ldrs: lost pl over 1f out* **50/1**
0504 **10** *3/4* **Behest**[6] 4734 5-8-10 **45** MickyFenton 11 30
(D G Bridgwater) *dwlt: in rr: gd hdwy on wd outside over 4f out: sn chsng ldrs: wknd over 1f out* **50/1**

2m 40.61s (0.81) **Going Correction** -0.125s/f (Firm)
WFA 3 from 4yo+ 11lb **10** Ran SP% **117.1**
Speed ratings (Par 101): **95,94,94,93,93 92,91,90,86,86**
toteswingers:1&2:£9.20, 1&3:£3.90, 2&3:£3.90. totesuper7: Win: Not won. Place: £69.00. CSF £46.56 CT £85.27 TOTE £10.80: £2.80, £1.60, £1.40; EX 58.90 Place 6 £64.75, Place 5 £32.09..

Owner Mel Brittain **Bred** C A Cyzer **Trained** Warthill, N Yorks
■ Stewards' Enquiry : Graham Gibbons caution: careless riding.

FOCUS
There wasn't much pace on in this second division, resulting in several of the runners taking a keen hold.
Maybeme Official explanation: jockey said filly was denied a clear run
T/Jkpt: Not won. T/Plt: £104.10 to a £1 stake. Pool:£54,664.71 - 383.01 winning tickets T/Qpdt: £28.90 to a £1 stake. Pool:£4,003.17 - 102.20 winning tickets WG

4580 HAMILTON (R-H)
Wednesday, August 11

OFFICIAL GOING: Good (good to soft in places; 8.9)
Far side rail in straight dolled out but all distances as advertised.
Wind: Breezy, across Weather: Overcast

4947 IRISH CRAIC "HANDS AND HEELS" APPRENTICE H'CAP (ROUND 4 OF HAMILTON PARK APPRENTICE RIDER SERIES) 6f 5y
5:20 (5:21) (Class 6) (0-65,65) 3-Y-O+ **£1,942** (£578; £288; £144) **Stalls** Centre

Form RPR
5202 **1** **Dickie Le Davoir**[14] 4478 6-9-9 **65** (b) AlexEdwards(5) 9 73
(R C Guest) *s.i.s: bhd: plenty to do 1/2-way: gd hdwy over 1f out: r.o strly to ld cl home* **6/1**
-010 **2** *hd* **Mayoman (IRE)**[36] 3761 5-9-9 **63** (v[1]) NeilFarley(3) 12 70
(D Carroll) *t.k.h: led at decent gallop: pushed clr over 1f out: no ex and hdd cl home* **9/2**[3]
5410 **3** *shd* **Two Turtle Doves (IRE)**[4] 4834 4-9-6 **62** JosephYoung(5) 3 69
(M Mullineaux) *prom: outpcd over 2f out: rallied fnl f: kpt on wl: jst hld* **8/1**
-523 **4** *1 3/4* **Residency (IRE)**[21] 4244 4-9-6 **60** AdamCarter(3) 4 61
(B Smart) *in tch: rdn and outpcd over 2f out: rallied appr fnl f: kpt on towards fin* **4/1**[2]
2220 **5** *2 1/2* **Botham (USA)**[13] 4515 6-9-6 **62** PaulNorton(5) 6 55
(J S Goldie) *sn towards rr: outpcd 1/2-way: rallied ins fnl f: nvr able to chal* **3/1**[1]
2340 **6** *2* **Fasliyanne (IRE)**[29] 3977 4-8-13 **53** (v) JulieBurke(3) 1 40
(K A Ryan) *disp ld 1f: cl up tl wknd ent fnl f* **8/1**
0500 **7** *hd* **Future Gem**[7] 4706 4-8-7 **49** (p) MarzenaJeziorek(5) 11 35
(N Wilson) *chsd ldrs tl wknd over 1f out* **16/1**
050 **8** *3 1/4* **Royal Cheer**[8] 4674 3-8-3 **49** ShaneBKelly(5) 8 25
(Mrs A Duffield) *towards rr: outpcd 1/2-way: n.d after* **66/1**
323 **9** *3 1/4* **Kristen Jane (USA)**[11] 4584 3-8-7 **48** ow1 DaleSwift 2 14
(Miss L A Perratt) *s.i.s: bhd and outpcd: nvr on terms* **14/1**
600- **10** *1 1/4* **Captain Peachey**[370] 4690 4-8-4 **48** oh1 ow2 DavidSimmonson(7) 10 10
(P Monteith) *t.k.h: hld up: hung rt and wknd fr over 3f out* **100/1**

1m 12.8s (0.60) **Going Correction** +0.075s/f (Good)
WFA 3 from 4yo+ 4lb **10** Ran SP% **114.7**
Speed ratings (Par 101): **99,98,98,96,92 90,90,85,81,79**
toteswingers:1&2:£5.50, 1&3:£9.00, 2&3:£9.00 CSF £32.59 CT £222.60 TOTE £10.60: £2.70, £3.60, £5.70; EX 37.80.
Owner Stan Wright **Bred** P And Mrs A G Venner **Trained** Stainforth, S Yorks

FOCUS
Modest sprinting fare. They ended up converging towards the stands' side, Mayoman soon having the field well stretched out with few ever getting in a serious blow. The form looks straightforward rated around the first three.

4948 RACING UK AUCTION NURSERY 6f 5y
5:50 (5:50) (Class 5) 2-Y-O **£3,238** (£963; £481; £240) **Stalls** Low

Form RPR
14 **1** **Alaskan Spirit (IRE)**[19] 4332 2-9-2 **81** BarryMcHugh(3) 5 93+
(Mrs A Duffield) *prom: effrt and rdn over 2f out: led appr fnl f: drew clr ins fnl f: readily* **10/3**[2]
516 **2** *6* **Blaze Of Thunder (IRE)**[18] 4388 2-9-7 **83** PaulHanagan 4 76
(R A Fahey) *t.k.h early: cl up: rdn to ld over 2f out: hdd appr fnl f: kpt on same pce fnl f* **8/11**[1]
400 **3** *hd* **Finn's Rainbow**[39] 3658 2-7-8 **63** oh3 ow3 JulieBurke(7) 6 55
(K A Ryan) *wnt rt s: bhd: outpcd 1/2-way: rallied appr fnl f: nvr able to chal* **16/1**
662 **4** *1 3/4* **Damascus Symphony**[18] 4368 2-8-7 **69** AndrewElliott 3 55
(J D Bethell) *cl up: ev ch and rdn over 2f out: no ex over 1f out* **8/1**[3]
154 **5** *1/2* **Roodee Queen**[29] 3986 2-8-6 **68** PJMcDonald 1 53
(Patrick Morris) *led: rdn and hdd over 2f out: wknd over 1f out* **11/1**

1m 13.13s (0.93) **Going Correction** +0.075s/f (Good) **5** Ran SP% **106.3**
Speed ratings (Par 94): **96,88,87,85,84**
CSF £5.75 TOTE £5.10: £4.10, £1.02; EX 6.20.
Owner John Gatenby **Bred** Mountarmstrong Stud **Trained** Constable Burton, N Yorks

FOCUS
Hard to believe there was much depth to this small-field nursery. The winner was impressive but the level is fluid with the runner-up below his best.

NOTEBOOK
Alaskan Spirit(IRE), who is now 2-3, was most impressive here, pulling right away in the final furlong. He's useful already and should be up to holding his own in conditions events, even if the inevitable hefty rise for this makes life hard for him in nurseries. (op 11-4)
Blaze Of Thunder(IRE) hasn't quite gone on as expected since his Haydock maiden win. He had seemingly found 5f too sharp for him last time, albeit in a strong nursery, but went as though a drop back to the minimum trip may suit here, moving powerfully for a long way but all out to hold second in the end. (tchd Evens in places)
Finn's Rainbow seems to be progressing steadily and this performance from 3lb out of the weights on his nursery bow was a step up on his maiden efforts. He was keeping on after being outpaced.
Damascus Symphony had improved when runner-up in a 7f maiden at Newcastle last time, but failed to reproduce it on her nursery bow, not lacking for speed back down in trip but weakening in the final 2f. (op 9-1 tchd 6-1)
Roodee Queen is exposed and has yet to make any impact in nurseries. (op 10-1 tchd 8-1)

4949 GIANT'S CAUSEWAY CLAIMING STKS 1m 65y
6:20 (6:20) (Class 6) 3-Y-O+ **£2,047** (£604; £302) **Stalls** High

Form RPR
5311 **1** **Sunnyside Tom (IRE)**[4] 4852 6-9-13 82 PaulHanagan 4 88
(R A Fahey) *mde all at ordinary gallop: rdn over 2f out: hld on gamely* **1/1**[1]
2636 **2** *3/4* **Finsbury**[13] 4514 7-8-10 65 TomEaves 6 69
(Miss L A Perratt) *reluctant to leave paddock and walked to s: s.i.s: hld up: hdwy to chse wnr over 1f out: no imp fnl f* **16/1**
-622 **3** *1 3/4* **Flying Valentino**[27] 4053 6-8-2 70 ow1 BillyCray(5) 8 62
(Ian Williams) *trckd ldrs: rdn and outpcd over 2f out: rallied fnl f: kpt on fin* **3/1**[2]
1600 **4** *nse* **Just Five (IRE)**[17] 4403 4-9-0 77 DaleSwift(5) 3 74
(M Dods) *hld up in tch: effrt and rdn over 2f out: one pce fnl f* **10/1**
-542 **5** *4 1/2* **Kashimin (IRE)**[4] 4822 5-8-10 69 (b) PJMcDonald 5 55
(G A Swinbank) *sn trcking wnr: rdn over 2f out: sn hung rt: wknd appr fnl f* **5/1**[3]
-005 **6** *1 3/4* **Strevelyn**[11] 4581 4-8-7 45 BarryMcHugh(3) 2 51?
(Mrs A Duffield) *hld up: rdn and hung lft fr 3f out: sn struggling* **80/1**
-005 **7** *1 3/4* **Wigwam Willie (IRE)**[56] 3089 8-9-10 78 (tp) AmyRyan(3) 7 64
(K A Ryan) *chsd ldrs tl rdn and wknd fr over 2f out* **25/1**

1m 48.13s (-0.27) **Going Correction** +0.075s/f (Good) **7** Ran SP% **111.7**
Speed ratings (Par 101): **104,103,101,101,96 95,93**
toteswingers:1&2:£5.20, 1&3:£1.90, 2&3:£5.10 CSF £19.01 TOTE £3.30: £1.40, £10.50; EX 20.70.
Owner The Sunnyside Racing Partnership **Bred** S W D McIlveen **Trained** Musley Bank, N Yorks
■ Stewards' Enquiry : Amy Ryan caution: used whip down shoulder in the forehand.

FOCUS
An at least fair claimer but the winner did not need to improve on recent form to score.

4950 EBF CAPTAIN J.C. STEWART FILLIES' H'CAP 1m 65y
6:55 (7:01) (Class 3) (0-95,87) 3-Y-O+ **£9,714** (£2,890; £1,444; £721) **Stalls** High

Form RPR
0654 **1** **Medici Pearl**[25] 4154 6-9-9 **82** DavidAllan 1 89+
(T D Easterby) *pressed ldr: shkn up to ld appr fnl f: r.o wl* **2/1**[2]
-000 **2** *1 1/2* **She's A Character**[13] 4509 3-9-0 **80** PaulHanagan 3 83
(R A Fahey) *chsd ldrs: rdn and outpcd over 2f out: rallied over 1f out: styd on fnl f: tk 2nd nr fin* **7/1**
3213 **3** *nk* **Avonrose**[11] 4603 3-8-11 **77** GregFairley 2 79
(M Johnston) *led: rdn over 2f out: hdd appr fnl f: edgd lft and nt qckn ins fnl f* **11/8**[1]
4222 **4** *7* **Seradim**[14] 4472 4-10-0 **87** TomEaves 4 74
(P F I Cole) *s.s: sn rcvrd and in tch: effrt over 2f out: edgd rt and wknd wl over 1f out* **4/1**[3]

1m 48.56s (0.16) **Going Correction** +0.075s/f (Good)
WFA 3 from 4yo+ 7lb **4** Ran SP% **107.9**
Speed ratings (Par 104): **102,100,100,93**
CSF £13.58 TOTE £4.60; EX 14.70.
Owner Ryedale Partners No 3 **Bred** Larkwood Stud **Trained** Great Habton, N Yorks

FOCUS
A rather disappointing turnout numbers-wise considering the prize on offer. Predictably, the gallop was by no means strong and the form is a bit muddling, although the third is rated to this year's level.

NOTEBOOK
Medici Pearl had won a stronger renewal of this last year off a 5lb higher mark and took this in the manner of a mare back to her best. She'll still be competitive once reassessed, though the ground is vital to her - all her wins having come on good or softer. (op 5-2 tchd 11-4)
She's A Character's performance in a small field probably isn't one to be going overboard about, but it was clearly a step in the right direction compared to previous efforts this term. She was briefly hemmed in towards the rail and may have finished a little closer had she got out sooner. She saw out the longer trip well, though this was hardly a test. (op 13-2 tchd 6-1)
Avonrose is in a consistent vein of form but had no excuses after enjoying the run of things from the front and will need to pull out more if she's to defy this mark. (op 15-8 tchd 5-4 and 2-1 in places)
Seradim missed the break badly but was able to close up in plenty of time with the gallop not strong and this has to go down as disappointing, as she came into this on the back of three good efforts. (op 5-2 tchd 9-2)

4951 EMERALD ISLE H'CAP 1m 65y
7:30 (7:31) (Class 6) (0-65,65) 3-Y-O **£2,047** (£604; £302) **Stalls** High

Form RPR
5005 **1** **Key Breeze**[27] 4061 3-8-9 **53** (t) PJMcDonald 5 60
(K A Ryan) *s.i.s: t.k.h: hld up: smooth hdwy over 2f out: led over 1f out: rdn clr ins fnl f* **10/1**
-001 **2** *2 1/4* **Gadobout Dancer**[7] 4707 3-7-9 **46** oh1 NeilFarley(7) 9 47+
(D Carroll) *hld up ins: hdwy to chse ldrs and rdn whn nt clr run over 1f out and ent fnl f: swtchd lft and styd on to take 2nd towards fin: nt rch wnr* **3/1**[1]
2023 **3** *hd* **North Central (USA)**[11] 4581 3-9-6 **64** LNewman 8 65
(J S Goldie) *hld up in tch: hdwy and ev ch over 1f out: sn rdn: one pce fnl f: lost 2nd towards fin* **7/1**
033 **4** *1 1/2* **Forks**[12] 4556 3-9-7 **65** TomEaves 1 63
(B Smart) *led: rdn over 2f out: edgd rt: hdd over 1f out: kpt on same pce* **5/1**[3]
0325 **5** *2* **Queen's Scholar (USA)**[19] 4335 3-9-7 **65** GregFairley 2 58
(M Johnston) *chsd ldr: rdn on outside over 2f out: sn outpcd: no imp fr over 1f out* **4/1**[2]
000 **6** *3/4* **Zamid (FR)**[67] 2741 3-8-5 **49** PaulHanagan 6 40
(R A Fahey) *hld up in midfield: drvn and outpcd over 2f out: n.d after* **14/1**
0050 **7** *3 3/4* **Acol**[27] 4061 3-8-4 **48** oh1 ow2 AndrewElliott 3 31
(A G Foster) *trckd ldrs tl rdn and wknd fr 2f out* **28/1**

456 **8** 3/4 **Lord's Seat**[11] 4581 3-7-9 **46** oh1 .... VictorSantos(7) 4 27
(A Berry) *hld up in midfield on outside: struggling 3f out: sn btn* **50/1**

1m 49.43s (1.03) **Going Correction** +0.075s/f (Good) **8** Ran SP% **95.3**
Speed ratings (Par 98): **97,94,94,93,91 90,86,85**
toteswingers:1&2:£4.70, 1&3:£7.60, 2&3:£3.10 CSF £27.61 CT £117.71 TOTE £11.50: £3.60, £1.02, £1.70; EX 44.90.
Owner Allan Kerr Peter McGivney **Bred** Farmers Hill Stud **Trained** Hambleton, N Yorks

FOCUS
Just a modest handicap. The pace steadied early on, the race not really beginning in earnest until the final 3f, the runner-up looking unlucky after meeting trouble. The third to latest course form is the best guide.
Gadobout Dancer Official explanation: jockey said filly was denied a clear run
Forks Official explanation: trainer's rep said gelding had been struck into
Lord's Seat Official explanation: jockey said gelding finished lame right-fore

4952 LUCK OF THE IRISH H'CAP 5f 4y
8:05 (8:06) (Class 5) (0-75,75) 3-Y-0+ **£3,238** (£963; £481; £240) **Stalls** Centre

Form RPR
5245 **1** **Verinco**[17] 4415 4-8-9 **65** ....(v) AdamCarter(7) 11 76
(B Smart) *w ldr: led 1/2-way: drvn and hung lft ins fnl f: kpt on wl* **16/1**
5223 **2** nk **Mandarin Spirit (IRE)**[4] 4820 10-9-2 **65** ....(b) PJMcDonald 6 75
(Miss L A Perratt) *hld up: hdwy on outside to chse wnr over 1f out: rdn and kpt on fnl f* **12/1**
3544 **3** 2 **Sandwith**[13] 4516 7-8-7 **56** ....(v) LNewman 2 59
(A G Foster) *trckd ldrs: drvn over 2f out: kpt on same pce fnl f* **12/1**
4614 **4** 1 **Poppy's Rose**[12] 4542 6-9-5 **73** .... DaleSwift(5) 5 72
(T J Etherington) *towards rr: rdn after 2f: hdwy over 1f out: nvr able to chal* **12/1**
0041 **5** nk **River Falcon**[4] 4820 10-9-0 **70** .... PaulNorton(7) 1 68
(J S Goldie) *outpcd and sn wl bhd: gd hdwy fnl f: fin wl* **5/2**[1]
5400 **6** 1 3/4 **Rothesay Dancer**[23] 4192 7-9-3 **69** .... GaryBartley(3) 4 61
(J S Goldie) *hld up: hdwy over 1f out: no imp fnl f* **25/1**
4215 **7** nse **Lesley's Choice**[18] 4372 4-9-10 **73** ....(v) PaulHanagan 9 65
(Miss L A Perratt) *led to 1/2-way: rdn and wknd over 1f out* **7/2**[2]
143 **8** shd **Distant Sun (USA)**[13] 4513 6-9-5 **71** .... BarryMcHugh(3) 10 62
(Miss L A Perratt) *t.k.h: prom tl rdn and wknd wl over 1f out* **14/1**
6230 **9** 1/2 **Mulglen**[21] 4243 4-9-10 **73** ....(tp) DavidAllan 3 62
(T D Easterby) *bhd and sn outpcd: rdn 1/2-way: nvr able to chal* **8/1**
4203 **10** 6 **Cheyenne Red (IRE)**[4] 4834 4-9-6 **69** .... TomEaves 8 37
(M Dods) *chsd ldrs tl rdn and wknd fr 2f out* **6/1**[3]

60.00 secs **Going Correction** +0.075s/f (Good) **10** Ran SP% **115.7**
Speed ratings (Par 103): **103,102,99,97,97 94,94,94,93,83**
toteswingers:1&2:£18.90, 1&3:£16.60, 2&3:£7.50 CSF £191.57 CT £2427.78 TOTE £29.40: £7.30, £4.50, £7.20; EX 139.00.
Owner B Smart **Bred** Mrs M Gutkin **Trained** Hambleton, N Yorks

FOCUS
Just a run-of-the-mill sprint but straightforward form rated around the principals. As in the opener, the field edged over towards the stands' rail, with not that many actually getting in a meaningful blow.

4953 DUBLIN H'CAP 1m 4f 17y
8:35 (8:35) (Class 5) (0-70,75) 3-Y-0+ **£3,238** (£963; £481; £240) **Stalls** High

Form RPR
0010 **1** **Epic (IRE)**[13] 4520 3-9-4 **70** ....(b) GregFairley 2 85+
(M Johnston) *chsd ldr: rdn to ld over 2f out: edgd rt and drew clr over 1f out* **5/1**[3]
2104 **2** 2 3/4 **Regent's Secret (USA)**[11] 4582 10-8-10 **58** .... PaulNorton(7) 5 66
(J S Goldie) *hld up and bhd: plenty to do 4f out: gd hdwy over 1f out: chsd wnr ins fnl f: nvr able to chal* **10/1**
31 **3** 3 3/4 **George Adamson (IRE)**[9] 4656 4-10-6 **75** 6ex .... PJMcDonald 1 77
(G A Swinbank) *prom: effrt and chsd ldr 2f out: no ex and lost 2nd ins fnl f* **11/8**[1]
2333 **4** 2 1/2 **Mohawk Ridge**[23] 4190 4-9-9 **64** .... TomEaves 6 62
(M Dods) *trckd ldrs: drvn and outpcd over 2f out: n.d after* **11/4**[2]
000- **5** 1/2 **Louisa (GER)**[338] 5734 6-8-7 **51** oh5 ow1 .... BarryMcHugh(3) 3 48
(P Monteith) *hld up in tch: rdn and outpcd over 3f out: sme late hdwy: n.d* **25/1**
4510 **6** 1 1/4 **Balwearie (IRE)**[23] 4190 9-9-2 **57** .... PaulHanagan 4 52
(Miss L A Perratt) *led tl over 2f out: sn rdn: wknd over 1f out* **17/2**

2m 38.47s (-0.13) **Going Correction** +0.075s/f (Good)
WFA 3 from 4yo+ 11lb **6** Ran SP% **108.9**
Speed ratings (Par 103): **103,101,98,97,96 95**
toteswingers:1&2:£9.10, 1&3:£2.40, 2&3:£2.90 CSF £46.56 TOTE £6.60: £1.80, £1.70; EX 38.10 Place 6 £245.36, Place 5 £93.73..
Owner Racegoers Club Owners Group **Bred** P D Savill **Trained** Middleham Moor, N Yorks

FOCUS
This probably didn't take that much winning but the form appears sound enough rated through the second.
T/Plt: £474.60 to a £1 stake. Pool £38,329.38 - 58.95 winning tickets T/Qpdt: £127.00 to a £1 stake. Pool £4,773.67 - 27.80 winning tickets RY

4382 SALISBURY (R-H)
Wednesday, August 11

OFFICIAL GOING: Good (good to firm in places; 8.6)
Rail erected up to 5m off permanent far side rail between 6.5f and 2f.
Wind: Slight breeze, variable Weather: Overcast but warm

4954 E B F MOLSON COORS MAIDEN STKS 6f
2:30 (2:31) (Class 4) 2-Y-0 **£4,209** (£1,252; £625; £312) **Stalls** High

Form RPR
2 **1** **Big Issue (IRE)**[15] 4460 2-9-3 0 .... RichardHughes 11 93+
(R Hannon) *trckd ldrs: led on bit wl over 1f out: qcknd clr ent fnl f: easily: impressive* **1/4**[1]
0 **2** 2 **Fists And Stones**[15] 4460 2-9-3 0 .... ChrisCatlin 2 81+
(M R Channon) *mid-div: rdn 3f out: r.o fnl f: wnt 2nd fnl 75yds: no ch w easy wnr* **33/1**
3 1 1/2 **Another Laugh** 2-9-3 0 .... MichaelHills 12 76+
(B W Hills) *mid-div: pushed along over 3f out: nt clr run briefly 2f out: swtchd rt: r.o ins fnl f* **33/1**
4 hd **Glanusk** 2-9-3 0 .... WilliamBuick 13 76+
(R M Beckett) *hld up bhd: nt clr run 3f out: pushed along and hdwy fr over 1f out: fin strly: improve* **33/1**
05 **5** hd **Buddy Miracle**[10] 4622 2-8-12 0 .... DavidProbert 7 70
(A M Balding) *led: rdn whn edgd lft and hdd wl over 1f out: kpt on chsng wnr tl no ex and lost 3 pls fnl 75yds* **9/1**[2]
0 **6** 2 3/4 **Sluggsy Morant**[19] 4323 2-9-3 0 .... DaneO'Neill 3 66
(H Candy) *trckd ldr: rdn 3f out: wknd fnl f* **14/1**[3]
7 2 **Danceyourselfdizzy (IRE)** 2-9-3 0 .... PatDobbs 6 60
(R Hannon) *hld up towards rr: swtchd to centre over 2f out: sn drvn: little imp* **20/1**
0 **8** shd **Appyjack**[30] 3961 2-9-3 0 .... LukeMorris 8 59
(J S Moore) *a towards rr* **100/1**
60 **9** 1 1/2 **Hero From Zero (IRE)**[12] 4549 2-9-3 0 .... MartinDwyer 1 55
(B J Meehan) *trckd ldrs: rdn 3f out: wknd over 1f out* **20/1**
10 shd **Farlow (IRE)** 2-9-3 0 .... JimCrowley 4 54
(R M Beckett) *a towards rr* **16/1**
4 **11** 1 1/4 **Basilica**[99] 1793 2-9-0 0 .... JamesMillman(3) 9 50
(B R Millman) *cl up: rdn 2f out: wknd ent fnl f* **16/1**

1m 16.39s (1.59) **Going Correction** +0.175s/f (Good) **11** Ran SP% **127.8**
Speed ratings (Par 96): **96,93,91,91,90 87,84,84,82,82 80**
toteswingers:1&2:£8.90, 1&3:£4.20, 2&3:£50.90 CSF £26.44 TOTE £1.20: £1.02, £12.00, £7.20; EX 20.20.
Owner Malih L Al Basti **Bred** Tinnakill Bloodstock & P Lawlor **Trained** East Everleigh, Wilts

FOCUS
A few of these are open to plenty of improvement and the race should produce winners.

NOTEBOOK
Big Issue(IRE) confirmed the promise he showed when runner-up in a decent Goodwood maiden on debut with a nice performance. His jockey didn't have to get particularly serious and he looked to take this with plenty to spare. He holds no fancy entries, but will obviously be well worth his place in better company. (op 3-10 tchd 4-11 in places)
Fists And Stones is flattered to get so close to the winner, but this was still an improvement on the form he showed behind that rival on debut. He shaped as though he'll come on again and should improve for a step up in trip.
Another Laugh, the first foal of a dual 7f winner, was under pressure before halfway, running green, but kept on nicely and should have learnt plenty.
Glanusk ◆, a 58,000gns half-brother to 1m-1m1f winner Ethics Girl, is another who looks set to come on a bundle for this. He lacked the required speed and knowhow of some his rivals, but ran on nicely.
Buddy Miracle, one of only two fillies in the line up, ran with credit. Now eligible for a mark, she should find her level. (op 10-1)
Sluggsy Morant, reported to have stopped quickly when beaten at 5-4 on debut, fared better this time but still didn't see his race out.
Danceyourselfdizzy(IRE) shaped as though he'll come on a lot for the run. (op 25-1)

4955 STEVENS GARNIER LTD NURSERY 6f 212y
3:00 (3:00) (Class 4) (0-85,82) 2-Y-0 **£3,561** (£1,059; £529; £264) **Stalls** Centre

Form RPR
4534 **1** **Orientalist**[10] 4623 2-9-0 **75** .... KierenFallon 2 80
(Eve Johnson Houghton) *trckd ldr: chal over 2f out: rdn over 1f out: led ins fnl f: r.o wl towards fin* **5/2**[1]
126 **2** 1/2 **Shewalksinbeauty (IRE)**[10] 4623 2-8-12 **73** .... PatDobbs 1 77
(R Hannon) *sn led: rdn 2f out: hdd ins fnl f: kpt on but no ex* **15/2**
5051 **3** 1 3/4 **Rosina Grey**[8] 4677 2-8-13 **77** 6ex .... JamesMillman(3) 7 76
(B R Millman) *hld up: racd keenly early: hdwy 2f out: sn rdn: hung rt: kpt on but nt gng pce to get on terms* **4/1**[3]
0103 **4** 1/2 **Liberty Cap (USA)**[16] 4429 2-9-7 **82** ....(p) WilliamBuick 8 80+
(J H M Gosden) *v awkward leaving stalls: hld up: swtchd to centre and rdn 2f out: styd on ins fnl f: snatched 4th fnl stride* **8/1**
0210 **5** hd **Whodathought (IRE)**[10] 4623 2-8-10 **71** .... RichardHughes 6 68
(R Hannon) *trckd ldrs: rdn over 2f out: kpt on same pce fnl f: lost 4th fnl stride* **10/3**[2]
444 **6** 1 1/4 **Cathcart Castle**[39] 3657 2-8-4 **65** .... ChrisCatlin 9 59
(M R Channon) *hld up: hdwy wl over 1f out: sn rdn: kpt on same pce fnl f* **8/1**
1456 **7** 1 1/2 **Alfraamsey**[12] 4539 2-8-9 **70** .... SamHitchcott 3 60
(M R Channon) *trckd ldrs: rdn to chal briefly over 2f out: one pce fr over 1f out* **20/1**
0040 **8** hd **Salvationist**[8] 4677 2-7-12 **59** oh2 ....(b[1]) DavidProbert 5 48
(J L Dunlop) *trckd ldrs for over 2f: in tch: rdn over 2f out: one pce fr over 1f out* **50/1**

1m 32.4s (3.40) **Going Correction** +0.175s/f (Good) **8** Ran SP% **112.4**
Speed ratings (Par 96): **87,86,84,83,83 82,80,80**
toteswingers:1&2:£4.40, 1&3:£3.30, 2&3:£5.50 CSF £21.14 CT £71.59 TOTE £3.80: £1.50, £1.80, £1.90; EX 21.80.
Owner Eden Racing IV **Bred** Whitsbury Manor Stud **Trained** Blewbury, Oxon
■ Stewards' Enquiry : Pat Dobbs one-day ban: careless riding (Aug 25)

FOCUS
The pace seemed to slow significantly after a couple of furlongs or so.

NOTEBOOK
Orientalist was always well placed considering the lack of pace and found enough for pressure. He would probably prefer a stronger-run race and might defy a rise. (op 7-2 tchd 9-4)
Shewalksinbeauty(IRE) was given a good ride from the front and had her chance, but she couldn't reverse recent Newbury placings with Orientalist. (op 11-2)
Rosina Grey was 3lb well in under the penalty picked up for her recent Chepstow victory, but she's not straightforward and gave herself little chance of following up. Again wanting to hang right, she didn't have a rail to help this time, and also carried her head high. Earlier in the race she had been much too keen, with the steady pace not suiting, and she's not one to rely on. (op 6-1)
Liberty Cap(USA) isn't progressing, but the steady pace didn't suit considering he raced out the back, and he can be given another chance. Official explanation: jockey said colt reared as stalls opened (op 6-1)
Whodathought(IRE) offered little, although he is already due to be eased 2lb. (tchd 3-1, 7-2 and 4-1 in places)

4956 GOLDRING SECURITY SERVICES PEMBROKE CUP (H'CAP) 1m
3:35 (3:37) (Class 4) (0-85,82) 3-Y-0 **£4,209** (£1,252; £625; £312) **Stalls** High

Form RPR
0420 **1** **Mr Irons (USA)**[33] 3867 3-9-5 **80** ....(v[1]) KierenFallon 4 87
(Sir Michael Stoute) *cl up: chal u.p over 2f out: drvn ahd fnl 110yds: styd on wl* **9/2**[2]
2234 **2** 1 1/4 **Faithful One (IRE)**[32] 3890 3-9-7 **82** .... ChrisCatlin 2 87
(D R Lanigan) *trckd ldr: led over 2f out: sn hrd pressed and rdn: hdd fnl 110yds: no ex* **8/1**
2201 **3** nk **Red Yarn**[11] 4588 3-8-13 **74** ....(b) SamHitchcott 9 78
(G L Moore) *led for 1f: trckd ldrs: swtchd off far rails over 2f out: sn rdn: styd on ins fnl f* **22/1**
0042 **4** shd **Our Boy Barrington (IRE)**[9] 4660 3-8-12 **73** .... RichardHughes 10 77
(R Hannon) *cl up: hdwy on far rails 2f out: sn rdn: swtchd lft jst ins fnl f: styd on* **9/2**[2]

4351 **5** *shd* **Jubail (IRE)**[14] 4479 3-8-11 **72**.................................... FergusSweeney 1 75+
(A King) *led after 1f: hdd over 2f out: sn rdn and ct flat-footed: styd on again ins fnl f* **5/2**[1]

0203 **6** *1 ½* **White Devil**[36] 3766 3-9-3 **78**..(p) LiamKeniry 6 78
(A M Balding) *s.i.s: towards rr: swtchd lft for effrt over 2f out: kpt on same pce: nvr threatened ldrs* **8/1**

3434 **7** *shd* **Be A Devil**[27] 4058 3-9-0 **75**... MartinDwyer 8 77+
(W R Muir) *hld up: rdn whn nt clr run over 2f out: swtchd rt to far rails: nvr clr passage ins fnl f: unable to get on terms* **5/1**[3]

36-6 **8** *8* **Poor Prince**[14] 4491 3-9-2 **77**... LukeMorris 3 58
(C G Cox) *s.i.s: towards rr: effrt 3f out: wknd over 1f out* **20/1**

10-0 **9** *31* **Running Mate (IRE)**[113] 1453 3-9-2 **77**.............................. IanMongan 7 —
(Miss Jo Crowley) *trckd ldrs: rdn 3f out: wknd over 1f out: eased fnl f* **50/1**

1m 44.46s (0.96) **Going Correction** +0.175s/f (Good) **9** Ran SP% **114.9**
Speed ratings (Par 102): **102,100,100,100,100 98,98,90,59**
toteswingers: 1&2 £4.80, 1&3 £11.20, 2&3 £18.50 CSF £38.71 CT £715.44 TOTE £5.40: £2.10, £2.30, £4.60; EX 35.90.
Owner Mrs Elizabeth Moran **Bred** Hunter Valley Farm & Hatta Bldstk **Trained** Newmarket, Suffolk

FOCUS
There was a bunch finish in behind the winnner and this probably isn't strong form.
Red Yarn Official explanation: jockey said filly hung right-handed
Poor Prince Official explanation: jockey said gelding was slowly away

4957 EUROPEAN BREEDERS' FUND UPAVON FILLIES' STKS (LISTED RACE) 1m 1f 198y
4:05 (4:06) (Class 1) 3-Y-0+
£25,546 (£9,684; £4,846; £2,416; £1,210; £607) **Stalls** High

Form RPR

-143 **1** **Alsace Lorraine (IRE)**[19] 4319 5-9-0 105.......................... KierenFallon 7 105
(J R Fanshawe) *s.i.s: sn in tch: nt clr run fr 3f out tl wl over 1f out: qcknd up wl to squeeze through gap ent fnl f: sn led: hung lft: drvn out* **11/8**[1]

535 **2** *nk* **Gallic Star (IRE)**[10] 4624 3-8-5 110.. ChrisCatlin 6 104
(M R Channon) *hld up in last pair: hdwy 2f out: sn rdn: edgd rt but chal ins fnl f: styd on: hld nr fin* **10/1**

5402 **3** *nk* **Mudaaraah**[19] 4347 3-8-6 96 ow1.. RichardHills 3 105
(J L Dunlop) *hld up in last: swtchd to centre and hdwy wl over 1f out: sn rdn: styd on wl ins fnl f but nvr quite getting there* **7/2**[2]

4050 **4** *2 ¾* **Three Moons (IRE)**[25] 4143 4-9-0 98............................ RichardHughes 9 98
(H J L Dunlop) *trckd ldrs: nt clr run on rails tl cutaway wl over 1f out: qcknd up to chal: rdn and led briefly jst ins fnl f: kpt on same pce fnl 100yds* **16/1**

1043 **5** *4 ½* **Totally Ours**[19] 4347 3-8-5 94.. MartinDwyer 8 89
(W R Muir) *trckd ldrs: rdn to chal 3f out: fdd ins fnl f* **20/1**

1260 **6** *1* **Fatanah (IRE)**[40] 3632 3-8-5 107.. TadhgO'Shea 4 87
(M P Tregoning) *in tch: rdn to chal 3f out: wknd ent fnl f* **12/1**

1420 **7** *1 ¼* **Pink Symphony**[28] 4037 3-8-6 100 ow1........................ JamieSpencer 1 86
(P F I Cole) *sn led: rdn over 2f out: wandering sltly whn hdd and bmpd jst ins fnl f: wknd* **6/1**[3]

46-3 **8** *19* **Chantilly Tiffany**[130] 1084 6-9-0 98................................... WilliamBuick 5 47
(J H M Gosden) *in tch: rdn to chse ldrs 3f out: wknd jst over 1f out: eased* **10/1**

2m 9.17s (-0.73) **Going Correction** 0.0s/f (Good)
WFA 3 from 4yo+ 9lb **8** Ran SP% **115.1**
Speed ratings (Par 108): **102,101,101,99,95 94,93,78**
toteswingers: 1&2 £5.40, 1&3 £1.90, 2&3 £7.80 CSF £16.83 TOTE £2.00: £1.10, £3.20, £1.30; EX 19.20.
Owner Merry Fox Stud Limited **Bred** 6c Stallions Ltd **Trained** Newmarket, Suffolk

FOCUS
A weak fillies' Listed contest, and the early pace was steady, resulting in a time 0.12 seconds slower than the 59-rated Bramalea recorded in the following handicap.

NOTEBOOK
Alsace Lorraine(IRE), a beaten favourite behind the promising Field Day at this level over 1m last time, had to be worth another try over this trip judged on her breeding (possibly unlucky only previous try) and she just proved good enough. She looks worth persevering with over this sort of distance, especially as she might do better off a stronger pace, and she may now go for a Group 3 abroad. (op 13-8)
Gallic Star(IRE) was probably unsuited by the lack of pace on this drop back in trip, especially as the winner had been racing over 1m. She ran well in the circumstances. (op 17-2 tchd 8-1)
Mudaaraah, carrying 1lb overweight, probably ran to a similar level as when runner-up in this grade at York last time. (op 9-2)
Three Moons(IRE) was suited by the drop in trip and ran about as well as could have been expected considering she had something to find at the weights. (op 14-1)
Totally Ours was another who faced a stiff task at the weights and she couldn't make a telling impression, finishing further behind Mudaaraah than at York last time. William Muir reported afterwards that the filly was in season. Official explanation: trainer's rep said filly was in season (op 16-1)
Pink Symphony, carrying 1lb overweight, was allowed a soft enough lead and better could have been expected. She was on the retreat when becoming unbalanced around 1f out. (op 7-1)

4958 CHAMPAGNE JOSEPH PERRIER H'CAP 1m 1f 198y
4:40 (4:40) (Class 5) (0-70,70) 3-Y-0+ **£3,238** (£963; £481; £240) **Stalls** High

Form RPR

204 **1** **Bramalea**[33] 3865 5-9-3 **59**.. IanMongan 12 75
(B W Duke) *w ldr: led over 3f out: styd on strly fnl 2f: rdn out* **15/2**

02-2 **2** *2 ¼* **Three Ducks**[6] 4756 4-10-0 **70**.................................... RichardHughes 10 82
(R Hannon) *in tch: swtchd lft for effrt 2f out: sn rdn to chse wnr: kpt on for clr 2nd but a being hld* **10/3**[2]

-005 **3** *3 ¾* **Finch Flyer (IRE)**[54] 3155 3-7-7 **51** oh4.....................(p) HarryBentley[(7)] 7 55
(G L Moore) *hld up towards rr of midfield: struggling 4f out: styd on fr wl over 1f out to chse ldng pair ent fnl f but nvr any ch* **8/1**

000 **4** *1 ¾* **Rio Prince**[21] 4257 3-8-1 **52** oh3 ow1................................ NeilChalmers 9 53
(J J Bridger) *s.i.s: towards rr: rdn 3f out: no imp tl styd on fr 2f out* **100/1**

0035 **5** *7* **Smart Endeavour (USA)**[16] 4422 4-9-12 **68**...............(v[1]) ChrisCatlin 4 55
(W R Swinburn) *trckd ldrs: rdn 2f out: fdd jst ins fnl f* **14/1**

6032 **6** *2* **Gallego**[10] 4620 8-9-5 **61**.. JimCrowley 3 44
(R J Price) *hld up: rdn and stdy hdwy on rails fr over 3f out: swtchd lft 2f out: nvr rchd ldrs: wknd ent fnl f* **11/4**[1]

-043 **7** *4* **Recalcitrant**[23] 4201 7-9-4 **60**.. KierenFallon 8 35
(S Dow) *s.i.s: towards rr: hdwy into midfield over 4f out: rdn and nt clr run whn squeezed out wl over 1f out: wknd ent fnl f* **7/2**[3]

-002 **8** *1 ¾* **Qaraqum (USA)**[20] 4281 3-8-4 **55**...................................... TadhgO'Shea 1 26
(D J Coakley) *in tch: rdn 3f out: sn btn* **20/1**

-605 **9** *¾* **Merrymadcap (IRE)**[5] 4794 8-9-4 **65**................................. JohnFahy[(5)] 11 35
(Miss Tor Sturgis) *led tl over 3f out: sn rdn: wknd 2f out* **33/1**

2042 **10** *2 ½* **Markhesa**[13] 4498 4-8-13 **62**.. JamesRogers[(7)] 5 27
(J R Boyle) *hld up towards rr: hdwy over 3f out: sn rdn: wknd wl over 1f out* **14/1**

2m 9.05s (-0.85) **Going Correction** 0.0s/f (Good)
WFA 3 from 4yo+ 9lb **10** Ran SP% **116.9**
Speed ratings (Par 103): **103,101,98,96,91 89,86,85,84,82**
toteswingers: 1&2 £7.10, 1&3 £14.20, 2&3 £8.10 CSF £32.34 CT £209.09 TOTE £11.60: £3.40, £1.10, £3.10; EX 42.90.
Owner P J Cave **Bred** P J Cave **Trained** Lambourn, Berks

FOCUS
The time was 0.12 seconds quicker than earlier steadily run Listed contest won by Alsace Lorraine.
Recalcitrant Official explanation: jockey said gelding was denied a clear run

4959 AXMINSTER CARPETS RACING EXCELLENCE APPRENTICE H'CAP (WHIPS SHALL BE CARRIED BUT NOT USED) 6f 212y
5:10 (5:11) (Class 5) (0-70,69) 3-Y-0+ **£3,238** (£963; £481; £240) **Stalls** Centre

Form RPR

4005 **1** **Foxtrot Alpha (IRE)**[22] 4232 4-8-11 **53**..................... JamesRogers[(3)] 10 59
(P Winkworth) *mde all: kpt on gamely ins fnl f: hld on* **4/1**[2]

-534 **2** *nk* **Pebblesonthebeach**[16] 4425 3-9-7 **69**..........................(p) HollyHall[(3)] 11 72
(J W Hills) *unsettled stalls: slowly away: towards rr: swtchd lft to centre over 2f out: str run nrest stands' side fnl f: wnt 2nd nr fin: jst failed to rch wnr* **9/2**[3]

0300 **3** *¾* **Rio Royale (IRE)**[25] 4130 4-9-0 **56**...........................(p) NatashaEaton[(3)] 5 59
(Mrs A J Perrett) *wnt rt s: chsd wnr: ch over 1f out: kpt on ins fnl f: hld fnl 110yds: lost 2nd nr fin* **10/1**

0-00 **4** *½* **Sir Tom**[18] 4382 5-8-9 **48** oh2... RyanClark 1 50
(J J Bridger) *towards rr: pushed along after 2f: stdy prog fr over 2f out: swtchd rt over 1f out: styd on* **33/1**

2655 **5** *2 ¾* **Song To The Moon (IRE)**[28] 4022 3-9-5 **69**........(v[1]) FrancisHayes[(5)] 12 61
(A M Balding) *mid-div: styd on same pce fnl 2f: nvr threatened ldrs* **7/1**

0230 **6** *hd* **Eye For The Girls**[25] 4130 4-9-1 **54**.. AmyScott 9 48
(M R Channon) *chsd ldrs: rdn 3f out: kpt on same pce fnl f* **6/1**

6-00 **7** *½* **Croeso Ynol**[8] 4681 4-8-4 **48** oh3.............................. MatthewCosham[(5)] 4 41
(H J Evans) *chsd ldrs: rdn over 3f out: one pce fnl 2f* **33/1**

3050 **8** *2 ¾* **Shaded Edge**[27] 4044 6-10-0 **67**... DebraEngland 8 52
(D W P Arbuthnot) *mid-div: hdwy 2f out: wknd fnl f* **7/2**[1]

0400 **9** *2* **So Surreal (IRE)**[63] 2871 3-9-4 **66**............................(b) HarryBentley[(3)] 3 44
(G L Moore) *chsd ldrs: rdn 3f out: edgd lft over 1f out: wknd* **8/1**

5060 **10** *5* **Louie's Lad**[29] 3979 4-8-6 **48** oh3...........................(v) SophieSilvester[(3)] 6 14
(J J Bridger) *squeezed up sn after s: sn in mid-div: wknd 2f out* **40/1**

00-0 **11** *39* **Manchestermaverick (USA)**[11] 4591 5-8-9 **51**...(bt[1]) RichardRowe[(3)] 7 —
(Dr J R J Naylor) *squeezed out s: a struggling in rr* **40/1**

1m 30.63s (1.63) **Going Correction** +0.175s/f (Good)
WFA 3 from 4yo+ 6lb **11** Ran SP% **118.2**
Speed ratings (Par 103): **97,96,95,95,92 91,91,88,85,80 35**
toteswingers: 1&2 £5.20, 1&3 £7.70, 2&3 £7.40 CSF £21.87 CT £170.24 TOTE £4.30: £1.20, £1.20, £4.00; EX 28.30 Place 6 £50.25, Place 5 £37.39..
Owner Looks A Bright Prospect Racing & Partner **Bred** Irish National Stud **Trained** Chiddingfold, Surrey

FOCUS
A modest handicap in which these apprentices were not allowed to use their whips.
Pebblesonthebeach ◆ Official explanation: jockey said gelding hung left-handed
Manchestermaverick(USA) Official explanation: vet said gelding bled from the nose
T/Plt: £36.00 to a £1 stake. Pool: £50,927.14. 1,030.63 winning tickets. T/Qpdt: £18.50 to a £1 stake. Pool: £3,445.87. 137.70 winning tickets. TM

4753 SANDOWN (R-H)
Wednesday, August 11

OFFICIAL GOING: Good (good to soft in places)
Rail dolled out 4yds from mile to winning post adding about 5yds to races on round course.
Wind: Virtually nil Weather: Bright early

4960 BERRYLANDS MAIDEN STKS 5f 6y
5:30 (5:33) (Class 5) 2-Y-0 **£2,590** (£770; £385; £192)

Form RPR

1 **Jerrazzi (IRE)** 2-9-3 0.. GeorgeBaker 13 73
(G L Moore) *trckd ldrs: rdn and qcknd to ld fnl 120yds: hld on wl* **10/1**

6 **2** *hd* **Cruiser**[10] 4622 2-9-3 0.. FrankieDettori 8 72
(W R Muir) *chsd ldr: led wl over 1f out: rdn and hdd fnl 120yds: rallied last strides but a jst hld* **11/8**[1]

60 **3** *1 ½* **Forty Proof (IRE)**[10] 4622 2-9-3 0...................................... ShaneKelly 7 67
(W J Knight) *chsd ldrs: rdn and hdwy to take 3rd ins fnl f: kpt on but no imp* **15/2**[3]

4 *½* **Cristaliyev** 2-9-3 0.. PatCosgrave 1 65
(J R Boyle) *in tch: rdn 2f out: styd on wl fnl f to cl on 3rd but no imp on ldng duo* **66/1**

5 *1 ½* **Ma Quillet** 2-8-12 0.. DaneO'Neill 14 54+
(H Candy) *slowly away: in rr: gd prog and pushed along fr 1/2-way: styd on fnl f* **16/1**

5 **6** *¾* **Hackett (IRE)**[11] 4590 2-9-3 0.. SebSanders 6 57
(M Quinn) *chsd ldrs in 3rd: rdn 2f out: wknd ins fnl f* **40/1**

00 **7** *nk* **High Avon**[26] 4110 2-9-3 0.................................... FrankieMcDonald 5 56
(D K Ivory) *s.i.s: rdn 1/2-way: sme hdwy and swtchd lft over 1f out: kpt on same pce ins fnl f* **80/1**

0 **8** *nk* **Tweenie (IRE)**[23] 4203 2-8-12 0.. PatDobbs 11 50
(R Hannon) *in rr: sme hdwy 2f out: nvr rchd ldrs* **28/1**

9 *2 ¼* **Whistle On By** 2-9-3 0.. MichaelHills 4 48+
(B W Hills) *in rr: sme late prog* **12/1**

5 **10** *½* **High Class Lady**[14] 4474 2-8-12 0.................................... AdamKirby 12 40
(W R Swinburn) *s.i.s: nt rcvr and a outpcd* **5/1**[2]

0 **11** *2 ¾* **Shostakovich (IRE)**[89] 2078 2-9-3 0.................................. SteveDrowne 2 38
(S Kirk) *covered 2f after false s: sn led: hdd wl over 1f out: rn green and wknd ins fnl f* **16/1**

12 *2 ½* **Ganesa** 2-8-12 0.. TobyAtkinson[(5)] 10 41+
(M Botti) *v.s.a: sme prog 1/2-way but nt rcvr* **10/1**

30 **13** *nse* **Callipygos**[118] 1324 2-8-5 0.. LeonnaMayor[(7)] 9 21
(P S McEntee) *racd wd: a outpcd* **100/1**

62.98 secs (1.38) **Going Correction** +0.125s/f (Good) **13** Ran SP% **117.8**
Speed ratings (Par 94): **93,92,90,89,87 85,85,84,81,80 76,72,72**
toteswingers:1&2:£6.10, 1&3:£5.10, 2&3:£2.80 CSF £23.28 TOTE £14.00: £2.60, £1.70, £2.60; EX 36.20.
Owner Philip V Simpson **Bred** Jaykayenn Syndicate **Trained** Lower Beeding, W Sussex

FOCUS
There was 10mm of rain the previous day and the going was officially described as good, good to soft in places. The rail was moved out four yards from 1m to the winning post, adding approximately five yards to races on the round course. There did not seem to be much strength in depth in this maiden. There was a flag start because the stall handlers had not arrived due to traffic problems. After one false start they eventually got going but the bare form looks ordinary rated around the placed horses.

NOTEBOOK
Jerrazzi(IRE) did well to manoeuvre himself away from potential traffic problems and put in a professional display to make a winning debut. He is closely related to useful sprinter Parisian Pyramid and his sales price shot up to 46,000euros in May after being led out unsold at 2,000euros as a foal. The form is probably not very strong, but he looks to have a decent attitude and could go on to better things. (op 8-1)
Cruiser was not beaten far in midfield in a 6f Newbury maiden on debut this month, form which gave him strong claims in this weaker event. Always well positioned after the flag start, it looked like he was going to collect after hitting the front but he was overhauled after being matched at 1.07 in-running on the exchanges. He should be able to gain compensation if switched to slightly more patient tactics next time and a Mill Reef entry suggests he is highly regarded. (op 15-8 tchd 2-1 in places)
Forty Proof(IRE) put in his third respectable effort. He is a half-brother to Sirenuse, a progressive dual 5f winner, but on the evidence so far he looks more of a nursery type than a potential maiden winner. Official explanation: jockey said colt ran green (op 7-1 tchd 8-1)
Cristaliyev, a first foal of a 7f/1m2f winner, did some good late work out wide and should improve for his first run.
Ma Quillet also showed some debut promise on debut, staying on steadily from some way back. She is related to a couple of fair winners at up to 1m. (op 12-1)
High Class Lady showed up well for a long way when 16-1 for a Leicester maiden on debut, but she was never involved dropped back in trip on her second run. (op 11-2)
Ganesa was still circling and lost about five lengths when the runners set off. She can be forgiven this debut effort. (op 9-1)

4961 WATCH RACING UK ON SKY CHANNEL 432 H'CAP — 5f 6y
6:00 (6:04) (Class 4) (0-80,76) 4-Y-O+ **£3,885** (£1,156; £577; £288) **Stalls** High

Form				RPR
0003	**1**		**Tagula Night (IRE)**[35] 3779 4-9-8 **75**.....(vt) AdamKirby 11 (W R Swinburn) *trckd ldrs: wnt 2nd wl over 1f out: drvn to ld ins fnl f: r.o strly* **5/1**[2]	87
3523	**2**	1 ½	**Cape Royal**[10] 4625 10-9-7 **74**.....(bt) PatCosgrave 13 (J M Bradley) *led: rdn and hdd ins fnl f: sn nt pce of wnr but kpt on wl for 2nd* **13/2**[3]	81
4015	**3**	1 ¾	**The Wee Chief (IRE)**[32] 3914 4-9-1 **68**..... PatDobbs 10 (J C Fox) *s.i.s: in rr: hdwy on ins over 1f out: fin wl to take 3rd ins fnl f but no imp on ldng duo* **7/1**	68
6000	**4**	nse	**Even Bolder**[17] 4401 7-9-1 **73**..... KierenFox(5) 8 (E A Wheeler) *mid-div: rdn and hdwy fr 2f out: styd on to take 4th ins fnl f but nvr gng pce to chal* **16/1**	73
4006	**5**	3	**The Jobber (IRE)**[13] 4518 9-8-11 **64**..... SebSanders 7 (M Blanshard) *towards rr: effrt and nt clr run over 1f out: r.o ins fnl f but nt trble ldrs* **16/1**	53
532	**6**	hd	**Doctor Hilary**[9] 4659 8-8-12 **65**..... FrankieDettori 1 (M R Hoad) *towards rr: rdn 1/2-way: styd on fnl f but nvr gng pce to get into contention* **12/1**	54+
5261	**7**	hd	**Brynfa Boy**[20] 4292 4-9-0 **76**.....(t) TonyCulhane 9 (P W D'Arcy) *in tch: trckd ldrs and rdn ins fnl 2f: no imp and wknd ins fnl f* **4/1**[1]	64
1340	**8**	1	**Tubby Isaacs**[12] 4551 6-9-9 **76**..... SteveDrowne 4 (D K Ivory) *s.i.s: outpcd: mod prog fnl f* **7/1**	60+
2310	**9**	7	**Triple Dream**[4] 4836 5-9-8 **75**.....(p) LiamKeniry 2 (J M Bradley) *chsd ldrs 3f* **16/1**	34
1012	**10**	2	**Ajjaadd (USA)**[60] 2973 4-9-4 **71**..... GeorgeBaker 6 (T E Powell) *chsd ldr: rdn 2f out: wknd qckly appr fnl f* **13/2**[3]	23

61.48 secs (-0.12) **Going Correction** +0.125s/f (Good) **10** Ran SP% **113.7**
Speed ratings (Par 105): **105,102,99,99,94 94,94,92,81,78**
toteswingers:1&2:£5.30, 1&3:£7.30, 2&3:£7.20 CSF £36.48 CT £190.37 TOTE £6.70: £2.50, £2.90, £4.00; EX 34.00.
Owner Hufford, Moss & Papworth **Bred** Carpet Lady Partnership **Trained** Aldbury, Herts

FOCUS
A competitive handicap, in which several of the runners were dropping back from 6f. The pace was not particularly strong and hardly anything got into it from behind. The first two set the level.
Ajjaadd(USA) Official explanation: trainer said gelding finished distressed

4962 CHAMPAGNE LANSON ROSE BRUT N.V. MEDIAN AUCTION MAIDEN STKS — 7f 16y
6:35 (6:40) (Class 5) 2-Y-O **£3,238** (£963; £481; £240) **Stalls** High

Form				RPR
03	**1**		**Mr Perceptive (IRE)**[14] 4490 2-9-3 0..... RichardHughes 3 (R Hannon) *mde all: drvn and qckned fr 2f out: rdn and kpt on wl fnl f and a jst doing enough* **9/4**[2]	79
0	**2**	hd	**Gay Gallivanter**[42] 3562 2-8-12 0..... WilliamBuick 8 (J H M Gosden) *chsd wnr: rdn appr fnl 2f and one pce but styd in 2nd: rallied and kpt on wl thrght fnl f: clsng on line but a jst hld* **11/2**[3]	73
	3	5	**Torun City** 2-9-3 0..... SebSanders 2 (Eve Johnson Houghton) *hld up towards rr: gd hdwy on outside over 2f out: sn rdn: edgd rt and rn green whn taking 3rd over 1f out but nvr any ch w ldng duo* **33/1**	65
0	**4**	1 ¼	**All The Evil (IRE)**[32] 3915 2-9-3 0..... MartinDwyer 10 (B J Meehan) *s.i.s: sn chsng ldrs and wnt 3rd 4f out: rdn and one pce over 2f out: wknd into 4th over 1f out* **8/1**	62
	5	½	**Tanfeeth** 2-9-3 0..... RichardHills 4 (E A L Dunlop) *s.i.s: in rr: shkn up and r.o fnl 2f: nvr any threat* **13/8**[1]	62+
000	**6**	1 ¾	**Cantonese Cat (IRE)**[25] 4131 2-9-3 0..... ShaneKelly 6 (B J Meehan) *racd in 3rd 3f: rdn over 2f out wknd wl over 1f out* **50/1**	56
	7	nse	**Norse Blues** 2-9-3 0..... LiamKeniry 5 (S Kirk) *plld hrd in rr: rdn: green and no prog whn nt clr run over 2f out: sn wknd* **20/1**	55+
	8	1 ½	**Geordie Iris (IRE)** 2-8-12 0..... PatDobbs 7 (R Hannon) *towards rr most of way* **10/1**	46

1m 33.3s (3.80) **Going Correction** +0.325s/f (Good) **8** Ran SP% **114.1**
Speed ratings (Par 94): **91,90,85,83,83 81,81,79**
toteswingers:1&2:£2.70, 1&3:£4.50, 2&3:£32.40 CSF £14.71 TOTE £4.90: £1.90, £1.90, £10.70; EX 14.80.
Owner One More Time **Bred** Barnane Stud **Trained** East Everleigh, Wilts

FOCUS
A maiden severely weakened by the withdrawal of the two leading form contenders. The pace was fairly steady. The first two filled those positions throughout and finished a long way clear of the rest with the winner rated a slight improver on latest course form.

NOTEBOOK
Mr Perceptive(IRE) left his debut form well behind when third in a C&D maiden last month. He set the standard for the others to aim at and put in a feisty front-running display, despite racing a bit awkwardly around the final bend. It is hard to gauge the value of this form, but he looks a scopey and progressive type who should stay a bit further than this. (tchd 2-1 and 11-4)
Gay Gallivanter compromised her chance by pulling hard on debut at Kempton in June. She was again keen early on, but gave it a good shot to try and run down the all-the-way winner. This represents a decent step forward and there could be quite a bit more to come from the half-sister to fairly useful dual 6f winner Pumpkin. (op 7-1)
Torun City shaped with quite a bit of promise on debut, doing best of the runners who came from behind. By Sulamani out of an unraced half-sister to a Middle Park winner, there are mixed messages on breeding regarding trip requirements, but on this initial evidence it looks like 7f-1m could suit this season. (op 20-1)
All The Evil(IRE) was always towards rear after a slow start on debut, but there were signs of ability this time from a colt who is related to a stack of winners at distances ranging from 5f-1m4f. (tchd 15-2)
Tanfeeth ◆ could never got involved under a patient ride on debut, but it was very interesting that the Royal Lodge-entered colt was a big market mover throughout the day. He should have learned a lot and could step up significantly next time. (op 2-1 tchd 9-4)
Norse Blues took a strong hold and was never a factor on debut. (op 18-1 tchd 25-1 and 33-1 in a place)

4963 CHELSEA FC EDUCATION CENTRE'S H'CAP — 7f 16y
7:10 (7:10) (Class 3) (0-90,88) 3-Y-O **£5,828** (£1,734; £866; £432) **Stalls** High

Form				RPR
310-	**1**		**Thrill**[284] 7187 3-9-2 **81**..... WilliamBuick 6 (J H M Gosden) *trckd ldrs: drvn to ld jst ins fnl 2f: drvn and hld on wl thrght fnl f* **4/1**[2]	92+
1-	**2**	nk	**Asraab (IRE)**[285] 7145 3-9-6 **85**..... FrankieDettori 8 (Saeed Bin Suroor) *trckd ldrs: nt clr run 2f out: swtchd lft and hdwy over 1f out and chsd wnr sn after: kpt on wl fnl f and clsng nr fin but a jst hld* **6/5**[1]	95+
0131	**3**	1	**Merchant Of Medici**[18] 4365 3-8-9 **74**..... MartinDwyer 3 (W R Muir) *t.k.h towards rr: rdn over 2f out: styd on to take 3rd cl home but no imp on ldng duo* **28/1**	81
2240	**4**	nk	**Rule Of Nature**[12] 4541 3-9-3 **82**..... ShaneKelly 4 (Sir Michael Stoute) *hld up towards rr: hdwy and nt clr run appr fnl 2f: stl n.m.r whn drvn to take 3rd over 1f out: sn fnd no ex u.p ins fnl f and lost 3rd cl home* **12/1**	88
3322	**5**	1	**First Cat**[18] 4377 3-9-6 **85**..... RichardHughes 2 (R Hannon) *stdd s: hld up in rr: hdwy on outside over 2f out: no imp whn edgd rt u.p over 1f out* **6/1**[3]	89
1301	**6**	3	**Whirly Dancer**[20] 4287 3-9-6 **85**..... IanMongan 11 (H R A Cecil) *s.i.s: in rr: hdwy on outside over 2f out: no imp and hung rt u.p over 1f out and sn btn* **8/1**	81
0221	**7**	nk	**Rolling Hills (IRE)**[18] 4364 3-8-5 **70**..... FrankieMcDonald 9 (H Candy) *chsd ldr: chal fr 4f out: rdn and upsides fr over 2f out: wknd over 1f out* **33/1**	65
162-	**8**	2 ¼	**Brick Red**[304] 6693 3-9-5 **84**..... LiamKeniry 5 (A M Balding) *chsd ldrs: rdn over 2f out: wknd and bmpd sn after* **12/1**	73+
5020	**9**	7	**Planet Red (IRE)**[23] 4204 3-9-5 **84**.....(b¹) PatDobbs 10 (R Hannon) *led: jnd fr 4f out: hdd jst ins fnl 2f: sn btn* **40/1**	54

1m 31.04s (1.54) **Going Correction** +0.325s/f (Good) **9** Ran SP% **115.1**
Speed ratings (Par 104): **104,103,102,102,101 97,97,94,86**
toteswingers:1&2:£2.70, 1&3:£21.80, 2&3:£4.80 CSF £8.98 CT £114.80 TOTE £4.90: £1.30, £1.10, £6.40; EX 11.90.
Owner Cheveley Park Stud **Bred** Cheveley Park Stud Ltd **Trained** Newmarket, Suffolk

FOCUS
A fascinating handicap which was dominated by two well-related runners who were both returning from a lengthy layoff. It was a bit of a messy race but the form looks sound overall and probably worth following.

NOTEBOOK
Thrill won a soft-ground Salisbury maiden with plenty in hand last October before being well held in a Listed race. She was a springer in the market for her comeback/handicap debut and showed a resilient attitude to get back in the groove. A sister to high-class 7f/1m performer Infallible, she should not go up much for this second win and could have quite a bit more scope to successfully operate in handicaps for a powerful yard. She has shown her best form on a slow surface, but has a fluent action and may not be inconvenienced by fast ground. (op 8-1 tchd 7-2)
Asraab(IRE) ◆ had numerous winners behind when justifying favouritism in a 6f Newmarket maiden on debut last October. He was a heavily backed favourite in his bid to defy an absence and strike on handicap debut, but he ran into some traffic problems and couldn't quite reel in the winner after a gap appeared. The 220,000euros colt has a good cruising speed and shouldn't have too much trouble gaining compensation for this hard-luck story. (op 5-4 tchd Evens and 6-4 in a place and 11-8 in places)
Merchant Of Medici also found some trouble before finishing well to snatch third. This was big effort in his bid to defy a 6lb rise for his Lingfield win in a lower grade last time. (op 22-1 tchd 33-1 in a place)
Rule Of Nature had a brief barging match with a couple of rivals before staying on steadily. She found things happening too quickly at 5f last time, but this was a decent effort back at 7f. She is still chasing a first win, but her form stacks up quite well and she should be able to strike away from progressive types. (op 9-1)
First Cat put in another respectable effort. He is a reliable type and the reason he tilts his head to one side is probably a result of him being blind in his right eye. (op 11-2 tchd 13-2)
Whirly Dancer put a rare blip behind her when reeling in a subsequent winner at Doncaster last time, but she was a drifter in her bid to defy a 3lb rise and could never land a serious blow before fading out wide. Official explanation: jockey said filly hung left final furlong (op 15-2 tchd 10-1)

4964 RUSSELL DURNFORD 40TH BIRTHDAY H'CAP — 1m 2f 7y
7:45 (7:45) (Class 4) (0-80,80) 3-Y-O **£3,885** (£1,156; £577; £288) **Stalls** High

Form				RPR
6124	**1**		**Scottish Boogie (IRE)**[12] 4532 3-8-13 **70**..... LiamKeniry 6 (S Kirk) *in tch: hdwy to chse ldrs 4f out: rdn: hung rt and led wl over 1f out: drvn and styd on strly ins fnl f* **16/1**	79
4220	**2**	1 ½	**Valiant Knight (FR)**[11] 4573 3-9-9 **80**..... RichardHughes 4 (R Hannon) *hld up towards rr: hdwy on ins fr 3f out: drvn to chse wnr ins fnl f but no imp* **5/2**[2]	85
2060	**3**	½	**Paintball (IRE)**[13] 4504 3-9-6 **77**..... MartinDwyer 1 (W R Muir) *in rr: hdwy on outside over 2f out: styd on u.p to go 3rd ins fnl f: one pce* **4/1**[3]	81
1303	**4**	2	**Ostentation**[13] 4501 3-8-10 **70**..... MatthewDavies(3) 5 (R A Teal) *chsd ldr: rdn to chal fr over 2f out: one pce whn hmpd wl over 1f out: wknd ins fnl f* **8/1**	70
320	**5**	5	**Blitzed**[18] 4360 3-9-1 **72**..... GeorgeBaker 2 (G L Moore) *towards rr: rdn over 2f out: nvr in contention* **25/1**	62
303	**6**	6	**Weathervane**[54] 3173 3-9-5 **76**..... WilliamBuick 8 (J H M Gosden) *led: rdn over 2f out: hdd wl over 1f out and sn btn* **13/8**[1]	54

54-5 **7** *40* **Seaside Sizzler**[16] 4425 3-9-3 **74** .... JimCrowley 7 —
(R M Beckett) *chsd ldrs: rdn and wknd over 3f out: eased whn no ch fr over 1f out: t.o* **16/1**

2m 13.59s (3.09) **Going Correction** +0.325s/f (Good) **7** Ran SP% **113.4**
Speed ratings (Par 102): **100,98,98,96,92 88,56**
toteswingers:1&2:£2.90, 1&3:£12.40, 2&3:£2.70 CSF £55.11 CT £196.25 TOTE £18.10: £8.10, £1.10; EX 71.80.
Owner J C Smith **Bred** Littleton Stud **Trained** Upper Lambourn, Berks

FOCUS
They went a fair pace for this three-year-old handicap, which was won in good style by one of the more exposed runners. The form looks solid rated around the first three.

4965 J20 WHITE BLEND SUMMER SERIES H'CAP 1m 6f
8:15 (8:15) (Class 4) (0-80,75) 3-Y-O **£3,885** (£1,156; £577; £288) **Stalls** High

Form RPR

-042 **1** **Sidney Melbourne (USA)**[32] 3909 3-9-9 **75** .... SteveDrowne 2 81
(J R Best) *racd in 3rd: drvn and styd on fr over 2f out: led wl over 1f out: pushed out fnl f* **7/1**[3]

-221 **2** *1 3/4* **Tuscan Gold**[14] 4493 3-9-9 **75** .... SebSanders 5 79+
(Sir Mark Prescott) *hld up in rr: swtchd lft to outside and stdy hdwy fr 3f out: rdn to chse ldrs 2f out: nvr quite on terms and styd on same pce fnl f* **8/11**[1]

0-01 **3** *1/2* **Killusty Fancy (IRE)**[66] 2792 3-9-1 **67** .... JamesDoyle 1 70
(D J S Ffrench Davis) *chsd clr ldr: rdn to ld over 2f out: hdd wl over 1f out: one pce fnl f* **33/1**

0232 **4** *1* **Yankee Bright (USA)**[12] 4557 3-9-4 **70** .... LeeVickers 6 72+
(J G Given) *led: 10 l clr 1/2-way: rdn and hdd over 2f out: hmpd on ins: lost pl and swtchd lft sn after: r.o again ins fnl f* **20/1**

0352 **5** *1/2* **Old Hundred (IRE)**[20] 4290 3-9-9 **75** .... AdamKirby 4 76
(J R Fanshawe) *in rr: hdwy 3f out: one pce whn hung rt wl over 1f out: n.d after* **11/4**[2]

2-02 **6** *15* **Cast Of Stars (IRE)**[22] 4227 3-9-6 **72** ....(p) JimCrowley 3 52
(R M Beckett) *chsd ldrs: wknd fr 2f out* **12/1**

3m 16.09s (11.59) **Going Correction** +0.325s/f (Good) **6** Ran SP% **112.5**
Speed ratings (Par 102): **79,78,77,77,76 68**
toteswingers:1&2:£1.20, 1&3:£18.50, 2&3:£4.10 CSF £12.73 TOTE £8.90: £2.50, £1.50; EX 16.80 Place 6 £40.66, Place 5 £26.21..
Owner Mrs A M Riney **Bred** Sun Valley Farm & Jeffrey Johnson **Trained** Hucking, Kent

FOCUS
An interesting staying handicap involving mostly unexposed runners. However, on the downside the time was over 17 seconds slower than standard and they finished in a bit of a bunch. Not surprisingly the form is muddling.
T/Plt: £268.00 to a £1 stake. Pool £49,854.17 - 135.79 winning tickets. T/Qpdt: £31.60 to a £1 stake. Pool £6,885.10 - 161.20 winning tickets. ST

4759 YARMOUTH (L-H)
Wednesday, August 11

OFFICIAL GOING: Good to soft (good in places) changing to good (good to soft in places) after race 1 (2.20)
Back straight and bend dolled out 3m, increasing races on round course by about 10yds.
Wind: Fresh across Weather: Cloudy with sunny spells

4966 EUROPEAN BREEDERS' FUND MAIDEN FILLIES' STKS 6f 3y
2:20 (2:22) (Class 5) 3-Y-O **£2,849** (£847; £423; £211) **Stalls** High

Form RPR

1 **Queen Of Mean** 3-9-0 0 .... NickyMackay 7 86+
(J H M Gosden) *chsd ldrs: pushed along 1/2-way: shkn up to ld ins fnl f: r.o wl* **5/2**[2]

P0 **2** *3 1/2* **Ming Meng (IRE)**[21] 4251 3-9-0 0 .... EddieAhern 9 75
(M L W Bell) *chsd ldr: rdn to ld and hung lft over 1f out: hdd and no ex ins fnl f* **12/1**

0- **3** *1* **Maany (USA)**[368] 4797 3-9-0 0 .... RichardMullen 5 72
(M A Jarvis) *edgd lft s: chsd ldrs: rdn over 1f out: no ex ins fnl f* **9/4**[1]

4 *4 1/2* **Meia Noite** 3-9-0 0 .... AlanMunro 2 57
(C F Wall) *hld up in tch: pushed along 1/2-way: wknd over 1f out* **16/1**

5 *1/2* **Rosie Gem** 3-9-0 0 .... RichardKingscote 6 56
(Tom Dascombe) *led: rdn: hung lft and hdd over 1f out: wknd fnl f* **7/1**[3]

6 *shd* **Citadella** 3-9-0 0 .... StevieDonohoe 8 55
(D M Simcock) *dwlt: sn prom: rdn and wknd over 1f out* **20/1**

0 **7** *1* **Bouncy Bouncy (IRE)**[21] 4251 3-9-0 0 .... TomQueally 1 52
(M L W Bell) *prom: rdn over 2f out: wknd over 1f out* **12/1**

0- **8** *2 1/2* **Arabian Jewel**[438] 2490 3-9-0 0 .... CathyGannon 3 44
(D M Simcock) *s.i.s: sn pushed along in rr: hdwy over 2f out: rdn and wknd over 1f out* **40/1**

9 *1* **Maid To Dream** 3-9-0 0 .... SaleemGolam 4 41
(J H M Gosden) *s.i.s and hmpd s: a in rr: wknd over 2f out* **7/1**[3]

1m 13.2s (-1.20) **Going Correction** +0.025s/f (Good) **9** Ran SP% **112.8**
Speed ratings (Par 97): **109,104,103,97,96 96,94,91,90**
toteswingers:1&2:£8.10, 1&3:£1.70, 2&3:£5.50 CSF £31.65 TOTE £3.20: £1.10, £4.50, £1.40; EX 20.50 Trifecta £52.90 Pool £444.73 - 6.21 winning units..
Owner Normandie Stud Ltd **Bred** Normandie Stud Ltd **Trained** Newmarket, Suffolk

FOCUS
A dry night after 5mm of rain during Tuesday meant that conditions had dried out and were good to soft (good in places) from good to soft overnight.Three Newmarket yards were doubly represented in this fillies' maiden and, with the runners with racecourse experience having shown little meaningful form, much interest concerned the newcomers.
Maany(USA) Official explanation: jockey said filly lost its action final furlong
Rosie Gem Official explanation: jockey said filly hung left

4967 GREAT YARMOUTH ADVERTISER CLAIMING STKS 7f 3y
2:50 (2:51) (Class 6) 2-Y-O **£1,813** (£539; £269; £134) **Stalls** High

Form RPR

0 **1** **History Repeating**[11] 4568 2-7-5 0 .... IanBurns(7) 1 53+
(M L W Bell) *s.i.s and drvn along early: swvd lft and hdwy over 5f out: led 2f out: edgd rt over 1f out: rdn and hung lft wl ins fnl f: r.o* **10/1**

350 **2** *1 1/4* **Ajaafa**[9] 4645 2-8-5 0 .... RichardMullen 4 56
(J G Given) *a.p: rdn to chse wnr ins fnl f: no ex towards fin* **7/4**[1]

0005 **3** *1 1/4* **Jealousy Defined (IRE)**[4] 4848 2-8-0 44 ....(p) JimmyQuinn 5 48
(N Tinkler) *chsd ldrs: rdn over 1f out: styd on same pce ins fnl f* **8/1**

0350 **4** *2* **Ivan's A Star (IRE)**[10] 4623 2-8-5 60 .... CathyGannon 6 48
(J S Moore) *led: rdn and hdd 2f out: no ex fnl f* **7/2**[2]

500 **5** *1 1/2* **Angle Knight (USA)**[75] 2493 2-8-10 51 ....(b[1]) Louis-PhilippeBeuzelin(3) 8 52
(B J Meehan) *hld up: rdn over 2f out: styd on: nt trble ldrs* **7/1**[3]

55 **6** *5* **Onlyfoalsandhorses (IRE)**[12] 4528 2-7-11 0 .... RyanPowell(7) 7 29
(J S Moore) *prom: racd keenly: rdn and wknd over 1f out* **20/1**

0060 **7** *1 3/4* **Ad Vitam (IRE)**[8] 4678 2-7-12 50 ....(t) SophieDoyle(5) 2 23
(S Kirk) *sn pushed along in rr: bhd fr 1/2-way* **33/1**

063 **8** *1/2* **Cinq Heavens (IRE)**[38] 3712 2-8-13 59 ....(p) RichardKingscote 3 32
(Tom Dascombe) *chsd ldrs: rdn 1/2-way: wknd over 2f out* **15/2**

1m 28.1s (1.50) **Going Correction** +0.025s/f (Good) **8** Ran SP% **110.8**
Speed ratings (Par 92): **92,90,89,86,85 79,77,76**
toteswingers:1&2:£5.80, 1&3:£28.30, 2&3:£2.50 CSF £26.20 TOTE £16.40: £5.70, £1.02, £1.90; EX 40.10 Trifecta £251.30 Part won. Pool £339.64 - 0.62 winning units..History Repeating was claimed by M. D. Usher for £4,000.
Owner C Wright & The Hon Mrs J M Corbett **Bred** Usk Valley Stud **Trained** Newmarket, Suffolk

FOCUS
A modest contest with some of the runners already beaten in selling grade.

NOTEBOOK
History Repeating attracted support in the morning, but drifted back out in price on course. She is related to three winners and has entries in the big sales races later in the season. It probably says plenty that she was dropped to this level having finished tailed off on her debut. She was by far the most talented performer in this race and overcame an eccentric passage to score with something in hand. She quite obviously is not straightforward and was later claimed by Mark Usher. She will need to be less erratic if she is going to progress to better races. (op 8-1)
Ajaafa was also trying this claiming grade for the first time. A little disappointing after a good effort on debut, he caught a tartar here in that the winner is far more talented than most animals he would come up against at this level. The trip looked perfectly suitable and he should manage a small race. (op 2-1)
Jealousy Defined(IRE) puts the race in perspective, having been beaten in a seller last time. The step up in trip looked ideal and she was ridden from the front. She just came up against two better horses, and a seller is within her abilities. (op 10-1)
Ivan's A Star(IRE) puts even more credence to the modest level of the form. This was his eighth start having been beaten in two sellers here on his two previous outings. He is probably better suited to 6f and a drop to selling grade again offers his best chance. (tchd 4-1)
Angle Knight(USA), despite the first-time blinkers, continues to regress after his initial outing. (tchd 17-2)
Onlyfoalsandhorses(IRE) was too keen early and faded tamely at the business end of the race. (op 16-1)

4968 CLIFF HOTEL "FOR ALL YOUR NEEDS" H'CAP 7f 3y
3:25 (3:25) (Class 5) (0-75,75) 3-Y-O+ **£2,201** (£655; £327; £163) **Stalls** High

Form RPR

5331 **1** **Sir Mozart (IRE)**[49] 3322 7-9-5 **65** .... TomQueally 2 74+
(B J Curley) *hld up and bhd: swtchd rt and hdwy over 1f out: shkn up to ld wl ins fnl f: readily* **11/4**[1]

4010 **2** *3/4* **Maze (IRE)**[33] 3863 5-9-13 **73** .... EddieAhern 7 80
(A W Carroll) *trckd ldr: plld hrd: led over 4f out: rdn: edgd rt and hdd wl ins fnl f* **8/1**

5146 **3** *1 3/4* **Rough Rock (IRE)**[7] 4717 5-9-0 **67** .... AdamBeschizza(7) 5 69
(C A Dwyer) *chsd ldrs: rdn over 1f out: styd on* **9/2**[3]

4054 **4** *1* **French Art**[18] 4354 5-9-7 **67** ....(p) KirstyMilczarek 4 67
(N Tinkler) *hld up: pushed along 4f out: hdwy 1/2-way: rdn and edgd rt over 1f out: no ex ins fnl f* **3/1**[2]

0306 **5** *3/4* **Cheddar George**[12] 4547 4-8-13 **62** ....(b[1]) Louis-PhilippeBeuzelin(3) 3 60
(B J Meehan) *awkward leaving stalls: hld up: hdwy over 4f out: rdn over 2f out: no ex fnl f* **5/1**

0604 **6** *1 1/2* **Lordship (IRE)**[8] 4681 6-9-0 **65** .... SophieDoyle(5) 6 59
(A W Carroll) *led: hdd over 4f out: styd on same pce appr fnl f* **9/1**

1100 **7** *1/2* **Catherines Call (IRE)**[76] 2475 3-9-4 **75** .... SimonPearce(5) 8 65
(D Donovan) *hld up: hdwy over 2f out: rdn over 1f out: wknd ins fnl f* **16/1**

1m 27.29s (0.69) **Going Correction** +0.025s/f (Good)
WFA 3 from 4yo+ 6lb **7** Ran SP% **113.5**
Speed ratings (Par 103): **97,96,94,93,92 90,89**
toteswingers:1&2:£3.50, 1&3:£1.80, 2&3:£5.60 CSF £24.52 CT £94.72 TOTE £3.50: £1.10, £5.70; EX 37.30 Trifecta £94.90 Pool £289.96 - 2.26 winning units..
Owner P A Byrne **Bred** Western Bloodstock **Trained** Newmarket, Suffolk

FOCUS
A tight looking handicap with morning support on the exchanges for three of the contestants. The pace was only fair but the winner showed a good trun of foot to score.
Rough Rock(IRE) Official explanation: trainer said gelding had been struck into

4969 MERRIVALE MODEL VILLAGE GREAT YARMOUTH H'CAP 1m 3y
3:55 (3:56) (Class 6) (0-65,65) 3-Y-O+ **£2,072** (£616; £308; £153) **Stalls** High

Form RPR

5065 **1** **Cool Kitten (IRE)**[16] 4439 3-8-2 **53** ....(v) AdamBeschizza(7) 15 62
(W J Knight) *mde all: rdn over 1f out: edgd rt: styd on* **17/2**

-000 **2** *1/2* **Big Sur**[16] 4439 4-9-1 **52** .... StevieDonohoe 12 61
(T Keddy) *chsd ldrs: rdn over 2f out: sn outpcd: rallied over 1f out: r.o* **20/1**

0/01 **3** *1 1/2* **Colinca's Lad (IRE)**[7] 4715 8-9-2 **53** .... EddieCreighton 10 59
(P Charalambous) *hld up in tch: plld hrd: rdn over 1f out: styd on* **11/8**[1]

3030 **4** *1* **Easy Wonder (GER)**[6] 4763 5-8-9 **46** oh1 .... RichardMullen 16 49
(I A Wood) *mid-div: hdwy 1/2-way: rdn over 1f out: hung lft and styd on ins fnl f* **20/1**

-000 **5** *1 1/2* **Grand Vizier (IRE)**[100] 1767 6-10-0 **65** .... KirstyMilczarek 3 65
(C F Wall) *hld up: hdwy 1/2-way: rdn over 1f out: edgd rt and no ex fnl f* **7/1**[2]

-000 **6** *5* **Trecase**[16] 4425 3-8-12 **56** .... TomQueally 2 43+
(A W Carroll) *hld up: rdn over 2f out: styd on ins fnl f: nvr nrr* **8/1**[3]

6204 **7** *1* **Clearing House**[13] 4498 5-8-10 **47** .... SaleemGolam 14 33
(J Ryan) *chsd ldrs: rdn over 2f out: wknd over 1f out* **8/1**[3]

0350 **8** *3 1/4* **Charpoy Cobra**[19] 4335 3-8-5 **52** .... Louis-PhilippeBeuzelin(3) 1 30
(J A R Toller) *prom: rdn 1/2-way: wknd 2f out* **7/1**[2]

500- **9** *3/4* **Toballa**[242] 7727 5-8-9 **46** oh1 ....(t) JimmyQuinn 5 23
(H J Collingridge) *prom: racd keenly: lost pl 4f out: in rr whn nt clr run wl over 2f out: styd on ins fnl f* **25/1**

0-00 **10** *hd* **Hilltop Alchemy**[23] 4213 4-8-6 **46** oh1 ....(b) AndrewHeffernan(3) 11 22
(J R Jenkins) *s.i.s: hld up: sme hdwy 1/2-way: wknd 2f out* **100/1**

5000 **11** *shd* **Whotsit (IRE)**[7] 4715 4-9-0 **51** ....(b) JerryO'Dwyer 13 27
(Miss Amy Weaver) *s.s: hld up: rdn 1/2-way: sme hdwy u.p over 2f out: sn wknd* **25/1**

0050 **12** *1 3/4* **Tipperary Tickle**[3] 4864 3-7-11 **46** oh1 ....(v) SimonPearce(5) 4 17
(J R Weymes) *hld up: bhd fr 1/2-way* **40/1**

065 **13** *2* **Slap And Tickle (IRE)**[11] 4596 4-8-11 **48** .... WilliamCarson 8 15
(M D Squance) *stdd s: hld up: plld hrd: rdn over 2f out: a in rr* **33/1**

-000 **14** *7* **Hilltop Legacy**[83] 2257 7-8-3 **47** ....(b) DannyBrock(7) 6 —
(J R Jenkins) *edgd rt sn after s: chsd ldrs tl wknd over 2f out* **66/1**

54-0 **15** 2 1/2 **Avec Moi**[106] 1605 3-8-2 **46** oh1 NickyMackay 7 —
(Mrs C A Dunnett) *prom: hmpd and lost pl sn after s: racd keenly in rr: rdn and wknd over 2f out* **66/1**

1m 41.24s (0.64) **Going Correction** +0.025s/f (Good)
WFA 3 from 4yo+ 7lb **15** Ran SP% **126.4**
Speed ratings (Par 101): **97,96,95,94,92 87,86,83,82,82 82,80,78,71,68**
toteswingers:1&2:£52.30, 1&3:£4.70, 2&3:£18.70 CSF £174.33 CT £381.33 TOTE £5.80: £1.60, £9.10, £1.10; EX 170.70 TRIFECTA Not won..
Owner G Roddick **Bred** David Jamison Bloodstock **Trained** Patching, W Sussex

FOCUS
A weak looking handicap, with ten of the 15 starters still retaining their maiden status.
Whotsit(IRE) Official explanation: jockey said gelding moved poorly closing stages

4970 FREE RACING WITH ODDSCHECKER.COM WEDNESDAYS H'CAP 7f 3y
4:30 (4:32) (Class 6) (0-55,55) 3-Y-O **£2,072** (£616; £308; £153) **Stalls** High

Form				RPR
5-50	**1**		**Franki J**[5] 4775 3-8-1 **47** SophieDoyle(5) 10 (D Donovan) *mde all: rdn and hung rt over 1f out: styd on wl* **14/1**	56
30-0	**2**	2 1/4	**Hellenio**[23] 4210 3-8-12 **53** (t) AndreaAtzeni 14 (M G Quinlan) *chsd ldrs: rdn and ev ch over 1f out: styd on same pce ins fnl f* **8/1**	56
030	**3**	3	**Dreamacha**[45] 3484 3-8-12 **53** WilliamCarson 16 (S C Williams) *chsd ldrs: rdn and ev ch over 1f out: no ex ins fnl f* **7/1**[3]	48
0505	**4**	3/4	**Zelos Spirit**[8] 4687 3-8-0 **46** oh1 SimonPearce(5) 7 (Rae Guest) *hld up: hdwy over 2f out: sn rdn: styd on u.p: nt trble ldrs* **14/1**	39
6100	**5**	shd	**Nurai**[19] 4335 3-8-13 **54** (tp) TomQueally 2 (P W D'Arcy) *chsd wnr: rdn over 2f out: styd on same pce fnl f* **11/2**[2]	47
-602	**6**	1	**Major Monty (IRE)**[9] 4649 3-9-0 **55** (v1) RichardKingscote 6 (Tom Dascombe) *trckd ldrs: rdn and hung rt over 1f out: styd on same pce* **2/1**[1]	45
345	**7**	1	**Lady Brickhouse**[44] 3515 3-8-5 **46** oh1 SaleemGolam 12 (M D Squance) *s.i.s: hld up: rdn over 2f out: nvr on terms* **33/1**	33
0344	**8**	1 3/4	**Marafong**[6] 4761 3-8-5 **53** (b1) AdamBeschizza(7) 3 (Miss J Feilden) *sn drvn along in rr: hung rt over 5f out: n.d* **17/2**	35
5005	**9**	1/2	**Mororless**[13] 4502 3-8-11 **52** (p) KirstyMilczarek 8 (Miss Z C Davison) *chsd ldrs: rdn over 2f out: sn wknd* **20/1**	33
0330	**10**	3	**Monsieur Pontaven**[19] 4344 3-8-7 **48** RichardMullen 1 (R Bastiman) *s.i.s: hld up: rdn 1/2-way: n.d* **7/1**[3]	21
0-00	**11**	shd	**The Midshipmaid**[36] 3766 3-8-2 **46** oh1 (v1) AndrewHeffernan(3) 11 (Lucinda Featherstone) *prom: racd keenly: rdn over 2f out: wknd over 1f out* **40/1**	19
0006	**12**	13	**Rileys Crane**[23] 4210 3-8-11 **52** MarcHalford 4 (Mrs C A Dunnett) *hld up: sme hdwy 1/2-way: rdn and wknd over 2f out* **25/1**	—

1m 27.78s (1.18) **Going Correction** +0.025s/f (Good) **12** Ran SP% **122.7**
Speed ratings (Par 98): **94,91,88,87,87 85,84,82,82,78 78,63**
toteswingers:1&2:£17.30, 1&3:£20.60, 2&3:£16.20 CSF £120.81 CT £869.80 TOTE £18.80: £4.60, £2.90, £3.80; EX 353.50 TRIFECTA Not won..
Owner River Racing **Bred** Mrs A M Upsdell **Trained** Newmarket, Suffolk

FOCUS
An extremely modest event, with the top-weight only rated 55.
Franki J Official explanation: trainer said, regarding apparent improvement in form, that the filly was better suited by the flat track and easier race.

4971 SEALIFE CENTRE GREAT YARMOUTH H'CAP 1m 2f 21y
5:00 (5:01) (Class 5) (0-70,76) 3-Y-O **£2,266** (£674; £337; £168) **Stalls** Low

Form				RPR
6003	**1**		**Wood Fair**[18] 4374 3-7-12 **52** SimonPearce(5) 3 (J R Weymes) *dwlt: hld up: hdwy over 2f out: rdn ins fnl f: r.o to ld post* **15/2**	58
3261	**2**	hd	**Granite Girl**[10] 4626 3-9-6 **76** 6ex AdamBeschizza(7) 5 (P J McBride) *s.i.s: sn chsng ldrs: rdn over 1f out: led ins fnl f: hdd post* **15/8**[1]	82
35	**3**	1	**Bizarrely (IRE)**[6] 4763 3-9-2 **65** StevieDonohoe 8 (J Pearce) *chsd ldr tl led 3f out: rdn over 1f out: hdd and unable qck ins fnl f* **14/1**	69
0264	**4**	1 1/2	**Wavertree Bounty**[6] 4763 3-8-2 **51** JimmyQuinn 1 (J Ryan) *hld up: hdwy over 2f out: rdn and swtchd lft over 1f out: styd on* **5/1**	52
4454	**5**	7	**Invitee**[20] 4290 3-9-3 **66** RichardMullen 2 (E A L Dunlop) *hld up: hdwy over 2f out: sn rdn: wknd over 1f out* **4/1**[2]	53
0260	**6**	5	**Underworld Dandy**[121] 1264 3-8-9 **58** (p) KirstyMilczarek 4 (Miss Z C Davison) *prom: rdn over 3f out: wknd over 2f out* **50/1**	35
4040	**7**	nk	**Strong Vigilance (IRE)**[11] 4571 3-9-7 **70** (v1) EddieAhern 6 (M L W Bell) *led after 1f: rdn and hdd 3f out: wknd 2f out* **9/2**[3]	46
500-	**8**	3 1/2	**Carlcol Girl**[288] 7097 3-8-2 **51** oh6 NickyMackay 7 (Mrs C A Dunnett) *led 1f: chsd ldrs: rdn over 2f out: wknd wl over 1f out* **66/1**	20

2m 10.88s (0.38) **Going Correction** +0.025s/f (Good) **8** Ran SP% **111.5**
Speed ratings (Par 100): **99,98,98,96,91 87,87,84**
toteswingers:1&2:£4.30, 1&3:£6.40, 2&3:£5.20 CSF £20.89 CT £188.46 TOTE £12.60: £3.20, £1.40, £2.00; EX 19.80 Trifecta £241.60 Part won. Pool £326.58 - 0.62 winning units..
Owner The Wood Fair Partnership **Bred** Redmyre Bloodstock & Gareth Jones Bloodstock **Trained** Middleham Moor, N Yorks

FOCUS
An interesting little handicap, and a decent gallop was set.

4972 NORFOLK NELSON MUSEUM H'CAP 1m 3f 101y
5:35 (5:36) (Class 5) (0-70,68) 3-Y-O **£2,266** (£674; £337; £168) **Stalls** Low

Form				RPR
-001	**1**		**Kathleen Frances**[62] 2909 3-9-2 **68** AshleyMorgan(5) 8 (M H Tompkins) *hld up in tch: led 3f out: rdn and hung lft over 1f out: styd on wl: eased nr fin* **7/2**[2]	78+
306	**2**	2 1/2	**Joan D'Arc (IRE)**[11] 4572 3-9-4 **65** WilliamCarson 5 (M G Quinlan) *hld up: hdwy over 3f out: rdn to chse wnr over 1f out: styd on same pce ins fnl f* **20/1**	70
000	**3**	1	**Marcus Antonius**[46] 3443 3-8-2 **49** oh2 NickyMackay 3 (J R Boyle) *sn pushed along and prom: rdn over 2f out: styd on same pce fnl f* **16/1**	52
0354	**4**	1/2	**Chicane**[12] 4557 3-9-6 **67** RichardMullen 4 (W J Haggas) *pushed along to ld after 1f: hdd over 8f out: chsd ldrs: rdn over 3f out: styd on same pce fr over 1f out* **7/2**[2]	69
000	**5**	2 3/4	**Mandate**[16] 4425 3-8-10 **57** KirstyMilczarek 2 (J A R Toller) *hld up: rdn over 3f out: styd on: nt pce to chal* **12/1**	55
2006	**6**	nse	**Fairy Flight (USA)**[21] 4259 3-9-6 **67** (v1) EddieAhern 7 (W J Knight) *led1f: chsd ldr: led again over 4f out: hdd 3f out: sn rdn: no ex fr over 1f out* **8/1**	64
2543	**7**	9	**One Cool Poppy (IRE)**[47] 3404 3-8-6 **53** JimmyQuinn 1 (H J Collingridge) *hld up in tch: shkn up over 3f out: wknd over 2f out* **11/2**[3]	35
00-0	**8**	34	**Ildiko (USA)**[25] 4134 3-9-3 **64** StevieDonohoe 6 (Sir Mark Prescott) *s.i.s: sn prom: led over 8f out: rdn and hdd over 4f out: wknd over 3f out: t.o* **11/4**[1]	—

2m 30.31s (1.61) **Going Correction** +0.025s/f (Good) **8** Ran SP% **115.9**
Speed ratings (Par 100): **95,93,92,92,90 90,83,58**
toteswingers:1&2:£7.00, 1&3:£5.90, 2&3:£17.40 CSF £68.36 CT £992.26 TOTE £4.10: £3.80, £9.10, £9.90; EX 61.90 TRIFECTA Not won. Place 6 £59.73, Place 5 £45.74..
Owner Russell Trew Ltd **Bred** Russell Trew Ltd **Trained** Newmarket, Suffolk

FOCUS
A modest contest.
Ildiko(USA) Official explanation: trainer said filly got upset in stalls and never travelled
T/Plt: £80.00 to a £1 stake. Pool:£55,850.91 - 509.43 winning tickets T/Qpdt: £45.30 to a £1 stake. Pool:£3,466.21 - 56.60 winning tickets CR

4973 - 4979a (Foreign Racing) - See Raceform Interactive

4939 BEVERLEY (R-H)
Thursday, August 12

OFFICIAL GOING: Good to firm (firm in places in the back straight; 9.4)
Rail moved out around bottom bend increasing distances by about 6yards on round course.
Wind: Light against Weather: Cloudy and showers

4980 HOLD YOUR CHRISTMAS PARTY HERE (S) H'CAP 1m 4f 16y
2:10 (2:10) (Class 6) (0-60,59) 3-Y-O+ **£2,104** (£626; £312; £156) **Stalls** High

Form				RPR
0045	**1**		**Always Dixie (IRE)**[6] 4800 3-8-3 **46** JoeFanning 6 (M Johnston) *trckd ldrs: smooth hdwy wl over 2f out: led wl over 1f out and sn rdn: drvn ins fnl f and kpt on gamely* **8/1**	54
4403	**2**	nk	**Tivers Song (USA)**[16] 4454 6-8-13 **48** (b) BarryMcHugh(3) 10 (John A Harris) *hld up towards rr: stdy hdwy over 4f out: rdn 2f out: chsd wnr over 1f out: drvn and ev ch ins fnl f tl no ex towards fin* **7/1**	56
0644	**3**	1 1/2	**Dimashq**[14] 4511 8-9-1 **47** PaulHanagan 12 (P T Midgley) *hld up in rr: hdwy on inner over 4f out: swtchd lft wl over 1f out: rdn to chse ldng pair ent fnl f: kpt on same pce* **11/2**[3]	53
3-00	**4**	3 1/2	**Miss Wendy**[64] 2853 3-9-2 **50** AshleyMorgan(5) 7 (M H Tompkins) *chsd ldrs: pushed along 1/2-way: sn lost pl and bhd: rdn 3f out: styd on fnl 2f: nrst fin* **18/1**	50
5402	**5**	1/2	**Quince (IRE)**[8] 4689 7-9-4 **50** (v) SaleemGolam 11 (J Pearce) *trckd ldrs on inner: pushed along and lost pl 3f out: rdn and hdwy wl over 1f out: swtchd lft and kpt on ins fnl f: nrst fin* **5/1**[2]	49
3400	**6**	1/2	**Without Equal**[10] 4648 4-8-13 **45** (p) DanielTudhope 4 (N Wilson) *dwlt: sn cl up: led after 4f: rdn along and jnd over 4f out: drvn over 2f out: hdd wl over 1f out and grad wknd* **50/1**	43
3454	**7**	3/4	**What A Day**[5] 4854 4-8-11 **48** IanBrennan(5) 3 (J J Quinn) *led 4f: cl up: disp ld over 4f out: rdn wl over 2f out: ev ch tl drvn wl over 1f out and grad wknd* **10/3**[1]	45
2565	**8**	4 1/2	**New England**[3] 4912 8-9-4 **50** GrahamGibbons 1 (N J Vaughan) *dwlt: sn chsng ldng pair: rdn along 3f out: sn drvn and wknd* **11/2**[3]	40
0000	**9**	nk	**Sitwell**[16] 4454 4-9-6 **52** (p) DavidAllan 5 (I W McInnes) *hld up in rr: sme hdwy on outer 4f out: rdn along 3f out: sn wknd* **33/1**	42
0400	**10**	3 1/4	**Slip**[6] 4793 5-9-8 **59** (b) DaleSwift(5) 9 (C R Dore) *hld up: a in rr* **15/2**	43

2m 37.19s (-2.61) **Going Correction** -0.35s/f (Firm)
WFA 3 from 4yo+ 11lb **10** Ran SP% **116.1**
Speed ratings (Par 101): **98,97,96,94,94 93,93,90,90,87**
toteswingers: 1&2 £10.80, 1&3 £5.50, 2&3 £6.30 CSF £62.63 CT £336.66 TOTE £12.00: £2.60, £2.40, £1.50; EX 71.50.There was no bid for the winner.
Owner Always Trying Partnership VII **Bred** Mark Johnston Racing Ltd **Trained** Middleham Moor, N Yorks
■ Stewards' Enquiry : David Allan caution: used whip down shoulder in the forehand.

FOCUS
A day of sunshine and showers but the ground remained on the quicker side of good. A standard selling handicap run at a sensible pace. Limited form, with modest improvement from the winner.

4981 E B F BEVERLEY ANNUAL BADGEHOLDERS MAIDEN FILLIES' STKS 5f
2:40 (2:40) (Class 4) 2-Y-O **£4,047** (£1,204; £601; £300) **Stalls** High

Form				RPR
	1		**Barefoot Lady (IRE)** 2-9-0 0 PaulHanagan 1 (R A Fahey) *chsd ldrs: pushed along 1/2-way: rdn and hdwy over 1f out: styd on to ld jst ins fnl f: sn rdn clr* **11/4**[2]	82+
03	**2**	6	**Infectious (IRE)**[26] 4149 2-9-0 0 GrahamGibbons 5 (D H Brown) *wnt lft s: chsd ldr: rdn along 2f out: drvn and ev ch over 1f out: kpt on same pce ins fnl f: tk 2nd nr line* **15/8**[1]	61
3403	**3**	hd	**Misscomplacent**[10] 4650 2-8-11 67 (v) BarryMcHugh(3) 9 (Mrs A Duffield) *led: rdn over 1f out: hdd jst ins fnl f and wknd: lost 2nd nr line* **3/1**[3]	60
	4	3	**Cottam Stella** 2-9-0 0 DavidAllan 4 (M Brittain) *green and sn outpcd in rr tl styd on fnl 2f* **14/1**	49
	5	2 3/4	**Oldmeldrum (IRE)** 2-9-0 0 PhillipMakin 7 (B M R Haslam) *chsd ldrs: rdn along 2f out: sn wknd* **9/1**	39
00	**6**	2 3/4	**Snow Legend (IRE)**[13] 4543 2-8-9 0 RossAtkinson(5) 8 (Tom Dascombe) *broke wl: stdd s and hld up in rr: keen and hit ins rail after 1/2f: a in rr after* **22/1**	29
	7	30	**Belles Boudier** 2-9-0 0 DuranFentiman 2 (G Woodward) *v s.i.s and lost many l s: a wl bhd* **66/1**	—

63.27 secs (-0.23) **Going Correction** -0.20s/f (Firm) **7** Ran SP% **109.0**
Speed ratings (Par 93): **93,83,83,78,73 69,21**
toteswingers: 1&2 £1.30, 2&3 £2.00, 1&3 not won. CSF £7.47 TOTE £2.60: £1.10, £2.30; EX 8.30.
Owner Mrs H Steel **Bred** Arbawny Ventures 2000uc **Trained** Musley Bank, N Yorks

FOCUS
A weak maiden, but the first-time out winner looks a filly of real potential.

NOTEBOOK
Barefoot Lady(IRE) ◆, daughter of a tough race mare, had the worst of the draw. She took time to get into full stride but won going right away in the end. She deserves a crack at a much higher grade after this auspicious debut. (op 2-1)

The Form Book, Raceform Ltd, Compton, RG20 6NL

Infectious(IRE), who recorded an RPR of just 51 when third at Ripon on her second start, struggled to master the pacesetter and they were both left for dead in the end. (op 5-2 tchd 11-4)
Misscomplacent, having her fifth start and with an official rating of 67, had finished well behind Infectious at Ripon on her third start. Third there since in a first-time visor, she took them along but looks strictly limited and nurseries may prove a better option now. (tchd 5-2)
Cottam Stella showed a glimmer of ability on her debut keeping on late in the day. (op 12-1)
Oldmeldrum(IRE) showed speed on her debut but she tired appreciably late on and looks as though she will need more time. (tchd 10-1)

4982 MRS ANNE CORKELL'S BIRTHDAY CELEBRATION FILLIES' H'CAP 5f
3:15 (3:15) (Class 5) (0-70,68) 3-Y-0+ **£2,914** (£867; £433; £216) **Stalls** High

Form RPR
160 **1** **Caranbola**[8] 4712 4-9-9 **65** SilvestreDeSousa 7 74
(M Brittain) *mde most: rdn wl over 1f out: drvn and edgd lft ins fnl f: kpt on strly towards fin* **7/2**[2]
2113 **2** *2* **Comptonspirit**[18] 4415 6-9-12 **68** J-PGuillambert 2 70
(B P J Baugh) *prom: rdn to chse wnr wl over 1f out: drvn to chal ent fnl f and ev ch tl one pce last 100yds* **11/2**
006 **3** *shd* **Best Known Secret (IRE)**[22] 4251 4-8-2 **49** oh4 IanBrennan(5) 4 50
(C C Bealby) *in tch: swtchd rt to inner 1/2-way: effrt and n.m.r wl over 1f out: sn swtchd lft and rdn: styd on strly ins fnl f* **28/1**
000 **4** *nk* **Accamelia**[80] 2393 4-8-8 **50** PaulMulrennan 5 50
(C W Fairhurst) *sltly hmpd s and in rr: hdwy over 1f out: str run ins fnl f: nrst fin* **33/1**
4010 **5** *½* **Miss Daawe**[19] 4373 6-9-0 **61** DaleSwift(5) 3 60
(B Ellison) *chsd ldrs: rdn 2f out: drvn over 1f out: kpt on same pce* **9/2**[3]
0032 **6** *hd* **Midget**[5] 4826 3-8-7 **59** NeilFarley(7) 8 56
(D Carroll) *chsd ldrs: rdn along 2f out: drvn over 1f out: sn one pce* **9/2**[3]
1431 **7** *2 ¼* **Arriva La Diva**[6] 4799 4-9-7 **63** 6ex PaulHanagan 1 53
(J J Quinn) *in tch on outer: rdn along wl over 1f out and sn btn* **10/3**[1]
2000 **8** *2* **Piste**[4] 4868 4-9-2 **58** PJMcDonald 9 41
(Miss T Jackson) *chsd ldrs on inner: rdn along wl over 1f out: sn drvn and wknd* **8/1**
0-00 **9** *10* **Princess Charlmane (IRE)**[86] 2213 7-8-7 **49** oh1..(tp) PatrickMathers 6 —
(C J Teague) *cl up: rdn along 2f out: sn wknd* **100/1**

62.46 secs (-1.04) **Going Correction** -0.20s/f (Firm)
WFA 3 from 4yo+ 3lb **9** Ran SP% **115.5**
Speed ratings (Par 100): **100,96,96,96,95 95,91,88,72**
toteswingers: 1&2 £8.30, 1&3 £9.00, 2&3 £39.00 CSF £22.80 CT £462.05 TOTE £4.70: £1.80, £2.30, £4.90.
Owner Mel Brittain **Bred** T E Pocock **Trained** Warthill, N Yorks

FOCUS
A tight fillies-only sprint handicap. Straightforward form, the winner rated to last year's best.

4983 TAKE THAT 2 HERE ON SATURDAY H'CAP 2m 35y
3:50 (3:50) (Class 4) (0-85,85) 3-Y-0+ **£5,180** (£1,541; £770; £384) **Stalls** High

Form RPR
200 **1** **Keenes Day (FR)**[20] 4320 5-10-0 **85** JoeFanning 3 93
(M Johnston) *trckd ldr: cl up 4f out: led 2f out: and sn rdn: edgd rt and drvn ins fnl f: kpt on wl* **5/2**[1]
1606 **2** *½* **Rawnaq (IRE)**[12] 4571 3-8-3 **75** SilvestreDeSousa 4 82
(M Johnston) *led: rdn along over 3f out: hdd 2f out: drvn over 1f out: edgd lft and rallied ins fnl f: kpt on wl* **11/4**[2]
3125 **3** *1 ¾* **Rare Ruby (IRE)**[33] 3896 6-9-1 **72** PaulHanagan 1 77
(Jennie Candlish) *hld up in rr: niggled along after 5f: pushed along 6f out: rdn 3f out: hdwy 2f out: drvn to chse ldrs over 1f out: kpt on: tk 3rd nr line* **6/1**
6254 **4** *hd* **Bollin Greta**[12] 4604 5-8-12 **69** (t) DavidAllan 5 74
(T D Easterby) *hld up in rr: smooth hdwy over 3f out: rdn to chse ldng pair 2f out: drvn over 1f out and kpt on same pce* **5/1**
051- **5** *14* **No Rules**[159] 7084 5-8-8 **70** AshleyMorgan(5) 2 58
(M H Tompkins) *trckd ldrs: pushed along over 4f out: rdn 3f out and sn wknd* **14/1**
4253 **6** *2 ½* **French Hollow**[12] 4604 5-8-9 **66** oh1 PaulMulrennan 6 51
(T J Fitzgerald) *trckd ldng pair on inner: tk clsr order over 4f out: rdn along wl over 2f out: drvn and wknd wl over 1f out* **4/1**[3]

3m 31.98s (-7.82) **Going Correction** -0.35s/f (Firm)
WFA 3 from 5yo+ 15lb **6** Ran SP% **112.9**
Speed ratings (Par 105): **105,104,103,103,96 95**
toteswingers: 1&2 £2.00, 1&3 £4.30, 2&3 £3.70 CSF £9.80 TOTE £4.70: £3.50, £2.00; EX 7.70.
Owner Mrs R J Jacobs **Bred** Newsells Park Stud Ltd **Trained** Middleham Moor, N Yorks

FOCUS
A stayers' handicap and the gallop was unrelenting. Pretty solid form.
French Hollow Official explanation: jockey said gelding ran flat

4984 RACING UK ON SKY 432 NURSERY 7f 100y
4:25 (4:25) (Class 5) (0-75,74) 2-Y-0 **£2,914** (£867; £433; £216) **Stalls** High

Form RPR
056 **1** **Kalkan Bay**[16] 4447 2-9-1 **68** PJMcDonald 2 71
(Jedd O'Keeffe) *cl up: led over 2f out: rdn wl over 1f out: drvn and edgd rt jst ins fnl f: kpt on gamely* **7/1**
536 **2** *1* **Countrywide Flame**[20] 4336 2-8-0 **53** SilvestreDeSousa 6 54
(K A Ryan) *trckd ldrs: hdwy to chse ldng pair over 2f out: rdn wl over 1f out: drvn and kpt on ins fnl f* **9/1**
0625 **3** *½* **Witzend (IRE)**[34] 3872 2-9-5 **72** PaulMulrennan 4 71+
(Jedd O'Keeffe) *trckd ldng pair: hdwy 2f out: rdn and nt clr run 1f out: swtchd lft and drvn ins fnl f: kpt on same pce* **5/1**[2]
0436 **4** *½* **Sheila's Star (IRE)**[34] 3872 2-8-9 **65** RussKennemore(3) 9 63
(J S Moore) *in tch: hdwy over 2f out: rdn wl over 1f out: kpt on u.p ins fnl f: nrst fin* **11/2**[3]
4042 **5** *1 ¾* **Dark Dune (IRE)**[40] 3657 2-9-1 **68** DavidAllan 5 62
(T D Easterby) *in tch: hdwy over 2f out: rdn to chse ldrs over 1f out: sn drvn and kpt on same pce* **7/1**
3211 **6** *1* **Mica Mika (IRE)**[22] 4242 2-9-4 **71** PaulHanagan 7 63
(R A Fahey) *trckd ldrs: effrt over 2f out: hdwy on inner and n.m.r over 1f out: sn swtchd lft and rdn: kpt on same pce* **7/2**[1]
1534 **7** *1 ½* **Tro Nesa (IRE)**[11] 4615 2-9-4 **74** BarryMcHugh(3) 8 61
(Mrs A Duffield) *hld up: effrt and sme hdwy on outer 2f out: sn rdn and no imp ins fnl f* **10/1**
0000 **8** *1 ½* **Bonjour Bongee**[11] 4614 2-8-7 **60** (v[1]) GrahamGibbons 3 44
(A J McCabe) *led: rdn along and hdd over 2f out: drvn over 1f out: edgd rt and grad wknd appr fnl f* **40/1**
3534 **9** *1 ¾* **Little Miss Take**[39] 3705 2-8-11 **69** RossAtkinson(5) 1 48
(Tom Dascombe) *stdd and swtchd rt s: hld up: a in rr* **25/1**
035 **10** *3 ½* **Hi Ho Ron**[71] 2654 2-8-12 **65** PhillipMakin 10 36
(D H Brown) *hld up: a towards rr* **15/2**

1m 33.79s (-0.01) **Going Correction** -0.35s/f (Firm) **10** Ran SP% **116.4**
Speed ratings (Par 94): **86,84,84,83,81 80,78,77,75,71**
toteswingers: 1&2 £10.20, 1&3 £7.40, 2&3 £9.50 CSF £68.23 CT £345.19 TOTE £7.30: £2.30, £3.40, £1.60; EX 114.50.
Owner Ken & Delia Shaw-KGS Projects Management **Bred** N J Hughes **Trained** Middleham Moor, N Yorks

FOCUS
An ordinary nursery and the pace was sound.

NOTEBOOK
Kalkan Bay, who wore blinkers on his first two starts, is settling better. On his nursery bow, he dived right entering the final furlong but in the end did more than enough. The extended 7f seemed to suit him. Official explanation: trainer said, regarding apparent improvement in form, that the gelding was having its first run in a handicap and had run well on its previous run. (op 9-1)
Countrywide Flame, whose three qualifying runs were over 5f, moved up looking a real threat but was being held by the winner at the line. The big step up in trip clearly suited him. (op 10-1)
Witzend(IRE), carrying the same colours as the winner, his stable companion, came in for plenty of support. He was pushed sideways by his stablemate at a crucial stage but cannot be counted in anyway unlucky. (tchd 9-2)
Sheila's Star(IRE), dropped 3lb after her nursery debut, stayed on when it was all over and will be suited by a return to 1m. (op 6-1 tchd 13-2)
Dark Dune(IRE), who had Kalkan Bay three places behind him when runner-up on his fourth start here six weeks ago, travelled strongly before flatting out. He might just have needed it. (op 6-1 tchd 11-2)
Mica Mika(IRE) was racing from a 4lb higher mark and was making hard work of it when tightened up coming to the final furlong. (op 3-1 tchd 11-4)
Hi Ho Ron Official explanation: jockey said gelding never travelled

4985 WHITE ROSE SADDLERY CHRIS HOGGARD MEMORIAL H'CAP (FOR AMATEUR RIDERS) (DIV I) 1m 100y
5:00 (5:00) (Class 6) (0-65,65) 4-Y-0+ **£1,717** (£532; £266; £133) **Stalls** High

Form RPR
3453 **1** **Strike Force**[7] 4740 6-9-10 **52** (t) MissALHutchinson(5) 11 65
(Miss Olivia Maylam) *hld up and bhd: swtchd outside and hdwy wl over 2f out: rdn over 1f out: str run ent fnl f to ld last 75yds and kpt on wl* **10/1**
6666 **2** *2* **Mr Udagawa**[11] 4620 4-10-1 **59** (p) MrRJWilliams(7) 9 67
(B J Llewellyn) *t.k.h early: trckd ldrs: hdwy over 2f out: rdn to chse ldr over 1f out: ev ch ins fnl f: kpt on* **22/1**
3231 **3** *½* **Call Of Duty (IRE)**[10] 4644 5-10-9 **65** 6ex MissECSayer(5) 1 72
(Mrs Dianne Sayer) *sn led: clr 3f out: rdn wl over 1f out: hdd and one pce last 75yds* **9/2**[2]
0506 **4** *nk* **Mojeerr**[4] 4857 4-9-9 **46** oh1 (v) MissSBrotherton 3 52
(A J McCabe) *trckd ldrs: hdwy on inner 2f out: rdn over 1f out: swtchd lft and ch ent fnl f: sn one pce* **11/1**
0403 **5** *3 ¼* **Lujano**[15] 4485 5-10-5 **63** MissVCoates(7) 12 62
(Ollie Pears) *trckd ldng pair: pushed along on inner and lost pl wl over 2f out: swtchd lft and kpt on ins fnl f* **8/1**
3222 **6** *hd* **Silly Gilly (IRE)**[10] 4644 6-9-13 **55** MissVBarr(5) 8 53
(R E Barr) *chsd ldrs: rdn along over 2f out: drvn wl over 1f out and kpt on same pce* **7/2**[1]
1402 **7** *½* **Bajan Pride**[14] 4514 6-10-9 **65** MissWGibson(5) 6 62
(P T Midgley) *midfield: hdwy and in tch over 2f out: sn rdn and no imp appr fnl f* **11/1**
2521 **8** *¾* **Royal Composer (IRE)**[16] 4454 7-9-8 **50** MissRKneller(5) 5 45
(T D Easterby) *hld up towards rr: effrt and hdwy on outer wl over 2f out: sn rdn and no imp fr over 1f out* **8/1**
0453 **9** *¾* **Lucayan Dancer**[9] 4673 10-10-9 **65** MrSebSpencer(5) 4 59
(N Bycroft) *stdd and swtchd rt s: hld up and bhd: sme hdwy 2f out: styng on whn n.m.r over 1f out: nvr a factor* **25/1**
60-4 **10** *shd* **Richo**[12] 4596 4-10-8 **64** (p) MrCAHarris(5) 14 57
(S A Harris) *a in rr* **25/1**
-000 **11** *3* **Royal Applord**[26] 4156 5-9-9 **46** oh1 MissADeniel 13 32
(N Tinkler) *a towards rr* **22/1**
6053 **12** *½* **Emperor's Well**[10] 4644 11-9-4 **46** oh1 (b) MissJoannaMason(5) 7 31
(M W Easterby) *sn chsng ldr: rdn along over 2f out: drvn wl over 1f out and sn wknd* **14/1**
6003 **13** *½* **Whipma Whopma Gate (IRE)**[5] 4824 5-10-5 **63** (v) MrJHarney(7) 10 47
(D Carroll) *in tch: effrt 3f out: sn rdn along and wknd wl over 1f out* **15/2**[3]

1m 46.15s (-1.45) **Going Correction** -0.35s/f (Firm) **13** Ran SP% **123.2**
Speed ratings (Par 101): **93,91,90,90,86 86,86,85,84,84 81,81,80**
toteswingers: 1&2 £47.20, 1&3 £10.70, 2&3 £32.70 CSF £221.41 CT £1171.80 TOTE £14.80: £3.90, £9.50, £1.10; EX 274.00.
Owner Miss A L Hutchinson **Bred** Cheveley Park Stud Ltd **Trained** Newmarket, Suffolk
■ Stewards' Enquiry : Miss A Deniel one-day ban: used whip when out of contention (tbn)

FOCUS
Part one of a low-grade amateur riders' handicap and the early pace was strong, with the time coming out 5lb faster than division two. The third is the best guide to the form.

4986 WHITE ROSE SADDLERY CHRIS HOGGARD MEMORIAL H'CAP (FOR AMATEUR RIDERS) (DIV II) 1m 100y
5:30 (5:31) (Class 6) (0-65,65) 4-Y-0+ **£1,717** (£532; £266; £133) **Stalls** High

Form RPR
5-66 **1** **Postman**[55] 3149 4-10-9 **65** MrJNewman(5) 8 71
(B Smart) *trckd ldrs: hdwy to ld 2f out: rdn and hdd ins fnl f: rallied to ld again nr line* **11/1**
5220 **2** *shd* **Rowan Lodge (IRE)**[10] 4656 8-10-6 **64** (b) MissVCoates(7) 3 70
(Ollie Pears) *hld up in rr: hdwy on wd outside 1/2-way: chsd ldrs over 2f out: chal over 1f out: led ins fnl f: hdd and no ex nr line* **5/1**[2]
3004 **3** *3 ¼* **Kings Point (IRE)**[14] 4514 9-10-7 **65** MissJWalker(7) 13 64
(D Nicholls) *hld up in tch: hdwy over 2f out: rdn wl over 1f out: styd on ins fnl f* **5/1**[2]
5004 **4** *1 ¾* **Mountain Pass (USA)**[8] 4708 8-9-9 **53** (t) MrRJWilliams(7) 11 48
(B J Llewellyn) *hld up in rr: hdwy 3f out: swtchd ins and rdn wl over 1f out: styd on ins fnl f: nrst fin* **14/1**
3643 **5** *¾* **Vertigo On Course (IRE)**[167] 719 5-10-2 **60** MrJButterfield(7) 5 53
(R A Fahey) *hld up and bhd: hdwy 1/2-way: rdn to chse ldrs wl over 1f out: no imp ins fnl f* **5/1**[2]
5304 **6** *nse* **Just Timmy Marcus**[10] 4644 4-10-5 **56** MissSBrotherton 2 49
(B P J Baugh) *in tch: hdwy 3f out: rdn to chal wl over 1f out and ev ch tl wknd ent fnl f* **9/4**[1]
0600 **7** *4* **Officer Mor (USA)**[12] 4606 4-9-4 **46** oh1 MissECSayer(5) 10 29
(Mrs Dianne Sayer) *led: rdn along 3f out: hdd 2f out and grad wknd* **33/1**
0140 **8** *1* **Ivestar (IRE)**[10] 4644 5-10-7 **63** (bt) MissCharlotteHolmes(5) 1 44
(B M R Haslam) *prom: effrt to chal over 2f out: sn rdn and edgd rt over 1f out: wknd* **8/1**[3]

5-00 **9** *1* **Noble Attitude**[12] 4582 4-9-6 **50** MissLWilson(7) 9 29
(N Tinkler) *a towards rr* **40/1**

0/00 **10** *1 ¾* **High Window (IRE)**[21] 4285 10-9-4 **46** oh1 MissJoannaMason(5) 7 21
(G P Kelly) *a towards rr* **66/1**

0-00 **11** *2* **Apurna**[40] 3684 5-9-10 **47** (p) MissADeniel 12 17
(John A Harris) *bhd fr 1/2-way* **40/1**

0600 **12** *¾* **Pacific Bay (IRE)**[16] 4454 4-9-6 **46** MissPernillaHermansson(3) 6 15
(R Ford) *prom: rdn along over 2f out and sn wknd* **25/1**

1m 46.81s (-0.79) **Going Correction** -0.35s/f (Firm) 12 Ran SP% **120.0**
Speed ratings (Par 101): **89,88,85,83,83 83,79,78,77,75 73,72**
toteswingers:1&2:£12.30, 2&3:£13.40, 1&3:£10.90. totesuper7: Win: Not won. Place: Not won. CSF £63.67 CT £320.95 TOTE £14.20: £2.80, £1.50, £2.50; EX 44.20 Place 6: £164.06 Place 5: 48.98 .
Owner Crossfields Racing **Bred** Newsells Park Stud **Trained** Hambleton, N Yorks

FOCUS
Part two and more of the same with the early pace frenetic, but it was the slower of the divisions. The winner was back close to his 3yo form.
Ivestar(IRE) Official explanation: vet said gelding had been struck into
T/Plt: £771.60 to a £1 stake. Pool of £48,241.39 - 45.64 winning tickets. T/Qpdt: £243.90 to a £1 stake. Pool of £3,033.28 - 9.20 winning tickets. JR

4675 CHEPSTOW (L-H)
Thursday, August 12

OFFICIAL GOING: Good to soft (soft in places) changing to good to soft after race 1 (5.45)
Wind: Virtually nil Weather: Bright early

4987 RED DRAGON FM H'CAP — 1m 14y
5:45 (5:47) (Class 6) (0-55,55) 3-Y-O+ **£2,460** (£732; £365; £182) **Stalls** High

Form RPR

5002 **1** **Belle Park**[7] 4733 3-8-9 **51** JerryO'Dwyer 3 61
(Karen George) *in tch: hdwy over 2f out: qcknd to ld over 1f out: pushed out* **9/2**[1]

6056 **2** *1 ½* **Fly By Nelly**[23] 4232 4-9-5 **54** TravisBlock 17 62
(H Morrison) *chsd ldrs: led over 2f out: sn rdn: hdd over 1f out and sn outpcd* **9/1**

400- **3** *1 ¾* **Master Mahogany**[357] 5179 9-9-0 **49** SamHitchcott 13 53
(R J Hodges) *sn led: rdn and hdd over 2f out: styd on same pce appr fnl f* **12/1**

-060 **4** *1 ¾* **On The Feather**[28] 4044 4-9-6 **55** TomMcLaughlin 11 55
(B R Millman) *pressed ldrs: ev ch over 2f out: wknd ins fnl f* **16/1**

046 **5** *2 ¼* **Aggbag**[45] 3521 6-8-7 **47** DeclanCannon(5) 6 42
(A W Carroll) *chsd ldrs: rdn and ev ch over 2f out: wknd over 1f out* **6/1**[2]

0000 **6** *nk* **Lily Wood**[3] 4913 4-9-0 **49** LiamJones 12 43
(J W Unett) *in rr: pushed along 1/2-way: styd on fr over 1f out: nt trble ldrs* **25/1**

5054 **7** *1 ½* **Lucas Pitt**[17] 4428 3-8-5 **54** HarryBentley(7) 1 44
(M J Scudamore) *chsd ldrs: rdn and wknd over 2f out* **15/2**[3]

0506 **8** *hd* **Barataria**[17] 4439 8-9-0 **52** MatthewDavies(3) 10 42
(R Bastiman) *fly j. s: in rr styd on fnl 2f: kpt on ins fnl f* **18/1**

0165 **9** *1 ¾* **Bold Diva**[17] 4428 5-8-10 **50** (v) BillyCray(5) 2 36
(A W Carroll) *pressed ldrs over 5f* **12/1**

2606 **10** *hd* **Dancing Welcome**[17] 4428 4-9-6 **55** (b) LukeMorris 8 41
(J M Bradley) *chsd ldrs: rdn 3f out: wknd 2f out* **28/1**

0400 **11** *1 ¼* **Hilbre Court (USA)**[15] 4488 5-9-3 **52** (p) JimmyQuinn 5 35
(B P J Baugh) *pressed ldrs over 5f* **8/1**

42-0 **12** *4* **Captain Oats (IRE)**[11] 4620 7-8-13 **53** SophieDoyle(5) 7 27
(Mrs P Ford) *towards rr most of way* **22/1**

0004 **13** *3* **Fiancee (IRE)**[20] 4324 4-9-1 **53** (v) JamesSullivan(3) 9 20
(R Brotherton) *bhd fr 1/2-way* **14/1**

0250 **14** *7* **Pretty Orchid**[34] 3854 5-9-2 **51** (p) TonyCulhane 4 2
(P T Midgley) *bhd fr 1/2-way* **9/1**

000- **15** *8* **Key To Love (IRE)**[290] 7069 4-8-10 **50** MarkCoumbe(5) 14 —
(A J Chamberlain) *s.i.s: a bhd* **50/1**

1m 34.63s (-1.57) **Going Correction** -0.15s/f (Firm)
WFA 3 from 4yo+ 7lb 15 Ran SP% **122.1**
Speed ratings (Par 101): **101,99,97,96,93 93,91,91,90,89 88,84,81,74,66**
toteswingers:1&2 £4.90, 2&3:£22.70, 1&3 £14.60 CSF £42.70 CT £476.30 TOTE £5.00: £1.10, £1.40, £4.50; EX 68.30.
Owner Eastington Racing Club **Bred** C A Green **Trained** Higher Eastington, Devon

FOCUS
Pretty demanding conditions, as at the last meeting here, and the jockeys who rode in the opener came back reporting it to be generally good to soft all round. This was an open low-grade handicap in which not many got into the contest. The winner is on the upgrade and the form seems sound.
Barataria Official explanation: jockey said gelding hung right-handed

4988 KAM AND SALLY AT BREAKFAST FILLIES' H'CAP — 1m 14y
6:20 (6:20) (Class 5) (0-75,73) 3-Y-O+ **£4,144** (£1,233; £616; £307) **Stalls** High

Form RPR

0033 **1** **Ashkalara**[15] 4492 3-8-5 **57** JimmyQuinn 12 66
(H S Howe) *stdd s: t.k.h in rr tl gd hdwy over 3f out: chal over 1f out: slt ld jst ins fnl f: drvn out* **13/2**

-042 **2** *nk* **My Sister**[34] 3852 3-8-0 **59** AdamBeschizza(7) 11 67
(M D I Usher) *led 1f: styd chsng ldr: led again over 2f out: rdn and jnd over 1f out: narrowly hdd jst ins fnl f: kpt on: a jst hld* **9/2**[2]

0016 **3** *2 ¾* **Angelena Ballerina (IRE)**[13] 4534 3-8-7 **59** (v) JerryO'Dwyer 7 61
(Karen George) *chsd ldrs: rdn 3f out: outpcd by ldng duo ins fnl f* **18/1**

0524 **4** *3 ¼* **Sweet Secret**[24] 4201 3-8-10 **62** SamHitchcott 4 56
(R Hannon) *chsd ldrs: rdn 3f out: wknd fr 2f out* **11/2**[3]

3413 **5** *¾* **Gemma's Delight (IRE)**[14] 4515 3-8-6 **58** (p) LiamJones 6 50
(J W Unett) *chsd ldrs: led 6f out: hdd over 2f out: sn btn* **9/1**

3041 **6** *3 ¼* **Croeso Cusan**[9] 4680 5-9-0 **64** 6ex SophieDoyle(5) 3 50
(J L Spearing) *s.i.s: in rr: pushed along over 3f out and no rspnse* **5/2**[1]

5424 **7** *3 ¾* **Magenta Strait**[22] 4249 3-8-4 **59** KellyHarrison(3) 1 35
(R Hollinshead) *bhd most of way* **28/1**

0-01 **8** *2* **Polar Annie**[20] 4324 5-9-8 **67** TomMcLaughlin 10 45
(M S Saunders) *sn in tch: hdwy to chse ldrs 4f out: wknd ins fnl 3f* **11/2**[3]

4-00 **9** *30* **Chat De Soie (IRE)**[62] 2935 3-8-4 **56** LukeMorris 5 —
(J S Moore) *s.i.s: a in rr: eased fnl f: t.o* **50/1**

3030 **10** *½* **Diapason (IRE)**[31] 3947 4-9-7 **73** (t) SoniaEaton(7) 8 —
(Tom Dascombe) *chsd ldrs tl wknd bef 1/2-way: eased fnl f: t.o* **25/1**

1m 35.02s (-1.18) **Going Correction** -0.15s/f (Firm)
WFA 3 from 4yo+ 7lb 10 Ran SP% **115.4**
Speed ratings (Par 100): **99,98,95,92,91 88,84,82,52,52**
CSF £34.83 CT £502.83 TOTE £9.40: £3.10, £2.70, £6.90; EX 28.00.
Owner Roly Roper **Bred** R G Levin **Trained** Oakford, Devon

FOCUS
A race dominated by the three-year-olds, who filled the first five places. They finished quite well strung out and it turned into a duel in the final furlong. It was slower than the earlier Class 6 handicap. Improvement from the first two.

4989 LINDLEY CATERING H'CAP — 6f 16y
6:50 (6:50) (Class 6) (0-65,65) 3-Y-O **£2,590** (£770; £385; £192) **Stalls** High

Form RPR

0-00 **1** **Up At Last**[13] 4556 3-8-6 **50** LiamJones 4 72
(W J Haggas) *hld up towards rr: hdwy over 2f out: drvn and str run to chse ldr 1f out: led fnl 120yds: kpt on wl* **8/1**

0344 **2** *2 ¼* **Bathwick Xaara**[7] 4730 3-8-7 **58** (p) AdamBeschizza(7) 1 73
(J G Portman) *chsd ldrs: rdn to ld 2f out: hdd and outpcd fnl 120yds* **9/1**

2456 **3** *6* **Dazeen**[10] 4647 3-9-7 **65** (p) TonyCulhane 13 61
(P T Midgley) *hld up in tch: rdn and styd on fr 2f out: chsd ldng duo fnl f but nvr any ch* **9/2**[1]

2323 **4** *½* **Rosiliant (IRE)**[8] 4692 3-8-10 **54** (b) LukeMorris 8 48
(C G Cox) *chsd ldrs: rdn over 2f out: styd on same pce wl over 1f out* **13/2**[2]

0000 **5** *¾* **Fashion Tycoon (IRE)**[6] 4791 3-8-8 **55** AndrewHeffernan(3) 16 47
(M F Harris) *in tch: rdn and styd on fnl 2f but nvr gng pce to get into contention* **28/1**

4-00 **6** *1* **Knowledgeable**[31] 3957 3-7-13 **48** oh1 ow2 (p) DeclanCannon(5) 5 37
(B Palling) *in tch: rdn over 2f out: styd on same pce* **22/1**

0260 **7** *¾* **Captain Bluebird (IRE)**[18] 4406 3-8-9 **58** (b[1]) KierenFox(5) 3 44
(D Donovan) *s.i.s: sn led: rdn over 3f out: hdd 2f out: sn btn* **25/1**

3036 **8** *2* **Nadinska**[6] 4775 3-9-7 **65** SamHitchcott 12 45
(M R Channon) *chsd ldrs: rdn 3f out: wknd 2f out* **9/1**

0002 **9** *nse* **Gilderoy**[8] 4692 3-7-13 **48** BillyCray(5) 6 28
(D J S Ffrench Davis) *mid-div: rdn 1/2-way and nvr gng pce to trble ldrs* **7/1**[3]

000- **10** *2 ¾* **Dudley**[377] 4478 3-7-11 **48** HarryBentley(7) 10 19
(J G Portman) *in tch 4f* **28/1**

0 **11** *¾* **Silent Annie**[8] 4692 3-8-4 **51** ow1 MatthewDavies(3) 17 19
(Matthew Salaman) *chsd ldrs over 3f* **16/1**

0600 **12** *nk* **Quaestor (IRE)**[40] 3680 3-9-0 **65** (v[1]) SoniaEaton(7) 11 32
(Tom Dascombe) *pressed ldrs 3f* **20/1**

6500 **13** *hd* **My Meteor**[87] 2185 3-8-12 **56** TravisBlock 14 23
(A G Newcombe) *s.i.s: outpcd most of way* **22/1**

4-56 **14** *3 ¾* **Madam Isshe**[110] 1535 3-8-11 **55** TomMcLaughlin 7 10
(M S Saunders) *bhd fr 1/2-way* **20/1**

0-00 **15** *1* **Outshine**[15] 4478 3-9-4 **62** JerryO'Dwyer 9 14
(Karen George) *in tch 3f* **18/1**

4000 **16** *½* **Dolly Will Do**[7] 4733 3-7-13 **46** oh1 KellyHarrison(3) 15 —
(N P Mulholland) *in tch 3f* **40/1**

0-00 **P** **Greenore Gordon**[110] 1535 3-8-2 **46** oh1 JimmyQuinn 2 —
(M S Saunders) *pressed ldr 3f: sn wknd: t.o whn p.u over 1f out* **33/1**

1m 11.12s (-0.88) **Going Correction** -0.15s/f (Firm) 17 Ran SP% **120.6**
Speed ratings (Par 98): **99,96,88,87,86 85,84,81,81,77 76,76,75,70,69 68,—**
toteswingers:1&2 £18.00, 2&3 £14.00, 1&3 £12.30 CSF £64.97 CT £381.92 TOTE £11.10: £3.50, £2.30, £1.50, £1.10; EX 118.70.
Owner P D Player **Bred** Whatton Manor Stud **Trained** Newmarket, Suffolk

FOCUS
No strength in depth to this low-grade handicap and, given most of these are disappointing types, it is not form to be taking literally. They were spread right across the track but the pace was towards the middle, and that is where the race evolved as two came clear. The improved winner can probably do better again.
Up At Last Official explanation: trainer said, regarding apparent improvement in form, that the filly had been very disappointing and this was going to be its last race if it did not improve and may have been suited by the straight course

4990 WYVERN ICES MAIDEN H'CAP — 2m 2f
7:25 (7:26) (Class 6) (0-65,65) 3-Y-O+ **£2,590** (£770; £385; £192) **Stalls** Low

Form RPR

0603 **1** **Torran Sound**[14] 4519 3-8-0 **47** ow2 LukeMorris 11 58
(J M P Eustace) *trckd ldr: led 4f out: rdn 3f out: styd on strly fr over 1f out: readily* **4/1**[2]

44/ **2** *½* **Cubism**[11] 6147 4-9-12 **55** (t) SamHitchcott 10 65
(M F Harris) *in tch: hdwy 1/2-way: drvn to chse ldrs 4f out: wnt 2nd wl over 1f out: styd on wl ins fnl f: a hld* **9/2**[3]

-502 **3** *8* **Miniyamba (IRE)**[23] 4223 3-9-4 **65** JimmyQuinn 1 66
(J L Dunlop) *in rr: rdn over 5f out: stl plenty to do and pushed along 4f out: plugged on fnl 2f to take wl hld 3rd last strides* **7/4**[1]

606 **4** *hd* **Deejan (IRE)**[22] 4258 5-9-9 **57** DeclanCannon(5) 6 58
(B Palling) *chsd ldrs: rdn to chal 4f out: outstyd over 2f out and lost 2nd wl over 1f out: ct for wl hld 3rd last strides* **14/1**

2053 **5** *1* **Prickles**[21] 4279 5-9-3 **46** JerryO'Dwyer 7 46
(Karen George) *hld up in rr: hdwy fr 5f out to chse ldrs over 4f out: nvr any ch: btn fnl 2f* **9/1**

0 **6** *20* **Aughcarra (IRE)**[20] 4327 5-9-9 **52** NeilChalmers 3 30
(Harry Chisman) *chsd ldrs tl wknd qckly 4f out* **33/1**

50-4 **7** *3* **Eastwell Smiles**[23] 1758 6-9-10 **53** (bt) MattieBatchelor 4 28
(R T Phillips) *led tl hdd & wknd 4f out* **5/1**

0000 **8** *27* **Aston Boy**[9] 4676 5-8-11 **45** KierenFox(5) 2 —
(M Blanshard) *a in rr: lost tch fnl 5f* **40/1**

00 **9** *1 ½* **Finzi Contini (FR)**[34] 3848 6-9-11 **54** (v[1]) FrannyNorton 8 —
(Tim Vaughan) *a in rr: lost tch fnl 5f* **20/1**

4m 2.19s (-1.41) **Going Correction** -0.05s/f (Good)
WFA 3 from 4yo+ 18lb 9 Ran SP% **118.0**
Speed ratings (Par 101): **101,100,97,97,96 87,86,74,73**
toteswingers:1&2 £3.70, 2&3 £4.80, 1&3 £2.90 CSF £22.45 CT £42.49 TOTE £6.40: £3.80, £2.10, £1.02; EX 23.80.
Owner The MacDougall Two **Bred** R E Crutchley **Trained** Newmarket, Suffolk

FOCUS
A low-grade staying event run at an even gallop. It was quite a staying test and may not be form to take too literally, but the winner posted a clear personal best at face value.

4991 FOREST OF DEAN WYE VALLEY REVIEW H'CAP — 1m 4f 23y
7:55 (7:57) (Class 6) (0-60,58) 3-Y-O+ **£1,942** (£578; £216; £216) **Stalls** Low

Form RPR

0-01 **1** **Bute Street**[9] 4676 5-9-9 **52** 6ex WilliamCarson 8 64
(R J Hodges) *trckd ldr: led 4f out: rdn 2f out: hld on wl ins fnl f* **5/1**[1]

-304 **2** ½ **Fine Lace (IRE)**[13] 4545 3-9-2 **56** .... JamesDoyle 4 67
(D J S Ffrench Davis) *in rr: rdn along fr 5f out: styd on fr over 2f out to chse wnr over 1f out: styd on to cl u.p fnl 120yds: a hld* **5/1**[1]

26 **3** 8 **Red Current**[17] 984 6-9-3 **46** .... TonyCulhane 3 44
(M J Scudamore) *s.i.s: sn chsng ldrs: rdn to chse wnr ins fnl 3f: no ch 2f out and lost 2nd over 1f out* **28/1**

0044 **3** dht **Princess Flame (GER)**[9] 4676 8-8-13 **47** .... KylieManser(5) 12 45
(B G Powell) *towards rr whn rdn and n.m.r bnd 6f out: rdn over 3f out: styd on fr over 1f out to share wl hld 3rd on line* **10/1**[3]

03 **5** shd **Suor Angelica (IRE)**[9] 4676 5-8-13 **45** .... MatthewDavies(3) 6 43
(George Baker) *sn slt ld: rdn and hdd 4f out: sn one pce but kpt on u.p fnl f to press for wl hld 3rd nr fin* **16/1**

5004 **6** ¾ **Special Cuvee**[8] 4689 4-9-7 **55** .... GemmaGracey-Davison(5) 11 52
(Mrs A M Thorpe) *in rr: rdn over 3f out: styd on fr over 1f out to cl on wl hld plcd horse nr fin* **16/1**

6665 **7** ¾ **Highland Cadett**[13] 4552 3-8-3 **50** ....(v) AdamBeschizza(7) 7 46
(B R Millman) *chsd ldrs: rdn over 3f out: styd on same pce fnl 2f* **11/1**

6460 **8** 15 **Dulce Domum**[37] 3760 4-8-11 **45** .... DeclanCannon(5) 15 17
(A B Haynes) *in rr whn awkward and rdn bnd 6f out: sme hdwy 5f out: wknd fr 4f out* **12/1**

2240 **9** 11 **Port Hill**[45] 3519 3-9-4 **58** .... TomMcLaughlin 5 12
(W M Brisbourne) *a towards rr* **18/1**

-146 **10** 29 **It's A Deal (IRE)**[61] 2953 3-8-13 **53** .... LukeMorris 16 —
(P Winkworth) *pressed ldrs tl wknd 4f out: t.o* **17/2**[2]

2m 40.69s (1.69) **Going Correction** -0.05s/f (Good)
WFA 3 from 4yo+ 11lb **10** Ran SP% **89.5**
Speed ratings (Par 101): **92,91,86,86,86 85,85,75,67,48**PL: Princess Flame £2.10, Red Current £2.60 TRI: Bute Street/Fine Lace/PF £49.66. BS/FL/RC £128.46 toteswingers: 1&2 £3.60, 1& Princess Flame £2.10, 1& Red Current £2.20, PF&2 £2.20, RC&2 £8.60 CSF £PL: Princess Flame £2.10, Red Current £2.60 TRI: Bute Street/Fine Lace/PF £49.66. BS/FL/RC £128.46 toteswingers: 1&2 £3.60, 1& Princess Flame £2.10, 1& Red Current £2.20, PF&2 £2.20, RC&2 £8.60.

Owner J W Mursell **Bred** J W Mursell **Trained** Charlton Mackrell, Somerset
■ Green Energy (5/2F) and Gold Ring (28/1) were withdrawn after proving unruly in the stalls. Deduct 25p in the £ under R4.

FOCUS
Another weak contest, even more so when well-backed favourite Green Energy was withdrawn at the start. The winner built on his latest C&D win but the form does not look that solid.

4992 LINDLEY CATERING H'CAP 1m 2f 36y
8:25 (8:28) (Class 6) (0-55,55) 3-Y-O+ **£2,460** (£732; £365; £182) **Stalls** Low

Form RPR

4040 **1** **Pennfield Pirate**[8] 4689 3-8-11 **55** .... TravisBlock 7 64
(H Morrison) *chsd ldrs: led appr fnl 3f: drvn and styd on wl fr over 1f out* **8/1**

-404 **2** 1¼ **Oriental Girl**[20] 4327 5-8-13 **55** .... RyanPowell(7) 16 62+
(J S Moore) *reluctant to enter stalls: hood removed late and lost 10 l: stdy hdwy on outside fr 4f out: clsng on ldrs whn hung lft 2f out: styd on to chse wnr fnl 120yds: no imp: unlucky* **4/1**[1]

0513 **3** ¾ **Corrib (IRE)**[17] 4434 7-9-1 **50** ....(p) NeilChalmers 9 55
(B Palling) *in tch: hdwy 3f out: drvn to chse wnr 1f out: no imp and lost 2nd fnl 120yds* **11/2**[3]

0530 **4** 1½ **Aspirational (IRE)**[56] 3128 4-8-8 **48** .... DeclanCannon(5) 2 50
(B Palling) *sn led: hdd appr fnl 3f: styd on same pce: lost 2nd 1f out: wknd fnl 120yds* **10/1**

4263 **5** hd **Farncombe (IRE)**[19] 4361 4-9-2 **51** .... TonyCulhane 4 53
(M J Scudamore) *chsd ldrs: rdn 3f out: styd on same pce fnl 2f* **14/1**

0006 **6** ¾ **Oak Leaves**[8] 4689 3-8-0 **50** ow1 .... AdamBeschizza(7) 1 51
(J G Portman) *chsd ldrs: rdn and outpcd over 2f out: sn swtchd rt to outside and styd on again ins fnl f* **5/1**[2]

0045 **7** 1 **Catholic Hill (USA)**[10] 3473 5-8-9 **47** .... MichaelStainton(3) 3 47
(Mark Gillard) *pressed ldr 3f: styd front rnk tl wknd fr 2f out: no ch whn hmpd on rail ins fnl f* **18/1**

-400 **8** hd **Glan Y Mor (IRE)**[52] 3263 3-8-0 **49** .... KierenFox(5) 6 47
(A W Carroll) *t.k.h: stdd towards rr after 3f: hdwy 4f out: chsd ldrs 3f out: wknd over 1f out* **14/1**

1550 **9** ¾ **Under Fire (IRE)**[6] 4793 7-9-6 **55** .... JamesDoyle 11 51
(A W Carroll) *chsd ldrs: rdn 3f out: wknd fr 2f out* **10/1**

500 **10** 7 **Kitty Koo (IRE)**[162] 768 3-8-5 **52** .... AndrewHeffernan(3) 15 34
(A W Carroll) *nvr bttr than mid-div* **50/1**

0-40 **11** 2 **Carnival Time (IRE)**[21] 4289 3-8-10 **54** .... LukeMorris 12 32
(C G Cox) *s.i.s: sn in tch: rdn 5f out: sn bhd* **12/1**

1250 **12** 2½ **Jackie Kiely**[59] 3028 9-8-12 **50** ....(vt[1]) JamesSullivan(3) 10 23
(R Brotherton) *sn bhd* **10/1**

5000 **13** ¾ **Tigers Charm**[9] 4679 3-8-2 **46** oh1 ....(t) FrannyNorton 14 18
(J M Bradley) *bhd most of way* **40/1**

0510 **14** 15 **Market Puzzle (IRE)**[24] 4212 3-8-9 **53** .... TomMcLaughlin 13 —
(W M Brisbourne) *bhd most of way* **16/1**

2m 11.56s (0.96) **Going Correction** -0.05s/f (Good)
WFA 3 from 4yo+ 9lb **14** Ran SP% **127.0**
Speed ratings (Par 101): **94,93,92,91,91 90,89,89,88,83 81,79,79,67**
CSF £42.16 CT £201.37 TOTE £9.70: £3.00, £2.10, £1.50; EX 45.90 Place 6: £42.27 Place 5: £15.76.

Owner Beahan, Morrison **Bred** Whatton Manor Stud **Trained** East Ilsley, Berks

FOCUS
An ordinary handicap won in decent style by the winner, but that would surely not have been the outcome had Oriental Girl not completely blown the start. The form is rated around the winner and third.

Oriental Girl Official explanation: jockey said, regarding running, that the blindfold was difficult to remove and the mare missed the break

T/Plt: £49.50 to a £1 stake. Pool:£64,263.54 - 946.57 winning tickets T/Qpdt: £4.00 to a £1 stake. Pool:£6,667.88 - 1,231.30 winning tickets ST

4498 EPSOM (L-H)
Thursday, August 12

OFFICIAL GOING: Good to soft (good in places; 7.5 home straight: far side 7.2; stands' side 7.4)
Rail dolled out 6yds from 1m to 6f, thereafter dolled out 3- 4yds down hill and up home straight increasing distances by about 8yds
Wind: fresh, half against Weather: overcast

4993 RACEHORSE SANCTUARY "ZIGAURA" EBF MAIDEN STKS 1m 114y
2:20 (2:24) (Class 4) 2-Y-O **£4,533** (£1,348; £674; £336) **Stalls** Low

Form RPR

1 **Suzy Wong** 2-8-12 0 .... SebSanders 9 78+
(J Akehurst) *s.i.s: sn in midfield on outer: hdwy to chse ldng pair over 2f out: led and rn green over 1f out: r.o strly and drew wl clr ins fnl f* **33/1**

0 **2** 5 **Time To Work (IRE)**[62] 2932 2-9-3 0 .... LiamKeniry 8 71
(A M Balding) *s.i.s: bhd in last trio: pushed along and hdwy 3f out: kpt on u.p fr over 1f out: wnt 2nd ins fnl f: no ch w wnr* **12/1**

533 **3** 1¾ **Zakon (IRE)**[28] 4054 2-9-3 69 .... ShaneKelly 1 67
(D J Coakley) *sn bustled up to chse ldr: pushed into ld wl over 2f out: rdn and hdd over 1f out: drvn and nt gng pce of wnr ent fnl f: lost 2nd ins fnl f* **5/1**[3]

634 **4** 3¾ **Il Battista**[16] 4447 2-9-3 71 ....(v[1]) JamesDoyle 7 59
(A J McCabe) *reminders sn after s: in tch in midfield: effrt and rdn to chse clr ldng pair over 2f out: sn no imp after: 4th and wl btn 1f out* **14/1**

5 ¾ **Swaninstockwell (IRE)** 2-9-3 0 .... IanMongan 5 57
(P M Phelan) *s.i.s: bhd: stl plenty to do ent fnl 2f: styd on steadily fr wl over 1f out: nvr trbld ldrs* **50/1**

000 **6** 5 **Seas Of Sorrow (IRE)**[51] 3296 2-8-12 0 .... DaneO'Neill 10 42
(B W Duke) *t.k.h: chsd ldrs: rdn and racd awkwardly wl over 2f out: sn struggling: no ch fr wl over 1f out* **100/1**

45 **7** nk **Swift Alhaarth (IRE)**[20] 4346 2-9-3 0 .... GregFairley 11 46
(M Johnston) *led tl rdn and hdd wl over 2f out: wknd 2f out and sn wl btn* **4/1**[2]

63 **8** 2¾ **Book Keeper**[14] 4499 2-9-3 0 .... AhmedAjtebi 4 40
(Mahmood Al Zarooni) *nvr looked happy in midfield: effrt: unbalanced and hanging lft fr 3f out: no prog and nvr trbld ldrs: wl bhd and eased ins fnl f* **5/4**[1]

0 **9** ½ **Orange Ketchup (IRE)**[41] 3631 2-9-3 0 .... AlanMunro 3 39
(P F I Cole) *a bhd: struggling on downhill run over 4f out: wl bhd fnl 3f* **8/1**

6523 **10** 3 **Pigeon Hollow**[7] 4741 2-9-3 70 .... SamHitchcott 6 33
(M R Channon) *chsd ldrs: pushed along after 2f: lost pl u.p 3f out: sn bhd: eased ins fnl f* **8/1**

1m 48.63s (2.53) **Going Correction** +0.125s/f (Good) **10** Ran SP% **123.6**
Speed ratings (Par 96): **93,88,87,83,83 78,78,75,75,72**
toteswingers:1&2 £26.60, 2&3 £9.50, 1&3 £12.50 CSF £400.72 TOTE £42.30: £7.20, £4.00, £1.30; EX 260.10 TRIFECTA Not won..

Owner Giles W Pritchard-Gordon **Bred** Giles W Pritchard-Gordon (farming) Ltd **Trained** Epsom, Surrey

FOCUS
This didn't look a strong maiden, so even though the winner was an outsider, it wasn't a surprise that a newcomer was successful.

NOTEBOOK
Suzy Wong ◆, the first foal of a useful maiden mare, settled in midfield early before coming with a sweeping effort round the outside of the field to win in good style. It's debatable that she beat much, but she was visually impressive and looks a useful prospect.
Time To Work(IRE) finished up well beaten on debut at Sandown but seemingly learnt plenty from that run, and stayed on in promising style to get into second. (op 9-1)
Zakon(IRE), third at this course last time, attracted support and was ridden prominently to have every chance. He hit the front over 2f out and kept going, but was unable to match the winner's kick in the latter stages, and lost second place inside the final furlong. (op 13-2 tchd 7-1)
Il Battista, visored for the first time, was one of many in trouble turning in and never posed a threat. (op 12-1 tchd 11-1)
Swaninstockwell(IRE), related to a couple of winners, got behind on his debut but made pleasing progress from 3f out, and hinted at ability.
Swift Alhaarth(IRE), up in trip, got to an easy lead but offered nothing once joined. (op 5-1 tchd 7-2)
Book Keeper, who gave a little trouble at the start, has only ever raced at this course (over 7f), but didn't seem to handle the track this time once under pressure. (op 6-4 tchd 13-8 in a place)
Pigeon Hollow, who finished in front of Book Keeper at the end of July, was never going and was most disappointing. (op 9-1 tchd 10-1)

4994 THOROUGHBRED GENETICS H'CAP 1m 114y
2:50 (2:52) (Class 5) (0-75,71) 3-Y-O **£4,209** (£1,252; £625; £312) **Stalls** Low

Form RPR

0331 **1** **Super Duplex**[3] 4907 3-9-0 **62** 6ex .... IanMongan 4 71+
(P M Phelan) *stdd s: hld up in last pair: gd hdwy to join ldrs 4f out: led wl over 2f out: sn edgd lft u.p: styd on wl ins fnl f: rdn out* **10/3**[2]

-055 **2** 2 **Rodrigo De Freitas (IRE)**[6] 4791 3-8-10 **58** .... PatCosgrave 6 62
(J R Boyle) *s.i.s: sn rcvrd and in tch: rdn and effrt over 3f out: chsd wnr over 1f out: edgd lft and no imp fnl 100yds* **11/1**

2313 **3** 3 **The Shuffler**[15] 4491 3-9-9 **71** .... GeorgeBaker 1 68+
(G L Moore) *stdd s: hld up in last: shkn up 3f out: rdn and hdwy to chse ldng pair jst over 1f out: one pce and no imp ins fnl f* **11/4**[1]

5223 **4** 4½ **Catchanova (IRE)**[7] 4756 3-8-11 **59** .... SebSanders 5 46
(Eve Johnson Houghton) *sn chsng ldr: ev ch over 3f out: rdn and nt gng pce of wnr ent fnl 2f: hung lft and wknd jst over 1f out* **11/4**[1]

5630 **5** hd **Mountrath**[17] 4422 3-9-9 **71** .... LiamKeniry 2 57
(B R Johnson) *chsd ldng pair: rdn and unable qck over 2f out: struggling whn short of room 2f out: sn edging rt and lft and wl btn ins fnl f* **11/2**[3]

6035 **6** 2½ **Lou Bear (IRE)**[6] 4793 3-8-7 **55** .... AlanMunro 3 36
(J Akehurst) *led tl rdn and hdd over 2f out: wknd wl over 1f out: bhd ins fnl f* **9/1**

1m 47.42s (1.32) **Going Correction** +0.125s/f (Good) **6** Ran SP% **110.1**
Speed ratings (Par 100): **99,97,94,90,90 88**
toteswingers:1&2 £5.40, 2&3 £6.50, 1&3 £2.30 CSF £34.99 TOTE £3.90: £2.40, £7.00; EX 33.20.

Owner Special Piping Materials Ltd **Bred** Ermyn Lodge Stud Limited **Trained** Epsom, Surrey

FOCUS
A weak-looking handicap, with four of these were maidens coming into it, but the form reads sound. The early pace didn't seem strong, and the winner may have nicked it off the home bend. He built on his Windsor win.

4995 TOTEPOOL FLEXI BETTING H'CAP 7f
3:25 (3:25) (Class 3) (0-90,90) 3-Y-O+ **£6,476** (£1,927; £963; £481) **Stalls** Low

Form RPR

6022 **1** **Woodcote Place**[21] 4296 7-9-4 **82** GeorgeBaker 4 91
(P R Chamings) *hld up in tch in midfield: hdwy and edging out rt over 2f out: rdn to ld over 1f out: styd on wl ins fnl f: rdn out* **8/1**

0246 **2** 1 **Mishrif (USA)**[2] 4929 4-9-0 **78** (b) SebSanders 11 84
(J R Jenkins) *in tch in midfield on outer: hdwy u.p ent fnl 2f: kpt on to chse wnr ins fnl f: no imp fnl 75yds* **15/2**

5-04 **3** 1 ½ **Suffolk Punch (IRE)**[27] 4104 3-8-13 **83** LiamKeniry 9 83
(A M Balding) *chsd ldrs: effrt u.p ent fnl 2f: kpt on u.p ins fnl f: nt gng pce to rch ldrs* **11/2**[2]

0015 **4** 1 **Guilded Warrior**[23] 4224 7-9-12 **90** IanMongan 5 89
(W S Kittow) *chsd ldr tl wnt upsides 4f out: rdn ent fnl 3f: chalng whn bumping match w rival over 2f out: led over 1f out: sn hdd: wknd ins fnl f* **14/1**

2441 **5** ¾ **Hot Spark**[12] 4593 3-8-13 **83** (t) DaneO'Neill 10 78+
(J Akehurst) *in rr: rdn and effrt over 2f out: styd on ins fnl f: nvr trbld ldrs* **15/2**

0633 **6** ½ **Viking Spirit**[20] 4333 8-9-0 **78** AdamKirby 6 74
(W R Swinburn) *hld up in last trio: rdn and effrt 2f out: kpt on same pce ins fnl f: nvr trbld ldrs* **9/1**

0001 **7** 1 **Golden Shaheen (IRE)**[19] 4369 3-9-4 **88** (b) GregFairley 1 79
(M Johnston) *dwlt: sn bustled up to chse ldrs: rdn 3f out: bumping match w rival and chal over 2f out: led 2f out: tl over 1f out: wknd ins fnl f* **7/2**[1]

6000 **8** 1 ½ **Cornus**[5] 4832 8-9-7 **85** (be) JamesDoyle 8 74
(A J McCabe) *stdd and dropped in bhd after s: bhd: effrt on inner whn nt clr run and swtchd rt over 2f out: no prog after and n.d* **33/1**

-040 **9** 3 ½ **Aye Aye Digby (IRE)**[13] 4536 5-9-10 **88** PatCosgrave 7 68
(J R Boyle) *hld up in tch in midfield: rdn and fnd little 2f out: wl btn ins fnl f* **9/1**

0663 **10** 5 **Hi Shinko**[35] 3813 4-8-7 **71** ChrisCatlin 3 37
(B R Millman) *led tl rdn and hdd 2f out: sn btn: wknd over 1f out: eased wl ins fnl f* **6/1**[3]

1m 24.46s (1.16) **Going Correction** +0.125s/f (Good)
WFA 3 from 4yo+ 6lb **10** Ran SP% **116.1**
Speed ratings (Par 107): **98,96,95,94,93 92,91,89,85,80**
toteswingers:1&2 £7.10, 2&3 £7.50, 1&3 £8.90 CSF £66.40 CT £368.37 TOTE £12.20: £4.30, £1.60; £2.30; EX 86.60 TRIFECTA Not won..
Owner The Foxford House Partnership **Bred** Mrs Ann Jenkins **Trained** Baughurst, Hants

FOCUS
As one would expect, the pace seemed sound for a competitive handicap. However, quite a few of these didn't appear to handle the track inside the final 3f and the form may not be that reliable. The winner produced his best effort for a year.

NOTEBOOK
Woodcote Place, beaten a nose last time over C&D, doesn't win that often and seemed on a high enough mark but, after being dropped into middle of the pack, he got a trademark Baker hold-up ride to be produced at the right time just over 1f out. Given his overall record, he won't appeal as one to back to follow up. (op 17-2 tchd 9-1)
Mishrif(USA), down in trip after running over 1m114yd at this course last time, likes to get on with things but was ridden with a bit of restraint here from the widest draw. He kept on well towards the centre of the track but didn't help his cause by hanging. (op 10-1)
Suffolk Punch(IRE), dropped a couple of pounds since his last run, was less exposed that most and has threatened to be better than his current mark on occasions. A juvenile C&D winner, he could not get on terms because he edged right a little under pressure.
Guilded Warrior, back down to 7f, looks high in the weights on his winning form but had run well on his one previous outing at this course last season, again over this trip. He helped to force the pace with Hi Shinko and kept on at the one speed after holding every chance. (tchd 16-1)
Hot Spark looked a surprise winner in late July at Newmarket on his first outing for this stable, and was raised 6lb for that success. He wasn't going anywhere quickly 3f out but picked up well inside the final furlong to be closing at the end. (op 13-2 tchd 6-1)
Viking Spirit ◆, without a win since May 2008, is certainly well treated now on his winning handicap form and hinted that he is not far off a success with a fair effort from off the pace. (op 15-2)
Golden Shaheen(IRE), raised 8lb for winning at Newcastle over 6f on his previous start, dropped away after hitting the front briefly. He seems to win or be well beaten. (op 4-1 tchd 9-2)
Aye Aye Digby(IRE) was back down to his last winning handicap mark, and had run well at this track in the past, albeit over 6f. He appeared to lose his footing on the bend and needed riding along from that point to stay in contention. Official explanation: jockey said gelding lost its action coming down the hill (op 15-2)

4996 RACEHORSE SANCTUARY "MOORCROFT BOY" H'CAP 1m 2f 18y
4:00 (4:01) (Class 4) (0-85,85) 3-Y-O+ **£5,180** (£1,541; £770; £384) **Stalls** Low

Form RPR

2033 **1** **Resurge (IRE)**[21] 4306 5-9-9 **80** IanMongan 7 93
(W S Kittow) *hld up in last pair: hdwy to chse ldrs 3f out: rdn and qcknd to ld 2f out: sn clr: r.o wl: comf* **6/1**[3]

4351 **2** 4 **Wiggy Smith**[15] 4476 11-9-8 **79** DaneO'Neill 8 84
(H Candy) *hld up towards rr: hdwy on outer 3f out: sn rdn: kpt on to chse wnr ins fnl f: no imp* **20/1**

4560 **3** nk **Laudatory**[41] 3632 4-9-7 **78** AdamKirby 4 82
(W R Swinburn) *hld up wl in tch: rdn and unable qck jst over 2f out: no ch w wnr and kpt on same pce u.p ins fnl f* **8/1**

0603 **4** 1 ½ **Majuro (IRE)**[10] 4660 6-10-0 **85** GeorgeBaker 1 86
(C F Wall) *stdd after s: hld up in rr: shkn up over 2f out: no prog tl kpt on ins fnl f: no ch w wnr* **16/1**

0-60 **5** 2 ½ **Sanctuary**[11] 4619 4-9-8 **79** TomEaves 9 75
(B Smart) *restless in stalls: hld up in tch towards rr: pushed and racing awkwardly on downhill run 4f out: hdwy and disputing 2nd wl over 1f out: sn hung lft and no prog: wknd ins fnl f* **9/1**

4125 **6** 3 **Inspirina (IRE)**[18] 4405 6-9-7 **78** AlanMunro 6 68
(R Ford) *t.k.h: chsd ldr tl led wl over 2f out: hdd and nt gng pce of wnr 2f out: lost 2nd ent fnl f: sn wknd* **8/1**

5421 **7** 3 ¼ **Flying Destination**[21] 4306 3-9-4 **84** ShaneKelly 5 68
(W J Knight) *chsd ldrs: unable qck u.p over 2f out: wknd wl over 1f out: wl bhd ins fnl f* **3/1**[1]

6551 **8** 11 **Fame Is The Spur**[19] 4381 3-8-2 **71** MartinLane(3) 2 33
(J W Hills) *chsd ldrs tl lost pl u.p 3f out: bhd whn nt clr run and swtchd rt over 2f out: sn lost tch: eased ins fnl f* **5/1**[2]

11-2 **P** **Kaleo**[35] 3814 6-9-9 **80** SebSanders 3 —
(S Dow) *led tl hdd and eased wl over 2f out: sn t.o: p.u and dismntd nr fin* **5/1**[2]

2m 9.59s (-0.11) **Going Correction** +0.125s/f (Good)
WFA 3 from 4yo+ 9lb **9** Ran SP% **115.5**
Speed ratings (Par 105): **105,101,101,100,98 95,93,84,—**
toteswingers:1&2 £7.20, 2&3 £18.50, 1&3 £9.40 CSF £114.73 CT £964.14 TOTE £8.20: £3.50, £6.70, £5.80; EX 60.20 TRIFECTA Not won..
Owner Chris & David Stam **Bred** Sweetmans Bloodstock **Trained** Blackborough, Devon

FOCUS
The early pace was far from strong and only appeared to significantly increase on the home bend. The runner-up is the best guide to the form.
Wiggy Smith Official explanation: jockey said gelding hung left
Kaleo Official explanation: jockey said gelding lost its action

4997 ROB MAYALL BIRTHDAY BASH MAIDEN FILLIES' STKS 1m 114y
4:35 (4:36) (Class 5) 3-Y-O+ **£3,238** (£963; £481; £240) **Stalls** Low

Form RPR

062 **1** **Fork Lightning (USA)**[20] 4339 3-8-12 73 SebSanders 6 79+
(Sir Mark Prescott) *stdd s: hld up wl in tch: rdn to chse ldng pair ent fnl 2f: led and rn green over 1f out: r.o strly and clr ins fnl f: comf* **4/5**[1]

3 **2** 4 **Shamardal Phantom (IRE)**[18] 4397 3-8-9 0 MartinLane(3) 4 70
(D M Simcock) *stdd s: hld up in last: hdwy and swtchd rt jst over 2f out: kpt on u.p to chse wnr jst ins fnl f: no imp after* **4/1**[2]

5356 **3** 2 **Treasure Way**[15] 4492 3-8-12 66 LiamKeniry 7 65
(P R Chamings) *chsd ldr: ev ch and rdn ent fnl 3f: led over 2f out: hdd over 1f out: sn outpcd by wnr: wl hld ins fnl f* **8/1**

00-5 **4** 2 **Child Of Our Time (IRE)**[18] 4397 3-8-12 69 AlanMunro 1 61
(P W Chapple-Hyam) *in tch: rdn and effrt over 2f out: outpcd jst over 2f out: one pce and wl hld fr over 1f out* **14/1**

50 **5** 1 **Mexican Deb**[18] 4397 3-8-12 0 DaneO'Neill 3 59
(W R Muir) *t.k.h early: hld up in tch towards rr: effrt and rdn over 2f out: sn outpcd and no ch fr over 1f out* **25/1**

06 **6** nk **Hotfoot**[17] 4425 3-8-12 0 IvaMilickova 8 58?
(John Berry) *in tch: rdn and effrt over 2f out: sn outpcd and wl hld fr over 1f out* **66/1**

66 **7** 3 ¼ **Bill's Story**[21] 4307 3-8-12 0 AdamKirby 2 50
(M R Channon) *chsd ldrs tl wknd u.p ent fnl 2f: wl btn over 1f out* **25/1**

35-2 **8** 3 **Sasheen**[17] 4425 3-8-12 70 PatCosgrave 5 43
(J R Boyle) *led tl over 2f out: wknd qckly wl over 1f out: wl bhd ins fnl f: eased towards fin* **6/1**[3]

1m 47.72s (1.62) **Going Correction** +0.125s/f (Good) **8** Ran SP% **116.8**
Speed ratings (Par 100): **97,93,91,89,89 88,85,83**
toteswingers: 1&2 £2.00, 1&3 £2.70, 2&3 £5.30 CSF £4.28 TOTE £1.60: £1.10, £2.40, £2.00; EX 4.70 Trifecta £18.50 Pool: £702.78 - 27.99 winning units..
Owner Denford Stud **Bred** Belgrave Bloodstock Limited **Trained** Newmarket, Suffolk

FOCUS
A modest fillies' maiden, rated around the runner-up. The winner probably didn't need to improve.

4998 KENWARD GROUNDWORKS H'CAP 6f
5:10 (5:10) (Class 5) (0-70,68) 3-Y-O **£4,209** (£1,252; £625; £312) **Stalls** High

Form RPR

-631 **1** **Micky P**[61] 2962 3-9-7 **66** JackMitchell 5 67+
(S C Williams) *bmpd s: in tch: hdwy over 3f out: rdn to chse ldr 2f out: ev ch over 1f out: drvn to ld jst ins fnl f: edgd lft fnl 100yds: hld on u.p towards fin* **11/10**[1]

6053 **2** nk **Gessabelle**[7] 4760 3-7-11 **49** oh4 (t) LeonnaMayor(7) 3 49
(P S McEntee) *dwlt and bmpd s: in tch in last: rdn and hanging lft over 2f out: swtchd rt and hdwy over 1f out: hung lft ent fnl f: r.o to press wnr fnl 50yds: hld towards fin* **20/1**

4221 **3** 2 **Admirable Duchess**[13] 4531 3-9-9 **68** JamesDoyle 6 62
(D J S Ffrench Davis) *broke wl: led: rdn 2f out: drvn and hdd jst ins fnl f: keeping on same pce and hld whn short of room and swtchd rt towards fin* **5/2**[2]

3453 **4** 3 ¾ **Annia Galeria (IRE)**[8] 4720 3-7-13 **51** oh2 ow2 MatthewCosham(7) 1 33
(C A Dwyer) *chsd ldr tl 2f out: wknd qckly ins fnl f* **10/1**

2032 **5** 2 ¼ **Mrs Mogg**[26] 4151 3-9-3 **62** SebSanders 2 36
(Tom Dascombe) *chsd ldrs: rdn and chsd ldr over 2f out tl 2f out: unbalanced and wknd qckly jst over 1f out* **4/1**[3]

1m 12.39s (2.99) **Going Correction** +0.125s/f (Good) **5** Ran SP% **110.0**
Speed ratings (Par 100): **85,84,81,76,73**
CSF £21.68 TOTE £1.70: £2.30, £7.10; EX 32.60 Place 6: £561.05 Place 5: £121.48.
Owner O Pointing **Bred** O Pointing **Trained** Newmarket, Suffolk

FOCUS
A weak sprint handicap. The second lends doubts to the form and it is unlikely the winner had to improve.
T/Plt: £823.10 to a £1 stake. Pool of £45,778.07 - 40.60 winning tickets. T/Qpdt: £42.60 to a £1 stake. Pool of £4,179.37 - 72.57 winning tickets. SP

4573 GOODWOOD (R-H)
Thursday, August 12

OFFICIAL GOING: Good (good to soft in places on straight course; 7.8)
Rail from 6f on lower bend to winning post dolled out 8yds. Top bend dolled out 4yds increasing distances on round course by about 15yds
Wind: Moderate, half against Weather: Fine but cloudy

4999 IWC MAIDEN AUCTION STKS 6f
4:55 (4:55) (Class 4) 2-Y-O **£3,238** (£963; £481; £240) **Stalls** Low

Form RPR

5 **1** **Winter's Night (IRE)**[27] 4095 2-8-6 0 PhilipRobinson 8 72+
(C G Cox) *pressed ldr: led over 2f out: rdn over 1f out: styd on wl to assert ins fnl f* **4/6**[1]

36 **2** 1 ½ **Hard Bargain (IRE)**[26] 4131 2-8-11 0 EddieAhern 4 72
(D J Coakley) *trckd ldrs: rdn to chse wnr over 1f out: tried to cl ent fnl f: no imp last 150yds and jst pushed along* **9/2**[2]

05 **3** 2 ½ **Bouzy**[29] 4029 2-8-4 0 FrankieMcDonald 3 57+
(P Winkworth) *hld up towards rr: rdn wl over 2f out: prog wl over 1f out: stl looked green: kpt on to hold 3rd ins fnl f* **40/1**

6 **4** nk **Secret Tycoon (IRE)**[13] 4543 2-9-1 0 StephenCraine 9 67
(Patrick Morris) *trckd ldng pair: rdn and nt qckn 2f out: outpcd ins fnl f* **14/1**

5 1 ¾ **Song Of The Siren** 2-8-4 0 DavidProbert 6 50
(A M Balding) *trckd ldrs: shkn up over 2f out: outpcd fr over 1f out* **8/1**

00 **6** *4* **Only Ten Per Cent (IRE)**[17] 4437 2-8-9 0 CathyGannon 2 43
(J S Moore) *settled in rr: shkn up over 2f out: sn outpcd: n.d after* **100/1**

0 **7** *3* **Music News (USA)**[101] 1749 2-8-13 0 WilliamBuick 7 37
(M Johnston) *led and trckd across to nr side rail: hdd over 2f out: wknd over 1f out: eased* **7/1**[3]

00 **8** *5* **Titan Diamond (IRE)**[11] 4622 2-8-11 0 EddieCreighton 1 19
(M D I Usher) *a in rr: rdn on outer over 2f out: sn wknd* **100/1**

9 *4 1/2* **Juarla (IRE)** 2-8-4 0 JohnFahy(5) 5 3
(R A Harris) *s.v.s: a last: wknd 2f out* **25/1**

1m 13.56s (1.36) **Going Correction** +0.025s/f (Good) **9** Ran SP% **116.7**
Speed ratings (Par 96): **91,89,85,85,82 77,73,66,60**
toteswingers:1&2 £1.90, 2&3 £6.80, 1&3 £7.80 CSF £3.94 TOTE £1.60: £1.10, £1.10, £4.00; EX 4.20.
Owner J T Thomas **Bred** J T And Mrs Thomas **Trained** Lambourn, Berks

FOCUS
No rain overnight and a dry, breezy day saw the ground dry out to good, good to soft in places. A couple of the riders described the going as "lovely, good ground". The running rail from the 6f marker on the lower bend to the winning post was dolled out approximately 8 yards and the top bend was dolled out approximately 4 yards, increasing distances on the round course by about 15 yards. As the betting suggested, there was very little depth in an uncompetitive maiden and the proximity of the third and fourth confirms this bare form is nothing special. The field headed for the stands' rail after a furlong or so and the two market leaders pulled clear in the closing stages on the back of just an ordinary gallop.

NOTEBOOK
Winter's Night(IRE) had shaped well on her debut in a race that has thrown up winners and fully confirmed that promise, despite racing with the choke out, to justify the market confidence. She should have no problems with 7f and, although this was not a strong race, she is open to improvement and will be an interesting runner in nurseries. (op 4-5)
Hard Bargain(IRE) showed his latest running to be all wrong and posted an effort in keeping with his fair debut effort. He's likely to remain vulnerable to the better types in this grade but should be able to pick up an uncompetitive event.
Bouzy hadn't achieved much on her first two outings but fared a good deal better returned to turf. She should be even better suited by 7f on this evidence and should be seen to better effect in run-of-the mill nurseries.
Secret Tycoon(IRE) again showed ability at an ordinary level on this second start. He is capable of a little better in ordinary nursery company. (op 16-1)
Song Of The Siren, a half-sister to numerous winners from 5f-1m4f, is a leggy type who wasn't totally disgraced on this racecourse debut. She was not unduly knocked about and may do better with time and experience.
Music News(USA), nibbled at in the market, was again soundly beaten but did show up for a longer time. He has a bit of size and scope, is in good hands and may do better as he matures. (op 8-1)

5000 KENWOOD STKS (NURSERY H'CAP) 5f
5:25 (5:26) (Class 5) (0-70,70) 2-Y-O **£2,590** (£770; £385; £192) **Stalls** Low

Form RPR

662 **1** **Jameela Girl**[26] 4149 2-9-6 **67** EddieAhern 9 81+
(R M H Cowell) *pressed ldr: rdn to ld over 1f out: readily drew clr ins fnl f* **7/2**[1]

1602 **2** *3* **Johnny Hancocks (IRE)**[8] 4688 2-9-0 **61** CathyGannon 12 63
(P D Evans) *led: drvn and hdd over 1f out: no ch w wnr: jst hld on for 2nd* **13/2**

0600 **3** *shd* **Robber Stone**[12] 4587 2-8-8 **55** ChrisCatlin 11 57
(M R Channon) *stdd s but sn trckd ldrs: outpcd and shkn up 2f out: styd on wl ins fnl f: nrly snatched 2nd* **16/1**

004 **4** *1* **Till Dawn (IRE)**[17] 4432 2-8-6 **53** DavidProbert 14 51
(A W Carroll) *s.i.s but sn trckd ldng pair: outpcd 2f out: one pce after* **5/1**[2]

053 **5** *2 1/4* **Dubai Affair**[12] 4590 2-9-6 **67** SteveDrowne 1 59+
(H Morrison) *hld up in midfield: already outpcd whn shkn up over 1f out: kpt on same pce after* **7/1**

3323 **6** *1 1/2* **Upark Flyer**[9] 4675 2-9-5 **66** RichardHughes 3 51
(Patrick Morris) *stdd s: hld up wl in rr: gng wl but plenty to do 2f out: shkn up and kpt on: no ch* **15/2**

0556 **7** *1 3/4* **Sarandjam**[9] 4678 2-8-8 **55** EddieCreighton 6 33
(M R Channon) *rdr tk two attempts to remove blindfold and horse slowly away: rdn in rr 1/2-way: kpt on: no ch* **40/1**

0000 **8** *hd* **Three Scoops**[61] 2951 2-8-0 **47** FrankieMcDonald 10 25
(D J S Ffrench Davis) *chsd ldrs: rdn 1/2-way: wknd fnl 2f* **40/1**

5331 **9** *1 1/2* **Scommettitrice (IRE)**[9] 4675 2-9-9 **70** 6ex StephenCraine 5 42
(R A Harris) *chsd ldrs: rdn and steadily wknd fnl 2f* **6/1**[3]

003 **10** *3* **Ignore The Advice (IRE)**[13] 4528 2-8-9 **56** TadhgO'Shea 2 17
(J S Moore) *nvr bttr than midfield: struggling bdly fr 2f out: wknd* **20/1**

U4 **11** *2 3/4* **Chestival (IRE)**[27] 4083 2-8-1 **53** JohnFahy(5) 4 4
(Patrick Morris) *t.k.h: chsd ldrs tl wknd qckly 2f out* **25/1**

6364 **12** *6* **Crazy In Love**[28] 4067 2-8-6 **56** JackDean(3) 8 —
(W G M Turner) *nvr gng wl: sn rdn to stay in tch: wknd 1/2-way: t.o* **50/1**

444 **13** *5* **Novabridge**[12] 4580 2-9-7 **68** WilliamBuick 7 —
(A B Haynes) *dwlt: nvr gng wl and sn bhd: t.o* **12/1**

59.14 secs (0.74) **Going Correction** +0.025s/f (Good) **13** Ran SP% **119.8**
Speed ratings (Par 94): **95,90,90,88,84 82,79,79,76,72 67,58,50**
toteswingers: 1&2 £5.80, 1&3 £12.10, 2&3 £13.20 CSF £24.60 CT £269.71 TOTE £3.30: £1.10, £3.00, £8.00.
Owner Lone Oak Stud/Mrs J Morley/Foulkes **Bred** Lone Oak Stud Mare Syndicate **Trained** Six Mile Bottom, Cambs
■ Stewards' Enquiry : Eddie Creighton jockey said he was slow to remove the blindfold and the colt missed the break

FOCUS
An ordinary nursery on paper, but one that saw a much-improved effort from the winner. The whole field avoided the stands' rail this time and, although the gallop seemed sound throughout, those held up were at a disadvantage.

NOTEBOOK
Jameela Girl ◆ has improved with every run and, after attracting support, turned in easily her best effort on this nursery debut. She is unlikely to be inconvenienced by the return to 6f and will be of obvious interest if turned out before reassessment. (op 4-1)
Johnny Hancocks(IRE), 4lb lower than when returning to form at Brighton last week, had the run of the race and, while no match for the progressive winner, seemed to give it his best shot and should be a reasonable guide to this form. He'll be 4lb higher in future and is exposed but is capable of winning again for this yard. (tchd 11-2)
Robber Stone's maiden form is patchy but he seemed to run creditably, despite edging right when pressure was applied on this nursery debut. He'll be suited by the return to 6f and it will be interesting to see if this can be built on. (op 25-1)
Till Dawn(IRE) was the subject of market support and was far from disgraced returned to turf on this nursery debut. There will be easier opportunities in this grade, she should be equally at home over 6f and she may be capable of a little better. (op 15-2 tchd 8-1)
Dubai Affair ◆ looks better than the bare form after faring the best of those held up and after racing more towards the stands' side than the ones that finished ahead of her on this nursery debut. She was not knocked about, will be better suited by 6f and is one to keep an eye on in similar company, either on turf or Polytrack. (op 9-2 tchd 15-2)
Upark Flyer has been a reliable yardstick in maidens but, even though her opening mark looks a shade high, she wasn't at her best in a race that suited the prominent-racers, but she did reverse recent Chepstow placings with easy-to-back Scommettitrice. Official explanation: jockey said filly hung right (tchd 8-1)
Scommettitrice(IRE)'s run of progressive efforts came to a halt under her penalty on this nursery debut. Life will be tougher in future as she is due to go up another 4lb. (op 5-1 tchd 13-2)
Novabridge Official explanation: jockey said colt never travelled

5001 DELONGHI MAIDEN STKS 1m 1f 192y
5:55 (5:56) (Class 5) 3-Y-O+ **£2,590** (£770; £385; £192) **Stalls** High

Form RPR

4-02 **1** **Lunar Victory (USA)**[24] 4205 3-9-3 84 WilliamBuick 3 89+
(J H M Gosden) *led after 2f: shkn up and stretched wl clr fr over 2f out: eased last 75yds* **1/4**[1]

5 **2** *8* **Priors Gold**[21] 4307 3-9-3 0 RichardHughes 5 67
(M P Tregoning) *hld up in 3rd: shkn up to go 2nd over 2f out: vain pursuit of wnr after* **6/1**[2]

3 *2 1/4* **Pursuit Of Reason** 3-8-12 0 EddieAhern 6 58
(G L Moore) *trckd ldng trio: shkn up and effrt over 3f out: kpt on in modest 3rd fnl 2f* **16/1**

00 **4** *3 3/4* **Voysey (IRE)**[22] 4257 3-9-3 0 PhilipRobinson 7 55
(Mrs A J Perrett) *led 2f: chsd wnr to over 2f out: pushed along and steadily wknd* **18/1**

5 *nk* **Ahaazeeg** 3-9-3 0 TadhgO'Shea 4 54
(J L Dunlop) *s.i.s: a in 5th: outpcd over 3f out: n.d after* **12/1**[3]

0-0 **6** *11* **Bravo Bravo**[10] 4661 3-9-3 0 ChrisCatlin 1 32
(M R Channon) *a in last pair: lft bhd fr over 4f out: t.o* **50/1**

0-0 **7** *18* **Pivotal Express (IRE)**[42] 3593 4-9-9 0 JackDean(3) 2 —
(J F Panvert) *a in last pair: lft bhd fr over 4f out: t.o* **100/1**

2m 8.69s (0.69) **Going Correction** -0.05s/f (Good)
WFA 3 from 4yo 9lb **7** Ran SP% **116.1**
Speed ratings (Par 103): **95,88,86,83,83 74,60**
toteswingers:1&2 £1.20, 2&3 £2.90, 1&3 £2.40 CSF £2.54 TOTE £1.30: £1.10, £2.00; EX 2.40.
Owner K Abdulla **Bred** Willian Parson Jr & David S Howe **Trained** Newmarket, Suffolk

FOCUS
A one-sided maiden with the 84-rated winner proving in a different league to his modest rivals. The gallop was a moderate one. The winner had little to beat but is rated to form.

5002 BUTLINS STKS (H'CAP) 1m 4f
6:30 (6:30) (Class 4) (0-85,84) 3-Y-O+ **£3,885** (£1,156; £577; £288) **Stalls** Low

Form RPR

5216 **1** **Nave (USA)**[3] 4891 3-8-10 **77** GregFairley 4 88
(M Johnston) *hld up in 4th: shkn up and clsd over 3f out: rdn to ld over 2f out: styd on wl* **7/2**[2]

0543 **2** *2 1/4* **Dakiyah (IRE)**[2] 4933 6-9-11 **81** (p) IanMongan 3 88
(Mrs L J Mongan) *hld up in last trio: clsd on ldrs over 3f out: rdn to chse wnr 2f out: fnd nil and sn hld: kpt on* **15/2**

33-5 **3** *5* **Fanditha (IRE)**[69] 2703 4-10-0 **84** KierenFallon 1 83
(L M Cumani) *settled in last trio: rdn and prog over 3f out: disp 2nd 2f out: sn btn: wknd ins fnl f* **9/2**[3]

-434 **4** *1 1/4* **Rockfella**[26] 4147 4-9-4 **74** EddieAhern 7 71
(D J Coakley) *trckd ldng pair: lost pl but stl gng wl enough 3f out: shkn up over 2f out: sn btn* **5/1**

04 **5** *8* **Missionaire (USA)**[19] 4360 3-8-10 **77** ShaneKelly 2 61
(W J Knight) *trckd ldr: led over 3f out to over 2f out: wknd* **3/1**[1]

21/0 **6** *16* **Pathos (GER)**[61] 2975 6-9-8 **78** GeorgeBaker 8 37
(G L Moore) *led to over 3f out: wknd* **15/2**

-116 **7** *62* **Mister New York (USA)**[187] 447 5-9-10 **80** WilliamBuick 5 —
(Noel T Chance) *s.i.s: a last: wknd over 4f out: t.o* **14/1**

2m 36.02s (-2.38) **Going Correction** -0.05s/f (Good)
WFA 3 from 4yo+ 11lb **7** Ran SP% **112.3**
Speed ratings (Par 105): **105,103,100,99,94 83,42**
toteswingers: 1&2 £4.60, 1&3 £2.70, 2&3 £10.40 CSF £28.15 CT £117.61 TOTE £2.60: £1.20, £6.00; EX 37.00.
Owner Anthony Hogarth **Bred** Mineola Farm II Llc Et Al **Trained** Middleham Moor, N Yorks

FOCUS
An open-looking handicap on paper but one in which the market leader disappointed. Although the gallop looked no more than fair, the field finished well strung out. Sound form, the runner-up a solid guide.
Fanditha(IRE) Official explanation: jockey said filly hung right

5003 TANQUERAY STKS (H'CAP) 1m
7:00 (7:01) (Class 4) (0-85,81) 3-Y-O+ **£3,885** (£1,156; £577; £288) **Stalls** High

Form RPR

0406 **1** **Kavachi (IRE)**[16] 4459 7-9-10 **77** GeorgeBaker 1 86+
(G L Moore) *hld up bhd ldrs: clsd over 2f out: rdn to ld 1f out: styd on wl* **9/4**[1]

4010 **2** *1 1/2* **L'Hirondelle (IRE)**[16] 4459 6-9-9 **76** NeilCallan 2 82
(M J Attwater) *t.k.h: reluctant ldr 1f: trckd ldr after: led jst over 2f out: hdd 1f out: nt qckn* **13/2**

3420 **3** *1/2* **Spiritual Art**[21] 4306 4-9-1 **68** RichardHughes 5 73
(L A Dace) *t.k.h: hld up last: cl enough over 2f out: pushed along whn pce lifted 2f out: styd on same pce* **9/2**[3]

1561 **4** *1/2* **Roman Glory (IRE)**[14] 4501 4-10-0 **81** WilliamBuick 4 85
(B J Meehan) *t.k.h: trckd ldng pair: pushed along whn pce lifted 2f out: nt qckn* **3/1**[2]

4063 **5** *2* **Magroom**[28] 4044 6-9-2 **69** SteveDrowne 6 68
(R J Hodges) *hld up in tch: pushed along whn pce lifted 2f out: nt qckn and sn btn* **7/1**

0-04 **6** *1/2* **Marsh Warbler**[40] 3661 3-9-1 **78** MartinLane(3) 3 76
(D M Simcock) *led after 1f at stdy pce: tried to kick on 3f out: hdd jst over 2f out: wknd* **7/1**

1m 41.27s (1.37) **Going Correction** -0.05s/f (Good)
WFA 3 from 4yo+ 7lb **6** Ran SP% **112.3**
Speed ratings (Par 105): **91,89,89,88,86 86**
toteswingers:1&2 £4.20, 2&3 £3.60, 1&3 £2.10 CSF £17.12 TOTE £4.50: £2.60, £5.40; EX 21.70.
Owner Pink Punters & Partners **Bred** Gainsborough Stud Management Ltd **Trained** Lower Beeding, W Sussex

FOCUS

Exposed performers in a fair handicap, but one in which the gallop was moderate. The winner had slipped to a good mark.

5004 TALK TALK STKS (H'CAP) 1m 1f 192y

7:35 (7:36) (Class 3) (0-95,95) 3-Y-O+ **£5,828** (£1,734; £866; £432) **Stalls** High

Form RPR

5-21 **1** **Mirror Lake**[57] 3080 3-8-12 **88**... PatDobbs 8 100+
(Mrs A J Perrett) *trckd ldng pair: wnt 2nd over 2f out: led wl over 1f out: r.o wl: comf* **7/2**[1]

1060 **2** *3 ¼* **Moynahan (USA)**[16] 4455 5-9-8 **89**..............................(p) NeilCallan 7 94
(P F I Cole) *hld up in rr: taken to outer and effrt over 2f out: prog wl over 1f out: wnt 2nd last 100yds: no ch w wnr* **9/2**[2]

-340 **3** *1* **Togiak (IRE)**[55] 3142 3-9-5 **95**............................. RichardHughes 11 98
(E A L Dunlop) *led to over 6f out: chsd ldr to over 2f out: wnt 2nd again jst over 1f out to last 100yds: one pce* **7/1**

01-0 **4** *shd* **Braveheart Move (IRE)**[27] 4100 4-9-13 **94**...................... IanMongan 9 97
(Jonjo O'Neill) *trckd ldr: led over 6f out: drvn and hdd wl over 1f out: outpcd* **25/1**

400/ **5** *3 ¼* **Levera**[652] 4504 7-9-9 **90**.. WilliamBuick 6 86
(A King) *hld up in tch: rdn wl over 2f out: sn outpcd: fdd insd fnl f* **16/1**

0133 **6** *2 ¼* **South Cape**[46] 3483 7-9-5 **86**....................................... GeorgeBaker 5 78
(G L Moore) *dwlt: hld up in last pair: shkn up briefly over 2f out: no prog* **8/1**

0303 **7** *3 ¾* **Mujood**[12] 4579 7-9-5 **89**.. PatrickHills(3) 4 73+
(Eve Johnson Houghton) *chsd ldrs: rdn 3f out: struggling after: eased whn no ch ins fnl f* **12/1**

021- **8** *6* **Botanist**[303] 6759 3-8-11 **87**..................................... RichardMullen 1 59+
(Sir Michael Stoute) *dwlt: hld up in last trio: effrt on outer over 3f out: no prog and btn over 2f out: wknd* **7/2**[1]

-630 **9** *3* **Luc Jordan**[53] 3239 4-9-6 **87**.................................... KierenFallon 2 53+
(L M Cumani) *in tch: effrt over 3f out to chse ldrs: btn 2f out: virtually p.u ins fnl f* **6/1**[3]

2m 7.19s (-0.81) **Going Correction** -0.05s/f (Good)
WFA 3 from 4yo+ 9lb **9** Ran SP% **117.9**
Speed ratings (Par 107): **101,98,97,97,94 93,90,85,82**
toteswingers:1&2 £6.00, 2&3 £8.60, 1&3 £6.50 CSF £19.72 CT £105.61 TOTE £3.30: £1.10, £2.30, £3.80; EX 17.70.
Owner K Abdulla **Bred** Millsec Limited **Trained** Pulborough, W Sussex

FOCUS

The best event quality wise on the card and one in which the winner, a progressive 3-y-o, turned in a performance bordering on smart. The next three home set the standard. The gallop was only fair.

NOTEBOOK

Mirror Lake ◆ has improved with every outing and, after being well placed in a race run at just an ordinary gallop on this first run after a short break, showed a good turn of foot to register a career-best effort. She is only lightly raced, is fully effective on Polytrack, is open to further progress and, although a mark in the mid-90s now looks likely, she appeals strongly as the type to win more races. (tchd 4-1)

Moynahan(USA), with the cheekpieces refitted, didn't look an easy ride but he looks a bit better than the bare fact suggest after faring easily the best of those to come from off the pace after attracting a bit of support. However his record is one of inconsistency, he's not a regular winner and he wouldn't be one to go in head down for at single-figure odds next time. (op 6-1 tchd 4-1)

Togiak(IRE) had been well beaten in a Group 2 over 1m4f at Royal Ascot but fared better after enjoying the run of the race back in trip and returned to this more realistic company. However this illustrated that he may have to drop in the weights before he is able to win a competitive handicap. (op 8-1 tchd 9-1)

Braveheart Move(IRE) was easy to back but who had the run of the race and fared a good deal better than on his previous Flat run at Newbury. He'll be suited by the return to 1m4f but he will be of more interest when getting a sound surface over hurdles (all form over hurdles so far on easy and in soft ground). (op 20-1)

Levera, absent since winning over hurdles in October 2008, should be better for this outing but is another that looks plenty high enough in the weights. He may be suited by a more truly race back over shorter but he'll have to show a fair bit more before he's worth a bet in a competitive handicap.

Botanist had a progressive profile last year and promised to be suited by this sort of trip but he ran as though this race was needed on this handicap debut and first start since. However he is in very good hands, is only lightly raced and is almost certainly worth another chance. (tchd 4-1)

Luc Jordan has yet to match the progressive form he showed last year but, while again well beaten - this time under suitable conditions - his rider reported he had lost his action. Official explanation: jockey said gelding lost its action (op 11-2 tchd 13-2)

5005 VINTAGE CURATORS H'CAP 6f

8:05 (8:06) (Class 5) (0-75,74) 3-Y-O+ **£2,590** (£770; £385; £192) **Stalls** High

Form RPR

0161 **1** **Slip Sliding Away (IRE)**[18] 4398 3-9-5 **73**....................... JohnFahy(5) 4 85+
(P R Hedger) *s.i.s: hld up in last pair: prog on outer over 2f out: rdn to ld jst over 1f out: r.o strly* **15/8**[1]

0400 **2** *3 ½* **Speak The Truth (IRE)**[2] 4930 4-9-6 **65**.................(p) PatCosgrave 7 68
(J R Boyle) *racd on outer: pressed ldr: led 2f out: drvn and hdd jst over 1f out whn wl clr of rest: no ch w wnr after* **7/1**

1203 **3** *2 ½* **Alfresco**[10] 4662 6-10-0 **73**...(b) KierenFallon 1 67
(J R Best) *hld up in last pair: plld out wd 2f out but sn outpcd: kpt on to take modest 3rd ins fnl f* **9/2**[3]

6445 **4** *2 ¾* **Kyllachy Storm**[34] 3851 6-9-9 **68**...............................(b) GeorgeBaker 2 53
(R J Hodges) *t.k.h: hld up bhd ldrs against rail: shkn up and no rspnse 2f out: btn after: tk modest 4th nr fin* **5/1**

-126 **5** *¾* **Pose (IRE)**[24] 4204 3-9-11 **74**.................................... RichardHughes 3 56
(R Hannon) *trckd ldng pair: cl enough and shkn up 2f out: wknd over 1f out: eased ins fnl f* **10/3**[2]

0000 **6** *½* **Goodwood Maestro**[13] 4541 3-9-6 **69**............................ EddieAhern 5 49
(J L Dunlop) *led and crossed to rail: rdn and hdd 2f out: wknd* **10/1**

1m 11.86s (-0.34) **Going Correction** +0.025s/f (Good)
WFA 3 from 4yo+ 4lb **6** Ran SP% **114.3**
Speed ratings (Par 103): **103,98,95,91,90 89**
toteswingers:1&2 £4.40, 2&3 £7.10, 1&3 £1.10 CSF £15.99 TOTE £3.50: £1.70, £4.60; EX 19.60 Place 6: £24.18 Place 5: £18.62 .
Owner Bernard Keay & Partners **Bred** S Holt & A C Beggan & R J Beggan **Trained** Dogmersfield, Hampshire

FOCUS

A fair handicap but one that saw a useful performance from the progressive winner. None of the others are on the upgrade and the form is not rated that solidly. The gallop was a reasonable one and the field raced close to the stands rail.

Pose(IRE) Official explanation: jockey said filly finished lame

T/Plt: £38.10 to a £1 stake. Pool of £34,753.35 - 664.93 winning tickets. T/Qpdt: £12.20 to a £1 stake. Pool of £3,339.40 202.00 winning tickets. JN

4954 SALISBURY (R-H)

Thursday, August 12

OFFICIAL GOING: Good to firm (good in places)

Wind: mild breeze against Weather: overcast with sunny spells

5006 RSM TENON MAIDEN AUCTION STKS 6f 212y

2:30 (2:31) (Class 5) 2-Y-O **£3,238** (£963; £481; £240) **Stalls** Centre

Form RPR

4 **1** **Catalyze**[36] 3785 2-8-9 0...(t) FrannyNorton 7 84+
(A M Balding) *mde all: edgd lft whn rdn 2f out: r.o strly to assert fnl 110yds* **3/1**[2]

5 **2** *4* **Sagramor**[12] 4577 2-8-9 0.. SteveDrowne 5 73
(H Morrison) *trckd ldrs: rdn to chal fr over 2f out: kpt on for clr 2nd: comf hld fnl 110yds* **9/4**[1]

4 **3** *3* **Cornish Quest**[73] 2598 2-8-9 0...................................... DarryllHolland 2 65
(M H Tompkins) *s.i.s: sn mid-div: hdwy 3f out: sn rdn: styd on to chse ldng pair fr wl over 1f out: no further imp* **18/1**

0 **4** *2 ½* **Frederick William**[15] 4490 2-8-13 0................................ NeilCallan 8 62
(P J Makin) *cl up tl short of room whn lost pl after 1f: mid-div: rdn 3f out: styd on ins fnl f* **12/1**

5 *nse* **Mountain Range (IRE)** 2-8-13 0...................................... EddieAhern 9 62+
(J L Dunlop) *sn outpcd in rr: swtchd lft 2f out: styd on fr over 1f out: nvr trbld ldrs* **20/1**

0 **6** *1* **Alshazah**[60] 3000 2-9-2 0... TomMcLaughlin 3 63
(B R Millman) *prom: rdn 3f out: kpt on same pce fr 2f out tl no ex fnl 75yds* **66/1**

7 *½* **Major Domo (FR)** 2-8-9 0... JamieSpencer 13 54
(H J L Dunlop) *trckd ldrs: rdn 3f out: sn edgd lft: one pce fnl 2f* **22/1**

0 **8** *nk* **Boogie Star**[8] 4716 2-8-9 0.. LukeMorris 11 53
(J S Moore) *s.i.s: towards rr: sme late prog: nvr a factor* **25/1**

9 *1 ¼* **Classic Voice (IRE)** 2-9-2 0....................................... RichardHughes 4 57
(R Hannon) *prom tl rdn over 2f out: wknd jst over 1f out* **11/2**[3]

0 **10** *nse* **Beach Babe**[29] 4021 2-8-4 0... NeilChalmers 14 45
(J G Portman) *nvr bttr than mid-div* **50/1**

5 **11** *3 ¼* **Les Landes (IRE)**[7] 4736 2-8-13 0.............................. FergusSweeney 6 45
(J A Osborne) *mid-div: rdn over 3f out: wknd 2f out* **50/1**

00 **12** *7* **Highcliffe**[34] 3861 2-8-6 0... RichardMullen 10 20
(R Hannon) *trckd ldrs tl rdn 3f out* **25/1**

04 **13** *3 ¼* **Fastada (IRE)**[27] 4103 2-8-8 0.. JimCrowley 1 12
(J G Portman) *prom tl wknd over 2f out* **8/1**

00 **14** *3* **Blue Cossack (IRE)**[8] 4695 2-8-11 0............................ LeeNewnes(5) 12 12
(M D I Usher) *sn pushed along: a towards rr* **100/1**

1m 29.54s (0.54) **Going Correction** +0.15s/f (Good) **14** Ran SP% **118.4**
Speed ratings (Par 94): **102,97,94,91,91 89,89,89,87,87 83,75,72,68**
toteswingers:1&2 £2.30, 2&3 £11.10, 1&3 £11.70 CSF £8.98 TOTE £3.10: £1.30, £1.70, £3.80; EX 9.80.
Owner Robert Hanson & Partners **Bred** The Hon Robert Hanson **Trained** Kingsclere, Hants

FOCUS

The ground had dried out since the previous day, with it officially described as good to firm, good in places. Just an ordinary juvenile maiden auction.

NOTEBOOK

Catalyze had made a promising debut on the Polytrack last month, but he seemed more at home on turf and really improved for the additional furlong, drawing right away in the final 150 yards to provide his trainer with a first juvenile winner of the year. He looks a promising type for nurseries. (op 10-3 tchd 7-2)

Sagramor looked in need of the experience when fifth on debut at Glorious Goodwood, and this represented a step forward, but he challenged on the far rail and found himself not quite on terms with the winner down the centre of the track. (op 5-2 tchd 11-4)

Cornish Quest, last of four over 5f on debut at Leicester, kept on late and seemed effective over the longer trip. He will be one for handicaps down the line. (op 14-1)

Frederick William again shaped with promise and will be interesting once given a mark.

Mountain Range(IRE) made a promising start. A 17,000gns gelding who is bred to need further, he stayed on late and looks likely to improve. (op 16-1)

Alshazah was another who shaped with promise and will be interesting once given a mark.

Classic Voice(IRE), out of a sister to high-class sprinter Pip's Pride, was green beforehand and dropped away rather quickly but should improve. (op 6-1 tchd 13-2)

5007 MARY WORT MEMORIAL MAIDEN STKS 6f 212y

3:05 (3:09) (Class 4) 3-4-Y-O **£3,885** (£1,156; £577; £288) **Stalls** Centre

Form RPR

3-2 **1** **Barq (IRE)**[23] 4238 3-9-3 0...(t) FrankieDettori 5 79+
(Saeed Bin Suroor) *trckd ldrs: led over 2f out: pushed clr over 1f out: rdn ins fnl f: enough in hand to hold on: all out* **2/5**[1]

2 *hd* **Magic Jack** 3-9-3 0.. PatDobbs 3 79+
(R Hannon) *in tch: hdwy on far rails over 2f out: rdn over 1f out: swtchd off rails ent fnl f: r.o wl: jst hld* **14/1**

433 **3** *3 ¼* **Danehill Sunset (IRE)**[41] 3635 3-9-3 72............................ MichaelHills 2 70
(B W Hills) *squeezed out s: sn trcking ldrs: rdn and ev ch over 2f out: kpt on for clr 3rd: nt gng pce of ldng pair fr over 1f out* **7/2**[2]

5 **4** *7* **Brewers Boy**[19] 4385 3-9-0 0....................................... JamesMillman(3) 6 51
(B R Millman) *hld up: rdn and hdwy over 3f out: nvr gng pce to get on terms* **20/1**

205 **5** *4* **Warm Memories**[27] 4107 3-9-3 75................................. RichardMullen 1 40
(Sir Michael Stoute) *sn led: rdn and hdd over 2f out: wknd over 1f out* **13/2**[3]

00 **6** *6* **Kargarann (IRE)**[19] 4385 3-9-3 0..................................... MickyFenton 9 24
(Stef Higgins) *a towards rr* **50/1**

0- **7** *1 ¼* **Far View (IRE)**[267] 7429 3-9-3 0....................................... EddieAhern 4 21
(J W Hills) *plld hrd early: trckd ldr tl wknd 2f out* **40/1**

00 **8** *2 ¼* **Miss Tenacious**[46] 3477 3-8-12 0..................................... TravisBlock 7 10
(R J Hodges) *slowly away and wnt rt s: a towards rr* **66/1**

1m 28.96s (-0.04) **Going Correction** +0.15s/f (Good)
WFA 3 from 4yo 6lb **8** Ran SP% **124.3**
Speed ratings (Par 105): **106,105,102,94,89 82,81,78**
toteswingers: 1&2 £3.50, 1&3 £1.40, 2&3 £3.90 CSF £9.51 TOTE £1.30: £1.10, £3.00, £1.20.
Owner Godolphin **Bred** Darley **Trained** Newmarket, Suffolk

The Form Book, Raceform Ltd, Compton, RG20 6NL

FOCUS
An ordinary maiden but run at a good pace. Sound form, rated around the winner.

5008 EUROPEAN BREEDERS' FUND FILLIES' H'CAP 1m 4f
3:40 (3:40) (Class 4) (0-80,80) 3-Y-O+ £5,828 (£1,734; £866; £432) Stalls High

Form RPR

-113 1 **Aktia (IRE)**[15] 4476 3-9-8 80 ... KierenFallon 7 95+
(L M Cumani) *mid-div: pushed along on far rails fr over 3f out: rdn whn swtchd lft over 2f out: drvn and str run ins fnl f: led line* 11/2[3]

2-12 2 *nse* **Calatrava Cape (IRE)**[48] 3414 3-9-7 79 ... TedDurcan 11 94+
(J L Dunlop) *in tch: smooth hdwy to join ldrs over 2f out: sn rdn: led ent fnl f: kpt on: ct line* 3/1[1]

-531 3 *2 1/2* **Silent Act (USA)**[6] 4794 4-9-13 74 6ex ... NeilCallan 9 85
(Mrs A J Perrett) *trckd ldr: nudged along over 3f out: rdn to chal over 2f out: ev ch ent fnl f: no ex fnl 110yds* 11/1

5421 4 *4* **Sula Two**[11] 4621 3-8-8 66 6ex ... WilliamCarson 2 70
(R J Hodges) *s.i.s: nudged along in last: swtchd to centre and rdn 3f out: styd on fr 2f out: wnt 4th ins fnl f: nvr trbld ldrs* 16/1

-100 5 *3/4* **Countess Comet (IRE)**[19] 4360 3-9-7 79 ... JimCrowley 5 82+
(R M Beckett) *mid-div: rdn over 3f out: no imp whn short of room and snatched up over 2f out: styd on same pce* 33/1

6111 6 *1* **Goldtrek (USA)**[36] 3789 3-9-8 80 ... SteveDrowne 1 81
(R Charlton) *led: rdn and hrd pressed fr over 2f out: hdd ent fnl f: fdd fnl 100yds* 11/2[3]

-104 7 *1 1/2* **Marie De Guise (IRE)**[65] 2843 3-9-7 79 ... RichardMullen 10 78
(Sir Michael Stoute) *in tch tl outpcd 3f out: nvr bk on terms* 4/1[2]

-323 8 *8* **Donna Elvira**[20] 4330 3-9-6 78 ... RichardHughes 8 64
(R Hannon) *hld up towards rr: rdn and nt clr run whn swtchd rt over 2f out: no imp* 14/1

0560 9 *1 3/4* **Featherweight (IRE)**[26] 4125 4-10-0 75 ... MichaelHills 6 58
(B W Hills) *trckd ldr: rdn and ev ch fr over 2f out tl wknd ent fnl f: eased* 25/1

10 10 *6* **Balletlou (IRE)**[19] 4360 3-9-0 77 ... KierenFox(5) 3 51
(J R Best) *hld up towards rr: pushed along and hdwy over 4f out: sn rdn: wknd over 2f out* 14/1

3411 11 *2 1/2* **Shy**[33] 3917 5-9-4 68 ... JamesMillman(3) 4 38
(B R Millman) *trckd ldrs on outer: effrt over 3f out: wkng whn bmpd over 2f out: eased ins fnl f* 16/1

2m 35.84s (-2.16) **Going Correction** -0.125s/f (Firm)
WFA 3 from 4yo+ 11lb 11 Ran SP% **116.0**
Speed ratings (Par 102): **102,101,100,97,97 96,95,90,88,84 83**
toteswingers: 1&2 £4.30, 1&3 £10.80, 2&3 £8.30 CSF £21.96 CT £176.29 TOTE £5.00: £1.60, £1.60, £4.00; EX 23.20.
Owner Mrs M Marinopoulos **Bred** Swordlestown Stud **Trained** Newmarket, Suffolk

FOCUS
A good fillies' handicap for the grade, with several in-form and progressive sorts taking part. A clear personal best from the winner.

5009 TOTESPORT.COM SOVEREIGN STKS (GROUP 3) 1m
4:15 (4:17) (Class 1) 3-Y-O+
£34,062 (£12,912; £6,462; £3,222; £1,614; £810) Stalls High

Form RPR

0111 1 **Sea Lord (IRE)**[13] 4537 3-8-7 115 ... KierenFallon 3 115
(M Johnston) *mde all: wound pce up fr over 3f out: kpt on v gamely: all out: jst hld on* 7/2[2]

4-00 2 *nse* **Poet's Voice**[40] 3704 3-8-7 110 ... (t) TedDurcan 10 115+
(Saeed Bin Suroor) *awkward leaving stalls: hld up last: pushed along in 8th whn swtchd lft over 1f out: rdn and r.o strly fnl 175yds: only narrowly failed* 16/1

31-3 3 *3/4* **Secrecy**[188] 440 4-9-0 110 ... FrankieDettori 9 114
(Saeed Bin Suroor) *stmbld leaving stalls: in tch: swtchd lft for effrt 2f out: sn rdn: nvr quite got on terms w wnr: kpt on ins fnl f: lost 2nd nr fin* 13/2

1002 4 *hd* **Fair Trade**[35] 3827 3-8-7 104 ... JamieSpencer 7 113+
(D R C Elsworth) *in tch: nt clr run whn swtchd lft jst over 1f out: sn rdn and short of room briefly: r.o* 9/1

-034 5 *nk* **Hearts Of Fire**[39] 3719 3-8-7 118 ... (t) RichardHughes 1 112
(Pat Eddery) *mid-div: crept clsr over 2f out: sn rdn: nt gng pce to chal: kpt on ins fnl f* 5/2[1]

3335 6 *1/2* **Dream Eater (IRE)**[15] 4469 5-9-0 117 ... (t) FrannyNorton 2 112
(A M Balding) *racd keenly early: trckd wnr: rdn 2f out: nt pce to chal: kpt on but no ex fnl 75yds* 11/2[3]

-231 7 *3/4* **Pressing (IRE)**[74] 2576 7-9-5 117 ... NeilCallan 6 115
(M A Jarvis) *trckd wnr: rdn 2f out: nt pce to chal: kpt on: no ex fnl 100yds* 8/1

2144 8 *hd* **Fanunalter**[47] 3455 4-9-0 106 ... DarryllHolland 8 113+
(M Botti) *hld up: pushed along but travelling wl enough on heels of ldrs over 1f out: absolutely no run at all bhd wall of horses fr there on in* 22/1

4065 9 *4 1/2* **Freeforaday (USA)**[12] 4574 3-8-7 102 ... SteveDrowne 5 98
(J R Best) *mid-div: rdn over 2f out: sn hld* 50/1

1m 41.82s (-1.68) **Going Correction** +0.15s/f (Good)
WFA 3 from 4yo+ 7lb 9 Ran SP% **112.8**
Speed ratings: **114,113,113,113,112 112,111,111,106**
toteswingers: 1&2 £10.70, 1&3 £3.50, 2&3 £13.10 CSF £55.70 TOTE £3.20: £1.10, £5.30, £1.30; EX 59.90.
Owner Sheikh Hamdan Bin Mohammed Al Maktoum **Bred** Darley **Trained** Middleham Moor, N Yorks

FOCUS
A really competitive Group 3 contest that was run at a good gallop. Despite this the field finished quite well bunched. Sea Lord probably didn't have to improve on his Goodwood form, and the second is rated back to his 2yo best.

NOTEBOOK
Sea Lord(IRE) was responsible for setting the tempo, one which the rapidly progressive colt had no trouble maintaining right the way to the line, just holding on from the fast-finishing runner-up. Successful off a mark of 106 in the totesport Mile at Glorious Goodwood last time, this habitual front-runner looked a ready made Group winner that day and the manner of this success very much points to him staying a little further in future. He's now won six of his last seven, and it will be interesting to see where this thoroughly likeable individual goes next. It would come as no surprise to see him join Godolphin at some stage. (op 10-3, tchd 4-1 in places)
Poet's Voice, a smart juvenile, he had disappointed on both previous starts this season, albeit they were against good opposition in France, but he settled much better this time and produced a taking late burst out wide, just failing to get there. He's well up to winning races at this level assuming he can go on from this. (op 25-1 tchd 28-1)
Secrecy, the choice of Dettori, is reportedly best fresh, looked fit and he ran an improved race on this first try at Group level, coming out best of the older horses. (op 6-1 tchd 11-2)
Fair Trade, who played up a bit in the paddock, is a fine, big, galloping type and he did well to finish so close considering he met with an interrupted passage. He can be rated a tad better than the bare form and remains a horse to keep on-side, with him almost certain to develop into a better 4-y-o. (op 12-1)
Hearts Of Fire was the standout pick on form, having finished third in the St James's Palace Stakes and fourth in the Prix Jean Prat latest, but he looked dull in his coat and was unable to quicken when asked for his effort, and proved rather disappointing. He isn't the biggest and it won't be easy getting his head in front again at Group level. Official explanation: jockey said colt jumped right and hung right-handed throughout (op 9-4)
Dream Eater(IRE) is often thereabouts in good company, but he finds it tough to win and didn't quite get home having been a touch keen. (op 9-2)
Pressing(IRE) has never won in this country and it was no surprise to see him come up short once more under his Group 2 penalty. (tchd 15-2)
Fanunalter had plenty to find, but he received a luckless passage, being trapped with nowhere to go on the inner, and never had a chance to show what he could have produced. Official explanation: jockey said gelding was denied a clear run (op 28-1 tchd 33-1)
Freeforaday(USA) stood little chance on form and was duly outclassed.

5010 BILL GARNETT MEMORIAL FILLIES' H'CAP 6f
4:50 (4:51) (Class 5) (0-70,67) 3-Y-O+ £3,238 (£963; £481; £240) Stalls High

Form RPR

0242 1 **Russian Rave**[23] 4236 4-9-11 65 ... JamieSpencer 4 77
(J G Portman) *in tch: trckd ldrs 3f out: rdn to ld jst over 1f out: drifted rt: r.o strly: readily* 3/1[1]

0443 2 *2 1/2* **Silvee**[7] 4739 3-8-10 54 ... NeilChalmers 7 57
(J J Bridger) *w ldr: led over 3f out: rdn over 2f out: hdd jst over 1f out: sltly hmpd sn after: kpt on: nt gng pce of wnr* 11/1

6564 3 *nk* **Blue Again**[22] 4248 3-9-7 65 ... TedDurcan 5 67+
(W R Swinburn) *in tch on far rails: rdn 2f out: disputing cl 3rd whn squeezed up on rails jst ins fnl f: kpt on* 15/2

006- 4 *3/4* **Gooseberry Bush**[297] 6903 3-9-8 66 ... NeilCallan 1 66
(P J Makin) *hld up in last pair: nt clr run over 2f out: swtchd lft wl over 1f out: sn rdn: styd on ins fnl f* 14/1

42 5 *3/4* **Miss Firefly**[7] 4744 5-9-6 60 ... WilliamCarson 6 58
(R J Hodges) *racd keenly early: trckd ldrs: nt best of runs fr over 2f out: kpt on same pce whn gap appeared jst over 1f out* 13/2

6641 6 *2 1/4* **Dualagi**[7] 4744 6-9-2 56 6ex ... FergusSweeney 2 47
(M R Bosley) *hld up: rdn 2f out: nt gng pce to get on terms* 6/1[3]

0215 7 *6* **Thalia Grace**[14] 4503 3-9-2 60 ... KirstyMilczarek 8 31
(L Montague Hall) *racd keenly w ldr: rdn 2f out: hung rt and wknd ent fnl f* 9/1

3620 8 *2 1/2* **Pragmatist**[27] 4099 6-9-4 61 ... JamesMillman(3) 3 25
(B R Millman) *sn trcking ldrs: rdn over 2f out: wknd ent fnl f* 4/1[2]

0003 9 *2* **Candyfloss Girl**[13] 4529 3-9-9 67 ... (p) RichardMullen 9 23
(H J L Dunlop) *led tl over 3f out: struggling whn squeezed up on rails over 2f out: sn wknd* 25/1

1m 15.67s (0.87) **Going Correction** +0.15s/f (Good)
WFA 3 from 4yo+ 4lb 9 Ran SP% **113.2**
Speed ratings (Par 100): **100,96,96,95,94 91,83,79,77**
toteswingers:1&2 £8.60, 2&3 £10.20, 1&3 £5.20 CSF £36.23 CT £224.16 TOTE £2.90: £1.10, £4.60, £3.70; EX 32.60.
Owner The Traditionalists **Bred** P A & M J Reditt & Morton Bloodstock **Trained** Compton, Berks

FOCUS
A moderate enough sprint handicap for fillies. Sound form, the winner rated back to her best.
Thalia Grace Official explanation: jockey said filly hung right

5011 PAT BOAKES MEMORIAL H'CAP 1m 6f 21y
5:20 (5:21) (Class 5) (0-70,67) 3-Y-O+ £3,238 (£963; £481; £240)

Form RPR

-244 1 **Arab League (IRE)**[33] 3896 5-9-12 67 ... WilliamCarson 7 82
(R J Price) *trckd ldr wl clr of chsng gp: led over 2f out: rdn clr sn after: styd on strly* 6/1[3]

0002 2 *9* **Lombok**[6] 4780 4-9-10 65 ... JamieSpencer 1 67+
(M L W Bell) *mid-div in main gp: effrt to make hdwy on cutaway whn snatched up over 3f out: sn rdn: wnt 3rd 2f out: styd on to go 2nd ins fnl f: nvr any ch w wnr* 11/4[1]

-655 3 *1* **Yonder**[29] 4026 6-9-3 58 ... (bt) MickyFenton 2 59
(H Morrison) *led at gd pce: sn clr w one other: rdn and hdd over 2f out: sn hld by wnr: tiring whn lost 2nd ins fnl f* 20/1

1332 4 *nk* **Seventh Hill**[19] 4386 5-9-12 67 ... FergusSweeney 13 67
(M Blanshard) *slowly away: reminders: towards rr: rdn and stdy prog fr 3f out: styd on same pce fnl 2f: nvr a danger* 5/1[2]

5353 5 *1* **Zaif (IRE)**[19] 4386 7-8-13 57 ... AshleyHamblett(3) 6 56+
(D J S Ffrench Davis) *hld up towards rr: rdn 3f out: styd on past btn horses fnl 2f: nvr a factor* 10/1

5-05 6 *nse* **Colonel Flay**[46] 3475 6-9-9 64 ... KirstyMilczarek 8 63
(Mrs P N Dutfield) *mid-div of main gp: rdn 3f out: 5th of gp 2f out but nvr any imp on clr ldrs* 16/1

430 7 *4* **Hidden**[37] 3754 4-9-7 65 ... Louis-PhilippeBeuzelin(3) 5 58
(B J Meehan) *mid-div of main gp: rdn over 4f out: no imp* 22/1

-050 8 *2 3/4* **Gearbox (IRE)**[20] 4327 4-9-6 61 ... TedDurcan 14 50
(H J L Dunlop) *chsd clr ldrs at hd of main gp tl 2f out: sn wknd* 40/1

30-1 9 *2 1/4* **Abulharith**[21] 4279 4-9-0 58 ... PatrickHills(3) 10 44
(M J Scudamore) *prom in chsng gp tl wknd over 1f out: nvr rchd ldrs* 16/1

1/3 10 *nk* **Blue Eyed Eloise**[20] 868 8-9-7 62 ... DarryllHolland 11 48
(B J McMath) *reluctant to line up: a towards rr* 8/1

654 11 *13* **Businessmoney Judi**[49] 3347 4-9-7 65 ... JamesMillman(3) 9 32
(B R Millman) *mid-div of main gp: rdn 5f out: sltly hmpd over 3f out: wknd over 2f out* 20/1

/ 12 *2* **Grand Bay (USA)**[29] 3899 9-9-8 63 ... (t) JimCrowley 3 28
(Jonjo O'Neill) *mid-div of main gp: rdn over 3f out: sn wknd* 16/1

406 13 *3/4* **Shooting Party (IRE)**[17] 4426 4-9-6 61 ... PatDobbs 4 25
(R Hannon) *prom in chsng gp tl wknd 2f out: nvr rchd ldrs* 11/1

3m 4.59s (-2.81) **Going Correction** -0.125s/f (Firm) 13 Ran SP% **120.1**
Speed ratings (Par 103): **103,97,97,97,96 96,94,92,91,91 83,82,82**
toteswingers:1&2 £5.00, 2&3 £17.10, 1&3 £22.20 CSF £21.65 CT £319.71 TOTE £6.90: £2.50, £2.10, £6.70; EX 20.40 Place 6: £25.23 Place 5: £17.61.
Owner Mrs P A Wallis **Bred** D G Iceton **Trained** Ullingswick, H'fords

FOCUS
This staying handicap was a funny sort of race as two raced in a clear lead and their rivals allowed them too much rope, as it proved almost impossible to land a serious blow from off the pace. A clear personal best from the winner at face value, but maybe not form to take too literally.
Seventh Hill Official explanation: jockey said gelding planted at the start
T/Jkpt: Not won. T/Plt: £44.20 to a £1 stake. Pool of £56,075.29 - 924.71 winning ticket. T/Qpdt: £18.40 to a £1 stake. Pool of £3,208.65 - 128.40 winning tickets. TM

5012 - 5015a (Foreign Racing) - See Raceform Interactive

4766 LEOPARDSTOWN (L-H)
Thursday, August 12

OFFICIAL GOING: Good to firm (good in places)

5016a DESMOND STKS (GROUP 3) 1m
7:30 (7:31) 3-Y-O+ £34,513 (£10,088; £4,778; £1,592)

RPR
1 **Beethoven (IRE)**[15] 4469 3-9-7 117 (b[1]) JPO'Brien 4 117+
(A P O'Brien, Ire) *chsd ldr: 2nd 1/2-way: impr to ld 1 1/2f out: rdn out hands and heels ins fnl f: comf* 2/1[1]
2 3/4 **Dandy Boy (ITY)**[26] 4160 4-9-7 102 CO'Donoghue 2 109
(David Marnane, Ire) *hld up and t.k.h: 4th 1/2-way: rdn into 3rd 1f out: styd on to go 2nd ins fnl f: nt match wnr* 5/1
3 1 1/4 **Emulous**[25] 4177 3-8-11 103 PJSmullen 1 102
(D K Weld, Ire) *chsd ldr: 3rd 1/2-way: rdn 1 1/2f out: no imp in 2nd 1f out: no ex in 3rd ins fnl f: kpt on same pce* 10/3[3]
4 2 1/2 **King Jock (USA)**[57] 3069 9-9-7 106 PShanahan 5 100
(Tracey Collins, Ire) *hld up in rr: rdn in 4th 2f out: no imp in 5th 1 1/2f out: kpt on one pce* 8/1
5 1 1/4 **Akdarena**[25] 4178 3-9-0 114 (bt) KJManning 3 97
(J S Bolger, Ire) *led: rdn and hdd 1 1/2f out: no ex in 4th 1f out: wknd* 5/2[2]

1m 39.52s (-1.68) **Going Correction** -0.075s/f (Good)
WFA 3 from 4yo+ 7lb 5 Ran SP% **112.8**
Speed ratings: **105,104,103,100,99**
CSF £12.46 TOTE £2.50: £1.60, £2.30; DF 15.20.
Owner M Tabor, D Smith & Mrs John Magnier **Bred** Whisperview Trading Ltd **Trained** Ballydoyle, Co Tipperary

FOCUS
The first two are rated more or less to their best.

NOTEBOOK
Beethoven(IRE) had a Group 1 penalty for his Dewhurst Stakes win to contend with and his apprentice rider, who had ridden him at Royal Ascot and at Goodwood, was again unable to claim his 5lb allowance. Both horse and rider acquitted themselves well and, under a hands-and-heels ride, he was well on top in the closing stages having been sent to the front over 1f out. (op 7/4 tchd 9/4)
Dandy Boy(ITY), unproven at this trip, never figured in the Royal Hunt Cup due to an unfavourable draw and was back up in trip here following a creditable third in a 7f Group 3 event at the Curragh last month. Held up and quite keen for much of the race, he was last into the straight before closing to press the winner inside the final furlong. He kept on but was always being held. (op 7/1 tchd 8/1)
Emulous, winner of a 7f maiden on soft ground at the Curragh on her only start last season, was up in class following second placings, one at Listed level, on her two previous attempts this year. She had every chance, but could raise no extra in second from over 1f out. (op 3/1 tchd 7/2)
King Jock(USA), now nine and with ten victories to his credit, had produced a fine effort when beaten a short head by Famous Name in a similar type event to this over the same C&D in May. Well beaten in the Royal Hunt Cup, he was ridden in fourth place turning for home and was never able to get in a serious challenge. (op 9/1 tchd 10/1)
Akdarena, down in class following three efforts at Group 1 level, two of them at 1m4f, had shown her best form when third in the 1m2f Pretty Polly Stakes. This was her first attempt over 1m since last season and, predictably, she made the running. She never got more than three lengths clear and while she was shaken up to try and stretch her rivals turning for home, she was soon headed and done with. (op 2/1)

5017 - 5018a (Foreign Racing) - See Raceform Interactive

4668 CATTERICK (L-H)
Friday, August 13

OFFICIAL GOING: Good (8.7)
Wind: fresh 1/2 against Weather: damp and very breezy

5019 PIN POINT RECRUITMENT AMATEUR RIDERS' H'CAP 1m 3f 214y
5:50 (5:51) (Class 5) (0-75,78) 3-Y-O+ £1,936 (£600; £300; £150) Stalls Low

Form RPR
6142 1 **Maneki Neko (IRE)**[23] 4246 8-10-11 69 MissSBrotherton 7 79
(E W Tuer) *hld up in mid-div: hdwy 4f out: led on ins over 1f out: drew clr: comf* 7/2[1]
0/15 2 6 **Daytime Dreamer (IRE)**[15] 4511 6-10-10 71 MrJHamer(3) 9 71
(M Todhunter) *chsd ldrs: outpcd over 2f out: styd on to take modest 2nd post* 16/1
6443 3 shd **Dimashq**[1] 4980 8-9-4 53 oh6 MissWGibson(5) 4 53
(P T Midgley) *mid-div: hdwy to chse wnr over 1f out: kpt on same pce* 22/1
0121 4 3/4 **Umverti**[9] 4708 5-11-1 78 6ex MrSebSpencer(5) 5 77
(N Bycroft) *led tl over 7f out: led over 5f out: hdd over 2f out: one pce* 7/2[1]
022 5 1 1/2 **River Ardeche**[28] 4088 5-10-9 72 MrJMQuinlan(5) 3 69
(B M R Haslam) *w ldr: led over 7f out tl over 5f out: led over 2f out: hdd over 1f out: sn wknd* 13/2
00 6 2 **Tropical Duke (IRE)**[73] 2625 4-9-8 57 MissVBarr(5) 11 50
(R E Barr) *hld up in rr: hdwy over 4f out: hung lft over 2f out: nvr nr ldrs* 18/1
2266 7 1 **Night Knight (IRE)**[16] 4484 4-10-0 58 (tp) MissLHorner 6 50
(C Grant) *in rr: hdwy over 4f out: hung lft and one pce fnl 2f* 33/1
2512 8 2 1/4 **Hurricane Thomas (IRE)**[15] 4511 6-9-12 61 MissPhillipaTutty(5) 2 49
(R A Fahey) *mid-div: outpcd over 2f out: no threat after* 5/1[3]
500/ 9 2 1/2 **Airedale Lad (IRE)**[7] 7605 9-9-2 53 oh8 MissGTutty(7) 10 37
(N Wilson) *chsd ldrs: lost pl after 3f: no threat after* 100/1
-421 10 1/2 **Astronomical (IRE)**[29] 4070 8-10-4 65 (p) MrStephenHarrison(3) 12 48
(R Hollinshead) *sn chsg ldrs: lost pl 2f out* 4/1[2]
0646 11 2 **Masterofceremonies**[8] 4740 7-9-4 55 (p) MissALMurphy(7) 8 35
(W M Brisbourne) *dwlt: in rr: drvn over 6f out: nvr on terms* 66/1
04/0 12 2 3/4 **Follow On**[15] 4511 8-9-4 53 oh8 (t) MissAngelaBarnes(5) 1 29
(M A Barnes) *hld up: a last* 50/1

2m 43.75s (4.85) **Going Correction** +0.275s/f (Good) 12 Ran SP% **117.3**
Speed ratings (Par 103): **94,90,89,89,88 87,86,84,83,82 81,79**
toteswingers: 1&2 £29.30, 1&3 £12.90, 2&3 £29.30. CSF £58.24 CT £1079.61 TOTE £2.80: £1.10, £9.20, £9.20; EX 64.10.
Owner Mr & Mrs C Tompkins & E Tuer **Bred** Mrs Orlagh Sherry **Trained** Great Smeaton, N Yorks

FOCUS
An ordinary amateur riders' handicap. The winner reversed latest C&D form with the runner-up. The winner is rated back to his best but the third limits the form.
Hurricane Thomas(IRE) Official explanation: jockey said gelding was unsuited by the good ground
Astronomical(IRE) Official explanation: trainer had no explanation for the poor form shown

5020 REBECCA RIPLEY WEDDING (S) STKS 7f
6:20 (6:21) (Class 6) 2-Y-O £1,706 (£503; £252) Stalls Low

Form RPR
1 **Mary Boyle** 2-8-1 0 DeclanCannon(5) 4 58
(A J McCabe) *s.i.s: hdwy over 2f out: swtchd rt 1f out: wandered: styd on wl to ld nr fin: slipped and fell whn pulling up* 25/1
3021 2 1/2 **Chilworth Lass (IRE)**[7] 4788 2-8-6 57 (v) SamHitchcott 3 57
(M R Channon) *t.k.h: trckd ldrs: styd on ins fnl f: tk 2nd nr fin* 2/1[1]
2233 3 nk **Alhoni**[14] 4554 2-7-13 54 (b[1]) ShaneBKelly(7) 8 56
(J J Quinn) *trckd ldrs: t.k.h: led over 2f out: hung violently lft over 1f out: ended up alone far side: hdd nr fin* 11/2[3]
0305 4 2 **Karafuse (IRE)**[14] 4554 2-8-6 50 (b) DuranFentiman 5 51
(T D Easterby) *led tl over 2f out: swtchd rt 1f out: one pce* 14/1
5600 5 8 **Louis Girl**[9] 4701 2-8-9 56 ow6 BarryMcHugh(3) 12 37
(R A Fahey) *w ldrs: hung bdly rt bnd 3f out: wkng whn hmpd over 1f out* 8/1
6300 6 4 **Imperial Waltzer**[9] 4701 2-8-11 61 DanielTudhope 6 26
(G M Moore) *in rr div: nvr on terms* 20/1
0 7 3 **Antipas (IRE)**[73] 2623 2-8-6 0 AndrewElliott 9 14
(Mrs K Burke) *dwlt: sn chsng ldrs: outpcd 4f out: lost pl over 2f out* 28/1
0061 8 6 **He's The Star (IRE)**[14] 4554 2-9-3 63 CathyGannon 7 10
(P D Evans) *t.k.h in midfield: edgd lft sn after s: drvn 4f out: wknd over 2f out* 11/4[2]
9 9 **Legal Heights (IRE)** 2-8-11 0 EddieCreighton 11 —
(T T Clement) *s.i.s: in rr: bhd fnl 3f* 12/1
046 10 nse **Commander Veejay**[8] 4747 2-8-11 0 (p) GregFairley 1 —
(B S Rothwell) *dwlt: in rr and sn drvn along: bhd fnl 3f* 25/1
000 11 15 **Land Bank**[20] 4368 2-8-6 41 LanceBetts(5) 2 —
(T D Easterby) *sltly hmpd sn after s: in rr: bhd 4f out: t.o over 2f out* 100/1

1m 30.24s (3.24) **Going Correction** +0.275s/f (Good) 11 Ran SP% **117.7**
Speed ratings (Par 92): **92,91,91,88,79 75,71,64,54,54 37**
toteswingers:1&2 £7.40, 2&3 £2.60, 1&3 £15.30 CSF £72.25 TOTE £36.90: £7.30, £1.90, £1.10; EX 148.00.There was no bid for winner.
Owner Mrs M J McCabe **Bred** Brendan Boyle **Trained** Averham Park, Notts

FOCUS
The whole field came over to the stands' side on this occasion, which often happens here when rain has eased the ground. This was very much low-grade fare overall.

NOTEBOOK
Mary Boyle did well to overcome inexperience on her debut, running on strongly as she got the hang of things. She did get rid of her rider soon after the line and crashed through the rails when loose, but she is open to progress if that nasty experience does not leave a mark. The second and third are both rated in the mid-50s so the handicapper certainly can't go overboard with her. (op 16-1)
Chilworth Lass(IRE) has been consistent since the visor was applied and looks to have run right up to her Lingfield form here. (op 3-1 tchd 10-3)
Alhoni, blinkered instead of visored this time, probably would have won had she not hung markedly left in the straight, though this is not the first time she has looked less than straightforward. (op 9-2)
Karafuse(IRE) fared a little better than previously, particularly as he was impeded by the hanging Alhoni, but it is still only poor stuff. (op 12-1)
He's The Star(IRE) Official explanation: trainer's rep said colt was struck into

5021 SAM WARD HAPPY BIRTHDAY NURSERY 5f 212y
6:55 (6:55) (Class 4) (0-85,82) 2-Y-O £3,238 (£963; £481; £240) Stalls Low

Form RPR
1034 1 **First Class Favour (IRE)**[13] 4600 2-8-10 71 DavidAllan 4 72+
(T D Easterby) *mde all: hld on gamely* 7/1[3]
2133 2 nk **Orchid Street (USA)**[13] 4600 2-9-0 78 BarryMcHugh(3) 3 78+
(Mrs A Duffield) *dwlt: in rr: hdwy over 2f out: chal over 1f out: no ex nr fin* 15/8[2]
065 3 6 **Downtown Boy (IRE)**[28] 4089 2-8-4 65 AndrewMullen 5 47
(T P Tate) *drvn to chse ldrs: outpcd 3f out: kpt on fnl 2f: tk modest 3rd nr fin* 25/1
344 4 nk **Dunmore Boy (IRE)**[34] 3897 2-8-6 67 PaulHanagan 6 48
(R A Fahey) *chsd ldrs: styd on same pce fnl 2f* 7/4[1]
2144 5 3 1/4 **Defence Council (IRE)**[20] 4367 2-9-7 82 TomEaves 1 53
(J Howard Johnson) *s.i.s: effrt 3f out: swtchd lft over 1f out: sn wknd* 9/1
0324 6 2 **Just For Leo (IRE)**[10] 4677 2-8-10 71 (v[1]) CathyGannon 2 36
(P D Evans) *t.k.h: sn trcking ldrs: drvn over 2f out: wknd 1f out* 8/1

1m 15.85s (2.25) **Going Correction** +0.275s/f (Good) 6 Ran SP% **108.6**
Speed ratings (Par 96): **96,95,87,87,82 80**
CSF £19.26 TOTE £6.20: £2.90, £1.10; EX 18.70.
Owner S A Heley **Bred** Oghill House Stud **Trained** Great Habton, N Yorks

FOCUS
It is hard to believe there was much depth to this small-field nursery, but the leading pair need crediting for coming clear. Once again they all came stands' side in the straight.

NOTEBOOK
First Class Favour(IRE) had not really progressed since her maiden win here (5f) in May, though she did pay for trying to match strides with the useful Face The Problem at Thirsk last time and turned round form with Orchid Street from that occasion, clearly seeing out this longer trip well. Her immediate prospects depend to a large degree on how the handicapper reacts to the front two pulling so far clear. (op 6-1)
Orchid Street(USA) has now finished placed on all three starts in nurseries. The step up to 6f suited but she found the winner pulling out more after moving through smoothly from the back. She will look well treated if connections can find her a race before she is reassessed. (op 7-4 tchd 13-8)
Downtown Boy(IRE) did not find any improvement switched to nurseries for the first time, shaping as though a return to 7f may suit if anything. (op 22-1)
Dunmore Boy(IRE) was clearly expected to do better if the market was any guide, but failed even to match his maiden form, and the writing was on the wall from early in the straight. (op 5-2)
Defence Council(IRE) has not progressed and looks on a stiff mark. (op 8-1)
Just For Leo(IRE) dropped away tamely in a first-time visor and is another who could do with some leniency from the handicapper. Official explanation: jockey said gelding ran too free (op 15-2)

5022 HAPPY BIRTHDAY DENYS SMITH MAIDEN STKS 1m 3f 214y
7:25 (7:26) (Class 5) 3-Y-O+ £2,072 (£616; £308; £153) Stalls Low

Form RPR
3422 1 **Ceoil An Aith (IRE)**[11] 4655 4-9-8 78 GregFairley 7 76+
(M Johnston) *chsd ldrs: wnt 2nd over 7f out: drvn and sltly outpcd over 2f out: hung lft: styd on to ld last 100yds* 7/4[2]

The Form Book, Raceform Ltd, Compton, RG20 6NL

633 **2** *2* **Mutanaker**[13] 4572 3-9-2 76 ... TadhgO'Shea 6 78
(Sir Michael Stoute) *trckd ldrs: led after 2f: qcknd over 4f out: edgd lft and hdd ins fnl f: no ex* **5/4**[1]
0 **3** *2 ½* **Maroon**[64] 2891 3-8-11 0 ... PaulHanagan 2 71+
(B W Hills) *trckd ldrs: chal over 2f out: one pce whn nt clr run and eased 100yds out* **9/2**[3]
6- **4** *6* **Tayacoba (CAN)**[296] 6930 3-8-13 0 ... GaryBartley(3) 1 64
(J S Goldie) *hld up towards rr: outpcd 4f out: kpt on fnl 2f* **14/1**
5 *16* **Just Nod (IRE)** 4-9-8 0 ... PJMcDonald 5 33
(Mrs R A Carr) *s.i.s: drvn and outpcd 4f out: sn lost pl* **66/1**
6 *1 ½* **Good Bye Day** 3-8-11 0 ... DavidAllan 3 31
(T D Easterby) *s.i.s: modest 4th whn slipped over 2f out: sn wknd* **40/1**
00 **7** *11* **Secret Sortie (IRE)**[19] 4407 5-9-3 0 ... DaleSwift(5) 4 13
(T J Etherington) *led 2f: drvn over 5f out: lost pl over 4f out: sn bhd* **66/1**

2m 44.94s (6.04) **Going Correction** +0.275s/f (Good)
WFA 3 from 4yo+ 11lb 7 Ran SP% **111.1**
Speed ratings (Par 103): **90,88,87,83,72 71,64**
toteswingers:1&2 £1.02, 2&3 £1.80, 1&3 £2.20 CSF £4.00 TOTE £3.80: £3.80, £1.02; EX 3.30.
Owner Mrs Joan Keaney **Bred** Mrs Joan Keaney **Trained** Middleham Moor, N Yorks
■ Stewards' Enquiry : Tadhg O'Shea two day ban: careless riding (Aug 27-28)

FOCUS
No depth to this maiden and it was predictably fought out by the market leaders, with the runner-up the best guide. The pace was only modest.

5023 HAPPY 7TH BIRTHDAY GEORGIA H'CAP 5f
8:00 (8:00) (Class 6) (0-65,65) 3-Y-O+ **£2,047** (£604; £302) **Stalls** Low

Form RPR
0102 **1** **Mayoman (IRE)**[2] 4947 5-9-10 **63** ... (v) DavidNolan 8 82
(D Carroll) *mde all: rdn and hung lft over 1f out: forged clr* **11/4**[1]
0035 **2** *5* **Liberty Ship**[25] 4199 5-9-12 **65** ... (bt) SilvestreDeSousa 4 66
(J D Bethell) *chsd wnr thrght: kpt on same pce ins fnl f* **9/2**[3]
5250 **3** *1 ¾* **Speedy Senorita (IRE)**[13] 4583 5-9-7 **60** ... PaulHanagan 5 55
(J J Quinn) *wnt rt s: chsd ldrs: kpt on same pce fnl 2f* **15/2**
4402 **4** *1* **Rio Sands**[17] 4452 5-9-1 **57** ... AmyRyan(3) 11 48
(R M Whitaker) *chsd ldrs: one pce fnl 2f* **12/1**
015 **5** *1 ½* **Tamarind Hill (IRE)**[3] 4938 3-9-2 **63** ... (b) DeclanCannon(5) 3 48
(A J McCabe) *mid-div: hung rt and kpt on fnl 2f: nvr a threat* **12/1**
0522 **6** *½* **Raccoon (IRE)**[10] 4672 10-9-7 **60** ... PJMcDonald 1 44
(Mrs R A Carr) *prom on outside: fdd over 1f out* **4/1**[2]
500 **7** *1 ¼* **Embra (IRE)**[20] 4373 5-8-9 **53** ... DaleSwift(5) 12 32
(T J Etherington) *mid-div: sn drvn along: nvr a factor* **16/1**
0-54 **8** *½* **Windjammer**[23] 4245 6-8-11 **53** ... (b) KellyHarrison(3) 6 31
(L A Mullaney) *hmpd s: a in rr* **14/1**
-061 **9** *hd* **Alacity (IRE)**[10] 4672 4-9-8 **61** 6ex ... FrannyNorton 2 38
(N Bycroft) *racd on outside: in rr over 2f out* **12/1**
000/ **10** *2* **Archilini**[735] 4808 5-8-9 **48** ... SamHitchcott 7 18
(M Sheppard) *a in rr* **66/1**

60.38 secs (0.58) **Going Correction** +0.15s/f (Good)
WFA 3 from 4yo+ 3lb 10 Ran SP% **113.7**
Speed ratings (Par 101): **101,93,90,88,86 85,83,82,82,79**
toteswingers:1&2 £3.80, 2&3 £7.60, 1&3 £12.10 CSF £14.44 CT £81.27 TOTE £2.70: £1.02, £1.60, £4.30; EX 24.60.
Owner Tom Tuohy **Bred** James Cosgrove **Trained** Sledmere, E Yorks

FOCUS
Few got into this sprint, the winner soon having the rest at it and the whole field coming towards the stands' side. A clear personal best from Mayoman, and this could underrate him.
Windjammer Official explanation: jockey said gelding missed the break

5024 DURHAM CHESHIRE HOMES H'CAP 7f
8:30 (8:31) (Class 6) (0-60,66) 3-Y-O+ **£2,047** (£604; £302) **Stalls** Low

Form RPR
0000 **1** **Hot Rod Mamma (IRE)**[19] 4408 3-8-4 **46** oh1 ... DuranFentiman 6 50
(Mrs Dianne Sayer) *in rr: gd hdwy 2f out: r.o to ld fnl stride* **50/1**
0334 **2** *shd* **Needy McCredie**[5] 4869 4-9-0 **50** ... PJMcDonald 14 55
(J R Turner) *chsd ldrs on outside: led jst ins fnl f: hdd post* **7/2**[1]
5150 **3** *½* **Nuit Sombre (IRE)**[4] 4897 10-9-10 **60** ... (p) SilvestreDeSousa 2 64
(G A Harker) *led: hdd jst ins fnl f: kpt on same pce* **13/2**[3]
3455 **4** *1* **Northern Flyer (GER)**[16] 4485 4-9-1 **56** ... (v[1]) IanBrennan(5) 15 57
(J J Quinn) *prom on outside: effrt over 2f out: styd on ins fnl f* **9/2**[2]
0040 **4** *dht* **No Quarter (IRE)**[13] 4581 3-8-8 **53** ... AndrewHeffernan(3) 11 52+
(Miss Tracy Waggott) *s.i.s: mid-div: hdwy and hmpd over 2f out: nt clr run over 1f out: kpt on wl ins fnl f* **16/1**
5500 **6** *3 ¾* **Wotatomboy**[5] 4868 4-8-8 **47** ... AmyRyan(3) 9 38
(R M Whitaker) *mid-div: drvn over 2f out: nvr nr ldrs* **14/1**
0654 **7** *1 ¾* **Regal Emperor (IRE)**[10] 4674 3-8-10 **55** ... MichaelGeran(3) 4 40
(D Nicholls) *chsd ldrs: kpt on one pce fnl 2f* **12/1**
0106 **8** *½* **Choc'A'Moca (IRE)**[10] 4674 3-8-10 **52** ... (v) DavidNolan 12 35
(D Carroll) *chsd ldrs: wknd appr fnl f* **8/1**
0650 **9** *6* **Karate Queen**[5] 4868 5-8-7 **46** oh1 ... (v) MichaelStainton(3) 10 15
(R E Barr) *dwlt: in rr: effrt in centre over 2f out: nvr on terms* **33/1**
4440 **10** *11* **Zabeel Tower**[7] 4796 7-9-7 **57** ... TomEaves 7 —
(R Allan) *chsd ldrs: lost pl over 2f out* **18/1**
0-00 **11** *8* **Psychopathicsandra (IRE)**[60] 3027 3-8-1 **46** oh1 ... KellyHarrison(3) 8 —
(Joss Saville) *v s.i.s: a detached and bhd* **100/1**
0/50 **12** *nk* **Wainwright (IRE)**[68] 2791 10-8-5 **46** oh1 ... (tp) DeclanCannon(5) 3 —
(J Mackie) *in tch: drvn and lost pl over 2f out* **50/1**
0000 **13** *6* **Royal Crest**[14] 4559 4-8-10 **46** oh1 ... (b) GregFairley 1 —
(A Crook) *mid-div: lost pl 3f out* **50/1**
6101 **14** *12* **Ellies Image**[10] 4674 3-9-10 **66** 6ex ... PaulHanagan 13 —
(B P J Baugh) *dwlt: in rr: wl bhd fnl 3f: virtually p.u* **7/2**[1]

1m 29.98s (2.98) **Going Correction** +0.275s/f (Good)
WFA 3 from 4yo+ 6lb 14 Ran SP% **122.4**
Speed ratings (Par 101): **93,92,92,91,91 86,84,84,77,64 55,55,48,34**
toteswingers:1&2 £24.10, 2&3 £8.90, 1&3 not won. CSF £221.70 CT £1379.49 TOTE £97.70: £19.20, £1.40, £5.50; EX 413.00 Place 6: £38.06, Place 5: £11.58..
Owner A Slack **Bred** Philip Hore Jnr **Trained** Hackthorpe, Cumbria

FOCUS
Decidedly run-of-the-mill fare, the blanket finish suggesting it did not feature any noticeably ahead of their marks. The third is the best guide.
Hot Rod Mamma(IRE) Official explanation: trainer said, regarding apparent improvement in form, that the filly settled better having been dropped back in distance and appeared to appreciate the easier ground.
Ellies Image Official explanation: jockey said filly was unsuited by the good ground
T/Plt: £124.70 to a £1 stake. Pool of £37,769.60 - 220.99 winning tickets. T/Qpdt: £15.00 to a £1 stake. Pool of £4,000.09 - 197.00 winning tickets. WG

4694 KEMPTON (A.W) (R-H)
Friday, August 13

OFFICIAL GOING: Standard
Wind: Light, against Weather: Heavy rain before meeting; sunshine and showers during racing

5025 DIGIBET.COM H'CAP 5f (P)
6:10 (6:12) (Class 5) (0-75,75) 3-Y-O+ **£2,590** (£770; £385; £192) **Stalls** High

Form RPR
2603 **1** **Island Legend (IRE)**[23] 4256 4-9-1 **64** ... (p) LiamKeniry 3 74
(J M Bradley) *mde all: maintained gallop and decisive advantage fr over 1f out* **11/4**[2]
340 **2** *2 ¼* **Steelcut**[27] 4148 6-9-6 **69** ... J-PGuillambert 6 71
(Andrew Reid) *a chsng wnr: no imp over 1f out: jst hld on for 2nd* **5/2**[1]
0430 **3** *hd* **Little Edward**[21] 4326 12-9-7 **70** ... GeorgeBaker 8 71
(R J Hodges) *chsd ldrs in 6th: pushed along 1/2-way: styd on fnl f to battle out minor placings* **9/1**
2224 **4** *hd* **Cavitie**[18] 4431 4-8-7 **56** ... DarryllHolland 2 56
(Andrew Reid) *chsd ldng pair and racd towards outer: nt qckn over 1f out: kpt on same pce* **13/2**
3200 **5** *nk* **Fromsong (IRE)**[23] 4255 12-8-12 **64** ... RussKennemore(3) 9 63
(D K Ivory) *chsd ldrs: nt qckn over 1f out: kpt on same pce ins fnl f* **17/2**
0650 **6** *2 ½* **Lord Of The Reins (IRE)**[21] 4343 6-9-12 **75** ... SebSanders 5 65
(J G Given) *sn pushed along in 7th: reminders over 1f out: threatened to make prog ent fnl f but didn't* **5/1**[3]
0666 **7** *4 ½* **Spic 'n Span**[21] 4326 5-9-0 **63** ... (b) LukeMorris 4 37
(R A Harris) *tried evthing he could to avoid gng to post: dwlt: t.k.h and rushed up on outer to go prom 1/2-way: wknd rapidly over 1f out* **16/1**
00 **8** *4* **Spring Horizon (IRE)**[62] 2964 4-8-7 **56** oh10 ... FrankieMcDonald 7 16
(Miss Z C Davison) *rel to r: a detached in last* **100/1**

59.36 secs (-1.14) **Going Correction** -0.075s/f (Stan) 8 Ran SP% **112.6**
Speed ratings (Par 103): **106,102,102,101,101 97,90,83**
toteswingers: 1&2 £3.00, 1&3 £6.20, 2&3 £4.20. CSF £9.73 CT £51.62 TOTE £5.40: £2.30, £1.10, £3.80; EX 15.50.
Owner J M Bradley **Bred** Jerome Casey **Trained** Sedbury, Gloucs
■ Stewards' Enquiry : Darryll Holland three-day ban: weighed-in 2lb heavy (Aug 27-29)

FOCUS
They went a decent pace in this sprint handicap but hardly anything got involved behind an all-the-way winner, who is rated back to his best. The time was 0.14 seconds faster than standard.
Spring Horizon(IRE) Official explanation: jockey said filly was slowly away

5026 DIVERSITY AT KEMPTON TONIGHT MAIDEN STKS 1m 2f (P)
6:45 (6:47) (Class 4) 3-Y-O **£4,533** (£1,348; £674; £336) **Stalls** High

Form RPR
1 **Ferdoos** 3-8-12 0 ... NeilCallan 6 86+
(M A Jarvis) *trckd ldrs: prog 2f out: sn wnt 2nd: led jst over 1f out: pushed wl clr fnl f* **15/2**[3]
2 *5* **Invincibility (IRE)** 3-9-3 0 ... SebSanders 8 81
(S Dow) *pressed ldr: pushed along over 3f out: led 2f out: drvn and hdd jst over 1f out: styd on but easily outpcd* **40/1**
3243 **3** *6* **Azimuth (USA)**[28] 4107 3-9-3 83 ... (t) DarryllHolland 1 69+
(J Noseda) *settled in tch: pushed along over 2f out: styd on to take modest 3rd fnl f* **4/1**[2]
044- **4** *3* **Palio Square (USA)**[289] 7121 3-9-3 83 ... EddieAhern 11 63+
(H R A Cecil) *hld up in tch: disputing 6th and gng wl whn nowhere to go and snatched up sharply jst over 2f out: no ch after but styd on to take modest 4th* **3/1**[1]
5 *7* **Doon Kalal (IRE)** 3-9-3 0 ... MartinDwyer 3 49
(M P Tregoning) *n.m.r sn after s: mostly in last pair: rn wd bnd 3f out to 2f out: nvr a factor but passed a few rivals fnl f* **22/1**
05 **6** *3 ¼* **Tobernea (IRE)**[19] 4407 3-9-3 0 ... J-PGuillambert 5 43
(M Johnston) *chsd ldng pair: pushed along 3f out: wknd qckly wl over 1f out* **16/1**
7 *¾* **Rhythm Stick** 3-9-3 0 ... IvaMilickova 2 41
(John Berry) *settled in rr: stl there 2f out and sn outpcd: keeping on whn rn up blind alley fnl f and snatched up* **80/1**
0 **8** *1 ½* **Hoodie (IRE)**[25] 4205 3-9-3 0 ... FrankieDettori 9 38
(Saeed Bin Suroor) *led: shkn up and hdd 2f out: wknd v rapidly* **4/1**[2]
5 **9** *3 ½* **Pickwick**[29] 4069 3-9-3 0 ... RichardMullen 10 31
(Sir Michael Stoute) *t.k.h: trckd ldng pair: wknd rapidly wl over 1f out* **3/1**[1]
0 **10** *32* **Shemita's Song (USA)**[30] 4028 3-8-12 0 ... DaraghO'Donohoe 4 —
(George Baker) *n.m.r sn after s: a last and struggling: t.o* **200/1**

2m 6.18s (-1.82) **Going Correction** -0.075s/f (Stan) 10 Ran SP% **116.2**
Speed ratings (Par 102): **104,100,95,92,87 84,84,82,80,54**
toteswingers: 1&2 £8.50, 1&3 £5.00, 2&3 £7.80. CSF £261.76 TOTE £11.80: £3.50, £9.40, £1.20; EX 296.90.
Owner Sheikh Ahmed Al Maktoum **Bred** Miss A Shaykhutdinova **Trained** Newmarket, Suffolk
■ Stewards' Enquiry : Iva Milickova four-day ban: careless riding (Aug 27-30)

FOCUS
It was raining heavily. A number of these were closely matched on form in what looked a competitive maiden but a well-bred newcomer stormed clear of another debutant who was a long way ahead of the rest. The runner-up will set the level.
Azimuth(USA) Official explanation: jockey said colt became unbalanced on bend
Palio Square(USA) Official explanation: jockey said colt was denied a clear run
Pickwick Official explanation: jockey said colt ran too freely

5027 LADIES DAY SEPTEMBER 4TH CLAIMING STKS 6f (P)
7:15 (7:19) (Class 6) 3-5-Y-O **£2,047** (£604; £302) **Stalls** High

Form RPR
600 **1** **C'Mon You Irons (IRE)**[11] 4662 5-8-10 71 ... (v[1]) KierenFox(5) 5 80
(M R Hoad) *chsd ldng pair: wnt 2nd over 2f out: drvn over 1f out: styd on dourly to ld nr fin* **16/1**
5450 **2** *½* **Defector (IRE)**[15] 4501 4-9-0 71 ... (p) MartinDwyer 12 78
(W R Muir) *wnt lft s: pressed ldr: led over 3f out: drvn 2f out: kpt on but hdd nr fin* **7/1**
-300 **3** *4* **Cape Kimberley**[10] 4684 3-8-7 73 ... RichardMullen 4 61
(J G Given) *chsd ldrs: rdn over 2f out: kpt on to take 3rd jst ins fnl f: no ch w ldng pair* **14/1**
1205 **4** *1 ½* **Caprio (IRE)**[29] 4053 5-9-7 81 ... StephenCraine 9 67
(J R Boyle) *sn in last trio: shuffled along fr 3f out: styd on steadily to take 4th last strides: nvr remotely nr ldrs* **13/2**[3]

0564 **5** *nk* **Lutine Charlie (IRE)**[7] 4775 3-8-5 70............................(p) LukeMorris 3 53
(P Winkworth) *t.k.h early: hld up in tch: prog over 2f out: drvn into 3rd briefly 1f out: one pce after* **10/1**

1602 **6** *3/4* **Maoi Chinn Tire (IRE)**[22] 4298 3-8-9 70..........................(p) LiamKeniry 1 55
(J S Moore) *led to over 3f out: lost 2nd over 2f out: steadily wknd* **6/1[2]**

0440 **7** *3/4* **Berbice (IRE)**[15] 4510 5-8-10 73...............................(e) RichardHughes 11 50
(S Kirk) *given slt nudge s: hld up towards rr: gng easily but plenty to do 2f out: sme prog on bit over 1f out: no ch fnl f and effrt flattened out* **13/8[1]**

3000 **8** *hd* **Imperial House**[6] 4839 4-8-10 63..................................(b) DavidProbert 10 50
(R A Harris) *s.i.s: rousted along early in last trio: no prog tl kpt on fnl f* **25/1**

4-06 **9** *3* **Magnus Thrax (USA)**[11] 4660 3-8-7 78............................ SteveDrowne 6 40
(R Hannon) *rrng bdly in stalls bef s: mostly in midfield: shkn up and no prog 2f out: fdd* **10/1**

0600 **10** *1 1/4* **Tarita (IRE)**[20] 4378 3-8-6 70...................................... FrankieMcDonald 7 35
(R Hannon) *pushed up into midfield: rdn and no prog over 2f out: wknd over 1f out* **28/1**

1560 **11** *1 1/2* **Avow (USA)**[19] 4398 3-8-7 65...(b) NeilChalmers 8 31
(J J Bridger) *a towards rr: effrt on inner over 2f out: sn no prog and wknd* **50/1**

00 **12** *9* **Rubbinghouse Com**[116] 1432 3-8-11 0............................ SebSanders 2 —
(P M Phelan) *dwlt: a in last trio: wknd over 2f out: t.o* **66/1**

1m 12.05s (-1.05) **Going Correction** -0.075s/f (Stan)
WFA 3 from 4yo+ 4lb 12 Ran SP% **119.7**
Speed ratings (Par 101): **104,103,98,96,95 94,93,93,89,87 85,73**
toteswingers: 1&2 £19.80, 1&3 £40.60, 2&3 £11.20. CSF £121.90 TOTE £23.10: £7.20, £3.00, £7.00; EX 71.30.Berbice was claimed by Ken McGarrity for £5,000. Defector was claimed by Milton Bradley for £9,000. Lutine Charlie was claimed by J L Flint for £4,000.
Owner double-r-racing.com **Bred** Airlie Stud **Trained** Lewes, E Sussex

FOCUS
Nine of the runners had a BHA rating of between 70 and 81 in this competitive claimer. It was run at a decent pace but the hold-up performers struggled to land a blow. The form is rated at something like face value.

5028 OLLY MURS LIVE ON LADIES DAY MEDIAN AUCTION MAIDEN STKS 7f (P)
7:50 (7:53) (Class 6) 3-5-Y-O **£2,047** (£604; £302) **Stalls** High

Form RPR

00 **1** **Spanish Island (USA)**[10] 4679 3-9-3 0.......................... GeorgeBaker 14 79
(M A Magnusson) *chsd ldrs: rdn over 2f out: wnt 3rd over 1f out: clsd qckly to ld jst ins fnl f: sn clr* **4/1[2]**

06 **2** *4* **Dirakh Shan**[15] 4521 3-9-3 0.. J-PGuillambert 4 68
(L M Cumani) *mde most: jnd 3f out: battled it out tl wnr stormed by ins fnl f* **7/2[1]**

53 **3** *nk* **Wise Up**[53] 3258 3-9-3 0.. DarryllHolland 3 67
(C A Dwyer) *pressed ldr: chal fr 3f out: upsides after tl wnr stormed past ins fnl f* **4/1[2]**

00 **4** *3 3/4* **Queenie's Star (IRE)**[19] 4397 3-8-7 0.................... JemmaMarshall(5) 2 52
(M J Attwater) *t.k.h: prom: outpcd and shkn up 2f out: kpt on* **33/1**

5 *nk* **Catching Zeds** 3-8-12 0.. EddieAhern 13 51+
(Ian Williams) *stdd in rr after s: pushed along over 2f out: styd on steadily after: nrly snatched 4th: fair debut* **14/1**

0 **6** *2 1/4* **Marksbury**[86] 2227 3-8-12 0.. LukeMorris 12 45
(J M P Eustace) *towards rr: reminder after 3f and pushed along after: sme prog 2f out: nvr on terms* **22/1**

0 **7** *nk* **Noisy Noverre (IRE)**[98] 1878 3-8-12 0.................... DaraghO'Donohoe 8 44
(George Baker) *mostly chsd ldng pair tl wknd over 1f out* **66/1**

8 *5* **Fastinthestraight (IRE)** 3-9-3 0.................................. SteveDrowne 11 36
(J R Boyle) *dwlt: detached in last: effrt on inner over 2f out: sn no prog: wknd over 1f out* **14/1**

9 *3/4* **Flying Cherry (IRE)** 3-8-12 0.. LiamKeniry 5 29
(Miss Jo Crowley) *dwlt: towards rr: rdn and sme prog over 2f out: no hdwy wl over 1f out: wknd* **12/1**

0- **10** *1 3/4* **Starstreamer (IRE)**[363] 5026 3-8-5 0........................ KatiaScallan(7) 10 24
(M P Tregoning) *racd wd: nvr beyond midfield: wknd over 2f out* **10/1**

00- **11** *nk* **Seeker Rainbow**[387] 4200 3-8-12 0.......................... FrankieMcDonald 7 23
(Mrs L C Jewell) *t.k.h: prom: rdn 3f out: sn wknd* **66/1**

12 *18* **Zarius** 3-9-3 0.. JimCrowley 6 —
(C F Wall) *a wl in rr: t.o* **7/1[3]**

13 *4* **Mr Shammie** 3-9-3 0.. AdamKirby 1 —
(M G Quinlan) *wnt lft s: a wl in rr: t.o* **22/1**

1m 27.15s (1.15) **Going Correction** -0.075s/f (Stan) 13 Ran SP% **119.5**
Speed ratings (Par 101): **90,85,85,80,80 77,77,71,70,68 68,48,43**
toteswingers: 1&2 £6.30, 1&3 £3.90, 2&3 £2.70. CSF £17.43 TOTE £5.40: £1.60, £1.80, £1.10; EX 23.00.
Owner Eastwind Racing Ltd And Martha Trussell **Bred** E T Buckley, S Varney & A O'Donnell **Trained** Upper Lambourn, Berks

FOCUS
There didn't seem to be much strength in depth in this maiden. However, the winner produced a fast-finishing effort to forge clear of the two main form contenders who were a long way ahead of the rest and the form looks solid enough. It has been rated around the second and third.
Catching Zeds Official explanation: vet said filly bled from the nose
Fastinthestraight(IRE) Official explanation: jockey said gelding was slowly away
Seeker Rainbow Official explanation: jockey said filly became upset at start
Mr Shammie Official explanation: jockey said colt ran green

5029 EUROPEAN BREEDERS' FUND MAIDEN FILLIES' STKS 7f (P)
8:20 (8:24) (Class 4) 2-Y-O **£4,468** (£1,329; £664; £331) **Stalls** High

Form RPR

22 **1** **Ragsah (IRE)**[35] 3871 2-9-0 0.. FrankieDettori 8 86+
(Saeed Bin Suroor) *trckd ldrs: plld out and effrt 2f out: pushed firmly into ld ent fnl f: in command after* **4/9[1]**

2 *1 1/4* **Secret Love (IRE)** 2-9-0 0.. GeorgeBaker 14 81+
(M A Magnusson) *trckd ldrs on inner: prog to ld wl over 1f out: r.o but hdd and outpcd ent fnl f* **16/1**

02 **3** *3 3/4* **Fly By White (IRE)**[13] 4587 2-9-0 0.............................. RichardHughes 5 72
(R Hannon) *trckd ldrs on outer: shkn up and cl up 2f out: sn outpcd: pushed along to take 3rd ins fnl f* **4/1[2]**

4 *nk* **Winged Valkyrie (IRE)** 2-9-0 0.................................... MichaelHills 6 72+
(B W Hills) *dwlt: hld up in midfield: 8th 2f out: pushed along and styd on steadily after* **12/1[3]**

0 **5** *1 1/4* **Star Concert (USA)**[15] 4508 2-9-0 0.............................. EddieAhern 4 68
(Mrs A J Perrett) *trckd ldr: shkn up and upsides jst over 2f out: outpcd over 1f out: wl btn 3rd ent fnl f: lost 2 pls after* **14/1**

0 **6** *3* **Luv U Too**[18] 4421 2-9-0 0.. DarryllHolland 13 61
(F J Brennan) *led to wl over 1f out: wknd fnl f* **40/1**

53 **7** *1 1/2* **Rosa Midnight (USA)**[22] 4299 2-9-0 0........................ J-PGuillambert 9 57+
(M L W Bell) *hld up in midfield on inner: n.m.r after 2f: effrt over 2f out: fdd over 1f out* **18/1**

0 **8** *2 1/4* **Memory Lane**[9] 4695 2-9-0 0.. SebSanders 1 51
(Sir Mark Prescott) *nvr beyond midfield on outer: outpcd fr 2f out* **50/1**

0 **9** *nk* **Talkhees (IRE)**[37] 3778 2-9-0 0.................................... MartinDwyer 7 51
(B J Meehan) *wl in tch in midfield: nudged along over 2f out: wknd over 1f out* **33/1**

10 *1/2* **Gypsy Legend (IRE)** 2-9-0 0.. LiamKeniry 11 49
(S Kirk) *dwlt: wl in rr and rn green: taken wd in st: nvr a factor but kpt on fnl f* **50/1**

11 *1/2* **Silbury (IRE)** 2-9-0 0.. SteveDrowne 3 48
(R Charlton) *pressed ldrs tl wknd qckly jst over 2f out* **40/1**

12 *nse* **Notify** 2-9-0 0.. JimCrowley 2 48
(P R Chamings) *settled wl in rr and racd wd thrght: no ch fnl 2f: pushed along and kpt on* **66/1**

13 *3* **Disturbia (IRE)** 2-9-0 0.. AdamKirby 12 40
(J W Hills) *dwlt: a in last trio: wl bhd fnl 2f* **66/1**

00 **14** *9* **Avon Causeway**[10] 4678 2-9-0 0.................................. FrankieMcDonald 10 18
(J M Bradley) *rdn and dropped to last bef 1/2-way: t.o* **125/1**

1m 26.57s (0.57) **Going Correction** -0.075s/f (Stan) 14 Ran SP% **130.3**
Speed ratings (Par 93): **93,91,87,86,85 82,80,77,77,76 76,76,72,62**
toteswingers: 1&2 £4.90, 1&3 £1.20, 2&3 £9.50. CSF £11.96 TOTE £1.60: £1.10, £5.00, £1.10; EX 16.30.
Owner Godolphin **Bred** Darley **Trained** Newmarket, Suffolk

FOCUS
A fair maiden fillies' event. It was run at a decent pace and the hot favourite did the job in good style.

NOTEBOOK
Ragsah(IRE) set the standard on her runner-up efforts at short prices in a pair of 6f Newmarket maidens. She was sent off at prohibitive odds again and displayed a low head-carriage and willing attitude to surge into the lead under a confident ride. It is hard to rate the value of the form but the half-sister to brilliant 1m-1m2f winner Dubai Millennium should continue to progress with time and distance and could have a bright future. (tchd 8-15 in a place)
Secret Love(IRE) moved smoothly and kicked into the lead approaching the furlong marker before being overhauled. This was a very promising debut from an 80,000gns half-sister to 7f winners Illustrious Prince and Mastoora. She finished clear of the rest and should not have too much trouble winning a similar event next time. (op 14-1)
Fly By White(IRE) shaped with promise out wide and wasn't given a hard time when the front two got away. She seems to be quietly progressing after three runs and should be able to wins races. (op 6-1)
Winged Valkyrie(IRE) showed signs of inexperience before flashing home for fourth on debut. She should have learned a lot and is a very well-bred filly being a Hawk Wing half-sister to Group 3 2-yo winner/1,000 Guineas fourth Sent From Heaven. (tchd 11-1)
Star Concert(USA) ran a bit better than market expectations when staying-on eighth in a 7f Goodwood maiden last month. There was no big improvement on her second start but she kept plugging away and should find her niche in nurseries. (op 12-1)

5030 PANORAMIC BAR & RESTAURANT H'CAP 1m (P)
8:50 (8:51) (Class 3) (0-95,92) 3-Y-O
£6,854 (£2,052; £1,026; £513; £256; £128) **Stalls** High

Form RPR

1132 **1** **Kajima**[53] 3271 3-9-2 87.. RichardHughes 6 96
(R Hannon) *hld up in 6th: gng easily 2f out: weaved through over 1f out: produced to ld last 120yds: r.o* **7/1**

-350 **2** *3/4* **Colepeper**[35] 3867 3-9-6 91.. JoeFanning 8 98
(M Johnston) *trckd ldng pair: rdn to go between them fr 2f out: nt qckn jst over 1f out: r.o once wnr wnt by last 100yds* **6/1**

4200 **3** *1* **High Twelve (IRE)**[57] 3103 3-9-7 92.............................. SteveDrowne 7 97
(J H M Gosden) *trckd ldrs gng wl: rdn and nt qckn over 1f out: kpt on to take 3rd last strides* **9/2[2]**

4210 **4** *nk* **Zakiy**[20] 4357 3-8-8 79..(t) EddieAhern 2 83
(W J Haggas) *disp ld after 2f to 2f out: stl chalng ent fnl f: outpcd last 100yds* **16/1**

331 **5** *hd* **Linnens Star (IRE)**[28] 4107 3-9-3 88............................ JimCrowley 3 92
(R M Beckett) *led or disp: narrow advantage fr 2f out: hdd & wknd last 120yds* **8/1**

1420 **6** *1 1/4* **Hypnotized (USA)**[57] 3103 3-9-6 91.............................(p) FrankieDettori 1 92
(M L W Bell) *hld up in last trio: shkn up over 2f out: no prog over 1f out: plugged on* **5/2[1]**

1100 **7** *1/2* **Edinburgh Knight (IRE)**[107] 1616 3-9-3 88.................. NeilCallan 5 88
(P W D'Arcy) *hld up in last trio: rdn over 2f out: limited prog over 1f out: fdd fnl f* **5/1[3]**

10-3 **8** *3/4* **Spying**[20] 4371 3-9-5 90.. SebSanders 4 88
(Mrs A Duffield) *trckd ldrs: rdn wl over 2f out: fdd over 1f out* **10/1**

-000 **9** *17* **Kalypso King (USA)**[20] 4357 3-9-7 92.......................... StephenCraine 9 51
(S Kirk) *stdd s: hld up in last trio: rdn over 2f out: sn wknd: t.o* **50/1**

1m 37.86s (-1.94) **Going Correction** -0.075s/f (Stan) 9 Ran SP% **118.3**
Speed ratings (Par 104): **106,105,104,103,103 102,102,101,84**
toteswingers: 1&2 £13.70, 1&3 £5.70, 2&3 £7.90. CSF £49.74 CT £212.88 TOTE £5.50: £1.70, £3.30, £3.00; EX 51.20.
Owner Miss Yvonne Jacques **Bred** F J O' Connor **Trained** East Everleigh, Wilts

FOCUS
A decent handicap. The pace was not particularly strong and they finished a bit bunched. The form seems sound and the winner continues on the up.

NOTEBOOK
Kajima scythed his way through the pack to defy a market drift and gain compensation for his narrow defeat in a Windsor handicap when last seen in June. His mark will take another hit after this third win of the season but he has a good cruising speed and decent turn foot and could continue to climb up the ranks. (op 5-1)
Colepeper put in a gritty effort and nearly gave the winner a scare on Polytrack debut. This was his first strongly competitive effort in a handicap since his 6f Catterick maiden win last September and could be the springboard to success in a similar race. (op 8-1 tchd 5-1)
High Twelve(IRE) looked a big threat halfway up the straight but got caught a bit flat-footed when the pace quickened before staying on again. He has not lived up to expectations since a fourth in the Royal Lodge last autumn but has dropped 13lb in the weights this season and should be able to build on this encouraging return from a short break and gelding operation. (op 6-1 tchd 13-2)
Zakiy, tailed off on handicap debut at Ascot last time, bounced back with a fair effort under a prominent ride and has probably run close to the form of his York maiden win in June.
Linnens Star(IRE) ran his rivals into submission when a clear-cut winner of a 1m Newmarket maiden on his third run but couldn't repeat the front-running trick off a tough opening mark on handicap/AW debut. (op 7-1)
Hypnotized(USA) couldn't get into out wide in his bid to make it 3-3 at this track. He probably doesn't have much margin for error off his current mark but should be more potent from a better draw in a more strongly run race next time. Official explanation: jockey said colt hung left (op 3-1 tchd 10-3)

Edinburgh Knight(IRE) was never dangerous back in a handicap after two unsuccessful raids in Group 3/Listed company. (op 11-2 tchd 4-1)

5031 STAVROS FLATLEY AT KEMPTON TONIGHT H'CAP 7f (P)
9:20 (9:20) (Class 4) (0-80,80) 3-Y-O **£4,533** (£1,348; £674; £336) **Stalls** High

Form RPR

3215 **1** **Belgique (IRE)**[14] 4548 3-9-4 **77**.................... RichardHughes 1 81
(R Hannon) *wl away fr wd draw and pressed ldr: shkn up to ld 1f out: a in command after* **5/1**[2]

-440 **2** ½ **Saharia (IRE)**[35] 3876 3-9-6 **79**.................... DarryllHolland 5 82+
(J Noseda) *t.k.h: hld up in midfield: tried to creep clsr 2f out: urged along jst over 1f out: r.o fnl f: tk 2nd nr fin* **8/1**

4306 **3** nk **Ongoodform (IRE)**[23] 4264 3-9-7 **80**.................... NeilCallan 8 82
(P W D'Arcy) *t.k.h: trckd ldrs: cl enough 2f out: nt qckn over 1f out: styd on to take 3rd last strides* **7/1**[3]

0304 **4** hd **Fivefold (USA)**[23] 4264 3-9-5 **78**.................... J-PGuillambert 4 80
(J Akehurst) *plld hrd: led: kicked on 2f out: hdd 1f out: fdd nr fin* **8/1**

366 **5** hd **Fazza**[13] 4588 3-8-11 **70**.................... LiamKeniry 11 73+
(D W P Arbuthnot) *hld up in midfield: gng strly 2f out: nt clr run over 1f out and lost pl: swtchd lft and styd on fnl f: nt rcvr* **20/1**

1330 **6** 1 ¼ **Vanilla Rum**[20] 4387 3-9-3 **76**.................... DaneO'Neill 7 74
(H Candy) *dwlt: hld up in last trio: rdn 2f out: styd on fnl f: no threat* **10/1**

015- **7** ½ **Pittodrie Star (IRE)**[254] 7611 3-9-1 **74**.................... DavidProbert 3 70
(A M Balding) *dwlt: t.k.h: hld up in last trio: rdn and struggling over 2f out: no prog tl styd on ins fnl f* **8/1**

6041 **8** ½ **Master Mylo (IRE)**[30] 4025 3-9-0 **73**.................... JimCrowley 2 68
(D K Ivory) *t.k.h: hld up towards rr and racd wd: rdn and nt qckn 2f out: one pce after* **11/4**[1]

-406 **9** hd **Dark Eyes (IRE)**[50] 3361 3-9-5 **78**.................... EddieAhern 10 72
(D J Coakley) *trckd ldrs: cl enough 2f out: nt qckn over 1f out: fdd ins fnl f* **9/1**

2200 **10** ¾ **Torres Del Paine**[65] 2868 3-8-5 **69**.................... JemmaMarshall(5) 6 61
(J C Fox) *hld up in rr: looking for room over 2f out: one pce and no prog over 1f out* **16/1**

4456 **11** ½ **Bidruma**[23] 4250 3-8-2 **61** oh1.................... AndreaAtzeni 9 52
(Mike Murphy) *t.k.h: trckd ldng pair to jst over 1f out: wknd* **40/1**

3205 **12** ¾ **Poppy Golightly**[14] 4529 3-8-8 **67**.................... FrankieMcDonald 12 56
(R J Hodges) *t.k.h: trckd ldrs on inner: lost pl fr 2f out* **33/1**

1m 25.98s (-0.02) **Going Correction** -0.075s/f (Stan) **12 Ran SP% 124.3**
Speed ratings (Par 102): **97,96,96,95,95 94,93,93,92,91 91,90**
toteswingers: 1&2 £6.10, 1&3 £7.50, 2&3 £19.90. CSF £46.30 CT £293.73 TOTE £6.10: £1.90, £3.70, £3.50; EX 46.70 Place 6: £132.18, Place 5: £84.68..
Owner Philip F Myerscough **Bred** Philip And Mrs Jane Myerscough **Trained** East Everleigh, Wilts

FOCUS
Not a strong handicap for the grade. It was run at a fair pace but they finished in a bit of a bunch. Improvement from the winner with the runner-up to form.
Master Mylo(IRE) Official explanation: jockey said gelding ran too freely
T/Plt: £225.70 to a £1 stake. Pool of £44,199.49 - 142.92 winning tickets. T/Qpdt: £51.40 to a £1 stake. Pool of £4,586.88 - 66.00 winning tickets. JN

4620 NEWBURY (L-H)
Friday, August 13

OFFICIAL GOING: Good to firm changing to good after race 1 (1.30)
Rail moved out from 7f to 5f increasing distances on round course by about 20m.
Wind: Moderate ahead Weather: Overcast

5032 DON DEADMAN MEMORIAL EUROPEAN BREEDERS' FUND MAIDEN STKS (DIV I) 7f (S)
1:30 (1:32) (Class 4) 2-Y-O **£4,857** (£1,445; £722; £360) **Stalls** Centre

Form RPR

1 **Saamidd** 2-9-3 0.................... FrankieDettori 8 97+
(Saeed Bin Suroor) *hld up towards rr but in tch shkn up and rapid hdwy to ld wl over 1f out: c readily clr ins fnl f: impressive* **11/4**[2]

6 **2** 7 **Yair Hill (IRE)**[37] 3794 2-9-3 0.................... EddieAhern 3 77
(J L Dunlop) *chsd ldrs: slt advantage ins fnl 2f: hdd wl over 1f out and styd on: nvr any ch w easy wnr* **7/2**[3]

3 **3** 1 ¼ **Buckland (IRE)**[12] 4622 2-9-3 0.................... MartinDwyer 2 74
(B J Meehan) *stdd towards rr but in tch: drvn and hdwy over 2f out: chal: hung rt and stl green wl over 1f out: wknd ins fnl f* **11/10**[1]

4 ¾ **Musawama (IRE)** 2-9-3 0.................... RichardHills 10 72+
(J H M Gosden) *trckd ldr: shkn up and ev ch 2f out: outpcd ins fnl f* **14/1**

5 4 **Dressing Room (USA)** 2-9-3 0.................... KierenFallon 9 62
(M Johnston) *chsd ldrs: rdn 3f out: one pce fnl 2f* **25/1**

6 ¾ **Midnight Maasai** 2-9-3 0.................... PhilipRobinson 4 60
(C G Cox) *led tl hdd ins fnl 2f: sn outpcd* **50/1**

6 **7** ½ **Brandy Alexander**[18] 4421 2-9-3 0.................... RichardHughes 1 59+
(R Hannon) *trckd ldrs: outpcd over 1f out: fdd fnl 120yds* **33/1**

00 **8** 2 ½ **Erythrina (IRE)**[22] 4299 2-8-12 0.................... FergusSweeney 11 48
(B G Powell) *chsd ldrs: rdn 3f out: wknd ins fnl 2f* **100/1**

9 ½ **Pivot Bridge** 2-9-3 0.................... MichaelHills 12 51+
(B W Hills) *s.i.s: in rr tl mod late prog ins fnl f* **40/1**

10 4 **Jan Smuts (IRE)** 2-9-3 0.................... WilliamBuick 6 41
(B J Meehan) *bhd fr 1/2-way* **66/1**

11 ½ **Waterborne** 2-9-3 0.................... SteveDrowne 5 40
(R Charlton) *green in rr: sme hdwy: stl green 1/2-way: sn wknd* **100/1**

12 shd **Talking Back** 2-9-3 0.................... LiamKeniry 7 40
(S Kirk) *s.i.s: a in rr* **100/1**

1m 29.04s (3.34) **Going Correction** +0.40s/f (Good) **12 Ran SP% 118.8**
Speed ratings (Par 96): **96,88,86,85,81 80,79,76,76,71 71,71**
toteswingers: 1&2 £2.70, 1&3 £2.60, 2&3 £2.10 CSF £12.38 TOTE £4.20: £1.70, £1.10, £1.50; EX 16.60.
Owner Godolphin **Bred** Darley **Trained** Newmarket, Suffolk

FOCUS
Following 4.4mm of rain overnight and steady drizzle leading up to the meeting, the ground had eased to good, though a couple of the jockeys in the opener thought it was riding softer than that. Won by the subsequent Breeders' Cup Juvenile Turf winner Pounced last year, this looked the stronger of the two divisions on paper and it may have unearthed another superstar. The field raced as one group down the centre and only three mattered according to the market.

NOTEBOOK
Saamidd ◆, out of a 1m2f winner and from the family of Barathea and Gossamer, travelled well behind the leaders towards the nearside of the field and once asked for his effort, produced an astonishing turn of foot to shoot right away from his rivals inside the last furlong. He should have no problem staying 1m at least and looks set to go a long way. He was immediately best quoted at 25-1 for next year's 2,000 Guineas by Hills. (tchd 5-2)
Yair Hill(IRE), an eyecatching sixth of 14 on his Newmarket debut last month, improved from that and was always there or thereabouts. Although no match for the winner, he kept on going to finish a clear second best and he should get further in due course. (tchd 4-1)
Buckland(IRE), a promising third of 11 on his debut over 6f here at the start of the month, was making hard work of it when delivered with his effort towards the far side of the track 2f from home, and that was as close as he got. He is entered for both the Dewhurst and Racing Post Trophy and, although this effort suggests he isn't up to that level, it's too early to be giving up on him. (op 5-4 tchd 11-8 and 6-4 in places)
Musawama(IRE) ◆, a half-brother to a winning sprinter in Greece and representing last year's winning stable, was keen enough in a handy position early and, although completely outpaced when the winner went for home over a furlong out, still showed enough to suggest that this Royal Lodge and Racing Post Trophy entry has a future.
Dressing Room(USA), a 140,000gns half-brother to two winners at up to 1m including the high-class Lord Shanakill, was having to be shoved along from before halfway so is likely to come on a good deal for this. (op 20-1)
Midnight Maasai, already gelded and out of a multiple winner at up to 1m as a juvenile, set the pace until entering the last 2f and is another likely to improve with racing. (op 66-1)
Brandy Alexander ◆, green when unplaced on his Windsor debut, travelled well off the pace and was by no means knocked about over the last couple of furlongs. There is better still to come from him.

5033 DON DEADMAN MEMORIAL EUROPEAN BREEDERS' FUND MAIDEN STKS (DIV II) 7f (S)
2:00 (2:05) (Class 4) 2-Y-O **£4,857** (£1,445; £722; £360) **Stalls** Centre

Form RPR

1 **Treasury Devil (USA)** 2-9-3 0.................... WilliamBuick 1 84+
(J H M Gosden) *trckd ldrs: led over 2f out: pushed along and green ins fnl f: styd on strly* **9/4**[2]

2 ¾ **General Synod** 2-9-3 0.................... RichardHughes 7 76+
(R Hannon) *hld up in tch: drvn and hdwy wl over 1f out: styd on to u.p to chse wnr fnl 120yds: a readily hld* **5/4**[1]

242 **3** 3 ¼ **Cocohatchee**[36] 3811 2-9-3 **77**.................... FergusSweeney 6 74
(P M Phelan) *chsd ldrs: rdn to chse wnr ins fnl 2f: hung lft u.p ins fnl f: wknd and lost 2nd fnl 120yds* **11/1**

4 1 ¼ **Red Eyes** 2-9-3 0.................... MartinDwyer 5 71+
(B J Meehan) *s.i.s: in rr: rdn 2f out: green but hdwy appr fnl f: kpt on: nt trble ldrs* **16/1**

5 1 ¼ **Charles Camoin (IRE)** 2-9-3 0.................... LiamKeniry 4 68
(S Kirk) *led tl hdd over 2f out: rdn and outpcd sn after: styd on again ins fnl f* **50/1**

6 ¾ **Traffic Sister (USA)** 2-8-12 0.................... NeilCallan 2 61
(J S Moore) *chsd ldrs: rdn over 2f out: wknd over 1f out* **33/1**

7 9 **Reflect (IRE)** 2-9-3 0.................... SteveDrowne 9 43
(R Hannon) *s.i.s: sn chsng ldrs: rdn over 2f out hung lft and wknd sn after* **33/1**

8 nk **Reach Out** 2-9-0 0.................... RussKennemore(3) 8 43
(B G Powell) *chsd ldrs: rdn over 2f out: hung lft and wknd sn after* **100/1**

9 1 ½ **Colebrooke** 2-9-3 0.................... KierenFallon 11 39
(M Johnston) *sn rdn along in rr: a outpcd* **6/1**[3]

10 3 ½ **Fleeting Tiger** 2-9-3 0.................... EddieAhern 3 30
(J L Dunlop) *s.i.s: in rr: sme hdwy over 3f out: sn wknd* **33/1**

11 nk **Ollywood** 2-9-3 0.................... SebSanders 10 29
(A W Carroll) *s.i.s: a outpcd* **100/1**

1m 30.64s (4.94) **Going Correction** +0.40s/f (Good) **11 Ran SP% 116.5**
Speed ratings (Par 96): **87,83,82,81,79 78,68,68,66,62 62**
toteswingers: 1&2 £1.70, 1&3 £3.70, 2&3 £3.40 CSF £5.13 TOTE £2.90: £1.20, £1.30, £2.20; EX 7.10.
Owner Lord Lloyd-Webber **Bred** Watership Down Stud **Trained** Newmarket, Suffolk

FOCUS
They went a much steadier early pace in this division and the winning time was 1.6 seconds slower.

NOTEBOOK
Treasury Devil(USA) ◆, a $1,000,000 half-brother to the useful Crystany, held an entry in the Listed race here on Saturday which indicates the regard in which he is held. He travelled strongly behind the leaders, quickened up nicely when asked over 2f from home and, once in front, was always doing more than enough. He holds an entry in the Racing Post Trophy, and with improvement to come it will be interesting to see where he goes next. (op 5-2)
General Synod ◆, a half-brother to four winners at up to 1m2f, came off the bridle much earlier than the winner and took time to respond, but he got the hang of things and stayed on right to the line. Another Racing Post Trophy entry, he should take long in going one better. (op 6-4)
Cocohatchee was the only one in the field with previous experience, but was surprisingly restrained at the back of the field early and took a keen grip. He tried to make an effort towards the far side of the field over 2f from home, but started to hang and could make little impression on the front pair. His official rating of 77 provides some sort of benchmark for the form. (op 17-2)
Red Eyes ◆, a 48,000gns half-brother to five winners including the smart King's County, made eyecatching late progress under hands-and-heels riding. His trainer had warned beforehand that he would probably need it, and this Royal Lodge entry is definitely worth keeping an eye out for.
Charles Camoin(IRE), a 32,000euros half-brother to two winners at up to 7f, made much of the early running before tiring and hanging once headed over 2f from home. He is very likely to improve.
Traffic Sister(USA), a sister to the smart Traffic Guard, showed enough on this debut to suggest she has a future in her own right. (tchd 40-1)
Colebrooke, like the Johnston representative in the first division, was needing to be ridden along from an early stage. A 90,000gns half-brother to four winners at up to 1m4f including the useful Hazeymm, he looks one for later on. (op 5-1)

5034 CHRISTOPHER SMITH ASSOCIATES CLAIMING STKS 1m 3f 5y
2:35 (2:35) (Class 5) 3-Y-O+ **£3,238** (£963; £481; £240) **Stalls** Low

Form RPR

-306 **1** **Foxhaven**[51] 3329 8-9-12 **78**.................... (v) JimCrowley 3 81
(P R Chamings) *hld up in tch: hdwy on bit to trck ldrs 2f out: drvn to ld and hung lft ins fnl f: pushed out* **11/8**[1]

1150 **2** 1 **Lang Shining (IRE)**[13] 4579 6-9-9 **85**.................... SophieDoyle(5) 7 81
(J A Osborne) *hld up in rr: stdy hdwy on outside over 2f out: shkn up and hung lft ins fnl f: kpt on to take 2nd cl home but no ch w wnr* **10/3**[3]

5600 **3** ½ **Tammela**[12] 4626 3-8-3 **59**.................... DavidProbert 1 65
(A P Jarvis) *slt ld: jnd 6f out: rdn and kpt slt advantage fr 3f out: hdd and hung rt ins fnl f: sn outpcd by wnr: lost 2nd cl home* **40/1**

12-0 **4** 3 **Penton Hook**[58] 3079 4-8-13 **75**.................... LukeMorris 6 60
(P Winkworth) *chse ldrs: outpcd 4f out: styd on again ins fnl f: nvr any threat* **8/1**

04-4 **5** ½ **Grande Caiman (IRE)**[16] 4489 6-8-6 **85**.................... CharlesEddery(7) 2 59
(R Hannon) *chsd ldr: chal fr 6f out and stl upsides ins fnl 2f: wkng whn hmpd ins fnl f* **11/4**[2]

3166 **6** 3 **Sgt Schultz (IRE)**[28] 4101 7-9-2 68 .... RyanPowell(7) 4 63
(J S Moore) *in rr: hdwy to chse ldrs 3f out: wknd ins fnl 2f* **14/1**

2m 26.17s (4.97) **Going Correction** +0.35s/f (Good)
WFA 3 from 4yo+ 10lb **6** Ran SP% **112.1**
Speed ratings (Par 103): **95,94,93,91,91 89**
toteswingers: 1&2 £1.80, 1&3 £9.20, 2&3 £9.40 CSF £6.26 TOTE £2.30: £1.30, £1.60; EX 6.50.Grande Caiman was claimed by G. A. Harker for £5000.
Owner Inhurst Players **Bred** Highclere Stud Ltd **Trained** Baughurst, Hants
■ Stewards' Enquiry : David Probert two-day ban:careless riding (Aug 27-28)

FOCUS
An ordinary claimer run at a modest pace and the six runners were within a length or so of each other passing the 2f pole. The proximity of the third casts some doubt over the form.

5035 PUNTER SOUTHALL TRANSACTION SERVICES H'CAP 1m 5f 61y
3:10 (3:10) (Class 3) (0-90,89) 3-Y-0+ **£6,476** (£1,927; £963; £481) **Stalls** Low

Form RPR

-051 **1** **Kansai Spirit (IRE)**[23] 4257 4-9-8 **83** .... WilliamBuick 6 97+
(J H M Gosden) *hld up in tch: hdwy and swtchd rt wl over 1f out: drvn and qckd to ld ins fnl f: r.o strly* **5/1**[2]

05-0 **2** 2 ¼ **Lethal Glaze (IRE)**[103] 1736 4-10-0 **89** .... RichardHughes 11 97
(R Hannon) *chsd ldrs: rdn to ld 1f out: hdd and outpcd ins fnl f* **12/1**

0403 **3** 3 **Cool Strike (UAE)**[32] 3955 4-9-11 **86** ....(v) LiamKeniry 3 89
(A M Balding) *led: rdn 2f out: hdd 1f out: sn wknd* **16/1**

3551 **4** hd **Goodwood Starlight (IRE)**[29] 4055 5-9-7 **85** .... RobertLButler(3) 4 88
(Miss Sheena West) *hdwy to trck ldrs 6f out: travelleing wl appr fnl 2f: rdn over 1f out: styd on same pce* **9/1**

2511 **5** 2 ¼ **Yemeni Princess (IRE)**[27] 4141 4-8-12 **76** .... RussKennemore(3) 8 75
(B G Powell) *in rr: hdwy to chse ldrs fr 3f out: rdn over 2f out: wknd over 1f out* **13/2**[3]

0531 **6** 10 **Incendo**[23] 4252 4-9-9 **84** ....(vt) AdamKirby 2 68
(J R Fanshawe) *t.k.h: in tch: rdn ins fnl 2f: wknd qckly* **8/1**

0411 **7** ½ **Fantino**[35] 3865 4-8-11 **72** .... DavidProbert 1 56
(J Mackie) *chsd ldrs tl rdn and wknd 2f out* **14/1**

3512 **8** 2 ½ **Strathcal**[27] 4141 4-9-6 **81** .... SteveDrowne 12 61
(H Morrison) *chsd ldrs: rdn over 2f out: sn btn* **9/2**[1]

1000 **9** 78 **Brett Vale (IRE)**[13] 4597 4-9-3 **78** ....(p) FergusSweeney 9 —
(P R Hedger) *slowly away: in rr: rdn: hung lft and wknd 4f out* **50/1**

2m 54.2s (2.20) **Going Correction** +0.35s/f (Good)
WFA 3 from 4yo+ 12lb **9** Ran SP% **91.5**
Speed ratings (Par 107): **107,105,103,103,102 96,95,94,46**
toteswingers:1&2 £6.10, 2&3 £7.80, 1&3 £8.90 CSF £37.92 CT £371.64 TOTE £4.60: £1.80, £3.10, £2.80; EX 36.10.
Owner R Van Gelder **Bred** Keatly Overseas Ltd **Trained** Newmarket, Suffolk

FOCUS
A decent handicap featuring some in-form and progressive stayers, but weakened when the favourite Mountain Hiker was withdrawn at the start after he refused to enter the stalls (5/2, deduct 25p in the £ under R4). The remaining runners went a fair enough pace in the conditions and came down the centre of the track once into the home straight. Solid form, with the winner backing up his AW improvement.

NOTEBOOK
Kansai Spirit(IRE) ◆ was back in a handicap after beating a subsequent winner in a Polytrack maiden last month and was 2lb well-in compared with his new mark. He travelled very nicely in the middle of the field throughout and was still on the bridle when brought to challenge towards the nearside of the field a furlong from home. He found plenty once in front and, on this evidence, still appears to be improving. (op 9-2 tchd 11-2)
Lethal Glaze(IRE) ◆, not seen since a modest reappearance effort in May, was always up there and kept on going, even though he was completely outpaced by the winner inside the last furlong. He appreciates cut, so the rain would have been welcome and he should be able to find a winning opportunity or two this autumn. (op 14-1)
Cool Strike(UAE), who set a solid pace from the start, took some catching and it wasn't until passing the furlong pole that he was overhauled. The rain wouldn't have been in his favour, so this was a good effort. (op 14-1)
Goodwood Starlight(IRE) raced too keenly for his own good early on and, although he put himself in with every chance a furlong from home, he didn't see his race out. He was bumped up 9lb for last month's Epsom romp, so will need to find improvement from somewhere in order to defy this sort of mark. (op 8-1 tchd 10-1)
Yemeni Princess(IRE), up 4lb in her bid for a hat-trick, tried to put in an effort from off the pace coming to the last 2f but lacked a turn of foot and probably needs a return to further. (op 8-1)
Incendo had been raised 9lb for his easy success in a four-runner event at Leicester last month when visored for the first time. He travelled well off the pace, but didn't find as much off the bridle as had looked likely, and he looks to be on a stiff mark now. (op 12-1)
Fantino, bidding for a hat-trick off a 6lb higher mark, raced prominently for a long way but faded after coming under pressure 3f out and he could have done without the rain. (tchd 12-1)
Strathcal, up another 2lb following his good effort in defeat here last month, was inclined to race in snatches and his rider reported that he had no more to give. Official explanation: jockey said gelding had no more to give (op 6-1 tchd 4-1)

5036 BATHWICK TYRES ST HUGH'S STKS (LISTED RACE) 5f 34y
3:45 (3:47) (Class 1) 2-Y-0
£13,340 (£5,057; £2,530; £1,261; £632; £317) **Stalls** Centre

Form RPR

4211 **1** **Electric Waves (IRE)**[27] 4124 2-8-12 88 .... RichardMullen 7 101+
(E S McMahon) *sn in tch: drvn and hdwy fr 2f out to ld appr fnl f: drvn out* **10/1**

215 **2** 1 ¼ **Sweet Cecily (IRE)**[20] 4356 2-8-12 99 .... RichardHughes 11 97
(R Hannon) *in tch: pushed along 2f out: hdwy over 1f out: styd on ins fnl f to take 2nd nr fin: no imp on wnr* **7/2**[2]

1222 **3** ¾ **The Thrill Is Gone**[22] 4278 2-8-12 90 .... NeilCallan 10 94
(M R Channon) *chsd ldrs: rdn and edgd lft 2f out: styd on to chse wnr 1f out: no imp and lost 2nd nr fin* **25/1**

4600 **4** 5 **Serena's Pride**[17] 4458 2-8-12 90 .... KierenFallon 4 76
(A P Jarvis) *chsd ldrs: rdn 2f out: outpcd by ldng trio ins fnl f* **10/1**

4021 **5** ¾ **Overwhelm**[18] 4432 2-8-12 69 .... RussKennemore 8 73
(Andrew Reid) *chsd ldrs: rdn and bmpd 2f out: hung lft sn after and wknd appr fnl f* **66/1**

103 **6** nse **Hooray**[37] 3792 2-8-12 103 .... SebSanders 13 73
(Sir Mark Prescott) *carried rt s: sn rcvrd: towards rr: rdn and styd on fnl 2f: nvr in contention* **6/5**[1]

1011 **7** 2 **Marlinka**[23] 4275 2-9-1 93 .... SteveDrowne 6 69
(R Charlton) *led tl hdd appr fnl f: sn wknd* **11/2**[3]

1040 **8** ¾ **Primo Lady**[17] 4458 2-9-1 89 ....(v) DavidProbert 9 66
(Miss Gay Kelleway) *rdn 1/2-way: a outpcd* **33/1**

6100 **9** hd **The Sydney Arms (IRE)**[5] 4872 2-8-12 85 .... JimCrowley 3 62
(R Hannon) *chsd ldrs over 3f* **66/1**

0134 **10** 5 **Excello**[47] 3482 2-8-12 96 .... TomMcLaughlin 12 44
(M S Saunders) *swtchd rt s and racd alone on stands' side: on terms tl wknd ins fnl 2f* **20/1**

1 **11** 7 **Mayfair Princess**[127] 1180 2-8-12 0 ....(t) JohnFahy 2 19
(P S McEntee) *unruly stalls: sn bhd* **50/1**

441 **12** 1 ½ **Mortitia**[16] 4471 2-8-12 81 .... MartinDwyer 5 14
(B J Meehan) *s.i.s: hung lft 2f out: a bhd* **20/1**

63.02 secs (1.62) **Going Correction** +0.40s/f (Good) **12** Ran SP% **122.5**
Speed ratings (Par 102): **103,101,99,91,90 90,87,86,85,77 66,64**
CSF £43.77 TOTE £12.20: £2.60, £1.70, £3.90; EX 51.30.
Owner J C Fretwell **Bred** Ms Michelle Lyons **Trained** Lichfield, Staffs

FOCUS
There was a sharp downpour of rain before this race. A competitive Listed sprint for 2-y-o fillies and the last two winners of the race, Madame Trop Vite and Sand Vixen, went on to win the Flying Childers at the St Leger meeting. The bulk of the field raced centre-to-stands' side with Excello running a solo up the stands' rail.

NOTEBOOK
Electric Waves(IRE) ◆ has improved with every run and was upped in class in her bid for a hat-trick following her successes in a Warwick maiden and under top weight in a Haydock nursery, and that last victory showed that she could handle an easy surface. Having travelled strongly just behind the leaders, she put the race to bed after hitting the front a furlong out and there may well be a lot more to come from her this autumn, especially when there is give underfoot. (op 15-2 tchd 7-1)
Sweet Cecily(IRE), slightly disappointing when only fifth in the Princess Margaret, was doing all her best work late but the winner got first run on her and wasn't for catching. On this evidence a return to 6f is needed. (tchd 10-3)
The Thrill Is Gone tries hard, but she was the most exposed in the field so was always vulnerable to an improver. As it turned out she ran a blinder having been up on the pace the whole way. She deserves to win again, but may be a filly who will always find one to beat her, irrespective of the level she is running at. (tchd 22-1)
Serena's Pride was dropping to Listed class having been held in Group company since finishing a fair fourth in the Queen Mary. A springer in the market beforehand, she ran well for a long way before fading but is not proving the easiest filly to place. (op 22-1)
Overwhelm, back on turf following her Wolverhampton maiden victory, is only rated 69 so ran with a lot of credit having shown decent early speed, but she may not have helped her handicap mark with this performance.
Hooray, down to the minimum trip for the first time, set the standard on her third behind Memory and Soraaya in the Cherry Hinton, but she didn't enjoy the rub of the green here. She was slightly intimidated when Excello dived across her at the start in order to get across to the stands' rail and, as a result, soon found herself well out of her ground. Over this shorter trip that was always going to be a problem, and she didn't get going until it was far too late. She can be forgiven this, but probably needs to go back up in distance. (op 7-4 tchd 15-8)
Marlinka, bidding for a hat-trick but carrying a 3lb penalty for winning a Listed race at Vichy the previous month, showed her usual early speed but faded dramatically after being headed over a furlong from home. Her rider reported that she was unsuited by the ground. Official explanation: jockey said filly was unsuited by the good ground (op 9-2)
Excello ran a solo up the stands' rail, but it didn't appear to do her many favours. (tchd 22-1)

5037 M C SEAFOODS H'CAP 6f 8y
4:20 (4:20) (Class 4) (0-80,79) 3-Y-0 **£4,209** (£1,252; £625; £312) **Stalls** Centre

Form RPR

2-12 **1** **Desert Poppy (IRE)**[12] 4625 3-9-7 **79** .... ShaneKelly 2 96+
(W R Swinburn) *disp ld tl nosed ahd 3f out: c readily clr appr fnl f: v easily* **2/1**[1]

5412 **2** 4 ½ **Flouncing (IRE)**[15] 4503 3-9-2 **74** .... RichardHughes 3 73
(W J Haggas) *t.k.h: trckd ldrs: rdn and styd on ins fnl f to take 2nd cl home: nvr any ch w v easy wnr* **7/2**[2]

14 **3** hd **Pin Cushion**[15] 4503 3-9-5 **77** .... MartinDwyer 4 75
(B J Meehan) *ponied to s: c to stands' side and disp ld 3f: styd chsng wnr tl rdn and easily outpcd ins fnl f: lost 2nd cl home* **5/1**[3]

221 **4** 1 ½ **Valencha**[20] 4385 3-9-1 **73** .... SteveDrowne 5 67
(H Morrison) *t.k.h: towards rr: in tch: rdn 2f out: sn outpcd* **7/2**[2]

0355 **5** ¾ **Chinese Democracy (USA)**[3] 4922 3-7-12 **61** .... SophieDoyle(5) 6 52
(P D Evans) *plunged s: t.k.h: in rr but in tch: rdn and outpcd fnl 2f* **22/1**

5623 **6** 6 **Key Light (IRE)**[18] 4424 3-9-2 **74** .... MichaelHills 1 46
(J W Hills) *chsd ldrs: rdn 2f out: wknd over 1f out* **15/2**

1m 15.02s (2.02) **Going Correction** +0.40s/f (Good) **6** Ran SP% **110.6**
Speed ratings (Par 102): **102,96,95,93,92 84**
toteswingers:1&2 £2.00, 2&3 £3.30, 1&3 £2.50 CSF £8.90 TOTE £2.80: £1.40, £2.30; EX 8.50.
Owner Oasis Dreamers **Bred** Kildaragh Stud **Trained** Aldbury, Herts

FOCUS
This fair 3-y-o sprint handicap was only contested by fillies. They did not go that quick early as they came to race on the stands' rail, but this became a one-horse race. The winner impressed and the form is rated around the runner-up.

5038 RUTHY SMITH MEMORIAL MAIDEN FILLIES' STKS 1m 2f 6y
4:55 (4:59) (Class 5) 3-Y-0+ **£3,238** (£963; £481; £240) **Stalls** Low

Form RPR

03-3 **1** **Red Intrigue (IRE)**[12] 4626 3-8-12 72 .... JimCrowley 10 79
(Mrs A J Perrett) *hld up towards rr: in tch: n.m.r and swtchd lft ins fnl 2f: hung lft and styd on wl ins fnl f to ld fnl 75yds* **9/2**[3]

2 ¾ **Dark Promise** 3-8-12 0 .... PhilipRobinson 2 78+
(M A Jarvis) *trckd ldrs: pushed along and styd on to ld wl over 1f out: drvn: green and hung lft ins fnl f: hdd and no ex fnl 75yds* **6/4**[1]

3625 **3** 4 ½ **Easy Terms**[42] 3628 3-8-9 72 .... JamesMillman(3) 7 69
(B R Millman) *chsd ldrs: rdn over 2f out: styd on same pce fr over 1f out* **12/1**

4 **4** hd **Piano**[28] 4114 3-8-12 0 .... WilliamBuick 12 68
(J H M Gosden) *towards rr but in tch: drvn and hdwy over 2f out: styd on same pce u.p fr over 1f out* **7/2**[2]

-200 **5** 4 ½ **Silent Oasis**[62] 2961 4-9-7 71 .... ShaneKelly 8 59
(B G Powell) *sn led: rdn and hung lft 1f out: hdd wl over 1f out and sn btn* **33/1**

6 hd **Kashmiriana (IRE)** 3-8-12 0 .... KierenFallon 6 59
(L M Cumani) *in rr: hdwy fr 3f out: nvr quite rchd ldrs: wknd ins fnl f* **14/1**

0 **7** nk **Spring Stock**[28] 4115 3-8-12 0 .... FergusSweeney 9 58
(B G Powell) *swtchd lft s: in rr: pushed along 3f out: styd on to 2f out: nvr quite on terms: wknd ins fnl f* **100/1**

35 **8** 3 **Wasara**[69] 2755 3-8-13 0 ow1 .... AdamKirby 5 53
(Miss Amy Weaver) *chsd ldrs rdn over 2f out: sn wknd* **100/1**

5426 **9** 4 **Shades Of Grey**[51] 3337 3-8-12 70 .... RichardThomas 3 44
(C G Cox) *reluctant to enter stalls: chsd ldrs tl wknd over 2f out* **25/1**

10 nse **Land And Sea** 3-8-12 0 .... MichaelHills 1 44+
(B W Hills) *s.i.s: t.k.h: towards rr most of way* **33/1**

4 **11** *36* **Personified (GER)**[25] 4207 3-8-12 0 .... RichardHughes 4 —
(E F Vaughan) *reluctant stalls entry: t.k.h: chsd ldrs tl wknd fr 3f out: eased: t.o* **10/1**
60 **12** *15* **Tulle (IRE)**[64] 2891 3-8-12 0 .... MartinDwyer 11 —
(B J Meehan) *swtchd lft stalls: a towards rr: no ch fnl 3f: eased: t.o* **33/1**
2m 12.11s (3.31) **Going Correction** +0.35s/f (Good)
WFA 3 from 4yo 9lb **12** Ran SP% **118.5**
Speed ratings (Par 100): **100,99,95,95,92 91,91,89,86,86 57,45**
toteswingers:1&2 £3.10, 2&3 £7.20, 1&3 £8.60 CSF £11.08 TOTE £5.00: £1.30, £1.50, £4.10; EX 17.60.
Owner Lady Clague **Bred** Newberry Stud Company **Trained** Pulborough, W Sussex

FOCUS

An interesting older-fillies' maiden with a few that had already shown ability up against some fascinating newcomers. Some of these proved a handful to load into the stalls, however, and the winner and third rated 72 and the fifth rated 71 gives a guide to the level of the form. The winner is rated up 4lb. The runners made a beeline for the stands' rail on reaching the home straight.
Personified(GER) Official explanation: jockey said filly stopped quickly

5039 BETTOR RACING TIPS AT BETTOR.COM APPRENTICE H'CAP 1m 1f

5:25 (5:27) (Class 5) (0-70,70) 4-Y-0+ **£2,590** (£770; £288; £288) **Stalls** Low

Form RPR
-040 **1** **Gross Prophet**[56] 3160 5-9-6 **66** .... SophieDoyle 7 76
(A J Lidderdale) *mde all: styd far side: pushed along over 2f out: kpt on strly fnl f: unchal* **8/1**
0-05 **2** *2 1/4* **Becuille (IRE)**[60] 3036 5-9-7 **67** ....(b) BillyCray 6 72
(B J Meehan) *t.k.h: chsd ldrs: c centre crse over 4f out: rdn to chse wnr and hung lft fr 3f out: no imp fr over 1f out* **7/1**
3640 **3** *2 3/4* **Having A Ball**[16] 4488 6-8-2 **51** oh1 .... AmyScott(3) 3 50
(P D Cundell) *chsd ldrs: styd far side and chsd wnr over 4f out: rdn and styd on same pce fnl 2f: jnd for 3rd on line* **13/2**
0304 **3** *dht* **Cape Quarter (USA)**[23] 4260 4-9-3 **63** ....(t) AshleyMorgan 9 62+
(W J Haggas) *t.k.h: hld up in rr: c centre crse over 4f out: stl plenty to do whn pushed along and hdwy fr 2f out: styd on fnl f to join 3rd on line but no ch w ldng duo* **4/1**[2]
0360 **5** *3 1/2* **War And Peace (IRE)**[16] 4488 6-9-5 **65** .... RichardEvans 2 56
(P D Evans) *in rr: racd in centre crse fr over 4f out: rdn over 2f out and nvr in contention* **11/2**[3]
54 **6** *2 1/2* **Miss Bounty**[20] 4366 5-9-1 **61** .... RossAtkinson 4 47
(George Baker) *chsd ldrs: racd in centre crse over 4f out: rdn 3f out: hung lft and wknd fr 2f out* **3/1**[1]
-400 **7** *3* **Chantilly Dancer (IRE)**[24] 4236 4-8-2 **51** oh6 .... RyanPowell(3) 10 30
(M Quinn) *chsd ldr tl c to r in centre crse over 4f out: wknd wl over 2f out* **33/1**
2-00 **8** *hd* **San Antonio**[28] 4112 10-9-3 **70** .... ChristyMews(7) 5 49
(Mrs P Sly) *t.k.h: chsd ldrs: styd towards far side over 4f out: wknd 3f out* **16/1**
000- **9** *8* **Addikt (IRE)**[304] 6760 5-9-4 **69** .... RichardRowe(5) 1 30
(H J Evans) *awkward leaving stalls and slowly away: plld hrd: racd centre crse over 4f out: a bhd* **12/1**
1m 59.01s (3.51) **Going Correction** +0.35s/f (Good) **9** Ran SP% **113.8**
Speed ratings (Par 103): **98,96,93,93,90 88,85,85,78**PL: Cape Quarter £0.50, Having a Ball £1.40 TRICAST: GP/B/CQ £128.63 GP/B/Having a Ball £194.12 toteswingers: 1&2 6.90, 2&Cape Quarter £2.10, 2&Having a Ball £3.80, 1&CP £2.20, 1&HAB £3.70 CSF £61.74 CT £194.12 TOTE £10.00: £3.10, £3.00; EX 33.70 Place 6: £30.5327 Owner.
■ Stewards' Enquiry : Richard Evans one-day ban: used whip down shoulder in the forehand (Aug 27)

FOCUS

A moderate apprentice handicap and a difference of opinion as to where the best ground was, as the main group came up the centre once into the straight whilst two, including the winner, stayed against the inside rail. Not form to be positive about.
T/Jkpt: Part won. Pool of £17314.35 - 0.50 winning units. T/Plt: £34.80 to a £1 stake. Pool of £53,526.52 - 1,122.53 winning tickets. T/Qpdt: £15.40 to a £1 stake. Pool of £3141.46 - 150.50 winning tickets. ST

4701 NEWCASTLE (L-H)

Friday, August 13

OFFICIAL GOING: Good to soft changing to soft after race 1 (2.10)
Wind: Fresh, half behind Weather: Overcast, raining

5040 E B F / WATERAID MAIDEN STKS 7f

2:10 (2:10) (Class 5) 2-Y-O **£3,238** (£963; £481; £240) **Stalls** Low

Form RPR
00 **1** **Newport Arch**[23] 4240 2-8-12 0 .... IanBrennan(5) 11 71+
(J J Quinn) *hld up: shkn up over 2f out: hdwy over 1f out: edgd lft and styd on ins fnl f: led cl home* **50/1**
2 *hd* **Ventura Sands (IRE)** 2-9-3 0 .... PaulHanagan 10 70+
(R A Fahey) *in tch: pushed along over 2f out: hdwy to ld over 1f out: sn rdn: kpt on ins fnl f: hdd cl home* **6/4**[1]
3 *2* **Old Possum (USA)** 2-9-3 0 .... AhmedAjtebi 7 65+
(Mahmood Al Zarooni) *prom: rdn and outpcd over 2f out: rallied over 1f out: edgd rt u.p and styd on ins fnl f: nt rch first two* **5/1**[3]
4 *hd* **Defence Of Duress (IRE)** 2-9-3 0 .... MickyFenton 1 65+
(T P Tate) *dwlt: hld up towards rr: hdwy u.p 2f out: kpt on same pce ins fnl f* **12/1**
5 *3 1/2* **Hawdyerwheesht** 2-9-3 0 .... GregFairley 12 56+
(M Johnston) *trckd ldrs: led briefly and rn green over 1f out: outpcd ins fnl f* **12/1**
50 **6** *nk* **Microlight**[11] 4645 2-9-3 0 .... DavidAllan 9 55
(T D Easterby) *slt ld to over 1f out: sn rdn and edgd lft: wknd ins fnl f* **40/1**
6 **7** *2 3/4* **Chagal (IRE)**[11] 4650 2-9-3 0 .... PhillipMakin 8 48
(K A Ryan) *w ldr tl rdn and wknd over 1f out* **20/1**
8 *1* **Bosambo** 2-9-3 0 .... PJMcDonald 3 46
(G A Swinbank) *chsd ldrs: rdn over 2f out: edgd lft and wknd over 1f out* **4/1**[2]
0 **9** *2* **Sandpipers Dream**[28] 4089 2-9-3 0 .... DuranFentiman 4 41
(T D Walford) *hld up: rdn over 2f out: nvr able to chal* **80/1**
45 **10** *shd* **Chibchan (IRE)**[16] 4477 2-8-10 0 .... AntiocoMurgia(7) 6 40
(Mahmood Al Zarooni) *trckd ldrs tl wknd fr 2f out* **7/1**
0 **11** *1 1/4* **Byron Bear (IRE)**[28] 4089 2-9-3 0 .... TonyCulhane 2 37
(P T Midgley) *dwlt: hld up: hdwy and prom over 1f out: wknd ent fnl f* **66/1**
1m 32.94s (4.24) **Going Correction** +0.55s/f (Yiel) **11** Ran SP% **116.4**
Speed ratings (Par 94): **97,96,94,94,90 89,86,85,83,83 81**
toteswingers: 1&2 £9.80, 1&3 £27.30, 2&3 £2.10 CSF £122.74 TOTE £86.40: £12.00, £1.10, £2.20; EX 338.50 TRIFECTA Not won..
Owner Alan Mann **Bred** R P Williams **Trained** Settrington, N Yorks

FOCUS

Several likely newcomers on show in a fair maiden but the rain-softened ground ended up catching one or two out, and the race went to one of the two horses with most experience. The runners were well bunched to past halfway and came down the centre of the track.

NOTEBOOK

Newport Arch had looked more one for modest nurseries down the line, but he proved suited by the stiffer test of stamina he encountered here and put his experience to good use to run down the eventual second close home. He's a half-brother to a 1m2f winner and will stay further in time. (op 66-1 tchd 40-1)

Ventura Sands(IRE) ◆, a 92,000gns yearling and the second foal of a maiden half-sister to the smart miler Soviet Flash, was all the rage in the betting and for much of the way looked like making a winning debut, only to be run down in the closing strides. There was much to like about the way he travelled through the race after being a bit keen early on, and he looks certain to improve and get off the mark before too long in similar company. This trip is probably right for now. (op 13-8 tchd 15-8 and 2-1 in a place)

Old Possum(USA), a costly yearling by More Than Ready with a US dirt pedigree, also shaped promisingly on his debut, losing his place when the tempo increased before staying on strongly. He showed palpable signs of greenness and probably has a fair amount of improvement in him. (op 6-1 tchd 13-2 and 9-2)

Defence Of Duress(IRE) had plenty to recommend him on pedigree, being a half brother to several winners out of a smart half-sister to the Arc winner Suave Dancer, while also holding a Derby entry. He too shaped encouragingly, making eyecatching progress to challenge, only to then leave the impression he needed the run badly. Plenty of improvement should be forthcoming, and he too appeals as a likely winner of a staying maiden. (tchd 14-1)

Hawdyerwheesht is out of a 5f winner and shaped as if this trip is probably as far as he wants for now. His yard has had very few first time out juvenile winners this season, but most newcomers have improved for the run. (op 14-1 tchd 11-1)

Microlight ran a better race with blinkers left off, but his experience probably gave him something of an advantage in the conditions, and it might be that he will get a stiffish nursery mark if the handicapper takes this at face value. (op 50-1 tchd 33-1)

Bosambo, a half-brother to a couple of winners, one smart, was prominent in the market but ultimately left the impression he needed the run. He should improve. (op 11-4)

Sandpipers Dream came with a promising looking challenge in the penultimate furlong but ran then as if he either still needed the race or didn't stay. He might be an interesting one for nurseries after another run. (tchd 100-1)

5041 JOSHUA BENTLEY IS 16 FILLIES' H'CAP 1m 3y(S)

2:45 (2:45) (Class 5) (0-75,74) 3-Y-O **£2,072** (£616; £308; £153) **Stalls** Low

Form RPR
0332 **1** **Gifted Apakay (USA)**[21] 4335 3-9-7 **74** .... PaulHanagan 6 82
(E A L Dunlop) *chsd ldrs: rdn to ld over 1f out: sn hrd pressed: hld on wl ins fnl f* **5/4**[1]
0512 **2** *1 1/4* **Luv U Noo**[21] 4344 3-8-10 **63** .... TomEaves 4 68
(B Ellison) *t.k.h: in tch smooth hdwy and pressed wnr appr fnl f: sn rdn: one pce last 100yds* **2/1**[2]
2061 **3** *8* **Excellent Day (IRE)**[16] 4475 3-9-3 **70** .... SamHitchcott 2 57
(M R Channon) *hld up last but in tch: effrt over 2f out: rdn over 1f out: wknd ins fnl f* **3/1**[3]
0550 **4** *3 1/2* **Colamandis**[11] 4649 3-8-2 **55** .... PatrickMathers 7 34
(H A McWilliams) *led: rdn over 2f out: hdd over 1f out: sn wknd* **28/1**
4605 **5** *6* **Kirkby's Gem**[10] 4674 3-7-9 **55** oh10 .... VictorSantos(7) 3 20
(A Berry) *chsd ldr tl lost pl over 3f out: struggling fnl 2f* **50/1**
1m 49.66s (6.26) **Going Correction** +0.55s/f (Yiel) **5** Ran SP% **108.2**
Speed ratings (Par 97): **90,88,80,77,71**
CSF £3.87 TOTE £1.90: £1.10, £2.70; EX 3.40.
Owner V I Araci **Bred** R D Hubbard **Trained** Newmarket, Suffolk
■ Stewards' Enquiry : Patrick Mathers one-day ban: failed to ride to draw (Aug 27)

FOCUS

A weakish handicap that was run at a steady gallop and turned into a game of cat and mouse, though the result was still the right one on the day. The runners again came down the centre. The winner is progressing but only the first two ran their race.

5042 GOWLAND & DAWSON NURSERY 5f

3:20 (3:21) (Class 6) (0-65,65) 2-Y-O **£1,554** (£462; £231; £115) **Stalls** Low

Form RPR
0050 **1** **Bellemere**[34] 3923 2-9-4 **65** .... JamesSullivan(3) 1 67
(M W Easterby) *racd alone far rail: in tch: hdwy to ld over 1f out: hld on wl ins fnl f* **9/2**
403 **2** *1/2* **Eilean Mor**[15] 4512 2-9-2 **60** .... PaulHanagan 4 60
(J S Goldie) *hld up: effrt and hdwy over 1f out: chsd wnr ins fnl f: r.o: hld nr fin* **3/1**[1]
0205 **3** *3* **Reel Amber**[25] 4195 2-8-12 **56** ....(b) DavidAllan 8 45
(T D Easterby) *trckd ldrs: effrt and rdn over 1f out: one pce ins fnl f* **17/2**
0060 **4** *nse* **Key To The Motion (IRE)**[25] 4195 2-8-8 **52** .... TonyCulhane 5 41
(P T Midgley) *t.k.h: prom: hdwy 1/2-way: rdn and led briefly over 1f out: no ex ins fnl f* **12/1**
3003 **5** *1 1/4* **Look'N'Listen (IRE)**[38] 3757 2-8-9 **53** .... SilvestreDeSousa 6 38
(A D Brown) *led: drifted lft and hdd over 1f out: wknd ins fnl f* **7/2**[2]
3560 **6** *7* **Dotty Darroch**[17] 4451 2-9-1 **59** .... PhillipMakin 2 19
(R Bastiman) *chsd ldrs: rdn 1/2-way: wknd over 1f out* **7/1**
0445 **7** *1 1/4* **Roman Ruler (IRE)**[20] 4367 2-8-8 **52** .... TomEaves 3 7
(C W Fairhurst) *chsd ldrs tl rdn and wknd fr 1/2-way* **4/1**[3]
64.85 secs (3.75) **Going Correction** +0.55s/f (Yiel) **7** Ran SP% **116.1**
Speed ratings (Par 92): **92,91,86,86,84 73,71**
toteswingers:1&2 £3.10, 2&3 £3.60, 1&3 £5.60 CSF £18.97 CT £110.69 TOTE £4.00: £1.50, £2.40; EX 11.80 Trifecta £95.10 Pool: £288.11 - 2.24 winning units..
Owner Lady Manton Mr & Mrs R Congreve S Bowett **Bred** The Rt Hon Mary, Lady Manton **Trained** Sheriff Hutton, N Yorks

FOCUS

A very modest nursery but one at least run at a good gallop and the first two brought up the rear at halfway. The winner stayed hard on the far rail but that strip didn't look any quicker than the centre.

NOTEBOOK

Bellemere held just about the best claims on his York run two starts before, and was well ridden in that didn't get involved in the early scuffle for the lead. He just had enough to hang on close home with the rail possibly helping him but he won't find many easier winning opportunities in nurseries than this one. Official explanation: trainer's rep said, regarding apparent improvement in form, that it was the weakest race the filly had run in and also stayed on the fastest ground. (op 3-1)

Eilean Mor stepped up on his previous efforts on this nursery debut, putting in a sustained challenge inside the last. He's yet to try 6f but gives the impression it will bring about a bit of improvement. (op 4-1)

Reel Amber appeared to have no excuses other than not being good enough at the weights, and is going to be very hard to place outside of selling nurseries. (tchd 9-1)

Key To The Motion(IRE), like the third, appeared to have no excuses other than not being good enough at the weights, and is going to be very hard to place outside of selling nurseries. (tchd 10-1)

Look'N'Listen(IRE) has plenty of early pace and might have gone a bit hard early in the conditions. She might be seen to better effect in nurseries on quicker ground. (op 9-2 tchd 5-1 in a place)

Dotty Darroch hasn't gone on since her debut and looks on far too stiff a mark. (tchd 13-2)
Roman Ruler(IRE) was disappointing considering he'd hinted at better to come in stronger nurseries than this on his two previous starts. He may have found conditions too soft. Official explanation: jockey said colt was unsuited by the soft ground (op 5-1)

5043 FASTFLOW H'CAP 7f
3:55 (3:55) (Class 4) (0-85,85) 3-Y-O+ **£3,626** (£1,079; £539; £269) **Stalls** Low

Form RPR

0100 **1** **Northern Fling**35 3876 6-9-6 **82** GaryBartley(3) 13 91
(J S Goldie) *hld up: pushed along 2f out: qcknd to ld 1f out: rdn out* **16/1**

0463 **2** ½ **Imperial Djay (IRE)**6 4850 5-9-2 **75** PJMcDonald 8 83
(Mrs R A Carr) *hld up in tch: hdwy and ev ch 1f out: kpt on ins fnl f* **12/1**

0642 **3** 1 **Zomerlust**20 4394 8-9-4 **82** (v) IanBrennan(5) 11 87
(J J Quinn) *hld up in tch: effrt on outside over 1f out: kpt on ins fnl f: nrst fin* **5/1**3

3412 **4** ½ **Rosko**9 4704 6-8-9 **73** (b) DaleSwift(5) 12 77
(B Ellison) *t.k.h: sn cl up: effrt and ch 1f out: nt qckn ins fnl f* **11/4**1

2214 **5** hd **Ancient Cross**20 4370 6-9-12 **85** (t) PhillipMakin 1 88
(M W Easterby) *trckd ldrs: effrt and shkn up over 1f out: nt qckn ins fnl f* **8/1**

2602 **6** 1 ½ **Mandalay King (IRE)**10 4670 5-8-4 **68** DeanHeslop(5) 6 67
(Mrs Marjorie Fife) *trckd ldrs: rdn and outpcd 2f out: no imp ins fnl f* **11/1**

5013 **7** 2 ¼ **Last Sovereign**13 4598 6-9-4 **82** JamesO'Reilly(5) 7 75
(J O'Reilly) *cl up: rdn over 2f out: wknd ins fnl f* **14/1**

2200 **8** 1 **Dark Moment**13 4602 4-8-10 **72** BarryMcHugh(3) 2 62
(Ollie Pears) *dwlt: hld up: rdn 2f out: nvr able to chal* **20/1**

5002 **9** ¾ **Game Lad**20 4370 8-9-8 **81** (tp) DavidAllan 10 69
(T D Easterby) *dwlt: hld up: rdn along over 2f out: nvr on terms* **7/1**

0120 **10** ¾ **Sailorman (IRE)**23 4264 3-9-6 **85** GregFairley 3 71
(M Johnston) *upset in stalls: led at ordinary gallop: rdn and hdd 1f out: wknd qckly* **4/1**2

1m 31.87s (3.17) **Going Correction** +0.55s/f (Yiel)
WFA 3 from 4yo+ 6lb **10** Ran SP% **120.3**
Speed ratings (Par 105): **103,102,101,100,100 98,96,95,94,93**
toteswingers: 1&2 £28.70, 1&3 £19.40, 2&3 £12.60 CSF £198.74 CT £1113.21 TOTE £24.70: £6.70, £4.00, £2.60; EX 200.80 TRIFECTA Not won..
Owner Paul Moulton **Bred** Lady Juliet Tadgell **Trained** Uplawmoor, E Renfrews

FOCUS
A steadily-run handicap but despite that the first three all came from off the pace. The field hugged the far rail. Fair form for the grade, the winner looking the best guide.
Game Lad Official explanation: jockey said gelding missed the break

5044 LUMSDEN & CARROLL FILLIES' H'CAP 6f
4:30 (4:31) (Class 5) (0-70,66) 3-Y-O **£2,072** (£616; £308; £153) **Stalls** Low

Form RPR

0650 **1** **Fair Bunny**19 4406 3-8-7 **52** (b) SilvestreDeSousa 1 57
(A D Brown) *mde all: rdn over 2f out: hld on wl ins fnl f* **16/1**

1042 **2** ½ **Red Scintilla**9 4714 3-9-7 **66** TomEaves 7 69
(N Tinkler) *prom: effrt 2f out: chsd wnr ins fnl f: kpt on u.p* **9/4**2

03-2 **3** ½ **Sparking**204 253 3-9-0 **59** PhillipMakin 5 60
(T D Barron) *hld up: hdwy over 2f out: kpt on ins fnl f: one pce towards fin* **6/1**

-304 **4** 1 ½ **Praesepe**14 4553 3-8-13 **58** PaulHanagan 3 55
(W J Haggas) *prom: rdn and hdwy to chse wnr over 1f out to ins fnl f: one pce* **2/1**1

2354 **5** 13 **Shaluca**21 4342 3-9-7 **66** RobertWinston 2 21
(E S McMahon) *chsd wnr to over 1f out: sn struggling* **10/3**3

30-6 **6** 8 **Precious Coral (IRE)**16 4482 3-9-3 **65** (bt1) JamesSullivan(3) 4 —
(Mrs R A Carr) *hld up in tch: rdn and outpcd over 2f out: edgd lft and sn btn* **25/1**

0-0 **7** 7 **Somewhere Else**11 4649 3-7-9 **47** oh2 VictorSantos(7) 8 —
(A Berry) *dwlt: bhd: struggling over 2f out: sn btn* **100/1**

1m 18.24s (3.64) **Going Correction** +0.55s/f (Yiel) **7** Ran SP% **112.2**
Speed ratings (Par 97): **97,96,95,93,76 65,56**
toteswingers:1&2 £4.30, 2&3 £2.70, 1&3 £5.00 CSF £50.30 CT £246.55 TOTE £18.50: £7.50, £1.30; EX 64.40 Trifecta £309.70 Part won. Pool of £418.61 - 0.50 winning units..
Owner Mrs Susan Johnson **Bred** Mrs S Johnson **Trained** Yedingham, N Yorks

FOCUS
A modest fillies' handicap. The pace was steady initially and the winner stole something of a march on her rivals but proved game in a tight finish. The field kept to the far rail. The form is rated around the runner-up, and there is a bit of doubt over it given the ground and lack of pace.
Shaluca Official explanation: jockey said filly was unsuited by the soft ground

5045 NORTHUMBRIAN WATER H'CAP 6f
5:05 (5:05) (Class 6) (0-60,60) 3-Y-O+ **£1,554** (£462; £231; £115) **Stalls** Low

Form RPR

4042 **1** **Lake Chini (IRE)**9 4706 8-9-2 **57** (b) JamesSullivan(3) 3 70
(M W Easterby) *t.k.h: chsd ldr: rdn 2f out: led ins fnl f: r.o strly* **7/2**3

-000 **2** 1 ½ **Captain Royale (IRE)**9 4706 5-8-13 **51** (p) RobertWinston 2 59
(Miss Tracy Waggott) *led: rdn and qcknd 2f out: hdd ins fnl f: kpt on same pce* **12/1**

6060 **3** 4 **Ingleby King (USA)**16 4485 4-9-6 **58** (b1) PhillipMakin 5 53
(T D Barron) *dwlt: hld up in tch: effrt over 2f out: no imp ins fnl f* **6/1**

-025 **4** 2 ½ **Elkhorn**60 3027 8-8-8 **51** ow2 (b) DaleSwift(5) 9 38
(Julie Camacho) *hld up: effrt over 2f out: no imp fr over 1f out* **3/1**2

0200 **5** 7 **Tanley**31 3976 5-8-13 **54** GaryBartley(3) 8 19
(I W McInnes) *hld up: shortlived effrt 2f out: sn btn* **18/1**

0402 **6** 3 **He's A Humbug (IRE)**3 4936 6-9-2 **59** (p) JamesO'Reilly(5) 7 14
(J O'Reilly) *stall opened fractionally early: t.k.h: hld up in tch: rdn over 2f out: sn wknd* **2/1**1

-005 **7** 3 ¼ **One Cat Diesel (IRE)**16 4482 3-8-8 **50** PatrickMathers 6 —
(H A McWilliams) *cl up tl rdn and wknd over 2f out* **14/1**

1m 17.11s (2.51) **Going Correction** +0.55s/f (Yiel)
WFA 3 from 4yo+ 4lb **7** Ran SP% **114.5**
Speed ratings (Par 101): **105,103,97,94,85 81,76**
toteswingers:1&2 £4.40, 2&3 £5.80, 1&3 £6.60 CSF £42.88 CT £243.55 TOTE £4.10: £2.30, £4.40; EX 20.70 Trifecta £121.10 Part won. Pool of £163.69 - 0.61 winning units..
Owner Mrs Jean Turpin **Bred** Paul McEnery **Trained** Sheriff Hutton, N Yorks

FOCUS
A weak handicap run at a steady pace in which the first two held those positions throughout. The action again took place on the far rail. The winner looks the best guide.
Tanley Official explanation: jockey saisd gelding was unsuited by the soft ground
He's A Humbug(IRE) Official explanation: jockey said gelding was unsuited by the soft ground

5046 WATERAID H'CAP 5f
5:40 (5:40) (Class 5) (0-70,73) 3-Y-O **£2,072** (£616; £308; £153) **Stalls** Low

Form RPR

-321 **1** **Jack Luey**19 4406 3-9-2 **68** IanBrennan(5) 8 72+
(L A Mullaney) *cl up gng wl: hdwy to ld over 1f out: rdn and r.o wl ins fnl f* **7/2**3

0500 **2** 1 ¾ **Areeg (IRE)**6 4826 3-7-9 **49** oh4 VictorSantos(7) 2 47
(A Berry) *s.s: bhd: gd hdwy over 1f out: chsd wnr and hung lft ins fnl f: r.o* **33/1**

0342 **3** 2 ¾ **Mottley Crewe**8 4749 3-8-10 **57** PhillipMakin 4 45
(M Dods) *prom: rdn and outpcd over 2f out: rallied appr fnl f: sn no imp* **15/8**1

0100 **4** 2 ½ **Thinking**10 4674 3-8-13 **60** RobertWinston 6 39
(T D Easterby) *cl up: rdn and ev ch over 1f out: wknd ins fnl f* **8/1**

3001 **5** ¾ **Mark Anthony (IRE)**9 4714 3-9-7 **73** 6ex MichaelO'Connell(5) 7 49
(K A Ryan) *led to over 1f out: sn rdn and btn* **2/1**2

0003 **6** shd **Lieu Day Louie (IRE)**11 4649 3-7-13 **49** JamesSullivan(3) 5 25
(N Wilson) *s.s: bhd: hdwy over 1f out: sn rdn and edgd rt: wknd ins fnl f* **9/1**

63.93 secs (2.83) **Going Correction** +0.55s/f (Yiel) **6** Ran SP% **114.4**
Speed ratings (Par 100): **99,96,91,87,86 86**
toteswingers:1&2 £6.90, 2&3 £8.50, 1&3 £2.20. totesuper7: Win: Not won. Place: £1334.20. CSF £83.39 CT £276.25 TOTE £2.90: £1.10, £10.50; EX 126.90 Trifecta £196.10 Part won. Pool of £265.05 - 0.41 winning units. Place 6: £216.90 Place 5: £131.53 .
Owner The Jack Partnership & S Rimmer **Bred** Miss D A Johnson **Trained** Great Habton, N Yorks

FOCUS
Two late withdrawals left this race looking a bit light and the eventual winner perhaps wasn't left with a lot to beat after two of the market leaders failed to come up to expectations. The field again stuck to the far rail. The bare form is limited by the runner-up.
Mark Anthony(IRE) Official explanation: jockey said gelding was unsuited by the soft ground
T/Plt: £98.00 to a £1 stake. Pool of £60,670.28 - 451.90 winning tickets. T/Qpdt: £74.30 to a £1 stake. Pool of £5,051.08 50.30 winning tickets. RY

4841
NEWMARKET (July Course) (R-H)
Friday, August 13

OFFICIAL GOING: Good to soft (soft in places) changing to soft after race 1 (5.30)
Far side section of July Course utilised.
Wind: Fresh half-behind Weather: Showers

5047 RACING UK MEDIAN AUCTION MAIDEN STKS 7f
5:30 (5:33) (Class 5) 2-Y-O **£3,238** (£963; £481; £240) **Stalls** Low

Form RPR

542 **1** **Diamond Penny (IRE)**21 4346 2-9-3 78 JamieSpencer 15 84+
(P F I Cole) *w'like: scope: rangy: lw: led centre gp tl wnt far side over 4f out: chsd ldr: shkn up to ld over 2f out: rdn and hung lft over 1f out: r.o: eased nr fin* **7/4**1

2 3 ¼ **Auden (USA)** 2-9-3 0 AhmedAjtebi 3 75
(Mahmood Al Zarooni) *athletic: lw: racd far side: chsd ldrs: swtchd rt over 2f out: sn rdn: styng on same pce whn wnt 2nd ins fnl f* **5/1**2

0 **3** ½ **Rocky Rebel**16 4490 2-9-3 0 JackMitchell 16 74+
(R M Beckett) *racd centre tl wnt far side over 4f out: hld up: hdwy and hung lft fr over 1f out: styd on* **6/1**3

04 **4** nk **Aciano (IRE)**16 4490 2-9-0 0 Louis-PhilippeBeuzelin(3) 2 73
(B J Meehan) *racd far side: chsd ldrs: rdn over 2f out: styd on same pce appr fnl f* **10/1**

03 **5** 6 **Loch Ordie**7 4802 2-9-3 0 JerryO'Dwyer 14 58
(M G Quinlan) *leggy: racd centre tl wnt far side over 4f out: hld up: swtchd lft over 2f out: nvr trbld ldrs* **40/1**

6 **6** ½ **Miss Exhibitionist**62 2958 2-8-12 0 RichardHills 1 52
(P W Chapple-Hyam) *w'like: overall ldr far side tl hdd over 2f out: wknd ins fnl f* **6/1**3

00 **7** shd **Focail Maith**14 4549 2-9-3 0 MarcHalford 5 56
(J Ryan) *str: racd far side: chsd ldrs: rdn over 2f out: wknd over 1f out* **18/1**

65 **8** ½ **Nettis**24 4233 2-9-3 0 SaleemGolam 13 55
(G Prodromou) *racd centre tl wnt far side over 4f out: chsd ldrs tl rdn and wknd over 1f out* **66/1**

0 **9** ¾ **Bouggatti**9 4716 2-9-3 0 AlanMunro 8 53
(W Jarvis) *str: racd centre tl wnt far side over 4f out: dwlt: hld up: pushed along 1/2-way: nvr on terms* **28/1**

0 **10** hd **Beating Harmony**25 4208 2-9-3 0 PatCosgrave 10 53
(J R Fanshawe) *w'like: leggy: racd centre tl wnt far side over 4f out: chsd ldrs: rdn over 2f out: wknd over 1f out* **66/1**

11 ½ **Kiss My Tiara (IRE)** 2-8-12 0 PaulEddery 18 47
(B J Meehan) *w'like: racd centre tl wnt far side over 4f out: dwlt: hld up: n.d* **25/1**

4 **12** 1 ¼ **Olynthos (IRE)**20 4375 2-9-3 0 LiamJones 6 48
(Jane Chapple-Hyam) *lengthy: racd far side: chsd ldrs: rdn over 3f out: wknd over 1f out* **16/1**

13 3 ½ **Twice Bitten** 2-9-3 0 KirstyMilczarek 7 40
(J A R Toller) *w'like: racd far side: s.i.s: hld up: a in rr* **40/1**

20 **14** 8 **Alantina**25 4208 2-8-10 0 DannyBrock(7) 20 20
(J R Jenkins) *bit bkwd: racd centre tl wnt far side over 4f out: chsd ldrs tl rdn and wknd over 2f out* **100/1**

15 5 **Be Amazing (IRE)** 2-8-12 0 ChrisCatlin 19 2
(D R Lanigan) *leggy: racd centre tl wnt far side over 4f out: s.i.s: outpcd* **33/1**

5 **16** 1 ¾ **Rural Pursuits**9 4716 2-8-5 0 AdamBeschizza(7) 9 —
(Mrs C A Dunnett) *leggy: swtchd to racd far side after 1f: hld up: a in rr: wknd over 2f out* **50/1**

0 **17** 16 **Unex Monet**20 4379 2-9-3 0 AdrianNicholls 11 —
(M L W Bell) *str: bit bkwd: racd centre tl wnt far side over 4f out: hld up: bhd fnl 3f* **33/1**

1m 27.91s (2.21) **Going Correction** +0.175s/f (Good) **17** Ran SP% **125.8**
Speed ratings (Par 94): **94,90,89,89,82 81,81,81,80,80 79,78,74,65,59 57,39**
toteswingers: 1&2 £3.20, 1&3 £5.80, 2&3 £8.00. CSF £9.30 TOTE £2.60: £1.40, £2.50, £2.50; EX 11.40.
Owner Mrs Fitri Hay **Bred** Theo Waddington And Mrs Theo Waddington **Trained** Whatcombe, Oxon

FOCUS
Several heavy showers during the day saw the ground change to soft and the testing ground sorted out these two-year-olds, with experience and fitness coming to the fore.

NOTEBOOK

Diamond Penny(IRE) ran out a convincing winner. The race initially saw a group of seven head to the far rail and from over 4f out they were joined by the others, who raced up the centre early on. Diamond Penny, rated 78, proved he handled cut with a professional display. He seems to handle all surfaces and it would be no surprise if he went on to further success. (op 11-4)
Auden(USA), a half-brother to last year's St Leger winner Mastery and high-class stayer Kirklees, gave a promising debut. He was one of the few to stay on, shaping like a horse who will progress over further. (op 11-2 tchd 13-2)
Rocky Rebel, only beaten just over 3l at Sandown on debut, ran respectably and should pick up a maiden. He finished behind Aciano last time, but turned the tables. (op 8-1)
Aciano(IRE) still ran with credit, some six lengths clear of the fifth home, and may prefer better ground. (op 8-1)
Loch Ordie had finished placed in a seller over course and distance a week earlier and is likely to have run to a similar level here. (op 50-1)
Miss Exhibitionist, making her second career start, showed up well but tired badly late on. (op 5-1)
Bouggatti impressed in the paddock and might be a nice prospect for nurseries later in the season. (op 25-1 tchd 33-1)
Beating Harmony showed considerably more than his debut and is bred to come into his own from next year, so could make an interesting long-term project.
Twice Bitten Official explanation: jockey said colt was unsuited by the good to soft (soft in places) ground

5048 NGK SPARK PLUGS H'CAP 6f
6:00 (6:01) (Class 4) (0-85,82) 3-Y-0+ **£4,533** (£1,348; £674; £336) **Stalls** Low

Form RPR
00-3 **1** **Rash Judgement**[49] 3401 5-9-11 **82** ChrisCatlin 5 91
(W S Kittow) *led: hdd over 1f out: rallied to ld ins fnl f: hung lft nr fin: r.o* **8/1**[3]
1231 **2** ½ **Pirate's Song**[14] 4553 3-8-10 **71** (t) RichardHills 2 77
(J A R Toller) *lw: chsd ldrs: rdn and ev ch ins fnl f: r.o* **9/2**[1]
6202 **3** 2¼ **Simple Rhythm**[9] 4715 4-8-5 **65** Louis-PhilippeBeuzelin(3) 8 65
(J Ryan) *trckd wnr: racd keenly: led over 1f out: rdn and hdd ins fnl f: no ex* **6/1**[2]
1020 **4** 2 **The Strig**[55] 3218 3-9-1 **76** WilliamCarson 9 68
(S C Williams) *plld hrd and prom: rdn over 1f out: styd on same pce* **28/1**
2021 **5** ¾ **Dickie Le Davoir**[2] 4947 6-8-8 **65** (b) PaulEddery 6 56+
(R C Guest) *hld up: pushed along over 1f out: r.o ins fnl f: nvr trbld ldrs* **6/1**[2]
026 **6** 1 **Ginger Ted (IRE)**[7] 4806 3-9-5 **80** (p) LiamJones 3 67+
(R C Guest) *pitched bdly and nrly uns rdr leaving stalls: sn pushed along in rr: nvr on terms* **6/1**[2]
2504 **7** ¾ **Requisite**[3] 4930 5-9-4 **75** (v) PatCosgrave 10 60
(I A Wood) *hld up: rdn 1/2-way: n.d* **9/2**[1]
0040 **8** ½ **Leverage (IRE)**[16] 4489 4-9-3 **74** TomQueally 1 58
(M Wigham) *hld up in tch: racd keenly: rdn and wknd over 1f out* **12/1**
5000 **9** 3¾ **Earlsmedic**[49] 3401 5-8-13 **70** SaleemGolam 4 42
(S C Williams) *hld up: a in rr: wknd over 1f out* **20/1**
430 **10** 2 **Distant Sun (USA)**[2] 4952 6-9-0 **71** AlanMunro 7 36
(Miss L A Perratt) *trckd ldrs: plld hrd: rdn over 2f out: wknd over 1f out* **11/1**
2350 **11** 3¼ **Tell Halaf**[13] 4593 3-8-11 **72** JerryO'Dwyer 11 26
(M G Quinlan) *hld up: a in rr: wknd 2f out* **25/1**

1m 14.72s (2.22) **Going Correction** +0.50s/f (Yiel)
WFA 3 from 4yo+ 4lb **11** Ran SP% **118.4**
Speed ratings (Par 105): **105,104,101,98,97 96,95,94,89,87 82**
toteswingers: 1&2 £5.00, 1&3 £9.00, 2&3 £4.10. CSF £43.12 CT £240.23 TOTE £9.90: £2.20, £2.00, £2.20; EX 50.80.
Owner Reg Gifford **Bred** D R Tucker **Trained** Blackborough, Devon
■ Stewards' Enquiry : Chris Catlin caution: used whip without giving gelding time to respond

FOCUS
It paid to race handily in this competitive-looking race, in which nothing came from off the pace. The first three home were never out of those positions. The form makes sense and the time was respectable for the soft conditions, being 4.42 seconds outside standard.
Ginger Ted(IRE) Official explanation: jockey said gelding stumbled leaving stalls

5049 EUROPEAN BREEDERS' FUND MAIDEN STKS 1m
6:35 (6:36) (Class 4) 2-Y-0 **£4,533** (£1,348; £674; £336) **Stalls** Low

Form RPR
1 **Frankel** 2-9-3 0 TomQueally 10 95+
(H R A Cecil) *gd sort: w'like: scope: dwlt: hld up: hdwy over 2f out: led ins fnl f: shkn up and r.o: readily* **7/4**[1]
2 ½ **Nathaniel (IRE)** 2-9-3 0 WilliamBuick 8 92+
(J H M Gosden) *w'like: scope: tall: chsd ldr tl led over 2f out: rdn over 1f out: hdd ins fnl f: r.o* **3/1**[2]
3 5 **Genius Beast (USA)** 2-9-3 0 AhmedAjtebi 2 81
(Mahmood Al Zarooni) *w'like: scope: lw: chsd ldrs: outpcd over 2f out: styd on to go 3rd wl ins fnl f* **15/2**[3]
225 **4** hd **Dortmund**[48] 3449 2-8-10 83 AntiocoMurgia(7) 4 81
(Mahmood Al Zarooni) *led over 5f: sn rdn: no ex fnl f* **15/2**[3]
6 **5** 1¾ **Bonita Star**[15] 4508 2-8-12 0 AlanMunro 9 72
(M R Channon) *prom: rdn over 1f out: hung lft and wknd ins fnl f* **20/1**
30 **6** 5 **Maher (USA)**[29] 4054 2-9-3 0 KierenFallon 5 66
(D M Simcock) *trckd ldrs: racd keenly: edgd lft and wknd over 1f out* **8/1**
7 ½ **Elrasheed** 2-9-3 0 RichardHills 12 65
(J L Dunlop) *lengthy: hld up: hdwy over 2f out: sn wknd* **25/1**
8 ½ **Man Of God (IRE)** 2-9-3 0 SaleemGolam 6 64
(J H M Gosden) *str: scope: bit bkwd: hld up: hdwy over 2f out: wknd over 1f out* **16/1**
6 **9** shd **Lemon Drop Red (USA)**[21] 4318 2-9-3 0 TomMcLaughlin 7 64
(E A L Dunlop) *chsd ldrs: rdn over 2f out: hung lft and wknd over 1f out* **33/1**
10 14 **Castlemorris King** 2-8-10 0 AdamBeschizza(7) 1 33
(M C Chapman) *w'like: cl cpld: s.s: sn prom: wknd over 2f out* **100/1**
11 1¾ **Colour Vision (FR)** 2-9-3 0 AdrianNicholls 3 29
(M Johnston) *leggy: s.s: sn pushed along and rn green in rr: lost tch over 2f out* **25/1**
12 3½ **Breton Star** 2-9-3 0 ChrisCatlin 11 21
(D M Simcock) *leggy: s.s: a in rr: wknd over 2f out* **66/1**

1m 43.69s (3.69) **Going Correction** +0.50s/f (Yiel) **12** Ran SP% **119.8**
Speed ratings (Par 96): **101,100,95,95,93 88,88,87,87,73 71,68**
toteswingers:1&2 £2.30, 2&3 £3.90, 1&3 £3.50 CSF £6.30 TOTE £3.10: £1.60, £1.70, £2.70; EX 7.80.
Owner K Abdulla **Bred** Juddmonte Farms Ltd **Trained** Newmarket, Suffolk

FOCUS
This looked an above average maiden that will throw up a stack of winners. The first two home left the impression that they are more than entitled to their lofty entries.

NOTEBOOK
Frankel ◆ is closely related to the stable's Lingfield Derby winner Bullet Train and is out of a Listed winner. A February foal, the manner in which he travelled up to challenge the eventual second was visually impressive. Barely off the bridle, he only needed to be nudged out by his rider to settle this and will have learnt plenty from the experience. He is in the Royal Lodge Stakes and, with the programme book not full of options for a horse who certainly won't have been missed by the handicapper, that could be an interesting target. (op 13-8 tchd 11-8)
Nathaniel(IRE) ◆, closely related to Playful Act and Percussionist, looks sure to enhance the family's reputation. If it hadn't been for the winner, he'd have been a five-length Newmarket maiden winner and grabbing the headlines himself. He is undoubtedly a smart prospect and, on breeding, looks sure to improve as he matures from this very pleasing debut. (op 7-1)
Genius Beast(USA), a February foal out of the top-class Shawanda, impressed as really good mover on his way to post. He won't meet rivals like the first two every day and is likely to make his mark in maiden company before progressing. (op 11-2 tchd 8-1)
Dortmund, second on his first two starts but then beaten too far to be true as favourite at Newcastle 48 days ago, also ran a good race. Markedly stepped up in trip, he saw it out and is certainly capable of winning a maiden. (op 7-1 tchd 8-1)
Bonita Star is a half-sister to several winners and again showed some promise after finishing sixth on her debut over 7f at Goodwood a fortnight ago. (tchd 16-1)
Maher(USA) was keen early and is now eligible for a mar, should connections opt to head down the nurseries route, but he is well up to winning in maiden company if settling a little better. (tchd 7-1)
Elrasheed is a half-brother to high-class middle-distance performer Akmal and should improve over further as he matures. (op 16-1)
Man Of God(IRE), who cost 290,000gns, was green and is sure to come on for the experience. (op 20-1 tchd 25-1)

5050 HUGHES H'CAP 1m
7:05 (7:09) (Class 5) (0-75,73) 3-Y-0+ **£3,238** (£963; £481; £240) **Stalls** Low

Form RPR
-503 **1** **Oh So Saucy**[9] 4715 6-9-10 **69** AlanMunro 13 77
(C F Wall) *a.p: chsd ldr over 5f out: rdn to ld ins fnl f: r.o* **7/1**
3551 **2** ¾ **Beaumont's Party (IRE)**[21] 4335 3-9-6 **72** PatCosgrave 8 77
(R Hannon) *lw: trckd ldrs: plld hrd: led over 1f out: rdn and hdd ins fnl f: styd on* **4/1**[2]
0602 **3** nk **Ilie Nastase (FR)**[9] 4713 6-10-0 **73** RichardHills 12 79+
(C R Dore) *hld up: hdwy over 1f out: sn rdn: edgd lft and r.o* **9/2**[3]
01 **4** 2½ **Bell's Ocean (USA)**[10] 4687 3-8-6 **61** 6ex Louis-PhilippeBeuzelin(3) 5 60
(J Ryan) *set stdy pce tl qcknd over 2f out: rdn and hdd over 1f out: no ex ins fnl f* **12/1**
6353 **5** 1½ **Tanforan**[14] 4547 8-9-3 **62** TomMcLaughlin 4 58
(B P J Baugh) *trckd ldrs: plld hrd: rdn over 1f out: styd on same pce* **9/1**
0101 **6** ¾ **Aviso (GER)**[28] 4108 6-9-13 **72** TomQueally 9 67
(B J Curley) *hld up in tch: plld hrd: rdn over 1f out: no ex* **5/2**[1]
066 **7** shd **Plan A (IRE)**[27] 4146 3-8-5 **57** WilliamCarson 6 50
(M G Quinlan) *dwlt: hld up: effrt over 1f out: no imp fnl f* **33/1**
-031 **8** 1 **Sonny Parkin**[14] 4548 8-9-9 **68** (v) KierenFallon 11 62
(J Pearce) *s.i.s: hld up: rdn over 1f out: nvr trbld ldrs: eased whn btn ins fnl f* **11/2**
4006 **9** 14 **Half Sister (IRE)**[8] 4762 3-8-10 **69** LeonnaMayor(7) 3 28
(M E Rimmer) *prom: rdn: hung lft and wknd 2f out* **50/1**

1m 46.4s (6.40) **Going Correction** +0.65s/f (Yiel)
WFA 3 from 5yo+ 7lb **9** Ran SP% **117.2**
Speed ratings (Par 103): **94,93,92,90,88 88,88,87,73**
toteswingers:1&2 £6.70, 2&3 £3.90, 1&3 £4.70 CSF £35.71 CT £143.03 TOTE £4.90: £1.80, £1.60, £1.70.
Owner The Eight Of Diamonds **Bred** Mrs C J Walker **Trained** Newmarket, Suffolk

FOCUS
A fair handicap, but it was slowly run and the form is muddling. The third is rated to his recent best.

5051 CLIFF WATERMAN MEMORIAL H'CAP 1m 2f
7:40 (7:42) (Class 5) (0-70,70) 3-Y-0+ **£3,238** (£963; £481; £240) **Stalls** Centre

Form RPR
0212 **1** **Grams And Ounces**[22] 4289 3-9-9 **65** KierenFallon 8 74
(Miss Amy Weaver) *prom: hmpd over 8f out: wnt centre ent st: led that gp over 3f out: rdn and edgd rt over 1f out: styd on to ld overall wl ins fnl f: hung lft nr fin* **11/4**[2]
3300 **2** 1¾ **Orpen Wide (IRE)**[20] 4374 8-9-6 **58** (b) GemmaGracey-Davison(5) 4 63
(M C Chapman) *led: clr 8f out and racd alone on stands' side rail: hung lft fr 3f out: rdn over 1f out: hdd wl ins fnl f* **20/1**
2112 **3** nk **Sunley Spinalonga**[4] 4907 3-10-0 **70** WilliamBuick 12 74
(D R C Elsworth) *hld up: wnt centre ent st: hdwy over 2f out: sn hung rt: rdn over 1f out: hung lft and styd on ins fnl f* **3/1**[3]
0441 **4** 1¼ **Noah Jameel**[9] 4689 8-9-0 **54** 6ex AdamBeschizza(7) 3 56
(A G Newcombe) *prom: wnt centre ent st: rdn over 2f out: styd on same pce ins fnl f* **12/1**
2323 **5** 2 **Broughtons Paradis (IRE)**[7] 4804 4-9-9 **61** JohnFahy(5) 2 59
(W J Musson) *s.i.s: hld up: wnt centre ent st: hdwy over 2f out: sn rdn: no imp ins fnl f* **2/1**[1]
/6- **6** 2½ **Ptolomeos**[410] 3447 7-9-4 **58** IanBurns(7) 6 51
(S Regan) *chsd ldrs: wnt centre ent st: rdn hung lft and wknd over 1f out* **50/1**
0250 **7** 4½ **Hierarch (IRE)**[21] 4335 3-10-0 **70** PatCosgrave 11 54
(R Hannon) *chsd ldrs: wnt centre ent st: rdn over 2f out: hung lft and wknd over 1f out* **10/1**
000 **8** 3½ **Telescopic**[21] 4330 3-8-6 **51** Louis-PhilippeBeuzelin(3) 7 28
(W Jarvis) *chsd ldr tl wnt centre ent st: led that gp tl over 3f out: wknd 2f out* **25/1**
-406 **9** 12 **Petsas Pleasure**[49] 3405 4-9-10 **57** (p) ChrisCatlin 10 10
(Ollie Pears) *hld up: a in rr: wnt centre ent st: lost tch fr over 2f out* **25/1**

2m 14.06s (8.56) **Going Correction** +0.65s/f (Yiel)
WFA 3 from 4yo+ 9lb **9** Ran SP% **116.2**
Speed ratings (Par 103): **91,89,89,88,86 84,81,78,68**
toteswingers:1&2 £7.10, 2&3 £12.20, 1&3 £1.70 CSF £58.87 CT £176.97 TOTE £3.90: £1.50, £3.30, £1.20; EX 45.10.
Owner Miss A Weaver **Bred** Brook Stud Bloodstock Ltd **Trained** Newmarket, Suffolk
■ Stewards' Enquiry : Adam Beschizza five-day ban: careless riding (Aug 27-31)

FOCUS
This was contested by several horses who have been competitive at their level this summer. A clear personal best from the winner with the next three close to their recent form.

Petsas Pleasure Official explanation: jockey said gelding lost its action

5052 SINGH SKIPS, SAFE BET FILLIES' H'CAP 7f
8:10 (8:12) (Class 3) (0-95,93) 3-Y-0+ £9,066 (£2,697; £1,348; £673) Stalls Low

Form RPR
4-43 1 **Perfect Silence**[22] 4287 5-8-7 79....(b) JohnFahy(5) 5 86
(C G Cox) *s.i.s: shkn up to trck ldrs: rdn to ld ins fnl hung lft: r.o* 7/2[3]
0-56 2 1 1/2 **Mistic Magic (IRE)**[16] 4473 3-9-5 92....(b[1]) KierenFallon 7 93
(P F I Cole) *set stdy pce tl qcknd over 2f out: rdn over 1f out: hdd ins fnl f: styd on same pce* 8/1
000 3 3 1/4 **Jeninsky (USA)**[12] 4617 5-9-2 90.... AdamBeschizza(7) 3 84
(Rae Guest) *chsd ldrs: rdn over 1f out: no ex ins fnl f* 10/3[2]
033 4 hd **What's Up Pussycat (IRE)**[6] 4828 4-9-12 93.... TomQueally 1 87+
(D M Simcock) *hld up: rdn over 1f out: styd on same pce* 11/8[1]
6506 5 nk **Fly Silca Fly (IRE)**[5] 4865 3-8-8 81.... AlanMunro 2 72
(M R Channon) *lw: chsd ldrs: rdn over 1f out: no ex ins fnl f* 14/1
0303 6 18 **Souter's Sister (IRE)**[81] 2387 4-9-3 89.... TobyAtkinson(5) 4 33
(M Botti) *hld up: rdn and wknd over 2f out* 16/1

1m 29.4s (3.70) **Going Correction** +0.65s/f (Yiel)
WFA 3 from 4yo+ 6lb 6 Ran SP% **111.1**
Speed ratings (Par 104): **104,102,98,98,98 77**
toteswingers:1&2 £2.30, 2&3 £5.70, 1&3 £3.30 CSF £29.20 TOTE £4.50: £2.20, £2.90; EX 25.50 Place 6: £64.11, Place 5: £48.00..
Owner Wild Beef Racing (Mr & Mrs R J Vines) **Bred** R J Vines **Trained** Lambourn, Berks
■ Stewards' Enquiry : John Fahy two-day ban: used whip with excessive frequency (Aug 27-28)

FOCUS
The rain continued to get into the ground as the card unfolded and this was 1.49 seconds slower than the opening juvenile maiden. Muddling form, the winner probably only running to her latest form.

NOTEBOOK
Perfect Silence duly put this race to bed in determined fashion. It was the best performance of her career to date, as she won off a 4lb higher mark than her last winning mark. The other point to note is that she appears to have struck up a good relationship with her up-and-coming apprentice. (tchd 4-1)
Mistic Magic(IRE), dropped 3lb after failing to get competitive on two previous starts, was given a canny front-running ride by Fallon but is unlikely to be granted a similarly easy time of it in front in future engagements. (op 15-2 tchd 7-1)
Jeninsky(USA) is due to drop 3lb with immediate effect and that will help as she has not played a part at the business end of her races this season. (op 7-2 tchd 4-1)
What's Up Pussycat(IRE) was completely unsuited by the slow pace. She has useful form over 1m in the soft and likes to come past horses late on in a truly-run race as she did at both Haydock and Newbury in her previous two assignments. She should be given another chance, especially if there appears to be obvious early speed among the opposition. (op 7-4 tchd 5-4)
Fly Silca Fly(IRE) has been in the grip of the handicapper since scoring on the Rowley Mile back in May. She is probably stretched at this trip, having failed to make the three in five runs over it. (op 10-1 tchd 16-1)
Souter's Sister(IRE) has three wins on decent surfaces, so the rain-eased ground was unlikely to assist, especially as this was her first run for 81 days. (op 10-1)
T/Plt: £67.50 to a £1 stake. Pool of £54,102.29 - 584.50 winning tickets. T/Qpdt: £23.80 to a £1 stake. Pool of £4,495.37 - 139.29 winning tickets. CR

4932 NOTTINGHAM (L-H)
Friday, August 13

OFFICIAL GOING: Good (good to soft in places)
All races on outer course. Rail moved out 5m from 2nd dog leg 4.5f out and then 2m as far as 10f start, increasing distances on round course by 24yds.
Wind: Light across Weather: Overcast

5053 EUROPEAN BREEDERS' FUND MAIDEN STKS 6f 15y
2:20 (2:22) (Class 5) 2-Y-0 £3,561 (£1,059; £529; £264) Stalls Centre

Form RPR
1 **My Freedom (IRE)** 2-9-3 0.... TedDurcan 1 87+
(Saeed Bin Suroor) *trckd ldrs: swtchd rt and smooth hdwy 2f out: led 1 1/2f out: pushed clr ins fnl f* 7/4[2]
22 2 3 **Enthusing (IRE)**[20] 4379 2-9-3 0.... DaneO'Neill 5 75
(D R C Elsworth) *t.k.h early: trckd ldr: led over 3f out: rdn and hdd 1 1/2f out: kpt on same pce* 1/1[1]
00 3 6 **Major Return (IRE)**[46] 3517 2-9-3 0.... JamesDoyle 3 57
(A J McCabe) *sn pushed along in rr: rdn and hdwy 1/2-way: chsd ldng pair over 1f out: sn no imp* 100/1
4 2 1/4 **Chokidar (IRE)** 2-9-3 0.... FrannyNorton 6 50
(J A Glover) *trckd ldrs: rdn along wl over 2f out: sn outpcd* 100/1
4 5 hd **Supermarine**[28] 4089 2-9-3 0.... PaulMulrennan 4 50
(J A Glover) *led: hdd over 3f out and sn rdn along: edgd lft over 2f out and sn wknd* 16/1
6 14 **Fimias (IRE)** 2-9-3 0.... KirstyMilczarek 2 —
(L M Cumani) *sn pushed along and a in rr: bhd fnl 2f* 33/1
6 7 14 **Elusive Love (IRE)**[9] 4702 2-9-3 0.... JoeFanning 7 —
(M Johnston) *wnt rt s: sn cl up: rdn along 1/2-way: sn wknd and eased wl over 1f out* 7/1[3]

1m 16.38s (1.48) **Going Correction** +0.05s/f (Good) 7 Ran SP% **109.7**
Speed ratings (Par 94): **92,88,80,77,76 58,39**
toteswingers: 1&2 £1.10, 1&3 £15.90, 2&3 £14.20 CSF £3.46 TOTE £3.30: £2.20, £1.10; EX 4.30.
Owner Godolphin **Bred** Skymarc Farm **Trained** Newmarket, Suffolk

FOCUS
There wasn't much strength in depth to this maiden and the two market leaders dominated. The winner looks one to follow.

NOTEBOOK
My Freedom(IRE) ◆ cost 260,000euros and is out of a mare who is half-sister to 1m1f-1m4f winner Press The Button. He travelled sweetly into contention and, despite initially showing his inexperience when asked to win the race, soon had matters in control passing the furlong marker. The easy ground was evidently to his liking and really he won without having to be asked a serious question so, using the runner-up as a guide, could well prove to be a very useful colt. He has an entry in the Group 2 Mill Reef next month and a run there looks viable, granted normal improvement from this outing. (op 15-8 tchd 6-4)
Enthusing(IRE) had shaped as though easier ground may be more in his favour, and could've been considered a winner without a penalty after his near miss at Newmarket last time. He had every chance, but bumped into one in the winner and has now become expensive to follow. Some will assume he is ungenuine as he has now finished second in his three outings, and he does still have something to learn, but he did appear to do his best here. (op 10-11 tchd 11-10)
Major Return(IRE) posted a carer-best on this third outing. He got badly outpaced around halfway and it's not hard to see why he was tried over 7f last time. Things should be easier for him now he can enter nurseries.
Chokidar(IRE) cost little and is bred to enjoy racing over further in due course. He just got the better of his more-experienced stablemate Supermarine and ought to know a deal more next time.
Fimias(IRE) is the first foal of a half-sister to Halicarnassus, who herself stayed 1m4f. He ran distinctly green, lacking anything like the pace for this test, and is more of a long-term project. (op 28-1 tchd 40-1)
Elusive Love(IRE) had run as though in need of the experience on debut at Newcastle nine days earlier. He was up there early, but his rider was sending out distress signals from halfway and he was eased right off in the end. This obviously wasn't his true running. (op 8-1 tchd 9-1)

5054 DIGIBET.COM FILLIES' H'CAP 6f 15y
2:55 (2:55) (Class 4) (0-80,80) 3-Y-0+ £4,209 (£1,252; £625; £312) Stalls Centre

Form RPR
2100 1 **Revue Princess (IRE)**[6] 4834 5-8-9 64....(b) TedDurcan 4 73
(T D Easterby) *in tch on outer: hdwy over 2f out: rdn to chse ldng pair over 1f out: styd on to ld last 100yds* 5/1[3]
5440 2 1 3/4 **Feelin Foxy**[15] 4510 6-9-9 78.... PaulMulrennan 3 82
(J G Given) *led: rdn wl over 1f out: drvn and edgd lft ent fnl f: hdd and one pce last 100yds* 8/1
12 3 2 1/2 **Supreme Spirit (IRE)**[28] 4091 3-9-2 75.... FrannyNorton 1 70
(D Nicholls) *trckd ldrs: hdwy wl over 2f out: rdn to chse ldr over 1f out: sn drvn: edgd lft and kpt on same pce ins fnl f* 13/8[1]
0254 4 2 1/4 **Angus Newz**[4] 4892 7-9-11 80.... AndreaAtzeni 6 68
(M Quinn) *trckd ldrs: hdwy 1/2-way: rdn 2f out: drvn and edgd lft over 1f out: sn one pce* 15/2
6200 5 4 **Absa Lutte (IRE)**[10] 4684 7-9-11 80....(t) DaneO'Neill 9 56
(Dr R D P Newland) *in tch: rdn along wl over 2f out and sn outpcd* 14/1
5366 6 1/2 **Leonid Glow**[32] 3947 5-9-4 76.... PatrickDonaghy(3) 8 50
(M Dods) *hld up: stmbld after 1f: a in rr* 4/1[2]
6002 7 19 **Posy Fossil (USA)**[41] 3677 3-8-3 62....(vt) WilliamCarson 2 —
(S C Williams) *prom: rdn along and lost pl after 2f: in rr and hung rt 1/2-way: sn outpcd and bhd* 16/1

1m 14.85s (-0.05) **Going Correction** +0.05s/f (Good)
WFA 3 from 4yo+ 4lb 7 Ran SP% **110.2**
Speed ratings (Par 102): **102,99,96,93,88 87,62**
toteswingers:1&2 £13.30, 2&3 £2.10, 1&3 £2.50 CSF £40.08 CT £85.66 TOTE £7.10: £3.60, £4.10; EX 31.90.
Owner S A Heley **Bred** Raymond Shanahan **Trained** Great Habton, N Yorks

FOCUS
A modest fillies' handicap was run at a sound tempo and the main action developed down the middle to far side. The winner is rated back to her best.

5055 CHARLES HORNER 70TH BIRTHDAY H'CAP 5f 13y
3:30 (3:30) (Class 6) (0-55,55) 3-Y-0+ £1,619 (£481; £240; £120) Stalls Centre

Form RPR
5001 1 **Gracie's Games**[8] 4760 4-8-7 51 6ex....(v) TobyAtkinson(5) 3 62+
(R J Price) *chsd ldrs: pushed along 1/2-way: hdwy on wd outside to ld wl over 1f out: clr whn hung bdly lft ins fnl f: kpt on* 7/1[3]
0-00 2 1 **Sleepy Blue Ocean**[9] 4706 4-8-12 54.... MartinLane(3) 12 59
(J Balding) *in tch: hdwy 2f out: rdn to chse wnr ins fnl f: kpt on* 16/1
00 3 2 **D'Allziance (IRE)**[23] 4256 4-8-13 52.... RichardKingscote 10 50+
(Jonjo O'Neill) *in tch: pushed along over 2f out: sn rdn and styd on strly ins fnl f: nrst fin* 20/1
3121 4 nk **You'relikemefrank**[24] 4239 4-9-2 55....(p) AndrewElliott 11 52
(J Balding) *led 2f: cl up: rdn wl over 1f out: drvn and one pce ins fnl f* 9/2[2]
0500 5 1/2 **Lithaam (IRE)**[21] 4326 6-8-9 55....(p) RyanClark(7) 5 50
(J M Bradley) *cl up: led after 2f: rdn and hdd wl over 1f out: drvn and wknd ent fnl f* 9/1
0600 6 1/2 **What Katie Did (IRE)**[7] 4789 5-9-2 55....(p) DaneO'Neill 17 48
(J M Bradley) *chsd ldrs on outer: hdwy 2f out and sn rdn: drvn over 1f out and no imp ins fnl f* 7/1[3]
1000 7 1 1/2 **Pinball (IRE)**[5] 4869 4-9-0 53....(v) PaulMulrennan 9 41
(Mrs L Williamson) *cl up: rdn and ev ch 2f out: sn drvn and wknd* 12/1
/404 8 2 3/4 **Emma's Secrets**[3] 4938 5-8-7 46 oh1.... JimmyQuinn 14 24
(D Shaw) *a in rr* 9/1
0000 9 1 **Cookie Galore**[10] 4674 3-8-5 47....(be[1]) JamieMackay 2 20
(J A Glover) *s.i.s: a in rr* 50/1
6414 10 nse **Fashion Icon (USA)**[10] 4672 4-8-10 49.... TedDurcan 13 23
(D O'Meara) *chsd ldrs: rdn along bef 1/2-way: sn lost pl and bhd* 3/1[1]
6664 11 14 **Turf Time**[11] 4651 3-8-8 50.... FrannyNorton 16 —
(J A Glover) *a in rr* 7/1[3]

61.77 secs (0.77) **Going Correction** +0.20s/f (Good)
WFA 3 from 4yo+ 3lb 11 Ran SP% **121.0**
Speed ratings (Par 101): **101,99,96,95,94 94,91,87,85,85 63**
toteswingers:1&2 £27.80, 2&3 £58.30, 1&3 £17.50 CSF £116.21 CT £2182.77 TOTE £8.90: £3.30, £4.90, £7.40; EX 161.70.
Owner David Prosser & Keith Warrington **Bred** David Prosser & Keith Warrington **Trained** Ullingswick, H'fords

FOCUS
This moderate sprint was decimated by non-runners. They went a solid enough pace and those drawn low seemed at more of an advantage. Sound form for the grade.
Fashion Icon(USA) Official explanation: jockey said filly was unsuited by the good (good to soft places) ground

5056 MITIE FILLIES' H'CAP 1m 2f 50y
4:05 (4:06) (Class 4) (0-85,85) 3-Y-0 £5,828 (£1,734; £866; £432) Stalls Low

Form RPR
6442 1 **Bahamian Music (IRE)**[15] 4520 3-8-5 74.... LeeTopliss(5) 2 86
(R A Fahey) *trckd ldng pair: smooth hdwy on inner over 3f out: rdn to ld wl over 1f out: drvn and edgd rt ins fnl f: jst hld on* 10/1
6011 2 shd **Snoqualmie Star**[21] 4329 3-8-13 77....(b) RichardKingscote 3 89
(D R C Elsworth) *trckd ldr: cl up 4f out: rdn along and ev ch 2f out: drvn and styd on ins fnl f: jst failed* 7/1
61 3 1 1/2 **Sea Of Galilee**[28] 4115 3-9-3 81.... DaneO'Neill 1 90
(H Candy) *led: rdn along 3f out: hdd and drvn wl over 1f out: edgd lft and one pce ent fnl f* 11/10[1]
0-64 4 11 **Craighall**[64] 2891 3-8-2 66.... AndreaAtzeni 4 53
(D M Simcock) *chsd ldrs: pushed along and lost pl 1/2-way: kpt on fnl 2f: n.d* 33/1
314 5 17 **Viewing**[20] 4389 3-9-0 78.... NickyMackay 5 31
(J H M Gosden) *chsd ldrs: rdn along over 4f out: sn wknd* 4/1[2]
2123 6 nk **Sumerian**[14] 4532 3-9-3 81....(b[1]) PaulMulrennan 7 33
(Sir Mark Prescott) *hld up in rr: hdwy to chse ldrs over 4f out: rdn along over 3f out: sn wknd* 6/1[3]

The Form Book, Raceform Ltd, Compton, RG20 6NL

4150 **7** *21* **Bakongo (IRE)**[28] 4098 3-8-7 **74**..................................... MartinLane(3) 6 —
(M L W Bell) *t.k.h early: hld up: a in rr: outpcd and bhd fnl 3f* **25/1**

2m 15.47s (3.77) **Going Correction** +0.375s/f (Good) 7 Ran SP% **110.3**
Speed ratings (Par 99): **99,98,97,88,75 75,58**
toteswingers:1&2 £5.10, 2&3 £2.00, 1&3 £3.60 CSF £70.59 CT £130.16 TOTE £13.00: £5.90, £3.90; EX 39.00.
Owner R A Fahey **Bred** Genesis Green Stud Ltd **Trained** Musley Bank, N Yorks
■ Stewards' Enquiry : Lee Topliss two-day ban: used whip with excessive frequency (Aug 27-28)

FOCUS
A fillies' handicap that had the makings of a decent affair for the grade. However, it was shame the highly progressive Sparkling Smile failed to show up and deteriorating ground conditions found out most of the field a long way out. The first three finished clear and a fairly positive view has been taken of the form.
Viewing Official explanation: trainer had no explanation for the poor form shown

5057 MITIE MAIDEN STKS 1m 75y
4:40 (4:41) (Class 5) 3-Y-O **£2,590** (£770; £385; £192) **Stalls** Centre

Form RPR
0- **1** **Taqleed (IRE)**[309] 6617 3-9-3 0.. NickyMackay 9 86+
(J H M Gosden) *led 1f: prom tl led again over 2f out: rdn clr over 1f out: easily* **13/2**[2]
56 **2** *9* **Tasza (USA)**[13] 4601 3-8-12 0.. JamesDoyle 3 60
(A J McCabe) *midfield: hdwy and in tch over 3f out: rdn 2f out: styd on wl ins fnl f: no ch w wnr* **66/1**
2-2 **3** *½* **Forest Runner**[28] 4107 3-9-3 0.. TedDurcan 4 64
(Saeed Bin Suroor) *trckd ldng pair: hdwy to chse ldr 1/2-way: rdn over 2f out: sn drvn and one pce fr wl over 1f out* **1/4**[1]
36 **4** *nse* **Swiftly Done (IRE)**[21] 4339 3-9-3 0.. DavidNolan 5 64
(D Carroll) *hld up: hdwy wl over 2f out: rdn over 1f out: kpt on ins fnl f: nrst fin* **25/1**
0 **5** *2 ¼* **Swingle**[10] 4679 3-8-12 0.. DaneO'Neill 6 54
(D Haydn Jones) *chsd ldrs: rdn along over 2f out: sn drvn and grad wknd* **80/1**
0 **6** *8* **Chief Storm Eagle (IRE)**[29] 4069 3-8-12 0.............. TobyAtkinson(5) 10 40
(M Botti) *plld hrd: led after 1f: rdn over 3f out: sn hdd and grad wknd* **40/1**
0 **7** *2* **The Chester Giant**[21] 4339 3-8-12 0.. PaulMulrennan 8 31
(Patrick Morris) *a in rr* **100/1**
0 **8** *2 ½* **Floridita (USA)**[163] 776 3-8-12 0.. JoeFanning 2 25
(M Johnston) *chsd ldrs: green and pushed along after 3f: lost pl 1/2-way and bhd fnl 3f* **11/1**[3]
0 **9** *16* **Gypsy Style**[77] 2517 3-8-9 0.. PatrickDonaghy(3) 1 —
(Mrs K Walton) *dwlt: a in rr: bhd fnl 3f* **100/1**
10 *30* **Smashing Brasses (IRE)** 3-9-4 0 ow1..................(t) DarrenWilliams 7 —
(Miss Amy Weaver) *s.i.s: a bhd* **100/1**

1m 52.11s (6.51) **Going Correction** +0.375s/f (Good) 10 Ran SP% **113.6**
Speed ratings (Par 100): **82,73,72,72,70 62,60,57,41,11**
toteswingers:1&2 £8.60, 2&3 £3.60, 1&3 £1.50 CSF £301.38 TOTE £7.80: £1.70, £7.20, £1.02; EX 251.00.
Owner Hamdan Al Maktoum **Bred** Shadwell Estate Co Ltd **Trained** Newmarket, Suffolk

FOCUS
A modest maiden with an easy winner. It was steadily run and there is a bit of doubt over the form, but the winner impressed.
Swiftly Done(IRE) Official explanation: jockey said, regarding running and riding, that his orders were to jump out, get an early position and do his best, he was unable to get a position early and had to race wide, deciding to drop the gelding in at the end of the back straight, having been happy with the way it travelled early off a slow pace, it was outpaced and ran green turn into straight, running past beaten horses, adding that it might be suited by further.
Smashing Brasses(IRE) Official explanation: trainer's rep said gelding had a breathing problem

5058 DIGIBET.COM H'CAP 1m 6f 15y
5:15 (5:16) (Class 6) (0-60,63) 3-Y-O **£1,619** (£481; £240; £120) **Stalls** Low

Form RPR
-062 **1** **Albeed**[22] 4301 3-9-1 **60**.. MartinLane(3) 1 69+
(J L Dunlop) *hld up in tch: hdwy on inner over 3f out: swtchd rt and rdn to chse ldng pair over 2f out: drvn to chal over 1f out: styd on to ld ins fnl f: drvn out* **9/4**[1]
504 **2** *¾* **Sheikhtothemusic**[37] 3776 3-8-13 **55**.. LeeVickers 15 63
(J G Given) *hld up: hdwy on outer 1/2-way: led 3f out: rdn over 2f out: drvn and hdd ins fnl f: kpt on* **50/1**
5003 **3** *4 ½* **Jennerous Blue**[8] 4765 3-8-5 **47**..................................(p) PaulQuinn 3 49
(D K Ivory) *hld up towards rr: hdwy on outer wl over 2f out: sn rdn and styd on wl ins fnl f: nrst fin* **8/1**
0454 **4** *nk* **New Code**[25] 4212 3-9-4 **60**.. DaneO'Neill 5 62
(W R Muir) *trckd ldrs on inner: hdwy over 3f out: rdn over 2f out and ev ch tl drvn and one pce appr fnl f* **16/1**
2142 **5** *2 ¾* **Dubawi King**[15] 4519 3-8-12 **54**.. RichardKingscote 10 52
(N Tinkler) *bhd: hdwy over 3f out: rdn along over 2f out: kpt on ins fnl f: nvr nr ldrs* **4/1**[3]
000 **6** *shd* **Namehim**[20] 4364 3-8-13 **55**.. AndreaAtzeni 14 53
(E F Vaughan) *hld up: hdwy on outer over 3f out: rdn and edgd lft over 2f out: sn no imp* **66/1**
-003 **7** *½* **Cheyenne Chant**[30] 4015 3-8-5 **47**.. FrannyNorton 7 44
(D O'Meara) *chsd ldrs: rdn along over 3f out: grad wknd* **10/1**
6606 **8** *1 ½* **Joe Rua (USA)**[26] 3273 3-7-11 **46** oh1........................ NatashaEaton(7) 9 41
(J Ryan) *led: rdn along and hdd 3f out: sn drvn and wknd 2f out* **66/1**
-004 **9** *3 ¾* **Footsie (IRE)**[19] 4408 3-9-1 **57**.. PaulMulrennan 12 47
(J G Given) *chsd ldrs: rdn along over 3f out: sn wknd* **16/1**
00-0 **10** *10* **Fireflash (IRE)**[27] 4156 3-8-1 **46**.. PatrickDonaghy(3) 8 22
(N Tinkler) *a towards rr* **33/1**
050- **11** *nk* **Always Roses**[267] 7450 3-7-13 **46** oh1........................ RosieJessop(5) 13 21
(C C Bealby) *prom: rdn along over 3f out: sn drvn and wknd* **50/1**
0056 **12** *nk* **Red Eddie**[22] 4295 3-8-7 **49**.. TedDurcan 6 24
(S Dow) *in tch: rdn along over 4f out and sn wknd* **25/1**
0-51 **13** *30* **Budva**[10] 4683 3-9-7 **63** 6ex.. JimmyQuinn 11 —
(H Morrison) *trckd ldr: effrt and cl up over 4f out: sn rdn and wknd over 3f out: bhd and eased fnl 2f* **7/2**[2]

3m 16.19s (8.89) **Going Correction** +0.60s/f (Yiel) 13 Ran SP% **118.7**
Speed ratings (Par 98): **98,97,95,94,93 93,92,92,89,84 84,83,66**
toteswingers:1&2 £22.10, 2&3 £31.30, 1&3 £4.30 CSF £148.75 CT £790.39 TOTE £3.50: £1.50, £10.60, £2.30; EX 137.60 Place 6: £700.21 Place 5: £637.50.
Owner J L Dunlop **Bred** Shadwell Estate Company Limited **Trained** Arundel, W Sussex

FOCUS
A poor staying handicap which was unevenly run. The form is rated around the third and fourth.
Dubawi King Official explanation: jockey said gelding was denied a clear run
Budva Official explanation: trainer had no explanation for the poor form shown

T/Plt: £1,953.30 to a £1 stake. Pool of £44,151.63 - 16.50 winning tickets. T/Qpdt: £162.50 to a £1 stake. Pool of £3,909.16 - 17.80 winning tickets. JR

5059 - 5062a (Foreign Racing) - See Raceform Interactive

CLAIREFONTAINE (R-H)
Friday, August 13

OFFICIAL GOING: Turf: very soft

5063a PRIX CINEMA MORNY CLUB DEAUVILLE (PRIX DES FUSCHIAS) (CLAIMER) (2YO FILLIES) (TURF) 1m
1:40 (12:00) 2-Y-O **£11,061** (£4,424; £3,318; £2,212; £1,106)

RPR
1 **Jetfire**[21] 4338 2-8-13 0.. ChristopheSoumillon 2 77
(P F I Cole) *towards rr initially along rail: rdn to ld on ins ent st 2 1/2f out whn field racd wd: sn swtchd towards stands' rail: qckng wl to go clr: r.o wl: comf* **6/4**[1]
2 *2* **Goldtara (FR)**[17] 2-8-6 0.. WilliamsSaraiva(3) 6 69
(Mme J Bidgood, Spain) **11/1**
3 *½* **A Moment With You (IRE)**[32] 2-8-9 0........................(b) MaximeGuyon 8 68
(K Borgel, France) **58/10**[3]
4 *2* **Livia Noire (FR)**[32] 2-8-9 0.. FlavienPrat 10 63
(P Bary, France) **43/10**[2]
5 *2* **Taysa (USA)**[10] 2-9-2 0.. GregoryBenoist 3 66
(X Nakkachdji, France) **11/1**
6 *3* **Bella Cara (FR)**[107] 2-8-4 0.. MatthieuAutier(5) 4 52
(M Boutin, France) **25/1**
7 *1* **Mindsia (FR)** 2-8-9 0.. IoritzMendizabal 9 50
(C Boutin, France) **15/1**
8 *3* **Holly Rose (FR)**[10] 2-8-8 0.. StevanBourgois(8) 5 50
(Robert Collet, France) **8/1**
9 *5* **Mensonge (IRE)** 2-8-8 0.. EddyHardouin(8) 1 39
(Robert Collet, France) **41/1**
10 *4* **Massilly (FR)** 2-8-9 0.. MickaelForest 11 24
(P Vidotto, France) **76/1**
11 **Mara Damdam (FR)** 2-9-2 0.. TonyPiccone 7 31
(C Boutin, France) **31/1**

1m 41.4s (101.40) **11 Ran SP% 118.3**
WIN (incl. 1 euro stake): 2.50. PLACES: 1.40, 2.40, 1.90. DF: 14.00. SF: 23.20.
Owner R A Instone **Bred** R A Instone **Trained** Whatcombe, Oxon

NOTEBOOK
Jetfire, who had been in the frame in all four starts in Britain, handled the step up in trip and soft ground to get off the mark under a good ride, picking up some decent prizemoney in this claimer.

4567 DONCASTER (L-H)
Saturday, August 14

OFFICIAL GOING: Good (good to firm in places)
Wind: Moderate across Weather: Cloudy - sunny periods

5064 CENTURION EUROPE H'CAP (DIV I) 7f
1:50 (1:50) (Class 5) (0-70,70) 3-Y-O+ **£2,914** (£867; £433; £216) **Stalls** High

Form RPR
0354 **1** **Sea Salt**[10] 4706 7-8-12 **60**.. LanceBetts(5) 3 67
(R E Barr) *mde all: rdn 2f out: hung bdly lft ins fnl f: drvn and kpt on wl towards fin* **10/1**
0-22 **2** *1* **Master Of Song**[11] 4687 3-8-3 **52**..................................(p) JimmyQuinn 9 54
(S R Bowring) *hld up in rr: pushed along 3f out: rdn over 2f out: gd hdwy over 1f out: drvn and styd on strly ins fnl f: tk 2nd on line* **6/1**[3]
1460 **3** *nse* **Sairaam (IRE)**[10] 4715 4-9-6 **63**.. RobertWinston 6 67
(C Smith) *a.p: chal 2f out: sn rdn and ev ch whn carried bdly lft ins fnl f: hld whn hmpd and no ex towards fin: lost 2nd on line* **6/1**[3]
4030 **4** *shd* **Piquante**[21] 4354 4-9-7 **64**.. SilvestreDeSousa 10 68
(N Tinkler) *hld up in rr: hdwy on outer 2f out: rdn to chse ldrs over 1f out: drvn and kpt on ins fnl f: nrst fin* **5/1**[2]
6100 **5** *1 ¾* **Piccolo Express**[17] 4485 4-8-10 **53**.. J-PGuillambert 7 52
(B P J Baugh) *chsd ldrs: hdwy 2f out: sn rdn: drvn and one pce fnl f* **22/1**
60 **6** *shd* **Bid For Gold**[30] 4063 6-8-13 **59**.. PatrickDonaghy(3) 8 58
(Jedd O'Keeffe) *hld up: effrt wl over 2f out and sn pushed along: rdn and hdwy wl over 1f out: kpt on same pce ins fnl f* **14/1**
0060 **7** *2* **Pearly Wey**[21] 4394 7-9-12 **69**.. PatrickMathers 4 63
(I W McInnes) *chsd ldrs: rdn along over 2f out: drvn over 1f out: no imp* **12/1**
4060 **8** *nk* **Southandwest (IRE)**[22] 4333 6-9-13 **70**..............................(p) LukeMorris 1 63
(A M Hales) *in tch: rdn along over 2f out: n.d* **18/1**
3300 **9** *2* **Bajan Flash**[71] 2700 3-9-6 **69**..............................(v[1]) RoystonFfrench 11 54
(B Smart) *hld up: a towards rr* **10/1**
2551 **10** *shd* **Rainy Night**[17] 4478 4-9-9 **66**..............................(p) JackMitchell 2 53
(R Hollinshead) *trckd ldng pair: effrt over 2f out: sn rdn and wknd wl over 1f out* **3/1**[1]
006 **11** *2 ¼* **Le Reve Royal**[6] 4868 4-8-5 **51** oh2........................ JamesSullivan(3) 5 32
(G R Oldroyd) *a in rr* **28/1**

1m 23.21s (-3.09) **Going Correction** -0.40s/f (Firm)
WFA 3 from 4yo+ 6lb 11 Ran SP% **115.8**
Speed ratings (Par 103): **101,99,99,99,97 97,95,94,92,92 89**
Tote Swingers: 1&2 £9.30, 1&3 £8.70, 2&3 £6.70 CSF £67.86 CT £401.93 TOTE £9.50: £2.20, £1.80, £2.30; EX 33.10.
Owner R E Barr **Bred** D R Tucker **Trained** Seamer, N Yorks
■ Stewards' Enquiry : Lance Betts four-day ban: careless riding (Aug 28-31)

FOCUS
A moderate handicap, rated around the third's recent efforts. Despite the runners sticking towards the stands' side early, the main action took place more towards the far side as the winner hung across.
Rainy Night Official explanation: trainer had no explanation for the poor form shown

5065 CROWNHOTEL-BAWTRY.COM MAIDEN STKS 6f
2:20 (2:24) (Class 5) 3-4-Y-O **£3,238** (£963; £481; £240) **Stalls** High

Form RPR
0 **1** **Ardent**[22] 4339 3-8-12 0.. NickyMackay 6 84+
(J H M Gosden) *qckly away: mde all: rdn over 1f out and kpt on strly* **7/2**[2]
2 **2** *4* **Al Muthanaa**[28] 4146 3-9-3 0.. LiamJones 4 76
(W J Haggas) *t.k.h: trckd ldrs: hdwy to chse wnr 2f out: rdn wl over 1f out: drvn and edgd lft ent fnl f: sn no imp* **8/13**[1]

2 **3** 1 1/2 **Self Employed**43 3621 3-9-3 0 RobertWinston 9 71
(G Woodward) *dwlt and in rr: hdwy and pushed along wl over 2f out: rdn wl over 1f out: kpt on ins fnl f* **13/2**3

5- **4** 2 3/4 **Tsar Bomba (USA)**446 2339 3-8-12 0 DeanHeslop(5) 2 62
(T D Barron) *chsd ldrs: rdn along over 2f out: drvn over 1f out and grad wknd* **20/1**

5 3 1/2 **Miss Blink** 3-8-12 0 SilvestreDeSousa 8 46
(R Bastiman) *chsd ldrs: outpcd and n.m.r 1/2-way: sn swtchd lft and rdn: kpt on appr fnl f* **50/1**

3004 **6** 1/2 **Nativity**14 4589 4-9-2 52 JimmyQuinn 3 45
(J L Spearing) *chsd ldrs: rdn along over 2f out: sn outpcd* **14/1**

-602 **7** 7 **Red Roar (IRE)**14 4584 3-8-7 53 MarkCoumbe(5) 11 22
(A Berry) *chsd ldrs: rdn along 1/2-way: sn wknd* **20/1**

0 **8** 2 3/4 **Clearly Cryptonite (USA)**74 2627 3-9-3 0 LeeVickers 7 18
(T J Pitt) *sn rdn along and a in rr* **66/1**

0 **9** 2 1/4 **Premier Contender (IRE)**22 4339 3-8-12 0 MichaelO'Connell(5) 10 11
(D Nicholls) *cl up: rdn wl over 2f out: sn wknd* **22/1**

00 **10** *shd* **Barton Bounty**15 4556 3-9-0 0 JamesSullivan(3) 5 11
(P D Niven) *sn outpcd and wl bhd fr 1/2-way* **100/1**

11 20 **Bigern** 3-9-3 0 RoystonFfrench 1 —
(M Mullineaux) *wnt lft s: sn outpcd and wl bhd fr 1/2-way* **66/1**

69.89 secs (-3.71) **Going Correction** -0.40s/f (Firm)
WFA 3 from 4yo 4lb **11** Ran SP% **123.9**
Speed ratings (Par 103): **108,102,100,97,92 91,82,78,75,75 48**
Tote Swingers: 1&2 £1.10, 1&3 £3.20, 2&3 £2.00 CSF £6.00 TOTE £4.50: £1.40, £1.02, £2.40; EX 6.70.
Owner Cheveley Park Stud **Bred** Cheveley Park Stud Ltd **Trained** Newmarket, Suffolk

FOCUS
An uncompetitive maiden with little depth. The form is taken at face value, with the winner a big improver.
Premier Contender(IRE) Official explanation: jockey said gelding hung left throughout

5066 ROYAL BRITISH LEGION E B F MAIDEN FILLIES' STKS 1m (S)
2:50 (2:54) (Class 5) 2-Y-O £3,238 (£963; £481; £240) Stalls High

Form RPR

2 **1** **Blue Bunting (USA)**14 4595 2-9-0 0 AhmedAjtebi 1 89+
(Mahmood Al Zarooni) *cl up on outer: led 3f out: rdn 2f out: drvn and hdd jst ins fnl f: rallied to ld last 50yds* **6/4**1

2 1/2 **Midnight Caller** 2-9-0 0 NickyMackay 11 89+
(J H M Gosden) *trckd ldrs: hdwy to chse ldr wl over 2f out: rdn to chal over 1f out: led jst ins fnl f: edgd lft then jinked rt and hdd last 50yds* **5/1**3

0 **3** 11 **Slight Advantage (IRE)**31 4021 2-9-0 0 LukeMorris 7 64
(C G Cox) *a.p: rdn along wl over 2f out: drvn over 1f out: kpt on same pce* **66/1**

4 *nk* **Alareen (USA)** 2-9-0 0 (t) DaraghO'Donohoe 9 64+
(Saeed Bin Suroor) *s.i.s and bhd: hdwy over 2f out: swtchd outside and rdn over 1f out: styd on ins fnl f* **6/1**

5 3/4 **Miss Villefranche** 2-9-0 0 HayleyTurner 4 61
(M L W Bell) *sltly hmpd s: in tch: hdwy to chse ldrs 3f out: rdn along over 2f out: drvn wl over 1f out and kpt on same pce* **20/1**

0 **6** 1 1/4 **Sokolka**22 4338 2-9-0 0 RobertWinston 13 59
(T D Easterby) *led: rdn along 1/2-way: hdd 3f out: sn drvn and grad wknd* **66/1**

4 **7** 1 **Phoenix Flame**11 4668 2-9-0 0 AndrewMullen 2 56
(A J McCabe) *in tch: hdwy to chse ldrs 1/2-way: rdn along wl over 2f out and grad wknd* **12/1**

8 1 1/4 **Chesnut Coffee** 2-9-0 0 LiamJones 8 54+
(D M Simcock) *midfield: hdwy and in tch 3f out: rdn over 2f out and sn wknd* **33/1**

0 **9** 3/4 **Rudegirl (IRE)**21 4392 2-9-0 0 SilvestreDeSousa 12 52
(N Tinkler) *a towards rr* **28/1**

10 1/2 **Palitana (USA)** 2-9-0 0 SaleemGolam 5 51
(J H M Gosden) *dwlt and in rr: hdwy to chse ldrs 1/2-way: rdn and hung lft 3f out: sn lost pl and bhd* **3/1**2

0 **11** 3/4 **Princesse Fleur**35 3915 2-9-0 0 JimmyQuinn 10 49
(M J Scudamore) *chsd ldrs: rdn along 1/2-way: sn wknd* **100/1**

12 2 3/4 **Lady Chloe** 2-9-0 0 LeeVickers 3 43
(P A Kirby) *hmpd and wnt lft s: towards rr: hdwy to chse ldrs 1/2-way: rdn along over 3f out and sn wknd* **100/1**

13 12 **Karmarouge (IRE)** 2-9-0 0 (t) RoystonFfrench 6 17
(B S Rothwell) *wnt lft s: a towards rr* **100/1**

000 **14** 1 1/4 **Be My Spy**18 4447 2-8-9 42 TobyAtkinson(5) 14 14
(P Salmon) *in tch: rdn along 1/2-way and sn wknd* **100/1**

1m 37.39s (-1.91) **Going Correction** -0.40s/f (Firm) 2y crse rec **14** Ran SP% **121.7**
Speed ratings (Par 91): **93,92,81,81,80 79,78,76,76,75 74,72,60,58**
Tote Swingers: 1&2 £1.90, 1&3 £36.20, 2&3 £51.50 CSF £9.00 TOTE £2.10: £1.10, £2.10, £15.50; EX 7.10.
Owner Godolphin **Bred** B M Kelley **Trained** Newmarket, Suffolk

FOCUS
A fair juvenile fillies' maiden. The first pair dominated and finished a long way clear.

NOTEBOOK
Blue Bunting(USA) just looked held by the runner-up for most of the final furlong, but her previous experience was a notable advantage as she found extra to get up near the line. She ran with promise over 7f on debut at Newmarket a fortnight earlier and this extra furlong looked sure to suit. She ultimately needed every yard to score and she looks a useful middle-distance performer in the making. This also pays a compliment to her impressive debut conqueror Theysken's Theory, who could be bound for the Fillies' Mile next month. (tchd 11-8 and 7-4)
Midnight Caller ◆ looked her stable's first string on jockey bookings, but was weaker in the market than stablemate Palitana. She knew her job as she was never far away and was able to bag the stands' rail when locking horns with the winner. She appeared to be holding that rival half a furlong out and her rider appeared the more confident, but she jinked right near the finish and threw it away. That had to be down to her inexperience and it was nearing the paddick exit, so this choicely bred newcomer shouldn't be long in making amends. (op 11-2 tchd 13-2)
Slight Advantage(IRE) didn't get a great run early on her debut at Kempton a month previously and, showing the clear benefit of that outing, ran a much improved race over this extra furlong. She should go forward again for the run.
Alareen(USA) ◆ hails from a decent middle-distance family. She missed the break, but there was a lot to like about the way she finished under an educational ride. She is bred to come into her own next year, but she could well find an opening in the coming weeks, especially if faced with slightly easier ground. (op 8-1)
Miss Villefranche has a pedigree that suggests a mix of speed and stamina. She looked to have inherited more of the staying side of the family, however, and this was a pleasing introduction. (op 18-1)
Palitana(USA) is a half-sister to 2,000 Guineas winner Footstepsinthesand and a winner over 2m. She made a sluggish start, though, and ultimately proved far too green to show her true colours. Expect her to know more next time. (op 5-2)

Be My Spy Official explanation: vet said filly finished lame

5067 CENTURION EUROPE H'CAP (DIV II) 7f
3:25 (3:25) (Class 5) (0-70,70) 3-Y-O+ £2,914 (£867; £433; £216) Stalls High

Form RPR

0065 **1** **Commando Scott (IRE)**15 4547 9-8-10 60 NeilFarley(7) 4 73
(D Carroll) *cl up: led after 3f: rdn along 2f out: hdd and drvn over 1f out: rallied to ld again last 100yds* **6/1**3

0322 **2** 3/4 **El Dececy (USA)**57 3149 6-9-5 62 RobertWinston 8 73
(J Balding) *led 3f: cl up tl rdn to ld again over 1f out: drvn and edgd lft ins fnl f: hdd and nt qckn fnl 100yds* **7/2**1

0420 **3** 3/4 **Elijah Pepper (USA)**16 4515 5-9-1 63 DeanHeslop(5) 3 72
(T D Barron) *trckd ldrs: hdwy over 2f out: rdn to chse ldng pair ent fnl f: sn drvn and kpt on* **4/1**2

5504 **4** 3 1/2 **Nacho Libre**15 4555 5-9-6 66 (b) JamesSullivan(3) 1 66
(M W Easterby) *trckd ldrs: effrt 3f out: rdn over 2f out: edgd rt and drvn over 1f out on same pce* **7/1**

-050 **5** 1 3/4 **Olympic Dream**20 4404 4-9-3 65 MichaelO'Connell(5) 6 60
(M Herrington) *chsd ldrs: rdn along over 2f out: swtchd lft and drvn over 1f out: no imp* **25/1**

4436 **6** 1 **Powerful Pierre**3 4939 3-8-12 64 (vt) PatrickDonaghy(3) 9 54+
(Jedd O'Keeffe) *s.i.s and bhd: rdn over 2f out: sme late hdwy* **8/1**

0066 **7** 3 1/2 **The Scorching Wind (IRE)**48 3483 4-9-13 70 (t) RoystonFfrench 10 53+
(S C Williams) *v.s.a: a bhd* **7/2**1

5500 **8** 4 1/2 **Royal Patriot (IRE)**42 3682 3-8-7 56 SilvestreDeSousa 2 25
(Paul Green) *t.k.h: chsd ldrs: rdn along wl over 2f out and sn wknd* **20/1**

0203 **9** 6 **Shannon Golden**39 3768 4-8-8 51 oh2 JimmyQuinn 5 —
(S R Bowring) *chsd ldrs: rdn along wl over 2f out: sn wknd* **10/1**

1m 23.04s (-3.26) **Going Correction** -0.40s/f (Firm)
WFA 3 from 4yo+ 6lb **9** Ran SP% **120.0**
Speed ratings (Par 103): **102,101,100,96,94 93,89,84,77**
Tote Swingers: 1&2 £7.20, 1&3 £32.90, 2&3 £2.00 CSF £28.49 CT £96.88 TOTE £7.60: £2.40, £1.40, £1.60; EX 30.10.
Owner Mrs Ann Morris **Bred** Noel Finegan **Trained** Sledmere, E Yorks

FOCUS
This second division of the 7f handicap was stronger than the first, and worked out at a length faster. Coincidently, it was another race where the first two ended up more towards the far side. The form looks sound.
Powerful Pierre Official explanation: jockey said gelding missed the break
The Scorching Wind(IRE) Official explanation: jockey said gelding missed the break
Royal Patriot(IRE) Official explanation: jockey said gelding ran too free
Shannon Golden Official explanation: jockey said gelding hit its head on leaving stalls

5068 CLOSE BUILDING SERVICES, DONCASTER H'CAP 7f
4:00 (4:03) (Class 2) (0-105,100) 4-Y-O+ £9,714 (£2,890; £1,444; £721) Stalls High

Form RPR

0331 **1** **Smarty Socks (IRE)**21 4394 6-8-6 85 SilvestreDeSousa 12 96
(D O'Meara) *trckd ldrs: smooth hdwy over 2f out: led wl over 1f out: rdn ent fnl f and kpt on strly* **11/2**2

2060 **2** 1 1/4 **Swift Gift**21 4358 5-9-4 97 RobertWinston 2 105
(B J Meehan) *midfield: hdwy over 2f out: rdn to chal wl over 1f out and ev ch tl drvn ins fnl f and kpt on same pce* **11/2**2

0000 **3** *nk* **Spirit Of Sharjah (IRE)**7 4843 5-8-12 98 AdamBeschizza(7) 1 105
(Miss J Feilden) *hld up in rr: hdwy on outer over 2f out: rdn to chse ldrs over 1f out: drvn and kpt on ins fnl f* **9/1**

230 **4** 1 1/2 **Flowing Cape (IRE)**21 4354 5-8-3 82 LukeMorris 8 85
(R Hollinshead) *chsd ldrs: rdn along and sltly outpcd 2f out: drvn and kpt on ins fnl f* **16/1**

0000 **5** 3/4 **Axiom**36 3869 6-9-7 100 J-PGuillambert 5 101
(L M Cumani) *midfield: hdwy to chse ldrs 3f out: rdn wl over 1f out: sn edgd rt and one pce fnl f* **12/1**

-025 **6** 1 3/4 **Horatio Carter**21 4370 5-8-10 89 (p) JimmyQuinn 4 85
(K A Ryan) *hld up: hdwy over 2f out: rdn to chse ldrs wl over 1f out: sn drvn and one pce* **12/1**

0600 **7** 1/2 **Dubai Dynamo**7 4816 5-8-13 95 JamesSullivan(3) 3 90
(Mrs R A Carr) *hld up and bhd: hdwy wl over 1f out: sn rdn and kpt on ins fnl f: nt rch ldrs* **18/1**

4205 **8** 1/2 **Aldermoor (USA)**43 3619 4-8-7 86 SaleemGolam 6 80
(S C Williams) *prom: hdwy to ld over 2f out: rdn and hdd wl over 1f out: sn drvn and wknd ent fnl f* **25/1**

-60 **9** *nk* **Decent Fella (IRE)**21 4358 4-8-2 86 SimonPearce(5) 7 79
(A M Balding) *hld up in tch: effrt 3f out: sn rdn along and wkng whn n.m.r wl over 1f out* **4/1**1

0303 **10** 4 1/2 **Bonnie Charlie**14 4569 4-9-5 98 LiamJones 13 79
(W J Haggas) *led: rdn along and hdd over 2f out: sn wknd* **12/1**

1033 **11** *shd* **Opus Maximus (IRE)**13 4617 5-8-9 88 RoystonFfrench 9 68
(M Johnston) *hld up in tch: pushed along 3f out: rdn over 2f out and sn wknd* **17/2**3

5-01 **12** 23 **Arteus**37 3833 4-8-2 88 (b) LewisWalsh(7) 10 6
(Jane Chapple-Hyam) *cl up: rdn along over 2f out: wkng whn sddle slipped and eased wl over 1f out* **10/1**

1m 21.92s (-4.38) **Going Correction** -0.40s/f (Firm) **12** Ran SP% **118.5**
Speed ratings (Par 109): **109,107,107,105,104 102,102,101,101,96 95,69**
Tote Swingers: 1&2 £5.20, 1&3 £10.30, 2&3 £10.20 CSF £34.34 CT £241.35 TOTE £5.00: £1.90, £2.40, £2.70; EX 32.60.
Owner R G Fell **Bred** Mick McGinn **Trained** Nawton, N Yorks
■ Beauchamp Xerxes was withdrawn (14/1, unruly in stalls). Deduct 5p in the £ under R4.

FOCUS
A very competitive handicap. It was run at a solid pace and the form should work out.The first two posted personal bests.

NOTEBOOK
Smarty Socks(IRE) didn't give away too much ground from the gates as can often be the case, and followed up his York success last month off a 5lb higher mark. He had his ideal conditions here, was well drawn and again partnered by the bang in-form Silvestre De Sousa. Obviously thriving at present, this rates a career-best display and there is every chance he can go in again despite another rise in the weights. (op 5-1)
Swift Gift posted his best outing since resuming on the all-weather earlier this term. He deserves a little extra credit, as he had to race wide, and should find another winning turn before the season's end. (op 7-1 tchd 5-1)
Spirit Of Sharjah(IRE) got a very patient ride and came mid-track with his challenge. He ran on strongly inside the final furlong. This was one of his better efforts and he just looks held by the handicapper. (op 11-1)
Flowing Cape(IRE) ran a solid race in defeat and can certainly find less competitive assignments from his current mark. (op 18-1 tchd 20-1)
Axiom ◆ really wants more cut in the ground and there was enough in his display here to think he will come good when faced with a suitably softer surface. (op 11-1 tchd 10-1)

Decent Fella(IRE) didn't get a great passage through the race, but he found nothing when put under maximum pressure and something might have gone amiss. (op 5-1 tchd 6-1)

Opus Maximus(IRE) Official explanation: jockey said gelding missed the break

Arteus Official explanation: jockey said saddle slipped

5069 UNIVERSAL RECYCLING H'CAP 5f

4:35 (4:35) (Class 3) (0-90,85) 3-Y-O+

£6,231 (£1,866; £933; £467; £233; £117) **Stalls** High

Form				RPR
6520	**1**		**Tabaret**[8] 4806 7-9-10 **85** (v[1]) J-PGuillambert 2 (R M Whitaker) *racd wd: chsd ldrs: hdwy wl over 1f out: rdn to ld jst ins fnl f: drvn out* **10/1**	94
0364	**2**	½	**Doctor Parkes**[8] 4798 4-9-9 **84** RobertWinston 11 (E J Alston) *trckd ldrs: hdwy over 1f out: rdn and styd on to have ev ch ins fnl f: drvn and nt qckn towards fin* **15/2**	91
2030	**3**	¾	**The Nifty Fox**[7] 4832 6-9-10 **85** DavidNolan 3 (T D Easterby) *trckd ldrs: hdwy over 1f out: rdn to chal ent fnl f and ev ch tl drvn and nt qckn last 75yds* **7/1**[3]	89
1252	**4**	¾	**Brierty (IRE)**[14] 4583 4-8-12 **80** NeilFarley[(7)] 12 (D Carroll) *hld up: swtchd lft and hdwy over 1f out: sn rdn and styd on ins fnl f: nrst fin* **4/1**[1]	82
2201	**5**	½	**Solemn**[13] 4625 5-9-9 **84** (b) NickyMackay 4 (J M Bradley) *a.p: effrt wl over 1f out: sn rdn and ev ch tl grad wknd ins fnl f* **6/1**[2]	84
0110	**6**	¾	**Ryan Style (IRE)**[29] 4118 4-8-13 **81** AdamBeschizza[(7)] 6 (Mrs L Williamson) *chsd ldrs: hdwy whn n.m.r over 1f out: sn rdn and kpt on same pce ins fnl f* **14/1**	78
3110	**7**	shd	**Nickel Silver**[8] 4798 5-9-5 **80** (v) RoystonFfrench 13 (B Smart) *led: rdn over 1f out: hdd & wknd ent fnl f* **10/1**	77
6030	**8**	¾	**Sir Geoffrey (IRE)**[29] 4090 4-8-7 **71** (b) PatrickDonaghy[(3)] 5 (J A Glover) *trckd ldrs: hdwy and cl up 1/2-way: rdn and ev ch over 1f out: drvn and wknd ent fnl f* **33/1**	65
6210	**9**	nk	**Frognal (IRE)**[3] 4942 4-8-13 **77** (b) JamesSullivan[(3)] 9 (Mrs R A Carr) *dwlt: sltly hmpd and swtchd rt to stands' rail sn after s: a towards rr* **12/1**	70
0546	**10**	2¾	**Le Toreador**[24] 4243 5-9-4 **84** (tp) MichaelO'Connell[(5)] 10 (K A Ryan) *cl up: effrt 2f out: sn rdn and ev ch tl drvn and wknd ent fnl f* **8/1**	67
6110	**11**	1¼	**Atlantic Beach**[29] 4118 5-9-3 **78** SilvestreDeSousa 7 (D O'Meara) *in tch: rdn along 2f out: sn drvn and wknd* **15/2**	57
6550	**12**	8	**Canadian Danehill (IRE)**[20] 4401 8-9-7 **82** (p) HayleyTurner 1 (R M H Cowell) *racd wd: chsd ldrs to 1/2-way: sn wknd and bhd* **18/1**	32

57.31 secs (-3.19) **Going Correction** -0.40s/f (Firm) **12** Ran SP% **122.2**

Speed ratings (Par 107): **109,108,107,105,105 103,103,102,101,97 95,82**

Tote Swingers: 1&2 £16.40, 1&3 £12.90, 2&3 £12.10 CSF £85.68 CT £579.12 TOTE £15.70: £4.20, £3.20, £1.90; EX 59.80.

Owner T L Adams **Bred** The P B T Group And G F Pemberton **Trained** Scarcroft, W Yorks

FOCUS

Not the strongest of sprint handicaps for the class, but it was still typically competitive and the form is fair for the grade. There didn't appear to be any bias with the draw as the pace was solid and the winner came widest of all.

NOTEBOOK

Tabaret's hopes rested on a change of headgear having the desired effect. It did just that as he ran out a determined winner, despite getting no cover through the race, and rates value for a bit further as he was idling near the finish. His two wins this year have been at this venue and he deserves a crack at the Portland back here next month. (op 9-1)

Doctor Parkes ran right up to his mark at Musselburgh last time and this represents another improved effort, but he is just struggling to find his ideal trip this season. He also looks well worth a shot at the Portland, though, as the distance there could prove to be spot on for him and his course form figures now read 32. (tchd 8-1)

The Nifty Fox enjoyed the decent pace on this drop back to the minimum, but continues his battle with the handicapper. (tchd 15-2)

Brierty(IRE) caught the eye staying on strongly towards the finish and looks worth another try over 6f again. She helps to set the level. (op 9-2 tchd 5-1)

Solemn was 3lb higher than when beating a subsequent winner at Newbury 13 days earlier and he ran a solid race in defeat. (tchd 11-2)

Ryan Style(IRE) returned to something near his best.

Nickel Silver again tired nearing the business end having shown real dash on the stands' rail.

5070 ZESTBARANDGRILL.COM H'CAP 1m 6f 132y

5:10 (5:10) (Class 4) (0-85,82) 3-Y-O+ **£5,180** (£1,541; £770; £384) **Stalls** Low

Form				RPR
5260	**1**		**Crocus Rose**[28] 4125 4-9-7 **75** JimmyQuinn 3 (H J L Dunlop) *hld up in tch: hdwy over 3f out: trckd ldr 2f out: rdn to ld appr fnl f: kpt on wl* **8/1**	84
4023	**2**	2¼	**Akbabend**[11] 4671 4-10-0 **82** (b[1]) RoystonFfrench 2 (M Johnston) *trckd ldr: cl up 4f out: led 3f out: rdn and hdd appr fnl f: sn drvn and kpt on same pce* **7/2**[2]	88
2132	**3**	shd	**Forrest Flyer (IRE)**[26] 4190 6-9-4 **72** LNewman 4 (J S Goldie) *trckd ldrs on inner: swtchd rt and hdwy over 3f out: rdn to chse ldng pair over 1f out: drvn and kpt on ins fnl f* **5/1**[3]	78
3131	**4**	1¾	**Simple Jim (FR)**[14] 4604 6-8-11 **65** SilvestreDeSousa 1 (D O'Meara) *hld up in rr: hdwy on outer 3f out: rdn to chse ldrs over 1f out: drvn ent fnl f and sn no imp* **11/8**[1]	69+
123	**5**	3¾	**Kames Park (IRE)**[22] 4348 8-9-2 **75** MarkCoumbe[(5)] 7 (R C Guest) *dwlt and swtchd lft s: hld up in rr: hdwy on inner 3f out: chsd ldrs 2f out: sn rdn and wknd over 1f out* **11/1**	74
1403	**6**	5	**Hallstatt (IRE)**[50] 3398 4-8-10 **69** DeclanCannon[(5)] 5 (J Mackie) *trckd ldrs: effrt over 3f out: rdn wl over 2f out: sn drvn and grad wknd* **8/1**	61
30-0	**7**	6	**Motafarred (IRE)**[10] 4713 8-9-4 **72** PatrickMathers 6 (Miss T Jackson) *led: rdn along 4f out: hdd 3f out: sn drvn and wknd* **33/1**	56

3m 6.07s (-1.33) **Going Correction** -0.275s/f (Firm) **7** Ran SP% **114.5**

Speed ratings (Par 105): **90,88,88,87,85 83,79**

Tote Swingers: 1&2 £4.80, 1&3 £6.00, 2&3 £3.30 CSF £36.06 TOTE £10.20: £3.10, £2.40; EX 53.70.

Owner When Harry Met Rosie Partnership **Bred** Biddestone Stud **Trained** Lambourn, Berks

FOCUS

Not a bad staying handicap for the class, but a bit of a muddling race. The second and third set the standard.

5071 LOVELL RESPOND APPRENTICE H'CAP 1m 2f 60y

5:45 (5:46) (Class 5) (0-75,75) 4-Y-O+ **£2,590** (£770; £385; £192) **Stalls** Low

Form				RPR
-013	**1**		**Mistoffelees**[36] 3847 4-9-3 **73** TalibHussain[(5)] 6 (L M Cumani) *in tch on inner: hdwy 3f out: cl up over 1f out: rdn to chal ent fnl f: styd on to ld last 100yds* **4/1**[1]	83+
1124	**2**	1¼	**Marjury Daw (IRE)**[17] 4492 4-9-9 **74** RossAtkinson 2 (J G Given) *led 1f: trckd ldr tl led again over 2f out: rdn wl over 1f out: drvn ins fnl f: hdd and no ex last 100yds* **17/2**	81
4122	**3**	1	**Bavarica**[12] 4657 8-9-7 **75** AdamBeschizza[(3)] 3 (Miss J Feilden) *trckd ldrs: hdwy 3f out: rdn to chal over 1f out: drvn and ev ch ins fnl f: one pce last 100yds* **9/1**	80
5000	**4**	2¼	**Rosbay (IRE)**[14] 4603 6-9-9 **74** LanceBetts 9 (T D Easterby) *hld up in rr: hdwy 3f out: rdn to chse ldrs wl over 1f out: drvn and kpt on ins fnl f* **9/2**[2]	75+
/1-0	**5**	½	**More Than Many (USA)**[20] 4404 4-9-4 **72** LeeTopliss[(3)] 7 (R A Fahey) *trckd ldrs: effrt and hdwy 3f out: rdn over 2f out and sn one pce* **4/1**[1]	72
1012	**6**	1¼	**King Zeal (IRE)**[9] 4752 6-9-0 **70** JamesRogers[(5)] 5 (B D Leavy) *led after 1f: rdn along over 3f out: hdd over 2f out and grad wknd* **11/2**	67
6111	**7**	12	**Count Ceprano (IRE)**[17] 4481 6-9-1 **66** SimonPearce 8 (J Pearce) *hld up towards rr: effrt and sme hdwy 3f out: sn rdn and wknd* **5/1**[3]	39
3010	**8**	20	**Border Owl (IRE)**[29] 4093 5-9-3 **68** TobyAtkinson 4 (P Salmon) *hld up: a in rr* **25/1**	1

2m 7.51s (-1.89) **Going Correction** -0.275s/f (Firm) **8** Ran SP% **114.6**

Speed ratings (Par 103): **103,102,101,99,99 98,88,72**

Tote Swingers: 1&2 £7.00, 1&3 £6.00, 2&3 £7.50 CSF £38.18 CT £287.36 TOTE £3.90: £1.60, £2.10, £3.30; EX 34.10 Place 6: £58.00 Place 5: £20.90..

Owner Mrs Luca Cumani **Bred** The Kingwood Partnership **Trained** Newmarket, Suffolk

■ Stewards' Enquiry : Talib Hussain one-day ban: used whip down shoulder in the forehand without giving colt time to respond (Aug 28)

FOCUS

This was a very competitive handicap of its type, run at a sound pace. The winer resumed his progression and the next two also ran as well as ever.

Count Ceprano(IRE) Official explanation: jockey said gelding lost its action

Border Owl(IRE) Official explanation: jockey said gelding finished lame

T/Plt: £64.50 to a £1 stake. Pool of £67,708 - 765.22 winning tickets. T/Qpdt: £21.50 to a £1 stake. Pool of £4,114 - 141.10 winning tickets. JR

4926 LINGFIELD (L-H)

Saturday, August 14

OFFICIAL GOING: Turf course - good changing to soft after race 3 (6.30); all-weather - standard

5072 BETFAIR RACING EXCELLENCE APPRENTICE TRAINING SERIES H'CAP 1m 2f (P)

5:30 (5:31) (Class 6) (0-62,62) 3-Y-O+ **£2,047** (£604; £302) **Stalls** Low

Form				RPR
-533	**1**		**Josr's Magic (IRE)**[25] 4227 6-9-10 **56** AmyScott 6 (P R Hedger) *stdd s: t.k.h: rapid hdwy to chse ldr over 8f out tl led 5f out: mde rest: clr 3f out: rdn over 1f out: kpt on wl* **7/1**	65
0203	**2**	1¾	**Amends (USA)**[14] 4586 3-9-0 **60** IanBurns[(5)] 2 (J R Best) *in tch in midfield: rdn and swtchd rt and bmpd rival 3f out: chsd clr wnr over 2f out: kpt on u.p fnl f: nvr gng pce to rch wnr* **12/1**	66
0445	**3**	1¾	**Aurora Sky (IRE)**[23] 4295 4-9-10 **59** NathanAlison[(3)] 4 (J Akehurst) *t.k.h: hld up towards rr: hdwy over 3f out: rdn and chsd ldng trio ent fnl 2f: wnt 3rd 1f out: styd on steadily fnl f: nt rch ldrs* **6/1**[3]	61
00	**4**	3¼	**Search For The Key (USA)**[22] 4327 3-9-7 **62** (b[1]) DuilioDaSilva 1 (P F I Cole) *chsd ldr tl over 8f out: styd chsng ldrs: 3rd and stuggling u.p jst over 2f out and no ch w ldrs after: lost 3rd 1f out* **14/1**	58
3-24	**5**	2	**Privy Speech (IRE)**[25] 4229 3-9-2 **62** AlexEdwards[(5)] 10 (Rae Guest) *dwlt: racd off the pce in last pair: nt clr run wl over 2f out tl 2f out: rdn plugged on same pce after: nvr trbld ldrs* **16/1**	54
4232	**6**	6	**Rosy Dawn**[9] 4740 5-8-8 **45** MatthewCosham[(5)] 9 (J J Bridger) *led and crossed to rail: hdd 5f out: rdn 4f out: wknd u.p and slighlty hmpd bnd over 2f out: sn wl btn* **5/1**[2]	25
-110	**7**	¾	**Usquaebach**[69] 2792 3-9-7 **62** RyanClark 8 (M G Quinlan) *in tch in midfield: rdn and effrt to chse ldrs over 3f out: sn outpcd by wnr: wknd and wl btn fnl 2f* **7/2**[1]	40
0524	**8**	11	**Green Community (USA)**[28] 4156 3-9-7 **62** RyanPowell 3 (E F Vaughan) *in tch in midfield: nt clr run on inner and shuffled bk to rr 3f out: no ch after: wl bhd and eased ins fnl f* **10/1**	18
5154	**9**	6	**Dark Ranger**[35] 3894 4-10-0 **60** JohnFahy 7 (T J Pitt) *hld up towards rr: prog into midfield and rdn over 4f out: struggling whn bmpd ent fnl 3f: sn wl btn: eased ins fnl f: t.o: fin 10th: plcd 9th* **7/2**[1]	4
-306	**D**	10	**Generous Lad (IRE)**[5] 4912 7-8-13 **50** (p) MarkPower[(5)] 5 (A B Haynes) *dwlt: rdn along in last tl sddle slipped 6f out: continued on outer wout irons: fin 9th: disqualified* **25/1**	—

2m 6.42s (-0.18) **Going Correction** -0.10s/f (Stan)

WFA 3 from 4yo+ 9lb **10** Ran SP% **121.1**

Speed ratings (Par 101): **96,94,93,90,89 84,83,74,62,66**

Tote Swingers: 1&2 £11.30, 1&3 £8.00, 2&3 £11.90 CSF £90.85 CT £542.68 TOTE £11.30: £3.40, £4.30, £3.00; EX 89.80.

Owner Ken Tyre & Lee Tyre **Bred** Bryan Ryan **Trained** Dogmersfield, Hampshire

■ Stewards' Enquiry : Ian Burns two-day ban: careless riding (Aug 28-29)

FOCUS

Rain fell throughout the day and only stopped about half an hour before this modest opener. Rosy Dawn ensured a generous pace from the outset. The winner produced her best form since late 2008.

Generous Lad(IRE) Official explanation: jockey said saddle slipped

5073 EAST GRINSTEAD CLAIMING STKS 1m (P)
6:00 (6:01) (Class 6) 3-Y-O £1,706 (£503; £252) Stalls High

Form RPR

4620 1 **Syrian**[29] 4104 3-9-7 80 GeorgeBaker 8 82+
(M L W Bell) *stdd s: hld up in last trio: smooth hdwy on outer to trck ldrs on bit over 2f out: led over 1f out: sn qcknd wl clr: v easily* **11/4**[1]

2500 2 7 **Stef And Stelio**[28] 4133 3-9-7 65 (t) TadhgO'Shea 9 66
(G A Butler) *led for 1f: chsd ldr after: rdn and ev ch over 2f out: led 2f out tl hdd and nt pce of wnr over 1f out: no ch after but kpt on for clr 2nd* **28/1**

4000 3 2 **So Surreal (IRE)**[3] 4959 3-8-12 66 (b) PatDobbs 5 52
(G L Moore) *hld up towards rr: rdn and hdwy wl over 1f out: no ch w wnr but kpt on u.p to go modest 3rd ins fnl f: n.d* **14/1**

-062 4 nk **Sabatini (IRE)**[28] 4133 3-8-12 74 MickyFenton 2 54+
(J Pearce) *hld up in rr: hdwy but no ch w wnr whn nt clr run on inner over 1f out: swtchd rt ent fnl f: r.o to press for 3rd cl home: nvr trbld ldrs* **11/4**[1]

0030 5 1 ½ **Gra Adhmhar (IRE)**[30] 4058 3-9-3 65 JimCrowley 11 53
(D J Coakley) *bhd: effrt on outer whn wd bnd over 2f out: plugged on u.p but no ch w wnr* **16/1**

-000 6 nk **Rainsborough**[27] 3557 3-8-13 53 (p) JamesDoyle 7 49
(S Curran) *in tch: no ch w wnr but sme hdwy on inner wl over 1f out: plugged on same pce fnl f* **66/1**

0006 7 hd **Wigan Lane**[35] 3910 3-8-1 50 ow2 AndrewHeffernan(3) 3 39
(P Howling) *chsd ldrs: rdn and struggling wl over 2f out: outpcd and no ch w wnr fr over 1f out: plugged on same pce fnl f* **50/1**

0000 8 ¾ **Ultravox (USA)**[9] 4751 3-8-7 68 (b) RichardMullen 4 40
(B J Meehan) *in tch in midfield: rdn and nt qckn ent fnl 2f: hanging lft and wl btn ent fnl f* **13/2**[3]

6256 9 ¾ **Caldermud (IRE)**[10] 4714 3-8-13 73 SebSanders 6 45
(J R Best) *chsd ldr tl led after 1f: rdn over 2f out: hdd 2f out: sn no ch w wnr: wknd over 1f out: wl btn fnl f* **11/2**[2]

55 10 4 ½ **Daneside (IRE)**[10] 4718 3-8-6 0 JosephineBruning(7) 12 34
(W G Harrison) *stdd and dropped in bhd after s: a bhd: nt clr run and swtchd rt wl over 1f out: no prog and nvr on terms* **40/1**

0020 11 ½ **Takajan (IRE)**[13] 4618 3-8-13 64 TomMcLaughlin 10 33
(W M Brisbourne) *hld up in midfield on outer: effrt to chse ldrs over 2f out: wknd u.p 2f out: wl btn and eased ins fnl f* **10/1**

3065 12 3 **Transfixed (IRE)**[8] 4779 3-8-1 57 ow2 JohnFahy(5) 1 19
(P D Evans) *dwlt: sn bustled up to chse ldrs: struggling u.p over 2f out: wl bhd fnl f* **20/1**

1m 36.9s (-1.30) **Going Correction** -0.10s/f (Stan) 12 Ran SP% 117.8
Speed ratings (Par 98): **102,95,93,92,91 90,90,89,89,84 84,81**
Tote Swingers: 1&2 £15.90, 1&3 £13.30, 2&3 £26.30 CSF £96.28 TOTE £3.10: £1.10, £10.70, £4.50; EX 53.80.Syrian was claimed by Ian Williams for £12,000.
Owner Highclere Thoroughbred Racing (Donoghue) **Bred** Barry Walters **Trained** Newmarket, Suffolk

FOCUS
Nothing entered this claimer with recent winning form, and few got into it. The winner did it easily but there are doubts over the worth of the form.
Sabatini(IRE) Official explanation: jockey said filly was denied a clear run
Rainsborough Official explanation: jockey said gelding was denied a clear run

5074 EUROPEAN BREEDERS' FUND MAIDEN STKS 6f
6:30 (6:30) (Class 5) 2-Y-O £2,914 (£867; £433; £216) Stalls High

Form RPR

3 1 **Sharnberry**[17] 4471 2-8-12 0 KierenFallon 1 84+
(E A L Dunlop) *trckd ldng pair: wnt 2nd jst over 2f out: pushed into ld over 1f out: in command and r.o wl fnl f: easily* **4/5**[1]

0 2 3 **Hoot (IRE)**[43] 3624 2-9-3 0 TadhgO'Shea 4 80
(Saeed Bin Suroor) *chsd ldng trio: rdn and effrt over 1f out: chsd wnr 1f out: kpt on but no imp on wnr* **4/1**[3]

0 3 4 **Christmas Aria (IRE)**[28] 4131 2-9-3 0 SebSanders 7 68
(S Dow) *led tl 4f out: chsd wnr tl jst over 2f out: outpcd u.p over 1f out: no ch w wnr fnl f* **33/1**

2 4 1 ½ **Latin Lashes (USA)**[12] 4658 2-8-12 0 PatDobbs 3 59
(R Hannon) *w ldr tl led 4f out: rdn and hdd over 1f out: wknd qckly fnl f* **9/4**[2]

54 5 6 **Lord Of Persia (USA)**[17] 4477 2-9-3 0 JimCrowley 2 46
(R M Beckett) *swtchd rt after s: a towards rr: rdn and struggling over 2f out: wl btn over 1f out* **10/1**

0065 6 1 ¼ **Marmaduke**[35] 3913 2-8-12 45 JohnFahy(5) 6 42
(J J Bridger) *stdd s: sn wl outpcd and detached in last: passed btn horses ins fnl f: nvr on terms* **50/1**

0 7 ½ **Dorothy's Dancing (IRE)**[12] 4658 2-8-12 0 RichardMullen 5 35
(G L Moore) *stdd s: hld up in rr: sme hdwy int midfield 1/2-way: rdn and wl btn over 2f out* **25/1**

0 8 11 **Mi Sun Donk**[24] 4263 2-9-3 0 EddieCreighton 8 7
(B R Johnson) *t.k.h early: in tch tl swvd lft and lost pl over 4f out: rn green after and lost tch wl over 2f out* **50/1**

1m 12.95s (1.75) **Going Correction** +0.15s/f (Good) 8 Ran SP% 126.1
Speed ratings (Par 94): **94,90,84,82,74 73,72,57**
Tote Swingers: 1&2 £1.70, 1&3 £6.80, 2&3 £11.30 CSF £5.23 TOTE £2.00: £1.10, £1.20, £9.70; EX 4.50.
Owner St Albans Bloodstock LLP **Bred** Rabbah Bloodstock Limited **Trained** Newmarket, Suffolk

FOCUS
The going on the turf course had changed from good to firm to good to soft before racing on account of the appreciable rain in between. Following feedback from the riders after this maiden, it was further changed to soft.

NOTEBOOK
Sharnberry's fine Goodwood third on debut had already received two boosts with the fourth and sixth winning since. Still available at even-money in places mid-afternoon, confidence in her joining that list of scorers proved well founded, as Fallon didn't have to exert much effort to get her upsides the leader with over a furlong to travel. He settled the issue with a few shakes of the reins. A well-regarded filly with entries in a plethora of Tattersalls Auction races later this season, she may be aimed next at the Listed EBF Dick Poole Fillies' Stakes at Salisbury's early September meeting. Going as soft as this is not regarded as a prerequisite. (tchd 8-11)
Hoot(IRE) ◆'s challenge on debut at Haydock had ended almost as soon as it started after completely missing the break, but he got all the basics right this time. It's unlikely that racing wider than a smart-looking prospect made any difference to the outcome, but the ability to land a fair maiden, possibly around a tougher 6f, looks to be there. (op 6-1)
Christmas Aria(IRE) stepped up appreciably on his debut at this course last month, remaining thereabouts until giving way just before the furlong pole. The softened going didn't appear to inconvenience and he can be placed to advantage in handicaps once getting a mark after his next run.
Latin Lashes(USA) raced keen early and paid for it, fading out of matters pretty tamely in the end. A decent second on debut at Windsor, she can prove better than this effort again next time if more relaxed. (op 2-1 tchd 11-4 and 3-1 in a place)
Dorothy's Dancing(IRE) Official explanation: jockey said filly was unsuited by the good to soft ground

5075 TRYST - EAST GRINSTEAD'S ULTIMATE NIGHT CLUB (S) STKS 6f
7:00 (7:00) (Class 6) 3-Y-O+ £1,706 (£503; £252) Stalls High

Form RPR

1633 1 **Anjomarba (IRE)**[23] 4298 3-8-9 62 (p) JackDean(3) 2 63
(W G M Turner) *chsd ldr tl rdn to ld over 1f out: r.o wl and in command fnl 100yds: comf* **11/2**[3]

0002 2 2 ½ **Hart Of Gold**[8] 4790 6-9-2 48 (b) TomMcLaughlin 4 56
(R A Harris) *led and crossed to stands' rail: rdn and hdd over 1f out: no ex and btn ins fnl f* **8/1**

0052 3 hd **Timeteam (IRE)**[8] 4776 4-9-7 74 PatDobbs 5 60
(G L Moore) *s.i.s: bhd but in tch: rdn and effrt wl over 1f out: drvn and kpt on u.p fnl f: nvr gng pce to trble wnr* **13/8**[1]

0006 4 5 **Joss Stick**[8] 4778 5-8-13 39 (p) AndrewHeffernan(3) 7 39
(J J Bridger) *t.k.h early: chsd ldrs: swtchd lft and effrt u.p wl over 1f out: wknd ent fnl f* **50/1**

-000 5 1 **James Barrymore**[8] 4791 3-8-12 57 MickyFenton 6 35
(Miss J R Tooth) *awkward leaving stalls: bhd: rdn and no prog whn hung lft over 1f out: n.d* **16/1**

0006 6 1 ½ **Dynamo Dave (USA)**[8] 4776 5-8-11 44 LeeNewnes(5) 3 31
(M D I Usher) *in tch in midfield: rdn and struggling over 2f out: wl btn over 1f out* **33/1**

4000 7 nse **Twilight Star (IRE)**[10] 4690 6-8-11 64 (b) JohnFahy(5) 1 31
(R A Teal) *wnt bdly lft s and slowly away: reminders sn after: hdwy to chse ldrs after 2f: rdn and no rspnse 2f out: sn wknd: wl btn fnl f* **9/4**[2]

0004 8 nk **Briannsta (IRE)**[8] 4789 8-8-11 43 SophieDoyle(5) 8 30
(J E Long) *in tch in midfield tl n.m.r on rail and lost pl after 1f: struggling u.p 2f out: sn wl btn* **14/1**

1m 13.07s (1.87) **Going Correction** +0.30s/f (Good)
WFA 3 from 4yo+ 4lb 8 Ran SP% 112.8
Speed ratings (Par 101): **99,95,95,88,87 85,85,84**
Tote Swingers: 1&2 £5.90, 1&3 £1.50, 2&3 £4.00 CSF £46.95 TOTE £5.50: £1.40, £2.70, £1.02; EX 47.30.Anjomarba was bought by Brett Johnson for 6,600gns.
Owner Marbary Partnership **Bred** Tally-Ho Stud **Trained** Sigwells, Somerset

FOCUS
An ordinary seller in which the first two home got over to the stands' rail at an early stage. The form is rated around them, with the favourite disappointing.

5076 CORAL.CO.UK H'CAP 6f
7:30 (7:33) (Class 5) (0-70,70) 4-Y-O+ £2,388 (£529; £529) Stalls High

Form RPR

0221 1 **Titus Gent**[14] 4589 5-9-4 67 KirstyMilczarek 8 73
(R A Harris) *broke wl and crossed to r on stands' rail: mde all: rdn ent fnl f: kpt on wl* **3/1**[2]

6060 2 ½ **White Shift (IRE)**[6] 4875 4-8-11 65 KierenFox(5) 9 69
(P Howling) *hld up in tch towards rr on stands' rail: hdwy and chsng ldrs whn n.m.r over 1f out tl ins fnl f: styd on u.p fnl 100yds* **14/1**

5406 2 dht **Commandingpresence (USA)**[14] 4589 4-8-1 55 oh4 ow4 JohnFahy(5) 2 59
(J J Bridger) *w ldr: rdn over 1f out: unable qck and a jst hld fnl f* **25/1**

5006 4 nk **Desert Icon (IRE)**[15] 4551 4-9-0 70 (v) HarryBentley(7) 4 73
(W J Knight) *taken down early: t.k.h: chsd ldrs: rdn and effrt wl over 1f out: drvn and styd on same pce fnl f* **9/4**[1]

6450 5 ¾ **Memphis Man**[7] 4834 7-8-9 65 KevinLundie(7) 10 66
(P D Evans) *taken down early and led to post: in tch in rr: pushed along and hdwy over 1f out: styd on same pce and no imp fnl 100yds* **15/2**

3066 6 ¾ **Charles Darwin (IRE)**[6] 4875 7-9-1 64 GeorgeBaker 7 62
(M Blanshard) *chsd ldrs: rdn and unable qck wl over 1f out: styd on same pce u.p fnl f* **9/2**[3]

4020 7 1 ¾ **Talamahana**[9] 4735 5-8-1 55 (v) AmyBaker(5) 5 48
(A B Haynes) *v.s.a and sn pushed along: hdwy and in tch 1/2-way: no imp u.p fr over 1f out* **14/1**

5305 8 ½ **Lord Deevert**[8] 4790 5-8-6 58 ow1 (p) JackDean(3) 3 49
(W G M Turner) *in tch: rdn and unable qck ent fnl 2f: no prog and btn 1f out: eased wl ins fnl f* **8/1**

1m 13.6s (2.40) **Going Correction** +0.30s/f (Good) 8 Ran SP% 114.0
Speed ratings (Par 103): **96,95,95,94,93 92,90,89**
Place: White Shift £6.10 Commandingpresence £8.20. Ex: Titus Gent-WS £13.70 TG-C £28.90. Tricast: TG-WS-C £441.20 TG-C-WS £456.26 Tote Swingers: TG&WS £12.90, TG&C £17.10, WS&C £30.00. TOTE £3.00: £1.10.
Owner Alan & Adam Darlow, A Darlow Productions **Bred** Heather Raw **Trained** Earlswood, Monmouths

FOCUS
A slower winning time was recorded than in the earlier seller and juvenile maiden both over the same C&D, though the deteriorating underfoot conditions were entitled to have played a part in that. The proximity of Commandingpresence limits the form.

5077 CORAL TV H'CAP 7f 140y
8:00 (8:02) (Class 6) (0-65,65) 3-Y-O+ £2,047 (£604; £302) Stalls Centre

Form RPR

0404 1 **Sonny G (IRE)**[14] 4586 3-7-13 49 ow3 KierenFox(5) 16 57
(J R Best) *mde all on stands' rail: rdn clr 2f out: tiring ins fnl f: jst lasted: all out* **9/2**[1]

0043 2 hd **Resuscitator (USA)**[23] 4300 3-9-3 62 (v[1]) TadhgO'Shea 11 69
(Mrs H S Main) *chsd wnr thrght: rdn and outpcd ent fnl 2f: hung lft ent fnl f: kpt on u.p fnl 100yds: nt quite rch wnr* **9/1**

4020 3 6 **Art Market (CAN)**[23] 4308 7-9-13 65 (p) RichardMullen 4 57
(Miss Jo Crowley) *in tch: rdn and chsd ldng pair over 1f out: no imp and wl hld fnl f* **20/1**

0000 4 ½ **Pictures (IRE)**[9] 4756 3-8-10 62 RyanClark(7) 2 51
(J J Bridger) *hld up in midfield: effrt on outer over 2f out: no ch w ldng pair but pressing for 3rd ins fnl f: kpt on* **20/1**

0306 5 nk **Orangeleg**[10] 4715 4-9-7 59 (t) WilliamCarson 9 49
(S C Williams) *chsd ldrs: rdn and unable qck ent fnl 2f: one pce and no ch w ldng pair fr over 1f out* **12/1**

0050 6 2 ¼ **Abhainn (IRE)**[22] 4326 4-9-0 52 DavidProbert 14 36
(B Palling) *in tch: rdn and unable qck ent fnl 2f: hung lft and wl btn over 1f out* **6/1**[2]

1300 7 ¾ **Goodbye Cash (IRE)**[14] 4589 6-9-4 59 AndrewHeffernan(3) 1 41
(R J Smith) *awkward s and slowly away: towards rr: hdwy 1/2-way: kpt on same pce and no imp u.p fr over 1f out* **20/1**

5452 **8** 1 1/4 **Safari Guide**[10] 4700 4-9-12 **64**........ JimCrowley 6 42
(P Winkworth) *hld up towards rr: hdwy into midfield 1/2-way: no prog and wl btn over 1f out* **6/1**[2]

000 **9** 1/2 **Woolston Ferry (IRE)**[25] 4232 4-9-4 **56**........(p) EddieCreighton 7 33
(David Pinder) *s.i.s: sn rdn along in rr: kpt on past btn horses fnl f: n.d* **33/1**

-600 **10** 2 1/4 **Brody's Boy**[24] 4248 3-8-10 **55**........(p) SamHitchcott 8 25
(G L Moore) *in tch in midfield: rdn and struggling 1/2-way: wl btn fnl 2f* **50/1**

00-0 **11** 9 **Five Gold Rings (IRE)**[184] 501 4-8-12 **55**........(t) JohnFahy(5) 3 —
(F J Brennan) *t.k.h: hld up towards rr: rdn and wl btn over 2f out: wl bhd over 1f out: eased ins fnl f* **20/1**

0100 **12** 3/4 **Lord Of The Dance (IRE)**[15] 4547 4-9-10 **62**........ GeorgeBaker 12 —
(W M Brisbourne) *s.i.s: hld up in midfield: struggling 1/2-way: wl btn fnl 2f* **16/1**

0-62 **13** nk **Accountable**[23] 4300 3-8-12 **60**........ RussKennemore(3) 10 —
(B G Powell) *a in rr: rdn and struggling 1/2-way: wl bhd fnl 2f* **10/1**

0500 **14** 9 **Medici Brave**[10] 4700 3-8-12 **57**........(p) PatDobbs 15 —
(Mrs A J Perrett) *stdd s: hld up in rr: rdn 1/2-way: sn wl btn: eased ins fnl f: t.o* **10/1**

0020 **15** 7 **Crystallize**[10] 4715 4-9-7 **59**........ TomMcLaughlin 13 —
(A B Haynes) *chsd ldrs tl rdn and wknd over 2f out: t.o and eased ins fnl f* **7/1**[3]

1m 34.32s (2.02) **Going Correction** +0.30s/f (Good)
WFA 3 from 4yo+ 7lb **15** Ran SP% **125.0**
Speed ratings (Par 101): **101,100,94,94,94 91,91,89,89,87 78,77,76,67,60**
Tote Swingers: 1&2 £11.50, 1&3 £12.90, 2&3 £12.10 CSF £41.40 CT £775.82 TOTE £6.10: £2.30, £4.40, £6.40; EX 62.10 Place 6: £229.72 Place 5: £40.25..
Owner Martin Long **Bred** G G Racing **Trained** Hucking, Kent

FOCUS
A moderate handicap in which the draw played its part. The winner had slipped to a good mark and was another to make all against the rail. The runner-up was also well placed.
Accountable Official explanation: trainer said colt was unsuited by the soft ground
T/Plt: £219.70 to a £1 stake. Pool of £65,198 - 216.60 winning tickets. T/Qpdt: £19.10 to a £1 stake. Pool of £6,737 - 260.92 winning tickets. SP

5032 NEWBURY (L-H)

Saturday, August 14

OFFICIAL GOING: Good to soft (good in places)
Rail realignment increased distances on round course by about 12m.
Wind: Virtually nil Weather: Overcast

5078 BATHWICK TYRES EUROPEAN BREEDERS' FUND MAIDEN FILLIES' STKS 6f 8y

1:25 (1:25) (Class 4) 2-Y-O **£4,857** (£1,445; £722; £360) **Stalls** Centre

Form RPR

6 **1** **Attracted To You (IRE)**[17] 4471 2-9-0 0........ RichardHughes 11 86+
(R Hannon) *t.k.h: trckd ldrs on rail: drvn to ld 1f out: styd on strly* **10/3**[2]

2 2 1/2 **Darajaat (USA)** 2-9-0 0........ RichardHills 10 79+
(M P Tregoning) *led after 1f: pushed along 2f out: hdd 1f out: sn outpcd by wnr: kpt on wl for 2nd* **5/1**[3]

43 **3** 1 1/2 **Layla Jamil (IRE)**[22] 4317 2-9-0 0........ FrankieDettori 13 74
(M R Channon) *chsd ldrs: rdn 2f out: styd on same pce ins fnl f: tk 3rd last strides* **3/1**[1]

04 **4** hd **Saskia's Dream**[22] 4317 2-9-0 0........ ShaneKelly 6 73
(Jane Chapple-Hyam) *led 1f: pressed ldrs: rdn and hung lft over 2f out: kpt on same pce fr over 1f out: lost 3rd last strides* **13/2**

6 **5** 1 **Choral**[47] 3509 2-9-0 0........ PatDobbs 14 70+
(R Hannon) *in rr: pushed along and hdwy fr 2f out: styd on and swtchd lft ins fnl f: nvr gng pce of ldrs* **28/1**

6 3 **Heavenly Song (IRE)** 2-9-0 0........ LiamKeniry 12 61
(S Kirk) *chsd ldrs: rdn 1/2-way: hung lft 2f out: wknd over 1f out* **28/1**

7 1/2 **Etarre (IRE)** 2-9-0 0........ MickyFenton 4 60+
(Mrs P Sly) *in rr: pushed along 1/2-way: c to stands' side and r.o fnl f: gng on cl home: nvr a threat* **28/1**

8 3/4 **Bavarian Princess (USA)** 2-9-0 0........ JimCrowley 9 58
(R M Beckett) *chsd ldrs: rdn over 2f out: wknd over 1f out* **12/1**

9 1 1/4 **Thunda** 2-9-0 0........ EddieAhern 3 54
(Eve Johnson Houghton) *chsd ldrs: rdn over 2f out: wknd wl over 1f out* **40/1**

10 1 3/4 **Fire Crystal** 2-9-0 0........ EddieCreighton 2 49
(M R Channon) *outpcd most of way* **33/1**

11 3 1/4 **Shim Sham (IRE)** 2-9-0 0........ MartinDwyer 7 39
(B J Meehan) *slowly away: t.k.h: in tch w main gp 1/2-way: sn wknd* **15/2**

1m 15.34s (2.34) **Going Correction** +0.35s/f (Good) **11** Ran SP% **113.3**
Speed ratings (Par 93): **98,94,92,92,91 87,86,85,83,81 77**
toteswingers:1&2 £2.50, 2&3 £4.80, 1&3 £1.50 CSF £18.24 TOTE £3.30: £1.20, £2.20, £1.70; EX 16.40.
Owner W P Drew **Bred** Lynn Lodge Stud **Trained** East Everleigh, Wilts

FOCUS
Rain in the 24 hours leading up to racing resulted in the going being changed from good to firm (good in places) to good to soft (good in places), which produced a number of withdrawals. This maiden has not produced anything particularly of note, although it has thrown up the odd Listed performer. That said, the 2007 winner Rinterval recently gave the mighty Zenyatta a good race in a Grade 1 in the USA. The field all came to race towards the stands' side, suggesting the ground was on the soft side.

NOTEBOOK
Attracted To You(IRE), who pulled too hard on her debut at Goodwood, a race from which the fourth had won since, showed the benefit of that experience. Racing close to the pace from her high draw, she asserted inside the last and came away for a cosy success. She has no fancy entries but can be expected to go on again from this. (op 3-1)
Darajaat(USA) ◆, a half-sister of a dual winner at up to 1m out of a very useful mare who won the equivalent race on her debut at this meeting in 2001, nearly emulated her dam. Always in the leading trio, she showed in front 2f out but found the more experienced winner too strong late on. She has a Cheveley Park entry and should not be long in getting off the mark. (op 9-2)
Layla Jamil(IRE), third behind a subsequent Group 3 winner on her second start, set the standard on that but both her outings were on fast ground. She was under pressure 2f out before staying on in the closing stages without ever threatening to trouble the principals. (op 10-3)
Saskia's Dream finished 2l behind Layla Jamil on her second start so had a bit to find. She ran pretty well though under a positive ride, and only just lost third to her old rival. She now qualifies for handicaps and might be seen to better effect in that sphere. (op 8-1)
Choral, a market drifter on her debut in an ordinary maiden, was the stable second string behind the winner. She was held up at the back on the rail before staying on quite takingly in the last furlong, finishing on the heels of those in the frame, and is one to bear in mind. (op 33-1)
Heavenly Song(IRE), a half-sister to several winners out of the top-class Lochangel, showed promise on this debut before fading. Her close relatives have been better as 3-y-os plus, so we may not see the best of her until next season. (op 33-1)
Etarre(IRE), a 75,000gns breeze-up buy from a speedy family, hinted at ability on this debut and should be better for the experience. (op 25-1)
Shim Sham(IRE), an 180,000gns sibling to winners at 7f-1m2f, including Irish 2000 Guineas third Decado, lost her chance on this debut with a slow start. She has a Fillies' Mile entry, so is clearly held in some regard, and can be expected to do better with this behind her.

5079 MATALAN STKS (REGISTERED AS THE WASHINGTON SINGER STAKES) (LISTED RACE) 7f (S)

2:00 (2:00) (Class 1) 2-Y-O **£13,340** (£5,057; £2,530; £1,261) **Stalls** Centre

Form RPR

1 **1** **Janood (IRE)**[15] 4549 2-9-0 0........ FrankieDettori 1 100+
(Saeed Bin Suroor) *racd alone 2f: trckd ldrs 5f out: drvn to ld over 1f out: pushed out: edgd rt nr fin* **2/1**[2]

561 **2** 1 3/4 **Slim Shadey**[36] 3844 2-9-0 90........ LiamKeniry 2 96
(J S Moore) *led tl narrowly hdd over 3f out: slt ld again ins fnl 2f: hdd over 1f out: one pce u.p ins fnl f* **9/1**

1 **3** 3 1/2 **Sensei (IRE)**[32] 3985 2-9-0 0........ RichardHughes 3 87
(M G Quinlan) *stdd s: t.k.h: hld up trcking ldng duo: rdn over 2f out and sn outpcd: hung lft u.p over 1f out and tk wl hld 3rd ins fnl f* **9/2**[3]

11 **4** 3 **Zaidan (USA)**[56] 3190 2-9-3 0........ SebSanders 4 83
(C E Brittain) *trckd ldr tl slt ld over 3f out: rdn and hdd ins fnl 2f: wknd over 1f out and lost wl hld 3rd ins fnl f* **1/1**[1]

1m 28.82s (3.12) **Going Correction** +0.35s/f (Good) **4** Ran SP% **111.5**
Speed ratings (Par 102): **96,94,90,86**
CSF £16.24 TOTE £3.20; EX 16.60.
Owner Godolphin **Bred** Lodge Park Stud **Trained** Newmarket, Suffolk

FOCUS
This long-established Listed race has produced some decent performers in recent seasons, but the best by far was the subsequent 2000 Guineas and Champion Stakes winner Haafhd. This year's renewal looked an interesting contest, despite the small field, with four of the five runners coming here unbeaten.

NOTEBOOK
Janood(IRE), well backed when getting up close home to beat another Godolphin colt on his debut over 6f at Newmarket, raced wide of the others in the early stages as that trio crossed towards the stands' rail. He made his way across and settled behind the leaders by halfway and, when asked to make his effort, did it well and scored with something in hand. He is entered in several sales races but has no group entries at this stage. (op 5-2 tchd 11-4)
Slim Shadey is steadily progressive, although he finished behind Zaidan on his second start in the Chesham. He scored over slightly shorter at Ascot last time and built on that from the front here, although he was no match for the winner. (op 13-2 tchd 6-1)
Sensei(IRE), a cheaply bought colt who scored on his debut over 7f on fast ground, was taking a big step up in grade. He was the first under pressure before picking up when switched to the outside, only for his effort to peter out late on. (tchd 5-1)
Zaidan(USA), an impressive winner of Chesham Stakes on his second start, got a bit warm beforehand and was the big disappointment. He raced up with the pace from the start but dropped away tamely under pressure in the closing stages. Presumably the soft ground was the problem, a view backed up by connections subsequently, but he will have to bounce back to justify big-race entries later in the season. Official explanation: jockey said colt was unsuited by the good to soft (good in places) ground (tchd 11-10 in places)

5080 CGA GEOFFREY FREER STKS (GROUP 3) 1m 5f 61y

2:30 (2:30) (Class 1) 3-Y-O+

£32,358 (£12,266; £6,138; £3,060; £1,533; £769) **Stalls** Low

Form RPR

6641 **1** **Sans Frontieres (IRE)**[37] 3825 4-9-8 117........(tp) JMurtagh 1 123
(J Noseda) *trckd ldrs: chal over 2f out: shkn up: led and wnt rt wl over 1f out: pushed out ins fnl f* **3/1**[2]

-321 **2** 2 1/4 **Laaheb**[49] 3454 4-9-4 111........ RichardHills 7 116
(M A Jarvis) *pressed ldr 7f out tl led ins fnl 4f: pushed along and jnd over 2f out: hdd and bmpd wl over 1f out: styd on same pce ins fnl f* **5/1**[3]

-125 **3** 1 1/4 **Saptapadi (IRE)**[49] 3470 4-9-4 106........ KierenFallon 9 114
(Sir Michael Stoute) *plld hrd towards rr: in tch: stl t.k.h over 5f out: drvn and hdwy over 2f out: styng on whn pushed rt and hmpd wl over 1f out: hung lft and one pce ins fnl f* **9/1**

0300 **4** 1 3/4 **Golden Sword**[15] 4535 4-9-4 105........ RichardHughes 5 111
(Jane Chapple-Hyam) *chsd ldrs: rdn 3f out: btn whn eged lft 1f out: hld on for wl hld 4th last strides* **10/1**

3401 **5** shd **Pompeyano (IRE)**[16] 4500 5-9-4 110........ TadhgO'Shea 3 111
(Saeed Bin Suroor) *in rr: drvn and hdwy over 2f out: styd on fr over 1f out and clsng for wl hld 4th last strides* **12/1**

2-10 **6** 18 **Kite Wood (IRE)**[58] 3102 4-9-8 116........ FrankieDettori 4 88
(Saeed Bin Suroor) *led: rdn and narrowly hdd ins fnl 4f: wknd over 3f out* **6/4**[1]

3-60 **7** 1 **Blizzard Blues (USA)**[91] 2116 4-9-4 100........(b) EddieAhern 2 82
(H R A Cecil) *hld up in rr rdn over 3f out and no rspnse* **16/1**

6302 **8** 2 **Aaim To Prosper (IRE)**[22] 4320 6-9-4 87........(p) KJManning 6 79
(B J Meehan) *chsd ldrs: rdn 5f out: wknd fr 3f out* **25/1**

2m 52.22s (0.22) **Going Correction** +0.30s/f (Good) **8** Ran SP% **118.2**
Speed ratings (Par 113): **111,109,108,107,107 96,96,94**
toteswingers:1&2 £3.10, 2&3 £4.50, 1&3 £6.50 CSF £19.20 TOTE £4.30: £1.50, £1.80, £2.60; EX 17.80 Trifecta £78.90 Pool: £741.75 - 6.95 winning units..
Owner Sir Robert Ogden **Bred** The Lavington Stud **Trained** Newmarket, Suffolk

FOCUS
This Group 3 has a long history and has been won by plenty of established Group performers. Kite Wood was a relatively rare 3-y-o winner when taking this last year en-route to the St Leger, and was a major contender to repeat that success. Sans Frontieres more than confirmed his Newmarket improvement and the runner-up ran to form.

NOTEBOOK
Sans Frontieres(IRE) ◆ put up an improved effort to win the Princess Of Wales's Stakes last month in a first-time tongue tie and cheekpieces and followed up here on this softer surface. He travelled well throughout and, although doing the runner-up no favours when striking the front, came away to win in good style. He was officially the highest-rated on 117 going into this but has not had much racing and looks to be on the upgrade. The Irish St Leger is likely to be his next target, with the Melbourne Cup the aim at the end of the year. (op 4-1)
Laaheb, a dual Listed winner at shorter trips who had won on his only run on soft ground, was up in distance but ran his race, despite being no match for the winner. He is probably the best guide to the level. (tchd 13-2)
Saptapadi(IRE), a lightly raced half-brother to Patkai from the family of Islington, has been progressive this season, finishing runner-up in a Group 2 over 2m. Having had a break since disappointing last time, he ran much better without being able to get to the principals. (op 8-1 tchd 12-1)

Golden Sword, winner of Chester Vase in 2009 and runner-up in Irish Derby on easy ground for Aidan O'Brien, had produced a decent effort for Mike de Kock in Dubai early in the year. He ran better on this second start for his new trainer, but had a lot to find with the winner through Redwood, and in truth had every chance here before fading. (op 14-1)

Pompeyano(IRE), a winner at Listed level on soft in France, was successful on his first start in Britain over 1m2f but had been placed over 2m. Held up early, he made some headway in the straight but never threatened the main players. (tchd 11-1)

Kite Wood(IRE), last year's winner of this, went on to win a Group 2 earlier this year over further and had won both starts on ground softer than good. He made the running but dropped out pretty tamely once put under pressure, although he did pick up again past the two outsiders near the finish. Connections later reported that the colt had lost his action. Official explanation: jockey said colt lost its action (op 11-8 tchd 5-4 and 13-8 in places)

5081 CGA HUNGERFORD STKS (GROUP 2) 7f (S)
3:05 (3:05) (Class 1) 3-Y-O+

£51,093 (£19,368; £9,693; £4,833; £2,421; £1,215) **Stalls** Centre

Form				RPR
-165	1		**Shakespearean (IRE)**[28] 4166 3-8-11 110 (t) FrankieDettori 6 (Saeed Bin Suroor) *dictated pce: drvn and qcknd over 2f out: in command after and styd on strly ins fnl f: unchal* 3/1[2]	118
0402	2	1 ½	**Cat Junior (USA)**[18] 4457 5-9-3 113 (vt) KJManning 9 (B J Meehan) *t.k.h: trckd ldrs: rdn over 2f out: hd to one side and styd on ins fnl f to take wl hld 2nd fnl 120yds* 9/2[3]	116
-204	3	½	**Ouqba**[35] 3888 4-9-3 117 (b[1]) RichardHills 2 (B W Hills) *hld up in rr drvn and hdwy over 2f out: chsd wnr over 1f out: a readily hld: styd on same pce and lost 2nd fnl 120yds* 5/2[1]	115
2223	4	2	**Himalya (IRE)**[21] 4358 4-9-3 110 (p) JMurtagh 8 (J Noseda) *ponied to s: t.k.h: chsd wnr: rdn and outpcd over 1f out: btn whn hung rt ins fnl f* 9/2[3]	109
6252	5	2 ½	**Golden Stream (IRE)**[15] 4540 4-9-0 103 ShaneKelly 5 (Sir Michael Stoute) *t.k.h: trckd ldrs: rdn over 2f out and no imp: wknd 1f out* 12/1	100
10-0	6	1 ¾	**Summer Fete (IRE)**[15] 4540 4-9-0 103 RichardMullen 4 (B Smart) *t.k.h: hld up in rr: rdn 2f out: mod prog but nvr rchd ldrs and sn wknd* 14/1	95
0-00	7	2 ¼	**Finjaan**[18] 4457 4-9-3 115 TadhgO'Shea 3 (M P Tregoning) *plld hrd and stdd s: t.k.h in rr: rdn over 2f out and little rspnse* 10/1	92

1m 26.38s (0.68) **Going Correction** +0.35s/f (Good)
WFA 3 from 4yo+ 6lb 7 Ran SP% **113.4**
Speed ratings (Par 115): **110,108,107,105,102 100,98**
toteswingers:1&2 £3.20, 2&3 £3.00, 1&3 £2.40 CSF £16.57 TOTE £4.00: £2.00, £2.70; EX 17.80 Trifecta £28.40 Pool: £1216.14 - 31.59 winning units..
Owner Godolphin **Bred** Mrs H Owen **Trained** Newmarket, Suffolk

FOCUS
This is usually a competitive Group 2 and has been won by Group 1 winners Red Evie and Paco Boy in recent seasons. This year's line-up was not the strongest on paper, especially with three withdrawals, and the pace looked fairly steady early, although the time was nearly a second and a half faster than the earlier juvenile race. The winner made all for a length personal best. They raced about eight horse-widths off the stands' rail.

NOTEBOOK
Shakespearean(IRE), a 7f Listed winner who had also scored over 1m, had been a winner on easy ground on his racecourse debut and had the credentials for this, despite being the only 3-y-o in the race. Dettori was allowed to dictate the pace and did it perfectly, with his mount never looking likely to be headed at any stage. He is a useful sort at this trip and the Park Stakes could be next. (op 4-1)

Cat Junior(USA), a winner of a 1m Group 3 in Dubai earlier in the year on Tapeta, bounced back to form when runner-up in Goodwood Group 2 with a visor on for the first time on his previous start. He tracked the leaders but was unable to pick up sufficiently under pressure to trouble the winner. Faster ground and a better pace probably brings out the best in him. (tchd 5-1)

Ouqba had not won since taking the Jersey Stakes in 2009 but had run a decent second in the Lockinge this season and had won on easy ground. Fitted with blinkers for the first time, he was held up before making his effort on the outside and could never land a serious blow at the winner. He might have done better ridden closer to the pace. (op 11-4)

Himalya(IRE) has not won since his debut in 2008 but had run some good races in big handicaps under welter burdens. He had never raced on soft ground and had a bit to find up in grade. He was ponied to the start to keep him settled and had every chance in the race, but could not respond when the winner quickened. (tchd 4-1)

Golden Stream(IRE), a dual Listed winner at 7f and running well of late, mainly contests fillies' races and had finished well beaten on her only try on soft ground. She appeared to run her race but was out of her depth against colts at this level. (op 10-1)

Summer Fete(IRE), a 7f Group 3 winner last season but returning from long absence when well beaten in the same race this season, was a Listed winner over C&D on soft ground as a juvenile. However, she was another who could not compete in this grade.

Finjaan finished behind today's runner-up at Goodwood but that was his first run after returning from Dubai. He was always at the rear and probably needs faster ground, although he has something to prove now. (op 15-2)

5082 CGA LADIES DAY H'CAP 7f (S)
3:40 (3:40) (Class 3) (0-95,96) 3-Y-O+

£7,477 (£2,239; £1,119; £560; £279; £140) **Stalls** Centre

Form				RPR
3103	1		**Fleeting Echo**[24] 4264 3-8-12 86 RichardHughes 2 (R Hannon) *trckd ldrs: drvn and qcknd appr fnl f: str run to ld fnl 120yds: readily* 5/1[3]	96
4141	2	2 ¼	**Watch Amigo (IRE)**[14] 4598 4-9-3 85 ShaneKelly 7 (W R Swinburn) *chsd ldr: rdn and one pce over 1f out: styd on ins fnl f to take 2nd cl home: no imp on wnr* 7/2[1]	91+
0442	3	nk	**Manassas (IRE)**[7] 4843 5-10-0 96 (b) MartinDwyer 4 (B J Meehan) *led cl to stands' rail: shkn up and travelling wl appr fnl f: rdn and hdd fnl 120yds: sn no ch w wnr: lost 2nd cl home* 7/2[1]	101
-432	4	3 ¾	**Oil Strike**[21] 4387 3-9-0 88 JimCrowley 10 (P Winkworth) *stdd in rr: sn trcking ldrs: rdn 2f out: wknd ins fnl f* 4/1[2]	81
0450	5	nse	**Nezami (IRE)**[22] 4322 5-9-1 83 DaneO'Neill 1 (J Akehurst) *chsd ldrs: wknd over 1f out: btn whn hung rt ins fnl f* 14/1	78
1610	6	1 ¾	**Kingswinford (IRE)**[50] 3396 4-8-9 77 RichardMullen 11 (P D Evans) *chsd ldrs: rdn over 2f out: sn btn* 12/1	67
100	7	½	**Averoo**[15] 4536 5-8-9 77 (p) KierenFallon 3 (M D Squance) *s.i.s: rdn 3f out: a towards rr* 16/1	66
0061	8	1	**Stevie Gee (IRE)**[20] 4413 6-8-9 77 (v) TadhgO'Shea 5 (Ian Williams) *hld up: hdwy and n.m.r 2f out: rdn and nt clr run over 1f out and ins fnl f: nt rcvr* 10/1	63
00	9	1 ½	**Prince Apollo**[7] 4830 5-9-3 85 EddieAhern 8 (Ian Williams) *a in rr* 16/1	67

1m 27.38s (1.68) **Going Correction** +0.35s/f (Good)
WFA 3 from 4yo+ 6lb 9 Ran SP% **116.3**
Speed ratings (Par 107): **104,101,101,96,96 94,94,93,91**
toteswingers:1&2 £3.80, 2&3 £2.70, 1&3 £3.40 CSF £23.06 CT £69.82 TOTE £6.80: £2.20, £1.90, £1.50; EX 27.00 Trifecta £62.80 Pool: £663.83 - 7.81 winning units..
Owner P J & Mrs J P Haycock **Bred** P J Haycock **Trained** East Everleigh, Wilts

FOCUS
A decent handicap that had been spread pretty evenly among the age groups as regards previous winners. The field came to race towards the stands' side, the first three finished clear and the time was a second slower than the feature race. The winner produced a clear personal best.

NOTEBOOK
Fleeting Echo ran out a comfortable winner. She took a while to settle but was dropped into the pack and then picked up really well when asked. She cut down the leader entering the final furlong and drew away to score well. Her previous wins have been on a sound surface or Polytrack but she seemed suited by the cut in the ground, and could be capable of improvement on the surface this autumn. (op 15-2 tchd 9-2)

Watch Amigo(IRE), 5lb higher following his recent success, had never encountered easy ground before. He was never far away but could not go with the winner when that one quickened and only stayed on past the long-time leader late on. (op 4-1)

Manassas(IRE) made the running and brought the field to the stands' side. He looked like holding on over 1f out but had nothing left when challenged. He has rediscovered his form since blinkers were applied but has been a little unlucky with the ground the last twice, and might last home if he gets a fast surface. (tchd 4-1)

Oil Strike was held up on the rail and did not appear to have much room when the pace was quickening in front of him. However, when he did get into clear the response was less than looked likely and, as his earlier form suggests, softer ground does not suit him as well as a sound surface. (tchd 7-2 and 9-2)

Nezami(IRE) ran arguably his best race since returning from injury earlier this year. He can be given extra credit as he raced on the outside of his field throughout. (op 16-1)

Kingswinford(IRE) might have needed this first run following a break.

Averoo was a market springer but was the first under pressure and never posed a threat. The ground might not have suited. Official explanation: jockey said gelding lost its action (op 11-1 tchd 10-1)

Stevie Gee(IRE), raised 6lb for his recent success and back up in trip, was held up and found himself with nowhere to go over 1f out, by which time the principals had gone for home anyway. His rider confirmed his mount was denied a clear run and did not give him a hard time after it was clear his chance had gone. He is likely to perform better back on a sound surface. Official explanation: jockey said gelding was denied a clear run (op 6-1)

5083 BRIARS DENTAL CENTRE H'CAP 1m 2f 6y
4:15 (4:15) (Class 4) (0-85,82) 3-Y-O **£4,857** (£1,445; £722; £360) **Stalls** Low

Form				RPR
316	1		**Sharedah (IRE)**[29] 4106 3-9-2 77 RichardHills 5 (Sir Michael Stoute) *sn led: pushed along and edgd rt ins fnl f stmbld fnl 120yds: styd on wl* 9/2[3]	89
1460	2	½	**Finest Reserve (IRE)**[14] 4573 3-9-4 79 (v) KierenFallon 8 (M R Channon) *trckd ldr: drvn to chal over 1f out: rdn and kpt on ins fnl f: a jst hld* 4/1[2]	90
-056	3	5	**Mingun Bell (USA)**[30] 4068 3-9-5 80 (b[1]) EddieAhern 7 (H R A Cecil) *chsd ldrs: rdn and styng on same pce and no ch w ldng duo whn edgd rt ins fnl f: swtchd lft sn after* 8/1	81
1640	4	1 ¼	**Hulcote Rose (IRE)**[36] 3866 3-8-9 70 LiamKeniry 6 (S Kirk) *in rr: drvn and hdwy over 1f out: styng on same pce and no ch w ldng duo whn pushed rt ins fnl f* 20/1	69
0-11	5	2 ¼	**Hidden Fire**[33] 3962 3-9-2 77 PhilipRobinson 1 (D R C Elsworth) *plld hrd chsd ldrs: rdn over 2f out: nvr rchd ldrs and wknd over 1f out* 4/1[2]	71
1	6	5	**Jivry**[29] 4114 3-9-7 82 DaneO'Neill 4 (H Candy) *in rr: in tch: rdn over 2f out: sn wknd* 10/3[1]	66
0-31	7	5	**Flotation (USA)**[49] 3428 3-9-2 77 MichaelHills 3 (B W Hills) *in rr: in tch: rdn and sme hdwy 3f out: sn wknd* 5/1	51

2m 9.58s (0.78) **Going Correction** +0.30s/f (Good) 7 Ran SP% **113.8**
Speed ratings (Par 102): **108,107,103,102,100 96,92**
toteswingers:1&2 £2.90, 2&3 £6.60, 1&3 £6.70 CSF £22.50 CT £138.12 TOTE £4.80: £2.40, £1.90; EX 19.80.
Owner Hamdan Al Maktoum **Bred** Shadwell Estate Company Limited **Trained** Newmarket, Suffolk

FOCUS
A decent 3-y-o handicap with most unexposed, but the pace was steady and the first two held those positions throughout. The form looks sound though.

Hidden Fire Official explanation: jockey said filly ran too free

Jivry Official explanation: jockey said filly was unsuited by the good to soft (good in places) ground

Flotation(USA) Official explanation: jockey said filly was unsuited by the good to soft (good in places) ground

5084 UK HYGIENE LADIES DERBY H'CAP (FOR LADY AMATEUR RIDERS) 1m 4f 5y
4:50 (4:50) (Class 4) (0-80,79) 3-Y-O+ **£4,684** (£1,452; £726; £363) **Stalls** Low

Form				RPR
331	1		**Eastern Paramour (IRE)**[23] 4294 5-10-4 76 MissIsabelTompsett 1 (B R Millman) *mde all: rdn and c persistently rt fr ins fnl f: styd on* 11/2[2]	86
0135	2	½	**Kerchak (USA)**[21] 4360 3-9-4 73 MissSBrotherton 7 (W Jarvis) *chsd ldrs: wnt 2nd 2f out: styng on whn persistently carried rt ins fnl f and intimidated by winning rdrs whip fnl 120yds: kpt on* 5/2[1]	82
-321	3	1	**Kings Troop**[23] 4295 4-9-12 75 MissRachelKing[(5)] 6 (A King) *hld up in rr: stl plenty to do 2f out: rapid hdwy over 1f out: swtchd lft and fin strly fnl 120yds* 7/1[3]	82+
0221	4	2 ¼	**Dashing Doc (IRE)**[9] 4740 3-9-3 75 MissLAllan[(3)] 12 (D R C Elsworth) *t.k.h: chsd ldrs: rdn and styd on same pce fnl 2f: wl hld whn hung lft ins fnl f* 5/2[1]	79
0-20	5	3 ½	**All The Winds (GER)**[23] 4306 5-10-5 77 MissGAndrews 5 (S Lycett) *s.i.s: in rr: rdn and hdwy fr 3f out: nvr rchd ldrs: wknd ins fnl f* 10/1	75
41-0	6	nk	**King Supreme (IRE)**[223] 25 5-9-10 73 MissRKneller[(5)] 9 (R Hannon) *in rr: pushed along and hdwy fr 2f out: kpt on ins fnl f: nvr a threat* 8/1	71
0005	7	2 ¾	**Bon Spiel**[24] 4266 6-9-8 71 (tp) MissCLWills[(5)] 4 (C Gordon) *chsd wnr: rdn 2f out: wknd appr fnl f* 18/1	64
2-26	8	3 ½	**Taste The Wine (IRE)**[143] 280 4-9-7 65 MrsEEvans 2 (J S Moore) *t.k.h: chsd ldrs: rdn and wknd over 2f out* 12/1	53

The Form Book, Raceform Ltd, Compton, RG20 6NL

5200 **9** *10* **Wind Star**[13] 4619 7-10-7 **79**.............................. MissCharmaineO'Neill 11 51
(M F Harris) *a in rr* **33/1**

2m 41.89s (6.39) **Going Correction** +0.30s/f (Good)
WFA 3 from 4yo+ 11lb **9** Ran SP% **121.1**
Speed ratings (Par 105): **90,89,89,87,85 84,83,80,74**
toteswingers:1&2 £5.10, 2&3 £5.00, 1&3 £6.90 CSF £20.71 CT £101.19 TOTE £9.20: £2.40, £1.60, £1.90; EX 30.90 Place 6: £66.87 Place 5: £51.48..
Owner W A Harrison-Allan **Bred** Masaichiro Abe **Trained** Kentisbeare, Devon
■ Stewards' Enquiry : Miss Isabel Tompsett one-day ban: careless riding (tbn)

FOCUS
A tightly knit handicap for lady amateurs. Unusually, they went very steadily early on, and ability in the saddle proved important. The form is still taken at face value.
T/Jkpt: Not won. T/Plt: £274.30 to a £1 stake. Pool of £115,246.93 - 306.63 winning tickets. T/Qpdt: £31.00 to a £1 stake. Pool of £7,666.39 - 182.87 winning tickets. ST

5047 NEWMARKET (July Course) (R-H)

Saturday, August 14

OFFICIAL GOING: Soft (5.8)
Far side section of July Course utilised.
Wind: Light half-against becoming fresher race 3 onwards Weather: Sunshine and showers

5085 EUROPEAN BREEDERS' FUND MAIDEN STKS 6f
1:45 (1:48) (Class 4) 2-Y-O **£4,533** (£1,348; £674; £336) **Stalls** Low

Form RPR
0 **1** **Signs In The Sand**[100] 1845 2-9-3 0.............................. TedDurcan 9 90+
(Saeed Bin Suroor) *mde all: rdn over 1f out: r.o wl* **1/1**[1]
523 **2** *6* **Baransky**[24] 4263 2-9-3 79.............................. JimmyFortune 4 72
(Mahmood Al Zarooni) *a.p: rdn to chse wnr over 1f out: styd on same pce* **11/4**[2]
3 *6* **Fast Samurai (USA)** 2-9-3 0.............................. FergusSweeney 7 54+
(D M Simcock) *chsd ldrs: rdn over 1f out: hung lft and wknd fnl f* **9/1**
0 **4** *3 1/4* **Abadejo**[20] 4396 2-9-3 0.............................. DavidProbert 8 44
(J R Jenkins) *plld hrd early: trckd wnr tl rdn: hung lft and wknd over 1f out* **40/1**
0 **5** *4 1/2* **Jeeran**[58] 3112 2-9-3 0.............................. ChrisCatlin 5 31
(C E Brittain) *hld up: rdn over 2f out: wknd over 1f out* **40/1**
6 *2 1/2* **Dictionary** 2-9-3 0.............................. JamieSpencer 3 23
(W J Haggas) *hld up: shkn up and wknd wl over 1f out* **11/2**[3]
7 *19* **Red Jacaranda** 2-8-12 0.............................. WilliamCarson 6 —
(C A Dwyer) *dwlt: sn pushed along in rr: hung lft and wknd wl over 2f out: t.o* **33/1**

1m 16.51s (4.01) **Going Correction** +0.70s/f (Yiel) **7** Ran SP% **109.9**
Speed ratings (Par 96): **101,93,85,80,74 71,46**
Tote Swingers: 1&2 £1.70, 1&3 £3.80, 2&3 £4.50 CSF £3.49 TOTE £2.30: £1.10, £2.20; EX 4.60.
Owner Godolphin **Bred** Darley **Trained** Newmarket, Suffolk

FOCUS
This wasn't the strongest or most competitive two-year-old maiden ever staged on the July Course and they finished well spread out. The quotes regarding the ground from the jockeys after this race ranged from "poached" to "very tacky".

NOTEBOOK
Signs In The Sand ◆ was a disappointing favourite when only ninth of 11 on his Goodwood debut back in May when he apparently got jarred up, but has obviously thrived in the meantime. Well backed once again, he was sent straight into the lead and, relishing the easy ground, had no trouble in pulling clear from the runner-up inside the last furlong. He holds a Mill Reef entry, so is clearly highly regarded. (op 5-4 tchd 11-8 in places)
Baransky, another Godolphin-owned colt, was as weak in the market as Signs In The Sand was strong. Rated 79 after showing ability in three 7f maidens, he looked a bit soft in a battle last time but never got involved in a fight here as the winner was running all over him from some way out. Nurseries may be the way to go with him now. (op 9-4)
Fast Samurai(USA) tried to get on terms with the Godolphin pair over the last two furlongs, but was firmly put in his place and their previous experience was a big advantage in these conditions. This 75,000gns two-year-old and half-brother to six winners in the US still showed enough to suggest he has a future, however. (op 8-1)
Abadejo, a well-beaten last of seven on his Ascot debut, showed a bit more this time but he was keen early and then hung all over the place inside the last two furlongs, suggesting the experience was still needed. He looks more of a long-term handicap prospect. (op 50-1)
Jeeran, a well-beaten last of eight in a 7f Leicester maiden on debut, didn't show much more here. (op 33-1)
Dictionary, a 72,000euros 2-y-o and half-brother to a winner at up to 1m4f in Scandinavia, offered little encouragement on this racecourse debut. His rider reported that he was unsuited by the ground. Official explanation: jockey said colt was unsuited by the soft ground (op 5-1)

5086 BURGHLEY HORSE TRIALS H'CAP 1m
2:15 (2:15) (Class 4) (0-85,81) 3-Y-O **£6,476** (£1,927; £963; £481) **Stalls** Low

Form RPR
41 **1** **Kalk Bay (IRE)**[11] 4679 3-8-11 74.............................. JohnFahy(5) 2 89+
(W J Haggas) *racd centre: hld up: hdwy over 2f out: edgd rt and chsd wnr over 1f out: led ins fnl f: r.o wl: hung lft towards fin* **11/4**[1]
3000 **2** *2 1/4* **Ingleby Spirit**[16] 4504 3-9-8 80.............................. TedDurcan 1 88
(R A Fahey) *trckd ldr far side: rdn over 3f out: hung rt fr over 2f out: styd on to go 2nd wl ins fnl f: no ch w wnr* **9/2**[2]
4022 **3** *2 3/4* **Yes Chef**[22] 4325 3-9-1 73.............................. ChrisCatlin 6 75
(J Gallagher) *s.i.s: racd alone on stands' side: rcvrd to ld overall over 6f out: sn wl clr: rdn over 1f out: edgd lft: hdd and no ex ins fnl f* **5/1**[3]
666 **4** *2 1/2* **Flighty Frances (IRE)**[56] 3217 3-9-4 76.............................. DarryllHolland 4 72
(D R C Elsworth) *racd centre: hld up: rdn over 2f out: hung rt: styd on: nt trble ldrs* **11/1**
-410 **5** *nk* **Veni Vedi Veci (IRE)**[42] 3697 3-9-4 76.............................. JimmyFortune 3 71
(A M Balding) *led duo on far side and overall ldr to over 6f out: rdn over 2f out: sn hung rt: wknd fnl f* **10/1**
221- **6** *3/4* **Dahaam**[304] 6772 3-9-9 81.............................. JamieSpencer 7 75
(B J Meehan) *led centre: rdn over 2f out: wknd fnl f* **6/1**
5154 **7** *7* **Yabtree (IRE)**[22] 4335 3-8-13 71.............................. SteveDrowne 9 48
(R Charlton) *chsd ldrs in centre tl rdn and wknd wl over 1f out* **8/1**
4220 **8** *5* **Marosh (FR)**[22] 4335 3-8-13 74.............................. (p) MartinLane(3) 8 40
(R M H Cowell) *chsd ldr in centre tl rdn 3f out: wknd over 2f out* **12/1**
4005 **9** *6* **Whisper Wind**[22] 4325 3-8-11 69.............................. FergusSweeney 5 21
(G L Moore) *prom in centre tl rdn and wknd over 2f out* **40/1**

1m 43.91s (3.91) **Going Correction** +0.70s/f (Yiel) **9** Ran SP% **114.5**
Speed ratings (Par 102): **108,105,103,100,100 99,92,87,81**
Tote Swingers: 1&2 £4.70, 1&3 £3.40, 2&3 £6.40 CSF £14.77 CT £57.98 TOTE £3.60: £1.50, £1.80, £1.60; EX 18.30 Trifecta £108.50 Pool: £488.56 - 3.33 winning units..
Owner Bernard Kantor **Bred** Wentworth Racing **Trained** Newmarket, Suffolk

FOCUS
Only nine runners in this decent handicap, but they still managed to split into three groups with six coming up the centre, two up the far side and one against the stands' rail. This looked hard work for these three-year-olds in the ground. The form is rated around the runner-up and the winner looks destined for better things.

5087 RACING WELFARE GREY HORSE H'CAP (FOR GREY HORSES ONLY) 6f
2:45 (2:46) (Class 4) (0-85,85) 3-Y-O+
£12,462 (£3,732; £1,866; £934; £466; £234) **Stalls** Low

Form RPR
0-03 **1** **Witchry**[23] 4283 8-7-12 59 oh1.............................. DavidProbert 3 66
(A G Newcombe) *chsd ldrs: rdn to ld over 1f out: styd on gamely* **5/1**[2]
4464 **2** *hd* **Billberry**[7] 4839 5-7-12 59 oh3.............................. (vt) CathyGannon 13 65
(S C Williams) *hld up: hdwy over 1f out: sn rdn: r.o* **6/1**[3]
0000 **3** *hd* **Sunshine Always (IRE)**[31] 4023 4-8-9 70.............................. (p) KirstyMilczarek 16 76
(T D McCarthy) *hld up: hdwy and nt clr run over 1f out: swtchd rt: r.o wl* **12/1**
4030 **4** *hd* **Sakhee's Pearl**[23] 4287 4-9-0 75.............................. (b[1]) JimmyFortune 15 80
(Miss Gay Kelleway) *chsd ldrs: rdn and ev ch fr over 1f out: styd on* **9/2**[1]
1134 **5** *1* **Sutton Veny (IRE)**[28] 4148 4-9-9 84.............................. SteveDrowne 5 86
(J R Gask) *led: rdn and hdd over 1f out: styd on same pce ins fnl f* **9/2**[1]
2602 **6** *4* **Chapter And Verse (IRE)**[58] 3117 4-9-5 80.............................. AndreaAtzeni 6 69
(Mike Murphy) *hld up: hdwy over 2f out: rdn over 1f out: wknd fnl f* **8/1**
0121 **7** *1 1/2* **Lady Florence**[9] 4735 5-8-8 72 ow3.............................. RussKennemore(3) 11 56
(A B Coogan) *chsd ldr tl rdn over 2f out: wknd over 1f out* **13/2**
1006 **8** *3/4* **Ride A White Swan**[5] 4910 5-8-0 64 ow2.............................. (p) MartinLane(3) 8 46
(D Shaw) *dwlt: hld up: rdn and wknd over 1f out* **10/1**
-000 **9** *5* **Zowington**[63] 2973 8-8-9 70.............................. (v) WilliamCarson 4 36
(S C Williams) *s.i.s: hld up: hdwy over 3f out: wknd fnl f* **10/1**

1m 15.86s (3.36) **Going Correction** +0.70s/f (Yiel)
WFA 3 from 4yo+ 4lb **9** Ran SP% **117.6**
Speed ratings (Par 105): **105,104,104,104,102 97,95,94,87**
Tote Swingers: 1&2 £8.40, 1&3 £17.80, 2&3 £19.80 CSF £35.75 CT £346.54 TOTE £7.10: £2.20, £2.40, £4.20; EX 38.60 Trifecta £436.90 Part won. Pool £590.52 - 0.94 winning units..
Owner White Swan Racing & A G Newcombe **Bred** Darley **Trained** Yarnscombe, Devon
■ Stewards' Enquiry : David Probert one-day ban: used whip with excessive frequency (Aug 29)

FOCUS
A race decimated by seven non-runners, but still a thrilling contest with barely a length covering the first four home. This time the runners stayed against the stands' rail. The form looks reasonably sound.
Lady Florence Official explanation: jockey said mare hung left throughout

5088 NATIONAL STUD STKS (H'CAP) 6f
3:20 (3:20) (Class 2) (0-105,105) 3-Y-O
£18,693 (£5,598; £2,799; £1,401; £699; £351) **Stalls** Low

Form RPR
1422 **1** **Dafeef**[28] 4140 3-9-4 102.............................. (p) TedDurcan 13 110
(Saeed Bin Suroor) *hld up: hdwy to ld 1f out: rdn out* **8/1**
2102 **2** *nk* **Deacon Blues**[22] 4333 3-8-8 92.............................. DarryllHolland 12 99+
(J R Fanshawe) *trckd ldrs: nt clr run fr over 2f out tl shkn up over 1f out: r.o wl* **7/1**
111 **3** *1/2* **Bated Breath**[42] 3673 3-9-7 105.............................. JimmyFortune 5 110+
(R Charlton) *hld up: swtchd lft and hdwy over 1f out: r.o u.p* **9/4**[1]
15-5 **4** *1/2* **Amitola (IRE)**[63] 2960 3-8-1 85.............................. DavidProbert 3 89
(T D Barron) *chsd ldrs: rdn and ev ch over 1f out: styd on* **20/1**
-204 **5** *3/4* **Coolminx (IRE)**[21] 4369 3-8-3 87.............................. FrankieMcDonald 8 88
(R A Fahey) *led: rdn and hdd 1f out: styd on same pce* **33/1**
2020 **6** *3/4* **Bagamoyo**[15] 4536 3-9-2 100.............................. PatCosgrave 11 99
(J R Fanshawe) *chsd ldrs: rdn over 1f out: styd on same pce ins fnl f* **13/2**[3]
6500 **7** *nk* **Iver Bridge Lad**[14] 4576 3-9-4 102.............................. (b) MarcHalford 2 100
(J Ryan) *hld up: racd keenly: hdwy over 2f out: rdn over 1f out: no ex ins fnl f* **20/1**
6211 **8** *1/2* **Gramercy (IRE)**[7] 4819 3-9-1 99.............................. JamieSpencer 10 95+
(M L W Bell) *trckd ldrs: rdn over 2f out: nt clr run over 1f out: styd on same pce* **11/4**[2]
6566 **9** *9* **Jira**[28] 4140 3-8-8 92.............................. (t) ChrisCatlin 1 60
(C E Brittain) *chsd ldrs: rdn over 2f out: wknd fnl f* **40/1**
0-43 **10** *1/2* **Capercaillie (USA)**[7] 4819 3-8-4 91.............................. MartinLane(3) 6 57
(M Johnston) *w ldr tl rdn and wknd over 1f out* **20/1**

1m 16.07s (3.57) **Going Correction** +0.70s/f (Yiel) **10** Ran SP% **114.0**
Speed ratings (Par 106): **104,103,102,102,101 100,99,99,87,86**
Tote Swingers: 1&2 £10.40, 1&3 £5.40, 2&3 £1.90 CSF £55.67 CT £170.42 TOTE £10.40: £2.80, £2.30, £1.40; EX 71.50 Trifecta £111.80 Pool: £953.85 - 6.31 winning units..
Owner Godolphin **Bred** Shadwell Estate Company **Trained** Newmarket, Suffolk

FOCUS
A decent handicap containing several in-form and progressive sorts, but it wasn't strong run. They raced centre-to-stands' side and the winning time was 0.21sec slower than the older handicappers in the greys' race.

NOTEBOOK
Dafeef was 12lb higher than when winning his last start in a handicap at Salisbury in May and hasn't looked straightforward on occasions, but he was given a cracking ride here. Held up off the pace, his jockey produced him through the gap tight against the stands' rail to lead inside the final furlong, which gave him little time to start thinking about it. Perhaps the return to 6f and the softer ground helped him, so it will be interesting to see if he can back this up.
Deacon Blues hadn't enjoyed much luck in either start since his impressive win off 11lb lower at Yarmouth in June, but returned to form here and finished in great style to snatch second. This effort shows that he remains capable off this sort of mark. (op 6-1)
Bated Breath was racing off a 10lb higher mark in his bid to extend his unbeaten record to four, but his trainer had expressed some reservations over the ground and in his defence events also conspired against him here. Settled in last, he still held that position passing the 2f pole travelling well, but he was forced to make his final effort out wide whilst the front pair were produced closer to the stands' rail and he was never quite getting there. He remains a decent prospect and should still develop into a Pattern-class performer in due course. (op 2-1)
Amitola(IRE) ◆, a well-beaten fifth of seven on her belated return and handicap debut at Leicester in June, was 3lb lower here and fared best of the trio that disputed the early advantage. She remains unexposed and can find other opportunities. (op 18-1)
Coolminx(IRE), well held in handicaps the last twice and down another 3lb, was another of the early pacesetters to hang in there for longer than might have been expected and there will be other days.
Bagamoyo, on soft ground for the first time since winning on his racecourse debut, was close enough starting up the hill but he didn't find as much as had looked likely. (op 7-1 tchd 15-2)

Gramercy(IRE), up another 7lb in his bid for a hat-trick, was well backed beforehand but his finishing effort was tame and he didn't appear to be handling the ground, which was later confirmed by his rider. Official explanation: jockey said colt was unsuited by the soft ground (op 4-1)

5089 WT'S SNOOKER & SPORTING CLUB NURSERY 5f
3:55 (3:57) (Class 4) (0-85,77) 2-Y-0 £4,533 (£1,348; £674; £336) Stalls Low

Form				RPR
2453	1		**Loki's Revenge**[4] 4927 2-8-10 66 SteveDrowne 4 (W Jarvis) *trckd ldrs: led over 1f out: rdn and hung lft ins fnl f: r.o* 5/2[2]	72
45U3	2	1 ½	**So Is She (IRE)**[20] 4409 2-8-9 70 BillyCray(5) 1 (A Bailey) *a.p: rdn and ev ch over 1f out: styd on same pce ins fnl f* 11/2[3]	71
31	3	1 ½	**Normandy Maid**[14] 4599 2-9-1 71 JamieSpencer 3 (R A Fahey) *hld up in tch: plld hrd: hung lft fr 1/2-way: rdn over 1f out: styd on same pce ins fnl f: wnt 3rd towards fin* 11/10[1]	66
6140	4	nk	**Instructress**[14] 4592 2-9-0 73 (p) MartinLane(3) 8 (R M H Cowell) *disp ld: rdn and hdd over 1f out: edgd lft and no ex ins fnl f: lost 3rd towards fin* 13/2	67
4030	5	5	**Sirens**[5] 4890 2-8-5 61 (t) ChrisCatlin 6 (P S McEntee) *w ldr tl rdn over 1f out: wknd fnl f* 25/1	37

63.70 secs (4.60) **Going Correction** +0.70s/f (Yiel) 5 Ran SP% 108.8
Speed ratings (Par 96): **91,88,86,85,77**
CSF £15.32 TOTE £3.90: £1.90, £2.30; EX 15.00.
Owner Dr J Walker **Bred** The Athenians **Trained** Newmarket, Suffolk

FOCUS
A weak nursery and another race affected by non-runners, with the one colt proving too good for the four fillies. Again they raced centre-to-stands' side and the race bore similarities to the preceding contest with the winner being produced against the stands' rail, whilst the beaten favourite was forced to make her effort out towards the centre of the track.

NOTEBOOK
Loki's Revenge had made the frame in all four previous starts over this trip, including on Polytrack four days earlier. He settled well behind the two pacesetters here and once produced to hit the front against the nearside rail a furlong out, he quickened up well despite hanging away to his left in the latter stages. (op 11-4 tchd 9-4)
So Is She(IRE), making her nursery debut after showing ability in her first three (completed) starts, ran on up the hill to finished a clear second-best. She has the ability to win a race, but she did carry her head a little high in the closing stages here. (op 13-2 tchd 7-1)
Normandy Maid, who still looked green when winning a Thirsk maiden last time, was settled off the pace after taking a bump from the winner exiting the gates. She probably wasn't helped but having to make her finishing effort wide, but neither did she convince that she handled this much slower ground. (op Evens tchd 10-11 and 6-5 in places)
Instructress, who didn't get home when stepped up to 6f here last time and had cheekpieces on for the first time, didn't help her chances by taking Sirens on for the early lead. (op 15-2 tchd 8-1)

5090 MICKEY FLYNN'S AMERICAN POOL HALL CONDITIONS STKS 1m 2f
4:30 (4:35) (Class 2) 3-Y-0+
£9,969 (£2,985; £1,492; £747; £372; £187) Stalls Centre

Form				RPR
5033	1		**Traffic Guard (USA)**[15] 4535 6-9-4 108 JamieSpencer 6 (P F I Cole) *chsd ldrs tl led and edgd rt over 2f out: clr fnl f: easily* 2/1[1]	114
05-0	2	11	**Balius (IRE)**[21] 4390 7-9-4 112 (b) TedDurcan 1 (Saeed Bin Suroor) *hld up: hdwy over 2f out: rdn to chse wnr over 1f out: wknd and eased ins fnl f* 4/1[3]	95
125-	3	2 ¾	**Nideeb**[317] 6426 3-8-6 106 ChrisCatlin 2 (C E Brittain) *chsd ldrs: shkn up over 3f out: wknd 2f out* 8/1	84
0221	4	4 ½	**Classic Punch (IRE)**[21] 4376 7-9-1 105 DarryllHolland 4 (D R C Elsworth) *chsd clr ldr tl led 1/2-way: rdn and hdd over 2f out: wknd over 1f out* 9/4[2]	75
621-	5	4 ½	**Libel Law**[371] 4781 4-9-1 107 JimmyFortune 3 (Saeed Bin Suroor) *prom: chsd ldr 5f out tl rdn over 2f out: wknd over 1f out: eased* 5/1	66
0650	6	121	**Slap And Tickle (IRE)**[3] 4969 4-8-10 48 WilliamCarson 5 (M D Squance) *led and sn clr: racd alone in centre tl wknd and hdd 1/2-way: t.o* 150/1	—

2m 12.0s (6.50) **Going Correction** +0.70s/f (Yiel)
WFA 3 from 4yo+ 9lb 6 Ran SP% 112.5
Speed ratings (Par 109): **102,93,91,87,83** —
Tote Swingers: 1&2 £2.00, 1&3 £3.20, 2&3 £4.70 CSF £10.49 TOTE £2.90: £1.30, £2.80; EX 11.70.
Owner Mrs Fitri Hay **Bred** Frank Penn And John R Penn **Trained** Whatcombe, Oxon

FOCUS
Some talented performers contested this conditions event, but two of them were reappearing from long absences whilst another was rated just 48, so the form may not add up to very much. The modest time and the winner are the most likely guides.

NOTEBOOK
Traffic Guard(USA) may have been unlucky not to have done even better than third in a Goodwood Group 3 last time and although all his wins have come on faster ground, conditions were yielding when he was beaten just half a length by New Approach in the 2008 Irish Champion Stakes. Having cruised to the front over 2f from home, he quickly put daylight between himself and his rivals and although the value of the form is hard to gauge, this success can only have done his confidence a power of good. (op 9-4 tchd 15-8)
Balius(IRE), last of eight in a York Group 2 last month on his first start since November, stayed on from the back of the field over the last 2f, but was never a threat to the winner and he is still to prove that he is as good as he was. (tchd 9-2)
Nideeb, the only 3-y-o in the field, hadn't been seen since finishing fifth of nine in a Group 3 on the Rowley Mile last October. The ground had come right for him, but he proved awkward going to post and eventually had to be walked to the stalls. He didn't run at all badly in the race itself and was by no means knocked about when his chance had gone, but he will have to come on a ton for this in order to justify an entry in the Champion Stakes. (op 10-1)
Classic Punch(IRE) has gained three of his five wins on the July Course, including on soft ground, and can be a very hard horse to catch if able to establish an uncontested lead. With the outsider and tearaway leader soon becoming an irrelevance, he basically got his own way out in front but he was made to look very slow when the winner went past him over two furlongs out and found these better rivals too much for him. Official explanation: jockey said gelding was unsuited by the soft ground (op 5-2 tchd 11-4)
Libel Law, making his debut for Godolphin, hadn't been seen since winning a valuable Haydock handicap off 99 for Michael Jarvis a year ago and was another to be given an easy time of it once his winning chance had gone. (op 9-2)

5091 NEWMARKETRACECOURSES.CO.UK H'CAP 1m 4f
5:05 (5:07) (Class 4) (0-85,85) 3-Y-0+ £4,533 (£1,348; £674; £336) Stalls Centre

Form				RPR
-605	1		**Magicalmysterytour (IRE)**[22] 4334 7-10-0 83 ChrisCatlin 8 (W J Musson) *hld up: hdwy 1/2-way: swtchd rt over 2f out: rdn to ld over 1f out: hung lft insde fnl f: styd on* 5/2[1]	94
0	2	2 ½	**Pool Of Knowledge (FR)**[9] 4758 4-9-6 75 DarryllHolland 6 (Miss Venetia Williams) *prom: lost pl over 3f out: hdwy over 2f out: rdn and ev ch over 1f out: sn hung lft: styd on same pce ins fnl f* 16/1	82
3012	3	4	**North Cape (USA)**[14] 4597 4-9-10 79 FergusSweeney 5 (H Candy) *prom: chsd ldr over 3f out: led over 2f out: sn hung rt: rdn and hdd over 1f out: no ex fnl f* 9/2	80
-015	4	10	**Munsarim (IRE)**[29] 4106 3-9-5 85 JamieSpencer 3 (J L Dunlop) *led: rdn and hdd over 2f out: hung rt and wknd over 1f out* 11/4[2]	70
0142	5	5	**Chain Of Events**[14] 4594 3-8-10 76 JackMitchell 4 (N B King) *hld up: hdwy over 3f out: rdn and wknd over 1f out* 7/2[3]	53
3531	6	18	**Rowan Tiger**[25] 4226 4-9-9 78 PatCosgrave 2 (J R Boyle) *chsd ldr tl rdn over 3f out: wknd 2f out: t.o* 7/1	26

2m 39.93s (7.03) **Going Correction** +0.70s/f (Yiel)
WFA 3 from 4yo+ 11lb 6 Ran SP% 114.0
Speed ratings (Par 105): **104,102,99,93,89 77**
Tote Swingers: 1&2 £5.90, 1&3 £2.50, 2&3 £4.70 CSF £39.35 CT £171.06 TOTE £4.30: £2.30, £4.90; EX 54.80 Place 6: £35.60 Place 5: £30.94..
Owner Broughton Thermal Insulation **Bred** Premier Bloodstock **Trained** Newmarket, Suffolk

FOCUS
A fair handicap run at just an ordinary pace and this time all six runners went over to race against the far rail in the home straight. The winner's best run since late last year.
Chain Of Events Official explanation: jockey said gelding was unsuited by the soft ground
T/Plt: £61.70 to a £1 stake. Pool of £92,782 - 1,096.01 winning tickets. T/Qpdt: £34.70 to a £1 stake. Pool of £4,544 - 96.90 winning tickets. CR

4650 RIPON (R-H)
Saturday, August 14

OFFICIAL GOING: Good to soft (8.3)
Rail on bend from back to home straight moved out 4m adding 9yds to races on round course.
Wind: light against Weather: dull

5092 MIKE BURTON MEMORIAL MAIDEN AUCTION STKS (DIV I) 6f
1:55 (2:20) (Class 4) 2-Y-0 £3,561 (£1,059; £529; £264) Stalls Low

Form				RPR
0	1		**Mariachi Man**[93] 2059 2-8-11 0 DavidAllan 11 (T D Easterby) *swtchd rt to r far side: led gp over 3f out: overall ldr over 1f out: drvn clr* 5/1[3]	81+
4322	2	3 ½	**Intrusion**[14] 4580 2-8-8 68 PaulHanagan 4 (R A Fahey) *prom stands' side: rdn to ld over 2f out: hdd over 1f out: kpt on: 1st of 9 in gp* 4/1[1]	68
3	3	1 ½	**Fieldgunner Kirkup (GER)**[29] 4116 2-8-13 0 PhillipMakin 10 (T D Barron) *trckd ldrs stands' side: rdn over 2f out: kpt on fr over 1f out: 2nd of 9 in gp* 4/1[1]	68
4532	4	1	**Brave Dream**[21] 4388 2-8-13 68 NeilCallan 6 (K A Ryan) *in tch stands' side: rdn along whn swtchd rt over 2f out: ev ch over 1f out: kpt on same pce fnl f: 3rd of 9 in gp* 5/1[3]	65
4	5	nk	**Flash City (ITY)**[20] 4409 2-9-3 0 TomEaves 9 (B Smart) *chsd ldrs stands' side: rdn over 2f out: kpt on tl no ex ins fnl f: 4th of 9 in gp* 10/1	68
00	6	1 ½	**The Oboist (IRE)**[43] 3624 2-8-10 0 JoeFanning 8 (M Johnston) *in tch stands' side: rdn and outpcd over 2f out: kpt on fnl f: 5th of 9 in gp* 20/1	57
6	7	2 ½	**Ryedale Dancer (IRE)**[21] 4392 2-8-6 0 (t) DuranFentiman 1 (T D Easterby) *led stands' side: hdd over 2f out: wknd over 1f out: 6th of 9 in gp* 50/1	45
00	8	2 ¼	**Mayan Flight (IRE)**[22] 4346 2-9-0 0 MichaelStainton(3) 13 (R M Whitaker) *swtchd rt to r far side: led gp to over 3f out: sn rdn and wknd: 2nd of 2 in gp* 100/1	49
0	9	9	**Wandering Lad**[39] 3756 2-8-11 0 DavidNolan 5 (D Carroll) *chsd ldrs stands' side: rdn over 2f out: sn wknd: 7th of 9 in gp* 28/1	16
5	10	10	**Jonelha**[12] 4658 2-8-6 0 FrannyNorton 12 (P W D'Arcy) *chsd ldrs stands' side: wknd over 2f out: 8th of 9 in gp* 9/2[2]	—
	11	8	**Brilliant Disguise** 2-8-4 0 AdrianNicholls 2 (B M R Haslam) *slowly away: a bhd stands' side: 9th of 9 in gp* 80/1	—

1m 15.51s (2.51) **Going Correction** +0.30s/f (Good) 11 Ran SP% 113.0
Speed ratings (Par 96): **95,90,88,87,86 84,81,78,66,52 42**
toteswingers:1&2 £4.30, 2&3 £3.80, 1&3 £6.20 CSF £23.27 TOTE £5.40: £1.80, £1.60, £1.70; EX 23.90 Trifecta £46.10 Pool: £276.76 - 4.44 winning units..
Owner Jeremy Gompertz **Bred** Jeremy Gompertz **Trained** Great Habton, N Yorks

FOCUS
There was 4mm of overnight rain, and the going eased to good to soft - the Goingstick read 8.3. As a result, quite a few horses came out of the races during the day due to the easing ground.There was an approximate 25-minute delay to this race because of a problem getting the ambulance to the course, which may have unsettled some of these juveniles.

NOTEBOOK
Mariachi Man ◆ galloped on strongly down the far-side, and won by a wide margin. Absent since a promising effort back in May, this looked a decent performance from the winner, but it remains to seen whether he was flattered by the advantage of racing near the far rail. (op 9-1)
Intrusion, rated 68, raced prominently down the stands' side and once again ran well without getting her head in front. (op 3-1tchd 11-4 in places)
Fieldgunner Kirkup(GER) travelled nicely up the near-side rail for the majority of the race but could not quicken when he needed to. (op 5-1 tchd 13-2)
Brave Dream stayed towards the stands' side and probably ran up to his level, giving those who stayed on his side of the course another decent form marker. (op 7-2 tchd 11-2)
Flash City(ITY) didn't seem to obviously progress a lot from his first outing but certainly did not indicate he had regressed from it. (op 8-1)
Ryedale Dancer(IRE), fitted with a tongue-tie after a moderate first start last time, showed good pace but tired before the furlong pole. (op 80-1)
Jonelha showed ability at a long price on her initial outing but wasn't able to back that up here on much different going. (op 11-2 tchd 6-1 in places)

5093 SIS LIVE H'CAP 1m 4f 10y
2:25 (2:40) (Class 5) (0-75,73) 3-Y-0 £3,885 (£1,156; £577; £288) Stalls High

Form				RPR
2501	1		**Emerald Glade (IRE)**[12] 4648 3-8-6 58 DavidAllan 4 (T D Easterby) *hld up: smooth hdwy over 3f out: swtchd rt over 2f out: rdn to ld over 1f out: kpt on wl* 3/1[1]	69+
4244	2	2	**Aegean Destiny**[71] 2704 3-8-2 59 DeclanCannon(5) 3 (J Mackie) *midfield: hdwy to ld over 2f out: drvn whn hdd over 1f out: no ex fnl 100yds* 13/2	67

3255 **3** *9* **Danceintothelight**[12] 4656 3-8-7 **59**.................... TomEaves 7 52
(Micky Hammond) *hld up: hdwy to r promly over 7f out: led over 3f out: hdd over 2f out: sn wknd* **7/2**[2]

0555 **4** *7* **Brooklands Bay (IRE)**[13] 4618 3-9-1 **67**.................... PaulMulrennan 8 49
(J R Weymes) *hld up: rdn over 4f out: sn no imp* **10/1**

4226 **5** *3/4* **Sheiling (IRE)**[15] 4557 3-8-12 **64**.................... PaulHanagan 5 45
(R A Fahey) *hld up: rdn wl over 3f out: sn no imp* **7/2**[2]

0355 **6** *3/4* **Munaawer (USA)**[58] 3123 3-9-7 **73**.................... PhillipMakin 1 53
(J D Bethell) *trckd ldr: rdn over 3f out: sn wknd* **9/1**

1100 **7** *24* **Lovers Causeway (USA)**[14] 4573 3-9-5 **71**..................(b[1]) JoeFanning 6 12
(M Johnston) *led: hdd wl over 3f out: sn wknd* **11/2**[3]

2m 40.16s (3.46) **Going Correction** +0.30s/f (Good) **7** Ran SP% **117.3**
Speed ratings (Par 100): **100,98,92,88,87 87,71**
toteswingers:1&2 £22.80, 2&3 £6.90, 1&3 £2.50 CSF £23.79 CT £71.48 TOTE £3.30: £2.50, £4.10; EX 18.70 Trifecta £52.00 Part won. Pool of £70.30 - 0.60 winning units..
Owner D A West **Bred** J T And Mrs Thomas **Trained** Great Habton, N Yorks

FOCUS
A tight-looking contest which was well run. It is rated around the runner-up.

5094 RIPON HORN BLOWER CONDITIONS STKS 6f
2:55 (3:01) (Class 3) 2-Y-O **£6,308** (£1,888; £944; £472; £235) **Stalls** Low

Form RPR

214 **1** **Mayson**[18] 4458 2-9-5 95.................... PaulHanagan 1 98+
(R A Fahey) *trckd ldrs: swtchd rt over 2f out: sn rdn: led over 1f out: edgd rt ins fnl 100yds: kpt on* **5/4**[1]

2544 **2** *1/2* **Chilworth Lad**[17] 4468 2-9-5 100.................... AlanMunro 5 97+
(M R Channon) *dwlt: hld up: hdwy to chal over 1f out: kpt on: a jst hld ins fnl f* **9/4**[2]

2400 **3** *2* **Bathwick Bear (IRE)**[15] 4539 2-9-7 87.................... RichardEvans(3) 3 96
(P D Evans) *prom: rdn to ld 2f out: hdd over 1f out: no ex ins fnl f* **25/1**

321 **4** *5* **Malgoof (IRE)**[10] 4702 2-9-0 81.................... TomEaves 2 71
(B Smart) *led: rdn 3f out: hdd 2f out: wknd over 1f out* **7/2**[3]

6213 **5** *3 3/4* **King Of Aquitaine (IRE)**[30] 4066 2-9-5 82.................... NeilCallan 4 64
(K A Ryan) *prom: rdn over 2f out: wknd over 1f out: eased ins fnl f* **11/1**

1m 15.0s (2.00) **Going Correction** +0.30s/f (Good) **5** Ran SP% **109.6**
Speed ratings (Par 98): **98,97,94,88,83**
CSF £4.27 TOTE £2.20: £1.20, £1.80; EX 3.50.
Owner David W Armstrong **Bred** Highfield Farm Llp **Trained** Musley Bank, N Yorks

FOCUS
A solid bunch of horses lined up for this contest, and the form looks sure to be sound, although it was achieved on what the winning rider described as gluey going.

NOTEBOOK
Mayson shaped nicely in the Group 3 Molecomb Stakes, and was trying this trip for the first time. He took a while to really find his stride, but got going inside the final furlong and did just enough to hold on once in front. Connections indicated that he may make a quick return in the Roses Stakes at York. (tchd 6-5)
Chilworth Lad ran respectably in the Group 2 Vintage Stakes at Glorious Goodwood after another sound effort at that level in Ireland. Slightly hampered leaving the stalls by King Of Aquitaine in this, he needed bustling along in rear quite early but, with the winner, came through on the outside to hold every chance. (tchd 5-2 in places)
Bathwick Bear(IRE), beaten in a nursery last time, was the beaten odds-on favourite in Chester's Lily Agnes Stakes back in May after winning his first two starts, so clearly has ability as his double penalty showed. He travelled strongly for a lot of the race and probably came off the bridle last, but could not quicken away once given the opportunity. A drop to 5f again will do him no harm, especially if decent ground can be found for him (op 20-1)
Malgoof(IRE), a recent 6f maiden winner at Newcastle getting weight from all of his rivals here, showed good pace down the stands' rail and was unfortunate not to be a bit closer, as King Of Aquitaine tended to lean on him, while he himself appeared to be edging away from the rail, and then got chopped for room again when Bathwick Bear started to edge across. He would not have won, but is better than his final position suggests. Official explanation: jockey said colt hung right-handed throughout (op 4-1 tchd 9-2)
King Of Aquitaine(IRE), third in a Leicester nursery on his previous start, raced up with the pace but failed to go on when his jockey wanted him to lengthen. (op 9-1 tchd 12-1)

5095 WILLIAM HILL GREAT ST WILFRID (HERITAGE H'CAP) 6f
3:30 (3:31) (Class 2) 3-Y-0+
£40,501 (£12,129; £6,064; £3,035; £1,514; £760) **Stalls** Low

Form RPR

6203 **1** **Damika (IRE)**[7] 4832 7-8-10 **94**.................... MichaelStainton(3) 15 103
(R M Whitaker) *racd far side: midfield: swtchd lft over 1f out: rdn and gd hdwy to ld ins fnl f: hld on wl* **18/1**

1040 **2** *nk* **Tajneed (IRE)**[21] 4391 7-8-13 **94**.................... AdrianNicholls 20 102
(D Nicholls) *racd far side: sn led: drvn and overall ldr appr fnl 1f: hdd ins fnl f: kpt on: 2nd of 10 in gp* **3/1**[1]

2460 **3** *3/4* **Signor Peltro**[15] 4537 7-9-4 **99**.................... TonyCulhane 13 105
(H Candy) *racd far side: hld up: swtchd lft wl over 1f out: sn rdn: kpt on strly: nrst fin: 3rd of 10 in gp* **16/1**

0024 **4** *hd* **Rileyskeepingfaith**[14] 4576 4-9-7 **102**....................(v) AlanMunro 18 107
(M R Channon) *racd far side: hld up: rdn over 2f out: kpt on wl ins fnl f: 4th of 10 in gp* **15/2**[3]

5352 **5** *3/4* **Quest For Success (IRE)**[13] 4616 5-9-0 **100**.................... LeeTopliss(5) 1 103+
(R A Fahey) *prom stands' side: rdn to ld overall over 1f out: hdd ent fnl f: 1st of 7 in gp* **28/1**

000 **6** *nk* **Hitchens (IRE)**[14] 4576 5-9-2 **97**.................... PhillipMakin 19 99
(T D Barron) *racd far side: hld up: rdn over 2f out: kpt on fnl f: nrst fin: 5th of 10 in gp* **16/1**

3044 **7** *shd* **Tiddliwinks**[15] 4536 4-8-13 **94**.................... NeilCallan 10 95
(K A Ryan) *racd far side: midfield: gd hdwy to chal over 1f out: sn drvn: no ex ins fnl 100yds: 6th of 10 in gp* **6/1**[2]

0602 **8** *1* **Pavershooz**[26] 4191 5-8-7 **91**.................... MichaelGeran(3) 6 89
(N Wilson) *led on stands' side tl over 1f out: kpt on once hdd: 2nd of 7 in gp* **22/1**

0000 **9** *nk* **Advanced**[14] 4576 7-8-13 **97**.................... AmyRyan(3) 17 94
(K A Ryan) *prom far side: rdn over 2f out: wknd appr fnl f: 7th of 10 in gp* **17/2**

1000 **10** *shd* **Johannes (IRE)**[14] 4576 7-9-0 **98**.................... BarryMcHugh(3) 7 95
(R A Fahey) *chsd ldrs stands' side: rdn over 2f out: kpt on same pce: 3rd of 7 in gp* **25/1**

2111 **11** *1* **Favourite Girl (IRE)**[26] 4191 4-8-13 **94**....................(v) DuranFentiman 3 88
(T D Easterby) *racd stands' side: chsd ldrs: rdn over 2f out: sn one pce: 4th of 7 in gp* **20/1**

064 **12** *shd* **Fullandby (IRE)**[7] 4832 8-8-7 **93** ow2.................... DaleSwift(5) 2 86
(T J Etherington) *racd stands' side: hld up: rdn over 2f out: sn no imp: 5th of 7 in gp* **22/1**

0000 **13** *2 3/4* **Everymanforhimself (IRE)**[14] 4576 6-8-13 **94**..........(v) FrannyNorton 8 78
(K A Ryan) *racd stands' side: sn prom: rdn over 2f out: wknd over 1f out: eased ins fnl f: 6th of 7 in gp* **50/1**

1100 **14** *3/4* **Lowdown (IRE)**[15] 4536 3-9-1 **100**.................... JoeFanning 9 81
(M Johnston) *racd far side: prom: rdn over 2f out: wknd over 1f out: 8th of 10 in gp* **25/1**

1450 **15** *1 1/2* **Novellen Lad (IRE)**[7] 4832 5-8-11 **92**.................... PJMcDonald 12 69
(E J Alston) *racd far side: prom tl wknd over 1f out: 9th of 10 in gp* **11/1**

0440 **16** *3/4* **Knot In Wood (IRE)**[14] 4576 8-9-10 **105**.................... PaulHanagan 4 80
(R A Fahey) *racd stands' side: hld up: nvr a factor: 7th of 7 in gp* **28/1**

2200 **17** *1 1/2* **Midnight Martini**[12] 4653 3-8-8 **93**....................(t) DavidAllan 16 62
(T D Easterby) *racd far side: prom tl wknd over 1f out: last of 10 in gp* **12/1**

1m 13.31s (0.31) **Going Correction** +0.30s/f (Good)
WFA 3 from 4yo+ 4lb **17** Ran SP% **124.6**
Speed ratings (Par 109): **109,108,107,107,106 105,105,104,104,103 102,102,98,97,95 94,92**
toteswingers:1&2 £7.40, 2&3 £20.10, 1&3 £59.90 CSF £64.63 CT £933.11 TOTE £19.20: £3.80, £2.10, £3.30, £2.60; EX 55.80 Trifecta £1472.30 Pool: £39593.74 - 19.90 winning units..
Owner G B Bedford **Bred** Patrick J Monahan **Trained** Scarcroft, W Yorks

FOCUS
Most of these have been clashing or will be coming up against each other during this season. The difference between defeat and success in these big sprints can often depend on how much of a clear run you get and whether you're drawn on the right side at some courses. Ripon can often have a favoured rail when the going is on the easy side, which was borne out in this year's renewal. However, this looked a fairly clean contest with regards to problems in running, so the form should be fairly reliable. The winner ran his best race since late 2008.

NOTEBOOK
Damika(IRE) has enjoyed a mainly consistent season and collected a couple of victories back in May. By no means the quickest away, he sat in behind when back on an even keel and cut down the runner-up inside the final half-furlong. Connections pointed to the fact that the winner enjoys ground with ease in it, and thought that had played to his strengths. The Portland Handicap and Ayr Gold Cup are obvious targets, but the trainer also mentioned that he would not mind finding a race for him in France if he could, because the going is likely to be ideal over there. (op 16-1)
Tajneed(IRE), the winner of this race in 2008 off a 2lb lower mark, and defending an unbeaten three-from-three record at this course, broke smartly and was soon in front rank. He ran right up to his best but was mugged late on by the fast-finishing Damika. (op 11-4)
Signor Peltro ◆, whose trainer supplied last year's winner Markab off a similar official rating, appeared to be travelling well in behind a wall of horses and may have been slightly unlucky not to have played a bigger part in the finish, as he needed switching into space to make an effort. (op 14-1 tchd 18-1)
Rileyskeepingfaith, a solid fourth in the Stewards' Cup last time, was at the rear of his group with about two furlongs to go but kept on well to pass plenty of his rivals in the latter stages. (op 8-1 tchd 7-1)
Quest For Success(IRE) ◆, said to want soft ground, emerged from stall 1 and did the best of the group that had to stay that side. He has been in good form and is entitled to respect next time given an equal chance. (op 25-1)
Hitchens(IRE) ◆, sixth in this last year, was reunited with Phillip Makin - the jockey who had ridden him to his last two victories - and he raced with plenty of zest, hinting that he is on his way back. Better ground is needed, however. (op 14-1)
Tiddliwinks was less exposed than many he took on here and had every chance from over a furlong out, but he was unable to get to the front. He had no obvious excuses. (op 15-2)
Pavershooz, who was narrowly beaten by Favourite Girl last time after having a wind operation, showed good pace on the stands' side and is in good heart. (tchd 20-1 in places)
Advanced, a close third off this mark in the race last year, travelled strongly in his bunch but was one paced at the business end. (op 11-1 tchd 8-1)
Favourite Girl(IRE) appeared to travel too strongly early. (op 16-1)
Novellen Lad(IRE) found his price halve at one stage before the off but was comfortably held on the favoured side. (op 20-1 tchd 9-1)
Midnight Martini had her chance up the far rail, but weakened. (op 14-1)

5096 EUROPEAN BREEDERS' FUND FILLIES' H'CAP 1m 1f 170y
4:05 (4:05) (Class 4) (0-80,80) 3-Y-O+ **£5,992** (£1,793; £896; £448; £223) **Stalls** High

Form RPR

0350 **1** **Starla Dancer (GER)**[21] 4389 4-9-10 **71**.................... PaulHanagan 6 85
(R A Fahey) *trckd ldrs: rdn and hdwy to chal fr over 2f out: kpt on to ld ins fnl f: drvn out* **15/2**

0012 **2** *1 1/2* **Anacopa (USA)**[32] 3995 3-9-3 **80**.................... AntiocoMurgia(7) 2 91
(Mahmood Al Zarooni) *hld up: smooth hdwy fr over 3f out: rdn to ld over 1f out: hdd and no ex ins fnl f* **9/2**[3]

1-50 **3** *4* **Cherry Bee**[7] 4823 3-8-13 **69**.................... JoeFanning 4 72
(M Johnston) *prom: rdn to ld wl over 2f out: hdd over 1f out: sn no ex* **13/2**

4113 **4** *3* **Ailsa Craig (IRE)**[18] 4450 4-10-0 **75**.................... PaulMulrennan 5 72
(E W Tuer) *led: hdd wl over 2f out: grad wknd* **6/1**

2120 **5** *5* **Ice Diva**[14] 4571 3-9-7 **77**.................... TonyCulhane 8 63
(P W D'Arcy) *trckd ldrs: rdn and sn lost pl over 3f out* **4/1**[2]

5112 **6** *1 1/4* **Akhmatova**[21] 4389 3-9-9 **79**.................... TomEaves 7 63
(G A Butler) *hld up: rdn wl over 3f out: sn no hdwy* **11/4**[1]

3146 **7** *nk* **Layla's Lexi**[13] 4618 3-9-1 **71**.................... PJMcDonald 3 54
(Ian Williams) *hld up: rdn wl over 3f out: a bhd* **10/1**

2m 6.92s (1.52) **Going Correction** +0.30s/f (Good)
WFA 3 from 4yo 9lb **7** Ran SP% **113.3**
Speed ratings (Par 102): **105,103,100,98,94 93,92**
toteswingers:1&2 £8.60, 2&3 £13.40, 1&3 £7.40 CSF £40.00 CT £231.00 TOTE £9.30: £3.80, £1.80; EX 34.20 Trifecta £64.30 Part won. Pool of £87.00 - 0.50 winning units..
Owner Aricabeau Racing Limited **Bred** Hof Ittlingen & Morton Bloodstock **Trained** Musley Bank, N Yorks

FOCUS
A competitive-looking contest, in which the older generation just prevailed. Sound form.
Akhmatova Official explanation: jockey said filly was unsuited by the good to soft ground

5097 E-TECH GROUP TOTAL ELECTRICAL SOLUTIONS MAIDEN STKS 5f
4:40 (4:41) (Class 5) 3-Y-0+ **£3,885** (£1,156; £577; £288) **Stalls** Low

Form RPR

6203 **1** **Pelmanism**[28] 4151 3-9-3 63....................(b) NeilCallan 7 66
(K A Ryan) *prom: led over 1f out: rdn clr* **10/3**[3]

5440 **2** *3 1/4* **Sea Crest**[23] 4285 4-9-1 54.................... AlanMunro 9 50
(M Brittain) *sn chsd along to keep in tch: drvn 2f out: kpt on to take 2nd fnl 50yds* **11/4**[1]

6-34 **3** *3/4* **Ballarina**[8] 4799 4-9-1 45.................... DavidAllan 1 48
(E J Alston) *led: hdd over 1f out: wknd ins fnl f: lost 2nd fnl 50yds* **3/1**[2]

0040 **4** *3 3/4* **Happy The Man (IRE)**[17] 4485 3-9-3 38..............(b[1]) DuranFentiman 10 38
(T D Easterby) *chsd ldrs: rdn over 2f out: sn no imp* **20/1**

5 *5* **Appleby Fair** 3-9-3 0.................... PhillipMakin 4 20
(T D Barron) *hld up: rdn over 2f out: sn no imp* **9/2**

0 **6** *2 1/4* **Grey Crystal**[22] 4339 4-8-8 0 .... JohnCavanagh(7) 5 7
(M Brittain) *slowly away: a towards rr* **40/1**

0-0 **7** *5* **Grant Me A Wish**[42] 3663 4-9-3 0 .... MichaelStainton(3) 2 —
(S P Griffiths) *in tch: rdn and sn lost pl over 2f out* **40/1**

00 **8** *3/4* **The Nifty Belle**[22] 4340 4-9-1 0 .... PaulMulrennan 11 —
(N Wilson) *chsd ldrs: wknd qckly fr 2f out* **33/1**

62.11 secs (1.41) **Going Correction** +0.30s/f (Good)
WFA 3 from 4yo 3lb **8** Ran SP% **105.5**
Speed ratings (Par 103): **100,94,93,87,79 76,68,66**
toteswingers:1&2 £2.20, 2&3 £1.70, 1&3 £2.20 CSF £10.41 TOTE £3.80: £1.50, £1.30, £1.20; EX 6.60 Trifecta £16.30 Pool: £205.83 - 9.34 winning units..
Owner Guy Reed **Bred** Guy Reed **Trained** Hambleton, N Yorks

FOCUS
A weak affair, rated through the winner who showed slightly improved form. Captain Sachin proved to be unruly in the stalls and was withdrawn (8/1, deduct 10p in the £ under R4).

5098 VW VAN CENTRE WEST YORKSHIRE H'CAP 1m
5:15 (5:15) (Class 3) (0-90,88) 3-Y-O+ **£6,308** (£1,888; £944; £472; £235) **Stalls** High

Form RPR

1424 **1** **Sir George (IRE)**[14] 4603 5-9-5 **82** .... BarryMcHugh(3) 13 91
(Ollie Pears) *midfield: hdwy over 2f out: rdn to ld over 1f out: kpt on wl* **7/2**[1]

6012 **2** *1/2* **City Of The Kings (IRE)**[7] 4849 5-10-0 **88** .... (p) TomEaves 9 96
(G A Harker) *hld up: rdn over 3f out: hdwy over 2f out: kpt on wl ins fnl f: nvr rch wnr* **8/1**

5-44 **3** *hd* **Faithful Ruler (USA)**[18] 4450 6-9-9 **83** .... PaulHanagan 10 91+
(R A Fahey) *hld up: stl last over 2f out: hdwy on inner over 1f out: swtchd lft 1f out: swtchd rt ins fnl f: r.o wl: nrst fin* **6/1**[3]

2623 **4** *1 1/4* **Bolodenka (IRE)**[7] 4849 8-8-8 **75** .... MarzenaJeziorek(7) 7 80
(R A Fahey) *s.i.s: hld up: hdwy on outer fr over 3f out: chal 2f out: stl ev ch 1f out: no ex fnl 100yds* **14/1**

6020 **5** *1* **Keys Of Cyprus**[18] 4459 8-9-9 **83** .... AdrianNicholls 15 86
(D Nicholls) *midfield: rdn over 2f out: kpt on ins fnl f* **7/1**

0321 **6** *3/4* **Licence To Till (USA)**[10] 4690 3-9-2 **83** .... JoeFanning 14 83
(M Johnston) *trckd ldrs: rdn over 2f out: kpt on same pce* **11/2**[2]

0404 **7** *1/2* **Exit Smiling**[29] 4112 8-9-6 **80** .... TonyCulhane 11 80
(P T Midgley) *prom: led 3f out: rdn and hdd over 1f out: sn no ex* **13/2**

6530 **8** *3/4* **Come And Go (UAE)**[12] 4652 4-9-3 **77** .... PJMcDonald 8 75
(G A Swinbank) *trckd ldrs: rdn over 2f out: wknd ins fnl f* **17/2**

-000 **9** *6* **Charlie Tipple**[52] 3318 6-9-1 **75** .... DuranFentiman 2 59
(T D Easterby) *midfield: rdn over 3f out: sn wknd* **22/1**

0600 **10** *nk* **Wigram's Turn (USA)**[7] 4828 5-9-6 **80** .... DavidAllan 12 64
(M W Easterby) *midfield: rdn over 3f out: sn wknd* **28/1**

0-00 **11** *11* **Jack Dawkins (USA)**[67] 2835 5-9-10 **87** .... MichaelGeran(3) 1 45
(D Nicholls) *led: hdd 3f out: wknd qckly* **25/1**

1m 42.6s (1.20) **Going Correction** +0.30s/f (Good)
WFA 3 from 4yo+ 7lb **11** Ran SP% **117.7**
Speed ratings (Par 107): **106,105,105,104,103 102,101,101,95,94 83**
toteswingers:1&2 £8.00, 2&3 £11.40, 1&3 £9.40 CSF £31.00 CT £164.72 TOTE £4.70: £2.00, £3.60, £2.10; EX 44.70 Trifecta £248.70 Part won. Pool of £336.14 - 0.20 winning units..
Owner Ian Bishop **Bred** Bernard Colclough **Trained** Norton, N Yorks

FOCUS
A competitive handicap which was well run. The form looks pretty solid.

NOTEBOOK
Sir George(IRE), who was well backed prior to the off, must be one of the most consistent horses in training, and he once again got his head in front after battling on bravely for success. His ability to handle the going would have been an advantage, and he must be a great horse to own. (op 9-2 tchd 5-1 in places)
City Of The Kings(IRE), twice a winner at this course but over further, has been in good heart and almost claimed another victory. He threaded his way through the pack in the final two furlongs but couldn't get his head to the front. (op 9-1 tchd 10-1)
Faithful Ruler(USA) ◆, a fair fourth last time on his first outing since the start of January, flew home once the gaps opened. He looks ready to strike soon. (op 13-2 tchd 7-1)
Bolodenka(IRE), without a win on the Flat since September 2008, came through to look a potential winner but failed to get home as strongly as a few around him. (tchd 16-1)
Keys Of Cyprus has plenty of good form when there is ease in the ground, and he finished well after taking a while to hit top gear. (op 6-1)
Licence To Till(USA), 6lb higher for dead-heating at Brighton recently, had every chance but was ultimately one-paced, probably because he seemed a bit keen whilst in behind. (op 5-1)
Exit Smiling, who has run well at this course in the past, and had a C&D victory in soft ground to his credit, may have been a little keen while sat just behind the early leader, but he still kept running on after getting to the head of affairs. (op 6-1)
Come And Go(UAE), back down in trip after a modest effort at this course behind City Of Kings, was almost in front two furlongs out but had no extra gears once there. (op 9-1)

5099 MIKE BURTON MEMORIAL MAIDEN AUCTION STKS (DIV II) 6f
5:50 (5:51) (Class 4) 2-Y-O **£3,561** (£1,059; £529; £264) **Stalls** Low

Form RPR

1 **Zenella** 2-8-7 0 .... MatthewDavies(3) 10 91+
(Mrs A Duffield) *hld up: swtchd rt over 1f out: sn gd hdwy to ld his gp over 1f out: led overall ins fnl f: drvn clr* **20/1**

3552 **2** *3 3/4* **No Poppy (IRE)**[8] 4783 2-8-4 71 .... (b) DuranFentiman 12 74
(T D Easterby) *swtchd rt to r far side: overall ldr over 1f out: hdd ins fnl f: 1st of 2 in gp* **4/1**[2]

422 **3** *2 1/2* **Chevise (IRE)**[23] 4293 2-8-4 75 .... RichardKingscote 11 67
(R M Beckett) *swtchd rt to r far side: hdd over 1f out: wknd ins fnl f* **10/11**[1]

032 **4** *2 3/4* **Bajan Bear**[29] 4116 2-8-9 71 .... NeilCallan 3 63
(M Blanshard) *racd stands' side: prom: led over 2f out: hdd over 1f out: sn no ex: 2nd of 8 in gp* **13/2**[3]

0 **5** *5* **Rocky Coast**[33] 3945 2-8-9 0 .... TomEaves 7 48
(B Smart) *racd stands' side: prom: rdn over 2f out: wknd over 1f out: 3rd of 8 in gp* **28/1**

0 **6** *3 1/4* **Vetvey (IRE)**[14] 4599 2-9-3 0 .... PaulMulrennan 1 47
(M Johnston) *racd stands' side: led: rdn and hdd over 2f out: sn wknd: 4th of 8 in gp* **12/1**

56 **7** *3/4* **Hal Of A Lover**[24] 4240 2-9-1 0 .... PaulHanagan 9 42
(R A Fahey) *racd stands' side: hld up: rdn over 2f out: sn no hdwy: 5th of 8 in gp* **18/1**

05 **8** *1/2* **Say A Prayer**[10] 4702 2-8-8 0 .... (b) DavidAllan 6 34
(T D Easterby) *racd stands' side: hld up: n.d: 6th of 8 in gp* **20/1**

0 **9** *13* **Bigalo's Vera B**[82] 2376 2-8-6 0 ow3 .... BarryMcHugh(3) 4 —
(L A Mullaney) *racd stands' side: prom tl wknd fnl 2f: 7th of 8 in gp* **100/1**

10 *18* **Investment World (IRE)** 2-8-13 0 .... JoeFanning 5 —
(M Johnston) *racd stands' side: hld up: a bhd: eased fnl 2f: last of 8 in gp* **14/1**

1m 15.66s (2.66) **Going Correction** +0.30s/f (Good) **10** Ran SP% **119.3**
Speed ratings (Par 96): **94,89,85,82,75 71,70,69,52,28**
toteswingers:1&2 £29.80, 2&3 £1.02, 1&3 £29.80 CSF £97.62 TOTE £23.60: £4.10, £1.20, £1.70; EX 250.00 Trifecta £148.50 Part won. Pool of £200.70 - 0.40 winning units. Place 6: £40.11 Place 5: £24.33..
Owner S E Sangster **Bred** Dukes Stud & Vanquish Bloodstock Ltd **Trained** Constable Burton, N Yorks

FOCUS
The second division of the juvenile maiden was won in impressive style by a winner that came down what was considered the 'wrong' side. There wasn't a great deal between the winning times of each race, although this was slightly slower.

NOTEBOOK
Zenella, a half-sister to a 2yo 1m winner in Italy and 7f-1m1f winner Hoh Wotanite, saw her sales price increase to 20,000euros as a yearling, but even that looks a bargain judged on this performance. She stormed home down what had been perceived to be the unfavoured stands' side, and won going away. She doesn't hold any fancy entries yet but looks well worth a try in a decent contest next time when considering how well she beat two horses rated in the 70s. (op 16-1)
No Poppy(IRE) was one of the most experienced in this field and readily beat the only horse to go with her down the far side of the course. (op 9-2)
Chevise(IRE) was disappointing, as she was only second-best of the two that headed to the far side of the course. (op 11-10 tchd 5-4 in places)
Bajan Bear has been progressing nicely and stayed on to give an indication that he will win in time. (op 8-1)
Rocky Coast ended up well beaten on the stands' side and probably needs more time. (op 33-1)
Vetvey(IRE) is still in the Group 1 Middle Park Stakes as well as valuable sales races, but will need to improve significantly on this effort to justify those entries. (tchd 16-1)
Investment World(IRE), a half-brother to winners, is bred to need much longer trips and failed to make an impact. (op 8-1)
T/Plt: £24.10 to a £1 stake. Pool of £82,915.83 - 2,504.58 winning tickets. T/Qpdt: £7.00 to a £1 stake. Pool of £3,555.78 - 375.42 winning tickets. AS

5100 - 5106a (Foreign Racing) - See Raceform Interactive

5137 DEAUVILLE (R-H)
Saturday, August 14

OFFICIAL GOING: Turf: very soft; fibresand: standard

5107a PRIX GONTAUT-BIRON - HONG KONG JOCKEY CLUB (GROUP 3) (4YO+) (TURF) 1m 2f
1:05 (12:00) 4-Y-O+ **£35,398** (£14,159; £10,619; £7,079; £3,539)

RPR

1 **Vision D'Etat (FR)**[140] 1027 5-8-10 0 ow1 .... OlivierPeslier 3 119
(E Libaud, France) *racd towards rr on ins: rdn 2f out: qcknd wl: grabbed ld 1f out: r.o wl* **37/10**[2]

2 *1* **Budai (GER)**[46] 3548 4-8-9 0 .... DominiqueBoeuf 9 116
(W Hickst, Germany) *racd towards rr on outer: rdn 1 1/2f out: mde swift prog and r.o wl ins fnl f: wnt 2nd fnl 50yds* **11/1**

3 *1 1/2* **Cirrus Des Aigles (FR)**[181] 558 4-8-9 0 .... FranckBlondel 6 113
(Mme C Barande-Barbe, France) *led fr s: swtchd to centre of trck ent st: r.o wl: hdd 1f out: styd on wl* **17/1**

4 *1 1/2* **Starlish (IRE)**[61] 3045 5-8-11 0 .... AnthonyCrastus 7 112
(E Lellouche, France) *racd in 4th: gng wl ent st: rdn but fnd no ex: styd on fnl f* **35/1**

5 *hd* **Court Canibal**[24] 4276 5-8-11 0 .... GeraldMosse 8 112
(M Delzangles, France) *racd towards rr: racd wdst of all ent st: r.o wl fnl f* **18/1**

6 *4* **Un Air De Salsa (FR)**[31] 4-8-9 0 .... RaphaelMarchelli 1 102
(S Wattel, France) *racd towards rr: rdn early in st: no ex: styd on* **9/1**[3]

7 *nk* **Agent Secret (IRE)**[24] 4276 4-9-1 0 .... Francois-XavierBertras 11 107
(F Rohaut, France) *racd in midfield: ev ch ent st: rdn 2f out: no ex: fdd* **1/1**[1]

8 *shd* **Russian Cross (IRE)**[24] 4276 5-8-11 0 .... MaximeGuyon 2 103
(A Fabre, France) *racd in 2nd towards ins: rdn ent st: grad fdd* **13/1**

9 *1* **Silver Frost (IRE)**[28] 4166 4-8-11 0 .... StephanePasquier 5 101
(Y De Nicolay, France) *racd towards rr: rdn early in st: grad wknd* **18/1**

10 *15* **Mores Wells**[48] 3494 6-8-11 0 .... (b) PJSmullen 10 71
(R Gibson, France) *racd in 3rd: rdn early in st: sn wknd* **35/1**

2m 12.1s (1.90) **Going Correction** +0.525s/f (Yiel) **10** Ran SP% **118.4**
Speed ratings: **113,112,111,109,109 106,106,106,105,93**
WIN (incl. 1 euro stake): 4.70. PLACES: 2.20, 3.80, 4.40. DF: 31.90. SF: 67.90.
Owner Jacques Detre **Bred** Gaetan Gilles **Trained** France

NOTEBOOK
Vision D'Etat(FR) was having on his first start since jarring himself up on the Tapeta in the Dubai World Cup in March, but showed his usual change of gear to score cosily. His trainer intends to go for the Champion Stakes at Newmarket next before another attempt to win the Hong Kong Cup next December.
Budai(GER), successful on two previous start in France, was stepping up in grade and recorded a personal best. He will be of interest in similar races this autumn.
Cirrus Des Aigles(FR), having his first start since February, ran pretty well, aided by the soft ground.

5108a PRIX DE POMONE - HARAS D'ETREHAM (GROUP 2) (3YO+ FILLIES & MARES) (TURF) 1m 4f 110y
1:35 (12:00) 3-Y-O+ **£65,575** (£25,309; £12,079; £8,053; £4,026)

RPR

1 **Peinture Rare (IRE)**[103] 1792 4-9-4 0 .... AnthonyCrastus 4 111
(E Lellouche, France) *racd promly bhd ldrs: qcknd wl to chal for ld fnl 150yds: grabbed ld 100yds out: r.o wl* **11/1**

2 *1* **High Heeled (IRE)**[48] 3494 4-9-4 0 .... WilliamBuick 8 110
(J H M Gosden) *bkmarker fr s: qcknd wl on wd outside in st: r.o strly fnl f to grab 2nd on line* **14/5**[2]

3 *nse* **Burn The Breeze (IRE)**[20] 5-9-4 0 .... ChristopheSoumillon 10 110
(Mlle H Van Zuylen, France) *sent st to ld: stl in front ent fnl f: chal 150yds out: surrendered ld 100yds out: styd on wl: lost 2nd on line* **10/1**

4 *1* **Eastern Aria (UAE)**[16] 4507 4-9-4 0 .... GregFairley 7 108
(M Johnston) *a.p: styd on wl in st* **58/10**[3]

5 *1 1/2* **Pearl Banks**[80] 2447 4-9-4 0 .... Francois-XavierBertras 1 106
(F Rohaut, France) *w.w: rdn early in st on inner: r.o but no threat to ldrs* **5/2**[1]

6 *3/4* **La Boum (GER)**[20] 7-9-4 0 .... ThierryJarnet 2 105
(Robert Collet, France) *racd towards rr: effrt early in st: no ex* **17/2**

7 *1* **Soberania (GER)**[61] 3045 4-9-4 0 (p) MircoDemuro 3 103
(J De Roualle, France) *racd towards rr: rdn early in st: no ex* **39/1**
8 *¾* **Polly's Mark (IRE)**[16] 4507 4-9-4 0 OlivierPeslier 6 102
(C G Cox) *racd promly tl early in st: no ex* **17/2**
9 *3* **One Clever Cat (IRE)**[20] 4-9-4 0 FlavienPrat 9 98
(T Clout, France) *nvr figured and qckly wknd in st* **22/1**
10 *10* **Coronata (ITY)**[48] 4-9-4 0 FabioBranca 5 83
(P A Picchi, Italy) *nvr figured: wknd qckly in st* **93/1**
2m 53.1s (6.70) **Going Correction** +0.525s/f (Yiel) **10** Ran SP% **116.0**
Speed ratings: **100,99,99,98,97 97,96,96,94,88**
WIN (incl. 1 euro stake): 12.20. PLACES: 3.10, 1.90, 3.00. DF: 22.40. SF: 39.10.
Owner Ecurie Wildenstein **Bred** Dayton Investments Ltd **Trained** Lamorlaye, France

NOTEBOOK
Peinture Rare(IRE) was always beautifully placed and took command a furlong out before staying on well to the line. The daughter of Sadler's Wells had not raced since early May and the very soft ground certainly suited. The plan now is to run her in the Prix Vermeille and the distances of around 1m4f is ideal for her.
High Heeled(IRE) came from way back and the trainer reported that the lack of early pace was against her.
Burn The Breeze(IRE), who is in-foal to Naaqoos, made the running and stuck on well when headed.
Eastern Aria(UAE) was never far away and stuck to her task but proved less effective on this very soft surface.
Polly's Mark(IRE), who is usually pretty consistent, was another who was found out by the soft ground.

5109a LE GALOP HERMES 3EME MANCHE (CONDITIONS) (4YO+) (INTERNATIONAL JOCKEYS CHALLENGE) (FIBRESAND) 1m 4f
3:55 (12:00) 4-Y-0+ **£15,486** (£6,194; £4,646; £3,097; £1,548)

RPR
1 **Dansant**[364] 5023 6-9-0 0 OlivierPeslier 4 95
(G A Butler) *settled towards rr fr s: smooth prog into st: swtchd to wd outside: qcknd wl u.p to chal for ld 100yds out: r.o wl to take ld in fnl 25yds* **17/5**[1]
2 *snk* **Gentoo (FR)**[27] 6-9-0 0 (p) MircoDemuro 1 94
(A Lyon, France) **63/10**
3 *2½* **Diodoros (FR)**[43] 4-9-3 0 AStarke 7 93
(C Laffon-Parias, France) **6/1**
4 *nk* **Bookend**[105] 6-9-0 0 StephanePasquier 9 90
(D Smaga, France) **7/2**[2]
5 *1½* **Kimble (FR)**[27] 8-9-0 0 MaximeGuyon 2 88
(N Leenders, France) **13/2**
6 *6* **Terre Du Vent (FR)**[104] 1748 4-8-10 0 ChristopheSoumillon 3 74
(Y De Nicolay, France) **9/2**[3]
7 *6* **Major D'Helene (FR)**[42] 5-9-0 0 CoreyBrown 8 68
(F-X De Chevigny, France) **37/1**
8 *10* **Oroveso (BRZ)**[140] 1023 4-8-11 0 GeraldMosse 6 49
(P Bary, France) **16/1**
9 *15* **Satwa Prince (FR)**[126] 7-9-3 0 PJSmullen 5 31
(J De Roualle, France) **21/1**
2m 37.3s (157.30) **9** Ran SP% **117.5**
WIN (incl. 1 euro stake): 4.40. PLACES: 2.00, 2.00, 2.00. DF: 22.40. SF: 35.10.
Owner Mrs Barbara M Keller **Bred** Mrs Cino Del Duca **Trained** Newmarket, Suffolk

NOTEBOOK
Dansant took the third leg of this Hermes-sponsored International Jockeys' Challenge at Deauville on Saturday. He was running his first race for exactly a year after an enforced break due to injury having finished fourth in the Geoffrey Freer Stakes at Newbury. He badly injured both knees in that race and then he nearly died of colic over Christmas, so his trainer did well to get him back in such good form. His trainer reported that he came here as he had no other options before running in the Anatolia Trophy in Turkey on the all-weather, which is were he goes now.

4728 BATH (L-H)
Sunday, August 15

OFFICIAL GOING: Good (good to firm in places; 7.5)
Wind: quite strong breeze behind Weather: Sunny

5111 BATH ORGANICS NURSERY 5f 161y
2:30 (2:31) (Class 6) (0-65,69) 2-Y-O **£1,554** (£462; £231; £115) **Stalls** Centre

Form RPR
0452 1 **Magic Cross**[5] 4935 2-8-0 48 NickyMackay 7 57+
(P J McBride) *worked up bef loading: hld up towards rr: hdwy over 2f out: sn rdn: led jst ins fnl f: r.o wl* **9/4**[1]
213 2 *1½* **Stunning In Purple (IRE)**[31] 4040 2-9-3 65 EddieAhern 4 68
(A B Haynes) *led: rdn 2f out: hdd jst ins fnl f: kpt on but nt pce of wnr* **5/1**[2]
0631 3 *1¼* **Diamond Vine (IRE)**[12] 4678 2-9-7 69 (p) TomMcLaughlin 13 68
(R A Harris) *in tch: hdwy to chal over 2f out: sn rdn: ev ch ent fnl f: kpt on same pce* **11/2**[3]
004 4 *2* **Local Diktator**[24] 4277 2-7-12 46 oh1 AndreaAtzeni 2 38
(R A Harris) *trckd ldrs: rdn over 2f out: nt quite pce to chal: kpt on same pce fnl f: jockey said rein broke 2f out* **25/1**
2353 5 *¾* **Crown Ridge (IRE)**[12] 4678 2-8-10 58 ChrisCatlin 15 48
(M R Channon) *mid-div on outer: rdn over 3f out: no imp tl styd on fnl f* **8/1**
060 6 *nk* **Suave Character**[16] 4543 2-8-2 50 LukeMorris 6 39
(M Blanshard) *trckd ldrs: rdn 3f out: kpt on same pce fnl 2f* **33/1**
0000 7 *nk* **Magical Star**[12] 4675 2-8-0 48 oh1 ow2 FrankieMcDonald 8 36
(R Hannon) *towards rr: rdn 3f out: sme late prog: nvr trbld ldrs* **50/1**
0156 8 *2¾* **Melodize**[11] 4688 2-9-1 63 MartinDwyer 12 42
(W R Muir) *in tch: clsd on ldrs over 2f out: sn rdn: wknd fnl f* **16/1**
0546 9 *hd* **Moorland Boy**[54] 3288 2-9-1 63 FergusSweeney 14 41
(J A Osborne) *hld up towards rr: swtchd rt wl over 2f out: sn rdn and hdwy: wknd fnl f* **14/1**
050 10 *nk* **Striking Love**[9] 4802 2-8-0 53 ow3 JohnFahy[(5)] 3 30
(R Charlton) *s.i.s: towards rr: rdn 3f out: little imp: wknd over 1f out* **8/1**
6522 11 *¾* **Ruby Alexander (IRE)**[31] 4067 2-8-12 60 (p) JimCrowley 5 35
(R M Beckett) *mid-div: rdn over 2f out: wknd ent fnl f* **9/1**
0450 12 *1* **River Blade**[12] 4678 2-8-5 53 TadhgO'Shea 9 24
(W M Brisbourne) *trckd ldrs: rdn 3f out: wknd 2f out* **50/1**
1m 11.81s (0.61) **Going Correction** -0.05s/f (Good) **12** Ran SP% **118.3**
Speed ratings (Par 92): **93,91,89,86,85 85,84,81,80,80 79,78**
Tote Swingers: 1&2 £2.90, 1&3 £4.70, 2&3 £3.10 CSF £12.43 CT £55.94 TOTE £3.60: £1.10, £1.20, £3.50; EX 18.10 Trifecta £31.50 Pool: £152.71 - 3.58 winning units..
Owner Peter Charter **Bred** J W P Clark **Trained** Newmarket, Suffolk

FOCUS
Most of the meetings at Bath during the summer had been on firm ground, with dust kicking up at times, but after plenty of rain over the past week, the going was good, good to firm in places. This was a very moderate nursery.

NOTEBOOK
Magic Cross gave some trouble at the start, and needed to be led without her rider behind the stalls. She went in without too much fuss and proved too strong for her rivals inside the final furlong. Second when running off an official mark of 52 in a similar race last time, she is moderate but capable. (tchd 5-2)
Stunning In Purple(IRE) continued her fine record of never being out of the first three with another solid performance. She got clear of the stalls really well and is a precocious sort. (tchd 9-2)
Diamond Vine(IRE) won a seller by a clear margin on his last run, which helps to put the form into perspective. (tchd 6-1)
Local Diktator, a stablemate of the third, showed promise, especially as the reins broke over 2f out, and may be good enough to win a low-grade affair Official explanation: jockey said rein broke 2 1/2f out (op 28-1)
Crown Ridge(IRE) stayed on but was forced to make his bid on the outside after breaking from a wide stall. (op 9-1)
Suave Character showed plenty of early pace, but lost his position quite quickly about two furlongs out before running on again in the latter stages. (op 40-1)

5112 ALEX MCCRINDLE MEMORIAL APPRENTICE H'CAP 5f 161y
3:00 (3:00) (Class 5) (0-75,74) 3-Y-O+ **£2,007** (£597; £298; £149) **Stalls** Centre

Form RPR
5132 1 **Vhujon (IRE)**[11] 4693 5-9-9 74 AdamBeschizza[(5)] 1 84
(P D Evans) *trckd ldrs: rdn 2f out: led ins fnl f: r.o: rdn out* **4/1**[3]
3462 2 *2¾* **Stamford Blue**[23] 4326 9-8-8 57 (b) JohnFahy[(3)] 6 58
(R A Harris) *trckd ldrs: led wl over 2f out: rdn wl over 1f out: edgd lft ent fnl f: sn hdd: no ex* **10/3**[1]
3404 3 *2* **Bateleur**[7] 4875 6-8-9 60 AmyScott[(5)] 9 54
(M R Channon) *hld up: hdwy over 2f out: sn rdn: kpt on to go 3rd ent fnl f but nt pce to chal* **13/2**
4210 4 *1¾* **The Name Is Frank**[14] 4625 5-9-2 65 (t) SimonPearce[(3)] 8 54
(Mark Gillard) *s.i.s: towards rr: rdn and hdwy on outer fr 3f out: nvr able to get on terms: styd on same pce fnl 2f* **7/2**[2]
6550 5 *1½* **The Tatling (IRE)**[13] 4659 13-9-1 64 BillyCray[(3)] 2 48
(J M Bradley) *hld up: rdn wl over 2f out: no imp* **10/1**
4454 6 *nk* **Kyllachy Storm**[3] 5005 6-9-8 68 MartinLane 4 51
(R J Hodges) *trckd ldr: rdn wl over 2f out: one pce fnl f* **7/2**[2]
00-0 7 *8* **Orpen Lady**[53] 3308 4-8-9 55 oh10 AndreaAtzeni 5 11
(J M Bradley) *led tl wl over 2f out: sn rdn: kpt chsng ldrs tl wknd ent fnl f: eased* **66/1**
0-00 8 *28* **Steeple Caster**[52] 3374 4-8-4 55 oh10 (p) RyanPowell[(5)] 3 —
(J M Bradley) *awkward leaving stalls: a in last pair: lost tch 2f out: t.o* **100/1**
1m 10.72s (-0.48) **Going Correction** -0.05s/f (Good) **8** Ran SP% **112.4**
Speed ratings (Par 103): **101,97,94,92,90 89,79,41**
Tote Swingers: 1&2 £3.00, 1&3 £3.80, 2&3 £4.50 CSF £17.12 CT £82.94 TOTE £4.40: £1.10, £1.20, £2.90; EX 17.80 Trifecta £57.70 Pool: £369.06 - 4.73 winning units..
Owner Nick Shutts **Bred** Robert Berns **Trained** Pandy, Monmouths

FOCUS
An ordinary sprint handicap.

5113 ALLEN FORD FILLIES' H'CAP 1m 5y
3:30 (3:31) (Class 5) (0-70,72) 3-Y-O+ **£2,007** (£597; £298; £149) **Stalls** Low

Form RPR
3502 1 **Tap Dance Way (IRE)**[22] 4365 3-9-4 68 LiamKeniry 1 74
(P R Chamings) *mde all: rdn and hrd pressed fr over 2f out: kpt finding for press ins fnl f: all out: game* **11/4**[1]
4103 2 *shd* **Mellifera**[18] 4479 3-9-3 67 (b[1]) EddieAhern 5 73
(W R Swinburn) *trckd wnr: chal fr over 2f out: sn rdn: ev ch thrght fnl f: jst hld* **3/1**[2]
2052 3 *3¼* **Perfect Friend**[10] 4735 4-9-8 72 AdamBeschizza[(7)] 2 71
(S Kirk) *trckd ldrs: rdn over 2f out: swtchd rt ent fnl f: kpt on same pce* **7/2**[3]
4002 4 *nk* **Egmarey (IRE)**[11] 4705 3-9-4 68 (b[1]) TedDurcan 7 66
(D R Lanigan) *hld up in tch: rdn 2f out: no imp tl kpt on ins fnl f* **4/1**
3643 5 *2¼* **Lathaat**[22] 4364 3-9-3 67 TadhgO'Shea 6 60
(J L Dunlop) *trckd ldrs: rdn to chal 2f out: wknd fnl f* **8/1**
6-50 6 *3¾* **Avon Castle**[191] 425 3-8-7 57 LukeMorris 3 41
(R A Harris) *v reluctant on way to s: awkward leaving stalls: hld up in tch: rdn over 3f out: nvr gng pce to get on terms* **33/1**
-006 7 *6* **Lilly Blue (IRE)**[20] 4427 4-8-3 51 oh3 (p) JohnFahy[(5)] 8 21
(R Brotherton) *cl up early: dropped to last pair but in tch after 2f: hdwy 3f out: sn rdn: wknd ent fnl f* **16/1**
1m 42.63s (1.83) **Going Correction** -0.05s/f (Good)
WFA 3 from 4yo+ 7lb **7** Ran SP% **113.8**
Speed ratings (Par 100): **88,87,84,84,82 78,72**
Tote Swingers: 1&2 £2.50, 1&3 £1.20, 2&3 £3.50 CSF £11.20 CT £28.22 TOTE £4.30: £1.10, £1.40; EX 12.20 Trifecta £43.10 Pool: £352.88 - 6.05 winning units..
Owner Mrs Alexandra J Chandris **Bred** Mrs J Chandris **Trained** Baughurst, Hants

FOCUS
The early pace was not strong, which meant there was a sprint up the home straight. A couple of them also did not look straightforward characters, so the value of this form has to be dubious for future races.

5114 EUROPEAN BREEDERS' FUND DICK HERN FILLIES' STKS (LISTED RACE) 1m 5y
4:00 (4:01) (Class 1) 3-Y-O+
£19,869 (£7,532; £3,769; £1,879; £941; £472) **Stalls** Low

Form RPR
104 1 **Sajjhaa**[52] 3368 3-8-7 93 (t) PhilipRobinson 3 108+
(M A Jarvis) *mde all: styd on strly to assert fr over 1f out: rdn out* **3/1**[1]
6503 2 *3¾* **Kinky Afro (IRE)**[18] 4472 3-8-7 92 LiamKeniry 7 99
(J S Moore) *hld up towards rr: hdwy over 2f out: sn rdn: chsd wnr ent fnl f: kpt on but a being hld* **25/1**
-216 3 *½* **Forest Crown**[29] 4137 3-8-7 90 JimCrowley 12 98+
(R M Beckett) *settled towards rr: hdwy on outer fr over 2f out: rdn to dispute 2nd fr over 1f out: kpt on but no ex ins fnl f* **12/1**
1131 4 *1* **Dance East**[18] 4472 3-8-7 96 DarryllHolland 10 96
(J Noseda) *trckd wnr: rdn in clr 2nd over 1f out tl ent fnl f: no ex* **7/2**[2]
1260 5 *1¼* **Carioca (IRE)**[42] 3720 3-8-12 106 AndreaAtzeni 11 98
(M Botti) *trckd ldrs: rdn over 2f out: kpt on same pce fr over 1f out* **11/1**

0564 **6** ½ **Good Again**8 4816 4-9-0 91 (p) HayleyTurner 1 93
(G A Butler) *trckd wnr: rdn wl over 2f out: kpt on same pce fr over 1f out* **12/1**

5220 **7** ½ **Bahati (IRE)**29 4145 3-8-7 91 RichardKingscote 6 91+
(J G Portman) *hld up towards rr: rdn whn nt clr run over 1f out: kpt on ins fnl f: nvr trbld ldrs* **40/1**

-364 **8** 2 ¼ **Sweet Sonnet (USA)**38 3827 3-8-7 97 TedDurcan 9 86
(Saeed Bin Suroor) *in tch: rdn over 2f out: wknd ins fnl f* **15/2**

1142 **9** 1 ¾ **Dr Wintringham (IRE)**16 4533 4-9-0 78 JerryO'Dwyer 5 83
(Karen George) *hld up towards rr: rdn wl over 2f out: no imp* **66/1**

2201 **10** 1 **First City**29 4137 4-9-0 101 ShaneKelly 2 86
(D M Simcock) *mid-div: rdn to chse ldrs 2f out: wknd fnl f* **9/2**3

6025 **11** 1 ¼ **Carcinetto (IRE)**7 4860 8-9-0 72 CathyGannon 4 77
(P D Evans) *trckd ldrs tl losing pl whn squeezed out on bnd over 5f out: nvr bk on terms: wknd over 1f out* **66/1**

4024 **12** 4 **Please Sing**23 4319 4-9-0 98 ChrisCatlin 8 68
(M R Channon) *mid-div: rdn wl over 2f out: wknd over 1f out* **12/1**

1m 38.75s (-2.05) **Going Correction** -0.05s/f (Good)
WFA 3 from 4yo+ 7lb **12** Ran SP% **117.8**
Speed ratings (Par 108): **108,104,103,102,101 101,100,98,96,95 94,90**
Tote Swingers: 1&2 £22.40, 1&3 £8.60, 2&3 £59.50 CSF £85.01 TOTE £4.10: £2.00, £8.60, £5.20; EX 128.30 TRIFECTA Not won..
Owner Sheikh Ahmed Al Maktoum **Bred** Darley **Trained** Newmarket, Suffolk

FOCUS
This looked well up to scratch for a Listed contest, but the value of the form may be a little bit suspect at the gallop set by the winner looked to be start-stop and then quicken.

NOTEBOOK
Sajjhaa, absent since being beaten at 5-6 in a Listed event at Newcastle in June, was wearing a tongue-tie for the first time, which possibly made a difference as she simply outclassed her rivals. Sent straight to the front, Phillip Robinson appeared to set a gallop to suit his mount and the pair readily outpaced the challengers in the latter stages. Good ground is what connections say she needs, and they will look for Group races again now. (op 7-2)
Kinky Afro(IRE), closely matched with Dance East on their Goodwood meeting, kept on but was never going to make the winner sweat for victory. (op 16-1)
Forest Crown, evens favourite but well behind First City at Newbury, was one of a few that pulled hard towards the rear, which almost certainly did not help her in the latter stages. However, this was a much better effort by the Ralph Beckett horse and she can progress again. (op 17-2)
Dance East found this jump in class a bit too much on this occasion, but should be given another chance. (op 9-2)
Carioca(IRE) was the highest rated of these on official figures and had been given a small break since a couple of fair efforts in French Group races. Close up, she tended to wander a little under pressure and may be better for this run. (op 16-1 tchd 10-1)
Good Again, fitted with cheekpieces for the first time, had no obvious excuses for being well beaten.
Bahati(IRE) ◆, well beaten in a handicap on her previous outing, caught the eye as she was still travelling strongly when a few were starting to weaken. She is still, however, searching for a first success since making a winning racecourse debut. Official explanation: jockey said filly was denied a clear run
Sweet Sonnet(USA) played up a little on the way to the start and showed little when asked to make a challenge. (op 8-1 tchd 7-1)
First City was slightly hampered on a number of occasions from the home bend, and is no doubt better than she showed. Official explanation: vet said filly lost a right-hind shoe and had been struck into
Please Sing has been running well in Listed races and came into this off a good effort in the Valiant Stakes at Ascot. Weak in the betting, she pulled really hard under restraint and dropped away tamely. (op 10-1)

5115 PARK GARDEN CENTRES FRIENDS & FAMILY H'CAP — 1m 2f 46y
4:30 (4:31) (Class 4) (0-80,80) 3-Y-O+ **£3,626** (£1,079; £539; £269) **Stalls** Low

Form RPR

041 **1** **Bramalea**4 4958 5-8-13 **65** 6ex TadhgO'Shea 12 72+
(B W Duke) *trckd ldrs: rn wd on bnd over 4f out: led wl over 2f out: styd on gamely: drvn out* **4/1**2

3143 **2** nk **Sunny Future (IRE)**55 3257 4-9-3 **69** TomMcLaughlin 3 75
(M S Saunders) *unsettled stalls: hld up bhd: hdwy fr 3f out: rdn 2f out: styd on fnl f: wnt 2nd fnl stride: nt quite rch wnr* **7/1**

6500 **3** shd **Bold Cross (IRE)**7 4859 7-9-2 **68** PaulFitzsimons 11 74
(E G Bevan) *mid-div: hdwy 3f out: rdn to chal fr over 2f out: kpt on but no ex fnl 75yds: lost 2nd fnl stride* **12/1**

1345 **4** 1 **Tamtara**18 4492 3-8-12 **73** PatDobbs 8 77
(Mrs A J Perrett) *trckd ldrs: rdn over 2f out: kpt on same pce fr over 1f out* **9/1**

1365 **5** ½ **Welsh Anthem**7 4859 4-9-3 **69** (p) MartinDwyer 4 72
(W R Muir) *in tch: rdn over 2f out: kpt on same pce fr over 1f out* **17/2**

0443 **6** 2 **Pelham Crescent (IRE)**5 4923 7-9-6 **72** LukeMorris 6 71
(B Palling) *rdn over 2f out: nvr bttr than mid-div* **13/2**3

4521 **7** 4 **Sandy Shaw**24 4282 3-8-8 **69** EddieAhern 10 60
(J W Hills) *led tl rdn wl over 2f out: styd chsng ldrs: wknd fnl f* **7/2**1

3020 **8** ½ **Celtic Dragon**13 4657 5-8-9 **61** oh1 (b) CathyGannon 1 51
(P D Evans) *racd keenly in midfield: effrt over 2f out: wknd fnl f* **20/1**

5043 **9** 2 ¼ **Aflaam (IRE)**16 4548 5-9-2 **71** AndrewHeffernan(3) 5 56
(R A Harris) *mid-div tl dropped to rr over 4f out: nvr bk on terms* **9/1**

0354 **10** 2 **Faith Jicaro (IRE)**14 4618 3-8-1 **67** SimonPearce(5) 2 48
(N J Vaughan) *trckd ldrs: rdn 3f out: wknd 2f out* **16/1**

50-0 **11** ¾ **Alpen Glen**15 4603 4-10-0 **80** DarryllHolland 7 60
(John Berry) *hld up and a towards rr* **20/1**

0650 **12** 10 **Goose Green (IRE)**10 4756 6-8-9 **61** oh3 LiamKeniry 9 21
(R J Hodges) *a towards rr* **33/1**

2m 9.13s (-1.87) **Going Correction** -0.05s/f (Good)
WFA 3 from 4yo+ 9lb **12** Ran SP% **124.6**
Speed ratings (Par 105): **105,104,104,103,103 101,98,98,96,94 94,86**
Tote Swingers: 1&2 £5.80, 1&3 £19.10, 2&3 £24.10 CSF £33.25 CT £322.26 TOTE £5.10: £1.10, £3.40, £7.20; EX 54.40 TRIFECTA Not won..
Owner P J Cave **Bred** P J Cave **Trained** Lambourn, Berks

FOCUS
Ordinary handicap form.
Welsh Anthem Official explanation: vet said filly lost its left-hind shoe
Sandy Shaw Official explanation: vet said filly lost a left-fore shoe

5116 PARKGARDENCENTRES.CO.UK MAIDEN STKS — 1m 3f 144y
5:00 (5:01) (Class 5) 3-Y-O+ **£2,007** (£597; £298; £149) **Stalls** Low

Form RPR

5333 **1** **First Fandango**18 4493 3-9-2 73 EddieAhern 4 81
(J W Hills) *trckd ldrs: rdn over 2f out: styd on ins fnl f: led fnl 75yds: rdn out* **3/1**2

26 **2** ½ **Vibrant Force (USA)**8 4845 3-8-9 0 AntiocoMurgia(7) 5 80
(Mahmood Al Zarooni) *trckd ldr: rdn over 2f out: styd on to hold ev ch fnl 75yds: hld nr fin* **7/4**1

423 **3** 2 ½ **Sensationally**38 3829 3-8-11 74 JimCrowley 1 71
(R M Beckett) *led: rdn over 1f out: no ex whn hdd fnl 75yds* **9/2**3

4 hd **Hibba (USA)** 3-8-11 0 TadhgO'Shea 3 70+
(M P Tregoning) *hld up bhd ldrs: rn green and pushed along over 4f out: outpcd 3f out: styd on fr over 1f out: nvr trbld ldrs* **9/2**3

5 1 ¾ **Garth Mountain** 3-9-2 0 PatDobbs 2 72
(Mrs A J Perrett) *trckd ldr: rdn 3f out: one pce fnl f* **16/1**

6 6 **Eurasian** 3-9-2 0 ShaneKelly 6 62
(D M Simcock) *hld up bhd ldrs: outpcd 3f out: wknd fnl f* **12/1**

2m 31.31s (0.71) **Going Correction** -0.05s/f (Good) **6** Ran SP% **111.3**
Speed ratings (Par 103): **95,94,93,92,91 87**
Tote Swingers: 1&2 £2.00, 1&3 £1.50, 2&3 £2.10 CSF £8.53 TOTE £4.10: £1.90, £1.40; EX 10.30 Place 6: £34.06 Place 5: £24.07.
Owner Nick Hubbard & Richard Tufft **Bred** Aylesfield Farms Stud Ltd **Trained** Upper Lambourn, Berks
■ Stewards' Enquiry : Antioco Murgia one-day ban: careless riding (Aug 29)

FOCUS
Probably only a modest maiden.
T/Plt: £97.00 to a £1 stake. Pool of £79,076 - 594.59 winning tickets. T/Qpdt: £40.60 to a £1 stake. Pool of £4,545 - 82.81 winning tickets. TM

4708 PONTEFRACT (L-H)
Sunday, August 15

OFFICIAL GOING: Good (7.6)
Wind: light across Weather: fine

5117 E B F NOVA DISPLAY MAIDEN STKS — 5f
2:10 (2:16) (Class 4) 2-Y-O **£5,180** (£1,541; £770; £384) **Stalls** Low

Form RPR

3322 **1** **Lexi's Hero (IRE)**16 4543 2-9-3 83 JamieSpencer 9 90
(K A Ryan) *mde all: dived rt over 1f out: sn drew clr: eased towards fin* **6/4**1

2 6 **Podgies Boy (IRE)** 2-9-3 0 PaulHanagan 6 69
(R A Fahey) *chsd ldrs: effrt over 2f out: chsd wnr over 1f out: styd on same pce* **8/1**

4 **3** ½ **Jack Smudge**34 3945 2-9-3 0 PaulMulrennan 4 68
(J G Given) *chsd ldrs: drvn over 2f out: hmpd appr fnl f: kpt on wl fnl f* **3/1**2

06 **4** ¾ **Reachtothestars (USA)**83 2376 2-9-3 0 PhillipMakin 1 64
(M Dods) *s.i.s: effrt over 2f out: swtchd rt and styd on appr fnl f* **6/1**3

4U33 **5** 4 ½ **Novalist**33 3971 2-9-3 68 NeilCallan 5 48
(R Bastiman) *chsd ldrs: reminders after 1f: hung rt and wknd appr fnl f* **16/1**

6 **6** 3 ½ **Icy Blue**18 4480 2-9-0 0 MichaelStainton(3) 2 35
(R M Whitaker) *s.i.s: drvn along: nvr a factor* **50/1**

0 **7** hd **Silver Angel (IRE)**20 4421 2-8-12 0 SamHitchcott 10 29
(M R Channon) *swvd bdly rt s: a in rr* **33/1**

8 2 **Rhal (IRE)** 2-8-12 0 TomEaves 7 22
(B Smart) *s.s: nvr on terms* **16/1**

9 5 **Christine's Gold (IRE)** 2-8-12 0 DavidAllan 8 —
(E J Alston) *v free to post: chsd ldrs: wkng whn hmpd appr fnl f* **40/1**

63.99 secs (0.69) **Going Correction** -0.10s/f (Good) **9** Ran SP% **109.5**
Speed ratings (Par 96): **90,80,79,78,71 65,65,62,54**
Tote Swingers: 1&2 £2.80, 1&3 £1.90, 2&3 £3.90 CSF £12.94 TOTE £2.30: £1.10, £2.00, £1.40; EX 12.50.
Owner Dr Marwan Koukash **Bred** T J Pabst **Trained** Hambleton, N Yorks

FOCUS
A fair juvenile maiden won by the subsequent Group 2 winner Our Jonathan last season.

NOTEBOOK
Lexi's Hero(IRE), whose trainer had taken the race twice in the last three years, put his experience to good use, jumping well from his wide draw and making all the running to win unchallenged. The drop back in trip proved no problem for the winner, and this should help his confidence, but he will not find things easy in handicaps off his current mark, and he might be better off in novice events for now. (tchd 11-8)
Podgies Boy(IRE), a half-brother to a smart French-trained juvenile Ascot Glory, put up a promising effort on this debut. He tracked the pace before trying to chase the winner and, although making no impression in the straight, did enough to suggest he can win a similar contest before long. (op 13-2)
Jack Smudge had run promisingly on his debut at Ayr but seemed to find the drop in trip against him here, despite the stiffer track. He kept on late and a return to 6f seems likely now. (op 7-2, tchd 4-1 in a place)
Reachtothestars(USA) had been a disappointing favourite when last seen in May, but that turned out to be a hot race, with the winner going on to score at Royal Ascot. He had been given a break since, but rather sweated up at the start here and spoilt his chance with a tardy break. He now qualifies for a handicap mark and will be of interest in that sphere with this under his belt. (op 15-2)
Novalist had to be bustled along to hold his early pitch and then wandered under pressure in the closing stages. He does not look straightforward. Official explanation: jockey said gelding hung right-handed final 2f
Christine's Gold(IRE) has reportedly shown an aversion to the stalls, but she had no problems on this debut. However, she was free to the start before showing good early pace in the race, although she stopped quickly in the straight. (op 33-1)

5118 FAMILY FUNDAY H'CAP — 1m 4f 8y
2:40 (2:43) (Class 3) (0-90,88) 3-Y-O+
£6,231 (£1,866; £933; £467; £233; £117) **Stalls** Low

Form RPR

0264 **1** **La Vecchia Scuola (IRE)**22 4393 6-10-0 **87** KierenFallon 7 97
(J S Goldie) *chsd ldr: led 2f out: forged clr fnl f* **7/1**

6255 **2** 3 ½ **Trip The Light**23 4348 5-9-13 **86** (v) PaulHanagan 1 90
(R A Fahey) *chsd ldrs: wnt 2nd over 1f out: no imp* **6/1**

-04 **3** ¾ **Red Fama**9 4785 6-8-9 **68** oh3 DanielTudhope 4 71
(N Bycroft) *hld up in rr: effrt on ins over 2f out: styd on wl fnl f* **33/1**

60-5 **4** 1 **Folk Tune (IRE)**120 1151 7-9-5 **78** PhillipMakin 5 80
(J J Quinn) *hld up in mid-div: hdwy over 4f out: kpt on same pce fnl 2f* **66/1**

2131 **5** 1 ½ **Roxy Flyer (IRE)**15 4573 3-9-4 **88** JimmyQuinn 8 87+
(Mrs A J Perrett) *hld up wl in tch: hdwy 5f out: rdn and hung lft 2f out: kpt on same pce* **10/3**2

0102 **6** ½ **Sir Royal (USA)**[12] 4671 5-9-4 **77** .... TomEaves 9 75
(G A Swinbank) *swtchd lft s: hld up in rr: nt clr run 2f out tl 1f out: kpt on: nvr trbld ldrs* **22/1**

4-31 **7** shd **Blissful Moment (USA)**[27] 4205 3-9-2 **86** .... RichardMullen 10 84
(Sir Michael Stoute) *chsd ldrs: hrd drvn and outpcd over 2f out: kpt on ins fnl f* **3/1**[1]

5030 **8** ½ **Record Breaker (IRE)**[21] 4400 6-9-13 **86** ....(v) GregFairley 6 83
(M Johnston) *in rr: pushed along 5f out: nt clr run over 1f out: nvr nr ldrs* **9/2**[3]

-562 **9** shd **Knight's Victory (IRE)**[18] 4481 4-8-6 **68** oh2 .... MichaelStainton(3) 3 65
(Michael Smith) *t.k.h: trckd ldrs: effrt over 2f out: one pce* **18/1**

6200 **10** 4½ **Eton Fable (IRE)**[10] 4737 5-9-1 **74** ....(p) TravisBlock 2 67
(W J H Ratcliffe) *led: hdd 2f out: wknd qckly jst ins fnl f: eased nr fin* **12/1**

2m 38.93s (-1.87) **Going Correction** -0.10s/f (Good)
WFA 3 from 4yo+ 11lb **10** Ran SP% **114.8**
Speed ratings (Par 107): **102,99,99,98,97 97,97,96,96,93**
Tote Swingers: 1&2 £4.60, 1&3 £10.90, 2&3 £7.60 CSF £46.99 CT £1293.56 TOTE £8.90: £3.50, £1.70, £9.30; EX 47.00.
Owner Johnnie Delta Racing **Bred** Maurice Craig **Trained** Uplawmoor, E Renfrews

FOCUS
A decent and pretty competitive handicap.

NOTEBOOK
La Vecchia Scuola(IRE) missed all of last season but had shown the ability was still there in her races over longer trips this term. She was ridden positively over a distance that looked on the short side for her, but asserted turning for home and was never going to be reeled in from that point. She could reappear at York later in the week. (op 15-2 tchd 8-1)
Trip The Light had a successful time earlier in the year but had struggled in recent starts. He was backed this time, though, and bounced back, running on late without troubling La Vecchia Scuola. He often contests claimers and might win another one before long. (op 9-1)
Red Fama ◆ has been lightly raced and has struggled for form in the last two years, but was a good horse with some cut in the ground at one time and the easier conditions here enabled him to run his best race for a long time. He was 3lb out of the handicap here so is likely to go up a pound or two, but could be one to bear in mind if the rains continue. (op 20-1)
Folk Tune(IRE) is better known as a jumper, but he ran creditably on this comeback from a four-month break. This should put him right for a return to chasing.
Roxy Flyer(IRE) was 8lb higher than when winning a handicap at Glorious Goodwood, but she did not really look at home on the track and failed to land a blow. Both her successes have been at the Sussex track and she might be better on a right-handed course. (tchd 3-1 and 7-2)
Blissful Moment(USA) was making his handicap debut having beaten a subsequent winner in a Windsor maiden over 1m2f last time. He was never far away, but was being ridden before the home turn and backed out of it. He looks to need a drop in the weights and might be happier on a fast surface. Official explanation: jockey said colt never travelled (op 7-2)
Record Breaker(IRE) was trying to repeat his 2007 success, but he does not look as good as he was and never got involved. (op 5-1)
Knight's Victory(IRE) Official explanation: jockey said gelding ran too free early stages

5119 TOTEPOOL FLEXI BETTING H'CAP 2m 1f 22y
3:10 (3:13) (Class 5) (0-70,68) 3-Y-0+ **£3,238** (£963; £481; £240) **Stalls** Low

Form RPR

0641 **1** **Lava Lamp (GER)**[12] 4669 3-8-10 **65** ....(v) SilvestreDeSousa 7 76
(G A Harker) *s.i.s: in rr: hdwy on ins over 2f out: chsng ldr over 1f out: led last 100yds: styd on strly* **5/1**[3]

321 **2** 2½ **Stage Acclaim (IRE)**[20] 4441 5-9-3 **57** ....(p) JamieSpencer 10 65
(Dr R D P Newland) *chsd ldr: led after 5f: hdd ins fnl f: no ex* **9/2**[2]

3213 **3** 1¾ **Petella**[8] 4825 4-8-7 **50** .... KellyHarrison(3) 1 56
(C W Thornton) *hld up towards rr: hdwy over 2f out: swtchd rt jst ins fnl f: styd on wl* **8/1**

1125 **4** nk **Tillietudlem (FR)**[15] 4604 4-10-0 **68** .... KierenFallon 11 74
(J S Goldie) *chsd ldrs: chal over 2f out: styd on same pce appr fnl f* **9/2**[2]

40/1 **5** hd **Fair Spin**[64] 1424 10-8-9 **49** ....(v) PaulMulrennan 9 54
(Micky Hammond) *hld up in rr: hdwy over 5f out: effrt over 2f out: keeping on same pce whn hmpd twice ins fnl f* **14/1**

1461 **6** 3¼ **Dubara Reef (IRE)**[17] 4519 3-8-7 **62** .... SteveDrowne 5 64
(Paul Green) *chsd ldrs: drvn over 5f out: rallied over 3f out: wknd over 1f out* **4/1**[1]

2065 **7** 1¼ **Chocolate Caramel (USA)**[8] 4825 8-9-6 **60** .... PaulHanagan 4 61
(R A Fahey) *chsd ldrs: drvn 3f out: wknd appr fnl f* **14/1**

6026 **8** 3¾ **Bandanaman (IRE)**[15] 4604 4-9-8 **62** .... PJMcDonald 6 58
(G A Swinbank) *hld up towards rr: hdwy to trck ldrs 5f out: wknd over 1f out* **8/1**

4560 **9** 7 **Planetarium**[8] 4825 5-9-1 **58** ....(p) JamesSullivan(3) 14 47
(P Monteith) *chsd ldrs: wknd 2f out* **40/1**

0642 **10** nk **Spiritonthemount (USA)**[23] 4328 5-8-10 **50** ....(b) WilliamCarson 2 38
(P W Hiatt) *mid-div: drvn 6f out: hmpd and lost pl over 2f out* **20/1**

4255 **11** 14 **Spring Breeze**[78] 2533 9-8-10 **49** oh1 ow1 .... PhillipMakin 12 23
(J J Quinn) *led 5f: chsd ldrs: lost pl over 2f out: bhd whn eased fnl 2f* **25/1**

26-5 **12** 2¼ **Carmela Maria**[28] 4174 5-9-1 **55** ....(p) TomEaves 8 25
(M E Sowersby) *in rr: lost pl 3f out: sn bhd* **66/1**

3m 50.12s (5.52) **Going Correction** -0.10s/f (Good)
WFA 3 from 4yo+ 15lb **12** Ran SP% **121.1**
Speed ratings (Par 103): **83,81,81,80,80 79,78,76,73,73 66,65**
Tote Swingers: 1&2 £4.60, 1&3 £10.90, 2&3 £7.60 CSF £27.44 CT £182.32 TOTE £6.20: £2.20, £2.80, £3.10; EX 41.80.
Owner An Englishman, Irishman & Scotsman **Bred** Graf And Grafin Von Stauffenberg **Trained** Thirkleby, N Yorks
■ Stewards' Enquiry : Kelly Harrison two-day ban: careless riding (Aug 29-30)
Silvestre De Sousa caution: used whip down shoulder in the forehand.

FOCUS
A modest staying handicap featuring several regulars in similar contests around here.

5120 E B F FLYING FILLIES' STKS (LISTED RACE) 6f
3:40 (3:43) (Class 1) 3-Y-0+
£22,708 (£8,608; £4,308; £2,148; £1,076; £540) **Stalls** Low

Form RPR

4144 **1** **Bounty Box**[14] 4616 4-9-0 **93** .... GeorgeBaker 3 107
(C F Wall) *trckd ldrs: t.k.h: led 3f out: shkn up and wnt clr over 1f out: styd on wl* **6/1**[3]

1131 **2** 2½ **Dever Dream**[29] 4145 3-8-10 **96** .... MichaelHills 10 99+
(W J Haggas) *s.s: swtchd lft after s: hdwy over 3f out: nt clr run over 1f out: styd on wl to chse wnr last 100yds* **6/1**[3]

-132 **3** 2½ **Flambeau**[29] 4145 3-8-10 **98** .... DaneO'Neill 4 91
(H Candy) *led 3f: kpt on same pce over 1f out* **4/1**[2]

4U00 **4** 1½ **Sea Of Leaves (USA)**[16] 4536 4-9-0 **90** .... KierenFallon 1 86
(J S Goldie) *chsd ldrs: styd on same pce fnl 2f* **10/1**

1-50 **5** 1½ **Electric Feel**[58] 3143 3-8-10 **99** .... JamieSpencer 12 81+
(M Botti) *in rr: swtchd lft after 1f: swtchd outside and gd hdwy 2f out: styd on ins fnl f* **20/1**

1355 **6** 3 **Little Scotland**[22] 4369 3-8-10 **82** .... BarryMcHugh 13 72
(R A Fahey) *in tch: effrt over 2f out: wknd appr fnl f* **66/1**

-300 **7** ½ **Anglezarke (IRE)**[85] 2326 4-9-0 **97** ....(b[1]) PaulHanagan 5 70
(R A Fahey) *trckd ldrs: t.k.h: effrt over 2f out: hung lft and wknd over 1f out* **14/1**

4-12 **8** ½ **Beyond Desire**[66] 2912 3-9-0 **100** .... NeilCallan 11 78+
(M A Jarvis) *trckd ldrs: t.k.h: wknd 1f out: 5th and hld whn eased 75yds out* **5/2**[1]

5030 **9** nk **Ishiadancer**[8] 4832 5-9-0 **83** .... DavidAllan 14 68+
(E J Alston) *swtchd lft after s: towards rr: sme hdwy 2f out: nvr nr ldrs* **66/1**

0415 **10** 1½ **Pretty Bonnie**[29] 4145 5-9-0 **84** .... NataliaGemelova 9 63
(A E Price) *in rr: sme hdwy over 2f out: lost pl over 1f out* **80/1**

32-1 **11** 1 **Vitoria (IRE)**[15] 4569 4-9-0 **96** .... RichardMullen 6 60
(B Smart) *chsd ldrs: wkng whn nt clr run 1f out* **12/1**

0000 **12** hd **Look Busy (IRE)**[14] 4616 5-9-0 **97** .... TomEaves 7 59
(A Berry) *mid-div: effrt over 2f out: wknd over 1f out* **33/1**

-040 **13** 28 **Queen's Grace**[14] 4616 3-8-10 **95** .... SteveDrowne 2 —
(H Morrison) *s.i.s: in rr and drvn along: bhd fnl 2f: eased: wl t.o* **28/1**

1m 14.92s (-1.98) **Going Correction** -0.10s/f (Good)
WFA 3 from 4yo+ 4lb **13** Ran SP% **116.0**
Speed ratings (Par 108): **109,105,102,100,98 94,93,93,92,90 89,89,51**
Tote Swingers: 1&2 £8.00, 1&3 £5.10, 2&3 £4.60 CSF £38.27 TOTE £6.10: £1.90, £2.30, £1.70.
Owner John E Sims **Bred** Farmers Hill Stud **Trained** Newmarket, Suffolk

FOCUS
A typically competitive renewal of this Listed fillies' sprint on paper, but in the end a quite decisive winner. The time was better than standard.

NOTEBOOK
Bounty Box likes an uphill finish and goes well on Newmarket's July course, but she had been held in a three previous tries at this level. However, she travelled well throughout, went clear off the home turn and was never going to be reeled in. The black type will be important from a breeding point of view, but she gives the impression there is more to come.
Dever Dream ◆ is a progressive hold-up filly, but she rather blew the start before running on well in the closing stages. She confirmed previous form with the third on worse terms and, with not much mileage on the clock, looks capable of scoring at this level before long. (op 7-1)
Flambeau showed good speed early on and kept going under pressure. She at least earns black type, but is likely to be stronger next year and could to be more of a player in this grade. (op 9-2)
Sea Of Leaves(USA) beat today's winner in a handicap at Newmarket last October and ran quite well here, but she is not quite up to this level, although she has been unlucky to miss out on black type by one place on three separate occasions now. (op 9-1)
Electric Feel had given the impression in two previous starts - one admittedly at the top level - that she had not trained on this season. However, helped by a break and dropping in trip, she put up a decent effort, finishing well having been held up and racing wide on a day when it was better to be close to the pace near the rail. She looks one to bear in mind for a similar contest this autumn. (op 16-1)
Little Scotland has been running well in handicaps, and she ran with credit in this grade. Hopefully the assessor will not take the form at face value or her mark might suffer. (op 50-1)
Anglezarke(IRE) ran too free early in the first-time blinkers. (tchd 12-1)
Beyond Desire, a Listed winner earlier this season, was found to be dehydrated after travelling badly when beaten in Ireland next time. She tried to race up with the pace from her wide draw early, but dropped away in the straight. Official explanation: jockey said he thought something was amiss with filly having hung both ways in straight and eased final furlong (op 11-4 tchd 3-1)

5121 SUNDAY PLATE H'CAP 1m 4y
4:10 (4:11) (Class 3) (0-95,88) 3-Y-0
£6,231 (£1,866; £933; £467; £233; £117) **Stalls** Low

Form RPR

2115 **1** **Aattash (IRE)**[17] 4504 3-9-5 **86** .... SamHitchcott 8 101
(M R Channon) *mde all: shkn up and qcknd over 1f out: rdn clr: styd on strly: unchal* **4/1**[1]

154 **2** 4½ **Qanoon (USA)**[37] 3846 3-9-4 **85** .... RichardHills 3 88
(W J Haggas) *chsd ldrs: drvn 3f out: styd on on ins to take 2nd last 50yds* **4/1**[1]

4 **3** ½ **Aghadoe (IRE)**[15] 4593 3-9-4 **85** .... KierenFallon 7 87
(A M Balding) *w wnr: t.k.h: rdn over 1f out: kpt on same pce* **4/1**[1]

2444 **4** ¾ **Ejteyaaz**[37] 3878 3-8-13 **80** .... PaulHanagan 1 80
(R A Fahey) *hld up in midfield: effrt over 2f out: styd on fnl 100yds* **6/1**[2]

2102 **5** 1½ **Vito Volterra (IRE)**[11] 4710 3-8-8 **78** .... MichaelStainton(3) 10 75
(Michael Smith) *racd wd: trckd ldrs: t.k.h: effrt 2f out: kpt on one pce* **16/1**

6103 **6** 2 **Sir Frank Wappat**[11] 4710 3-8-7 **74** .... JoeFanning 2 66
(M Johnston) *dwlt: in rr: effrt on inner and n.m.r over 1f out: nvr nr ldrs* **16/1**

0113 **7** 2 **Rasselas (IRE)**[11] 4704 3-9-1 **82** .... AdrianNicholls 4 70
(D Nicholls) *in rr: drvn 3f out: nvr a factor* **13/2**[3]

-504 **8** 1¾ **Tominator**[31] 4068 3-9-7 **88** .... JackMitchell 9 72
(R Hollinshead) *w ldrs on outer: tk fierce hold: wknd over 1f out* **16/1**

3134 **9** shd **Law To Himself (IRE)**[29] 4153 3-8-8 **75** .... PJMcDonald 5 58
(G A Swinbank) *prom: effrt 3f out: lost pl over 1f out* **10/1**

4061 **10** 3¾ **Stags Leap (IRE)**[69] 2820 3-9-1 **85** .... JamesSullivan(3) 6 60
(P Monteith) *in rr: pushed along over 3f out: wknd 2f out* **50/1**

1m 44.2s (-1.70) **Going Correction** -0.10s/f (Good) **10** Ran SP% **116.3**
Speed ratings (Par 104): **104,99,99,98,96 94,92,91,90,87**
Tote Swingers: 1&2 £4.00, 1&3 £4.50, 2&3 £3.00 CSF £19.30 CT £69.15 TOTE £4.60: £1.50, £2.70, £2.10; EX 24.50.
Owner Sheikh Ahmed Al Maktoum **Bred** Oghill House Stud **Trained** West Ilsley, Berks

FOCUS
A good 3-y-o handicap that fell to the subsequent Royal Hunt Cup winner Invisible Man last season. Following the earlier trend, it was best to be close to the pace and only one got involved from the back.

NOTEBOOK
Aattash(IRE) has improved for forcing tactics and ran a fine race in a hot handicap at Goodwood on his previous start. He set off in front and his rider dictated a fair gallop, before his mount picked up off the home bend and came right away. He remains progressive and is difficult to get past, so might be able to go in again off his revised mark. (op 7-2 tchd 9-2)
Qanoon(USA) chased the leaders from the start but could not pick up as well as the winner. He stayed on to get second and this slightly easier surface appeared to suit. (op 7-2)
Aghadoe(IRE) ran well on his first start for his new trainer but was ridden more positively this time. However he was keen early on and paid for it in the closing stages. (op 5-1)
Ejteyaaz ◆ has been running over all sorts of distances this season, but his best effort was over 1m, and the return to that trip suited as he did best of those held up off the pace. He looks one to keep an eye on this autumn, as his form in Ireland last season was on soft ground. (op 7-1)
Vito Volterra(IRE) ran well considering he raced towards the outside of the field. (tchd 14-1)

Tominator also ran well considering he raced towards the outside of the field, although he raced more prominently and dropped out in the straight. (op 14-1 tchd 18-1)

5122 BETFAIR MAIDEN STKS — 1m 4y

4:40 (4:41) (Class 4) 3-Y-O+ £3,885 (£1,156; £577; £288) Stalls Low

Form RPR

40- 1 **Lucky Windmill**[310] 6646 3-9-0 0 PJMcDonald 10 84
(G A Swinbank) *mde all: t.k.h: styd on strly to forge clr fnl f* **12/1**

1 2 8 **Sunbow (USA)**[99] 1927 3-9-0 0 AhmedAjtebi 4 65
(Mahmood Al Zarooni) *trckd ldrs: effrt over 2f out: chsng wnr whn ducked rt over 1f out: hung lft and kpt on same pce* **4/5**[1]

3 nk **Edelweiss** 3-8-9 0 PaulHanagan 1 60
(R A Fahey) *chsd ldrs: drvn 3f out: edgd rt appr fnl f: kpt on ins fnl f* **7/1**[3]

4 4 nk **Crimson Empire (USA)**[23] 4340 3-8-9 0 RichardMullen 5 59
(B Smart) *chsd ldrs: drvn over 3f out: hmpd over 1f out: styd on fnl 100yds* **12/1**

0- 5 2 ¾ **Sory**[292] 7099 3-9-0 0 SilvestreDeSousa 2 58
(Miss T Jackson) *s.i.s: drvn over 3f out: kpt on fnl f: nvr nr ldrs* **50/1**

204 6 1 ¼ **Cookie Crumbles (IRE)**[17] 4521 3-8-9 79 JackMitchell 9 50
(C F Wall) *in tch: hdwy to chse ldrs 5f out: hung lft and one pce over 1f out* **5/1**[2]

7 18 **Talent Scout (IRE)** 4-9-7 0 DuranFentiman 6 13
(T D Walford) *s.i.s: in rr: sme hdwy over 3f out: wknd 2f out: sn bhd* **66/1**

04 8 hd **Corky Dancer**[21] 4407 5-9-4 0 JamesSullivan(3) 7 13
(P Monteith) *s.i.s: in rr: bhd fnl 3f* **16/1**

9 ¾ **Three Bay Leaves** 3-8-9 0 JoeFanning 8 —
(M Johnston) *chsd ldrs: drvn 3f out: hung lft and lost pl over 1f out* **14/1**

0-0 10 ¾ **Princeofthedesert**[6] 4893 4-9-4 0 BarryMcHugh(3) 11 —
(G Woodward) *in rr: drvn 6f out: bhd fnl 3f* **66/1**

0-0 11 11 **Makarthy**[195] 372 3-8-7 0 ShaneBKelly(7) 3 —
(Paul Green) *in rr: drvn 4f out: bhd fnl 2f: eased clsng stages* **100/1**

1m 44.97s (-0.93) **Going Correction** -0.10s/f (Good)
WFA 3 from 4yo+ 7lb 11 Ran SP% **118.6**
Speed ratings (Par 105): **100,92,91,91,88 87,69,69,68,67 56**
Tote Swingers: 1&2 £7.60, 1&3 £2.50, 2&3 £3.90 CSF £22.21 TOTE £13.70: £3.50, £1.10, £1.40; EX 37.80.
Owner Porter, Watson, Valentine **Bred** R V Young **Trained** Melsonby, N Yorks

FOCUS
A fair maiden at best in which the disqualified debut winner Sunbow and Cookie Crumbles set a fair standard. There were also a couple of interesting newcomers from major northern yards.

5123 TREVOR WOODS MEMORIAL H'CAP — 5f

5:10 (5:10) (Class 5) (0-70,75) 3-Y-O+ £2,914 (£867; £433; £216) Stalls Low

Form RPR

0040 1 **Bosun Breese**[19] 4452 5-9-10 **70** JackMitchell 4 82
(T D Barron) *chsd ldr: led over 1f out: kpt on wl* **12/1**

4024 2 2 **Rio Sands**[2] 5023 5-8-8 **57** AmyRyan(3) 2 62
(R M Whitaker) *hdwy over 3f out: chsng ldrs over 2f out: kpt on to take 2nd jst ins fnl f: styd on same pce* **6/1**

3251 3 nk **King Of Swords (IRE)**[11] 4712 6-9-3 **63** (p) RichardMullen 6 67
(N Tinkler) *chsd ldrs: kpt on same pce fnl f* **9/2**[3]

4505 4 ½ **Select Committee**[11] 4712 5-8-12 **65** ShaneBKelly(7) 11 67
(J J Quinn) *in rr: hdwy on outside 2f out: kpt on same pce fnl f: styd on towards fin* **11/1**

2231 5 1 ¼ **Foreign Rhythm (IRE)**[7] 4869 5-8-9 **60** 6ex DaleSwift(5) 3 57
(R E Barr) *in rr: hdwy 3f out: n.m.r and swtchd rt 1f out: kpt on same pce* **11/4**[1]

5412 6 4 **Mr Wolf**[11] 4712 9-9-13 **73** PaulHanagan 9 56
(J J Quinn) *led tl over 1f out: wknd jst ins fnl f* **3/1**[2]

4100 7 2 ½ **Hitches Dubai (BRZ)**[19] 4452 5-9-4 **64** SilvestreDeSousa 7 38
(G A Harker) *chsd ldrs on outside: hung lft and lost pl over 1f out* **10/1**

0340 8 1 ¼ **Greek Secret**[7] 4869 7-8-11 **62** ow3 (b) JamesO'Reilly(5) 1 32
(J O'Reilly) *dwlt: hmpd and dropped detached last after 1f: nvr on terms* **14/1**

63.68 secs (0.38) **Going Correction** -0.10s/f (Good) 8 Ran SP% **115.9**
Speed ratings (Par 103): **92,88,88,87,85 79,75,73**
Tote Swingers: 1&2 £11.00, 1&3 £9.50, 2&3 £5.10 CSF £82.59 CT £378.15 TOTE £13.80: £2.80, £2.10, £1.60; EX 87.10 Place 6: £51.74 Place 5: £40.40. totesuper7: Win: Not won. Place: £371.30. .
Owner Estio Capital Racing **Bred** Lady Lonsdale **Trained** Maunby, N Yorks

FOCUS
An ordinary handicap featuring a couple of course regulars, and the early pace was frenetic.
T/Jkpt: Not won. T/Plt: £67.50 to a £1 stake. Pool of £87,233 - 942.83 winning tickets. T/Qpdt: £7.80 to a £1 stake. Pool of £4,750 - 446.55 winning tickets. WG

5124 - 5126a (Foreign Racing) - See Raceform Interactive

3997 DUNDALK (A.W) (L-H)

Sunday, August 15

OFFICIAL GOING: Standard

5127a BAR ONE RACING H'CAP — 6f (P)

3:45 (3:46) 3-Y-O+ £23,008 (£6,725; £3,185; £1,061)

RPR

1 **Bajan Tryst (USA)**[17] 4510 4-9-1 89 PJSmullen 7 103
(K A Ryan) *chsd ldrs: 3rd 1/2-way: impr to ld under 2f out: rdn and kpt on wl fr over 1f out* **4/1**[2]

2 1 ¼ **Luisant**[7] 4882 7-9-11 104 JPO'Brien(5) 6 114
(J A Nash, Ire) *mid-div: 7th 1/2-way: rdn into 5th 1 1/2f out: 4th 1f out: kpt on into 2nd ins fnl f: nt rch wnr* **7/2**[1]

3 2 ½ **Tellelle (IRE)**[7] 4883 4-8-5 84 MHarley(5) 11 86
(Liam McAteer, Ire) *chsd ldrs: 4th 1/2-way: rdn 2f out: styd on to 2nd 1f out: no ex ins fnl f and kpt on same pce* **10/1**

4 1 ¾ **Miss Gorica (IRE)**[7] 4882 6-10-0 102 (p) WMLordan 8 98
(Ms Joanna Morgan, Ire) *led: rdn and hdd under 2f out: no ex in 3rd over 1f out: kpt on same pce ins fnl f* **8/1**[3]

5 ½ **Arganil (USA)**[49] 3489 5-9-11 106 (p) LFRoche(7) 2 101
(K A Ryan) *chsd ldrs: 6th 1/2-way: rdn 2f out: no ex 1 1/2f out: 7th 1f out: kpt on same pce ins fnl f* **9/1**

6 ½ **Cape Vale (IRE)**[11] 4723 5-8-11 85 CDHayes 4 78
(Kevin Prendergast, Ire) *chsd ldrs: 5th 1/2-way: rdn in 7th and no ex 1 1/2f out: 6th 1f out: kpt on same pce* **14/1**

7 1 ¼ **Calm Bay (IRE)**[9] 4809 4-8-13 94 (b) DCByrne(7) 9 83
(H Rogers, Ire) *chsd ldr in 2nd: chal 2f out: rdn in 2nd 1 1/2f out: no ex in 5th 1f out: kpt on one pce* **20/1**

8 ¾ **Copper Dock (IRE)**[49] 3489 6-9-3 94 BACurtis(3) 10 81
(T G McCourt, Ire) *hld up towards rr: hdwy into 8th 2f out: rdn and no imp 1 1/2f out: kpt on one pce* **14/1**

9 1 **The Tooth Fairy (IRE)**[98] 1953 4-9-1 92 GFCarroll(3) 13 76
(Michael Mulvany, Ire) *in rr of mid-div: rdn and no imp over 2f out: kpt on one pce* **20/1**

10 2 ½ **Bashir Biyoum Zain (IRE)**[39] 3800 3-8-10 88 (p) WJSupple 12 64
(P D Deegan, Ire) *a towards rr* **12/1**

11 nk **Dawn Eclipse (IRE)**[7] 4883 5-8-13 87 KJManning 5 62
(T G McCourt, Ire) *a towards rr* **8/1**[3]

12 3 ½ **Tarrsille (IRE)**[10] 4767 4-8-12 86 (b) DPMcDonogh 1 49
(Mrs John Harrington, Ire) *a towards rr* **20/1**

13 2 ½ **Airspace (IRE)**[28] 4180 4-9-2 90 JMurtagh 3 45
(M Halford, Ire) *a towards rr* **8/1**[3]

1m 11.6s (71.60)
WFA 3 from 4yo+ 4lb 13 Ran SP% **130.0**
CSF £19.60 CT £133.98 TOTE £5.50: £2.30, £1.80, £2.90; DF 22.80.
Owner Mrs Margaret Forsyth & Mrs R G Hillen **Bred** William Patterson & James Glenn **Trained** Hambleton, N Yorks

NOTEBOOK
Bajan Tryst(USA) had been in fine form lately in the Rockingham and again at Goodwood and appreciated the step up to this trip. He got a nice tow from the leaders and found plenty under Pat Smullen, never looking as though he would be caught. Clearly an improving sprinter, he has surely earned himself a try at pattern level now and takes his racing well. (op 9/2)

Luisant ran another cracker without winning. He still has only two wins to his name (both recorded here) and ultimately made no real impression on Bajan Tryst, but he made mincemeat of everything else and deserves a break now. Connections suggested afterwards that he might get one too. (op 9/2)

Tellelle(IRE) had more on her plate here after a Curragh victory, but ran a cracking race. She is obviously in great heart. (op 14/1)

Miss Gorica(IRE) is a credit to her connections and gave a good account of herself The weight probably found her out in such a competitive heat. (op 7/1)

Arganil(USA) had plenty on his plate off top weight and never really figured, but ran a solid race.

Cape Vale(IRE) might be up to winning a lesser handicap. (op 14/1 tchd 12/1)

Calm Bay(IRE) travelled well and would probably be better over the minimum trip.

Bashir Biyoum Zain(IRE) has become disappointing and was getting reminders very early on.

Tarrsille(IRE) Official explanation: jockey said gelding ran short of room in the early stages

5129a CUCHULAINN CRYSTAL H'CAP (DIV II) — 1m (P)

4:45 (4:46) (50-70,70) 3-Y-O+ £3,823 (£868; £366; £199)

RPR

1 **Buaiteoir (FR)**[24] 4311 4-9-10 66 FMBerry 13 71
(David Marnane, Ire) *chsd ldrs: 7th 1/2-way: hdwy in 4th 2f out: sn led: rdn and narrowly hdd 1f out: kpt on ins fnl f: led again on line* **6/1**[2]

2 shd **Rambling Dancer (IRE)**[24] 4311 6-9-7 66 SMGorey(3) 10 71
(Mrs Valerie Keatley, Ire) *mid-div: 9th 1/2-way: hdwy in 5th 2f out: sn chal: rdn to ld narrowly 1f out: strly pressed: hdd on line* **4/1**[1]

3 1 ½ **Cloud Fire (IRE)**[23] 4351 4-9-9 65 DPMcDonogh 7 67
(Kevin Prendergast, Ire) *chsd ldrs: 4th 1/2-way: rdn in cl 6th 2f out: 4th 1 1/2f out: no ex in 3rd 1f out: kpt on same pce ins fnl f* **4/1**[1]

4 ¾ **Kammaan**[29] 4159 4-9-11 67 WMLordan 4 67
(David Peter Nagle, Ire) *chsd ldrs: 6th 1/2-way: rdn in 8th 2f out: styd on to 5th 1 1/2f out: 4th and no ex 1f out: kpt on same pce ins fnl f* **14/1**

5 4 **Moonlight Rock (IRE)**[46] 3573 3-9-0 63 (p) PJSmullen 9 53
(P D Deegan, Ire) *chsd ldrs: 5th 1/2-way: rdn to chal in 3rd 2f out: no ex in 5th 1f out: kpt on same pce ins fnl f* **11/1**

6 ¾ **Trotting Weasel (IRE)**[9] 4811 7-9-0 56 (tp) JMurtagh 3 45
(M Halford, Ire) *mid-div: 8th 1/2-way: rdn 2f out: 7th 1f out: kpt on same pce ins fnl f* **13/2**[3]

7 2 **Richelieu**[29] 4162 8-9-1 62 MHarley(5) 12 46
(J J Lambe, Ire) *hld up towards rr: rdn in 10th 2f out: styd on to 6th 1f out: no ex ins fnl f: kpt on same pce* **16/1**

8 1 **Fandango Boy**[18] 4495 9-9-4 60 MCHussey 8 42
(J P Broderick, Ire) *chsd ldrs: 3rd 1/2-way: rdn in 7th 2f out: no ex 1 1/2f out: 8th 1f out: kpt on one pce* **12/1**

9 ½ **Cullofane (IRE)**[13] 4667 5-9-3 66 KarenKenny(7) 1 47
(Patrick Martin, Ire) *towards rr for most: nvr a factor* **12/1**

10 hd **Adam's Return (IRE)**[10] 4771 4-10-0 70 CDHayes 6 50
(W T Farrell, Ire) *in rr of mid-div for most: rdn and no ex ent st* **12/1**

11 nk **Gleaming Silver (IRE)**[77] 2572 4-9-4 70 DJBenson(10) 14 50
(G M Lyons, Ire) *a towards rr* **14/1**

12 ¾ **Strandhill (IRE)**[27] 4219 3-8-12 68 (b) RPWhelan(7) 11 45
(Brian Nolan, Ire) *led: hdd after 2 1/2f out: 2nd 1/2-way: chal 3f out: rdn and no ex under 2f out: sn wknd* **14/1**

13 4 ½ **Five Two**[3] 5017 7-9-2 58 (bt) WJSupple 5 26
(Gavin Patrick Cromwell, Ire) *hld up towards rr early: swift hdwy to ld after 2 1/2f out: rdn and hdd under 2f out: wknd* **14/1**

1m 39.02s (99.02)
WFA 3 from 4yo+ 7lb 13 Ran SP% **131.6**
CSF £33.48 CT £118.84 TOTE £5.40: £2.00, £2.00, £2.10; DF 22.50.
Owner Eugene McDermott **Bred** Ruthlyn Bloodstock Limited **Trained** Bansha, Co Tipperary

NOTEBOOK
Buaiteoir(FR) showed a game attitude to win this and continue his trainer's fine recent run. Those held up off the gallop were well placed here and the Buailteoir came to win his race, but seemed to be losing the battle to the runner-up. He found plenty to get up again close home and his trainer intends keeping him to this surface and looking for something similar next time. (op 13/2 tchd 7/1)

Rambling Dancer(IRE) took the eye a long way out and came there travelling well to seemingly win his race. He was worn down in the end but gave his all. (op 9/2)

Cloud Fire(IRE), who led early, was then settled behind the leaders. She was given a sensible ride and had no excuses. (op 11/2)

Kammaan showed up quite well and might to be able to pick up a small handicap. (op 12/1)

Moonlight Rock(IRE) has generally been very disappointing. (op 10/1)

5128 - 5131a (Foreign Racing) - See Raceform Interactive

3018 COLOGNE (R-H)

Sunday, August 15

OFFICIAL GOING: Turf: soft

5132a RHEINLAND-POKAL (GROUP 1) (3YO+) (TURF) 1m 4f

4:00 (4:18) 3-Y-O+ £88,495 (£29,203; £13,274; £6,194)

RPR

1 **Campanologist (USA)**[29] 4164 5-9-6 0 ADeVries 7 115+
(Saeed Bin Suroor) *settled in 4th then dropped bk to last at end of bk st: mde smooth prog on fnl turn: swept to ld 2f out: drew clr ins fnl f: easily* **5/4**[1]

2 3 1/2 **Appel Au Maitre (FR)**[90] 2195 6-9-6 0 FJohansson 5 109
(Wido Neuroth, Norway) *broke fast to ld: setting mod pce initially: increasing tempo down bk st: gng 2 l clr: r.o wl in st: hdd 2f out: styd on wl to take 2nd on line* **12/1**

3 shd **Zazou (GER)**[28] 4184 3-8-10 0 THellier 4 110
(Mario Hofer, Germany) *last fr s: prog arnd fnl turn on outside and tk 2nd: wknd ins fnl f: lost 2nd on line* **13/8**[2]

4 4 **Quijano (GER)**[29] 4164 8-9-6 0 AStarke 2 102
(P Schiergen, Germany) *settled in 3rd: proged along bk st but could only stay on in st* **7/1**[3]

5 8 **Lyssio (GER)**[28] 4184 3-8-10 0 EPedroza 6 91
(P Schiergen, Germany) *racd in 2nd fr s and stl prom ent st: wknd in st* **12/1**

2m 40.81s (7.91)
WFA 3 from 4yo+ 11lb 5 Ran SP% **110.4**
WIN (incl.10 euro stake): 30. PLACES: 19, 22. SF: 158.
Owner Godolphin **Bred** Darley **Trained** Newmarket, Suffolk

FOCUS
Adrie De Vries replaced Frankie Dettori, who was caught in traffic on his way to the course. Titurel and Wiener Walzer were absentees because of the testing ground.

NOTEBOOK
Campanologist(USA) ploughed through the mud and rain to follow up his win in this grade in the Grosser Preis von Lotto Hamburg. Seeing off Zazou's challenge for a comfortable victory, he may return to Germany next month for the Grosser Preis von Baden.
Zazou(GER)

5107 DEAUVILLE (R-H)

Sunday, August 15

OFFICIAL GOING: Turf: very soft; fibresand: standard

5133a PRIX FRANCOIS BOUTIN (LISTED RACE) (2YO) (TURF) 7f

1:35 (12:00) 2-Y-O £24,336 (£9,734; £7,300; £4,867; £2,433)

RPR

1 **Hung Parliament (FR)**[16] 4565 2-9-2 0 DavyBonilla 1 102
(Tom Dascombe) *racd in 5th fr s: mde prog 2 1/2f out: chal for ld 1 1/2f out: grabbed ld 1f out: r.o wl* **22/1**

2 1 **Split Trois (FR)**[21] 4419 2-8-13 0 StephanePasquier 7 96
(Y De Nicolay, France) **73/10**

3 snk **King David (FR)**[4] 2-9-2 0 IoritzMendizabal 5 99
(M Boutin, France) **13/1**

4 nk **Private Jet (FR)**[17] 4527 2-9-2 0 MaximeGuyon 4 98
(H-A Pantall, France) **10/1**

5 3/4 **Ares Flight (IRE)**[19] 2-8-13 0 FlavienPrat 2 93
(P Bary, France) **9/1**

6 6 **Major Art**[18] 4468 2-9-2 0 RichardHughes 3 81
(R Hannon) *led fr s: rdn 2 1/2f out: wknd* **1/1**[1]

7 1/2 **Colorado Gold**[16] 4550 2-9-2 0 OlivierPeslier 6 80
(P F I Cole) *racd in 2nd fr s: rdn 1/2-way: sn wknd* **63/10**[2]

8 1/2 **Trebetherick (IRE)**[19] 2-9-2 0 ChristopheSoumillon 8 79
(J E Hammond, France) **13/2**[3]

1m 28.4s (0.10) **Going Correction** +0.175s/f (Good) 8 Ran SP% **119.7**
Speed ratings: **106,104,104,104,103 96,96,95**
WIN (incl. 1 euro stake): 23.30. PLACES: 5.30, 2.30, 3.30. DF: 71.80. SF: 214.10.
Owner The Tipperary Partners **Bred** Team Hogdala A B **Trained** Malpas, Cheshire

NOTEBOOK
Hung Parliament(FR) came into this a maiden and was stepping up in grade, but the softer surface suited and he scored well. A French-bred who cost €48,000 at the Arqana Sales last October, in addition to the prizemoney he also earned an owner's premium of 75 per cent. He could be aimed at the Group 3 Prix La Rochette at Longchamp next month over the same distance.
Major Art made the running but could not handle this much softer ground than he had previously encountered, and dropped away having been eased.
Colorado Gold also raced close to the pace but was another to struggle in the soft ground.

5134a PRIX DU HARAS DE FRESNAY-LE-BUFFARD - JACQUES LE MAROIS (GROUP 1) (3YO+ COLTS & FILLIES) (TURF) 1m (R)

2:40 (12:00) 3-Y-O+ £303,398 (£121,380; £60,690; £30,318; £15,185)

RPR

1 **Makfi**[61] 3048 3-8-11 0 ChristopheSoumillon 5 128
(M Delzangles, France) *settled in 6th: smoothly tk clsr order ins fnl 3f: 2nd 2f out: rdn to ld appr fnl 110yds: r.o wl* **7/1**[3]

2 2 1/2 **Goldikova (IRE)**[14] 4639 5-9-1 0 OlivierPeslier 6 121
(F Head, France) *trckd the two pcemakers travelling wl: led 2f out: rdn and hdd appr fnl 100yds: no ex* **4/6**[1]

3 nk **Paco Boy (IRE)**[61] 3046 5-9-4 0 RichardHughes 2 123
(R Hannon) *settled in last pl: hdwy 2 1/2f out: went 2nd and ev ch fnl f: no ex last 100yds* **9/4**[2]

4 6 **Fuisse (FR)**[29] 4166 4-9-4 0 StephanePasquier 8 109
(Mme C Head-Maarek, France) *settled in share of 4th on outside: in tch w front three 1 1/2f out: sn rdn and wknd* **8/1**

5 3 **Royal Bench (IRE)**[36] 3933 3-8-11 0 IoritzMendizabal 4 101
(Robert Collet, France) *racd in 7th: strly rdn 3f out: kpt on at one pce: n.d* **50/1**

6 1 **Runaway**[84] 2374 8-9-4 0 ThierryJarnet 3 100
(R Pritchard-Gordon, France) *disp 4th tl pushed along and fdd ins fnl 2f* **100/1**

7 6 **Only Green (IRE)**[14] 4639 4-9-1 0 DavyBonilla 7 83
(F Head, France) *pressed ldr: disp ld 2 1/2f out: sn led but hdd 2f out and dropped out qckly u.p: eased fnl 100yds* **200/1**

8 15 **Saying (USA)**[39] 3-8-8 0 (b) MickaelBarzalona 1 48
(F Head, France) *led: pushed along 3f out: jnd 2 1/2f out and dropped away qckly: eased fnl f* **100/1**

1m 39.4s (-1.40) **Going Correction** +0.175s/f (Good)
WFA 3 from 4yo+ 7lb 8 Ran SP% **118.8**
Speed ratings: **114,111,111,105,102 101,95,80**
PARI-MUTUEL (all including 1 euro stakes): WIN 5.40; PLACE 1.30, 1.10, 1.20; DF 8.80; SF 17.70.
Owner Mathieu Offenstadt **Bred** Shadwell Estate Company Limited **Trained** France

FOCUS
Makfi improved on his Guineas form but Goldikova was not at her best in the ground. Paco Boy improved on his previous best form in soft ground.

NOTEBOOK
Makfi proved he is one of the best of the Classic generation. He put his disappointing effort in the St James's Palace Stakes to behind him, when he was reportedly suffering from a throat infection, in swamping two very classy rivals. His 2000 Guineas victory from Dick Turpin and Canford Cliffs had been rubber stamped, with the runner-up gaining a Group 1 success in the Prix Jean Prat and the third taking the Irish 2000 Guineas, St James's Palace Stakes and the Sussex Stakes. Settled off the pace in the early stages, he was soon moving smoothly through the opposition and went to the front over 100m out. He picked up impressively in the easy ground to score a comfortable success, and it will be fascinating if he and Canford Cliffs meet again in the Queen Elizabeth II Stakes at Ascot next month.
Goldikova(IRE), bidding for a record-breaking 11th Group 1 victory, was put firmly in her place by the three-year-old Makfi, as she tried to follow up her success in this event 12 months earlier. Everything appeared to be panning out perfectly as she was held up tracking her pacemakers. However, the turn of foot she had shown to brush aside her rivals on her previous start in the Prix Rothschild (ex Prix D'Astarte) over C&D at the beginning of the month was not in evidence back against the colts. She picked up to lead over a furlong and a half out but she was soon being run down by the winner and Paco Boy. Maybe the very soft ground was against her, but she did outstay Paco Boy to claim the runner-up spot. She remains a top class mare and it should be only a matter of time before she notches another success at the highest level.
Paco Boy(IRE) wasn't held up as far back as when beaten by Goldikova in the Queen Anne at Royal Ascot and made a bold bid to gain his revenge. The winner of the Lockinge Stakes readily went past Goldikova 200m out, before being put in his place by the winner, but then lost out for second when the mare stayed on. He has proven on plenty of occasions that he gets the mile well enough but in these testing conditions he may not have got home quite as well as he should. This was third time that Goldikova has finished in front of him but he is a very classy horse and was well clear of the rest.
Fuisse(FR) has been on an upward curve with victories in Group 3 events at Maisons-Laffitte and Chantilly in the past two months and he ran a reasonable race taking this major step up in class but was left behind by the first three entering the closing stages. He has plenty of ability and can soon return to winning form in a lower grade than this.

5135a PRIX GUILLAUME D'ORNANO (GROUP 2) (3YO) (TURF) 1m 2f

3:15 (12:00) 3-Y-O £65,575 (£25,309; £12,079; £8,053; £4,026)

RPR

1 **Scalo**[28] 4184 3-9-2 0 MaximeGuyon 7 113
(A Wohler, Germany) *settled in bk three: 4th st: sn pushed along and mde hdwy to ld 1 1/2f out: styd on strly* **15/2**

2 2 **Wealthy (IRE)**[43] 3703 3-8-11 0 Pierre-CharlesBoudot 6 104
(A Fabre, France) *racd in 3rd: followed wnr through 1 1/2f out: kpt on wout having pce to go w wnr* **7/2**[2]

3 1 1/2 **Black Spirit (USA)**[21] 4420 3-8-11 0 RichardHughes 5 101
(C G Cox) *racd in bk three: 5th st: rdn 2f out: styd on to take 3rd ins fnl f* **7/1**[3]

4 2 **Mellon Martini (USA)**[43] 3703 3-8-11 0 GeraldMosse 3 97
(A De Royer-Dupre, France) *hld up towards rr: last st: rdn and outpcd over 2f out: styd on u.p fnl f: r.o strly fnl 50yds to take 4th cl home* **5/2**[1]

5 shd **Circumvent**[19] 4456 3-8-11 0 IoritzMendizabal 9 97
(P F I Cole) *led: 2l clr st: rdn over 2f out: hdd 1 1/2f out: no ex* **7/1**[3]

6 3/4 **Marceti (IRE)**[28] 4186 3-8-11 0 DominiqueBoeuf 2 95
(E Leenders, France) *trckd ldr: 2nd st gng wl: rdn and wknd fnl 300yds* **16/1**

7 3 **Lumineux**[21] 4420 3-8-11 0 OlivierPeslier 8 89
(A Fabre, France) *nvr plcd to chal* **7/2**[2]

2m 13.0s (2.80) **Going Correction** +0.35s/f (Good) 7 Ran SP% **115.7**
Speed ratings: **102,100,99,97,97 96,94**
PARI-MUTUEL (all including 1 euro stakes): WIN 9.80; PLACE 3.10, 2.10, 4.30; DF 27.40; SF 55.80.
Owner Gestut Ittlingen **Bred** Gestut Hof Ittlingen **Trained** Germany

NOTEBOOK
Scalo finished ninth in the Deutsches Derby last time out and fifth in a German Group 2 before that, but he left that well behind on the soft turf, conditions that clearly brought out the best in him. His trainer opted to run him here instead of a Group 1 at Cologne against older horses. There are no plans for the colt.
Wealthy(IRE) was never far away and ranged up on the leader's flank, but when the winner asserted he could only keep on at one-pace.
Black Spirit(USA) pleased his trainer with a decent third and handled the soft ground pretty well. He might come back to France for a race like La Coupe at Maisons-Laffitte next month.
Mellon Martini(USA) was sent off favourite but raced in the rear until late, and could only stay on past the backmarkers.
Circumvent finished fifth after attempting to make all and kicking on at the turn to the straight. His trainer might consider dropping him back to a mile and running in the Prix Daniel Wildenstein on Arc weekend.

5136a PRIX MICHEL HOUYVET (LISTED RACE) (3YO) (TURF) 1m 7f

3:50 (12:00) 3-Y-O £24,336 (£9,734; £7,300; £4,867; £2,433)

RPR

1 **Le Larron (IRE)**[63] 3014 3-8-11 0 ChristopheSoumillon 9 89
(A De Royer-Dupre, France) **5/2**[1]

2 snk **Brampour (IRE)**[49] 3-8-11 0 IoritzMendizabal 2 89
(J-C Rouget, France) **11/1**

3 2 **Amarak**[18] 3-8-11 0 (b) OlivierPeslier 5 87
(F Head, France) **17/2**

4 3 **Tazmiyna (FR)**[35] 3-8-8 0 GeraldMosse 3 80
(A De Royer-Dupre, France) **7/2**[2]

5 snk **Nobel (GER)**[83] 3-8-11 0 (b) DavyBonilla 8 83
(Andreas Lowe, Germany) **14/1**

6 3 **Plenty Pocket (FR)**[49] 3-8-11 0 AnthonyCrastus 7 79
(E Lellouche, France) **8/1**

7 15 **Bedouin Bay**[26] 3-8-11 0 Pierre-CharlesBoudot 6 61
(A Fabre, France) **8/1**

8 10 **Admission**93 2070 3-8-11 0 RichardHughes 1 49
(M L W Bell) *settled towards rr of field: dropped bk to last ent st: rdn and sn wknd: eased* **43/10**3

3m 21.1s (2.00) **Going Correction** +0.35s/f (Good) 8 Ran SP% **117.4**
Speed ratings: **108,107,106,105,105 103,95,90**
WIN (incl. 1 euro stake): 3.50. PLACES: 1.60, 2.60, 2.50. DF: 14.30. SF: 24.20.
Owner Marquesa De Moratalla **Bred** P Nataf **Trained** Chantilly, France

NOTEBOOK
Admission never looked dangerous and eventually tailed off, having been eased.

4884 DEAUVILLE (R-H)
Thursday, August 12
OFFICIAL GOING: Turf: good to soft; fibresand: standard

5137a PRIX ETALON NAAQOOS (CONDITIONS) (2YO) (FIBRESAND) 6f 110y
3:25 (12:00) 2-Y-0 **£12,831** (£5,132; £3,849; £2,566; £1,283)

RPR
1 **Nova Step**32 2-8-0 0 EddyHardouin(6) 6 90
(F Rohaut, France) **33/10**3
2 2 **Kagura (USA)**34 2-8-13 0 OlivierPeslier 4 91
(G Henrot, France) **5/2**2
3 2 ½ **Footsteppy (IRE)**27 2-8-6 0 RaphaelMarchelli 2 77
(S Wattel, France) **9/5**1
4 1 **Venetien (FR)** 2-8-13 0 (b) StephanePasquier 1 81
(R Gibson, France) **73/10**
5 nk **Allez Les Bleus (FR)**22 4274 2-8-9 0 WilliamsSaraiva(4) 8 81
(Mme J Bidgood, Spain) **10/1**
6 8 **Aglaia (IRE)** 2-8-6 0 ThomasHuet 3 52
(J E Pease, France) **17/1**
7 10 **Allegorio (FR)**27 4089 2-8-9 0 DavyBonilla 7 27
(Tom Dascombe) *swtchd to rails sn after s: sn rdn: u.p ent st: qckly wknd: t.o* **33/1**
8 ¾ **Kiss Doll (IRE)**48 2-8-3 0 MorganDelalande(3) 5 22
(C Lerner, France) **58/1**

1m 20.7s (80.70) 8 Ran SP% **118.9**
WIN (incl., 1 euro stake): 4.30. PLACES: 1.30, 1.20, 1.20. DF: 8.90. SF: 18.60.
Owner A Mouknass & A Forde **Bred** Dreosan Et Associates **Trained** Sauvagnon, France

NOTEBOOK
Allegorio(FR) was never going and finished well beaten on this first try on Polytrack.

5138a PRIX MINERVE - SHADWELL (GROUP 3) (3YO FILLIES) (TURF) 1m 4f 110y
4:35 (12:00) 3-Y-0 **£35,398** (£14,159; £10,619; £7,079; £3,539)

RPR
1 **Announce**29 4037 3-8-9 0 MaximeGuyon 5 104
(A Fabre, France) *racd in 2nd: qcknd u.p to take ld 1 1/2f out: wandered off st line ins fnl f but r.o wl to line to hold runner-up* **11/4**2
2 nk **Shamanova (IRE)**46 3493 3-8-9 0 GeraldMosse 4 104
(A De Royer-Dupre, France) *racd in 3rd: rdn 1 1/2f out: r.o wl: appeared to be hmpd briefly by wnr 100yds out: qcknd wl: failed only narrowly* **10/11**1
3 1 ½ **Middle Club**56 3101 3-8-9 0 IoritzMendizabal 6 102
(R Hannon) *led fr s: set mod pce: hdd 1 1/2f out: hrd rdn and styd on wl* **8/1**3
4 nk **Sarah Lynx (IRE)**26 3-8-9 0 ChristopheSoumillon 1 101
(J E Hammond, France) *s.i.s: racd in 5th upon settling: hrd rdn early in st: qcknd wl ent fnl f: styd on wl* **12/1**
5 1 ½ **Bikini Babe (IRE)**12 4612 3-8-9 0 DominiqueBoeuf 2 99
(M Johnston) *racd in 4th: rdn 1 1/2f out: failed to qckn: styd on ins fnl f* **9/1**
6 4 **Maria Royal (IRE)**19 4395 3-8-9 0 MorganDelalande 3 93
(A De Royer-Dupre, France) *settled at rr: rdn early in st: fnd no ex: fdd* **11/1**

2m 46.8s (0.40) **Going Correction** +0.225s/f (Good) 6 Ran SP% **116.2**
Speed ratings: **107,106,105,105,104 102**
WIN (incl. 1 euro stake): 2.90. PLACES: 1.40, 1.30. SF: 5.70.
Owner K Abdulla **Bred** Juddmonte Farms **Trained** Chantilly, France

NOTEBOOK
Announce won her third successive race and first Group race with a more comfortable victory than the margin suggests. She is likely to be aimed at the Prix Vermeille now.
Shamanova(IRE) has now been a beaten favourite in both her Group races but she remains on the upgrade. She might prefer a slightly faster surface.
Middle Club made the running but could have done with a better pace, according to connections, as she stayed on again having been headed. The Prix de Royallieu at the Arc meeting is her likely target.
Bikini Babe(IRE) never got involved and is probably happier on a sounder surface.

5139a PRIX DE LIEUREY - SHADWELL (GROUP 3) (3YO FILLIES) (TURF) 1m (R)
5:05 (12:00) 3-Y-0 **£35,398** (£14,159; £10,619; £7,079; £3,539)

RPR
1 **Via Medici (IRE)**68 2777 3-8-11 0 Francois-XavierBertras 14 100
(F Rohaut, France) *settled in last: rdn st: r.o wl fnl 1 1/2f to ld fnl 50yds* **13/2**3
2 1 **Field Day (IRE)**20 4319 3-8-11 0 MartinDwyer 10 97
(B J Meehan) *hld up towards rr: hdwy 2f out: 7th and hmpd by rival 1 1/2f out: swtchd and r.o wl u.p* **4/1**1
3 snk **Rockatella (IRE)**53 3-8-11 0 DominiqueBoeuf 1 97
(W Hefter, Germany) *racd in midfield: 5th 3f out: rdn ins fnl 2f: swtchd 1 1/2f out and r.o: hmpd 1f out: r.o wl fnl 100yds* **20/1**
4 ½ **Naadrah**28 3-8-11 0 DavyBonilla 5 96
(J E Hammond, France) *racd towards rr: 10th st (jst over 2f out): swtchd ins appr fnl f and r.o to chal ldr 100yds out: led briefly: hdd and no ex fnl 50yds* **25/1**
5 hd **Evading Tempete**55 3143 3-9-2 0 (p) OlivierPeslier 8 100
(F Rohaut, France) *racd in midfield: 10th 3f out: pushed along 2f out and sltly impeded by rival: hmpd again 1f out: styd on u.p fnl 50yds* **5/1**2
6 nk **Aslana (IRE)**29 4035 3-9-2 0 AStarke 6 100
(P Schiergen, Germany) *racd in midfield: 7th st: pushed along and disp 3rd ins fnl f: no ex last 75yds* **9/1**
7 shd **Disclose**32 3944 3-8-11 0 MaximeGuyon 2 94
(A Fabre, France) *hld up: last st: hdwy u.p 1 1/2f out: no imp fnl 100yds: fin 8th: plcd 7th* **14/1**
8 ¾ **Ercolini (IRE)**18 3-8-11 0 J-LMartinez 3 93
(F Rodriguez Puertas, Spain) *a.p: 4th st: sn rdn and unable qck: fin 9th: plcd 8th* **18/1**
9 hd **Kilo Alpha**18 3-8-11 0 StephanePasquier 13 92
(Mme C Head-Maarek, France) *chsd ldr: disp 2nd st: sn rdn and wknd: fin 10th: plcd 9th* **8/1**
10 **Corcovada (IRE)**32 3944 3-8-11 0 GregoryBenoist 7 —
(V Luka Jr, Czech Republic) *chsd ldng quartet: 4th 3f out: drifted lft u.p and hmpd rival 1 1/2f out: sn wknd: fin 11th: plcd 10th* **20/1**
11 **Khelwa (FR)**28 3-8-11 0 GeraldMosse 11 —
(R Gibson, France) *hld up towards rr: disp 8th 3f out: c wd fnl bnd: kpt on at one pce: n.d: fin 12th: plcd 11th* **10/1**
12 **Thai Haku (IRE)**49 3385 3-8-11 0 PhilippeSogorb 12 —
(M Delzangles, France) *a bhd: hmpd 1f out: eased: fin 13th: plcd 12th* **20/1**
13 **Mahamaya (GER)**39 3720 3-8-11 0 ADeVries 9 —
(A Trybuhl, Germany) *settled in midfield: 6th 3f out: drifted lft and impeded rival ins fnl 2f: bdly hmpd 1f out: eased: fin 14th: plcd 13th* **14/1**
D ½ **It's Midnight (USA)**42 3-8-11 0 ChristopheSoumillon 4 94
(P Bary, France) *led: swvd bdly lft 1f out: hdd ins fnl 100yds: no ex: fin 7th: disqualified* **7/1**

1m 41.3s (0.50) **Going Correction** +0.225s/f (Good) 14 Ran SP% **129.4**
Speed ratings: **106,105,104,104,104 103,103,102,102,102 102,102,102,103**
WIN (incl. 1 euro stake): WIN 6.20; PLACE 2.30, 2.30, 7.90; DF 15.80; SF 47.00.
Owner Scea Haras De Saint Pair **Bred** 6c Racing **Trained** Sauvagnon, France

NOTEBOOK
Via Medici(IRE) came from last to first to beat the favourite. She won a Listed race at Longchamp in June and stepped up again here. She is reportly being aimed at the Flower Bowl Invitational at Belmont in October.
Field Day(IRE) was held up early but was short of room at the top of the straight as she tried to make progress from the rear and was hampered and had to be snatched up a furlong and a half from home. She recovered and ran on well but the winner got first run. Her trainer believes she is a Group 1 filly and so she will be aimed at either the Sun Chariot or the Prix de l'Opera over the first weekend in October with a race in between.
Rockatella(IRE), a Listed winner in Italy in June, was another who was hampered by the errant It's Midnight and also finished well.

5025 KEMPTON (A.W) (R-H)
Monday, August 16
OFFICIAL GOING: Standard
Wind: Nil Weather: Sunny

5140 DIGIBET.COM NURSERY 6f (P)
2:30 (2:31) (Class 4) (0-85,80) 2-Y-0 **£3,238** (£963; £481; £240) **Stalls High**

Form RPR
3324 1 **Fifth Ave**50 3476 2-8-13 77 SophieDoyle(5) 3 80
(J A Osborne) *trckd ldr: led over 1f out: shkn up and styd on strly fnl f* **8/1**
244 2 1 ¾ **Hortensia (IRE)**12 4696 2-9-7 80 ChrisCatlin 5 78
(M R Channon) *trckd ldrs: drvn and styd on to chse wnr appr fnl f: no imp* **4/1**2
61 3 2 **Majestic Dream (IRE)**21 4421 2-9-4 77 ShaneKelly 2 69
(W R Swinburn) *awkward leaving stalls: trckd ldrs: rdn and one pce ins fnl 2f: kpt on u.p ins fnl f: nvr any threat to ldng duo* **11/8**1
4551 4 1 ½ **Volcanic Dust (IRE)**12 4688 2-8-10 69 WilliamBuick 6 57
(E A L Dunlop) *stdd s: plld hrd chsng ldrs: rdn and effrt on ins 2f out: rdn: edgd lft and wknd appr fnl f* **9/2**3
6250 5 3 ¼ **Inagh River**16 4592 2-8-13 72 (b1) RichardHughes 4 50
(R Hannon) *t.k.h: led: pushed along and hdd over 1f out: sn wknd* **9/2**3

1m 13.88s (0.78) **Going Correction** +0.075s/f (Slow) 5 Ran SP% **109.6**
Speed ratings (Par 96): **97,94,92,90,85**
CSF £37.62 TOTE £3.20: £2.90, £1.90; EX 24.60.
Owner Pennick, Durkan, Hearn **Bred** Llety Stud **Trained** Upper Lambourn, Berks

FOCUS
A lack of progressive types made for an ordinary nursery and the profiles of front two limits things.

NOTEBOOK
Fifth Ave, freshened up by a 50-day break, showed herself on a good mark, running on well without her rider having to go for everything. She should remain competitive. (op 9-1)
Hortensia(IRE) found this easier that the C&D nursery she contested last time, but she was no match for the winner. A sluggish start didn't help matters and she could make no impression. (op 7-1)
Majestic Dream(IRE) probably didn't beat much when winning his maiden at Windsor, and he failed to justify skinny odds on this switch to nursery company. His chance wasn't helped by racing wide, but even so this was disappointing. (op 11-10)
Volcanic Dust(IRE) won despite pulling hard over 5f at Brighton on her previous start, but she couldn't get away with it this time, in better company off a 6lb higher mark, and over a slightly longer trip. She looks one to avoid. (op 7-2)
Inagh River, fitted with blinkers for the first time, didn't settle in front and weakened quickly in the straight. She was reported to have hung right. Official explanation: jockey said filly hung right-handed (op 11-2 tchd 4-1 after 13-2 in places)

5141 OLLY MURS LIVE ON LADIES DAY MAIDEN FILLIES' STKS 1m 4f (P)
3:00 (3:00) (Class 5) 3-Y-0+ **£2,286** (£675; £337) **Stalls High**

Form RPR
2 1 **Flower Fairy (USA)**14 4661 3-8-12 0 WilliamBuick 5 74+
(J H M Gosden) *trckd ldrs in 3rd: wnt 2nd ins fnl 4f: pushed along to ld jst ins fnl 2f: shkn up ins fnl f: comf* **1/1**1
2623 2 2 **Wulfrida (IRE)**7 4893 3-8-12 79 PatCosgrave 1 71
(J R Fanshawe) *hld up towards rr in tch: rdn and hung rt 2f out: stl hanging whn rdn to chse wnr jst ins fnl f: a readily hld* **7/4**2
04 3 2 ½ **Tigress Hill**10 4792 3-8-12 0 PatDobbs 3 67
(Mrs A J Perrett) *led: pushed along and hdd jst ins fnl 2f: lost 2nd jst ins fnl f: sn wknd* **20/1**
64 4 shd **Silver Colors (USA)**28 4205 3-8-12 0 JimmyFortune 4 67
(J Noseda) *chsd ldrs: puhed along and outpcd over 2f out: kpt on again ins fnl f but nvr a threat* **6/1**3

66 **5** *37* **Utern**[10] 4792 6-9-8 0............................ LiamKeniry 2 —
(Miss Venetia Williams) *trckd ldr tl ins fnl 4f: hung lft bnd 3f out: sn no ch and wnt rt to far rail over 2f out: eased: t.o* **50/1**

2m 35.55s (1.05) **Going Correction** +0.075s/f (Slow)
WFA 3 from 6yo 10lb 5 Ran SP% **107.4**
Speed ratings (Par 100): **99,97,96,95,71**
CSF £2.79 TOTE £1.90: £1.10, £1.10; EX 2.70.
Owner H R H Princess Haya Of Jordan **Bred** Indian Creek, H Lascelles, A Stroud & W B Isaa **Trained** Newmarket, Suffolk

FOCUS
An uncompetitive fillies' maiden and the time was modest. The form looks fluid and could prove unreliable.

5142 LADIES DAY SEPTEMBER 4TH H'CAP 1m (P)
3:30 (3:30) (Class 4) (0-85,85) 3-Y-0+ **£3,885** (£1,156; £577; £288) **Stalls** High

Form RPR

5440 **1** **Sweet Clementine (IRE)**[16] 4593 3-9-3 **82**.................. ShaneKelly 1 90+
(W J Knight) *hld up in rr: swtchd lft over 2f out and str run fr over 1f out: styd on wl u.p ins ins fnl f to ld last stride* **8/1**

2000 **2** *nse* **Red Somerset (USA)**[11] 4756 7-9-12 **85**.................. AndreaAtzeni 3 94
(Mike Murphy) *sn in tch: hdwy 3f out: chsd ldrs over 2f out: chsd ldr appr fnl f: styd on to chal fnl 120yds: disp ld last strides: hdd on line* **40/1**

11-6 **3** *shd* **Mustakmil (IRE)**[40] 3782 4-9-5 **78**.................. WilliamBuick 11 87
(S Dow) *chsd ldr: led over 2f out: rdn and styd on gamely whn strly chal thrght fnl f: hdd last stride* **6/1**[3]

2400 **4** *2* **Dinner Date**[61] 3079 8-8-8 **74**.................. SophieSilvester(7) 5 78
(T Keddy) *s.i.s: hld up in rr: stdy hdwy over 2f out: kpt on wl fnl f and gng on cl home but nt trbld ldng trio* **20/1**

2-30 **5** *2* **Walcot Square (IRE)**[16] 4593 3-8-10 **75**.................. SteveDrowne 9 73
(R Charlton) *chsd ldrs: rdn 2f out: styd on same pce fnl f* **7/1**

0310 **6** *1 1/4* **Cobo Bay**[33] 4023 5-9-10 **83**.................. (b) LiamKeniry 2 80
(C R Dore) *chsd ldrs over 2f out tl appr fnl f: wknd fnl 120yds* **25/1**

0526 **7** *1/2* **Prince Of Thebes (IRE)**[11] 4756 9-9-1 **79**.................. KierenFox(5) 4 75
(M J Attwater) *chsd ldrs: rdn over 2f out: wknd fnl f* **16/1**

6403 **8** *nse* **Having A Ball**[3] 5039 6-8-7 **66**.................. ChrisCatlin 10 61
(P D Cundell) *in rr: pushed along and r.o fr over 1f out: kpt on cl home* **20/1**

1133 **9** *2 1/4* **Warning Song (USA)**[12] 4699 3-8-12 **77**.................. PatDobbs 14 65
(Mrs A J Perrett) *chsd ldrs: rdn over 2f out: wknd fnl f* **9/2**[2]

5-00 **10** *1* **Hurricane Hymnbook (USA)**[61] 3083 5-9-8 **81**.................. TonyCulhane 13 69
(W J Musson) *in rr: sme prog fnl f* **14/1**

2261 **11** *3/4* **Kiss A Prince**[9] 4839 4-9-0 **73**.................. (b) TomQueally 12 59
(D K Ivory) *s.i.s: rdn and hung rt 2f out: a in rr* **4/1**[1]

0004 **12** *nk* **Arachnophobia (IRE)**[16] 4598 4-9-10 **83**.................. RichardHughes 7 69
(Pat Eddery) *chsd ldrs: rdn 2f out: sn wknd* **15/2**

0002 **13** *2* **Elusive Fame (USA)**[7] 4894 4-9-0 **80**.................. (b) CharlesPerkins(7) 6 61
(M Johnston) *led tl hdd & wknd over 2f out* **16/1**

1m 37.99s (-1.81) **Going Correction** +0.075s/f (Slow)
WFA 3 from 4yo+ 6lb 13 Ran SP% **122.1**
Speed ratings (Par 105): **112,111,111,109,107 106,106,106,103,102 102,101,99**
toteswingers:1&2:£54.20, 1&3:£13.40, 2&3:£53.10 CSF £308.79 CT £2132.63 TOTE £17.20: £5.20, £14.30, £1.10; EX 487.50.
Owner D G Hardisty Bloodstock **Bred** D G Hardisty Bloodstock **Trained** Patching, W Sussex

FOCUS
A good, competitive handicap run at a quick gallop. There was a thrilling finish, with three horses in a line giving their all. The form loos sound but limited by the proximity of the second.
Hurricane Hymnbook(USA) Official explanation: jockey said gelding moved poorly

5143 EPSOM TRAINERS OPEN DAY AUGUST 22ND H'CAP 7f (P)
4:00 (4:01) (Class 2) (0-100,95) 3-Y-0
£9,221 (£2,761; £1,380; £691; £344; £173) **Stalls** High

Form RPR

2111 **1** **Kakatosi**[26] 4264 3-9-6 **94**.................. JimmyFortune 6 107+
(A M Balding) *t.k.h early: chsd ldrs: drvn over 2f out: styd on to ld ins fnl f: r.o strly* **13/2**

2241 **2** *1 3/4* **Bohemian Melody**[27] 4231 3-9-2 **90**.................. JerryO'Dwyer 3 100+
(M Botti) *bmpd and wnt lft s: in rr: hdwy over 2f out: styng on whn nt clr run on ins 1f out: swtchd lft and kpt on wl to chse wnr ins fnl f but no imp* **13/2**

2000 **3** *2* **Al Farahidi (USA)**[23] 4358 3-9-1 **89**.................. (b) AndrewMullen 4 92
(M Johnston) *vered lft s: chsd ldrs: led over 2f out: rdn over 1f out and hdd ins fnl f: sn wknd* **12/1**

1-24 **4** *1/2* **Mass Rally (IRE)**[23] 4357 3-9-6 **94**.................. WilliamBuick 1 96+
(J H M Gosden) *s.i.s: in rr: pushed along 3f out: hdwy on outside fr 2f out: edgd lft and kpt on to take readily hld 4th ins fnl f* **9/4**[1]

-111 **5** *nk* **The Confessor**[7] 4894 3-8-13 **87** 6ex.................. DaneO'Neill 2 88
(H Candy) *bmpd s: sn rcvrd to chse ldrs: rdn and one pce 2f out: kpt on again fnl f* **3/1**[2]

531 **6** *1 1/2* **Avenuesnalleyways (IRE)**[38] 3876 3-9-2 **90**.................. RichardKingscote 9 87
(R M Beckett) *led: rdn and hdd over 2f out: wknd fnl f* **5/1**[3]

-000 **7** *hd* **Quarrel (USA)**[16] 4574 3-9-7 **95**.................. GeorgeBaker 8 91
(W J Haggas) *in rr tl styd on fnl f* **28/1**

66-5 **8** *1/2* **Florio Vincitore (IRE)**[128] 1221 3-8-8 **82**.................. EddieCreighton 5 77
(E J Creighton) *chsd ldrs tl wknd over 2f out* **100/1**

1-00 **9** *3/4* **Rum King (USA)**[9] 4819 3-9-5 **93**.................. RichardHughes 7 86
(R Hannon) *stdd s: shkn up over 2f out: a in rr* **40/1**

1m 24.97s (-1.03) **Going Correction** +0.075s/f (Slow) 9 Ran SP% **113.7**
Speed ratings (Par 106): **108,106,103,103,102 101,100,100,99**
toteswingers:1&2:£5.50, 1&3:£11.60, 2&3:£10.90 CSF £46.68 CT £493.09 TOTE £9.80: £3.30, £2.00, £4.70; EX 44.70.
Owner Robert E Tillett **Bred** T E Pocock **Trained** Kingsclere, Hants

FOCUS
A decent 3-y-o handicap full of progressive types, and they went a good pace. The winner recorded a personal best and the form looks decent.

NOTEBOOK
Kakatosi defied a 6lb higher mark than when winning at Sandown on his previous start. He was keen, but in a manner that suggests he thoroughly enjoys his racing, as opposed to wanting to get it over and done with, and displayed an exuberant action, basically just showing a really willing attitude. He can surely keep progressing, and is likely to be stepped up to pattern company next time (may be given a Challenge Stakes entry), although it's fair to say he should have been given more to do on this occasion by Bohemian Melody. (op 7-1 tchd 15-2)
Bohemian Melody ◆ received a poor ride. Raised 5lb for his recent 6f course win, was initially well placed considering the quick gallop, but was taken towards the inside early in the straight, rather than going wide of Kakatosi, and following a shrewd bit of race riding from the winner's jockey, he became short of room around 1f out. He was going well at the time, but that incident cost him vital momentum. Whatever, his form figures on Polytrack read 21212, and also effective on turf, he's very much one to keep on-side. (tchd 7-1)
Al Farahidi(USA) appreciated the return to Polytrack - form figures on the surface now 213 - and ran a good race, keeping on after chasing the hot pace. (op 20-1)
Mass Rally(IRE) was 7lb better off with Kakatosi than when just a head behind that rival at Sandown on July 3, but he produced a rather laboured effort. He was being pushed along in rear by about halfway and simply got going much too late. On this evidence he'll be suited by a return to around 1m. (op 2-1 tchd 5-2)
The Confessor ◆ couldn't defy a penalty for his impressive Fibresand success, but this was by no means a bad performance. He was trying both a right-handed track and Polytrack for the first time, had a far from ideal draw, and couldn't dominate, yet still finished close up. There should be more to come. (tchd 11-4)
Avenuesnalleyways(IRE) went off fast and couldn't defy a 12lb rise for his York win. (op 11-2)

5144 DIGIBET CASINO H'CAP 2m (P)
4:30 (4:31) (Class 4) (0-85,79) 4-Y-0+ **£3,885** (£1,156; £577; £288) **Stalls** High

Form RPR

4300 **1** **Satwa Gold (USA)**[9] 4846 4-9-6 **78**.................. TomQueally 1 86+
(Stef Higgins) *trckd ldrs: slt ld 2f out: shkn up and r.o strly fnl f* **10/3**[1]

4636 **2** *1 3/4* **Alnwick**[30] 4141 6-9-4 **76**.................. DaneO'Neill 5 82
(P D Cundell) *in rr but in tch: hdwy 3f out: rdn and styd on fr over 1f out: kpt on fnl f to take 2nd clsng stages but no ch w wnr* **9/2**

065 **3** *hd* **William's Way**[15] 4620 8-8-9 **67**.................. (t) LiamKeniry 4 73
(I A Wood) *hld up in rr: hdwy on ins to press wnr 2f out: outpcd fnl f and lost 2nd clsng stages* **16/1**

1100 **4** *1 1/4* **On Terms (USA)**[19] 4467 4-9-5 **77**.................. WilliamBuick 2 81
(S Dow) *led 3f: trckd ldr: slt ld again over 4f out: rdn and hdd 2f out: styd on same pce fr over 1f out* **7/2**[2]

31-3 **5** *8* **Count Of Tuscany (USA)**[17] 4530 4-9-3 **75**.................. RichardHughes 6 74
(C R Egerton) *led after 3f: narrowly hdd over 3f out: styd pressing ldr to 2f out: wknd qckly 1f out: eased whn btn* **9/2**

4410 **6** *17* **Curacao**[19] 4467 4-9-7 **79**.................. PatDobbs 3 53
(Mrs A J Perrett) *chsd ldrs: rdn stable bnd 9f out: styd chsng ldrs tl rdn 6f out: wknd 3f out* **4/1**[3]

30/- **7** *9* **Noddies Way**[786] 3250 7-8-2 **60**.................. DavidProbert 7 23
(J F Panvert) *in tch tl rdn and wknd over 3f out* **20/1**

3m 29.79s (-0.31) **Going Correction** +0.075s/f (Slow) 7 Ran SP% **112.3**
Speed ratings (Par 105): **103,102,102,101,97 88,84**
toteswingers:1&2:£3.70, 1&3:£5.50, 2&3:£6.50 CSF £17.90 TOTE £6.00: £3.70, £2.20; EX 18.90.
Owner Mrs Anne & Fred Cowley **Bred** B P Walden, L Taylor Et Al **Trained** Lambourn, Berks

FOCUS
A fair staying handicap run at a modest gallop early but the time was reasonable and the runner-up represents a solid guide.
Alnwick Official explanation: vet said gelding returned distressed
Count Of Tuscany(USA) Official explanation: jockey said filly hung left-handed

5145 DIGIBET.COM FILLIES' H'CAP 7f (P)
5:00 (5:01) (Class 4) (0-80,78) 3-Y-0 **£3,885** (£1,156; £577; £288) **Stalls** High

Form RPR

0-62 **1** **Falling Angel**[26] 4250 3-9-4 **75**.................. JamieSpencer 9 77
(P F I Cole) *mde all: hrd rdn fnl f: all out* **3/1**[2]

0613 **2** *1* **Excellent Day (IRE)**[3] 5041 3-8-13 **70**.................. ChrisCatlin 4 68
(M R Channon) *in rr: hdwy on ins 2f out: styd on u.p to disp 2nd fnl f: kpt on to chse wnr cl home but a hld* **10/1**

0125 **3** *nk* **Lenkiewicz**[26] 4250 3-9-2 **76**.................. JamesMillman(3) 8 74
(B R Millman) *chsd ldrs: wnt 2nd 2f out: rdn and effrt over 1f out: nvr quite on terms and one pce ins fnl f: lost 2nd cl home* **8/1**

1500 **4** *2* **Water Gipsy**[19] 4472 3-9-5 **76**.................. GeorgeBaker 5 69
(G L Moore) *chsd wnr to 2f out: wknd fnl f* **16/1**

0-33 **5** *nk* **Night Sky**[54] 3333 3-8-12 **69**.................. JimmyFortune 2 61
(P J Makin) *s.i.s: towards rr but in tch: rdn over 3f out: edgd rt fr 2f out: styd on fnl f but nvr a threat* **6/1**

2153 **6** *7* **Our Drama Queen (IRE)**[13] 4680 3-8-13 **70**.................. RichardHughes 7 43
(R Hannon) *chsd ldrs: rdn over 2f out: sn btn* **11/4**[1]

1645 **P** **Al Khimiya (IRE)**[25] 4308 3-8-13 **70**.................. RichardMullen 6 —
(S Woodman) *p.u sn after leaving stalls* **4/1**[3]

1m 26.92s (0.92) **Going Correction** +0.075s/f (Slow) 7 Ran SP% **112.0**
Speed ratings (Par 99): **97,95,95,93,92 84,—**
toteswingers:1&2:£3.90, 1&3:£4.10, 2&3:£6.00 CSF £30.61 CT £213.87 TOTE £3.70: £2.70, £6.30; EX 28.10 Place 6 £456.62; Place 5 £131.46.
Owner C M Budgett **Bred** Kirtlington Stud Ltd And C M Budgett **Trained** Whatcombe, Oxon

FOCUS
A fair fillies' handicap but the time was slow and the form could be muddling, although it is taken at face value for now.
Our Drama Queen(IRE) Official explanation: jockey said filly ran flat
T/Plt: £948.90 to a £1 stake. Pool:£59,273.78 - 45.60 winning tickets T/Qpdt: £153.60 to a £1 stake. Pool:£5,244.43 - 25.25 winning tickets ST

4902 WINDSOR (R-H)
Monday, August 16

OFFICIAL GOING: Good (good to soft in places; 7.2)
Stands' rail dolled out 3yds at 6f and 1/2yd at winning post. Top bend dolled out 3yds from innermost line, adding 4yds to races of one mile and over.
Wind: Light to moderate, half behind Weather: Fine

5146 ROYAL WINDSOR RACING CLUB APPRENTICE H'CAP 1m 2f 7y
5:40 (5:40) (Class 5) (0-75,75) 3-Y-0+ **£2,593** (£765; £383) **Stalls** Low

Form RPR

0342 **1** **Higgy's Ragazzo (FR)**[37] 3917 3-9-1 **75**.................. CharlesEddery(5) 3 84+
(R Hannon) *rousted along early: hld up in last pair: stl there over 2f out: gd prog on outer after: sustained run to ld last 100yds* **9/2**[1]

5233 **2** *1 1/4* **Beauchamp Xiara**[21] 4422 4-9-5 **71**.................. AmyScott(5) 8 77
(H Candy) *stdd s: hld up in last pair: prog over 3f out to trck ldrs 2f out: rdn to chal over 1f out: upsides ins fnl f: outpcd* **11/2**[3]

5056 **3** *3/4* **Halyard (IRE)**[86] 2321 3-8-6 **64**.................. JohnFahy(3) 9 69
(W R Swinburn) *hld up in rr: pushed along and gd prog on inner fr 3f out: rdn to ld narrowly jst over 1f out: hdd and fdd last 100yds* **6/1**

244 **4** *1 1/2* **Marching Song (USA)**[26] 4258 4-9-11 **75**.................. TobyAtkinson(3) 6 77
(Andrew Turnell) *mde most: rdn over 2f out: hdd and fdd jst over 1f out* **6/1**

6654 **5** *8* **Meydan Dubai (IRE)**[11] 4756 5-9-4 **68**.................. KierenFox(3) 2 54
(J R Best) *cl up: prog to press ldr 4f out: drvn over 2f out: wknd qckly over 1f out* **12/1**

-562 **6** 2½ **Starry Mount**[16] 4585 3-9-0 72 AmyBaker(3) 5 53
(A B Haynes) *struggling in rr fr 1/2-way: no real prog u.str.p over 2f out* 5/1²

4453 **7** 1¼ **Zero Cool (USA)**[65] 2966 6-9-5 71 (p) HarryBentley(5) 11 49
(G L Moore) *t.k.h: trckd ldrs: rdn 3f out: sn wknd* 13/2

-060 **8** 2¾ **Manshoor (IRE)**[40] 3781 5-9-13 74 Louis-PhilippeBeuzelin 7 47
(Mrs L Wadham) *chsd ldrs: rdn and lost pl over 3f out: sn no ch* 20/1

00-6 **9** 4 **Akula (IRE)**[88] 2250 3-8-8 66 AshleyMorgan(3) 1 31
(M H Tompkins) *cl up: rdn over 3f out: sn wknd: eased fnl f* 12/1

650- **10** 17 **Royal Box**[252] 7669 3-8-9 67 SophieDoyle(3) 10 —
(D Burchell) *pressed ldr to 4f out: wknd rapidly: t.o* 33/1

2m 7.22s (-1.48) **Going Correction** -0.125s/f (Firm)
WFA 3 from 4yo+ 8lb **10** Ran SP% **115.2**
Speed ratings (Par 103): **100,99,98,97,90 88,87,85,82,68**
toteswingers:1&2:£7.60, 1&3:£12.40, 2&3:£9.80 CSF £28.73 CT £149.29 TOTE £7.10: £2.40, £2.10, £2.80; EX 27.00 Trifecta £547.70 Pool: £814.25 - 1.10 winning units..
Owner I Higginson **Bred** Thierry Grandsir & Patrick Bruneau **Trained** East Everleigh, Wilts

FOCUS
After a dry day the going was changed to good, good to soft in places. The rails were dolled out which added four yards to race distances at 1m-plus. There was a lively market for this apprentices' handicap which involved a few unexposed types. The early pace was steady but it quickened at halfway and the first four pulled a long way clear of the rest. The form is ordinary rated around those in the frame behind the winner.

5147 E B F SPORTINGBET.COM MAIDEN FILLIES' STKS 6f
6:10 (6:11) (Class 5) 2-Y-O **£3,207** (£947; £473) **Stalls** High

Form RPR

1 **Winnie Dixie (USA)** 2-9-0 0 JamieSpencer 2 73+
(P F I Cole) *trckd ldrs gng wl: shkn up to ld jst over 1f out: in command and rdn out* 9/2²

0 **2** 1¼ **Humdrum**[55] 3296 2-9-0 0 RichardHughes 3 70+
(R Hannon) *dwlt: wl in rr: pushed along and prog wl over 1f out: styd on wl fnl f to take 2nd nr fin* 7/2¹

4 **3** nk **Imogen Louise (IRE)**[82] 2440 2-9-0 0 DaneO'Neill 9 69
(D Haydn Jones) *trckd ldrs: effrt over 1f out: rdn to go 2nd briefly wl ins fnl f: kpt on* 15/2

0 **4** 1¾ **Talkative Guest (IRE)**[14] 4658 2-9-0 0 PhilipRobinson 8 64
(G G Margarson) *mde most to jst over 1f out: fdd ins fnl f* 12/1

0 **5** 1½ **Indiracer (IRE)**[19] 4471 2-9-0 0 PatCosgrave 14 59
(A Bailey) *early reminder: chsd ldrs: rdn 2f out: styd on same pce fnl f against rail* 16/1

0 **6** nk **Cloud Illusions (USA)**[14] 4658 2-8-9 0 JohnFahy(5) 13 58
(Mrs H S Main) *racd against rail: pressed ldng pair to over 1f out: fdd* 20/1

00 **7** 5 **Complicate**[14] 4658 2-8-11 0 RussKennemore(3) 1 43
(Andrew Reid) *racd on outer: chsd ldrs: shkn up and fdd over 1f out* 50/1

0 **8** ¾ **Volcanic Lady (IRE)**[7] 4909 2-9-0 0 CathyGannon 12 41
(D M Simcock) *dwlt: wl in rr: pushed along 2f out: stdy late prog: n.d* 50/1

0 **9** hd **Bint Mazyouna**[19] 4471 2-9-0 0 ChrisCatlin 11 40
(M R Channon) *nvr bttr than midfield: wknd wl over 1f out* 7/2¹

10 ½ **One Cool Chick** 2-8-9 0 DeclanCannon(5) 4 39
(J J Bridger) *dwlt: rn green in rr: nvr a factor* 66/1

0 **11** 3¾ **Burnem Green**[11] 4759 2-9-0 0 IanMongan 7 28
(A Bailey) *in tch towards outer: no prog 2f out: wknd qckly over 1f out* 66/1

0 **12** nse **Tymismoni (IRE)**[24] 4317 2-9-0 0 DavidProbert 10 27
(R J Smith) *pressed ldr tl wknd u.p 2f out* 25/1

0 **13** 6 **Porthgwidden Beach (USA)**[54] 3331 2-9-0 0 (t) AndreaAtzeni 5 9
(S C Williams) *in tch in rr tl wknd 2f out* 66/1

14 1¾ **Symi (IRE)** 2-9-0 0 WilliamBuick 16 4
(J H M Gosden) *dwlt: rchd midfield after 2f: pushed along and wknd 2f out: eased* 5/1³

00 **15** 54 **Hazy Ridge**[54] 3332 2-9-0 0 FrankieMcDonald 6 —
(M Madgwick) *sn struggling: t.o fr 1/2-way* 200/1

1m 13.68s (0.68) **Going Correction** +0.075s/f (Good) **15** Ran SP% **122.1**
Speed ratings (Par 91): **98,96,95,93,91 91,84,83,83,82 77,77,69,67,—**
toteswingers:1&2:£3.20, 1&3:£13.80, 2&3:£5.60 CSF £19.76 TOTE £6.40: £2.90, £1.70, £1.80; EX 27.30 Trifecta £144.30 Pool: £1,762.83 - 9.04 winning units..
Owner Mrs Fitri Hay **Bred** Woodlawn Breeding Inc & W S Farish **Trained** Whatcombe, Oxon

FOCUS
This fillies' maiden did not look particularly strong but it was won in good style by a newcomer who was prominent in the betting, and a Richard Hannon-trained runner shaped with plenty of promise to finish runner-up on her second start.

NOTEBOOK
Winnie Dixie(USA) ◆ was a big gamble during the day. Her price slipped into reverse on course but she broke well from a difficult draw and travelled smoothly for most of the way before winning with something in hand on this debut. This $400,000 filly is from a very successful US sprinting family and looks a promising prospect. (op 7-2 tchd 5-1)
Humdrum ◆ had plenty of work to do in a bid to justify strong support after another slow start but finished strongly from a long way back, and almost gave the winner a scare. This was an eyecatching second run by a half-sister to 1m winner Life's A Whirl and quite useful 7f-1m3f winner Full Toss. (op 11-2 tchd 6-1)
Imogen Louise(IRE) also attracted support and stayed on steadily down the centre of the track to step up significantly on her debut effort at 5f. She is a half-sister to a 1m2f winner and a winning hurdler, so should continue to progress as the emphasis on stamina increases. (op 10-1 tchd 7-1)
Talkative Guest(IRE), a half-sister to a 1m2f winner in France by High Chaparral, showed up well for a long way on her second start and could take another step forward next time. (op 14-1)
Indiracer(IRE) did some good late work against the stands' rail and has managed to reverse debut form with Bint Mazyouna.
Bint Mazyouna put in a laboured effort, which was a bit disappointing considering she set the standard on her three-length seventh in a Goodwood fillies' maiden on her debut. (op 5-1)
Symi(IRE), a late withdrawal at Newbury over the previous weekend, was a drifter on course and was never anywhere near the pace after a very slow start on this debut. However, this very well-bred Cheveley Park-entered filly should know a lot more next time and could leave this form well behind. Official explanation: jockey said filly had no more to give (op 3-1)

5148 SPORTINGBET.COM (S) STKS 1m 3f 135y
6:40 (6:40) (Class 6) 3-Y-O+ **£1,774** (£523; £262) **Stalls** Low

Form RPR

0-35 **1** **Talenti (IRE)**[14] 4657 7-9-11 72 (t) DaneO'Neill 6 63+
(Mrs Lawney Hill) *hld up in 5th: stdy prog on outer over 2f out: led over 1f out: rdn clr: readily* 13/8²

1111 **2** 2½ **Timocracy**[28] 4202 5-10-2 68 RichardHughes 2 63+
(A B Haynes) *led: styd against rail fr 3f out: hdd u.p over 1f out: one pce* 6/5¹

0046 **3** ¾ **Special Cuvee**[4] 4991 4-9-11 53 WilliamBuick 4 57
(Mrs A M Thorpe) *trckd ldr to 6f out: disp 2nd again over 2f out: sn rdn and nt qckn* 9/1³

2545 **4** ¾ **Bussell Along (IRE)**[12] 4689 4-9-6 50 (tp) TomQueally 7 51
(Stef Higgins) *s.s: hld up in last pair: clsd on ldrs over 2f out: reminders over 1f out: one pce* 10/1

6443 **5** 7 **Resplendent Ace (IRE)**[7] 4912 6-10-2 48 IanMongan 5 49
(P Howling) *hld up in 4th: rdn over 2f out: cl enough wl over 1f out: wknd qckly* 28/1

0- **6** ¾ **Green Army**[304] 6821 3-9-1 0 ChrisCatlin 3 43
(M R Channon) *a in last pair: pushed along fr 1/2-way: outpcd fr over 2f out* 33/1

0 **7** ½ **Commanche Luke**[7] 4912 7-9-11 0 (b¹) DavidProbert 1 42
(C Roberts) *trckd ldr 6f out to over 2f out: wknd rapidly* 100/1

2m 32.78s (3.28) **Going Correction** -0.125s/f (Firm)
WFA 3 from 4yo+ 10lb **7** Ran SP% **110.0**
Speed ratings (Par 101): **84,82,81,81,76 76,75**
toteswingers:1&2:£1.02, 1&3:£3.30, 2&3:£4.80 CSF £3.55 TOTE £3.00: £2.40, £1.10; EX 4.50.There was no bid for the winner. Timocracy was subject to a friendly claim of £6,000.
Owner Alan Hill **Bred** Watership Down Stud **Trained** Aston Rowant, Oxon

FOCUS
An uncompetitive seller, run at a fair pace. The two market leaders filled the first two places but the third and fourth hold the form down.

5149 TRINIDAD AND TOBAGO STEEL PAN FILLIES' H'CAP 1m 67y
7:10 (7:10) (Class 4) (0-85,82) 3-Y-O+ **£4,209** (£1,252; £625; £312) **Stalls** High

Form RPR

-413 **1** **Miss Antonia (IRE)**[10] 4784 3-9-0 75 TomQueally 2 85+
(H R A Cecil) *hld up in 7th: shkn up over 3f out: prog on outer 2f out: rdn to ld ins fnl f: styd on wl* 6/1²

103 **2** 1¼ **Chica Whopa (IRE)**[7] 4905 3-9-5 80 RichardHughes 4 87
(R Hannon) *hld up in 6th: effrt against rail over 2f out: styd on fnl f to take 2nd last stride* 8/1

4402 **3** nse **Ken's Girl**[13] 4680 6-8-11 66 IanMongan 11 74
(W S Kittow) *led: styd against rail fr 3f out: hrd rdn and edgd lft over 1f out: hdd and one pce ins fnl f* 17/2

3601 **4** 2 **Queen Of Wands**[32] 4058 3-8-9 70 SteveDrowne 10 72
(H Morrison) *chsd ldr: rdn wl over 2f out: lost 2nd and fdd fnl f* 16/1

2621 **5** 1 **Night Lily (IRE)**[17] 4533 4-9-13 82 TonyCulhane 5 83
(P W D'Arcy) *trckd ldrs: pushed along over 2f out: nt qckn over 1f out: kpt on* 8/1

2132 **6** 2 **Cabal**[19] 4491 3-9-1 79 Louis-PhilippeBeuzelin(3) 7 75
(Sir Michael Stoute) *trckd ldrs: rdn wl over 2f out: nt qckn over 1f out: fdd fnl f* 8/1

5262 **7** 2 **Steel Free (IRE)**[19] 4492 4-8-13 68 ChrisCatlin 1 60
(M Madgwick) *t.k.h: mostly trckd ldng pair: rdn wl over 2f out: btn over 1f out: wknd ins fnl f* 25/1

0001 **8** ½ **Hip Hip Hooray**[11] 4756 4-8-8 63 oh3 CathyGannon 3 54
(L A Dace) *s.s: mostly in last trio: effrt 4f out: no prog and btn 2f out* 25/1

1102 **9** ¾ **Right Rave (IRE)**[17] 4548 3-9-4 79 ShaneKelly 6 67
(P J McBride) *t.k.h: hld up towards rr: rdn and no prog over 3f out* 7/1³

3-00 **10** hd **Club Tahiti**[24] 4322 4-9-13 82 PatCosgrave 9 71
(A W Carroll) *dwlt: a in last trio: rdn and no prog 3f out* 10/1

3031 **11** 4½ **Wild Rockette**[11] 4762 3-8-11 72 (b) JamieSpencer 12 49
(B J Meehan) *dwlt: a wl in rr: pushed along and no prog 3f out: eased* 11/4¹

1m 41.87s (-2.83) **Going Correction** -0.125s/f (Firm)
WFA 3 from 4yo+ 6lb **11** Ran SP% **120.0**
Speed ratings (Par 102): **109,107,107,105,104 102,100,100,99,99 94**
toteswingers:1&2:£8.60, 1&3:£8.50, 2&3:£21.10 CSF £54.60 CT £416.52 TOTE £7.90: £2.50, £2.30, £4.50; EX 40.90 Trifecta £503.20 Pool: £2,135.49 - 3.14 winning units..
Owner Gestut Ammerland **Bred** Ammerland Verwaltung Gmbh **Trained** Newmarket, Suffolk

FOCUS
A competitive handicap, involving four last-time-out winners and four others who finished runner-up on their latest start. The pace was solid and the form should work out.
Hip Hip Hooray Official explanation: jockey said filly missed the break
Wild Rockette Official explanation: trainer's rep said filly was unsuited by the track

5150 YES EVENTS MAIDEN STKS 1m 67y
7:40 (7:41) (Class 5) 3-4-Y-O **£2,456** (£725; £362) **Stalls** High

Form RPR

-502 **1** **Official Style**[46] 3586 3-9-3 81 RichardMullen 6 83+
(Sir Michael Stoute) *t.k.h early: trckd ldrs: rdn over 2f out: wnt 2nd over 1f out: drvn and styd on to ld ins fnl f* 5/4¹

6-20 **2** 1¾ **Aultcharn (FR)**[12] 4699 3-9-3 79 JamieSpencer 10 79
(B J Meehan) *led: wound it up fr 3f out: hrd rdn w hd at awkward angle over 1f out: hdd and nt qckn ins fnl f* 4/1²

-262 **3** 4 **Battle Honour**[18] 4521 3-9-3 80 DaneO'Neill 1 70
(H Candy) *trckd ldr: rdn over 2f out: lost 2nd and outpcd fr over 1f out* 15/2

54 **4** nse **Perfect Point (IRE)**[25] 4307 3-9-3 0 ShaneKelly 9 70
(W R Swinburn) *trckd ldrs: outpcd fr 2f out: reminder 1f out: styd on and nrly snatched 3rd* 16/1

4220 **5** ¾ **Streets Of War (USA)**[74] 2682 3-9-0 76 PatrickHills(3) 7 68
(P W Chapple-Hyam) *trckd ldrs: shkn up over 2f out: outpcd fr wl over 1f out: kpt on* 10/1

00 **6** 3¼ **Epernay**[14] 4661 3-8-12 0 SteveDrowne 11 55+
(Ian Williams) *hld up: gng wl enough but last over 2f out: tk modest 6th over 1f out: one reminder sn after: possible improver* 66/1

7 3 **Sun Seeker (IRE)** 3-8-12 0 RichardHughes 4 49+
(J Noseda) *s.v.s: detached in last to 1/2-way: effrt on outer 3f out: wknd wl over 1f out* 11/2³

6 **8** 10 **Equine Science**[12] 4697 3-8-12 0 SophieDoyle(5) 3 31
(G D Blake) *hld up in midfield: shkn up 3f out: wknd over 2f out* 66/1

9 4 **Chris's Ridge** 3-9-0 0 Louis-PhilippeBeuzelin(3) 8 21
(B J Meehan) *dwlt: a in rr: shkn up 3f out: wknd over 2f out* 16/1

1m 43.45s (-1.25) **Going Correction** -0.125s/f (Firm)
WFA 3 from 4yo 6lb **9** Ran SP% **115.4**
Speed ratings (Par 103): **101,99,95,95,94 91,88,78,74**
toteswingers:1&2:£4.50, 1&3:£5.40, 2&3:£2.60 CSF £6.23 TOTE £2.10: £1.10, £1.80, £1.70; EX 8.00 Trifecta £23.20 Pool: £502.24 - 15.99 winning units..
Owner K Abdulla **Bred** Juddmonte Farms Ltd **Trained** Newmarket, Suffolk

FOCUS
A fairly useful maiden. It was run at a stop-start gallop and developed into a bit of a sprint, but the two market leaders pulled clear of an 80-rated third. The winner looks the best guide to the level.
Aultcharn(FR) Official explanation: jockey said colt hung right under pressure
Sun Seeker(IRE) Official explanation: jockey said filly missed the break and ran green

Equine Science Official explanation: jockey said gelding was unsuited by the good (good to soft places) ground
Chris's Ridge Official explanation: jockey said gelding was unsuited by the good (good to soft places) ground and ran green

5151 IT DOESN'T GET BETTER THAN BARBADOS H'CAP 5f 10y
8:10 (8:10) (Class 4) (0-85,85) 3-Y-0+ **£4,209** (£1,252; £625; £312) **Stalls** High

Form RPR
5232 1 **Cape Royal**[5] 4961 10-8-12 **74**..........(bt) PatCosgrave 4 85
(J M Bradley) *mde all: pushed along firmly fr over 1f out: styd on wl* **11/4**[1]
0202 2 1 1/2 **Secret Witness**[7] 4904 4-9-9 **85**..........(b) SteveDrowne 5 91
(R A Harris) *stdd s: t.k.h and sn chsd wnr: rdn over 1f out: no imp fnl f* **11/4**[1]
3040 3 2 1/2 **Master Lightfoot**[25] 4292 4-9-0 **76**.......... ShaneKelly 8 73
(W R Swinburn) *t.k.h early: trckd ldng pair: rdn 2f out: lft bhd fr over 1f out* **11/2**[3]
314 4 1 3/4 **Gwilym (GER)**[14] 4662 7-8-10 **72**.......... DaneO'Neill 6 62
(D Haydn Jones) *hld up: rdn 2f out: outpcd fr over 1f out: fdd* **5/1**[2]
23-1 5 4 **Noble Greek (USA)**[173] 683 3-8-13 **82**.......... KierenFox(5) 2 58
(J R Best) *chsd ldrs on outer: rdn 2f out: wknd over 1f out* **11/2**[3]
1343 6 nk **Wanchai Whisper**[14] 4659 3-8-2 **66** oh2..........(p) CathyGannon 3 41
(P R Hedger) *in tch in rr: rdn 2f out: wknd over 1f out* **8/1**

60.00 secs (-0.30) **Going Correction** +0.075s/f (Good)
WFA 3 from 4yo+ 2lb **6** Ran SP% **111.9**
Speed ratings (Par 105): **105,102,98,95,89 88**
toteswingers:1&2:£1.10, 1&3:£5.10, 2&3:£6.50 CSF £10.23 CT £36.31 TOTE £3.40: £1.70, £2.20; EX 8.50 Trifecta £28.60 Pool: £350.62 - 9.06 winning units. Place 6 £14.76; Place 5 £8.11.
Owner E A Hayward **Bred** D R Brotherton **Trained** Sedbury, Gloucs

FOCUS
A competitive sprint handicap run at a fair pace and this was the winner's best effort for two years.
Wanchai Whisper Official explanation: jockey said filly was unsuited by the good (good to soft places) ground
T/Jkpt: £5,856.20. Pool:£65,986.43 - 8.00 winning tickets T/Plt: £39.00 to a £1 stake. Pool:£88,587.72 - 1,656.37 winning tickets T/Qpdt: £7.80 to a £1 stake.Pool:£8,073.44 - 760.40 winning tickets JN

4908 WOLVERHAMPTON (A.W) (L-H)
Monday, August 16

OFFICIAL GOING: Standard
Wind: Fresh across Weather: Fine

5152 FREE HORSE RACING TIPS @ BIGTIPS.CO.UK H'CAP 5f 20y(P)
2:15 (2:15) (Class 6) (0-60,60) 3-Y-O **£1,706** (£503; £252) **Stalls** Low

Form RPR
4534 1 **Annia Galeria (IRE)**[4] 4998 3-8-5 **47**..........(b) CathyGannon 3 54
(C A Dwyer) *mde all: clr 2f out: rdn over 1f out: jst hld on* **9/1**
0300 2 nk **Flaxen Lake**[25] 4284 3-9-1 **57**..........(tp) NeilCallan 2 63
(J M Bradley) *a.p: hmpd over 3f out: sn rdn: chsd wnr over 1f out: r.o* **7/1**
4342 3 hd **Vilnius**[6] 4920 3-8-13 **55**.......... SamHitchcott 5 60
(M R Channon) *prom: drvn along 3f out: edgd lft and r.o wl u.p ins fnl f* **5/1**[2]
50U0 4 2 1/4 **Music Lover**[11] 4760 3-9-4 **60**.......... LukeMorris 6 57+
(R A Harris) *s.i.s and hmpd s: in rr whn rdn and hung rt over 3f out: hdwy u.p and hung lft fr over 1f out: nrst fin* **25/1**
4-40 5 1 1/2 **Burnt Cream**[58] 3228 3-9-1 **57**.......... TomEaves 4 49
(B Smart) *s.i.s: hdwy over 3f out: rdn 1/2-way: styd on same pce appr fnl f* **8/1**
6053 6 nk **Duke Of Rainford**[14] 4651 3-8-11 **53**..........(b) PaulHanagan 12 44+
(M Herrington) *hld up: hmpd 3f out: hdwy over 1f out: nt trble ldrs* **8/1**
1542 7 2 1/2 **Rathbawn Girl (IRE)**[11] 4739 3-8-7 **56**.......... AdamBeschizza(7) 10 38+
(Miss J Feilden) *s.i.s: sn pushed along in rr: nvr nrr* **6/1**
0205 8 1 **Thewinnatakesitall**[11] 4760 3-8-5 **47**..........(p) SilvestreDeSousa 7 25+
(N Tinkler) *sn pushed along and a in rr* **11/2**[3]
0500 9 nk **Rightcar**[10] 4791 3-8-10 **52**.......... RobertWinston 11 29+
(Peter Grayson) *s.i.s: a in rr* **50/1**
0326 10 3/4 **Midget**[4] 4982 3-8-11 **60**.......... NeilFarley(7) 1 34
(D Carroll) *unruly in stalls: chsd ldr: rdn 1/2-way: wknd over 1f out* **9/2**[1]
-600 11 52 **Rightcar Marian**[28] 4194 3-8-4 **46** oh1.......... FrankieMcDonald 8 —
(Peter Grayson) *chsd ldrs: hung lft and lost action over 3f out: wknd 1/2-way: eased: t.o* **80/1**

62.59 secs (0.29) **Going Correction** -0.05s/f (Stan) **11** Ran SP% **116.3**
Speed ratings (Par 98): **95,94,94,90,88 87,83,82,81,80** —
toteswingers:1&2:£16.00, 1&3:£6.90, 2&3:£7.60 CSF £69.08 CT £353.35 TOTE £14.10: £3.00, £3.20, £2.20; EX 89.30 Trifecta £143.80 Part won. Pool: £194.40 - 0.30 winning units..
Owner S B Components Ltd & Mrs Shelley Dwyer **Bred** Jay Gee Partnership **Trained** Burrough Green, Cambs

FOCUS
It doesn't come much more open than this low-grade sprint handicap. It was run at a decent early pace, but proved to be a messy race in behind and the form should be treated with some caution, with the winner the best guide.
Music Lover ◆ Official explanation: jockey said gelding hung badly right
Burnt Cream Official explanation: trainer said filly bled from the nose
Thewinnatakesitall Official explanation: jockey said filly suffered interference in running
Rightcar Official explanation: jockey said gelding hung right-handed
Rightcar Marian Official explanation: vet said filly finished lame behind

5153 FREE HORSE RACING TIPS @ BIGTIPS.CO.UK MAIDEN STKS 5f 216y(P)
2:45 (2:45) (Class 5) 3-Y-0+ **£2,115** (£624; £312) **Stalls** Low

Form RPR
2224 1 **Advertisement (USA)**[13] 4679 3-9-3 75..........(t) PaulHanagan 3 81
(J Noseda) *mde all: pushed clr fnl 2f* **1/4**[1]
0 2 13 **Katmai River (IRE)**[13] 4679 3-8-12 0.......... LeeNewnes(5) 2 39
(M D I Usher) *prom: rdn 1/2-way: sn lost tch: wnt 2nd ins fnl f: nvr any ch w wnr* **50/1**
3 4 **Xeralda (IRE)** 3-8-12 0.......... LukeMorris 1 22
(C G Cox) *chsd ldrs: drvn along thrght: outpcd fr over 2f out: wnt mod 3rd ins fnl f* **17/2**[3]
5 4 2 1/4 **Sonia Girl (IRE)**[7] 4908 3-8-12 0.......... StephenCraine 4 14
(Patrick Morris) *hld up: swished tail over 2f out: nvr nr to chal* **22/1**
0660 5 8 **Riggs (IRE)**[11] 4760 4-9-6 30.......... FergusSweeney 7 —
(Peter Grayson) *chsd wnr: rdn over 2f out: hung lft and wknd wl over 1f out: lost 2nd ins fnl f* **100/1**

R **Delaware Dancer (IRE)** 3-8-12 0..........(t) NeilCallan 5 —
(J R Gask) *c out of stalls: hung rt and ref to r* **7/1**[2]

1m 13.62s (-1.38) **Going Correction** -0.05s/f (Stan)
WFA 3 from 4yo 3lb **6** Ran SP% **110.3**
Speed ratings (Par 103): **107,89,84,81,70** —
toteswingers:1&2:£5.10, 1&3:£1.50, 2&3:£7.60 CSF £22.41 TOTE £1.40: £1.02, £15.40; EX 14.70.
Owner M Barber, Tom Ludt & Winstar Farm **Bred** Dr & Mrs Walter Zent & Tony Holmes **Trained** Newmarket, Suffolk

FOCUS
A most uncompetitive maiden, although the winner clocked a good time and sets the standard.

5154 BIGTIPS.CO.UK FOR FREE BETS AND TIPS H'CAP 5f 216y(P)
3:15 (3:15) (Class 3) (0-95,90) 3-Y-0+ **£5,677** (£1,699; £849; £424; £211) **Stalls** Low

Form RPR
0215 1 **Arabian Mirage**[23] 4378 4-9-10 **90**.......... KierenFallon 3 102
(B J Meehan) *hld up: hdwy over 2f out: led 1f out: edgd lft: r.o* **7/2**[2]
1566 2 2 1/2 **Baby Strange**[9] 4832 6-9-4 **84**.......... FrannyNorton 9 88
(D Shaw) *hld up: hdwy over 1f out: r.o: nt rch wnr* **12/1**
-366 3 shd **Excellerator (IRE)**[45] 3629 4-9-7 **90**..........(t) MatthewDavies(3) 7 94
(George Baker) *hld up: hdwy over 1f out: sn rdn: r.o* **12/1**
222- 4 1/2 **Gouray Girl (IRE)**[282] 7290 3-9-4 **87**.......... EddieAhern 5 89+
(W R Swinburn) *a.p: chsd ldr 2f out: led over 1f out: sn rdn and hdd: no ex ins fnl f* **11/2**[3]
3620 5 2 **Green Park (IRE)**[5] 4942 7-8-11 **77**..........(v) DavidNolan 10 73
(D Carroll) *chsd ldrs: rdn over 2f out: styd on same pce fnl f* **20/1**
0600 6 1 1/4 **Imprimis Tagula (IRE)**[13] 4685 6-9-10 **90**..........(v) RobertWinston 4 82
(A Bailey) *led: hdd over 4f out: chsd ldr tl rdn over 2f out: no ex fnl f* **25/1**
-600 7 shd **Captain Ramius (IRE)**[31] 4085 4-9-10 **90**..........(b[1]) NeilCallan 11 81
(K A Ryan) *reminder sn after s: prom: led over 4f out: rdn and hdd over 1f out: wknd ins fnl f* **11/1**
2206 8 nk **Ivory Silk**[126] 1266 5-9-6 **86**.......... LukeMorris 2 76
(J R Gask) *hld up: rdn 1/2-way: nvr on terms* **20/1**
1-25 9 nk **Summerinthecity (IRE)**[96] 2028 3-9-5 **88**.......... PaulHanagan 8 77
(J Noseda) *chsd ldrs: rdn and hung rt fr over 2f out: wknd ins fnl f* **2/1**[1]
5360 10 1 1/4 **Coleorton Choice**[24] 4345 4-8-8 **74**..........(p) JackMitchell 1 59
(R Hollinshead) *chsd ldrs: rdn over 3f out: wknd over 2f out* **25/1**
00-6 11 1 3/4 **Soap Wars**[9] 4814 5-9-10 **90**.......... FergusSweeney 6 70
(J A Osborne) *hld up: a in rr* **8/1**

1m 13.53s (-1.47) **Going Correction** -0.05s/f (Stan)
WFA 3 from 4yo+ 3lb **11** Ran SP% **123.0**
Speed ratings (Par 107): **107,103,103,102,100 98,98,98,97,95 93**
toteswingers:1&2:£7.50, 1&3:£14.90, 2&3:£21.50 CSF £44.36 CT £470.08 TOTE £4.40: £2.40, £5.20, £5.00; EX 53.00 Trifecta £207.70 Part won. Pool: £280.78 - 0.10 winning units..
Owner David F O'Rourke **Bred** Minster Stud **Trained** Manton, Wilts

FOCUS
This was an interesting sprint handicap and it proved to be a vibrant betting heat. They went a frantic early pace and that suited the closers. The placed horses set the level.

NOTEBOOK
Arabian Mirage ◆ found the strong early tempo right up her street as she was able to settle better and got produced full of running at the top of the home straight. She could have been called the winner at the 1f marker and obviously likes this venue as she is now 2-2 here. It was her first win over 6f, but granted a real test over the trip she remains open to further improvement as a sprinter. Connections will now look to gain some black type with her. (op 11-2)
Baby Strange had yet to shine on artificial surfaces and his best efforts away from turf had been at Kempton. He ran a decent race, though, proving well suited by the strong early pace and was very close to his recent level. (op 8-1)
Excellerator(IRE), back up a furlong, took a keen hold to post so it wasn't surprising to see her restrained out the back. She found herself with plenty to do nearing the home bend, but was helped by the way the race unfolded on that front and finished her race strongly to grab third. She is another that obviously enjoys the AW as her form figures indicate, and this was a definite step back in the right direction. (tchd 11-1)
Gouray Girl(IRE), who won over C&D on her debut last term, is one to take from the race. She attracted support on this belated 3-y-o return and only felt the pinch late on, posting a very pleasing effort against her elders. Providing she goes the right way from this as is expected, she could reach even greater heights this season as she has few miles on the clock. (op 8-1)
Green Park(IRE) turned in one of his better efforts for the return to Polytrack, and helps to set the standard as he is held by the handicapper.
Summerinthecity(IRE) failed to get home over 7f on his previous outing 96 days earlier, but had run a career-best on his AW debut over this trip on his seasonal return when an unlucky looking second. He showed decent early pace, but hung his chance away when coming right off the home bend and ending up towards the stands' rail. This leaves him with a bit to prove, but he is entitled to come on for the run and is too lightly raced to abandon. Official explanation: jockey said colt hung right-handed throughout (tchd 5-2)

5155 £1000 IN FREE BETS @ BIGTIPS.CO.UK H'CAP (DIV I) 1m 1f 103y(P)
3:45 (3:45) (Class 6) (0-60,66) 3-Y-0+ **£1,364** (£403; £201) **Stalls** Low

Form RPR
6-05 1 **Lyric Poet (USA)**[51] 3444 3-8-12 **54**..........(t) WilliamCarson 10 82
(G C Bravery) *hld up: hdwy over 4f out: led over 3f out: rdn clr fr over 2f out* **9/2**[2]
0000 2 17 **Cherri Fosfate**[84] 2392 6-9-3 **59**.......... NeilFarley(7) 6 52+
(D Carroll) *hld up: hdwy u.p over 1f out: wnt 2nd ins fnl f: no ch w wnr* **3/1**[1]
0040 3 2 1/4 **Formidable Guest**[21] 4433 6-9-11 **60**.......... MickyFenton 4 48
(J Pearce) *hld up: hdwy over 3f out: rdn over 2f out: sn outpcd* **5/1**[3]
-500 4 1/2 **Empress Leizu (IRE)**[24] 4325 3-8-13 **55**.......... PaulHanagan 5 42
(A W Carroll) *led: hdd over 3f out: sn rdn: wknd over 1f out* **7/1**
4624 5 1/2 **Douchkette (FR)**[18] 2487 4-9-6 **55**.......... NeilCallan 11 41
(John Berry) *prom: rdn over 2f out: wknd over 1f out* **8/1**
0401 6 1 **Rebellious Spirit**[7] 4914 7-9-10 **66** 6ex..........(p) AnthonyFreeman(7) 3 50
(S Curran) *prom: rdn over 3f out: wknd over 1f out* **15/2**
3500 7 3/4 **Business Bay (USA)**[47] 3564 3-9-4 **60**..........(b[1]) JackMitchell 9 42
(E F Vaughan) *chsd ldr tl rdn over 3f out: hung lft and wknd wl over 1f out* **12/1**
4004 8 9 **Mississippian (IRE)**[7] 4897 6-9-0 **49**.......... DuranFentiman 7 12
(Mrs D J Sanderson) *hld up: hdwy over 4f out: rdn 3f out: wknd wl over 1f out: t.o* **10/1**
0000 9 9 **Hannah Hawk**[24] 4340 3-8-4 **46** oh1.......... LukeMorris 1 —
(Lucinda Featherstone) *s.s: sn drvn along and a in rr: lost tch fnl 3f: t.o* **100/1**
0605 10 2 1/4 **Musigny (USA)**[29] 4173 4-8-12 **50**..........(p) MichaelStainton(3) 8 —
(Miss S E Hall) *chsd ldrs: rdn over 3f out: sn wknd: t.o* **50/1**

5300 **11** *27* **Royal Torbo (ISR)**[18] 4519 3-8-7 **52**........................ MatthewDavies(3) 2 —
(George Baker) *prom: rdn over 5f out: wknd 4f out: t.o* **25/1**

2m 0.19s (-1.51) **Going Correction** -0.05s/f (Stan)
WFA 3 from 4yo+ 7lb **11** Ran SP% **118.8**
Speed ratings (Par 101): **104,88,86,86,86 85,84,76,68,66 42**
toteswingers:1&2:£6.20, 1&3:£6.00, 2&3:£7.40 CSF £18.42 CT £71.15 TOTE £9.80: £3.00, £2.60, £1.10; EX 31.00 Trifecta £84.80 Part won. Pool: £114.61 - 0.50 winning units..
Owner George Houghton **Bred** B Wayne Hughes **Trained** Cowlinge, Suffolk

FOCUS
What looked a fairly open handicap on paper was turned into an absolute procession. The winner is rated a big improver with everything else below their marks.

5156 REGISTER FOR FREE TODAY AT BIGTIPS.CO.UK MAIDEN STKS 7f 32y(P)
4:15 (4:16) (Class 5) 2-Y-O **£2,115** (£624; £312) **Stalls** High

Form RPR
0 **1** **Layali Al Arab (IRE)**[20] 4447 2-9-3 0.............................. FrankieDettori 3 80+
(Saeed Bin Suroor) *mde all: rdn over 1f out: r.o: readily* **8/11**[1]
6 **2** *2 ¼* **Avid Kale**[11] 4741 2-9-3 0... NeilCallan 4 72
(M Botti) *a.p: rdn to chse wnr 2f out: no imp ins fnl f* **40/1**
63 **3** *1 ¼* **Bearheart (IRE)**[26] 4254 2-9-3 0............................. PaulHanagan 7 69
(E A L Dunlop) *chsd ldrs: rdn 2f out: styd on same pce fnl f* **11/4**[2]
0 **4** *1 ¾* **Royal Reverie**[19] 4477 2-9-3 0.. EddieAhern 2 65
(W R Swinburn) *s.i.s: sn prom: rdn over 1f out: styd on same pce* **25/1**
5 *2 ½* **Proenza (USA)** 2-8-12 0.. KierenFallon 5 54
(B J Meehan) *chsd wnr 5f: wknd fnl f* **7/1**[3]
6 *¾* **Silk Bounty** 2-9-3 0... PaulMulrennan 12 57
(J G Given) *prom: pushed along 2f out: hung lft over 1f out: wknd fnl f* **66/1**
50 **7** *¾* **Echos Of Motivator**[30] 4131 2-9-3 0............................... LukeMorris 10 55
(R A Harris) *hld up: drvn along over 2f out: nt clr run sn after: swtchd lft over 1f out: nt trble ldrs* **100/1**
8 *1 ¾* **Baileys Moneypenny** 2-8-12 0....................................... LeeVickers 11 46
(J G Given) *sn pushed along in rr: nvr on terms* **100/1**
9 *nk* **All In A Paddy** 2-9-3 0.. FrannyNorton 9 50
(E S McMahon) *hld up: a in rr* **50/1**
50 **10** *½* **Les Landes (IRE)**[4] 5006 2-9-3 0................................ FergusSweeney 6 49
(J A Osborne) *hld up: effrt over 2f out: sn wknd* **100/1**
63 **11** *5* **Ivan Vasilevich (IRE)**[11] 4743 2-8-10 0........................ LewisWalsh(7) 8 36+
(Jane Chapple-Hyam) *s.i.s: hld up: last and stl gng wl enough leaving bk st: shkn up over 1f out: nvr nr to chal* **20/1**
12 *13* **Saturday Sam** 2-9-3 0.......................................(t) SilvestreDeSousa 1 5+
(M G Rimell) *s.s: outpcd* **66/1**

1m 30.78s (1.18) **Going Correction** -0.05s/f (Stan) **12** Ran SP% **116.0**
Speed ratings (Par 94): **91,88,87,85,82 81,80,78,78,77 71,56**
toteswingers:1&2:£9.50, 1&3:£2.10, 2&3:£10.60 CSF £50.75 TOTE £1.70: £1.60, £6.30, £1.20; EX 31.20 Trifecta £69.30 Pool: £410.77 - 4.38 winning units..
Owner Godolphin **Bred** Darley **Trained** Newmarket, Suffolk

FOCUS
Probably a fair maiden for the track with the winner much improved from his debut.

NOTEBOOK
Layali Al Arab(IRE) proved all the rage and opened his account at the second time of asking. This half-brother to Court Masterpiece had run well below market expectations on debut at Newmarket last month, but had presumably been doing the right things at home since and made all with something left up his sleeve. He essentially looks more of a staying type, despite his dam being a triple winner over 5f, and should progress again for this experience. Where he goes from here is uncertain, though. (op 4-6 tchd 8-13)
Avid Kale ◆ badly needed his debut outing at Folkestone 11 days earlier and he showed the benefit of that experience with a much-improved effort. He was the only one to give the winner a serious race off the home turn, but eventually got outstayed by that rival. His dam was a triple AW winner so the switch to this surface clearly helped and he can be found a winning turn before that long. (tchd 33-1)
Bearheart(IRE), third over this trip on his AW debut at Lingfield last month, had his chance yet failed to see it out like the first pair. His future looks to lie with the handicapper as he is now eligible for a mark. (tchd 7-2)
Royal Reverie came under pressure nearing the home turn, but kept on and this was a nice improvement on his debut over 6f on turf last time. He is entitled to come on again and will be qualified for nurseries after his next outing. (op 28-1)
Proenza(USA), whose yard won this last year, was soon racing just off the pace in a nice rhythm. She weakened out of things soon after turning in, though, and the debut outing looked needed. A stiffer test will suit her down the line. (op 10-1)
Silk Bounty wasn't helped by the outside stall for his debut and there was a fair bit to like about his display. He travelled sweetly before feeling the pinch around 1f out and should be plenty sharper for this initial experience. His pedigree also suggests dropping back a furlong may suit ideally.
Echos Of Motivator came under pressure a fair way out, but kept on and this was a little better again back on Polytrack. He shouldn't be overburdened when switching to nurseries, for which he is now qualified.

5157 REGISTER FOR FREE TODAY AT BIGTIPS.CO.UK H'CAP 7f 32y(P)
4:45 (4:47) (Class 4) (0-80,79) 4-Y-O+ **£3,626** (£1,079; £539; £269) **Stalls** High

Form RPR
4-02 **1** **Greensward**[84] 2399 4-9-7 **79**.. KierenFallon 4 91
(B J Meehan) *hld up: nt clr run over 2f out: hdwy over 1f out: led ins fnl f: r.o wl* **11/4**[1]
6603 **2** *2 ½* **Buxton**[25] 4308 6-9-0 **72**...(t) PaulHanagan 3 77
(R Ingram) *mid-div: hdwy over 1f out: led ins fnl f: sn hdd: styd on* **15/2**
0-00 **3** *2 ¼* **Mister Tinktastic (IRE)**[17] 4558 4-9-2 **74**......................... PhillipMakin 1 73
(N J Vaughan) *chsd ldr to over 5f out: remained handy: rdn over 2f out: styd on same pce fnl f* **33/1**
0000 **4** *¾* **Shaws Diamond (USA)**[9] 4847 4-8-10 **68**................(v[1]) FrannyNorton 5 65
(D Shaw) *hld up: rdn over 1f out: r.o ins fnl f: nrst fin* **28/1**
0115 **5** *nk* **Kipchak (IRE)**[12] 4690 5-8-11 **69**....................................(p) SamHitchcott 8 65
(C R Dore) *hdwy to chse ldr over 5f out: rdn over 2f out: no ex ins fnl f* **16/1**
4506 **6** *shd* **Hatta Stream (IRE)**[68] 2877 4-8-12 **70**............................ MickyFenton 7 66
(J Pearce) *hld up: rdn over 1f out: nvr trbld ldrs* **33/1**
3156 **7** *2 ¼* **Smalljohn**[16] 4602 4-9-2 **74**...(v) TomEaves 6 64
(B Smart) *chsd ldrs: rdn over 2f out: wknd fnl f* **8/1**
0311 **8** *2 ¼* **Glenridding**[17] 4555 6-8-13 **71**..................................(p) PaulMulrennan 2 55
(J G Given) *led: rdn over 1f out: hdd & wknd ins fnl f* **3/1**[2]
600 **9** *1 ½* **Mountain Cat (IRE)**[54] 3318 6-9-5 **77**...............................(p) NeilCallan 10 57
(K A Ryan) *hld up: hdwy 4f out: rdn over 2f out: wknd over 1f out* **7/2**[3]
0056 **U** **Emeebee**[35] 3970 4-8-8 **66**.. JamieMackay 9 —
(W J Musson) *uns rdr leaving stalls* **11/1**

1m 28.23s (-1.37) **Going Correction** -0.05s/f (Stan) **10** Ran SP% **120.3**
Speed ratings (Par 105): **105,102,99,98,98 98,95,93,91,—**
toteswingers:1&2:£5.30, 1&3:£11.90, 2&3:£19.10 CSF £24.55 CT £467.85 TOTE £5.10: £1.50, £2.10, £8.20; EX 19.90 TRIFECTA Not won..
Owner Lady Rothschild **Bred** Kincorth Investments Inc **Trained** Manton, Wilts

FOCUS
Unsurprisingly there was no hanging about here and three of the first four were nearer last than first turning into the home straight. the runner-up is the best guide to the level.
Shaws Diamond(USA) Official explanation: jockey said filly hung right-handed

5158 £1000 IN FREE BETS @ BIGTIPS.CO.UK H'CAP (DIV II) 1m 1f 103y(P)
5:15 (5:15) (Class 6) (0-60,60) 3-Y-O+ **£1,364** (£403; £201) **Stalls** Low

Form RPR
0-36 **1** **Love In The West (IRE)**[29] 4172 4-9-8 **57**..................... RobertWinston 1 67
(G A Swinbank) *chsd ldr 7f out: rdn to ld over 1f out: styd on gamely* **6/1**
3653 **2** *nk* **Tres Froide (FR)**[7] 4914 5-8-12 **47**.............................(p) SilvestreDeSousa 6 56
(N Tinkler) *hld up: hdwy over 1f out: rdn and ev ch ins fnl f: styd on* **9/2**[2]
2022 **3** *4* **Join Up**[6] 4932 4-9-4 **53**... KierenFallon 2 54
(W M Brisbourne) *hld up in tch: rdn over 1f out: hung lft and styd on same pce ins fnl f* **2/1**[1]
0000 **4** *1 ¼* **Rocky Mood (IRE)**[35] 3963 3-9-0 **56**............................(v[1]) EddieAhern 8 54
(W R Swinburn) *chsd ldr tl 7f out: remained handy: rdn over 2f out: hung rt and ev ch 1f out: no ex ins fnl f* **10/1**
2245 **5** *hd* **Wavertree Warrior (IRE)**[11] 4740 8-9-11 **60**.................(b) LukeMorris 3 58
(N P Littmoden) *rrd s: bhd: styd on u.p fr over 1f out: nt trble ldrs* **14/1**
-063 **6** *2 ¼* **Rebel Woman**[42] 3723 4-8-13 **48**.. NeilCallan 10 41
(J A Osborne) *dwlt: hld up: racd keenly: hdwy 3f out: rdn over 1f out: wknd ins fnl f* **6/1**
00-0 **7** *nk* **Mister Fantastic**[22] 4407 4-9-10 **59**.................................... PhillipMakin 9 52
(N J Vaughan) *led: rdn and hdd over 1f out: wknd ins fnl f* **50/1**
4034 **8** *4* **Location**[11] 4740 4-9-5 **54**...(v[1]) PaulHanagan 5 38
(Ian Williams) *chsd ldrs: rdn over 2f out: wknd over 1f out* **11/2**[3]
4046 **9** *¾* **Truly Magic**[35] 3957 3-8-9 **51**.. MickyFenton 4 34
(H J L Dunlop) *hld up: a in rr: bhd fnl 2f* **25/1**

2m 1.69s (-0.01) **Going Correction** -0.05s/f (Stan)
WFA 3 from 4yo+ 7lb **9** Ran SP% **117.0**
Speed ratings (Par 101): **98,97,94,93,92 90,90,87,86**
toteswingers:1&2:£4.90, 1&3:£3.90, 2&3:£2.60. totesuper7: Win: Not won. Place: £553.70. CSF £33.64 CT £73.26 TOTE £5.60: £1.90, £1.30, £1.10; EX 33.00 Trifecta £158.30 Part won. Pool: £213.94 - 0.70 winning units. Place 6 £44.61; Place 5 £10.57.
Owner John P Jones **Bred** Noel Brosnan **Trained** Melsonby, N Yorks

FOCUS
A moderate handicap, run at a fair pace and the third sets the level to previous course form.
T/Plt: £60.70 to a £1 stake. Pool:£68,223.22 - 820.20 winning tickets T/Qpdt: £24.10 to a £1 stake. Pool:£5,159.06 - 158.40 winning tickets CR

4966 YARMOUTH (L-H)
Monday, August 16

OFFICIAL GOING: Good (good to soft in places; 6.7)
Back straight and bend dolled out 3m adding 11yds to distances on round course.
Wind: very blustery Weather: overcast and very dull and chilly

5159 BETFAIR RACING EXCELLENCE APPRENTICE TRAINING SERIES H'CAP 1m 3y
5:30 (5:31) (Class 6) (0-60,60) 3-Y-O+ **£2,331** (£693; £346; £173) **Stalls** High

Form RPR
6446 **1** **Tallawalla (IRE)**[25] 4282 3-8-7 **49**.. RyanClark 11 57
(M R Channon) *chsd ldrs on stands' rails: drvn to ld over 2f out: 2 l clr over 1f out: rdn out and nvr in danger* **20/1**
6006 **2** *3 ¾* **Crocodile Bay (IRE)**[10] 4795 7-9-3 **58**......................... SeanPalmer(5) 10 58
(R C Guest) *led at str pce and sn 4 l clr: hdd over 2f out: sn outpcd by wnr but kpt on steadily and jst hld on to 2nd* **12/1**
0304 **3** *hd* **Easy Wonder (GER)**[5] 4969 5-8-10 **46** oh1................. AntiocoMurgia 1 46
(I A Wood) *midfield: effrt 2f out: 4th over 1f out: kpt on ins fnl f: catching runner-up cl home but no ch w wnr* **8/1**
0-02 **4** *½* **Hellenio**[5] 4970 3-8-6 **53**...(t) IanBurns(5) 9 50
(M G Quinlan) *prom: wnt 2nd 1/2-way tl wl over 2f out: bmpd along after: kpt on gamely but no match for wnr fnl f* **5/1**[2]
2211 **5** *1 ¼* **Fire King**[11] 4738 4-9-4 **59**..(p) MarkPower(5) 12 55
(A B Haynes) *swtchd lft after s and racd in midfield: brought bk to stands' rails over 2f out and tried to improve: racd idly and no imp ins fnl f* **4/1**[1]
5503 **6** *nk* **Al Rayanah**[27] 4236 7-8-9 **50**...(p) RichardOld(5) 3 45
(G Prodromou) *s.i.s: t.k.h in rr: bmpd along and mod prog on outside 2f out: no imp ins fnl f* **9/1**
364 **7** *5* **Bookiebasher Babe (IRE)**[28] 4213 5-8-8 **47**............ NatashaEaton(3) 4 30
(M Quinn) *awkward in paddock and rdn to s wout irons: nvr bttr than midfield and on outside: rdn over 3f out: sn struggling* **16/1**
4405 **8** *nse* **Battle Study (IRE)**[18] 4522 3-8-8 **55**................................. NoraLooby(5) 7 37
(A J McCabe) *s.i.s: a bhd: no ch fnl 3f* **8/1**
6050 **9** *1* **Tt's Dream**[6] 4931 3-8-13 **60**.. KatiaScallan(5) 2 40
(A J Lidderdale) *chsd clr ldr tl 1/2-way: sn lost pl* **14/1**
040 **10** *7* **Clearing House**[5] 4969 5-8-6 **47**...................................... LeonnaMayor(5) 6 12
(J Ryan) *s.i.s: a bhd: t.o* **14/1**
5150 **11** *1 ½* **Unlimited**[31] 4108 8-9-10 **60**.. LeeTopliss 8 21
(A W Carroll) *s.v.s: nvr rcvrd: drvn w no rspnse 3f out: eased 1f out: t.o* **15/2**[3]

1m 39.57s (-1.03) **Going Correction** -0.075s/f (Good)
WFA 3 from 4yo+ 6lb **11** Ran SP% **112.3**
Speed ratings (Par 101): **102,98,98,97,96 96,91,90,89,82 81**
toteswingers:1&2:£57.00, 1&3:£22.60, 2&3:£17.40 CSF £230.38 CT £2109.84 TOTE £33.50: £14.60, £7.40, £4.90; EX 111.10.
Owner M Channon **Bred** John Connaughton **Trained** West Ilsley, Berks

FOCUS
Despite half a millimetre of rain overnight the official ground was changed early morning to good (good to soft in places). The runners had to contend with a blustery wind, mainly from behind, and the back straight and bend had been dolled out three metres, adding 10m to races run on the round course. The leader Crocodile Bay set a good gallop and soon had the field stretched in this modest apprentices' handicap. The form is rated around the placed horses.
Unlimited Official explanation: jockey said gelding lost its action

5160 EUROPEAN BREEDERS' FUND MEDIAN AUCTION MAIDEN STKS 6f 3y
6:00 (6:02) (Class 6) 2-Y-O **£2,590** (£770; £385; £192) **Stalls** High

Form RPR
3 **1** **Biaraafa (IRE)**[19] 4474 2-8-12 0.. HayleyTurner 3 72+
(M L W Bell) *pressed ldr: rdn over 1f out: led ins fnl f: had matters in hand fnl 50yds* **2/1**[1]

02 **2** ¾ **His Grace (IRE)**[11] 4759 2-9-3 0 JimmyQuinn 16 73
(A B Haynes) *led and racd enthusiastically: rdn 2f out: hdd ins fnl f: kpt on gamely* **5/1**[3]
04 **3** 2½ **Eyes On**[11] 4759 2-8-12 0 NickyMackay 1 61
(P J McBride) *pressed ldrs: rdn 2f out: nt qckn fnl f* **18/1**
44 **4** 1 **Tamareen (IRE)**[86] 2312 2-9-3 0 (t) RichardHills 8 63
(E A L Dunlop) *prom: rdn and tending to edge rt 2f out: one pce fnl f* **7/2**[2]
5 ½ **Flying Phoenix** 2-8-12 0 KirstyMilczarek 4 56+
(W J Haggas) *midfield: looked green and rdn and outpcd over 2f out: effrt over 1f out: styng on stoutly ins fnl f: promising* **20/1**
6 **6** nk **Cinderkamp**[97] 1986 2-9-3 0 AlanMunro 12 60+
(E F Vaughan) *towards rr early: kpt on over 1f out: nvr able to chal: do bttr* **33/1**
04 **7** hd **Silent Blessing**[7] 4890 2-9-0 0 MartinLane(3) 9 61
(R M H Cowell) *chsd ldrs: drvn over 2f out: kpt on same pce and n.d after* **14/1**
06 **8** 1¼ **Exchange**[18] 4499 2-9-3 0 LiamJones 7 56
(W J Haggas) *chsd ldrs: drvn over 2f out: no imp ins fnl f* **8/1**
9 ½ **Honkers Bonkers** 2-9-3 0 JamesDoyle 14 54+
(A J McCabe) *towards rr: no ch fr 1/2-way* **50/1**
50 **10** 1¼ **Toparichi**[11] 4759 2-9-3 0 DarryllHolland 2 51
(M H Tompkins) *chsd ldrs: drvn over 2f out: wknd over 1f out* **9/1**
11 4½ **Lady Ellice** 2-8-12 0 TomMcLaughlin 15 32
(P S McEntee) *chsd ldrs: rdn 1/2-way: sn btn* **100/1**
12 3½ **Icelady** 2-8-12 0 AndrewElliott 11 22
(R M H Cowell) *unruly leaving paddock and uns rdr: dwlt: rdn in rr: nvr gng wl* **100/1**
0 **13** ¾ **Fajer Al Kuwait**[27] 4233 2-9-3 0 SaleemGolam 5 24
(G Prodromou) *a bhd: no ch fr 1/2-way* **150/1**
14 3 **Colzium** 2-9-3 0 SebSanders 10 15
(M H Tompkins) *s.s: a struggling in rr: t.o fnl 2f* **50/1**
15 2¼ **Blazing Apostle (IRE)** 2-8-12 0 MarcHalford 6 —
(Mrs C A Dunnett) *a wl bhd and looked v green: t.o fnl 2f* **150/1**

1m 14.36s (-0.04) **Going Correction** -0.075s/f (Good) **15** Ran SP% **120.2**
Speed ratings (Par 92): **97,96,92,91,90 90,90,88,87,86 80,75,74,70,67**
toteswingers:1&2:£4.10, 1&3:£9.40, 2&3:£25.30 CSF £11.32 TOTE £2.60: £1.10, £3.30, £8.90; EX 16.70.
Owner R L W Frisby **Bred** Palm Tree Thoroughbreds **Trained** Newmarket, Suffolk

FOCUS
A fairly competitive median auction event. The gallop looked solid enough.

NOTEBOOK
Biaraafa(IRE) confirmed the promise of her debut run three weeks earlier, chasing the pacesetting His Grace and readily finding enough to score. She's entered in the big-money sales races at Doncaster and Redcar later in the season, and is certainly going in the right direction. This was a professional performance. (op 9-4 tchd 15-8)
His Grace(IRE) posted another solid effort to follow up his good run here last time out, confirming form with Eyes On. He's a keen-going sort who made a bee-line for the centre of the course from his stall on the stands' rail. He is related to winners and should have no trouble in finding a race. (op 8-1)
Eyes On was a long way behind the winner when both made their debuts at Leicester. She virtually repeated her last run here (with His Grace and Toparichi). She will be competitive in nurseries having now qualified for a mark. (op 16-1 tchd 20-1)
Tamareen(IRE) came back from a longish break here, and was tongue-tied. Prominent throughout, he could muster only one pace when coming under pressure and this was an unconvincing effort. (op 9-2)
Flying Phoenix ◆ did best of the newcomers and was staying on in eyecatching fashion in the final furlong. Not overly expensive and with 1m2f and 1m4f winners (at a fairly modest level) in his pedigree, it is obvious a step up in trip will suit. Jockey bookings suggested he wasn't expected to go better than Exchange, so this was a promising debut and he looks a likely winner over further. (op 16-1)
Cinderkamp was also staying on late having looked green and racing awkwardly over a furlong out. This was a much better effort than his debut, but he's been given time since that run and showed plenty of promise here. (tchd 40-1)
Exchange is a strong sort and was all at sea on the undulations at Epsom last time, but this has to go down as a disappointment as he never looked likely to be involved in the finish. He is related to three winners at up to 1m and this trip looked too sharp side already. (op 11-2)

5161 THRIGBY HALL WILDLIFE PARK CLAIMING STKS 1m 2f 21y
6:30 (6:30) (Class 6) 3-4-Y-0 **£2,201** (£655; £327; £163) **Stalls** Low

Form RPR
304 **1** **Managua**[24] 4348 4-9-9 78 AlanMunro 2 70
(M R Channon) *settled 3rd: wnt 2nd gng best ent st: led over 3f out: a being kpt up to work but looked wnr after: 2 l clr 1f out: all out cl home but probably idling* **8/11**[1]
0000 **2** ½ **Motirani**[30] 4156 3-8-4 50 HayleyTurner 3 58
(M L W Bell) *chsd ldr tl ent st: rdn and changing legs and racing w high hd carriage after: fnd v little but wnt 2nd nr fin: flattered by proximity to wnr* **12/1**
-010 **3** nk **Northern Acres**[66] 2941 4-9-4 69 BillyCray(5) 5 68
(D Nicholls) *settled 4th: drvn ent st: wnt 2nd over 3f out: chsd wnr vainly tl fnl strides* **5/2**[2]
0106 **4** 28 **Fasette**[12] 4718 3-7-13 56 (b[1]) JimmyQuinn 1 —
(M H Tompkins) *drvn to ld: sn 5 l clr: rdn and hdd over 3f out: immediately gave up: eased and t.o* **8/1**[3]
3600 **5** 99 **Seek The Cash (USA)**[65] 2962 3-8-10 55 NickyMackay 4 —
(M Quinn) *a last: hrd drvn and t.o 1/2-way: virtually p.u fnl 4f* **50/1**

2m 12.14s (1.64) **Going Correction** -0.075s/f (Good)
WFA 3 from 4yo 8lb **5** Ran SP% **107.2**
Speed ratings (Par 101): **90,89,89,66,—**
CSF £9.84 TOTE £1.40: £1.10, £7.90; EX 6.60.Motirani was claimed by Jeff Pearce for £4,000.
Owner Capital **Bred** Brook Stud Bloodstock Ltd **Trained** West Ilsley, Berks

FOCUS
A modest claimer and muddling form, so not a race to be positive about.

5162 HALLS GROUP MAIDEN H'CAP 6f 3y
7:00 (7:01) (Class 5) (0-70,69) 3-Y-0+ **£2,719** (£809; £404; £202) **Stalls** High

Form RPR
234 **1** **Cardinal**[12] 4715 5-9-0 55 HayleyTurner 10 75
(R M H Cowell) *hld up gng wl towards rr: smooth prog on bit 2f out: led 1f out: sn qcknd clr: pushed out* **2/1**[1]
0003 **2** 6 **Rigid**[10] 4791 3-8-2 51 BillyCray(5) 8 52
(A W Carroll) *prom but racing awkwardly: led over 2f out: drvn and hdd 1f out: immediately outpcd by wnr* **9/1**
0360 **3** ¾ **Nadinska**[4] 4989 3-9-4 62 AlanMunro 9 60
(M R Channon) *towards rr: rdn over 2f out: effrt over 1f out: one pce and n.d* **9/1**
206 **4** 1½ **Young Simon**[33] 4025 3-9-5 63 SebSanders 6 57
(G G Margarson) *midfield: rdn 1/2-way: one pce and n.d over 1f out: snatched 4th* **11/1**
3224 **5** nk **Frequency**[67] 2892 3-9-11 69 TomMcLaughlin 4 62
(E A L Dunlop) *trckd ldrs gng wl: shkn up whn carried sltly lft over 2f out: rdn over 1f out: sn wknd* **5/1**[2]
6000 **6** 1¼ **Pavement Games**[30] 4151 3-8-3 47 oh2 PaulEddery 5 36
(R C Guest) *dwlt and stdd: stl last 2f out: mod late prog but nt gng freely* **66/1**
-043 **7** 1¼ **Swansea Jack**[8] 4861 3-8-7 51 (t) SaleemGolam 3 36
(S C Williams) *plld hrd and racd v awkwardly: led after 2f tl rdn and veered lft over 2f out: sn lost pl and nt run on* **15/2**[3]
060 **8** 3 **Midnight M**[9] 4835 3-8-3 47 oh2 (t) NickyMackay 2 22
(Rae Guest) *sn pushed along: effrt to chse ldrs 1/2-way: sltly impeded over 2f out: sn btn: eased fnl f* **40/1**
4025 **9** 2¾ **Frontline Boy (IRE)**[37] 3904 3-9-4 62 (t) AndrewElliott 7 28
(Mrs K Burke) *slt ld 2f: lost pl 1/2-way: drvn and btn over 2f out* **14/1**
0532 **10** ¾ **Gessabelle**[4] 4998 3-8-0 47 oh2 (t) MartinLane(3) 1 11
(P S McEntee) *taken down early: s.s: drvn to chse ldrs after 2f: sn looking awkward: btn whn sltly impeded over 2f out* **8/1**

1m 13.45s (-0.95) **Going Correction** -0.075s/f (Good)
WFA 3 from 5yo 3lb **10** Ran SP% **111.8**
Speed ratings (Par 103): **103,95,94,92,91 89,88,84,80,79**
toteswingers:1&2:£4.40, 1&3:£3.90, 2&3:£13.40 CSF £19.79 CT £120.55 TOTE £2.10: £1.10, £7.10, £5.10; EX 21.40.
Owner Mrs J May **Bred** The Queen **Trained** Six Mile Bottom, Cambs

FOCUS
The ten-strong field for this maiden handicap had contested 92 races between them.
Rigid Official explanation: jockey said gelding hung left

5163 EAST COAST TRUCKERS 25TH ANNIVERSARY H'CAP 7f 3y
7:30 (7:31) (Class 5) (0-70,69) 3-Y-0 **£2,978** (£886; £442; £221) **Stalls** High

Form RPR
0356 **1** **Perfect Ch'I (IRE)**[22] 4398 3-9-7 69 TomMcLaughlin 7 74
(I A Wood) *mde all: rdn and hanging lft fr over 1f out and hampering her main rival: in command ins fnl f* **8/1**
3255 **2** 1¼ **Leitzu (IRE)**[23] 4382 3-9-0 62 AlanMunro 8 64+
(M R Channon) *pressed ldr: rdn over 2f out: trying to chal whn n.m.r over 1f out: bdly squeezed for room 1f out: unable to regain momentum tl rallied gamely to snatch 2nd: wnr beyond recall* **9/2**[3]
0322 **3** shd **Piddie's Power**[19] 4482 3-9-7 69 SebSanders 2 70
(E S McMahon) *taken down early: cl up: rdn 2f out: chsd wnr over 1f out: fnd little and lost 2nd on line* **9/4**[1]
1000 **4** shd **Miss Kitty Grey (IRE)**[10] 4791 3-8-12 60 NickyMackay 5 61
(J R Boyle) *pressed ldng pair: pushed along over 2f out: kpt on ins fnl f but a hld: ev ch of 2nd tl last strides* **16/1**
-245 **5** 2 **Via Aurelia (IRE)**[24] 4324 3-8-9 57 HayleyTurner 3 52
(J R Fanshawe) *rather keen early: hld up in last pair: rdn over 2f out: chsng ldrs 1f out: unable to chal* **7/2**[2]
0031 **6** 1 **Mack's Sister**[10] 4791 3-8-13 61 JimmyQuinn 6 54
(D K Ivory) *t.k.h in midfield: rdn over 2f out: no ex 1f out* **6/1**
225 **7** hd **Jemima Nicholas**[16] 4584 3-9-2 64 LiamJones 4 56
(W J Haggas) *last pair tl 1/2-way: effrt and rdn over 2f out: no ex 1f out* **14/1**
44-0 **8** 8 **Silken Aunt**[72] 2754 3-8-12 60 KirstyMilczarek 1 30
(J A R Toller) *towards rr: drvn and struggling over 2f out* **28/1**

1m 27.23s (0.63) **Going Correction** -0.075s/f (Good) **8** Ran SP% **112.6**
Speed ratings (Par 100): **93,91,91,91,89 87,87,78**
toteswingers:1&2:£4.50, 1&3:£5.40, 2&3:£2.60 CSF £42.36 CT £107.69 TOTE £17.30: £4.40, £2.10, £1.10; EX 38.60.
Owner Paddy Barrett **Bred** Glencarrig Stud **Trained** Upper Lambourn, Berks
■ Stewards' Enquiry : Tom McLaughlin one-day ban: careless riding (Aug 30)

FOCUS
A modest, but tightly contested handicap and the form looks fairly sound, rated around the first four.

5164 ATI TANK HIRE MAIDEN H'CAP 1m 6f 17y
8:00 (8:03) (Class 5) (0-70,68) 3-Y-0+ **£2,719** (£809; £404; £202) **Stalls** Low

Form RPR
4252 **1** **Head Hunted**[17] 4545 3-9-9 66 MartinLane(3) 11 73
(D M Simcock) *settled midfield: prog 4f out: rdn to ld over 2f out: a holding rivals after: pushed out* **5/1**[2]
5335 **2** 1¾ **Pena Dorada (IRE)**[17] 4545 3-9-11 65 (p) AndrewElliott 8 70
(Mrs K Burke) *virtually a 2nd: rdn and ev ch 3f out: chsd wnr vainly fnl 2f* **9/2**[1]
5002 **3** 3¼ **Iron Condor**[12] 4698 3-10-0 68 SebSanders 7 68
(J M P Eustace) *hld up in rr: stl disputing last ent st: prog 3f out: chsd ldng pair over 2f out: fnd nil whn rdn and nvr got in a blow* **9/2**[1]
4060 **4** 3¾ **Juwireya**[17] 4557 3-9-9 68 (b) BillyCray(5) 12 63
(P W Hiatt) *midfield: outpcd by ldrs over 3f out: hrd rdn 2f out: nvr able to chal first trio* **20/1**
3-50 **5** ½ **Dubai Phantom (USA)**[66] 2924 3-9-10 64 LiamJones 6 59
(D M Simcock) *hld up and bhd: plugged on past stragglers fnl 2f: nvr rchd ldrs* **25/1**
6060 **6** 1 **Dovedon Earl**[11] 4765 4-9-3 45 (b[1]) DaraghO'Donohoe 13 38
(T Keddy) *drvn leaving stalls: sn pulling and racing in 3rd: rdn and fdd over 3f out: fin v weakly* **40/1**
2633 **7** nk **Red Barcelona (IRE)**[17] 4552 3-9-1 55 DarryllHolland 10 48
(M H Tompkins) *led after 1f: rdn and hdd over 2f out: grad lost pl* **9/2**[1]
-623 **8** 1¼ **Little Oz (IRE)**[17] 4557 3-9-9 63 TomMcLaughlin 1 54
(E A L Dunlop) *drvn to ld for 1f: prom: rdn and little rspnse over 3f out: sn btn: eased clsng stages* **9/2**[1]
0422 **9** 5 **Tower**[23] 4362 3-9-9 63 AlanMunro 5 47
(G Prodromou) *hld up: brief effrt 4f out: sn rdn and struggling* **8/1**[3]
6060 **10** 4½ **Joe Rua (USA)**[3] 5058 3-8-5 45 MarcHalford 3 23
(J Ryan) *midfield: rdn and fdd 4f out: t.o* **66/1**
/000 **11** 10 **Sensible**[97] 2012 5-9-8 50 JimmyQuinn 2 14
(H J Collingridge) *midfield: rdn and fdd 4f out: t.o fnl 2f* **50/1**
0000 **12** 7 **Melinoise**[13] 4683 3-8-6 51 (b[1]) SimonPearce(5) 4 5
(Rae Guest) *bhd: pushed along and struggling 1/2-way: disp last st: t.o fnl 2f* **66/1**

3m 11.93s (4.33) **Going Correction** -0.075s/f (Good)
WFA 3 from 4yo+ 12lb **12** Ran SP% **116.5**
Speed ratings (Par 103): **84,83,81,79,78 78,77,77,74,71 66,62**
toteswingers:1&2:£5.40, 1&3:£3.80, 2&3:£6.10 CSF £25.62 CT £108.13 TOTE £4.10: £1.30, £1.40, £1.70; EX 21.70 Place 6 £56.35; Place 5 £6.42.
Owner J M Cook **Bred** Rabbah Bloodstock Limited **Trained** Newmarket, Suffolk

FOCUS
A wide-open staying handicap in which a testing gallop was set from the outset. The third is rated to his latest form.
T/Plt: £187.10 to a £1 stake. Pool:£58,136.45 - 226.81 winning tickets T/Qpdt: £8.80 to a £1 stake. Pool:£6,403.14 - 533.90 winning tickets IM

5165 - 5168a (Foreign Racing) - See Raceform Interactive

4774 BRIGHTON (L-H)

Tuesday, August 17

OFFICIAL GOING: Good to firm (good in places) changing to good (good to firm in places) after race 3 (3.10)
Rail realignment increased distances by about 10yds.
Wind: fresh, against Weather: overcast, breezy

5169 HARDINGS CATERING SERVICES H'CAP (DIV I) 5f 213y
2:00 (2:00) (Class 6) (0-60,60) 3-Y-O+ £1,295 (£385; £192; £96) Stalls Centre

Form RPR
3003 1 **Rio Royale (IRE)**[6] 4959 4-9-3 56....(p) SebSanders 7 63
(Mrs A J Perrett) *t.k.h: trckd ldrs: rdn and ev ch wl over 1f out: hrd drvn to ld ins fnl f: kpt on: all out* 5/2[1]
0303 2 shd **Shakespeare's Son**[35] 3977 5-8-4 48.... JohnFahy(5) 9 55
(H J Evans) *t.k.h: hld up in tch in midfield: hdwy jst over 2f out: rdn and ev ch ent fnl f: hrd drvn and kpt on fnl 100yds: jst hld* 4/1[3]
4000 3 nk **Avoncreek**[20] 4487 6-8-7 46 oh1.... KirstyMilczarek 6 52
(B P J Baugh) *led tl over 3f out: led again 2f out: sn rdn: hdd ins fnl f: no ex towards fin* 16/1
4043 4 1 **Bateleur**[2] 5112 6-9-7 60.... CathyGannon 5 64+
(M R Channon) *stdd s: hld up in rr: hdwy jst over 2f out: chsng ldrs and edging lft whn nt clr run 1f out tl swtchd rt ins fnl f: kpt on: unable to chal* 3/1[2]
-000 5 1 3/4 **If Only**[75] 2678 4-8-12 51....(p) LukeMorris 1 48
(D Morris) *wnt rt s: chsd ldrs: rdn and unable qck wl over 1f out: styd on same pce ins fnl f* 14/1
1010 6 3 1/2 **Boldinor**[20] 4478 7-9-6 59.... GeorgeBaker 4 45
(M R Bosley) *restless in stalls: sn niggled along in last trio: hdwy towards inner 2f out: rdn and wknd ent fnl f* 5/1
0-00 7 6 **Calabaza**[11] 4790 8-8-2 46.... JemmaMarshall(5) 3 13
(M J Attwater) *taken down early: bmpd and short of room s: a struggling in rr: n.d* 66/1
5301 8 2 1/2 **Ellen Vannin (IRE)**[13] 4692 3-8-12 57....(p) PatrickHills(3) 10 16
(Eve Johnson Houghton) *w ldr tl led over 3f out tl hdd 2f out: wknd rapidly and sn bhd* 9/1

1m 11.92s (1.72) **Going Correction** +0.275s/f (Good)
WFA 3 from 4yo+ 3lb 8 Ran SP% **114.3**
Speed ratings (Par 101): **99,98,98,97,94 90,82,78**
toteswingers: 1&2 £2.00, 1&3 £6.90, 2&3 £9.80 CSF £12.79 CT £128.24 TOTE £2.70: £1.40, £1.90, £5.70; EX 11.90 Trifecta £153.40 Pool: £339.99 - 1.64 winning units..
Owner Mrs Amanda Perrett **Bred** Glending Bloodstock **Trained** Pulborough, W Sussex
■ Stewards' Enquiry : Seb Sanders one-day ban: used whip with excessive frequency (Aug 31)

FOCUS
The ground had quickened up after only getting 1mm of rain overnight and was now described as good to firm, good on places with the jockeys reporting that it was riding "good" with a very strong headwind. The rails had been pushed right out on the top bend to provide fresh ground, adding roughly a further ten yards. A run-of-the-mill sprint handicap which lost a little of its interest when Clerical was withdrawn after spooking at a dog and unseating his rider beforehand. It is hard to be positive about this form.
Ellen Vannin(IRE) Official explanation: jockey said filly hung right

5170 EUROPEAN BREEDERS' FUND MEDIAN AUCTION MAIDEN STKS 6f 209y
2:35 (2:36) (Class 5) 2-Y-O £3,217 (£962; £481; £240; £119) Stalls Centre

Form RPR
5 1 **Mubtadi**[52] 3433 2-9-3 0.... LiamKeniry 3 78+
(D M Simcock) *stdd s: t.k.h early: hld up in last trio: hdwy over 2f out: rdn to chse ldr over 1f out: led ins fnl f: in command and pushed out fnl 75yds* 5/2[3]
2 3/4 **Makeynn** 2-9-3 0.... TedDurcan 5 76+
(Saeed Bin Suroor) *chsd ldr tl led over 2f out: rdn clr w wnr over 1f out: hdd ins fnl f: kpt on same pce and btn fnl 75yds* 2/1[1]
5 3 4 1/2 **Thomas Tompion (IRE)**[8] 4902 2-9-3 0.... GeorgeBaker 6 64
(G L Moore) *t.k.h early: chsd ldrs: bmpd over 2f out: rdn to chse ldng pair over 1f out: no imp and btn whn edgd lft ins fnl f* 9/4[2]
06 4 2 1/4 **Papas Fritas**[8] 4902 2-9-0 0.... Louis-PhilippeBeuzelin(3) 2 59
(B J Meehan) *chsd ldrs: effrt and hung rt over 2f out: outpcd and rdn ent fnl 2f: wl btn over 1f out* 20/1
0 5 3 1/2 **Ihavenotime (IRE)**[10] 4844 2-8-12 0.... SamHitchcott 8 44
(M R Channon) *dwlt: in tch in midfield: struggling u.p 3f out: wl btn fnl 2f* 50/1
0 6 1 **Munro's Dragon**[11] 4802 2-9-3 0.... PatCosgrave 7 47
(M H Tompkins) *in tch in midfield tl rdn and dropped to rr 4f out: wl bhd fnl 2f* 100/1
0 7 3/4 **Kalgoolie**[13] 4695 2-8-12 0.... ChrisCatlin 4 40
(Rae Guest) *stdd after s: nvr gng wl or handling the trck: sn rdn in last: wl bhd fr over 2f out* 40/1
03 8 1 1/4 **Educated Son**[17] 4587 2-9-3 0.... DavidProbert 1 42
(W R Muir) *taken down early: fly-jmpd leaving stalls: sn rcvrd and led: hdd and rdn over 2f out: wknd qckly wl over 1f out: wl btn and eased ins fnl f* 12/1

1m 25.03s (1.93) **Going Correction** +0.275s/f (Good) 8 Ran SP% **110.5**
Speed ratings (Par 94): **99,98,93,90,86 85,84,83**
toteswingers:1&2 £2.50, 2&3 £2.10, 1&3 £2.00 CSF £7.27 TOTE £3.60: £1.30, £1.10, £1.10; EX 8.70 Trifecta £18.20 Pool: £621.81 - 25.21 winning units..
Owner Abdulla Al Mansoori **Bred** Whitsbury Manor Stud **Trained** Newmarket, Suffolk

FOCUS
An interesting maiden for the track and the winner built on his nice start.

NOTEBOOK
Mubtadi built on his previous eyecatching racecourse debut to get off the mark. He was a little slowly away, but was soon travelling on an even keel before coming through to take it up just inside the distance. He is a nice type who looks to be a strong traveller which should hold him in good stead in the future if he is to contest some of the lofty entries he holds. (op 11-4 tchd 3-1)
Makeynn, a half-brother to seven winners including triple Group 2 winner Iffraaj, made a respectable debut. He knew his job well, as you would expect from the stable, but he looks an uncomplicated, promising type who can only build on this (op 7-4)
Thomas Tompion(IRE) had come in for good support throughout the day, but could not match the pace of the leading pair after holding a chance over a furlong out. He is going the right way and should be off the mark before long as he might have been unlucky to have bumped into a useful-looking pair. (tchd 2-1)
Papas Fritas had struggled to go the pace over 6f in previous efforts and again was under pressure a fair way out. This was a fair effort and he should now do better in nurseries. (tchd 25-1)
Kalgoolie Official explanation: vet said filly finished lame

5171 ABF THE SOLDIERS CHARITY H'CAP 7f 214y
3:10 (3:10) (Class 6) (0-65,64) 3-Y-O £1,554 (£462; £231; £115) Stalls Low

Form RPR
0-00 1 **Ermyntrude**[16] 4621 3-7-13 47 ow2.... JemmaMarshall(5) 12 56
(P M Phelan) *chsd ldrs: swtchd lft and effrt ent fnl 2f: led ent fnl f: kpt on wl u.p* 33/1
6-30 2 1 3/4 **Farmers Dream (IRE)**[18] 4534 3-8-12 55.... LiamKeniry 10 60
(J L Spearing) *hld up in tch towards rr: rdn and effrt wl over 1f out: kpt on u.p to chse wnr fnl 100yds: no imp after* 10/1
1220 3 3/4 **Eye Of Eternity**[12] 4746 3-8-11 54.... DavidProbert 1 57+
(Rae Guest) *in tch in midfield: rdn and hdwy to chse ldrs ent fnl 2f: drvn to ld over 1f out: sn hdd: no ex and btn ins fnl f* 12/1
0402 4 1 **King's Approach (IRE)**[11] 4791 3-9-1 58....(p) TomMcLaughlin 9 59
(R A Harris) *led: rdn and hdd over 1f out: wknd ins fnl f* 14/1
3U43 5 1 1/4 **Little Meadow (IRE)**[11] 4779 3-8-2 45.... CathyGannon 3 43+
(Miss J Feilden) *in tch: whn bdly hmpd and lost pl after 1f: bhd after: styd on u.p fr over 1f out: nvr trbld ldrs* 16/1
0122 6 3/4 **Lady Of Garmoran (USA)**[11] 4774 3-9-1 58.... TedDurcan 11 54
(P F I Cole) *in tch in midfield: rdn and effrt 2f out: keeping on same pce whn n.m.r ent fnl f: no imp after* 10/3[2]
5650 7 7 **Tiger Hawk (USA)**[42] 3759 3-8-9 52....(b) SamHitchcott 7 32
(Jim Best) *chsd ldr tl wl over 2f out: sn struggling u.p: wl btn over 1f out* 33/1
0636 8 4 **Take My Hand**[11] 4791 3-9-1 58.... ChrisCatlin 6 29
(M R Channon) *hld up in tch: hdwy to chse ldr over 2f out: wknd qckly u.p over 1f out: wl btn ins fnl f* 11/1
006 9 15 **Proud Tuscan**[24] 4383 3-8-4 47.... LukeMorris 2 —
(J S Moore) *in tch in midfield: rdn and losing pl 4f out: wkng whn hmpd ent fnl 2f: wl bhd and eased ins fnl f* 50/1
0-40 10 5 **Power Of Dreams (IRE)**[47] 3607 3-9-7 64.... PatCosgrave 8 —
(M H Tompkins) *hld up in tch towards rr: short-lived effrt u.p wl over 1f out: wl btn 1f out: eased ins fnl f: t.o* 16/1
0320 11 64 **Motty's Gift**[18] 4534 3-9-0 57....(v) ShaneKelly 5 —
(W R Swinburn) *towards rr whn hmpd after 1f: sn detached fr field and nvr travelling after: virtually p.u fr over 1f out: t.o* 5/1[3]
0432 P **Resuscitator (USA)**[3] 5077 3-9-5 62....(v) GeorgeBaker 4 —
(Mrs H S Main) *dwlt: busted along and in tch whn squeezed out and clipped heels after 1f: detached in last and nvr gng after: eased fr over 2f out: p.u and dismntd ins fnl f* 3/1[1]

1m 37.51s (1.51) **Going Correction** +0.275s/f (Good) 12 Ran SP% **116.1**
Speed ratings (Par 98): **103,101,100,99,98 97,90,86,71,66 2,—**
toteswingers:1&2 £49.20, 2&3 £24.80, 1&3 £65.70 CSF £325.31 CT £4216.94 TOTE £51.10: £14.40, £4.60, £3.80; EX 385.00 TRIFECTA Not won..
Owner Timesquare Ltd **Bred** Ermyn Lodge Stud Limited **Trained** Epsom, Surrey

FOCUS
A rough passage for many in this ordinary handicap, but it was sound run and the surprise winner seemed no fluke.
Little Meadow(IRE) Official explanation: jockey said filly suffered interference in running; vet said filly was struck into and lost right-hind shoe
Proud Tuscan Official explanation: vet said colt was lame left-hind
Motty's Gift Official explanation: vet said gelding returned distressed
Resuscitator(USA) Official explanation: jockey said colt suffered interference in running

5172 SUPPORT THE ABF THE SOLDIERS CHARITY H'CAP 1m 1f 209y
3:45 (3:45) (Class 5) (0-70,70) 3-Y-O+ £2,201 (£655; £327; £163) Stalls High

Form RPR
204 1 **Librettista (AUS)**[28] 4238 4-9-12 69.... KirstyMilczarek 6 78
(L M Cumani) *chsd ldrs: ev ch u.p 1f out: led ins fnl f: edgd lft: r.o wl fnl 100yds* 8/1
2623 2 1 3/4 **The Hague**[27] 4261 4-9-9 70....(v[1]) DeanHeslop(5) 3 76
(P D Evans) *hld up in tch: chsng ldrs u.p 1f out: wnt 2nd fnl 100yds: kpt on same pce after* 8/1
4412 3 3/4 **Ubiquitous**[17] 4591 5-8-8 55....(t) SimonPearce(5) 2 60
(S Dow) *led tl 4f out: in ld again and drvn 1f out: sn hdd: no ex fnl 100yds* 14/1
5431 4 1 **Shianda**[11] 4774 3-8-8 58....(b) FergusSweeney 7 61
(G L Moore) *hld up in tch: chsng ldrs u.p 1f out: styd on same pce after* 4/1[2]
2511 5 1 3/4 **Celestial Girl**[35] 3983 3-9-1 65.... ChrisCatlin 8 64
(H Morrison) *hld up in tch: wkng u.p 1f out: wl hld ins fnl f* 11/10[1]
504 6 4 1/2 **Yourgolftravel Com**[22] 4439 5-9-0 61....(e[1]) JohnFahy(5) 4 51
(M Wigham) *t.k.h: hld up in last: wl btn 1f out* 6/1[3]
0400 7 3 3/4 **Illuminative (USA)**[19] 4498 4-9-4 60....(b[1]) SamHitchcott 5 43
(Miss Z C Davison) *t.k.h: chsd ldrs: in ld 4f out: wl bhd 1f out* 40/1

2m 5.56s (1.96) **Going Correction** +0.275s/f (Good)
WFA 3 from 4yo+ 8lb 7 Ran SP% **113.2**
Speed ratings (Par 103): **103,101,101,100,98 95,92**
toteswingers:1&2 £6.30, 2&3 £7.10, 1&3 £8.00 CSF £66.56 CT £877.47 TOTE £10.70: £4.60, £3.00; EX 52.70 Trifecta £322.20 Part won. Pool: £435.45 - 0.41 winning units..
Owner S Stuckey **Bred** Darley Australia Pty Ltd **Trained** Newmarket, Suffolk

FOCUS
The sea fret had emerged so visibility was very poor for this competitive little 51-70 handicap. The favourite disappointed but the form still looks sound.
Ubiquitous Official explanation: vet said mare lost a right-fore shoe
Shianda Official explanation: jockey said filly was denied a clear run 1f out

5173 RDF I.T. SOLUTIONS H'CAP 1m 3f 196y
4:20 (4:20) (Class 5) (0-70,61) 3-Y-O £2,201 (£655; £327; £163) Stalls High

Form RPR
5212 1 **Baoli**[31] 4134 3-9-7 61.... KirstyMilczarek 6 66
(L M Cumani) *trckd ldrs early: ev ch ent fnl 2f: rdn: hung lft and bmpd rival over 1f out: kpt hanging lft u.p: led wl ins fnl f: kpt on* 7/4[2]
231 2 1/2 **Rockweiler**[7] 4925 3-9-4 61 6ex....(v) RichardEvans(3) 4 65
(P D Evans) *led: jnd over 2f out: rdn and bmpd over 1f out: carried lft after: hdd and no ex wl ins fnl f* 4/6[1]
054 3 nse **River Tease**[13] 4718 3-9-3 57.... LukeMorris 7 61
(J S Moore) *bhd: chsng ldng pair u.p ent fnl 2f: hung lft fr over 1f out: styd on fnl 100yds to press for 2nd cl home* 16/1[3]

0-40 **4** *18* **Astrovenus**[18] 4557 3-9-1 **55** .... SaleemGolam 1 30
(M H Tompkins) *chsd ldrs: struggling u.p over 2f out: wl btn over 1f out* **20/1**

6465 **5** *4 ½* **Vadition (IRE)**[11] 4774 3-8-5 **45** .... NeilChalmers 2 13
(J J Bridger) *chsd ldr tl 4f out: sn struggling u.p: wl btn over 1f out* **50/1**

2m 38.21s (5.51) **Going Correction** +0.275s/f (Good) **5** Ran SP% **109.0**
Speed ratings (Par 100): **92,91,91,79,76**
CSF £3.16 TOTE £3.10: £1.60, £1.10; EX 3.30.
Owner Andrew Patey **Bred** W M Johnstone **Trained** Newmarket, Suffolk
■ Stewards' Enquiry : Richard Evans one-day ban: used whip with excessive frequency (Aug31)

FOCUS
A much depleted field for this 1m4f handicap with conditions again very poor. Weak form.

5174 FOOD FESTIVAL LAUNCHES HERE 1ST SEPTEMBER H'CAP 6f 209y
4:55 (4:55) (Class 5) (0-70,69) 3-Y-0+ **£2,201** (£655; £327; £163) **Stalls** Centre

Form RPR

1210 **1** **Lady Florence**[3] 5087 5-9-9 **69** .... RussKennemore(3) 8 79
(A B Coogan) *mde all: styd on far rail 3f out: rdn ent fnl 2f: styd on wl and clr ins fnl f* **3/1**[2]

1211 **2** *2 ¼* **Eager To Bow (IRE)**[28] 4232 4-9-7 **64** .... GeorgeBaker 7 68
(P R Chamings) *stdd s: hld up in last: c stands' side 3f out: drvn and effrt 2f out: chsd wnr ins fnl f: nvr able to chal* **6/4**[1]

-535 **3** *nk* **Phluke**[9] 4870 9-9-1 **58** .... (v) LiamKeniry 5 61
(Eve Johnson Houghton) *in tch: c stands' side 3f out: rdn and edgd rt wl over 2f out: kpt on u.p fnl f: nvr gng pce to chal wnr* **15/2**

1541 **4** *¾* **Amber Sunset**[19] 4502 4-9-11 **68** .... LukeMorris 3 69
(D Morris) *t.k.h: trckd ldrs: wnt 2nd and c stands' side 3f out: drvn wl over 1f out: no imp on wnr: lost 2 pls ins fnl f* **9/2**[3]

0012 **5** *5* **Dvinsky (USA)**[11] 4777 9-9-8 **65** .... (b) IanMongan 9 53
(P Howling) *sn bustled along to chse ldr: c stands' side and lost pl over 3f out: wkng whn hmpd over 2f out: wl btn ins fnl f* **15/2**

0050 **6** *2 ½* **Mororless**[6] 4970 3-8-6 **54** ow2 .... (b[1]) SamHitchcott 6 33
(Miss Z C Davison) *bustled along leaving stalls: in tch: rdn and struggling whn c stands' side 3f out: wl btn over 1f out* **50/1**

1m 24.48s (1.38) **Going Correction** +0.275s/f (Good)
WFA 3 from 4yo+ 5lb **6** Ran SP% **108.7**
Speed ratings (Par 103): **103,100,100,99,93 90**
toteswingers:1&2 £1.80, 2&3 £2.90, 1&3 £4.20 CSF £7.38 CT £24.02 TOTE £4.90: £3.20, £1.10; EX 8.40 Trifecta £67.20 Pool: £184.50 - 2.03 winning units..
Owner A B Coogan **Bred** The National Stud **Trained** Soham, Cambs

FOCUS
The fog had cleared for this competitive 7f handicap that was run at a decent pace, with all but one of the runners racing up the stands' side. The winner is rated up 7lb.
Dvinsky(USA) Official explanation: vet said gelding lost an off-fore shoe

5175 HARDINGS CATERING SERVICES H'CAP (DIV II) 5f 213y
5:25 (5:25) (Class 6) (0-60,59) 3-Y-0+ **£1,295** (£385; £192; £96) **Stalls** Centre

Form RPR

4065 **1** **Pipers Piping (IRE)**[13] 4715 4-8-7 **48** .... (p) MichaelStainton(3) 9 61
(P Howling) *stdd s: hld up in tch in rr: hdwy towards inner 2f out: rdn to chse ldr ent fnl f: led ins fnl f: r.o wl* **5/1**[3]

0350 **2** *1 ½* **Avonlini**[20] 4486 4-8-8 **46** .... JackMitchell 2 54
(B P J Baugh) *led: rdn and edgd rt over 2f out: hdd and no ex ins fnl f* **10/1**

1544 **3** *2 ¼* **Bermondsey Bob (IRE)**[7] 4936 4-9-5 **57** .... SamHitchcott 10 58
(J L Spearing) *chsd ldr: rdn and unable qck wl over 1f out: styd on one pce u.p fnl f* **9/4**[1]

0650 **4** *3* **Mandhooma**[7] 4936 4-9-7 **59** .... LukeMorris 6 50
(P W Hiatt) *hld up in tch in midfield: rdn and effrt 2f out: outpcd and drvn over 1f out: one pce and wl hld ins fnl f* **14/1**

5500 **5** *nse* **Super Frank (IRE)**[17] 4589 7-9-3 **55** .... (p) DaneO'Neill 7 46
(J Akehurst) *bustled along leaving stalls: chsd ldrs: unable qck u.p over 1f out: wknd ent fnl f* **7/2**[2]

0000 **6** *nk* **Lilli Palmer (IRE)**[17] 4589 3-8-11 **52** .... PaulFitzsimons 3 42
(Miss J R Tooth) *chsd ldrs: rdn and btn over 1f out: wknd ins fnl f* **66/1**

521 **7** *2 ½* **Loyal Royal (IRE)**[11] 4790 7-9-1 **53** .... (bt) LiamKeniry 8 35
(J M Bradley) *t.k.h: hld up in tch: rdn and no hdwy over 1f out: nvr trbld ldrs: eased fnl 50yds* **7/2**[2]

00 **8** *19* **Spirit Of Normandy**[91] 2197 3-8-4 **52** ow7 .... LauraSimpson(7) 5 —
(R Ingram) *taken down early and led to post: s.i.s: a detached in last: lost tch over 2f out* **50/1**

1m 11.91s (1.71) **Going Correction** +0.275s/f (Good)
WFA 3 from 4yo+ 3lb **8** Ran SP% **111.1**
Speed ratings (Par 101): **99,97,94,90,89 89,86,60**
toteswingers:1&2 £9.20, 2&3 £4.40, 1&3 £3.90 CSF £49.93 CT £138.01 TOTE £7.50: £2.40, £3.70, £1.10; EX 60.00 TRIFECTA Not won..
Owner C N Wright **Bred** Drumhass Stud **Trained** Newmarket, Suffolk

FOCUS
A very ordinary sprint, run in a similar time to division one.

5176 FESTIVAL WAITERS HERE 1ST SEPTEMBER H'CAP 5f 59y
5:55 (5:55) (Class 6) (0-65,65) 3-Y-0+ **£1,554** (£462; £231; £115) **Stalls** Low

Form RPR

5053 **1** **Magical Speedfit (IRE)**[9] 4875 5-9-2 **62** .... SimonPearce(5) 10 74
(G G Margarson) *hld up in tch towards rr: c stands' side 3f out: rdn and hdwy to ld ent fnl f: r.o wl: eased towards fin* **10/3**[1]

-000 **2** *2* **Elhamri**[19] 4518 6-9-9 **65** .... LiamKeniry 1 70
(S Kirk) *stdd after s: hld up in tch in rr: styd on far side 3f out: hdwy wl over 1f out: rdn 1f out: chsd wnr ins fnl f: nvr able to chal* **12/1**

4261 **3** *1 ¼* **Maryolini**[11] 4778 5-9-2 **58** .... StevieDonohoe 9 58
(T Keddy) *in tch: c stands' side 3f out: effrt and rdn to press ldrs over 1f out: no ex and btn fnl 150yds* **7/2**[2]

1043 **4** *½* **Best One**[11] 4778 6-8-12 **54** .... (b) LukeMorris 6 53
(R A Harris) *dwlt: sn chsng ldrs: styd far side and led that gp 3f out: chsd wnr ent fnl f: wknd fnl 100yds* **6/1**[3]

5005 **5** *2 ½* **Lithaam (IRE)**[4] 5055 6-8-6 **55** .... (p) RyanClark(7) 7 45
(J M Bradley) *dwlt: in tch: c stands' side a 3f out: rdn and effrt wl over 1f out: wknd ent fnl f* **7/1**

5650 **6** *3* **Green Lagonda (AUS)**[33] 4041 8-9-1 **60** .... RichardEvans(3) 5 39
(P D Evans) *chsd ldrs: c stands' side 3f out: ev ch over 1f out: wknd qckly 1f out* **9/1**

0226 **7** *1 ¼* **Pocket's Pick (IRE)**[22] 4435 4-9-5 **61** .... IanMongan 8 35
(Jim Best) *led: c stands' side 3f out: hdd ent fnl f: wknd qckly ins fnl f* **6/1**[3]

000 **8** *2 ½* **Spring Horizon (IRE)**[4] 5025 4-8-4 **46** .... KirstyMilczarek 3 11
(Miss Z C Davison) *awkward leaving stalls and s.i.s: a bhd: styd towards far side 3f out: wl btn fnl 2f* **40/1**

6055 **9** *2 ½* **Slasi**[13] 4692 3-8-8 **52** .... (b) JackMitchell 4 8
(C E Brittain) *chsd ldr: styd far side and lost pl 3f out: wknd and wl btn fnl 2f* **10/1**

63.18 secs (0.88) **Going Correction** +0.275s/f (Good)
WFA 3 from 4yo+ 2lb **9** Ran SP% **115.6**
Speed ratings (Par 101): **103,99,97,97,93 88,86,82,78**
toteswingers:1&2 £8.50, 2&3 £8.50, 1&3 £4.60. totesuper7: WIN: Not won. PLACE £75.40. CSF £43.53 CT £149.64 TOTE £4.80: £1.20, £4.70, £1.40; EX 33.90 Trifecta £103.20 Part won. Pool of £139.57 - 0.30 winning units. Place 6: £177.26 Place 5: £94.15.
Owner Exors of the Late John Guest **Bred** John Malone **Trained** Newmarket, Suffolk

FOCUS
A competitive low-grade sprint run at a decent clip, with the field splitting into two groups from over 2f out. The winner probably did not need to match his early-season form.
Spring Horizon(IRE) Official explanation: jockey said filly reared in stalls and was slowly away
T/Plt: £126.40 to a £1 stake. Pool of £62,525.20 - 360.90 winning tickets. T/Qpdt: £82.80 to a £1 stake. Pool of £4,409.53 - 39.40 winning tickets. SP

5140 KEMPTON (A.W) (R-H)
Tuesday, August 17

OFFICIAL GOING: Standard
Wind: Light, behind Weather: Fine

5177 DIGIBET.COM NURSERY 7f (P)
6:50 (6:51) (Class 4) (0-85,83) 2-Y-0 **£3,238** (£963; £481; £240) **Stalls** High

Form RPR

6411 **1** **Byrony (IRE)**[25] 4331 2-9-7 **82** .... PatDobbs 1 87
(R Hannon) *trckd ldr: led over 2f out: hung lft over 1f out: hung rt ins fnl f: r.o wl* **11/4**[2]

4151 **2** *2 ¼* **Miss Clairton**[8] 4911 2-9-8 **83** 6ex .... SebSanders 2 82
(Sir Mark Prescott) *hld up last: shkn up to chse wnr over 1f out: forced to switch twice after: r.o but no imp ins fnl f* **8/13**[1]

0424 **3** *6* **Prophet In A Dream**[11] 4801 2-8-4 **65** .... ChrisCatlin 3 49
(M R Channon) *t.k.h: hld up in 3rd: sltly hmpd over 2f out: effrt to dispute 2nd sn after: wknd over 1f out* **8/1**

604 **4** *6* **George Woolf**[27] 4254 2-8-8 **69** .... JamesDoyle 4 40
(A J McCabe) *reluctant to enter stalls: led: hit rail: stmbld and hdd over 2f out: wknd rapidly over 1f out* **11/2**[3]

1m 25.85s (-0.15) **Going Correction** -0.075s/f (Stan) **4** Ran SP% **115.1**
Speed ratings (Par 96): **97,94,87,80**
CSF £5.30 TOTE £3.20; EX 4.50.
Owner Axom XXIII **Bred** Mr & Mrs C Booth **Trained** East Everleigh, Wilts

FOCUS
Three of the four were previous winners but this was not a competitive event and one in which the market leader proved a bit disappointing. The gallop was a modest one and the winner came down the centre in the straight.

NOTEBOOK
Byrony(IRE) is a progressive individual who was well placed considering the way things unfolded but showed a good attitude, despite jinking left, to beat a rival who is due to go up 11lb in future and maintain her unbeaten record in nurseries returned to Polytrack. This race lacked any strength in depth and she will be up again in the weights, but she is going the right way and may be capable of a little better. (op 9-4)
Miss Clairton looked the one to beat after running away with a Wolverhampton nursery but she failed to match that effort from only a 4lb higher mark returned to the scene of her only other previous defeat on Polytrack. She's clearly useful but, while the return to a left-handed track (both wins that way round) may suit better, life will be tougher from an 11lb higher mark in future. (op 8-11 tchd 4-5 and 5-6 in a place)
Prophet In A Dream failed to settle and had her limitations exposed in the closing stages against a couple of useful types after attracting a bit of support at double-figure odds. There will be easier opportunities than this one but she needs to settle better if she is to progress. (op 14-1)
George Woolf, who was nibbled at in the market, dropped out tamely after becoming unbalanced approaching the intersection on this nursery debut and was disappointing. He'd been steadily progressive in maidens, has a bit of physical scope and is probably worth another chance. (op 7-1)

5178 EUROPEAN BREEDERS' FUND MAIDEN STKS 1m (P)
7:20 (7:20) (Class 4) 2-Y-0 **£4,209** (£1,252; £625; £312) **Stalls** High

Form RPR

5 **1** **Bawaab (USA)**[27] 4263 2-9-3 0 .... TedDurcan 4 76+
(Saeed Bin Suroor) *dwlt: sn trckd ldng pair: shkn up over 2f out: grad clsd to ld over 1f out: sn drew clr* **8/15**[1]

5 **2** *3 ½* **Mark Harbour (IRE)**[13] 4695 2-9-3 0 .... PatDobbs 2 66
(R Hannon) *w ldr: shkn up over 2f out: stl upsides over 1f out: sn outpcd by wnr: kpt on to take 2nd nr fin* **4/1**[2]

04 **3** *shd* **All The Evil (IRE)**[6] 4962 2-9-0 0 .... Louis-PhilippeBeuzelin(3) 1 66
(B J Meehan) *narrow ldr: modest pce to 1/2-way: shkn up over 2f out: hdd over 1f out: outpcd by wnr: lost 2nd nr fin* **15/2**[3]

40 **4** *2* **Ice Magic**[25] 4346 2-9-3 0 .... PatCosgrave 3 61
(M H Tompkins) *dwlt: settled in last: pushed along fr 1/2-way: outpcd over 2f out: plugged on to take 4th ins fnl f* **16/1**

0 **5** *¾* **Luckyreno**[32] 4096 2-9-3 0 .... (v[1]) RichardMullen 5 60
(Sir Michael Stoute) *chsd ldng trio: rdn over 2f out: sn outpcd: n.d after* **20/1**

1m 41.15s (1.35) **Going Correction** -0.075s/f (Stan) **5** Ran SP% **107.6**
Speed ratings (Par 96): **90,86,86,84,83**
CSF £2.76 TOTE £1.60: £1.10, £2.10; EX 2.60.
Owner Godolphin **Bred** Stoneway Farm **Trained** Newmarket, Suffolk

FOCUS
Not much strength in depth to an ordinary maiden but the winner posted an improved effort and may be able to progress further. The gallop was an ordinary one and the winner came down the centre.

NOTEBOOK
Bawaab(USA) ◆, who had shaped with a degree of promise on his debut, still looked inexperienced and took a few strides to grasp what was required in this moderately run race but picked up well to win with more in hand than the official margin suggests to justify the market confidence on this Polytrack debut. More of an end-to-end gallop will suit, he's open to further improvement and is the type to win again. (op 1-2)
Mark Harbour(IRE) had shown modest form from an ordinary draw over 7f at this course on his debut but he bettered that effort after being well placed in a race run at just an ordinary gallop. While he may be vulnerable to the better types in this grade, he will be of more interest in run-of-the-mill nurseries. (op 10-3)

All The Evil(IRE), who has improved steadily with every outing, was far from disgraced after being allowed to set his own gallop on this all-weather debut. He is almost certainly capable of a bit better when switched to nurseries. (op 10-1)

Ice Magic had failed to confirm the bit of debut promise shown on his latest start but fared better on this first run on an artificial surface. He left the strong impression that a much stiffer test of stamina would have played to his strengths and he is now qualified for a handicap mark. (op 20-1 tchd 12-1)

Luckyreno hadn't shown much on his debut at Newbury but fared better with the visor fitted on this all-weather debut, despite travelling with little fluency. He is likely to remain vulnerable in this grade but may do better in ordinary nuseries granted a stiffer test of stamina. (tchd 25-1)

5179 BOOK LADIES DAY TICKETS ON 0844 579 3008 H'CAP 2m (P)

7:50 (7:50) (Class 5) (0-70,70) 4-Y-0+ **£2,286** (£675; £337) **Stalls** High

Form				RPR
4522	1		**Saute**[8] 4915 4-9-1 **64**....(p) AdamKirby 4 (W R Swinburn) *led 5f: led again 5f out: kicked on over 3f out: only one possible rival after: drvn and styd on wl* **3/1**[1]	78
0012	2	3	**Perception (IRE)**[18] 4530 4-9-5 **68**.... FergusSweeney 2 (A King) *trckd ldrs: prog to go 2nd 3f out: clr of rest over 2f out: drvn and kpt on: no imp on wnr* **8/1**	78
0145	3	4	**Uncle Keef (IRE)**[31] 4141 4-8-11 **60**....(b) PatDobbs 8 (M P Tregoning) *hld up and sn last: stdy prog fr 3f out to take 3rd wl over 1f out: ldng pair long gone: styd on wl* **4/1**[2]	66+
3536	4	9	**Free Falling**[11] 4780 4-8-2 **51** oh5....(b) DavidProbert 3 (Miss Gay Kelleway) *early reminder: settled midfield: pushed along over 4f out: outpcd fr 3f out: no ch after* **25/1**	46
0-22	5	nk	**The Composer**[12] 4731 8-8-2 **51** oh1.... WilliamCarson 13 (M Blanshard) *settled in last trio: outpcd over 3f out: no ch after: plugged on past wkng rivals* **14/1**	45
0054	6	3/4	**Honorable Endeavor**[12] 4745 4-8-2 **51** oh1....(v) FrankieMcDonald 5 (E F Vaughan) *dwlt: mostly in midfield: drvn over 4f out: v wd bnd 3f out and already outpcd: no ch after* **16/1**	45
0-32	7	nk	**Gandalf**[28] 4226 8-9-7 **70**.... HayleyTurner 11 (Miss Amy Weaver) *hld up wl in rr: swtchd out wd bnd 3f out: drvn to chal for 3rd 2f out but ldng pair already flown: fdd* **5/1**[3]	63
00	8	4	**Suhailah**[27] 4258 4-8-2 **51** oh6.... NickyMackay 7 (M J Attwater) *prom: rdn 5f out: outpcd over 3f out: stl chalng for 3rd 2f out: wknd* **66/1**	39
3310	9	1 3/4	**Graylyn Ruby (FR)**[31] 4141 5-8-12 **61**.... MickyFenton 10 (R Dickin) *prog to ld after 5f: hdd 5f out: stl 3rd 2f out but wl outpcd: sn wknd* **11/2**	47
0262	10	2 3/4	**Chincoteague (IRE)**[12] 4734 4-9-4 **70**....(b1) Louis-PhilippeBeuzelin(3) 9 (B J Meehan) *t.k.h: trckd ldrs: rdn 5f out: wknd over 2f out* **9/1**	53
0065	11	13	**Anis Etoile**[8] 4915 5-8-6 **55**.... IvaMilickova 1 (John Berry) *ldng trio tl wknd rapidly wl over 2f out: t.o* **25/1**	22

3m 27.1s (-3.00) **Going Correction** -0.075s/f (Stan) 11 Ran SP% **119.9**

Speed ratings (Par 103): **104,102,100,96,95 95,95,93,92,91 84**

CSF £27.87 CT £99.53 TOTE £3.10: £1.10, £2.50, £2.00; EX 32.50.

Owner P W Harris **Bred** Azienda Agricola Rosati Colarieti **Trained** Aldbury, Herts

FOCUS

An ordinary handicap in which the gallop was on the steady side to the home straight but the first three pulled clear of the rest. The winner edged towards the far rail in the closing stages. The form is rated around the first two.

Chincoteague(IRE) Official explanation: jockey said filly hung left-handed

5180 PANORAMIC BAR & RESTAURANT H'CAP 1m 4f (P)

8:20 (8:20) (Class 6) (0-65,65) 3-Y-0+ **£1,637** (£483; £241) **Stalls** High

Form				RPR
0306	1		**Rowan Light**[17] 4591 4-9-3 **54**....(b1) PatCosgrave 6 (J R Boyle) *trckd ldng pair: wnt 2nd over 3f out: drvn to ld wl over 1f out: kpt on stoutly* **20/1**	63
0660	2	1 3/4	**Eseej (USA)**[34] 4019 5-9-13 **64**.... TomMcLaughlin 12 (P W Hiatt) *chsd ldr: led 5f out and maintained str pce: drvn and hdd wl over 1f out: kpt on* **7/1**	70
4445	3	2	**Stadium Of Light (IRE)**[20] 4493 3-9-4 **65**....(t) TravisBlock 11 (H Morrison) *chsd ldrs: drvn in 5th 4f out: styd on u.p to take 3rd over 1f out: no imp after* **5/1**[2]	68
3125	4	1	**Dazzling Begum**[11] 4780 5-9-2 **58**.... SimonPearce(5) 1 (J Pearce) *settled in last quartet: stl there and wl off the pce 4f out: shkn up and sme prog fr 3f out: styd on to take 4th nr fin: nvr nrr* **11/1**	59+
0462	5	1/2	**Champagne Fizz (IRE)**[69] 2870 4-9-3 **54**.... DaneO'Neill 9 (Miss Jo Crowley) *wnt lft s: settled midfield: gng bttr than most in 6th 4f out: tried to cl on ldrs 2f out: fnd nil and sn btn* **4/1**[1]	54
003	6	2 1/2	**Beat Route**[13] 4698 3-8-12 **64**.... JemmaMarshall(5) 5 (M J Attwater) *prom: rdn to chse ldng pair over 3f out: no imp 2f out: fdd ins fnl f* **7/1**	60
25-3	7	1/2	**Eagle Nebula**[22] 4433 6-9-9 **60**.... LiamKeniry 13 (B R Johnson) *hld up in midfield: plenty to do whn pushed along in 7th over 3f out: no imp on ldrs 2f out* **13/2**[3]	56
0200	8	hd	**Storm Hawk (IRE)**[9] 4870 3-8-9 **63**.... JamesRogers(7) 8 (Pat Eddery) *crowded s: a towards rr: rdn and struggling 4f out: plugged on fnl 2f* **20/1**	58
464/	9	shd	**Spaceman**[144] 4069 7-9-5 **56**....(v) PaulMulrennan 7 (M R Bosley) *dwlt: towards rr: rdn in 9th and struggling 4f out: nvr on terms after: plugged on* **33/1**	51
00-0	10	30	**Allanit (GER)**[13] 4719 6-10-0 **65**.... JerryO'Dwyer 14 (B J Curley) *led at v str pce: hdd and hanging 5f out: pushed along and lost pl rapidly over 3f out: eased 2f out: t.o* **12/1**	12
00-0	11	13	**Monaadi (IRE)**[14] 4676 5-8-13 **50**....(p) FergusSweeney 3 (B G Powell) *dwlt: sn rdn in last: wl t.o over 3f out* **40/1**	—
5005	12	3 1/4	**Love In The Park**[22] 4433 5-9-5 **56**....(p) SebSanders 4 (R Brotherton) *in tch in midfield: reminders 7f out: wknd u.p over 3f out: sn wl t.o* **14/1**	—
145/	13	1 1/2	**Adorabella (IRE)**[692] 6203 7-9-11 **62**....(t) GeorgeBaker 2 (Simon Earle) *dwlt: a in last quartet: wknd 4f out: sn wl t.o* **14/1**	—

2m 31.93s (-2.57) **Going Correction** -0.075s/f (Stan) 13 Ran SP% **119.3**

WFA 3 from 4yo+ 10lb

Speed ratings (Par 101): **105,103,102,101,101 99,99,99,99,79 70,68,67**

CSF £148.62 CT £824.77 TOTE £60.60: £14.60, £2.00, £4.60; EX 155.60.

Owner Rowan Stud Partnership 1 **Bred** Rowan Farm Stud **Trained** Epsom, Surrey

■ Stewards' Enquiry : Pat Cosgrave caution: used whip without giving filly time to respond.

FOCUS

A modest handicap in which the gallop was only fair and those held up could never get competitive. The winner came down the centre in the straight and the third looks the best guide to the level.

Allanit(GER) Official explanation: jockey said gelding hung right-handed

Adorabella(IRE) Official explanation: jockey said mare had a breathing problem

5181 BOOK ON LINE AT KEMPTON.CO.UK FILLIES' H'CAP 1m 3f (P)

8:50 (8:50) (Class 4) (0-80,79) 3-Y-0+ **£3,885** (£1,156; £577; £288) **Stalls** High

Form				RPR
0413	1		**On Her Way**[20] 4483 3-9-2 **75**.... IanMongan 5 (H R A Cecil) *trckd ldr: led 4f out: sn kicked on: hung lft fr over 2f out and ended against nr side rail: cajoled along and a in command* **11/4**[1]	87
1242	2	1 3/4	**Marjury Daw (IRE)**[3] 5071 4-9-10 **74**.... PaulMulrennan 1 (J G Given) *hld up in 6th: prog to go 3rd over 4f out: chsd wnr over 3f out: styd on but readily hld fnl 2f* **5/1**[3]	83
3012	3	1 1/4	**Woodford Belle (USA)**[17] 4571 3-9-2 **78**..(b) Louis-PhilippeBeuzelin(3) 6 (B J Meehan) *trckd ldng pair to over 4f out: sltly outpcd over 3f out: drvn up inner to go 3rd again over 2f out: styd on but no imp* **10/3**[2]	85
6-13	4	5	**Love Action (IRE)**[32] 4098 3-9-3 **76**.... PatDobbs 2 (R Hannon) *trckd ldrs on outer: rdn and nt qckn over 3f out: disp 4th 2f out: sn lft bhd* **5/1**[3]	74
1532	5	2	**Hel's Angel (IRE)**[9] 4859 4-9-13 **77**.... SebSanders 3 (Mrs A Duffield) *hld up last: rdn and effrt over 3f out: no hdwy 2f out and sn lft bhd* **11/2**	71
54-4	6	3 3/4	**Panto Princess**[13] 4694 4-9-6 **70**.... FrankieMcDonald 4 (H Candy) *hld up in 5th: dropped to last 5f out: pushed along over 3f out: nvr on terms after* **12/1**	57
-165	7	8	**Lucky Breeze (IRE)**[7] 4923 3-9-5 **78**.... GeorgeBaker 8 (W J Knight) *t.k.h: led to 4f out: wkng whn bdly hmpd over 2f out* **16/1**	56

2m 20.29s (-1.61) **Going Correction** -0.075s/f (Stan)

WFA 3 from 4yo 9lb 7 Ran SP% **112.0**

Speed ratings (Par 102): **102,100,99,96,94 92,86**

toteswingers:1&2 £3.10, 2&3 £2.30, 1&3 £2.90 CSF £16.06 CT £45.55 TOTE £3.20: £2.20, £1.10; EX 16.40.

Owner Malih L Al Basti **Bred** Whatton Manor Stud **Trained** Newmarket, Suffolk

FOCUS

Several in-form types in what had looked an open fillies' handicap but an improved effort from the winner, who drifted to the stands side in the closing stages. As with the majority of races on this card, the gallop was just an ordinary one. The placed horses set the level.

5182 EPSOM TRAINERS OPEN DAY SUNDAY COMING H'CAP 6f (P)

9:20 (9:21) (Class 4) (0-85,84) 3-Y-0 **£3,885** (£1,156; £577; £288) **Stalls** High

Form				RPR
0510	1		**Hairspray**[29] 4204 3-9-4 **81**.... CathyGannon 7 (M R Channon) *led 1f: chsd ldr: drvn to ld over 1f out: edgd rt: styd on wl* **7/1**	87
5313	2	1	**Starwatch**[11] 4777 3-8-2 **65** oh2.... NeilChalmers 2 (J J Bridger) *led after 1f: drvn over 2f out: hdd over 1f out: one pce* **9/2**[3]	68
0322	3	2 3/4	**Bougainvilia (IRE)**[10] 4837 3-9-6 **83**.... PatDobbs 4 (R Hannon) *plld ahd early: restrained into 4th: trckd ldng pair gng easily over 2f out: swtchd ins sn after: nt qckn and hld whn short of room and swtchd lft 1f out* **1/1**[1]	77
-001	4	1/2	**Crown (IRE)**[41] 3779 3-9-7 **84**.... IanMongan 1 (Miss Jo Crowley) *awkward s: sn chsd ldng pair: rdn over 2f out and nt qckn: wl hld after* **7/2**[2]	77
0404	5	2 1/4	**Minortransgression (USA)**[12] 4738 3-8-4 **70**.... MartinLane(3) 6 (P D Evans) *hld up in last pair: shuffled along fr over 2f out: nvr nr ldrs* **20/1**	55
1060	6	3/4	**Private Olley**[60] 3154 3-8-4 **67**.... NickyMackay 5 (J Akehurst) *dwlt: mostly in last pair and racd wd: wd bnd 3f out: rdn and struggling over 2f out* **11/1**	50
5600	7	shd	**Avow (USA)**[4] 5027 3-8-2 **65**.... WilliamCarson 3 (J J Bridger) *nvr bttr than 5th: rdn and struggling over 2f out* **33/1**	48

1m 12.18s (-0.92) **Going Correction** -0.075s/f (Stan) 7 Ran SP% **118.9**

Speed ratings (Par 102): **103,101,98,97,94 93,93**

toteswingers:1&2 £2.90, 2&3 £2.60, 1&3 £2.80 CSF £40.22 TOTE £5.60: £1.50, £2.70; EX 17.50 Place 6: £200.27 Place 5: £47.03.

Owner John Breslin **Bred** J Breslin **Trained** West Ilsley, Berks

FOCUS

A couple of in-form types in just a reasonable handicap. The gallop was fair but this was another race where those up with the pace held the edge. The winner edged towards the far rail in the closing stages. The winner is rated to his juvenile best with the runner-up a slight improver and the form could rate higher.

T/Plt: £171.70 to a £1 stake.Pool of £61,677.50 - 262.22 winning units. T/Qpdt: £49.50 to a £1 stake. Pool of £5,554.30 - 83.00 winning units. JN

4388 YORK (L-H)

Tuesday, August 17

OFFICIAL GOING: Good (6.6)

Course at inner configuration and all distances as advertised.

Wind: moderate 1/2 against Weather: fine

5183 SYMPHONY GROUP H'CAP 5f 89y

1:45 (1:47) (Class 2) 3-Y-0+ **£25,904** (£7,708; £3,852; £1,924) **Stalls** Low

Form				RPR
1346	1		**Hamish McGonagall**[23] 4401 5-9-6 **104**.... DavidAllan 15 (T D Easterby) *chsd ldrs towards stands' side: styd on wl to ld last 150yds: r.o wl* **9/1**	112
6000	2	1 1/2	**Judge 'n Jury**[10] 4814 6-8-11 **95**.... JoeFanning 16 (R A Harris) *t.k.h: led after 1f towards stands' side: hdd over 1f out: kpt on same pce ins fnl f* **25/1**	98
3525	3	hd	**Quest For Success (IRE)**[3] 5095 5-9-2 **100**.... PaulHanagan 8 (R A Fahey) *lw: chsd ldrs: led over 1f out: hdd jst ins fnl f: no ex* **9/2**[1]	102+
3143	4	shd	**Haajes**[24] 4372 6-7-13 **86** ow1.... PaulPickard(3) 4 (P T Midgley) *mid-div: hdwy far side over 1f out: styd on wl towards fin* **20/1**	88+
0200	5	shd	**Captain Dunne (IRE)**[19] 4505 5-9-9 **107**.... JimmyFortune 17 (T D Easterby) *trckd ldrs towards stands' side: effrt 2f out: styd on same pce ins fnl f* **16/1**	108
30	6	1 3/4	**Cheveton**[8] 4904 6-8-3 **87**.... WilliamCarson 10 (R J Price) *s.i.s: hdwy stands' side over 1f out: hung lft: nvr nr to chal* **10/1**	82
3531	7	1 1/4	**Walvis Bay (IRE)**[15] 4654 3-8-0 **86**.... AndrewMullen 14 (T P Tate) *chsd ldrs: kpt on same pce fnl 2f* **8/1**[3]	76
0001	8	nk	**Rasaman (IRE)**[11] 4798 6-8-1 **85**....(v) JimmyQuinn 13 (J S Goldie) *mid-div: kpt on fnl 2f: hmpd jst ins fnl f: nvr trbld ldrs* **20/1**	74+

The Form Book, Raceform Ltd, Compton, RG20 6NL

1050 **9** ½ **Sir Gerry (USA)**[17] 4576 5-9-0 **105** AdamBeschizza(7) 3 93+
(C A Dwyer) *lw: dwlt: in rr: hdwy far side 2f out: kpt on: nvr nr ldrs* **9/1**
0000 **10** 1 ½ **Oldjoesaid**[18] 4536 6-8-1 **85** FrannyNorton 9 67
(K A Ryan) *mid-div: drvn over 2f out: nvr a factor* **14/1**
0000 **11** nk **Strike Up The Band**[29] 4191 7-8-6 **90** AdrianNicholls 11 71
(D Nicholls) *led 1f: w ldrs: wknd over 1f out* **20/1**
2006 **12** 1 **Damien (IRE)**[24] 4391 4-9-2 **100** MichaelHills 5 78
(B W Hills) *mid-div: drvn over 2f out: nvr a factor* **6/1**[2]
1601 **13** nk **Hotham**[38] 3919 7-8-8 **95** BarryMcHugh(3) 7 71
(N Wilson) *s.s: a in rr* **14/1**
0010 **14** nk **Barney McGrew (IRE)**[31] 4136 7-9-10 **108** PhillipMakin 1 83
(M Dods) *trckd ldrs towards far side: effrt 2f out: wknd fnl 150yds* **33/1**
5500 **15** ¾ **Saucy Brown (IRE)**[18] 4536 4-8-1 **85** (t) PaulQuinn 6 58
(D Nicholls) *a towards rr* **18/1**

63.48 secs (-0.82) **Going Correction** +0.05s/f (Good)
WFA 3 from 4yo+ 2lb **15** Ran SP% **118.2**
Speed ratings (Par 109): **108,105,105,105,104 102,100,99,98,96 96,94,93,93,92**
toteswingers: 1&2 £52.80, 1&3 £6.60, 2&3 £28.60 CSF £222.74 CT £1175.43 TOTE £10.40: £3.70, £7.90, £2.00; EX 246.20 Trifecta £526.30 Pool: £3201.06 - 4.50 winning units..
Owner Reality Partnerships I **Bred** J P Coggan And Whitsbury Manor Stud **Trained** Great Habton, N Yorks

FOCUS
A typically competitive sprint handicap for the course, with all the pace coming from the high-drawn runners. They came centre-field for this opening contest. The third sets the level.

NOTEBOOK
Hamish McGonagall kept on strongly to register course win number three. Already twice victorious this term, including here, he was 5lb higher than when scoring at Musselburgh in June and had been comfortably held of late, but is evidently still improving and recorded a career-best in winning off 104. He's in a race at the Curragh on Sunday week, but the Portland Handicap will presumably be his main aim now.
Judge 'n Jury, now 3lb below his last winning mark, has been struggling for form of late, but he came right back to something like his best with the tongue-tie left off, just holding on for second having shown bright early speed. He will be of interest for something similar. (op 20-1)
Quest For Success(IRE) remains 5lb above his last winning mark, but has still been competitive and he again ran well, clearly being none the worse for his Ripon effort three days earlier. (op 11-2)
Haajes, narrowly denied off this mark at Newcastle latest, raced away from the pace and did really well to finish so close, especially considering his rider was putting up 1lb overweight. He can be rated second-best and should continue to give a good account. (op 16-1)
Captain Dunne(IRE), beaten just 2l in a Group 2 at Glorious Goodwood latest, is still 7lb above his last winning mark and ran about as well as could have been expected.
Cheveton, who wasn't the best away, finished close-up on the heels of the leaders and remains well weighted. (op 9-1 tchd 8-1)
Walvis Bay(IRE), raised 8lb for his Ripon success, found this a bit too competitive against his elders for the first time, but it's still early days for him, and he remains capable of better. (op 15-2)
Rasaman(IRE), up 3lb for winning at Musselburgh, could never quite get into it, being hampered late on when already held. (op 18-1)
Sir Gerry(USA) was always struggling following a slow start. (op 12-1)
Damien(IRE) is creeping down the weights, but could make no impression over the shortest trip he has tackled to date. (op 15-2)

5184 SPORTINGBET.COM ACOMB STKS (GROUP 3) 7f
2:15 (2:16) (Class 1) 2-Y-O **£29,630** (£11,205; £5,600; £2,800) **Stalls** High

Form RPR
621 **1** **Waiter's Dream**[32] 4096 2-9-0 88 KierenFallon 9 105+
(B J Meehan) *lw: trckd ldr: edgd rt and led on wd outside 1f out: styd on strly: v readily* **5/2**[2]
1 **2** 4 ½ **Silvertrees (IRE)**[32] 4089 2-9-0 0 PJMcDonald 3 93+
(G A Swinbank) *w'like: hdwy over 3f out: sn chsng ldrs: upsides and hung lft over 1f out: styd on same pce* **8/1**
31 **3** 1 **Timothy T**[17] 4587 2-9-0 85 FrankieDettori 2 90
(M Botti) *w'like: led: hdd and edgd rt 1f out: no ex* **9/1**
4 1 ¾ **Lake Ontario (USA)**[15] 4663 2-9-0 0 JMurtagh 5 87
(A P O'Brien, Ire) *in rr: drvn over 5f out: reminders 3f out: styd on over 1f out: hmpd and swtchd lft nr fin: nvr a factor* **2/1**[1]
12 **5** 5 **Katell (IRE)**[7] 4934 2-9-0 0 TomEaves 10 73
(Mrs L Stubbs) *chsd ldrs: drvn over 3f out: hung lft and lost pl over 1f out* **40/1**
15 **6** 2 ¼ **Satin Love (USA)**[18] 4538 2-9-0 0 JoeFanning 6 68
(M Johnston) *lw: t.k.h: trckd ldrs: hung lft over 2f out: wknd over 1f out* **4/1**[3]
21 **7** 1 **Rigolleto (IRE)**[16] 4614 2-9-0 83 RichardHughes 1 65
(M R Channon) *trckd ldrs: drvn over 2f out: wknd over 1f out* **10/1**

1m 24.82s (-0.48) **Going Correction** +0.05s/f (Good) **7** Ran SP% **114.5**
Speed ratings (Par 104): **104,98,97,95,90 87,86**
toteswingers:1&2 £4.80, 2&3 £4.70, 1&3 £2.50 CSF £22.59 TOTE £3.20: £1.80, £4.40; EX 23.80 Trifecta £111.10 Pool: £1240.59 - 8.26 winning units..
Owner R P Foden **Bred** Ridgecourt Stud **Trained** Manton, Wilts
■ Stewards' Enquiry : Kieren Fallon caution: used whip down shoulder in the forehand.

FOCUS
Two of the last six winners of this (no race in 2008) subsequently won at the top level, including Rule Of Law, who took the 2004 St Leger. However, this looked an ordinary running, and Waiter's Dream was a class apart. The pace seemed reasonable, and the main action was middle-to-stands' side in the straight and the fourth looks the best guide to the form.

NOTEBOOK
Waiter's Dream was beaten on his first two starts, but impressed when taking a Newbury maiden by 4l last time and continued his progression with an authoritative display on this step up in class. It remains to be seen exactly what he achieved, with the opposition not looking particularly strong for the level, but he seems likely to go on improving, and may stay further. Brian Meehan mentioned the Dewhurst as a possible target, and this promising colt will be well worth his place in the line up. (op 7-2)
Silvertrees(IRE) stepped up on the form he showed when winning his maiden over this trip at Haydock. He was no match at all for the winner, but is obviously pretty useful and might be able to pick up a Listed race this term. The Stardom Stakes at Goodwood on September 7 could be a suitable target. (op 11-2)
Timothy T, off the mark over 71/2f on turf at Lingfield, again went from the front and had his chance, but although running well he wasn't quite up to this level. He was reported to have hung right. Official explanation: jockey said gelding hung right-handed (op 10-1 tchd 17-2)
Lake Ontario(USA) looked good when winning a Naas maiden by 5l, but he ran a lazy race in this better company. Not moving with any real fluency through the early stages, he was soon last and was still there by the time the field reached the straight. Once under strong pressure, he took an age to pick up before finally running on near the line, and would have been about 1l closer had he not been short of room late on. He seems to have an awful lot of learning to do, and it would not be a surprise to see him do significantly better in time, probably over further. (op 9-4 tchd 11-4)
Katell(IRE) ran creditably enough without proving his stamina, or that he's up to this class. (op 33-1)
Satin Love(USA) wasn't beaten that far in the Richmond Stakes, but probably didn't achieve a great deal all the same and he failed to improve for this step up in trip. (tchd 7-2 and 9-2)
Rigolleto(IRE) was outclassed. Official explanation: jockey said colt ran flat (tchd 8-1)

5185 SPORTINGBET.COM GREAT VOLTIGEUR STKS (GROUP 2) (C&G) 1m 4f
2:50 (2:50) (Class 1) 3-Y-O **£82,964** (£31,374; £15,680; £7,840) **Stalls** Centre

Form RPR
213 **1** **Rewilding**[73] 2746 3-8-12 113 FrankieDettori 8 124+
(Mahmood Al Zarooni) *hld up in rr: smooth hdwy 4f out: shkn up to ld appr fnl f: qcknd clr: v readily* **6/4**[1]
-152 **2** 4 **Midas Touch**[51] 3491 3-9-1 118 JMurtagh 6 120
(A P O'Brien, Ire) *trckd ldrs: led over 2f out: hdd appr fnl f: styd on same pce* **5/2**[2]
1- **3** 2 ¼ **Joshua Tree (IRE)**[325] 6268 3-8-12 113 JamieSpencer 10 114+
(A P O'Brien, Ire) *str: lw: hld up: smooth hdwy over 3f out: shkn up over 2f out: styd on same pce over 1f out* **14/1**
3-10 **4** 6 **Ted Spread**[73] 2746 3-8-12 105 DarryllHolland 5 104
(M H Tompkins) *in tch: hdwy to chse ldrs over 4f out: edgd lft over 2f out: one pce* **20/1**
1140 **5** 7 **Monterosso**[30] 4184 3-9-1 115 KierenFallon 2 96
(M Johnston) *in rr: sn drvn along: nvr a factor* **8/1**[3]
3444 **6** ¾ **Simenon (IRE)**[40] 3822 3-8-12 97 JimmyFortune 4 92
(A M Balding) *trckd ldrs: effrt over 3f out: wknd over 1f out* **100/1**
1212 **7** 6 **Harris Tweed**[40] 3822 3-8-12 105 LiamJones 1 82
(W J Haggas) *drvn to ld: racd keenly and tended to hang rt: hdd over 2f out: wknd over 1f out* **12/1**
-220 **8** nk **Dancing David (IRE)**[72] 2802 3-8-12 108 MartinDwyer 7 82
(B J Meehan) *trckd ldrs: drvn over 3f out: wknd 2f out* **22/1**
-413 **9** 10 **Total Command**[60] 3145 3-8-12 107 OlivierPeslier 3 66
(Sir Michael Stoute) *hld up in mid-div: effrt over 3f out: wknd 2f out* **14/1**
3 **10** 6 **Momkinzain (USA)**[122] 1386 3-8-12 0 RichardHughes 9 56
(M R Channon) *dwlt: swtchd lft after s: in rr: hung lft 3f out: sn bhd* **50/1**

2m 28.93s (-4.27) **Going Correction** +0.05s/f (Good) **10** Ran SP% **112.8**
Speed ratings (Par 112): **116,113,111,107,103 102,98,98,91,87**
toteswingers:1&2 £1.60, 2&3 £7.00, 1&3 £5.00 CSF £4.69 TOTE £2.50: £1.20, £1.30, £3.50; EX 6.20 Trifecta £32.30 Pool: £8884.83 - 203.25 winning units..
Owner Godolphin **Bred** Watership Down Stud **Trained** Newmarket, Suffolk

FOCUS
A race that is often the key St Leger trial, with six of the last ten winners of the season's final classic contesting this en route - only three of which won - and this year's running looked a strong one, with the Derby third, Irish Derby runner-up and King Edward VII winner on show. It could hardly have been a better trial, with Harris Tweed setting a searching gallop, which resulted in a very good time, and the 'big' two in the market coming to the fore. The form is rated around the second and fourth.

NOTEBOOK
Rewilding ◆, despite winning with ease at Goodwood on his debut for Godolphin, looked unhappy on the track at Epsom, only getting going in the final 2f once finding his stride, and immediately afterwards was earmarked as an ideal type for the Leger. Dettori never looked in any doubt aboard the son of Tiger Hill, closing readily with 4f to run and, having sat in a stalking position until 2f out, he showed tidy change of pace to assert inside the final furlong, staying on strongly in the manner of a horse unlikely to have any trouble with a stiffer test. The last Godolphin horse to win this was Rule Of Law, who followed up in the Leger, and Mastery also took the same route last year (albeit he was beaten in this under a penalty), but it's safe to assume this fellow is a good deal better than either of those, with him already being spoken of as a horse for next year's Arc. He looks the one to beat next month. (op 15-8)
Midas Touch, two places and just over 4l behind Rewilding at Epsom, recorded a career-best when second to Cape Blanco at the Curragh, but it's very hard to defy a penalty in this race and in hindsight probably left himself vulnerable in tracking the fast pace, hence it was a very decent effort to be beaten an almost identical distance by the winner once more. Although it's hard to visualise him reversing form at Doncaster, he will be better off at the weights and could give him more of a fight, with the extra yardage certain to suit. (op 11-4)
Joshua Tree(IRE) hadn't been seen since winning last season's Royal Lodge. He had been kept off with a few hold-ups, and was expected to come on nicely for the run, so to see him shape so well was encouraging. He tracked the winner through, appearing to be travelling strongly also, but was unable to find when asked and the lack of an outing ultimately took its toll. He will be entitled to take his chance in the Leger on the back of this, but needs to make marked improvement if he's to reverse form with either of the first two. (tchd 16-1)
Ted Spread, the Chester Vase winner who hadn't run since finishing down the field in the Derby, kept boxing on for fourth, but lacked the class to make an impact on the principals. He's also Leger-bound. (op 16-1)
Monterosso, the other penalised runner, ran a good race when fourth at the Curragh just eight days after his Royal Ascot success, but not a lot went right in Germany last time and this run very much suggested he's lost his edge, a busy campaign possibly catching up with him. He was the first under pressure and, although plugging on, never looked like featuring.
Simenon(IRE) isn't up to this level and slowly faded having been up there early.
Harris Tweed, running here instead of the Ebor, for which he had failed to make the cut, intended to make full use of his stamina, but went a bit too hard and ultimately dropped right out. (op 10-1)
Dancing David(IRE) failed to stay. (op 20-1)
Total Command, who looked dull in his coat, proved most disappointing, stopping quickly and clearly failing to run his race. (op 10-1)
Momkinzain(USA) was hanging and eased right off late on. (tchd 40-1)

5186 JUDDMONTE INTERNATIONAL STKS (GROUP 1) 1m 2f 88y
3:25 (3:25) (Class 1) 3-Y-O+
£393,699 (£149,241; £74,689; £37,240; £18,655; £9,362) **Stalls** Low

Form RPR
0-62 **1** **Rip Van Winkle (IRE)**[20] 4469 4-9-5 125 JMurtagh 7 128+
(A P O'Brien, Ire) *swtg: hld up towards rr: effrt 3f out: styd on strly fnl 150yds: led nr fin* **7/4**[1]
-021 **2** ½ **Twice Over**[45] 3693 5-9-5 123 TomQueally 1 127
(H R A Cecil) *trckd ldrs: led over 1f out: kpt on wl: hdd nr fin* **6/1**
-121 **3** ¾ **Byword**[62] 3068 4-9-5 124 MaximeGuyon 8 125
(A Fabre, France) *lw: trckd ldrs: led over 2f out: hdd appr fnl f: styd on same pce* **11/4**[2]
0550 **4** 4 **Cavalryman**[62] 3068 4-9-5 118 FrankieDettori 4 117
(Saeed Bin Suroor) *hld up in rr: effrt on wd outside 3f out: styd on same pce over 1f out* **14/1**
2221 **5** 2 ½ **Dick Turpin (IRE)**[44] 3719 3-8-11 124 RichardHughes 2 112
(R Hannon) *t.k.h: hld up: effrt over 3f out: rdn 2f out: no imp* **5/1**[3]
-161 **6** 3 **Jakkalberry (IRE)**[65] 3019 4-9-5 120 (t) OlivierPeslier 3 106
(E Botti, Italy) *dwlt: t.k.h in rr early: sme hdwy 3f out: nvr nr ldrs* **20/1**
-115 **7** 2 ¼ **Cutlass Bay (UAE)**[86] 2369 4-9-5 119 KierenFallon 5 102
(Saeed Bin Suroor) *chsd ldrs: drvn over 3f out: wknd over 1f out* **33/1**
-640 **8** ¾ **Stimulation (IRE)**[31] 4139 5-9-5 117 DarryllHolland 6 100
(H Morrison) *led: qcknd over 4f out: hdd over 2f out: lost pl over 1f out* **100/1**

-112 **9** *9* **Bushman**[24] 4390 6-9-5 110.. WilliamBuick 9 82
(D M Simcock) *trckd ldrs: t.k.h: effrt over 3f out: lost pl over 1f out: eased whn bhd ins fnl f* **66/1**

2m 8.58s (-3.92) **Going Correction** +0.05s/f (Good)
WFA 3 from 4yo+ 8lb **9** Ran SP% **110.8**
Speed ratings (Par 117): **117,116,116,112,110 108,106,106,98**
CSF £11.78 TOTE £3.50: £1.20, £1.90, £1.10; EX 16.70 Trifecta £52.60 Pool: £14224.49- 199.75 winning units..
Owner Mrs John Magnier, M Tabor & D Smith **Bred** Roberto Brogi **Trained** Ballydoyle, Co Tipperary

FOCUS

It's a real shame Harbinger was denied the chance to confirm the brilliance of his King George win, but in his absence this year's International Stakes still attracted a top-quality field, with seven of the nine runners previous Group 1 winners. The early pace was modest, resulting in some of these racing a little keenly, but the big names still came to the fore and this is strong form. The main action was towards the stands' rail in the straight. The winner is rated to his Sussex Stakes form, with the third to his mark.

NOTEBOOK

Rip Van Winkle(IRE) ◆ has been brought along steadily this year, needing the run in the Queen Anne, and his connections predicting he'd improve again from his second to Canford Cliffs in the Sussex Stakes, and so it proved. Trying 1m2f on turf for the first time since giving Sea The Stars a fright in last year's Eclipse, he was a little keen off the steady gallop, but it was nothing to be too concerned about. Once in the straight, the Khalid Abdulla-owned pair got first run on him, and being a horse who can't call on a change of pace, he took a while to respond. However, he produced a sustained challenge inside the final furlong to get up near the line, possibly being helped by racing closest to the stands' rail of the front three. His career hasn't gone entirely to plan, with persistent hoof problems not helping his progress last season, but this was his third Group 1 success, and he's long looked a cut above the average for this level when at his best. Both Aidan O'Brien and Johnny Murtagh seemed convinced that there will be more to come, and a more positive ride and/or a stronger-run race is likely to see him in an even better light. There are any number of options open to him, and the most intriguing of all is the Breeders' Cup Classic, for the impression is that he may well be suited to dirt. (tchd 13-8 and 2-1 in a place)

Twice Over produced a tremendous performance to reverse Royal Ascot form with Byword, but was caught with a sucker punch near the line. He's had plenty of hard races on quick ground, including when winning the Eclipse last time, and the impression is he probably appreciated this slightly more forgiving surface. It's hard to argue with Cecil's assessment that this was a career-best performance from the 5-y-o, who may now defend his Champion Stakes crown. The Breeders' Cup and another crack at the Dubai World Cup were also mentioned as possible targets. (op 11-2)

Byword, just as when winning at Royal Ascot, was ideally placed by Maxime Guyon, and although a touch keen early on, had every chance. This looks as far as he wants to go, and he could probably even drop back to 1m. Maybe he'll have a 'decider' against Twice Over in the Champion Stakes. (op 10-3 tchd 5-2)

Cavalryman ◆'s optimum conditions appear to be 1m4f on easy ground, making this a noteworthy effort against three quicker rivals, especially considering the lack of early pace. He made good headway to get on the heels of the front three inside the final 2f, but ultimately lacked the speed of that trio, and he was eased near the line, adding about 1l to the beaten margin. He's struggled to find his best form since joining this yard (lost action at Royal Ascot), but appears well on the way back now and it wouldn't surprise to see him improve on last year's third placing in the Arc. (op 16-1)

Dick Turpin(IRE), the only 3-y-o having been supplemented at a cost of £50,000 following his impressive Prix Jean Prat win, had stamina to prove on his first outing against older horses, and didn't help himself by racing keenly for the first furlong or so. He could make no impression in the straight and looked a non-stayer. (tchd 11-2)

Jakkalberry(IRE), a 1m4f Group 1 winner in Italy in June, was unsuited by a steadily run race over this shorter trip on quickish ground. He can do better.

Cutlass Bay(UAE) had looked so promising when trained in France, but he ran a shocker on his debut for this yard (first-time tongue-tie) in the Tattersalls Gold Cup, and this was another tame effort. He probably wants genuinely soft ground, but still has plenty to prove. (op 25-1)

Stimulation(IRE) was clearly flattered by his fourth in the Prince Of Wales's Stakes.

Bushman was out his depth and didn't help himself by racing keenly. (op 50-1)

5187 SPORTINGBET.COM NURSERY 6f

4:05 (4:06) (Class 2) 2-Y-O £12,952 (£3,854; £1,926; £962) **Stalls** Low

Form RPR

5153 **1** **Puddle Duck**[10] 4851 2-8-8 **76**.. JamieSpencer 12 89+
(K A Ryan) *hld up in rr: gd hdwy and swtchd stands' side over 2f out: str run to ld appr fnl f: drvn clr* **6/1**[3]

125 **2** *3 ½* **Azzurra Du Caprio (IRE)**[27] 4242 2-8-5 **76**............... KellyHarrison(3) 9 79
(B M R Haslam) *lw: hld up in midfield: effrt over 2f out: styd on fnl f: tk n.d 2nd nr fin* **33/1**

2211 **3** *½* **Madany (IRE)**[18] 4544 2-9-7 **89**.. RichardHills 1 91+
(B W Hills) *lw: hld up: hdwy on outside to trck ldrs over 2f out: chal over 1f out: kpt on same pce* **11/2**[2]

21 **4** *½* **Regal Approval**[26] 4293 2-8-13 **81**................................ SteveDrowne 14 82
(H Morrison) *hld up in rr: effrt and n.m.r over 2f out: kpt on wl stands' side fnl f* **5/1**[1]

3103 **5** *shd* **Barista (IRE)**[14] 4677 2-8-0 **68** ow2............................... FrannyNorton 11 68
(M R Channon) *in rr: effrt over 2f out: nt clr run over 1f out: swtchd lft and styd on wl last 150yds* **14/1**

514 **6** *½* **Da Ponte**[25] 4331 2-8-7 **75**.. AndreaAtzeni 6 73
(Pat Eddery) *chsd ldrs: kpt on same pce ins fnl f* **14/1**

1340 **7** *nk* **Meandmyshadow**[63] 3051 2-8-8 **76**......................... SilvestreDeSousa 15 73
(A D Brown) *hld up in rr stands' side: hdwy over 2f out: kpt on: nvr nr ldrs* **33/1**

041 **8** *1* **Thirteen Shivers**[15] 4645 2-8-8 **79**.............................. JamesSullivan(3) 3 73
(M W Easterby) *led tl appr fnl f: sn wknd* **33/1**

10 **9** *1 ¾* **Honeymead (IRE)**[60] 3141 2-9-0 **82**................................ PaulHanagan 4 71
(R A Fahey) *chsd ldrs: rdn over 2f out: wknd over 1f out* **7/1**

2144 **10** *shd* **Lady Del Sol**[10] 4851 2-8-9 **77**.. JimmyQuinn 7 65
(G R Oldroyd) *s.i.s: hdwy over 2f out: nvr nr ldrs* **25/1**

6033 **11** *2 ¼* **Magic Stella**[17] 4592 2-8-2 **77**.. HarryBentley(7) 8 59
(A P Jarvis) *chsd ldrs: wknd over 1f out* **16/1**

0341 **12** *1 ¼* **First Class Favour (IRE)**[4] 5021 2-8-9 **77** 6ex..................... DavidAllan 2 55
(T D Easterby) *w ldr on outside: wknd fnl 150yds* **16/1**

1210 **13** *1 ¼* **Bilko Pak (IRE)**[31] 4138 2-9-6 **88**................................... JimmyFortune 5 62
(R Hannon) *in rr: sn drvn along: nvr a factor* **40/1**

2314 **14** *1 ¼* **Sir Lunchalott**[18] 4539 2-8-0 **75**...................................... RyanPowell(7) 13 45
(J S Moore) *in tch stands' side: effrt over 2f out: sn lost pl* **22/1**

2210 **15** *nk* **Jaahiz (IRE)**[31] 4138 2-9-1 **83**... RichardHughes 10 52
(R Hannon) *trckd ldrs stands' side: effrt 2f out: sn lost pl* **11/2**[2]

1m 12.11s (0.21) **Going Correction** +0.05s/f (Good) **15** Ran SP% **118.8**
Speed ratings (Par 100): **100,95,94,94,93 93,92,91,89,89 86,84,82,81,80**
toteswingers:1&2 £29.30, 2&3 £39.40, 1&3 £6.60 CSF £203.47 CT £1181.09 TOTE £7.30: £2.40, £10.30, £2.10; EX 283.70 TRIFECTA Not won..
Owner Mrs S J Barker **Bred** Cecil And Miss Alison Wiggins **Trained** Hambleton, N Yorks

FOCUS

A wide-open nursery and it again appeared to be a slight advantage to have a high draw.

NOTEBOOK

Puddle Duck has been shaping as though ready for 7f, but he got a decent gallop to chase and, having been held up right at the back by Spencer, picked up strongly once switched right and drew clear inside the final furlong, winning with plenty in hand. An additional furlong may well bring about further improvement and he remains one to keep on-side. (op 7-1)

Azzurra Du Caprio(IRE), dropping in distance, stayed on strongly inside the final furlong, having been outpaced, and looks to need a step back up in trip. She looks capable of better. (op 25-1)

Madany(IRE), drawn in stall one, challenged away from the winner in this bid for a hat-trick and never quite looked to be on terms. Racing from a mark of 89, she is still progressing and should stay 7f. (op 5-1)

Regal Approval was short of room 2f out and lacked the speed to get himself back in the race. He was edging nearer as they crossed the line, and remains capable of winning off this sort of mark. (tchd 11-2)

Barista(IRE), whose rider was putting up 2lb overweight, was held by the winner on Glorious Goodwood form, but again ran well, keeping on late, and looks certain to win a nursery at some stage. He was reported to have been denied a clear run. Official explanation: jockey said gelding was denied a clear run (op 12-1)

Da Ponte, dropping in trip, showed good early speed, but couldn't quicken inside the final 2f and slowly faded. (op 16-1)

Meandmyshadow, dropping in grade, did well considering how hard she pulled early.

Honeymead(IRE) was disappointing on this nursery debut, quickly losing her pitch and ending up well held. (tchd 15-2)

Jaahiz(IRE) won his maiden here, but bombed out in the Super Sprint last time and he dropped right away here having shown early pace. Official explanation: trainer had no explanation for the poor form shown (op 7-1 tchd 5-1)

5188 PATRINGTON HAVEN LEISURE PARK H'CAP 1m 2f 88y

4:40 (4:40) (Class 2) (0-105,102) 3-Y-O+ £12,952 (£3,854; £1,926; £962) **Stalls** Low

Form RPR

1250 **1** **Sweet Lightning**[38] 3921 5-9-8 **95**.. TomEaves 9 106+
(M Dods) *hld up in mid-div: stdy hdwy 3f out: led jst ins fnl f: hld on towards fin* **14/1**

-500 **2** *hd* **Royal Destination (IRE)**[18] 4537 5-9-6 **93**.................... OlivierPeslier 12 104
(J Noseda) *w ldrs: led narrowly over 1f out: hdd jst ins fnl f: rallied and no ex nr fin* **7/1**[2]

021 **3** *1* **Be Invincible (IRE)**[15] 4660 3-8-4 **85**............................ FrannyNorton 10 94
(B W Hills) *trckd ldrs: t.k.h: chal over 1f out: edgd lft and styd on same pce ins fnl f* **12/1**

3110 **4** *2* **Jutland**[20] 4470 3-8-12 **93**... GregFairley 15 98+
(M Johnston) *lw: chsd ldrs: outpcd over 2f out: styd on ins fnl f* **12/1**

1033 **5** *1 ¼* **Arlequin**[17] 4570 3-8-11 **92**.. PhilipRobinson 19 95
(J D Bethell) *mid-div: effrt over 3f out: kpt on same pce ins fnl f* **14/1**

10-4 **6** *3 ¼* **Sirvino**[23] 4412 5-10-0 **101**.. PhillipMakin 8 98
(T D Barron) *hld up towards rr: effrt over 2f out: kpt on ins fnl f* **12/1**

-104 **7** *nse* **Red Jade**[74] 2710 5-8-13 **86**.. PaulHanagan 2 83
(R A Fahey) *chsd ldrs: chal over 3f out: wknd ins fnl f* **8/1**[3]

2544 **8** *nk* **Almiqdaad**[21] 4455 4-9-12 **99**...................................(b) RichardHills 14 95
(M A Jarvis) *chsd ldrs: wknd ins fnl f* **8/1**[3]

5155 **9** *1 ½* **Reve De Nuit (USA)**[32] 4100 4-9-1 **88**............................... TomQueally 4 81
(A J McCabe) *in rr: hdwy over 2f out: nvr a factor* **25/1**

0026 **10** *nk* **Right Step**[12] 4757 3-8-2 **90**.. HarryBentley(7) 17 83
(A P Jarvis) *s.s: in rr: swtchd to stands' side rail over 3f out: nvr nr ldrs* **25/1**

0300 **11** *nk* **Charlie Cool**[10] 4830 7-9-3 **93**................................(p) JamesSullivan(3) 11 85
(Mrs R A Carr) *in rr: sme hdwy over 2f out: nvr a factor* **50/1**

1-23 **12** *1* **Splinter Cell (USA)**[184] 553 4-9-7 **94**............................ WilliamBuick 18 84
(M Botti) *in rr: effrt on outside over 3f out: nvr a factor* **25/1**

1-00 **13** *½* **Tipperary Boutique (IRE)**[24] 4389 3-8-3 **84**.................... JoeFanning 6 73
(B W Hills) *hld up in mid-div: effrt over 3f out: btn whn n.m.r over 1f out* **18/1**

1636 **14** *1* **Party Doctor**[40] 3827 3-9-7 **102**................................ RichardKingscote 1 89
(Tom Dascombe) *chsd ldrs: rdn over 3f out: wknd 2f out* **33/1**

1120 **15** *¾* **Caldercruix (USA)**[40] 3824 3-8-11 **92**........................... JamieSpencer 3 78
(T P Tate) *led: drvn along 7f out: hdd over 1f out: sn lost pl* **10/1**

-300 **16** *7* **Roman Republic (FR)**[21] 4455 4-9-10 **97**..................... FrankieDettori 5 70
(Saeed Bin Suroor) *mid-div: drvn over 3f out: sn chsng ldrs: hung rt and wknd over 1f out: eased ins fnl f* **9/2**[1]

0-00 **17** *19* **Markazzi**[19] 4504 3-8-7 **88**..(t) TadhgO'Shea 13 25
(Sir Michael Stoute) *swtchd lft after s: in rr: bhd over 3f out: t.o* **25/1**

043 **18** *80* **Hanson'D (IRE)**[11] 4805 3-8-10 **91**................................ KierenFallon 7 —
(K A Ryan) *trckd ldrs: tk fierce hold: lost pl 4f out: sn wl bhd: virtually p.u: hopelessly t.o: struck into* **16/1**

2m 10.6s (-1.90) **Going Correction** +0.05s/f (Good)
WFA 3 from 4yo+ 8lb **18** Ran SP% **129.8**
Speed ratings (Par 109): **109,108,108,106,105 102,102,102,101,101 100,100,99,98,98 92,77,13**
toteswingers:1&2 £28.90, 2&3 £20.10, 1&3 £49.60 CSF £106.19 CT £1253.30 TOTE £19.80: £4.30, £2.30, £3.70, £4.10; EX 189.90 TRIFECTA Not won. Place 6: £101.68 Place 5: £37.84 .
Owner Andrew Tinkler **Bred** Mrs M Lavell **Trained** Denton, Co Durham

FOCUS

A good, competitive handicap, but they didn't go that quick through the opening stages, and the time was 2.02 seconds slower than the International Stakes, which was also run at a modest early gallop. The main action was up the middle of the track in the straight and the form looks sound rated around those in the frame behind the winner.

NOTEBOOK

Sweet Lightning ◆ returned to form following a disappointing effort over this C&D in the John Smith's Cup. A strong traveller who doesn't always find that much off the bridle, he was in front sooner than ideal, such was the ease with which he moved through the field, but did enough. His target is the Cambridgeshire, and he could well be a big player, with a strongly run 1m1f likely to suit. Beforehand he could go to Newbury for the John Smith's Stakes, a good trial for the Newmarket contest, and a race in which he finished third last year off a mark of 88 when with William Muir.

Royal Destination(IRE), whose last success came in this race off a 1lb lower mark last year, was beautifully positioned by Peslier and was just denied the follow up, albeit he was probably flattered to finish so close to the idling winner. (op 8-1)

Be Invincible(IRE), 8lb higher than when winning a lesser race over 1m1/2f at Windsor, did well to finish so close considering he was keen early on.

Jutland plugged on in a manner than suggests the steady early pace didn't help, and he probably has more to offer. (op 16-1 tchd 11-1)

Arlequin doesn't seem to have much in hand off his current sort of mark.

Sirvino posted a creditable effort under top weight on only his second start of the campaign. (op 10-1 tchd 9-1)

Red Jade was simply too keen. (tchd 15-2)

Roman Republic(FR) ran as though something was amiss. Official explanation: jockey said colt hung right (op 5-1 tchd 11-2)

Markazzi Official explanation: jockey said colt had no more to give
Hanson'D(IRE) Official explanation: jockey said colt had been struck into behind
T/Jkpt: Not won. T/Plt: £149.70 to a £1 stake. Pool of £269,353.00 - 1,312.68 winning tickets. T/Qpdt: £13.90 to a £1 stake. Pool of £14,167.89 - 749.00 winning tickets. WG

5189 - 5195a (Foreign Racing) - See Raceform Interactive

4644 CARLISLE (R-H)
Wednesday, August 18

OFFICIAL GOING: Good to firm (good in places)
Wind: moderate 1/2 against Weather: overcast becoming fine and sunny

5196 PES-SECURITY.COM E B F MEDIAN AUCTION MAIDEN STKS 5f 193y
1:30 (1:30) (Class 4) 2-Y-O £4,196 (£1,239; £619) **Stalls** High

Form RPR
3 **1** **Glen's Diamond**[19] 4543 2-8-12 0................................ LeeTopliss(5) 6 84+
(R A Fahey) *sltly hmpd s: chsd ldrs: hung lft over 1f out: styd on to ld nr fin* **5/2**[2]
5 **2** *nk* **Candys Girl**[26] 4317 2-8-12 0.. MickyFenton 3 77
(M L W Bell) *w ldr: led 2f out: no ex and hdd towards fin* **11/8**[1]
3453 **3** *3* **Lady Platinum Club**[12] 4783 2-8-12 67..........................(p) LeeVickers 2 68
(G R Oldroyd) *chsd ldrs: kpt on same pce appr fnl f* **12/1**
4222 **4** *1 1/4* **Boundaries**[11] 4831 2-9-3 76.. DavidAllan 8 69
(T D Easterby) *swvd bdly lft s: t.k.h: led: hung lft: hdd 2f out: fdd ins fnl f* **11/4**[3]
00 **5** *2 1/2* **Black Annis Bower**[26] 4336 2-8-9 0.......................... JamesSullivan(3) 1 57
(M W Easterby) *dwlt: prom: drvn over 2f out: edgd rt and sn wknd* **150/1**
5 **6** *4* **Itzakindamagic (IRE)**[36] 3985 2-8-12 0...................... RoystonFfrench 5 47
(M Johnston) *hmpd s: sn drvn along: a outpcd* **22/1**
7 *1 1/4* **Henrys Gift (IRE)** 2-9-0 0.................................... PatrickDonaghy(3) 4 46
(M Dods) *s.i.s: t.k.h: drvn over 2f out: sn lost pl* **80/1**
00 **8** *11* **Pinotage**[50] 3536 2-9-0 0.. MichaelStainton(3) 7 14
(R M Whitaker) *dwlt and sltly hmpd s: outpcd and lost pl over 2f out: sn bhd* **100/1**

1m 13.78s (0.08) **Going Correction** +0.025s/f (Good) 8 Ran SP% 112.3
Speed ratings (Par 96): **100,99,95,93,90 85,83,68**
toteswingers:1&2 £1.60, 2&3 £4.30, 1&3 £6.30 CSF £6.06 TOTE £4.50: £1.10, £1.20, £2.30; EX 6.80.
Owner Morebrooke Ltd **Bred** Doverlane Finance Ltd **Trained** Musley Bank, N Yorks

FOCUS
It was dry overnight and the ground was on the quick side, officially described as good to firm, good down the hill, with a GoingStick reading of 8.5. An ordinary maiden, with the 67-rated third possibly the best guide to the form.

NOTEBOOK
Glen's Diamond confirmed the promise he showed when third on debut at Haydock. He did well to win over 6f seeing as he seems sure to improve when stepped up in trip, as his breeding suggests. (op 3-1)
Candys Girl, a Cheveley Park entrant who had finished fifth on her debut at Ascot. She was simply outstayed by the winner and may be better suited by 5f. (op 11-10)
Lady Platinum Club might prefer easier ground but this was a respectable effort nonetheless.
Boundaries looked a thoroughly awkward ride, diving left as the stalls opened and then wanting to hang in that direction, carrying his head to one side through the first couple of furlongs or so. He didn't pick up in the straight and looks one to avoid. Official explanation: jockey said colt hung left-handed throughout (op 10-3 tchd 5-2)
Black Annis Bower improved significantly on her two previous starts and nurseries are now an option
Itzakindamagic(IRE) was never going after being hampered on leaving the stalls. (op 25-1 tchd 20-1)

5197 FANTAILS RESTAURANT BOYS DAY OUT CLAIMING STKS 5f 193y
2:05 (2:05) (Class 6) 3-Y-O+ £1,619 (£481; £240; £120) **Stalls** High

Form RPR
26-0 **1** **Silaah**[21] 4473 6-9-10 83...(p) AdrianNicholls 7 83
(D Nicholls) *t.k.h in last: nt clr run and swtchd outside over 1f out: carried hd high and led 1f out: edgd rt drvn clr* **5/2**[2]
0036 **2** *3 1/2* **Esprit De Midas**[9] 4894 4-9-10 87....................................... DavidAllan 3 72
(K A Ryan) *w ldr: narow ld and edgd lft over 1f out: hdd 1f out: kpt on same pce* **11/10**[1]
0004 **3** *3/4* **Beckermet (IRE)**[12] 4795 8-8-13 77........................... JamesSullivan(3) 5 62
(Mrs R A Carr) *chsd ldrs: n.m.r over 1f out tl ins fnl f: kpt on same pce* **4/1**[3]
5303 **4** *1/2* **Red River Boy**[10] 4868 5-8-11 50............................. KellyHarrison(3) 1 58
(C W Fairhurst) *hmpd s: hld up in rr: hdwy to chse ldrs 3f out: kpt on same pce ins fnl f* **20/1**
240 **5** *1 1/4* **Craicattack (IRE)**[35] 4031 3-8-11 71.............................(p) MickyFenton 2 54
(Mrs S A Watt) *swvd lft s: led: hdd over 1f out: wknd ins fnl f* **12/1**
3130 **6** *3 3/4* **Artsu**[34] 4060 5-8-12 66.. RoystonFfrench 4 40
(M Dods) *trckd ldrs: t.k.h: wknd over 1f out* **14/1**
600 **7** *26* **Orpenia (IRE)**[108] 1722 4-8-4 46.................................. PatrickMathers 6 —
(J A McShane) *dwlt: t.k.h: chsd ldrs: drvn 3f out: sn lost pl and bhd: t.o* **100/1**

1m 12.89s (-0.81) **Going Correction** +0.025s/f (Good)
WFA 3 from 4yo+ 3lb 7 Ran SP% 116.3
Speed ratings (Par 101): **106,101,100,99,98 93,58**
toteswingers:1&2 £1.10, 2&3 £1.10, 1&3 £3.50 CSF £5.81 TOTE £4.70: £3.70, £1.10; EX 8.20.
Owner Mrs Jackie Love & David Nicholls **Bred** Bearstone Stud **Trained** Sessay, N Yorks

FOCUS
A fair claimer, despite abysmal prize money, although the proximity of the 50-rated Red River Boy, who took the eye in the paddock, limits the form. They went a strong pace.

5198 STOBART GROUP & HOSPICE AT HOME H'CAP 5f
2:40 (2:41) (Class 4) (0-80,78) 3-Y-O+ £3,885 (£1,156; £577; £288) **Stalls** High

Form RPR
1132 **1** **Comptonspirit**[6] 4982 6-8-13 68................................... MickyFenton 14 79
(B P J Baugh) *chsd ldrs: led over 1f out: styd on wl* **8/1**
1615 **2** *2* **The Bear**[12] 4798 7-9-3 72.. LeeVickers 9 76
(Miss L A Perratt) *led: hdd over 1f out: styd on same pce* **20/1**
010 **3** *1/2* **Captain Scooby**[11] 4834 4-8-10 68............................ MichaelStainton(3) 5 70
(R M Whitaker) *in rr: hdwy 2f out: styd on wl ins fnl f* **12/1**
1623 **4** *3/4* **Hazelrigg (IRE)**[19] 4542 5-9-4 73...................................(bt) DavidAllan 3 73
(T D Easterby) *in rr: hdwy over 2f out: hung bdly lft: n.m.r over 1f out: kpt on ins fnl f* **7/2**[1]
0316 **5** *1* **Galpin Junior (USA)**[14] 4712 4-9-3 72.......................... AdrianNicholls 1 68
(D Nicholls) *swtchd rt after 1f to r w main body of field: in rr: hdwy over 2f out: kpt on: nt rch ldrs* **6/1**[2]
0061 **6** *3/4* **Timber Treasure (USA)**[19] 4559 6-8-1 59..............(b) PaulPickard(3) 11 52
(Paul Green) *s.i.s: in rr tl hdwy fnl 2f* **11/1**
0413 **6** *dht* **Chosen One (IRE)**[14] 4712 5-9-0 72........................... JamesSullivan(3) 8 65
(Mrs R A Carr) *chsd ldrs: kpt on same pce over 1f out* **9/1**
1324 **8** *nk* **Sir Nod**[31] 4171 8-9-8 77.. RoystonFfrench 12 69
(Julie Camacho) *chsd ldrs: kpt on same pce fnl 2f* **11/1**
3120 **9** *1/2* **Ursus**[14] 4706 5-8-1 59...(p) KellyHarrison(3) 10 49
(C R Wilson) *mid-div: hdwy over 1f out: nvr a factor* **33/1**
6201 **10** *2* **Rio Cobolo (IRE)**[11] 4834 4-9-3 75.....................(v) PatrickDonaghy(3) 13 58
(Paul Green) *s.i.s: hdwy over 2f out: hung rt: nvr nr ldrs* **17/2**
1556 **11** *1 1/2* **Argentine (IRE)**[12] 4798 6-9-1 75...............................(b) LeeTopliss(5) 4 53
(J A McShane) *chsd ldrs: lost pl wl over 1f out* **14/1**
0-00 **12** *4 1/2* **Sharp Bullet (IRE)**[69] 2883 4-8-12 67...................(b[1]) PatrickMathers 6 29
(Bruce Hellier) *in tch: lost pl 2f out* **125/1**
0006 **13** *1 1/2* **Rievaulx World**[16] 4653 4-9-6 78..................................(p) AmyRyan(3) 2 34
(K A Ryan) *swtchd lft after 1f and racd alone stands' side: chsd ldrs: lost pl over 1f out* **7/1**[3]

60.26 secs (-0.54) **Going Correction** +0.025s/f (Good) 13 Ran SP% 120.2
Speed ratings (Par 105): **105,101,101,99,98 97,97,96,95,92 90,82,80**
toteswingers:1&2 £28.20, 2&3 £62.70, 1&3 £14.50 CSF £160.64 CT £1971.11 TOTE £7.80: £3.40, £7.90, £4.80; EX 137.70.
Owner G B Hignett **Bred** Mrs F Wilson **Trained** Audley, Staffs

FOCUS
A fair sprint handicap. They all raced far side in the straight and not many got involved. The form is rated around the runner-up.
Sharp Bullet(IRE) Official explanation: trainer said gelding lost its near-fore shoe

5199 WHYTE & MACKAY FILLIES' H'CAP 6f 192y
3:15 (3:16) (Class 4) (0-80,80) 3-Y-O+ £5,180 (£1,541; £770; £384) **Stalls** High

Form RPR
0324 **1** **Amethyst Dawn (IRE)**[11] 4847 4-9-9 73............................ DavidAllan 7 81
(T D Easterby) *chsd ldrs: led over 1f out: hld on wl* **9/4**[2]
1150 **2** *1/2* **Rascal In The Mix (USA)**[11] 4824 4-8-11 64...............(p) AmyRyan(3) 5 71
(R M Whitaker) *s.i.s: hld up in rr: hdwy over 2f out: styd on to chse wnr last 100yds: no ex* **15/2**
2630 **3** *3/4* **Elusive Sue (USA)**[39] 3919 3-9-3 77................................ LeeTopliss(5) 4 78
(R A Fahey) *trckd ldrs: chal and hung rt over 1f out: styd on same pce last 100yds* **13/2**[3]
-262 **4** *3 1/2* **Dylanesque**[21] 4483 3-9-8 80.. JamesSullivan(3) 9 72
(M A Jarvis) *towards rr: drvn and hdwy over 2f out: nvr nr ldrs* **2/1**[1]
0601 **5** *1 3/4* **Who's Shirl**[14] 4706 4-9-3 70...................................... KellyHarrison(3) 1 61+
(C W Fairhurst) *s.s: swtchd rt after s: hld up detached in last: hdwy over 2f out: hmpd and swtchd lft jst ins fnl f: nvr rchd ldrs* **16/1**
0-30 **6** *3 3/4* **Solitary**[41] 3806 4-9-3 67.. MickyFenton 3 48
(Mrs Marjorie Fife) *led: edgd lft and hdd over 1f out: sn wknd* **40/1**
0025 **7** *1/2* **Salerosa (IRE)**[16] 4644 5-8-13 66.........................(v) MichaelStainton(3) 2 45
(Mrs A Duffield) *hld up towards rr: hdwy over 2f out: wknd appr fnl f* **9/1**
6200 **8** *1/2* **Battlemaiden (IRE)**[18] 4593 3-9-9 78.............................. RoystonFfrench 6 52
(M Johnston) *chsd ldrs: edgd rt over 1f out: sn wknd* **18/1**

1m 26.33s (-0.77) **Going Correction** -0.05s/f (Good)
WFA 3 from 4yo+ 5lb 8 Ran SP% 112.8
Speed ratings (Par 102): **102,101,100,96,94 90,89,89**
toteswingers:1&2 £2.30, 2&3 £8.70, 1&3 £3.60 CSF £18.99 CT £93.82 TOTE £2.50: £1.10, £2.60, £3.60; EX 17.80.
Owner D A West **Bred** W Kane **Trained** Great Habton, N Yorks

FOCUS
A fair fillies' handicap run at a strong pace. Sound form.
Who's Shirl Official explanation: jockey said filly was denied a clear run

5200 J20 WHITE BLEND SUMMER SERIES H'CAP 1m 6f 32y
3:50 (3:50) (Class 4) (0-80,74) 3-Y-O+ £4,174 (£1,445) **Stalls** High

Form RPR
5223 **1** **Simonside**[15] 4686 7-9-7 70... DavidAllan 4 81
(B Ellison) *chsd ldr: led after 3f: shkn up over 3f out: clr over 1f out: eased towards fin* **6/5**[1]
26-0 **2** *7* **Rosewin (IRE)**[18] 4604 4-8-13 65............................ JamesSullivan(3) 3 66
(Ollie Pears) *trckd ldng pair: hung bdly lft thrght: c stands' side over 2f out: eased whn wl btn ins fnl f* **5/1**[3]
0202 **P** **Interdiamonds**[8] 4923 4-9-11 74................................. RoystonFfrench 1 —
(M Johnston) *t.k.h to ld: hdd after 3f: broke hind leg and immediately p.u: fatally injured* **5/4**[2]

3m 11.26s (3.76) **Going Correction** -0.05s/f (Good) 3 Ran SP% 106.6
Speed ratings (Par 105): **87,83,—**
CSF £5.92 TOTE £1.90; EX 4.50.
Owner Racing Management & Training Ltd **Bred** Keith Richardson **Trained** Norton, N Yorks

FOCUS
Meaningless form, with one pulled up and the other pair split by the entire width of the track in the straight. The winner probably only had to run to form.

5201 TEXT 55MISSCUMBRIA ON 81118 H'CAP 7f 200y
4:25 (4:26) (Class 6) (0-60,65) 3-Y-O £1,619 (£481; £240; £120) **Stalls** High

Form RPR
-200 **1** **Jozafeen**[25] 4374 3-8-13 58.. PaulPickard(3) 4 65
(R Bastiman) *s.i.s: hld up towards rr: racd wd: hdwy over 2f out: chal 1f out: styd on to ld last stride* **11/1**
-001 **2** *nse* **Madame Excelerate**[10] 4864 3-9-9 65 6ex.................... FrannyNorton 12 72
(W M Brisbourne) *trckd ldrs: t.k.h: styd on to ld last 100yds: hdd post* **11/4**[1]
6554 **3** *1 3/4* **Military Call**[10] 4864 3-8-13 60...........................(p) MichaelO'Connell(5) 9 63
(A C Whillans) *trckd ldrs: chal 2f out: led 1f out: hdd and no ex ins fnl f* **10/1**
0511 **4** *3/4* **Gee Major**[13] 4733 3-9-0 56.. RoystonFfrench 5 57
(N J Vaughan) *led: hdd 1f out: kpt on one pce* **7/2**[2]
0550 **5** *2 1/4* **Hairy Maclary**[26] 4344 3-8-12 54....................................... DavidAllan 11 49
(T D Easterby) *chsd ldrs: rdn and outpcd over 2f out: one pce fnl f* **7/2**[2]
0000 **6** *1* **Patricks Lodge**[12] 4786 3-8-1 46 oh1..................... JamesSullivan(3) 8 39
(Mrs R A Carr) *sn chsng ldrs: chal over 2f out: wknd jst ins fnl f* **66/1**
-334 **7** *2 1/4* **Uddy Mac**[14] 4714 3-8-13 58....................................... KellyHarrison(3) 2 45
(N Bycroft) *hld up in rr: hdwy over 2f out: chsng ldrs 1f out: sn wknd* **7/1**[3]
4000 **8** *10* **Dispol Kabira**[10] 4864 3-8-4 46.............................(b[1]) PatrickMathers 7 8
(D W Thompson) *dwlt: t.k.h sn trcking ldrs: drvn to chal over 2f out: sn wknd* **40/1**

0006 9 4 **Zamid (FR)**[7] 4951 3-8-7 **49**....(p) AdrianNicholls 10 —
(R A Fahey) *sn detached in last: reminders 4f out: sn bhd* **11/1**

1m 40.97s (0.97) **Going Correction** -0.05s/f (Good) **9** Ran SP% **113.3**
Speed ratings (Par 98): **93,92,91,90,88 87,84,74,70**
toteswingers:1&2 £9.30, 2&3 £4.00, 1&3 £12.40 CSF £40.64 CT £317.42 TOTE £12.80: £3.40, £2.10, £3.00; EX 62.50.
Owner Mrs C Steel **Bred** Steel's Thoroughbred Breeding **Trained** Cowthorpe, N Yorks

FOCUS
A moderate handicap. The winner was back to her reappearance form.

5202 BARNARDO'S BELIEVE IN CHILDREN AMATEUR RIDERS' H'CAP (DIV I) 1m 6f 32y
5:00 (5:00) (Class 6) (0-60,52) 4-Y-0+ **£1,318** (£405; £202) **Stalls** High

Form RPR
4532 1 **Jenny Soba**[15] 4673 7-10-13 **51**.... MrSWalker 1 61+
(Lucinda Featherstone) *trckd ldrs: effrt on ins to ld over 4f out: sn drvn clr: eased towards fin* **5/2**[2]
4000 2 5 **Chateauneuf (IRE)**[11] 4854 4-10-0 **46** oh1.... MissBeckyBrisbourne[(7)] 9 48
(W M Brisbourne) *trckd ldrs: dropped bk after 5f: hdwy on wd outside over 2f out: styd on to take modest 2nd post* **28/1**
3306 3 nse **Knock Three Times (IRE)**[11] 4825 4-10-7 **46** oh1.... MissLHorner 2 48
(W Storey) *in rr: hdwy to trck ldrs over 4f out: wnt modest 2nd over 2f out: hung lft: kpt on same pce* **13/2**
5511 4 3 ½ **Ballade De La Mer**[11] 4825 4-10-7 **50**....(p) MrGJCockburn[(5)] 3 48
(A G Foster) *trckd ldrs: drvn over 2f out: wknd jst ins fnl f* **9/4**[1]
0640 5 8 **Parchment (IRE)**[11] 4854 8-10-7 **46** oh1....(b) MissADeniel 10 32
(A J Lockwood) *hld up in rr: hmpd bnd after 2f: hdwy over 4f out: hung rt 2f out: sn wknd* **9/2**[3]
0401 6 19 **Media Stars**[10] 4863 5-10-7 **52** 6ex....(t) MissEYoung[(7)] 6 12
(R Johnson) *t.k.h: sn trcking ldrs: outpcd over 3f out: wknd 2f out* **18/1**
0-20 7 38 **Orpen Bid (IRE)**[18] 4582 5-10-4 **46** oh1.... MissMMullineaux[(3)] 8 —
(M Mullineaux) *mid-div: hdwy to ld after 5f: hdd over 4f out: wknd over 2f out: sn bhd: heavily eased last 100yds: t.o* **16/1**
550- 8 10 **Samizdat (FR)**[65] 6769 7-10-5 **48**.... MissECSayer[(5)] 5 —
(Mrs Dianne Sayer) *led 5f: lost pl 5f out: t.o 3f out* **12/1**

3m 10.7s (3.20) **Going Correction** -0.05s/f (Good) **8** Ran SP% **113.1**
Speed ratings (Par 101): **88,85,85,83,78 67,45,40**
toteswingers:1&2 £13.00, 2&3 £8.80, 1&3 £4.20 CSF £63.81 CT £407.42 TOTE £3.80: £1.10, £6.60, £4.10; EX 71.70.
Owner J Roundtree **Bred** Theakston Stud **Trained** Atlow, Derbyshire

FOCUS
The top weight was rated just 52, so the form's clearly limited, though the time was 1.47 seconds quicker than the modestly run second division. The winner was basically back to her best.
Knock Three Times(IRE) Official explanation: jockey said filly hung left-handed throughout

5203 BARNARDO'S BELIEVE IN CHILDREN AMATEUR RIDERS' H'CAP (DIV II) 1m 6f 32y
5:35 (5:36) (Class 6) (0-60,52) 4-Y-0+ **£1,318** (£405; £202) **Stalls** High

Form RPR
050 1 **Dream Risk (FR)**[21] 3760 4-11-0 **52**....(t) MissSBrotherton 4 60
(Mrs K Walton) *trckd ldrs: wnt 2nd over 3f out: led 2f out: 3 l clr ins fnl f: jst lasted* **4/1**[3]
-240 2 nse **Winged Farasi**[18] 4604 6-10-5 **50**.... MissHBethell[(7)] 3 58
(Miss J E Foster) *hld up: reminders 4f out: gd hdwy over 1f out: wnt 2nd 100yds out: styd on wl: jst failed* **13/2**
4643 3 4 **Snowberry Hill (USA)**[23] 4441 7-10-7 **46** oh1.... MrSWalker 5 47
(Lucinda Featherstone) *led tl 9f out: led over 6f out tl 2f out: styd on same pce* **3/1**[2]
-503 4 2 **Heart Of Dubai (USA)**[11] 4854 5-10-4 **47**.... HenryBrooke[(5)] 10 47
(Micky Hammond) *hld up in rr: hdwy 7f out: chsng ldrs over 3f out: one pce fnl 2f* **5/2**[1]
6435 5 2 **Dechiper (IRE)**[9] 4900 8-10-4 **49**....(t) MissCWalton[(7)] 7 46
(R Johnson) *trckd ldrs: led 9f out tl over 6f out: outpcd over 2f out: one pce* **6/1**
3654 6 3 ¼ **Perez (IRE)**[9] 4900 8-10-7 **46** oh1....(vt) MissLHorner 6 37
(W Storey) *hld up: lost pl over 4f out: hung lft and sn bhd: kpt on fnl 2f* **9/1**
000/ 7 17 **Bronze Dancer (IRE)**[623] 3642 8-11-0 **52**....(tp) MissJCoward 1 20
(B Storey) *chsd ldrs: lost pl over 4f out: sn bhd* **50/1**
0000 8 19 **Sacco D'Oro**[8] 4932 4-10-4 **46** oh1....(p) MissMMullineaux[(3)] 2 —
(M Mullineaux) *swewrved bdly lft leaving stalls: detached in rr: drvn along 8f out: sn bhd: t.o* **80/1**

3m 12.17s (4.67) **Going Correction** -0.05s/f (Good) **8** Ran SP% **114.4**
Speed ratings (Par 101): **84,83,81,80,79 77,67,56**
toteswingers:1&2 £6.40, 2&3 £5.30, 1&3 £3.90 . totesuper7: Win: Not won. Place: Not won. CSF £30.02 CT £87.68 TOTE £4.50: £2.40, £3.20, £1.10; EX 31.60 Place 6: £94.54 Place 5: £68.62.
Owner Keep The Faith Partnership **Bred** Trainers House Enterprises Ltd **Trained** Middleham Moor, N Yorks

FOCUS
Like the first division, the highest official mark on offer was just 52. The pace was steady, resulting in a time 1.47 seconds slower than the previous leg. The form is rated around the third.
T/Plt: £129.10 to a £1 stake. Pool of £38,332.75 - 216.70 winning tickets. T/Qpdt: £47.20 to a £1 stake. Pool of £2,972.88 - 46.60 winning tickets. WG

4741 FOLKESTONE (R-H)
Wednesday, August 18

OFFICIAL GOING: Good to firm (8.2)
Wind: medium, half behind Weather: bright spells

5204 ADAMSON'S LABORATORY SERVICES MAIDEN AUCTION STKS 7f (S)
5:30 (5:32) (Class 6) 2-Y-0 **£2,047** (£604; £302) **Stalls** Low

Form RPR
1 **Cloud Rock** 2-8-9 0.... AlanMunro 6 83+
(P W Chapple-Hyam) *trckd ldng pair gng wl: wnt 2nd 3f out: rdn to ld jst over 1f out: pushed clr ins fnl f: easily* **5/6**[1]
55 2 3 ¾ **Ice Cold Bex**[19] 4549 2-8-9 0.... DaneO'Neill 11 71
(P J McBride) *t.k.h: chsd ldrs: wnt 3rd 3f out: rdn and pressing ldrs over 1f out: nt gng pce of wnr and wl hld ins fnl f* **9/2**[3]
2202 3 hd **Kissing Clara (IRE)**[13] 4736 2-7-11 68....(p) RyanPowell[(7)] 9 66
(J S Moore) *restless in stalls: led: sddle slipped 1/2-way: rdn wl over 1f out: hdd jst over 1f out: no ch w wnr ins fnl f* **7/2**[2]
50 4 15 **Laffraaj (IRE)**[28] 4247 2-8-4 0.... TobyAtkinson[(5)] 2 33
(Pat Eddery) *racd in midfield and jst in tch: outpcd wl over 2f out: 4th and wl btn whn hung rt and hld hd high wl over 1f out* **16/1**
5 3 ½ **Beautiful Lando (FR)** 2-8-9 0.... ChrisCatlin 1 24
(Mrs H S Main) *v.s.a: wl bhd in last: styd on past btn horses fnl f: nvr on terms* **66/1**
6 1 ¼ **Skeleton (IRE)** 2-8-8 0.... GilmarPereira[(3)] 4 23
(W J Haggas) *sn outpcd in rr: lost tch 4f out: hmpd wl over 1f out: n.d* **16/1**
7 1 ¾ **Safari Sunbeam** 2-8-9 0.... FrankieMcDonald 10 17
(P Winkworth) *in midfield tl rdn and struggling after 2f: wl bhd fr 1/2-way* **33/1**
06 8 10 **Dells Breezer**[10] 4871 2-8-4 0.... JemmaMarshall[(5)] 3 —
(P M Phelan) *rrd s and v.s.a: a wl bhd: t.o fr 1/2-way* **22/1**
9 9 **Pipit Nest (IRE)** 2-7-11 0.... NoelGarbutt[(7)] 12 —
(T B P Coles) *racd keenly: w ldr after 1f tl 3f out: dropped out rapidly and sn bhd: wl t.o ins fnl f* **80/1**

1m 26.09s (-1.21) **Going Correction** -0.325s/f (Firm) **9** Ran SP% **116.7**
Speed ratings (Par 92): **93,88,88,71,67 65,63,52,42**
toteswingers:1&2 £2.20, 2&3 £2.30, 1&3 £2.00 CSF £4.86 TOTE £2.30: £1.60, £1.10, £1.10; EX 5.40.
Owner The Coalition **Bred** Lofts Hall Stud **Trained** Newmarket, Suffolk

FOCUS
This was just a moderate juvenile maiden.

NOTEBOOK
Cloud Rock readily made a winning debut. Breeding points to him needing a stiffer test, but a Racing Post Trophy entry suggests he's thought a bit of, and judging by the ease with which he won, it would be no surprise to see him pitched into Group company before long. (op 8-11 tchd 4-6-, 1-1 and 10-11 in a place)
Ice Cold Bex, up to 7f for the first time, had twice run well in Newmarket maidens and he again did enough here to suggest he can win a modest maiden before sent handicapping. (op 6-1)
Kissing Clara(IRE) has now finished either second or third on six of her nine starts. Rated 68, she did well considering the saddle slipped, just failing to hold on for second, but is going to remain vulnerable to less-exposed types. Official explanation: jockey said saddle slipped (op 9-2)
Laffraaj(IRE) finished well back, but is at least now qualified for nurseries (op 20-1)
Beautiful Lando(FR), whose dam was a winning sprinter on dirt in the US, shaped with some promise considering he got so far behind following a slow start. (tchd 50-1)
Skeleton(IRE) was another who failed to get into it having been behind, also getting hampered. (op 14-1)

5205 ENVEX COMPANY H'CAP 7f (S)
6:00 (6:02) (Class 4) (0-80,80) 3-Y-0 **£4,533** (£1,348; £674; £336) **Stalls** Low

Form RPR
3414 1 **Aleqa**[18] 4588 3-8-11 **70**.... AlanMunro 4 76
(C F Wall) *wnt rt s: sn trcking ldrs: rdn and qcknd to ld jst over 1f out: edgd lft to stands' rail ins fnl f: r.o wl* **15/2**
-000 2 1 ¼ **Fardyieh**[28] 4255 3-8-8 **67**....(t) ChrisCatlin 2 70
(C E Brittain) *led and set stdy gallop: qcknd: hanging rt 2f out: hdd jst over 1f out: kpt hanging and n.m.r ins fnl f: styd on same pce* **12/1**
2124 3 shd **Love Match**[39] 3918 3-9-7 **80**.... SteveDrowne 5 83+
(R Charlton) *stdd after s: hld up wl in tch in last: hdwy over 1f out: chsd ldrs and rdn ins fnl f: kpt on same pce and no imp fnl 75yds* **5/1**[3]
03-1 4 nk **Boogie Diva**[16] 4662 3-9-7 **80**.... IvaMilickova 7 82
(Jane Chapple-Hyam) *hld up wl in tch: effrt on outer wl over 1f out: chsd ldrs 1f out: styd on same pce and no imp fnl 100yds* **6/1**
0562 5 1 **Fawley Green**[18] 4588 3-8-13 **72**.... DaneO'Neill 1 71+
(W R Muir) *t.k.h: trckd ldrs on stands' rail: nt clr run fr over 1f out: nvr able to chal* **4/1**[2]
1000 6 nk **Catherines Call (IRE)**[7] 4968 3-8-11 **75**.... KierenFox[(5)] 3 73
(D Donovan) *hld up wl in tch in last pair: effrt over 1f out: kpt on same pce and nvr enough room ins fnl f* **12/1**
1-15 7 2 **Cloud's End**[11] 4847 3-9-7 **80**.... LiamJones 6 73
(W J Haggas) *hld up in tch: rdn and edgd rt wl over 1f out: wknd ins fnl f* **2/1**[1]
-200 8 2 ¾ **Ocean Rosie (IRE)**[20] 4515 3-8-1 **67**.... AdamBeschizza[(7)] 8 53
(Miss J Feilden) *sn crossed to press ldr towards stands' rail: rdn and edgd rt 2f out: wknd u.p over 1f out* **50/1**

1m 27.91s (0.61) **Going Correction** -0.325s/f (Firm) **8** Ran SP% **113.4**
Speed ratings (Par 102): **83,81,81,81,79 79,77,74**
toteswingers:1&2 £8.80, 2&3 £11.50, 1&3 £7.60 CSF £89.26 CT £491.32 TOTE £7.60: £2.00, £9.50, £1.30; EX 56.50.
Owner Ms Aida Fustoq **Bred** Deerfield Farm **Trained** Newmarket, Suffolk

FOCUS
Just a moderate 3yo handicap. It was slowly run and the form is dubious.

5206 PERSONNEL HEALTH AND SAFETY CONSULTANTS H'CAP 6f
6:30 (6:31) (Class 6) (0-65,65) 3-Y-0 **£2,047** (£604; £302) **Stalls** Low

Form RPR
4032 1 **Dream Number (IRE)**[10] 4861 3-9-4 **62**.... DaneO'Neill 1 72+
(W R Muir) *w ldrs tl led 2f out: pushed clr over 1f out and in command ins fnl f: pushed out: easily* **7/2**[2]
306 2 2 ¼ **Stratton Banker (IRE)**[113] 1601 3-9-1 **59**....(t) SaleemGolam 5 61
(S C Williams) *led: hdd 2f out: sn rdn and nt pce of wnr: kpt on: no ch w wnr ins fnl f* **7/2**[2]
-004 3 1 ¼ **Freedom Pass (USA)**[29] 4237 3-8-5 **56**....(t) AdamBeschizza[(7)] 2 54
(J A R Toller) *in tch: effrt to chse ldng pair 2f out: no imp u.p fr over 1f out* **5/2**[1]
06-2 4 3 ¾ **Elsie's Orphan**[62] 3125 3-9-3 **61**.... LiamKeniry 3 47
(P R Chamings) *restless in stalls: s.i.s: in tch in rr: rdn and unable qck 2f out: sn outpcd and wl btn* **7/2**[2]
5134 5 1 ½ **Watch Chain (IRE)**[10] 4861 3-8-12 **56**.... DarrylHolland 9 37
(M H Tompkins) *stdd and dropped in bhd after s: in tch: effrt and rdn ent fnl 2f: sn no imp and wl btn over 1f out* **8/1**[3]
-046 6 5 **Going French (IRE)**[19] 4529 3-9-2 **65**.... RossAtkinson[(5)] 7 30
(F J Brennan) *t.k.h early: chsd ldrs tl wl over 2f out: sn struggling u.p: wl btn over 1f out* **33/1**
6064 7 ¾ **Princess Shamal**[30] 4210 3-8-5 **49**.... IvaMilickova 10 12
(J R Jenkins) *in tch on outer: rdn and struggling 1/2-way: wl btn fr wl over 1f out* **25/1**
000- 8 28 **Diamond Affair (IRE)**[316] 6554 3-8-4 **48**.... KirstyMilczarek 8 —
(M G Quinlan) *restless in stalls: w ldrs tl rdn and struggling over 2f out: bhd and eased fr over 1f out: t.o* **66/1**

1m 10.92s (-1.78) **Going Correction** -0.325s/f (Firm) **8** Ran SP% **114.6**
Speed ratings (Par 98): **98,95,93,88,86 79,78,41**
toteswingers:1&2 £3.60, 2&3 £3.40, 1&3 £2.10 CSF £15.99 TOTE £6.60: £2.90, £1.10, £2.20; EX 20.60.
Owner Linkslade Lottery **Bred** James Waldron **Trained** Lambourn, Berks

FOCUS
Few got into this weakish handicap and the first pair were always 1-2 on the rail.
Freedom Pass(USA) Official explanation: jockey said filly hung left-handed

Elsie's Orphan Official explanation: jockey said filly lost an off-fore shoe

5207 INSPECTION SERVICES (UK) H'CAP 5f

7:00 (7:02) (Class 5) (0-75,74) 3-Y-O+ **£2,388** (£529; £529) **Stalls** Low

Form				RPR
346	1		**Love You Louis**[77] 2639 4-9-11 **74**........ PatDobbs 1 (J R Jenkins) *chsd ldrs and hld stands' rail: rdn and ev ch wl over 1f out: led 1f out: hld on wl u.p* **7/2**[2]	79
4010	2	hd	**Littlemisssunshine (IRE)**[47] 3637 5-9-5 **68**........(t) LiamKeniry 6 (T B P Coles) *trckd ldrs gng wl: ev ch ent fnl 2f: led over 1f out: rdn and hdd 1f out: kpt on u.p: a jst hld ins fnl f* **20/1**	72
-414	2	dht	**Luminous Gold**[20] 4518 5-9-11 **74**........ AlanMunro 4 (C F Wall) *sn niggled along in tch in last pair: swtchd rt and hdwy over 1f out: kpt on wl u.p ins fnl f: nt quite rch wnr* **13/8**[1]	78+
3436	4	3/4	**Wanchai Whisper**[2] 5151 3-8-8 **64**........(p) KierenFox[(5)] 5 (P R Hedger) *stdd and short of room sn after s: in tch in last: nt clr run ent fnl 2f tl hmpd and lost grnd over 1f out: rdn and rallied 1f out: keeping on whn nt clr run again fnl 75yds: nvr able to chal* **10/1**	65+
0000	5	3	**Step It Up (IRE)**[27] 4292 6-9-3 **66**........ PatCosgrave 2 (J R Boyle) *led tl rdn and hdd over 1f out: wknd ins fnl f* **7/2**[2]	57
0520	6	9	**Edith's Boy (IRE)**[27] 4292 4-8-5 **61**........ AdamBeschizza[(7)] 7 (S Dow) *chsd ldrs on outer: rdn ent fnl 2f: wknd qckly over 1f out: wl btn ins fnl f* **5/1**[3]	19

59.60 secs (-0.40) **Going Correction** -0.325s/f (Firm)
WFA 3 from 4yo+ 2lb **6** Ran SP% **113.1**
CSF £29.83 CT £75.84 TOTE £2.80: £1.10; EX 37.70 27.

FOCUS
A competitive sprint handicap, but it was steadily run with a bunch finish. The winner was back to his early-season form.
Wanchai Whisper Official explanation: jockey said filly slipped and stumbled 1 1/2f out
Edith's Boy(IRE) Official explanation: jockey said gelding ran flat

5208 RSA ENVIRONMENTAL HEALTH H'CAP 1m 4f

7:30 (7:30) (Class 5) (0-70,66) 3-Y-O+ **£2,388** (£705; £352) **Stalls** Low

Form				RPR
443	1		**Minikin (IRE)**[16] 4661 3-9-6 **66**........ SteveDrowne 10 (H Morrison) *t.k.h: chsd ldr tl led 9f out: set stdy gallop tl rdn and qcknd 2f out: sn clr w runner-up: r.o wl and in command fnl 100yds: readily* **11/4**[1]	76+
003	2	2	**Isobar (GER)**[24] 4414 4-9-12 **62**........ J-PGuillambert 2 (L M Cumani) *led after 1f tl 9f out: chsd wnr tl over 6f out: trckd ldrs after tl rdn and qcknd to press wnr over 1f out: no ex and btn ins fnl f* **11/4**[1]	69+
062	3	3	**Joan D'Arc (IRE)**[7] 4972 3-8-12 **65**........ AdamBeschizza[(7)] 7 (M G Quinlan) *in tch in midfield: rdn and unable qck w ldng pair 2f out: kpt on ins fnl f: nvr gng pce to threaten ldrs* **7/1**[3]	67+
4504	4	3/4	**Thundering Home**[12] 4793 3-9-1 **61**........ FergusSweeney 6 (M J Attwater) *stdd s: t.k.h: hld up in last trio: hdwy 6f out: rdn and chsd ldng pair over 1f out: sn no imp: lost 3rd wl ins fnl f* **16/1**	62
0621	5	1 3/4	**Diamond Twister (USA)**[12] 4793 4-9-9 **64**........ KierenFox[(5)] 8 (J R Best) *t.k.h: chsd ldrs: wnt 2nd over 6f out tl rdn and nt gng pce of ldng pair 2f out: wl hld ins fnl f* **7/1**[3]	62
4346	6	1 3/4	**Locum**[40] 3860 5-9-11 **61**........ DarryllHolland 9 (M H Tompkins) *hld up in tch in last pair: rdn and outpcd ent fnl 2f: no ch w ldrs after* **4/1**[2]	56
406	7	2 1/2	**Aegean King**[29] 4227 4-9-9 **59**........ StephenCraine 1 (M Wigham) *s.i.s: hld up in last pair: rdn and immediately outpcd whn pce qcknd 2f out: no ch after* **12/1**	50
1/0-	8	1 1/4	**Yab Adee**[324] 6342 6-9-4 **61**........ KatiaScallan[(7)] 3 (M P Tregoning) *hld up wl in tch: c wd and rdn ent fnl 2f: sn outpcd and wl btn over 1f out* **40/1**	50

2m 46.62s (5.72) **Going Correction** +0.175s/f (Good)
WFA 3 from 4yo+ 10lb **8** Ran SP% **114.3**
Speed ratings (Par 103): **87,85,83,83,82 80,79,78**
CSF £10.23 CT £46.02 TOTE £2.90: £1.10, £1.40, £2.70; EX 11.20.
Owner Mrs Sonia Rogers **Bred** Airlie Stud **Trained** East Ilsley, Berks

FOCUS
There wasn't much pace on here and little got into it with the front pair nearly always 1-2. Both can do better.
Locum Official explanation: jockey said gelding ran too freely

5209 QUALITY LEISURE MANAGEMENT LEISURESAFE MAIDEN STKS 1m 1f 149y

8:00 (8:00) (Class 5) 3-Y-O+ **£2,729** (£806; £403) **Stalls** Centre

Form				RPR
4333	1		**Best Intent**[27] 4294 3-8-12 73........ JackMitchell 4 (M A Jarvis) *chsd ldr: rdn to chal over 2f out: led wl over 1f out: edgd lft u.p ent fnl f: kpt on: rdn out* **15/8**[2]	72+
422	2	3/4	**Fascination (IRE)**[43] 3754 3-8-12 75........ PatDobbs 6 (M L W Bell) *led tl rdn and hdd wl over 1f out: rallied u.p ins fnl f: no imp fnl 75yds* **4/6**[1]	70+
/0-0	3	4 1/2	**Derby Desire (IRE)**[27] 4298 6-8-13 33........ AdamBeschizza[(7)] 2 (D Donovan) *chsd ldng pair thrght: rdn and outpcd over 2f out: kpt on same pce after* **100/1**	61?
3	4	3	**Astound**[15] 4679 3-8-9 70........ MartinLane[(3)] 1 (P D Evans) *stdd s: hld up in last pair: hdwy 4f out: outpcd and rdn over 2f out: no ch w ldrs fnl 2f* **9/1**[3]	55
0000	5	21	**Kalligal**[12] 4776 5-9-6 40........ SteveDrowne 5 (R Ingram) *taken down early: t.k.h: hld up in midfield: rdn over 2f out: sn btn: wl bhd and eased ins fnl f* **100/1**	—
	6	1 1/4	**Cotton King** 3-9-3 0........(t) TomMcLaughlin 3 (T B P Coles) *s.i.s: alway last: pushed along over 6f out: lost tch wl over 2f out* **33/1**	—

2m 5.85s (0.95) **Going Correction** +0.175s/f (Good)
WFA 3 from 5yo+ 8lb **6** Ran SP% **109.7**
Speed ratings (Par 103): **103,102,98,96,79 78**
CSF £3.28 TOTE £5.10: £3.00, £1.02; EX 3.50 Place 6: £7.57 Place 5: £6.91 .
Owner Lordship Stud **Bred** Lordship Stud **Trained** Newmarket, Suffolk

FOCUS
A straight match on paper. Neither was at their best in a slowly run race.
T/Plt: £10.90 to a £1 stake. Pool of £54,825.59 - 3,643.72 winning units. T/Qpdt: £2.40 to a £1 stake. Pool of £5,006.44 -1,482.23 winning units. SP

4947 HAMILTON (R-H)

Wednesday, August 18

OFFICIAL GOING: Good (good to firm in places; 9.3)
Straight course far rail dolled out to rest ground and all distances as advertised.
Wind: Almost nil Weather: Overcast, showery

5210 EUROPEAN BREEDERS' FUND MAIDEN STKS 6f 5y

1:55 (1:55) (Class 5) 2-Y-O **£3,561** (£1,059; £529; £264) **Stalls** Low

Form				RPR
5	1		**Cape Of Dance (IRE)**[12] 4782 2-8-12 0........ JoeFanning 5 (M Johnston) *w ldr: rdn over 1f out: led ins fnl f: styd on wl* **11/4**[2]	74
62	2	1/2	**Calypso Magic (IRE)**[37] 3945 2-8-12 0........ IanBrennan[(5)] 4 (J Howard Johnson) *t.k.h: led: edgd rt thrght: rdn over 1f out: hdd ins fnl f: hld towards fin* **1/3**[1]	78
0	3	1 3/4	**Ted's Brother (IRE)**[14] 4702 2-8-12 0........ MarkCoumbe[(5)] 2 (R C Guest) *t.k.h: cl up: rdn and edgd rt over 1f out: kpt on same pce fnl f* **125/1**	72
	4	9	**Moonboughie** 2-8-12 0........ DuranFentiman 3 (T D Walford) *dwlt and wnt bdly rt s: outpcd and bhd: lost tch fnl 2f* **33/1**[3]	40

1m 13.17s (0.97) **Going Correction** -0.10s/f (Good) **4** Ran SP% **105.4**
Speed ratings (Par 94): **89,88,86,74**
CSF £3.93 TOTE £2.90; EX 4.90.
Owner Sheikh Hamdan Bin Mohammed Al Maktoum **Bred** Peter And Jackie Grimes **Trained** Middleham Moor, N Yorks

FOCUS
A modest maiden, run at a fair pace.

NOTEBOOK
Cape Of Dance(IRE), who comes from the family of Main Aim, certainly improved from her debut run at Haydock where she ran very green. Showing a willing attitude, she can improve from this and should stay 7f in due course. (op 3-1)
Calypso Magic(IRE), who had made the running last time out, still looked green in front and continued to hang towards the centre of the track. He should be able to shed his maiden tag in nurseries, which looks the route to go with him (op 2-7 tchd 4-11 in places)
Ted's Brother(IRE), who failed to beat a horse home on his debut at Newcastle recently, showed up a lot better here and he also looks the type for nurseries.
Moonboughie was always struggling after a slow start and can only be watched for the time being.

5211 TENTS & EVENTS H'CAP 6f 5y

2:30 (2:31) (Class 6) (0-65,65) 3-Y-O **£2,047** (£604; £302) **Stalls** Centre

Form				RPR
31	1		**Henry Morgan**[18] 4584 3-9-2 **60**........ JoeFanning 4 (B Smart) *pressed ldr: rdn to ld over 1f out: kpt on wl ins fnl f: comf* **9/4**[1]	67
2434	2	1	**Monte Mayor One**[11] 4820 3-8-12 **61**........(p) DaleSwift[(5)] 6 (P Monteith) *prom: effrt and rdn 2f out: chsd wnr ins fnl f: r.o* **5/1**[3]	65
0201	3	3/4	**Amoureuse**[16] 4649 3-7-11 **48**........ NeilFarley[(7)] 1 (D Carroll) *t.k.h: led tl edgd rt and hdd over 1f out: kpt on same pce ins fnl f* **6/1**	49
-006	4	3 3/4	**Pycian**[25] 4365 3-9-2 **65**........ IanBrennan[(5)] 2 (Mrs L Stubbs) *trckd ldrs: drvn over 2f out: one pce fr over 1f out* **9/1**	54
3043	5	hd	**Weetentherty**[11] 4826 3-8-3 **47**........ DuranFentiman 5 (J S Goldie) *chsd ldng gp: rdn and outpcd 1/2-way: rallied u.p over 1f out: nvr able to chal* **12/1**	36
0366	6	4	**Saxby (IRE)**[10] 4866 3-9-5 **63**........(v[1]) SilvestreDeSousa 3 (G A Harker) *prom tl rdn and wknd fr 2f out: eased whn no ch ins fnl f* **5/2**[2]	39
-600	7	3/4	**Olympic Ceremony**[21] 4482 3-9-6 **64**........ AndrewMullen 8 (Miss Tracy Waggott) *dwlt: bhd: rdn 1/2-way: nvr on terms* **33/1**	38

1m 11.48s (-0.72) **Going Correction** -0.10s/f (Good) **7** Ran SP% **110.9**
Speed ratings (Par 98): **100,98,97,92,92 87,86**
toteswingers:1&2 £3.00, 2&3 £2.00, 1&3 £2.60 CSF £13.02 CT £54.84 TOTE £3.20: £1.60, £3.80; EX 10.90.
Owner Mrs F Denniff **Bred** A S Denniff **Trained** Hambleton, N Yorks

FOCUS
A weak handicap, run at an even pace. Sound form.

5212 BOOK NOW FOR FORCES AND SERVICES NIGHT CLAIMING STKS 5f 4y

3:05 (3:06) (Class 6) 3-Y-O+ **£2,047** (£604; £302) **Stalls** Centre

Form				RPR
2150	1		**Lesley's Choice**[7] 4952 4-9-4 73........(b) LNewman 7 (Miss L A Perratt) *prom: rdn and drifted rt over 1f out: led ins fnl f: hld on wl* **4/1**[3]	80
0002	2	hd	**Northern Bolt**[11] 4833 5-8-10 75........(b[1]) DaleSwift[(5)] 5 (I W McInnes) *prom: rdn over 2f out: hdwy over 1f out: kpt on ins fnl f: jst hld* **5/1**	76
2232	3	1/2	**Mandarin Spirit (IRE)**[7] 4952 10-8-12 65........(b) SilvestreDeSousa 1 (Miss L A Perratt) *led stands' side: rdn 2f out: hdd ins fnl f: no ex towards fin* **11/4**[2]	71
0121	4	2 3/4	**Desperate Dan**[12] 4776 9-9-0 77........(v) JoeFanning 2 (A B Haynes) *hld up in tch: rdn over 2f out: edgd rt over 1f out: r.o: nvr able to chal* **2/1**[1]	64
4300	5	1/2	**Distant Sun (USA)**[5] 5048 6-8-13 71........ IanBrennan[(5)] 6 (Miss L A Perratt) *stdd s: hld up in tch: rdn and edgd rt 2f out: sn no imp* **9/1**	66
4006	6	3 1/2	**Rothesay Dancer**[7] 4952 7-8-8 69........ GaryBartley[(3)] 4 (J S Goldie) *bhd: drvn and outpcd 1/2-way: nvr on terms* **11/1**	46
-030	7	3 1/2	**Angelofthenorth**[20] 4516 8-8-6 45........ AndrewElliott 3 (C J Teague) *in tch: outpcd and hung rt 1/2-way: sn wknd* **66/1**	29
000	8	hd	**Princess Charlmane (IRE)**[6] 4982 7-8-2 48 ow1..(vt[1]) DeanHeslop[(5)] 8 (C J Teague) *chsd ldrs tl rdn and wknd wl over 1f out* **150/1**	29

59.11 secs (-0.89) **Going Correction** -0.10s/f (Good) **8** Ran SP% **117.2**
Speed ratings (Par 101): **103,102,101,97,96 91,85,85**
toteswingers:1&2 £3.10, 2&3 £3.30, 1&3 £2.50 CSF £24.97 TOTE £5.30: £1.10, £2.60, £1.30; EX 22.30.
Owner Jackton Racing Club **Bred** B C Allen **Trained** East Kilbride, South Lanarks

FOCUS
A competitive claimer and a tight three-way finish. The winner is the best guide to the form.

5213 COSMIC CASES SCOTTISH TROPHY SERIES FINAL STKS (H'CAP) 1m 1f 36y
3:40 (3:42) (Class 3) 3-Y-0+ £7,771 (£2,312; £1,155; £577) Stalls High

Form RPR
06-1 1 **Belle Noverre (IRE)**[6] 5015 6-9-2 70 MHarley(5) 10 84
(Shaun Harley, Ire) *in tch: smooth hdwy to ld 3f out: rdn clr over 1f out: edgd lft ins fnl f: kpt on wl* 6/1[3]
1634 2 2 **Raleigh Quay (IRE)**[14] 4710 3-9-2 72 JoeFanning 13 82+
(Micky Hammond) *midfield: effrt and swtchd over 2f out: hdwy to chse wnr over 1f out: kpt on: no imp* 16/1
4403 3 4 ½ **Veroon (IRE)**[18] 4585 4-9-5 73 DaleSwift(5) 8 74
(J G Given) *prom: effrt and chsd wnr over 2f out to over 1f out: sn no ex* 4/1[2]
1431 4 1 ¾ **Daring Dream (GER)**[18] 4602 5-9-4 70 GaryBartley(3) 3 67
(J S Goldie) *dwlt: bhd: hdwy on outside over 2f out: no imp ins fnl f* 9/1
0211 5 1 ¼ **Fujin Dancer (FR)**[7] 4939 5-9-8 78 6ex (p) JulieBurke(7) 7 72
(K A Ryan) *hld up: smooth hdwy and in tch over 3f out: rdn and one pce fnl 2f* 12/1
113 6 2 ¼ **Applaude**[11] 4852 5-9-2 65 (b) PaulEddery 11 55
(R C Guest) *hld up: hdwy and in tch over 2f out: sn rdn and nt qckn* 20/1
3111 7 ½ **High Resolution**[18] 4585 3-9-5 75 SilvestreDeSousa 14 63
(Miss L A Perratt) *hld up: effrt on outside over 2f out: nvr able to chal* 11/4[1]
6362 8 ½ **Finsbury**[7] 4949 7-9-2 65 AndrewElliott 12 52
(Miss L A Perratt) *taken early to post: hld up: rdn over 3f out: sme hdwy over 1f out: n.d* 16/1
2346 9 10 **Royal Straight**[18] 4585 5-9-7 70 LNewman 1 36
(Miss L A Perratt) *prom: effrt and ev ch 3f out: wknd 2f out* 16/1
3665 10 ½ **King Of The Moors (USA)**[26] 4088 7-8-11 65 (b) MarkCoumbe(5) 5 30
(R C Guest) *missed break: bhd: rdn over 2f out: nvr on terms* 25/1
6062 11 1 **Shy Glance (USA)**[11] 4823 8-8-8 62 (p) DeanHeslop(5) 2 25
(P Monteith) *trckd ldrs tl rdn and wknd over 2f out* 22/1
-300 12 4 **Cigalas**[108] 1717 5-8-6 55 AndrewMullen 16 10
(Mrs J C McGregor) *led tl edgd lft and hdd 3f out: sn wknd* 66/1
6000 13 6 **Al Wasef (USA)**[11] 4824 5-8-2 56 (v[1]) IanBrennan(5) 6 —
(J S Goldie) *in tch: rdn over 4f out: wknd over 2f out* 80/1
5255 14 32 **Talk Of Saafend (IRE)**[11] 4823 5-8-5 59 (p) LanceBetts(5) 4 —
(P Monteith) *w ldr tl wknd qckly over 3f out: lost tch and eased fnl 2f* 16/1

1m 56.17s (-3.53) **Going Correction** -0.20s/f (Firm)
WFA 3 from 4yo+ 7lb 14 Ran SP% **117.9**
Speed ratings (Par 107): **107,105,101,99,98 96,96,95,86,86 85,81,76,48**
toteswingers:1&2 £11.80, 2&3 £16.40, 1&3 £4.90 CSF £90.07 CT £432.67 TOTE £6.90: £2.30, £4.30, £1.70; EX 119.60.
Owner Lough Derg Syndicate **Bred** Rozelle Bloodstock **Trained** Letterkenny, Co. Donegal

FOCUS
A modest handicap, run at a frantic pace. The winner is rated back to her old Irish best.

NOTEBOOK
Belle Noverre(IRE) deserves plenty of credit as she was never too far away and won with plenty in hand. A previous C&D winner, the 6-y-o has been busy of late but is holding her form very well. However, she will be set for a fair hike in the weights and it will require a career best once the handicapper has had his say. (op 17-2)
Raleigh Quay(IRE), 3lb higher for his win at Musselburgh in June, ran a solid race. Still lightly raced, he can win again and was unlucky to run into a well handicapped horse. (op 14-1)
Veroon(IRE), back to his last winning mark, ran up to form here but holds no secrets from the handicapper. (op 9-2 tchd 7-2)
Daring Dream(GER), 3lb higher for his Thirsk win, stayed on well and remains in good form. (op 8-1)
Fujin Dancer(FR), a winner of a seller and a claimer on his last two starts, ran well under top weight. (op 11-1)
High Resolution was looking for his fourth straight win, but could never get involved and will need to bounce back. Official explanation: jockey said gelding never travelled (op 7-2)
King Of The Moors(USA) Official explanation: jockey said gelding was reluctant to race

5214 HAMILTON-PARK.CO.UK MAIDEN STKS 6f 5y
4:15 (4:16) (Class 5) 3-Y-0+ £2,729 (£806; £403) Stalls Centre

Form RPR
030- 1 **Stellarina (IRE)**[436] 2769 4-8-8 63 JulieBurke(7) 1 59
(K A Ryan) *mde virtually all: rdn and edgd rt fr 2f out: hld on wl ins fnl f* 11/2[3]
06-3 2 nk **Hambleton**[11] 4853 3-9-3 58 JoeFanning 6 63
(B Smart) *disp ld thrght: rdn over 1f out: blkd ins fnl f: kpt on: hld nr fin* 11/8[1]
34- 3 ¾ **Benny The Bear**[364] 5157 3-8-12 0 IanBrennan(5) 5 61
(James Moffatt) *rrd s: t.k.h and sn prom: effrt and rdn over 1f out: hung rt: kpt on ins fnl f* 6/1
0240 4 2 ¾ **Bahamian Jazz (IRE)**[14] 4714 3-9-3 70 SilvestreDeSousa 2 52
(R Bastiman) *in tch: sn drvn along: rallied wl over 1f out: no imp ins fnl f* 85/40[2]
0-06 5 8 **Frill A Minute**[34] 4064 6-8-10 32 DaleSwift(5) 4 21
(Miss L C Siddall) *chsd ldrs tl rdn and wknd over 2f out* 80/1
2460 6 8 **Clare Harrier (IRE)**[32] 4127 3-8-10 56 VictorSantos(7) 3 —
(A Berry) *dwlt: bhd and sn struggling: no ch fr 1/2-way* 25/1

1m 12.63s (0.43) **Going Correction** -0.10s/f (Good)
WFA 3 from 4yo+ 3lb 6 Ran SP% **108.9**
Speed ratings (Par 103): **93,92,91,87,77 66**
toteswingers:1&2 £2.10, 2&3 £2.00, 1&3 £2.40 CSF £12.74 TOTE £5.90: £2.20, £1.10; EX 19.20.
Owner S Rudolf **Bred** Patrick F Kelly **Trained** Hambleton, N Yorks

FOCUS
A weak maiden run in a slow time. It has been rated around the runner-up.

5215 GRIFFITHS & ARMOUR H'CAP 1m 4f 17y
4:50 (4:51) (Class 5) (0-70,76) 3-Y-0+ £2,914 (£867; £433; £216) Stalls High

Form RPR
0101 1 **Epic (IRE)**[7] 4953 3-9-10 76 6ex (b) JoeFanning 2 85+
(M Johnston) *prom: rdn over 2f out: led over 1f out: edgd rt: styd on strly* 5/2[1]
4126 2 1 ¾ **Graceful Descent (FR)**[17] 4619 5-9-11 70 GaryBartley(3) 9 76
(J S Goldie) *cl up: led over 2f out to over 1f out: kpt on u.p ins fnl f* 5/1[2]
3005 3 nk **Red Kestrel (USA)**[12] 4781 5-9-4 67 JulieBurke(7) 12 73
(K A Ryan) *led 2f: cl up: drvn and outpcd over 4f out: rallied 2f out: styd on wl towards fin* 16/1
6313 4 ½ **Patavium (IRE)**[22] 4449 7-9-9 70 DaleSwift(5) 11 75
(E W Tuer) *led after 2f to over 3f out: rallied: kpt on same pce ins fnl f* 12/1
1213 5 1 ¼ **Amir Pasha (UAE)**[7] 4945 5-9-3 66 (p) AdamCarter(7) 6 69
(Micky Hammond) *trckd ldrs: drvn 3f out: kpt on same pce over 1f out* 15/2[3]
52-1 6 1 ¾ **Sovento (GER)**[32] 4158 6-9-0 61 MHarley(5) 1 61
(Shaun Harley, Ire) *hld up: drvn and effrt on outside over 2f out: edgd rt and no imp over 1f out* 15/2[3]
1042 7 shd **Regent's Secret (USA)**[7] 4953 10-8-11 58 IanBrennan(5) 7 58
(J S Goldie) *s.i.s: hld up: rdn over 2f out: sme late hdwy: nvr rchd ldrs* 8/1
4-45 8 shd **Helieorbea**[21] 4481 4-9-10 66 (b[1]) DuranFentiman 5 66
(T D Easterby) *in tch tl edgd rt and outpcd fr 2f out* 25/1
5630 9 hd **King's Head (IRE)**[24] 4405 7-9-5 61 LNewman 8 60
(Miss L A Perratt) *hld up: pushed along 3f out: styd on ins fnl f: nvr on terms* 40/1
5504 10 3 **Casino Night**[13] 4752 5-9-1 57 SilvestreDeSousa 3 51
(G A Harker) *in tch tl drvn and wknd fr 2f out* 5/1[2]
00-5 11 57 **Decimus Meridius (IRE)**[103] 1866 3-8-8 60 AndrewElliott 10 —
(J Howard Johnson) *t.k.h: midfield: rdn and struggling over 5f out: t.o* 50/1

2m 35.72s (-2.88) **Going Correction** -0.20s/f (Firm)
WFA 3 from 4yo+ 10lb 11 Ran SP% **118.4**
Speed ratings (Par 103): **101,99,99,99,98 97,97,97,97,95 57**
toteswingers:1&2 £4.10, 2&3 £16.70, 1&3 £15.50 CSF £14.45 CT £167.23 TOTE £3.60: £2.50, £2.30, £8.30; EX 16.80.
Owner Racegoers Club Owners Group **Bred** P D Savill **Trained** Middleham Moor, N Yorks

FOCUS
Not a bad handicap for the grade, and it was well run. Sound form but the winner only needed to match his previous best.

5216 RACING UK H'CAP 1m 3f 16y
5:20 (5:21) (Class 6) (0-55,55) 3-Y-0+ £2,047 (£604; £302) Stalls High

Form RPR
2333 1 **Sharp Sovereign (USA)**[18] 4582 4-9-3 52 SilvestreDeSousa 13 64
(T D Barron) *t.k.h: led 3f: led again 1/2-way: rdn and edgd rt 2f out: hld on gamely fnl f* 11/8[1]
4462 2 ¾ **Vittachi**[50] 3532 3-8-5 54 LanceBetts(5) 7 65
(A C Whillans) *hld up: rdn and hdwy 3f out: chsd wnr over 1f out: r.o fnl f* 5/1[3]
5440 3 4 ½ **Croix Rouge (USA)**[196] 383 8-9-2 54 RobertLButler(3) 4 57
(R J Smith) *hld up in midfield: smooth hdwy to trck ldrs over 3f out: rdn and edgd rt 2f out: sn outpcd* 14/1
5043 4 6 **Roman History (IRE)**[21] 4484 7-8-13 48 (p) AndrewMullen 8 41
(Miss Tracy Waggott) *in tch: drvn over 3f out: outpcd fnl 2f* 14/1
0003 5 3 ¼ **Real Desire**[11] 4823 4-8-13 51 PatrickDonaghy(3) 6 38
(P Monteith) *hld up: rdn over 3f out: plugged on fnl f: nvr on terms* 14/1
5640 6 1 ¼ **Papa's Princess**[28] 4246 6-8-10 45 PaulEddery 9 30
(James Moffatt) *bhd: drvn over 3f out: nvr rchd ldrs* 20/1
5400 7 ½ **Goodison Park**[11] 4823 3-8-3 52 ow6 (p) DeanHeslop(5) 1 36
(A G Foster) *dwlt: hdwy into midfield after 4f: rdn and wknd over 3f out* 25/1
4400 8 2 ¼ **Step To It (IRE)**[15] 4687 3-8-1 52 (p) JulieBurke(7) 12 33
(K A Ryan) *led after 3f to 1/2-way: cl up tl wknd 2f out* 40/1
6000 9 ½ **Fantastic Favour**[33] 4120 3-8-11 55 AndrewElliott 5 35
(Jedd O'Keeffe) *t.k.h: trckd ldrs tl wknd fr 3f out* 40/1
-051 10 1 ¼ **Short Supply (USA)**[18] 4582 4-9-2 51 DuranFentiman 11 29
(T D Walford) *in tch: lost pl 1/2-way: effrt u.p over 3f out: sn btn* 9/2[2]
3000 11 hd **Henry Havelock**[11] 4854 3-8-1 50 ow1 (p) IanBrennan(5) 3 27
(C Grant) *chsd ldrs: rdn over 4f out: wknd over 3f out* 10/1

2m 22.86s (-2.74) **Going Correction** -0.20s/f (Firm)
WFA 3 from 4yo+ 9lb 11 Ran SP% **119.5**
Speed ratings (Par 101): **101,100,97,92,90 89,89,87,87,86 86**
toteswingers:1&2 £2.40, 2&3 £8.30, 1&3 £6.50 CSF £7.90 CT £68.17 TOTE £2.30: £1.10, £2.60, £4.30; EX 9.40 Place 6: £84.40 Place 5: £20.81.
Owner Raymond Miquel **Bred** James Sumter Carter **Trained** Maunby, N Yorks

FOCUS
A weak handicap and the first pair came clear. The form is not that solid and cannot be rated that positively.
Short Supply(USA) Official explanation: jockey said filly never travelled
T/Plt: £162.70 to a £1 stake. Pool of £38,549.57 - 172.86 winning tickets. T/Qpdt: £21.90 to a £1 stake. Pool of £3,956.95 - 133.30 winning tickets. RY

5183 YORK (L-H)
Wednesday, August 18

OFFICIAL GOING: Good (good to firm in places; 7.2)
Course at inner configuration and all distances as advertised.
Wind: Moderate across Weather: Cloudy with sunny periods

5217 TOTESPORT.COM STKS (H'CAP) 1m 4f
1:45 (1:45) (Class 2) (0-100,100) 3-Y-0+ £19,428 (£5,781; £2,889; £1,443) Stalls Centre

Form RPR
6210 1 **The Fonz**[46] 3672 4-9-5 87 KierenFallon 10 97
(Sir Michael Stoute) *lw: hld up towards rr: hdwy on outer 3f out: effrt over 2f out: rdn to ld wl over 1f out: drvn ent fnl f: edgd lft and hld on wl towards fin* 10/1
6600 2 ½ **Dazzling Light (UAE)**[25] 4393 5-8-9 77 TedDurcan 8 86
(J S Goldie) *hld up in rr: hdwy 3f out: chsd ldrs and n.m.r over 1f out: rdn and nt clr run ent fnl f: sn drvn and ev ch tl no ex towards fin* 33/1
2042 3 ¾ **Life And Soul (IRE)**[11] 4815 3-8-10 88 PhilipRobinson 17 96
(Mrs A J Perrett) *lw: t.k.h: trckd ldrs: hdwy 3f out: chal 2f out: sn rdn and ev ch whn edgd rt ent fnl f: drvn and one pce last 100yds* 5/1[1]
-514 4 1 ¼ **Times Up**[24] 4400 4-9-13 95 JamieSpencer 2 101+
(J L Dunlop) *hld up and bhd: hdwy over 2f out: effrt whn nt clr run and swtchd lft over 1f out: nt clr run again ins fnl f: sn swtchd lft and kpt on wl towards fin* 10/1
1323 5 1 ½ **Satwa Moon (USA)**[22] 4455 4-9-2 84 JimCrowley 16 87
(E A L Dunlop) *chsd ldrs on outer: cl up 4f out: rdn along 3f out: drvn and n.m.r over 1f out: kpt on same pce ins fnl f* 7/1[2]
-130 6 nk **Thin Red Line (IRE)**[46] 3672 4-9-12 94 TomEaves 3 97+
(M Dods) *hld up and bhd: hdwy over 2f out: nt clr run wl over 1f out: sn rdn and kpt on ins fnl f: nrst fin* 20/1

4121 **7** *hd* **Tepmokea (IRE)**[18] 4570 4-9-4 **86** WilliamBuick 4 89
(R A Fahey) *t.k.h: chsd ldrs: rdn along and n.m.r over 2f out: kpt on ins fnl f* **8/1**

4255 **8** *1 1/2* **Antigua Sunrise (IRE)**[25] 4389 4-8-10 **78** PaulMulrennan 13 78
(R A Fahey) *in tch: rdn along and sltly outpcd over 2f out: kpt on ins fnl f* **16/1**

-510 **9** *hd* **Anhar (USA)**[22] 4461 3-9-8 **100** (t) FrankieDettori 5 100+
(Saeed Bin Suroor) *s.i.s and bhd: hdwy on inner over 3f out: rdn to chal 2f out: sn drvn and ch tl wknd ent fnl f* **17/2**

2121 **10** *nse* **Chilly Filly (IRE)**[8] 4933 4-9-7 **89** 6ex GregFairley 14 89
(M Johnston) *lw: trckd ldrs: hdwy 3f out: rdn to ld briefly over 2f out: drvn and hdd wl over 1f out: wknd ent fnl f* **15/2**[3]

346 **11** *hd* **Sedgwick**[18] 4594 8-8-3 **76** oh1 DeclanCannon(5) 11 75
(S A Harris) *hld up towards rr: effrt and sme hdwy 3f out: rdn along over 2f out: n.d* **50/1**

6066 **12** *3 3/4* **Sohcahtoa (IRE)**[26] 4320 4-9-1 **83** (b) RichardHughes 9 76
(R Hannon) *prom: hdwy and cl up 3f out: sn rdn and wknd 2f out* **25/1**

3030 **13** *5* **Crackentorp**[25] 4393 5-9-7 **89** RobertWinston 6 74
(T D Easterby) *in tch: hdwy 3f out: rdn along over 2f out: sn drvn and wknd* **12/1**

4163 **14** *1/2* **Aphrodisia**[25] 4389 6-9-1 **83** EddieAhern 15 68+
(Ian Williams) *in tch: rdn along to chse ldrs 3f out: wkng whn hmpd over 1f out* **40/1**

1011 **15** *1 1/2* **Yorgunnabelucky (USA)**[11] 4818 4-9-12 **94** (p) HayleyTurner 18 76
(M Johnston) *lw: led: rdn along 3f out: drvn and hdd over 2f out: sn wknd* **12/1**

5010 **16** *1 1/4* **Think Its All Over (USA)**[13] 4751 3-8-0 **78** ow1 FrannyNorton 1 58
(T P Tate) *chsd ldrs: hdwy over 3f out: rdn over 2f out: sn drvn and wknd* **25/1**

2m 33.06s (-0.14) **Going Correction** +0.125s/f (Good)
WFA 3 from 4yo+ 10lb 16 Ran SP% **121.8**
Speed ratings (Par 109): **105,104,104,103,102 102,102,101,100,100 100,98,94,94,93 92**
toteswingers:1&2 £87.80, 2&3 £45.20, 1&3 £11.10 CSF £321.97 CT £1855.26 TOTE £10.70: £2.30, £8.40, £1.60, £3.90 Trifecta £1451.90 Pool: £3198.15 - 1.63 winning units..
Owner Anthony & David de Rothschild **Bred** Southcourt Stud **Trained** Newmarket, Suffolk
■ Stewards' Enquiry : Philip Robinson two-day ban: careless riding (Sep 1-2)

FOCUS
The breeze had a drying effect on the racing surface, which was described as good, good to firm in places before the opening event. Four different jockeys after the race offered differing views on the ground. This decent handicap was run at nothing more than an even gallop, which resulted in plenty of the field taking a strong grip in behind. As had seemed to be the case of the previous day, racing up the stands' side looked an advantage. Solid form which should work out. The progressive winner is up 4lb.

NOTEBOOK
The Fonz, down the field when last seen in the Old Newton Cup, a place in front of Thin Red Line, was under pressure over 3f out, but Fallon kept pushing his mount along and steadily drew his rivals off the bridle as he edged to the front. This performance strongly suggests he has stamina rather than speed, and a step up in trip may be ideal, possibly with a race like the Mallard Handicap at Doncaster an ideal target. However, connections reported afterwards that his poor effort at Haydock had been put down to the horse returning too quickly to the track after a success seven days previously, so there is a chance he will be given plenty of time to get over this. Official explanation: trainer said, regarding apparent improvement in form, that the gelding was suited by a more experienced rider. (op 12-1)
Dazzling Light(UAE), who was well beaten over 2m last time when racing too freely, kept on bravely throughout the latter stages despite being crowded between two horses. She is an infrequent winner, and this good effort will see her go up the weights, which will make her life hard.
Life And Soul(IRE), running against his elders for the first time, has form tied in with St Leger fancy Dandino, so it was not difficult so see why he attracted support. Close up but keen throughout, this was almost certainly a good performance and he can win a decent race if learning to settle much better. (op 11-2)
Times Up, representing a trainer with a fair record in this contest, might have won had Spencer been able to get a clear run, but the combination was blocked in behind the three that finished in front of him at a crucial stage over 1f out. Official explanation: jockey said gelding suffered interference in running (op 11-1)
Satwa Moon(USA) has proved to be consistent this season and was back up in trip after a good effort over shorter at Glorious Goodwood. Kept towards the centre of the course, he found more for pressure and appeared to stay this trip, which should give connections more options. (op 13-2)
Thin Red Line(IRE) could be spotted going really well up the home straight, but lacked a bit of room at stages. This was a better run than last time, and he will be of interest in a large-field contest before the end of the season, although he is reported to be not the biggest and may struggle to carry big weights in decent events. (op 14-1)
Tepmokea(IRE), raised 4lb for winning last time, does virtually all of his racing over shorter trips but may have been a bit closer in this had his jockey been able to press on when he wanted to. He was another horse forced to sit in for a while before seeing clear space. (op 10-1)
Antigua Sunrise(IRE) has gone well at York in the past, including a win over C&D in 2009, but seemed anchored off this mark.
Anhar(USA), with the visor taken off this time but tongue-tie reapplied, was the highest-rated 3-y-o in this but ruined his chance with a slow start. He did have his chance but never got involved. (op 10-1)
Chilly Filly(IRE), beaten half a length by her stable companion Yorgunnabelucky at Pontefract in August, won over 1m6f last time (raised 9lb for that) but faded here after being in front rank over 2f out. (op 7-1)
Sedgwick, the winner of a C&D amateur riders' handicap off a 10lb lower mark in May, appeared to run well but may have been slightly flattered by coming up what looked the favoured side of the course. Official explanation: jockey said gelding lost a shoe (op 40-1)

5218 WEATHERBYS INSURANCE LONSDALE CUP (GROUP 2) 2m 88y

2:15 (2:15) (Class 1) 3-Y-O+

£79,478 (£30,128; £15,078; £7,518; £3,766; £1,890) **Stalls** Low

Form RPR

1313 **1** **Opinion Poll (IRE)**[46] 3695 4-9-1 107 FrankieDettori 6 116
(M A Jarvis) *lw: hld up towards rr: hdwy 3f out: chal on outer wl over 1f out: sn rdn and edgd rt ent fnl f: sn led and kpt on* **9/2**[2]

12/4 **2** *1/2* **Samuel**[46] 3695 6-9-1 110 EddieAhern 8 115
(J H M Gosden) *lw: hld up in tch: hdwy to trck ldrs 6f out: effrt and cl up 3f out: rdn to ld 2f out: drvn over 1f out: hdd ins fnl f: kpt on* **11/2**[3]

-141 **3** *3/4* **King Of Wands**[46] 3695 4-9-1 106 WilliamBuick 10 114
(J H M Gosden) *hld up in rr: hdwy 4f out: chsd ldrs over 2f out and sn rdn: nt clr run and swtchd lft ent fnl f: sn drvn and kpt on towards fin* **3/1**[1]

0-32 **4** *hd* **Electrolyser (IRE)**[20] 4506 5-9-1 114 PhilipRobinson 5 114
(C G Cox) *chsd ldr: hdwy 3f out: sn rdn along: drvn whn n.m.r ent fnl f: kpt on* **9/2**[2]

1421 **5** *1/2* **Illustrious Blue**[20] 4506 7-9-4 116 JimCrowley 4 116
(W J Knight) *hld up in rr: hdwy 3f out: rdn along 2f out: styd on appr fnl f: nrst fin* **7/1**

-020 **6** *3* **Tastahil (IRE)**[62] 3102 6-9-1 111 TadhgO'Shea 7 110
(B W Hills) *t.k.h: chsd ldrs: rdn along 3f out: drvn 2f out and grad wknd* **16/1**

0010 **7** *3/4* **Akmal**[62] 3102 4-9-4 109 RichardHills 2 112
(J L Dunlop) *led: jnd and rdn along 3f out: hdd 2f out and sn drvn: wknd ent fnl f* **11/2**[3]

6-4 **8** *3 1/4* **Moon Indigo**[39] 3922 4-9-1 92 PaulMulrennan 3 105?
(J Howard Johnson) *trckd ldrs: rdn along 3f out: sn wknd* **66/1**

3m 34.84s (0.34) **Going Correction** +0.125s/f (Good) 8 Ran SP% **112.0**
Speed ratings (Par 115): **104,103,103,103,103 101,101,99**
toteswingers:1&2 £5.30, 2&3 £3.90, 1&3 £2.80 CSF £28.07 TOTE £5.70: £2.30, £2.20, £1.50; EX 35.10 Trifecta £165.20 Pool: £5562.71 - 24.91 winning units..
Owner Sheikh Ahmed Al Maktoum **Bred** Darley **Trained** Newmarket, Suffolk
■ Stewards' Enquiry : Frankie Dettori caution: careless riding and use of whip

FOCUS
This Group 2 is now firmly established in the calendar for the top stayers, having been won by some of the most famous names in the sphere. This season's renewal did not look quite up to the normal level, especially with the absence of Ask, but the majority were closely matched judged on previous form and it was a relatively open betting market. The early pace was moderate and the field came up the stands' rail in the straight. The form makes sense.

NOTEBOOK
Opinion Poll(IRE), a progressive sort in 2009, had taken a Listed race in France this time. Suited by soft going, the drying ground would not have been ideal, but he was able to come from last of all on the home turn to pick up his rivals over a furlong out and reverse Sandown form with the third and fifth. The flat, left-handed course suited - he is now 3-3 on that sort of track - and this consistent sort can be expected to improve again. Connections will pick from the remaining major staying races with him, but his targets will be ground-dependent. It would no surprise to see him back here next season for the Yorkshire Cup, possibly in Godolphin silks. Official explanation: jockey said colt hung right (op 7-2 tchd 5-1)
Samuel, a Listed winner here back in 2008, missed 2009 due to a hole in a tendon but was not far behind today's third and winner in another Listed race at Sandown on his return. His rider made a sensible forward move (given the slow early pace) at around halfway, and got to the stands' rail first. He kept on gamely under pressure but found the winner too strong. He should be up to winning in Group company on this evidence, and might go for the Prix du Cadran if the ground is not soft. (op 6-1)
King Of Wands had beaten the fifth and the first two in a Listed race at Sandown last time, his first try at the trip. He was held up early but looked the likely winner when produced over a furlong out, only for his effort to peter out late on. He might need genuinely fast ground to get home at this distance. (op 7-2 tchd 4-1 in a place)
Electrolyser(IRE), a Listed winner over 2m in 2009, had finished behind Illustrious Blue both at Ascot and Goodwood this season but was 3lb better off this time. He was in the right place from the start but took a keen grip then stuck to his task under pressure, and was staying on again at the finish. He looks as if a stiffer test will be in his favour, and the Doncaster Cup seems likely to suit and could be on the agenda now. (op 5-1)
Illustrious Blue beat today's fourth in the Goodwood Cup but was 3lb worse off, and had finished behind King Of Wands and Akmal in two races at Sandown before that. He was held up early, but came under pressure as the pace increased early in the straight and only ran on late. He seems ideally suited by going the other way around, especially Goodwood, so might be worth sending to Longchamp for the Prix du Cadran. (op 11-2)
Tastahil(IRE), a 1m5f Listed winner in 2009, had finished runner-up in the Chester Cup this year but looked the owner's second string on jockey bookings. He was held up at the back before staying on, and is another who might appreciate a stiffer test.
Akmal, a progressive front runner last season, had stepped up on that when winning the Henry II Stakes at Sandown. However, he had finished well beaten in the Gold Cup and had been off since. He made the running at a steady pace but tended to mess about, spooking at people by the rails and jumping paths in the early stages. His rider tried to wind things up from the home turn but he failed to get the rail, and the pair faded out of things in the last quarter-mile. Cheekpieces might be worth a try to help him to concentrate. (op 7-1)
Moon Indigo, a dual winner over 1m6f in Ireland last season, finished well held in a Listed handicap over 1m6f here on his first start for the yard. He looked out of his depth at this level. (op 50-1)

5219 IRISH THOROUGHBRED MARKETING GIMCRACK STKS (GROUP 2) (C&G) 6f

2:50 (2:51) (Class 1) 2-Y-O

£89,962 (£34,020; £17,002; £8,501) **Stalls** Low

Form RPR

4143 **1** **Approve (IRE)**[24] 4419 2-9-1 107 EddieAhern 3 112
(W J Haggas) *a.p: chal 2f out: and sn rdn: drvn over 1f out: styd on wl to ld last 100yds* **8/1**

116 **2** *3/4* **Crown Prosecutor (IRE)**[21] 4468 2-8-12 0 (t) MartinDwyer 7 107
(B J Meehan) *led 2f: cl up: rdn to chal 2f out: drvn to ld jst ins fnl f: hdd and no ex last 100yds* **15/2**

213 **3** *2 1/2* **Sir Reginald**[33] 4097 2-8-12 93 FrankieDettori 10 99
(R A Fahey) *towards rr: pushed along 1/2-way: rdn and n.m.r wl over 1f out: styd on strly ins fnl f: nrst fin* **14/1**

11 **4** *shd* **Temple Meads**[32] 4138 2-8-12 0 JimmyFortune 9 99
(E S McMahon) *racd freely: cl up: led after 2f: rdn wl over 1f out: drvn and hdd jst ins fnl f: sn wknd* **5/2**[1]

1313 **5** *nk* **Premier Clarets (IRE)**[25] 4355 2-8-12 95 PaulMulrennan 11 98
(R A Fahey) *chsd ldrs: rdn along and sltly outpcd 2f out: swtchd lft over 1f out and kpt on ins fnl f* **33/1**

421 **6** *3/4* **Trade Storm**[69] 2887 2-8-12 87 TadhgO'Shea 1 96
(J Gallagher) *sn pushed along and outpcd in rr: rdn over 2f out: hdwy on wd outside over 1f out: kpt on wl fnl f: nrst fin* **50/1**

0103 **7** *5* **Move In Time**[32] 4138 2-8-12 93 TomEaves 2 81
(B Smart) *hld up in tch: hdwy to chse ldrs 1/2-way: rdn 2f out: sn drvn and edgd rt: wknd over 1f out* **33/1**

151 **8** *1/2* **Casual Glimpse**[41] 3826 2-8-12 101 RichardHughes 5 79
(R Hannon) *chsd ldrs: rdn along 1/2-way: sn wknd* **6/1**[3]

21 **9** *5* **Gold Pearl (USA)**[9] 4902 2-8-12 0 JimCrowley 6 64
(S C Williams) *lengthy: chsd ldrs: rdn along 1/2-way: drvn and wknd whn n.m.r over 1f out* **25/1**

1 **10** *1* **Shropshire (IRE)**[32] 4123 2-8-12 0 MichaelHills 4 61
(B W Hills) *in tch: hdwy to chse ldrs over 2f out: rdn and carried rt over 1f out: sn wknd* **4/1**[2]

120 **11** *12* **Dubawi Gold**[62] 3100 2-8-12 94 KierenFallon 12 25
(M Dods) *outpcd: hdwy whn hmpd over 2f out and over 1f out: sn eased* **8/1**

1m 11.67s (-0.23) **Going Correction** 0.0s/f (Good) 11 Ran SP% **115.2**
Speed ratings (Par 106): **101,100,96,96,96 95,88,87,81,79 63**
toteswingers:1&2 £13.60, 2&3 £14.90, 1&3 £12.30 CSF £62.98 TOTE £6.90: £1.90, £2.00, £3.00; EX 55.90 Trifecta £687.00 Pool: £6573.22 - 7.08 winning units..
Owner Highclere Thoroughbred Racing (Bahram) **Bred** Abbeville And Meadow Court Partners **Trained** Newmarket, Suffolk
■ Stewards' Enquiry : Eddie Ahern one-day ban: used whip with excessive frequency (Sep 1)

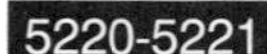

FOCUS
This looked a solid set of contenders for a well-established and prestigious juvenile contest, so the form should be reliable during the rest of this campaign, although it is worth noting that even though they broke from stalls on the far side of the course, the whole field headed stands' side well over 3f from home. All of the winners in the last ten years have been sprinters pure and simple, apart from Rock Of Gibraltar, and it's difficult to imagine this year's victor doing anything other than following in their footsteps.

NOTEBOOK
Approve(IRE), beaten twice at Group 2 level since landing the Norfolk Stakes at Royal Ascot, and reunited with Ahern who missed the ride in the Prix Robert Papin (the horse reportedly lost his concentration in that), was the only runner carrying a penalty but that did not stop him collecting this valuable prize - he became only the second horse in the last 15 years to win this giving weight away, a feat only matched by Rock Of Gibraltar. Just behind the leaders on their outside, he needed pushing along to make sure he kept in contact and things didn't look good about a furlong out when under pressure, but he stayed on well, needing every yard of the 6f trip to assert. It's easy to see why connections feel he'll get further, but it will be a surprise if he doesn't head to the Group 1 Middle Park Stakes next time, although he has some valuable sales entries as well, notably the 7f £500,000 Tattersalls Millions 2YO Trophy a day after the Middle Park. (op 12-1)
Crown Prosecutor(IRE), down in trip after pulling far too hard in the early stages of the Group 2 Vintage Stakes at Glorious Goodwood (he reportedly finished distressed), raced prominently and came back to the sort of promise he showed in his first two outings. His trainer feels that the step up to 7f last time was probably a mistake in hindsight and it came too early in his career, but there was a lot to like about this performance and he looks sure to head to towards races like the Mill Reef and Champagne Stakes, both of which are Group 2s, with a leading chance - he also holds sales race entries. (op 13-2 tchd 8-1)
Sir Reginald looked to be heavily restrained leaving the stalls and only made inroads on the leading two inside the final furlong after finding some traffic problems. It looked a decent effort and connections hope to win a Listed contest with him next if a suitable opportunity could be found. He also has sales race entries, which look a good option later on in the year. (tchd 16-1)
Temple Meads, trying 6f for the first time, made an impressive debut at Newmarket before getting spots in this throat, which kept him from running at Royal Ascot. He landed the valuable Super Sprint last time and looked a leading contender here when considering the pace he had shown. Fortune took the ride for the first time as his regular rider was forced to miss this due to a one-day ban, and he soon had his mount towards the head of affairs, racing a bit freely, which probably compromised his finishing effort even though he came down what looked the favoured stands' rail. There was still a lot to like about the natural ability he showed and, considering he has already won at Newbury, the Mill Reef looks a good opportunity for him. Official explanation: jockey said colt ran too free (op 11-4 tchd 3-1 in a place)
Premier Clarets(IRE), twice beaten in Listed company, was dropping in trip after a run over 7f at Ascot and kept on after showing early dash. (op 40-1)
Trade Storm got outpaced at around halfway but made pleasing late progress. He can win at this distance at a lower level, but ought to benefit from a step up in trip. (op 40-1)
Move In Time, beaten just over a length by Temple Meads in the Super Sprint, was another to find the early pace a stride too quick, and faded inside the final furlong.
Casual Glimpse, already beaten in Listed company, was soon in trouble and got knocked into by the third at one stage when in behind. If anything, he still looked like he was a bit green despite this being his fourth outing. (op 4-1)
Gold Pearl(USA), the winner of a Windsor maiden on the previous start, is a half-brother to Group 1-placed Arch Swing and showed good speed to about the 2f pole. He is worth another chance at a lower level. (op 22-1)
Shropshire(IRE), related to plenty of smart performers at a range of trips, including his brother Arctic, a Group 3 winning 2-y-o in Ireland last year, showed plenty of promise when winning on his racecourse debut at Haydock, but failed to pick up here after travelling nicely for the majority of the contest. Official explanation: jockey said colt hung right throughout (tchd 9-2)
Dubawi Gold, absent since finishing behind Approve in the Norfolk Stakes after being in front of him at Epsom in the Woodcote Stakes, was awkward to load and then found quite a bit of trouble in running when trying to make a challenge up the stands' rail. He is far better than he was allowed to show (his rider eased off in the final stages whilst looking down at his mount) and might be one for a nurseries off what might be a good mark. Official explanation: jockey said colt hung badly right (op 12-1)

5220 TOTESPORT EBOR (HERITAGE H'CAP) 1m 6f
3:25 (3:28) (Class 2) 3-Y-0+

£130,851 (£39,186; £19,593; £9,807; £4,893; £2,457) Stalls Low

Form				RPR
01-1	1		**Dirar (IRE)**[20] 3198 5-9-1 **100** JamieSpencer 22 (Gordon Elliott, Ire) *hld up: hdwy 4f out: effrt and n.m.r on inner 2f out: sn swtchd lft and hdwy over 1f out: drvn and styd on to ld ins fnl f: kpt on* **14/1**	111
-304	2	1 1/4	**Rosika**[20] 4507 4-8-12 **97** KierenFallon 8 (Sir Michael Stoute) *hld up in midfield: hdwy over 3f out: chsd ldrs 2f out: swtchd lft and rdn over 1f out: led 1f out: drvn and hdd ins fnl f no ex towards fin* **12/1**	106
-100	3	shd	**Bridge Of Gold (USA)**[174] 706 4-9-2 **101** GeorgeBaker 9 (M A Magnusson) *in tch: hdwy to chse ldrs 4f out: rdn to ld wl over 1f out: sn drvn and hdd 1f out: ev ch tl no ex last 75yds* **33/1**	110
6524	4	4	**Salute Him (IRE)**[19] 4564 7-9-6 **105** JMurtagh 21 (A J Martin, Ire) *lw: hld up towards rr: gd hdwy over 5f out: led wl over 2f out and sn rdn: hdd wl over 1f out: sn drvn and kpt on same pce* **25/1**	109
45-0	5	1	**Ajaan**[105] 1821 6-9-1 **100** (b) TomQueally 16 (H R A Cecil) *stdd and swtchd lft s: hld up towards rr: hdwy 3f out and sn rdn: drivern wl over 1f out: styd on strly ins fnl f: nrst fin* **20/1**	102
0-63	6	nk	**Desert Sea (IRE)**[53] 3447 7-8-10 **95** NeilCallan 1 (D W P Arbuthnot) *lw: chsd ldrs: hdwy 4f out: cl up 3f out: rdn and ch 2f out: sn drvn and wknd over 1f out* **22/1**	97
2-30	7	1/2	**Sopranist**[39] 3921 4-9-2 **101** TedDurcan 11 (Saeed Bin Suroor) *in tch: hdwy to chse ldrs 3f out: edgd rt and rdn 2f out: sn drvn and no imp* **40/1**	102
661	8	3/4	**Dangerous Midge (USA)**[46] 3672 4-9-10 **109** MartinDwyer 12 (B J Meehan) *lw: trckd ldrs: hmpd on inner over 4f out: hdwy 3f out: rdn along 2f out: sn drvn and grad wknd* **11/1**	109
4104	9	nk	**Hillview Boy (IRE)**[39] 3921 6-9-0 **99** PhillipMakin 7 (J S Goldie) *hld up in rr: stdy hdwy over 3f out: rdn to chse ldrs 2f out: sn drvn and no imp* **16/1**	99
1311	10	nk	**Martyr**[22] 4461 5-9-1 **100** 4ex RichardHughes 4 (R Hannon) *lw: hld up in tch on inner: hdwy 4f out: chsd ldrs 3f out: effrt and ch over 2f out: sn rdn and grad wknd* **9/2**[1]	99
/3-2	11	1/2	**Elyaadi**[64] 3050 6-8-8 **96** GFCarroll(3) 3 (John Queally, Ire) *midfield: hdwy and in tch over 3f out: rdn over 2f out and n.d* **9/1**[3]	94
1-30	12	1 3/4	**Darley Sun (IRE)**[62] 3102 4-9-7 **106** FrankieDettori 5 (Saeed Bin Suroor) *in tch: hdwy to chse ldrs over 3f out: rdn over 2f out: drvn and wknd wl over 1f out* **14/1**	102
5265	13	shd	**Nanton (USA)**[25] 4390 8-9-0 **106** PaulNorton(7) 6 (J S Goldie) *hld up: a towards rr* **33/1**	102
15-0	14	3 1/2	**The Betchworth Kid**[20] 4506 5-9-4 **103** HayleyTurner 10 (A King) *hld up: a towards rr* **25/1**	94
4-01	15	nk	**Fortuni (IRE)**[74] 2747 4-8-11 **96** SebSanders 13 (Sir Mark Prescott) *chsd ldr: pushed along whn hmpd over 4f out: racd alone far side in home st: sn wknd* **9/1**[3]	86
0423	16	5	**Demolition**[39] 3921 6-8-9 **94** TomEaves 17 (R A Fahey) *prom: hdwy 4f out: led over 3f out: drvn and hdd over 2f out: sn wknd* **16/1**	77
-001	17	3/4	**Bernie The Bolt (IRE)**[11] 4817 4-8-11 **96** 4ex JimmyFortune 2 (A M Balding) *hld up: a towards rr* **11/1**	78
0-60	18	10	**Centennial (IRE)**[26] 4320 5-8-13 **98** (b) RichardKingscote 15 (Jonjo O'Neill) *prom: trckd ldr 1/2-way: led over 5f out: rdn and hdd over 3f out: sn wknd* **66/1**	66
00-1	19	8	**Prospect Wells (FR)**[59] 3240 5-9-9 **108** PaulMulrennan 19 (J Howard Johnson) *t.k.h: chsd ldrs: rdn along 4f out: sn wknd* **50/1**	65
21-1	20	30	**Overturn (IRE)**[20] 3447 6-9-0 **99** EddieAhern 18 (D McCain Jnr) *sn led: rdn along and hdd over 5f out: wknd qckly over 3f out: sn bhd and eased* **8/1**[2]	14

2m 57.13s (-3.07) **Going Correction** +0.125s/f (Good) **20** Ran SP% **127.3**
Speed ratings (Par 109): **113,112,112,109,109 109,108,108,108,108 107,106,106,104,104 101,101,95,91,73**
toteswingers:1&2 £47.90, 2&3 £123.50, 1&3 £109.40 CSF £157.81 CT £5408.47 TOTE £20.70: £4.20, £3.50, £6.70, £6.60; EX 339.80 Trifecta £5234.60 Part won. Pool: £7073.90 - 0.24 winning units..

Owner Mick White, Dale White & Marcus Reeder **Bred** His Highness The Aga Khan's Studs S C **Trained** Capranny, Co. Meath

■ Stewards' Enquiry : Jamie Spencer one-day ban: used whip with excessive frequency without giving gelding time to respond (Sep 1)

FOCUS
One of the most valuable handicaps of the season, it has been won by unexposed 3-y-os and seasoned handicappers or, as with last year's winner, horses better known as hurdlers. This year's contest looked typically competitive but they went a strong early gallop, the field mainly came to race towards the stands' side and the first three finished clear. Solid form, with the winner better than ever.

NOTEBOOK
Dirar(IRE), better known as a hurdler, having finished third behind Overturn in the Galway Hurdle last time, was a 1m5f winner at Ayr in June. Racing off 6lb higher, he was settled off the early pace and, after switching off the stands' rail well over 2f out, gradually weaved his way through and struck the front when back nearest the rail inside the last. The good gallop suited, and the trainer reported that the gelding could go to Dubai this winter, before being brought back next summer with the Galway Hurdle in mind. (op 12-1)

Rosika appeared not to get home at this trip last time but had been placed at Listed level over shorter. Despite being 11lb above her last winning mark, she ran well having been held up, only finding the winner too strong late on. Connections will be looking for more black type with her and, with her stamina now assured, the Park Hill at Doncaster looks a feasible target for her. (op 14-1)

Bridge Of Gold(USA) ◆ is lightly raced and was having his first run since a spell in Dubai over the winter, having come back with a virus. Taking a big step up in trip, he was never far away and battled on gamely in the closing stages. He might need time to get over this, but this talented individual looks sure to win a good race before too long, and connections are considering the Canadian International.

Salute Him(IRE), the winner of an amateurs' race in Ireland this season but a good fourth in a Listed race at Royal Ascot, had to prove he stays this trip having been held over it last time and, after joining the leaders travelling strongly on the rail 2f out, he weakened entering the last furlong. (op 33-1)

Ajaan, a winner at 1m6f in 2008 and placed in the Chester Cup in 2009, had not been seen since finishing tailed off in the same race this season. Held up early, he was one of the first under pressure early in the straight but ran on well late on. It will be no surprise if his target is again the Cesarewitch, a race in which he finished fifth last season. (op 33-1)

Desert Sea(IRE), third to Overturn in the Northumberland Plate, was 5lb better off but his best form is at 2m and he was well beaten in this last year. However, he was much better drawn this time around and came to have every chance before tiring in the last furlong. He is another for whom the Cesarewitch could be on the agenda, although he will not want the ground any worse than good.

Sopranist, lightly raced and a 1m2f winner on fast ground, had a recent run following a break since returning from Dubai. Taking a big step up in trip, he stayed on steadily in the last 2f and is worth another try at the trip. (op 50-1)

Dangerous Midge(USA), an impressive winner of the Old Newton Cup from Demolition, was 13lb higher and up in trip. He ran a fine race under his welter burden, especially as he ended up on the outside of his field. Pattern company looks likely for him now.

Hillview Boy(IRE), in good form last season as a result of which he had climbed the handicap, finished a close fourth in the John Smith's Cup here in July having finished last behind Dangerous Midge at Haydock. He was held up early before moving into contention halfway up the straight, but he failed to last home. He is one to bear in mind for a race over 1m4f.

Martyr, in good form this season having been a winner at this trip, 1m4f and 2m, was 13lb higher than for the first of those wins. Ideally suited by fast ground, he came to have every chance 2f out but then dropped away. (op 13-2)

Elyaadi was well backed, having won a handicap over this trip at Leopardstown and then finished second in the Ascot Stakes. She stayed on towards the end without being given a hard time once her chance had gone, and remains in good heart.

Darley Sun(IRE), an impressive winner of the Cesarewitch last season, had since joined Godolphin but had been held in Group races at staying trips. Racing off 12lb higher than for his last success, he travelled well enough just off the pace but failed to pick up when the race began in earnest. (op 16-1)

Nanton(USA) won the Mallard handicap over this trip at Doncaster last year off 8lb lower, and also finished fourth in this race and third in the Cambridgeshire. He had been running creditably in mainly pattern races this year but was out the back from the start here, and only stayed on past beaten horses late on.

Fortuni(IRE) beat a subsequent Royal Ascot winner in a handicap at the Epsom Derby meeting, but was 11lb higher and up in trip. He raced up with the pace but stuck more towards the far rail in the straight, and could not sustain his effort. He can be rated better than the bare form.

Centennial(IRE), a Group 2 winner back in 2008 and placed at that level last year, had been a bit below that form for his current trainer but had dropped in the weights. He was in the leading group from the start and committed off the home turn, but paid for his earlier efforts in the closing stages.

Prospect Wells(FR) Official explanation: jockey said gelding ran too free

Overturn(IRE) has developed into a really good hurdler, winning the Scottish Champion Hurdle and Galway Hurdle, and also made all from a bad draw to win the Northumberland Plate on the Flat in between. Racing off 6lb higher, he tried to adopt the same tactics but was taken on turning for home, and was quickly beaten. He was allowed to come home in his own time, and it looked as if his earlier efforts this season had caught up with him. Official explanation: jockey said gelding finished distressed (op 7-1)

5221 JULIA GRAVES ROSES STKS (LISTED RACE) 5f
4:05 (4:06) (Class 1) 2-Y-O **£17,778** (£6,723; £3,360; £1,680) **Stalls** Low

Form RPR

1 **1** **New Planet (IRE)**[24] 4409 2-9-0 0 KierenFallon 9 104+
(J J Quinn) *in tch stands' side: hdwy wl over 1f out: rdn and styd on ins fnl f to ld last 50yds* **17/2**

51 **2** *nk* **Pabusar**[22] 4460 2-9-0 0 JimCrowley 13 103+
(R M Beckett) *hld up stands' side: swtchd rt and hdwy 2f out: rdn to ld and overall ldr ent fnl f: drvn: hdd and no ex last 50yds: 2nd of 9 in gp* **5/1**[2]

041 **3** *2 1/2* **Julius Geezer (IRE)**[105] 1819 2-9-0 90 RichardKingscote 6 94
(Tom Dascombe) *chsd ldrs stands' side: hdwy to ld that gp 2f out: sn rdn and ev ch whn hung lft over 1f out: drvn and kpt on same pce ins fnl f: 3rd of 9 in gp* **28/1**

4003 **4** *3/4* **Bathwick Bear (IRE)**[4] 5094 2-9-0 87 RichardEvans 5 91
(P D Evans) *prom stands' side: rdn to chal 2f out and ev ch tl drvn and one pce ent fnl f: 4th of 9 in gp* **66/1**

3153 **5** *shd* **Choose Wisely (IRE)**[22] 4458 2-9-0 100 NeilCallan 1 91+
(K A Ryan) *chsd ldng pair far side: rdn along 2f out: kpt on u.p ins fnl f 1st of 4 in gp* **6/1**[3]

021 **6** *shd* **Arctic Feeling (IRE)**[12] 4797 2-9-0 96 PaulMulrennan 7 91
(R A Fahey) *cl up stands' side: rdn and ev ch 2f out: drvn and wknd over 1f out: 5th of 9 in gp* **16/1**

0102 **7** *2 3/4* **Black Moth (IRE)**[12] 4787 2-9-0 97 MartinDwyer 12 86+
(B J Meehan) *lw: hld up towards rr: effrt whn hmpd 2f out: sn rdn and n.d: 6th of 9 in gp* **12/1**

4111 **8** *1 3/4* **Face The Problem (IRE)**[18] 4600 2-9-0 108 MichaelHills 2 74+
(B W Hills) *chsd ldr far side: led and overall ldr 1/2-way: rdn wl over 1f out: hdd & wknd ent fnl f: 2nd of 4 in gp* **13/8**[1]

2561 **9** *4* **Foghorn Leghorn**[18] 4590 2-9-0 85 JimmyFortune 10 62
(P W Chapple-Hyam) *swtg: in tch stands' side: rdn along whn hmpd 2f out: sn in rr: 7th of 9 in gp* **33/1**

523 **10** *1* **Abzolutely (IRE)**[9] 4896 2-8-9 0 RobertWinston 4 51
(D O'Meara) *qckly away and overall ldr far side: hdd 1/2-way: sn rdn and wknd: 3rd of 4 in gp* **100/1**

1126 **11** *3/4* **Leiba Leiba**[22] 4458 2-9-0 93 SebSanders 3 54+
(M Botti) *a in rr far side: 4th of 4 in gp* **18/1**

1320 **12** *hd* **On The High Tops (IRE)**[19] 4544 2-9-0 85 JamieSpencer 8 53
(T P Tate) *dwlt: a in rr stands' side: 8th of 9 in gp* **66/1**

521 **13** *1/2* **Cadeaux Pearl**[27] 4303 2-9-0 95 RichardHughes 11 51
(R Hannon) *lw: prom stands' side gp: rdn along after 2f: sn hdd and bhd fnl 2f: last of 9 in gp* **8/1**

58.93 secs (-0.37) **Going Correction** 0.0s/f (Good) **13** Ran SP% **119.9**
Speed ratings (Par 102): **102,101,97,96,96 96,91,88,82,80 79,79,78**
toteswingers:1&2 £8.80, 2&3 £37.20, 1&3 £27.60 CSF £49.72 TOTE £10.30: £2.80, £2.20, £5.30; EX 45.90 Trifecta £1192.10 Pool: £2013.81 - 1.25 winning units..
Owner Ross Harmon **Bred** Mrs Diane Williams **Trained** Settrington, N Yorks
■ Stewards' Enquiry : Jim Crowley three-day ban: careless riding (Sep 1-3)

FOCUS
Plenty of speed was shown by these juveniles,

NOTEBOOK
New Planet(IRE), with Fallon replacing the 5lb claimer who rode him to victory on his racecourse debut, looked to have a bit to find against these, but he knuckled down under pressure and won in good style. Nicely supported in the betting, his trainer said afterwards that his horse had been working really well coming into this, and feels that New Planet is worthy of a chance at the Group 2 Flying Childers at Doncaster. (op 9-1)
Pabusar showed that his debut run at Ffos Las, when he was seemingly well fancied, was all wrong with a winning performance at Glorious Goodwood next time. Trapped in a pocket for a while here, he did manage to get to the front for a few strides but was passed again by the winner in the final stages. He is entitled to renew rivalry with New Planet at Doncaster, but does hold an entry in the Group 2 Mill Reef Stakes. (op 9-2 tchd 11-2)
Julius Geezer(IRE), not seen on the racecourse since beating today's fourth in the Lily Agnes Stakes at Chester in May, hit the front on his side quite early and ran respectably. His early-season form had come with some ease in the ground, so a race like the Listed Harry Rosebery at Ayr in September might be ideal for him, where he is likely to find some give. (op 25-1)
Bathwick Bear(IRE) again showed good speed, and looks a 5f horse pure and simple.
Choose Wisely(IRE), whose owner reportedly fancied a crack at the Nunthorpe after his good run in the Molecomb Stakes, can probably feel unfortunate that their horses stayed towards the far side of the course, a route that had looked heavily unfavoured during the previous races. He came home strongly inside the final furlong and it is possible that he may have won had he been handed a higher draw. (op 7-1)
Arctic Feeling(IRE), behind Gimcrack winner Approve at Royal Ascot, and second to today's sixth at Beverley in early July, got back to winning ways at Musselburgh on his previous outing, and may have briefly headed his side before finding only one pace. (op 16-1)
Black Moth(IRE) tracked the runner-up up the stands' rail, but found his progress momentarily checked when hampered over 2f out.
Face The Problem(IRE), officially the highest-rated runner taking part, may have been unfortunate as he stayed towards the far side of the course, a route that had looked heavily unfavoured during the previous races. He showed good speed, but didn't quite get home. (op 7-4 tchd 6-4)
Foghorn Leghorn was staying on when getting involved in the scrimmaging 2f out. It's unlikely he would have won, but he was just behind New Planet when getting knocked sideways. Official explanation: jockey said colt was struck into
Abzolutely(IRE) showed tons of early toe and will be hard to catch in a nursery at a speed-favouring track.
Cadeaux Pearl, absent since winning a modest maiden by ten lengths at Sandown, showed up early but was readily left behind when the tempo increased.

5222 EBF TOTEPOOL FILLIES' STKS (H'CAP) 1m
4:40 (4:40) (Class 2) (0-100,92) 3-Y-O **£12,952** (£3,854; £1,926; £962) **Stalls** Low

Form RPR

641 **1** **Conciliatory**[14] 4697 3-8-4 75 MartinDwyer 1 83
(Rae Guest) *lengthy: trckd ldng pair: effrt and cl up over 2f out: rdn to ld ent fnl f: edgd rt and kpt on* **8/1**

4152 **2** *3/4* **Gobama**[32] 4137 3-9-4 89 SebSanders 2 95
(J W Hills) *towards rr: pushed along 3f out: rdn wl over 1f out: styd on to chal ins fnl f: sn drvn and edgd rt: nt qckn towards fin* **6/1**

1106 **3** *1/2* **Maid In Heaven (IRE)**[17] 4617 3-9-7 92 ShaneKelly 4 97
(W R Swinburn) *swtg: sn led: rdn along over 2f out: drvn over 1f out: hdd ent fnl f: kpt on same pce* **11/2**[3]

-515 **4** *nk* **Path Of Peace**[64] 3063 3-8-4 75 JimmyQuinn 6 79
(J D Bethell) *lw: trckd ldrs: hdwy over 2f out: rdn and n.m.r over 1f out: swtchd lft and drvn ent fnl f: kpt on same pce* **10/1**

0112 **5** *1* **Sooraah**[13] 4762 3-8-12 83 KierenFallon 3 85
(W J Haggas) *hld up in rr: pushed along 1/2-way: rdn along wl over 2f out: kpt on u.p ins fnl f* **2/1**[1]

0116 **6** *nk* **Admire The View (IRE)**[27] 4296 3-9-0 85 TedDurcan 8 86
(D R Lanigan) *hld up in tch: effrt 3f out: rdn along over 2f out: drvn over 1f out and no imp* **12/1**

4165 **7** *1* **Christmas Light**[13] 4750 3-8-6 77 HayleyTurner 5 76
(D O'Meara) *cl up: rdn along over 2f out: drvn wl over 1f out: sn wknd* **9/2**[2]

0002 **8** *3 1/4* **She's A Character**[7] 4950 3-8-9 80 PaulMulrennan 7 71
(R A Fahey) *chsd ldrs: rdn along and outpcd over 2f out: sn in rr* **14/1**

1m 39.84s (1.04) **Going Correction** +0.125s/f (Good) **8** Ran SP% **115.7**
Speed ratings (Par 103): **99,98,97,97,96 96,95,91**
toteswingers:1&2 £6.30, 2&3 £3.60, 1&3 £7.80 CSF £55.61 CT £288.65 TOTE £10.60: £2.50, £1.70, £2.30; EX 60.00 Trifecta £431.90 Pool: £2194.73 - 3.76 winning units.Place 6: £1578.17 Place 5: £510.26 .
Owner Miss K Rausing **Bred** Miss K Rausing **Trained** Newmarket, Suffolk

FOCUS
A relatively new addition to the meeting, this looked a decent fillies' handicap and it produced a good race. The field again raced nearest the stands' rail in the straight. The winner improved to the tune of 4lb.

NOTEBOOK
Conciliatory has progressed with racing, having got off the mark over 1m on Polytrack on her previous start. Making her handicap debut off a reasonable mark, she raced up with the leaders from the start, and battled on gamely to get the better of several challengers. She is out of a mare who scored over 1m6f, so it will be no surprise if she is tried over longer trips at some time in the future, and is likely to stay in training next season. (op 9-1 tchd 7-1)
Gobama is not the most straightforward but is consistent enough, and sets the standard for this form. She came under pressure 2f out before keeping on well in the last furlong, although she was always being held by the winner.
Maid In Heaven(IRE), a three-time winner at shorter trips, was given a positive rider on her first try over this distance and stayed on gamely under pressure. She is another that represents a good guide to the form and could win over this trip, although she appears to need a sound surface, so her chances might be limited by the weather.
Path Of Peace, a winner at this trip before finishing behind today's runner-up at Thirsk, was 11lb better off but could not reverse the placings. She raced just behind the leaders and did not appear to have much room in the last 2f, but did not really pick up when a gap appeared and might be high enough in the handicap. (op 11-1 tchd 12-1)
Sooraah, another improving sort, had Fallon replacing her regular apprentice rider. She was never travelling at the rear of the field and was one of the first under pressure. She only began to run when the race was over. Official explanation: jockey said filly ran flat (op 9-4)
Admire The View(IRE) was held up off the pace and could only stay on in her own time in the latter stages. (op 10-1)
Christmas Light did not appear to get home over 1m2f here last time, and the soft ground conspired against her on her last start. She raced prominently and her rider got the rail, but she faded in the last furlong. (op 6-1)
She's A Character has returned to form of late, but dropped away late on after travelling well. (op 11-1)
T/Jkpt: Not won. T/Plt: £2,267.90 to a £1 stake. Pool of £286,544.22 - 92.23 winning tickets. T/Qpdt: £431.20 to a £1 stake. Pool of £12,587.75 - 21.60 winning tickets. JR

5223 - 5225a (Foreign Racing) - See Raceform Interactive

5133 DEAUVILLE (R-H)
Wednesday, August 18

OFFICIAL GOING: Turf: soft; fibresand: standard

5226a PRIX DE LA VALLEE D'AUGE (LISTED RACE) (2YO) (TURF) 5f
4:00 (12:00) 2-Y-O **£24,336** (£9,734; £7,300; £4,867; £2,433)

RPR

1 **Chinese Wall (IRE)**[28] 4275 2-8-8 0 ThierryJarnet 11 104
(D Guillemin, France) **68/10**[3]

2 *3* **Boccalino (GER)**[28] 4275 2-8-11 0 GeraldMosse 3 96
(H-A Pantall, France) **9/2**[2]

3 *nse* **Dingle View (IRE)**[11] 4831 2-8-8 0 CathyGannon 6 93
(P D Evans) *broke wl: sn prom: 3rd 2f out: rdn and outpcd 1f out: c again to fin strly u.p fnl 100yds: jst missed 2nd* **78/10**

4 *shd* **Concealing**[15] 2-8-8 0 MaximeGuyon 1 93
(A Fabre, France) **1/1**[1]

5 *snk* **Magic Potion (FR)**[45] 3718 2-8-8 0 GregoryBenoist 8 92
(P Bary, France) **17/1**

6 *1 1/2* **Matreshka (IRE)**[28] 4274 2-8-8 0 StephanePasquier 5 87
(N Clement, France) **11/1**

7 *1 1/2* **Americaine Cat (FR)**[15] 2-8-8 0 MaximeFoulon 9 81
(J-V Toux, France) **104/1**

8 *1 1/2* **Moranda (FR)**[24] 2-8-8 0 FranckBlondel 10 76
(C Boutin, France) **27/1**

9 *4* **Scarlet Rocks (IRE)**[10] 4872 2-8-8 0 DominiqueBoeuf 4 62
(P D Evans) *broke wl and led: hdd 2 1/2f out: rdn 2f out: sn wknd* **24/1**

10 *3/4* **Lady Jak (FR)**[45] 3718 2-8-8 0 WilliamsSaraiva 2 59
(J-V Toux, France) **33/1**

0 **Carata (FR)**[24] 2-8-8 0 (b) RaphaelMarchelli 7 —
(C Boutin, France) **31/1**

59.40 secs (1.90) **11** Ran SP% **120.8**
PARI-MUTUEL (all including 1 euro stakes): WIN: 7.80. PLACES: 2.00, 1.70, 2.40. DF: 11.70. SF: 36.60.
Owner Marquesa De Moratalla **Bred** Mise De Moratalla **Trained** France

NOTEBOOK
Dingle View(IRE), a nursery winner off 85 last time out, showed good speed to lead and knuckled down well when hard ridden to secure some valuable black type.

4987 CHEPSTOW (L-H)
Thursday, August 19

5227 Meeting Abandoned - grass root damage

[4993]EPSOM (L-H)

Thursday, August 19

OFFICIAL GOING: Good

Rail dolled out up to 8yds from 6f, to winning post increasing distances by about 10yds.

Wind: fresh, across Weather: bright spells,light clouds

5233 WATCH RACING UK ON SKY 432 CLAIMING STKS 1m 2f 18y

5:10 (5:11) (Class 5) 3-Y-0+ **£3,238** (£963; £481; £240) **Stalls** Low

Form RPR

3106 **1** **Cobo Bay**[3] 5142 5-9-9 86..(b) DarrylHolland 6 78
(C R Dore) *chsd ldr: effrt to join ldr and rdn over 2f out: led 1f out: styd on wl and drew clr ins fnl f: eased towards fin* **6/4**[1]

00 **2** *4 ½* **Beck's Bolero (IRE)**[10] 4912 4-8-12 0........................ FergusSweeney 1 58
(J A Osborne) *led: jnd and rdn over 2f out: hdd 1f out: wknd ins fnl f* **66/1**

1502 **3** *nk* **Lang Shining (IRE)**[6] 5034 6-9-8 85............................ SophieDoyle(5) 2 72
(J A Osborne) *in tch in last pair: shkn up to chse ldng pair ent fnl 2f: rdn and hung lft fnl f: no imp on wnr* **6/4**[1]

2023 **4** *9* **Orchard Supreme**[22] 4489 7-9-3 75.................................... PatDobbs 5 44
(R Hannon) *chsd ldng pair tl rdn and fnd nil ent 2f out: wl btn over 1f out: eased ins fnl f* **3/1**[2]

4-00 **5** *6* **Pursestrings**[94] 2189 3-7-11 55............................... CharlotteJenner(7) 3 27
(Mrs L J Mongan) *hld up in last pair: dropped to last 6f out: lost tch and edgd lft ent fnl 2f* **50/1**[3]

2m 10.35s (0.65) **Going Correction** +0.125s/f (Good)
WFA 3 from 4yo+ 8lb 5 Ran SP% **108.5**
Speed ratings (Par 103): **102,98,98,90,86**
CSF £51.26 TOTE £2.60: £2.40, £17.20; EX 44.40.
Owner Patrick Wilmott **Bred** The C H F Partnership **Trained** Cowbit, Lincs

FOCUS
The rail was dolled out up to eight yards from the winning post adding approximately ten yards to race distances. The ground was officially described as good. Three of the runners had BHA ratings between 75 and 86 in this decent claimer. It was run at a good pace, despite the small field. The runner-up is a doubt and it is likely the winner and third were below their best.
Orchard Supreme Official explanation: trainer's rep said gelding was unsuited by the track

5234 JRA NURSERY 7f

5:40 (5:40) (Class 4) (0-85,83) 2-Y-0 **£4,533** (£1,348; £674; £336) **Stalls** Low

Form RPR

21 **1** **Ardour (IRE)**[26] 4384 2-9-7 83... PatDobbs 2 88+
(R Hannon) *mde all: set stdy gallop tl pushed along and qcknd over 2f: edgd rt over 1f out: pushed along and in command ins fnl f: comf* **1/1**[1]

034 **2** *1 ½* **High On The Hog (IRE)**[37] 3981 2-8-2 67.... Louis-PhilippeBeuzelin(3) 6 67
(J L Dunlop) *t.k.h: sn chsng wnr: ev ch and rdn 3f out: nt gng pce of wnr over 1f out: styd on same pce ins fnl f* **14/1**

525 **3** *3* **Tokum (IRE)**[41] 3874 2-8-9 71.. DarrylHolland 1 64
(J Noseda) *t.k.h early: rdn and unable qck over 2f out: edgd lft and styd on same pce fr over 1f out* **6/1**[3]

2461 **4** *15* **Arabian Star (IRE)**[18] 4623 2-8-11 73................................ AlanMunro 5 28+
(M R Channon) *a in last: rdn and unable qck over 2f out: wknd 2f out: wl bhd and eased ins fnl f* **7/4**[2]

1m 26.56s (3.26) **Going Correction** +0.125s/f (Good) 4 Ran SP% **107.3**
Speed ratings (Par 96): **86,84,80,63**
CSF £12.55 TOTE £1.50; EX 18.30.
Owner Miss Yvonne Jacques **Bred** Old Carhue Stud **Trained** East Everleigh, Wilts

FOCUS
Not many runners but there were some unexposed types in this interesting nursery.

NOTEBOOK
Ardour(IRE) went close behind a highly progressive rival on debut before landing the odds in a 6f Salisbury maiden. A well backed favourite for his nursery debut, he travelled smoothly out in front and found plenty for pressure to score with quite a bit in hand. A couple behind were quite keen and the form may not be very solid but this 100,000gns son of Danehill Dancer looks a scopey and well organised type, who has plenty of potential and could shoot up the ranks. (op 11-8)
High On The Hog(IRE) put in a more dynamic effort stepped up in trip on nursery debut, particularly as he took a strong hold early on. He still has a bit to learn but a stronger pace will suit and his dam was placed at 2m, so he should continue to improve with an emphasis on stamina. (op 10-1)
Tokum(IRE) disappointing at 11-4 in a 7f York maiden last time, was weak in the market and never really involved on his first try off a mark. (op 4-1 tchd 7-2)
Arabian Star(IRE) appreciated the step up to 7f when staying on strongly to make a winning nursery debut at Newbury. A 4lb rise looked fair but he got warm beforehand and put in a very laboured effort in his bid for a double. There is a good deal of ability there but it is a worry that this was a second major blip in his last three starts. Official explanation: trainer's rep said gelding was unsuited by the track (tchd 13-8 and 15-8)

5235 TOMPKINS & MAY PARTNERSHIP LADIES' DERBY H'CAP (FOR LADY AMATEUR RIDERS) 1m 4f 10y

6:15 (6:16) (Class 4) (0-80,78) 4-Y-0+ **£5,621** (£1,743; £871; £435) **Stalls** Centre

Form RPR

256 **1** **Inspirina (IRE)**[7] 4996 6-10-7 78............... MissPernillaHermansson(3) 7 86
(R Ford) *t.k.h: sn chsng ldr tl led 8f out: mde rest: rdn ent fnl clr: drew clr 1f out: styd on wl* **9/2**[3]

21/5 **2** *4* **Top Mark**[21] 4520 8-10-0 73....................................... MissRachelKing(5) 2 75
(A King) *t.k.h early: chsd ldng pair: shuffled bk and swtchd rt ent fnl 4f: hdwy u.p 2f out: chsd wnr ins fnl f: no imp* **7/1**

0534 **3** *1 ½* **Lord Theo**[13] 4804 6-10-6 74.................................. MrsEmmaLittmoden 8 74
(N P Littmoden) *taken down early: t.k.h early: chsd ldrs: chsd wnr over 4f out: ev ch whn rdn and unable qck ent fnl 2f: plugged on same pce ins fnl f* **9/2**[3]

6566 **4** *4 ½* **Dani's Girl (IRE)**[29] 4266 7-10-7 75............................ MissSBrotherton 4 67
(P M Phelan) *t.k.h early: hld up in midfield: hdwy to chse ldng pair wl over 3f out: pressed ldr and rdn 2f out: btn over 1f out: wknd ins fnl f* **10/3**[1]

06-2 **5** *2 ¼* **Sir Boss (IRE)**[10] 4912 5-10-3 74..........................(t) MissMMullineaux(3) 3 63
(M Mullineaux) *hld up in last pair: effrt to chse ldng trio and rdn over 3f out: no prog and nvr trbld ldrs* **16/1**

0633 **6** *1 ¾* **Potentiale (IRE)**[14] 4737 6-10-1 74.....................(p) MissPhillipaTutty(5) 6 60
(J W Hills) *in tch in last trio: outpcd and rdn wl over 3f out: wl btn whn hung lft ent fnl 2f* **7/2**[2]

3106 **7** *3* **Hustle (IRE)**[24] 4438 5-10-1 69.................................... MissGAndrews 5 50
(Miss Gay Kelleway) *stdd s: hld up in tch in rr: rdn and no rspnse over 2f out: n.d* **14/1**

6525 **8** *21* **Profit's Reality (IRE)**[10] 4891 8-10-7 75........................ MissEJJones 1 23
(M J Attwater) *set v stdy gallop for 2f: hdd 8f out: chsd wnr tl racd awkwardly downhill and lost pl qckly over 4f out: wl bhd fnl 2f: virtually p.u after* **10/1**

2m 49.19s (10.29) **Going Correction** +0.125s/f (Good) 8 Ran SP% **115.8**
Speed ratings (Par 105): **70,67,66,63,61 60,58,44**
toteswingers:1&2 £5.20, 2&3 £5.30, 1&3 £4.80 CSF £36.20 CT £149.88 TOTE £4.00: £1.30, £1.10, £2.20.
Owner Miss Gill Quincey **Bred** Mohammad Al-Qatami **Trained** Butterton, Staffs
■ Pernilla Hermansson's first winner in Britain.

FOCUS
A competitive handicap for lady amateur riders. It was run at a very steady early pace and not many got into it. The form has been rated around the runner-up and looks a bit dubious.
Profit's Reality(IRE) Official explanation: trainer said gelding lost both front shoes and was struck into

5236 TOTEPOOL FLEXI BETTING H'CAP 1m 114y

6:45 (6:45) (Class 4) (0-85,85) 3-Y-0 **£5,828** (£1,734; £866; £432) **Stalls** Low

Form RPR

4322 **1** **Rare Tern (IRE)**[9] 4931 3-8-6 70.................................... StevieDonohoe 1 80
(Sir Mark Prescott) *pushed along after s to ld after 1f: rdn and hdd 2f out: led again over 1f out: styd on wl to assert jst ins fnl f: rdn out* **11/8**[1]

4406 **2** *2* **Dream On Buddy (IRE)**[13] 4784 3-8-1 70................ AshleyMorgan(5) 5 76
(B W Hills) *hld up in last pair: rdn and effrt ent fnl 2f: chsd ldng pair over 1f out: kpt on to go 2nd fnl 50yds: no threat to wnr* **10/1**

-043 **3** *¾* **Suffolk Punch (IRE)**[7] 4995 3-9-5 83................................. LiamKeniry 6 87
(A M Balding) *led for 1f: w wnr after tl led 2f out: sn rdn and hdd over 1f out: btn jst ins fnl f: lost 2nd fnl 50yds* **2/1**[2]

3034 **4** *8* **Ostentation**[8] 4964 3-8-6 70.. AlanMunro 3 57
(R A Teal) *broke wl: stdd and hld up in last pair after 1f: rdn and effrt over 2f out: sn hung lft and no real prog: wl btn whn nt clr run ent fnl f: swtchd rt ins fnl f and wnt 4th towards fin* **9/2**[3]

150 **5** *½* **Mejd (IRE)**[19] 4603 3-9-7 85.. SamHitchcott 7 71
(M R Channon) *dwlt: sn rcvrd to chse ldrs: rdn and wnt 3rd wl over 3f out: wknd u.p and hung lft over 1f out: wl hld ins fnl f* **10/1**

36-0 **6** *11* **Sir William Orpen**[57] 3325 3-8-3 67.............................(t) NeilChalmers 2 28
(P M Phelan) *t.k.h: chsd ldrs: swtchd rt and rdn over 2f out: sn hung bk lft and btn: wl bhd fr over 1f out* **25/1**

1m 44.99s (-1.11) **Going Correction** +0.125s/f (Good) 6 Ran SP% **115.6**
Speed ratings (Par 102): **109,107,106,99,99 89**
toteswingers:1&2 £4.60, 2&3 £4.40, 1&3 £1.70 CSF £16.71 CT £27.78 TOTE £3.10: £1.80, £8.90; EX 21.20.
Owner Sir Edmund Loder **Bred** Sir E J Loder **Trained** Newmarket, Suffolk

FOCUS
A decent handicap run at a reasonable pace. The first and third had a sustained duel for most of the way and none of the others got into a dangerous position. The first three came clear and a slightly positive view has been taken of the form.

5237 WEATHERBYS PRINTING H'CAP 1m 114y

7:20 (7:20) (Class 5) (0-75,74) 4-Y-0+ **£3,238** (£963; £481; £240) **Stalls** Low

Form RPR

466 **1** **Ahlawy (IRE)**[17] 4652 7-9-9 74...(t) LeeVickers 7 81
(F Sheridan) *v.s.a: hld up in last pair: rdn and gd hdwy on outer wl over 1f out: kpt edging lft: r.o wl to ld fnl 100yds: eased nr fin* **12/1**

6023 **2** *½* **Ilie Nastase (FR)**[6] 5050 6-9-9 74....................................... LiamKeniry 4 80
(C R Dore) *chsd ldr: rdn to chal over 2f out: drvn to ld over 1f out tl hdd and one pce fnl 100yds* **7/2**[1]

-005 **3** *2* **Young Dottie**[42] 3813 4-8-13 64.. IanMongan 8 66
(P M Phelan) *t.k.h: hld up in tch towards rr: hdwy to chse ldrs wl over 3f out: drvn to chse ldr over 1f out tl ins fnl f: one pce fnl 150yds* **4/1**[2]

4203 **4** *1 ¼* **Spiritual Art**[7] 5003 4-9-3 68.. FergusSweeney 5 67+
(L A Dace) *in tch in midfield: hdwy to chse ldrs and n.m.r ent fnl 2f: swtchd rt over 1f out: styd on same pce ins fnl f* **9/1**

0123 **5** *1 ¼* **Jewelled**[20] 4533 4-9-9 74...(v) GeorgeBaker 3 70
(J W Hills) *chsd ldrs: n.m.r on inner and swtchd rt jst over 2f out: kpt on same pce ins fnl f* **6/1**[3]

0026 **6** *¾* **Trafalgar Square**[11] 4870 8-8-4 58........................(v) MatthewDavies(3) 6 52
(M J Attwater) *hld up towards rr: swtchd rt and effrt ent fnl 2f: no prog and styd on same pce fr over 1f out* **8/1**

3334 **7** *¾* **Ocean Countess (IRE)**[15] 4690 4-9-5 70......................... CathyGannon 9 63
(Miss J Feilden) *in tch in midfield: pushed along 4f out: rdn and unable qck ent fnl 3f: no imp after* **8/1**

6030 **8** *¾* **Full Victory (IRE)**[31] 4201 8-8-10 61.................................... AlanMunro 1 52
(R A Farrant) *led: rdn and hrd pressed jst over 2f out: hdd over 1f out: btn whn nt clr run ins fnl f: eased towards fin* **7/1**

5034 **9** *1 ¼* **Musical Script (USA)**[13] 4777 7-8-7 58................(b) FrankieMcDonald 2 46
(Mouse Hamilton-Fairley) *stdd s: t.k.h: hld up in rr: rdn and no prog ent fnl 2f: n.d* **20/1**

1m 46.56s (0.46) **Going Correction** +0.125s/f (Good) 9 Ran SP% **113.7**
Speed ratings (Par 103): **102,101,99,98,97 96,96,95,94**
toteswingers:1&2 £13.60, 2&3 £4.20, 1&3 £9.00 CSF £52.99 CT £202.17 TOTE £18.00: £2.80, £2.80, £1.30; EX 102.20.
Owner Frank Sheridan **Bred** Castlemartin Stud And Skymarc Farm **Trained** Averham Park, Notts

FOCUS
A fairly competitive handicap, but ordinary form with the winner close to last year's turf best. Full Victory set a decent pace before fading and the winner came from last to first in the straight.
Musical Script(USA) Official explanation: jockey said gelding ran too free

5238 CHANTILLY H'CAP 7f

7:50 (7:51) (Class 5) (0-75,71) 3-Y-0+ **£3,238** (£963; £481; £240) **Stalls** Low

Form RPR

6630 **1** **Hi Shinko**[7] 4995 4-9-10 71.. DarrylHolland 8 84
(B R Millman) *taken down early: mde all: rdn ent fnl 2f: kpt on wl ins fnl f* **9/2**[2]

6521 **2** *1 ¼* **Another Try (IRE)**[12] 4836 5-9-6 70......................... MatthewDavies(3) 7 80
(A P Jarvis) *chsd wnr: rdn jst over 2f out: pressed wnr wl over 1f out: no ex and btn fnl 100yds* **7/2**[1]

0620 **3** *2 ½* **Leadenhall Lass (IRE)**[15] 4690 4-9-7 68..........................(v) IanMongan 1 71
(P M Phelan) *taken down early: wnt rt s: chsd ldng pair: drvn and unable qck wl over 1f out: edgd lft u.p and btn 1f out* **5/1**[3]

5560 **4** *½* **Spinning Bailiwick**[21] 4502 4-9-9 70................................. GeorgeBaker 4 72
(G L Moore) *taken down early: chsd clr ldng trio: rdn and no prog over 2f out: kpt on u.p ins fnl f: nvr trbld ldrs* **14/1**

652- **5** *1 ¾* **Dancing Queen (IRE)**[327] 6284 3-9-5 71.............................. LiamKeniry 5 66
(M A Magnusson) *broke wl: plld hrd early: grad stdd bk to last trio over 4f out: rdn and no prog ent fnl 2f: kpt on ins fnl f: nvr threatened ldrs* **13/2**

1241 **6** *3* **Dutiful**[13] 4779 3-9-5 **71** AlanMunro 3 58
(M R Channon) *bmpd s: hld up wl off the pce in last pair: rdn and effrt ent fnl 2f: no real prog: n.d* **7/2**[1]

0 **7** *4 ½* **Big Boom**[100] 1998 5-8-11 **58** StevieDonohoe 6 35
(M Quinn) *racd in midfield: rdn and struggling wl over 3f out: lost pl and bhd fnl 2f* **20/1**

42 **8** *nk* **Sermons Mount (USA)**[13] 4775 4-9-1 **62** FrankieMcDonald 2 38
(Mouse Hamilton-Fairley) *short of room and stdd s: hld up wl off pce in last pair: rdn and no hdwy over 2f out: nvr on terms* **7/1**

1m 23.55s (0.25) **Going Correction** +0.125s/f (Good)
WFA 3 from 4yo+ 5lb **8** Ran SP% **116.6**
Speed ratings (Par 103): **103,101,98,98,96 92,87,87**
toteswingers:1&2 £4.20, 2&3 £3.20, 1&3 £3.90 CSF £21.10 CT £82.28 TOTE £6.10: £1.90, £1.10, £3.40; EX 29.30 Place 6: £39.36 Place 5: £16.67.
Owner Always Hopeful Partnership **Bred** Mrs Laura Grasby **Trained** Kentisbeare, Devon

FOCUS
A couple of last-time-out winners lined up for this handicap. It was run at a strong pace but the first three filled those positions throughout and none of the others posed a threat. The first two are rated close to form.
T/Plt: £132.90 to a £1 stake. Pool of £37,733.64 - 207.11 winning ticket. T/Qpdt: £26.00 to a £1 stake. Pool of £5,803.43 - 164.80 winning tickets. SP

4795 MUSSELBURGH (R-H)

Thursday, August 19

OFFICIAL GOING: Good (good to firm in places on round course; 6.5)
Wind: Fairly strong, against Weather: Sunny

5239 SCOTTISH RACING MAIDEN AUCTION STKS 5f

1:55 (1:55) (Class 6) 2-Y-O **£1,942** (£578; £288; £144) **Stalls** Low

Form RPR

2352 **1** **Crimson Knot (IRE)**[13] 4797 2-8-6 77 PatrickMathers 1 70
(A Berry) *trckd ldrs: rdn to ld 1f out: styd on strly* **9/4**[1]

3064 **2** *2 ½* **Surely This Time (IRE)**[8] 4941 2-8-13 67 (p) TomEaves 7 68
(K A Ryan) *led: rdn and hdd 1f out: carried hd high: kpt on same pce fnl f* **4/1**[3]

0230 **3** *nse* **Saltergate**[8] 4941 2-8-9 69 (p) SilvestreDeSousa 5 64
(N Tinkler) *sn w ldr: ev ch and rdn over 1f out: nt qckn fnl f* **5/2**[2]

06 **4** *1* **Rothesay Chancer**[17] 4645 2-8-8 0 GaryBartley(3) 6 62
(J S Goldie) *in tch on outside: effrt over 1f out: kpt on same pce fnl f* **8/1**

54 **5** *2 ¼* **Myjestic Melody (IRE)**[17] 4650 2-8-6 0 DuranFentiman 2 49
(N Wilson) *trckd ldrs: effrt and ev ch over 1f out: wknd ins fnl f* **7/1**

50 **6** *3 ¼* **Rylee Mooch**[22] 4477 2-8-10 0 PaulEddery 3 41
(R C Guest) *dwlt: bhd and outpcd: nvr on terms* **22/1**

7 *3 ¾* **Come On Eileen (IRE)** 2-8-2 0 JamesSullivan(3) 4 23
(R C Guest) *chsd ldng gp: rdn 1/2-way: wknd wl over 1f out* **25/1**

61.22 secs (0.82) **Going Correction** +0.075s/f (Good) **7** Ran SP% **111.1**
Speed ratings (Par 92): **96,92,91,90,86 81,75**
toteswingers:1&2:£3.00, 1&3:£1.80, 2&3:£3.00 CSF £10.93 TOTE £3.10: £1.10, £3.30; EX 11.80.
Owner William Burns **Bred** Iona Equine **Trained** Cockerham, Lancs

FOCUS
A modest maiden auction in which the winner set the standard and probably didn't need to improve. The pace was just fair and the result overall looks the right one.

NOTEBOOK
Crimson Knot(IRE) held a solid chance on all her form at 5f, including over this C&D last time, and she won as she was entitled to, in little danger once pushed to the front inside the last. This is her trip, and she should be competitive at it in nurseries given quickish conditions. (op 6-4)
Surely This Time(IRE) seemed more settled in the cheekpieces this time, not blazing off as fast as he had done the last twice, and ran a better race as a result. Though it was easy to see from his finishing effort why headgear has been called upon so soon. (op 6-1)
Saltergate also looked a bit quirky (as he has done before) towards the finish, but form-wise his effort can't be faulted, and this looks about as good as he is for now at this trip. (op 3-1)
Rothesay Chancer needed this run for a mark and shaped as if she will need further when going into nurseries, struggling to go with the placed horses once the pace lifted. (op 9-1 tchd 10-1)
Myjestic Melody(IRE) didn't perhaps improve as much as seemed likely for the drop back to 5f but should find easier opportunities in modest nurseries. (tchd 13-2 and 15-2)
Rylee Mooch once again failed to show any of the speed possessed by his half brother Nickel Silver. (op 50-1)
Come On Eileen(IRE), from a stable not known for debut 2yo winners, is bred to need much further and was always struggling. (op 20-1)

5240 SCOTTISH RACING YOUR BETTER BET H'CAP 5f

2:30 (2:31) (Class 5) (0-70,68) 4-Y-O+ **£3,238** (£963; £481; £240) **Stalls** Low

Form RPR

2323 **1** **Mandarin Spirit (IRE)**[1] 5212 10-9-6 **65** (b) SilvestreDeSousa 3 74
(Miss L A Perratt) *prom: drvn over 2f out: styd on wl u.p fnl f: led nr fin* **2/1**[1]

0-00 **2** *¾* **Francis Albert**[9] 4938 4-7-13 **51** oh1 ow2 (b) JosephYoung(7) 2 57
(M Mullineaux) *t.k.h: led: rdn over 1f out: hung rt ins fnl f: hdd nr fin* **40/1**

0502 **3** *2* **Highland Warrior**[21] 4513 11-9-6 **68** PaulPickard(3) 5 67
(P T Midgley) *dwlt: bhd and rdn 1/2-way: hdwy over 1f out: kpt on: nt rch first two* **8/1**

5443 **4** *1* **Sandwith**[8] 4952 7-8-11 **56** (v) LNewman 4 52
(A G Foster) *chsd ldrs: drvn 1/2-way: one pce fnl f* **4/1**[3]

0333 **5** *4* **Wicked Wilma (IRE)**[13] 4798 6-9-7 **66** FrannyNorton 6 47
(A Berry) *cl up: effrt and drvn wl over 1f out: wknd ent fnl f* **7/2**[2]

0042 **6** *1 ¾* **Secret Venue**[9] 4938 4-9-6 **65** TomEaves 7 40
(Jedd O'Keeffe) *prom on outside tl rdn and wknd wl over 1f out* **9/2**

60.35 secs (-0.05) **Going Correction** +0.075s/f (Good) **6** Ran SP% **107.3**
Speed ratings (Par 103): **103,101,98,97,90 87**
toteswingers:1&2:£11.30, 1&3:£4.00, 2&3:£12.40 CSF £59.83 TOTE £3.40: £2.00, £11.10; EX 45.00.
Owner Peter Tsim **Bred** W Haggas And W Jarvis **Trained** East Kilbride, South Lanarks

FOCUS
A modest handicap in which the first two raced nearest the stands' rail throughout. The pace again seemed no more than a fair one. The form is suspect but rated through the winner.

5241 RACING UK CLASSIFIED CLAIMING STKS 1m

3:05 (3:06) (Class 6) 3-Y-O+ **£1,942** (£578; £288; £144) **Stalls** High

Form RPR

4140 **1** **Zubova**[13] 4804 3-8-10 70 (t) SilvestreDeSousa 8 77
(Rae Guest) *trckd ldr: shkn up to ld wl over 1f out: qcknd clr fnl f* **2/1**[1]

2251 **2** *6* **Bed Fellow (IRE)**[12] 4824 6-8-10 63 PatrickDonaghy(3) 2 61
(P Monteith) *stdd s: hld up: hdwy on outside over 2f out: styd on fnl f to take 2nd nr fin: no ch w wnr* **7/1**

4020 **3** *nk* **Bajan Pride**[7] 4985 6-8-13 65 MickyFenton 1 60
(P T Midgley) *hld up on outside: hdwy over 2f out: edgd rt and chsd wnr ins fnl f: no imp and lost 2nd nr fin* **6/1**[3]

3104 **4** *hd* **Stellite**[12] 4822 10-8-5 67 KellyHarrison(3) 4 55+
(J S Goldie) *t.k.h: hld up: hdwy whn n.m.r over 1f out: swtchd lft and styd on towards fin: n.d* **4/1**[2]

5406 **5** *2* **Makbullet**[29] 4245 3-8-9 67 TomEaves 7 56
(J Howard Johnson) *prom: rdn over 2f out: no ex over 1f out* **12/1**

5000 **6** *½* **Flores Sea (USA)**[20] 4547 6-8-5 62 (b) JamesSullivan(3) 9 49
(Mrs R A Carr) *t.k.h: led to wl over 1f out: wknd ent fnl f* **20/1**

0040 **7** *nk* **Lakeman (IRE)**[12] 4833 4-8-8 62 DaleSwift(5) 3 53
(B Ellison) *hld up towards rr: drvn over 3f out: effrt on outside over 1f out: nvr able to chal* **12/1**

-046 **8** *9* **Jibrrya**[26] 4377 3-8-11 70 FrannyNorton 5 36
(D Nicholls) *t.k.h: in tch tl rdn and wknd fr 2f out* **8/1**

1m 39.77s (-1.43) **Going Correction** -0.025s/f (Good)
WFA 3 from 4yo+ 6lb **8** Ran SP% **111.4**
Speed ratings (Par 101): **106,100,99,99,97 97,96,87**
toteswingers:1&2:£3.00, 1&3:£3.10, 2&3:£4.20 CSF £15.56 TOTE £3.00: £1.10, £1.50, £2.10; EX 14.00.Zubova was claimed by J. Weymes for £11,000.
Owner J M Duggan & T P Duggan **Bred** D A Yardy **Trained** Newmarket, Suffolk

FOCUS
An uncompetitive claimer and a ready win for the most reliable horse in the field, who rated a 5lb personal best. The gallop wasn't an overly strong one, and those dropped out were set quite a task.

5242 EAST LOTHIAN COUNCIL H'CAP 7f 30y

3:40 (3:47) (Class 3) (0-90,90) 3-Y-O+ **£6,476** (£1,927; £963; £481) **Stalls** High

Form RPR

6120 **1** **Jeannie Galloway (IRE)**[21] 4524 3-8-9 **83** LeeTopliss(5) 9 92
(R A Fahey) *trckd ldrs: rdn to ld over 1f out: edgd lft and hrd pressed ins fnl f: hld on gamely* **5/1**[3]

1341 **2** *shd* **Gap Princess (IRE)**[17] 4653 6-9-8 **86** SilvestreDeSousa 2 97
(G A Harker) *hld up: gd hdwy on outside over 1f out: edgd rt and chal ins fnl f: kpt on: jst hld* **8/1**

1346 **3** *2 ½* **Glen Shiel (USA)**[12] 4843 3-9-2 **85** GregFairley 7 87
(M Johnston) *midfield: effrt over 2f out: prom appr fnl f: kpt on same pce ins fnl f* **4/1**[2]

1341 **4** *2* **Polish World (USA)**[21] 4515 6-8-11 **75** MickyFenton 11 74
(P T Midgley) *led tl rdn and hdd over 1f out: no ex fnl f* **7/1**

1512 **5** *1 ¼* **Silver Rime (FR)**[12] 4828 5-9-10 **88** LNewman 5 83
(Miss L A Perratt) *hld up: effrt over 2f out: hung rt: no imp over 1f out* **17/2**

4331 **6** *¾* **Malcheek (IRE)**[12] 4850 8-9-4 **82** DuranFentiman 3 75
(T D Easterby) *t.k.h: sn cl up: effrt and ev ch 2f out: wknd ent fnl f* **25/1**

0126 **7** *3* **Mr Rainbow**[26] 4370 4-9-12 **90** TomEaves 1 75
(G A Swinbank) *in tch: rdn and outpcd whn hmpd 2f out: sn btn* **12/1**

0330 **8** *shd* **King's Wonder**[20] 4536 5-9-4 **85** MichaelGeran(3) 12 70
(D Nicholls) *hld up ins: effrt whn hung lft 2f out: sn btn* **7/2**[1]

-102 **9** *8* **Prince Of Vasa (IRE)**[11] 4865 3-8-7 **79** MichaelStainton(3) 8 40
(Michael Smith) *trckd ldrs tl rdn and wknd fr 2f out* **25/1**

0215 **10** *1 ¾* **Dickie Le Davoir**[6] 5048 6-8-7 **71** oh6 (b) PaulEddery 10 30
(R C Guest) *dwlt: bhd: rdn over 3f out: nvr on terms* **33/1**

0060 **11** *1 ½* **Deadly Encounter (IRE)**[26] 4394 4-8-7 **78** MarzenaJeziorek(7) 4 32
(R A Fahey) *dwlt: bhd and sn pushed along: nvr on terms* **20/1**

1m 27.44s (-1.56) **Going Correction** -0.025s/f (Good)
WFA 3 from 4yo+ 5lb **11** Ran SP% **116.1**
Speed ratings (Par 107): **107,106,104,101,100 99,96,95,86,84 83**
toteswingers:1&2:£13.90, 1&3:£7.30, 2&3:£6.80 CSF £41.63 CT £179.01 TOTE £6.60: £2.30, £2.80, £2.30; EX 61.40.
Owner David Renwick **Bred** G And J Bloodstock **Trained** Musley Bank, N Yorks
■ Nufoudh (17/2) was withdrawn after unseating his rider and bolting before the start. Deduct 10p in the £ under R4.
■ Stewards' Enquiry : Lee Topliss caution: used whip with excessive frequency

FOCUS
A well-contested handicap that was run at a good clip and favoured those ridden from just off the pace. The runner-up can be counted the moral winner. Personal bests from the first two.

NOTEBOOK
Jeannie Galloway(IRE) goes well here and put her Galway disappointment behind her with a game effort, rallying after being headed briefly inside the last. She might have a bit more to give this autumn, particularly on easier ground than this, and shapes as if she will prove just as good at 1m. (old market op 11-1 new market)
Gap Princess(IRE) ◆ is thriving and turned in another career-best for her current yard, while leaving the impression the effort of making her run from so far back just found her out. She's unlikely to be dropped so far out next time now connections are more sure of her stamina, and she can win again either at 6f or 7f. (old market op 8-1 new market)
Glen Shiel(USA) had things go more his way here than has been the case elsewhere since his last win, and seemed to run up to his best with no excuses. He's not yet been tried at 1m and that trip might turn out to suit him. (old market tchd 5-1 new market)
Polish World(USA) is in the form of his life, and did well to last so long having been harried in front up in a much higher grade than normal. He can win another handicap back at a lower level when he gets things more his own way. (new market)
Silver Rime(FR) ran a fair race considering 7f round here on quickish ground is plenty sharp enough for him nowadays. (old market tchd 17-2 new market)
Malcheek(IRE) pulled too hard for his own good in the early stages and shouldn't be judged too harshly on this. (old market op 16-1 new market)
Mr Rainbow was weak in the market and backers knew their fate even before he was squeezed for room. For all he's won a race this season, he's not quite developed into the horse that it looked he might at the end of 2009. Official explanation: jockey said gelding hung right throughout (old market op 8-1 new market)
King's Wonder was well backed and, though short of room at one point, failed to impress with his head carriage and probably isn't one to be making too many excuses for. (old market op 9-2 tchd 7-2 new market)

5243 RACING UK SHOWING BEST RACECOURSES LIVE H'CAP 1m 4f 100y

4:15 (4:17) (Class 4) (0-85,77) 3-Y-O+ **£5,828** (£1,734; £866; £432) **Stalls** High

Form RPR

4614 **1** **Line Of Duty (IRE)**[14] 4751 3-9-8 **77** AndrewElliott 2 92+
(G A Swinbank) *unruly bef s: cl up: led after 4f: mde rest: rdn 3f out: sn hrd pressed: styd on wl fnl f* **2/1**[1]

511 **2** *5* **Amazing King (IRE)**[21] 3403 6-9-8 **70** RussKennemore(3) 4 77
(P A Kirby) *trckd ldrs: hdwy to chal over 2f out: sn rdn: no ex ins fnl f* **7/2**[3]

0254 **3** *5* **Ethics Girl (IRE)**[14] 4737 4-9-13 **72** .... FrannyNorton 1 71
(John Berry) *hld up in tch: hdwy to chse ldng pair over 2f out: edgd rt: wknd over 1f out* **9/4**[2]

4655 **4** *11* **Grey Granite (IRE)**[34] 4086 4-10-0 **73** .... TomEaves 5 54
(W Jarvis) *t.k.h: trckd ldrs tl edgd rt and wknd over 2f out* **6/1**

6-42 **5** *hd* **Leopard Hills (IRE)**[31] 4200 3-8-8 **66** .... JamesSullivan(3) 3 47
(J Howard Johnson) *led 4f: cl up tl drvn and wknd fr 3f out* **8/1**

2m 40.61s (-1.39) **Going Correction** -0.025s/f (Good)
WFA 3 from 4yo+ 10lb **5** Ran SP% **111.7**
Speed ratings (Par 105): **103,99,96,89,88**
CSF £9.45 TOTE £2.50: £1.30, £2.60; EX 8.10.
Owner J N Swinbank **Bred** Olive O'Connor And Raymond Gaffney **Trained** Melsonby, N Yorks

FOCUS
Just a fair handicap and though the winner is progressive, he wasn't left with much to beat with a couple of his rivals not giving their running. He rates a 7lb personal best. The pace was reasonable but no more.

5244 SCOTTISH RACING H'CAP 1m 1f
4:50 (4:51) (Class 5) (0-70,70) 3-Y-0+ **£3,238** (£963; £481; £240) **Stalls** High

Form RPR

050 **1** **Kimberley Downs (USA)**[12] 4825 4-9-3 **60** .... GaryBartley(3) 10 70
(N Wilson) *mde all: rdn and qcknd 2f out: kpt on strly fnl f* **8/1**[3]

4264 **2** *2* **Grand Diamond (IRE)**[12] 4823 6-9-5 **66** ....(p) PaulNorton(7) 9 72
(J S Goldie) *in tch: rdn over 2f out: hdwy to chse wnr appr fnl f: kpt on same pce* **4/1**[2]

3-00 **3** *1 ¼* **Social Rhythm**[46] 3707 6-9-3 **57** .... LNewman 7 60
(A C Whillans) *hld up in midfield: hdwy on outside 2f out: kpt on same pce fnl f* **16/1**

5040 **4** *2* **Casino Night**[1] 5215 5-9-3 **57** .... SilvestreDeSousa 12 57
(G A Harker) *trckd ldrs: drvn over 2f out: kpt on same pce appr fnl f* **3/1**[1]

1140 **5** *2 ¾* **Bernix**[52] 3502 8-8-12 **57** ....(p) DaleSwift(5) 5 50
(N Tinkler) *midfield: rdn and outpcd over 3f out: rallied over 1f out: nvr able to chal* **18/1**

24-0 **6** *1* **Fantastic Strike (IRE)**[51] 3537 3-9-9 **70** .... GregFairley 6 61
(M Johnston) *sn cl up: rdn: edgd lft and outpcd over 2f out: n.d after* **4/1**[2]

5425 **7** *2 ¼* **Coole Dodger (IRE)**[8] 4939 5-8-10 **50** .... PatrickMathers 13 36
(B Ellison) *s.v.s: t.k.h and sn jnd main gp: rdn over 2f out: sme late hdwy: nvr on terms* **17/2**

044 **8** *3 ¼* **Ra Junior (USA)**[31] 4198 4-10-0 **68** .... MickyFenton 4 48
(P T Midgley) *t.k.h: hld up: rdn over 2f out: sn n.d* **16/1**

2460 **9** *1* **Classic Descent**[12] 4823 5-9-1 **58** ....(tp) JamesSullivan(3) 2 35
(Mrs R A Carr) *hld up: shkn up over 2f out: nvr nr ldrs* **10/1**

-000 **10** *1 ¼* **Funky Munky**[19] 4582 5-8-13 **53** .... AndrewElliott 1 28
(A C Whillans) *bhd: drvn over 3f out: nvr on terms* **25/1**

600- **11** *15* **Sams Spirit**[491] 1281 4-8-5 **50** .... LeeTopliss(5) 8 —
(J A McShane) *prom tl rdn and wknd qckly 3f out: t.o* **80/1**

1m 51.89s (-2.01) **Going Correction** -0.025s/f (Good)
WFA 3 from 4yo+ 7lb **11** Ran SP% **117.8**
Speed ratings (Par 103): **107,105,104,102,99 99,97,94,93,92 78**
toteswingers:1&2:£6.00, 1&3:£25.30, 2&3:£15.70. totesuper7: Win: Not won. Place: Not won. CSF £40.09 CT £508.89 TOTE £8.00: £3.40, £1.10, £6.40; EX 34.20 Place 6 £56.71; Place 5 £34.82.
Owner Far 2 Many Sues **Bred** Gaines-Gentry Thoroughbreds **Trained** Sandhutton, N Yorks

FOCUS
A modest finale contested by largely out-of-form horses. The field were soon well strung out and only the third got into things from off the pace. The winner only had to match his early-season form.
Kimberley Downs(USA) Official explanation: trainer's rep said, regarding the apparent improvement in form shown, gelding was suited by the drop back in trip
T/Plt: £100.70 to a £1 stake. Pool:£34,405.67 - 249.32 winning tickets T/Qpdt: £16.50 to a £1 stake. Pool:£2,428.85 - 108.75 winning tickets RY

5217 YORK (L-H)
Thursday, August 19

OFFICIAL GOING: Good (good to firm in places; 7.4)
Rails moved out 3m on back straight and home bend adding 8yards to races of one mile and over.
Wind: Moderate, half behind Weather: Cloudy and dry

5245 DBS PREMIER YEARLING STKS 6f
1:45 (1:46) (Class 2) 2-Y-0
£147,720 (£59,100; £29,550; £14,760; £7,380; £7,380) **Stalls** Low

Form RPR

11 **1** **Wootton Bassett**[35] 4049 2-8-11 0 .... PaulHanagan 15 106+
(R A Fahey) *w ldr: led over 3f out: hdd over 1f out: led ins fnl f: won gng away* **5/4**[1]

1102 **2** *1 ¾* **Galtymore Lad**[26] 4355 2-9-2 99 .... KierenFallon 10 106
(M R Channon) *chsd ldrs: narrow ld over 1f out: hdd and no ex last 75yds* **12/1**

1201 **3** *4 ½* **Chiswick Bey (IRE)**[26] 4367 2-8-11 92 .... PaulMulrennan 5 87
(R A Fahey) *mid-div: hdwy over 2f out: edgd rt and styd on fnl f: tk modest 3rd nr line* **33/1**

1201 **4** *¾* **Reckless Reward (IRE)**[13] 4787 2-8-11 103 .... JimmyFortune 13 85
(R Hannon) *sn w ldrs: kpt on same pce fnl 2f* **8/1**[2]

4112 **5** *½* **Majestic Myles (IRE)**[19] 4578 2-8-11 94 .... BarryMcHugh 16 83
(R A Fahey) *mid-div: hdwy 2f out: kpt on ins fnl f* **10/1**[3]

4012 **6** *hd* **Diamond Geezah (IRE)**[20] 4539 2-8-11 90 .... MichaelHills 19 83
(B W Hills) *in rr: hdwy and edgd lft 2f out: kpt on fnl f* **18/1**

1260 **7** *1 ¾* **Shoshoni Wind**[26] 4356 2-8-7 94 ow1 .... PJSmullen 20 76
(K A Ryan) *b.hind: dwlt: hld up in rr: nt clr run over 1f out: styd on ins fnl f* **22/1**

32 **8** *nk* **Indieslad**[10] 4896 2-8-11 0 .... PhillipMakin 12 77
(Mrs A Duffield) *s.i.s: hld up in mid-div: one pce fnl 2f* **50/1**

114 **9** *½* **Bahceli (IRE)**[34] 4097 2-8-11 94 .... SteveDrowne 9 75
(R Hannon) *s.i.s: in rr: hdwy over 1f out: nvr nr ldrs* **33/1**

5324 **10** *nk* **Mappin Time (IRE)**[33] 4138 2-8-11 91 ....(b) DavidAllan 3 74
(T D Easterby) *chsd ldrs on outside: one pce fnl 2f* **33/1**

104 **11** *hd* **Al Madina (IRE)**[12] 4842 2-8-6 94 .... RoystonFfrench 6 69
(B Smart) *chsd ldrs on outside: one pce fnl 2f* **33/1**

1230 **12** *1 ¼* **My Son Max**[20] 4550 2-8-11 85 .... TedDurcan 11 70
(R Hannon) *in rr: sn drvn along: nvr a factor* **50/1**

2010 **13** *1 ¼* **Remotelinx (IRE)**[33] 4138 2-8-11 93 .... DaneO'Neill 4 66
(J W Hills) *mid-div on outside: nvr a threat* **28/1**

1132 **14** *½* **Cape To Rio (IRE)**[34] 4097 2-9-2 107 .... RichardHughes 7 70
(R Hannon) *chsd ldrs: lost pl over 1f out* **8/1**[2]

15 *3 ¾* **Tom Sawyer**[13] 4807 2-8-11 0 .... JMurtagh 8 55
(A P O'Brien, Ire) *hld up towards rr: effrt and nt clr run over 2f out: nvr on terms* **10/1**[3]

4216 **16** *7* **Capaill Liath (IRE)**[40] 3887 2-8-11 86 .... LiamKeniry 17 32
(B W Hills) *trckd ldrs: lost pl over 2f out* **50/1**

6410 **17** *2 ¼* **Dubai Celebration**[26] 4388 2-8-11 83 .... PJMcDonald 1 26
(Jedd O'Keeffe) *chsd ldrs on wd outside: drvn and lost pl over 2f out* **100/1**

0414 **18** *8* **Bussa**[20] 4544 2-8-11 85 .... RobertWinston 18 2
(P D Evans) *led tl over 3f out: lost pl over 2f out: heavily eased ins fnl f* **80/1**

1m 10.19s (-1.71) **Going Correction** -0.05s/f (Good) **18** Ran SP% **125.5**
Speed ratings (Par 100): **109,106,100,99,99 98,96,96,95,94 94,93,91,90,85 76,73,62**
toteswingers:1&2:£8.00, 1&3:£32.70, 2&3:£76.80 CSF £15.59 TOTE £2.30: £1.40, £3.00, £10.20; EX 26.40 Trifecta £726.40 Pool: £3,141.49 - 3.20 winning units..
Owner Frank Brady & The Cosmic Cases **Bred** Laundry Cottage Stud Farm **Trained** Musley Bank, N Yorks

FOCUS
The ground remained good, good to firm in places, but it certainly appeared to be riding quicker than the previous day, which was confirmed by the winning time for this opening contest. These big-field sales races are often nowhere near as competitive as the numbers suggest, and for the fifth time in eight years, this particular one went the way of the favourite. He would probably have won the Gimcrack had he run in that. The first two finished well clear and the form is solid.

NOTEBOOK
Wootton Bassett had a lot going for him and was backed as though defeat was unthinkable. Nicely drawn in 15, his Doncaster win had been boosted by the subsequent victory of runner-up Forjatt, and he showed himself to possess both speed and stamina, running on strongly inside the final furlong to assert from the runner-up. He's thought quite a bit of and will reportedly take his chance at Group level before long (entered in the Mill Reef and Middle Park), but connections are inclined to chase another big pot first, with the valuable sales race at Doncaster's St Leger meeting next on the agenda. (op 6-4)
Galtymore Lad, shouldering a 3lb penalty, improved for the step up to 7f latest, finding only the well-regarded Toolain too good in Listed company at Ascot, but he showed himself equally effective at this distance with a cracking effort in defeat, readily drawing clear with the favourite but just lacking his speed. He seems to be progressing all the time and is entitled to re-oppose at Doncaster, where the extra half a furlong and turnaround at the weights will obviously be in his favour. (op 16-1)
Chiswick Bey(IRE), a cosy winner off 85 latest, had earlier finished down the field in the Coventry and he ran well considering he came from stall five, staying on centre-track for third. A step up to 7f now looks in order.
Reckless Reward(IRE), runner-up in the Norfolk, had enjoyed mixed fortunes since, bouncing back from his Super Sprint flop when winning at odds of 1-6 latest, but he promised to be suited by 6f and kept on at the one pace to hold fourth. (op 9-1 tchd 10-1)
Majestic Myles(IRE), the third and final Fahey runner, has been progressing well in nurseries, finishing second off 90 at Glorious Goodwood latest, but this proved a step too far. He was far from disgraced, but is clearly just a handicapper. (op 11-1)
Diamond Geezah(IRE), runner-up in a 7f nursery at Glorious Goodwood, was always likely to find the drop in trip against him, so didn't run badly. (op 16-1)
Shoshoni Wind, whose rider was putting up 1lb overweight, wasn't the best away and as a result was always going to struggle to get a clear run through, having been drawn in 20. (op 20-1)
Indieslad didn't get the best of starts, but did keep on late. This was his first try at 6f, and he should have no trouble breaking his duck at some stage. (op 40-1)
Bahceli(IRE), held in Listed company latest, couldn't get into it having been sluggish leaving the stalls.
Remotelinx(IRE)'s rider reported that the colt hung right. Official explanation: jockey said colt hung right (op 25-1)
Cape To Rio(IRE) has twice finished placed at Listed level, but he never looked like making an impact from his single-figure draw and was disappointing, although his rider reported he was unsuited by the ground. Official explanation: jockey said colt was unsuited by the good (good to firm in places) ground (op 15-2 tchd 9-1)
Tom Sawyer, who failed to leave the rear, was denied a clear run according to the jockey. Official explanation: jockey said colt was denied a clear run (op 11-1)
Bussa Official explanation: jockey said gelding was unsuited by the good (good to firm in places) ground

5246 JAGUAR CARS LOWTHER STKS (GROUP 2) (FILLIES) 6f
2:15 (2:16) (Class 1) 2-Y-0
£56,770 (£21,520; £10,770; £5,370; £2,690; £1,350) **Stalls** Low

Form RPR

1036 **1** **Hooray**[6] 5036 2-8-12 103 .... SebSanders 5 110
(Sir Mark Prescott) *mde all: rdn and qcknd wl over 1f out: styd on wl fnl f* **11/1**

1122 **2** *¾* **Margot Did (IRE)**[26] 4356 2-8-12 105 .... HayleyTurner 7 108
(M L W Bell) *lw: hld up towards rr: effrt and n.m.r over 1f out: rdn and styd on ent fnl f: sn drvn to chse wnr: kpt on* **10/3**[2]

1 **3** *2 ¼* **Rimth**[101] 1972 2-8-12 0 .... JamieSpencer 4 101
(P F I Cole) *str: in tch on outer: hdwy to chse ldrs 2f out: sn rdn and kpt on u.p ins fnl f* **4/1**[3]

11 **4** *nk* **Maqaasid**[64] 3070 2-9-1 0 .... RichardHills 3 103
(J H M Gosden) *trckd ldrs: slt bump after 2f and sn keen: effrt to chal wl over 1f out: sn rdn and wknd ins fnl f* **11/8**[1]

4134 **5** *1 ¾* **Imperialistic Diva (IRE)**[26] 4356 2-8-12 99 .... DavidAllan 8 95
(T D Easterby) *trckd wnr on inner: rdn along 2f out: drvn wl over 1f out and sn wknd* **28/1**

06 **6** *2 ¾* **Queen Of Spain (IRE)**[26] 4356 2-8-12 0 .... JMurtagh 1 87
(A P O'Brien, Ire) *stdd s: hld up in rr: effrt 2f out: sn rdn and n.d* **14/1**

13 **7** *½* **Perfect Tribute**[26] 4356 2-8-12 0 .... LukeMorris 6 85
(C G Cox) *trckd ldrs: rdn along over 2f out: sn drvn and wknd wl over 1f out* **11/1**

2321 **8** *7* **Joyously**[69] 2918 2-8-12 80 .... PaulHanagan 2 64
(P D Evans) *cl up: rdn along over 2f out: sn wknd* **100/1**

1m 10.14s (-1.76) **Going Correction** -0.05s/f (Good) **8** Ran SP% **113.0**
Speed ratings (Par 103): **109,108,105,104,102 98,97,88**
toteswingers:1&2:£4.80, 1&3:£6.10, 2&3:£2.60 CSF £46.46 TOTE £12.50: £3.00, £1.30, £1.60; EX 57.10 Trifecta £258.40 Pool: £9,955.73 - 28.50 winning units..
Owner Cheveley Park Stud **Bred** Cheveley Park Stud Ltd **Trained** Newmarket, Suffolk
■ Stewards' Enquiry : Luke Morris five-day ban: careless riding (Sep 2-6)

FOCUS
This had the look of an up-to-scratch renewal of this Group 2 prize beforehand, with the Albany, Queen Mary, Cherry Hinton and Princess Margaret Stakes form all represented, but it turned into a slightly unsatisfactory affair with the field quickly making for the stands' side again and one or two of them encountering trouble. Russian Rhythm, successful here in 2002, was the last Lowther winner to go on to land the 1,000 Guineas the following year.

NOTEBOOK

Hooray had proved a disappointing favourite in the Listed St Hugh's Stakes at Newbury the previous Friday, some early buffeting and the rain-eased ground contributing to her defeat, but had earlier shown smart form when a close-up third to Memory and Soraaya in the Cherry Hinton. She has been a touch keen at times in her races and new tactics were employed on this return to 6f. Quickly securing a place against the stands' rail, she made all the running and stayed on well to hold the late flourish of the unlucky runner-up. Her trainer described her as 'very much a 2-y-o' and she doesn't strike as the type to stay much further than this, so makes little appeal as a Guineas prospect. She will be aimed at the Cheveley Park Stakes at Newmarket in the autumn. (op 14-1 tchd 10-1)

Margot Did(IRE), held up two from the rear going well, found herself stuck behind the labouring Imperialistic Diva at just the time the race was coming to the boil. Her rider had to sit and suffer while the winner went for home, and although the filly ran on strongly inside the last, the line was always going to beat her. She has now finished second on each of her three ventures into Group company, and thoroughly deserves to pick up a good race. The Cheveley Park is the obvious target and she could take in Salisbury's Dick Poole Stakes along the way. She will definitely get further and looks the only realistic 1,000 Guineas prospect in this field, having gone down by only a head to current favourite Memory in the Albany Stakes. (op 3-1 tchd 7-2)

Rimth had been off the track with shin problems since her impressive winning debut at Windsor in May, but she has always been well regarded and she ran a nice race despite a less than ideal preparation. She was dropped in before improving on the outside of the bunch, and although she was running on late she never promised to get to the winner. She was still green and there is improvement to come. (op 13-2)

Maqaasid was conceding a 3lb penalty all round for her victory in the Queen Mary Stakes. She took a bump from Perfect Tribute before halfway which rather lit her up, and seeing a good deal of daylight on the outside didn't help. She was still in second spot inside the final furlong but was tiring and lost two places from there. Her stamina for this trip remains open to debate. (op 11-10)

Imperialistic Diva(IRE) was soon well placed on the fence but was in trouble with two to run, fading to finish further behind Margot Did than she had at Ascot. She should get another furlong. (op 25-1)

Queen Of Spain(IRE), another who was dropped in leaving the stalls, made only modest late headway. She has now been held in three tries at Group level and the quest for black type continues. (op 16-1)

Perfect Tribute had reportedly improved physically since finishing third in the Princess Margaret Stakes, but was unable to build on that effort, fading after tracking the pace.

Joyously, winner of a Chepstow novice event when last seen over two months ago, was predictably found wanting in this company.

5247 ADDLESHAW GODDARD STKS (H'CAP) 1m

2:50 (2:51) (Class 2) 3-Y-0+ **£32,380** (£9,635; £4,815; £2,405) **Stalls** Low

Form					RPR
2100	**1**		**Ransom Note**^{20} 4537 3-9-0 **100** (B W Hills) *lw: trckd ldrs: edgd rt and led over 1f out: styd on strly ins fnl f* **8/1**^{3}	MichaelHills 1	112+
4020	**2**	*2*	**Acrostic**^{20} 4537 5-9-10 **104** (L M Cumani) *lw: mid-div: effrt 4f out: chal and edgd rt over 1f out: styd on same pce ins fnl f* **8/1**^{3}	KierenFallon 10	112
0554	**3**	*¾*	**Proponent (IRE)**^{20} 4537 6-9-3 **97** (R Charlton) *lw: trckd ldrs: t.k.h: effrt over 2f out: swtchd lft over 1f out: kpt on fnl f* **6/1**^{2}	RichardHughes 3	103
3100	**4**	*¾*	**Navajo Chief**^{40} 3886 3-8-12 **98** (A P Jarvis) *sn trcking ldrs: bmpd over 1f out: kpt on same pce ins fnl f* **28/1**	TedDurcan 2	101
6036	**5**	*¾*	**Light From Mars**^{25} 4412 5-9-1 **98** (B R Millman) *trckd ldrs: effrt and n.m.r over 2f out: kpt on same pce appr fnl f* **16/1**	JamesMillman$^{(3)}$ 12	101
2400	**6**	*1 ¼*	**Stoic (IRE)**^{64} 3069 4-9-10 **104** (J Noseda) *hld up towards rr: hdwy over 2f out: kpt on fnl f* **9/1**	JMurtagh 9	104
3320	**7**	*nk*	**Balcarce Nov (ARG)**^{64} 3069 5-9-9 **103** (T P Tate) *led hung lft and hdd over 1f out: kpt on same pce* **16/1**	JamieSpencer 11	102
3552	**8**	*1*	**Vainglory (USA)**^{12} 4816 6-8-11 **94** (D M Simcock) *mid-div: effrt and nt clr run over 2f out: kpt on fnl f: nvr trbld ldrs* **28/1**	MartinLane$^{(3)}$ 13	91+
1400	**9**	*nse*	**Classic Colori (IRE)**^{76} 2707 3-8-13 **99** (Tom Dascombe) *dwlt: mid-div: effrt over 2f out: nvr a threat* **25/1**	RichardKingscote 14	95
0000	**10**	*½*	**Extraterrestrial**^{23} 4463 6-8-12 **92** (R A Fahey) *in rr: nt clr run stands' side over 2f out: swtchd lft: styd on fnl f* **20/1**	PaulHanagan 15	87
0104	**11**	*shd*	**Tiger Reigns**^{12} 4828 4-9-4 **98** (M Dods) *t.k.h in tch: effrt over 2f out: nvr a factor* **18/1**	PhillipMakin 18	93
2110	**12**	*¾*	**Capponi (IRE)**^{21} 4504 3-9-0 **100** (M Johnston) *lw: chsd ldrs on outer: nt clr run stands' side rail and lost pl over 2f out: kpt on steadily fnl f* **9/2**^{1}	FrankieDettori 20	92+
5300	**13**	*4 ½*	**Greyfriarschorista**^{40} 3886 3-9-2 **102** (M Johnston) *chsd ldrs: wknd over 2f out* **33/1**	JoeFanning 19	84
1000	**14**	*1 ¾*	**Tartan Gigha (IRE)**^{23} 4455 5-9-8 **102** (M Johnston) *a towards rr* **33/1**	RichardHills 17	81
0650	**15**	*¾*	**Freeforaday (USA)**^{7} 5009 3-9-2 **102** (J R Best) *hmpd sn after s: t.k.h in rr: nvr on terms* **28/1**	SteveDrowne 5	78
0006	**16**	*2 ¼*	**Al Muheer (IRE)**^{20} 4537 5-9-3 **97** (D Nicholls) *a towards rr* **12/1**	AdrianNicholls 6	69
0120	**17**	*3*	**Mahadee (IRE)**^{20} 4537 5-9-1 **95** (R M Beckett) *in rr-div: drvn over 3f out: nvr on terms* **25/1**	(b) JimCrowley 4	60

1m 37.46s (-1.34) **Going Correction** +0.075s/f (Good)

WFA 3 from 4yo+ 6lb **17** Ran SP% **118.1**

Speed ratings (Par 109): **109,107,106,105,104 103,103,102,102,101 101,100,96,94,93 91,88**

toteswingers:1&2:£12.40, 1&3:£8.30, 2&3:£7.00 CSF £57.01 CT £372.57 TOTE £7.50: £2.20, £2.10, £1.70, £8.80; EX 59.10 Trifecta £308.50 Pool: £4,315.03 - 10.34 winning units..Suruor was withdrawn. Price at time of withdrawal 12/1. Rule 4 applies to all bets - deduction 5p in the pound.

Owner H R Mould **Bred** Rabbah Bloodstock Limited **Trained** Lambourn, Berks

FOCUS

A wide-open handicap, or at least it was on paper anyway, as little came from off the pace to challenge. As a result the form is not as positively rated as it might have been. The solid third is a good guide. The field headed for the stands' rail on straightening.

NOTEBOOK

Ransom Note, 8lb higher than when winning the Britannia Stakes, had a poor draw to overcome at Glorious Goodwood last time and it was no surprise to see him come right back to top form here, always holding a prominent position and staying on strongly having hit the front 1f out. Although appearing not to stay on one previous try at 1m2f, Barry Hills expects him to have no trouble with it in future, and the Cambridgeshire over 1m1f will be his main aim now. (op 9-1)

Acrostic, behind the winner at Goodwood when also poorly drawn (got no run when trying to stay on), had earlier run well in defeat off 3lb lower at Sandown, but once again met a 3-y-o with pretensions of being a Group horse. (op 9-1)

Proponent(IRE) has been running well, finishing ahead of the front two at Goodwood last time, but as is often the case, he was found wanting for a finishing kick. (op 8-1)

Navajo Chief, below par the last twice, including behind the winner in the Britannia, looked a player on his earlier Haydock win and was keeping on for pressure when bumped by the winner 1f out. He did manage to keep on for fourth. (op 25-1)

Light From Mars, best suited by a strongly run 7f, didn't have much room against the rail from over 2f out, but could only stay on at the one pace once in the clear late on anyway. (op 18-1)

Stoic(IRE), mid-division in the Hunt Cup latest, made some late headway but is going to remain vulnerable off this sort of mark. (op 8-1)

Balcarce Nov(ARG), badly hampered in the Hunt Cup, gave more of an idea as to what he is capable of here, only giving way 1f out.

Vainglory(USA), runner-up at the Shergar Cup, would have been closer with a clear run.

Classic Colori(IRE), gelded since last seen, was another going on at the finish. (op 33-1)

Extraterrestrial, who ideally needs softer ground, stayed on late having been denied a clear run. (op 25-1)

Capponi(IRE), progressive until appearing not to last 1m2f at Goodwood latest, was tight for room against the stands' rail and, having been shuffled back, kept on late under considerate handling. He can be rated better than the bare form and deserves another chance. (op 5-1)

Freeforaday(USA)'s rider reported the colt suffered interference. Official explanation: jockey said colt suffered interference early on

Al Muheer(IRE) failed to build on his unlucky looking Goodwood run, being eased late on once his chance had gone, but he continues to ease down the weights and seems sure to come good at some stage for connections. (op 10-1)

5248 DARLEY YORKSHIRE OAKS (GROUP 1) (F&M) 1m 4f

3:25 (3:27) (Class 1) 3-Y-O+

£175,987 (£66,712; £33,387; £16,647; £8,339; £4,185) **Stalls** Centre

Form					RPR
1-21	**1**		**Midday**^{19} 4575 4-9-7 120 (H R A Cecil) *lw: hld up in tch: smooth hdwy over 3f out: led 2f out: qcknd clr over 1f out: rdn and hung lft ins fnl f: kpt on strly* **11/4**^{3}	TomQueally 6	124+
-111	**2**	*3*	**Snow Fairy (IRE)**^{32} 4178 3-8-11 119 (E A L Dunlop) *hld up in tch: hdwy over 3f out: effrt 2f out: rdn to chse wnr over 1f out: drvn and kpt on ins fnl f: no imp* **5/2**^{2}	RichardHughes 8	118
-231	**3**	*2*	**Eleanora Duse (IRE)**^{70} 2889 3-8-11 104 (Sir Michael Stoute) *hld up in rr: hdwy over 3f out: rdn 2f out: chsd ldng pair over 1f out: kpt on same pce* **25/1**	OlivierPeslier 5	115
-124	**4**	*1 ½*	**Meeznah (USA)**^{32} 4178 3-8-11 113 (D R Lanigan) *hld up towards rr: hdwy 3f out: rdn to chse ldrs 2f out: drvn over 1f out and kpt on same pce* **10/1**	KierenFallon 1	113
-325	**5**	*8*	**Flying Cloud (IRE)**^{21} 4507 4-9-7 114 (Saeed Bin Suroor) *chsd ldr: rdn over 3f out: cl up over 2f out: sn drvn and wknd* **25/1**	(t) TedDurcan 4	100
4316	**6**	*3 ¼*	**Barshiba (IRE)**^{19} 4575 6-9-7 110 (D R C Elsworth) *led: rdn clr 4f out: drvn over 2f out: sn hdd & wknd* **33/1**	PaulHanagan 2	95
3100	**7**	*30*	**Hibaayeb**^{18} 4640 3-8-11 114 (Saeed Bin Suroor) *trckd ldng pair: hdwy over 3f out and sn rdn: wknd qckly over 2f out: sn heavily eased* **16/1**	(t) FrankieDettori 7	47
3-12	**R**		**Sariska**^{76} 2709 4-9-7 118 (M L W Bell) *lw: ref to r* **85/40**^{1}	JamieSpencer 3	—

2m 30.53s (-2.67) **Going Correction** +0.075s/f (Good)

WFA 3 from 4yo+ 10lb **8** Ran SP% **112.8**

Speed ratings (Par 117): **111,109,107,106,101 99,79,—**

toteswingers:1&2:£2.00, 1&3:£10.60, 2&3:£10.10 CSF £9.67 TOTE £4.10: £1.40, £1.50, £2.80; EX 13.00 Trifecta £74.90 Pool: £17,455.66 - 172.41 winning units..

Owner K Abdulla **Bred** Juddmonte Farms Ltd **Trained** Newmarket, Suffolk

FOCUS

A tremendous edition of the Yorkshire Oaks appeared in prospect, featuring two Epsom Oaks winners in opposition for the first time since Love Divine and Ramruma found Petrushka too good in this race a decade ago. It was weakened when Sariska refused to race, but Midday put up a fine performance and a small personal best. The pace was solid and the first four home comprised the last quartet when the field turned into the home straight, where they headed for the stands' side once more.

NOTEBOOK

Midday had been beaten by Sariska on each of the three times they had met, but came out just the better filly at the weights on their running here in May and it is a shame we were denied a fourth clash. With her old rival out of the way the path was smoothed for her to pick up her fourth win in the highest grade, but she produced a brilliant performance and Sariska might well have had her work cut out to beat her. Tackling 1m4f for the first time since last year's Irish Oaks, she travelled strongly, quickened up in awesome style and was already clear when drifting to her left inside the final furlong. She still looks to be improving and is well up to adding further successes at the top level. Her trainer is keen to keep her against her own sex, which would rule out the Arc, but she is in the Prix Vermeille and the Prix l'Opera, both at Longchamp, and her primary target is another Breeders' Cup Filly & Mare Turf at Churchill Downs. That race is over 1m3f this year, which is another plus. (op 3-1 tchd 5-2)

Snow Fairy(IRE) had not been totally at home in yielding conditions at the Curragh despite bolting up there by eight lengths. With Richard Hughes replacing the injured Ryan Moore, she travelled as strongly as the winner into the straight, but after following the older filly through she had no answer to her turn of foot. The seventh Epsom Oaks winner to be beaten here since 1997 - it happened to Sariska 12 months ago - she was unable to complete the Oaks 'treble' most recently achieved by Alexandrova four years ago, but lost nothing in defeat against a top-notch opponent and cemented her superiority over Meeznah. The St Leger remains an option, but there might be stronger stayers there. (op 3-1 tchd 10-3 in places)

Eleanora Duse(IRE)'s trainer persuaded the owners that she should run here rather than in the Galtres Stakes, and the filly repaid their faith with a fine effort. She was taking a big hike in class after winning her owners' money back in the Listed Ballymacoll Stud Stakes at Newbury in June, but is clearly an improving filly who was well at home with the step up to 1m4f for the first time. (op 20-1)

Meeznah(USA) stayed on from the back of the field in the straight without really getting to grips with the big two. Perhaps not quite at her best here, although she ran better than she had in easy ground at the Curragh, she will step up over 2f in trip in the Park Hill Stakes at Doncaster. She promises to stay and deserves to pick up her first Group victory.

Flying Cloud(IRE), who had been held by Sariska and Midday in the Middleton Stakes at the May fixture here, did the better of the Godolphin pair. There was nothing wrong with the way she applied herself under pressure, but she is not proving an easy filly to place successfully.

Barshiba(IRE) showed a bit of reluctance to enter the stalls. She set a generous gallop and tried to kick clear entering the straight, only to be readily worn down. She owes her connections nothing, but has now run in a dozen Group 1s and has never been placed. (op 28-1)

Hibaayeb dropped away rather quickly in the straight with Dettori glancing down before easing her. She has disappointed three times now since her Ribblesdale triumph and, unlike her runs in Ireland and Germany, could not use the ground as an excuse. Her rider reported the filly was never travelling. Official explanation: jockey said filly was never travelling (op 14-1)

Sariska decided to plant herself in the stalls, stripping the race of a fair bit of interest. She has not done anything like this before and hopefully she can still enjoy a fruitful autumn campaign. (op 2-1 tchd 5-2)

5249 EUROPEAN BREEDERS' FUND GALTRES STKS (LISTED RACE) (F&M) 1m 4f

4:05 (4:05) (Class 1) 3-Y-0+ **£23,704** (£8,964; £4,480; £2,240) **Stalls** Centre

Form RPR

4116 **1** **Brushing**[12] 4830 4-9-4 86 .... KierenFallon 10 105
(M H Tompkins) *hld up in rr: smooth hdwy on outer over 2f out: rdn to ld appr fnl f and sn hung lft: drvn out* **20/1**

4 **2** 2 **Sense Of Purpose (IRE)**[18] 4631 3-8-8 95 ....(v[1]) PJSmullen 5 102
(D K Weld, Ire) *a.p: chsd ldr 5f out: rdn to ld 2f out: drvn and hdd appr fnl f: kpt on same pce* **12/1**

23-5 **3** 2 **Copperbeech (IRE)**[27] 4347 4-9-4 99 .... FrankieDettori 7 99
(Saeed Bin Suroor) *a.p: hdwy 3f out: rdn and ev ch 2f out: drvn whn sltly hmpd appr fnl f: kpt on same pce* **10/1**

4634 **4** 2 ¾ **Honimiere (IRE)**[33] 4143 4-9-4 100 .... PJMcDonald 3 95
(G A Swinbank) *lw: set gd pce: rdn along 3f out: drvn and hdd 2f out: grad wknd* **14/1**

5020 **5** ½ **Snoqualmie Girl (IRE)**[18] 4624 4-9-4 100 .... JimmyFortune 8 94
(D R C Elsworth) *hld up towards rr: hdwy 3f out: rdn over 2f out: n.d* **22/1**

-120 **6** ¾ **Eldalil**[32] 4178 3-8-8 108 .... RichardHills 2 93
(Sir Michael Stoute) *in tch: hdwy over 3f out: rdn to chse ldrs over 2f out: sn drvn and grad wknd* **9/2**[2]

1321 **7** 2 **Destinys Dream (IRE)**[26] 4389 5-9-4 86 .... AndrewMullen 4 89
(Miss Tracy Waggott) *in tch: hdwy to chse ldrs 3f out: rdn along over 2f out: sn drvn and grad wknd* **28/1**

-403 **8** 14 **Saphira's Fire (IRE)**[18] 4624 5-9-4 100 .... MartinDwyer 6 67
(W R Muir) *chsd ldrs: rdn along wl over 2f out: sn drvn and wknd* **8/1**[3]

1-30 **9** 29 **Ceilidh House**[76] 2711 3-8-8 98 .... JimCrowley 11 21
(R M Beckett) *chsd ldrs: rdn along over 3f out: wknd qckly and eased over 2f out* **9/1**

3 **10** 28 **Zarebiya (IRE)**[18] 4631 3-8-8 0 .... JamieSpencer 9 —
(John M Oxx, Ire) *w'like; scope: rrd: hit hd on stalls and lost many l s: a bhd: eased fnl 3f* **11/8**[1]

2m 31.97s (-1.23) **Going Correction** +0.075s/f (Good)
WFA 3 from 4yo+ 10lb **10** Ran SP% **117.4**
Speed ratings (Par 111): **107,105,104,102,102 101,100,91,71,53**
toteswingers:1&2:£28.70, 1&3:£9.10, 2&3:£15.90 CSF £235.19 TOTE £24.90: £5.30, £3.50, £2.40; EX 395.10 Trifecta £1981.40 Part won. Pool: £2,677.65 - 0.30 winning units..
Owner John Brenchley **Bred** Dullingham Park **Trained** Newmarket, Suffolk
■ Stewards' Enquiry : Kieren Fallon caution: careless riding

FOCUS
It didn't look the strongest race for the grade, with several of the other fancied ones disappointing also, so the form may not be worth much. They went a good gallop, so it was no surprise to see the winner come from off the pace. The form is rated around the third, with improvement from the first two.

NOTEBOOK
Brushing had been comfortably held in a handicap at Haydock last time, albeit a well-contested one. A dual winner at Carlisle earlier in the season, once for Fallon, she evidently relished every yard of the trip, sweeping to the front over 1f out and saying on well. She deserves a chance to show this wasn't a one-off, and it will be interesting to see where she goes next, with the valuable John Smith's Handicap at Newbury under consideration. (tchd 22-1)
Sense Of Purpose(IRE), beaten at this level on three occasions in Ireland and behind the favourite in a Group 3 last time, appeared to show improved form in a first-time visor, chasing the early pace and keeping on all the way to the line in second. (op 14-1)
Copperbeech(IRE), comfortably held in a Listed race over shorter at the course last time, was briefly checked in her stride when the winner took over, but it didn't affect her finishing position. (op 12-1)
Honimiere(IRE) led them over to the stands' rail and again ran well, but she's still seeking her first win of the year. (op 12-1)
Snoqualmie Girl(IRE) stayed on inside the final 2f, but never looked like reaching the leaders. (op 20-1)
Eldalil, unsuited by the soft ground in the Irish Oaks, found little once coming under pressure and slowly faded. This effort leaves her with plenty to prove. (op 5-1)
Destinys Dream(IRE) was outclassed on this rise in grade. (op 20-1)
Saphira's Fire(IRE) was below form for no obvious reason. Official explanation: jockey said mare scoped dirty post race (op 15-2)
Ceilidh House just hasn't come up to expectations this year. The trainer reported that the filly scoped dirty after the race. Official explanation: jockey said filly had no more to give (op 8-1)
Zarebiya(IRE) may well have won but for the stalls incident. Her trainer has won this three times in the recent past, including last year, but she could never get out of last and was eased right down by Spencer in the straight. Official explanation: jockey said filly reared up at the start (op 13-8)

5250 EVENTMASTERS.CO.UK 25TH ANNIVERSARY H'CAP 5f

4:40 (4:40) (Class 2) (0-100,98) 3-Y-O **£12,952** (£3,854; £1,926; £962) **Stalls** Low

Form RPR

1205 **1** **Monsieur Joe (IRE)**[12] 4814 3-9-6 97 .... EddieAhern 2 104
(W R Swinburn) *midfield: hdwy on outer 2f out: sn rdn: drvn and styd on ins fnl f to ld nr fin* **14/1**

2211 **2** shd **La Fortunata**[12] 4837 3-8-2 79 oh1 .... AndreaAtzeni 5 86
(Mike Murphy) *mde most and sn crossed to stands' rail: rdn wl over 1f out: drvn and edgd lft ins fnl f: hdd and no ex nr fin* **20/1**

4344 **3** 1 ¼ **Duchess Dora (IRE)**[31] 4191 3-8-12 94 .... IanBrennan(5) 11 97
(J J Quinn) *chsd ldrs on inner: hdwy 2f out: rdn over 1f out: drvn and kpt on ins fnl f* **9/1**

3000 **4** shd **Singeur (IRE)**[19] 4576 3-9-7 98 ....(b) NeilCallan 9 100
(R Bastiman) *s.i.s and bhd: hdwy and n.m.r over 1f out: swtchd outside and drvn: fin strly* **9/1**

0110 **5** nse **Kingsgate Choice (IRE)**[43] 3791 3-8-13 90 .... RobertWinston 17 92
(J R Best) *in tch whn sltly hmpd after 1f: hdwy to chse ldrs 2f out: sn rdn and kpt on u.p fnl f* **5/1**[2]

-306 **6** shd **Skylla**[20] 4541 3-9-0 91 .... PaulHanagan 1 93
(R A Fahey) *cl up: rdn wl over 1f out and ev ch tl drvn and nt qckn ins fnl f* **20/1**

1105 **7** 1 ½ **Hoof It**[41] 3856 3-9-1 92 .... KierenFallon 12 94+
(M W Easterby) *sn pushed along in rr: hdwy wl over 1f out: swtchd rt and rdn ent fnl f: styng on whn hmpd and snatched up last 100yds* **9/2**[1]

1111 **8** ½ **Perfect Blossom**[20] 4541 3-8-11 91 .... AmyRyan(3) 3 86+
(K A Ryan) *prom: rdn to chal wl over 1f out and ev ch tl drvn and wknd ins fnl f* **8/1**[3]

0535 **9** ½ **Tawaabb**[20] 4541 3-9-4 95 ....(v) RichardHughes 15 88+
(M R Channon) *hld up towards rr: hdwy wl over 1f out: nt clr run ent fnl f: sn swtchd lft and kpt on: nrst fin* **14/1**

3522 **10** ½ **Confessional**[16] 4685 3-8-12 89 ....(e) DavidAllan 4 80
(T D Easterby) *chsd ldrs: rdn 2f out: drvn and wknd appr fnl f* **16/1**

4002 **11** 1 **Magical Macey (USA)**[10] 4901 3-8-7 84 ....(b) RoystonFfrench 6 71
(T D Barron) *chsd ldrs: rdn along 2f out: grad wknd* **28/1**

-032 **12** ¾ **Above Limits (IRE)**[32] 4185 3-8-13 95 .... JohnFahy(5) 7 80
(D M Simcock) *chsd ldrs: n.m.r and swtchd lft after 1f: rdn 2f out: sn drvn and grad wknd ent fnl f* **14/1**

5201 **13** nk **Mon Brav**[10] 4901 3-8-7 84 6ex ....(v) JamieSpencer 16 67
(D Carroll) *bhd: hdwy over 1f out: nt clr run and swtchd lft ins fnl f: nvr a factor* **11/1**

-101 **14** ½ **Beat Baby (IRE)**[32] 4171 3-8-11 88 .... PaulMulrennan 13 70+
(J Howard Johnson) *chsd ldrs on inner whn bdly hmpd after 1f: bhd after* **20/1**

4205 **15** 6 **The Only Boss (IRE)**[61] 3218 3-8-13 90 .... JMurtagh 10 50
(W J Haggas) *in tch whn hmpd after 1f: t.k.h after: rdn 2f out: n.m.r and sn wknd* **16/1**

1216 **16** 2 ½ **Lewyn**[117] 1523 3-8-9 86 .... PJMcDonald 14 37
(K A Ryan) *dwlt: sn outpcd and a bhd* **66/1**

58.21 secs (-1.09) **Going Correction** -0.05s/f (Good) **16** Ran SP% **125.3**
Speed ratings (Par 106): **106,105,103,103,103 103,101,100,99,98 97,95,95,94,84 80**
toteswingers:1&2:£6.00, 1&3:£25.30, 2&3:£15.70 CSF £280.90 CT £2775.65 TOTE £16.70: £3.20, £3.80, £2.80, £3.00; EX 418.70 TRIFECTA Not won. Place 6 £569.71; Place 5 £320.35.
Owner Mrs Helen Checkley **Bred** Nicola And Eleanor Kent **Trained** Aldbury, Herts
■ Stewards' Enquiry : Andrea Atzeni ten-day ban: careless riding (Sep 2-10)
Paul Hanagan one-day ban: careless riding (Sep 2)

FOCUS
A highly competitive sprint handicap for 3-y-os. A number of them found trouble in a fast and furious race, but the form still has a sound look to it. It has been rated around the third.

NOTEBOOK
Monsieur Joe(IRE), who came out of stall 2, delivered his challenge widest on the track, his rider having made no attempt to get him over to the fence. Snatching the race in the dying strides, the colt came here on the back of three good efforts against older sprinters at Ascot. He did well to win this from off the pace and is still on the upgrade.
La Fortunata arrived here in top form and nearly landed the hat-trick, but after blazing a trail on the stands' rail she edged to her left close home and was just picked off. She was racing from 1lb out of the handicap, which theoretically cost her victory.
Duchess Dora(IRE) tracked the runner-up on the fence, moving well, and had to be switched twice for a clear run as the other filly edged off a line. She still secured third and is pretty consistent. (tchd 8-1)
Singeur(IRE), racing in the winner's slipstream down the outside, flew home for fourth. This was another creditable effort in blinkers but he really needs 6f. (op 11-1)
Kingsgate Choice(IRE) was one of several involved in a chain reaction early on but was keeping on well at the end. He made his effort alongside the winner and should not be classed as unlucky. On this evidence he might appreciate a return to 6f. (op 6-1)
Skylla reverted to prominent tactics and showed bright pace to get over from the lowest stall. The runner-up just edged across her late on, but for which she might have made the frame.
Hoof It was outpaced through the early parts but was coming home well after weaving his way through, only to have to be snatched up late on. Although 11lb above his last win, he gives the impression that he has not stopped winning when things fall for him.
Perfect Blossom was previously unbeaten in six 5f handicaps this term and had accounted for a number of these along the way, including four of them at Glorious Goodwood on her latest start, and La Fortunata at Epsom the time before. Another 7lb rise put her on a mark no less than 35lb higher than for her first win, but she ran well for a long way and was still in second place entering the last before fading out of the picture. (op 7-1)
Tawaabb ran better than the bare result and remains in good heart. (op 16-1 tchd 18-1)
Confessional, who was runner-up in Perfect Blossom's Goodwood race, weakened after chasing the pace. (tchd 18-1)
Mon Brav, who was 4lb wrong under his penalty, did not get the breaks but gave the impression he remains in form, and another whose performance here can probably be written off. (tchd 12-1)
The Only Boss(IRE) was reported as having been a denied a clear run. Official explanation: jockey said gelding was denied a clear run (op 20-1)
T/Jkpt: Not won. T/Plt: £920.70 to a £1 stake. Pool:£288,903.94 - 229.05 winning tickets T/Qpdt: £148.10 to a £1 stake. Pool:£12,735.42 - 63.60 winning tickets JR

5063 CLAIREFONTAINE (R-H)

Thursday, August 19

OFFICIAL GOING: Turf: soft

5251a PRIX BOURDIN & CO (PRIX D'AUBERVILLE) (MAIDEN) (2YO COLTS & GELDINGS) (TURF) 7f

1:10 (12:00) 2-Y-O **£10,619** (£4,247; £3,185; £2,123; £1,061)

RPR

1 **Yarubo (FR)**[16] 2-9-2 0 .... ChristopheSoumillon 6 90
(J-C Rouget, France) **2/5**[1]

2 4 **Point Du Jour (FR)**[27] 4332 2-9-2 0 .... DominiqueBoeuf 7 80
(I A Wood) *trckd the ldr: led ins fnl 2f: hdd ins fnl f: no ex* **4/1**[2]

3 2 **Victorian Number (FR)** 2-9-2 0 .... JulienAuge 2 75
(E J O'Neill, France) **12/1**[3]

4 6 **Allegorio (FR)**[7] 5137 2-9-2 0 ....(b[1]) DavyBonilla 8 60
(Tom Dascombe) *qckly away: led fr s: hdd ins fnl 2f: wknd fnl f* **15/1**

5 2 **Kourdo (FR)** 2-9-2 0 .... RomainLeDren-Doleuze 3 55
(J Parize, France) **30/1**

6 5 **Far Far Away (FR)** 2-9-2 0 .... MathiasSautjeau 5 43
(B Barbier, France) **16/1**

7 8 **Alighieri (FR)** 2-9-2 0 .... YannLerner 1 23
(Mme M-C Naim, France) **37/1**

1m 26.4s (86.40) **7** Ran SP% **117.1**
PARI-MUTUEL (all including 1 euro stakes): WIN 1.40; PLACE 1.10, 1.10, 1.10; DF 1.80; SF 2.40.
Owner Jean-Claude Gour **Bred** F Bayrou & P McNulty **Trained** Pau, France

NOTEBOOK
Point Du Jour(FR), runner-up in a decent little heat at Newmarket last time, ran well in defeat once more, but couldn't live with the winner, who's considered a Group horse in the making by connections.
Allegorio(FR) showed early speed in the first-time blinkers.

5252a PRIX LES GRANDES GUEULES (PRIX DE VAUVILLE) (MAIDEN) (2YO FILLIES) (TURF) 7f

1:45 (12:00) 2-Y-O **£10,619** (£4,247; £3,185; £2,123; £1,061)

RPR

1 **Darling Story (FR)** 2-9-0 0 .... ChristopheSoumillon 10 79
(J-C Rouget, France) **37/10**[2]

2 1½ **Celenza (FR)** 2-9-0 0 ..... GeraldMosse 6 75
(A De Royer-Dupre, France) **68/10**
3 nk **Beginnings (USA)**^{16} 2-9-0 0 ..... StephanePasquier 4 75
(D Smaga, France) **9/5**^{1}
4 1 **Hoppy's Flyer (FR)**^{11} 4884 2-9-0 0 ..... MaximeGuyon 5 72
(Tom Dascombe) *broke wl and led: qcknd st: hdd ins fnl 2f: no ex fnl 100yds: jst hld on for 4th* **5/1**^{3}
5 shd **Gwenhwyfar (IRE)** 2-9-0 0 ..... Pierre-CharlesBoudot 7 72
(A Fabre, France) **73/10**
6 ¾ **Nonsuch Way (IRE)**^{18} 2-9-0 0 ..... SylvainRuis 8 70
(F Vermeulen, France) **12/1**
7 3 **Liberty Gree (IRE)**^{16} 2-9-0 0 ..... GregoryBenoist 9 62
(Mme C Head-Maarek, France) **48/1**
8 2½ **Venise Jelois (FR)**^{7} 2-8-6 0 ..... EddyHardouin$^{(8)}$ 1 56
(Robert Collet, France) **58/1**
9 2 **Good Society** 2-9-0 0 ..... KarlMartin 2 51
(Alex Fracas, France) **42/1**
10 8 **Azarra (IRE)** 2-9-0 0 ..... YannLerner 3 31
(C Lerner, France) **79/1**
P **Taquawin (FR)** 2-9-0 0 ..... FranckBlondel 11 —
(D Prod'Homme, France) **28/1**

1m 28.0s (88.00) **11** Ran SP% **117.0**
PARI-MUTUEL (all including 1 euro stakes): WIN 4.70; PLACE 1.70, 2.30, 1.50; DF 22.50; SF 45.30.
Owner Mme B Hermelin & J C Rouget S A **Bred** Y Fremiot & Mme Y Fremiot **Trained** Pau, France

NOTEBOOK
Hoppy's Flyer(FR) was again given a positive ride and probably ran to a similar level as at Deauville last time.

5006 SALISBURY (R-H)
Friday, August 20

OFFICIAL GOING: Good to soft (good in places) changing to soft after race 2 (5.25pm)
Rail erected up to 20ft off permanent far side rail between 6.5f and 1f.
Wind: Strong, across. Weather: light rain

5254 DAVID BROAD "40 YEARS" LADY AMATEUR RIDERS' H'CAP 1m
4:55 (4:55) (Class 5) (0-70,70) 3-Y-O+ **£3,123** (£968; £484; £242) **Stalls** High

Form RPR
0401 1 **Gross Prophet**^{7} 5039 5-10-4 **66** ..... MissZoeLilly$^{(3)}$ 4 76
(A J Lidderdale) *trckd ldrs in centre: rdn over 2f out: kpt on ins fnl f: led nr fin* **6/1**^{2}
1412 2 nse **Calypso Star (IRE)**^{27} 4383 3-9-12 **70** .....(b) MissDaisySharp$^{(7)}$ 3 79
(R Hannon) *prom in centre: overall ldr over 3f out: sn 3 l clr: rdn ent fnl f: hdd fnl stride* **5/1**^{1}
4531 3 1¾ **Strike Force**^{8} 4985 6-9-6 **56** 6ex .....(t) MissALHutchinson$^{(5)}$ 8 62
(Miss Olivia Maylam) *hld up in rr of centre gp: hdwy fr over 2f out: styd on to go 3rd ins fnl f: nt quite rch ldrs: hld whn eased nr fin* **6/1**^{2}
3360 4 3¼ **King Columbo (IRE)**^{27} 4382 5-9-12 **64** ..... MissSBirkett$^{(7)}$ 2 62
(Miss J Feilden) *prom in centre: rdn to chse clr ldr over 2f out: drifted rt over 1f out: no ex ins fnl f* **10/1**^{3}
3453 5 4 **Alqaahir (USA)**^{17} 4681 8-10-1 **65** ..... MissMBryant$^{(5)}$ 9 54
(P Butler) *racd centre: sn outpcd in rr: styd on steadily fr 2f out: nvr trbld ldrs* **14/1**
3605 6 1½ **War And Peace (IRE)**^{7} 5039 6-10-6 **65** ..... MrsEEvans 6 51
(P D Evans) *in tch in centre: rdn over 2f out: sn one pce* **14/1**
-004 7 6 **Sir Tom**^{9} 4959 5-9-3 **48** oh1 ow1 ..... MissGAndrews 10 20
(J J Bridger) *s.i.s: towards rr of centre: sme late prog: nvr a factor* **20/1**
5342 8 2½ **Pebblesonthebeach**^{9} 4959 3-9-13 **69** .....(p) MissPhillipaTutty$^{(5)}$ 1 34
(J W Hills) *nvr bttr than mid-div in centre* **6/1**^{2}
2001 9 ½ **Sovereignty (JPN)**^{16} 4700 8-9-10 **62** ..... MissECrossman$^{(7)}$ 12 27
(D K Ivory) *overall ldr: racd on far side: hdd over 3f out: sn btn* **25/1**
030 10 ½ **My Jeanie (IRE)**^{58} 3323 6-8-11 **47** oh2 ..... MissRKneller$^{(5)}$ 7 11
(J C Fox) *trckd ldrs in centre tl wknd over 2f out* **33/1**
4230 11 6 **Cottonfields (USA)**^{16} 4700 4-10-2 **61** .....(p) MissEJJones 5 11
(Mrs H S Main) *sn pushed along in tch: wknd over 2f out* **18/1**
30/0 12 6 **Wrecking Crew (IRE)**^{17} 4681 6-9-8 **60** ..... MissDO'Brien$^{(7)}$ 11 —
(B R Millman) *restrained s: a bhd* **40/1**
053 13 2 **Lady Willa (IRE)**^{73} 2844 3-9-10 **61** ..... MissSBrotherton 13 —
(Mark Gillard) *chsd ldr on far side tl wknd 3f out* **6/1**^{2}

1m 46.15s (2.65) **Going Correction** +0.125s/f (Good)
WFA 3 from 4yo+ 6lb **13** Ran SP% **115.5**
Speed ratings (Par 103): **91,90,89,85,81 80,74,71,71,70 64,58,56**
Tote Swingers: 1&2 £5.10, 1&3 £8.60, 2&3 £3.80 CSF £33.15 CT £188.46 TOTE £7.40: £3.00, £2.20, £1.90; EX 22.70.
Owner Lambourn Valley Racing **Bred** A David Solomon **Trained** Eastbury, Berks

FOCUS
They finished well strung out.

5255 MARGARET MILLS RETIREMENT MAIDEN AUCTION STKS 6f
5:25 (5:31) (Class 5) 2-Y-O **£3,238** (£963; £481; £240) **Stalls** High

Form RPR
2 1 **Morache Music**^{46} 3735 2-8-13 0 ..... PatCosgrave 6 88+
(P J Makin) *s.i.s: towards rr: smooth hdwy to trck ldrs over 3f out: led wl over 1f out: r.o strly to draw clr fnl f: comf* **2/1**^{1}
2 2 5 **Choose The Moment**^{15} 4753 2-8-4 0 ..... AdrianNicholls 17 64
(Eve Johnson Houghton) *prom: rdn and ev ch over 2f out tl outpcd by wnr jst over 1f out* **11/2**^{2}
52 3 1¼ **Park Ballet (IRE)**^{16} 4716 2-8-5 0 ow8 ..... CharlesEddery$^{(7)}$ 2 68
(J G Portman) *racd keenly in tch: rdn over 2f out: ch over 1f out: kpt on same pce fnl f* **15/2**
20 4 1½ **Royalorien**^{23} 4471 2-8-8 0 ..... MartinDwyer 12 60
(W J Knight) *prom: rdn and ev ch wl over 1f out: one pce fnl f* **7/1**
0 5 shd **Homeboy (IRE)**^{12} 4871 2-8-4 0 ..... KatiaScallan$^{(7)}$ 7 62
(M P Tregoning) *s.i.s: towards rr: nt clr run over 2f out: hdwy over 1f out: kpt on: nvr trbld ldrs* **40/1**
6 3 **Cultural Desert** 2-9-2 0 ..... JackMitchell 15 58
(R M Beckett) *hld up towards rr: prog whn short of room and snatched up over 3f out: swtchd lft: styd on fnl f: nvr trbld ldrs* **12/1**
7 hd **Neytiri** 2-8-4 0 ..... HayleyTurner 3 46
(R M Beckett) *chsd ldrs: rdn over 2f out: one pce fnl f* **28/1**
6 8 nk **Queen Of Cash (IRE)**^{18} 4658 2-8-11 0 ..... AdrianLayt 5 52
(H Morrison) *chsd ldrs: rdn over 2f out: wknd fnl f* **13/2**^{3}
6 9 1 **Shutupandrive**^{15} 4729 2-7-13 0 ..... SophieDoyle$^{(5)}$ 9 42
(M D I Usher) *led: rdn and hdd wl over 1f out: wknd ent fnl f* **80/1**
10 1¼ **Shaman Dancer (GER)** 2-9-2 0 ..... LiamKeniry 4 50
(A M Balding) *chsd ldrs: rdn over 2f out: wknd over 1f out* **12/1**
00 11 1¼ **Tweenie (IRE)**^{9} 4960 2-8-11 0 ..... SteveDrowne 13 41
(R Hannon) *a towards rr* **33/1**
03 12 1 **May's Boy**^{28} 4323 2-8-9 0 ..... TravisBlock 10 36
(M D I Usher) *mid-div: rdn whn short of room over 1f out: sn wknd* **40/1**
00 13 shd **Bathwick Siesta**^{64} 3106 2-8-11 0 ow5 ..... JackDean$^{(3)}$ 16 41
(J G Portman) *hld up: hdwy over 3f out: effrt over 2f out: sn wknd* **80/1**

1m 16.53s (1.73) **Going Correction** +0.125s/f (Good) **13** Ran SP% **115.4**
Speed ratings (Par 94): **93,86,84,82,82 78,78,77,76,74 73,71,71**
Tote Swingers: 1&2 £3.90, 1&3 £3.90, 2&3 £6.90 CSF £11.30 TOTE £3.20: £1.60, £1.70, £1.50; EX 12.40.
Owner R P Marchant D M Ahier Mrs E Lee **Bred** Michael E Broughton **Trained** Ogbourne Maisey, Wilts

FOCUS
This had the feel of a slightly stronger than average auction maiden.

NOTEBOOK
Morache Music proved far too good for his rivals and went some way in justifying connections high opinion of him. He looks to have learnt plenty from his promising Windsor maiden and, despite being held up since having scoped dirty, he took a step forward here, getting off the mark in emphatic style. He holds an entry in the Two-Year-Old Trophy at Redcar and connections are apparently keen to keep him at 6f for the time being. (tchd 15-8 and 9-4)
Choose The Moment also confirmed the promise of her debut effort, appreciating the extra furlong and keeping on well. She'll not be long in winning. (op 7-1 tchd 8-1)
Park Ballet(IRE) coped with the drop back to 6f fine and can break her duck soon, probably in a nursery, for which she is now qualified. (op 7-1 tchd 6-1)
Royalorien was a bit too keen early but wasn't disgraced and looks the type to do better in time. (op 13-2)
Homeboy(IRE) made some late headway once switched towards the middle of the track and looks an interesting longer term project. (op 33-1 tchd 50-1)

5256 MANOR FARM MEATS NURSERY 1m
6:00 (6:04) (Class 5) (0-75,74) 2-Y-O **£3,238** (£963; £481; £240) **Stalls** High

Form RPR
005 1 **Piceno (IRE)**^{26} 4409 2-8-12 **65** ..... JackMitchell 7 79+
(L M Cumani) *racd keenly: mde all: r.o strly ent fnl f: comf* **7/1**^{3}
0622 2 5 **Jacobs Son**^{17} 4682 2-9-7 **74** ..... SteveDrowne 4 76
(R A Mills) *trckd ldrs: rdn over 2f out: kpt on to go clr 2nd ins fnl f: no ch w wnr* **7/2**^{1}
005 3 1¼ **Mediplomat**^{36} 4054 2-8-10 **63** ..... MartinDwyer 11 62
(M Botti) *prom: rdn over 2f out: outpcd by wnr jst over 1f out: lost 2nd ins fnl f* **9/1**
6525 4 shd **Presto Volante (IRE)**^{19} 4623 2-8-13 **66** ..... HayleyTurner 8 65
(Mrs A J Perrett) *trckd ldrs: effrt wl over 2f out: kpt on same pce fnl f* **7/1**^{3}
032 5 nk **Sixty Roses (IRE)**^{32} 4208 2-9-5 **72** ..... LiamKeniry 1 70
(J L Dunlop) *hld up towards rr: rdn and stdy prog fr 2f out: styd on: nvr trbld ldrs* **15/2**
514 6 1¾ **Sceal Nua (IRE)**^{42} 3872 2-9-4 **71** ..... PatCosgrave 12 66
(R Hannon) *mid-div: rdn over 2f out: effrt over 1f out: kpt on same pce fnl f* **4/1**^{2}
000 7 2¼ **King Bling (IRE)**^{34} 4131 2-8-4 **57** ..... AdrianNicholls 2 47
(S Kirk) *restrained towards rr after 1f: swtchd rt and hdwy over 2f out: sn rdn: no further imp fr over 1f out* **50/1**
035 8 2½ **Dubai Glory**^{24} 4447 2-8-13 **66** ..... TomMcLaughlin 9 50
(E A L Dunlop) *mid-div: rdn and hdwy wl over 1f out: wknd fnl f* **9/1**
2105 9 ½ **Whodathought (IRE)**^{9} 4955 2-8-9 **69** ..... CharlesEddery$^{(7)}$ 5 52
(R Hannon) *trckd ldrs: rdn over 2f out: nt clr run ent fnl f: wknd* **14/1**
0204 10 4 **Gower Rules (IRE)**^{35} 4111 2-8-5 **63** ..... SophieDoyle$^{(5)}$ 3 37
(M D I Usher) *s.i.s: a towards rr* **40/1**
326 11 11 **A Little Bit Dusty**^{32} 4208 2-9-0 **70** ..... JackDean$^{(3)}$ 6 20
(W G M Turner) *rdn after being bmpd 4f out: a towards rr* **33/1**
006 12 2¾ **Irie Ute**^{62} 3209 2-8-12 **65** ..... AdrianLayt 10 9
(S Kirk) *mid-div: rdn wl over 2f out: wknd over 1f out* **40/1**

1m 44.82s (1.32) **Going Correction** +0.125s/f (Good) **12** Ran SP% **115.4**
Speed ratings (Par 94): **98,93,91,91,91 89,87,84,84,80 69,66**
Tote Swingers: 1&2 £8.90, 1&3 £22.30, 2&3 £6.40 CSF £30.08 CT £227.26 TOTE £6.40: £4.10, £1.80, £5.00; EX 40.00.
Owner Team Spirit 2 **Bred** Miss Wendy Fox **Trained** Newmarket, Suffolk

FOCUS
A steadily run nursery dominated by the horse who was allowed to dictate the pace.

NOTEBOOK
Piceno(IRE) fairly hacked up. These were new tactics for the winner who has been held up in his three maiden runs but his jockey managed to bag the stands' rail and, although keen enough initially, he soon got into a good rhythm and the further they went the further clear he went clear. He had earned a modest mark of 65 for this handicap debut but the form of his latest Pontefract has worked out well (winner won Listed race at Yorkthis week) and this colt is clearly going to be hit hard for this success. Official explanation: trainer's representative said, that the colt is an improving young horse, who would have appreciated the soft ground today (op 5-1 tchd 9-2)
Jacobs Son has shown improved form since on the all-weather recently and he confirmed himself just as effective back on turf by keeping on for second, although the winner was in a different league. (op 9-2)
Mediplomat, backed beforehand, has begun handicap life on a modest mark and on this evidence he has the ability to take advantage of it. (op 20-1)
Presto Volante(IRE) also appreciated the step up to 1m and he didn't shape too badly. (op 11-2)
Sixty Roses(IRE), whose pedigree is chock full of stamina, was noted putting in some good late work from way off the pace. She was unsuited by the way this panned out so her performance deserves marking up a couple of notches. (op 13-2)
Sceal Nua(IRE) could never get competitive. (op 7-2)
A Little Bit Dusty Official explanation: jockey said that the gelding slipped after two furlongs

5257 WEATHERBYS BANK STONEHENGE STKS (LISTED RACE) 1m
6:30 (6:36) (Class 1) 2-Y-O
£13,624 (£5,164; £2,584; £1,288; £645; £324) **Stalls** High

Form RPR
2211 1 **Royal Exchange**^{21} 4539 2-8-13 **97** ..... RichardHughes 6 100+
(R Hannon) *hld up: bit slipped through mouth after 1f: smooth hdwy over 2f out: swtchd rt to join ldrs gng wl jst over 1f out: led ins fnl f: pushed out: comf* **5/4**^{1}
5631 2 1¾ **Sonoran Sands (IRE)**^{10} 4928 2-8-13 **89** ..... LiamKeniry 5 92
(J S Moore) *led tl 3f out: styd prom: sn rdn: rallied ins fnl f to regaind 2nd but a being hld* **14/1**
0421 3 nk **Ahlaain (USA)**^{16} 4691 2-8-13 **85** ..... ShaneKelly 1 91
(D M Simcock) *trckd ldrs: led 3f out: rdn whn hrd pressed fr 2f out: hdd ins fnl f: no ex whn lost 2nd nr fin* **6/1**

1410 **4** ¾ **Memen (IRE)**[21] 4539 2-8-13 91 .... HayleyTurner 3 90
(P F I Cole) *hld up: hdwy 3f out: rdn over 1f out: ev ch jst ins fnl f: no ex fnl 75yds* **11/2**[3]

1 **5** 7 **Beyeh (IRE)**[59] 3281 2-8-8 0 .... AdrianNicholls 4 69
(C E Brittain) *racd green and in snatches chsng ldrs: rdn 4f out: lost pl 3f out: nvr bk on terms* **33/1**

1 **6** ½ **Borug (USA)**[23] 4490 2-8-13 0 .... SteveDrowne 2 73
(Saeed Bin Suroor) *sn pushed along to trck ldr: rdn wl over 2f out: sn one pce: wknd ent fnl f* **5/2**[2]

1m 44.46s (0.96) **Going Correction** +0.125s/f (Good) **6** Ran SP% **112.3**
Speed ratings (Par 102): **100,98,97,97,90 89**
Tote Swingers: 1&2 £6.00, 1&3 £2.80, 2&3 £17.60 CSF £19.98 TOTE £1.80: £1.10, £8.20; EX 22.50.
Owner The Queen **Bred** The Queen **Trained** East Everleigh, Wilts

FOCUS
This was a cakewalk for Royal Exchange.

NOTEBOOK
Royal Exchange cruised into contention, with his rider pulling double, and found enough when shaken up inside the final 100 yards to go clear and win with seemingly a ton in hand. Things didn't look quite so rosy early on in the contest as Richard Hughes didn't appear overly happy on the colt, but he reported afterwards that the bit had slipped through the horse's mouth which he was trying to remedy. Once back on an even keel, his mount travelled strongly and handled the rain-softened ground fine. He is being targeted at the Horris Hill at Newbury. (tchd 11-8 and 6-4 in a place)
Sonoran Sands(IRE) had little chance of beating Royal Exchange on these terms (rated 8lb inferior), but he kept on well enough to reclaim second from Ahlaain and run with credit. He'll need to improve to find success at this level though. (op 16-1 tchd 12-1)
Ahlaain(USA) saw out the trip no problem having done his racing over 7f previously, and this was another step forward. He'll improve again when settling better. (op 9-1)
Memen(IRE) wasn't disgraced, although he didn't look overly happy on the track as he rolled out towards the centre in the final furlong, while his best form has come on faster ground. (op 13-2 tchd 15-2)
Borug(USA) ran badly and Steve Drowne reported afterwards that he was never travelling. Official explanation: jockey said that the colt was never travelling (op 85-40)

5258 JULIE PACKWOOD 50TH BIRTHDAY MAIDEN STKS — 1m 1f 198y
7:00 (7:01) (Class 4) 3-4-Y-0 — **£3,885** (£1,156; £577; £288) **Stalls** High

Form — RPR

0656 **1** **Balatoma (IRE)**[16] 4698 3-8-12 66 .... (b¹) MartinDwyer 3 71
(M P Tregoning) *trckd ldrs: rdn to chal fr over 2f out: kpt on ins fnl f: led fnl 50yds: drvn out* **11/1**

04 **2** ¾ **Warlu Way**[18] 4661 3-9-3 0 .... RichardHughes 2 75
(J L Dunlop) *sn led: rdn and hrd pressed fr 3f out: kpt on gamely but no ex whn hdd fnl 50yds* **4/1**[3]

32 **3** ½ **My Manikato**[32] 4207 3-9-3 0 .... J-PGuillambert 4 74
(L M Cumani) *trckd ldr: rdn to chal over 3f out: ev ch ent fnl f: no ex fnl 75yds* **5/2**[1]

4 nk **Almarmooq (USA)** 3-9-3 0 .... NickyMackay 7 73+
(J H M Gosden) *s.i.s: last: hdwy to join ldrs 4f out: rdn 3f out: ev ch ent fnl f: kpt on but no ex fnl 100yds* **5/2**[1]

0/ **5** 2½ **Rising Star**[658] 7105 4-9-11 0 .... PatDobbs 8 68
(Mrs A J Perrett) *trckd ldrs: rdn 3f out: kpt on but nvr gng pce to mount chal* **40/1**

6 29 **Sentosa** 3-8-12 0 .... IanMongan 5 —
(H R A Cecil) *trckd ldrs tl outpcd 3f out: eased fr over 1f out* **7/2**[2]

2m 12.99s (3.09) **Going Correction** +0.125s/f (Good)
WFA 3 from 4yo 8lb **6** Ran SP% **110.1**
Speed ratings (Par 105): **92,91,91,90,88 65**
Tote Swingers:1&2:£9.40, 2&3:£2.90, 1&3:£2.80 CSF £51.47 TOTE £4.90: £1.40, £2.30; EX 30.70.
Owner Nurlan Bizakov **Bred** Giacinto Guglielmi **Trained** Lambourn, Berks

FOCUS
A modest maiden.
Sentosa Official explanation: jockey said that the filly stumbled 3 ½ furlongs out

5259 WEATHERBYS BANK H'CAP — 1m 4f
7:35 (7:36) (Class 4) (0-85,84) 3-Y-O — **£4,209** (£1,252; £625; £312) **Stalls** High

Form — RPR

1 **1** **Vita Nova (IRE)**[51] 3563 3-9-3 80 .... IanMongan 2 92+
(H R A Cecil) *hld up bhd ldrs: hdwy to join ldrs and snatched stands' side rail over 4f out: rdn 3f out: led jst ins fnl f: styd on wl* **5/2**[1]

-426 **2** 3¾ **Valid Reason**[27] 4360 3-9-3 80 .... PatDobbs 8 86
(Mrs A J Perrett) *trckd ldr: rdn over 2f out: sltly hmpd ent fnl f: styd on to go 2nd fnl 100yds but a being hld* **15/2**

6321 **3** nk **Joseph Lister**[15] 4751 3-9-4 81 .... NickyMackay 1 87
(J H M Gosden) *trckd ldr: rdn 3f out: swtchd rt ent fnl f: chsd wnr sn after: styd on: lost 2nd fnl 100yds* **11/4**[2]

2630 **4** ½ **Issabella Gem (IRE)**[23] 4470 3-8-8 76 .... JohnFahy(5) 4 81+
(C G Cox) *hld up in last pair: outpcd over 3f out: hdwy over 1f out: styd on fnl f* **8/1**

-405 **5** 1½ **Tiger Star**[53] 3519 3-8-8 71 .... HayleyTurner 7 73
(J M P Eustace) *led: rdn whn hrd pressed fr over 2f out: hdd jst ins fnl f: no ex* **10/1**

1402 **6** hd **Hayzoom**[15] 4751 3-9-4 81 .... JackMitchell 6 83
(P W Chapple-Hyam) *trckd ldrs: rdn wl over 2f out: styd on same pce fnl f* **4/1**[3]

1201 **7** 93 **Mawaddah (IRE)**[65] 3081 3-9-7 84 .... RichardHughes 3 —
(R Hannon) *little slow away: hld up in last: racd wd after 2f tl 6f out: rdn 3f out: no imp: virtually p.u fnl f* **16/1**

2m 38.67s (0.67) **Going Correction** +0.125s/f (Good) **7** Ran SP% **113.1**
Speed ratings (Par 102): **102,99,99,98,97 97,35**
Tote Swingers: 1&2 £6.80, 1&3 £1.10, 2&3 £6.20 CSF £21.08 CT £53.63 TOTE £4.00: £2.00, £5.50; EX 21.70.
Owner H E Sheikh Sultan Bin Khalifa Al Nahyan **Bred** Paget Bloodstock **Trained** Newmarket, Suffolk

FOCUS
A fair handicap.

5260 WESTOVER GROUP H'CAP — 1m 6f 21y
8:05 (8:05) (Class 5) (0-70,71) 3-Y-O+ — **£3,238** (£963; £481; £240)

Form — RPR

6352 **1** **The Starboard Bow**[15] 4728 3-9-3 70 .... LiamKeniry 14 80
(S Kirk) *mid-div: rdn 3f out: hdwy over 2f out: styd on wl fnl f: led towards fin: drvn out* **10/1**

0411 **2** ½ **Bramalea**[5] 5115 5-10-2 71 12ex .... IanMongan 9 80
(B W Duke) *mid-div: hdwy over 3f out: rdn to take narrow advantage 2f out: sn hung rt: styd on: hdd towards fin* **7/1**[3]

50 **3** ½ **Kalamill (IRE)**[64] 3116 3-9-0 70 .... RussKennemore(3) 13 79
(S Lycett) *trckd ldrs: racd centre and led over 4f out: rdn and edgd to far rail whn narrowly hdd 2f out: remained w ev ch: no ex towards fin* **14/1**

05-5 **4** 6 **Viviani (IRE)**[16] 4698 3-8-9 62 .... (t) PatDobbs 10 62
(Mrs A J Perrett) *mid-div: rdn 3f out: styd on to go 4th ent fnl f: nvr trbld ldrs* **10/1**

606 **5** 4½ **Genes Of A Dancer (AUS)**[30] 4257 4-8-7 60 .... LucyBarry(7) 6 49
(M Appleby) *racd keenly: trckd ldr: rdn and ev ch 3f out: one pce fnl 2f* **40/1**

1326 **6** 1½ **Blinka Me**[23] 4493 3-8-7 60 .... HayleyTurner 7 52
(A M Hales) *led tl over 4f out: sn rdn: one pce fnl 2f* **8/1**

15-0 **7** 1½ **Kokkokila**[44] 3780 6-9-2 57 .... RichardHughes 8 47
(Lady Herries) *hld up towards rr: hdwy 3f out: sn rdn: wknd over 1f out* **9/2**[2]

0100 **8** ½ **Marju King (IRE)**[18] 4657 4-9-9 69 .... (t) JohnFahy(5) 12 58
(W S Kittow) *shortlived effrt 3f out: mainly towards rr* **14/1**

0026 **9** 9 **Jewellery (IRE)**[15] 4764 3-8-11 64 .... PatCosgrave 4 40
(J R Fanshawe) *trckd ldrs: rdn over 3f out: wknd 2f out* **16/1**

/031 **10** ¾ **Erdeli (IRE)**[11] 4915 6-9-6 61 .... (tp) DavidProbert 5 36
(Tim Vaughan) *mid-div: pushed along to chse ldrs over 4f out: sn rdn: wknd 2f out* **5/2**[1]

1634 **11** nk **Mountain Forest (GER)**[35] 4101 4-8-10 51 .... SteveDrowne 11 26
(H Morrison) *trckd ldrs: rdn 3f out: wknd 2f out* **10/1**

3m 9.02s (1.62) **Going Correction** +0.125s/f (Good)
WFA 3 from 4yo+ 12lb **11** Ran SP% **119.3**
Speed ratings (Par 103): **100,99,99,96,93 92,91,91,86,85 85**
Tote Swingers:1&2:£10.50, 2&3:£12.40, 1&3:£48.60 CSF £79.49 CT £994.18 TOTE £17.20: £5.10, £3.30, £7.60; EX 83.50 Place 6 £106.05; Place 5 £54.24.
Owner C Wright & The Hon Mrs J M Corbett **Bred** Stratford Place Stud **Trained** Upper Lambourn, Berks

FOCUS
The front three finished a long way clear, but they were spread right across the track.
Kalamill(IRE) Official explanation: jockey said that the gelding hung right handed
Erdeli(IRE) Official explanation: jockey said that the gelding was unsuited by the soft ground
Mountain Forest(GER) Official explanation: jockey said that the gelding ran too free
T/Plt: £377.30 to a £1 stake. Pool:£29,719.98 - 57.49 winning tickets . T/Qpdt: £103.00 to a £1 stake. Pool:£4,804.22 - 34.50 winning tickets . TM

4960 SANDOWN (R-H)
Friday, August 20

OFFICIAL GOING: Round course - good to firm (good in places); sprint course - good (good to firm in places; sprint 8.4, round 8.7)
Home bend 3yds off innermost configuration with drop in at 3f pole increasing distances on round course by about 4yds. Sprint course at full width.
Wind: Moderate across Weather: Low cloud

5261 EPSOM TRAINERS OPEN DAY 22ND AUGUST NURSERY — 5f 6y
2:05 (2:05) (Class 4) (0-85,83) 2-Y-O — **£3,238** (£963; £481; £240) **Stalls** High

Form — RPR

6621 **1** **Jameela Girl**[8] 5000 2-8-11 73 6ex .... J-PGuillambert 4 81+
(R M H Cowell) *disp ld tl def advantage ins fnl 2f: drvn and styd on strly fnl f* **15/8**[1]

3425 **2** 1¼ **Whoateallthepius (IRE)**[12] 4872 2-9-0 76 .... AdamKirby 7 79
(D K Ivory) *chsd ldrs: rdn to go 2nd over 1f out: styd on fnl f but no imp on wnr* **11/1**

4611 **3** 1 **Millyluvstobouggie**[10] 4927 2-8-9 71 6ex .... LukeMorris 2 70
(C G Cox) *in tch: hdwy and drvn 2f out: styd on to go 3rd ins fnl f but no imp on ldng duo fnl 120yds* **9/1**

1405 **4** ¾ **Twist Of Silver (USA)**[42] 3844 2-9-7 83 .... DarryllHolland 1 79
(J Noseda) *s.i.s: in rr: pushed along 1/2-way: rdn and swtchd lft appr fnl f: styd on wl fnl 120yds and gng on cloes home but nt rch ldng trio* **10/1**

0215 **5** nse **Overwhelm**[7] 5036 2-8-7 69 .... ShaneKelly 6 65
(Andrew Reid) *disp ld: rdn 3f out: hdd ins fnl 2f: wknd ins fnl f* **3/1**[2]

5636 **6** 2 **Star Today**[20] 4600 2-8-1 67 ow1 .... (b) JohnFahy(5) 8 57
(B J Meehan) *s.i.s: sn in tch: rdn 2f out: wknd appr fnl f* **7/1**[3]

1623 **7** nk **Master Macho (IRE)**[16] 4688 2-8-12 74 .... ChrisCatlin 5 62
(M R Channon) *chsd ldrs: rdn 3f out: wknd appr fnl f* **16/1**

4530 **8** 3¼ **Golden Taurus (IRE)**[20] 4578 2-8-9 71 .... DaneO'Neill 3 47
(J W Hills) *s.i.s: a outpcd* **14/1**

62.43 secs (0.83) **Going Correction** +0.20s/f (Good) **8** Ran SP% **112.3**
Speed ratings (Par 96): **101,99,97,96,96 92,92,87**
toteswingers:1&2:£5.70, 1&3:£2.10, 2&3:£5.90 CSF £22.88 CT £148.11 TOTE £2.80: £1.10, £3.80, £2.30; EX 31.50.
Owner Lone Oak Stud/Mrs J Morley/Foulkes **Bred** Lone Oak Stud Mare Syndicate **Trained** Six Mile Bottom, Cambs

FOCUS
A fair nursery. It was run at a good pace with the action taking place on the far rail.

NOTEBOOK
Jameela Girl is clearly very much on the upgrade and, theoretically 4lb well in despite a penalty, wasn't made to work too hard to follow up her Goodwood success and that despite being harried for the lead for the first 3f. She's going to be of interest kept to this trip even after another rise in her mark. (op 7-4 tchd 2-1)
Whoateallthepius(IRE) was probably suited by the good pace on her first attempt at 5f, but despite that still wasn't able to put in a challenge to the winner. All in all it was a good effort, but one that suggests she will continue to be vulnerable to the really progressive types. (op 8-1)
Millyluvstobouggie ran respectably in her bid for a three-timer, but found this more competitive than the nursery she won last time. Due to race off a 2lb higher mark from tomorrow, she'll find easier opportunities back in a lower grade. (tchd 11-1)
Twist Of Silver(USA) did herself few favours with a slow start and though she stayed on to be nearest at the finish, she displayed a rather awkward head carriage before she did so. This trip, even on a stiff track, looks too sharp for her even in this grade. (op 8-1)
Overwhelm looks a speedy sort and probably wasn't helped by being taken on for the lead up in this grade. Back at a sharper 5f with an uncontested lead, she'd make some appeal in something like a 0-70 or 0-75 for which she will still be eligible after this. (op 4-1)
Star Today was soon playing catch-up after a sluggish start. (op 9-1 tchd 10-1)
Master Macho(IRE) had been exposed in a weaker nursery than this at Brighton last time and will struggle to add to his maiden win kept to this grade. (tchd 14-1)

Golden Taurus(IRE) was soon playing catch-up after a sluggish start. (op 16-1)

5262 KAIZEN PARTNERSHIP H'CAP — 5f 6y

2:40 (2:41) (Class 5) (0-75,75) 3-Y-O+ **£3,238** (£963; £481; £240) **Stalls High**

Form				RPR
0543	**1**		**Efistorm**[9] 4942 9-9-11 **75** .... HayleyTurner 8	85
			(C R Dore) *in rr: nt clr run and swtchd lft appr fnl f: qcknd ins fnl f to ld fnl 80yds: pushed out* **8/1**
144	**2**	*1*	**Gwilym (GER)**[4] 5151 7-9-8 **72** .... DaneO'Neill 15	78
			(D Haydn Jones) *led: rdn 2f out: hdd and outpcd fnl 80yds* **11/2**[2]
0004	**3**	*nk*	**Even Bolder**[9] 4961 7-9-4 **73** .... KierenFox(5) 12	78
			(E A Wheeler) *chsd ldrs: rdn ins fnl 2f: one pce jst ins fnl f: kpt on again to take 3rd cl home* **7/1**
2013	**4**	*shd*	**Grudge**[55] 3440 5-9-9 **73** ....(be) ShaneKelly 13	78
			(C R Dore) *chsd ldrs: rdn 2f out: styd on same pce fnl 100yds* **13/2**[3]
3100	**5**	*¾*	**Triple Dream**[9] 4961 5-9-11 **75** ....(b[1]) AdamKirby 6	77
			(J M Bradley) *chsd ldr: rdn 2f out: wknd fnl 50yds* **28/1**
0065	**6**	*hd*	**The Jobber (IRE)**[9] 4961 9-9-0 **64** .... LukeMorris 3	65
			(M Blanshard) *chsd ldrs: rdn over 1f out: sn one pce: kpt on again cl home* **16/1**
0153	**7**	*½*	**The Wee Chief (IRE)**[9] 4961 4-9-4 **68** .... PatDobbs 11	67+
			(J C Fox) *s.i.s: hld up in rr: nt clr run fr 2f out: stl no daylight whn swtchd lft over 1f out: hdwy ins fnl f but stl n.m.r: gng on cl home but nt rcvr* **7/2**[1]
4002	**8**	*hd*	**Speak The Truth (IRE)**[8] 5005 4-9-1 **65** ....(p) PatCosgrave 7	64
			(J R Boyle) *in rr: rdn and sme hdwy on outside over 1f out: kpt on fnl 100yds: nvr a threat* **12/1**
1436	**9**	*hd*	**Silvanus (IRE)**[22] 4513 5-9-4 **68** .... TadhgO'Shea 10	66+
			(P T Midgley) *plld hrd in rr: continually denied a clr run fr over 1f out: fin on bridle* **16/1**
0050	**10**	*nk*	**Rocker**[22] 4510 6-9-10 **74** .... GeorgeBaker 5	71+
			(G L Moore) *in tch: chse ldrs and hmpd fr over 1f out and ins fnl f: nt rcvr and eased* **20/1**
3600	**11**	*½*	**Captain Kallis (IRE)**[20] 4589 4-8-1 **56** .... JohnFahy(5) 9	51
			(D J S Ffrench Davis) *chsd ldr: rdn 2f out: wknd ins fnl f* **16/1**
-056	**12**	*2½*	**Adventure Story**[15] 4754 3-9-6 **72** .... JimmyFortune 14	58+
			(R Hannon) *hld up towards rr on ins: sme hdwy whn hmpd 1f out stl tight whn snatched up and eased fnl 100yds* **12/1**

62.90 secs (1.30) **Going Correction** +0.20s/f (Good)
WFA 3 from 4yo+ 2lb **12** Ran SP% **115.8**
Speed ratings (Par 103): **97,95,94,94,93 93,92,92,91,91 90,86**
toteswingers:1&2:£5.70, 1&3:£26.70, 2&3:£10.90 CSF £50.32 CT £330.76 TOTE £7.70: £2.50, £2.40, £3.10; EX 34.60.
Owner Sean J Murphy **Bred** E Duggan And D Churchman **Trained** Cowbit, Lincs

FOCUS

A competitive sprint but a very messy race with plenty of trouble in running and the result probably isn't one to take at face value. The field again raced far side.

The Wee Chief(IRE) Official explanation: jockey said gelding denied a clear run

Silvanus(IRE) ◆ Official explanation: jockey said gelding denied a clear run

Rocker ◆ Official explanation: jockey said gelding denied a clear run

Adventure Story Official explanation: jockey said filly denied a clear run

5263 EUROPEAN BREEDERS' FUND MAIDEN STKS — 7f 16y

3:15 (3:17) (Class 4) 2-Y-O **£4,533** (£1,348; £674; £336) **Stalls High**

Form				RPR
0	**1**		**Cai Shen (IRE)**[19] 4622 2-9-3 .... PatDobbs 10	87+
			(R Hannon) *mde all: shkn up 2f out: styd on strly fr over 1f out: unchal* **12/1**
52	**2**	*2*	**Noonenose**[28] 4318 2-9-3 .... ShaneKelly 8	82
			(W J Knight) *chsd ldrs: drvn to dispute 2nd fr ins fnl f tl chsd comf wnr cl home* **4/1**[3]
5	**3**	*½*	**Arc Light (IRE)**[14] 4803 2-9-3 .... AhmedAjtebi 12	81
			(Mahmood Al Zarooni) *s.i.s: sn mid-div: hdwy on ins over 2f out: disp 2nd ins fnl f but nvr any ch w comfortable wnr: outpcd into 3rd cl home* **11/4**[1]
6	**4**	*2¾*	**Labarinto**[21] 4549 2-9-3 .... DarryllHolland 9	74
			(Sir Michael Stoute) *t.k.h hold early: chsd ldrs: rdn ins fnl 2f: no imp and one pce fnl f* **3/1**[2]
2	**5**	*hd*	**Muntasib (USA)**[16] 4691 2-9-3 .... TadhgO'Shea 7	73
			(M P Tregoning) *chsd wnr: drvn and no imp 2f out: wknd fnl f* **6/1**
6	*3½*	**Oversteer (USA)** 2-9-3 .... NickyMackay 13	65+
			(J H M Gosden) *s.i.s: sn chsng ldrs: drvn ins fnl 3f: wknd ins fnl 2f* **12/1**
00	**7**	*nk*	**Prince Freddie**[30] 4263 2-9-0 .... RussKennemore(3) 1	64
			(P A Kirby) *in rr: pushed along 3f out: styd on fnl 2f but nvr in contention* **100/1**
8	*nk*	**Ari Gold (IRE)** 2-9-3 .... RichardKingscote 4	63+
			(Tom Dascombe) *in rr pushed along 2f out: styd on fnl f but nvr in contention* **40/1**
9	*½*	**Spartan King (IRE)** 2-9-3 .... DaneO'Neill 2	62+
			(H J L Dunlop) *s.i.s: in rr tl sme late prog* **66/1**
10	*¾*	**Perfect Mission** 2-9-3 .... JimmyFortune 6	60
			(A M Balding) *mid-div: pushed along over 2f out: wknd ins fnl 2f* **33/1**
0	**11**	*shd*	**Four Nations (USA)**[71] 2887 2-9-3 .... AdamKirby 11	60
			(Mrs A J Perrett) *mid-div: rdn ins fnl 3f: wknd ins fnl 2f* **40/1**
12	*7*	**Acute (IRE)** 2-9-3 .... LiamJones 3	42
			(B J Meehan) *slowly away: sn drvn in rr: a bhd* **80/1**
13	*1*	**Violet Ray (USA)** 2-9-0 .... EJMcNamara(3) 14	40
			(R M Beckett) *chsd ldrs tl wknd 3f out* **50/1**
14	*1¾*	**Holy Mackerel (IRE)** 2-9-3 .... ChrisCatlin 5	35
			(M R Channon) *s.i.s: a bhd* **66/1**

1m 30.1s (0.60) **Going Correction** +0.075s/f (Good) **14** Ran SP% **116.3**
Speed ratings (Par 96): **99,96,96,93,92 88,88,88,87,86 86,78,77,75**
toteswingers:1&2:£15.50, 1&3:£13.80, 2&3:£2.60 CSF £55.91 TOTE £17.90: £6.10, £2.20, £1.20; EX 94.50.
Owner Mrs J Wood **Bred** Wardstown Stud Ltd **Trained** East Everleigh, Wilts

FOCUS

A mixture of lightly-raced and unexposed types and form probably bordering on fairly useful from the winner. The field weren't as well strung out here as they can get, but little still got involved from behind.

NOTEBOOK

Cai Shen(IRE) had clearly benefited from his debut at Newbury and left that form behind with an emphatic success, soon in front and drawing clear readily without recourse to strong pressure and value for more than his winning margin. He's no fancy entries, but promises to be useful and is best kept to this trip for his next run.

Noonenose set the standard on his second at Ascot in a maiden that has thrown up two winners, but he had his lack of tactical pace exposed halfway up the straight and left the impression that despite his pedigree, he might need 1m already. He's not up to his Dewhurst entry. (op 10-3, tchd 9-2 in a place)

Arc Light(IRE) was well backed after his initial promising run at Newmarket and can be rated better than this, having been asked to make his effort from further back than the other principals but looking likely to come through and get second until that effort told. He can improve again and win a maiden. (op 7-2)

Labarinto, a brother to the top-class 7f/1m winner Price Tag, fared best of the newcomers. He held just about every chance 2f out but was given a largely educational ride once his winning chance had gone and shaped as if capable of a fair bit better next time. He holds a clutch of big-race entries and is clearly well regarded. (op 4-1 after 6-1 in a place)

Muntasib(USA) is another that holds multiple Group races entries. Significant among those perhaps is the Middle Park, as a drop to 6f might suit him in the short term, being plenty keen enough early on (as well as to post) and then fading late. He still looks as if he has some growing up to do, and might yet turn out to be decent. (op 4-1)

Oversteer(USA), a late foal out of a French 7f/1m winner, is in the Royal Lodge and Racing Post Trophy and looked one for later in the season as he dropped away probably needing the race on top of the signs of inexperience he showed. (op 16-1 tchd 11-1)

Prince Freddie is eligible for nurseries now and should do better in that sphere.

Ari Gold(IRE), a colt by Motivator and a half-brother to a US Grade 2 winner, made some late headway after looking very inexperience early in the straight and should improve. (op 33-1, tchd 66-1 in a place)

Spartan King(IRE) is a half-brother to St Leger runner-up Unsung Heroine and is sure to be of more interest over further.

5264 CHARLOTTE AND DAMIAN SADLER'S WEDDING DAY H'CAP — 1m 14y

3:50 (3:51) (Class 3) (0-90,89) 3-Y-O+ **£6,476** (£1,927; £963; £481) **Stalls High**

Form				RPR
4U12	**1**		**First Post (IRE)**[28] 4322 3-8-6 **74** .... AndreaAtzeni 1	85
			(D Haydn Jones) *chsd ldrs: rdn over 2f out: styd on appr fnl f: kpt on wl fnl f to ld last strides* **20/1**
3220	**2**	*hd*	**Directorship**[44] 3796 4-9-6 **82** .... RichardKingscote 2	94
			(P R Chamings) *towards rr: hdwy over 3f out: drvn to ld insde fnl 2f: kpt on u.p fnl f: hdd last strides* **8/1**
2120	**3**	*1¾*	**Major Phil (IRE)**[35] 4100 4-9-12 **88** .... J-PGuillambert 8	96+
			(L M Cumani) *in rr: swtchd lft to outside and hdwy fr 2f out: str run and edgd rt to take 3rd ins fnl f but no imp on ldng duo* **8/1**
5310	**4**	*½*	**Kay Gee Be (IRE)**[24] 4459 6-9-10 **86** .... LiamJones 10	93
			(W Jarvis) *led tl hdd ins fnl 2f: wknd ins fnl f* **20/1**
4-1	**5**	*1*	**Julienas (IRE)**[25] 4425 3-9-2 **84** .... AdamKirby 5	88+
			(W R Swinburn) *mid-div: rdn and hdwy over 2f out: sn hrd drvn styd on fnl f but nvr a danger* **6/1**[1]
1336	**6**	*½*	**South Cape**[8] 5004 7-9-10 **86** .... GeorgeBaker 6	89
			(G L Moore) *in rr: hdwy over 2f out styng on whn sltly hmpd ins fnl f: kpt on again cl home* **25/1**
4052	**7**	*¾*	**Rule Breaker (IRE)**[11] 4905 3-8-13 **81** .... RoystonFfrench 14	82
			(M Johnston) *chsd ldrs: rdn 2f out: wknd fnl f* **15/2**[3]
0250	**8**	*½*	**Summer Dancer (IRE)**[20] 4598 6-9-5 **81** .... JimmyFortune 7	82
			(P T Midgley) *in rr: hdwy on ins fr 2f out: kpt on same pce ins fnl f* **40/1**
2001	**9**	*1¼*	**Black N Brew (USA)**[23] 4488 4-8-7 **74** .... KierenFox(5) 3	72
			(J R Best) *s.i.s: in rr: pushed along 2f out: hdwy over 1f out: fin wl fnl 50yds* **20/1**
5406	**10**	*½*	**Halsion Chancer**[30] 4265 6-8-11 **73** .... ChrisCatlin 4	69
			(J R Best) *in rr tl late prog fnl f* **33/1**
6-61	**11**	*½*	**Mufti (IRE)**[16] 4705 3-8-10 **78** .... DarryllHolland 9	72
			(J Noseda) *chsd ldrs: rdn 3f out: sltly hmpd over 2f out: sn drvn but n.d after* **12/1**
05	**12**	*1¼*	**General Eliott (IRE)**[55] 3431 5-9-11 **87** ....(b) TadhgO'Shea 11	79
			(P F I Cole) *in rr: hdwy and hung bdly rt 2f out: tried to improve again but hung bdly rt over 1f out: nt rcvr* **33/1**
3332	**13**	*1½*	**Truism**[20] 4579 4-9-10 **86** .... PatDobbs 13	75
			(Mrs A J Perrett) *mid-div: hdwy to chse ldrs 3f out: sn rdn and wknd 2f out* **7/1**[2]
1400	**14**	*¾*	**Cape Rock**[24] 4459 5-9-9 **85** .... ShaneKelly 12	72
			(W J Knight) *t.k.h: chsd ldrs: rdn and hung rt over 2f out: continued hanging and wknd over 1f out* **7/1**[2]
2021	**15**	*14*	**Clockmaker (IRE)**[51] 3565 4-9-13 **89** .... NickyMackay 15	44
			(J H M Gosden) *s.i.s: sn wl there: drvn and faltered 4f out: wknd qckly ins fnl 3f* **7/1**[2]

1m 42.31s (-0.99) **Going Correction** +0.075s/f (Good)
WFA 3 from 4yo+ 6lb **15** Ran SP% **119.9**
Speed ratings (Par 107): **107,106,105,104,103 103,102,101,100,100 99,98,96,96,82**
toteswingers:1&2:£30.90, 1&3:£15.20, 2&3:£10.30 CSF £159.18 CT £1434.89 TOTE £28.10: £7.10, £3.00, £3.20; EX 240.20.
Owner Llewelyn, Runeckles **Bred** D Llewelyn & J Runeckles **Trained** Efail Isaf, Rhondda C Taff

FOCUS

A competitive handicap despite some of the market leaders and more reliable types running below form. The pace was sound and there wasn't an advantage to be had ridden either way

NOTEBOOK

First Post(IRE) overcame an outside draw and being forced wide on the home turn to make steady progress and put his head in front on the post. Despite his recent form figures, things arguably haven't fallen right for him in his last two races and it wouldn't be a surprise if he is capable of further improvement. He shaped once again as if he might worth a try over a bit further (op 25-1 tchd 28-1)

Directorship goes well here and put a poor run at Newmarket behind him to run his best race of the season, just being edged out after making impressive headway to look the likely winner for most of the last 2f. This is his best trip. (op 10-1)

Major Phil(IRE) probably deserves his effort upgrading as he got further back than ideal and then found his run petering out after nearly making up all the leeway. He might yet stay 1m2f. (tchd 17-2)

Kay Gee Be(IRE) did best of those up in the van throughout, but the pace he set wasn't a breakneck one and though he ran well, he didn't really have any excuse other than not being good enough.

Julienas(IRE) had been set a stiff task by the assessor on the basis of his Windsor maiden form, but he once again came in for good support and might have fared much better had inexperience not held him back, tending to carry his head to once side and wander around. This run should have taught him more than his Windsor win and he remains open to improvement. (op 11-2 tchd 13-2)

South Cape was hampered by Major Phil as that one made his challenge, but was held at the time anyway and wasn't in any way unlucky.

Rule Breaker(IRE) headed the list of disappointments and for all he is capable of much better as his recent Windsor second showed, his overall profile is a very inconsistent one. That said, it might be this stiff 1m is more of a test than suits him ideally. (op 6-1 tchd 8-1)

Black N Brew(USA) can be rated a bit better than the result as he was just beginning to stay on when hampered. (op 18-1)

General Eliott(IRE) Official explanation: jockey said gelding hung badly right handed

Truism has been a model of consistency this year, but turned in a below-par performance away from Goodwood for the first time this year. (tchd 6-1)

Clockmaker(IRE) was another to perform well below expectations, leaving the impression all was not right as he was the first to drop away. Official explanation: jockey said was never travelling (op 6-1)

5265 SIVARAJAH AND BOUCHARE MAIDEN FILLIES' STKS — 1m 14y

4:25 (4:27) (Class 5) 3-Y-O — **£2,590** (£770; £385; £192) **Stalls** High

Form — RPR

23 **1** **Calipatria**[16] 4697 3-9-0 0 ... NickyMackay 3 — 80+
(J H M Gosden) *chsd ldrs: drvn over 3f out: styd on to chse ldr and edgd rt 2f out: rdn to ld fnl 100yds: won gng away* **10/11**[1]

363 **2** 3/4 **Madonna Dell'Orto**[12] 4874 3-9-0 0 ... ShaneKelly 6 — 78
(W R Swinburn) *led: 3 l clr 3f out: rdn over 1f out: hdd fnl 100yds: no ex cl home* **3/1**[2]

0 **3** 9 **Lalika**[126] 1358 3-9-0 0 ... AdamKirby 8 — 57
(C G Cox) *chsd ldr: rdn and wkng into 3rd whn pushed lft 2f out* **20/1**

4 3 **Royal Assent** 3-9-0 0 ... JimmyFortune 2 — 50
(A M Balding) *in tch: rdn over 3f out: no ch w ldrs fnl 2f* **15/2**[3]

5 2 1/4 **Sennybridge** 3-9-0 0 ... DaneO'Neill 7 — 45
(J W Hills) *in rr: rdn along over 3f out and nvr in contention* **50/1**

6 3 1/2 **Ijaaza (USA)** 3-9-0 0 ... TadhgO'Shea 9 — 37
(E A L Dunlop) *chsd ldrs: rdn: green and wknd fr 3f out* **8/1**

7 4 1/2 **Fair Breeze** 3-9-0 0 ... LiamJones 5 — 27
(R T Phillips) *s.i.s: a in rr* **50/1**

8 3 **Regency Girl (IRE)** 3-9-0 0 ... ChrisCatlin 1 — 20
(M P Tregoning) *slowly away: green and in rr thrght* **16/1**

1m 44.92s (1.62) **Going Correction** +0.075s/f (Good) — 8 Ran SP% **114.8**
Speed ratings (Par 97): **94,93,84,81,79 75,71,68**
toteswingers:1&2:£1.40, 1&3:£5.70, 2&3:£8.70 CSF £3.66 TOTE £1.70: £1.10, £1.30, £4.20; EX 4.10.
Owner H R H Princess Haya Of Jordan **Bred** Aldridge Racing Partnership **Trained** Newmarket, Suffolk

FOCUS
Not much strength in depth to this maiden and the two market principals pulled well clear at the end of a moderately-run race.

5266 HAMPTON COURT H'CAP — 1m 2f 7y

5:00 (5:00) (Class 4) (0-80,79) 3-Y-O — **£3,885** (£1,156; £577; £288) **Stalls** High

Form — RPR

0253 **1** **Aquarius Star (IRE)**[34] 4134 3-9-6 **76** ... DaneO'Neill 7 — 83
(Pat Eddery) *chsd ldrs: rdn to dispute ld in 3-way chal ins fnl f: led last strides* **8/1**

1232 **2** hd **Park View**[21] 4532 3-9-9 **79** ... JimmyFortune 4 — 85
(B W Hills) *led: rdn and kpt slt advantage tl narrowly hdd in 3-way chal ins fnl f: rallied gamely to retake 2nd last stride but nt quite get to wnr* **3/1**[1]

0041 **3** nse **Frontline Phantom (IRE)**[26] 4408 3-8-4 **60** oh2 ... AndrewElliott 1 — 66
(Mrs K Burke) *chsd ldr: chal fr 2f out: slt ld u.p in 3-way chal ins fnl f: hdd last strides and lost 2nd on line* **11/1**

-602 **4** 1/2 **Brigadoon**[14] 4793 3-8-9 **65** ... LiamJones 11 — 70+
(W Jarvis) *in rr: hdwy u.p fr 2f out: styd on ins fnl f: clsng on ldng trio nr fin* **8/1**

-130 **5** 1 3/4 **Eltheeb**[21] 4546 3-9-4 **74** ... TadhgO'Shea 10 — 76
(J L Dunlop) *chsd ldrs: rdn and styd on fr over 1f out: one pce ins fnl f* **8/1**

2-10 **6** 1/2 **Cornish Beau (IRE)**[15] 4751 3-9-1 **71** ... DarryllHolland 6 — 72
(M H Tompkins) *chsd ldrs: rdn and outpcd insde fnl 3f: styd on again u.p fr over 1f out* **14/1**

0603 **6** dht **Paintball (IRE)**[9] 4964 3-9-0 **77** ... JamesRogers(7) 5 — 78
(W R Muir) *in tch: rdn and styd on fr 2f out: kpt on fnl f but nvr gng pce to get into contention* **7/1**[3]

610 **8** 1 1/2 **Kensei (IRE)**[20] 4573 3-9-5 **75** ... GeorgeBaker 3 — 73
(R M Beckett) *stdd s: in rr: hdwy over 3f out: chsd ldrs 2f out: wknd ins fnl f* **7/2**[2]

544- **9** 9 **Henry San (IRE)**[319] 6548 3-9-2 **77** ... SimonPearce(5) 8 — 57
(A King) *t.k.h: in rr: brief effrt over 2f out: sn wknd* **20/1**

2m 10.29s (-0.21) **Going Correction** +0.075s/f (Good) — 9 Ran SP% **112.8**
Speed ratings (Par 102): **103,102,102,102,101 100,100,99,92**
toteswingers:1&2:£3.50, 1&3:£9.00, 2&3:£6.10. totesuper7: Win: Not won. Place: Not won. CSF £31.43 CT £264.56 TOTE £10.30: £2.90, £1.50, £2.70; EX 28.40 Place 6 £137.38; Place 5 £68.76.
Owner Mrs Gay Smith **Bred** J Hanly **Trained** Nether Winchendon, Bucks

FOCUS
Not a great deal to choose between several of these beforehand and the result confirmed what a tight-knit handicap it was. The pace was uneven and the fourth can be counted unlucky.
Brigadoon ◆ Official explanation: jockey said gelding was denied a clear run
T/Plt: £88.80 Pool:£47,329.43 388.67 winning tickets T/Qpdt: £30.10 Pool:£4,025.70 98.80 winning tickets ST

5152 WOLVERHAMPTON (A.W) (L-H)

Friday, August 20

OFFICIAL GOING: Standard
Wind: Fresh half-behind Weather: Showery

5267 SPONSOR A RACE BY CALLING 01902 390000 H'CAP — 5f 216y(P)

6:45 (6:46) (Class 6) (0-60,60) 3-Y-O+ — **£1,876** (£554; £277) **Stalls** Low

Form — RPR

2244 **1** **Cavitie**[7] 5025 4-9-2 **56** ... JamesDoyle 1 — 68
(Andrew Reid) *chsd ldrs: rdn to ld 1f out: r.o* **7/2**[1]

5343 **2** nk **Fantasy Fighter (IRE)**[14] 4789 5-9-1 **60** ... IanBrennan(5) 4 — 71
(J J Quinn) *s.i.s: hld up: hdwy over 2f out: nt clr run and swtchd lft ins fnl f: swished tail and r.o wl* **4/1**[2]

0205 **3** 1 1/2 **Cwmni**[23] 4478 4-8-13 **58** ... DeclanCannon(5) 10 — 64
(B Palling) *sn pushed along in rr: nt clr run and swtchd rt over 1f out: r.o ins fnl f: wnt 3rd nr fin: nt rch ldrs* **16/1**

0303 **4** 1/2 **Downhill Skier (IRE)**[10] 4936 6-9-0 **57** ... PaulPickard(3) 13 — 62
(W M Brisbourne) *chsd ldrs: rdn to ld over 1f out: sn hdd: styd on same pce ins fnl f* **8/1**

0066 **5** 1/2 **Desert Falls**[16] 4706 4-9-3 **57** ... (v) CathyGannon 6 — 60
(R M Whitaker) *chsd ldrs: rdn over 1f out: styd on u.p* **10/1**

0650 **6** 3/4 **Figaro Flyer (IRE)**[13] 4839 7-9-3 **60** ... MichaelStainton(3) 2 — 61+
(P Howling) *hld up in tch: nt clr run wl over 1f out: hmpd jst over 1f out: r.o: nvr able to chal* **9/2**[3]

5001 **7** 1/2 **Only A Game (IRE)**[95] 2184 5-8-13 **58** ... (vt) DaleSwift(5) 8 — 57
(I W McInnes) *hld up: hdwy over 2f out: rdn and hung lft fr over 1f out: no ex ins fnl f* **16/1**

0500 **8** 1 3/4 **Not My Choice (IRE)**[16] 4712 5-9-4 **58** ... (t[1]) DavidNolan 7 — 51
(D C Griffiths) *chsd ldrs: led 4f out: rdn and hdd over 1f out: no ex fnl f* **28/1**

3000 **9** 2 3/4 **Charlie Delta**[10] 4936 7-9-4 **58** ... (b) LukeMorris 9 — 43
(R A Harris) *prom: rdn 1/2-way: hmpd over 1f out: sn wknd* **50/1**

5232 **10** 4 1/2 **Faithful Duchess (IRE)**[14] 4789 3-9-3 **60** ... RichardMullen 11 — 30
(E A L Dunlop) *hld up: rdn over 2f out: a in rr* **9/1**

6006 **11** 2 **What Katie Did (IRE)**[7] 5055 5-9-4 **58** ... (p) PaulMulrennan 3 — 22
(J M Bradley) *sn led: hdd 4f out: rdn over 1f out: sn wknd* **16/1**

0424 **12** 5 **Bentley**[20] 4606 6-9-5 **59** ... (v) TonyCulhane 12 — 7
(B P J Baugh) *mid-div: sn pushed along: lost pl 5f out: wknd over 2f out* **10/1**

040- **13** nse **Gabriel's Spirit (IRE)**[40] 3938 3-9-3 **60** ... (t) StevieDonohoe 5 — 8
(Joseph Quinn, Ire) *sn pushed along in rr: bhd fr 1/2-way* **40/1**

1m 13.94s (-1.06) **Going Correction** -0.025s/f (Stan)
WFA 3 from 4yo+ 3lb — 13 Ran SP% **125.2**
Speed ratings (Par 101): **106,105,103,102,102 101,100,98,94,88 85,79,79**
toteswingers:1&2:£5.60, 1&3:£9.00, 2&3:£4.90 CSF £17.81 CT £214.05 TOTE £3.20: £1.10, £1.10, £8.80; EX 19.30.
Owner A S Reid **Bred** A S Reid **Trained** Mill Hill, London NW7

FOCUS
Mainly exposed performers in a moderate handicap. The gallop was reasonable and the winner was close to the inside rail throughout.
Cwmni Official explanation: jockey said that the filly was denied a clear run

5268 DINE IN THE HORIZONS RESTAURANT FILLIES' (S) STKS — 5f 20y(P)

7:15 (7:15) (Class 6) 2-Y-O — **£1,706** (£503; £252) **Stalls** Low

Form — RPR

1500 **1** **Two Feet Of Snow (IRE)**[12] 4872 2-9-1 78 ... PatrickHills(3) 5 — 70
(R Hannon) *chsd ldrs: shkn up to ld over 1f out: sn clr* **8/11**[1]

4603 **2** 3 3/4 **Bendigedig**[14] 4788 2-8-5 54 ... AdamBeschizza(7) 10 — 51
(S Kirk) *chsd ldrs: rdn 1/2-way: wnt 2nd and edgd lft ins fnl f: styd on* **5/1**[3]

040 **3** 1/2 **Venus Empress**[24] 4451 2-8-12 61 ... RichardMullen 8 — 49
(E S McMahon) *chsd ldrs: rdn over 1f out: sn hung lft: styd on same pce ins fnl f* **7/2**[2]

6034 **4** 5 **Livia Quarta (IRE)**[38] 3992 2-8-12 49 ... StevieDonohoe 2 — 31
(E J Creighton) *chsd ldr: led 1/2-way: rdn and hdd over 1f out: wknd fnl f* **12/1**

0055 **5** 2 **Minus Tolerance**[14] 4788 2-8-7 36 ... AmyBaker(5) 6 — 24
(Miss S L Davison) *prom: rdn and wknd over 1f out* **80/1**

00 **6** 6 **Royal Classy Cleo**[14] 4802 2-8-12 0 ... CathyGannon 9 — 2
(P D Evans) *sn pushed along and a in rr* **50/1**

7 hd **Kachiri (IRE)** 2-8-12 0 ... PaulEddery 4 — 1
(Peter Grayson) *s.i.s: a in rr* **66/1**

6500 **8** 1 1/4 **Sister June (IRE)**[38] 3992 2-8-12 30 ... (b) EddieCreighton 1 — —
(E J Creighton) *sn outpcd* **66/1**

40 **9** 3 **Isontonic (IRE)**[11] 4890 2-8-12 0 ... TonyCulhane 3 — —
(P T Midgley) *led to 1/2-way: sn hung rt: wknd over 1f out* **16/1**

62.32 secs (0.02) **Going Correction** -0.025s/f (Stan) — 9 Ran SP% **116.5**
Speed ratings (Par 89): **98,92,91,83,80 70,70,68,63**
toteswingers:1&2:£1.60, 2&3:£3.60, 1&3:£1.90 CSF £4.91 TOTE £1.40: £1.02, £1.60, £1.10; EX 4.80.The winner was sold to I McGuinness for 5,500 guineas.
Owner Alpine Racing **Bred** Paulyn Limited **Trained** East Everleigh, Wilts

FOCUS
An uncompetitive fillies' seller in which the market leaders dominated. The pace was reasonable and the winner raced close to the inside rail in the straight.

NOTEBOOK
Two Feet Of Snow(IRE) appreciated the drop in grade for this all-weather debut and didn't have to improve to beat a 54-rated rival with a fair bit in hand over this shorter trip. Life will be much tougher back in nurseries from her current mark of 78 but she should be able to win if kept to this grade. She now joins Ian McInnes. (tchd 10-11)
Bendigedig isn't very reliable and has yet to win a race but fared best of the remainder from her double-figure draw. The return to 6f ought to be to her liking on this evidence but she doesn't look one to place maximum faith in. (op 9-2 tchd 4-1 and 11-2)
Venus Empress, a half-sister to a Polytrack scorer, attracted support and wasn't disgraced on this all-weather debut and first run in selling company. Low-grade nurseries may be the way forward with her and she is probably worth another chance. (op 9-2 tchd 3-1)
Livia Quarta(IRE), who had been well beaten on her nursery debut, was readily swept aside in the face of a stiffish task dropped in distance for this all-weather debut. Official explanation: vet said the filly appeared tied up and had lost a left hind shoe
Royal Classy Cleo Official explanation: jockey said that the filly lost action
Sister June(IRE) Official explanation: jockey said that the filly lost a left front shoe
Isontonic(IRE) Official explanation: jockey said that the filly hung right

5269 ENJOY A PITCHER OF PIMM'S CLAIMING STKS — 7f 32y(P)

7:45 (7:49) (Class 5) 2-Y-O — **£3,412** (£1,007; £504) **Stalls** High

Form — RPR

2310 **1** **Captain Loui (IRE)**[13] 4848 2-8-10 63 ... (p) NeilCallan 4 — 64
(K A Ryan) *mde all: rdn over 1f out: edgd lft ins fnl f: r.o* **2/1**[1]

0 **2** 2 1/4 **Lindo Erro**[22] 4517 2-8-2 0 ... DeclanCannon(5) 6 — 55
(J Mackie) *prom: rdn over 2f out: chsd wnr ins fnl f: r.o* **20/1**

1154 **3** 1 **Bachelor Knight (IRE)**[25] 4429 2-9-0 70 ... PaulMulrennan 11 — 60
(R A Fahey) *chsd ldrs: rdn over 1f out: no ex ins fnl f* **2/1**[1]

00 **4** 3/4 **Elusive Vine (IRE)**[53] 3517 2-8-1 0 ... AndrewHeffernan(3) 9 — 48
(R A Harris) *hld up: racd keenly: hdwy over 2f out: rdn over 1f out: styd on same pce fnl f* **33/1**

0 **5** 1/2 **Cool Land (IRE)**[28] 4323 2-8-10 0 ... LukeMorris 1 — 53
(R A Harris) *pushed along early to chse ldrs: rdn over 1f out: edgd lft and no ex ins fnl f* **28/1**

6 1 **Bathwick Scanno (IRE)** 2-8-10 0 ... RichardMullen 10 — 50
(P D Evans) *mid-div: rdn 3f out: no ex fnl f* **12/1**[3]

50 **7** 4 **Miss Nimbus**[20] 4587 2-8-4 0 ow1 ... MatthewDavies(3) 2 — 38
(George Baker) *prom: hmpd bnd over 6f out: rdn over 1f out: wknd fnl f* **50/1**

1506 **8** 1/2 **Little Libretto (IRE)**[42] 3859 2-8-5 64 ... CathyGannon 7 — 34
(P D Evans) *chsd ldr tl rdn over 2f out: wknd fnl f* **6/1**[2]

00 **9** 6 **Petronilla**[14] 4802 2-8-6 0 ... JamieMackay 5 — 21
(W J Musson) *hld up: a in rr: bhd fnl 3f* **66/1**

10 1 3/4 **Generale (IRE)** 2-8-12 0 ... (bt[1]) LeeVickers 3 — 22
(F Sheridan) *s.i.s: a in rr: bhd fnl 3f* **25/1**

11 nk **Ivanov (IRE)** 2-8-11 0 ... StevieDonohoe 8 — 21
(W J Musson) *dwlt: a in rr: bhd fnl 3f* **14/1**

The Form Book, Raceform Ltd, Compton, RG20 6NL

00 **12** *1 1/4* **Hannah Cann**[78] 2677 2-8-2 0.......... PaulEddery 12 9
(Peter Grayson) *hld up: a in rr: bhd fnl 3f* **150/1**

1m 32.07s (2.47) **Going Correction** -0.025s/f (Stan) **12** Ran SP% **114.4**
Speed ratings (Par 94): **84,81,80,79,78 77,73,72,65,63 63,61**
toteswingers:1&2:£8.30, 1&3:£1.50, 2&3:£7.70 CSF £49.56 TOTE £3.50: £1.10, £7.30, £1.02; EX 51.90.Captain Loui was claimed by T. R. Pearson for £6,000.

Owner Dr Marwan Koukash **Bred** Denis McDonnell **Trained** Hambleton, N Yorks

FOCUS
Another uncompetitive event in which the proximity of the runner-up, fourth and fifth holds down the form. The gallop was ordinary and the winner came down the centre in the straight.

NOTEBOOK
Captain Loui(IRE), who had the cheekpieces refitted and was one of the few with a good chance at the weights, was allowed a fairly easy time of it in front on this Polytrack debut and first start over 7f and did not have to improve to beat a rival that had been soundly beaten on her debut. Apart from a blip on his penultimate run, he's been fairly consistent and he now joins Dai Burchell. (op 7-2)

Lindo Erro, well beaten at a big price over 6f after a slow start on his debut, had a stiff task on these terms but fared a good deal better on this all-weather debut. She should be suited by the step up to 1m but low-grade handicaps will be the way forward with her in due course. (op 16-1)

Bachelor Knight(IRE) looked a leading player on his turf form but, although dropped in grade in an uncompetitive event, he was again below his best over this course and distance. The return to turf should suit but he looks high enough in the weights. (op 13-8)

Elusive Vine(IRE), tailed off on both previous starts in maidens, including over course and distance last time, fared a good deal better in this lesser event, despite failing to settle but it may not be wise to take this race at face value. (op 25-1)

Cool Land(IRE) had the run of the race up in trip on this all-weather debut and was another to show much improved form but is another that is likely to remain vulnerable in this type of event or in maiden company. (op 22-1 tchd 16-1)

Little Libretto(IRE), who had a good chance at the weights, has been disappointing since winning on soft ground in spring and failed to get home over this longer trip on this all-weather debut. She has plenty to prove at present. (op 8-1)

Generale(IRE) Official explanation: jockey said that the colt was slow away

5270 STAY AT THE WOLVERHAMPTON HOLIDAY INN MEDIAN AUCTION MAIDEN STKS 1m 141y(P)
8:15 (8:15) (Class 6) 3-4-Y-O **£1,706** (£503; £252) **Stalls** Low

Form RPR
2234 **1** **City Ground (USA)**[34] 4146 3-9-3 78.......... NeilCallan 4 77
(M A Jarvis) *mde all: set stdy pce tl qcknd over 2f out: rdn and hung lft ins fnl f: r.o* **10/11**[1]

32 **2** *1 1/4* **Broadway Dancer**[20] 4601 3-8-12 0.......... PaulMulrennan 5 69
(R A Fahey) *chsd wnr: rdn over 2f out: swtchd lft over 1f out: hung lft ins fnl f: unable qck towards fin* **2/1**[2]

2 **3** *1/2* **Norman Orpen (IRE)**[27] 4364 3-9-3 0.......... LukeMorris 2 73
(N P Littmoden) *chsd ldrs: rdn over 2f out: r.o* **11/2**[3]

06 **4** *11* **Bedouin Princess (IRE)**[12] 4874 3-8-5 0.......... AdamBeschizza(7) 1 43
(Lucinda Featherstone) *prom: lost pl 6f out: rdn and wknd over 2f out* **33/1**

5 *2 1/4* **I Spy Baileys** 3-8-12 0.......... LeeVickers 3 38
(J G Given) *dwlt: hdwy 6f out: rdn and wknd over 2f out* **25/1**

1m 51.67s (1.17) **Going Correction** -0.025s/f (Stan) **5** Ran SP% **107.9**
Speed ratings (Par 101): **93,91,91,81,79**
CSF £2.79 TOTE £1.10: £1.02, £3.50; EX 2.90.

Owner R J Baines **Bred** Mrs E Scott Jr & Mrs L Macelree **Trained** Newmarket, Suffolk

FOCUS
Little strength to this ordinary maiden and one in which the three market leaders pulled clear. The pace was a moderate one and the winner raced centre to far side in the straight.

Norman Orpen(IRE) Official explanation: jockey said that the gelding lost a left hind shoe

5271 GREAT OFFERS AT WOLVERHAMPTON-RACECOURSE.CO.UK H'CAP 1m 141y(P)
8:50 (8:51) (Class 6) (0-60,60) 3-Y-O+ **£1,876** (£554; £277) **Stalls** Low

Form RPR
0360 **1** **Aussie Blue (IRE)**[14] 4804 6-9-4 56..........(v) MichaelStainton(3) 9 66
(R M Whitaker) *chsd ldrs: rdn to ld over 1f out: styd on* **12/1**

0351 **2** *1* **Mr Chocolate Drop (IRE)**[23] 4485 6-9-6 55..........(t) AdamKirby 2 63
(Miss M E Rowland) *hld up: hdwy over 2f out: rdn over 1f out: r.o* **7/1**

0002 **3** *nk* **Big Sur**[9] 4969 4-9-3 52.......... StevieDonohoe 6 59
(T Keddy) *a.p: rdn over 2f out: r.o* **9/2**[1]

032 **4** *nk* **Out Of Nothing**[11] 4914 7-8-11 51.......... KierenFox(5) 12 57
(D Burchell) *chsd ldr tl led over 2f out: rdn and hdd over 1f out: styd on same pce ins fnl f* **5/1**[2]

0045 **5** *nk* **Kenyan Cat**[15] 4762 3-9-1 60.......... MatthewDavies(3) 13 66+
(George Baker) *hld up: hdwy over 1f out: swtchd lft ins fnl f: r.o: nt rch ldrs* **16/1**

0223 **6** *1 3/4* **Join Up**[4] 5158 4-8-13 53.......... RossAtkinson(5) 8 55
(W M Brisbourne) *mid-div: hdwy over 5f out: rdn over 3f out: styd on same pce ins fnl f* **6/1**[3]

-455 **7** *4 1/2* **Nicholas Pocock (IRE)**[16] 4707 4-9-4 58.......... DaleSwift(5) 1 49
(B Ellison) *led: rdn and hdd over 2f out: wknd fnl f* **9/2**[1]

5060 **8** *7* **Athboy Auction**[16] 4715 5-8-13 48.......... CathyGannon 10 23
(H J Collingridge) *s.i.s: rdn over 3f out: alwsays in rr* **40/1**

2500 **9** *1 1/2* **Naseby (USA)**[17] 4687 3-8-6 55.......... AdamBeschizza(7) 4 27
(Miss S L Davison) *hld up: rdn 1/2-way: a in rr* **50/1**

6060 **10** *3/4* **Dancing Welcome**[8] 4987 4-9-6 55..........(b) NeilCallan 3 57+
(J M Bradley) *mid-div: hdwy over 2f out: cl 5th and styng on whn clipped heels and nrly uns rdr over 1f out: nt rcvr and eased* **28/1**

0410 **11** *1* **Bob Stock (IRE)**[25] 4427 4-9-11 60.......... TonyCulhane 5 28
(W J Musson) *hld up: hdwy 5f out: wknd 3f out* **15/2**

0450 **12** *2* **Decree Absolute (USA)**[16] 4700 3-9-2 58..........(v[1]) PaulFitzsimons 7 21
(Miss J R Tooth) *mid-div: rdn and wknd over 3f out* **33/1**

0546 **13** *3* **Diamondgeezer Luke (IRE)**[26] 4408 3-9-4 60.......... StephenCraine 11 16
(Patrick Morris) *chsd ldrs tl rdn and wknd over 2f out* **28/1**

1m 48.57s (-1.93) **Going Correction** -0.025s/f (Stan)
WFA 3 from 4yo+ 7lb **13** Ran SP% **119.4**
Speed ratings (Par 101): **107,106,105,105,105 103,99,93,92,91 90,88,86**
toteswingers:1&2:£12.00, 1&3:£12.20, 2&3:£6.50 CSF £89.45 CT £458.97 TOTE £15.30: £6.80, £4.40, £1.70; EX 82.00.

Owner G F Pemberton **Bred** T L Adams & G F Pemberton **Trained** Scarcroft, W Yorks

FOCUS
A modest but open handicap run at a decent gallop in driving rain. The gallop was sound and the winner came down the centre in the straight.

5272 CORAL TV H'CAP 1m 4f 50y(P)
9:20 (9:21) (Class 5) (0-70,70) 3-Y-O+ **£3,412** (£1,007; £504) **Stalls** Low

Form RPR
0613 **1** **Moscow Oznick**[11] 4915 5-9-1 64..........(v) AdamBeschizza(7) 3 70
(D Donovan) *chsd ldr: rdn over 2f out: edgd rt and styd on u.p to ld wl ins fnl f* **4/1**[2]

/2-1 **2** *nk* **Matjar (IRE)**[38] 4009 7-9-10 66.......... AdamKirby 2 72
(Joseph Quinn, Ire) *trckd ldrs: rdn and ev whn hmpd ins fnl f: styd on* **7/2**[1]

3500 **3** *3/4* **Hindu Kush (IRE)**[50] 3588 5-10-0 70.......... StevieDonohoe 1 75
(R A Mills) *led: rdn over 1f out: hdd wl ins fnl f* **4/1**[2]

4500 **4** *2 1/4* **Carter**[15] 4752 4-9-1 57..........(p) PaulMulrennan 5 58
(W M Brisbourne) *hld up: plld hrd: hdwy over 4f out: rdn over 2f out: no ex fnl f* **6/1**[3]

3414 **5** *1/2* **Kyle Of Bute**[24] 4454 4-9-5 61.......... TonyCulhane 7 61
(B P J Baugh) *hld up: hdwy over 2f out: rdn over 2f out: no ex fnl f* **10/1**

41-2 **6** *3 1/2* **Babilu**[109] 1768 5-8-13 60.......... KierenFox(5) 4 55
(D Burchell) *s.i.s: hld up: hdwy over 2f out: wknd fnl f* **6/1**[3]

330 **7** *1* **Bid For Glory**[168] 814 6-10-0 70..........(v) JerryO'Dwyer 6 63
(H J Collingridge) *hld up: hdwy u.p over 1f out: wknd fnl f* **16/1**

3004 **8** *9* **Ancient Times (USA)**[25] 4433 3-8-12 64..........(p) DuranFentiman 8 43
(Joss Saville) *chsd ldrs: rdn over 3f out: wknd over 2f out* **11/1**

2m 41.3s (0.20) **Going Correction** -0.025s/f (Stan)
WFA 3 from 4yo+ 10lb **8** Ran SP% **114.1**
Speed ratings (Par 103): **98,97,97,95,95 93,92,86**
toteswingers:1&2:£3.40, 1&3:£6.30, 2&3:£2.10 CSF £18.33 CT £58.44 TOTE £8.60: £2.90, £1.02, £2.30; EX 14.00 Place 6 £5.12; Place 5 £2.70.
Owner W P Flynn **Bred** Llety Stud **Trained** Newmarket, Suffolk
■ Stewards' Enquiry : Adam Beschizza caution: careless riding

FOCUS
A modest handicap in which the gallop was only fair. The first two came down the centre in the straight.
Bid For Glory Official explanation: jockey said that the gelding hung right
T/Plt: £10.60 to a £1 stake. Pool:£70,454.76 - 4,844.55 winning tickets T/Qpdt: £5.00 to a £1 stake. Pool:£5,105.10 - 747.20 winning tickets CR

5245 YORK (L-H)
Friday, August 20

OFFICIAL GOING: Good to firm (good in places) changing to good to firm after race 3 (2:50)
Rails moved out 3m on back straight and home bend adding 8yards to races of one mile and over.
Wind: Moderate,half-behind Weather: overcast

5273 SKY BET MELROSE STKS (H'CAP) 1m 6f
1:45 (1:50) (Class 2) (0-105,104) 3-Y-O **£42,094** (£12,525; £6,259; £3,126) **Stalls** Low

Form RPR
4115 **1** **Mount Athos (IRE)**[23] 4470 3-8-1 84.......... FrannyNorton 1 101+
(J W Hills) *t.k.h on inner: trckd ldrs: hdwy 3f out: led 2f out: rdn: hung bdly rt ins fnl f and sn hdd: rallied u.p to ld again last 50yds: styd on wl* **8/1**[1]

-102 **2** *1/2* **Tactician**[29] 4304 3-8-0 86.......... MartinLane(3) 14 101
(M L W Bell) *dwlt and bhd: hdwy 5f out: effrt to chse ldrs over 2f out: rdn to chse wnr over 1f out: styd on to ld ins fnl f: sn drvn and hdd last 50yds* **20/1**

1610 **3** *2 3/4* **Christopher Wren (USA)**[13] 4815 3-8-3 86.......... JimmyQuinn 15 97
(J R Best) *lw: hld up: stdy hdwy 5f out: trckd ldrs 3f out: rdn to chse wnr 2f out: drvn over 1f out and kpt on same pce* **20/1**

3101 **4** *3 1/2* **Zuider Zee (GER)**[20] 4571 3-8-6 89.......... RichardMullen 9 95+
(J H M Gosden) *lw: hld up in rr: hdwy on outer 3f out: rdn 2f out: kpt on fnl f: nrst fin* **8/1**[1]

0611 **5** *3 3/4* **Montparnasse (IRE)**[41] 3909 3-7-11 83.......... Louis-PhilippeBeuzelin(3) 6 84
(B J Meehan) *trckd ldrs: hdwy over 3f out: rdn over 2f out: kpt on same pce* **11/1**

-431 **6** *1 1/2* **Green Lightning (IRE)**[97] 2125 3-8-0 83..........(b) JoeFanning 4 82+
(M Johnston) *midfield: hdwy 5f out: chsd ldrs over 3f out: rdn and ch wl over 2f out: sn drvn and wknd* **9/1**[3]

2105 **7** *11* **Bowdler's Magic**[13] 4815 3-8-9 92.......... KierenFallon 8 75
(M Johnston) *chsd ldrs: hdwy and cl up over 3f out: sn rdn and wknd over 2f out* **12/1**

-410 **8** *14* **Desert Sage**[33] 4178 3-8-9 92.......... JimCrowley 7 56
(R M Beckett) *midfield: effrt and sme hdwy 3f out: rdn over 2f out and n.d* **20/1**

1230 **9** *8* **Grey Bunting**[23] 4470 3-8-0 83.......... DavidProbert 11 35
(B W Hills) *midfield: hdwy and in tch 1/2-way: effrt on outer 5f out: sn rdn along and wknd 3f out* **20/1**

3212 **10** *1/2* **Comedy Act**[13] 4827 3-8-3 86.......... SilvestreDeSousa 3 38
(Sir Mark Prescott) *cl up: led over 3f out: rdn wl over 2f out: sn wknd and eased over 1f out* **8/1**[1]

1164 **11** *1 1/4* **Desert Recluse (IRE)**[28] 4320 3-8-8 91.......... RichardHughes 12 41
(Pat Eddery) *hld up and bhd: sme hdwy wl over 2f out: nvr a factor* **16/1**

1540 **12** *16* **Berling (IRE)**[23] 4470 3-8-7 90..........(b[1]) EddieAhern 13 18
(J L Dunlop) *a towards rr: bhd fnl 3f* **17/2**[2]

3135 **13** *30* **Moose Moran (USA)**[63] 3145 3-9-7 104.......... TomQueally 5 —
(H R A Cecil) *chsd ldrs: rdn along 4f out: sn wknd* **16/1**

4121 **14** *2 1/2* **Bay Willow (IRE)**[26] 4400 3-9-5 102.......... FrankieDettori 10 —
(M Johnston) *a towards rr: wl bhd fnl 3f* **8/1**[1]

1411 **15** *19* **Trovare (USA)**[27] 4380 3-8-1 84.......... PaulHanagan 2 —
(Mrs A J Perrett) *led: rdn along over 4f out: hdd over 3f out and wknd qckly* **11/1**

2210 **16** *3* **Deauville Post (FR)**[92] 2252 3-8-0 83.......... FrankieMcDonald 17 —
(R Hannon) *prom: rdn along over 4f out: wknd qckly and sn bhd* **50/1**

2m 58.19s (-2.01) **Going Correction** +0.025s/f (Good) **16** Ran SP% **122.1**
Speed ratings (Par 106): **106,105,104,102,100 99,92,84,80,80 79,70,53,51,40 39**
toteswingers:1&2:£44.70, 1&3:£55.50, 2&3:£92.60 CSF £168.56 CT £3089.62 TOTE £10.10: £3.00, £5.70, £6.40, £2.00; EX 297.50 TRIFECTA Not won..
Owner Corinthian **Bred** David Magnier And Cobra Bloodstock **Trained** Upper Lambourn, Berks
■ Stewards' Enquiry : Martin Lane two-day ban: used whip with excessive frequency

FOCUS
This is usually a red-hot 3-y-o handicap and the form should work out. The pace was honest and the action was middle-to- stands' side in the straight.

NOTEBOOK

Mount Athos(IRE) ◆, upped in trip and returned to a galloping course, would have won convincingly had he not veered away from the whip over 1f out. He had travelled through the race easily and, although he was running off a mark of just 84, it's no exaggeration to say he looked a colt of pattern-class potential, provided his waywardness can either be corrected or managed. After all, he's closely related to Derby runner-up The Great Gatsby, and it turns out he's currently being leased by these connections from David Magnier. The type to keep improving, he's one to follow. (op 9-1 tchd 10-1)

Tactician ran a fine race in defeat, but is flattered to finish so close to the errant winner. He's on the up, and should stay even further, but had a hard enough race with his rider banned for two days for using his whip with excessive frequency. (tchd 22-1, 25-1 in a place)

Christopher Wren(USA) appreciated the return to a left-handed track, as well as the step up in trip, and is still improving. He has the scope to make a nice 4-y-o. (tchd 25-1 in a place)

Zuider Zee(GER), 7lb higher than when winning over 1m4f on his previous outing, lacked the pace of some of these and couldn't seriously threaten. A return to more positive tactics might suit. (op 7-1 tchd 10-1)

Montparnasse(IRE) was bidding for a hat-trick, but couldn't defy a 7lb rise for his success over this trip in lesser company last time. (op 17-2)

Green Lightning(IRE), 5lb higher than when making all over 1m4f at the July course, had no chance of dominating this time after missing the break. He recovered to have a chance, but had got quite warm and didn't see his race out. (op 8-1 tchd 10-1)

Comedy Act wasn't at his best back on quick ground and seems best suited by an easy surface. (op 10-1)

Berling(IRE) wasn't at his best back on quick ground and seems best suited by an easy surface. (op 9-1)

Bay Willow(IRE) disappointed off a 4lb higher mark than when winning from the front over 1m4f at Ascot on his previous start, getting nowhere near the lead. Official explanation: trainer was unable to offer any explanation for the poor performance shown (tchd 15-2)

Trovare(USA), the winner of three of his last four starts, was kept honest up front, but even so he weakened as though something was amiss. (op 14-1)

5274 SKY BET STRENSALL STKS (GROUP 3) 1m 208y

2:15 (2:20) (Class 1) 3-Y-O+

£48,254 (£18,292; £9,154; £4,564; £2,286; £1,147) **Stalls** Low

Form	Pos	Dist	Horse / details	RPR
0110	1		**Rio De La Plata (USA)**[13] 4829 5-9-5 114 .... FrankieDettori 8 (Saeed Bin Suroor) *lw: trckd ldrs: hdwy 3f out: cl up 2f out: rdn to ld 1f out: drvn and kpt on wl towards fin* **7/1**[2]	118
1-21	2	nk	**Rainbow Peak (IRE)**[63] 3144 4-9-5 115 .... NeilCallan 7 (M A Jarvis) *trckd ldrs: hdwy 3f out: swtchd rt and effrt wl over 1f out: rdn to chal ent fnl f: sn drvn and ev ch: nt qckn nr fin* **5/4**[1]	117+
4522	3	¾	**Kings Gambit (SAF)**[41] 3921 6-9-5 110 .... JamieSpencer 12 (T P Tate) *trckd ldng pair: hdwy to ld over 3f out: rdn 2f out: drvn and hdd 1f out: kpt on gamely u.p tl no ex towards fin* **7/1**[2]	116
6021	4	¾	**Vesuve (IRE)**[20] 4596 4-9-5 110 .... TedDurcan 6 (Saeed Bin Suroor) *trckd ldrs: rdn along and sltly outpcd over 2f out: kpt on u.p appr fnl f: nrst fin* **20/1**	114
0606	5	6	**Confront**[27] 4359 5-9-5 111 .... OlivierPeslier 1 (Sir Michael Stoute) *trckd ldr: racd alone far side in st: rdn along over 3f out and grad wknd fnl 2f* **8/1**[3]	102
1013	6	½	**Harrison George (IRE)**[26] 4412 5-9-5 114 .... PaulHanagan 10 (R A Fahey) *in tch: hdwy to chse ldrs over 3f out and sn rdn: drvn over 2f out and sn one pce* **20/1**	101
0511	7	nk	**Critical Moment (USA)**[20] 4574 3-8-12 108 .... MichaelHills 11 (B W Hills) *led: rdn along and hdd over 3 out: drvn over 2f out and grad wknd* **9/1**	100
64-1	8	8	**Cesare**[36] 4050 9-9-5 111 .... JMurtagh 4 (J R Fanshawe) *hld up and bhd: effrt and sme hdwy 3f out: sn rdn and nvr a factor* **20/1**	83
5153	9	1 ½	**Field Of Dream**[20] 4574 3-8-12 109 .... KierenFallon 2 (L M Cumani) *in tch on inner: pushed along 4f out: rdn 3f out: sn outpcd and bhd* **11/1**	80
5400	10	3	**Halicarnassus (IRE)**[63] 3144 6-9-5 106 .... AlanMunro 9 (M R Channon) *a in rr: rdn along 3f out and sn bhd* **66/1**	74

1m 49.04s (-2.96) **Going Correction** +0.025s/f (Good)

WFA 3 from 4yo+ 7lb **10** Ran SP% **114.7**

Speed ratings (Par 113): **114,113,113,112,107 106,106,99,97,95**

toteswingers:1&2:£2.90, 1&3:£4.40, 2&3:£2.50 CSF £15.08 TOTE £6.20: £1.70, £1.50, £2.20; EX 19.10 Trifecta £84.00 Pool: £8,617.66 - 75.84 winning units..

Owner Godolphin **Bred** Jose De Camargo, Robert N Clay Et Al **Trained** Newmarket, Suffolk

FOCUS

A very competitive Group 3 event, run at a sound pace. The majority of the field came down the middle of the track, with only the well-beaten Confront sticking to the far rail. Eventually the first four came clear in a tight finish and the form looks up to scratch.

NOTEBOOK

Rio De La Plata(USA) landed his third win from five outings this season with a game effort under a strong ride from Frankie Dettori. He was well positioned to strike when it mattered and, in front throughout the final furlong, knuckled down pleasingly to repel challengers at the business end. He came unstuck on testing ground at Haydock last time, but when dead-heating at Pontefract on quick ground on his penultimate outing his rider that day was of the definite opinion he would've won clearly with a little more cut underfoot. Therefore ground this firm was of a little concern beforehand, but he obviously acted on it without fuss and it also enabled him to find the sufficient stamina for this trip. He didn't stay in the 2008 Derby behind New Approach, but this was just his second third outing beyond 1m and he is open to further improvement over this sort of trip before the season's end. His connections have done very well to get him back firing after he lost his way last year and it wouldn't be surprising to see him go for a big one again in something like the Champion Stakes at Newmarket later on. (op 8-1)

Rainbow Peak(IRE) looked all over a Group performer when taking the Listed Wolferton Handicap on his previous run at Royal Ascot in June, but was originally due to reappear in the Group 2 Sky Bet York Stakes over C&D last month before a hiccup prevented him turning up there. He was officially raised 8lb for his Ascot success which made him top rated here, despite it being his debut in such company, and he was heavily backed. He was produced for everything at the furlong pole and ended up closest to the near side, which has been the favoured place to be in previous races here this week. He couldn't get on top of the winner try as he might, though, and indeed took time to master the third. It still rates a career-best from this late-maturing son of Hernando and he left the impression the ground was probably as quick as he wants it. He ought to win races of this nature with a little more ease underfoot and will be better off getting back over a stiffer test. He may well have even more to offer as a 5-y-o. Connections later said the Prix Dollar over 1m2f in France during Arc weekend may be next for him. (tchd 11-8)

Kings Gambit(SAF) was so narrowly denied in the John Smith's Cup over 1m2f last month and had finished second to Rainbow Peak on his penultimate outing in the Wolferton at Royal Ascot. He just failed to reverse that form, but was 2lb worse off and he too produced a career-best in defeat. He certainly deserves to get his head back in front. (op 8-1)

Vesuve(IRE) ◆ was very much the second string here. He showed the clear benefit of his confidence-boosting success over 1m at Newmarket 20 days earlier and performed right up to his best. He may find it tricky to win one of these, but is certainly capable of winning a Listed race and will likely appreciate returning to easier ground.

Confront, used a pacemaker for Harbinger last time out, had won a Listed race at this meeting last term and came in for support. He was disadvantaged in going solo on the far side, but is yet another here that is still to convince he wants to go this far. (op 11-1)

Harrison George(IRE) was closely matched with the winner on his last-time-out Pontefract form and likes this venue as his three-career wins indicate. He got tapped for toe as the tempo got serious here, however, due to being ridden with greater restraint over this longer trip and was never seriously involved. It's most probable he needs dropping back to 1m. (op 16-1 tchd 14-1)

Critical Moment(USA) found this a lot tougher taking on his elders for the first time and is another that wants dropping back to 1m. (op 17-2 tchd 15-2)

Cesare narrowly beat Vesuve on his comeback last month, but that was the fourth consecutive occasion he has won first time out and he wasn't nearly as effective on this return to Group company over the extra distance. (op 14-1)

Field Of Dream was in trouble turning for home after being restrained. (op 12-1)

Halicarnassus(IRE) proved very unruly on this return to action, never figuring from out the back.

5275 SKY BET CITY OF YORK STKS (LISTED RACE) 7f

2:50 (2:51) (Class 1) 3-Y-O+ **£23,704** (£8,964; £4,480; £2,240) **Stalls** Low

Form	Pos	Dist	Horse / details	RPR
1214	1		**Yaa Wayl (IRE)**[27] 4358 3-8-9 106 .... PhilipRobinson 6 (M A Jarvis) *trckd ldrs: chal over 1f out: styd on wl to ld ins fnl f: r.o* **5/1**[2]	115
1533	2	½	**Skysurfers**[90] 2318 4-9-0 113 .... FrankieDettori 15 (Saeed Bin Suroor) *trckd ldrs: led over 1f out: hdd and no ex last 100yds* **7/1**	116
0205	3	nk	**Fravashi (AUS)**[34] 4136 5-9-0 112 .... TedDurcan 2 (Saeed Bin Suroor) *stdd s: hld up: hdwy on stands' side over 2f out: styd on fnl f: tk 3rd nr fin* **16/1**	115
5320	4	1 ½	**Palace Moon**[20] 4576 5-9-0 110 ....(t) KierenFallon 13 (W J Knight) *stmbld s: sn drvn along: hdwy over 3f out: chal over 1f out: styd on same pce* **5/1**[2]	111
2220	5	hd	**Red Jazz (USA)**[24] 4457 3-9-0 113 .... MichaelHills 7 (B W Hills) *lw: led after 1f: hdd over 1f out: kpt on same pce* **4/1**[1]	114
414-	6	5	**Mr David (USA)**[366] 5172 3-8-9 104 .... JamieSpencer 1 (B J Meehan) *chsd ldrs: hung rt and wknd fnl f* **16/1**	95
1010	7	1 ¾	**Oasis Dancer**[22] 4537 3-8-9 106 .... JimCrowley 4 (R M Beckett) *hld up: hdwy over 3f out: chsng ldrs over 1f out: sn wknd* **8/1**	90
-300	8	2 ¼	**Carnaby Street (IRE)**[64] 3103 3-8-9 99 .... RichardHughes 5 (R Hannon) *led 1f: w ldrs: wknd appr fnl f* **28/1**	84
2210	9	4	**Treadwell (IRE)**[20] 4574 3-8-9 105 .... FergusSweeney 9 (J A Osborne) *s.i.s: hld up towards rr: rdn 2f out: no rspnse* **17/2**	74
0310	10	2 ¾	**Castles In The Air**[20] 4576 5-9-0 105 .... PaulHanagan 3 (R A Fahey) *trckd ldrs: effrt over 2f out: wknd over 1f out* **13/2**[3]	68

1m 21.93s (-3.37) **Going Correction** -0.20s/f (Firm)

WFA 3 from 4yo+ 5lb **10** Ran SP% **116.0**

Speed ratings (Par 111): **111,110,110,108,108 102,100,97,93,90**

toteswingers:1&2:£7.00, 1&3:£17.70, 2&3:£15.50 CSF £39.72 TOTE £5.80: £1.90, £2.40, £4.90; EX 45.20 Trifecta £980.00 Pool: £2,291.11 - 1.73 winning units..

Owner Sheikh Ahmed Al Maktoum **Bred** Ballylinch Stud **Trained** Newmarket, Suffolk

FOCUS

The ground was changed to good to firm all over following this contest. A good, competitive Listed contest, run at a decent pace, and the race unfolded middle-to-stands' side in the straight.

NOTEBOOK

Yaa Wayl(IRE), fourth behind Castles In The Air in the International Stakes handicap at Ascot on his previous start, coped with the return to Listed company and displayed a game attitude to hold off the two Godolphin runners. He can remain competitive at this level, and maybe even in Group 3s. (op 6-1)

Skysurfers, who looked so promising on synthetics in Dubai earlier in the year, had disappointed on his turf debut when returned to Britain at Goodwood in May, but this was better, with him clearly having benefited from a short break. He stays further and should build on this. (op 9-2)

Fravashi(AUS), dropped in grade and upped in trip, stayed on towards the stands' rail but was never quite getting there. He's not easy to win with, but can probably be found an ordinary Listed or conditions race before presumably going back to Dubai.

Palace Moon, seemingly unsuited by well-watered ground in the Stewards' Cup, fared better this time, but still appeared below his very best. He was never going that well following an awkward start and it's to his credit he finished so close. (op 9-2)

Red Jazz(USA) couldn't take advantage of the return to Listed company. He's not progressing, which leaves him vulnerable in pattern company. (op 11-2)

Mr David(USA) ran a noteworthy race on his first start since finishing fourth in last year's Gimcrack. He still looked inexperienced under pressure, and didn't help himself by hanging right, yet still ran well for a long way. There should be better to come. (tchd 20-1 in a place)

Oasis Dancer was switched towards the outside with his challenge and didn't pick up. He had also disappointed at Goodwood last time and has a bit to prove now. (op 17-2 tchd 9-1 in a place)

Treadwell(IRE) started slowly and failed to respond to pressure. (op 8-1)

Castles In The Air was another to run well below form. (op 8-1)

5276 COOLMORE NUNTHORPE STKS (GROUP 1) 5f

3:25 (3:26) (Class 1) 2-Y-O+

£136,248 (£51,648; £25,848; £12,888; £6,456; £3,240) **Stalls** Low

Form	Pos	Dist	Horse / details	RPR
-146	1		**Sole Power**[14] 4808 3-9-9 104 .... WMLordan 11 (Edward Lynam, Ire) *hld up: hdwy over 2f out: r.o to ld last 75yds* **100/1**	119
511	2	1 ¼	**Starspangledbanner (AUS)**[42] 3870 4-9-11 121 .... JMurtagh 13 (A P O'Brien, Ire) *racd stands' side: sn drvn along and outpcd: hdwy over 2f out: chsng ldrs 1f out: styd on same pce fnl 75yds* **6/4**[1]	114
0-24	3	1 ¼	**Piccadilly Filly (IRE)**[54] 3486 3-9-6 106 .... EddieCreighton 2 (E J Creighton) *chsd ldrs: edgd rt after 1f: led appr fnl f: hdd ins fnl f: no ex* **100/1**	107
1005	4	nse	**Prime Defender**[12] 4885 6-9-11 111 .... RobertWinston 8 (B W Hills) *lw: chsd ldrs: styd on same pce fnl f* **40/1**	110
1261	5	¾	**Rose Blossom**[42] 3875 3-9-6 103 ....(v[1]) PaulHanagan 9 (R A Fahey) *lw: led: hdd appr fnl f: fdd last 100yds* **20/1**	104
3331	6	½	**Borderlescott**[22] 4505 8-9-11 112 .... NeilCallan 7 (R Bastiman) *mid-div: effrt and edgd lft 2f out: styd on same pce fnl f* **11/1**	105
116	7	nse	**Dinkum Diamond (IRE)**[64] 3100 2-8-1 101 .... FrankieMcDonald 5 (H Candy) *chsng ldrs whn hmpd after 1f: in rr: hdwy over 1f out: kpt on: nt rch ldrs* **20/1**	97
4055	8	1	**Spin Cycle (IRE)**[22] 4505 4-9-11 107 ....(v) RichardMullen 6 (B Smart) *mid-div: hdwy 2f out: nvr nr ldrs* **40/1**	101
-164	9	¾	**Kingsgate Native (IRE)**[42] 3870 5-9-11 116 .... KierenFallon 1 (Sir Michael Stoute) *hld up towards rr: hdwy over 2f out: n.m.r: nvr nr ldrs* **9/2**[3]	99
F004	10	2 ½	**Mister Hughie (IRE)**[22] 4505 3-9-9 105 .... AlanMunro 10 (M R Channon) *sn outpcd and in rr* **28/1**	90
2442	11	2 ¼	**Stone Of Folca**[24] 4458 2-8-1 101 .... JimmyQuinn 12 (J R Best) *trckd ldrs: wknd over 1f out* **10/1**	74

1212 **12** *8* **Equiano (FR)**[42] 3870 5-9-11 120.. MichaelHills 3 53
(B W Hills) *lw: s.i.s: sn chsng ldrs: hmpd after 1f: wknd 2f out: eased appr fnl f* **7/2**[2]

57.14 secs (-2.16) **Going Correction** -0.20s/f (Firm) **12** Ran SP% **117.7**
Speed ratings: **109,107,105,104,103 102,102,101,100,96 92,79**
toteswingers:1&2:£37.50, 1&3:£59.90, 2&3:£30.30 CSF £239.61 TOTE £122.80: £14.90, £1.20, £11.40; EX 417.60 Trifecta £6311.40 Pool: £14,584.63 - 1.71 winning units..
Owner Mrs S Power **Bred** G Russell **Trained** Dunshaughlin, Co Meath
■ Only the second 100/1 Group 1 winner in the history of the pattern, after Hittite Glory in the 1975 Flying Childers Stakes.
■ Stewards' Enquiry : Eddie Creighton two day ban: careless riding (Sept 3 - 4)

FOCUS
This looked a strong renewal beforehand, but the draw was of importance and it proved to be a messy race after a scorcing early pace found out most. There was a shock result and the form is suspect.

NOTEBOOK
Sole Power struck another blow for the Classic generation this season and came home a ready winner. Restrained early on, he made smooth headway from halfway and took it up going powerfully 1f out. He was briefly threatened by the strong-finishing Starspangledbanner, but he was always doing enough and looked to have a little up his sleeve at the finish. It's difficult to see where this vast improvement has come from considering he came into this with just two wins on Polytrack at Dundalk to his name, and he had not been at his best on his last three outings. He did run very well at this meeting last year in the St Leger Yearling Stakes over 6f, but an official mark of 104 did seem about right for him. He did produce a career-best when fourth to Equiano in the Palace House at Newmarket, however, and obviously bettered that form here. The only two 3-y-o winners of this event in the past decade were the outstanding Oasis Dream and Mozart, so it's not hard to see that it has required a top-notch sprinter of that age to succeed. While there appeared to be little fluke about the way he performed, with his past record it's most unlikely he is in the same class as that pair, but he must be given a chance to prove he is a worthy winner. A tilt at the Prix De L'Abbaye on Arc day at Longchamp in October could figure next, and a run in that should reveal more as to whether he can back this form up. It would have to be a sound surface for him to turn up there, though. (tchd 66-1)
Starspangledbanner(AUS)'s progression since he made his British debut over this C&D in May has been fantastic and he once again proved very popular on this drop back from 6f. He was drawn on the outside in stall 13 and, racing alone towards the nearside, got markedly outpaced through the early parts. He showed his class when finishing strongly inside the final furlong, but the winner was gone beyond recall. Ultimately dropping back to this quick 5f found him out, but he probably wasn't helped by racing where he did and he continues as Europe's leading sprinter. It remains to be seen whether he now heads off to stud in his native Australia or indeed has another outing before doing so. (op 13-8)
Piccadilly Filly(IRE), rated 106, looked to be faced with a near-impossible task but she ran the race of her life to grab third. She got warm beforehand, but her proven early dash stood her in really good stead and this will have delighted her connections, who have always held her in high regard. It was just her third outing of the year and a tenth career start, so there could well be some more to come. Her proximity does little for the overall form and sums up how messy the race was, but it will be fascinating to see how she goes on her next assignment. (op 80-1)
Prime Defender had been comfortably held in all his previous attempts at this level. He wasn't done any favours in the July Cup, but shaped better in France last time on ground easier than he cares for. He kept on respectably without ever threatening over this much sharper test and deserves a drop down in grade to get his head back in front.
Rose Blossom, a dual winner at the course this season, was lit up by a first-time visor and unsurprisingly paid the price from the furlong marker. She would be interesting if kept in training next year. (op 16-1)
Borderlescott was bidding to emulate Tag End (1928-1930) and Sharpo (1980-82) in winning this for the third time. His participation was down to a miraculous recovery from the injury he sustained when resuming winning ways at Glorious Goodwood 22 days earlier and connections believed they had him back near his best. He lacked the early toe to play a part, though, and was keeping on too late near the finish. It's hard to judge just how much his injury played a part in this display, but he wasn't at all disgraced and looks likely to head for another crack at the Prix De L'Abbeye. (op 10-1 tchd 9-1)
Dinkum Diamond(IRE) ◆, having his first outing since a beaten favourite in the Norfolk Stakes, fared best of two juveniles and he was doing some decent work late. It looks a good idea to try him over 6f now and it wouldn't be at all surprising to see him win a Group event before the season's end. (op 16-1)
Kingsgate Native(IRE), well backed, wasn't helped by the scorching early pace and didn't get the best of passages, but wasn't on a going day in any case. (op 13-2)
Stone Of Folca was representing the trainer who won this with Kingsgate Native as a juvenile in 2007 and, like that one, he too came into the race a maiden. His fate was sealed before halfway, though, and surely a maiden would be best for him now. (op 9-1)
Equiano(FR) had been in the form of his life coming here and was a big fancy to turn around July Cup form with Starspangledbanner, over what has appeared his optimum trip. He was easy to back largely on account of his low draw, but was never really going after a poor start and his rider eased him off soon after halfway. This obviously wasn't anything like his true running, but it does leave him with something to prove. (op 4-1 tchd 9-2 in a place)

5277 RACING POST CONVIVIAL MAIDEN STKS 7f
4:05 (4:07) (Class 2) 2-Y-O **£16,190** (£4,817; £2,407; £1,202) Stalls Low

Form RPR
02 **1** **Moriarty (IRE)**[19] 4622 2-9-3 0.. JMurtagh 4 90+
(R Hannon) *trckd ldrs: effrt 2f out: r.o to ld wl ins fnl f* **12/1**
4 **2** *1 1/4* **El Muqbil (IRE)**[44] 3794 2-9-3 0.. RichardHills 12 87
(B J Meehan) *lw: hmpd s: w ldrs: led over 1f out: hdd and no ex last 75yds* **2/1**[1]
6 **3** *4* **Star Of Dance (IRE)**[23] 4490 2-9-3 0........................ KierenFallon 13 77+
(Sir Michael Stoute) *w'like: lw: dwlt and wnt rt s: in rr: hdwy 3f out: styd on fnl f* **9/1**[2]
02 **4** *3/4* **Flodden (USA)**[27] 4375 2-9-3 0.. JamieSpencer 11 75
(P F I Cole) *swvd rt s: trckd ldrs: drvn 3f out: kpt on same pce over 1f out* **33/1**
2 **5** *nk* **Edmaaj (IRE)**[23] 4490 2-9-3 0.. MichaelHills 15 74+
(B W Hills) *w'like: scope: s.i.s: in rr: hdwy over 2f out: styd on wl fnl f* **10/1**[3]
00 **6** *1* **Smart Step**[22] 4508 2-8-12 0.. GregFairley 14 67
(M Johnston) *leggy: led tl over 1f out: grad wknd* **100/1**
0 **7** *3 3/4* **The Bells O Peover**[55] 3452 2-9-3 0.. JoeFanning 3 62
(M Johnston) *leggy: chsd ldrs: wknd over 1f out* **22/1**
2 **8** *1 3/4* **Bahri Sheen (IRE)**[12] 4871 2-9-3 0........................ RobertWinston 16 58
(J R Best) *str: w ldrs on wd outside: lost pl over 1f out* **33/1**
9 *1 3/4* **Ashva (USA)** 2-9-3 0.. PhillipMakin 2 54
(M Dods) *lengthy: trckd ldrs: t.k.h: effrt over 2f out: wknd over 1f out* **33/1**
10 *shd* **Terdaad (IRE)** 2-9-3 0.. FrankieDettori 5 53+
(Saeed Bin Suroor) *gd sort: dwlt: mid-div: drvn and hdwy 4f out: chsng ldrs over 1f out: sn wknd* **2/1**[1]
2 **11** *nse* **Ollon (USA)**[33] 4167 2-9-3 0.. PaulHanagan 6 53
(R A Fahey) *unf: scope: dwlt: hld up in rr: sme hdwy 2f out: nvr on terms* **12/1**
12 *hd* **Spey Song (IRE)** 2-8-12 0.. TomQueally 1 48
(J D Bethell) *leggy: dwlt: hdwy on ins to chse ldrs over 3f out: wknd 2f out* **100/1**
50 **13** *1/2* **Oliver's Gold**[77] 2715 2-9-3 0.. PhilipRobinson 9 52
(Mrs A J Perrett) *w ldrs: lost pl over 2f out* **66/1**
6 **14** *8* **Syncopated Lady (IRE)**[12] 4862 2-8-12 0............ SilvestreDeSousa 17 27
(D O'Meara) *unf: s.i.s: a in rr* **100/1**
15 *1 3/4* **Tees And Cees (IRE)** 2-9-3 0.. NeilCallan 10 27
(R Hannon) *leggy: mid-div: drvn over 2f out: sn wknd* **50/1**
16 *5* **Marc De Savoie (IRE)** 2-9-3 0.. TomEaves 8 15
(K A Ryan) *unf: s.i.s: a bhd* **100/1**
60 **17** *9* **Pitkin**[27] 4392 2-9-3 0.. JamesSullivan 7 —
(M W Easterby) *sn bhd: t.o 2f out* **100/1**

1m 23.4s (-1.90) **Going Correction** -0.20s/f (Firm) **17** Ran SP% **122.7**
Speed ratings (Par 100): **102,100,96,95,94 93,89,87,85,85 85,84,84,75,73 67,57**
toteswingers:1&2:£6.00, 1&3:£10.20, 2&3:£4.60 CSF £34.54 TOTE £12.10: £3.40, £1.20, £2.80; EX 47.90 Trifecta £173.60 Pool: £2.210.15 - 9.42 winning units..
Owner Justin Dowley & Michael Pescod **Bred** Rathasker Stud **Trained** East Everleigh, Wilts

FOCUS
This maiden has produced some decent types in years gone by and was run over 7f for the first time this season, upped from 6f. The race should produce its share of nice winners. They were well spread out in the straight, but the middle was the place to be.

NOTEBOOK
Moriarty(IRE) probably would have won had he stayed straight when runner-up over 6f at Newbury last time, but he made no mistake on this step back up in trip. He's improved with every start so far - this was a very useful performance - and he'll be well worth his place in better company. (tchd 14-1)
El Muqbil(IRE), who holds a number of big-race entries, confirmed the promise he showed when fourth on debut at the July course, but simply found one too good. Clear of the remainder, this was a decent performance in defeat and he should be tough to beat in maiden company next time. (op 9-4 tchd 5-2)
Star Of Dance(IRE) ◆, a Champagne Stakes entrant, needed the experience on debut at Sandown, and although this was better, he again shaped as though he's still got a lot of learning to do. He looks one to get onside. (op 10-1)
Flodden(USA) couldn't reverse debut placings with El Muqbil, but still ran well. He can find a lesser maiden, and also now has the option of nurseries.
Edmaaj(IRE), who's in the Dewhurst, had Star Of Dance behind when an unlucky runner-up on debut at Sandown, but he didn't learn much from that experienced judged by this display. He took an age to work out what was required, but was running on well at the line and will surely improve for the run (tchd 9-1)
Smart Step ◆ had shown only modest form at best, but she's in the Fillies' Mile and Cheveley Park. Although well held, this was a respectable effort against males, especially as she raced towards the unfavoured far side in the straight.
The Bells O Peover ◆, another with major entires, ran to just a moderate level on debut but this time wasn't helped by racing towards the far side in the closing stages. (tchd 20-1)
Ashva(USA) ◆ showed up well for a fair way until getting tired and has ability.
Terdaad(IRE), a brother to 1m2f winner Mortbet, out of 7f scorer who's a sister to Iffraaj, has been entered in the Beresford, as well as the Mill Reef, and seemed well fancied to make a winning debut. He was comfortably held, but raced far side in the straight, which probably wasn't ideal, and can certainly be given another chance. Official explanation: jockey said the colt was unsuited by he good/firm ground. (tchd 7-4)
Ollon(USA) had a hard enough race when beaten favourite on debut and struggled in this tougher company. (op 10-1 tchd 14-1)
Spey Song(IRE) ◆ shaped nicely. She showed her inexperience with a slow start, and then wasn't helped by racing far side in the closing stages, so she's open to plenty of improvement.

5278 STOWE FAMILY LAW LLP STKS (H'CAP) 2m 88y
4:40 (4:40) (Class 3) (0-95,93) 4-Y-O+ **£12,952** (£3,854; £1,926; £962) Stalls Low

Form RPR
-500 **1** **Hawk Mountain (UAE)**[70] 2938 5-8-7 **79**........................ JamieSpencer 8 87
(J J Quinn) *lw: prom: hrd rdn and c towards stands' side over 3f out: edgd rt over 1f out: styd on to ld last 75yds* **8/1**
231 **2** *1 3/4* **Wicked Daze (IRE)**[27] 4393 7-8-9 **81**........................ PhillipMakin 15 87
(Miss L A Perratt) *led: kpt on gamely: hdd wl ins fnl f* **12/1**
0565 **3** *1* **Becausewecan (USA)**[13] 4817 4-9-1 **87**........................ JoeFanning 5 92
(M Johnston) *trckd ldrs: chal over 1f out: styd on same pce last 100yds* **20/1**
-000 **4** *1 3/4* **Mith Hill**[23] 4467 9-7-10 **75**........................(v) RyanPowell[(7)] 3 78
(Ian Williams) *hmpd bnd after 1f: mid-div: hdwy to chse ldrs over 6f out: styd towards far side over 4f out: kpt on one pce appr fnl f* **28/1**
1323 **5** *nk* **Forrest Flyer (IRE)**[6] 5070 6-8-2 **74** oh2................ SilvestreDeSousa 14 76
(J S Goldie) *chsd ldrs: outpcd over 3f out: one pce fnl 2f* **20/1**
5100 **6** *nk* **Perfect Shot (IRE)**[24] 4461 4-9-4 **90**........................ EddieAhern 12 92
(J L Dunlop) *hld up in rr: rapid hdwy over 6f out: drvn and outpcd over 3f out: c stands' side: swtchd lft over 1f out: nvr trbld ldrs* **20/1**
1153 **7** *4 1/2* **Deauville Flyer**[41] 3922 4-9-7 **93**........................ RobertWinston 7 89
(T D Easterby) *lw: hld up in rr: drvn and hdy over 3f out: one pce fnl 2f* **11/4**[1]
3435 **8** *nk* **Palomar (USA)**[27] 4393 8-8-6 **78**........................ PJMcDonald 11 74
(B Ellison) *dwlt: hld up in rr: hdwy over 2f out: styng on at fin* **12/1**
-332 **9** *2 3/4* **Lady Luachmhar (IRE)**[35] 4086 4-8-13 **85**........................ PaulHanagan 6 78
(R A Fahey) *lw: t.k.h towards rr: hdwy 10f out: drvn 3f out: sn wknd* **10/1**
-102 **10** *nse* **Dazinski**[27] 4393 4-9-1 **87**........................ TedDurcan 2 80
(M H Tompkins) *hld up in rr: hmpd bnd after 1f: effrt far side 3f out: nvr a factor* **7/1**[3]
-106 **11** *nk* **Hollins**[23] 4467 6-8-8 **80**........................ KierenFallon 9 72
(Micky Hammond) *chsd ldrs: drvn along 7f out: lost pl over 2f out* **11/2**[2]
536/ **12** *1/2* **Osolomio (IRE)**[24] 105 7-8-3 **75**........................(e[1]) JimmyQuinn 1 67
(Jennie Candlish) *chsd ldrs: chal over 3f out: lost pl over 2f out* **50/1**
0044 **13** *3/4* **Cosmic Sun**[19] 4619 4-8-8 **85**........................ LeeTopliss[(5)] 10 76
(R A Fahey) *in rr: hdwy 6f out: drvn over 3f out: wknd over 1f out* **12/1**
2120 **14** *3* **The Last Alzao (IRE)**[26] 4405 4-8-5 **80**........................ BarryMcHugh[(3)] 4 67
(R A Fahey) *hld up in rr: effrt over 3f out: sn wknd* **14/1**

3m 35.79s (1.29) **Going Correction** +0.025s/f (Good) **14** Ran SP% **124.2**
Speed ratings (Par 107): **97,96,95,94,94 94,92,92,90,90 90,90,89,88**
toteswingers:1&2:£29.00, 1&3:£41.70, 2&3:£25.10 CSF £95.95 CT £1880.49 TOTE £9.60: £3.60, £3.60, £3.80; EX 135.20 Trifecta £2134.30 Part won. Place 6 £313.77; Place 5 £89.83.
Owner P Morrison & N Luck **Bred** Darley **Trained** Settrington, N Yorks
■ Stewards' Enquiry : Jamie Spencer two day ban: used whip with excessive frequency

FOCUS
A good staying handicap, run at an uneven gallop and it proved hard to sufficiently make up ground from off the pace.

NOTEBOOK

Hawk Mountain(UAE) bounced back to his best and ran out a game winner. He arrived with plenty to prove having run below par on his three previous outings this term, but his yard is now back in much better form and he did finish fourth in this race last season off a 5lb higher mark. He proved keen early on, but Jamie Spencer soon had him settled in mid-field and really got stuck into him when delivering towards the near rail from 3f out. He mastered the runner-up in the closing stages and was nicely on top at the line, so is clearly back in decent heart. There is still room for further improvement in him this term and he evidently stays better this year, this being his first win over 2m. His connections will now aim him at the Cesarewitch and he may well go straight there, with a 4lb penalty for this helping to ensure a run in that. Official explanation: trainer said, regarding the apparent improvement in form, gelding benefited from having a break of 70 days since its last run and stable's runners had been under a cloud (op 10-1 tchd 14-1)

Wicked Daze(IRE), 2lb higher, got very much the run of things when making all over C&D last month and, again getting an uncontested lead, very nearly got away with it once more. He gave his all when challenged from 3f out and only gave way to the winner late on. He will go up again for this, but did win off a mark of 92 in 2008 and his consistency should continue to hold him in decent stead. (op 14-1)

Becausewecan(USA) ◆ was never far away and looked to be travelling best of all around 2f out. He ultimately failed to get home like the first pair, but this was a decent effort on ground quick enough for him and, fairly handicapped at present, looks well worth another try over a slightly sharper test. (op 16-1)

Mith Hill, who made his effort more towards the far side, fared best of those given waiting rides. This was his best effort of the season with a visor back on and returning to more positive handling could see him get closer over this distance. (op 33-1 tchd 25-1)

Forrest Flyer(IRE), 2lb out of the handicap, was suited by racing close to the pace but he turned in a creditable effort in this better company. The handicapper just looks to have his measure. (op 16-1)

Perfect Shot(IRE), whose stable won this last term, is a confirmed hold-up performer who was never going to be seen at his best due to the way the race unfolded. (tchd 18-1)

Deauville Flyer finished third over 1m6f in Listed company at the track on his previous outing. He was another that couldn't get involved due to being held up, but he was staying on late in the day and is worth another chance. (op 3-1 tchd 10-3)

Palomar(USA) was 2lb better off with the winner on their last-time-out C&D form, but once again he got caught out by the way the race was run. He didn't look too willing at times, but he too is entitled to another chance. (op 16-1 tchd 20-1)

Dazinski was just behind the winner here last time out, but ran a tame race. (op 6-1)

Hollins dropped away 2f out and may be in need of a break. (op 7-1 tchd 15-2)

T/Jkpt: Not won. T/Plt: £287.50 to a £1 stake. Pool:£288,624.69 - 732.65 winning tickets T/Qpdt: £83.00 to a £1 stake. Pool:£12,691.56 - 113.14 winning tickets WG

5279 - 5283a (Foreign Racing) - See Raceform Interactive

5111 BATH (L-H)

Saturday, August 21

OFFICIAL GOING: Good (good to soft in places) changing to good to soft after race 2 (6:05)

Wind: Moderate across Weather: Overcast

5284 SWINDON DESIGNER OUTLET JAEGER NOVICE STKS — 5f 161y

5:35 (5:36) (Class 4) 2-Y-O — £3,561 (£1,059; £529; £264) Stalls Centre

Form				RPR
1052	1		**Penny's Pearl (IRE)**[11] 4928 2-9-0 90 PatDobbs 2 (R Hannon) *trckd ldr 3f out: led ins fnl 2f: shkn up and styd on strly fnl f* **1/1**[1]	89
14	2	1 1/4	**Nordic Spruce (USA)**[11] 4934 2-9-0 77 TomQueally 4 (H R A Cecil) *s.i.s: sn in tch: chsd wnr ins fnl 2f: no imp fnl f* **9/4**[2]	85
1	3	3	**Child Bride**[116] 1603 2-8-11 0 SamHitchcott 3 (P F I Cole) *led: rdn and hdd ins fnl 2f: wknd appr fnl f* **5/1**[3]	72
3230	4	4	**Button Moon (IRE)**[35] 4138 2-8-9 80 TomMcLaughlin 1 (I A Wood) *chsd ldr to 3f out: sn rdn: wknd 2f out* **8/1**	57

1m 11.15s (-0.05) **Going Correction** -0.10s/f (Good) 4 Ran SP% **108.5**

Speed ratings (Par 96): **96,94,90,85**

CSF £3.51 TOTE £1.90; EX 3.70.

Owner Malcolm Brown & Mrs Penny Brown **Bred** Liam O'Neill **Trained** East Everleigh, Wilts

FOCUS

An interesting novice event featuring three previous winners and, after a single defection, an all-filly line-up.

NOTEBOOK

Penny's Pearl(IRE), second on her latest start and officially rated 90, set a standard none of her rivals could match. Third in the early stages, she went second at halfway and led over a furlong out. She had something in hand at the finish and probably did not need to run to her rating. Her pedigree suggests she will et further but, as she does not look Listed class, she may be obliged to take on tough tasks in nurseries. (tchd 10-11)

Nordic Spruce(USA) had disappointed on her second run, having won cosily at Nottingham first time out, but returned to her best here. Held up early, she made rapid progress to grab the lead two furlongs out, but could not match the winner's pace inside the last. Nurseries beckon for her too. (op 3-1)

Child Bride, successful on debut in April, was having her first race since and the manner in which her price eased suggested she was expected to need this outing. She messed around at the start but, after breaking quickly, took the field along until well after halfway. She faded from there. (op 7-2)

Button Moon(IRE) lined up with a trio of creditable placed finishes to her name, but the best of her form indicated she was up against it in this company. Second early, she was soon outpaced and never threatened to collect. (tchd 7-1)

5285 SWINDON DESIGNER OUTLET HUGO BOSS H'CAP — 5f 161y

6:05 (6:05) (Class 4) (0-85,87) 3-Y-O+ — £3,885 (£1,156; £577; £288) Stalls Centre

Form				RPR
1-32	1		**Hot Pursuits**[22] 4531 3-8-8 72 SteveDrowne 4 (H Morrison) *chsd ldrs: led appr fnl 2f: drvn out fnl f* **9/2**[2]	83
2022	2	1	**Secret Witness**[5] 5151 4-9-12 87 (b) TomMcLaughlin 6 (R A Harris) *in rr: rdn and hdwy 3f out: chsd wnr ins fnl 2f: styd on u.p fr over 1f out and kpt on ins fnl f but a hld* **4/1**[1]	95
1321	3	8	**Vhujon (IRE)**[6] 5112 5-8-13 74 PatDobbs 2 (P D Evans) *in rr: rdn and hdwy over 2f out: styd on to take poor 3rd 1f out* **4/1**[1]	55
1105	4	3	**Brandywell Boy (IRE)**[20] 4625 7-8-9 75 BillyCray(5) 3 (D J S Ffrench Davis) *in tch: drvn and hdwy 3f out: nvr on terms and wknd wl over 1f out* **5/1**[3]	46
3402	5	4 1/2	**Steelcut**[8] 5025 6-8-10 74 RussKennemore(3) 1 (Andrew Reid) *chsd ldrs: rdn and wknd over 2f out* **17/2**	30
0000	6	3	**Kerrys Requiem (IRE)**[11] 4930 4-9-9 84 SamHitchcott 5 (M R Channon) *rdn 3f out: a bdly outpcd* **12/1**	30
0563	7	hd	**Ocean Blaze**[16] 4730 6-9-0 75 (b) TomQueally 8 (B R Millman) *chsd ldr: led over 3f out and racd wd: hdd appr fnl 2f: sn wknd* **7/1**	20
4141	8	5	**Spanish Acclaim**[16] 4739 3-8-10 74 NeilChalmers 7 (A M Balding) *led tl hdd over 3f out: sn wknd* **8/1**	—

1m 10.52s (-0.68) **Going Correction** -0.05s/f (Good)

WFA 3 from 4yo+ 3lb 8 Ran SP% **116.7**

Speed ratings (Par 105): **102,100,90,86,80 76,75,69**

toteswingers:1&2:£3.30, 1&3:£4.60, 2&3:£2.40 CSF £23.38 CT £78.56 TOTE £7.80: £3.00, £1.30, £2.30; EX 42.50.

Owner Mrs I Eavis **Bred** M Channon B/Stck & G Richardson B/Stck **Trained** East Ilsley, Berks

FOCUS

A competitive handicap, but run in a deluge of rain and hailstones, so the form may not be entirely reliable. Such was the ferocity of the storm, all eight jockeys weighed in 4lb higher than they had weighed out. The first two finished clear.

5286 SWINDON DESIGNER OUTLET PHASE EIGHT H'CAP — 1m 3f 144y

6:35 (6:35) (Class 4) (0-80,80) 3-Y-O+ — £3,885 (£1,156; £577; £288) Stalls Low

Form				RPR
3546	1		**Mons Calpe (IRE)**[16] 4737 4-8-11 62 (p) TomQueally 4 (P F I Cole) *led after 1f: c towards stands' side and narrowly hdd jst ins fnl 2f: rallied to take slt ld again ins fnl f: hld on all out* **9/1**	73
1260	2	nse	**Abergavenny**[14] 4841 3-9-5 80 MartinDwyer 2 (M Johnston) *chsd wnr after 2f: c to r on stands' rail and drvn to tale slt ld jst ins fnl 2f: narrowly hdd ins fnl f: styd upsides: no ex last stride* **4/1**[2]	91
1-06	3	3	**King Supreme (IRE)**[7] 5084 5-9-7 72 PatDobbs 7 (R Hannon) *chsd ldrs: c to r on stands' side 3f out: styng on same pce whn nt clr run and swtchd lft ins fnl f: no imp* **9/1**	78
1432	4	1 1/2	**Sunny Future (IRE)**[6] 5115 4-9-4 69 TomMcLaughlin 1 (M S Saunders) *t.k.h in rr: drvn and hdwy fr 3f out: racd towards centre crse: styd on same pce fnl 2f* **7/2**[1]	72+
4002	5	2 1/2	**Resplendent Light**[16] 4737 5-9-7 79 JamesRogers(7) 11 (W R Muir) *chsd ldrs: rdn towards centre crse and styd on fr 3f out: wknd over 1f out* **15/2**[3]	78
340	6	4 1/2	**Citizenship**[20] 4619 4-9-5 70 (t) SteveDrowne 12 (Ian Williams) *stdd towards rr: c to stands' side and rdn 3f out: no rspnse and wknd fr 2f out* **7/2**[1]	61
3-30	7	nk	**Wild Desert (FR)**[37] 4051 5-9-13 78 LiamKeniry 8 (A King) *led 1f: styd chsng ldrs: c to stands' side and rdn 3f out: wknd 2f out* **8/1**	69
1-12	8	28	**Danger Mulally**[199] 386 3-9-2 77 (t) DavidProbert 6 (A M Balding) *a in rr: no ch fnl 3f* **16/1**	—

2m 32.7s (2.10) **Going Correction** +0.30s/f (Good)

WFA 3 from 4yo+ 10lb 8 Ran SP% **113.2**

Speed ratings (Par 105): **105,104,102,101,100 97,97,78**

toteswingers:1&2:£4.80, 1&3:£11.90, 2&3:£8.20 CSF £43.92 CT £334.62 TOTE £10.00: £2.60, £1.20, £2.70; EX 44.40.

Owner H R H Sultan Ahmad Shah **Bred** Swettenham Stud **Trained** Whatcombe, Oxon

FOCUS

The ground was officially changed to good to soft before this race. It was just an average handicap.

Citizenship Official explanation: jockey said that the gelding hung right

5287 SWINDON DESIGNER OUTLET TOMMY HILFIGER H'CAP — 1m 5y

7:05 (7:05) (Class 4) (0-80,77) 3-Y-O+ — £3,885 (£1,156; £577; £288) Stalls Low

Form				RPR
5111	1		**One Scoop Or Two**[22] 4547 4-9-0 68 RussKennemore(3) 14 (R Hollinshead) *chsd ldrs: rdn to go 2nd ins fnl 3f: led 2f out: styd on u.p fr over 1f out* **7/1**	79+
5531	2	1/2	**Advertise**[28] 4382 4-9-6 71 DavidProbert 11 (A M Balding) *in tch: hdwy 3f out: styd on u.p fr 2f out to chse wnr 1f out: kpt on but a jst hld* **5/2**[1]	81
0300	3	2	**Full Victory (IRE)**[2] 5237 8-8-10 61 MartinDwyer 10 (R A Farrant) *in rr: hrd drvn and hdwy over 2f out: styd on to take narrow 3rd ins fnl f but no imp on ldng duo* **10/1**	66
2556	4	shd	**Effigy**[23] 4501 6-9-11 76 DaneO'Neill 5 (H Candy) *in rr: hdwy towards centre crse over 2f out: styd on to disp one pce 3rd ins fnl f: dropped to 4th last stride* **13/2**[3]	81
4210	5	6	**Flying Silks (IRE)**[23] 4522 4-9-7 72 (v) TomQueally 6 (J R Gask) *s.i.s: in rr: sme hdwy fr 2f out: nvr nr ldrs* **8/1**	63
4000	6	2	**Carnivore**[25] 4450 8-9-4 69 SamHitchcott 12 (T D Barron) *chsd ldr: led ins fnl 3f: hdd 2f out: wknd appr fnl f* **33/1**	56
-220	7	1/2	**Petomic (IRE)**[13] 4870 5-8-9 65 RossAtkinson(5) 1 (M Hill) *s.i.s: in rr: drvn and sme hdwy over 2f out: nvr rchd ldrs and wknd over 1f out* **18/1**	51
36	8	3 1/4	**Peaceful Means (IRE)**[3] 4873 7-9-2 67 RichardThomas 7 (A W Carroll) *s.i.s: towards rr most of way* **40/1**	45
3010	9	1 3/4	**Kilburn**[21] 4579 6-9-11 76 (p) SteveDrowne 2 (A J Lidderdale) *chsd ldrs: rdn over 2f out: wkng and n.m.r over 1f out: eased sn after* **11/1**	50
4510	10	1	**Very Well Red**[17] 4690 7-9-5 75 BillyCray(5) 9 (P W Hiatt) *chsd ldrs tl wknd wl over 2f out* **14/1**	47
0004	11	15	**Captain Macarry (IRE)**[30] 4306 5-9-8 73 (v) LiamKeniry 4 (J J Quinn) *led tl hdd ins fnl 3f: sn wknd* **9/2**[2]	10

1m 42.25s (1.45) **Going Correction** +0.30s/f (Good)

WFA 3 from 4yo+ 6lb 11 Ran SP% **118.4**

Speed ratings (Par 105): **104,103,101,101,95 93,92,89,87,86 71**

toteswingers:1&2:£2.80, 1&3:£16.40, 2&3:£8.40 CSF £24.95 CT £163.57 TOTE £5.60: £1.70, £1.10, £5.60; EX 23.90.

Owner Showtime Ice Cream Concessionaire **Bred** S And R Ewart **Trained** Upper Longdon, Staffs

FOCUS

Another run-of-the-mill handicap, run at a strong early pace.

Flying Silks(IRE) Official explanation: jockey said gelding hung badly right

Kilburn Official explanation: jockey said gelding had no more to give

5288 SWINDON DESIGNER OUTLET LK BENNETT MAIDEN STKS — 1m 5y

7:35 (7:35) (Class 5) 3-Y-O+ — £2,590 (£770; £385; £192) Stalls Low

Form				RPR
020	1		**Youm Jamil (USA)**[63] 3215 3-9-3 76 MartinDwyer 3 (B J Meehan) *led after 1f: t.k.h: pushed along and styd on strly fr over 1f out: pushed out: readily* **9/4**[2]	75
4333	2	1	**Danehill Sunset (IRE)**[9] 5007 3-9-3 70 LiamKeniry 2 (B W Hills) *plld hrd: in tch: hrd rdn and styd on fr 2f out: chsd wnr 1f out: sn hung lft and fnd no ex* **7/1**	73
2	3	3 1/4	**Magic Jack**[9] 5007 3-9-3 0 PatDobbs 4 (R Hannon) *chsd ldrs: hrd drvn over 2f out: styd on same pce fnl f to take one pce 3rd last strides* **6/5**[1]	66

The Form Book, Raceform Ltd, Compton, RG20 6NL

6 **4** *hd* **Politbureau**[37] [4069] 3-9-3 0 ..... TomQueally 5 65
(M Johnston) *led 1f: styd chsng wnr: hrd rdn: hung rt and lost 2nd 1f out: dropped to wl hld 4th last strides* **6/1**[3]

52 **5** *4* **Priors Gold**[9] [5001] 3-9-3 0 ..... DaneO'Neill 1 56
(M P Tregoning) *chsd ldrs: rdn over 2f out: sn btn* **7/1**

1m 43.57s (2.77) **Going Correction** +0.35s/f (Good) **5** Ran SP% **115.5**
Speed ratings (Par 103): **100,99,95,95,91**
CSF £17.93 TOTE £2.20: £1.10, £2.50; EX 16.90.
Owner Jaber Abdullah **Bred** Ashleigh Stud Farm **Trained** Manton, Wilts

FOCUS
A modest little 3-y-o maiden.

5289 SWINDON DESIGNER OUTLET T.M. LEWIN H'CAP — 1m 5f 22y
8:05 (8:05) (Class 6) (0-55,57) 3-Y-O+ — **£1,619** (£481; £240; £120) **Stalls** High

Form				RPR
0620 **1** **Jasmeno**[18] [4676] 3-8-8 **53** ..... (t) SteveDrowne 2 66+
(H Morrison) *hld up in rr: gd hdwy over 2f out: drvn to ld appr fnl f: pushed clr: comf* **9/2**[2]

1-44 **2** *4* **Zelos Diktator**[25] [3989] 4-9-7 **55** ..... (p) GeorgeBaker 11 62
(G L Moore) *sn chsng ldr: rdn over 2f out: kpt on to chse wnr ins fnl f but nvr any ch* **9/2**[2]

-060 **3** *¾* **Annelko**[16] [4764] 3-8-7 **52** ..... NeilChalmers 13 58
(A B Haynes) *led after 1f: hdd u.p appr fnl f: sn no ch and outpcd into 3rd* **28/1**

5321 **4** *1 ¼* **Jenny Soba**[3] [5202] 7-9-6 **57** 6ex ..... RussKennemore(3) 7 61
(Lucinda Featherstone) *led 1f: chsd ldrs: rdn and styd on over 2f out: wknd ins fnl f* **15/8**[1]

2303 **5** *2 ¼* **Filun**[15] [4794] 5-8-6 **47** ..... RichardRowe(7) 6 49
(A Middleton) *in rr: hdwy 4f out: sme prog on stands' rail whn nt clr run and swtchd lft ins fnl 2f: n.d after* **10/1**

/004 **6** *17* **Hareem (IRE)**[12] [4915] 6-9-7 **55** ..... (v) MartinDwyer 9 30
(W R Muir) *led 1f: styd chsng ldrs tl rdn 3f out: sn wknd: eased whn no ch fnl f* **12/1**

0003 **7** *hd* **Bethlehem (IRE)**[32] [4230] 3-8-7 **52** ..... (t) DavidProbert 10 27
(H Morrison) *in tch: rdn to chse ldrs 3f out: wknd qckly ins fnl 2f: eased whn no ch fnl f* **11/2**[3]

5463 **8** *2 ½* **Laura Land**[18] [4683] 4-8-8 **47** ..... RossAtkinson(5) 8 18
(W M Brisbourne) *chsd ldrs tl wknd qckly over 2f out: eased whn no ch fnl f* **11/1**

0-00 **9** *35* **Manchestermaverick (USA)**[10] [4959] 5-8-13 **47** ..(v) RichardThomas 14 —
(Dr J R J Naylor) *lost tch after 5f and sn t.o* **33/1**

2m 56.95s (4.95) **Going Correction** +0.35s/f (Good)
WFA 3 from 4yo+ 11lb **9** Ran SP% **118.0**
Speed ratings (Par 101): **98,95,95,94,92 82,82,80,59**
toteswingers:1&2:£6.60, 1&3:£30.90, 2&3:£18.10 CSF £25.72 CT £512.47 TOTE £4.90: £1.80, £1.50, £8.70; EX 32.00 Place 6 £103.95; Place 5 £51.39.
Owner Melksham Craic **Bred** Melksham Craic **Trained** East Ilsley, Berks

FOCUS
A modest staying handicap to end proceedings, with the top-weight rated just 57.
Manchestermaverick(USA) Official explanation: jockey said gelding slipped on the first bend
T/Plt: £294.90 to a £1 stake. Pool:£51,892.73 - 128.45 winning tickets T/Qpdt: £80.70 to a £1 stake. Pool:£5,215.88 - 47.82 winning tickets ST

4614 CHESTER (L-H)
Saturday, August 21

OFFICIAL GOING: Good to soft (soft in places between 6f and 4f; 6.4)
Rail out 8yds from 6f to 4f, and 3yds from 4f to top of home straight adding 20yds to races over 6f, 6.5f and 7f, 37yds to 1m 5f race and 40yds to 2m race.
Wind: Almost nil Weather: Cloudy

5290 TOTEPOOL H'CAP (DIV I) — 6f 18y
2:20 (2:20) (Class 4) (0-85,85) 3-Y-O+ — **£5,180** (£1,541; £770; £384) **Stalls** Low

Form				RPR
31-0 **1** **Great Charm (IRE)**[18] [4684] 5-9-4 **77** ..... PatCosgrave 14 87+
(E J Alston) *a.p: rdn to ld over 1f out: kpt on gamely ins fnl f* **33/1**

0005 **2** *½* **Roker Park (IRE)**[28] [4371] 5-9-9 **82** ..... (p) DarryllHolland 2 90
(K A Ryan) *chsd ldrs: pushed along to go pce over 3f out: rdn and nt qckn over 1f out: r.o ins fnl f: gng on at fin* **4/1**[1]

0251 **3** *½* **Bahamian Lad**[22] [4558] 5-9-3 **76** ..... (p) JerryO'Dwyer 1 82
(R Hollinshead) *led for 1f: continued to chse ldrs: rdn over 1f out: styd on ins fnl f: nt quite gng pce of ldrs at fin* **7/1**

2321 **4** *nk* **Tyfos**[15] [4806] 5-9-11 **84** ..... JoeFanning 4 89
(B P J Baugh) *led after 1f: rdn and hdd over 1f out: continued to press wnr and ev ch ins fnl f: no ex fnl strides* **4/1**[1]

3446 **5** *nk* **Victorian Bounty**[43] [3845] 5-9-4 **77** ..... JackMitchell 3 81
(Stef Higgins) *racd keenly: a.p: rdn 2f out: swtchd lft whn chsng ldrs over 1f out: nt qckn ins fnl f* **11/2**[2]

001 **6** *¾* **Ursula (IRE)**[40] [3947] 4-9-7 **80** ..... TedDurcan 10 82
(Mrs K Burke) *in tch: pushed along 2f out: kpt on same ins fnl f* **12/1**

2100 **7** *hd* **Frognal (IRE)**[7] [5069] 4-8-13 **77** ..... (b) DaleSwift(5) 7 78
(Mrs R A Carr) *s.i.s: hld up: rdn over 1f out: kpt on ins fnl f: nt pce to chal* **33/1**

3442 **8** *shd* **Lucky Dan (IRE)**[22] [4542] 4-9-5 **78** ..... FrannyNorton 5 79
(Paul Green) *midfield: rdn over 1f out: hdwy u.p ins fnl f: kpt on but nt pce to rch ldrs* **6/1**[3]

0005 **9** *2* **Indian Trail**[23] [4510] 10-9-8 **81** ..... (v) AdrianNicholls 12 76
(D Nicholls) *midfield: lost pl 3f out: rdn over 1f out: no imp after* **20/1**

12-0 **10** *2 ¼* **Conry (IRE)**[147] [1006] 4-9-5 **85** ..... NeilFarley(7) 9 73
(Patrick Morris) *s.i.s: a bhd: rdn over 1f out: nvr on terms* **40/1**

01 **11** *1 ½* **Luscivious**[18] [4685] 6-9-9 **82** ..... (b) JimmyFortune 6 65
(J A Glover) *hld up: rdn over 1f out: nvr on terms: eased whn n.d wl ins fnl f* **7/1**

0000 **12** *5* **Falasteen (IRE)**[43] [3856] 3-9-9 **85** ..... ShaneKelly 11 52
(R A Fahey) *s.i.s: a bhd* **33/1**

1m 18.44s (4.64) **Going Correction** +0.825s/f (Soft)
WFA 3 from 4yo+ 3lb **12** Ran SP% **118.4**
Speed ratings (Par 105): **102,101,100,100,99 98,98,98,95,92 90,84**
toteswingers:1&2:£15.10, 1&3:£92.70, 2&3:£9.20 CSF £155.08 CT £1077.68 TOTE £55.80: £10.40, £2.10, £2.50; EX 370.10 Trifecta £596.60 Part won. Pool: £806.24 - 0.10 winning units..
Owner Mr & Mrs G Middlebrook **Bred** G And Mrs Middlebrook **Trained** Longton, Lancs

FOCUS
The first division of the 6f sprint looked a competitive affair and was quicker than the second. After riding in the opener Joe Fanning felt the ground was tacky, and Jerry O'Dwyer agreed it was tacky and holding.

Falasteen(IRE) Official explanation: jockey said gelding missed the break

5291 TOTESPORT.COM CHESTER H'CAP (LISTED RACE) — 1m 5f 89y
2:50 (2:50) (Class 1) (0-110,106) 3-Y-O+
£21,004 (£7,962; £3,984; £1,986; £995; £499) **Stalls** Low

Form				RPR
1144 **1** **Lady Eclair (IRE)**[14] [4817] 4-8-12 **93** ..... JoeFanning 6 101+
(M Johnston) *chsd ldrs: rdn to ld narrowly over 1f out: gamely fnd ex cl home* **13/2**[3]

0104 **2** *nk* **Red Cadeaux**[17] [4711] 4-8-11 **92** oh2 ..... MichaelHills 3 100+
(E A L Dunlop) *midfield: hdwy over 3f out: chal 4 wd 2f out: moved upsides wnr u.p over 1f out: hld cl home fin* **6/1**[2]

4142 **3** *1 ¾* **Jedi**[25] [4461] 4-8-11 **92** oh1 ..... ShaneKelly 7 97
(Sir Michael Stoute) *midfield: rdn and hdwy whn swtchd rt over 1f out: styd on to cl ins fnl f: nt rch front duo* **10/3**[1]

0-02 **4** *hd* **Chock A Block (IRE)**[23] [4500] 4-9-9 **104** ..... TedDurcan 5 109
(Saeed Bin Suroor) *in tch: trckd ldrs 4f out: effrt 2f out: styd on same pce and no imp on ldrs ins fnl f* **10/1**

1-06 **5** *1 ½* **Precision Break (USA)**[17] [4711] 5-8-13 **94** ..... (t) PatCosgrave 4 97
(P F I Cole) *hld up in midfield: u.p fr 3f out: stdy prog fr over 1f out: kpt on ins fnl f: no imp on ldrs* **20/1**

2641 **6** *¾* **La Vecchia Scuola (IRE)**[6] [5118] 6-8-11 **90** 3ex ..... GaryBartley 11 94
(J S Goldie) *sn led: rdn over 2f out: hdd over 1f out: wknd fnl 75yds* **8/1**

2152 **7** *4* **Emerging Artist (FR)**[14] [4818] 4-9-1 **96** ..... AdrianNicholls 10 92
(M Johnston) *chsd ldr after 2f: chalng 3f out: rdn over 2f out: sn lost 2nd: wknd fnl f* **8/1**

1146 **8** *9* **Into Wain (USA)**[69] [3014] 3-8-0 **92** ..... FrannyNorton 12 74
(D M Simcock) *hld up: pushed along over 5f out: nvr able to trble ldrs* **25/1**

5/4- **9** *1 ¾* **Numide (FR)**[112] [7237] 7-9-3 **98** ..... JamesMillman 2 78
(B R Millman) *s.s: a bhd: nvr on terms* **33/1**

0035 **10** *3 ¼* **Mojave Moon**[42] [3922] 4-9-5 **100** ..... AhmedAjtebi 1 75
(Mahmood Al Zarooni) *midfield: outpcd 3f out: toiling after* **16/1**

34/P **11** *19* **Bouguereau**[50] [3632] 5-9-11 **106** ..... JackMitchell 8 52
(P W Chapple-Hyam) *hld up: u.p over 2f out: nvr on terms* **25/1**

5-02 **12** *6* **Lethal Glaze (IRE)**[8] [5035] 4-8-11 **92** ..... JimmyFortune 9 29
(R Hannon) *w ldr early: chsd ldrs after: niggled along fr over 4f out: rdn and wknd over 2f out: eased whn wl btn fnl f* **7/1**

3m 1.81s (8.61) **Going Correction** +0.825s/f (Soft)
WFA 3 from 4yo+ 11lb **12** Ran SP% **115.8**
Speed ratings (Par 111): **106,105,104,104,103 103,100,95,94,92 80,76**
toteswingers:1&2:£10.10, 1&3:£4.00, 2&3:£2.10 CSF £41.86 CT £153.21 TOTE £7.50: £2.40, £2.50, £1.60; EX 46.50 Trifecta £105.90 Pool: £1,271.61 - 8.88 winning units..
Owner Netherfield House Stud **Bred** Lynch Bages Ltd & Samac Ltd **Trained** Middleham Moor, N Yorks

FOCUS
Probably not a really strong line-up for the grade despite the BHA ratings on show, but it produced a tremendous finish.

NOTEBOOK
Lady Eclair(IRE) had enjoyed a fantastic season, landing six races after making her racecourse debut back in March of this year. A good fourth in the 2m5f Goodwood Stakes two runs previous, she took that winning total to seven victories with a hard-fought success on the softest ground she has encountered. She looks all guts, the type for which her stable is renowned, and it wouldn't be a surprise to see her aimed towards the Park Hill Stakes at Doncaster next month in search of some Group form. (op 7-1 tchd 15-2)
Red Cadeaux, running from 2lb out of the handicap, finished eighth in the Chester Cup towards the start of the year but was disappointing on his return to action recently over 1m4f, albeit at Pontefract. Settled quite close to the leaders, he battled all the way to the line with the winner but was unable to get past her. (op 11-2)
Jedi, a pound out of the weights, ran well on his first try over a similar trip at Goodwood, and did so again, although without looking likely to win from a midfield position. He deserves another chance. (op 4-1)
Chock A Block(IRE), trying this sort of distance for the first time, plugged on but looked very one-paced. He probably doesn't want ground with ease in it. (op 9-1)
Precision Break(USA), fitted with a tongue-tie for the first time, has been disappointing this year, so this was a bit better after being settled towards the rear.
La Vecchia Scuola(IRE), 3lb higher than when winning at Pontefract six days previously, was handed an uncontested lead but did not get home as strongly as those in front of her.
Into Wain(USA), the only 3-y-o in the race, had been absent since finishing just over 8 lengths last of six in the Group 3 Prix Du Lys at Chantilly in June (the winner Goldwaki has subsequently run well in the Group 1 Grand Prix De Paris), and ran as though he needed this. He wasn't given a hard time in the latter stages.
Numide(FR), having his first start since leaving Gary Moore, was always towards the back and passed a couple of rivals late on.
Mojave Moon pulled much too hard again. (op 25-1)
Lethal Glaze(IRE) reportedly was never travelling. Official explanation: jockey said gelding ran flat (tchd 13-2)

5292 TOTESCOOP6 H'CAP — 7f 122y
3:25 (3:31) (Class 2) 3-Y-O+
£21,808 (£6,531; £3,265; £1,634; £815; £409) **Stalls** Low

Form				RPR
6513 **1** **Side Glance**[28] [4357] 3-8-12 **96** ..... JimmyFortune 11 107+
(A M Balding) *midfield: hdwy on outer over 1f out: r.o to ld ins fnl f: rdn out* **9/2**[2]

1-34 **2** *1 ½* **Tamaathul**[106] [1858] 3-9-5 **103** ..... MichaelHills 5 110+
(B W Hills) *in tch: hdwy on outer 2f out: edgd lft and led over 1f out: hdd u.p ins fnl f: no ex cl home* **4/1**[1]

000 **3** *nk* **Redford (IRE)**[14] [4843] 5-9-4 **96** ..... AdrianNicholls 15 103
(D Nicholls) *bmpd s: hld up: hdwy whn nt clr run over 1f out: styd on to take 3rd ins fnl f: clsd on front duo towards fin* **10/1**

0351 **4** *4 ½* **Kyllachy Star**[20] [4617] 4-8-13 **91** ..... DarryllHolland 13 87
(R A Fahey) *hld up: hdwy over 1f out: styd on u.p ins fnl f: n.d to front trio* **10/1**

5210 **5** *½* **Lucky Numbers (IRE)**[18] [4685] 4-8-11 **89** ..... FrannyNorton 16 83
(Paul Green) *w ldr: led over 2f out: hdd over 1f out: sn wnt sltly rt: one pce and btn whn edgd rt ins fnl f* **33/1**

1002 **6** *1 ¼* **Brae Hill (IRE)**[20] [4617] 4-9-5 **97** ..... PatCosgrave 7 88
(R A Fahey) *trckd ldrs: rdn over 1f out: nt qckn: one pce ins fnl f* **5/1**[3]

2111 **7** *½* **Cameroonev**[56] [3448] 7-8-8 **91** ..... DaleSwift(5) 6 81
(B Ellison) *trckd ldrs: rdn over 2f out: wknd fnl f* **8/1**

1-60 **8** *1 ¼* **Big Audio (IRE)**[23] [4504] 3-9-2 **100** ..... (vt) TedDurcan 3 85
(Saeed Bin Suroor) *in tch: pushed along and outpcd 2f out: no imp after* **10/1**

3005 **9** *4* **Thebes**[24] 4473 5-8-12 **93** ... PatrickHills(3) 9 69
(M Johnston) *in tch: effrt to chal over 2f out: wknd 1f out* **20/1**

3010 **10** *4 ½* **Something (IRE)**[28] 4358 8-9-2 **94** ... PaulQuinn 4 58
(D Nicholls) *missed break: a bhd: nvr on terms* **14/1**

0000 **11** *½* **Everymanforhimself (IRE)**[7] 5095 6-8-12 **90**...(b) DaraghO'Donohoe 14 53
(K A Ryan) *pushed along towards rr: hdwy on outer over 3f out: nt trble ldrs: wknd 2f out* **33/1**

4100 **12** *4 ½* **Below Zero (IRE)**[14] 4819 3-8-11 **95** ... JoeFanning 10 45
(M Johnston) *led: hdd over 2f out: wknd over 1f out* **20/1**

1116 **13** *8* **Ezdeyaad (USA)**[51] 3585 6-9-2 **94** ... AhmedAjtebi 8 25
(G A Swinbank) *s.i.s: midfield: pushed along and wknd 2f out* **16/1**

1m 38.6s (4.80) **Going Correction** +0.825s/f (Soft)
WFA 3 from 4yo+ 6lb 13 Ran SP% **121.2**
Speed ratings (Par 109): **109,107,107,102,102 100,100,99,95,90 90,85,77**
toteswingers:1&2:£3.70, 1&3:£10.10, 2&3:£9.60 CSF £22.01 CT £178.02 TOTE £5.40: £1.70, £2.10, £4.50; EX 22.00 Trifecta £155.10 Pool: £1,251.78 - 5.97 winning units..
Owner Kingsclere Racing CLub **Bred** Kingsclere Stud **Trained** Kingsclere, Hants

FOCUS
A competitive handicap despite the four non-runners.

NOTEBOOK
Side Glance ◆, who was taking on his elders for the first time, settled off the pace in a good tracking position. Jimmy Fortune played safe and came wide with his mount off the bend to claim the runner-up inside the final furlong. It's unlikely that this will be Side Glance's last win of the year considering how tidily he took this. (op 6-1 tchd 4-1 and 13-2 in places)
Tamaathul, absent since running at this course over 1m2f in the Dee Stakes back in May, represented a trainer with a good record in this contest and went close to enhancing it. He got to the front at what looked the right time but was swallowed up by a strong-finishing Side Glance. (op 6-1 tchd 13-2 in places)
Redford(IRE) ◆, who is steadily coming down the weights, was restrained in rear early but could be spotted going really well in behind. He was not able to get to the two in front of him but is showing signs of coming back to form. (op 12-1 tchd 14-1)
Kyllachy Star got behind and couldn't make progress until it was all too late. (tchd 9-1)
Lucky Numbers(IRE), who needed attention from the farrier before the off, does most of his racing over sprint trips and didn't seem to get home after racing prominently. (op 22-1)
Brae Hill(IRE) kept going at only the one pace after being prominent. (op 11-2 tchd 6-1)
Camerooney has enjoyed a terrific season but had been given a short break since landing his third successive victory in June. He came under pressure on the home bend, and may have needed this. (op 13-2)
Big Audio(IRE), down in trip after a disappointing effort at Goodwood, didn't really make much impression and was soundly beaten. (op 9-1 tchd 8-1)
Ezdeyaad(USA) started his winning spree off a 12lb lower mark in May, but gave the impression last time, when chasing a fourth successive victory over C&D at Haydock, that the handicapper had caught up with him. After appearing to race keenly along side the winner in the early stages, he dropped right out. (op 12-1)

5293 TOTEPOOL FLEXI BETTING E B F COMBERMERE FILLIES' CONDITIONS STKS 6f 18y
3:55 (4:00) (Class 2) 2-Y-O **£10,092** (£3,020; £1,510; £755; £376) **Stalls** Low

Form RPR

2211 **1** **Belle Royale (IRE)**[15] 4783 2-9-1 81 ... FrannyNorton 5 93
(W M Brisbourne) *trckd ldrs: wnt 2nd 3f out: rdn to ld over 1f out: kpt on wl towards fin* **9/4**[2]

16 **2** *1 ¼* **Admirable Spirit**[30] 4305 2-9-1 0 ... JimmyFortune 3 89
(R Hannon) *hld up: hdwy on outer 2f out: rdn to chse wnr over 1f out: edgd lft ins fnl f: nt qckn and hld towards fin* **2/1**[1]

1643 **3** *3* **Tipsy Girl**[30] 4278 2-8-12 80 ... ShaneKelly 2 77
(D J Coakley) *hld up: nt clr run 3f out: effrt to chse ldrs 2f out: outpcd fnl f* **9/1**[3]

1003 **4** *1 ½* **Turn The Tide**[16] 4748 2-9-1 80 ... AdrianNicholls 6 76
(A Bailey) *led over 5f out: rdn and hdd over 1f out: wknd ins fnl f* **14/1**

1011 **5** *9* **Fifth Commandment (IRE)**[12] 4903 2-9-3 88 ... SophieDoyle 1 51
(J A Osborne) *led: hdd over 5f out: chsd ldr to 3f out: rdn and wknd wl over 1f out* **9/4**[2]

1m 20.07s (6.27) **Going Correction** +0.95s/f (Soft) 5 Ran SP% **111.5**
Speed ratings (Par 97): **96,94,90,88,76**
CSF £7.28 TOTE £3.70: £1.50, £1.60; EX 7.30.
Owner Peter Mort **Bred** Dxb Ltd **Trained** Great Ness, Shropshire

FOCUS
A tight-looking conditions event, as only 8lb covered the four with an official handicap mark.

NOTEBOOK
Belle Royale(IRE), a C&D winner, has had plenty of racing but that doesn't stop her holding her form, and she completed a hat-trick with a gutsy display. There is possibly a nursery for her at Doncaster, but she is also worthy of taking her chance in the Group 3 Firth Of Clyde Stakes at the Ayr Gold Cup meeting. (op 11-4)
Admirable Spirit, not beaten far when sent off joint-favourite for the Listed Star Stakes last time, travelled strongly into contention but found that the vastly more experienced Belle Royale was in no mood to give up. (tchd 9-4)
Tipsy Girl had been looking in need of 7f previously and got outpaced at a crucial stage. (op 8-1 tchd 10-1)
Turn The Tide, whose trainer sent Aspen Darlin out to take this race in 2008, ruined her chance at Haydock by pulling too hard early, so seemingly was allowed to stride on in this. She led into the home straight but couldn't quicken again. (op 9-1 tchd 8-1)
Fifth Commandment(IRE) was chasing a hat-trick after victories at Newmarket and Windsor. Giving weight to all her rivals, she encountered a couple of bits of minor trouble in running while stuck in a pocket, and lost valuable ground at a time the tempo was increasing. The jockey reported afterwards that her mount didn't like the ground. Official explanation: jockey said filly was unsuited by the ground (op 5-2 tchd 11-4)

5294 TOTESWINGER FLEXI BETTING E B F MAIDEN STKS 7f 2y
4:30 (4:32) (Class 4) 2-Y-O **£5,180** (£1,541; £770; £384) **Stalls** Low

Form RPR

1 **Cosmic Moon** 2-8-12 0 ... JackMitchell 8 72+
(R A Fahey) *dwlt: hld up: hdwy over 3f out: wnt 2nd 1f out: styd on to ld wl ins fnl f: on top at fin* **16/1**

5U32 **2** *½* **So Is She (IRE)**[7] 5089 2-8-12 72 ...(v[1]) MarcHalford 7 71
(A Bailey) *midfield: hdwy 1f out: tried to chal 3 wd over 2f out: rdn and nt qckn over 1f out: edgd lft ent fnl f: styd on u.p to take cl 2nd towards fin* **8/1**[3]

4 **3** *¾* **Night Carnation**[17] 4695 2-8-12 0 ... JimmyFortune 3 69+
(A M Balding) *led and travelled wl: looked in control over 1f out: rdn and hdd wl ins fnl f: no ex cl home* **10/3**[2]

5 **4** *6* **Hawdyerwheesht**[8] 5040 2-9-3 0 ... JoeFanning 10 59
(M Johnston) *prom: rdn over 2f out: wknd and lost tch w ldrs over 1f out* **8/1**[3]

0 **5** *½* **Barwick**[15] 4803 2-9-3 0 ... PatCosgrave 11 58
(M H Tompkins) *upset in stalls: late removal of blindfold and missed break: towards rr: kpt on fr over 1f out: nvr on terms w ldrs* **22/1**

03 **6** *9* **Power Punch (IRE)**[20] 4614 2-9-3 0 ... MichaelHills 12 35
(B W Hills) *trckd ldrs: rdn 2f out: wknd wl over 1f out: eased whn wl btn fnl f* **2/1**[1]

04 **7** *6* **Yachtmaster (IRE)**[15] 4782 2-9-3 0 ... DarryllHolland 2 20
(J J Quinn) *trckd ldrs: pushed along and lost pl 3f out: n.d after* **17/2**

5 **8** *2* **Safe Haven (IRE)**[107] 1835 2-8-12 0 ... FrannyNorton 5 10
(A Bailey) *racd keenly: prom: pushed along 3f out: wknd over 2f out* **11/1**

60 **9** *1* **Brandy Alexander**[8] 5032 2-9-3 0 ... TedDurcan 4 13
(R Hannon) *sn pushed along in midfield: wknd over 2f out* **9/1**

10 *49* **Lady Goodricke** 2-8-12 0 ... PaulQuinn 6 —
(W M Brisbourne) *missed break: a bhd: tail flashed whn niggled along over 4f out: t.o fnl 3f* **33/1**

1m 33.5s (7.00) **Going Correction** +0.95s/f (Soft) 10 Ran SP% **120.7**
Speed ratings (Par 96): **98,97,96,89,89 78,72,69,68,12**
toteswingers:1&2:£8.00, 1&3:£5.30, 2&3:£4.50 CSF £142.53 TOTE £12.60: £4.30, £3.20, £1.02; EX 103.40.
Owner The Cosmic Cases **Bred** The Cosmic Cases **Trained** Musley Bank, N Yorks
■ Stewards' Enquiry : Michael Hills two-day ban: careless riding (Sep 5-6)

FOCUS
Not many of these could be seriously fancied on what they had shown on a racecourse, and two dominated the market, but it wasn't a massive surprise to see a newcomer prove good enough. The pace did not seem that quick in the early stages.

NOTEBOOK
Cosmic Moon, a Doyen half-sister to Royal Ascot winner Cosmic Sun, who finished second in this maiden back in 2008, quickened in the manner of a useful sort and got her career off to the best possible start. She enjoyed a good education during the contest, which will stand her in good stead for the future. (op 8-1)
So Is She(IRE), visored for the first time and officially rated 72, took a strong hold under her rider and was going a bit quicker than he would have liked rounding the bend. Edging towards the inside rail in the final stages, she stayed on well and almost got to the front. (op 15-2 tchd 7-1)
Night Carnation showed promise in a Polytrack maiden on her first outing but didn't quite get home here in this ground after possibly being a bit keen at the head of affairs. (op 4-1 tchd 3-1)
Hawdyerwheesht only showed mild promise on his debut and here again. (tchd 11-1)
Barwick ◆, well beaten when starting at 66-1 on his debut at Newmarket, got upset in the stalls and started slowly. He made encouraging late progress and is possibly one for middle-distance handicaps next year. Official explanation: jockey said colt had been difficult in stalls and he found it difficult to remove the blindfold (op 25-1 tchd 28-1)
Power Punch(IRE), third over C&D last time when looking the stable's second string, represented a trainer with a 6 wins and 1 place from 8 runners record in this maiden, which included this year's Britannia Handicap winner Ransom Note. Drawn wide, he ran a shocker after readily getting across. The jockey reported that his mount did not like the going. Official explanation: jockey said colt was unsuited by the ground (op 5-2 tchd 11-4 and 3-1 in places)
Lady Goodricke Official explanation: jockey said filly ran green

5295 TOTETRIFECTA FLEXI BETTING E B F CONDITIONS STKS 6f 18y
5:05 (5:05) (Class 2) 2-Y-O **£9,462** (£2,832; £1,416; £708) **Stalls** Low

Form RPR

3214 **1** **Fight The Chance (IRE)**[12] 4903 2-9-1 90 ... TedDurcan 1 92
(M R Channon) *hld up: impr to ld over 1f out: drvn out and r.o ins fnl f* **2/1**[1]

10 **2** *1 ¼* **Little Lion Man**[65] 3100 2-8-12 77 ... JackMitchell 3 85
(P W Chapple-Hyam) *trckd ldrs: effrt over 1f out: sn wnt 2nd: no imp on wnr ins fnl f* **4/1**

1304 **3** *3 ¾* **Jamesway (IRE)**[14] 4831 2-9-4 90 ... PatCosgrave 4 80
(R A Fahey) *led after 1f: hdd 2f out: one pce u.p fnl f* **3/1**[3]

221 **4** *1 ½* **Major Muscari (IRE)**[12] 4896 2-9-1 84 ... ShaneKelly 2 73
(A J McCabe) *led for 1f: racd in cl 2nd pl: regained ld 2f out: hdd over 1f out: wknd ins fnl f* **9/4**[2]

1m 20.77s (6.97) **Going Correction** +1.075s/f (Soft) 4 Ran SP% **109.1**
Speed ratings (Par 100): **96,94,89,87**
CSF £9.75 TOTE £2.40; EX 8.50.
Owner Jaber Abdullah **Bred** J Cullinan **Trained** West Ilsley, Berks

FOCUS
Tactics were always likely to play a part in this small-field contest, and all of them looked tired passing the post.

NOTEBOOK
Fight The Chance(IRE), who looked the biggest of these, settled in behind and needed pushing along to get back on the bridle turning in. His jockey threaded his way through rivals to hit the front over 1f out, and the pair did just enough to hold on. (tchd 15-8)
Little Lion Man, absent since finishing last of 12 in the Norfolk Stakes are Royal Ascot, had 13lb to find with the best of these on official figures, so ran respectably. One would imagine nurseries will be next. (op 9-2 tchd 5-1)
Jamesway(IRE), trying 6f for the first time, showed good speed, possibly travelling a bit keen, and didn't seem to get home in this ground. He might be one for a switch to Polytrack at the minimum distance. (op 11-4)
Major Muscari(IRE), up 1f in trip after getting off the mark at Thirsk, was soon passed here by the third for the lead and didn't seem to enjoy conditions. (op 5-2)

5296 BET TOTEPOOL AT TOTESPORT.COM H'CAP 1m 7f 195y
5:40 (5:41) (Class 4) (0-85,84) 3-Y-O+ **£5,180** (£1,541; £770; £384) **Stalls** Low

Form RPR

6042 **1** **Rangefinder**[20] 4619 6-10-0 **84** ... ShaneKelly 1 96
(Jane Chapple-Hyam) *trckd ldrs: wnt 2nd over 3f out: led 2f out: rdn and edgd rt 1f out: styd on wl to draw clr ins fnl f* **4/1**[2]

0022 **2** *7* **Omokoroa (IRE)**[14] 4846 4-9-10 **80** ... PatCosgrave 2 84
(M H Tompkins) *hld up: hdwy over 3f out: rdn to take 2nd over 1f out: no imp on wnr ins fnl f* **5/2**[1]

2042 **3** *2 ¾* **Royal Trooper (IRE)**[15] 4785 4-9-0 **75** ... DaleSwift(5) 6 75
(J G Given) *prom: led 5f out: rdn and hdd 2f out: wknd fnl f* **4/1**[2]

2301 **4** *¾* **Calculating (IRE)**[18] 4686 6-8-12 **68** oh1 ... FrannyNorton 5 67
(M D I Usher) *hld up: u.p over 2f out: styd on ins fnl f: no imp on ldrs* **11/1**

1054 **5** *½* **Veloso (FR)**[12] 4891 8-9-8 **81** ... KellyHarrison(3) 7 80
(J A Glover) *in tch: pushed along and lost pl over 4f out: tried to stay on for press 1f out: no imp* **16/1**

-633 **6** *1 ¾* **Puy D'Arnac (FR)**[15] 4785 7-9-1 **71** ... JimmyFortune 3 68
(G A Swinbank) *in rr: struggling 2f out: tried to stay on for press 1f out: no imp: eased whn wl btn wl ins fnl f* **11/2**[3]

The Form Book, Raceform Ltd, Compton, RG20 6NL

2321 **7** *hd* **Never Can Tell (IRE)**[15] 4792 3-8-5 **80**........................ SophieDoyle(5) 4 76
(J A Osborne) *led: hdd 5f out: chsd ldr to over 3f out: wknd 2f out: edgd rt whn btn 1f out* **11/2**[3]

3m 43.11s (15.11) **Going Correction** +1.075s/f (Soft)
WFA 3 from 4yo+ 14lb **7** Ran SP% **113.6**
Speed ratings (Par 105): **105,101,100,99,99 98,98**
toteswingers:1&2:£3.20, 1&3:£3.10, 2&3:£3.50 CSF £14.23 TOTE £5.30: £2.30, £2.50; EX 13.00 Place 6 £57.52; Place 5 £21.70.
Owner Dr Marwan Koukash **Bred** Aston House Stud **Trained** Dalham, Suffolk

FOCUS
A decent staying handicap.

5297 TOTEPOOL H'CAP (DIV II) 6f 18y
6:10 (6:12) (Class 4) (0-85,84) 3-Y-0+ **£5,180** (£1,541; £770; £384) **Stalls** Low

Form RPR
3030 **1** **Fathsta (IRE)**[14] 4832 5-9-12 **84**........................ JimmyFortune 8 96
(D M Simcock) *hld up in midfield: hmpd over 4f out: hdwy 2f out: r.o to ld wl ins fnl f: won gng away* **6/1**[2]
3600 **2** *2 1/2* **Coleorton Choice**[5] 5154 4-9-5 **77**........................(p) ShaneKelly 14 81
(R Hollinshead) *chsd ldrs: effrt on outer to ld 2f out: hdd u.p wl over 1f out: edgd rt and continued to chal ins fnl f: nt pce of wnr fnl 75yds* **28/1**
6205 **3** *3/4* **Green Park (IRE)**[5] 5154 7-8-12 **77**........................(b) NeilFarley(7) 12 79
(D Carroll) *midfield: hdwy over 3f out: rdn to ld wl over 1f out: hdd wl ins fnl f: no ex towards fin* **11/1**
2300 **4** *6* **Mullglen**[10] 4952 4-8-11 **72**........................(tp) KellyHarrison(3) 6 54
(T D Easterby) *hld up: rdn over 1f out: prog to take 3rd wl ins fnl f: unable to trble front trio* **20/1**
1106 **5** *1* **Ryan Style (IRE)**[7] 5069 4-9-8 **80**........................ JoeFanning 4 59
(Mrs L Williamson) *midfield: rdn over 1f out: kpt on u.p: nt pce to chal* **8/1**
0004 **6** *3/4* **Green Manalishi**[10] 4942 9-9-10 **82**........................(tp) DarryllHolland 7 59
(K A Ryan) *prom: rdn over 1f out: nt pce to get on terms w ldrs: wl btn ins fnl f* **11/2**[1]
0130 **7** *1/2* **Last Sovereign**[8] 5043 6-9-5 **82**........................ JamesO'Reilly(5) 1 57
(J O'Reilly) *pushed along towards rr: nvr able to get on terms* **11/2**[1]
0060 **8** *3 3/4* **Rievaulx World**[3] 5198 4-9-6 **78**........................(p) AdrianNicholls 3 41
(K A Ryan) *led: rdn and hdd 2f out: wknd over 1f out* **14/1**
4-00 **9** *shd* **Rahya Cass (IRE)**[32] 4231 3-9-2 **82**........................(t) TobyAtkinson(5) 9 45
(J R Gask) *chsd ldr tl over 2f out: sn n.m.r and hmpd: wknd over 1f out* **28/1**
310- **10** *9* **Mister Laurel**[383] 4598 4-9-10 **82**........................ JackMitchell 2 16
(R A Fahey) *prom: pushed along 4f out: sn lost pl: struggling and n.d after* **7/1**
2010 **11** *20* **Rio Cobolo (IRE)**[3] 5198 4-9-3 **75**........................(v) DaraghO'Donohoe 5 —
(Paul Green) *bmpd sn after s: a bhd: eased whn n.d fnl 2f* **13/2**[3]

1m 19.96s (6.16) **Going Correction** +1.075s/f (Soft)
WFA 3 from 4yo+ 3lb **11** Ran SP% **108.7**
Speed ratings (Par 105): **101,97,96,88,87 86,85,80,80,68 41**
toteswingers:1&2:£29.40, 1&3:£8.70, 2&3:£75.70 CSF £138.17 CT £929.14 TOTE £5.60: £1.80, £9.30, £3.30; EX 175.80.
Owner Dr Marwan Koukash **Bred** Brian Miller **Trained** Newmarket, Suffolk
■ Legal Eagle was withdrawn (9/1, burst out of stalls.) Deduct 10p in the £ under R4.
■ Stewards' Enquiry : Shane Kelly two-day ban: careless riding (Sep 5-6)

FOCUS
The second division of this sprint was slightly delayed when Legal Eagle burst through the stalls. He was withdrawn as a result. The winning time was slower than the opener, probably because the ground appeared to get steadily slower during the eight-race card.
T/Jkpt: Not won. T/Plt: £80.30 to a £1 stake. Pool:£112,453.19 - 1,021.36 winning tickets T/Qpdt: £15.60 to a £1 stake. Pool:£4,738.29 - 224.44 winning tickets DO

5092 RIPON (R-H)
Saturday, August 21

OFFICIAL GOING: Good (good to firm in places; 8.6)
Rails at inner configuration and distances as advertised.
Wind: Virtually nil Weather: Bright and dry

5298 AT THE RACES SKY 415 MAIDEN STKS 6f
2:00 (2:02) (Class 5) 2-Y-0 **£3,238** (£963; £481; £240) **Stalls** Low

Form RPR
5522 **1** **No Poppy (IRE)**[7] 5099 2-8-12 74........................(b) DuranFentiman 3 72
(T D Easterby) *overall ldr stands' side: rdn clr over 1f out: drvn ins fnl f: hld on wl* **4/1**[1]
02 **2** *1* **Moral Issue**[10] 4941 2-9-3 0........................ PaulMulrennan 15 74
(Jedd O'Keeffe) *led far side gp: rdn along 2f out and ev ch: drvn ins fnl f: kpt on: 1st of 9 in gp* **4/1**[1]
3 *1 3/4* **New Springs** 2-8-12 0........................ PaulHanagan 16 64
(R A Fahey) *prom far side: hdwy to chse ldr of that gp 2f out: rdn over 1f out: kpt on: 2nd of 9 in gp* **6/1**[2]
4 *2 3/4* **Jade** 2-8-12 0........................ PhillipMakin 9 56
(Ollie Pears) *in tch far side: hdwy 2f out: swtchd lft over 1f out: kpt on ins fnl f: nrst fin: 3rd of 9 in gp* **13/2**[3]
03 **5** *1/2* **Mossgorda (IRE)**[71] 2939 2-8-12 0........................ MichaelO'Connell(5) 2 59
(Mrs K Burke) *trckd ldrs stands' side: effrt 2f out: sn rdn and one pce: 2nd of 7 in gp* **16/1**
050 **6** *3/4* **Grazeon Again (IRE)**[25] 4447 2-8-12 70........................ IanBrennan(5) 11 57
(J J Quinn) *hld up far side: hdwy 2f out: rdn over 1f out: kpt on ins fnl f: 4th of 9 in gp* **16/1**
3 **7** *1 3/4* **City Legend**[26] 4421 2-9-3 0........................(v) NeilCallan 1 52
(A J McCabe) *chsd ldrs stands' side: rdn along 2f out: wknd over 1f out: 3rd of 7 in gp* **6/1**[2]
0 **8** *2* **Breezolini**[12] 4896 2-8-9 0........................ MichaelStainton(3) 13 41
(R M Whitaker) *in tch far side: effrt over 2f out: rdn whn hmpd over 1f out: sn one pce: 5th of 9 in gp* **28/1**
03 **9** *3* **Je Suis Unrockstar**[12] 4890 2-9-3 0........................ DavidAllan 14 37
(J A Glover) *cl up far side: rdn along wl over 2f out: sn wknd: 6th of 9 in gp* **12/1**
10 *hd* **Ballinargh Boy** 2-9-3 0........................ AndrewElliott 5 36
(R D Wylie) *chsd wnr stands' side: effrt 2f out: sn rdn and one pce appr fnl f: 4th of 7 in gp* **22/1**
6050 **11** *nk* **West Stand**[40] 3945 2-8-9 70........................ JamesSullivan(3) 12 32
(Mrs K Walton) *chsd ldrs far side: rdn along over 2f out: grad wknd: 7th of 9 in gp* **40/1**
12 *2* **Barnet Fair** 2-9-3 0........................ PaulEddery 8 29
(R C Guest) *a in rr stands' side: outpcd and bhd fr 1/2-way: 5th of 7 in gp* **100/1**
0 **13** *4* **False Promises**[12] 4890 2-9-3 0........................ PatrickMathers 17 17
(D Shaw) *chsd ldrs far side: rdn along 1/2-way: sn wknd: 8th of 9 in gp* **80/1**
60 **14** *nse* **Dreamweaving (IRE)**[100] 2059 2-8-9 0........ Louis-PhilippeBeuzelin(3) 4 12
(N Tinkler) *in tch stands' side: rdn along wl over 2f out and sn wknd: 6th of 7 in gp* **28/1**
00 **15** *7* **Tigerino (IRE)**[15] 4782 2-9-3 0........................ DanielTudhope 10 —
(C W Thornton) *a in rr far side: 9th of 9 in gp* **100/1**
16 *22* **Vanessa My Girl** 2-8-10 0 ow3........................ MarkCoumbe(5) 7 —
(R C Guest) *a outpcd and bhd stands' side: last of 7 in gp* **100/1**

1m 13.43s (0.43) **Going Correction** -0.10s/f (Good) **16** Ran SP% **119.3**
Speed ratings (Par 94): **93,91,89,85,85 84,81,79,75,74 74,71,66,66,56 27**
toteswingers: 1&2 £3.10, 1&3 £4.60, 2&3 £4.80. CSF £17.15 TOTE £3.80: £1.40, £1.90, £2.80; EX 20.60 Trifecta £47.10 Pool: £252.86 - 3.97 winning units..
Owner Mrs M H Easterby **Bred** Michael O'Mahony **Trained** Great Habton, N Yorks

FOCUS
A dry day left the official going unchanged, and the ground was described as "lovely" by a couple of jockeys in the first. Despite the good-sized field this was a pretty moderate maiden, particularly for a Racing Post Yearling Bonus race. They split into two groups from the start, nine racing on the far side and the other seven, who came from a separate block of stalls, coming down the stands' rail. Neither flank seemed especially favoured.

NOTEBOOK
No Poppy(IRE) made all the running on the near flank, but only late on was it apparent that she was the overall leader. She set a fair standard with a BHA rating of 74 and had been placed four times previously, so was not winning this out of turn. Nurseries look the way forward for her and she doesn't mind easier ground than this. (op 7-2)
Moral Issue was always in front on the opposite side of the track to the winner and this Beverley runner-up lost little in defeat. He could have done with a bit of company and saw out the sixth furlong well enough. (op 5-1)
New Springs is a sprint-bred filly out of a winning half-sister to smart sprinter Ringmoor Down. Normal improvement from this should see her land a maiden for her leading yard.
Jade, whose dam, a half-sister to smart sprinter Ashdown Express, has already produced a 1m2f winner, was well supported. She showed signs of inexperience, but was running on nicely late in the day and will be better for the experience. (op 6-1)
Mossgorda(IRE) travelled strongly in the slipstream of the winner for some way and finished clear second best on his side. Third in a valuable York seller on his final outing for John Weymes, he looks the type for nurseries.
Grazeon Again(IRE) came home in nice style and looks the type to improve when allowed to tackle further again in handicap company. (tchd 20-1)
City Legend probably gave his running, but he was under pressure by halfway and may not be straightforward. (op 13-2 tchd 7-1)
Je Suis Unrockstar showed pace in the larger far-side bunch and is now eligible for nurseries. (op 16-1)
Dreamweaving(IRE) Official explanation: jockey said filly was never travelling and was unsuited by the undulations

5299 M J SHARMAN CELEBRATION APPRENTICE (S) STKS 6f
2:30 (2:32) (Class 6) 3-4-Y-O **£2,590** (£770; £385; £192) **Stalls** Low

Form RPR
0334 **1** **Apache Ridge (IRE)**[13] 4857 4-9-12 72........................(p) AmyRyan 14 64
(K A Ryan) *chsd ldrs far side: swtchd lft and hdwy 2f out: rdn to ld jst ins fnl f: drvn out* **9/4**[1]
4040 **2** *1* **Sharp Shoes**[23] 4516 3-8-13 51........................(p) RosieJessop(5) 12 56
(Mrs A Duffield) *prom far side: hdwy to ld over 2f out and sn rdn: drvn over 1f out: hdd jst ins fnl f: kpt on: 2nd of 6 in gp* **40/1**
3326 **3** *2* **Minturno (USA)**[18] 4670 4-9-4 63........................ IanBrennan(3) 2 50
(Mrs A Duffield) *chsd ldrs stands' side: hdwy 2f out: sn rdn and styd on fnl f: nrst fin: 1st of 6 in gp* **4/1**[2]
1005 **4** *shd* **Collect Art (IRE)**[24] 4475 3-9-6 65........................(v) AmyBaker(3) 15 54
(A B Haynes) *prom far side: rdn along over 2f out: drvn over 1f out and sn one pce: 3rd of 6 in gp* **10/1**
0564 **5** *1 1/2* **Klynch**[18] 4670 4-9-7 63........................(b) JamesSullivan 10 44
(Mrs R A Carr) *chsd ldrs far side: hdwy 2f out: sn rdn and no imp fnl f: 4th of 6 in gp* **13/2**[3]
1104 **6** *1 1/2* **Thaliwarru**[78] 2722 3-9-9 67........................ AndreaAtzeni 7 45
(J R Gask) *in tch stands' side: hdwy over 2f out: sn rdn and no imp: 2nd of 6 in gp* **13/2**[3]
155 **7** *3/4* **Tamarind Hill (IRE)**[8] 5023 3-9-6 62........................(b) TobyAtkinson(3) 3 42
(A J McCabe) *overall ldr stands' side: rdn and hung bdly rt over 2f out: sn hdd and drvn: wknd over 1f out: 3rd of 6 in gp* **16/1**
3406 **8** *3 3/4* **Fasliyanne (IRE)**[10] 4947 4-8-11 52........................(v) JulieBurke(5) 9 20
(K A Ryan) *prom stands' side: pushed along whn sltly hmpd over 2f out: sn rdn and grad wknd: 4th of 6 in gp* **12/1**
2000 **9** *1/2* **Saucy Girl (IRE)**[10] 4939 3-8-10 50........................(b[1]) LanceBetts(3) 5 19
(T D Easterby) *a in rr stands' side: 5th of 6 in gp* **20/1**
0036 **10** *1* **Lieu Day Louie (IRE)**[8] 5046 3-9-1 45........................(b[1]) DeanHeslop(3) 11 20
(N Wilson) *a towards rr far side: 5th of 6 in gp* **40/1**
0000 **11** *9* **Account Closed**[12] 4893 3-8-6 35........................(b) DavidSimmonson(7) 8 —
(M W Easterby) *a in rr stands' side: last of 6 in gp* **100/1**
0250 **12** *1 3/4* **Frontline Boy (IRE)**[5] 5162 3-9-1 62........................(v[1]) MichaelO'Connell(3) 13 —
(Mrs K Burke) *led far side gp: rdn along 1/2-way: sn hdd & wknd: last of 6 in gp* **14/1**

1m 12.5s (-0.50) **Going Correction** -0.10s/f (Good)
WFA 3 from 4yo 3lb **12** Ran SP% **117.4**
Speed ratings (Par 101): **99,97,95,94,92 90,89,84,84,82 70,68**
toteswingers: 1&2 £8.70, 1&3 £2.10, 2&3 £40.50. CSF £117.64 TOTE £3.00: £1.40, £7.50, £1.90; EX 156.10 TRIFECTA Not won..There was no bid for the winner.
Owner Aidan Heeney **Bred** Allevamento Ficomontanino Srl **Trained** Hambleton, N Yorks
■ Stewards' Enquiry : Amy Baker one-day ban: failed to ride to draw (Sep 5)

FOCUS
A very modest apprentice seller. It produced an even split and the far-side group emerged on top, although the winner finished up down the centre.
Saucy Girl(IRE) Official explanation: jockey said filly reared in the stalls

5300 AT THE RACES VIRGIN 534 H'CAP 1m 1f 170y
3:05 (3:06) (Class 4) (0-80,81) 3-Y-O **£5,046** (£1,510; £755; £377; £188) **Stalls** High

Form RPR
0-24 **1** **The Caped Crusader (IRE)**[37] 4052 3-8-3 **67**........................ IanBrennan(5) 6 78
(Ollie Pears) *trckd ldrs on inner: hdwy over 2f out: rdn over 1f out: styd on ent fnl f: squeezed through and kpt on to ld last 40yds* **6/1**[3]
621 **2** *nk* **Lord Raglan (IRE)**[20] 4618 3-9-2 **75**........................ AndrewElliott 10 85
(Mrs K Burke) *led: rdn along and hdd 2f out: drvn over 1f out: rallied to ld again ins fnl f: hdd and no ex last 40yds* **11/2**[2]
2031 **3** *1/2* **Hail Bold Chief (USA)**[13] 4867 3-8-9 **68**........................ JimmyQuinn 8 77
(G A Swinbank) *cl up: rdn along 2f out: drvn to chal ent fnl f and ev ch tl no ex last 50yds* **11/2**[2]

4602 **4** *1 1/4* **Finest Reserve (IRE)**[7] 5083 3-9-8 **81**..............................(v) NeilCallan 9 88
(M R Channon) *trckd ldrs on inner: hdwy 3f out: led 2f out and sn rdn: drvn and hdd ins fnl f: wknd towards fin* **5/2**[1]

6066 **5** *4* **Muwalla**[49] 3697 3-8-12 **71**.. PhillipMakin 7 70
(J D Bethell) *hld up in rr: hdwy on inner wl over 2f out: rdn along wl over 1f out: kpt on fnl f: nt rch ldrs* **14/1**

5452 **6** *1 3/4* **Mason Hindmarsh**[15] 4796 3-8-0 **62**......................... JamesSullivan[(3)] 3 57
(Karen McLintock) *in tch: rdn along wl over 2f out: sn one pce* **8/1**

4340 **7** *3/4* **Beneath**[54] 3519 3-9-3 **76**.. StephenCraine 2 70
(K A Ryan) *a in rr* **14/1**

2-50 **8** *1* **Flipping**[17] 4698 3-8-7 **66**.. TadhgO'Shea 5 58
(W S Kittow) *chsd ldrs: rdn along 3f out: drvn over 2f out and sn wknd* **14/1**

0160 **9** *25* **City Vaults Girl (IRE)**[21] 4573 3-8-13 **72**........................ PaulHanagan 1 14
(R A Fahey) *hld up: sme hdwy on outer 4f out: rdn along over 3f out and sn wknd* **12/1**

2m 3.12s (-2.28) **Going Correction** -0.175s/f (Firm) **9** Ran SP% **112.4**
Speed ratings (Par 102): **102,101,101,100,97 95,95,94,74**
toteswingers: 1&2 £6.90, 1&3 £5.00, 2&3 £2.10. CSF £37.62 CT £189.92 TOTE £7.40: £2.90, £2.80, £2.70; EX 37.90 Trifecta £138.20 Pool: £209.20 - 1.12 winning units..
Owner David Silversides **Bred** Ballylinch Stud **Trained** Norton, N Yorks

FOCUS
An interesting and open 3yo handicap. Not many got into it and the first four came clear to contest a fine finish. The form amongst the principals seems sound.
Finest Reserve(IRE) Official explanation: jockey said colt hung badly left in final 2f

5301 DBS ST LEGER YEARLING STKS 6f
3:40 (3:43) (Class 2) 2-Y-O

£24,620 (£9,850; £4,925; £2,460; £1,230; £1,230) **Stalls** Low

Form RPR

1 **1** **Murbeh (IRE)**[20] 4622 2-8-11 0... TadhgO'Shea 8 91+
(B J Meehan) *trckd ldrs stands' side: smooth hdwy 1/2-way: led 2f out: qcknd clr over 1f out: comf* **11/4**[1]

4 **2** *2 3/4* **Gentle Lord**[20] 4622 2-8-11 0.................................... RichardKingscote 5 80
(Tom Dascombe) *overall ldr stands' side: rdn along 2f out: sn hdd: drvn and edgd rt ins fnl f: kpt on: 2nd of 7 in gp* **7/1**[3]

15 **3** *nk* **Berberana (IRE)**[11] 4934 2-8-6 78..................................... DavidAllan 20 74
(T D Easterby) *prom far side: hdwy to ld that gp 2f out and sn rdn: drvn over 1f out: kpt on same pce: 1st of 9 in gp* **6/1**[2]

6343 **4** *nk* **Mother Jones**[20] 4615 2-8-6 69.................................. MichaelStainton 1 73
(D H Brown) *hld up towards rr stands' side: swtchd rt and hdwy over 2f out: rdn over 1f out: styd on ins fnl f: nrst fin: 3rd of 7 in gp* **33/1**

321 **5** *nk* **Cathedral Spires**[29] 4336 2-8-11 79.......................... PaulMulrennan 14 77
(J Howard Johnson) *prom far side: rdn to chal 2f out: drvn over 1f out: kpt on same pce: 2nd of 9 in gp* **14/1**

21 **6** *3/4* **Riverdale (IRE)**[10] 4941 2-8-11 77.................................. PhillipMakin 18 75
(Mrs A Duffield) *chsd ldrs far side: hdwy over 2f out: rdn wl over 1f out: kpt on same pce fnl f: 3rd of 9 in gp* **11/4**[1]

0150 **7** *hd* **Believe It Or Not (IRE)**[36] 4111 2-8-11 70.................... JimmyQuinn 13 74
(J S Moore) *towards rr far side: hdwy over 2f out: rdn over 1f out: kpt on ins fnl f: 4th of 9 in gp* **50/1**

0155 **8** *1/2* **Lizzie (IRE)**[14] 4851 2-8-6 66.......................................(p) AndrewElliott 3 68
(T D Easterby) *chsd ldrs stands' side: rdn along 2f out: drvn and kpt on same pce fr over 1f out: 4th of 7 in gp* **25/1**

20 **9** *3 1/4* **El Viento (FR)**[36] 4116 2-8-11 0..................................... PaulHanagan 17 63
(R A Fahey) *towards rr far side: effrt and sme hdwy 2f out: n.d: 5th of 9 in gp* **20/1**

5022 **10** *1* **West Leake Bridge (IRE)**[15] 4782 2-8-11 75................. PaulEddery 16 60
(B W Hills) *led far side gp: rdn along over 2f out: sn drvn and hdd: wknd wl over 1f out: 6th of 9 in gp* **22/1**

4213 **11** *3 1/4* **Royal Opera**[20] 4623 2-8-11 76...................................... HayleyTurner 15 50
(B R Millman) *chsd ldrs far side: rdn along over 2f out: sn drvn and wknd: 7th of 9 in gp* **9/1**

0304 **12** *1 1/2* **May Be Some Time**[29] 4323 2-8-11 70................................ NeilCallan 6 46
(W S Kittow) *a towards rr stands' side: 5th of 7 in gp* **80/1**

04 **13** *1/2* **Climaxfortackle (IRE)**[16] 4748 2-8-6 0......................... PatrickMathers 4 39
(D Shaw) *dwlt: a in rr stands' side: 6th of 7 in gp* **100/1**

2262 **14** *1 1/4* **Sea Flower (IRE)**[47] 3729 2-8-6 70............................... DuranFentiman 7 36
(T D Easterby) *cl up stands' side: rdn along wl over 2f out: sn wknd: last of 7 in gp* **28/1**

54 **15** *3/4* **Close To The Edge (IRE)**[49] 3658 2-8-6 0................. AndrewMullen 11 33
(A J McCabe) *dwlt and a towards rr far side: 8th of 9 in gp* **40/1**

030 **16** *7* **Alexs Rainbow (USA)**[93] 2251 2-8-6 67............................ AmyRyan 9 12
(J Gallagher) *a towards rr far side: rdn along and bhd fr 1/2-way: last of 9 in gp* **80/1**

1m 12.17s (-0.83) **Going Correction** -0.10s/f (Good) **16** Ran SP% **124.0**
Speed ratings (Par 100): **101,97,96,96,96 95,94,94,89,88 84,82,81,79,78 69**
toteswingers: 1&2 £6.10, 1&3 £5.00, 2&3 £20.20. CSF £20.94 TOTE £4.00: £1.90, £2.80, £3.00; EX 18.10 Trifecta £103.80 Pool: £412.39 - 2.94 winning units..
Owner Hamdan Al Maktoum **Bred** Ann & Joe Hallinan **Trained** Manton, Wilts

FOCUS
A consolation race for horses who missed the cut in Thursday's big sales race at York, won by Wootton Bassett. The field split into two groups and this time the first two home both came from the seven drawn lowest, who raced on the stands' side. The form looks sound and the winner would appear to be very useful.

NOTEBOOK
Murbeh(IRE)'s Newbury debut win received a hefty boost when runner-up Moriarty won a York maiden on Friday, and he represented a yard successful in this race 12 months ago with Hold Your Colour. Ponied to the start around 15 minutes early, the gelding was always travelling well and proved much too good for some decent opposition, quickening clear before the final furlong. He will be sent in search of some black type now. (op 2-1)
Gentle Lord had been fourth to Murbeh on his debut at Newbury and although beaten a little further here he ran another nice race, running on to good purpose through the final furlong. He should not be long in getting off the mark. (op 13-2 tchd 15-2)
Berberana(IRE), the pick on official pre-race figures, was drawn highest and came through to lead her group late on. She is held in some regard, as a Cheveley Park Stakes entry would suggest, and this run confirms her effectiveness on turf. (op 10-1)
Mother Jones, still a maiden, ran well on this better ground and might be ready for an extra furlong now. (op 20-1)
Cathedral Spires, another taken to the start early, ran a reasonable race without entirely convincing that the return to 6f was what he wanted. (tchd 12-1)
Riverdale(IRE)'s Beverley maiden win was at the chief expense of Moral Issue, who was runner-up in the first race on this card. He looked in fine shape in the paddock and ran creditably on a track which might not have entirely suited him. (op 11-2)
Believe It Or Not(IRE) kept on without quite getting to the leaders and appeared to get the 6f well enough this time. Official explanation: jockey said colt suffered interference at the start (op 66-1)
Lizzie(IRE) seems to be exposed as modest but was putting in some fair late work.

Close To The Edge(IRE) Official explanation: jockey said filly suffered interference at the start

5302 RIPON CATHEDRAL CITY OF DALES H'CAP 6f
4:10 (4:17) (Class 2) (0-100,98) 4-Y-0+

£9,969 (£2,985; £1,492; £747; £372; £187) **Stalls** Low

Form RPR

0402 **1** **Tajneed (IRE)**[7] 5095 7-9-1 **97**............................... MichaelO'Connell[(5)] 3 111
(D Nicholls) *overall ldr stands' side: mde all: rdn and qcknd clr over 1f out: kpt on strly* **4/1**[1]

5130 **2** *2 1/2* **Parisian Pyramid (IRE)**[21] 4576 4-9-7 **98**..................... StephenCraine 8 104
(K A Ryan) *trckd ldrs stands' side: hdwy to chse wnr 2f out: rdn and edgd rt over 1f out: kpt on same pce ins fnl f: 2nd of 8 in gp* **12/1**

2111 **3** *hd* **Piazza San Pietro**[15] 4777 4-8-9 **86** ow1........................... NeilCallan 14 91
(A B Haynes) *chsd ldrs far side: hdwy over 2f out: rdn wl over 1f out: drifted lft ent fnl f: styd on: 1st of 7 in gp* **14/1**

1222 **4** *shd* **Misplaced Fortune**[27] 4413 5-8-9 **89**.......... Louis-PhilippeBeuzelin[(3)] 11 94
(N Tinkler) *prom far side: hdwy 1/2-way: rdn to chal 2f out: drvn and edgd lft ent fnl f: kpt on same pce: 2nd of 7 in gp* **16/1**

0010 **5** *3/4* **Medicean Man**[63] 3193 4-9-5 **96**....................................(p) JimmyQuinn 1 98+
(J R Gask) *in rr stands' side: swtchd rt and hdwy 2f out: rdn over 1f out: styd on fnl f: n.m.r towards fin: 3rd of 8 in gp* **11/2**[2]

6242 **6** *1* **Discanti (IRE)**[10] 4942 5-8-9 **86**.......................................(t) DavidAllan 5 85
(T D Easterby) *chsd ldrs stands' side: rdn along over 2f out: drvn and one pce fr over 1f out: 4th of 8 in gp* **9/1**

60-2 **7** *1/2* **Sioux Rising (IRE)**[19] 4653 4-8-7 **84**............................ PaulHanagan 13 81
(R A Fahey) *prom far side: effrt to chal over 2f out: sn rdn and wknd over 1f out: 3rd of 7 in gp* **6/1**[3]

4351 **8** *1 1/4* **Joseph Henry**[22] 4536 8-8-12 **89**................................ PhillipMakin 15 82
(D Nicholls) *led far side gp: rdn along over 2f out: drvn and edgd lft ent fnl f: wknd: 4th of 7 in gp* **16/1**

3412 **9** *nse* **Gap Princess (IRE)**[2] 5242 6-8-6 **86**.......................... PaulPickard[(3)] 16 79
(G A Harker) *in tch far side: hdwy to chse ldrs 1/2-way: sn rdn and one pce fnl 2f: 5th of 7 in gp* **6/1**[3]

5000 **10** *nk* **Sonny Red (IRE)**[21] 4576 6-9-1 **92**................................ AndrewMullen 6 84
(D Nicholls) *hld up in tch stands' side: effrt and sme hdwy over 2f out: sn rdn and btn: 5th of 8 in gp* **25/1**

0256 **11** *1 3/4* **Horatio Carter**[7] 5068 5-8-11 **88**..............................(p) PaulMulrennan 9 75
(K A Ryan) *chsd ldrs stands' side: rdn along over 2f out: sn drvn and one pce: 6th of 8 in gp* **33/1**

40-0 **12** *shd* **Mastership (IRE)**[19] 4653 6-8-3 **85**..........................(p) IanBrennan[(5)] 12 71
(J J Quinn) *racd far side: bhd fr 1/2-way: 6th of 7 in gp* **16/1**

3003 **13** *1/2* **Wildcat Wizard (USA)**[22] 4536 4-9-3 **94**........................ TadhgO'Shea 10 79
(P F I Cole) *in tch stands' side: rdn along over 2f out: sn btn: 7th of 8 in gp* **14/1**

0305 **14** *1 3/4* **Red Cape (FR)**[19] 4653 7-8-3 **83**............................... JamesSullivan[(3)] 2 62
(Mrs R A Carr) *prom stands' side: rdn along over 2f out: sn wknd: last of 8 in gp* **20/1**

4006 **15** *5* **Ishetoo**[10] 4942 6-8-4 **81**..(t) DuranFentiman 17 44
(Ollie Pears) *in tch far side: rdn along bef 1/2-way: drvn and wknd over 2f out: sn bhd: last of 7 in gp* **28/1**

1m 10.95s (-2.05) **Going Correction** -0.10s/f (Good) **15** Ran SP% **127.6**
Speed ratings (Par 109): **109,105,105,105,104 102,102,100,100,100 97,97,97,94,88**
toteswingers: 1&2 £13.60, 1&3 £8.60, 2&3 £23.00. CSF £53.71 CT £653.20 TOTE £4.20: £2.20, £5.40, £4.40; EX 73.50 TRIFECTA Not won..
Owner Alex Nicholls And Finola Devaney **Bred** R Hodgins **Trained** Sessay, N Yorks
■ Stewards' Enquiry : Phillip Makin four-day ban: careless riding (Sep 5-8)
Duran Fentiman one-day ban: failed to ride to draw (Sep 5)

FOCUS
The fourth running of this good sprint handicap. Once again they split into two similarly sized groups.

NOTEBOOK
Tajneed(IRE) just failed to land a gamble in the Great St Wilfrid over course and distance a week earlier, being picked off late by Damika, but he loves this venue and that is his only defeat in five visits now. Making pretty much all the running under the stands' fence here, the winner was never seriously in danger and won in fine style. Likely to head for the Ayr Gold Cup this autumn, he looks better than ever and deserves a crack at a Listed race at some point. (op 5-1 tchd 7-2 and 13-2 in a place early)
Parisian Pyramid(IRE)'s Stewards' Cup effort could be safely scrubbed out as he was badly drawn, and he returned to form despite racing from a career-high mark. He was not able to claim the lead with Tajneed in opposition, but chased him through for second. (op 16-1)
Piazza San Pietro drifted into the centre of the course late on but stuck his neck out willingly. Currently 20lb higher than when winning at Yarmouth in June, he has had a terrific season and has not finished out of the first three in any of his last 11 starts. (tchd 12-1)
Misplaced Fortune has edged up the weights to a career-high mark despite not winning and she ran another thoroughly creditable race, especially as she was carried to her left in the latter stages. She should continue to give a good account of herself. (tchd 20-1)
Medicean Man finished strongly once switched away from the stands' rail. It appears that he is still progressing and may be capable of picking up another handicap this year. (op 13-2 tchd 15-2)
Discanti(IRE), another on a career-high mark, ran a solid race back up in trip. (op 18-1 tchd 8-1)
Sioux Rising(IRE) had her chance and did manage to turn around course form with Gap Princess. (op 8-1)
Joseph Henry, up 5lb after Goodwood, led his group before edging into the centre of the track and fading. (op 14-1)
Gap Princess(IRE) never really made an impact on this quick reappearance. (tchd 13-2)
Sonny Red(IRE) ◆, who represented the same conections as the winner, has become well handicapped and he shaped as if he could be ready to strike before long. (op 18-1)

5303 TOTEPOOL FLEXI BETTING MAIDEN STKS 1m 1f 170y
4:45 (4:50) (Class 5) 3-Y-O+ **£3,238** (£963; £481; £240) **Stalls** High

Form RPR

20 **1** **Mainland (USA)**[64] 3176 4-9-11 0................................ PaulMulrennan 11 76
(K A Ryan) *in tch: hdwy on outer over 3f out: led 2f out: rdn and hung lft over 1f out: drvn and kpt on fnl f* **3/1**[3]

2 **2** *2 1/2* **Tarooq (USA)**[22] 4556 4-9-11 0....................................... PaulHanagan 2 71
(R A Fahey) *in tch: hdwy to trck ldrs over 4f out: effrt over 2f out: sn rdn and chsd wnr over 1f out: drvn and no imp ins fnl f* **11/4**[2]

3 *2 1/4* **Rio's Rosanna (IRE)** 3-8-9 0................................ MichaelStainton[(3)] 14 62
(R M Whitaker) *hld up: hdwy on inner 3f out: swtchd lft and rdn wl over 1f out: sn chsng ldrs: kpt on ins fnl f* **20/1**

3 **4** *2* **Waheed**[30] 4307 3-9-3 0... TadhgO'Shea 15 63
(M P Tregoning) *prom: cl up over 4f out: led 3f out: sn rdn and hdd 2f out: grad wknd* **9/4**[1]

00 **5** *hd* **Hedonist (IRE)**[23] 4521 3-9-3 0....................................... JimmyQuinn 18 62
(J R Gask) *led: rdn along and hdd 3f out: drvn 2f out and sn one pce* **28/1**

The Form Book, Raceform Ltd, Compton, RG20 6NL

00 **6** ½ **Red Storm Rising**[27] 4407 3-9-3 0 AndreaAtzeni 4 61
(K A Morgan) *hld up towards rr: hdwy over 2f out: rdn and kpt on fnl f: nt rch ldrs* **100/1**

64 **7** 4 **Wolf Rock**[27] 4414 3-9-3 0 PhillipMakin 16 53
(T D Barron) *t.k.h: trckd ldrs: effrt 3f out: rdn over 2f out and sn wknd* **20/1**

43 **8** 1 ½ **La Bacouetteuse (FR)**[27] 4407 5-9-11 0 LNewman 12 50
(A G Foster) *a towards rr* **12/1**

53 **9** 5 **Fantastic Storm**[19] 4655 3-9-3 0 HayleyTurner 9 40
(R Bastiman) *chsd ldrs: rdn along 3f out: wknd over 2f out* **50/1**

6 **10** 2 **Good Bye Day**[8] 5022 3-8-12 0 DavidAllan 17 31
(T D Easterby) *towards rr: hdwy 4f out: in tch 3f out: sn rdn and wknd* **50/1**

11 1 **Just Zak** 5-9-4 0 AndrewYoxall(7) 8 34
(O Brennan) *s.i.s: a bhd* **80/1**

12 10 **Penny Bazaar** 3-8-12 0 AndrewElliott 6 —
(G M Moore) *a outpcd in rr* **50/1**

13 1 ¾ **Harsh But Fair**[48] 4-9-8 0 JamesSullivan(3) 7 —
(M W Easterby) *v.s.a and a bhd* **16/1**

00 **14** 4 **Denison Flyer**[10] 4939 3-8-12 0 IanBrennan(5) 1 —
(L A Mullaney) *a outpcd and bhd* **66/1**

15 1 ½ **Strong Aim** 3-8-12 0 LeeVickers 13 —
(M W Easterby) *s.i.s: a bhd* **66/1**

2m 5.25s (-0.15) **Going Correction** -0.175s/f (Firm)
WFA 3 from 4yo+ 8lb **15** Ran SP% **120.1**
Speed ratings (Par 103): **93,91,89,87,87 87,83,82,78,77 76,68,66,63,62**
toteswingers: 1&2 £4.00, 1&3 £15.70, 2&3 £17.10. CSF £10.58 TOTE £4.30: £1.20, £1.90, £5.50; EX 13.80 Trifecta £188.30 Pool: £495.38 - 1.94 winning units.
Owner Kennerley Brydon Collins **Bred** Juddmonte Farms Inc **Trained** Hambleton, N Yorks

FOCUS
An ordinary maiden containing quite a range of abilities. A number missed the break and the field was soon stretched out despite a moderate pace.
Mainland(USA) Official explanation: trainer said, regarding apparent improvement of form, that the gelding broke quicker and travelled better.

5304 SIS LIVE H'CAP 1m
5:15 (5:18) (Class 4) (0-80,78) 3-Y-O **£5,046** (£1,510; £755; £377; £188) **Stalls** High

Form RPR

6001 **1** **Tukitinyasok (IRE)**[17] 4704 3-8-12 **74** (p) IanBrennan(5) 4 82
(R F Fisher) *mde all: rdn along wl over 2f out: drvn over 1f out: kpt on gamely ins fnl f* **12/1**

321- **2** nk **Medicinal Compound**[309] 6821 3-9-7 **78** NeilCallan 5 85+
(K A Ryan) *hld up in rr: hdwy on outer over 2f out: sn rdn and edgd rt wl over 1f out: drvn and styd on ins fnl f* **7/2**[2]

4640 **3** 1 ½ **Bin Shamardal (IRE)**[24] 4491 3-9-2 **73** PaulEddery 1 77
(B W Hills) *chsd wnr: rdn along wl over 2f out: drvn over 1f out: edgd lft ent fnl f: sn edgd rt and kpt on same pce* **11/2**[3]

U306 **4** nse **Koo And The Gang (IRE)**[12] 4898 3-8-5 **62** PatrickMathers 7 66
(B Ellison) *chsd ldrs: hdwy 3f out: rdn 2f out: drvn over 1f out: kpt on same pce* **16/1**

5413 **5** 2 ¼ **Squall**[31] 4265 3-9-7 **78** PaulHanagan 6 77
(J Noseda) *trckd ldrs: hdwy over 2f out: effrt and n.m.r over 1f out: rdn and hmpd ins fnl f: nt rcvr* **11/8**[1]

1054 **6** ½ **Master Of Dance (IRE)**[40] 3949 3-9-2 **73** PaulMulrennan 8 71
(J G Given) *hld up in rr: effrt 2f out: sn rdn and no imp* **10/1**

3244 **7** ¾ **Raqeeb (USA)**[15] 4784 3-9-3 **77** (b) JamesSullivan(3) 3 73
(Mrs R A Carr) *trckd ldng pair: hdwy over 3f out: rdn to chal over 2f out: drvn and ev ch tl wknd appr fnl f* **15/2**

1m 39.6s (-1.80) **Going Correction** -0.175s/f (Firm) **7** Ran SP% **114.1**
Speed ratings (Par 102): **102,101,100,100,97 97,96**
toteswingers: 1&2 £4.40, 1&3 £8.70, 2&3 £2.30. CSF £53.29 CT £261.45 TOTE £18.20: £6.70, £2.80; EX 53.50 Trifecta £178.60 Pool: £296.90 - 1.23 winning units. Place 6 £48.99; Place 5 £32.52.
Owner Des Johnston **Bred** Newlands House Stud **Trained** Ulverston, Cumbria

FOCUS
A fair handicap but a bit of a messy race. A strong initial pace soon slowed up and the field was rather compressed at the line.
T/Plt: £69.80 to a £1 stake. Pool:£62,956.85 - 657.79 winning tickets T/Qpdt: £24.20 to a £1 stake. Pool:£3,452.84 - 105.50 winning tickets JR

5261 SANDOWN (R-H)
Saturday, August 21

OFFICIAL GOING: Good to firm (good in places on sprint course: sprint 8.5, round 8.8)
Course at innermost configuration and distances as advertised. Sprint course at full width
Wind: virtually nil Weather: overcast, muggy

5305 DANEPAK ATALANTA STKS (LISTED RACE) (F&M) 1m 14y
2:05 (2:13) (Class 1) 3-Y-O+
£19,869 (£7,532; £3,769; £1,879; £941; £472) **Stalls** High

Form RPR

-011 **1** **Seta**[58] 3375 3-8-12 107 J-PGuillambert 1 111+
(L M Cumani) *sn chsng ldr: wnt upsides ldr and rdn ent fnl 2f: led over 1f out: drvn and styd on gamely fnl f: jst hld on* **11/4**[2]

40-4 **2** shd **Long Lashes (USA)**[21] 4574 3-8-8 102 (p) FrankieDettori 5 106+
(Saeed Bin Suroor) *chsd ldrs: swtchd lft and effrt wl over 1f out: sn chsd ldng pair: kpt on wl u.p to chse wnr wl ins fnl f: clsng at fin: jst hld* **7/1**

4146 **3** 1 **Flora Trevelyan**[29] 4319 4-9-0 97 AdamKirby 4 105
(W R Swinburn) *led: jnd and rdn ent fnl 2f: hdd and drvn over 1f out: stl ev ch tl no ex and lost 2nd wl ins fnl f* **8/1**

2004 **4** 1 **Blue Angel (IRE)**[22] 4540 3-8-8 102 RichardHughes 7 102
(R Hannon) *stdd after s: hld up in tch in last pair: effrt on inner ent fnl 2f: kpt on u.p fnl f: nvr quite gng pce to rch ldrs* **10/1**

-102 **5** hd **Chachamaidee (IRE)**[29] 4319 3-8-12 105 EddieAhern 8 105
(H R A Cecil) *dwlt: sn chsng ldng trio: rdn and effrt ent fnl 2f: kpt on same pce u.p fnl f* **3/1**[3]

1-1 **6** 2 ¾ **Decorative (IRE)**[72] 2898 3-8-8 96 PhilipRobinson 9 95+
(M A Jarvis) *t.k.h: hld up in tch in last: hdwy on outer to chse ldrs 4f out: rdn and unable qck ent fnl 2f: outpcd wl over 1f out: n.d fnl f* **5/2**[1]

1m 41.95s (-1.35) **Going Correction** -0.10s/f (Good)
WFA 3 from 4yo 6lb **6** Ran SP% **112.9**
Speed ratings (Par 111): **102,101,100,99,99 96**
toteswingers:1&2:£2.50, 1&3:£4.80, 2&3:£5.70 CSF £21.79 TOTE £4.10: £2.00, £2.20; EX 14.80 Trifecta £92.10 Pool: £797.03 - 6.40 winning units..
Owner Miss Sarah J Leigh **Bred** Sarah J Leigh And Robin S Leigh **Trained** Newmarket, Suffolk

FOCUS
A quality Listed contest, although they went just a modest gallop and it paid to race handy. Still, the time was respectable.

NOTEBOOK
Seta benefited from a fine ride from JP Guillambert, who had her well placed throughout and kept the runner-up hemmed in at a crucial stage, and she was just able to complete the hat-trick. The return to 1m did not inconvenience the winner, but this big filly still needs to strengthen up and mature - she was rather climbing in the closing stages, just generally looking ungainly. She is entered in the Matron Stakes, as well as the Sun Chariot, but it is unlikely she will fully realise her potential this year, whereas she should be well up to Group class next season. (op 9-4 tchd 3-1 and 7-2 in places)
Long Lashes(USA) ◆, tried in cheekpieces for the first time, improved significantly on the form she showed at Goodwood on her reappearance and arguably should have won. She travelled with enthusiasm for the most part, but had to wait longer than ideal for a run, being stuck behind Flora Trevelyan and kept in by Seta, and the manner in which she stayed on when finally in the clear suggests she was unlucky. Whatever, this was a pleasing return to form from a filly who looked potentially Group 1 class last year, and she can improve again, enough to win a nice prize. (op 5-1 tchd 9-2)
Flora Trevelyan had won both her previous starts over C&D, but in lesser company. She had the run of the race in front, and although no match for the front two, stuck on well to pick up some black type. (op 10-1)
Blue Angel(IRE) was not good enough, although a stronger-run race might have suited better. (op 12-1 tchd 7-1)
Chachamaidee(IRE) was keen when finishing ahead of today's third and fourth in a similar event at Ascot on her previous start, but despite settling better this time, she failed to pick up. This was a disappointing effort. (op 9-2)
Decorative(IRE) had to be re-shod at the start after spreading a plate, and pulled much too hard in the race itself. She ended up swinging four-wide around the bend into the straight and soon faded. She looked a nice prospect when winning her first two starts, a maiden last year and a handicap off 87 on her sole previous outing this year, and holds Group 1 entries, but she has something to prove now. Official explanation: jockey said filly hung left (op 11-4 tchd 3-1)

5306 ALEXIS CATCHPOLE CELEBRATION SOLARIO STKS (GROUP 3) 7f 16y
2:35 (2:41) (Class 1) 2-Y-O
£21,288 (£8,070; £4,038; £2,013; £1,008; £506) **Stalls** High

Form RPR

1 **1** **Native Khan (FR)**[45] 3794 2-9-0 0 EddieAhern 4 105+
(E A L Dunlop) *hld up in tch in last pair: hdwy ent fnl 2f: rdn and effrt between horses to press ldr jst over 1f out: led ins fnl f: kpt on u.p: rdn out* **6/5**[1]

11 **2** ½ **Measuring Time**[35] 4135 2-9-0 0 RichardHughes 3 103
(R Hannon) *short of room sn after s: sn niggled along in last: hdwy into midfield 5f out: rdn and unable qck ent fnl 2f: rallied u.p 1f out: chsd wnr fnl 100yds: kpt on but a hld* **6/1**[3]

0210 **3** ½ **Surrey Star (IRE)**[24] 4468 2-9-0 96 LiamKeniry 6 102
(R A Teal) *t.k.h early: led for 1f: chsd ldr after tl led again over 2f out: rdn wl over 1f out: hdd ins fnl f: styd on same pce u.p fnl 150yds* **20/1**

1333 **4** 3 ½ **Roayh (USA)**[22] 4538 2-9-0 105 FrankieDettori 8 93
(Saeed Bin Suroor) *plld hrd: w ldr for 1f: chsd ldng pair after: rdn and effrt wl over 1f out: keeping on same pce whn n.m.r ent fnl f: wknd ins fnl f* **3/1**[2]

115 **5** 2 ¼ **Waltz Darling (IRE)**[24] 4468 2-9-0 98 TomEaves 5 88
(R A Fahey) *in tch in last pair: rdn and effrt on rail wl over 2f out: sn struggling and outpcd: plugged on ins fnl f: nvr trbld ldrs* **14/1**

5122 **6** 1 ½ **Stentorian (IRE)**[24] 4468 2-9-0 100 GregFairley 1 84
(M Johnston) *sn bustled along: led after 1f: rdn and hdd over 2f out: wknd over 1f out: fdd fnl f* **13/2**

1m 29.19s (-0.31) **Going Correction** -0.10s/f (Good) **6** Ran SP% **109.5**
Speed ratings (Par 104): **97,96,95,91,89 87**
toteswingers:1&2:£1.90, 1&3:£5.30, 2&3:£10.30 CSF £8.45 TOTE £2.00: £1.10, £3.00; EX 7.40 Trifecta £99.10 Pool: £672.82 - 5.02 winning units.
Owner V I Araci **Bred** Aliette Forien And Gilles Forien **Trained** Newmarket, Suffolk

FOCUS
A race with a mixed history, but it has been won by some class horses, notably Raven's Pass in 2007. The bare form of the latest running does not look anything special, with the pace having been just ordinary (time only 0.63 seconds quicker than 79-rated Orientalist managed in later nursery), but the likable Native Khan seems considerably better than the result indicates.

NOTEBOOK
Native Khan(FR) ◆, who impressed when taking a decent July course maiden on his debut, travelled like a high-class individual, still cruising when looking for a run between rivals over 1f out. Once in the clear, he did not find as much as had seemed likely, still appearing inexperienced and idling, but was always doing enough. He seems sure to keep improving and is particularly exciting considering his breeding suggests he may stay middle distances, being by Azamour, out of a Kendor mare, albeit the dam was a 6f winner. According to Ed Dunlop, Native Khan will only have one or two more starts this year, and he holds a number of big-race entries, including the Grand Criterium, the Dewhurst and the Racing Post Trophy. The Longchamp race will make particular appeal to his connections seeing as he is a French-bred, although soft ground would be an unknown. (op 11-8 tchd 11-10 and 6-4 in places)
Measuring Time, the winner of his first two starts, ran well on this step up in class, although he was possibly flattered to get so close to the winner. He should improve for a step up in trip. (op 9-2)
Surrey Star(IRE) made no impression in the Vintage Stakes, but this was better. He is progressing into a smart colt and his breeding suggests he may do even better over further. (op 25-1)
Roayh(USA) raced keenly on this step up in trip and did not prove his stamina. He was third in the Richmond Stakes last time, but that form is not working out. (op 7-2)
Waltz Darling(IRE) could not confirm Vintage Stakes form with Surrey Star and does not look up to this level. (op 12-1)
Stentorian(IRE), representing last year's winning trainer, took them along but found disappointingly little for pressure, running below the form he showed when runner-up in the Vintage Stakes. (op 11-2 tchd 7-1)

5307 SUNDERLANDS H'CAP 1m 2f 7y
3:10 (3:12) (Class 2) 3-Y-O+
£31,155 (£9,330; £4,665; £2,335; £1,165; £585) **Stalls** High

Form RPR

1410 **1** **Forte Dei Marmi**[42] 3921 4-9-6 **98** J-PGuillambert 5 109
(L M Cumani) *hld up towards rr: hdwy over 2f out: chsng ldrs over 1f out: swtchd lft and rdn jst ins fnl f: r.o wl to ld fnl 50yds* **6/1**[1]

2101 **2** 1 **Hanoverian Baron**[29] 4321 5-8-13 **91** SteveDrowne 9 100
(A G Newcombe) *racd off the pce in midfield: rdn and clsd on ldrs 2f out: led ent fnl f tl jst ins fnl f: sn carried sltly lft: stl ev ch tl nt pce of wnr fnl 75yds* **13/2**[2]

1053 **3** *nk* **Sandor**[27] 4400 4-9-0 **92** .... GregFairley 15 100
(P J Makin) *hld up off the pce in midfield: rdn and gd hdwy over 2f out: led and edgd lft jst ins fnl f: hdd fnl 50yds: one pce after* **8/1**

0514 **4** *hd* **Cumulus Nimbus**[23] 4504 3-8-7 **93** .... RichardHughes 10 101
(R Hannon) *s.i.s: bhd: hdwy u.p on outer ent fnl 2f: chsd ldrs 1f out: kpt on u.p fnl f* **15/2**[3]

2401 **5** *shd* **Elliptical (USA)**[21] 4579 4-9-1 **93** .... DaneO'Neill 6 101
(G A Butler) *hld up off the pce towards rr: hdwy and switching rt over 1f out: styng on whn swtchd lft ins fnl f: gng on wl fin: nt rch ldrs* **16/1**

1120 **6** *shd* **Jo'Burg (USA)**[25] 4455 6-8-5 **86** .... MartinLane(3) 14 94+
(Lady Herries) *stdd s: hld up wl off the pce in last pair: c to stands' rail and rdn along over 3f out: hdwy and rt on terms w ldrs over 1f out: styd on same pce fnl f* **10/1**

0014 **7** *1 ¾* **Greylami (IRE)**[29] 4321 5-9-2 **94** .... EddieAhern 4 98
(R A Mills) *racd off the pce in midfield: rdn and effrt over 2f out: styng on same pce whn sltly hmpd 1f out: no imp after* **16/1**

-100 **8** *½* **Kings Destiny**[35] 4139 4-9-10 **102** .... PhilipRobinson 13 105
(M A Jarvis) *chsd ldrs: allowed ldng pair to go clr 8f out: clsd and rdn ent fnl 2f: pressing ldrs u.p jst over 1f out: wknd ins fnl f* **12/1**

0425 **9** *½* **Australia Day (IRE)**[25] 4455 7-9-2 **94** .... MartinDwyer 8 96
(P R Webber) *led: drew clr w rival 8f out: rdn 2f out: hdd ent fnl f: wknd ins fnl f* **8/1**

2303 **10** *1 ¾* **Ramona Chase**[14] 4841 5-7-13 **77** ....(t) LukeMorris 12 76
(M J Attwater) *wl off the pce towards rr: rdn over 3f out: styd on fnl f: nvr trbld ldrs* **25/1**

1005 **11** *1 ¼* **Dansili Dancer**[56] 3462 8-8-12 **95** .... JohnFahy(5) 11 91
(C G Cox) *racd wl off the pce in midfield: effrt u.p over 2f out: no imp ent fnl f* **14/1**

3542 **12** *3 ¾* **Changing The Guard**[25] 4455 4-8-9 **87** .... TomEaves 16 76
(R A Fahey) *racd wl off the pce in midfield: rdn and effrt over 2f out: no real prog: nvr trbld ldrs* **18/1**

0012 **13** *7* **Geneva Geyser (GER)**[47] 3737 4-8-10 **88** .... SebSanders 3 63
(J M P Eustace) *racd keenly: w ldr and drew clr of field 8f out: rdn over 2f out: wknd qckly over 1f out: wl btn and eased ins fnl f* **28/1**

0112 **14** *3 ¼* **Fontley**[49] 3694 3-8-11 **97** .... JimCrowley 17 65
(Eve Johnson Houghton) *prom in main gp tl wknd u.p wl over 1f out: wl btn and eased ins fnl f* **10/1**

0003 **15** *1 ¾* **Submariner (USA)**[14] 4818 4-8-10 **88** .... FrankieDettori 7 53
(M Johnston) *prom in main gp tl wknd wl over 1f out: wl btn and eased fnl f* **9/1**

2m 7.21s (-3.29) **Going Correction** -0.10s/f (Good)
WFA 3 from 4yo+ 8lb **15** Ran SP% **128.5**
Speed ratings (Par 109): **109,108,107,107,107 107,106,105,105,104 103,100,94,91,90**
toteswingers:1&2:£7.10, 1&3:£10.80, 2&3:£8.60 CSF £46.35 CT £329.19 TOTE £7.40: £3.10, £2.00, £3.20; EX 52.90 Trifecta £698.50 Pool: £76,339.98 - 80.86 winning units..
Owner Fittocks Stud **Bred** Fittocks Stud **Trained** Newmarket, Suffolk
■ Stewards' Enquiry : Martin Lane two-day ban: used whip with excessive frequency (Sep 6-7)

FOCUS
A decent, competitive handicap. There was something of a bunch finish, but the gallop was quick and this is strong form.

NOTEBOOK
Forte Dei Marmi ◆ has a good cruising speed but only a short finishing burst, so a waiting ride off a strong pace was ideal and he produced his best performance yet. He disappointed in the John Smith's Cup last time (reported to have lost action), but that was the second time he had run below form at York, from only two starts at the track, and he showed himself to still be on the upgrade. He looks a Pattern performer in the making, although his connections may be tempted to aim him at the Cambridgeshire, presumably after going for the Dubai Duty Free Stakes at Newbury (impressive winner only previous start at the track). In the longer term, he looks an ideal type for Dubai. (op 8-1)
Hanoverian Baron came here after missing the cut for the Ebor. He ran a fine race off a 3lb higher mark than when winning at Ascot on his previous start and is clearly still improving, with the possibility of even more to come when he goes back up in trip. (op 7-1 tchd 15-2 in places)
Sandor seemed to have every chance and ran a good race on this drop in trip. (tchd 15-2 in places)
Cumulus Nimbus, who again missed the break, got the strong pace he needs but was not quite good enough. He might get further. (op 10-1)
Elliptical(USA) ◆, 6lb higher than when winning a lesser race over 1m1f at Goodwood, very much caught the eye running on strongly at the line. He surely has more to offer and would be interesting in races like the Dubai Duty Free Stakes at Newbury and the Cambridgeshire, although he may ultimately need 1m4f. (op 14-1)
Jo'Burg(USA), just as when winning over C&D in June, was taken towards the stands' side in the straight and raced alone. He certainly was not on slower ground and briefly looked set to win (he would have picked up a £100,000 bonus having already won twice at Sandown this season), but he got tired late on. This was a fine effort in defeat.
Greylami(IRE) ran respectably off a 5lb higher mark than when third in this last year. (tchd 20-1 in a place)
Australia Day(IRE) went off too fast and did well to finish as close as he did, especially with Geneva Geyser, who hassled him for the lead, finishing well behind. (op 9-1)
Fontley, another chasing the £100,000 bonus, was well below form on this step back up in trip.
Official explanation: trainer said filly was found to be in season

5308 S. NORTON H'CAP 5f 6y
3:45 (3:50) (Class 2) (0-100,95) 3-Y-0+
£9,346 (£2,799; £1,399; £700; £349; £175) **Stalls** High

Form RPR

0000 **1** **Sohraab**[12] 4904 6-9-1 **85** .... JimCrowley 14 95
(H Morrison) *chsd ldrs: effrt to chse clr ldr ent fnl f: r.o wl to ld wl ins fnl f: sn in command* **10/1**

0002 **2** *1* **Judge 'n Jury**[4] 5183 6-9-11 **95** .... LukeMorris 10 102
(R A Harris) *racd keenly: led: rdn clr wl over 1f out: drvn ins fnl f: hdd and no ex wl ins fnl f* **11/2**[2]

0050 **3** *½* **Drawnfromthepast (IRE)**[22] 4536 5-9-2 **86** .... DaneO'Neill 11 91
(J A Osborne) *in tch: rdn and effrt to chse ldng pair 1f out: kpt on u.p fnl f* **16/1**

1446 **4** *nk* **Medici Time**[23] 4510 5-9-0 **84** ....(v) TomEaves 9 88
(T D Easterby) *wnt lft s: bhd: hdwy on far rail wl over 1f out: kpt on u.p fnl f: nt gng pce to rch ldrs* **12/1**

5355 **5** *1 ½* **Invincible Lad (IRE)**[18] 4685 6-8-13 **83** ....(b[1]) RichardHughes 4 82+
(E J Alston) *stdd s: t.k.h: hld up in last trio: hdwy ent fnl f: styd on but nvr gng pce to rch ldrs* **8/1**

125 **6** *¾* **Ziggy Lee**[77] 2759 4-9-2 **86** .... WilliamCarson 5 82+
(S C Williams) *in tch in midfield: rdn and sltly outpcd wl over 1f out: kpt on again ins fnl f but nvr threatened ldrs* **12/1**

3223 **7** *1 ¾* **Rocket Rob (IRE)**[12] 4904 4-9-6 **90** ....(p) FrankieDettori 6 80
(M Botti) *in tch in midfield: rdn and outpcd wl over 1f out: kpt on same pce and n.d fnl f* **5/1**[1]

6020 **8** *½* **Pavershooz**[7] 5095 5-9-2 **89** .... MichaelGeran(3) 2 77
(N Wilson) *chsd ldrs: rdn to chse ldr 2f out tl ent fnl f: hung lft and wknd fnl f* **11/2**[2]

0164 **9** *¾* **Piscean (USA)**[23] 4510 5-9-2 **86** .... AdamKirby 1 71
(T Keddy) *stdd after s: hld up in last trio: rdn and effrt over 1f out: nvr trbld ldrs* **16/1**

2162 **10** *¾* **Five Star Junior (USA)**[11] 4937 4-9-10 **94** .... EddieAhern 7 76
(Mrs L Stubbs) *hmpd s: a in rr after and nvr able to rcvr: nvr trbld ldrs* **15/2**[3]

201 **11** *6* **Tabaret**[7] 5069 7-9-4 **88** ....(v) J-PGuillambert 13 49
(R M Whitaker) *chsd ldr: rdn and struggling ent fnl 2f: wknd over 1f out: wl bhd and eased ins fnl f* **8/1**

61.18 secs (-0.42) **Going Correction** +0.15s/f (Good) **11** Ran SP% **117.7**
Speed ratings (Par 109): **109,107,106,106,103 102,99,98,97,96 86**
toteswingers:1&2:£17.00, 1&3:£33.70, 2&3:£21.50 CSF £64.22 CT £643.55 TOTE £12.70: £3.20, £2.50, £5.80; EX 79.20 Trifecta £1200.20 Part won. Pool: £1,621.92 - 0.78 winning units..

Owner Pangfield Racing **Bred** T J Billington **Trained** East Ilsley, Berks

FOCUS
A good sprint handicap, although there was a bias towards those drawn high.

NOTEBOOK
Sohraab had been having a poor season, but as a consequence was 13lb lower than at the start of the campaign and he finally returned to form, with his draw a help. He will still look well handicapped next time and may be hard to oppose, especially considering he might regain some confidence from this. (op 12-1 tchd 14-1 in places)
Judge 'n Jury ◆, from stall ten, set out to make all against the far rail and, despite racing freely, looked set to win, touching 1.14 in running. The stiff track ultimately found him out, but this was another good effort, following on from his back-to-form second at York four days earlier, and he could pick up a nice prize when returned to a quicker track, even allowing for an inevitable weight rise. (op 7-1 tchd 8-1)
Drawnfromthepast(IRE), another well drawn, had his chance and ran respectably. (tchd 20-1)
Medici Time ran on after a slow start but was never getting there. (op 16-1)
Invincible Lad(IRE) did not face the first-time blinkers, missing the break and then racing keenly. (op 9-1 tchd 15-2)
Rocket Rob(IRE) came into this in good form, but he proved pretty disappointing in first-time cheekpieces. (op 9-2 tchd 4-1)
Pavershooz was poorly drawn and is easily excused his modest effort. Official explanation: jockey said gelding hung left (op 7-1 tchd 8-1)
Five Star Junior(USA), who was sweating beforehand, could not recover from being short of room at the start. (tchd 7-1)
Tabaret Official explanation: jockey said gelding lost its action when crossing the path

5309 LIFE BUILD H'CAP 5f 6y
4:15 (4:21) (Class 4) (0-85,82) 3-Y-0 **£5,180** (£1,541; £770; £384) **Stalls** High

Form RPR

5060 **1** **Italian Tom (IRE)**[117] 1584 3-8-13 **72** .... LukeMorris 8 80
(R A Harris) *racd in midfield: rdn and hdwy to press ldrs on far rail ent fnl f: led fnl 100yds: r.o wl* **33/1**

111 **2** *½* **Captain Coke (IRE)**[57] 3417 3-9-8 **81** .... PhilipRobinson 9 87
(M A Jarvis) *chsd ldr: clsd over 2f out: led over 1f out: sn rdn: hdd and unable qck fnl 100yds* **11/8**[1]

2621 **3** *1 ¾* **Diman Waters (IRE)**[29] 4349 3-9-9 **82** .... RichardHughes 7 82
(E J Alston) *stdd s: hld up in last trio: hdwy 1/2-way: chsd ldrs and rdn ent fnl f: no ex and btn fnl 100yds* **9/4**[2]

2010 **4** *2 ¼* **Mon Brav**[2] 5250 3-9-7 **80** ....(v) DavidNolan 5 72
(D Carroll) *in tch in midfield: rdn to chse ldrs over 1f out: wknd jst ins fnl f* **8/1**[3]

1012 **5** *¾* **Panpiper**[13] 4875 3-8-7 **69** .... MartinLane(3) 6 58
(G L Moore) *chsd ldrs: sn rdn along: clsd on ldr u.p 2f out: ev ch ent fnl f: wknd fnl 150yds and btn whn hung rt wl ins fnl f* **12/1**

3144 **6** *2 ½* **Special Quality (USA)**[52] 3561 3-9-0 **73** .... FrankieDettori 2 53
(R M H Cowell) *stdd sn after s: hld up in last trio: hdwy and nt clr run on far rail over 1f out: sn swtchd lft and rdn 1f out: no imp and btn whn nt clr run wl ins fnl f* **9/1**

6410 **7** *4 ½* **Diamond Johnny G (USA)**[22] 4541 3-9-5 **78** ....(t) EddieCreighton 4 42
(E J Creighton) *in midfield sn rdn along and lost pl: dropped to rr 1/2-way wl bhd fnl f* **25/1**

2622 **8** *3* **Superior Edge**[11] 4922 3-8-9 **73** .... JohnFahy(5) 1 26
(B Palling) *racd in midfield struggling u.p and dropped to rr 1/2-way: wl bhd fnl f* **20/1**

513- **9** *8* **Wellington Fair**[320] 6550 3-9-5 **78** ....(v) AdamKirby 3 2
(Miss Tor Sturgis) *sn led and clr: c bk to field 2f out: hdd over 1f out: sn dropped out and wl bhd fnl f* **22/1**

61.79 secs (0.19) **Going Correction** +0.15s/f (Good) **9** Ran SP% **117.6**
Speed ratings (Par 102): **104,103,100,96,95 91,84,79,66**
toteswingers:1&2:£15.20, 1&3:£19.80, 2&3:£1.40 CSF £77.82 CT £157.79 TOTE £30.80: £5.40, £1.20, £1.50; EX 76.00.
Owner S & A Mares **Bred** Tom Radley **Trained** Earlswood, Monmouths

FOCUS
A decent 3yo sprint handicap run at a strong pace, courtesy of the free-going Wellington Fair. Like in the earlier 5f contest, a high draw was a help, even with only nine runners.

5310 VARIETY CLUB ANDREWS CLASSIC NURSERY 7f 16y
4:50 (4:51) (Class 4) (0-85,85) 2-Y-0 **£4,533** (£1,348; £674; £336) **Stalls** High

Form RPR

5341 **1** **Orientalist**[10] 4955 2-9-1 **79** .... EddieAhern 1 85+
(Eve Johnson Houghton) *hld up in tch in last pair: hdwy on far rail to trck ldrs but nt clr run over 1f out: fnlly in the clr and swtchd lft ins fnl f: qcknd to ld nr fin* **10/1**

231 **2** *hd* **Introvert (IRE)**[31] 4253 2-9-3 **81** .... FrankieDettori 2 85
(Mahmood Al Zarooni) *led: and grad crossed to rail: rdn 2f out: kpt on wl u.p fnl f tl hdd and no ex nr fin* **5/2**[2]

241 **3** *2* **Jehanbux (USA)**[16] 4755 2-9-7 **85** .... RichardHughes 3 84
(R Hannon) *stdd s: hld up in last pair: hdwy into midfield over 4f out: rdn to chse ldrs 2f out: n.m.r ent fnl f: styd on same pce fnl 100yds* **2/1**[1]

01 **4** *¾* **Bloodsweatandtears**[26] 4437 2-9-4 **82** .... JimCrowley 8 79
(W J Knight) *t.k.h: chsd ldr: ev ch and rdn 2f out: drvn and unable qck over 1f out: wknd ins fnl f* **3/1**[3]

0330 **5** *¾* **Silken Thoughts**[22] 4539 2-8-3 **67** .... IvaMilickova 4 62
(John Berry) *t.k.h early: in midfield tl rn wd and lost pl bnd over 4f out: hdwy to chse ldrs over 1f out: drvn 1f out: wknd ins fnl f* **28/1**

0103 **6** *4 ½* **Las Verglas Star (IRE)**[22] 4544 2-8-8 **72** .... TomEaves 5 56
(R A Fahey) *t.k.h early: in tch: rdn and wknd wl over 1f out* **20/1**

0521 **7** *nk* **Titus Two (IRE)**[17] 4716 2-8-11 **80**.................................. JohnFahy(5) 6 63
(P W Chapple-Hyam) *chsd ldrs: rdn over 2f out: wknd u.p over 1f out* **8/1**
1m 29.82s (0.32) **Going Correction** -0.10s/f (Good) 7 Ran SP% **115.3**
Speed ratings (Par 96): **94,93,91,90,89 84,84**
toteswingers:1&2:£3.10, 1&3:£4.70, 2&3:£1.50 CSF £35.90 CT £71.63 TOTE £12.10: £3.80, £1.50; EX 42.10.
Owner Eden Racing IV **Bred** Whitsbury Manor Stud **Trained** Blewbury, Oxon

FOCUS
A fair nursery and the time was a respectable 0.63 seconds slower than Native Khan recorded in the Solario Stakes.

NOTEBOOK
Orientalist defied a 4lb rise for his Salisbury success and had more in hand than the margin suggests. He was trapped away towards the inside for much of the straight, only getting in the open inside the final furlong, but he picked up well. Considering he should not go up too much for this, the hat-trick is a distinct possibility. (op 15-2)
Introvert(IRE) improved on the form he showed when winning a weak Polytrack maiden on his previous start and is going the right way. (op 4-1)
Jehanbux(USA), off the mark over 1m here last time, proved unsuited by the drop in trip. He did not have a great deal of room in the closing stages and otherwise would have finished closer. He can do better back over further. (op 15-8 tchd 9-4 in places)
Bloodsweatandtears holds a number of Group-race entries, but he failed to confirm the promise of his Yarmouth maiden victory, not picking up after racing keenly. (op 11-4 tchd 10-3)
Silken Thoughts ◆ was keen, racing much wider than ideal without cover, and is better than she showed. (op 25-1 tchd 40-1 in a place)
Titus Two(IRE) Official explanation: jockey said colt was never travelling

5311 VARIETY CLUB MILES COMMERCIAL H'CAP — 1m 2f 7y
5:25 (5:28) (Class 4) (0-80,80) 3-Y-O+ **£4,533** (£1,348; £674; £336) **Stalls** High

Form RPR
0444 **1** **Sequillo**[28] 4376 4-9-11 **77**...(b1) RichardHughes 6 88
(R Hannon) *mde all: gng best 2f out: pushed along and a jst doing enough fnl f* **8/1**
5603 **2** *nk* **Laudatory**[9] 4996 4-9-11 **77**..(p) AdamKirby 8 87
(W R Swinburn) *in tch in midfield: effrt on inner wl over 1f out: swtchd lft and bmpd rival jst over 1f out: sn chsng wnr: kpt on but a hld fnl f* **4/1**[1]
0365 **3** *½* **Monte Cavallo (SAF)**[21] 4597 5-9-10 **76**..................... EddieCreighton 1 85+
(M Wigham) *stdd s: t.k.h: hld up wl bhd: hdwy on outer 2f out: chsd ldrs jst ins fnl f: sn chalng: edging rt and no ex fnl 75yds* **6/1**[3]
0020 **4** *3¼* **Rumble Of Thunder (IRE)**[14] 4841 4-10-0 **80**................. JimCrowley 4 83
(D W P Arbuthnot) *in tch in midfield: rdn and hdwy to chse ldrs ent fnl 2f: drvn over 1f out: wknd jst ins fnl f* **15/2**
1-03 **5** *1¼* **Spensley (IRE)**[13] 4859 4-9-4 **70**...................................... EddieAhern 12 70+
(J R Fanshawe) *hld up in last trio: rdn ent fnl 2f: hdwy u.p towards inner over 1f out: nvr trbld ldrs* **9/2**[2]
0013 **6** *3¾* **Ballinteni**[17] 4713 8-9-4 **75**.. KierenFox(5) 5 68
(Miss Gay Kelleway) *in tch in midfield: effrt to chse ldrs u.p ent fnl 2f: wknd ent fnl f* **10/1**
3446 **7** *hd* **Touch Of Style (IRE)**[16] 4758 6-8-4 **61** oh1.................... JohnFahy(5) 10 54
(Matthew Salaman) *chsd ldrs tl wknd u.p wl over 1f out* **12/1**
40-0 **8** *3¼* **Summer Winds**[23] 4520 5-10-0 **80**.................................(v1) FrankieDettori 7 66
(R A Mills) *chsd wnr: rdn ent fnl 2f: bmpd jst over 1f out: wknd ent fnl f: wl btn and eased fnl 75yds* **10/1**
5264 **9** *5* **Addwaitya**[13] 4859 5-9-13 **79**...(v1) IanMongan 2 55
(Mrs L J Mongan) *in tch on outer: chsd ldrs over 4f out: rdn wl over 2f out: hrd drvn and wkng whn squeezed out jst over 1f out: fdd fnl f* **12/1**
1555 **10** *1* **Archie Rice (USA)**[12] 4907 4-9-6 **72**................................. TomEaves 11 46
(T Keddy) *hld up towards rr: rdn and no prog ent fnl 2f: n.d* **16/1**
21-0 **11** *1* **Burma Rock (IRE)**[19] 4652 4-9-12 **78**........................ J-PGuillambert 9 50
(L M Cumani) *plld hrd: chsd ldrs tl wknd u.p 2f out: wl bhd fnl f* **8/1**
2m 9.13s (-1.37) **Going Correction** -0.10s/f (Good) 11 Ran SP% **125.9**
Speed ratings (Par 105): **101,100,100,97,96 93,93,91,87,86 85**
toteswingers:1&2:£9.70, 1&3:£18.50, 2&3:£13.10 CSF £43.01 CT £216.04 TOTE £9.80: £3.50, £2.00, £3.80; EX 54.50 Place 6 £102.18; Place 5 £44.43.
Owner White Beech Farm **Bred** Redmyre Bloodstock And S Hillen **Trained** East Everleigh, Wilts
■ Stewards' Enquiry : Adam Kirby two-day ban: careless riding (Sep 5-6)

FOCUS
They went a steady pace (time was 1.92 seconds slower than Forte Dei Marmi recorded earlier on card), with Sequillo making all under a fine front-running ride from Richard Hughes.
T/Plt: £133.30 to a £1 stake. Pool:£155,181.66 - 849.72 winning tickets T/Qpdt: £44.40 to a £1 stake. Pool:£6,909.77 - 115.05 winning tickets SP

5312 - 5315a (Foreign Racing) - See Raceform Interactive

4876 CURRAGH (R-H)
Saturday, August 21

OFFICIAL GOING: Good to firm

5316a GALILEO EUROPEAN BREEDERS FUND FUTURITY STKS (GROUP 2) — 7f
4:25 (4:26) 2-Y-O
£53,097 (£16,814; £7,964; £2,654; £1,769; £884)

RPR
1 **Pathfork (USA)**[34] 4175 2-9-1 .... FMBerry 7 115+
(Mrs John Harrington, Ire) *a.p: trckd ldr in 2nd: led under 2f out: rdn and pressed 1f out: styd on wl ins fnl f* **10/11**[1]
2 *1½* **Glor Na Mara (IRE)**[13] 4880 2-9-1 .... KJManning 1 112
(J S Bolger, Ire) *settled towards rr: hdwy on outer 1/2-way: wnt 3rd 2f out: 2nd and chal 1f out: no imp u.p ins fnl f* **2/1**[2]
3 *2½* **Samuel Morse (IRE)**[13] 4880 2-9-1 107............................... JMurtagh 2 105
(A P O'Brien, Ire) *settled in rr: hdwy on inner into 5th 2f out: 4th u.p 1f out: 3rd ins fnl f but no imp on principals* **8/1**[3]
4 *½* **High Ruler (USA)**[30] 4310 2-9-1 99................................. JAHeffernan 6 104
(A P O'Brien, Ire) *chsd ldrs: 4th 1/2-way: 6th and pushed along fr 2f out: kpt on same pce wout threatening to regain 4th fnl f* **25/1**
5 *1½* **Rudolf Valentino**[34] 4176 2-9-1 .... CO'Donoghue 4 100
(A P O'Brien, Ire) *led: drvn along fr 1/2-way: hdd under 2f out: sn wknd and dropped to 5th ins fnl f* **25/1**
6 *nk* **Longhunter**[55] 3488 2-9-1 .... DPMcDonogh 5 100
(Kevin Prendergast, Ire) *trckd ldrs on far rail: travelling wl in 4th under 3f out: swtchd lft 2f out: sn rdn and no ex fr over 1f out* **8/1**[3]
7 *5* **Robin Hood (IRE)**[26] 4442 2-9-1 .... JPO'Brien 3 87
(A P O'Brien, Ire) *trckd ldrs in 3rd: rdn and wknd qckly fr 2f out* **9/1**
1m 23.45s (-7.35) **Going Correction** -0.90s/f (Hard) 7 Ran SP% **125.6**
Speed ratings: **106,104,101,100,99 98,93**
CSF £3.45 TOTE £2.10: £1.50, £1.60; DF 6.10.
Owner Silverton Hill Partnership **Bred** Flaxman Holdings Limited **Trained** Moone, Co Kildare

FOCUS
A race with a history of being won by a top-notch performer, notably St Jovite, Hawk Wing, Giant's Causeway, Oratorio, Teofilo, New Approach and Cape Blanco.

NOTEBOOK
Pathfork(USA) ◆ broke in front but was soon headed and remained prominent until being sent to the lead soon after passing the 2f marker. He travelled well through the race and went about his business in good style, finding more than enough to see off the runner-up inside the final furlong, and was well on top at the finish. His trainer said "He's not in the National Stakes, but he is in the Dewhurst and the Beresford, while I know his owners, who are from Kentucky, would like him to go to the Breeders' Cup. We will have to have a few conferences before any decisions are made." (op 11/8)
Glor Na Mara(IRE) had shown dramatic improvement from his first run to split Zoffany and Strong Suit in the Group 1 Phoenix Stakes here early this month and was expected to improve again. Whether that improvement didn't happen or he was simply beaten by a better horse is debatable, but he appeared to be beaten fair and square after being held up before arriving with his effort over 1f out. He ran on but was always being well held by the winner. He will next appear in the National Stakes next month. (op 7/4 tchd 9/4)
Samuel Morse(IRE), like the runner-up, was trying 7f for the first time. This was his seventh start of the season and he had finished approximately 6l off Glor Na Mara in the Phoenix Stakes on his previous start. Held up in rear, he was switched to the inside and got a clear run up the inside from 1½f out. He ran on but never posed a threat to the first two. (op 8/1 tchd 7/1)
High Ruler(USA), a maiden winner over the trip at Roscommon before finishing second to Zoffany in the four-runner Group 3 Tyros Stakes at Leopardstown, stayed on from over over 1f out to be nearest at the finish despite appearing to lean right. (op 16/1)
Rudolf Valentino was in front on settling down and made the running until coming under pressure and giving best under 2f out. (op 16/1)
Longhunter, back over the trip at which he won his maiden first time out at Leopardstown having been slowly away and never in contention dropped to 6f in the Group 2 Railway Stakes, looked as if he might get involved when closing 2f out but he found nothing when asked to raise his effort and faded out of contention.

5317 - 5318a (Foreign Racing) - See Raceform Interactive

ARLINGTON PARK (L-H)
Saturday, August 21

OFFICIAL GOING: Turf: good

5319a SECRETARIAT STKS (GRADE 1) (3YO) (TURF) — 1m 2f
9:37 (9:45) 3-Y-O
£148,148 (£49,382; £24,691; £12,345; £7,407; £4,938)

RPR
1 **Paddy O'Prado (USA)**[35] 3-9-0 0.................................. KDesormeaux 1 118
(Dale Romans, U.S.A) *broke wl and settled in 3rd on the rail: pushed along 3f out: cl 3rd and three wd turning for hom: lef jst ins fnl f: r.o wl* **1/2**[1]
2 *1¼* **Wigmore Hall (IRE)**[15] 4805 3-8-11 0............................ JamieSpencer 4 112
(M L W Bell) *settled towards rr: relegated to last 4f out: asked to cl and 4th 2f out: r.o st to take 2nd ins fnl f: styd on wl but always hld* **31/10**[2]
3 *¾* **Workin For Hops (USA)**[35] 3-8-11 0.. FTorres 6 111
(Michael Stidham, U.S.A) *chsd the ldr: pressed him fron 3f out but did nt master him tl after the first two had gone past ins the fnl f: kpt on gamely* **42/10**[3]
4 *nk* **Cherokee Lord (USA)**[23] 3-8-7 0.. JEFelix 3 106
(Charlie Livesay, U.S.A) *broke wl and sn led: responded wl whn pressed fr 3f out: hdd ins fnl f: unable qck but kpt on willingly* **50/1**
5 *2½* **Dean's Kitten (USA)**[35] 3-8-11 0..................................(b) JRLeparoux 5 105
(Michael J Maker, U.S.A) *settled in rr: mde sme hdwy 4f out: rdn and unable qck fnl 2f* **122/10**
6 *1¾* **Mister Marti Gras (USA)**[35] 3-8-11 0....................................... EPerez 2 101
(Chris Block, U.S.A) *chsd ldrs: rdn and wknd fnl 2f* **189/10**
2m 4.71s (3.07) 6 Ran SP% **124.8**
PARI-MUTUEL (all including $2 stake): WIN 3.00; PLACE (1-2) 2.20, 3.40; SHOW (1-2-3): 2.10, 2.40, 2.40; SF 9.80.
Owner Donegal Racing **Bred** Winchell Thoroughbreds LLC **Trained** USA

FOCUS
The time was 1.70 seconds slower than the Arlington Million.

NOTEBOOK
Paddy O'Prado(USA), the Kentucky Derby third, has now won all three of his starts since returning to turf. He was always doing enough to hold off the runner-up and is by far the best of his generation on this surface in the States. The Grade 2 Joe Hirsch Turf Classic at Belmont on October 2 will probably be his next race, ahead of the Breeders' Cup Turf.
Wigmore Hall(IRE), the John Smith's Cup winner who landed a July course conditions race last time, used first-time Lasix and ran on well to take second, but he could not match the winner's speed. Michael Bell hopes the gelding could be a bit of a globetrotter, and will consider races in the likes of Hong Kong, Singapore and Dubai.

5320a BEVERLY D. STKS (GRADE 1) (3YO+ FILLIES & MARES) (TURF) — 1f 110y(T)
10:24 (10:29) 3-Y-O+
£269,444 (£89,814; £44,907; £22,453; £13,472; £8,981)

RPR
1 **Eclair De Lune (GER)**[35] 4-8-11 0..................................... JAlvarado 5 112
(Ronald McAnally, U.S.A) *smartly away and sn settled in 2nd: racd 3 to 4 l off the ldr: clsd that gap fr over 2f out: led st and grad plld clr fnl f* **32/5**
2 *1½* **Hot Cha Cha (USA)**[35] 4-8-11 0.................................. JamesGraham 2 109
(Phillip A Sims, U.S.A) *chsd the ldng pair: clsd up but stl 3rd st: wnt 2nd ins fnl 100yds but nvr threatened wnr* **41/10**[3]
3 *nk* **Gypsy's Warning (SAF)**[34] 5-8-11 0.............................. WilliamBuick 4 108
(H Graham Motion, U.S.A) *hld up: seventh over 3f out: 5th and c wd st: styd on wl fnl f* **92/10**
4 *1* **Romacaca (USA)**[49] 4-8-11 0..(b) MCBaze 7 106
(N Canani, U.S.A) *broke wl and sn led: hdd st and sn wknd* **11/1**
5 *hd* **Treat Gently**[35] 5-8-11 0.. KDesormeaux 8 106
(William Mott, U.S.A) *hld up towards rr: sme hdwy 2f out: 4th st: no ex* **39/10**[2]
6 *2¾* **Pachattack (USA)**[20] 4624 4-8-11 0................................ KierenFallon 1 100
(G A Butler) *slowly away: steadily mde up lost grnd but stl last over 3f out: mde sme late hdwy: n.d* **71/10**
7 *2¼* **Acoma (USA)**[49] 5-8-11 0.. JRLeparoux 3 96
(David M Carroll, U.S.A) *broke wl: settled in 4th: rdn and grad wknd fr 3f out* **84/10**
8 *¾* **Ave**[34] 4-8-11 0.. RADominguez 9 94
(Roger L Attfield, Canada) *a in last two pls: nvr in contention having been bmpd and forced wd on last turn* **16/5**[1]

9 ¾ **Biased**27 4-8-11 0 GregoryBenoist 6 93
(M Delzangles, France) *dwlt: racd in midfield: 4th 3f out: sn rdn and lost pl* **34/1**

1m 56.56s (1.09) **9** Ran SP% **121.3**
PARI-MUTUEL (all including $2 stake): WIN 14.80; PLACE (1-2) 7.40, 5.40; SHOW (1-2-3): 4.80, 3.40, 5.80; SF 65.40.
Owner Richard L Duchossois **Bred** Thomas Kohler **Trained** USA

NOTEBOOK
Eclair De Lune(GER)'s success strongly suggests Tuscan Evening would have won this had she not sadly collapsed and died after a recent workout. Ron McAnally's runner was ½l behind that filly when getting 11lb in the C&D Modesty Handicap last time.
Pachattack(USA), who came into this off the back of a couple of Listed wins, lost several lengths with a slow start and did well to get so close. She used Lasix for the first time.

5321a ARLINGTON MILLION XXVIII (GRADE 1) (3YO+) (TURF) 1m 2f
11:14 (11:19) 3-Y-O+
£359,259 (£119,753; £59,876; £29,938; £17,962; £11,975)

RPR
1 **Debussy (IRE)**28 [4390] 4-9-0 0 WilliamBuick 1 122
(J H M Gosden) **11/1**
2 ½ **Gio Ponti (USA)**42 5-9-0 0 RADominguez 5 121
(Christophe Clement, U.S.A) **9/10**1
3 2 **Tazeez (USA)**44 [3825] 6-9-0 0 RichardHills 8 117
(J H M Gosden) **32/5**3
4 ½ **Rahystrada (USA)**35 6-9-0 0 IKarlsson 6 116
(Byron G Hughes, U.S.A) **92/10**
5 1 **Summit Surge (IRE)**28 [4390] 6-9-0 0 KierenFallon 9 114
(L M Cumani) **119/10**
6 3½ **Tajaaweed (USA)**35 5-9-0 0 MCBaze 7 107
(Daniel Peitz, U.S.A) **153/10**
7 nk **General Quarters (USA)**35 4-9-0 0 JamesGraham 2 106
(Thomas R McCarthy, U.S.A) **104/10**
8 nk **Just As Well (USA)**35 7-9-0 0 JRLeparoux 3 106
(Jonathan Sheppard, U.S.A) **63/10**2
9 1 **Quite A Handful (USA)**40 4-9-0 0 TRiggs 4 104
(Andrew Hansen, U.S.A) **45/1**

2m 3.01s (1.37) **9** Ran SP% **122.8**
PARI-MUTUEL (all including $2 stake): WIN 24.00; PLACE (1-2) 8.20, 2.80; SHOW (1-2-3): 5.60, 2.40, 4.00; SF 77.60.
Owner H R H Princess Haya Of Jordan **Bred** Darley **Trained** Newmarket, Suffolk

FOCUS
The time was 1.70 seconds quicker than the Secretariat Stakes.
NOTEBOOK
Debussy(IRE), using first-time Lasix, was shuffled back when short of room around the turn into the straight, but showed superb acceleration when finally getting a run against the far rail and gained an unlikely victory. He's now 4-6 going left-handed over 1m2f on turf.
Gio Ponti(USA) probably would have become only the second horse to win this race twice, following on from John Henry, had his rider been more patient. Desperate to ensure an uninterrupted trip, Dominguez asked Gio Ponti to make his move six wide around the sharp bend into the straight, and despite the gelding showing a tremendous burst of speed to go clear, looking the winner for much of the straight, his exertions told late on. It's true to say he might not have got a run otherwise, but he was picked off by a rival who saved ground around the final turn, having waited for a gap.
Tazeez(USA), racing on Lasix for the first time, was forced to work to get the lead from Quite A Handful, so this was a good effort.
Summit Surge(IRE) had Debussy behind when landing a Group 2 at York over this trip last time, but he was not good enough to confirm form. Like the winner, he used Lasix for the first time, but the outside draw was not ideal.

5226 DEAUVILLE (R-H)
Saturday, August 21
OFFICIAL GOING: Turf: good to soft; fibresand: standard

5322a PRIX DU CALVADOS - HARAS DES CAPUCINES (GROUP 3) (2YO FILLIES) (TURF) 7f
1:35 (12:00) 2-Y-O **£35,398** (£14,159; £10,619; £7,079; £3,539)

RPR
1 **Mambia**23 [4527] 2-8-9 0 DavyBonilla 2 105
(J Boisnard, France) *led fr s along rail: rdn 1 1/2f out: chal 100yds out: r.o strly* **4/1**3
2 1½ **Miss Fifty (IRE)**19 2-8-9 0 MaximeGuyon 3 101
(U Suter, France) *racd in 4th on rail: following ldr: rdn 1 1/2f out: qcknd wl: chal for ld ins fnl 100yds: r.o wl* **23/1**
3 1½ **Fork Handles**14 [4842] 2-8-9 0 GeraldMosse 5 98
(M R Channon) *racd in 3rd on outer: rdn 2f out: r.o wl wout threatening ldrs ins fnl f* **12/1**
4 1½ **Crying Lightening (IRE)**14 [4842] 2-8-10 0 ow1 OlivierPeslier 4 95
(P W Chapple-Hyam) *broke wl to r in 2nd: ev ch whn rdn 2f out: no ex: styd on fnl f* **9/10**1
5 1½ **Hello Fuji**20 2-8-9 0 ChristopheSoumillon 1 90
(L A Urbano-Grajales, France) *broke slowly: racd in 5th: rdn 2 1/2f out: no ex fnl f* **19/5**2
6 3 **Militante (IRE)**21 [4611] 2-8-9 0 StephanePasquier 6 83
(Y De Nicolay, France) *bkmarker to 1/2-way: rdn 2 1/2f out on outside: no ex: fdd* **13/2**

1m 24.0s (-4.30) **6** Ran SP% **118.7**
WIN (incl. 1 euro stake): 5.00. PLACES: 2.70, 6.30. SF: 51.50.
Owner Raymond Luce **Bred** Scea Haras Du Ma **Trained** France

NOTEBOOK
Mambia made all the running and now has the Marcel Boussac as her main aim.
Fork Handles, seventh in the Sweet Solera last time, reversed form with a below-par Crying Lightening but wasn't in the same class as the winner.
Crying Lightening(IRE), second in the Sweet Solera last time out, ran way below her best and the suspicion was that she may have been in season.

5323a CRITERIUM DU FONDS EUROPEEN DE L'ELEVAGE (LISTED RACE) (TURF) 1m (R)
2:40 (12:00) 2-Y-O **£53,982** (£21,592; £16,194; £10,796; £5,398)

RPR
1 ¾ **Klammer**43 [3868] 2-8-11 0 OlivierPeslier 3 101
(Jane Chapple-Hyam) *towards rr fr s: wnt 3rd after 2f: wnt 2nd arnd fnl turn: rdn early in st: tk ld 1 1/2f out: wandered off st line wl ins fnl f: hdd 50yds out: r.o wl: fin 2nd: awrdd r* **5/2**1
2 snk **Temps Au Temps (IRE)**19 2-8-11 0 GeraldMosse 1 99
(M Delzangles, France) *fin 3rd: plcd 2nd* **14/5**2
3 **Danedream (GER)**27 [4416] 2-8-8 0 MaximeGuyon 5 98
(P Schiergen, Germany) *fin 1st: plcd 3rd* **21/1**
4 2 **Nitza (FR)**22 2-8-8 0 JohanVictoire 2 92
(Mme C Head-Maarek, France) **6/1**3
5 ½ **Borysthene (FR)**38 [4036] 2-8-11 0 ChristopheSoumillon 7 94
(J-C Rouget, France) **5/2**1
6 snk **The Mole Catcher (IRE)** 2-8-11 0 IoritzMendizabal 4 93
(D De Watrigant, France) **83/10**
7 2½ **Nashi (FR)**22 [4565] 2-8-11 0 JulienAuge 6 88
(E J O'Neill, France) **17/1**

1m 42.3s (1.50) **7** Ran SP% **118.6**
WIN (incl. 1 euo stake): 3.50. PLACES: 2.40, 1.90. SF: 14.40.
Owner Yan Wah Wu **Bred** Ermyn Lodge Stud Limited **Trained** Dalham, Suffolk

NOTEBOOK
Klammer, third in the Superlative Stakes last time, benefited from a Stewards enquiry which resulted in the demotion of the original winner Danedream to third place. The softer ground really suited him, and he may now go for the Royal Lodge or come back to France for the Prix La Rochette or Prix des Chenes at Longchamp next month.

5204 FOLKESTONE (R-H)
Sunday, August 22
OFFICIAL GOING: Good (good to firm in places) changing to good after race 1 (2.10) changing to soft after race 2 (2.40)
Wind: Medium, across Weather: Raining

5324 ELLIE DEBLING E B F MAIDEN FILLIES' STKS 7f (S)
2:10 (2:11) (Class 5) 2-Y-O **£3,302** (£982; £491; £245) **Stalls** Low

Form RPR
43 1 **Apace (IRE)**39 [4029] 2-9-0 0 RichardMullen 1 80+
(Sir Michael Stoute) *mde all: rdn and qcknd wl over 1f out: styd on wl fnl f* **9/2**2
22 2 1½ **Dubawi Gulf**24 [4508] 2-9-0 0 TomQueally 2 76
(E A L Dunlop) *chsd wnr: rdn and tried to chal over 1f out: styd on same pce and btn ins fnl f* **4/7**1
3 2¾ **Menha** 2-9-0 0 AhmedAjtebi 3 69+
(Mahmood Al Zarooni) *trckd ldng pair: edging out rt ent fnl 2f: rdn and nt pce of ldng pair wl over 1f out: kpt on fnl f* **9/2**2
0 4 1¼ **Hello Tomorrow (USA)**22 [4595] 2-9-0 0 TedDurcan 5 66
(D R Lanigan) *chsd ldrs: rdn and outpcd by ldng pair over 1f out: styd on same pce fnl f* **33/1**
5 hd **Mazagee (FR)** 2-9-0 0 LiamKeniry 6 66+
(D R Lanigan) *stdd s: hld up in tch in last pair: rdn and outpcd ent fnl 2f: kpt on same pce and n.d after* **66/1**
6 1½ **Flying Arch (USA)** 2-9-0 0 KirstyMilczarek 8 62
(L M Cumani) *wnt rt s: t.k.h: hld up in tch in last pair: rdn and outpcd wl over 1f out: n.d after* **18/1**3

1m 30.48s (3.18) **Going Correction** +0.25s/f (Good) **6** Ran SP% **109.7**
Speed ratings (Par 91): **91,89,86,84,84 82**
toteswingers: 1&2 £1.02, 1&3 £2.60, 2&3 £1.20. CSF £7.14 TOTE £4.00: £2.40, £1.10; EX 3.80 Trifecta £14.30 Pool: £387.27 - 20.04 winning units..
Owner Cheveley Park Stud **Bred** Grangecon Stud **Trained** Newmarket, Suffolk

FOCUS
An interesting maiden, and fair form, but as is so often the case as Folkestone, the stands' rail looked advantageous.
NOTEBOOK
Apace(IRE) made all from stall one. She was turned over at odds of 8-13 in a 6f Polytrack maiden last time, but benefited from the step up in trip and showed a professional attitude. While she might be flattered, she's bred to be smart (cost 350,000gns) and there should be more to come. (op 7-2 tchd 11-2)
Dubawi Gulf was runner-up for the third race in succession, but she did nothing wrong, simply bumping into a useful type. Her action suggests she may prefer a faster surface and an ordinary race can come her way. (op 8-13 tchd 1-2)
Menha, out of a useful German performer, showed some knee action, so the rain-eased ground probably suited. Outpaced when first coming under pressure and not looking totally comfortable on the undulations, she made pleasing late progress. There should be improvement to come. (op 10-1)
Hello Tomorrow(USA) stepped up on the form she showed on debut, but was still well held. (op 16-1 tchd 14-1)
Mazagee(FR), a 65,000euros purchase, needed the experience. (op 40-1)
Flying Arch(USA), out of a 1m winner, raced wide without cover and didn't settle. She can leave this form behind. (op 14-1)

5325 HOBBS PARKER TELECOM (S) STKS 7f (S)
2:40 (2:42) (Class 6) 3-Y-O+ **£1,910** (£564; £282) **Stalls** Low

Form RPR
6641 1 **Fault**14 [4857] 4-9-10 68 (t) TomQueally 2 79
(Stef Higgins) *stdd s: hld up in rr: switching rt and hdwy 2f out: nt clr run and swtchd lft wl over 1f out: sn pushed along to chse ldr: led ins fnl f: sn clr: pushed out: comf* **4/1**3
6330 2 2½ **I Confess**32 [4260] 5-9-5 68 (b) RichardMullen 4 67
(Jim Best) *led tl over 5f out: chsd ldrs after: rdn and outpcd wl over 2f out: rallied and carried rt ent fnl f: styd on u.p to go 2nd nr fin: no ch w wnr* **7/4**1
6603 3 nk **Lodi (IRE)**15 [4836] 5-9-5 65 (tp) AdamKirby 9 66
(J Akehurst) *w ldrs: led and crossed to stands' rail over 5f out: pushed along and qcknd clr 3f out: rdn: edgd rt and flashed tail over 1f out: hdd ins fnl f: sn btn: lost 2nd nr fin* **10/3**2
3U0 4 1¾ **Landucci**27 [4427] 9-9-0 65 (p) SophieDoyle(5) 6 62
(S Curran) *stdd s: hld up in tch: effrt and rdn to chse ldng trio over 1f out: drvn and styd on same pce fnl f* **20/1**

The Form Book, Raceform Ltd, Compton, RG20 6NL

00-5 **5** 7 **Voortrekker**[20] 4660 4-9-5 65........(v[1]) TadhgO'Shea 3 43
(D J Coakley) *hld up in tch in rr: rdn and fnd little ent fnl 2f: no ch w ldrs whn hung lft fnl f* **11/1**

4520 **6** ½ **Safari Guide**[8] 5077 4-9-5 64........ LukeMorris 8 41
(P Winkworth) *taken down early: in tch: rdn and effrt 2f out: wknd u.p wl over 1f out: wl btn fnl f* **9/1**

0356 **7** 4½ **Lou Bear (IRE)**[10] 4994 3-9-0 52........(b[1]) LiamKeniry 1 27
(J Akehurst) *stdd s: t.k.h: hld up in rr: rdn and btn ent fnl 2f: sn wl bhd* **14/1**

00-0 **8** ¾ **Mumtaz Begum**[117] 1591 5-9-0 40........(v) KirstyMilczarek 7 22
(J E Long) *mostly chsd ldr tl wl over 1f out: sn wknd u.p: wl bhd fnl f* **100/1**

1m 29.93s (2.63) **Going Correction** +0.475s/f (Yiel)
WFA 3 from 4yo+ 5lb **8** Ran SP% **110.2**
Speed ratings (Par 101): **103,100,99,97,89 89,84,83**
toteswingers: 1&2 £1.40, 1&3 £2.70, 2&3 £1.70. CSF £10.52 TOTE £4.60: £1.20, £1.10, £1.10; EX 8.60 Trifecta £8.40 Pool: £345.46 - 30.34 winning units..There was no bid for the winner.
Owner David Gilbert **Bred** Mrs A M Vestey **Trained** Lambourn, Berks

FOCUS
After this contest the ground was changed to soft. They went a strong pace, with a few of these keen to get a position against the possibly favoured stands' rail.
Voortrekker Official explanation: jockey said gelding was unsuited by the ground; trainer confirmed this

5326 WIN A SHARE IN SUSPENDER BELT H'CAP 7f (S)
3:10 (3:11) (Class 6) (0-60,60) 3-Y-0+ **£2,047** (£604; £302) **Stalls** Low

Form RPR
0051 **1** **Foxtrot Alpha (IRE)**[11] 4959 4-9-4 **57**........ LukeMorris 3 67
(P Winkworth) *racd stands' side: mde all: rdn over 1f out: kpt on u.p fnl f: a hanging on* **11/4**[1]

0622 **2** hd **Hellbender (IRE)**[13] 4910 4-9-7 **60**........(t) LiamKeniry 2 69
(S Kirk) *racd stands' side: hld up wl in tch: drvn and effrt to chse wnr over 1f out: edgd rt ent fnl f: kpt on wl u.p and pressing wnr nr fin: a jst hld: 2nd of 8 in gp* **7/1**[3]

0000 **3** 1¾ **Resplendent Alpha**[12] 4936 6-8-13 **52**........ TomQueally 1 57
(P Howling) *racd stands' side: stdd s: hld up in tch in rr: rdn and hdwy wl over 1f out: chsd ldng pair jst ins fnl f: kpt on but nt pce to rch ldng pair: 3rd of 8 in gp* **12/1**

3453 **4** 2½ **Fathey (IRE)**[11] 4939 4-8-13 **55**........ MartinLane(3) 6 53
(C Smith) *chsd wnr: rdn over 2f out lost 2nd over 1f out: wknd fnl f: 4th of 8 in gp* **3/1**[2]

004 **5** 2½ **Lordsbury Pride (USA)**[99] 2121 3-8-11 **60**........ KierenFox(5) 12 49
(J R Best) *racd in far side pair: in tch overall: rdn and edgd lft wl over 1f out: wknd 1f out: 1st of 2 in gp* **20/1**

1000 **6** 1½ **Munich (IRE)**[18] 4700 6-9-5 **58**........ AdamKirby 9 45
(R Curtis) *racd stands' side: dwlt and early reminders: sn chsng ldrs: rdn ent fnl 3f: wknd u.p ent fnl f: 5th of 8 in gp* **12/1**

0363 **7** shd **Thoughtful (IRE)**[16] 4775 3-8-2 **46**........ DavidProbert 7 31
(J W Hills) *racd stands' side: hld up in tch in last trio: rdn and sme hdwy 3f out: wknd 2f out: wl btn fnl f: 6th of 8 in gp* **10/1**

-000 **8** nk **Croeso Ynol**[11] 4959 4-8-2 **46** oh1........(v[1]) JohnFahy(5) 5 32
(H J Evans) *racd stands' side: s.i.s: hld up in rr: rdn and effrt wl over 2f out: sn struggling: wl btn over 1f out: 7th of 8 in gp* **25/1**

0004 **9** nk **Ayam Zainah**[17] 4733 3-8-8 **52**........ TedDurcan 10 35
(M R Channon) *racd in far side pair: in tch overall: rdn ent fnl 2f: sn struggling: wl btn ent fnl f: 2nd of 2 in gp* **10/1**

3043 **10** 8 **Easy Wonder (GER)**[6] 5159 5-8-8 **47** oh1 ow1........ RichardMullen 4 11
(I A Wood) *racd stands' side: chsd ldrs tl lost pl u.p ent fnl 3f: wl bhd and eased ent fnl f: 8th of 8 in gp* **7/1**[3]

1m 30.2s (2.90) **Going Correction** +0.475s/f (Yiel)
WFA 3 from 4yo+ 5lb **10** Ran SP% **118.8**
Speed ratings (Par 101): **102,101,99,96,94 92,92,91,91,82**
toteswingers: 1&2 £3.20, 1&3 £11.70, 2&3 £11.20. CSF £23.06 CT £178.68 TOTE £3.50: £1.10, £2.30, £5.50 Trifecta £79.50 Pool: £150.49 - 1.40 winning units..
Owner Looks A Bright Prospect Racing & Partner **Bred** Irish National Stud **Trained** Chiddingfold, Surrey

FOCUS
The near-side rail was once again advantageous.

5327 HR GO RECRUITMENT - PASSIONATE ABOUT PEOPLE H'CAP 6f
3:40 (3:41) (Class 5) (0-75,75) 3-Y-0+ **£2,388** (£705; £352) **Stalls** Low

Form RPR
536U **1** **Liberty Lady (IRE)**[12] 4922 3-9-9 **75**........ DavidProbert 3 83
(D Donovan) *hld up in last pair: niggled along 1/2-way: rdn and hdwy wl over 1f out: swtchd rt and wnt between horses wl ins fnl f: edgd rt u.p but r.o wl to ld towards fin* **7/2**[1]

4432 **2** ½ **Silvee**[10] 5010 3-8-2 **54**........ NeilChalmers 6 60
(J J Bridger) *w ldr: rdn ent fnl 2f: edgd rt u.p and led wl ins fnl f: sn hdd and carried sltly rt: no ex towards fin* **6/1**

1251 **3** hd **Ace Of Spies (IRE)**[13] 4895 5-9-10 **73**........ ShaneKelly 7 78
(C R Dore) *sn pushed along to ld and cross to stands' rail: rdn 2f out: drvn and edgd rt fnl f: hdd and no ex wl ins fnl f* **9/2**[3]

0064 **4** 1¼ **Sweet Gale (IRE)**[27] 4424 6-8-11 **60**........ AndreaAtzeni 5 61
(Mike Murphy) *s.i.s: hld up in last pair: rdn and hdwy over 1f out: pressed ldrs ins fnl f tl wknd fnl 50yds* **5/1**

0266 **5** 4½ **Farmers Wish (IRE)**[12] 4922 3-9-4 **70**........(p) LiamKeniry 1 57
(J L Spearing) *chsd ldrs: rdn and no rspnse wl over 2f out: dropped to rr and wl btn wl over 1f out* **9/2**[3]

5005 **6** shd **Super Frank (IRE)**[5] 5175 7-8-6 **55**........ LukeMorris 4 42
(J Akehurst) *in tch in midfield: rdn to chse ldrs 1/2-way: wknd u.p over 1f out* **4/1**[2]

1m 15.01s (2.31) **Going Correction** +0.475s/f (Yiel)
WFA 3 from 4yo+ 3lb **6** Ran SP% **109.5**
Speed ratings (Par 103): **103,102,102,100,94 94**
toteswingers: 1&2 £20.50, 1&3 £3.90, 2&3 £1.30 CSF £22.93 CT £86.11 TOTE £6.70: £3.50, £3.00 Trifecta £156.00 Part won. Pool: £210.83 - 0.50 winning units..
Owner Mark Jones **Bred** Chris Giblett **Trained** Newmarket, Suffolk

FOCUS
A competitive handicap despite the small field, but the form looks limited. The near rail was again a help.
Ace Of Spies(IRE) Official explanation: jockey said gelding hung right

5328 CHURCH & DWIGHT EMPLOYEE SUGGESTION SCHEME MEDIAN AUCTION MAIDEN STKS 5f
4:10 (4:16) (Class 6) 2-Y-0 **£2,217** (£654; £327) **Stalls** Low

Form RPR
423 **1** **Cocohatchee**[9] 5033 2-9-3 77........ ShaneKelly 10 74
(P M Phelan) *chsd ldr: rdn and ev ch 2f out: led and hung lft u.p jst ins fnl f: kpt on wl fnl 100yds* **7/4**[1]

4 **2** ½ **Cristaliyev**[11] 4960 2-9-3 0........ TomQueally 3 72
(J R Boyle) *chsd ldng pair: rdn along and sltly outpcd wl over 2f out: swtchd rt and hdwy over 1f out: ev ch ins fnl f: no ex fnl 75yds* **2/1**[2]

3 1 **Whitstable Native** 2-8-12 0........ KierenFox(5) 8 69+
(J R Best) *s.i.s and hmpd s: wl bhd: sme hdwy 2f out: rdn and r.o wl fr over 1f out: wnt 3rd wl ins fnl f: gng on wl at fin* **9/1**

04 **4** 4½ **King Cobra (IRE)**[27] 4423 2-9-3 0........ SimonWhitworth 6 52
(J W Hills) *wnt rt s: sn outpcd in last trio: rdn and styd on fr over 1f out: swtchd rt ins fnl f: kpt on to go 4th nr fin: nvr trbld ldrs* **20/1**

00 **5** nk **Silver Angel (IRE)**[7] 5117 2-8-12 0........ TedDurcan 1 46
(M R Channon) *chsd ldng trio: rdn and struggling 3f out: kpt on same pce fnl 2f: wl hld whn hung rt ins fnl f* **13/2**[3]

0204 **6** shd **Welsh Inlet (IRE)**[12] 4927 2-8-12 69........ WilliamCarson 5 49
(S C Williams) *hung rt thrght: broke fast and led: jnd and hanging 2f out: hdd jst ins fnl f: sn short of room and hmpd: hung bdly rt and fdd fnl 100yds* **7/1**

7 11 **Soviet Suspect (IRE)** 2-8-10 0........ LauraPike(7) 9 11
(Miss Amy Weaver) *a wl outpcd in last* **25/1**

62.91 secs (2.91) **Going Correction** +0.475s/f (Yiel) **7** Ran SP% **114.1**
Speed ratings (Par 92): **95,94,92,85,84 84,67**
toteswingers: 1&2 £2.00, 1&3 £4.30, 2&3 £3.90. CSF £5.48 TOTE £2.20: £1.20, £1.70; EX 5.60 Trifecta £30.40 Pool: £445.93 - 10.85 winning units..
Owner John James (Cranborne) **Bred** Henry And Mrs Rosemary Moszkowicz **Trained** Epsom, Surrey

FOCUS
An ordinary juvenile maiden.

NOTEBOOK
Cocohatchee proved suited by the drop in trip from 7f, with the easy ground probably helping, and did well to overcome the outside stall. He hung left on to the stands' rail in the closing stages, but was always doing enough. His main target is a sales race at Doncaster on September 9. (tchd 11-8)
Cristaliyev confirmed the promise he showed on debut over this trip at Sandown, but probably needs another furlong. (op 11-4)
Whitstable Native raced out the back for much of the way following a slow start, but he made encouraging late headway. This should sharpen him up a good deal. (op 13-2)
King Cobra(IRE) clearly needs further and will be a different proposition when upped in trip and sent handicapping. (op 16-1 tchd 22-1)
Silver Angel(IRE) is another who may need further and she's now eligible for a mark. (op 16-1)
Welsh Inlet(IRE), for the third race in succession, hung right. She was in trouble when short of room inside the final furlong. (op 5-1)

5329 EUROPEAN BREEDERS' FUND FILLIES' H'CAP 1m 1f 149y
4:40 (4:40) (Class 3) (0-90,87) 3-Y-0+ **£7,123** (£2,119; £1,059; £529) **Stalls** Centre

Form RPR
-521 **1** **Fastback (IRE)**[38] 4046 4-9-9 **76**........ JimCrowley 2 86
(R M Beckett) *sn pressing ldr: pushed ahd ent fnl 2f: rdn clr wl over 1f out: edgd rt u.p fnl f: kpt on wl* **9/4**[2]

-432 **2** 1½ **Nafura**[61] 3298 3-9-12 **87**........(v) TedDurcan 7 94
(Saeed Bin Suroor) *led: hdd jst over 2f out: rdn and nt pce of wnr wl over 1f out: plugging on u.p whn nt clr run and swtchd lft ins fnl f: no imp* **15/8**[1]

0122 **3** 2¼ **Anacopa (USA)**[8] 5096 3-9-3 **85**........ AntiocoMurgia(7) 1 87
(Mahmood Al Zarooni) *stdd s: hld up in last: hdwy to trck ldng pair 2f out: rdn and fnd little over 1f out: btn and edgd rt ins fnl f* **3/1**[3]

031 **4** 6 **Ishraaqat**[28] 4397 3-9-2 **77**........ TadhgO'Shea 4 67
(M P Tregoning) *chsd ldng pair: rdn and hanging rt 2f out: sn btn* **9/2**

2m 9.52s (4.62) **Going Correction** +0.575s/f (Yiel)
WFA 3 from 4yo+ 8lb **4** Ran SP% **108.7**
Speed ratings (Par 104): **104,102,101,96**
toteswinger: 1&2 £1.60. CSF £6.82 TOTE £3.70; EX 7.90.
Owner Mrs R J Jacobs **Bred** Newsells Park Stud Limited **Trained** Whitsbury, Hants

FOCUS
Only four runners and it paid to race handy.

NOTEBOOK
Fastback(IRE), a winner on really firm ground at Bath last time, had no trouble with these vastly different conditions and defied a 2lb rise in convincing fashion. Although she only defeated three rivals, the form is still reasonable. However, she's said to be in foal, so it remains to be seen just how much more we see of her. (tchd 11-4)
Nafura, returning from two months off, ran her usual sort of race, looking set to finish well held when coming off the bridle, only to run on again all too late. This idle filly surely needs a more aggressive ride, or maybe she'll be worth a shot at 1m4f. (op 2-1 tchd 6-4)
Anacopa(USA) once again travelled well before finding little off the bridle. Out of a Green Desert mare, this trip seems to be stretching her, even though she managed to win a maiden over the distance. (op 4-1)
Ishraaqat, a winner over quick ground over 1m on her previous start, was the first one beaten. (op 3-1)

5330 STAR SPORTS WELCOME VICKERS CLIENTS H'CAP 1m 4f
5:10 (5:10) (Class 6) (0-65,65) 3-Y-0 **£2,047** (£604; £302) **Stalls** Low

Form RPR
0422 **1** **Now What**[21] 4626 3-9-5 **63**........ JimCrowley 5 70
(J G Portman) *chsd ldrs: hdwy to press ldr gng wl over 2f out: rdn to ld 2f out: drvn and kpt on wl fnl f* **11/4**[2]

5044 **2** 3½ **Thundering Home**[4] 5208 3-9-3 **61**........ ShaneKelly 4 62
(M J Attwater) *hld up in tch in rr: hdwy to trck ldrs over 2f out: rdn to chse wnr over 1f out: hung rt u.p jst ins fnl f: no prog and wl hld fnl 100yds* **11/2**

6532 **3** 2¾ **Rose Aurora**[17] 4746 3-8-6 **50**........ HayleyTurner 2 47
(M P Tregoning) *hld up in last pair: hdwy to chse ldrs over 2f out: rdn and hung rt 2f out: sn no prog and btn over 1f out: plugged on fnl f to go 3rd nr fin* **7/4**[1]

000 **4** hd **Jovial (IRE)**[27] 4425 3-8-8 **52**........ TadhgO'Shea 3 48
(D J Coakley) *w ldr tl led 3f out: sn rdn: hdd 2f out: wknd u.p over 1f out* **9/2**[3]

P-64 **5** 15 **Roar Talent (USA)**[15] 4840 3-9-2 **65**........ KierenFox(5) 6 37
(J R Best) *led tl rdn and hdd 3f out: lost pl over 2f out: wl btn fnl 2f* **14/1**

-104 **6** *1 ½* **Nom De La Rosa (IRE)**[17] 4746 3-9-0 58........................(p) LiamKeniry 7 28
(Miss Sheena West) *chsd ldrs: rdn 4f out: lost pl qckly and dropped to rr 3f out: sn lost tch* **12/1**

0000 **7** *51* **Farmer Palmer**[34] 4200 3-8-2 46 oh1..........................(b[1]) AndreaAtzeni 1 —
(Louise Best) *chsd ldrs tl rn wd bnd and dropped to last after over 9f out: rn in snatches after: lost tch 3f out: virtually p.u fnl 2f: t.o* **22/1**

2m 48.11s (7.21) **Going Correction** +0.575s/f (Yiel) 7 Ran SP% **115.3**
Speed ratings (Par 98): **98,95,93,93,83 82,48**
toteswingers: 1&2 £3.40, 1&3 £1.30, 2&3 £2.20. CSF £18.53 CT £32.73 TOTE £3.70: £2.00, £2.80; EX 14.50 Trifecta £21.20 Pool: £256.74 - 8.95 winning units. Place 6: £25.72, Place 5: £19.89..
Owner Mrs D Joly **Bred** Mrs D O Joly **Trained** Compton, Berks

FOCUS
A moderate contest run at a reasonable gallop.
Nom De La Rosa(IRE) Official explanation: jockey said filly was unsuited by the ground; confimed by the trainer
T/Plt: £15.90 to a £1 stake. Pool:£65,776.30 - 3,015.66 winning tickets T/Qpdt: £16.00 to a £1 stake. Pool:£3,711.42 - 171.20 winning tickets SP

5239 MUSSELBURGH (R-H)
Sunday, August 22

OFFICIAL GOING: Good (6.5)
Wind: Fairly strong, half against Weather: Sunny

5331 RACING UK APPRENTICE H'CAP 1m
2:20 (2:20) (Class 6) (0-60,59) 4-Y-0+ **£1,942** (£578; £288; £144) **Stalls** High

Form RPR

3650 **1** **Cold Quest (USA)**[34] 4188 6-8-4 47.................................. BillyCray(3) 13 56
(Miss L A Perratt) *prom: lost pl after 3f: rallied over 2f out: led ent fnl f: kpt on strly* **16/1**

0-00 **2** *2* **Second Reef**[20] 4644 8-8-0 45.. SoniaEaton(5) 2 49
(T A K Cuthbert) *cl up: effrt and ev ch over 1f out: edgd lft ins fnl f: r.o: nt rch wnr* **66/1**

4044 **3** *½* **Chichen Daawe**[65] 3147 4-8-7 52 ow4.............................. DaleSwift(5) 11 55
(B Ellison) *in tch: effrt over 2f out: swtchd lft and styd on fnl f: no imp* **4/1[2]**

0406 **4** *1* **Fortunate Bid (IRE)**[13] 4897 4-9-0 54......................(p) JamesSullivan 12 55
(Mrs L Stubbs) *bhd tl hdwy 2f out: kpt on fnl f: nvr able to chal* **8/1**

-005 **5** *nk* **Broughtons Silk**[15] 4820 5-8-5 45.............................. AndrewHeffernan 3 45
(A C Whillans) *led: rdn over 2f out: hdd ent fnl f: no ex* **25/1**

4554 **6** *2 ¼* **Northern Flyer (GER)**[9] 5024 4-8-13 56......................(v) IanBrennan(3) 9 51
(J J Quinn) *trckd ldrs: effrt over 1f out: edgd rt: wknd ins fnl f* **5/2[1]**

0002 **7** *2 ½* **Cherri Fosfate**[6] 5155 6-9-0 59.. NeilFarley(5) 5 48
(D Carroll) *bhd on outside: rdn over 2f out: sn no imp* **8/1**

6-64 **8** *hd* **Bourse (IRE)**[15] 4824 5-8-0 45.................................... NathanAlison(5) 7 34
(A G Foster) *towards rr: rdn over 2f out: nvr able to chal* **5/1[3]**

6600 **9** *3* **Blue Charm**[11] 4939 6-9-0 57.......................................(v[1]) LanceBetts(3) 14 39
(I W McInnes) *s.s: bhd on ins: rdn over 3f out: nvr on terms* **10/1**

0303 **10** *1 ¼* **Barraland**[15] 4822 5-8-8 51.. DeanHeslop(3) 10 30
(J S Goldie) *towards rr on ins: pushed along over 3f out: nvr on terms* **16/1**

6000 **11** *3* **Officer Mor (USA)**[10] 4986 4-7-12 45............................ ShaneBKelly(7) 4 17
(Mrs Dianne Sayer) *s.i.s: plld hrd and sn midfield: rdn and wknd over 2f out* **40/1**

0000 **12** *11* **Ensign's Trick**[22] 4606 6-8-5 45.. PaulPickard 8 —
(W M Brisbourne) *prom tl rdn and wknd fr 3f out* **66/1**

1m 41.29s (0.09) **Going Correction** +0.05s/f (Good) 12 Ran SP% **117.6**
Speed ratings (Par 101): **101,99,98,97,97 94,92,92,89,88 85,74**
toteswingers: 1&2 £82.70, 1&3 £15.40, 2&3 £60.60. CSF £807.51 CT £5030.77 TOTE £21.30: £6.30, £20.50, £2.10; EX 812.10.
Owner Ken McGarrity **Bred** Carwell Equities Ltd **Trained** East Kilbride, South Lanarks

Cherri Fosfate Official explanation: jockey said gelding stumbled shortly after the start and lost an iron
Bourse(IRE) Official explanation: jockey said saddle slipped
Ensign's Trick Official explanation: jockey said saddle slipped

5332 RACING UK IN YOUR HOME MAIDEN AUCTION STKS 7f 30y
2:50 (2:50) (Class 6) 2-Y-0 **£1,942** (£578; £288; £144) **Stalls** High

Form RPR

0 **1** **Fairlie Dinkum**[29] 4368 2-8-5 0.. GregFairley 3 71+
(B Smart) *t.k.h: trckd ldr: rdn to ld over 2f out: carried hd high and edgd rt over 1f out: pushed out fnl f* **8/1**

022 **2** *1 ½* **Janet's Pearl (IRE)**[19] 4668 2-8-4 71 ow2.................. BarryMcHugh(3) 6 67
(Mrs A Duffield) *cl up: effrt and chsd wnr over 1f out: edgd rt: kpt on ins fnl f* **11/10[1]**

30 **3** *6* **Good Boy Jackson**[19] 4682 2-8-9 0.............................. PaulHanagan 4 54
(K A Ryan) *t.k.h: trckd ldrs: rdn and outpcd 2f out: no imp after* **11/4[2]**

00 **4** *¾* **Arashone**[20] 4645 2-8-4 0.. DuranFentiman 1 47
(J R Weymes) *led to over 2f out: rdn and wknd over 1f out* **80/1**

5 *nse* **History Girl (IRE)** 2-8-7 0.. JoeFanning 2 50
(M Johnston) *slowly away: bhd: hdwy on outside over 2f out: sn no imp* **7/1[3]**

40 **6** *¾* **Purkab**[18] 4702 2-8-12 0.. LNewman 5 53
(J S Goldie) *chsd ldng gp: rdn over 2f out: nvr able to chal* **20/1**

030 **7** *10* **Princess Izzy**[33] 4233 2-8-9 64.. LeeVickers 7 25
(P A Kirby) *hld up on ins: drvn over 2f out: edgd rt and sn wknd* **20/1**

1m 30.75s (1.75) **Going Correction** +0.05s/f (Good) 7 Ran SP% **108.7**
Speed ratings (Par 92): **92,90,83,82,82 81,70**
toteswingers: 1&2 £2.70, 1&3 £2.80, 2&3 £1.80. CSF £15.65 TOTE £11.40: £5.80, £1.10; EX 18.30.
Owner Minster Horseboxes **Bred** Lesley Winn And Reveley Farms **Trained** Hambleton, N Yorks

FOCUS
A moderate maiden.

NOTEBOOK
Fairlie Dinkum, never involved at Newcastle on debut, had clearly learned a lot and, despite displaying a fairly awkward head carriage, she kept on well for pressure to score. A step up to 1m shouldn't be a problem and she remains capable of better in nurseries. (tchd 15-2)
Janet's Pearl(IRE) has now finished runner-up on three straight occasions. Not helped by her rider putting up 3lb overweight, was ridden quite as aggressively as last time and, although keeping on well, she never looked like reaching the winner. (op 6-4 tchd Evens)
Good Boy Jackson, ineffective on Fibresand latest, ran much better and should find easier opportunities in nurseries. (op 3-1 tchd 10-3)
Arashone made the early running and improved markedly on what she had previously achieved.
History Girl(IRE), half-sister to a couple of middle-distance winners, was very slow to break and made enough late headway to suggest she has a future over further. (op 5-1)

5333 DAILY RECORD H'CAP 1m 6f
3:20 (3:20) (Class 5) (0-75,74) 3-Y-0+ **£3,238** (£963; £481; £240) **Stalls** High

Form RPR

4401 **1** **Cat O' Nine Tails**[23] 4557 3-8-13 67.................................. JoeFanning 5 74
(M Johnston) *chsd ldr: rn wd bnd ent st: sn rdn: effrt over 2f out: led ins fnl f: edgd lft: styd on wl* **4/1[3]**

334 **2** *¾* **Ahmedy (IRE)**[72] 2941 7-9-9 70.................................. IanBrennan(5) 4 76
(J J Quinn) *prom: effrt over 2f out: pressed wnr ins fnl f: r.o: hld towards fin* **11/4[1]**

1223 **3** *2* **Park's Prodigy**[11] 4946 6-9-9 65.................................. PaulHanagan 1 68
(G A Harker) *trckd ldrs: carried wd bnd ent st: led over 2f out: edgd rt and hdd ins fnl f: no ex* **3/1[2]**

0-04 **4** *6* **Yossi (IRE)**[13] 4907 6-9-12 68...................................(p) PhillipMakin 2 63
(R C Guest) *hld up: effrt over 2f out: plugged on fnl f: nvr able to chal* **16/1**

5014 **5** *½* **Gulf Coast**[20] 4648 5-9-3 59......................................(p) DuranFentiman 3 53
(T D Walford) *hld up in tch: drvn and outpcd 3f out: n.d after* **12/1**

0224 **6** *4 ½* **Cloudy City (USA)**[39] 4026 3-9-6 74..............................(b[1]) GregFairley 7 62
(M Johnston) *t.k.h: led: rdn: hung rt and hdd over 2f out: wknd over 1f out* **4/1[3]**

364 **7** *17* **Valdan (IRE)**[44] 3860 6-9-8 67................................(t) AndrewHeffernan(3) 6 31
(M A Barnes) *plld hrd: hld up: rdn over 2f out: sn struggling: t.o* **9/1**

3m 3.83s (-1.47) **Going Correction** +0.05s/f (Good)
WFA 3 from 5yo+ 12lb 7 Ran SP% **115.2**
Speed ratings (Par 103): **106,105,104,101,100 98,88**
toteswingers: 1&2 £3.50, 1&3 £2.30, 2&3 £2.50. CSF £15.70 TOTE £6.60: £2.60, £2.90; EX 21.70.
Owner S And D Richards, N Browne And M Broke **Bred** The Duke Of Devonshire & Floors Farming **Trained** Middleham Moor, N Yorks

FOCUS
An ordinary staying handicap.

5334 EVENT-A-LOO LTD (S) STKS 5f
3:50 (3:51) (Class 6) 2-Y-0 **£1,942** (£578; £288; £144) **Stalls** Low

Form RPR

3236 **1** **Upark Flyer**[10] 5000 2-8-1 65.. IanBrennan(5) 3 63
(Patrick Morris) *s.i.s: sn prom: effrt over 1f out: led ins fnl f: edgd rt: hld on wl* **4/1[3]**

4033 **2** *¾* **Misscomplacent**[10] 4981 2-8-6 65................................(v) PaulHanagan 1 60
(Mrs A Duffield) *led to over 1f out: sn outpcd: r.o fnl f to take 2nd cl home: nt rch wnr* **9/4[2]**

2133 **3** *shd* **Madam Markievicz (IRE)**[36] 4124 2-8-12 72..............(p) PhillipMakin 2 66
(M Dods) *w ldr: led over 1f out: rdn and hdd ins fnl f: fnd little: lost 2nd cl home* **2/1[1]**

430 **4** *4 ½* **Glenns Princess**[20] 4645 2-8-5 65 ow2.......................... BarryMcHugh(3) 4 46
(R A Fahey) *prom: drvn and outpcd 2f out: no imp fnl f* **5/1**

2053 **5** *nse* **Reel Amber**[9] 5042 2-8-6 53......................................(b) DavidAllan 5 44
(T D Easterby) *hld up in tch: drvn and outpcd 1/2-way: n.d after* **16/1**

6 *2 ¼* **Katiesister** 2-8-3 0.. JamesSullivan(3) 7 35
(J S Goldie) *sn outpcd and wl bhd: sme late hdwy: nvr on terms* **18/1**

62.52 secs (2.12) **Going Correction** +0.275s/f (Good) 6 Ran SP% **111.9**
Speed ratings (Par 92): **94,92,92,85,85 81**
toteswingers: 1&2 £2.10, 1&3 £1.10, 1&3 £2.10. CSF £13.35 TOTE £4.90: £1.90, £4.00; EX 16.30.There was no bid for the winner.
Owner Mrs Helen Jane Lloyd **Bred** Mrs D O Joly **Trained** Tarporley, Cheshire

FOCUS
A modest juvenile seller.

NOTEBOOK
Upark Flyer, ridden too far out of her ground in a nursery at Goodwood latest, looked a big player down to this level for the first time and she battled on well to register her first success. She remains capable of better back in nurseries. (tchd 9-2)
Misscomplacent has shown improved form the last twice and again ran well dropped to this level for the first time. (op 7-2)
Madam Markievicz(IRE), already a winner at this level, was conceding weight all round, but she's run well in nurseries the last twice and looked the one to beat. She didn't find for pressure, though, and was run out of it inside the final furlong. (op 13-8)
Glenns Princess, whose rider was putting up 2lb overweight, proved a little disappointing on this drop in grade. (tchd 6-1)

5335 TOTEEXACTA H'CAP 5f
4:20 (4:21) (Class 3) (0-90,89) 3-Y-0+
£6,231 (£1,866; £933; £467; £233; £117) **Stalls** Low

Form RPR

0010 **1** **Rasaman (IRE)**[5] 5183 6-9-4 85.................................. GaryBartley(3) 3 96
(J S Goldie) *bhd and sn pushed along: gd hdwy over 1f out: swtchd rt and qcknd to ld ins fnl f: comf* **4/1[2]**

0-00 **2** *2 ¼* **Titus Andronicus (IRE)**[11] 4942 4-9-2 80.......................... PaulHanagan 4 86+
(R A Fahey) *trckd ldrs: effrt whn nt clr run over 1f out to ins fnl f: r.o wl to take 2nd towards fin: nt rch wnr* **7/1[3]**

0303 **3** *½* **The Nifty Fox**[8] 5069 6-9-7 85.. DavidAllan 5 86
(T D Easterby) *hld up in tch: smooth hdwy over 1f out: ev ch and rdn ent fnl f: kpt on same pce* **2/1[1]**

6152 **4** *nk* **The Bear**[4] 5198 7-8-8 72.. PJMcDonald 8 72
(Miss L A Perratt) *dwlt: sn chsng ldrs: effrt and led briefly ent fnl f: kpt on same pce* **7/1[3]**

1501 **5** *2 ¼* **Lesley's Choice**[4] 5212 4-9-0 78 6ex..........................(b) LNewman 6 70
(Miss L A Perratt) *cl up: drvn over 2f out: kpt on same pce fnl f* **7/1[3]**

0536 **6** *1 ¼* **Jargelle (IRE)**[65] 3165 4-9-11 89.................................. AdrianNicholls 9 76
(D Nicholls) *w ldr: led and edgd lft over 1f out: wknd ins fnl f* **12/1**

4-36 **7** *½* **Eternal Instinct**[22] 4583 3-8-5 74.............................. JamesSullivan(3) 2 60
(J S Goldie) *bhd and outpcd: hdwy and edgd rt over 1f out: nvr able to chal* **25/1**

040- **8** *½* **Sloop Johnb**[387] 4490 4-8-12 79.............................. BarryMcHugh(3) 1 63
(R A Fahey) *in tch tl rdn and wknd wl over 1f out* **16/1**

3103 **9** *½* **Ignatieff (IRE)**[13] 4901 3-9-0 80.............................. DuranFentiman 10 62
(Mrs L Stubbs) *led tl rdn and hdd over 1f out: sn wknd* **18/1**

6240 **10** *3 ¼* **Living It Large (FR)**[23] 4541 3-9-8 88.............................. TomEaves 11 58
(R F Fisher) *chsd ldng gp on outside: struggling over 2f out: sn wknd* **25/1**

60.84 secs (0.44) **Going Correction** +0.275s/f (Good)
WFA 3 from 4yo+ 2lb 10 Ran SP% **117.4**
Speed ratings (Par 107): **107,103,102,102,98 96,95,94,94,88**
toteswingers: 1&2 £6.40, 1&3 £3.10, 1&3 £4.60. CSF £32.48 CT £70.54 TOTE £5.50: £1.60, £3.50, £1.02; EX 52.20.

Owner Paul Moulton **Bred** Rasana Partnership **Trained** Uplawmoor, E Renfrews

FOCUS
A competitive handicap sprint.

NOTEBOOK
Rasaman(IRE), who got going too late when also hampered at York just five days earlier, had earlier won over C&D off 3lb lower and, despite still being at the back of the field and ridden with 2f to run, he produced a powerful burst once switched right and ended up winning with a bit to spare. He's clearly in top form at present. (op 5-1)
Titus Andronicus(IRE) ◆ ran easily his most encouraging race of the season so far, keeping on well for second having briefly been denied a clear run. He's not at all badly weighted and could soon be back winning. (op 8-1 tchd 9-1 in a place)
The Nifty Fox travelled well and had his chance, but couldn't match the winners burst. (tchd 9-4 in a place)
The Bear has been running well, winning over C&D last month, but he couldn't lead after missing the start, and was always being held. (op 6-1)
Lesley's Choice, narrow winner of a Hamilton claimer four days earlier, faced a stiffer task here under the 6lb penalty and wasn't up to it. (op 17-2)
Jargelle(IRE) Official explanation: jockey said filly hung left throughout

5336 SCOTTISH RACING H'CAP — 1m 4f 100y
4:50 (4:50) (Class 6) (0-65,64) 3-Y-O+ — **£2,590** (£770; £385; £192) **Stalls** High

Form / RPR

4052 **1** **Miss Ferney**[15] 4854 6-8-13 **52** ... PaulPickard(3) 6 — 65
(A Kirtley) *t.k.h: hld up: hdwy over 2f out: rdn to ld ins fnl f: sn clr: eased nr fin* **11/4**[2]

5106 **2** *5* **Balwearie (IRE)**[11] 4953 9-9-5 **55** ... LNewman 1 — 60
(Miss L A Perratt) *trckd ldrs: rdn to ld over 2f out: clr whn edgd rt over 1f out: hdd ins fnl f: no ch w wnr* **8/1**

5201 **3** *2* **Golden Future**[16] 4800 7-9-6 **56** ... PaulHanagan 9 — 58
(P D Niven) *trckd ldrs: rdn over 3f out: kpt on same pce fnl 2f* **11/8**[1]

2060 **4** *¾* **Oddsmaker (IRE)**[83] 2579 9-9-9 **62** ...(t) AndrewHeffernan(3) 2 — 63
(M A Barnes) *cl up: led after 4f to over 2f out: wknd over 1f out* **8/1**

0500 **5** *11* **Acol**[11] 4951 3-7-12 **47** ow2 ... JamesSullivan(3) 4 — 30
(A G Foster) *hld up in tch: rdn over 3f out: shortlived effrt over 2f out: sn edgd rt and wknd* **28/1**

600 **6** *23* **Barra Raider**[28] 4407 3-8-9 **55** ... TomEaves 5 — —
(R F Fisher) *hld up in tch: struggling over 3f out: t.o* **20/1**

1/04 **7** *4 ½* **Banquet (IRE)**[11] 4946 5-9-4 **54** ...(b) DuranFentiman 8 — —
(T D Walford) *led 4f: cl up: rdn over 4f out: sn struggling: t.o* **15/2**[3]

2m 42.48s (0.48) **Going Correction** +0.05s/f (Good)
WFA 3 from 4yo+ 10lb — **7 Ran SP% 111.0**
Speed ratings (Par 101): **100,96,95,94,87 72,69**
toteswingers: 1&2 £4.30, 1&3 £1.20, 2&3 £3.50. CSF £23.03 CT £39.06 TOTE £3.50: £2.20, £3.00; EX 27.50.
Owner Mrs P J Taylor-Garthwaite **Bred** K And P J Garthwaite **Trained** West Auckland, Co Durham

FOCUS
A very moderate middle-distance handicap and there was an easy winner.
Banquet(IRE) Official explanation: trainer had no explanation for the poor form shown

5337 TURFTV H'CAP — 1m
5:20 (5:22) (Class 5) (0-70,68) 3-Y-O — **£3,238** (£963; £481; £240) **Stalls** High

Form / RPR

5543 **1** **Military Call**[4] 5201 3-8-6 **58** ...(p) IanBrennan(5) 5 — 64
(A C Whillans) *t.k.h early: hld up in tch: hdwy on outside 2f out: styd on fnl f to ld nr fin* **5/1**

0012 **2** *hd* **Madame Excelerate**[4] 5201 3-9-3 **64** ... TomEaves 3 — 70
(W M Brisbourne) *led: rdn over 2f out: hung lft ins fnl f: hdd nr fin* **7/4**[1]

6445 **3** *2 ¼* **Coolella (IRE)**[20] 4649 3-8-2 **52** ... JamesSullivan(3) 7 — 53
(J R Weymes) *trckd ldrs: effrt and rdn wl over 1f out: nt qckn fnl f* **11/1**

445 **4** *¾* **Spread Boy (IRE)**[30] 4340 3-9-4 **65** ... PhillipMakin 4 — 64
(A Berry) *dwlt: hld up: hdwy on ins 2f out: kpt on fnl f: nrst fin* **25/1**

0233 **5** *1* **North Central (USA)**[11] 4951 3-9-4 **65** ... PaulHanagan 1 — 62
(J S Goldie) *t.k.h early: chsd ldrs: effrt over 2f out: no ex fnl f* **4/1**[2]

335 **6** *10* **Shethoughtshewas (IRE)**[22] 4601 3-9-6 **67** ... PJMcDonald 8 — 41
(G A Swinbank) *dwlt: in tch on ins: drvn and outpcd over 2f out: sn btn* **9/2**[3]

000 **7** *2 ¾* **Royal Holiday (IRE)**[29] 4374 3-8-6 **53** ow1 ...(b[1]) DavidAllan 6 — 20
(B Ellison) *s.i.s: hld up in tch: struggling over 2f out: sn btn* **15/2**

420- **8** *46* **Brisbane (IRE)**[434] 2940 3-9-7 **68** ... DuranFentiman 2 — —
(Mrs Dianne Sayer) *plld hrd: cl up tl wknd over 2f out: t.o* **40/1**

1m 41.79s (0.59) **Going Correction** +0.05s/f (Good) — **8 Ran SP% 117.6**
Speed ratings (Par 100): **99,98,96,95,94 84,82,36**
toteswingers: 1&2 £2.30, 1&3 £8.30, 2&3 £6.20. totesuper7: Win: Not won. Place: £939.10 CSF £14.64 CT £93.74 TOTE £5.40: £1.20, £1.20, £3.60; EX 16.90 Place 6: £86.85, Place 5: £22.58..

Owner Play Fair Partnership **Bred** Southill Stud **Trained** Newmill-On-Slitrig, Borders

FOCUS
A moderate handicap which saw the first pair come clear.
T/Plt: £292.80 to a £1 stake. Pool: £54,112.01 - 134.88 winning tickets T/Qpdt: £25.90 to a £1 stake. Pool: £4,289.04 - 122.50 winning tickets RY

5338 - 5344a (Foreign Racing) - See Raceform Interactive

BREMEN
Sunday, August 22

OFFICIAL GOING: Turf: good

5345a WALTHER J JACOBS-STUTENPREIS (GROUP 3) (3YO+ FILLIES & MARES) (TURF) — 1m 3f
4:10 (12:00) 3-Y-O+
£28,318 (£9,734; £4,867; £2,654; £1,769; £1,327)

RPR

1 *nk* **Ovambo Queen (GER)**[42] 3943 3-8-10 0 ... HenkGrewe 3 — 102
(Dr A Bolte, Germany) *broke wl: settled in 4th: mde move in st: chal strly: r.o wl u.p: locked in battle fnl 1 1/2f and bmpd: fin 2nd: awrdd r* **63/10**[3]

2 **Superstition (FR)**[28] 4-9-5 0 ... AHelfenbein 6 — 103
(A De Royer-Dupre, France) *racd in 2nd: swift prog to ld early in st: led 1 1/2f out: wandered off st line: bmpd runner-up: r.o wl to win: fin 1st: disqualified for interference: plcd 2nd* **43/10**[2]

3 *1 ¼* **Tech Exceed (GER)**[21] 4640 3-8-10 0 ... EPedroza 1 — 100
(A Wohler, Germany) *racd in 3rd: qcknd early in st: r.o wl wout threatening ldrs* **2/1**[1]

4 *3* **Nianga (GER)**[21] 4640 3-8-10 0 ... AStarke 10 — 95
(P Schiergen, Germany) *bkmarker fr s: mde gd prog towards end of bk st: threatened briefly early in st: no ex* **107/10**

5 *1 ¾* **Amare**[21] 4640 3-8-10 0 ... EFrank 4 — 91
(T Mundry, Germany) *settled in midfield: nvr figured in st* **32/5**

6 *½* **Ephigenie (IRE)**[14] 4-9-5 0 ... ManuelaMurke 9 — 91
(T Mundry, Germany) *racd in midfield: nvr threatened in st* **26/1**

7 *1 ¼* **Serienhoehe (IRE)**[36] 4-9-5 0 ... AGoritz 2 — 88
(P Schiergen, Germany) *racd in 5th: qcknd wl early in st: sn fdd* **39/1**

8 *nk* **Lunduv (IRE)**[98] 2155 5-9-5 0 ... AndreBest 7 — 88
(C Von Der Recke, Germany) *led tl into st: sn btn* **42/1**

9 *8* **That's Me (GER)**[372] 7-9-5 0 ... JLinek 8 — 73
(Jozef Roszival, Hungary) *in rr: nvr figured* **65/1**

10 *10* **Kalla**[343] 5929 4-9-5 0 ... ADeVries 5 — 55
(J Hirschberger, Germany) *settled in midfield: mde move ent st: qcknd wl but v qckly wknd and dropped away* **2/1**[1]

2m 18.52s (138.52)
WFA 3 from 4yo+ 9lb — **10 Ran SP% 131.3**
WIN (incl. 10 euro stake): 73. PLACES: 14, 14, 13. SF: 467..
Owner Dr H H Leimbach **Bred** Gestut Rietberg **Trained** Germany

5322 DEAUVILLE (R-H)
Sunday, August 22

OFFICIAL GOING: Turf: good; fibresand: standard

5346a DARLEY PRIX DE LA NONETTE (GROUP 3) (3YO FILLIES) (TURF) — 1m 2f
1:35 (12:00) 3-Y-O — **£35,398** (£14,159; £10,619; £7,079; £3,539)

RPR

1 **Lily Of The Valley (FR)**[49] 3720 3-9-0 0 ... ChristopheSoumillon 5 — 111
(J-C Rouget, France) *settled in 3rd: travelling easily ent fnl f: qcknd wl u.p 100yds out: got up on line* **7/4**[1]

2 *hd* **Contredanse (IRE)**[22] 4575 3-9-0 0 ... KierenFallon 1 — 111
(L M Cumani) *broke wl to ld: rdn 1 1/f out: qcknd wl: r.o strly: hdd on line* **4/1**[3]

3 *hd* **Zagora (FR)**[22] 4612 3-9-0 0 ... IoritzMendizabal 3 — 111
(J-C Rouget, France) *settled in 4th: rdn 1f out: chal on outside: qcknd wl: jst failed to get 2nd* **5/2**[2]

4 *1* **Silver Grey (IRE)**[22] 4612 3-9-0 0 ...(p) OlivierPeslier 4 — 109?
(R Ingram) *chsd ldr fr s: ev ch 1 1/2f out: r.o wl u.p: no ex fnl 100yds* **16/1**

5 *2* **Never Forget (FR)**[56] 3493 3-9-0 0 ... AnthonyCrastus 6 — 105
(E Lellouche, France) *settled towards rr: rdn early in st: no ex fnl f: styd on* **6/1**

6 *¾* **Gallic Star (IRE)**[11] 4957 3-9-0 0 ... RichardHughes 2 — 103
(M R Channon) *broke slowly: racd at rr: rdn 1 1/2f out: no ex fnl f: styd on* **12/1**

2m 11.8s (1.60) **Going Correction** 0.0s/f (Good) — **6 Ran SP% 112.8**
Speed ratings: **93,92,92,91,90 89**
WIN (incl. 1 euro stake); 2.40. PLACES; 1.60, 1.80. SF; 9.50..
Owner Bernard Barsi **Bred** Dunmore Stud Limited **Trained** Pau, France

NOTEBOOK
Lily Of The Valley(FR) completed a five-timer under an all-out ride from Soumillon. She will now be stepped up to Group 1 company, with the Prix de l'Opera being targeted, even though her trainer considers her a length or so better on a left-handed track.
Contredanse(IRE), who ran with credit in the Nassau last time out, appreciated the drop in class and was given a good front-running ride by Fallon. The EP Taylor Stakes is being considered for her.
Zagora(FR), a stablemate of the winner, is considered by her trainer to be a better horse over shorter, despite staying on strongly to win over the C&D last time out. The Queen Elizabeth II Stakes and the Queen Elizabeth II Cup at Keeneland are likely to be her next targets.
Silver Grey(IRE) is another now likely to be dropped back in trip.
Gallic Star(IRE) is not really up to this class. (op 10-1)

5347a DARLEY PRIX MORNY (GROUP 1) (2YO COLTS & FILLIES) (TURF) — 6f
2:40 (12:00) 2-Y-O — **£176,982** (£70,805; £35,402; £17,685; £8,858)

RPR

1 **Dream Ahead (USA)**[37] 4110 2-9-0 0 ... WilliamBuick 10 — 116+
(D M Simcock) *racd in midfield on outer: swtchd arnd horses 2f out: qcknd wl 1 1/2f out: chal for ld 1f out: tk ld 150yds out: wnt clr despite wandering off st line: comf* **8/1**

2 *1 ½* **Tin Horse (IRE)**[28] 4419 2-9-0 0 ... ThierryJarnet 6 — 112
(D Guillemin, France) *towards rr fr s: short of room 1 1/2f out: qcknd wl between horses 1f out: r.o wl towards fin to take 2nd fnl strides* **33/1**

3 *nk* **Pontenuovo (FR)**[21] 4637 2-8-10 0 ... StephanePasquier 5 — 107
(Y De Nicolay, France) *settled bhd ldr on stands' side: rdn and qcknd into ld 1 1/2f out: styd on wl: hdd 150yds out: lost 2nd fnl strides* **8/1**

4 *1* **Broox (IRE)**[28] 4419 2-9-0 0 ... OlivierPeslier 9 — 108
(E J O'Neill, France) *settled bhd ldr in centre of trck: rdn 1 1/2f out: styd on wl* **16/1**

5 *¾* **Irish Field (IRE)**[28] 4419 2-9-0 0 ... ChristopheSoumillon 2 — 105
(J W Hills) *towards rr early on stands' side: hrd rdn 1 1/2f out: styd on wl* **7/1**[3]

6 *hd* **Libranno**[23] 4538 2-9-0 0 ... RichardHughes 3 — 105
(R Hannon) *broke wl to ld stands' side: rdn 2f out: no ex fnl f* **9/4**[1]

7 *nk* **Captain Chop (FR)**[21] 4637 2-9-0 0 ... MaximeGuyon 11 — 104
(D Guillemin, France) *towards rr on outside: rdn 1 1/2f out: no ex fnl f* **40/1**

8 *½* **Soraaya (IRE)**[29] 4356 2-8-10 0 ... JimmyFortune 4 — 98
(M R Channon) *racd towards rr on outer: rdn 1 1/2f out: no ex fnl f: eased* **5/1**[2]

9 *2 ½* **Keratiya (FR)**[49] 3718 2-8-10 0 ... GeraldMosse 7 — 91
(J-C Rouget, France) *racd in midfield in centre of trck: rdn 1 1/2f out: no ex fnl f: eased* **5/1**[2]

10 *5* **Al Aasifh (IRE)**[37] 4097 2-9-0 0 ... FrankieDettori 1 — 80
(Saeed Bin Suroor) *towards rr on stands' rail fr s: nvr figured* **10/1**

11 *½* **Monsieur Le Prince (FR)**[22] 2-9-0 0 ... JulienAuge 8 — 78
(E J O'Neill, France) *broke wl to ld in centre of trck: hrd rdn at 1/2-way: grad wknd: eased fnl f* **66/1**

69.60 secs (-1.40) **Going Correction** 0.0s/f (Good) — **11 Ran SP% 120.7**
Speed ratings: **109,107,106,105,104 104,103,102,99,92 92**
WIN (incl. 1 euro stake); 14.10. PLACES; 5.60, 6.40, 3.00. DF; 237.30. SF; 424.60..
Owner Khalifa Dasmal **Bred** Darley **Trained** Newmarket, Suffolk
■ David Simcock's first Group 1 winner.

FOCUS
A race that has been dominated by British-trained winners, with only three French-trained winners in the previous 16 years.

NOTEBOOK
Dream Ahead(USA) impressively lived up to his trainer's high expectations of him. He had waltzed in on his debut at Nottingham a month earlier and had been destined to take his chance in the Acomb Stakes at York until the ground dried out, but he vindicated his trainer's decision to run in this event with a display of pure class. He was the least experienced member of the field but was soon travelling easily held up towards the rear and smoothly made up ground before hitting the front a furlong out. He quickened clear in the way only a class individual can and this was as impressive a performance as we have seen from a juvenile this season. The ground had dried out a little to good, which dispelled thoughts that he must have soft ground to show his best, and he will have no problems stepping up to 7f as he settles so well. His trainer has earmarked the Middle Park and then the Dewhurst, and provided the ground isn't riding too fast it is going to take a very smart colt to lower his colours as he should be capable of further improvement from only his second run. (op 15-2)
Tin Horse(IRE) had won his first two races and had finished behind Irish Field in the Prix Robert Papin, but was able to reverse the placing with the winner and Broox this time. He was another held up in mid-division in the early stages of the race and kept on in the closing stages, but he was no match for the winner. He's clearly going the right way and simply met a tartar on this occasion. (op 25-1)
Pontenuovo(FR), who won the Prix de Cabourg over C&D earlier in the month, easily came out best of the three fillies in the race. She was another held up before being asked for her effort in the final 2f and kept on well. She improved on her previous efforts and could well be worth her place in the Cheveley Park, as last year's winner of the Newmarket race, Special Duty, split Arcano and Canford Cliffs in this event 12 months ago.
Broox(IRE) had finished runner-up in the Papin and was another to reverse placings with the winner. He was given a lovely tow towards the centre of the course by his stablemate Monsieur Le Prince and had every chance inside the final furlong but, like the others, had nothing to offer against the finishing burst of Dream Ahead. He finished ahead of the Gimcrack winner Approve in the Papin, which gives a good indicator to the value of this form.
Irish Field(IRE) had joined John Hills after his Prix Robert Papin win and was unable to confirm the placings. He was in mid-division in the early stages of the race and kept on in the closing stages but could only really maintain the same pace. He may just need a little more time to settle in to his new surroundings and it would be dangerous to write him off as he had looked very much on the upgrade beforehand.
Libranno had won his three races to date, which included the July Stakes and the Richmond Stakes, but the form had taken a little knock the previous day when the Goodwood third had finished only fourth to Native Khan in the Solario Stakes at Sandown, and he never looked likely to maintain his sequence. He was smartly out of the stalls towards the stands' side but the distress signals were out with 2f to go and he never picked up. He has had to do it the hard way in his races and may just need freshening up. (op 11-4)
Captain Chop(FR) had finished behind Pontenuovo in the Prix de Cabourg and ran as well as could be expected. (op 33-1)
Soraaya(IRE) was a major disappointment and never landed a blow. She had beaten the unlucky Lowther runner-up Margot Did at Ascot and this was clearly not her running. (op 9-2)
Keratiya(FR) had beaten Irish Field when last seen out at Chantilly in July but she was another to disappoint badly. She was held up but was another to make little impression in the closing stages, and is surely better than she showed on this occasion. (op 9-2)
Al Aasifh(IRE) had bounced back to winning form in a Listed event at Newbury on his latest start but dropped out in the closing stages after chasing Libranno towards the stands' side. He was probably just out of his depth in Group 1 company.
Monsieur Le Prince(FR) faced a tall order and, after giving a good lead to stablemate Brook, dropped out in the closing stages. (op 50-1)

5348a DARLEY PRIX JEAN ROMANET (GROUP 1) (4YO+ FILLIES & MARES) (TURF) 1m 2f
3:15 (12:00) 4-Y-0+ **£126,415** (£50,575; £25,287; £12,632; £6,327)

RPR

1 **Stacelita (FR)**[22] 4575 4-9-0 0 ChristopheSoumillon 3 112
(J-C Rouget, France) *racd in 2nd fr s: rdn to ld 1 1/2f out: hrd rdn fnl 50yds: jst hld on* **1/1**[1]

2 *hd* **Antara (GER)**[22] 4575 4-9-0 0 FrankieDettori 4 112
(Saeed Bin Suroor) *racd in 3rd: mde prog on outside early in st: r.o wl u.p fnl f: jst failed* **3/1**[2]

3 *1* **Board Meeting (IRE)**[28] 4-9-0 0 AnthonyCrastus 1 110
(E Lellouche, France) *led: hdd 1 1/2f out: styd on wl* **16/1**

4 *1/2* **Fleur Enchantee (FR)**[8] 6-9-0 0 (p) StephanePasquier 5 109?
(P Van De Poele, France) *racd in 5th: hrd rdn 1 1/2f out: styd on wl fnl f* **33/1**

5 *3/4* **Reggane**[31] 4316 4-9-0 0 MaximeGuyon 6 108
(A De Royer-Dupre, France) *slowly away and racd towards rr: rdn 1 1/2f out: styd on wl fnl f* **12/1**

6 *3/4* **Celimene (IRE)**[56] 3494 4-9-0 0 (p) OlivierPeslier 7 106
(C Lerner, France) *racd in 4th: rdn early in st: u.p 1 1/2f out: no ex fnl f* **9/1**

7 *1* **Shalanaya (IRE)**[67] 3068 4-9-0 0 GeraldMosse 8 104
(M Delzangles, France) *in rr fr s: no ex fnl 2f: styd on* **11/2**[3]

8 *6* **Rainbow Dancing**[54] 3548 5-9-0 0 DominiqueBoeuf 2 92
(Mlle H Van Zuylen, France) *racd towards rr: u.p early in st: no ex fnl 2f: wknd* **50/1**

2m 9.30s (-0.90) **Going Correction** 0.0s/f (Good) **8** Ran SP% **118.9**
Speed ratings: **103,102,102,101,101 100,99,94**
WIN (incl. 1 euro stake); 1.80. PLACES 1.10, 1.50, 2.50. DF 4.60. SF 5.00..
Owner Martin S Schwartz **Bred** J P J Dubois **Trained** Pau, France

NOTEBOOK
Stacelita(FR) confirmed Nassau Stakes form with Antara to gain a fourth Group 1 success. The Monsun filly had given Midday a few worrying moments before the subsequent Darley Yorkshire Oaks winner pulled away again in the closing stages at Goodwood, and this went very much according to plan for her. Christophe Soumillon always had his mount tracking the front-runner and she was always finding enough on the run to the line after hitting the front 2f out. She is a tough, classy filly who will no doubt be placed to further advantage in similar company.
Antara(GER) had won the Princess Elizabeth Stakes on her debut for Godolphin at Epsom on Oaks day and had finished a length behind Stacelita when the pair occupied the places in the Nassau. She narrowed that deficit further on this occasion, as she tracked the winner throughout and followed her through. She kept on well to the line and could well be up to winning a Group 1 event confined to fillies over this trip when the ground eases even more.
Board Meeting(IRE) has been placed in Group 1s behind Stacelita and Shalanaya last season, and ran her best race this term. She adopted a front-running role and gave best to the first two only inside the final 2f, and kept on courageously to hold third place. She has possibly just come to herself now and looks capable of finding success at a level just a notch or two below this grade.
Fleur Enchantee(FR) put up a career-best performance to stay on for fourth place. She won on the AW here on her latest visit and picked up some valuable prize-money.
Reggane had finished only a neck behind Antara at Epsom but she never looked to be travelling that well on the ground and could never get in the hunt.
Celimene(IRE) chased the front three for much of the way but was outpaced in the closing stages and would probably welcome a return to 1m4f. (op 8-1)
Shalanaya(IRE) was the major disappointment in the race as she never got into it after being held up in last place. It is hard to know what to make of this performance. (tchd 5-1)

5349a DARLEY PRIX KERGORLAY (GROUP 2) (3YO+) (TURF) 1m 7f
3:50 (12:00) 3-Y-0+ **£65,575** (£25,309; £12,079; £8,053; £4,026)

RPR

1 **Americain (USA)**[23] 4566 5-9-4 0 GeraldMosse 3 111
(A De Royer-Dupre, France) *racd in midfield on rail: rdn 1 1/2f out: qcknd wl between horses to take ld 150yds out: hld on wl fnl 50yds* **3/1**[2]

2 *snk* **Manighar (FR)**[23] 4535 4-9-6 0 KierenFallon 4 113
(L M Cumani) *in rr fr s: rdn early in st: short of room 1 1/2f out: swtchd towards outside: c between horses 1f out: fin strly* **11/2**[3]

3 *2 1/2* **Blek (FR)**[39] 4038 5-9-6 0 AnthonyCrastus 7 110
(E Lellouche, France) *racd in 2nd: rdn 1 1/2f out to ld briefly: hdd under 1f out: styd on* **9/4**[1]

4 *1/2* **Los Cristianos (FR)**[39] 4038 4-9-4 0 ThomasHuet 8 107
(A Couetil, France) *racd in 4th: rdn early in st to be prom: hrd rdn 1f out: styd on* **10/1**

5 *hd* **Tres Rock Danon (FR)**[40] 4012 4-9-4 0 DominiqueBoeuf 6 107
(W Hickst, Germany) *led: rdn early in st: hdd 1 1/2f out: styd on* **7/1**

6 *1* **Green Tango (FR)**[23] 4566 7-9-4 0 RonanThomas 5 106
(P Van De Poele, France) *racd towards rr: swtchd towards outer early in st: styd on fnl f* **16/1**

7 *3* **Watar (IRE)**[23] 4566 5-9-4 0 DavyBonilla 2 102
(F Head, France) *broke slowly and racd in rr: rdn early in st on wd outside: mde prog 1 1/2f out: sn fdd* **9/1**

8 *shd* **Sybelio (FR)**[23] 4566 6-9-4 0 ChristopheSoumillon 1 102
(J Rossi, France) *racd in 3rd on rail: lost position early in st and sn wknd: eased* **14/1**

3m 13.2s (-5.90) **Going Correction** 0.0s/f (Good) **8** Ran SP% **115.3**
Speed ratings: **115,114,113,113,113 112,111,111**
WIN (incl. 1 euro stake); 2.90. PLACES; 1.30, 2.10, 1.20. DF; 18.20. SF; 33.30..
Owner Gerard Thomas Ryan **Bred** Wertheimer Et Frere **Trained** Chantilly, France

NOTEBOOK
Americain(USA) picked up well once he found a gap and booked his ticket to the Melbourne Cup. He won't run again before going into quarantine.
Manighar(FR) finished well after seeing the winner get first run on him. He'll now join Americain in going into quarantine prior to a Melbourne Cup bid. (op 5-1)

4526 OVREVOLL (R-H)
Sunday, August 22

OFFICIAL GOING: Turf: soft

5350a MARIT SVEAAS MINNELOP (GROUP 3) (3YO+) (TURF) 1m 1f
3:00 (12:00) 3-Y-0+ **£85,561** (£27,807; £12,834; £7,700; £5,133)

RPR

1 **Touch Of Hawk (FR)**[45] 4-9-4 0 LennartHammer-Hansen 5 95
(Wido Neuroth, Norway) *racd in 2nd: hrd rdn 3f out: kep on wl: led 2f out: r.o* **7/2**[2]

2 *nk* **Entangle**[31] 4-9-0 0 KimAndersen 10 90
(Arnfinn Lund, Norway) *racd in 3rd: chal for ld 2f out: no ex ins fnl f* **23/10**[1]

3 *1/2* **Theatrical Award (NOR)**[10] 5-9-0 0 CarlosLopez 1 89
(Michael Taylor, Norway) *slowly away: in rr ent st: hrd rdn: kpt on* **43/10**

4 *1/2* **Tertullus (FR)**[43] 3934 7-9-6 0 EspenSki 3 94
(Rune Haugen, Norway) *racd in midfield: nvr threatened ldrs in st* **68/10**

5 *1/2* **Handsome Hawk (IRE)**[45] 4-9-4 0 (b) FJohansson 9 91
(Wido Neuroth, Norway) *bkmarker fr s: mde prog ent st: hrd rdn: no ex fnl f* **41/10**[3]

6 *5 1/2* **Volo Cat (FR)**[21] 4641 6-9-4 0 JerryO'Dwyer 8 79
(Bent Olsen, Denmark) *racd in midfield: hrd rdn 3f out: no ex* **25/1**

7 *1/2* **Alnitak (USA)**[21] 4641 9-9-4 0 (b) JacobJohansen 11 78
(Bent Olsen, Denmark) *towards rr fr s: nvr figured in st* **50/1**

8 *1/2* **Peas And Carrots (DEN)**[21] 4641 7-9-4 0 EddieAhern 2 77
(Lennart Reuterskiold Jr, Sweden) *racd in midfield: proged bef st: hrd rdn: fdd* **78/10**

9 *1/2* **Prince Fasliyev**[21] 6-9-4 0 (b) Per-AndersGraberg 6 76
(Niels Petersen, Norway) *led fr s and stl in front ent st: hdd 2f out and sn wknd* **189/10**

1m 51.7s (1.80) **9** Ran SP% **126.0**
WIN (incl. 1 kroner stake): 4.57. PLACES: 1.31, 1.42, 1.62. DF: 11.20.
Owner Stall E & F **Bred** Dieter Burkle **Trained** Norway

4887 DEL MAR (L-H)
Sunday, August 22

OFFICIAL GOING: Turf: firm

5351a DEL MAR OAKS (GRADE 1) (3YO FILLIES) (TURF) 1m 1f (T)
2:25 (2:27) 3-Y-0 **£111,111** (£37,037; £22,222; £11,111; £3,703)

RPR

1 **Evening Jewel (USA)**[27] 3-8-10 0 VEspinoza 4 110
(James Cassidy, U.S.A) *qckly away and led briefly: sn settled in 3rd: styd there travelling wl: 3rd and short of room fnl turn: qckly swtchd ins to be 2nd st: led ins fnl f: r.o but drifted rt: hld on gamely* **7/5**[1]

2 *1/2* **Harmonious (USA)**[49] 3-8-10 0 MESmith 6 109
(John Shirreffs, U.S.A) *racd in bk two: hdwy over 2f out: 5th st (c five wd fnl turn): styd on strly down wd outside to take 2nd fnl 80yds: r.o wl* **33/10**[2]

3 *1 1/4* **Perfect Shirl (USA)**[25] 3-8-10 0 ChantalSutherland 3 106
(Roger L Attfield, Canada) *plld early and racd in midfield: 4th and c wd st: sltly hmpd fnl f: swtchd and r.o wl* **26/5**[3]

4 *1 1/4* **Antares World (USA)**[49] 3-8-10 0 FAlvarado 2 104
(Steve Specht, U.S.A) *stmbld leaving stalls but sn rcvrd to take ld: pressed ins fnl 2f: led st: hdd ins fnl f: wknd last 100yds* **184/10**

5 *1* **Crisp (USA)**[27] 3-8-10 0 (b) RBejarano 9 102
(John W Sadler, U.S.A) *dwlt: sn chsng ldr: pressed ldr fr 2f out: 3rd st: sn rdn and wknd* **31/5**

6 ½ **Berg Bahn (IRE)**53 3571 3-8-10 0 .... ASolis 1 101
(G M Lyons, Ire) *settled towards rr: nowhere to go 3 1/2f out to 2 1/2f out: fnd racing room and 6th st: no ex fnl f* **223/10**

7 1 **Weekend Magic (USA)**27 3-8-10 0 .... (b) AQuinonez 8 99
(Myung Kwon Cho, U.S.A) *broke wl but sn settled in midfield: 4th 3f out: rdn 2f out and wknd st* **246/10**

8 1 ¼ **It Tiz (USA)**27 3-8-10 0 .... DFlores 7 96
(Mark Glatt, U.S.A) *in rr: 7th st: fdd fnl f* **119/10**

9 4 ¾ **Distinctive**53 3571 3-8-10 0 .... BBlanc 5 86
(B Smart) *smartly away: sn settled towards rr: bhd fr 3f out* **28/1**

1m 47.27s (0.18) **9 Ran SP% 119.5**
PARI-MUTUEL (all including $2 stakes): WIN 4.80 PLACE (1-2) 2.80, 3.20 SHOW (1-2-3) 2.20, 2.60, 3.20; DF 8.60; SF 16.60.
Owner Braly Family Trust **Bred** Betty L Mabee & Larry Mabee **Trained** USA

NOTEBOOK
Distinctive, trying her longest trip to date, never got competitive from off the pace.

5196 CARLISLE (R-H)
Monday, August 23

OFFICIAL GOING: Good (good to soft in places) changing to soft after race 1 (5.30)
Old Stable bend moved out 3m up to 4f adding 8m to races on round course.
Wind: Light, half-against. Weather: persistent rain before racing, changeable and unsettled, showers last 3

5352 RACING UK CHANNEL 432 MEDIAN AUCTION MAIDEN STKS 5f 193y
5:30 (5:30) (Class 5) 2-Y-O **£2,729** (£806; £403) **Stalls High**

Form RPR

5324 1 **Brave Dream**9 5092 2-9-3 68 .... PJMcDonald 1 72
(K A Ryan) *mde all: styd on wl fnl f* **15/8**1

0002 2 1 ¾ **Indian Giver**21 4645 2-8-12 70 .... PatrickMathers 4 62
(H A McWilliams) *chsd ldrs: edgd lft over 1f out: styd on wl last 150yds: tk 2nd on line* **13/2**3

3 3 shd **Inside**19 4702 2-8-12 0 .... PaulHanagan 6 61
(R A Fahey) *w wnr: kpt on same pce last 150yds* **11/4**2

05 4 2 ½ **Rocky Coast**9 5099 2-9-3 0 .... DavidAllan 7 59
(B Smart) *chsd ldrs: chal over 2f out: wknd fnl 100yds* **7/1**

0 5 1 **Cheeky Wee Red**12 4941 2-8-9 0 .... BarryMcHugh(3) 8 50
(R A Fahey) *s.i.s: in rr: hdwy to chse ldrs 3f out: wknd over 1f out* **20/1**

05 6 1 ¼ **Tapis Libre**12 4940 2-9-0 0 .... JamesSullivan(3) 9 52
(M W Easterby) *mid-div: outpcd over 2f out: sn wknd* **33/1**

7 1 ½ **Buddy Twosocks** 2-9-0 0 .... PaulPickard(3) 3 47
(S G West) *s.i.s: hung lft and lost pl over 2f out* **16/1**

8 8 **Always De Man (IRE)** 2-9-3 0 .... AdrianNicholls 5 22
(M Johnston) *s.i.s: reminders after s: sn drvn along and outpcd: bhd fnl 3f* **8/1**

1m 18.19s (4.49) **Going Correction** +0.60s/f (Yiel) **8 Ran SP% 112.0**
Speed ratings (Par 94): **94,91,91,88,86 85,83,72**
Tote Swingers:1&2:£2.20, 2&3:£1.90, 1&3:£1.70 CSF £14.02 TOTE £2.10: £1.10, £4.30, £1.10; EX 11.90.
Owner Hokey Cokey Partnership **Bred** Emma Thorman & Trickledown Stud **Trained** Hambleton, N Yorks

FOCUS
After a wet afternoon the ground was changed to good, good to soft in places. Probably just an ordinary maiden which was run at an ordinary gallop and the race developed towards the far side of the track. The first three pulled well clear.

NOTEBOOK
Brave Dream, the most experienced runner, found a good opportunity to lose his maiden tag at the seventh attempt. Never far off the pace, he showed a willing attitude close home and appears versatile regarding the ground. He should continue to pay his way in nurseries. (op 9-4)
Indian Giver, second over C&D last time out at a massive price, proved that run was no fluke and she has ability. She could have done with some company down the centre of the track. Rated 70, a fillies' maiden should be within her grasp in the coming weeks. (op 9-1)
Inside, from a respected yard, had shown clear ability on her debut at Newcastle and backed it up here with another solid effort. A fillies' maiden should also be the way forward for her. (tchd 5-2 and 3-1)
Rocky Coast, well backed beforehand, raced prominently before getting tired close home. All three of his runs have come over 6f and he can make his mark in nurseries. (op 14-1)
Always De Man(IRE) comes from a top yard, but was very easy to back and was the first off the bridle and can only be watched after this ordinary debut run. (op 4-1)

5353 IAN STAPLETON CLAIMING STKS 7f 200y
6:00 (6:00) (Class 6) 3-Y-O **£1,706** (£503; £252) **Stalls High**

Form RPR

5113 1 **Miami Gator (IRE)**15 4866 3-9-2 68 .... (v) AndrewElliott 2 73
(Mrs K Burke) *mde all: styd on wl fnl f: drvn out* **9/4**1

0012 2 2 ½ **Jupiter Fidius**21 4646 3-8-7 68 .... DaleSwift(5) 8 63
(Mrs K Walton) *chsd wnr: drvn over 3f out: kpt on same pce fnl 2f* **5/2**2

4563 3 ½ **Dazeen**11 4989 3-9-0 64 .... TonyCulhane 1 64
(P T Midgley) *dwlt: swtchd rt after s: hld up: hdwy over 2f out: sn rdn: kpt on same pce* **17/2**

1060 4 2 ¾ **Maison Brillet (IRE)**26 4483 3-9-0 70 .... PaulHanagan 7 57
(J Howard Johnson) *chsd ldrs: drvn over 4f out: one pce fnl 2f* **12/1**

1252 5 3 ¼ **Cono Zur (FR)**15 4866 3-8-8 70 .... (p) JamesSullivan(3) 6 47
(Mrs R A Carr) *chsd ldrs: effrt over 2f out: lost pl over 1f out* **3/1**3

1-00 6 37 **Chardonnay**74 2884 3-8-11 73 .... PJMcDonald 5 —
(G A Swinbank) *hld up towards rr: hdwy 4f out: wknd 2f out: sn eased: t.o* **14/1**

1m 44.16s (4.16) **Going Correction** +0.60s/f (Yiel) **6 Ran SP% 109.2**
Speed ratings (Par 98): **103,100,100,97,94 57**
Tote Swingers:1&2:£2.60, 2&3:£6.10, 1&3:£2.60 CSF £7.68 TOTE £3.40: £1.10, £4.00; EX 9.20.
Owner Mrs Elaine M Burke **Bred** Newlands House Stud **Trained** Middleham Moor, North Yorks

FOCUS
The ground was changed to soft before this claimer which was run at a sound pace thanks to the winner. Once again the jockeys stuck to the far side rail and it probably didn't take much winning with a few of the runners not running up to form.

Cono Zur(FR) Official explanation: jockey said colt was unsuited by the soft ground

5354 CARIBBEAN COMES TO CARLISLE NURSERY 5f
6:30 (6:30) (Class 5) (0-75,73) 2-Y-O **£3,412** (£1,007; £504) **Stalls High**

Form RPR

4012 1 **Indian Ballad (IRE)**13 4927 2-9-5 71 .... AdrianNicholls 3 75+
(E S McMahon) *trckd ldrs travelling strly: led over 1f out: edgd lft: kpt on wl towards fin* **5/1**2

5340 2 nk **Tro Nesa (IRE)**11 4984 2-9-2 71 .... BarryMcHugh(3) 8 74
(Mrs A Duffield) *sn outpcd in rr and drvn along: hdwy on outside over 2f out: chsd wnr fnl f: kpt on same pce last 50yds* **11/1**

4214 3 1 ¾ **Fantasy Fry**17 4783 2-9-4 70 .... PJMcDonald 9 67
(H Morrison) *dwlt: in rr: hung lft after 1f: swtchd rt and hdwy on outside over 1f out: styd on wl last 150yds* **7/2**1

1040 4 shd **Mini Bon Bon**22 4615 2-8-5 57 .... (v1) PaulHanagan 1 54
(A Bailey) *swvd lft s: sn chsng ldrs on wd outside: kpt on same pce fnl f* **7/1**

1406 5 1 **Sacrosanctus**16 4831 2-9-2 73 .... DaleSwift(5) 4 66
(J A Glover) *wnt rt s: chsd ldrs: wknd fnl f* **6/1**3

4151 6 1 **Nellie Ellis (IRE)**35 4195 2-9-1 67 .... JamieSpencer 2 56
(K A Ryan) *led: hdd over 1f out: hmpd 1f out: wknd rapidly last 150yds* **7/2**1

3444 7 ¾ **Dunmore Boy (IRE)**10 5021 2-8-8 67 .... MarzenaJeziorek(7) 5 54
(R A Fahey) *bmpd s: chsd ldrs: outpcd over 2f out: wknd over 1f out* **17/2**

050 8 1 **Guinea Seeker**48 3767 2-7-12 50 .... DuranFentiman 6 33
(T D Easterby) *bmpd s: chsd ldrs: lost pl over 1f out* **12/1**

63.79 secs (2.99) **Going Correction** +0.60s/f (Yiel) **8 Ran SP% 114.4**
Speed ratings (Par 94): **100,99,96,96,94 93,92,90**
Tote Swingers:1&2:£13.40, 2&3:£2.70, 1&3:£3.30 CSF £57.44 CT £217.60 TOTE £10.00: £1.70, £8.20, £1.40; EX 61.30.
Owner R L Bedding **Bred** J M Beever **Trained** Lichfield, Staffs

FOCUS
A 0-75 nursery in which the top weight was 2lb below the ceiling rating. It was run at a sound pace and the race developed down the centre of the track.

NOTEBOOK
Indian Ballad(IRE), a winner over this trip on firm ground at Bath on his penultimate start, showed the softer ground was no hindrance with a very pleasing performance. Never far away, there should be more to come from him. (op 4-1)
Tro Nesa(IRE), a winner at this track on her debut over 6f, stayed on well. She appears all heart but the handicapper hasn't been that kind and might still be vulnerable to an improver. (op 14-1 tchd 18-1)
Fantasy Fry ran a very strange race, struggling after a sluggish start before running on strongly close home. He didn't convince with his head carriage, although that might have been the soft ground as he lost his maiden tag on firm going. With his yard going very well, he is worth another chance. (tchd 4-1 in a place)
Mini Bon Bon, wearing a visor for the first time, was well held on this easier ground. Her win came in selling company. (op 6-1 tchd 9-2)
Nellie Ellis(IRE), who scored in claiming company last time out, might have just run into a very well handicapped horse on the night. (tchd 3-1)

5355 TEXT 55MISSCUMBRIA ON 81118 H'CAP 1m 3f 107y
7:00 (7:00) (Class 4) (0-85,82) 3-Y-O+ **£5,118** (£1,511; £756) **Stalls Low**

Form RPR

2161 1 **Nave (USA)**11 5002 3-9-7 82 .... JoeFanning 8 92
(M Johnston) *trckd ldr: hung lft and chsd ldr over 2f out: racd stands' side and styd on to ld last 75yds* **9/4**1

0022 2 1 ½ **Amazing Blue Sky**17 4781 4-9-3 72 .... JamesSullivan(3) 7 80
(Mrs R A Carr) *led: styd far side in st and ended up racing alone: hdd and no ex ins fnl f* **6/1**3

3460 3 4 **Royal Straight**5 5213 5-9-4 70 .... LNewman 4 71
(Miss L A Perratt) *hld up in rr: hdwy 3f out: styd on same pce fnl f* **16/1**

300 4 2 ¾ **Persian Peril**16 4830 6-9-11 77 .... PJMcDonald 2 73
(G A Swinbank) *sn trcking ldrs: t.k.h: wknd fnl f* **11/2**2

/152 5 5 **Daytime Dreamer (IRE)**10 5019 6-9-2 68 .... PhillipMakin 1 56
(M Todhunter) *hld up: racd keenly: hdwy to trck ldrs over 5f out: wknd 2f out* **16/1**

6415 6 nk **High Office**29 4400 4-9-11 77 .... PaulHanagan 3 65
(R A Fahey) *t.k.h in rr: effrt 3f out: lost pl 2f out* **9/4**1

64-0 7 8 **Robby Bobby**191 536 5-9-10 76 .... AdrianNicholls 5 50
(M Johnston) *chsd ldrs: effrt over 3f out: lost pl 2f out: sn bhd* **12/1**

2m 31.16s (8.06) **Going Correction** +0.60s/f (Yiel)
WFA 3 from 4yo+ 9lb **7 Ran SP% 110.7**
Speed ratings (Par 105): **94,92,90,88,84 84,78**
Tote Swingers:1&2:£2.30, 2&3:£18.60, 1&3:£6.00 CSF £15.32 CT £159.62 TOTE £2.70: £1.20, £4.30; EX 12.10.
Owner Anthony Hogarth **Bred** Mineola Farm II Llc Et Al **Trained** Middleham Moor, N Yorks

FOCUS
A handicap open to horses rated 66-85 but the top weight was 8lb below the ceiling rating. The seven runners were only split by 9lb and it went to the progressive 3yo Nave.
High Office Official explanation: jockey said gelding ran flat

5356 CHRISTMAS PARTY NIGHT AT CARLISLE RACECOURSE H'CAP 5f
7:30 (7:30) (Class 5) (0-75,75) 3-Y-O+ **£2,590** (£770; £385; £192) **Stalls High**

Form RPR

2451 1 **Verinco**12 4952 4-8-11 68 .... (v) AdamCarter(7) 8 78
(B Smart) *mde all racing towards far side: 4 l clr 1f out: unchal* **6/1**2

6045 2 1 ¾ **Rowayton**12 4942 4-9-11 75 .... PhillipMakin 7 79
(J D Bethell) *hld up in mid-div: hdwy 2f out: styd on wl to take 2nd nr fin* **4/1**1

2431 3 ½ **Sharp Eclipse**19 4703 3-9-8 74 .... JamieSpencer 9 76
(K A Ryan) *chsd ldrs: styd on fnl f* **4/1**1

3335 4 nse **Wicked Wilma (IRE)**4 5240 6-9-2 66 .... PatrickMathers 1 68
(A Berry) *chsd ldrs racing towards stands' side: chsd wnr over 1f out: kpt on same pce fnl f* **16/1**

2034 5 3 ¼ **Ingleby Star (IRE)**19 4712 5-9-8 75 .... (p) GaryBartley(3) 12 65
(N Wilson) *chsd ldrs towards far side: wknd fnl f* **9/1**

3202 6 1 ¾ **Ryedane (IRE)**24 4559 8-9-6 70 .... (b) DavidAllan 3 54
(T D Easterby) *s.i.s: brought to r stands' side: sn outpcd and detached in last: hdwy over 1f out: nvr nr ldrs* **10/1**

02 7 ¾ **La Capriosa**14 4892 4-9-7 71 .... PJMcDonald 11 52
(J A Glover) *chsd wnr towards far side: wknd fnl f* **8/1**3

-510 8 1 **Bahamian Ballet**27 4452 8-9-9 73 .... AdrianNicholls 10 50
(E S McMahon) *dwlt: racd far side: nvr a factor* **10/1**

6005 9 1 **Dispol Grand (IRE)**67 3119 4-9-1 65 .... TonyCulhane 5 39
(P T Midgley) *chsd ldrs: wknd over 1f out* **22/1**

4144 **10** 2 1/4 **Six Diamonds**[18] 4754 3-9-9 75.....(t) PaulHanagan 6 41
(H Morrison) *trckd ldrs: drvn over 2f out: sn lost pl* **8/1**[3]
5560 **11** 6 **Argentine (IRE)**[5] 5198 6-9-11 75.....(b) PaulMulrennan 2 19
(J A McShane) *trckd ldrs racing towards stands' side: wknd over 1f out: eased towards fin* **22/1**
63.34 secs (2.54) **Going Correction** +0.60s/f (Yiel)
WFA 3 from 4yo+ 2lb 11 Ran SP% **119.3**
Speed ratings (Par 103): **103,100,99,99,94 91,90,88,86,83 73**
Tote Swingers:1&2:£6.30, 2&3:£4.00, 1&3:£5.90 CSF £30.68 CT £107.49 TOTE £6.50: £1.90, £1.10, £1.10; EX 54.80.
Owner B Smart **Bred** Mrs M Gutkin **Trained** Hambleton, N Yorks
FOCUS
This 56-75 sprint handicap was run during a heavy shower. It was run at a sound pace with most of the runners coming towards the stands side, the winner an exception.

5357 CARLISLE-RACES.CO.UK H'CAP 6f 192y
8:00 (8:00) (Class 5) (0-70,70) 3-Y-0+ **£2,590** (£770; £385; £192) **Stalls** High

Form RPR
006 **1** **Cara's Request (AUS)**[25] 4515 5-9-8 66..... AdrianNicholls 5 78
(D Nicholls) *mde all centre: clr over 1f out: unchal* **9/1**
0-33 **2** 3 **Diggeratt (USA)**[17] 4796 4-9-7 65..... PaulHanagan 2 69
(R A Fahey) *chsd ldrs: chsd wnr on outer over 1f out: edgd lft ins fnl f: no imp* **4/1**[1]
0U04 **3** 1/2 **Toby Tyler**[16] 4833 4-9-4 62..... TonyCulhane 3 65
(P T Midgley) *s.i.s: sn last: hdwy on outer over 2f out: styd on fnl f* **16/1**
6404 **4** nse **Peter's Gift (IRE)**[16] 4834 4-8-12 56.....(p) JamieSpencer 1 58
(K A Ryan) *in rr: hdwy stands' side over 2f out: n.m.r ins fnl f: styd on same pce* **15/2**
0651 **5** 6 **Commando Scott (IRE)**[9] 5067 9-9-0 65..... NeilFarley(7) 6 51
(D Carroll) *chsd ldrs: wknd over 1f out* **5/1**[3]
0150 **6** nk **Dhhamaan (IRE)**[19] 4704 5-8-10 57.....(b) JamesSullivan(3) 4 42
(Mrs R A Carr) *chsd wnr: wnt 2nd over 2f out: wknd appr fnl f* **18/1**
606 **7** 1 1/4 **Bid For Gold**[9] 5064 6-8-13 57.....(p) PaulMulrennan 9 39
(Jedd O'Keeffe) *in rr: kpt on fnl 2f: nvr a factor* **14/1**
6423 **8** 2 1/2 **Lindoro**[40] 4014 5-9-7 70..... DaleSwift(5) 10 45
(K M Prendergast) *s.i.s: t.k.h in rr: sme hdwy over 2f out: nvr on terms* **12/1**
4250 **9** 3/4 **Bold Marc (IRE)**[30] 4394 8-9-5 63.....(p) AndrewElliott 13 36
(Mrs K Burke) *chsd ldrs towards far side: wknd wl over 1f out* **9/2**[2]
0135 **10** 3 1/4 **Stonehaugh (IRE)**[17] 4795 7-9-5 68.....(t) IanBrennan(5) 11 32
(J Howard Johnson) *mid-div far side: nvr trbld ldrs: heavily eased last 100yds* **16/1**
0034 **11** 3/4 **Final Salute**[60] 3357 4-8-12 56.....(v) TomEaves 7 18
(B Smart) *s.i.s: mid-div: hung rt and lost pl 2f out* **25/1**
560- **12** nse **Dialogue**[324] 6490 4-9-7 70..... MichaelO'Connell(5) 14 32
(G A Harker) *t.k.h in rr towards far side: nvr on terms* **20/1**
0544 **13** 1 1/4 **King's Sabre**[15] 4866 4-9-4 62.....(e) PhillipMakin 12 21
(R C Guest) *s.i.s: a in rr* **14/1**
0560 **14** 19 **Deely Plaza**[73] 2919 3-9-0 63..... PJMcDonald 8 —
(J A Glover) *mid-div: lost pl over 1f out: heavily eased* **50/1**
1m 30.93s (3.83) **Going Correction** +0.60s/f (Yiel)
WFA 3 from 4yo+ 5lb 14 Ran SP% **125.2**
Speed ratings (Par 103): **102,98,98,97,91 90,89,86,85,81 81,80,79,57**
Tote Swingers:1&2:£3.60, 2&3:£14.50, 1&3:£30.80. totesuper7: Win: Not won. Place: £218.50. CSF £45.75 CT £452.99 TOTE £11.90: £8.10, £1.10, £12.60; EX 32.80 Place 6 £13.47, Place 5 £10.91..
Owner Stewart Aitken **Bred** S Aitken **Trained** Sessay, N Yorks
■ Stewards' Enquiry : Paul Hanagan caution: careless riding.
FOCUS
This competitive, wide-open 51-70 handicap, which had four previous course winners in the line-up, was run at a furious pace.
T/Plt: £19.50 to a £1 stake. Pool:£54,043.33. 2,020.90 winning tickets T/Qpdt: £11.50 to a £1 stake. Pool:£5,101.82. 328.00 winning tickets WG

5210 HAMILTON (R-H)
Monday, August 23

OFFICIAL GOING: Good (9.2) changing to good to soft after race 3 (3.30)
The ground seemed softer than the official descrption, even after being changed to good to soft.
Wind: Almost nil Weather: Overcast, raining

5358 ACF CLEANING LTD 2YO CLAIMING STKS 6f 5y
2:30 (2:32) (Class 6) 2-Y-0 **£1,942** (£578; £288) **Stalls** Low

Form RPR
2442 **1** **Hortensia (IRE)**[7] 5140 2-8-9 80..... SamHitchcott 3 76+
(M R Channon) *pressed ldr: rdn 2f out: led ins fnl f: edgd lft: hld on wl* **2/5**[1]
545 **2** shd **Roodee Queen**[12] 4948 2-7-10 65..... NeilFarley(7) 1 70
(Patrick Morris) *t.k.h: led: rdn and edgd rt over 2f out: hdd ins fnl f: kpt on towards fin: jst hld* **5/1**[3]
53 **3** 14 **Norwegian Liberty (IRE)**[21] 4645 2-8-7 0..... AndrewElliott 2 32
(B M R Haslam) *trckd ldrs: drvn over 2f out: sn struggling: t.o* **9/2**[2]
1m 13.05s (0.85) **Going Correction** +0.05s/f (Good) 3 Ran SP% **106.3**
Speed ratings (Par 92): **96,95,77**
CSF £2.63 TOTE £1.40; EX 2.80.
Owner Box 41 **Bred** River Downs Stud **Trained** West Ilsley, Berks
FOCUS
Only three runners and Hortensia did not seem to run up to her official mark of 80, seeing as she had 9lb in hand of the runner-up at the weights.
NOTEBOOK
Hortensia(IRE) may have found the ground possibly easier than ideal, but whatever, having been pushed out with mainly hands and heels for much of the way, she was ultimately all out, with her rider going for his whip near the line. She's not very big and will probably struggle to progress. (op 4-11)
Roodee Queen, despite racing keenly, nearly upset the favourite. She seemed to run up to her official mark of 65 at the very least. (tchd 9-2)
Norwegian Liberty(IRE) disappointed on this drop in grade, but she might not have appreciated the ground. (op 6-1)

5359 HOWARD AND NANCY MCDOWALL MEMORIAL MEDIAN AUCTION MAIDEN STKS 6f 5y
3:00 (3:02) (Class 5) 3-4-Y-0 **£2,590** (£770; £385; £192) **Stalls** Low

Form RPR
P02 **1** **Ming Meng (IRE)**[12] 4966 3-8-12 0..... PaulMulrennan 5 82+
(M L W Bell) *pressed ldr: led 2f out: drew clr fnl f: readily* **1/1**[1]
6020 **2** 7 **Red Roar (IRE)**[9] 5065 3-8-12 53..... FrannyNorton 4 60
(A Berry) *prom: effrt and chsd wnr over 1f out: no imp fnl f* **13/2**[3]
6-32 **3** 7 **Hambleton**[5] 5214 3-9-3 58..... TomEaves 2 42
(B Smart) *led: rdn and hdd 2f out: lost 2nd and wknd over 1f out* **15/8**[2]
4 9 **Curious Ciara (IRE)** 3-8-12 0..... JoeFanning 3 —
(Anthony Mulholland, Ire) *trckd ldrs: hung rt and outpcd over 3f out: btn whn hung lft over 1f out* **18/1**
0 **5** 6 **Prince Of Fife (IRE)**[108] 1868 3-9-3 0..... LNewman 1 —
(Miss L A Perratt) *taken down early to post: unruly bef s: missed break: hdwy and in tch after 2f: rdn and wknd over 2f out* **40/1**
1m 12.67s (0.47) **Going Correction** +0.05s/f (Good) 5 Ran SP% **105.8**
Speed ratings (Par 103): **98,88,79,67,59**
CSF £7.31 TOTE £1.90: £1.30, £2.20; EX 6.00.
Owner Paddy Barrett **Bred** Mount Coote Stud **Trained** Newmarket, Suffolk
FOCUS
A weak maiden - the runner-up was officially rated only.

5360 ISLE OF SKYE BLENDED SCOTCH WHISKY CLAIMING STKS 1m 1f 36y
3:30 (3:30) (Class 5) 3-5-Y-0 **£2,590** (£770; £385; £192) **Stalls** High

Form RPR
1202 **1** **Honest Broker (IRE)**[17] 4795 3-9-0 73..... JoeFanning 6 78
(M Johnston) *prom: effrt whn nt clr run over 2f out: sn rdn: hdwy to chse ldr over 1f out: styd on wl fnl f: led nr fin* **9/4**[2]
2115 **2** nk **Fujin Dancer (FR)**[5] 5213 5-9-5 72.....(p) JamieSpencer 1 74
(K A Ryan) *hld up: hdwy on bit to chse ldrs over 2f out: rdn and led over 1f out: kpt on fnl f: hdd nr fin* **6/4**[1]
5234 **3** 4 **Plus Ultra (IRE)**[15] 4867 3-8-12 71..... RussKennemore(3) 2 68
(P A Kirby) *trckd ldrs: effrt over 2f out: edgd rt over 1f out: sn outpcd* **9/2**[3]
4154 **4** 3 1/4 **Prime Circle**[13] 4932 4-9-4 63.....(p) SilvestreDeSousa 5 57
(A D Brown) *cl up: led over 3f out to over 1f out: sn btn* **7/1**
001/ **5** 4 1/2 **Tayarat (IRE)**[307] 5571 5-9-4 72.....(tp) PaulMulrennan 3 47
(D Burchell) *led to over 3f out: rdn and wknd over 2f out* **20/1**
00 **6** 21 **Shamo Hill Theatre**[24] 4556 3-9-0 0..... TomEaves 4 4
(C J Teague) *hld up in tch: struggling 4f out: t.o* **100/1**
2m 1.91s (2.21) **Going Correction** +0.125s/f (Good)
WFA 3 from 4yo+ 7lb 6 Ran SP% **107.2**
Speed ratings (Par 103): **95,94,91,88,84 65**
Tote Swingers:1&2:£1.10, 2&3:£1.20, 1&3:£2.60 CSF £5.41 TOTE £3.10: £2.20, £1.20; EX 5.20.
Owner F Towey **Bred** Frank Towey **Trained** Middleham Moor, N Yorks
FOCUS
Following this contest the ground was changed to good to soft, but it's highly questionable whether there was any good in the ground - the time was 6.51 seconds outside standard. A fair claimer, although it proved quite a test.

5361 LONDON HILL DRY GIN H'CAP 1m 65y
4:00 (4:02) (Class 6) (0-60,59) 3-Y-0 **£2,266** (£674; £337; £168) **Stalls** High

Form RPR
0012 **1** **Gadobout Dancer**[12] 4951 3-8-4 52..... NeilFarley(7) 2 60
(D Carroll) *t.k.h early: pressed ldr: led over 3f out: edgd lft over 1f out: styd on wl* **5/1**[3]
0003 **2** 1 **Miss Chaumiere**[20] 4687 3-8-8 49.....(v) JamieSpencer 7 55
(M L W Bell) *chsd clr ldrs: hdwy to go 2nd over 2f out: sn drvn: edgd rt over 1f out: kpt on fnl f: hld nr fin* **7/1**
0051 **3** 4 1/2 **Key Breeze**[12] 4951 3-9-4 59.....(t) PaulMulrennan 8 54
(K A Ryan) *hld up: smooth hdwy and prom 2f out: sn rdn: no ex fnl f* **4/1**[2]
550 **4** 2 1/4 **Daneside (IRE)**[9] 5073 3-8-11 52..... DuranFentiman 9 42
(W G Harrison) *hld up: drvn and outpcd over 3f out: rallied over 1f out: nvr able to chal* **33/1**
4461 **5** 1 1/2 **Tallawalla (IRE)**[7] 5159 3-8-8 49..... SamHitchcott 6 36
(M R Channon) *prom: outpcd and wandered fr over 2f out: sn btn* **9/4**[1]
0002 **6** 1 1/4 **Bring Sweets (IRE)**[15] 4864 3-8-8 49.....(b) TomEaves 5 33
(B Ellison) *hld up in tch: rdn and outpcd over 2f out: sn btn* **12/1**
0300 **7** 10 **North Shadow**[12] 4944 3-8-12 53..... SilvestreDeSousa 3 14
(A D Brown) *led to over 3f out: wknd fr 2f out* **4/1**[2]
-000 **8** 8 **Chardonnay Star (IRE)**[29] 4407 3-8-3 49 ow4.....(p) DeanHeslop(5) 1 —
(C J Teague) *hld up: outpcd and hung rt 4f out: sn struggling* **50/1**
1m 49.7s (1.30) **Going Correction** +0.125s/f (Good) 8 Ran SP% **112.5**
Speed ratings (Par 98): **98,97,92,90,88 87,77,69**
Tote Swingers:1&2:£3.70, 2&3:£5.20, 1&3:£4.40 CSF £38.18 CT £152.88 TOTE £6.90: £2.30, £2.70, £1.40; EX 18.00 Trifecta £80.40 Pool £402.30 - 3.70 winning units..
Owner White Rose & Thistle **Bred** P Cutler **Trained** Sledmere, E Yorks
FOCUS
A moderate handicap.

5362 DAVID MURRAY - A LIFETIME IN RACING H'CAP 5f 4y
4:35 (4:36) (Class 6) (0-60,59) 4-Y-0+ **£2,266** (£674; £337; £168) **Stalls** Low

Form RPR
2306 **1** **Eye For The Girls**[12] 4959 4-8-11 52..... SamHitchcott 4 58
(M R Channon) *sn outpcd and drvn along towards rr: gd hdwy over 1f out: styd on to ld nr fin* **11/2**[3]
5050 **2** nk **Cayman Fox**[30] 4373 5-8-13 54..... LNewman 8 59
(Miss L A Perratt) *led and sn clr: rdn 2f out: tired ins fnl f: hdd nr fin* **7/2**[1]
0646 **3** hd **Monsieur Harvey**[119] 1569 4-8-4 45..... SilvestreDeSousa 5 49
(B Smart) *prom: hung rt thrght: rdn 1/2-way: hdwy over 1f out: styd on wl towards fin* **7/2**[1]
005 **4** 2 1/4 **Almaty Express**[24] 4559 8-8-6 50.....(b) KellyHarrison(3) 2 46
(J R Weymes) *midfield: sn outpcd and drvn along: hdwy appr fnl f: nt rch first 3* **4/1**[2]
0000 **5** 3/4 **Norse Warrior (USA)**[17] 4789 4-8-4 45.....(b) FrannyNorton 7 38
(Peter Grayson) *wnt rt s: bhd and outpcd: hdwy over 1f out: no imp ins fnl f* **10/1**
2106 **6** 7 **Tournedos (IRE)**[17] 4799 8-9-4 59.....(b) TomEaves 6 27
(Mrs R A Carr) *chsd clr ldr: rdn and hung lft 2f out: sn wknd* **13/2**
0056 **7** hd **Handsinthemist (IRE)**[50] 3711 5-8-4 45..... JoeFanning 1 12
(Anthony Mulholland, Ire) *sn outpcd and drvn along: struggling fr 1/2-way* **14/1**

4000 **8** *1* **Mr Rooney (IRE)**[23] 4605 7-7-11 **45**..........................(b) VictorSantos(7) 3 9
(A Berry) *dwlt: bhd and outpcd: nvr on terms* **33/1**
61.87 secs (1.87) **Going Correction** +0.375s/f (Good) **8** Ran SP% **111.9**
Speed ratings (Par 101): **100,99,99,95,94 83,82,81**
Tote Swingers:1&2:£4.10, 2&3:£3.70, 1&3:£3.70 CSF £23.93 CT £75.80 TOTE £4.20: £1.90, £2.60, £1.30; EX 26.90 Trifecta £135.70 Pool £298.96 - 1.63 winning units..
Owner Heart Of The South Racing **Bred** John And Caroline Penny **Trained** West Ilsley, Berks

FOCUS
A moderate sprint handicap run at a furious pace.

5363 GLENGOYNE HIGHLAND SINGLE MALT SCOTCH WHISKY H'CAP 1m 3f 16y
5:05 (5:05) (Class 5) (0-75,75) 4-Y-O+ **£3,238** (£963; £481; £240) **Stalls** High

Form RPR
1262 **1** **Graceful Descent (FR)**[5] 5215 5-9-2 **70**.......................... FrannyNorton 6 78+
(J S Goldie) *trckd ldrs: drvn and sltly outpcd 2f out: rallied to ld ins fnl f: styd on wl* **5/4**[1]
1405 **2** *2* **Magnitude**[14] 4914 5-8-2 **56** oh2.......................... PaulQuinn 5 60
(B P J Baugh) *hld up in tch: drvn over 3f out: hdwy over 1f out: styd on fnl f to chse wnr towards fin* **20/1**
-605 **3** *3/4* **Sanctuary**[11] 4996 4-9-7 **75**.......................... TomEaves 1 78
(B Smart) *t.k.h: hld up in tch: smooth hdwy to ld over 2f out: rdn and edgd rt over 1f out: hdd ins fnl f: one pce* **10/3**[2]
6042 **4** *2* **Hurlingham**[21] 4656 6-8-13 **67**..........................(b) PaulMulrennan 3 66
(M W Easterby) *led to over 2f out: sn rdn and rallied: no ex fnl f* **7/2**[3]
2331 **5** *12* **Maslak (IRE)**[21] 4657 6-9-1 **72**.......................... RussKennemore(3) 7 49
(P W Hiatt) *cl up tl rdn and wknd over 3f out* **11/2**
2m 28.86s (3.26) **Going Correction** +0.375s/f (Good) **5** Ran SP% **109.9**
Speed ratings (Par 103): **103,101,101,99,90**
CSF £24.16 TOTE £2.40: £2.10, £8.10; EX 30.70 Trifecta £46.80 Pool £181.08 - 2.86 winning units..
Owner Eric Nisbet & Stan Moffat **Bred** Castleton Group **Trained** Uplawmoor, E Renfrews

FOCUS
A modest handicap.

5364 SCOTTISH RACING ON BIG SCREEN AMATEUR RIDERS' H'CAP 1m 5f 9y
5:35 (5:35) (Class 6) (0-65,65) 4-Y-O+ **£1,977** (£608; £304) **Stalls** High

Form RPR
0-40 **1** **Terenzium (IRE)**[14] 4900 8-9-10 **50**..........................(p) MrJHamer(3) 4 59
(Micky Hammond) *hld up: smooth hdwy over 2f out: rdn to ld ins fnl f: sn clr* **5/1**
0220 **2** *3* **Hi Dancer**[23] 4604 7-10-9 **65**.......................... MissCharlotteHolmes(5) 1 70
(B M R Haslam) *prom: effrt over 2f out: chsd wnr ins fnl f: kpt on* **9/1**
0 **3** *3* **Front Rank (IRE)**[27] 3122 10-9-4 **46** oh1.......................... MissECSayer(5) 10 46
(Mrs Dianne Sayer) *led 2f: cl up: ev ch and rdn over 3f out: drifted lft fr over 1f out: sn one pce* **4/1**[2]
6240 **4** *2* **Tilos Gem (IRE)**[20] 4683 4-10-9 **60**.......................... MrSWalker 6 57
(M Johnston) *cl up: led over 3f out: rdn and edgd rt 2f out: hdd ins fnl f: sn btn* **10/3**[1]
0420 **5** *hd* **Regent's Secret (USA)**[5] 5215 10-10-9 **60**.......................... MrsCBartley 7 57
(J S Goldie) *s.i.s: hld up: pushed along over 3f out: hdwy over 1f out: nvr able to chal* **9/2**[3]
00-5 **6** *nk* **Louisa (GER)**[12] 4953 6-9-4 **46** oh1.......................... MissHCuthbert(5) 5 42
(P Monteith) *bhd: pushed along and outpcd over 4f out: styd on fnl f: nrest at fin* **14/1**
06-0 **7** *2* **Shanavaz**[12] 4945 4-9-9 **46**..........................(p) MissADeniel 3 39
(C J Teague) *hld up in tch: drvn and outpcd over 2f out: n.d after* **50/1**
6024 **8** *18* **Back To Paris (IRE)**[26] 4481 8-9-7 **51**..........................(t) MrTGarner(7) 8 17
(P A Kirby) *plld hrd: led after 2f to over 3f out: rdn and wknd over 1f out* **11/1**
4433 **9** *2 1/2* **Dimashq**[10] 5019 8-9-5 **47**.......................... MissWGibson(5) 9 10
(P T Midgley) *t.k.h: cl up: ev ch over 3f out: wknd over 2f out* **10/1**
3m 2.69s (8.79) **Going Correction** +0.375s/f (Good) **9** Ran SP% **114.0**
Speed ratings (Par 101): **87,85,83,82,81 81,80,69,67**
Tote Swingers:1&2:£8.90, 2&3:£7.70, 1&3:£7.70 CSF £48.42 CT £196.08 TOTE £4.60: £1.60, £4.80, £2.80; EX 40.40 TRIFECTA Not won. Place 6 £12.00, Place 5 £8.43..
Owner O'Sunburn Partnership **Bred** Azienda Agricola Patrizia **Trained** Middleham Moor, N Yorks

FOCUS
A moderate contest run at a decent enough pace in the conditions. They were spread out across the track in the closing stages.
T/Plt: £15.30 to a £1 stake. Pool £52,478.26. 2,500.29 winning tickets. T/Qpdt: £4.60 to a £1 stake. Pool £3,710.20. 588.14 winning tickets. RY

5177 KEMPTON (A.W) (R-H)
Monday, August 23

OFFICIAL GOING: Standard
Wind: Virtually nil. Weather: Overcast

5365 LADIES DAY SATURDAY SEPTEMBER 4TH NURSERY 5f (P)
2:15 (2:15) (Class 6) (0-65,65) 2-Y-O **£1,637** (£483; £241) **Stalls** High

Form RPR
0535 **1** **Dubai Affair**[11] 5000 2-9-7 **65**.......................... SteveDrowne 8 71
(H Morrison) *trckd ldrs: nt clr run bnd 2f out: qcknd over 1f out: pushed along to ld fnl 100yds: comf* **4/1**[2]
335 **2** *3/4* **Kokojo (IRE)**[51] 3686 2-9-5 **63**.......................... FergusSweeney 12 66
(B G Powell) *sn led: rdn over 1f out: hdd fnl 100yds: sn outpcd by wnr but kpt on wl for 2nd* **10/1**
0044 **3** *3/4* **Till Dawn (IRE)**[11] 5000 2-8-9 **53**.......................... EddieAhern 11 54
(A W Carroll) *t.k.h: chsd ldrs: wnt 2nd over 1f out and chal sn after: outpcd ins fnl f* **5/1**[3]
1365 **4** *nse* **Silly Billy (IRE)**[14] 4911 2-9-7 **65**.......................... RichardHughes 9 65
(S Kirk) *trckd ldr: upsides and pushed along 2f out: one pce u.p ins fnl f* **15/2**
6022 **5** *1 1/4* **Johnny Hancocks (IRE)**[11] 5000 2-9-2 **65**.......................... JohnFahy(5) 10 61
(P D Evans) *s.i.s: in rr: pushed along and hdwy 2f out: styd on but nvr gng pce to get into contention* **4/1**[2]
6642 **6** *hd* **Avalon Bay**[19] 4696 2-9-5 **63**.......................... DaneO'Neill 7 58
(Pat Eddery) *s.i.s: in rr: plld hrd: hdwy on outside: rdn and hung lft wl over 1f out: styd on but nvr a threat* **7/2**[1]
6003 **7** *3* **Robber Stone**[11] 5000 2-8-12 **56**.......................... ChrisCatlin 2 40+
(M R Channon) *s.i.s: plld hrd and sn chsd ldrs: rdn 2f out: hung rt u.p and wknd ins fnl 2f* **14/1**
6032 **8** *4* **Bendigedig**[3] 5268 2-8-9 **53**.......................... LiamKeniry 4 23
(S Kirk) *rdn 3f out: a in rr* **16/1**
000 **9** *8* **Blade Pirate**[19] 4716 2-8-11 **55**..........................(be) PatCosgrave 6 —
(J Ryan) *rdn 3f out: a in rr* **33/1**
60.94 secs (0.44) **Going Correction** +0.05s/f (Slow) **9** Ran SP% **115.2**
Speed ratings (Par 92): **98,96,95,95,93 93,88,82,69**
Tote Swingers:1&2:£9.20, 2&3:£8.60, 1&3:£5.80 CSF £43.30 CT £205.35 TOTE £5.20: £1.50, £3.60, £1.90; EX 68.20.
Owner G B Balding **Bred** Miss B Swire **Trained** East Ilsley, Berks

FOCUS
This moderate sprint nursery was the first of four races on the card run round the inside loop, where a high draw is usually a distinct advantage. Racing handily is also often favoured on this course, and being near the front end was no doubt a help here.

NOTEBOOK
Dubai Affair dug deep to get on top and shed her maiden tag at the fifth attempt. She obviously goes well on Polytrack, having finished a fair third at Lingfield on her only previous try on the AW, and is certainly bred to be better than this grade. A return to 6f shouldn't inconvenience her too much looking at the way she finished this off and there could be more to come. (op 7-2)
Kokojo(IRE), having her first outing for 51 days, proved easy to back on this nursery debut. She had the plum draw, though, and racing from the front was much in her favour. She has now clearly found her sort of level. (op 8-1)
Till Dawn(IRE), well backed, was 2lb worse off with the winner on their last-time-out Goodwood form. She too had a decent draw and held every chance on the inside. (op 13-2)
Silly Billy(IRE), who came out of stall nine, unsurprisingly raced positively on this drop back from 7f yet lacked the tactical pace from the furlong marker. Stepping back up a furlong should help and this was more like it again from him. (op 8-1)
Johnny Hancocks(IRE) finished ahead of the winner and the third when second at Goodwood 11 days earlier, and was 4lb higher, but looked to have excellent claims here from stall ten. He proved easy to back, though, and really lost the race due to having to come from behind after a messy start. (op 7-2)
Avalon Bay looked worth a try over the minimum trip and attracted support. He can race freely and did so again early on here, but being restrained over this sharper test was the wrong move. (tchd 10-3)

5366 DIGIBET MAIDEN FILLIES' STKS 1m 2f (P)
2:45 (2:49) (Class 5) 3-Y-O+ **£2,286** (£675; £337) **Stalls** High

Form RPR
23- **1** **Cheetah**[304] 6992 3-8-12 0.......................... KierenFallon 12 90+
(L M Cumani) *trckd ldrs: wnt 2nd 3f out: led 2f out: rdn and flashed tail over 1f out: edgd rt to far rail 1f out: styd on strly* **6/5**[1]
5 **2** *3* **Kristalette (IRE)**[38] 4114 3-8-12 0.......................... AdamKirby 10 84+
(W R Swinburn) *led: rdn and hdd 2f out btn whn crossed and swtchd lft 1f out* **7/1**[3]
222 **3** *3 1/2* **Dolphina (USA)**[14] 4893 3-8-12 75.......................... TomQueally 1 77
(H R A Cecil) *chsd ldr tl rdn 3f out and sn outpcd: plugged on again fr over 1f out but nvr any threat* **9/4**[2]
4 *4* **Star Hill** 3-8-12 0.......................... FergusSweeney 6 69
(A King) *chsd ldrs: rdn and one pce 4f out: styd on again fr 2f out but nvr a threat* **40/1**
5 *3/4* **Moonlight Mischief (IRE)** 3-8-12 0.......................... MartinDwyer 3 68
(B J Meehan) *chsd ldrs: rdn over 3f out: wknd over 2f out* **20/1**
2-50 **6** *4* **Inner Angel**[53] 3581 3-8-12 68.......................... LiamKeniry 13 60
(R A Teal) *chsd ldrs: rdn over 3f out: wknd 2f out* **10/1**
0-0 **7** *2 1/2* **Danvilla**[15] 4874 3-8-12 0.......................... EddieAhern 8 55
(P R Webber) *in rr: styd on fnl 2f but nvr nr ldrs* **40/1**
0 **8** *2* **She's Untouchable**[34] 4238 3-8-8 0 ow1.......................... MarkCoumbe(5) 5 52
(P Leech) *in rr: modest prog fnl 2f* **66/1**
0 **9** *7* **Sea Tobougie**[30] 4364 3-8-12 0.......................... TravisBlock 4 37
(M D I Usher) *s.i.s: mid-div 1/2-way: sn towards rr* **66/1**
03 **10** *shd* **Distant Waters**[112] 1782 3-8-12 0.......................... TedDurcan 11 36
(A P Jarvis) *s.i.s: mid-div 1/2-way: wknd over 3f out* **20/1**
0-5 **11** *1/2* **Dongola (IRE)**[16] 4840 3-8-12 0.......................... LukeMorris 2 35
(P Winkworth) *s.i.s: a towards rr* **50/1**
12 *2* **Beseech (USA)** 3-8-12 0.......................... JimmyQuinn 7 31
(Miss J Feilden) *slowly away: a in rr* **66/1**
00 **13** *3 1/4* **Floridita (USA)**[10] 5057 3-8-12 0.......................... GregFairley 9 25
(M Johnston) *rdn and lost tch 1/2-way* **33/1**
2m 7.28s (-0.72) **Going Correction** +0.05s/f (Slow) **13** Ran SP% **121.6**
Speed ratings (Par 100): **104,101,98,95,95 91,89,88,82,82 82,80,77**
Tote Swingers: 1&2 £3.50, 1&3 £1.40, 2&3 £2.90 CSF £9.75 TOTE £2.30: £1.30, £1.90, £1.10; EX 11.70.
Owner Fittocks Stud **Bred** Fittocks Stud **Trained** Newmarket, Suffolk
■ Stewards' Enquiry : Kieren Fallon caution: careless riding.

FOCUS
A fillies' maiden featuring largely late-maturing 3-y-os. It was run at a fair enough pace and the form looks straightforward.

5367 DIGIBET SPORTS BETTING H'CAP 1m 2f (P)
3:15 (3:18) (Class 5) (0-70,70) 3-Y-O+ **£2,286** (£675; £337) **Stalls** High

Form RPR
-005 **1** **Classically (IRE)**[14] 4910 4-9-8 **65**.......................... SteveDrowne 8 75
(H Morrison) *trckd ldrs: drvn and styd on to dispute ld in three-way chal thrght fnl f: led last stride* **4/1**[1]
3205 **2** *nse* **Blitzed**[12] 4964 3-9-4 **69**.......................... GeorgeBaker 7 79
(G L Moore) *led: rdn 2f out: jnd in three-way chal thrght fnl f: hdd last stride* **5/1**[2]
6/5- **3** *nse* **Ateeb**[508] 1087 4-9-8 **65**.......................... TadhgO'Shea 1 75
(E A L Dunlop) *trckd ldr to 5f out: wnt 2nd again ins fnl 2f: disp ld in three-way chal thrght fnl f: no ex last stride* **13/2**
0051 **4** *2 3/4* **Dream Of Fortune (IRE)**[37] 4132 6-9-7 **64**.......................... TomQueally 6 68
(P D Evans) *in rr: hdwy and rdn fr 2f out: styd on fnl f: no imp on ldng trio* **6/1**[3]
-300 **5** *1/2* **Watchmaker**[135] 1241 7-9-6 **63**.......................... FergusSweeney 10 66
(Miss Tor Sturgis) *chsd ldrs: rdn 3f out: outpcd fnl f* **8/1**
0031 **6** *2 3/4* **Beat Up**[14] 4913 4-9-7 **64**.......................... SaleemGolam 4 62
(G D Blake) *t.k.h: in tch: styng on at one pce whn hmpd on ins over 1f out: kpt on again but nvr in contention* **5/1**[2]
0/0- **7** *3* **Given A Choice (IRE)**[275] 7475 8-9-3 **65**.......................... SimonPearce(5) 9 57
(J Pearce) *s.i.s: in rr: styd on same pce fnl 2f* **25/1**
3450 **8** *2* **Saviour Sand (IRE)**[17] 4804 6-9-4 **66**..........................(t) KylieManser(5) 12 54
(Miss Olivia Maylam) *slowly away: t.k.h in rr tl rapid hdwy on outside to chse wnr 5f out: rdn 2f out and sn wknd* **25/1**
046 **9** *3/4* **Aldo**[21] 4661 3-9-5 **70**..........................(t) TedDurcan 13 56
(A J Lidderdale) *chsd ldrs tl rdn and wknd ins fnl 2f* **11/1**
0424 **10** *6* **Khajaaly (IRE)**[19] 4705 3-9-2 **67**.......................... JimmyQuinn 11 41
(Miss J Feilden) *chsd ldrs tl wknd 2f out* **14/1**

56-0 **11** *24* **Trifti**194 485 9-9-13 **70**............ DaneO'Neill 14 —
(Miss Jo Crowley) *s.i.s: a in rr* **33/1**

2m 8.01s (0.01) **Going Correction** +0.05s/f (Slow)
WFA 3 from 4yo+ 8lb 11 Ran SP% **117.7**
Speed ratings (Par 103): **101,100,100,98,98 96,93,92,91,86 67**
Tote Swingers:1&2:£6.70, 2&3:£9.00, 1&3:£6.00 CSF £23.10 CT £128.53 TOTE £4.90: £1.70, £2.50, £2.90; EX 26.30.
Owner Ben Arbib **Bred** Bridgewater Equine Ltd **Trained** East Ilsley, Berks
FOCUS
A moderate handicap. It was run at an average pace and proved to be another race where racing handily was a must, with the first three fighting out a blanket finish.
Beat Up Official explanation: vet said gelding had been struck into
Saviour Sand(IRE) Official explanation: jockey said gelding was slowly away

5368 DIGIBET.COM H'CAP 5f (P)
3:45 (3:45) (Class 4) (0-80,77) 3-Y-0+ £3,885 (£1,156; £577; £288) Stalls High

Form RPR
2065 **1** **Danzoe (IRE)**15 4858 3-8-11 **65**............ DavidProbert 8 73
(Mrs C A Dunnett) *in rr: drvn along 1/2-way: hdwy u.p appr fnl f: str run to ld fnl 25yds: won gng away* **20/1**
6031 **2** *1* **Island Legend (IRE)**10 5025 4-9-2 **68**............(p) LiamKeniry 6 72
(J M Bradley) *led: rdn over 2f out: kpt on u.p: hdd and outpcd fnl 25yds* **6/4**1
4303 **3** *½* **Little Edward**10 5025 12-9-3 **69**............ GeorgeBaker 4 71
(R J Hodges) *chsd ldrs: rdn and styd on fr over 1f out: kpt on ins fnl f* **12/1**
0120 **4** *nk* **Ajjaadd (USA)**12 4961 4-9-5 **71**............ SteveDrowne 3 72+
(T E Powell) *stdd s: in rr: rdn and hdwy on outside over 1f out: styd on strly ins fnl f: gng on cl home* **9/1**
6506 **5** *nk* **Lord Of The Reins (IRE)**10 5025 6-9-6 **72**............ TomQueally 5 72
(J G Given) *in rr: rdn and hdwy over 1f out: kpt on ins fnl f: one pce cl home* **8/1**
0465 **6** *½* **Riflessione**16 4836 4-9-6 **72**............(b) LukeMorris 7 70
(R A Harris) *chsd ldrs: rdn and hung rt over 1f out: wknd ins fnl f* **11/2**3
513 **7** *1 ¾* **Ask Jenny (IRE)**35 4209 8-8-9 **61**............ RichardHughes 2 53
(Patrick Morris) *s.i.s: hld up: sme hdwy fnl f* **12/1**
2005 **8** *hd* **Absa Lutte (IRE)**10 5054 7-9-11 **77**............(t) DaneO'Neill 1 68+
(Dr R D P Newland) *chsd ldrs: rdn over 2f out: wknd appr fnl f* **14/1**
1061 **9** *4 ½* **Night Affair**18 4730 4-9-11 **77**............ AdamKirby 9 52
(D W P Arbuthnot) *chsd ldrs: wkng whn hmpd appr fnl f* **5/1**2

60.20 secs (-0.30) **Going Correction** +0.05s/f (Slow)
WFA 3 from 4yo+ 2lb 9 Ran SP% **120.0**
Speed ratings (Par 105): **104,102,101,101,100 99,97,96,89**
Tote Swingers:1&2:£9.80, 2&3:£3.30, 1&3:£18.10 CSF £52.54 CT £413.58 TOTE £33.00: £7.10, £1.10, £3.00; EX 96.60.
Owner The Smart Syndicate **Bred** Miss Anne Ormsby **Trained** Hingham, Norfolk
FOCUS
A tight-looking sprint handicap. Unsurprisingly it was run at a strong early pace.

5369 EUROPEAN BREEDERS' FUND MAIDEN FILLIES' STKS 1m (P)
4:20 (4:20) (Class 5) 2-Y-0 £3,076 (£915; £457; £228) Stalls High

Form RPR
04 **1** **Wafeira**75 2861 2-9-0 0............ TomQueally 8 79+
(H R A Cecil) *t.k.h and stdd in rr after 1f: hdwy: nt clr run and swtchd lft 2f out: str run fr over 1f out and qcknd ins fnl f: upsides in four-way chal fnl 75yds: led last strides* **4/1**1
65 **2** *hd* **Choral**9 5078 2-8-11 0............ PatrickHills(3) 6 77
(R Hannon) *chsd ldrs: rdn to dispute ld in four-way chal ins fnl f: stl pressing clsng stages: no ex last strides* **16/1**
3 **3** *nse* **Poplin**25 4517 2-9-0 0............ KierenFallon 14 76+
(L M Cumani) *s.i.s: in rr: hdwy 3f out: str run fr over 1f out to press for ld in four-way chal fnl 75yds: sn slt advantage: hdd last strides* **13/2**
034 **4** *¾* **Opera Dancer**25 4508 2-9-0 **79**............ LiamKeniry 4 75
(S Kirk) *chsd ldr: drvn to ld over 1f out: jnd in four-way chal fnl 75yds: sn narrowly hdd: wknd nr fin* **9/2**2
0 **5** *1 ¾* **Magical Flower**25 4508 2-9-0 0............ FrankieDettori 10 71
(W J Knight) *led: rdn and jnd 2f out: hdd over 1f out: wknd ins fnl f* **9/2**2
00 **6** *¾* **Memory Lane**10 5029 2-9-0 0............ SebSanders 3 69+
(Sir Mark Prescott) *chsd ldrs on outside: stl wl there fr 2f out: kpt on same pce fnl f* **50/1**
65 **7** *hd* **Bonita Star**10 5049 2-9-0 0............ AlanMunro 12 69
(M R Channon) *chsd ldrs: pushed along over 2f out: wknd ins fnl f* **8/1**
8 *nk* **Cool Wind (IRE)** 2-9-0 0............ AhmedAjtebi 11 68+
(Mahmood Al Zarooni) *s.i.s: in rr: pushed along and kpt on fnl 2f* **7/1**
4 **9** *½* **Set To Music (IRE)**16 4844 2-9-0 0............ HayleyTurner 1 67
(M L W Bell) *stdd s: in rr: pushed along and hdwy on ins over 2f out: one pce fnl f* **6/1**3
0 **10** *7* **Dolcezza (IRE)**23 4595 2-8-11 0............ Louis-PhilippeBeuzelin(3) 2 52
(B J Meehan) *in rr but in tch tl wknd 3f out* **25/1**
11 *7* **Handicraft (IRE)** 2-9-0 0............ GregFairley 7 36
(M Johnston) *rdn and bhd fnl 3f* **25/1**

1m 42.07s (2.27) **Going Correction** +0.05s/f (Slow) 11 Ran SP% **123.1**
Speed ratings (Par 91): **90,89,89,89,87 86,86,86,85,78 71**
Tote Swingers:1&2:£15.90, 2&3:£12.60, 1&3:£7.40 CSF £71.45 TOTE £5.40: £2.10, £4.60, £2.20; EX 83.10.
Owner K Abdulla **Bred** Juddmonte Farms Ltd **Trained** Newmarket, Suffolk
FOCUS
The betting suggested this fillies' maiden was wide open. There were some choicely bred sorts on show, and the distance would've provided quite a test for these juveniles at this stage of their careers. There was just an uneven pace on, though, which resulted in a tight finish and another race where racing prominently was an advantage.
NOTEBOOK
Wafeira hit top gear half a furlong out down the centre of the track and got in front nearing the line. She was a beaten favourite on her two previous outings, but was returning from a 75-day absence and this longer trip proved more to her liking. This was her AW debut and she is a half-sister to Stand Guard, a four-time winner at this venue, so the switch of surface clearly helped. Her stable tends to excel with such fillies but she is probably more of one for next season, when a longer trip will be well within her compass. (op 11-2)
Choral was also stepping up from 6f and she got a positive ride. She responded well to pressure and very nearly made it third time lucky. She is now eligible for nurseries and is obviously open to improvement over this sort of trip.
Poplin was a well-beaten third on her debut at Nottingham, but is bred to enjoy this sort of test and her yard's juveniles most often improve with racing. Drawn highest of all, she got a strong ride from Kieren Fallon and only just lost out. It shouldn't be long before she finds a race, but her entry in the Fillies' Mile looks to optimistic. (op 5-1)
Opera Dancer, another in the Fillies' Mile, was having her fourth outing and her previous experience saw her get into a decent early position from her moderate draw. She paid for her early exertions late on, but again ran well and deserves to win. (op 5-1)
Magical Flower, who attracted support, proved keen to post. She got pretty much the run of the race on the front end and failed to see out the extra furlong under such tactics, but this was still an improved effort. (op 6-1)
Memory Lane was caught wide for most of the race, but posted a much-improved effort for the stiffer test and will now be handicapped on this effort. (op 66-1)
Bonita Star was another keen to post and through the early parts of the race. She is related to AW winners, though, and does stay well. Nurseries are now an option.
Cool Wind(IRE), whose dam was a debut winner over 5f, missed the break and ran distinctly green. She caught the eye staying on for pressure late on, however, and should be plenty wiser for this debut experience. (op 9-1)
Set To Music(IRE) ran with promise on her debut over 7f at Newmarket and is another entered in the Fillies' Mile. Friendless in the betting ring, she was dropped in from her outside stall and tried her best to close on the inside 2f out, but lacked a sufficient gear change. (op 9-2)

5370 EUROPEAN BREEDERS' FUND CONDITIONS STKS 1m (P)
4:50 (4:51) (Class 3) 3-Y-0+
£7,290 (£2,183; £1,091; £546; £272; £136) Stalls High

Form RPR
1-33 **1** **Secrecy**11 5009 4-9-3 110............ TedDurcan 2 111+
(Saeed Bin Suroor) *hld up in rr but in tch: hdwy and hung rt 2f out: edgd rt u.p and styd on to ld ins fnl f: kpt on wl* **15/8**2
0362 **2** *1 ¼* **Sirocco Breeze**37 4126 5-9-3 115............ FrankieDettori 4 108+
(Saeed Bin Suroor) *slowly away and lost 8 l s: sn in tch w main gp: rapid hdwy fr 2f out to ld over 1f out: hdd and one pce ins fnl f* **7/4**1
4-1 **3** *½* **Capital Attraction (USA)**93 2335 3-8-11 88............ TomQueally 5 106
(H R A Cecil) *chsd ldrs tl rdn and outpcd over 2f out: styd on again to chse ldrs ins fnl f: one pce nr fin* **9/2**3
-530 **4** *1 ¾* **Cloudy Start**104 2020 4-9-3 108............ FergusSweeney 1 103
(J A Osborne) *led tl hdd over 1f out: outpcd fnl f* **14/1**
4600 **5** *1 ¼* **Viva Vettori**16 4843 6-9-8 99............ DaneO'Neill 6 105
(D R C Elsworth) *chsd ldr: rdn over 2f out: wknd over 1f out* **9/1**
0000 **6** *1 ¼* **Ceremonial Jade (UAE)**136 1206 7-8-12 99............ TobyAtkinson(5) 3 97
(M Botti) *s.i.s: in rr: rdn and hdwy on ins to chse ldrs ins fnl 2f: wknd fnl f* **25/1**

1m 38.9s (-0.90) **Going Correction** +0.05s/f (Slow)
WFA 3 from 4yo+ 6lb 6 Ran SP% **109.8**
Speed ratings (Par 107): **106,104,104,102,101 100**
Tote Swingers:1&2:£1.60, 2&3:£2.10, 1&3:£1.80 CSF £5.28 TOTE £2.90: £1.10, £1.10; EX 5.40.
Owner Godolphin **Bred** Whatton Manor Stud **Trained** Newmarket, Suffolk
FOCUS
A decent little conditions event for the class. It was something of a strange race, but the three market leaders still fought it out.
NOTEBOOK
Secrecy was passed over by Frankie Dettori, but he received a good ride from Ted Durcan and ultimately his proven stamina won him the day on this AW debut. He performed near his previous best when third in Group 3 company on his return 11 days earlier and, showing the benefit of that run here, this rates another forward step. He doesn't have many miles on the clock and could just nick a Group event before the year is out. (op 2-1)
Sirocco Breeze, the winner's stablemate, was unproven over this far, but otherwise had a lot going for him on this return to an artificial surface. However, he completely missed the break and then proved keen when jumping out. The average pace helped him recover and he showed his class by quickening smartly to lead in the home straight. He really made his move too soon, though, as he was swamped by the winner at the business end. It would be hard to blame Dettori for that as he must have been going very well 2f out and, while a more patient ride could see him winning over this trip in due course, he does look a 7f specialist. (op 5-4)
Capital Attraction(USA) was having his first outing since winning his maiden at Lingfield back in May and was obviously faced with a much stiffer task. He was a little free early on and lacked an immediate change of pace when it mattered, but still posted a decent effort in defeat. He remains open to further progression, but his official mark will now shoot up as a result of this. (op 11-2 tchd 7-2)
Cloudy Start, returning from a 103-day break without headgear, has won from the front over C&D before and set out to make all. He is entitled to come on for the run, but got a freebie out in front and didn't look that willing under maximum pressure. (op 20-1)
Viva Vettori likes this venue, but faced a stiff task conceding weight to classier rivals. (op 12-1)
Ceremonial Jade(UAE) was never a threat, but should improve for the run.

5371 DAY TIME, NIGHT TIME, GREAT TIME H'CAP 1m 4f (P)
5:20 (5:20) (Class 2) (0-100,90) 3-Y-0
£9,221 (£2,761; £1,380; £691; £344; £173) Stalls High

Form RPR
0451 **1** **Wild Rose**19 4698 3-8-13 **82**............(t) HayleyTurner 1 96
(M L W Bell) *hld up in rr: stdy hdwy over 2f out: qcknd to ld appr fnl f: drvn clr* **11/1**
2-21 **2** *6* **Fourth Generation (IRE)**29 4407 3-8-9 **78**............ KierenFallon 3 82
(G A Swinbank) *w ldr 3f: styd trcking ldrs: rdn to take slt ld ins fnl 2f: hddappr fnl f and sn no ch w wnr* **7/1**
13 **3** *1* **Shubaat**16 4827 3-9-2 **85**............ PhilipRobinson 7 87
(M A Jarvis) *t.k.h: led after 4f: hdd 4f out: stl chalng but n.m.r between horses over 2f out: no ch w wnr fnl f and styd on same pce for 3rd* **5/1**3
3316 **4** *1* **Sing Sweetly**16 4815 3-9-1 **84**............ TomQueally 2 85
(G A Butler) *hld up in rr: stdy hdwy 3f out: rdn to chse ldrs and fnd no ex wl over 1f out* **5/1**3
21 **5** *6* **Sagamore**13 4926 3-9-7 **90**............ NeilCallan 6 81
(J H M Gosden) *led 4f: styd pressing ldr tl led again 4f out: rdn ins fnl 3f: hdd ins fnl 2f: sn btn* **11/4**1
0423 **6** *2 ¼* **Dromore (IRE)**23 4573 3-9-4 **87**............ JimmyFortune 5 75
(A M Balding) *s.i.s: in rr: rdn 4f out: no imp on ldrs: wknd over 2f out* **5/1**3
0004 **7** *14* **Fareej (USA)**16 4815 3-9-3 **86**............ FrankieDettori 4 51
(Saeed Bin Suroor) *chsd ldrs: rdn 3f out: wknd over 2f out* **4/1**2

2m 33.11s (-1.39) **Going Correction** +0.05s/f (Slow) 7 Ran SP% **117.5**
Speed ratings (Par 106): **106,102,101,100,96 95,85**
Tote Swingers: 1&2 £9.20, 1&3 £7.10, 2&3 £5.10 CSF £86.42 TOTE £11.90: £4.40, £3.60; EX 36.10 Place 6 £20.35, Place 5 £5.71..
Owner Saif Ali & Saeed H Altayer **Bred** Biddestone Stud **Trained** Newmarket, Suffolk
FOCUS
What looked a competitive 3-y-o middle-distance handicap was turned into a procession.
NOTEBOOK
Wild Rose didn't have to come out of third gear to score as she pleased and is now 4-5 on Polytrack. Settled in rear early on, she made stylish headway around 2f out and eventually went clear without needing to be extended. She was 7lb higher than when taking a lesser race at the track 19 days earlier, and the handicapper will react accordingly for this, so her best option is probably to look for something under a penalty in this sphere. It may be that connections look to gain some valuable black type, though. (op 9-1)
Fourth Generation(IRE), off the mark at Carlisle last month, was second on his penultimate outing when making his AW debut. He had stamina to prove in this better race and, while no match for the easy winner, turned in an improved effort in defeat. (op 6-1)

Shubaat, having his first taste of the AW, increased the tempo when going to the front on the back straight. He was made to look very one-paced, but it's not hard to see why he was tried over further last time and he is too lightly raced to write off yet. (op 4-1)
Sing Sweetly was returning to the C&D that saw her win her maiden effortlessly two runs back. She travelled sweetly into contention with the winner, but was firmly put in her place when that one asserted and looks held by the handicapper.
Sagamore created a decent impression when off the mark at Lingfield over this trip at Lingfield 13 days earlier. He was conceding weight all round, but was cooked 2f out and may just have found the run coming a bit too soon. He is another that is too lightly raced to be writing off. (op 4-1)
Dromore(IRE) was the first beat turning for home and was some way below his recent level. (op 7-1)
Fareej(USA) had returned to form of late and had previously scored on Polytrack, but he turned in a tame effort. Official explanation: jockey had no explanation for the poor form shown (op 7-2)
T/Plt: £37.60 to a £1 stake. Pool £72,742.06. 1,411.59 winning tickets. T/Qpdt: £9.10 to a £1 stake. Pool £5,043.80. 409.20 winning tickets. ST

5146 WINDSOR (R-H)
Monday, August 23

OFFICIAL GOING: Good to soft (soft in places) changing to soft (good to soft in places) after race 1 (5.15)
Stands' rail dolled out 3yds at 6f and 1/2yd at winning post. Top bend dolled out 6yds from innermost line, adding 14yds to races of one mile and over.
Wind: Strong, behind. Weather: Mostly fine

5372 E B F SPORTINGBET.COM MAIDEN STKS 6f
5:15 (5:15) (Class 5) 2-Y-O £3,821 (£1,128; £564) Stalls High

Form RPR
2 **1** **Invincible Ridge (IRE)**[14] 4902 2-9-3 0 RichardHughes 10 84+
(R Hannon) trckd ldrs: smooth prog to go 2nd over 1f out: pushed along to ld last 100yds: comf **8/13**[1]
2 *1* **Valerius Maximus** 2-8-10 0 DuilioDaSilva(7) 13 79
(P F I Cole) led: styd towards centre fr 1/2-way: rdn and hung lft 2f out: kpt on wl despite hanging lft: hdd and wl hld last 100yds **40/1**
6 **3** *6* **Babich Bay (IRE)**[139] 1136 2-8-12 0 JohnFahy(5) 8 61
(F J Brennan) w ldrs: shkn up over 2f out: outpcd over 1f out: jst hld on for 3rd **12/1**[3]
0 **4** *nk* **Whistle On By**[12] 4960 2-9-3 0 MichaelHills 15 60
(B W Hills) dwlt: pushed along in rr 1/2-way: stdy prog over 1f out: styd on wl to press for 3rd nr fin **25/1**
5 *1/2* **Dusty Bluebells (IRE)** 2-8-12 0 LukeMorris 16 54
(J S Moore) wl in rr: prog in centre fr 2f out: kpt on same pce fnl f **40/1**
6 *1/2* **Les Verguettes (IRE)** 2-8-12 0 PatCosgrave 7 52
(Stef Higgins) s.s: rcvrd to chse ldrs: disp 2nd over 1f out: sn wknd **20/1**
5 **7** *3 1/2* **Swaninstockwell (IRE)**[11] 4993 2-9-3 0 IanMongan 12 47
(P M Phelan) dwlt: sn in tch bhd ldrs: shkn up and wknd over 1f out **33/1**
8 *1 1/4* **L'Astre De Choisir (IRE)** 2-9-3 0 ShaneKelly 14 43
(W R Swinburn) dwlt: a in rr: rn green 1/2-way: no prog 2f out **12/1**[3]
54 **9** *1* **Proper Charlie**[24] 4549 2-9-3 0 (t) JimCrowley 4 40
(W J Knight) mostly chsd ldr to over 1f out: wknd rapidly **5/1**[2]
10 *2 1/4* **Special Endeavour (IRE)** 2-9-3 0 MartinDwyer 6 33
(W R Muir) w ldrs: shkn up 1/2-way: wknd over 2f out **33/1**
11 *1/2* **Looney Les (IRE)** 2-9-3 0 KevinGhunowa 1 32
(F J Brennan) s.v.s: mostly last and a struggling **66/1**

1m 14.91s (1.91) **Going Correction** +0.20s/f (Good) 11 Ran SP% **114.8**
Speed ratings (Par 94): **95,93,85,85,84 83,79,77,76,73 72**
Tote Swingers:1&2:£10.80, 2&3:£65.90, 1&3:£4.00 CSF £43.14 TOTE £1.80: £1.10, £4.40, £3.30; EX 21.40 Trifecta £99.00 Pool £2,640.39 - 19.73 winning units..
Owner Con Harrington **Bred** Con Harrington **Trained** East Everleigh, Wilts

FOCUS
Just an ordinary pace for this maiden but the front pair look to have potential as they drew well clear of the field.

NOTEBOOK
Invincible Ridge(IRE) was given a typically confident ride from Richard Hughes and got off the mark with the minimum of fuss. The jockey was fairly confident that the son of Invincible Spirit would handle the conditions and he only had to be ridden out hands and heels to assert his authority in the closing stages. He will probably take the nursery route now but also has the option of one of the Newmarket Sales races and looks a fair prospect. (op 4-6 tchd 1-2)
Valerius Maximus ran with plenty of promise and should be off the mark before long. He is entitled to come on a bundle for this experience as he ran green when hitting the front and hung left, but he finished clear of the remainder.
Babich Bay(IRE) had been gelded and switched yards after his debut run at Ffos Las in similar conditions. He produced a respectable effort but could not match the pace of the front pair when they kicked on a furlong out. (op 16-1)
Whistle On By appreciated being upped in distance after staying on at Sandown on debut over 5f and looks to be capable of finding an opportunity if building on this. (op 14-1)
Dusty Bluebells(IRE) shaped with promise. He was soon being pushed along in the rear but, when the penny dropped, stayed on well in the closing stages. (op 50-1)
Les Verguettes(IRE) was another who shaped with a degree of promise and showed good early speed before fading in the final furlong.

5373 HARLEQUINS RUGBY SCRUM DOWN (S) STKS 1m 67y
5:45 (5:45) (Class 6) 2-Y-O £1,774 (£523; £262) Stalls High

Form RPR
2 **1** **Rather Cool**[17] 4788 2-8-7 0 EddieAhern 10 58
(A B Haynes) chsd clr ldr: clsd to ld over 2f out: drvn and hrd pressed fr over 1f out: hld on wl **6/1**[2]
0 **2** *nk* **Areopagitica**[61] 3332 2-8-2 0 JohnFahy(5) 9 57+
(C G Cox) hld up in 9th: prog over 3f out and prom over 2f out: rdn to chal wl over 1f out: nrly upsides after: nt qckn last 100yds **12/1**
0 **3** *2 3/4* **Red Jacaranda**[9] 5085 2-8-7 0 WilliamCarson 12 51
(C A Dwyer) chsd ldrs: rdn over 2f out and cl enough: nt qckn wl over 1f out: styd on to take 3rd last stride **20/1**
3504 **4** *shd* **Ivan's A Star (IRE)**[12] 4967 2-8-12 56 (p) LukeMorris 6 56
(J S Moore) hld up in tch: prog to chse ldrs 3f out: rdn and cl enough 2f out: no imp on ldng pair over 1f out: lost 3rd last stride **14/1**
0540 **5** *nk* **Blaze On By**[22] 4623 2-8-8 55 ow1 RichardHughes 5 51
(R Hannon) hld up in last pair: pushed along over 3f out: styd on fr over 1f out: nrest at fin **6/1**[2]
05 **6** *1* **Indiracer (IRE)**[7] 5147 2-8-7 0 GregFairley 11 48
(A Bailey) settled in midfield: outpcd over 2f out: kpt on but nvr on terms w ldrs **6/4**[1]
0 **7** *2 1/2* **Senor Sassi (USA)**[17] 4802 2-8-12 0 AlanMunro 4 48
(J S Moore) hld up in last pair: pushed along over 3f out: nvr on terms: modest late prog **40/1**
0656 **8** *1 1/4* **Ventose**[24] 4554 2-8-7 56 ChrisCatlin 2 40
(M R Channon) free to post: led and sn clr: c bk and hdd over 2f out: sn btn but didn't weaken tl fnl f **25/1**
000 **9** *3* **Bathwick Siesta**[3] 5255 2-8-12 0 (p) JimCrowley 7 38
(J G Portman) chsd ldrs: rdn and cl enough 3f out: wknd jst over 2f out **8/1**[3]
006 **10** *14* **Only Ten Per Cent (IRE)**[11] 4999 2-8-12 51 LiamKeniry 13 8
(J S Moore) in tch to 3f out: wknd rapidly: t.o **16/1**
004 **11** *54* **Endorser**[20] 4682 2-8-12 60 (b) MartinDwyer 1 —
(W R Muir) chsd ldng pair to 4f out: wknd v rapidly and sn wl t.o **14/1**

1m 48.27s (3.57) **Going Correction** +0.375s/f (Good) 11 Ran SP% **117.6**
Speed ratings (Par 92): **97,96,93,93,93 92,90,88,85,71 17**
Tote Swingers:1&2:£14.00, 2&3:£96.00, 1&3:£7.00 CSF £73.74 TOTE £4.50: £1.60, £5.50, £3.10; EX 83.90 Trifecta £616.40 Pool £2,082.76 - 2.50 winning units..The winner was bought in for £11,400.
Owner P Cook **Bred** R J Barber And T E Pocock **Trained** Limpley Stoke, Bath
■ Stewards' Enquiry : John Fahy one-day ban: used whip with excessive frequency (Sep 6)

FOCUS
This seller was run at a decent pace.

NOTEBOOK
Rather Cool had performed with credit when runner-up on debut for Ron Hodges in a seller and was subsequently claimed by Andy Haynes for £6,000. She has a very willing attitude as she looked as though she would be swallowed up over 2f out but kept finding for pressure and ran out a determined winner. This should hold her in good stead for the future, as well as being open to further improvement when stepped up in class. There was plenty of interest at the auction and connections had to go to £11,200 to retian her, so she is clearly held in some regard. (op 9-2 tchd 3-1)
Areopagitica was unable to go the pace over 6f on debut but aprreciated the step up in distance and gave the winner most to do throughout the final furlong. She looks capable of being competitive at this level. (op 9-1 tchd 14-1)
Red Jacaranda was quite highly tried on debut but looked far better suited being dropped to this level. He had his chance but could only muster the same pace from over a furlong out. (op 14-1)
Ivan's A Star(IRE) had been performing with some promise in this grade and again ran to that level of form. (op 11-1)
Blaze On By had been disappointing when dropped to selling company and off a low mark in a nursery last time. She could never get involved from well off the pace but she did stay on in the closing stages. (op 13-2 tchd 8-1)
Indiracer(IRE) was a strong favourite, but looked very one-paced in the rain-softened conditions and could not land a blow. (op 9-4)
Ventose ensured this seller was run at a decent pace and was soon clear of the field before getting headed over 2f out. (op 16-1)

5374 SPORTINGBET.COM NURSERY 1m 67y
6:15 (6:16) (Class 3) (0-85,83) 2-Y-O £3,885 (£1,156; £577; £288) Stalls High

Form RPR
01 **1** **Pisco Sour (USA)**[20] 4682 2-9-0 **76** EddieAhern 6 84+
(H Morrison) trckd ldng pair: wnt 2nd 3f out: rdn to ld wl over 1f out: edgd rt sn after: drew clr fnl f **5/4**[1]
1034 **2** *2 1/4* **Liberty Cap (USA)**[12] 4955 2-9-6 **82** (p) SteveDrowne 7 84
(J H M Gosden) led: veered rt at intersection over 3f out: hdd wl over 1f out: sltly impeded after: one pce fnl f **9/1**
4364 **3** *5* **Sheila's Star (IRE)**[11] 4984 2-8-3 **65** LukeMorris 3 57
(J S Moore) chsd ldr to 3f out: hrd rdn and steadily fdd **10/1**
031 **4** *2 1/4* **Menadati (USA)**[12] 4940 2-9-4 **80** TedDurcan 8 67+
(D R Lanigan) t.k.h: hld up in 4th: shkn up over 2f out: fnd nil and sn btn **4/1**[2]
4466 **5** *3/4* **Dazzling Valentine**[22] 4614 2-8-1 **68** JohnFahy(5) 9 53
(A Bailey) prom briefly but sn heavily restrained to last: effrt 3f out: no prog and wl btn 2f out **8/1**
3002 **6** *7* **Takeaway**[17] 4801 2-9-7 **83** RichardHughes 4 54
(R Hannon) hld up in 5th: rdn wl over 2f out: sn wknd **5/1**[3]
540 **7** *29* **Algurayn (IRE)**[28] 4437 2-8-7 **69** (p) SaleemGolam 5 —
(G Prodromou) rdn in 6th 1/2-way: sn wknd: t.o **40/1**

1m 47.29s (2.59) **Going Correction** +0.375s/f (Good) 7 Ran SP% **113.8**
Speed ratings (Par 98): **102,99,94,92,91 84,55**
Tote Swingers:1&2:£4.10, 2&3:£13.10, 1&3:£3.50 CSF £13.62 CT £78.61 TOTE £3.00: £2.80, £4.10; EX 17.50 Trifecta £90.60 Pool £3,225.47 - 26.34 winning units..
Owner Michael Kerr-Dineen **Bred** Hascombe Stud **Trained** East Ilsley, Berks

FOCUS
An interesting nursery with a good pace.

NOTEBOOK
Pisco Sour(USA) was making his handicap debut off what appeared to be an attractive mark and duly landed the spoils with enough in hand. He was strongly pressed by the runner-up and wandered around a bit but was comfortably on top in the latter stages. His yard are in fine form at present and this clearly progressive son of Lemon Drop Kid looks an exciting prospect. (op 15-8 tchd 2-1)
Liberty Cap(USA) had been nibbled at early but was a big drifter before the off. He ran with plenty of credit and was a serious threat when making his challenge before getting slighty impeded when the winner hung into him. He stuck to his task well and was slighty unlucky to bump into a promising sort. (op 5-1 tchd 12-1)
Sheila's Star(IRE) has been running consistently in nurseries and again performed with credit, although readily held by the front two. (op 16-1 tchd 18-1)
Menadati(USA) had been progressing well and got off the mark at the third time of asking in a Beverley maiden. He had his chance but the soft ground probably found him out. (op 5-1)
Dazzling Valentine was heavily restrained off the pace, but could not get to the leaders when asked to do so. (op 9-1 tchd 10-1 and 15-2)
Takeaway probably failed to see out the step up to a mile in the conditions. Official explanation: trainer's rep said colt was unsuited by the soft (good to soft places) ground (op 4-1 tchd 11-2)

5375 WESTONS CIDER H'CAP 1m 2f 7y
6:45 (6:45) (Class 4) (0-85,83) 3-Y-O+ £4,403 (£1,310; £654; £327) Stalls Low

Form RPR
2-31 **1** **Absinthe (IRE)**[18] 4758 4-10-0 **83** AdamKirby 4 101+
(W R Swinburn) hld up in 6th: prog to ld over 2f out: shkn up and drew clr over 1f out: eased last 100yds **9/4**[1]
3121 **2** *2* **Urban Space**[15] 4873 4-9-8 **77** WilliamCarson 6 86
(J L Flint) hld up in 8th: prog 3f out: rdn and cl up over 2f out: chsd wnr wl over 1f out: kpt on but no imp **11/2**[3]
30-0 **3** *1* **Green Wadi**[18] 4758 5-9-2 **71** GeorgeBaker 11 78
(G L Moore) t.k.h: trckd ldng pair: chsd wnr over 2f out to wl over 1f out: kpt on **22/1**

3132 **4** 2 **Peace Corps**[15] 4873 4-9-6 75 ....(vt) PatCosgrave 8 78
(J R Boyle) *hld up in 5th: rdn and effrt over 2f out: kpt on same pce fnl 2f: nvr able to threaten* **12/1**

2-06 **5** 3/4 **Spirit Of A Nation (IRE)**[40] 4023 5-9-13 82 .... ChrisCatlin 2 84
(D H Brown) *chsd ldr: chal 3f out: lost pl u.p over 2f out: wl btn over 1f out* **8/1**

04 **6** 3/4 **At Wits End**[47] 3782 4-9-3 72 .... KirstyMilczarek 1 72
(J A R Toller) *hld up in last pair: stl there 3f out: prog on outer and reminder over 1f out: kpt on: nvr nr ldrs* **7/1**

0005 **7** 5 **Wing Play (IRE)**[18] 4758 5-9-10 79 ....(p) ShaneKelly 9 69
(H Morrison) *hld up in 9th: pushed along 3f out: modest prog past wkng rivals and one reminder over 1f out: wknd fnl f* **11/1**

2363 **8** 3 3/4 **Hidden Glory**[18] 4758 3-9-2 79 ....(b[1]) DaneO'Neill 10 62
(Pat Eddery) *chsd ldng trio: lost pl qckly over 2f out: sn struggling* **4/1**[2]

30-6 **9** 1 3/4 **Blaise Tower**[41] 3995 4-9-4 73 ....(v[1]) NeilCallan 3 52
(A B Haynes) *mde most to over 2f out: sn wknd* **40/1**

2000 **10** 3/4 **Wind Star**[9] 5084 7-9-2 76 .... MarkCoumbe(5) 7 54
(M F Harris) *hld up in 7th: rdn over 3f out: wknd over 2f out* **50/1**

21-0 **11** 23 **Mirabella (IRE)**[109] 1850 3-9-5 82 .... RichardHughes 5 —
(R Hannon) *dwlt: a in last pair: wknd and eased over 2f out: t.o* **16/1**

2m 11.04s (2.34) **Going Correction** +0.375s/f (Good)
WFA 3 from 4yo+ 8lb **11** Ran SP% **120.4**
Speed ratings (Par 105): **105,103,102,101,100 99,95,92,91,90 72**
Tote Swingers: 1&2 £2.00, 1&3 £11.20, 2&3 £34.70 CSF £14.80 CT £222.91 TOTE £2.70: £1.90, £2.10, £9.40; EX 10.60 Trifecta £213.70 Pool £3,668.84 - 12.70 winning units..
Owner P W Harris **Bred** Moyglare Stud Farm Ltd **Trained** Aldbury, Herts

FOCUS
An ordinary pace for this competitive handicap.

5376 TALKSPORT MAIDEN STKS 1m 2f 7y
7:15 (7:16) (Class 5) 3-Y-O+ **£2,456** (£725; £362) **Stalls** Low

Form RPR

1 **Roberto Pegasus (USA)** 4-9-11 0 .... IanMongan 3 72
(P M Phelan) *dwlt: sn chsd ldng trio: shkn up over 2f out: wnt 3rd over 1f out: drvn and styd on wl fnl f to ld last strides* **16/1**

-456 **2** nk **Santa Margherita**[22] 4626 3-8-12 62 .... DaneO'Neill 7 66
(H J L Dunlop) *led: rdn and narrowly hdd 2f out: hanging lft after but pressed ldr: upsides nr fin: nt qckn* **7/1**[3]

0 **3** hd **Shallow Bay**[14] 4906 3-9-3 0 .... ShaneKelly 4 71
(W R Swinburn) *trckd ldr: led narrowly 2f out: hrd pressed after: hdd and nt qckn last strides* **9/4**[2]

4 7 **Sense Of Pride** 3-8-12 0 .... SteveDrowne 9 52+
(J H M Gosden) *rn green in 5th: pushed along and lost tch w ldrs 4f out: no ch after: kpt on fnl f* **2/1**[1]

0 **5** 3 1/4 **Zawadi**[21] 4661 3-8-12 0 .... JimCrowley 11 45
(R M Beckett) *trckd ldng pair: shkn up over 2f out and cl enough: wknd qckly fr over 1f out* **12/1**

0 **6** 15 **Falcun**[93] 2334 3-9-3 0 .... J-PGuillambert 6 20
(L M Cumani) *hld up in rr: pushed along and lost tch 4f out: sn wl bhd: t.o* **9/1**

7 1 **Mister Bit (IRE)** 3-9-3 0 .... GeorgeBaker 1 18
(J R Best) *a in last pair: shkn up and lost tch 4f out: t.o* **33/1**

8 7 **Dalanoni (IRE)** 3-9-3 0 .... PatCosgrave 8 —
(J R Fanshawe) *rn green in rr: pushed along and lost tch 4f out: sn wl bhd: wl t.o* **8/1**

0 **9** 18 **Fashion Lady (IRE)**[21] 4661 3-8-12 0 .... TedDurcan 2 —
(C F Wall) *a towards rr: pushed along and lost tch 4f out: t.o* **20/1**

2m 11.87s (3.17) **Going Correction** +0.375s/f (Good)
WFA 3 from 4yo 8lb **9** Ran SP% **119.0**
Speed ratings (Par 103): **102,101,101,96,93 81,80,75,60**
Tote Swingers:1&2:£15.90, 2&3:£1.90, 1&3:£11.30 CSF £126.52 TOTE £29.30: £7.00, £2.20, £1.60; EX 113.30 Trifecta £1140.70 Pool £2,003.96 - 1.30 winning units..
Owner J Daniels **Bred** Gigginstown House Stud **Trained** Epsom, Surrey

FOCUS
A fair pace for this interesting maiden that produced a three-way finish.
Fashion Lady(IRE) Official explanation: jockey said filly had no more to give

5377 METRIC OFFICE FURNITURE H'CAP 5f 10y
7:45 (7:50) (Class 5) (0-70,70) 3-Y-O+ **£2,593** (£765; £383) **Stalls** High

Form RPR

0300 **1** **Sir Geoffrey (IRE)**[9] 5069 4-9-11 70 ....(b) IanMongan 1 84
(J A Glover) *mde all: led most of gp to far side after 2f: in command fnl 2f: styd on wl* **5/1**[1]

2341 **2** 2 1/4 **Matterofact (IRE)**[31] 4326 7-9-9 68 .... TomMcLaughlin 3 74
(M S Saunders) *sn chsd wnr: followed him far side after 2f: kpt on but no imp over 1f out* **5/1**[1]

6-01 **3** 2 **Imaginary Diva**[21] 4659 4-8-3 53 .... SimonPearce(5) 14 52+
(G G Margarson) *snatched up nr side over 3f out: swtchd to far side 1/2-way: prog over 1f out: styd on to take 3rd fnl f* **8/1**[3]

5505 **4** 1 1/4 **The Tatling (IRE)**[8] 5112 13-9-5 64 .... DaneO'Neill 12 58
(J M Bradley) *in tch: wnt far side after 2f to chse ldng pair: no imp 2f out: lost 3rd fnl f* **16/1**

-300 **5** 2 **Convince (USA)**[197] 451 9-8-13 58 ....(p) WilliamCarson 5 45
(J L Flint) *pushed along in rr early: wnt far side after 2f: nvr rchd ldrs: kpt on* **16/1**

-031 **6** hd **Scottish Glen**[33] 4256 4-9-5 64 .... LiamKeniry 4 50
(P R Chamings) *towards rr: wnt far side after 2f: nvr on terms w ldrs* **15/2**[2]

2005 **7** 3/4 **Fromsong (IRE)**[10] 5025 12-9-0 59 .... AdamKirby 9 43
(D K Ivory) *one of two that racd nr side thrght: nt on terms fr 1/2-way* **14/1**

0602 **8** 1/2 **White Shift (IRE)**[9] 5076 4-9-6 65 .... J-PGuillambert 10 47
(P Howling) *racd alone towards centre after 2f: nvr on terms after* **16/1**

6000 **9** hd **Captain Kallis (IRE)**[3] 5262 4-8-6 56 ....(b) JohnFahy(5) 8 37
(D J S Ffrench Davis) *led pair that remained nr side thrght: nt on terms fr 1/2-way* **8/1**[3]

500 **10** hd **Know No Fear**[30] 4366 5-8-5 57 ....(p) KatiaScallan(7) 13 37
(A J Lidderdale) *dwlt: wl in rr: swtchd to far side 1/2-way: nvr on terms after* **16/1**

0-05 **11** 3/4 **Dancing Again**[16] 4835 4-7-13 51 oh6 .... HarryBentley(7) 7 29
(E A Wheeler) *swtchd to r far side 1/2-way: nvr on terms w ldrs there* **33/1**

2250 **12** 2 1/4 **Ginobili (IRE)**[58] 3463 4-9-7 66 .... MartinDwyer 2 36
(Andrew Reid) *prom: wnt far side after 2f: wknd 2f out* **15/2**[2]

60.82 secs (0.52) **Going Correction** +0.20s/f (Good) **12** Ran SP% **112.2**
Speed ratings (Par 103): **103,99,96,94,91 90,89,88,88,88 86,83**
Tote Swingers:1&2:£5.00, 2&3:£2.50, 1&3:£6.50 CSF £24.23 CT £150.56 TOTE £6.70: £2.90, £1.10, £1.90; EX 19.60 Trifecta £121.80 Pool £396.98 - 2.41 winning units. Place 6 £66.62, Place 5 £48.03..
Owner Dixon, Howlett & The Chrystal Maze Ptn **Bred** P Rabbitte **Trained** Babworth, Notts

FOCUS
A very tight sprint handicap which lost some of its interest when Elhamri broke out of the stalls before being withdrawn. However, it still featured plenty of in-form sorts with the three horses racing up the stands' side rail being well held entering the final furlong.
White Shift(IRE) Official explanation: trainer said filly was unsuited by the soft (good to soft places) ground
T/Jkpt: £34,479.50 to a £1 stake. Pool:£1,116,944.12. 23.00 winning tickets. T/Plt: £140.80 to a £1 stake. Pool:£98,720.93. 511.57 winning tickets. T/Qpdt: £22.50 to a £1 stake. Pool:£7,942.29. 260.99 winning tickets. JN

5251 CLAIREFONTAINE (R-H)
Monday, August 23

OFFICIAL GOING: Turf: very soft

5378a PRIX DON DU SANG (PRIX DES GARDENIAS) (CLAIMER) (4YO+) (TURF) 1m 6f 110y
2:30 (12:00) 4-Y-O+ **£7,964** (£3,185; £2,389; £1,592; £796)

RPR

1 **Benjamin (FR)**[190] 558 5-9-4 0 ....(b) ChristopheSoumillon 1 79
(L A Urbano-Grajales, France) **37/10**[2]

2 2 1/2 **Clear Reef**[23] 4597 6-9-4 0 ....(p) OlivierPeslier 5 76
(Jane Chapple-Hyam) *racd in midfield: dropped bk towards rr whn field c wd into st: u.p 2f out: picked up wl in centre of trck: mde gd prog ent fnl f: r.o wl* **23/10**[1]

3 1 1/2 **Twester (FR)**[76] 8-8-11 0 ....(p) IoritzMendizabal 12 66
(J Thibault, France) **15/2**[3]

4 3/4 **Frantz De Galais (FR)**[303] 7037 4-8-8 0 .... WilliamsSaraiva(3) 11 65
(Y Fouin, France) **27/1**

5 shd **Montebella (FR)**[74] 4-8-11 0 .... YohannBourgois 10 65
(Mme L Audon, France) **20/1**

6 1/2 **Trulamani (IRE)**[292] 4-8-13 0 .... SylvainRuis 2 67
(J-P Roman, France) **20/1**

7 5 **Miss Naline (FR)**[51] 5-8-3 0 .... MathieuTavaresDaSilva(5) 3 55
(Mlle S Sine, France) **11/1**

8 1/2 **Star Star (FR)** 7-8-11 0 .... TonyPiccone 13 57
(M Ramin, France) **84/1**

9 5 **Lamborgino (FR)**[51] 7-8-11 0 ....(b) RomainLeDren-Doleuze 14 50
(J Parize, France) **55/1**

10 1 1/2 **Weipert (GER)** 4-9-1 0 .... JohanVictoire 4 52
(H Blume, Germany) **78/10**

0 **Licato (GER)**[42] 11-9-1 0 .... SebastienMaillot 6 —
(Robert Collet, France) **27/1**

0 **Royal Breeze (FR)**[85] 8-8-11 0 .... RonanThomas 9 —
(M Seror, France) **63/1**

0 **War Queen (FR)**[11] 4-8-8 0 .... GregoryBenoist 8 —
(Mme P Alexanian, France) **43/1**

0 **Mafra (IRE)**[123] 4-8-8 0 .... MorganDelalande(3) 15 —
(Y Fouin, France) **9/1**

3m 22.4s (202.40) **14** Ran SP% **116.5**
WIN (incl. 1 euro stake): 4.70. PLACES: 1.70, 1.60, 2.00. DF: 6.40. SF: 10.80.
Owner Luis A Urbano Grajales **Bred** Haras De Manneville **Trained** Pau, France

NOTEBOOK
Clear Reef, who stays further than this, ran on well at the end of the race and could probably have done with a stronger all-round gallop.

5365 KEMPTON (A.W) (R-H)
Tuesday, August 24

OFFICIAL GOING: Standard
Wind: Strong, across (away from stands) Weather: Fine

5379 BOOK KEMPTON TICKETS ON 0844 579 3008 CLASSIFIED STKS 7f (P)
6:40 (6:40) (Class 6) 3-Y-O+ **£1,637** (£483; £241) **Stalls** High

Form RPR

-500 **1** **Fitz**[48] 3783 4-9-3 55 .... TedDurcan 10 65
(Matthew Salaman) *hld up in 7th: plld out over 2f out and shkn up: gd prog wl over 1f out: sustained effrt to ld last 150yds: styd on wl* **10/1**[2]

6450 **2** 2 **Aqua Vitae (IRE)**[56] 3534 3-8-12 55 .... JimCrowley 11 58
(Miss Tor Sturgis) *trckd ldng trio: rdn and prog to ld wl over 1f out: hdd and one pce last 150yds* **12/1**

0026 **3** 1 **A Pocketful Of Rye (IRE)**[19] 4760 3-8-9 55 .... MichaelStainton(3) 8 55
(P Howling) *hld up in 8th: shkn up over 2f out: prog over 1f out: styd on wl to take 3rd last 150yds* **11/1**[3]

660 **4** 1 **Youm Al Mizayin**[30] 4397 3-8-12 55 .... ChrisCatlin 7 53
(M R Channon) *dwlt: hld up in 9th: gd prog on inner over 2f out to press ldrs over 1f out: nt qckn and sn hld: kpt on last 150yds* **25/1**

341 **5** 1 1/4 **Cardinal**[8] 5162 5-9-9 55 .... RichardHughes 14 57
(R M H Cowell) *hld up in 5th: gng easily over 2f out: shkn up and nt qckn wl over 1f out: wnt 3rd sn after: one pce and lost 2 pls fnl 150yds* **8/13**[1]

0006 **6** nk **Trecase**[13] 4969 3-8-12 54 .... JimmyFortune 6 48
(A W Carroll) *dwlt: wl off the pce in 10th: shkn up and stl there over 2f out: styd on fr over 1f out: nrst fin* **16/1**

350 **7** 7 **Mount Acclaim (IRE)**[20] 4697 4-9-3 54 .... FergusSweeney 9 32
(J A Osborne) *trckd ldrs in 6th: shkn up 2f out: tried to cl briefly over 1f out: wknd rapidly ins fnl f* **33/1**

0-06 **8** 1 1/2 **Avon Rock**[16] 4861 3-8-5 49 ....(tp) KatiaScallan(7) 13 25
(A J Lidderdale) *trckd ldng pair to 2f out: nudged along and wknd* **66/1**

3366 **9** 3 1/2 **Mini Max**[6] 3716 3-8-7 55 ....(b) SophieDoyle(5) 12 16
(B W Duke) *led to wl over 1f out: wknd rapidly* **20/1**

5000 **10** hd **Medici Brave**[10] 5077 3-8-12 53 ....(p) MartinDwyer 1 15
(Mrs A J Perrett) *dwlt: a wl in rr: struggling fr 1/2-way* **25/1**

5-56 **11** 2 1/4 **Cils Blancs (IRE)**[39] 4082 4-9-3 54 .... TomEaves 4 11
(B Smart) *t.k.h: pressed ldr to 2f out: wknd rapidly* **12/1**

000 **12** 2 1/4 **Final Try**[31] 4364 3-8-9 44 .... RobertLButler(3) 5 3
(P Butler) *a in last trio: rdn and struggling 3f out* **100/1**

0-00 **13** 5 **Dovedon Diva**[122] 1522 3-8-12 52 .... SteveDrowne 3 —
(T Keddy) *rn v wd bnd 4f out whn already in last trio: wl bhd after* **66/1**

1m 26.16s (0.16) **Going Correction** +0.025s/f (Slow)
WFA 3 from 4yo+ 5lb **13** Ran SP% **120.0**
Speed ratings (Par 101): **100,97,96,95,94 93,85,83,79,79 77,74,68**
toteswingers:1&2 £15.80, 2&3 £17.90, 1&3 £8.40 CSF £116.06 TOTE £16.90: £3.60, £2.50, £3.50; EX 137.30.

Owner Mrs Victoria Keen **Bred** Bearstone Stud **Trained** Upper Lambourn, Berks

FOCUS

As befits a race with a 55-rating ceiling this was modest event with only three of the 13 starters managing a win, and that was one apiece in a total of 35 starts.

Cardinal Official explanation: trainer's rep had no explanation for the poor form shown

Dovedon Diva Official explanation: jockey said filly hung badly left-handed on bend

5380 LAURA MACMILLAN BIRTHDAY MEDIAN AUCTION MAIDEN STKS 1m 4f (P)

7:10 (7:11) (Class 6) 3-5-Y-O **£1,637** (£483; £241) **Stalls** High

Form RPR

50-3 **1** **Baralaka**[59] 3443 3-9-3 75 SebSanders 7 81
(Sir Mark Prescott) *settled in midfield: rousted along and prog over 3f out: wnt 3rd over 2f out and 2nd over 1f out: led last 150yds: styd on wl* **7/4**[2]

2322 **2** 1 1/2 **Astral Flower**[27] 4493 3-8-12 71 RichardMullen 1 74
(Sir Michael Stoute) *led: kicked on over 3f out: 3 l clr over 2f out: hdd and outpcd last 150yds* **6/4**[1]

2 **3** 5 **Bull Five**[17] 4840 3-9-3 0 JimCrowley 12 71
(N P Littmoden) *t.k.h: hld up in 5th: prog to chse ldr 3f out: no imp and lost 2nd over 1f out: kpt on* **8/1**[3]

043 **4** 2 3/4 **Chasse Coeur**[17] 4840 3-8-12 67 JimmyFortune 3 62
(A M Balding) *t.k.h: racd wd in tch: outpcd over 3f out: rdn and kpt on fr over 2f out: tk 4th ins fnl f* **9/1**

0 **5** 5 **Jubilant Lady (USA)**[66] 3207 3-8-12 0 (v[1]) TomEaves 2 54
(B Smart) *chsd ldr: rdn over 3f out: steadily wknd fr over 2f out* **33/1**

/2-5 **6** 4 1/2 **Repealed**[15] 4893 4-9-13 65 (t) SteveDrowne 4 51
(H Morrison) *trckd ldng trio: rdr looking down at various times fr 1/2-way: nudged along and steadily lost pl fr over 4f out: sddle slipped* **10/1**

00 **7** 4 **Southwark Newsman**[82] 2684 3-9-3 0 TomMcLaughlin 5 45
(Mrs C A Dunnett) *dwlt: racd wd towards rr: effrt over 3f out but sn outpcd: no ch after* **66/1**

00- **8** 2 1/2 **Laid Bare**[297] 7177 3-8-7 0 SophieDoyle(5) 11 36
(Mrs P N Dutfield) *chsd ldng pair: rdn over 3f out: wknd over 2f out* **100/1**

000 **9** 1/2 **Jenny Dawson (IRE)**[17] 4840 4-9-8 43 IvaMilickova 6 35
(John Berry) *a wl in rr: bmpd along and struggling 3f out* **100/1**

00-6 **10** 3 3/4 **Bonamassa**[17] 4840 3-8-12 55 JemmaMarshall(5) 10 34
(M J Attwater) *lost midfield pl and pushed along 1/2-way: struggling in rr 3f out* **66/1**

11 10 **Mlini (IRE)**[118] 4-9-13 0 LeeVickers 9 18
(T J Etherington) *sn last: pushed along 5f out: wl bhd fnl 4f: t.o* **100/1**

0 **P** **Stuff Of Legends**[36] 4205 3-8-12 0 JimmyQuinn 8 —
(H J L Dunlop) *dwlt: a in rr: broke down and p.u over 2f out* **66/1**

2m 36.24s (1.74) **Going Correction** +0.025s/f (Slow)
WFA 3 from 4yo 10lb **12** Ran SP% **117.0**
Speed ratings (Par 101): **95,94,90,88,85 82,79,78,77,75 68,—**
toteswingers:1&2 £1.10, 2&3 £4.00, 1&3 £3.10 CSF £4.56 TOTE £3.20: £2.80, £1.02, £1.60; EX 3.90.

Owner Mrs S L Warman **Bred** Watership Down Stud **Trained** Newmarket, Suffolk

FOCUS

A maiden that lacked any strength in depth.

Repealed Official explanation: jockey said saddle slipped

Bonamassa Official explanation: jockey said gelding hung both ways

5381 EUROPEAN BREEDERS' FUND MAIDEN STKS 6f (P)

7:40 (7:41) (Class 4) 2-Y-O **£4,209** (£1,252; £625; £312) **Stalls** High

Form RPR

02 **1** **Hoot (IRE)**[10] 5074 2-9-3 0 TedDurcan 8 81
(Saeed Bin Suroor) *trckd ldr: shkn up to ld over 1f out: r.o wl ins fnl f: readily* **15/8**[2]

2 2 1/2 **Desert Law (IRE)** 2-9-3 0 JimmyFortune 11 76+
(A M Balding) *hld up in 6th: pushed along and prog to chse wnr jst over 1f out: styd on wl: no imp* **6/4**[1]

022 **3** 3 1/2 **Barking (IRE)**[19] 4743 2-9-3 73 RichardHughes 10 63
(R Hannon) *led at gd slip: hdd over 1f out: wl btn ins fnl f and jst hld on for 3rd* **5/1**[3]

4 nk **Silver Ocean (USA)** 2-9-3 0 JimCrowley 4 65+
(R M Beckett) *dwlt: hld up last: stl there 2f out: gd prog after: pushed along and nrly tk 3rd fin* **33/1**

0 **5** 2 1/4 **Sleeping Brave**[16] 4871 2-9-3 0 StephenCraine 6 55
(J R Boyle) *dwlt: in tch towards rr: outpcd fr over 2f out: plugged on* **100/1**

4 **6** 1 3/4 **Silver Age (IRE)**[21] 4678 2-8-10 0 RyanPowell(7) 2 50
(J S Moore) *racd wd: wl in tch: appeared gng strly over 2f out: hanging rt after and no prog* **66/1**

7 hd **Zahraan (IRE)** 2-9-3 0 MartinDwyer 9 53+
(M P Tregoning) *rn green in rr: shkn up and no prog over 2f out: modest late hdwy ins fnl f* **13/2**

0 **8** nk **Legal Heights (IRE)**[11] 5020 2-9-3 0 EddieCreighton 5 49
(T T Clement) *chsd ldng pair to over 2f out: steadily wknd* **200/1**

00 **9** nk **Burnem Green**[8] 5147 2-8-12 0 FergusSweeney 3 43
(A Bailey) *chsd ldrs: rdn over 2f out: sn lost pl and btn* **150/1**

0 **10** 1/2 **Mirabile Visu**[91] 2413 2-8-12 0 SebSanders 12 41
(Mrs H S Main) *racd awkwardly: chsd ldrs to over 2f out: sn btn* **150/1**

11 nk **Konstantin (IRE)** 2-9-3 0 ChrisCatlin 1 45
(M P Tregoning) *a in last trio: rdn 1/2-way: n.d after* **50/1**

1m 12.98s (-0.12) **Going Correction** +0.025s/f (Slow) **11** Ran SP% **114.0**
Speed ratings (Par 96): **101,97,93,92,89 87,87,86,86,85 85**
toteswingers:1&2 £1.60, 2&3 £2.80, 1&3 £1.50 CSF £4.82 TOTE £2.90: £1.10, £1.10, £1.10; EX 5.90.

Owner Godolphin **Bred** Shortgrove Manor Stud **Trained** Newmarket, Suffolk

FOCUS

Time might show that this was a decent maiden.

NOTEBOOK

Hoot(IRE) is learning with each run and had all moves covered from a good tactical position throughout. The switch to Polytrack was certainly not a hindrance and it will be interesting to see what nursery mark he gets. (op 2-1 tchd 9-4)

Desert Law(IRE) ◆ was strong in the market despite the lack of a first-time-out juvenile winner from his stable so far this season. However, this was a debut full of promise and any losses are surely lent as he is clearly smart like his dam, Speed Cop. Tardy at the start, he was a touch keen and travelled like a horse that has probably been able to do everything on the bit at home. He was still travelling very nicely up the home straight, but lacked the track sense of the winner. He'll be hard to beat next time. (op 7-4 tchd 2-1 in a place)

Barking(IRE) set the standard having been alloted a rating of 73. He tried to make his experience count from the front, but he was readily run down. He shouldn't move for this and a nursery over this trip might be the right option next time. (op 9-2 tchd 4-1)

Silver Ocean(USA) ◆ was the eyecatcher in the race. Slow at the gate from a moderate draw, he had plenty to do when switched from a wide position to the inside, but really rattled home. He's another that will be a handful next time.

Sleeping Brave belied his odds and stayed on nicely, an improvement on his Windsor debut. He looks one for nurseries after another appearance.

Silver Age(IRE) caught the eye last time in a seller at Chepstow and was ridden closer to the pace here and again made a good impression. He looked awkward, losing his stride up the home straight when possibly clipping heels, but showed more than enough to suggest he can win a nursery once given a rating after his next start. Official explanation: jockey said gelding ran green (op 50-1 tchd 40-1)

Zahraan(IRE) was green from the gate and still showed enough to suggest it will be worth keeping an eye on him next time. The Elusive City colt was given a sensible introduction on the inside and will have learned plenty for this. (op 6-1 tchd 15-2)

5382 DIGIBET CASINO H'CAP 2m (P)

8:10 (8:10) (Class 5) (0-75,72) 3-Y-O+ **£2,286** (£675; £337) **Stalls** High

Form RPR

4-33 **1** **Sir Freddie**[38] 4141 4-9-12 **69** SebSanders 8 74
(Lady Herries) *trckd ldr: led after 7f: kicked on 4f out: hdd over 2f out: dropped to 3rd ins fnl f: rallied between rivals u.str.p to ld post* **4/1**[3]

5221 **2** nse **Saute**[7] 5179 4-10-0 **71** 6ex (p) AdamKirby 2 76
(W R Swinburn) *led at stdy pce for 7f: trckd ldr: rdn to ld again over 2f out: drvn 2 l clr 1f out: hdd post* **9/4**[1]

2211 **3** shd **Corr Point (IRE)**[31] 4362 3-9-1 **72** FergusSweeney 1 77
(J A Osborne) *trckd ldng trio: wnt 3rd and rdn over 2f out: clsd fnl f to chal last 100yds: nt qckn nr fin* **7/1**

2313 **4** 3 1/2 **Spice Fair**[15] 4907 3-9-0 **71** RichardHughes 6 72
(M D I Usher) *t.k.h: hld up bhd ldrs: rdn over 2f out: sn wnt 4th: nt qckn over 1f out: wl hld after* **5/2**[2]

3324 **5** 1 1/4 **Seventh Hill**[12] 5011 5-9-9 **66** MartinDwyer 3 65
(M Blanshard) *stdd s: hld up towards rr: pushed along over 3f out: outpcd over 2f out: nvr on terms after* **16/1**

653 **6** hd **William's Way**[8] 5144 8-9-10 **67** (t) TomMcLaughlin 5 66
(I A Wood) *stdd s: hld up last: effrt 3f out: sn outpcd: no imp after* **25/1**

3100 **7** 2 1/2 **Graylyn Ruby (FR)**[7] 5179 5-9-4 **61** JimmyQuinn 7 57
(R Dickin) *t.k.h: hld up: dropped to last briefly 3f out and outpcd: n.d after* **20/1**

6540 **8** 1/2 **Businessmoney Judi**[12] 5011 4-9-0 **60** JamesMillman(3) 4 55
(B R Millman) *hld up: a in last trio: outpcd fr wl over 2f out* **33/1**

3211 **9** 1 **Where's Susie**[19] 4734 5-10-0 **71** (p) ChrisCatlin 9 65
(M Madgwick) *chsd ldng pair: rdn over 3f out: wknd 2f out* **16/1**

3m 32.39s (2.29) **Going Correction** +0.025s/f (Slow)
WFA 3 from 4yo+ 14lb **9** Ran SP% **115.2**
Speed ratings (Par 103): **95,94,94,93,92 92,91,90,90**
toteswingers:1&2 £3.00, 2&3 £5.10, 1&3 £7.20 CSF £13.04 CT £60.05 TOTE £3.90: £1.60, £1.10, £2.20; EX 12.70.

Owner Lady Herries and Friends **Bred** Lady Herries **Trained** Patching, W Sussex

FOCUS

A tricky handicap on paper and a three-way photo.

Spice Fair Official explanation: jockey said gelding ran too free

5383 GOODBYE AND GOOD LUCK LAUREN PALAU H'CAP 7f (P)

8:40 (8:42) (Class 4) (0-85,85) 3-Y-O **£3,885** (£1,156; £577; £288) **Stalls** High

Form RPR

62-0 **1** **Brick Red**[13] 4963 3-9-4 **82** JimmyFortune 2 90
(A M Balding) *racd wd early: trckd ldrs: cl up and rdn over 1f out: drvn ahd last 100yds: hld on* **11/1**

0410 **2** hd **Master Mylo (IRE)**[11] 5031 3-8-9 **73** WilliamCarson 1 80
(D K Ivory) *dwlt: swtchd fr wd draw to inner and hld up wl in rr: taken wd and rdn 3f out: gd prog over 1f out: clsd on wnr fin* **25/1**

4402 **3** 1/2 **Saharia (IRE)**[11] 5031 3-9-2 **80** DarryllHolland 4 86
(J Noseda) *hld up in midfield on inner: looking for room over 2f out: swtchd ins and gd prog over 1f out: pressed ldrs ins fnl f: styd on* **10/1**

1000 **4** nk **Edinburgh Knight (IRE)**[11] 5030 3-9-7 **85** TonyCulhane 11 90
(P W D'Arcy) *hld up towards rr: smooth prog to chal 2f out: shkn up to ld jst over 1f out but fnd little: hdd and folded last 100yds* **10/3**[2]

2060 **5** nk **Master Leon**[36] 4193 3-8-11 **75** (v) TomEaves 5 79
(B Smart) *trckd ldr: led jst over 2f out: sn rdn: hdd jst over 1f out: nt qckn* **40/1**

5244 **6** 1 1/2 **Red Gulch**[14] 4929 3-8-9 **76** AshleyHamblett(3) 6 76
(E A L Dunlop) *trckd ldng trio: tried to chal over 1f out: jst lacked pce ent fnl f: hld whn short of room last 100yds* **15/2**[3]

-053 **7** 3/4 **Flip Flop (IRE)**[64] 3271 3-9-1 **79** MichaelHills 12 77
(B W Hills) *trckd ldng pair: tried to chal over 2f out: lost pl and btn over 1f out: one pce after* **9/1**

6132 **8** 3/4 **Excellent Day (IRE)**[8] 5145 3-8-3 **67** ChrisCatlin 9 63
(M R Channon) *hld up wl in rr: pushed along 3f out: prog over 1f out: effrt flattened out ins fnl f* **16/1**

01-4 **9** 2 **Kings Bayonet**[89] 2479 3-9-3 **81** TomQueally 8 72
(H R A Cecil) *hld up in tch: rdn and nt qckn over 2f out: no prog after: fdd ins fnl f* **2/1**[1]

0330 **10** 4 1/2 **Law Of Attraction (IRE)**[25] 4547 3-8-8 **72** SteveDrowne 10 50
(J R Gask) *led to jst over 2f out: wknd over 1f out* **28/1**

5335 **11** 1 1/2 **Kurtanella**[31] 4387 3-9-2 **80** RichardHughes 3 54
(R Hannon) *hld up in detached last: pushed along over 2f out: sme limited prog over 1f out: no ch and sn eased* **22/1**

001 **12** 8 **Spanish Island (USA)**[11] 5028 3-9-4 **82** GeorgeBaker 7 35
(M A Magnusson) *a in rr: u.p and struggling 3f out: sn bhd* **8/1**

2-16 **13** 1/2 **Mutafajer**[89] 2450 3-9-7 **85** TedDurcan 13 36
(Saeed Bin Suroor) *trckd ldrs: lost pl on inner over 2f out: sn wknd: eased ins fnl f* **12/1**

1m 25.52s (-0.48) **Going Correction** +0.025s/f (Slow) **13** Ran SP% **134.4**
Speed ratings (Par 102): **103,102,102,101,101 99,98,98,95,90 88,79,79**
toteswingers:1&2 £60.10, 2&3 £53.00, 1&3 £30.70 CSF £282.48 CT £1809.01 TOTE £16.90: £4.40, £10.30, £3.60; EX 422.40.

Owner Brick Racing **Bred** Raimon Bloodstock **Trained** Kingsclere, Hants

FOCUS

A good-quality handicap.

Kurtanella Official explanation: jockey said filly moved poorly

5384 KEMPTON.CO.UK H'CAP 1m (P)

9:10 (9:10) (Class 5) (0-75,72) 3-Y-O **£2,286** (£675; £337) **Stalls** High

Form RPR

5244 **1** **Sweet Secret**[12] 4988 3-8-10 **61** RichardHughes 5 66
(R Hannon) *in tch: pushed along over 3f out: prog u.p over 2f out: chal ins fnl f: drvn ahd last strides* **11/2**[3]

0104 **2** *hd* **Abhar (USA)**[27] 4491 3-9-3 **68** .... JimmyQuinn 3 72
(J R Best) *trckd ldr: rdn 2f out: clsd to ld ent fnl f: kpt on: hdd last strides* **8/1**

0436 **3** *1* **Rain On The Wind (IRE)**[58] 3479 3-9-0 **65** ....(t) WilliamCarson 9 67
(S C Williams) *led: drvn and pressed 2f out: hdd ent fnl f: hld in 3rd whn short of room last strides* **8/1**

5653 **4** *1 1/4* **Al Jaadi**[19] 4735 3-9-4 **69** .... SebSanders 4 68
(W Jarvis) *hld up in last pair: rdn and prog fr over 2f out: tried to cl on ldrs 1f out: one pce after* **4/1**[2]

14 **5** *6* **Bell's Ocean (USA)**[11] 5050 3-8-11 **62** .... JimmyFortune 6 47
(J Ryan) *chsd ldrs: outpcd and struggling over 2f out: no ch after* **15/2**

042- **6** *2 1/2* **Plenty O'Toole**[271] 7538 3-9-7 **72** .... EddieCreighton 2 51
(Mrs D J Sanderson) *t.k.h: trckd ldng trio: wknd over 2f out* **8/1**

5-20 **7** *hd* **Sasheen**[12] 4997 3-9-5 **70** .... StephenCraine 8 49
(J R Boyle) *trckd ldng pair: rdn over 2f out: wknd rapidly on inner over 1f out* **16/1**

0-05 **8** *3 3/4* **Suzhou**[73] 2968 3-8-11 **62** .... DarryllHolland 1 32
(D J Coakley) *t.k.h: hld up last: awkward bnd 4f out: swtchd lft over 2f out: sn rdn and fnd nil* **9/4**[1]

1m 39.08s (-0.72) **Going Correction** +0.025s/f (Slow) **8** Ran SP% **117.1**
Speed ratings (Par 100): **104,103,102,101,95 93,92,89**
toteswingers:1&2 £7.00, 2&3 £7.80, 1&3 £4.80. totesuper7: Win: Not won. Place: £613.90. CSF £49.55 CT £356.31 TOTE £7.60: £1.10, £1.90, £4.60; EX 32.70 Place 6: £212.96 Place £51.85.
Owner Carmel Stud **Bred** Carmel Stud **Trained** East Everleigh, Wilts
■ Stewards' Enquiry : Jimmy Quinn two-day ban: used whip in incorrect place (Sep 7-8)

FOCUS
An ordinary handicap.
T/Plt: £179.30 to a £1 stake. Pool of £56,869.06 - 231.50 winning tickets. T/Qpdt: £17.90 to a £1 stake. Pool of £6,595.84 - 271.60 winning tickets. JN

4856 LEICESTER (R-H)

Tuesday, August 24

OFFICIAL GOING: Soft (heavy in places; 6.3)
Wind: Strong half-behind Weather: Overcast

5385 INCHCAPE TOYOTA DERBY MAIDEN AUCTION STKS 7f 9y
5:20 (5:20) (Class 5) 2-Y-O £2,655 (£790; £394; £197) Stalls Low

Form RPR

05 **1** **Persian Herald**[34] 4253 2-8-10 0 .... ShaneKelly 15 81+
(Pat Eddery) *chsd ldrs: pushed along 1/2-way: outpcd over 2f out: rallied to ld over 1f out: rdn and hung lft ins fnl f: r.o wl* **22/1**

04 **2** *5* **Standout**[77] 2839 2-8-10 0 .... DaneO'Neill 9 67
(R Hannon) *chsd ldrs: led over 5f out: hdd 4f out: outpcd over 2f out: rallied over 1f out: styd on same pce ins fnl f* **5/2**[2]

3 *1/2* **Songsmith** 2-8-13 0 .... GregFairley 7 69
(Mrs L Wadham) *chsd ldrs: rdn over 2f out: styd on same pce ins fnl f* **10/1**

0 **4** *2 1/4* **Callie's Angel**[15] 4909 2-8-6 0 .... DeclanCannon(5) 10 61
(B Palling) *racd keenly: led: hdd over 5f out: chsd ldrs: rdn over 2f out: wknd ins fnl f* **50/1**

05 **5** *3 1/4* **Al Rannan**[19] 4747 2-9-0 0 .... EddieAhern 4 56+
(M L W Bell) *hld up: hdwy 1/2-way: shkn up over 1f out: nvr nr to chal* **7/1**[3]

6 *1* **Rainbows Reach** 2-8-6 0 .... PaulHanagan 14 46+
(Miss Gay Kelleway) *s.i.s: hdwy over 5f out: outpcd 1/2-way: n.d after* **25/1**

4 **7** *1/2* **Soldiers Point**[40] 4059 2-8-9 0 .... PaulMulrennan 2 47
(B Smart) *w ldrs: led 4f out: rdn and hdd 2f out: wknd ins fnl f* **11/1**

3 **8** *hd* **Lowawatha**[31] 4384 2-9-0 0 .... JackMitchell 12 52
(R M Beckett) *chsd ldrs: led 2f out: rdn and hdd over 1f out: wknd ins fnl f: eased nr fin* **7/4**[1]

0 **9** *4* **Caledonia Prince**[34] 4247 2-8-4 0 .... RossAtkinson(5) 3 37
(F J Brennan) *hld up: a in rr: bhd fr 1/2-way* **100/1**

10 *3 1/2* **Laafhd** 2-8-4 0 .... LukeMorris 17 23
(A G Newcombe) *s.i.s: a in rr: bhd fr 1/2-way* **40/1**

0 **11** *2 1/2* **Mrs G**[32] 4336 2-8-4 0 .... PaulEddery 5 17
(R C Guest) *a in rr: bhd fr 1/2-way* **80/1**

12 *1 3/4* **Precious Diamond** 2-8-9 0 .... SamHitchcott 16 17
(M R Channon) *s.i.s: sn drvn along and a in rr: bhd fr 1/2-way* **40/1**

1m 28.81s (2.61) **Going Correction** +0.125s/f (Good) **12** Ran SP% **112.1**
Speed ratings (Par 94): **90,84,83,81,77 76,75,75,70,66 64,62**
toteswingers:1&2 £8.50, 2&3 £6.30, 1&3 £16.00 CSF £70.77 TOTE £15.50: £3.40, £2.10, £3.40; EX 99.90.
Owner Pat Eddery (Colorspin) **Bred** J W P Clark **Trained** Nether Winchendon, Bucks

FOCUS
There had been 50mm of rain in the previous three days and the testing conditions saw a raft of horses taken out during the day. There was a fairly strong tailwind behind the runners in the straight and the winning rider described the ground as soft. An ordinary event in which those with previous experience were only modest at best and one in which the market leader didn't get home in the conditions. The gallop was fair and the field raced towards the stands' side.

NOTEBOOK
Persian Herald had shown only moderate form in two starts on quick ground and on Polytrack but turned in a much-improved effort, despite carrying his head high. This testing ground clearly suited and he may be able to win again granted similar conditions. (op 16-1 tchd 25-1)
Standout had shown ability at a modest level and was far from disgraced in this much softer ground up in distance. He is now qualified for nurseries, is in good hands and leaves the impression the step up to 1m will suit. He should be able to pick up a small event. (tchd 9-4)
Songsmith, a half-brother to fast-ground debut winner Businessman, attracted support and ran creditably on this racecourse debut. He should have no problems with 1m and, although the overall level of this form isn't special, he is entitled to improve for the experience. (op 7-1 tchd 12-1)
Al Rannan ◆ couldn't get competitive after attracting a bit of support but he wasn't unduly knocked about and may do better in ordinary nursery company when returned to 1m. (op 11-1)
Rainbows Reach, the first foal of a 7f Fibresand winner, hinted at ability and her future lies in ordinary handicaps. (op 22-1)
Soldiers Point ran well for a long way on this first run over 7f and should fare better in nurseries. (op 14-1)
Lowawatha's encouraging debut run has thrown up winners but he failed to build on that in these much softer conditions. He'll be worth another chance back on a soundish surface. (tchd 13-8)

5386 TMS VOLVO HINCKLEY H'CAP 7f 9y
5:50 (5:50) (Class 4) (0-80,80) 3-Y-O+ £3,626 (£1,079; £539; £269) Stalls Low

Form RPR

0326 **1** **Tevez**[67] 3168 5-8-7 **61** ....(p) CathyGannon 8 77
(D Donovan) *s.s: sn drvn along in rr: hdwy 1/2-way: led over 2f out: sn hung rt: styd on u.p to assert towards fin* **10/1**

1560 **2** *3/4* **Justonefortheroad**[28] 4459 4-9-10 **78** .... PaulHanagan 4 92
(R A Fahey) *led: hdd over 5f out: chsd ldrs: rdn and ev ch fr over 2f out tl no ex towards fin* **5/1**[2]

423 **3** *5* **Lochan Mor**[18] 4806 4-9-12 **80** .... JamieSpencer 10 80
(M L W Bell) *hld up: hdwy over 2f out: rdn and hung lft over 1f out: styd on same pce* **9/4**[1]

2213 **4** *1 1/2* **Gracie's Gift (IRE)**[15] 4895 8-8-12 **66** .... DaneO'Neill 6 62
(R C Guest) *chsd ldrs: rdn over 2f out: wknd ins fnl f* **12/1**

5240 **5** *1/2* **You've Been Mowed**[15] 4905 4-8-11 **72** .... HarryBentley(7) 12 67
(R J Price) *sat down in stalls: chsd ldrs: led over 5f out: rdn and hdd over 2f out: wknd over 1f out* **7/1**

0060 **6** *2 1/4* **Tamasou (IRE)**[48] 3779 5-9-2 **70** .... ShaneKelly 1 59
(F J Brennan) *s.i.s: hdwy 1/2-way: rdn and hung rt over 2f out: wknd over 1f out* **13/2**[3]

1001 **7** *3 1/2* **West End Lad**[26] 4522 7-9-11 **79** ....(b) RobertWinston 7 59
(S R Bowring) *chsd ldrs: rdn 1/2-way: wknd over 1f out* **8/1**

0-0 **8** *8* **Spring Secret**[104] 2024 4-8-12 **66** .... LukeMorris 5 24
(B Palling) *prom: rdn 1/2-way: wknd over 2f out* **25/1**

3150 **9** *1 3/4* **Neduardo**[5] 4684 3-9-2 **75** .... JackMitchell 13 26
(P W Chapple-Hyam) *hld up in tch: rdn over 2f out: sn wknd* **16/1**

0 **10** *12* **Big Boom**[5] 5238 5-8-7 **61** oh3 .... FrannyNorton 9 —
(M Quinn) *chsd ldrs: rdn 1/2-way: sn wknd: t.o* **16/1**

1m 26.16s (-0.04) **Going Correction** +0.125s/f (Good)
WFA 3 from 4yo+ 5lb **10** Ran SP% **116.8**
Speed ratings (Par 105): **105,104,98,96,96 93,89,80,78,64**
toteswingers:1&2 £12.30, 2&3 £2.80, 1&3 £6.70 CSF £59.50 CT £157.40 TOTE £17.20: £3.70, £3.20, £1.10; EX 88.10.
Owner River Racing **Bred** P A And Mrs D G Sakal **Trained** Newmarket, Suffolk

FOCUS
Exposed performers in a fair handicap. The gallop was a good one in the conditions and the field raced in the centre this time. The first two pulled clear.

5387 FENWICK LEICESTER H'CAP 1m 3f 183y
6:20 (6:20) (Class 3) (0-95,95) 3-Y-O+ £5,677 (£1,699; £849; £424; £211) Stalls High

Form RPR

-103 **1** **Senate**[19] 4757 3-8-9 **87** .... PaulHanagan 2 100+
(J H M Gosden) *mde all: rdn and hung rt wl over 1f out: sn clr: comf* **2/1**[1]

6051 **2** *2 1/2* **Magicalmysterytour (IRE)**[10] 5091 7-9-8 **90** .... EddieAhern 3 99
(W J Musson) *hld up: hdwy over 3f out: outpcd over 2f out: rallied to chse wnr ins fnl f: r.o* **8/1**

-004 **3** *2 1/2* **All Annalena (IRE)**[17] 4841 4-9-0 **82** .... DaneO'Neill 8 87
(Mrs L Wadham) *hld up in tch: plld hrd: rdn over 2f out: styd on* **33/1**

5501 **4** *1 3/4* **Topolski (IRE)**[24] 4597 4-9-4 **86** ....(p) LiamKeniry 1 88
(A M Balding) *chsd wnr tl rdn over 4f out: outpcd over 2f out: styd on ins fnl f* **12/1**

5 *3* **Ella**[111] 1829 6-9-11 **93** .... RobertWinston 5 90
(G A Swinbank) *prom: chsd wnr 4f out: rdn over 2f out: hmpd wl over 1f out: wknd ins fnl f* **9/2**[2]

2-42 **6** *6* **Prince Of Dreams**[85] 2585 3-7-9 **80** .... HarryBentley(7) 10 68
(W J Knight) *hld up in tch: rdn over 3f out: sn wknd* **6/1**[3]

6/2- **7** *1/2* **Cool Judgement (IRE)**[478] 1709 5-9-13 **95** .... PhilipRobinson 11 82
(M A Jarvis) *hld up: hdwy over 2f out: wknd over 1f out* **7/1**

10- **8** *61* **Burnett (IRE)**[304] 7030 3-8-7 **85** .... DaraghO'Donohoe 4 —
(Saeed Bin Suroor) *racd green and bustled along early: hdwy over 10f out and racd keenly: rdn 4f out: wknd 3f out: eased t.o* **8/1**

2m 35.99s (2.09) **Going Correction** +0.35s/f (Good)
WFA 3 from 4yo+ 10lb **8** Ran SP% **111.2**
Speed ratings (Par 107): **107,105,103,102,100 96,96,55**
toteswingers:1&2 £2.80, 2&3 £14.30, 1&3 £18.70 CSF £17.62 CT £376.63 TOTE £3.20: £1.10, £2.50, £7.10; EX 22.90.
Owner H R H Princess Haya Of Jordan **Bred** Watership Down Stud **Trained** Newmarket, Suffolk

FOCUS
A decent-quality handicap but one run at just an ordinary gallop till the last 3f. The field again raced towards the centre in the straight.

NOTEBOOK
Senate ◆ is a lightly raced and progressive individual who had the run of the race under ideal conditions and he turned in a career-best effort to beat a previous winner on his first outing over this trip. He handles quicker ground, is in very good hands, is open to further improvement and appeals strongly as the sort to win a decent handicap before the season is out. (op 15-8 tchd 9-4)
Magicalmysterytour(IRE), who had slipped in the weights prior to returning to winning ways at Newmarket on his previous start, ran creditably against a progressive type from this 7lb higher mark. As with many from this yard, his style of racing means he will be ideally suited by more of an end-to-end gallop, and he's capable of adding to his tallly, especially away from the less-exposed types. (tchd 7-1)
All Annalena(IRE), Listed placed in Germany last year, has slipped in the weights for her current yard this year and she ran creditably to confirm her effectiveness over this trip. There will be easier opportunities than this one but she may need to drop further in the weights before winning a competitive handicap. (tchd 28-1)
Topolski(IRE), 4lb higher than his Newmarket good-ground victory at the end of last month, couldn't build on that with the cheekpieces on again but he may do better returned to a sound surface and he's also worth another try on Polytrack. (op 14-1)
Ella has been raced sparingly in recent times and was a bit of a disappointment under her optimum conditions on this first start since early May. However, while she may remain vulnerable to more progressive types from this mark, she is usually consistent and is probably worth another chance. (op 10-3)
Prince Of Dreams was nibbled at in the market for this handicap debut but failed to build on the form he had shown in maidens. It's too soon to be writing him off and, although he ran creditably on soft ground on his debut, he may be ideally suited by better ground. (op 9-1)
Cool Judgement(IRE) wasn't at all knocked about on this first run since last May and should be all the better for this experience. He's in very good hands and, although he'll have to show a fair bit more before he is a solid betting proposition, it will be interesting to see if his trainer can get him anywhere near back to his best this term. Official explanation: jockey said gelding became very tired on the soft ground (op 15-2 tchd 13-2)

Burnett(IRE), reportedly unsuited by the soft ground when well beaten in the Horris Hill on his final run last October, was virtually pulled up after taking a good hold on this reappearance and handicap debut. Better ground may suit ideally but he'll have to settle better if he is to progress. (tchd 9-1)

5388 TAYLOR WIMPEY EAST MIDLANDS CLAIMING STKS 5f 218y
6:50 (6:51) (Class 5) 3-Y-0+ £2,266 (£674; £337; £168) Stalls Low

Form				RPR
1053	1		**Basle**[15] 4892 3-8-4 73 PaulHanagan 12	70
			(Miss Gay Kelleway) *hld up in tch: plld hrd: led over 1f out: rdn out* **7/2**[2]	
3003	2	2 ¼	**Cape Kimberley**[11] 5027 3-8-2 68 JamesSullivan(3) 13	64
			(J G Given) *a.p: rdn over 2f out: chsd wnr ins fnl f: styd on* **12/1**	
0412	3	2 ¼	**Daddy's Gift (IRE)**[16] 4857 4-8-13 62 DaneO'Neill 11	62
			(R Hannon) *chsd ldrs: led over 3f out: rdn and hdd over 1f out: styd on same pce ins fnl f* **9/2**[3]	
0005	4	½	**If Only**[7] 5169 4-8-8 51 (p) LukeMorris 14	55
			(D Morris) *led: hdd over 3f out: rdn and ev ch wl over 1f out: no ex ins fnl f* **33/1**	
0623	5	2	**Mata Hari Blue**[27] 4478 4-8-13 58 EddieAhern 7	54
			(J R Holt) *chsd ldrs: rdn over 2f out: wknd ins fnl f* **13/2**	
0051	6	6	**Universal Circus**[14] 4922 3-8-10 76 SamHitchcott 8	34
			(M R Channon) *sn drvn along in rr: bhd fr 1/2-way* **11/1**	
001	7	2 ½	**C'Mon You Irons (IRE)**[11] 5027 5-9-3 75 (v) IanBrennan(5) 3	35
			(M R Hoad) *chsd ldrs: rdn over 2f out: hung rt and wknd over 1f out* **5/1**	
5000	8	2 ¼	**Stonecrabstomorrow (IRE)**[14] 4936 7-8-7 57 (b) MarkCoumbe(5) 10	18
			(John A Harris) *s.i.s: a in rr: bhd fr 1/2-way* **50/1**	
050	9	7	**Aeroplane**[14] 4924 7-9-0 89 JamieSpencer 6	—
			(P D Evans) *hld up: a in rr: bhd fr 1/2-way: eased over 1f out* **10/3**[1]	

1m 13.6s (0.60) **Going Correction** +0.125s/f (Good)
WFA 3 from 4yo+ 3lb 9 Ran SP% 114.4
Speed ratings (Par 103): **101,98,95,94,91 83,80,77,68**
toteswingers:1&2 £8.50, 2&3 £7.60, 1&3 £7.60 CSF £44.24 TOTE £3.30: £1.10, £4.10, £2.80; EX 38.40.Basle was subject to a friendly claim. Cape Kimberley was claimed by A. G. Newcombe for £5000.
Owner Raymond Tooth **Bred** W H R John And Partners **Trained** Exning, Suffolk

FOCUS
A couple of fair sorts but one in which the market leader disappointed. The gallop was reasonable and the field raced centre to stands' side.
Aeroplane Official explanation: jockey said horse moved poorly throughout; vet said horse returned lame

5389 POTTERS SUPERSTORE NURSERY 1m 60y
7:20 (7:21) (Class 6) (0-65,65) 2-Y-O £1,942 (£578; £288; £144) Stalls High

Form				RPR
650	1		**Imperial Look**[29] 4432 2-9-0 58 AdrianNicholls 10	66+
			(E S McMahon) *chsd ldrs: rdn over 1f out: styd on u.p to ld nr fin* **11/2**	
005	2	nk	**Regimental (IRE)**[21] 4668 2-8-13 57 PhillipMakin 4	62
			(Mrs A Duffield) *sn chsng ldr: rdn to ld over 1f out: hung lft: hdd nr fin* **5/1**[3]	
040	3	2	**Fastada (IRE)**[12] 5006 2-9-7 65 RobertWinston 11	66
			(J G Portman) *led: rdn: hdd and hung lft over 1f out: no ex wl ins fnl f* **14/1**	
446	4	3	**Cathcart Castle**[13] 4955 2-9-6 64 EddieAhern 14	58
			(M R Channon) *prom: rdn over 2f out: no ex ins fnl f* **4/1**[2]	
035	5	1	**Loch Ordie**[11] 5047 2-9-7 65 JerryO'Dwyer 5	57
			(M G Quinlan) *hld up: hdwy over 2f out: rdn over 1f out: one pce* **15/2**	
020	6	2 ½	**Pahente**[17] 4838 2-9-4 62 LukeMorris 9	49
			(J S Moore) *hld up in tch: rdn over 3f out: wknd over 1f out* **20/1**	
2040	7	2 ¾	**Gower Rules (IRE)**[4] 5256 2-9-0 63 (p) LeeNewnes(5) 13	44
			(M D I Usher) *hld up: hdwy 1/2-way: rdn over 3f out: wknd 2f out* **28/1**	
043	8	½	**Eduardo**[21] 4682 2-9-6 64 JackMitchell 8	44
			(Jedd O'Keeffe) *hld up in tch: plld hrd: rdn and wknd over 1f out* **7/2**[1]	
4260	9	1 ¾	**Bajan Bullet**[23] 4615 2-9-7 65 CathyGannon 3	41
			(P D Evans) *prom: rdn over 2f out: edgd rt and wknd over 1f out* **18/1**	
4230	10	2 ½	**Lady Morganna (IRE)**[20] 4716 2-9-0 63 JohnFahy(5) 6	33
			(Miss Gay Kelleway) *s.s: sn drvn along: hdwy 3f out: wknd over 2f out* **14/1**	
0040	11	71	**Endorser**[1] 5373 2-9-2 60 (b) PaulHanagan 7	—
			(W R Muir) *sn pushed along in rr: bhd fr 1/2-way: t.o* **22/1**	

1m 50.42s (5.32) **Going Correction** +0.35s/f (Good) 11 Ran SP% 117.2
Speed ratings (Par 92): **87,86,84,81,80 78,75,74,73,70** —
toteswingers:1&2 £9.40, 2&3 £17.90, 1&3 £19.30 CSF £32.10 CT £375.02 TOTE £6.40: £2.30, £2.40, £5.40; EX 33.50.
Owner S L Edwards **Bred** S L Edwards **Trained** Lichfield, Staffs

FOCUS
A modest nursery in which the gallop was on the steady side and those up with the pace held the edge. The field came down the centre in the straight.

NOTEBOOK
Imperial Look failed to settle in the early stages on this turf and nursery debut on this first run beyond 6f but turned in an improved effort to justify the market support. There may be a bit more to come, especially as he learns to settle. Official explanation: trainer said, regarding apparent improvement in form, that the colt was suited by the step up in trip. (op 7-1)
Regimental(IRE), also popular in the market, had the run of the race and turned in his best effort on this nursery debut up to this trip for the first time. On this evidence he should be able to pick up a similar event. (op 8-1)
Fastada(IRE) had been well beaten on two of her three starts but she was allowed a fairly easy time of it in front over this longer trip on this nursery debut and ran her best race on this first run away from quick ground. Things went her way and it remains to be seen whether this will be built on next time. (tchd 16-1)
Cathcart Castle has been running creditably on a sound surface but, while he wasn't disgraced in this much softer ground over this longer trip, a return to a sounder surface may be more to his liking. (op 9-2)
Loch Ordie fared best of those ridden with a bit of patience on this nursery debut and first run over this trip but he left the impression that a return to 7f on better ground will suit ideally. (op 4-1)
Eduardo's last run at Southwell had been franked by the subsequent win of Pisco Sour but he failed to improve for the switch to soft ground on turf. He is probably worth another chance returned to Fibresand. (op 9-2)

5390 HEART 106 H'CAP 5f 218y
7:50 (7:50) (Class 3) (0-90,90) 3-Y-O £5,677 (£1,699; £849; £424; £211) Stalls Low

Form				RPR
0002	1		**Colonel Mak**[31] 4369 3-9-7 88 JamieSpencer 5	98
			(T D Barron) *hld up: swtchd lft and hdwy over 1f out: r.o to ld post* **6/4**[1]	
2460	2	nse	**Flaneur**[31] 4369 3-8-10 77 (b) DavidAllan 9	87
			(T D Easterby) *led: rdn and edgd rt over 1f out: hdd ins fnl f: r.o* **9/2**[2]	
266	3	hd	**Ginger Ted (IRE)**[11] 5048 3-8-9 79 (p) AndrewHeffernan(3) 8	88
			(R C Guest) *chsd ldr 2f: remained handy: rdn and edgd lft over 1f out: led ins fnl f: hdd post* **9/2**[2]	
1140	4	1 ¾	**Joe Packet**[17] 4819 3-9-3 89 JohnFahy(5) 7	92
			(J G Portman) *hld up: hdwy over 2f out: rdn over 1f out: no ex wl ins fnl f* **7/1**[3]	
1005	5	1	**Ventura Cove (IRE)**[32] 4349 3-8-9 76 (p) PaulHanagan 2	76
			(R A Fahey) *s.i.s: sn prom: rdn and n.m.r over 1f out: no ex ins fnl f* **11/1**	
0033	6	2	**Edgewater (IRE)**[14] 4930 3-9-0 81 DaneO'Neill 4	75
			(J Akehurst) *chsd ldrs: rdn over 1f out: no ex ins fnl f* **8/1**	
2403	7	26	**Bilash**[47] 3808 3-8-4 71 oh3 LukeMorris 1	—
			(R Hollinshead) *chsd ldrs: rdn 1/2-way: wknd over 1f out: t.o* **33/1**	

1m 14.16s (1.16) **Going Correction** +0.125s/f (Good) 7 Ran SP% 111.2
Speed ratings (Par 104): **97,96,96,94,93 90,55**
toteswingers:1&2 £2.10, 2&3 £4.50, 1&3 £2.30 CSF £7.91 CT £22.64 TOTE £2.60: £2.30, £1.20; EX 9.20 Place6: £7.37 Place 5: £27.98.
Owner Norton Common Farm Racing **Bred** Peter Baldwin **Trained** Maunby, N Yorks

FOCUS
A couple of useful, if exposed, performers in a reasonable handicap and the field again raced in the centre of the track. The gallop was only an ordinary one for a sprint and the first three finished in a line.

NOTEBOOK
Colonel Mak is a useful sprinter who did well to come from just off the pace in a race where the leaders weren't stopping to poke his head in front on the line. A strongly run race over this trip with give in the ground are his ideal requirements and he'll be worth keeping an eye out for if connections opt to send him for the Silver or Bronze Cup at Ayr's Western Meeting. (op 2-1 tchd 11-8)
Flaneur finished a long way behind Colonel Mak after helping to force too strong a pace at Newcastle on his previous start but he was allowed to do his own thing for a long way and got much closer this time. He's usually a consistent sort who won't be going up too much for this and he's capable of winning again away from progressive sorts. (op 8-1)
Ginger Ted(IRE) goes particularly well on a soft surface and returned to something like his best after being well placed throughout. He has little margin for error from this mark but should continue to give it his best shot when he gets his ground. (op 7-2 tchd 5-1)
Joe Packet, who again travelled strongly, fared better than at Ascot on his previous start returned to a soft surface for the first time in over a year. He's high enough in the weights but remains worth a try over the minimum trip. (op 5-1)
Ventura Cove(IRE) hasn't been at his best since beating Flaneur at level weights at Thirsk in early May and the first-time cheekpieces failed to spark him back into life. He is in very good hands but is going to have to show a bit more before he is a solid betting proposition. (op 12-1)
Edgewater(IRE) had run creditably with the cheekpieces left off on Polytrack on his previous start but failed to build on that on this first run on a soft surface. He is on the same mark as for his last win and should do better back on Polytrack. (op 6-1)
T/Jkpt: Not won. T/Plt: £323.40 to a £1 stake. Pool of £71,305.03 - 160.91 winning tickets.
T/Qpdt: £56.50 to a £1 stake. Pool of £6,132.90 - 80.20 winning tickets. CR

5159 YARMOUTH (L-H)
Tuesday, August 24

OFFICIAL GOING: Good to soft (6.5)
Back straight and bend dolled out 3m increasing distances on round course by about 10yds.
Wind: strong, across Weather: dry, showers threatening, windy

5391 AVENUE PUB H'CAP 1m 3y
2:30 (2:31) (Class 5) (0-70,70) 3-Y-O+ £2,590 (£770; £385; £192) Stalls High

Form				RPR
0103	1		**Shesells Seashells**[19] 4762 3-9-6 69 HayleyTurner 7	78
			(M L W Bell) *hld up in tch towards rr: hdwy over 2f out: chsd ldr over 1f out: pushed into ld 1f out: kpt on wl: comf* **7/2**[1]	
6330	2	1 ½	**Cat Hunter**[50] 3739 3-9-4 67 TomQueally 5	73
			(H R A Cecil) *stdd s: hld up in rr: gd hdwy ent fnl 2f: rdn to ld over 1f out: hdd 1f out: styd on same pce fnl 100yds* **7/2**[1]	
0-54	3	½	**Child Of Our Time (IRE)**[12] 4997 3-9-5 68 AlanMunro 13	73
			(P W Chapple-Hyam) *in tch in rr: pushed along 1/2-way: rdn and hdwy wl over 1f out: kpt on u.p to chse ldng pair fnl 100yds: nt rch ldng pair* **25/1**	
06-0	4	2 ¼	**Montelissima (IRE)**[54] 3586 3-9-3 66 GeorgeBaker 1	66
			(E A L Dunlop) *t.k.h: prom: chsd ldr over 5f out tl led over 2f out: rdn and hdd over 1f out: wknd ent fnl f* **9/1**[3]	
2660	5	5	**Iptkaar (USA)**[27] 4479 3-8-11 67 (b) AhmedAjtebi(7) 6	55
			(C E Brittain) *chsd ldrs: rdn and lost pl wl over 2f out: plugged on again fr over 1f out: no threat to ldrs* **25/1**	
2106	6	1 ¼	**Eastern Gift**[20] 4690 5-9-8 70 KylieManser(5) 10	56
			(Miss Gay Kelleway) *hld up wl in tch: hdwy and ev ch ent fnl 2f: rdn and wknd qckly jst over 1f out: wl btn fnl f* **16/1**	
206	7	1 ¾	**Calahonda**[18] 4804 4-9-11 68 NeilCallan 12	50
			(P W D'Arcy) *chsd ldr tl over 5f out: styd prom: ev ch and rdn ent fnl 2f: wknd qckly over 1f out: no ch fnl f* **7/2**[1]	
-602	8	¾	**Profligate (IRE)**[58] 3484 3-9-4 67 JackMitchell 15	47
			(W Jarvis) *chsd ldrs: rdn and unable qck ent fnl 2f: sn struggling: wl btn whn edgd rt over 1f out* **11/1**	
4050	9	nk	**Astrodonna**[19] 4763 5-8-13 61 AshleyMorgan(5) 14	41
			(M H Tompkins) *stdd s: hld up in rr: hdwy to chse ldrs enteering fnl 2f: rdn wl over 1f out: sn btn and no ch fnl f* **8/1**[2]	
1004	10	3 ¾	**Scruffy Skip (IRE)**[15] 4895 5-9-8 65 (p) TomMcLaughlin 8	36
			(Mrs C A Dunnett) *led tl over 2f out: sn lost pl: wl bhd wl over 1f out* **18/1**	

1m 43.15s (2.55) **Going Correction** +0.325s/f (Good)
WFA 3 from 4yo+ 6lb 10 Ran SP% 114.9
Speed ratings (Par 103): **100,98,98,95,90 89,87,87,86,82**
toteswingers:1&2 £3.30, 2&3 £7.80, 1&3 £7.90 CSF £14.35 CT £259.18 TOTE £5.00: £2.40, £1.40, £4.50; EX 17.60 Trifecta £144.50 Pool: £449.23 - 2.30 winning units..
Owner Get To The Bar Racing **Bred** G A E And J Smith Bloodstock Ltd **Trained** Newmarket, Suffolk

FOCUS
Just a modest handicap, and the main action was up the centre of the track.

5392 AVENUE PUB & RESTAURANT NOVICE STKS 1m 3y
3:00 (3:00) (Class 4) 2-Y-O £5,046 (£1,510; £755; £377; £188) Stalls High

Form				RPR
2	1		**Buthelezi (USA)**[18] 4803 2-9-0 0 NeilCallan 5	89
			(J H M Gosden) *t.k.h hold: trckd ldng pair: rdn and qcknd to ld wl over 1f out: kpt on wl ins fnl f* **10/11**[1]	
4	2	hd	**Dux Scholar**[25] 4550 2-9-0 0 RichardMullen 3	89+
			(Sir Michael Stoute) *t.k.h: hld up in tch in last pair: rdn and effrt ent fnl 2f: chsd wnr ins fnl f: r.o wl and clsng at fin* **4/1**[2]	

0223 3 1 3/4 **Amwell Pinot**[25] 4550 2-9-5 89 HayleyTurner 2 90
(A Bailey) *chsd ldr: rdn and chsng wnr over 1f out tl ins fnl f: one pce fnl 100yds* **7/1**
1 4 7 **Mutual Force (USA)**[28] 4447 2-8-12 0 AntiocoMurgia(7) 1 74
(Mahmood Al Zarooni) *led at stdy gallop: rdn ent fnl 2f: hdd wl over 1f out: sn outpcd and wl btn ins fnl f* **12/1**
153 5 nk **Deep South**[14] 4928 2-9-5 92 (p) AhmedAjtebi 6 74
(Mahmood Al Zarooni) *t.k.h: hld up wl in tch in last pair: effrt ent fnl 2f: rdn and hld hd high wl over 1f out: sn btn* **5/1**[3]
1m 41.7s (1.10) **Going Correction** +0.325s/f (Good) 5 Ran SP% **109.2**
Speed ratings (Par 96): **107,106,105,98,97**
CSF £4.73 TOTE £2.00: £1.10, £2.70; EX 5.10.
Owner H R H Princess Haya Of Jordan **Bred** Dr John A Chandler **Trained** Newmarket, Suffolk
FOCUS
Strong form, with the very useful Amwell Pinot taking third behind two promising types, and the time was 1.45 seconds quicker than the 69-rated Shesells Seashells recorded in the earlier handicap. They raced up the middle of the track.
NOTEBOOK
Buthelezi(USA) ◆, a Royal Lodge and Racing Post Trophy entry, confirmed the promise he showed when runner-up on debut over 7f at the July course. He didn't win as convincingly as had appeared likely at one stage, still looking green in front, but was always doing enough. His action suggests he may do better on a faster surface and he'll surely be stepped up in class next time. (op 6-5 after early 5-4 in places)
Dux Scholar ◆ showed a knee action, really grabbing the ground, so the easy surface suited and he finished powerfully, building on the form he showed when behind Amwell Pinot over 7f on debut. Likely to stay further next year, he can keep progressing and could be smart in time. (tchd 5-1)
Amwell Pinot ran a fine race considering he was conceding 5lb to the front pair, both progressive and potentially smart. Alan Bailey's colt may be better than his official mark of 89 suggests. (op 9-2)
Mutual Force(USA) did not progress from his winning debut, gained in an ordinary contest on quick ground. (op 10-1)
Deep South also disappointed, racing keenly in first-time cheekpieces before finding nothing for pressure. (op 11-2 tchd 6-1)

5393 AVENUE PUB & RESTAURANT H'CAP 6f 3y
3:30 (3:31) (Class 3) (0-95,94) 3-Y-O+ **£6,799** (£2,023; £1,011; £505) **Stalls** High

Form RPR
/3-2 1 **Harry Patch**[17] 4832 4-9-6 87 NeilCallan 3 99+
(M A Jarvis) *stdd s: t.k.h: trckd ldr tl pushed into ld over 1f out: rdn and qcknd ins fnl f: comf* **1/1**[1]
2100 2 1 1/2 **Mac's Power (IRE)**[31] 4358 4-9-5 86 (t) GeorgeBaker 6 93
(J R Fanshawe) *stdd s: t.k.h: trckd ldrs: shkn up to chal over 1f out: drvn jst ins fnl f: nt qng pce of wnr fnl 100yds* **4/1**[3]
-100 3 3/4 **Spitfire**[17] 4832 5-9-6 87 StephenCraine 1 92
(J R Jenkins) *hld up wl in tch: rdn and effrt wl over 1f out: kpt on same pce ins fnl f* **11/1**
0500 4 1/2 **Doric Lady**[21] 4685 5-8-10 77 KirstyMilczarek 7 80
(J A R Toller) *stdd s: t.k.h: hld up in tch in last pair: rdn and hdwy 2f out: kpt on same pce ins fnl f* **18/1**
3003 5 1/2 **Imperial Guest**[17] 4843 4-9-12 93 TomQueally 2 95
(G G Margarson) *stdd s: hld up in tch in last pair: rdn and effrt 2f out: styd on same pce fr over 1f out* **7/2**[2]
6201 6 6 **Waveband**[16] 4858 3-9-7 91 RichardHills 9 73
(M Johnston) *led: rdn and qcknd ent fnl 2f: hdd over 1f out: wknd qckly ent fnl f* **10/1**
1m 15.16s (0.76) **Going Correction** +0.325s/f (Good)
WFA 3 from 4yo+ 3lb 6 Ran SP% **114.9**
Speed ratings (Par 107): **107,105,104,103,102 94**
toteswingers:1&2 £1.70, 2&3 £5.60, 1&3 £3.60 CSF £5.59 CT £26.49 TOTE £1.90: £1.10, £2.80; EX 6.60 Trifecta £21.70 Pool: £891- 30.34 winning units..
Owner Mrs Gay Jarvis **Bred** Red House Stud **Trained** Newmarket, Suffolk
FOCUS
Possibly not that strong a race for the grade. The pace was not particularly quick, and they raced middle to far side.
NOTEBOOK
Harry Patch ◆ was a cut above his rivals. He had shaped well in a stronger race than this on his return from a 15-month absence at Haydock earlier this month and showed he's gone the right way subsequently with a straightforward success, taking this with more authority than the margin suggests. Seeing as this was only his fifth start, there really should be plenty to come, provided of course that he continues to stand training,. He has a significant knee action and the softer the ground the better for him. He's 16-1 from 25-1 for the Ayr Gold Cup. (op 5-6 tchd 6-5)
Mac's Power(IRE) probably wasn't suited by the modest pace as he stays further and was always being held, but this was a good effort nonetheless. (op 15-2)
Spitfire had the ground to suit but was a bit keen early on and, not for the first time, held his head high under pressure. (op 17-2 tchd 12-1)
Doric Lady returned to form following a couple of poor efforts, but she made no real impression and probably would have preferred a quicker gallop. (op 20-1)
Imperial Guest seemed to handle similar ground when a good third at the July Course last time, and his four wins have been gained over this trip, so this was a disappointing showing. (op 5-1)
Waveband, 5lb higher than when winning at Leicester, took them along in a soft enough lead but found nothing for pressure and clearly needs a quicker surface. (op 17-2 tchd 8-1)

5394 FLORAL DESIGNS FLORIST GORLESTON H'CAP 1m 1f
4:00 (4:00) (Class 4) (0-80,78) 3-Y-O **£4,533** (£1,348; £674; £336) **Stalls** Low

Form RPR
0401 1 **Nelson's Bounty**[14] 4931 3-9-4 75 TonyCulhane 4 88
(P W D'Arcy) *hld up in last pair: hdwy gng wl 4f out: led 2f out: sn rdn: styd on wl ins fnl f: rdn out* **5/2**[2]
6604 2 1 1/4 **Osgood**[19] 4732 3-8-10 67 AlanMunro 1 77
(M R Channon) *hld up in last pair: hdwy wl over 2f out: rdn to chse wnr over 1f out: styd on same pce ins fnl f* **8/1**
3000 3 3 **Aquarian Spirit**[24] 4603 3-9-4 78 BarryMcHugh(3) 6 81
(R A Fahey) *led after 1f: rdn and hdd ent fnl 2f: wknd u.p jst over 1f out* **85/40**[1]
4520 4 nse **Opening Nite (IRE)**[15] 4898 3-8-8 68 (p) MartinLane(3) 5 71
(R A Fahey) *s.i.s: reminders after s: hdwy to press ldr after 1f: rdn ent fnl 3f: wknd u.p jst over 1f out* **8/1**
510 5 1 **Law Of The Range**[31] 4389 3-9-0 76 TobyAtkinson(5) 3 77
(M Botti) *led for 1f: short of room and hmpd sn after: chsd ldrs: n.m.r on inner fr 3f out tl swtchd rt over 1f out: no ch w ldrs after: plugged on* **9/1**
5626 6 2 **Starry Mount**[8] 5146 3-9-1 72 NeilCallan 2 69
(A B Haynes) *chsd ldrs: rdn ent fnl 3f: drvn and wknd wl over 1f out* **9/2**[3]
1m 58.97s (3.17) **Going Correction** +0.425s/f (Yiel) 6 Ran SP% **111.0**
Speed ratings (Par 102): **102,100,98,98,97 95**
toteswingers:1&2 £3.50, 2&3 £3.00, 1&3 £2.30 CSF £21.30 TOTE £2.90: £1.40, £4.70; EX 14.50.

Owner The Newmarket Pirates **Bred** Slatch Farm Stud **Trained** Newmarket, Suffolk
■ Stewards' Enquiry : Alan Munro caution: used whip without giving colt time to respond.
FOCUS
The back straight and bend was dolled out 3m, adding 10m to the distance. This was a weak-looking handicap for the class.
Law Of The Range Official explanation: jockey said filly was denied a clear run

5395 YARMOUTH GREYHOUND STADIUM MAIDEN FILLIES' STKS 7f 3y
4:30 (4:31) (Class 5) 3-Y-O+ **£3,238** (£963; £481; £240) **Stalls** High

Form RPR
3-2 1 **Hamloola**[20] 4697 3-9-0 0 RichardHills 4 78+
(W J Haggas) *a.p: pushed into ld wl over 1f out: sn wl clr: v easily* **1/2**[1]
00 2 8 **Chaqueta**[39] 4114 3-9-0 0 AlanMunro 7 56
(C F Wall) *dwlt: hld up in tch in rr: rdn and effrt on far side wl over 1f out: no ch w wnr: kpt on to go modest 2nd ins fnl f* **66/1**
3 nk **Fun Affair (USA)** 3-9-0 0 SaleemGolam 11 56
(J H M Gosden) *hld up in tch towards rr: no ch w wnr: kpt on u.p fr over 1f out: hmpd and swtchd rt ins fnl f: wnt modest 3rd nr fin* **14/1**
0-60 4 1/2 **Stargazing (IRE)**[32] 4339 4-9-2 41 (b[1]) Louis-PhilippeBeuzelin(3) 1 56
(B J Meehan) *t.k.h: in tch: rdn and wl outpcd by wnr: wnt 2nd over 1f out: hung rt u.p and lost 2 pls ins fnl f* **33/1**
5 5 2 1/4 **Alioonagh (USA)**[20] 4697 3-9-0 0 MickyFenton 6 48
(N P Littmoden) *racd keenly: w ldrs tl led wl over 2f out: rdn and hdd wl over 1f out: no ch w wnr after: wl btn whn hmpd ins fnl f* **7/2**[2]
6 6 1 1/4 **Citadella**[13] 4966 3-9-0 0 PatCosgrave 8 45
(D M Simcock) *dwlt: hld up in tch: rdn and outpcd ent fnl 2f: plugged on same pce and wl btn after* **28/1**
0-3 7 1 1/2 **Maany (USA)**[13] 4966 3-9-0 0 TadhgO'Shea 9 41
(M A Jarvis) *prom: rdn jst over 2f out: sn struggling: wl btn over 1f out* **8/1**[3]
0-0 8 1 1/4 **Arabian Jewel**[13] 4966 3-9-0 0 AndreaAtzeni 2 37
(D M Simcock) *dwlt: hld up in tch in rr: rdn and btn ent fnl 2f: wl bhd ins fnl f* **80/1**
00 9 5 **Bouncy Bouncy (IRE)**[13] 4966 3-9-0 0 HayleyTurner 3 24
(M L W Bell) *t.k.h: wl in tch tl rdn and btn ent fnl 2f: sn wl bhd* **28/1**
4-00 10 1 1/4 **Avec Moi**[13] 4969 3-9-0 43 MarcHalford 13 20
(Mrs C A Dunnett) *led tl wl over 2f out: sn lost pl u.p: wl bhd over 1f out* **100/1**
1m 27.16s (0.56) **Going Correction** +0.325s/f (Good)
WFA 3 from 4yo 5lb 10 Ran SP% **120.2**
Speed ratings (Par 100): **109,99,99,98,96 94,93,91,86,84**
CSF £76.47 TOTE £1.50: £1.10, £10.70, £5.10; EX 52.10 Trifecta £691.20 Part won. Pool: £934.14 - 0.50 winning units..
Owner Hamdan Al Maktoum **Bred** Floors Farming And Dominic Burke **Trained** Newmarket, Suffolk
FOCUS
An uncompetitive fillies' maiden, but the time was decent, being 1.67 seconds quicker than the progressive 81-rated 4-y-o Wake Up Call recorded in the following handicap. The action was middle to far side.

5396 NORFOLK AND SUFFOLK ANIMAL TRUST FILLIES' H'CAP 7f 3y
5:00 (5:01) (Class 4) (0-85,83) 3-Y-O+ **£4,533** (£1,348; £674; £336) **Stalls** High

Form RPR
3-11 1 **Wake Up Call**[29] 4438 4-9-10 81 GeorgeBaker 6 96
(C F Wall) *trckd ldng pair: led gng wl over 1f out: sn shkn up and wandered: clr 1f out: rdn and r.o wl ins fnl f: comf* **13/8**[1]
6513 2 1 1/2 **Avon Lady**[17] 4847 3-8-10 72 PatCosgrave 5 81
(J R Fanshawe) *wl in tch: rdn and effrt over 1f out: n.m.r and carried lft ent fnl f: drvn and chsd wnr ins fnl f: no imp fnl 75yds* **11/4**[2]
5103 3 2 **Starclass**[31] 4387 3-8-13 78 MartinLane(3) 8 82
(W R Swinburn) *s.i.s: wl in tch in midfield: rdn and effrt to chse ldr over 1f out: edgd rt 1f out: kpt on same pce ins fnl f* **5/1**[3]
3556 4 shd **Little Scotland**[9] 5120 3-9-3 82 BarryMcHugh(3) 7 85
(R A Fahey) *restless in stalls: in tch in rr: rdn over 2f out: styng on same pce u.p and btn whn short of room wl ins fnl f* **11/2**
2-16 5 1 3/4 **Mainstay**[89] 2475 4-9-12 83 SaleemGolam 2 84
(J H M Gosden) *s.i.s: t.k.h: sn rcvrd and chsd ldr: rdn and ev ch 2f out: nt gng pce of wnr over 1f out: wknd ins fnl f* **11/1**
-430 6 nk **Blue Lyric**[17] 4847 3-8-10 72 KirstyMilczarek 10 70
(L M Cumani) *hld up in tch towards rr: rdn and unable qck 2f out: drvn and kpt on same pce fr over 1f out* **22/1**
2005 7 13 **The Hermitage (IRE)**[14] 4930 3-8-13 75 RichardHills 4 38
(M Johnston) *led: rdn ent fnl 2f: hdd over 1f out: wl btn and eased ins fnl f* **16/1**
1m 28.83s (2.23) **Going Correction** +0.325s/f (Good)
WFA 3 from 4yo 5lb 7 Ran SP% **115.4**
Speed ratings (Par 102): **100,98,96,95,93 93,78**
toteswingers:1&2 £2.00, 2&3 £2.60, 1&3 £2.80 CSF £6.38 CT £17.35 TOTE £2.60: £1.20, £2.70; EX 5.80 Trifecta £26.90 Pool: £590.70 - 16.19 winning units. Place 6: £9.41 Place 5: £4.96 .
Owner J G Lambton **Bred** Whatton Manor Stud **Trained** Newmarket, Suffolk
FOCUS
A good fillies' handicap, but the early pace was steady, resulting in a time 1.67 seconds slower than earlier maiden won by Hamloola. They raced towards the far side in the closing stages, with a strong cross-wind encouraging them in that direction.
T/Plt: £13.70 to a £1 stake. Pool of £78,605.98 - 4,166.37 winning tickets. T/Qpdt: £4.70 to a £1 stake. Pool of £4,622.95 - 719.92 winning tickets. SP

5397 - 5403a (Foreign Racing) - See Raceform Interactive

4820 AYR (L-H)
Wednesday, August 25
OFFICIAL GOING: Good (9.0)
Straight course stands side rail moved in 5m. Round course back straight out 4m, home bend out 6m adding about 18yds to distances on round course.
Wind: Slight, half against Weather: Sunny, hot

5404 E.B.F./COCA COLA MAIDEN STKS 7f 50y
2:10 (2:12) (Class 4) 2-Y-O **£4,306** (£1,281; £640; £319) **Stalls** High

Form RPR
2 1 **Man Of The Match (IRE)**[17] 4856 2-9-3 0 RobertWinston 6 79+
(A Bailey) *mde all: set stdy pce: rdn 2f out: hld on wl fnl f* **1/1**[1]
3 2 nk **Red Riverman**[26] 4549 2-9-3 0 TonyCulhane 5 78
(W J Haggas) *hld up in tch: smooth hdwy to chal over 1f out: sn rdn: kpt on fnl f: hdd nr fin* **13/8**[2]

The Form Book, Raceform Ltd, Compton, RG20 6NL

04 **3** 2 1/4 **Perignon (IRE)**60 3449 2-9-3 0 PJMcDonald 4 73
(G A Swinbank) *trckd ldrs: rdn and edgd rt over 1f out: kpt on fnl f: nt rch first two* **12/1**

5 **4** 2 **Dressing Room (USA)**12 5032 2-9-3 0 JoeFanning 10 68
(M Johnston) *pressed wnr: rdn over 2f out: edgd lft and no ex 1f out* **8/1**3

620 **5** 3 **Cotton Spirit**33 4346 2-9-3 72 PaulHanagan 7 61
(R A Fahey) *t.k.h: trckd ldrs: rdn and outpcd over 2f out: kpt on fnl f: no imp* **25/1**

06 **6** 4 1/2 **Monel**18 4821 2-9-3 0 LNewman 1 49
(J S Goldie) *t.k.h: hld up in tch: rdn and outpcd over 2f out: sn btn* **100/1**

0 **7** 1 1/4 **Coracle**40 4110 2-8-12 0 (t) DaleSwift(5) 3 46
(J A Glover) *plld hrd: hld up on ins: rdn over 2f out: sn btn* **100/1**

8 *hd* **Sam Nombulist** 2-9-0 0 MichaelStainton(3) 2 46
(R M Whitaker) *s.s: sn rcvrd off slow pce to join pack: rdn over 2f out: sn wknd* **66/1**

9 3 3/4 **Subramaniam** 2-9-3 0 PaulMulrennan 8 37
(J G Given) *hld up: rdn over 2f out: sn wknd* **100/1**

1m 35.51s (2.11) **Going Correction** -0.225s/f (Firm) **9** Ran SP% **115.2**
Speed ratings (Par 96): **78,77,75,72,69 64,62,62,58**
toteswingers: 1&2 £1.20, 1&3 £3.00, 2&3 £3.40 CSF £2.75 TOTE £1.80: £1.02, £1.10, £3.60; EX 3.10.
Owner Rathordan Partnership **Bred** Michael Dalton **Trained** Newmarket, Suffolk

FOCUS
This maiden was won in 2008 by subsequent Group 1 scorer Zafisio, and although there was probably not anything of that calibre in this year's field, the first two look decent prospects.

NOTEBOOK
Man Of The Match(IRE) had to bow to the greater experience of Azrael on his debut at Leicester but was well supported to make amends. Adopting different tactics, he made all and responded willingly to hold off the runner-up. A good-looking colt, he can hold his own in better company. (tchd 11-10 and 11-8 early)
Red Riverman was a promising third on his debut at Newmarket behind subsequent Washington Singer Stakes winner Janood. Last off the bridle, he had every chance but was always just being held. He still looked a little unsure what to do when asked to put his head down and battle and should come on again for this. (tchd 7-4)
Perignon(IRE) was briefly outpaced by the principals before running on nicely. The step up to 7f suited him and he is now eligible for nurseries, but a cautionary note is that he has been entered in selling company. (op 14-1)
Dressing Room(USA) has a bit of scope about him, but he was unable to build on his debut fifth at Newbury behind the impressive Saamidd. (tchd 9-1)
Cotton Spirit has been gelded since his last appearance a month ago. He saw out the trip but looks exposed as modest. (tchd 22-1)
Coracle, who has been gelded, was fitted with a tongue tie. He did not seem to appreciate being held up and was rather keen.
Sam Nombulist is a half-brother to five winners, the best of them being the smart sprinter Ratio, who dead-heated for the Wokingham. He missed the break badly and, although the slow pace meant he was quickly in touch with the bunch, he was never out of the last pair. (op 80-1)

5405 WALLACES EXPRESS H'CAP (DIV I) 7f 50y
2:40 (2:41) (Class 6) (0-65,65) 3-Y-O+ **£1,706** (£503; £252) **Stalls** High

Form RPR
3-40 **1** **Scrapper Smith (IRE)**18 4834 4-9-11 **64** PJMcDonald 8 81+
(A C Whillans) *hld up: hdwy on outside to ld over 1f out: pushed clr fnl f* **13/2**

3030 **2** 8 **Barraland**3 5331 5-8-9 **51** GaryBartley(3) 4 46
(J S Goldie) *led to over 1f out: kpt on same pce fnl f* **16/1**

-000 **3** *nse* **This Ones For Eddy**36 4237 5-9-2 **55** AndrewElliott 2 50
(J Balding) *cl up: effrt and ev ch over 1f out: kpt on same pce fnl f* **11/2**2

0403 **4** *shd* **Spin Again (IRE)**19 4795 5-9-12 **65** AndrewMullen 7 60
(D Nicholls) *prom: effrt over 2f out: edgd lft: one pce fnl f* **6/1**3

00-4 **5** 4 **Nolecce**37 4188 3-8-2 **46** oh1 PaulEddery 10 28
(R C Guest) *hld up: rdn over 2f out: kpt on fnl f: nvr able to chal* **4/1**1

5234 **6** 2 3/4 **Residency (IRE)**14 4947 4-9-7 **60** TomEaves 9 37
(B Smart) *hld up in tch: drvn and outpcd over 2f out: n.d after* **11/2**2

1554 **7** 3 **Mr Lu**44 3948 5-9-10 **63** (p) PaulHanagan 3 32
(J S Goldie) *hld up: rdn and hung lft over 2f out: sn no imp* **11/2**2

2500 **8** 5 **Hosanna**18 4824 4-8-11 **50** PaulMulrennan 1 —
(J Barclay) *t.k.h: trckd ldrs tl rdn and wknd over 1f out* **16/1**

-000 **9** 20 **Maxwell Hawke (IRE)**95 2331 4-9-10 **63** (t) RichardKingscote 5 —
(Tom Dascombe) *cl up tl wknd over 2f out: t.o* **9/1**

1m 30.97s (-2.43) **Going Correction** -0.225s/f (Firm)
WFA 3 from 4yo+ 5lb **9** Ran SP% **115.5**
Speed ratings (Par 101): **104,94,94,94,90 86,83,77,54**
toteswingers: 1&2 £11.10, 1&3 £7.50, 2&3 £17.90 CSF £102.72 CT £612.53 TOTE £5.80: £1.70, £4.90, £2.40; EX 94.90.
Owner A C Whillans **Bred** John Costello **Trained** Newmill-On-Slitrig, Borders

FOCUS
Division one of this low-grade handicap. It was run at a solid pace and the time was the best part of five seconds quicker than the earlier 2-y-o race. Much-improved form from the emphatic winner, and the race could be out a few pounds either way.

5406 COORS LIGHT H'CAP (DIV II OF 2.40PM) 7f 50y
3:10 (3:10) (Class 6) (0-65,65) 3-Y-O+ **£1,706** (£503; £252) **Stalls** High

Form RPR
3222 **1** **El Dececy (USA)**11 5067 6-9-12 **65** (p) RobertWinston 8 75
(J Balding) *mde all: set stdy pce: qcknd over 2f out: clr over 1f out: kpt on wl: unchal* **9/4**1

0055 **2** 3 3/4 **Broughtons Silk**3 5331 5-8-7 **46** oh1 PJMcDonald 3 46
(A C Whillans) *in tch: rdn and hdwy on ins to chse wnr over 1f out: no imp fnl f* **7/1**

2663 **3** 1 **Hansomis (IRE)**21 4706 6-9-2 **60** DaleSwift(5) 7 57
(B Mactaggart) *hld up in tch on outside: rdn over 2f out: kpt on fnl f: nrst fin* **8/1**

0043 **4** 1/2 **Kings Point (IRE)**13 4986 9-9-5 **63** BillyCray(5) 2 59
(D Nicholls) *chsd wnr to over 1f out: kpt on same pce u.p* **7/2**2

0256 **5** 3/4 **Shunkawakhan (IRE)**18 4824 7-8-12 **51** PaulHanagan 5 45
(Miss L A Perratt) *t.k.h: hld up in tch: drvn over 2f out: nvr able to chal* **11/2**3

2205 **6** *nk* **Botham (USA)**14 4947 6-9-1 **61** PaulNorton(7) 10 54
(J S Goldie) *hld up last in steadily run r: effrt on ins over 1f out: kpt on fnl f: nvr able to chal* **10/1**

4400 **7** 3 1/4 **Zabeel Tower**12 5024 7-9-2 **55** TomEaves 1 39
(R Allan) *cl up tl rdn and wknd over 1f out* **25/1**

1005 **8** 1 1/4 **Piccolo Express**11 5064 4-8-13 **52** MickyFenton 6 33
(B P J Baugh) *prom tl rdn and wknd wl over 1f out* **12/1**

1m 33.26s (-0.14) **Going Correction** -0.225s/f (Firm)
WFA 3 from 4yo+ 5lb **8** Ran SP% **112.6**
Speed ratings (Par 101): **91,86,85,85,84 83,80,78**
toteswingers: 1&2 £3.30, 1&3 £3.80, 2&3 £7.90 CSF £17.96 CT £105.38 TOTE £2.60: £1.10, £3.10, £1.90; EX 18.30.
Owner Brian Morton & Willie McKay **Bred** Shadwell Farm LLC **Trained** Scrooby, Notts

FOCUS
This was run in a time 2.29 seconds slower than the first division. The winner dictated and is rated to his best form of the past year.

5407 SMIRNOFF VODKA H'CAP 1m
3:40 (3:40) (Class 4) (0-80,80) 3-Y-O+ **£4,533** (£1,348; £674; £336) **Stalls** Low

Form RPR
3003 **1** **Arabian Spirit**40 4093 5-9-8 **75** PaulHanagan 8 86
(R A Fahey) *hld up in tch: hdwy on outside 2f out: drvn to ld ins fnl f: styd on wl* **5/1**1

4203 **2** 1 **Elijah Pepper (USA)**11 5067 5-8-12 **65** PaulMulrennan 3 74
(T D Barron) *midfeld on ins: hdwy 2f out: sn rdn: chsd wnr ins fnl f: r.o* **12/1**

4314 **3** 2 **Daring Dream (GER)**7 5213 5-9-0 **70** GaryBartley(3) 13 74
(J S Goldie) *hld up towards rr: hdwy over 1f out: kpt on ins fnl f* **6/1**2

2030 **4** *hd* **Thunderball**49 3796 4-9-7 **79** DaleSwift(5) 4 83
(J A Glover) *cl up: led over 2f out to ins fnl f: kpt on same pce* **8/1**

0230 **5** 3/4 **Espero (IRE)**32 4371 4-9-9 **76** LNewman 2 78
(Miss L A Perratt) *prom: stdy hdwy over 2f out: rdn over 1f out: one pce fnl f* **10/1**

1315 **6** *nk* **Glenluji**19 4796 5-8-5 **65** NoraLooby(7) 11 66
(J S Goldie) *dwlt: bhd tl hdwy fnl f: nrst fin* **14/1**

6650 **7** 1 **King Of The Moors (USA)**7 5213 7-8-12 **65** (p) MickyFenton 12 64
(R C Guest) *towards rr: rdn and hung lft 2f out: kpt on fnl f: nvr able to chal* **40/1**

0004 **8** 1 **Mr Macattack**41 4065 5-9-10 **77** (t) RichardKingscote 9 74
(Tom Dascombe) *hld up on ins: drvn over 2f out: nvr able to chal* **12/1**

2400 **9** 1 **Moheebb (IRE)**18 4828 6-9-13 **80** (b) PJMcDonald 10 74
(Mrs R A Carr) *bhd: rdn over 2f out: sn no imp* **10/1**

005 **10** 2 3/4 **Billy Dane (IRE)**25 4603 6-9-12 **79** RobertWinston 6 67
(F P Murtagh) *led to over 2f out: wknd over 1f out* **5/1**1

6046 **11** 3 **Lordship (IRE)**14 4968 6-8-1 **61** JakePayne(7) 1 42
(A W Carroll) *t.k.h: trckd ldrs tl wknd fr 2f out* **20/1**

4-51 **12** 11 **Midwestern (USA)**21 4710 3-9-5 **78** TomEaves 5 33
(B Smart) *prom: drvn over 3f out: wknd over 2f out* **7/1**3

1m 40.84s (-2.96) **Going Correction** -0.225s/f (Firm)
WFA 3 from 4yo+ 6lb **12** Ran SP% **118.7**
Speed ratings (Par 105): **105,104,102,101,101 100,99,98,97,95 92,81**
toteswingers: 1&2 £11.20, 1&3 £4.40, 2&3 £12.10 CSF £65.67 CT £378.35 TOTE £4.80: £2.30, £5.80, £1.60; EX 62.60.
Owner Timeform Betfair Racing Club Ltd **Bred** Malih Lahij Al Basti **Trained** Musley Bank, N Yorks

FOCUS
A fair handicap run at a sound pace. The winner posted his best form for this yeard, with the third a solid guide.
Billy Dane(IRE) Official explanation: jockey said gelding ran too free
Midwestern(USA) Official explanation: trainer's rep had no explanation for the poor form shown

5408 WHYTE & MACKAY H'CAP 1m 2f
4:10 (4:10) (Class 4) (0-85,85) 3-Y-O+
£4,673 (£1,399; £699; £350; £174; £87) **Stalls** Low

Form RPR
0211 **1** **Northside Prince (IRE)**18 4823 4-10-0 **78** PJMcDonald 1 91
(G A Swinbank) *in tch on ins: hdwy to ld over 1f out: hrd pressed ins fnl f* **7/2**1

2422 **2** *nk* **Marjury Daw (IRE)**8 5181 4-9-12 **76** PaulMulrennan 10 88
(J G Given) *hld up in tch: effrt and rdn over 2f out: ev ch ins fnl f: kpt on: hld cl home* **7/1**

1110 **3** *hd* **High Resolution**7 5213 3-8-12 **75** DaleSwift(5) 12 87
(Miss L A Perratt) *hld up in last: plld out and gd hdwy on outside over 1f out: ev ch ins fnl f: hld towards fin* **11/2**2

2642 **4** 3 **Grand Diamond (IRE)**6 5244 6-8-9 **66** (p) PaulNorton(7) 11 72+
(J S Goldie) *hld up: smooth hdwy over 2f out: rdn over 1f out: kpt on fnl f: nt rch first three* **7/1**

5-31 **5** 4 **Accompanist**10 5128 7-9-1 **68** (p) BACurtis(3) 8 66
(T G McCourt, Ire) *hld up: rdn over 2f out: styd on fnl f: nvr able to chal* **12/1**

610 **6** *hd* **Stags Leap (IRE)**10 5121 3-9-10 **85** PatrickDonaghy(3) 3 82
(P Monteith) *trckd ldrs tl rdn and wknd wl over 1f out* **50/1**

2010 **7** 3/4 **Monkton Vale (IRE)**25 4573 3-9-4 **76** PaulHanagan 5 72
(R A Fahey) *led: rdn over 2f out: hdd wl over 1f out: sn wknd* **13/2**3

0650 **8** 3 **French Applause (IRE)**26 4546 4-8-10 **60** MickyFenton 9 50
(T P Tate) *sn w ldr: rdn and led briefly wl over 1f out: sn wknd* **18/1**

3115 **9** 1 1/4 **That'll Do Nicely (IRE)**41 4051 7-9-13 **77** TomEaves 4 64
(N G Richards) *t.k.h: in tch: rdn over 2f out: wknd over 1f out* **13/2**3

2550 **10** 1/2 **Talk Of Saafend (IRE)**7 5213 5-8-9 **59** AndrewElliott 7 45
(P Monteith) *prom on outside tl hung lft and wknd wl over 1f out* **20/1**

0620 **11** 2 3/4 **Shy Glance (USA)**7 5213 8-8-12 **62** (p) RobertWinston 6 43
(P Monteith) *trckd ldrs: drvn over 2f out: wknd over 1f out* **16/1**

0000 **12** 16 **Suburbia (USA)**18 4823 4-8-9 **59** oh14 (b) LNewman 2 —
(J Barclay) *hld up: rdn over 2f out: sn lost tch* **100/1**

2m 9.30s (-2.70) **Going Correction** -0.225s/f (Firm)
WFA 3 from 4yo+ 8lb **12** Ran SP% **115.8**
Speed ratings (Par 105): **101,100,100,98,95 94,94,91,90,90 88,75**
toteswingers: 1&2 £4.50, 1&3 £4.80, 2&3 £8.00 CSF £26.63 CT £132.36 TOTE £3.40: £1.20, £2.00, £3.30; EX 18.20.
Owner S S Anderson **Bred** F Dunne **Trained** Melsonby, N Yorks
■ Stewards' Enquiry : P J McDonald caution: used whip down shoulder in the forehand.
Paul Mulrennan one-day ban: used whip with excessive frequency (Sep 8)

FOCUS
Quite a well contested handicap, although the top weight - the winner - was 7lb below the ceiling rating. The pace was sound. The progressive winner was rated up 4lb.

Talk Of Saafend(IRE) Official explanation: jockey said mare had a breathing problem

5409 TENNENT'S LAGER H'CAP 6f
4:40 (4:41) (Class 5) (0-75,74) 3-Y-O £2,590 (£770; £385; £192) Stalls Centre

Form				RPR
0363	1		**Music Festival (USA)**[44] 3951 3-8-6 59 JoeFanning 3 (J S Goldie) *in tch: effrt and pushed along over 2f out: led ins fnl f: styd on wl* 7/1	65
4342	2	nk	**Monte Mayor One**[7] 5211 3-8-8 61 PaulHanagan 7 (P Monteith) *prom: effrt over 1f out: rdn and ev ch ins fnl f: kpt on: hld nr fin* 5/1	66
3561	3	3/4	**Chushka**[39] 4155 3-9-3 70 (v) TomEaves 9 (B Smart) *led: rdn over 1f out: hdd ins fnl f: one pce towards fin* 2/1[1]	73
-360	4	1 1/4	**Eternal Instinct**[3] 5335 3-9-0 74 PaulNorton(7) 2 (J S Goldie) *sn wl bhd: shkn up and hdwy over 1f out: kpt on strly under hands and heels riding fnl f: nvr nr to chal* 9/2[3]	73+
4000	5	1/2	**Coolree Star (IRE)**[18] 4834 3-8-12 65 RobertWinston 4 (J A Glover) *cl up: drvn over 2f out: one pce appr fnl f* 12/1	62
0501	6	9	**Spinning Spirit (IRE)**[20] 4749 3-8-11 64 PaulMulrennan 5 (J G Given) *prom: rdn over 2f out: wknd over 1f out* 7/2[2]	32
3200	7	3/4	**Reach For The Sky (IRE)**[20] 4749 3-7-9 55 oh2 VictorSantos(7) 1 (A Berry) *cl up tl rdn and wknd fr 2f out* 33/1	21
0-66	8	1 1/2	**Precious Coral (IRE)**[12] 5044 3-8-7 60 (bt) PJMcDonald 6 (Mrs R A Carr) *hld up in tch: drvn over 2f out: sn wknd* 33/1	21

1m 12.64s (-0.96) **Going Correction** -0.225s/f (Firm) 8 Ran SP% 116.5
Speed ratings (Par 100): **97,96,95,93,93 81,80,78**
toteswingers: 1&2 £5.40, 1&3 £4.30, 2&3 £2.70 CSF £42.55 CT £95.89 TOTE £13.80: £2.10, £1.70, £1.10; EX 33.10.
Owner W M Johnstone **Bred** Gainsborough Farm Llc **Trained** Uplawmoor, E Renfrews
■ Stewards' Enquiry : Paul Norton 12-day ban: failed to take all reasonable and permissible measures (dates tbn)

FOCUS
A moderate sprint handicap for 3yos. The form is rated around the second, with the winner up 6lb.
Eternal Instinct Official explanation: jockey said, regarding running and riding, that his orders were to drop the filly in and get it settled and come with a late run; trainer confirmed but added that in his opinion the jockey had overdone the waiting tactics and should have sat closer to the pace once it had settled.

5410 J20 WHITE BLEND H'CAP 5f
5:10 (5:11) (Class 6) (0-65,62) 3-Y-O £2,047 (£604; £302) Stalls Centre

Form				RPR
404	1		**Lees Anthem**[27] 4513 3-9-0 60 DaleSwift(5) 3 (C J Teague) *w ldrs: rdn over 1f out: styd on to ld towards fin* 10/1	67
5511	2	nk	**Rio's Girl**[18] 4826 3-9-2 57 PaulQuinn 7 (R M Whitaker) *cl up: led and rdn 2f out: edgd lft ins fnl f: kpt on: hdd towards fin* 5/4[1]	63
0466	3	hd	**Tartufo Dolce (IRE)**[20] 4749 3-9-2 57 PaulMulrennan 11 (J G Given) *in tch: rdn 2f out: kpt on u.p fnl f* 16/1	62
510	4	3 3/4	**Tabiet**[31] 4406 3-9-6 61 PaulHanagan 10 (James Moffatt) *midfield: effrt and rdn over 1f out: kpt on fnl f: nt rch first three* 9/1[3]	53
0004	5	3	**Hold On Tiger (IRE)**[18] 4826 3-9-3 58 PJMcDonald 9 (N G Richards) *in tch: drvn over 2f out: wknd over 1f out* 10/1	39
066	6	1 1/4	**Bombay Mist**[27] 4516 3-8-4 45 (e) PaulEddery 2 (R C Guest) *led to 2f out: sn rdn and wknd* 18/1	21
2060	7	nk	**Taborcillo**[18] 4826 3-9-5 60 TomEaves 6 (T D Barron) *chsd ldrs: drvn and outpcd 1/2-way: n.d after* 22/1	35
5002	8	1 1/4	**Areeg (IRE)**[12] 5046 3-8-1 49 VictorSantos(7) 8 (A Berry) *bhd: drvn along 1/2-way: nvr on terms* 28/1	20
0066	9	1/2	**Classlin**[18] 4826 3-8-6 47 JoeFanning 5 (J S Goldie) *towards rr: drvn along 1/2-way: nvr able to chal* 12/1	16
604	10	3 1/4	**Six Wives**[23] 4659 3-9-7 62 RobertWinston 1 (J A Glover) *dwlt: bhd and sn drvn along: no ch fr 1/2-way* 8/1[2]	19
230	R		**Kristen Jane (USA)**[14] 4947 3-8-1 47 BillyCray(5) 4 (Miss L A Perratt) *ref to r* 11/1	—

59.48 secs (-0.62) **Going Correction** -0.225s/f (Firm) 11 Ran SP% 118.7
Speed ratings (Par 98): **95,94,94,88,83 81,80,78,78,72** —
toteswingers: 1&2 £3.90, 1&3 £21.00, 2&3 £6.70 CSF £22.99 CT £218.00 TOTE £10.30: £3.00, £1.10, £7.90; EX 28.30.
Owner A Rice **Bred** Silvano Scanu **Trained** Station Town, Co Durham

FOCUS
Another moderate sprint handicap for 3-y-os and they raced down the centre. The winner improved by a length on this year's form.
Six Wives Official explanation: jockey said filly never travelled

5411 KOPPARBERG H'CAP 1m 2f
5:45 (5:45) (Class 6) (0-65,64) 3-Y-O £2,047 (£604; £302) Stalls Low

Form				RPR
056	1		**Tobernea (IRE)**[12] 5026 3-9-0 57 JoeFanning 1 (M Johnston) *led to over 2f out: sn rdn: rallied and regained ld wl ins fnl f: hld on wl* 6/1[3]	66+
3000	2	hd	**Bajan Flash**[11] 5064 3-9-7 64 (p) TomEaves 3 (B Smart) *cl up: led and rdn over 2f out: hdd wl ins fnl f: kpt on* 16/1	73
4622	3	1 1/2	**Vittachi**[7] 5216 3-8-11 54 PJMcDonald 9 (A C Whillans) *prom: drvn over 2f out: edgd lft: kpt on fnl f: nt pce of first two* 5/2[1]	60
5100	4	1/2	**Market Puzzle (IRE)**[13] 4992 3-8-8 51 RichardKingscote 11 (W M Brisbourne) *trckd ldrs: effrt and hung lft over 2f out: kpt on same pce fnl f* 33/1	56
	5	nse	**Horsewithnoname (IRE)**[21] 4726 3-8-11 57 (v[1]) BACurtis(3) 5 (T G McCourt, Ire) *hld up in midfield: rdn over 2f out: kpt on u.p fnl f: no imp* 12/1	62
0031	6	1/2	**Wood Fair**[14] 4971 3-8-7 55 SimonPearce(5) 13 (Mrs K Burke) *hld up: nt clr run fr 2f out: hmpd ins fnl f: kpt on wl whn clr last 50yds: nt rcvr* 4/1[2]	59+
0660	7	3/4	**Hong Kong Island (IRE)**[55] 3597 3-9-1 58 PaulHanagan 12 (N G Richards) *hld up on outside: rdn and effrt over 2f out: no imp fnl f* 12/1	60
0014	8	1 1/2	**Catawollow**[66] 3238 3-8-1 49 (e) BillyCray(5) 7 (R C Guest) *hld up: rdn over 2f out: sme late hdwy: nvr rchd ldrs* 6/1[3]	48
5503	9	1/2	**Red Skies (IRE)**[21] 4705 3-9-2 64 DaleSwift(5) 8 (Mrs L Stubbs) *in tch on ins: rdn over 2f out: sn outpcd* 20/1	62
350	10	2 1/4	**Wasara**[12] 5038 3-9-3 60 AndrewElliott 6 (Miss Amy Weaver) *hld up: effrt on outside 2f out: nvr able to chal* 12/1	54
0350	11	5	**Mary Helen**[34] 4289 3-8-12 55 PaulMulrennan 4 (W M Brisbourne) *hld up in tch: rdn over 3f out: wknd over 2f out* 33/1	39
12	6		**Rappletrap Car**[16] 4918 3-8-6 49 (v[1]) PaulEddery 10 (T G McCourt, Ire) *cl up tl rdn and wknd qckly over 2f out* 66/1	21

2m 9.82s (-2.18) **Going Correction** -0.225s/f (Firm) 12 Ran SP% 118.2
Speed ratings (Par 98): **99,98,97,97,97 96,96,95,94,92 88,84**
toteswingers: 1&2 £17.60, 1&3 £3.80, 2&3 £12.60. totesuper7: Win: Not won, Place: £59.00 CSF £93.20 CT £303.40 TOTE £5.30: £1.70, £10.40, £1.70; EX 126.50 Place 6 £41.00, Place 5 £36.48.
Owner Mrs Joan Keaney **Bred** Mrs Joan Keaney **Trained** Middleham Moor, N Yorks
■ Stewards' Enquiry : Joe Fanning caution: used whip down shoulder in the forehand.

FOCUS
A moderate handicap, but the first two came into this relatively unexposed and should have more to offer. The winner is rated up 10lb but the form is not entirely convincing.
Tobernea(IRE) Official explanation: trainer's rep said, regarding apparent improvement in form, that this was the colt's first run in a handicap and, in their opinion, was given a handicap mark it could win off.
Horsewithnoname(IRE) Official explanation: jockey said gelding hung left
Wood Fair Official explanation: jockey said filly was denied a clear run
T/Jkpt: Not won. T/Plt: £59.40 to a £1 stake. Pool: £69,943.24. 859.31 winning tickets. T/Qpdt: £7.70 to a £1 stake. Pool: £4,360.16. 416.30 winning tickets. RY

5169 BRIGHTON (L-H)
Wednesday, August 25

OFFICIAL GOING: Good (good to soft in places) changing to good to soft (soft in places) after race 1 (2.30) changing to soft after race 3 (3.30)
Wind: Virtually nil Weather: Raining

5412 ODDSCHECKER.COM WEDNESDAY NURSERY 5f 213y
2:30 (2:30) (Class 6) (0-65,64) 2-Y-O £1,942 (£578; £288; £144) Stalls Low

Form				RPR
545	1		**Spennymoor (IRE)**[20] 4741 2-9-7 64 AhmedAjtebi 4 (Mahmood Al Zarooni) *hld up in tch: c stands' side and hdwy over 2f out: rdn to ld wl over 1f out: styd on wl fnl f* 5/1[3]	70
0000	2	1 1/4	**Three Scoops**[13] 5000 2-7-13 47 ow2 (t) SophieDoyle(5) 10 (D J S Ffrench Davis) *chsd ldr tl over 2f out: sn c stands' side and stydhandy: drvn and chsd wnr jst over 1f out: kpt on same pce ins fnl f* 14/1	49
3205	3	shd	**Jambo Bibi (IRE)**[19] 4802 2-9-6 63 RichardHughes 2 (R Hannon) *in tch: grad switching rt fr over 2f out to r against stands' rail wl over 1f out: kpt on u.p ins fnl f: snatched 3rd on post* 9/4[1]	65
004	4	nk	**Country Waltz**[63] 3310 2-8-11 54 ChrisCatlin 3 (M R Channon) *in tch in last trio: effrt u.p to chse ldrs wl over 1f out: styd on same pce fnl f* 7/1	55
3535	5	2	**Crown Ridge (IRE)**[10] 5111 2-9-1 58 EddieCreighton 7 (M R Channon) *chsd ldrs early: sn bustled along and lost pl and in last trio: rdn and c stands' side over 2f out: styd on ins fnl f: nvr trbld ldrs* 9/2[2]	53
600	6	2 1/4	**Miss Toldyaso (IRE)**[19] 4802 2-8-3 46 WilliamCarson 9 (M G Quinlan) *chsd ldrs: pushed to ld and c stands' side over 2f out: hdd and rdn wl over 1f out: drvn and wknd ent fnl f* 8/1	34
0045	7	2 1/4	**Fairy Tales**[30] 4423 2-8-4 47 NeilChalmers 8 (J J Bridger) *a in rr: c stands' side over 2f out: rdn and no prog wl over 1f out* 50/1	29
060	8	hd	**Place And Chips**[44] 3959 2-8-13 56 SebSanders 5 (Tom Dascombe) *dwlt: sn rcvrd to ld: styd far side and hdd over 2f out: btn over 1f out: wknd fnl f* 11/2	37

1m 11.75s (1.55) **Going Correction** +0.075s/f (Good) 8 Ran SP% 113.2
Speed ratings (Par 92): **92,90,90,89,87 84,81,80**
toteswingers: 1&2 £11.90, 1&3 £1.70, 2&3 £12.50 CSF £68.68 CT £199.65 TOTE £4.10: £1.10, £3.90, £1.20; EX 76.00 Trifecta £167.90 Pool: £392.71 - 1.73 winning units..
Owner Godolphin **Bred** Derek Veitch **Trained** Newmarket, Suffolk

FOCUS
A moderate nursery and, as is nearly always the case when conditions are on the easy side at Brighton, the main action was stands' side in the straight.

NOTEBOOK
Spennymoor(IRE), reported to have hung right over 7f on quick ground last time, found these conditions more suitable and won well enough on her nursery debut, finding plenty after travelling well. She'll be forced up in class when reassessed, however, and that may be enough to deny her the follow-up. (op 4-1)
Three Scoops, 5lb wrong including 2lb overweight, ran respectably in a first-time tongue-tie, with the soft ground seemingly in her favour. (op 12-1)
Jambo Bibi(IRE), switched to the stands' rail in the straight, was never getting to the winner but would surely have been second had she been pushed out more vigorously, although the winner did edge into her path in the final strides. She is limited. (op 5-2 tchd 11-4)
Country Waltz emerges with credit considering she raced widest of all of those stands' side. (op 13-2 tchd 15-2)
Crown Ridge(IRE) was well backed, but offered little and is due to be eased 4lb. (op 11-2 tchd 4-1)
Place And Chips traded as low as 2.2 in running after being able to dominate, but bizarrely stayed far side. He had no chance. (op 6-1)

5413 ODDSCHECKER.COM MAIDEN STKS 7f 214y
3:00 (3:01) (Class 5) 2-Y-O £2,266 (£674; £337; £168) Stalls Low

Form				RPR
42	1		**Profondo Rosso (IRE)**[24] 4614 2-9-3 0 KierenFallon 5 (Sir Michael Stoute) *chsd ldrs: wnt 2nd jst over 3f out: rdn and hung lft fr 2f out: drvn to ld ins fnl f: styd on strly and drew clr fnl 75yds* 4/6[1]	82+
03	2	2 1/4	**Enabling (IRE)**[17] 4856 2-9-3 0 RichardHughes 6 (R Hannon) *w ldr tl led over 4f out: pushed along and qcknd ent fnl 3f: clr w wnr wl over 1f out: drvn and hdd ins fnl f: btn and eased fnl 50yds* 10/3[2]	76
20	3	9	**U A E Storm (USA)**[35] 4247 2-9-3 0 ShaneKelly 2 (D M Simcock) *stdd s: hld up in tch in last pair: effrt to chse ldng trio ent fnl 2f: sn outpcd and no ch w ldrs: kpt on same pce fnl f* 8/1[3]	56
0	4	3/4	**Fine Style (IRE)**[19] 4803 2-9-3 0 HayleyTurner 3 (M L W Bell) *dwlt: bhd: nt clr run and swtchd lft 2f out: sn rdn: no ch w ldng pair but pressing for 3rd 1f out: kpt on same pce* 9/1	55
03	5	nk	**Freehand (USA)**[14] 4940 2-9-3 0 (t) AhmedAjtebi 9 (Mahmood Al Zarooni) *chsd ldng trio: lost pl qckly and bhd jst over 3f out: no ch w ldrs fnl 2f: plugged on again u.p ins fnl f* 33/1	54
0	6	1 1/4	**Droxford (USA)**[21] 4695 2-9-3 0 (b[1]) FergusSweeney 7 (J A Osborne) *stdd s: t.k.h: hld up in tch towards rr: rdn and outpcd by ldng pair 3f out: wl btn whn edgd lft over 1f out* 100/1	51

The Form Book, Raceform Ltd, Compton, RG20 6NL

0 **7** *7* **Drumadoon (IRE)**[20] 4741 2-9-3 0 EddieAhern 1 36
(J L Dunlop) *led tl over 4f out: rdn and lost pl 3f out: no ch w ldng pair after: wknd ent fnl f: eased fnl 75yds* **50/1**

1m 37.27s (1.27) **Going Correction** +0.075s/f (Good) **7** Ran SP% **110.1**
Speed ratings (Par 94): **96,93,84,84,83 82,75**
toteswingers: 1&2 £1.02, 1&3 £1.80, 2&3 £4.80 CSF £2.78 TOTE £1.40: £1.10, £1.70; EX 2.70 Trifecta £5.60 Pool: £638.52 - 84.07 winning units..
Owner Ballymacoll Stud **Bred** Ballymacoll Stud Farm Ltd **Trained** Newmarket, Suffolk

FOCUS
The race unfolded stands' side, and two fair types pulled a long way clear.

NOTEBOOK
Profondo Rosso(IRE) was keen early and needed a typically persuasive Fallon ride in the closing stages, carrying his head awkwardly when first coming under pressure and then hanging left, appearing unsuited by the track. Although this was hard work, his waywardness meant he raced away from the favoured stands' rail in the straight, and all things considered he may be better than the bare result. It would probably be unwise to underestimate him when he goes handicapping. (op 4-7 tchd 8-15)
Enabling(IRE) was given every chance by Hughes, grabbing the stands' rail in the straight, ahead of the favourite, and can have few excuses. He was well clear of the others and can find an ordinary maiden, with nurseries also now an option. (op 7-2 tchd 9-2)
U A E Storm(USA), reported to have been unsuited by ground on the fast side last time, never threatened the front two. It would be no surprise to see him do better now he's qualified for a mark. (op 12-1)
Fine Style(IRE) was never involved and looks one for handicaps in due course. (op 15-2)
Freehand(USA) did not improve for a first-time tongue-tie, or the switch to easy ground, but he's now eligible for an official mark. (op 22-1 tchd 20-1)

5414 JIMMY HEAL MEMORIAL H'CAP — 1m 1f 209y
3:30 (3:33) (Class 6) (0-60,60) 3-Y-O **£1,942** (£578; £288; £144) **Stalls** High

Form RPR

0660 **1** **Plan A (IRE)**[12] 5050 3-8-13 **55** WilliamCarson 4 71+
(M G Quinlan) *led for 1f: chsd ldr after tl led ent fnl 3f: rdn ent fnl 2f: hld on wl u.p fnl f* **10/1**

00-2 **2** *nk* **Honoured (IRE)**[68] 3153 3-8-10 **52** SebSanders 3 67+
(Sir Mark Prescott) *wnt rt s: hdwy to ld after 1f: hdd and rdn ent fnl 3f: drvn over 2f out: rallied and ev ch 1f out: kpt on but no ex nr fin* **7/4**[1]

0053 **3** *nse* **Finch Flyer (IRE)**[14] 4958 3-7-12 **47** (p) HarryBentley(7) 6 62
(G L Moore) *hld up in tch: rdn to chse ldng pair over 2f out: drvn and ev ch 1f out: kpt on same pce fnl 75yds* **7/2**[2]

-001 **4** *11* **Ermyntrude**[8] 5171 3-8-4 **51** 6ex JemmaMarshall(5) 12 44
(P M Phelan) *chsd ldrs: rdn wl over 2f out: outpcd by ldng pair over 2f out: 4th and wl btn over 1f out* **10/1**

3440 **5** *2 ¼* **Marafong**[14] 4970 3-8-4 **51** AdamBeschizza(5) 13 39
(Miss J Feilden) *hld up in tch towards rr: hdwy and chsng ldrs 4f out: rdn and btn over 2f out:* **25/1**

0003 **6** *2 ¾* **Blue Zealot (IRE)**[19] 4774 3-9-1 **57** HayleyTurner 2 40
(M L W Bell) *chsd ldrs: rdn 3f out: sn struggling and wl btn: no ch fnl 2f* **9/1**

0543 **7** *5* **River Tease**[8] 5173 3-9-1 **57** (p) LukeMorris 7 30
(J S Moore) *in tch in midfield: rdn 4f out: sn struggling: wl btn whn edgd lft over 1f out* **16/1**

0004 **8** *9* **Pictures (IRE)**[11] 5077 3-9-4 **60** NeilChalmers 1 15
(J J Bridger) *hld up in tch towards rr: rdn and btn ent fnl 3f: wl bhd fnl 2f* **25/1**

0000 **9** *2* **Many A Slip**[19] 4791 3-8-13 **55** EddieAhern 14 —
(J L Dunlop) *stdd s: hld up in tch in rr: lost tch ent 3f out: n.d* **33/1**

0563 **10** *7* **Cuckoo Rock (IRE)**[20] 4733 3-8-10 **52** NeilCallan 5 —
(J G Portman) *t.k.h: in tch tl rdn and btn ent fnl 3f: wl bhd fnl 2f: t.o and eased ins fnl f* **14/1**

066 **11** *16* **Hotfoot**[13] 4997 3-9-3 **59** KierenFallon 15 —
(John Berry) *t.k.h: chsd ldrs tl lost pl 4f out: rdn and lost tch 3f out: t.o and eased ins fnl f* **7/1**[3]

06 **12** *3* **Chief Storm Eagle (IRE)**[12] 5057 3-8-4 **51** TobyAtkinson(5) 8 —
(M Botti) *stdd s: t.k.h: hld up in tch in last trio: rdn and toiling over 3f out: t.o fnl 2f: eased ins fnl f* **16/1**

-000 **13** *1 ¼* **Chat De Soie (IRE)**[13] 4988 3-8-9 **51** (b[1]) CathyGannon 11 —
(J S Moore) *hld up in rr: rdn and toiling over 4f out: wl bhd fnl 3f: t.o fover 2f out: eased ins fnl f* **66/1**

2m 4.25s (0.65) **Going Correction** +0.075s/f (Good) **13** Ran SP% **129.8**
Speed ratings (Par 98): **100,99,99,90,89 86,82,75,74,68 55,53,52**
toteswingers: 1&2 £7.10, 1&3 £9.50, 2&3 £2.00 CSF £29.41 CT £82.25 TOTE £13.70: £4.10, £1.10, £1.80; EX 57.80 Trifecta £316.20 Part won. Pool: £427.38 - 0.61 winning units..
Owner Liam Mulryan **Bred** L Mulryan **Trained** Newmarket, Suffolk

FOCUS
A moderate contest and, with the pace steady and the action again unfolding nearside in the closing stages, it paid to race prominently. The unexposed winner was up a stone on his maiden form.
Plan A(IRE) Official explanation: trainer's rep said, regarding apparent improvement in form, that the gelding appreciated the step up in trip.
Cuckoo Rock(IRE) Official explanation: trainer said gelding did not handle the track

5415 BRIGHTON FOOD AND DRINK FESTIVAL H'CAP — 7f 214y
4:00 (4:02) (Class 3) (0-90,87) 3-Y-O+
£7,227 (£2,164; £1,082; £541; £270; £135) **Stalls** Low

Form RPR

2420 **1** **Secretive**[20] 4750 3-9-6 **86** (b) NeilCallan 3 94
(M Johnston) *mde all: rdn ent fnl 2f: hung lft but forged clr over 1f out: stl hanging but kpt on wl ins fnl f* **4/1**[2]

6231 **2** *1* **Purple Gallery (IRE)**[20] 4732 3-8-4 **77** (p) RyanPowell(7) 5 82
(J S Moore) *in tch in midfield: effrt against stands' rail ent fnl 2f: hung lft over 1f out: kpt on u.p to go 2nd wl ins fnl f: nt rch wnr* **8/1**

4201 **3** *1* **Mr Irons (USA)**[14] 4956 3-9-3 **83** (v) KierenFallon 1 86
(Sir Michael Stoute) *chsd wnr: rdn over 2f out: unable qck over 1f out: hung lft ent fnl f: kpt on same pce after* **7/2**[1]

3340 **4** *4 ½* **Ocean Countess (IRE)**[6] 5237 4-8-10 **70** CathyGannon 6 64
(Miss J Feilden) *in tch in last pair: rdn and no prog 3f out: no ch w ldrs but plugged on past btn horses ins fnl f* **16/1**

1052 **5** *½* **Satwa Laird**[29] 4459 4-9-13 **87** RichardHughes 7 80
(E A L Dunlop) *in tch: chsd ldng pair 3f out tl wl over 1f out: edgd lft u.p and wknd jst over 1f out* **7/2**[1]

101 **6** *1 ¼* **Dajen**[44] 3956 4-9-5 **86** LauraPike(7) 4 76
(D M Simcock) *in tch in midfield: rdn and effrt wl over 2f out: hung bdly lft fr 2f out: no prog and wl btn over 1f out* **9/2**[3]

2462 **7** *13* **Mishrif (USA)**[13] 4995 4-9-6 **80** (b) SebSanders 8 40
(J R Jenkins) *hld up in rr: rdn and btn 3f out: wl bhd fnl 2f* **6/1**

1m 38.03s (2.03) **Going Correction** +0.275s/f (Good)
WFA 3 from 4yo+ 6lb **7** Ran SP% **113.9**
Speed ratings (Par 107): **100,99,98,93,93 91,78**
toteswingers: 1&2 £5.40, 1&3 £3.20, 2&3 £3.30 CSF £34.70 CT £121.30 TOTE £5.50: £1.90, £4.00; EX 41.50 Trifecta £142.90 Pool: £486.80 - 2.52 winning units..
Owner Sheikh Hamdan Bin Mohammed Al Maktoum **Bred** T A Scothern **Trained** Middleham Moor, N Yorks

FOCUS
A potentially decent handicap, but few of the runners handled the ground and/or the track and it was not a strong race for the grade. They raced middle to stands' side in the straight.

NOTEBOOK
Secretive ran inexplicably poorly at Haydock on his previous start, but there was good money around for him this time and he returned to form with a ready success, despite hanging towards the middle of the course late on. Having been allowed a soft time up front, he simply coped with the ground and track better than most. Official explanation: trainer's rep had no explanation for the poor form shown (op 15-2 tchd 8-1)
Purple Gallery(IRE), 4lb higher than when winning a lesser race on quick ground last time, couldn't go with the winner early in the straight but stuck on well against the favoured near rail. (op 12-1)
Mr Irons(USA), 3lb higher than when winning at Salisbury on his previous start, didn't look totally comfortable on the ground and/or the track, and can be given another chance. (tchd 9-2)
Ocean Countess(IRE), the only runner proven at the track coming into the race, got going much too late to challenge. She's not applying herself in the early stages of her races and may need headgear. (op 11-1 tchd 10-1)
Satwa Laird was reported by the vet to have finished lame. Official explanation: vet said colt returned lame (op 10-3)
Dajen, up 5lb for his latest win, goes on soft ground but did not handle the track. A big horse, he showed a scratchy action on the way to the start and did not cope the undulations at all, losing his place early in the straight before hanging left, all the way over the middle of the course. (op 10-3 tchd 3-1)

5416 FOOD FESTIVAL LAUNCHES HERE 1ST SEPTEMBER H'CAP — 6f 209y
4:30 (4:30) (Class 3) (0-95,94) 3-Y-O+ **£7,227** (£2,164; £1,082; £541) **Stalls** Centre

Form RPR

3502 **1** **Colepeper**[12] 5030 3-9-4 **93** KierenFallon 6 101
(M Johnston) *mde all: rdn wl over 1f out: drvn and styd on wl ins fnl f: in command and eased towards fin* **13/8**[1]

6604 **2** *1 ¾* **Layla's Hero (IRE)**[20] 4750 3-9-5 **94** RichardHughes 1 97
(D M Simcock) *trckd ldrs: n.m.r over 4f out: hdwy to chse wnr 3f out: rdn and pressed wnr jst over 1f out: drvn and no ex ins fnl f* **13/8**[1]

003 **3** *1 ¾* **Jeninsky (USA)**[12] 5052 5-9-3 **87** TedDurcan 5 88
(Rae Guest) *t.k.h: hld up wl in tch: rdn and effrt 2f out: drvn and styd on same pce fr over 1f out* **6/1**[3]

3030 **4** *6* **Mujood**[13] 5004 7-9-3 **87** (v) NeilCallan 3 75
(Eve Johnson Houghton) *chsd wnr tl 3f out: sn rdn: drvn and btn over 1f out: wl btn and eased ins fnl f* **5/1**[2]

1m 24.3s (1.20) **Going Correction** +0.275s/f (Good)
WFA 3 from 4yo+ 5lb **4** Ran SP% **107.1**
Speed ratings (Par 107): **104,102,100,93**
toteswingers: 1&2 £2.20 CSF £4.39 TOTE £1.80; EX 4.00.
Owner Sheikh Hamdan Bin Mohammed Al Maktoum **Bred** Whitley Stud **Trained** Middleham Moor, N Yorks

FOCUS
A poor turnout and ordinary form for the level. The winner produced a length personal best.

NOTEBOOK
Colepeper grabbed the favoured stands' rail in the straight and ran on well, confirming himself to be a versatile, progressive colt. (op 6-4 tchd 11-8 and 7-4)
Layla's Hero(IRE), last to come over to the stands' side, raced off the rail and was always being held by the winner. (op 7-4 tchd 15-8)
Jeninsky(USA) failed to build on her recent third at the July course. (op 5-1)
Mujood probably didn't appreciate the ground. (op 7-1 tchd 9-2)

5417 FESTIVAL WAITERS HERE 1ST SEPTEMBER H'CAP — 5f 59y
5:00 (5:01) (Class 4) (0-80,78) 3-Y-O **£4,100** (£1,227; £613; £306; £152) **Stalls** Low

Form RPR

6122 **1** **Humidor (IRE)**[63] 3311 3-9-3 **77** MatthewDavies(3) 1 76
(George Baker) *taken down early: chsd clr ldr: effrt and rdn over 1f out: hung bdly lft and racd awkwardly ins fnl f but kpt on to ld fnl 75yds* **9/4**[2]

5341 **2** *¾* **Annia Galeria (IRE)**[9] 5152 3-8-2 **59** 6ex (b) CathyGannon 5 55
(C A Dwyer) *led and sn clr: rdn and hung bdly lft fr over 1f out: hdd and no ex fnl 75yds* **13/2**

3132 **3** *2 ¼* **Starwatch**[8] 5182 3-8-6 **63** NeilChalmers 3 51
(J J Bridger) *sn niggled along in last pair: rdn to go modest 3rd over 1f out: kpt on ins fnl f: nvr gng pce to rch ldrs* **15/8**[1]

243 **4** *5* **Angel Of Fashion (IRE)**[21] 4717 3-8-4 **61** ow1 ChrisCatlin 6 32
(P Charalambous) *chsd ldrs: rdn and no prog wl over 1f out: 4th and wl btn ent fnl f* **3/1**[3]

4100 **5** *½* **Diamond Johnny G (USA)**[4] 5309 3-9-4 **78** (t) AlanCreighton(3) 2 47
(E J Creighton) *taken down early: a last and sn pushed along: rdn and no prog over 1f out: n.d* **10/1**

63.40 secs (1.10) **Going Correction** +0.275s/f (Good) **5** Ran SP% **113.0**
Speed ratings (Par 102): **102,100,97,89,88**
toteswingers: 1&2 £3.90, 1&3 £9.20, 2&3 £14.20 CSF £16.59 TOTE £3.60: £1.10, £5.70; EX 16.50 Place 6 £63.56, Place 5 £39.79.
Owner M Khan X2 **Bred** Yeomanstown Stud **Trained** Moreton Morrell, Warwicks

FOCUS
A moderate sprint and the runner-up looks the best guide. The first two hung over to the far side late on.
Annia Galeria(IRE) Official explanation: jockey said filly hung left

T/Plt: £133.00 to a £1 stake. Pool: £56,690.80. 311.13 winning tickets. T/Qpdt: £92.20 to a £1 stake. Pool £4,215.54. 33.82 winning tickets. SP

[5019]CATTERICK (L-H)

Wednesday, August 25

OFFICIAL GOING: Good to firm (good in places; 8.9)

Wind: Virtually nil Weather: Cloudy with sunny periods

5418 RACINGUK.COM MEDIAN AUCTION MAIDEN STKS 5f

2:20 (2:21) (Class 6) 2-Y-O **£1,842** (£544; £272) **Stalls** Low

Form RPR

43 **1** **Jack Smudge**[10] 5117 2-9-0 0 JamesSullivan(3) 14 75
(J G Given) *in tch: hdwy 2f out: sn edgd lft: rdn and slipped through on inner ins fnl f to ld last 50yds* **5/1[3]**

2 *1* **Plume De Ma Tante (IRE)** 2-8-12 0 DuranFentiman 4 66
(J A Glover) *led 1 1/2f: cl up: rdn to ld again briefly ins fnl f: hdd and nt qckn last 50yds* **66/1**

5230 **3** *hd* **Abzolutely (IRE)**[7] 5221 2-8-12 71 SilvestreDeSousa 12 66
(D O'Meara) *chsd ldrs: led after 1 1/2f out: rdn 2f out: drvn and hdd ins fnl f: one pce* **11/4[2]**

63 **4** *hd* **Key Lago (IRE)**[50] 3756 2-9-3 0 PhillipMakin 6 70
(M Dods) *trckd ldrs: swtchd rt and smooth hdwy 2f out: cl up on bit over 1f out: shkn up and led briefly ins fnl f: sn hdd and fnd nil* **5/2[1]**

005 **5** *½* **Black Annis Bower**[7] 5196 2-8-7 0 LanceBetts(5) 9 63
(M W Easterby) *chsd ldrs: rdn along 2f out: drvn over 1f out and kpt on same pce* **50/1**

6 **6** *4 ½* **Crucis Abbey (IRE)**[14] 4941 2-9-3 0 AdrianNicholls 15 52
(J W Unett) *dwlt and wnt rt s: sn chsd along and in tch: rdn to chse ldrs 2f out: sn one pce* **16/1**

64 **7** *1 ½* **Secret Tycoon (IRE)**[13] 4999 2-9-3 0 StephenCraine 7 47
(Patrick Morris) *nvr bttr than midfield* **17/2**

8 *1* **Mujapiste (IRE)** 2-8-9 0 BarryMcHugh(3) 1 38
(L A Mullaney) *outpcd and in rr tl sme late hdwy* **50/1**

05 **9** *3 ½* **Mr Mo Jo**[16] 4896 2-9-0 0 PaulPickard(3) 13 30
(R Bastiman) *chsd ldrs: rdn along 1/2-way: sn wknd* **16/1**

10 *3 ¾* **Jay Jays Joy** 2-8-12 0 DeanHeslop(5) 11 17
(T D Barron) *s.i.s: sn rdn along and a in rr* **9/1**

50 **11** *nk* **Tancred Spirit**[56] 3549 2-8-12 0 FrannyNorton 10 11
(P T Midgley) *in tch: rdn along over 2f out and sn wknd* **40/1**

12 *15* **Lloydy Lumps** 2-9-3 0 DavidNolan 2 —
(Peter Grayson) *sn outpcd and a in rr* **100/1**

13 *1 ¾* **Tea And Sympathy** 2-8-12 0 KirstyMilczarek 5 —
(J R Holt) *a in rr* **50/1**

59.56 secs (-0.24) **Going Correction** -0.15s/f (Firm) **13** Ran SP% **115.0**

Speed ratings (Par 92): **95,93,93,92,91 84,82,80,75,69 68,44,41**

toteswingers: 1&2 £51.50, 1&3 £4.30, 2&3 £27.60 CSF £313.77 TOTE £5.70: £1.70, £18.60, £1.10; EX 245.20.

Owner Danethorpe Racing Partnership **Bred** P And Mrs A G Venner **Trained** Willoughton, Lincs

FOCUS

Quite an interesting median auction maiden race and they raced in one group towards the far side.

NOTEBOOK

Jack Smudge, having his third start, gave his trainer his first juvenile success this time with his 33rd runner. Fourth over 6f at Ayr and third over 5f at Pontefract, he had an outside draw to overcome. He drifted left over a furlong out and made the most of an opening on the inside. He is now qualified for nurseries and should improve again, especially given a slightly stiffer test. (op 4-1)

Plume De Ma Tante(IRE), bred for speed, was an unconsidered outsider on her debut but she knew her job and went down fighting. She is sure to improve and go one better.

Abzolutely(IRE), rated 71 and out of her depth in Listed company at York, was having her fifth start. She helped force the pace from her double-figure draw, but left the door open for the winner on her inside. She deserves to break her duck. (op 5-2 tchd 3-1)

Key Lago(IRE) ◆, from a yard back on the scoresheet after a lean summer, was having his first outing since finishing third on the AW at Southwell on his second start seven weeks earlier. Quite keen, he moved upsides on the bridle, but was found lacking in the closing stages. He looks all speed and is one to bear in mind for a 5f nursery. (op 4-1)

Black Annis Bower was another eye-catcher as she finished with quite a flourish down the outside. This was her fourth outing and she looks set to land a nursery stepped up to 6f.

Crucis Abbey(IRE) again showed ability from the worst of the draw, but he will need another outing under his belt before he qualifies for a handicap mark. (tchd 14-1)

Jay Jays Joy made a tardy start, which is fatal here when the ground rides fast. (op 17-2 tchd 8-1)

Tea And Sympathy Official explanation: jockey said filly missed the break

5419 ZETLAND MAIDEN STKS 5f 212y

2:50 (2:52) (Class 5) 3-Y-O+ **£2,072** (£616; £308; £153) **Stalls** Low

Form RPR

6235 **1** **Mata Hari Blue**[1] 5388 4-9-1 58 KirstyMilczarek 7 55
(J R Holt) *t.k.h: trckd ldrs: hdwy on outer 2f out: rdn to chal over 1f out: drvn to ld wl ins fnl f* **8/1[2]**

6222 **2** *nk* **Engulf (IRE)**[61] 3397 3-9-3 78 LiamJones 5 59
(W J Haggas) *t.k.h: trckd ldrs: hdwy to chse ldr 1/2-way: chal 2f out and sn rdn: drvn and ev ch whn edgd rt ins fnl f: no ex towards fin* **1/8[1]**

00 **3** *1 ¼* **Premier Contender (IRE)**[11] 5065 3-9-3 0 AdrianNicholls 6 56
(D Nicholls) *led: rdn and green 2f out: drvn over 1f out: hdd wl ins fnl f* **20/1[3]**

00- **4** *¾* **Rose Bed (IRE)**[21] 4726 3-8-12 43 FrannyNorton 2 48?
(M G Quinlan) *t.k.h: chsd ldr to 1/2-way: rdn 2f out: drvn over 1f out: keeping on whn n.m.r towards fin* **50/1**

00 **5** *1* **Clearly Cryptonite (USA)**[11] 5065 3-9-0 0 BarryMcHugh(3) 1 50?
(T J Pitt) *hld up in tch: hdwy 2f out: rdn to chse ldrs over 1f out: drvn and one pce fnl f* **66/1**

4606 **6** *16* **Clare Harrier (IRE)**[7] 5214 3-9-3 56 (b[1]) PatrickMathers 4 —
(A Berry) *s.i.s: sn rdn along and a bhd* **100/1**

1m 13.66s (0.06) **Going Correction** -0.325s/f (Firm)

WFA 3 from 4yo 3lb **6** Ran SP% **109.2**

Speed ratings (Par 103): **86,85,83,82,81 60**

toteswingers: 1&2 £1.10, 1&3 £1.30, 2&3 £2.00 CSF £9.52 TOTE £8.20: £1.60, £1.10; EX 10.60.

Owner M J Golding **Bred** R T And Mrs Watson **Trained** Peckleton, Leics

FOCUS

What looked a penalty kick for the 78-rated Engulf turned out otherwise.

Rose Bed(IRE) Official explanation: jockey said filly was denied a clear run

5420 TOTEPOOL A BETTER WAY TO BET H'CAP 1m 7f 177y

3:20 (3:21) (Class 5) (0-70,70) 3-Y-O+ **£2,183** (£644; £322) **Stalls** Low

Form RPR

121 **1** **Andorn (GER)**[18] 4854 6-9-9 60 PaulPickard(3) 6 71+
(P A Kirby) *trckd ldrs: effrt: nt clr run and hmpd over 2f out and again 2f out: nt clr run over 1f out and sn swtchd rt: rdn and styd on ins fnl f: edgd lft and led nr fin* **11/2**

3262 **2** *nk* **Zefooha (FR)**[16] 4900 6-9-11 59 (p) DuranFentiman 4 67
(T D Walford) *led: rdn and qcknd over 2f out: drvn over 1f out: hdd and no ex towards fin* **7/1**

2603 **3** *1 ¼* **They All Laughed**[16] 4900 7-9-6 54 (p) PhillipMakin 2 60
(Mrs Marjorie Fife) *hld up: hdwy on inner 3f out: rdn to chse ldr over 1f out: n.m.r and drvn ins fnl f: kpt on* **5/1[3]**

553 **4** *½* **Naughty Naughty**[19] 4792 5-9-11 62 RussKennemore(3) 3 68
(B G Powell) *trckd ldng pair on inner: effrt to chse ldr over 2f out: rdn over 1f out: drvn and ev ch ent fnl f: wknd towards fin* **10/1**

3214 **5** *6* **Light The City (IRE)**[19] 4800 3-8-6 57 JamesSullivan(3) 10 55
(Mrs R A Carr) *hld up: hdwy and in tch 1/2-way: chsd ldrs 3f out: rdn to chal and ch wl over 1f out: sn drvn and wknd engtering fnl f* **10/1**

4616 **6** *8* **Dubara Reef (IRE)**[10] 5119 3-9-0 62 SilvestreDeSousa 11 51
(Paul Green) *chsd ldrs: rdn along and lost pl 1/2-way: n.d after* **4/1[2]**

2324 **7** *11* **Yankee Bright (USA)**[14] 4965 3-9-8 70 DavidAllan 5 46
(J G Given) *sn trcking ldr: rdn along 3f out: drvn over 2f out and sn wknd* **7/2[1]**

5106 **8** *1 ½* **Brave Bugsy (IRE)**[41] 4042 7-9-8 56 LiamJones 7 30
(M Appleby) *dwlt: a in rr: outpcd and bhd fnl 3f* **16/1**

240- **9** *½* **King's Majesty (IRE)**[61] 7888 8-9-11 62 BarryMcHugh(3) 12 35
(T J Pitt) *hld up: a towards rr* **40/1**

3m 26.7s (-5.30) **Going Correction** -0.325s/f (Firm)

WFA 3 from 5yo+ 14lb **9** Ran SP% **113.3**

Speed ratings (Par 103): **100,99,99,98,95 91,86,85,85**

toteswingers: 1&2 £7.10, 1&3 £5.70, 2&3 £6.30 CSF £42.70 CT £203.11 TOTE £6.50: £2.60, £3.10, £1.10; EX 33.00.

Owner Preesall Garage **Bred** Gestut Schlenderhan **Trained** Castleton, N Yorks

FOCUS

A modest event, but a dramatic finish to this 57-62 stayers' handicap.

Dubara Reef(IRE) Official explanation: jockey said gelding never travelled

Yankee Bright(USA) Official explanation: trainer's rep had no explanation for the poor form shown

5421 CAROL ALLARDYCE BIRTHDAY H'CAP 7f

3:50 (3:54) (Class 4) (0-80,80) 3-Y-O **£3,691** (£1,098; £548; £274) **Stalls** Low

Form RPR

3320 **1** **Kilt Rock (IRE)**[16] 4898 3-8-8 70 AndrewHeffernan(3) 1 77
(R C Guest) *in tch: hdwy on inner 3f out: swtchd rt and rdn to chse ldr over 1f out: drvn to chal ins fnl f: kpt on to ld nr line* **11/1**

0011 **2** *shd* **Tukitinyasok (IRE)**[4] 5304 3-9-4 80 6ex (p) BarryMcHugh(3) 3 87
(R F Fisher) *led: rdn 2f out: drvn ent fnl f: edgd rt towards fin: hdd nr line* **5/1[3]**

4354 **3** *2 ½* **Dancing Red Devil (IRE)**[17] 4858 3-8-11 70 SilvestreDeSousa 5 70
(Paul Green) *hld up in rr: hdwy over 2f out: rdn along wl over 1f out: kpt on ins fnl f: nrst fin* **15/2**

3051 **4** *2 ¼* **Night Trade (IRE)**[22] 4670 3-9-0 78 (p) JamesO'Reilly(5) 10 72+
(Mrs D J Sanderson) *t.k.h: chsd ldrs: hdwy over 2f out: rdn and hung lft wl over 1f out: sn drvn and one pce* **4/1[1]**

-055 **5** *3 ½* **Wisecraic**[35] 4264 3-9-7 80 RichardMullen 2 65
(Tom Dascombe) *in rr: hdwy on outer 2f out: sn rdn and kpt on ins fnl f: nrst fin* **14/1**

2460 **6** *½* **Breathless Kiss (USA)**[23] 4647 3-9-5 78 (v[1]) FrannyNorton 4 61
(K A Ryan) *hld up in rr: hdwy to chse ldrs wl over 2f out: sn rdn and wknd wl over 1f out* **10/1**

0113 **7** *6* **Lutine Bell**[26] 4531 3-9-4 77 (b) PhillipMakin 9 44
(Sir Mark Prescott) *dwlt: sn cl up: rdn along and edgd lft over 2f out: drvn whn n.m.r and hmpd wl over 1f out: bhd after* **9/2[2]**

6034 **8** *6* **Transmit (IRE)**[23] 4647 3-8-12 71 (b) DavidAllan 7 22
(T D Easterby) *cl up: rdn 2f out and ev ch whn sltly hmpd wl over 1f out: sn drvn and wknd* **5/1[3]**

1010 **R** **Just The Tonic**[16] 4898 3-8-2 66 (t) DeanHeslop(5) 11 —
(Mrs Marjorie Fife) *unruly in preliminaries: resddled s: ref to r* **20/1**

1m 24.28s (-2.72) **Going Correction** -0.325s/f (Firm) **9** Ran SP% **112.1**

Speed ratings (Par 102): **102,101,99,96,92 91,85,78,—**

toteswingers: 1&2 £5.20, 1&3 £11.70, 2&3 £6.90 CSF £62.70 CT £442.18 TOTE £10.50: £2.80, £2.10, £2.90; EX 57.60.

Owner EERC **Bred** Strategy Bloodstock **Trained** Stainforth, S Yorks

FOCUS

A tight 70-80 handicap.

Transmit(IRE) Official explanation: jockey said gelding ran too free early

5422 YORKSHIRE4X4.COM ADVENTURE ACTIVITIES H'CAP 5f

4:20 (4:21) (Class 6) (0-65,65) 3-Y-O+ **£2,047** (£604; £302) **Stalls** Low

Form RPR

3034 **1** **Red River Boy**[7] 5197 5-8-7 50 KellyHarrison(3) 3 58
(C W Fairhurst) *trckd ldrs: hdwy and nt clr run over 1f out: swtchd rt ent fnl f: rdn and qcknd to ld and hung lft last 50yds: kpt on* **7/1**

2503 **2** *hd* **Speedy Senorita (IRE)**[12] 5023 5-9-2 59 BarryMcHugh(3) 4 66
(J J Quinn) *trckd ldrs: hdwy 2f out: rdn over 1f out: led ins fnl f: drvn: hdd and no ex last 40yds* **11/2[3]**

5000 **3** *1 ¼* **Spirit Of Coniston**[22] 4672 7-8-13 53 PhillipMakin 5 56
(P T Midgley) *led: rdn wl over 1f out: drvn and hdd ins fnl f: no ex towards fin* **14/1**

5651 **4** *nk* **Drumpellier (IRE)**[23] 4651 3-9-1 60 PaulPickard(3) 9 62
(S G West) *cl up: rdn to chal 2f out and ev ch tl drvn ins fnl f: hld whn n.m.r and hmpd towards fin* **20/1**

0500 **5** *shd* **Miacarla**[26] 4542 7-8-6 46 oh1 (p) PatrickMathers 2 47
(H A McWilliams) *midfield: hdwy wl over 1f out: styng on wl whn n.m.r ins fnl f and hmpd nr fin* **66/1**

0014 **6** *1 ¾* **Arch Walker (IRE)**[21] 4703 3-9-4 65 MichaelO'Connell(5) 10 60
(Jedd O'Keeffe) *towards rr: hdwy over 2f out: sn rdn and kpt on ins fnl f: nrst fin* **20/1**

0200 **7** *1 ¾* **On The Piste (IRE)**[17] 4869 3-8-9 51 (p) DavidAllan 7 40
(L A Mullaney) *chsd ldrs: rdn along 2f out: drvn and hld whn hmpd wl ins fnl f* **22/1**

5226 **8** *shd* **Raccoon (IRE)**[12] 5023 10-9-2 59 JamesSullivan(3) 8 47
(Mrs R A Carr) *chsd ldrs: rdn along wl over 1f out: sn one pce* **11/1**

The Form Book, Raceform Ltd, Compton, RG20 6NL

6110 **9** *shd* **Cross Of Lorraine (IRE)**[23] 4644 7-9-5 **64**................(b) LanceBetts[(5)] 6 52
(C Grant) *a towards rr* **4/1**[1]
4060 **9** *dht* **Fasliyanne (IRE)**[4] 5299 4-8-12 **52**...........................(v) RichardMullen 11 40
(K A Ryan) *sltly hmpd s: a towards rr* **17/2**
0352 **11** *3* **Liberty Ship**[12] 5023 5-9-11 **65**............................(bt) SilvestreDeSousa 14 42
(J D Bethell) *dwlt and sn swtchd lft to inner: effrt 1/2-way: sn rdn along and nvr a factor* **5/1**[2]
0610 **12** *2 3/4* **Alacity (IRE)**[12] 5023 4-9-2 **56**....................................... FrannyNorton 13 23
(N Bycroft) *dwlt: a in rr* **20/1**
0041 **13** *5* **Braille**[17] 4868 5-9-2 **56**.. DuranFentiman 12 5
(T D Walford) *dwlt: a in rr* **14/1**
00-0 **14** *4* **Countrywide City (IRE)**[19] 4776 4-8-12 **55**......(b[1]) RussKennemore[(3)] 1 —
(A B Coogan) *dwlt: sn chsng ldrs: rdn along 1/2-way: drvn 2f out and sn wknd* **28/1**

58.88 secs (-0.92) **Going Correction** -0.15s/f (Firm)
WFA 3 from 4yo+ 2lb **14** Ran SP% **120.3**
Speed ratings (Par 101): **101,100,98,98,98 95,92,92,92,92 87,82,74,68**
toteswingers: 1&2 £7.60, 1&3 £23.60, 2&3 £19.90 CSF £40.61 CT £402.13 TOTE £9.30: £3.50, £1.60, £8.10; EX 30.90.
Owner John Gibb **Bred** Southill Stud **Trained** Middleham Moor, N Yorks
■ Stewards' Enquiry : Kelly Harrison one-day ban: careless riding (Sep 8)

FOCUS
A modest 46-65 handicap and a tight five-horse finish.
Miacarla Official explanation: jockey said mare was denied a clear run
Liberty Ship Official explanation: trainer's rep said gelding never travelled
Braille Official explanation: jockey said gelding missed the break

5423 GO RACING AT REDCAR ON SATURDAY H'CAP 1m 3f 214y
4:50 (4:52) (Class 6) (0-60,57) 3-Y-O **£2,047** (£604; £302) **Stalls** Low

Form RPR
0030 **1** **Cheyenne Chant**[12] 5058 3-8-6 **45**.........................(t) SilvestreDeSousa 8 56
(D O'Meara) *mde all: pushed along over 3f out: rdn over 2f out: drvn and styd on wl fnl f* **5/1**[2]
0451 **2** *2* **Always Dixie (IRE)**[13] 4980 3-8-10 **49**.............................. GregFairley 9 56
(M Johnston) *trckd wnr: effrt and cl up 3f out: rdn 2f out: drvn over 1f out: one pce ins fnl f* **11/2**[3]
3464 **3** *1 1/4* **Miss Whippy**[19] 4774 3-8-10 **49**.. KirstyMilczarek 1 54
(P Howling) *trckd ldrs on inner: hdwy to chse ldng pair 5f out: rdn along 3f out: drvn and one pce appr fnl f* **12/1**
2553 **4** *shd* **Danceintothelight**[11] 5093 3-9-4 **57**.................................. PhillipMakin 3 62
(Micky Hammond) *chsd ldrs: effrt 3f out: rdn along over 2f out and sn one pce* **9/2**[1]
6200 **5** *3 1/2* **Electric City (IRE)**[22] 4687 3-8-10 **49**............................. FrannyNorton 5 48
(M G Quinlan) *midfield: stdy hdwy 4f out: chsd ldrs 2f out: sn rdn and no imp* **17/2**
0040 **6** *3 1/4* **Footsie (IRE)**[12] 5058 3-8-11 **53**................................. BarryMcHugh[(3)] 12 47
(J G Given) *in rr: hdwy 3f out: rdn and kpt on fnl 2f: nvr nr ldrs* **11/1**
6250 **7** *4 1/2* **Second Brook (IRE)**[141] 1145 3-8-11 **53**....................... PaulPickard[(3)] 2 40
(R Hollinshead) *in rr tl sme late hdwy* **33/1**
6653 **8** *2* **Miereveld**[29] 4448 3-8-11 **50**....................................(b[1]) PatrickMathers 15 34
(B Ellison) *s.i.s: a towards rr* **20/1**
00-5 **9** *2 1/2* **Bollin Andrew**[141] 1145 3-8-10 **49**..................................(t) DavidAllan 14 29
(T D Easterby) *in tch: rdn along 1/2-way: drvn and wknd over 3f out* **13/2**
0633 **10** *2* **Venture Girl (IRE)**[41] 4052 3-9-0 **53**............................ DuranFentiman 10 29
(T D Easterby) *midfield: hdwy over 4f out: in tch and rdn over 2f out: sn wknd* **8/1**
0-00 **11** *12* **Fireflash (IRE)**[12] 5058 3-8-3 **45**................................ KellyHarrison[(3)] 13 —
(N Tinkler) *a towards rr: bhd fnl 3f* **80/1**
660- **12** *1 1/4* **Ariel Bender**[13] 4327 3-8-4 **46** ow1........................ AndrewHeffernan[(3)] 7 —
(Peter Grayson) *a towards rr: bhd fnl 3f* **150/1**
0000 **13** *9* **Dispol Kabira**[7] 5201 3-8-6 **45**.. AdrianNicholls 11 —
(D W Thompson) *a in rr: bhd fnl 4f* **66/1**
0000 **14** *12* **Fantastic Favour**[7] 5216 3-8-11 **55**...................(b[1]) MichaelO'Connell[(5)] 6 —
(Jedd O'Keeffe) *chsd ldrs: rdn along 1/2-way: sn lost pl and bhd fnl 3f* **40/1**
0-50 **P** **Ilkley**[66] 3238 3-8-6 **48**.. JamesSullivan[(3)] 4 —
(M W Easterby) *towards rr: lost pl and bhd whn p.u bef 1/2-way* **25/1**

2m 34.7s (-4.20) **Going Correction** -0.325s/f (Firm) **15** Ran SP% **118.6**
Speed ratings (Par 98): **101,99,98,98,96 94,91,89,88,86 78,78,72,64,—**
toteswingers: 1&2 £3.90, 1&3 £9.20, 2&3 £14.20 CSF £30.17 CT £317.60 TOTE £6.40: £2.60, £3.10, £5.10; EX 32.70.
Owner R Naylor **Bred** Stanley Estate And Stud Co **Trained** Nawton, N Yorks

FOCUS
A low-grade 45-57 handicap and a seller in all but name. The pace was strong and the first five were up there throughout.
Dispol Kabira Official explanation: jockey said filly ran too free
Ilkley Official explanation: jockey said filly lost its action; vet said filly returned lame left-hind

5424 BOOK NOW FOR 18TH SEPTEMBER H'CAP 5f 212y
5:25 (5:27) (Class 5) (0-75,75) 3-Y-O+ **£2,072** (£616; £308; £153) **Stalls** Low

Form RPR
4126 **1** **Mr Wolf**[10] 5123 9-9-7 **73**..(p) BarryMcHugh[(3)] 6 83
(J J Quinn) *mde all: rdn wl over 1f out: kpt on strly* **14/1**
5500 **2** *2 3/4* **Real Diamond**[16] 4895 4-8-8 **57**....................................... FrannyNorton 3 58
(Ollie Pears) *prom on inner: effrt to chse wnr over 2f out and sn rdn: drvn over 1f out: kpt on same pce* **12/1**
0022 **3** *3* **Solar Spirit (IRE)**[88] 2534 5-9-4 **74**.............................. ShaneBKelly[(7)] 4 66
(J J Quinn) *chsd ldrs: rdn along 2f out: drvn over 1f out: sn one pce* **7/2**[1]
1200 **4** *3/4* **Ursus**[7] 5198 5-8-7 **59**...(p) KellyHarrison[(3)] 1 48
(C R Wilson) *stmbld s: hld up towards rr: hdwy over 2f out: rdn to chse ldrs over 1f out: sn drvn and no imp* **14/1**
2024 **5** *1 1/2* **Avontuur (FR)**[99] 2206 8-9-4 **70**.................................. JamesSullivan[(3)] 12 54+
(Mrs R A Carr) *chsd ldrs on outer: hdwy to chse wnr 1/2-way: rdn over 2f out and grad wknd* **16/1**
5025 **6** *shd* **Just Sam (IRE)**[26] 4558 5-9-0 **68**...................................... LanceBetts[(5)] 8 52
(R E Barr) *towards rr: hdwy 2f out: sn rdn and sme hdwy approachinjg fnl f: n.d* **11/1**
0010 **7** *1/2* **Feeling Fresh (IRE)**[16] 4910 5-9-12 **75**..................... SilvestreDeSousa 2 57
(Paul Green) *dwlt and towards rr: hdwy on wd outside 2f out: sn rdn and nvr nr ldrs* **7/2**[1]
5000 **8** *3/4* **Royal Patriot (IRE)**[11] 5067 3-8-1 **56** oh2........................ PaulPickard[(3)] 7 36
(Paul Green) *s.i.s: a in rr* **50/1**
5560 **9** *1/2* **Timeless Elegance (IRE)**[21] 4712 3-9-6 **72**..................... PhillipMakin 11 50
(J Howard Johnson) *chsd ldrs: rdn along 2f out: sn drvn and wknd wl over 1f out* **10/1**[3]
2026 **10** *2 1/2* **Ryedane (IRE)**[2] 5356 8-9-7 **70**...(b) DavidAllan 9 40
(T D Easterby) *sn rdn along and a towards rr* **6/1**[2]
3303 **11** *2* **Jigajig**[23] 4654 3-9-2 **71**.. AmyRyan[(3)] 10 35
(K A Ryan) *chsd ldrs: rdn along wl over 2f out: sn wknd* **10/1**[3]
405 **12** *9* **Craicattack (IRE)**[7] 5197 3-9-0 **71**......................(p) MichaelO'Connell[(5)] 5 6
(Mrs S A Watt) *prom: rdn along 1/2-way: drvn 2f out: sn wknd* **33/1**

1m 11.14s (-2.46) **Going Correction** -0.325s/f (Firm)
WFA 3 from 4yo+ 3lb **12** Ran SP% **117.1**
Speed ratings (Par 103): **103,99,95,94,92 92,91,90,89,86 83,71**
toteswingers: 1&2 £27.80, 1&3 £8.10, 2&3 £11.20 CSF £169.65 CT £723.90 TOTE £17.60: £5.30, £3.80, £1.60; EX 212.80 Place 6 £100.86, Place 5 £49.69.
Owner Andrew Turton & David Barker **Bred** P Asquith **Trained** Settrington, N Yorks

FOCUS
A competitive 56-75 sprint handicap, but the remarkable winner turned it into a procession.
T/Plt: £109.30 to a £1 stake. Pool: £49,706.49. 331.96 winning tickets. T/Qpdt: £36.20 to a £1 stake. Pool £3,328.66. 67.90 winning tickets. JR

5431 - 5432a (Foreign Racing) - See Raceform Interactive

5404 AYR (L-H)
Thursday, August 26

OFFICIAL GOING: Good to firm (good in places; 9.2)
Round course back straight out 4m, home bend out 6m adding about 18yds to distances on round course.
Wind: Breezy, half against Weather: Sunny, hot

5433 VICTORCHANDLER.COM MAIDEN AUCTION STKS 6f
2:10 (2:11) (Class 5) 2-Y-O **£2,590** (£770; £385; £192) **Stalls** High

Form RPR
3222 **1** **Intrusion**[12] 5092 2-8-8 70.. PaulHanagan 1 75
(R A Fahey) *pressed ldr: shkn up to ld over 1f out: drvn out fnl f* **5/4**[1]
U322 **2** *1 1/2* **So Is She (IRE)**[5] 5294 2-8-1 72....................................(v) BillyCray[(5)] 4 69
(A Bailey) *s.i.s: sn pushed along in last pl: hdwy over 2f out: chsd wnr ent fnl f: r.o* **5/4**[1]
3 *5* **Elusive Prince** 2-8-13 0... PhillipMakin 3 61+
(T D Barron) *trckd ldrs: shkn up appr fnl f: sn outpcd by ldng pair* **12/1**[3]
00 **4** *3 1/2* **Music News (USA)**[14] 4999 2-9-1 0...................................... JoeFanning 2 52
(M Johnston) *led to over 1f out: wknd ins fnl f* **10/1**[2]

1m 12.1s (-1.50) **Going Correction** -0.30s/f (Firm) **4** Ran SP% **105.7**
Speed ratings (Par 94): **98,96,89,84**
CSF £2.87 TOTE £1.80; EX 2.90.
Owner T G & Mrs M E Holdcroft **Bred** Bearstone Stud **Trained** Musley Bank, N Yorks

FOCUS
Straightforward maiden form.

NOTEBOOK
Intrusion, runner-up on her last three starts, had something to find in conceding 2lb to the runner-up, but she showed a much more resolute attitude than that one and was well on top at the finish. Her future now lies back in nurseries and, although a mark of 70 has her about right, this should boost her confidence nicely. (op Evens)
So Is She(IRE), sporting a second-time visor, has now finished second on her last three outings and her attitude will now rightly come into question. It must be noted she played up a little before loading up and is proving a tricky filly to place successfully, but returning to 7f ought to help. (op 11-8 tchd 11-10)
Elusive Prince is an already gelded son of Storming Home and related to winners at around this distance. He looked a bit backward and was easy to back, but showed definite ability. There ought to be a deal of improvement in him for the initial experience, but he is more of one for nurseries in due course. (op 14-1)
Music News(USA) faded tamely after making the early running against the stands' rail. He is now eligible for a handicap mark, but needs to step up big time on what he has shown thus far. (op 11-1 tchd 12-1)

5434 SENATE ELECTRICAL NURSERY 6f
2:40 (2:41) (Class 6) (0-65,64) 2-Y-O **£2,266** (£674; £337; £168) **Stalls** High

Form RPR
066 **1** **Fleet Captain**[59] 3498 2-9-7 **64**... TomEaves 3 69+
(K A Ryan) *prom: drvn over 2f out: led ins fnl f: hld on wl* **5/1**[2]
3502 **2** *1/2* **Ajaafa**[15] 4967 2-9-6 **63**.. PaulMulrennan 7 66
(J G Given) *in tch on outside: effrt over 2f out: pressed wnr ins fnl f: r.o* **14/1**
4032 **3** *1 1/2* **Eilean Mor**[13] 5042 2-9-6 **63**... PaulHanagan 14 62+
(J S Goldie) *hld up: swtchd rt and hdwy over 1f out: kpt on fnl f: nt rch first two* **5/1**[2]
0000 **4** *1/2* **Miss Cosette (IRE)**[40] 4150 2-8-6 **49**............................... FrannyNorton 6 46
(T D Barron) *bhd tl hdwy over 1f out: kpt on wl fnl f: nrst fin* **12/1**
0404 **5** *3/4* **Mini Bon Bon**[3] 5354 2-8-7 **57**....................................(v) NatashaEaton[(7)] 5 52
(A Bailey) *led: rdn over 1f out: hung lft and hdd ins fnl f: no ex* **12/1**
550 **6** *3/4* **Dark Times (IRE)**[40] 4150 2-8-7 **50**................................. AndrewElliott 9 43
(Mrs K Burke) *prom: rdn and edgd lft over 1f out: sn one pce* **8/1**
0300 **7** *2 1/2* **Peters Spirit (IRE)**[20] 4783 2-9-1 **61**........................ BarryMcHugh[(3)] 15 46
(R A Fahey) *hld up in midfield: hung lft thrght: effrt over 1f out: sn no imp* **7/1**[3]
0006 **8** *1 1/4* **Whats For Pudding (IRE)**[19] 4848 2-7-11 **47**.................. NeilFarley[(7)] 8 28
(D Carroll) *trckd ldrs tl rdn and wknd over 1f out* **50/1**
030 **9** *3/4* **Volcanic Ash (USA)**[50] 3794 2-9-0 **57**.............................. JoeFanning 12 36
(M Johnston) *midfield: drvn and outpcd over 2f out: n.d after* **5/2**[1]
5606 **10** *1 1/2* **Dotty Darroch**[13] 5042 2-8-12 **55**.....................(b[1]) SilvestreDeSousa 10 30
(R Bastiman) *cl up tl rdn and wknd over 1f out* **50/1**
506 **11** *3* **Microlight**[13] 5040 2-9-5 **62**... DavidAllan 13 28
(T D Easterby) *midfield: drvn and outpcd after 2f: n.d after* **16/1**
300 **12** *1 3/4* **Shy Bird**[51] 3756 2-9-0 **57**.. PJMcDonald 2 17
(J A Glover) *dwlt: bhd on outside: hdwy 1/2-way: wknd 2f out* **25/1**
0000 **13** *3/4* **Aprication (IRE)**[17] 4899 2-8-7 **50**.......................(b[1]) DuranFentiman 4 8
(J R Weymes) *dwlt: bhd on outside: struggling 1/2-way: nvr on terms* **66/1**

1m 13.62s (0.02) **Going Correction** -0.30s/f (Firm) **13** Ran SP% **122.7**
Speed ratings (Par 92): **87,86,84,83,82 81,78,76,75,73 69,67,66**
toteswingers:1&2:£10.70, 1&3:£5.20, 2&3:£9.40 CSF £73.57 CT £388.09 TOTE £5.90: £2.60, £4.40, £1.10; EX 71.40.
Owner Clipper Logistics **Bred** Mrs C R Philipson & Mrs H G Lascelles **Trained** Hambleton, N Yorks
■ Stewards' Enquiry : Tom Eaves one-day ban: used whip with excessive frequency (Sep 9)

FOCUS
A moderate nursery dominated by the topweights.

NOTEBOOK

Fleet Captain disappointed when eased to 5f on his previous outing, but he has always been well thought of and showed his true colours on this nursery debut. He has evidently benefited for his recent time off the track and this return to the extra furlong was much more to his liking. He remains open to improvement and can rate higher as he matures. Official explanation: trainer's rep had no explanation for the apparent improvement in form.

Ajaafa, held in a claimer last time, again found one too good but ran his race and sets the standard. This drop to 6f suited and he deserves to get his head in front. (tchd 16-1)

Eilean Mor showed his hand when second on his nursery debut 13 days earlier and looked interesting over this stiffer test. He got going all too late, but is in good hands and worth persevering with over this distance. (tchd 9-2)

Miss Cosette(IRE) caught the eye running on with purpose late in the day, but she was well beaten in a seller last time out and does put the form into some perspective. It was a clear personal-best, though, and she deserves a chance to prove herself an improver. (op 14-1)

Volcanic Ash(USA) was making his nursery debut off a perch of just 57 despite having shown some ability in three previous runs. The drop back in trip may have been against him, but he was really one of the first beaten and now has it all to prove. Official explanation: trainer had no explanation for the poor form shown (tchd 3-1)

5435 PATRICK DROMGOOLE OF PENKILL 80TH BIRTHDAY H'CAP — 7f 50y

3:10 (3:10) (Class 4) (0-85,85) 3-Y-O+ £4,857 (£1,445; £722; £360) Stalls High

Form RPR

6423 1 **Zomerlust**[13] 5043 8-9-9 **82**............(v) TomEaves 10 92
(J J Quinn) *hld up in tch: hdwy over 1f out: led ins fnl f: rdn out* **6/1**[2]

3463 2 ¾ **Glen Shiel (USA)**[7] 5242 3-9-7 **85**............ JoeFanning 11 91
(M Johnston) *cl up: led over 1f out to ins fnl f: kpt on same pce* **7/4**[1]

0415 3 nse **River Falcon**[15] 4952 10-8-11 **77**............ PaulNorton(7) 6 85
(J S Goldie) *hld up: plenty to do 1/2-way: gd hdwy on outside over 1f out: kpt on towards fin* **16/1**

0020 4 nk **Game Lad**[13] 5043 8-9-7 **80**............(tp) DavidAllan 9 87
(T D Easterby) *hld up: hdwy over 1f out: r.o fnl f: nrst fin* **8/1**

0-00 5 1 ¼ **Dhaular Dhar (IRE)**[110] 1900 8-9-9 **85**............ GaryBartley(3) 5 89
(J S Goldie) *hld up: effrt and rdn over 2f out: no imp appr fnl f* **6/1**[2]

4402 6 5 **Feelin Foxy**[13] 5054 6-9-5 **78**............ PaulMulrennan 7 68
(J G Given) *t.k.h: led to over 1f out: sn wknd* **11/1**

6006 7 ¾ **Imprimis Tagula (IRE)**[10] 5154 6-8-10 **76**............(v) NatashaEaton(7) 8 64
(A Bailey) *trckd ldrs: ev ch over 2f out: wknd over 1f out* **20/1**

0000 8 1 ¾ **Quanah Parker (IRE)**[40] 4154 4-9-3 **79**............(p) MichaelStainton(3) 4 62
(R M Whitaker) *in tch on ins: effrt and hdwy over 2f out: wknd over 1f out* **7/1**[3]

0040 9 6 **Deadly Secret (USA)**[17] 4894 4-9-1 **74**............ PaulHanagan 3 41
(R A Fahey) *trckd ldrs: rdn over 2f out: sn wknd* **14/1**

1m 30.4s (-3.00) **Going Correction** -0.30s/f (Firm)

WFA 3 from 4yo+ 5lb 9 Ran SP% **114.2**

Speed ratings (Par 105): **105,104,104,103,102 96,95,93,86**

toteswingers:1&2:£10.70, 1&3:£5.20, 2&3:£9.40 CSF £16.67 CT £159.82 TOTE £7.20: £2.70, £1.10, £5.00; EX 12.70.

Owner Dawson And Quinn **Bred** The Lavington Stud **Trained** Settrington, N Yorks

FOCUS

A fair handicap, run at a decent pace.

5436 GORDON SCOTT'S 60TH BIRTHDAY H'CAP — 1m 1f 20y

3:40 (3:40) (Class 4) (0-85,84) 4-Y-O+ £4,857 (£1,445; £722; £360) Stalls Low

Form RPR

6424 1 **Grand Diamond (IRE)**[1] 5408 6-7-10 **66**............(p) NeilFarley(7) 4 74
(J S Goldie) *hld up: hdwy on outside over 3f out: rdn to ld over 1f out: hld on wl fnl f* **5/1**[2]

4033 2 ½ **Veroon (IRE)**[8] 5213 4-8-10 **73**............(p) PaulMulrennan 5 79
(J G Given) *cl up: ev ch 2f out: sn rdn: kpt on fnl f: hld nr fin* **9/2**[1]

6500 3 1 ¼ **King Of The Moors (USA)**[1] 5407 7-8-2 **65**............(p) FrannyNorton 12 69
(R C Guest) *prom: effrt over 2f out: edgd lft over 1f out: kpt on same pce fnl f* **28/1**

5206 4 1 ¼ **Bullet Man (USA)**[30] 4450 5-9-3 **80**............ PaulHanagan 10 81
(R A Fahey) *hld up in tch: rdn and outpcd over 2f out: kpt on fnl f: nvr able to chal* **11/2**[3]

-065 5 1 ¼ **Spirit Of A Nation (IRE)**[3] 5375 5-9-0 **82**............ DaleSwift(5) 2 80
(D H Brown) *trckd ldrs: drvn over 2f out: kpt on same pce fnl f* **11/2**[3]

0046 6 ¾ **Jewelled Dagger (IRE)**[5] 4823 6-8-4 **67**............(p) JoeFanning 7 63
(J S Goldie) *trckd ldr: led over 2f to 1f out: sn no ex* **9/1**

-000 7 2 ½ **Nevada Desert (IRE)**[34] 4348 10-8-6 **72**............ MichaelStainton(3) 6 63
(R M Whitaker) *dwlt: t.k.h: hld up: rdn over 2f out: nvr rchd ldrs* **40/1**

501 8 shd **Kimberley Downs (USA)**[7] 5244 4-8-0 **66** 6ex............ JamesSullivan(3) 8 57
(N Wilson) *led to over 2f out: wknd over 1f out* **9/2**[1]

0004 9 ¾ **Rosbay (IRE)**[12] 5071 6-8-9 **72**............ DuranFentiman 9 61
(T D Easterby) *dwlt: hld up on ins: drvn over 2f out: sn btn* **11/1**

36 10 3 ¼ **Applaude**[8] 5213 5-8-2 **65**............(b) PaulEddery 1 47
(R C Guest) *hld up: rdn over 2f out: sn btn* **20/1**

1m 55.08s (-3.32) **Going Correction** -0.30s/f (Firm) 10 Ran SP% **112.8**

Speed ratings (Par 105): **102,101,100,99,98 97,95,95,94,91**

toteswingers:1&2:£3.50, 1&3:£27.70, 2&3:£17.90 CSF £26.13 CT £562.39 TOTE £5.00: £1.80, £1.20, £7.60; EX 31.50.

Owner Jim Goldie Racing Club **Bred** Newberry Stud Company **Trained** Uplawmoor, E Renfrews

FOCUS

A run-of-the-mill handicap, run at a decent pace.

Kimberley Downs(USA) Official explanation: trainer said, regarding running, that the gelding was unsuited by being taken on for the lead.

5437 BET LIVE AT VICTORCHANDLER.COM H'CAP — 1m 5f 13y

4:10 (4:10) (Class 6) (0-65,65) 3-Y-O+ £2,047 (£604; £302) Stalls Low

Form RPR

3334 1 **Mohawk Ridge**[15] 4953 4-9-11 **62**............(p) PhillipMakin 6 67
(M Dods) *cl up: rdn to ld over 2f out: edgd lft u.p ins fnl f: hld on wl* **5/1**

0650 2 nk **Chocolate Caramel (USA)**[11] 5119 8-9-9 **60**............ PaulHanagan 5 65
(R A Fahey) *midfield: drvn over 2f out: styd on wl fnl f: tk 2nd cl home* **15/2**

3556 3 shd **The Mighty Mod (USA)**[15] 4945 3-7-13 **47**............(b) SilvestreDeSousa 1 51
(M Johnston) *in tch: drvn over 3f out: rallied over 2f out: ev ch ins fnl f: kpt on: hld nr fin* **9/2**[3]

66-0 4 ¾ **Lady Bluesky**[78] 2864 7-9-1 **52**............ PJMcDonald 8 55
(A C Whillans) *hld up: hdwy on outside over 2f out: kpt on fnl f: no ex towards fin* **7/2**[1]

3433 5 1 ½ **Maid Of Meft**[20] 4800 3-9-2 **64**............ LNewman 12 65
(Miss L A Perratt) *bhd tl rdn and hdwy over 1f out: nvr able to chal* **11/1**

043- 6 nk **Dramatic Jewel (USA)**[5] 6497 4-9-13 **64**............ JoeFanning 2 65
(Miss Lucinda V Russell) *trckd ldrs: drvn over 2f out: one pce fnl f* **50/1**

/030 7 1 ¼ **Black Coffee**[20] 4781 5-10-0 **65**............ TomEaves 7 64
(W M Brisbourne) *bhd tl hdwy over 1f out: nvr able to chal* **16/1**

-403 8 1 **Almutaham (USA)**[55] 3639 3-8-5 **53**............ FrannyNorton 10 50
(James Moffatt) *prom: rdn and outpcd over 2f out: n.d after* **9/1**

5042 9 2 **Sheikhtothemusic**[13] 5058 3-8-13 **61**............ PaulMulrennan 3 55
(J G Given) *hld up in midfield: hdwy and prom over 2f out: wknd appr fnl f* **4/1**[2]

3000 10 nk **Cigalas**[8] 5213 5-9-4 **55**............ AndrewMullen 9 49
(Mrs J C McGregor) *bhd: drvn over 3f out: nvr on terms* **80/1**

0056 11 nk **Quitao (GER)**[20] 4800 3-7-12 **49** oh1 ow3............ JamesSullivan(3) 14 42
(P Monteith) *prom tl rdn and wknd over 2f out* **100/1**

00 12 2 ¾ **Sri Kuantan (IRE)**[70] 3122 6-8-9 **46** oh1............(t) PaulEddery 13 35
(R C Guest) *led tl rdn and hdd over 2f out: wknd over 1f out* **25/1**

2m 56.28s (2.28) **Going Correction** -0.30s/f (Firm)

WFA 3 from 4yo+ 11lb 12 Ran SP% **121.1**

Speed ratings (Par 101): **80,79,79,79,78 78,77,76,75,75 75,73**

toteswingers:1&2:£7.00, 1&3:£5.40, 2&3:£7.70 CSF £42.71 CT £184.96 TOTE £4.50: £1.20, £3.20, £2.50; EX 34.80.

Owner Doug Graham **Bred** Old Mill Stud Ltd And Oomswell Ltd **Trained** Denton, Co Durham

FOCUS

A weak staying handicap that had a wide-open look about it. There was a sound enough pace on, but things did rather steady up nearing the home turn.

Sheikhtothemusic Official explanation: trainer said filly was unsuited by the good to firm (good in places) ground

Cigalas Official explanation: jockey said gelding ran too free

5438 VAL & HUGH'S PRESTWICK CENTRAL BAR H'CAP — 6f

4:40 (4:41) (Class 6) (0-60,60) 3-Y-O £2,047 (£604; £302) Stalls High

Form RPR

3300 1 **Monsieur Pontaven**[15] 4970 3-8-5 **47**............(b[1]) SilvestreDeSousa 7 56
(R Bastiman) *dwlt: sn prom: hdwy and led over 1f out: jnd ins fnl f: kpt on wl u.p* **9/2**[3]

0006 2 hd **Pavement Games**[10] 5162 3-8-4 **46** oh1............ PaulEddery 11 54
(R C Guest) *hld up: hdwy whn nt clr run briefly over 1f out: effrt and str chal fnl f: jst hld* **22/1**

5046 3 4 ½ **Itsthursdayalready**[24] 4651 3-9-1 **57**............ PaulMulrennan 4 51
(W M Brisbourne) *cl up: effrt and ev ch over 1f out: outpcd fnl f* **11/2**

5-64 4 1 ¼ **Billionaire Boy (IRE)**[26] 4584 3-8-10 **52**............ DanielTudhope 8 42
(Patrick Morris) *t.k.h: slt ld tl edgd lft and hdd over 1f out: sn btn* **4/1**[2]

0435 5 1 ½ **Weetentherty**[8] 5211 3-8-5 **47**............(p) PaulHanagan 5 32
(J S Goldie) *cl up: drvn over 2f out: wknd over 1f out* **4/1**[2]

3-23 6 ½ **Sparking**[13] 5044 3-9-3 **59**............ PhillipMakin 6 42
(T D Barron) *disp ld: rdn over 2f out: wknd over 1f out* **2/1**[1]

000- 7 1 ½ **Sumay Buoy (IRE)**[329] 6408 3-8-12 **54**............ AndrewMullen 3 32
(Mrs J C McGregor) *cl up tl rdn and wknd over 1f out* **40/1**

1m 12.32s (-1.28) **Going Correction** -0.30s/f (Firm) 7 Ran SP% **113.7**

Speed ratings (Par 98): **96,95,89,88,86 85,83**

toteswingers:1&2:£7.20, 1&3:£4.70, 2&3:£9.90 CSF £85.71 CT £552.70 TOTE £5.90: £2.90, £9.50; EX 78.90.

Owner Ms M Austerfield **Bred** Whitsbury Manor Stud **Trained** Cowthorpe, N Yorks

FOCUS

A very weak 3-y-o handicap, run at a decent pace and two came well clear.

5439 BET LIVE AT VICTORCHANDLER.COM APPRENTICE H'CAP — 1m

5:15 (5:16) (Class 6) (0-60,58) 4-Y-O+ £1,942 (£578; £288; £144) Stalls Low

Form RPR

-003 1 **Social Rhythm**[7] 5244 6-9-4 **57**............ GarryWhillans 3 74
(A C Whillans) *hld up: gd hdwy on outside to ld over 1f out: edgd lft: pushed clr fnl f* **4/1**[1]

53 2 6 **Morocchius (USA)**[38] 4188 5-9-1 **57**............(p) NeilFarley(3) 9 60
(Julie Camacho) *hld up: hdwy on outside to ld briefly 2f out: hung lft: nt pce of wnr fnl f* **4/1**[1]

102 3 ½ **Red Skipper (IRE)**[19] 4824 5-9-1 **57**............ JulieBurke(3) 10 59
(N Wilson) *led tl hdd 2f out: sn drvn: one pce fnl f* **9/2**[2]

062 4 ¾ **Crocodile Bay (IRE)**[10] 5159 7-9-0 **58**............ SeanPalmer(5) 12 58
(R C Guest) *cl up: rdn over 2f out: one pce over 1f out* **10/1**

-640 5 hd **Bourse (IRE)**[4] 5331 5-8-3 **45**............ NathanAlison(3) 5 45
(A G Foster) *hld up in midfield: drvn and outpcd over 2f out: rallied fnl f: nvr able to chal* **6/1**[3]

0035 6 ½ **Real Desire**[8] 5216 4-8-7 **51**............ DavidSimmonson(5) 14 50
(P Monteith) *t.k.h in midfield: rdn and outpcd over 2f out: n.d after* **18/1**

150- 7 1 **Whaston (IRE)**[336] 5513 5-9-0 **53**............ DaleSwift 13 49
(Miss P Robson) *trckd ldrs: drvn over 2f out: edgd lft and no ex over 1f out* **6/1**[3]

8 3 ¼ **Pecavi (IRE)**[401] 7569 5-8-4 **48**............ CPHoban(5) 1 37
(John C McConnell, Ire) *trckd ldrs tl rdn and wknd fr 2f out* **13/2**

64/0 9 3 ¾ **Bella's Story**[22] 4706 4-8-6 **50**............ PaulNorton(5) 2 30
(J S Goldie) *hld up on ins: drvn over 2f out: sn btn* **11/1**

0600 10 ¾ **Sendreni (FR)**[28] 4515 6-8-5 **49**............(p) JakePayne(5) 4 27
(Mrs J C McGregor) *t.k.h in midfield: rdn over 2f out: sn btn* **40/1**

1m 41.45s (-2.35) **Going Correction** -0.30s/f (Firm) 10 Ran SP% **125.2**

Speed ratings (Par 101): **99,93,92,91,91 91,90,86,83,82**

toteswingers:1&2:£5.70, 1&3:£5.90, 2&3:£3.70. totesuper7: Win: Not won, Place: Not won CSF £21.64 CT £78.61 TOTE £6.60: £2.60, £1.20, £1.30; EX 19.00 Place 6 £345.80; Place 5 £164.86.

Owner Mrs L M Whillans **Bred** A And B Fairfields **Trained** Newmill-On-Slitrig, Borders

FOCUS

A moderate handicap, run at a sound pace.

T/Plt: £718.60 to a £1 stake. Pool:£55,476.44 - 56.35 winning tickets T/Qpdt: £248.30 to a £1 stake. Pool:£3,925.92 - 11.70 winning tickets RY

4920 FFOS LAS (L-H)

Thursday, August 26

OFFICIAL GOING: Soft (good to soft in places; 7.2)

Wind: Light behind Weather: Overcast

5440 BURNS PET NUTRITION MAIDEN STKS — 1m (R)

2:20 (2:21) (Class 5) 2-Y-O £2,590 (£770; £385; £192) Stalls Low

Form RPR

2 1 **Marzante (USA)**[47] 3915 2-9-3 0............ SteveDrowne 8 79+
(R Charlton) *chsd ldr tl led over 2f out: rdn and hung lft fr over 1f out: r.o* **8/11**[1]

2 1 ¼ **Cobbs Quay** 2-9-3 0.. NickyMackay 3 76+
(J H M Gosden) *s.i.s: hdwy over 5f out: rdn to chse wnr and hung lft fr over 1f out: r.o* **4/1**[2]

52 3 4 ½ **Mark Harbour (IRE)**[9] 5178 2-9-3 0............................ RichardHughes 1 66
(R Hannon) *sn pushed along to ld: rdn and hdd over 2f out: hung lft and wknd ins fnl f* **9/2**[3]

0 4 1 ¼ **Mirradores**[52] 3735 2-9-3 0.. PhilipRobinson 7 64
(W R Muir) *chsd ldrs: rdn over 3f out: hung lft and wknd over 1f out* **40/1**

5 49 **Embezzle** 2-9-3 0.. TadhgO'Shea 6 —
(R Charlton) *s.s: outpcd: t.o* **17/2**

1m 42.47s (1.97) **Going Correction** +0.15s/f (Good) **5** Ran SP% **109.1**
Speed ratings (Par 94): **96,94,90,89,40**
CSF £3.87 TOTE £1.50: £1.10, £3.40; EX 4.50 Trifecta £15.20 Pool: £338.31 - 16.45 winning units..
Owner K Abdulla **Bred** Juddmonte Farms Inc **Trained** Beckhampton, Wilts

FOCUS
After 18 hours of non-stop rain (nearly 30mm in all) the ground was officially given as soft early on, before being changed to soft, good to soft in places prior to the opener. The jockey who rode the winner of the first race reported afterwards that the ground was not testing despite the heavy rain over the past 24 hours. He felt the going was just about soft, but certainly no worse than that.

NOTEBOOK
Marzante(USA), a brother to a Grade 1 winner in America who started his career for this trainer/owner combination, had a clear chance on his debut effort and duly got off the mark after racing prominently. The step up in trip proved to be no problem but it remains to be seen how well he does in handicaps or conditions events. One would imagine he'll be seen on Polytrack at some stage, considering how well his sibling went on it. (tchd 4-6 and 4-5 in places)
Cobbs Quay, who cost 270,000gns at the sales and is entered in next year's Derby, made an eyecatching debut after unseating his rider on the way to the start. Said to be noisy and green in the paddock, he wasn't the quickest away but looked a potential winner a furlong out, so should be good enough to win an ordinary maiden. (op 6-1 tchd 13-2)
Mark Harbour(IRE), running for the first time on turf after two starts on Polytrack, was driven to the lead and did a good job of taking the winner along in the early stages. He was easily passed once joined but plugged on inside the final furlong. (op 11-4)
Mirradores probably ran as well as he did on his first outing at Windsor over 6f, and is probably one for handicaps.
Embezzle, the winner's stable companion, who had already been gelded prior to his debut, was slowly away and soon out of contention. His trainer had reported on his website before this run that the horse had looked lazy and not shown a great deal, so was hoping the penny would drop when on the racecourse, which it seemingly didn't. (op 16-1)

5441 E.B.F./6 IN 6 MAIDEN FILLIES' STKS 6f
2:50 (2:50) (Class 5) 2-Y-O **£3,238** (£963; £481; £240) **Stalls** High

Form RPR
06 1 **Luv U Too**[13] 5029 2-9-0 0.. TadhgO'Shea 1 76
(F J Brennan) *mde all: rdn over 1f out: styd on* **20/1**

02 2 1 ¼ **Humdrum**[10] 5147 2-9-0 0.. RichardHughes 7 72
(R Hannon) *hld up: hdwy 1/2-way: rdn to chse wnr ins fnl f: hung lft: r.o* **1/1**[1]

3 shd **Carrignavar (USA)** 2-8-11 0...................................... EJMcNamara(3) 3 72+
(R M Beckett) *s.s: bhd: hdwy over 1f out: shkn up ins fnl f: r.o* **14/1**

4 4 2 **My Little Star (IRE)**[24] 4658 2-9-0 0............................... MichaelHills 4 66
(B W Hills) *trckd ldrs: rdn over 1f out: edgd lft and no ex ins fnl f* **15/8**[2]

00 5 1 **Bint Mazyouna**[10] 5147 2-9-0 0...................................... EddieCreighton 6 63
(M R Channon) *prom: rdn 1/2-way: wknd ins fnl f* **8/1**[3]

6 6 1 ¼ **Duquesa (IRE)**[28] 4517 2-9-0 0....................................... CathyGannon 2 59
(P D Evans) *chsd ldr tl rdn over 2f out: wknd fnl f* **50/1**

7 6 **Burst Of Stardust** 2-8-11 0.. MartinLane(3) 5 41
(B Palling) *chsd ldrs: rdn 1/2-way: wknd over 1f out* **40/1**

1m 11.39s (1.69) **Going Correction** +0.025s/f (Good) **7** Ran SP% **111.7**
Speed ratings (Par 91): **89,87,87,84,83 81,73**
toteswingers:1&2:£6.60, 1&3:£24.50, 2&3:£3.90 CSF £39.10 TOTE £26.20: £6.20, £1.60; EX 72.60 Trifecta £292.20 Part won. Pool: £394.95 - 0.41 winning units..
Owner Phones Direct Partnership **Bred** Richard Hunt **Trained** Lambourn, Berks

FOCUS
An ordinary looking maiden and punters centred their attention on only two runners, but both ran below expectations and an outsider collected.

NOTEBOOK
Luv U Too, who looked the biggest in the field, hadn't been disgraced in two previous outings, including once on Polytrack, but didn't look ready to win on those efforts. Sent straight into the lead, she had her own way out in front and was a comfortable victor after facing very little challenge. (tchd 18-1)
Humdrum appeared to be the one to beat when considering her previous start, but never looked like winning here, despite finishing second. Out of an Alzao mare, she probably needs further. (op 10-11and 11-10 and 4-5 in a place)
Carrignavar(USA) ◆, a $35,000 half-sister to an American 2-y-o winner, lost lots of ground after fly-jumping out of the stalls but still came through to be a threat over a furlong out. Her jockey was not hard on her, and it's not difficult to think she may have won had she got away on terms. (op 20-1 tchd 22-1)
My Little Star(IRE) showed a degree of promise on her debut but failed to reproduce it, even though she was given every chance. This was most disappointing. (op 2-1)
Bint Mazyouna never featured, as she was pushed along from an early stage. (op 11-1 tchd 12-1)
Duquesa(IRE) still looked as though this experience would bring her on. (op 66-1)
Burst Of Stardust, a half-brother to a winner, raced prominently but tended to hang whilst doing so. She soon dropped away once off the bridle. (op 33-1 tchd 50-1)

5442 BET ON LIVE GOLF AT TOTESPORT.COM H'CAP 6f
3:20 (3:20) (Class 2) (0-100,98) 3-Y-O **£9,714** (£2,890; £1,444; £721) **Stalls** High

Form RPR
1120 1 **Cansili Star**[28] 4509 3-9-2 **93**.. PhilipRobinson 9 102
(M A Jarvis) *chsd ldr: rdn to ld ins fnl f: r.o* **11/2**[3]

2110 2 ½ **Jack My Boy (IRE)**[89] 2545 3-8-13 **93**......................(b) MartinLane(3) 1 100
(P D Evans) *led: rdn and hdd ins fnl f: styd on* **12/1**

1000 3 ¾ **Lowdown (IRE)**[12] 5095 3-9-7 **98**...................................... GregFairley 5 103
(M Johnston) *hld up: rdn over 2f out: hdwy over 1f out: r.o* **6/1**

3100 4 hd **Sunraider (IRE)**[19] 4843 3-9-3 **94**..................................... MichaelHills 4 98
(B W Hills) *hld up: hdwy 1/2-way: rdn 2f out: r.o* **3/1**[2]

-121 5 4 ½ **Desert Poppy (IRE)**[13] 5037 3-8-13 **90**............................ ShaneKelly 2 80
(W R Swinburn) *chsd ldrs: rdn over 1f out: wknd ins fnl f* **2/1**[1]

3000 6 1 **Duplicity**[54] 3696 3-9-1 **92**... RichardHughes 7 78
(R Hannon) *hld up in tch: rdn and wknd over 1f out* **13/2**

5065 7 6 **Fly Silca Fly (IRE)**[13] 5052 3-8-2 **79**............................. CathyGannon 10 46
(M R Channon) *hld up: rdn 1/2-way: wknd 2f out* **25/1**

68.94 secs (-0.76) **Going Correction** +0.025s/f (Good) **7** Ran SP% **112.9**
Speed ratings (Par 106): **106,105,104,104,98 96,88**
toteswingers:1&2:£9.10, 1&3:£8.40, 2&3:£6.70 CSF £63.74 CT £405.81 TOTE £7.60: £5.10, £4.50; EX 45.70 Trifecta £173.90 Pool: £378.39 - 1.61 winning units..
Owner A D Spence **Bred** Hascombe And Valiant Studs **Trained** Newmarket, Suffolk

FOCUS
A competitive handicap.

NOTEBOOK
Cansili Star, down in trip and his trainer's first runner at this course, travelled nicely just behind the winner and made his bid at the right time to hold off all rivals. He seems to handle most ground, which should give his connections a few options this autumn. (op 6-1)
Jack My Boy(IRE) led, slightly away from his rivals, and kept on all the way to the line. If his previous effort at Newmarket can be forgotten, which was back in late May, he is holding his form well this season. (op 10-1)
Lowdown(IRE) was soon pushed along and behind rivals with a bit to do, but he picked up after a couple of reminders 2f out and was closing with every stride in the final stages. (op 9-1)
Sunraider(IRE), who ran moderately last time at Newmarket over 7f, was always thereabouts and appeared to run up to his best form. (op 5-2)
Desert Poppy(IRE), 11lb higher than last time, travelled well alongside the winner in the early stages but started to wander once off the bridle. She didn't look very co-operative once asked for maximum effort, but it's hard to fault a horse with the form she possesses. The easiest conclusion to draw is that she didn't handle the ground. (op 5-2)
Duplicity was never involved and is struggling. (op 6-1 tchd 8-1)

5443 40 LIVE FOOTBALL MARKETS AT TOTESPORT.COM H'CAP 1m 6f (R)
3:50 (3:50) (Class 4) (0-85,81) 3-Y-O+ **£4,533** (£1,348; £674; £336) **Stalls** Low

Form RPR
2533 1 **Admirable Duque (IRE)**[24] 4657 4-9-1 **71**..................(p) MartinLane(3) 1 79
(D J S Ffrench Davis) *a.p: chsd ldr 2f out: led over 1f out: rdn and hung lft wl ins fnl f: styd on* **10/1**

3326 2 ½ **Act Of Kalanisi (IRE)**[19] 4846 4-9-6 **73**............................ GregFairley 2 80
(M Johnston) *led: rdn and hdd over 1f out: styd on gamely* **9/4**[2]

2222 3 1 **Saggiatore**[22] 4719 3-8-10 **75**.. PhilipRobinson 3 82
(E A L Dunlop) *chsd ldrs: wnt 2nd 3f out to 2f out: sn rdn: styng on same pce whn n.m.r wl ins fnl f* **15/8**[1]

3014 4 5 **Calculating (IRE)**[5] 5296 6-8-9 **67**................................. LeeNewnes(5) 4 66
(M D I Usher) *chsd ldr tl rdn over 3f out: n.m.r sn after: styd on same pce fnl 2f* **15/2**

0551 5 11 **Mabuya (UAE)**[16] 4923 4-10-0 **81**.................................. RichardHughes 5 71
(P J Makin) *hld up: hdwy 3f out: rdn and wknd over 1f out: eased ins fnl f* **7/2**[3]

3m 8.66s (4.86) **Going Correction** +0.15s/f (Good)
WFA 3 from 4yo+ 12lb **5** Ran SP% **108.6**
Speed ratings (Par 105): **92,91,91,88,82**
CSF £31.65 TOTE £12.20: £5.80, £1.70; EX 30.60.
Owner Brian W Taylor **Bred** Airlie Stud And R N Clay **Trained** Lambourn, Berks

FOCUS
Despite the small field, the pace was respectable.
Mabuya(UAE) Official explanation: jockey said gelding ran flat

5444 GET LIVE FOOTBALL STATS AT TOTESPORT.COM FILLIES' H'CAP 1m 4f (R)
4:20 (4:20) (Class 4) (0-85,85) 3-Y-O+ **£4,533** (£1,348; £674; £336) **Stalls** Low

Form RPR
2513 1 **Mujdeya**[61] 3427 3-9-4 **85**... TadhgO'Shea 6 99+
(J H M Gosden) *hld up: hdwy over 3f out: led over 2f out: shkn up over 1f out: styd on wl: eased nr fin* **9/4**[1]

-100 2 2 ½ **Serafina's Flight**[105] 2047 3-8-10 **77**.............................. RichardHughes 3 84
(W R Muir) *a.p: chsd ldr over 4f out: rdn and ev ch over 2f out: no ex and flashed tail fnl f* **10/1**

4221 3 1 ½ **Ceoil An Aith (IRE)**[13] 5022 4-9-5 **76**.............................. GregFairley 1 81
(M Johnston) *chsd ldr tl pushed along over 4f out: rdn and hung lft fr over 3f out: ev ch over 2f out: styd on same pce appr fnl f* **8/1**

5321 4 1 **Chelsea Morning (USA)**[24] 4655 3-8-9 **76**........................ MichaelHills 4 79
(B W Hills) *chsd ldrs: rdn over 3f out: n.m.r over 2f out: styd on same pce appr fnl f* **5/2**[2]

3230 5 nk **Donna Elvira**[14] 5008 3-8-7 **74** ow1................................ ShaneKelly 2 77
(R Hannon) *led: rdn and hdd over 2f out: styd on same pce* **13/2**

5-60 6 4 ½ **Anice Stellato (IRE)**[83] 2703 4-9-11 **85**.......................... EJMcNamara(3) 5 80
(R M Beckett) *hld up: hdwy over 4f out: wknd over 2f out* **14/1**

1365 7 11 **Hollow Green (IRE)**[62] 3388 4-9-10 **81**............................ CathyGannon 8 59
(P D Evans) *hld up: rdn over 4f out: wknd 3f out* **6/1**[3]

2m 41.29s (4.49) **Going Correction** +0.15s/f (Good)
WFA 3 from 4yo 10lb **7** Ran SP% **113.8**
Speed ratings (Par 102): **91,89,88,87,87 84,77**
toteswingers:1&2:£5.30, 1&3:£3.10, 2&3:£7.40 CSF £24.79 CT £152.49 TOTE £3.60: £1.50, £7.00; EX 28.30 Trifecta £148.10 Pool: £446.52 - 2.23 winning units..
Owner Hamdan Al Maktoum **Bred** Shadwell Estate Company Limited **Trained** Newmarket, Suffolk

FOCUS
A fair handicap.

5445 WALTERS UK CIVIL ENGINEERING & CONSTRUCTION MAIDEN FILLIES' STKS 1m 4f (R)
4:50 (4:50) (Class 5) 3-Y-O+ **£2,590** (£770; £385; £192) **Stalls** Low

Form RPR
5-22 1 **Western Pearl**[19] 4845 3-8-12 74...................................... ShaneKelly 5 87+
(W J Knight) *chsd ldrs: led over 9f out: rdn clr over 1f out: easily* **11/4**[2]

5-3 2 5 **Strictly Lambada**[61] 3437 3-8-12 0.................................. NickyMackay 1 76
(J H M Gosden) *chsd ldrs: styng on same pce whn rdn and hung lft fr over 1f out: wnt 2nd ins fnl f* **4/1**[3]

022 3 ¾ **La Concorde (FR)**[34] 4330 3-8-12 76.............................. RichardHughes 4 75
(Sir Michael Stoute) *sn led: hdd over 9f out: remained handy: rdn to chse wnr over 2f out: hung lft over 1f out: wknd ins fnl f* **1/1**[1]

34 4 2 ½ **Astound**[8] 5209 3-8-12 70.. CathyGannon 6 71
(P D Evans) *hld up: plld hrd: hdwy over 7f out: rdn over 3f out: hung lft and wknd over 1f out* **25/1**

000/ 5 63 **Beshairt**[35] 3595 6-9-8 40.. SteveDrowne 3 —
(D Burchell) *led early: chsd ldrs tl lost tch fnl 8f: t.o* **16/1**

0 6 49 **Tiscaline (FR)**[23] 4679 3-8-9 0....................................... MartinLane(3) 2 —
(B Palling) *dwlt: plld hrd in rr: hdwy over 9f out: wknd over 6f out: t.o* **66/1**

2m 39.26s (2.46) **Going Correction** +0.15s/f (Good)
WFA 3 from 6yo 10lb **6** Ran SP% **107.9**
Speed ratings (Par 100): **97,93,93,91,49 16**
toteswingers:1&2:£1.70, 1&3:£1.40, 2&3:£1.30 CSF £12.86 TOTE £2.90: £1.20, £2.00; EX 9.60 Place 6 £168.00; Place 5 £143.88.
Owner Mrs N Welby **Bred** Mrs A K H Ooi **Trained** Patching, W Sussex

FOCUS
This is form to be wary of, as the early pace was far from strong until the winner took command.
T/Plt: £200.60 to a £1 stake. Pool:£58,802.45 - 213.96 winning tickets T/Qpdt: £78.40 to a £1 stake. Pool:£3,455.34 - 32.60 winning tickets CR

[5072]LINGFIELD (L-H)

Thursday, August 26

OFFICIAL GOING: Turf course - soft (good to soft in places; 7.3); all-weather - standard

5452 JACKSBRIDGE NURSERY 7f (P)

2:30 (2:31) (Class 5) (0-75,75) 2-Y-0 **£2,388** (£705; £352) **Stalls** Low

Form RPR

2134 **1** **Spartic**[20] 4801 2-9-0 **68** JamesDoyle 4 75
(A J McCabe) *in tch: hdwy to chse ldrs 3f out: pushed along to chse ldr over 2f out: rdn to ld over 1f out: clr and idling ins fnl f: jst hld on* **16/1**

3343 **2** *shd* **Malpas Missile (IRE)**[37] 4221 2-9-6 **74** RichardKingscote 3 81
(Tom Dascombe) *chsd ldrs: rdn to chse clr ldng pair wl over 1f out: chsd wnr ins fnl f: styd on wl and clsng qckly on idling wnr at fin: jst hld* **5/1**[3]

6000 **3** *2 ¼* **Ree's Rascal (IRE)**[45] 3959 2-7-13 **53** oh1 ow1 AndreaAtzeni 8 54+
(J R Boyle) *in tch in midfield: pushed along over 4f out: hdwy to chse ldng trio wl over 1f out: kpt on wl to go 3rd ins fnl f: nt rch ldrs* **8/1**

0331 **4** *2 ¼* **Rutterkin (USA)**[36] 4254 2-9-7 **75** (t) AhmedAjtebi 11 71
(Mahmood Al Zarooni) *racd keenly: chsd ldrs tl wnt 2nd over 4f out: pushed into ld over 2f out: rdn and hdd over 1f out: fdd ins fnl f* **4/1**[1]

343 **5** *2 ¼* **Out Of The Storm**[22] 4691 2-8-12 **66** SebSanders 13 58+
(S Dow) *stdd and dropped in bhd after s: hld up in rr: looking for run over 1f out: hdwy ent fnl f: kpt on wl fnl f: nvr trbld ldrs* **12/1**

6100 **6** *nk* **Danube Dancer (IRE)**[26] 4592 2-9-2 **70** LiamKeniry 12 59
(J S Moore) *hld up in rr: rdn and effrt wl over 1f out: styd on fnl f: nvr trbld ldrs* **40/1**

505 **7** *½* **Sodashy (IRE)**[21] 4743 2-9-0 **68** JerryO'Dwyer 9 56
(Miss Amy Weaver) *hld up in last trio: rdn and effrt on outer bnd 2f out: kpt on fr over 1f out: nvr trbld ldrs* **9/1**

0001 **8** *2 ¼* **Rafella (IRE)**[43] 4029 2-9-3 **71** JimCrowley 6 53
(R M Beckett) *in midfield whn n.m.r on bnd 5f out and pushed along: towards rr and nt gng wl after: rdn and no rspnse ent fnl 2f: n.d* **9/2**[2]

3010 **9** *nk* **Miss Moneypenni**[26] 4592 2-9-2 **70** NeilCallan 7 52
(N P Littmoden) *led for 1f: chsd ldr after tl over 4f out: wknd qckly u.p over 2f out* **25/1**

053 **10** *½* **Bouzy**[14] 4999 2-8-10 **64** FrankieMcDonald 5 44
(P Winkworth) *bmpd s and s.i.s: a towards rr and sn pushed along: n.d* **25/1**

0306 **11** *1 ¾* **Memorabilia**[26] 4580 2-9-2 **70** KierenFallon 10 46
(M Johnston) *chsd ldr tl led after 1f: rdn and hdd over 2f out: wknd qckly over 1f out* **9/1**

5144 **12** *1 ½* **Wotsthehurry**[18] 4872 2-9-0 **68** SamHitchcott 2 40
(M R Channon) *hld up in tch in midfield: rdn and no rspnse jst over 2f out: wl bhd fnl f* **25/1**

4613 **13** *3 ¾* **Our Way Only (IRE)**[22] 4696 2-9-5 **73** PatDobbs 1 36
(R Hannon) *in tch in midfield tl rdn and struggling over 2f out: wl bhd over 1f out: eased wl ins fnl f: sddle slipped* **8/1**

1m 26.07s (1.27) **Going Correction** +0.05s/f (Slow) 13 Ran SP% **124.6**
Speed ratings (Par 94): **94,93,91,88,86 85,85,82,82,81 79,78,73**
toteswingers:1&2:£17.00, 1&3:£27.60, 2&3:£17.70 CSF £94.74 CT £714.08 TOTE £21.00: £3.40, £2.40, £3.00; EX 130.70.
Owner Derek Buckley **Bred** D J Buckley **Trained** Averham Park, Notts

FOCUS

An ordinary nursery in which most of the main players were handy throughout.

NOTEBOOK

Spartic, making his AW debut, gained his previous win from the front but was content with a stalking role this time. He seemed likely to win comfortably when hitting the front over a furlong out, but he drifted to the inside rail and, in the end, just held on by the skin of his teeth under strong pressure. He took to the surface well enough, however, and there should be other opportunities. (op 14-1 tchd 12-1)

Malpas Missile(IRE), disappointing since finishing third in the Hilary Needler, was stepping up in trip for this AW debut. She came off the bridle behind the leaders at halfway, but found her stride once into the straight and she would have got up in another stride. Despite her string of placings, she can be given another chance on this surface. (op 13-2 tchd 7-1)

Ree's Rascal(IRE), making his nursery debut after finishing well held in four maidens, had been shaping as though worth a try over this longer trip and he was another to finish well after coming off the bridle a long way out. (op 12-1tchd 16-1 in a place)

Rutterkin(USA), another making his nursery debut after getting off the mark in a C&D maiden last month, had the tongue tie on for the first time. He went to the front easily enough on the home turn, but folded tamely once the winner headed him over a furlong out. (op 9-2)

Out Of The Storm, yet another making her nursery debut after showing ability in three maidens, is the one to take from the race as she was given plenty to do and was still last turning in, but she stayed on over the last furlong or so with her rider never going for his whip. She is one to watch. (op 11-1)

Danube Dancer(IRE), beaten a long way in two starts since winning a Warwick fillies' maiden on her second outing, is another to keep an eye on as she was also given a lot to do and didn't take the home bend too well, but made some late progress down the wide outside to suggest that she isn't a lost cause.

Bouzy Official explanation: jockey said filly never travelled

Our Way Only(IRE) Official explanation: jockey said saddle slipped

5453 SWEETWOODS PARK GOLF CLUB MEDIAN AUCTION MAIDEN STKS 6f (P)

3:00 (3:01) (Class 6) 2-Y-O **£2,047** (£604; £302) **Stalls** Low

Form RPR

0 **1** **Days Of Summer (IRE)**[38] 4203 2-8-12 0 JimCrowley 3 78+
(R M Beckett) *chsd ldrs: rdn and effrt to press ldr and carried wd bnd 2f out: sn ld: drvn and styd on wl fnl f* **12/1**

4 **2** *1 ½* **Fityaan**[49] 3826 2-9-3 0 RichardHills 10 79
(B W Hills) *in tch in midfield: hdwy to chse ldng pair and carried wd bnd 2f out: chsd wnr over 1f out: drvn and styd on same pce fnl f* **5/6**[1]

50 **3** *2* **Jonelha**[12] 5092 2-8-7 0 KierenFox(5) 9 68
(P W D'Arcy) *bmpd s and s.i.s: hld up towards rr: hdwy 3f out: chsd ldng trio and rdn 2f out: wnt 3rd jst ins fnl f: kpt on: nt rch ldng pairs* **33/1**

4 *3 ¼* **Jinky** 2-9-3 0 SamHitchcott 4 63+
(M R Channon) *sn bustled along towards rr: rdn and hdwy on inner over 1f out: kpt on to go 4th ins fnl f: nvr trbld ldrs* **40/1**

022 **5** *1 ½* **His Grace (IRE)**[10] 5160 2-9-3 0 NeilCallan 7 58
(A B Haynes) *hung rt thrght: w ldr tl led 3f out: hung rt and rn wd bnd 2f out: sn hdd: fdd fnl f* **13/2**[3]

6 **6** *¾* **Fimias (IRE)**[13] 5053 2-9-3 0 KierenFallon 11 59+
(L M Cumani) *wnt rt s: t.k.h: hld up towards rr: hdwy on outer ent fnl 3f: wd and outpcd bnd 2f out: n.d and plugged on same pce fnl f* **33/1**

35 **7** *1* **King Of The Desert (IRE)**[18] 4871 2-9-3 0 EddieAhern 2 53
(E A L Dunlop) *in tch in midfield: lost pl and dropped towards rr over 2f out: nudged along and kpt on same pce fr over 1f out: nvr trbld ldrs* **16/1**

0 **8** *1* **Ebony Song (USA)**[20] 4803 2-9-3 0 DarryllHolland 5 50
(J Noseda) *restless in stalls: awkward leaving stalls and s.i.s: in tch towards rr: pushed along and outpcd over 2f out: no ch fnl 2f* **7/2**[2]

0230 **9** *nk* **Henrys Air**[70] 3106 2-9-0 70 PatrickHills(3) 8 49
(D G Bridgwater) *chsd ldrs: rdn 3f out: wknd u.p jst over 2f out: wl btn fnl f* **50/1**

10 *2 ¼* **Arrow Storm (USA)** 2-9-3 0 RichardKingscote 6 42
(Tom Dascombe) *s.i.s: a in rr: pushed along and no prog ent fnl 2f: n.d* **50/1**

00 **11** *11* **Mi Sun Donk**[12] 5074 2-9-3 0 JackMitchell 1 9
(B R Johnson) *racd keenly: led tl 3f out: rdn and wknd qckly ent fnl 2f: wl bhd and eased ins fnl f* **100/1**

1m 12.84s (0.94) **Going Correction** +0.05s/f (Slow) 11 Ran SP% **116.9**
Speed ratings (Par 92): **95,93,90,86,84 83,81,80,79,76 62**
toteswingers:1&2:£4.00, 1&3:£48.30, 2&3:£14.20 CSF £21.91 TOTE £16.70: £3.10, £1.10, £12.40; EX 11.90.
Owner Clipper Logistics **Bred** Ballylinch Stud **Trained** Whitsbury, Hants

FOCUS

Not a bad maiden and winners should come out of it. The main action unfolded towards the nearside of the track once the runners had reached the home straight.

NOTEBOOK

Days Of Summer(IRE) had been well backed when well beaten on her Windsor debut, but she was a different proposition this time as she travelled nicely behind the leaders and, once in front over a furlong out, knuckled down gamely to ward off the market leader. She is entitled to improve again from this and connections may look for a Listed race with her now. (op 9-1 tchd 8-1)

Fityaan had finished fourth of six against previous winners on his Newmarket debut and looked likely to score himself when moving up smoothly to challenge off the home bend, but he either couldn't or wouldn't go past the filly. It's still early days, but this did look a winning opportunity spurned. (op 5-4 tchd 4-5)

Jonelha, who showed plenty of ability on her debut before disappointing on softer ground next time, bounced back with a pleasing effort as she stayed on well in the home straight, despite hanging right, having been well back early. She now gets a mark and could be interesting in nurseries. (op 40-1)

Jinky's jockey was after him as soon as the combination left the stalls and he remained animated throughout the contest. He stayed on strongly from the home turn, however, and his effort deserves even more credit as he made his run tight against the inside rail. He should do much better in due course. Official explanation: jockey said colt ran green (op 33-1)

His Grace(IRE), runner-up at Yarmouth in his last two starts, made much of the running but the game was up for him before reaching the furlong pole. (op 11-2 tchd 7-1)

Ebony Song(USA), well beaten on his Newmarket debut, is bred to act on sand and holds entries in the Middle Park and Dewhurst amongst other big races, but having missed the break he never figured at all. Official explanation: jockey said colt missed the break (op 5-2)

Henrys Air Official explanation: jockey said colt hung badly left

5454 FORD MANOR ROAD H'CAP 6f (P)

3:30 (3:31) (Class 4) (0-80,80) 3-Y-O+ **£4,209** (£1,252; £625; £312) **Stalls** Low

Form RPR

2021 **1** **Dubai Media (CAN)**[19] 4835 3-9-8 **80** KierenFallon 11 88+
(E A L Dunlop) *dwlt: sn rcvrd and in tch on outer: outpcd and wd bnd 2f out: pushed along and gd hdwy ent fnl f: r.o wl under hands and heed to ld towards fin* **9/4**[1]

5402 **2** *¾* **Freddie's Girl (USA)**[16] 4930 3-9-3 **75** SebSanders 7 81
(Stef Higgins) *chsd ldr: rdn ent fnl 2f: drvn and ev ch ins fnl f: led wl ins fnl f: sn hdd and unable qck towards fin* **4/1**[2]

5360 **3** *nk* **Chief Exec**[138] 1238 8-9-2 **71** NeilCallan 5 76
(J R Gask) *led: rdn and qcknd ent fnl 2f: drvn jst over 1f out: hdd and no ex wl ins fnl f* **33/1**

1043 **4** *½* **Sheer Force (IRE)**[16] 4922 3-9-2 **74** (v[1]) JimCrowley 2 77
(W J Knight) *hld up in tch in midfield: rdn and swtchd lft over 1f out: ev ch ins fnl f tl unable qck and btn fnl 50yds* **11/2**

5040 **5** *3* **Requisite**[13] 5048 5-9-6 **75** (v) GeorgeBaker 9 69
(I A Wood) *hld up in tch in midfield: rdn and outpcd ent fnl 2f: kpt on same pce and no threat to ldrs fnl f* **9/1**

3213 **6** *nk* **Vhujon (IRE)**[5] 5285 5-9-0 **74** AdamBeschizza(5) 8 67
(P D Evans) *chsd ldng pair tl drvn and unable qck 2f out: one pce and wl hld fr over 1f out* **5/1**[3]

1016 **7** *2 ½* **Hinton Admiral**[19] 4836 6-8-12 **74** LeonnaMayor(7) 1 59
(P Howling) *in tch on inner: rdn and struggling whn edgd rt wl over 1f out: sn wknd and no ch fnl f* **25/1**

5140 **8** *shd* **Knightfire (IRE)**[57] 3567 3-8-11 **74** (t) JohnFahy(5) 3 59
(W R Swinburn) *hld up in last pair: rdn and effrt on inner wl over 1f out: drvn and no prog ent fnl f: n.d* **16/1**

344 **9** *½* **Punching**[23] 4684 6-9-4 **73** LiamKeniry 12 56
(C R Dore) *t.k.h: hld up in last tio: rdn and btn ent fnl 2f: nvr trbld ldrs* **20/1**

4060 **10** *nk* **Dark Eyes (IRE)**[13] 5031 3-9-4 **76** DarryllHolland 6 58
(D J Coakley) *stdd s: hld up in rr: rdn and no prog jst over 2f out: n.d* **12/1**

1m 12.74s (0.84) **Going Correction** +0.05s/f (Slow)
WFA 3 from 5yo+ 3lb 10 Ran SP% **117.9**
Speed ratings (Par 105): **96,95,94,93,89 89,86,86,85,85**
toteswingers:1&2:£4.20, 1&3:£10.50, 2&3:£17.50 CSF £10.87 CT £237.88 TOTE £2.20: £1.10, £2.10, £9.10; EX 14.80.
Owner Ahmad Al Shaikh **Bred** Kinghaven Farms Limited **Trained** Newmarket, Suffolk

■ Stewards' Enquiry : John Fahy one-day ban: used whip when out of contention (Sep 9)
Darryll Holland caution: used whip when out of contention.

FOCUS

A fair sprint handicap and there were four in a line well inside the last furlong.

Dark Eyes(IRE) Official explanation: jockey said filly missed the break

5455 FELBRIDGE CLAIMING STKS 1m 1f

4:00 (4:00) (Class 6) 3-Y-O+ **£1,706** (£503; £252) **Stalls** Low

Form RPR

5023 **1** **Lang Shining (IRE)**[7] 5233 6-9-9 83 SophieDoyle(5) 5 68
(J A Osborne) *hld up in last: hdwy on inner 2f out: pushed along to press ldr ent fnl f: rdn and qcknd to ld fnl 100yds: sn in command: comf* **2/5**[1]

6060 **2** *1 ¼* **Red Willow**[36] 4257 4-9-1 44 KirstyMilczarek 1 52
(J E Long) *t.k.h: chsd ldrs: rdn and effrt over 2f out: nt clr run and swtchd rt 2f out: pressed ldrs u.p 1f out: kpt on to go 2nd wl ins fnl f: no threat to wnr* **16/1**

3640 **3** ¾ **Bookiebasher Babe (IRE)**[10] 5159 5-8-12 47 .... JerryO'Dwyer 6 47
(M Quinn) chsd ldr: rdn and jnd ldr over 2f out: drvn to ld wl over 1f out: hdd fnl 100yds: sn no ch w wnr: lost 2nd wl ins fnl f **8/1**[3]

4050 **4** 4 ½ **Battle Study (IRE)**[10] 5159 3-8-11 55 .... JamesDoyle 3 43
(A J McCabe) hld up in last pair: rdn and effrt over 2f out: drvn and btn wl over 1f out: plugged on to go 4th ins fnl f: nvr trbld ldrs **11/2**[2]

5 1 **Guppy's Girl (IRE)** 3-8-1 0 .... JohnFahy(5) 8 36
(Miss S L Davison) t.k.h: hld up in tch: rdn and effrt over 2f out: struggling whn sltly hmpd 2f out: sn hung lft and wknd over 1f out **16/1**

0006 **6** 2 ½ **Rainsborough**[12] 5073 3-8-13 48 ....(p) LiamKeniry 7 38
(S Curran) led: rdn over 2f out: hdd wl over 1f out: hung rt and wknd qckly over 1f out **25/1**

2m 0.93s (4.33) **Going Correction** +0.475s/f (Yiel)
WFA 3 from 4yo+ 7lb **6** Ran SP% **113.5**
Speed ratings (Par 101): **99,97,97,93,92 90**
toteswingers:1&2:£2.90, 1&3:£1.90, 2&3:£3.80 CSF £9.11 TOTE £1.70: £1.40, £4.70; EX 10.00.
Owner A Taylor **Bred** Ballymacoll Stud Farm Ltd **Trained** Upper Lambourn, Berks

FOCUS
Following 33mm of rain overnight, the ground on the turf course was soft, good to soft in places. A weak and uncompetitive claimer with a predictable result.

5456 MARTIN LONG 60TH BIRTHDAY H'CAP 1m 2f
4:30 (4:30) (Class 5) (0-75,75) 3-Y-O **£2,266** (£674; £337; £168) **Stalls** Low

Form RPR

-051 **1** **Lyric Poet (USA)**[10] 5155 3-8-6 **60** 6ex ....(t) WilliamCarson 7 74+
(G C Bravery) chsd ldr tl pushed into ld 3f out: sn clr and in n.d after: pushed along and kpt on wl fnl f: easily **2/1**[1]

0452 **2** 4 **Southern Cape (IRE)**[21] 4732 3-8-12 **66** .... EddieAhern 5 72
(D J Coakley) chsd ldrs: rdn and hung rt over 2f out: chsd clr wnr ent fnl 2f: no imp but kpt on to hold 2nd fnl f **12/1**

1241 **3** ¾ **Scottish Boogie (IRE)**[15] 4964 3-9-6 **74** .... LiamKeniry 10 79
(S Kirk) t.k.h: hld up in tch in midfield: effrt but wl outpcd by wnr whn carried rt ent fnl 2f: wnt 3rd over 1f out: kpt on but no ch w wnr **7/1**

3421 **4** ½ **Higgy's Ragazzo (FR)**[10] 5146 3-9-0 **75** .... CharlesEddery(7) 1 79
(R Hannon) s.i.s and pushed along in last early: clsd and in tch 8f out but stl in last pair: rdn and edging lft ent fnl 2f: no ch w wnr after: wnt modest 4th 1f out **7/2**[2]

1-46 **5** 6 **Forgotten Army (IRE)**[80] 2816 3-9-0 **68** .... PatCosgrave 6 60
(M H Tompkins) in tch in midfield: rdn and outpcd wl over 2f out: drvn and wl btn fr over 1f out **15/2**

0-00 **6** ½ **Lady Slippers (IRE)**[29] 4492 3-8-4 **58** ow1 .... ChrisCatlin 4 49
(H J L Dunlop) led: rdn and hdd 3f out: sn no ch w wnr: wknd over 1f out **40/1**

6201 **7** 4 **Ancient Greece**[22] 4718 3-9-3 **74** ....(t) MatthewDavies(3) 3 57
(George Baker) in tch whn bdly hmpd and dropped to last trio after 1f: swtchd wd and rdn ent fnl 3f: no hdwy and wl btn fnl 2f **16/1**

2360 **8** 1 ¾ **Green Earth (IRE)**[99] 2225 3-9-3 **71** .... NeilCallan 9 50
(Mrs A J Perrett) chsd ldrs: rdn and outpcd by wnr whn edgd rt over 2f out: no ch after: wknd and wl btn wl over 1f out **33/1**

0655 **9** 22 **Whistleinthewind (IRE)**[21] 4757 3-9-3 **71** ....(b) GeorgeBaker 2 6
(G L Moore) in tch whn bdly hmpd and hit rail after 1f: bhd after: lost tch 3f out: virtually p.u fr over 1f out: t.o **6/1**[3]

2m 14.81s (4.31) **Going Correction** +0.475s/f (Yiel) **9** Ran SP% **113.1**
Speed ratings (Par 100): **101,97,97,96,92 91,88,87,69**
toteswingers:1&2:£6.10, 1&3:£5.00, 2&3:£12.50 CSF £27.38 CT £140.12 TOTE £3.40: £1.70, £3.40, £2.80; EX 26.80.
Owner George Houghton **Bred** B Wayne Hughes **Trained** Cowlinge, Suffolk

FOCUS
An ordinary handicap and something of a rough race with Southern Cape badly interfering with Ancient Greece on the inside after 2f, who in turn sent Whistleinthewind crashing into the rail. The performances of the latter pair can be forgiven to a degree.
Higgy's Ragazzo(FR) Official explanation: jockey said colt was slowly away

5457 HOLLOW LANE H'CAP 1m 2f
5:00 (5:00) (Class 6) (0-65,65) 4-Y-0+ **£2,047** (£604; £302) **Stalls** Low

Form RPR

4453 **1** **Aurora Sky (IRE)**[12] 5072 4-9-0 **58** .... LiamKeniry 6 70
(J Akehurst) in tch: rdn to chse ldrs 3f out: chsd ldr wl over 1f out: ev ch ent fnl f: drvn to ld nr fin **7/2**[1]

0430 **2** nk **Recalcitrant**[15] 4958 7-8-11 **60** .... SimonPearce(5) 3 71
(S Dow) led: rdn ent fnl 2f: hrd pressed wl over 1f out: kpt on tl hdd and no ex nr fin **8/1**

2023 **3** 2 ½ **Vinces**[20] 4793 6-9-3 **61** .... KirstyMilczarek 1 67
(T D McCarthy) chsd ldr for 2f: styd handy: rdn to chse ldr again 3f out tl wl over 1f out: drvn over 1f out: wknd fnl 100yds **6/1**

6215 **4** 1 ¾ **Diamond Twister (USA)**[8] 5208 4-9-1 **64** ....(t) KierenFox(5) 2 67
(J R Best) in tch in midfield: pushed along 5f out: effrt to chse ldng trio ent fnl 2f: wknd u.p ent fnl f **11/2**[3]

1003 **5** 9 **Beaubrav**[20] 4780 4-9-3 **61** ....(t) ChrisCatlin 9 46
(M Madgwick) s.i.s: sn niggled in rr: c wd and rdn over 3f out: no prog and wl btn fnl 2f **9/2**[2]

0006 **6** 2 **Sleep Over**[25] 4621 5-8-8 **52** ow1 .... NeilCallan 11 33
(D Morris) chsd ldrs: wnt 2nd after 2f tl 3f out: sn rdn and btn: wl bhd over 1f out **10/1**

0005 **7** 1 **Una Pelota (IRE)**[83] 2690 4-9-7 **65** ....(t) RichardKingscote 8 44
(Tom Dascombe) stdd s: hld up in last pair: rdn and no prog over 3f out: wl bhd fnl 2f **10/1**

3005 **8** 1 ¼ **Felicia**[40] 4132 5-7-9 **46** oh1 .... RichardRowe(7) 10 22
(J E Long) stdd s: in tch in midfield: hdwy on outer to chse ldrs 4f out: wd and lost pl bnd over 3f out: sn rdn and wknd: wl bhd fnl 2f **8/1**

0-56 **9** 1 ¼ **Christophers Quest**[84] 2676 5-8-7 **51** ow1 ....(t) PaulFitzsimons 4 25
(Miss N A Lloyd-Beavis) hld up in last pair: rdn and short-lived effrt over 3f out: wl bhd fr over 2f out **16/1**

40-0 **10** 8 **Bonnie Bea**[23] 4676 4-8-3 **47** ....(b[1]) AndreaAtzeni 7 5
(B I Case) in tch tl lost pl qckly over 3f out: sn wl bhd: eased ins fnl f **25/1**

2m 14.96s (4.46) **Going Correction** +0.475s/f (Yiel) **10** Ran SP% **120.2**
Speed ratings (Par 101): **101,100,98,97,90 88,87,86,85,79**
toteswingers:1&2:£8.20, 1&3:£3.40, 2&3:£11.00 CSF £33.15 CT £166.91 TOTE £3.30: £1.10, £3.30, £1.90; EX 38.60 Place 6 £ 30.75; Place 5 £6.96.
Owner M Chandler **Bred** Roland Alder & Morton Bloodstock **Trained** Epsom, Surrey

FOCUS
A moderate handicap and very few ever got into the race. The winning time was 0.15 seconds slower than the 3-y-os in the preceding handicap, but it did provide a stirring finish between the front pair.
T/Plt: £41.70 to a £1 stake. Pool:£71,545.83 - 1,251.14 winning tickets T/Qpdt: £4.10 to a £1 stake. Pool:£4,743.98 - 846.76 winning tickets SP

5458 - 5464a (Foreign Racing) - See Raceform Interactive

5284 BATH (L-H)
Friday, August 27

OFFICIAL GOING: Soft
Wind: virtually nil Weather: sunny

5465 RAJPOOT INDIAN RESTAURANT MAIDEN AUCTION STKS 5f 161y
4:45 (4:46) (Class 5) 2-Y-O **£2,072** (£616; £308; £153) **Stalls** Centre

Form RPR

0 **1** **Majestic Dubawi**[66] 3296 2-8-10 0 .... ChrisCatlin 4 82+
(M R Channon) a.p: led 2f out: r.o wl: rdn out **9/4**[1]

45 **2** 2 ¼ **Laugh Or Cry**[67] 3269 2-8-11 0 ow1 .... SebSanders 1 76
(P J Makin) hld up towards rr: hdwy over 2f out: sn rdn: chsd wnr over 1f out: kpt on but a hld fnl f **8/1**

3 2 ¾ **Whitecrest** 2-8-5 0 .... FrannyNorton 15 61
(J L Spearing) mid-div: hdwy over 2f out: rdn and ev ch wl over 1f out: kpt on same pce fnl f **33/1**

0 **4** 1 **Brave Battle**[62] 3459 2-9-0 0 .... PatrickHills(3) 2 69
(R Hannon) chsd ldrs: rdn over 2f out: styd on same pce **25/1**

64 **5** 4 ½ **Swendab (IRE)**[99] 2238 2-8-11 0 .... LukeMorris 11 48
(J G M O'Shea) mid-div: hdwy to chse ldrs over 2f out: sn rdn: styd on same pce **9/1**

02 **6** ½ **Poetically**[18] 4890 2-8-10 0 .... RichardKingscote 7 46
(J G Portman) prom: rdn over 2f out: wknd over 1f out: edgd lft fnl f **5/1**[3]

0 **7** 3 **West Leake Melody**[17] 4934 2-9-1 0 .... JimmyFortune 8 41
(B W Hills) s.i.s: towards rr: sme late hdwy: nvr a factor **12/1**

53 **8** 1 ¼ **Green Pearl (IRE)**[19] 4871 2-9-2 0 .... JimCrowley 6 38
(R M Beckett) led tl rdn over 2f out: sn btn **4/1**[2]

54 **9** ¾ **Miskin Diamond (IRE)**[17] 4921 2-8-12 0 ow1 .... IanMongan 14 31
(B Palling) chsd ldrs: rdn over 2f out: wknd over 1f out **16/1**

10 1 ¼ **Uppercut** 2-8-10 0 .... FrankieMcDonald 12 25
(W S Kittow) mid-div: rdn over 3f out: wknd 2f out **66/1**

00 **11** 1 ½ **Appyjack**[16] 4954 2-9-1 0 .... GeorgeBaker 10 25
(J S Moore) mid-div: rdn over 3f out: wknd over 2f out **20/1**

00 **12** ½ **Shostakovich (IRE)**[16] 4960 2-8-12 0 .... EddieAhern 5 29+
(S Kirk) t.k.h: hld up: hdwy over 3f out: wknd 2f out **20/1**

13 nk **Taverners Jubilee** 2-9-2 0 .... StephenCraine 13 23
(Patrick Morris) s.i.s: a towards rr **66/1**

00 **14** 13 **Commercial (IRE)**[99] 2238 2-8-13 0 .... FergusSweeney 3 —
(J A Osborne) hld up: hdwy over 3f out: sn rdn: wknd 2f out **50/1**

1m 12.59s (1.39) **Going Correction** +0.20s/f (Good) **14** Ran SP% **123.4**
Speed ratings (Par 94): **98,95,91,90,84 83,79,77,76,75 73,72,71,54**
Tote Swingers: 1&2 £5.50, 1&3 £34.30, 2&3 £30.30 CSF £19.95 TOTE £3.20: £1.40, £2.10, £9.80; EX 18.60.
Owner Jaber Abdullah **Bred** P A Mason **Trained** West Ilsley, Berks

FOCUS
Soft ground, although the times suggested it wasn't quite that bad, and they finished well strung out so easy to forgive the efforts of plenty of these. Jockeys said after the first that it was quite tacky in places.

NOTEBOOK
Majestic Dubawi, by a sire whose progeny handle cut well, showed the benefit of her encouraging Newbury debut and, having travelled sweetly down the middle of the track, found plenty for pressure in the final furlong to score fairly impressively. Clearly these conditions suit her well and an entry in the Two-Year-Old Trophy at Redcar suggests connections think a bit of her. (op 9-2)
Laugh Or Cry also has a pedigree that suggests soft ground was fine and he confirmed the promise of his first two runs by keeping on nicely and coming clear of the rest. He's qualified for nurseries now and looks capable of winning races.
Whitecrest is a cheap purchase but this was an encouraging first run.
Brave Battle stepped up markedly on his tame effort first time. (op 20-1 tchd 28-1)
Green Pearl(IRE) dropped away having been front rank early, and was disappointing. (op 3-1 tchd 5-1)
Shostakovich(IRE) Official explanation: vet said colt had been struck into on its right-fore and lost the shoe

5466 E B F & RAJPOOT AT BATH MAIDEN FILLIES' STKS 5f 11y
5:15 (5:16) (Class 5) 2-Y-O **£3,238** (£963; £481; £240) **Stalls** Centre

Form RPR

3 **1** **Yasmeena (USA)**[22] 4753 2-9-0 0 .... JimmyFortune 9 74+
(B W Hills) trckd ldrs: led wl over 2f out: kpt on wl fnl f: pushed out **7/4**[1]

6026 **2** 1 ¾ **Silca Conegliano (IRE)**[17] 4927 2-9-0 67 .... FrannyNorton 1 67
(M R Channon) chsd ldrs: rdn over 2f out: kpt on to chse wnr over 1f out but a being hld **5/1**[3]

0 **3** 1 **Shes Rosie**[115] 1793 2-9-0 0 .... LukeMorris 2 63
(J G M O'Shea) prom: rdn over 2f out: nt pce of wnr but kpt on fnl f **20/1**

4 2 ½ **Shugar Rhi (IRE)** 2-9-0 0 .... IanMongan 4 54
(B Palling) s.i.s: towards rr: rdn over 2f out: styd on fnl f: nvr trbld ldrs **50/1**

2 **5** 1 **Kilk**[24] 4675 2-9-0 0 .... FergusSweeney 6 51
(A G Newcombe) prom: rdn over 2f out: kpt on same pce fr over 1f out **4/1**[2]

5 **6** ½ **Illmindu (IRE)**[29] 4517 2-8-11 0 .... JamesMillman(3) 7 51+
(B R Millman) s.i.s: towards rr: sme late prog: nvr a danger **14/1**

7 ¾ **Arabella Fenella** 2-9-0 0 .... EddieAhern 8 46
(R M H Cowell) led tl over rdn wl over 2f out: wknd ent fnl f **12/1**

50 **8** ¾ **High Class Lady**[16] 4960 2-9-0 0 .... ChrisCatlin 5 44
(W R Swinburn) chsdldrs: sn pushed along: rdn wl over 2f out: wknd jst over 1f out **8/1**

9 2 ¼ **Deveze (IRE)** 2-9-0 0 .... SebSanders 3 36
(J W Hills) s.i.s: a towards rr **11/1**

64.27 secs (1.77) **Going Correction** +0.20s/f (Good) **9** Ran SP% **113.6**
Speed ratings (Par 91): **93,90,88,84,83 82,81,79,76**
Tote Swingers: 1&2 £4.20, 1&3 £3.70, 2&3 £13.00 CSF £10.29 TOTE £2.20: £1.10, £1.70, £8.50; EX 9.50.
Owner Hamdan Al Maktoum **Bred** Colts Neck Stable **Trained** Lambourn, Berks

FOCUS
They came up the stands' side in this modest maiden.

NOTEBOOK
Yasmeena(USA) bagged the stands' rail first and stayed on strongly to get off the mark at the second time of asking. She is the first foal of top-class sprinter La Cucaracha so she is bred to go a bit, and she built on an encouraging debut effort, racing much more professionally and seeing this out strongly. She has an entry in the Cheveley Park Stakes, suggesting connections have a very high opinion of her, and she has the potential to go a long way. (op 11-8 tchd 2-1)
Silca Conegliano(IRE) set a modest standard with an official mark of 67 and, given she appears to have run her race once again, looks the one to rate the race around. She is vulnerable to anything remotely progressive, but has the ability to win races. (tchd 9-2)

Shes Rosie hadn't been seen since her modest C&D debut in May, but she improved on that here and, given the way she stuck to her task, looks sure to improve again for a slightly stiffer test of stamina. (op 16-1)
Shugar Rhi(IRE) needs marking up for she didn't get a clear run up the stands' rail when still travelling and the front three had flown by the time she saw daylight. She picked up quite nicely without being given too hard a time and obviously has ability. (op 33-1)
Kilk took a step backwards from her good Chepstow debut and perhaps the slower conditions here were to blame. (op 15-2)
Illmindu(IRE) Official explanation: jockey said filly missed the break

5467 RAJPOOT.COM H'CAP — 1m 5f 22y
5:45 (5:46) (Class 5) (0-70,72) 3-Y-O — £2,007 (£597; £298; £149) Stalls High

Form — RPR

4214 **1** **Sula Two**[15] 5008 3-9-4 **66**.......... GeorgeBaker 6 — 73
(R J Hodges) *mid-div: hdwy over 2f out: sn rdn: chal jst over 1f out: edgd lft: led ins fnl f: styd on gamely: drvn out* **4/1**[2]

2301 **2** *nk* **Raktiman (IRE)**[22] 4728 3-9-5 **67**..........(p) RichardKingscote 5 — 74
(Tom Dascombe) *in tch: rdn over 2f out: chal ent fnl f: styd on but no ex towards fin* **11/1**

3544 **3** *1 3/4* **Chicane**[16] 4972 3-9-3 **65**.......... LiamJones 8 — 69
(W J Haggas) *led after 1f: rdn 3f out: hrd pressed fr over 1f out: hdd ins fnl f: no ex* **7/1**

430 **4** *nk* **Elvira Madigan**[23] 4698 3-9-7 **69**.......... JimmyFortune 1 — 72
(A M Balding) *mid-div: hdwy whn rdn wl over 2f out to chse ldrs: styd on fnl f* **5/1**[3]

4431 **5** *3/4* **Minikin (IRE)**[9] 5208 3-9-10 **72** 6ex.......... JimCrowley 3 — 74+
(H Morrison) *hld up towards rr: rdn wl over 2f out: nt gng pce to get on terms: styd on fnl f* **5/2**[1]

-400 **6** *1 3/4* **Carnival Time (IRE)**[15] 4992 3-8-3 **51**..........(p) LukeMorris 7 — 51
(C G Cox) *t.k.h: trckd ldrs: rdn wl over 2f out: styd on same pce fnl fr over 1f out* **25/1**

3320 **7** *1 3/4* **Septemberintherain**[41] 1433 3-9-7 **69**..........(v) EddieAhern 4 — 66
(R A Mills) *rdn over 2f out: nvr gng pce to cl: a towards rr* **12/1**

-013 **8** *1 1/4* **Killusty Fancy (IRE)**[16] 4965 3-9-1 **68**.......... BillyCray(5) 9 — 63
(D J S Ffrench Davis) *in tch: rdn over 3f out: wknd over 1f out* **5/1**[3]

5-66 **9** *6* **Groove Master**[29] 4519 3-8-3 **51**.......... FrankieMcDonald 10 — 37
(A King) *led for 1f: chsd ldr: rdn wl over 2f out: wknd over 1f out* **50/1**

-004 **10** *9* **Lady Christie**[17] 4925 3-8-2 **50** oh5.......... FrannyNorton 2 — 23
(M Blanshard) *a towards rr* **66/1**

2m 58.21s (6.21) **Going Correction** +0.275s/f (Good) — **10** Ran SP% **117.7**
Speed ratings (Par 100): **91,90,89,89,89 88,86,86,82,76**
Tote Swingers: 1&2 £8.30, 1&3 £3.50, 2&3 £5.80 CSF £47.10 CT £302.21 TOTE £4.60: £1.10, £4.10, £3.20; EX 61.50.
Owner Richard Prince **Bred** D R Tucker **Trained** Charlton Mackrell, Somerset

FOCUS
Just an ordinary staying handicap and the pace was moderate.

5468 RAJPOOT CLASSIC CUISINE H'CAP — 1m 3f 144y
6:15 (6:15) (Class 6) (0-60,58) 4-Y-O+ — £1,813 (£539; £269; £134) Stalls Low

Form — RPR

6064 **1** **Deejan (IRE)**[15] 4990 5-9-2 **56**.......... NeilChalmers 3 — 67
(B Palling) *led: rdn and hdd 3f out: rallied gamely: led jst ins fnl f: styd on: hld on wl* **8/1**

60-2 **2** *nk* **Dancing Storm**[24] 4676 7-9-3 **57**.......... IanMongan 7 — 67
(W S Kittow) *hld up in last pair: hdwy over 3f out: rdn over 2f out: ev ch ent fnl f: styd on: hld nr fin* **9/4**[2]

3212 **3** *2 3/4* **Stage Acclaim (IRE)**[12] 5119 5-9-3 **57**..........(p) SebSanders 5 — 62
(Dr R D P Newland) *prom: led 3f out: sn rdn and hrd pressed: hdd jst ins fnl f: no ex* **6/4**[1]

1254 **4** *2 1/4* **Dazzling Begum**[10] 5180 5-9-4 **58**.......... ChrisCatlin 1 — 60
(J Pearce) *in tch: rdn wl over 2f out: nt pce to chal: styd on fnl f* **7/1**[3]

5320 **5** *hd* **Foxtrot Bravo (IRE)**[21] 4780 4-8-1 **46**..........(b) AmyBaker(5) 6 — 47
(Miss S L Davison) *trckd ldrs: rdn over 4f out: ev ch 2f out: sn hung lft: styd on same pce* **14/1**

5610 **6** *28* **Ocean Of Peace (FR)**[18] 4913 7-8-9 **49**.......... LukeMorris 2 — —
(M R Bosley) *awkward leaving stalls: a last: rdn 3f out: wknd over 2f out: eased fnl f* **10/1**

2m 33.41s (2.81) **Going Correction** +0.275s/f (Good) — **6** Ran SP% **110.1**
Speed ratings (Par 101): **101,100,98,97,97 78**
Tote Swingers: 1&2 £3.80, 1&3 £3.20, 2&3 £1.30 CSF £25.36 CT £38.75 TOTE £16.20: £9.70, £1.10; EX 32.00.
Owner The Bill & Ben Partnership **Bred** Vincent T Lawler **Trained** Tredodridge, Vale Of Glamorgan

FOCUS
A moderate handicap run at a fair gallop in the conditions.
Ocean Of Peace(FR) Official explanation: jockey said gelding was unsuited by the soft (good to soft places) ground

5469 DIGIBET.COM H'CAP — 1m 5y
6:45 (6:47) (Class 6) (0-65,65) 3-Y-O — £1,619 (£481; £240; £120) Stalls Low

Form — RPR

0122 **1** **Madame Excelerate**[5] 5337 3-9-6 **64**.......... TomMcLaughlin 15 — 74
(W M Brisbourne) *a.p: led over 4f out: rdn and hrd pressed fr 3f out: kpt on gamely: hld on wl: all out* **9/4**[1]

6555 **2** *nk* **Song To The Moon (IRE)**[16] 4959 3-9-7 **65**..........(v) JimmyFortune 7 — 74
(A M Balding) *led for over 3f: remained pressing wnr: hrd rdn fr over 2f out: ev ch thrght fnl f: hld nr fin* **9/2**[2]

0020 **3** *2 3/4* **Qaraqum (USA)**[16] 4958 3-8-11 **55**.......... EddieAhern 9 — 58
(D J Coakley) *mid-div: hdwy 3f out: sn rdn to chse ldrs: kpt on ins fnl f: snatched 3rd fnl stride* **9/1**

6035 **4** *nse* **Michael's Nook**[22] 4732 3-8-11 **55**.......... IanMongan 10 — 58
(W S Kittow) *trckd ldrs: rdn and ev ch wl over 2f out: no ex ent fnl f: lost 3rd fnl stride* **8/1**

615 **5** *1 1/4* **Tallawalla (IRE)**[4] 5361 3-8-5 **49**.......... ChrisCatlin 12 — 49
(M R Channon) *trckd ldrs: rdn over 2f out: kpt on but nt pce to chal* **7/1**

0021 **6** *1* **Belle Park**[15] 4987 3-9-0 **58**.......... JamieMackay 3 — 56
(Karen George) *trckd ldrs: rdn over 3f out: nt pce to chal: fdd ins fnl f* **13/2**[3]

406 **7** *2 3/4* **Sunset Place**[18] 4906 3-9-7 **65**.......... LukeMorris 4 — 56
(C G Cox) *mid-div: rdn over 3f out: no imp* **16/1**

0600 **8** *3* **Midnight M**[11] 5162 3-8-2 **46** oh1..........(t) FrannyNorton 2 — 30
(Rae Guest) *s.i.s: a towards rr* **20/1**

5005 **9** *2 1/4* **Future Regime (IRE)**[24] 4680 3-8-4 **48**.......... CathyGannon 8 — 27
(Patrick Morris) *slowly away: a towards rr* **50/1**

-006 **10** *3 1/2* **Knowledgeable**[15] 4989 3-7-11 **46** oh1..........(p) SimonPearce(5) 6 — 17
(B Palling) *lost pl on bnd over 4f out: mainly towards rr* **33/1**

060 **11** *4* **Avon Rock**[3] 5379 3-7-12 **49**..........(t) KatiaScallan(7) 5 — 11
(A J Lidderdale) *mid-div: rdn 3f out: sn wknd* **40/1**

0005 **12** *20* **Fashion Tycoon (IRE)**[15] 4989 3-8-3 **50**.......... AndrewHeffernan(3) 1 — —
(M F Harris) *mid-div: rdn 3f out: sn wknd* **25/1**

0040 **P** **First Term**[80] 2844 3-9-2 **60**.......... FergusSweeney 16 — —
(M S Saunders) *slowly away: sn detached: p.u over 3f out: lame* **25/1**

1m 43.36s (2.56) **Going Correction** +0.275s/f (Good) — **13** Ran SP% **121.6**
Speed ratings (Par 98): **98,97,94,94,93 92,89,86,84,81 77,57,—**
Tote Swingers: 1&2 £5.50, 1&3 £8.10, 2&3 £8.80 CSF £10.91 CT £79.73 TOTE £3.20: £1.10, £2.80, £3.20; EX 16.60.
Owner Equiform Nutrition Limited **Bred** Brown Moss Stud **Trained** Great Ness, Shropshire

FOCUS
Not a great race and it was dominated by those that raced on or close to the pace.
Future Regime(IRE) Official explanation: jockey said filly was slowly away
First Term Official explanation: vet said filly pulled up lame right-hind

5470 LAS IGUANAS H'CAP — 5f 11y
7:15 (7:15) (Class 5) (0-70,67) 3-Y-O — £2,007 (£597; £298; £149) Stalls Centre

Form — RPR

-560 **1** **Madam Isshe**[15] 4989 3-8-6 **52**.......... LiamJones 5 — 58
(M S Saunders) *a.p: rdn over 2f out: edgd rt over 1f out: narrow advantage whn edgd lft ins fnl f: kpt on: all out* **16/1**

3160 **2** *hd* **Sweet Avon**[133] 1347 3-9-0 **60**.......... ShaneKelly 9 — 65
(Matthew Salaman) *chsd ldrs: rdn to chal 2f out: ev ch ent fnl f: kpt on but no ex* **6/1**

3022 **3** *1 1/2* **Rebecca Romero**[23] 4720 3-8-5 **51**.......... CathyGannon 6 — 51+
(D J Coakley) *little slowly away and squeezed out s: sn pushed along: hdwy to chse ldrs over 2f out: kpt on fnl f but no ex fnl 100yds* **10/3**[2]

5003 **4** *1* **Nepotism**[36] 4284 3-9-7 **67**.......... TomMcLaughlin 1 — 63
(M S Saunders) *prom: led 3f out: rdn over 2f out: hdd ent fnl f: no ex fnl 100yds* **5/2**[1]

2200 **5** *1* **Pherousa**[22] 4754 3-9-3 **63**.......... FrannyNorton 2 — 56
(M Blanshard) *chsd ldrs: rdn wl over 2f out: nvr gng pce to get on terms* **4/1**[3]

50-0 **6** *4* **Royal Box**[11] 5146 3-9-2 **67**.......... SophieDoyle(5) 7 — 46
(D Burchell) *sn outpcd in rr: nvr on terms* **12/1**

2464 **7** *9* **Morgans Choice**[17] 4920 3-8-11 **60**.......... JackDean(3) 8 — 7
(J L Spearing) *wnt sltly rt s: led tl 3f out: sn rdn: wknd over 1f out* **7/1**

00-0 **8** *9* **Chill Out Charley**[20] 4835 3-8-2 **48** oh3.......... NeilChalmers 4 — —
(J J Bridger) *a outpcd in rr* **33/1**

63.46 secs (0.96) **Going Correction** +0.20s/f (Good) — **8** Ran SP% **115.0**
Speed ratings (Par 100): **100,99,97,95,94 87,73,58**
Tote Swingers: 1&2 £23.20, 1&3 £11.90, 2&3 £2.10 CSF £108.39 CT £405.80 TOTE £22.70: £5.40, £1.20, £1.10; EX 160.10.
Owner M S Saunders **Bred** Miss Jackie Penny **Trained** Green Ore, Somerset

FOCUS
A modest contest but a close finish with four in line entering the final furlong.
Madam Isshe Official explanation: trainer said, regarding apparent improvement in form, that the filly appeared better suited by 5f and the soft (good to soft places) ground

5471 UNIVERSITY OF BATH PARADE BAR H'CAP — 5f 11y
7:45 (7:46) (Class 6) (0-60,60) 4-Y-O+ — £1,489 (£443; £221; £110) Stalls Centre

Form — RPR

5020 **1** **Namir (IRE)**[33] 4415 8-9-4 **60**..........(vt) JimCrowley 4 — 68
(H J Evans) *rrd leaving stalls and squeezed out: towards rr: hdwy 2f out: led ins fnl f: r.o strly: rdn out* **4/1**[2]

4062 **2** *1 3/4* **Commandingpresence (USA)**[13] 5076 4-8-13 **55**.......... NeilChalmers 3 — 57
(J J Bridger) *sn pushed along towards rr: hdwy 2f out: sn rdn: r.o to chse wnr ins fnl f but a hld* **11/2**[3]

5352 **3** *1/2* **The Jailer**[21] 4778 7-8-11 **56**..........(p) RussKennemore(3) 8 — 56
(J G M O'Shea) *trckd ldrs rdn to ld on stand-side rails wl over 1f out: hdd ins fnl f: no ex* **5/2**[1]

-005 **4** *1 1/4* **Like For Like (IRE)**[21] 4776 4-8-4 **46** oh1.......... FrankieMcDonald 7 — 42
(R J Hodges) *trckd ldrs: rdn and kpt on same pce fnl 2f* **9/1**

0400 **5** *1/2* **Mazzola**[45] 3994 4-8-12 **54**..........(p) ChrisCatlin 9 — 48
(J M Bradley) *in tch: travelling wl to chal 2f out: sn rdn: nt qckn* **15/2**

000 **6** *1* **Know No Fear**[4] 5377 5-8-8 **57**..........(p) KatiaScallan(7) 6 — 48
(A J Lidderdale) *in tch: rdn over 2f out: nt pce to chal* **7/1**

0064 **7** *1 1/2* **Joss Stick**[13] 5075 5-8-1 **46** oh1..........(p) AndrewHeffernan(3) 2 — 31
(J J Bridger) *wnt rt s: in tch: rdn over 2f out: no imp: fdd ins fnl f* **20/1**

0-00 **8** *4* **Orpen Lady**[12] 5112 4-8-4 **46** oh1.......... CathyGannon 1 — 17
(J M Bradley) *trckd ldrs: effrt over 2f out: wknd fnl f* **16/1**

0040 **9** *8* **Hatman Jack (IRE)**[158] 967 4-8-10 **52**.......... FergusSweeney 5 — —
(B G Powell) *led: rdn and hdd wl over 1f out: sn wknd* **16/1**

63.37 secs (0.87) **Going Correction** +0.20s/f (Good) — **9** Ran SP% **114.7**
Speed ratings (Par 101): **101,98,97,95,94 93,90,84,71**
Tote Swingers: 1&2 £3.30, 1&3 £2.10, 2&3 £3.40 CSF £26.12 CT £65.33 TOTE £5.50: £1.30, £1.10, £1.10; EX 23.80 Place 6: £94.32 Place 5: £48.03.
Owner ownaracehorse.co.uk (Shakespeare) **Bred** B Kennedy **Trained** Broadwas, Worcs

FOCUS
Weak form and winning doesn't come naturally to any of these.
The Jailer Official explanation: jockey said mare hung right-handed
Know No Fear Official explanation: jockey said gelding lost a near-fore shoe
T/Plt: £151.30 to a £1 stake. Pool:£44,677.16 - 21.50 winning tickets T/Qpdt: £35.70 to a £1 stake. Pool:£4,406.92 - 91.20 winning tickets TM

5440 FFOS LAS (L-H)
Friday, August 27

OFFICIAL GOING: Flat course - good to soft (7.7); jumps courses - good (good to soft in places; 7.9)
Wind: Fresh across Weather: Fine

5472 TOTEPLACEPOT NURSERY — 6f
2:00 (2:04) (Class 4) (0-85,81) 2-Y-O — £4,533 (£1,348; £674; £336) Stalls High

Form — RPR

4010 **1** **Veil Of Night**[26] 4623 2-8-1 **68**.......... HarryBentley(7) 4 — 70
(D Haydn Jones) *sn prom: rdn over 1f out: r.o to ld wl ins fnl f* **22/1**

1252 **2** *3/4* **Captain Dimitrios**[26] 4615 2-9-0 **74**.......... CathyGannon 7 — 74
(P D Evans) *led to 1/2-way: led again over 1f out: hdd ins fnl f: r.o* **7/2**[2]

6415 **3** *nk* **Arctic Mirage**[21] 4783 2-9-1 **75**.......... ShaneKelly 3 — 74
(M Blanshard) *s.i.s: sn pushed along in rr: hdwy over 1f out: sn rdn: r.o* **11/1**

553 **4** *hd* **Red Marling (IRE)**[56] 3624 2-9-1 **75**............................ RobertWinston 9 73
(B W Hills) *chsd ldrs: rdn over 1f out: edgd lft and led ins fnl f: sn hdd and unable qck* **9/4**[1]

0513 **5** *1 ½* **Rosina Grey**[16] 4955 2-9-1 **80**.. SophieDoyle(5) 5 74
(B R Millman) *dwlt: in rr tl hdwy over 1f out: r.o: nt rch ldrs* **15/2**

0104 **6** *½* **Reginald Claude**[17] 4935 2-8-7 **74**........................ MatthewCosham(7) 2 66
(M D I Usher) *hld up: rdn 1/2-way: nt clr run over 2f out: styd on same pce fr over 1f out* **10/1**

031 **7** *¾* **Cruise Tothelimit (IRE)**[21] 4782 2-9-7 **81**.................... StephenCraine 1 71
(Patrick Morris) *hung lft almost thrght: chsd ldrs: led 1/2-way: rdn and hdd over 1f out: no ex ins fnl f* **6/1**[3]

5260 **8** *9* **Good Morning Dubai (IRE)**[23] 4696 2-9-1 **75**.......(b[1]) EddieCreighton 8 38
(B J Meehan) *plld hrd and prom: rdn over 2f out: wknd over 1f out* **16/1**

011 **9** *15* **Tedious**[43] 4040 2-9-1 **75**.. JamesDoyle 6 —
(S Kirk) *chsd ldrs: rdn over 2f out: sn wknd* **8/1**

1m 10.96s (1.26) **Going Correction** +0.125s/f (Good) **9** Ran SP% **117.8**
Speed ratings (Par 96): **96,95,94,94,92 91,90,78,58**
Tote Swingers: 1&2 £11.80, 1&3 £11.10, 2&3 £16.00 CSF £99.77 CT £926.51 TOTE £23.80: £4.30, £1.50, £4.00; EX 115.80 Trifecta £200.20 Part won. Pool: £270.60 - 0.41 winning units..
Owner Mrs M L Parry **Bred** Mrs M L Parry **Trained** Efail Isaf, Rhondda C Taff

FOCUS
A mixed meeting to end the three-day 'festival' at the track. The ground had dried out from the previous days, and was officially changed to Good to soft on the Flat track before racing. A quite competitive nursery and they appeared to go a decent pace early but there was a surprise result.

NOTEBOOK
Veil Of Night had beaten today's runner-up at Leicester earlier in the season but, after a below-par effort on her second start, was 3lb better off. She settled in behind the leaders before hitting the front over a furlong out, then battled on gamely when challenged on either side. Clearly suited by a little cut in the ground, she looks to have more to offer. (op 20-1 tchd 25-1)
Captain Dimitrios is a consistent sort and ran his race, despite meeting the winner on worse times compared with their previous meeting. He raced up with the pace throughout and probably sets the standard. (op 9-2)
Arctic Mirage, another who appreciates some cut, came to have his chance on the outside entering the final furlong but could not sustain his effort. (op 14-1)
Red Marling(IRE) was a well-backed favourite on this nursery debut. Held up early, he arrived on the scene at the right time but had no more to offer, so possibly the softer ground was not ideal. (op 10-3)
Rosina Grey has been progressive of late but missed the break and was hampered leaving the stalls. She ran on late and can be given a chance to atone. (op 8-1 tchd 7-1)
Cruise Tothelimit(IRE), who made all when scoring on his turf debut last time, was on his toes beforehand and was too keen in front, lugging to the left under restraint. He was also taken on for the lead but, after being headed, did not drop away until late on. (op 9-2 tchd 4-1)
Tedious took on the top weight for the early lead and faded quickly once put under pressure. He probably needs the minimum trip and a sound surface on turf. (op 7-1)

5473 UHY PEACHEYS H'CAP 6f
2:30 (2:35) (Class 5) (0-70,70) 4-Y-0+ **£3,238** (£963; £481; £240) **Stalls** High

Form RPR

0360 **1** **George Thisby**[49] 3863 4-9-2 **65**.. HayleyTurner 5 73
(B R Millman) *chsd ldr: led over 1f out: rdn and hung rt ins fnl f: r.o* **6/1**

0064 **2** *1 ¼* **Desert Icon (IRE)**[13] 5076 4-9-0 **70**............................(v) HarryBentley(7) 6 74
(W J Knight) *plld hrd and prom: rdn over 1f out: hung rt ins fnl f: r.o* **3/1**[3]

0011 **3** *1 ¼* **Gracie's Games**[14] 5055 4-8-3 **57** ow2....................(v) TobyAtkinson(5) 2 57
(R J Price) *led: rdn: hung lft and hdd over 1f out: hung rt and styd on same pce ins fnl f* **11/4**[2]

0000 **4** *nk* **Croeso Ynol**[5] 5326 4-7-11 **51** oh6................................ SophieDoyle(5) 3 50
(H J Evans) *hld up: hdwy over 2f out: rdn and hung lft ins fnl f: styd on same pce* **16/1**

4505 **5** *¾* **Memphis Man**[13] 5076 7-8-9 **65**.............................. MatthewCosham(7) 1 62
(P D Evans) *sn prom: drvn along 1/2-way: hung lft ins fnl f: styd on same pce* **9/1**

20/1 **6** *1 ¼* **San Jose City (IRE)**[2] 5426 5-9-2 **65**........................(p) RobertWinston 4 58
(Muredach Kelly, Ire) *hld up: rdn over 2f out: edgd rt ins fnl f: nvr trbld ldrs: b.b.v* **9/4**[1]

1m 11.04s (1.34) **Going Correction** +0.125s/f (Good) **6** Ran SP% **112.6**
Speed ratings (Par 103): **99,97,95,95,94 92**
Tote Swingers: 1&2 £4.80, 1&3 £3.40, 2&3 £1.10 CSF £24.31 TOTE £8.00: £4.20, £2.10; EX 26.60.
Owner Robert Thisby **Bred** Meon Valley Stud **Trained** Kentisbeare, Devon

FOCUS
A small field for this modest sprint handicap but they ended up spread right across the track and the time was fractionally slower than the opening nursery. The first two came more towards the stands' side.
San Jose City(IRE) Official explanation: trainer said gelding bled from the nose

5474 FRUBOB MAIDEN FILLIES' STKS 1m (R)
3:05 (3:07) (Class 4) 3-Y-0+ **£4,533** (£1,348; £674; £336) **Stalls** Low

Form RPR

423 **1** **Sennockian Storm (USA)**[27] 4601 3-8-12 75........... J-PGuillambert 11 73
(M Johnston) *led: hdd 7f out: chsd ldr tl led again over 2f out: rdn over 1f out: styd on wl* **15/8**[1]

0 **2** *2 ½* **Land And Sea**[14] 5038 3-8-12 0.................................. RobertWinston 6 67
(B W Hills) *s.i.s: sn prom: rdn over 2f out: chsd wnr and hung lft over 1f out: styd on same pce fnl f* **11/4**[2]

3 *1 ¾* **Holiday Snap**[284] 4-9-1 0.. EJMcNamara(3) 8 63
(Mrs Mary Hambro) *led 7f out: rdn and hdd over 2f out: edgd lft over 1f out: no ex fnl f* **10/1**

044 **4** *½* **Only You Maggie (IRE)**[18] 4906 3-8-10 63 ow3......... MarkCoumbe(5) 4 65
(W G Harrison) *sn pushed along in rr: styd on fr over 1f out: nt rch ldrs* **9/1**

00 **5** *½* **Spring Stock**[14] 5038 3-8-9 0...................................... RussKennemore(3) 1 61
(B G Powell) *s.i.s: sn pushed along in rr: styd on appr fnl f: nvr rchd ldrs* **20/1**

6 **6** *3 ¼* **Mackenzie Spiers**[34] 4364 3-8-12 0................................ JamesDoyle 10 53
(B R Millman) *in rr and pushed along: rdn over 3f out: nvr on terms* **25/1**

05 **7** *7* **Swingle**[14] 5057 3-8-12 0.. AndreaAtzeni 7 37
(D Haydn Jones) *chsd ldrs: rdn over 2f out: sn wknd* **12/1**

00 **8** *7* **Wizzacus**[37] 4249 3-8-7 0.. TobyAtkinson(5) 9 21
(R J Price) *hld up: rdn over 3f out: a in rr* **40/1**

40- **9** *5* **Enjoyment**[387] 4666 3-8-12 0.. HayleyTurner 3 10
(M L W Bell) *chsd ldrs tl rdn and wknd over 2f out: wknd over 1f out* **7/2**[3]

1m 42.32s (1.82) **Going Correction** +0.325s/f (Good)
WFA 3 from 4yo+ 6lb **9** Ran SP% **121.5**
Speed ratings (Par 102): **103,100,98,98,97 94,87,80,75**
Tote Swingers: 1&2 £2.00, 1&3 £4.00, 2&3 £6.00 CSF £7.42 TOTE £2.10: £1.10, £1.70, £2.80; EX 8.20 Trifecta £36.40 Pool: £417.43 - 8.47 winning units..
Owner The Vine Accord **Bred** Overbrook Farm **Trained** Middleham Moor, N Yorks

FOCUS
A modest maiden for fillies with the majority of the field looking likely to find their level once qualified for handicaps. The pace was pretty sound and they finished fairly strung out.

5475 TOTESWINGER FLEXI BETTING H'CAP 1m 4f (R)
3:40 (3:40) (Class 3) (0-95,93) 3-Y-0+ **£7,569** (£2,265; £1,132; £566) **Stalls** Low

Form RPR

51 **1** **Herculean**[18] 4893 3-8-12 **84**.. ShaneKelly 4 94+
(W J Haggas) *hld up: hdwy over 3f out: led over 1f out: hung lft ins fnl f: r.o* **7/2**[3]

3311 **2** *2 ¾* **Resentful Angel**[23] 4694 5-9-11 **87**........................... RobertWinston 7 92
(Pat Eddery) *prom: chsd ldr over 8f out: led over 3f out: rdn and hdd over 1f out: styd on same pce* **5/1**

1104 **3** *½* **Jutland**[10] 5188 3-9-7 **93**.. J-PGuillambert 3 97
(M Johnston) *chsd ldr over 3f: remained handy: rdn over 4f out: no ex fnl f* **6/4**[1]

6311 **4** *2* **Denton (NZ)**[21] 4804 7-9-4 **85**..................................(t) SimonPearce(5) 6 86
(J R Gask) *led: hdd over 3f out: sn rdn: wknd fnl f* **2/1**[2]

2m 38.58s (1.78) **Going Correction** +0.325s/f (Good)
WFA 3 from 4yo+ 10lb **4** Ran SP% **112.2**
Speed ratings (Par 107): **107,105,104,103**
CSF £18.83 TOTE £3.10; EX 12.40.
Owner Highclere Thoroughbred Racing Tudor Min **Bred** Meon Valley Stud **Trained** Newmarket, Suffolk

FOCUS
Three withdrawals cut the field for this decent handicap almost in half. The pace was relatively steady until the straight.

NOTEBOOK
Herculean ◆, by far the least experienced runner in the line-up, missed the break but was able to settle at the back. It was clear 2f out he was going best of all, but his rider did not ask him to settle the issue until entering the last furlong. He came away to win decisively and looks to have more improvement to come. He should prove a decent prospect for next season. (op 9-4)
Resentful Angel, a five-time winner on Polytrack in the last year, was racing off a mark 13lb higher than when last seen on turf. She was never far away and stuck to her task in the straight to hold off the favourite, but the winner was far too good. (op 9-2)
Jutland has some solid form this season and was sent off favourite, but this was his first try on ground this soft and he did not look as effective. (op 9-4)
Denton(NZ) came into this in good form but had gone up 12lb for his last two successes and was up in grade. He made the running and tried to kick from the front but weakened out of contention once the winner went for home. (op 9-4)

5358 HAMILTON (R-H)
Friday, August 27

OFFICIAL GOING: Good (8.9)
Wind: Breezy, across Weather: Overcast

5476 BUILDING CRAFTSMEN NURSERY 6f 5y
5:35 (5:35) (Class 4) (0-80,79) 2-Y-0 **£5,180** (£1,541; £770; £384) **Stalls** Low

Form RPR

252 **1** **Azzurra Du Caprio (IRE)**[10] 5187 2-9-4 **76**.................... PJMcDonald 3 79
(B M R Haslam) *cl up: led and rdn over 1f out: hrd pressed ins fnl f: kpt on gamely* **4/1**[3]

6430 **2** *nk* **Top Care (USA)**[20] 4851 2-9-3 **75**.. GregFairley 4 77
(M Johnston) *dwlt: in tch: rdn over 2f out: hdwy and ev ch ins fnl f: jst hld* **7/1**

035 **3** *1 ½* **Barista (IRE)**[10] 5187 2-8-8 **66**.. SamHitchcott 2 64
(M R Channon) *trckd ldrs: rdn over 2f out: kpt on u.p fnl f* **11/4**[2]

3400 **4** *4* **Meandmyshadow**[10] 5187 2-9-4 **76**......................... SilvestreDeSousa 1 62
(A D Brown) *led to over 1f out: wknd ins fnl f* **11/1**

314 **5** *2 ¾* **Bahamian Sunset**[27] 4578 2-9-4 **79**............................ BarryMcHugh(3) 5 56
(R A Fahey) *t.k.h: cl up tl rdn and wknd over 1f out* **6/4**[1]

1m 13.18s (0.98) **Going Correction** +0.075s/f (Good) **5** Ran SP% **107.5**
Speed ratings (Par 96): **96,95,93,88,84**
CSF £27.50 TOTE £3.70: £1.20, £4.90; EX 28.80.
Owner Blue Lion Racing VIII **Bred** Glending Bloodstock **Trained** Middleham Moor, N Yorks
■ Stewards' Enquiry : P J McDonald one-day ban: used whip with excessive frequency (Sep 10)

FOCUS
A fair nursery.

NOTEBOOK
Azzurra Du Caprio(IRE) had finished second in a competitive nursery at York last week and went one better off the same mark, carrying her head a bit to one side under pressure but pulling out more when the runner-up got upsides. She shouldn't go up much more than the 2lb she's already due to rise for York, and will continue to be of interest. (op 7-2)
Top Care(USA) wasted little time putting a blip on his nursery bow behind him, making a well-treated rival pull out all the stops. He's in excellent hands and there could easily be more to come from him after just a handful of starts, with 7f likely to suit him before long. (op 8-1)
Barista(IRE) has had a fair bit of racing but this isn't the first time he's shaped as if he's got a win in him off this sort of mark, particularly when tried at 7f, once again leaving the impression that trip is sure to suit him. (op 3-1 tchd 9-4)
Meandmyshadow faded after cutting out the running, and needs to come down in the weights on the evidence of her two nursery starts. (op 10-1 tchd 12-1)
Bahamian Sunset had gone the right way before this, her fourth in a Glorious Goodwood nursery almost certainly solid form, and she can't have been right, fading tamely. She deserves another chance. Official explanation: trainer had no explanation for the poor form shown (tchd 13-8)

5477 DALUCIANO RESTAURANT & BAR H'CAP 5f 4y
6:05 (6:06) (Class 5) (0-70,73) 3-Y-0+ **£3,238** (£963; £481; £240) **Stalls** Centre

Form RPR

0502 **1** **Cayman Fox**[4] 5362 5-8-10 **54**.. PJMcDonald 7 67
(Miss L A Perratt) *mde all: rdn over 1f out: styd on strly fnl f* **5/4**[1]

0413 **2** *1 ¾* **Angelo Poliziano**[54] 3711 4-9-5 **66**.........................(v) BarryMcHugh(3) 4 73
(Mrs A Duffield) *hld up: hdwy over 2f out: hung rt: edgd lft and chsd wnr ins fnl f: r.o* **13/2**[3]

4400 **3** *2 ¼* **Berbice (IRE)**[14] 5027 5-9-11 **69**.. LNewman 1 67
(Miss L A Perratt) *hld up in tch: effrt and rdn over 1f out: kpt on same pce fnl f* **9/1**

-000 **4** *hd* **Sharp Bullet (IRE)**[9] 5198 4-9-9 **67**................................(b) GregFairley 5 65
(Bruce Hellier) *chsd wnr: effrt and rdn over 1f out: no ex ins fnl f* **33/1**

0066 **5** *3 ¼* **Rothesay Dancer**[9] 5212 7-9-0 **65**.................................. PaulNorton(7) 3 51
(J S Goldie) *hld up: outpcd 1/2-way: hdwy and edgd rt 1f out: nvr rchd ldrs: fin lame* **7/1**

0666 **6** *7* **Bombay Mist**[2] 5410 3-8-4 **50** oh5....................................(e) PaulEddery 2 —
(R C Guest) *chsd ldrs tl rdn and wknd wl over 1f out* **28/1**

3231 **7** 33 **Mandarin Spirit (IRE)**[8] 5240 10-10-1 **73** 6ex.......(b) SilvestreDeSousa 6 —
(Miss L A Perratt) *rrd and blindfold stl on as stalls opened: t.o thrght* **11/4**[2]

59.97 secs (-0.03) **Going Correction** +0.075s/f (Good)
WFA 3 from 4yo+ 2lb **7** Ran SP% **113.3**
Speed ratings (Par 103): **103,100,96,96,91 79,27**
Tote Swingers:1&2:£2.20, 1&3:£3.00, 2&3:£5.80 CSF £9.99 TOTE £2.70: £1.40, £3.20; EX 8.20.
Owner R R Whitton **Bred** R R Whitton **Trained** East Kilbride, South Lanarks

FOCUS
Essentially a weak handicap, particularly with second favourite Mandarin Spirit effectively taking no part after rearing as the stalls opened.
Rothesay Dancer Official explanation: jockey said, regarding running and riding, that his orders were to jump handy, keep the mare balanced and and gradually make a run from about 2 1/2f out, adding that it broke well and attempted to get cover, but was outpaced from 3f out and stayed on one paced to the line; vet said mare returned lame right-fore.
Mandarin Spirit(IRE) Official explanation: jockey said gelding reared as stalls opened and was unable to remove blindfold

5478 VARIETY CLUB OPEN MAIDEN STKS — 1m 1f 36y
6:35 (6:35) (Class 5) 3-4-Y-O **£3,238** (£963; £481; £240) **Stalls** High

Form RPR
5245 **1** **Tamarillo Grove (IRE)**[21] 4784 3-9-3 73................. SilvestreDeSousa 6 77
(B Smart) *mde all: shkn up over 2f out: kpt on strly to go clr over 1f out* **8/13**[1]
0 **2** 8 **Wild Geese (IRE)**[18] 4906 3-9-3 0....................................... GregFairley 1 60
(M Johnston) *cl up: rdn and rn green fr 3f out: no imp fnl 2f* **3/1**[2]
6-4 **3** 5 **Tayacoba (CAN)**[14] 5022 3-9-0 0................................ GaryBartley(3) 3 49
(J S Goldie) *hld up in tch: effrt over 2f out: sn no imp* **25/1**
4 7 **Sartingo (IRE)** 3-9-3 0... PJMcDonald 4 34
(G A Swinbank) *cl up tl rdn and outpcd over 2f out: btn over 1f out* **5/1**[3]
5 4 **Psalm Twentythree**[171] 4-9-10 0................................... DavidAllan 2 25
(J A McShane) *s.i.s: t.k.h and sn prom: rdn and wknd over 2f out* **50/1**
5 **6** 21 **Just Nod (IRE)**[14] 5022 4-9-2 0.................................. BarryMcHugh(3) 5 —
(Mrs R A Carr) *bhd: struggling whn hung lft 4f out: sn btn: eased whn no ch* **80/1**

1m 58.49s (-1.21) **Going Correction** +0.075s/f (Good)
WFA 3 from 4yo 7lb **6** Ran SP% **110.6**
Speed ratings (Par 103): **108,100,96,90,86 68**
Tote Swingers:1&2:£1.10, 1&3:£2.80, 2&3:£4.10 CSF £2.61 TOTE £1.50: £1.10, £2.50; EX 2.50.
Owner H E Sheikh Rashid Bin Mohammed **Bred** Darley **Trained** Hambleton, N Yorks

FOCUS
No depth to this maiden and it was plain sailing for the odds-on favourite.
Just Nod(IRE) Official explanation: jockey said filly hung left-handed throughout

5479 ROBERT WISEMAN DAIRIES FRESH "N" LO STKS (H'CAP) — 1m 65y
7:05 (7:06) (Class 5) (0-70,69) 3-Y-O **£4,209** (£1,252; £625; £312) **Stalls** High

Form RPR
0313 **1** **Hail Bold Chief (USA)**[6] 5300 3-9-6 **68**.......................... PJMcDonald 5 74
(G A Swinbank) *mde all: rdn over 2f out: hld on wl fnl f* **3/1**[1]
003 **2** 1 1/4 **Dandarrell**[52] 3758 3-8-5 **56**... BarryMcHugh(3) 4 59
(Julie Camacho) *hld up in tch: effrt and edgd rt over 2f out: kpt on to chse wnr wl ins fnl f: r.o* **13/2**
0140 **3** nk **Catawollow**[2] 5411 3-8-2 **50** oh1.............................(e) SilvestreDeSousa 7 52
(R C Guest) *trckd ldrs: effrt over 2f out: kpt on same pce ins fnl f* **4/1**[2]
0-45 **4** nk **Nolecce**[2] 5405 3-8-2 **50** oh5.. PaulEddery 8 52+
(R C Guest) *dwlt: hld up: effrt over 2f out: kpt on same pce fnl f* **7/1**
2335 **5** 1/2 **North Central (USA)**[5] 5337 3-9-3 **65**............................... LNewman 6 66
(J S Goldie) *in tch: rdn over 2f out: kpt on same pce fnl f* **8/1**
-503 **6** nk **Cherry Bee**[13] 5096 3-9-7 **69**.. GregFairley 3 69
(M Johnston) *pressed wnr: rdn 3f out: one pce fnl f* **9/2**[3]
664 **7** 2 **Hades (IRE)**[20] 4853 3-8-12 **60**.. DavidAllan 1 55
(T D Easterby) *trckd ldrs: rdn and outpcd whn hmpd over 2f out: n.d after* **7/1**
5504 **8** 3/4 **Daneside (IRE)**[4] 5361 3-7-11 **52**............................. VictorSantos(7) 2 46
(W G Harrison) *hld up: nt clr run and swtchd over 2f out: nvr able to chal* **40/1**

1m 48.98s (0.58) **Going Correction** +0.075s/f (Good) **8** Ran SP% **115.1**
Speed ratings (Par 100): **100,98,98,98,97 97,95,94**
Tote Swingers:1&2:£2.60, 1&3:£2.50, 2&3:£2.80 CSF £23.13 CT £78.28 TOTE £2.90: £1.10, £1.30, £2.50; EX 11.80.
Owner Solway Stayers **Bred** Tracy Farmer **Trained** Melsonby, N Yorks

FOCUS
Run-of-the-mill fare, none of these obviously ahead of their marks. The winner dictated what was no more than a modest gallop for most part.

5480 FREEBETS.CO.UK H'CAP — 6f 5y
7:35 (7:36) (Class 4) (0-80,79) 3-Y-O+ **£7,123** (£2,119; £1,059; £529) **Stalls** Centre

Form RPR
2304 **1** **Legal Eagle (IRE)**[28] 4558 5-9-2 **76**..........................(p) DuilioDaSilva(7) 5 86
(Paul Green) *mde virtually all: rdn over 2f out: hld on wl fnl f* **13/2**[3]
-226 **2** 1/2 **Fishforcompliments**[34] 4354 6-9-8 **78**....................... BarryMcHugh(3) 8 86
(R A Fahey) *cl up: rdn over 2f out: hdwy to press wnr fnl f: kpt on: hld towards fin* **3/1**[2]
6026 **3** 1 1/4 **Mandalay King (IRE)**[14] 5043 5-8-12 **68**.................... RobertLButler(3) 4 72
(Mrs Marjorie Fife) *bhd tl hdwy and edgd rt over 1f out: kpt on u.p fnl f: nrst fin* **16/1**
6260 **4** 1/2 **Melundy**[20] 4826 3-7-12 **61** ow1.................................. NathanAlison(7) 11 64
(Miss L A Perratt) *chsd ldng gp on outside: hdwy over 2f out: edgd lft over 1f out: r.o same pce wl ins fnl f* **50/1**
0102 **5** 1 1/2 **Maze (IRE)**[16] 4968 5-9-8 **75**.. SamHitchcott 13 73
(A W Carroll) *cl up: effrt over 2f out: one pce fnl f* **12/1**
1113 **6** shd **King Of Eden (IRE)**[35] 4345 4-9-11 **78**.............................. DavidAllan 7 76
(E J Alston) *towards rr: rdn and hdwy over 2f out: edgd rt over 1f out: edgd lft and kpt on same pce fnl f* **9/4**[1]
0022 **7** 1 1/4 **Northern Bolt**[9] 5212 5-9-5 **75**.................................(b) MichaelGeran(3) 6 69
(I W McInnes) *prom: drvn and outpcd over 2f out: n.d after* **14/1**
3005 **8** 1 **Distant Sun (USA)**[9] 5212 6-9-3 **70**...................................... LNewman 9 60
(Miss L A Perratt) *chsd ldng gp: effrt over 2f out: no imp over 1f out* **40/1**
1100 **9** 3/4 **Atlantic Beach**[13] 5069 5-9-10 **77**............................... SilvestreDeSousa 2 65
(D O'Meara) *in tch: drvn over 2f out: wknd over 1f out* **12/1**
6040 **10** 4 **Floor Show**[20] 4850 4-9-10 **77**..(p) PJMcDonald 1 52
(N Wilson) *hung rt thrght: hld up in tch: rdn and wknd fr 2f out* **8/1**
054- **11** 5 **Blown It (USA)**[279] 7478 4-9-2 **72**................................ GaryBartley(3) 3 31
(J S Goldie) *hld up: drvn over 2f out: btn over 1f out* **16/1**

30-0 **12** 2 1/4 **Burnwynd Boy**[232] 71 5-9-12 **79**....................................... GregFairley 10 31
(J A McShane) *cl up on outside tl rdn and wknd over 1f out* **40/1**

1m 12.09s (-0.11) **Going Correction** +0.075s/f (Good)
WFA 3 from 4yo+ 3lb **12** Ran SP% **120.9**
Speed ratings (Par 105): **103,102,100,100,98 97,96,94,93,88 81,78**
Tote Swingers:1&2:£4.70, 1&3:£18.50, 2&3:£13.00 CSF £26.55 CT £309.47 TOTE £5.80: £1.50, £1.40, £7.80; EX 26.60.
Owner Paul Boyers **Bred** John Cooke **Trained** Lydiate, Merseyside
■ Stewards' Enquiry : Barry McHugh one-day ban: used whip with excessive frequency (Sep 10)

FOCUS
Competitive enough fare and no reason why the form won't hold up for the level. The main action unfolded towards the centre, the leaders edging towards the near rail late on. Most of the principals were handy throughout.

5481 EXECUTIVE BENEFIT CONSULTANCY H'CAP — 6f 5y
8:05 (8:05) (Class 6) (0-65,62) 3-Y-O **£3,070** (£906; £453) **Stalls** Centre

Form RPR
3423 **1** **Vilnius**[11] 5152 3-9-1 **56**... SamHitchcott 5 62
(M R Channon) *mde all: rdn over 1f out: styd on strly fnl f* **9/1**[3]
3423 **2** 2 1/2 **Mottley Crewe**[14] 5046 3-9-7 **62**..................................... PJMcDonald 1 60
(M Dods) *chsd ldrs: effrt over 1f out: kpt on fnl f: nt rch wnr* **4/1**[2]
3422 **3** 2 **Monte Mayor One**[2] 5409 3-9-6 **61**..............................(p) DavidAllan 6 53
(P Monteith) *in tch: effrt over 1f out: no ex fnl f* **4/1**[2]
-001 **4** 3 1/2 **Up At Last**[15] 4989 3-9-3 **58**................................... SilvestreDeSousa 7 38
(W J Haggas) *t.k.h: cl up tl rdn and outpcd wl over 1f out: n.d after* **11/10**[1]
5-00 **5** 2 **Maragna (IRE)**[19] 4861 3-8-4 **45**.. GregFairley 3 19
(Paul Green) *t.k.h: cl up tl rdn and wknd 2f out* **16/1**
6105 **6** 15 **Ya Boy Sir (IRE)**[20] 4826 3-9-3 **61**................................ GaryBartley(3) 2 —
(N Wilson) *cl up: edgd to stands' side 1/2-way: rdn and wknd over 1f out* **12/1**
2000 **7** 1/2 **Reach For The Sky (IRE)**[2] 5409 3-8-5 **53**................. VictorSantos(7) 4 —
(A Berry) *hmpd s and sn wl bhd: nvr on terms* **33/1**

1m 12.7s (0.50) **Going Correction** +0.075s/f (Good) **7** Ran SP% **114.1**
Speed ratings (Par 98): **99,95,93,88,85 65,65**
Tote Swingers:1&2:£2.80, 1&3:£4.10, 2&3:£3.10 CSF £44.36 TOTE £9.90: £6.90, £1.80; EX 47.50 Place 6: £128.31 Place 5: £23.54..
Owner P Trant **Bred** P Trant & Mike Channon Bloodstock Limited **Trained** West Ilsley, Berks

Reach For The Sky(IRE) Official explanation: jockey said filly missed the break
T/Plt: £107.90 to a £1 stake. Pool:£44,113.87 - 298.27 winning tickets T/Qpdt: £13.10 to a £1 stake. Pool:£4,705.42 - 264.10 winning tickets RY

5040 NEWCASTLE (L-H)
Friday, August 27

OFFICIAL GOING: Good to soft (stands' side 6.1; far side 6.4)
Wind: Virtually nil Weather: Cloudy with showers

5482 6BOX SUPPORTS JAMES MOFFATT RACING "HANDS AND HEELS" APPRENTICE SERIES H'CAP — 6f
5:25 (5:25) (Class 6) (0-65,65) 3-Y-O+ **£2,201** (£655; £327; £163) **Stalls** Centre

Form RPR
0413 **1** **Angaric (IRE)**[27] 4605 7-9-6 **55**.. AdamCarter 8 67
(B Smart) *cl up: led 1/2-way: rdn wl over 1f out: styd on wl fnl f* **7/1**[3]
3342 **2** 2 **Needy McCredie**[14] 5024 4-8-13 **51**............................ ShaneBKelly(3) 4 57
(J R Turner) *trckd ldrs: hdwy over 2f out: rdn to chse wnr wl over 1f out: no imp fnl f* **9/4**[1]
5060 **3** 7 **Cheery Cat (USA)**[36] 4285 6-9-0 **49**.............................(p) RichardRowe 6 32
(J Balding) *a.p: effrt and ev ch 2f out: sn rdn and grad wknd* **16/1**
060 **4** 5 **Bid For Gold**[4] 5357 6-9-3 **57**..............................(p) EleanorMcGowan(5) 3 24
(Jedd O'Keeffe) *chsd ldrs: hdwy and cl up over 2f out: sn rdn and wknd wl over 1f out* **4/1**[2]
5005 **5** 4 1/2 **My One Weakness (IRE)**[18] 4901 3-9-13 **65**.................(be) DaleSwift 9 18
(B Ellison) *s.i.s and sn rdn along in rr: hdwy 1/2-way: drvn 2f out and n.d* **8/1**
0100 **6** hd **Crianza**[23] 4706 4-9-2 **54**... IanBurns(3) 1 6
(N Tinkler) *s.i.s and sn rdn along in rr: sme hdwy fnl 2f: n.d* **28/1**
000 **7** 1 1/2 **Quaker Parrot**[41] 4127 3-9-10 **62**............................(p) SoniaEaton 11 9
(Tom Dascombe) *chsd ldrs: rdn along wl over 2f out: grad wknd* **15/2**
6500 **8** 1 1/4 **City For Conquest (IRE)**[19] 4869 7-8-10 **45**..............(p) JamesRogers 5 —
(John A Harris) *s.i.s: a in rr* **20/1**
422- **9** nk **Magical Song**[412] 3852 5-8-13 **53**..............................(p) AndrewSmith(5) 7 —
(J Balding) *led to 1/2-way: sn wknd* **9/1**
-065 **10** 6 **Frill A Minute**[9] 5214 6-8-10 **45**.. AlexEdwards 2 —
(Miss L C Siddall) *sn outpcd and a in rr* **125/1**
0000 **11** 3 **Lujiana**[111] 1928 5-9-2 **51**... JulieBurke 10 —
(M Brittain) *chsd ldrs: rdn along bef 1/2-way: sn lost pl and bhd* **25/1**

1m 15.98s (1.38) **Going Correction** +0.125s/f (Good)
WFA 3 from 4yo+ 3lb **11** Ran SP% **114.9**
Speed ratings (Par 101): **95,92,83,76,70 70,68,66,66,58 54**
Tote Swingers: 1&2:£1.60, 1&3:£10.20, 2&3:£38.20 CSF £21.68 CT £245.34 TOTE £6.00: £2.60, £1.60, £3.00; EX 12.40.
Owner B Smart **Bred** Humphrey Okeke **Trained** Hambleton, N Yorks

FOCUS
After a heavy shower early afternoon the ground was described as good to soft all around. A wide-open, run of the mill, 46-65 apprentice handicap which was full of out of form horses. It was run at an even pace and the race developed down the centre of the track. The first two pulled well clear of the reminder.

5483 6BOX SPONSORS GARY BARTLEY NURSERY — 5f
5:55 (5:55) (Class 5) (0-70,70) 2-Y-O **£2,590** (£770; £385; £192) **Stalls** Centre

Form RPR
643 **1** **Watts Up Son**[16] 4941 2-9-5 **68**......................................(t) DavidNolan 5 78+
(D Carroll) *cl up: led after 1f: rdn wl over 1f out: kpt on strly* **9/2**[3]
0501 **2** 2 1/4 **Bellemere**[14] 5042 2-9-4 **70**.. JamesSullivan(3) 3 71
(M W Easterby) *a.p: hdwy to chal wl over 1f out: sn rdn and one pce fnl f* **4/1**[2]
5000 **3** 1 **Ever Roses**[33] 4409 2-7-8 **50**.. RichardRowe(7) 1 48+
(P T Midgley) *t.k.h: trckd ldrs tl lost pl and in rr 1/2-way: hdwy wl over 1f out: rdn to chse ldng pair and wandered ins fnl f: kpt on towards fin* **50/1**
401 **4** 5 **Ingleby Exceed (IRE)**[30] 4480 2-9-4 **67**............................ PhillipMakin 2 46
(T D Barron) *dwlt: trckd ldrs 1/2-way: rdn 2f out: sn one pce* **5/1**
6525 **5** 3 1/4 **Wild Hysteria (IRE)**[41] 4124 2-8-10 **59**........................... MickyFenton 8 27
(T P Tate) *chsd ldrs on outer: rdn along over 2f out: sn wknd* **7/1**

0006 **6** *5* **Back For Tea (IRE)**[18] 4890 2-8-3 **52**........................(v[1]) NickyMackay 6 2
(Tom Dascombe) *led 1f: cl up tl rdn 2f out and sn wknd* **7/1**

0535 **7** *2 ½* **Reel Amber**[5] 5334 2-8-1 **53**....................................(b) KellyHarrison(3) 10 —
(T D Easterby) *a towards rr* **12/1**

4560 **8** *7* **Alfraamsey**[16] 4955 2-9-4 **67**... JoeFanning 11 —
(M R Channon) *wnt rt s: in tch: rdn along 1/2-way and sn wknd* **10/3**[1]

62.69 secs (1.59) **Going Correction** +0.125s/f (Good) **8** Ran SP% **112.6**
Speed ratings (Par 94): **92,88,86,78,73 65,61,50**
Tote Swingers:1&2:£2.30, 1&3:£40.60, 2&3:£73.90 CSF £22.09 CT £774.96 TOTE £5.30: £1.90, £1.10, £8.90; EX 13.90.
Owner L Ibbotson & D Watts **Bred** West Dereham Abbey Stud **Trained** Sledmere, E Yorks

FOCUS
It proved hard work on this ground for these juveniles, including two previous course winners in the line-up. Again they raced towards the centre of the track. The first three pulled well clear.

NOTEBOOK
Watts Up Son, coming from a yard going very well, was running here in a nursery for the first time. He travelled well throughout and it was a pleasing performance. He's rated 68 and the handicapper will have his say but he looks the type who should continue to improve and can score again. (tchd 4-1)
Bellemere, 5lb higher for her course-and-distance success, again ran bang up to form and time might prove she ran into a smart and well handicapped winner. (op 7-2 tchd 9-2)
Ever Roses was coming back from a slight break. Although well beaten in a seller on her penultimate start, this was a step forward and she can lose her maiden tag in similar company at some point.
Ingleby Exceed(IRE) lost her maiden tag at Redcar in very different conditions. Rated 67, the handicapper has taken no chances and, although she might prefer better ground, she could remain vulnerable until the handicapper relents. (op 9-2 tchd 13-2)
Alfraamsey was the disappointment of the race. He was always towards the rear and will need to bounce back after this tame effort. Official explanation: jockey said colt never travelled (op 9-2)

5484 6BOX PROMOTIONS 01270 213476 H'CAP 7f
6:25 (6:26) (Class 5) (0-75,75) 3-Y-O £2,590 (£770; £385; £192) **Stalls** Centre

Form RPR

0422 **1** **Red Scintilla**[14] 5044 3-8-13 67.. PaulMulrennan 6 75
(N Tinkler) *dwlt: hld up in tch: hdwy 3f out: chsd ldrs wl over 1f out: rdn and edgd lft ent fnl f: sn drvn and styd on wl to ld nr fin* **5/1**[2]

1044 **2** *nk* **Whispered Times (USA)**[23] 4704 3-9-2 73...........(p) JamesSullivan(3) 2 80
(Miss Tracy Waggott) *prom: led over 4f out: rdn over 1f out: drvn ins fnl f: edgd rt and hdd nr fin* **9/1**

0122 **3** *6* **Jupiter Fidius**[4] 5353 3-8-9 68.. DaleSwift(5) 1 59
(Mrs K Walton) *trckd ldrs on outer: hdwy over 2f out: rdn to chal over 1f out: drvn and one pce ent fnl f* **7/1**[3]

5300 **4** *1 ¼* **William Morgan (IRE)**[34] 4394 3-9-4 72........................ PaulHanagan 3 59
(R A Fahey) *trckd ldrs: hdwy over 2f out: rdn over 1f out and grad wknd* **2/1**[1]

0221 **5** *6* **Viking Warrior (IRE)**[20] 4853 3-9-2 70............................ PhillipMakin 7 41
(M Dods) *prom: rdn along 3f out: grad wknd* **15/2**

5510 **6** *1 ¼* **Kielder (IRE)**[25] 4647 3-9-1 69... JoeFanning 5 37
(T D Barron) *prom: pushed along 1/2-way: sn rdn and lost pl: bhd fnl 2f* **18/1**

3105 **7** *2 ¾* **Verluga (IRE)**[23] 4704 3-8-4 61..................................(b) KellyHarrison(3) 4 21
(T D Easterby) *trckd ldrs: prom 1/2-way: rdn along wl over 2f out and sn wknd* **10/1**

002 **8** *1 ¼* **Tombellini (IRE)**[20] 4853 3-8-5 59.................................. AndrewMullen 9 16
(D Nicholls) *chsd ldrs: rdn along 1/2-way: wknd wl over 2f out* **10/1**

350 **9** *13* **Electioneer (USA)**[16] 4942 3-9-7 75.. LeeVickers 8 —
(M W Easterby) *led: hdd over 4f out: sn rdn along and wknd wl over 2f out* **7/1**[3]

1m 29.62s (0.92) **Going Correction** +0.125s/f (Good) **9** Ran SP% **120.2**
Speed ratings (Par 100): **99,98,91,90,83 82,78,77,62**
Tote Swingers:1&2:£9.60, 1&3:£6.40, 2&3:£11.30 CSF £51.30 CT £322.65 TOTE £4.80: £1.30, £8.30, £6.00; EX 39.80.
Owner Philip A Jarvis **Bred** Philip A Jarvis **Trained** Langton, N Yorks

FOCUS
An interesting 56-75 handicap which was run at a sound pace. The race developed down the centre of the track and the first two pulled clear.

5485 6BOX CORPORATE HOSPITALITY 6BOX.CO.UK H'CAP 5f
6:55 (6:55) (Class 6) (0-55,55) 3-Y-O+ £2,331 (£693; £346; £173) **Stalls** Centre

Form RPR

0002 **1** **Captain Royale (IRE)**[14] 5045 5-8-11 **51**....................(p) AndrewMullen 1 68
(Miss Tracy Waggott) *mde all: rdn clr over 1f out: kpt on strly* **9/2**[1]

000 **2** *3 ½* **Embra (IRE)**[1] 5023 5-8-7 **52** ow1.................................. DaleSwift(5) 7 56
(T J Etherington) *dwlt and hmpd s: sn pushed along in rr: swtchd to outer and hdwy 2f out: rdn over 1f out: chsd wnr ins fnl f: no imp* **14/1**

0600 **3** *2 ¾* **Prigsnov Dancer (IRE)**[18] 4897 5-8-3 **46** oh1...........(p) PaulPickard(3) 3 41
(O Brennan) *chsd ldrs: hdwy and cl up 1/2-way: rdn wl over 1f out and kpt on same pce* **20/1**

553 **4** *nse* **Divine Spirit**[34] 4373 9-8-10 **53**................................. PatrickDonaghy(3) 5 47
(M Dods) *wnt rt s: towards rr: pushed along and hdwy 1/2-way: rdn to chse ldrs wl over 1f out: drvn and kpt on ins fnl f* **17/2**

4350 **5** *½* **Tenancy (IRE)**[18] 4895 6-8-1 **48**.. SoniaEaton(7) 13 41
(S A Harris) *hmpd s: chsd ldrs: rdn along 2f out: drvn over 1f out and sn one pce* **17/2**

0402 **6** *3 ¾* **Sharp Shoes**[6] 5299 3-8-4 **51**.. RosieJessop(5) 11 30
(Mrs A Duffield) *hld up towards rr: hdwy 2f out: swtchd rt and rdn over 1f out: kpt on: nvr nr ldrs* **9/1**

6463 **7** *2* **Monsieur Harvey**[4] 5362 4-8-6 **46** oh1.................................. JoeFanning 4 18
(B Smart) *cl up: rdn along over 2f out: sn drvn and wknd* **13/2**[3]

4402 **8** *3 ½* **Sea Crest**[13] 5097 4-8-11 **51**.. PaulHanagan 12 10
(M Brittain) *wnt rt s: racd alone stands' rail: prom: rdn along 1/2-way and sn wknd* **5/1**[2]

-002 **9** *½* **Sleepy Blue Ocean**[14] 5055 4-9-1 **55**............................ AndrewElliott 10 12
(J Balding) *prom: rdn along over 2f out: sn wknd* **7/1**

500 **10** *5* **Royal Cheer**[16] 4947 3-8-2 **47**..(p) AmyRyan(3) 8 —
(Mrs A Duffield) *outpcd and bhd fr 1/2-way* **66/1**

0063 **11** *½* **Best Known Secret (IRE)**[15] 4982 4-8-5 **48**........... JamesSullivan(3) 14 —
(C C Bealby) *hmpd s: outpcd and bhd fr 1/2-way* **10/1**

5-00 **12** *1* **Joyeaux**[79] 2849 8-9-1 **55**..(p) DuranFentiman 9 —
(Ollie Pears) *a towards rr: bhd fr 1/2-way* **14/1**

61.53 secs (0.43) **Going Correction** +0.125s/f (Good)
WFA 3 from 4yo+ 2lb **12** Ran SP% **120.4**
Speed ratings (Par 101): **101,95,91,90,90 84,80,75,74,66 65,64**
Tote Swingers:1&2:£17.20, 1&3:£41.40, 2&3:£85.40 CSF £69.43 CT £1161.21 TOTE £7.60: £1.80, £6.40, £14.80; EX 101.00.
Owner H Conlon **Bred** Skymarc Farm Inc **Trained** Spennymoor, Co Durham
■ Stewards' Enquiry : Paul Hanagan three-day ban: careless riding (Sep 10,12-13)

FOCUS
A wide-open 46-55 sprint handicap which was full of horses who haven't found winning easy this season. It was run at a sound pace and most of the field came up the centre of the track.
Sleepy Blue Ocean Official explanation: jockey said gelding was unsuited by the good to soft ground

5486 RISING KHELEYF SHARES AVAILABLE WITH 6BOX H'CAP 1m 3y(S)
7:25 (7:26) (Class 5) (0-70,70) 3-Y-O+ £2,590 (£770; £385; £192) **Stalls** Centre

Form RPR

4012 **1** **Frontline Girl (IRE)**[39] 4188 4-9-10 **67**.............................. AndrewElliott 1 77
(Mrs K Burke) *mde most: rdn clr over 1f out: drvn ins fnl f and kpt on* **11/2**[1]

0001 **2** *1 ¾* **Rising Kheleyf (IRE)**[19] 4866 4-9-9 **66**............................ PhillipMakin 2 72
(John A Harris) *in tch: hdwy over 2f out and sn rdn: drvn to chse wnr ins fnl f: no imp towards fin* **20/1**

0605 **3** *1 ¼* **Geojimali**[20] 4824 8-9-2 **59**.. PaulHanagan 3 62
(J S Goldie) *midfield: hdwy over 2f out: rdn over 1f out: kpt on ins fnl f* **11/2**[1]

-036 **4** *1 ¾* **Scarab (IRE)**[22] 4752 5-9-5 **62**... DuranFentiman 8 61
(T D Walford) *cl up: rdn along and sltly outpcd 2f out: drvn and rallied ent fnl f: sn wknd* **17/2**

0400 **5** *2 ½* **Lakeman (IRE)**[8] 5241 4-9-5 **62**....................................(b[1]) LeeVickers 14 55
(B Ellison) *racd alone stands' rail: cl up: rdn and ev ch 2f out: sn drvn and grad wknd appr fnl f* **22/1**

2000 **6** *1* **Dark Moment**[14] 5043 4-9-8 **70**....................................... IanBrennan(5) 6 61
(Ollie Pears) *hld up in rr: hdwy over 2f out: rdn wl over 1f out: kpt on ins fnl f: nvr rchd ldrs* **10/1**

0030 **7** *2 ¼* **Whipma Whopma Gate (IRE)**[15] 4985 5-9-6 **63**..........(v) DavidNolan 9 49
(D Carroll) *trckd ldrs: effrt over 2f out: sn rdn and grad wknd* **11/2**[1]

10 **8** *nk* **Celtic Step**[42] 4119 6-8-12 **58**...................................... PaulPickard(3) 10 43
(A Kirtley) *chsd ldrs: rdn along over 2f out: grad wknd* **6/1**[2]

50-0 **9** *½* **Hartshead**[33] 4404 11-9-3 **60**.. AndrewMullen 7 44
(Miss Tracy Waggott) *in tch: rdn along over 2f out: sn wknd* **25/1**

4006 **10** *2 ¾* **Ninth House (USA)**[23] 4713 8-9-1 **61**.................(t) JamesSullivan(3) 12 39
(Mrs R A Carr) *nvr bttr than midfield* **15/2**[3]

002 **11** *1 ¼* **Navajo Joe (IRE)**[23] 4707 5-8-5 **51** oh2...................(t) KellyHarrison(3) 11 26
(R Johnson) *rrd s: a in rr* **12/1**

2500 **12** *7* **Pretty Orchid**[15] 4987 5-8-8 **51** oh2...............................(p) JoeFanning 13 10
(P T Midgley) *hld up: a in rr* **25/1**

0300 **13** *24* **Miss Flash Dancer**[28] 4546 4-8-9 **55**...................... PatrickDonaghy(3) 5 —
(C C Bealby) *prom: rdn along over 3f out: sn wknd* **40/1**

1m 44.99s (1.59) **Going Correction** +0.125s/f (Good) **13** Ran SP% **118.8**
Speed ratings (Par 103): **97,95,94,92,89 88,86,86,85,82 81,74,50**
Tote Swingers:1&2:£12.60, 1&3:£3.40, 2&3:£15.00 CSF £118.93 CT £489.34 TOTE £3.80: £1.10, £6.30, £1.10; EX 82.60.
Owner M A Roden **Bred** J Donnelly **Trained** Middleham Moor, North Yorks

FOCUS
Probably just an ordinary 51-70 handicap, which was run at a sound pace and it proved hard to make ground off the pace.
Miss Flash Dancer Official explanation: jockey said filly hung left throughout

5487 6BOX SUPPORTS JOHN HARRIS RACING MAIDEN STKS 7f
7:55 (7:58) (Class 5) 3-4-Y-O £2,590 (£770; £385; £192) **Stalls** Centre

Form RPR

1 **Bella Noir** 3-8-12 0.. AndrewElliott 7 79
(Mrs K Burke) *mde most: rdn clr over 1f out: styd on strly* **16/1**

200 **2** *9* **Fifty Moore**[22] 4750 3-9-3 80.. PaulHanagan 3 60
(Jedd O'Keeffe) *a.p: effrt over 2f out: sn rdn and ev ch tl drvn and one pce appr fnl f* **9/2**[2]

00 **3** *nk* **Gypsy Style**[14] 5057 3-8-12 0...(t) AndrewMullen 4 54
(Mrs K Walton) *in rr: pushed along 1/2-way: hdwy wl over 1f out: styd on ins fnl f: nrst fin* **100/1**

2 **4** *2 ¾* **African Wave (USA)**[152] 1029 3-9-3 0.............................. NickyMackay 8 52
(J H M Gosden) *trckd ldrs: pushed along 3f out: rdn over 2f out: sn edgd lft and one pce* **8/13**[1]

5 **5** *nk* **Deferto Delphi**[25] 4646 3-8-12 0...................................... IanBrennan(5) 6 51
(F P Murtagh) *in tch: hdwy to chse ldrs over 2f out: sn rdn and wknd ent fnl f* **40/1**

364 **6** *2 ¾* **Swiftly Done (IRE)**[14] 5057 3-9-3 0................................. DavidNolan 9 44
(D Carroll) *chsd ldrs: rdn along and prom 2f out: drvn over 1f out: sn wknd* **8/1**[3]

7 *8* **Moorgate Lad** 3-9-3 0... PaulMulrennan 10 22
(O Brennan) *sn outpcd and bhd: sme late hdwy* **100/1**

0 **8** *6* **Talent Scout (IRE)**[12] 5122 4-9-8 0............................... DanielTudhope 1 6
(T D Walford) *in tch: rdn along 1/2-way and sn outpcd* **50/1**

9 *1 ½* **Stella Marris** 3-8-12 0... PhillipMakin 11 —
(C R Wilson) *t.k.h and cl up: rdn along 1/2-way: sn lost pl and bhd* **80/1**

10 *nk* **Jingoism (USA)**[13] 4-9-3 0..(b[1]) DaleSwift(5) 2 —
(B Ellison) *sn outpcd and a bhd* **28/1**

0 **11** *30* **Opera Cat (USA)**[112] 1868 3-9-3 0..................................... JoeFanning 5 —
(M Johnston) *in tch: rdn along and outpcd 1/2-way: sn bhd* **8/1**[3]

1m 30.74s (2.04) **Going Correction** +0.125s/f (Good)
WFA 3 from 4yo 5lb **11** Ran SP% **119.3**
Speed ratings (Par 103): **93,82,82,79,78 75,66,59,58,57 23**
Tote Swingers:1&2:£28.20, 1&3:£39.70, 2&3:£17.60 CSF £85.72 TOTE £33.00: £4.20, £1.10, £29.70; EX 134.40 Place 6: £433.49 Place 5: £230.02.
Owner Mrs Elaine M Burke **Bred** M E Broughton **Trained** Middleham Moor, North Yorks

FOCUS
A maiden lacking strength in depth and it was weakened further with a couple running well below-par. Again it helped to race up with the pace and it developed down the centre of the track.
African Wave(USA) Official explanation: jockey said colt was unsuited by the good to soft ground
Moorgate Lad Official explanation: jockey said gelding ran green
Talent Scout(IRE) Official explanation: jockey said gelding was unsuited by the good to soft ground

T/Plt: £590.60 to a £1 stake. Pool:£51,824.47 - 64.05 winning tickets T/Qpdt: £266.10 to a £1 stake. Pool:£6,042.96 - 16.80 winning tickets JR

5085 **NEWMARKET** (July Course) (R-H)

Friday, August 27

OFFICIAL GOING: Soft (5.2)

Stands' side section of July Course utilised.

Wind: virtualy nil Weather: cloudy, brighter spells

5488 EUROPEAN BREEDERS' FUND MAIDEN FILLIES' STKS (DIV I) 7f

1:50 (1:51) (Class 4) 2-Y-O £4,209 (£1,252; £625; £312) Stalls Low

Form RPR

1 **Lucy Limelites** 2-9-0 0 SteveDrowne 11 73
(R Charlton) *wnt rt s: sn chsng ldr: rdn to ld ent fnl f: kpt on wl fnl f* **10/1**[2]

0 2 1 1/2 **Grecian Goddess (IRE)**[20] 4844 2-9-0 0 MarcHalford 9 69
(J Ryan) *led: sn clr: rdn and edgd rt over 1f out: hdd ent fnl f: styd on same pce after* **25/1**

3 2 **Abergeldie (USA)** 2-9-0 0 RichardMullen 6 64
(Sir Michael Stoute) *a chsng ldng pair: rdn along 2f out: kpt on same pce and no imp fnl f* **7/1**[1]

4 3 1/2 **Dancerella** 2-9-0 0 NeilCallan 7 55
(D R C Elsworth) *racd in last pair: pushed along 1/2-way: rdn to chse ldng trio over 2f out: sn no prog and wl hld fr over 1f out* **11/1**[3]

5 6 **Dubawi Dancer** 2-9-0 0 SimonWhitworth 4 40
(W J Haggas) *stdd s: hld up in tch: pushed along and struggling 1/2-way: lost tch wl over 1f out* **16/1**

6 7 **Amazon Twilight** 2-9-0 0 AdamKirby 3 23
(B R Johnson) *stdd s: hld up mn last: pushed along and rn green 1/2-way: hung lft and struggling 3f out: lost tch 2f out* **14/1**

1m 31.42s (5.72) **Going Correction** +0.65s/f (Yiel) 6 Ran SP% **46.3**

Speed ratings (Par 93): **93,91,89,85,78 70**

Tote Swingers: 1&2 £5.00, 1&3 £1.60, 2&3 £3.50 CSF £33.41 TOTE £4.20: £2.00, £2.70; EX 24.00.

Owner Lady Richard Wellesley **Bred** Marston Stud And Fleming Thoroughbreds **Trained** Beckhampton, Wilts

FOCUS

Plenty of rain earlier in the week and another 13mm overnight meant the going was given as soft, with a GoingStick reading of 5.2. There were four non-runners and the forecast 4/7 favourite Quiet Oasis was withdrawn at the start after losing both her front plates (deduct 60p in the £ under R4), so this maiden ended up a pretty weak affair.

NOTEBOOK

Lucy Limelites, who's out of a mare who won at Listed level over a mile at three, wore a sheepskin noseband but she still carried her head high. She picked up well when given a slap, though, and clearly has a future, although this bare form is probably nothing special. (op 8-1)

Grecian Goddess(IRE), the only one in the line-up with the benefit of a previous run, put her previous experience to good use and once again made the running. She had no answer when the winner quickened up, though. (op 28-1 tchd 20-1)

Abergeldie(USA), whose dam is a half-sister to Barathea and Gossamer, ran all right on her debut and might do better granted a sounder surface. (op 13-2 tchd 6-1)

Dancerella is bred to come into her own next year over middle distances. She was keeping on at the finish, will appreciate a step up to a mile and will improve for this. (op 12-1)

Dubawi Dancer looks the type that will do better in time once eligible for handicaps. (tchd 14-1)

5489 EUROPEAN BREEDERS' FUND MAIDEN FILLIES' STKS (DIV II) 7f

2:20 (2:20) (Class 4) 2-Y-O £4,209 (£1,252; £625; £312) Stalls Low

Form RPR

1 **Havant** 2-9-0 0 KierenFallon 4 84+
(Sir Michael Stoute) *trckd ldrs: wnt 2nd 3f out: rdn to ld wl over 1f out: styd on strly and drew clr fnl f: eased towards fin* **7/4**[1]

2 5 **Mia Madonna** 2-9-0 0 MartinDwyer 1 70+
(B J Meehan) *sltly hmpd and wnt lft sn after s: chsd ldr after 1f tl 3f out: rdn and outpcd 2f out: kpt on again ins fnl f to go 2nd towards fin: no ch w wnr* **7/1**

3 3/4 **Lucky Meadows (IRE)** 2-9-0 0 RichardHughes 9 68
(R Hannon) *led at stdy gallop and flashing tail: rdn and qcknd ent fnl 2f: hdd wl over 1f out: btn jst ins fnl f: lost 2nd towards fin* **7/2**[2]

4 nk **Schism** 2-9-0 0 DaneO'Neill 5 67+
(H Candy) *stdd s hld up in tch: rdn and hdwy to chse ldrs 2f out: outpcd jst over 1f out: kpt on same pce and no ch w wnr fnl f* **9/2**[3]

5 1 1/4 **Scented** 2-9-0 0 PhilipRobinson 8 64
(W J Haggas) *stdd and awkward leaving stalls: hld up in tch: rdn and rn green jst over 2f out: sn outpcd: kpt on same pce and no ch fnl f* **9/2**[3]

6 5 **Corvette** 2-9-0 0 JimmyQuinn 6 53
(J R Jenkins) *dwlt: hld up in tch in last: rdn ent fnl 2f: sn struggling and btn over 1f out: eased wl ins fnl f* **33/1**

1m 32.82s (7.12) **Going Correction** +0.65s/f (Yiel) 6 Ran SP% **110.4**

Speed ratings (Par 93): **85,79,78,78,76 70**

Tote Swingers: 1&2 £3.10, 1&3 £1.70, 2&3 £4.00 CSF £14.08 TOTE £2.70: £1.80, £2.70; EX 16.30.

Owner Mr & Mrs James Wigan **Bred** Mrs James Wigan & London TB Services Ltd **Trained** Newmarket, Suffolk

FOCUS

They went a steady early pace here, resulting in a time 1.4sec slower than the first division.

NOTEBOOK

Havant impressed in quickening right away up the hill to score easily. A half-sister to Italian Group 1 1m4f winner Leadership, she clearly enjoyed the soft ground and, while it's anyone's guess what the form is worth, she's entitled to respect when stepped up in grade. A mile should be within her compass this year, and middle distances next season. (tchd 13-8 and 15-8)

Mia Madonna, representing a stable whose 2-y-os rarely win first time up, couldn't live with the winner when that one quickened up, but she stayed on steadily to take second. She'll surely come on for the run and, given her dam won first time up on fast ground, a quicker surface may well help. (tchd 6-1)

Lucky Meadows(IRE) is by a sire whose stock generally prefer quick ground and out of a filly who was a fast-ground sprinter, so conditions were probably not ideal for her. Her tail went round like a windmill during the first half of the race, and she didn't get home up the hill. Quicker ground and possibly a drop back to 6f might suit her. (op 10-3 tchd 3-1)

Schism has a middle-distance pedigree and is bred to do a lot better at three than two. This race proved too much of a test of speed but a stronger all-round gallop, and a step up to a mile will suit. (op 11-2)

Scented is a sister to a couple of middle-distance winners and is another bred to do better next year. She didn't look that comfortable on this ground. (op 5-1)

5490 BREHENY NURSERY 1m

2:55 (2:57) (Class 4) (0-85,84) 2-Y-O £5,180 (£1,541; £770; £384) Stalls Low

Form RPR

0051 1 **Piceno (IRE)**[7] 5256 2-8-8 71 6ex KierenFallon 3 77
(L M Cumani) *led: rdn wl over 2f out: hrd pressed and hung rt u.p fr 2f out: hdd jst over 1f out: kpt on gamely to ld again fnl 100yds: continued to hang and bmpd rival nr fin: hld on wl* **4/5**[1]

21 2 nk **Askaud (IRE)**[18] 4899 2-8-10 73 TomQueally 4 78+
(J A Glover) *t.k.h: hld up wl in tch: rdn to chse wnr wl over 2f out: ev ch and carried rt fr 2f out: led jst over 1f out tl hdd fnl 100yds: stl ev ch and battling on whn bmpd and no ex nr fin* **7/1**[3]

01 3 1 1/2 **Kalahaag (IRE)**[29] 4508 2-9-4 81 RichardHughes 6 84
(R Hannon) *in tch in midfield: rdn and effrt to chse ldng pair over 2f out: edging rt u.p fr wl over 1f out: keeping on same pce and hld whn nt clr run and eased nr fin* **7/1**[3]

404 4 1/2 **Roi Du Boeuf (IRE)**[21] 4802 2-7-6 62 oh4 ow1 RyanPowell(7) 5 63
(D M Simcock) *in tch towards rr: rdn and effrt to chse ldng trio ent fnl 2f: no imp tl styd on wl ins fnl f: nt pce to rch ldrs* **20/1**

0051 5 6 **Buzz Law (IRE)**[21] 4801 2-8-3 66 JimmyQuinn 8 54
(Mrs K Burke) *after and dropped in bhd after s: t.k.h: hld up in tch in rr: rdn and effrt 3f out: sn struggling: wknd and wl btn fr wl over 1f out* **14/1**

4400 6 11 **On Wings Of Love (IRE)**[27] 4592 2-8-5 68 (p) RichardMullen 1 32
(A Bailey) *s.i.s: hld up in tch in rr: rdn and effrt 3f out: sn struggling and wl btn fnl 2f* **20/1**

30 7 4 **Honourable Knight (IRE)**[21] 4801 2-8-8 71 MartinDwyer 2 26
(M D I Usher) *sn bustled along: chsd ldrs tl lost pl qckly u.p 3f out: sn wl bhd* **33/1**

621 8 8 **Tinkertown (IRE)**[69] 3222 2-9-7 84 JamieSpencer 7 21
(P F I Cole) *sn w wnr: rdn ent fnl 3f: lost 2nd wl over 2f out and sn wknd: wl bhd fr wl over 1f out: eased ins fnl f* **13/2**[2]

1m 44.22s (4.22) **Going Correction** +0.525s/f (Yiel) 8 Ran SP% **113.0**

Speed ratings (Par 96): **99,98,97,96,90 79,75,67**

Tote Swingers: 1&2 £2.90, 1&3 £2.70, 2&3 £3.30 CSF £6.48 CT £23.30 TOTE £2.00: £1.10, £2.10, £1.50; EX 8.30.

Owner Team Spirit 2 **Bred** Miss Wendy Fox **Trained** Newmarket, Suffolk

■ Stewards' Enquiry : Kieren Fallon three-day ban: careless riding (Sep 10, 12-13); two-day ban: used whip down shoulder in the forehand (Sep14-15)

FOCUS

A fair nursery.

NOTEBOOK

Piceno(IRE) made hard work of landing the odds and was forced to survive a 'stewards enquiry. He was 6lb well in under his penalty for his Salisbury success and, proven in the ground, looked to hold obvious claims. Having made much of the running towards the far rail, he started to drift right under pressure, carrying Askaud with him, and eventually ended up nearer the stands' side rail. He bumped Askaud near the line, but looked on top at the time and the stewards rightly left the result to stand. On this evidence he'll struggle off his revised mark, but the second and third came into this on the back of maiden wins and perhaps the race was more competitive than it had looked. (tchd 8-11 tchd 5-6 and 10-11 in places)

Askaud(IRE), runner-up to the smart Toolain on debut and a winner at Thirsk second time up, ran a fine race in defeat against a well-handicapped rival. There were concerns about the ground, but she coped with it well and she shouldn't be long in winning something similar. (op 11-2 tchd 15-2)

Kalahaag(IRE), a winner at the Glorious Goodwood meeting, is like the runner-up a daughter of Iffraaj. It's questionable whether this soft ground was ideal for her but she ran a solid race and is another quite capable of defying her current mark in similar company. Official explanation: jockey said filly was whinnying from 2f out (tchd 11-2)

Roi Du Boeuf(IRE), debuting for a new stable and 4lb out of the handicap, put up his best effort to date, clearly improving for the step up to a mile on soft ground. He can expect a hike in the weights now, so he might have to be turned out quickly. (tchd 18-1 and 22-1)

Buzz Law(IRE), who won over 7f here last time, was having his first start for a new stable. He seemed to find this longer trip in softer ground a bit too much of a test. (op 16-1 tchd 20-1)

Tinkertown(IRE) raced alongside the winner through the first half of the race but dropped out quite tamely, and perhaps he needed this following a two-month break. (op 15-2)

5491 EUROPEAN BREEDERS' FUND MAIDEN STKS 7f

3:30 (3:32) (Class 4) 2-Y-O £4,533 (£1,348; £674; £336) Stalls Low

Form RPR

1 **Seattle Drive (IRE)** 2-9-0 0 DaneO'Neill 9 83+
(D R C Elsworth) *s.i.s: in tch in last early: pushed along and gd hdwy over 1f out: led ins fnl f: immediately rn green and edgd lft but sn in command: comf* **33/1**

2 2 **Fulgur** 2-9-0 0 KierenFallon 19 78+
(L M Cumani) *t.k.h: chsd ldrs: rdn and sltly outpcd wl over 1f out: kpt on again and n.m.r ins fnl f: kpt on to take 2nd fnl 75yds: no imp on wnr* **8/1**[3]

3 1 1/4 **Double Dealer** 2-9-0 0 TedDurcan 15 75
(Mahmood Al Zarooni) *led: rdn and edgd rt fr 2f out: hdd ins fnl f: sn outpcd by wnr and lost 2nd fnl 75yds* **8/1**[3]

4 1 1/4 **Marden (IRE)** 2-9-0 0 MartinDwyer 3 72
(B J Meehan) *racd keenly: hld up wl in tch: rdn and effrt 2f out: ev ch ent fnl f: nt pce of ldng trio fnl 100yds: kpt on* **14/1**

5 1 1/4 **Utley (USA)** 2-9-0 0 WilliamBuick 7 69
(J H M Gosden) *chsd ldrs: effrt to chse ldr 3f out: rdn and ev ch over 1f out tl wknd ins fnl f* **10/3**[1]

6 1 1/2 **Chilled** 2-9-0 0 RichardMullen 5 65+
(Sir Michael Stoute) *in tch: rdn and effrt ent fnl 2f: ev ch u.p ent fnl f: wknd fnl 150yds* **10/1**

7 1 3/4 **Adone (IRE)** 2-8-11 0 Louis-PhilippeBeuzelin(3) 1 61+
(Sir Michael Stoute) *wnt rt s: hld up wl in tch towards rr: hdwy 1/2-way: chsd ldrs and rdn 2f out: wknd over 1f out and wl btn fnl f* **20/1**

8 6 **Odin (IRE)** 2-9-0 0 NeilCallan 4 46
(D R C Elsworth) *s.i.s: hld up wl in tch towards rr: hdwy into midfield 1/2-way: rdn and btn ent fnl 2f* **28/1**

9 1 1/2 **Sergeant Troy (IRE)** 2-9-0 0 SteveDrowne 6 42
(R Charlton) *stdd s: hld up in midfield tl shuffled bk towards rr 4f out: sme hdwy 3f out: sn rdn and struggling: wl btn fnl 2f* **16/1**

10 hd **Three Sparrows (IRE)** 2-9-0 0 RichardHughes 8 41
(R Hannon) *s.i.s: sn wl in tch in midfield: losing pl and pushed along whn swtchd lft wl over 2f out: sn wl btn* **8/1**[3]

11 1/2 **Deny** 2-9-0 0 RichardHills 14 40
(Sir Michael Stoute) *in tch in midfield: rdn 4f out: struggling whn rn green 3f out: bhd and wl btn fnl 2f* **9/1**

12 3/4 **My Mate Les (IRE)** 2-9-0 0 AlanMunro 10 38
(J R Best) *s.i.s: in tch in rr: rdn and struggling whn edgd lft wl over 2f out: wl bhd fnl 2f* **40/1**

The Form Book, Raceform Ltd, Compton, RG20 6NL

13 1 **Ugo (USA)** 2-9-0 0 LiamKeniry 20 36
(Mrs H S Main) *wl in tch towards rr: rdn ent fnl 3f: sn btn and wl bhd fnl 2f* **100/1**
14 2 1/2 **Tanjung Agas (IRE)** 2-9-0 0 PhilipRobinson 18 29
(M A Jarvis) *s.i.s: sn niggled along and rn green in rr: wknd and wl bhd wl over 2f out* **11/2[2]**
15 3 1/2 **Diocese (USA)** 2-9-0 0 PatDobbs 13 21
(Sir Michael Stoute) *chsd ldr tl 3f out: sn rdn and losing pl: wl bhd fr wl over 1f out* **25/1**

1m 30.27s (4.57) **Going Correction** +0.525s/f (Yiel) **15** Ran SP% **121.9**
Speed ratings (Par 96): **94,91,90,88,87 85,83,76,75,74 74,73,72,69,65**
Tote Swingers: 1&2 £41.30, 1&3 £61.80, 2&3 £13.30 CSF £268.19 TOTE £45.30: £10.50, £2.80, £3.40; EX 429.30.
Owner J C Smith **Bred** Littleton Stud **Trained** Newmarket, Suffolk

FOCUS
A decent looking maiden on paper, run in a time 1.15sec quicker than the faster of the two divisions of the fillies' maiden earlier on the card. It should throw up a few winners.

NOTEBOOK
Seattle Drive(IRE) is a half-brother to Listed winners Snoqualmie Boy and Snoqualmie Girl but his jockey carried the owner's second colours and he was fairly dismissed in the betting. Having been held up at the back of the field, though, he came through to challenge 2f out and quickened up smartly once he hit the rising ground. He won with a degree of ease and, although he holds no significant entries, looks well worth a try in a conditions race now. He'll get a mile no problem. (op 25-1)
Fulgur, who has a middle-distance pedigree and is entered in the Racing Post Trophy, was prominent throughout and stayed on well towards the finish. He'll appreciate a step up to a mile. (tchd 17-2)
Double Dealer, who is not really bred to want much further than this as a 2-y-o, ran a sound race on his debut and should not have too much difficult winning a similar race. (op 11-1)
Marden(IRE) ◆ did best of those that raced more towards the far side. A half-brother to Grade 1 winning miler Luas Line, he holds Royal Lodge and Racing Post Trophy entries, and shaped like a sure-fire next-time-out winner. (op 20-1)
Utley(USA) ◆ is a half-brother to the owner's top-class filly Rainbow View, who made a winning debut over this C&D. Well entered up, he showed enough to suggest he can win his maiden before stepping up in class. (op 4-1 tchd 3-1)
Chilled, a half-brother to the owners' Group 1 placed miler Infallible, showed up well to a furlong out before getting a little tired. He's fully entitled to come on for this debut effort. (op 9-1)
Adone(IRE) ◆, a half-brother to Group 3 winning sprinter Greek Renaissance, is by Irish Guineas winner Araafa, who coped well with soft ground. He looked very much in need of this beforehand and plenty of improvement can be expected for the outing. (op 16-1)
Odin(IRE), stablemate of the winner, was on edge a bit beforehand and didn't pick up under pressure. He looks more of a long-term prospect. (op 25-1)
Three Sparrows(IRE) struggled to land a blow from off the pace but his dam won four times, including at Listed level, and he might do better on quicker ground. (op 15-2 tchd 7-1)
Deny is by Mr Greeley, whose stock tend to prefer a sounder surface. He ran green here and looks sure to have learnt plenty for the outing. (tchd 17-2)
Tanjung Agas(IRE) was another who looked pretty clueless on his debut. He cost 250,000gns, holds numerous Group race entries and was sent off second-favourite, though, so the chances are he'll soon leave this form well behind. Official explanation: jockey said colt ran green (op 9-2)

5492 J20 WHITE BLEND H'CAP 1m 6f 175y
4:05 (4:08) (Class 3) (0-95,94) 3-Y-0+ **£9,066** (£2,697; £1,348; £673) **Stalls** Centre

Form RPR
136 1 **Maxim Gorky (IRE)**[65] 3335 3-8-3 **82** JimmyQuinn 11 97+
(Sir Michael Stoute) *stdd s: hld up in last trio: hdwy 4f out: chsd ldr gng wl 3f out: led 2f out: sn pushed clr and in command 1f out: rdn along hands and heels and readily fnd ex ins fnl f: comf* **11/4[2]**
2423 2 1 1/4 **Plymouth Rock (IRE)**[20] 4846 4-9-9 **89** (v) WilliamBuick 9 99
(J Noseda) *stdd s: hld up in last pair: rdn and effrt ent fnl 3f: swtchd rt over 1f out: chsd wnr 1f out: edgd lft u.p and no imp fnl 100yds* **2/1[1]**
0546 3 3 1/4 **Ocean's Minstrel**[34] 4393 4-9-6 **86** AlanMunro 1 91
(J Ryan) *stdd s: hld up in last pair: hdwau over 4f out: rdn over 2f out: kpt on u.p and chsd clr wnr briefly jst over 1f out: 3rd and no prog fnl f* **16/1**
2530 4 13 **Hevelius**[20] 4817 5-9-8 **88** AdamKirby 8 75
(W R Swinburn) *led and sn clr: c to r in centre fr 8f out: rdn and hdd 2f out: sn no ch w wnr: fdd ent fnl f: fin tired* **14/1**
60-0 5 10 **Wells Lyrical (IRE)**[20] 4846 5-9-8 **88** TomEaves 3 61
(B Smart) *chsd ldr after 2f and sn clr of field: c to r in centre 8f out: rdn and lost 2nd 3f out: sn drvn and struggling: wl btn over 1f out: eased fnl f* **14/1**
1060 6 2 1/2 **Hollins**[7] 5278 6-9-0 **80** KierenFallon 10 50
(Micky Hammond) *t.k.h: prom in main gp tl rdn and lost pl over 3f out: wl bhd fnl 2f: eased fnl f: hmpd and swtchd rt nr fin* **6/1[3]**
206 7 1 1/2 **Kid Charlemagne (IRE)**[29] 4506 7-9-13 **93** TomQueally 5 61
(W J Greatrex) *stdd s: t.k.h: hld up off the pce in midfield: swtchd lft to r in centre 5f out: rdn and struggling 4f out: drvn and wl btn wl over 1f out: eased fnl f:* **10/1**
-020 8 nk **Lethal Glaze (IRE)**[6] 5291 4-9-12 **92** RichardHughes 7 59
(R Hannon) *chsd ldr for 2f: chsd clr ldng pair after: clsd 4f out: rdn 3f out: hung lft and wknd over 1f out: v tired fnl f and virtually p.u fnl 100yds* **9/1**

3m 16.3s (5.00) **Going Correction** +0.525s/f (Yiel)
WFA 3 from 4yo+ 13lb **8** Ran SP% **112.6**
Speed ratings (Par 107): **107,106,104,97,92 91,90,90**
Tote Swingers: 1&2 £2.40, 1&3 £7.80, 2&3 £5.50 CSF £8.36 CT £68.16 TOTE £3.90: £1.60, £1.30, £3.80; EX 9.70.
Owner Mrs John Magnier, M Tabor & D Smith **Bred** Ecurie De Meautray, Skymarc Farm & Castl **Trained** Newmarket, Suffolk

FOCUS
A fair staying handicap, run at a sound pace. The main action developed more away from the stands' rail, despite all bar two of the field starting off on it entering the home straight, and eventually three pulled clear.

NOTEBOOK
Maxim Gorky(IRE) ran out a ready winner and landed good support in the process. Sir Michael Stoute's colt was having his first outing since running below par at Salisbury 65 days earlier on quick ground. Being faced with some cut underfoot once more proved right up his street and he saw out the longer trip without that much fuss. There was plenty to like about the manner in which he travelled into contention and he was probably idling near the finish, having been out in front plenty long enough. The winner was getting plenty of weight all round, but this race has been won by some decent 3-y-o stayers in the past and he could well be up to making his mark in better company as he has very few miles on the clock. The Mallard Handicap at Doncaster's St Leger meeting may be a viable target for him, although that may come soon enough, but either way he should make a nice staying handicapper next season. (op 4-1 tchd 5-2)
Plymouth Rock(IRE) finished strongly, but the bird had flown and he again managed to find one too good. More positive handling over this slightly sharper test may have suited, but it's most unlikely it would have changed the result as he does find it hard to get his head in front. (op 15-8 tchd 7-4 tchd 9-4 in places)
Ocean's Minstrel is on a losing run, but he's improved since being upped to this sort of trip recently and ran another sound race on ground plenty soft enough. He deserves a change of fortune. (op 14-1 tchd 20-1)
Hevelius was given an aggressive ride and was the first to go mid-track off the home bend. He was cooked 3f out, though, and really wants quicker ground. (tchd 16-1)
Wells Lyrical(IRE) was well held, but this was a bit more encouraging and he's entitled to come on again for the run so he's one to keep an eye on if getting respite from the handicapper. (tchd 8-1)
Hollins, who does act on this ground, has now shaped on his last two outings as though he would benefit from a break. (tchd 15-2)

5493 NEWMARKETRACECOURSES.CO.UK MAIDEN STKS 1m
4:35 (4:37) (Class 4) 3-Y-0+ **£4,533** (£1,348; £674; £336) **Stalls** Low

Form RPR
2- 1 **Call To Reason (IRE)**[300] 7182 3-8-12 0 RichardHughes 1 82+
(J Noseda) *hld up wl in tch: smooth hdwy to trck ldrs 2f out: ev ch ent fnl f: pushed ahd ins fnl f: edgd rt but sn clr: easily* **4/6[1]**
23 2 2 3/4 **Significant Move**[97] 2334 3-9-3 0 (t) SteveDrowne 12 73+
(R Charlton) *chsd ldrs: wnt 2nd 1/2-way: rdn ent fnl 2f: ev ch u.p ent fnl f: nt pce of wnr ins fnl f: wnt 2nd fnl 50yds* **10/3[2]**
04 3 1/2 **Present Story**[17] 4926 3-8-12 0 DaraghO'Donohoe 8 67
(P Leech) *led at stdy gallop: rdn and qcknd over 2f out: drvn ent fnl f: hdd and nt pce of wnr ins fnl f: lost 2nd fnl 50yds* **100/1**
4 2 **Transeggselence** 3-8-9 0 AshleyHamblett(3) 13 62
(P Leech) *t.k.h: hld up wl in tch: chsd ldng trio and rdn wl over 1f out: edgd lft and no imp ent fnl f* **100/1**
5 5 **Annuity (IRE)** 3-9-3 0 NeilCallan 10 54
(W J Knight) *in tch in midfield: rdn 1/2-way: wl outpcd and no ch w ldrs 2f out: plugged on steadily fnl f* **25/1**
6 1 **Jaldarshaan (IRE)** 3-8-12 0 TravisBlock 3 46
(W J H Ratcliffe) *hld up in tch in midfield: hdwy 3f out: chsd ldrs and rdn wl over 1f out: no prog and wl btn ent fnl f* **66/1**
6 7 1/2 **Cotton King**[9] 5209 3-9-3 0 (t) TomQueally 7 50
(T B P Coles) *s.i.s: bhd: rdn and struggling wl over 2f out: no ch fr wl over 1f out: sme modest hdwy ins fnl f: n.d* **100/1**
03-P 8 5 **En Fuego**[104] 2122 3-9-3 0 JackMitchell 9 37
(P W Chapple-Hyam) *t.k.h: chsd ldrs: rdn and struggling ent fnl 2f: wkng whn edgd rt over 1f out: wl btn fnl f* **14/1**
5 9 7 **Red Flash (IRE)**[126] 1500 3-9-3 0 AdrianLayt 4 19
(P Leech) *w ldr tl 1/2-way: sn rdn and losing pl: wl bhd fr wl over 1f out* **100/1**
10 6 **Launchpad** 3-9-3 0 KierenFallon 6 —
(L M Cumani) *s.i.s: a in rr: pushed along 1/2-way: lost tch ent fnl 2f* **12/1**
0 11 nk **Chateau Galliard (IRE)**[23] 4697 4-9-9 0 AdamKirby 11 —
(T T Clement) *a in rr: rdn and btn over 2f out: wl bhd fnl 2f* **150/1**
12 shd **Longsword** 3-9-3 0 WilliamBuick 5 —
(Mahmood Al Zarooni) *t.k.h: hld up in midfield: rdn and struggling 1/2-way: in rr and wl btn 2f out* **10/1[3]**

1m 44.44s (4.44) **Going Correction** +0.525s/f (Yiel)
WFA 3 from 4yo 6lb **12** Ran SP% **116.5**
Speed ratings (Par 105): **98,95,94,92,87 86,86,81,74,68 67,67**
Tote Swingers: 1&2 £2.10, 1&3 £13.60, 2&3 £20.90 CSF £2.79 TOTE £1.70: £1.10, £1.20, £13.20; EX 3.40.
Owner The Socrates Partnership **Bred** J Hanly, T Stewart & A Stroud **Trained** Newmarket, Suffolk

FOCUS
The performance of the third holds down the value of this form.
Cotton King Official explanation: jockey said gelding became upset in stalls

5494 NGK SPARK PLUGS CLAIMING STKS 7f
5:10 (5:10) (Class 5) 3-Y-0 **£3,238** (£963; £481; £240) **Stalls** Low

Form RPR
2245 1 **Frequency**[11] 5162 3-8-7 69 KierenFallon 3 67
(E A L Dunlop) *chsd ldrs: rdn over 1f out: drvn to ld 1f out: styd on wl* **7/2[2]**
2210 2 1 1/2 **Rolling Hills (IRE)**[16] 4963 3-9-1 70 DaneO'Neill 2 71
(H Candy) *led: rdn and hung rt fr over 1f out: hdd 1f out: styd on same pce after* **4/1[3]**
664 3 nk **Flighty Frances (IRE)**[13] 5086 3-8-13 74 WilliamBuick 7 68
(D R C Elsworth) *stdd s: hld up in tch: rdn 3f out: no real prog tl styd on to go 3rd ins fnl f: drvn and pressing for 2nd nr fin: nvr gng pce to chal wnr* **15/8[1]**
2500 4 2 **Hierarch (IRE)**[14] 5051 3-9-3 68 RichardHughes 5 67
(R Hannon) *stdd s: hld up in tch in last trio: rdn and effrt 2f out: drvn over 1f out: kpt on same pce ins fnl f* **7/1**
0023 5 1 **Ginger Grey (IRE)**[57] 3580 3-8-13 67 (b) NeilCallan 6 60
(D R C Elsworth) *chsd ldr tl over 1f out: wknd u.p jst ins fnl f* **7/1**
145 6 13 **Bell's Ocean (USA)**[3] 5384 3-8-8 59 MichaelHills 1 20
(J Ryan) *stdd s: hld up in tch in last trio: rdn wl over 2f out: wknd over 1f out: wl btn and eased ins fnl f* **12/1**

1m 29.65s (3.95) **Going Correction** +0.40s/f (Good) **6** Ran SP% **109.7**
Speed ratings (Par 100): **93,91,90,88,87 72**
Tote Swingers: 1&2 £2.60, 1&3 £2.50, 2&3 £2.30 CSF £16.80 TOTE £4.50: £2.00, £2.90; EX 16.70.Frequency was claimed by Mr Paul Howling for £4,000.
Owner Thurloe Thoroughbreds XXV **Bred** Manor Farm Stud (rutland) **Trained** Newmarket, Suffolk

FOCUS
They went a good pace in this claimer and the winning time was the quickest of the four races run over the distance on the card.

5495 TURFTV H'CAP 6f
5:40 (5:40) (Class 4) (0-85,84) 3-Y-0+ **£5,180** (£1,541; £770; £384) **Stalls** Low

Form RPR
1423 1 **R Woody**[29] 4503 3-9-7 **82** AlanMunro 20 96
(D K Ivory) *racd in pair nrest stands' rail: hld up in tch: rdn and effrt over 1f out: 1f out: r.o strly and drew clr ins fnl f: comf* **16/1**
3 2 2 1/4 **Avertor**[42] 4090 4-9-8 **80** SteveDrowne 19 87
(R Charlton) *racd in pair nrest stnds' rail: chsd ldrs: rdn and edgd lft fr over 1f out: ev ch ent fnl f: nt pce of wnr fnl f: kpt on for clr 2nd* **4/1[1]**
2002 3 2 1/2 **New Leyf (IRE)**[27] 4598 4-9-7 **79** JamieSpencer 14 78
(J R Gask) *chsd ldrs: rdn 1/2-way: chsd ldr u.p over 2f out: ev ch and hrd drvn over 1f out: outpcd by ldng pair fnl f: kpt on to hold 3rd* **7/1[3]**
5142 4 3/4 **Arabian Pearl (IRE)**[32] 4440 4-9-4 **76** (b) JackMitchell 9 73
(P W Chapple-Hyam) *led: rdn and edgd rt ent fnl 2f: hdd 1f out: sn outpcd and wl hld fnl f* **10/1**
0215 5 1/2 **Kings 'n Dreams**[33] 4398 3-8-13 **74** (b) TomQueally 1 69+
(D K Ivory) *in tch in midfield: rdn and effrt ent fnl 2f: styd on same pce and no prog ent fnl f* **28/1**

0066 **6** *1 ¼* **Getcarter**[18] 4904 4-9-10 **82** PatDobbs 17 73
(R Hannon) *hld up in tch in midfield: rdn and effrt ent fnl 2f: outpcd by ldrs wl over 1f out and n.d after: plugged on ins fnl f* **16/1**

0610 **7** *nse* **Stevie Gee (IRE)**[13] 5082 6-8-12 **77** (v) RyanPowell(7) 10 68
(Ian Williams) *s.i.s: bhd: rdn 1/2-way: hdwy over 1f out: styd on ins fnl f: nvr trbld ldrs* **14/1**

0000 **8** *nk* **Cornus**[15] 4995 8-9-4 **83** (be) NoraLooby(7) 15 73
(A J McCabe) *bhd: rdn over 2f out: hdwy over 1f out: styd on past btn horses fnl f: nvr trbld ldrs* **50/1**

6336 **9** *2 ¾* **Viking Spirit**[15] 4995 8-9-5 **77** AdamKirby 8 58
(W R Swinburn) *in tch in midfield: rdn and effrt 2f out: rdn and btn over 1f out: wknd fnl f* **9/1**

6002 **10** *1 ½* **Coleorton Choice**[6] 5297 4-9-5 **77** (p) WilliamBuick 4 53
(R Hollinshead) *chsd ldrs: rdn 1/2-way: wknd over 1f out: wl btn and eased wl ins fnl f* **12/1**

003 **11** *nse* **Sunshine Always (IRE)**[13] 5087 4-8-12 **70** (p) KirstyMilczarek 11 46
(T D McCarthy) *in tch towards rr: rdn 1/2-way: no prog and wl btn over 1f out: nvr trbld ldrs* **12/1**

5066 **12** *nk* **Hatta Stream (IRE)**[11] 5157 4-8-12 **70** SaleemGolam 7 45
(J Pearce) *a bhd: rdn and no real prog over 2f out: no ch whn hmpd and swtchd rt 1f out: n.d* **50/1**

2050 **13** *2 ¾* **Aldermoor (USA)**[13] 5068 4-9-12 **84** WilliamCarson 18 50
(S C Williams) *chsd ldrs: rdn and struggling over 2f out: wkng whn sltly hmpd 2f out: wl btn over 1f out* **20/1**

0440 **14** *1* **Mrs Penny (AUS)**[62] 3435 6-9-7 **79** LiamKeniry 5 42
(J R Gask) *in tch in midfield: rdn and struggling 1/2-way: wl bhd fr wl over 1f out* **28/1**

3044 **15** *1 ½* **Fivefold (USA)**[14] 5031 3-9-1 **76** DaneO'Neill 3 34
(J Akehurst) *chsd ldr tl 1/2-way: sn rdn and struggling: wl bhd over 1f out: eased wl ins fnl f* **25/1**

0050 **16** *1 ½* **Cyflymder (IRE)**[31] 4459 4-9-12 **84** RichardHughes 13 38
(R Hannon) *stdd s: hld up in rr: struggling fr 1/2-way: wl bhd fr wl over 1f out* **12/1**

011 **17** *3 ½* **Signore Momento (IRE)**[38] 4225 4-9-7 **79** (tp) KierenFallon 6 21
(Miss Amy Weaver) *hld up towards rr: rdn and no prog over 2f out: wl btn whn edgd rt over 1f out: eased ins fnl f* **5/1**[2]

1m 14.07s (1.57) **Going Correction** +0.40s/f (Good)
WFA 3 from 4yo+ 3lb **17** Ran SP% **129.2**
Speed ratings (Par 105): **105,102,98,97,97 95,95,94,91,89 89,88,85,83,81 79,75**
Tote Swingers: 1&2 £18.70, 1&3 £24.00, 2&3 £7.90. totesuper7: Win: Not won, Place: £1,360.80 CSF £77.59 CT £399.56 TOTE £24.60: £4.60, £1.70, £1.40, £2.80; EX 107.60 Place 6:£57.28 Place 5: £11.46..
Owner Quintessential Thoroughbreds Solar Syn **Bred** R, D And M Close **Trained** Radlett, Herts

FOCUS
Those drawn high and racing nearest the stands' side dominated here.
Signore Momento(IRE) Official explanation: jockey said gelding never travelled
T/Jkpt: Not won. T/Plt: £426.70 to a £1 stake. Pool:£64,855.39 - 110.95 winning tickets T/Qpdt: £12.00 to a £1 stake. Pool:£6,282.78 - 385.82 winning tickets SP

4896 THIRSK (L-H)
Friday, August 27
OFFICIAL GOING: Good to firm (good in places; 10.0)
Wind: light 1/2 behind Weather: fine

5496 GORMIRE (S) STKS 6f
1:40 (1:41) (Class 5) 3-Y-O+ **£3,238** (£963; £481; £240) **Stalls** High

Form RPR

3300 **1** **King's Wonder**[8] 5242 5-8-13 85 AdrianNicholls 1 65
(D Nicholls) *sn w ldr on outside: led over 2f out: edgd rt over 1f out: hld on towards fin* **4/6**[1]

0043 **2** *nk* **Beckermet (IRE)**[9] 5197 8-8-10 77 JamesSullivan(3) 3 64
(Mrs R A Carr) *led tl over 3f out: chsd wnr: swtchd lft and styd on ins fnl f: no ex nr fin* **5/1**[2]

4036 **3** *3* **Forzarzi (IRE)**[19] 4869 6-8-13 45 PhillipMakin 9 54
(H A McWilliams) *hld up in rr: hdwy stands' side 2f out: chsd ldng pair over 1f out: kpt on same pce* **50/1**

0665 **4** *4* **Desert Falls**[7] 5267 4-8-10 57 (v) MichaelStainton(3) 4 41
(R M Whitaker) *chsd ldrs: drvn 3f out: wknd over 1f out* **16/1**

0204 **5** *¾* **Errigal Lad**[19] 4868 5-8-13 60 (p) AndrewElliott 8 39
(J Balding) *sn drvn along: chsd ldrs: wknd over 1f out* **12/1**

0200 **6** *1 ¼* **Musca (IRE)**[19] 4868 6-8-13 59 PaulHanagan 6 35
(C Grant) *prom: wknd over 1f out* **14/1**

0600 **7** *3* **Pearly Wey**[13] 5064 7-8-8 65 DaleSwift(5) 2 25
(I W McInnes) *chsd ldrs on wd outside: sn drvn along: wknd 2f out* **7/1**[3]

0560 **8** *5* **Soto**[19] 4869 7-9-5 57 (b) PaulMulrennan 7 15
(M W Easterby) *trckd ldrs: t.k.h: lost pl and eased over 1f out* **40/1**

1m 10.93s (-1.77) **Going Correction** -0.15s/f (Firm) **8** Ran SP% **113.8**
Speed ratings (Par 103): **105,104,100,95,94 92,88,81**
Tote Swingers: 1&2 £2.00, 1&3 £9.70, 2&3 £9.60 CSF £4.25 TOTE £1.40: £1.02, £2.10, £10.20; EX 4.00.No bid for winner.
Owner Middleham Park Racing XXXII **Bred** Bearstone Stud **Trained** Sessay, N Yorks

FOCUS
An uncompetitive seller dominated by the two horses with the best chances on official ratings.

5497 TOTEPOOL H'CAP 2m
2:10 (2:10) (Class 4) (0-80,77) 3-Y-O+ **£3,885** (£1,156; £577; £288) **Stalls** Low

Form RPR

-114 **1** **Lady Hestia (USA)**[46] 3955 5-10-0 **73** FrankieDettori 2 80
(M P Tregoning) *mde all: qcknd over 2f out: sn hrd drvn: hld on gamely* **7/1**

6321 **2** *1* **Blazing Desert**[37] 4266 6-9-9 **73** IanBrennan(5) 5 79+
(J J Quinn) *hld up: hdwy to chal over 3f out: wnt 2nd appr fnl f: no real imp* **9/2**[3]

6062 **3** *1 ½* **Rawnaq (IRE)**[15] 4983 3-9-4 **77** JoeFanning 7 81
(M Johnston) *chsd wnr: kpt on same pce fnl 2f* **13/8**[1]

1254 **4** *2 ¼* **Tillietudlem (FR)**[12] 5119 4-9-9 **68** PaulHanagan 3 70
(J S Goldie) *sn trckng ldrs: outpcd 4f out: one pce fnl 2f* **7/2**[2]

/151 **5** *½* **Jeu De Roseau (IRE)**[18] 4900 6-9-2 **61** PaulMulrennan 6 62
(C Grant) *trckd ldrs: chal over 3f out: sn rdn: one pce fnl 2f* **5/1**

3m 29.11s (-3.69) **Going Correction** -0.10s/f (Good)
WFA 3 from 4yo+ 14lb **5** Ran SP% **107.7**
Speed ratings (Par 105): **105,104,103,102,102**
CSF £34.61 TOTE £4.80: £2.60, £1.40; EX 16.70.
Owner Mr And Mrs A E Pakenham **Bred** Shadwell Farm LLC **Trained** Lambourn, Berks

FOCUS
A fair staying handicap that was run at a steady pace for the most part.

5498 EUROPEAN BREEDERS' FUND MAIDEN STKS 1m
2:40 (2:41) (Class 4) 2-Y-O **£4,338** (£1,291; £645; £322) **Stalls** Low

Form RPR

0 **1** **Colour Vision (FR)**[14] 5049 2-9-3 0 JoeFanning 10 80+
(M Johnston) *in rr-div: outpcd over 4f out: hdwy and swtchd outside over 2f out: hung lft: chsd wnr appr fnl f: styd on to ld nr fin* **18/1**

2 *½* **Ru'Oud** 2-9-3 0 FrankieDettori 8 79+
(Saeed Bin Suroor) *led 1f: trckd ldrs: smooth hdwy to chal over 2f out: shkn up to ld over 1f out: hdd and no ex towards fin* **2/1**[2]

2 **3** *3 ¼* **Grand Duchy**[16] 4940 2-9-3 0 AhmedAjtebi 6 72
(Mahmood Al Zarooni) *chsd ldrs: swtchd rt over 2f out: edgd lft 1f out: one pce* **6/1**[3]

4 *3 ¾* **Mojolika** 2-9-3 0 DavidNolan 4 64+
(T D Easterby) *in rr-div: effrt over 3f out: kpt on fnl 2f* **66/1**

0365 **5** *4 ½* **Anddante (IRE)**[69] 3222 2-9-3 70 DuranFentiman 7 54
(T D Easterby) *led after 1f: hdd over 1f out: sn wknd* **20/1**

0 **6** *hd* **Illustrious Forest**[22] 4755 2-9-3 0 PaulMulrennan 11 53
(J Mackie) *chsd ldrs: effrt over 3f out: hmpd over 2f out and over 1f out: one pce* **25/1**

2 **7** *5* **Ventura Sands (IRE)**[14] 5040 2-9-3 0 PaulHanagan 3 42
(R A Fahey) *trckd ldrs: t.k.h: lost pl over 1f out* **6/5**[1]

8 *1 ½* **Smart Violetta (IRE)** 2-8-12 0 PhillipMakin 2 34+
(Mrs A Duffield) *dwlt: in rr and drvn along: nvr on terms* **50/1**

9 *nk* **One Of Twins** 2-9-0 0 JamesSullivan(3) 5 38
(M W Easterby) *s.i.s: a in rr* **100/1**

00 **10** *nse* **Sandpipers Dream**[14] 5040 2-9-3 0 DanielTudhope 9 38
(T D Walford) *trckd ldrs: hung lft and wknd over 1f out* **100/1**

00 **11** *44* **Bodie**[19] 4856 2-9-3 0 AdrianNicholls 12 —
(Mrs P Sly) *chsd ldrs on outside: lost pl over 2f out: sn bhd and eased: virtually p.u ins fnl f: t.o* **50/1**

1m 40.06s (-0.04) **Going Correction** -0.10s/f (Good) **11** Ran SP% **114.3**
Speed ratings (Par 96): **96,95,92,88,84 83,78,77,77,76 32**
Tote Swingers: 1&2 £10.40, 1&3 £13.20, 2&3 £2.30 CSF £51.41 TOTE £18.40: £3.00, £1.30, £1.20; EX 81.40.
Owner Sheikh Hamdan Bin Mohammed Al Maktoum **Bred** Capricorn Stud **Trained** Middleham Moor, N Yorks

FOCUS
An interesting maiden but one that produced something of a surprise result after the pace had been no more than fair. The form is probably decent for the track.

NOTEBOOK
Colour Vision(FR) is a well-bred colt with plenty of scope and, in company with several youngsters from his yard this year, left his debut running behind. Noticeably green throughout still, he only asserted late on and will be seen to much better effect again next time, with a step up to 1m2f also likely to suit. He's the sort that might well develop into a contender for the Zetland Stakes later in the season, though judging by the way he moved here, soft ground possibly had something to do with his modest debut performance too. (tchd 20-1)
Ru'Oud, who is out of a sister to the top-class Dubai Millennium and was well supported in the betting, took the eye beforehand, showing a fluent action, and ran well enough to suggest he should be able to break his maiden before long. Lack of previous experience probably caught him out late after he'd been left in front, but he'd travelled strongly to that point and looks to have a high natural level of ability. (op 7-4)
Grand Duchy probably ran to a similar standard as on his debut while performing in near-identical fashion, keeping on well despite carrying his head a shade high. The progeny of his sire have a good record on Fibresand and he'd be interesting if sent for a staying maiden or nursery (after one more run) at Southwell. (op 7-1)
Mojolika, a January foal out of an unraced mare, shaped well first time considering he was hampered on the turn and kept on in taking fashion once finally finding his stride. He's going to stay well this year, and promises to improve quite a lot. (op 80-1)
Anddante(IRE) might have needed his first run for well over two months, but he probably wouldn't have been good enough even if at peak fitness given his previous form and his action suggests he needs more give in the ground anyway. (tchd 18-1)
Illustrious Forest didn't really go on for his Sandown debut, but wasn't knocked about and shapes as if he is more of a long-term prospect. (op 22-1)
Ventura Sands(IRE) was a disappointing favourite. His Newcastle debut had been fill of promise, for all that race lacked strength, but he was too keen early and dropped out tamely when asked for his effort. He still has some growing up to do, and will probably be dropped back to 7f next time.
Official explanation: jockey said colt ran too free (op 11-8 tchd 11-10)
Smart Violetta(IRE), a half-sister to her yard's middle-distance winner Bavarian Nordic, looked to have something about her beforehand but never threatened after getting behind. She's entitled to improve.
Bodie Official explanation: jockey said colt had a breathing problem

5499 TOTEEXACTA THIRSK STKS (H'CAP) (DIV I) 7f
3:15 (3:16) (Class 4) (0-80,79) 3-Y-O+ **£3,561** (£1,059; £529; £264) **Stalls** Low

Form RPR

6515 **1** **Commando Scott (IRE)**[4] 5357 9-8-10 **65** NeilFarley(7) 4 73
(D Carroll) *hld up towards rr: effrt over 2f out: sn w ldrs: hung lft and led 1f out: hld on towards fin* **4/1**[1]

0300 **2** *½* **Champain Sands (IRE)**[27] 4602 11-8-6 **57** oh4 PaulPickard(3) 6 64
(E J Alston) *s.i.s: hld up in rr: swtchd outside over 2f out: styd on to chse ldr wl ins fnl f: no ex* **25/1**

4560 **3** *¾* **Legal Legacy**[20] 4850 4-9-9 **71** PhillipMakin 9 76
(M Dods) *trckd ldrs: t.k.h: kpt on wl ins fnl f* **11/2**[3]

0434 **4** *nk* **Kings Point (IRE)**[2] 5406 9-9-1 **63** AdrianNicholls 2 67
(D Nicholls) *chsd ldrs: styd on same pce ins fnl f* **5/1**[2]

5440 **5** *½* **King's Sabre**[4] 5357 4-8-10 **63** ow1 (e) MichaelO'Connell(5) 10 65
(R C Guest) *in rr: hdwy over 2f out: kpt on same pce fnl f* **16/1**

2515 **6** *nk* **Nufoudh (IRE)**[34] 4394 6-9-9 **71** AndrewMullen 7 73
(Miss Tracy Waggott) *gave problems s: led: hdd 1f out: kpt on same pce* **10/1**

0000 **7** *½* **Steel Stockholder**[34] 4394 4-9-5 **67** PaulHanagan 8 67
(M Brittain) *chsd ldrs: kpt on one pce appr fnl f* **5/1**[2]

5414 **8** *½* **Amber Sunset**[10] 5174 4-9-3 **68** MartinLane(3) 1 67
(D Morris) *t.k.h in rr: nt clr run over 2f out: kpt on fnl f* **12/1**

4000 **9** *9* **Baybshambles (IRE)**[23] 4704 6-8-10 **61** MichaelStainton(3) 11 36
(R E Barr) *t.k.h on wd outside: sn w ldrs: lost pl over 1f out* **16/1**

3-60 **10** *8* **Trailblazing**[42] 4112 3-9-12 **79** JoeFanning 3 30
(M Johnston) *chsd ldrs: lost pl over 1f out: sn bhd* **14/1**

3110 **11** 2 **Glenridding**[11] 5157 6-10-0 **76**....(p) PaulMulrennan 5 24
(J G Given) *in rr: lost pl over 2f out: sn bhd* **7/1**

1m 26.79s (-0.41) **Going Correction** -0.10s/f (Good)
WFA 3 from 4yo+ 5lb 11 Ran SP% **120.3**
Speed ratings (Par 105): **98,97,96,96,95 95,94,94,83,74 72**
Tote Swingers: 1&2 £22.70, 1&3 £9.10, 2&3 £12.50 CSF £110.68 CT £572.05 TOTE £5.10: £1.70, £8.70, £2.20; EX 142.30.
Owner Mrs Ann Morris **Bred** Noel Finegan **Trained** Sledmere, E Yorks

FOCUS
A modest handicap though one perhaps not run at quite the frantic tempo that seemed likely beforehand given the number of usual front runners in opposition.
Amber Sunset Official explanation: jockey said filly was denied a clear run
Glenridding Official explanation: jockey said gelding never travelled

5500 TOTEEXACTA THIRSK STKS (H'CAP) (DIV II) 7f
3:50 (3:51) (Class 4) (0-80,76) 3-Y-0+ **£3,561** (£1,059; £529; £264) **Stalls** Low

Form RPR
6000 **1** **Mujaadel (USA)**[26] 4619 5-9-9 **70**.... PaulMulrennan 6 81
(D Nicholls) *hmpd s: hld up towards rr: hdwy and n.m.r over 2f out: led 1f out: r.o strly* **5/1**[3]
0100 **2** 2 ½ **Chambers (IRE)**[24] 4670 4-8-7 **57**.... PaulPickard[(3)] 5 61
(E J Alston) *wnt rt s: in rr: hdwy on ins 3f out: nt clr run and swtchd rt 2f out: styd on to chse wnr jst ins fnl f* **16/1**
043/ **3** nk **Amazing Star (IRE)**[26] 4634 5-9-3 **71**.... NeilFarley[(7)] 2 74+
(D Carroll) *stdd s: t.k.h in rr: nt clr run over 2f out: styd on steadily fnl f* **15/2**
3201 **4** 1 ½ **Kilt Rock (IRE)**[2] 5421 3-9-10 **76** 6ex.... FrankieDettori 1 73
(R C Guest) *sn chsng ldrs: kpt on same pce fnl 2f* **5/2**[1]
3541 **5** hd **Sea Salt**[13] 5064 7-8-10 **62**.... LanceBetts[(5)] 3 61
(R E Barr) *led: hdd 1f out: fdd fnl 100yds* **9/1**
0160 **6** 2 ½ **Trans Sonic**[18] 4894 7-9-11 **75**.... JamesSullivan[(3)] 8 67
(D O'Meara) *chsd ldrs on outside: wknd fnl f* **10/1**
0623 **7** ¾ **Tobrata**[163] 911 4-9-1 **62**.... PaulHanagan 4 52
(M Brittain) *chsd ldrs: outpcd over 3f out: one pce fnl 2f* **10/1**
0020 **8** nk **Methaaly (IRE)**[28] 4558 7-9-8 **72**....(be) AmyRyan[(3)] 9 61
(M Mullineaux) *hld up in rr: hdwy on outer 3f out: sn chsng ldrs: wknd fnl f* **18/1**
0006 **9** 2 ½ **Violent Velocity (IRE)**[34] 4394 7-9-1 **67**.... IanBrennan[(5)] 7 50
(J J Quinn) *wnt lft s: sn chsng ldrs: wknd over 1f out* **4/1**[2]

1m 26.63s (-0.57) **Going Correction** -0.10s/f (Good)
WFA 3 from 4yo+ 5lb 9 Ran SP% **116.3**
Speed ratings (Par 105): **99,96,95,94,93 91,90,89,86**
Tote Swingers: 1&2 £29.90, 1&3 £11.90, 2&3 £34.50 CSF £80.71 CT £600.19 TOTE £5.50: £1.80, £3.20, £2.90; EX 122.60.
Owner W R B Racing 49 **Bred** Lawrence Goichman **Trained** Sessay, N Yorks

FOCUS
The second division and another modest affair, though the good early pace on this occasion set things up for those ridden patiently.
Amazing Star(IRE) Official explanation: jockey said gelding was denied a clear run

5501 TURFTV H'CAP 6f
4:25 (4:25) (Class 5) (0-75,75) 3-Y-0 **£3,238** (£963; £481; £240) **Stalls** High

Form RPR
3313 **1** **Jimmy The Poacher (IRE)**[23] 4714 3-9-4 **75**.... AdrianNicholls 1 84
(E S McMahon) *trckd ldrs on outside: edgd rt over 4f out: led on stands' side rail over 3f out: hld on towards fin* **11/4**[1]
6604 **2** hd **Tasmeem (IRE)**[19] 4865 3-9-3 **74**....(b) PaulHanagan 8 82+
(R A Fahey) *hld up in rr: nt clr run and swtchd lft over 2f out: swtchd rt over 1f out: hdwy to chse wnr ins fnl f: jst hld* **4/1**[3]
3314 **3** 2 ¾ **Offspring**[22] 4749 3-8-13 **70**.... DuranFentiman 5 70
(T D Easterby) *t.k.h: sn trcking ldrs: effrt 2f out: styd on same pce* **11/2**
3212 **4** 1 ¾ **Grand Zafeen**[28] 4529 3-8-13 **75**.... IanBrennan[(5)] 3 69
(M R Channon) *swtchd rt after s: hld up towards rr: swtchd lft 2f out: hung lft: one pce* **10/3**[2]
4016 **5** ½ **Melody In The Mist (FR)**[35] 4349 3-8-13 **73**.... MartinLane[(3)] 7 65
(T D Barron) *wl away: led 1f: lost pl over 3f out: hdwy 2f out: kpt on same pce* **9/1**
2031 **6** 4 **Pelmanism**[13] 5097 3-8-7 **64** ow1....(p) PaulMulrennan 2 44
(K A Ryan) *trckd ldrs: wknd appr fnl f* **7/1**
6540 **7** 3 ¼ **Briary Mac**[19] 4864 3-8-4 **61** oh4.... AndrewMullen 4 30
(N Bycroft) *swtchd rt after s: led after 1f: hdd over 3f out: lost pl 2f out* **22/1**

1m 12.13s (-0.57) **Going Correction** -0.15s/f (Firm) 7 Ran SP% **112.0**
Speed ratings (Par 100): **97,96,93,90,90 84,80**
Tote Swingers: 1&2 £3.30, 1&3 £4.20, 2&3 £2.30 CSF £13.37 CT £54.11 TOTE £3.10: £1.70, £1.90; EX 15.30.
Owner Stephen Lee & James McDonald **Bred** Jim McDonald **Trained** Lichfield, Staffs

FOCUS
A fairly useful handicap run at something of an uneven pace with the winner stealing it with a decisive move mid race.

5502 TOTEPOOL FLEXI BETTING APPRENTICE STKS (H'CAP) 5f
5:00 (5:00) (Class 5) (0-70,70) 3-Y-0+ **£3,238** (£963; £481; £240) **Stalls** High

Form RPR
1021 **1** **Mayoman (IRE)**[14] 5023 5-9-7 **70**....(v) NeilFarley[(5)] 3 81+
(D Carroll) *w ldrs on outside: led and wnt lft over 1f out: drvn rt out* **5/4**[1]
1214 **2** 1 ½ **You'relikemefrank**[14] 5055 4-8-11 **55**....(p) AshleyMorgan 1 61
(J Balding) *s.i.s: sn chsng ldrs on outside: styd on same pce ins fnl f* **10/1**
0426 **3** nk **Secret Venue**[8] 5240 4-9-9 **67**....(v[1]) MichaelO'Connell 5 72
(Jedd O'Keeffe) *w ldrs: styd on same pce fnl f* **20/1**
-002 **4** nk **Francis Albert**[8] 5240 4-8-2 **51** oh6....(b) JosephYoung[(5)] 9 54
(M Mullineaux) *s.s: hdwy on stands' side to ld over 3f out: hdd over 1f out: kpt on same pce* **16/1**
4310 **5** 3 **Arriva La Diva**[15] 4982 4-9-5 **63**.... IanBrennan 8 56
(J J Quinn) *hld up towards rr: effrt 2f out: nvr nr ldrs* **11/2**[2]
4140 **6** nse **Fashion Icon (USA)**[14] 5055 4-8-4 **51** oh3.... RosieJessop[(3)] 6 43
(D O'Meara) *chsd ldrs: lost pl 2f out* **16/1**
-000 **7** ½ **Sea Rover (IRE)**[28] 4559 6-8-13 **60**.... JohnCavanagh[(3)] 10 51
(M Brittain) *led over 1f: lost pl over 1f out* **12/1**
3422 **8** 2 ¾ **Micky Mac (IRE)**[20] 4820 6-9-8 **66**.... RossAtkinson 7 47
(C J Teague) *chsd ldrs: outpcd and lost pl over 2f out: edgd lft over 1f out* **14/1**
5005 **9** 1 ½ **Miacarla**[2] 5422 7-8-7 **51** oh6....(p) PatrickDonaghy 2 26
(H A McWilliams) *in rr: edgd lft over 1f out: nvr on terms* **22/1**

0505 **U** **Lucky Art (USA)**[59] 3540 4-9-0 **63**.... SophieSilvester[(5)] 11 —
(Mrs R A Carr) *dwlt: rdr lost iron sn after s and sddle sn slipped: in rr whn uns rdr 150yds out* **7/1**[3]

58.41 secs (-1.19) **Going Correction** -0.15s/f (Firm) 10 Ran SP% **116.7**
Speed ratings (Par 103): **103,100,100,99,94 94,93,89,87,—**
Tote Swingers: 1&2 £4.40, 1&3 £8.40, 2&3 £13.30 CSF £14.86 CT £171.32 TOTE £2.10: £1.10, £2.10, £4.90; EX 18.10 Place 6:£239.46 Place 5: £184.31..
Owner Tom Tuohy **Bred** James Cosgrove **Trained** Sledmere, E Yorks

FOCUS
Several in-form rivals and quite a competitive race for the grade. The winner came down the middle but there seemed no advantage anywhere overall.
Lucky Art(USA) Official explanation: jockey said saddle slipped
T/Plt: £479.20 to a £1 stake. Pool:£46,124.34 - 70.25 winning tickets T/Qpdt: £47.60 to a £1 stake. Pool:£3,582.60 - 55.60 winning tickets WG

5503 - 5508a (Foreign Racing) - See Raceform Interactive

4980 BEVERLEY (R-H)
Saturday, August 28

OFFICIAL GOING: Good (8.3)
Wind: Gusty against Weather: Cloudy with sunny periods and showers

5509 EUROPEAN BREEDERS' FUND SPECIOSA MAIDEN FILLIES' STKS 7f 100y
1:55 (2:10) (Class 4) 2-Y-0 **£4,209** (£1,252; £625; £312) **Stalls** High

Form RPR
05 **1** **Kalleidoscope**[36] 4338 2-9-0 0.... SamHitchcott 9 74
(M R Channon) *mde all: edgd lft home turn: rdn wl over 1f out: drvn ins fnl f and kpt on* **20/1**
6 **2** nk **The Shrew**[73] 3082 2-9-0 0.... J-PGuillambert 2 73
(J H M Gosden) *towards rr: hdwy over 2f out: rdn to chse ldrs over 1f out: swtchd lft ins fnl f and kpt on wl towards fin* **8/1**
3 ¾ **Question Times** 2-9-0 0.... JoeFanning 8 72+
(P W Chapple-Hyam) *trckd wnr: effrt 2f out: rdn to chal over 1f out: sn drvn and ev ch tl one pce wl ins fnl f* **13/8**[1]
4 ½ **Abdicate (IRE)** 2-9-0 0.... PaulMulrennan 1 73+
(R A Fahey) *s.i.s and bhd: hdwy over 2f out: swtchd ins and effrt to chse ldrs over 1f out: swtchd lft ins fnl f and kpt on wl: nrst fin* **33/1**
5 2 ½ **Sovereign Street** 2-8-11 0.... BarryMcHugh[(3)] 10 64
(Mrs A Duffield) *trckd ldng pair on inner: hdwy over 2f out: rdn and green whn n.m.r over 1f out: kpt on same pce fnl f* **18/1**
44 **6** 1 ½ **El Torbellino (IRE)**[19] 4899 2-9-0 0.... SilvestreDeSousa 4 61
(D O'Meara) *chsd ldrs: hdwy over 2f out: rdn wl over 1f out and sn one pce* **14/1**
0 **7** nk **Lady Chloe**[14] 5066 2-8-11 0.... RussKennemore[(3)] 11 60
(P A Kirby) *chsd ldrs on inner: rdn along 2f out: sn drvn and one pce* **66/1**
62 **8** nk **Lady Amakhala**[21] 4821 2-9-0 0.... PJMcDonald 6 60
(G M Moore) *sn rdn along and a towards rr* **13/2**[3]
06 **9** 1 ¼ **Auburn Lady**[17] 4940 2-8-9 0.... DaleSwift[(5)] 5 57
(A D Brown) *a towards rr* **80/1**
42 **10** 2 ½ **Pandoro De Lago (IRE)**[20] 4862 2-9-0 0.... PaulHanagan 3 51
(R A Fahey) *chsd ldrs: effrt on outer over 2f out: sn rdn and wknd over 1f out* **2/1**[2]

1m 33.58s (-0.22) **Going Correction** -0.125s/f (Firm) 10 Ran SP% **118.2**
Speed ratings (Par 93): **96,95,94,94,91 89,89,88,87,84**
toteswingers:1&2:£25.80, 1&3:£10.90, 2&3:£7.40 CSF £169.41 TOTE £27.70: £5.80, £2.30, £1.30; EX 140.80.
Owner Jackie & George Smith **Bred** G A E And J Smith Bloodstock Ltd **Trained** West Ilsley, Berks

FOCUS
The bottom bend had been moved so that the course was back at its widest configuration. A modest maiden, especially as the original favourite Sahafh was withdrawn after unseating her rider on the way to the start (9/4, deduct 30p in the £ under R4, new market formed.)

NOTEBOOK
Kalleidoscope had shown some ability in her first two starts, but this was still a big step up on those efforts. A half-sister to five winners, she was ridden positively and, despite running a little wide off the bend into the straight, dug deep to repel all challengers. She looks a tough sort who will pay her way in nurseries. (old market op 28-1 tchd 33-1, new market op 18-1)
The Shrew, absent 73 days since her debut, was a little on edge beforehand and ran a little green but finished her race off well. She should be able to find an ordinary maiden before stepping into handicap company. (old market op 12-1 tchd 10-1 and 14-1, new market tchd 7-1 and 9-1)
Question Times, who showed signs of greenness in the prelims, was well supported on her debut and travelled like the best horse through the race, only to find less than required off the bridle. It was still a good effort, though, and she should come on for the run. (old market op 11-4, new market op 6-4)
Abdicate(IRE) ◆ caught the eye as she was drawn worst of all, settled out the back and stayed on nicely without enjoying the clearest of runs. It was a very pleasing introduction and it'll be a surprise if she doesn't build on it. Official explanation: jockey said filly ran green and hung right (old market op 50-1)
Sovereign Street, a half-sister to three winners, has the pedigree to do well at two, and this was a perfectly acceptable debut effort. (old market op 25-1, new market op 16-1)
El Torbellino(IRE) Official explanation: jockey said filly hung left
Pandoro De Lago(IRE) was being niggled along from an early stage and clearly failed to run to the form of her previous two starts. Handicaps are now open to her, however. (old market op 4-1 tchd 7-2)

5510 BET ON TOTESCOOP6 AT TOTESPORT.COM H'CAP 7f 100y
2:25 (2:34) (Class 4) (0-85,84) 3-Y-0+ **£4,209** (£1,252; £625; £312) **Stalls** High

Form RPR
000 **1** **Shotley Mac**[27] 4617 6-9-3 **75**....(b) FrannyNorton 9 85
(N Bycroft) *trckd ldng pair: hdwy 2f out: rdn to ld over 1f out: drvn and kpt on wl fnl f* **8/1**
2500 **2** 2 ¼ **Summer Dancer (IRE)**[8] 5264 6-9-8 **80**.... PhillipMakin 4 84
(P T Midgley) *hld up towards rr: hdwy 2f out: rdn to chse ldrs ent fnl f: kpt on wl towards fin* **14/1**
131 **3** nk **Dabbers Ridge (IRE)**[24] 4713 8-9-2 **77**.... GaryBartley[(3)] 7 80
(I W McInnes) *hld up in rr: swtchd wd and hdwy over 2f out: rdn to chse ldrs over 1f out: drvn ent fnl f: kpt on same pce* **8/1**
612- **4** shd **Guest Book (IRE)**[335] 6305 3-9-6 **83**.... JoeFanning 1 84+
(M Johnston) *in tch: hdwy on outer over 2f out: rdn to chse ldrs over 1f out: drvn and kpt on same pce ins fnl f* **4/1**[1]
0400 **5** ½ **Euston Square**[28] 4579 4-9-3 **75**....(p) AndrewMullen 11 77
(D Nicholls) *dwlt: sn in tch on inner: hdwy wl over 2f out: rdn to chse ldrs wl over 1f out: drvn and kpt on same pce ent fnl f* **18/1**
3602 **6** 2 ¼ **My Gacho (IRE)**[18] 4929 8-9-12 **84**....(v) J-PGuillambert 5 80
(M Johnston) *midfield: hdwy and in tch 1/2-way: rdn 2f out: n.m.r and swtchd lft over 1f out: drvn and no imp fnl f* **9/1**

-000 **7** *nse* **Inheritor (IRE)**71 3150 4-9-10 **82** .... TomEaves 3 78
(B Smart) *chsd ldrs: rdn along 2f out: drvn over 1f out and grad wknd* **20/1**

0450 **8** *1 ½* **Istiqdaam**24 4704 5-8-11 **72** ....(b) JamesSullivan(3) 10 64
(M W Easterby) *hld up towards rr: n.m.r on inner after 2f: sme hdwy 2f out: sn rdn and n.d* **16/1**

3241 **8** *dht* **Amethyst Dawn (IRE)**10 5199 4-9-5 **77** .... DavidAllan 2 69+
(T D Easterby) *towards rr: effrt and sme hdwy over 2f out: sn rdn and n.d* **11/2**2

0200 **10** *1* **Montego Breeze**30 4522 4-8-5 **66** oh15 ow1........ BarryMcHugh(3) 6 56?
(John A Harris) *in tch: hdwy to chse ldrs wl over 2f out: drvn over 1f out: wkng whn n.m.r appr fnl f* **100/1**

5340 **11** *hd* **She's In The Money**31 4472 4-9-10 **82** .... PaulHanagan 12 71
(R A Fahey) *chsd ldr: c lose up 1/2-way: rdn 2f out and ev ch tl drvn and wknd over 1f out* **6/1**3

5000 **12** *2 ¼* **Saucy Brown (IRE)**11 5183 4-9-10 **82** ....(t) AdrianNicholls 13 66
(D Nicholls) *led: rdn over 2f out: drvn and hdd over 1f out: sn wknd* **12/1**

1656 **13** *½* **Indian Skipper (IRE)**34 4413 5-9-8 **83** ....(be) AndrewHeffernan(3) 8 65
(R C Guest) *s.i.s: a in rr* **14/1**

1m 32.25s (-1.55) **Going Correction** -0.125s/f (Firm)
WFA 3 from 4yo+ 5lb **13 Ran SP% 119.8**
Speed ratings (Par 105): **103,100,100,99,99 96,96,95,95,93 93,91,90**
toteswingers:1&2:£21.00, 1&3:£10.00, 2&3:£30.10 CSF £115.42 CT £934.78 TOTE £11.50: £4.00, £4.70, £2.20; EX 114.60 TRIFECTA Not won..
Owner J A Swinburne **Bred** N Bycroft **Trained** Brandsby, N Yorks

FOCUS
An ordinary but competitive handicap.
Amethyst Dawn(IRE) Official explanation: jockey said filly was denied a clear run

5511 TOTESPORT.COM HOME OF POOL BETTING H'CAP 1m 1f 207y
3:00 (3:01) (Class 2) (0-105,95) 3-Y-O **£22,666** (£6,744; £3,370; £1,683) **Stalls High**

Form RPR

1151 **1** **Aattash (IRE)**13 5121 3-9-7 **95** .... SamHitchcott 12 105
(M R Channon) *mde all: pushed along and qcknd 2f out: rdn over 1f out: styd on strly* **11/1**

4022 **2** *1* **Bonfire Knight**28 4570 3-8-3 **82** .... IanBrennan(5) 13 90
(J J Quinn) *in tch whn edgd lft after 2f: hdwy to trck ldrs 3f out: rdn and edgd lft 2f out: drvn and edgd rt over 1f out: styd on to chse wnr ins fnl f: no imp towards fin* **15/2**3

3204 **3** *1 ¾* **Averroes (IRE)**28 4573 3-9-2 **90** .... LukeMorris 9 95+
(C G Cox) *midfield: whn hmpd and edgd rt after 2f: sn towards rr: hdwy over 2f out: swtchd rt and rdn to chse ldrs over 1f out: drvn and styd on ins fnl f: tk 3rd nr line* **10/1**

2313 **4** *hd* **Gritstone**17 4943 3-8-8 **82** .... PaulHanagan 4 86+
(R A Fahey) *midfield whn n.m.r and hmpd after 2f: hdwy and in tch 4f out: rdn to chse ldrs whn n.m.r and swtchd rt over 1f out: drvn and kpt on same pce fnl f* **5/1**1

0411 **5** *1* **Spoken**30 4520 3-9-4 **92** ....(p) SteveDrowne 1 94
(R Charlton) *prom: hdwy to chse ldng pair 4f out: rdn over 2f out: drvn over 1f out and kpt on same pce* **10/1**

40-1 **6** *1 ½* **Lucky Windmill**13 5122 3-8-9 **83** .... PJMcDonald 8 82
(G A Swinbank) *chsd wnr: hdwy 2f out: rdn wl over 1f out: drvn and wknd appr fnl f* **16/1**

6201 **7** *4* **Syrian**14 5073 3-8-6 **80** .... SilvestreDeSousa 7 71
(Ian Williams) *dwlt: stdd and hld up on inner in rr: n.m.r and hmpd over 4f out: hdwy 3f out: swtchd rt and rdn 2f out: n.d* **25/1**

530 **8** *¾* **Take It To The Max**21 4830 3-9-0 **88** .... DavidAllan 11 78
(G M Moore) *chsd ldng pair: rdn along on inner over 3f out: grad wknd* **33/1**

1-12 **9** *1 ½* **Psychic Ability (USA)**21 4841 3-9-5 **93** ....(p) FrannyNorton 10 80
(Saeed Bin Suroor) *in tch on outer: whn bmpd and edgd rt after 2f: rdn to chse ldrs over 2f out: drvn and wknd over 1f out* **10/1**

6111 **10** *2 ¼* **Don't Call Me (IRE)**35 4357 3-9-2 **90** ....(t) TomEaves 5 72+
(B Smart) *hld up towards rr: hdwy 3f out: rdn along 2f out and sn swtchd lft: swtchd rt and drvn wl over 1f out: wknd* **10/1**

2612 **11** *¾* **Granite Girl**17 4971 3-8-4 **78** .... NickyMackay 3 59
(P J McBride) *in tch on outer: hdwy over 3f out: rdn along to chse ldrs over 2f out: sn drvn and wknd over 1f out* **40/1**

4333 **12** *3* **Layla's Dancer**23 4751 3-7-13 **76** .... JamesSullivan(3) 6 51
(R A Fahey) *hld up in rr: swtchd wd and hdwy 4f out: rdn to chse ldrs 2f out: sn drive: edgd rt and wknd* **12/1**

1310 **13** *20* **Gold Rules**51 3824 3-9-1 **89** .... J-PGuillambert 14 24
(L M Cumani) *dwlt: hdwy on inner 4f out: in tch 3f out: rdn along 2f out and sn wknd* **7/1**2

21-2 **14** *14* **Medicinal Compound**7 5304 3-8-7 **81** .... PaulMulrennan 16 —+
(K A Ryan) *dwlt: hld up on inner whn hmpd after 2f: effrt and sme hdwy over 3f out: rdn and btn 2f out: sn bhd and eased* **9/1**

14-2 **15** *9* **Pallantes Cross**18 4924 3-9-7 **95** .... JoeFanning 15 —
(M Johnston) *trckd ldrs on inner: rdn along 4f out: drvn over 2f out: wknd qckly and bhd whn eased wl over 1f out* **10/1**

2m 3.48s (-3.52) **Going Correction** -0.125s/f (Firm) **15 Ran SP% 127.5**
Speed ratings (Par 106): **109,108,106,106,105 104,101,100,99,97 97,94,78,67,60**
toteswingers:1&2:£45.50, 1&3:£73.50, 2&3:£25.90 CSF £94.53 CT £879.58 TOTE £16.10: £4.20, £3.40, £3.50; EX 163.10 Trifecta £1710.70 Pool: £14,194.57 - 6.14 winning units..
Owner Sheikh Ahmed Al Maktoum **Bred** Oghill House Stud **Trained** West Ilsley, Berks

FOCUS
Not as high class a handicap as the rating band would have one believe, as the top weight was rated 10lb below the ceiling for the race. It was also run at a fairly steady early pace and the winner was able to dictate throughout.

NOTEBOOK
Aattash(IRE) had a good draw and likes to front-run, so it was no surprise to see him bounced out in front. Nothing seriously took him on in front and he made the most of it, leading all the way to the line. He's been on a big upward curve this summer, had no trouble with the return to 1m2f, and, if he continues to be allowed to dominate, further wins are sure to come his way. (op 10-1)
Bonfire Knight kept on well from midfield to take second but never really threatened to catch the winner. Largely consistent this term, he deserves to win a handicap before the season is out, and the fact that he'll probably prefer softer ground might help on that score. (op 8-1 tchd 9-1)
Averroes(IRE) has run well from the front in the past but was ridden patiently here. He was staying on really well at the finish, but the steady pace had been all against him and the win was beyond reach. (op 12-1)
Gritstone got bumped about a bit back in the pack during the early stages as they all jostled for position off the steady pace, and didn't get the smoothest of passages up the straight either. He was unlucky last time and didn't have much go his way here so remains one to be interested in. (op 9-1)
Spoken, who made all to win his last two races, was drawn worst of all and had no hope of taking up a front-running role this time. He raced wider than ideal the whole way round, so it wasn't a bad effort in the circumstances. (op 12-1)
Lucky Windmill, running in a handicap for the first time, tracked the winner through the race, and the only excuse he can have is that the longer trip was too far. (op 22-1)
Syrian Official explanation: jockey said gelding ran too free
Layla's Dancer Official explanation: jockey said colt missed the break
Gold Rules, who's been gelded since he last ran, just wouldn't settle out the back off the ordinary early gallop. He can do better in a stronger-run race. (op 11-2)
Medicinal Compound Official explanation: jockey said gelding never travelled

5512 TOTESPORT.COM BEVERLEY BULLET SPRINT STKS (LISTED RACE) 5f
3:30 (3:31) (Class 1) 3-Y-O+ **£23,704** (£8,964; £4,480; £2,240) **Stalls High**

Form RPR

0040 **1** **Mister Hughie (IRE)**8 5276 3-8-12 **105** .... SamHitchcott 12 108+
(M R Channon) *dwlt: hdwy to trck ldrs 1/2-way: nt clr run over 1f out: swtchd rt and rdn ins fnl f: qcknd wl to ld nr line* **7/1**

3431 **2** *shd* **Prohibit**21 4814 5-9-0 **105** ....(p) J-PGuillambert 7 108+
(R M H Cowell) *trckd ldrs: swtchd lft and hdwy over 1f out: rdn to chal ins fnl f: sn drvn and ev ch tl nt qckn nr line* **7/2**1

2005 **3** *shd* **Captain Dunne (IRE)**11 5183 5-9-0 **107** .... DavidAllan 5 107
(T D Easterby) *prom: effrt to ld 1 1/2f out: rdn ent fnl f: sn drvn: hdd and nt qckn nr fin* **11/2**3

3000 **4** *1 ½* **Anglezarke (IRE)**13 5120 4-8-9 **94** ....(b) PaulHanagan 10 97
(R A Fahey) *dwlt and towards rr: hdwy 1/2-way: rdn to chse ldrs over 1f out: drvn and kpt on ins fnl f* **9/1**

5010 **5** *nk* **Nosedive**21 4819 3-8-12 **94** .... PhillipMakin 4 101
(R C Guest) *hld up in rr: hdwy wl over 1f out: rdn and kpt on ins fnl f: nrst fin* **40/1**

0000 **6** *nk* **Look Busy (IRE)**13 5120 5-8-9 **93** .... PatrickMathers 1 95+
(A Berry) *s.i.s and bhd: swtchd outside and hdwy over 1f out: rdn and styd on ins fnl f: nrst fin* **20/1**

0550 **7** *1* **Spin Cycle (IRE)**8 5276 4-9-0 **105** ....(v) TomEaves 2 96
(B Smart) *chsd ldrs: hdwy on outer 2f out: rdn over 1f out: wknd ins fnl f* **5/1**2

2-63 **8** *½* **Noble Storm (USA)**18 4937 4-9-0 **100** .... FrannyNorton 8 94
(E S McMahon) *cl up: effrt wl over 1f out: rdn and ev ch appr fnl f: sn wknd* **15/2**

2501 **9** *2 ¾* **Masta Plasta (IRE)**18 4937 7-9-0 **101** .... AdrianNicholls 9 84
(D Nicholls) *led: rdn along 2f out: drvn and hdd 1 1/2f out: sn wknd* **6/1**

2500 **10** *1 ¼* **Fol Hollow (IRE)**21 4814 5-9-0 **96** .... AndrewMullen 6 80
(D Nicholls) *prom: rdn along 1/2-way: sn wknd* **28/1**

6211 **11** *¾* **Mey Blossom**17 4942 5-8-9 **80** .... MichaelStainton 13 72
(R M Whitaker) *chsd ldrs on inner: rdn along 2f out: sn wknd* **14/1**

62.84 secs (-0.66) **Going Correction** +0.10s/f (Good)
WFA 3 from 4yo+ 2lb **11 Ran SP% 120.1**
Speed ratings (Par 111): **109,108,108,106,105 105,103,102,98,96 95**
toteswingers:1&2:£7.30, 1&3:£6.40, 2&3:£5.50 CSF £31.78 TOTE £8.80: £2.60, £1.10, £2.10; EX 39.10 Trifecta £320.00 Pool: £1,634.74 - 3.78 winning units..
Owner Mulryan Partnership **Bred** Mcmac Syndicate **Trained** West Ilsley, Berks

FOCUS
A competitive sprint in which few could be confidently ruled out. However, just nine 3-y-os have competed in the race over the past four years, and yet the Classic generation has provided the winner each time.

NOTEBOOK
Mister Hughie(IRE) didn't run much of a race in the Nunthorpe last time out, but then again a number of horses disappointed at York. His previous fourth in the King George Stakes at Goodwood gave him every chance in this company, though, and this stiffer track was always going to suit him better. He had an unfortunate experience on his last visit here in May, but travelled best of all this time and quickened up smartly to settle the issue. He's an improving sprinter, deserving of another crack at Group company, but it's worth noting he's yet to race on ground worse than good. (tchd 15-2)
Prohibit, winner of a handicap off 100 last time out, ran well back up in grade and is clearly at the top of his game right now. He's another for whom softer ground this autumn would be a worry, though. (op 4-1)
Captain Dunne(IRE), officially best in at the weights, albeit narrowly, was never too far off the pace and perhaps could have had his challenge delayed a touch longer, as he quickened to lead but was then there to be shot at by Mister Hughie and Prohibit. (op 5-1)
Anglezarke(IRE) has been out of form lately but she showed a bit more on this return to 5f. Perhaps her retirement will be put on hold now for the time being. (op 14-1)
Nosedive looked to find this test on the sharp side, and will appreciate returning to 6f.
Look Busy(IRE), who won this race last year and came into the race having won three of her four starts over this C&D, hasn't been in anything like the same form this time around. This was a little more promising, though, as she was poorly drawn but kept on well after fluffing the start. (op 25-1 tchd 28-1)
Spin Cycle(IRE)'s effort flattened out inside the last and an easier 5f probably suits him best. (op 11-2 tchd 6-1)
Noble Storm(USA) was pulling for his head and did far too much early on to have a chance of getting home. (op 8-1)
Masta Plasta(IRE) set too fast a pace and is another probably at his most effective over a sharper/easier 5f. (op 11-2 tchd 5-1)

5513 40 LIVE FOOTBALL MARKETS AT TOTESPORT.COM H'CAP 5f
4:05 (4:05) (Class 5) (0-75,74) 3-Y-O+ **£2,849** (£847; £423; £211) **Stalls High**

Form RPR

1601 **1** **Caranbola**16 4982 4-9-6 **69** .... PaulHanagan 13 77
(M Brittain) *mde most: rdn over 1f out: drvn and hdd ins fnl f: rallied gamely to ld nr line* **10/3**1

5054 **2** *shd* **Select Committee**13 5123 5-9-1 **64** ....(v) TomEaves 7 72
(J J Quinn) *t.k.h: hld up in tch: smooth hdwy to join ldrs 2f out: rdn and slt ld ins fnl f: drvn and hdd nr line* **7/1**3

6234 **3** *nk* **Hazelrigg (IRE)**10 5198 5-9-10 **73** ....(bt) DavidAllan 1 80
(T D Easterby) *hld up in rr: hdwy pon outer 2f out: chal ins fnl f: sn rdn and ev ch whn put hd in air and fnd little nr fin* **9/1**

3165 **4** *nk* **Galpin Junior (USA)**10 5198 4-9-6 **72** .... MichaelGeran(3) 5 78
(D Nicholls) *s.i.s: hdwy 2f out: rdn over 1f out: styd on wl fnl f: nrst fin* **14/1**

1000 **5** *2* **Espy**17 4942 5-8-8 **60** .... GaryBartley(3) 2 59
(I W McInnes) *stdd and swtchd rt s: in rr tl hdwy wl over 1f out: sn rdn and styd on ins fnl f: nrst fin* **40/1**

4136 **6** *1* **Chosen One (IRE)**10 5198 5-9-5 **71** .... JamesSullivan(3) 3 66
(Mrs R A Carr) *trckd ldrs towards outer: effrt and n.m.r 2f out: rdn over 1f out: kpt on ins fnl f: n.d* **20/1**

3354 **7** *nk* **Wicked Wilma (IRE)**5 5356 6-8-9 **65** .... VictorSantos(7) 4 59
(A Berry) *trckd ldrs: pushed along and sltly outpcd whn n.m.r wl over 1f out: one pce after* **16/1**

0105 8 3/4 **Miss Daawe**[16] 4982 6-8-11 60 .... LeeVickers 12 51+
(B Ellison) *dwlt: hdwy on inner whn n.m.r and hmpd over 1f out: kpt on ins fnl f: nrst fin* 20/1

1321 9 1/2 **Comptonspirit**[10] 5198 6-9-6 74 .... IanBrennan(5) 10 64
(B P J Baugh) *cl up: rdn along 2f out: sn drvn and wknd over 1f out* 5/1[2]

2513 10 1 **King Of Swords (IRE)**[13] 5123 6-9-0 63 .... (p) J-PGuillambert 11 49
(N Tinkler) *chsd wnr: rdn along wl over 1f out: sn drvn and wknd* 8/1

4360 11 3/4 **Silvanus (IRE)**[8] 5262 5-9-5 68 .... PhillipMakin 6 51
(P T Midgley) *dwlt and in rr: hdwy 1/2-way: swtchd ins and effrt whn nt clr run over 1f out: nt rcvr* 12/1

6144 12 3/4 **Poppy's Rose**[17] 4952 6-9-4 72 .... DaleSwift(5) 8 53
(T J Etherington) *chsd ldrs: rdn 2f out: sn drvn and wknd* 9/1

U00 13 1 1/4 **Azygous**[17] 4942 7-8-2 58 oh6 ow3 .... JamesRogers(7) 14 34
(G P Kelly) *chsd ldrs on inner: rdn along wl over 1f out: sn wknd* 50/1

0242 14 nk **Rio Sands**[13] 5123 5-8-8 57 .... PaulQuinn 9 32
(R M Whitaker) *prom: rdn along 1/2-way: sn wknd* 12/1

63.52 secs (0.02) **Going Correction** +0.10s/f (Good) 14 Ran SP% 125.2
Speed ratings (Par 103): **103,102,102,101,98 97,96,95,94,93 91,90,88,88**
toteswingers:1&2:£3.50, 1&3:£8.30, 2&3:£25.20 CSF £26.13 CT £207.34 TOTE £4.00: £1.20, £2.90, £4.50; EX 30.80.
Owner Mel Brittain **Bred** T E Pocock **Trained** Warthill, N Yorks
■ Stewards' Enquiry : J-P Guillambert caution: careless riding

FOCUS
An ordinary handicap.
Espy Official explanation: jockey said gelding was denied a clear run
Silvanus(IRE) Official explanation: jockey said gelding was denied a clear run

5514 GET LIVE FOOTBALL STATS AT TOTESPORT.COM MAIDEN STKS 5f
4:40 (4:40) (Class 5) 3-Y-O+ £2,752 (£818; £409; £204) Stalls High

Form RPR
0202 1 **Red Roar (IRE)**[5] 5359 3-8-12 53 .... FrannyNorton 8 63
(A Berry) *trckd ldrs: hdwy whn n.m.r and squeezed through to chal 1 1/2f out: rdn to ld appr fnl f: edgd lft and kpt on* 7/2[3]

2 2 3/4 **Bushwhacker (AUS)**[283] 5-9-5 75 .... PaulHanagan 1 58
(W R Muir) *cl up: led and edgd rt 1 1/2f out: sn rdn and hdd ent fnl f: one pce* 5/2[2]

6454 3 nk **Ruler's Honour (IRE)**[52] 3773 3-9-3 58 .... (p) LeeVickers 5 57
(T J Etherington) *dwlt: hdwy 1/2-way: trcking ldrs whn nt clr run and hmpd over 1f out: swtchd lft and rdn ent fnl f: kpt on* 13/2

3603 4 2 **Nadinska**[12] 5162 3-8-12 60 .... SamHitchcott 4 45
(M R Channon) *trckd ldrs: hdwy over 1f out: sn ev ch tl rdn and wknd jst ins fnl f* 9/4[1]

5 5 11 **Appleby Fair**[14] 5097 3-9-3 0 .... PhillipMakin 6 10
(T D Barron) *led: rdn: edgd rt and hdd whn bdly hmpd 1 1/2f out: bhd after* 9/1

6 9 **Bluegrass Gal (USA)** 4-9-0 0 .... TomEaves 2 —
(Mrs L Williamson) *cl up: rdn along bef 1/2-way: sn lost pl and bhd* 16/1

06 7 7 **Grey Crystal**[14] 5097 4-8-7 0 .... JohnCavanagh(7) 3 —
(M Brittain) *s.i.s and veered bdly lft s: a in rr: bhd fr 1/2-way* 40/1

64.69 secs (1.19) **Going Correction** +0.10s/f (Good)
WFA 3 from 4yo+ 2lb 7 Ran SP% 113.2
Speed ratings (Par 103): **94,89,89,85,68 53,42**
toteswingers:1&2:£2.80, 1&3:£4.00, 2&3:£4.20 CSF £12.43 TOTE £4.00: £2.50, £1.60; EX 14.40.
Owner Sporting Kings **Bred** Tally-Ho Stud **Trained** Cockerham, Lancs
■ Stewards' Enquiry : Paul Hanagan caution: careless riding.

FOCUS
This looked a pretty poor maiden.

5515 STARS OF THE FUTURE APPRENTICE H'CAP 1m 1f 207y
5:15 (5:15) (Class 6) (0-65,62) 4-Y-O+ £2,266 (£674; £337; £168) Stalls High

Form RPR
0020 1 **Cherri Fosfate**[6] 5331 6-9-6 60 .... NeilFarley 1 69
(D Carroll) *prom: hdwy to ld 2f out: rdn over 1f out: styd on wl fnl f* 5/1[3]

102 2 1 1/2 **Avitus**[24] 4708 4-9-2 56 .... JamesRogers 2 62
(Micky Hammond) *trckd ldrs: hdwy over 3f out: rdn to chse wnr over 1f out: drvn and kpt on fnl f* 4/1[2]

4032 3 1/2 **Tivers Song (USA)**[16] 4980 6-8-10 50 .... (b) SoniaEaton 7 55
(John A Harris) *hld up towards rr: hdwy over 3f out: rdn to chse ldrs wl over 1f out: drvn and kpt on same pce fnl f* 15/2

4530 4 1 1/4 **Lucayan Dancer**[16] 4985 10-9-5 62 .... AnthonyBetts(3) 9 65
(N Bycroft) *hld up in rr: hdwy 1/2-way: rdn to chse ldrs wl over 1f out: kpt on ins fnl f: nrst fin* 16/1

0640 5 1 **Kingaroo (IRE)**[30] 4522 4-8-5 45 .... AlexEdwards 8 46
(G Woodward) *hld up in rr: swtchd lft and hdwy 2f out: rdn over 1f out: kpt on ins fnl f: nrst fin* 25/1

6405 6 1 1/4 **Parchment (IRE)**[10] 5202 8-8-5 45 .... (b) NathanAlison 6 43
(A J Lockwood) *trckd ldrs on inner: hdwy 3f out: rdn along wl over 1f out: drvn and no imp appr fnl f* 12/1

6500 7 hd **Grey Command (USA)**[17] 4945 5-8-11 51 .... JulieBurke 11 49
(M Brittain) *chsd ldr: rdn along over 2f out: sn wknd* 4/1[2]

5/-0 8 7 **Jetta Joy (IRE)**[87] 2659 5-8-7 50 .... LucyBarry(3) 3 34
(Mrs A Duffield) *hld up towards rr: hdwy on outer to chse ldrs 1/2-way: rdn 3f out and sn wknd* 25/1

-000 9 3 **Princess Aliuska**[17] 4946 5-8-5 45 .... RichardRowe 10 23
(C Smith) *led: rdn along 3f out: hdd 2f out and sn wknd* 28/1

6135 10 19 **Highland Love**[23] 4752 5-8-12 57 .... EleanorMcGowan(5) 5 —
(Jedd O'Keeffe) *a towards rr* 11/4[1]

2m 5.82s (-1.18) **Going Correction** -0.125s/f (Firm) 10 Ran SP% 119.8
Speed ratings (Par 101): **99,97,97,96,95 94,94,88,86,71**
toteswingers:1&2:£5.60, 1&3:£9.30, 2&3:£5.20 CSF £25.53 CT £152.26 TOTE £5.90: £2.00, £1.40, £2.30; EX 34.50 Place 6: £225.21 Place 5: £116.73 .
Owner Stoppers **Bred** The Newchange Syndicate **Trained** Sledmere, E Yorks

FOCUS
A moderate handicap.
Highland Love Official explanation: vet said gelding finished distressed
T/Plt: £213.00 to a £1 stake. Pool:£77,166.49 - 264.42 winning tickets T/Qpdt: £39.10 to a £1 stake. Pool:£4,828.91 - 91.31 winning tickets JR

4999 GOODWOOD (R-H)
Saturday, August 28

OFFICIAL GOING: Soft (7.1)
Fresh ground on last 6f of mile course but all distances as advertised.
Wind: Moderate across Weather: Bright periods

5516 HARWOODS RACING CLUB STKS (H'CAP) 7f
2:00 (2:01) (Class 2) (0-105,104) 3-Y-O+
£9,346 (£2,799; £1,399; £700; £349; £175) Stalls High

Form RPR
0005 1 **Axiom**[14] 5068 6-9-7 99 .... KierenFallon 6 110+
(L M Cumani) *hld up in rr: hdwy 2f out: nt clr run 1f out and swtchd lft: qcknd wl fnl 120yds to ld last stride* 10/3[1]

0655 2 shd **Desert Creek (IRE)**[21] 4828 4-8-11 89 .... EddieAhern 1 98
(Sir Michael Stoute) *chsd ldrs: led over 1f out: styd on u.p: hdd last stride* 9/2[3]

35 3 1 **Suruor (IRE)**[35] 4358 4-9-8 100 .... JimCrowley 4 106+
(D M Simcock) *in rr: hdwy 2f out: hmpd jst ins fnl f: swtchd rt and r.o wl fnl 100yds: nt rch ldng duo* 9/2[3]

4-43 4 1 1/2 **City Style (USA)**[87] 2651 4-9-12 104 .... FrankieDettori 2 106
(Mahmood Al Zarooni) *awkward stalls: in tch: drvn and hdwy over 2f out: styd on same pce fnl f* 16/1

421 5 1 1/4 **Mata Keranjang (USA)**[29] 4556 3-8-8 91 .... (p) JamieSpencer 3 88
(P F I Cole) *chsd ldr: rdn to chal wl over 1f out: wknd ins fnl f* 5/1

0060 6 3 1/4 **Gallagher**[21] 4843 4-9-7 99 .... EddieCreighton 8 89
(B J Meehan) *t.k.h: in tch: rdn 2f out: wknd wl over 1f out* 11/1

1330 7 3 1/4 **Seek The Fair Land**[19] 4894 4-8-11 89 .... (p) PatCosgrave 7 70
(J R Boyle) *chsd ldr: rdn 2f out: sn wknd* 33/1

4423 8 nk **Manassas (IRE)**[14] 5082 5-9-4 96 .... (b) MartinDwyer 5 76
(B J Meehan) *led: sn 4 l clr: hdd & wknd wl over 1f out* 4/1[2]

1m 27.45s (0.55) **Going Correction** +0.325s/f (Good)
WFA 3 from 4yo+ 5lb 8 Ran SP% 113.3
Speed ratings (Par 109): **109,108,107,106,104 100,97,96**
toteswingers:1&2:£3.80, 1&3:£3.30, 2&3:£4.10 CSF £18.14 CT £66.98 TOTE £3.50: £1.60, £1.60, £1.90; EX 11.80 Trifecta £57.20 Pool: £792.13 - 10.23 winning units..
Owner Samanda Racing **Bred** Cheveley Park Stud Ltd **Trained** Newmarket, Suffolk

FOCUS
A good handicap that usually falls to a high-class handicapper. Victories in the last ten years have been spread evenly across the age groups, and those drawn in the three highest stalls have had the best record, a trend that was upheld.

NOTEBOOK
Axiom, a C&D winner here last season who handles good or softer ground, had not had his favoured surface since November 2008. Having been belatedly gelded prior to his previous start, he was sent off a well-backed favourite. He settled at the back early and made steady progress through the middle of the pack before being produced late, and won with a little more in hand than the margin suggests. His yard is in good form and he could go in again, as he should not go up much, although he is due to go to the sales this autumn. (tchd 11-4 and 7-2 in a place)
Desert Creek(IRE) had looked on the way back at Haydock last time and had the ground in his favour. He was held up going well before striking for home over a furlong out, only to be run down near the line. His winning turn should not be long delayed. (tchd 5-1)
Suruor(IRE), a C&D winner on easy ground here last season, had been running well recently. He was held up right at the back and then followed the winner through. His rider had to wait for a gap to appear over a furlong out, and he picked up well when asked. It could be argued that he was unlucky in that the winner got first run, but he was unable to close the margin on that rival once in the clear. (op 7-2)
City Style(USA), a dual winner in Dubai in the winter at around this trip and placed in Listed company since returning here, was having his first try on soft ground. He was one of the first to be ridden along but kept going, although unable to change pace with his rivals. A try over further looks in order. (op 14-1)
Mata Keranjang(USA), the only 3-y-o in line-up, got off the mark last time over 1m on fast ground when he wore blinkers for the first time. The cheekpieces were back on here though, and he performed well on this handicap debut until fading in the last furlong. Fast ground probably suits him better. (op 15-2)
Gallagher was 4lb better off with Suruor for 3/4l compared with their recent Ascot running but finished further behind after being unable to pick up in the ground. (op 12-1)
Seek The Fair Land, a useful Polytrack handicapper, has had limited tries on turf and had never raced on soft. He chased the leader from the start but faded once the principals got involved. (op 25-1 tchd 20-1)
Manassas(IRE) had been running well from the front since blinkers were applied, and had been unlucky that the ground had gone against him the last twice. The same happened here but in truth his rider allowed him to go too fast in the conditions. (op 11-2 tchd 6-1)

5517 WINDFLOWER MARCH STKS (LISTED RACE) 1m 6f
2:30 (2:30) (Class 1) 3-Y-O+
£22,708 (£8,608; £4,308; £2,148; £1,076; £540) Stalls High

Form RPR
5322 1 **Drunken Sailor (IRE)**[49] 3922 5-9-7 112 .... (b) KierenFallon 2 109
(L M Cumani) *hld up in rr: stdy hdwy 2f out: rdn: edgd rt and qckând ins fnl f: str run to ld last stride* 5/4[1]

2/51 2 shd **Bergo (GER)**[70] 3195 7-9-7 109 .... GeorgeBaker 6 109
(G L Moore) *trckd ldr tl led over 3f out: rdn fr over 2f out: styd on gamely whn chal ins fnl f: hdd last stride* 14/1

-133 3 1 **Caucus**[51] 3822 3-8-7 97 .... EddieAhern 4 106
(H Morrison) *hld up in tch: hdwy 3f out: str run on ins to chal ins fnl f: no ex and wknd fnl 75yds* 8/1

-305 4 3 1/4 **Wajir (FR)**[30] 4506 4-9-7 110 .... FrankieDettori 7 103
(Saeed Bin Suroor) *in rr: hdwy fr 2f out: drvn to press ldrs 2f out: wknd fnl f* 5/2[2]

3004 5 12 **Golden Sword**[14] 5080 4-9-7 106 .... JamieSpencer 1 86
(Jane Chapple-Hyam) *chsd ldrs: rdn 3f out and sn hanging rt: wknd over 2f out* 4/1[3]

1-40 6 15 **Deportment**[104] 2155 4-9-2 85 .... JimCrowley 5 60
(S C Williams) *led tl hdd over 3f out: sn wknd* 50/1

3m 7.34s (3.74) **Going Correction** +0.325s/f (Good)
WFA 3 from 4yo+ 12lb 6 Ran SP% 112.8
Speed ratings (Par 111): **102,101,101,99,92 84**
toteswingers:1&2:£2.20, 1&3:£2.30, 2&3:£5.40 CSF £20.26 TOTE £1.90: £1.40, £3.80; EX 13.40.
Owner Samanda Racing & Tony Bloom **Bred** Cyril Kiernan **Trained** Newmarket, Suffolk

FOCUS
This Listed race has been dominated by three trainers in the last ten years but none of the trio was represented this time. It looked a bog standard race for the grade beforehand, and Kieren Fallon adopted very similar tactics to those used on the first winner in the same colours.

NOTEBOOK

Drunken Sailor(IRE), a progressive ex-Irish gelding, had finished runner-up in the Northumberland Plate and a Listed race over this trip at York since returning from a successful spell in Dubai in the winter. He had got to the front too soon on his last start, and his rider was at pains to make sure that did not happen again. The soft ground proved no problem and, after being niggled along running downhill half a mile out, he came back on the bridle and picked up well to snatch the race near the line. He will go into quarantine next week, and will be sent to Australia with the Melbourne Cup as the target, with the Caulfield Cup beforehand. (op 6-5 tchd 11-10 and 11-8 and 6-4 in places)

Bergo(GER) is better known as hurdler/chaser but had won Queen Alexandra at Royal Ascot on his previous start. The ground was the question with him but, with his stamina for much further proven, he was ridden positively and committed for home over 3f out. He held off all challengers and kept finding more until the winner's late thrust deprived him the race. He now has the Cesarewitch as the target, where he is likely to carry top weight. (op 10-1)

Caucus, a 1m4f fast ground maiden winner this year, had subsequently been placed in a Royal Ascot handicap and a Group 3. Taking a slight rise in trip, he ran his race on ground that he was unproven on, having every chance entering the last furlong before fading. He will be aimed at the Prix Jean de Chaudenay at Longchamp over the Arc weekend. (op 10-1 tchd 12-1)

Wajir(FR), the winner of a Group 3 over 1m7f in France last year, has struggled since joining Godolphin. He travelled well into contention but failed to pick up to any great effect off the bridle. (tchd 11-4)

Golden Sword had not gone on from his second in the Irish Derby last year, and had joined his current trainer after a spell with Mike De Kock. He had his chance in the straight but backed out of contention over a furlong from home. He was later reported as having finished lame. Official explanation: vet said colt returned lame (op 11-2)

Deportment, the winner of a 1m2f handicap off 75 for James Fanshawe last season, had been well held for her current trainer in Listed company so far and was so again, merely setting the pace until the race began in earnest. (op 40-1)

5518 TOTESPORT.COM CELEBRATION MILE (GROUP 2) 1m

3:05 (3:05) (Class 1) 3-Y-O+ **£56,770** (£21,520; £10,770; £5,370) **Stalls** High

Form				RPR
-002	1		**Poet's Voice**[16] 5009 3-8-9 112.....(t) FrankieDettori 3	121
			(Saeed Bin Suroor) *stdd s: hld up in last pl tl stdy hdwy to take 3rd 3f out: drvn and qcknd to ld wl over 1f out and edgd rt: pushed clr ins fnl f: comf* **2/1**[2]	
3104	2	4 ½	**Main Aim**[32] 4457 5-9-1 113..... EddieAhern 2	111
			(Sir Michael Stoute) *trckd ldr: drvn to chal wl over 1f out: sn pushed rt: comf outpcd by wnr ins fnl f* **4/5**[1]	
0-06	3	6	**Summer Fete (IRE)**[14] 5081 4-8-12 101..... KierenFallon 4	94
			(B Smart) *t.k.h: led tl hdd wl over 1f out: wkng whn hmpd over 1f out* **7/1**[3]	
2655	4	10	**Vitznau (IRE)**[21] 4816 6-9-1 99..... PatDobbs 1	74
			(R Hannon) *chsd ldr to 3f out: wknd sn after* **10/1**	

1m 39.22s (-0.68) **Going Correction** +0.325s/f (Good)
WFA 3 from 4yo+ 6lb **4 Ran SP% 110.5**
Speed ratings (Par 115): **116,111,105,95**
CSF £4.12 TOTE £3.00; EX 3.90.
Owner Godolphin **Bred** Darley **Trained** Newmarket, Suffolk
■ Stewards' Enquiry : Frankie Dettori caution: careless riding.

FOCUS

A disappointing turnout numbers-wise for this Group 2. Sir Michael Stoute has dominated this race in recent years, and was bidding for his seventh success in the last 11 runnings.

NOTEBOOK

Poet's Voice, a dual 7f winner and narrowly beaten in a 1m Group 3 last time, finished well beaten on his only previous try on soft ground. Held up at the back, he closed up comfortably on the favourite and came right away once asked for his effort. The Queen Elizabeth II Stakes and possibly the Breeders' Cup Mile could both figure in plans. (op 7-4 tchd 9-4)

Main Aim, sent off an odds-on favourite, he tracked the leader from the start but, when asked for maximum effort, could not pick up nearly as well as the winner. It looks as if 7f is his optimum trip but he would not have won at that distance either. (op 10-11 tchd 8-11 and Evens in a place)

Summer Fete(IRE) won a fillies' Group 3 here in 2009 but was off for a long time afterwards. She had not made much impression in two runs since her return but soft ground suited. She set off in front but was a little keen and had nothing more to offer when the older horses challenged. She was done no favours as they crossed her going into the last furlong but it made no difference to the result. (tchd 15-2)

Vitznau(IRE) had not won on turf since June 2007 but stays this trip well and handles cut in the ground. He had a good bit to find on the ratings but this still looked a below-par effort, as he never got involved having been held up. (op 16-1)

5519 CHICHESTER OBSERVER PRESTIGE STKS (GROUP 3) 7f

3:40 (3:40) (Class 1) 2-Y-O

£22,708 (£8,608; £4,308; £2,148; £1,076; £540) **Stalls** High

Form				RPR
01	1		**Theyskens' Theory (USA)**[28] 4595 2-9-0 0..... MartinDwyer 4	105+
			(B J Meehan) *mde all: pushed along and styd on strly fr over 1f out: unchal* **11/10**[1]	
12	2	1 ¼	**Cochabamba (IRE)**[37] 4305 2-9-0 0..... JackMitchell 6	97
			(R A Teal) *t.k.h early: chsd ldr: n.m.r on ins and jnd for 2nd appr fnl 2f: no ch w wnr fnl f but styd on for clr 2nd fnl 100yds* **11/1**	
31	3	½	**Cape Dollar (IRE)**[67] 3296 2-9-0 85..... KierenFallon 1	96
			(Sir Michael Stoute) *t.k.h early: chsd ldrs and disp 2nd over 2f out: sn rdn: no imp on wnr appr fnl f but nvr any ch: outpcd into 3rd fnl 100yds* **4/1**[2]	
102	4	1 ½	**Masaya**[28] 4592 2-9-0 75..... SebSanders 7	92
			(C E Brittain) *t.k.h early: sn chsng ldrs: rdn over 2f out: outpcd fnl f* **33/1**	
1	5	hd	**Princess Severus (IRE)**[31] 4474 2-9-0 0..... JimCrowley 3	92
			(R M Beckett) *in rr: rdn and effrt on outside fr 2f out: nvr rchd ldrs and styd on same pce fnl f* **25/1**	
1	6	¾	**Date With Destiny (IRE)**[50] 3861 2-9-0 0..... PatDobbs 2	90
			(R Hannon) *towards rr but in tch rdn over 2f out: kpt on but nvr gng pce to get into contention* **9/2**[3]	
212	7	½	**Sonning Rose (IRE)**[70] 3190 2-9-0 98..... AlanMunro 5	88
			(M R Channon) *in rr: rdn over 2f out and nvr gng pce to get into contention* **13/2**	

1m 28.9s (2.00) **Going Correction** +0.325s/f (Good) **7 Ran SP% 114.3**
Speed ratings (Par 104): **101,99,99,97,97 96,95**
toteswingers:1&2:£4.10, 1&3:£2.20, 2&3:£4.20 CSF £15.03 TOTE £2.10: £1.10, £5.40; EX 16.50.
Owner Andrew Rosen **Bred** Ar Enterprises Llc **Trained** Manton, Wilts

FOCUS

This fillies' Group 3 has proved a jumping-off point for several high-class sorts in recent seasons, Gossamer, Nannina and Fantasia probably being the best of them. Last season the subsequent dual Oaks winner Snow Fairy could finish only third here. This year's line-up looked solid enough but the placings barely changed throughout the race.

NOTEBOOK

Theyskens' Theory(USA) ◆ had shown the benefit of her debut when winning her maiden over 7f at Newmarket. The runner-up had won since and she was expected to build on that in this higher grade. She set off in front and looked in trouble when challenged on either side around the quarter-mile pole, but she found more and came away to win somewhat cosily. She looks a decent prospect, and might be more impressive back on better ground. She will now be aimed at the Meon Valley Stud Fillies' Mile with the Rockfel as an alternative. We will know much more about her after that. She was quoted at 8/1 for next year's 1000 Guineas after the race. (op 11-8 tchd 6-4 in places)

Cochabamba(IRE), the winner of a 6f Polytrack maiden on her debut, had been narrowly beaten in a Listed race last time. The form had not really been boosted since but she proved her quality by chasing the winner from the start and trying to challenge up the rail before her rival found more. She looks capable of picking up a Pattern race on this evidence. (op 10-1 tchd 9-1)

Cape Dollar(IRE) improved from her debut to win a 7f fast-ground maiden on her second start, with two subsequent winners behind. She was always close to the winner and looked a big threat when coming to challenge on the outside, but her effort petered out entering the last furlong, and she could only keep on at one pace. (op 9-2 tchd 5-1 in a place)

Masaya, a 5f winner on her debut, had been beaten a head by a subsequent winner in a Newbury nursery after being well held in the Queen Mary. She did not run badly on this step up in grade but was one-paced in the last 2f. (tchd 25-1)

Princess Severus(IRE), a winner over 6f on officially fast ground in a Leicester maiden on her debut (the rider reported it was on the easy side though), made her move from the back after halfway but when put under pressure had no more to offer. (op 16-1)

Date With Destiny(IRE), the only progeny of George Washington, had been a 7f winner on fast ground on her debut, form that had closely matched her with Cape Dollar. Held up early, she made her effort in the straight but seemed to sprawl in the soft ground and faded. She can be given another chance on a sound surface. (op 4-1 tchd 6-1)

Sonning Rose(IRE), runner-up to Crown Prosecutor here on her debut over 6f, had won her maiden before finishing second in the Chesham over this trip, again against colts. Having had a break since and back against fillies, she set the standard but failed to make any impression from the rear. (tchd 11-2)

5520 DAVID WILSON HOMES MAIDEN AUCTION STKS 1m

4:15 (4:16) (Class 5) 2-Y-O **£2,655** (£790; £394; £197) **Stalls** High

Form				RPR
	1		**Devoted (IRE)** 2-8-6 0 ow2..... JackMitchell 7	76+
			(R M Beckett) *hld up in rr: stdy hdwy on outside over 2f out: pushed along to ld appr fnl f: sn drvn: r.o strly* **7/1**	
0	2	1 ½	**Strictly Rhythm**[50] 3861 2-8-9 0..... JimCrowley 3	77+
			(R Hannon) *wnt lft s: in rr but in tch: hdwy on ins whn n.m.r over 2f out: swtchd lft and rdn over 1f out: styd on wl fnl f to take 2nd fnl 75yds but no imp on wnr* **16/1**	
05	3	1	**Levantera (IRE)**[37] 4286 2-8-1 0..... SimonPearce(5) 4	71
			(C G Cox) *led: rdn 2f out: hdd over 1f out: one pce ins fnl f and lost 2nd fnl 75yds* **9/2**[2]	
440	4	2 ¼	**Piccarello**[33] 4437 2-8-10 75..... KierenFallon 1	70
			(M H Tompkins) *wnt rt s: chsd ldrs: rdn 2f out: wknd fnl f* **3/1**[1]	
5	5	¾	**Mountain Range (IRE)**[16] 5006 2-8-12 0..... EddieAhern 2	70
			(J L Dunlop) *crossed and wnt lft s: sn chsng ldr: rdn 2f out: outpcd over 1f out* **3/1**[1]	
	6	10	**Tourmaline (IRE)** 2-8-4 0..... MartinDwyer 6	40
			(P W Chapple-Hyam) *t.k.h: a in rr: lost tch over 1f out* **10/1**	
50	7	7	**Sir Rocky (IRE)**[49] 3915 2-9-0 0..... PatDobbs 5	35+
			(R Hannon) *chsd ldrs: rdn and hmpd over 2f out: wknd sn after* **5/1**[3]	

1m 43.34s (3.44) **Going Correction** +0.325s/f (Good) **7 Ran SP% 112.3**
Speed ratings (Par 94): **95,93,92,90,89 79,72**
toteswingers:1&2:£21.00, 1&3:£8.40, 2&3:£20.70 CSF £99.29 TOTE £8.80: £4.60, £7.00; EX 117.00.
Owner Landmark Racing Limited **Bred** Maddenstown Equine Enterprise Ltd **Trained** Whitsbury, Hants

FOCUS

A modest juvenile race, by far the best recent winner being Youmzain. Ralph Beckett won this last season with a newcomer and repeated the trick.

NOTEBOOK

Devoted(IRE) ◆ is from the family of Classic Cliché and has a fair amount of speed on the dam's side. Held up early by her rider who was putting up 2lb overweight, she made smooth progress in the straight and, when asked for more, found extra to settle the issue and scored comfortably. She appeared to know her job, although connections felt she was a little green, but she could be the sort to thrive over further next season. (op 8-1 tchd 6-1)

Strictly Rhythm was too green to do herself justice on her debut but the experience had clearly been of benefit, evidenced by an improved effort here. She tried for a run up the rail in the straight but had to switch before staying on in the wake of the winner. She should be up to winning a similar race. (op 12-1 tchd 20-1)

Levantera(IRE) finished behind today's runner-up on their respective debuts but had built on that next time. She made the running and stuck on under pressure when headed. She now qualifies for a handicap mark and can find a race in that sphere. (op 4-1 tchd 11-2)

Piccarello set the standard off a mark of 75 but had his chance and was unable to pick up. He might have found the ground softer than ideal, but is another whose future probably lies in handicaps. (op 7-2 tchd 15-4 in a place)

Mountain Range(IRE) was sent off favourite on the strength of an encouraging debut but failed to step up on that having been somewhat difficult to load into the stalls. (op 7-2 tchd 11-4)

Sir Rocky(IRE), the better fancied stable companion of the runner-up, was held up before being denied a run in the straight and then faded disappointingly, as though something might have been amiss. The ground might not have suited and he is another that qualifies for handicaps now. (op 6-1 tchd 4-1)

5521 E B F PORTSMOUTH NEWS FILLIES' STKS (H'CAP) 6f

4:50 (4:50) (Class 3) (0-95,92) 3-Y-O+ **£7,771** (£2,312; £1,155; £577) **Stalls** Low

Form				RPR
0435	1		**Alice Alleyne (IRE)**[28] 4593 3-9-2 **82**..... KierenFallon 7	90
			(Sir Michael Stoute) *sn trcking ldrs: led ins fnl 2f: rdn fnl f: jst hld on* **4/1**[1]	
22-4	2	shd	**Gouray Girl (IRE)**[12] 5154 3-9-7 **87**..... EddieAhern 1	95+
			(W R Swinburn) *hld up in rr: hdwy over 1f out: rdn and styd on to chse wnr fnl 120yds: fin wl: nt quite get up* **4/1**[1]	
1505	3	2	**Yer Woman (IRE)**[29] 4551 3-9-10 **90**..... JimCrowley 2	92
			(R Hannon) *s.i.s: in rr: hdwy over 1f out: styd on ins fnl f but nvr gng pce to rch ldng duo* **25/1**	
0006	4	1 ¼	**Kerrys Requiem (IRE)**[7] 5285 4-9-5 **82**..... AlanMunro 8	80
			(M R Channon) *chsd ldrs: rdn to chse wnr wl over 1f out but no imp: wknd fnl 120yds* **8/1**	
2114	5	½	**Rio Mist**[64] 3415 3-9-10 **90**..... PatDobbs 4	86
			(R Hannon) *chsd ldrs: rdn and outpcd over 1f out: kpt on again cl home* **5/1**[3]	
2	6	2 ¾	**Miss Faustina (IRE)**[22] 4806 3-9-4 **84**..... PatCosgrave 5	71
			(P J McBride) *led tl hdd ins fnl 2f: sn edgd rt u.p and wknd over 1f out* **9/2**[2]	

The Form Book, Raceform Ltd, Compton, RG20 6NL

020 **7** 1 3/4 **Perfect Flight**[19] 4904 5-9-5 **82** ShaneKelly 6 64
(M Blanshard) *chsd ldrs over 3f* **8/1**

-562 **8** 6 **Mistic Magic (IRE)**[15] 5052 3-9-12 **92** (b) MartinDwyer 3 54
(P F I Cole) *chsd ldrs tl wknd qckly 1/2-way* **17/2**

1m 14.28s (2.08) **Going Correction** +0.45s/f (Yiel)
WFA 3 from 4yo+ 3lb **8** Ran SP% **111.4**
Speed ratings (Par 104): **104,103,101,99,98 95,92,84**
toteswingers:1&2:£3.60, 1&3:£10.60, 2&3:£8.40 CSF £18.95 CT £339.60 TOTE £4.90: £1.80, £1.80, £3.30; EX 22.20.
Owner Plantation Stud **Bred** Plantation Stud **Trained** Newmarket, Suffolk

FOCUS
A decent fillies' handicap.

NOTEBOOK
Alice Alleyne(IRE), who has been running mainly over 7f, was well backed this first try on soft ground and justified the support. Coming though to lead inside the last 2f, she ran on well under pressure and just did enough. (op 6-1 tchd 7-2)
Gouray Girl(IRE) ◆, whose reappearance was delayed by a back problem, was sent off favourite and looked the unlucky one in the race. Held up at the back early, she had to wait for a gap before picking up and then was closing down on the winner all the way to the line. She would have been in front in a few more strides and deserves to go one better. (op 10-3 tchd 11-4)
Yer Woman(IRE) missed the break slightly and was held up before making headway just behind the runner-up. She stayed on steadily to the line, and will be of particular interest when returned to Polytrack. (op 16-1)
Kerrys Requiem(IRE) gained her only win of the season over C&D in June and ran pretty well from her outside stall until fading in the last furlong. (op 10-1)
Rio Mist had a successful time earlier in the year but was having her first run for nine weeks after a below-par effort. She ran as if the outing will bring her on, but her best form has been on fast ground, and she might need an indian summer if she is to build on this. (op 9-2 tchd 4-1)
Miss Faustina(IRE) made the running having won over further in Ireland. The tactics did not work and she might be better off ridden less forcefully over further. (op 6-1)
Perfect Flight was bidding to repeat her success of two years previously. She showed up for some way but dropped out in the closing stages.
Mistic Magic(IRE) failed to fire in the second-time blinkers on ground she has handled in the past. (op 7-1 tchd 10-1)

5522 TURFTV IS FOR BETTING SHOPS MAIDEN STKS (H'CAP) 2m
5:25 (5:25) (Class 5) (0-70,70) 3-Y-O **£2,590** (£770; £385; £192) **Stalls** High

Form RPR

0-06 **1** **Bravo Bravo**[16] 5001 3-8-4 **51** oh4 LiamJones 5 59+
(M R Channon) *s.i.s: in rr: hdwy on outside over 2f out: str run to ld fnl 120yds: won gng away* **25/1**

5-54 **2** 1 1/4 **Viviani (IRE)**[8] 5260 3-8-13 **60** (t) PatDobbs 1 66
(Mrs A J Perrett) *trckd ldrs: pushed along to chse wnr over 2f out: rdn to ld over 1f out: hdd and outpcd fnl 120yds* **11/4**[1]

2-03 **3** 1 1/2 **Mighty Mambo**[44] 4062 3-9-9 **70** PatCosgrave 10 74
(Jane Chapple-Hyam) *chsd ldr: rdn over 3f out: led over 2f out: hdd over 1f out: styd on same pce* **4/1**[2]

5023 **4** 4 **Miniyamba (IRE)**[16] 4990 3-9-3 **64** (b[1]) EddieAhern 7 63
(J L Dunlop) *chsd ldrs: rdn 3f out: no imp on ldrs over 2f out: wknd fnl f* **11/4**[1]

-004 **5** 2 1/2 **Weliketobougie**[33] 4426 3-7-13 **51** oh1 SimonPearce(5) 6 47
(A M Hales) *stdd towards rr: rdn and sme hdwy 3f out: nvr rchd ldrs and wknd ins fnl 2f* **11/1**

0604 **6** 1/2 **Juwireya**[12] 5164 3-9-4 **65** JimCrowley 4 60
(P W Hiatt) *in tch 1/2-way: rdn 3f out: no ch fr over 2f out* **14/1**

644 **7** 2 3/4 **Silver Colors (USA)**[12] 5141 3-9-6 **67** ShaneKelly 2 59
(J Noseda) *stdd towards rr 6f out: rdn over 3f out and little rspnse* **8/1**[3]

-065 **8** hd **Lis Pendens**[25] 4683 3-8-4 **51** oh2 MartinDwyer 9 43
(W R Muir) *sn led: rdn over 3f out: hdd over 2f out: sn wknd* **10/1**

5000 **9** 8 **Business Bay (USA)**[12] 5155 3-8-10 **57** JackMitchell 8 39
(E F Vaughan) *in rr: sme hdwy over 3f out: sn wknd* **20/1**

3m 39.32s (10.32) **Going Correction** +0.325s/f (Good) **9** Ran SP% **117.1**
Speed ratings (Par 100): **87,86,85,83,82 82,80,80,76**
toteswingers:1&2:£23.50, 1&3:£14.10, 2&3:£3.90 CSF £94.62 CT £348.28 TOTE £27.20: £6.00, £1.80, £2.30; EX 114.20 Place 6: £547.51 Place 5: £344.31.
Owner Derek And Jean Clee **Bred** D & Jean Clee & Burlington Bloodstock **Trained** West Ilsley, Berks

FOCUS
A modest maiden handicap which local trainer John Dunlop was bidding to win for the third time since 2004 but his representative could not improve his record. The gallop looked even and the winner was the only one to come from off the pace.
Bravo Bravo Official explanation: ttrainer said, regarding apparent improvement in form, that the gelding has matured and appeared better suited by the longer trip.
T/Plt: £347.20 to a £1 stake. Pool:£83,598.90 - 175.74 winning tickets T/Qpdt: £321.80 to a £1 stake. Pool:£3,544.99 - 8.15 winning tickets ST

5488
NEWMARKET (July Course) (R-H)
Saturday, August 28

OFFICIAL GOING: Good to soft
Stands' side section of July Course utilised.
Wind: Light behind Weather: Cloudy with sunny spells

5523 MERCEDES-BENZ OF BURY ST EDMUNDS & CAMBRIDGE E B F MAIDEN STKS 6f
1:45 (1:45) (Class 4) 2-Y-O **£4,533** (£1,348; £674; £336) **Stalls** High

Form RPR

2 **1** **Codemaster**[35] 4384 2-9-3 0 DaneO'Neill 3 90+
(H Candy) *chsd ldrs: led over 1f out: rdn clr fnl f* **7/4**[2]

2 6 **Blue Tiger's Eye (IRE)** 2-9-3 0 TedDurcan 12 75+
(Saeed Bin Suroor) *dwlt: hld up: racd keenly: hdwy: nt clr run and swtchd lft over 1f out: sn hung lft: r.o to go 2nd wl ins fnl f: no ch w wnr* **6/4**[1]

3 3/4 **State Of Mind** 2-9-3 0 TomQueally 14 70+
(P F I Cole) *hld up: hdwy over 2f out: swtchd lft over 1f out: styd on same pce fnl f* **20/1**

4 2 3/4 **St Augustine (IRE)** 2-8-12 0 KierenFox(5) 2 62+
(J R Best) *hld up: hdwy over 4f out: rdn over 1f out: wknd fnl f* **20/1**

06 **5** 3/4 **Elusivity (IRE)**[57] 3624 2-9-3 0 WilliamBuick 8 59+
(B J Meehan) *prom: rdn over 2f out: hung lft and wknd over 1f out* **11/1**

60 **6** nk **Granny Anne (IRE)**[29] 4549 2-8-5 0 NatashaEaton(7) 1 53
(A Bailey) *hdwy over 4f out: led and hung lft over 3f out: hdd over 2f out: wknd fnl f* **66/1**

5 **7** hd **Tijori (IRE)**[33] 4421 2-9-3 0 RichardHughes 11 58
(R Hannon) *led: hdd over 3f out: rdn over 2f out: wknd fnl f* **8/1**[3]

8 1 3/4 **Monsieur Jamie** 2-8-10 0 DannyBrock(7) 5 53
(J R Jenkins) *s.i.s: hdwy over 4f out: rdn over 2f out: wknd over 1f out* **100/1**

05 **9** 3/4 **Aquilifer (IRE)**[24] 4691 2-9-3 0 TonyCulhane 7 50
(W Jarvis) *hld up: shkn up over 2f out: nvr nr to chal* **100/1**

66 **10** 1 1/4 **Cinderkamp**[12] 5160 2-9-3 0 LiamKeniry 4 47
(E F Vaughan) *w ldr: racd keenly: led over 2f out: rdn: edgd lft and hdd over 1f out: sn wknd* **33/1**

00 **11** 1/2 **Bouggatti**[15] 5047 2-9-3 0 JimmyFortune 6 45
(W Jarvis) *s.i.s: a in rr: wknd over 2f out* **33/1**

06 **12** 1 **Munro's Dragon**[11] 5170 2-8-12 0 AshleyMorgan(5) 9 42
(M H Tompkins) *mid-div: sn pushed along: wknd over 2f out* **100/1**

03 **13** nk **Good Timin'**[22] 4782 2-9-3 0 RobertWinston 13 41
(D H Brown) *trckd ldrs: plld hrd: wknd over 1f out* **20/1**

1m 13.99s (1.49) **Going Correction** +0.25s/f (Good) **13** Ran SP% **120.4**
Speed ratings (Par 96): **100,92,91,87,86 85,85,83,82,80 80,78,78**
Tote Swingers: 1&2 £1.30, 1&3 £4.10, 2&3 £4.40 CSF £4.23 TOTE £2.30: £1.10, £1.70, £3.40; EX 5.60 Trifecta £30.60 Pool: £599.69 - 14.48 winning units..
Owner J J Byrne **Bred** J Byrne And Partners **Trained** Kingston Warren, Oxon

FOCUS
This didn't look the strongest maiden by Newmarket standards with several of these qualifying for a nursery mark after this. It was a two-horse race, according to the market, and they duly filled the first two places, but in reality there was only one horse in it.

NOTEBOOK
Codemaster ◆ had been beaten narrowly by a subsequent winner on his Salisbury debut last month and was on slower ground here, but it made no difference to him. Never far away, he was sent to the front over a furlong out and quickly bounded right away for an impressive success. It remains to be seen what he has beaten, but he still looks a nice prospect and may be given just one more run this season. (op 9-4)
Blue Tiger's Eye(IRE), a 110,000gns half-brother to a couple of winning milers, did everything wrong as he missed the break and then race erratically near the back of the field with his head held high. He did eventually manage to zigzag his way through to snatch the runner-up spot, but he cannot be supported with any confidence to go one better next time and it now seems clear as to why he had already been gelded. (op 13-8 tchd 7-4)
State Of Mind ◆, a 43,000euros half-brother to a 1m2f winner in France, made a pleasing debut and the way he stayed on suggests he will appreciate further in his own right.
St Augustine(IRE), a £20,000 half-brother to a dual winning sprinter, was never too far away on the outside of the pack and should have learned plenty from this. (op 16-1 tchd 25-1 in places)
Elusivity(IRE), making his debut for the yard after showing some ability in two starts for Richard Hannon, had been gelded since last seen. He was never a threat, but did make some late progress and is one of those for whom nurseries now become a possibility. (op 10-1 tchd 12-1)
Granny Anne(IRE), who hinted at ability in her first two starts on quick ground, didn't fare badly as she saw plenty of daylight on the wide outside and also now gets a mark. (op 100-1)
Tijori(IRE), fifth of nine when a short-priced favourite for an ordinary Windsor maiden on debut, made the early running before hanging right and fading entering the last 2f. This effort suggests that the market support at Windsor was more down to the reputation of the yard rather than his true ability. (tchd 7-1)
Good Timin' Official explanation: jockey said colt ran too free

5524 CHRIS BLACKWELL MEMORIAL H'CAP 7f
2:15 (2:16) (Class 3) (0-90,90) 3-Y-O **£9,066** (£2,697; £1,348; £673) **Stalls** High

Form RPR

6606 **1** **Bullwhip (IRE)**[23] 4750 3-9-9 **90** WilliamBuick 14 103
(J H M Gosden) *hld up: hdwy over 2f out: rdn to ld 1f out: r.o wl* **6/1**[2]

4415 **2** 4 **Hot Spark**[16] 4995 3-9-2 **83** (t) DaneO'Neill 3 85
(J Akehurst) *prom: rdn over 2f out: styd on same pce fnl f* **14/1**

-062 **3** 1/2 **Waabel**[25] 4679 3-8-10 **77** HayleyTurner 1 78
(Jim Best) *w ldrs: rdn 2f out: no ex ins fnl f* **16/1**

0054 **4** shd **Take Ten**[52] 3791 3-9-5 **86** GregFairley 12 86
(M Johnston) *chsd ldrs: rdn and ev ch over 1f out: no ex ins fnl f* **15/2**

-120 **5** 1 3/4 **Bintalwaadi**[45] 4030 3-9-8 **89** RichardHills 16 85
(E A L Dunlop) *led: rdn and hdd 1f out: hung rt and wknd ins fnl f* **13/2**[3]

01-0 **6** 1 1/2 **Leviathan**[19] 4894 3-9-7 **88** MickyFenton 15 80
(T P Tate) *prom: rdn over 2f out: wknd over 1f out* **10/1**

1032 **7** 1/2 **Chica Whopa (IRE)**[12] 5149 3-9-0 **81** RichardHughes 9 71
(R Hannon) *hld up: hdwy over 2f out: sn rdn: wkng whn hmpd ins fnl f* **8/1**

1232 **8** 2 **Tesslam**[28] 4593 3-9-7 **88** PhilipRobinson 4 73
(M A Jarvis) *chsd ldrs: rdn and hung rt over 2f out: wknd over 1f out* **6/1**[2]

02-6 **9** 1/2 **Paradise Spectre**[58] 3587 3-8-13 **80** NeilCallan 2 64
(Mrs K Burke) *hld up in tch: rdn over 2f out: wknd over 1f out* **33/1**

-212 **10** 1 **Tartan Trip**[24] 4699 3-9-2 **83** JimmyFortune 5 64
(A M Balding) *hld up: swtchd rt 1/2-way: hdwy over 2f out: sn rdn: wknd over 1f out* **9/2**[1]

0000 **11** 3/4 **Amary (IRE)**[42] 4137 3-8-13 **80** (p) ChrisCatlin 8 59
(C E Brittain) *chsd ldrs: rdn over 2f out: edgd rt and wknd over 1f out* **66/1**

4660 **12** 2 **Kumbeshwar**[117] 1776 3-8-10 **77** CathyGannon 11 50
(P D Evans) *prom: rdn over 3f out: wkng whn n.m.r over 1f out* **66/1**

-505 **13** 1 1/2 **Exceedingly Bold**[98] 2348 3-9-4 **85** (t) JimmyQuinn 13 54
(Miss Gay Kelleway) *s.i.s: hld up: rdn over 2f out: a in rr* **40/1**

10-0 **14** 5 **Abriachan**[137] 1279 3-8-8 **75** WilliamCarson 7 31
(M G Quinlan) *s.i.s: sn pushed along and a in rr* **66/1**

35-1 **15** 2 **Ghost (IRE)**[36] 4340 3-9-1 **82** MichaelHills 6 32
(B W Hills) *w ldrs: rdn over 2f out: wknd over 1f out* **14/1**

1m 26.7s (1.00) **Going Correction** +0.25s/f (Good) **15** Ran SP% **121.1**
Speed ratings (Par 104): **104,99,98,98,96 95,94,92,91,90 89,87,85,79,77**
Tote Swingers: 1&2 £22.60, 1&3 £23.70, 2&3 £28.00 CSF £85.17 CT £1305.88 TOTE £7.30: £2.60, £5.00, £5.40; EX 113.30 Trifecta £1074.70 Part won. Pool: £1,452.41 - 0.30 winning units..
Owner H R H Princess Haya Of Jordan **Bred** John O'Connor **Trained** Newmarket, Suffolk

FOCUS
A competitive handicap and they used the full width of the track. The result suggests there was no track bias at this meeting.

NOTEBOOK
Bullwhip(IRE) ◆ had found life tough, including in the face of some stiff tasks, since making a winning racecourse debut at Doncaster in March, but he is proven on a testing surface and relished these conditions. He was off the bridle over 2f from home, but really found his stride up the hill and eventually pulled away from his rivals. He still doesn't have that many miles on the clock and there should be more to come from him under suitable conditions, either this year or next. (op 15-2 tchd 8-1)
Hot Spark had finished unplaced in both previous starts on a soft surface, but this was a lot better and he did really well as he was one of those to race more towards the far side of the track, well away from the winner. This removed any doubts over his ability to handle soft ground and he should find another opportunity before the season is out.

Waabel ◆, beaten narrowly in a Chepstow maiden earlier this month that has worked out well, was on soft ground for the first time and he deserves a lot of credit as he raced closest to the far rail up with the pace and saw plenty of daylight. He seemed likely to drop away, but kept on going to just lose out on second place and he will surely break his duck sooner rather than later.
Take Ten ran a cracker here at the July Meeting last month, but he had never previously encountered ground softer than good and, although he had every chance and put in a solid effort, he may be happier back on a sounder surface. (op 8-1)
Bintalwaadi, who is still unexposed, has run well in both previous turf outings in soft ground and she seemed to be in the ideal position up with the pace against the stands' rail, but she didn't see her race out. She was found to have bled from the nose. Official explanation: jockey said filly bled from the nose (op 6-1 tchd 7-1)
Leviathan ◆ was entitled to need his belated reappearance on Fibresand earlier this month and tracked Bintalwaadi up the stands' rail, but he seemed likely to drop away when coming under pressure over 2f from home. However, he ran on again up the hill and, as he is getting fitter all the time, is one to note for the autumn. (tchd 11-1 in places)
Tesslam was reportedly unsuited by the ground. Official explanation: jockey said gelding was unsuited by the good to soft ground (op 7-1)
Tartan Trip stays further than this and the conditions should have helped compensate for that, but he may not have appreciated this first try on soft ground as he didn't get home Jimmy Fortune reported that the gelding was never travelling. Official explanation: jockey said gelding never travelled (op 11-2)
Ghost(IRE) had reportedly bolted to post. Official explanation: jockey said gelding bolted going to post

5525 BET365 NURSERY — 7f
2:45 (2:45) (Class 2) 2-Y-O — **£10,361** (£3,083; £1,540; £769) **Stalls** High

Form				RPR
31	**1**		**Glen's Diamond**[10] 5196 2-9-0 **83** — JimmyFortune 9	87
			(R A Fahey) *s.i.s: hld up: hdwy over 2f out: nt clr run over 1f out: hrd rdn to ld nr fin* **7/2**[2]	
21	**2**	¾	**Belgian Bill**[63] 3433 2-9-0 **83** — TonyCulhane 6	85
			(George Baker) *chsd ldrs: led over 2f out: rdn over 1f out: hung lft and hdd nr fin* **11/4**[1]	
21	**3**	¾	**Byronic (IRE)**[54] 3735 2-9-2 **85** — AdamKirby 3	85
			(C G Cox) *chsd ldrs: pushed along 1/2-way: rdn and hung rt over 2f out: ev ch over 1f out: styng on same pce whn hmpd nr fin* **8/1**[3]	
3434	**4**	¾	**Mother Jones**[7] 5301 2-8-6 **75** — JimmyQuinn 4	73
			(D H Brown) *s.i.s: hld up: hdwy 2f out: sn ev ch: no ex towards fin* **10/1**	
41	**5**	4 ½	**Whaileyy (IRE)**[46] 3991 2-9-3 **86** — RichardMullen 8	73
			(Sir Michael Stoute) *chsd ldrs: ev ch fr over 2f out: tl wknd ins fnl f* **7/2**[2]	
1050	**6**	2 ¾	**Planet Waves (IRE)**[35] 4355 2-8-10 **79** — (t) ChrisCatlin 10	59
			(C E Brittain) *sn led: hdd over 2f out: wknd over 1f out* **20/1**	
120	**7**	9	**Clarke Lane (USA)**[70] 3190 2-9-7 **90** — (b[1]) NeilCallan 11	48
			(M A Jarvis) *chsd ldrs: rdn 1/2-way: wknd over 1f out* **10/1**	
1006	**8**	28	**Molly Mylenis**[37] 4278 2-7-12 **67** oh2 — CathyGannon 1	—
			(P D Evans) *w ldrs tl rdn 3f out: hmpd over 2f out: wknd over 1f out: t.o* **50/1**	
1410	**9**	7	**Geesala (IRE)**[82] 2828 2-8-13 **82** — RichardHughes 7	—
			(K A Ryan) *hld up in tch: plld hrd: nt clr run over 2f out: wknd and eased over 1f out: t.o* **10/1**	

1m 27.06s (1.36) **Going Correction** +0.25s/f (Good) — **9** Ran SP% **116.2**
Speed ratings (Par 100): **102,101,100,99,94 91,80,48,40**
Tote Swingers: 1&2 £2.70, 1&3 £5.40, 2&3 £5.20 CSF £13.67 CT £71.74 TOTE £4.20: £1.60, £1.10, £3.20; EX 14.80 Trifecta £163.40 Pool: £401.74 - 1.81 winning units..
Owner Morebrooke Ltd **Bred** Doverlane Finance Ltd **Trained** Musley Bank, N Yorks

FOCUS
A decent nursery with eight of the nine runners previous winners, but although there wasn't much covering the first four at the line, the others finished well strung out and this looked hard work for these youngsters.

NOTEBOOK
Glen's Diamond ◆, making his nursery debut after winning an ordinary Carlisle maiden ten days earlier, is bred to be suited by this extra furlong and this looked a case of him outstaying his rivals. Held up early, he still had a bit to do starting up the hill, but he relished the stiff finish and flashed past his rivals in the dying strides. He looks a nice handicapper in the making. (op 5-1 tchd 11-2)
Belgian Bill, making his nursery debut after easily winning a Doncaster maiden last time filled with subsequent winners, ran a brave race. He looked to have done enough to see off his two nearest challengers inside the last furlong, especially when slightly hampering the pair as he drifted left under a right-hand drive, but he left himself vulnerable to the winner's late flourish. He had only raced on fast ground before and may be happier back a sounder surface. (op 9-4)
Byronic(IRE) was up in trip for this nursery debut having won a fast-ground Windsor maiden last month in which subsequent winners filled four of the next six places. He was always close to the pace on the outside of the field and had every chance, but he too may be better off back on better ground. (op 7-1 tchd 9-1 in places)
Mother Jones, the only maiden in the field, had been shaping as though this extra furlong would suit. She gave away plenty of ground with a slow start and was forced to make her effort widest, but she still gave herself every chance and seemed to have run her race when receiving a bump close to the line. This was still a good effort and she deserves to get her head in front. (tchd 17-2)
Whaileyy(IRE), making his nursery debut after edging out a subsequent winner when long odds-on for a Yarmouth maiden last month, went off well backed and he was close enough passing the 2f pole, but he didn't seem to get home in the ground. (op 9-2)
Planet Waves(IRE), who has faced some stiff tasks and not been up to it since winning a Nottingham maiden in May, disputed the early lead against the stands' rail but was another to get tired in the conditions. (tchd 25-1)
Geesala(IRE) Official explanation: jockey said filly moved poorly

5526 NOVAE BLOODSTOCK INSURANCE HOPEFUL STKS (LISTED RACE) — 6f
3:20 (3:20) (Class 1) 3-Y-O+ — **£21,004** (£7,962; £3,984; £1,986; £995; £499) **Stalls** High

Form				RPR
2346	**1**		**Doncaster Rover (USA)**[27] 4616 4-9-0 107 — RobertWinston 6	111
			(D H Brown) *chsd ldrs: rdn over 2f out: led ins fnl f: edgd rt: drvn out* **9/2**[3]	
0000	**2**	1 ¼	**Advanced**[14] 5095 7-9-0 95 — AmyRyan 5	107
			(K A Ryan) *led: hdd over 2f out: rdn and ev ch ins fnl f: styd on same pce* **14/1**	
4221	**3**	shd	**Dafeef**[14] 5088 3-8-11 106 — (p) RichardHills 8	107
			(Saeed Bin Suroor) *trckd ldrs: racd keenly: shkn up over 1f out: styd on* **4/1**[2]	
1113	**4**	1 ½	**Bated Breath**[14] 5088 3-8-11 107 — RichardHughes 4	102+
			(R Charlton) *hld up: racd keenly: hdwy over 2f out: edgd lft over 1f out: styd on: nt trble ldrs* **7/4**[1]	
1303	**5**	¾	**Rodrigo De Torres**[42] 4140 3-8-11 103 — TomQueally 7	99
			(H R A Cecil) *chsd ldr tl led over 2f out: rdn and hdd ins fnl f: no ex* **8/1**	
0500	**6**	4 ½	**Sir Gerry (USA)**[11] 5183 5-9-4 104 — TedDurcan 1	89
			(C A Dwyer) *hld up: rdn over 1f out: nvr trbld ldrs* **14/1**	
3030	**7**	1	**Mon Cadeaux**[73] 3066 3-8-11 98 — JimmyFortune 3	82
			(A M Balding) *hld up: rdn over 2f out: n.d* **8/1**	
0111	**8**	½	**Caledonia Princess**[19] 4904 4-8-9 78 — RossAtkinson 2	75
			(F J Brennan) *chsd ldrs tl rdn and wknd over 1f out* **50/1**	

1m 13.02s (0.52) **Going Correction** +0.25s/f (Good)
WFA 3 from 4yo+ 3lb — **8** Ran SP% **112.1**
Speed ratings (Par 111): **106,104,104,102,101 95,93,93**
Tote Swingers: 1&2 £10.20, 1&3 £4.50, 2&3 £11.00 CSF £60.85 TOTE £5.00: £1.60, £3.90, £1.20; EX 59.70 Trifecta £687.70 Pool: £1,254.73 - 1.35 winning units..
Owner P Holling I Raeburn S Halsall S Bolland **Bred** Coffeepot Stable **Trained** Maltby, S Yorks
■ Stewards' Enquiry : Amy Ryan one-day ban: used whip with excessive frequency (Sep 12)

FOCUS
An interesting Listed sprint, but although 3-y-os made up half the field no member of the Classic generation had been successful in this race since 2001 and that trend continued. Unusually, for a contest of this class, they didn't seem to go a great pace early and the runners spurned the nearside rail on this occasion.

NOTEBOOK
Doncaster Rover(USA) was one of those best in at these weights and had returned from his previous outing at Chester with an infection, but his wins had come on a quicker surface, though he does have placed form on soft ground. He looked an unlikely winner coming to the last 2f as he was the first off the bridle and under strong pressure, but he responded gamely and powered up the hill on the wide outside to hit the front inside the last furlong. He will now take his chance in next Saturday's Betfred Sprint Cup at Haydock. (op 6-1)
Advanced has been placed a few times in Pattern company and goes on the ground, so perhaps it wasn't such a surprise to see him run a big race even though he had plenty on at the weights. He impressed with the way he battled back after losing the advantage and still has what it takes to win a decent prize. (op 18-1 tchd 20-1)
Dafeef enjoyed the run of the race when beating Bated Breath by under a length in soft ground over C&D earlier this month. He travelled very powerfully from the off, if perhaps a little keenly, but he found nothing like as much off the bridle as had seemed likely. He has plenty of ability, but does have his quirky side also. (op 7-2 tchd 10-3)
Bated Breath didn't find the race panning out for him when losing his unbeaten record behind Dafeef over C&D last time and enjoyed a 3lb pull with the Godolphin colt. He had a scare coming into this when suffering an abscess in his near-fore the previous evening, but he was allowed to take his chance. Tucked in at the back of the field early and a bit keen, he didn't find a great deal when coming under pressure over a furlong out and could only make modest late headway. Whether the foot problem was greater than had been thought, or whether he isn't so effective on soft ground, remains to be seen. Either way, he is well worth another chance to confirm the impression he made in his first three starts. (op 15-8 tchd 2-1)
Rodrigo De Torres, down to this trip for the first time since last October, was on soft ground for the first time and showed up for a long way before getting tired inside the last furlong. (op 13-2)
Sir Gerry(USA) made no impression from off the pace. (op 11-1 tchd 10-1)
Mon Cadeaux also failed to pick up when asked. (op 9-1 tchd 10-1 in places)
Caledonia Princess, who was seeking a four-timer, showed up for some of the way but she ended up where she should have on official ratings. (tchd 66-1)

5527 £100,000 TATTERSALLS MILLIONS AUCTION STKS — 6f
3:55 (3:56) (Class 2) 2-Y-O — **£55,769** (£25,341; £10,142; £5,066; £3,047; £2,028) **Stalls** High

Form				RPR
1511	**1**		**Zebedee**[32] 4458 2-9-3 103 — RichardHughes 4	94+
			(R Hannon) *hld up: hdwy over 1f out: shkn up to ld nr fin: cosily* **1/1**[1]	
2304	**2**	hd	**Button Moon (IRE)**[7] 5284 2-8-2 74 — (p) MartinLane 3	78
			(I A Wood) *chsd ldrs: led over 1f out: sn rdn: hdd nr fin* **40/1**	
0163	**3**	1 ¾	**Mayhab**[22] 4801 2-8-13 75 — NeilCallan 12	84
			(C E Brittain) *led: rdn: edgd lft and hdd over 1f out: styd on same pce ins fnl f* **25/1**	
62	**4**	nk	**Cruiser**[17] 4960 2-8-9 0 — RichardMullen 6	79
			(W R Muir) *chsd ldrs: rdn over 1f out: styd on same pce ins fnl f* **16/1**	
0	**5**	1 ½	**Queen O'The Desert (IRE)**[43] 4095 2-8-4 0 — GregFairley 1	69
			(A M Balding) *a.p: rdn over 1f out: no ex ins fnl f* **50/1**	
5	**6**	½	**Yashila (IRE)**[31] 4471 2-8-8 0 — DaneO'Neill 10	72
			(R Hannon) *hmpd s: hld up: hdwy over 4f out: rdn over 1f out: styd on same pce* **16/1**	
432	**7**	hd	**Shafgaan**[114] 1835 2-8-5 84 — ChrisCatlin 9	68
			(C E Brittain) *prom: rdn over 1f out: styd on same pce appr fnl f* **6/1**[3]	
1	**8**	1 ¼	**Malthouse (GER)**[34] 4396 2-9-1 0 — RichardHills 8	75
			(M Johnston) *w ldr: rdn and ev ch over 1f out: wknd ins fnl f* **10/3**[2]	
13	**9**	shd	**Child Bride**[7] 5284 2-8-0 79 — JimmyQuinn 7	59
			(P F I Cole) *hld up: rdn over 1f out: nvr on terms* **16/1**	
0	**10**	2	**Firstknight**[18] 4934 2-8-11 0 — WilliamBuick 11	64
			(Tom Dascombe) *trckd ldrs: plld hrd: wknd over 1f out* **25/1**	
005	**11**	8	**Freedom Trail**[82] 2813 2-8-2 64 — HayleyTurner 2	31
			(D R C Elsworth) *sn pushed along and a in rr: lost tch fnl 2f* **100/1**	

1m 14.69s (2.19) **Going Correction** +0.25s/f (Good) — **11** Ran SP% **118.1**
Speed ratings (Par 100): **95,94,92,92,90 89,89,87,87,84 73**
Tote Swingers: 1&2 £11.60, 1&3 £7.60, 2&3 £47.00 CSF £67.38 TOTE £1.80: £1.10, £7.10, £7.20; EX 67.00 Trifecta £538.80 Pool: £1,567.95 - 2.15 winning units..
Owner Mrs J Wood **Bred** Hascombe & Valiant Studs **Trained** East Everleigh, Wilts

FOCUS
They raced down the centre of the track this time. Few could be seriously considered in this valuable sales race, which revolved around the winner.

NOTEBOOK
Zebedee found himself under top weight after two wins in Pattern company, including a cheeky success in the Molecomb. However, he was trying beyond 5f for the first time and had never encountered ground softer than good before, so he was ridden with that in mind. Making his ground up gradually from off the pace, he was produced with his effort in plenty of time and scored another slightly cheeky victory. He seemed to get the trip well enough in the holding ground, albeit against just fair opposition, and he is in both the Mill Reef and the Middle Park over this trip. The Flying Childers over the minimum would, however, still seem the most attractive option at this stage. (op 11-10 tchd 10-11)
Button Moon(IRE) showed plenty of promise earlier in the season, but hadn't beaten a rival in her previous two starts. Sporting first-time cheekpieces here, she proved a revelation and having been handy from the start, was only cut down in the last 50 yards. She picked up a nice prize for finishing second, but she deserves to win a race if she can maintain this form.
Mayhab, narrowly beaten in a 7f nursery here earlier this month, had 24lb to find with the winner on these terms and the way he kept on suggests he will be suited by a return to further.
Cruiser, narrowly beaten in an ordinary Sandown maiden last time, was never far away and ran well. He shouldn't be long in finding a race. (tchd 20-1 in places)
Queen O'The Desert(IRE) ran much better than when beaten a long way on her Newbury debut and she will find easier opportunities than this. (tchd 66-1)
Yashila(IRE), surrounded by subsequent winners when an eye-catching fifth of nine on her Goodwood debut and representing the same owner/trainer as the winner, is another who should be able to win a routine maiden. (op 18-1 tchd 20-1)
Shafgaan has improved with each outing and was trying an extra furlong on this first start since his unlucky defeat at Chester in May. He never got into it, but should come on for the run. (op 7-1 tchd 11-2)

Malthouse(GER), winner of an ordinary Ascot newcomers' race on faster ground on debut, dropped away after showing up early and better might have been expected, but he was coltish beforehand so may have had his mind on other things. (tchd 4-1)
Firstknight Official explanation: jockey said colt ran too free

5528 UNIVERSITY OF CAMBRIDGE VETERINARY SCHOOL TRUST H'CAP 5f
4:30 (4:31) (Class 4) (0-85,85) 3-Y-O+ **£5,180** (£1,541; £770; £384) **Stalls** High

Form				RPR
2544	1		**Angus Newz**[15] 5054 7-9-2 **78** (v) WilliamBuick 9 (M Quinn) *chsd ldrs: rdn over 1f out: hung lft ins fnl f: r.o to ld towards fin* **11/1**	88
3001	2	½	**Sir Geoffrey (IRE)**[5] 5377 4-9-0 **76** 6ex (b) IanMongan 6 (J A Glover) *chsd ldr: rdn and hung rt over 1f out: led ins fnl f: hdd towards fin* **7/1**	84
0031	3	1 ¼	**Tagula Night (IRE)**[17] 4961 4-9-4 **80** (vt) AdamKirby 1 (W R Swinburn) *hld up: hdwy over 1f out: sn rdn: r.o* **6/1**[2]	84
5051	4	1 ½	**Billy Red**[24] 4693 6-9-1 **77** (b) FergusSweeney 7 (J R Jenkins) *led: rdn over 1f out: hdd and no ex ins fnl f* **16/1**	75
06	5	½	**Cheveton**[11] 5183 6-9-9 **85** RobertWinston 8 (R J Price) *dwlt: sn pushed along in rr: rdn and n.m.r over 1f out: r.o ins fnl f: nt rch ldrs* **9/4**[1]	81
1331	6	nk	**Boogie Waltzer**[19] 4892 3-8-6 **75** (t) AshleyMorgan(5) 2 (S C Williams) *in rr: hdwy and hung lft over 1f out: styd on same pce ins fnl f* **14/1**	70
0040	7	¾	**Equuleus Pictor**[27] 4625 6-8-12 **77** JackDean(3) 11 (J L Spearing) *sn pushed along and prom: rdn over 1f out: hung lft and no ex ins fnl f* **13/2**[3]	70
5060	8	nk	**Bel Cantor**[19] 4894 7-8-5 **70** (p) KellyHarrison(3) 13 (W J H Ratcliffe) *chsd ldrs: rdn over 1f out: styd on same pce* **33/1**	61
3223	9	shd	**Bougainvilia (IRE)**[11] 5182 3-9-5 **83** RichardHughes 5 (R Hannon) *chsd ldrs: rdn 1/2-way: no ex fnl f* **8/1**	74
5023	10	¾	**Highland Warrior**[9] 5240 11-8-2 **67** PaulPickard(3) 12 (P T Midgley) *s.i.s: outpcd: sme hdwy u.p over 1f out: nvr on terms* **16/1**	55
4450	11	¾	**Spanish Bounty**[21] 4832 5-9-6 **82** (p) StephenCraine 3 (J G Portman) *mid-div: rdn halgway: wknd fnl f* **20/1**	68
000-	12	1	**Magic Cat**[322] 6678 4-9-9 **85** NeilCallan 10 (Mrs K Burke) *sn pushed along in rr: nvr on terms* **12/1**	67

60.40 secs (1.30) **Going Correction** +0.25s/f (Good)
WFA 3 from 4yo+ 2lb **12** Ran SP% **124.2**
Speed ratings (Par 105): **99,98,96,93,93 92,91,90,90,89 88,86**
Tote Swingers: 1&2 £15.70, 1&3 £10.80, 2&3 £5.60 CSF £90.16 CT £528.65 TOTE £14.50: £4.00, £1.90, £1.80; EX 128.80 Trifecta £635.80 Pool: £1,116.99 - 1.30 winning units..
Owner M J Quinn **Bred** Henry And Mrs Rosemary Moszkowicz **Trained** Newmarket, Suffolk

FOCUS
A decent sprint handicap and, with several trailblazers in opposition, this seemed set up for a closer, but in the event the pace held up better than might have been expected. The field was spread across the track, if not tight against either rail.

5529 JULY COURSE H'CAP 1m 2f
5:00 (5:02) (Class 3) (0-95,93) 3-Y-O+ **£9,066** (£2,697; £1,348; £673) **Stalls** Centre

Form				RPR
0-1	1		**Taqleed (IRE)**[15] 5057 3-9-0 **85** WilliamBuick 2 (J H M Gosden) *a.p: led over 1f out: hung rt ins fnl f: rdn clr* **7/1**[3]	103+
5244	2	3 ¾	**Sharaayeen**[23] 4757 3-8-5 **76** GregFairley 11 (B W Hills) *chsd ldrs: led over 2f out: rdn and hdd whn carried rt over 1f out: styd on same pce ins fnl f* **15/2**	86
3161	3	nk	**Sharedah (IRE)**[14] 5083 3-8-11 **82** RichardHills 3 (Sir Michael Stoute) *trckd ldrs: rdn and ev ch whn hung rt over 1f out: styd on same pce* **7/2**[1]	91
3511	4	1 ¾	**Christmas Carnival**[22] 4784 3-8-13 **84** (b) CO'Donoghue 5 (B J Meehan) *a.p: rdn over 1f out: no ex fnl f* **9/1**	90
0602	5	hd	**Moynahan (USA)**[16] 5004 5-9-13 **90** NeilCallan 12 (P F I Cole) *hld up: swtchd lft and hdwy over 2f out: nt clr run and swtchd rt over 1f out: styd on: nt trble ldrs* **14/1**	96
460	6	1 ¼	**Sedgwick**[10] 5217 8-8-6 **74** DeclanCannon(5) 8 (S A Harris) *hld up: rdn over 3f out: hdwy u.p 2f out: no ex ins fnl f* **33/1**	77
0-02	7	2 ½	**Qalahari (IRE)**[21] 4847 4-9-3 **80** JimmyQuinn 13 (D J Coakley) *chsd ldrs: rdn and hung lft over 1f out: wknd fnl f* **20/1**	78
3-53	8	½	**Fanditha (IRE)**[16] 5002 4-9-6 **83** KirstyMilczarek 6 (L M Cumani) *hld up: pushed along 1/2-way: sme hdwy and hung lft over 1f out: wknd ins fnl f* **10/1**	80
0-	9	5	**The Only Key**[262] 7697 4-9-11 **88** WilliamCarson 1 (S W James) *sn led: rdn and hdd over 2f out: wknd over 1f out* **50/1**	75
0051	10	¾	**Bencoolen (IRE)**[17] 4943 5-9-9 **91** MichaelO'Connell(5) 14 (D Nicholls) *awkward leaving stalls: sn chsng ldr: rdn and ev ch over 2f out: wknd over 1f out* **16/1**	77
1550	11	2 ¾	**Reve De Nuit (USA)**[11] 5188 4-9-10 **87** RobertWinston 10 (A J McCabe) *chsd ldrs tl wknd 2f out* **14/1**	67
5144	12	18	**Cumulus Nimbus**[7] 5307 3-9-8 **93** RichardHughes 4 (R Hannon) *s.i.s: hld up: hdwy and gng wl whn hmpd over 2f out: eased: t.o* **9/2**[2]	37+
2044	13	8	**Essexbridge**[23] 4758 3-8-4 **75** FrankieMcDonald 9 (R Hannon) *mid-div: pushed along 1/2-way: wknd over 2f out: t.o* **20/1**	—
4421	U		**Bahamian Music (IRE)**[15] 5056 3-8-9 **80** RichardMullen 7 (R A Fahey) *hld up: racd keenly: hdwy over 3f out: cl up whn clipped heels and uns rdr over 2f out* **11/1**	—

2m 6.16s (0.66) **Going Correction** +0.25s/f (Good)
WFA 3 from 4yo+ 8lb **14** Ran SP% **125.7**
Speed ratings (Par 107): **107,104,103,102,102 101,99,98,94,94 92,77,71,—**
CSF £58.97 CT £222.20 TOTE £6.80: £2.50, £2.80, £1.90; EX 65.00 Trifecta £53.00 Pool: £653.70 - 9.12 winning units. Place 6: £112.57 Place 5: £88.90.
Owner Hamdan Al Maktoum **Bred** Shadwell Estate Co Ltd **Trained** Newmarket, Suffolk

FOCUS
A decent handicap which resulted in a Hamdan Al Maktoum benefit, with the owner having the first three home.

NOTEBOOK
Taqleed(IRE) ◆ wasn't the owner's first string on jockey bookings, but he was much the best of this lot. Making his handicap debut and up in trip after bolting up in a weak-looking Nottingham maiden earlier this month, he was taken widest once into the home straight and, after leading over a furlong out, powered right away. He still has plenty of scope with this only being his third start, so there should be more where this came from. He was cut as low as 14-1 for the Cambridgeshire, but would still need to step up a good deal on this in order to justify that entry. (op 6-1 tchd 5-1)
Sharaayeen ◆ didn't perform well in two previous starts on an easy surface, but he was a springer in the market here, so better was expected and he duly ran well, holding every chance entering the last 2f before the winner pounced. He is gradually returning to form after being gelded and should find another race in due course. (op 16-1)
Sharedah(IRE), who only saw the racecourse for the first time in May, had won two of her four starts and carried the owner's first colours. She travelled well and had her chance, but didn't find as much as had looked likely under pressure up the hill and perhaps she needs to be ridden more positively in order to show her best. (tchd 4-1)
Christmas Carnival handles testing ground, as his two recent narrow victories demonstrated, but he was trying this distance for the first time off a 4lb higher mark in his hat-trick bid. He was always up there, but didn't quite get home and this trip in the holding ground may have been a bigger problem to him than his current mark. (op 10-1)
Moynahan(USA) has two ways of running and ran poorly in his only previous try on genuinely soft ground. He made some late progress, but never looked like winning and is a hard horse to predict. (op 12-1 tchd 16-1)
Sedgwick handles the ground and made some modest late progress, but he remains 9lb higher than when winning an amateurs' event at York in May.
Cumulus Nimbus had twice run well off this mark since winning over C&D last month, but the ground was an issue. He was just trying to get into the race from off the pace when badly hampered by the fall of Bahamian Music right in front of him over 2f out, and that ended any chance he may have had. Official explanation: jockey said colt suffered interference in running (tchd 4-1 and 5-1)
T/Jkpt: Not won. T/Plt: £205.90 to a £1 stake. Pool:£106,073 - 375.97 winning tickets T/Qpdt: £19.70 to a £1 stake. Pool:£6,622 - 248.33 winning tickets CR

4862 REDCAR (L-H)
Saturday, August 28

OFFICIAL GOING: Good to firm (firm in places; watered; 8.8)
Wind: Fresh half against Weather: Dry but overcast

5530 HOME-TEK LADY AMATEUR RIDERS' H'CAP 1m 2f
5:20 (5:22) (Class 5) (0-75,75) 3-Y-O+ **£1,998** (£619; £309; £154) **Stalls** Low

Form				RPR
006	1		**Tropical Duke (IRE)**[15] 5019 4-9-1 **56** oh2 MissRKneller(5) 3 (R E Barr) *hld up towards inner: swtchd to outer 4f out: hdwy fr 3f out to chal over 1f out: kpt on to ld post* **18/1**	65
0401	2	shd	**Pennfield Pirate**[16] 4992 3-8-9 **60** MissNDumelow(7) 10 (H Morrison) *trckd ldrs on outer: hdwy to ld over 1f out: ct post* **14/1**	69
6435	3	2	**Vertigo On Course (IRE)**[16] 4986 5-9-6 **61** ow2 MrsVFahey(5) 5 (R A Fahey) *led: edgd rt and hdd 4f out: outpcd over 3f out: kpt on fr over 1f out* **9/1**	66
5120	4	2	**Hurricane Thomas (IRE)**[15] 5019 6-9-6 **61** MissPhillipaTutty(5) 4 (R A Fahey) *prom: chal fr over 3f out tl no ex ins fnl f* **12/1**	62
0632	5	¾	**Muftarres (IRE)**[21] 4852 5-9-11 **66** MissWGibson(5) 9 (P T Midgley) *trckd ldrs: rdn over 3f out: kpt on same pce* **11/1**	65
5343	6	¾	**Lord Theo**[9] 5235 6-10-8 **72** MrsEmmaLittmoden 1 (N P Littmoden) *midfield: hdwy on inner to ld 4f out: hdd over 1f out: no ex ins fnl f* **5/1**[2]	70
5532	7	½	**Leaving Alone (USA)**[20] 4867 3-9-4 **62** MissSBrotherton 8 (E W Tuer) *midfield: rdn over 3f out: kpt on same pce* **9/2**[1]	59
6050	8	nk	**Edas**[34] 4405 8-9-10 **65** MissHCuthbert(5) 6 (T A K Cuthbert) *slowly away: hld up towards rr: swtchd to outer 4f out: kpt on steadily wout threatening* **18/1**	61
6-25	9	½	**Sir Boss (IRE)**[9] 5235 5-10-3 **70** (t) MissMMullineaux(3) 13 (M Mullineaux) *v.s.a: rcvrd into midfield by 1/2-way: chsd ldrs 3f out: wknd ins fnl f* **33/1**	65
4145	10	1	**Kyle Of Bute**[8] 5272 4-9-10 **60** MissLHorner 15 (B P J Baugh) *s.i.s: hld up: brief hdwy on outer over 3f out: sn no imp* **18/1**	53
-450	11	½	**Helieorbea**[10] 5215 4-9-8 **63** MissJoannaMason(5) 14 (T D Easterby) *trckd ldrs: wknd over 2f out* **11/1**	55
30-6	12	½	**Follow The Sun (IRE)**[17] 4946 6-9-6 **56** oh4 MissGAndrews 12 (Ronald O'Leary, Ire) *hld up: a towards rr* **20/1**	47
5313	13	5	**Strike Force**[8] 5254 6-9-3 **58** (t) MissALHutchinson(5) 7 (Miss Olivia Maylam) *midfield: rdn over 3f out: sn no imp* **7/1**[3]	39
2202	14	1	**Rowan Lodge (IRE)**[16] 4986 8-9-9 **66** (b) MissVCoates(7) 11 (Ollie Pears) *midfield: wknd 2f out* **16/1**	45
0211	15	5	**Island Chief**[19] 4897 4-10-11 **75** (p) MissJCoward 2 (M W Easterby) *prom: rdn over 3f out: sn wknd* **12/1**	44

2m 8.26s (1.16) **Going Correction** +0.05s/f (Good)
WFA 3 from 4yo+ 8lb **15** Ran SP% **125.4**
Speed ratings (Par 103): **97,96,95,93,93 92,92,91,91,90 90,89,85,85,81**
toteswingers:1&2:£76.60, 1&3:£39.60, 2&3:£45.90 CSF £258.81 CT £2439.56 TOTE £30.70: £7.90, £5.60, £2.50; EX 522.70.
Owner Mrs R E Barr **Bred** George Ward **Trained** Seamer, N Yorks

FOCUS
Racing began with a competitive lady amateurs' event in which few could be confidently discounted.
Tropical Duke(IRE) Official explanation: trainer said, regarding apparent improvement in form, that the gelding was suited by the drop back in trip.
Kyle Of Bute Official explanation: jockey said gelding never travelled
Strike Force Official explanation: jockey said saddle slipped

5531 MARKET CROSS JEWELLERS MEDIAN AUCTION MAIDEN STKS 6f
5:50 (5:51) (Class 5) 2-Y-O **£2,719** (£809; £404; £202) **Stalls** High

Form				RPR
	1		**Robert The Painter (IRE)** 2-9-0 0 NataliaGemelova(3) 6 (R A Fahey) *in tch: rdn and rn green over 2f out: hdwy over 1f out: led ins fnl f: r.o strly* **16/1**	79+
4	2	¾	**Chokidar (IRE)**[15] 5053 2-9-3 0 PJMcDonald 4 (J A Glover) *chsd ldrs: rdn over 2f out: drvn over 1f out: kpt on wl fnl f* **50/1**	77
320	3	nk	**Indieslad**[9] 5245 2-9-0 85 BarryMcHugh(3) 13 (Mrs A Duffield) *trckd ldrs: hdwy to ld 1f out: sn hung lft: hdd ins fnl 100yds* **2/1**[1]	76
2224	4	shd	**Boundaries**[10] 5196 2-9-3 75 DuranFentiman 7 (T D Easterby) *prom: led over 1f out: hdd 1f out: kpt on* **14/1**	76
00	5	5	**Wandering Lad**[14] 5092 2-9-3 0 DavidNolan 5 (D Carroll) *chsd ldrs: rdn over 2f out: wknd ins fnl f* **66/1**	61
	6	hd	**Stilettoesinthemud (IRE)** 2-8-12 0 PaulMulrennan 16 (J G Given) *midfield: rdn and rn green over 2f out: kpt on fnl f* **40/1**	57+
22	7	½	**Nine Before Ten (IRE)**[43] 4083 2-8-12 0 SilvestreDeSousa 14 (Mrs D J Sanderson) *led: hdd 2f out: wknd ins fnl f* **6/1**[3]	54

2 **8** 2 ¾ **Podgies Boy (IRE)**[13] 5117 2-9-3 0 .... AdrianNicholls 15 51
(R A Fahey) *chsd ldrs: rdn 3f out: wknd over 1f out* **6/1**[3]

0 **9** 1 ½ **Geronimo Chief (IRE)**[17] 4941 2-9-0 0 .... AndrewHeffernan(3) 3 46
(B M R Haslam) *chsd ldrs on outer tl wknd over 1f out* **50/1**

44 **10** 2 ¾ **Plenty Power**[19] 4902 2-9-3 0 .... JoeFanning 9 38
(M R Channon) *trckd ldrs: rdn over 2f out: sn wknd* **9/4**[2]

11 nk **Finefrenzyrolling (IRE)** 2-8-12 0 .... AndrewElliott 12 32
(Mrs K Burke) *a towards rr* **22/1**

12 ¾ **Kwik Lightening** 2-8-12 0 .... DeanHeslop(5) 1 35
(B M R Haslam) *slowly away: a outpcd in rr* **66/1**

005 **13** ½ **Running Water**[17] 4941 2-8-12 0 .... PatrickMathers 11 28
(H A McWilliams) *a towards rr* **100/1**

14 11 **Wolds Agent** 2-9-3 0 .... LNewman 10 —
(T D Easterby) *a outpcd in rr* **80/1**

1m 12.69s (0.89) **Going Correction** +0.05s/f (Good) **14** Ran SP% **121.1**
Speed ratings (Par 94): **96,95,94,94,87 87,86,83,81,77 77,76,75,60**
toteswingers:1&2:£29.90, 1&3:£10.90, 2&3:£23.50 CSF £650.28 TOTE £21.20: £6.10, £13.20, £1.10; EX 459.80.
Owner Stephen Humphreys **Bred** Ballylinch Stud **Trained** Musley Bank, N Yorks
■ Stewards' Enquiry : Natalia Gemelova caution: careless riding.

FOCUS
Just an ordinary maiden, but a clutch had solid form and it featured a few promisingly bred newcomers.

NOTEBOOK
Robert The Painter(IRE), a 25,000 euros newcomer from a yard in great form, sprang something of a surprise. Easy to back beforehand, he was not the quickest away, but made progress from halfway and knuckled down nicely in the closing stages. It would be unwise to get carried away with the level of form needed to take this contest, but he ought to improve and collect again. (op 12-1)
Chokidar(IRE), a well-beaten fourth on his only previous outing, stepped up considerably on that form. Always close to the pace, he battled on well in the closing stages without quite showing the winner's finishing kick. (op 66-1)
Indieslad had twice gone close over 5f before finding himself out of his depth in a valuable York sales race and this represented a drop in class. It was all the more disappointing, then, that, after getting into contention at the two-furlong pole, he hung under pressure and found little when it really mattered. He will need to do better to take an average maiden and has a little to prove now. (op 11-4 tchd 3-1)
Boundaries, the most experienced in the line-up and with an official mark of 75, looks a feasible, though perhaps not rock-solid, marker for the form. He led early on and stayed prominent throughout, plugging on gamely without really promising to collect. (op 8-1)
Wandering Lad, who had shown next to nothing on two previous starts, improved on those efforts and may find a minor nursery in due course. (op 80-1)
Stilettoesinthemud(IRE), a half-sister to a multiple winner, showed a hint of promise by staying on in the closing stages. (op 50-1)

5532 BUY YOUR TICKETS ON-LINE @ REDCARRACING.CO.UK NOVICE MEDIAN AUCTION STKS 7f
6:20 (6:20) (Class 5) 2-Y-O **£2,072** (£616; £308) **Stalls** High

Form RPR

0 **1** **Red Presence (IRE)**[79] 2887 2-8-13 0 .... RichardKingscote 1 88
(Tom Dascombe) *trckd ldr: rdn over 2f out: led over 1f out: hld on wl ins fnl f* **14/1**[3]

141 **2** hd **Alaskan Spirit (IRE)**[17] 4948 2-9-0 93 .... BarryMcHugh(3) 3 91
(Mrs A Duffield) *led: edgd lft and hdd narrowly over 1f out: kpt on but a jst hld ins fnl f* **4/7**[1]

531 **3** 18 **Marston Moor (USA)**[24] 4695 2-9-1 85 .... AhmedAjtebi 2 44+
(Mahmood Al Zarooni) *hld up in 3rd: rdn over 2f out: sn no imp: eased ins fnl f* **15/8**[2]

1m 28.29s (3.79) **Going Correction** +0.05s/f (Good) **3** Ran SP% **105.1**
Speed ratings (Par 94): **80,79,59**
CSF £22.67 TOTE £6.30; EX 26.90.
Owner The Folly Racers **Bred** Martyn J McEnery **Trained** Malpas, Cheshire

FOCUS
A disappointingly small turnout, but an intriguing finish and a shock result for many punters.

NOTEBOOK
Red Presence(IRE), ninth of 14 in an ordinary Newbury maiden on his debut, showed much improved form to score. Keen in the early stages, he was soon tucked in behind the runner-up, but still obviously green. He needed to be niggled along at halfway and wandered when put under stronger pressure, but he kept finding a bit more and ultimately had too much for the odds-on second. He should learn from this and, while the form may not be completely reliable, did enough to suggest he can win again at some stage. His trainer rates him "a proper horse". (op 15-2)
Alaskan Spirit(IRE) had taken a 6f nursery by six lengths from a mark of 81 on his latest start and, although his revised official rating of 93 almost certainly flatters him, he seemed to have an excellent chance here. He led from the start, apparently going nicely, but did not look happy in the closing stages and hung to his left under driving, allowing the winner to worry him out of another success. He may require a drop back in trip. (op 8-11)
Marston Moor(USA), successful over this trip on Kempton's Polytrack early in the month, ran poorly back on turf. Always last, he was left well behind when the first two got down to their final-furlong battle. He is not progressing and was reported to have run flat. Official explanation: jockey said colt ran flat (op 7-4 tchd 2-1)

5533 JOHN SMITH'S REDCAR STRAIGHT-MILE CHAMPIONSHIP QUALIFIER (H'CAP) 1m
6:50 (6:51) (Class 4) (0-80,77) 3-Y-O+ **£3,626** (£1,079; £539; £269) **Stalls** High

Form RPR

6212 **1** **Dream Win**[38] 4261 4-9-5 70 .... BarryMcHugh(3) 9 79
(B Ellison) *hld up: hdwy over 2f out: rdn to chse ldrs over 1f out: led wl ins fnl f* **5/1**[2]

0000 **2** hd **Daaweitza**[63] 3450 7-9-7 74 .... DaleSwift(5) 10 82
(B Ellison) *midfield: hdwy over 2f out: chal 1f out: kpt on ins fnl f* **12/1**

1200 **3** ½ **Harriet's Girl**[28] 4603 4-9-12 74 .... AndrewElliott 2 81
(Mrs K Burke) *trckd ldrs: hdwy to ld 3f out: rdn 2f out: hdd fnl 75yds* **5/1**[2]

0001 **4** ½ **Mujaadel (USA)**[1] 5500 5-9-9 76 6ex .... (p) BillyCray(5) 8 82
(D Nicholls) *hld up: rdn over 2f out: edgd rt and hdwy over 1f out: kpt on ins fnl f: nrst fin* **10/1**

4135 **5** 2 ½ **Squall**[7] 5304 3-9-9 77 .... PaulHanagan 6 77
(J Noseda) *trckd ldrs: rdn over 2f out: hrd drvn and hung lft over 1f out: wknd ins fnl f* **3/1**[1]

2636 **6** hd **Wiseman's Diamond (USA)**[26] 4644 5-9-5 67 .... JoeFanning 7 67
(P T Midgley) *hld up in midfield: rdn wl over 2f out: kpt on same pce* **18/1**

0004 **7** shd **Shaws Diamond (USA)**[12] 5157 4-9-4 66 .... (v) FrannyNorton 3 65
(D Shaw) *midfield: rdn over 3f out: dropped to rr over 2f out: kpt on again ins fnl f* **33/1**

4433 **8** ¾ **Observatory Star (IRE)**[34] 4403 7-9-11 73 .... (p) PaulMulrennan 5 71
(T D Easterby) *in tch: rdn over 2f out: sn no imp* **10/1**

4124 **9** 4 **Rosko**[15] 5043 6-9-13 75 .... (v[1]) DavidAllan 4 63
(B Ellison) *hld up in tch: rdn wl over 2f out: sn no imp* **10/1**

1025 **10** 9 **Vito Volterra (IRE)**[13] 5121 3-9-6 77 .... MichaelStainton(3) 11 45
(Michael Smith) *led: hdd 3f out: sn wknd* **8/1**[3]

4035 **11** nk **Lujano**[16] 4985 5-8-11 62 .... JamesSullivan(3) 1 29
(Ollie Pears) *prom: racd freely initially: rdn wl over 3f out: sn wknd* **20/1**

1m 38.56s (0.56) **Going Correction** +0.05s/f (Good)
WFA 3 from 4yo+ 6lb **11** Ran SP% **117.4**
Speed ratings (Par 105): **99,98,98,97,95 95,95,94,90,81 80**
toteswingers:1&2:£13.40, 1&3:£7.70, 2&3:£15.20 CSF £63.57 CT £323.87 TOTE £4.50: £1.30, £6.90, £2.10; EX 57.90.
Owner Koo's Racing Club **Bred** Juddmonte Farms Ltd **Trained** Norton, N Yorks

FOCUS
A fair handicap, with the top-weight rated 76, and it looked ultra-competitive on paper.

5534 HOLD YOUR CHRISTMAS PARTY @ REDCAR RACECOURSE H'CAP 1m 6f 19y
7:20 (7:20) (Class 6) (0-65,67) 3-Y-O **£1,619** (£481; £240; £120) **Stalls** Low

Form RPR

1425 **1** **Dubawi King**[15] 5058 3-8-10 54 .... (v[1]) PaulHanagan 8 61
(N Tinkler) *hld up: chsd along over 4f out: gd hdwy on outer fr 2f out despite persistently hanging lft: led jst ins fnl f: kpt on* **4/1**[2]

3303 **2** 2 **Il Portico**[23] 4745 3-8-10 54 .... SamHitchcott 4 58
(M R Channon) *prom: led over 2f out: hdd jst ins fnl f* **10/1**

0-66 **3** hd **Pobs Trophy**[16] 4863 3-8-2 46 oh1 .... (p) PaulEddery 1 50
(R C Guest) *midfield: rdn and outpcd over 2f out: last over 1f out: kpt on wl ins fnl f: nrst fin* **20/1**

5534 **4** ¾ **Danceintothelight**[3] 5423 3-8-13 57 .... TomEaves 3 60
(Micky Hammond) *hld up: smooth hdwy to trck ldrs 3f out: rdn over 2f out: hmpd 1f out: kpt on same pce fnl f* **11/2**[3]

2651 **5** ¾ **Escape Artist**[40] 4200 3-8-9 53 .... (t[1]) DavidAllan 5 56
(T D Easterby) *led: hdd over 2f out: stl 3rd whn short of room against rail over 1f out: eased ins fnl 100yds* **5/2**[1]

2265 **6** 1 ½ **Sheiling (IRE)**[14] 5093 3-9-1 62 .... BarryMcHugh(3) 7 62
(R A Fahey) *midfield: rdn to chal 3f out: stl ev ch over 1f out: wknd ins fnl f* **12/1**

3352 **7** 1 ¼ **Pena Dorada (IRE)**[12] 5164 3-9-4 67 .... (p) IanBrennan(5) 2 65
(Mrs K Burke) *trckd ldrs on inner: rdn over 3f out: hmpd over 1f out: eased fnl f* **5/2**[1]

3m 6.74s (2.04) **Going Correction** +0.05s/f (Good) **7** Ran SP% **114.1**
Speed ratings (Par 98): **96,94,94,94,93 93,92**
toteswingers:1&2:£6.80, 1&3:£8.30, 2&3:£7.00 CSF £41.65 CT £707.58 TOTE £4.20: £2.90, £6.80; EX 23.40.
Owner D Bloy & P Beecroft **Bred** Cliveden Stud Ltd **Trained** Langton, N Yorks

FOCUS
A modest contest, with the top-weight rated just 67.
Pena Dorada(IRE) Official explanation: jockey said gelding was denied a clear run

5535 FOLLOW REDCAR RACING ON FACEBOOK H'CAP 6f
7:50 (7:51) (Class 6) (0-55,55) 3-Y-O+ **£1,706** (£503; £252) **Stalls** High

Form RPR

3623 **1** **Forever's Girl**[22] 4799 4-9-3 52 .... PaulMulrennan 7 64
(G R Oldroyd) *prom: led wl over 1f out: kpt on wl: drvn out* **5/1**[1]

2043 **2** 1 **French Fantasy**[18] 4920 3-9-0 52 .... (t) JoeFanning 12 61
(H Morrison) *prom: rdn 2f out: kpt on* **8/1**

0602 **3** 1 ¾ **Sweet Mirasol (IRE)**[25] 4674 3-8-13 51 .... (t) SilvestreDeSousa 6 54
(Miss M E Rowland) *chsd ldrs: rdn over 2f out: kpt on ins fnl f* **12/1**

0020 **4** ½ **Dream Express (IRE)**[20] 4869 5-8-12 50 .... MichaelStainton(3) 8 52
(D W Thompson) *trckd ldrs: rdn over 2f out: kpt on ins fnl f* **20/1**

4240 **5** 1 **Bentley**[8] 5267 6-9-0 49 .... PaulHanagan 1 47
(B P J Baugh) *towards rr: rdn over 2f out: kpt on ins fnl f: nrst fin* **7/1**[3]

0254 **6** ½ **Elkhorn**[15] 5045 8-8-9 49 .... (b) DaleSwift(5) 13 46
(Julie Camacho) *s.i.s: sn rcvrd to chse ldrs: rdn over 2f out: kpt on same pce fnl f* **11/2**[2]

4040 **7** ¾ **Emma's Secrets**[15] 5055 5-8-10 45 .... FrannyNorton 20 39
(D Shaw) *hld up: rdn and hdwy over 1f out: kpt on ins fnl f* **20/1**

026 **8** 1 ½ **Misterisland (IRE)**[28] 4606 5-9-1 50 .... (b) SamHitchcott 14 40
(M Mullineaux) *chsd ldrs: rdn bef 1/2-way: kpt on one pce* **20/1**

0032 **9** shd **Carnival Dream**[20] 4868 5-9-4 53 .... (p) PatrickMathers 3 42
(H A McWilliams) *in tch: rdn over 2f out: no imp* **11/1**

6026 **10** 1 ¾ **Major Monty (IRE)**[17] 4970 3-8-12 55 .... (p) RossAtkinson(5) 5 39
(Tom Dascombe) *chsd ldrs: rdn along over 2f out: wknd over 1f out* **9/1**

2005 **11** ½ **Tanley**[15] 5045 5-9-2 54 .... GaryBartley(3) 2 36
(I W McInnes) *hld up: rdn over 2f out: nvr threatened* **25/1**

000 **12** nk **Isle Of Ellis (IRE)**[31] 4485 3-8-5 46 ow1 .... BarryMcHugh(3) 11 27
(R E Barr) *sn chsd along towards rr: nvr a factor* **40/1**

0600 **13** ¾ **Port Ronan (USA)**[34] 4415 4-8-12 47 .... DanielTudhope 19 26
(J S Wainwright) *in tch: hdwy to chse ldrs over 1f out: wknd ins fnl f* **25/1**

6540 **14** 4 ½ **Regal Emperor (IRE)**[15] 5024 3-8-13 51 .... AdrianNicholls 9 15
(D Nicholls) *led: rdn over 2f out: hdd wl over 1f out: sn wknd* **15/2**

0000 **15** nk **Maison Dieu**[70] 3200 7-8-13 48 .... DavidAllan 10 11
(Joss Saville) *a towards rr* **25/1**

00-0 **16** nk **Silver In The Sand**[155] 991 3-9-0 52 .... PJMcDonald 18 14
(J D Bethell) *hld up: a towards rr* **22/1**

6640 **17** 4 **Turf Time**[15] 5055 3-8-11 49 .... (p) DuranFentiman 16 —
(J A Glover) *chsd ldrs: wknd over 1f out: eased ins fnl f* **33/1**

1m 11.86s (0.06) **Going Correction** +0.05s/f (Good)
WFA 3 from 4yo+ 3lb **17** Ran SP% **129.0**
Speed ratings (Par 101): **101,99,97,96,95 94,93,91,91,89 88,88,87,81,80 80,75**
toteswingers:1&2:£10.80, 1&3:£10.30, 2&3:£24.00 CSF £39.66 CT £478.60 TOTE £6.80: £1.10, £3.30, £3.80, £7.80; EX 36.40 Place 6 £9,727.12; Place 5 £1,235.55.
Owner R C Bond **Bred** R C Bond **Trained** Brawby, N Yorks

FOCUS
A weak finale, with the top-weight rated only 54, but it looked very open.
Regal Emperor(IRE) Official explanation: jockey said gelding ran too free
T/Plt: £18.50 to a £1 stake. Pool:£58,170.27 - 2,289.54 winning tickets T/Qpdt: £13.70 to a £1 stake. Pool:£7,864.47 - 422.45 winning tickets AS

5372 WINDSOR (R-H)

Saturday, August 28

OFFICIAL GOING: Soft (6.6)

Stands rail dolled out 3yd and ½yd at winning post, top bend dolled out 6yds from innermost line adding 14yds to races of one mile and over.

Wind: medium, behind Weather: cloudy, brighter spells

5536 AJA INSURE MEMBERS FEGENTRI WORLD CHAMPIONSHIP H'CAP (FOR GENTLEMAN AMATEUR RIDERS) 1m 3f 135y

5:10 (5:10) (Class 5) (0-70,70) 3-Y-O+ **£2,307** (£709; £354) **Stalls** Low

Form				RPR
-600	**1**		**Sancho Panza**[23] 4763 3-9-11 **45** ... MrJacobSmith 2	54
			(Miss J Feilden) *stdd after s: hld up wl in tch in last: pushed along and hdwy towards stands' rail ent fnl 2f: led jst ins fnl f: sn clr and r.o strly: pushed out* **33/1**	
3364	**2**	2 ½	**Gordon Flash**[38] 4259 3-11-3 **65** ... MrFlorentGuy 9	70
			(R Hannon) *stdd after s: hld up wl in tch in last trio: hdwy to trck ldrs 4f out: styd against stands' rail and rdn to ld over 2f out: hdd jst ins fnl f: sn outpcd by wnr* **3/1**[1]	
0215	**3**	1 ½	**Choral Festival**[20] 4873 4-11-10 **62** ... MrMarioBaratti 8	64
			(J J Bridger) *stdd after s: hld up wl in tch towards rr: hdwy to trck ldrs and wnt to r towards centre over 2f out: sn rdn and chsd ldr ent fnl 2f: tl over 1f out: kpt on one pce after* **4/1**[3]	
43	**4**	1	**Rare Malt (IRE)**[23] 4752 3-11-8 **70** ...(v) HarryChalloner 3	71
			(Miss Amy Weaver) *dwlt: sn rcvrd and chsng ldrs: rdn and wnt to r in centre over 2f out: chsd ldng pair and edgd rt ent fnl 2f: drvn and one pce fr over 1f out* **7/2**[2]	
3-	**5**	8	**Oddshoes (IRE)**[219] 194 8-11-7 **59** ... MrPatrickDeno 7	46
			(P J Hobbs) *t.k.h: in tch: hdwy to chse ldrs 6f out: wnt to r in centre and hung rt u.p over 2f out: wknd wl over 1f out* **7/1**	
0545	**6**	nse	**Stoical (IRE)**[22] 4792 3-11-5 **67** ... MrKKjaer 6	54
			(W Jarvis) *taken down early: chsd ldrs: pushed along and lost pl 4f out: no ch fnl 2f* **10/1**	
0004	**7**	½	**Rio Prince**[17] 4958 3-9-13 **47** ... MrRBirkett 5	33
			(J J Bridger) *t.k.h: w ldr tl led 8f out: wnt to r towards centre and rdn over 2f out: sn hdd: wknd 2f out* **8/1**	
523-	**8**	8	**Tecktal (FR)**[394] 4449 7-10-13 **51** ... MrPPower 4	23
			(P M Phelan) *led tl 8f out: chsd ldr after: wnt to r towards centre over 2f out: sn rdn and struggling whn n.m.r ent fnl 2f: sn wknd* **8/1**	
44-0	**9**	18	**Feeling (IRE)**[180] 753 6-10-7 **45** ... MrTimoDegel 1	—
			(D Burchell) *t.k.h: chsd ldrs tl lost pl qckly over 4f out: wl bhd fnl 3f: t.o* **20/1**	

2m 38.44s (8.94) **Going Correction** +0.35s/f (Good)

WFA 3 from 4yo+ 10lb **9** Ran SP% **118.7**

Speed ratings (Par 103): **84,82,81,80,75 75,74,69,57**

toteswingers:1&2:£19.50, 1&3:£33.40, 2&3:£3.10 CSF £134.05 CT £506.20 TOTE £35.60: £7.00, £1.10, £1.90; EX 163.40 Trifecta £1379.30 Pool: £4,659.96 - 2.50 winning units..

Owner Carol Bushnell & Partners **Bred** Harts Farm Stud **Trained** Exning, Suffolk

■ A winner on his first ride in Britain for American Jacob Smith.

FOCUS

Rail movements added 14 yards to all races at 1m or more.\n\x\x A novelty event and it might not be wise to take the form too literally with the field being well bunched for the most part and then fanning across almost the whole width of the home straight. The first two stayed nearest the stand rail.

Sancho Panza Official explanation: trainer said, regarding apparent improvement in form, that the gelding appeared better suited by being ridden just hands and heels.

Gordon Flash Official explanation: vet said colt returned lame in front

5537 BET TOTEPOOL AT TOTESPORT.COM NOVICE MEDIAN AUCTION STKS 6f

5:40 (5:40) (Class 5) 2-Y-O **£2,456** (£725; £362) **Stalls** High

Form				RPR
21	**1**		**Morache Music**[8] 5255 2-9-2 88 ... SebSanders 11	90+
			(P J Makin) *hld up wl in tch: hdwy to press ldrs gng wl ent fnl 2f: led and hung lft over 1f out: edgd rt u.p ins fnl f: qcknd clr fnl 100yds: r.o wl* **8/13**[1]	
1	**2**	1 ½	**Jerrazzi (IRE)**[17] 4960 2-9-5 0 ... GeorgeBaker 10	88
			(G L Moore) *led: rdn 2f out: hdd over 1f out: kpt on wl u.p tl nt pce of wnr and btn fnl 100yds* **9/1**	
3313	**3**	1 ¼	**Local Singer (IRE)**[36] 4332 2-9-2 81 ... TedDurcan 9	81
			(M R Channon) *t.k.h: hld up wl in tch: effrt to join ldrs 2f out: sn rdn: no ex and one pce u.p fnl f* **7/1**[2]	
1	**4**	1	**Sextons House (IRE)**[65] 3349 2-8-13 0 ... PatrickHills(3) 6	78
			(R Hannon) *wnt lft s and s.i.s: t.k.h: hld up in tch in rr: rdn and effrt wl over 1f out: kpt on u.p fnl f: nvr gng pce to rch ldrs* **8/1**[3]	
01	**5**	1 ¾	**Speedfit Girl (IRE)**[20] 4871 2-8-11 70 ... PhilipRobinson 2	68
			(G G Margarson) *w ldr: rdn over 2f out: wknd u.p 1f out* **14/1**	
0	**6**	3 ½	**Morermaloke**[19] 4902 2-8-11 0 ... Louis-PhilippeBeuzelin(3) 4	60
			(B J Meehan) *ponied to s and taken down early: stdd s: hld up in tch towards rr: effrt and rdn ent fnl 2f: btn over 1f out: wknd fnl f* **10/1**	
0	**7**	6	**Touch Of Red (USA)**[22] 4803 2-9-0 0 ... JimmyFortune 8	42
			(R Hannon) *chsd ldrs tl struggling ent fnl 2f: towards rr whn stmbld over 1f out: bhd and eased ins fnl f* **20/1**	
0	**8**	hd	**One Cool Chick**[12] 5147 2-8-9 0 ... NeilChalmers 1	36
			(J J Bridger) *wnt lft s: t.k.h: hld up in tch in rr: hung lft and rdn over 2f out: wknd 2f out: bhd fnl f* **66/1**	

1m 14.5s (1.50) **Going Correction** +0.10s/f (Good) **8** Ran SP% **117.5**

Speed ratings (Par 94): **94,92,90,89,86 82,74,73**

toteswingers:1&2:£2.80, 1&3:£2.10, 2&3:£3.70 CSF £7.59 TOTE £1.70: £1.10, £2.00, £1.40; EX 7.60 Trifecta £18.60 Pool: £7,805.14 - 308.89 winning units..

Owner R P Marchant D M Ahier Mrs E Lee **Bred** Michael E Broughton **Trained** Ogbourne Maisey, Wilts

FOCUS

A fair novice event. The pace was just fair for the most part as the field made their way steadily across to the far rail and the result is probably a bit muddling.

NOTEBOOK

Morache Music was well backed to make it 2-3 and though not overly impressive, might have found this race coming plenty soon enough after his romp in similar conditions last week. Pretty much the last off the bridle, he took some time to assert and still looked a bit inexperienced as he carried his head awkwardly, but he was comfortably on top late on and the result probably underestimates his real superiority. He'll stay 7f, and remains a useful prospect. (op 8-11tchd 4-5 in a place)

Jerrazzi(IRE) built on his promising Sandown debut and looked very much at home over the extra furlong. He was probably a bit flattered to get as close as he did to the winner, but in conceding 3lb readily to the third readily he has shown enough to suggest he can win something similar kept to this trip. (op 13-2 tchd 10-1)

Local Singer(IRE) handled the ground well enough but for all he has been progressing, his improvement has been only gradual and he looks vulnerable to faster improvers now he is out of maidens. (op 13-2)

Sextons House(IRE) was a bit keen early on his first run since winning at 7f at Goodwood in June but considering his stamina was proven it was surprising to see him a lot to so as the race was run, only really getting into his stride late. He's better than this and might be one for nurseries back at 7f or perhaps even 1m. (op 7-1)

Speedfit Girl(IRE) had won her maiden here under faster conditions but has an action that suggests the softer ground tonight wouldn't inconvenience her and she was beaten more because she wasn't good enough than anything else. (op 16-1)

Morermaloke, from a yard whose youngsters often improve a good deal second time out, was ponied to post and attracted some money at long odds but was left behind once the race began in earnest. He seemed to labour on the ground. (op 20-1)

Touch Of Red(USA) Official explanation: trainer's rep said colt was unsuited by the soft ground

5538 TOTEPOOL AUGUST STKS (LISTED RACE) 1m 3f 135y

6:10 (6:10) (Class 1) 3-Y-O+

£19,869 (£7,532; £3,769; £1,879; £941; £472) **Stalls** Low

Form				RPR
1420	**1**		**Whispering Gallery**[29] 4535 4-9-2 107 ... TedDurcan 5	113
			(Saeed Bin Suroor) *mde all: stdd gallop 5f out: rdn and qckná ent fnl 2f: r.o wl fnl f* **14/1**	
0331	**2**	1 ¼	**Traffic Guard (USA)**[14] 5090 6-9-2 110 ... JamieSpencer 4	111+
			(P F I Cole) *s.i.s: hld up in last: hdwy 4f out: swtchd rt and effrt whn hmpd ent fnl 2f: hdwy u.p jst over 1f out: hrd drvn and r.o to chse wnr fnl 75yds: no imp after* **6/5**[1]	
4015	**3**	2	**Pompeyano (IRE)**[14] 5080 5-9-2 109 ... FrankieDettori 8	107
			(Saeed Bin Suroor) *hld up in last pair: hdwy to chse ldrs over 3f out: rdn and effrt on far rail over 2f out: chsd wnr over 1f out tl fnl 75yds: wknd towards fin* **5/1**[3]	
0625	**4**	½	**Bikini Babe (IRE)**[16] 5138 3-8-1 105 ... LukeMorris 3	102
			(M Johnston) *in tch in midfield: effrt to chse ldrs over 3f out: rdn and edgd rt ent fnl 2f: hrd drvn and kpt on same pce fnl f* **16/1**	
2106	**5**	½	**Bullet Train**[71] 3142 3-8-13 108 ... TomQueally 1	113
			(H R A Cecil) *chsd wnr: ev ch and rdn over 2f out: hrd drvn over 1f out: wknd ins fnl f* **4/1**[2]	
5356	**6**	3 ½	**Kingdom Of Fife**[29] 4535 5-9-2 112 ...(v) JimmyFortune 6	100
			(Sir Michael Stoute) *chsd ldng pair: rdn and unable qck whn pushed rt ent fnl 2f: sn no prog and btn ent fnl f* **8/1**	
0-05	**7**	64	**Soul City (IRE)**[126] 1532 4-9-2 109 ... KierenFallon 7	—
			(R Hannon) *t.k.h: hld up wl in tch: dropped towards rr 5f out: pushed along and btn 4f out: wl t.o and virtually p.u fnl 2f* **10/1**	

2m 31.84s (2.34) **Going Correction** +0.35s/f (Good)

WFA 3 from 4yo+ 10lb **7** Ran SP% **114.9**

Speed ratings (Par 111): **106,105,103,103,103 100,58**

toteswingers:1&2:£4.50, 1&3:£6.00, 2&3:£1.60 CSF £31.82 TOTE £17.70: £5.20, £2.10; EX 48.20 Trifecta £558.10 Pool: £6,638.01 - 8.80 winning units..

Owner Godolphin **Bred** Darley **Trained** Newmarket, Suffolk

FOCUS

A decent Listed event but one in which the pace was rather uneven and the best place to be, as it often is under these conditions here, was in front. The field again made their way to the far rail.

NOTEBOOK

Whispering Gallery has had something of a chequered career since joining Godolphin and looked the second string here on jockey bookings, but he's a tough nut to crack on his day, not least when allowed an easy time of things in front as he was here, and as a guaranteed stayer was always going to see the trip out strongly. He clearly has no issues with soft ground and that ought to widen his options going into the autumn as he has looked more than good enough on occasions before to win a Group 3. (tchd 16-1)

Traffic Guard(USA) was bidding to follow up his win in this race in 2009. Bringing up the rear turning in, he was impeded when Kingdom Of Fife jinked out to his right halfway up the straight but it was more that he was set too much to do given the pace at which the race was run than that particular incident that cost him victory. He nearly followed up in another Listed race at Chester last year, and that might well be an option again if the ground stays on the easy side. (op 6-4 tchd 7-4 and 13-8 in a place)

Pompeyano(IRE) handles this ground and might perhaps have expected more help from his front-running stable-companion considering his proven stamina, and his performance seemed to confirm that he found the trip too sharp. His current merit isn't easy to establish exactly, and he might not be easy to place even in Listed company. (op 6-1)

Bikini Babe(IRE) is being kept busy and recorded a creditable third effort in a row. (op 14-1)

Bullet Train looked to have a bit to prove after a slightly disappointing effort at Royal Ascot. He had looked as if a forcing ride on this sort of ground might suit him, so it was a bit of a letdown to see him drop away late on. It might be that he's not such a strong stayer as initially thought and that he needs a drop down to 1m2f to get his career back on track. (op 7-2)

Kingdom Of Fife has shown his best form on faster ground but even so showed his darker side here, jinking out to his right when seemingly intimidated by Bikini Babe halfway up the straight but then throwing in the towel quickly after that. He's not won since May 2009. (op 7-1)

Soul City(IRE) Official explanation: jockey said colt finished lame but appeared sound when examined by vet

5539 TOTESPORT.COM WINTER HILL STKS (GROUP 3) 1m 2f 7y

6:40 (6:41) (Class 1) 3-Y-O+ **£36,900** (£13,988; £7,000; £3,490; £1,748) **Stalls** Low

Form				RPR
123	**1**		**Distant Memories (IRE)**[21] 4829 4-9-0 108 ... JamieSpencer 2	116
			(T P Tate) *mde all: rdn over 2f out: drvn over 1f out: hrd drvn and edgd rt u.p fnl f: kpt on gamely: all out* **6/1**	
3051	**2**	½	**Hot Prospect**[21] 4830 3-8-6 110 ... PhilipRobinson 4	115
			(M A Jarvis) *hld up in tch in last: pushed along over 2f out: rdn to chse ldng pair wl over 1f out: carried rt and chsd wnr wl ins fnl f: no ex towards fin* **5/4**[1]	
3255	**3**	½	**Flying Cloud (IRE)**[9] 5248 4-8-11 112 ...(t) FrankieDettori 1	111
			(Saeed Bin Suroor) *hld up in tch in last pair: hdwy to chse ldr 3f out: rdn 2f out: hrd drvn over 1f out: unable qck whn short of room and swtchd lft wl ins fnl f: kpt on one pce towards fin* **10/3**[3]	
0012	**4**	2	**Class Is Class (IRE)**[21] 4829 4-9-0 111 ...(v) KierenFallon 5	110
			(Sir Michael Stoute) *chsd ldng pair tl pushed along over 3f out: rdn and effrt over 2f out: styd on same pce fnl f* **5/2**[2]	
25-3	**5**	4	**Nideeb**[14] 5090 3-8-6 104 ... ChrisCatlin 3	102
			(C E Brittain) *dwlt: sn pushed up to chse wnr: pushed along and lost 2nd 3f out: drvn over 2f out: wknd u.p jst over 1f out* **25/1**	

2m 8.75s (0.05) **Going Correction** +0.35s/f (Good)

WFA 3 from 4yo 8lb **5** Ran SP% **114.2**

Speed ratings (Par 113): **113,112,112,110,107**

CSF £14.69 TOTE £8.60: £2.60, £1.40; EX 21.80.

Owner Mrs Fitri Hay **Bred** Kildaragh Stud **Trained** Tadcaster, N Yorks
■ Stewards' Enquiry : Jamie Spencer two-day ban: careless riding (Sep 12-13); one-day ban: used whip with excessive frequency (Sep 14)

FOCUS
A small field and no more than an ordinary race for the grade. Like the previous race, it was something of a tactical affair and had a similar outcome in that winner made all and the runner-up was set a lot to do. The field came centre to stands side.

NOTEBOOK
Distant Memories(IRE) had finished behind Class Is Class on his most recent outing when slightly disappointing upped to this level in the Rose Of Lancaster at Haydock, but he put that run behind him and resumed the progression he was showing before then with a gutsy success that owed plenty to a fine tactical ride that saw his rider judge the fractions just right. He's going to need to improve to make a further jump up the ladder, but he handles these conditions well and his stomach for a scrap will always stand him in good stead. The Prix Dollar on Arc day is a possible target. (op 7-1 tchd 11-2)
Hot Prospect had looked just that when an impressive winner of a good handicap at Haydock last time under conditions similar to these but he'd given handicappers less start then than he gave better rivals here and in hindsight his rider might wish that he'd have been wiser sooner to the likely ramifications of being so far off the pace on a track that favours front runners. His mount ended up having quite a hard race in the process, so the Select Stakes at Goodwood in a fortnight will almost certainly come too soon. The Listed Doonside Cup at the Ayr Western meeting looks a better option. (op 6-4 tchd 7-4 and 13-8 in places)
Flying Cloud(IRE) had been a bit disappointing on her last two starts but ran a better race here while leaving the impression that she'd have fared better had her stamina been tested even more. She really needs a step back up to 1m4f. (op 4-1)
Class Is Class(IRE) wasn't discredited in view of his last two efforts but didn't have any obvious excuses here and perhaps the effects of the visor which has sparked his recent improvement has worn off. (op 9-4)
Nideeb was able to hang in there for longer than on his recent return but that much was probably to do with the pace at which the race was run as anything else and he looks to need his sights lowering. (op 20-1)

5540 TOTESPORT.COM HOME OF POOL BETTING H'CAP — 1m 67y
7:10 (7:16) (Class 4) (0-85,83) 3-Y-0+ — £4,403 (£1,310; £654; £327) Stalls High

Form				RPR
310	1		**Autumn Riches**[21] 4828 3-9-5 **81** ... KierenFallon 4 (M Johnston) *chsd ldrs: pushed along 4f out: rdn and hdwy to chse clr ldr 2f out: kpt on u.p and str chal wl ins fnl f: led last strides* **3/1**[1]	93
1142	2	*hd*	**Play It Sam**[62] 3483 4-9-13 **83** ... AdamKirby 11 (W R Swinburn) *sn led: rdn and qcknd 3f out: clr and drvn 1f out: hrd pressed wl ins fnl f: hdd last strides* **3/1**[1]	95
15-0	3	*4*	**Pittodrie Star (IRE)**[15] 5031 3-8-10 **72** ... LiamKeniry 7 (A M Balding) *in tch in midfield: rdn and unable qck 3f out: kpt on u.p fr over 1f out: wnt 3rd wl ins fnl f: no imp after* **22/1**	74
0563	4	*nse*	**Mingun Bell (USA)**[14] 5083 3-9-1 **77** ... (b) TomQueally 3 (H R A Cecil) *dwlt: sn rcvrd to chse ldr: rdn and outpcd by ldr wl over 2f out: no imp on ldng pair fr over 1f out: lost 3rd nr fin* **15/2**	79
3431	5	½	**Lastkingofscotland (IRE)**[24] 4690 4-9-7 **77** ... (v) HayleyTurner 1 (C R Dore) *in tch in midfield: rdn and unable qck wl over 2f out: kpt on same pce fnl f* **14/1**	79
4061	6	1 ½	**Kavachi (IRE)**[16] 5003 7-9-12 **82** ... GeorgeBaker 9 (G L Moore) *chsd ldrs: rdn and outpcd 3f out: one pce u.p and no threat to ldrs after* **7/1**[3]	80
4122	7	½	**Calypso Star (IRE)**[8] 5254 3-8-13 **75** ... (b) JimmyFortune 6 (R Hannon) *stdd after s: hld up in last pair: pushed along and effrt 2f out: no real prog and nvr trbld ldrs* **4/1**[2]	71
6003	8	1 ¾	**Swift Chap**[39] 4224 4-9-7 **77** ... AlanMunro 8 (B R Millman) *in tch in midfield: rdn and unable qck 3f out: one pce and n.d fnl 2f* **16/1**	70
1405	9	3 ¾	**Compton Blue**[36] 4322 4-9-5 **75** ... (b) RichardHughes 5 (R Hannon) *hld up in last trio: effrt u.p but stl plenty to do whn nt clr run ent fnl f: sn swtchd rt and no where to go fnl f: no ch* **12/1**	73+
3500	10	*18*	**Tell Halaf**[15] 5048 3-8-8 **70** ... TedDurcan 2 (M G Quinlan) *stdd s: t.k.h: hld up in rr: lost tch 3f out: eased ins fnl f* **40/1**	12

1m 47.12s (2.42) **Going Correction** +0.35s/f (Good)
WFA 3 from 4yo+ 6lb — 10 Ran SP% **121.3**
Speed ratings (Par 105): **101,100,96,96,96 94,94,92,88,70**
toteswingers:1&2:£3.20, 1&3:£18.40, 2&3:£15.00 CSF £12.30 CT £175.47 TOTE £4.50: £1.50, £1.70, £5.80; EX 15.00 Trifecta £212.20 Pool: £2,810.22 - 9.80 winning units..
Owner Sheikh Hamdan Bin Mohammed Al Maktoum **Bred** Darley **Trained** Middleham Moor, N Yorks

FOCUS
An open handicap and one in which it proved very hard to come from off the pace.

5541 SOUNDS OF MOTOWN SUMMER CELEBRATION FILLIES' H'CAP — 1m 67y
7:40 (7:41) (Class 5) (0-75,77) 3-Y-0+ — £2,593 (£765; £383) Stalls High

Form				RPR
4023	1		**Ken's Girl**[12] 5149 6-9-5 **66** ... IanMongan 14 (W S Kittow) *taken down early: mde all: rdn and clr w rival ent fnl 2f: styd on wl ins fnl f* **7/2**[1]	76
5126	2	*2*	**Miss Bootylishes**[109] 1997 5-9-8 **74** ... AmyBaker(5) 8 (A B Haynes) *chsd wnr: rdn and clr w wnr ent fnl 2f out: no ex and btn ins fnl f* **16/1**	79
5031	3	*1*	**Oh So Saucy**[15] 5050 6-9-12 **73** ... AlanMunro 7 (C F Wall) *in tch in midfield: rdn and outpcd 3f out: rallied u.p over 1f out: wnt 3rd ins fnl f: kpt on but nt pce to rch ldrs* **9/2**[2]	76
/450	4	1 ¾	**Al Aqabah (IRE)**[42] 4134 5-8-13 **60** ... JackMitchell 10 (B Gubby) *hld up in rr: stl last over 2f out: rdn and hdwy wl over 1f out: kpt on wl u.p fnl f: wnt 4th nr fin* **20/1**	59+
0422	5	*nk*	**My Sister**[16] 4988 3-8-10 **63** ... TomQueally 2 (M D I Usher) *in tocuh: rdn and outpcd by ldrs over 2f out: chsd clr ldng pair u.p over 1f out: kpt on same pce and lost 2 pls ins fnl f* **5/1**[3]	61
-264	6	¾	**Zenarinda**[23] 4762 3-8-13 **66** ... PatCosgrave 5 (M H Tompkins) *plld hrd: hld up towards rr: rdn and unable qck wl over 2f out: drvn and kpt on fr over 1f out: nvr trbld ldrs* **10/1**	62
2005	7	¾	**Silent Oasis**[15] 5038 4-9-7 **68** ... SebSanders 12 (B G Powell) *chsd ldrs: rdn and unable qck over 2f out: hanging lft and styd on same pce fr over 1f out* **20/1**	63
2034	8	1 ¾	**Spiritual Art**[9] 5237 4-9-6 **67** ... RichardHughes 3 (L A Dace) *hld up in rr: pushed and stl plenty to do whn n.m.r jst over 2f out: no real prog fnl 2f: n.d* **7/1**	58
0514	9	3 ½	**Ajool (USA)**[35] 4381 3-9-4 **71** ... LiamKeniry 1 (P W D'Arcy) *hld up wl in tch: rdn and unable qck wl over 2f out: wl btn over 1f out* **20/1**	53

Form				RPR
-621	10	1 ½	**Falling Angel**[12] 5145 3-9-10 **77** ... JamieSpencer 11 (P F I Cole) *chsd ldrs: rdn and outpcd by ldng pair over 2f out: lost 3rd over 1f out and sn wknd: eased wl ins fnl f* **5/1**[3]	56
6605	11	1 ¾	**Iptkaar (USA)**[4] 5391 3-9-0 **67** ... (b) ChrisCatlin 9 (C E Brittain) *in tch tl lost pl and rdn 4f out: wl btn fnl 2f* **25/1**	42
15-0	12	*13*	**Kai Mook**[65] 3361 3-9-6 **73** ... CathyGannon 13 (Miss Olivia Maylam) *towards rr: rdn and struggling over 3f out: lost tch 2f out: eased ins fnl f* **40/1**	18

1m 47.61s (2.91) **Going Correction** +0.35s/f (Good)
WFA 3 from 4yo+ 6lb — 12 Ran SP% **121.8**
Speed ratings (Par 100): **99,97,96,94,93 93,92,90,87,85 83,70**
toteswingers:1&2:£13.60, 1&3:£3.60, 2&3:£9.20 CSF £58.41 CT £267.47 TOTE £4.70: £1.10, £5.80, £2.40; EX 102.60 Trifecta £276.10 Part won Pool: £373.13 - 0.40 winning units. Place 6 £12.37; Place 5 £6.22.
Owner Midd Shire Racing **Bred** D R Tucker **Trained** Blackborough, Devon

FOCUS
Seemingly a competitive affair on paper but a steady gallop once again played into the hands of the leaders and little got into the race from off the pace. The runners went far side.
T/Plt: £18.50 to a £1 stake. Pool:£58,170.27 - 2,289.54 winning tickets T/Qpdt: £13.70 to a £1 stake. Pool:£7,864.47 - 422.45 winning tickets SP

BADEN-BADEN (L-H)
Saturday, August 28

OFFICIAL GOING: Turf: soft

5542a PREIS DER SPARKASSEN-FINANZGRUPPE (GROUP 3) (4YO+) (TURF) — 1m 2f
4:15 (12:00) 4-Y-0+
£28,318 (£9,734; £4,867; £2,654; £1,769; £1,327)

			RPR
1		**Budai (GER)**[14] 5107 4-9-0 0 ... APietsch 8 (W Hickst, Germany) *broke wl: settled in 3rd: qcknd wl early in st: tk ld 2f out: r.o wl: ct ins fnl f: fought bk strly to regain ld ins fnl 50yds to win comf* **14/5**[1]	110
2	¾	**Scolari**[34] 4418 5-8-11 0 ... THellier 3 (T Mundry, Germany) *racd in midfield: dropped bk arnd fnl turn: fnd clr passage early in st: qcknd wl to ld ins fnl f: r.o wl: hdd and no ex fnl 50yds* **13/2**	105
3	*hd*	**Liang Kay (GER)**[34] 4418 5-9-2 0 ... YannLerner 4 (Uwe Ostmann, Germany) *settled towards rr: mde early move in st: threatened briefly 1/2-way down st: no ex cl home* **22/5**[3]	110
4	*1*	**Miss Europa (IRE)**[83] 2806 4-8-10 0 ... AStarke 1 (P Schiergen, Germany) *broke wl to r in midfield: hit traffic problems arnd fnl turn: picked up wl: styd on* **19/5**[2]	102
5	*1*	**Derwisch (IRE)**[55] 4-8-11 0 ... JBojko 9 (A Wohler, Germany) *one of the bkmarkers fr s: racd wd ent st: styd on wl* **35/1**	101
6	*nk*	**Illo (GER)**[27] 4-9-0 0 ... ADeVries 5 (J Hirschberger, Germany) *broke fast: settled in 4th: threatened early in st: no ex* **69/10**	103
7	1 ¼	**Falun (GER)**[27] 4-9-0 0 ... RoystonFfrench 6 (A Trybuhl, Germany) *racd in midfield: styd on in st: no threat* **17/1**	101
8	*4*	**Lamino (GER)**[77] 4-8-11 0 ... MickaelBarzalona 2 (P Vovcenko, Germany) *one of the bkmarkers: passed btn horses in st* **37/1**	90
9	*8*	**Ruten (USA)**[328] 6521 5-8-11 0 ... JiriPalik 11 (T Kluczynski, Poland) *broke wl to ld briefly: then settled in 3rd: r.o wl early in st: chal for ld briefly: sn wknd* **34/1**	74
10	¾	**Querari (GER)**[34] 4418 4-9-6 0 ... EPedroza 7 (A Wohler, Germany) *settled in midfield: nvr figured* **48/10**	81
11	1 ¾	**Schutzenjunker (GER)**[27] 5-9-2 0 ... DPorcu 10 (Uwe Ostmann, Germany) *racd in 5th: sn wknd in st* **30/1**	74
12	1 ¼	**Oriental Lion**[419] 3670 4-8-11 0 ... (b[1]) AHelfenbein 12 (Uwe Ostmann, Germany) *broke fast: plld hrd: led after a f: stl in front ent st: hdd 2f out: wknd qckly* **228/10**	66

2m 7.05s (2.06) — 12 Ran SP% **130.2**
WIN (incl. 10 euro stake): 38. PLACES: 17, 21, 18. SF: 277.
Owner PT Stable **Bred** Gestut Schlenderhan **Trained** Germany

5543 - (Foreign Racing) - See Raceform Interactive

4855
SARATOGA (R-H)
Saturday, August 28

OFFICIAL GOING: Dirt: fast

5544a SHADWELL TRAVERS STKS (GRADE 1) (3YO) (DIRT) — 1m 2f (D)
10:46 (10:50) 3-Y-0
£370,370 (£123,456; £61,728; £30,864; £18,518; £2,058)

			RPR
1		**Afleet Express (USA)**[28] 4613 3-9-0 0 ... JJCastellano 7 (James Jerkens, U.S.A) **7/1**	124
2	*nse*	**Fly Down (USA)**[28] 4613 3-9-0 0 ... JLezcano 8 (Nicholas Zito, U.S.A) **61/10**[3]	124+
3	6 ¾	**First Dude (USA)**[27] 4643 3-9-0 0 ... (b[1]) RADominguez 4 (Dale Romans, U.S.A) **67/10**	112
4	1 ½	**Afleet Again (USA)**[27] 4643 3-9-0 0 ... (b) CVelasquez 10 (Robert E Reid Jr, U.S.A) **47/1**	109
5	½	**A Little Warm (USA)**[28] 4613 3-9-0 0 ... JRVelazquez 5 (Anthony Dutrow, U.S.A) **48/10**[2]	108
6	1 ½	**Friend Or Foe (USA)**[28] 4613 3-9-0 0 ... RMaragh 9 (John C Kimmel, U.S.A) **236/10**	105
7	*nse*	**Miner's Reserve (USA)**[28] 4613 3-9-0 0 ... DCohen 1 (Nicholas Zito, U.S.A) **245/10**	105
8	¾	**Ice Box (USA)**[27] 4643 3-9-0 0 ... JRLeparoux 6 (Nicholas Zito, U.S.A) **76/10**	104
9	*12*	**Trappe Shot (USA)**[27] 4643 3-9-0 0 ... AGarcia 2 (Kiaran McLaughlin, U.S.A) **39/10**[1]	82
10	1 ¼	**Super Saver (USA)**[27] 4643 3-9-0 0 ... CHBorel 11 (Todd Pletcher, U.S.A) **69/10**	80

The Form Book, Raceform Ltd, Compton, RG20 6NL

11 7 1/4 **Admiral Alex (USA)**[28] 3-9-0 0 KDesormeaux 3 67
(L Blusiewicz, U.S.A) **113/10**

2m 3.28s (123.28) **11** Ran SP% **119.7**
PARI-MUTUEL (all including $2 stakes): WIN 16.00; PLACE (1-2) 7.80, 6.90; SHOW (1-2-3) 4.90, 5.20, 4.60; SF 114.50.
Owner Gainesway Farm & Martin L Cherry **Bred** Mcmillin Brothers & James Devaney **Trained** USA

NOTEBOOK
Afleet Express(USA) improved on his third in the Jim Dandy, with the step up in trip helping. He's progressing into a high-class colt, and though connections have yet to nominate his next target, perhaps the Jockey Club Gold Cup will be on his agenda, ahead of the Breeders' Cup Classic.
Fly Down(USA) stepped up on his Jim Dandy effort, returning to the sort of form that saw him take the Dwyer Stakes and finish runner-up in the Belmont Stakes. It's arguable that he was unlucky, having had to go wider than the winner into the straight, but then again he couldn't match that one's tactical speed.
First Dude(USA) ran well without improving for first-time blinkers. This big horse can be a real force next year.
Afleet Again(USA) ran on for fourth without threatening. A long-striding colt, he shapes as though well worth a shot over further on turf.
Super Saver(USA), the Kentucky Derby winner, hadn't performed too badly in the Haskell but ran abysmally this time. No excuse was forthcoming.

5509 BEVERLEY (R-H)
Sunday, August 29

OFFICIAL GOING: Good to firm (8.8)
Wind: strong and very blustery 1/2 against Weather: mainly fine but very breezy

5545 JOHN JENKINS MEMORIAL CLAIMING STKS 7f 100y
2:20 (2:21) (Class 5) 3-Y-0+ **£2,428** (£722; £361; £180) **Stalls** High

Form RPR
3111 **1** **Sunnyside Tom (IRE)**[18] 4949 6-9-10 84 PaulHanagan 6 92
(R A Fahey) *chsd ldrs: edgd lft and led over 1f out: drvn clr* **5/4**[1]
1113 **2** 6 **Fremen (USA)**[76] 3021 10-9-7 85 MichaelGeran(3) 3 77+
(D Nicholls) *dwlt: hdwy over 4f out: kpt on to take modest 2nd ins fnl f* **7/1**[3]
1350 **3** 1 **Stonehaugh (IRE)**[6] 5357 7-8-9 68 (t) IanBrennan(5) 14 65
(J Howard Johnson) *led tl 5f out: upsides over 1f out: kpt on same pce* **16/1**
1104 **4** 4 **Carlitos Spirit (IRE)**[18] 4939 6-8-12 72 (v) LeeTopliss(5) 15 58
(I W McInnes) *chsd ldr: led 5f out: hdd over 1f out: sn wknd* **8/1**
0000 **5** 1 **Nevada Desert (IRE)**[3] 5436 10-8-11 72 MichaelStainton(3) 12 52
(R M Whitaker) *dwlt: in rr: effrt on outer over 2f out: kpt on: nvr nr ldrs* **14/1**
1152 **6** 3 **Fujin Dancer (FR)**[6] 5360 5-9-2 72 (p) AmyRyan(3) 1 50
(K A Ryan) *hld up in rr: hdwy and swtchd outside 2f out: nvr on terms* **4/1**[2]
4-00 **7** 4 1/2 **Ubenkor (IRE)**[30] 4555 5-8-10 64 MichaelO'Connell(5) 11 34
(M Herrington) *in tch: effrt 3f out: wknd over 1f out* **40/1**
6500 **8** nk **Karate Queen**[16] 5024 5-8-6 40 BarryMcHugh(3) 10 28
(R E Barr) *in rr-div: sme hdwy 2f out: nvr a factor* **66/1**
2004 **9** 1 1/2 **Dragon Slayer (IRE)**[22] 4852 8-9-0 69 GaryBartley(3) 4 32
(John A Harris) *s.s: nvr on terms* **16/1**
60 **10** 1/2 **Grand Honour (IRE)**[78] 2967 4-9-5 49 PatCosgrave 7 33
(P Howling) *in rr: sme hdwy 2f out: nvr on terms* **80/1**
0000 **11** 3/4 **Royal Holiday (IRE)**[7] 5337 3-8-9 52 SilvestreDeSousa 5 24
(B Ellison) *hld up: a in rr* **66/1**
3004 **12** nse **Fol Liam**[54] 3765 4-8-13 60 (p) JamesDoyle 13 25
(A J McCabe) *prom: lost pl 2f out* **25/1**
35/0 **13** 2 **Gee Ceffyl Bach**[86] 2726 6-8-3 49 BillyCray(5) 8 15
(G Woodward) *in rr: sme hdwy over 2f out: sn wknd* **100/1**
0000 **14** 1/2 **Union Jack Jackson (IRE)**[18] 4939 8-8-12 45 (b) PJMcDonald 2 17
(John A Harris) *chsd ldrs: lost pl over 2f out* **40/1**

1m 31.11s (-2.69) **Going Correction** -0.375s/f (Firm)
WFA 3 from 4yo+ 5lb **14** Ran SP% **120.4**
Speed ratings (Par 103): **100,93,92,87,86 82,77,77,75,75 74,74,71,71**
Tote Swingers: 1&2 £2.80, 1&3 £6.80, 2&3 £18.30 CSF £9.96 TOTE £2.10: £1.10, £1.90, £4.90; EX 10.90.
Owner The Sunnyside Racing Partnership **Bred** S W D McIlveen **Trained** Musley Bank, N Yorks

FOCUS
The winning rider in the first race described the wind as "seriously strong". This claimer wasn't as competitive as the numbers would suggest and it paid to be handy, with the horses that raced in the first three places early finishing in the first four.

5546 E B F OLD CROSSLEYANS RUGBY UNION FOOTBALL CLUB MAIDEN STKS 1m 100y
2:55 (2:55) (Class 5) 2-Y-0 **£3,561** (£1,059; £529; £264) **Stalls** High

Form RPR
44 **1** **Golden Hinde**[33] 4460 2-9-3 0 SilvestreDeSousa 3 80+
(M Johnston) *sltly hmpd s: mde all: edgd lft ins fnl f: hld on wl* **11/8**[1]
2 1/2 **Sir Byron (IRE)** 2-9-3 0 PaulHanagan 7 79+
(R A Fahey) *chsd ldrs: rn green: drvn over 2f out: edgd lft over 1f out: styd on to take 2nd last 100yds: clsng at fin: will improve* **9/2**[3]
2254 **3** 2 1/4 **Dortmund**[16] 5049 2-9-3 83 AhmedAjtebi 1 74
(Mahmood Al Zarooni) *trckd wnr: chal over 2f out: one pce fnl f* **2/1**[2]
4 6 **Benidorm** 2-9-3 0 JamesDoyle 2 62
(A J McCabe) *in rr: drvn over 3f out: edgd lft: kpt on down wd outside fnl 2f: nvr nr ldrs* **25/1**
66 **5** 1 1/2 **Icy Blue**[14] 5117 2-9-0 0 MichaelStainton(3) 5 58
(R M Whitaker) *hmpd s: hld up: hdwy and hung lft 4f out: wknd over 1f out* **50/1**
6 4 1/2 **Already Basking (CAN)** 2-9-3 0 PhillipMakin 6 49
(P F I Cole) *wnt lft s: trckd ldrs: t.k.h: wknd 2f out* **10/1**
0 **7** 8 **Henry Chettle (IRE)**[86] 2701 2-9-0 0 AndrewHeffernan(3) 8 32
(D C Griffiths) *in rr: effrt 3f out: sn lost pl and bhd* **100/1**

1m 47.63s (0.03) **Going Correction** -0.375s/f (Firm) **7** Ran SP% **109.5**
Speed ratings (Par 94): **84,83,81,75,73 69,61**
Tote Swingers: 1&2 £1.80, 1&3 £1.20, 2&3 £2.00 CSF £7.27 TOTE £2.60: £1.70, £2.00; EX 9.50.
Owner Sheikh Hamdan Bin Mohammed Al Maktoum **Bred** Highclere Stud **Trained** Middleham Moor, N Yorks

FOCUS
The winning time was slow for this maiden, but this would have been quite a test of stamina for these juveniles, especially given the strong wind. The third horse's official rating of 83 gives some guide to the merit of the form.

NOTEBOOK
Golden Hinde, whose stable had won two of the previous three runnings of this race, was a disappointing favourite at Goodwood last month after his encouraging Redcar debut, but he was right back on track here having been well backed. Given a positive ride, he always had matters under control despite hanging about inside the final furlong and he looks one for staying nurseries during the autumn. (op 2-1)
Sir Byron(IRE) ◆, a £38,000 2-y-o and a half-brother to three winners including the useful Mass Rally, ran green throughout the contest and took a while to realise what was required, but he was really grabbing the ground in the latter stages and any improvement on this should see him going one better before long. (op 7-2)
Dortmund saw plenty of daylight from the outside stall and raced freely early, but although he had every chance he started to run about under strong pressure from over a furlong out and was never doing enough. His form seems to have levelled out. (tchd 9-4)
Benidorm ◆, an already gelded 10,000gns yearling out of a dual winning juvenile over 7f, proved clueless. Firstly, he missed the break, then had to be ridden along to stay in touch, and raced very wide around the home bend. He also looked ungainly on the ground, so the fact that he ran on into a respectable fourth suggests that connections have something to play with. (op 18-1)
Icy Blue, green when unplaced in his first two starts, will have more options now that he gets a mark. (op 40-1)
Already Basking(CAN), a $95,000 half-brother to smart performers in France and the US, showed up until folding under pressure over 2f out. He was weak in the market and should improve, but will need to. (op 15-2)

5547 RIVERSIDE VOLVO DEALER OF YEAR NURSERY 5f
3:30 (3:30) (Class 4) (0-85,84) 2-Y-0 **£5,180** (£1,541; £770; £384) **Stalls** High

Form RPR
1210 **1** **Krypton Factor**[22] 4851 2-9-6 **83** (b) SebSanders 5 90
(Sir Mark Prescott) *sn outpcd and in rr: hdwy over 2f out: nt clr run and swtchd far rail over 1f out: led last 100yds: styd on wl* **7/2**[2]
5514 **2** 1 3/4 **Volcanic Dust (IRE)**[13] 5140 2-8-3 **66** PaulHanagan 6 67
(E A L Dunlop) *t.k.h: trckd ldrs: edgd rt and led jst ins fnl f: sn hdd and no ex* **11/2**
1516 **3** 3 1/2 **Nellie Ellis (IRE)**[6] 5354 2-8-4 **67** SilvestreDeSousa 7 55
(K A Ryan) *led tl over 2f out: led over 1f out: edgd lft: hdd jst ins fnl f: fdd* **9/2**[3]
1445 **4** 3/4 **Defence Council (IRE)**[16] 5021 2-8-11 **79** IanBrennan(5) 2 64
(J Howard Johnson) *dwlt: reminders over 3f out: hdwy on outer 2f out: edgd rt and one pce* **16/1**
3410 **5** nk **First Class Favour (IRE)**[12] 5187 2-8-12 **75** DuranFentiman 4 59
(T D Easterby) *w ldrs: led over 2f out: hdd over 1f out: sn fdd* **12/1**
2155 **6** shd **Ballinargh Girl (IRE)**[22] 4831 2-8-11 **74** AndrewElliott 3 58
(R D Wylie) *sn chsng ldrs on outer: rdn 2f out: one pce* **9/2**[3]
6230 **7** 2 3/4 **Master Macho (IRE)**[9] 5261 2-8-7 **70** SamHitchcott 8 44
(M R Channon) *slowly into strde: hdwy to chse ldrs on inner over 2f out: wkng whn hmpd jst ins fnl f* **3/1**[1]

62.96 secs (-0.54) **Going Correction** -0.10s/f (Good) **7** Ran SP% **112.5**
Speed ratings (Par 96): **100,97,91,90,89 89,85**
Tote Swingers: 1&2 £3.30, 1&3 £2.40, 2&3 £5.40 CSF £22.08 CT £85.95 TOTE £3.90: £1.80, £4.20; EX 16.60.
Owner Lady Fairhaven & The Hon C & H Broughton **Bred** Lady Fairhaven **Trained** Newmarket, Suffolk

FOCUS
A decent nursery and the form should work out. The winning time was 0.28 seconds faster than the older handicappers in the following contest.

NOTEBOOK
Krypton Factor ran poorly off this mark in second-time blinkers at Redcar earlier this month having won in them first time, but he bounced right back to form here. He didn't travel all that well off the pace early, but the further they went the stronger he became and once switched to the inside over a furlong out, he quickened up in smart fashion. He still has more to offer. Official explanation: trainer's rep had no explanation for the apparent improvement in form (op 3-1)
Volcanic Dust(IRE) needs a strong pace as she can pull hard, but she travelled like the winner for much of the contest. She did quicken up when asked, but just hung away to her right under pressure and couldn't match the finishing effort of the winner. This stiff track just seemed to find her out and she should be winning again over a sharper 5f. (tchd 13-2)
Nellie Ellis(IRE), 2-2 over C&D with both wins coming in claimers, ran moderately on her nursery debut in soft ground at Carlisle six days earlier, but this was more like it. Always handy, she still had every chance entering the last furlong before the front pair left her behind. She can win an ordinary nursery. (tchd 7-2)
Defence Council(IRE) finished 10l behind First Class Favour over a furlong further at Catterick last time and managed to just about reverse that form on 7lb better terms, but his finishing effort was too little too late. (op 14-1 tchd 12-1)
First Class Favour(IRE) ended up well beaten after showing early pace in a hot 6f nursery at the York Ebor meeting and, having been weak in the market, she again didn't get home after showing good speed. She needs a sharper track. (op 8-1)
Ballinargh Girl(IRE), who didn't get home in a couple of much stronger nurseries at Newmarket and Haydock, was disappointing in this lesser grade though she did see plenty of daylight on the wide outside. (tchd 5-1)
Master Macho(IRE) was backed down into favouritism, but that may have been down to the hot current form of the yard. He was the first beaten and is now 1-18. (op 5-1)

5548 BEVERLEY LIONS H'CAP 5f
4:05 (4:07) (Class 6) (0-60,66) 3-Y-0 **£2,729** (£806; £403) **Stalls** High

Form RPR
0215 **1** **Oondiri (IRE)**[27] 4651 3-9-1 **57** PJMcDonald 8 65
(T D Easterby) *chsd ldrs: led over 1f out: edgd lft and kpt on wl* **13/2**
0536 **2** 1 1/4 **Duke Of Rainford**[13] 5152 3-8-7 **49** PaulHanagan 1 52
(M Herrington) *in rr: gd hdwy on outer outer over 1f out: styd on wl to take 2nd nr line* **16/1**
0052 **3** hd **Gower Sophia**[27] 4651 3-8-8 **50** SilvestreDeSousa 12 52
(M Brittain) *chsd ldrs: styd on same pce fnl 75yds* **9/2**[2]
41 **4** 2 **Lees Anthem**[4] 5410 3-9-5 **66** 6ex DaleSwift(5) 9 61+
(C J Teague) *s.s: hdwy over 1f out: styd on: nt rch ldrs* **6/1**[3]
2013 **5** 1 **Amoureuse**[11] 5211 3-7-13 **48** NeilFarley(7) 11 40
(D Carroll) *led tl over 1f out: fdd last 150yds* **4/1**[1]
3260 **6** 1 1/4 **Midget**[13] 5152 3-9-3 **59** DavidNolan 13 46
(D Carroll) *chsd ldrs: one pce appr fnl f: wknd towards fin* **8/1**
0043 **7** hd **Kalahari Desert (IRE)**[25] 4703 3-8-11 **56** AmyRyan(3) 5 42
(R M Whitaker) *chsd ldrs: one pce over 1f out* **9/1**
3000 **8** 1/2 **Media Jury**[57] 3663 3-8-2 **47** (p) JamesSullivan(3) 14 31
(J S Wainwright) *chsd ldrs: wknd appr fnl f* **28/1**
U **9** nk **Boy The Bell**[21] 4861 3-9-3 **59** (b[1]) SamHitchcott 3 42
(M Mullineaux) *in rr: sme hdwy over 1f out: hung lft: nvr a factor* **33/1**
000 **10** nk **The Midshipmaid**[18] 4970 3-8-2 **47** oh1 ow1 (v) AndrewHeffernan(3) 10 29
(Lucinda Featherstone) *mid-div: sn drvn along: nvr a factor* **66/1**
2050 **11** 1 1/2 **Thewinnatakesitall**[13] 5152 3-8-5 **47** (p) DuranFentiman 4 24
(N Tinkler) *in tch on outer: effrt over 2f out: fdd over 1f out* **40/1**

0-00 **12** *6* **Sue And Sue**[39] 4251 3-8-1 **46** oh1 .... PaulPickard(3) 6 —
(G Woodward) *s.s and hmpd s: in rr: bhd fnl 2f* **100/1**

000 **13** *1* **Gower Diva**[37] 4340 3-8-3 **50** .... BillyCray(5) 15 —
(D Nicholls) *s.s: in rr: bhd fnl 2f* **9/1**

41-5 **14** *26* **Point To Prove**[222] 222 3-9-4 **60** .... AndrewElliott 7 —
(J Balding) *rrd: wnt lft and s.s: a bhd: virtually p.u over 1f out: t.o* **28/1**

2000 **15** *11* **On The Piste (IRE)**[4] 5422 3-8-4 **51** .... IanBrennan(5) 2 —
(L A Mullaney) *in rr: hung bdly lft: sn bhd: virtually p.u over 1f out: t.o* **22/1**

63.24 secs (-0.26) **Going Correction** -0.10s/f (Good) 15 Ran SP% **121.9**
Speed ratings (Par 98): **98,96,95,92,90 88,88,87,87,86 84,74,73,31,14**
Tote Swingers: 1&2 £15.00, 1&3 £6.60, 2&3 £11.00 CSF £99.95 CT £535.13 TOTE £6.40: £2.60, £5.10, £2.20; EX 119.30.

Owner C H Stevens **Bred** Newlands House Stud **Trained** Great Habton, N Yorks

■ Stewards' Enquiry : Silvestre De Sousa one-day ban: used whip with excessive frequency (Sep 12)

FOCUS
A very moderate handicap with the winning time 0.28 seconds slower than the nursery. It was dominated by those that raced handily and very few made any headway from off the pace.

Boy The Bell Official explanation: jockey said gelding hung left

On The Piste(IRE) Official explanation: jockey said filly hung left

5549 CHARLES ELSEY MEMORIAL H'CAP 1m 4f 16y
4:40 (4:40) (Class 5) (0-75,75) 3-Y-O+ **£3,238** (£963; £481; £240) **Stalls** High

Form RPR

2125 **1** **Leader Of The Land (IRE)**[36] 4380 3-9-5 **75** .... PaulHanagan 12 88
(D R Lanigan) *led 1f: trckd ldrs: led over 1f out: hld on wl* **7/4**[1]

4-06 **2** *½* **Fantastic Strike (IRE)**[10] 5244 3-8-12 **68** .... SilvestreDeSousa 11 80
(M Johnston) *s.i.s: rr-div: hdwy to trck ldrs 7f out: chal over 1f out: no ex clsng stages* **11/2**[3]

3525 **3** *4* **Old Hundred (IRE)**[18] 4965 3-9-5 **75** .... (v[1]) PatCosgrave 1 81
(J R Fanshawe) *swtchd rt s: hdwy to trck ldrs 7f out: n.m.r and c outside over 2f out: kpt on one pce appr fnl f* **8/1**

0053 **4** *5* **Red Kestrel (USA)**[11] 5215 5-9-0 **67** .... JulieBurke(7) 6 65
(K A Ryan) *drvn to ld after 1f: hdd over 1f out: one pce* **8/1**

235 **5** *1* **Kames Park (IRE)**[15] 5070 8-9-13 **73** .... PaulEddery 10 69
(R C Guest) *s.i.s: hdwy over 2f out: nvr trbld ldrs* **12/1**

4036 **6** *6* **Hallstatt (IRE)**[15] 5070 4-9-5 **65** .... (p) SebSanders 8 52
(J Mackie) *jnd ldr after 3f: upsides over 4f out: wknd over 1f out* **14/1**

1-42 **7** *6* **Elite Land**[19] 2285 7-9-2 **67** .... DaleSwift(5) 2 44
(B Ellison) *in rr and sn drvn along: lost tch over 4f out: nvr on terms* **4/1**[2]

4210 **8** *7* **Astronomical (IRE)**[16] 5019 8-9-5 **65** .... (p) PhillipMakin 4 31
(R Hollinshead) *sn trcking ldrs: wknd 2f out* **25/1**

0/00 **9** *28* **Motarid (USA)**[29] 4604 5-9-0 **60** .... (v[1]) DavidNolan 5 —
(T D Walford) *chsd ldrs: hmpd bnd after 1f: lost pl over 4f out: sn bhd: virtually p.u: t.o* **33/1**

2m 35.46s (-4.34) **Going Correction** -0.375s/f (Firm) course record
WFA 3 from 4yo+ 10lb 9 Ran SP% **115.1**
Speed ratings (Par 103): **103,102,100,96,96 92,88,83,64**
Tote Swingers: 1&2 £2.00, 1&3 £5.20, 2&3 £6.00 CSF £11.49 CT £60.57 TOTE £3.00: £1.70, £2.40, £1.40; EX 10.90.

Owner Saeed H Altayer **Bred** Rabbah Bloodstock Limited **Trained** Newmarket, Suffolk

FOCUS
An ordinary handicap, but they went a solid pace and it produced a cracking finish. There were only three 3-y-os in the field and they filled the first three places.

5550 RACING AGAIN ON 15TH SEPTEMBER H'CAP 1m 1f 207y
5:15 (5:15) (Class 6) (0-60,59) 3-Y-O **£2,266** (£674; £337; £168) **Stalls** High

Form RPR

6503 **1** **Akamon**[24] 4763 3-9-0 **55** .... PaulHanagan 5 63
(E A L Dunlop) *mid-div: drvn 4f out: styd on to ld jst ins fnl f: hld on wl* **7/4**[1]

4-65 **2** *1* **Ella Grace (USA)**[21] 4867 3-8-13 **59** .... LeeTopliss(5) 4 65
(R A Fahey) *mid-div: effrt and swtchd lft over 2f out: styd on to take 2nd last 75yds: no real imp* **6/1**[3]

4464 **3** *1 ¾* **Straversjoy**[23] 4786 3-8-10 **51** .... PaulEddery 11 54
(R Hollinshead) *hld up in rr: hdwy on outer over 2f out: hmpd over 2f out: edgd rt over 1f out: kpt on to take 3rd last 50yds* **4/1**[2]

0504 **4** *1 ¾* **Battle Study (IRE)**[3] 5455 3-8-12 **53** .... JamesDoyle 3 52
(A J McCabe) *chsd ldr: led 3f out: hdd jst ins fnl f: one pce* **7/1**

0000 **5** *6* **Marsh's Gift**[37] 4337 3-8-4 **48** .... BarryMcHugh(3) 6 35
(R E Barr) *chsd ldrs: drvn over 4f out: wknd fnl f* **17/2**

055 **6** *12* **Nephele (IRE)**[22] 4853 3-9-1 **56** .... DuranFentiman 1 19
(T D Easterby) *trckd ldrs: t.k.h: drvn 4f out: c wd: wkng whn sltly hmpd over 2f out* **12/1**

-060 **7** *6* **Singing Scott (IRE)**[34] 4439 3-8-4 **45** .... SilvestreDeSousa 8 —
(R Bastiman) *in rr: sme hdwy whn swvd lft over 2f out: sn wknd* **16/1**

5000 **8** *11* **Penderyn**[21] 4857 3-8-1 **45** .... (v[1]) PaulPickard(3) 7 —
(C Smith) *led: set str pce: hdd 3f out: hung lft and sn lost pl* **33/1**

05 **9** *13* **Both Ends Burning (IRE)**[18] 4944 3-8-1 **45** .... (p) JamesSullivan(3) 2 —
(J S Wainwright) *chsd ldrs: wknd over 2f out: eased whn bhd clsng stages* **40/1**

000- **10** *24* **Check The Anchor (IRE)**[340] 6214 3-8-4 **45** .... AndrewElliott 10 —
(N Tinkler) *s.i.s: sn drvn along: bhd 7f out: virtually p.u over 1f out: t.o* **25/1**

2m 4.63s (-2.37) **Going Correction** -0.375s/f (Firm) 10 Ran SP% **116.5**
Speed ratings (Par 98): **94,93,91,90,85 76,71,62,52,32**
Tote Swingers: 1&2 £4.50, 1&3 £3.00, 2&3 £4.70 CSF £12.21 CT £37.41 TOTE £2.00: £1.10, £2.20, £2.00; EX 12.50 Place 6: £39.01 Place 5: £24.99 .

Owner Mrs J Ellis & Lady Derby **Bred** Stanley House Stud And New England Stud **Trained** Newmarket, Suffolk

■ Stewards' Enquiry : Lee Topliss interference to Straversjoy, and in turn to Nephele, by Ella Grace app 2f out. No action taken.

FOCUS
A very poor contest with all ten runners maidens coming into it and only three of them had been placed. They went a very strong pace early and that helped the hold-up horses.

T/Jkpt: £1,319.30 to a £1 stake. Pool:£42,739.14 - 23 winning tickets T/Plt: £26.10 to a £1 stake. Pool:£62,881.19 - 1,753.23 winning tickets T/Qpdt: £10.90 to a £1 stake. Pool:£4,517.62 - 306 winning tickets WG

5516 GOODWOOD (R-H)
Sunday, August 29

OFFICIAL GOING: Straight course - soft; round course - good to soft
Top bend moved out 4yds.
Wind: Brisk across Weather: Overcast

5551 BANK HOLIDAY STKS (H'CAP) 6f
2:10 (2:10) (Class 3) (0-95,88) 3-Y-O+ **£6,476** (£1,927; £963; £481) **Stalls** Low

Form RPR

-100 **1** **Definightly**[22] 4832 4-9-11 **88** .... (b[1]) SteveDrowne 6 112
(R Charlton) *mde all: pushed along and qcknd clr ins fnl f: unchal* **15/2**

1611 **2** *5* **Slip Sliding Away (IRE)**[17] 5005 3-8-11 **82** .... JohnFahy(5) 5 90
(P R Hedger) *s.i.s and wnt lft s: hld up in rr tl stdy hdwy 2f out: sn chsng wnr: rdn and nt qckn fr over 1f out* **2/1**[1]

0040 **3** *1 ¾* **Seamus Shindig**[23] 4806 8-8-11 **79** .... AmyScott(5) 4 81
(H Candy) *in rr: hdwy fr 2f out: styd on ins fnl f but nver a threat to ldng duo* **13/2**

0400 **4** *shd* **Aye Aye Digby (IRE)**[17] 4995 5-9-9 **86** .... (p) DaneO'Neill 3 88
(J R Boyle) *chsd ldrs: rdn over 2f out: styd on same pce fnl f* **6/1**[3]

1003 **5** *nk* **Spitfire**[5] 5393 5-9-10 **87** .... PhilipRobinson 2 88
(J R Jenkins) *chsd ldrs: shkn up and hung rt over 2f out: styd on same pce fnl f* **5/2**[2]

100 **6** *6* **Harlech Castle**[20] 4894 5-9-2 **79** .... (b) GeorgeBaker 1 61
(J R Boyle) *drvn to chse wnr fr stalls: wknd over 1f out* **20/1**

100 **7** *29* **Palisades Park**[53] 3791 3-9-7 **87** .... JimmyFortune 7 —
(R Hannon) *in rr: pushed along and no rspnse 2f out: eased fnl f* **25/1**

1m 14.21s (2.01) **Going Correction** +0.475s/f (Yiel)
WFA 3 from 4yo+ 3lb 7 Ran SP% **109.9**
Speed ratings (Par 107): **105,98,96,95,95 87,48**
Tote Swingers: 1&2 £2.70, 1&3 £10.50, 2&3 £4.20 CSF £21.15 TOTE £5.90: £3.10, £1.20; EX 18.60.

Owner S Emmet And Miss R Emmet **Bred** S Emmet And Miss R Emmet **Trained** Beckhampton, Wilts

FOCUS
Top bend moved out 4yds. Conditions had dried overnight and the ground, which looked rather tacky, was reported as dead by riders in the first. The time for the opener was just under four seconds outside the standard. Only a fair handicap, with doubts over most of these heading into the race. The runners kept away from the stands' rail and came down the centre of the track.

NOTEBOOK
Definightly, sharpened up by first-time blinkers, was in front throughout and came right away in the final furlong to slam his pursuers. He had been held up in most of his previous runs, including when winning here first time out this year, but he did make all at Lingfield as a juvenile. It will be interesting to see whether the headgear works so well again. He could go for the Ayr Silver Cup next, for which he picks up a penalty. (op 9-2)
Slip Sliding Away(IRE) had won three of his four starts on turf and was unbeaten in two runs at Goodwood, but was 9lb higher than when winning here last time. He recovered from his regular slow start to race smoothly, but after moving into second he could not get to the winner, who was drawing away from him late on. This easier ground was not a problem. (op 11-4)
Seamus Shindig kept on down the outer to shade third. He is not running badly at present and has been dropped a total of 10lb by the handicapper this season. (op 7-1 tchd 6-1)
Aye Aye Digby(IRE) had cheekpieces fitted for the first time following a disappointing run at Epsom, but the aids failed to bring out much improvement. (tchd 7-1)
Spitfire, third at Yarmouth five days earlier, ran his race but lacked a change of gear as he attempted to improve on the near side of the bunch. (op 3-1)
Harlech Castle could not claim the lead and faded badly after racing up with the pace. He has yet to recapture any worthwhile form after returning from a long break. (op 16-1)
Palisades Park found nothing when asked to pick up and has been well beaten in three runs since scoring on his reappearance. (op 16-1)

5552 FEGENTRI WORLD CUP OF NATIONS (AMATEUR RIDERS' H'CAP) (IN MEMORY OF THE LATE JOHN CIECHANOWSKI) 1m 1f
2:45 (2:46) (Class 5) (0-75,75) 3-Y-O+ **£3,123** (£968; £484; £242) **Stalls** High

Form RPR

0133 **1** **Pintura**[23] 4786 3-11-11 **74** .... (p) MrRBirkett 6 84
(D M Simcock) *trckd ldrs in 3rd: wnt 2nd over 2f out: chal over 1f out: sn led: drvn clr ins fnl f* **7/4**[1]

3244 **2** *3 ½* **Megalala (IRE)**[27] 4657 9-11-9 **65** .... MrMarioBaratti 5 67
(J J Bridger) *led: pushed along over 2f out: jnd over 1f out and sn hdd: no ch w wnr ins fnl f but hld on wl for 2nd* **15/8**[2]

4414 **3** *¾* **Noah Jameel**[16] 5051 8-10-10 **52** .... MrsAndreaHierer 3 53
(A G Newcombe) *racd in cl 4th: rdn over 2f out and styd on to take 3rd ins fnl f and clsng on 2nd nr fin but nvr any ch w wnr* **11/2**

0555 **4** *hd* **Mavalenta (IRE)**[24] 4756 3-11-0 **63** .... MrJean-PhilippeBoisgontier 4 63
(J W Hills) *chsd ldr: rdn over 2f out: lost 2nd over 1f out and styd on same pce ins fnl f* **3/1**[3]

2m 0.56s (4.26) **Going Correction** +0.25s/f (Good)
WFA 3 from 8yo+ 7lb 4 Ran SP% **111.5**
Speed ratings (Par 103): **91,87,87,87**
CSF £5.55 TOTE £2.30; EX 3.90.

Owner Dr Marwan Koukash **Bred** Dulverton Equine **Trained** Newmarket, Suffolk

FOCUS
The withdrawal of Trafalgar Square (new market formed) further reduced what was already a disappointing turnout for this international amateurs' race. The pace was a reasonable one but the form is very modest.

5553 HARWOODS RACING CLUB & EMPLOYEES E B F ALICE KEPPEL (FILLIES' & MARES' H'CAP) (LISTED RACE) 1m 1f 192y
3:20 (3:20) (Class 1) (0-110,100) 3-Y-O+
£19,869 (£7,532; £3,769; £1,879; £941; £472) **Stalls** High

Form RPR

-211 **1** **Mirror Lake**[17] 5004 3-9-2 **96** .... PatDobbs 4 106+
(Mrs A J Perrett) *trckd ldrs: shkn up and qcknd to take narrow ld 2f out: rdn and styd on strly fnl f: asserted fnl 120yds* **9/4**[1]

5211 **2** *¾* **Fastback (IRE)**[7] 5329 4-8-11 **83** 3ex oh1 .... JackMitchell 13 91
(R M Beckett) *chsd ldrs: drvn to press wnr 2f out and stl rt there but u.p 1f out: outpcd fnl 120yds* **8/1**[3]

0065 **3** *2 ½* **Marie De Medici (USA)**[29] 4612 3-9-6 **100** .... JoeFanning 6 103
(M Johnston) *in tch: rdn along on outside over 2f out: styd on wl fr over 1f out and kpt on to take 3rd fnl 75yds* **14/1**

551P **4** *hd* **Paquerettza (FR)**[76] 3031 4-9-4 **90** .... RobertWinston 12 93
(D H Brown) *chsd ldr: ev ch fr 3f out and stll upsides 2f out: wknd fnl f and lost 3rd fnl 75yds* **20/1**

0-21 **5** 1 1/4 **Warling (IRE)**[113] 1932 3-8-3 **83** oh5 .... JimmyQuinn 5 83+
(J Noseda) *s.i.s: in rr: drvn and hdwy on outside fr over 2f out: kpt on fnl f but nt rch ldrs* **8/1**[3]

-611 **6** 3/4 **Critical Path (IRE)**[29] 4594 4-8-11 **83** .... JimmyFortune 9 82
(A M Balding) *in rr: rdn and hdwy over 2f out: styd on fnl f but nt rch ldrs* **8/1**[3]

600 **7** nk **Victoria Sponge (IRE)**[64] 3457 4-8-11 **83** oh1 .... DaneO'Neill 7 81+
(S C Williams) *v.s.a and lost 8 l s: last but in tch w main gp 5f out: rdn and outpcd 3f out: statyed on again fr over 1f out: kpt on cl home* **25/1**

-300 **8** 1 3/4 **Ceilidh House**[10] 5249 3-9-4 **98** .... GeorgeBaker 3 93
(R M Beckett) *chsd ldrs: rdn and ev ch 3f out: styd front rnk tl over 1f out: wknd fnl f* **16/1**

53-3 **9** 1/2 **Clarietta**[148] 1082 3-8-13 **93** .... EddieAhern 8 87
(J L Dunlop) *in rr: rdn and no prog fr 3f out* **10/1**

-303 **10** 4 1/2 **Miss Glitters (IRE)**[20] 4891 5-8-11 **83** oh9 .... SteveDrowne 2 68
(H Morrison) *led: rdn 3f out: hdd and n.m.r on rails 2f out: sn btn* **33/1**

4-00 **11** hd **Wedding March (IRE)**[28] 4624 3-9-4 **98** .... FrankieDettori 11 82
(Saeed Bin Suroor) *in tch: hdwy 3f out: rdn to chse ldrs over 2f out: sn wknd* **7/1**[2]

334 **12** 6 **What's Up Pussycat (IRE)**[16] 5052 4-9-8 **94** .... NeilCallan 10 66
(D M Simcock) *in rr: hdwy on ins 3f out: n.m.r 2f out: sn wknd* **7/1**[2]

2m 8.45s (0.45) **Going Correction** +0.25s/f (Good)
WFA 3 from 4yo+ 8lb **12** Ran SP% **122.3**
Speed ratings (Par 108): **108,107,105,105,104 103,103,102,101,98 97,93**
Tote Swingers: 1&2 £3.70, 1&3 £10.40, 2&3 £21.00 CSF £20.56 CT £215.74 TOTE £3.40: £1.80, £3.30, £4.70; EX 22.50.
Owner K Abdulla **Bred** Millsec Limited **Trained** Pulborough, W Sussex

FOCUS
A competitive renewal of this Listed handicap, which looked to be run at an ordinary pace. There were a number in with a shout before the first two came clear.

NOTEBOOK
Mirror Lake came here with impressive wins in a Polytrack maiden and a course-and-distance handicap behind her, and the rise in grade could not prevent her from completing a hat-trick off this 8lb higher mark. She did not win as comfortably as she had threatened to once bursting through to lead, but she still did it well and there could easily be more to come from her in the remainder of the season. A Group 3 in Ireland could be her next port of call. The softer conditions posed her no problems. (tchd 15-8 and 5-2)
Fastback(IRE) ran on against the rail to make the winner work for her victory. She was 4lb out of the weights under the penalty for the second of her recent wins in four-runner handicaps, but has blossomed since getting in foal and picked up valuable black type with this career-best effort. (op 10-1 tchd 11-1)
Marie De Medici(USA) has a win at this level to her name, in the Pretty Polly Stakes at Newmarket in the spring, but she had looked out of sorts since and this represented something of a return to form. She failed to stay 1m4f in the Oaks but might be worth another try at that trip. (op 11-1)
Paquerettza(FR) was pulled up in a distressed state at Warwick in June and was found to have mucus in her lungs. Given a break since, she ran an honest race up with the pace and just missed out on third. (op 16-1 tchd 25-1)
Warling(IRE) ◆ had not been seen since winning a Warwick maiden back in May and was 5lb out of the weights here. After missing the break she was in rear until picking up when it was all over and coming home in taking fashion. The return to further will suit her and she is clearly a useful filly. Official explanation: jockey said filly was slowly away (op 10-1)
Critical Path(IRE) arrived on a hat-trick following a pair of handicap wins. This represented her stiffest test yet and she ran creditably if never threatening the principals. (tchd 10-1)
Victoria Sponge(IRE) was a pound out of the weights and blew the start badly before passing beaten opponents. Official explanation: jockey said filly was slowly away (op 33-1)
Ceilidh House ran a lot better than she had at York, but just as it looked as if she might play a part in the finish she dropped away. The easy ground ought to have suited her. Her rider reported that she hung right. Official explanation: jockey said filly hung right under pressure (tchd 14-1)
Clarietta, off the track since early April, was rather keen to post and could never get involved. (op 12-1)
Miss Glitters(IRE) was 9lb out of the weights on this return to turf and faded after making the running. (op 28-1)
Wedding March(IRE) was unproven in this sort of ground and ran another disappointing race. (op 8-1)
What's Up Pussycat(IRE) is proven in softish conditions and should have been suited by this longer trip, but could never get into the race. Official explanation: vet said filly returned lame (op 15-2 tchd 13-2)

5554 SUPREME STKS (GROUP 3) 7f
3:55 (3:55) (Class 1) 3-Y-O+
£32,358 (£12,266; £6,138; £3,060; £1,533; £769) **Stalls** High

Form RPR
6131 **1** **Tropical Paradise (IRE)**[30] 4540 4-9-1 105 .... IanMongan 1 111
(P Winkworth) *trckd ldrs: slt ld 2f out: rdn and styd on wl fnl f* **7/2**[2]

2010 **2** 1 1/4 **First City**[14] 5114 4-8-11 101 .... EddieAhern 5 104+
(D M Simcock) *trckd ldrs: nt clr run 2f out: squeezed through over out: sn hung lft but styd on to chse wnr ins fnl f but no imp* **8/1**

2234 **3** 3/4 **Himalya (IRE)**[15] 5081 4-9-0 110 .... ShaneKelly 3 105
(J Noseda) *hld up in tch: hdwy 2f out: pushed along over 1f out: styd on to take 3rd ins fnl f but readily hld by ldng duo* **5/2**[1]

1032 **4** 1/2 **Aldovrandi (IRE)**[64] 3460 3-8-9 105 .... MartinDwyer 2 101
(M Botti) *plld hrd and settled in rr after 1f: pushed along 2f out: styd on to take 4th ins fnl f but nvr a threat* **4/1**[3]

545 **5** 1 **Georgebernardshaw (IRE)**[50] 3893 5-9-0 102 .... NeilCallan 4 101
(D M Simcock) *t.k.h: led: hdd 2f out: wknd ins fnl f* **9/1**

1-00 **6** 1 **Prince Of Dance**[106] 2118 4-9-0 105 .... (t) SteveDrowne 6 98
(J R Gask) *chsd ldr: drvn to chal 2f out: wknd fnl f* **9/2**

1m 28.34s (1.44) **Going Correction** +0.25s/f (Good)
WFA 3 from 4yo+ 5lb **6** Ran SP% **110.1**
Speed ratings (Par 113): **101,99,98,98,97 95**
Tote Swingers: 1&2 £3.70, 1&3 £10.40, 2&3 £21.00 CSF £28.66 TOTE £3.60: £2.30, £4.10; EX 22.90.
Owner S Lovelace & R Muddle **Bred** George E McMahon **Trained** Chiddingfold, Surrey

FOCUS
A substandard Group 3 run at just a steady pace, and not strong form.

NOTEBOOK
Tropical Paradise(IRE), the only runner previously successful in this company, shouldered a penalty for that win in the Oak Tree Stakes at the Glorious meeting. Taking on male opposition this time, she was always well placed and showed a willing attitude once asked to go and win her race. An uncomplicated filly, she will stay in training next year and will doubtless be heading back to Goodwood as she clearly likes the place. (op 11-4 tchd 5-2)
First City put a disappointing effort at Bath behind her. She was short of room for a time before getting through a gap and running on to secure second. She is a smart filly when on song, but showed a high head carriage and is tricky. (op 13-2)
Himalya(IRE), another less than straightforward character, was ponied to the start again. He was briefly hemmed in when the race was developing, but was out in sufficient time had he been able to quicken up. This was a lost opportunity as he was 5lb best in on BHA figures, but he is notoriously hard to win with. (tchd 11-4)
Aldovrandi(IRE), the only three-year-old in the line-up, was running for the first time in two months. He raced very keenly early on, throwing his head about under restraint, but settled by the straight and did run on past a couple of rivals late on. Official explanation: jockey said colt ran too freely (op 6-1)
Georgebernardshaw(IRE), the runner-up's stablemate, became rather warm before the start. Proven in softish ground when trained by Aidan O'Brien, he made the running and was still in with a chance of a place inside the last. (tchd 8-1)
Prince Of Dance, last seen in the Lockinge Stakes in the spring when trained by Tom Dascombe, was fitted with a tongue tie for the first time and went to post early. Still in second place going to the final furlong, he dropped away to finish last and has now beaten only one opponent in three appearances this year, but is entitled to come on for this. (op 5-1 tchd 11-2)

5555 GOODWOOD REVIVAL H'CAP 7f
4:30 (4:30) (Class 5) (0-70,66) 3-Y-O+ **£2,590** (£770; £385; £192) **Stalls** High

Form RPR
-163 **1** **Leelu**[22] 4839 4-9-1 **54** .... LiamKeniry 6 66
(D W P Arbuthnot) *chsd ldrs: rdn to ld ins fnl 2f: drvn clr ins fnl f: readily* **9/2**[3]

2112 **2** 2 1/4 **Eager To Bow (IRE)**[12] 5174 4-9-12 **65** .... GeorgeBaker 1 71
(P R Chamings) *in rr: hdwy on outside over 2f out: rdn to chse wnr ins fnl f but no imp* **3/1**[1]

0005 **3** 1/2 **Grand Vizier (IRE)**[18] 4969 6-9-10 **63** .... EddieAhern 7 68
(C F Wall) *in rr: hdwy ins fnl 3f: n.m.r 2f out: sn drvn and swtchd rt to r on far side rail over 1f out: disp 2nd sn after: no ex and one pce into 3rd ins fnl f* **10/3**[2]

0000 **4** 1 3/4 **Ymir**[38] 4308 4-8-8 **47** .... (vt[1]) JoeFanning 4 47
(M J Attwater) *t.k.h: chsd ldrs: rdn over 2f out: wknd ins fnl f* **14/1**

0050 **5** 2 **Whisper Wind**[15] 5086 3-9-6 **64** .... (b[1]) FergusSweeney 5 58
(G L Moore) *towards rr but in tch: pushed along 3f out: styng on whn nt clr run jst ins fnl 2f: no ch after but kpt on fnl f* **12/1**

4123 **6** 1 **Daddy's Gift (IRE)**[5] 5388 4-9-9 **62** .... PatDobbs 10 54
(R Hannon) *chsd ldrs: hmpd jst ins fnl 2f: stl in tch whn hmpd again on ins over 1f out: no ch after* **9/2**[3]

-000 **7** 2 3/4 **Zazous**[185] 691 9-8-2 **46** oh1 .... KierenFox[(5)] 2 30
(J J Bridger) *in rr over 2f out and no imp on ldrs* **33/1**

0040 **8** 1 **Giulietta Da Vinci**[46] 4025 3-8-13 **62** .... JohnFahy[(5)] 9 44
(S Woodman) *chsd ldrs tl bdly hmpd jst ins fnl 2f: nt rcvr* **10/1**

0600 **9** 1 1/2 **Louie's Lad**[18] 4959 4-8-7 **46** oh1 .... NeilChalmers 8 24
(J J Bridger) *led tl hdd ins fnl 2f: sn btn* **33/1**

1m 28.8s (1.90) **Going Correction** +0.25s/f (Good)
WFA 3 from 4yo+ 5lb **9** Ran SP% **113.8**
Speed ratings (Par 103): **99,96,95,93,91 90,87,86,84**
Tote Swingers: 1&2 £3.30, 2&3 £3.00 CSF £18.10 CT £49.43 TOTE £5.20: £1.40, £2.10, £2.20; EX 20.00.
Owner Philip Banfield **Bred** P Banfield **Trained** Compton, Berks

FOCUS
Only a modest handicap, but the time was less than half a second slower than the earlier Group 3. Several runners encountered traffic problems.
Daddy's Gift(IRE) Official explanation: jockey said filly was denied a clear run

5556 GG CLUB STKS (H'CAP) 1m
5:05 (5:05) (Class 3) (0-95,94) 3-Y-O+ **£6,476** (£1,927; £963; £481) **Stalls** High

Form RPR
-030 **1** **Emirates Dream (USA)**[32] 4470 3-9-7 **93** .... FrankieDettori 7 103
(Saeed Bin Suroor) *trckd ldrs: led over 1f out: drvn and qcknd clr ins fnl f: comf* **11/2**

330 **2** 2 **Dunn'o (IRE)**[22] 4816 5-10-0 **94** .... PhilipRobinson 5 99
(C G Cox) *led: rdn 2f out: hdd over 1f out: styd on but no ch w wnr ins fnl f* **5/1**[3]

3366 **3** 3/4 **South Cape**[9] 5264 7-8-12 **85** .... HarryBentley[(7)] 4 88
(G L Moore) *slowly away: in rr: pushed along and clsd on ldrs 3f out: kpt on same pce tl r.o to take 3rd fnl 120yds* **8/1**

2141 **4** nk **Innocuous**[40] 4224 3-8-12 **87** .... MartinLane[(3)] 1 89+
(D M Simcock) *racd on outside: rdn and styd on fr over 2f out to take 3rd 1f out: no imp and outpcd into 4th fnl 120yds* **2/1**[1]

050 **5** shd **General Eliott (IRE)**[9] 5264 5-9-4 **84** .... (p) ShaneKelly 8 86
(P F I Cole) *chsd ldr: rdn and hung bdly rt fr over 2f out but styd disputing 2nd tl over 1f out: stl edging rt but kpt on same pce ins fnl f* **16/1**

051 **6** 3/4 **Salient**[19] 4929 6-8-7 **78** .... KierenFox[(5)] 2 79
(M J Attwater) *chsd ldrs: rdn 3f out: wknd fnl f* **25/1**

3320 **7** 11 **Truism**[9] 5264 4-9-0 **85** .... JohnFahy[(5)] 9 60
(Mrs A J Perrett) *in rr but in tch: rdn 3f out: no prog: wknd fr 2f out* **4/1**[2]

020 **P** **Smokey Oakey (IRE)**[22] 4828 6-9-12 **92** .... JimmyQuinn 3 —
(M H Tompkins) *in rr: rdn and no imp fr 3f out: bhd whn wknd qckly 2f out: p.u and dismntd over 1f out* **11/1**

1m 40.44s (0.54) **Going Correction** +0.25s/f (Good)
WFA 3 from 4yo+ 6lb **8** Ran SP% **114.6**
Speed ratings (Par 107): **107,105,104,103,103 103,92,—**
Tote Swingers: 1&2 £4.90, 1&3 £7.20, 2&3 £6.50 CSF £33.08 CT £218.68 TOTE £5.40: £1.80, £1.70, £3.00; EX 31.70.
Owner Godolphin **Bred** Kilroy Thoroughbred Partnership **Trained** Newmarket, Suffolk

FOCUS
It was raining heavily during this decent handicap, and it looked quite hard work for the runners. The pace was respectable.

NOTEBOOK
Emirates Dream(USA), who was down in trip and had been dropped 5lb after failing to get home over 1m4f here at the big meeting, was well supported. Ridden differently this time, he took it up going well and showed a good attitude to see out his race. He hold an entry in the Cambridgeshire. (op 6-1 tchd 13-2)
Dunn'o(IRE) ran his usual honest race from the front and refused to lie down when headed by the winner. He remains winless since May last year. (op 7-1 tchd 9-2)
South Cape badly missed the break and was still only sixth entering the final furlong, before staying on. He was a course winner the last time he encountered soft ground, nearly two years ago. Official explanation: jockey said gelding was slowly away (Tchd 9-1 in places)
Innocuous was 7lb higher than when winning at Ffos Las, but looked progressive and was proven in soft conditions. Caught wide from his low stall, he could never quite get to the principals and might not have been at home on this track. (op 11-8)
General Eliott(IRE) ran a bit better with the cheekpieces back on but he hung again and is far from an easy ride. He is 25lb lower than he was this time last year. Official explanation: jockey said gelding hung right under pressure (op 14-1)
Salient, a recent Lingfield winner, ran respectably on this return to turf. (op 16-1)
Truism, a course regular, was well beaten and the ground looked to blame. Official explanation: jockey said gelding was unsuited by the good to soft ground (op 6-1)

Smokey Oakey(IRE) had suitable conditions underfoot, but was eased down and pulled up with something seemingly amiss. Official explanation: jockey said gelding lost its action (op 12-1)

5557 GOODWOOD FREEPHONE 08000188191 APPRENTICE STKS (H'CAP) 6f
5:40 (5:40) (Class 5) (0-70,65) 3-Y-O+ £2,590 (£770; £385; £192) Stalls Low

Form RPR

0564 **1** **The Human League**[24] 4739 3-9-4 **62** RossAtkinson(3) 10 71
(M R Channon) *chsd ldrs: rdn over 2f out: led over 1f out: hdd fnl 120yds: rallied gamely to ld again last stride* **5/1**[2]

-031 **2** *shd* **Witchry**[15] 5087 8-9-9 **61** RussKennemore 4 70
(A G Newcombe) *in tch: hdwy fr 2f out: drvn to take narrow ld fnl 120yds: ct last stride* **4/1**[1]

2351 **3** *2* **Mata Hari Blue**[4] 5419 4-9-9 **64** 6ex TobyAtkinson(3) 5 67
(J R Holt) *chsd ldrs: rdn and kpt on fnl f tl outpcd by ldng duo fnl 120yds* **8/1**

4642 **4** *1 3/4* **Billberry**[15] 5087 5-9-5 **60** (vt) AshleyMorgan(3) 2 57
(S C Williams) *in rr: rdn 2f out: hdwy over 1f out: kpt on ins fnl f: nt rch ldrs* **4/1**[1]

0513 **5** *shd* **Avonvalley**[24] 4761 3-9-10 **65** MatthewDavies 12 62
(George Baker) *led tl hdd over 1f out: wknd ins fnl f* **12/1**

0640 **6** *5* **Joss Stick**[2] 5471 5-8-8 **46** oh1 Louis-PhilippeBeuzelin 9 27
(J J Bridger) *stdd s: sn in tch: rdn 2f out: nvr rchd ldrs and wknd ins fnl f* **25/1**

0-55 **7** *hd* **Bouggie Daize**[22] 4833 4-9-10 **65** JohnFahy(3) 1 45
(C G Cox) *racd alone stands' side: rdn 1/2-way: a outpcd* **15/2**

0111 **8** *1 1/2* **Clerical (USA)**[32] 4487 4-9-6 **58** (p) MartinLane 7 33
(R M H Cowell) *chsd ldrs: rdn over 2f out: sn btn* **6/1**[3]

6000 **9** *3/4* **Avow (USA)**[12] 5182 3-8-11 **57** HarryBentley(5) 6 30
(J J Bridger) *sn rdn in rr: a outpcd* **33/1**

5050 **10** *1/2* **Spiritofthewest (IRE)**[36] 4394 4-9-4 **63** ClaireMurray(7) 3 34
(D H Brown) *v.s.a: wnt rt sn after s and racd on outside: a struggling and no ch whn hung lft 2f out* **11/1**

-000 **11** *1* **Calabaza**[12] 5169 8-8-5 **46** oh1 (p) KierenFox(3) 8 14
(M J Attwater) *chsd ldrs over 3f* **40/1**

0-00 **12** *23* **Chill Out Charley**[2] 5470 3-8-0 **46** oh1 RyanPowell(5) 13 —
(J J Bridger) *showed spd for 3f: sn fdd* **66/1**

1m 14.5s (2.30) **Going Correction** +0.475s/f (Yiel)
WFA 3 from 4yo+ 3lb **12** Ran SP% **120.6**
Speed ratings (Par 103): **103,102,100,97,97 91,90,88,87,87 85,55**
Tote Swingers: 1&2 £8.90, 1&3 £16.00, 2&3 £9.00 CSF £25.10 CT £163.73 TOTE £7.80: £2.40, £2.00, £3.00; EX 31.00 Place 6: £126.53 Place 5: £55.02.
Owner M Channon **Bred** C J Murfitt **Trained** West Ilsley, Berks
■ Stewards' Enquiry : Russ Kennemore caution: used whip with excessive frequency.
Claire Murray one-day ban: used whip when out of contention (Sep 12)

FOCUS
An ordinary sprint handicap for apprentices, but the form seems sound enough. The runners all headed down the centre with the exception of topweight Bouggie Daize near the stands' rail.
Joss Stick Official explanation: jockey said gelding ran flat
T/Plt: £104.90 to a £1 stake. Pool:£63,949.16 - 444.69 winning tickets T/Qpdt: £16.80 to a £1 stake. Pool:£4,982.22 - 16.80 winning tickets ST

5391 YARMOUTH (L-H)
Sunday, August 29

OFFICIAL GOING: Soft (5.8)
Back and straight and bend dolled out 3m increasing distances on round course by about 10yds
Wind: strong, half behind later on Weather: showery, breezy

5558 E B F & EASTERN DAILY PRESS MAIDEN FILLIES' STKS 6f 3y
2:00 (2:00) (Class 5) 2-Y-O £3,217 (£962; £481; £240; £119) Stalls High

Form RPR

1 **Finoon (IRE)** 2-9-0 0 TedDurcan 7 79+
(Saeed Bin Suroor) *s.i.s: sn rcvrd and wl in tch: chsd ldr 3f out: edgd lft and drew clr w wnr jst over 2f out: led ins fnl f: kpt on wl* **11/10**[1]

2 **2** *1 3/4* **Celtic Sixpence (IRE)**[25] 4702 2-9-0 0 WilliamCarson 5 73+
(M G Quinlan) *led: hung lft thrght: rdn clr w wnr jst over 2f out: continued to hang bdly lft u.p: hdd and no ex ins fnl f* **13/8**[2]

0 **3** *10* **Icelady**[13] 5160 2-9-0 0 HayleyTurner 1 43
(R M H Cowell) *s.i.s: sn bustled along to chse ldrs: rdn and wl outpcd jst over 2f out: plugged on to go modest 3rd ins fnl f* **80/1**

00 **4** *1 1/4* **Millies Dancer (IRE)**[30] 4550 2-9-0 0 AndreaAtzeni 4 39
(M G Quinlan) *chsd ldr tl 4f out: rdn and wl outpcd by ldng pair jst over 2f out: wl btn over 1f out: lost 3rd ins fnl f* **50/1**

00 **5** *shd* **Volcanic Lady (IRE)**[13] 5147 2-9-0 0 NickyMackay 6 39
(D M Simcock) *s.i.s: hld up in tch in last pair: rdn and wl outpcd by ldng pair jst over 2f out: pressing for modest 3rd fr wl over 1f out: no ex ins fnl f* **40/1**

6 *nk* **Gainsboroughs Best (IRE)** 2-9-0 0 RichardHills 2 38
(W J Haggas) *s.i.s: hld up in tch in last pair: pushed along and btn jst over 2f out: wl bhd over 1f out* **7/1**[3]

05 **7** *11* **Kaifi (IRE)**[70] 3237 2-9-0 0 ChrisCatlin 3 —
(C E Brittain) *chsd ldrs: wnt 2nd 4f out tl 3f out: sn struggling and lost pl: wl bhd fnl 2f* **16/1**

1m 16.39s (1.99) **Going Correction** +0.25s/f (Good) **7** Ran SP% **109.7**
Speed ratings (Par 91): **96,93,80,78,78 78,63**
Tote Swingers: 1&2 £1.10, 1&3 £11.20, 2&3 £8.30 CSF £2.77 TOTE £2.00: £1.50, £1.10; EX 3.30.
Owner Godolphin **Bred** Darley **Trained** Newmarket, Suffolk

FOCUS
Despite a dry night the going was given as soft (GoingStick 5.8), which was confirmed by the jockeys after the first. The wind was also strong across the course. The back straight and bend were dolled out 3m, adding 10m to 1m2f and 1m6f races. The betting was concentrated on the front two in the market in this maiden, and they fought out the finish well clear of the rest.

NOTEBOOK
Finoon(IRE), a daughter of Pivotal, wasn't best away, but she soon recovered and got a nice tow through the race. While her more experienced market rival hung under pressure, she kept a straight line, and in the end that was enough to see her finish on top at the finish. It was nice introduction and she should come on for this. (op 5-4 tchd 11-8)
Celtic Sixpence(IRE) had the benefit of a run under her belt and tried to make it tell under a positive ride. She didn't help her cause by hanging under pressure, though, and had she kept straight she would surely have given the winner more to do. Official explanation: jockey said filly hung left (op 6-4 tchd 11-8)
Icelady, a half-sister to multiple winning stayer Callisto Moon, shaped better than on her debut but a longer trip will no doubt suit her in time. (tchd 66-1)
Millies Dancer(IRE) is at least now eligible for a mark. (op 20-1)
Gainsboroughs Best(IRE) was perhaps a bit disappointing but his sire's stock generally prefer quick ground. (op 8-1)

5559 AVENUE PUB H'CAP (DIV I) 1m 3y
2:35 (2:36) (Class 6) (0-60,60) 3-Y-O+ £1,295 (£385; £192; £96) Stalls High

Form RPR

6050 **1** **Tilsworth Glenboy**[26] 4687 3-9-0 **55** StephenCraine 5 71
(J R Jenkins) *stdd s: hld up in rr: smooth hdwy to trck ldr on bit over 1f out: led ent fnl f: c clr on bit fnl f: hrd hld* **15/2**

2233 **2** *5* **Harting Hill**[25] 4700 5-9-10 **59** TomQueally 10 63
(M P Tregoning) *stdd s: hld up in tch in rr: hdwy over 2f out: rdn to ld and edgd lft over 1f out: hdd ent fnl f: no ch w wnr fnl f: plugged on* **4/1**[2]

4/00 **3** *3 1/4* **Broughtons Dream**[54] 3765 4-9-1 **50** TonyCulhane 6 46
(W J Musson) *in tch towards rr: rdn 1/2-way: chsd ldng pair and drvn wl over 1f out: wl btn jst over 1f out* **12/1**

000 **4** *3 3/4* **Boundless Applause**[23] 4790 4-8-10 **45** TomMcLaughlin 9 32
(I A Wood) *chsd ldr tl led wl over 2f out: rdn over 2f out: hdd over 1f out: sn wknd and wl btn fnl f* **50/1**

6000 **5** *2 1/4* **Beauchamp Wizard**[84] 2790 5-9-9 **58** HayleyTurner 8 40
(G A Butler) *t.k.h: led tl wl over 2f out: wknd u.p wl over 1f out: wl btn whn edgd rt ins fnl f* **16/1**

5054 **6** *13* **Zelos Spirit**[18] 4970 3-7-13 **45** SimonPearce(5) 3 —
(Rae Guest) *chsd ldrs: rdn over 2f out: wknd qckly wl over 1f out: sn wl bhd* **5/1**[3]

0000 **7** *3* **Chandrayaan**[23] 4791 3-8-5 **49** (v) NataliaGemelova(3) 11 —
(J E Long) *nvr gng wl and sn niggled along in rr: toiling bdly fr 1/2-way: t.o* **14/1**

-455 **8** *3* **Zinjbar (USA)**[41] 4212 3-9-5 **60** ChrisCatlin 2 —
(C E Brittain) *in tch: hdwy to chse ldrs 1/2-way: pushed up and wknd rapidly 2f out: wl bhd and eased ins fnl f: t.o* **7/1**

0651 **9** *1 1/4* **Cool Kitten (IRE)**[18] 4969 3-9-2 **57** (v) WilliamBuick 1 —
(W J Knight) *in tch in midfield: hdwy to chse ldrs 1/2-way: wknd qckly u.p wl over 1f out: wl bhd and eased ins fnl f: t.o* **9/4**[1]

20-0 **10** *28* **Gone'N'Dunnett (IRE)**[103] 2196 11-8-10 **45** NickyMackay 4 —
(Mrs C A Dunnett) *chsd ldrs: rdn and struggling 1/2-way: wl bhd and virtually p.u fnl 2f: t.o* **40/1**

1m 43.99s (3.39) **Going Correction** +0.25s/f (Good)
WFA 3 from 4yo+ 6lb **10** Ran SP% **116.3**
Speed ratings (Par 101): **93,88,84,81,78 65,62,59,58,30**
Tote Swingers: 1&2 £4.20, 1&3 £36.20, 2&3 £13.60 CSF £37.51 CT £360.54 TOTE £7.90: £1.90, £1.30, £7.10; EX 39.40 TRIFECTA Not won..
Owner M Ng **Bred** Michael Ng **Trained** Royston, Herts

FOCUS
An ordinary handicap.
Tilsworth Glenboy Official explanation: trainer said, regarding apparent improvement in form, that the gelding was better suited by the soft ground
Chandrayaan Official explanation: trainer said gelding was unsuited by the soft ground
Cool Kitten(IRE) Official explanation: trainer's rep said, regarding running, the the filly was unsuited by the soft ground

5560 AVENUE PUB H'CAP (DIV II) 1m 3y
3:10 (3:11) (Class 6) (0-60,60) 3-Y-O+ £1,295 (£385; £192; £96) Stalls High

Form RPR

4050 **1** **Exopuntia**[24] 4763 4-8-11 **46** TonyCulhane 4 55
(Miss J Feilden) *chsd ldr: rdn to ld 2f out: kpt on wl u.p ins fnl f: rdn out* **7/1**

5036 **2** *1 1/2* **Al Rayanah**[13] 5159 7-9-0 **49** (p) SaleemGolam 1 55
(G Prodromou) *s.i.s: in tch in rr: hdwy wl over 1f out: n.m.r over 1f out: sn chsng wnr: rdn and chal ins fnl f: no ex and btn fnl 100yds* **4/1**[3]

1500 **3** *2 1/4* **Hi Spec (IRE)**[157] 984 7-9-0 **49** (p) AdamKirby 10 49
(Miss M E Rowland) *stdd s: hld up in last trio: hdwy over 2f out: rdn to chse wnr briefly over 1f out: edgd rt and wknd u.p ins fnl f* **14/1**

-024 **4** *1 1/2* **Hellenio**[13] 5159 3-9-1 **56** (t) AndreaAtzeni 7 52
(M G Quinlan) *chsd ldrs: pushed along and lost pl over 3f out: rdn and keeping on whn n.m.r over 1f out: no prog and btn ins fnl f* **9/4**[1]

0-00 **5** *1 1/2* **Pont De Nuit**[34] 4439 3-9-5 **60** (b[1]) PaulMulrennan 2 52
(A B Haynes) *in tch: hdwy to chse ldrs over 3f out: wknd u.p over jst over 1f out* **8/1**

1-40 **6** *hd* **Final Drive (IRE)**[121] 1653 4-9-10 **59** TomQueally 5 52
(J Ryan) *hld up in tch towards rr: hdwy and pushed along 3f out: chsd ldrs and drvn 2f out: wknd jst over 1f out* **7/2**[2]

00-0 **7** *2 1/4* **Toballa**[18] 4969 5-8-5 **45** (t) SimonPearce(5) 8 33
(H J Collingridge) *restless in stalls: chsd ldrs tl lost pl qckly over 3f out: bhd fnl 2f* **16/1**

056/ **8** *6* **Jack Jicaro**[746] 4986 4-8-10 **45** KirstyMilczarek 9 19
(N J Vaughan) *t.k.h: led tl 2f out: wknd qckly over 1f out: wl bhd and eased ins fnl f* **16/1**

1m 44.34s (3.74) **Going Correction** +0.25s/f (Good)
WFA 3 from 4yo+ 6lb **8** Ran SP% **115.0**
Speed ratings (Par 101): **91,89,87,85,84 84,81,75**
Tote Swingers: 1&2 £4.20, 1&3 £16.10, 2&3 £8.90 CSF £35.31 CT £387.92 TOTE £11.10: £3.40, £2.80, £2.60; EX 41.10 TRIFECTA Not won..
Owner John W Ford **Bred** J W Ford **Trained** Exning, Suffolk
■ Stewards' Enquiry : Andrea Atzeni caution: used whip down shoulder in the forehand.

FOCUS
The slower of the two divisions by 0.35sec.
Toballa Official explanation: trainer said mare had a breathing problem

5561 NORWICH EVENING NEWS H'CAP 7f 3y
3:45 (3:47) (Class 4) (0-80,79) 3-Y-O+ £3,532 (£1,057; £528; £264; £131) Stalls High

Form RPR

4044 **1** **Rosedale**[24] 4735 3-8-9 **62** TedDurcan 7 73
(J A R Toller) *hld up in tch towards rr: hdwy and rdn ent fnl 2f: chsd ldr over 1f out: ev ch 1f out: led fnl 75yds: r.o wl* **8/1**

4633 **2** *1* **Fantasy Gladiator**[20] 4894 4-9-7 **69** AdamKirby 4 79
(R M H Cowell) *sn pushed along towards rr: hdwy to chse ldrs 1/2-way: rdn to ld 2f out: hung rt u.p over 1f out: hrd pressed 1f out: hdd fnl 75yds: sn btn* **7/4**[1]

1463 **3** *6* **Rough Rock (IRE)**[18] 4968 5-9-4 **66** WilliamCarson 1 60
(C A Dwyer) *hld up in tch towards rr: rdn and effrt 2f out: outpcd and no ch w ldng pair jst over 1f out: kpt on to go modest 3rd wl ins fnl f* **9/1**

6135 **4** 1 **Cativo Cavallino**[19] 4929 7-8-11 **62**........................ NataliaGemelova(3) 5 53
(J E Long) *chsd ldrs: rdn 3f out: 3rd and wknd jst over 1f out: no ch w ldng pair fnl f: lost 3rd wl ins fnl f* **14/1**

1016 **5** 2½ **Aviso (GER)**[16] 5050 6-9-10 **72**........................ TomQueally 9 56
(B J Curley) *chsd ldr tl over 2f out: wknd over 1f out: wl btn fnl f* **5/1**[2]

0-00 **6** 3½ **Zebrano**[45] 4065 4-9-12 **74**........................(b[1]) PaulMulrennan 8 49
(A B Haynes) *led tl hdd and rdn 2f out: wknd over 1f out: tired ins fnl f* **25/1**

3561 **7** 4½ **Perfect Ch'I (IRE)**[13] 5163 3-9-5 **72**........................ TomMcLaughlin 6 33
(I A Wood) *chsd ldrs towards far side: rdn 3f out: sn struggling: wl btn over 1f out* **7/1**[3]

0002 **8** 1¾ **Fardyieh**[11] 5205 3-9-0 **67**........................(t) ChrisCatlin 3 23
(C E Brittain) *short of room sn after s: a in rr: rdn and struggling 1/2-way: wl bhd fnl 2f* **16/1**

6135 **9** 2½ **Scarcity (IRE)**[59] 3592 3-8-13 **66**........................ HayleyTurner 10 15
(E A L Dunlop) *hld up in tch: rdn and struggling 3f out: sn wknd and bhd fnl 2f* **8/1**

1m 27.37s (0.77) **Going Correction** +0.25s/f (Good)
WFA 3 from 4yo+ 5lb **9** Ran SP% **114.1**
Speed ratings (Par 105): **105,103,97,95,93 89,83,81,79**
Tote Swingers: 1&2 £6.40, 1&3 £19.50, 2&3 £2.40 CSF £22.11 CT £131.08 TOTE £8.50: £2.50, £1.10, £3.50; EX 27.10 Trifecta £164.00 Pool: £283.70 - 1.28 winning units..
Owner Alan Gibson **Bred** Alan Gibson **Trained** Newmarket, Suffolk

FOCUS
A fairly competitive handicap on paper, but the first two came well clear.
Fardyieh Official explanation: jockey said filly suffered interference in running shortly after start
Scarcity(IRE) Official explanation: trainer's rep had no explanation for the poor form shown

5562 GREAT YARMOUTH MERCURY H'CAP 5f 43y
4:20 (4:21) (Class 5) (0-70,71) 3-Y-O+ £2,072 (£616; £308; £153) Stalls High

Form RPR

2425 **1** **Wreningham**[27] 4659 5-9-3 **60**........................ WilliamCarson 6 66
(S C Williams) *led: rdn wl over 1f out: hdd ins fnl f: hrd drvn and rallied gamely fnl 100yds to ld again on post* **11/4**[1]

6060 **2** nse **Guto**[75] 3064 7-9-0 **57**........................ TravisBlock 1 63
(W J H Ratcliffe) *chsd wnr: rdn and ev ch over 1f out: drvn to ld ins fnl f: hdd on post* **9/1**

0243 **3** nk **Caramelita**[22] 4833 3-9-8 **67**........................ WilliamBuick 8 72
(J R Jenkins) *stdd after s: hld up in tch: rdn and unable qck ent 2f out: hdwy u.p ins fnl f: r.o wl: nt quite rch ldng pair* **5/1**[2]

0651 **4** 1¼ **Danzoe (IRE)**[6] 5368 3-9-12 **71** 6ex........................ TomMcLaughlin 3 71
(Mrs C A Dunnett) *in tch: rdn 1/2-way: hdwy and chsd ldng pair u.p over 1f out: no ex fnl 100yds* **15/2**[3]

013 **5** 2 **Imaginary Diva**[6] 5377 4-8-10 **53**........................ TomQueally 2 46
(G G Margarson) *stdd s: hld up in tch: hdwy to chse ldrs and rdn 2f out: btn over 1f out: wknd fnl f* **11/4**[1]

-110 **6** ½ **Replicator**[130] 1482 5-9-6 **66**........................(e) AshleyHamblett(3) 4 57
(P L Gilligan) *t.k.h: chsd ldrs tl rdn and btn over 1f out: wknd fnl f* **11/1**

0560 **7** 3 **Izzi Mill (USA)**[163] 937 4-8-11 **54**........................ TonyCulhane 5 34
(P W D'Arcy) *hld up in tch in rr: rdn and no rspnse 2f out: wl btn ent fnl f* **15/2**[3]

64.61 secs (1.91) **Going Correction** +0.25s/f (Good)
WFA 3 from 4yo+ 2lb **7** Ran SP% **111.9**
Speed ratings (Par 103): **94,93,93,91,88 87,82**
Tote Swingers: 1&2 £6.00, 1&3 £2.60, 2&3 £7.10 CSF £27.08 CT £114.73 TOTE £3.00: £1.10, £6.70; EX 35.10 Trifecta £129.40 Part won. Pool: £174.91 - 0.10 winning units..
Owner Mervyn Ayers **Bred** Executive Bloodlines Ltd **Trained** Newmarket, Suffolk

FOCUS
A tight little sprint handicap.
Izzi Mill(USA) Official explanation: jockey said filly hung right

5563 EAST COAST TRUCKERS CHARITY CONVOY H'CAP 1m 2f 21y
4:55 (4:56) (Class 5) (0-75,74) 3-Y-O+ £2,072 (£616; £308; £153) Stalls Low

Form RPR

2041 **1** **Librettista (AUS)**[12] 5172 4-9-12 **72**........................ KirstyMilczarek 6 80
(L M Cumani) *chsd ldrs: rdn over 2f out: ev ch and drvn wl over 1f out: led ent fnl f: kpt on wl fnl 100yds* **4/1**[3]

-401 **2** ½ **Starkat**[24] 4752 4-10-0 **74**........................ WilliamBuick 7 81
(Jane Chapple-Hyam) *stdd s: hld up in last trio: hdwy on outer over 3f out: rdn over 2f out: ev ch ent fnl f: edgd rt and sltly outpcd ins fnl f: rallied u.p to go 2nd nr fin* **3/1**[2]

500 **3** hd **Dream Of Olwyn (IRE)**[30] 4546 5-9-5 **65**........................ PaulMulrennan 3 72
(J G Given) *sn chsng ldr: rdn to ld 2f out: drvn and hdd ent fnl f: kpt on same pce fnl 100yds: lost 2nd nr fin* **20/1**

0503 **4** 1¾ **Top Tigress**[24] 4764 3-8-4 **58**........................ NickyMackay 1 61
(Sir Michael Stoute) *t.k.h early: chsd ldrs: rdn and unable qck 3f out: styng on and clsng whn nt clr run 1f out: sn swtchd rt and drvn: no imp after* **7/1**

-510 **5** 2 **Knotgarden (IRE)**[23] 4804 4-9-5 **70**........................ SimonPearce(5) 8 69
(J R Fanshawe) *stdd s: hld up in last: hdwy on outer over 3f out: rdn and pressed ldrs 2f out: wknd jst ins fnl f* **16/1**

4055 **6** 2 **Tiger Star**[9] 5259 3-9-3 **71**........................ HayleyTurner 2 66
(J M P Eustace) *led: hdd and rdn 2f out: wknd ent fnl f* **2/1**[1]

1105 **7** 19 **Agapanthus (GER)**[23] 4804 5-10-0 **74**........................ TomQueally 5 31
(B J Curley) *dwlt: in tch towards rr: rdn over 3f out: lost tch wl over 1f out: eased ins fnl f* **13/2**

2m 17.11s (6.61) **Going Correction** +0.55s/f (Yiel)
WFA 3 from 4yo+ 8lb **7** Ran SP% **114.8**
Speed ratings (Par 103): **95,94,94,93,91 89,74**
Tote Swingers: 1&2 £7.50, 2&3 £8.60 CSF £16.56 CT £210.75 TOTE £4.60: £2.80, £1.90; EX 13.60 Trifecta £181.00 Pool: £300.91 - 1.23 winning units..
Owner S Stuckey **Bred** Darley Australia Pty Ltd **Trained** Newmarket, Suffolk

FOCUS
There were one or two interesting, lightly raced types here.

5564 AVENUE PUB & RESTAURANT H'CAP 1m 6f 17y
5:30 (5:31) (Class 6) (0-60,59) 3-Y-O+ £1,554 (£462; £231; £115) Stalls High

Form RPR

0401 **1** **Fuzzypeg (IRE)**[24] 4765 3-8-7 **52**........................ WilliamBuick 4 64
(J R Fanshawe) *hld up towards rr: hdwy 5f out: rdn to chse ldng pair 4f out: led 2f out: kpt on u.p fnl f: drvn out* **4/1**[2]

0003 **2** 1½ **Marcus Antonius**[18] 4972 3-8-2 **47**........................ NickyMackay 14 57
(J R Boyle) *dwlt: sn pushed along and hld up in tch after 1f: hdwy to chse ldr 4f out: rdn 3f out: drvn and ev ch 2f out: chsd wnr after and styd on same pce fnl f* **12/1**

0060 **3** 4½ **Sparkaway**[24] 4765 4-9-5 **52**........................ TonyCulhane 11 56
(W J Musson) *hld up towards rr: rdn and hdwy over 4f out: 6th and no ch 2f out: plugged on to go 3rd ins fnl f: nvr trbld ldrs* **13/2**

1102 **4** 1 **Mediterranean Sea (IRE)**[26] 4683 4-9-10 **57**........................ StephenCraine 7 59+
(J R Jenkins) *hld up in last pair early: hdwy 10f out: chsd ldr over 5f out tl led wl over 4f out: drvn and hdd 2f out: btn over 1f out: wknd and lost 3rd ins fnl f* **12/1**

1453 **5** 2 **Uncle Keef (IRE)**[12] 5179 4-9-12 **59**........................(b) AdamKirby 9 58
(M P Tregoning) *bhd and rdn along early: hdwy u.p to chse ldng trio 4f out: drvn and no imp over 2f out: wl btn over 1f out* **9/4**[1]

5364 **6** 3¾ **Free Falling**[12] 5179 4-8-7 **45**........................(b) DeclanCannon(5) 1 39
(Miss Gay Kelleway) *chsd ldrs: short of room jst over 4f out: sn outpcd: swtchd rt and rdn: no prog and wl btn fnl 3f* **14/1**

4540 **7** 24 **What A Day**[17] 4980 4-8-12 **45**........................ TomQueally 12 —
(J J Quinn) *racd in midfield: rdn struggling 4f out: sn wl btn: t.o fnl 2f* **9/2**[3]

00-6 **8** 6 **Hippodrome (IRE)**[8] 2786 8-8-13 **46**........................(p) PaulMulrennan 5 —
(John A Harris) *a towards rr: struggling and lost tch over 4f out: t.o fr wl over 2f out* **50/1**

4320 **9** 3 **Davana**[138] 1283 4-8-12 **45**........................ TravisBlock 15 —
(W J H Ratcliffe) *chsd ldr tl over 5f out: rdn and swtchd rt over 4f out: sn wl btn: t.o fnl 2f* **33/1**

0 **10** 6 **River Danube**[24] 4765 7-8-12 **45**........................(b) MickyFenton 6 —
(T J Fitzgerald) *in tch: rdn and losing pl over 6f out: wl bhd over 4f out: t.o fnl 3f* **33/1**

4630 **11** 2¼ **Laura Land**[8] 5289 4-8-12 **45**........................ TomMcLaughlin 3 —
(W M Brisbourne) *led tl rdn and hdd wl over 4f out: sn dropped out: t.o fnl 3f* **33/1**

0002 **12** 20 **Chateauneuf (IRE)**[11] 5202 4-8-12 **45**........................ ChrisCatlin 8 —
(W M Brisbourne) *hld up in last pair: lost tch 5f out: wl t.o fnl 3f* **20/1**

3m 14.75s (7.15) **Going Correction** +0.55s/f (Yiel)
WFA 3 from 4yo+ 12lb **12** Ran SP% **119.9**
Speed ratings (Par 101): **101,100,97,97,95 93,80,76,74,71 70,58**
Tote Swingers: 1&2 £8.10, 1&3 £6.80, 2&3 £17.40 CSF £48.58 CT £311.96 TOTE £4.10: £1.90, £3.50, £2.50; EX 45.70 Trifecta £167.10 Part won. Pool: £225.90 - 0.41 winning units..
Owner Lord Halifax **Bred** Lord Halifax **Trained** Newmarket, Suffolk

FOCUS
Most of these looked pretty exposed.

5565 COASTAL LIFE MAGAZINE APPRENTICE H'CAP 1m 2f 21y
6:00 (6:00) (Class 6) (0-60,58) 4-Y-O+ £1,554 (£462; £231; £115) Stalls Low

Form RPR

/6-6 **1** **Ptolomeos**[16] 5051 7-8-11 **55**........................ LucyBarry(5) 3 60
(S Regan) *chsd ldr tl led over 3f out: rdn and clr over 1f out: racd awkwardly but in command fnl f: rdn out* **8/1**

0506 **2** 4 **Gheed (IRE)**[24] 4763 5-8-9 **53**........................(tp) MatthewCosham(5) 7 50
(K A Morgan) *s.i.s: bhd: pushed along and hdwy on outer 3f out: chsd wnr 2f out: sn unable qck and btn over 1f out: kpt on same pce fnl f* **11/2**[3]

0-60 **3** nk **Renege The Joker**[25] 4715 7-8-1 **45**........................ NoelGarbutt(5) 6 41
(S Regan) *stdd s: hld up in last pair: rdn and hdwy on inner 3f out: disp 2nd fr 2f out: sn no imp on wnr and one pce fnl f* **50/1**

0-00 **4** 3 **Kings On The Roof**[40] 4234 4-8-3 **45**........................ SophieSilvester(3) 4 35
(P Leech) *chsd ldrs: pushed along and effrt over 2f out: btn over 1f out: wknd ins fnl f* **18/1**

2554 **5** shd **Folio (IRE)**[21] 4873 10-9-2 **58**........................ JamesRogers(3) 1 48
(W J Musson) *in tch: lost pl and dropped to rr ent fnl 2f: pushed along and no prog fr over 1f out* **10/11**[1]

0000 **6** 5 **Sensible**[13] 5164 5-8-6 **45**........................ CharlesEddery 2 25
(H J Collingridge) *chsd ldrs: rdn and pushed rt 3f out: wknd 2f out: wl btn 1f out* **11/1**

106- **7** 11 **Credential**[383] 4880 8-8-12 **51**........................ JohnCavanagh 5 9
(John A Harris) *led tl hdd and rdn over 3f out: sn edgd rt u.p: wknd and bhd fnl 2f* **4/1**[2]

2m 19.02s (8.52) **Going Correction** +0.55s/f (Yiel) **7** Ran SP% **114.4**
Speed ratings (Par 101): **87,83,83,81,81 77,68**
Tote Swingers: 1&2 £4.90, 1&3 £16.60, 2&3 £27.20. totesuper7: Win: Not won, Place: £231 CSF £50.68 TOTE £9.80: £3.80, £2.60; EX 43.20 Place 6: £87.73 Place 5: £79.83.
Owner Mrs Connie Taylor **Bred** G Prodromou **Trained** Snetterton, Norfolk

FOCUS
A weak race.
Folio(IRE) Official explanation: jockey said gelding found nothing off the bridle
Credential Official explanation: jockey said gelding hung right
T/Plt: £60.40 to a £1 stake. Pool:£56,095.20 - 646.93 winning tickets T/Qpdt: £22.40 to a £1 stake. Pool:£4,838.58 - 159.75 winning tickets SP

5312 CURRAGH (R-H)
Sunday, August 29

OFFICIAL GOING: Round course - good to firm; straight course - good (good to firm places)

5567a GO AND GO ROUND TOWER STKS (GROUP 3) 6f
2:45 (2:45) 2-Y-O £34,513 (£10,088; £4,778; £1,592)

RPR

1 **Dingle View (IRE)**[11] 5226 2-8-12........................ CathyGannon 2 106
(P D Evans) *led: rdn and strly pressed fr 2f out: narrowly hdd ins fnl f: rallied u.p to regain ld cl home* **22/1**

2 hd **Glor Na Mara (IRE)**[8] 5316 2-9-1 113........................ KJManning 8 108
(J S Bolger, Ire) *trckd ldrs on outer: 5th early: tk clsr order in 3rd 2f out: 2nd and rdn to chal 1f out: sn led narrowly: kpt on u.p: hdd cl home* **4/5**[1]

3 2 **Big Issue (IRE)**[18] 4954 2-9-1........................ RichardHughes 3 102
(R Hannon) *cl up in 2nd: rdn to chal fr 2f out: 3rd 1f out: sn no ex: kpt on same pce* **11/4**[2]

4 1¼ **Emperor Hadrian (IRE)**[21] 4880 2-9-1 99........................(b) JMurtagh 5 98
(A P O'Brien, Ire) *hld up in 7th: kpt on wout threatening fr over 1f out* **12/1**

5 shd **Moonlit Garden (IRE)**[8] 5313 2-8-12 99........................(b) PJSmullen 4 95
(D K Weld, Ire) *trckd ldrs: 6th 1/2-way: impr into cl 4th and effrt 1 1/2f out: no imp fnl f* **12/1**

6 ½ **Sydney Harbour (IRE)**[59] 3645 2-9-1 90........................(b[1]) WMLordan 6 96
(David Wachman, Ire) *hld up towards rr: no imp fr 2f out* **25/1**

7 hd **Oor Jock (IRE)**[63] 3488 2-9-1 98........................ PShanahan 1 96
(D K Weld, Ire) *prom: 3rd 1/2-way: dropped to 5th 2f out: sn no ex* **16/1**

8 1 **Queen Of Spain (IRE)**[10] 5246 2-8-12........................ JAHeffernan 9 90
(A P O'Brien, Ire) *a towards rr* **16/1**

9 *9* **Fred Archer (IRE)**[17] 5013 2-9-1 .... CO'Donoghue 7 66+
(David Marnane, Ire) *trckd ldrs in 4th: wknd 2f out: sn trailing and eased* **7/1**[3]

1m 12.89s (-2.11) **Going Correction** -0.45s/f (Firm) **9** Ran SP% **130.1**
Speed ratings: **96,95,93,91,91 90,90,89,77**
CSF £45.49 TOTE £14.30: £2.50, £1.10, £1.60; DF 61.90.
Owner Mrs I M Folkes **Bred** Robert Berns **Trained** Pandy, Monmouths
■ Cathy Gannon's first Group winner.

FOCUS
This result willl, no doubt, raise question marks about the form of the better Irish juveniles, but it would be rash to read too much into Glor Na Mara's defeat on that score.

NOTEBOOK
Dingle View(IRE), a three-time winner over 5f, was stepping up to this trip for the first time having run third in a Listed event at Deauville on her previou start. She broke smartly and made all, digging deep and keeping on gamely when hard pressed from over a furlong out. (op 20/1)
Glor Na Mara(IRE) was clearly the form pick here having finished second to Zoffany at Group 1 level over this course and trip before filling the same position behind Pathfork in a 7f Group 2 here eight days previously. However, he was upstaged and beaten fair and square. He kept on but was always being held by the winner. (op 4/5 tchd 9/10)
Big Issue(IRE) was in the front rank all the way. Second under pressure over a furlong out, he was unable to raise his game thereafter. (op 11/4 tchd 10/3)
Emperor Hadrian(IRE) was having his eighth start. Well exposed over different distances, he never got into serious contenion although he did stay on in the closing stages. (op 10/1 tchd 14/1)
Moonlit Garden(IRE), a C&D winner of a maiden in May, has maintained a consistent level of form, without adding to her tally, since. Back up in trip here after a couple of runs over 5f, she was held up before arriving with her effort on the stands' side rail 1½f out. She kept on for pressure.
Fred Archer(IRE) Official explanation: jockey said colt lost its action and was eased

5568a DANCE DESIGN STKS (GROUP 3) (F&M) 1m 1f
3:15 (3:16) 3-Y-0+ **£40,265** (£11,769; £5,575; £1,858)

RPR

1 **Obama Rule (IRE)**[43] 4163 3-8-12 .... DPMcDonogh 7 100+
(Ms Joanna Morgan, Ire) *hld up towards rr: 11th into st: hdwy on inner 2f out: 4th 1f out: sn chal: qckn to ld 100yds out: r.o wl* **16/1**
2 *1* **Shareen (IRE)**[18] 4977 3-8-12 95.................................... NGMcCullagh 13 97
(John M Oxx, Ire) *attempted to make all: rdn and strly pressed fr under 2f out: hdd 100yds out: kpt on u.p* **13/2**
3 *hd* **Miss Laa Di Da**[42] 4177 3-8-12 100.........................(t) RichardHughes 12 97
(Noel Meade, Ire) *trckd ldrs in 4th: 3rd early st: 2nd and chal fr under 2f out: bmpd sltly ins fnl f: kpt on* **16/1**
4 *2* **Lush Lashes**[428] 3412 5-9-5 110..(t) KJManning 4 92
(J S Bolger, Ire) *mid-div on outer: 8th 1/2-way: prog 2f out: edgd rt 1 1/2f out: kpt on same pce fr over 1f out* **7/2**[1]
5 *¾* **Harriers Call (IRE)**[42] 4177 5-9-5 96.. WJLee 11 91
(J C Hayden, Ire) *hld up: prog early st: 7th and effrt 2f out: checked briefly over 1f out: kpt on* **20/1**
6 *hd* **Barbadine (USA)**[18] 4977 3-8-12 91.................................... WMLordan 8 91
(David Wachman, Ire) *mid-div: 7th 1/2-way: kpt on same pce fr under 2f out* **25/1**
7 *nk* **Rose Hip (IRE)**[18] 4977 6-9-5 101.. CDHayes 9 90
(Joseph G Murphy, Ire) *mid-div: 6th 1/2-way: effrt whn short of room 1 1/2f out: one pce ins fnl f* **16/1**
8 *1* **Mid Mon Lady (IRE)**[14] 5130 5-9-5 99.........................(b) KierenFallon 1 88+
(H Rogers, Ire) *hld up in rr: rdn and one pce st* **12/1**
9 *1* **Romie's Kastett (GER)**[51] 3884 3-8-12 .... FMBerry 10 88
(John M Oxx, Ire) *chsd ldr in 2nd: rdn early st: 3rd under 2f out: sn no ex and wknd* **7/1**
10 *½* **Barring Decree (IRE)**[18] 4977 5-9-5 100............................... KLatham 5 85
(F Dunne, Ire) *trckd ldrs in 5th: rdn and wknd fr over 2f out* **8/1**
11 *3* **You'll Be Mine (USA)**[154] 1036 3-8-12 105.......................... JMurtagh 6 79
(A P O'Brien, Ire) *hld up towards rr: no imp st* **9/2**[2]
12 *nk* **Enchanted Evening (IRE)**[99] 2355 4-9-5 99..................... PJSmullen 3 78
(D K Weld, Ire) *trckd ldrs in 3rd: 4th and rdn early st: wknd under 2f out: eased ins fnl f* **11/2**[3]

1m 56.09s (1.19) **Going Correction** +0.025s/f (Good)
WFA 3 from 4yo+ 7lb **12** Ran SP% **126.7**
Speed ratings: **95,94,93,92,91 91,91,90,89,89 86,86**
CSF £124.49 TOTE £26.10: £3.50, £2.70, £5.60; DF 205.20.
Owner Noel O'Callaghan **Bred** Sweetenham Stud **Trained** Ballivor, Co Meath

FOCUS
The fifth and seventh have been rated to their previous form, with the runner-up, third and sixth all to small personal bests.

NOTEBOOK
Obama Rule(IRE) ◆ did well to win here, on a few scores. She was the only maiden in the line-up and had raced only twice previously, and she had to come from the back of the field having had only one rival behind her into the straight. She began her run on the inside 2f out and ran on well before being switched to challenge between the second and third to lead well inside the final furlong. (op 14/1)
Shareen(IRE), a three-time winner and running in her first Group 3, made the running and, after being driven along early in the straight, kept on well, only giving best well inside the final furlong. On this evidence, going back up in trip will suit. (op 7/1)
Miss Laa Di Da ran her best race since finishing fourth in the Athasi Stakes here in May. Always close up, she went second well over a furlong out and soon had every chance. She appeared to be slightly hampered when the winner came through between her and the runner-up inside the final furlong.
Lush Lashes was returning to the track for the first time since June of last year having failed to hold on to a foal after being covered by Sea The Stars this year. She escaped any penalty here and, while failing to produce anything near her best form, it was a satisfactory run in view of her long absence. Held up in mid-division, she made headway on the outside in the straight before edging right 1½f out. She could make little impression thereafter but kept on. (op 9/4)
Harriers Call(IRE) began to make headway 2f out and did not have the clearest of runs approaching the final furlong before staying on in the closing stages.
Rose Hip(IRE) was under pressure and scrapping to get into contention for a possible first-four placing when she got squeezed between Lush Lashes and Enchanted Evening 1½f out.

5569a GOFFS FLYING FIVE STKS (GROUP 3) 5f
3:45 (3:50) 3-Y-0+ **£36,238** (£10,592; £5,017; £1,672)

RPR

1 **Astrophysical Jet**[31] 4505 3-8-12 .... GrahamGibbons 2 114
(E S McMahon) *mid-div on stand's side: hdwy 1 1/2f out: led under 1f out: r.o strly: comf* **9/2**[2]
2 *2* **Tax Free (IRE)**[24] 4773 8-9-3 .... AdrianNicholls 11 110
(D Nicholls) *hld up in tch: prog on outer 2f out: rdn to dispute ld briefly 1f out: 2nd and kpt on last 100yds* **10/1**
3 *hd* **Santo Padre (IRE)**[23] 4808 6-9-3 105.......................... CO'Donoghue 15 109
(David Marnane, Ire) *settled towards rr: prog on wd outside under 2f out: 4th 1f out: kpt on u.p* **14/1**
4 *nk* **Hamish McGonagall**[12] 5183 5-9-3 .... DAllen 13 108
(T D Easterby) *trckd ldrs: 6th 1/2-way: swtchd rt over 1f out: r.o wl cl home* **10/1**
5 *hd* **Triple Aspect (IRE)**[31] 4505 4-9-6 .... LiamJones 4 110
(W J Haggas) *hld up towards rr: last and rdn over 1f out: r.o strly last 100yds* **7/2**[1]
6 *¾* **Invincible Ash (IRE)**[23] 4808 5-9-0 104............................(p) GFCarroll 3 102
(M Halford, Ire) *prom on stand's rail: rdn to dispute ld 1 1/2f out: hdd under 1f out: kpt on same pce* **10/1**
7 *shd* **Moorhouse Lad**[31] 4505 7-9-3 .... TomEaves 8 104
(B Smart) *disp ld: rdn 1 1/2f out: hdd 1f out: no ex* **25/1**
8 *hd* **Judge 'n Jury**[8] 5308 6-9-3 .... CDHayes 1 104
(R A Harris) *cl up and disp ld: hdd & wknd fr over 1f out* **16/1**
9 *½* **Miss Gorica (IRE)**[3] 5461 6-9-0 100...........................(p) WMLordan 10 99
(Ms Joanna Morgan, Ire) *prom: 3rd 1/2-way: rdn under 2f out: no imp whn sltly hmpd over 1f out: no ex* **25/1**
10 *nk* **Rain Delayed (IRE)**[21] 4882 4-9-3 108...........................(b[1]) KLatham 7 101
(G M Lyons, Ire) *hld up in tch: effrt over 1 1/2f out: no imp: one pce* **20/1**
11 *hd* **Benbaun (IRE)**[63] 3486 9-9-3 ....(b) PJSmullen 16 100
(K A Ryan) *prom on outer: 3rd and chal 2f out: wknd fr over 1f out* **12/1**
12 *1* **Tropical Treat**[31] 4505 3-8-12 .... JimCrowley 5 94
(R M Beckett) *hld up: no imp fr under 2f out* **8/1**
13 *1 ¾* **Blue Jack**[50] 3895 5-9-3 ....(b) RichardKingscote 9 90
(Tom Dascombe) *nvr a factor* **7/1**[3]
14 *2 ½* **Reverence**[50] 3895 9-9-3 .... PShanahan 6 81
(E J Alston) *nvr a factor: eased fnl f* **25/1**
15 *4* **Glamorous Spirit (IRE)**[31] 4505 4-9-3 .... KierenFallon 12 67
(R A Harris) *cl up and disp ld: hdd & wknd fr 1 1/2f out: eased ins fnl f* **18/1**

58.56 secs (-3.94) **Going Correction** -0.45s/f (Firm)
WFA 3 from 4yo+ 2lb **15** Ran SP% **133.1**
Speed ratings: **113,109,109,109,108 107,107,107,106,105 105,103,101,97,90**
CSF £51.99 TOTE £4.90: £1.90, £2.90, £4.70; DF 63.90.
Owner Ladas **Bred** Grangecon Stud **Trained** Lichfield, Staffs
■ Stewards' Enquiry : Adrian Nicholls one-day ban: careless riding (Sep 12)

FOCUS
The in-form winner and third have been rated as running career bests, with the form rated through the sixth and eighth.

NOTEBOOK
Astrophysical Jet, third in a Group 2 at Goodwood on her previous start when she was repeatedly switched left and ended up near the stands' side rail, got on the Pattern race scoreboard here with an easy win. Soon tracking the leaders, she got an opening about 1½f out and hit the front early in the final furlong before quickening clear. According to trainer Ed McMahon, the winner will not race again this year and will have the Palace House Stakes as an early-season target next term. (op 4/1)
Tax Free(IRE) was bidding for win number 15 of his career. Soon close up towards the middle of the track, he began his effort under 2f out and soon had every chance before being unable to match the winner in the closing stages. His rider picked up a one-day careless riding ban after a stewards' inquiry into an incident with Moorhouse Lad, who finished seventh, inside the final furlong. (op 8/1)
Santo Padre(IRE) had run second to Invincible Ash, a rival again here, in a Listed event over this trip at Tipperary on his previous start. Done no favours by his high draw, he began his run from behind out wide 2f out and finished well. (op 12/1)
Hamish McGonagall, the winner of six handicaps, was raised to a mark of 109 following his most recent succes at York 12 days previously. He chased the leaders and, after being switched right over a furlong out, ran on well and was probably unlucky not to finish a place or two closer. (op 8/1)
Triple Aspect(IRE) unseated his rider due to a slipped saddle in the race Astrophysical Jet contested at Goodwood last time. A dual winner at this level and also in Listed company, he raced in rear and was still at the back of the field approaching the final furlong before finishing strongly. (op 5/1)
Benbaun(IRE), a course specialist whose seven wins at the track include three consecutive runnings of this event between 2005 and 2007, looked up against it from his high draw and, after racing close up, was done with well over a furlong out. (op 12/1 tchd 14/1)
Glamorous Spirit(IRE) Official explanation: jockey said filly was eased after shortening stride

5570a MOYGLARE STUD STKS (GROUP 1) (FILLIES) 7f
4:15 (4:18) 2-Y-0
£120,619 (£39,513; £18,716; £6,238; £4,159; £2,079)

RPR

1 **Misty For Me (IRE)**[21] 4879 2-8-12 109........................... JAHeffernan 8 113
(A P O'Brien, Ire) *mde all: rdn and strly pressed fr 1 1/2f out: styd on wl ins fnl f* **10/1**
2 *1* **Laughing Lashes (USA)**[21] 4879 2-8-12 111......................... FMBerry 2 110
(Mrs John Harrington, Ire) *sn trckd ldr in 2nd: chal fr under 2f out: no imp ins fnl f: kpt on u.p* **7/2**[2]
3 *nk* **Kissable (IRE)**[45] 4077 2-8-12 .... CDHayes 12 109
(Kevin Prendergast, Ire) *trckd ldrs: 4th fr 1/2-way: rdn and no imp fr under 2f out tl r.o wl last 100yds* **12/1**
4 *½* **Together (IRE)**[21] 4879 2-8-12 106...................................... JMurtagh 10 108
(A P O'Brien, Ire) *sn trckd ldrs in 3rd: rdn fr 2f out: kpt on same pce fr over 1f out* **4/1**[3]
5 *5* **Wild Wind (GER)**[64] 3465 2-8-12 .... CO'Donoghue 4 96+
(A P O'Brien, Ire) *hld up: 7th and prog under 3f out: mod 5th fr 2f out: one pce* **10/1**
6 *½* **Memory (IRE)**[53] 3792 2-8-12 .... RichardHughes 1 94+
(R Hannon) *hld up towards rr: 7th and sme prog over 2f out: mod 6th and no imp fr over 1f out* **1/1**[1]
7 *1 ¾* **Why (IRE)**[17] 5012 2-8-12 .... JPO'Brien 6 90
(A P O'Brien, Ire) *chsd ldrs: 6th over 2f out: sn rdn and no imp: one pce* **28/1**
8 *2 ½* **Gatamalata (IRE)**[21] 4879 2-8-12 96.................................... WMLordan 3 84+
(Joseph G Murphy, Ire) *hld up towards rr: kpt on one pce fr over 2f out* **33/1**
9 *½* **Negotiate**[17] 5012 2-8-12 .... PJSmullen 5 82
(Andrew Oliver, Ire) *mid-div: no imp fr over 2f out* **66/1**
10 *3* **Palinode (USA)**[45] 4077 2-8-12 93...................................... KJManning 9 75+
(J S Bolger, Ire) *in rr of mid-div on inner: rdn and no imp fr 2 1/2f out* **25/1**
11 *9* **Mrs Happy (IRE)**[109] 2035 2-8-12 ....(t) PShanahan 7 52
(Tracey Collins, Ire) *mid-div on outer: wknd fr 2 1/2f out* **66/1**
12 *1 ¾* **Light Footsteps (IRE)**[64] 3465 2-8-12 .... KierenFallon 11 48
(Eoin Griffin, Ire) *2nd early: 5th and rdn 1/2-way: sn wknd* **33/1**

1m 24.56s (-6.24) **Going Correction** -0.60s/f (Hard) **12** Ran SP% **134.3**
Speed ratings: **111,109,109,108,103 102,100,97,97,93 83,81**
CSF £49.13 TOTE £10.40: £2.80, £1.20, £6.50; DF 38.20.

The Form Book, Raceform Ltd, Compton, RG20 6NL

Owner Michael Tabor **Bred** March Thoroughbreds **Trained** Ballydoyle, Co Tipperary

NOTEBOOK

Misty For Me(IRE) ◆, runner-up to Laughing Lashes in the Group 2 Debutante Stakes over the same C&D early this month, turned the tables on that rival with a thoroughly game front-running performance. She made all and stuck to her task very well when pressed over the last 2f. Connections are planning to step up her up to 1m now, with the Fillies' Mile at Ascot and the Prix Marcel Boussac at Longchamp mentioned as possible targets. (op 8/1)

Laughing Lashes(USA) was attempting to become the seventh winner of the Debutante to follow up in this event in the past 20 years. In second place on settling down, she had every chance from 2f out but was unable to peg back the winner. She swished her tail once but she appears thoroughly genuine and just might have a preference for easier ground - it was yielding when she won the Debutante. (op 7/2 tchd 4/1)

Kissable(IRE), third behind Together and Laughing Lashes in the Group 3 Silver Flash Stakes at Leopardstown, got a bit closer to Laughing Lashes on this occasion and gave the impression that 1m and easier ground should play to her strengths. She tracked the leaders and, after making little impression when asked to raise her game well over 1f out, was warming to her task well inside the final furlong.

Together(IRE)'s form tied in closely with the first, second and third here. Having beaten Laughing Lashes and Kissable at Leopardstown, she had drifted badly left in the closing stages when third behind Laughing Lashes and Misty For Me in the Debutante. There was no repeat of that here and, after tracking the leaders on the inside, she kept on for pressure over the last 2f without raising her game sufficiently to mount a serious challenge. (op 6/1)

Wild Wind(GER), back from a break for her first run since beating Laughing Lashes, who was making her debut, in a maiden over the C&D in June, made headway over 2f out and kept on without troubling the leaders. (op 12/1)

Memory(IRE), the Albany Stakes and Cherry Hinton winner, was attempting to retain her unbeaten record on her first attempt over the trip. She proved very disappointing and the extra furlong cannot be put forward as an excuse as she was never travelling at any stage and never threatened to get involved. She was reportedly fine the following day, and her trainer was inclined to blame her low draw. She will go for the Cheveley Park Stakes now. (op 11/10)

5571a SOCIAL HARMONY EUROPEAN BREEDERS FUND IRISH CAMBRIDGESHIRE (PREMIER H'CAP) 1m

4:50 (4:55) 3-Y-O+

£53,097 (£16,814; £7,964; £2,654; £1,769; £884)

RPR

1 **Hujaylea (IRE)**[45] 4080 7-8-3 87 ....(p) CPHoban(7) 26 99
(M Halford, Ire) *trckd ldrs on inner: 5th 2 1/2f out: 4th and swtchd to chal 1 1/2f out: 2nd 1f out: sn led: styd on wl* **25/1**

2 1 1/4 **Kyllachy Star**[8] 5292 4-9-0 91 .... RichardHughes 24 100
(R A Fahey) *trckd ldrs on inner: 4th appr 1/2-way: impr into 2nd under 2f out: sn chal and led: hdd under 1f out: kpt on* **14/1**

3 1 **Separate Ways (IRE)**[18] 4975 5-9-2 93 ....(b) CO'Donoghue 6 100
(David Marnane, Ire) *mid-div: hdd 2f out: 8th over 1f out: r.o u.p* **16/1**

4 3/4 **Start Right**[33] 4459 3-9-1 98 .... KierenFallon 10 102
(L M Cumani) *reluctant to load: hld up: hdwy in centre 1 1/2f out: 9th under 1f out: r.o strly* **5/2**[1]

5 shd **Napa Starr (FR)**[52] 3837 6-8-11 88 ow1 .... FMBerry 21 93
(C Byrnes, Ire) *hld up in tch: hdwy under 2f out: 7th over 1f out: kpt on* **10/1**[3]

6 shd **Irish Heartbeat (IRE)**[30] 4537 5-9-2 93 .... JMurtagh 18 98
(R A Fahey) *chsd ldrs: 8th 1/2-way: prog over 2f out: 3rd appr fnl f: kpt on same pce* **9/1**[2]

7 1/2 **Excelerate (IRE)**[39] 4271 7-9-2 96 ....(t) GFCarroll(3) 23 99
(Edward Lynam, Ire) *s.i.s and hld up towards rr: styd on fr under 2 1/2f out* **28/1**

8 1 3/4 **Worldly Wise**[12] 5192 7-9-9 100 .... DMGrant 20 99
(Patrick J Flynn, Ire) *hld up: rdn and kpt on wout threatening fr 2f out* **16/1**

9 1/2 **Simla Sunset (IRE)**[24] 4768 4-8-3 85 ....(t) SMLevey(5) 3 83
(P J Prendergast, Ire) *prom: 3rd 1/2-way: rdn to chal fr 2f out: no ex fr over 1f out* **16/1**

10 nk **Douze Points (IRE)**[29] 4608 4-8-11 88 ....(p) CDHayes 19 86
(Joseph G Murphy, Ire) *s.i.s and hld up towards rr: kpt on wout threatening fr over 2f out* **20/1**

11 nk **Barack (IRE)**[99] 2351 4-8-12 94 ....(bt[1]) MHarley(5) 27 91
(Francis Ennis, Ire) *led: rdn and strly pressed 2f out: hdd over 1 1/2f out: sn no ex* **20/1**

12 1 3/4 **Drombeg Dawn (IRE)**[29] 4608 4-8-12 89 .... WJLee 16 82
(A J McNamara, Ire) *chsd ldrs: 6th 1/2-way: no imp fr over 2f out* **20/1**

13 1 **Romeo's On Fire (IRE)**[13] 5166 6-8-0 87 .... DJBenson(10) 25 77
(G M Lyons, Ire) *mid-div: rdn and no imp fr 2 1/2f out* **33/1**

14 1/2 **Scandal Sheet (IRE)**[18] 4977 4-9-4 95 ....(p) KJManning 2 84
(J S Bolger, Ire) *prom: 5th 1/2-way: rdn 2 1/2f out: no ex fr over 1 1/2f out* **16/1**

15 hd **Picture Perfect (IRE)**[23] 4813 3-8-5 93 .... MACleere(5) 4 81
(David Wachman, Ire) *chsd ldrs on outer: 8th appr 1/2-way: no ex fr over 2f out* **25/1**

16 2 1/2 **Bean Uasal (IRE)**[24] 4768 4-8-6 86 ....(b) BACurtis(3) 1 69
(John M Oxx, Ire) *mid-div on outer: wknd fr over 2f out* **20/1**

17 1/2 **Flameoftheforest (IRE)**[32] 4496 3-8-5 88 .... RPCleary 17 69
(C F Swan, Ire) *nvr bttr than mid-div* **20/1**

18 1 3/4 **Unaccompanied (IRE)**[9] 5280 3-8-12 95 .... PJSmullen 11 72
(D K Weld, Ire) *hld up: no imp fr 2 1/2f out* **10/1**[3]

19 1/2 **Prince Jock (USA)**[12] 5191 3-8-7 90 ....(b[1]) PShanahan 13 66
(Tracey Collins, Ire) *mid-div: 9th 3f out: sn no ex and wknd* **12/1**

20 1 3/4 **Castle Bar Sling (USA)**[18] 4975 5-8-8 85 ....(p) WMLordan 5 58
(T J O'Mara, Ire) *nvr a factor* **33/1**

21 1 1/4 **Rock And Roll Kid (IRE)**[33] 4463 5-9-9 103 .... DEMullins(3) 7 73
(Anthony Mullins, Ire) *nvr a factor: bhd fr over 2f out* **25/1**

22 8 **Ballivor (IRE)**[63] 3487 7-8-8 85 .... PBBeggy 14 37
(W T Farrell, Ire) *cl up in 2nd: wknd fr 2 1/2f out* **33/1**

23 3 1/2 **Big Robert**[33] 4463 6-8-8 90 ....(p) JPO'Brien(5) 12 33
(P D Deegan, Ire) *v.s.a and a bhd* **33/1**

24 4 **Mujaazef**[33] 4463 3-9-0 97 .... DPMcDonogh 15 30
(Kevin Prendergast, Ire) *nvr a factor: bhd fr 2 1/2f out* **16/1**

25 25 **Headford View (IRE)**[23] 4813 6-9-4 95 ....(p) JAHeffernan 22 —
(James Halpin, Ire) *a bhd: wknd after 1/2-way: t.o* **20/1**

1m 39.38s (-6.62) **Going Correction** -0.60s/f (Hard)
WFA 3 from 4yo+ 6lb **25 Ran SP% 155.8**
Speed ratings: **109,107,106,106,105 105,105,103,103,102 102,100,99,99,99 96,96,94,93,92 90,82,79,75,50**
CSF £331.83 TOTE £51.60: £7.50, £3.50, £5.50, £1.50; DF 1000.50.
Owner Gerard M O'Leary **Bred** Christopher Flynn **Trained** Doneany, Co Kildare

FOCUS

The first two home here came from high draws. The front-running runner-up has been rated to his best form, with the winner, third and fifth rated as running personal bests.

NOTEBOOK

Hujaylea(IRE) came out on top to record his fifth win. All but one of his previous victories were achieved at Dundalk but he has performed at a consistent level elsewhere since. After tracking the leaders on the inside, he was switched left to challenge over 1f out, hit the front early in the final furlong and kept on well.

Kyllachy Star, four of whose five wins were achieved over 7f, tracked the leaders on the inner, got to the front over 1f out and kept on, but he failed to match the winner inside the final furlong. (op 12/1 tchd 16/1)

Separate Ways(IRE), unlike the first two, was drawn towards the outside. He was on a hat-trick and had gone up a total of 12lb for his wins at Galway and Gowran Park. He made steady progress from 2f out and was eighth over 1f out, from where he stayed on well. (op 12/1)

Start Right, on a hat-trick after wins at Newmarket and Goodwood, was up 10lb since the latter win and was a rare handicap runner in Ireland for Luca Cumani. He appeared reluctant to lead and was being pushed along in the final third of the field at halfway, but began to close 2f out and finished the race well having been only ninth approaching the final furlong. (op 3/1 tchd 9/4)

Napa Starr(FR), another chasing a hat-trick on his return from a break, had gone up a total of 13lb for his two wins. Ridden along in mid-division over 2f out, he ran on to be nearest at the finish. (op 9/1 tchd 8/1)

Headford View(IRE) Official explanation: trainer said mare was found to be lame post-race

5572 - (Foreign Racing) - See Raceform Interactive

5542 BADEN-BADEN (L-H)

Sunday, August 29

OFFICIAL GOING: Turf: soft

5573a BESTWETTEN.DE GOLDENE PEITSCHE (GROUP 2) (3YO+) (TURF) 6f

3:35 (12:00) 3-Y-O+

£35,398 (£13,716; £5,752; £3,539; £2,212; £1,327)

RPR

1 **Amico Fritz (GER)**[21] 4885 4-9-4 0 .... FabriceVeron 9 116
(H-A Pantall, France) *racd in midfield: qcknd wl in st: ct ldrs 1f out: r.o wl to gain ld 50yds out* **5/1**[2]

2 1/2 **Contat (GER)**[21] 4888 7-9-4 0 .... RJuracek 14 114
(P Vovcenko, Germany) *broke wl: a.p in 3rd: swung wd ent st: mde gd hdwy: led ins fnl f: looked wnr 100yds out: ct cl home* **20/1**

3 3/4 **Gilt Edge Girl**[31] 4505 4-9-1 0 .... LukeMorris 12 109
(C G Cox) *broke wl: bmpd sn after s: settled bhd ldrs: qcknd wl in st: led 1 1/2f out: hdd ins fnl f: r.o wl* **12/1**

4 1 **Mood Music**[24] 4773 6-9-4 0 ....(b) RoystonFfrench 10 108
(Mario Hofer, Germany) *settled towards rr: short of room early in st: mde gd prog whn clr but too late* **33/1**

5 1/2 **Atlantic Sport (USA)**[35] 5-9-4 0 ....(b) AStarke 6 107
(P Schiergen, Germany) *settled in midfield: fnd a way through traffic in st: looked threatening: fdd* **66/1**

6 hd **Rock Jock (IRE)**[50] 3928 3-9-1 0 .... MCHussey 1 106
(Tracey Collins, Ire) *broke fast: trckd pce: btn early in st* **16/1**

7 2 1/2 **Overdose**[14] 5-9-4 0 .... ChristopheSoumillon 13 98
(Jozef Roszival, Hungary) *hrd to load then stmbld coming out of stalls: settled in 2nd: led briefly 2f out: hdd over 1 1/2f out: began to fade: wknd* **4/6**[1]

8 1 1/4 **Indomito (GER)**[21] 4885 4-9-4 0 .... FilipMinarik 7 94
(P Vovcenko, Germany) *settled towards rr: hit traffic problems: fnd no ex in st* **20/1**

9 1 1/4 **Walero (GER)**[84] 2805 4-9-4 0 .... AHelfenbein 4 90
(Uwe Ostmann, Germany) *settled in ldng gp: no ex in st: fdd* **20/1**

10 4 **Nareion (GER)**[44] 4122 4-9-4 0 .... DominiqueBoeuf 3 77
(W Baltromei, Germany) *nvr figured* **25/1**

11 3/4 **Smooth Operator (GER)**[21] 4885 4-9-4 0 .... THellier 5 75
(Mario Hofer, Germany) *nvr figured* **11/2**[3]

12 12 **Fenella Rose**[181] 3-8-10 0 .... JBojko 11 32
(P Vovcenko, Germany) *broke wl to ld: passed 2f out: fdd* **150/1**

1m 11.38s (1.09)
WFA 3 from 4yo+ 3lb **12 Ran SP% 128.8**
WIN (incl. 10 euro stake): 80. PLACES: 22, 44, 35. SF: 1,571..
Owner Alexandre Pereira **Bred** A Pereira **Trained** France

NOTEBOOK

Amico Fritz(GER), whose run in the Prix Maurice de Gheest could be written off as he was badly hampered, bounced back to the form which saw him finish fifth in the Golden Jubilee on his previous start. The soft ground certainly helped him - all of his five wins have now come on good ground or softer. He's now likely to be given a bit of a break before being prepared for the Hong Kong Sprint towards the end of the year.

Gilt Edge Girl ran well on this step up in class and really relished the underfoot conditions. She should be able to find a pattern race this autumn on this evidence.

Overdose lost his unbeaten record after proving very uncooperative at the start. He sweated up badly and refused to enter the stalls on several occasions, causing the start to be delayed by eight minutes. He was in front at halfway but could never get clear of his rivals and was swamped inside the last. His previous two successes this term following a bout of laminitis came against ordinary opposition in Hungary and Slovakia, and he has a bit to prove now, but the Abbaye is still the plan.

Smooth Operator(GER) was the chief sufferer of Overdose's antics at the start, as he twice reared up in the stalls and returned with serious cuts to his face.

5346 DEAUVILLE (R-H)

Sunday, August 29

OFFICIAL GOING: Turf: soft; fibresand: standard

5574a PRIX QUINCEY LUCIEN BARRIERE (GROUP 3) (3YO+) (TURF) 1m (R)

1:35 (12:00) 3-Y-O+ £35,398 (£14,159; £10,619; £7,079; £3,539)

RPR

1 **Elusive Wave (IRE)**[28] 4639 4-8-13 0 .... IoritzMendizabal 2 111
(J-C Rouget, France) *trckd ldr fr s: rdn 1 1/2f out: tk ld 1f out: r.o wl* **13/8**[1]

2 1 1/2 **Vertigineux (FR)**[50] 3888 6-9-2 0 .... PhilippeSogorb 6 111
(Mme C Dufreche, France) *trckd eventual wnr fr s: rdn 1 1/2f out: swtchd to chal for ld 100yds out: r.o wl: a hld by wnr* **7/4**[2]

3 1/2 **Arasin (IRE)**[28] 4638 3-8-10 0 .... GeraldMosse 4 109
(P Bary, France) *led fr s: rdn 1 1/2f out: lost ld 1f out: r.o wl fnl 50yds* **12/1**

4 3 **Too Nice Name (FR)**[14] 3-8-10 0 .... OlivierPeslier 7 102
(Robert Collet, France) *midfield on outside fr s: rdn 2f out: gd prog 1 1/2f out: no ex fnl f* **33/1**

5 1 1/2 **Blue Panis (FR)**28 4638 3-8-10 0 MaximeGuyon 1 99
(F Chappet, France) *racd in 3rd: rdn 2f out: no ex fnl f: styd on* **6/1**3
6 1 1/2 **Foreteller**77 3016 3-8-8 0 StephanePasquier 5 93
(D Smaga, France) *racd in 4th on outside: u.p 2f out: no ex: fdd* **11/1**
7 10 **Slickly Royal (FR)**57 3704 6-9-2 0 (b) AnthonyCrastus 3 73
(P Demercastel, France) *in rr fr s: rdn 2f out: no ex: fdd* **16/1**

1m 41.1s (0.30)
WFA 3 from 4yo+ 6lb 7 Ran SP% **113.6**
WIN (incl. 1 euro stake): 2.20. PLACES: 1.60, 1.40. SF: 5.60.
Owner Martin S Schwartz **Bred** Pier House Stud **Trained** Pau, France

NOTEBOOK
Elusive Wave(IRE) reversed Chantilly form with Vertigineux despite having to meet him on the same terms. It was her first win since taking the Poule d'Essai des Pouliches last year. The Prix Daniel Wildenstein is next on her agends, before being sent to the sales in December.

5575a LUCIEN BARRIERE GRAND PRIX DE DEAUVILLE (GROUP 2) (3YO+) (TURF) 1m 4f 110y
2:40 (12:00) 3-Y-0+ **£100,884** (£38,938; £18,584; £12,389; £6,194)

RPR
1 **Marinous (FR)**21 4886 4-9-3 0 DavyBonilla 6 114
(F Head, France) *racd in 4th on outer: rdn 2f out: chal for ld 1 1/2f: led 1f out: r.o wl fnl 50yds* **20/1**
2 1/2 **Redwood**30 4535 4-9-3 0 MichaelHills 9 113
(B W Hills) *racd in 6th: rdn 1 1/2f out: str chal for ld on wd outside 100yds out: no ex fnl 50yds* **7/1**3
3 1/2 **La Boum (GER)**15 5108 7-9-0 0 ThierryJarnet 1 109
(Robert Collet, France) *racd in midfield: rdn 1 1/2f: short of room 1f out: r.o wl whn fnd daylight fnl 100yds* **20/1**
4 3/4 **Shimraan (FR)**35 4420 3-8-9 0 GeraldMosse 5 114
(A De Royer-Dupre, France) *racd in midfield: rdn 1 1/2f out: following eventual runner-up: r.o wl fnl 100yds wout threatening ldrs* **13/8**1
5 shd **Goldwaki (GER)**46 4039 3-8-6 0 MickaelBarzalona 4 111
(A Fabre, France) *in rr fr s: rdn 1 1/2f out: short of room: fin wl fnl 100yds whn in clr: narrowly missed 4th* **5/2**2
6 snk **Monitor Closely (IRE)**36 4390 4-9-3 0 JamieSpencer 3 110
(M L W Bell) *led fr s: stl in front 1 1/2f out: hdd and rdn 1f out: r.o wl: no ex fnl 50yds* **8/1**
7 1 **Telluride**21 4886 4-9-3 0 (p) MaximeGuyon 2 109
(J E Hammond, France) *racd towards rr: rdn 1 1/2f out: styd on fnl f* **14/1**
8 hd **Pouvoir Absolu**63 3494 5-9-3 0 (b) AnthonyCrastus 7 108
(E Lellouche, France) *racd in 3rd: rdn 1 1/2f out: no ex fnl f* **9/1**
9 1 **Winter Dream (IRE)**21 4886 6-9-3 0 IoritzMendizabal 10 107
(Robert Collet, France) *racd in 2nd: rdn 1 1/2f out: no ex fnl f: fdd* **25/1**
10 1 1/2 **Hot Six (BRZ)**21 4886 5-9-3 0 BReis 8 104
(P Bary, France) *a towards rr: nvr figured* **25/1**

2m 46.8s (0.40)
WFA 3 from 4yo+ 10lb 10 Ran SP% **124.2**
WIN (incl. 1 euro stake): 23.00. PLACES: 4.80, 2.50, 7.00. DF: 54.90. SF: 306.80.
Owner Saeed Nasser Al Romaithi **Bred** David, Julien & Virginie Elias De Proenca **Trained** France

NOTEBOOK
Marinous(FR), only third in a Listed event last time out, caused a shock. His connections hope to run him in Dubai next year.
Redwood, who won the Group 3 Glorious Stakes at Goodwood on his previous start, ran well considering ground this soft was a new experience for him. The Canadian International will likely be next up for him.
Monitor Closely(IRE) may have found conditions too testing.

5576a PRIX DE MEAUTRY LUCIEN BARRIERE (GROUP 3) (3YO+) (TURF) 6f
3:10 (12:00) 3-Y-0+ **£35,398** (£14,159; £10,619; £7,079; £3,539)

RPR
1 **Swiss Diva**24 4773 4-8-11 0 IoritzMendizabal 12 108
(D R C Elsworth) *broke wl and led in centre of crse: pushed along and qcknd clr ins fnl 300yds: r.o wl fnl f: comf* **4/1**1
2 3 **Kachgai (IRE)**8 7-9-1 0 MickaelBarzalona 11 102
(Y De Nicolay, France) *dwlt and towards rr early on: stdy prog to disupte 4th 2 1/2f out: rdn 1 1/2f out and styd on to take 2nd fnl 110yds* **12/1**
3 hd **Tiza (SAF)**24 4773 8-9-1 0 (p) GregoryBenoist 9 101
(A De Royer-Dupre, France) *racd in midfield: disp 4th travelling wl 2 1/2f out: pushed along 2f out and rdn appr fnl f: styd on to take 3rd fnl 110yds* **5/1**2
4 1 **Letteratura (IRE)**51 3875 4-8-11 0 JohanVictoire 6 94
(J-C Rouget, France) *trckd ldr: 2nd and rdn 1 1/2f out: wknd fnl 100yds* **12/1**
5 1 1/2 **Nuit De Glace (FR)**8 6-8-11 0 SebastienMaillot 8 89
(Mlle Valerie Boussin, France) *hld up towards rr: hdwy 2f out: wnt 5th appr fnl f: kpt on wout qckning* **33/1**
6 2 1/2 **Kermiyan (FR)**30 3-8-11 0 GeraldMosse 5 84
(J-C Rouget, France) *settled towards rr: in midfield at 1/2-way: sn rdn and no imp* **6/1**3
7 1 1/2 **Eightfold Path (USA)**321 6752 3-8-11 0 StephanePasquier 7 80
(P Bary, France) *hld up in last two: rdn 2f out and mde sme hdwy: nvr in contention* **13/2**
8 2 **Mariol (FR)**21 4885 7-9-1 0 FranckBlondel 4 74
(Robert Collet, France) *broke wl and disp 4th: stl prom 2 1/2f out: sn rdn and grad wknd* **5/1**2
9 hd **Pietra Santa (FR)**57 3704 4-8-11 0 MichaelHills 10 70
(J-M Beguigne, France) *cl 3rd: pressed for 2nd 2 1/2f out: fdd u.p fnl 2f* **22/1**
10 hd **Top Music**65 3425 3-8-11 0 OlivierPeslier 2 72
(A Fabre, France) *dwlt and towards rr early: in midfield by 1/2-way: sn btn* **10/1**
11 **Salut L'Africain (FR)**24 4773 5-9-1 0 (p) MaximeGuyon 5 73
(Robert Collet, France) *a towards rr: n.d* **10/1**

1m 11.9s (0.90)
WFA 3 from 4yo+ 3lb 11 Ran SP% **121.8**
PARI-MUTUEL (all including 1 euro stakes): WIN 4.30; PLACE 2.00, 3.90, 2.90; DF 32.50; SF 56.50.
Owner Lordship Stud **Bred** Lordship Stud **Trained** Newmarket, Suffolk

NOTEBOOK
Swiss Diva made all the running and had this won at the 2f marker. She cruised home to score with plenty in hand and is now likely to be aimed at the Abbaye, with an outing in the race's trial (Petit-Couvert) in a couple of weeks' time also possible in the meantime.

5351 DEL MAR (L-H)
Sunday, August 29
OFFICIAL GOING: Polytrack: fast

5577a PACIFIC CLASSIC STKS PRESENTED BY TVG (GRADE 1) (3YO+) (POLYTRACK) 1m 2f
12:30 (12:49) 3-Y-0+ **£370,370** (£123,456; £74,074; £37,037; £12,345)

RPR
1 **Richard's Kid (USA)**29 5-8-12 0 (b) MESmith 6 118
(Bob Baffert, U.S.A) *hld up towards rr: clsd up 4f out: rapid hdwy on outside 3f out: cl 7th and five-wd fnl turn: r.o strly to ld fnl 40yds* **48/10**2
2 3/4 **Crowded House**35 4417 4-8-12 0 (b) CNakatani 8 116
(B Cecil, U.S.A) *racd in midfield: 5th 4f out: hdwy to go 3rd 2f out: disp 2nd st: led 1f out: hdd fnl 40yds: no ex* **126/10**
3 1/2 **Dakota Phone (USA)**28 5-8-12 0 JRosario 3 115
(Jerry Hollendorfer, U.S.A) *hld up towards rr: clsd up appr 2f out: 8th st: 7th 1f out: fin strly to take 3rd fnl 50yds* **87/10**
4 1 **Battle Of Hastings**28 4-8-12 0 BBlanc 1 113
(Jeff Mullins, U.S.A) *racd in midfield: 5th 2f out: no ex st* **103/10**
5 1/2 **The Usual Q. T. (USA)**35 4417 4-8-12 0 VEspinoza 10 112
(James Cassidy, U.S.A) *chsd ldrs: 4th 2f out: r.o u.p to ld briefly st: hdd 1f out: one pce* **5/2**1
6 1/2 **Temple City (USA)**29 5-8-12 0 (b) RBejarano 4 111
(Carla Gaines, U.S.A) *chsd ldr: led 2f out: hdd st: wknd fnl f* **31/5**
7 1 3/4 **Isle Of Giant's (USA)**28 5-8-12 0 PValenzuela 2 108
(B Cecil, U.S.A) *wl away and set pce: hdd 2f out: fdd* **211/10**
8 1/2 **Hold Me Back (USA)**59 4-8-12 0 GKGomez 7 107
(William Mott, U.S.A) *chsd ldng pair tl rdn and wknd 3f out* **26/5**3
9 nse **Unusual Suspect (USA)**29 6-8-12 0 (b) AQuinonez 5 106
(Barry Abrams, U.S.A) *nvr plcd to chal* **43/1**
10 1/2 **Awesome Gem (USA)**49 7-8-12 0 (b) DFlores 9 105
(Craig Dollase, U.S.A) *settled towards rr: hdwy 2 1/2f out to go 6th st: sn btn* **89/10**

2m 3.27s (123.27) 10 Ran SP% **119.2**
PARI-MUTUEL (all including $2 stakes): WIN 11.60; PLACE (1-2) 5.60, 10.60; SHOW (1-2-3) 3.80, 6.40, 4.80; DF 81.20; SF 144.20.
Owner Zabeel Racing International, Corp **Bred** Fitzhugh, LLC **Trained** USA

NOTEBOOK
Richard's Kid(USA) ran down Crowded House inside the last to repeat last year's success in this race.
Crowded House ran a fine race on his first start for his new stable. He got first run early in the straight and, although he was run down late by Richard's Kid, his connections were understandably thrilled.

5544 SARATOGA (R-H)
Sunday, August 29
OFFICIAL GOING: Dirt: fast

5578a PERSONAL ENSIGN INVITATIONAL STKS (GRADE 1) (3YO+ FILLIES & MARES) (DIRT) 1m 2f (D)
10:56 (12:00) 3-Y-0+ **£111,111** (£37,037; £18,518; £9,259; £5,555)

RPR
1 **Persistently (USA)**30 4-8-4 0 (b) AGarcia 3 108
(Claude McGaughey III, U.S.A) **215/10**
2 1 **Rachel Alexandra (USA)**36 4-8-10 0 CHBorel 2 112+
(Steven Asmussen, U.S.A) **9/20**1
3 10 1/4 **Life At Ten (USA)**43 5-8-8 0 JRVelazquez 4 92+
(Todd Pletcher, U.S.A) **37/20**2
4 5 1/4 **Miss Singhsix (IRE)**43 5-8-4 0 JValdiviaJr 1 78
(Martin D Wolfson, U.S.A) **92/10**3
5 14 1/2 **Classofsixtythree (USA)**28 4-8-4 0 (b) JJCastellano 5 52
(Gary Contessa, U.S.A) **31/1**

2m 4.49s (124.49) 5 Ran SP% **121.4**
PARI-MUTUEL (all including $2 stakes): WIN 45.00; PLACE (1-2) 8.10, 2.30; SHOW (1-2-3) 3.60, 2.10, 2.10; SF 94.00.
Owner Phipps Stable **Bred** Phipps Stable **Trained** USA

NOTEBOOK
Rachel Alexandra(USA) had plenty to prove on this step up to her furthest trip to date, having so failed to recapture her brilliance of 2009, but while again nowhere neat her best on RPRs and time figures, the result's misleading - she actually emerges with a deal of credit in defeat. Quite simply, she was given a terrible ride by Borel, setting off too fast in a speed dual with Life At Ten, and though picked off by a vastly inferior rival in the final strides, it's to her credit she pulled so far clear of the third-placed finisher, who had won her last six starts, including a Grade 1. It may also be worth remembering that Saratoga was the scene of Rachel's least impressive race of last year, when scraping home under a hard ride in the Woodward. She again had a tough race, but can still be a force at the top level judged on this showing.

5465 BATH (L-H)
Monday, August 30
OFFICIAL GOING: Good
Meeting switched from Chepstow, where the track was under repair.
Wind: Moderate across Weather: Sunny

5579 DIGIBET.COM H'CAP (DIV I) 5f 161y
1:35 (1:36) (Class 6) (0-55,58) 3-Y-0+ **£1,619** (£481; £240; £120) **Stalls** Centre

Form RPR
5325 1 **Wooden King (IRE)**39 4283 5-8-12 51 LiamJones 1 64
(M S Saunders) *mde virtually all: jnd over 1f out: styd on wl u.p fnl f* **6/1**
005 2 3/4 **Kinigi (IRE)**24 4789 4-8-5 47 (b) AndrewHeffernan(3) 7 58
(R A Harris) *sn chsng ldr: str chal fr over 1f out tl ins fnl f: no ex fnl 75yds* **11/2**3

006 **3** *hd* **Mushy Peas (IRE)**[27] 4679 3-7-11 **46** oh1 .... SophieSilvester(7) 8 56+
(P D Evans) *stmbld s and in rr: stdy hdwy fr 2f out: kpt on wl under hand-driving fnl f: gng on cl home and jst failed to take 2nd last strides* **33/1**

3061 **4** *6* **Eye For The Girls**[7] 5362 4-9-5 **58** 6ex .... SamHitchcott 9 48
(M R Channon) *in tch: chsd ldrs and rdn 2f out: outpcd fnl f* **9/2**[2]

3032 **5** *nk* **Shakespeare's Son**[13] 5169 5-8-5 **49** ....(v) JohnFahy(5) 4 38
(H J Evans) *s.i.s: in tch 1/2-way: sn rdn: outpcd fnl 2f* **3/1**[1]

5053 **6** *2 1/4* **Charlietoo**[22] 4857 4-8-11 **53** ow1 ....(p) JackDean(3) 6 35
(E G Bevan) *in tch tl rdn 2f out: wknd sn after* **10/1**

-050 **7** *shd* **It's A Mans World**[82] 2876 4-8-13 **55** .... MartinLane(3) 11 36
(Ian Williams) *in rr: rdn and sme hdwy on outside over 2f out: sn wknd* **14/1**

0003 **8** *2 3/4* **Avoncreek**[13] 5169 6-8-7 **46** .... KirstyMilczarek 3 18
(B P J Baugh) *chsd ldrs tl wknd fr 2f out* **7/1**

0005 **9** *2 3/4* **Norse Warrior (USA)**[7] 5362 4-8-2 **46** oh1 ....(b) SimonPearce(5) 5 9
(Peter Grayson) *reluctant to go to post: s.i.s: in rr: mod late prog* **28/1**

0054 **10** *1 1/4* **Like For Like (IRE)**[3] 5471 4-8-7 **46** oh1 .... FrankieMcDonald 10 —
(R J Hodges) *chsd ldrs to 1/2-way* **16/1**

0403 **11** *20* **Novastasia (IRE)**[24] 4790 4-8-7 **46** oh1 .... LukeMorris 2 —
(D K Ivory) *early spd: sn wl bhd* **20/1**

1m 10.59s (-0.61) **Going Correction** 0.0s/f (Good)
WFA 3 from 4yo+ 3lb **11** Ran SP% **118.1**
Speed ratings (Par 101): **104,103,102,94,94 91,91,87,83,82 55**
Tote Swingers:1&2:£11.60, 1&3:£15.80, 2&3:£22.30 CSF £38.28 CT £1030.40 TOTE £12.80: £2.70, £4.20, £6.00; EX 50.90.
Owner Pat Hancock **Bred** Terence E Connelly **Trained** Green Ore, Somerset

FOCUS
A decent pace for this low-grade sprint and fair form for the grade.
Norse Warrior(USA) Official explanation: jockey said gelding reared up leaving stalls

5580 LANCER SCOTT CONSTRUCTION APPRENTICE H'CAP 5f 11y
2:05 (2:05) (Class 6) (0-60,59) 3-Y-O+ **£1,942** (£578; £288; £144) **Stalls** Centre

Form RPR

4622 **1** **Stamford Blue**[15] 5112 9-9-2 **57** ....(b) JakePayne(3) 9 63
(R A Harris) *trckd ldrs: led wl over 1f out: drvn out fnl f* **9/4**[1]

3005 **2** *1/2* **Convince (USA)**[7] 5377 9-9-1 **58** ....(p) MatthewCosham(5) 10 62
(J L Flint) *drvn along to chse ldrs fr s: rdn 3f out and again whn hdwy on outside fr 2f out: r.o ins fnl f to take 2nd last strides but nt rch wnr* **8/1**

425 **3** *nk* **Miss Firefly**[18] 5010 5-9-7 **59** .... SophieSilvester 7 62
(R J Hodges) *chsd ldrs: wnt 2nd jst ins fnl f: no imp on wnr and lost 2nd last strides* **3/1**[2]

3006 **4** *1 1/2* **Cocktail Party (IRE)**[20] 4938 4-8-9 **47** ....(v) AlexEdwards 4 45
(J W Unett) *chsd ldrs: pushed along and one pce 2f out: kpt on again ins fnl f* **10/1**

1600 **5** *nk* **Helping Hand (IRE)**[31] 4559 5-8-6 **49** .... NicolaJackson(5) 5 45
(R Hollinshead) *chsd ldrs: led over 2f out: hdd wl over 1f out: wknd fnl 120yds* **7/1**[3]

0-00 **6** *1/2* **Five Gold Rings (IRE)**[16] 5077 4-8-12 **50** .... RichardRowe 1 45
(F J Brennan) *led tl hdd over 2f out: sn rdn: swtchd rt appr fnl f and styd on same pce* **25/1**

3010 **7** *1 1/2* **Ellen Vannin (IRE)**[13] 5169 3-9-3 **57** ....(p) NathanAlison 6 46
(Eve Johnson Houghton) *broke wl: sn outpcd: sme prog fnl f* **12/1**

-050 **8** *1* **Dancing Again**[7] 5377 4-8-7 **45** .... JamesRogers 3 31
(E A Wheeler) *s.i.s: outpcd in rr: mod prog fnl f* **33/1**

0000 **9** *2* **Pinball (IRE)**[17] 5055 4-9-0 **52** ....(v) HarryBentley 8 30
(Mrs L Williamson) *s.i.s: in rr: drvn and hdwy to chse ldrs 2f out: sn rdn and hung bdly rt to stands' side and no ch after* **7/1**[3]

62.79 secs (0.29) **Going Correction** 0.0s/f (Good)
WFA 3 from 4yo+ 2lb **9** Ran SP% **115.5**
Speed ratings (Par 101): **97,96,95,93,92 92,89,88,84**
Tote Swingers:1&2:£5.10, 1&3:£1.90, 2&3:£5.10 CSF £21.10 CT £54.68 TOTE £4.00: £1.50, £2.20, £1.50; EX 17.40.
Owner Brian Hicks **Bred** Mrs Wendy Miller **Trained** Earlswood, Monmouths

FOCUS
An ordinary apprentice sprint. The winner is rated to this year's form.

5581 LANCER SCOTT RETAIL NURSERY 5f 11y
2:40 (2:42) (Class 6) (0-60,60) 2-Y-O **£2,047** (£604; £302) **Stalls** Centre

Form RPR

5220 **1** **Ruby Alexander (IRE)**[15] 5111 2-9-2 **58** ....(b[1]) EJMcNamara(3) 7 62+
(R M Beckett) *s.i.s: in rr: hdwy ins fnl 2f: nt clr run and swtchd rt jst ins fnl f: str run to ld nr fin* **12/1**

000 **2** *3/4* **Regal Bullet (IRE)**[77] 3034 2-9-1 **54** .... SamHitchcott 9 54
(D K Ivory) *in rr: rdn and hdwy on outside fr 2f out: str run u.p fnl f to take 2nd nr fin but nt pce of wnr* **25/1**

030 **3** *hd* **One Cool Bex**[19] 4941 2-9-3 **56** ....(e) JackMitchell 12 55
(P J McBride) *chsd ldrs: rdn and styd on to chse wnr ins fnl f: no imp and one pce cl home* **7/1**[3]

0443 **4** *hd* **Till Dawn (IRE)**[7] 5365 2-8-11 **53** .... MartinLane(3) 13 51
(A W Carroll) *s.i.s: sn in tch and drvn to ld over 2f out: kpt on u.p fnl f tl hdd and lost 2 pls cl home* **4/1**[1]

5560 **5** *2 3/4* **Sarandjam**[18] 5000 2-8-10 **49** .... EddieCreighton 8 37
(M R Channon) *hood off late and s.i.s: drvn and hdwy on outside over 1f out: kpt on ins fnl f but no imp on ldrs* **5/1**[2]

600 **6** *hd* **Brave Tiger (IRE)**[22] 4856 2-8-6 **45** ....(t) LiamJones 4 33
(S C Williams) *chsd ldrs: rdn and one pce over 2f out: kpt on again ins fnl f* **22/1**

423 **7** *nk* **Liberty Ess (IRE)**[46] 4067 2-9-1 **54** ....(p) NickyMackay 15 41
(M Wigham) *chsd ldrs: drvn to chal appr fnl 2f: wknd fnl 50yds* **9/1**

1560 **8** *1/2* **Melodize**[15] 5111 2-9-7 **60** .... MartinDwyer 10 46
(W R Muir) *chsd ldrs: styng on same pce on ins whn hmpd jst ins fnl f: no ch after* **9/1**

0044 **9** *1* **Local Diktator**[15] 5111 2-8-6 **45** .... LukeMorris 6 27
(R A Harris) *t.k.h to s: chsd ldrs: styng on whn nt clr run and swtchd lft ins fnl f: one pce* **7/1**[3]

0600 **10** *1 3/4* **Place And Chips**[5] 5412 2-9-3 **56** ....(vt[1]) RichardKingscote 14 31
(Tom Dascombe) *t.k.h to post: sn led: hdd over 2f out: wknd fnl f* **10/1**

0220 **11** *hd* **Calormen**[58] 3678 2-9-3 **59** ....(b[1]) RussKennemore(3) 5 33
(A G Juckes) *in rr: sn rdn along: sme late hdwy* **25/1**

004 **12** *nk* **Alltherightmoves (IRE)**[70] 3260 2-9-4 **57** ....(b) LiamKeniry 1 30
(Eve Johnson Houghton) *in rr: rdn and hanging lft whn swtchd to outer and rdn over 1f out: hung lft sn after but sme prog nr fin* **20/1**

0555 **13** *nk* **Minus Tolerance**[10] 5268 2-8-1 **45** .... SophieDoyle(5) 11 17
(Miss S L Davison) *sn chsng ldrs: rdn and one pce whn hmpd appr fnl f and sn wknd* **66/1**

005 **14** *2 1/2* **Indian Dip**[77] 3035 2-8-11 **50** .... TadhgO'Shea 3 13
(F J Brennan) *chsd ldrs: rdn over 2f out: sn btn* **12/1**

500 **15** *2 3/4* **Capa Cruz (IRE)**[87] 2687 2-8-9 **51** .... AndrewHeffernan(3) 2 4
(R A Harris) *chsd ldrs over 3f* **33/1**

62.99 secs (0.49) **Going Correction** 0.0s/f (Good) **15** Ran SP% **127.4**
Speed ratings (Par 92): **96,94,94,94,89 89,88,88,86,83 83,82,82,78,74**
Tote Swingers:1&2:£38.40, 1&3:£38.40, 2&3:£38.40 CSF £299.32 CT £2283.30 TOTE £11.00: £3.50, £11.40, £2.60; EX 396.30.
Owner The Millennium Madness Partnership **Bred** Mountarmstrong Stud **Trained** Whitsbury, Hants
■ A first winner since coming to Britain for Emmet McNamara.

FOCUS
A modest nursery, but an open affair and a good test. Limited but sound form.

NOTEBOOK
Ruby Alexander(IRE) got the breaks late on to swoop through and open her account. She had blinkers replacing the cheekpieces she had worn when a respectable runner-up to an improver in a nursery before a disappointing run here last time. The blinkers obviously had the desired effect, but she has been beaten in sellers before and might just struggle to follow up when reassessed. (op 10-1)
Regal Bullet(IRE) had not shown a great deal to date but, under a power-packed ride, delivered a sound effort. He was finishing strongly and can build upon this. (op 40-1)
One Cool Bex had finished third in a Yarmouth seller, but had not shaped with too much promise either side although the form of the Beverley maiden has been working out well. He raced prominently throughout and kept on well enough in the closing stages. (op 8-1)
Till Dawn(IRE) had been well-supported and looked to have the measure of the field after taking it up at the 2f pole, but was eventually run out it in the closing stages. He ought to be capable of getting off the mark in a similar contest. (op 7-2 tchd 100-30 and 9-2)
Sarandjam could not get involved after sitting well off the pace, but finished well and looks capable of making his presence felt off current mark. (op 11-1)

5582 LANCER SCOTT M & E EUROPEAN BREEDERS' FUND MAIDEN STKS (C&G) 1m 5y
3:15 (3:19) (Class 5) 2-Y-O **£3,108** (£924; £462; £230) **Stalls** Low

Form RPR

4 **1** **Happy Today (USA)**[24] 4803 2-9-0 0 .... MartinDwyer 14 83+
(B J Meehan) *led after 1f tl awkward bnd and wnt v wd bnd ins fnl 5f: rcvrd to ld again ins fnl 3f: drvn over 1f out: styd on strly fnl f* **8/11**[1]

64 **2** *2 1/4* **El Mansour (USA)**[59] 3631 2-9-0 0 .... LukeMorris 11 74
(C G Cox) *led 1f: lft in ld on bnd ins fnl 5f: hdd ins fnl 3f: drvn and styd on fnl 2f but no imp on wnr: kpt on wl for 2nd ins fnl f* **9/2**[2]

3 *1 1/4* **Biographical (USA)** 2-9-0 0 .... NickyMackay 2 71
(J H M Gosden) *chsd ldrs: rdn and kpt on fr 2f out: one pce ins fnl f* **9/1**

0 **4** *hd* **Reflect (IRE)**[17] 5033 2-9-0 0 .... PatDobbs 6 71
(R Hannon) *chsd ldrs: pushed along and n.m.r between horses fnl f: kpt on cl home* **20/1**

0 **5** *11* **Holy Mackerel (IRE)**[10] 5263 2-9-0 0 .... EddieCreighton 13 47
(M R Channon) *chsng ldr whn carried v wd bnd ins fnl 5f: rdn to stay chsng ldrs over 3f out: wknd over 2f out* **50/1**

0 **6** *1 1/2* **Drummer Boy**[40] 4254 2-9-0 0 .... CathyGannon 8 43
(P Winkworth) *in rr: pushed along and styd on fr over 2f out: modest prog fnl f* **66/1**

7 *nse* **Plattsburgh (USA)** 2-9-0 0 .... AhmedAjtebi 4 43
(Mahmood Al Zarooni) *in tch: pushed along over 3f out: one pce and no ch sn after* **13/2**[3]

8 *3/4* **Hollow Tree** 2-9-0 0 .... LiamKeniry 3 42
(A M Balding) *chsd ldrs to 3f out* **20/1**

9 *2 1/4* **Phoenix Fantasy (IRE)** 2-9-0 0 .... RichardKingscote 1 37
(J G Portman) *slowly away and wl bhd tl styd on fnl 2f* **66/1**

10 *1/2* **Tileyf (IRE)** 2-8-9 0 .... JohnFahy(5) 12 36
(C G Cox) *in rr: mod late prog* **50/1**

11 *1 1/2* **Cunning Act** 2-9-0 0 .... StephenCraine 7 32
(J G Portman) *in rr: no ch whn hmpd over 2f out* **66/1**

12 *1 1/4* **Bumbling Bertie** 2-8-9 0 .... SimonPearce(5) 15 30
(A M Balding) *a in rr* **33/1**

13 *3/4* **Dust Cloud (IRE)** 2-9-0 0 .... FrankieMcDonald 9 28
(P Winkworth) *in rr: mod effrt on outside 3f out: sn wknd* **66/1**

0 **14** *8* **Wet Your Whistle**[23] 4838 2-9-0 0 .... TadhgO'Shea 16 10
(B J Meehan) *chsd ldrs: wnt wd bnd ins fnl 5f: wknd 3f out* **66/1**

15 *nk* **Striking Willow** 2-8-12 0 ow1 .... JamesMillman(3) 10 11
(B R Millman) *bhd most of way* **40/1**

1m 41.63s (0.83) **Going Correction** 0.0s/f (Good) **15** Ran SP% **125.7**
Speed ratings (Par 94): **95,92,91,91,80 78,78,78,75,75 73,72,71,63,63**
Tote Swingers:1&2:£2.20, 1&3:£3.10, 2&3:£8.50 CSF £3.79 TOTE £1.80: £1.10, £1.60, £2.80; EX 5.70.
Owner Jaber Abdullah **Bred** Rabbah Bloodstock Llc **Trained** Manton, Wilts

FOCUS
A fair maiden with only a few with racecourse experience and, despite not too many getting involved off a good pace, the form should stand up with the front four looking promising sorts as they finished well clear of the remainder. The winner is open to improvement.

NOTEBOOK
Happy Today(USA) had made an encouraging debut and was well supported to get off the mark here which he duly did. He did not cope particularly well with the bend after running wide, but there was plenty to like about the performance. There are no solid plans for him, but his jockey believes he will be all the better next season. (tchd 4-7 opened 8-11 after 10-11 in a place Evens in places, tchd 4-5)
El Mansour(USA) is progressing with experience, with this being another step forward after a further step up in trip and he looks capable of getting off the mark now he is eligible for nurseries. (op 15-2 tchd 8-1)
Biographical(USA), a $270,000 yearling out of a decent US mare, shaped with plenty of promise as he looked as though he would come on for the experience. (op 8-1 tchd 10-1)
Reflect(IRE) holds a Derby entry, but had to take a big leap forward after his debut at Newbury. He raced up with the leaders, but could only keep on at the same pace. (tchd 25-1)
Holy Mackerel(IRE) failed to get involved, but it was a better effort than on his debut.
Drummer Boy also ran better than on debut. (op 50-1)
Plattsburgh(USA), a $320,000 purchase out of a Group 3 winning mare, also holds a Derby entry but was another who will benefit from the experience. (op 8-1 tchd 10-1)

5583 FESTIVAL RACING ON COURSE EUROPEAN BREEDERS' FUND MEDIAN AUCTION MAIDEN FILLIES' STKS 1m 5y
3:50 (3:52) (Class 5) 2-Y-O **£3,108** (£924; £462; £230) **Stalls** Low

Form RPR

5 **1** **Masaraat (FR)**[30] 4595 2-9-0 0 .... TadhgO'Shea 2 77+
(J L Dunlop) *towards rr but in tch: pushed along and hdwy fr 3f out to chse ldr 2f out: str chal ins fnl f: led last stride* **11/4**[2]

3433 **2** *shd* **Galloping Queen (IRE)**[22] 4862 2-9-0 79 .... SamHitchcott 10 77
(M R Channon) *chsd ldr: drvn to ld appr fnl 2f: hrd drvn and styd on whn strly chal ins fnl f: hdd last stride* **3/1**[3]

02 **3** 4½ **Gay Gallivanter**[19] 4962 2-9-0 0 NickyMackay 3 67
(J H M Gosden) *t.k.h: trckd ldrs: pushed along fr 3f out: tk 3rd ins fnl 2f but no ch w ldng duo fnl f* **2/1**[1]

4 ½ **Norse Wing** 2-9-0 0 JackMitchell 6 66+
(R M Beckett) *s.i.s: in rr: hdwy on outside over 2f out: styd on fnl f to press for 3rd but no ch w ldng duo* **15/2**

00 **5** 2¼ **Beach Babe**[18] 5006 2-9-0 0 RichardKingscote 9 61
(J G Portman) *chsd ldrs: rdn and n.m.r 2f out: wknd sn after* **40/1**

6 1½ **Pandorica** 2-9-0 0 LukeMorris 8 58
(C G Cox) *broke wl: stdd in rr: rdn over 3f out: mod prog fnl f* **11/1**

7 4 **Glyn Ceiriog** 2-9-0 0 MartinDwyer 7 49
(George Baker) *s.i.s: a towards rr* **16/1**

0 **8** nk **Gypsy Legend (IRE)**[17] 5029 2-9-0 0 LiamKeniry 1 48
(S Kirk) *in tch: rdn over 2f out: sn wknd* **33/1**

004 **9** 11 **Elusive Vine (IRE)**[10] 5269 2-8-11 48 AndrewHeffernan(3) 4 24
(R A Harris) *t.k.h: sn led: hdd appr fnl 2f: sn wknd* **80/1**

0006 **10** 26 **Shesanindian (IRE)**[41] 4228 2-8-11 30 MartinLane(3) 5 —
(A W Carroll) *a bhd: t.o* **100/1**

1m 42.18s (1.38) **Going Correction** 0.0s/f (Good) **10** Ran SP% **118.6**
Speed ratings (Par 91): **93,92,88,87,85 84,80,79,68,42**
Tote Swingers:1&2:£2.60, 1&3:£1.80, 2&3:£1.30 CSF £11.58 TOTE £3.80: £1.60, £1.10, £1.60; EX 11.30.
Owner Hamdan Al Maktoum **Bred** Shadwell Estate Co Ltd **Trained** Arundel, W Sussex

FOCUS
A decent little maiden fillies' race which was run at a fair pace and featured some promising sorts. The runner-up sets the level.

NOTEBOOK
Masaraat(FR) had shown promise when staying on late in a Newmarket maiden, and showed a good attitude to get off the mark after a protracted battle with the runner-up. She ought to come into her own when stepped further up in trip, as there is plenty of stamina on the dam's side. She can only build on this. (tchd 3-1)
Galloping Queen(IRE) had been placed in a Listed contest at the Curragh and set a decent standard here stepping up to a mile. She lost little in defeat and saw out the trip well, only losing out on the nod. She can gain compensation and get off the mark soon. (op 11-4 tchd 7-2)
Gay Gallivanter had failed to settle when well beaten on her debut, but took a big step forward when narrowly beaten at Sandown. He was well backed here upped to a mile, but could only stay on at the same pace after racing rather keenly early on. (op 11-4)
Norse Wing, from the family of Lochsong, shaped with promise on this her debut. She was being pushed along from a fair way out, but stayed on nicely in the final 2f and can only benefit from the experience. (op 8-1 tchd 7-1)
Beach Babe had no more to give after racing up with the pace entering the final furlong, but now qualifies for a mark, and could be of interest when sent handicapping. (op 66-1)

5584 FESTIVAL RACING ON THE RAILS H'CAP 1m 5y
4:25 (4:29) (Class 5) (0-70,68) 3-Y-O+ £2,460 (£732; £365; £182) Stalls Low

Form RPR

5-54 **1** **Mr Money Maker**[41] 4222 3-9-2 68 RussKennemore(3) 13 77
(J L Flint) *mde virtually all: rdn over 2f out: styd on strly fr over 1f out: unchal* **8/1**

2200 **2** 1 **Petomic (IRE)**[9] 5287 5-9-6 63 TadhgO'Shea 1 71
(M Hill) *chsd wnr: rdn fr 3f out: no imp on wnr fr over 1f out* **12/1**

3003 **3** 3¼ **Full Victory (IRE)**[9] 5287 8-9-3 60 LiamKeniry 8 61+
(R A Farrant) *chsd ldrs: rdn 3f out: tk one-pce 3rd 1f out* **9/2**[1]

-335 **4** 2¼ **Night Sky**[14] 5145 3-8-13 67 SophieDoyle(5) 16 61+
(P J Makin) *in rr: rdn and hdwy on outside fr over 2f out: kpt on fnl f but nvr in contention* **6/1**[3]

0604 **5** nse **On The Feather**[18] 4987 4-8-7 53 MartinLane(3) 5 48
(B R Millman) *chsd ldrs: rdn over 3f out and sn one pce: sme prog fnl f* **11/1**

0635 **6** 2½ **Magroom**[18] 5003 6-9-11 68 GeorgeBaker 3 57
(R J Hodges) *chsd ldrs: rdn over 2f out: wknd over 1f out* **5/1**[2]

1512 **7** nk **Bidable**[27] 4681 6-9-5 67 AshleyMorgan(5) 4 56
(B Palling) *chsd ldrs: rdn over 2f out: sn wknd* **8/1**

0R- **8** 4 **The Winged Assasin (USA)**[329] 6547 4-9-11 68 NickyMackay 12 48
(M Wigham) *in rr: sme hdwy over 2f out: nvr rchd ldrs* **13/2**

3535 **9** 2 **Tanforan**[17] 5050 8-9-4 61 JackMitchell 2 36
(B P J Baugh) *chsd ldrs tl wknd ins fnl 2f* **12/1**

05- **10** 2 **Zagarock**[313] 6931 3-8-13 62 LukeMorris 11 31
(B Palling) *s.i.s: rdn and sme hdwy over 3f out: sn wknd* **28/1**

0/00 **11** nk **Wrecking Crew (IRE)**[10] 5254 6-8-12 58 ow2 JamesMillman(3) 15 28
(B R Millman) *s.i.s: a in rr* **28/1**

4000 **12** 10 **Glan Y Mor (IRE)**[18] 4992 3-8-0 49 oh3 CathyGannon 9 —
(A W Carroll) *a in rr* **16/1**

1m 41.06s (0.26) **Going Correction** 0.0s/f (Good)
WFA 3 from 4yo+ 6lb **12** Ran SP% **121.2**
Speed ratings (Par 103): **98,97,93,91,91 88,88,84,82,80 80,70**
Tote Swingers:1&2:£19.80, 1&3:£20.70, 2&3:£11.60 CSF £102.60 CT £494.86 TOTE £12.50: £3.20, £4.60, £2.20; EX 183.10.
Owner E R Griffiths **Bred** E R Griffiths **Trained** Kenfig Hill, Bridgend

FOCUS
A very open, if ordinary, mile handicap. The front pair were always 1-2 and the winner is rated up 10lb on his handicap debut.
Glan Y Mor(IRE) Official explanation: jockey said filly ran too free

5585 BET WITH FESTIVAL RACING ON COURSE H'CAP 1m 2f 46y
5:00 (5:02) (Class 6) (0-65,65) 3-Y-O+ £1,942 (£578; £288; £144) Stalls Low

Form RPR

4042 **1** **Oriental Girl**[18] 4992 5-10-0 58 (p) LiamKeniry 3 67
(J S Moore) *trckd ldrs: wnt 2nd and drvn 2f out: led 1f out: kpt on wl: readily* **9/2**[2]

4314 **2** 1¼ **Shianda**[13] 5172 3-9-6 58 (b) GeorgeBaker 7 65
(G L Moore) *in rr: hdwy over 2f out: styd on to chse wnr ins fnl f but a readily hld* **9/2**[2]

5133 **3** nk **Corrib (IRE)**[18] 4992 7-9-6 50 (p) TadhgO'Shea 8 56
(B Palling) *s.i.s in rr: hdwy on outside fr 3f out: styd on to dispute 2nd ins fnl f but no imp on wnr* **8/1**

312 **4** 3½ **Rockweiller**[13] 5173 3-9-13 65 (v) CathyGannon 12 64
(P D Evans) *chsd ldrs: rdn 4f out: led wl over 2f out: hdd 1f out and sn wknd* **10/3**[1]

3403 **5** shd **Alfredtheordinary**[42] 4213 5-9-7 51 SamHitchcott 9 50
(M R Channon) *hld up in rr: rdn and hdwy on ins 3f out: styd on to chse ldrs over 1f out: sn one pce* **12/1**

2635 **6** hd **Farncombe (IRE)**[18] 4992 4-9-6 50 EddieCreighton 10 48
(M J Scudamore) *in tch: drvn along fr 4f out: hdwy fr 3f out: styd on fnl f but nvr a threat* **20/1**

300 **7** 1½ **My Jeanie (IRE)**[10] 5254 6-8-10 45 SophieDoyle(5) 11 40
(J C Fox) *in rr tl hdwy over 2f out: mod prog fnl f* **50/1**

00-3 **8** 2 **Master Mahogany**[18] 4987 9-9-5 49 RichardKingscote 2 40
(R J Hodges) *chsd ldrs: rdn over 2f out: wknd over 1f out* **8/1**

6666 **9** 6 **Hounds Ditch**[40] 4249 3-9-2 54 (t) JackMitchell 6 33
(Eve Johnson Houghton) *s.i.s: in rr: sme hdwy whn hmpd on ins 3f out: n.d after* **25/1**

5304 **10** nk **Aspirational (IRE)**[18] 4992 4-9-3 47 LukeMorris 4 26
(B Palling) *sn led: hdd 7f out: led again appr fnl 3f: hdd wl over 2f out and wknd qckly* **7/1**[3]

-440 **11** 7 **Gwenllian (IRE)**[42] 4201 3-9-10 62 MartinDwyer 5 27
(Ian Williams) *chsd ldrs tl wknd 3f out* **16/1**

-005 **12** 8 **Iron Man Of Mersey (FR)**[25] 4731 4-8-12 45 (v1) MartinLane(3) 1 —
(A W Carroll) *led 7f out: hdd & wknd appr fnl 3f* **50/1**

2m 10.6s (-0.40) **Going Correction** 0.0s/f (Good)
WFA 3 from 4yo+ 8lb **12** Ran SP% **120.3**
Speed ratings (Par 101): **101,100,99,96,96 96,95,93,89,88 83,76**
Tote Swingers:1&2:£7.50, 1&3:£5.30, 2&3:£4.00 CSF £24.56 CT £159.50 TOTE £4.70: £2.30, £2.10, £2.70; EX 36.10.
Owner Kimpton Down Partnership **Bred** Aston Mullins Stud And D J Erwin **Trained** Upper Lambourn, Berks

FOCUS
A good pace for this tricky 46-65 1m2f handicap. Sound form.

5586 DIGIBET.COM H'CAP (DIV II) 5f 161y
5:35 (5:37) (Class 6) (0-55,55) 3-Y-O+ £1,619 (£481; £240; £120) Stalls Centre

Form RPR

0016 **1** **Emiratesdotcom**[39] 4283 4-8-13 52 LiamKeniry 8 60
(J M Bradley) *trckd ldrs: rdn to chse ldr and edgd lft 1f out: drvn to chal sn after: edgd lft u.p and led cl home* **9/4**[1]

3502 **2** nk **Avonlini**[13] 5175 4-8-9 48 JackMitchell 2 55
(B P J Baugh) *trckd ldr: led over 2f out: rdn and edgd rt 1f out: strly chal ins fnl f: pushed lft and hdd cl home* **11/2**[3]

6000 **3** 3 **Connor's Choice**[20] 4936 5-8-6 50 SimonPearce(5) 6 47
(Andrew Turnell) *t.k.h: trckd ldrs: shkn up ins fnl 2f: outpcd fnl f* **15/2**

0022 **4** hd **Hart Of Gold**[16] 5075 6-9-2 55 (b) LukeMorris 1 51
(R A Harris) *led tl hdd over 2f out: wknd fnl f* **4/1**[2]

000 **5** 1½ **Miss Tenacious**[18] 5007 3-8-2 47 oh1 ow1 MartinLane(3) 7 38
(R J Hodges) *s.i.s: in rr: pushed along over 2f out: kpt on fnl f but nvr a threat* **25/1**

-143 **6** ¾ **Mansii**[20] 4938 5-9-2 55 (t) EddieCreighton 4 44
(P J McBride) *s.i.s: in rr: rdn and styd on fr over 1f out: nvr in contention* **4/1**[2]

200- **7** 1 **White Ledger (IRE)**[254] 7815 11-8-2 46 SophieDoyle(5) 5 32
(R E Peacock) *s.i.s: in rr: sme late prog* **20/1**

00/0 **8** 11 **Doctor's Cave**[35] 4427 8-8-7 46 oh1 (b) SimonWhitworth 9 —
(K O Cunningham-Brown) *prom whn wnt rt after 1f: sn bhd* **40/1**

0000 **9** 6 **Warrior Nation (FR)**[56] 3723 4-8-7 46 oh1 (t) KirstyMilczarek 3 —
(A J Chamberlain) *chsd ldrs to 1/2-way* **22/1**

6000 **10** 7 **Pacific Bay (IRE)**[18] 4986 4-8-7 46 oh1 (p) CathyGannon 10 —
(R Ford) *bmpd after 1f: sn chsng ldrs: rdn and wknd over 2f out* **14/1**

1m 11.58s (0.38) **Going Correction** 0.0s/f (Good)
WFA 3 from 4yo+ 3lb **10** Ran SP% **120.0**
Speed ratings (Par 101): **97,96,92,92,90 89,88,73,65,56**
Tote Swingers:1&2:£2.90, 1&3:£3.70, 2&3:£13.30; totesuper7: Win: Not won Place:Not won. CSF £14.68 CT £83.70 TOTE £3.20: £1.30, £1.30, £2.80; EX 19.70 Place 6 £91.64; Place 5 £19.94.
Owner Ms S Howell **Bred** Newsells Park Stud Limited **Trained** Sedbury, Gloucs

FOCUS
The second leg of the 46-55 sprint which was run in a time a second slower than the first division. Ordinary form.
T/Plt: £117.10 to a £1 stake. Pool:£51,725.24 - 322.43 winning tickets T/Qpdt: £26.60 to a 1 stake. Pool:£3,571.83 - 99.10 winning tickets S

5233 EPSOM (L-H)
Monday, August 30

OFFICIAL GOING: Good
Wind: Light, across Weather: Fine but cloudy

5587 ASHLEY CENTRE E.B.F. MEDIAN AUCTION MAIDEN STKS 7f
2:00 (2:01) (Class 4) 2-Y-O £4,533 (£1,348; £674; £336) Stalls Low

Form RPR

1 **John Biscuit (IRE)** 2-9-3 0 JimmyFortune 11 80+
(A M Balding) *dwlt: hld up towards rr: 9th st: stdy prog on outer over 2f out: shkn up to ld jst over 1f out: hld on nr fin* **16/1**

522 **2** nk **Noonenose**[10] 5263 2-9-3 85 NeilCallan 5 79
(W J Knight) *trckd ldrs: 5th st: sn pushed along: nt qckn 2f out: drvn and r.o to take 2nd wl ins fnl f: clsd on wnr fin* **11/10**[1]

4 **3** ¾ **Winged Valkyrie (IRE)**[17] 5029 2-8-12 0 MichaelHills 4 72
(B W Hills) *led: hrd pressed 2f out: hdd jst over 1f out: styd on but hld after* **9/2**[2]

00 **4** 1¾ **Barathea Dancer (IRE)**[45] 4096 2-8-12 0 StevieDonohoe 6 68+
(R A Teal) *dwlt: in tch: 8th st: shkn up and wanting to hang lft 2f out: styd on wl fnl f to take 4th nr fin* **33/1**

40 **5** ¾ **Rowan Ridge**[41] 4221 2-9-3 0 PatCosgrave 3 71
(J R Boyle) *trckd ldng trio: shkn up and nt qckn 2f out: kpt on same pce fnl f* **66/1**

33 **6** nk **Sylas Ings**[100] 2319 2-9-3 0 (t) IanMongan 12 70
(P M Phelan) *trckd ldrs: 6th st: rdn and prog on outer to chal 2f out: upsides over 1f out: wknd fnl f* **13/2**[3]

3 **7** ¾ **Torun City**[19] 4962 2-9-3 0 TomQueally 1 68
(Eve Johnson Houghton) *in tch: 7th st: shkn up and no prog over 2f out: kpt on same pce after* **16/1**

044 **8** hd **Aciano (IRE)**[17] 5047 2-9-0 78 (b1) Louis-PhilippeBeuzelin(3) 7 68
(B J Meehan) *wl in rr: 10th st and pushed along: no prog tl styd on wl fnl f: nrst fin* **8/1**

50 **9** 7 **Oetzi**[25] 4755 2-9-0 0 MatthewDavies(3) 2 50
(A P Jarvis) *dwlt: t.k.h: hld up in 11th: pushed along and no prog over 2f out: sn wknd* **100/1**

30 **10** ¾ **City Legend**[9] 5298 2-9-3 0 AndreaAtzeni 8 48
(A J McCabe) *pressed ldr to 2f out: wknd rapidly* **25/1**

11 ½ **Valley Tiger** 2-9-3 0 TedDurcan 9 47+
(W R Muir) *dwlt: sn last: pushed along and nt handling trck 3f out: eased fnl f* **40/1**

The Form Book, Raceform Ltd, Compton, RG20 6NL

0 12 *19* **Investment World (IRE)**[16] 5099 2-9-3 0........................ SebSanders 10 —
(M Johnston) *prom: 3rd st: wknd rapidly wl over 2f out: t.o* **50/1**

1m 25.84s (2.54) **Going Correction** +0.10s/f (Good) **12** Ran SP% **115.7**
Speed ratings (Par 96): **89,88,87,85,84 84,83,83,75,74 74,52**
Tote Swingers:1&2:£7.50, 1&3:£12.70, 2&3:£2.70 CSF £32.32 TOTE £19.00: £3.60, £1.10, £1.80; EX 61.90.
Owner Dr Philip Brown **Bred** Dr Philip J Brown **Trained** Kingsclere, Hants

FOCUS
This was just an ordinary maiden.

NOTEBOOK
John Biscuit(IRE), representing last year's winning stable, wasn't best away and showed his inexperience, but came with a sweeping run out wide and, having got to the front 1f out, kept on well to just hold on. He holds no significant entries, but this was a promising start and he should improve.
Noonenose set the standard, having already twice finished runner-up, but his trainer was concerned beforehand about his ability to handle the track and he didn't look comfortable, especially running down the hill. He did stay on well to just miss out and a race will surely come his way before long. (op 5-4 tchd 10-11 and 6-4 and 11-8 in places)
Winged Valkyrie(IRE), a keeping-on fourth at Kempton on debut, had plenty of use made of her and kept on for pressure, but couldn't match the front pair late on. It's possible she was at a disadvantage in racing against the far rail. (tchd 5-1)
Barathea Dancer(IRE) didn't handle the track, but kept on nicely for fourth and will be interesting in a handicap. (op 40-1)
Rowan Ridge had run quite well at this track on debut and he fared better than his 66-1 odds suggested he would. Nurseries beckon.
Sylas Ings was a tad disappointing in the first-time tongue-tie. (op 15-2 tchd 8-1)
Torun City kept on late and should do better in nurseries. (tchd 20-1)
Aciano(IRE) never got into it in the first-time blinkers. (op 13-2)
Valley Tiger, a 30,000gns first foal, struggled badly on the undulations and should leave this form behind.
Investment World(IRE) Official explanation: jockey said colt stopped quickly

5588 TOMPKINS & MAY PARTNERSHIP NEWBUILD H'CAP 6f
2:35 (2:37) (Class 5) (0-75,73) 3-Y-O **£3,885** (£1,156; £577; £288) **Stalls** High

Form RPR
4322 **1** **Silvee**[8] 5327 3-8-2 **54**........................ NeilChalmers 6 59
(J J Bridger) *hld up in 7th: rdn and prog on outer jst over 2f out: wnt 2nd fnl f: styd on gamely to ld last strides* **5/1**[3]
5250 **2** *shd* **Yurituni**[35] 4424 3-9-7 **73**........................ TomQueally 8 78
(Eve Johnson Houghton) *trckd ldng pair: shkn up to ld 2f out: styd on fnl f: hdd last strides* **16/1**
062 **3** *1* **Stratton Banker (IRE)**[12] 5206 3-8-7 **59**........................ AndreaAtzeni 3 60
(S C Williams) *hld up in 5th: smooth prog to chal 2f out: rdn and fnd nil over 1f out: kpt on same pce after* **11/4**[1]
2226 **4** *2 3/4* **Pippbrook Ministar**[54] 3786 3-9-6 **72**........................ JimmyFortune 2 65
(J R Boyle) *trckd ldng trio: effrt to chal and upsides over 2f out: nt qckn wl over 1f out: fdd fnl f* **9/1**
-040 **5** *nk* **Royal Blade (IRE)**[25] 4754 3-8-8 **63**........................ MatthewDavies(3) 5 55
(A P Jarvis) *mde most to 2f out: grad fdd over 1f out* **22/1**
0321 **6** *3 3/4* **Dream Number (IRE)**[12] 5206 3-9-2 **68**........................ TedDurcan 7 48
(W R Muir) *chsd ldr to over 2f out: wknd* **10/3**[2]
0125 **7** *7* **Panpiper**[9] 5309 3-9-3 **69**........................ NeilCallan 4 26
(G L Moore) *stdd s: hld up in 6th: pushed along 1/2-way: struggling in rr fnl 2f* **6/1**
65 **8** *7* **Excellent Thought**[31] 4553 3-9-1 **67**........................ IanMongan 1 —
(P Howling) *hld up in last: shkn up and no prog 1/2-way: eased whn no ch over 1f out* **7/1**

1m 10.83s (1.43) **Going Correction** +0.10s/f (Good) **8** Ran SP% **113.4**
Speed ratings (Par 100): **94,93,92,88,88 83,74,64**
Tote Swingers:1&2:£11.60, 1&3:£4.90, 2&3:£12.20 CSF £76.93 CT £262.63 TOTE £6.30: £2.10, £4.50, £1.60; EX 50.00.
Owner Mr & Mrs K Finch **Bred** Mr And Mrs K Finch **Trained** Liphook, Hants

FOCUS
They appeared to go a fair gallop for what was a modest sprint handicap. The field came more centre-track in the straight.

5589 TOTESUPER7 H'CAP 5f
3:10 (3:10) (Class 2) (0-100,92) 3-Y-O+
£11,215 (£3,358; £1,679; £840; £419; £210) **Stalls** High

Form RPR
2321 **1** **Cape Royal**[14] 5151 10-8-9 **77**........................(bt) PatCosgrave 9 87
(J M Bradley) *racd against rail: mde all: styd on stoutly fr over 1f out* **8/1**
2112 **2** *1* **La Fortunata**[11] 5250 3-8-12 **82**........................ AndreaAtzeni 8 88
(Mike Murphy) *racd one off rail: chsd wnr: drvn over 1f out: styd on: a hld* **11/2**[2]
0000 **3** *3/4* **Strike Up The Band**[13] 5183 7-9-2 **87**........................ MichaelGeran(3) 5 91
(D Nicholls) *racd jst off rail: chsd ldrs: rdn over 1f out: kpt on fnl f* **12/1**
5620 **4** *nk* **City Dancer (IRE)**[52] 3875 4-9-6 **88**........................ TedDurcan 2 91+
(D Nicholls) *ponied to s: dwlt: hld up in last pair: swtchd out to centre and effrt over 2f out: prog over 1f out: tried to chal but fdd ins fnl f* **7/2**[1]
1000 **5** *2* **Fathom Five (IRE)**[23] 4814 6-9-10 **92**........................ AlanMunro 6 87
(C F Wall) *dwlt: hld up in last pair and racd against rail: plld out and rdn over 1f out: no imp* **11/2**[2]
0000 **6** *3/4* **Oldjoesaid**[13] 5183 6-9-1 **83**........................(b[1]) NeilCallan 7 76
(K A Ryan) *hld up bhd ldrs against rail: rdn and nt qckn over 1f out: wl btn after* **6/1**[3]
0016 **7** *7* **Bertoliver**[65] 3430 6-9-6 **88**........................ MichaelHills 4 56
(S C Williams) *racd four off the rail: chsd ldrs: wknd over 1f out* **10/1**
2015 **8** *1 1/2* **Solemn**[16] 5069 5-9-2 **84**........................(b) SebSanders 3 46
(J M Bradley) *racd in centre: nvr on terms w ldrs: bhd over 1f out* **15/2**
-002 **9** *1* **Titus Andronicus (IRE)**[8] 5335 4-8-12 **80**........................ JimmyFortune 1 39
(R A Fahey) *racd in centre: nvr on terms w ldrs: bhd over 1f out* **9/1**

55.06 secs (-0.64) **Going Correction** +0.10s/f (Good)
WFA 3 from 4yo+ 2lb **9** Ran SP% **116.9**
Speed ratings (Par 109): **109,107,106,105,102 101,90,87,86**
Tote Swingers:1&2:£2.80, 1&3:£19.40, 2&3:£14.30 CSF £52.15 CT £533.66 TOTE £7.60: £2.20, £1.70, £4.40; EX 14.60.
Owner E A Hayward **Bred** D R Brotherton **Trained** Sedbury, Gloucs

FOCUS
Plenty of trailblazers in opposition, so this was always going to be fast and furious.

NOTEBOOK
Cape Royal, with the rail to run against, came out on top, leading throughout and staying on strongly for course win number three. He has been a model of consistency of late but may struggle to defy much of a rise. (tchd 7-1)
La Fortunata, denied narrowly off 3lb lower when bidding for a hat-trick at York latest, had run well here earlier in the season and she battled on well without quite being able to match the winner. She remains on the up. (op 5-1 tchd 6-1)
Strike Up The Band is on a long losing run and this season's efforts haven't been good, but he's on a very handy mark these days and this was much more encouraging.
City Dancer(IRE) has good course form but she's hard to win with and, whereas in the past she's got going too late, this time she didn't get home so well having challenged a lot earlier. She was challenging a few off the rail, though, so perhaps was at a slight disadvantage. (op 5-1)
Fathom Five(IRE) ran a little better returned to his favourite course. (op 13-2)
Oldjoesaid showed a bit more in the first-time blinkers. (op 11-2)
Solemn reported to have hung left. Official explanation: jockey said gelding hung left (op 9-1 tchd 7-1)

5590 TOMPKINS & MAY PARTNERSHIP REACTIVE REPAIRS CONDITIONS STKS 1m 2f 18y
3:45 (3:47) (Class 3) 3-Y-O+ **£6,854** (£2,052; £1,026; £513; £256) **Stalls** Low

Form RPR
-426 **1** **Prince Siegfried (FR)**[44] 4139 4-9-2 110........................ FrankieDettori 4 114+
(Saeed Bin Suroor) *mde all: pressed over 1f out: shkn up and sn asserted: styd on wl* **4/6**[1]
511 **2** *1 1/2* **Jet Away**[25] 4757 3-8-8 92........................ TomQueally 5 111+
(H R A Cecil) *hld up last: prog on outer to take 2nd wl over 1f out: threatened briefly but sn nt qckn and readily hld* **7/2**[2]
-205 **3** *2* **Prompter**[46] 4068 3-8-8 102........................ NeilCallan 2 107
(M L W Bell) *hld up: trckd ldng pair 5f out: chsd wnr over 2f out to wl over 1f out: one pce* **20/1**
6065 **4** *2 1/2* **Confront**[10] 5274 5-9-2 107........................ JimmyFortune 1 102
(Sir Michael Stoute) *chsd ldr to over 2f out: nt qckn and wl btn 4th over 1f out* **13/2**[3]
20-4 **5** *2 1/4* **Layali Al Andalus**[108] 2070 3-8-8 110........................(t) TedDurcan 3 98
(Saeed Bin Suroor) *chsd ldng pair to 5f out: last and wl btn 2f out* **9/1**

2m 7.99s (-1.71) **Going Correction** +0.10s/f (Good)
WFA 3 from 4yo+ 8lb **5** Ran SP% **110.3**
Speed ratings (Par 107): **110,108,107,105,103**
CSF £3.29 TOTE £1.60: £1.10, £2.20; EX 3.90.
Owner Godolphin **Bred** Haras Saint Pair Du Mont **Trained** Newmarket, Suffolk

FOCUS
An interesting little conditions race that saw Frankie Dettori excel from the front on Prince Siegfried.

NOTEBOOK
Prince Siegfried(FR) appreciated the slight bit of give in the ground and was given a fine ride by Dettori to score. A horse who can be a tricky ride, the hold-up tactics didn't work at Newbury last time and he seemed much happier here bossing lesser opposition. He will presumably now return to Listed/Group 3 level. (op 11-10)
Jet Away, whose latest Sandown win had come off a mark of just 86, ran a race full of promise. Evidently held in some regard and very much viewed as a horse for next year, he picked up swiftly to challenge, but the winner had a bit left, and in the end he had to settle for second. He remains capable of better back on a more conventional track. (op 11-4)
Prompter, gelded since last seen, was ridden with more restraint than usual and ran well, although he's going to remain tough to place. (op 12-1)
Confront seems to have taken a step backwards this season and was again disappointing. (op 9-2 tchd 7-1)
Layali Al Andalus, bitterly disappointing at Hamilton on his debut for Godolphin, showed more here and should do better again, considering he appeared not to like the track. (tchd 11-1)

5591 TOMPKINS & MAY PARTNERSHIP AMATEUR DERBY (H'CAP) (FOR GENTLEMAN AMATEUR RIDERS) 1m 4f 10y
4:20 (4:22) (Class 4) (0-85,85) 4-Y-O+ **£6,246** (£1,937; £968; £484) **Stalls** Centre

Form RPR
2021 **1** **Maybe I Wont**[32] 4498 5-9-13 **66** oh1........................ MrPCollington(3) 7 74
(Lucinda Featherstone) *hld up last: prog on wd outside and 11th st: sustained effrt u.p fr 3f out: clsd to ld last 150yds: hld on* **14/1**
5462 **2** *1/2* **Arashi**[19] 4945 4-9-11 **66** oh5........................(v) MrJPFeatherstone(5) 13 73
(Lucinda Featherstone) *dwlt: hld up in last pair: 14th st: rdn over 2f out and stl plenty to do: wnt lft over 1f out and r.o: tk 2nd last 50yds and clsd on wnr fin* **25/1**
2341 **3** *1 1/4* **King's Masque**[22] 4859 4-10-11 **80**........................ MrRJWilliams(5) 9 85
(B J Llewellyn) *hld up in midfield: gd prog on inner and 4th st: led wl over 2f out: edgd rt over 1f out: hdd and one pce last 150yds* **12/1**
02 **4** *hd* **Pool Of Knowledge (FR)**[16] 5091 4-10-12 **76**........................ HarryChalloner 5 81
(Miss Venetia Williams) *trckd ldrs: prog on inner and cl 5th st: chal 3f out: chsd ldr sn after: carried sltly rt 1f out: one pce fnl f* **12/1**
4112 **5** *3/4* **Bramalea**[10] 5260 5-10-5 **74**........................ MrTGarner(5) 2 78+
(B W Duke) *prom: chsd ldr 5f out: led briefly 3f out: nt qckn over 2f out: styd on again ins fnl f* **14/1**
0/0- **6** *1/2* **Celticello (IRE)**[16] 584 8-10-0 **69**........................ MrJMQuinlan(5) 12 72
(M G Quinlan) *settled midfield: 9th st: shkn up and no prog 3f out: styd on u.p fr over 1f out: nrst fin* **18/1**
300- **7** *1 3/4* **Laughing Boy (IRE)**[12] 5225 4-11-7 **85**........................ MrPWMullins 4 85
(W P Mullins, Ire) *dwlt: hld up wl in rr: 10th and sing to make prog on inner st: hanging lft 2f out and nt qckn: plugged on* **6/1**[3]
1223 **8** *1 1/4* **Bavarica**[16] 5071 8-10-8 **75**........................ MrRBirkett(3) 1 73
(Miss J Feilden) *dwlt: sn prom: 3rd st: styd cl up but lost pl sn after: nt qckn over 2f out: fdd* **20/1**
5331 **9** *hd* **Admirable Duque (IRE)**[4] 5443 4-10-8 **77** 6ex..........(p) MrCMartin(5) 14 75
(D J S Ffrench Davis) *settled wl in rr: 13th st: rdn on wd outside 3f out: plugged on but nvr rchd ldrs* **16/1**
0050 **10** *1 1/2* **Wing Play (IRE)**[7] 5375 5-10-10 **79**........................ MrRPooles(5) 11 74
(H Morrison) *hld up in rr: 12th st: rdn on outer 3f out: plugged on but nvr on terms* **16/1**
3061 **11** *2 1/4* **Foxhaven**[17] 5034 8-10-9 **78**........................(v) MrNdeBoinville(5) 15 70
(P R Chamings) *trckd ldrs: 6th st: cl enough over 2f out: hanging bdly lft after: fdd over 1f out* **12/1**
0440 **12** *1/2* **Cosmic Sun**[10] 5278 4-11-5 **83**........................ MrMSeston 8 74
(R A Fahey) *led: hdd u.p 3f out: steadily wknd* **11/2**[2]
111- **13** *2 1/2* **The Last Don (IRE)**[10] 5283 4-11-4 **85**........................ MrPJMcMahon(3) 6 72
(Charles O'Brien, Ire) *chsd ldrs: lost pl fr 1/2-way: last and toiling bdly st: nvr on terms after* **18/1**
0445 **14** *8* **Strategic Mount**[23] 4818 7-11-5 **83**........................(p) MrSWalker 10 57
(P F I Cole) *trckd ldrs: 7th and sing to lose pl st: sn bhd* **5/1**[1]
4033 **15** *dist* **Cool Strike (UAE)**[17] 5035 4-11-7 **85**........................(v) MrDHDunsdon 3 —
(A M Balding) *chsd ldr to 5f out: 8th and wkng rapidly st: sn t.o* **7/1**

2m 41.0s (2.10) **Going Correction** +0.10s/f (Good) **15** Ran SP% **126.1**
Speed ratings (Par 105): **97,96,95,95,95 94,93,92,92,91 90,89,88,82,—**
Tote Swingers:1&2:£35.80, 1&3:£21.80, 2&3:£72.30 CSF £337.14 CT £4299.71 TOTE £14.30: £4.50, £10.70, £4.30; EX 442.90.
Owner J Roundtree **Bred** Wheelersland Stud **Trained** Atlow, Derbyshire
■ A 1-2 for Lucinda Featherstone.

FOCUS
This was an ultra-competitive amateur riders' handicap. The pace was a good one and those coming from off the pace were at a definite advantage, in fact the first two home were last and second-last on the approach to Tattenham Corner.
Cool Strike(UAE) Official explanation: jockey said gelding lost its action

5592 TOMPKINS & MAY PARTNERSHIP PLANNED MAINTENANCE H'CAP — 1m 2f 18y
4:55 (4:56) (Class 3) (0-90,89) 3-Y-O+ — £6,476 (£1,927; £963; £481) Stalls Low

Form				RPR
-600	1		**Plaisterer**[23] 4830 5-9-10 **85** ... AlanMunro 3 (C F Wall) *mde all: stdd pce after 4f: pushed along firmly and upped tempo over 2f out: styd on wl: rdr nvr used whip* **10/3**[2]	94
0331	2	1	**Resurge (IRE)**[18] 4996 5-9-12 **87** ... IanMongan 7 (W S Kittow) *stdd s: t.k.h: hld up in last pair: swtchd out wd over 2f out: drvn and prog to take 2nd jst ins fnl f: styd on but nvr able to chal* **11/4**[1]	94+
3030	3	1 ½	**Ramona Chase**[9] 5307 5-9-0 **75** ...(t) NeilCallan 6 (M J Attwater) *trckd ldng pair: t.k.h downhill 1/2-way: cl enough 2f out: nt qckn and hld after* **7/1**	79
1302	4	½	**Blues Music (IRE)**[25] 4758 3-8-11 **80** ... MichaelHills 5 (B W Hills) *trckd wnr: rdn and nt qckn 2f out: hld after: lost 2 pls fnl f* **11/4**[1]	83
5606	5	1 ½	**Tartan Gunna**[23] 4816 4-10-0 **89** ...(v) SebSanders 1 (M Johnston) *dwlt and rousted along early: hld up in last pair: nt qckn and wl outpcd over 2f out: n.d after* **4/1**[3]	89
0000	6	3 ¼	**Wind Star**[7] 5375 7-9-1 **76** ... StevieDonohoe 4 (M F Harris) *trckd ldng pair: pushed along wl over 2f out: lost pl and btn wl over 1f out: wknd* **25/1**	70

2m 14.05s (4.35) **Going Correction** +0.10s/f (Good)
WFA 3 from 4yo+ 8lb — **6** Ran SP% **112.8**
Speed ratings (Par 107): **86,85,84,83,82 79**
Tote Swingers:1&2:£2.60, 1&3:£3.20, 2&3:£2.70 CSF £13.03 TOTE £3.80: £2.60, £1.40; EX 12.80.
Owner David Andrews Plastering **Bred** Vogue Development Company (kent) Ltd **Trained** Newmarket, Suffolk

FOCUS
A decent handicap that turned into a bit of a dash for home.

NOTEBOOK
Plaisterer had been struggling this year, but was on a good mark and found plenty inside the final 2f to win with a bit in hand. She very much had the run of things, though, so how she gets on in the immediate future may depend on the handicapper. (op 7-2 tchd 4-1)
Resurge(IRE) dotted up off 7lb lower at the track last time and he may well have supplemented that win had there been more pace on early. The winner was always doing too much for him, but he did stay on well for second and remains capable of better. (tchd 3-1)
Ramona Chase has slipped back to a good mark but it's over three years now since he gained his sole victory. (op 11-2)
Blues Music(IRE) was disappointing off 2lb higher, fading out of it late on. Official explanation: jockey said colt did not handle the track (op 7-2 tchd 4-1)
Tartan Gunna was again slowly away and couldn't get involved. (tchd 7-2)

5593 TOMPKINS & MAY PARTNERSHIP VOID MANAGEMENT H'CAP — 1m 114y
5:30 (5:31) (Class 4) (0-80,76) 3-Y-O+ — £5,180 (£1,541; £770; £384) Stalls Low

Form				RPR
2121	1		**Mr Harmoosh (IRE)**[22] 4870 3-9-2 **71** ... AndreaAtzeni 9 (E F Vaughan) *hld up last: stl there 2f out: drvn and prog after: led last 100yds: styd on* **9/2**[3]	79+
3604	2	½	**King Columbo (IRE)**[10] 5254 5-9-1 **63** ... TomQueally 6 (Miss J Feilden) *hld up: 5th st: prog on inner to ld over 1f out: hdd and one pce last 100yds* **10/3**[2]	70
4105	3	½	**Veni Vedi Veci (IRE)**[16] 5086 3-9-6 **75** ... JimmyFortune 1 (A M Balding) *led: c wd in st: hdd over 2f out: stl cl enough u.p over 1f out: edgd rt and one pce* **11/4**[1]	81
50-2	4	shd	**Not In The Clock (USA)**[178] 805 3-8-2 **62** ... KierenFox[(5)] 2 (J R Best) *chsd ldr to over 4f out: cl 4th st: nt qckn over 2f out and struggling: styd on again fnl f* **8/1**	67
00	5	1 ¾	**Ermyn Express**[29] 4626 3-7-13 **59** ow2 ... JemmaMarshall[(5)] 8 (P M Phelan) *hld up in 6th: prog towards inner 2f out: chal and upsides 1f out: hanging lft and wknd last 100yds* **20/1**	60
0310	6	hd	**Zambuka (FR)**[30] 4585 3-8-2 **62** ... RossAtkinson[(5)] 3 (F J Brennan) *t.k.h: racd wd: trckd ldng trio: wnt 2nd over 4f out: carried to centre in st: nt qckn over 2f out: no imp after* **9/2**[3]	63
442	7	½	**Pha Mai Blue**[41] 4232 5-8-13 **61** ...(v) PatCosgrave 5 (J R Boyle) *awkward s: t.k.h: trckd ldng pair: led over 2f out to over 1f out: stl upsides ent fnl f: hld whn squeezed out last 100yds* **8/1**	61

1m 46.86s (0.76) **Going Correction** +0.10s/f (Good)
WFA 3 from 5yo 7lb — **7** Ran SP% **113.1**
Speed ratings (Par 105): **100,99,99,99,97 97,96**
Tote Swingers:1&2:£3.70, 1&3:£3.10, 2&3:£2.00 CSF £19.39 CT £47.64 TOTE £4.50: £2.30, £1.30; EX 17.70 Place 6 £175.06; Place 5 £129.86.
Owner Salem Rashid **Bred** Thomas G Cooke **Trained** Newmarket, Suffolk

FOCUS
There wasn't much to separate the seven runners, who ended up spread right across the track.
T/Plt: £163.30 to a £1 stake. Pool:£65,819.36 - 294.11 winning tickets T/Qpdt: £53.50 to a £1 stake. Pool:£3,421.95 - 47.30 winning tickets JN

5482 NEWCASTLE (L-H)
Monday, August 30

OFFICIAL GOING: Good to soft (good in places; 6.8)
Wind: Almost nil Weather: Overcast

5594 EUROPEAN BREEDERS' FUND MAIDEN STKS (DIV I) — 7f
2:15 (2:15) (Class 4) 2-Y-O
£3,832 (£1,147; £573; £287; £143; £71) Stalls Centre

Form				RPR
44	1		**Loukoumi**[42] 4187 2-8-12 0 ... TomEaves 12 (B Smart) *hld up: hdwy 1/2-way: led ins fnl f: drvn out* **11/1**	69+
00	2	1	**Rudegirl (IRE)**[16] 5066 2-8-9 0 ... BarryMcHugh[(3)] 10 (N Tinkler) *trckd ldrs: led over 2f out to ins fnl f: kpt on: hld towards fin* **100/1**	67
5	3	1 ¾	**Ibsaar**[29] 4614 2-9-3 0 ... FrannyNorton 6 (W J Haggas) *led to over 2f out: rallied and ev ch ent fnl f: kpt on same pce* **3/1**[1]	67
5	4	1 ½	**Deep Applause**[68] 3316 2-9-3 0 ... PJMcDonald 9 (M Dods) *hld up bhd ldng gp: shkn up over 2f out: kpt on fnl f: nvr nr to chal* **12/1**	63+
32	5	1 ¼	**Maverik**[51] 3923 2-9-3 0 ... PhillipMakin 4 (M Dods) *trckd ldrs: effrt and ev ch over 1f out: no ex ins fnl f* **4/1**[3]	60
00	6	2	**The Bells O Peover**[10] 5277 2-9-3 0 ... JoeFanning 2 (M Johnston) *cl up: edgd to far rail 3f out: ev ch tl wknd ins fnl f* **7/2**[2]	55
03	7	1 ¾	**Beer Flush (IRE)**[37] 4368 2-9-0 0 ... PatrickDonaghy[(3)] 5 (Jedd O'Keeffe) *dwlt: sn prom: effrt and ev ch over 1f out: wknd ins fnl f* **14/1**	51
	8	1 ¼	**Elysian Heights (IRE)** 2-9-3 0 ... DarryllHolland 8 (J Noseda) *dwlt: sn in tch: rdn and hung lft over 2f out: sn outpcd* **15/2**	48
	9	½	**Pink Diva (IRE)** 2-8-12 0 ... JamieSpencer 11 (T P Tate) *dwlt: hld up: rdn and outpcd 3f out: n.d after* **7/1**	42
04	10	10	**Solo Whisper (IRE)**[33] 4480 2-9-3 0 ... PaulMulrennan 1 (J Howard Johnson) *in tch tl rdn and wknd fr over 2f out* **40/1**	22
	11	6	**Big Zaf** 2-9-0 0 ... PaulPickard[(3)] 3 (P T Midgley) *dwlt: sn pushed along in rr: struggling after 3f* **100/1**	7
00	12	19	**Lady Of The Knight (IRE)**[22] 4862 2-8-12 0 ... PatrickMathers 7 (H A McWilliams) *sn in tch: struggling after 3f: sn btn: eased whn no ch* **150/1**	—

1m 28.6s (-0.10) **Going Correction** -0.075s/f (Good) — **12** Ran SP% **119.3**
Speed ratings (Par 96): **97,95,93,92,90 88,86,85,84,73 66,44**
Tote Swingers:1&2:£36.80, 1&3:£5.90, 2&3:£39.80 CSF £801.45 TOTE £14.60: £3.80, £12.00, £1.60; EX 615.80.
Owner Legard Sidebottom & Sykes **Bred** Lady Legard & Sir Tatton Sykes **Trained** Hambleton, N Yorks

FOCUS
All eight races were on the straight course, where the ground had dried out and was reckoned "slow, hard work". Part one of this 2-y-o maiden had plenty of interesting pedigrees. They raced middle to far side with the first two racing towards the centre.

NOTEBOOK
Loukoumi, who had raced too freely when a well-beaten fourth at Ayr on her second start, settled much better and came with a well-timed run to win quite decisively in the end. This sets her up for a nursery campaign.
Rudegirl(IRE) had shown little in two previous starts. She ran a lot better here and was just edged out, but this will have blown a potentially lenient nursery mark out of the water. (op 80-1)
Ibsaar showed plenty of toe towards the centre of the track, but did not see out the stiff 7f quite as well as the first two. (op 4-1)
Deep Applause, his trainer's second string, made up a deal of late ground on his first start for almost ten weeks. He has plenty of size and scope and should make his mark in handicap company at three. (tchd 14-1)
Maverik, his trainer's number one hope, chased the leader towards the far side but, slightly keen, did not truly see out the extra furlong. (op 9-2 tchd 7-2)
The Bells O Peover, seventh in a good-class maiden at York, took them along but edged towards the far-side rail and again did not see out the trip. (tchd 4-1)
Elysian Heights(IRE), a handsome son of Galileo, missed the break but showed signs of ability, improving to chase the leaders at halfway before tiring. (op 7-1)
Pink Diva(IRE), an expensive yearling purchase, missed a beat at the start and looked very inexperienced. She can surely do a fair bit better in due course. (op 11-2)
Lady Of The Knight(IRE) Official explanation: jockey said filly finished lame right-fore

5595 EUROPEAN BREEDERS' FUND MAIDEN STKS (DIV II) — 7f
2:50 (2:51) (Class 4) 2-Y-O
£3,832 (£1,147; £573; £287; £143; £71) Stalls Centre

Form				RPR
	1		**Sergeant Ablett (IRE)** 2-9-3 0 ... JoeFanning 5 (M Johnston) *in tch: hdwy to ld over 1f out: shkn up and styd on strly fnl f* **9/2**[2]	86+
	2	2 ¾	**Sud Pacifique (IRE)** 2-9-3 0 ... DarryllHolland 10 (J Noseda) *sn niggled along in rr: gd hdwy to chse wnr over 1f out: shkn up and no imp fnl f* **1/1**[1]	79+
0022	3	8	**Indian Giver**[7] 5352 2-8-12 69 ... PatrickMathers 1 (H A McWilliams) *w ldr: rdn and edgd rt over 1f out: sn outpcd by ldng pair* **12/1**	54
0	4	nk	**Face The Future**[42] 4187 2-9-3 0 ... PhillipMakin 4 (M Dods) *trckd ldrs: drvn over 2f out: kpt on same pce over 1f out* **18/1**	58
0	5	2 ¼	**White Fusion**[27] 4668 2-8-12 0 ... DaleSwift[(5)] 9 (J Howard Johnson) *prom: drvn and outpcd over 2f out: n.d after* **25/1**	53
335	6	nk	**Adlington**[23] 4821 2-9-0 73 ... BarryMcHugh[(3)] 3 (R A Fahey) *slt ld to over 1f out: sn n.m.r and wknd* **6/1**[3]	52
	7	nk	**Miss T** 2-8-12 0 ... PaulMulrennan 2 (J G Given) *in tch: drvn over 3f out: wknd over 2f out* **33/1**	46
00	8	3 ¼	**Byron Bear (IRE)**[17] 5040 2-9-3 0 ... PJMcDonald 8 (P T Midgley) *hld up towards rr: rdn 3f out: nvr able to chal* **40/1**	43
0500	9	nse	**West Stand**[9] 5298 2-8-12 65 ... AndrewMullen 11 (Mrs K Walton) *hld up in tch: rdn over 3f out: btn fnl 2f* **14/1**	38
	10	12	**Geordie Joe** 2-9-3 0 ... DuranFentiman 6 (J R Weymes) *missed break: bhd and pushed along: struggling fr 1/2-way* **40/1**	—
	11	5	**Margot De Medici (FR)** 2-8-12 0 ... TomEaves 7 (N Tinkler) *hld up in tch: struggling after 3f: sn btn* **25/1**	—

1m 28.6s (-0.10) **Going Correction** -0.075s/f (Good) — **11** Ran SP% **117.6**
Speed ratings (Par 96): **97,93,84,84,81 81,81,77,77,63 57**
Tote Swingers:1&2:£2.40, 1&3:£3.20, 2&3:£4.10 CSF £8.84 TOTE £6.00: £2.90, £1.02, £4.00; EX 10.10.
Owner J Barson **Bred** D G Hardisty Bloodstock **Trained** Middleham Moor, N Yorks

FOCUS
This looked much the stronger division of the maiden, though the time was very similar, and they raced in one group towards the centre.

NOTEBOOK
Sergeant Ablett(IRE) is a half-brother to the stable's useful stayer Drill Sergeant and cost 120,000gns as a yearling. A leggy colt with plenty of scope, he moved up towards the far side to take charge and, getting first run on the favourite, was never in any danger. He won going away and looks a fine prospect. (op 6-1 tchd 7-1)
Sud Pacifique(IRE), a laid-back newcomer, cost 600,000 euros. Out of a sister to a Marcel Boussac winner, he already holds Group 1 entries. Blanketed for stalls entry, he was held up at the back but could not land a blow when asked to go in pursuit of the winner. He looks certain to find a maiden at least. (op 11-10 tchd 6-5 in places)
Indian Giver, rated just 69, was having her sixth start and gives a good line to exactly what the first two achieved first time. (tchd 10-1)
Face The Future, who had been very green on his debut, was having his first run for six weeks. He shaped much better but will need another outing to qualify for a nursery mark. (tchd 20-1)
White Fusion, who made an awkward exit from the stalls, was soon in the firing line. He still looks very immature. (op 18-1 tchd 16-1)

Adlington, rated 73, took them along on his fourth start but he does not look to be progressing. (op 5-1)

5596 LA TAXIS CLAIMING STKS 1m 3y(S)
3:25 (3:25) (Class 6) 3-Y-O+ **£1,457** (£433; £216; £108) **Stalls** Centre

Form					RPR
1320	**1**		**Moody Tunes**[23] 4828 7-9-8 78	MichaelO'Connell(5) 2	83
			(Mrs K Burke) *cl up: led over 2f out: styd on strly fnl f* **9/4**[1]		
6004	**2**	3	**Just Five (IRE)**[19] 4949 4-9-8 76	DaleSwift(5) 3	76
			(M Dods) *in tch: rdn to chse wnr over 2f out: kpt on same pce fnl f* **6/1**[3]		
0050	**3**	3	**Wigwam Willie (IRE)**[19] 4949 8-9-13 73	(tp) JamieSpencer 6	69
			(K A Ryan) *hld up: rdn over 2f out: hdwy over 1f out: no imp fnl f* **13/2**		
0000	**4**	2 ¾	**Ten To The Dozen**[22] 4868 7-8-4 40	NeilFarley(7) 7	47
			(D W Thompson) *bhd: rdn 1/2-way: hdwy over 2f out: one pce over 1f out* **80/1**		
4250	**5**	½	**Coole Dodger (IRE)**[11] 5244 5-8-11 50	(b[1]) PJMcDonald 4	46
			(B Ellison) *led: swtchd to r alone stands' rail 4f out: hdd over 2f out: sn outpcd* **10/1**		
6234	**6**	4	**Bolodenka (IRE)**[16] 5098 8-9-8 75	(p) LeeTopliss(5) 8	53
			(R A Fahey) *in tch: effrt over 3f out: wknd fr 2f out* **3/1**[2]		
2525	**7**	1 ¾	**Cono Zur (FR)**[7] 5353 3-8-12 70	(b[1]) JamesSullivan(3) 10	42
			(Mrs R A Carr) *hld up in tch: drvn over 3f out: wknd over 2f out* **6/1**[3]		
4000	**8**	8	**Step To It (IRE)**[12] 5216 3-8-5 49	(b[1]) JoeFanning 1	13
			(K A Ryan) *chsd ldrs tl rdn and wknd over 2f out* **33/1**		
05-0	**9**	6	**Old Firm**[30] 4581 4-9-10 49	BarryMcHugh(3) 5	16
			(J A McShane) *in tch: drvn 1/2-way: btn over 2f out* **100/1**		
0203	**10**	1 ¾	**Bajan Pride**[11] 5241 6-9-9 63	PaulMulrennan 9	—
			(P T Midgley) *hld up in tch: stdy hdwy 1/2-way: wknd over 2f out* **16/1**		

1m 42.28s (-1.12) **Going Correction** -0.075s/f (Good)
WFA 3 from 4yo+ 6lb **10** Ran SP% **117.8**
Speed ratings (Par 101): **102,99,96,93,92 88,87,79,73,71**
Tote Swingers:1&2:£4.30, 1&3:£2.80, 2&3:£7.20 CSF £16.49 TOTE £3.30: £1.30, £2.70, £2.00; EX 16.10.
Owner Mrs Elaine M Burke **Bred** Llety Stud **Trained** Middleham Moor, North Yorks

FOCUS
A run-of-the-mill claimer and in the end very much a one-horse race.
Coole Dodger(IRE) Official explanation: jockey said gelding hung right-handed

5597 FREEBETTING.CO.UK BLAYDON NURSERY 1m 3y(S)
4:00 (4:01) (Class 2) 2-Y-O
£6,480 (£1,940; £970; £485; £242; £121) **Stalls** Centre

Form					RPR
561	**1**		**My Single Malt (IRE)**[28] 4650 2-8-12 74	JamieSpencer 6	82+
			(T P Tate) *hld up: swtchd lft and hdwy to ld appr fnl f: edgd rt ins fnl f: hld on wl* **5/1**[2]		
221	**2**	½	**Next Edition (IRE)**[43] 4167 2-9-2 83	DaleSwift(5) 10	88
			(J Howard Johnson) *led tl rdn and hdd appr fnl f: kpt on u.p towards fin* **4/1**[1]		
4614	**3**	1 ¼	**Arabian Star (IRE)**[11] 5234 2-8-11 73	FrannyNorton 11	75
			(M R Channon) *in tch: rdn and outpcd over 2f out: styd on wl fnl f: nrst fin* **15/2**[3]		
0052	**4**	hd	**Regimental (IRE)**[6] 5389 2-7-7 60 oh3	RosieJessop(5) 1	62
			(Mrs A Duffield) *cl up: effrt and ev ch over 1f out: kpt on same pce ins fnl f* **8/1**		
050	**5**	nse	**My Mate Jake (IRE)**[38] 4346 2-8-8 70	PaulMulrennan 12	71
			(J G Given) *hld up in midfield: drvn and outpcd over 2f out: no imp tl styd on fnl f: nvr able to chal* **14/1**		
01	**6**	1 ½	**Chin'n Tonic (IRE)**[37] 4368 2-9-4 80	PJMcDonald 2	78
			(G A Swinbank) *trckd ldrs: drvn and outpcd over 2f out: r.o ins fnl f: no imp* **4/1**[1]		
0561	**7**	¾	**Kalkan Bay**[18] 4984 2-8-10 72	TomEaves 5	69
			(Jedd O'Keeffe) *cl up tl rdn and outpcd over 1f out: no imp ins fnl f* **16/1**		
6624	**8**	1	**Damascus Symphony**[19] 4948 2-8-7 69	JoeFanning 4	63
			(J D Bethell) *prom: drvn over 2f out: no ex over 1f out* **28/1**		
2116	**9**	½	**Mica Mika (IRE)**[18] 4984 2-8-4 71	LeeTopliss(5) 9	64
			(R A Fahey) *in tch: rdn 3f out: btn over 1f out* **12/1**		
0425	**10**	2 ¼	**Dark Dune (IRE)**[18] 4984 2-8-5 67	DuranFentiman 3	55
			(T D Easterby) *in tch tl rdn and wknd wl over 1f out* **20/1**		
4644	**11**	1	**Golden Blaze**[26] 4701 2-7-5 60 oh3	NeilFarley(7) 8	46
			(James Moffatt) *bhd: pushed along over 2f out: nvr on terms* **16/1**		
006	**12**	3	**Rainbows Son**[73] 3162 2-7-12 62 oh15 ow3	(p) PaulPickard(3) 7	42
			(P T Midgley) *hld up: rdn over 2f out: edgd lft and sn btn* **100/1**		

1m 42.95s (-0.45) **Going Correction** -0.075s/f (Good) **12** Ran SP% **114.9**
Speed ratings (Par 100): **99,98,97,97,97 95,94,93,93,91 90,87**
Tote Swingers:1&2:£5.40, 1&3:£5.90, 2&3:£6.40 CSF £23.94 CT £150.20 TOTE £5.90: £1.60, £1.80, £2.50; EX 27.00.
Owner Mrs Fitri Hay **Bred** Ballylinch Stud **Trained** Tadcaster, N Yorks
■ Stewards' Enquiry : Rosie Jessop caution: careless riding.

FOCUS
A nursery that carried four times as much prize-money in the past, but a highly competitive renewal all the same.

NOTEBOOK
My Single Malt(IRE), a thick-set, well-made colt, had struggled to get off the mark at the third attempt in a modest 6f maiden at Ripon a month earlier. Clearly thriving, he came there strongly to take charge towards the far side. Idling in front, he had to be kept right up to his work. He will improve again and should make a useful handicapper at three. (op 6-1)
Next Edition(IRE), off the mark at the third attempt over 7f at Redcar, took them along and fought back bravely when headed. He deserves to go one better. (op 9-2)
Arabian Star(IRE), unsuited by the track when last of four at Epsom, was 4lb higher than when taking a nursery over 7f at Newbury. He was putting in all his best work at the finish and is clearly well suited by 1m. (op 8-1)
Regimental(IRE), runner-up at Leicester a week earlier, raced from 3lb out of the handicap and deserves credit.
My Mate Jake(IRE), stepping up to 1m for the first time, came from the back to finish in good style. Now his stamina has been proven, he will benefit from more forceful tactics.
Chin'n Tonic(IRE), an easy winner here on his second start, travelled strongly before getting outpaced. He was sticking on at the death and the experience will not be lost on him. (op 10-3 tchd 3-1)

5598 HANRO FILLIES' H'CAP 7f
4:35 (4:35) (Class 5) (0-75,73) 3-Y-O+ **£1,955** (£585; £292; £146; £72) **Stalls** Centre

Form					RPR
0430	**1**		**Clumber Place**[32] 4515 4-8-7 53 oh1	PaulEddery 4	63
			(R C Guest) *mde all: set ordinary gallop: rdn 2f out: flashed tail u.p ins fnl f: hld on wl* **12/1**		
0346	**2**	½	**Always Dazzling**[23] 4850 3-8-8 59	JoeFanning 6	66
			(M Johnston) *cl up: effrt over 1f out: ev ch and rdn ins fnl f: hld towards fin* **11/1**		
2552	**3**	3 ½	**Leitzu (IRE)**[14] 5163 3-8-11 62	FrannyNorton 1	59
			(M R Channon) *trckd ldrs: rdn and outpcd by ldng pair over 1f out: kpt on fnl f: no imp* **5/1**[2]		
5122	**4**	¾	**Luv U Noo**[17] 5041 3-8-7 63	DaleSwift(5) 5	58
			(B Ellison) *dwlt: t.k.h: hld up: hdwy on outside over 2f out: no imp over 1f out* **9/4**[1]		
2226	**5**	shd	**Silly Gilly (IRE)**[18] 4985 6-8-9 55	PatrickMathers 7	52
			(R E Barr) *trckd ldrs: drvn over 3f out: one pce fr 2f out* **11/2**[3]		
2650	**6**	shd	**Celtic Lynn (IRE)**[39] 4287 5-9-9 69	PhillipMakin 8	66+
			(M Dods) *t.k.h: hld up: rdn wl over 1f out: no imp fnl f* **7/1**		
500-	**7**	5	**Dubai Legend**[319] 6798 4-9-12 72	DarryllHolland 3	55
			(N Wilson) *hld up: rdn over 2f out: nvr able to chal* **33/1**		
1-40	**8**	1	**Tatiana Romanova (USA)**[89] 2652 3-9-5 73	BarryMcHugh(3) 10	51
			(R A Fahey) *trckd ldrs tl rdn and wknd fr 2f out* **7/1**		
0051	**9**	3 ¾	**Dolly Royal (IRE)**[66] 3407 5-9-0 65	LeeTopliss(5) 9	35
			(R Johnson) *in tch: drvn over 3f out: wknd over 2f out* **28/1**		
3350	**10**	3	**Refuse To Wait (IRE)**[67] 3371 3-8-9 60	DuranFentiman 2	20
			(T D Easterby) *in tch: rdn along 1/2-way: sn struggling* **20/1**		

1m 28.72s (0.02) **Going Correction** -0.075s/f (Good)
WFA 3 from 4yo+ 5lb **10** Ran SP% **115.0**
Speed ratings (Par 100): **96,95,91,90,90 90,84,83,79,75**
Tote Swingers:1&2:£35.70, 1&3:£9.20, 2&3:£6.60 CSF £130.45 CT £770.63 TOTE £15.70: £4.30, £4.30, £2.20; EX 198.50.
Owner The Clumber Park Syndicate **Bred** Worksop Manor Stud **Trained** Stainforth, S Yorks

FOCUS
A modest 53-72 fillies' handicap. They raced middle to far side and the first two home were one-two throughout.
Luv U Noo Official explanation: trainer said filly was in season
Dubai Legend Official explanation: jockey said filly was struck into behind

5599 ALEXANDRA CARS H'CAP 5f
5:10 (5:10) (Class 6) (0-65,65) 3-Y-O+ **£1,419** (£424; £212; £106; £52) **Stalls** Centre

Form					RPR
5021	**1**		**Cayman Fox**[3] 5477 5-9-4 60 6ex	PJMcDonald 6	77
			(Miss L A Perratt) *mde all: rdn over 1f out: styd on wl fnl f: unchal* **7/2**[2]		
3020	**2**	3 ¾	**Dispol Kylie (IRE)**[59] 3622 4-9-9 65	PhillipMakin 7	69
			(Mrs K Walton) *hld up: hdwy to chse wnr appr fnl f: kpt on: no imp* **8/1**[3]		
5000	**3**	1 ½	**Future Gem**[19] 4947 4-8-5 47	(p) JoeFanning 5	45
			(N Wilson) *chsd wnr to appr fnl f: kpt on same pce* **25/1**		
534	**4**	nk	**Divine Spirit**[3] 5485 9-8-8 53	PatrickDonaghy(3) 3	50
			(M Dods) *dwlt: hld up: rdn and hdwy over 1f out: nvr able to chal* **11/1**		
000	**5**	1	**Danum Dancer**[23] 4833 6-9-1 57	(b) DanielTudhope 1	50
			(N Bycroft) *in tch: rdn over 2f out: no ex fnl f* **10/1**		
0004	**6**	2 ¼	**Sharp Bullet (IRE)**[3] 5477 4-9-4 60	(b) PatrickMathers 9	45
			(Bruce Hellier) *blkd s: bhd: rdn and sme hdwy over 1f out: n.d* **20/1**		
0021	**7**	1	**Captain Royale (IRE)**[3] 5485 5-9-1 57 6ex	(p) AndrewMullen 4	39
			(Miss Tracy Waggott) *prom tl rdn and wknd appr fnl f* **7/4**[1]		
0003	**8**	3	**Spirit Of Coniston**[5] 5422 7-8-11 53	PaulMulrennan 11	24
			(P T Midgley) *towards rr: rdn and hung lft 1/2-way: sn btn* **12/1**		
6514	**9**	2 ¾	**Drumpellier (IRE)**[5] 5422 3-8-13 60	PaulPickard(3) 10	21
			(S G West) *in tch: drvn and outpcd 1/2-way: n.d after* **10/1**		
0000	**10**	nk	**Thunder Bay**[30] 4606 5-7-11 46 oh1	(v) NeilFarley(7) 8	6
			(R E Barr) *towards rr: struggling 1/2-way: sn btn* **25/1**		
0410	**11**	3 ¾	**Braille**[5] 5422 5-9-0 56	DuranFentiman 12	—
			(T D Walford) *awkward s: rdn in midfield 1/2-way: btn over 1f out* **25/1**		
4620	**12**	2 ¼	**First Order**[146] 1147 9-9-1 62	(v) AnnStokell(5) 2	—
			(Miss A Stokell) *in tch tl rdn and wknd fr 1/2-way* **40/1**		

60.49 secs (-0.61) **Going Correction** -0.075s/f (Good)
WFA 3 from 4yo+ 2lb **12** Ran SP% **122.6**
Speed ratings (Par 101): **101,95,92,92,90 86,85,80,76,75 69,66**
Tote Swingers:1&2:£5.10, 1&3:£4.60, 2&3:£54.40 CSF £30.47 CT £626.19 TOTE £4.60: £1.80, £1.70, £5.00; EX 34.80.
Owner R R Whitton **Bred** R R Whitton **Trained** East Kilbride, South Lanarks

FOCUS
A modest handicap.
Spirit Of Coniston Official explanation: jockey said gelding hung left throughout
First Order Official explanation: jockey said gelding was unsuited by the good to soft (soft in places) ground

5600 HAPPY 21ST BIRTHDAY LAURA JANE FENWICK H'CAP 5f
5:45 (5:45) (Class 5) (0-75,72) 3-Y-O **£1,955** (£585; £292; £146; £72) **Stalls** Centre

Form					RPR
3122	**1**		**Bronze Beau**[26] 4703 3-9-4 72	(t) JamesSullivan(3) 5	82
			(Mrs L Stubbs) *mde all: shkn up over 1f out: kpt on wl fnl f: comf* **11/4**[1]		
3030	**2**	1 ¾	**Jigajig**[5] 5424 3-9-6 71	(p) JamieSpencer 6	75
			(K A Ryan) *cl up: drvn and chsd wnr over 1f out: kpt on ins fnl f* **11/4**[1]		
6624	**3**	½	**Dancing Freddy (IRE)**[30] 4567 3-9-7 72	(b) PaulMulrennan 4	74
			(J G Given) *prom: effrt and rdn over 1f out: kpt on same pce fnl f* **9/2**[2]		
2453	**4**	2 ½	**Texas Queen**[94] 2494 3-9-6 71	FrannyNorton 3	64
			(M R Channon) *hld up in tch: drvn 1/2-way: effrt over 1f out: edgd lft and sn no imp* **9/2**[2]		
0020	**5**	1 ½	**Areeg (IRE)**[5] 5410 3-7-9 53 oh4	VictorSantos(7) 2	41
			(A Berry) *t.k.h: trckd ldrs: outpcd 1/2-way: n.d after* **20/1**		
3206	**6**	1	**Tillys Tale**[28] 4654 3-9-2 70	PaulPickard(3) 1	54
			(P T Midgley) *cl up: rdn 1/2-way: wknd over 1f out* **5/1**[3]		

60.41 secs (-0.69) **Going Correction** -0.075s/f (Good) **6** Ran SP% **111.1**
Speed ratings (Par 100): **102,99,98,94,92 90**
Tote Swingers:1&2:£1.70, 1&3:£2.70, 2&3:£2.80 CSF £10.17 TOTE £4.60: £1.10, £1.50; EX 13.10.
Owner D Arundale **Bred** Meon Valley Stud **Trained** Norton, N Yorks

FOCUS
A modest 53-72 5f handicap and another step up from the in-form winner.

5601 WAVERLEY TBS H'CAP 6f
6:15 (6:15) (Class 4) (0-80,80) 3-Y-O+ **£3,500** (£1,047; £523; £261; £130) **Stalls** Centre

Form					RPR
2663	**1**		**Ginger Ted (IRE)**[6] 5390 3-9-6 79	(p) JamieSpencer 4	93
			(R C Guest) *hld up: hdwy to ld over 1f out: rdn and r.o wl fnl f* **9/2**[1]		
0-20	**2**	2 ½	**Mango Music**[228] 171 7-8-10 69	BarryMcHugh(3) 10	75
			(R A Fahey) *t.k.h: slt ld to over 1f out: kpt on fnl f: nt rch wnr* **7/1**[3]		
1001	**3**	¾	**Revue Princess (IRE)**[17] 5054 5-8-13 69	(b) DuranFentiman 1	73
			(T D Easterby) *cl up: effrt and ev ch over 1f out: sn one pce* **10/1**		

0245 **4** ½ **Avontuur (FR)**[5] 5424 8-8-11 **70** JamesSullivan(3) 3 72
(Mrs R A Carr) *in tch: effrt over 2f out: kpt on same pce fnl f* **16/1**

0000 **5** ½ **Bond City (IRE)**[27] 4684 8-9-10 **80** PaulMulrennan 6 80
(G R Oldroyd) *prom: rdn over 2f out: no ex fnl f* **18/1**

0000 **6** 1 **Baybshambles (IRE)**[3] 5499 6-8-5 **61** PatrickMathers 2 58
(R E Barr) *hld up: effrt on outside over 2f out: no imp fnl f* **22/1**

0-02 **7** nk **Dubai Hills**[23] 4834 4-8-11 **67** TomEaves 12 63
(B Smart) *disp ld to 1/2-way: rdn wl over 1f out: one pce fnl f* **6/1**[2]

0243 **8** 1¼ **Bonnie Prince Blue**[27] 4685 7-8-13 **74** (b) DaleSwift(5) 11 66
(B Ellison) *t.k.h: cl up: ev ch tl wknd over 1f out* **6/1**[2]

0220 **9** ½ **Northern Bolt**[3] 5480 5-9-5 **75** (b) PJMcDonald 5 66
(I W McInnes) *dwlt: bhd: rdn over 2f out: kpt on fnl f: nvr able to chal* **6/1**[2]

2604 **10** nse **Melundy**[3] 5480 3-7-9 **61** oh1 NeilFarley(7) 7 51
(Miss L A Perratt) *t.k.h: bhd: shortlived effrt over 1f out: nvr rchd ldrs* **7/1**[3]

0-00 **11** 10 **Burnwynd Boy**[3] 5480 5-9-4 **79** LeeTopliss(5) 9 37
(J A McShane) *hld up in tch: struggling over 2f out: sn btn* **33/1**

00 **12** 6 **Knavesmire (IRE)**[136] 1361 4-9-0 **70** FrannyNorton 8 9
(M Brittain) *hld up: rdn 1/2-way: btn fnl 2f* **40/1**

3400 **13** 3½ **Pawan (IRE)**[145] 1174 10-9-5 **80** (b) AnnStokell(5) 13 —
(Miss A Stokell) *in tch tl rdn and wknd over 2f out* **40/1**

1m 13.59s (-1.01) **Going Correction** -0.075s/f (Good)
WFA 3 from 4yo+ 3lb **13** Ran SP% **118.4**
Speed ratings (Par 105): **103,99,98,98,97 96,95,93,93,93 79,71,67**
Tote Swingers:1&2:£4.60, 1&3:£10.80, 2&3:£49.80 CSF £33.84 CT £308.81 TOTE £5.70: £2.40, £3.00, £4.30; EX 38.80 Place 6 £106.76; Place 5 £37.68.
Owner Showhouse Furniture Ltd **Bred** T Counihan **Trained** Stainforth, S Yorks

FOCUS
A competitive 61-80 sprint handicap with plenty having every chance.
T/Jkpt: Not won. T/Plt: £188.10 to a £1 stake. Pool:£60,475.20 - 234.65 winning tickets T/Qpdt: £50.00 to a £1 stake. Pool:£4,100.89 - 60.60 winning tickets RY

5298 RIPON (R-H)
Monday, August 30

OFFICIAL GOING: Good (good to firm in places; 8.6)
Wind: Virtually nil Weather: Cloudy with sunny periods

5602 RACING AGAIN TOMORROW (S) STKS 6f
2:25 (2:26) (Class 5) 2-Y-O £2,729 (£806; £403) Stalls Low

Form RPR

2356 **1** **Fred Willetts (IRE)**[20] 4935 2-9-2 67 (b1) SilvestreDeSousa 16 71
(P D Evans) *cl up far side: led that gp 1/2-way: overall ldr 1 1/2f out: sn clr and styd on strly: 1st of 2 in gp* **15/2**

0060 **2** 8 **Whats For Pudding (IRE)**[4] 5434 2-8-11 47 DavidNolan 6 42
(D Carroll) *midfield stands' side: hdwy over 2f out: rdn wl over 1f out: styd on wl fnl f: 1st of 15 in gp* **80/1**

0212 **3** 2¾ **Chilworth Lass (IRE)**[17] 5020 2-9-2 56 (v) ChrisCatlin 2 39
(M R Channon) *prom stands' side: rdn 2f out and ev ch: sn drvn and kpt on same pce appr fnl f: 2nd of 15 in gp* **11/1**

50 **4** ¾ **Ad Value (IRE)**[76] 3058 2-9-2 0 ShaneKelly 1 37
(G A Swinbank) *in rr stands' side: rdn along over 2f out: hdwy wl over 1f out: styd on ins fnl f: nrst fin: 3rd of 15 in gp* **11/1**

0630 **5** 1 **Paragons Folly (IRE)**[19] 4941 2-8-11 69 IanBrennan(5) 17 34
(J J Quinn) *led far side gp to 1/2-way: sn rdn along and kpt on same pce fnl 2f: 2nd of 2 in gp* **6/1**[3]

0332 **6** 1¾ **Misscomplacent**[8] 5334 2-8-11 65 (v) JimCrowley 7 23
(Mrs A Duffield) *overall ldr stands' side: rdn and hdd 1 1/2f out: sn drvn and wknd ent fnl f: 4th of 15 in gp* **7/1**

1543 **7** 1 **Bachelor Knight (IRE)**[10] 5269 2-9-7 70 PaulHanagan 5 30
(R A Fahey) *towards rr stands' side: rdn over 2f out and sme late hdwy: 5th of 15 in gp* **8/1**

443 **8** 5 **Trading**[101] 2272 2-9-2 68 DavidAllan 8 10
(T D Easterby) *chsd ldrs stands' side: rdn along over 2f out: sn drvn and wknd: 6th of 15 in gp* **4/1**[1]

0200 **9** ½ **Kodibelle (IRE)**[23] 4848 2-8-11 55 (b) RoystonFfrench 12 4
(T D Easterby) *wnt lft s: chsd ldrs stands' side: rdn along over 2f out: sn wknd: 7th of 15 in gp* **100/1**

000 **10** 2 **Imaginary World (IRE)**[21] 4909 2-8-4 48 DavidKenny(7) 4 —
(E S McMahon) *s.i.s and a towards rr stands' side: 8th of 15 in gp* **40/1**

0430 **11** nk **Bigalo's Laura B (IRE)**[20] 4934 2-8-6 54 (be) DeclanCannon(5) 10 —
(L A Mullaney) *chsd ldrs stands' side: rdn along 1/2-way: sn wknd: 9th of 15 in gp* **66/1**

12 ¾ **Red Ears** 2-9-2 0 LNewman 13 —
(D O'Meara) *a in rr stands' side: 10th of 15 in gp* **66/1**

0426 **13** 1¼ **Blind Stag (IRE)**[37] 4367 2-9-2 59 TonyCulhane 3 —
(P T Midgley) *a towards rr stands' side: 11th of 15 in gp* **33/1**

032 **14** ½ **Infectious (IRE)**[18] 4981 2-8-11 65 RichardHills 9 —
(D H Brown) *chsd ldrs stands' side: rdn along over 2f out: sn wknd: 12th of 15 in gp* **5/1**[2]

0053 **15** 1¼ **Jealousy Defined (IRE)**[19] 4967 2-8-11 54 (p) AndrewElliott 11 —
(N Tinkler) *a bhd stands' side: 13th of 15 in gp* **50/1**

00 **16** ¾ **Alhoralhora (IRE)**[31] 4543 2-8-11 0 LeeVickers 15 —
(J G Given) *wnt lft s: a bhd on stands' side: 14th of 15 in gp* **80/1**

004 **17** 19 **Irelandisuperman**[23] 4848 2-9-2 53 AdrianNicholls 14 —
(D Nicholls) *hmpd s: sn in tch: chsd ldrs 1/2-way: sn rdn and wknd: bhd whn eased over 1f out: last of 15 in gp* **20/1**

1m 13.85s (0.85) **Going Correction** -0.05s/f (Good) **17** Ran SP% **121.5**
Speed ratings (Par 94): **92,81,77,76,75 73,71,65,64,61 61,60,58,57,56 55,29**
Tote Swingers:1&2:£103.60, 1&3:£13.00, 2&3:£64.90 CSF £538.81 TOTE £12.40: £3.70, £13.40, £4.40; EX 1132.00 TRIFECTA Not won..The winner was bought in for 3,200gns.
Owner 24 - 7 / Gap Personnel **Bred** Liam Queally **Trained** Pandy, Monmouths

FOCUS
A one-sided seller in the end. A few performed well below expectations, the reliable Chilworth Lass being probably the best guide to the form.

NOTEBOOK
Fred Willetts(IRE), one of only two who raced on the far side, came home well clear. He had finished placed in a couple of maidens earlier in the season, so it was hardly a shock he was capable of winning at this level, but there's little doubt he showed improved form in first-time blinkers. There are clearly more wins in him at this grade if the headgear contiues to have such a positive effect. (op 17-2 tchd 9-1)
Whats For Pudding(IRE) had looked decidedly limited previously, so this seemingly improved effort isn't easy to explain away, though there was no obvious fluke about it. She stuck on well having been under pressure from halfway, leaving the impression she's worth another try at 7f.
Chilworth Lass(IRE) has been most consistent since the visor was fitted but her merit is firmly established and she's always likely to be vulnerable under her penalty in these. (tchd 10-1)
Ad Value(IRE) is related to plenty of winners and shaped with a bit of promise in the end, being off the bridle from an early stage (presumably still due to greenness) but going on at the finish. He can't get much of a mark for nurseries and is worth looking out for, with 7f likely to suit him on this evidence. (tchd 10-1)
Paragons Folly(IRE) was left trailing in the winner's wake after halfway over on the far side, and was almost certainly below the pick of his form in maidens. (op 15-2 tchd 8-1)
Misscomplacent had been most consistent recently but it's hard to believe she was that close to her best here. (tchd 13-2)
Bachelor Knight(IRE), a previous C&D winner, was another who was below par. (op 13-2 tchd 6-1)
Trading had made the frame in three ordinary maidens earlier in the season and had plenty of market confidence behind him. However, he shaped as if possibly needing the run after a break, fading from prominence on his first try at this trip. (op 5-1 tchd 11-2)
Infectious(IRE) had progressed steadily in maidens, finishing placed the last twice, and clearly can't have been right, being beaten soon after halfway. Official explanation: jockey said saddle slipped (op 11-2 tchd 6-1)
Irelandisuperman Official explanation: jockey said gelding hung left-handed throughout

5603 RIPON LAND ROVER MAIDEN STKS 1m
3:00 (3:18) (Class 5) 3-4-Y-O £2,914 (£867; £433; £216) Stalls High

Form RPR

22 **1** **Al Muthanaa**[16] 5065 3-9-3 0 RichardHills 3 72+
(W J Haggas) *trckd ldrs: smooth hdwy 3f out: led 2f out: sn rdn and edgd rt: hdd briefly ent fnl f: sn drvn to ld again and styd on wl towards fin* **1/5**[1]

2 1 **Apache Warrior** 3-9-3 0 ShaneKelly 7 70+
(G M Moore) *hld up in tch: hdwy on outer over 2f out: chal over 1f out: rdn to ld briefly ent fnl f: sn drvn: hdd and no ex towards fin* **16/1**

00 **3** 1¼ **Norville (IRE)**[32] 4521 3-8-12 0 DeclanCannon(5) 9 67
(P D Evans) *trckd ldrs on inner: hdwy 3f out: squeezed through to chal 2f out and ev ch tl rdn and one pce ent fnl f* **66/1**

0-0 **4** 8 **Roman Sioux (IRE)**[97] 2425 3-8-10 0 JohnLawson(7) 5 49
(R Bastiman) *trckd ldng pair: hdwy to ld 1/2-way: rdn along and jnd over 2f out: sn hdd and grad wknd* **100/1**

5 ½ **Seven Sons** 3-9-3 0 LNewman 10 47
(I W McInnes) *led: pushed along and hdd 1/2-way: rdn 3f out: grad wknd* **100/1**

0 **6** ½ **Saffron Hick (IRE)**[100] 2334 3-9-3 0 DavidAllan 4 46
(G A Butler) *towards rr: hdwy on inner 3f out: rdn along 2f out: kpt on: n.d* **33/1**

0 **7** ½ **Three Bay Leaves**[15] 5122 3-8-12 0 RoystonFfrench 8 40+
(M Johnston) *chsd ldr: rdn along over 3f out: cl up and drvn whn n.m.r and squeezed out over 2f out: one pce after* **12/1**[3]

50 **8** 3½ **Fear Factor (IRE)**[21] 4906 3-9-3 0 PaulHanagan 6 37+
(G A Butler) *trckd ldrs: rdn along over 3f out and sn wknd* **14/1**

0-6 **9** 1¾ **Green Army**[14] 5148 3-9-3 0 ChrisCatlin 1 33
(M R Channon) *s.i.s: a in rr* **33/1**

10 9 **No Thank You** 3-9-3 0 SilvestreDeSousa 2 12
(K A Ryan) *v.s.a and green in rr: hdwy and in tch on outer 1/2-way: rdn along 3f out and sn wknd* **8/1**[2]

1m 42.7s (1.30) **Going Correction** -0.05s/f (Good) **10** Ran SP% **124.0**
Speed ratings (Par 103): **91,90,88,80,80 79,79,75,74,65**
Tote Swingers:1&2:£3.10, 1&3:£7.80, 2&3:£21.20 CSF £6.43 TOTE £1.20: £1.02, £3.60, £8.70; EX 9.10 Trifecta £177.20 Pool: £962.82 - 4.02 winning units..
Owner Hamdan Al Maktoum **Bred** Newsells Park Stud **Trained** Newmarket, Suffolk

FOCUS
Little depth to this maiden, the front three coming clear.

5604 RIPON CHAMPION TWO YRS OLD TROPHY, 2010 (LISTED RACE) 6f
3:35 (3:38) (Class 1) 2-Y-O
£17,031 (£6,456; £3,231; £1,611; £807; £405) Stalls Low

Form RPR

0034 **1** **Bathwick Bear (IRE)**[12] 5221 2-9-2 96 RichardEvans 8 99
(P D Evans) *cl up: chal over 2f out: rdn wl over 1f out: drvn and kpt on gamely ins fnl f to ld last 100yds* **16/1**

2141 **2** nk **Mayson**[16] 5094 2-9-2 100 PaulHanagan 7 98
(R A Fahey) *cl up: led after 2f: rdn over 1f out: drvn ent fnl f: hdd and nt qckn last 100yds* **7/4**[1]

1020 **3** 1¼ **Black Moth (IRE)**[12] 5221 2-9-2 97 KierenFallon 6 94
(B J Meehan) *hld up in tch: swtchd wd and hdwy over 2f out: rdn to chse ldrs over 1f out: drvn and ch ins fnl f: one pce towards fin* **8/1**

122 **4** 2¼ **Cocktail Charlie**[86] 2757 2-9-2 95 DavidAllan 3 88
(T D Easterby) *t.k.h: trckd ldrs: hdwy 2f out: rdn to chse ldng pair over 1f out: drvn and wknd ins fnl f* **4/1**[3]

5442 **5** 2 **Chilworth Lad**[16] 5094 2-9-2 98 ChrisCatlin 5 83
(M R Channon) *dwlt and sltly hmpd s: a in rr* **11/2**

120 **6** ½ **Lord Of The Stars (USA)**[34] 4458 2-9-2 95 JimCrowley 4 80
(R M Beckett) *wnt rt s: sn cl up: rdn along over 2f out and sn wknd* **3/1**[2]

5130 **7** 29 **Minch Man**[45] 4097 2-9-2 86 (b1) AndrewElliott 2 —
(Mrs K Burke) *led 2f: rdn along 1/2-way: sn lost pl and bhd fnl 2f* **50/1**

1m 13.65s (0.65) **Going Correction** -0.05s/f (Good) **7** Ran SP% **115.7**
Speed ratings (Par 102): **93,92,90,87,85 84,45**
Tote Swingers:1&2:£4.10, 1&3:£10.10, 2&3:£3.40 CSF £45.64 TOTE £20.80: £5.90, £1.20; EX 45.10 Trifecta £274.70 Pool: £556.88 - 1.50 winning units..
Owner Bathwick Gold Partnership **Bred** D Veitch & R O'Callaghan **Trained** Pandy, Monmouths

FOCUS
A Listed contest, but hard to believe the form is any better than useful, the winner and third both having had plenty of chances. The first two occupied those positions throughout, the pace probably being not overly strong in the first half of the contest.

NOTEBOOK
Bathwick Bear(IRE) had been over 2l behind Mayson when they met over C&D earlier in the month but a 5lb swing in the weights saw him turn the tables. A real credit to his trainer, the Redcar 2-y-o Trophy is the obvious next port of call for him. (op 14-1)
Mayson ran creditably but it's an effort which suggests he may have levelled off for the time being ,as he had no obvious excuses. His Pattern entries this autumn look beyond him, a rematch with Bathwick Bear in the Redcar 2-y-o Trophy being a more suitable target. (op 13-8 tchd 6-4 and 2-1 in a place)
Black Moth(IRE) has had plenty of chances but this was clearly one of his better efforts, particularly as he possibly came from a little further back than ideal. He's another who could be Redcar bound. (op 17-2)
Cocktail Charlie has potential but will need to settle better to prove fully effective at this trip, proving way too keen for his own good on his first attempt at it. Although this first outing in nearly three months may at least have taken a bit of the freshness out of him. Official explanation: jockey said colt ran too freely (op 9-2)
Chilworth Lad had been reliable previously, splitting Mayson and Bathwick Bear here earlier in the month, and possibly got unsettled by being slightly squeezed out at the start, as he was never going with much fluency thereafter. Official explanation: jockey said gelding was hampered at start (op 6-1 tchd 13-2)

Lord Of The Stars(USA) had shaped as if there might be more to come from him back at 6f after his effort in the Molecomb, but he was disappointing. (op 4-1)

5605 RIPON ROWELS H'CAP 1m

4:10 (4:10) (Class 2) (0-100,98) 3-Y-O+

£11,215 (£3,358; £1,679; £840; £419; £210) Stalls High

Form				RPR
5040	1		**Osteopathic Remedy (IRE)**[51] 3920 6-9-2 87 PaulHanagan 5 (M Dods) *t.k.h: in tch: hdwy to trck ldrs 1/2-way: pushed along on outer to chal 3f out: led 2f out: rdn clr over 1f out: drvn and edgd rt ins fnl f: kpt on wl* **18/1**	100
4040	2	1 ¾	**Exit Smiling**[16] 5098 8-8-3 79 DeclanCannon(5) 7 (P T Midgley) *a.p: hdwy 3f out: rdn along 2f out: drvn over 1f out: kpt on wl fnl f* **40/1**	88
0205	3	½	**Keys Of Cyprus**[16] 5098 8-8-11 82 AdrianNicholls 11 (D Nicholls) *midfield: effrt on inner 3f out: swtchd lft and pushed along over 2f out: rdn and swtchd rt appr fnl f: drvn to chse ldrs whn edgd lft ins fnl f: kpt on* **28/1**	90
3221	4	hd	**Cheers For Thea (IRE)**[23] 4849 5-9-0 85 (bt) DavidAllan 19 (T D Easterby) *midfield and n.m.r on inner after 2f: swtchd lft and hdwy 3f out: rdn to chse ldrs 2f out: drvn and kpt on ins fnl f* **12/1**	92
3311	5	¾	**Smarty Socks (IRE)**[16] 5068 6-9-5 90 SilvestreDeSousa 14 (D O'Meara) *dwlt: hld up in rr: hdwy over 2f out: effrt and n.m.r over 1f out: rdn and styng on whn n.m.r and sltly hmpd ins fnl f: nrst fin* **8/1**[3]	96+
6200	6	hd	**Collateral Damage (IRE)**[23] 4828 7-9-4 89 (t) DavidNolan 1 (T D Easterby) *midfield: effrt over 2f out: sn rdn and kpt on ins fnl f: nrst fin* **33/1**	94+
1412	7	hd	**Watch Amigo (IRE)**[16] 5082 4-9-1 86 ShaneKelly 8 (W R Swinburn) *midfield: hdwy on outer over 2f out: rdn wl over 1f out: kpt on ins fnl f: nrst fin* **11/1**	91
2120	8	nk	**Venutius**[32] 4509 3-9-1 92 GrahamGibbons 10 (E S McMahon) *led: rdn along 3f out: hdd and drvn 2f out: grad wknd* **12/1**	95
4304	9	1 ¾	**Gaily Noble (IRE)**[20] 4924 4-9-0 90 AmyBaker(5) 15 (A B Haynes) *towards rr: effrt and n.m.r over 2f out: swtchd outside and rdn over 1f out: kpt on ins fnl f: n.d* **50/1**	90
4334	10	½	**Sand Skier**[30] 4570 3-8-13 90 RoystonFfrench 16 (M Johnston) *midfield: rdn along and outpcd over 3f out: kpt on appr fnl f* **13/2**[2]	88
120	11	½	**Reel Buddy Star**[30] 4603 5-8-13 84 RichardHills 4 (G M Moore) *chsd ldrs: rdn along 3f out: drvn over 2f out: grad wknd* **28/1**	82
1040	12	¾	**Tiger Reigns**[11] 5247 4-9-10 98 MichaelStainton(3) 6 (M Dods) *prom: cl up 1/2-way: rdn along 3f out: grad wknd* **16/1**	94
4543	13	hd	**Webbow (IRE)**[31] 4537 8-9-6 91 (p) KierenFallon 18 (N Tinkler) *dwlt: a towards rr* **9/2**[1]	87
6000	14	hd	**Dubai Dynamo**[16] 5068 5-9-4 94 IanBrennan(5) 3 (Mrs R A Carr) *dwlt and in rr: sme hdwy on wd outside over 3f out: rdn along over 2f out: sn btn* **50/1**	89
0-11	15	3	**Uphold**[25] 4750 3-9-0 91 TonyCulhane 17 (B W Hills) *trckd ldrs on inner: rdn along 3f out: drvn 2f out: wkng whn hmpd and snatched up appr fnl f: eased after* **9/2**[1]	78+
0122	16	2	**City Of The Kings (IRE)**[16] 5098 5-9-5 90 (p) ChrisCatlin 12 (G A Harker) *a towards rr* **20/1**	74
1160	17	2	**Ezdeyaad (USA)**[9] 5292 6-9-8 93 AndrewElliott 13 (G A Swinbank) *in tch: effrt and sme hdwy over 3f out: rdn along over 2f out and sn wknd* **50/1**	72
6116	18	2 ½	**San Cassiano (IRE)**[30] 4574 3-8-13 90 JimCrowley 9 (Mrs R A Carr) *t.k.h: prom: chsd ldr 1/2-way: rdn along 3f out: drvn 2f out and sn wknd: towards rr whn hmpd appr fnl f: eased after* **20/1**	62+

1m 39.11s (-2.29) **Going Correction** -0.05s/f (Good)
WFA 3 from 4yo+ 6lb 18 Ran SP% **123.4**
Speed ratings (Par 109): **109,107,106,106,105 105,105,105,103,102 102,101,101,101,98 96,94,91**
Tote Swingers:1&2:£142.30, 1&3:£57.50, 2&3:£82.70 CSF £624.89 CT £18210.87 TOTE £23.10: £4.10, £8.50, £5.10, £3.00; EX 547.70 TRIFECTA Not won..
Owner Kevin Kirkup **Bred** Airlie Stud **Trained** Denton, Co Durham

FOCUS
A useful and competitive handicap though, as is often the case over this trip round here, it certainly paid to race handily.

NOTEBOOK
Osteopathic Remedy(IRE) obtained a good early position from a stall that was potentially lower than ideal and bettered even the form he showed when taking the Thirsk Hunt Cup earlier in the season. He'll be up in the 90s once reassessed for this, a mark he's usually struggled off in the past, but this is at least a further indication that Michael Dods has his team back in better heart after a quiet spell at the height of the summer. (op 20-1)
Exit Smiling is back below the mark he won off at Redcar earlier in the season, and signalled that he might be about to take advantage as there'll certainly be weaker races than this for him from his mark. (op 33-1)
Keys Of Cyprus has been pretty reliable this season but his consistency means he's not getting the leniency from the handicapper that he probably needs to get his head back in front.
Cheers For Thea(IRE) had gone up a further 7lb for Redcar but showed she can still be competitive. She's enjoying an excellent season and should continue to go well. (op 14-1 tchd 16-1)
Smarty Socks(IRE) remains in top form, his tendency to start slowly certainly catching him out here as he ended up with too much to do, doing very well to finish as close as he did. He's clearly still on a fair mark, despite his two recent wins. (op 9-1)
Collateral Damage(IRE) enjoyed a really good run around this time last year and shaped as if coming to hand, having the worst of the draw here but keeping on at the finish. He's down below his last winning mark now and is one to bear in mind.
Watch Amigo(IRE) has a steadily progressive profile and this shouldn't be taken to suggest the handicapper's got his measure, ending up with too much to do but shaping as if this longer trip wasn't a problem. (op 10-1)
Sand Skier had made the frame on all previous starts this year but this was more competitive and he didn't have any excuses. (op 15-2)
Webbow(IRE) is hard to win with but usually acquits himself with credit in races of this nature and is probably forgiven this, never being able to recover from a slow start. (tchd 7-2)
Uphold looked the one obviously improving type in the field, having won both starts this year, so this was disappointing, particularly as he was well enough positioned on the heels of the leaders. A 4lb rise for Haydock certainly didn't look excessive and he deserves another chance. (op 4-1)

5606 BILLY NEVETT MEMORIAL H'CAP 6f

4:45 (4:45) (Class 4) (0-85,84) 3-Y-O £4,533 (£1,348; £674; £336) Stalls Low

Form				RPR
3511	1		**Amenable (IRE)**[27] 4684 3-9-7 84 AdrianNicholls 5 (D Nicholls) *cl up: rdn to ld 1f out: drvn ent fnl f: hld on gamely towards fin* **11/2**[3]	94
6042	2	hd	**Tasmeem (IRE)**[3] 5501 3-8-11 74 (b) PaulHanagan 3 (R A Fahey) *trckd ldrs: hdwy 2f out: rdn to chse wnr over 1f out: drvn to chal ent fnl f and ev ch tl nt qckn nr fin* **4/1**[2]	84
3243	3	1 ¾	**Pepper Lane**[22] 4865 3-8-7 70 SilvestreDeSousa 1 (D O'Meara) *trckd ldrs on inner: effrt and nt clr run 2f out: rdn over 1f out: kpt on ins fnl f* **7/1**	74
0015	4	¾	**Mark Anthony (IRE)**[17] 5046 3-8-13 76 KierenFallon 4 (K A Ryan) *led: rdn along and hdd 2f out: drvn and wknd appr fnl f* **7/2**[1]	78
4602	5	1 ¾	**Flaneur**[6] 5390 3-9-0 77 (v[1]) DavidAllan 7 (T D Easterby) *trckd ldrs: hdwy 1/2-way: rdn to chse ldng pair over 1f out: drvn and wknd ins fnl f* **4/1**[2]	73
1654	6	1 ¼	**Thrust Control (IRE)**[28] 4646 3-8-13 76 LeeVickers 9 (B Ellison) *dwlt and in rr: hdwy 2f out: rdn wl over 1f out: sn no imp* **14/1**	68
5500	7	2 ¼	**Jarrow (IRE)**[28] 4653 3-9-6 83 RoystonFfrench 6 (M Johnston) *a towards rr* **16/1**	68
1020	8	2	**Prince Of Vasa (IRE)**[11] 5242 3-9-0 80 MichaelStainton(3) 2 (Michael Smith) *bmpd s and towards rr: hdwy to chse ldrs after 2f: rdn along wl over 2f out: sn wknd* **18/1**	58
2010	9	9	**Besty**[37] 4369 3-8-13 76 JimCrowley 8 (B Smart) *in tch on outer: rdn along 1/2-way: sn wknd* **12/1**	26

1m 12.61s (-0.39) **Going Correction** -0.05s/f (Good) 9 Ran SP% **115.6**
Speed ratings (Par 102): **100,99,97,96,94 92,89,86,74**
Tote Swingers:1&2:£3.40, 1&3:£4.50, 2&3:£5.40 CSF £27.82 CT £157.34 TOTE £7.10: £2.60, £1.90, £2.20; EX 35.10 Trifecta £136.60 Pool: £485.82 - 2.63 winning units..
Owner Turton Brown Williams Lindley **Bred** Michael Downey & Roalso Ltd **Trained** Sessay, N Yorks

FOCUS
A fair handicap.

5607 TOTEPOOL A BETTER WAY TO BET H'CAP 1m 1f 170y

5:20 (5:21) (Class 5) (0-70,70) 3-Y-O £2,914 (£867; £433; £216) Stalls High

Form				RPR
0214	1		**Sharakti (IRE)**[19] 4944 3-8-10 64 DeclanCannon(5) 6 (A J McCabe) *trckd ldrs: hdwy to ld over 3f out: rdn and hung rt 2f out: drvn and edgd over 1f out: hrd drvn and hung lft ins fnl f: hld on* **9/2**[2]	71
1353	2	nk	**Magic Millie (IRE)**[19] 4944 3-8-6 55 SilvestreDeSousa 8 (D O'Meara) *cl up on inner: led after 4f: pushed along and hdd over 3f out: swtchd lft and rdn 2f out: drvn to chal over 1f out: ev ch whn carried lft ins fnl f: kpt on* **9/4**[1]	61
0024	3	1	**Egmarey (IRE)**[15] 5113 3-9-4 67 (b) ChrisCatlin 3 (D R Lanigan) *bhd and rdn along 1/2-way: hdwy 3f out: rdn over 2f out: styd on to chse ldng pair 1f out: drvn and sltly hmpd ins fnl f: no ex towards fin* **12/1**	71
0413	4	3	**Frontline Phantom (IRE)**[10] 5266 3-8-13 62 AndrewElliott 5 (Mrs K Burke) *led 4f: cl up and rdn along 3f out: drvn over 2f out: kpt on same pce appr fnl f* **9/4**[1]	60
1040	5	7	**Petrocelli**[38] 4337 3-8-6 60 DeanHeslop(5) 1 (W Storey) *chsd ldrs: rdn along over 3f out: drvn over 2f out and sn wknd* **33/1**	44
322	6	19	**Broadway Dancer**[10] 5270 3-9-7 70 PaulHanagan 2 (R A Fahey) *in rr: pushed along 1/2-way: hdwy on outer 4f out: rdn and cl up 3f out: drvn and wknd over 2f out* **11/2**[3]	16
2354	7	6	**Layla's Boy**[65] 3428 3-9-5 68 GrahamGibbons 7 (J Mackie) *trckd ldrs: hdwy to chse ldng pair 1/2-way: rdn along over 3f out and sn wknd* **14/1**	2

2m 4.41s (-0.99) **Going Correction** -0.05s/f (Good) 7 Ran SP% **112.4**
Speed ratings (Par 100): **101,100,99,97,91 76,71**
Tote Swingers:1&2:£2.70, 1&3:£6.80, 2&3:£5.60 CSF £14.53 CT £109.93 TOTE £6.10: £3.20, £1.60; EX 16.70 Trifecta £66.20 Pool: £789.06 - 8.81 winning units. Place 6 £704.31; Place 5 £76.00..
Owner Mrs D E Sharp **Bred** John Foley **Trained** Averham Park, Notts

FOCUS
A handicap which was full of largely exposed types for a 3-y-o contest, and hard to believe the form is anything out of the ordinary for the grade.
T/Plt: £1,140.20 to a £1 stake. Pool:£68,728.48 - 44.00 winning tickets T/Qpdt: £199.30 to a £1 stake. Pool:£4,713.56 - 17.50 winning tickets JR

3829 WARWICK (L-H)

Monday, August 30

OFFICIAL GOING: Good to soft (soft in places)
Wind: Light half-against Weather: Cloudy with sunny spells

5608 EUROPEAN BREEDERS' FUND MAIDEN STKS 7f 26y

2:10 (2:12) (Class 5) 2-Y-O £3,238 (£963; £481; £240) Stalls Low

Form				RPR
66	1		**Kingarrick**[34] 4460 2-9-3 0 EddieAhern 1 (Eve Johnson Houghton) *chsd ldrs: rdn over 2f out: r.o to ld wl ins fnl f* **6/5**[1]	74
5	2	½	**Piece Of Mind**[25] 4753 2-8-12 0 RichardHughes 7 (R Hannon) *led 2f: chsd ldr: rdn over 2f out: led over 1f out: hdd wl ins fnl f* **6/1**[3]	68
04	3	¾	**Royal Reverie**[14] 5156 2-9-3 0 AdamKirby 4 (W R Swinburn) *chsd ldr tl led 5f out: rdn and hdd over 1f out: ev ch tl no ex wl ins fnl f* **6/1**[3]	71+
00	4	hd	**Aldwick Bay (IRE)**[56] 3735 2-9-0 0 PatrickHills(3) 2 (R Hannon) *hld up: hdwy over 2f out: sn rdn: r.o: nt rch ldrs* **4/1**[2]	70
	5	4	**Mr Dream Maker (IRE)** 2-9-3 0 SaleemGolam 5 (Ian Williams) *s.i.s: hld up: styd on fr over 1f out: n.d* **28/1**	60
0	6	nk	**Waterborne**[17] 5032 2-9-3 0 SteveDrowne 3 (R Charlton) *hld up: rdn over 1f out: n.d* **12/1**	60+
45	7	1	**Supermarine**[17] 5053 2-9-3 0 (t) DaneO'Neill 6 (J A Glover) *s.i.s: sn prom: rdn over 2f out: wknd over 1f out* **18/1**	57

1m 27.77s (3.17) **Going Correction** +0.10s/f (Good) 7 Ran SP% **110.4**
Speed ratings (Par 94): **85,84,83,83,78 78,77**
Tote Swingers:1&2:£2.70, 1&3:£2.50, 2&3:£2.80 CSF £8.19 TOTE £2.00: £1.10, £3.60; EX 8.60.

Owner Miss Yvonne Jacques **Bred** Southcourt Stud **Trained** Blewbury, Oxon

FOCUS

A modest renewal of a maiden that nearly always takes a fair bit more winning. The pace was steady and the race didn't begin in earnest until the straight.

NOTEBOOK

Kingarrick had easily the best form and ended up winning with more in hand than the winning margin suggests after settling matters with the best turn of foot. He might not have had to repeat his previous best to have taken this, and will need to improve to defy what might be a tough nursery mark given the subsequent achievements of some of those in front of him in his previous two races. He'll be suited by a step up to 1m. (op 7-4)

Piece Of Mind stepped up on her debut form and can have no excuses as the race was run, the first to grab the rail in the straight. She seemed to see the trip out well, for all that it wasn't a proper test of stamina, but, being by Mind Games she's not bred to be much better or stay much further than this and it remains to be seen how she progresses. (op 11-2 tchd 5-1)

Royal Reverie led the field into the straight and had every chance thereafter. He handled the ground well enough but looks limited on the evidence so far. (op 9-2)

Aldwick Bay(IRE) can have his effort upgraded since he wasn't really asked for more serious effort until the first three had already got first run on him. He was still closing at the line and looks one for nurseries after this, with a step up to 1m promising to suit. (op 6-1 tchd 13-2)

Mr Dream Maker(IRE) is quite well related on the female side of his pedigree, but his yard aren't known for their success with two-year-old newcomers, and he'll be of more interest after another run or so. (op 14-1)

Waterborne again looked as if he needs more time and probably distance as well. (op 8-1)

Supermarine, fitted with a tongue-tie, dropped away disappointingly considering the steady early pace. (op 16-1 tchd 14-1)

5609 WARWICK CONDITIONS STKS (FOR THE SYD MERCER MEMORIAL TROPHY) 7f 26y

2:45 (2:47) (Class 3) 3-Y-0+ **£6,476** (£1,927; £963; £481) **Stalls** Low

Form RPR

5-64 **1** **Ashram (IRE)**[51] 3893 4-9-0 110 (v) DaraghO'Donohoe 3 110
(Saeed Bin Suroor) *a.p: rdn to ld ins fnl f: r.o* **9/2**[3]

2-04 **2** *1 3/4* **Za Za Zoom (IRE)**[44] 4126 3-8-1 98 JimmyQuinn 7 95
(B W Hills) *chsd ldrs: rdn to ld over 1f out: hdd and unable qck ins fnl f* **11/4**[1]

0-00 **3** *hd* **Wannabe King**[109] 2057 4-8-11 100 (p) DaneO'Neill 2 101+
(D R Lanigan) *hld up: hdwy over 1f out: sn rdn: r.o* **11/4**[1]

0300 **4** *4 1/2* **Ishiadancer**[15] 5120 5-7-13 81 RyanPowell(7) 1 84
(E J Alston) *chsd ldr: styd far side to r alone over 2f out: sn rdn: no ex fnl f* **16/1**

P-56 **5** *3/4* **Welsh Emperor (IRE)**[44] 4126 11-8-11 102 (b) MickyFenton 5 87
(T P Tate) *sn pushed along to ld: rdn and hdd over 1f out: wknd ins fnl f* **12/1**

2055 **6** *1/2* **Asset (IRE)**[44] 4126 7-8-11 103 (b) RichardHughes 4 86
(Saeed Bin Suroor) *hld up: rdn over 1f out: a in rr* **3/1**[2]

0/2 **7** *1 1/2* **Supa Seeker (USA)**[81] 2900 4-8-11 0 JamesDoyle 6 82?
(A W Carroll) *hld up: rdn over 2f out: a in rr* **50/1**

1m 23.62s (-0.98) **Going Correction** +0.10s/f (Good)
WFA 3 from 4yo+ 5lb 7 Ran SP% **112.1**
Speed ratings (Par 107): **109,107,106,101,100 100,98**
Tote Swingers:1&2:£2.10, 1&3:£3.00, 2&3:£1.90 CSF £16.56 TOTE £5.90: £3.20, £1.10; EX 14.70.

Owner Godolphin **Bred** Waterford Hall Stud **Trained** Newmarket, Suffolk

FOCUS

A useful minor event, for all that the best of the older horses had seen better days. The gallop was a good one and the winner came from off the pace.

NOTEBOOK

Ashram(IRE) had disappointed in both his races this year, but he just about had the best chance at the weights if he could repeat his Dubai Duty Free Cup form from Newbury last October, and he ended up winning a shade cosily. Being ridden with more patience on easier ground than he has encountered so far than this season seemed to suit him, and there must be every chance that he'll head back to Newbury next month in a bid for back-to-back wins. (op 7-2 tchd 10-3 in places)

Za Za Zoom(IRE) seems a decent guide to the form as she is proven under the conditions and held every chance as the race was run. She might not be quite as good now as she was when second in a Listed race last year but won't mind a wet autumn. (op 3-1)

Wannabe King was the subject of good support during the day, and though he ran respectably, his effort can be upgraded seeing as he sat too far out of his ground against speedier rivals proven at this shorter trip. He's had very little racing this year but looked as good as ever at Newbury on his comeback and this run should tee him up nicely for a crack at a good handicap this autumn, with the Ayrshire Handicap at the Ayr Western meeting a possible target. (op 4-1)

Ishiadancer couldn't dominate and had little chance at the weights, but fared respectably. The fact that she stayed towards the far side in the straight was probably of little consequence. (op 20-1)

Welsh Emperor(IRE) had run well on his only previous try over course and distance, but he's not the force now he was then, and though the blinkers back on perked him up initially, he dropped away quickly when headed. His current ability is hard to assess accurately but is probably some way below his current official rating. (op 15-2)

Asset(IRE) stays this trip and handles this ground, but he was ridden as if both together might be a problem. That said, he never promised to get involved and this was another in a string of substandard efforts. He's one to treat with caution right now. (op 10-3 tchd 7-2)

5610 MERCIA - MADE FOR COVENTRY AND WARWICKSHIRE MAIDEN STKS 1m 2f 188y

3:20 (3:20) (Class 5) 3-Y-0+ **£2,590** (£770; £385; £192) **Stalls** Low

Form RPR

422 **1** **Marywell**[65] 3437 3-8-12 87 WilliamBuick 9 81+
(J H M Gosden) *chsd ldr: led over 1f out: rdn out* **4/9**[1]

50 **2** *3 1/2* **Pickwick**[17] 5026 3-9-3 0 DaneO'Neill 7 79
(Sir Michael Stoute) *led: racd keenly: rdn and hdd over 1f out: styd on same pce ins fnl f* **8/1**[3]

0 **3** *1 3/4* **Aneel**[94] 2507 3-9-3 0 RichardHughes 6 76
(J Noseda) *chsd ldrs: rdn over 2f out: hung lft and no ex fnl f* **12/1**

5 **4** *1 1/2* **Ahaazeeg**[18] 5001 3-9-3 0 EddieAhern 3 73
(J L Dunlop) *hld up in tch: rdn over 1f out: styd on same pce* **16/1**

64 **5** *nse* **Surface Tension (IRE)**[73] 3173 3-9-3 0 J-PGuillambert 2 73
(L M Cumani) *chsd ldrs: rdn over 2f out: styd on same pce appr fnl f* **9/2**[2]

6 *23* **Raghdaan** 3-9-3 0 MickyFenton 5 29
(P W Hiatt) *s.i.s: sme hdwy over 4f out: wknd over 3f out: t.o* **40/1**

7 *12* **Najca De Thaix (FR)**[181] 9-9-12 0 AdamKirby 8 7
(J L Spearing) *sn pushed along in rr: lost tch fnl 4f: t.o* **66/1**

8 *1 3/4* **Millie Mops** 3-8-12 0 SaleemGolam 1 —
(Ian Williams) *a in rr: bhd fnl 4f: t.o* **33/1**

2m 21.0s (-0.10) **Going Correction** +0.10s/f (Good)
WFA 3 from 4yo+ 9lb 8 Ran SP% **119.0**
Speed ratings (Par 103): **104,101,100,99,99 82,73,72**
Tote Swingers:1&2:£2.50, 1&3:£2.50, 2&3:£6.50 CSF £5.32 TOTE £1.40: £1.10, £2.10, £2.20; EX 5.70.

Owner Lady Rothschild **Bred** Carwell Equities Ltd **Trained** Newmarket, Suffolk

FOCUS

A one-sided maiden on the form book and that's pretty much how it turned out at the end of a race run at a stop-start gallop.

Aneel Official explanation: jockey said colt hung badly left

5611 LEAMINGTON FOOD AND DRINK FESTIVAL H'CAP 1m 2f 188y

3:55 (3:55) (Class 4) (0-80,80) 3-Y-0+ **£3,885** (£1,156; £577; £288) **Stalls** Low

Form RPR

6105 **1** **Broughtons Swinger**[25] 4764 3-8-0 61 JamieMackay 1 71
(W J Musson) *mde all: rdn over 1f out: styd on* **10/1**

1040 **2** *1* **Marie De Guise (IRE)**[18] 5008 3-9-3 78 WilliamBuick 11 86+
(Sir Michael Stoute) *chsd ldrs: pushed along 1/2-way: outpcd over 2f out: rallied and swtchd lft over 1f out: r.o: wnt 2nd towards fin* **4/1**[1]

/114 **3** *1/2* **Dolcetto (IRE)**[44] 4134 5-9-9 75 FergusSweeney 2 82
(A King) *a.p: rdn to chse wnr over 1f out: styd on same pce ins fnl f: lost 2nd towards fin* **4/1**[1]

0030 **4** *2 3/4* **It's Dubai Dolly**[108] 2093 4-9-5 71 JamesDoyle 3 73
(A J Lidderdale) *chsd wnr tl rdn over 1f out: styd on same pce ins fnl f* **8/1**[3]

1300 **5** *1 1/2* **Buddy Holly**[30] 4579 5-9-7 78 TobyAtkinson(5) 8 77
(Pat Eddery) *hld up: rdn over 2f out: styd on fr over 1f out: nt trble ldrs* **10/1**

6415 **6** *nk* **Ubi Ace**[24] 4785 4-9-8 74 J-PGuillambert 7 72
(T D Walford) *hld up: hdwy u.p and hmpd over 1f out: no imp ins fnl f* **9/1**

000 **7** *3 1/4* **Prince Apollo**[16] 5082 5-10-0 80 RichardHughes 9 72
(Ian Williams) *hld up: rdn over 1f out: n.d* **18/1**

6554 **8** *hd* **Grey Granite (IRE)**[11] 5243 4-9-5 71 SteveDrowne 5 63
(W Jarvis) *chsd ldrs: rdn over 2f out: wknd ins fnl f* **5/1**[2]

0-00 **9** *nk* **Alpen Glen**[15] 5115 4-9-9 75 (b[1]) EddieAhern 10 66
(John Berry) *hld up in tch: plld hrd: rdn and hung lft over 1f out: wknd fnl f* **22/1**

0600 **10** *1 1/2* **Manshoor (IRE)**[14] 5146 5-9-4 70 (b[1]) DaneO'Neill 4 58
(Mrs L Wadham) *dwlt: hdwy 8f out: rdn and hmpd over 1f out: wknd fnl f* **16/1**

1160 **11** *7* **Mister New York (USA)**[18] 5002 5-9-5 71 HayleyTurner 6 46
(Noel T Chance) *s.i.s: hld up: rdn over 2f out: a in rr* **16/1**

2m 20.7s (-0.40) **Going Correction** +0.10s/f (Good)
WFA 3 from 4yo+ 9lb 11 Ran SP% **117.3**
Speed ratings (Par 105): **105,104,103,101,100 100,98,98,97,96 91**
Tote Swingers:1&2:£7.20, 1&3:£6.00, 2&3:£4.00 CSF £49.68 CT £190.67 TOTE £12.80: £3.20, £1.70, £2.20; EX 61.30.

Owner Broughton Thermal Insulation **Bred** Michael E Broughton **Trained** Newmarket, Suffolk

FOCUS

A fair handicap, though not one chock full of obviously in-form horses, with none of the runners having been placed last time out. The winner was able to dictate and it was hard to come from well off the pace.

5612 J20 WHITE BLEND H'CAP 1m 6f 213y

4:30 (4:30) (Class 4) (0-85,74) 3-Y-0+ **£4,209** (£1,252; £625; £312) **Stalls** Low

Form RPR

3262 **1** **Act Of Kalanisi (IRE)**[4] 5443 4-9-13 73 GregFairley 4 81
(M Johnston) *mde all: rdn over 2f out: styd on wl* **10/3**[2]

0621 **2** *1* **Albeed**[17] 5058 3-8-9 68 JimmyQuinn 5 75+
(J L Dunlop) *a.p: rdn to chse wnr over 1f out: styd on* **3/1**[1]

3411 **3** *2 1/4* **Broughtons Point**[26] 4719 4-9-10 70 JamieMackay 6 74
(W J Musson) *hld up: hdwy over 1f out: styd on: nt rch ldrs* **12/1**

4224 **4** *3* **Mykingdomforahorse**[44] 4141 4-9-12 72 RichardHughes 1 72
(M R Channon) *hld up: hdwy over 1f out: wknd ins fnl f* **7/2**[3]

5011 **5** *1 1/2* **Saborido (USA)**[25] 4745 4-9-12 72 PhilipRobinson 3 70
(Mrs A J Perrett) *chsd wnr: rdn and bmpd over 2f out: wknd fnl f* **11/2**

6423 **6** *9* **Relative Strength (IRE)**[33] 4467 5-10-0 74 (v) DavidProbert 2 61
(A M Balding) *chsd ldrs: rdn and hung lft over 2f out: wknd over 1f out* **9/2**

3m 23.14s (4.14) **Going Correction** +0.10s/f (Good)
WFA 3 from 4yo+ 13lb 6 Ran SP% **111.6**
Speed ratings (Par 105): **92,91,90,88,87 83**
Tote Swingers:1&2:£2.80, 1&3:£6.00, 2&3:£6.30 CSF £13.52 TOTE £3.30: £1.20, £2.90; EX 16.00.

Owner Mrs Joan Keaney **Bred** Mrs Joan Keaney **Trained** Middleham Moor, N Yorks

FOCUS

Only six runners, but there was little to choose between them at the weights and they all came into it in good form. The pace was an honest one with the field soon strung out.

5613 CASTLE TOYS SMITH STREET WARWICK NURSERY 5f 110y

5:05 (5:07) (Class 5) (0-75,73) 2-Y-0 **£2,590** (£770; £385; £192) **Stalls** Low

Form RPR

4531 **1** **Loki's Revenge**[16] 5089 2-9-7 73 SteveDrowne 7 78
(W Jarvis) *hld up: nt clr run swtchd lft and hdwy over 1f out: rdn to ld cl home* **5/1**

254 **2** *hd* **Perfect Pastime**[49] 3959 2-9-5 71 AdamKirby 2 75
(W R Swinburn) *wnt rt s: prom: pushed along 1/2-way: rdn to ld ins fnl f: hung rt: hdd cl home* **9/2**[3]

055 **3** *1 1/2* **Buddy Miracle**[19] 4954 2-9-7 73 DavidProbert 4 72
(A M Balding) *led: rdn and hdd over 1f out: hung rt ins fnl f: styd on* **7/2**[2]

440 **4** *1/2* **Novabridge**[18] 5000 2-8-13 65 (b[1]) DaneO'Neill 8 63
(A B Haynes) *trckd ldrs: rdn to ld over 1f out: hung lft and hdd ins fnl f: no ex* **22/1**

4521 **5** *1 1/2* **Magic Cross**[15] 5111 2-8-3 55 HayleyTurner 6 48
(P J McBride) *s.i.s: hdwy 1/2-way: nt clr run and lost pl over 1f out: styd on ins fnl f* **8/1**

31 **6** *1 1/2* **Native Picture (IRE)**[28] 4658 2-9-7 73 RichardHughes 9 61
(R Hannon) *w ldr: rdn over 1f out: looked hld whn hmpd ins fnl f* **5/2**[1]

000 **7** *1 1/2* **Bernie's Tune**[30] 4587 2-8-0 52 ow2 JimmyQuinn 3 35
(J L Spearing) *hmpd s: a in rr* **40/1**

0240 **8** *2 1/2* **Kyncraighe (IRE)**[30] 4578 2-9-6 72 EddieAhern 5 47
(Eve Johnson Houghton) *chsd ldrs tl edgd lft and wknd over 1f out:* **14/1**

4602 **9** *2 3/4* **Maggie's Treasure (IRE)**[27] 4677 2-9-3 69 FergusSweeney 1 35
(J Gallagher) *chsd ldrs: rdn 1/2-way: wknd over 1f out* **14/1**

67.94 secs (2.04) **Going Correction** +0.35s/f (Good) 9 Ran SP% **116.9**
Speed ratings (Par 94): **100,99,97,97,95 93,91,87,84**
Tote Swingers:1&2:£3.30, 1&3:£6.30, 2&3:£4.30 CSF £28.15 CT £89.86 TOTE £5.70: £1.40, £1.40, £2.20; EX 29.60.

Owner Dr J Walker **Bred** The Athenians **Trained** Newmarket, Suffolk

■ Stewards' Enquiry : David Probert two-day ban: careless riding (Sep 13-14)

FOCUS

Three last-time-out winners in opposition, and though not a strong race numerically, the right horses in large part came to the fore and the form should stand up. The first two came from off the pace with the winner ending up in the centre of the track.

NOTEBOOK

Loki's Revenge comes from a Polytrack nursery at Lingfield two runs back that is working out well, but softer ground back on turf since seems to have been the making of him and he won this a shade cosily after having to be switched to his left before edging back right again. He'll probably stay 6f, but will be forced up in grade in his bid for a three-timer. (op 7-1)

Perfect Pastime ran well on his nursery debut as well as it being his first run on soft ground, looking the winner for most of the last furlong and doing little wrong. Gelded since his last run, he might yet have more progress in him. (op 5-1 tchd 4-1)

Buddy Miracle was another making her nursery debut, and though running well, left the impression that the drop back in trip wasn't to her advantage. She can do better again up at 6f and is clearly on a fair mark. (op 10-3 tchd 4-1)

Novabridge didn't look entirely straightforward in first-time blinkers and isn't the sort that can be relied upon to reproduce this running. (op 28-1)

Magic Cross didn't get the best of runs when going for a run on the rail, but lack of tactical speed caught her out and she might prefer more of a test. (op 7-1 tchd 13-2)

Native Picture(IRE) hadn't won much of a race at Windsor but seemed undone here more by soft ground than by her handicap mark, already held when hampered inside the last. The least experienced member of the field, she might still be open to a bit of improvement back under faster conditions. (op 11-4 tchd 9-4)

5614 WEDDING FAIR HERE ON 19TH SEPTEMBER H'CAP 6f

5:40 (5:40) (Class 5) (0-70,70) 3-Y-O+ £2,590 (£770; £385; £192) Stalls Low

Form RPR

0332 1 **Erebus (IRE)**[25] 4754 3-9-9 **67**........ RichardHughes 8 76
(S Kirk) *w ldrs: rdn to ld over 1f out: styd on* **3/1**[1]

3034 2 ¾ **Downhill Skier (IRE)**[10] 5267 6-9-1 **56**........ EddieAhern 5 62
(W M Brisbourne) *chsd ldrs: rdn and ev ch fr over 1f out: styd on* **4/1**[2]

0020 3 1 **Speak The Truth (IRE)**[10] 5262 4-9-9 **64**........(p) HayleyTurner 9 67
(J R Boyle) *hld up: hdwy u.p over 1f out: hung rt ins fnl f: styd on* **10/1**

326 4 1¼ **Doctor Hilary**[19] 4961 8-9-10 **65**........ J-PGuillambert 2 64
(M R Hoad) *chsd ldrs: rdn over 2f out: styd on same pce fnl f* **13/2**[3]

2665 5 3¾ **Farmers Wish (IRE)**[8] 5327 3-9-12 **70**........(b[1]) AdamKirby 4 57
(J L Spearing) *led: rdn and hdd over 1f out: wknd ins fnl f* **9/1**

0010 6 ¾ **Only A Game (IRE)**[10] 5267 5-9-0 **58**........(vt) GaryBartley[(3)] 10 43
(I W McInnes) *hld up: hdwy over 1f out: sn rdn: one pce fnl f* **14/1**

4103 7 nk **Two Turtle Doves (IRE)**[19] 4947 4-9-3 **65**........ JosephYoung[(7)] 11 49+
(M Mullineaux) *hld up: rdn and nt clr run 2f out: n.d* **9/1**

6620 8 nk **Valmina**[23] 4839 3-9-9 **67**........(tp) DavidProbert 6 50+
(Andrew Turnell) *chsd ldrs: rdn over 1f out: wknd fnl f* **16/1**

0200 9 nk **Takajan (IRE)**[16] 5073 3-9-0 **58**........ MickyFenton 1 40
(W M Brisbourne) *prom: rdn over 2f out: wknd fnl f* **20/1**

105 10 nk **Straboe (USA)**[140] 1258 4-9-9 **64**........(v) SaleemGolam 3 45+
(S C Williams) *hld up: hdwy and nt clr run over 1f out: wknd fnl f* **16/1**

0013 11 4 **Batgirl**[30] 4588 3-9-2 **60**........ DaneO'Neill 7 28
(John Berry) *chsd ldrs: nt clr run and lost pl over 2f out: n.d after* **8/1**

1m 13.39s (1.59) **Going Correction** +0.35s/f (Good)
WFA 3 from 4yo+ 3lb 11 Ran SP% **121.7**
Speed ratings (Par 103): **103,102,100,99,94 93,92,92,91,91 86**
Tote Swingers:1&2:£3.50, 1&3:£6.70, 2&3:£9.00 CSF £15.13 CT £110.15 TOTE £2.90: £1.10, £2.40, £4.80; EX 12.20 Place 6 £15.23; Place 5 £9.55.
Owner The Classics Partnership **Bred** R J Brennan And D Boocock **Trained** Upper Lambourn, Berks

FOCUS

Just an ordinary handicap that went to arguably the most in-form runner. The advantage was with those that raced handily.

Doctor Hilary Official explanation: jockey said gelding lost a near-hind shoe

T/Plt: £23.40 to a £1 stake. Pool:£30,182.16 - 939.89 winning tickets T/Qpdt: £10.20 to a £1 stake. Pool:£2,174.42 - 157.40 winning tickets CR

5574 DEAUVILLE (R-H)

Monday, August 30

OFFICIAL GOING: Turf: good to soft: fibresand: standard

5622a PRIX DE BLAY (CONDITIONS) (2YO FILLIES) (TURF) 1m (R)

11:50 (12:00) 2-Y-O £15,044 (£6,017; £4,513; £3,008; £1,504)

RPR

1 **Camelia Rose (FR)**[21] 2-9-0 **0**........ ChristopheSoumillon 6 94
(J-C Rouget, France) **9/10**[1]

2 1½ **Gypsy Highway (IRE)**[20] 2-8-10 **0**........ GregoryBenoist 8 87
(D Smaga, France) **13/2**[3]

3 ½ **Nosail (FR)**[20] 2-8-10 **0**........ OlivierPeslier 5 86
(F Head, France) **4/1**[2]

4 hd **Nova Hawk**[26] 2-8-8 **0**........ EddyHardouin[(6)] 3 90
(Rod Collet, France) **29/1**

5 2½ **Visinada (IRE)**[20] 2-8-5 **0**........ MorganDelalande[(5)] 7 80
(A De Royer-Dupre, France) **10/1**

6 hd **Madly In Love (FR)**[27] 2-8-10 **0**........ ThierryJarnet 10 80
(J-L Gay, France) **23/1**

7 1½ **Vauville (IRE)**[34] 2-8-10 **0**........ StephanePasquier 2 76
(Y De Nicolay, France) **21/1**

8 4 **Emerald Fields (IRE)** 2-8-10 **0**........ FranckBlondel 9 68
(Robert Collet, France) **66/1**

9 1½ **Hoppy's Flyer (FR)**[11] 5252 2-8-10 **0**........ MaximeGuyon 1 64
(Tom Dascombe) *broke wl: settled midfield on rail: dropped towards rr bef st: rdn 1 1/2f out: no prog: wknd: eased fnl 100yds* **20/1**

10 1½ **Amarilou (FR)** 2-9-0 **0**........ JulienAuge 4 65
(C Boutin, France) **21/1**

1m 46.8s (6.00) 10 Ran SP% **117.9**
WIN (incl. 1 euro stake): 1.90. PLACES: 1.20, 1.50, 1.30. DF: 7.50. SF: 11.70.
Owner Mme B Hermelin & A Holmes **Bred** J Aznar Rivero **Trained** Pau, France

NOTEBOOK

Hoppy's Flyer(FR) ran her best race over slightly shorter here earlier in the month so this has to go down as a disappointing effort.

5324 FOLKESTONE (R-H)

Tuesday, August 31

OFFICIAL GOING: Good (good to soft in places; 7.5)

5623 40 LIVE FOOTBALL MARKETS AT TOTESPORT.COM MAIDEN STKS 1m 1f 149y

4:50 (4:52) (Class 5) 3-Y-O+ £2,590 (£770; £385; £192) Stalls Centre

Form RPR

5 1 **Doon Kalal (IRE)**[18] 5026 3-9-3 **0**........(b[1]) PatDobbs 1 86+
(M P Tregoning) *mde all: clr and rdn over 1f out: styd on strly* **20/1**

2 3¾ **Nerves Of Steel (IRE)** 3-9-3 **0**........ JamieSpencer 2 78+
(P F I Cole) *dwlt: sn pushed up into mid field: rdn ent fnl 2f: swtchd lft over 1f out: styd to go 2nd nr fin: no ch w wnr* **15/2**

36 3 ½ **Snow Magic (IRE)**[37] 4397 3-8-12 **0**........ PatCosgrave 7 72
(J R Fanshawe) *chsd ldng pair: rdn over 2f out: chsd clr wnr and drvn over 1f out: no imp: lost 2nd towards fin* **10/1**

2 4 1¾ **Invincibility (IRE)**[18] 5026 3-9-3 **0**........ DarryllHolland 8 73
(S Dow) *chsd wnr: rdn over 2f out: drvn and no prog over 1f out: wknd ins fnl f* **2/1**[1]

5 shd **Qamar** 3-9-3 **0**........(t) TedDurcan 5 73+
(Saeed Bin Suroor) *short of room s and v.s.a: hld up bhd: hdwy and in tch 4f out: rdn and unable qck 2f out: kpt on: nvr gng pce to rch ldrs* **11/4**[2]

5 6 4½ **Toymaker**[31] 4572 3-9-3 **0**........ KierenFallon 6 64
(L M Cumani) *hld up towards rr: hdwy and in tch 4f out: rdn ent fnl 2f: sn btn: eased wl ins fnl f* **7/2**[3]

7 19 **Hecton Lad (USA)** 3-8-12 **0**........ KierenFox[(5)] 4 24
(J R Best) *stdd after s: hld up in last pair: lost tch 4f out* **50/1**

0440 8 27 **Durgan**[195] 587 4-9-11 **60**........ IanMongan 3 —
(Mrs L C Jewell) *stdd after s: hld up towards rr: lost tch qckly over 3f out: t.o* **40/1**

2m 6.44s (1.54) **Going Correction** +0.125s/f (Good)
WFA 3 from 4yo 8lb 8 Ran SP% **112.2**
Speed ratings (Par 103): **98,95,94,93,93 89,74,52**
toteswingers:1&2 £11.50, 2&3 £5.10, 1&3 £11.30 CSF £154.03 TOTE £42.70: £6.40, £3.00, £3.40; EX 123.10.
Owner Sheikh Ahmed Al Maktoum **Bred** Shadwell Estate Company Limited **Trained** Lambourn, Berks

FOCUS

A maiden made up of late-maturing horses. The decent pace had the field strung out early on and few landed a serious blow from out the back. The race should throw up its share of future winners in handicap company.

Qamar Official explanation: jockey said colt ran green early

5624 GET LIVE FOOTBALL STATS AT TOTESPORT.COM H'CAP 1m 1f 149y

5:25 (5:25) (Class 4) (0-80,77) 3-Y-O+ £3,885 (£1,156; £577; £288) Stalls Centre

Form RPR

2121 1 **Grams And Ounces**[18] 5051 3-8-12 **69**........ KierenFallon 5 80+
(Miss Amy Weaver) *broke wl and led: stdd and hdd after 1f: trckd ldrs after: swtchd rt and effrt wl over 1f out: qcknd to ld jst over 1f out: clr ins fnl f eased nr fin* **1/1**[1]

4011 2 1½ **Gross Prophet**[11] 5254 5-9-4 **72**........ SophieDoyle[(5)] 2 77
(A J Lidderdale) *led after 1f: drvn ent fnl 2f: hdd jst over 1f out: no ch w wnr ins fnl f: kpt on* **7/1**[3]

000S 3 nk **Truly Asia (IRE)**[23] 4859 4-9-7 **70**........ SteveDrowne 3 74+
(R Charlton) *stdd after s: hld up in last pair: hdwy and nt clr run 2f out: swtchd lft and hdwy u.p over 1f out: r.o: no ch w wnr* **14/1**

-205 4 ¾ **All The Winds (GER)**[17] 5084 5-9-9 **75**........(bt[1]) RussKennemore[(3)] 7 78
(S Lycett) *dwlt: hld up in last pair: hdwy 3f out: rdn on inner 2f out: styd on same pce ins fnl f* **12/1**

0232 5 1 **Ilie Nastase (FR)**[12] 5237 6-9-11 **77**........ EJMcNamara[(3)] 6 77
(C R Dore) *in tch in midfield: hdwy to chse ldng pair 4f out: rdn over 2f out: one pce fr over 1f out* **17/2**

3133 6 4½ **The Shuffler**[19] 4994 3-9-1 **72** ow1........ GeorgeBaker 1 63
(G L Moore) *hdwy to chse ldr over 7f out: ev ch 3f out: wknd u.p over 1f out* **5/1**[2]

2-04 7 14 **Penton Hook**[18] 5034 4-9-10 **73**........ IanMongan 8 34
(P Winkworth) *hld up in tch: rdn and wknd qckly 2f out: eased ins fnl f* **16/1**

2m 7.44s (2.54) **Going Correction** +0.125s/f (Good)
WFA 3 from 4yo+ 8lb 7 Ran SP% **109.9**
Speed ratings (Par 105): **94,92,92,91,91 87,76**
toteswingers:1&2 £2.50, 2&3 £16.70, 1&3 £5.00 CSF £7.75 CT £53.38 TOTE £2.20: £1.10, £2.30; EX 4.70.
Owner Miss A Weaver **Bred** Brook Stud Bloodstock Ltd **Trained** Newmarket, Suffolk

FOCUS

After riding the winner of the opener Pat Dobbs described the ground as being just on the easy side of good. This modest handicap proved a lively betting heat. It was run at a muddling pace, but the form still looks fair.

5625 BET ON LIVE TENNIS AT TOTESPORT.COM H'CAP 1m 4f

5:55 (5:56) (Class 6) (0-65,61) 3-Y-O+ £1,942 (£578; £288; £144) Stalls Low

Form RPR

6201 1 **Jasmeno**[10] 5289 3-9-5 **61**........(t) SteveDrowne 1 79+
(H Morrison) *towards rr: gd hdwy on outer over 2f out: rdn to ld over 1f out: sn clr: v easily* **4/1**[3]

0004 2 6 **Dove Cottage (IRE)**[25] 4794 8-9-11 **57**........ FergusSweeney 3 62
(W S Kittow) *taken down early: chsd ldrs tl led after 2f: jnd and rdn over 2f out: hdd over 1f out: no ch w wnr: hld on for 2nd ins fnl f* **14/1**

6040 3 ¾ **Barbirolli**[85] 2811 8-8-13 **45**........ ChrisCatlin 7 49
(W B Stone) *towards rr: hdwy to chse ldrs 5f out: pressed ldr over 2f out: nt gngpce of wnr over 1f out: kpt on* **33/1**

4403 4 1½ **Croix Rouge (USA)**[13] 5216 8-9-3 **52**........ RobertLButler[(3)] 9 54
(R J Smith) *in tch in midfield: rdn and unable qck over 2f out: styd on same pce fnl 2f* **22/1**

200 5 hd **Storming Redd**[27] 4697 3-9-4 **60**........ TomMcLaughlin 6 61
(J M P Eustace) *s.i.s: sn rdn in rr: kpt on u.p fnl 2f: nvr trbld ldrs* **50/1**

-000 6 1 **Whitley Bay (USA)**[25] 4793 3-8-1 **48**........ KierenFox[(5)] 10 48
(J R Best) *chsd ldrs 3f: rdn and lost pl 3f out: no imp ins fnl f* **50/1**

-011 7 nk **Bute Street**[19] 4991 5-10-0 **60**........ LiamKeniry 8 59
(R J Hodges) *chsd ldrs tl wknd u.p over 2f out* **4/1**[3]

-125 8 12 **Galiotto (IRE)**[68] 3348 4-9-12 **58**........ GeorgeBaker 2 54
(C F Wall) *restless in stalls: rrd s and v.s.a: a in rr* **10/3**[2]

2244 **9** *5* **Apache Kid (IRE)**[26] 4764 3-9-5 **61** .... KierenFallon 5 59
(D M Simcock) *midfield tl hdwy to chse ldr 7f out tl 3f out: sn rdn and wknd: eased ins fnl f* **9/4**[1]

06 **10** *30* **Aughcarra (IRE)**[19] 4990 5-9-3 **49** ....(p) DarrylHolland 4 —
(Harry Chisman) *led 2f: chsd ldr tl lost pl rapidly 7f out: virtually p.u fnl 4f: t.o* **50/1**

2m 42.03s (1.13) **Going Correction** +0.125s/f (Good)
WFA 3 from 4yo+ 10lb **10** Ran SP% **113.7**
Speed ratings (Par 101): **101,97,96,95,95 94,94,86,83,63**
CSF £51.49 CT £1585.49 TOTE £6.90: £3.40, £5.40, £9.40; EX 32.10.
Owner Melksham Craic **Bred** Melksham Craic **Trained** East Ilsley, Berks

FOCUS
An ordinary handicap, run at a sound pace.
Whitley Bay(USA) Official explanation: jockey said gelding hung left in straight
Galiotto(IRE) Official explanation: jockey said gelding reared in stalls and was slowly away
Apache Kid(IRE) Official explanation: jockey said colt hung right throughout
Aughcarra(IRE) Official explanation: jockey said gelding lost its action

5626 PLAY BLACKJACK AT TOTESPORT.COM MAIDEN AUCTION STKS 7f (S)
6:25 (6:29) (Class 5) 2-Y-O **£2,655** (£790; £394; £197) **Stalls** Low

Form RPR

5 **1** **Song Of The Siren**[19] 4999 2-8-4 0 .... DavidProbert 2 73+
(A M Balding) *mde all: rdn and edgd rt 2f out: styd on wl* **9/4**[1]

2 *2* **Copper Canyon** 2-8-9 0 .... FergusSweeney 3 71
(A B Haynes) *bhd: hdwy 2f out: chsd ldrs and rdn over 1f out: kpt on wl to go 2nd ins fnl f* **50/1**

4320 **3** *¾* **Rojo Boy**[52] 3887 2-9-1 76 .... JamieSpencer 6 75
(D R C Elsworth) *s.i.s: bhd: switching rt and hdwy 2f out: kpt on u.p* **7/2**[2]

0332 **4** *½* **Ransom Request**[22] 4911 2-8-10 73 .... LiamKeniry 9 69
(E F Vaughan) *in tch: hdwy to chse wnr 2f out: sn rdn: no ex ins fnl f* **15/2**

43 **5** *1 ½* **Cornish Quest**[19] 5006 2-8-10 0 .... DarrylHolland 14 65
(M H Tompkins) *bhd: hdwy over 2f out: rdn and chsd ldrs over 1f out: wknd ins fnl f* **13/2**[3]

0444 **6** *12* **Bright Applause**[26] 4736 2-8-6 69 .... HarryBentley(7) 8 38
(G L Moore) *prom tl wknd 2f out* **12/1**

5 **7** *½* **Beautiful Lando (FR)**[13] 5204 2-8-9 0 .... SteveDrowne 7 33
(Mrs H S Main) *chsd wnr to 2f out: sn wknd* **66/1**

5 **8** *1 ¾* **Hi Note**[26] 4729 2-8-7 0 .... ChrisCatlin 10 27
(M R Channon) *midfield struggling u.p 2f out* **33/1**

05 **9** *hd* **Sleeping Brave**[7] 5381 2-8-11 0 .... PatCosgrave 5 30
(J R Boyle) *midfield: struggling u.p 2f out: sn wl btn* **25/1**

0 **10** *5* **Tiberius Claudius (IRE)**[22] 4902 2-9-2 0 .... PhilipRobinson 4 23+
(G G Margarson) *midfield on stands' rail: shkn up whn stmbld and hit rail 2f out: nt pushed and no prog after* **7/1**

0 **11** *2* **Safari Sunbeam**[13] 5204 2-8-5 0 .... AshleyMorgan(5) 13 12
(P Winkworth) *midfield on outer: wknd 3f out* **50/1**

504 **12** *1 ¼* **Laffraaj (IRE)**[13] 5204 2-8-10 52 .... TedDurcan 1 14
(Pat Eddery) *s.i.s: a bhd: no ch whn hmpd 2f out* **12/1**

13 *½* **Dolly Colman (IRE)** 2-8-0 0 .... AmyBaker(5) 11 2
(A B Haynes) *midfield on outer: wknd 1/2-way* **66/1**

0 **14** *2 ¾* **Pipit Nest (IRE)**[13] 5204 2-7-13 0 .... SophieDoyle(5) 12 —
(T B P Coles) *s.i.s: a bhd* **100/1**

1m 29.12s (1.82) **Going Correction** +0.125s/f (Good) **14** Ran SP% **120.7**
Speed ratings (Par 94): **94,91,90,90,88 74,74,72,72,66 64,62,62,58**
toteswingers:1&2 £25.30, 2&3 £38.80, 1&3 £3.40 CSF £146.99 TOTE £4.10: £2.20, £14.10, £1.90; EX 146.90.
Owner Miss K Rausing **Bred** Miss K Rausing **Trained** Kingsclere, Hants

FOCUS
An average juvenile maiden, run at a solid pace. Those drawn low were at an advantage. The third to fifth set the level.

NOTEBOOK
Song Of The Siren proved all the rage in the market and shed her maiden tag at the second attempt with a decisive effort. She ran just moderately on her debut, but has clearly done well since and showed the clear benefit of that experience. The step up a furlong helped, as did being able to race against the stands' rail, and it will be interesting to see how the handicapper rates this. (op 4-1)
Copper Canyon ◆ looked a nice type in the paddock and he turned in a big run on this racecourse debut. Out of a dam who won over 1m4f, he looked to need all of this trip and connections evidently have a nice prospect on their hands.
Rojo Boy is a former stablemate of the winner and was making his debut for his new trainer. He attracted support on this sixth outing, but found himself with too much to do from off the pace and was always getting there too late. A more positive ride looks on the cards as connections now know he stays this far, and it was a step back in the right direction. Official explanation: jockey said colt was slowly away (op 4-1)
Ransom Request was easy to back, but stayed on stoutly from the furlong marker and rates a sound benchmark. She once again left the impression she wants a stiffer test and deserves to lose her maiden tag. (op 4-1)
Cornish Quest got himself behind and was noted doing some fair late work. He wasn't helped by being drawn on the outside here and better is expected from him when switching to nurseries, for which he is now qualified. (op 15-2 tchd 6-1)
Tiberius Claudius(IRE) was reported to have lost his action after hitting the stands' rail. Official explanation: jockey said colt lost its action (op 10-1)
Laffraaj(IRE) Official explanation: jockey said colt suffered interference in running

5627 PLAY ROULETTE AT TOTESPORT.COM H'CAP 7f (S)
6:55 (6:56) (Class 4) (0-85,81) 3-Y-O+ **£3,885** (£1,156; £577; £288) **Stalls** Low

Form RPR

6301 **1** **Hi Shinko**[12] 5238 4-9-7 **76** .... DarryllHolland 2 88
(B R Millman) *mde all: rdn 2f out: styd on wl ins fnl f* **7/2**[2]

3-21 **2** *¾* **Barq (IRE)**[19] 5007 3-9-4 **78** ....(t) TedDurcan 1 86
(Saeed Bin Suroor) *trckd ldng pair: swtchd rt and rdn to chse wnr over 1f out: drvn and one pce ins fnl f* **1/1**[1]

5300 **3** *2 ¾* **Midnight Fantasy**[25] 4806 4-9-1 **70** .... SteveDrowne 3 73
(Rae Guest) *in tch in last: rdn and outpcd 2f out: wnt 3rd 1f out: kpt on ins fnl f* **7/1**[3]

4505 **4** *4* **Nezami (IRE)**[17] 5082 5-9-12 **81** .... GeorgeBaker 5 73
(J Akehurst) *chsd wnr tl wl over 1f out: sn rdn and outpcd: no ch ins fnl f* **7/2**[2]

0006 **5** *1* **Safari Mischief**[40] 4292 7-9-6 **80** .... AshleyMorgan(5) 4 69
(P Winkworth) *in tch: rdn 2f out: sn outpcd* **22/1**

1m 27.14s (-0.16) **Going Correction** +0.125s/f (Good)
WFA 3 from 4yo+ 5lb **5** Ran SP% **111.3**
Speed ratings (Par 105): **105,104,101,96,95**
CSF £7.59 TOTE £4.30: £1.70, £1.20; EX 8.20.
Owner Always Hopeful Partnership **Bred** Mrs Laura Grasby **Trained** Kentisbeare, Devon

FOCUS
A modest little handicap, run at an uneven pace.

5628 LIPSCOMB.CO.UK H'CAP 5f
7:25 (7:25) (Class 4) (0-80,79) 3-Y-O+ **£3,885** (£1,156; £577; £288) **Stalls** Low

Form RPR

5431 **1** **Efistorm**[11] 5262 9-9-7 **79** .... EJMcNamara(3) 5 87
(C R Dore) *hld up bhd: nt clr run over 1f out: swtchd sharply rt and bmpd rival 1f out: pushed along and qcknd to ld fnl 75yds: r.o wl* **13/2**

0500 **2** *¾* **Rocker**[11] 5262 6-9-5 **74** .... GeorgeBaker 2 79
(G L Moore) *bmpd s: in tch: rdn to chse ldr over 1f out: led ins fnl f: hdd and one pce fnl 75yds* **11/4**[1]

3461 **3** *nk* **Love You Louis**[13] 5207 4-9-6 **75** .... PatDobbs 6 79
(J R Jenkins) *w ldr: rdn to ld over 1f out: hdd and one pce ins fnl f* **5/1**[3]

0531 **4** *hd* **Magical Speedfit (IRE)**[14] 5176 5-8-10 **70** .... SimonPearce(5) 7 74
(G G Margarson) *hld up in tch: hdwy on outer to chse ldrs whn bmpd 1f out: kpt on* **8/1**

5150 **5** *¾* **Ray Of Joy**[21] 4930 4-9-8 **77** .... PhilipRobinson 3 78
(J R Jenkins) *bmpd and squeezed out sn after s: in tch: switching rt 2f out: nt clr run and styd on same pce ins fnl f* **14/1**

05 **6** *½* **Step It Up (IRE)**[13] 5207 6-8-1 **63** .... NathanAlison(7) 4 62
(J R Boyle) *chsd ldrs: rdn 2f out: styd on same pce ins fnl f* **9/1**

1005 **7** *1* **Triple Dream**[11] 5262 5-9-4 **73** ....(b) LiamKeniry 1 68
(J M Bradley) *wnt rt s: led: rdn and hdd over 1f out: wknd ins fnl f* **9/2**[2]

0042 **8** *1* **Our Piccadilly (IRE)**[26] 4730 5-9-5 **74** .... FergusSweeney 8 66
(W S Kittow) *hld up in tch: rdn and hdwy to chse ldrs over 1f out: bmpd and pushed rt 1f out: nt rcvr* **13/2**

60.87 secs (0.87) **Going Correction** +0.125s/f (Good) **8** Ran SP% **116.0**
Speed ratings (Par 105): **98,96,96,96,94 94,92,90**
toteswingers:1&2 £5.40, 2&3 £4.70, 1&3 £6.50 CSF £25.14 CT £98.38 TOTE £11.50: £3.70, £1.10, £1.30; EX 24.60 Place 6: £114.06 Place 5: £12.72.
Owner Sean J Murphy **Bred** E Duggan And D Churchman **Trained** Cowbit, Lincs
■ Stewards' Enquiry : E J McNamara four-day ban: careless riding (Sep 14-17)

FOCUS
A run-of-the-mill sprint handicap that looked wide open. There was no hanging about early with the runners quick to get over to the stands' rail.
T/Plt: £156.10 to a £1 stake. Pool of £53,754.61 - 251.32 winning tickets. T/Qpdt: £14.40 to a £1 stake. Pool of £7,212.13 - 368.95 winning tickets. SP

5385 LEICESTER (R-H)
Tuesday, August 31

OFFICIAL GOING: Soft (good to soft in places; 6.4)
Wind: Almost nil Weather: Cloudy with sunny spells

5629 LADBROKES.COM E B F APOLLO MAIDEN STKS 7f 9y
2:10 (2:12) (Class 4) 2-Y-O **£4,533** (£1,348; £674; £336) **Stalls** Low

Form RPR

1 **Unex El Greco** 2-9-3 0 .... WilliamBuick 4 82+
(J H M Gosden) *s.s: hdwy over 4f out: led wl over 1f out: edgd lft ins fnl f: r.o: eased nr fin* **12/1**

4 **2** *2 ¼* **The Mongoose**[31] 4577 2-9-3 0 .... RichardMullen 7 72
(Sir Michael Stoute) *hld up in tch: rdn over 1f out: styd on* **6/4**[1]

0 **3** *½* **Number Theory**[23] 4856 2-9-3 0 .... NickyMackay 11 71
(J R Holt) *chsd ldr: rdn and ev ch wl over 1f out: styd on* **50/1**

0 **4** *1 ¾* **Cross Culture (IRE)**[41] 4263 2-9-3 0 .... JimmyFortune 5 66+
(A M Balding) *led: rdn and hdd wl over 1f out: styd on same pce ins fnl f* **22/1**

5 *shd* **Mutayaser** 2-9-3 0 .... RichardHills 3 66+
(Sir Michael Stoute) *prom: pushed along over 2f out: styd on same pce ins fnl f* **5/2**[2]

6 *nk* **Dumbarton (IRE)** 2-9-0 0 .... Louis-PhilippeBeuzelin(3) 8 65+
(Sir Michael Stoute) *hld up: hdwy 3f out: rdn over 1f out: no ex wl ins fnl f* **10/1**[3]

7 *1 ½* **Spyder** 2-9-3 0 .... LukeMorris 13 62
(S W James) *chsd ldrs: rdn over 2f out: styd on same pce appr fnl f* **200/1**

2445 **8** *3 ¾* **Restless Bay (IRE)**[23] 4856 2-9-3 70 .... PaulMulrennan 2 52
(R Hollinshead) *unruly on the way to post: hld up: rdn 1/2-way: styd on u.p fr over 1f out: n.d* **20/1**

6 **9** *½* **Sleeping Wolf**[103] 2245 2-9-3 0 .... RoystonFfrench 9 51
(R Hannon) *chsd ldrs: rdn over 2f out: wknd over 1f out* **14/1**

10 *¾* **Grumeti** 2-9-3 0 .... HayleyTurner 1 49
(M L W Bell) *dwlt: sn drvn along in rr: nvr on terms* **16/1**

11 *2 ¾* **Canaveral** 2-9-3 0 .... MartinDwyer 10 42
(B J Meehan) *chsd ldrs tl wknd over 2f out* **40/1**

12 *1 ¼* **No Larking (IRE)** 2-9-3 0 .... DaneO'Neill 14 39
(H Candy) *mid-div: rdn over 2f out: sn wknd* **50/1**

0 **13** *1 ¾* **Reach Out**[18] 5033 2-9-3 0 .... StevieDonohoe 6 35
(B G Powell) *in rr and sn pushed along: nvr on terms* **100/1**

0600 **14** *1 ¾* **Silver Writer**[28] 4682 2-9-3 53 .... PhillipMakin 15 30
(M W Easterby) *prom: lost pl 1/2-way: sn bhd* **200/1**

0 **15** *½* **Talking Back**[18] 5032 2-9-3 0 .... JamesDoyle 12 29
(S Kirk) *mid-div: rdn over 4f out: wknd 1/2-way* **100/1**

1m 28.33s (2.13) **Going Correction** +0.125s/f (Good) **15** Ran SP% **116.3**
Speed ratings (Par 96): **92,89,88,86,86 84,84,80,79,78 75,74,72,70,69**
toteswingers:1&2 £4.80, 2&3 £15.50, 1&3 £61.70 CSF £27.79 TOTE £7.90: £1.90, £1.10, £11.50; EX 34.60.
Owner W J Gredley **Bred** Middle Park Stud Ltd **Trained** Newmarket, Suffolk

FOCUS
This can be a good maiden - Ibn Khaldun the most notable recent winner - and plenty of powerful connections were represented. However, the time was only 0.49 seconds quicker than the following juvenile seller won by the 57-rated Sky Diamond. The winner impressed and the third is the long-term key.

NOTEBOOK
Unex El Greco, a half-brother to 7f-1m winner Foolin Myself, won nicely on debut. His head was a touch high in the closing stages, but that was probably through greenness and he still ran on well, having travelled best. He doesn't hold any fancy entries in Britain this year, but is clearly worth his place in decent company. (op 9-1)
The Mongoose lacked the winner's speed and didn't improve as much as expected on his debut effort. He holds some Group-race entries this year, but is highly unlikely to be seen at his best until tackling middle-distances next season. (op 13-8 tchd 11-8)
Number Theory stepped up hugely on his debut effort and evidently has a fair amount of ability. (op 40-1)
Cross Culture(IRE) was given a positive ride and showed up well for much of the way, improving on his first effort. (op 25-1)

Mutayaser, a 230,000gns purchase, was well backed despite his stable also sending out the favourite, but he was never seriously competitive. A half-brother to a number of winners over 1m4f-plus, he can be expected to do much better over longer trips in due course. (tchd 9-4)
Dumbarton(IRE), the first foal of a high-class 7f-1m4f winner, was the least fancied of the Stoute trio. He showed ability and is open to plenty of improvement. (op 12-1 tchd 16-1)

5630 LADBROKES.COM (S) STKS — 7f 9y
2:40 (2:40) (Class 6) 2-Y-O — **£1,942** (£578; £288; £144) **Stalls** Low

Form — RPR
0500 **1** — **Sky Diamond (IRE)**[48] 4020 2-8-12 57 — PaulMulrennan 14 — 60+
(J G Given) *hld up: swtchd lft 1/2-way: hdwy u.p to ld over 1f out: r.o wl* **8/1**
0 **2** 3 ¾ **Green With Envy (IRE)**[64] 3517 2-8-12 0 — (p) DaraghO'Donohoe 7 — 51
(George Baker) *hld up: hdwy u.p over 1f out: styd on to go 2nd wl ins fnl f: no ch w wnr* **25/1**
2600 **3** 1 **Bajan Bullet**[7] 5389 2-8-7 65 — JamesDoyle 15 — 43
(P D Evans) *prom: rdn over 2f out: styd on same pce ins fnl f* **15/2**
03 **4** nk **Red Jacaranda**[8] 5373 2-8-7 0 — LiamJones 4 — 42
(C A Dwyer) *hld up in tch: rdn and ev ch over 1f out: edgd lft: no ex ins fnl f* **5/1**[2]
00 **5** 3 **Mini's Destination**[34] 4474 2-8-7 0 — NickyMackay 2 — 35
(J R Holt) *prom: pushed along to join ldr 1/2-way: rdn and hung rt over 1f out: wknd ins fnl f* **16/1**
0 **6** nk **Nippy Nikki**[45] 4150 2-8-7 0 — AdrianNicholls 10 — 34
(J R Norton) *mid-div: outpcd 1/2-way: styd on u.p fr over 1f out* **100/1**
0 **7** nk **Nutley Copse**[85] 2819 2-8-7 0 — (v[1]) NeilChalmers 5 — 33
(A M Balding) *s.s: hdwy over 4f out: rdn over 2f out: wkng whn hung lft ins fnl f* **4/1**[1]
2006 **8** 1 ¼ **Dancing Tara**[25] 4802 2-8-7 57 — CathyGannon 3 — 30
(P D Evans) *mid-div: hdwy 1/2-way: rdn and wknd over 1f out* **7/1**[3]
0 **9** ½ **Ivanov (IRE)**[11] 5269 2-8-12 0 — StevieDonohoe 9 — 34
(W J Musson) *dwlt: outpcd: styd on ins fnl f: nvr nrr* **28/1**
0060 **10** nse **Muse To Use**[45] 4150 2-8-4 46 — KellyHarrison(3) 6 — 29
(I W McInnes) *chsd ldrs: led 1/2-way: hung rt over 2f out: rdn and hdd over 1f out: wknd ins fnl f* **25/1**
0604 **11** ½ **Livinadream**[20] 4940 2-8-4 52 — Louis-PhilippeBeuzelin(3) 1 — 28
(N Tinkler) *hld up: hdwy 1/2-way: rdn over 2f out: wkng whn hmpd ins fnl f* **20/1**
4304 **12** 11 **Glenns Princess**[9] 5334 2-8-7 65 — RoystonFfrench 17 — —
(R A Fahey) *chsd ldrs: rdn over 2f out: sn wknd* **9/1**
000 **13** 3 **Adzing (IRE)**[35] 4447 2-8-12 48 — LukeMorris 12 — —
(R A Harris) *chsd ldrs tl rdn and wknd over 2f out* **40/1**
5060 **14** 1 **Little Libretto (IRE)**[11] 5269 2-8-12 63 — RichardMullen 8 — —
(P D Evans) *prom: rdn 1/2-way: wknd over 2f out* **14/1**
000 **15** 6 **Kings Arms**[39] 4346 2-8-12 36 — (b[1]) PhillipMakin 16 — —
(M W Easterby) *s.i.s: sn rcvrd to ld: hdd 1/2-way: hmpd and wknd over 2f out* **28/1**

1m 28.82s (2.62) **Going Correction** +0.125s/f (Good) — **15** Ran SP% **117.4**
Speed ratings (Par 92): **90,85,84,84,80 80,80,78,78,78 77,64,61,60,53**
toteswingers:1&2 £60.40, 2&3 £30.50, 1&3 £10.10 CSF £196.38 TOTE £9.50: £4.00, £6.60, £2.00; EX 295.30.There was no bid for the winner.
Owner Danethorpe Racing Partnership **Bred** David Bourke **Trained** Willoughton, Lincs

FOCUS
A standard seller, although the time wasn't bad, being just 0.49 seconds slower than the earlier maiden won by Unex El Greco. The winner is rated back to his early-season course form.

NOTEBOOK
Sky Diamond(IRE) stepped up on his four previous efforts, taking advantage of the drop in grade with a clear-cut success after 48 days off. He could be competitive in nurseries. (op 7-1)
Green With Envy(IRE) showed nothing on Polytrack first time up, but this was a lot better, with the cheekpieces appearing to help. There might more to come. (op 20-1 tchd 18-1)
Bajan Bullet, dropped into a seller for the first time, didn't seem to run up to her official mark of 65. (op 13-2 tchd 6-1)
Red Jacaranda ran respectably without improving for the drop in trip (op 13-2 tchd 9-2)
Nutley Copse failed to justify market support, not improving for the first-time visor and step up in trip. (op 7-1)

5631 LADBROKES.COM MARKFIELD H'CAP — 1m 3f 183y
3:10 (3:10) (Class 5) (0-70,67) 3-Y-O+ — **£2,266** (£674; £337; £168) **Stalls** High

Form — RPR
-543 **1** — **Bondage (IRE)**[82] 2909 3-9-3 **66** — HayleyTurner 9 — 75+
(J R Fanshawe) *chsd ldr tl led over 4f out: shkn up over 1f out: styd on: idled towards fin* **7/2**[2]
0424 **2** 1 **Hurlingham**[8] 5363 6-10-0 **67** — (b) PhillipMakin 11 — 73+
(M W Easterby) *hld up: hdwy over 3f out: nt clr run and lost pl over 2f out: rallied and hung rt over 1f out: r.o to go 2nd nr fin: nt rch wnr* **7/1**[3]
1200 **3** nk **Red Wine**[56] 3760 11-9-4 **60** — KellyHarrison(3) 2 — 66
(J A Glover) *stdd s: hld up: hdwy over 2f out: rdn to chse wnr and hung rt fr over 1f out: styd on: lost 2nd nr fin* **18/1**
0-60 **4** 3 ¼ **Akula (IRE)**[15] 5146 3-9-0 **63** — LiamJones 13 — 63
(M H Tompkins) *hld up: plld hrd: hdwy over 7f out: rdn over 3f out: no ex ins fnl f* **14/1**
2232 **5** 4 **Ice Viking (IRE)**[25] 4786 3-9-2 **65** — PaulMulrennan 12 — 59+
(J G Given) *chsd ldrs: nt clr run and lost pl over 3f out: n.d after* **2/1**[1]
2500 **6** nk **Second Brook (IRE)**[6] 5423 3-8-4 **53** — LukeMorris 7 — 46
(R Hollinshead) *prom: chsd ldr over 3f out tl rdn wl over 1f out: nt clr run and swtchd lft ent fnl f: sn wknd* **16/1**
6065 **7** 1 **Genes Of A Dancer (AUS)**[11] 5260 4-8-8 **57** — LucyBarry(7) 8 — 46
(M Appleby) *plld hrd and prom: rdn over 2f out: wkng whn hmpd over 1f out* **10/1**
000 **8** 1 **Transfered (IRE)**[24] 4854 4-8-6 **48** oh3 — AndrewHeffernan(3) 1 — 38
(Lucinda Featherstone) *prom: hmpd over 7f out: rdn over 3f out: wknd over 1f out* **25/1**
0-00 **9** 24 **House Point**[76] 3091 3-8-11 **60** — WilliamBuick 3 — 12
(S C Williams) *hld up: rdn and wknd over 2f out: t.o* **7/1**[3]
00/0 **10** 16 **Real Dandy**[31] 4591 4-8-11 **50** — NeilChalmers 10 — —
(Lucinda Featherstone) *led: hdd over 4f out: wknd over 2f out: t.o* **100/1**
2030 **11** 24 **Pedasus (USA)**[19] 4120 4-9-7 **60** — (p) StevieDonohoe 6 — —
(T Keddy) *hld up: last and rdn 1/2-way: sn lost tch: t.o* **50/1**

2m 37.02s (3.12) **Going Correction** +0.325s/f (Good)
WFA 3 from 4yo+ 10lb — **11** Ran SP% **114.3**
Speed ratings (Par 103): **102,101,101,98,96 96,95,94,78,68 52**
toteswingers:1&2 £3.30, 2&3 £11.50, 1&3 £11.10 CSF £27.10 CT £382.98 TOTE £4.10: £1.20, £1.20, £5.30; EX 24.00.
Owner Mrs Andrew Crawshaw & Mrs J Fanshawe **Bred** Mesnil Investments Ltd & Carrigbeg Stud **Trained** Newmarket, Suffolk

FOCUS
Plenty of these have questionable attitudes and the form's probably not worth dwelling on.

Akula(IRE) Official explanation: jockey said colt ran too freely

5632 LADBROKES.COM PRESTWOLD CONDITIONS STKS — 5f 2y
3:40 (3:40) (Class 3) 3-Y-O+ — **£5,607** (£1,679; £839; £420; £209) **Stalls** Low

Form — RPR
3344 **1** — **Star Rover (IRE)**[21] 4937 3-8-7 94 — CathyGannon 1 — 94
(P D Evans) *chsd ldr: sn pushed along: rdn over 1f out: led ins fnl f: r.o* **7/2**[2]
5441 **2** 1 **Angus Newz**[3] 5528 7-8-7 78 — (v) MartinDwyer 3 — 88
(M Quinn) *led: rdn over 1f out: hdd and unable qck ins fnl f* **5/1**[3]
0004 **3** 1 ¾ **Singeur (IRE)**[12] 5250 3-8-7 98 — (b) RichardMullen 5 — 84
(R Bastiman) *sn outpcd: swtchd rt and styd on fr over 1f out: wnt 3rd nr fin: nvr trbld ldrs* **10/11**[1]
0600 **4** hd **Abraham Lincoln (IRE)**[37] 4401 6-8-9 86 — (p) LukeMorris 2 — 83
(R A Harris) *trckd ldrs: rdn over 1f out: no ex ins fnl f* **10/1**
0-03 **5** 23 **Red Avalanche (IRE)**[46] 4105 3-8-8 88 ow1 — (t) WilliamBuick 4 — —
(P F I Cole) *chsd ldrs: rdn 1/2-way: wknd and eased over 1f out* **11/1**

59.60 secs (-0.40) **Going Correction** +0.125s/f (Good)
WFA 3 from 6yo+ 2lb — **5** Ran SP% **108.7**
Speed ratings (Par 107): **108,106,103,103,66**
CSF £19.58 TOTE £5.20: £3.40, £1.80; EX 13.70.
Owner Christy Leo **Bred** Yeomanstown Stud **Trained** Pandy, Monmouths

FOCUS
An ordinary conditions race, though the time was highly respectable in the conditions.

NOTEBOOK
Star Rover(IRE), a five-time winner during his juvenile campaign, gained his first success of 2010 in straightforward fashion, taking advantage of a good opportunity considering he had 14lb in hand over the runner-up (although that one was due to go up 5lb). (op 4-1 tchd 10-3)
Angus Newz had a bit to find at the weights, but she was formerly very useful and might have gained confidence from her recent handicap win. She is due for a 5lb rise now. (op 4-1 tchd 11-2)
Singeur(IRE) caught the eye at York last time and was the pick of these weights - he had 4lb in hand over the winner - but he was never going the required speed. He has to be worth another shot at 6f. (tchd 5-6 and Evens)
Abraham Lincoln(IRE) didn't shape as though about to end his long losing run. (op 11-1 tchd 16-1 and 9-1)

5633 E B F LADBROKES.COM FILBERT MAIDEN FILLIES' STKS — 1m 60y
4:10 (4:13) (Class 4) 2-Y-O — **£4,533** (£1,348; £674; £336) **Stalls** High

Form — RPR
2 **1** — **Midnight Caller**[17] 5066 2-9-0 0 — WilliamBuick 7 — 83+
(J H M Gosden) *trckd ldrs: n.m.r and lost pl over 5f out: hdwy over 2f out: led on bit wl over 1f out: easily* **1/4**[1]
03 **2** 1 ½ **Slight Advantage (IRE)**[17] 5066 2-9-0 0 — LukeMorris 3 — 69
(C G Cox) *w ldr: rdn over 2f out: ev ch wl over 1f out: sn outpcd* **33/1**
05 **3** shd **Ihavenotime (IRE)**[14] 5170 2-9-0 0 — AlanMunro 4 — 69
(M R Channon) *chsd ldrs: outpcd over 1f out: styd on ins fnl f* **66/1**
0 **4** 1 ½ **Azlaa**[61] 3590 2-9-0 0 — JimmyFortune 6 — 65
(R Hannon) *led: rdn and hdd wl over 1f out: no ex ins fnl f* **10/1**[2]
5 **5** 2 ½ **Miss Villefranche**[17] 5066 2-9-0 0 — HayleyTurner 5 — 60
(M L W Bell) *hld up: hdwy over 5f out: rdn over 3f out: styd on same pce fr over 1f out* **16/1**[3]
6 27 **Magic Of The Sea (IRE)** 2-9-0 0 — MartinDwyer 2 — 1
(M Botti) *dwlt and swvd lft s: plld hrd and hdwy over 5f out: wknd over 2f out: t.o* **28/1**

1m 47.9s (2.80) **Going Correction** +0.325s/f (Good) — **6** Ran SP% **102.9**
Speed ratings (Par 93): **99,97,97,95,93 66**
toteswingers:1&2 £2.30, 2&3 £8.10, 1&3 £5.70 CSF £10.00 TOTE £1.10: £1.10, £5.70; EX 8.00.
Owner George Strawbridge **Bred** George Strawbridge **Trained** Newmarket, Suffolk

FOCUS
An uncompetitive fillies' maiden, but a well above-average looking winner, who looks potentially Group class.

NOTEBOOK
Midnight Caller ◆ had shaped with plenty of promise when second to a decent type on debut at Doncaster, a race she may have won had she not jinked late on, and confirmed that with a taking display. Although she didn't beat a great deal, she had much more in hand than the official margin suggests and it will be a surprise if she's not up to competing in Pattern company. (op 3-10 tchd 2-9 and 1-3 in a place)
Slight Advantage(IRE) was 11l behind Midnight Caller at Doncaster last time and although this was better, she's flattered to get so close to the winner. (tchd 40-1)
Ihavenotime(IRE) hadn't shown much in her first two starts, but this was better for all that the bare result is misleading. Nurseries are now an option. (op 80-1)
Azlaa shaped reasonably on debut over 6f at Newbury, but did not improve for this step up in trip. She might do better back over shorter. (op 12-1 tchd 14-1)
Miss Villefranche was held by today's winner and runner-up on debut Doncaster form and made no impression. (op 20-1)
Magic Of The Sea(IRE) was extremely green. (op 22-1 tchd 18-1)

5634 LADBROKESCASINO.COM H'CAP — 7f 9y
4:40 (4:40) (Class 5) (0-70,72) 3-Y-O+ — **£2,266** (£674; £337; £168) **Stalls** Low

Form — RPR
226 **1** — **Nisaal (IRE)**[46] 4088 5-9-10 **66** — AdamKirby 12 — 78
(A W Carroll) *hld up: hdwy over 1f out: rdn to ld wl ins fnl f* **10/1**
0430 **2** nk **Aflaam (IRE)**[16] 5115 5-9-11 **70** — AndrewHeffernan(3) 11 — 81
(R A Harris) *trckd ldrs: led 2f out: rdn over 1f out: hdd wl ins fnl f* **6/1**[3]
2633 **3** 2 ½ **Copperwood**[41] 4260 5-9-10 **66** — DaneO'Neill 6 — 70
(M Blanshard) *s.i.s: hdwy 1/2-way: rdn over 2f out: styd on to go 3rd wl ins fnl f: nt trble ldrs* **14/1**
061 **4** 1 **Cara's Request (AUS)**[8] 5357 5-10-2 **72** 6ex — AdrianNicholls 7 — 74
(D Nicholls) *led: rdn and hdd 2f out: no ex ins fnl f* **5/4**[1]
6040 **5** 2 ½ **Kensington (IRE)**[22] 4910 9-9-9 **65** — (p) JamesDoyle 9 — 60
(A J McCabe) *chsd ldrs: rdn over 2f out: styd on same pce appr fnl f* **28/1**
0606 **6** shd **Tamasou (IRE)**[7] 5386 5-9-9 **70** — (p) RossAtkinson(5) 10 — 65
(F J Brennan) *chsd ldrs: rdn 1/2-way: styd on same pce fnl 2f* **8/1**
2000 **7** 1 ½ **Montego Breeze**[3] 5510 4-8-9 **51** oh1 — RoystonFfrench 8 — 42
(John A Harris) *s.i.s: sn pushed along in rr: rdn 1/2-way: n.d* **33/1**
0006 **8** 2 **Kingsmaite**[90] 2653 9-8-2 **51** oh6 — (b) CharlesEddery(7) 3 — 36
(S R Bowring) *hld up: a in rr: bhd fr 1/2-way* **50/1**
3223 **9** 2 ¼ **Piddie's Power**[15] 5163 3-9-8 **69** — RichardMullen 2 — 46
(E S McMahon) *s.i.s: sn prom: rdn over 2f out: wknd over 1f out* **11/2**[2]
0-06 **10** nk **Sands Of Dee (USA)**[24] 4833 3-8-10 **57** — (bt) PaulMulrennan 1 — 33
(J A Glover) *hld up: rdn 1/2-way: a in rr* **33/1**
2303 **11** 3 ¾ **Liberty Trail (IRE)**[25] 4776 4-9-7 **63** — (b) CathyGannon 4 — 31
(P D Evans) *chsd ldrs: rdn 1/2-way: wknd over 2f out* **20/1**

0002 **12** *19* **First Blade**[36] 4427 4-9-9 **65**....................(b) LiamJones 5 —
(S R Bowring) *s.i.s: a in rr: bhd fr 1/2-way: t.o* **16/1**

1m 26.52s (0.32) **Going Correction** +0.125s/f (Good)
WFA 3 from 4yo+ 5lb 12 Ran SP% **122.9**
Speed ratings (Par 103): **103,102,99,98,95 95,93,91,89,88 84,62**
toteswingers:1&2 £12.50, 2&3 £15.30, 1&3 £9.40 CSF £67.78 CT £876.75 TOTE £11.90: £2.90, £2.10, £2.80; EX 86.80.
Owner Dark Horse Racing Partnership Three **Bred** Shadwell Estate Company Limited **Trained** Cropthorne, Worcs

FOCUS
A modest but competitive handicap.

5635 LADBROKESCASINO.COM APPRENTICE H'CAP 1m 1f 218y
5:15 (5:15) (Class 5) (0-70,68) 4-Y-0+ **£2,266** (£674; £337; £168) **Stalls** High

Form RPR
-241 **1** **High Five Society**[21] 4932 6-9-8 **66**....................(b) RyanClark 6 77+
(S R Bowring) *hld up: hdwy over 3f out: led over 2f out: clr fr over 1f out: comf* **7/2**[3]

/060 **2** *4* **Strategic Mission (IRE)**[22] 4907 5-9-10 **68**.............. DuilioDaSilva 2 71
(P F I Cole) *hld up: hdwy 6f out: led over 3f out: hdd over 2f out: styd on same pce appr fnl f* **9/2**

360 **3** *1 ¼* **Peaceful Means (IRE)**[10] 5287 7-9-1 **62**.............. SoniaEaton(3) 5 63
(A W Carroll) *chsd ldrs: hmpd 5f out: rdn over 1f out: styd on same pce* **11/1**

0201 **4** *hd* **Cherri Fosfate**[3] 5515 6-9-8 **66** 6ex.................... NeilFarley 1 66
(D Carroll) *hld up in tch: jnd ldr over 3f out: rdn over 1f out: styd on same pce* **5/2**[1]

550 **5** *shd* **Opera Prince**[53] 3853 5-9-6 **67**.................... JamesRogers(3) 3 67
(Lady Herries) *trckd ldrs: swtchd rt 2f out: styd on same pce fr over 1f out* **11/4**[2]

/0-0 **6** *8* **Given A Choice (IRE)**[8] 5367 8-9-1 **62**.............. SophieSilvester(3) 4 46
(J Pearce) *s.s: hld up: rdn and edgd lft over 2f out: sn wknd* **14/1**

0/ **7** *3 ¼* **Bogside Dancer**[881] 1159 8-8-12 **56**.................... JohnCavanagh 8 33
(John A Harris) *led over 6f: wknd over 2f out* **33/1**

000/ **8** *dist* **Always Baileys (IRE)**[613] 6798 7-8-3 **50**.............. NatashaEaton(3) 7 —
(Mrs P Ford) *chsd ldr tl wknd over 3f out: t.o* **33/1**

2m 10.32s (2.42) **Going Correction** +0.325s/f (Good) 8 Ran SP% **116.5**
Speed ratings (Par 103): **103,99,98,98,98 92,89,—**
toteswingers:1&2 £3.20, 2&3 £6.20, 1&3 £4.90 CSF £20.10 CT £153.84 TOTE £3.20: £1.10, £1.80, £7.50; EX 25.10 Place 6: £260.30 Place 5: £144.34.
Owner S R Bowring **Bred** A C M Spalding **Trained** Edwinstowe, Notts

FOCUS
A modest apprentice handicap.
T/Jkpt: Not won. T/Plt: £203.30 to a £1 stake. Pool of £55,798.93 - 200.36 winning tickets. T/Qpdt: £18.70 to a £1 stake. Pool of £3,597.70 - 141.90 winning tickets. CR

5602 RIPON (R-H)
Tuesday, August 31
OFFICIAL GOING: Good (good to firm in places; 8.7)
Wind: light 1/2 behind Weather: fine

5636 CATHY MARR MEMORIAL (S) STKS 1m 1f 170y
2:30 (2:30) (Class 5) 3-4-Y-0 **£2,590** (£770; £385; £192) **Stalls** High

Form RPR
1540 **1** **Dark Ranger**[17] 5072 4-9-12 59....................(p) EddieAhern 11 70
(T J Pitt) *hld up towards rr: hdwy over 3f out: chsd ldr 2f out: styd on to ld nr fin* **8/1**

3540 **2** *hd* **Chantilly Pearl (USA)**[22] 4913 4-9-7 58.................... PaulHanagan 2 65
(J G Given) *trckd ldrs: wnt 2nd over 3f out: led over 2f out: no ex and hdd cl home* **7/2**[2]

5633 **3** *3 ¾* **Dazeen**[8] 5353 3-8-12 64.................... TonyCulhane 9 56
(P T Midgley) *hld up in rr: effrt on outside 4f out: chsng ldrs over 1f out: kpt on same pce* **5/1**[3]

3056 **4** *¾* **Tom Wade (IRE)**[35] 4448 3-8-10 55 ow1..............(p) GaryBartley(3) 1 56
(John A Harris) *sn chsng ldrs: chal 2f out: one pce* **16/1**

1643 **5** *7* **Guga (IRE)**[23] 4863 4-9-12 62....................(v[1]) SilvestreDeSousa 8 47
(G A Harker) *led: hdd over 2f out: wknd over 1f out* **3/1**[1]

3304 **6** *¾* **Dane Cottage**[26] 4728 3-8-4 58.................... MartinLane(3) 7 34
(P D Evans) *dwlt: in rr: hdwy over 3f out: wknd 2f out* **6/1**

0056 **7** *¾* **Strevelyn**[20] 4949 4-9-6 46.................... StephenCraine 12 38
(Mrs A Duffield) *trckd ldrs: effrt over 3f out: hung rt: wknd 2f out* **25/1**

4064 **8** *3 ¾* **Fortunate Bid (IRE)**[9] 5331 4-9-9 54..............(p) JamesSullivan(3) 13 36
(Mrs L Stubbs) *s.i.s: hld up in rr: effrt 4f out: nvr on terms* **16/1**

-400 **9** *nse* **Power Of Dreams (IRE)**[14] 5171 3-8-12 60.............. NeilCallan 10 30
(M H Tompkins) *in tch: lost pl over 2f out* **14/1**

0040 **10** *18* **Duke Of Normandy (IRE)**[22] 4912 4-9-6 46............(v[1]) JamieMackay 4 —
(B P J Baugh) *trckd ldr: t.k.h: reminders and hung rt over 4f out: nt keen and wknd qckly over 3f out: bhd whn eased over 1f out: t.o* **50/1**

56 **11** *40* **Just Nod (IRE)**[4] 5478 4-9-1 0.................... PJMcDonald 5 —
(Mrs R A Carr) *dwlt: hung bdly lft and racd wd in last: swtchd rt over 6f out: bhd fnl 4f: t.o whn virtually p.u over 1f out* **100/1**

2m 3.33s (-2.07) **Going Correction** -0.175s/f (Firm)
WFA 3 from 4yo 8lb 11 Ran SP% **114.5**
Speed ratings (Par 103): **101,100,97,97,91 91,90,87,87,73 41**
toteswingers:1&2 £6.10, 2&3 £4.70, 1&3 £6.80 CSF £34.80 TOTE £10.40: £2.90, £1.10, £1.50; EX 34.60 Trifecta £88.00 Pool: £167.78 - 1.41 winning units..There was no bid for the winner.
Owner Recycled Products Limited **Bred** Thomas G N Burrage **Trained** Norton, N Yorks

FOCUS
The going was pretty much as the day before - good, good to firm in places. This was a modest seller.
Just Nod(IRE) Official explanation: jockey said filly hung left throughout

5637 THANK YOU PETER BATESON NURSERY 6f
3:00 (3:01) (Class 4) (0-85,80) 2-Y-O **£3,885** (£1,156; £577; £288) **Stalls** Low

Form RPR
461 **1** **Maggie Mey (IRE)**[24] 4848 2-8-3 **62**.................... SilvestreDeSousa 2 65
(D O'Meara) *led 1f: chsd ldrs stands' side: n.m.r 1f out: squeezed through and r.o to ld nr fin* **3/1**[1]

5221 **2** *nk* **No Poppy (IRE)**[10] 5298 2-9-1 **74**....................(b) DuranFentiman 5 76
(T D Easterby) *wnt lft s: prom on outer: drvn and upsides over 1f out: no ex nr fin* **11/2**

4353 **3** *nse* **Eland Ally**[27] 4701 2-8-8 **67**.................... AndrewMullen 7 69
(T P Tate) *w ldrs: swtchd lft and led after 1f: edgd rt fnl f: hdd towards fin* **9/1**

530 **4** *½* **Jibaal (IRE)**[50] 3945 2-8-10 **68**.................... TadhgO'Shea 1 72+
(M Johnston) *chsd ldrs: outpcd and lost pl over 3f out: hdwy 2f out: nt clr run over 1f out: swtchd rt jst ins fnl f: n.m.r: styd on fin* **9/2**[2]

3040 **5** *½* **Philharmonic Hall**[32] 4539 2-8-5 **67** ow1.............. BarryMcHugh(3) 4 66
(R A Fahey) *lft short of room s: in rr and sn outpcd: hdwy over 2f out: chsng ldrs on outside over 1f out: kpt on same pce last 150yds* **22/1**

5162 **6** *1 ½* **Blaze Of Thunder (IRE)**[20] 4948 2-9-7 **80**.............. PJMcDonald 3 74
(G A Swinbank) *trckd ldrs: sltly hmpd over 4f out: nt clr run over 1f out: kpt on same pce ins fnl f* **6/1**

313 **7** *nk* **Normandy Maid**[17] 5089 2-8-11 **70**.................... PaulHanagan 8 63
(R A Fahey) *w ldrs: fdding whn hmpd ins fnl f* **5/1**[3]

2656 **8** *4* **Falkland Flyer (IRE)**[24] 4851 2-9-1 **74**.............. SamHitchcott 6 55
(M R Channon) *chsd ldrs: drvn over 2f out: lost pl over 1f out* **15/2**

1m 12.52s (-0.48) **Going Correction** -0.25s/f (Firm) 8 Ran SP% **115.6**
Speed ratings (Par 96): **93,92,92,91,91 89,88,83**
toteswingers:1&2 £3.80, 2&3 £5.70, 1&3 £6.60 CSF £19.99 CT £133.24 TOTE £3.20: £1.20, £1.20, £3.50; EX 17.30 Trifecta £143.90 Pool: £429.88 - 2.21 winning units..
Owner The Ten Commandments **Bred** Roger O'Callaghan **Trained** Nawton, N Yorks

FOCUS
An ordinary nursery which saw five or six in with a chance inside the final 100 yards. A compressed finish and limited form. The fourth looked unlucky.

NOTEBOOK
Maggie Mey(IRE), winner of a seller at Redcar latest, looked reasonably treated for this nursery debut and she just prevailed. Having the rail to race again proved a massive advantage in the end, but she shouldn't go up much and can continue to give a good account. (op 9-2)

No Poppy(IRE), finally off the mark in a maiden at Ripon last time, was under strong pressure from over 2f out, but she kept finding and went down narrowly. (op 4-1)

Eland Ally wasn't inconvenienced by the drop in trip for this nursery debut, soon leading and keeping on right the way to the line without quite being able to match the winner. (op 10-1 tchd 12-1)

Jibaal(IRE) ◆ got no run at all and would surely have won with a clear run. Outpaced early on this nursery debut, he started to look for room 2f out and was stopped in his run at least twice. He couldn't pick up in time once in the clear, albeit it was very late, but he would surely have had he got rolling earlier. He should have no trouble gaining compensation upped to 7f. (op 6-1 tchd 13-2)

Philharmonic Hall had to challenge widest of all and ran well, but couldn't muster the speed to win inside the final 100 yards. A return to 7f will help. (op 25-1 tchd 16-1)

Blaze Of Thunder(IRE) was struggling to pick up from 2f out and looks in need of further. (op 9-2)

Normandy Maid, up to 6f for the first time, backed out of it inside the final furlong and appeared not to stay. (op 9-2 tchd 11-2)

5638 CITY OF RIPON H'CAP 1m 1f 170y
3:30 (3:30) (Class 3) (0-90,90) 3-Y-0+
£7,477 (£2,239; £1,119; £560; £279; £140) **Stalls** High

Form RPR
1134 **1** **Ailsa Craig (IRE)**[17] 5096 4-8-10 **75**.................... JamesSullivan(3) 12 82
(E W Tuer) *trckd ldrs: wnt 2nd over 2f out: chal over 1f out: led jst ins fnl f: hld on towards fin* **14/1**

0004 **2** *¾* **Fastnet Storm (IRE)**[20] 4943 4-9-11 **87**.................... NeilCallan 10 93
(T P Tate) *led: qcknd over 3f out: hdd jst ins fnl f: no ex towards fin* **7/1**[2]

2310 **3** *nk* **Granston (IRE)**[24] 4818 9-9-12 **88**.................... SilvestreDeSousa 8 93
(J D Bethell) *sn chsng ldrs: drvn over 3f out: styd on same pce ins fnl f* **12/1**

4636 **4** *nk* **Norwegian Dancer (UAE)**[20] 4943 4-9-3 **79**.............. GrahamGibbons 6 83
(E S McMahon) *mid-div: effrt over 2f out: styd on same pce ins fnl f* **7/1**[2]

1630 **5** *shd* **Arizona John (IRE)**[20] 4943 5-9-5 **81**.................... StephenCraine 5 85
(J Mackie) *hld up towards rr: stdy hdwy on outside over 2f out: kpt on same pce ins fnl f* **20/1**

5500 **6** *nk* **Reve De Nuit (USA)**[3] 5529 4-9-6 **87**.................... JohnFahy(5) 2 91
(A J McCabe) *hld up towards rr: hdwy and nt clr run 2f out: r.o ins fnl f* **12/1**

1026 **7** *2 ¼* **Sir Royal (USA)**[16] 5118 5-9-1 **77**.................... TomEaves 9 76
(G A Swinbank) *s.i.s: hdwy on ins over 3f out: sn chsng ldrs: wknd ins fnl f* **22/1**

0000 **8** *¾* **Mirrored**[20] 4943 4-10-0 **90**.................... DavidNolan 1 88+
(T D Easterby) *hld up towards rr: nt clr run fr over 2f out: nt rcvr* **9/1**[3]

0006 **9** *nk* **Alsahil (USA)**[56] 3750 4-8-9 **71** oh3.................... PaulHanagan 3 68
(Micky Hammond) *in rr: drvn 3f out: sme hdwy on ins over 1f out: nvr a factor* **33/1**

4106 **10** *1 ¼* **Bollin Dolly**[24] 4841 7-9-4 **80**.................... DavidAllan 4 74
(T D Easterby) *sn chsng ldrs: drvn over 3f out: lost pl 2f out* **20/1**

213 **11** *6* **Be Invincible (IRE)**[14] 5188 3-9-4 **88**.................... MichaelHills 11 77+
(B W Hills) *t.k.h: trckd ldr: wknd over 1f out: eased ins fnl f* **6/4**[1]

-000 **12** *1 ¾* **Jack Dawkins (USA)**[17] 5098 5-9-4 **80**.................... AndrewMullen 7 59
(D Nicholls) *chsd ldrs: reminders over 4f out: wknd 2f out* **33/1**

2m 2.65s (-2.75) **Going Correction** -0.175s/f (Firm)
WFA 3 from 4yo+ 8lb 12 Ran SP% **116.8**
Speed ratings (Par 107): **104,103,103,102,102 102,100,100,99,98 94,92**
toteswingers:1&2 £14.70, 2&3 £8.30, 1&3 £18.20 CSF £98.97 CT £1214.99 TOTE £16.60: £3.90, £3.00, £2.70; EX 135.20 TRIFECTA Not won..
Owner Far Distant Partnership **Bred** P J B O'Callaghan **Trained** Great Smeaton, N Yorks

FOCUS
A fair handicap.

NOTEBOOK
Ailsa Craig(IRE), a bit below par when making the running on slow ground over C&D latest, settled just in behind the speed this time and saw her race out much better, leading over 1f out and staying on well. This was her third victory of the season and she's clearly still on the up. (op 16-1)

Fastnet Storm(IRE), who ran a blinder at Beverley last time, was off the same mark here and ran every bit as well, just finding the one too strong.

Granston(IRE), too keen over 1m4f at Ascot last time, needs a decent gallop at this distance and he returned to something like his best, keeping on well to not be beaten far.

Norwegian Dancer(UAE) has proved consistent this year, albeit without winning, and this was another reasonable effort. (op 6-1)

Arizona John(IRE) came with a steady challenge out wide, but never quite looked like getting there. (op 16-1)

Reve De Nuit(USA), making a quick reappearance, didn't get the best of runs and should have finished closer. (op 14-1)

Mirrored will surely come good at some stage for connections. (op 7-1 tchd 13-2)

Be Invincible(IRE) proved most disappointing considering he had run so well off only 3lb lower in a competitive handicap at York last time, finding little and stopping quickly. Official explanation: trainer said, regarding running, that the colt was unsuited by the track (op 2-1)

5639 SAPPER CONDITIONS STKS 5f
4:00 (4:00) (Class 3) 2-Y-O **£5,296** (£1,586; £793; £396; £198) **Stalls** Low

Form RPR

3240 **1** **Mappin Time (IRE)**[12] 5245 2-9-2 90 (b) DavidAllan 5 90
(T D Easterby) *w ldrs on outside: drvn over 2f out: styd on to ld last 100yds: jst hld on* **9/2**[3]

6211 **2** *hd* **Jameela Girl**[11] 5261 2-8-9 79 EddieAhern 6 83
(R M H Cowell) *led: swtchd lft after 100yds: hrd rdn and hdd ins fnl f: no ex nr fin* **4/1**[2]

1535 **3** *nk* **Choose Wisely (IRE)**[13] 5221 2-9-2 100 NeilCallan 1 89
(K A Ryan) *w ldr: rdn over 2f out: hung rt fr over 1f out: styd on last 50yds* **4/7**[1]

4421 **4** *1 1/4* **Hortensia (IRE)**[8] 5358 2-8-13 82 (v[1]) SamHitchcott 4 81
(M R Channon) *chsd ldrs: drvn over 2f out: kpt on same pce appr fnl f* **20/1**

3521 **5** *nk* **Crimson Knot (IRE)**[12] 5239 2-8-9 77 PatrickMathers 2 76
(A Berry) *chsd ldrs: sn drvn along: nvr a threat* **40/1**

59.34 secs (-1.36) **Going Correction** -0.25s/f (Firm) **5** Ran SP% **109.0**
Speed ratings (Par 98): **100,99,99,97,96**
CSF £21.41 TOTE £5.10: £1.90, £1.70; EX 15.90.
Owner P Baillie **Bred** J Jamgotchian **Trained** Great Habton, N Yorks

FOCUS
A trappy little conditions race that produced a tight finish. It may pay not to take the form at face value, with the exposed fourth setting the level.

NOTEBOOK
Mappin Time(IRE), well held in a valuable sales race at York last time, had earlier finished fourth in the Super Sprint and he was good enough to take advantage of this easier assignment, just getting the better of the runner-up. (tchd 7-1)
Jameela Girl, a winner off 73 at Sandown latest, was soon in front and gave it a real go off the front, battling on well when headed by the winner. This was an excellent effort at the weights and she's clearly progressing fast. (op 7-2 tchd 9-2)
Choose Wisely(IRE), rated 100, set the standard on his Molecomb third, but he was below that form last time and, although not beaten far here, again proved a tad disappointing. (op 4-6 tchd 1-2 and 8-11 in places)
Hortensia(IRE), narrow winner of a 6f Hamilton claimer latest, never really looked like winning returned to 5f in this stronger heat. (op 16-1)
Crimson Knot(IRE) found this a lot tougher than the maiden she won last time. (op 28-1)

5640 GOTTOHAVEDIAMONDS.COM FILLIES' MAIDEN AUCTION STKS 5f
4:30 (4:30) (Class 5) 2-Y-O **£2,914** (£867; £433; £216) **Stalls** Low

Form RPR

2303 **1** **Abzolutely (IRE)**[6] 5418 2-8-4 71 SilvestreDeSousa 9 69+
(D O'Meara) *mde all: 4l clr whn swtchd to stands' side rail after 100yds: unchal* **1/1**[1]

4 **2** *4* **Kinlochrannoch**[37] 4402 2-8-4 0 PaulHanagan 5 52+
(B M R Haslam) *chsd wnr: kpt on fnl 2f: edgd rt ins fnl f: nvr on terms* **16/1**

00 **3** *1 3/4* **Breezolini**[10] 5298 2-8-1 0 AmyRyan(3) 6 45
(R M Whitaker) *towards rr: hdwy and hung lft over 1f out: styd on to take 3rd clsng stages* **12/1**

0 **4** *2* **Gunalt Joy**[20] 4941 2-8-1 0 (t) JamesSullivan(3) 4 38
(M W Easterby) *chsd ldrs: wknd fnl 75yds* **12/1**

005 **5** *6* **Silver Angel (IRE)**[9] 5328 2-8-4 0 SamHitchcott 1 17
(M R Channon) *chsd ldrs: hrd drvn and hung rt over 2f out: sn lost pl* **10/1**[3]

6 *1 1/2* **Cuddly** 2-8-7 0 EddieAhern 3 14+
(R M H Cowell) *rrd s: nvr on terms* **2/1**[2]

7 *10* **Maunby Rumba (IRE)** 2-8-7 0 AndrewElliott 8 —
(B M R Haslam) *swvd rt s: sn chsng ldrs: rdn and lost pl 2f out* **50/1**

60 **8** *50* **Immacolata (IRE)**[45] 4123 2-8-4 0 PatrickMathers 7 —
(A Berry) *dwlt: sn outpcd and in rr: wandered and t.o 2f out: virtually p.u* **150/1**

59.12 secs (-1.58) **Going Correction** -0.25s/f (Firm) **8** Ran SP% **116.3**
Speed ratings (Par 91): **102,95,92,89,80 77,61,—**
toteswingers:1&2 £3.10, 2&3 £11.90, 1&3 £3.80 CSF £20.86 TOTE £2.00: £1.10, £3.40, £2.90; EX 14.90 Trifecta £79.00 Pool: £587.22 - 5.50 winning units..
Owner Mike Kirby & Andrew Crowther **Bred** A F O'Callaghan **Trained** Nawton, N Yorks

FOCUS
A weak maiden. The winner was never in any danger but this may not be form to get carried away with.

NOTEBOOK
Abzolutely(IRE) had shown more than enough to win a race such as this and she had it in the bag after 1f, shooting into a clear lead having got across from her wide draw and maintaining a healthy advantage right the way to the line. (op 11-10 tchd 10-11 and 6-5 in a place)
Kinlochrannoch improved on her initial effort and will be of interest for a minor contest once upped in trip. (op 14-1)
Breezolini is now qualified for a handicap mark and should do better in that sphere. (tchd 16-1)
Gunalt Joy is one who we won't see the best of until handicapped. (op 16-1 tchd 20-1)
Cuddly, whose dam was a useful 5f winner, was strong in the market but blew her race at the start. She is clearly thought capable of better and can safely have this effort ignored. Official explanation: jockey said filly reared as stalls opened (tchd 9-4)

5641 RAYE WILKINSON "LIFETIME DEDICATED TO RACING" STABLESTAFF H'CAP 1m
5:05 (5:06) (Class 5) (0-75,75) 3-Y-O+ **£2,914** (£867; £433; £216) **Stalls** High

Form RPR

2004 **1** **Chief Red Cloud (USA)**[31] 4602 4-9-7 67 NeilCallan 5 76
(Mrs K Burke) *trckd ldr: led over 1f out: hld on towards fin* **2/1**[1]

3042 **2** *nk* **Ours (IRE)**[23] 4860 7-9-5 68 (p) BarryMcHugh(3) 3 76
(John A Harris) *mid-div: outpcd over 3f out: hdwy 2f out: carried hd high and hung rt: tk 2nd last 75yds: clsng at line* **12/1**

014 **3** *2* **Desert Hunter (IRE)**[46] 4119 7-8-11 60 PatrickDonaghy(3) 9 64
(Micky Hammond) *trckd ldrs: t.k.h: effrt over 2f out: styd on same pce appr fnl f* **11/2**[2]

3415 **4** *3/4* **Elmfield Giant (USA)**[34] 4496 3-9-9 75 PaulHanagan 1 76
(R A Fahey) *broke wl and sn crossed to rail: led: hdd over 1f out: one pce* **11/2**[2]

5200 **5** *1 3/4* **Betteras Bertie**[31] 4602 7-9-2 62 SilvestreDeSousa 2 60
(M Brittain) *sn chsng ldr: fdd fnl 150yds* **40/1**

0226 **6** *1 1/2* **Chosen Forever**[24] 4849 5-9-8 73 IanBrennan(5) 6 68
(G R Oldroyd) *in rr: drvn and hung rt 4f out: kpt on fnl 2f: nvr nr ldrs* **13/2**[3]

3064 **7** *nk* **Koo And The Gang (IRE)**[10] 5304 3-8-10 62 PatrickMathers 7 55
(B Ellison) *chsd ldrs: drvn over 2f out: hung rt and wknd fnl 150yds: struck into* **8/1**

1036 **8** *10* **Sir Frank Wappat**[16] 5121 3-9-7 73 JoeFanning 8 43
(M Johnston) *hld up towards rr: hdwy 4f out: shkn up 2f out: hung lft and sn eased* **15/2**

4600 **9** *3 1/2* **Classic Descent**[12] 5244 5-8-9 58 (b) JamesSullivan(3) 4 21
(Mrs R A Carr) *in rr: lost pl over 2f out: eased over 1f out: rn wout declared tongue strap* **22/1**

1m 39.31s (-2.09) **Going Correction** -0.175s/f (Firm)
WFA 3 from 4yo+ 6lb **9** Ran SP% **114.8**
Speed ratings (Par 103): **103,102,100,99,98 96,96,86,82**
toteswingers:1&2 £7.30, 2&3 £8.70, 1&3 £3.60 CSF £28.32 CT £116.44 TOTE £2.90: £1.30, £3.90, £1.30; EX 33.80 Trifecta £120.10 Pool: £521.03 - 3.21 winning units..
Owner Mrs Elaine M Burke **Bred** Lochlow Farm **Trained** Middleham Moor, North Yorks

FOCUS
A modest handicap.
Chosen Forever Official explanation: jockey said gelding never travelled
Koo And The Gang(IRE) Official explanation: trainer said gelding struck into its left-fore

5642 WAKEMAN STAYERS H'CAP 2m
5:35 (5:35) (Class 6) (0-65,65) 3-Y-O+ **£2,590** (£770; £385; £192) **Stalls** Low

Form RPR

026 **1** **Descaro (USA)**[35] 4453 4-9-8 59 SilvestreDeSousa 1 68+
(D O'Meara) *hld up in midfield: hdwy 4f out: sn drvn: hung rt: and wnt 2nd over 1f out: styd on to ld nr fin* **5/1**[2]

2133 **2** *1/2* **Petella**[16] 5119 4-8-13 50 PaulHanagan 12 58+
(C W Thornton) *sn detached in last: niggled along 11f out: rapid hdwy to ld over 3f out: edgd rt: hdd and no ex nr fin* **9/4**[1]

1033 **3** *2 1/4* **Capable Guest (IRE)**[29] 4656 8-9-11 62 EddieAhern 3 68
(G M Moore) *hld up in rr: gd hdwy 2f out: styd on to take 3rd last 150yds* **9/1**

2145 **4** *2 1/2* **Light The City (IRE)**[6] 5420 3-8-3 57 JamesSullivan(3) 10 60
(Mrs R A Carr) *chsd ldrs: effrt 4f out: chal over 2f out: wknd ins fnl f* **14/1**

2550 **5** *2 3/4* **Spring Breeze**[16] 5119 9-8-12 49 oh3 (p) NeilCallan 5 48
(J J Quinn) *reminders after s: sn chsng ldr: drvn over 4f out: wknd over 1f out* **16/1**

-634 **6** *1 1/4* **Unawatuna**[105] 2218 5-9-0 56 DaleSwift(5) 9 54
(Mrs K Walton) *mid-div: effrt over 3f out: nvr nr to chal* **6/1**[3]

2135 **7** *1* **Amir Pasha (UAE)**[13] 5215 5-9-7 65 (p) AdamCarter(7) 7 62+
(Micky Hammond) *chsd ldrs: nt clr run wl over 1f out: one pce* **8/1**

6233 **8** *1/2* **Strikemaster (IRE)**[21] 4669 4-9-11 62 PatrickMathers 2 58
(B Ellison) *s.i.s: hld up in rr: reminders after 1f: drvn 4f out: nvr a factor* **16/1**

5400 **9** *1/2* **Smugglers Bay (IRE)**[22] 4900 6-9-4 55 (b) DavidNolan 4 51+
(T D Easterby) *hld up in rr: sme hdwy over 3f out: nt clr run over 1f out: nvr a factor* **9/1**

/000 **10** *11* **Power Desert (IRE)**[24] 4854 5-8-12 49 oh4 (v) DavidAllan 6 31
(G A Harker) *led: qcknd over 4f out: hdd over 3f out: lost pl 2f out: eased in clsng stages* **28/1**

450 **11** *81* **Captain Cornelius (IRE)**[39] 4348 3-8-4 55 DuranFentiman 11 —
(Joss Saville) *no lft eye: chsd ldrs: lost pl 4f out: sn wl bhd: eased whn t.o over 1f out* **33/1**

3m 30.36s (-1.44) **Going Correction** -0.175s/f (Firm)
WFA 3 from 4yo+ 14lb **11** Ran SP% **117.7**
Speed ratings (Par 101): **96,95,94,93,92 91,90,90,90,84 44**
toteswingers:1&2 £4.70, 2&3 £5.70, 1&3 £5.70 CSF £16.58 CT £99.86 TOTE £5.10: £2.30, £1.50, £2.80; EX 30.40 Trifecta £57.70 Pool: £257.51 - 3.30 winning units. Place 6: £170.32 Place 5: £83.08.
Owner R Fell & K Everitt **Bred** Langley House Stud **Trained** Nawton, N Yorks

FOCUS
A low-grade staying handicap, run at a sound enough gallop.
T/Plt: £155.30 to a £1 stake. Pool of £66,885.32 - 314.30 winning tickets. T/Qpdt: £28.70 to a £1 stake. Pool of £4,150.24 - 106.70 winning tickets. WG

4890 SOUTHWELL (L-H)
Tuesday, August 31

OFFICIAL GOING: Standard
Wind: Virtually nil Weather: Fine and dry

5643 LORD LIGHTFOOT MAIDEN STKS 6f (F)
5:10 (5:10) (Class 5) 2-Y-O **£2,729** (£806; £403) **Stalls** Low

Form RPR

32 **1** **Golden Creek (USA)**[36] 4432 2-9-3 0 JimCrowley 9 71
(R M Beckett) *cl up: rdn to chal 2f out: drvn over 1f out: led ins fnl f: kpt on* **1/1**[1]

60 **2** *hd* **Queen Of Cash (IRE)**[11] 5255 2-8-12 0 RobertWinston 2 65
(H Morrison) *led pushed along and jnd over 2f out: rdn wl over 1f out: drvn and hdd ins fnl f: rallied and ev ch tl no ex nr fin* **11/4**[2]

5 **3** *2 1/2* **Zalano**[22] 4909 2-9-3 0 FrankieMcDonald 4 63
(D Haydn Jones) *t.k.h: chsd ldrs: hdwy on inner and cl up 1/2-way: rdn 2f out and ev ch tl drvn and one pce ent fnl f* **12/1**

5 **4** *2 3/4* **Scoglio**[22] 4890 2-9-3 0 LeeVickers 5 54
(F Sheridan) *dwlt and wnt rt s: sn chsng ldrs: rdn along over 2f out: swtchd rt wl over 1f out and sn one pce* **16/1**

5 *2* **Oceanway (USA)** 2-8-12 0 GregFairley 8 43+
(M Johnston) *dwlt: green and sn pushed along in rr: bhd 1/2-way: styd on fnl 2f* **5/1**[3]

6 *15* **Romantic Girl (IRE)** 2-8-12 0 VinceSlattery 7 —
(A G Juckes) *sltly hmpd s: sn rdn along in rr: outpcd and bhd fr 1/2-way* **28/1**

1m 16.14s (-0.36) **Going Correction** -0.15s/f (Stan) **6** Ran SP% **110.4**
Speed ratings (Par 94): **96,95,92,88,86 66**
toteswingers:1&2 £1.70, 2&3 £5.20, 1&3 £1.60 CSF £3.75 TOTE £1.50: £1.10, £1.70; EX 3.50.
Owner Mogeely Stud & Mrs Maura Gittins **Bred** Overrbook Farm **Trained** Whitsbury, Hants

FOCUS
An uncompetitive maiden and one run at just a fair gallop on standard ground. The first two came down the centre in the straight and the form in all probability is modest.

NOTEBOOK
Golden Creek(USA), who had a solid chance on previous form, has improved steadily with every outing and turned in his best effort on this Fibresand debut returned to 6f. This wasn't a strong race but he's open to a bit more improvement and should stay 7f. (op 6-5 tchd 10-11)

Queen Of Cash(IRE) had shown ability at a modest level on turf but turned in an improved effort after enjoying the run of the race out of the kickback on this Fibresand debut. She was not unduly knocked about and looks capable of picking up a similar event in this grade or an ordinary nursery on the surface. She should stay 7f. (op 3-1)

Zalano had hinted at ability on Polytrack on his debut and ran to a similar level, despite proving easy in the market and after racing with the choke out on this Fibresand debut. Run-of-the-mill nurseries will be the way forward with him. (op 9-1 tchd 16-1)

Scoglio wasn't totally disgraced after also proving easy in the market. He may do better in ordinary handicaps in due course. (op 10-1)

Oceanway(USA), the second foal of a 1m2f winner, attracted support but was too green to do herself justice on this debut. However, newcomers from this yard invariably improve a fair bit for their first run and better can be expected from this one, especially when granted a stiffer test of stamina. (op 7-1 tchd 15-2)

5644 IN MEMORY OF SHAUN "SHAKEY" ROEBUCK NURSERY 7f (F)
5:40 (5:40) (Class 5) (0-70,70) 2-Y-O £3,043 (£905; £452; £226) Stalls Low

Form RPR

6344 **1** **Il Battista**[19] 4993 2-9-2 **70**............(p) DeclanCannon(5) 7 85
(A J McCabe) *led 1f: trckd ldng pair: hdwy 1/2-way: led wl over 2f out and wd st: sn rdn: drvn and clr whn edgd lft ins fnl f: kpt on* **11/2**[3]

060 **2** *2* **Red Oleander**[28] 4668 2-8-1 **50**............(b[1]) JimmyQuinn 3 60
(Sir Mark Prescott) *dwlt and pushed along to chse ldrs: led after 1f: rdn along 3f out: sn hdd and drvn: kpt on same pce u.p appr fnl f* **7/4**[1]

046 **3** *10* **Sabratha (IRE)**[27] 4716 2-8-10 **59**............ MickyFenton 5 44
(B J Curley) *chsd ldrs: rdn along 3f out: kpt on u.p fnl 2f: n.d* **7/1**

000 **4** *7* **Louis Vee (IRE)**[56] 3767 2-8-1 **50**............ AndreaAtzeni 8 18
(J G Given) *chsd ldrs: rdn along 1/2-way: drvn 3f out and sn outpcd* **14/1**

442 **5** *4* **Alensgrove (IRE)**[29] 4650 2-9-4 **67**............ TonyCulhane 2 25
(P T Midgley) *sltly hmpd and stdd s: swtchd wd and bhd: rdn along and wd st: nvr a factor* **7/2**[2]

055 **6** *19* **Key West (IRE)**[26] 4759 2-9-4 **67**............(b) NickyMackay 1 —
(J H M Gosden) *cl up on inner: rdn along 1/2-way: sn drvn and wknd wl over 2f out* **6/1**

0000 **7** *3 3/4* **Gunalt Penny Sweet**[88] 2693 2-7-5 **47** oh2............ MarzenaJeziorek(7) 4 —
(M W Easterby) *sn rdn along and a in rr: bhd fr 1/2-way* **66/1**

004 **8** *4* **Bright Dictator (IRE)**[33] 4517 2-8-4 **53**............ SaleemGolam 6 —
(J G Given) *a towards rr: rdn along bef 1/2-way: sn outpcd and bhd* **16/1**

1m 29.17s (-1.13) **Going Correction** -0.15s/f (Stan) 8 Ran SP% **114.8**
Speed ratings (Par 94): **100,97,86,78,73 52,47,43**
toteswingers:1&2 £3.60, 2&3 £6.90, 1&3 £10.90 CSF £15.63 CT £68.47 TOTE £5.30: £2.50, £1.10, £4.00; EX 17.20.
Owner Alotincommon Partnership **Bred** Cheveley Park Stud Ltd **Trained** Averham Park, Notts
■ Stewards' Enquiry : Andrea Atzeni one-day ban: used whip down shoulder in the forehand (Sep 14)

FOCUS
No previous winners and a couple of disappointments but the first two, who raced in the centre, are relatively unexposed and pulled a long way clear. The gallop was sound and the form looks solid, but it remains to be seen if this Fibresand form can be transferred.

NOTEBOOK
Il Battista, well backed, hadn't been at his best in a visor on his previous start but turned in a much-improved display for his in-form stable on this all-weather debut in the first-time cheekpieces, despite edging both ways under pressure. Life will be tougher after reassessment but it will be interesting to see if he can improve again on this surface. (op 8-1 tchd 9-2)

Red Oleander ◆, well supported throughout the day, showed improved form on this Fibresand and nursery debut in the first time cheekpieces. She pulled a long way clear of the remainder and she is more than capable of winning a race on this surface. (op 5-2 tchd 11-4)

Sabratha(IRE) failed to build on the hint of ability shown on this all-weather and nursery debut. She is in good hands but will have to improve to win a similar event on either turf or Fibresand. (op 13-2 tchd 8-1)

Louis Vee(IRE) had been soundly beaten in maidens and the switch to nurseries and the switch to Fibresand brought about no improvement. This surface may not have been ideal but he will have to show a fair bit more before he is a solid betting proposition. (op 16-1 tchd 12-1)

Alensgrove(IRE) had shaped with a modicum of promise on each of her three turf starts but was soundly beaten on this all-weather and nursery debut after again failing to go the early pace. Presumably she will be switched back to grass. Official explanation: jockey said filly suffered interference leaving stalls (tchd 10-3)

Key West(IRE) failed by a long chalk to reproduce the form shown on his last two turf runs on this nursery and all-weather debut. The return to turf may suit but it will be a bit of a surprise if connections hold on to him for much longer. (op 7-2)

5645 PLAY BINGO AT TOTESPORT.COM MAIDEN STKS 1m (F)
6:10 (6:12) (Class 5) 3-Y-O £2,590 (£770; £385; £192) Stalls Low

Form RPR

-465 **1** **William Van Gogh**[34] 4491 3-9-3 77............ WilliamBuick 4 73+
(J H M Gosden) *cl up: led wl over 2f out: shkn up and clr over 1f out* **8/11**[1]

450 **2** *5* **Lady Brickhouse**[20] 4970 3-8-12 44............ SaleemGolam 3 49
(M D Squance) *prom: rdn along and outpcd over 3f out: wd st: hdwy u.p wl over 1f out: swtchd lft and drvn ent fnl f: styd on to take 2nd nr fin* **50/1**[3]

2-05 **3** *1/2* **Old Money**[82] 2890 3-8-12 74............ RobertWinston 1 48
(H Morrison) *trckd ldrs on inner: hdwy to ld wl over 3f out: rdn and hdd wl over 2f out: drvn and edgd rt over 1f out: sn one pce: lost 2nd nr fin* **2/1**[2]

-000 **4** *9* **Avec Moi**[7] 5395 3-8-12 43............ MarcHalford 2 27
(Mrs C A Dunnett) *led: rdn along and hdd wl over 3f out: sn wknd* **100/1**

0 **5** *30* **Mr Shammie**[18] 5028 3-9-3 0............ MickyFenton 6 —
(M G Quinlan) *dwlt: a in rr: outpcd and bhd fnl 3f* **80/1**

1m 43.9s (0.20) **Going Correction** -0.15s/f (Stan) 5 Ran SP% **95.4**
Speed ratings (Par 100): **93,88,87,78,48**
CSF £18.17 TOTE £1.40: £1.50, £10.10; EX 15.50.
Owner W J Gredley **Bred** Stetchworth Park Stud Ltd **Trained** Newmarket, Suffolk
■ Hoodie was withdrawn on vet's advice (6/1, deduct 10p in the £ under R4.)

FOCUS
A most uncompetitive event and one run at just an ordinary gallop. The winner again raced in the centre.
Old Money Official explanation: jockey said filly hung right

5646 PLAY BLACKJACK AT TOTESPORT.COM H'CAP 1m 6f (F)
6:40 (6:40) (Class 5) (0-75,75) 3-Y-O+ £2,729 (£806; £403) Stalls Low

Form RPR

1504 **1** **Bivouac (UAE)**[28] 4686 6-9-12 **70**............ PJMcDonald 8 81+
(G A Swinbank) *trckd ldrs: smooth hdwy on outer 1/2-way: cl up 4f out: chal 3f out: led 2f out and sn rdn: drvn ins fnl f and kpt on wl towards fin* **7/2**[2]

1333 **2** *3/4* **Lastroseofsummer (IRE)**[27] 4719 4-9-4 **62**............ WilliamBuick 4 72
(Rae Guest) *led: rdn along over 3f out: hdd over 2f out: drvn over 1f out: rallied and ch ins fnl f: no ex last 100yds* **9/2**[3]

-510 **3** *2* **Budva**[18] 5058 3-8-11 **67**............ RobertWinston 7 74
(H Morrison) *cl up: rdn along over 3f out: led briefly over 2f out: sn hdd: drvn wl over 1f out and ch tl edgd rt and one pce ent fnl f* **3/1**[1]

0-24 **4** *7* **Sir Walter Raleigh**[41] 4257 3-8-10 **69**......(vt[1]) Louis-PhilippeBeuzelin(3) 5 66
(Sir Michael Stoute) *hld up in tch: rdn along and outpcd 5f out: wd st and kpt on u.p fnl 2f: nvr a factor* **9/2**[3]

6/45 **5** *4 1/2* **Daylami Dreams**[21] 4933 6-9-11 **69**............ MickyFenton 1 60
(John A Harris) *chsd ldrs: rdn along over 3f out: drvn and outpcd fnl 2f* **12/1**

1664 **6** *23* **Keenes Royale**[52] 3909 3-9-5 **75**............(t) JimCrowley 6 34
(R M Beckett) *chsd ldrs: rdn along over 3f out: drvn and wknd wl over 2f out* **8/1**

4-3 **7** *21* **Ibrox (IRE)**[67] 3 5-9-13 **71**............(p) JimmyQuinn 3 —
(A D Brown) *trckd ldrs on inner: pushed along over 4f out: rdn wl over 3f out: sn lost pl: bhd and eased fnl 2f* **14/1**

000 **8** *30* **Pass The Port**[55] 3780 9-10-0 **72**............ DaneO'Neill 2 —
(D Haydn Jones) *v s.i.s and bhd: hdwy and in tch 1/2-way: rdn along over 4f out: sn wknd: bhd and eased fnl 3f* **28/1**

3m 7.33s (-0.97) **Going Correction** -0.15s/f (Stan)
WFA 3 from 4yo+ 12lb 8 Ran SP% **112.5**
Speed ratings (Par 103): **96,95,94,90,87 74,62,45**
toteswingers:1&2 £3.20, 2&3 £3.80, 1&3 £1.50 CSF £18.96 CT £50.91 TOTE £3.80: £1.10, £2.90, £2.20; EX 21.40.
Owner Mrs J M Penney **Bred** Darley **Trained** Melsonby, N Yorks

FOCUS
An ordinary handicap in which progressive performers were thin on the ground. The gallop was a steady one and the first three, who pulled clear in the straight, continued the trend of racing in the centre.
Sir Walter Raleigh Official explanation: jockey said gelding never travelled
Ibrox(IRE) Official explanation: vet said gelding finished lame right-fore

5647 PLAY ROULETTE AT TOTESPORT.COM H'CAP 6f (F)
7:10 (7:11) (Class 4) (0-80,80) 3-Y-O+ £3,885 (£1,156; £577; £288) Stalls Low

Form RPR

0132 **1** **Westwood**[28] 4684 5-9-4 **72**............ DaneO'Neill 4 87+
(D Haydn Jones) *mde all: rdn and qcknd clr wl over 1f out: kpt on strly* **11/4**[1]

0356 **2** *5* **Elusive Warrior (USA)**[22] 4895 7-8-4 **65**............(p) NoraLooby(7) 1 64
(A J McCabe) *prom on inner: chsd wnr over 2f out: rdn wl over 1f out: kpt on same pce ins fnl f* **40/1**

0020 **3** *1* **Elusive Fame (USA)**[15] 5142 4-9-5 **80**............(b) CharlesPerkins(7) 8 76+
(M Johnston) *towards rr: hdwy over 2f out: rdn and kpt on appr fnl f: nrst fin* **16/1**

0040 **4** *1 3/4* **Scruffy Skip (IRE)**[7] 5391 5-8-13 **67**............(p) RobertWinston 7 57
(Mrs C A Dunnett) *prom: chsd wnr after 2f: rdn over 2f out: drvn wl over 1f out: grad wknd* **25/1**

2513 **5** *2 1/2* **Ace Of Spies (IRE)**[9] 5327 5-9-0 **73**............ LeeTopliss(5) 5 55
(C R Dore) *chsd ldrs: rdn along over 2f out: drvn wl over 1f out and sn one pce* **15/2**

0134 **6** *2 1/2* **Grudge**[11] 5262 5-9-4 **72**............(be) ShaneKelly 11 46
(C R Dore) *towards rr: wd st and hdwy over 2f out: sn rdn and kpt on appr fnl f: nvr nr ldrs* **16/1**

2134 **7** *1 1/4* **Gracie's Gift (IRE)**[7] 5386 8-8-12 **66**............ GrahamGibbons 3 36
(R C Guest) *in tch whn n.m.r and lost pl 1/2-way: hdwy 2f out: sn rdn and no imp appr fnl f* **4/1**[2]

6-50 **8** *1/2* **Florio Vincitore (IRE)**[15] 5143 3-9-4 **78**............ AlanCreighton(3) 12 47
(E J Creighton) *nvr bttr than midfield* **33/1**

0605 **9** *1 1/2* **Master Leon**[7] 5383 3-9-4 **75**............(v) TomEaves 9 39
(B Smart) *dwlt: a in rr* **11/1**

-01 **10** *1 1/4* **Prince James**[22] 4908 3-8-9 **66**............ JimmyQuinn 13 26
(M W Easterby) *wnt rt s: racd wd: a towards rr* **16/1**

2513 **11** *1/2* **Bahamian Lad**[10] 5290 5-9-9 **80**............(p) KellyHarrison(3) 6 38
(R Hollinshead) *in rr fr 1/2-way* **16/1**

3540 **12** *1/2* **Solstice**[46] 4091 3-9-2 **76**............ BarryMcHugh(3) 10 33
(Julie Camacho) *chsd ldrs: rdn along over 2f out: sn wknd* **7/1**[3]

3252 **13** *hd* **Bookiesindex Boy**[22] 4895 6-9-4 **72**............(b) StephenCraine 2 28
(J R Jenkins) *in tch on inner: rdn along wl over 2f out and sn wknd* **14/1**

1m 14.52s (-1.98) **Going Correction** -0.15s/f (Stan)
WFA 3 from 4yo+ 3lb 13 Ran SP% **118.7**
Speed ratings (Par 105): **107,100,99,96,93 90,88,87,85,84 83,82,82**
toteswingers:1&2 £37.00, 2&3 £28.10, 1&3 £15.00 CSF £134.39 CT £1563.10 TOTE £3.30: £1.10, £14.70, £6.50; EX 108.60.
Owner Merry Llewelyn And Runeckles **Bred** D Llewelyn & J Runeckles **Trained** Efail Isaf, Rhondda C Taff

FOCUS
Mainly exposed performers in an ordinary handicap. The pace was sound but those held up were at a disadvantage. The winner came down the centre in the straight.
Grudge Official explanation: jockey said gelding hung left

5648 PLAY SLOTS AT TOTESPORT.COM APPRENTICE H'CAP 1m (F)
7:40 (7:40) (Class 5) (0-75,75) 3-Y-O £2,590 (£770; £385; £192) Stalls Low

Form RPR

0000 **1** **Royal Holiday (IRE)**[2] 5545 3-8-6 **57**............ TobyAtkinson 8 62
(B Ellison) *cl up on outer: hdwy over 2f out: rdn to ld and hung lft 1 1/2f out: drvn and hung lft ins fnl f: kpt on towards fin* **16/1**

-245 **2** *1/2* **Indian Valley (USA)**[88] 2725 3-8-13 **69**............ NoelGarbutt(5) 7 73
(Rae Guest) *trckd ldrs: effrt over 2f out: swtchd lft and hdwy 1 1/2f out: rdn to chal ins fnl f: ev ch whn n.m.r and hit in face w opponents whip: no ex last 75yds* **11/2**

4045 **3** *2 1/4* **Minortransgression (USA)**[14] 5182 3-8-9 **65**...... MatthewCosham(5) 5 64
(P D Evans) *chsd ldr: rdn whn n.m.r 2f out: sn swtchd rt and kpt on same pce appr fnl f* **25/1**

4363 **4** *shd* **Rain On The Wind (IRE)**[7] 5384 3-8-11 **65**............(t) RyanClark(3) 1 64
(S C Williams) *led: rdn and edgd rt 2f out: hdd and hmpd 1 1/2f out: sn drvn and one pce ins fnl f* **4/1**[3]

466- **5** *6* **Art Machine (USA)**[337] 6334 3-8-11 **65**............ RosieJessop(3) 4 50
(Sir Mark Prescott) *dwlt: rdn along in rr 1/2-way: n.d* **3/1**[2]

0515 **6** *6* **Amity (IRE)**[21] 4931 3-8-13 **64**............ IanBrennan 3 35
(M Johnston) *chsd ldrs on inner: rdn along over 3f out: sn wknd* **8/1**

1401 **7** *3 1/4* **Zubova**[12] 5241 3-9-7 **72**............(t) LeeTopliss 6 36
(D Shaw) *dwlt and in rr: effrt and sme hdwy: sn outpcd and bhd fnl 2f* **9/4**[1]

The Form Book, Raceform Ltd, Compton, RG20 6NL

-060 **8** 3/4 **Vegas Palace (IRE)**[22] 4894 3-9-10 **75**......................(p) RossAtkinson 2 37
(Tom Dascombe) *a in rr: bhd fnl 2f* **20/1**

1m 42.41s (-1.29) **Going Correction** -0.15s/f (Stan) **8** Ran SP% **116.8**
Speed ratings (Par 100): **100,99,97,97,91 85,81,81**
toteswingers:1&2 £16.50, 2&3 £22.20, 1&3 £23.50. totesuper7: Win: Not won. Place: Not won. CSF £102.77 CT £2208.72 TOTE £24.70: £8.30, £1.10, £9.90; EX 136.40 Place 6: £54.96 Place 5: £47.54 .
Owner C P Lowther **Bred** E Tynan **Trained** Norton, N Yorks

FOCUS
Progressive sorts were in a minority in this ordinary handicap in which the two market leaders disappointed. The gallop was a fair one and the first two ended up near the inside rail.
Minortransgression(USA) Official explanation: trainer's rep said gelding suffered a breathing problem
T/Plt: £191.00 to a £1 stake. Pool of £42,212.56 - 161.32 winning tickets. T/Qpdt: £168.50 to a £1 stake. Pool of £6,126.40 - 26.90 winning tickets. JR

5573 BADEN-BADEN (L-H)

Tuesday, August 31

OFFICIAL GOING: Turf: soft

5649a DARLEY OETTINGEN-RENNEN (GROUP 2) (3YO+) (TURF) 1m

4:50 (12:00) 3-Y-O+

£35,398 (£13,716; £5,752; £3,539; £2,212; £1,327)

RPR

1 **Emerald Commander (IRE)**[37] 4420 3-8-10 0............ FrankieDettori 7 116
(Saeed Bin Suroor) *broke wl: trckd ldr: qckly tk ld on outside ent st 3f out: r.o wl* **4/5**[1]

2 2 1/2 **Earl Of Fire (GER)**[52] 3934 5-9-2 0............................ DominiqueBoeuf 6 111
(W Baltromei, Germany) *racd in midfield: rdn 2 1/2f out: wnt 2nd 1 1/2f out: chsd wnr home* **104/10**

3 3/4 **Fabiana**[30] 4639 4-8-13 0... THellier 4 106+
(Andreas Lowe, Germany) *settled towards rr: qcknd through horses arnd fnl turn: r.o wl in st: fin strly to get 3rd fnl strides* **54/10**[3]

4 nk **Win For Sure (GER)**[23] 4888 5-9-2 0.................................... EPedroza 5 109
(A Wohler, Germany) *prom fr s: r.o wl in st: ev ch: failed to qckn ent fnl f: lost 3rd fnl strides* **26/5**[2]

5 4 **Le Big (GER)**[23] 4888 6-9-2 0.. AStarke 9 99
(U Stoltefuss, Germany) *bkmarker fr s: failed to qckn early in st but r.o wl u.p fnl f* **103/10**

6 2 **Rockatella (IRE)**[19] 5139 3-8-7 0.. JBojko 3 91
(W Hefter, Germany) *broke fast: settled in 3rd: qcknd on ins ent st: r.o but mde no impact ins fnl 2f* **66/10**

7 2 1/2 **Prakasa (FR)**[99] 2404 3-8-7 0.. FilipMinarik 2 85
(W Hickst, Germany) *racd in 4th fr s: nvr threatened in st* **162/10**

8 7 **Rock My Soul (IRE)**[48] 4035 4-8-13 0.................................. DPorcu 10 70
(Uwe Ostmann, Germany) *broke wl: grabbed ld after 2f: hdd ent st: r.o wl early in st but sn wknd* **203/10**

9 3 **Konig Bernard (FR)**[16] 4-9-2 0.. YannLerner 8 66
(W Baltromei, Germany) *broke fast to ld for 2f: sn hdd: nvr a threat thereafter* **25/1**

1m 39.54s (0.43)
WFA 3 from 4yo+ 6lb **9** Ran SP% **132.4**
WIN (incl. 10 euro stake): 18. PLACES: 13, 25, 15. SF: 189.
Owner Godolphin **Bred** Grangecon Stud **Trained** Newmarket, Suffolk

NOTEBOOK
Emerald Commander(IRE) impressed in dominating his rivals and gaining his first success at this level. Connections plan to step him up to Group 1 races now with the Premio Vittorio di Capua in Milan a possible target.

5412 BRIGHTON (L-H)

Wednesday, September 1

OFFICIAL GOING: Good (7.7)

Rail moved out 1m between 4.5f and 3.5f. Rail realignment added 5yds to advertised distances.
Wind: Moderate, half behind Weather: Sunny

5650 ENTREMETTIER H'CAP 5f 213y

2:30 (2:30) (Class 6) (0-55,55) 3-Y-O **£1,942** (£578; £288; £144) **Stalls** Low

Form RPR

0063 **1** **Mushy Peas (IRE)**[2] 5579 3-8-7 **46** oh1......................... CathyGannon 2 54+
(P D Evans) *led tl hrd rdn and hdd 2f out: pressed ldr after: rallied to ld on line* **15/8**[1]

2455 **2** nse **Via Aurelia (IRE)**[16] 5163 3-9-2 **55**............................(v) HayleyTurner 10 63
(J R Fanshawe) *mid-div: hdwy to slt ld 2f out: hrd rdn ins fnl f: hdd on line* **4/1**[2]

0303 **3** 1 1/2 **Dreamacha**[21] 4970 3-8-12 **51**... WilliamCarson 5 54+
(S C Williams) *towards rr: c alone towards stands' rail st: hdwy to press ldrs 2f out: nt qckn ins fnl f* **9/2**[3]

3234 **4** 1/2 **Rosiliant (IRE)**[20] 4989 3-8-10 **54**.................................(b) JohnFahy(5) 12 56
(C G Cox) *s.s: bhd: drvn along over 2f out: nrst fin* **4/1**[2]

0020 **5** hd **Gilderoy**[20] 4989 3-8-8 **50**.. AshleyHamblett(3) 6 51
(D J S Ffrench Davis) *4th early: lost pl 3f out: kpt on again fr over 1f out* **14/1**

00-4 **6** hd **Rose Bed (IRE)**[7] 5419 3-8-2 **46** oh1............................ SophieDoyle(5) 9 46
(M G Quinlan) *prom tl no ex ins fnl 2f* **22/1**

6000 **7** 1 1/4 **Brody's Boy**[18] 5077 3-8-11 **50**...................................(bt[1]) PatDobbs 3 46
(G L Moore) *pressed ldr tl outpcd ent fnl 2f* **16/1**

-000 **8** 2 3/4 **Kyoatee Kilt**[26] 4778 3-8-3 **49** oh1 ow3...................(bt) DuilioDaSilva(7) 11 37
(P F I Cole) *towards rr: hdwy 3f out: rdn and wknd 2f out* **40/1**

69.69 secs (-0.51) **Going Correction** -0.10s/f (Good) **8** Ran SP% **112.3**
Speed ratings (Par 99): **99,98,96,96,96 95,94,90**
toteswingers:1&2 £3.20, 2&3 £2.30, 1&3 £4.60 CSF £9.07 CT £28.06 TOTE £3.50: £2.10, £1.30, £1.90; EX 10.90 Trifecta £49.50 Pool: £415.43 - 6.21 winning units..
Owner Raymond N R Auld **Bred** R N Auld **Trained** Pandy, Monmouths

FOCUS
A moderate sprint handicap in which Dreamacha raced alone towards the stands' side in the straight.

Rosiliant(IRE) Official explanation: jockey said filly was slowly away and never travelled

5651 EUROPEAN BREEDERS' FUND MAIDEN STKS 6f 209y

3:00 (3:00) (Class 5) 2-Y-O **£3,469** (£1,038; £519; £259; £129) **Stalls** Centre

Form RPR

1 **Raucous Behaviour (USA)** 2-9-3 0................................ GregFairley 5 76+
(M Johnston) *rdn leaving stalls: sn chsng ldrs: outpcd and hrd rdn over 2f out: rallied over 1f out: styd on to ld fnl 50yds* **6/1**[2]

0 **2** 1 1/2 **Enlightening (IRE)**[42] 4263 2-9-3 0.................................. PatDobbs 2 72
(R Hannon) *led: rdn 3 l clr 2f out: hrd rdn fnl f: hdd fnl 50yds* **16/1**

2 **3** shd **Auden (USA)**[19] 5047 2-9-3 0.. AhmedAjtebi 1 72
(Mahmood Al Zarooni) *dwlt and shkn up s: sn pressing ldr: outpcd 2f out: hrd rdn and unbalanced on trck: styd on same pce* **1/3**[1]

0 **4** 3 3/4 **Classic Voice (IRE)**[20] 5006 2-9-0 0.............................. PatrickHills(3) 4 62
(R Hannon) *settled in 6th: pushed along 4f out: hdwy to dispute 2nd ins fnl 2f: wknd ins fnl f* **33/1**

06 **5** 5 **Indian Wish (USA)**[40] 4338 2-8-12 0.............................. HayleyTurner 6 44
(M L W Bell) *stdd in rr s: rdn and struggling 4f out: nvr trbld ldrs* **12/1**[3]

03 **6** 2 1/4 **Christmas Aria (IRE)**[18] 5074 2-9-3 0.............................. SebSanders 7 42
(S Dow) *prom tl wknd 2f out* **12/1**[3]

00 **7** 10 **Dreams Of Glory**[25] 4838 2-8-12 0.............................. SimonPearce(5) 9 15
(R J Hodges) *chsd ldrs tl hrd rdn and wknd 2f out* **80/1**

8 18 **Master Perfect** 2-9-3 0..(t) KirstyMilczarek 10 —
(L M Cumani) *sn wl bhd* **16/1**

1m 22.28s (-0.82) **Going Correction** -0.10s/f (Good) **8** Ran SP% **120.6**
Speed ratings (Par 95): **100,98,98,93,88 85,74,53**
toteswingers:1&2 £7.80, 2&3 £5.50, 1&3 £1.50 CSF £97.85 TOTE £5.40: £1.40, £4.00, £1.02; EX 69.80 Trifecta £150.90 Pool: £430.45 - 2.11winning units..
Owner Sheikh Hamdan Bin Mohammed Al Maktoum **Bred** Stonerside Stable **Trained** Middleham Moor, N Yorks

FOCUS
An interesting maiden, certainly by Brighton's usual standards, and it went to a potentially decent sort in raucous Behaviour, who looks sure to improve.

NOTEBOOK
Raucous Behaviour(USA) ◆, a half-brother to 2009 Lincoln victor Expresso Star, is a big horse with an abundance of scope, and overcame a few negatives to ultimately win in taking fashion. Carrying plenty of condition, he ran green and did not appear comfortable on the track, coming off the bridle running downhill into the straight, but he picked up really well once meting the rising ground. There should be significant improvement to come, and he may prove versatile ground-wise, for he's sired by a dirt horse, but showed a knee action and his aforementioned sibling appreciated ease underfoot. (op 10-1 tchd 11-1)
Enlightening(IRE) handled the track well under a positive ride and nearly nicked this. He stepped up significantly on his first effort and may find a similar race.
Auden(USA) did not improve on the form he showed when runner-up on debut at Newmarket. He still looked green, going left soon after starting slowly, and didn't look totally comfortable on the undulations in the closing stages. (op 1-4 tchd 2-9 and 4-9 in a place and 2-5 in places)
Classic Voice(IRE), a stable companion of the runner-up, never threatened but still improved on his debut showing. He looks a nursery/handicap type. Official explanation: jockey said colt hung left
Indian Wish(USA) was never going the required speed and still looked in need of the experience. She's now eligible for a handicap mark. (tchd 11-1)
Dreams Of Glory Official explanation: jockey said colt hung right
Master Perfect Official explanation: jockey said colt ran green

5652 HARDINGS CATERING H'CAP 6f 209y

3:30 (3:30) (Class 5) (0-75,75) 3-Y-O+ **£2,590** (£770; £385; £192) **Stalls** Centre

Form RPR

0046 **1** **Beaver Patrol (IRE)**[23] 4905 8-9-5 **75**..........................(v) JohnFahy(5) 6 83
(Eve Johnson Houghton) *reminder s: chsd ldr: rdn to dispute ld over 2f out: led ins fnl f: drvn out* **9/2**[3]

0523 **2** 3/4 **Timeteam (IRE)**[18] 5075 4-9-9 **74**.................................. DarrylHolland 4 80
(G L Moore) *hld up in 4th: effrt and hrd rdn over 1f out: wnt 2nd ins fnl f: r.o: a hld* **10/1**

2101 **3** 2 3/4 **Lady Florence**[15] 5174 5-9-7 **75**.............................. RussKennemore(3) 7 74
(A B Coogan) *led: set gd early pce and crossed to ins rail: jnd by wnr over 2f out: no ex ins fnl f* **11/4**[2]

6032 **4** shd **Buxton**[16] 5157 6-9-7 **72**...(t) SebSanders 5 71
(R Ingram) *stdd in rr s: rdn over 2f out: hdwy towards centre over 1f out: styd on ins fnl f* **5/2**[1]

-020 **5** 1 3/4 **Queen's Envoy**[42] 4250 3-9-0 **69**................................ KirstyMilczarek 1 61
(L M Cumani) *stdd s: hld up in 5th: hdwy and hrd rdn over 1f out: no ex ins fnl f* **11/2**

1006 **6** 4 1/2 **Highland Harvest**[26] 4777 6-9-1 **66**.............................. StevieDonohoe 2 48
(Jamie Poulton) *prom tl hrd rdn and wknd over 1f out* **12/1**

1146 **7** 2 1/4 **Athwaab**[111] 2046 3-9-0 **69**.. WilliamCarson 3 43
(M G Quinlan) *t.k.h: sn stdd towards rr: rdn and n.d fnl 2f* **18/1**

1m 21.98s (-1.12) **Going Correction** -0.10s/f (Good)
WFA 3 from 4yo+ 4lb **7** Ran SP% **110.9**
Speed ratings (Par 103): **102,101,98,97,95 90,88**
toteswingers:1&2 £4.70, 2&3 £4.40, 1&3 £2.50 CSF £43.90 TOTE £4.70: £2.60, £4.80; EX 36.10.
Owner G C Stevens **Bred** Kevin B Lynch **Trained** Blewbury, Oxon

FOCUS
A fair handicap.
Athwaab Official explanation: jockey said filly hit its head exiting stalls

5653 BRIGHTON JUICE 107.2 H'CAP 1m 3f 196y

4:00 (4:00) (Class 6) (0-60,60) 3-Y-O **£1,942** (£578; £288; £144) **Stalls** High

Form RPR

6105 **1** **Al Shababiya (IRE)**[44] 4211 3-9-1 **57**............................ MartinLane(3) 6 68
(D M Simcock) *towards rr: hrd rdn and hdwy 2f out: styd on to ld nr fin* **12/1**

4512 **2** 3/4 **Always Dixie (IRE)**[7] 5423 3-8-10 **49**.............................. GregFairley 8 59
(M Johnston) *led: wnt 3 l clr 4f out: hrd rdn and tired ins fnl f: kpt on gamely: ct nr fin* **9/2**[2]

4544 **3** 1 3/4 **New Code**[19] 5058 3-9-4 **57**.. MartinDwyer 7 64
(W R Muir) *mid-div: hdwy 4f out: wnt 2nd 2f out: one pce ins fnl f* **9/2**[2]

455 **4** 3 1/2 **Belle Boleyn**[24] 4874 3-9-5 **58**.. AlanMunro 2 59+
(C F Wall) *in tch: lost pl over 4f out: sn detached last and struggling: styd on wl fr over 1f out* **6/1**[3]

4600 **5** 4 **Captain Cool (IRE)**[40] 4327 3-9-7 **60**..............................(b) PatDobbs 1 55
(R Hannon) *mid-div: drvn along 3f out: btn wl over 1f out* **14/1**

4443 **6** 3 1/4 **Affirmable**[27] 4728 3-9-4 **57**..(p) SebSanders 12 47
(J W Hills) *chsd ldrs: wnt 2nd 4f out tl 2f out: wknd over 1f out* **16/1**

0005 **7** 8 **Mandate**[21] 4972 3-9-2 **55**.. KirstyMilczarek 9 32
(J A R Toller) *chsd ldr: rdn over 4f out: wknd 3f out* **20/1**

6330 **8** *6* **Red Barcelona (IRE)**[16] 5164 3-9-0 **53**....................(b[1]) DarryllHolland 3 20
(M H Tompkins) *dwlt: bhd: effrt in centre 3f out: sn hrd rdn and wknd* **13/2**

2005 **9** *hd* **Electric City (IRE)**[7] 5423 3-8-10 **49**........................... WilliamCarson 11 16
(M G Quinlan) *towards rr: hrd rdn and mod effrt 3f out: sn wknd* **20/1**

0631 **10** *9* **Green Energy**[26] 4780 3-9-4 **57**......................................(p) JimmyQuinn 4 —
(Mrs A J Perrett) *prom tl wknd 3f out: bhd whn eased over 1f out: fin lame* **3/1**[1]

2m 32.35s (-0.35) **Going Correction** -0.10s/f (Good) **10** Ran SP% **118.7**
Speed ratings (Par 99): **97,96,95,93,90 88,82,78,78,72**
toteswingers:1&2 £6.60, 2&3 £5.50, 1&3 £12.90 CSF £66.57 CT £283.19 TOTE £13.70: £3.10, £1.70, £1.90; EX 71.50 Trifecta £337.60 Part won. Pool: £456.22 - 0.16 winning units..
Owner Ahmad Al Shaikh **Bred** De Burgh Equine **Trained** Newmarket, Suffolk

FOCUS
A moderate contest.
Red Barcelona(IRE) Official explanation: jockey said colt was slowly away
Green Energy Official explanation: trainer's rep said gelding finished lame left-hind

5654 IAN CARNABY FILLIES' H'CAP 1m 1f 209y
4:30 (4:32) (Class 5) (0-70,70) 3-Y-0+ **£2,590** (£770; £385; £192) **Stalls** High

Form RPR

0-16 **1** **Dhan Dhana (IRE)**[21] 4944 3-9-4 **65**.................................... LiamJones 2 79+
(W J Haggas) *prom: led over 1f out: hld on wl ins fnl f: all out* **7/1**[3]

5322 **2** *hd* **Azaday (IRE)**[33] 4552 3-9-2 **63**.................................... AlanMunro 12 76+
(C F Wall) *bhd: pushed along 4f out: hdwy over 2f out: str chal ins fnl f: jst hld* **15/8**[1]

6014 **3** *5* **Queen Of Wands**[16] 5149 3-9-8 **69**........................... SteveDrowne 4 72
(H Morrison) *led: rdn and edgd rt 2f out: hdd over 1f out: no ex ins fnl f* **4/1**[2]

3255 **4** *2* **Queen's Scholar (USA)**[21] 4951 3-9-3 **64**......................... GregFairley 1 63
(M Johnston) *prom: hrd rdn over 2f out: no ex over 1f out* **8/1**

-030 **5** *3/4* **Lovely Eyes (IRE)**[33] 4557 3-9-0 **64**.............................. MartinLane(3) 3 62
(D M Simcock) *mid-div: outpcd and struggling in rr 3f out: styd on fr over 1f out* **16/1**

1460 **6** *2* **Layla's Lexi**[18] 5096 3-9-9 **70**... StevieDonohoe 5 64
(Ian Williams) *mid-div: hdwy over 3f out: wknd wl over 1f out* **33/1**

6235 **7** *1 3/4* **Quiquillo (USA)**[40] 4329 4-9-9 **66**......................(b) AndrewHeffernan(3) 6 56
(P D Evans) *bhd: rdn 3f out: nvr rchd ldrs* **33/1**

4123 **8** *hd* **Ubiquitous**[15] 5172 5-8-10 **55**......................................(t) SimonPearce(5) 9 45
(S Dow) *prom tl wknd over 1f out* **10/1**

0-04 **9** *4* **Quality Mover (USA)**[60] 3662 3-9-6 **67**...................... EddieCreighton 10 49
(D M Simcock) *bhd: hdwy into midfield over 3f out: btn over 2f out* **25/1**

506 **10** *5* **Nabari (JPN)**[47] 4114 3-9-8 **69**.............................. KirstyMilczarek 8 41
(L M Cumani) *mid-div: hrd rdn 3f out: edgd rt and wknd over 2f out* **25/1**

0032 **11** *2* **Miss Chaumiere**[9] 5361 3-8-5 **52** oh3...........................(v) HayleyTurner 7 20
(M L W Bell) *chsd ldr tl wknd over 2f out* **12/1**

2m 1.09s (-2.51) **Going Correction** -0.10s/f (Good)
WFA 3 from 4yo+ 7lb **11** Ran SP% **114.6**
Speed ratings (Par 100): **106,105,101,100,99 98,96,96,93,89 87**
toteswingers:1&2 £4.30, 2&3 £2.70, 1&3 £4.80 CSF £19.11 CT £59.03 TOTE £14.00: £5.10, £1.20, £1.60; EX 25.80 Trifecta £50.20 Pool: £670.69 - 9.88 winning units..
Owner Mohammed Jaber **Bred** Swordlestown Stud **Trained** Newmarket, Suffolk

FOCUS
A reasonable fillies' handicap for the grade in which two progressive types pulled clear, despite the early pace appearing just ordinary.
Queen Of Wands Official explanation: jockey said filly hung right

5655 BRIGHTON FOOD AND DRINK FESTIVAL APPRENTICE H'CAP 7f 214y
5:00 (5:00) (Class 6) (0-60,60) 4-Y-0+ **£1,942** (£578; £288; £144) **Stalls** Low

Form RPR

5353 **1** **Phluke**[15] 5174 9-9-5 **58**......................................(v) Louis-PhilippeBeuzelin 8 65
(Eve Johnson Houghton) *mde all: rdn over 2f out: hld on wl ins fnl f* **9/2**[2]

00-0 **2** *nk* **Isabella Romee (IRE)**[30] 4657 4-8-6 **52**...................... LewisWalsh(7) 7 58
(Jane Chapple-Hyam) *sn prom: drvn to chal ins fnl f: r.o: jst hld* **13/2**

420 **3** *1 1/2* **Markhesa**[21] 4958 4-9-2 **60**.. NathanAlison(5) 2 63
(J R Boyle) *bhd: hrd rdn over 2f out: styd on wl to take 3rd ins fnl f* **8/1**

5442 **4** *1* **Prince Valentine**[27] 4738 9-8-3 **47**..............................(p) HarryBentley(5) 5 47
(G L Moore) *hld up in rr: plld wd and hdwy over 2f out: no ex ins fnl f* **11/2**[3]

0-30 **5** *2* **Master Mahogany**[2] 5585 9-8-10 **49**................................ MartinLane 1 45
(R J Hodges) *prom: hrd rdn over 2f out: wknd 1f out* **3/1**[1]

1050 **6** *1 3/4* **Justcallmehandsome**[51] 3970 8-9-0 **56**.......................(v) SophieDoyle(3) 3 49
(D J S Ffrench Davis) *chsd ldrs: lost pl and rdn 3f out: 6th and n.d whn n.m.r ins fnl f* **12/1**

0430 **7** *3* **Easy Wonder (GER)**[10] 5326 5-8-2 **46**......................... AntiocoMurgia(5) 6 31
(I A Wood) *prom: hrd rdn 2f out: sn wknd* **14/1**

0054 **8** *3 3/4* **Dubai Gem**[29] 4680 4-8-10 **49**... WilliamCarson 4 32
(Jamie Poulton) *hld up in 5th: effrt and hrd rdn 2f out: wknd 1f out: eased whn btn* **11/2**[3]

1m 34.99s (-1.01) **Going Correction** -0.10s/f (Good) **8** Ran SP% **112.8**
Speed ratings (Par 101): **101,100,99,98,96 94,91,87**
toteswingers:1&2 £7.70, 2&3 £9.20, 1&3 £5.60 CSF £32.60 CT £226.01 TOTE £5.30: £1.50, £3.20, £3.60; EX 35.10 Trifecta £351.80 Part won. Pool of £475.54 - 0.61 winning units. Place 6: £55.58 Place 5: £45.37.
Owner Mrs R F Johnson Houghton **Bred** Mrs R F Johnson Houghton **Trained** Blewbury, Oxon

FOCUS
A moderate apprentice handicap.
T/Plt: £62.60 to a £1 stake. Pool of £67,033.56 - 781.02 winning tickets. T/Qpdt: £27.20 to a £1 stake. Pool of £3,838.74 - 104.38 winning tickets. LM

5379 KEMPTON (A.W) (R-H)
Wednesday, September 1

OFFICIAL GOING: Standard
Wind: Moderate, half behind Weather: Fine

5656 LADIES DAY THIS SATURDAY H'CAP 1m 2f (P)
5:20 (5:21) (Class 5) (0-70,70) 3-Y-0 **£2,286** (£675; £337) **Stalls** High

Form RPR

0563 **1** **Halyard (IRE)**[16] 5146 3-8-11 **65**......................................(v[1]) JohnFahy(5) 6 74
(W R Swinburn) *hld up in 9th: gd prog fr 3f out: rdn to chse ldr 1f out and sn chalng: drvn ahd last stride* **3/1**[1]

1123 **2** *shd* **Sunley Spinalonga**[19] 5051 3-9-7 **70**......................... RichardHughes 11 79
(D R C Elsworth) *trckd ldrs: wnt 3rd 3f out: squeezed through on inner to ld over 1f out gng wl: pushed along to maintain narrow advantage ins fnl f: hdd post* **3/1**[1]

000 **3** *1 1/2* **Kayaan**[62] 3587 3-8-10 **59**.. MickyFenton 1 65
(Mrs P Sly) *s.s: hld up in last pair: gd prog fr 3f out: wnt 3rd ins fnl f: styd on wl: no imp nr fin* **25/1**

4220 **4** *4 1/2* **Tower**[16] 5164 3-8-11 **60**... SaleemGolam 5 57
(G Prodromou) *dwlt: sn trckd ldrs: rdn in 4th 3f out: outpcd over 1f out: kpt on again ins fnl f* **16/1**

0640 **5** *1/2* **Shoot The Pot (IRE)**[51] 3960 3-8-5 **59**.................... DeclanCannon(5) 7 55
(J Mackie) *trckd ldrs: pushed along in 5th 3f out: effrt on inner over 1f out: sn outpcd: rdn and kpt on ins fnl f: no ch* **8/1**

5430 **6** *3/4* **One Cool Poppy (IRE)**[21] 4972 3-8-3 **52**...................... CathyGannon 8 47
(H J Collingridge) *mostly in last trio: rdn 3f out: kpt on fr over 1f out: n.d* **16/1**

353 **7** *hd* **Bizarrely (IRE)**[21] 4971 3-9-2 **65**.................................. TadhgO'Shea 9 59
(J Pearce) *t.k.h: led: hdd over 1f out: wknd ins fnl f* **10/1**

1226 **8** *1 1/2* **Lady Of Garmoran (USA)**[15] 5171 3-8-9 **58**..................(b) JoeFanning 3 49
(P F I Cole) *trckd ldr: rdn to try to chal over 1f out: wknd rapidly ins fnl f* **7/1**[3]

2435 **9** *14* **Big Wave Bay (IRE)**[28] 4719 3-9-2 **65**.......................... TomQueally 4 28
(A P Jarvis) *towards rr: pushed along after 3f: struggling u.p 3f out: sn wknd: t.o* **6/1**[2]

-645 **10** *6* **Roar Talent (USA)**[10] 5330 3-9-2 **65**............................ AndreaAtzeni 10 16
(J R Best) *chsd ldrs tl wknd 3f out: t.o* **25/1**

00-0 **11** *52* **Carlcol Girl**[21] 4971 3-7-9 **51** oh6.................................... RyanPowell(7) 2 —
(Mrs C A Dunnett) *racd wd: prom: wknd rapidly 4f out: sn wl t.o* **66/1**

2m 6.76s (-1.24) **Going Correction** -0.05s/f (Stan) **11** Ran SP% **117.9**
Speed ratings (Par 101): **102,101,100,97,96 96,95,94,83,78 37**
toteswingers:1&2 £2.20, 2&3 £24.50, 1&3 £16.70 CSF £10.81 CT £188.72 TOTE £4.60: £2.60, £2.00, £8.70; EX 15.00.
Owner Hall Of Fame Partnership **Bred** Mount Coote Stud And M H Dixon **Trained** Aldbury, Herts

FOCUS
A run-of-the-mill handicap in which the gallop was an ordinary one. The first two ended up towards the inside rail in the closing stages and the runner-up looks the best guide to the form.

5657 EUROPEAN BREEDERS' FUND MEDIAN AUCTION MAIDEN STKS 6f (P)
5:50 (5:51) (Class 5) 2-Y-0 **£3,076** (£915; £457; £228) **Stalls** High

Form RPR

1 **Karam Albaari (IRE)** 2-9-3 0.. JimmyQuinn 4 76+
(J R Jenkins) *towards rr and rn green: stl same pl 2f out: gd prog over 1f out: rdn to ld ins fnl f: edgd lft: styd on wl* **33/1**

6 **2** *nk* **Les Verguettes (IRE)**[9] 5372 2-8-12 0.............................. TomQueally 5 70
(Stef Higgins) *chsd ldng pair: shkn up 2f out: styd on to take 2nd and chal ins fnl f: edgd lft and jst hld* **4/1**[2]

0 **3** *1 3/4* **Tees And Cees (IRE)**[12] 5277 2-9-3 0...................... RichardHughes 12 70
(R Hannon) *led: shkn up over 2f out: hdd ins fnl f: fdd and jst hld on for 3rd* **5/1**

0 **4** *hd* **Farlow (IRE)**[21] 4954 2-9-3 0... JackMitchell 2 69
(R M Beckett) *chsd ldrs in 6th: rdn over 2f out: kpt on fnl f: nrst fin* **9/1**

3 **5** *nse* **Another Laugh**[21] 4954 2-9-3 0.. MichaelHills 7 69
(B W Hills) *chsd ldrs in 5th: shkn up over 2f out: nvr gng pce to threaten: kpt on ins fnl f* **11/4**[1]

42 **6** *nk* **Cristaliyev**[10] 5328 2-9-3 0.. PatCosgrave 8 68
(J R Boyle) *chsd ldr: rdn over 2f out: no imp and hld over 1f out: one pce and lost pl ins fnl f* **9/2**[3]

7 *shd* **Up In Time** 2-8-12 0.. ShaneKelly 10 63
(W J Knight) *settled in rr: prog on inner fr 2f out: chsd ldrs over 1f out: one pce after* **12/1**

4 **8** *nk* **Pearl Opera**[29] 4675 2-8-9 0...................................... EJMcNamara(3) 9 62
(R M Beckett) *dwlt: sn chsd ldng pair: couple of light reminders 2f out: nudged along and hanging over 1f out: lost pl sn after* **8/1**

9 *1* **Mister Ben Vereen** 2-9-3 0.. SebSanders 3 64+
(Eve Johnson Houghton) *dwlt: rn green and mostly last: shkn up on outer over 2f out: kpt on fnl f* **25/1**

10 *10* **Maureens Litlun (IRE)** 2-8-12 0................................... JamieMackay 1 29
(M Wigham) *s.s: rn green and a in last pair: wknd 2f out* **66/1**

1m 13.55s (0.45) **Going Correction** -0.05s/f (Stan) **10** Ran SP% **118.6**
Speed ratings (Par 95): **95,94,92,92,91 91,91,91,89,76**
toteswingers:1&2 £21.10, 2&3 £4.40, 1&3 £24.40 CSF £162.24 TOTE £58.20: £19.00, £3.80, £1.70; EX 289.70.
Owner Fhad Al Harthi **Bred** Morecool Stud **Trained** Royston, Herts

FOCUS
No more than a modest maiden with the first eight in a bit of a heap. The gallop was an ordinary one and the first two came down the centre in the straight.

NOTEBOOK
Karam Albaari(IRE), a £30,000 first foal of a 1m4f Polytrack maiden winner, was a big price but turned in a pleasing performance to give his trainer a rare first-time out winner. He'll be at least as effective over 7f and, although this wasn't much of a race, he can only improve for this experience. (op 28-1)

Les Verguettes(IRE) had hinted at ability on her debut and bettered that effort after attracting support on this all-weather debut. This isn't strong form and she's vulnerable to an improver in this type of event but she may be able to get off the mark in ordinary nursery company. (op 5-1 tchd 11-2)

Tees And Cees(IRE), who didn't show much in a traditionally strong maiden at York first time, had the run of the race and fared much better in this lesser race, despite proving easy in the market. Run-of-the-mill nurseries will be the way forward with him. (op 7-2)

Farlow(IRE) attracted support at double-figure odds and showed improved form to reverse debut Salisbury form with the below-par Another Laugh. He has a bit of physical scope and is another that should do better once handicapped. (op 14-1)

Another Laugh had shown fair form on his debut when third to one that has gone on to show smart form in an Irish Group 3 but he failed to build on that on this all-weather debut. However, he will be suited by the step up to 7f and he remains capable of winning a similar race. (op 3-1)

Cristaliyev had shown fair form in two turf starts but failed to match that form on this all-weather debut on this first run over a trip that should have suited, despite being ideally placed throughout. He too should do better now qualified for a mark. (tchd 5-1)

Up In Time, the first foal of a half-sister to a UAE Oaks winner and to a couple of other winners, hinted at ability on this racecourse debut and should improve for the experience. (tchd 14-1)

The Form Book, Raceform Ltd, Compton, RG20 6NL

Mister Ben Vereen, a 20,000gns purchase, wasn't knocked about at any stage and should benefit from this considerate introduction. (op 33-1)

5658 DIGIBET CASINO MAIDEN STKS 7f (P)
6:20 (6:23) (Class 5) 3-Y-0+ **£2,286** (£675; £337) **Stalls** High

Form RPR

3240 **1** **Spa's Dancer (IRE)**[39] 4357 3-9-3 79 MichaelHills 14 83
(J W Hills) *t.k.h: trckd ldrs: effrt to ld 2f out: shkn up and styd on wl* **1/1**[1]

3-06 **2** *2* **Tenessee**[85] 2842 3-9-3 78 AdamKirby 3 78
(C G Cox) *awkward s and reminders early: sn prom on outer: rdn 3f out: styd on to take 2nd jst over 1f out: no imp onwnr* **9/4**[2]

5 **3** *2 3/4* **Catching Zeds**[19] 5028 3-8-12 0 PaulMulrennan 7 65
(Ian Williams) *chsd ldr to jst over 2f out: styd cl up tl outpcd in 3rd ins fnl f* **14/1**

0-0 **4** *5* **Far View (IRE)**[20] 5007 3-9-3 0 RichardHughes 10 57
(J W Hills) *t.k.h: hld up bhd ldrs: 5th and in tch 1/2-way: rdn to cl on ldrs 2f out: wknd over 1f out* **28/1**

0 **5** *4 1/2* **Flying Cherry (IRE)**[19] 5028 3-8-13 0 ow1 IanMongan 9 41
(Miss Jo Crowley) *dwlt: sn chsd ldrs: rdn in 6th 1/2-way: wl outpcd fr over 2f out* **33/1**

0 **6** *1/2* **Fastinthestraight (IRE)**[19] 5028 3-9-3 0 DaneO'Neill 5 43
(J R Boyle) *dwlt: t.k.h: hld up wl in rr: wl bhd 1/2-way: shkn up and passed a few rivals fr over 1f out* **40/1**

02 **7** *1* **Katmai River (IRE)**[16] 5153 3-8-12 0 LeeNewnes(5) 13 40
(M D I Usher) *rdn in 7th and struggling to stay in tch 1/2-way: sn no ch* **25/1**

00 **8** *3* **Mistress Shy**[29] 4679 3-8-12 0 SebSanders 8 27
(R Dickin) *a abt same pl: u.p and wl off the pce 1/2-way: no prog* **66/1**

9 *nse* **Ice Road Trucker (IRE)** 3-9-3 0 StephenCraine 6 32
(J R Boyle) *a wl in rr: long way adrift by 1/2-way: no real prog* **40/1**

10 *3/4* **Cloth Ears** 4-8-9 0 LeonnaMayor(7) 11 27
(P S McEntee) *led: had most in trble by 1/2-way: hdd & wknd rapidly 2f out* **66/1**

00 **11** *5* **Noisy Noverre (IRE)**[19] 5028 3-8-12 0 DaraghO'Donohoe 1 12
(George Baker) *a wl in rr and sn wl bhd* **66/1**

0 **12** *1/2* **Zarius**[19] 5028 3-9-3 0 JackMitchell 4 15
(C F Wall) *dwlt: mostly in last pair and sn wl bhd* **25/1**

3- **13** *2 3/4* **Marie Cuddy (IRE)**[340] 6274 3-8-12 0 DarryllHolland 2 —
(Karen George) *a wl in rr and sn wl bhd* **8/1**[3]

1m 25.25s (-0.75) **Going Correction** -0.05s/f (Stan)
WFA 3 from 4yo 4lb 13 Ran SP% **122.0**
Speed ratings (Par 103): **102,99,96,90,85 85,84,80,80,79 73,73,70**
toteswingers:1&2 £1.20, 2&3 £6.90, 1&3 £5.70 CSF £2.93 TOTE £2.00: £1.10, £1.60, £3.80; EX 3.70.
Owner The Seventh Pheasant Inn Partnership **Bred** Giacinto Gugliemi **Trained** Upper Lambourn, Berks

FOCUS
A couple of fair performers in an otherwise ordinary maiden. The gallop was an ordinary one and the winner came down the centre in the straight.

5659 DIGIBET NURSERY (DIV I) 1m (P)
6:50 (6:51) (Class 6) (0-65,65) 2-Y-O **£1,364** (£403; £201) **Stalls** High

Form RPR

5362 **1** **Countrywide Flame**[20] 4984 2-8-11 55 PaulHanagan 9 63+
(K A Ryan) *mde all: rdn to assert 2f out: 3 l clr fnl f: edgd: a gng to hold on* **4/1**[2]

0003 **2** *nk* **Ree's Rascal (IRE)**[6] 5452 2-8-4 51 MatthewDavies(3) 14 58
(J R Boyle) *hld up towards rr: sme prog into midfield over 2f out: swtchd lft sn after and drvn: tk 2nd 1f out: clsd on wnr u.p: nvr gng to get there in time* **7/2**[1]

000 **3** *nk* **Futurism**[23] 4902 2-9-4 62 RichardHughes 5 68+
(R Hannon) *t.k.h: hld up in last trio: pushed along on outer and sme prog over 3f out: gd hdwy to take 3rd 1f out: clsd on wnr w runner-up: nvr gng to get there* **12/1**

5044 **4** *5* **Ivan's A Star (IRE)**[9] 5373 2-8-12 56 (p) LukeMorris 7 51
(J S Moore) *snatched up in midfield after 2f and dropped to rr: drvn over 2f out: styd on to take 4th ins fnl f* **16/1**

4363 **5** *1 3/4* **Not So Bright (USA)**[22] 4935 2-9-3 61 PaulMulrennan 2 52
(J G Given) *mostly chsd wnr to 1f out: wknd* **9/1**

0400 **6** *nk* **Salvationist**[21] 4955 2-8-5 52 (b) MartinLane(3) 12 43
(J L Dunlop) *chsd ldrs: rdn over 2f out: stl chsng over 1f out: sn wl outpcd* **28/1**

606 **7** *hd* **Whitby Jet (IRE)**[78] 3053 2-8-10 54 LiamKeniry 1 44
(E F Vaughan) *hld up but sn bustled to latch on to bk of main gp: effrt on inner over 2f out: no imp over 1f out: plugged on* **50/1**

030 **8** *2 1/2* **May's Boy**[12] 5255 2-8-12 61 LeeNewnes(5) 11 46
(M D I Usher) *dwlt: nvr bttr than midfield: rdn over 2f out: nt qckn and no prog* **50/1**

1 **9** *3/4* **Mary Boyle**[19] 5020 2-8-9 58 DeclanCannon(5) 6 41
(A J McCabe) *chsd ldrs in 5th: rdn and nt qckn over 2f out: sn lost pl and struggling* **13/2**[3]

0000 **10** *1/2* **King Bling (IRE)**[12] 5256 2-8-9 53 DavidProbert 13 35
(S Kirk) *prom: disp 2nd over 2f out: wknd rapidly over 1f out* **14/1**

004 **11** *3/4* **Captain Sharpe**[32] 4587 2-8-13 57 (b) TomQueally 4 37
(H J L Dunlop) *racd wd in midfield: nt look keen over 2f out: short of room briefly sn after: wknd* **20/1**

650 **12** *7* **Nettis**[19] 5047 2-9-5 63 SaleemGolam 10 28
(G Prodromou) *prom: disp 3rd and rdn over 3f out: wknd qckly over 2f out* **33/1**

600 **13** *10* **Hero From Zero (IRE)**[21] 4954 2-9-7 65 MartinDwyer 8 8
(B J Meehan) *pushed along in midfield 1/2-way: sn dropped to rr and wl btn: t.o* **7/2**[1]

500 **14** *1* **Echos Of Motivator**[16] 5156 2-9-1 59 TomMcLaughlin 3 —
(R A Harris) *racd v wd in last and allowed to trundle rnd: t.o* **33/1**

1m 40.05s (0.25) **Going Correction** -0.05s/f (Stan) 14 Ran SP% **126.0**
Speed ratings (Par 93): **96,95,95,90,88 88,88,85,84,84 83,76,66,65**
toteswingers:1&2 £3.70, 2&3 £13.00, 1&3 £12.70 CSF £18.08 CT £166.64 TOTE £4.40: £2.10, £1.90, £3.60; EX 21.10.
Owner Countrywide Racing **Bred** Michael Clarke **Trained** Hambleton, N Yorks

FOCUS
The first division of a modest nursery. The gallop was only fair and the first three, who finished clear, came down the centre in the straight. The winner stepped forward from his nursery effort and the form should be ok.

NOTEBOOK
Countrywide Flame is a steadily progressive individual who was allowed his own way in front and turned in his best effort up in trip on this all-weather debut. Things went his way but he is in good hands and he may be capable of further success, especially when allowed to dominate. (op 7-2 tchd 9-2)

Ree's Rascal(IRE) is also a steady improver and he did well to get as close as he did to a rival that was allowed his own way in front on his first run over this trip. A stronger end-to-end gallop would have suited and he is capable of making amends. Official explanation: jockey said colt hung left (op 10-3 tchd 3-1)

Futurism was also set a fair bit to do given the way things unfolded but he turned in an improved display on this nursery debut. He won't be inconvenienced by a stronger gallop back over 7f and he should be placed to best advantage.

Ivan's A Star(IRE) wasn't disgraced back on Polytrack and back in nursery company with the cheekpieces on again. He has yet to win but he is essentially consistent. Official explanation: jockey said gelding suffered interference at start

Not So Bright(USA) had the run of the race but failed to get home on his first run over this trip back on Polytrack. 7f may be his optimum distance at present and he has physical scope but he is probably best watched until getting his head in front where it matters. (op 8-1)

Whitby Jet(IRE) only hinted at ability on this nursery and all-weather debut from the widest draw and will have to show something more concrete before he is a solid betting proposition.

May's Boy Official explanation: jockey said colt missed the break

Hero From Zero(IRE) had shown ability in maidens and attracted support but found disappointingly little when asked for an effort turning for home on his all-weather and nursery debut and was beaten before stamina became an issue. The return to turf may suit better. (op 6-1 tchd 13-2)

Echos Of Motivator Official explanation: jockey said colt hung left

5660 DIGIBET NURSERY (DIV II) 1m (P)
7:20 (7:22) (Class 6) (0-65,63) 2-Y-O **£1,364** (£403; £201) **Stalls** High

Form RPR

530 **1** **Rosa Midnight (USA)**[19] 5029 2-9-1 57 HayleyTurner 10 61+
(M L W Bell) *nt that wl away: sn in midfield: rdn over 2f out: prog wl over 1f out: drvn to ld ent fnl f: sn in command* **5/2**[1]

000 **2** *1 3/4* **Highcliffe**[20] 5006 2-8-11 53 RichardHughes 11 54
(R Hannon) *trckd ldrs: rdn over 2f out: trying to cl whn nt clr run over 1f out: styd on ins fnl f to take 2nd last stride* **12/1**

064 **3** *hd* **Papas Fritas**[15] 5170 2-9-5 61 MartinDwyer 1 61
(B J Meehan) *prom on outer: pressed ldng pair 5f out: rdn over 3f out: led over 1f out: hdd and no ex ent fnl f* **13/2**[3]

0006 **4** *2* **Seas Of Sorrow (IRE)**[20] 4993 2-8-11 58 SophieDoyle(5) 6 54
(B W Duke) *pressed ldr: led over 3f out: hd high over 2f out: hdd and fdd over 1f out* **66/1**

0206 **5** *shd* **Pahente**[8] 5389 2-9-6 62 (p) LukeMorris 3 57
(J S Moore) *rousted along early in rr: prog on outer over 2f out: hrd rdn to cl on ldrs over 1f out: sn outpcd* **25/1**

0430 **6** *2 1/4* **Stacey**[31] 4623 2-9-6 62 NeilChalmers 8 52
(M Blanshard) *n.m.r in rr over 6f out: rdn and no prog over 2f out: kpt on fr over 1f out: nrst fin* **20/1**

040 **7** *1/2* **Climaxfortackle (IRE)**[11] 5301 2-9-7 63 DaneO'Neill 9 52
(D Shaw) *nt that wl away: towards rr: rdn over 2f out: kpt on fr over 1f out: no ch* **20/1**

635 **8** *1* **Spirit Of Oakdale (IRE)**[47] 4110 2-9-1 57 AdamKirby 4 44
(W R Swinburn) *t.k.h early: hld up in rr: rdn and struggling in last pair 3f out: kpt on fr over 1f out* **4/1**[2]

060 **9** *1/2* **Little Book**[29] 4682 2-9-4 60 ShaneKelly 12 46
(E F Vaughan) *led to over 3f out: wknd rapidly fnl f* **10/1**

006 **10** *nk* **Wanchai Minx**[32] 4587 2-8-13 55 NeilCallan 13 40
(A P Jarvis) *cl up on inner: rdn 3f out: wknd rapidly over 1f out* **9/1**

006 **11** *hd* **Amistress**[42] 4254 2-8-8 50 CathyGannon 5 35
(Eve Johnson Houghton) *a towards rr: u.p over 3f out: sn btn* **20/1**

000 **12** *1/2* **Complicate**[16] 5147 2-8-12 54 JamesDoyle 14 38
(Andrew Reid) *towards rr: effrt and prog on inner over 2f out: chsd ldrs over 1f out: sn wknd rapidly* **25/1**

000 **13** *1 1/2* **Thank You Joy**[30] 4658 2-8-10 52 JimmyQuinn 7 33
(J R Jenkins) *sn last: briefest of effrt over 2f out: sn wknd* **40/1**

000 **14** *9* **Erythrina (IRE)**[19] 5032 2-8-13 55 FergusSweeney 2 16
(B G Powell) *chsd ldrs tl wknd 3f out: t.o* **33/1**

1m 41.2s (1.40) **Going Correction** -0.05s/f (Stan) 14 Ran SP% **117.5**
Speed ratings (Par 93): **91,89,89,87,86 84,84,83,82,82 82,81,80,71**
toteswingers:1&2 £9.50, 2&3 £13.20, 1&3 £3.80 CSF £28.70 CT £182.31 TOTE £2.30: £1.10, £5.00, £4.10; EX 30.70.
Owner Colin Bryce **Bred** Edward P Evans **Trained** Newmarket, Suffolk

FOCUS
Division two of an ordinary nursery saw no more than a fair early gallop and those held up were at a disadvantage. The winner raced centre to far side in the closing stages. She should do better, and the placed horses were near to their marks.

NOTEBOOK
Rosa Midnight(USA) duly proved suited by the step into ordinary nursery company and the step up to 1m and turned in an improved display from a favourable draw. Although this wasn't much of a race, there was enough to like about the way she went about her business and she may be capable of further progress. (tchd 9-4)

Highcliffe proved suited by the step up to 1m on this all-weather and nursery debut and ran her best race yet after enjoying the run of the race from her favourable draw. She lacks much in the way of physical scope and may not be entirely straightforward but shaped as though a stronger end-to-end gallop would have suited. Official explanation: jockey said filly ducked in behind (op 9-1)

Papas Fritas was far from disgraced after racing four deep from his draw and ran up to his best on this nursery and all-weather debut on his first run over 1m. He shapes as though he will stay a bit further, has scope for further improvement and should be able to pick up a similar event. (op 6-1 tchd 7-1)

Seas Of Sorrow(IRE), who only hinted at ability in turf maidens, had the run of the race and was far from disgraced on this all-weather and nursery debut after being well-placed throughout. She'll have to progress further to win a similar race from this mark, though.

Pahente bettered the form of his nursery debut in the first-time cheekpieces and returned to Polytrack but, although the step up to 1m2f may suit in due course, he is another that is going to have to improve to defy his current rating. (tchd 33-1)

Spirit Of Oakdale(IRE) was well supported on this nursery debut but proved a disappointment. However, he shaped as though a much stiffer overall test of stamina would have suited, he is in good hands and would not be one to write off just yet. (tchd 7-2 and 9-2)

Thank You Joy Official explanation: jockey said filly missed the break

5661 DIGIBET.COM CLAIMING STKS — 1m (P)
7:50 (7:52) (Class 6) 3-Y-O — £1,637 (£483; £241) Stalls High

Form				RPR
0624	1		**Sabatini (IRE)**[18] 5073 3-8-6 70 ChrisCatlin 5 (J Pearce) *trckd ldng pair: shkn up 2f out: clsd to chal 1f out: led ins fnl f: styd on* 3/1[2]	61
-400	2	¾	**Lean Machine**[27] 4756 3-8-10 72 ow1 RichardHughes 6 (R Hannon) *t.k.h early: hld up in 7th: pushed along 1/2-way: prog to go 5th 2f out: no imp over 1f out: styd on wl last 150yds to take 2nd fnl strides* 9/2[3]	63+
540	3	½	**Fonterutoli (IRE)**[48] 4058 3-9-3 73 AndreaAtzeni 9 (M Botti) *fractious preliminaries: trckd ldrs in 5th: effrt on inner 2f out: drvn to chal and upsides 1f out: nt qckn: lost 2nd last strides* 7/4[1]	69
533	4	½	**Wise Up**[19] 5028 3-8-13 70 DarryllHolland 4 (C A Dwyer) *nt that wl away but sn led: drvn over 1f out: hdd and one pce ins fnl f* 5/1	64
0-40	5	1 ½	**Musical Delight**[53] 3907 3-8-6 50 MatthewDavies(3) 1 (A P Jarvis) *chsd ldr: hrd rdn wl over 1f out: fdd ins fnl f* 40/1	56
5002	6	3 ¼	**Stef And Stelio**[18] 5073 3-9-3 65 (t) NickyMackay 10 (G A Butler) *broke wl: heavily restrained and sn detached in last: shuffled along over 2f out: nvr remotely involved* 8/1	56+
0003	7	¾	**So Surreal (IRE)**[18] 5073 3-8-7 63 ow1 (b) FergusSweeney 3 (G L Moore) *hld up in 6th: rdn 3f out: no prog and struggling over 2f out* 12/1	44
0-00	8	10	**Impressioniste (IRE)**[127] 1594 3-8-6 82 (b[1]) TobyAtkinson(5) 2 (Luke Comer, Ire) *chsd ldng trio: nt keen u.p over 2f out: sn dropped out: t.o* 33/1	24

1m 40.39s (0.59) **Going Correction** -0.05s/f (Stan) 8 Ran SP% **120.4**
Speed ratings (Par 99): **95,94,93,93,91 88,87,77**
.Lean Machine was claimed by R. A. Harris for £8000.\n\x\x
Owner A Watford, D Leech, M Prince **Bred** O Bourke **Trained** Newmarket, Suffolk

FOCUS
A few fair sorts but a modest gallop, and the proximity of the fifth means this bare form isn't reliable. The winner raced towards the inside rail in the closing stages.
Impressioniste(IRE) Official explanation: jockey said colt ran too free

5662 OLLY MURS LIVE ON LADIES DAY H'CAP — 1m (P)
8:20 (8:20) (Class 4) (0-85,84) 3-Y-O — £3,885 (£1,156; £577; £288) Stalls High

Form				RPR
2342	1		**Faithful One (IRE)**[21] 4956 3-9-5 **82** ChrisCatlin 8 (D R Lanigan) *hld up in 5th: gng strly over 2f out: prog to 3rd sn after: drvn ahd jst ins fnl f: styd on wl* 9/1	91
4131	2	1	**Miss Antonia (IRE)**[16] 5149 3-9-3 **80** TomQueally 4 (H R A Cecil) *hld up in 6th and racd wd: shkn up 2f out: prog over 1f out: styd on ins fnl f to take 2nd last strides* 5/1	87
1-	3	hd	**Bramshaw (USA)**[279] 7537 3-9-3 **80** NeilCallan 6 (Mrs A J Perrett) *hld up in last pair: looking for room over 2f out: prog sn after: drvn to cl on ldrs 1f out: wnt 2nd briefly last 50yds: kpt on* 7/4[1]	87+
-221	4	¾	**Touch Tone**[40] 4339 3-9-1 **78** MichaelHills 5 (B W Hills) *racd wd: hld up and sn last: shkn up 2f out: prog over 1f out: styd on ins fnl f: nvr able to chal* 11/1	83+
6411	5	shd	**Conciliatory**[14] 5222 3-9-2 **79** MartinDwyer 3 (Rae Guest) *trckd ldr: shkn up 2f out: led over 1f out: hdd and one pce jst ins fnl f* 9/2[3]	84
2142	6	2	**King Of Windsor (IRE)**[39] 4357 3-9-7 **84** JackMitchell 11 (R M Beckett) *hld up and sn in last trio: drvn over 2f out: nvr gng pce to make any significant prog* 3/1[2]	84
01	7	¾	**Boom And Bust (IRE)**[23] 4906 3-8-9 **72** PatDobbs 9 (M P Tregoning) *sn chsd ldng trio: rdn over 2f out: no imp over 1f out: fdd* 12/1	70
0344	8	1 ¾	**Ostentation**[13] 5236 3-8-9 **75** MatthewDavies(3) 10 (R A Teal) *led: set mod pce to 1/2-way: hdd over 1f out: wknd ins fnl f* 33/1	69
0004	9	4 ½	**Toga Tiger (IRE)**[46] 4128 3-8-13 **76** TonyCulhane 2 (P T Midgley) *trckd ldng pair to jst over 2f out: wknd rapidly* 40/1	60

1m 39.04s (-0.76) **Going Correction** -0.05s/f (Stan) 9 Ran SP% **127.6**
Speed ratings (Par 103): **101,100,99,99,98 96,96,94,89**
toteswingers:1&2 £6.90, 2&3 £3.50, 1&3 £9.50 CSF £59.30 CT £120.25 TOTE £18.80: £4.90, £3.40, £1.10; EX 65.00.
Owner Saif Ali **Bred** Darley **Trained** Newmarket, Suffolk

FOCUS
The best quality event on the card but, although the overall time was just above the Racing Post Standard, a muddling gallop means this bare form is not entirely reliable. The winner raced down the centre in the straight.

5663 KEMPTON.CO.UK APPRENTICE H'CAP — 1m 3f (P)
8:50 (8:50) (Class 6) (0-60,60) 3-Y-O+ — £1,637 (£483; £241) Stalls High

Form				RPR
605	1		**Carlton Scroop (FR)**[29] 4681 7-9-9 55 (b) KierenFox 8 (A W Carroll) *hld up in 7th: shkn up and prog over 2f out: str burst over 1f out to ld ins fnl f: sn clr* 3/1[1]	66+
0500	2	2 ½	**Gearbox (IRE)**[20] 5011 4-9-6 57 RichardRowe(5) 5 (H J L Dunlop) *trckd ldr to over 5f out and over 3f out to over 1f out: kpt on ins fnl f to take 2nd again last stride* 25/1	63
5331	3	shd	**Josr's Magic (IRE)**[18] 5072 6-9-11 **60** AmyScott(3) 9 (P R Hedger) *led: 2 l clr over 1f out: hdd and no ex ins fnl f: lost 2nd last stride* 9/2[2]	66
2000	4	1 ¾	**Storm Hawk (IRE)**[15] 5180 3-9-1 **60** (p) JamesRogers(5) 13 (Pat Eddery) *dwlt: hld up in 8th: effrt on inner over 2f out: kpt on fr over 1f out: n.d* 14/1	63
5003	5	nk	**Two Oclock John**[51] 3965 4-9-11 **60** AdamBeschizza(3) 11 (T T Clement) *trckd ldrs: rdn to dispute 2nd over 2f out: grad fdd fr over 1f out* 8/1	62
3143	6	1 ¾	**Dovedon Angel**[27] 4734 4-9-4 **50** DeclanCannon 14 (Miss Gay Kelleway) *awkward s: hld up in last trio: prog fr over 3f out: chsd ldrs over 1f out: no ex and fdd* 6/1[3]	49
1046	7	1	**Nom De La Rosa (IRE)**[10] 5330 3-8-13 **58** (p) HarryBentley(5) 4 (Miss Sheena West) *prom: urged along furiously fnl 2f: grad fdd* 28/1	55
600	8	10	**Miss Formidable (IRE)**[105] 2231 3-9-1 **55** AmyBaker 3 (Luke Comer, Ire) *a towards rr: rdn and no prog over 2f out: sn bhd* 50/1	34
1026	9	nk	**Blackstone Vegas**[76] 3110 4-9-9 **55** (v) LeeTopliss 6 (D Shaw) *restrained s: hld up in last trio: sharp reminder 6f out: last whn hmpd over 2f out: nvr a factor* 15/2	34
0540	10	½	**Turner's Touch**[28] 4689 8-8-8 **47** (b) ChelseyBanks(7) 7 (G L Moore) *stdd s: hld up last: pushed along and no real prog over 2f out* 25/1	25
0403	11	1 ¾	**Formidable Guest**[16] 5155 6-9-13 **59** SimonPearce 10 (J Pearce) *chsd ldrs: rdn over 3f out: wknd rapidly over 2f out* 6/1[3]	34
0463	12	dist	**Special Cuvee**[16] 5148 4-9-8 **54** (vt) TobyAtkinson 1 (Mrs A M Thorpe) *prom: chsd ldr over 5f out to over 3f out: wknd v rapidly: virtually p.u ins fnl f* 16/1	—

2m 20.6s (-1.30) **Going Correction** -0.05s/f (Stan)
WFA 3 from 4yo+ 8lb 12 Ran SP% **120.3**
Speed ratings (Par 101): **102,100,100,98,98 97,96,89,89,88 87,—**
toteswingers:1&2 £26.30, 2&3 £11.10, 1&3 £2.90 CSF £90.41 CT £344.01 TOTE £6.20: £2.00, £7.90, £2.20; EX 98.30 Place 6: £14.16 Place 5: £8.36.
Owner S Hussain & P O'Neill **Bred** Jonathan Jay **Trained** Cropthorne, Worcs

FOCUS
A moderate handicap in which the gallop was reasonable. The winner raced centre to far side in the closing stages.
Special Cuvee Official explanation: jockey said gelding had a breathing problem
T/Plt: £24.80 to a £1 stake. Pool of £66,442.64 - 1,955.58 winning tickets. T/Qpdt: £5.50 to a £1 stake. Pool of £9,726.40 - 1,289.92 winning tickets. JN

5452 LINGFIELD (L-H)
Wednesday, September 1

OFFICIAL GOING: Turf course - good to firm (good in places; 8.5); all-weather - standard
Wind: virtually nil Weather: sunny

5664 GALLAGHER GROUP H'CAP — 1m 1f
2:20 (2:20) (Class 5) (0-70,70) 3-Y-O+ — £2,914 (£867; £433; £216) Stalls Low

Form				RPR
050	1		**First In The Queue (IRE)**[33] 4563 3-9-1 **66** TravisBlock 1 (S Kirk) *mde all: rdn ent fnl 2f: kpt on wl ins fnl f* 8/1	75
0001	2	1	**Negotiation (IRE)**[27] 4763 4-9-9 **68** PatCosgrave 14 (M Quinn) *chsd ldng pair: rdn to chse wnr over 1f out: styd on same pce and a hld ins fnl f* 10/1	75
2203	3	nse	**Eye Of Eternity**[15] 5171 3-8-4 **55** oh1 DavidProbert 7 (Rae Guest) *pushed along early: towards rr: rdn and sltly hmpd wl over 2f out: rdn and hdwy on outer ent fnl 2f: chsd ldrs 1f out: kpt on: no imp on wnr ins fnl f* 13/2[2]	62+
6042	4	1 ¼	**Osgood**[8] 5394 3-9-2 **67** SamHitchcott 4 (M R Channon) *in tch: rdn and effrt to chse ldrs 2f out: drvn and styd on same pce fr over 1f out* 13/2[2]	71
0240	5	½	**Free As A Lark**[27] 4762 3-9-2 **67** JackMitchell 12 (C F Wall) *racd towards rr: dropped to last over 4f out: rdn and hdwy ent fnl 2f: kpt on ins fnl f: nt rch ldrs* 11/1	70+
4266	6	½	**Fire Raiser**[28] 4700 3-8-9 **60** LiamKeniry 9 (A M Balding) *in tch: rdn and effrt to chse ldrs over 2f out: drvn and styd on same pce fr over 1f out* 13/2[2]	62
1032	7	2 ¾	**Mellifera**[17] 5113 3-9-5 **70** (b) AdamKirby 13 (W R Swinburn) *wnt lft s and s.i.s: nvr travelling wl and sn niggled along in rr: sme prog u.p ent fnl 2f: swtchd lft over 1f out: no imp ins fnl f* 6/1[1]	66
0552	8	1 ¼	**Rodrigo De Freitas (IRE)**[20] 4994 3-8-9 **60** (b[1]) NickyMackay 3 (J R Boyle) *s.i.s: bhd: rdn and no prog 3f out: sme hdwy and swtchd lft over 1f out: nvr trbld ldrs* 12/1	53
0010	9	2 ½	**Hip Hip Hooray**[16] 5149 4-9-1 **60** RichardHughes 6 (L A Dace) *s.i.s: bhd: swtchd rt and rdn wl over 2f out: no real prog and wl btn over 1f out: eased wl ins fnl f* 10/1	47
3606	10	2 ¾	**On The Cusp (IRE)**[33] 4552 3-8-10 **64** ow3 RobertLButler(3) 8 (P Butler) *hld up in rr: pushed along and no hdwy 3f out: n.d* 50/1	45
002	11	1	**Beck's Bolero (IRE)**[13] 5233 4-9-4 **63** FergusSweeney 10 (J A Osborne) *chsd wnr: rdn and effrt to press wnr 3f out: struggling 2f out: lost 2nd over 1f out and sn wknd* 20/1	42
0066	12	1	**Fairy Flight (USA)**[21] 4972 3-8-13 **64** (v) WilliamBuick 5 (W J Knight) *in tch: rdn and struggling whn edgd rt wl over 2f out: sn bhd* 7/1[3]	41

1m 54.88s (-1.72) **Going Correction** -0.10s/f (Good)
WFA 3 from 4yo+ 6lb 12 Ran SP% **118.8**
Speed ratings (Par 103): **103,102,102,100,100 100,97,96,94,91 90,90**
toteswingers:1&2 £16.10, 2&3 £7.10, 1&3 £18.30 CSF £85.82 CT £564.69 TOTE £10.90: £3.30, £3.00, £3.20; EX 133.30.
Owner Liam Breslin **Bred** Holborn Trust Co **Trained** Upper Lambourn, Berks

FOCUS
The turf track had dried out and was officially described as good to firm, good in places. The betting for this modest handicap was wide open with the favourite sent off at 6-1 and those that raced handily were at an advantage.
On The Cusp(IRE) Official explanation: jockey said gelding lost its action

5665 GALLAGHER GROUP MAIDEN STKS — 1m 3f 106y
2:50 (2:50) (Class 5) 3-Y-O+ — £2,729 (£806; £403) Stalls High

Form				RPR
2-	1		**Rock My World (IRE)**[280] 7522 3-8-12 0 NeilCallan 6 (M A Jarvis) *t.k.h early: chsd ldrs: rdn and short of room 3f out: chal ent fnl 2f: led 1f out: kpt on wl ins fnl f* 3/1[2]	75+
2244	2	½	**Bombadero (IRE)**[25] 4827 3-9-3 78 (p) TedDurcan 4 (J L Dunlop) *in tch: chsd ldng pair and swtchd rt wl over 3f out: sn wandered u.p and no imp: drvn and kpt on ins fnl f: wnt 2nd wl ins fnl f: nvr gng to rch wnr* 10/3[3]	79
6332	3	¾	**Mutanaker**[19] 5022 3-9-3 75 RichardHills 5 (Sir Michael Stoute) *led: rdn 3f out: jnd ent fnl 2f: drvn and hdd 1f out: styd on same pce ins fnl f* 7/1	78
44-4	4	1 ½	**Palio Square (USA)**[19] 5026 3-9-3 80 TomQueally 9 (H R A Cecil) *in tch in midfield: rdn and effrt to chse ldng trio wl over 1f out: kpt on ins fnl f: nvr gng pce to rch ldrs* 15/8[1]	75+
323	5	7	**My Manikato**[12] 5258 3-9-3 73 (v[1]) J-PGuillambert 11 (L M Cumani) *dwlt: sn rdn along and hdwy to chse ldr after 1f: rdn and ev ch 3f out tl ent fnl 2f: sn hung lft and wknd* 8/1	64
44	6	½	**My Galway Man (IRE)**[23] 4893 3-9-3 0 JoeFanning 7 (M Johnston) *chsd ldrs: rdn and struggling over 2f out: wknd wl over 1f out* 14/1	63
0-0	7	14	**Destiny Rules**[32] 4601 3-8-12 0 IvaMilickova 8 (John Berry) *s.i.s: a towards rr: lost tch 4f out* 150/1	36
6	8	4	**Eurasian**[17] 5116 3-9-3 0 WilliamBuick 2 (D M Simcock) *racd in midfield: rdn and lost tch 4f out* 40/1	35

9 26 **Les Andelys**[111] 4-9-11 0 TomMcLaughlin 3 —
(T T Clement) *v.s.a: a wl bhd: lost tch 5f out: t.o fnl 3f* **200/1**

3 10 13 **Pursuit Of Reason**[20] 5001 3-8-12 0 RichardHughes 10 —
(G L Moore) *stdd s: hld up in last pair: lost tch 5f out: c to stands' side: eased and t.o fnl 3f* **25/1**

2m 29.85s (-1.65) **Going Correction** -0.10s/f (Good)
WFA 3 from 4yo 8lb 10 Ran SP% **120.6**
Speed ratings (Par 103): **102,101,101,100,94 94,84,81,62,53**
toteswingers:1&2 £2.40, 2&3 £3.20, 1&3 £5.00 CSF £13.90 TOTE £4.50: £1.10, £1.30, £3.40; EX 16.70.
Owner Stephen Dartnell **Bred** Round Hill Stud **Trained** Newmarket, Suffolk

FOCUS
Not a strong maiden and again those that raced close to the pace were favoured.

5666 KIER H'CAP 2m
3:20 (3:22) (Class 6) (0-65,62) 3-Y-0+ **£2,047** (£604; £302) **Stalls** Low

Form RPR

-061 1 **Bravo Bravo**[4] 5522 3-8-6 **53** 6ex SamHitchcott 2 61+
(M R Channon) *hld up in midfield: hdwy on inner over 3f out: rdn to chse ldr over 2f out: drvn to ld 1f out: styd on wl* **7/2**[2]

3042 2 2 **Fine Lace (IRE)**[20] 4991 3-9-0 **61** JamesDoyle 13 67+
(D J S Ffrench Davis) *hld up towards rr: gd hdwy to ld 4f out: rdn ent fnl 3f: drvn and hdd 1f out: styd on same pce and btn ins fnl f* **5/1**[3]

-064 3 nk **Go Amwell**[43] 4223 7-8-7 **48** DannyBrock(7) 5 54
(J R Jenkins) *hld up bhd: hdwy and swtchd rt 3f out: styd on wl to chse ldng pair ins fnl f: gng on fin: nt rch ldrs* **16/1**

-225 4 3 3/4 **The Composer**[15] 5179 8-9-1 **49** NeilCallan 10 50
(M Blanshard) *hld up towards rr: hdwy over 4f out: chsd ldng trio u.p 2f out: kpt on same pce fr over 1f out* **16/1**

6420 5 1/2 **Spiritonthemount (USA)**[17] 5119 5-9-0 **48** (b) LukeMorris 7 49
(P W Hiatt) *dwlt: sn drvn: hdwy to ld after 1f: hdd and allowed ldr to go clr 10f out: clsd over 4f out: 3rd and hrd drvn whn swtchd rt 2f out: wknd over 1f out* **12/1**

4300 6 8 **Hidden**[20] 5011 4-10-0 **62** (b[1]) TadhgO'Shea 6 53
(B J Meehan) *stdd after s: t.k.h early: hld up bhd: wl bhd 4f out: sme hdwy u.p: racing awkwardly over 2f out: nvr trbld ldrs* **10/1**

6-40 7 18 **Astromoon**[33] 4545 3-8-13 **60** PatCosgrave 1 29
(M H Tompkins) *led for 1f: chsd ldrs after tl wknd qckly wl over 2f out: eased fnl f: t.o* **33/1**

000 8 12 **Suhailah**[15] 5179 4-8-11 **45** NickyMackay 9 —
(M J Attwater) *chsd ldrs: rdn and struggling over 3f out: sn wknd: t.o and eased ins fnl f* **66/1**

2000 9 2 1/2 **Zuwaar**[160] 982 5-9-3 **54** (tp) RobertLButler(3) 3 —
(P Butler) *racd in midfield: lost pl over 4f out: wl btn fnl 3f: t.o and eased ins fnl f* **33/1**

5563 10 5 **The Mighty Mod (USA)**[6] 5437 3-8-0 **47** (b) JoeFanning 4 —
(M Johnston) *dwlt: hmpd after 1f: hdwy on outer to ld 10f out: sn clr: hdd 4f out: 3rd and rdn over 3f out: sn btn: t.o and eased ins fnl f* **5/2**[1]

0401 11 45 **Sunny Spells**[69] 3348 5-10-0 **62** WilliamBuick 14 —
(S C Williams) *chsd ldrs tl wknd 4f out: bhd and eased fnl 3f: t.o fnl 2f* **11/2**

3m 33.97s (-0.83) **Going Correction** -0.10s/f (Good)
WFA 3 from 4yo+ 13lb 11 Ran SP% **118.8**
Speed ratings (Par 101): **98,97,96,94,94 90,81,75,74,71 49**
toteswingers:1&2 £2.40, 2&3 £11.70, 1&3 £19.20 CSF £21.44 CT £250.71 TOTE £3.60: £1.10, £1.10, £4.80; EX 22.20.
Owner Derek And Jean Clee **Bred** D & Jean Clee & Burlington Bloodstock **Trained** West Ilsley, Berks

FOCUS
A moderate staying handicap and the lead changed hands several times during the contest. This was an example of how going the shortest way can pay dividends.

5667 LINGFIELD PARK MARRIOTT HOTEL AND COUNTRY CLUB (S) STKS 6f (P)
3:50 (3:51) (Class 6) 2-Y-0 **£2,047** (£604; £302) **Stalls** Low

Form RPR

002 1 **Saxonette**[25] 4848 2-8-6 60 ChrisCatlin 2 61+
(M R Channon) *mde all: rdn clr over 1f out: styd on strly: rdn out* **2/1**[2]

0000 2 2 1/2 **Bonjour Bongee**[20] 4984 2-8-11 55 (b[1]) JamesDoyle 4 58
(A J McCabe) *t.k.h: hld up wl in tch: rdn and effrt ent fnl 2f: drvn to chse clr wnr ent fnl f: no imp* **16/1**

0030 3 2 **Ignore The Advice (IRE)**[20] 5000 2-8-11 56 LiamKeniry 1 52
(J S Moore) *chsd ldrs: rdn to chse wnr over 2f out: nt gng pce of wnr wl over 1f out: lost 2nd ent fnl f: one pce and wl hld after* **33/1**

5001 4 nk **Two Feet Of Snow (IRE)**[12] 5268 2-8-13 75 PaulHanagan 11 53
(I W McInnes) *dwlt: in midfield on outer: hdwy to chse ldrs and rdn bnd 2f out: unable qck u.p wl over 1f out: plugged on same pce and wl hld ins fnl f* **1/1**[1]

5 hd **Simmons** 2-8-6 0 NickyMackay 7 45
(Matthew Salaman) *s.i.s: bhd: rdn and effrt jst over 2f out: swtchd lft over 1f out: styd on wl ins fnl f: nvr trbld ldrs* **20/1**

5460 6 nk **Moorland Boy**[17] 5111 2-8-11 60 FergusSweeney 8 49
(J A Osborne) *t.k.h: hld up in midfield: sltly hmpd and rdn jst over 2f out: edging lft u.p over 1f out: kpt on ins fnl f: nvr trbld ldrs* **14/1**[3]

00 7 3 **Dorothy's Dancing (IRE)**[18] 5074 2-8-6 0 RichardMullen 6 35
(G L Moore) *stdd after s: hld up in midfield: rdn and unable qck over 1f out: one pce and wl hld ins fnl f* **18/1**

000 8 3/4 **Burnem Green**[8] 5381 2-8-1 0 AdamBeschizza(5) 5 33
(A Bailey) *s.i.s: a in rr: rdn and sme hdwy over 1f out: n.d* **20/1**

000 9 2 1/4 **Snapshott (IRE)**[29] 4678 2-8-11 35 LukeMorris 10 31
(R A Harris) *chsd ldrs: rdn and chsd ldng pair over 2f out: btn over 1f out: fdd ins fnl f* **100/1**

00 10 19 **Zafrina**[72] 3260 2-8-6 0 FrankieMcDonald 3 —
(Peter Grayson) *s.i.s: towards rr: nt clr run and hmpd ent fnl 3f: sn rdn and struggling: wl bhd over 1f out* **100/1**

436 11 10 **Welsh Dresser (IRE)**[50] 3985 2-8-6 54 PaulEddery 9 —
(Peter Grayson) *chsd ldr: rdn 1/2-way: lost 2nd over 2f out: sn dropped out: t.o ins fnl f* **40/1**

1m 14.78s (2.88) **Going Correction** +0.30s/f (Slow) 11 Ran SP% **118.0**
Speed ratings (Par 93): **92,88,86,85,85 84,80,79,76,51 38**
toteswingers:1&2 £6.60, 2&3 £25.70, 1&3 £6.50 CSF £30.36 TOTE £2.70: £1.20, £4.00, £6.20; EX 33.70.The winner was bought by L. Perratt for 7,000gns.
Owner M Channon **Bred** Mike Channon Bloodstock Ltd **Trained** West Ilsley, Berks

FOCUS
A moderate juvenile seller, in which only two counted according to the market. It was dominated by those that raced handily and those drawn low. The winner might have more to offer.

NOTEBOOK
Saxonette was narrowly beaten by a subsequent nursery winner in a Redcar seller last month and only needed to repeat that form to win this. Quick from the stalls, she never looked in any danger and won this with plenty of authority. She was snapped up by Linda Perratt for 7,000gns at the auction and can win in higher grade. (tchd 15-8)
Bonjour Bongee, well beaten all five starts on turf and with first-time blinkers replacing the visor on this drop in grade, ran much better here having always been handy, though he was never near the winner. He can win a seller if the headgear works again. (tchd 18-1)
Ignore The Advice(IRE), dropped in grade, had every chance against the inside rail and is another that can probably win a routine seller.
Two Feet Of Snow(IRE), making his debut for the yard after winning a Wolverhampton seller for Richard Hannon 12 days earlier, had it to do from the outside stall and the last thing he needed was to get a bump soon after the start. He had a chance turning in, but was never able to get cover at any stage and it may be wise to forgive him this. (op 6-5 tchd 5-4)
Simmons, a half-sister to a 1m winner whose dam was successful on Fibresand and over hurdles, made late progress from off the pace and, although this effort should be measured within the context of the contest, she should come on for it and may well improve for further. (op 16-1)

5668 BUILDING MAGAZINE JOSEPH ALOYSIUS HANSOM MAIDEN STKS 6f (P)
4:20 (4:22) (Class 5) 3-Y-0 **£3,238** (£963; £481; £240) **Stalls** Low

Form RPR

6-24 1 **Elsie's Orphan**[14] 5206 3-8-12 60 LiamKeniry 11 68+
(P R Chamings) *chsd ldr tl led over 2f out: rdn clr 2f out: in command ins fnl f: eased towards fin* **11/2**[2]

03 2 3/4 **Toms Return**[25] 4835 3-8-12 0 KierenFox(5) 5 71+
(J R Best) *s.i.s: towards rr: gd hdwy 2f out: rdn and chsd ldng pair jst over 1f out: chsd clr wnr ins fnl f: r.o wl and clsng qckly on eased wnr at fin* **12/1**

-442 3 6 **Millden**[25] 4835 3-8-12 67 (b) AmyScott(5) 9 51
(H Candy) *chsd ldng pair: rdn to chse wnr but unable qck ent fnl 2f: wl btn 1f out: lost 2nd and wknd ins fnl f* **15/2**

06-4 4 2 1/2 **Gooseberry Bush**[20] 5010 3-8-12 65 NeilCallan 8 38
(P J Makin) *in tch: rdn and effrt ent fnl 2f: outpcd and wl btn over 1f out: wknd ins fnl f* **13/8**[1]

5 nk **Speedy Xaara (IRE)** 3-8-12 0 DaneO'Neill 2 37+
(H Candy) *s.i.s: pushed along early: bhd: clsd and in tch 1/2-way: nt clr run and swtchd rt bnd 2f out: kpt on u.p ins fnl f: nvr trbld ldrs* **6/1**[3]

6 1 3/4 **Kentish (USA)** 3-9-3 0 ShaneKelly 3 37
(Jane Chapple-Hyam) *s.i.s: bhd: clsd and in tch 1/2-way: rdn and outpcd ent fnl 2f: edgd lft and wl hld fr over 1f out* **7/1**

0U04 7 nse **Music Lover**[16] 5152 3-9-3 60 LukeMorris 7 37
(R A Harris) *dwlt and short of room sn after s: in tch in midfield: rdn and effrt to chse ldr 2f out: wknd u.p over 1f out* **14/1**

-00 8 3 1/4 **Battleship Grey**[81] 2968 3-9-3 0 AdamKirby 1 26
(D K Ivory) *stdd s: hld up in rr: clsd and in tch 1/2-way: rdn and outpcd ent fnl 2f: wl btn 1f out* **66/1**

0-0 9 1 3/4 **Starstreamer (IRE)**[19] 5028 3-8-12 0 ChrisCatlin 10 16
(M P Tregoning) *racd in midfield: rdn and unable qck over 2f out: wl btn over 1f out* **25/1**

- 10 8 **Exceedingthestars** 3-8-12 0 MarcHalford 4 —
(M D Squance) *in tch on inner: rdn and struggling ent fnl 2f: wkng whn nt clr run and hmpd wl over 1f out: wl bhd after* **66/1**

000 11 4 1/2 **Natalie N G**[28] 4720 3-8-5 25 DannyBrock(7) 6 —
(J R Jenkins) *led tl over 2f out: wknd rapidly ent fnl 2f: wl bhd ins fnl f* **100/1**

1m 13.5s (1.60) **Going Correction** +0.30s/f (Slow) 11 Ran SP% **114.2**
Speed ratings (Par 101): **101,100,92,88,88 85,85,81,79,68 62**
toteswingers:1&2 £8.90, 2&3 £4.80, 1&3 £4.40 CSF £65.71 TOTE £4.60: £1.30, £3.10, £2.40; EX 67.90.
Owner Mrs J E L Wright **Bred** Wheelers Land Stud **Trained** Baughurst, Hants

FOCUS
An ordinary 3-y-o maiden, but a couple did catch the eye.

5669 DORMANS PARK H'CAP (DIV I) 7f (P)
4:50 (4:51) (Class 6) (0-65,65) 3-Y-0 **£1,706** (£503; £252) **Stalls** Low

Form RPR

0000 1 **Paphos**[56] 3788 3-8-7 **51** oh6 (v) DavidProbert 8 62
(S C Williams) *sn chsng ldr: led over 2f out: rdn clr wl over 1f out: in command ins fnl f: rdn out* **10/1**

2653 2 2 1/4 **Orsett Lad (USA)**[27] 4742 3-8-5 **54** KierenFox(5) 9 59
(J R Best) *in tch in midfield: rdn and effrt to chse wnr jst over 2f out: no imp u.p ins fnl f* **7/2**[1]

-300 3 nk **South African Gold (USA)**[94] 2566 3-9-5 **63** LukeMorris 3 67
(J M P Eustace) *in midfield whn n.m.r and swtchd rt after 1f: t.k.h and hld up towards rr after: hdwy over 2f out: chsd ldrs and edging lft u.p over 1f out: kpt on to go 3rd nr fin: no threat to wnr* **14/1**

1634 4 1 1/4 **Decency (IRE)**[27] 4744 3-9-7 **65** WilliamBuick 12 66
(H J L Dunlop) *s.i.s: bhd: hdwy on outer bnd 2f out: rdn and no real prog wl over 1f out: styd on ins fnl f: nvr trbld ldrs* **9/2**[2]

2000 5 hd **Ocean Rosie (IRE)**[14] 5205 3-8-13 62 (v[1]) AdamBeschizza(5) 6 62
(Miss J Feilden) *chsd ldrs: rdn to chse ldng pair over 1f out: drvn and no imp ent fnl f: lost 2 pls fnl 100yds* **12/1**

660 6 1 3/4 **Bill's Story**[20] 4997 3-9-4 **62** ChrisCatlin 10 58+
(M R Channon) *s.i.s: sn in last pair: stl bhd ent fnl 2f: hdwy over 1f out: styd on ins fnl f: nvr trbld ldrs* **10/1**

0550 7 hd **Ice Cool Lady (IRE)**[74] 3212 3-9-5 **63** AdamKirby 2 58
(W R Swinburn) *sn pushed along: a towards rr: n.m.r over 2f out: rdn 2f out: kpt on ins fnl f: nvr trbld ldrs* **8/1**

-064 8 1 1/2 **Verity Lane (USA)**[22] 4931 3-9-3 **61** (p) J-PGuillambert 1 52
(R M H Cowell) *sn bustled along to chse ldrs: rdn: unable qck whn hmpd shuffled lost pl jst over 2f out: nt rcvr and n.d after* **15/2**

0500 9 3 1/4 **Dilys Maud**[49] 4025 3-9-2 **60** PaulHanagan 5 42
(R Ingram) *in tch in midfield whn hmpd and dropped to last trio after 1f: rdn jst over 2f out: no prog: eased wl ins fnl f* **18/1**

4024 10 1 1/4 **King's Approach (IRE)**[15] 5171 3-9-0 **58** (b) TomMcLaughlin 7 37
(R A Harris) *led and crossed to rail: hdd over 2f out: wknd u.p ent fnl 2f* **11/2**[3]

004 11 1 1/4 **Queenie's Star (IRE)**[19] 5028 3-8-8 **57** JemmaMarshall(5) 11 32
(M J Attwater) *s.i.s: a bhd* **33/1**

1m 26.92s (2.12) **Going Correction** +0.30s/f (Slow) 11 Ran SP% **119.4**
Speed ratings (Par 99): **99,96,96,94,94 92,92,90,86,85 83**
toteswingers:1&2 £13.60, 2&3 £13.10, 1&3 £37.20 CSF £45.66 CT £513.57 TOTE £14.30: £6.00, £2.30, £5.00; EX 66.60.
Owner Stuart C Williams **Bred** L Ellinas And Old Mill Stud Ltd **Trained** Newmarket, Suffolk

FOCUS
A moderate handicap and a gamble landed.

5670 DORMANS PARK H'CAP (DIV II) 7f (P)
5:25 (5:25) (Class 6) (0-65,65) 3-Y-O £1,706 (£503; £252) Stalls Low

Form RPR

0325 1 **Mrs Mogg**[20] 4998 3-9-3 61 RichardKingscote 8 69
(Tom Dascombe) *s.i.s: bhd and sn niggled along: reminder after 1f: hdwy over 2f out: rdn to chse ldrs 2f out: drvn and ev ch ins fnl f led fnl 75yds: r.o wl* 8/1

-306 2 1 **Swift Return**[69] 3363 3-9-7 65 (v[1]) NeilCallan 2 70
(S C Williams) *s.i.s: sn bustled along: in midfield after 1f: hdwy over 2f out: chsd ldrs and rdn over 1f out: ev ch ins fnl f: no ex fnl 50yds* 6/1[3]

0045 3 3 **Lordsbury Pride (USA)**[10] 5326 3-8-11 60 KierenFox(5) 9 57
(J R Best) *chsd ldrs: wnt 2nd over 3f out: ev ch u.p over 1f out: led ins fnl f: hdd fnl 75yds: wknd towards fin* 11/1

560 4 ¾ **Bidruma**[19] 5031 3-8-13 57 RichardMullen 11 52
(Mike Murphy) *led and crossed to rail: rdn jst over 2f out: hrd pressed ent fnl f: hdd ins fnl f: wknd fnl 75yds* 16/1

-620 5 ¾ **Accountable**[18] 5077 3-9-1 59 FergusSweeney 1 52
(B G Powell) *in tch towards rr: n.m.r bnd jst over 2f out: rdn and hung lft fr over 1f out: styd on same pce after* 16/1

0004 6 shd **Miss Kitty Grey (IRE)**[16] 5163 3-8-10 54 NickyMackay 6 47
(J R Boyle) *chsd ldrs: rdn ent fnl 2f: wknd ins fnl f* 10/1

0316 7 2 ½ **Mack's Sister**[16] 5163 3-9-3 61 SamHitchcott 3 47
(D K Ivory) *broke wl: stdd and hld up in midfield after 1f: nt clr run and shuffled bk to rr over 2f out: swtchd rt and rdn ent fnl 2f: no prog* 11/4[1]

4004 8 14 **Ravens Rose**[29] 4687 3-8-2 51 oh3 AdamBeschizza(5) 7 —
(J G Portman) *s.i.s: sn pushed along and outpcd in last: hdwy on outer 3f out: rdn and btn ent fnl 2f: wl bhd ins fnl f* 8/1

000 9 6 **Immovable (USA)**[23] 4906 3-9-4 62 GeorgeBaker 5 —
(M A Magnusson) *chsd ldr tl over 3f out: sn lost pl u.p: bhd jst over 2f out: lost tch over 1f out: eased ins fnl f* 3/1[2]

1m 27.12s (2.32) **Going Correction** +0.30s/f (Slow) 9 Ran SP% **117.4**
Speed ratings (Par 99): **98,96,93,92,91 91,88,72,65**
toteswingers:1&2 £6.60, 2&3 £6.20, 1&3 £5.90. totesuper7: Win: Not won. Place: £2045.40. CSF £56.17 CT £538.59 TOTE £9.80: £3.10, £2.10, £3.40; EX 37.30 Place 6: £284.59 Place 5: £87.20.
Owner Owen Promotions Limited **Bred** Darley **Trained** Malpas, Cheshire

FOCUS
A race of changing fortunes and the winning time was 0.2 seconds slower than the first division.
T/Plt: £217.50 to a £1 stake. Pool of £60,412.41 - 202.68 winning tickets. T/Qpdt: £23.20 to a £1 stake. Pool of £4,285.45 - 136.30 winning tickets. SP

5649 BADEN-BADEN (L-H)
Wednesday, September 1

OFFICIAL GOING: Turf: soft

5671a BELMONDO-PREIS (GROUP 3) (3YO) (TURF) 1m 2f
5:20 (5:26) 3-Y-O

£28,318 (£9,734; £4,867; £2,654; £1,769; £1,327)

RPR

1 **Elle Shadow (IRE)**[31] 4640 3-8-10 0 AStarke 7 97
(P Schiergen, Germany) *racd in 4th fr s: travelled smoothly arnd fnl turn to sweep into ld 2 1/2f out: r.o wl u.p: won comf* 6/5[1]

2 2 **Empire Storm (GER)**[87] 3-9-0 0 EPedroza 5 97
(A Wohler, Germany) *in rr fr s: mde gd prog arnd fnl turn: qcknd wl to chse wnr home* 31/5[3]

3 1 **Neatico (GER)**[45] 4184 3-9-2 0 GaetanMasure 4 97
(P Schiergen, Germany) *a.p: trcking ldr: slow to qckn in st but r.o wl in clsng stages* 15/2

4 4 **Keep Cool**[45] 4184 3-8-11 0 THellier 1 84
(Andreas Lowe, Germany) *racd in midfield: threatened briefly early in st: no ex fnl 2f* 92/10

5 ¾ **Mulan (GER)**[67] 3-9-0 0 ADeVries 6 86
(W Hickst, Germany) *settled in midfield: mde prog arnd fnl turn then flattened out and nvr threatened* 21/10[2]

6 5 **Altair Star (IRE)**[37] 4446 3-8-11 0 FilipMinarik 8 73
(P Schiergen, Germany) *tk ld fr s: set gd pce: hld on wl early in st: hdd 2 1/2f out: wknd qckly 2f out* 83/10

7 1 ¾ **Wild Danger (GER)** 3-8-11 0 JiriPalik 3 69
(Andreas Lowe, Germany) *prom early: sn wknd in st* 29/1

8 34 **Wuhan (GER)**[111] 3-8-11 0 HenkGrewe 2 1
(S Smrczek, Germany) *a bkmarker: wknd qckly arnd fnl turn* 32/1

2m 6.26s (1.27) 8 Ran SP% **130.3**
WIN (incl. 10 euro stake): 22. PLACES: 11, 14, 16. SF: 82..
Owner Gestut Wittekindshof **Bred** Gestut Wittekindshof **Trained** Germany

5587 EPSOM (L-H)
Thursday, September 2

OFFICIAL GOING: Good (good to firm in places; (overall 8.3, home straight: stands side 8.1, centre 7.5, far side 7.6)
Rail dolled out up to 4yds from 6f to winning post adding about 5yds to distances.
Wind: light, across Weather: sunny

5675 CICERO NURSERY 7f
2:20 (2:20) (Class 5) (0-70,70) 2-Y-O £3,561 (£1,059; £529; £264) Stalls Low

Form RPR

002 1 **Cometh**[27] 4802 2-8-5 57 MartinLane(3) 3 63+
(N P Littmoden) *mde all: hung rt on bnd over 3f out: jnd and rdn 3f out: kpt on wl to forge ahd 1f out: styd on wl: rdn out* 7/1[2]

5146 2 1 ¼ **Sceal Nua (IRE)**[13] 5256 2-9-7 70 PatDobbs 13 73
(R Hannon) *hld up in tch: swtchd lft and effrt ent fnl 3f: chsd ldng pair over 2f out: styd on whn edging lft fr over 1f out: chsd wnr fnl 100yds: no imp after* 9/4[1]

500 3 1 ¼ **Oliver's Gold**[13] 5277 2-9-2 65 NeilCallan 4 66+
(Mrs A J Perrett) *bhd: nt clr run and hmpd over 4f out: rdn and hdwy jst over 2f out: modest 5th over 1f out: r.o wl to go 3rd wl ins fnl f: nvr able to chal* 8/1

464 4 1 ½ **Cathcart Castle**[9] 5389 2-9-1 64 SamHitchcott 1 60
(M R Channon) *chsd ldrs: hdwy on inner to chse wnr jst over 3f out: ev ch ent fnl 2f: rdn and btn ent fnl f: wknd fnl 150yds* 15/2[3]

040 5 3 ¾ **Cuban Quality (USA)**[32] 4614 2-9-2 65 (v[1]) RichardKingscote 10 52
(Tom Dascombe) *restless in stalls: reminder and wnt lft sn after s: in tch in midfield: rdn and outpcd over 3f out: edging lft but styd on fnl f: nvr gng pce to trble ldrs* 9/1

0100 6 1 ¼ **Miss Moneypenni**[7] 5452 2-9-7 70 GeorgeBaker 9 54
(N P Littmoden) *bmpd sn after s: prom: chsd ldr over 5f out tl carried wd and lost 2nd bnd over 3f out: sn rdn and outpcd: no ch w ldrs fr wl over 1f out* 16/1

043 7 3 **All The Evil (IRE)**[16] 5178 2-9-4 67 DaneO'Neill 7 43
(B J Meehan) *s.i.s: bhd: rdn and effrt jst over 2f out: no real hdwy: wl btn and edging lft over 1f out* 8/1

0406 8 1 ¾ **Mirror Lad**[77] 3106 2-8-9 58 SebSanders 5 30
(Tom Dascombe) *taken down early: t.k.h: hld up towards rr: unbalanced on downhill run and lost pl 4f out: rdn and struggling over 3f out: wl btn fnl 2f* 14/1

606 9 2 ½ **Amber Mist**[50] 4029 2-8-2 56 ow1 KierenFox(5) 8 22
(David Pinder) *taken down early: racd keenly: chsd wnr tl over 5f out: losing pl and rdn over 3f out: bhd fnl 2f* 25/1

003 10 1 **Better Offer (IRE)**[28] 4759 2-9-5 68 TomQueally 11 31
(Miss Amy Weaver) *a in rr: rdn and struggling over 3f out: wl btn fnl 2f* 25/1

623 11 1 **Zarazar**[55] 3849 2-9-6 69 CathyGannon 2 30+
(P D Evans) *t.k.h: hld up in tch towards rr: n.m.r and shuffled bk towards rr 4f out: short-lived effrt on inner over 2f out: sn btn and wl bhd over 1f out* 8/1

1m 24.83s (1.53) **Going Correction** +0.025s/f (Good) 11 Ran SP% **118.6**
Speed ratings (Par 95): **92,90,89,87,83 81,78,76,73,72 71**
toteswingers:1&2:£4.40, 1&3:£11.20, 2&3:£5.50 CSF £23.23 CT £131.74 TOTE £8.50: £3.30, £1.10, £4.00; EX 36.20 Trifecta £100.50 Pool: £525.76 - 3.87 winning units..
Owner Larry Stratton **Bred** Larry Stratton **Trained** Newmarket, Suffolk

FOCUS
While the whole field stayed centre to far side in the straight, the winner of this nursery came widest of all. The first four finished clear and the form has a sound feel.

NOTEBOOK
Cometh did by far the best of those who raced prominently when a close second in a Newmarket seller last time out, and was 2lb well in at the weights. Quickly away from her low draw, she was soon in front, and although she didn't take the bend into the straight particularly well and still looked quite green, she knuckled down well under pressure to win quite nicely in the end. There's probably better to come, and she'll remain of interest after reassessment. (op 5-1)
Sceal Nua(IRE) was drawn in the outside box and trapped wide until they entered the straight. It was a solid effort in the circumstances. (op 7-2 tchd 2-1)
Oliver's Gold, running in a handicap for the first time, was out the back early and got hampered heading to the first turn. He had plenty of ground to make up at the top of the straight but finished well and should be capable of better on a more conventional track. (op 15-2)
Cathcart Castle had a good draw and stuck to the fence the whole way round, but didn't quite see the trip out. His dam was a sprinter and perhaps he'll be suited by a drop back to 6f. (op 9-1)
Cuban Quality(USA), who wore a visor for the first time, did not look particularly comfortable on the track and can do better on a more galloping course. His rider reported that the colt hung left. Official explanation: jockey said the colt hung left in the straight (tchd 17-2)
All The Evil(IRE) didn't run up to expectations, but was another who didn't look entirely happy on this unconventional track. (op 10-1)
Mirror Lad was reported to have been too free early. Official explanation: jockey said gelding ran too free in the early stages (tchd 16-1)

5676 EUROPEAN BREEDERS' FUND MAIDEN STKS 1m 114y
2:50 (2:52) (Class 4) 2-Y-O £4,533 (£1,348; £674; £336) Stalls Low

Form RPR

02 1 **Time To Work (IRE)**[21] 4993 2-9-3 0 DavidProbert 1 81+
(A M Balding) *dwlt: sn rcvrd to chse ldrs: swtchd rt and effrt to chse ldr 3f out: rdn and ev ch 2f out: led fnl 150yds: kpt on wl: rdn out* 11/4[2]

2 2 1 **Tiger Webb**[26] 4838 2-9-3 0 TomQueally 2 79+
(H R A Cecil) *led: jnd 2f out: rdn over 1f out: hdd fnl 150yds: styd on same pce after* 4/6[1]

46 3 4 **Coachlight**[28] 4755 2-9-3 0 EddieAhern 5 71
(J L Dunlop) *racd off the pce in midfield: gd hdwy on outer to chse ldrs 4f out: rdn over 3f out: edgd lft and wknd over 1f out* 14/1

0 4 13 **Flinty**[34] 4549 2-9-3 0 PatDobbs 7 43+
(R Hannon) *s.i.s: sn rdn and wl outpcd in last pair: styd on past btn horses fnl f to go modest 4th ins fnl f: nvr on terms* 50/1

5230 5 2 ¼ **Pigeon Hollow**[21] 4993 2-9-3 66 SamHitchcott 9 39
(M R Channon) *s.i.s: sn pushed along and wl off the pce in last trio: rdn 1/2-way: plugged on past btn horses fr over 1f out: n.d* 20/1

0 6 2 ½ **Cuban Piece (IRE)**[43] 4263 2-9-3 0 RichardKingscote 8 33
(Tom Dascombe) *chsd ldrs tl 5f out: rdn and wknd rapidly over 3f out: no ch fnl 3f* 16/1

63 7 nk **El Maachi**[24] 4899 2-9-3 0 CathyGannon 3 33
(P D Evans) *racd keenly: w ldr tl rdn over 3f out: sn no ch w ldrs: wknd fnl f* 12/1[3]

0 8 10 **Hurricane Spear**[33] 4577 2-9-3 0 GeorgeBaker 4 12
(G L Moore) *hld up in tch: pushed along and dropped out rapidly over 3f out: t.o and eased ins fnl f* 25/1

0 9 11 **Precious Diamond**[9] 5385 2-8-12 0 ChrisCatlin 6 —
(M R Channon) *s.i.s: immediately outpcd in last: t.o 5f out* 66/1

1m 46.58s (0.48) **Going Correction** +0.025s/f (Good) 9 Ran SP% **119.0**
Speed ratings (Par 97): **98,97,93,82,80 77,77,68,58**
toteswingers:1&2:£1.10, 1&3:£4.70, 2&3:£4.10 CSF £4.90 TOTE £3.40: £1.60, £1.10, £2.30; EX 5.60 Trifecta £27.40 Pool: £828.98 - 22.34 winning units..
Owner Another Bottle Racing 2 **Bred** Scuderia San Pancrazio Sas **Trained** Kingsclere, Hants

FOCUS
The market made this a two-horse race and they fought out the finish. Straightforward maiden form.

NOTEBOOK
Time To Work(IRE) had the benefit of previous experience of this track and made it count, for while the runner-up got a bit unbalanced, he coped with it well and saw his race out the stronger. It's also worth noting that he has more size than Tiger Webb, and there was an element of intimidation in the closing stages which helped him seal victory. He looks the type who'll progress with time. (op 3-1 tchd 5-2)
Tiger Webb hit the front going best of all but was outbattled by his bigger rival inside the last. He shouldn't have too much difficulty winning a similar maiden on a more galloping track. (op 8-11 tchd 10-11 and evens in places)
Coachlight had every chance but was outclassed by the first two. However, handicaps are next up, and he could well find improvement in that sphere. (tchd 12-1)

Flinty, who finished last over 6f on his debut, needed a reminder or two early on in the contest but stayed on from an impossible position to take a poor fourth. He looks a handicap prospect after one more outing.

Pigeon Hollow, the most experienced in the line-up, was disappointing over this C&D last time and again showed little, being under pressure early and never getting involved. (tchd 22-1)

El Maachi, stepping up in trip, was in the mix till 3f out but then weakened. Handicaps are now open to him. (op 10-1 tchd 9-1)

5677 WEATHERBYS BLOODSTOCK INSURANCE H'CAP 7f

3:25 (3:25) (Class 4) (0-80,78) 3-Y-O **£4,857** (£1,445; £722; £360) **Stalls** Low

Form RPR

0042 **1** **Chat De La Burg (USA)**[26] 4836 3-8-10 **72** KierenFox[(5)] 4 83
(J R Best) *taken down early: mde all: jnd and rdn over 2f out: drvn and hld on gamely fnl f* **3/1**[2]

3302 **2** ½ **Cat Hunter**[9] 5391 3-8-10 **67** TomQueally 2 77
(H R A Cecil) *stdd s: hld up in rr: shkn up and hdwy over 2f out: rdn to chal jst over 1f out: drvn and styd on same pce ins fnl f and a jst hld after* **7/4**[1]

1-44 **3** 5 **Pan American**[26] 4837 3-9-3 **74** FergusSweeney 5 70
(P J Makin) *taken down early: chsd wnr: effrt to chal and rdn wl over 2f out: ev ch tl btn ent fnl f: wknd and edgd lft ins fnl f* **13/2**

-103 **4** 6 **Sard**[87] 2807 3-9-7 **78** NeilCallan 7 58
(M A Jarvis) *stdd s: hld up in last pair: hdwy over 3f out: rdn to chse ldrs wl over 2f out: sn struggling: 4th and wl btn over 1f out* **15/2**

3200 **5** 10 **Interakt**[28] 4735 3-8-9 **66** SamHitchcott 1 19
(M R Channon) *chsd ldrs: rdn and effrt over 3f out: wknd ent fnl 2f: sn wl btn: eased ins fnl f* **10/1**

-463 **6** 4 **Hooligan Sean**[47] 4146 3-9-4 **75** DaneO'Neill 3 17
(H Candy) *t.k.h: hld up in tch: rdn and lost pl qckly over 3f out: wl bhd fr over 2f out* **5/1**[3]

1m 23.06s (-0.24) **Going Correction** +0.025s/f (Good) **6** Ran SP% **112.2**
Speed ratings (Par 103): **102,101,95,88,77 72**
toteswingers:1&2:£1.60, 1&3:£4.20, 2&3:£3.00 CSF £8.69 TOTE £4.20: £2.30, £1.40; EX 9.30.
Owner Kent Bloodstock 2009 **Bred** S M D Ltd **Trained** Hucking, Kent

FOCUS
A fair little handicap. The field was well strung out and the winner rates a personal best.
Hooligan Sean Official explanation: jockey said gelding was unsuited by the track; confirmed by trainer

5678 TOTEPOOL FLEXI BETTING H'CAP 6f

4:00 (4:00) (Class 4) (0-85,84) 3-Y-O+ **£5,828** (£1,734; £866; £432) **Stalls** High

Form RPR

0000 **1** **Falasteen (IRE)**[12] 5290 3-9-3 **82** TomQueally 6 90
(R A Fahey) *stdd s: hld up wl off the pce in last pair: clsd on ldrs and swtchd rt wl over 1f out: chsd ldr 1f out: drvn and r.o wl to ld nr fin* **5/1**[3]

0141 **2** hd **Seneschal**[42] 4296 9-8-8 **78** LucyBarry[(7)] 4 85
(M Appleby) *hld up wl off the pce in last trio: clsd on ldrs 2f out: pushed into ld 1f out: kpt on under hands and heels tl hdd and no ex nr fin* **10/1**

0514 **3** 4 ½ **Billy Red**[5] 5528 6-9-0 **77** (b) FergusSweeney 2 70
(J R Jenkins) *led and sn clr w rival: rdn wl over 1f out: hdd 1f out: wknd fnl 150yds* **7/2**[2]

3214 **4** ¾ **Tyfos**[12] 5290 5-9-7 **84** TomMcLaughlin 5 74
(B P J Baugh) *sn clr w ldr: rdn wl over 1f out: btn whn n.m.r jst ins fnl f: wknd fnl 150yds* **6/4**[1]

0516 **5** 5 **Universal Circus**[9] 5388 3-8-11 **76** ChrisCatlin 1 50
(M R Channon) *taken down early: s.i.s: a outpcd in rr* **11/1**

0204 **6** ½ **The Strig**[20] 5048 3-8-10 **75** NeilCallan 3 48
(S C Williams) *stdd s: chsd clr ldng pair: rdn ent fnl 2f: clsd 2f out: drvn and wknd over 1f out* **5/1**[3]

1m 10.14s (0.74) **Going Correction** +0.025s/f (Good)
WFA 3 from 5yo+ 2lb **6** Ran SP% **113.0**
Speed ratings (Par 105): **96,95,89,88,82 81**
toteswingers: 1&2 £6.10, 1&3 £3.20, 2&3 £5.00 CSF £50.04 TOTE £8.50: £4.00, £4.80; EX 65.90.
Owner Dr Marwan Koukash **Bred** Mrs Anne Marie Burns **Trained** Musley Bank, N Yorks

FOCUS
With more than one front-runner in the race this always threatened to be run at a strong pace, and it was set up for closers. The winner ran to this year's best.

5679 J20 WHITE BLEND SUMMER SERIES H'CAP 1m 4f 10y

4:35 (4:36) (Class 5) (0-75,81) 3-Y-O+ **£3,885** (£1,156; £577; £288) **Stalls** Centre

Form RPR

0-31 **1** **Baralaka**[9] 5380 3-10-0 **81** 6ex SebSanders 10 95+
(Sir Mark Prescott) *stdd after s: hld up towards rr: hdwy to chse ldrs 4f out: rdn to ld over 2f out: clr fnl 2f: styd on wl ins fnl f: rdn out* **11/4**[1]

0442 **2** 1 ¾ **Barliffey (IRE)**[27] 4794 5-9-10 **68** TomQueally 4 75
(D J Coakley) *s.i.s: hld up in rr: rdn and hdwy whn n.m.r jst over 2f out: chsd ldng pair over 1f out: chsd wnr ins fnl f: kpt on but nvr gng to rch wnr* **16/1**

6040 **3** 2 **Aalya (IRE)**[62] 3626 3-8-2 **60** KierenFox[(5)] 1 66+
(P W Chapple-Hyam) *hld up wl in tch: nt clr run and shuffled bk to rr 4f out: rdn and hdwy on inner over 1f out: styd on wl ins fnl f to go 3rd towards fin: nt rch ldng pair* **33/1**

0-03 **4** ½ **Green Wadi**[10] 5375 5-9-13 **71** GeorgeBaker 8 74
(G L Moore) *stdd s: hld up in last trio: hdwy gng wl 4f out: chsd clr ldr and rdn ent fnl 2f: kpt on same pce and no imp after: lost 2 pls ins fnl f* **6/1**[3]

4110 **5** 2 ¼ **Shy**[21] 5008 5-9-7 **68** JamesMillman[(3)] 3 68
(B R Millman) *chsd ldr for 1f: sn dropped to rr: rdn and effrt on outer whn bmpd 2f out: styd on same pce fr over 1f out* **14/1**

6024 **6** 1 ¼ **Brigadoon**[13] 5266 3-9-0 **67** AlanMunro 6 65
(W Jarvis) *t.k.h: hld up in tch on outer: hdwy to chse ldrs over 3f out: rdn and unable qck over 2f out: no prog and wl hld fr over 1f out* **10/3**[2]

-063 **7** 1 **King Supreme (IRE)**[12] 5286 5-10-0 **72** PatDobbs 5 68
(R Hannon) *chsd ldng pair tl 3f out: sn struggling u.p: no ch w ldrs fr over 1f out* **9/1**

2164 **8** hd **Dream Spinner**[36] 4493 3-9-4 **71** EddieAhern 9 67
(J L Dunlop) *led tl hdd and rdn over 2f out: wknd over 1f out* **6/1**[3]

2326 **9** 4 ½ **Outland (IRE)**[29] 4719 4-9-3 **61** FergusSweeney 7 49
(J R Jenkins) *s.i.s: t.k.h: sn in tch: rdn and unable qck whn n.m.r over 2f out: bhd fnl 2f* **10/1**

4-30 **10** 97 **Dishdasha (IRE)**[23] 4399 8-9-11 **69** (t) NeilCallan 2 —
(Mrs A M Thorpe) *s.i.s: t.k.h and chsd ldr after 1f tl 5f out: sn lost pl u.p: lost tch and virtually p.u fnl 3f: wl t.o* **18/1**

2m 40.79s (1.89) **Going Correction** +0.025s/f (Good)
WFA 3 from 4yo+ 9lb **10** Ran SP% **118.2**
Speed ratings (Par 103): **94,92,91,91,89 88,88,88,85,20**
toteswingers:1&2:£6.70, 1&3:£16.60, 2&3:£37.50 CSF £49.66 CT £1209.92 TOTE £3.30: £1.10, £4.80, £10.40; EX 38.50 TRIFECTA Not won..
Owner Mrs S L Warman **Bred** Watership Down Stud **Trained** Newmarket, Suffolk

FOCUS
An ordinary handicap which was sound run. The winner is improving quickly.
Dishdasha(IRE) Official explanation: jockey said gelding moved poorly in the straight

5680 REIGATE APPRENTICE H'CAP 1m 2f 18y

5:10 (5:11) (Class 5) (0-75,75) 3-Y-O+ **£3,238** (£963; £481; £240) **Stalls** Low

Form RPR

6336 **1** **Potentiale (IRE)**[14] 5235 6-9-6 **72** (p) HollyHall[(5)] 3 80+
(J W Hills) *stdd s: hld up in last: hdwy over 2f out: nt clr run and swtchd rt 2f out: pushed into ld over 1f out: in command ins fnl f: eased nr fin* **9/2**[2]

2154 **2** ½ **Diamond Twister (USA)**[7] 5457 4-9-3 **64** KierenFox 4 71
(J R Best) *led: rdn 3f out: hdd over 1f out: rallied gamely ins fnl f: a hld* **9/2**[2]

6232 **3** 2 ½ **The Hague**[16] 5172 4-9-6 **70** (v) AntiocoMurgia[(3)] 6 72
(P D Evans) *hld up in tch: hdwy on outer to chse ldr 5f out: rdn to press ldr 2f out tl over 1f out: no ex and btn fnl f* **15/8**[1]

046 **4** 1 ½ **Marsh Warbler**[21] 5003 3-9-7 **75** TobyAtkinson 5 74
(D M Simcock) *hld up in tch: hmpd and lost pl 6f out: sn pushed along: swtchd lft and rallied u.p ent fnl 2f: no prog and one pce ent fnl f* **11/2**[3]

6013 **5** 2 ¾ **Blue Tango (IRE)**[29] 4694 4-9-12 **73** (v) SimonPearce 7 67
(Mrs A J Perrett) *dwlt: t.k.h: chsd ldrs: wnt 2nd 7f out tl ent fnl 2f: wknd u.p jst over 1f out* **7/1**

4530 **6** 3 **Zero Cool (USA)**[17] 5146 6-9-2 **68** (p) HarryBentley[(5)] 2 56
(G L Moore) *chsd ldrs: rdn and outpcd over 3f out: drvn and btn 2f out* **9/1**

-004 **7** 28 **Kings On The Roof**[4] 5565 4-8-7 **59** oh14 NoelGarbutt[(5)] 1 —
(P Leech) *chsd ldr tl 7f out: styd chsng ldrs tl rdn and struggling 3f out: wl btn over 1f out: eased ins fnl f* **50/1**

2m 11.5s (1.80) **Going Correction** +0.025s/f (Good)
WFA 3 from 4yo+ 7lb **7** Ran SP% **111.0**
Speed ratings (Par 103): **93,92,90,89,87 84,62**
toteswingers:1&2:£3.30, 1&3:£3.00, 2&3:£1.80 CSF £23.34 TOTE £6.80: £3.90, £2.10; EX 21.60 Place 6 £88.20; Place 5 £54.02.
Owner Tony Waspe Partnership & Luke Tofts **Bred** Copperhead Stable **Trained** Upper Lambourn, Berks

■ Stewards' Enquiry : Kieren Fox two-day ban: used whip with excessive frequency (16 -17 sep)

FOCUS
An ordinary handicap. The runner-up is a fair guide and the winner can probably do a bit better.
T/Plt: £135.50 to a £1 stake. Pool:£60,928.35 - 328.19 winning tickets T/Qpdt: £72.90 to a £1 stake. Pool:£4,178.56 - 42.40 winning tickets SP

5530 REDCAR (L-H)

Thursday, September 2

OFFICIAL GOING: Good to firm (firm in places; watered)
Wind: Virtually nil Weather: Fine and dry

5681 WIN A VIP DAY OUT @ REDCARRACING.CO.UK H'CAP (DIV I) 1m 6f 19y

1:30 (1:30) (Class 6) (0-65,65) 3-Y-O+ **£1,364** (£403; £201) **Stalls** Low

Form RPR

0364 **1** **Bollin Judith**[31] 4656 4-9-12 **63** (t) DavidAllan 10 74+
(T D Easterby) *trckd ldrs: hdwy over 3f out: swtchd rt and effrt to ld 2f out: rdn clr and edgd lft appr fnl f: styd on strly* **11/4**[1]

0060 **2** 3 **Finellas Fortune**[33] 4604 5-9-5 **56** PJMcDonald 2 61
(G M Moore) *hld up in rr: swtchd wd and hdwy over 2f out: rdn wl over 1f out: drvn and edgd lft ins fnl f: tk 2nd nr fin* **22/1**

6044 **3** ½ **Extremely So**[28] 4765 4-8-10 **52** AdamBeschizza[(5)] 12 56
(P J McBride) *hld up towards rr: hdwy on outer 3f out: rdn to chse ldrs 2f out: drvn and hld on to chse wnr ent fnl f: sn one pce and lost 2nd nr fin* **6/1**[3]

2531 **4** 1 **Master Nimbus**[22] 4945 10-9-8 **64** (t) IanBrennan[(5)] 6 67
(J J Quinn) *trckd ldng pair: hdwy over 3f out: swtchd rt and cl up over 2f out: sn rdn and ev ch tl drvn over 1f out and sn one pce* **11/2**[2]

0032 **5** 1 **Harcas (IRE)**[9] 4825 8-8-12 **49** (b) PhillipMakin 4 50
(M Todhunter) *trckd ldrs: rdn along and outpcd wl over 2f out: kpt on u.p ins fnl f* **8/1**

1350 **6** nk **Amir Pasha (UAE)**[2] 5642 5-9-7 **65** (p) AdamCarter[(7)] 1 66
(Micky Hammond) *trckd ldrs: hdwy over 3f out: cl up 2f out: sn rdn and ev ch tl drvn and one pce appr fnl f* **11/2**[2]

6645 **7** ¾ **Maybeme**[22] 4946 4-9-5 **56** DanielTudhope 3 56
(N Bycroft) *chsd ldng pair: pushed along over 3f out: rdn along 2f out: sn drvn and grad wknd* **8/1**

0000 **8** 6 **Power Desert (IRE)**[2] 5642 5-8-9 **46** oh1 (v) SilvestreDeSousa 8 39
(G A Harker) *trckd ldrs: hdwy to chse ldr after 4f: rdn along over 4f out: led over 3f out: drvn and hdd 2f out: sn wknd* **12/1**

4016 **9** 1 ¼ **Media Stars**[15] 5202 5-8-13 **55** (t) LeeTopliss[(5)] 5 45
(R Johnson) *hld up in rr: hdwy 3f out: rdn along 2f out: sn drvn and wknd* **50/1**

4006 **10** 11 **Without Equal**[21] 4980 4-8-9 **46** oh1 (p) PaulMulrennan 11 20
(N Wilson) *led: rdn along wl over 4f out: hdd over 3f out and sn wknd* **40/1**

6-00 **11** 20 **Shanavaz**[10] 5364 4-8-9 **46** (p) PatrickMathers 7 —
(C J Teague) *a in rr: bhd fnl 3f* **66/1**

3m 4.81s (0.11) **Going Correction** +0.05s/f (Good) **11** Ran SP% **111.9**
Speed ratings (Par 101): **101,99,99,98,97 97,97,93,93,86 75**
toteswingers:1&2:£17.70, 1&3:£4.20, 2&3:£25.40 CSF £68.34 CT £330.90 TOTE £3.60: £1.50, £8.10, £2.70; EX 106.10.
Owner Sir Neil Westbrook **Bred** Sir Neil & Exors Of Late Lady Westbrook **Trained** Great Habton, N Yorks

■ Stewards' Enquiry : David Allan caution: careless riding

FOCUS
A modest handicap run slightly quicker than division II. The form looks sound enough.

5682 BUY YOUR TICKETS ON-LINE @ REDCARRACING.CO.UK NURSERY 7f
2:00 (2:00) (Class 5) (0-75,74) 2-Y-O £2,072 (£616; £308; £153) Stalls High

Form RPR

0323 **1** **Regal Kiss**[26] 4821 2-9-6 **73** JoeFanning 6 76+
(M Johnston) *trckd ldrs: hdwy and cl up 1/2-way: led 2f out: rdn over 1f out: drvn ins fnl f and kpt on wl* **7/2**[2]

5020 **2** 3/4 **Bradbury (IRE)**[24] 4899 2-8-13 **66** (b[1]) GrahamGibbons 4 67
(J D Bethell) *in tch: hdwy to trck ldrs 1/2-way: effrt 2f out: sn rdn: drvn and kpt on ins fnl f: tk 2nd nr line* **22/1**

043 **3** nk **Eyes On**[17] 5160 2-8-6 **64** AdamBeschizza(5) 1 64
(P J McBride) *dwlt and hld up in rr: hdwy on outer 1/2-way: chsd ldrs 2f out: rdn to chal over 1f out: drvn and ev ch ins fnl f: no ex last 100yds: lost 2nd nr line* **10/1**

3432 **4** 3 1/2 **Malpas Missile (IRE)**[7] 5452 2-9-2 **74** RossAtkinson(5) 7 65
(Tom Dascombe) *cl up: led after 1 1/2f: rdn along and hdd 2f out: sn drvn and wknd 1f out* **15/8**[1]

2333 **5** 1 1/2 **Alhoni**[20] 5020 2-8-3 **56** (b) SilvestreDeSousa 9 43
(J J Quinn) *trckd ldrs: effrt over 2f out and sn rdn: drvn over 1f out and no imp* **11/2**[3]

5060 **6** 1 1/4 **Microlight**[7] 5434 2-8-9 **62** DavidAllan 3 46
(T D Easterby) *cl up: rdn along wl over 2f out: sn edgd lft and grad wknd* **50/1**

003 **7** nk **Better Self**[30] 4668 2-9-2 **69** PaulMulrennan 10 52
(Mrs A Duffield) *inb tch: rdn along 1/2-way: sn drvn and wknd fnl 2f* **14/1**

035 **8** 3 1/2 **Mossgorda (IRE)**[12] 5298 2-8-11 **64** AndrewElliott 5 38
(Mrs K Burke) *towards rr: rdn along 3f out: nvr a factor* **7/1**

000 **9** 2 **Mayan Flight (IRE)**[19] 5092 2-8-3 **56** PaulQuinn 2 25
(R M Whitaker) *a in rr* **28/1**

045 **10** 4 **Bernisdale**[25] 4862 2-8-10 **63** PJMcDonald 8 22
(G M Moore) *led 1 1/2f: cl up: rdn along 1/2-way: sn wknd* **25/1**

1m 25.0s (0.50) **Going Correction** -0.125s/f (Firm) 10 Ran SP% **114.3**
Speed ratings (Par 95): **92,91,90,86,85 83,83,79,77,72**
toteswingers:1&2:£10.70, 1&3:£7.10, 2&3:£4.90 CSF £80.21 CT £720.91 TOTE £5.70: £1.10, £6.00, £4.00; EX 39.20.
Owner Mrs R J Jacobs **Bred** Newsells Park Stud **Trained** Middleham Moor, N Yorks

FOCUS
This was a moderate nursery, run at an average pace and the first three, all handicap newcomers, came clear. The winner could have more to offer.

NOTEBOOK
Regal Kiss opened her account at the fifth time of asking on this first outing outside of maiden company and completed the task readily. She was never that far away and, finding plenty when asked to win the race, had something left in the tank passing the post. She is improving with racing, will get further down the line and could well follow up. (op 4-1)
Bradbury(IRE) returned to form for the fitting of first-time blinkers and finished his race with purpose. He has begun life in this sphere on a workable mark and would appreciate a stiffer test, but it remains to be seen if the headgear continues to hold a positive effect. (op 18-1)
Eyes On ◆ proved surprisingly easy to back on this nursery debut. She hit top gear nearing the final furlong and had every chance, but was eventually outstayed by the first pair. Dropping back to a stiff 6f can see her win a race. (op 14-1)
Malpas Missile(IRE), due to race off a 4lb higher future mark, was always on the front end and had her chance. She probably wants holding onto for longer over this far and is consistent, but is now winless after eight outings. (op 13-8 tchd 6-4)
Alhoni was well backed in this better company, but she was made to look very one-paced. (op 6-1 tchd 13-2)

5683 RACING UK ON CHANNEL 432 MAIDEN AUCTION STKS 5f
2:30 (2:30) (Class 6) 2-Y-O £1,706 (£503; £252) Stalls High

Form RPR

3340 **1** **Heartbreak**[22] 4941 2-8-13 72 PaulMulrennan 2 74
(R A Fahey) *mde most: rdn over 1f out: edgd lft and hdd briefly ins fnl f: drvn and rallied to ld last 75yds* **15/8**[2]

3 **2** 1/2 **Insolenceofoffice (IRE)**[100] 2420 2-8-12 0 MatthewDavies(3) 3 74
(Mrs A Duffield) *dwlt: sn chsng wnr: hdwy 1/2-way: rdn along 2f out: drvn over 1f out: led briefly ins fnl f: hdd and no ex last 75yds* **10/11**[1]

2303 **3** 9 **Saltergate**[14] 5239 2-8-9 68 (v[1]) SilvestreDeSousa 4 40
(N Tinkler) *cl up: swtchd lft and rdn along after 110yds: drvn 1/2-way and sn outpcd* **4/1**[3]

59.53 secs (0.93) **Going Correction** -0.125s/f (Firm) 3 Ran SP% **107.2**
Speed ratings (Par 93): **87,86,71**
CSF £3.97 TOTE £2.60; EX 3.40.
Owner T G & Mrs M E Holdcroft **Bred** Bearstone Stud **Trained** Musley Bank, N Yorks
■ Stewards' Enquiry : Matthew Davies two-day ban: used whip with excessive frequency (16-17 sep)

FOCUS
A moderate little juvenile maiden run in a slow time. The winner is rated to his Wolverhampton level.

NOTEBOOK
Heartbreak showed his previous flop at Beverley to be wrong and gamely shed his maiden tag at the fifth attempt. He raced more towards the centre of the track and, despite looking vulnerable at the furlong marker, was always holding the runner-up in the closing stages. An official mark of 72 probably flatters him at this stage so things will now be tougher, but he could find some improvement over a stiffer test as he matures. (op 5-2 tchd 7-4)
Insolenceofoffice(IRE) was last seen finishing third on debut 100 days earlier and was a big market mover on this belated return. He lacked the natural pace of the winner, to whom he was conceding 2lb, but still posted an improved effort and should come on for the run. (op 8-13 tchd evens in a place)
Saltergate looked most unwilling in a first-time visor (replacing cheekpieces) and he is one to swerve. (op 11-2 tchd 7-2)

5684 WEDDING RECEPTIONS @ REDCAR RACECOURSE H'CAP 6f
3:05 (3:06) (Class 5) (0-75,75) 3-Y-O+ £2,072 (£616; £308; £153) Stalls High

Form RPR

6015 **1** **Who's Shirl**[15] 5199 4-8-13 **70** KellyHarrison(3) 1 85
(C W Fairhurst) *trckd ldrs: hdwy on wd outside 1/2-way: led wl over 1f out: rdn clr whn edgd lft ent fnl f: kpt on wl* **10/1**

0000 **2** 3 **Wyatt Earp (IRE)**[30] 4670 9-9-4 **72** (p) GregFairley 4 77
(P Salmon) *trckd ldrs: hdwy over 2f out: rdn to chse wnr over 1f out: drvn and no imp fnl f* **16/1**

3240 **3** 3 **Sir Nod**[15] 5198 8-9-7 **75** TomEaves 3 71
(Julie Camacho) *led: rdn along 2f out: hdd wl over 1f out: drvn and kpt on same pce ent fnl f* **9/1**

4220 **4** hd **Micky Mac (IRE)**[6] 5502 6-8-6 **67** ow1 DaleSwift(5) 6 62
(C J Teague) *cl up: rdn along and sltly outpcd 2f out: kpt on u.p fnl f* **18/1**

0452 **5** 1/2 **Rowayton**[10] 5356 4-9-7 **75** PhillipMakin 8 69
(J D Bethell) *trckd ldrs: hdwy over 2f out: rdn along wl over 1f out: drvn and no imp appr fnl f* **5/2**[1]

3263 **6** 1/2 **Minturno (USA)**[12] 5299 4-8-8 **62** (p) PaulMulrennan 5 54
(Mrs A Duffield) *towards rr: hdwy 1/2-way: rdn to chse ldrs wl over 1f out: drvn and wknd ent fnl f* **5/1**[3]

0263 **7** 2 1/4 **Mandalay King (IRE)**[6] 5480 5-8-11 **68** RobertLButler(3) 7 53
(Mrs Marjorie Fife) *dwlt and in rr: hdwy wl over 2f out: rdn wl over 1f out: sn drvn and no imp* **9/2**[2]

0256 **8** 7 **Just Sam (IRE)**[8] 5424 5-8-11 **68** BarryMcHugh(3) 9 30
(R E Barr) *cl up on outer: rdn along wl over 2f out: sn wknd* **9/2**[2]

1m 10.9s (-0.90) **Going Correction** -0.125s/f (Firm) 8 Ran SP% **111.8**
Speed ratings (Par 103): **101,97,93,92,92 91,88,79**
toteswingers:1&2:£15.90, 1&3:£14.80, 2&3:£9.60 CSF £144.36 CT £1028.63 TOTE £13.50: £4.00, £2.80, £2.80; EX 70.00.
Owner Mrs Shirley France **Bred** Mrs S France **Trained** Middleham Moor, N Yorks

FOCUS
An ordinary sprint handicap. All of the runners were under pressure 2f out and those racing more towards the far side filled the places. Probably not form to take too positively.

5685 JOHN SMITH'S REDCAR STRAIGHT-MILE CHAMPIONSHIP (QUALIFIER) (H'CAP) 1m
3:40 (3:40) (Class 4) (0-85,84) 3-Y-O+ £3,626 (£1,079; £539; £269) Stalls Low

Form RPR

2120 **1** **Soviet Secret**[33] 4593 3-8-13 **83** AdamBeschizza(5) 4 94
(P J McBride) *cl up: effrt 2f out: rdn to ld over 1f out: drvn and edgd rt ins fnl f: kpt on wl* **9/2**[2]

200 **2** 1 1/4 **Reel Buddy Star**[3] 5605 5-9-10 **84** PJMcDonald 1 93
(G M Moore) *cl up: effrt 2f out: sn rdn and ev ch tl drvn ins fnl f and no ex last 100yds* **7/2**[1]

2262 **3** 3/4 **Fishforcompliments**[6] 5480 6-9-1 **78** BarryMcHugh(3) 2 85
(R A Fahey) *dwlt and reminders s: sn led: rdn along over 2f out: hdd wl over 1f out: drvn and kpt on fnl f* **7/2**[1]

1-20 **4** nk **Right Grand**[28] 4750 3-9-1 **80** JoeFanning 7 86
(W J Haggas) *hld up: effrt 3f out and sn pushed along rdn to chse ldrs 2f out: drvn and edgd lft ent fnl f: one pce* **5/1**[3]

5121 **5** 3/4 **Shadowtime**[37] 4450 5-9-9 **83** RobertWinston 5 88
(Miss Tracy Waggott) *trckd ldrs: swtchd lft and hdwy 3f out: rdn to chal 2f out and ev ch tl drvn over 1f out and grad wknd* **9/2**[2]

0442 **6** 1 1/2 **Whispered Times (USA)**[6] 5484 3-8-8 **73** (p) PaulMulrennan 3 73
(Miss Tracy Waggott) *trckd ldrs: effrt over 2f out and sn rdn along: drvn and wknd over 1f out* **12/1**

5045 **7** 1 3/4 **Just Bond (IRE)**[65] 3537 8-9-3 **82** IanBrennan(5) 6 79
(G R Oldroyd) *hld up in rr: pushed along 3f out: rdn and one pce fnl 2f* **20/1**

15-0 **8** 28 **In Footlights (USA)**[91] 2683 4-9-10 **84** DaraghO'Donohoe 8 17
(Saeed Bin Suroor) *hld up in rr: pushed along 1/2-way: sn rdn and bhd fnl 3f* **18/1**

1m 35.93s (-2.07) **Going Correction** -0.125s/f (Firm)
WFA 3 from 4yo+ 5lb 8 Ran SP% **115.2**
Speed ratings (Par 105): **105,103,103,102,101 100,98,70**
toteswingers:1&2:£4.30, 1&3:£6.60, 2&3:£3.00 CSF £20.82 CT £60.89 TOTE £10.00: £3.40, £1.10, £2.50; EX 27.70.
Owner PMRacing **Bred** Miss D Fleming **Trained** Newmarket, Suffolk

FOCUS
A fair handicap and good form for the grade.
In Footlights(USA) Official explanation: jockey said colt never travelled

5686 SUBSCRIBE TO RACING UK MAIDEN STKS 6f
4:15 (4:16) (Class 5) 3-Y-O+ £2,072 (£616; £308; £153) Stalls High

Form RPR

500 **1** **Kate Skate**[31] 4651 3-8-7 53 AdamBeschizza(5) 6 60
(Miss Gay Kelleway) *a cl up: chal over 2f out: rdn to ld wl over 1f out: edgd lft ins fnl f: rdn out* **12/1**

3340 **2** 2 1/2 **Uddy Mac**[15] 5201 3-8-9 56 KellyHarrison(3) 3 52
(N Bycroft) *trckd ldrs: hdwy on outer 1/2-way: rdn to chal wl over 1f out: drvn to chse wnr ins fnl f: no imp towards fin* **4/1**[2]

5000 **3** 1 **Romancea (USA)**[29] 4705 3-8-12 65 (v[1]) JoeFanning 1 49
(E F Vaughan) *a.p: cl up 1/2-way: rdn to chal 2f out and ev ch tl drvn and one pce ent fnl f* **6/1**[3]

5-4 **4** nk **Tsar Bomba (USA)**[19] 5065 3-8-12 0 DeanHeslop(5) 8 53
(T D Barron) *chsd ldrs: hdwy wl over 2f out: rdn wl over 1f out: drvn and no imp ent fnl f* **2/1**[1]

5 **5** 5 **Miss Blink**[19] 5065 3-8-12 0 SilvestreDeSousa 5 32
(R Bastiman) *towards rr: pushed along 1/2-way: rdn over 2f out: kpt on appr fnl f: n.d* **11/1**

003 **6** 1 1/2 **Premier Contender (IRE)**[8] 5419 3-9-3 0 AdrianNicholls 2 32
(D Nicholls) *led: rdn along over 2f out: hdd wl over 1f out and sn wknd* **6/1**[3]

34-3 **7** nk **Benny The Bear**[15] 5214 3-9-3 58 PJMcDonald 4 31
(James Moffatt) *a towards rr* **8/1**

0050 **8** 9 **One Cat Diesel (IRE)**[20] 5045 3-9-3 45 PatrickMathers 9 2
(H A McWilliams) *a in rr* **66/1**

54 **9** 9 **Sonia Girl (IRE)**[17] 5153 3-8-6 0 ow1 BarryAdams(7) 7 —
(Patrick Morris) *dwlt: a in rr* **50/1**

1m 12.02s (0.22) **Going Correction** -0.125s/f (Firm) 9 Ran SP% **112.5**
Speed ratings (Par 103): **93,89,88,87,81 79,78,66,54**
toteswingers: 1&2 £8.30, 1&3 £10.80, 2&3 £5.00 CSF £57.76 TOTE £18.70: £4.30, £2.30, £1.50; EX 59.90.
Owner Nightmare Partnership **Bred** R A Instone **Trained** Exning, Suffolk

FOCUS
A very weak maiden and the form isn't solid.
Premier Contender(IRE) Official explanation: jockey said the gelding hung left handed
Sonia Girl(IRE) Official explanation: jockey said the filly missed the break

5687 WIN A VIP DAY OUT @ REDCARRACING.CO.UK H'CAP (DIV II) 1m 6f 19y
4:50 (4:50) (Class 6) (0-65,64) 3-Y-O+ £1,364 (£403; £201) Stalls Low

Form RPR

211 **1** **Andorn (GER)**[8] 5420 6-9-11 **64** 6ex RussKennemore(3) 8 74+
(P A Kirby) *prom: hdwy to chse ldr 4f out: rdn to chal 2f out: drvn over 1f out: styd on to ld ins fnl f* **5/1**[3]

2622 **2** 1 1/4 **Zefooha (FR)**[8] 5420 6-9-9 **59** (p) GrahamGibbons 9 67
(T D Walford) *led: pushed along and qcknd over 3f out: rdn and jnd 2f out: drvn over 1f out: hdd and no ex ins fnl f* **9/2**[2]

The Form Book, Raceform Ltd, Compton, RG20 6NL

1314 **3** *5* **Simple Jim (FR)**[19] 5070 6-10-0 **64**.......................... SilvestreDeSousa 7 65+
(D O'Meara) *hld up in midfield: hdwy 3f out: rdn wl over 1f out: drvn and kpt on same pce* **11/4**[1]

-663 **4** *½* **Pobs Trophy**[5] 5534 3-7-5 **45**..........................(p) NeilFarley(7) 3 45+
(R C Guest) *hld up in rr: hdwy on wd outside 3f out: rdn 2f out: kpt on appr fnl f: nrst fin* **8/1**

5034 **5** *hd* **Heart Of Dubai (USA)**[15] 5203 5-8-9 **45**..........................(p) TomEaves 1 45
(Micky Hammond) *hld up: hdwy over 3f out: rdn to chse ldrs 2f out: sn drvn and one pce* **16/1**

2402 **6** *½* **Winged Farasi**[9] 5203 6-9-1 **56**.................. GemmaGracey-Davison(5) 6 55
(Miss J E Foster) *in tch: effrt over 3f out and sn pushed along: rdn 2f out and sn one pce* **16/1**

0402 **7** *2* **Mymateeric**[28] 4765 4-9-0 **50**.......................... RobertWinston 12 47
(J Pearce) *trckd ldrs: hdwy 4f out: rdn to chse ldng pair 2f out: drvn and wknd 1f out* **12/1**

3063 **8** *shd* **Knock Three Times (IRE)**[15] 5202 4-8-6 **45**..........(t) JamesSullivan(3) 5 41
(W Storey) *hld up: sme hdwy over 4f out: rdn along 3f out: n.d* **25/1**

4355 **9** *¾* **Dechiper (IRE)**[15] 5203 8-8-6 **47** ow1..........................(t) LeeTopliss(5) 2 42
(R Johnson) *reminders sn after s: towards rr: effrt and sme hdwy 3f out: rdn over 2f out and n.d* **22/1**

536- **10** *19* **Fossgate**[345] 6183 9-9-5 **55**.......................... PJMcDonald 11 24
(J D Bethell) *chsd ldr: rdn along over 4f out: drvn 3f out and sn wknd* **40/1**

06/0 **11** *30* **Noble Edge**[130] 791 7-8-9 **45**..........................(t) AndrewElliott 10 —
(L R James) *chsd ldrs: rdn along on inner over 3f out: sn wknd* **100/1**

0521 **12** *7* **Miss Ferney**[11] 5336 6-9-3 **56** 6ex.......................... PaulPickard(3) 4 —
(A Kirtley) *hld up towards rr: effrt and sme hdwy 3f out: rdn and lost pl over 2f out: bhd and eased fnl f: virtually p.u nr fin* **7/1**

3m 5.76s (1.06) **Going Correction** -0.125s/f (Firm)
WFA 3 from 4yo+ 11lb 12 Ran SP% **116.2**
Speed ratings (Par 101): **98,97,94,94,94 93,92,92,92,81 64,60**
toteswingers: 1&2 £5.90, 2&3 £3.40, 1&3 £4.10 CSF £26.24 CT £74.20 TOTE £3.40: £1.40, £2.10, £1.10; EX 22.50.
Owner Preesall Garage **Bred** Gestut Schlenderhan **Trained** Castleton, N Yorks

FOCUS
The second division of the staying handicap was more competitive than the first. In contrast to the opening race, though, it paid to be handy the two pace-setters dominated. The form is rated around the runner-up.
Miss Ferney Official explanation: vet said mare finished lame

5688 FOLLOW REDCAR RACING ON FACEBOOK APPRENTICE H'CAP 7f
5:20 (5:21) (Class 5) (0-70,64) 3-Y-O+ **£2,072** (£616; £308; £153) **Stalls** High

Form RPR

0304 **1** **Piquante**[19] 5064 4-9-10 **64**.......................... Louis-PhilippeBeuzelin 9 71
(N Tinkler) *hld up in rr: hdwy over 2f out: rdn to chse ldrs over 1f out: drvn ins fnl f: styd on to ld last stride* **8/1**[3]

4366 **2** *shd* **Powerful Pierre**[19] 5067 3-9-2 **63**.......................... MichaelO'Connell(3) 7 68
(Jedd O'Keeffe) *chsd ldrs: hdwy 3f out: cl up 2f out: drvn to ld ins fnl f: hdd and no ex last stride* **12/1**

5645 **3** *2 ½* **Klynch**[12] 5299 4-9-7 **61**..........................(b) JamesSullivan 8 61
(Mrs R A Carr) *trckd ldng pair: hdwy 3f out: cl up wl over 1f out: sn rdn and ev ch tl drvn and one pce ins fnl f* **25/1**

0340 **4** *hd* **Final Salute**[10] 5357 4-8-11 **56**..........................(v) AdamCarter(5) 1 56
(B Smart) *cl up: led after 3f: rdn along and jnd 2f out: hrd pressed and drvn over 1f out: hdd & wknd ins fnl f* **10/1**

2206 **5** *4* **Mister Jingles**[57] 3775 7-9-4 **58**..........................(v) AmyRyan 3 47
(R M Whitaker) *chsd ldrs: rdn along over 2f out: kpt on same pce* **9/1**

4603 **6** *½* **Sairaam (IRE)**[19] 5064 4-9-4 **63**.......................... AdamBeschizza(5) 4 51
(C Smith) *hld up towards rr: hdwy 3f out: rdn to chse ldrs 2f out: drvn wl over 1f out and sn btn* **3/1**[1]

143 **7** *1 ¾* **Desert Hunter (IRE)**[2] 5641 7-9-3 **60**.......................... PatrickDonaghy(3) 6 43
(Micky Hammond) *dwlt: a in rr* **3/1**[1]

1503 **8** *6* **Nuit Sombre (IRE)**[20] 5024 10-8-13 **60**..........................(p) KaseyLoftus(7) 5 27
(G A Harker) *hld up in tch: hdwy to chse ldrs 1/2-way: rdn along 3f out and sn wknd* **12/1**

5415 **9** *nk* **Sea Salt**[6] 5500 7-9-5 **62**.......................... LanceBetts(3) 2 28
(R E Barr) *set str pce: hdd after 3f and cl up tl rdn along wl over 2f out and sn wknd* **6/1**[2]

1m 24.53s (0.03) **Going Correction** -0.125s/f (Firm)
WFA 3 from 4yo+ 4lb 9 Ran SP% **113.7**
Speed ratings (Par 103): **94,93,91,90,86 85,83,76,76**
toteswingers:1&2:£11.70, 1&3:£12.60, 2&3:£13.30 CSF £96.78 CT £1522.06 TOTE £9.60: £2.30, £5.30, £6.00; EX 112.30 Place 6 £540.76; Place 5 £237.71.
Owner W F Burton **Bred** Aston House Stud **Trained** Langton, N Yorks
■ Stewards' Enquiry : James Sullivan one-day ban: failed to keep straight from draw (Sept 16)
Michael O'Connell two-day ban: careless riding (Sept 16-17) one-day ban: failed to ride to draw (Sept 18)

FOCUS
A typically moderate handicap for apprentice riders. The top weight was rated 6lb below the race ceiling and it was run at a strong early pace. The form is rated at face value.
T/Plt: £896.90 to a £1 stake. Pool:£47,614.60 - 38.75 winning tickets T/Qpdt: £151.00 to a £1 stake. Pool:£4,256.48 - 20.85 winning tickets JR

5254 SALISBURY (R-H)
Thursday, September 2

OFFICIAL GOING: Good to firm (watered; 8.7)
Wind: mild breeze against Weather: dry and sunny

5689 AXMINSTER CARPETS RACING EXCELLENCE APPRENTICE H'CAP (WHIPS SHALL BE CARRIED BUT NOT USED) 1m
1:40 (1:43) (Class 5) (60-92,68) 3-Y-O+ **£3,238** (£963; £481; £240) **Stalls** High

Form RPR

2234 **1** **Catchanova (IRE)**[21] 4994 3-8-7 **59**.......................... NathanAlison(3) 4 71
(Eve Johnson Houghton) *sn trcking ldrs: led 2f out: kpt on ins fnl f: pushed out* **7/1**[3]

5645 **2** *½* **Lutine Charlie (IRE)**[20] 5027 3-8-7 **61**..........................(p) MatthewCosham(5) 3 72
(J L Flint) *mid-div: hung rt and hdwy fr wl over 2f out: chsd wnr ent fnl f: kpt on* **14/1**

0326 **3** *3 ¼* **Gallego**[22] 4958 8-9-1 **62**.......................... JamesRogers(3) 9 66
(R J Price) *stdd s: hld up towards rr: stdy prog fr 2f out: wnt 3rd towards fin: nvr trbld ldng pair* **5/1**[2]

2155 **4** *½* **Strike A Deal (IRE)**[40] 4381 3-9-0 **68**.......................... RoryHanley(5) 10 70
(C F Wall) *lw: hld up towards rr: pushed along 3f out: edgd lft 2f out: kpt on fnl f: wnt 4th nr fin: nvr nrr* **12/1**

3056 **5** *1* **Flapper (IRE)**[26] 4847 4-9-10 **68**.......................... AmyScott 11 69
(J W Hills) *lw: led tl 2f out: kpt chsng wnr tl no ex ent fnl f* **11/4**[1]

0562 **6** *1* **Fly By Nelly**[21] 4987 4-8-13 **57**.......................... DavidKenny 5 56
(H Morrison) *lw: mid-div: hdwy to chal wl over 2f out: sn pushed along: wknd fnl f* **7/1**[3]

0000 **7** *1* **Transfer**[45] 4201 5-8-8 **55**..........................(v[1]) RichardRowe(3) 12 51
(C P Morlock) *t.k.h: trckd ldr: rdn over 2f out: wknd jst over 1f out* **11/1**

040- **8** *5* **Loden**[341] 6291 3-9-0 **68**.......................... TalibHussain(5) 8 52
(L M Cumani) *rrd leaving stalls: a towards rr* **9/1**

05/0 **9** *2 ½* **Raise Again (IRE)**[21] 4586 7-8-7 **45** oh9.......................... AlexEdwards(3) 1 33
(Mrs P N Dutfield) *mid-div tl dropped in rr over 3f out: nvr bk on terms* **66/1**

41-6 **10** *½* **Levitation (IRE)**[52] 3962 4-9-3 **66**.......................... JakePayne(5) 6 44
(W S Kittow) *trckd ldrs: rdn over 2f out: sn wknd* **16/1**

0040 **11** *3 ½* **Pictures (IRE)**[8] 5414 3-8-11 **60**.......................... RyanClark 7 29
(J J Bridger) *awkward leaving stalls: sn mid-div: effrt over 2f out: wknd over 1f out* **33/1**

2643 **12** *6* **Pastello**[25] 4870 3-9-3 **66**.......................... CharlesEddery 13 21
(R Hannon) *mid-div tl wknd 2f out* **17/2**

004 **P** **Into The Wind**[40] 4364 3-9-1 **64** ow4.......................... DebraEngland 2 —
(B R Millman) *a towards rr: lost action whn p.u 2f out* **25/1**

1m 41.34s (-2.16) **Going Correction** -0.35s/f (Firm)
WFA 3 from 4yo+ 5lb 13 Ran SP% **125.7**
Speed ratings (Par 103): **96,95,92,91,90 89,88,83,81,80 77,71,—**
toteswingers:1&2:£21.00, 1&3:£6.60, 2&3:£16.40 CSF £105.11 CT £563.20 TOTE £5.60: £2.20, £6.10, £1.90; EX 155.00.
Owner Andrew Wyer Darrell Blake Hugh Arthur **Bred** G J King **Trained** Blewbury, Oxon

FOCUS
A medium gallop gave everyone a chance but it wasn't lively enough to help those arriving from the rear to get there in time. Ordinary form, with a step forward from the winner.
Pictures(IRE) Official explanation: jockey said that the filly ran flat
Pastello Official explanation: jockey said that the filly ran flat
Into The Wind Official explanation: jockey said that the filly stumbled and felt wrong in front

5690 E B F WHITSBURY MANOR STUD NOVICE STKS 1m
2:10 (2:11) (Class 4) 2-Y-O **£4,533** (£1,348; £674; £336) **Stalls** High

Form RPR

01 **1** **Cai Shen (IRE)**[13] 5263 2-9-3 87.......................... RichardHughes 3 91
(R Hannon) *lw: trckd ldr: rdn to chal 2f out: sn drifted lft: led ins fnl f: kpt on wl: drifted rt towards fin* **7/4**[2]

5421 **2** *1 ¼* **Diamond Penny (IRE)**[20] 5047 2-9-0 89.......................... JamieSpencer 4 85
(P F I Cole) *lw: nudged along to ld: qcknd pce 3f out: sn rdn: hdd ins fnl f: no ex towards fin* **6/4**[1]

3 *1 ¼* **Zain Shamardal (IRE)** 2-8-12 0.......................... MartinDwyer 2 84+
(B J Meehan) *unf: scope : lw: s.i.s: trckd ldng pair: rdn over 2f out: nt pce to chal: kpt on ins fnl f* **4/1**[3]

4 *17* **Mantoba** 2-8-12 0.......................... FrankieDettori 5 43+
(B J Meehan) *str: lw: s.i.s: chsd ldng trio: nudged along 4f out: rdn to chal for 3rd 3f out: wknd over 1f out* **10/1**

1m 41.41s (-2.09) **Going Correction** -0.35s/f (Firm) 4 Ran SP% **105.5**
Speed ratings (Par 97): **96,94,93,76**
CSF £4.51 TOTE £3.00; EX 4.10.
Owner Mrs J Wood **Bred** Wardstown Stud Ltd **Trained** East Everleigh, Wilts

FOCUS
The pace was nothing special, but this looks strong novice form rated around the front pair.

NOTEBOOK
Cai Shen(IRE) took the step up to 1m in his stride and showed he does not have to make the running. Placing him will be a challenge from his likely new mark, but he has a good attitude and should give it his best shot. (op 9-4)
Diamond Penny(IRE)'s previous four races had all been at 7f and, while he stayed 1m well enough, he did have the run of the race and was eventually worn down. A drop back in trip would not be a problem. (op 5-4 tchd 11-10)
Zain Shamardal(IRE) ◆ most recently changed hands for £51,000 and this Shamardal colt with Group-race entries made a promising debut. Closing on the two leaders at the finish, he looks above typical maiden standard and was not out of his depth in this novice company. (tchd 9-2)
Mantoba has some good entries at 7f-1m. However, this son of Noverre has mixed messages on his dam's side regarding distance and needs to be monitored for further clues. (op 7-1 tchd 11-1)

5691 EUROPEAN BREEDERS' FUND QUIDHAMPTON MAIDEN FILLIES' STKS (DIV I) 6f 212y
2:40 (2:44) (Class 3) 2-Y-O **£6,152** (£1,830; £914; £456) **Stalls** High

Form RPR

1 **Azameera (IRE)** 2-9-0 0.......................... AdamKirby 18 78+
(C G Cox) *str: bit bkwd: little slowly away: sn trcking ldrs: swtchd lft 2f out: sn rdn: led ent fnl f: r.o wl* **33/1**

2 *1 ¼* **Aneedah (IRE)** 2-9-0 0.......................... WilliamBuick 1 75
(J H M Gosden) *leggy: scope: mid-div: hdwy 3f out: shkn up to chal whn rn green 2f out: kpt on ins fnl f: wnt 2nd nr fin* **6/1**[2]

23 **3** *hd* **Sylvestris (IRE)**[33] 4595 2-8-11 0.......................... EJMcNamara(3) 17 75
(R M Beckett) *lw: a.p: led over 2f out: rdn whn hdd ent fnl f: kpt on but no ex* **7/4**[1]

4 *1 ½* **Inimitable Romanee (USA)** 2-9-0 0.......................... JimmyFortune 5 72+
(Mrs A J Perrett) *w'like: scope: bit bkwd: s.i.s and hmpd s: towards rr: hdwy after switching lft 2f out: c wd and kpt on wl fnl f: clsng at fin* **25/1**

0 **5** *½* **Baqaat (USA)**[26] 4844 2-9-0 0.......................... RichardHills 12 70
(E A L Dunlop) *w'like: in tch: rdn 3f out: kpt on fnl f* **10/1**

0 **6** *1* **Spade**[26] 4844 2-9-0 0.......................... HayleyTurner 8 67
(D R C Elsworth) *w'like: str: s.i.s: towards rr of midfield: rdn and hdwy 2f out: hung rt but kpt on fnl f* **8/1**[3]

7 *1 ½* **Sultah (USA)** 2-9-0 0.......................... TadhgO'Shea 6 65+
(B W Hills) *w'like: leggy: t.k.h: towards rr of midfield: nt clr run fr 2f out tl jst over 1f out: kpt on ins fnl f* **8/1**[3]

8 *1 ½* **Beatrice Aurore (IRE)** 2-9-0 0.......................... RichardMullen 16 60
(J L Dunlop) *w'like: leggy: bit bkwd: s.i.s: towards rr: nt clr run fr wl over 1f out: kpt on ins fnl f* **50/1**

00 **9** *¾* **Dolcezza (IRE)**[10] 5369 2-9-0 0.......................... EddieCreighton 3 58
(B J Meehan) *str: led: rdn and hdd over 2f out: wknd fnl f* **100/1**

10 *¾* **Saint Helena (IRE)** 2-9-0 0.......................... JamieSpencer 4 56
(H J L Dunlop) *leggy: s.i.s: towards rr: hung rt fr 2f out: sme late prog: nvr trbld ldrs* **50/1**

11 *nk* **Tidal Run** 2-9-0 0.......................... IanMongan 11 55
(M R Channon) *athletic: lw: trckd ldrs: rdn whn squeezed up 2f out: sn wknd* **14/1**

12 *1 ¼* **Full Footage** 2-9-0 0.......................... SteveDrowne 15 52
(R Charlton) *unf: scope: lw: nvr bttr than mid-div* **16/1**

6 **13** *hd* **Heavenly Song (IRE)**[19] 5078 2-9-0 0 .... LiamKeniry 2 51
(S Kirk) *str: in tch: effrt 3f out: stl cl up whn squeezed out 2f out: wknd sn after* **22/1**

0 **14** *2 ¼* **Kiss My Tiara (IRE)**[20] 5047 2-9-0 0 .... MartinDwyer 9 46
(B J Meehan) *nvr bttr than mid-div* **16/1**

15 *½* **Heart Felt** 2-9-0 0 .... RichardHughes 14 45
(R Hannon) *w'like: scope: lw: s.i.s: a towards rr* **33/1**

0 **16** *3 ½* **Disturbia (IRE)**[20] 5029 2-8-9 0 .... AmyScott(5) 13 36
(J W Hills) *leggy: a towards rr* **100/1**

17 *hd* **Miss Thea** 2-9-0 0 .... FrankieDettori 10 35
(M P Tregoning) *w'like: bit bkwd: in tch: rdn 3f out: wknd 2f out* **14/1**

1m 27.44s (-1.56) **Going Correction** -0.35s/f (Firm) **17** Ran SP% **127.0**
Speed ratings (Par 96): **94,92,92,90,90 88,87,85,84,83 83,82,81,79,78 74,74**
toteswingers:1&2:£46.40, 1&3:£22.40, 2&3:£3.80 CSF £220.68 TOTE £42.00: £11.00, £1.80, £1.10; EX 151.50.
Owner H E Sheikh Sultan Bin Khalifa Al Nahyan **Bred** P Byrne, Eimear Mulhern & B Grassick **Trained** Lambourn, Berks

FOCUS
Although the field was soon strung out, the pace was ordinary and it was hard to come from too far back. There was little experience on show and debutantes from either side of the course filled the first two places. A nice dtart from the winner, but limited form.

NOTEBOOK
Azameera(IRE), sister to two juvenile 7f winners and the smart 6f-1m US performer No Explaining, followed in their footsteps at the first attempt. Though the high draw and the fact that she sat handy both helped, runners from her stable tend to improve from their debuts, so she must be treated with respect. (op 25-1)
Aneedah(IRE), a tallish Invincible Spirit debutante out of an easy-ground winner in Ireland, had no problems with the fast conditions. Fit for this debut, she did well from her low stall and is one to note next time. (op 7-1 tchd 15-2)
Sylvestris(IRE) set the standard, having been placed in two maidens on good tracks. She was edgy leaving the paddock and needs to mature mentally, but there are races to won with her if she calms down. (op 5-2)
Inimitable Romanee(USA) ◆, a $210,000 US-bred yearling whose dam won at 1m2f, is likely to need at least that far in the long run. However, this was an excellent debut in which she did best of the hold-up runners, and she looks to have a future. (op 16-1)
Baqaat(USA) stepped up on her debut but needs a bit more time. She might just scrape a maiden but looks ideally suited to late-season nurseries or handicaps next year. (op 9-1)
Spade has shown ability in her two races and will come into her own when handicapped. (tchd 7-1)
Sultah(USA), a neatly-made newcomer, had a troubled passage almost from the word go. She will probably need at least one more run to reach her peak but lacks the scope of other late developers. (op 15-2)
Tidal Run Official explanation: jockey said the the filly was hampered a furlong out

5692 EUROPEAN BREEDERS' FUND QUIDHAMPTON MAIDEN FILLIES' STKS (DIV II) 6f 212y
3:15 (3:17) (Class 3) 2-Y-0 **£6,152** (£1,830; £914; £456) **Stalls** High

Form RPR

0 **1** **Shim Sham (IRE)**[19] 5078 2-9-0 0 .... MartinDwyer 13 78+
(B J Meehan) *unf: scope: travelled wl most of way: mde all: clr 3f out: pushed out* **33/1**

2 *¾* **Khawlah (IRE)** 2-9-0 0 .... FrankieDettori 15 78+
(Saeed Bin Suroor) *w'like: scope: slowly away: sn mid-div on rails: pushed along whn nt clr run and swtchd lft to centre over 2f out: sn rdn: kpt on wl ins fnl f but nvr gng pce to catch wnr* **1/1**[1]

0 **3** *1 ½* **Chinook Wind (IRE)**[55] 3871 2-9-0 0 .... AdamKirby 11 72
(B W Hills) *w'like: leggy: chsd wnr: rdn 3f out: nvr gng pce to chal: kpt on but no ex whn lost 2nd ins fnl f* **20/1**

4 *nk* **Caraboss** 2-9-0 0 .... RyanMoore 16 73+
(Sir Michael Stoute) *w'like: scope: bit bkwd: mid-div: rdn 3f out: hdwy 2f out: styd on fnl f* **8/1**[3]

5 *1* **Lay Time** 2-9-0 0 .... JimmyFortune 8 69
(A M Balding) *w'like: leggy: trckd ldrs: rdn 3f out: 4th whn stmbld jst ins fnl f: no ex* **16/1**

6 *½* **Sister Red (IRE)** 2-9-0 0 .... FrankieMcDonald 7 67
(R Hannon) *str: bit bkwd: in tch: rdn 3f out: kpt on same pce fnl 2f* **100/1**

6 **7** *1 ½* **Tameen**[26] 4844 2-9-0 0 .... RichardHills 3 64+
(J L Dunlop) *w'like: towards rr of midfield: styd on fr over 1f out: nvr trbld ldrs* **7/1**[2]

8 *3 ½* **Emperor's Princess (FR)** 2-9-0 0 .... RichardHughes 6 54+
(R Hannon) *w'like: a mid-div* **16/1**

0 **9** *shd* **Bavarian Princess (USA)**[19] 5078 2-8-11 0 .... EJMcNamara(3) 9 54+
(R M Beckett) *w'like: trckd ldrs: rdn 3f out: wknd jst over 1f out* **25/1**

10 *nk* **Isolate** 2-9-0 0 .... SteveDrowne 14 57+
(H Morrison) *leggy: hmpd whn snatched up over 2f out: nvr bttr than mid-div* **40/1**

11 *½* **Mrs Greeley** 2-9-0 0 .... LiamKeniry 12 52
(Eve Johnson Houghton) *leggy: scope: nvr bttr than mid-div* **80/1**

12 *2 ¼* **Vita Lika** 2-9-0 0 .... EddieCreighton 5 46
(B J Meehan) *w'like: scope: bit bkwd: towards rr of mid-div: rdn 3f out: little imp* **66/1**

13 *¾* **Sandtail (IRE)** 2-9-0 0 .... HayleyTurner 1 44
(J W Hills) *leggy: sn swtchd rt: a towards rr* **100/1**

14 *nk* **Abeer (USA)** 2-9-0 0 .... TadhgO'Shea 18 45
(E A L Dunlop) *w'like: bit bkwd: slowly away: squeezed up on rails shortly after s: a towards rr* **40/1**

15 *¾* **Wilaya (USA)** 2-9-0 0 .... WilliamBuick 4 42
(J H M Gosden) *w'like: athletic: mid-div: edgd rt 2f out: wknd over 1f out* **8/1**[3]

16 *1 ½* **Melancholy Hill (IRE)** 2-8-7 0 .... DuilioDaSilva(7) 17 38
(P F I Cole) *unf: scope: trckd ldrs: rdn 3f out: wknd over 1f out* **50/1**

17 *1 ½* **Catch Light** 2-9-0 0 .... IanMongan 2 34
(Mrs A J Perrett) *leggy: sn pushed along: a towards rr* **66/1**

18 *7* **Nutshell** 2-9-0 0 .... JamieSpencer 10 16
(H J L Dunlop) *w'like: leggy: s.i.s: a bhd* **80/1**

1m 27.07s (-1.93) **Going Correction** -0.35s/f (Firm) **18** Ran SP% **122.3**
Speed ratings (Par 96): **97,96,94,94,92 92,90,86,86,86 85,83,82,81,81 79,77,69**
toteswingers:1&2:£15.60, 1&3:£61.20, 2&3:£7.30 CSF £63.05 TOTE £36.90: £7.30, £1.30, £5.80; EX 146.10.
Owner B E Nielsen **Bred** D Noonan & Carragh Bloodstock **Trained** Manton, Wilts
■ Stewards' Enquiry : Frankie Dettori two-day ban: careless riding (Sep 16, 17)

FOCUS
In contrast to division 1, there was a good tempo but the times were similar and the winner managed to make all. Tricky form to pin down.

NOTEBOOK
Shim Sham(IRE) got away much better than on her debut and was allowed to stride on, having been too keen that day. A Fillies' Mile entry, this daughter of Danehill Dancer travelled comfortably for most of the trip despite going off at a decent pace, and she looks a useful prospect. (op 28-1)
Khawlah(IRE) ◆, a Cape Cross filly, had a difficult debut, being slowly away and then having to switch wide after getting caught up in the ruck. However, the manner in which she finished clearly advertised her prospects, with longer trips sure to suit as she matures. Official explanation: jockey said that the filly missed the break (op 5-4)
Chinook Wind(IRE), 125,000gns Encosta De Lago half-sister to some smart performers, confirmed the promise of her debut. She is good enough to win a maiden and there is probably better to come next year. (op 16-1)
Caraboss, a Cape Cross half-sister to two smart sorts, one at 1m and the other over middle-distances, made an encouraging debut. She should appreciate an extra test of stamina. (tchd 9-1)
Lay Time, a Galileo half-sister to winners from 6f to 1m4f, ran well for a long way but did not quite last home. She may stay 7f better with this race behind her, especially as the pace was testing. (op 20-1)
Sister Red(IRE) was soon struggling to go the pace and appears to need more time. A Diamond Green half-sister to a 7f-1m2f winner, she may do better with the winter behind her.
Tameen, expected to appreciate this faster ground compared with her debut, was not ideally drawn but she was beaten on merit and needs to improve to make an impact. (op 13-2 tchd 6-1)
Wilaya(USA), prominent in the market, ran respectably for a long way and can improve on this debut. (tchd 10-1)

5693 EUROPEAN BREEDERS' FUND DICK POOLE FILLIES' STKS (LISTED RACE) 6f
3:50 (3:51) (Class 1) 2-Y-0
£17,031 (£6,456; £3,231; £1,611; £807; £405) **Stalls** High

Form RPR

41 **1** **Brevity (USA)**[23] 4921 2-8-12 85 .... MartinDwyer 2 101
(B J Meehan) *trckd ldrs: swtchd lft 2f out: r.o u.str.p thrght fnl f: led line* **10/1**

13 **2** *nse* **Rimth**[14] 5246 2-8-12 102 .... JamieSpencer 3 101
(P F I Cole) *broke wl: trckd ldr: led 3f out: sn rdn: kpt on gamely fnl f: ct line* **10/3**[2]

1222 **3** *nk* **Margot Did (IRE)**[14] 5246 2-8-12 108 .... HayleyTurner 9 100
(M L W Bell) *lw: trckd ldrs: swtchd lft 2f out: rdn ent fnl f: r.o w wnr: no ex nr fin* **11/10**[1]

2152 **4** *1* **Sweet Cecily (IRE)**[20] 5036 2-8-12 99 .... RichardHughes 6 97
(R Hannon) *sn led: narrowly hdd 3f out: sn rdn: kpt pressing ldr: no ex fnl 100yds* **6/1**[3]

1 **5** *½* **Tale Untold (USA)**[57] 3778 2-8-12 83 .... RyanMoore 1 96
(R Hannon) *hld up: rdn over 2f out: kpt on but nt pce to chal* **20/1**

4410 **6** *hd* **Mortitia**[20] 5036 2-8-12 86 .... FrankieDettori 7 95
(B J Meehan) *hld up but cl up: rdn 2f out: r.o ent fnl f: no ex fnl 100yds* **50/1**

211 **7** *1* **Ishbelle**[25] 4872 2-8-12 85 .... JimmyFortune 10 92
(R M Beckett) *trckd ldrs: short of room on rails briefly 3f out: sn rdn: kpt on but nt pce to chal* **14/1**

10 **8** *2 ¼* **Ladyanne (IRE)**[76] 3141 2-8-12 82 .... LiamKeniry 8 85
(S Kirk) *s.i.s: last but in tch: rdn over 2f out: nt pce to get on terms* **100/1**

1m 13.37s (-1.43) **Going Correction** -0.35s/f (Firm) **8** Ran SP% **108.5**
Speed ratings (Par 100): **95,94,94,93,92 92,90,87**
toteswingers: 1&2 £4.30, 1&3 £3.80, 2&3 £1.90 CSF £38.26 TOTE £10.30: £2.50, £1.60, £1.10; EX 49.60.
Owner Mrs Lucinda Freedman **Bred** Cliveden Stud Ltd **Trained** Manton, Wilts
■ Perfect Tribute was withdrawn after proving unruly in the stalls. (12/1, deduct 5p in the £ under R4.)

FOCUS
A high-quality race but three crossed the line together and it remains to be seen how good they all are. The form has been given a chance and rated on the positive side.

NOTEBOOK
Brevity(USA) scraped home and may have been a shade fortunate to win, having had a better passage than the third. Her trainer Brian Meehan, who rates her as an improving sort, believes she will stay 7f but this may yet prove to be her best trip. (op 7-1)
Rimth had looked progressive in her previous run and confirmed that she is at home in Listed grade. Only just touched off, she did not appear to be inconvenienced by being ridden more positively and should continue to make her mark at this level and even back in Group company. (op 7-2 tchd 4-1)
Margot Did(IRE) was messed around at halfway, ending up in a pocket, and ultimately that may have cost her the race. She had previously shown her credentials in three Group races and deserves a change of luck. (tchd Evens and 6-5)
Sweet Cecily(IRE) ran a sound race but was beaten by three smart sorts. She stays 6f but would be able to handle a drop back to 5f. (op 17-2)
Tale Untold(USA), whose only previous run was a win on Polytrack, just fell short in this hot company. (op 16-1 tchd 22-1)
Mortitia had creditable form in maidens but has been found out twice in Listed company. (tchd 40-1)
Ishbelle, stepping up from handicap company, just lacked what was required at this level but probably ran her best race yet. (op 12-1 tchd 16-1)
Ladyanne(IRE) has been highly tried since making a winning debut at Warwick.

5694 EUROPEAN BREEDERS' FUND LOCHSONG FILLIES' STKS (H'CAP) 6f 212y
4:25 (4:26) (Class 2) (0-100,92) 3-Y-0+
£14,954 (£4,478; £2,239; £1,120; £559; £280) **Stalls** High

Form RPR

212 **1** **Sarasota Sunshine**[54] 3890 4-9-8 **86** .... (v) FrankieDettori 1 99+
(J Noseda) *lw: hld up: hdwy fr over 2f out: rdn over 1f out: r.o fnl f: led towards fin* **5/2**[2]

10-1 **2** *¾* **Thrill**[22] 4963 3-9-4 **86** .... WilliamBuick 6 95+
(J H M Gosden) *disp ld tl rdn and outrt ldr 2f out: kpt on: no ex whn hdd towards fin* **2/1**[1]

1013 **3** *1 ¾* **Folly Bridge**[40] 4378 3-9-10 **92** .... SteveDrowne 9 96
(R Charlton) *trckd ldrs: rdn over 2f out: kpt on but nt pce to chal* **15/2**[3]

4150 **4** *½* **Pretty Bonnie**[18] 5120 5-9-3 **84** .... NataliaGemelova(3) 3 89
(A E Price) *sn prom: rdn over 2f out: ev ch over 1f out: no ex ins fnl f* **50/1**

2200 **5** *½* **Bahati (IRE)**[18] 5114 3-9-8 **90** .... JamieSpencer 8 92
(J G Portman) *in tch: rdn over 3f out: kpt on but nt pce to chal* **14/1**

-431 **6** *½* **Perfect Silence**[20] 5052 5-8-13 **82** .... (b) JohnFahy(5) 10 84
(C G Cox) *in tch: rdn over 2f out: kpt on but no imp on ldrs* **10/1**

-430 **7** *½* **Capercaillie (USA)**[19] 5088 3-9-6 **88** .... RichardHills 7 87
(M Johnston) *in tch: rdn 3f out: one pce fnl f* **14/1**

206- **8** *nse* **Roodle**[307] 7147 3-9-8 **90** .... LiamKeniry 2 89
(Eve Johnson Houghton) *hld up: rdn whn swtchd lft 2f out: nvr gng pce to get on terms* **25/1**

1220 **9** 3 ½ **Strictly Dancing (IRE)**[34] 4540 3-9-9 **91** .... JimmyFortune 11 80
(A M Balding) *disp ld tl rdn 2f out: hung rt and sn short of room: wknd jst over 1f out* **12/1**

6-00 **10** 2 ¼ **Don't Tell Mary (IRE)**[57] 3790 3-9-0 **82** .... HayleyTurner 4 65
(Tom Dascombe) *squeezed out s: sn struggling: nvr on terms* **20/1**

1m 25.4s (-3.60) **Going Correction** -0.35s/f (Firm)
WFA 3 from 4yo+ 4lb **10** Ran SP% **114.4**
Speed ratings (Par 96): **106,105,103,102,102 101,100,100,96,94**
toteswingers:1&2:£2.10, 1&3:£5.00, 2&3:£4.20 CSF £7.49 CT £31.59 TOTE £3.30: £1.60, £1.30, £2.00; EX 7.80.
Owner Franconson Partners **Bred** London Thoroughbred S'Vces Ltd & West Bl **Trained** Newmarket, Suffolk

FOCUS
A valuable and well contested handicap for the course, and form to view positively. There was just a routine gallop, so the winner did well to come from the rear.

NOTEBOOK
Sarasota Sunshine continues to thrive and the way she passed her rivals was impressive. Shrugging off a much higher mark than in the past, she recorded a fast time and there is plenty more to come. (op 9-4 tchd 2-1)
Thrill ran a solid race off a 5lb higher mark than last time but could not hold off the progressive winner. She is lightly raced and has a bit more to give. (op 11-4 tchd 3-1)
Folly Bridge remains in good shape but the hike in the weights since winning at Newmarket seems to having its effect. (op 6-1 tchd 8-1)
Pretty Bonnie ran respectably over an extra furlong than usual, but she is more exposed that those who beat her. (op 66-1)
Bahati(IRE), who has not won since her juvenile debut, is several pounds too high at present. (op 12-1)
Perfect Silence did her best, but she is on a stiff mark now. (op 9-1)
Capercaillie(USA), having her first try at 7f, was not far off her usual level of form. (op 16-1)
Roodle gave the impression that she stays 7f, if not being quite good enough off this mark in this company. (op 50-1)
Strictly Dancing(IRE) Official explanation: jockey said that the filly hung badly right handed

5695 SYDENHAMS H'CAP — 5f
5:00 (5:00) (Class 5) (0-70,70) 3-Y-O+ **£3,238** (£963; £481; £240) **Stalls** High

Form RPR
3412 **1** **Matterofact (IRE)**[10] 5377 7-9-5 **68** .... JimmyFortune 5 77
(M S Saunders) *mde all: r.o gamely to assert fnl 75yds: rdn out* **9/4**[2]

0656 **2** 1 ½ **The Jobber (IRE)**[13] 5262 9-8-13 **62** .... JamieSpencer 8 66
(M Blanshard) *w wnr thrght: rdn wl over 1f out: ev ch ins fnl f: no ex fnl 75yds* **7/2**[3]

1530 **3** ½ **The Wee Chief (IRE)**[13] 5262 4-9-5 **68** .... RichardHughes 6 70
(J C Fox) *trckd ldrs: swtchd lft 2f out: sn rdn: nt quite pce to chal: kpt on* **2/1**[1]

2030 **4** 4 **Nollaig Shona (IRE)**[43] 4256 3-8-12 **62** .... LiamKeniry 4 49
(J W Mullins) *trckd ldrs: rdn over 2f out: kpt on same pce* **25/1**

322 **5** ¾ **Green Velvet**[43] 4256 5-8-11 **60** .... WilliamBuick 2 45
(P J Makin) *hld up last but in tch: rdn 3f out: nvr gng pce to get on terms* **7/2**[3]

60.12 secs (-0.88) **Going Correction** -0.35s/f (Firm)
WFA 3 from 4yo+ 1lb **5** Ran SP% **112.4**
Speed ratings (Par 103): **93,90,89,83,82**
CSF £10.63 TOTE £3.30: £2.40, £4.00; EX 10.50.
Owner Prempro Racing **Bred** Tony Gleeson **Trained** Green Ore, Somerset

FOCUS
Two runners dominated at a fair sprint gallop from the outset, with the fast ground making it hard for the others to get into it. The form looks solid.

5696 IRISH THOROUGHBRED MARKETING "PERSIAN PUNCH" CONDITIONS STKS — 1m 6f 21y
5:30 (5:30) (Class 2) 3-Y-O+ **£9,969** (£2,985; £1,492; £747; £372)

Form RPR
414 **1** **Free Agent**[35] 4506 4-9-2 102 .... RichardHughes 3 110
(R Hannon) *trckd ldr: rdn 5f out: clsd on ldr over 2f out: chal over 1f out: led narrowly fnl 100yds: drvn out* **7/2**[2]

/1-1 **2** hd **La De Two (IRE)**[55] 3877 4-9-2 110 .... (t) FrankieDettori 1 109
(Saeed Bin Suroor) *lw: trckd ldng pair: pushed along 4f out: rdn to cl on ldr over 2f out: narrow advantage over 1f out: hdd fnl 100yds: styd on* **8/11**[1]

0530 **3** 6 **Swingkeel (IRE)**[34] 4566 5-9-2 98 .... (p) JimmyFortune 6 101
(J L Dunlop) *trckd ldrs: pushed along 5f out: rdn 3f out: styd on same pce fnl 2f: wnt 3rd ins fnl f* **20/1**

-200 **4** 1 ½ **Peligroso (FR)**[47] 4139 4-9-5 107 .... RichardHills 4 102
(Saeed Bin Suroor) *led: rdn over 2f out: hdd over 1f out: fdd ins fnl f* **8/1**

012/ **5** 43 **Bauer (IRE)**[667] 7188 7-9-2 108 .... WilliamBuick 2 39
(L M Cumani) *hld up 5th: pushed along over 4f out: rdn over 2f out: sn wknd: eased* **13/2**[3]

3m 2.91s (-4.49) **Going Correction** -0.35s/f (Firm) **5** Ran SP% **109.3**
Speed ratings (Par 109): **98,97,94,93,69**
totesuper7: Win: Not won, Place: £274.10 CSF £6.42 TOTE £3.70: £2.50, £1.30; EX 6.80 Place 6 £42.82; Place 5 £10.06.
Owner The Queen **Bred** The Queen **Trained** East Everleigh, Wilts

FOCUS
They went a respectable gallop, with the pacemaker stepping it up joining the straight, 7f out, and for a while looking as if he might hold on. The form is rated around the third.

NOTEBOOK
Free Agent found the return to Group 2 company too much last time, and the drop to this level gave him a better chance. He runs as if that trip of 2m should suit him, but distances of 1m6f and slightly less have served him well and his will-to-win helped him home. (op 4-1)
La De Two(IRE), winner of a 1m4f handicap last time, showed he has the ability to win over this extra 2f, only to be worn down by a tough customer. Lightly raced, he has plenty more to offer. (op 4-6)
Swingkeel(IRE) had a few pounds to find on official ratings, and so it proved. In any case, this is a bit sharp for him these days. (tchd 25-1)
Peligroso(FR) seemed to be bowling along in the style of a potential winner for a long way, only to hit the wall 2f from home. He did his pacemaking job well enough but clearly failed to stay. (tchd 9-1)
Bauer(IRE), unseen since just failing to win the 2008 Melbourne Cup, looked a shadow of himself here. (op 7-1 tchd 6-1)
T/Jkpt: Not won. T/Plt: £61.30 to a £1 stake. Pool:£63,659.34 - 756.93 winning tickets T/Qpdt: £3.60 to a £1 stake. Pool:£4,705.85 - 947.50 winning tickets TM

5267 WOLVERHAMPTON (A.W) (L-H)
Thursday, September 2

OFFICIAL GOING: Standard
Wind: Light across Weather: Fine and sunny

5697 MOBILE.WILLIAMHILL.COM - BET ON MOVE H'CAP — 5f 20y(P)
5:45 (5:46) (Class 6) (0-60,59) 3-Y-O+ **£1,706** (£503; £252) **Stalls** Low

Form RPR
3241 **1** **Towy Boy (IRE)**[27] 4789 5-8-12 **53** .... (bt) MartinLane(3) 5 65
(I A Wood) *chsd ldrs: led over 1f out: r.o* **7/1**[3]

2142 **2** 1 ¼ **You'relikemefrank**[6] 5502 4-8-9 **52** .... (p) AshleyMorgan(5) 8 60
(J Balding) *mid-div: hdwy 1/2-way: rdn to chse wnr fnl f: r.o* **7/2**[1]

2600 **3** 1 ¼ **Captain Bluebird (IRE)**[21] 4989 3-9-0 **53** .... (b) CathyGannon 7 56
(D Donovan) *hld up: swtchd rt over 1f out: r.o wl ins fnl f: nt rch ldrs* **33/1**

205 **4** 1 ¼ **Double Carpet (IRE)**[42] 4285 7-9-5 **57** .... KirstyMilczarek 11 56
(G Woodward) *hld up: hdwy u.p over 1f out: nt rch ldrs* **25/1**

0055 **5** hd **Lithaam (IRE)**[16] 5176 6-9-1 **53** .... (p) JimmyQuinn 13 51
(J M Bradley) *hld up: hdwy over 1f out: r.o: nt trble ldrs* **20/1**

5636 **6** 2 ½ **Desert Strike**[34] 4542 4-8-11 **54** .... (v[1]) DeclanCannon(5) 10 43
(A J McCabe) *chsd ldrs: rdn over 1f out: wknd ins fnl f* **11/2**[2]

6506 **7** ½ **Figaro Flyer (IRE)**[13] 5267 7-9-7 **59** .... J-PGuillambert 3 46
(P Howling) *mid-div: sn pushed along: nt clr run 1/2-way: rdn whn hmpd 1f out: nvr trbld ldrs* **7/2**[1]

5032 **8** hd **Speedy Senorita (IRE)**[8] 5422 5-9-7 **59** .... PatCosgrave 9 45
(J J Quinn) *prom: rdn 1/2-way: edgd lft 1f out: wknd ins fnl f* **8/1**

0546 **9** 2 ½ **Pressed For Time (IRE)**[30] 4672 4-9-1 **53** .... (vt) DarryllHolland 6 30
(E J Creighton) *led: rdn and hdd over 1f out: wknd ins fnl f* **9/1**

U0 **10** 1 ¾ **Boy The Bell**[4] 5548 3-8-13 **59** .... JosephYoung(7) 2 30
(M Mullineaux) *sn outpcd* **25/1**

4404 **11** 1 ¼ **Flow Chart (IRE)**[51] 3988 3-9-4 **57** .... (b) DavidNolan 4 23
(Peter Grayson) *sn pushed along in rr: hmpd over 3f out: nvr on terms* **66/1**

4005 **12** 7 **Mazzola**[6] 5471 4-9-2 **54** .... (p) NickyMackay 1 —
(J M Bradley) *chsd ldrs: rdn 1/2-way: wkng whn hmpd 1f out* **12/1**

61.80 secs (-0.50) **Going Correction** 0.0s/f (Stan)
WFA 3 from 4yo+ 1lb **12** Ran SP% **118.0**
Speed ratings (Par 101): **104,102,100,98,97 93,92,92,88,85 83,72**
toteswingers:1&2:£3.70, 1&3:£30.00, 2&3:£37.60 CSF £29.66 CT £770.00 TOTE £6.30: £2.60, £1.80, £12.60; EX 39.90.
Owner C R Lambourne **Bred** R W K Lewis **Trained** Upper Lambourn, Berks

FOCUS
There were very few in-form horses in this modest opener and it was no surprise the finish was fought out by two of them. The race was run at a good clip and there seemed few excuses. Straightforward form.
Figaro Flyer(IRE) Official explanation: jockey said that the gelding ran flat

5698 WILLIAMHILL.COM/BONUS25 H'CAP — 5f 216y(P)
6:20 (6:20) (Class 5) (0-70,70) 3-Y-O+ **£2,115** (£624; £312) **Stalls** Low

Form RPR
2052 **1** **Darcey**[44] 4237 4-9-0 **63** .... CathyGannon 12 77
(Miss Amy Weaver) *broke wl sn lost pl: hdwy over 2f out: rdn over 1f out: led ins fnl f: r.o u.p* **16/1**

0660 **2** nk **Hatta Stream (IRE)**[6] 5495 4-9-5 **68** .... SaleemGolam 4 81
(J Pearce) *s.i.s: hld up: hdwy over 1f out: rdn and r.o wl: jst failed* **25/1**

5510 **3** 1 ¼ **Rainy Night**[19] 5064 4-9-3 **66** .... JackMitchell 11 75
(R Hollinshead) *broke wl: sn lost pl: hdwy over 2f out: hung lft over 1f out: rdn and ev ch ins fnl f: styd on same pce* **10/1**

2211 **4** 3 ¾ **Titus Gent**[19] 5076 5-9-6 **69** .... KirstyMilczarek 2 66+
(R A Harris) *chsd ldrs: led over 1f out: rdn: hdd and no ex ins fnl f* **8/1**[3]

2541 **5** nk **Bobs Dreamflight**[25] 4875 4-9-4 **67** .... WilliamCarson 9 63
(D K Ivory) *mid-div: dropped in rr over 3f out: r.o ins fnl f: nvr trbld ldrs* **7/1**[2]

6200 **6** 1 ¾ **Valmina**[3] 5614 3-9-2 **67** .... (b[1]) FrannyNorton 7 57
(Andrew Turnell) *hdwy over 4f out: rdn and hung lft over 1f out: wknd ins fnl f* **22/1**

2230 **7** ½ **Volito**[26] 4833 4-9-3 **66** .... RichardKingscote 10 55
(Jonjo O'Neill) *chsd ldrs: rdn over 1f out: wknd ins fnl f* **16/1**

2124 **8** 4 **Romantic Queen**[38] 4430 4-9-4 **67** .... (t) TedDurcan 13 43
(George Baker) *sn bhd: sme hdwy over 1f out: eased ins fnl f: nvr on terms* **11/1**

0211 **9** 2 **Mayoman (IRE)**[6] 5502 5-9-7 **70** .... (v) DavidNolan 1 40+
(D Carroll) *led: hdd over 1f out: wknd fnl f* **15/8**[1]

5210 **10** 2 ¼ **Loyal Royal (IRE)**[16] 5175 7-9-1 **64** .... (bt) PatCosgrave 6 26
(J M Bradley) *chsd ldrs: rdn over 2f out: hung lft and wknd over 1f out* **25/1**

5100 **11** 2 **Athaakeel (IRE)**[38] 4431 4-9-4 **67** .... MarcHalford 8 23
(R A Harris) *s.s: outpcd* **28/1**

0435 **12** 6 **Perlachy**[29] 4717 6-9-6 **69** .... (v) J-PGuillambert 5 —
(D Shaw) *mid-div: rdn and wknd over 2f out* **10/1**

1m 14.3s (-0.70) **Going Correction** 0.0s/f (Stan)
WFA 3 from 4yo+ 2lb **12** Ran SP% **112.2**
Speed ratings (Par 103): **104,103,101,96,96 94,93,88,85,82 79,71**
toteswingers:1&2:£23.50, 1&3:£13.60, 2&3:£23.40 CSF £358.65 CT £4176.25 TOTE £29.90: £8.70, £9.80, £2.00; EX 510.70.
Owner Bringloe & Lennox **Bred** Raymond Cowie **Trained** Newmarket, Suffolk

FOCUS
Quite a competitive handicap with a number of in-form runners, but it was run at as strong a gallop as might have been expected with two front-runners in the inside stalls, who set it up for some of those ridden with more patience and who were produced wide. The winner is rated to this year's form.
Titus Gent Official explanation: vet said gelding inished lame on his right fore
Athaakeel(IRE) Official explanation: jockey said that the filly was slow away

5699 MOBILE.WILLIAMHILL.COM - NEW IPHONE APP NOVICE AUCTION STKS — 1m 141y(P)
6:50 (6:51) (Class 5) 2-Y-O **£2,115** (£624; £312) **Stalls** Low

Form RPR
0 **1** **Geordie Iris (IRE)**[22] 4962 2-8-7 0 .... FrankieMcDonald 5 75+
(R Hannon) *trckd ldrs: racd keenly: rdn and r.o to ld cl home: cosily* **25/1**

0222 **2** nk **Janet's Pearl (IRE)**[11] 5332 2-8-4 71 .... JimmyQuinn 3 70
(Mrs A Duffield) *led: hdd wl over 6f out: chsd ldr tl led again over 2f out: rdn and hung rt fnl f: hdd cl home* **4/1**

4665 **3** *1 ¼* **Dazzling Valentine**10 5374 2-8-4 68 CathyGannon 4 68
(A Bailey) *s.i.s: hld up: hdwy over 2f out: sn rdn: r.o* **7/2**3

1 **4** *3 ¼* **Fifth Dimension (IRE)**58 3767 2-8-8 75 SophieDoyle(5) 1 70
(J A Osborne) *hld up in tch: nt clr run wl over 1f out: sn rdn: no imp fnl f* **2/1**1

2313 **5** *shd* **Fabiello**24 4911 2-8-11 74 RichardKingscote 2 67
(Tom Dascombe) *prom: pushed along over 3f out: rdn over 1f out: styd on same pce* **5/2**2

0 **6** *7* **Patricia's Hope**38 4437 2-8-4 0 FrannyNorton 6 46
(P W D'Arcy) *plld hrd and prom: led wl over 6f out: rdn and hdd over 2f out: wknd over 1f out* **50/1**

1m 52.51s (2.01) **Going Correction** 0.0s/f (Stan) **6** Ran SP% **109.9**
Speed ratings (Par 95): **91,90,89,86,86 80**
toteswingers:1&2:£10.30 CSF £114.50 TOTE £28.40: £21.30, £1.50; EX 84.50.
Owner D R Mean **Bred** Anthony Kirwin **Trained** East Everleigh, Wilts
■ Stewards' Enquiry : Jimmy Quinn caution: careless riding

FOCUS
A novice event in name but a modest race of its type and it promises to be muddling form given it was run at a steady pace. The second and third set the level.

NOTEBOOK
Geordie Iris(IRE) was dismissed in the betting but she'd not been beaten all that far despite finishing last on her debut at Sandown and she isn't the first youngster from this yard to leave its debut form well behind second time up. Never far away, she always looked like coming out on top in the straight despite a less vigorous ride than the second and will improve again. Her dam is a close relative of the top German middle-distance horse Tiger Hill and she too looks as if she will have no trouble with 1m2f this year. (op 18-1)
Janet's Pearl(IRE) has been running well and probably rates as a good guide to the level of the form. Once again she was a shade unfortunate to run into an improver, but that was to have been expected in a contest like this and though she tended to roll around a little off a straight line, she looked resolute in the finish. (op 5-2)
Dazzling Valentine held every chance on adjusted official ratings and ran well, not least considering she rather let the first two get first run on her but she wasn't making any impression close home and didn't look unlucky in any way. (op 11-2)
Fifth Dimension(IRE) had made an encouraging debut here in July at 7f but this race was run at a completely different tempo and a lack of tactical speed was probably as much to blame for his final position as a shortage of room on the home turn. He'll probably get things run more to suit in nurseries. (tchd 5-2)
Fabiello again left the impression this surface perhaps doesn't show him to best advantage, though on the evidence of his previous record a steadily-run race round here wouldn't have shown him to best advantage anyway. (op 11-4 tchd 3-1 and 9-4)
Patricia's Hope was allowed to dictate but had no answer when the pace lifted turning for home.

5700 QUINN RADIATORS MEDIAN AUCTION MAIDEN STKS 1m 141y(P)
7:20 (7:21) (Class 6) 3-5-Y-0 **£1,706** (£503; £252) **Stalls** Low

Form RPR
3 **1** **Status Symbol (IRE)**134 1479 5-9-9 0 WilliamCarson 1 76+
(G C Bravery) *s.i.s: hdwy to chse ldrs over 7f out: led over 2f out: edgd rt over 1f out: styd on wl* **7/4**1

23 **2** *1 ¼* **Norman Orpen (IRE)**13 5270 3-9-3 0 DarryllHolland 2 73
(N P Littmoden) *trckd ldrs: racd keenly: ev ch 2f out: sn rdn: styd on* **10/3**3

4- **3** *3 ½* **Spirit Of Love (IRE)**279 7556 3-9-3 0 StephenCraine 4 65
(M Wigham) *hld up: hdwy over 2f out: rdn over 1f out: styd on: nt trble ldrs* **7/1**

062 **4** *nse* **Dirakh Shan**20 5028 3-9-3 70 J-PGuillambert 9 65
(L M Cumani) *hld up: hdwy over 2f out: hrd rdn over 1f out: styd on: nt trble ldrs* **5/2**2

06 **5** *2 ½* **Marksbury**20 5028 3-8-12 0 MickyFenton 7 54
(J M P Eustace) *s.i.s: sn prom: chsd ldr over 6f out: led over 3f out: rdn and hdd over 2f out: hung lft and wknd fnl f* **50/1**

5004 **6** *hd* **Superstitious Me (IRE)**24 4913 4-9-4 45 DavidProbert 8 54?
(B Palling) *hld up: hdwy over 3f out: rdn and wknd over 1f out* **14/1**

0060 **7** *24* **Knowledgeable**6 5469 3-8-12 41 (p) DeclanCannon(5) 10 —
(B Palling) *led: hdd over 3f out: wknd over 2f out: t.o* **66/1**

0 **8** *16* **Shesasnip**90 2706 3-8-12 0 PaulEddery 3 —
(R Hollinshead) *hld up: a in rr: bhd fnl 3f: t.o* **66/1**

1m 51.03s (0.53) **Going Correction** 0.0s/f (Stan)
WFA 3 from 4yo+ 6lb **8** Ran SP% **112.1**
Speed ratings (Par 101): **97,95,92,92,90 90,69,54**
toteswingers:1&2:£2.00, 1&3:£2.80, 2&3:£5.20 CSF £7.54 TOTE £3.80: £1.80, £1.10, £2.70; EX 9.60.
Owner W H Carson **Bred** Darley **Trained** Cowlinge, Suffolk
■ Stewards' Enquiry : William Carson caution: careless riding

FOCUS
A weak maiden lacking strength in depth and run at a steady pace. The form makes sense around the principals and the winner looks the type to rate higher given more regular racing.

5701 HORIZONS RESTAURANT, THE PLACE TO DINE CLAIMING STKS 7f 32y(P)
7:50 (7:52) (Class 6) 2-Y-O **£1,706** (£503; £252) **Stalls** High

Form RPR
1630 **1** **Malice Or Mischief (IRE)**32 4623 2-8-10 74 JackMitchell 9 74
(R M Beckett) *hld up in tch: rdn to ld 2f out: r.o wl* **2/1**1

3510 **2** *2 ¼* **Daas Rite (IRE)**83 2939 2-8-7 70 JulieBurke(7) 12 70
(K A Ryan) *hld up: racd keenly: hdwy over 2f out: hung lft over 1f out: r.o wl ins fnl f: nt trble wnr* **9/2**3

0026 **3** *½* **Takeaway**10 5374 2-9-12 83 PatDobbs 5 81
(R Hannon) *chsd ldr: ev ch 2f out: sn rdn: styd on same pce fnl f* **3/1**2

6 **4** *2 ½* **Bathwick Scanno (IRE)**13 5269 2-8-8 0 CathyGannon 2 57
(P D Evans) *led: rdn and hdd 2f out: wknd ins fnl f* **7/1**

3260 **5** *½* **A Little Bit Dusty**13 5256 2-8-10 69 ow1 JackDean(3) 1 61
(W G M Turner) *chsd ldrs: rdn over 1f out: wknd ins fnl f* **16/1**

5420 **6** *1 ¼* **Majestic Style (IRE)**27 4802 2-8-5 57 FrannyNorton 7 50
(A P Jarvis) *chsd ldrs: ev ch 2f out: sn rdn: wknd fnl f* **18/1**

0040 **7** *2* **Elusive Vine (IRE)**3 5583 2-8-2 48 DavidProbert 10 42
(R A Harris) *s.i.s: hld up: styd on ins fnl f: nvr nrr* **25/1**

05 **8** *hd* **Cool Land (IRE)**13 5269 2-8-5 0 AndrewHeffernan(3) 6 47
(R A Harris) *trckd ldrs: plld hrd: rdn: hung lft and wknd over 1f out* **33/1**

9 *3 ¾* **Ameliana** 2-8-3 0 WilliamCarson 11 33
(M G Quinlan) *dwlt: rdn 1/2-way: a in rr* **33/1**

5400 **10** *¾* **Algurayn (IRE)**10 5374 2-9-0 69 (v1) SaleemGolam 8 42
(G Prodromou) *hld up: hmpd over 5f out: hdwy over 4f out: rdn over 2f out: sn wknd* **50/1**

0 **11** *2* **Generale (IRE)**13 5269 2-9-0 0 (t) LeeVickers 3 38
(F Sheridan) *s.i.s: sn pushed along into midfield: wknd 3f out* **100/1**

1m 30.76s (1.16) **Going Correction** 0.0s/f (Stan) **11** Ran SP% **112.8**
Speed ratings (Par 93): **93,90,89,87,86 85,82,82,78,77 75**
toteswingers:1&2:£3.00, 1&3:£2.10, 2&3:£2.00 CSF £10.07 TOTE £3.40: £1.20, £1.10, £1.30; EX 12.30.Malice Or Mischief was claimed by A. W. Carroll for £8,000.
Owner Mrs Carolyn Thornton Roberts **Bred** Kilnamoragh Stud **Trained** Whitsbury, Hants

FOCUS
An uncompetitive claimer that went to the runner best in on adjusted official ratings despite a modest early pace which saw plenty of bunching and some pulling hard. Straightforward form.

NOTEBOOK
Malice Or Mischief(IRE) had a very good chance at the weights down at this level for the first time and won pretty much as he was entitled to after showing the best turn of foot. A Newbury nursery such as he ran in last time is probably a bit hot for him, but he took this well enough to think a small race of that type can come his way. He was claimed by Tony Carroll for £8,000. (op 5-2)
Daas Rite(IRE) didn't look the easiest of rides and spoiled his chance by hanging before finally buckling down, but the ability is there to win at this level at this trip if he can focus his efforts and find some more consistency. (tchd 4-1)
Takeaway had been contesting much better races than this but he'd been entered him on the welter burden of 9st12lb and found the concession of 12lb and more to the first two beyond him. Nonetheless, this was a good race all the same at the weights. (op 5-2 tchd 9-4)
Bathwick Scanno(IRE) emerged best of the quartet who contested a similar event here last time, and given this was a stronger event, his effort for his in-form yard probably represents a step forward. (op 9-1)
A Little Bit Dusty never promised to finish any closer and has been disappointing since his Folkestone maiden second.
Majestic Style(IRE) wasn't discredited considering her task at the weights but she was well positioned as the race was run. (op 16-1 tchd 20-1)
Cool Land(IRE) spoiled his chance by racing much too freely early. Official explanation: jockey said that the gelding ran too free (op 28-1)
Ameliana Official explanation: jockey said that the filly was slowly away.

5702 GET BEST ODDS GUARANTEED AT WILLIAMHILL.COM H'CAP (DIV I) 7f 32y(P)
8:20 (8:20) (Class 3) (0-95,95) 3-Y-O+ **£5,361** (£1,604; £802; £401; £199) **Stalls** High

Form RPR
0000 **1** **Hajoum (IRE)**26 4843 4-9-3 88 GregFairley 5 97
(M Johnston) *chsd ldr: rdn and r.o to ld nr fin* **4/1**2

0105 **2** *nk* **Medicean Man**12 5302 4-9-10 95 (p) JimmyQuinn 4 103+
(J R Gask) *a.p: led on bit over 1f out: edgd rt ins fnl f: sn rdn: hdd nr fin* **9/2**3

0100 **3** *¾* **Celtic Sultan (IRE)**40 4371 6-9-3 88 (b) MickyFenton 8 94
(T P Tate) *led: rdn and hdd over 1f out: styd on u.p* **25/1**

4536 **4** *3* **Jordaura**26 4828 4-8-13 84 NickyMackay 7 82
(J R Holt) *s.i.s: sn pushed along in rr: swtchd lft and hdwy over 1f out: r.o: nt rch ldrs* **7/1**

5662 **5** *1 ½* **Baby Strange**17 5154 6-8-13 84 FrannyNorton 6 78
(D Shaw) *mid-div: hdwy over 2f out: rdn over 1f out: no ex ins fnl f* **8/1**

-120 **6** *shd* **Dance And Dance (IRE)**76 3146 4-9-6 91 TedDurcan 3 85
(E F Vaughan) *s.s: hld up: r.o ins fnl f: nvr nrr* **9/1**

3300 **7** *1 ¼* **Seek The Fair Land**5 5516 4-9-4 89 (p) PatCosgrave 10 79
(J R Boyle) *chsd ldrs: rdn over 2f out: wknd ins fnl f* **12/1**

2-00 **8** *2 ¾* **Badiat Alzaman (IRE)**117 1899 4-9-3 88 TomMcLaughlin 9 71
(E A L Dunlop) *hld up: hdwy over 2f out: sn rdn: wknd ins fnl f* **28/1**

0000 **9** *½* **Spectait**26 4830 8-9-2 87 GeorgeBaker 2 68
(Jonjo O'Neill) *dwlt: sn pushed along in rr: nvr on terms* **16/1**

4401 **10** *4* **Sweet Clementine (IRE)**17 5142 3-8-11 86 ShaneKelly 1 55
(W J Knight) *mid-div: rdn over 2f out: wknd over 1f out* **11/4**1

1m 27.46s (-2.14) **Going Correction** 0.0s/f (Stan)
WFA 3 from 4yo+ 4lb **10** Ran SP% **119.3**
Speed ratings (Par 107): **112,111,110,107,105 105,104,100,100,95**
toteswingers:1&2:£5.80, 1&3:£30.70, 2&3:£20.90 CSF £23.03 CT £404.10 TOTE £4.20: £1.30, £2.50, £10.60; EX 23.00.
Owner Sheikh Hamdan Bin Mohammed Al Maktoum **Bred** Darley **Trained** Middleham Moor, N Yorks

FOCUS
The stronger division of the feature handicap and despite the runners being well strung out from an early stage, little got into the race from off the pace. The form has been rated around the third and promises to stand up.

NOTEBOOK
Hajoum(IRE) is probably more at home on this surface than he is on turf for all he was fourth in the Buckingham Palace at Ascot, and he put some recent modest efforts behind him with a strong rally after looking held for much of the last furlong. Consistency hasn't been his strong suit as he has chased bigger prizes on turf, but that has kept his handicap mark down and he could be a good acquisition for the winter for someone at one of the autumn sales. (op 9-1)
Medicean Man had his stamina to prove at the trip but it wasn't lack of that that beat him but being out in front too long. He looked the likely winner well inside the last but was bullied out of it in the last couple of strides. For all this probably rates as a career-best effort, a strongly-run 5f or 6f will probably turn out to suit him ideally and he'll be worth a second look if he turns up again at Ascot this autumn. (tchd 5-1)
Celtic Sultan(IRE) has been hit and miss this season but he looked worthy of respect here given it was near certain he was going to get his own way in front and he battled on valiantly after setting a strong pace. This run opens up the options of a winter campaign.
Jordaura ran respectably considering he was soon a long way behind and still poorly positioned on the home turn over a trip on the sharp side. Though the patience of his supporters might be wearing thin, it's arguable he is still capable of better when things drop right. (tchd 13-2)
Baby Strange's effort seemed to confirm he is probably better at 6f on this surface. (tchd 12-1)
Dance And Dance(IRE) never threatened on his first run since being gelded. His rider reported he became unbalanced leaving the stalls. Official explanation: jockey said the gelding became unbalanced leaving the stalls and was slowly away (op 11-1)
Seek The Fair Land hadn't been at his best in two recent turf starts following a break and even a return to his favoured surface couldn't spark a revival. (tchd 11-1)
Spectait showed more than of late over a trip on the sharp side and might soon become of interest if dropped further in the weights and sent back up in trip. (op 12-1)
Sweet Clementine(IRE) Official explanation: trainer's representative was unable to offer any explanation for the poor performance shown

5703 GET BEST ODDS GUARANTEED AT WILLIAMHILL.COM H'CAP (DIV II) 7f 32y(P)
8:50 (8:52) (Class 3) (0-95,93) 3-Y-O+ **£5,361** (£1,604; £802; £401; £199) **Stalls** High

Form RPR
3316 **1** **Malcheek (IRE)**14 5242 8-9-2 84 DavidAllan 10 94
(T D Easterby) *mde all: rdn up over 1f out: styd on* **14/1**

-020 **2** *2 ¼* **Layline (IRE)**36 4473 3-9-7 93 (b1) JackMitchell 5 95
(R M Beckett) *hld up in tch: chsd wnr 2f out: sn rdn: styd on same pce fnl f* **9/2**2

0010 **3** 3/4 **Golden Shaheen (IRE)**[21] 4995 3-9-2 **88**......................(b) GregFairley 9 90+
(M Johnston) *s.s: last and rdn 1/2-way: sn outpcd: r.o u.p ins fnl f: nrst fin* **7/1**[3]

0050 **4** 1 1/4 **Titan Triumph**[26] 4843 6-9-5 **87**..........................(t) ShaneKelly 1 86
(W J Knight) *hld up: hdwy over 1f out: rdn over 1f out: styd on same pce* **16/1**

304 **5** 1 **Flowing Cape (IRE)**[19] 5068 5-9-6 **88**.......................... DavidProbert 4 84
(R Hollinshead) *chsd ldrs: rdn over 2f out: no ex ins fnl f* **11/4**[1]

0060 **6** nk **Imprimis Tagula (IRE)**[7] 5435 6-8-13 **88**......................(v) HobieGill(7) 6 83
(A Bailey) *chsd ldrs: rdn over 2f out: styd on same pce appr fnl f* **25/1**

200 **7** 1 **Nightjar (USA)**[40] 4371 5-9-10 **92**.......................... DarryllHolland 7 84
(K A Ryan) *chsd ldr 6f out tl rdn 2f out: sn outpcd* **33/1**

1m 28.21s (-1.39) **Going Correction** 0.0s/f (Stan)
WFA 3 from 5yo+ 4lb 7 Ran SP% **76.7**
Speed ratings (Par 107): **107,104,103,102,101 100,99**
toteswingers:1&2:£4.10, 1&3:£3.90, 2&3:£3.00 CSF £32.10 CT £121.63 TOTE £6.90: £2.40, £2.20; EX 40.70.
Owner Habton Farms **Bred** Carrigbeg Stud **Trained** Great Habton, N Yorks
■ Bronze Prince was withdrawn (7/4F, unruly in stalls). Deduct 35p in the £ under R4.

FOCUS
What looked the weaker of the two divisions beforehand was rendered even more so by three withdrawals, including that of the forecast favourite Bronze Prince, who was taken out after sitting down in the stalls, and a very slow start for one of the remaining runners who had seemingly been affected by that same incident. Altogether an unsatisfactory affair in which the winner was able to dictate a steady pace. The winner is rated back to his best at face value.

NOTEBOOK
Malcheek(IRE) goes well here (now 3 from 5) and, reverting to more usual tactics after a wasted run tried held up last time, was always in control once he was allowed an uncontested lead at a modest gallop. He probably wasn't left with a lot to beat and, after a rise in the weights, is likely to be one to take on in bigger fields or in more competitive affairs for the rest of the autumn. (op 12-1 tchd 10-1)
Layline(IRE) seemed to be travelling well 3f out but didn't find quite what it had looked he might. He'd probably have been suited by a stronger pace, but is probably not one to be making too many excuses for anyway and it's easy to see why he was tried in blinkers. (op 15-2 tchd 8-1)
Golden Shaheen(IRE) ran quite well to finish where he did as he became upset in the stalls and, quite possibly as a consequence, lost many lengths at the start. He looked to be labouring turning in, but stuck it out well, although it might be that his proximity says more about the immediate prospects of those behind than it does for his. Official explanation: vet said that the gelding lost a near hind shoe (op 5-1)
Titan Triumph, having his first run here, looks to be a light of other days, but he, too, would have preferred a stronger pace and might be worth one last chance back at Lingfield.
Flowing Cape(IRE) was disappointing considering his good record here.'s series of substandard runs continues. (op 4-1)
Imprimis Tagula(IRE)'s series of substandard runs continues.
Nightjar(USA)'s first run since being gelded was a quiet one, but this isn't really his surface and the success of that operation is best judged after he's been back on Fibresand.

5704 MOBILE.WILLIAMHILL.COM - LATEST ODDS ON YOUR IPHONE H'CAP 1m 1f 103y(P)
9:20 (9:20) (Class 6) (0-55,55) 3-Y-O+ **£1,706** (£503; £252) **Stalls** Low

Form RPR
-143 **1** **Pattern Mark**[23] 4932 4-9-2 **53**..........................(p) BarryMcHugh(3) 3 61
(Ollie Pears) *a.p: rdn: nt clr run and swtchd rt over 1f out: led ins fnl f: r.o* **7/2**[1]

6460 **2** 1/2 **Masterofceremonies**[20] 5019 7-9-4 **52**..................(v) TomMcLaughlin 6 59
(W M Brisbourne) *dwlt: hld up: rdn over 2f out: hdwy over 1f out: hung lft and r.o ins fnl f: nt rch wnr* **25/1**

0362 **3** 1 **Al Rayanah**[4] 5560 7-9-1 **49**..........................(p) SaleemGolam 10 55+
(G Prodromou) *hld up: hdwy over 2f out: hmpd over 1f out: r.o ins fnl f: nrst fin* **11/1**

1333 **4** hd **Corrib (IRE)**[3] 5585 7-9-2 **50**..........................(p) NeilChalmers 7 54+
(B Palling) *hld up: hdwy and nt clr run over 1f out: r.o* **8/1**

6532 **5** 1/2 **Tres Froide (FR)**[17] 5158 5-9-3 **51**......................(p) SilvestreDeSousa 11 54
(N Tinkler) *hld up: hdwy over 2f out: rdn over 1f out: unable qck towards fin* **6/1**[3]

4463 **6** shd **Lunar River (FR)**[24] 4913 7-9-0 **55**..........................(tp) DavidKenny(7) 13 60+
(David Pinder) *s.i.s: hld up: last turning for home: r.o ins fnl f: nrst fin* **20/1**

0052 **7** 3 **Herecomethegirls**[24] 4913 4-8-13 **50**..........................(p) JackDean(3) 12 46
(W G M Turner) *chsd ldrs: rdn and edgd lft over 1f out: led briefly ins fnl f: wknd towards fin* **12/1**

0013 **8** shd **Litenup (IRE)**[33] 4591 4-9-7 **55**..........................(t) TedDurcan 5 51
(A J Lidderdale) *led: hdd over 2f out: sn rdn: wknd ins fnl f* **6/1**[3]

0340 **9** hd **Location**[17] 5158 4-8-11 **52**.......................... RyanPowell(7) 2 48
(Ian Williams) *hld up: nt clr run over 1f out: r.o ins fnl f: n.d* **33/1**

0600 **10** 1/2 **Dancing Welcome**[13] 5271 4-9-5 **53**..........................(b) PatCosgrave 4 48
(J M Bradley) *chsd ldrs: rdn over 2f out: wknd ins fnl f* **33/1**

2236 **11** nse **Join Up**[13] 5271 4-9-2 **50**..........................(p) ShaneKelly 8 45
(W M Brisbourne) *trckd ldr: plld hrd: led over 2f out: rdn and hung lft over 1f out: wknd ins fnl f* **9/2**[2]

0000 **12** 2 1/2 **Achromatic**[93] 2636 4-8-10 **49**.......................... JohnFahy(5) 1 38
(W R Swinburn) *chsd ldrs: rdn over 2f out: wknd over 1f out* **14/1**

2m 2.57s (0.87) **Going Correction** 0.0s/f (Stan) 12 Ran SP% **117.3**
Speed ratings (Par 101): **96,95,94,94,94 93,91,91,91,90 90,88**
toteswingers:1&2:£20.20, 1&3:£12.20, 2&3:£40.60 CSF £100.18 CT £870.16 TOTE £6.40: £2.70, £7.90, £3.20; EX 163.90 Place 6 £579.73; Place 5 £223.40.
Owner David Scott and Co (Pattern Makers) Ltd **Bred** D Scott **Trained** Norton, N Yorks

FOCUS
A low-grade handicap, but, for the grade, a competitive one. The pace wasn't strong and the field were well bunched for a long way. The fourth is the best guide.
T/Plt: £715.00 to a £1 stake. Pool:£74,420.91 - 75.98 winning tickets T/Qpdt: £19.00 to a £1 stake. Pool:£9,664.31 - 374.60 winning tickets CR

5705 - 5708a (Foreign Racing) - See Raceform Interactive

5650 BRIGHTON (L-H)
Friday, September 3

OFFICIAL GOING: Good to firm (good in places; 8.1)
Rail realignment added 10yds to advertised distances
Wind: modest, across Weather: bright and sunny

5709 BUDDIES RESTAURANT BRIGHTON MAIDEN AUCTION STKS 7f 214y
2:30 (2:32) (Class 6) 2-Y-O **£2,590** (£770; £385; £192) **Stalls** Low

Form RPR
03 **1** **Ninfea (IRE)**[30] 4716 2-8-4 0.......................... DavidProbert 2 63
(S Kirk) *t.k.h: chsd ldr: rdn to chal 2f out: led over 1f out: kpt on wl and in command ins fnl f* **11/4**[2]

660 **2** 1 **Masonic Lady (IRE)**[25] 4899 2-8-3 65..........................(b[1]) JohnFahy(5) 9 65
(W J Haggas) *chsd ldng pair: rdn over 2f out: drvn and chsd wnr ins fnl f: kpt on but a hld by wnr* **7/1**

0500 **3** 2 1/2 **Dew Reward (IRE)**[28] 4802 2-8-11 50.......................... FergusSweeney 4 63
(Eve Johnson Houghton) *hld up in tch towards rr: hdwy 3f out: rdn and unable qck 2f out: plugged on ins fnl f to snatch 3rd on post: nvr gng pce to threaten wnr* **50/1**

0342 **4** nse **High On The Hog (IRE)**[15] 5234 2-8-10 67.. Louis-PhilippeBeuzelin(3) 7 64
(J L Dunlop) *led: clr 5f out: rdn ent fnl 2f: hdd over 1f out: wknd and lost 2 pls ins fnl f* **10/3**[3]

042 **5** 1/2 **Standout**[10] 5385 2-8-9 0.......................... PatDobbs 10 59
(R Hannon) *hld up in last pair: hdwy to chse ldng trio 4f out: rdn and unable qck over 2f out: drvn and kpt on same pce fr over 1f out* **15/8**[1]

500 **6** 14 **Bonniebridge**[39] 4437 2-8-2 53 ow3.......................... AdamBeschizza(5) 1 26
(Miss J Feilden) *chsd ldrs tl over 3f out: sn struggling u.p: wl bhd and eased ins fnl f* **25/1**

0656 **7** 18 **Marmaduke**[20] 5074 2-8-11 50.......................... NeilChalmers 3 —
(J J Bridger) *plld hrd early: hld up in tch in rr tl lost tch over 4f out: t.o fnl 2f: eased ins fnl f* **66/1**

0 **U** **Blue Vinney**[53] 3961 2-8-9 0.......................... TadhgO'Shea 6 —
(M P Tregoning) *rrd as stalls opened and uns rdr sn after s* **11/1**

1m 34.68s (-1.32) **Going Correction** -0.225s/f (Firm) 8 Ran SP% **112.7**
Speed ratings (Par 93): **97,96,93,93,92 78,60,—**
toteswingers:1&2:£5.20, 1&3:£19.00, 2&3:£29.00 CSF £21.27 TOTE £2.70: £1.10, £3.10, £15.80; EX 29.30 TRIFECTA Not won..
Owner Miss A Jones **Bred** Kilco Builders **Trained** Upper Lambourn, Berks

FOCUS
Just a run-of-the-mill maiden, and weak form with questionable improvement from the third.

NOTEBOOK
Ninfea(IRE) has now shown improved form on each start. Still green when third at Yarmouth last time, she showed here that she is learning her job quickly as she raced much more professionally and saw this out well having hit the front inside the final furlong. She looks to have the right attitude for the game and, given she is still apparently a bit on the weak side, has the scope to make a much better 3-y-o. (op 4-1)
Masonic Lady(IRE) posted her best performance so far with the first-time blinkers proving the catalyst to a much improved showing. She is qualified for nurseries and may improve again for a step up in trip (backed up by pedigree), providing the headgear continues to work. (op 6-1 tchd 11-2)
Dew Reward(IRE) had shown very little in four previous starts but there is ability there for he travelled well for a long way and although there was no noticeable change of gear when shaken up, he kept on to edge third. He might find his mark of 50 going up a bit given he's beaten a couple of much higher rated horses. (op 66-1)
High On The Hog(IRE) is becoming a little frustrating. (op 3-1)
Standout set the standard but proved a little disappointing. His best effort prior to this had come on soft ground and perhaps these quicker conditions proved his undoing. (op 2-1 tchd 7-4)

5710 BUDDIES RESTAURANT CAFE BAR H'CAP 7f 214y
3:00 (3:00) (Class 6) (0-65,66) 3-Y-O+ **£2,331** (£693; £346; £173) **Stalls** Low

Form RPR
6020 **1** **Cavendish Road (IRE)**[27] 4839 4-9-10 **66**..................(t) DarryllHolland 8 76
(N J Vaughan) *chsd wnr tl led over 2f out: rdn ent fnl 2f: styd wl u.p and drew clr ins fnl f: eased nr fin* **9/2**[2]

2115 **2** 2 3/4 **Fire King**[18] 5159 4-9-3 **59**..........................(p) StevieDonohoe 1 63
(A B Haynes) *hld up in tch in rr: hdwy over 2f out: chsd ldng pair and rdn 2f out: no imp on wnr ins fnl f: kpt on to snatch 2nd on post* **7/2**[1]

0355 **3** nse **Smart Endeavour (USA)**[23] 4958 4-9-4 **65**.......................... JohnFahy(5) 5 69
(W R Swinburn) *reminders to ld sn after s: hdd over 2f out: drvn and one pce fr over 1f out: wknd jst ins fnl f: lost 2nd on post* **7/2**[1]

4-00 **4** 2 3/4 **Destiny Blue (IRE)**[91] 2697 3-8-11 **58**.......................... FergusSweeney 6 56
(J A Osborne) *dwlt: t.k.h: hld up in tch in last trio: hdwy over 2f out: rdn to chse ldng trio wl over 1f out: no prog and btn 1f out* **16/1**

3062 **5** 3/4 **Swift Return**[2] 5670 3-9-4 **65**..........................(v) GeorgeBaker 9 61
(S C Williams) *in tch: c to r alone on stands' rail 3f out: rdn and effrt over 2f out: hung lft u.p and btn 1f out* **5/1**[3]

32-6 **6** nse **Mnasikia (USA)**[214] 374 3-9-3 **64**.......................... KirstyMilczarek 4 60
(L M Cumani) *chsd ldrs: rdn and unable qck over 2f out: drvn and btn over 1f out* **15/2**

2F24 **7** 12 **Louisiana Gift (IRE)**[28] 4779 3-8-10 **60**..........................(p) PatrickHills(3) 3 42
(J W Hills) *hld up in tch: rdn and effrt jst over 2f out: btn over 1f out: eased ins fnl f* **12/1**

-302 **8** 7 **Farmers Dream (IRE)**[17] 5171 3-8-10 **57**.......................... WilliamCarson 7 23
(J L Spearing) *t.k.h: chsd ldrs tl lost pl and rdn 3f out: wknd 2f out: wl btn and eased fnl f* **9/1**

1m 33.84s (-2.16) **Going Correction** -0.225s/f (Firm)
WFA 3 from 4yo+ 5lb 8 Ran SP% **114.6**
Speed ratings (Par 101): **101,98,98,95,94 94,82,75**
toteswingers:1&2:£3.90, 1&3:£3.00, 2&3:£3.90 CSF £20.71 CT £61.11 TOTE £7.40: £1.80, £1.90, £1.40; EX 26.00 Trifecta £36.00 Pool: £287.72 - 5.90 winning units..
Owner Mrs Lynn Vaughan **Bred** Garry Chong **Trained** Helshaw Grange, Shropshire

FOCUS
Sound but weakish form, with a length personal best from the winner.
Farmers Dream(IRE) Official explanation: vet said filly was distressed post race

5711 BEN SHAWS TASTE OF TRADITION H'CAP 6f 209y
3:30 (3:33) (Class 6) (0-60,60) 3-Y-O+ **£2,072** (£616; £308; £153) **Stalls** Centre

Form RPR
6200 **1** **Signora Frasi (IRE)**[58] 3783 5-9-2 **52**.......................... StevieDonohoe 12 65
(A G Newcombe) *hld up in last pair: rdn and effrt ent fnl 2f: swtchd rt and hdwy u.p over 1f out: chsd wnr fnl 100yds: r.o wl to ld nr fin* **9/1**

0651 **2** nk **Pipers Piping (IRE)**[17] 5175 4-9-1 **54**..................(p) MichaelStainton(3) 5 66
(P Howling) *w ldr tl led 4f out: rdn over 1f out: r.o wl u.p ins fnl f tl hdd and no ex nr fin* **4/1**[2]

6222 **3** 4 1/2 **Hellbender (IRE)**[12] 5326 4-9-5 **60**..........................(t) AdamBeschizza(5) 3 60
(S Kirk) *chsd ldng pair: effrt and rdn 2f out: drvn to chse ldr and hung lft 1f out: wknd ins fnl f* **2/1**[1]

0200 **4** 1 1/2 **Crystallize**[20] 5077 4-9-9 **59**.......................... FergusSweeney 9 55
(A B Haynes) *in tch: rdn and unable qck ent fnl 2f: kpt on u.p fnl f: no threat to ldrs* **15/2**

5114 **5** 2 **Gee Major**[16] 5201 3-9-2 **56**.......................... DarryllHolland 2 45
(N J Vaughan) *led tl 4f out: styd pressing ldr: hung lft and wknd ent fnl f* **9/2**[3]

0050 **6** 1 3/4 **Future Regime (IRE)**[7] 5469 3-8-5 **48**........ Louis-PhilippeBeuzelin(3) 10 32
(Patrick Morris) *bhd: rdn over 3f out: n.d* **40/1**

0440 **7** 3/4 **Song Of Praise**[45] 4232 4-8-13 **49**.......................... NeilChalmers 6 33
(M Blanshard) *dwlt: sn in tch in midfield: rdn and effrt to chse ldrs over 1f out: pushed lft and wknd qckly ent fnl f* **15/2**

645 8 ½ **Satin Princess (IRE)**35 4534 3-8-6 **46** oh1............ FrankieMcDonald 8 26
(A M Hales) *s.i.s: t.k.h: sn chsng ldrs: rdn ent fnl 2f: pushed lft and wknd qckly ent fnl f* **14/1**

1m 21.7s (-1.40) **Going Correction** -0.225s/f (Firm)
WFA 3 from 4yo+ 4lb **8** Ran SP% **114.2**
Speed ratings (Par 101): **99,98,93,91,89 87,86,86**
toteswingers:1&2:£9.10, 1&3:£4.80, 2&3:£1.10 CSF £44.68 CT £101.64 TOTE £9.80: £2.50, £1.80, £1.30; EX 45.40 Trifecta £192.30 Pool: £335.23 - 1.29 winning units..
Owner Kenneth Eastup **Bred** Mrs Clodagh McStay **Trained** Yarnscombe, Devon

FOCUS
Low-grade stuff, but run at a decent gallop and the first two came clear in the final furlong. The form is taken at face value.

5712 BRIGHTON AND HOVE CITY CABS APPRENTICE (S) STKS 6f 209y
4:00 (4:00) (Class 6) 3-4-Y-O **£1,942** (£578; £288; £144) **Stalls** Centre

Form RPR
5232 1 **Timeteam (IRE)**2 5652 4-9-3 74.............................. HarryBentley(5) 4 75
(G L Moore) *t.k.h: sn pressing ldr: rdn and ev ch fr wl over 1f out: lft in ld jst ins fnl f: rdn out* **8/11**1
5165 2 nk **Universal Circus**1 5678 3-8-10 76.............................. RyanClark(3) 6 67
(M R Channon) *stdd after s: trckd ldng pair: rdn and effrt over 2f out: ev ch ent fnl f: hmpd and pushed rt jst ins fnl f: rallied fnl 75yds: kpt on* **9/4**2
0400 3 nk **Giulietta Da Vinci**5 5555 3-8-5 62.............................. AdamBeschizza(3) 8 61
(S Woodman) *led: rdn over 1f out: wnt rt: hmpd rival and hdd jst ins fnl f: styd on same pce after* **11/2**3
0506 4 8 **Mororless**17 5174 3-8-13 48..............................(p) AshleyMorgan 7 47?
(Miss Z C Davison) *s.i.s: a in last: rdn over 3f out: wl btn over 1f out* **20/1**

1m 22.47s (-0.63) **Going Correction** -0.225s/f (Firm)
WFA 3 from 4yo 4lb **4** Ran SP% **108.8**
Speed ratings (Par 101): **94,93,93,84**
CSF £2.64 TOTE £1.40; EX 2.20.There was no bid for the winner.
Owner Tony Hind **Bred** R N Auld **Trained** Lower Beeding, W Sussex

FOCUS
A weak race decimated by non-runners. The winner did not need to match his recent form.

5713 BUDDIES CAFE FILLIES' H'CAP 6f 209y
4:30 (4:30) (Class 5) (0-75,72) 3-Y-O+ **£3,108** (£924; £462; £230) **Stalls** Centre

Form RPR
-130 1 **Progress (IRE)**69 3441 3-9-4 **70**.............................. DarryllHolland 7 75
(J Noseda) *mde all: rdn over 1f out: pushed along hands and heels ins fnl f: jst hld on* **9/1**
4500 2 nse **Ivory Lace**34 4579 9-9-2 **67**.............................. AndrewHeffernan(3) 8 74
(S Woodman) *stdd after s: hld up in tch: effrt and rdn 2f out: drvn and chsd ldrs 1f out: r.o wl and str chal fnl 50yds: jst failed* **8/1**3
2421 3 ½ **Russian Rave**22 5010 4-9-5 **72**.............................. AdamBeschizza(5) 4 78
(J G Portman) *t.k.h: chsd ldrs: rdn to chse wnr over 1f out: pressed wnr ins fnl f: no ex towards fin* **2/1**2
404 4 1 ½ **Hulcote Rose (IRE)**20 5083 3-9-0 **66**.............................. DavidProbert 2 66
(S Kirk) *hld up in tch: rdn and effrt 2f out: pressed wnr jst ins fnl f: wknd fnl 75yds* **15/8**1
1304 5 4 ½ **Lady Kent (IRE)**50 4053 4-9-4 **69**.............................. MatthewDavies(3) 5 58
(J R Boyle) *t.k.h: chsd ldrs: wnt 2nd 4f out: rdn ent fnl 2f: lost 2nd over 1f out: wknd ent fnl f* **8/1**3
30 6 2 **Lady Willa (IRE)**14 5254 3-8-8 **60**.............................. NeilChalmers 6 42
(Mark Gillard) *stdd s: hld up in tch in last: rdn and effrt ent fnl 2f: no prog and wl hld ent fnl f* **22/1**
6435 7 ¾ **Lathaat**19 5113 3-8-12 **64**..............................(b1) TadhgO'Shea 3 44
(J L Dunlop) *chsd wnr tl 4f out: rdn and dropped to rr ent fnl 3f: wl btn over 1f out* **12/1**

1m 21.7s (-1.40) **Going Correction** -0.225s/f (Firm)
WFA 3 from 4yo+ 4lb **7** Ran SP% **112.4**
Speed ratings (Par 100): **99,98,98,96,91 89,88**
toteswingers:1&2:£4.90, 1&3:£2.70, 2&3:£3.40 CSF £73.46 CT £199.65 TOTE £8.50: £4.60, £5.20; EX 49.20 Trifecta £161.20 Pool: £315.88 - 1.45 winning units..
Owner The Honorable Earle I Mack **Bred** Darley **Trained** Newmarket, Suffolk

FOCUS
Question marks over all of these on one count or another coming into this. The second and third are sound enough guides.

5714 BRIGHTON AND HOVE CITY CABS H'CAP 5f 213y
5:00 (5:00) (Class 6) (0-60,59) 3-Y-O+ **£2,072** (£616; £308; £153) **Stalls** Centre

Form RPR
5443 1 **Bermondsey Bob (IRE)**17 5175 4-9-4 **56**.............................. DarryllHolland 2 66
(J L Spearing) *mde all: rdn over 1f out: styd on wl fnl f* **11/4**1
0434 2 1 ½ **Bateleur**17 5169 6-9-4 **59**.............................. MatthewDavies(3) 3 64+
(M R Channon) *s.i.s: bhd: rdn and hdwy over 1f out: drvn and chsd wnr ins fnl f: no imp fnl 75yds* **13/2**3
6504 3 nk **Mandhooma**17 5175 4-9-6 **58**.............................. WilliamCarson 9 62
(P W Hiatt) *racd in last pair: hmpd over 4f out: rdn and effrt over 2f out: styd on wl u.p ins fnl f: wnt 3rd last stride* **14/1**
6221 4 shd **Stamford Blue**4 5580 9-8-12 **57**..............................(b) JakePayne(7) 7 61
(R A Harris) *chsd ldrs: wnt 2nd 4f out: rdn and styd on same pce fr wl over 1f out: lost 2 pls ins fnl f* **4/1**2
6416 5 nk **Dualagi**22 5010 6-9-4 **56**.............................. GeorgeBaker 4 59
(M R Bosley) *hld up towards rr: hmpd over 4f out: effrt on far side 2f out: rdn to chse ldrs ent fnl f: no ex and no imp fnl 150yds* **8/1**
3251 6 2 ½ **Wooden King (IRE)**4 5579 5-9-5 **57** 6ex.............................. LiamJones 6 52
(M S Saunders) *chsd ldrs: hmpd by loose horse over 4f out: rdn and unable qck 3f out wknd over 1f out* **4/1**2
0622 7 ½ **Commandingpresence (USA)**7 5471 4-9-3 **55**.......... NeilChalmers 1 48
(J J Bridger) *chsd wnr tl hmpd by loose horse over 4f out: styd chsng ldrs: rdn 2f out: struggling whn n.m.r ent fnl f: sn wknd* **12/1**
0600 8 hd **Tamino (IRE)**83 2964 7-8-12 **50**.............................. J-PGuillambert 5 43
(P Howling) *a towards rr: hmpd over 4f out: rdn and unable qck over 2f out: styd on same pce fr over 1f out: nvr trbld ldrs* **20/1**
0106 U **Boldinor**17 5169 7-9-0 **59**.............................. RyanPowell(7) 8 —
(M R Bosley) *uns rdr sn after s* **12/1**

69.70 secs (-0.50) **Going Correction** -0.225s/f (Firm) **9** Ran SP% **117.9**
Speed ratings (Par 101): **94,92,91,91,91 87,87,86,—**
toteswingers:1&2:£4.10, 1&3:£10.60, 2&3:£5.00 CSF £21.62 CT £216.68 TOTE £4.30: £1.80, £2.90, £3.30; EX 23.60 Trifecta £141.10 Pool: £337.72 - 1.77 winning units..
Owner A A Campbell **Bred** Pier House Stud **Trained** Kinnersley, Worcs

FOCUS
A low-grade handicap. The form is rated at face value but the winner may not have been as good as the margin suggests.
Dualagi Official explanation: jockey said mare suffered interference in running
Wooden King(IRE) Official explanation: jockey said gelding suffered interference in running
Commandingpresence(USA) Official explanation: jockey said filly suffered interference in running

5715 BEN SHAWS H'CAP 5f 59y
5:30 (5:30) (Class 6) (0-52,58) 3-Y-O+ **£2,072** (£616; £308; £153) **Stalls** Centre

Form RPR
052 1 **Kinigi (IRE)**4 5579 4-8-7 **47**..............................(b) AndrewHeffernan(3) 9 69
(R A Harris) *racd in midfield: hdwy ent fnl 2f: chsd ldr wl over 1f out: edgd lft u.p: led jst over 1f out: sn clr: r.o strly* **9/4**2
5601 2 6 **Madam Isshe**7 5470 3-9-6 **58** 6ex.............................. LiamJones 1 60
(M S Saunders) *led: sn hdd: chsd ldr after: rdn ent fnl 2f: drvn over 1f out: chsd clr wnr jst ins fnl f: no imp* **8/1**
0054 3 1 ½ **If Only**10 5388 4-8-12 **49**..............................(p) WilliamCarson 2 46
(D Morris) *towards rr: rdn and effrt over 2f out: no ch w wnr but kpt on u.p fnl f to go 3rd nr fin* **4/1**3
0000 4 hd **Spring Horizon (IRE)**17 5176 4-8-8 **45**.............................. KirstyMilczarek 4 41
(Miss Z C Davison) *chsd ldrs: rdn over 2f out: drvn and wl outpcd over 1f out: plugged on same pce fnl f: lost 3rd nr fin* **33/1**
3412 5 3 ¼ **Annia Galeria (IRE)**9 5417 3-8-6 **49**..............................(b) AdamBeschizza(5) 6 34
(C A Dwyer) *sn led and clr: styd on far rail 3f out: rdn wl over 1f out: hdd jst over 1f out: sn btn: fdd qckly ins fnl f* **7/4**1
020- 6 nk **Cane Cat (IRE)**263 7749 3-9-0 **52**.............................. MickyFenton 7 36
(A W Carroll) *taken down early: wnt rt s and s.i.s: a towards rr: rdn over 2f out: no hdwy and n.d* **14/1**
6000 7 1 ¼ **Louie's Lad**5 5555 4-8-8 **45**.............................. NeilChalmers 8 25
(J J Bridger) *racd in midfield: struggling u.p 1/2-way: bhd wl over 1f out* **20/1**
000 8 2 **Rubbinghouse Com**21 5027 3-8-6 **49**..............1 JemmaMarshall(5) 10 22
(P M Phelan) *stdd s: t.k.h: hld up in rr: shkn up and no rspnse 2f out: n.d* **14/1**

61.04 secs (-1.26) **Going Correction** -0.225s/f (Firm)
WFA 3 from 4yo+ 1lb **8** Ran SP% **119.3**
Speed ratings (Par 101): **101,91,89,88,83 83,81,77**
toteswingers:1&2:£3.70, 1&3:£2.10, 2&3:£4.60. totesuper7: Win: Not won, Place: Not won. CSF £21.84 CT £71.07 TOTE £2.60: £1.20, £2.10, £1.50; EX 19.00 Trifecta £48.80 Pool: £364.62 - 5.52 winning units. Place 6 £221.23; Place 5 £56.87.
Owner Brian Hicks **Bred** Corduff Stud **Trained** Earlswood, Monmouths

FOCUS
Little depth to this handicap.
T/Jkpt: Part won. £43,499.20 to a £1 stake. Pool:£61,266.53 - 0.50 winning tickets. T/Plt: £190.80 to a £1 stake. Pool:£76,792.69 - 293.69 winning tickets T/Qpdt: £17.10 to a £1 stake. Pool:£5,320.57 - 229.73 winning tickets SP

5656 KEMPTON (A.W) (R-H)
Friday, September 3

OFFICIAL GOING: Standard
Wind: Moderate, half behind Weather: Fine

5716 MIDLAND FACILITIES APPRENTICE H'CAP 1m (P)
5:45 (5:45) (Class 4) (0-85,85) 3-Y-O+ **£3,885** (£867; £867; £288) **Stalls** High

Form RPR
3240 1 **My Best Bet**27 4847 4-9-1 **78**.............................. JohnFahy(3) 11 85
(Stef Higgins) *hld up in last trio: rdn and prog on wd outside fr 2f out: styd on wl to ld last 100yds* **9/2**2
1560 2 1 **Expensive Problem**50 4057 7-8-6 **71**.............................. NathanAlison(5) 5 76
(R J Smith) *settled in 7th: pushed along 3f out: prog over 2f out: chal and upsides jst ins fnl f: kpt on same pce* **40/1**
400 2 dht **Rock Anthem (IRE)**41 4354 6-8-10 **70** oh1.............. RussKennemore 7 75
(Mike Murphy) *dwlt: hld up in last trio: prog fr 2f out: rdn to chal and nrly upsides ent fnl f: kpt on same pce* **10/1**
40 4 nk **Hazzard County (USA)**36 4501 6-8-11 **78**.............................. AliceHaynes(7) 2 82
(D M Simcock) *hld up in 6th: stdy prog on outer 2f out: led briefly ins fnl f: nudged along and fdd last 100yds* **20/1**
30-0 5 1 **Cool Hand Jake**51 4023 4-9-5 **79**.............................. JamesMillman 10 81
(P J Makin) *trckd ldng trio: effrt to cl over 1f out: nrly upsides ent fnl f: fdd* **5/1**3
6000 6 1 ½ **Wigram's Turn (USA)**20 5098 5-9-6 **80**.............................. JamesSullivan 3 78
(M W Easterby) *led: hdd & wknd ins fnl f* **15/2**
4010 7 nk **Zubova**3 5648 3-8-4 **72**..............................(t) SimonPearce(3) 4 70
(D Shaw) *chsd ldr to 1f out: wknd* **14/1**
6506 8 ¾ **Gallantry**142 1306 8-8-10 **77**.............................. IanBurns(7) 6 73
(P Howling) *chsd ldng trio: no imp 2f out: lost pl and btn over 1f out* **25/1**
5000 9 nk **Striding Edge (IRE)**51 4023 4-8-9 **74**.............................. JamesRogers(5) 8 69
(W R Muir) *settled in 8th: shkn up 3f out: sme prog on inner 2f out: no imp over 1f out: fdd* **20/1**
1004 10 10 **Stand Guard**140 1348 6-9-3 **84**.............................. LauraSimpson(7) 1 56
(P Howling) *racd wd: hld up in last pair: lost tch over 2f out: wl bhd after* **25/1**
4632 P **Glen Shiel (USA)**8 5435 3-9-6 **85**.............................. Louis-PhilippeBeuzelin 9 —
(M Johnston) *trckd ldr 3f: cl 3rd whn p.u over 2f out: fatally injured* **11/8**1

1m 39.22s (-0.58) **Going Correction** +0.075s/f (Slow)
WFA 3 from 4yo+ 5lb **11** Ran SP% **124.1**
Speed ratings (Par 105): **105,104,104,103,102 101,100,100,99,89** —PL: Expensive Problem £21.80, Rock Anthem £2.80 EX: MBB&EP £97.20 MBB&RA £30.90 CSF: MBB&EP £93.41 MBB&RA £23.64. T/C: MBB&EP&RA £887.57, MBB&RA&EP £830.97.
toteswingers:MBB&EP:£31.30, EP&RA:£72.60, MBB&RA:£10.00 CSF £23.64 CT £830.97 TOTE £3.90: £1.50; EX 97.20 27 Owner.

FOCUS
A modest handicap for apprentice riders. It was run to suit the closers and there were eight runners in with every chance at the furlong marker. The form looks sound.

5717 LETCHWORTH COURIERS E B F MAIDEN STKS (DIV I) 1m (P)
6:15 (6:15) (Class 4) 2-Y-O **£3,950** (£1,175; £587; £293) **Stalls** High

Form RPR
32 1 **Tick Tock Lover**49 4096 2-9-3 0.............................. FergusSweeney 8 81
(Miss Jo Crowley) *lw: led after 1f: mde rest: shkn up over 1f out: edgd lft but styd on wl fnl f* **7/4**1
2 2 1 ½ **Splash Point (USA)**49 4089 2-9-3 0.............................. AhmedAjtebi 2 78
(Mahmood Al Zarooni) *w'like: lw: prom: chsd wnr 1/2-way: rdn 2f out: keeping on but wl hld whn sltly impeded ins fnl f* **9/4**2
3 ½ **Halfsin (IRE)** 2-9-3 0.............................. RyanMoore 6 78+
(M Botti) *str: scope: bit bkwd: in tch in midfield: urged along fr over 3f out: prog over 2f out: wnt 3rd over 1f out: styd on wl fnl f* **9/2**3

The Form Book, Raceform Ltd, Compton, RG20 6NL

4 *5* **Aloneinthestreet (USA)** 2-9-3 0....................................... JoeFanning 9 66
(M Johnston) *athletic: lw: led 1f: chsd wnr to 1/2-way: outpcd fr 2f out: lost 3rd and wl btn over 1f out* **15/2**

0 5 *nse* **Acute (IRE)**[14] 5263 2-9-3 0... MartinDwyer 10 66+
(B J Meehan) *leggy: in tch: pushed along on inner over 3f out: n.m.r and snatched up sn after: nvr on terms after: kpt on* **22/1**

6 *2* **If You Whisper (IRE)** 2-9-3 0.. TonyCulhane 4 61
(Mike Murphy) *str: bit bkwd: hld up and racd wd: shuffled along fr over 2f out: nvr on terms* **28/1**

7 *3 3/4* **Warrant** 2-9-3 0.. JimmyQuinn 1 53
(P Howling) *str: scope: dwlt: a in rr: outpcd fr 3f out: no ch after* **66/1**

8 *2 1/4* **Chillie Peppar** 2-9-3 0... SaleemGolam 5 48
(G Prodromou) *w'like: bit bkwd: dwlt: hld up: a in last trio but travelled wl to over 2f out: wknd* **100/1**

9 *2* **Storm Runner (IRE)** 2-9-3 0... SebSanders 7 43
(G G Margarson) *w'like: bit bkwd: s.i.s: mostly in last trio: no ch fr over 2f out* **40/1**

10 *19* **Champagne Princess** 2-8-12 0............................... TomMcLaughlin 3 —
(P S McEntee) *w'like: chsd ldrs to 3f out: wknd rapidly: t.o* **80/1**

1m 40.5s (0.70) **Going Correction** +0.075s/f (Slow) **10** Ran SP% **111.0**
Speed ratings (Par 97): **99,97,97,92,91 89,86,83,81,62**
toteswingers:1&2:£1.10, 1&3:£2.20, 2&3:£2.80 CSF £5.17 TOTE £2.70: £1.10, £1.40, £2.00; EX 6.50.
Owner Kilstone Limited **Bred** Mrs R I Nelson **Trained** Whitcombe, Dorset

FOCUS
The first three came clear in this average juvenile maiden and the form should work out. The winner is rated pretty much to form in success.

NOTEBOOK
Tick Tock Lover got an aggressive ride and deservedly made it third time lucky on this return to Polytrack. He was entitled to score on the form of his previous second at Newbury to subsequent Acomb Stakes winner Waiter's Dream and is obviously a very useful prospect. He was drifting left under maximum pressure, but had been in front long enough and clearly stays well. He certainly has the size to make up into a better 3-y-o and connections reportedly plan to give him one more run before putting him away for the year. (op 15-8 tchd 2-1)
Splash Point(USA), second on debut at Haydock 49 days earlier, proved easy enough to back on this step up in trip and switch to the AW, despite his pedigree suggesting the surface would suit. He tracked the winner throughout and held every chance, but got outstayed where it mattered. He wasn't really helped by that rival drifting in front of him and he should soon find an opening. (op 7-4 tchd 13-8)
Halfsin(IRE) ◆'s dam was a decent miler in France that has already thrown up a 10f winner at this venue. He got markedly outpaced before staying on strongly all too late in the day and will surely go very close on his next assignment, but already looks in need of a stiffer test. (op 11-2 tchd 4-1)
Aloneinthestreet(USA) was starting off over a trip plenty far enough looking at his pedigree and shaped as though the run was needed. A drop to 7f may prove best in the short term and he has a future. (op 8-1 tchd 9-1)
If You Whisper(IRE) ◆ was a first-ever juvenile runner for his trainer. He lacked the pace to land a serious blow, but moved nicely through the race and is one to keep an eye on with a view to nurseries in due course. He too may be better off over a sharper test for the time being. (op 25-1)

5718 LETCHWORTH COURIERS E B F MAIDEN STKS (DIV II) 1m (P)
6:45 (6:47) (Class 4) 2-Y-0 **£3,950** (£1,175; £587; £293) **Stalls** High

Form RPR

1 **Boxeur Des Rues (USA)** 2-9-3 0.................................... MichaelHills 5 73+
(W J Haggas) *w'like: swtg: b.hind: s.v.s: wl bhd: poor 7th over 2f out: stl same pl over 1f out: styd on wl to take 2nd last 50yds: led post* **9/1**

0 2 *nse* **A Boy Named Suzi**[28] 4803 2-9-3 0................................ JackMitchell 4 73
(T T Clement) *chsd ldrs: pushed along and prog over 2f out: drvn to ld over 1f out: over a l clr whn veered lft 75yds out and jockey nrly off: nt rcvr and hdd post* **13/2**[3]

025 3 *2* **Tagansky**[27] 4838 2-9-3 73.. SebSanders 8 68
(S Dow) *chsd ldr: clsd to ld jst over 2f out: hdd over 1f out: hld whn sltly hmpd 50yds out* **8/1**

4 *1/2* **Gentleman Is Back (USA)** 2-9-3 0.............................. WilliamBuick 2 67+
(J H M Gosden) *w'like: scope: trckd ldng pair: pushed along 3f out: effrt to chal and w ldr 2f out: tired fnl f* **9/2**[2]

5 *shd* **Divine Rule (IRE)** 2-9-3 0.. SteveDrowne 1 67
(H Morrison) *w'like: s.i.s: sn chsd ldrs on outer: pushed along 3f out: tired and no ex fnl f* **14/1**

00 6 *3/4* **Orange Ketchup (IRE)**[22] 4993 2-8-10 0.................... DuilioDaSilva(7) 7 65
(P F I Cole) *chsd ldrs: shkn up 3f out: tried to cl 2f out: tired and no ex fnl f* **50/1**

622 7 *17* **Busker (USA)**[25] 4909 2-9-3 79...................................... AhmedAjtebi 9 28+
(Mahmood Al Zarooni) *lw: led at str pce: hdd & wknd rapidly jst over 2f out: t.o* **1/1**[1]

0 8 *nk* **Jan Smuts (IRE)**[21] 5032 2-9-3 0.................................... MartinDwyer 3 27
(B J Meehan) *leggy: t.o in last by 1/2-way* **25/1**

9 *1/2* **Brezza Di Mare (IRE)** 2-9-0 0................... Louis-PhilippeBeuzelin(3) 10 26
(B J Meehan) *str: sn struggling: wl bhd fr 1/2-way: t.o* **20/1**

500 10 *6* **Helen Of Toy**[126] 1660 2-8-12 42.................................(t) FergusSweeney 6 8
(B G Powell) *sn struggling: wl bhd 1/2-way: t.o* **100/1**

1m 40.82s (1.02) **Going Correction** +0.075s/f (Slow) **10** Ran SP% **120.9**
Speed ratings (Par 97): **97,96,94,94,94 93,76,76,75,69**
toteswingers:1&2:£5.30, 1&3:£9.20, 2&3:£6.20 CSF £66.38 TOTE £10.70: £2.40, £2.00, £3.50; EX 81.00.
Owner Equine Breeding & The Strikers **Bred** Grapestock Llc **Trained** Newmarket, Suffolk

FOCUS
The second division of the 1m juvenile maiden and it was run at a strong early pace, but resulted in a marginally slower time than the first. The winner should be able to progress from this.

NOTEBOOK
Boxeur Des Rues(USA) ◆ walked out of the gates, losing around six lengths, and looked like being one of the back numbers rounding the home turn as he displayed his inexperience. As the leaders began to wilt, though, he really found his stride and began to mow them down, but he was then slightly hampered by the runner-up near the finish. All considered he has to rate value for further and he should prove a lot sharper with the experience under his belt, so it will be very interesting to see where it is entered next. (tchd 14-1)
A Boy Named Suzi was delivered between horses at the furlong pole and looked sure to land some decent bets. However, he began to wander after smacked by the whip and then badly jinked to his left near the finish, causing his rider to nearly unseat. He was mugged late on and would've surely scored had he kept a true line. It may have been down to his rider being overly hard on him, or still down to greenness, but should he learn from this there ought to be a maiden for him before he switches to nurseries. (op 10-1)
Tagansky rates the benchmark for the race. He fared best of those racing handily and this was a fair effort, but he will probably need to go handicapping before tasting success. (op 9-1 tchd 15-2)
Gentleman Is Back(USA) ◆, a half-brother to 6f-1m winners, got across early from his wide draw and looked a big threat when switching to the inside 2f out. He couldn't find an extra gear thereafter, but should improve a deal for this initial outing and looks one to side with next time out. (op 4-1)
Divine Rule(IRE) is clearly thought to stay well by connections and proved easy to back. He was another slow to break, but recovered well and had his chance as the race developed. His trainer's juveniles always come on for their debut runs and this scopey colt can win races this year. (op 16-1 tchd 12-1)
Orange Ketchup(IRE) hit a flat spot before staying on again and is one to become more interested in now he qualifies for a mark. (op 40-1)
Busker(USA), second the last twice, did far too much early on over this longer trip and was made to pay from 2f out. He is probably worth another chance. Official explanation: jockey said colt stopped quickly (op 11-10 tchd 5-4)
Brezza Di Mare(IRE) Official explanation: jockey said gelding hung left

5719 WILDE CHILD 25TH ANNIVERSARY E B F MAIDEN FILLIES' STKS 6f (P)
7:15 (7:16) (Class 4) 2-Y-0 **£4,274** (£1,271; £635; £317) **Stalls** High

Form RPR

2 1 **Darajaat (USA)**[20] 5078 2-9-0 0.. RichardHills 7 85+
(M P Tregoning) *w'like: angular: trckd ldr: led over 2f out: pushed along and grad drew clr fr over 1f out: readily* **4/7**[1]

2 *2 3/4* **Blanche Dubawi (IRE)** 2-9-0 0..................................... TomQueally 4 74+
(M G Quinlan) *leggy: sn chsd ldng pair: chal over 2f out: chsd wnr after and sn clr of rest: wl hld fnl f* **16/1**

60 3 *2 1/4* **Polar Auroras**[26] 4871 2-9-0 0....................................... ShaneKelly 1 67
(Pat Eddery) *wnt lft s: sn chsd ldng trio: outpcd over 2f out: styd on to take 3rd ins fnl f* **25/1**

4 *1 1/4* **Blessed Biata (USA)** 2-9-0 0.................................... MichaelHills 10 63+
(W J Haggas) *w'like: leggy: settled in 9th: pushed along over 2f out: styd on steadily fr over 1f out: tk 4th nr fin* **14/1**

5 *3/4* **Bint Alakaaber (IRE)** 2-9-0 0.. EddieAhern 3 61
(J R Jenkins) *w'like: led to over 2f out: sn outpcd by ldng pair: wknd fnl f* **12/1**[3]

6 *1 1/2* **Bird In The Wind (USA)** 2-8-11 0........................... EJMcNamara(3) 11 57
(R M Beckett) *unf: hld up in 8th: sme prog on inner over 2f out: nvr a threat: no hdwy fnl f* **25/1**

2 7 *1/2* **Azzoom (IRE)**[49] 4103 2-9-0 0... RyanMoore 8 55
(C E Brittain) *unf: scope: tall: chsd ldrs in 6th: outpcd and wl btn over 2f out: no prog after* **4/1**[2]

8 *1/2* **Melbury** 2-9-0 0.. JimmyQuinn 5 54
(P Howling) *w'like: bit bkwd: dwlt: a in rr: outpcd fr 1/2-way: no ch after: plugged on* **100/1**

00 9 *3/4* **Talkhees (IRE)**[21] 5029 2-9-0 0................................... TadhgO'Shea 12 51
(B J Meehan) *chsd ldng quartet: outpcd over 2f out: grad wknd* **33/1**

10 *4* **Pink Cat** 2-9-0 0.. SteveDrowne 9 39
(J R Gask) *unf: dwlt: racd wd: a in last trio: no ch fr over 2f out* **66/1**

000 11 *11* **Veuveveuvevoom**[32] 4658 2-8-11 25............ Louis-PhilippeBeuzelin(3) 6 6
(G P Enright) *t.k.h in midfield: wknd rapidly over 2f out: t.o* **100/1**

12 *2* **Rio Belle (IRE)** 2-8-11 0.. RussKennemore(3) 2 —
(Andrew Reid) *neat: detached in last after 2f: t.o* **100/1**

1m 13.25s (0.15) **Going Correction** +0.075s/f (Slow) **12** Ran SP% **119.0**
Speed ratings (Par 94): **102,98,95,93,92 90,90,89,88,83 68,65**
toteswingers:1&2:£4.20, 2&3:£36.50, 1&3:£9.10 CSF £11.97 TOTE £1.90: £1.10, £4.70, £7.60; EX 11.90.
Owner Hamdan Al Maktoum **Bred** Shadwell Farm LLC **Trained** Lambourn, Berks

FOCUS
A decent opportunity for the odds-on winner in this ordinary maiden.

NOTEBOOK
Darajaat(USA) was found a decent opportunity to go one better than her promising second on debut at Newbury last month and she completed the task readily. She was never far away and, while taking a little time to master the runner-up, was fully in command at the finish, easing off near the line. She will need to step up again plenty on this to justify her entry in the Group 1 Cheveley Park Stakes, but rates a smart prospect and ought to learn again from this experience. (tchd 8-15 and 8-13)
Blanche Dubawi(IRE) ◆, who attracted late support, is the first foal of a dam that proved a real money spinner for her yard, winning at up to Group 3 level. She knew her job and made the winner work 2f out, but was put in her place from the furlong pole. She looks a sure-fire winner of one of these before setting her sights on something more valuable. (op 25-1)
Polar Auroras again went out markedly to her left from the gates but was soon racing handily. She lacked the tactical pace to land a serious blow, but kept on encouragingly late on and this rates a clear personal-best. Nurseries are now an option.
Blessed Biata(USA) ◆ is closely related to five previous winners and from a family her yard knows very well. Easy to back, it took time for the penny to drop, but she really caught the eye staying on late under an educational ride. Her entry in the Cheveley Park, while too ambitious at this stage, indicates she is highly regarded, and she ought to go close on her next assignment.
Bint Alakaaber(IRE) is another highly regarded filly entered in the Cheveley Park Stakes. She showed real early pace, but did too much on the front end and unsurprisingly paid in the home straight. This should teach her plenty and she obviously has a future. (op 10-1)
Azzoom(IRE) was the chief danger to the winner on paper, but she was undone by the drop to this trip and ran well below the level of her Newmarket debut second. (tchd 9-2)
Pink Cat Official explanation: jockey said filly hung left

5720 EVENTMASTERS 25TH ANNIVERSARY NURSERY 6f (P)
7:45 (7:47) (Class 5) (0-70,70) 2-Y-0 **£2,286** (£675; £337) **Stalls** High

Form RPR

333 1 **Golden Tempest (IRE)**[29] 4729 2-9-3 **66**.......................... ShaneKelly 3 79+
(W R Swinburn) *hld up in 8th: rdn and gd prog fr 2f out to ld jst over 1f out: sn clr* **10/1**

3320 2 *3* **Freckenham (IRE)**[34] 4592 2-9-6 **69**............................... HayleyTurner 9 72
(M L W Bell) *lw: hld up in 7th: effrt on inner over 2f out: hrd rdn over 1f out: styd on to take 2nd last 100yds: no ch w wnr* **4/1**[2]

303 3 *1 1/2* **My Love Fajer (IRE)**[41] 4363 2-9-2 **70**........................... KierenFox(5) 8 69
(G Prodromou) *chsd ldr: reminder over 3f out: drvn to ld 2f out: hdd jst over 1f out: fdd last 100yds* **28/1**

U605 4 *1/2* **Blackleyf (IRE)**[35] 4543 2-9-3 **66**........................(b[1]) RichardKingscote 4 63
(Tom Dascombe) *dwlt: wl off the pce in last: rdn 3f out: no prog tl styd on wl fr over 1f out: nrst fin* **25/1**

6426 5 *shd* **Avalon Bay**[11] 5365 2-9-0 **63**... KierenFallon 5 60
(Pat Eddery) *racd wd: pressed ldrs: drvn to chal over 2f out: nt qckn over 1f out: sn btn* **7/2**[1]

2523 6 *3/4* **Never Can Stop**[26] 4872 2-8-8 **64**.............................. HarryBentley(7) 11 58
(J G Portman) *wl off the pce in last trio: sme prog fr 2f out: kpt on one pce fnl f: n.d* **8/1**

6202 7 *3/4* **Delira (IRE)**[29] 4729 2-9-1 **64**.. DavidProbert 2 56
(J G Portman) *lw: sn off the pce in 9th: rdn and clsd grad fr over 2f out: rchd 6th ent fnl f: one pce after* **10/1**

355 8 *3/4* **Paco Belle (IRE)**[44] 4254 2-9-3 **66**.............................. RichardHughes 1 58
(R Hannon) *lw: stdd s and dropped on fr wd draw: hld up in last pair and wl off the pce: rdn on wd outside and struggling over 2f out: styd on fnl f: nrst fin* **14/1**

444 **9** ½ **Tamareen (IRE)**[18] 5160 2-9-4 **67**....................(t) RichardHills 7 55
(E A L Dunlop) *lw: chsd ldng pair: tried to chal on outer over 2f out: nt qckn over 1f out: wknd fnl f* **13/2**

060 **10** 3¾ **Dells Breezer**[16] 5204 2-9-1 **64**.................... IanMongan 12 42
(P M Phelan) *rousted along to ld: hdd 2f out: wknd rapidly jst over 1f out: eased last 100yds* **33/1**

003 **11** 3½ **Red Lite (IRE)**[32] 4658 2-9-3 **66**.................... MartinDwyer 6 33
(B J Meehan) *chsd ldrs in 6th tl wknd wl over 1f out: eased ins fnl f* **11/2**[3]

063 **12** 9 **Aurivorous**[81] 3029 2-9-4 **67**.................... SteveDrowne 10 7
(Jonjo O'Neill) *chsd ldrs and cl up: wknd rapidly over 2f out: eased over 1f out: t.o* **33/1**

1m 13.06s (-0.04) **Going Correction** +0.075s/f (Slow) 12 Ran SP% **120.1**
Speed ratings (Par 95): **103,99,97,96,96 95,94,93,92,87 82,70**
toteswingers:1&2:£9.80, 1&3:£16.10, 2&3:£20.70 CSF £48.68 CT £1118.11 TOTE £14.50: £3.80, £1.60, £9.40; EX 43.90.
Owner Silver Linings **Bred** Rathasker Stud **Trained** Aldbury, Herts

FOCUS
A low-grade nursery, but it was littered with potential improvers. There was a solid pace on and the form looks pretty good for the grade. The third and fourth help cement the level.

NOTEBOOK
Golden Tempest(IRE) ◆ got her head in front at the fourth time of asking on this nursery debut and ran out a taking winner. She came into this having finished third on each of her previous outings, but wasn't happy on the firm ground at Bath last time and this kinder surface showed her in a decent light. She would've won with more authority had she not had to wait for her challenge nearing the final furlong and, with a pedigree suggesting further will suit in due course, is one to keep on side until her level becomes truly apparent. (op 8-1)
Freckenham(IRE) stayed on well on the inside from 2f out without threatening the winner and has now posted her two best efforts on Polytrack. She can find one of these before too long and may now appreciate another furlong, but the handicapper clearly has her about right. (tchd 7-2)
My Love Fajer(IRE), again on the front end and, getting the extra furlong well enough, turned in a sound effort under top weight on this nursery debut. (op 25-1)
Blackleyf(IRE) would have no doubt gone closer had he not made a tardy start, but it's not hard to see why connections have reached for the headgear and he looks one to tread carefully with.
Avalon Bay was ridden more positively on this return to 6f and held every chance on the outside in the home straight. He can win off this mark, but connections haven't quite found the key to him yet. (tchd 10-3 and 4-1)
Paco Belle(IRE), making her nursery debut, deserves a mention. She found herself with plenty to do and covered a lot of ground, staying on steadily as though in need of a return to 7f.

5721 AMDOCS MANAGEMENT E B F FILLIES' CONDITIONS STKS 7f (P)
8:15 (8:15) (Class 3) 2-Y-O

£6,542 (£1,959; £979; £490; £244; £122) **Stalls** High

Form RPR
3 **1** **Quiet Oasis (IRE)**[27] 4844 2-8-12 0.................... MartinDwyer 4 84+
(B J Meehan) *w'like: scope: restless stalls: prom: w ldr after 1f: led over 2f out: jst pushed along whn chal over 1f out: one reminder fnl f and in command* **2/5**[1]

2 ½ **Zing Wing** 2-8-12 0.................... TomQueally 5 80+
(P F I Cole) *w'like: lw: t.k.h: trckd ldrs: effrt to chal over 1f out: pressed wnr hrd but a fighting losing battle* **12/1**[3]

1 **3** 2 **Fluvial (IRE)**[29] 4741 2-8-12 0.................... AhmedAjtebi 1 74
(Mahmood Al Zarooni) *leggy: athletic: lw: trckd ldng pair over 4f out: tried to chal 2f out: sn rdn and nt qckn: styd on* **11/4**[2]

4 3 **Adorable Choice (IRE)** 2-8-12 0.................... RichardKingscote 7 66+
(Tom Dascombe) *w'like: bit bkwd: settled in last: pushed along over 2f out: one reminder over 1f out: wl outpcd but styd on encouragingly fnl f* **25/1**

50 **5** 3¼ **Rural Pursuits**[21] 5047 2-8-12 0.................... NickyMackay 3 57
(Mrs C A Dunnett) *w'like: led after 1f to over 2f out: wknd fnl f:* **100/1**

0 **6** 2¼ **Blazing Apostle (IRE)**[18] 5160 2-8-12 0.................... DavidProbert 2 51
(Mrs C A Dunnett) *w'like: a in last trio: rdn 3f out: wknd over 1f out* **150/1**

0 **7** ¾ **Lady Ellice**[18] 5160 2-8-12 0.................... TomMcLaughlin 6 49
(P S McEntee) *w'like: t.k.h: led 1f: lost pl on inner over 4f out: in tch tl wknd qckly over 1f out* **100/1**

1m 27.88s (1.88) **Going Correction** +0.075s/f (Slow) 7 Ran SP% **112.3**
Speed ratings (Par 96): **92,91,89,85,82 79,78**
toteswingers:1&2:£11.30, 1&3:£1.02, 2&3:£12.40 CSF £6.49 TOTE £1.30: £1.10, £2.40; EX 7.70.
Owner Sangster Family **Bred** Breeding Capital Plc & Swettenham Stud **Trained** Manton, Wilts

FOCUS
An interesting conditions event. There is more to come from the winner and the standard of the form is fluid.

NOTEBOOK
Quiet Oasis(IRE) was backed almost to the exclusion of her rivals on this step up in grade and she duly obliged at the second attempt. She ran with promise when third on her debut at Newmarket last month and is clearly held in high regard by her in-form operation. She found herself on the front end due to none of her rivals wanting to go off in front and settled well. That held her in good stead from 2f out as she had to fight to shake off the runner-up, and she was always doing enough where it mattered. She is entitled to improve again for this experience, which ought to teach her plenty, and it wouldn't be at all surprising to see her tried in Pattern company next time out. Should that be the case, the Oh So Sharp Stakes back at Newmarket next month looks the logical choice. (op 8-15)
Zing Wing ◆'s dam was a dual Listed winner over 1m for the yard. She travelled sweetly and threw down a strong challenge to the winner, but that rival just knew that bit too much for her at the business end. Winning a maiden ought to prove a formality in the coming weeks. (op 11-1)
Fluvial(IRE), off the mark on debut at Folkestone, was produced with every chance from the top of the home straight and gives the form a solid look. She could be very interesting dropped to 6f looking at her pedigree and the way she fared here. (op 5-2)
Adorable Choice(IRE) ◆ is a half-sister to a smart 6f winner and was faced with a tough task on this racecourse debut. She took time to get the hang of things, but stayed on nicely under a considerate ride late on and looks sure to improve.

5722 BORN TO BE WILDE 25TH ANNIVERSARY H'CAP 2m (P)
8:45 (8:45) (Class 5) (0-70,70) 4-Y-O+ **£2,286** (£675; £337) **Stalls** High

Form RPR
0122 **1** **Perception (IRE)**[17] 5179 4-9-7 **70**.................... FergusSweeney 10 79
(A King) *lw: trckd ldng trio in moderately run contest: rdn over 2f out: clsd on wd outside over 1f out: drvn ahd last 100yds* **4/1**[1]

454- **2** ½ **Wester Ross (IRE)**[138] 6622 6-8-7 **56**.................... JoeFanning 12 64
(J M P Eustace) *trckd ldr: rdn 3f out: clsd grad on outer to ld 1f out: hdd and one pce last 100yds* **9/1**

-056 **3** 2½ **Colonel Flay**[22] 5011 6-8-7 **61**.................... SophieDoyle(5) 1 66
(Mrs P N Dutfield) *t.k.h: hld up in last pair in steadily run r: plenty to do after pce lifted 4f out: prog 2f out: styd on to take 3rd nr fin* **9/1**

-320 **4** ½ **Gandalf**[17] 5179 8-9-1 **69**.................... JohnFahy(5) 9 73
(Miss Amy Weaver) *mde most: set stdy pce to over 4f out: drvn over 2f out: edgd lft: hdd and fdd 1f out* **8/1**

0022 **5** 3¾ **Lombok**[22] 5011 4-9-7 **70**.................... HayleyTurner 11 70
(M L W Bell) *trckd ldng pair to 6f out and again over 3f out gng wl: rdn and nt qckn over 2f out: fdd over 1f out* **9/2**[2]

-334 **6** 2¼ **Dark Energy**[16] 4386 6-8-6 **55**....................(t) JimmyQuinn 7 52
(M J Scudamore) *lw: t.k.h: trckd ldrs: rdn and struggling over 3f out: effrt over 2f out: no prog over 1f out* **8/1**

220- **7** 1¼ **Ramora (USA)**[316] 6975 4-9-7 **70**.................... SteveDrowne 3 66
(Miss Olivia Maylam) *hld up in tch: rdn and nt qckn whn pce lifted over 3f out: no prog after: fdd over 1f out* **25/1**

1-26 **8** 2¾ **Babilu**[14] 5272 5-8-5 **59**....................(p) KierenFox(5) 2 51
(D Burchell) *t.k.h: hld up in last pair: drvn and effrt over 3f out: no prog over 2f out: fdd* **7/1**

0546 **9** ¾ **Honorable Endeavor**[17] 5179 4-8-2 **51** oh4..........(v) FrankieMcDonald 5 43
(E F Vaughan) *hld up: reminders 5f out: dropped to last over 3f out: sn btn* **33/1**

5534 **10** 3¾ **Naughty Naughty**[9] 5420 5-8-13 **62**.................... SebSanders 6 49
(B G Powell) *hld up in rr: prog on outer to go 3rd 6f out to over 3f out: sn wknd* **11/2**[3]

3m 32.98s (2.88) **Going Correction** +0.075s/f (Slow) 10 Ran SP% **115.1**
Speed ratings (Par 103): **95,94,93,93,91 90,89,88,87,86**
toteswingers:1&2:£8.50, 1&3:£7.90, 2&3:£15.90 CSF £39.74 CT £305.06 TOTE £5.30: £2.60, £1.20, £5.30; EX 43.20.
Owner Incipe Partnership **Bred** Zanim Ralphy Meahjohn **Trained** Barbury Castle, Wilts

FOCUS
A moderate and wide-open staying handicap. It paid to race handily due to the modest gallop. The form is rated around the winner.

5723 BUNGE UK H'CAP 1m 3f (P)
9:15 (9:16) (Class 3) (0-95,95) 3-Y-O+

£6,044 (£1,810; £905; £452; £226; £113) **Stalls** High

Form RPR
120- **1** **Ottoman Empire (FR)**[323] 6795 4-9-7 **90**.................... TedDurcan 9 103+
(D R Lanigan) *trckd ldrs: prog to go 2nd over 2f out: rdn to ld over 1f out: styd on strly* **7/2**[2]

6300 **2** 2 **Luc Jordan**[22] 5004 4-9-4 **87**.................... KierenFallon 4 94
(L M Cumani) *prom: led over 5f out: drvn and hdd over 1f out: one pce* **14/1**

0140 **3** 1¼ **Greylami (IRE)**[13] 5307 5-9-10 **93**.................... EddieAhern 2 98
(R A Mills) *sn prom: trckd ldr 5f out to over 2f out where stl gng strly: one reminder over 1f out: styd on: nvr chal* **7/1**[3]

1-5 **4** 2¼ **Hymnsheet**[112] 2076 3-8-13 **90**....................(t) RyanMoore 3 91+
(Sir Michael Stoute) *s.s: hld up in last pair in steadily run r: effrt 3f out: styd on to take 4th ins fnl f: no ch* **8/1**

0460 **5** ½ **Desert Vision**[69] 3450 6-9-2 **88**....................(vt) JamesSullivan(3) 12 88
(M W Easterby) *t.k.h in midfield: lost pl on inner 5f out: effrt again over 3f out: outpcd fnl 2f* **25/1**

1031 **6** 1 **Proud Times (USA)**[25] 4891 4-9-4 **87**.................... AndrewElliott 6 85
(G A Swinbank) *hld up in tch on outer: rdn and nt qckn over 2f out: sn btn* **8/1**

3403 **7** 2 **Togiak (IRE)**[22] 5004 3-9-4 **95**.................... RichardHughes 11 90
(E A L Dunlop) *lw: trckd ldrs: shkn up and nt qckn over 2f out: grad fdd over 1f out* **8/1**

0300 **8** ½ **Record Breaker (IRE)**[19] 5118 6-9-12 **95**....................(b) JoeFanning 8 89
(M Johnston) *hld up in rr in steadily run r: rdn 3f out: one pce and no prog* **10/1**

2340 **9** ¾ **Dance The Star (USA)**[34] 4594 5-9-5 **88**.................... TomQueally 10 81
(E A L Dunlop) *s.s: hld up towards rr: rdn over 2f out: no real prog* **14/1**

-230 **10** 1 **Lucky Punt**[80] 3050 4-9-7 **90**.................... FergusSweeney 1 81
(B G Powell) *led to over 5f out: rdn over 3f out: wknd 2f out* **40/1**

4511 **11** 2¼ **Wild Rose**[11] 5371 3-8-11 **88** 6ex....................(t) HayleyTurner 7 75
(M L W Bell) *stdd s: hld up in last pair in steadily run r: effrt on inner over 2f out: sn no prog and btn: wknd over 1f out* **2/1**[1]

2m 21.4s (-0.50) **Going Correction** +0.075s/f (Slow)
WFA 3 from 4yo+ 8lb 11 Ran SP% **130.1**
Speed ratings (Par 107): **104,102,101,100,99 98,97,97,96,95 94**
toteswingers:1&2:£5.50, 1&3:£5.00, 2&3:£12.60 CSF £58.39 CT £347.80 TOTE £6.20: £2.70, £7.80, £1.80; EX 60.70 Place 6 £97.00; Place 5 £24.34.
Owner Plantation Stud **Bred** S C E A Haras De La Perelle **Trained** Newmarket, Suffolk

FOCUS
This was a good, competitive handicap. However, the uneven pace dictated it was another race where those held up were at a real disadvantage and the overall form is worth treating with a degree of caution. The winner is progressive.

NOTEBOOK
Ottoman Empire(FR) ran out a ready winner on his belated seasonal return and looks a big improver this year. There was a lot to like about his attitude when asked to pick up and he has always looked the sort that would do better at four. It wouldn't be surprising to see him defy a higher mark on the AW as all of his three wins have now been in this sphere, but he could just have more to offer on turf this season. He could be just the sort for the November Handicap at the end of term. Official explanation: jockey said gelding hung in home straight (op 5-1)
Luc Jordan, previously unbeaten in two previous outings on the AW, posted a much better effort in defeat. He put some pace into the race when going on down the far side and didn't go down without a fight once headed by the winner. (op 20-1)
Greylami(IRE) moved up on the back straight and ultimately held every chance, but just looked to be racing a little awkwardly from the two-furlong pole. He helps to set the standard. (op 15-2)
Hymnsheet was the interesting one here, as she was thought of as a possible Oaks horse earlier in the year and has been patiently handled by connections. Easy to back and equipped with a first-time tongue on this return to action, she did best of those waited with out the back and is no doubt better than the bare form. (tchd 10-1)
Wild Rose loves this venue and was entitled to plenty of respect under her penalty. She found herself with far too much to do off the stop-start pace, though, and couldn't get into the race when eventually asked for her effort. (op 11-4 tchd 3-1)

T/Plt: £276.50 to a £1 stake. Pool:£61,276.97 - 161.75 winning tickets T/Qpdt: £44.70 to a £1 stake. Pool:£7,354.14 - 121.60 winning tickets JN

5664 LINGFIELD (L-H)

Friday, September 3

OFFICIAL GOING: Standard

Wind: Virtually nil Weather: Sunny intervals

5724 MSS INTERIORS MEDIAN AUCTION MAIDEN STKS 1m (P)

1:50 (1:52) (Class 6) 2-Y-O £2,729 (£806; £403) Stalls High

Form				RPR
43	1		**Safari Team (IRE)**^{30} 4695 2-9-3 0 ... IanMongan 8 (P Winkworth) *trckd ldrs: led 3f out: drvn over 1f out: styd on strly fnl f* **7/2^{2}**	76
	2	½	**Charles Fosterkane** 2-8-12 0 ... KierenFox$^{(5)}$ 10 (J R Best) *chsd ldrs: rdn and kpt on to go 2nd ins fnl f: gaining on wnr cl home but a readily hld* **40/1**	75+
03	3	¾	**Rocky Rebel**^{21} 5047 2-9-3 0 ... JackMitchell 4 (R M Beckett) *in rr: wd into st: sn drvn: effrt and hung lft fr over 1f out: r.o fnl f and fin wl to take 3rd cl home but nt rch ldng duo* **11/8^{1}**	73
62	4	1	**Avid Kale**^{18} 5156 2-9-3 0 ... NeilCallan 6 (M Botti) *chsd ldrs: rdn to go 2nd over 1f out: hung rt and one pce fnl 75yds* **6/1^{3}**	71
	5	nk	**Haylaman (IRE)** 2-9-3 0 ... KierenFallon 11 (E A L Dunlop) *chsd ldr: wnt 2nd 2f out: sn rdn: lost 2nd over 1f out: outpcd ins fnl f* **11/1**	70
0	6	2½	**Major Domo (FR)**^{22} 5006 2-9-3 0 ... EddieAhern 3 (H J L Dunlop) *in rr: pushed along over 1f out: styd on ins fnl f but nt rch ldrs* **33/1**	65
	7	½	**Kelinni (IRE)** 2-9-3 0 ... DaneO'Neill 9 (Mrs A J Perrett) *s.i.s: sn mid-div on outer: hdwy 3f out: nvr quite rchd ldrs and wknd ins fnl f* **12/1**	64
0	8	½	**Lady Barastar (IRE)**^{51} 4021 2-8-12 0 ... AdamKirby 5 (W R Swinburn) *chsd ldrs: rdn and outpcd 3f out: n.d after* **40/1**	58
00	9	1	**Four Nations (USA)**^{14} 5263 2-9-3 0 ... SebSanders 1 (Mrs A J Perrett) *s.i.s: in rr: nvr gng pce to get into contention* **14/1**	60+
	10	11	**O Ma Lad (IRE)** 2-9-3 0 ... LiamKeniry 7 (S Kirk) *slowly away: green and a in rr* **50/1**	36
	11	22	**Honor Breeze (USA)** 2-8-12 0 ... SamHitchcott 12 (Louise Best) *led tl hdd & wknd 3f out* **66/1**	—

1m 40.04s (1.84) **Going Correction** +0.175s/f (Slow) 11 Ran SP% **112.6**

Speed ratings (Par 93): **97,96,95,94,94 91,91,90,89,78 56**

toteswingers:1&2:£29.50, 1&3:£2.30, 2&3:£11.90 CSF £140.49 TOTE £4.40: £1.70, £6.10, £1.10; EX 108.70.

Owner P Winkworth **Bred** Fortbarrington Stud **Trained** Chiddingfold, Surrey

FOCUS

No more than a fair maiden, rated around the winner, third and time.

NOTEBOOK

Safari Team(IRE), up in trip, confirmed the promise of his first two efforts with a straightforward success. According to connections he may now be gelded and kept for next year, when he should make a reasonable handicapper. (op 4-1)

Charles Fosterkane had a sheepskin noseband fitted and carried his head a bit high under pressure, but he still ran on well after being a little short of room around the turn into the straight. This first foal of a dual winner on dirt in the US is open to improvement.

Rocky Rebel was set a bit to do and then didn't help himself by hanging left after being brought widest of all into the straight, but he still finished well. The form of his recent third at the July course is not really working out (runner-up beaten at 1-3 next time), but he's now eligible for a mark. (op 13-8 tchd 7-4 in places)

Avid Kale ran okay without improving for the step up in trip. Handicaps are now an option. (op 7-2)

Haylaman(IRE), a 14,000gns gelded half-brother to, among others, 1m-1m2f winner and fairly useful staying hurdler Football Crazy, ran to just a modest level but may improve. (op 10-1 tchd 12-1)

Major Domo(FR) was not given a hard time and should do better in handicaps over middle-distance/staying trips next year.

Kelinni(IRE) ◆ ran green, starting slowly and then taking a while to get balanced once in the straight, but he showed ability. He should do okay over further next year. (op 14-1 tchd 16-1)

Four Nations(USA) ◆ stuck towards the often unfavoured inside rail in the straight and was not subjected to a particularly tough race. Now eligible for an official rating, he should come into his own over further, probably next year. (op 16-1 tchd 18-1)

5725 CLIVE & JOAN SHRIMPTON 85TH BIRTHDAY NURSERY 5f (P)

2:20 (2:21) (Class 4) (0-85,77) 2-Y-O £5,180 (£1,541; £770; £384) Stalls High

Form				RPR
61	1		**Sadafiya**^{25} 4909 2-9-6 **76** ... RichardHills 6 (E A L Dunlop) *s.i.s: sn in tch: hdwy appr fnl f: rdn and qcknd to ld fnl 40yds: edgd lft: drvn out* **11/4^{1}**	82
6113	2	½	**Millyluvstobouggie**^{14} 5261 2-9-3 **73** ... AdamKirby 2 (C G Cox) *chsd ldrs: rdn to chal between horses over 1f out: led ins fnl f: hdd and outpcd fnl 40yds* **7/2^{2}**	77
1	3	1½	**Winnie Dixie (USA)**^{18} 5147 2-9-5 **75** ... KierenFallon 5 (P F I Cole) *chsd ldrs: rdn to chal 2f out: stl ev ch appr fnl f: one pce whn crossed and swtchd rt nr fin* **11/4^{1}**	74
3414	4	1	**Second Encore**^{56} 3849 2-9-4 **74** ... LiamKeniry 8 (J S Moore) *in rr: racd on outside: drvn and styd on fnl f: gng on cl home but nvr gng pce to get into contention* **33/1**	70
005	5	½	**Saucy Buck (IRE)**^{24} 4927 2-8-13 **69** ... SamHitchcott 1 (M R Channon) *s.i.s: in rr and pushed along tl styd on fnl f: nt rch ldrs* **33/1**	62
5351	6	nk	**Dubai Affair**^{11} 5365 2-9-1 **71** 6ex ... SteveDrowne 4 (H Morrison) *chsd ldrs: racd on outside: rdn 2f out: styd on same pce fnl f* **13/2**	63
4252	7	nk	**Whoateallthepius (IRE)**^{14} 5261 2-9-2 **72** ... RichardHughes 7 (D K Ivory) *led tl hdd ins fnl f: eased whn btn cl home* **11/2^{3}**	63+

60.24 secs (1.44) **Going Correction** +0.175s/f (Slow) 7 Ran SP% **110.2**

Speed ratings (Par 97): **95,94,91,90,89 88,88**

toteswingers:1&2:£2.90, 1&3:£3.50, 2&3:£2.80 CSF £11.63 CT £25.38 TOTE £3.00: £2.20, £2.10; EX 8.40.

Owner Hamdan Al Maktoum **Bred** Shadwell Estate Company Limited **Trained** Newmarket, Suffolk

■ Stewards' Enquiry : Richard Hills caution: careless riding

FOCUS

A fair sprint nursery run at a strong pace. The form should prove reliable.

NOTEBOOK

Sadafiya, off the mark over 6f on Wolverhampton's Polytrack last time, soon recovered from a slow start, travelling powerfully off the decent pace, and picked up well in the straight to take this with more authority than the margin suggests. She's not very big, but is quite a nippy type who looks capable of winning again. (op 9-2)

Millyluvstobouggie was always well placed and had every chance, but the progressive winner was too good. (op 10-3 tchd 11-4)

Winnie Dixie(USA), a winner on debut over 6f at Windsor, ran respectably but gave the impression that the drop to the minimum distance was not ideal, with her having to be rushed up to sit handy and then lacking the pace of the front two late on. (op 7-4)

Second Encore ran on after getting behind, giving the impression she's now ready for a step up to 6f. (op 25-1)

Saucy Buck(IRE) didn't help himself with a slow start and got going too late.

Dubai Affair disappointed under the penalty picked up for her recent Kempton win, and perhaps she's better going right-handed. (tchd 15-2)

Whoateallthepius(IRE) went off fast and didn't see her race out. (op 15-2 tchd 8-1 and 5-1)

5726 LINGFIELD PARK MARRIOTT HOTEL & COUNTRY CLUB MEDIAN AUCTION MAIDEN STKS 5f (P)

2:50 (2:50) (Class 6) 3-5-Y-O £2,729 (£806; £403) Stalls High

Form				RPR
3362	1		**Fear Nothing**^{25} 4908 3-9-0 72 ... (b) RichardMullen 8 (E S McMahon) *chsd ldrs: led jst ins fnl f: kpt on u.p cl home* **5/2^{1}**	67
6034	2	½	**Nadinska**^{6} 5514 3-8-9 60 ... ChrisCatlin 5 (M R Channon) *in rr and racd on outside: rdn and styd on strly fnl f to go 2nd fnl 50yds: nt rch wnr* **7/2^{2}**	60
4603	3	1¾	**Papageno**^{25} 4908 3-9-0 61 ... RichardHughes 7 (J R Jenkins) *in tch: rdn and hdwy fnl f: styd on to take 3rd cl home but no ch w ldng duo* **5/1^{3}**	59
0026	4	½	**Socceroo**^{25} 4892 5-8-10 51 ... (e) SteveDrowne 6 (D C Griffiths) *led tl hdd jst ins fnl f: sn one pce and lost 3rd cl home* **7/1**	52
4-	5	2¼	**Little Rufus**^{404} 4349 3-9-0 0 ... PatCosgrave 3 (K A Morgan) *chsd ldrs: rdn 2f out: wknd fnl f* **10/1**	49
4600	6	nk	**Final Turn**^{43} 4284 3-9-0 60 ... (b^{1}) DaneO'Neill 2 (H Candy) *chsd ldrs tl wknd appr fnl f* **11/2**	48
0-66	7	½	**Rosetta Hill**^{30} 4720 3-8-9 42 ... EddieAhern 4 (J R Jenkins) *hld up in tch: rdn and effrt to chse ldrs over 1f out: wknd ins fnl f* **20/1**	41
00-0	8	11	**Diamond Affair (IRE)**^{16} 5206 3-8-9 45 ... LiamKeniry 1 (M G Quinlan) *s.i.s: a in rr: eased fnl f* **66/1**	1

60.45 secs (1.65) **Going Correction** +0.175s/f (Slow)

WFA 3 from 5yo 1lb 8 Ran SP% **110.7**

Speed ratings (Par 101): **93,92,89,88,85 84,83,66**

toteswingers:1&2:£2.20, 1&3:£1.70, 2&3:£3.40 CSF £10.49 TOTE £2.40: £1.70, £1.30, £1.90; EX 13.70.

Owner J C Fretwell **Bred** Houghton Bloodstock Uk Ltd **Trained** Lichfield, Staffs

FOCUS

This lot had run 70 times between them without success, so clearly not form to dwell on. The winner has been disappointing.

5727 BRITANNIACREST RECYCLING H'CAP 1m 4f (P)

3:20 (3:20) (Class 4) (0-85,88) 3-Y-O+ £5,828 (£1,734; £866; £432) Stalls Low

Form				RPR
111	1		**Sparkling Smile (IRE)**^{63} 3618 3-9-6 **85** ... TedDurcan 1 (D R Lanigan) *hld up in rr: in tch: hdwy on outside 4f out: led 2f out: pushed along over 1f out: styd on strly: comf* **7/1**	100+
126	2	2¼	**Akhmatova**^{20} 5096 3-8-13 **78** ... DaneO'Neill 4 (G A Butler) *t.k.h ealy: in rr: hdwy on outside 2f out: drvn to chse wnr appr fnl f: kpt on but nvr any ch* **13/2^{3}**	88
4123	3	2¼	**Domination**^{49} 4092 3-8-12 **77** ... RichardHughes 6 (H Morrison) *chsd ldrs: rdn over 2f out: no ch w wnr over 1f out: styd on same pce fnl f* **3/1^{1}**	83
1611	4	1¼	**Nave (USA)**^{11} 5355 3-9-9 **88** 6ex ... RichardHills 7 (M Johnston) *led 2f: styd chsng ldr: upsides 4f out tl slt ld ins fnl 3f: hdd 2f out: wknd fnl f* **7/2^{2}**	92
0025	5	11	**Resplendent Light**^{13} 5286 5-9-9 **79** ... MartinDwyer 5 (W R Muir) *chsd ldrs: rdn over 3f out: wknd 2f out: eased fnl f* **16/1**	66
6-15	6	6	**Oriental Cat**^{96} 2562 3-9-4 **83** ... WilliamBuick 3 (J H M Gosden) *plld v hrd and led after 2f: hdd ins fnl 3f: wknd 2f out: eased fnl f* **7/2^{2}**	60
5514	7	2¼	**Goodwood Starlight (IRE)**^{21} 5035 5-9-9 **82** ... RobertLButler$^{(3)}$ 8 (Miss Sheena West) *plld hrd early: in rr: rdn 3f out: sn wknd* **9/1**	56
006	8	½	**Officer In Command (USA)**^{42} 4322 4-9-10 **80** ... LiamKeniry 2 (J S Moore) *in rr: rdn 4f out and sn wknd* **50/1**	53

2m 32.24s (-0.76) **Going Correction** +0.175s/f (Slow)

WFA 3 from 4yo+ 9lb 8 Ran SP% **113.1**

Speed ratings (Par 105): **109,107,106,105,97 93,92,92**

toteswingers:1&2:£9.10, 1&3:£2.40, 2&3:£5.50 CSF £50.31 CT £164.64 TOTE £8.30: £2.50, £1.60, £1.40; EX 52.30.

Owner Saif Ali & Saeed H Altayer **Bred** Georgestown Stud **Trained** Newmarket, Suffolk

FOCUS

A decent handicap which was well run, and form to be positive about with another clear step up from Sparkling Smile.

5728 FELBRIDGE H'CAP 1m 2f (P)

3:50 (3:54) (Class 3) (0-90,90) 3-Y-O £7,771 (£2,312; £1,155; £577) Stalls Low

Form				RPR
-133	1		**Sarrsar**^{32} 4652 3-9-3 **86** ... FrankieDettori 6 (M A Jarvis) *trckd ldr: drvn to ld over 1f out: sn pushed clr: readily* **7/2^{2}**	103+
-021	2	3	**Lunar Victory (USA)**^{22} 5001 3-9-2 **85** ... WilliamBuick 4 (J H M Gosden) *in tch: hdwy over 2f out: styd on to take 2nd ins fnl f but nvr any ch w wnr* **9/1**	94
1-50	3	1¼	**Muwakaba (USA)**^{83} 2970 3-9-2 **85** ... RichardHills 8 (Sir Michael Stoute) *sn led: rdn over 2f out: hdd over 1f out: sn no ch w wnr: hung rt and lost 2nd ins fnl f* **33/1**	92
0011	4	nk	**Lost In The Moment (IRE)**^{25} 4905 3-9-6 **89** ... RyanMoore 2 (J Noseda) *in rr: pushed along 3f out: hdwy towards outside fr 2f out: rdn and styd on fr over 1f out: tk one pce 4th ins fnl f* **1/1^{1}**	95+
011	5	4½	**Titbit**^{27} 4847 3-9-1 **84** ... TomQueally 7 (H R A Cecil) *chsd ldrs tl wknd over 1f out* **5/1^{3}**	81
6060	6	4	**Exceedthewildman**^{27} 4815 3-8-10 **84** ... (p) KierenFox$^{(5)}$ 1 (J S Moore) *rdn over 3f out: a bhd* **33/1**	73
0105	7	4½	**Nurture (IRE)**^{62} 3670 3-9-4 **90** ... EJMcNamara$^{(3)}$ 3 (R M Beckett) *s.i.s: a towards rr* **50/1**	70
0120	8	1¼	**If I Were A Boy (IRE)**^{34} 4573 3-8-9 **78** ... JamesDoyle 5 (D J S Ffrench Davis) *chsd ldrs towards outside: rdn over 3f out: wknd over 2f out* **33/1**	55

2m 6.34s (-0.26) **Going Correction** +0.175s/f (Slow) 8 Ran SP% **109.7**

Speed ratings (Par 105): **108,105,104,104,100 97,93,92**

toteswingers:1&2:£4.40, 1&3:£9.30, 2&3:£20.70 CSF £27.48 CT £646.06 TOTE £2.70: £1.10, £2.50, £7.60; EX 20.90.

Owner Sheikh Ahmed Al Maktoum **Bred** Darley **Trained** Newmarket, Suffolk
■ Autumn Riches was withdrawn on vet's advice (15/2, deduct 10p in the £ under R4).

FOCUS
A decent handicap but it was not strong run. The form is rated on the positive side.

NOTEBOOK
Sarrsar ◆ had been a beaten favourite on his last two turf starts, but he landed a maiden around here on reappearance and won impressively returned to what may prove to be his favoured surface. Indeed, it's interesting to note that his sire Shamardal is now 18-72 (25%) with his runners on Polytrack in Britain, while his dam has produced three other winners on either dirt on Poly, including Baharah, a Listed winner around here. He could be an ideal type for the Dubai Carnival, but whatever, clearly progressing, he should still be competitive on the grass. He was understandably shortened in the betting for the Cambridgeshire (now around 16-1), and Michael Jarvis is said to be keen to run him, but he requires a lot of horses to come out in order to make the cut, even with a 4lb penalty. (op 9-2 tchd 5-1)
Lunar Victory(USA), off the mark at Goodwood last time, ran a good race on his handicap/Polytrack debut, finishing a clear second behind a potentially smart rival. (op 12-1 tchd 14-1)
Muwakaba(USA) offered encouragement on this step up in trip after nearly three months off, proving no match for the winner but only losing second inside the final furlong after sticking towards the usually unfavoured far rail.
Lost In The Moment(IRE) was one of the favourites for the Cambridgeshire coming into this, but he produced a laboured performance off a 9lb higher mark than when winning at Windsor last time. His sire has only a modest record on the surface, so he could well resume his progress back on turf. (op 6-5 tchd 11-8 in a place)
Titbit had won her last two starts, creating a particularly good impression at the July course on her latest outing but, 9lb higher, she struggled. The step up trip certainly didn't help. (op 9-2 tchd 15-2)

5729 BUILDING MAGAZINE JOSEPH ALOYSIUS HANSOM H'CAP (DIV I) 7f (P)
4:20 (4:21) (Class 6) (0-55,55) 3-Y-O £1,706 (£503; £252) Stalls Low

Form RPR
000- 1 **True To Form (IRE)**[307] 7177 3-8-11 50 SebSanders 4 65+
(Sir Mark Prescott) *trckd ldr: slt ld fr 4f out: pushed clr wl over 1f out: easily* 11/10[1]
00-0 2 3 ¼ **No Complaining (IRE)**[149] 1165 3-8-9 48 ow1 TomQueally 2 51
(B J Curley) *chsd ldrs: wnt 2nd ins fnl 2f: sn rdn and no ch w wnr: hld on for 2nd cl home* 7/2[2]
5630 3 nk **Cuckoo Rock (IRE)**[9] 5414 3-8-13 52 (p) RichardKingscote 6 54
(J G Portman) *chsd ldrs: rdn 3f out: outpcd wl over 2f out: styd on again fnl f to take 3rd fnl 120yds: clsng on 2nd nr fin but nvr any ch w wnr* 10/1
6604 4 2 ¼ **Youm Al Mizayin**[10] 5379 3-9-2 55 SamHitchcott 7 51
(M R Channon) *bmpd s: rdn and outpcd in rr: drvn and styd on fr 1f out: kpt on ins fnl f but nvr any threat* 5/1[3]
0056 5 hd **Barberhoney**[28] 4774 3-8-13 52 EddieAhern 9 48
(J R Jenkins) *wnt lft s: hld up towards rr: drvn over 2f out: sme prog fr over 1f out but nvr gng pce to rch ldrs* 33/1
0560 6 2 ¾ **Red Eddie**[21] 5058 3-8-2 46 oh1 SimonPearce(5) 10 34
(S Dow) *in tch on outside: rdn over 3f out: sn outpcd: mod prog fnl f* 20/1
050 7 1 ¾ **Sparkys Gift (IRE)**[58] 3786 3-8-11 50 IanMongan 5 34
(P M Phelan) *s.i.s: sn drvn along: a towards rr* 25/1
5000 8 4 **Trelicia**[72] 3325 3-9-2 55 DaneO'Neill 11 28
(S C Williams) *chsd ldrs on outside: rdn over 2f out: wknd over 1f out* 40/1
0550 9 1 ¼ **Slasl**[17] 5176 3-9-1 54 ChrisCatlin 3 23
(C E Brittain) *led tl narrowly hdd 4f out: wknd qckly wl over 1f out* 14/1
4-00 10 29 **Silken Aunt**[18] 5163 3-9-2 55 RichardHughes 1 —
(J A R Toller) *a in rr: no ch whn eased* 28/1

1m 26.08s (1.28) **Going Correction** +0.175s/f (Slow) 10 Ran SP% 119.7
Speed ratings (Par 99): **99,95,94,92,92 89,87,82,81,47**
toteswingers:1&2:£2.30, 1&3:£3.50, 2&3:£4.40 CSF £4.70 CT £26.07 TOTE £2.60: £1.10, £2.00, £2.80; EX 8.00.
Owner G Moore - Osborne House **Bred** Sir E J Loder **Trained** Newmarket, Suffolk

FOCUS
A moderate contest with only two of the ten runners ever having been placed before, but the time was respectable, being 0.23 seconds quicker than the progressive Paphos managed in the second division. Interesting form to a modest race.
True To Form(IRE) Official explanation: trainer said regarding apparent improvement in form gelding had developed since last run and had improved for being gelded

5730 BUILDING MAGAZINE JOSEPH ALOYSIUS HANSOM H'CAP (DIV II) 7f (P)
4:50 (4:51) (Class 6) (0-55,55) 3-Y-O £1,706 (£503; £252) Stalls Low

Form RPR
0001 1 **Paphos**[2] 5669 3-8-12 51 6ex (v) ChrisCatlin 3 64+
(S C Williams) *sn chsng ldr: led ins fnl 2f: sn rdn: kpt on wl u.p fnl f* 7/4[1]
0040 2 2 ¾ **Ayam Zainah**[12] 5326 3-8-13 52 (v[1]) SamHitchcott 6 58
(M R Channon) *chsd ldrs: wnt 2nd u.p wl over 1f out: kpt on same pce fnl f* 20/1
-501 3 2 **Franki J**[23] 4970 3-8-11 55 SophieDoyle(5) 11 56
(D Donovan) *sn led: hdd ins fnl 2f: wknd ins fnl f* 14/1
0263 4 ½ **A Pocketful Of Rye (IRE)**[10] 5379 3-8-9 55 LeonnaMayor(7) 4 54
(P Howling) *in rr: stl plenty to do 2f out: sn gd hdwy on ins and kpt on wl fnl f to take 4th but no imp on ldng trio* 25/1
0006 5 2 ½ **Dancing Poppy**[43] 4281 3-8-9 48 (t) LiamKeniry 7 41
(R A Farrant) *chsd ldrs: rdn over 2f out: styd on same pce* 25/1
4502 6 4 ½ **Aqua Vitae (IRE)**[10] 5379 3-9-2 55 KierenFallon 10 35
(Miss Tor Sturgis) *sn drvn and in tch: chsd ldrs on outside but u.p 2f out: nvr quite on terms and wknd over 1f out* 5/1
0032 7 nk **Rigid**[18] 5162 3-8-12 51 NeilCallan 8 31
(A W Carroll) *chsd ldrs: rdn over 2f out: wknd and hung lft fnl f* 4/1[2]
6230 8 1 **Cheshire Lady (IRE)**[129] 1605 3-8-13 52 TedDurcan 9 29
(W M Brisbourne) *s.i.s: pushed along 1/2-way: sn outpcd* 25/1
6532 9 2 **Orsett Lad (USA)**[2] 5669 3-8-10 54 KierenFox(5) 1 25
(J R Best) *outpcd most of way* 9/2[3]
5000 10 shd **Rightcar**[18] 5152 3-8-11 50 DaneO'Neill 5 21
(Peter Grayson) *in tch: rdn 3f out: wknd ins fnl 2f* 50/1
3630 11 10 **Thoughtful (IRE)**[12] 5326 3-8-7 46 EddieAhern 2 —
(J W Hills) *a in rr* 20/1

1m 26.31s (1.51) **Going Correction** +0.175s/f (Slow) 11 Ran SP% 120.9
Speed ratings (Par 99): **98,94,92,92,89 84,83,82,80,80 68**
toteswingers:1&2:£11.80, 1&3:£4.80, 2&3:£33.10 CSF £47.36 CT £403.69 TOTE £3.60: £1.70, £8.50, £1.70; EX 70.90.
Owner Stuart C Williams **Bred** L Ellinas And Old Mill Stud Ltd **Trained** Newmarket, Suffolk

FOCUS
A moderate handicap in which a few of the fancied runners disappointed, but in fairness the winner is clearly progressing. Straightforward form.

5731 BURSTOW H'CAP 6f (P)
5:20 (5:20) (Class 3) (0-95,95) 3-Y-O+ £7,771 (£2,312; £1,155; £577) Stalls Low

Form RPR
4324 1 **Oil Strike**[20] 5082 3-8-12 88 IanMongan 5 98+
(P Winkworth) *chsd ldrs: led 2f out: drvn 2 l clr over 1f out: rdn out* 5/1[2]
0030 2 hd **Wildcat Wizard (USA)**[13] 5302 4-9-6 94 RichardHughes 2 103
(P F I Cole) *in rr: hdwy over 1f out: rdn and str run fnl f: tk 2nd cl home and gaining on wnr: nt quite get up* 8/1[3]
1220 3 ½ **Little Garcon (USA)**[35] 4541 3-8-12 88 TedDurcan 4 95
(M Botti) *in rr: gd hdwy over 1f out and kpt on to chse wnr ins fnl f: kpt on same pce and ct for 2nd cl home* 4/1[1]
2060 4 4 ½ **Ivory Silk**[18] 5154 5-8-10 84 (v[1]) ChrisCatlin 11 77
(J R Gask) *in rr and racd on outside: rdn over 2f out: kpt on fnl f but nvr gng pce to rch ldrs* 25/1
0535 5 ½ **Bella Swan**[27] 4819 3-9-0 90 AdamKirby 10 81
(W R Swinburn) *in tch: rdn and one pce 2f out: styd on fnl f but nvr a threat* 16/1
010 6 2 ¼ **Arteus**[20] 5068 4-9-0 88 (b) PatCosgrave 8 72
(Jane Chapple-Hyam) *chsd ldrs: wnt 2nd over 1f out but no imp: wknd fnl f* 14/1
0104 7 ¾ **Olynard (IRE)**[25] 4904 4-9-3 91 JackMitchell 3 73+
(R M Beckett) *boke wl: n.m.r on ins and lost pl after 1f: hdwy on ins whn nt clr run over 1f out: nvr in contention after* 8/1[3]
1400 8 2 ½ **Bravo Echo**[95] 2595 4-9-6 94 NeilCallan 6 68
(M J Attwater) *chsd ldrs: rdn 3f out: wknd wl over 1f out* 12/1
0-60 9 3 **Soap Wars**[18] 5154 5-8-13 87 DaneO'Neill 1 51
(J A Osborne) *chsd ldrs: wknd wl over 1f out* 33/1
0-00 10 2 ½ **Ancien Regime (IRE)**[34] 4576 5-9-7 95 (vt[1]) FrankieDettori 9 51
(Saeed Bin Suroor) *drvn to press ldr and led after 2f: hdd 2f out: sn btn* 8/1[3]
0003 11 2 ¾ **Al Farahidi (USA)**[18] 5143 3-8-13 89 (b) AndrewMullen 7 36
(M Johnston) *drvn and slt ld 2f: styd chsng ldr tl wknd qckly ins fnl 2f* 5/1[2]

1m 12.47s (0.57) **Going Correction** +0.175s/f (Slow)
WFA 3 from 4yo+ 2lb 11 Ran SP% 113.7
Speed ratings (Par 107): **103,102,102,96,95 92,91,88,84,80 77**
toteswingers:1&2:£10.90, 1&3:£3.80, 2&3:£10.00 CSF £43.16 CT £174.02 TOTE £5.00: £2.20, £5.00, £1.02; EX 57.20 Place 6 £18.39; Place 5 £13.15.
Owner David Holden **Bred** Cobhall Court Stud **Trained** Chiddingfold, Surrey

FOCUS
Few of these came into the race in form and this looked an ordinary sprint handicap for the class. The pace was perhaps overly strong and the winner is perhaps better than the bare form having raced prominently.

NOTEBOOK
Oil Strike won his maiden over C&D on his only previous start on Polytrack and both the trip and surface clearly provides his optimum conditions. He did well to hang on considering he was in front sooner than ideal, and he's one to keep in mind. (op 11-2 tchd 9-2 and 6-1 in a place)
Wildcat Wizard(USA), debuting on Polytrack, raced in a detached last early on, but he finally found his stride in the second half of the contest and finished well. It remains to be seen whether he'll build on this, though. (op 7-1)
Little Garcon(USA), the winner of two of his previous four starts on Polytrack, travelled well a fair way off the pace, and looked a real threat when produced with his chance, but his effort flattened out late on. (op 9-2)
Ivory Silk, visored for the first time (has worn blinkers), emerges with credit considering she was caught wide early on, with stall 11 no help.
Bella Swan did not improve for the removal of the visor and return to Polytrack. (op 12-1)
Olynard(IRE) Official explanation: jockey said gelding was denied a clear run
Al Farahidi(USA) proved totally unsuited by the drop in trip. (op 8-1)
T/Plt: £35.80 to a £1 stake. Pool:£58,775.77 - 1,197.19 winning tickets T/Qpdt: £14.50 to a £1 stake. Pool:£4,245.86 - 216.40 winning tickets ST

5331 MUSSELBURGH (R-H)
Friday, September 3

OFFICIAL GOING: Straight course - good (good to firm in places); round course - good to firm (good in places)
Bottom bend moved out 2m.
Wind: Virtually nil Weather: Fine and dry

5732 KLEINWORT BENSON H'CAP 7f 30y
2:10 (2:13) (Class 5) (0-70,71) 3-Y-O+ £3,238 (£963; £481; £240) Stalls High

Form RPR
0031 1 **Social Rhythm**[8] 5439 6-8-11 56 PJMcDonald 10 62
(A C Whillans) *hld up in rr: hdwy on outer 3f out: rdn wl over 1f out: drvn and styd on ins fnl f to ld on line* 15/8[1]
4044 2 nse **Peter's Gift (IRE)**[11] 5357 4-8-8 56 (p) AmyRyan(3) 8 62
(K A Ryan) *chsd ldrs: hdwy 3f out: cl up 2f out: rdn to ld 1f out: drvn ins fnl f: hdd on line* 10/1
4003 3 nk **Berbice (IRE)**[7] 5477 5-9-10 69 LNewman 7 74
(Miss L A Perratt) *trckd ldrs: hdwy 3f out: led 2f out: rdn and hdd over 1f out: drvn and ev ch ins fnl f tl no ex last 75yds* 14/1
6501 4 nk **Cold Quest (USA)**[12] 5331 6-8-5 55 oh8 BillyCray(5) 12 59
(Miss L A Perratt) *s.i.s and bhd: rdn along 3f out: hdwy on inner 2f out: drvn and kpt on ins fnl f: nrst fin* 6/1[2]
1002 5 1 ½ **Chambers (IRE)**[7] 5500 4-8-9 57 PaulPickard(3) 11 57
(E J Alston) *hld up: hdwy over 2f out: swtchd rt and rdn to chse ldrs over 1f out: drvn and kpt on fnl f* 7/1[3]
1044 6 1 **Stellite**[15] 5241 10-9-4 66 GaryBartley(3) 1 63
(J S Goldie) *stdd s and hld up in rr: hdwy wl over 2f out: rdn along over 1f out: kpt on ins fnl f: nrst fin* 33/1
00-0 7 3 ¼ **Captain Peachey**[23] 4947 4-8-10 55 oh10 PaulMulrennan 6 44?
(P Monteith) *chsd ldrs: rdn along wl over 2f out: drvn wl over 1f out and grad wknd* 100/1
2006 8 1 ¾ **Ansells Pride (IRE)**[28] 4796 7-9-7 66 TomEaves 3 50
(B Smart) *chsd ldrs: rdn along over 2f out: drvn wl over 1f out: grad wknd* 14/1
1506 9 3 ¼ **Dhhamaan (IRE)**[11] 5357 5-8-12 57 (b) PaulHanagan 4 32
(Mrs R A Carr) *set str pce: rdn along and hung lft 3f out: hdd 2f out: grad wknd* 16/1
-306 10 1 ¼ **Solitary**[16] 5199 4-9-6 65 PhillipMakin 5 37
(Mrs Marjorie Fife) *cl up: rdn along over 2f out: sn drvn and wknd* 25/1

2221 **11** *7* **El Dececy (USA)**[9] 5406 6-9-12 **71** 6ex......................(p) RobertWinston 2 24
(J Balding) *cl up: swtchd rt 3f out and sn rdn: drvn over 2f out and sn wknd* **6/1**[2]

1m 27.54s (-1.46) **Going Correction** -0.15s/f (Firm)
WFA 3 from 4yo+ 4lb **11** Ran SP% **111.9**
Speed ratings (Par 103): **102,101,101,101,99 98,94,92,88,87 79**
toteswingers:1&2:£6.10, 1&3:£6.90, 2&3:£18.30 CSF £20.04 CT £198.37 TOTE £2.40: £1.40, £3.20, £3.80; EX 20.40.
Owner Mrs L M Whillans **Bred** A And B Fairfields **Trained** Newmill-On-Slitrig, Borders

FOCUS
After a dry spell the ground was described as 'quick but no jar and a good cover of grass'. A modest 55-71 handicap run at a breakneck pace and the two leaders finished third last and last. The winner did not need to match her Ayr win.
Chambers(IRE) Official explanation: jockey said gelding hung left throughout
Dhhamaan(IRE) Official explanation: jockey said gelding hung left
El Dececy(USA) Official explanation: trainer said gelding was unable to dominate

5733 CALA HOMES MAIDEN AUCTION STKS 5f
2:40 (2:40) (Class 6) 2-Y-O **£1,942** (£578; £288; £144) **Stalls** Low

Form RPR
2244 **1** **Boundaries**[6] 5531 2-8-12 75.. PaulHanagan 4 70
(T D Easterby) *mde all: rdn over 1f out: drvn and kpt on ins fnl f* **4/9**[1]
6060 **2** *2 ½* **Dotty Darroch**[8] 5434 2-8-5 55..............................(b) SilvestreDeSousa 1 53
(R Bastiman) *chsd wnr whn n.m.r on inner after 1f: trckd ldng pair: effrt 2f out: rdn to chse wnr ent fnl f: sn drvn and one pce last 100yds* **12/1**
040 **3** *¾* **Silent Blessing**[18] 5160 2-8-11 63.................................(v[1]) PhillipMakin 3 56
(R M H Cowell) *chsd wnr: rdn to chal wl over 1f out: drvn ent fnl f and sn one pce* **7/1**[3]
4 *4* **Indian Arrow** 2-8-12 0.. TomEaves 5 43
(J J Quinn) *s.i.s and in rr: effrt and rn green 2f out: sn rdn and no imp* **4/1**[2]

60.76 secs (0.36) **Going Correction** 0.0s/f (Good) **4** Ran SP% **109.4**
Speed ratings (Par 93): **97,93,91,85**
CSF £6.55 TOTE £1.40; EX 7.30.
Owner T G & Mrs M E Holdcroft **Bred** Bearstone Stud **Trained** Great Habton, N Yorks

FOCUS
Two exposed platers and a speedily bred newcomer but a golden opportunity for the favourite. This is form to be slightly against.

NOTEBOOK
Boundaries made it tenth time lucky and the added bonus of picking up the £10,000 yearling bonus. A real good-looker, this colt had not always looked straightforward. Fast away and able to cross over to the stands' side rail, he hung right and ended up towards the middle without ever being threatened in any way. This was a golden opportunity safely tucked away, but he will not be easy to place from now on. Official explanation: caution; careless riding (op 4-7 tchd 8-13 in places)
Dotty Darroch, rated just 52 and having her seventh start, had to be checked early on when Boundaries moved over to take the rail position. She stuck on to claim second spot late on, but is clearly fully exposed. A return to 6f will be more in her favour. (op 20-1)
Silent Blessing, well beaten on his first try on turf on his third start, hunted up the winner but in the end did not get home. Rated 62, he had 4lb in hand of the runner-up, suggesting he will struggle in low-grade nurseries. (op 15-2 tchd 8-1)
Indian Arrow, a laid-back speedily-bred newcomer, missed the break and on this lightning fast track could never get into contention. He is surely capable of a fair bit better. (op 11-4)

5734 RACING UK H'CAP 5f
3:10 (3:11) (Class 3) (0-90,91) 3-Y-O+ **£6,476** (£1,927; £963; £481) **Stalls** Low

Form RPR
3632 **1** **Secret Millionaire (IRE)**[32] 4654 3-9-7 **87**.................... StephenCraine 4 96
(Patrick Morris) *trckd ldrs: hdwy 2f out: rdn to chal over 1f out: drvn to ld ins fnl f: jst hld on* **12/1**
1100 **2** *shd* **Nickel Silver**[20] 5069 5-9-0 **79**...(v) TomEaves 5 88
(B Smart) *led: rdn along over 1f out: drvn and hdd ins fnl f: rallied nr fin: jst hld* **16/1**
3033 **3** *nk* **The Nifty Fox**[12] 5335 6-9-6 **85**.. DavidAllan 10 93+
(T D Easterby) *dwlt and towards rr: swtchd to inner and hdwy 1/2-way: chsd ldrs and swtchd rt over 1f out: rdn to chal and ev ch ins fnl f: sn drvn and no ex towards fin* **9/2**[1]
120 **4** *¾* **Beat The Bell**[70] 3401 5-9-5 **84**.................................. GrahamGibbons 14 89+
(T D Barron) *s.i.s and in rr: hdwy 2f out: rdn over 1f out: styd on ins fnl f: nrst fin* **10/1**
0101 **5** *½* **Rasaman (IRE)**[12] 5335 6-9-9 **91** 6ex............................. GaryBartley[(3)] 8 94
(J S Goldie) *qckly away: sn restrained and dropped bk last after 1f: sn rdn along and outpcd after 2f: swtchd rt and hdwy wl over 1f out: rdn and styd on wl fnl f: nrst fin* **5/1**[2]
5460 **6** *nk* **Le Toreador**[20] 5069 5-9-0 **82**...(tp) AmyRyan[(3)] 3 84
(K A Ryan) *cl up: rdn along wl over 1f out: grad wknd* **12/1**
3642 **7** *¾* **Doctor Parkes**[20] 5069 4-9-6 **85**................................... RobertWinston 12 85
(E J Alston) *trckd ldrs: swtchd rt and rdn over 1f out: ev ch tl drvn and one pce ent fnl f* **6/1**
5366 **8** *1 ¼* **Jargelle (IRE)**[12] 5335 4-9-5 **84**.. BillyCray[(5)] 7 84
(D Nicholls) *in tch: rdn along 2f out: sn no imp* **20/1**
0020 **9** *¾* **Titus Andronicus (IRE)**[4] 5589 4-9-1 **80**.................. PaulHanagan 11 72
(R A Fahey) *hld up towards rr: effrt 2f out: sn rdn and n.d* **11/2**[3]
5600 **10** *½* **Argentine (IRE)**[11] 5356 6-8-7 **72**...............................(b) PaulMulrennan 1 63
(J A McShane) *cl up on inner: rdn along wl over 1f out: grad wknd* **40/1**
-000 **11** *2* **Burnwynd Boy**[4] 5601 5-8-9 **79**.. LeeTopliss[(5)] 13 62
(J A McShane) *prom towards outer: rdn along wl over 1f out: wkng whn hmpd appr fnl f* **40/1**
1524 **12** *1 ¼* **The Bear**[12] 5335 7-8-6 **74** ow2.. BarryMcHugh[(3)] 6 53
(Miss L A Perratt) *cl up: rdn along 2f out: drvn whn edgd rt and wknd over 1f out* **12/1**
0012 **13** *5* **Sir Geoffrey (IRE)**[6] 5528 4-8-11 **76** 6ex.......................(b) PJMcDonald 9 37
(J A Glover) *chsd ldrs: hdwy on wd outside wl over 1f out: sn rdn and wknd* **8/1**

59.43 secs (-0.97) **Going Correction** 0.0s/f (Good)
WFA 3 from 4yo+ 1lb **13** Ran SP% **123.3**
Speed ratings (Par 107): **107,106,106,105,104 103,102,100,99,98 95,93,85**
toteswingers:1&2:£40.40, 1&3:£16.00, 2&3:£25.90 CSF £192.54 CT £1038.09 TOTE £16.80: £4.40, £5.40, £1.90; EX 189.50.
Owner H & R Lloyd Syndicate **Bred** James Delaney **Trained** Tarporley, Cheshire
■ Stewards' Enquiry : Stephen Craine caution; used whip with excessive frequency

FOCUS
A highly competitive 72-91 £10,000 5f handicap and the pace, as expected, was very strong. The winner improved 5lb on his Ascot run.

NOTEBOOK
Secret Millionaire(IRE), who has found it tough going in handicap company this year after winning twice as a juvenile, was put up 5lb after finishing runner-up at Ripon. Favourably drawn and loaded last into the stalls, he showed real battling qualities to put his head in front right on the line. (op 11-1 tchd 14-1)
Nickel Silver, who has won from a 13lb higher mark on the all-weather, was drawn next to the winner and showed blinding speed to take them along. He drifted right in the closing stages and was nailed right on the line. (op 14-1)
The Nifty Fox, drawn in double figures, made a tardy start then had to bide his time for an opening to appear. He was just held in the end and can be accounted a shade unlucky. (op 17-2)
Beat The Bell ◆ was the one that was desperately unlucky. Gambled-on having his first outing for this yard, he was worst drawn, blew the start but finished fast to take fourth place on the heels of the first three. His three wins last year for another stable were over 6f, and he has won from a 2lb higher mark in the past, so will be a warm order when he seeks compensation. (op 25-1)
Rasaman(IRE), under a 6lb penalty for his course success 12 days earlier when he had The Nifty Fox behind, will need another penalty to guarantee his place in the Silver Cup at Ayr. Soon last and forced to switch wide, he is crying out for a return to 6f.
Le Toreador, drawn three, has slipped down the ratings and ran much better, but he reserves his best for Polytrack. (op 11-1)

5735 CORNHILL BUILDING SERVICES CLAIMING STKS 5f
3:40 (3:40) (Class 6) 3-Y-O+ **£1,942** (£578; £288; £144) **Stalls** Low

Form RPR
3105 **1** **Arriva La Diva**[7] 5502 4-8-5 63.. PaulHanagan 3 70
(J J Quinn) *cl up: swtchd rt and hdwy over 1f out: sn rdn and styd on to ld ins fnl f: drvn out* **9/4**[2]
1000 **2** *nk* **Atlantic Beach**[7] 5480 5-9-0 77...............................(v) SilvestreDeSousa 6 78
(D O'Meara) *cl up: rdn to ld wl over 1f out: drvn and hdd ins fnl f: kpt on same pce* **5/4**[1]
0014 **3** *4 ½* **Mercers Row**[51] 4016 3-8-6 68.................................... BarryMcHugh[(3)] 2 58
(N Wilson) *cl up: effrt 2f out: sn rdn and ev ch tl drvn and one pce ent fnl f* **18/1**
2260 **4** *1 ¼* **Raccoon (IRE)**[9] 5422 10-8-6 59.................................(b[1]) PJMcDonald 1 49
(Mrs R A Carr) *led: rdn along 2f out: sn hdd & wknd over 1f out* **8/1**
2310 **5** *12* **Mandarin Spirit (IRE)**[7] 5477 10-8-10 69.................(b) RobertWinston 5 10
(Miss L A Perratt) *v s.i.s and a wl bhd* **4/1**[3]

59.73 secs (-0.67) **Going Correction** 0.0s/f (Good)
WFA 3 from 4yo+ 1lb **5** Ran SP% **111.6**
Speed ratings (Par 101): **105,104,97,95,76**
CSF £5.57 TOTE £3.50: £1.20, £1.10; EX 4.90.Arriva La Diva was claimed by Ken McGarrity for £6,000.
Owner Allan Stennett **Bred** Mickley Stud, Stennett, Hillside Racing **Trained** Settrington, N Yorks

FOCUS
A modest claimer and unconvincing form.

5736 GRAHAM THE PLUMBERS MERCHANT H'CAP 1m 1f
4:10 (4:10) (Class 2) (0-100,93) 3-Y-O+
£10,592 (£3,172; £1,586; £793; £396; £198) **Stalls** High

Form RPR
-005 **1** **Dhaular Dhar (IRE)**[8] 5435 8-8-11 **85**............................ PaulNorton[(7)] 2 95
(J S Goldie) *s.i.s: in rr tl hdwy over 2f out: swtchd lft and rdn over 1f out: drvn to chal and edgd lft ent fnl f: styd on to ld last 100yds* **14/1**
3115 **2** *¾* **Smarty Socks (IRE)**[4] 5605 6-9-9 **90**.................. SilvestreDeSousa 7 98
(D O'Meara) *hld up towards rr: hdwy on outer 3f out: rdn 2f out: drvn and styd on to chal ins fnl f: ev ch tl no ex nr fin* **3/1**[2]
-443 **3** *1 ¾* **Faithful Ruler (USA)**[20] 5098 6-9-4 **88**........................ PaulHanagan 6 89
(R A Fahey) *trckd ldrs: hdwy over 2f out: rdn to chal over 1f out: drvn and ev ch ins fnl f: no ex last 50yds* **12/1**
1 **4** *¾* **Fox Hunt (IRE)**[32] 4661 3-9-4 **91**...................................... GregFairley 8 94
(M Johnston) *trckd ldrs: hdwy 3f out: rdn to chse ldrs 2f out: drvn and hld whn n.m.r ent fnl f: one pce after* **2/1**[1]
5646 **5** *shd* **Good Again**[19] 5114 4-9-4 **90**...(p) DaleSwift[(5)] 4 93
(G A Butler) *trckd ldrs: hdwy wl over 2f out and sn rdn: drvn over 1f out: kpt on same pce* **7/1**
1260 **6** *1* **Templetuohy Max (IRE)**[48] 4152 5-8-10 **77**...........(v) GrahamGibbons 9 77
(J D Bethell) *set stdy pce: pushed along: rdn 2f out: drvn over 1f out: hdd & wknd last 100yds* **16/1**
661 **7** *2 ¼* **Ahlawy (IRE)**[15] 5237 7-8-5 **79**..(t) NeilFarley[(7)] 5 75
(F Sheridan) *s.i.s and bhd: hdwy on outer 2f out: rdn over 1f out: n.d* **16/1**
2141 **8** *nse* **Jonny Lesters Hair (IRE)**[23] 4943 5-9-2 **83**............... DavidNolan 10 79
(T D Easterby) *trckd ldng pair: rdn along wl over 2f out: drvn and wknd over 1f out* **6/1**[3]
1600 **9** *1 ¾* **Ezdeyaad (USA)**[4] 5605 6-9-12 **93**................................... PJMcDonald 1 85
(G A Swinbank) *chsd ldr: rdn along over 2f out: sn drvn and wknd* **20/1**

1m 50.42s (-3.48) **Going Correction** -0.15s/f (Firm) course record
WFA 3 from 4yo+ 6lb **9** Ran SP% **116.0**
Speed ratings (Par 109): **109,108,106,106,106 105,103,103,101**
toteswingers:1&2:£8.40, 1&3:£13.40, 2&3:£6.00 CSF £56.22 CT £536.47 TOTE £22.50: £3.90, £1.10, £4.50; EX 85.90.
Owner Middleham Park Racing XLV **Bred** Gainsborough Stud Management Ltd **Trained** Uplawmoor, E Renfrews
■ Stewards' Enquiry : P J McDonald one-day ban; used whip without giving mount time to respond (17th Sept)

FOCUS
A £17,000, 77-93 handicap and though the early pace did not look strong, the time was below standard. The form is rated at face value.

NOTEBOOK
Dhaular Dhar(IRE), who has won from a 9lb higher mark in the past, showed the benefit of last week's Ayr outing, his first for three months. Stepping up in trip he was anchored in the rear before coming with a sustained run to show ahead. This was his first win for almost two and a half years, and he will now head for a 1m2f handicap at Ayr in two weeks' time. His rider is excellent value for his 7lb claim. (op 12-1)
Smarty Socks(IRE), who can be tricky at the start, jumped out on terms. Having his second outing in five days, he made his effort on the outer with the winner and deserves credit for this. Connections are eyeing a crack at the Cambridgeshire. (tchd 7-2)
Faithful Ruler(USA) ran another sound race without ever threatening to land the spoils. He is still 4lb higher than his sole turf success at Ayr a year ago, but he has three all-weather wins to his credit. (op 10-1)
Fox Hunt(IRE), who accounted for two subsequent winners when running away with a maiden at Windsor on his sole previous outing, looked to have plenty on from a rating of 91. Quite keen early, he hit a flat spot and his inexperience was there for all to see halfway up the home straight. Sticking on at the finish, this will have taught him plenty. (op 5-2)
Good Again, who was keen to get on with it, stayed on in her own time. Often quite highly tried, she is now 1lb below her last success at Pontefract almost a year ago. (op 8-1)
Templetuohy Max(IRE), absent for seven weeks, took them along and ran much better than on his two previous starts. (tchd 18-1)

Ahlawy(IRE), backed at long odds, blew his chance at the start and was always unsuccessfully playing catch-up. (op 25-1)
Jonny Lesters Hair(IRE) didn't fire under a much more patient ride than normal.

5737 SCOTTISH RACING YOUR BETTER BET H'CAP 1m
4:40 (4:40) (Class 4) (0-80,79) 3-Y-0+ **£5,180** (£1,541; £770; £384) **Stalls** High

Form RPR

5602 **1** **Justonefortheroad**[10] 5386 4-9-9 **78** PaulHanagan 11 90
(R A Fahey) *trckd ldr to 1/2-way: cl up on inner: effrt whn nt clr run and hmpd wl over 1f out: swtchd lft and rdn ent fnl f: drvn and styd on to ld last 50yds* **3/1**[1]

0304 **2** *3/4* **Thunderball**[9] 5407 4-9-5 **79** DaleSwift(5) 9 89
(J A Glover) *prom: chsd ldr 1/2-way: rdn 2f out: led ent fnl f: sn drvn: hdd and no ex last 50yds* **11/1**

2032 **3** *2 3/4* **Elijah Pepper (USA)**[9] 5407 5-8-10 **65** GrahamGibbons 8 69
(T D Barron) *in tch: hdwy to chse ldrs 3f out: effrt 2f out: rdn to chse ldng trio over 1f out: drvn and edgd rt whn rdr dropped whip ins fnl f: one pce* **9/2**[2]

050 **4** *1 1/2* **Billy Dane (IRE)**[9] 5407 6-9-5 **79** (v[1]) IanBrennan(5) 1 79
(F P Murtagh) *led: rdn 2f out: drvn over 1f out: hdd ent fnl f: wknd* **11/1**

2133 **5** *4* **Avonrose**[23] 4950 3-9-3 **77** GregFairley 7 68
(M Johnston) *in tch: effrt to chse ldrs 3f out: rdn over 2f out and sn no imp* **7/1**

3156 **6** *1/2* **Glenluji**[9] 5407 5-8-10 **65** LNewman 3 55
(J S Goldie) *hld up towards rr: hdwy over 2f out: swtchd lft and rdn wl over 1f out: sn no imp* **12/1**

3620 **7** *1* **Finsbury**[16] 5213 7-8-10 **65** PhillipMakin 5 53
(Miss L A Perratt) *nvr bttr than midfield* **33/1**

-401 **8** *hd* **Scrapper Smith (IRE)**[9] 5405 4-9-1 **70** 6ex PJMcDonald 6 57
(A C Whillans) *dwlt: hld up: a in rr* **5/1**[3]

-661 **9** *3/4* **Postman**[22] 4986 4-8-13 **68** TomEaves 2 53
(B Smart) *chsd ldrs: rdn along wl over 2f out: grad wknd* **25/1**

2305 **10** *hd* **Espero (IRE)**[9] 5407 4-9-7 **76** SilvestreDeSousa 4 61
(Miss L A Perratt) *hld up: a towards rr* **8/1**

2512 **11** *17* **Bed Fellow (IRE)**[15] 5241 6-8-7 **65** oh2 PatrickDonaghy(3) 10 11
(P Monteith) *s.i.s: a in rr* **40/1**

1m 37.79s (-3.41) **Going Correction** -0.15s/f (Firm) course record
WFA 3 from 4yo+ 5lb **11** Ran SP% **117.0**
Speed ratings (Par 105): **111,110,107,106,102 101,100,100,99,99 82**
toteswingers:1&2:£7.40, 1&3:£3.70, 2&3:£7.30 CSF £36.72 CT £136.83 TOTE £6.20: £1.10, £3.80, £2.70; EX 35.10.
Owner The Pontoon Partnership **Bred** Wellsummers Farm & Hammarsfield B'Stock **Trained** Musley Bank, N Yorks

FOCUS
A competitive 65-79 handicap and even though the pace was unrelenting, it was very difficult to make ground from the rear. The winner is rated back to his best.
Scrapper Smith(IRE) Official explanation: jockey said gelding was unsuited by going

5738 RACING UK IN YOUR HOME H'CAP 1m 4f 100y
5:10 (5:10) (Class 6) (0-65,65) 3-Y-0 **£1,942** (£578; £288; £144) **Stalls** High

Form RPR

0301 **1** **Cheyenne Chant**[9] 5423 3-8-9 **51** 6ex (t) SilvestreDeSousa 6 57+
(D O'Meara) *mde all: rdn 2f out: drvn ent fnl f: kpt on strly* **11/8**[1]

6223 **2** *1 1/4* **Vittachi**[9] 5411 3-9-3 **59** PJMcDonald 5 62
(A C Whillans) *trckd wnr: effrt over 2f out: rdn to chal wl over 1f out and ev ch tl drvn and one pce ins fnl f* **10/3**[3]

4251 **3** *3/4* **Dubawi King**[6] 5534 3-9-4 **60** 6ex (v) PaulHanagan 1 62
(N Tinkler) *t.k.h: hld up in rr: hdwy on outer 3f out: chsd ldrs 2f out: drvn and ch ent fnl f: one pce last 100yds* **9/4**[2]

5005 **4** *8* **Acol**[12] 5336 3-8-4 **46** oh1 GregFairley 3 35
(A G Foster) *chsd ldrs: rdn along 3f out: drvn over 2f out and sn wknd* **40/1**

5554 **5** *2* **Brooklands Bay (IRE)**[20] 5093 3-9-9 **65** TomEaves 4 51
(J R Weymes) *trckd ldng pair: rdn along over 2f out: sn drvn and wknd* **12/1**

050 **6** *12* **Converre**[29] 4764 3-8-3 **50** (p) IanBrennan(5) 2 17
(G A Butler) *hld up: a towards rr* **14/1**

2m 42.2s (0.20) **Going Correction** -0.15s/f (Firm) **6** Ran SP% **112.8**
Speed ratings (Par 99): **93,92,91,86,85 77**
toteswingers:1&2:£1.80, 1&3:£1.50, 2&3:£1.60 CSF £6.42 TOTE £2.70: £1.30, £1.60; EX 8.20 Place 6 £36.38; Place 5 £19.27.
Owner R Naylor **Bred** Stanley Estate And Stud Co **Trained** Nawton, N Yorks

FOCUS
A low-grade 46-65 middle-distance handicap and the pace was even. The form makes sense amongst the first three.
T/Plt: £62.80 to a £1 stake. Pool:£56,861.05 - 659.92 winning tickets T/Qpdt: £18.80 to a £1 stake. Pool:£3,685.21 - 144.32 winning tickets JR

5671 BADEN-BADEN (L-H)
Friday, September 3

OFFICIAL GOING: Turf: good

5739a COOLMORE STUD - BADEN-BADEN CUP (LISTED RACE) (3YO+ FILLIES & MARES) (TURF) 7f
3:45 (4:04) 3-Y-0+ **£10,619** (£4,424; £1,769; £884)

RPR

1 **Golden Whip (GER)**[12] 3-8-10 0 ow1 ADeVries 4 95
(W Hickst, Germany) **187/10**

2 *hd* **Western Mystic (GER)**[40] 3-9-0 0 APietsch 11 98
(W Hickst, Germany) **108/10**

3 *hd* **Aslana (IRE)**[22] 5139 3-9-2 0 AStarke 7 100
(P Schiergen, Germany) **19/10**[1]

4 *1* **Douala**[12] 3-9-0 0 FilipMinarik 5 95
(P Schiergen, Germany) **66/10**

5 *nse* **Green Dandy (IRE)**[40] 3-9-2 0 JulienAuge 2 97
(E J O'Neill, France) **17/5**[2]

6 *1 3/4* **Magic Eye (IRE)**[12] 5-9-4 0 THellier 10 92
(Andreas Lowe, Germany) **49/10**[3]

7 *shd* **Aujiang (GER)**[12] 3-8-11 0 EFrank 9 87
(P Schiergen, Germany) **28/1**

8 *1 1/4* **Amazing Beauty (GER)** 3-8-9 0 EPedroza 3 81
(A Wohler, Germany) **126/10**

9 *hd* **Lady Areia (GER)**[102] 4-9-2 0 VSchulepov 8 86
(H J Groschel, Germany) **185/10**

10 *3/4* **Devilish Lips (GER)**[33] 3-9-0 0 (b) AndreBest 12 84
(Andreas Lowe, Germany) **98/10**

11 *4 1/2* **Arrivederla (IRE)**[24] 4924 4-8-11 0 HenkGrewe 1 67
(H J L Dunlop) *broke slowly: rdn to ld on ins after 1f: set gd pce: led into st: r.o wl: hdd 2f out: wknd qckly* **226/10**

1m 25.68s (1.78)
WFA 3 from 4yo+ 4lb **11** Ran SP% **130.3**
WIN (incl. 10 euro stake): 197. PLACES: 43, 24, 13. SF: 1,638..
Owner Graf & Grafin von Stauffenberg **Bred** Comte P Von Stauffenberg & Ctsse M Von Stauffenber **Trained** Germany

NOTEBOOK
Arrivederla(IRE), stepping up from handicaps, was riiden to lead after a slow start but appeared to do too much too soon and dropped right away once headed.

5740a PREIS DES FERIENLAND TIROL (ZUKUNFTS-RENNEN) (GROUP 3) (2YO) (TURF) 7f
4:20 (4:36) 2-Y-0
£28,318 (£9,734; £4,867; £2,654; £1,769; £1,327)

RPR

1 *1/2* **Salona (GER)**[40] 4416 2-8-13 0 FilipMinarik 2 95
(J-P Carvalho, Germany) *broke fast: hrd to settle: trckd pce: mde swift move early in st: r.o wl to chal and take ld 1f out: ct in fnl strides* **61/10**

2 **Nice Danon**[40] 4416 2-9-2 0 EPedroza 1 99
(A Wohler, Germany) *sent st to ld: set str pce: r.o wl u.p in st: hdd over 1f out: rallied gamely to regain ld in fnl strides* **92/10**

3 *2 1/2* **Fort Hastings (IRE)**[19] 2-9-2 0 ADeVries 6 92
(Mario Hofer, Germany) *racd towards rr: mde gd prog arnd fnl turn and into st to go 3rd: r.o wl* **53/10**[3]

4 *1/2* **Night Of Dubai (IRE)** 2-8-13 0 THellier 7 88
(Mario Hofer, Germany) *settled at rr: mde gd prog arnd fnl turn: threatened briefly at top of st: fdd fnl f* **2/1**[2]

5 *6* **Mackensaw (IRE)** 2-9-2 0 AStarke 4 76
(P Schiergen, Germany) *a.p: racing cl 3rd: full of running ent st: faltered u.p 2f out: rallied but no threat fnl f* **6/5**[1]

6 *1 3/4* **Diego (GER)** 2-9-2 0 (b) EFrank 5 71
(T Mundry, Germany) *racd in 4th: threatened briefly turning for home: sn btn* **73/10**

1m 26.9s (3.00) **6** Ran SP% **130.6**
WIN (incl. 10 euro stake): 102. PLACES: 39, 32. SF: 339.
Owner Stall Lucky Owner **Bred** Klaus Hoffman **Trained** Germany

NOTEBOOK
Nice Danon had to survive an objection from connections of the runner-up.

4827 HAYDOCK (L-H)
Saturday, September 4

OFFICIAL GOING: 5f & 6f - good to firm (9.1); 1m and further - good (good to soft in places; 8.0)
Sprints on inner course. Races on round course were run on the outer home straight and consequently were run over 65yards shorter than advertised.
Wind: Light, half-behind Weather: Fine

5741 BETFRED "GOALS GALORE" SUPERIOR MILE (LISTED RACE) 1m 30y
2:00 (2:00) (Class 1) 3-Y-0+
£22,708 (£8,608; £4,308; £2,148; £1,076; £540) **Stalls** Low

Form RPR

0-42 **1** **Cityscape**[129] 1614 4-9-2 **108** SteveDrowne 1 119+
(R Charlton) *hld up in midfield: hdwy over 2f out: rdn to ld over 1f out: pressed ins fnl f: r.o and in command fnl 75yds* **9/2**[2]

-331 **2** *1 1/4* **Secrecy**[12] 5370 4-9-2 **110** JamieSpencer 6 116
(Saeed Bin Suroor) *hld up towards rr: hdwy over 1f out: sn wnt 2nd: str chal and upsides wnr ins fnl f: no ex fnl 75yds* **5/2**[1]

11-0 **3** *2 3/4* **Awzaan**[126] 1699 3-8-11 **117** TadhgO'Shea 7 109+
(M Johnston) *hld up in midfield: hdwy over 2f out: sn rdn to chal: wnt lft sltly and nt qckn over 1f out: outpcd by front pair fnl 100yds* **7/1**[3]

1522 **4** *1 1/2* **Desert Myth (USA)**[35] 4574 3-8-11 **107** RyanMoore 8 105
(Sir Michael Stoute) *trckd ldrs: effrt 2f out: nt qckn 1f out: sn swtchd rt: one pce after* **9/2**[2]

2200 **5** *2 1/2* **Dancing David (IRE)**[18] 5185 3-8-11 **108** (bt[1]) MartinDwyer 4 99
(B J Meehan) *led after 1f: hdd over 2f out: rdn and wknd over 1f out* **15/2**

6266 **6** *nk* **Ordnance Row**[70] 3460 7-9-2 **103** PhilipRobinson 5 100
(M A Jarvis) *broke wl: led for 1f: continued to chse ldr: regained ld over 2f out: rdn and hdd over 1f out: wknd ins fnl f* **16/1**

1440 **7** *2* **Fanunalter**[23] 5009 4-9-5 **106** WilliamBuick 3 104
(M Botti) *hld up in rr: effrt over 1f out: nvr able to chal ldrs: eased whn no imp fnl 100yds* **7/1**[3]

4-13 **8** *1 1/2* **Capital Attraction (USA)**[12] 5370 3-8-11 **100** EddieAhern 2 91
(H R A Cecil) *trckd ldrs: pushed along and outpcd by ldrs 3f out: wknd wl over 1f out* **16/1**

1m 39.44s (-5.26) **Going Correction** -0.325s/f (Firm) course record
WFA 3 from 4yo+ 5lb **8** Ran SP% **113.5**
Speed ratings (Par 111): **113,111,109,107,105 104,102,101**
Tote Swingers: 1&2 £3.70, 1&3 £4.90, 2&3 £3.30 CSF £15.91 TOTE £5.30: £1.90, £1.40, £2.20; EX 18.40 Trifecta £127.40 Pool: £528.83 - 3.07 winning units..
Owner K Abdulla **Bred** Juddmonte Farms Ltd **Trained** Beckhampton, Wilts

FOCUS
The going was officially good, good to soft in places, but there was a following wind in the straight. A competitive Listed event.

NOTEBOOK
Cityscape has endured a couple of absences which have affected him in the last two seasons since returning lame from the 2009 2000 Guineas. Having his first start since April, although the absence was due to the ground rather than any other problem, the winner travelled well throughout and picked up again when challenged by the favourite. He could be up to winning at Group level, and is also a possible for the Cambridgeshire (for which he will incur a 4lb penalty), and he was quoted as short as 12-1 for that race. (op 11-2 tchd 6-1)
Secrecy came into this in good form and, after needing to be ridden to get into contention, looked set to score before Cityscape found extra. Time may show there was no disgrace in this defeat. (tchd 9-4 and 11-4 in places)

The Form Book, Raceform Ltd, Compton, RG20 6NL

Awzaan, the highest-rated runner, was unbeaten as a juvenile, winning the Mill Reef and Middle Park, but had finished well behind on his sole start this season in the 2000 Guineas. He ran pretty well on this first outing since, but faded in the final furlong, and gives the impression a drop back in trip might suit him best. (op 6-1 tchd 11-2)

Desert Myth(USA), a 1m2f winner on his debut (next three home all won next time), had not really built on that until dropped to this trip last time. However, he was doing his best work at the finish here and might need a stiffer test at this trip. (op 4-1)

Dancing David(IRE), the winner of a 1m race on good ground last season, had finished well beaten in the French Derby and when tried over 1m4f this summer. Taking a big drop in trip and fitted with tongue tie and blinkers for the first time, he made the running but dropped out when headed, only to rally a little in the final furlong. (op 11-1)

Ordnance Row, a tough performer at this level over the years, had not scored for over a year and was having his first run since a below-par effort in June. He raced up with the pace but weakened when the race began in earnest. (op 18-1)

Fanunalter had a bit to find with Secrecy on previous form and on ratings, and never figured. (op 8-1)

Capital Attraction(USA) improved on his maiden win on Polytrack when third behind Secrecy at Kempton, but had something to find on that form. He dropped out in the straight and this dirt-bred colt does not look as effective on turf. (op 12-1)

5742 BETFRED "THE BONUS KING" BE FRIENDLY H'CAP 5f

2:30 (2:31) (Class 2) (0-100,98) 3-Y-0+

£15,577 (£4,665; £2,332; £1,167; £582; £292) **Stalls** Centre

Form RPR

5220 **1** **Confessional**[16] 5250 3-8-10 **88**..........(e) DavidAllan 7 100
(T D Easterby) *mde all: rdn over 1f out: edgd lft ins fnl f: r.o wl: in command towards fin* **14/1**

0002 **2** 1 ½ **Golden Destiny (IRE)**[28] 4814 4-9-7 **98**..........(b) RyanMoore 2 104
(P J Makin) *chsd ldrs: rdn 2f out: wnt 2nd jst over 1f out: r.o ins fnl f: run flattened out and nt pce of wnr fnl 75yds* **6/1**[1]

0040 **3** *shd* **Courageous (IRE)**[37] 4510 4-8-4 **86**.......... BillyCray(5) 16 92+
(D Nicholls) *in rr: pushed along to go pce over 2f out: hdwy ins fnl f: r.o: gng on at fin* **6/1**[1]

0004 **4** ½ **Anglezarke (IRE)**[7] 5512 4-9-1 **95**..........(b) BarryMcHugh(3) 9 99
(R A Fahey) *in tch: pushed along to go pce over 2f out: u.p and no real imp 1f out tl styd on towards fin* **15/2**

1434 **5** ¾ **Haajes**[18] 5183 6-8-6 **86**.......... PaulPickard(3) 17 88
(P T Midgley) *towards rr: rdn over 1f out: styd on u.p ins fnl f: nt pce to chal* **12/1**

1110 **6** *nse* **Favourite Girl (IRE)**[21] 5095 4-9-1 **92**..........(v) DuranFentiman 8 93
(T D Easterby) *gd spd and prom: rdn 2f out: kpt on same pce u.p fnl 100yds* **15/2**

-104 **7** ½ **Archers Road (IRE)**[36] 4541 3-9-3 **95**.......... PaulMulrennan 3 95
(T D Barron) *prom: rdn over 1f out: nt qckn ins fnl f: wl hld towards finno ex* **22/1**

1640 **8** *nk* **Piscean (USA)**[14] 5308 5-8-8 **85**.......... MartinDwyer 12 83
(T Keddy) *towards rr: pushed along 3f out: hdwy ins fnl f: nt pce to rch ldrsonside* **22/1**

0003 **9** ¾ **Strike Up The Band**[5] 5589 7-8-10 **87**.......... AdrianNicholls 14 83
(D Nicholls) *midfield: hdwy to chse ldrs over 2f out: rdn over 1f out: fdd fnl 75yds* **13/2**[2]

4464 **10** 1 ¾ **Medici Time**[14] 5308 5-8-7 **84**..........(v) GrahamGibbons 10 73
(T D Easterby) *midfield: u.p over 1f out: btn ins fnl f* **7/1**[3]

2105 **11** ½ **Lucky Numbers (IRE)**[14] 5292 4-8-12 **89**.......... JamieSpencer 11 77
(Paul Green) *gd spd and prom: rdn and btn over 1f out: n.m.r briefly whn hld fnl 100yds: eased* **8/1**

-425 **12** ¾ **Reignier**[63] 3691 3-9-3 **95**.......... AndrewElliott 5 80
(Mrs K Burke) *midfield: rdn under 2f out: wknd fnl f* **14/1**

58.38 secs (-2.62) **Going Correction** -0.275s/f (Firm) course record
WFA 3 from 4yo+ 1lb **12** Ran SP% **118.8**
Speed ratings (Par 109): **109,106,106,105,104 104,103,103,101,99 98,97**
Tote Swingers: 1&2 £19.60, 1&3 £17.00, 2&3 £9.20 CSF £95.97 CT £572.53 TOTE £16.40: £4.70, £2.30, £2.30; EX 142.00 Trifecta £1081.80 Part won. Pool: £1,461.90 - 0.74 winning units..

Owner T G & Mrs M E Holdcroft **Bred** Bearstone Stud **Trained** Great Habton, N Yorks

FOCUS

The ground had dried out and was officially good to firm on the inner sprint track, which resulted in a number of non-runners. This good, competitive handicap run in memory of Sir Peter O'Sullevan's champion sprinter usually falls to a battle-hardened type. Sound form, and like the other two sprint winners on the day the winner made all.

NOTEBOOK

Confessional has been running well since the eyeshield was fitted and aided by the tail wind, managed to make all and beat off the runner-up's challenge in the final furlong. (op 20-1)

Golden Destiny(IRE), a four-time winner last summer on fast ground, had not won since but had been placed in Listed company, and she put up a decent effort in a handicap last time with blinkers fitted. She ran well again under top weight here, but the winner proved just too strong. (op 7-1)

Courageous(IRE) ◆ had not won since scoring on his debut in 2008 but had finished placed in Listed company since and had produced fair efforts in a visor off similar marks the last twice. Since then he had been sold for £28,000, and the headgear was left off on this first run for his new yard. He was unable to go the early gallop, but finished with a real flourish and might have won in another half-furlong. The Ayr Gold (or Silver) Cup is the obvious target, but the Portland Handicap at Doncaster next week could be another option if he comes out of this well enough. (tchd 5-1)

Anglezarke(IRE) is well suited by 5f on a flat track. She had not won since May 2009, but had been campaigned almost exclusively in Pattern company and had placed at Group level. She was fairly weighted for this handicap debut, and stayed on well having chased the leaders throughout. (op 8-1)

Haajes handles most ground and had been running consistently of late. He was another who could not go the early pace but was finishing well and remains in good heart. (op 9-1 tchd 14-1)

Favourite Girl(IRE) was in good form earlier in the summer once a visor was applied, winning four times in five starts. She ran well again before fading and, having gone up 18lb in all and being 4lb above her last winning mark, the handicapper might have caught up for now. (op 8-1 tchd 7-1)

Archers Road(IRE), a tough, reliable sort who handles most ground, is suited by a sharp 5f, but he could not get to the front and weakened out of it in the closing stages. (op 18-1)

Strike Up The Band was rated in the 100s last season but has been struggling mostly this year. Dropped to a reasonable mark, he put up a better effort at Epsom earlier in the week, and his final placing here does not reflect the merit of this performance. (op 7-1)

Reignier was Group 2 placed as a juvenile and was making his handicap debut off a fair mark. Back from nine weeks off and back in his old yard, he struggled to go the pace from the start and was soon ridden along, then eventually paid the price for his efforts in the closing stages. (op 16-1)

5743 BETFRED KINGSPIN OLD BOROUGH CUP (HERITAGE H'CAP) 1m 6f

3:05 (3:06) (Class 2) (0-105,100) 3-Y-0**£45,332** (£13,489; £6,741; £3,367) **Stalls** Low

Form RPR

0511 **1** **Kansai Spirit (IRE)**[22] 5035 4-9-2 **92**.......... WilliamBuick 10 102+
(J H M Gosden) *hld up: hdwy over 2f out: led wl over 1f out: styd on gamely ins fnl f* **4/1**[1]

1042 **2** ¾ **Red Cadeaux**[14] 5291 4-9-5 **95**.......... RyanMoore 14 104
(E A L Dunlop) *hld up: hdwy over 2f out: sn chalng: rdn over 1f out: styd on for press tl no ex fnl strides* **13/2**[3]

1-04 **3** *nk* **Braveheart Move (IRE)**[23] 5004 4-9-3 **93**.......... RichardKingscote 3 102
(Jonjo O'Neill) *led for 1f: continued to chse ldr: regained ld 3f out: hdd over 2f out: styd on u.p thrght fnl f: a hld* **25/1**

0300 **4** *hd* **Crackentorp**[17] 5217 5-8-11 **87**.......... GrahamGibbons 8 95
(T D Easterby) *midfield: hdwy 3f out: rdn to chal over 2f out: styd on u.p thrght fnl f but a hld* **18/1**

1210 **5** ¾ **Chilly Filly (IRE)**[17] 5217 4-8-13 **89**.......... GregFairley 19 96
(M Johnston) *hld up: hdwy on outer over 2f out: pressed ldrs ins fnl f: one pce fnl strides* **14/1**

0421 **6** 2 ½ **Rangefinder**[14] 5296 6-9-2 **92**.......... ShaneKelly 12 96
(Jane Chapple-Hyam) *in tch: effrt to chal over 2f out: styd on same pce fr over 1f out* **20/1**

2514 **7** *shd* **Cotillion**[28] 4846 4-8-11 **87**.......... TomEaves 6 91
(Ian Williams) *missed break: bhd: rdn 2f out: hdwy over 1f out: styd on ins fnl f: nt rch ldrs* **16/1**

5-05 **8** 1 ¼ **Ajaan**[17] 5220 6-9-10 **100**..........(b) EddieAhern 18 102
(H R A Cecil) *missed break: bhd: u.p 2f out: kpt on ins fnl f: nvr able to chal* **15/2**

1441 **9** *hd* **Lady Eclair (IRE)**[14] 5291 4-9-7 **97**.......... JoeFanning 4 99
(M Johnston) *in tch: led over 2f out: rdn and hdd wl over 1f out: fdd fnl f* **6/1**[2]

5-50 **10** ½ **Recession Proof (FR)**[91] 2747 4-8-12 **88**.......... PatCosgrave 17 89
(J J Quinn) *midfield: u.p 2f out: no imp* **18/1**

1006 **11** ¾ **Perfect Shot (IRE)**[15] 5278 4-9-0 **90**.......... MartinDwyer 7 90
(J L Dunlop) *hld up in midfield: pushed along 3f out: sme hdwy 2f out: no imp on ldrs: wknd ins fnl f* **25/1**

3000 **12** ½ **Macarthur**[28] 4818 6-8-8 **91**.......... LewisWalsh(7) 16 90
(Jane Chapple-Hyam) *racd freely: led after 1f: hdd 3f out: stl ev ch u.p 2f out: wknd over 1f out* **28/1**

5653 **13** 4 ½ **Becausewecan (USA)**[15] 5278 4-8-13 **89**.......... RobertWinston 2 82
(M Johnston) *chsd ldrs: rdn over 2f out: wknd over 1f out* **14/1**

0142 **14** 2 ½ **Woolfall Treasure**[28] 4817 5-9-5 **95**..........(v) GeorgeBaker 9 84
(G L Moore) *hld up: pushed along over 3f out: sn wknd* **14/1**

3014 **15** 1 ¼ **Porgy**[28] 4830 5-8-12 **88**.......... JamieSpencer 15 76
(R A Fahey) *chsd ldrs: chal 3f out: rdn and wknd 2f out* **10/1**

1P/6 **16** 3 ¾ **Shipmaster**[150] 1176 7-9-10 **100**.......... SteveDrowne 5 82
(A King) *midfield: pushed along 3f out: wknd 2f out: eased whn btn over 1f out* **50/1**

2m 55.64s (-5.56) **Going Correction** -0.325s/f (Firm) course record **16** Ran SP% **122.7**
Speed ratings (Par 109): **102,101,101,101,100 99,99,98,98,98 97,97,94,93,92 90**
Tote Swingers: 1&2 £7.60, 1&3 £20.90, 2&3 £40.50 CSF £26.41 CT £593.00 TOTE £5.00: £2.00, £2.10, £4.50, £3.90; EX 30.00 Trifecta £732.30 Pool: £16,200.59 - 16.37 winning units..

Owner R Van Gelder **Bred** Keatly Overseas Ltd **Trained** Newmarket, Suffolk

FOCUS

This valuable handicap has been dominated in recent seasons by Mark Johnston, and he had three representatives this year, but this time none of them could make the frame. The form makes a fair bit of sense.

NOTEBOOK

Kansai Spirit(IRE) has been progressive in recent starts, winning twice at up to 1m5f and was proven on a sound surface. Up 9lb but relatively unexposed, he was sent off favourite. He tended to hang left most of the way up the straight, but William Buick managed to keep him going forward and relatively straight, and he found plenty for pressure, getting the better of the runner-up inside the last. He looks capable of making up into a Listed or Group performer if continuing to progress as he has. (op 9-2)

Red Cadeaux had not won beyond 1m4f but had appeared to stay the trip. Despite being 5lb above his last winning mark he showed plenty of dash, coming from off the pace to lead entering the final quarter-mile and then battling on, but just losing out to a progressive sort. He deserves to win one of these. (op 6-1)

Braveheart Move(IRE) was progressive at up to 1m5f for Sir Mark Prescott but had a moderate season over hurdles on soft going for his new yard. He put up a better effort recently at 1m2f on good ground and ran well, having been in the leading group throughout. He could be up to winning a decent middle-distance handicap before too long. (op 20-1 tchd 33-1 in a place)

Crackentorp, a dual 1m2f Polytrack winner but placed over 2m, had been a little off the boil of late but had dropped in the weights and bounced back to something like his best. (op 20-1 tchd 22-1)

Chilly Filly(IRE), generally in good form at up to this trip since her return to action but disappointing last time after hike in the weights, looked a big threat halfway up the straight, but she could not sustain the run and might be in the handicapper's grip now. (op 12-1)

Rangefinder, a winner at just short of 2m last time, travelled well for a long way, but he was up 8lb in a higher grade race and that eventually found him out. (op 16-1)

Cotillion, a C&D winner in July with Rangefinder behind on his only previous try at the trip, was 11lb higher and, after a slow start, was running on when the race was over.

Ajaan, very useful at up to this trip on good and easy ground and a running-on fifth in the Ebor last time, missed the break and trailed the field throughout. He did make some late progress and it would not be the biggest surprise if he consented to put his best foot forward in the Cesarewitch over further, a race in which he was fifth last season. (op 12-1 tchd 16-1 in a place)

Lady Eclair(IRE) has been in fine form from 1m5f to 2m and beat Red Cadeaux a neck on easy ground in a Listed race last time. She should have finished in the frame on that form but failed to pick up as might have been expected.

Porgy showed up for a long way but dropped right out in the last quarter-mile. (op 16-1 tchd 20-1 in a place)

Shipmaster Official explanation: jockey said gelding had no more to give

5744 BETFRED SPRINT CUP (GROUP 1) 6f

3:35 (3:38) (Class 1) 3-Y-0+

£163,809 (£62,095; £31,076; £15,495; £7,762; £3,895) **Stalls** Centre

Form RPR

1126 **1** **Markab**[49] 4136 7-9-3 113.......... PatCosgrave 14 121+
(H Candy) *racd on stands' side: mde all: rdn and edgd lft over 1f out: r.o wl fnl f: a in control: 1st of 6 in gp* **12/1**

-366 **2** 1 ¼ **Lady Of The Desert (USA)**[78] 3143 3-8-12 111.......... MartinDwyer 7 114
(B J Meehan) *ponied to s: racd on far side: a.p: led gp under 2f out: r.o u.p ins fnl f but a hld by stand's side wnr: 1st of 7 in gp* **9/1**[3]

4610 **3** *1* **Genki (IRE)**[35] [4576] 6-9-3 103 ....(v) SteveDrowne 4 114
(R Charlton) *racd on far side: hld up: rdn and hdwy ent fnl f: r.o: no further imp fnl strides: 2nd of 7 in gp* **20/1**

1640 **4** *3/4* **Kingsgate Native (IRE)**[15] [5276] 5-9-3 116 .... RyanMoore 8 111
(Sir Michael Stoute) *racd on far side: midfield: rdn and hdwy over 1f out: styd on ins fnl f: one pce and no further imp cl home: 3rd of 7 in gp* **6/1**[2]

5112 **5** *3/4* **Starspangledbanner (AUS)**[15] [5276] 4-9-3 121 .... CO'Donoghue 5 109
(A P O'Brien, Ire) *racd on far side: led gp tl u.p 2f out: rdn and nt qckn over 1f out: no ex fnl 100yds: 4th of 7 in gp* **11/8**[1]

0011 **6** *1* **Regal Parade**[27] [4885] 6-9-3 118 .... AdrianNicholls 6 106
(D Nicholls) *racd on far side: prom: pushed along over 2f out: rdn and nt qckn over 1f out: wknd fnl 100yds: 5th of 7 in gp* **9/1**[3]

3461 **7** *1/2* **Doncaster Rover (USA)**[7] [5526] 4-9-3 108 .... WilliamBuick 10 104
(D H Brown) *racd on stands' side: towards rr: rdn over 2f out: hdwy to chse ldrs over 1f out: one pce ins fnl f: 2nd of 6 in gp* **18/1**

3316 **8** *nk* **Borderlescott**[15] [5276] 8-9-3 112 .... NeilCallan 3 103
(R Bastiman) *racd on far side: chsd ldrs: edgd rt 2f out: rdn and nt qckn over 1f out: wknd ins fnl f: 6th of 7 in gp* **10/1**

5006 **9** *nk* **Sir Gerry (USA)**[7] [5526] 5-9-3 103 .... GeorgeBaker 12 102
(C A Dwyer) *racd on stands' side: hld up: rdn over 1f out: no imp on ldrs: 3rd of 6 in gp* **50/1**

5000 **10** *hd* **Iver Bridge Lad**[21] [5088] 3-9-1 100 ....(v[1]) EddieAhern 2 102
(J Ryan) *racd on far side: in rr: pushed along over 1f out: kpt on ins fnl f: nt pce to chal: 7th of 7 in gp* **100/1**

0100 **11** *2 3/4* **Barney McGrew (IRE)**[18] [5183] 7-9-3 105 .... TomEaves 9 93
(M Dods) *racd keenly on stands' side: prom: rdn over 2f out: wknd 1f out: 4th of 6 in gp* **66/1**

0054 **12** *3/4* **Prime Defender**[15] [5276] 6-9-3 109 .... RobertWinston 13 90
(B W Hills) *racd on stands' side: w ldr tl rdn over 1f out: sn wknd: 5th of 6 in gp* **16/1**

1-60 **13** *1/2* **Our Jonathan**[34] [4616] 3-9-1 105 .... JamieSpencer 16 89
(K A Ryan) *racd on stands' side: hld up: effrt to chse ldrs 2f out: hung lft over 1f out: wknd fnl f: 6th of 6 in gp* **33/1**

69.40 secs (-4.10) **Going Correction** -0.275s/f (Firm) course record
WFA 3 from 4yo+ 2lb **13** Ran SP% **116.5**
Speed ratings (Par 117): **116,114,113,112,111 109,109,108,108,107 104,103,102**
Tote Swingers: 1&2 £13.80, 1&3 £26.20, 2&3 £20.90 CSF £108.73 CT £2209.50 TOTE £18.50: £4.40, £3.20, £8.70; EX 154.60 Trifecta £1125.10 Pool: £7,602.16 - 5 winning units..
Owner Tight Lines Partnership **Bred** Shadwell Estate Company Limited **Trained** Kingston Warren, Oxon

FOCUS
One of the major sprints of the season and a decent renewal with plenty of runners, despite the withdrawals, although only one overseas challenger. They split into two virtually equal groups. The winner raced on the stands' side but drifted in the closing stages and ended up nearer the far rail, and the time surpassed the previous best, recorded by Iktamal on the old sprint track in 1996. Probably ordinary form for the race, with Markab continuing this year's progress but Sparspangledbanner below his summer form.

NOTEBOOK
Markab has improved this season, having won a Group 3 at the Curragh and finished runner-up in the King's Stand. He put behind him a poor effort at Newbury, where he reportedly had failed to recover sufficiently from getting jarred up at Ascot, and ran too free on rain-softened ground behind Regal Parade last time. Back on his favoured fast ground, he travelled well in the stands' side group and left them behind as he drifted across towards the far side. He scored with a bit in hand, and he is likely to go for the Prix de l'Abbaye next. (op 11-1 tchd 10-1)
Lady Of The Desert(USA), the Lowther winner in 2009 but held despite good efforts in both the Nell Gwyn and French Guineas this season, was dropping back in distance to the trip over which her last two wins were gained. She looked to have a bit to do against hardened sprinters, but travelled really well and ran down the pacemaking favourite before finding the winner too strong. She is unlikely to go for the Abbaye but could win a good race before the end of the season. (op 10-1)
Genki(IRE), a former Stewards' Cup winner but well beaten in that race this year (in a first-time visor), won over course and distance in first-time blinkers on his previous start. He was unable to go the early pace but finished well for the minor placing, and a race like the Diadem or Ayr Gold Cup could provide a suitable opportunity next. (op 18-1)
Kingsgate Native(IRE) is top-class on his day and is capable of popping up in one of these races. He won the Temple Stakes over 5f here in May and put up a creditable effort on the fast ground that suits. (op 15-2)
Starspangledbanner(AUS) made a big impression and was arguably the leading 6f sprinter in Europe going into this, having won the Golden Jubilee and July Cup before finishing runner-up in Nunthorpe. He jumped fast and made the running on the far side, but the runner-up cruised up to join him two furlongs out, and he had nothing in reserve. Official explanation: jockey said colt had no more to give (op 6-4)
Regal Parade caused a surprise when taking this in 2009 and had hardly looked back since. However, he was a market drifter on this fast ground and could not get involved having been under pressure to hold his place at halfway. (op 7-1)
Doncaster Rover(USA) is a reliable type who stays further. He did second best of the group that raced on the stands' side, but in truth never got into contention. (op 20-1 tchd 16-1)
Borderlescott finished behind Starspangledbanner and Prime Defender at York in his bid for a three-timer in the Nunthorpe, but had not run at 6f since Sha Tin in December. He was struggling from around halfway and has not looked quite the same since sustaining an injury when winning the King George Stakes at Glorious Goodwood. Reportedly that is it for the season and he will be roughed off now. Official explanation: jockey said gelding was never travelling
Our Jonathan Official explanation: jockey said colt hung left

5745 BETFRED "10 BEST ODDS RACES DAILY" NURSERY 6f
4:10 (4:12) (Class 2) 2-Y-O
£12,462 (£3,732; £1,866; £934; £466; £234) **Stalls** Centre

Form RPR

212 **1** **Easy Ticket (IRE)**[28] [4851] 2-9-2 83 .... RichardMullen 3 96+
(D H Brown) *racd on far side: mde all: clr over 1f out: r.o wl: a wl in command fnl f* **7/2**[1]

153 **2** *2 1/2* **Berberana (IRE)**[14] [5301] 2-8-9 76 .... DavidAllan 6 82+
(T D Easterby) *racd on stands' side: pressed gp ldr: led gp wl over 1f out: styd on u.p: no imp on far side ldr and all out cl home to hold on in gp: 1st of 8 in gp* **7/1**

21 **3** *hd* **Man Of The Match (IRE)**[10] [5404] 2-9-0 81 .... RobertWinston 13 86+
(A Bailey) *racd on stands' side: chsd ldrs: rdn 2f out: nt qckn over 1f out: r.o towards fin and clsd rapidly on gp ldr: 2nd of 8 in gp* **4/1**[2]

3241 **4** *3/4* **Brave Dream**[12] [5352] 2-8-1 68 .... JoeFanning 11 71+
(K A Ryan) *racd on stands' side: chsd ldrs: rdn 2f out: nt qckn over 1f out: styd on to chal in gp fnl 100yds: one pce fnl strides: 3rd of 8 in gp* **14/1**

3200 **5** *nk* **On The High Tops (IRE)**[17] [5221] 2-9-1 82 .... MickyFenton 7 84
(T P Tate) *racd on stands' side: led gp: hdd wl over 1f out: continued to chal gp ldr: no ex fnl 75yds: 4th of 8 in gp* **66/1**

411 **6** *1 1/4* **Talley Close**[28] [4851] 2-9-4 85 .... PaulMulrennan 8 83
(R A Fahey) *racd on stands' side: chsd ldrs: rdn over 1f out: one pce fnl 100yds: 5th of 8 in gp* **6/1**[3]

211 **7** *3/4* **Morache Music**[7] [5537] 2-9-7 88 .... PatCosgrave 1 84
(P J Makin) *racd on far side: chsd ldrs: wnt 2nd in gp 1/2-way: u.p and outpcd by wnr over 1f out: no ex fnl 100yds* **6/1**[3]

353 **8** *4 1/2* **Barista (IRE)**[8] [5476] 2-8-0 67 .... DuranFentiman 2 49
(M R Channon) *racd on far side: in tch: rdn over 2f out: outpcd over 1f out* **20/1**

2135 **9** *2 1/2* **King Of Aquitaine (IRE)**[21] [5094] 2-9-1 82 .... JamieSpencer 10 57
(K A Ryan) *racd on stands' side: a bhd: nvr on terms: 6th of 8 in gp* **28/1**

0322 **10** *1* **Point Du Jour (FR)**[16] [5251] 2-8-9 79 ....(t) MartinLane(3) 9 51
(I A Wood) *missed break: racd in centre of trck: in rr: pushed along and outpcd 1/2-way* **12/1**

4110 **11** *1* **Major Conquest (IRE)**[36] [4539] 2-9-4 85 .... MichaelHills 4 54
(J W Hills) *racd on far side: in tch: rdn 2f out: no imp: wknd ins fnl f: eased fnl 150yds* **25/1**

400 **12** *1 1/2* **Welsh Dancer**[39] [4460] 2-9-1 82 .... RyanMoore 14 46
(R Hannon) *racd on stands' side: a bhd: nvr on terms: 8th of 8 in gp* **16/1**

3210 **13** *4* **Joyously**[16] [5246] 2-8-13 80 .... SteveDrowne 5 32
(P D Evans) *racd in centre of trck and off the pce: outpcd 1/2-way: edgd lft over 2f out: n.d* **33/1**

1m 10.72s (-2.78) **Going Correction** -0.275s/f (Firm) 2y crse rec **13** Ran SP% **120.0**
Speed ratings (Par 101): **107,103,103,98,98 96,95,89,86,84 83,81,76**
Tote Swingers: 1&2 £9.70, 1&3 £4.70, 2&3 £8.60 CSF £26.49 CT £107.52 TOTE £4.90: £1.90, £3.00, £2.00; EX 28.30 Trifecta £72.90 Pool: £437.88 - 4.44 winning units..
Owner J C Fretwell **Bred** A Butler **Trained** Maltby, S Yorks

FOCUS
A competitive nursery with a number of these coming into the race in good form and/or unexposed as handicappers. The time was a respectable, being 1.32secs slower than the preceding Group 1. The race was a mirror image of that contest, with the winner racing well clear of his rivals on the far side, but chased home by the bunch on the stands' side. The winner impressed and the form looks solid with the first trio clear.

NOTEBOOK
Easy Ticket(IRE) has always been well regarded and showed what he was capable of, being fitted with a cross noseband and allowed to stride on this time. He blitzed his rivals on the far side of the track, and won in the manner of a sprinter with a future. He has entries in a couple of sales races and the Middle Park, but the target is reportedly the Rockingham Stakes at York. (op 4-1 tchd 9-2 in a place)
Berberana(IRE), a 5f winner on Fibresand on her debut, did best of those on the wrong side in a sales race last time. She was on the wrong side again, but battled on well to come out best of her group. A race like the Jersey Lily nursery at Newmarket or the Firth of Clyde Stakes at Ayr, against fillies, appeal as suitable targets. (op 12-1 tchd 13-2)
Man Of The Match(IRE), both of whose previous runs were over 7f, ran on late as if finding this trip on the short side. He can be given another chance back over further. (op 5-1)
Brave Dream likes fast ground but had looked exposed at a lower level and did well to make the frame. He helps set the level of the form. (op 12-1 tchd 16-1)
On The High Tops(IRE), dropping back from Listed class, showed good early pace up the stands' side and stuck to his task under pressure, proving that he is much better on fast going.
Talley Close, beat today's winner on their previous meeting and was closely matched with him on the revised terms. He failed to run his race and might have found the ground faster than ideal. Official explanation: jockey said colt ran flat (op 9-2)
Morache Music had won his two previous starts, both times when there was cut in the ground. He made a bold bid to chase the winner from halfway but paid for it in the closing stages, despite beating everything else in his group. Official explanation: trainer said colt coughed following race and a subsequent scope showed significant mucus in his lungs (op 13-2 tchd 7-1 in a place)
Joyously Official explanation: jockey said filly had no more to give

5746 BETFRED.COM STKS (REGISTERED AS THE ASCENDANT STAKES) (LISTED RACE) 1m 30y
4:45 (4:45) (Class 1) 2-Y-O £17,031 (£6,456; £3,231; £1,611; £807) **Stalls** Low

Form RPR

0003 **1** **Singapore Lilly (IRE)**[36] [4539] 2-8-9 80 .... ChrisCatlin 3 99
(M R Channon) *hld up: shkn up 3f out: hdwy over 1f out: sn chsd ldr: r.o to ld wl ins fnl f: on top at fin* **16/1**

112 **2** *nk* **Measuring Time**[14] [5306] 2-9-0 106 .... RyanMoore 8 103
(R Hannon) *chsd ldr: led over 3f out: rdn over 1f out: hdd wl ins fnl f: hld fnl strides* **11/10**[1]

20 **3** *8* **Robin Hood (IRE)**[14] [5316] 2-9-0 0 .... CO'Donoghue 6 85
(A P O'Brien, Ire) *led: hdd over 3f out: rdn and outpcd 2f out: wnt 3rd u.p 1f out: no ch w front pair fnl f* **5/2**[2]

5 **4** *3 1/2* **Claret'N'Blue (USA)**[36] [4550] 2-9-0 0 .... JamieSpencer 4 78+
(B J Meehan) *hld up: rdn under 4f out: hdwy to chal 3f out: stl ev ch 2f out: wknd over 1f out* **11/2**[3]

1 **5** *1 1/4* **Rhythm Of Light**[36] [4543] 2-8-9 82 .... RichardKingscote 7 70
(Tom Dascombe) *t.k.h: trckd ldrs: effrt 3f out: wanted to hang lft whn chalng 2f out: wknd over 1f out* **8/1**

1m 41.27s (-3.43) **Going Correction** -0.325s/f (Firm) **5** Ran SP% **108.6**
Speed ratings (Par 103): **104,103,95,92,90**
CSF £33.83 TOTE £10.90: £3.10, £1.10; EX 30.80 Trifecta £69.50 £425.49 - 4.53 winning units..

Owner Mrs T Burns **Bred** Troy Cullen **Trained** West Ilsley, Berks

FOCUS
An ordinary looking juvenile Listed race that fell to subsequent dual Group winner Emerald Commander last season. The pace looked sound but it produced a shock result, Singapore Lilly producing a huge step up. The first two finished well clear and the form looks sound.

NOTEBOOK
Singapore Lilly(IRE) had looked exposed prior to this, having been held at this level and beaten in a nursery since her win in May. However, she had gained that previous success on her only other encounter with a flat track, and the step up in trip might also have helped. Held up in the rear, she was caught out briefly as the pace quickened, but she came through to deliver her challenge entering the last furlong and got the better of the runner-up late on. This seals her paddock value but connections will presumably look for a similar race for her now. (op 14-1)
Measuring Time won his first two starts and built on that when runner-up in the Group 3 Solario last time. He looked the winner when going past the favourite over two furlongs out but could not hold off the filly in the last furlong. That said, he drew a long way clear of the rest, and it is hard to say that he did not run to somewhere near his form. (op 4-5)
Robin Hood(IRE) was well beaten in a Group 2 on his previous start, but before that won on easy ground at Galway. He made the running but was quickly in trouble when the runner-up took him for the lead, and could only keep going at the one pace. The drying ground was probably against him. (op 10-3 tchd 9-4)
Claret'N'Blue(USA) ran a fair race in a novice event on his debut but this was a big step up in grade, and he was well held in the straight. He probably needs more time. (op 8-1)

Rhythm Of Light cost next to nothing and looked a bargain after beating two subsequent winners on her debut. She was well backed earlier in the day but could not pick up in the straight, having had her chance. She might be better off at a lower level against her own sex. Official explanation: jockey said filly ran green (op 15-2)

5747 FRED'S LUCKY NUMBERS H'CAP 1m 6f
5:15 (5:16) (Class 3) (0-90,91) 3-Y-O **£8,095** (£2,408; £1,203; £601) **Stalls** Low

Form RPR

1235 **1** **Activate**[30] 4751 3-8-9 **78** .... HayleyTurner 3 91+
(M L W Bell) *midfield: hdwy 6f out: wnt 2nd 3f out: led wl over 1f out: edgd lft ins fnl f: styd on wl towards fin* **8/1**[3]

514 **2** 1 ½ **Nezhenka**[44] 4304 3-9-1 **84** .... PatCosgrave 8 95+
(Sir Mark Prescott) *n.m.r sn after s: bustled along early: led after 1f: rdn over 2f out: hdd wl over 1f out: styd on u.p ins fnl f: one pce cl home* **20/1**

6115 **3** *hd* **Montparnasse (IRE)**[15] 5273 3-8-13 **82** .... MartinDwyer 13 93+
(B J Meehan) *hld up: hdwy over 2f out: rdn to chse ldrs over 1f out: styd on ins fnl f: clsd on front 2 towards fin* **10/1**

5511 **4** 3 ¾ **Zigato**[28] 4827 3-9-4 **87** ....(p) WilliamBuick 4 93
(J H M Gosden) *bhd: niggled along 6f out: swtchd rt wl over 1f out: hdwy sn after: styd on ins fnl f: nt trble ldrs* **4/1**[1]

1336 **5** ½ **Boston Blue**[38] 4470 3-8-13 **82** ....(p) ShaneKelly 11 87
(W J Knight) *hld up: pushed along over 4f out: rdn over 2f out: kpt on over 1f out: no imp on ldrs* **13/2**[2]

-122 **6** *hd* **Calatrava Cape (IRE)**[23] 5008 3-9-2 **85** .... JamieSpencer 2 90+
(J L Dunlop) *t.k.h: hld up and bhd: hdwy 3f out: rdn 2f out: chsng ldrs over 1f out: hung lft and no imp ins fnl f* **4/1**[1]

4026 **7** 1 ¾ **Hayzoom**[15] 5259 3-8-12 **81** .... RyanMoore 12 83
(P W Chapple-Hyam) *hld up: rdn over 2f out: kpt on fr over 1f out: nvr able to chal* **16/1**

1050 **8** 1 **Bowdler's Magic**[15] 5273 3-9-8 **91** .... JoeFanning 7 92
(M Johnston) *chsd ldrs: lost pl after 6f out: clsd over 3f out: rdn whn chsng ldrs over 2f out: one pce over 1f out: wknd ins fnl f* **20/1**

4011 **9** 5 **Cat O' Nine Tails**[13] 5333 3-8-3 **72** .... GregFairley 6 66
(M Johnston) *t.k.h: chsd ldrs: rdn and outpcd over 3f out: wl btn 2f out* **14/1**

0352 **10** 1 ¾ **Istidlaal**[29] 4792 3-8-5 **74** ....(v) TadhgO'Shea 1 65
(Sir Michael Stoute) *led for 1f: chsd ldrs after: rdn 3f out: wknd over 1f out* **40/1**

4321 **11** ½ **Plato (JPN)**[28] 4845 3-9-2 **85** .... EddieAhern 10 76
(H R A Cecil) *midfield: rdn 4f out: no imp: wl btn over 1f out* **9/1**

3400 **12** 6 **Beneath**[14] 5300 3-8-1 **73** .... MartinLane(3) 5 55
(K A Ryan) *chsd ldrs: rdn over 3f out: wknd over 2f out* **50/1**

6141 **13** 4 **Line Of Duty (IRE)**[16] 5243 3-9-1 **84** .... AndrewElliott 9 61
(G A Swinbank) *n.m.r s: chsd ldr after 1f: rdn and lost 2nd 3f out: wknd 2f out* **9/1**

0421 **14** 16 **Sidney Melbourne (USA)**[24] 4965 3-8-11 **80** .... SteveDrowne 14 34
(J R Best) *s.i.s: midfield: rdn along and lost pl 5f out: bhd after* **25/1**

0-10 **15** 18 **Lajidaal (USA)**[25] 4933 3-9-2 **85** ....(b[1]) ChrisCatlin 15 14
(M P Tregoning) *midfield: hdwy after 2f: chsd ldrs: rdn and lost pl after 6f: bhd fnl 5f out* **50/1**

2m 54.6s (-6.60) **Going Correction** -0.325s/f (Firm) course record **15 Ran SP% 125.8**
Speed ratings (Par 105): **105,104,104,101,101 101,100,99,97,96 95,92,90,80,70**
Tote Swingers: 1&2 £55.10, 1&3 £20.20, 2&3 £49.70 CSF £170.07 CT £1636.60 TOTE £9.20: £3.20, £11.80, £4.20; EX 399.50 TRIFECTA Not won. Place 6: £114.70 Place 5: £71.29 .
Owner Highclere Thoroughbred Racing Tudor Min **Bred** Card Bloodstock **Trained** Newmarket, Suffolk

FOCUS
The 3yo version of the earlier staying handicap and a decent contest in its own right. The pace was good and the time was over a second faster than that race. The first three were unexposed and the form looks sound.

NOTEBOOK
Activate, whose best form earlier in the season was on Polytrack and fast ground, had disappointed here on soft going on his return from a break. He tracked the pace early before going after the leader three furlongs out, and managed to overhaul her inside the last. The longer trip here held no fears for him and he might even get further on this evidence.

Nezhenka, who was loaded with a blindfold and blanket, set out to make it a good gallop. Her rider kicked early in the straight and she soon had most of her rivals in trouble. However, she could not shake off the winner, with that rival proving too strong late on. (tchd 25-1)

Montparnasse(IRE), a dual winner on fast ground, including over this trip earlier in the year, was held up early before staying on steadily. However, he looked to be hanging left most of the way up the straight, but for which he would have gone close. (tchd 12-1)

Zigato, a winner over course and distance last time on soft ground, was fitted with cheekpieces in this bid for a hat-trick. However, he was being given reminders at the halfway mark and looked well held until passing a number of his rivals late on. A half-brother to Sariska, who has revealed some quirks of late, it is too soon to say he has temperament problems, as the drying ground may have been against him. Official explanation: jockey said colt hung badly left (op 9-2)

Boston Blue has displayed a tendency to hang and to not put everything in under pressure in the past. He was fitted with cheekpieces for the first time, but he seemed to be going nowhere before staying on late, and ran below previous form with the runner-up. (op 7-1)

Calatrava Cape(IRE), stepping up in trip, was another who seemed to be hanging in the straight, and she also ran into traffic problems before staying on. Official explanation: jockey said filly ran too free (op 6-1 tchd 13-2)

Bowdler's Magic seemed to run his race, but he is 7lb higher than for his last success and the handicapper seems to have got hold of him at present. (op 25-1)

T/Jkpt: Not won. T/Plt: £172.90 to a £1 stake. Pool:£152,318.39 - 643.04 winning tickets. T/Qpdt: £45.40 to a £1 stake. Pool:£8,037.21 - 130.88 winning tickets DO

5716 KEMPTON (A.W) (R-H)
Saturday, September 4

OFFICIAL GOING: Standard
Wind: Light, half behind Weather: Fine but cloudy

5748 TOTEPOOL SIRENIA STKS (GROUP 3) 6f (P)
2:15 (2:17) (Class 1) 2-Y-O **£22,708** (£8,608; £4,308; £2,148; £1,076) **Stalls** High

Form RPR

0361 **1** **Hooray**[16] 5246 2-9-2 110 .... SebSanders 1 113
(Sir Mark Prescott) *mde all: stretched clr fr over 1f out: v readily* **5/2**[2]

2014 **2** 3 ¾ **Reckless Reward (IRE)**[16] 5245 2-9-0 98 .... RichardHughes 6 100
(R Hannon) *lw: chsd wnr: tried to chal 2f out: sn nt qckn and safely hld* **7/1**[3]

01 **3** 6 **Signs In The Sand**[21] 5085 2-9-0 0 .... FrankieDettori 8 84
(Saeed Bin Suroor) *t.k.h: hld up: wnt 3rd over 2f out: nt qckn over 1f out: wknd fnl f* **7/4**[1]

4024 **4** 2 ½ **Grandmas Dream**[38] 4474 2-8-11 77 .... WilliamCarson 2 72
(G C Bravery) *mostly last: struggling fr 1/2-way: no ch after* **66/1**

102 **5** ¾ **Little Lion Man**[14] 5295 2-9-0 85 .... JimCrowley 5 72
(P W Chapple-Hyam) *dwlt: chsd ldng pair to over 2f out: sn wknd* **22/1**

1m 11.5s (-1.60) **Going Correction** -0.075s/f (Stan) **5 Ran SP% 83.3**
Speed ratings (Par 105): **107,102,94,90,89**
CSF £9.75 TOTE £2.50: £1.30, £1.30; EX 5.70 Trifecta £9.10 Pool: £169.82 - 13.80 winning units..
Owner Cheveley Park Stud **Bred** Cheveley Park Stud Ltd **Trained** Newmarket, Suffolk
■ Fifth Commandment (33/1, upset in stalls) & The Paddyman (25/1, unruly in stalls) were withdrawn. R4, Deduct 25p in the &.

FOCUS
A fair renewal and with pace holding up on the day they broke the 2-y-o course record set by Elnawin in this race two years ago. A quality performance from Hooray despite the race cutting up.

NOTEBOOK
Hooray, proven over C&D, was carrying a 5lb penalty for her all-the-way Lowther success and had the outside stall to overcome, but the withdrawal of two horses on her inside would have been a help and she showed decent early speed to cut across to get to the rail in front before the first bend. Although pressed on both sides after the intersection, she pulled out plenty more when asked and didn't have a hard race by any means. She obviously thrives on racing and may now head for the Group 3 Prix d'Arenberg at Maisons-Laffitte on September 13 before the Cheveley Park, though she wouldn't run at Newmarket if the ground came up soft. (op 2-1)

Reckless Reward(IRE), 2-2 on Polytrack before this (albeit over 5f at Lingfield), travelled well behind the winner and looked a big danger when ranging alongside inside the last 2f, but he couldn't stop the filly from stretching away from him and he didn't seem to quite get home. (op 8-1)

Signs In The Sand, making his AW debut after his impressive soft-ground success at Newmarket, was disappointing. He made his move towards the inside of the track after the intersection, but his finishing effort was weak to say the least and he was left well behind. He had got warm and edgy and been awkward to load beforehand, so may not have been on top form. (op 2-1)

Grandmas Dream, a beaten favourite in maidens the last twice and making her AW debut, had no chance in this company and was always struggling.

Little Lion Man faded after showing up early, but he may not have been helped by the antics of the pair berthed immediately to his left in the gates. (op 20-1)

5749 TOTESPORT.COM SEPTEMBER STKS (GROUP 3) 1m 4f (P)
2:45 (2:45) (Class 1) 3-Y-O+
£34,062 (£12,912; £6,462; £3,222; £1,614; £810) **Stalls** High

Form RPR

3212 **1** **Laaheb**[21] 5080 4-9-4 111 .... RichardHills 1 118
(M A Jarvis) *swtg: mde virtually all: kicked clr jst over 2f out: styd on powerfully: eased fnl 75yds* **11/4**[2]

1-15 **2** 3 ½ **Holberg (UAE)**[58] 3825 4-9-4 115 .... FrankieDettori 4 112
(Saeed Bin Suroor) *trckd ldrs: pushed along over 3f out: prog over 2f out: drvn into 2nd 1f out: no ch w wnr* **7/4**[1]

2214 **3** 2 ¼ **Classic Punch (IRE)**[21] 5090 7-9-4 105 .... DaneO'Neill 7 109
(D R C Elsworth) *lw: trckd ldng pair: gng bttr than most 3f out: chsd wnr over 2f out: no imp: lost 2nd 1f out* **28/1**

1253 **4** 1 ¾ **Saptapadi (IRE)**[21] 5080 4-9-4 109 .... SebSanders 9 106+
(Sir Michael Stoute) *lw: hld up in last trio: rdn over 3f out: prog over 2f out: rchd 4th over 1f out: no impact after: swtchd lft ins fnl f* **7/1**[3]

1-30 **5** 1 **Man Of Iron (USA)**[58] 3825 4-9-4 116 .... J-PGuillambert 5 104+
(L M Cumani) *hld up in last trio: rdn over 3f out: kpt on to take modest 5th 1f out: no ch* **8/1**

2145 **6** ¾ **Les Fazzani (IRE)**[28] 4829 6-9-1 108 .... PatDobbs 3 100
(K A Ryan) *lw: mostly chsd wnr to 5f out: sn u.p and dropped to midfield 4f out: n.d after: plugged on* **8/1**

6343 **7** 7 **Heliodor (USA)**[37] 4500 4-9-4 105 .... RichardHughes 2 92+
(R Hannon) *hld up in midfield: quick move to chse wnr 5f out: wknd qckly over 2f out* **33/1**

1156 **8** 2 ¼ **Buxted (IRE)**[104] 2375 4-9-4 103 .... StevieDonohoe 6 88
(R A Mills) *swtg: dwlt: chsd ldrs: rdn over 3f out: wknd over 2f out: sn bhd* **11/1**

5145 **9** 15 **Once More Dubai (USA)**[64] 3632 5-9-4 110 ......(bt) DaraghO'Donohoe 8 64
(Saeed Bin Suroor) *s.s: hld up in last trio: rdn and sme prog over 3f out: wknd rapidly over 2f out: t.o* **18/1**

2m 30.74s (-3.76) **Going Correction** -0.075s/f (Stan) **9 Ran SP% 117.7**
Speed ratings (Par 113): **109,106,105,104,103 102,98,96,86**
Tote Swingers: 1&2 £1.40, 1&3 £10.90, 2&3 £15.30 CSF £8.13 TOTE £3.80: £1.10, £1.40, £6.60; EX 8.40 Trifecta £245.00 Pool: £758.37 - 2.29 winning units..
Owner Hamdan Al Maktoum **Bred** Darley **Trained** Newmarket, Suffolk

FOCUS
This was the fifth running of the race on Polytrack and an interesting line-up, but the pace was ordinary and the way the race panned out once again demonstrated the dangers of allowing Richard Hills an uncontested lead.

NOTEBOOK
Laaheb, a progressive and consistent gelding making his AW debut, was able to dominate from the start. An injection of pace from the front passing the 2f pole had all of his rivals in trouble and he went further and further clear. He now goes for the Cumberland Lodge, although whether he will be allowed his own way out in front there is anyone's guess. (op 3-1 tchd 5-2)

Holberg(UAE), representing last year's winning connections and 2-2 on the AW before this, put his Newmarket disappointment well behind him with a better effort, but he was having to be niggled along to make headway over 3f from home and although he stayed on, he was never going to get to the winner. As the winner of a Queen's Vase, he needed a much stronger gallop than he got here and may take the winner on again in the Cumberland Lodge, with the Melbourne Cup still a possibility. (op 9-4 tchd 5-2)

Classic Punch(IRE), having his second try on sand on his 37th start, was always in about the same place and lacked a finishing kick, but he probably needs a more galloping track than this. (op 25-1)

Saptapadi(IRE), held by Laaheb on Newbury running, looks more of a stayer, so the modest tempo was no good to him and all he could do was plug on late from the back of the field. (tchd 13-2)

Man Of Iron(USA), winner of last season's Breeders' Cup Marathon for Aidan O'Brien, was held by both Laaheb and Holberg on his two turf efforts this year for his new yard and he was another that merely plodded on from well back in the latter stages. (op 9-1 tchd 10-1)

Les Fazzani(IRE), 3-5 on Polytrack and proven over C&D, was up there early but her replacement rider was sending out distress signals passing the 4f pole. (op 17-2)

Heliodor(USA) was also close to the pace early, but he was being niggled over 5f from home and eventually faded right out of it. He has shown his very best form over shorter.

Buxted(IRE), 3-3 on Polytrack but held in two turf Group races since, was reappearing from four months off after getting jarred up at Longchamp in May and he ran as though needing it. (op 12-1)

Once More Dubai(USA), winner of a C&D Listed event last November but apparently the stable's second string here, gave his rivals a start and a modest effort on the wide outside over 2f from home fizzled out as quickly as it had started. (op 20-1 tchd 16-1)

5750 TOTESCOOP6 LONDON MILE H'CAP (SERIES FINAL) 1m (P)
3:20 (3:20) (Class 2) 3-Y-0+

£37,386 (£11,196; £5,598; £2,802; £1,398; £702) Stalls High

Form RPR

6026 1 **Chapter And Verse (IRE)**[21] 5087 4-9-8 87 TonyCulhane 7 101
(Mike Murphy) *hld up in last gp: stl in last pair over 2f out: rapid prog through rivals over 1f out: stormed into ld last 100yds: sn clr* **25/1**

0002 2 2 1/4 **Red Somerset (USA)**[19] 5142 7-9-6 88 EJMcNamara(3) 15 97
(Mike Murphy) *dwlt: hld up in last gp: gd prog fr 2f out: drvn ahd briefly 150yds out: outpcd by wnr sn after* **25/1**

0102 3 1 **L'Hirondelle (IRE)**[23] 5003 6-9-5 84 JimCrowley 11 91
(M J Attwater) *lw: dwlt: hld up in 10th: plld out and prog jst over 2f out: r.o to take 3rd ins fnl f: nt pce of ldng pair* **16/1**

0210 4 3/4 **Clockmaker (IRE)**[15] 5264 4-9-10 89 FrankieDettori 8 94
(J H M Gosden) *lw: s.s: mostly in last pair: rdn over 3f out: stl last 2f out: styd on fr over 1f out on wd outside: nrst fin* **11/2**[2]

2120 5 nk **Tartan Trip**[7] 5524 3-8-13 83 (v[1]) DavidProbert 10 86
(A M Balding) *lw: prom: wnt 2nd over 2f out: drvn to cl on ldr 1f out: outpcd ins fnl f* **5/1**[1]

5314 6 nk **State Gathering**[31] 4699 3-8-13 83 DaneO'Neill 2 86
(H Candy) *hld up in midfield in abt 9th: prog over 2f out: clsd on ldrs 1f out: one pce fnl f* **9/1**

0105 7 hd **Den's Gift (IRE)**[52] 4030 6-9-3 87 (b) JohnFahy(5) 3 90
(C G Cox) *sn led at str pce: drvn clr over 2f out: stl 2 l clr over 1f out: swamped ins fnl f* **14/1**

0666 8 1 1/2 **Getcarter**[8] 5495 4-9-1 80 PatDobbs 9 83
(R Hannon) *dwlt: hld up in last trio: prog on inner over 2f out: nt qckn over 1f out: keeping on and ch of a pl whn nt clr run ins fnl f* **14/1**

0040 9 1/2 **Highly Regal (IRE)**[39] 4459 5-9-5 84 (b) JackMitchell 6 83
(R A Teal) *hld up in rr gp: rdn over 3f out: nt qckn and no prog over 2f out: hdwy at one pce over 1f out: effrt flattened out fnl f* **8/1**

5260 10 3 **Prince Of Thebes (IRE)**[19] 5142 9-8-7 77 KierenFox(5) 12 69
(M J Attwater) *chsd ldr 3f: styd prom: disp 2nd over 2f out: wknd over 1f out* **40/1**

625 11 2 **Swiss Cross**[94] 2644 3-8-9 79 (p) RichardHughes 5 65
(G A Butler) *hld up in midfield: rdn and no prog over 2f out: fdd over 1f out* **15/2**

U130 12 1 **Samarinda (USA)**[52] 4030 7-9-7 86 AdamKirby 14 71
(Mrs P Sly) *fast away but sn shuffled bnack to midfield on inner: rdn in 8th over 3f out: tried to cl briefly 2f out: sn wknd and eased* **25/1**

2312 13 6 **Purple Gallery (IRE)**[10] 5415 3-8-2 79 (p) RyanPowell(7) 1 49
(J S Moore) *prom: gng wl and chalng for 2nd 3f out: wknd rapidly over 2f out: eased* **33/1**

4151 14 1 1/4 **Shamir**[31] 4699 3-9-2 86 IanMongan 4 53
(Miss Jo Crowley) *nvr bttr than midfield: u.p and struggling over 3f out: wknd over 1f out: eased* **7/1**[3]

2033 15 11 **Alfresco**[23] 5005 6-8-12 77 (b) JimmyQuinn 13 20
(J R Best) *t.k.h: chsd ldr after 3f to over 2f out: wknd rapidly: eased* **25/1**

1m 37.16s (-2.64) **Going Correction** -0.075s/f (Stan)
WFA 3 from 4yo+ 5lb 15 Ran SP% **121.3**
Speed ratings (Par 109): **110,107,106,106,105 105,105,103,103,100 98,97,91,89,78**
Tote Swingers: 1&2 £51.60, 1&3 £10.60, 2&3 £52.30 CSF £287.58 CT £5019.05 TOTE £26.60: £6.30, £4.90, £3.60; EX 246.50 TRIFECTA Not won..

Owner D J Ellis **Bred** Stuart Weld **Trained** Westoning, Beds

■ Stewards' Enquiry : John Fahy one-day ban: used whip with excessive frequency (Sep 18)

FOCUS

The early pace was generous, perhaps too much so, as the first four horses home were among the last half-dozen at halfway and those near the front early got tired late on. The race proved a triumph for trainer Mike Murphy, who saddled the first two home. Sound form, with a clear personal best from the winner.

NOTEBOOK

Chapter And Verse(IRE) had finished in the frame in all four previous visits here without winning, but he is a winner over 1m2f, so a strongly run race over this trip played into his hands. His rider did very well to find a route through the field and he was able to weave his way through his rivals in the home straight, maintaining the run to collar his stablemate around 50 yards from the line. His future prospects will depend on a decent pace over this trip, though he has the option of going back up to 1m2f. (op 20-1)

Red Somerset(USA) was raised 3lb for a narrow defeat in a strongly run event over C&D last time. Held up early alongside his stablemate, he made his effort closer to the inside rail and looked to have timed it right when hitting the front inside the last, but his stablemate had other ideas and swamped him well inside the last half-furlong. He still has what it takes to win off this sort of mark. (op 14-1)

L'Hirondelle(IRE), 5lb higher than when successful over C&D on his last visit, had this race as his target for some time and ran a blinder, making his move from well off the pace down the outside and holding every chance over a furlong from home before his effort flattened out. (op 14-1)

Clockmaker(IRE), disappointing on turf last time but an impressive off 8lb lower over C&D before that, could be considered unfortunate not to have finished closer as he was very awkward from the gates and in a competitive event like this that was one handicap too many. He then took far too long to respond to pressure turning for home and his strong late effort down the wide outside was always going to be far too late. (tchd 5-1)

Tartan Trip ◆ had a visor on for the first time after his disappointing Newmarket effort. Having travelled well just behind the leaders against the inside rail, he had every chance over a furlong from home and deserves credit as he did best of those that raced nearer the front. He has a nice handicap in him. (op 7-1)

State Gathering, still 5lb higher than when winning over C&D two starts ago, had his chance and kept plugging away. He still has relatively few miles on the clock. (op 17-2 tchd 8-1)

Den's Gift(IRE), 4lb higher than when successful over C&D on his last visit and prepared with this race in mind, wasn't ideally drawn for an established front-runner, so under the circumstances he ran a blinder, especially as he had to work hard to get to the front after a furlong. He still had a lead of a couple of lengths coming to the last furlong, but it was no surprise that he soon became tired and got swamped. (op 12-1)

Getcarter, another held up early before making his effort towards the inside over 2f from home, may have finished a length or two closer had he not got stopped when staying on entering the last furlong, but he has shown his very best form over shorter. (op 12-1)

Highly Regal(IRE), a six-time winner over C&D and 7lb higher than when taking this last year, was the subject of strong market support earlier in the day but although he stayed on late down the outside, he never looked likely to get there. (op 12-1)

5751 TOTESPORT 0800 221 221 CONDITIONS STKS (C&G) 7f (P)
3:50 (3:51) (Class 3) 2-Y-O £5,504 (£1,637; £818) Stalls High

Form RPR

1 1 **Biondetti (USA)**[29] 4803 2-9-2 0 FrankieDettori 3 89+
(Mahmood Al Zarooni) *w'like: scope: lw: mde all: sedate pce tl qcknd 1/2-way: shrugged off rivals over 1f out: comf* **1/2**[1]

1 2 1 **Darej (USA)**[30] 4759 2-9-2 0 RichardHills 2 84
(W J Haggas) *w'like: scope: tall: chsd wnr: chal 3f out: rdn and outpcd over 1f out: n.d after* **5/2**[2]

3 5 **Above All** 2-8-12 0 RichardHughes 4 68+
(W J Haggas) *unf: scope: hld up last: effrt on outer 4f out: sn outpcd: clsd again 2f out: wknd fnl f* **8/1**[3]

1m 28.06s (2.06) **Going Correction** -0.075s/f (Stan) 3 Ran SP% **106.3**
Speed ratings (Par 99): **85,83,78**
CSF £1.99 TOTE £1.40; EX 1.40.

Owner Godolphin **Bred** Palides Investments N V Inc **Trained** Newmarket, Suffolk

FOCUS

An already small field was reduced even further when Ari Gold was withdrawn after bursting out the front of his stall, but this was still an interesting clash between two expensive and highly regarded colts. The winner made his own running and this is not form to put too mych faith in.

NOTEBOOK

Biondetti(USA), winner of a Newmarket maiden on debut last month that is working out well, cost $350,000 as a yearling and is a half-brother to several winners, including some smart performers in the US, so the surface was unlikely to be a problem. Left alone in front, his rider only needed to let out an inch of rein over a furlong out for him to stretch clear and he was value for much more than the winning margin. Still a big baby, he won't be over-raced this year and is likely to come into his own at three. (op 4-7 tchd 8-13 in places and 4-6 in a place)

Darej(USA), a $170,000 foal and entered for the Middle Park and Dewhurst, landed the odds on his debut at Yarmouth last month, but no winners have emerged from that race after nine attempts. He tried to serve it up to the favourite over 2f out, but was then outclassed and his lofty entries now look rather optimistic. (op 11-4 tchd 3-1 in places)

Above All, a half-brother to two winners at this trip, ran freely enough at the back of the field early and had dragged himself into a handy position three-wide rounding the turn, but couldn't respond when the front pair quickened. He wasn't disgraced, however, and this Royal Lodge entry should have learned from the experience. (tchd 15-2)

5752 40 LIVE FOOTBALL MARKETS AT TOTESPORT.COM H'CAP 2m (P)
4:20 (4:21) (Class 4) (0-80,78) 3-Y-O £3,885 (£1,156; £577; £288) Stalls High

Form RPR

2212 1 **Tuscan Gold**[24] 4965 3-9-5 76 SebSanders 7 91+
(Sir Mark Prescott) *lw: mde all: clr w one rival fr over 3f out: maintained gallop fnl 2f: unchal* **11/8**[1]

3521 2 3 1/2 **The Starboard Bow**[15] 5260 3-8-12 74 JohnFahy(5) 1 85
(S Kirk) *hld up last: prog 5f out: chsd wnr over 3f out: drvn and unable to cl fr 2f out: kpt on* **8/1**

2204 3 29 **Tower**[3] 5656 3-8-3 60 JimmyQuinn 3 36
(G Prodromou) *cl up tl wknd over 3f out: t.o* **7/1**

1510 4 10 **Sir Pitt**[107] 2252 3-9-5 76 FrankieDettori 5 40
(J H M Gosden) *chsd wnr after 4f to over 3f out: wknd rapidly: t.o* **9/2**[3]

-426 5 1/2 **Prince Of Dreams**[11] 5387 3-9-7 78 JimCrowley 4 42
(W J Knight) *chsd wnr 4f: rdn and wknd over 5f out: wl t.o* **12/1**

2113 P **Corr Point (IRE)**[11] 5382 3-9-4 75 FergusSweeney 2 —
(J A Osborne) *in tch: reminder 1/2-way: wknd rapidly and p.u 5f out* **4/1**[2]

3m 28.05s (-2.05) **Going Correction** -0.075s/f (Stan) 6 Ran SP% **111.6**
Speed ratings (Par 103): **102,100,85,80,80** —
Tote Swingers: 1&2 £2.60, 1&3 £3.20, 2&3 £6.90 CSF £12.99 TOTE £2.00: £1.10, £5.50; EX 12.70.

Owner The Green Door Partnership **Bred** Mrs James Wigan & London TB Services Ltd **Trained** Newmarket, Suffolk

FOCUS

A real war of attrition for these 3-y-o stayers with margins more akin to a 3m heavy ground novice chase in January. The front pair did well to pull well clear of the others but the form is not the strongest.

The Starboard Bow Official explanation: vet said gelding lost an off-hind shoe

Sir Pitt Official explanation: vet said gelding finished distressed

Corr Point(IRE) Official explanation: jockey said gelding ran flat and was pulled up

5753 GET LIVE FOOTBALL STATS AT TOTESPORT.COM H'CAP 1m 3f (P)
4:55 (4:55) (Class 4) (0-85,82) 3-Y-O+ £3,885 (£1,156; £577; £288) Stalls High

Form RPR

0340 1 **Spiritual Art**[7] 5541 4-8-13 69 PatDobbs 5 79
(L A Dace) *hld up in rr: clsd 2f out: swtchd sharply lft wl over 1f out and effrt: drvn to join ldr nr fin: jst prevailed* **33/1**

0112 2 nse **Snoqualmie Star**[22] 5056 3-9-4 82 (b) DaneO'Neill 11 92
(D R C Elsworth) *t.k.h early: trckd ldrs: prog over 2f out: drvn to ld jst over 1f out: jnd nr fin: btn on the nod* **10/3**[1]

0204 3 2 3/4 **Rumble Of Thunder (IRE)**[14] 5311 4-9-8 78 SebSanders 8 83
(D W P Arbuthnot) *cl up: prog to go 2nd 7f out: narrow ld over 2f out: hdd and one pce jst over 1f out* **13/2**

1020 4 1 1/4 **Ellemujie**[35] 4594 5-9-4 79 SophieDoyle(5) 4 82
(D K Ivory) *lw: racd wd: trckd ldrs: cl enough 2f out: sn nt qckn u.p: plugged on to take 4th nr fin* **6/1**[3]

1000 5 1/2 **Lovers Causeway (USA)**[21] 5093 3-9-0 78 RoystonFfrench 10 80
(M Johnston) *led 2f: rdn in 3rd 5f out: styd chsng ldrs u.p: one pce over 1f out* **12/1**

3660 6 hd **Mannlichen**[73] 3319 4-9-3 73 FrankieDettori 3 75
(M Johnston) *lw: led after 2f: rdn and hdd over 2f out: kpt on and upsides over 1f out: fdd ins fnl f* **7/2**[2]

1005 7 4 1/2 **Countess Comet (IRE)**[23] 5008 3-9-0 78 JimCrowley 13 71
(R M Beckett) *trckd ldrs: rdn and cl enough over 2f out: wknd over 1f out* **8/1**

1061 8 4 **Cobo Bay**[16] 5233 5-9-11 81 (b) DarryllHolland 9 67
(C R Dore) *pressed ldrs: rdn and cl up over 2f out: sn lost pl and wknd* **10/1**

442 9 32 **Encircled**[150] 1161 6-9-12 82 IanMongan 7 11
(J R Jenkins) *lw: in tch tl wknd u.p over 3f out: t.o* **12/1**

0442 10 2 3/4 **Thundering Home**[13] 5330 3-8-11 75 FergusSweeney 12 —
(M J Attwater) *in tch tl wknd rapidly u.p wl over 2f out: t.o* **33/1**

The Form Book, Raceform Ltd, Compton, RG20 6NL

300 P **Bid For Glory**[15] 5272 6-8-13 **69**......................(v) JimmyQuinn 2 —
(H J Collingridge) *b: restrained s: hld up in detached last: wknd and eased 4f out: p.u 2f out* **25/1**

2m 18.43s (-3.47) **Going Correction** -0.075s/f (Stan)
WFA 3 from 4yo+ 8lb **11** Ran SP% **118.2**
Speed ratings (Par 105): **109,108,106,106,105 105,102,99,76,74** —
Tote Swingers: 1&2 £24.90, 1&3 £32.20, 2&3 £6.00 CSF £139.65 CT £831.17 TOTE £37.20: £8.40, £1.70, £2.90; EX 263.60.
Owner Copped Hall Farm & Stud **Bred** R Haim **Trained** Five Oaks, W Sussex

FOCUS
A competitive handicap run at a fair tempo and the front two came from off the pace. The winner is rated back to her best.
Bid For Glory Official explanation: jockey said horse hung right

5754 BET ON LIVE TENNIS AT TOTESPORT.COM H'CAP 7f (P)
5:25 (5:25) (Class 4) (0-85,85) 3-Y-0+ **£3,885** (£1,156; £577; £288) **Stalls** High

Form RPR
-161 **1** **Parvaaz (IRE)**[33] 4647 3-9-2 **81**...................... FrankieDettori 6 90
(M A Jarvis) *lw: hld up bhd ldng pair: wnt 2nd over 2f out: rdn to ld over 1f out: styd on wl* **7/4**[1]

2254 **2** 3/4 **Mambo Spirit (IRE)**[26] 4905 6-9-2 **77**...................... SebSanders 4 86
(Stef Higgins) *led at gd pce: drvn and hdd over 1f out: fought on wl to press wnr fnl f: a hld* **9/1**

054 **3** 2 **Internationaldebut (IRE)**[34] 4617 5-9-10 **85**.............. TonyCulhane 1 89
(P T Midgley) *lw: hld up in 8th: effrt over 2f out: rdn and styd on to take 3rd ins fnl f: no threat to ldng pair* **6/1**[3]

4023 **4** 3/4 **Saharia (IRE)**[11] 5383 3-9-2 **81**...................... DarryllHolland 7 81
(J Noseda) *hld up in 7th: rdn over 2f out: effrt and swtchd rt over 1f out: kpt on: nt pce to threaten* **13/2**

-100 **5** 1/2 **Primaeval**[28] 4843 4-9-7 **82**...................... JimCrowley 2 82
(J R Fanshawe) *hld up last: rdn 3f out: no prog tl kpt on fnl f on outer: nrst fin* **11/2**[2]

5113 **6** 1/2 **Yankee Storm**[25] 4929 5-8-13 **74**......................(v) JimmyQuinn 3 73
(H J Collingridge) *trckd ldrs: rdn and prog to chse ldng pair over 1f out: no imp: wknd ins fnl f* **14/1**

4620 **7** hd **Mishrif (USA)**[10] 5415 4-9-5 **80**......................(b) IanMongan 5 78
(J R Jenkins) *chsd ldng pair: rdn and cl up over 2f out: nt qckn wl over 1f out: sn lost pl* **22/1**

0336 **8** 4 1/2 **Edgewater (IRE)**[11] 5390 3-9-2 **81**......................(p) PatDobbs 9 65
(J Akehurst) *trckd ldrs: shkn up wl over 1f out: sn lost pl and wknd* **20/1**

6026 **9** 6 **My Gacho (IRE)**[7] 5510 8-9-7 **82**......................(v) J-PGuillambert 8 52
(M Johnston) *pressed ldr: urged along over 3f out: wknd over 2f out* **10/1**

1m 24.49s (-1.51) **Going Correction** -0.075s/f (Stan)
WFA 3 from 4yo+ 4lb **9** Ran SP% **114.2**
Speed ratings (Par 105): **105,104,101,101,100 99,99,94,87**
Tote Swingers: 1&2 £5.20, 1&3 £3.30, 2&3 £10.10 CSF £18.27 CT £78.54 TOTE £2.20: £1.80, £2.90, £1.90; EX 19.80 Place 6: £203.12 Place 5: £64.03.
Owner Sheikh Ahmed Al Maktoum **Bred** Darley **Trained** Newmarket, Suffolk

FOCUS
A fair handicap run at a good pace with a contested lead. The form is sound with the unexposed winner rated up 8lb.
T/Plt: £81.60 to a £1 stake. Pool:£82,931.92 - 1,432.37 winning tickets T/Qpdt: £19.40 to a £1 stake. Pool:£3,921.85 - 149.23 winning tickets JN

5496 THIRSK (L-H)
Saturday, September 4

OFFICIAL GOING: Good to firm (9.3)
Wind: light across Weather: fine and sunny

5755 COW HOUSE BANK MAIDEN AUCTION STKS 6f
1:55 (1:57) (Class 4) 2-Y-O **£3,691** (£1,098; £548; £274) **Stalls** High

Form RPR
0 **1** **Picabo (IRE)**[50] 4095 2-8-4 0...................... PaulHanagan 2 65+
(Mrs L Wadham) *trckd ldrs on outer: cl up 1/2-way: led 2f out: shkn up over 1f out: rdn ins fnl f and kpt on wl* **5/4**[1]

22 **2** 2 **Choose The Moment**[15] 5255 2-8-4 0...................... SilvestreDeSousa 1 59
(Eve Johnson Houghton) *wnt lft s and sn pushed along on wd outside: edging lft and outpcd bef 1/2-way: tk clsr order over 2f out: rdn to chse ldrs over 1f out: kpt on ins fnl f* **11/8**[2]

4450 **3** 1/2 **Roman Ruler (IRE)**[22] 5042 2-8-13 49...................... PhillipMakin 6 66
(C W Fairhurst) *cl up: rdn along and outpcd 2f out: kpt on ins fnl f* **40/1**

0500 **4** 3/4 **Guinea Seeker**[12] 5354 2-8-8 45 ow4...................... LanceBetts[(5)] 9 64
(T D Easterby) *sn led: rdn along and hung lft 2f out: sn hdd: edgd lft and wknd ins fnl f* **25/1**

60 **5** 3 1/4 **Syncopated Lady (IRE)**[15] 5277 2-8-4 0...................... AndrewMullen 4 45
(D O'Meara) *chsd ldrs: rdn along over 2f out: sn one pce* **14/1**

6 2 3/4 **Spin A Wish** 2-8-1 0...................... AmyRyan[(3)] 7 37
(R M Whitaker) *s.i.s: sn outpcd and bhd tl sme late hdwy* **12/1**[3]

660 **7** 2 **Sleights Boy (IRE)**[24] 4941 2-8-4 64...................... IanBrennan[(5)] 5 38
(I W McInnes) *prom: rdn along 1/2-way: sn wknd* **20/1**

0 **8** 2 **Kwik Lightening**[7] 5531 2-8-9 0...................... PJMcDonald 3 30
(B M R Haslam) *prom: rdn along 1/2-way: sn wknd* **33/1**

1m 13.35s (0.65) **Going Correction** -0.125s/f (Firm) **8** Ran SP% **114.9**
Speed ratings (Par 97): **90,87,86,85,81 77,75,72**
toteswingers:1&2 £1.10, 2&3 £3.60, 1&3 £9.20 CSF £3.05 TOTE £2.10: £1.10, £1.10, £6.00; EX 3.20.
Owner Tom Ford **Bred** A B Mulholland **Trained** Newmarket, Suffolk

FOCUS
It had been dry overnight and the weather at the start of racing was no worse than overcast, but the ground had officially eased slightly since the previous day's forecast and was given as good to firm all round. The action began with a juvenile maiden that lacked depth. The winner is rated to her pre-race mark but the proximity of the third and fourth limits the form.

NOTEBOOK
Picabo(IRE) had shown promise when eighth in a fair Newbury event on her debut and stepped up on that performance to register a cosy success. Given time to find her feet, she made progress at halfway and challenged wide of the leader 2f out. She got to the front passing the one pole and, despite carrying her head slightly to one side, gamely drew away. A first ever 2yo winner for her trainer, her future in nurseries will now depend on the handicapper. (tchd 11-8)
Choose The Moment, runner-up in ordinary maidens on both her previous starts, again found one too good and is already looking exposed as no better than modest. She never threatened to win this, needing to be driven at halfway to get into contention, but ought to find life slightly easier in nurseries. (tchd 5-4 and 6-4 in a place)
Roman Ruler(IRE), officially rated 49, puts the form into perspective. He plugged on in the closing stages, having chased the pace from the outset, but is clearly no great shakes and may well end up in claimers or sellers. (op 50-1)
Guinea Seeker, with an official mark of 45, ran as well as could be expected. He was not the quickest away, but soon led and set a fair pace until overhauled by the winner. (op 33-1)
Spin A Wish, an inexpensively-bought sprint-bred newcomer, looked very green, losing ground from the stalls and struggling to stay with the rest. (op 10-1)
Kwik Lightening, who had shown little when 12th of 14 on his only previous outing, exhibited slightly more here, chasing the pace early on. (op 50-1)

5756 ADORN HATS H'CAP 1m
2:25 (2:25) (Class 5) (0-75,75) 4-Y-0+ **£3,497** (£1,040; £520; £259) **Stalls** Low

Form RPR
5603 **1** **Legal Legacy**[8] 5499 4-9-2 **70**...................... PhillipMakin 1 79+
(M Dods) *sn trcking ldrs: nt clr run fr over 2f out tl swtchd rt appr fnl f: r.o to ld fnl 50yds* **4/1**[2]

0040 **2** nk **Rosbay (IRE)**[9] 5436 6-8-11 **70**...................... LanceBetts[(5)] 3 78
(T D Easterby) *sn trcking ldrs: led 1f out: hdd and no ex clsng stages* **6/1**

0160 **3** 2 **Seldom (IRE)**[31] 4704 4-8-9 **63**...................... SilvestreDeSousa 2 66
(M Brittain) *led tl 1f out: kpt on same pce* **9/1**

0136 **4** 1 3/4 **Ballinteni**[14] 5311 8-9-6 **74**...................... PaulHanagan 7 73
(Miss Gay Kelleway) *chsd ldrs: pushed along 5f out: outpcd over 2f out: kpt on same pce appr fnl f* **8/1**

3002 **5** 1 **Champain Sands (IRE)**[8] 5499 11-8-7 **61** oh3.......... PatrickMathers 4 58
(E J Alston) *s.i.s: in rr: hdwy over 3f out: nt clr run and swtchd rt over 1f out: nvr trbld ldrs* **18/1**

1502 **6** 2 1/4 **Rascal In The Mix (USA)**[17] 5199 4-8-9 **66**..........(p) AmyRyan[(3)] 5 58
(R M Whitaker) *in rr: hdwy on outside 2f out: nvr nr ldrs: struck into* **5/1**[3]

5300 **7** 1/2 **Come And Go (UAE)**[21] 5098 4-9-7 **75**...................... PJMcDonald 9 66
(G A Swinbank) *w ldrs: wknd appr fnl f* **3/1**[1]

0544 **8** 3 1/4 **French Art**[24] 4968 5-8-9 **66**......................(p) KellyHarrison[(3)] 10 49
(N Tinkler) *hld up towards rr: drvn 3f out: sn bhd* **7/1**

1m 38.37s (-1.73) **Going Correction** -0.125s/f (Firm) **8** Ran SP% **114.8**
Speed ratings (Par 103): **103,102,100,98,97 95,95,91**
toteswingers:1&2:£5.50, 2&3:£17.80, 1&3:£7.50 CSF £28.25 CT £175.21 TOTE £4.90: £1.80, £2.30, £3.50; EX 31.30.
Owner D Vic Roper **Bred** D Dowling **Trained** Denton, Co Durham

FOCUS
Just a run-of-the-mill handicap and the form looks pretty straightforward rated around the first two.
Rascal In The Mix(USA) Official explanation: vet said filly was struck into behind

5757 HAMBLETON CUP H'CAP 1m 4f
2:55 (2:55) (Class 4) (0-85,84) 3-Y-0+ **£5,828** (£1,734; £866; £432) **Stalls** Low

Form RPR
2543 **1** **Ethics Girl (IRE)**[16] 5243 4-8-12 **70**...................... FrannyNorton 4 80+
(John Berry) *trckd ldng pair on inner: hdwy 3f out: rdn to ld over 1f out and sn edgd lft: drvn ins fnl f and kpt on* **9/1**

3320 **2** 1/2 **Lady Luachmhar (IRE)**[15] 5278 4-9-12 **84**...................... PaulHanagan 5 92
(R A Fahey) *t.k.h early: trckd ldrs: pushed along over 3f out: rdn and sltly outpcd wl over 2f out: drvn over 1f out: styd on strly ins fnl f* **11/2**[3]

13 **3** 1 **George Adamson (IRE)**[24] 4953 4-9-2 **74**...................... PJMcDonald 6 81
(G A Swinbank) *hld up in tch: hdwy 3f out: rdn 2f out: styng on whn sltly hmpd ins fnl f: drvn and kpt on towards fin* **9/2**[2]

225 **4** 1 1/4 **River Ardeche**[22] 5019 5-8-9 **70**......................(t) PatrickDonaghy[(3)] 7 75
(B M R Haslam) *trckd ldr: led over 3f out: rdn and edgd lft over 2f out: drvn and hdd over 1f out: n.m.r and swtchd rt ins fnl f: one pce* **20/1**

1205 **5** hd **Snow Dancer (IRE)**[24] 4943 6-9-4 **76**...................... PatrickMathers 1 80
(H A McWilliams) *hld up in rr: effrt and pushed along 3f out: rdn and hdwy on wd outside wl over 1f out: kpt on ins fnl f: nrst fin* **16/1**

1420 **6** hd **Brouhaha**[41] 4405 6-9-6 **83**...................... RossAtkinson[(5)] 8 87
(Tom Dascombe) *hld up towards rr: effrt and rdn along 3f out: n.m.r 2f out: sn drvn and kpt on ins fnl f: nrst fin* **20/1**

355 **7** 1/2 **Kames Park (IRE)**[6] 5549 8-9-1 **73**...................... PaulEddery 3 76
(R C Guest) *hld up in rr: hdwy on inner 3f out: effrt to chse ldrs over 1f out: n.m.r and hmpd jst ins fnl f: one pce after* **20/1**

4316 **8** 1 3/4 **Green Lightning (IRE)**[15] 5273 3-9-2 **83**............(b) SilvestreDeSousa 2 83
(M Johnston) *led: rdn along over 3f out and sn hdd: drvn over 2f out and sn wknd* **10/11**[1]

2m 36.11s (-0.09) **Going Correction** -0.125s/f (Firm)
WFA 3 from 4yo+ 9lb **8** Ran SP% **116.1**
Speed ratings (Par 105): **95,94,94,93,93 92,92,91**
toteswingers:1&2 £7.80, 2&3 £4.00, 1&3 £7.90 CSF £56.09 CT £251.57 TOTE £13.50: £2.70, £1.50, £1.90; EX 53.90 Trifecta £462.70.
Owner The 1997 Partnership **Bred** Newsells Park Stud **Trained** Newmarket, Suffolk
■ Stewards' Enquiry : Patrick Donaghy caution: used whip down the shoulder in the forehand position

FOCUS
An ultra-competitive handicap in which the major disappointment was the odds-on favourite. The form is muddling and not that solid.

5758 HUMPHREY AND TILLY H'CAP 1m
3:30 (3:32) (Class 5) (0-70,70) 3-Y-O **£3,497** (£1,040; £520; £129; £129) **Stalls** Low

Form RPR
5036 **1** **Cherry Bee**[8] 5479 3-9-4 **67**...................... SilvestreDeSousa 6 73
(M Johnston) *in rr div: drvn and hdwy on outside 3f out: edgd lft fnl f: styd on to ld last stride* **4/1**[1]

4062 **2** shd **Dream On Buddy (IRE)**[16] 5236 3-9-2 **70**.............. AshleyMorgan[(5)] 11 76+
(B W Hills) *hld up towards rr: smooth hdwy over 3f out: led over 2f out: hdd post* **9/2**[2]

0405 **3** 1 1/2 **Petrocelli**[5] 5607 3-8-8 **60**...................... JamesSullivan[(3)] 14 62
(W Storey) *chsd ldrs on outside: edgd rt and styd on same pce fnl 150yds* **50/1**

0404 **4** shd **No Quarter (IRE)**[22] 5024 3-8-0 **56** oh3...................... NeilFarley[(7)] 10 58
(Miss Tracy Waggott) *s.i.s: swtchd lft s: in rr: gd hdwy on outside over 2f out: hung lft over 1f out: kpt on one pce* **11/1**

1221 **4** dht **Madame Excelerate**[8] 5469 3-9-6 **69**...................... FrannyNorton 8 71
(W M Brisbourne) *chsd ldrs: effrt on ins 3f out: hmpd jst ins fnl f: styd on same pce* **5/1**[3]

0055 **6** 1 1/4 **My One Weakness (IRE)**[8] 5482 3-8-11 **60**.............. PaulHanagan 2 59
(B Ellison) *trckd ldrs: one pce appr fnl f* **5/1**[3]

1050 **7** 3 1/2 **Verluga (IRE)**[8] 5484 3-8-11 **60**...................... DavidNolan 13 51
(T D Easterby) *in rr and sn drvn along: hdwy over 2f out: chsng ldrs whn hmpd jst ins fnl f: wknd towards fin* **25/1**

0152 **8** 2 1/4 **Emeralds Spirit (IRE)**[26] 4898 3-8-4 **56** oh2.............. KellyHarrison[(3)] 1 42
(J R Weymes) *s.i.s: t.k.h: sn trcking ldrs: led over 5f out tl over 2f out: wkng whn edgd lft jst ins fnl f* **7/1**

5044 **9** 2 1/4 **Battle Study (IRE)**[6] 5550 3-8-8 **57** oh7 ow1.............. JamesDoyle 3 38
(A J McCabe) *mid-div: sn drvn along: outpcd over 2f out: no threat after* **14/1**

0000 **10** *5* **Russian Brigadier**[87] 2853 3-8-7 **56** oh11 .... AndrewMullen 4 25
(M Brittain) *w ldrs: t.k.h: hung rt bnd over 4f out: lost pl over 2f out* **100/1**
000 **11** *4 1/2* **Barton Bounty**[21] 5065 3-8-7 **56** oh6 .... PatrickMathers 7 15
(P D Niven) *in rr and sn drvn along: nvr on terms* **66/1**
5505 **12** *3/4* **Hairy Maclary**[17] 5201 3-8-7 **56** oh4 .... PJMcDonald 9 13
(T D Easterby) *led tl over 5f out: wknd 2f out* **20/1**
0435 **13** *18* **Director General (USA)**[60] 3755 3-8-13 **62** .... PhillipMakin 12 —
(Julie Camacho) *in rr: detached last and reminders over 4f out: t.o 2f out* **18/1**
0064 **14** *38* **Pycian**[17] 5211 3-8-6 **60** .... IanBrennan(5) 5 —
(Mrs L Stubbs) *chsd ldrs: lost pl 3f out: sn bhd and virtually p.u: t.o* **25/1**

1m 39.23s (-0.87) **Going Correction** -0.125s/f (Firm) 14 Ran SP% **121.2**
Speed ratings (Par 101): **99,98,97,97,97 96,92,90,88,83 78,77,59,21**
toteswingers:1&2 £3.20, 2&3 £73.60, 1&3 £62.20 CSF £20.43 CT £821.12 TOTE £4.90: £1.70, £2.10, £13.00; EX 14.60.
Owner Favourites Racing IV **Bred** Mount Coote Stud **Trained** Middleham Moor, N Yorks
■ Stewards' Enquiry : Kelly Harrison caution: careless riding
Ashley Morgan caution: used whip with excessive frequency

FOCUS
A modest contest, with the top weight rated 70 and almost half the field out of the handicap. The form seems sound rated around the fourth to sixth.
Russian Brigadier Official explanation: jockey said gelding failed to handle the bend

5759 "DRESSED OF HARROGATE" H'CAP 1m
4:05 (4:06) (Class 3) (0-95,95) 3-Y-O **£6,929** (£2,061; £1,030; £514) **Stalls** Low

Form RPR
103 **1** **Oriental Scot**[50] 4112 3-8-9 **83** .... PJMcDonald 3 96
(W Jarvis) *dwlt: hld up in rr: hdwy on inner 3f out: led wl over 1f out and sn rdn clr: styd on wl* **4/1**[2]
0003 **2** *3* **Aquarian Spirit**[11] 5394 3-8-2 **76** .... PaulHanagan 7 82
(R A Fahey) *trckd ldrs: hdwy 3f out: swtchd outside and cl up over 2f out: sn rdn and one pce* **11/2**
6110 **3** *1 1/4* **Ginger Jack**[42] 4357 3-9-4 **92** .... SilvestreDeSousa 8 95
(M Johnston) *chsd ldrs on outer: rdn along and lost pl 1/2-way: sn in rr: hdwy on wd outside 2f out: drvn and kpt on ins fnl f* **11/4**[1]
1040 **4** *2 1/4* **Hacienda (IRE)**[42] 4358 3-9-7 **95** .... AndrewMullen 4 93
(M Johnston) *trckd ldrs on inner: hdwy 3f out: rdn to ld briefly 2f out: sn hdd and drvn: wknd appr fnl f* **5/1**
1650 **5** *shd* **Christmas Light**[17] 5222 3-7-13 **76** oh1 .... JamesSullivan(3) 5 74
(D O'Meara) *trckd ldr: cl up over 3f out: rdn 2f out and ev ch: sn drvn and wknd over 1f out* **20/1**
4124 **6** *1 3/4* **Rule Maker**[42] 4377 3-9-0 **88** .... FrannyNorton 1 82
(J Noseda) *hld up in tch on inner: hdwy 3f out: rdn to chse ldrs 2f out: drvn and no imp whn n.m.r on inner over 1f out: wknd after* **9/2**[3]
0163 **7** *1 3/4* **Tres Coronas (IRE)**[35] 4593 3-8-9 **83** ow1 .... PhillipMakin 6 73
(T D Barron) *sn led: rdn along 3f out: drvn and hdd 2f out: grad wknd* **9/1**

1m 37.49s (-2.61) **Going Correction** -0.125s/f (Firm) 7 Ran SP% **114.6**
Speed ratings (Par 105): **108,105,103,101,101 99,97**
toteswingers:1&2 £7.40, 2&3 £1.30, 1&3 £2.20 CSF £26.07 CT £69.53 TOTE £4.60: £2.10, £2.70; EX 33.50.
Owner Dr J Walker **Bred** Miss K Rausing **Trained** Newmarket, Suffolk

FOCUS
A decent handicap and none could be confidently discounted. The form is rated around the placed horses.

NOTEBOOK
Oriental Scot, up just 1lb since his solid third at Nottingham in July and making his first appearance since, scored decisively. Held up in the early stages, he raced close to the rail on the turn for home and, as the field fanned out coming into the straight, he got a dream run up the inside. Quickening stylishly, he swept to the front approaching the final furlong and was well on top at the finish. This was his first outing for 50 days and it appears he goes exceptionally well fresh. That would seem to discount any prospect of his running again under a penalty, so his prospects next time out are likely to depend on the handicapper's response to this smooth victory. (op 9-2 tchd 5-1)
Aquarian Spirit lined up with a 0-10 record in handicaps, but ran well enough to indicate he is no forlorn hope to break his duck. Held up in touch in the early stages, he was fourth at halfway and kept on gamely all the way to the line. (tchd 6-1)
Ginger Jack, successful over this trip at Haydock and Musselburgh in July, ran a peculiar race. Second early on, he lost ground quickly on the home turn and appeared to be dropping out of contention. He got going again late on, though, making ground out towards the middle of the course, and was battling on well in the closing stages. (op 3-1)
Hacienda(IRE) was contesting a Class 3 race for the first time since his last victory and, not surprisingly, he found the opposition less exacting than in higher grades. He was not quite good enough at the weights to make the first three, though, despite racing close to the pace from the start. It may be that a mark of 95 is just too high for him. (op 7-1 tchd 9-2)
Christmas Light, the only filly in the line-up and racing from 1lb out of the handicap, was another prominent from the outset. She could not maintain her challenge, however, and faded late on. (op 9-1)
Rule Maker had the trip and ground to suit but looked held when short of space in the straight. (op 7-2)
Tres Coronas(IRE), whose best form has been registered when setting his own pace, adopted his favoured tactics. He was unable to dominate these rivals comprehensively, though, and once the winner struck for home he dropped away rather tamely. (op 10-1)

5760 SEE YOU NEXT YEAR H'CAP 6f
4:40 (4:41) (Class 5) (0-70,70) 4-Y-O+ **£3,497** (£1,040; £520; £259) **Stalls** High

Form RPR
3151 **1** **Divertimenti (IRE)**[25] 4936 6-9-2 **68** .... (b) RussKennemore(3) 10 83
(S R Bowring) *sn led: shkn up and styd on strly ins fnl f* **4/1**[1]
2454 **2** *3 1/4* **Avontuur (FR)**[5] 5601 8-9-3 **69** .... JamesSullivan(3) 12 74
(Mrs R A Carr) *rrd s: hld up in rr: hdwy and nt clr run over 2f out: chsd wnr jst ins fnl f: no imp* **9/2**[2]
0542 **3** *1 1/4* **Select Committee**[7] 5513 5-8-11 **65** .... (v) IanBrennan(5) 4 66
(J J Quinn) *swtchd rt s: hld up: hdwy over 2f out: sn chsng wnr: rdn over 1f out: kpt on same pce* **13/2**[3]
5502 **4** *1 1/4* **Secret City (IRE)**[27] 4869 4-8-11 **60** .... (b) SilvestreDeSousa 9 57
(R Bastiman) *chsd ldrs: sn drvn along: one pce fnl 2f* **4/1**[1]
1100 **5** *hd* **Cross Of Lorraine (IRE)**[10] 5422 7-9-0 **63** .... (b) PaulHanagan 13 59
(C Grant) *chsd ldrs: rdn and outpcd over 2f out: hung lft and kpt on fnl 100yds* **15/2**
2315 **6** *1 1/2* **Foreign Rhythm (IRE)**[20] 5123 5-8-8 **62** .... DaleSwift(5) 11 53
(R E Barr) *chsd ldrs: fdd ins fnl f* **13/2**[3]
3004 **7** *1/2* **Mullglen**[14] 5297 4-9-4 **70** .... (tp) KellyHarrison(3) 6 60
(T D Easterby) *s.i.s: hung lft and reminders over 3f out: hdwy on wd outside 2f out: nvr nr ldrs* **14/1**
-060 **8** *5* **Avertuoso**[42] 4373 6-8-2 **58** ow1 .... AdamCarter(7) 7 32
(B Smart) *in rr: hdwy on outer over 2f out: wknd appr fnl f: eased towards fin* **20/1**
0000 **9** *8* **Sea Rover (IRE)**[8] 5502 6-8-3 **59** .... JohnCavanagh(7) 5 7
(M Brittain) *racd wd: led early: hung rt and lost pl over 2f out: eased towards fin* **16/1**

1m 11.4s (-1.30) **Going Correction** -0.125s/f (Firm) 9 Ran SP% **113.9**
Speed ratings (Par 103): **103,98,97,95,95 93,92,85,75**
toteswingers:1&2 £4.90, 2&3 £5.80, 1&3 £3.80 CSF £21.64 CT £113.79 TOTE £3.70: £1.10, £1.40, £1.80; EX 22.60.
Owner K Nicholls **Bred** Airlie Stud **Trained** Edwinstowe, Notts

FOCUS
A modest handicap, although seemingly quite competitive on paper. The first two set the level.
Mullglen Official explanation: jockey said gelding hung left-handed throughout
Avertuoso Official explanation: jockey said gelding reared as stalls opened

5761 EUROPEAN BREEDERS' FUND MAIDEN STKS (DIV I) 7f
5:10 (5:10) (Class 4) 2-Y-O **£4,468** (£1,329; £664; £331) **Stalls** Low

Form RPR
043 **1** **Perignon (IRE)**[10] 5404 2-9-3 75 .... PJMcDonald 7 78
(G A Swinbank) *cl up: led over 2f out:: rdn over 1f out: drvn ins fnl f: kpt on wl towards fin* **7/2**[3]
422 **2** *1 1/2* **Midnight Rider (IRE)**[35] 4568 2-9-3 80 .... PhillipMakin 6 74
(C F Wall) *trckd ldrs: smooth hdwy 3f out: chal 2f out: sn rdn and ev ch: drvn: edgd lft and put hd in air ins fnl f: one pce towards fin* **11/4**[2]
44 **3** *1* **Chosen Character (IRE)**[31] 4702 2-8-12 0 .... RossAtkinson(5) 9 72
(Tom Dascombe) *chsd ldrs: hdwy over 2f out: sn rdn: kpt on ins fnl f* **14/1**
0 **4** *1 1/4* **Baileys Moneypenny**[19] 5156 2-8-12 0 .... LeeVickers 3 63
(J G Given) *led: rdn along 3f out: hdd over 2f out: drvn wl over 1f out and kpt on same pce* **50/1**
20 **5** *1/2* **Ollon (USA)**[15] 5277 2-9-3 0 .... PaulHanagan 2 67
(R A Fahey) *dwlt: sn trcking ldrs: effrt 3f out: rdn 2f out and kpt on same pce* **6/5**[1]
6 *3 1/4* **Muroona (IRE)** 2-8-12 0 .... SilvestreDeSousa 4 54
(M Johnston) *chsd ldrs: rdn along 3f out: wknd fnl 2f* **17/2**
0 **7** *1/2* **Honkers Bonkers**[19] 5160 2-9-3 0 .... JamesDoyle 11 58
(A J McCabe) *towards rr: hdwy on outer wl over 2f out: rdn and styng on whn edgd lft and rdn dropped reins ent fnl f: wknd after* **22/1**
0 **8** *14* **Rasteau (IRE)**[64] 3631 2-9-3 0 .... FrannyNorton 8 23
(T Keddy) *dwlt: a towards rr* **100/1**
9 *1 1/2* **Karens Legacy (IRE)** 2-8-7 0 .... (t) LeeTopliss(5) 1 14
(I W McInnes) *dwlt: a towards rr* **40/1**
0 **10** *3/4* **Somebody Loves You**[95] 2623 2-8-7 0 .... IanBrennan(5) 10 12
(Mrs A Duffield) *stdd s and swtchd lft to inner: hld up: hung rt a in rr* **50/1**

1m 26.95s (-0.25) **Going Correction** -0.125s/f (Firm) 10 Ran SP% **123.2**
Speed ratings (Par 97): **96,94,93,91,91 87,86,70,69,68**
toteswingers:1&2 £2.50, 2&3 £6.00, 1&3 £8.80 CSF £14.10 TOTE £5.90: £1.50, £1.40, £2.80; EX 17.60.
Owner Mrs J Porter **Bred** Miss Carmel McGinn **Trained** Melsonby, N Yorks

FOCUS
An ordinary maiden, weakened by the defection of the likely favourite. The form looks pretty straightforward rated around the first two.

NOTEBOOK
Perignon(IRE), whose official mark of 75 suggested he could take a race of this type, duly did so. Always disputing the lead, he took a clear advantage 2f out and stayed on resolutely. The handicapper may well raise him for this and, if that does happen, he will probably struggle in nurseries. He is game enough, but limited in ability. (op 11-4)
Midnight Rider(IRE), in the frame on all three of his previous starts and beaten just a nose last time out, looks absurdly flattered by his official mark of 80. He gave his all here, making ground from midfield to chase the winner in the last 2f, but was simply not good enough to bridge the gap. A drop in his rating looks called for. (tchd 3-1)
Chosen Character(IRE) had shown some promise when fourth on his two previous outings and again ran creditably. Never too far away, he stayed on well enough and improved a little on those earlier achievements. His future now lies in nurseries. (op 12-1)
Baileys Moneypenny, beaten 11 lengths when eighth of 12 in a Polytrack maiden first time out, fared better here and is another who will almost certainly be contesting two-year-old handicaps before too long.
Ollon(USA), a promising runner-up on debut but disappointing on his only subsequent outing, is beginning to look a risky betting proposition. Well backed beforehand, he never travelled like a winner and this run was more in keeping with his last flop than his first encouraging outing. (op 9-4)
Muroona(IRE), a £50,000 newcomer from a decent family, showed a hint of promise. She was prominent early, before fading in the closing stages. (op 8-1)
Somebody Loves You Official explanation: jockey said filly hung right-handed throughout

5762 EUROPEAN BREEDERS' FUND MAIDEN STKS (DIV II) 7f
5:40 (5:41) (Class 4) 2-Y-O **£4,468** (£1,329; £664; £331) **Stalls** Low

Form RPR
40 **1** **Mutajare (IRE)**[64] 3631 2-9-3 0 .... SilvestreDeSousa 3 78+
(M Johnston) *mde all: drvn clr appr fnl f: eased towards fin: v readily* **9/4**[2]
2 *6* **Corsicanrun (IRE)** 2-9-3 0 .... PaulHanagan 2 60+
(R A Fahey) *s.s: hdwy to chse ldrs after 2f: rdn to chse wnr 2f out: no imp* **1/1**[1]
0 **3** *1 3/4* **Colebrooke**[22] 5033 2-9-3 0 .... PJMcDonald 5 56+
(M Johnston) *chsd ldrs: drvn and outpcd over 3f out: styd on to go 3rd over 1f out: one pce* **9/2**[3]
0 **4** *5* **Kodicil (IRE)**[99] 2498 2-9-3 0 .... DanielTudhope 10 46+
(T D Walford) *hld up in mid-div: drvn and outpcd over 3f out: hdwy over 2f out: n.m.r over 1f out: sn wknd* **80/1**
0 **5** *1/2* **Marc De Savoie (IRE)**[15] 5277 2-9-3 0 .... FrannyNorton 6 50+
(K A Ryan) *t.k.h: w ldrs: lost pl bnd over 4f out: hdwy on outside over 2f out: edgd lft and hmpd over 1f out: sn wknd* **25/1**
60 **6** *2* **Sister Sioux (IRE)**[82] 3020 2-8-9 0 .... JamesSullivan(3) 4 32
(R Bastiman) *trckd ldrs: t.k.h: edgd lft and wknd over 1f out* **66/1**
7 *5* **Our Mate Joe (IRE)** 2-8-12 0 .... MichaelO'Connell(5) 7 24
(G A Harker) *s.i.s: in rr: bhd fnl 2f* **20/1**
0 **8** *1* **Smart Violetta (IRE)**[8] 5498 2-8-9 0 .... AmyRyan(3) 8 17
(Mrs A Duffield) *chsd ldrs: lost pl bnd over 4f out: bhd fnl 2f* **25/1**
9 *9* **Blake Dean** 2-9-3 0 .... PhillipMakin 1 —
(B M R Haslam) *s.v.s: a wl bhd* **28/1**

1m 27.18s (-0.02) **Going Correction** -0.125s/f (Firm) 9 Ran SP% **117.6**
Speed ratings (Par 97): **95,88,86,80,79 77,71,70,60**
toteswingers:1&2 £1.40, 2&3 £2.30, 1&3 £2.10 CSF £4.64 TOTE £3.30: £1.20, £1.02, £1.90; EX 5.30 Place 6: 88.50 Place 5: £75.68 .
Owner Hamdan Al Maktoum **Bred** Epona Bloodstock Ltd **Trained** Middleham Moor, N Yorks

FOCUS
This looked to have less depth than the first division. The winner impressed though.

The Form Book, Raceform Ltd, Compton, RG20 6NL

NOTEBOOK

Mutajare(IRE), whose second run had been a step backwards after his promising Redcar debut, made a leap forward this time. He led from the start and, after setting a decent pace, drew well clear inside the final furlong. Exactly what he achieved here is open to debate, but he should go into nurseries with his confidence high and may well stay further.

Corsicanrun(IRE), a well-bred newcomer who cost 175,000gns as a yearling, was all the rage beforehand but never threatened to collect. Fifth in the early stages, he had worked his way into third by halfway, but was always fighting a losing battle in his quest to hunt down the winner. (op 11-10 tchd 5-6)

Colebrooke had looked in need of the experience when ninth of 11 on his only previous outing and stepped up on that effort. Second in the early stages, he needed to be ridden to maintain his place at halfway and then dropped back to fourth. He stayed on again late and, as he still appeared rather green, may improve further for this outing. (op 13-2 tchd 7-1)

Kodicil(IRE), down the field first time out, was another to show he is progressing with racing, even if his achievement here does not suggest he is yet ready to break his duck in maiden company. He should eventually find his niche in low-level nurseries.

Marc De Savoie(IRE) had shown little when beating just one rival in a decent York maiden on debut, so his display must be viewed as a step up. It remains to be seen, however, in what grade he will make a mark. (op 28-1)

T/Plt: £81.60 to a £1 stake. Pool of £62,026.15 - 554.42 winning tickets. T/Qpdt: £23.20 to a £1 stake. Pool of £3,337.36 - 106.20 winning tickets. JR

5697 WOLVERHAMPTON (A.W) (L-H)

Saturday, September 4

OFFICIAL GOING: Standard

Wind: Light behind Weather: Overcast

5763 EUROPEAN BREEDERS' FUND MAIDEN STKS 5f 20y(P)

5:50 (5:51) (Class 5) 2-Y-O £2,978 (£886; £442; £221) Stalls Low

Form RPR

0 1 **Secret Gold (IRE)**[38] 4474 2-8-9 0 Louis-PhilippeBeuzelin(3) 9 67+
(B J Meehan) *trckd ldrs: racd keenly: rdn and r.o to ld towards fin* **7/2**[2]

40 2 ½ **Look Who's Kool**[26] 4896 2-9-3 0 GrahamGibbons 1 70
(E S McMahon) *led: rdn over 1f out: hung rt ins fnl f: hdd towards fin* **6/1**

66 3 nk **Crucis Abbey (IRE)**[10] 5418 2-9-3 0 WilliamCarson 8 70
(J W Unett) *chsd ldrs: nt clr run and hmpd over 1f out: sn rdn: r.o wl* **12/1**

66 4 1 **Fimias (IRE)**[9] 5453 2-9-3 0 KirstyMilczarek 12 65
(L M Cumani) *mid-div: hdwy 1/2-way: rdn over 1f out: hung lft and rdr dropped whip wl ins fnl f: styd on* **12/1**

2 5 1½ **Plume De Ma Tante (IRE)**[10] 5418 2-8-12 0 DuranFentiman 6 55
(J A Glover) *chsd ldr: rdn and ev ch wl over 1f out: swtchd lft ins fnl f: styd on same pce* **10/3**[1]

56 6 2¼ **Illmindu (IRE)**[8] 5466 2-8-9 0 JamesMillman(3) 2 47+
(B R Millman) *s.i.s: in rr tl r.o ins fnl f: nrst fin* **14/1**

06 7 1 **Lord Cornwall (IRE)**[29] 4782 2-8-12 0 SimonPearce(5) 4 48
(J R Gask) *hld up: r.o ins fnl f: nvr nr to chal* **33/1**

0 8 3 **Jay Jays Joy**[10] 5418 2-8-12 0 DeanHeslop(5) 5 37
(T D Barron) *s.i.s: styd on ins fnl f: nvr nrr* **20/1**

0 9 4 **Tsarina Louise**[36] 4543 2-8-12 0 PaulMulrennan 10 18+
(J G Given) *sn pushed along and a in rr* **28/1**

10 hd **Sea Of Love (IRE)** 2-8-12 0 TomMcLaughlin 7 17
(R A Harris) *mid-div: rdn 1/2-way: sn wknd* **28/1**

0 11 3½ **Ganesa**[24] 4960 2-9-3 0 GeorgeBaker 13 10
(M Botti) *prom: hung rt fr over 3f out: wknd and eased 2f out* **5/1**[3]

00 12 9 **Zohan (IRE)**[94] 2638 2-9-3 0 FrankieMcDonald 3 —
(Peter Grayson) *prom: rdn over 3f out: wknd 1/2-way* **100/1**

62.37 secs (0.07) **Going Correction** -0.05s/f (Stan) 12 Ran SP% 113.9

Speed ratings (Par 95): **97,96,95,94,91 88,86,81,75,75 69,55**

Tote Swingers: 1&2 £4.30, 1&3 £11.50, 2&3 £9.70 CSF £22.19 TOTE £4.20: £2.10, £1.70, £3.40; EX 32.80.

Owner Jaber Abdullah **Bred** Rabbah Bloodstock Limited **Trained** Manton, Wilts

■ Stewards' Enquiry : Duran Fentiman one-day ban: failed to keep straight from stalls (Sep 18)

FOCUS

A moderate maiden rated around the time and the balance of the principals.

NOTEBOOK

Secret Gold(IRE) needed until well into the final furlong to get on top of the pacesetting Look Who's Kool, and it is this trip, rather than the 6f of both the Cheveley Park Stakes and Redcar Two-Year-Old Trophy (for which she holds entries) that should continue to serve her best in the short term. (op 5-1)

Look Who's Kool enjoyed spinning off these sharp bends out in front before being collared close home. He ought to have a small nursery in him (for which he is now qualified) around this sort of course under similarly assertive tactics. (op 7-1)

Crucis Abbey(IRE)'s below-par second run last time owed much to a poor start and lingering greenness. He shaped better in every respect this time, and but for some interference at the furlong pole might have finished a place higher. He, too, can be sent the nursery route from now on with fair prospects of picking up a routine contest. (op 11-1 tchd 14-1)

Fimias(IRE), dropped to 5f for his AW debut, secured the inner rail halfway up the straight but could make only modest gains with its assistance. He'll need 6f on this surface. (tchd 11-1 and 14-1)

Plume De Ma Tante(IRE), second at rewarding odds on her debut at Catterick, once again showed both early speed and late greenness, hanging for pressure. She remains capable of better once working out fully what the job entails. (op 11-4)

Illmindu(IRE) Official explanation: jockey said filly mised the break

Ganesa lost all chance hanging around the turn for home. Official explanation: jockey said colt did no handle the bend (tchd 4-1)

5764 FREE BETTING WITH FREEBETTING.CO.UK H'CAP 5f 216y(P)

6:20 (6:21) (Class 6) (0-65,65) 3-Y-O+ £1,706 (£503; £252) Stalls Low

Form RPR

3432 1 **Fantasy Fighter (IRE)**[15] 5267 5-9-5 62 TomEaves 8 73
(J J Quinn) *hld up: plld hrd: hdwy over 2f out: led 1f out: shkn up and edgd lft ins fnl f: r.o* **11/4**[1]

4402 2 1¼ **Mrs Boss**[36] 4553 3-9-3 65 JamesMillman(3) 10 72
(B R Millman) *hld up: hdwy over 1f out: rdn to chse wnr and hung lft ins fnl f: r.o* **14/1**

3030 3 1¼ **Liberty Trail (IRE)**[4] 5634 4-8-13 59 Louis-PhilippeBeuzelin(3) 4 62
(P D Evans) *mid-div: sn pushed along: outpcd over 2f out: rallied and hung lft over 1f out: r.o* **7/1**[3]

0005 4 nse **Espy**[7] 5513 5-9-0 60 GaryBartley(3) 3 63+
(I W McInnes) *s.i.s: hld up: hdwy over 1f out: r.o* **7/2**[2]

2100 5 1½ **Loyal Royal (IRE)**[2] 5698 7-9-7 64 (bt) GeorgeBaker 1 62
(J M Bradley) *led 5f out: rdn edgd rt and hdd 1f out: no ex ins fnl f* **12/1**

0666 6 1 **Charles Darwin (IRE)**[21] 5076 7-9-6 63 PaulMulrennan 6 58
(M Blanshard) *led 1f: chsd ldr: rdn over 1f out: no ex ins fnl f* **10/1**

0060 7 hd **Ride A White Swan**[21] 5087 5-9-5 62 (p) GrahamGibbons 7 56
(D Shaw) *hld up: r.o fnl f: eased whn hld nr fin: nvr trbld ldrs* **15/2**

0360 8 1½ **Plumage**[66] 3556 5-9-6 63 KirstyMilczarek 5 52
(Miss Tor Sturgis) *s.i.s: hld up: nvr nrr* **12/1**

06 9 1½ **Avongate**[44] 4284 3-9-4 63 (b) TomMcLaughlin 2 48
(R A Harris) *chsd ldrs: rdn over 2f out: wknd ins fnl f* **33/1**

550 10 shd **Tamarind Hill (IRE)**[14] 5299 3-8-11 61 (b) DeclanCannon(5) 9 45
(A J McCabe) *chsd ldrs: rdn over 2f out: wknd over 1f out* **14/1**

26-0 11 7 **Braddock (IRE)**[40] 4430 7-9-2 59 (t) JackMitchell 11 21
(K O Cunningham-Brown) *hld up in tch: rdn and wknd over 2f out* **50/1**

1m 14.53s (-0.47) **Going Correction** -0.05s/f (Stan)

WFA 3 from 4yo+ 2lb 11 Ran SP% 115.9

Speed ratings (Par 101): **101,99,97,97,95 94,94,92,90,89 80**

Tote Swingers: 1&2 £2.40, 1&3 £7.10, 2&3 £9.40 CSF £42.58 CT £250.71 TOTE £2.30: £1.10, £3.70, £1.70; EX 21.90.

Owner The Fantasy Fellowship F **Bred** T C Clarke **Trained** Settrington, N Yorks

FOCUS

A tight handicap, run at an average pace. Modest form with the winner rated back to his best.

Charles Darwin(IRE) Official explanation: jockey said gelding hung left

Plumage Official explanation: jockey said mare missed the break and was hampered on the bend

5765 ENJOY THE RINGSIDE ENTERTAINMENT (S) STKS 1m 4f 50y(P)

6:50 (6:50) (Class 6) 3-5-Y-O £1,706 (£503; £252) Stalls Low

Form RPR

4304 1 **Country Road (IRE)**[24] 4945 4-9-4 64 (be) PaulMulrennan 1 72
(M W Easterby) *trckd ldrs: plld hrd: led over 1f out: rdn clr ins fnl f: comf* **3/1**[3]

-052 2 6 **Into The Light**[24] 4946 5-9-4 65 GrahamGibbons 9 62
(E S McMahon) *chsd ldr: rdn and ev ch over 1f out: no ex ins fnl f* **11/2**

6214 3 2¾ **Hypnotic Gaze (IRE)**[31] 4719 4-9-9 75 SteveDrowne 8 63
(J Mackie) *set stdy pce tl qcknd over 2f out: hdd over 1f out: hung lft and no ex ins fnl f* **15/8**[1]

-021 4 nk **Shannersburg (IRE)**[26] 4912 5-9-9 61 (t) EddieAhern 5 62
(Ian Williams) *s.i.s: hld up: hdwy 3f out: rdn over 1f out: styd on same pce* **11/4**[2]

5 5 2½ **Guppy's Girl (IRE)**[9] 5455 3-7-13 0 DeclanCannon(5) 6 48?
(Miss S L Davison) *trckd ldrs: plld hrd: rdn over 2f out: hung lft and wknd over 1f out* **40/1**

/-00 6 1¾ **Jetta Joy (IRE)**[7] 5515 5-8-13 48 JackMitchell 2 45?
(Mrs A Duffield) *hld up: racd keenly: rdn and wknd over 2f out* **25/1**

600 7 11 **Avon Rock**[8] 5469 3-8-9 44 (tp) KirstyMilczarek 7 33
(A J Lidderdale) *hld up: rdn over 3f out: wknd over 2f out* **100/1**

8 30 **Leomode (USA)**[48] 4-9-4 0 (t) GeorgeBaker 10 —
(L Corcoran) *s.i.s: a in rr: lost tch fnl 3f: t.o* **50/1**

2m 41.38s (0.28) **Going Correction** -0.05s/f (Stan)

WFA 3 from 4yo+ 9lb 8 Ran SP% 111.1

Speed ratings (Par 101): **97,93,91,90,89 88,80,60**

Tote Swingers: 1&2 £2.60, 1&3 £2.20, 2&3 £1.90 CSF £18.11 TOTE £4.50: £1.20, £1.20, £1.10; EX 18.90.The winner was sold to S. Hussain & P. O'Neill for 9,000gns. Hypnotic Gaze was claimed by M. Keighley for £6,000.

Owner K Wreglesworth **Bred** Brittas House Stud & Lynch Bages & Samac **Trained** Sheriff Hutton, N Yorks

FOCUS

A moderate staying seller, run at a crawl until the final half mile. Muddling form, rated around the winner.

5766 NEW RENAULT MEGANE COUPE CABRIOLET H'CAP (DIV I) 1m 141y(P)

7:20 (7:22) (Class 6) (0-60,60) 3-Y-O+ £1,364 (£403; £201) Stalls Low

Form RPR

24 1 **Out Of Nothing**[15] 5271 7-8-12 53 SimonPearce(5) 2 60
(D Burchell) *mde all: rdn and edgd rt over 1f out: r.o* **4/1**[1]

3046 2 ½ **Just Timmy Marcus**[23] 4986 4-9-10 60 (b[1]) GrahamGibbons 12 66+
(B P J Baugh) *s.i.s: hld up: hdwy over 2f out: rdn and r.o wl ins fnl f* **6/1**

3402 3 1 **Blue Moon**[42] 4374 3-8-11 60 JulieBurke(7) 13 64
(K A Ryan) *hld up: hdwy over 3f out: hung lft over 1f out: sn rdn and hung rt: hung lft again ins fnl f: r.o* **8/1**

0006 4 ¾ **Lily Wood**[23] 4987 4-8-10 46 WilliamCarson 7 48
(J W Unett) *prom: chsd wnr 5f out: rdn over 1f out: no ex ins fnl f* **28/1**

0216 5 1¾ **Belle Park**[8] 5469 3-8-10 57 KierenFox(5) 5 55
(Karen George) *chsd wnr over 3f: remained handy: rdn over 2f out: no ex ins fnl f* **9/2**[2]

2510 6 hd **Tomintoul Star**[26] 4914 4-9-9 59 TomEaves 11 57+
(Mrs R A Carr) *s.i.s: hld up: r.o ins fnl f: nvr nrr* **11/1**

0004 7 1½ **Rocky Mood (IRE)**[19] 5158 3-8-11 53 (p) EddieAhern 4 47
(W R Swinburn) *hld up: pushed along 5f out: styd on ins fnl f: nvr nrr* **5/1**[3]

-400 8 shd **Peckforton Castle**[49] 4127 3-8-10 52 PaulMulrennan 10 46
(Patrick Morris) *prom: rdn 3f out: hung rt over 1f out: styd on same pce* **33/1**

4000 9 nse **Trade Centre**[40] 4428 5-9-10 60 (p) TomMcLaughlin 6 54
(R A Harris) *hld up in tch: rdn over 2f out: wknd fnl f* **12/1**

0000 10 nse **Trading Nation (USA)**[23] 3511 4-9-0 50 (b[1]) DarrenWilliams 3 44
(P W Hiatt) *hld up: plld hrd: rdn over 1f out: nvr trbld ldrs* **33/1**

1650 11 3½ **Bold Diva**[23] 4987 5-9-7 57 (v) KirstyMilczarek 8 43
(A W Carroll) *hld up: rdn over 2f out: a in rr* **14/1**

0000 12 10 **Tigers Charm**[23] 4992 3-8-2 47 oh1 ow1 (t) AndrewHeffernan(3) 1 10
(J M Bradley) *prom: rdn over 3f out: wknd over 2f out* **66/1**

1m 50.19s (-0.31) **Going Correction** -0.05s/f (Stan)

WFA 3 from 4yo+ 6lb 12 Ran SP% 113.8

Speed ratings (Par 101): **99,98,97,97,95 95,93,93,93,93 90,81**

Tote Swingers: 1&2 £3.80, 1&3 £4.00, 2&3 £5.70 CSF £25.73 CT £183.76 TOTE £4.10: £2.30, £1.50, £3.40; EX 31.00.

Owner Phoenix Brothers **Bred** E Young And Sons **Trained** Briery Hill, Blaenau Gwent

FOCUS

A weak handicap, run a bit quicker than division II but still muddling. The winner probably only ran to recent form.

Peckforton Castle Official explanation: jockey said gelding hung right

Bold Diva Official explanation: jockey said mare had a breathing problem

5767 NEW RENAULT MEGANE COUPE CABRIOLET H'CAP (DIV II) 1m 141y(P)

7:50 (7:50) (Class 6) (0-60,60) 3-Y-O+ £1,364 (£403; £201) Stalls Low

Form RPR

000 1 **Woolston Ferry (IRE)**[21] 5077 4-9-4 54 EddieAhern 8 64
(David Pinder) *chsd ldrs: rdn to ld 1f out: hung lft ins fnl f: r.o* **20/1**

3512 2 nk **Mr Chocolate Drop (IRE)**[15] 5271 6-9-7 57 (t) AdamKirby 6 66
(Miss M E Rowland) *hld up: hdwy over 1f out: rdn and ev ch ins fnl f: r.o* **7/2**[1]

5046 **3** 2 1/2 **Yourgolftravel Com**[18] 5172 5-9-9 **59** GeorgeBaker 1 62
(M Wigham) *hld up: hdwy 1f out: sn rdn: styd on to go 3rd nr fin* **5/1**[3]
0530 **4** 1/2 **Emperor's Well**[23] 4985 11-8-10 **46** GrahamGibbons 7 48
(M W Easterby) *s.i.s: hdwy over 6f out: led over 2f out: rdn and hdd 1f out: styd on same pce* **16/1**
3400 **5** 1 **Mullitovermaurice**[119] 1920 4-9-0 **50** StephenCraine 11 50
(Patrick Morris) *led 1f: chsd ldrs: rdn and ev ch whn hung rt over 1f out: no ex ins fnl f* **8/1**
3601 **6** 1 1/2 **Aussie Blue (IRE)**[15] 5271 6-9-7 **60** (v) MichaelStainton(3) 2 56
(R M Whitaker) *hld up: hdwy over 1f out: sn rdn: no ex ins fnl f* **9/2**[2]
4000 **7** 3/4 **Hilbre Court (USA)**[23] 4987 5-9-10 **60** (b) TomMcLaughlin 3 55
(B P J Baugh) *trckd ldrs: racd keenly: rdn over 2f out: no ex fnl f* **14/1**
465 **8** shd **Aggbag**[23] 4987 6-8-5 **46** KierenFox(5) 9 40
(A W Carroll) *hld up: rdn over 1f out: nvr trbld ldrs* **9/2**[2]
4240 **9** 1 1/4 **Magenta Strait**[23] 4988 3-8-10 **57** SimonPearce(5) 4 49
(R Hollinshead) *hld up: hdwy over 1f out: wknd ins fnl f* **14/1**
0060 **10** 9 **Lilly Blue (IRE)**[20] 5113 4-8-10 **46** oh1 (tp) TomEaves 10 17
(R Brotherton) *led over 7f out: hdd over 2f out: wknd over 1f out* **40/1**

1m 50.98s (0.48) **Going Correction** -0.05s/f (Stan)
WFA 3 from 4yo+ 6lb 10 Ran SP% **112.8**
Speed ratings (Par 101): **95,94,92,92,91 89,89,89,87,79**
Tote Swingers: 1&2 £13.90, 1&3 £25.00, 2&3 £4.80 CSF £86.22 CT £423.02 TOTE £29.20: £6.90, £2.00, £2.50; EX 127.40.
Owner Ms L Burns **Bred** Tim Taylor **Trained** Kingston Lisle, Oxon
■ Stewards' Enquiry : Stephen Craine one-day ban: failed to keep straight from stalls (Sep 18)

FOCUS
The slower of the two divisions of the handicap by 0.8sec and another weak affair. The form is not too solid.

5768 FOLEY FOR ALL YOUR STEEL REQUIREMENTS CLAIMING STKS 7f 32y(P)
8:20 (8:20) (Class 5) 3-Y-O+ **£2,115** (£624; £312) **Stalls** High

Form RPR
0600 **1** **Southandwest (IRE)**[21] 5064 6-8-9 75 EddieAhern 5 68+
(A M Hales) *hld up in tch: lost pl 4f out: hdwy over 1f out: rdn to ld ins fnl f: r.o* **8/1**
0163 **2** hd **Angelena Ballerina (IRE)**[23] 4988 3-8-3 56 (v) KirstyMilczarek 4 63
(Karen George) *chsd ldr: rdn to ld over 1f out: hdd ins fnl f: r.o* **16/1**
0501 **3** 1/2 **Dingaan (IRE)**[38] 4489 7-9-7 86 DavidProbert 10 78+
(A M Balding) *hld up: rdn over 2f out: hdwy over 1f out: edgd lft ins fnl f: r.o wl: nt rch ldrs* **11/4**[1]
2504 **4** nk **Cape Melody**[28] 4836 4-9-5 72 TravisBlock 11 75
(H Morrison) *hld up in tch: rdn and ev ch fr over 2f out: styd on* **12/1**
3306 **5** nse **Vanilla Rum**[22] 5031 3-9-0 75 DaneO'Neill 8 72+
(H Candy) *s.i.s: hld up: rdn 1/2-way: r.o u.p ins fnl f: nrst fin* **4/1**[3]
0040 **6** 1 1/2 **Fol Liam**[6] 5545 4-8-4 67 (p) DeclanCannon(5) 12 61
(A J McCabe) *chsd ldrs: rdn over 1f out: styd on same pce ins fnl f* **25/1**
0125 **7** nse **Dvinsky (USA)**[18] 5174 9-8-12 72 (b) MichaelStainton(3) 7 67
(P Howling) *led: rdn and hdd over 1f out: no ex wl ins fnl f* **14/1**
0060 **8** 1/2 **Ninth House (USA)**[8] 5486 8-8-9 59 (t) TomEaves 9 59
(Mrs R A Carr) *s.i.s: hdwy 1/2-way: no ex fnl f* **33/1**
0113 **9** 3/4 **Orpenindeed (IRE)**[40] 4430 7-9-7 85 (b[1]) AndrewHeffernan(3) 2 72
(Jim Best) *chsd ldrs: rdn over 1f out: wknd ins fnl f* **10/3**[2]
0655 **10** 3 1/4 **Ravi River (IRE)**[65] 3595 6-8-9 65 (v) GrahamGibbons 1 48
(P D Evans) *mid-div: pushed along 1/2-way: outpcd fr over 2f out* **14/1**

1m 29.06s (-0.54) **Going Correction** -0.05s/f (Stan)
WFA 3 from 4yo+ 4lb 10 Ran SP% **114.6**
Speed ratings (Par 103): **101,100,100,99,99 98,98,97,96,92**
Tote Swingers: 1&2 £13.50, 1&3 £3.90, 2&3 £11.90 CSF £124.78 TOTE £11.80: £3.10, £4.20, £2.40; EX 172.50.Vanilla Run was claimed by J Mackie for £8,000.
Owner A M Hales **Bred** Paul Hardy **Trained** Wardington, Oxon

FOCUS
A steadily run claimer and the runner-up clouds the form. The winner, third and fifth are better than the bare form.

5769 ADVANCED DRIVER SOLUTIONS LTD AT WOLVERHAMPTON H'CAP 7f 32y(P)
8:50 (8:50) (Class 5) (0-75,74) 3-Y-O **£2,115** (£624; £312) **Stalls** High

Form RPR
-305 **1** **Walcot Square (IRE)**[19] 5142 3-9-5 **73** SteveDrowne 3 78
(R Charlton) *hld up: hdwy 2f out: sn rdn: r.o to ld wl ins fnl f* **15/8**[1]
0006 **2** nk **Catherines Call (IRE)**[17] 5205 3-8-13 **72** SophieDoyle(5) 4 76
(D Donovan) *a.p: rdn to chse ldr over 1f out: ev ch wl ins fnl f: r.o* **10/1**
3300 **3** 3/4 **Law Of Attraction (IRE)**[11] 5383 3-8-11 **70** SimonPearce(5) 2 72
(J R Gask) *hld up: hdwy 2f out: sn rdn: r.o* **12/1**
3523 **4** hd **Lay Claim (USA)**[42] 4385 3-9-6 **74** (p) DarrenWilliams 8 76
(A J McCabe) *a.p: chsd ldr over 5f out: led 3f out: rdn over 1f out: hdd wl ins fnl f* **11/1**
2200 **5** nk **Marosh (FR)**[21] 5086 3-9-4 **72** GeorgeBaker 7 73
(R M H Cowell) *hld up: hdwy u.p and hung lft over 1f out: r.o* **7/2**[2]
5610 **6** 1 1/2 **Perfect Ch'l (IRE)**[6] 5561 3-9-1 **72** MartinLane(3) 5 69
(I A Wood) *led over 6f out: rdn and hdd 3f out: no ex ins fnl f* **11/1**
3665 **7** 3 1/4 **Fazza**[22] 5031 3-9-2 **70** DavidProbert 6 58
(D W P Arbuthnot) *hld up in tch: rdn over 2f out: hung lft and wknd over 1f out* **9/2**[3]
5310 **8** 5 **St Ignatius**[87] 2868 3-9-3 **71** (b) JackMitchell 1 45
(K O Cunningham-Brown) *led early: chsd ldrs: rdn over 2f out: wknd over 1f out* **33/1**

1m 28.59s (-1.01) **Going Correction** -0.05s/f (Stan) 8 Ran SP% **111.6**
Speed ratings (Par 101): **103,102,101,101,101 99,95,90**
Tote Swingers: 1&2 £5.50, 1&3 £7.50, 2&3 £19.70 CSF £20.82 CT £169.68 TOTE £2.50: £1.50, £2.60, £2.40; EX 24.80.
Owner De La Warr Racing **Bred** Barouche Stud Ireland Ltd **Trained** Beckhampton, Wilts

FOCUS
A very tight 3-y-o handicap which produced a bunch finish. Ordinary form.

5770 WOLVERHAMPTON HOLIDAY INN H'CAP 1m 4f 50y(P)
9:20 (9:20) (Class 6) (0-60,60) 3-Y-O+ **£1,706** (£503; £252) **Stalls** Low

Form RPR
0002 **1** **Pertemps Networks**[40] 4433 6-9-9 **58** GrahamGibbons 3 73
(M W Easterby) *led: rdn and hdd over 1f out: rallied to ld ins fnl f: r.o* **11/4**[2]
051 **2** 2 1/4 **Carlton Scroop (FR)**[3] 5663 7-9-1 **55** (b) KierenFox(5) 9 66
(A W Carroll) *s.i.s: hld up: hdwy over 3f out: led over 1f out: sn rdn and hung lft: hdd and no ex ins fnl f* **7/4**[1]
0455 **3** 5 **Kenyan Cat**[15] 5271 3-8-13 **60** MatthewDavies(3) 10 63
(George Baker) *s.i.s: hld up: hdwy over 2f out: rdn and hung lft fr over 1f out: styd on same pce* **12/1**
5004 **4** 2 **Carter**[15] 5272 4-9-6 **55** EddieAhern 2 55
(W M Brisbourne) *prom: rdn over 2f out: styd on same pce* **7/1**[3]
4000 **5** nse **Carnac (IRE)**[77] 3221 4-9-6 **60** (b) DeclanCannon(5) 11 60
(A J McCabe) *chsd ldrs: rdn and ev ch over 2f out: wknd over 1f out* **12/1**
0430 **6** 1 1/4 **Motarjm (USA)**[26] 4912 6-9-8 **57** (t) DaneO'Neill 5 57
(J Pearce) *hld up: nt clr run over 2f out: nvr trbld ldrs* **20/1**
4550 **7** 3/4 **Nicholas Pocock (IRE)**[15] 5271 4-9-6 **55** TomEaves 7 52
(B Ellison) *hld up: nt clr run over 2f out: nvr on terms* **14/1**
-605 **8** 5 **Why Nee Amy**[30] 4746 4-8-13 **53** KylieManser(5) 4 42
(Miss Olivia Maylam) *prom: rdn over 2f out: sn wknd* **66/1**
6400 **9** 1 1/4 **Paint The Town Red**[14] 2961 5-9-7 **56** JackMitchell 8 43
(H J Collingridge) *hld up: hdwy over 2f out: rdn and wknd over 1f out* **25/1**
4435 **10** 1 1/4 **Resplendent Ace (IRE)**[19] 5148 6-9-6 **58** MichaelStainton(3) 1 43
(P Howling) *hld up: rdn over 2f out: a in rr* **14/1**
665 **11** 10 **Utern**[19] 5141 6-9-6 **55** PaulMulrennan 12 24
(Miss Venetia Williams) *chsd ldr: pushed along 6f out: rdn over 3f out: wknd over 2f out* **66/1**
64/0 **12** 26 **Spaceman**[18] 5180 7-9-4 **53** (v) GeorgeBaker 6 —
(M R Bosley) *chsd ldrs: rdn over 5f out: wknd over 3f out: t.o* **33/1**

2m 38.22s (-2.88) **Going Correction** -0.05s/f (Stan)
WFA 3 from 4yo+ 9lb 12 Ran SP% **118.8**
Speed ratings (Par 101): **107,105,102,100,100 99,99,96,95,94 87,70**
Tote Swingers: 1&2 £3.50, 1&3 £8.30, 2&3 £6.10 CSF £7.50 CT £47.91 TOTE £5.80: £2.20, £1.10, £3.90; EX 12.50 Place 6: £47.80 Place 5: £15.08.
Owner E A Brook **Bred** H G Llewellyn **Trained** Sheriff Hutton, N Yorks

FOCUS
A moderate handicap, run at a decent pace. Probably fair form for the grade.
Spaceman Official explanation: jockey said gelding had no more to give
T/Plt: £62.00 to a £1 stake. Pool of £66,943.54 - 787.90 winning tickets. T/Qpdt: £7.10 to a £1 stake. Pool of £8,954.87 - 924.65 winning tickets. CR

5771 - 5778a (Foreign Racing) - See Raceform Interactive

5012 LEOPARDSTOWN (L-H)
Saturday, September 4

OFFICIAL GOING: Good to firm (good in places) changing to good after race 1 (1.40)

5772a KILTERNAN STKS (GROUP 3) 1m 2f
2:10 (2:10) 3-Y-O+ **£34,513** (£10,088; £4,778; £1,592)

RPR
1 **Await The Dawn (USA)**[13] 5341 3-9-1 JMurtagh 8 114+
(A P O'Brien, Ire) *trckd ldr in 2nd: impr to ld ent st: sn drew clr: styd on strly: eased fr over 100yds out: impressive* **7/2**[1]
2 9 **South Easter (IRE)**[77] 3191 4-9-8 (b[1]) TomQueally 10 96
(W J Haggas) *led: rdn and hdd ent st: sn outpcd: mod 2nd and kpt on u.p fr 1 1/2f out* **5/1**[2]
3 1/2 **Nanton (USA)**[17] 5220 8-9-8 KierenFallon 9 95+
(J S Goldie) *chsd ldrs in 6th: drvn along 1/2-way: 8th u.p ent st: styd on wl to go mod 3rd fr 1f out* **15/2**
4 2 **Indiana Gal (IRE)**[24] 4977 5-9-5 99 (p) JAHeffernan 5 88
(Patrick Martin, Ire) *hld up towards rr: 9th appr st: prog into mod 5th 1 1/2f out: kpt on* **16/1**
5 1/2 **Icon Dream (IRE)**[28] 4829 3-9-1 (v) DPMcDonogh 7 90+
(David Wachman, Ire) *hld up in rr: last ent st: styd on fr 2f out* **14/1**
6 4 1/2 **Cashelgar (IRE)**[405] 4367 4-9-8 110 PJSmullen 2 81
(D K Weld, Ire) *trckd ldrs in 3rd: rdn 3f out: no imp st: no ex fr over 1f out* **7/2**[1]
7 3 **Vitruvian Man**[9] 5464 4-9-8 95 (t) FMBerry 1 75
(John M Oxx, Ire) *trckd ldrs in 5th: rdn over 3f out: no ex st* **8/1**
8 1 1/4 **Rose Hip (IRE)**[6] 5568 6-9-5 101 CDHayes 4 70
(Joseph G Murphy, Ire) *t.k.h early: settled 4th: rdn and wknd fr 3f out* **16/1**
9 2 1/2 **Noll Wallop (IRE)**[105] 2354 3-9-4 109 WMLordan 6 71
(T Stack, Ire) *hld up: 8th 1/2-way: no ex ent st* **6/1**[3]
10 9 **Carazam (IRE)**[20] 5130 3-9-1 90 KJManning 3 50
(T Stack, Ire) *chsd ldrs: 7th 1/2-way: wknd fr 3f out* **33/1**

2m 5.24s (-2.96) **Going Correction** +0.10s/f (Good)
WFA 3 from 4yo+ 7lb 10 Ran SP% **119.6**
Speed ratings: **115,107,107,105,105 101,99,98,96,89**
CSF £21.47 TOTE £3.70: £1.60, £2.20, £2.20; DF 35.50.
Owner Michael Tabor **Bred** Juddmonte Farms Inc **Trained** Ballydoyle, Co Tipperary

FOCUS
The winner rates a big personal best with the fourth and fifth rated close to recent marks.

NOTEBOOK
Await The Dawn(USA) ◆, still entered in the St Leger and Champion Stakes, looked a Group 1 horse against handicappers here. Tracking the runner-up, he quickened up smartly to challenge in the straight and then quickened again over a furlong out, drawing right away for a most impressive success. It was somewhat out of the blue, but he was very much an unexposed horse, although this level of improvement couldn't have been expected. In the light of that it's not hard to question the form of the race, and that will only be answered when this horse steps up to Group 1 company, which is surely inevitable after this. (op 4/1)
South Easter(IRE) ◆ was beaten almost as far here as he was by Fame And Glory in the Coronation Cup at Epsom if you believe in form lines like that. He had the run of the race, dictating a mostly steady pace before the winner left him standing in the straight. Take the winner out of the race and it would be lauded as a good performance.
Nanton(USA), a horse who ran in the Cesarewitch last year, doesn't give the bare form a terrifically encouraging look although it does suggest his handler is fairly shrewd, and fully justified his decision to bring him here. He was being ridden from a long way out and never really travelled but just stayed on very effectively in the straight to be never nearer. (op 13/2)
Indiana Gal(IRE) was held up and looked to be struggling a bit when they turned out of the back straight, but to her credit she ran on pretty well.
Icon Dream(IRE) kept on late but never really was close enough to make an impression.
Cashelgar(IRE) failed to settle and found little for pressure in the straight, finishing quite tired. (op 3/1)
Vitruvian Man was well placed to get involved but couldn't make any impression. (op 8/1 tchd 9/1)
Noll Wallop(IRE) was held up but was being hard driven well before the straight. He made no impression. (op 5/1)

The Form Book, Raceform Ltd, Compton, RG20 6NL

Carazam(IRE) Official explanation: trainer said colt was found to have a trapped epiglotis following a post-race vet's examination

5773a COOLMORE FUSAICHI PEGASUS MATRON STKS (GROUP 1) (F&M) 1m

2:40 (2:41) 3-Y-O+ £115,044 (£33,628; £15,929; £5,309)

RPR

1 **Lillie Langtry (IRE)**59 3793 3-8-12 118 JMurtagh 4 117+
(A P O'Brien, Ire) *hld up in rr: hdwy on outer ent st: 2nd 1 1/2f out: chal fr over 1f out: r.o wl to ld cl home* **7/2**3

2 *nk* **Spacious**59 3793 5-9-3 KierenFallon 7 117
(J R Fanshawe) *trckd ldr in 2nd: impr to ld appr st: rdn and strly pressed fr over 1f out: kpt on wl u.p: hdd cl home* **11/4**2

3 *1 ¼* **Music Show (IRE)**34 4639 3-8-12 FMBerry 5 113
(M R Channon) *trckd ldrs: drvn along 3f out: 5th appr st: prog into 4th 2f out: 3rd and styd on ins fnl f* **2/1**1

4 *3* **Hen Night (IRE)**34 4630 3-8-12 101 WMLordan 2 107
(David Wachman, Ire) *chsd ldrs on inner: 4th 1/2-way: dropped in rr ent st: kpt on same pce u.p fr 1 1/2f out* **22/1**

5 *1 ½* **Bethrah (IRE)**104 2370 3-8-12 112 PJSmullen 6 103
(D K Weld, Ire) *trckd ldrs in 3rd: 2nd early st: 3rd u.p 1 1/2f out: no ex fnl f* **4/1**

6 *3* **Gile Na Greine (IRE)**9 5461 3-8-12 115 KJManning 1 96
(J S Bolger, Ire) *led: rdn and hdd appr st: lost pl under 2f out: sn no ex: eased last 100yds* **16/1**

1m 39.68s (-1.52) **Going Correction** +0.10s/f (Good)
WFA 3 from 5yo 5lb **6** Ran SP% **112.5**
Speed ratings: **111,110,109,106,104 101**
CSF £13.57 TOTE £4.20: £1.90, £1.80; DF 15.90.
Owner Michael Tabor **Bred** K B Lynch **Trained** Ballydoyle, Co Tipperary

FOCUS

The first race of the day run on the inside track, and the effect of the rain was obvious. The time was a shade quicker than that recorded by Rainbow View last year, when the ground was officially good to yielding. Spacious is a good marker and Lillie Langtry is rated to her Ascot form.

NOTEBOOK

Lillie Langtry(IRE) was travelling easily approaching the straight on the heels of the other five, and was then pulled out wide to make her move widest of all. Murtagh only gave her the first crack of the whip just over a furlong out and she just wore down Spacious close home, but it was a cosy enough neck victory in the end. This was not a furious gallop by any means so the winner is no way flattered by the form. A stronger pace would probably suit her better, and she should be hard to beat next time in the Prix De l'Opera. (op 3/1)

Spacious remains the bridesmaid at the top level. Fallon purposely decided not to make the running, perhaps recalling that she may have done a little too much in front at Newmarket, but she got quite a nice lead off Gile Na Greine. Fallon kicked her into the lead around the home bend and, for a while it appeared as though she might last it out, but she could give no extra when joined close home. Ultimately, Spacious lacks the turn of foot that sets the really good ones apart from the remainder, but she went down fighting again. (op 3/1 tchd 9/4)

Music Show(IRE)'s performance was noteworthy. Things were never going to pan out for her as favourably as they did at Newmarket, but she was well-positioned just ahead of the winner for much of the race. She hit a flat spot fully 3f out, and had to be briefly shaken up to keep with the first three. To her credit, she ran on very well under hand riding in the final furlong, and probably wants a stronger pace. The score is now 2-2 between her and Lillie Langtry, but the Ballydoyle filly probably has her measure when they're both at their best (op 9/4 tchd 5/2)

Hen Night(IRE) ran a fine race, though she never got remotely involved. Considering she was running in a handicap earlier this season off a mark of 85, her progression has been admirable. (op 25/1)

Bethrah(IRE) was ultimately disappointing, but seems better than the bare form. She looked at one stage to be perhaps the biggest threat to Spacious when they turned in, but she seemed to get tired. She will probably struggle to beat these again, but in mitigation she had not run since winning the Irish Guineas and may have got tired.

Gile Na Greine(IRE) has now run three poor races on the bounce and had no excuses. It seems hard to think she can make the breakthrough at Group 1 level, for all that she came so close at Newmarket.

5774a WWW.THETOTE.COM SEPTEMBER H'CAP (PREMIER HANDICAP) 7f

3:10 (3:12) 3-Y-O+ £48,893 (£14,292; £6,769; £2,256)

RPR

1 **Hujaylea (IRE)**6 5571 7-8-8 94 (p) CPHoban(7) 6 101
(M Halford, Ire) *hld up towards rr: prog on inner ent st: 6th and hdwy 2f out: led over 1f out: styd on wl* **8/1**2

2 *¾* **Barack (IRE)**6 5571 4-8-12 94 (bt) BACurtis(3) 3 98
(Francis Ennis, Ire) *trckd ldrs: 5th 1/2-way: 4th under 2f out: 2nd and kpt on u.p ins fnl f* **12/1**

3 *½* **Douze Points (IRE)**6 5571 4-8-9 88 (p) WMLordan 12 91
(Joseph G Murphy, Ire) *hld up towards rr: nt clr run ent st: 9th and hdwy whn checked 1f out: r.o strly: nrest at fin* **14/1**

4 *¾* **Photo Opportunity**18 5189 3-7-13 89 LFRoche(7) 7 88
(D K Weld, Ire) *mid-div: 10th 1/2-way: 8th and hdwy 2f out: 5th whn swtchd 1f out: kpt on* **8/1**2

5 *nk* **Ask Jack (USA)**18 5192 6-9-7 103 (p) DEMullins(3) 14 103
(Joseph G Murphy, Ire) *trckd ldrs in 4th: 3rd early st: kpt on u.p fr 1 1/2f out* **8/1**2

6 *½* **Finicius (USA)**18 5192 6-9-12 105 (t) JMurtagh 18 103
(Eoin Griffin, Ire) *hld up towards rr: 17th appr st: styd on wl on outer fr 2f out* **14/1**

7 *shd* **Hard Rock City (USA)**30 4767 10-9-1 94 KJManning 2 92
(M J Grassick, Ire) *mid-div: 7th and prog appr st: 5th under 1 1/2f out: kpt on same pce* **12/1**

8 *¾* **Bay Knight (IRE)**29 4808 4-9-4 97 DPMcDonogh 11 93
(K J Condon, Ire) *hld up: 8th and prog on outer 2f out: 7th 1f out: kpt on same pce* **16/1**

9 *¾* **Toufan Express**35 4608 8-8-10 89 CDHayes 5 83
(Adrian McGuinness, Ire) *towards rr: kpt on wout threatening st* **9/1**3

10 *shd* **Rain Rush (IRE)**34 4630 7-8-9 93 JPO'Brien(5) 15 87
(David Marnane, Ire) *hld up in rr: last appr st: kpt on wout threatening fr under 2f out* **16/1**

11 *½* **Excelerate (IRE)**6 5571 7-9-2 95 (t) WJLee 10 88
(Edward Lynam, Ire) *hld up towards rr: 16th appr st: kpt on one pce fr 2f out* **14/1**

12 *½* **Brae Hill (IRE)**14 5292 4-9-3 96 TomQueally 9 87
(R A Fahey) *cl up in 2nd: chal ent st: led under 2f out: hdd 1f out: no ex and wknd* **6/1**1

13 *3 ½* **Six Of Hearts**30 4767 6-9-0 98 (p) MHarley(5) 16 80
(Cecil Ross, Ire) *trckd ldrs: prog into 5th appr st: sn rdn: no ex fr under 1 1/2f out* **20/1**

14 *shd* **Maundy Money**35 4608 7-9-1 94 JAHeffernan 4 75
(David Marnane, Ire) *mid-div: 8th appr st: sn rdn and no imp: checked ent fnl f* **11/1**

15 *1 ¼* **Anam Chara (IRE)**9 5461 4-8-4 90 DCByrne(7) 1 68
(Andrew Oliver, Ire) *led: strly pressed st: hdd under 2f out: sn wknd* **25/1**

16 *11* **The Tooth Fairy (IRE)**20 5127 4-8-10 92 (t) GFCarroll(3) 17 40
(Michael Mulvany, Ire) *mid-div: 9th appr 1/2-way: no ex ent st: wknd* **25/1**

17 *14* **Jembatt (IRE)**30 4767 3-8-13 96 (b1) FMBerry 13 5
(Edward Lynam, Ire) *prom: 3rd 1/2-way: wknd qckly ent st: eased over 1f out* **12/1**

18 *5* **Broad Meaning**35 4608 4-9-0 93 (b) PJSmullen 8 —
(D K Weld, Ire) *chsd ldrs in 6th: wknd ent st: eased fnl f* **20/1**

1m 27.74s (-0.96) **Going Correction** +0.10s/f (Good)
WFA 3 from 4yo+ 4lb **18** Ran SP% **138.0**
Speed ratings: **109,108,107,106,106 105,105,104,103,103 103,102,98,98,97 84,68,62**
CSF £107.24 CT £1409.51 TOTE £8.50: £2.40, £3.00, £3.80, £2.10; DF 127.70.
Owner Gerard M O'Leary **Bred** Christopher Flynn **Trained** Doneany, Co Kildare

NOTEBOOK

Hujaylea(IRE) was adding this to Sunday's win in the Cambridgeshire - not bad for a horse rated 48 when he won his first race. What was notable here was that he won despite being tardy at the gates and Conor Hoban had to wake him up in the first furlong, but it may have been a disguised blessing as they were probably going too fast up front. Hujaylea was able to save ground on the rail and got a dream run alongside it as they approached the straight. He very quickly made up such ground that he took it up probably earlier than ideal, but he was always holding on and had the race already won when the placed horses came at him. In strongly run big-field handicaps, he has developed into a very good performer and a durable one too. (op 9/1)

Barack(IRE) ran an extremely good race, considering he was never far off the pace. He surely needed the run in the Cambridgeshire when beaten over six lengths and could have won this if the race had been run a little differently. Against that, he just held on for second, but has a distinct liking for this track. (op 16/1)

Douze Points(IRE) remains something of an enigma but was clearly very unlucky. Just like in the big 7f handicap at Galway, he was running on strongly without getting there and that sums up his career. He was held up on the outside and travelled very well. He lost considerable ground early in the straight when snatched up and again ran into trouble over a furlong out before finishing very well. He looked very unlucky, but you could not bank on him making amends. Official explanation: jockey said gelding ran short of room throughout the last 2f but stayed on well at the finish (op 14/1 tchd 16/1)

Photo Opportunity had to switch to Barack's inner when making his run less than two furlongs out and was not at all knocked about by his jockey. This confirmed the suspicion that he will prove better than his mark and the experience of such a hurly-burly race will bring him on. Official explanation: jockey said colt ran green throughout, checked and became momentarily unbalanceed out of the back straight before staying on in the closing stages

Ask Jack(USA), winner of the Galway Mile and just touched off in that festival's big 7f handicap, ran another fine race. He was always up there and kept going, losing a couple of places close home. He is as tough as they come. (op 10/1)

Brae Hill(IRE) raced too close to the strong pace. (op 5/1)

5775a TATTERSALLS MILLIONS IRISH CHAMPION STKS (GROUP 1) 1m 2f

3:45 (3:47) 3-Y-O+

£384,513 (£125,663; £59,292; £19,469; £12,831; £6,194)

RPR

1 **Cape Blanco (IRE)**42 4359 3-9-0 119 JAHeffernan 1 127
(A P O'Brien, Ire) *mde all: set str pce: rdn clr ent st: styd on wl u.p: unchal* **6/1**3

2 *5 ½* **Rip Van Winkle (IRE)**18 5186 4-9-7 126 JMurtagh 6 116+
(A P O'Brien, Ire) *hld up in 5th: prog early st: mod 4th over 1f out: kpt on* **8/11**1

3 *shd* **Twice Over**18 5186 5-9-7 TomQueally 4 116+
(H R A Cecil) *hld up in 4th: prog 4f out: 3rd 3f out: rdn and no imp early st: kpt on same pce u.p fr over 1f out* **10/3**2

4 *shd* **Beethoven (IRE)**23 5016 3-9-0 117 (b) JPO'Brien 3 116
(A P O'Brien, Ire) *trckd ldrs in 3rd: 4th 3f out: sme prog into mod 3rd over 1f out: kpt on same pce* **33/1**

5 *½* **Sea Lord (IRE)**23 5009 3-9-0 KierenFallon 5 115
(M Johnston) *chsd ldr in 2nd: rdn under 3f out: outpcd ent st: kpt on same pce fr over 1f out* **20/1**

6 *1* **Famous Name**44 4312 5-9-7 117 PJSmullen 2 113+
(D K Weld, Ire) *hld up in rr: drvn along over 3f out: kpt on same pce u.p st* **12/1**

2m 3.89s (-4.31) **Going Correction** +0.10s/f (Good)
WFA 3 from 4yo+ 7lb **6** Ran SP% **110.7**
Speed ratings: **121,116,116,116,116 115**
CSF £10.57 TOTE £5.80: £2.70, £1.02; DF 12.60.
Owner Derrick Smith **Bred** Jack Ronan & Des Vere Hunt Far **Trained** Ballydoyle, Co Tipperary

FOCUS

A career best effort from Cape Blanco to make all. The fourth and fifth are the best guides to the form.

NOTEBOOK

Cape Blanco(IRE) ridden like a 1m4f horse, turned the race into a test of stamina on the rain-softened surface, exploited the relative lack of stamina in the opposition to the full, and it worked perfectly. Setting off at close to pacemaker fractions, he had everything on the stretch as they turned into the straight and the only chance for the chasing group was if he stopped, but it was always going to be the case that the stamina of the opposition was going to run out before his did. He's a very good horse, and he probably has more speed than the average 1m4f horse at this level. He brought everything into play today under conditions ideal for the way he set about his task. (op 11/2 tchd 5/1)

Rip Van Winkle(IRE) was settled as best as Murtagh could from off the pace and if he was ridden any handier he might have finished tailed off. He still travelled on the approach to the straight but he was going to have to find reserves of stamina previously unknown for to catch the winner. In the end he kept on as well as he could. Perhaps connections should drop him back to a mile and stick to that trip as it's clearly his best. (op 8/11 tchd 4/5)

Twice Over is undoubtedly a very good horse, but perhaps he just falls marginally short at the very top level over this trip. This distance does seem to be his optimum, but he was struggling to make any impression on the winner before the straight and ultimately he couldn't. He's tough and game and that will continue to paper over some of the shortcomings he has at this level. (op 7/2)

Beethoven(IRE) was ridden on his merits and didn't perform in a pacemaking role. It must be said that he probably ran above himself as it turned out and kept going in the straight despite coming under pressure early enough. The way he saw out the trip should give connections a few options with him.

Sea Lord(IRE), a supplementary entry, ran with great credit as he was the horse that gave chase to the winner for much of the race and was probably the first to come under pressure about half a mile from the finish. For all that, his stamina lasted probably better than most of those around him.

Famous Name was not in his comfort zone from about halfway and despite making up some ground in the straight he never looked likely to make an impression. He has picked up a fair few soft races this season, and credit to his trainer for campaigning him to maximum effect in that way, but it's probably fair to say that those sort of races wouldn't have prepared him for what he had to face in this race. (op 10/1)

5578 SARATOGA (R-H)

Saturday, September 4

OFFICIAL GOING: Dirt: fast

5779a FOREGO STKS (GRADE 1) (3YO+) (DIRT) 7f

10:14 (10:16) 3-Y-0+

£92,592 (£30,864; £15,432; £7,716; £4,629; £771)

RPR

1 **Here Comes Ben (USA)**[71] 4-8-12 0....................................(b) ASolis 5 122
(Charles Lopresti, U.S.A) *settled towards rr: clsd up and 7th 2 1/2f out: 6th and rdn st (jst ins fnl 2f): r.o to dispute 3rd 1f out: styd on strly to ld cl home* **99/10**

2 *3/4* **Big Drama (USA)**[27] 4-8-12 0..(b) ECoa 4 120
(David Fawkes, U.S.A) *broke wl: settled in 3rd on quarters of vineyard haven: wnt 2nd 4f out: pressed ldr and led appr 2f out: rdn over 1f out and r.o wl: ct cl home* **51/10**[3]

3 *1 1/2* **Vineyard Haven (USA)**[43] 4-8-12 0....................................(b) AGarcia 2 116
(Saeed Bin Suroor) *wl away and chsd ldr: relegated to 3rd on rail 4f out: 4th and ev ch 2 1/2f out: rdn st and tk 2nd on rail: no ex fnl f* **1/1**[1]

4 *nk* **Warrior's Reward (USA)**[96] 4-8-12 0.............................. JRLeparoux 7 115
(Ian Wilkes, U.S.A) *hld up in rr: tk clsr order gng wl 3f out: 8th st: r.o u.p up the outside: tk 3rd ins last 100yds* **23/5**[2]

5 *2* **Girolamo (USA)**[301] 7311 4-8-12 0.................................... CVelasquez 3 110
(Saeed Bin Suroor) *settled in 4th: win 2l of ld 3 1/2f out: 3rd and ev ch 2f out: rdn st: no ex* **1/1**[1]

6 *hd* **Bribon (FR)**[27] 7-8-12 0... GKGomez 1 109
(Todd Pletcher, U.S.A) *hld up towards rr: last but clsng 2f out: rdn and r.o st: disp 3rd 1 1/2f out: one pce fnl f* **58/10**

7 *4 3/4* **Omniscient (USA)**[34] 4-8-12 0.. CHBorel 6 96
(Steven Asmussen, U.S.A) *racd in 6th: a cl 5th 2 1/2f out: sn fdd* **28/1**

8 *1 1/4* **You And I Forever (USA)**[43] 5-8-12 0.................................. JJCastellano 9 93
(Thomas Bush, U.S.A) *racd in midfield til rdn and wknd st* **245/10**

9 *37* **Checklist (USA)**[61] 4-8-12 0... JRVelazquez 8 —
(Todd Pletcher, U.S.A) *rdn on outside to ld and swtchd to rail: hdd appr 2f out: wknd qckly st and heavily eased appr fnl f* **239/10**

1m 22.5s (82.50) **9** Ran SP% **169.5**

PARI-MUTUEL (all including $2 stakes): WIN 21.80; PLACE (1-2) 8.50, 6.70; SHOW (1-2-3) 3.70, 3.30, 2.10; SF 114.50.

Owner Brandon L & Marianne Chase **Bred** Marianne I Chase & Brandon L Chase **Trained** USA

NOTEBOOK

Here Comes Ben(USA) gained his fourth straight win on his Graded stakes debut. He could be a contender for the Breeders' Cup Dirt Mile.

Big Drama(USA) was outstayed by the winner. He should be a player in the Breeders' Cup Sprint.

Vineyard Haven(USA) impressed when winning a minor contest over C&D on reappearance, but he hasn't gone forward from that success, proving a little bit disappointing on his return to the top level. Perhaps he bounced - he set quick fractions last time and probably had a hard race.

Girolamo(USA) ran creditably on his first run since finishing well beaten in last year's Breeders' Cup Classic and is entitled to improve.

5780a WOODWARD STKS (GRADE 1) (3YO+) (DIRT) 1m 1f (D)

10:48 (10:51) 3-Y-0+

£277,777 (£92,592; £46,296; £23,148; £13,888; £4,629)

RPR

1 **Quality Road (USA)**[28] 4855 4-9-0 0.............................. JRVelazquez 3 122+
(Todd Pletcher, U.S.A) *pressed ldr: led 3f out: pushed along st: drew clr fnl f* **30/100**[1]

2 *4 3/4* **Mythical Power (USA)**[34] 4-9-0 0....................................(b) GKGomez 7 111
(Bob Baffert, U.S.A) *racd in 3rd: followed wnr through 3f out: pressed ldr 2f out: rdn st: kpt on but no imp on wnr* **122/10**

3 *1/2* **Tranquil Manner (USA)**[92] 4-9-0 0....................................... AGarcia 6 110
(Kiaran McLaughlin, U.S.A) *hld up: last st: styd on u.p on outside to take 3rd ins fnl 100yds* **192/10**

4 *1 1/4* **Convocation (USA)**[63] 4-9-0 0.. JJCastellano 1 108
(James Jerkens, U.S.A) *racd in 5th: nrly 10l off the pce 4f out: pushed along to take clsr order 3f out: 4th st and sn rdn: no ex ins fnl f* **54/10**[2]

5 *1 1/4* **Indian Dance (USA)**[34] 4-9-0 0....................................(b) RADominguez 5 105
(Lawrence E Murray, U.S.A) *settled in 6th: 5th st: sn rdn and unable qck* **35/1**

6 *11 3/4* **Arcodoro (USA)**[35] 4-9-0 0...(b) DCohen 4 83
(Eric J Guillot, U.S.A) *led: hdd 3f out: rdn 2f out and wknd qckly* **29/1**

7 *1 3/4* **Mine That Bird (USA)**[28] 4855 4-9-0 0............................(b[1]) RMaragh 2 80
(D Wayne Lukas, U.S.A) *racd on heels of two ldrs in 4th: remained cl up til rdn and outpcd 3 1/2f out: grad wknd u.p fnl 2f* **107/10**[3]

1m 50.0s (110.00) **7** Ran SP% **119.7**

PARI-MUTUEL (all including $2 stakes): WIN 2.60; PLACE (1-2) 2.10, 5.90; SHOW (1-2-3) 2.10, 4.40, 4.80; SF 14.00.

Owner Edward P Evans **Bred** Edward P Evans **Trained** USA

NOTEBOOK

Quality Road(USA), narrowly turned over by Blame in the Whitney Handicap last time, returned to winning form with a straightforward victory over six inferior rivals. He's being targeted at the Breeders' Cup Classic, but it's with confidence that he's predicted to not stay the 1m2f trip.

Mine That Bird(USA) had Maragh replacing Borel, as well as blinkers on for the first time, but he ran poorly. Last year's shock Kentucky Derby winner seems unlikely to make an impression at this level again.

VELIEFENDI

Saturday, September 4

OFFICIAL GOING: Polytrack: standard; turf: good

5781a INTERNATIONAL FRANCE GALOP-FRBC ANATOLIA TROPHY (GROUP 2) (3YO+) (POLYTRACK) 1m 2f (P)

5:00 (12:00) 3-Y-0+ **£101,769** (£40,707; £20,353; £10,176)

RPR

1 **Dervis Aga (TUR)**[19] 5-9-6 0...(b) HalisKaratas 1 111
(S Mutlu, Turkey) *hld up in 7th: clsd up fr 2f out but stl 6th appr fnl f: styd on strly u.p fnl 200yds to ld 40yds out* **5/4**[2]

2 *1/2* **Cutlass Bay (UAE)**[18] 5186 4-9-6 0.................................... TedDurcan 7 110
(Saeed Bin Suroor) *dwlt and last away: sn settled in 5th: styd trcking ldrs travelling wl: clsd up appr st: cl 4th 2f out: sn rdn and styd on u.p to ld 1f out: r.o but hdd fnl 40yds: no ex* **4/5**[1]

3 *4* **Boom Boom (TUR)**[10] 4-9-6 0...(b) ErhanYavuz 8 102
(M H Esin, Turkey) *racd in 4th: plld hrd: settled whn pce qcknd 7f out: moved up to dispute ld in line of three turning for home: led briefly appr fnl f: hdd 1f out: no ex* **596/100**

4 *1/2* **Dansant**[21] 5109 6-9-6 0.. OlivierPeslier 4 101
(G A Butler) *settled in 6th: 6th and ev ch st: sn pushed along: 5th and rdn 2f out: kpt on at same pce* **12/5**

5 *1/2* **Doku (TUR)**[24] 4-9-3 0.. SelimKaya 2 97
(D Ergin, Turkey) *a in the first three win 1 l of the ld: disp ld in line of three turning for home: led u.p 2f out: hdd appr fnl f: wknd* **29/20**[3]

6 *3* **Sinkasen (IRE)** 3-8-12 0 ow1..................(b) PanagiotisDimitsanis 3 93
(M Loannidas, Greece) *broke wl and let at stdy pce: hdd 7f out: styd prom: disp ld in line of three turning for home: sn rdn and wknd u.p fnl 300yds* **123/10**

7 *18* **Babayigit (TUR)**[43] 6-9-6 0.. GokhanKocakaya 6 58
(Z B Cinar, Turkey) *settled in last 10 l off the pce: rdn 3f out: nvr in contention* **155/10**

8 *1* **Kader Firtinasi (TUR)**[36] 6-9-6 0.................................... SadettinBoyraz 5 56
(M Tekdemir, Turkey) *broke wl and settled in 3rd bhd stdy pce: rushed up on outside to ld 7f out: rdn over 2 1/2f out: hdd turning for home: wknd qckly* **216/10**

2m 6.32s (1.32)

WFA 3 from 4yo+ 7lb **8** Ran SP% **202.6**

PARI-MUTUEL (all including 1Turkish lira stakes): WIN: 2.25; no place betting; DF 2.75; SF 6.75.

Owner Nevzat Unlu **Bred** H Somturk **Trained** Turkey

NOTEBOOK

Cutlass Bay(UAE) showed that he retained a degree of his ability after a couple of dismal efforts in better grade, and he looked sure to win after being produced to hit the front over a furlong out but was just outfought by his Turkish rival. He handled the surface and quickened up well but he possibly just idled a bit. He is likely to stay in training, with a winter at the Dubai Carnival now on the agenda.

Dansant needs further than this nowadays and the moderate early gallop was against him.

5782a INTERNATIONAL ISTANBUL EUROPEAN CAPITAL OF CULTURE TROPHY (GROUP 2) (3YO+ FILLIES & MARES) (TURF) 1m

7:00 (12:00) 3-Y-0+ **£101,769** (£40,707; £20,353; £10,176)

RPR

1 **Vanjura (GER)**[28] 3-8-13 0... APietsch 9 111
(R Dzubasz, Germany) *wl away and settled in 3rd: pushed along in st (2 1/2f out): wnt 3 l 2nd 2f out: led appr fnl f: grad drew clr* **29/20**[1]

2 *3 1/2* **Evading Tempete**[23] 5139 3-8-13 0..............................(p) OlivierPeslier 7 102
(F Rohaut, France) *trckd wnr in 5th: wnt 4th st on heels of wnr: pushed along and nt qckn appr 2f out: styd on u.p to take 2nd ins fnl f: kpt on but no ch w wnr* **5/2**[3]

3 *1 1/2* **Kinky Afro (IRE)**[20] 5114 3-8-13 0....................................... LiamKeniry 5 99
(J S Moore) *chsd ldrs and settled in 6th on rail: wnt 5th turning for home: sn rdn: styd on u.p ins fnl f to take 3rd cl home* **134/10**

4 *2 1/2* **Ravenel (GER)**[118] 4-9-6 0.. MEsposito 6 96
(R Rohne, Germany) *chsd clr ldr: 7 l 2nd turning for home: kpt on at same pce fr 2f out: lost 3rd cl home* **51/20**

5 *1/2* **Please Sing**[20] 5114 4-9-6 0.. TedDurcan 8 95
(M R Channon) *hld up towards rr: tk clsr order 4f out: 6th st: hmpd and swtchd 2f out: kpt on fnl f wout qckning* **7/1**

6 *1/2* **Actionmax (TUR)**[24] 5-9-6 0.......................................(t) HalisKaratas 10 94
(B Dag, Turkey) *racd in rr: r.o fnl 2f: n.d* **51/10**

7 *1 1/2* **Chi (TUR)**[24] 4-9-6 0... AyhanKursun 2 91
(A Ozgen, Turkey) *dwlt: rdn along to ld after 1f: sn clr: 7 l ahd turning for home: rdn 2f out and tiring: hdd appr fnl f: wknd* **127/20**

8 *1* **The Rising (TUR)**[24] 6-9-6 0...(t) AkinSozen 11 88
(C Filiksac, Turkey) *a bhd: 8th st: no imp* **41/20**[2]

9 *1* **Amarama (IRE)**[370] 5490 5-9-6 0............................. PanagiotisDimitsanis 4 86
(V Bariamoglou, Greece) *nvr out of rr quartet: n.d* **21/1**

10 *11 1/2* **Mayuska (TUR)**[24] 5-9-6 0...(b) OzcanYildirim 12 59
(A K Aksoy, Turkey) *broke wl and led: hdd and stdd after 1f: racd in midfield: wknd st* **101/20**

11 *1* **Lovely Doyoun (TUR)**[24] 7-9-6 0...................................... FuatCakar 3 57
(A K Aksoy, Turkey) **101/20**

1m 34.26s (-1.07)

WFA 3 from 4yo+ 5lb **11** Ran SP% **217.4**

PARI-MUTUEL (all including 1Turkish lira stakes): WIN: 2.45; PLACE (first two): 1.15, 1.25; DF 3.55; SF 5.80.

Owner German Racing Club **Bred** M Barth **Trained** Germany

NOTEBOOK

Kinky Afro(IRE) is really tough and was having her 13th run of a season that began with three all-weather successes, and has now encompassed racing in four countries. She is set for a break now before a possible trip to Dubai.

Please Sing was never really involved, but she was not helped by suffering trouble in running.

5273 YORK (L-H)

Sunday, September 5

OFFICIAL GOING: Good to firm (watered; 7.8)

Rail moved out 3m from 9f to entrance to home straight adding 8m to races of one mile and over.

Wind: moderate 1/2 behind Weather: fine and sunny

5784 JUDITH MARSHALL MEMORIAL STKS (NURSERY) 7f

2:00 (2:00) (Class 4) (0-85,83) 2-Y-O **£6,540** (£1,946; £972; £242; £242) **Stalls** Low

Form RPR

3411 **1** **Orientalist**[15] 5310 2-9-7 **83** SebSanders 2 87
(Eve Johnson Houghton) *hld up in mid-div: hdwy on ins to trck ldrs over 3f out: led over 1f out: hld on gamely* **7/2**[2]

446 **2** *hd* **El Torbellino (IRE)**[8] 5509 2-8-2 **69** ow3 JohnFahy(5) 6 73
(D O'Meara) *chsd ldrs: wnt 2nd over 1f out: kpt on wl fnl f: jst hld* **16/1**

0515 **3** *3/4* **Buzz Law (IRE)**[9] 5490 2-8-3 **65** AndrewElliott 11 67
(Mrs K Burke) *chsd ldrs: effrt over 2f out: styd on ins fnl f: clsng at fin* **8/1**

1 **4** *1* **Common Touch (IRE)**[43] 4392 2-9-5 **81** PaulHanagan 9 80
(R A Fahey) *trckd ldrs: effrt 2f out: kpt on ins fnl f* **9/4**[1]

056 **4** *dht* **Tapis Libre**[13] 5352 2-7-12 **63** oh4 ow3 JamesSullivan(3) 12 62
(M W Easterby) *s.i.s: sn chsng ldrs on outside: effrt over 2f out: one pce* **50/1**

006 **6** *1 3/4* **Smart Step**[16] 5277 2-8-8 **70** RoystonFfrench 10 65
(M Johnston) *led tl over 1f out: one pce* **11/2**

4404 **7** *2 3/4* **Piccarello**[8] 5520 2-8-6 **73** AshleyMorgan(5) 7 61
(M H Tompkins) *in rr: drvn 3f out: nvr nr ldrs* **25/1**

044 **8** *1/2* **Saskia's Dream**[22] 5078 2-8-12 **74** SilvestreDeSousa 4 61
(Jane Chapple-Hyam) *s.i.s: hld up in rr: hdwy over 3f out: sn rdn and hung bdly lft over 1f out: wknd over 1f out* **4/1**[3]

0506 **9** *shd* **Grazeon Again (IRE)**[15] 5298 2-8-6 **68** PJMcDonald 3 54
(J J Quinn) *hld up in rr: effrt over 2f out: wknd fnl f* **20/1**

1m 26.49s (1.19) **Going Correction** 0.0s/f (Good) **9 Ran SP% 115.9**
Speed ratings (Par 97): **93,92,91,90,90 88,85,85,84**
toteswingers:1&2:£9.50, 1&3:£5.00, 2&3:£12.40 CSF £55.07 CT £423.48 TOTE £5.10: £1.90, £5.10, £2.40; EX 78.20 TRIFECTA Not won..
Owner Eden Racing IV **Bred** Whitsbury Manor Stud **Trained** Blewbury, Oxon
■ Stewards' Enquiry : John Fahy one-day ban: used whip with excessive frequency (Sep 19)

FOCUS
The pace didn't look strong early, the race not really beginning in earnest until after halfway.

NOTEBOOK
Orientalist has really taken off in nurseries, completing the hat-trick in gutsy style. The narrow margin of this success means the handicapper can't go overboard, while his likeable attitude is sure to continue to hold him in good stead. (op 10-3 tchd 4-1)
El Torbellino(IRE) hails from an in-form yard and found some improvement switched to nurseries, making a thriving rival pull out all the stops. There'll be weaker races than this for her to contest, and she has over a fortnight to run before she's reassessed for this. (op 20-1)
Buzz Law(IRE) possibly failed to get home on soft ground last time and was back to the sort of level she showed when winning at Newmarket without having any excuses. (op 12-1)
Common Touch(IRE)'s winning debut form over 6f here isn't any great shakes and he emerges with credit on his nursery bow, despite never looking like justifying favouritism. He was tapped a little for speed when the race really began in earnest, then kept on. He has had only two starts so it's reasonable to expect further progress. (op 2-1)
Tapis Libre ran creditably on his nursery bow as he was 4lb wrong at the weights. He stuck to his task well and it won't be hard to find weaker races than this for him from his low rating. (op 2-1)
Smart Step had contested some quite strong maidens but failed to improve switched to nurseries, having no extra after cutting out a lot of the running. (op 5-1 tchd 6-1)
Saskia's Dream failed to cut any ice, but better was clearly expected from her given her prominence in the market. Official explanation: jockey said filly hung left in the final three furlongs (op 5-1)

5785 EUROPEAN BREEDERS' FUND MAIDEN STKS 5f 89y

2:35 (2:38) (Class 3) 2-Y-O **£6,799** (£2,023; £1,011; £505) **Stalls** Centre

Form RPR

200 **1** **El Viento (FR)**[15] 5301 2-9-3 74 (b[1]) PaulHanagan 11 89
(R A Fahey) *dwlt and reminders early: sn chsng ldrs: hdwy on outer over 2f out: rdn to ld over 1f out: clr ins fnl f* **8/1**

2230 **2** *3 1/2* **Bunce (IRE)**[65] 3624 2-9-3 78 RyanMoore 2 77
(R Hannon) *chsd ldrs: rdn along 1/2-way: drvn wl over 1f out: kpt on ins fnl f: nrst fin* **5/1**[2]

2 **3** *3/4* **Valerius Maximus**[13] 5372 2-9-3 0 SilvestreDeSousa 4 74
(P F I Cole) *trckd ldrs: hdwy over 2f out: rdn to chal wl over 1f out: sn drvn and kpt on same pce* **7/4**[1]

603 **4** *2* **Forty Proof (IRE)**[25] 4960 2-9-3 72 WilliamBuick 9 67
(W J Knight) *chsd ldrs: rdn along over 2f out: sn drvn and one pce ent fnl f* **7/1**[3]

0424 **5** *1/2* **Wolf Slayer**[27] 4909 2-8-12 76 RichardKingscote 5 60
(Tom Dascombe) *led: pushed along over 2f out: rdn and hung lft over 1f out: sn hdd & wknd* **7/1**[3]

3203 **6** *1 1/2* **Rojo Boy**[5] 5626 2-9-3 76 HayleyTurner 7 60+
(D R C Elsworth) *towards rr: rdn along 1/2-way: sme hdwy fnl 2f: n.d* **5/1**[2]

0 **7** *2 3/4* **Ice Girl**[86] 2939 2-8-9 0 JamesSullivan(3) 1 46
(M W Easterby) *a towards rr* **100/1**

6 **8** *3* **Katiesister**[14] 5334 2-8-12 0 PJMcDonald 8 35
(J S Goldie) *a towards rr* **25/1**

0 **9** *1 1/2* **Christine's Gold (IRE)**[21] 5117 2-8-12 0 DavidAllan 3 30
(E J Alston) *prom: rdn along 1/2-way: sn wknd* **40/1**

4 **10** *10* **Cottam Stella**[24] 4981 2-8-12 0 TomEaves 6 —
(M Brittain) *s.i.s: a outpcd and bhd* **50/1**

63.81 secs (-0.49) **Going Correction** 0.0s/f (Good) **10 Ran SP% 115.0**
Speed ratings (Par 99): **103,97,96,93,92 89,85,80,78,62**
toteswingers:1&2:£4.60, 1&3:£3.70, 2&3:£2.40 CSF £46.03 TOTE £9.50: £2.60, £1.70, £1.50; EX 35.10 Trifecta £73.00 Pool: £951.18 - 9.63 winning units..
Owner John Nicholls Ltd/David Kilburn **Bred** Ballykilbride Stud **Trained** Musley Bank, N Yorks

FOCUS
Not a strong maiden for the track, with the second, fourth and fifth all pretty exposed.

NOTEBOOK
El Viento(FR) had been a little disappointing since his debut. He clearly took to the first-time blinkers, starting slowly but coming well clear inside the final furlong. (op 9-1)
Bunce(IRE) can't have been right at Haydock (given couple of months off since) but bounced back to form here. He is thoroughly exposed but sprint maidens do at least tend to get a bit weaker at this time of year. (tchd 6-1)
Valerius Maximus confirmed he has a fair level of ability without going on quite in the manner that might have been expected after a promising debut second at Windsor. He should still pick up a similar event before too long, though. (op 2-1 tchd 9-4 in places)
Forty Proof(IRE) ran at least as well as previously, but has had a few chances now and it will be an ordinary maiden he wins. (op 6-1 tchd 11-2)
Wolf Slayer didn't really see her race out for the second consecutive start, edging left as her challenge petered out. With the speed she shows, she has got to be worth a try at a bare 5f. (op 8-1 tchd 9-1)
Rojo Boy was almost certainly unsuited by the step back in trip, having finished third over 7f at Folkestone earlier in the week, but isn't one to be making any real excuses for. (op 9-2 tchd 11-2)

5786 CONSTANT SECURITY CLAIMING STKS 1m 2f 88y

3:10 (3:10) (Class 3) 3-Y-O+ **£6,540** (£1,946; £972; £485) **Stalls** Low

Form RPR

1206 **1** **Jo'Burg (USA)**[15] 5307 6-9-3 86 SebSanders 7 92+
(Lady Herries) *s.s: hld up in last: stdy hdwy on ins over 3f out: shkn up to ld over 1f out: rdn out* **3/1**[1]

6034 **2** *1 3/4* **Majuro (IRE)**[24] 4996 6-9-1 83 GeorgeBaker 8 86
(C F Wall) *trckd ldr: upsides over 1f out: styd on to take 2nd ins fnl f: no imp* **13/2**

0660 **3** *1 1/2* **Sohcahtoa (IRE)**[18] 5217 4-9-4 81 (b) RyanMoore 9 86
(R Hannon) *chsd ldrs: drvn 4f out: upsides over 1f out: kpt on same pce* **9/1**

3000 **4** *3 1/2* **Charlie Cool**[19] 5188 7-8-11 91 (b) JamesSullivan(3) 6 75
(Mrs R A Carr) *hld up in mid-div: effrt over 3f out: kpt on: nvr nr to chal* **4/1**[3]

6366 **5** *1* **Wiseman's Diamond (USA)**[8] 5533 5-8-4 65 PaulPickard(3) 12 66
(P T Midgley) *in rr: kpt on fnl 2f: nvr nr ldrs* **40/1**

1111 **6** *3/4* **Sunnyside Tom (IRE)**[7] 5545 6-9-5 84 PaulHanagan 3 77
(R A Fahey) *t.k.h: led: hdd over 1f out: sn wknd* **7/2**[2]

2552 **7** *3/4* **Trip The Light**[21] 5118 5-9-2 87 (v) LeeTopliss(5) 2 77
(R A Fahey) *chsd ldrs: drvn 4f out: one pce* **8/1**

5003 **8** *1* **Bold Cross (IRE)**[21] 5115 7-8-12 72 PaulMulrennan 5 67
(E G Bevan) *mid-div: effrt over 3f out: nvr a factor* **25/1**

-404 **9** *8* **Autumn Harvest**[33] 4671 6-8-11 70 (t) SilvestreDeSousa 11 50
(G A Harker) *in rr: drvn over 3f out: hung rt and wknd over 2f out: eased clsng stages* **28/1**

0300 **10** *5* **Whipma Whopma Gate (IRE)**[9] 5486 5-7-13 62 (v) NeilFarley(7) 4 36
(D Carroll) *sn chsng ldrs: lost pl 2f out* **40/1**

-654 **11** *2 1/2* **Sceilin (IRE)**[85] 2961 6-8-6 64 (t) JoeFanning 1 31
(J Mackie) *chsd ldrs: lost pl 3f out* **25/1**

0436 **12** *3 1/4* **General Tufto**[48] 4196 5-8-9 73 (b) BarryMcHugh(3) 10 31
(C Smith) *lost pl after 1f: drvn over 4f out: wknd over 2f out* **33/1**

2m 11.33s (-1.17) **Going Correction** +0.075s/f (Good) **12 Ran SP% 120.6**
Speed ratings (Par 107): **107,105,104,101,100 100,99,98,92,88 86,83**
toteswingers:1&2:£6.00, 1&3:£9.00, 2&3:£5.60 CSF £21.56 TOTE £4.00: £1.30, £2.50, £2.90; EX 24.20 Trifecta £116.00 Pool: £801.36 - 5.11 winning units..Jo'burg was claimed by J. O'Reilly for £22,000.
Owner Lady Herries **Bred** Tim Cooper **Trained** Patching, W Sussex

FOCUS
A good-class claimer, with a few pretty useful types in opposition. The pace looked a fair one and the first three were close to their recent marks.

NOTEBOOK
Jo'Burg(USA) has enjoyed a good season and is always going to be a force to be reckoned with at this level. The long straight here suited his running style well and he was firmly on top at the finish. (op 7-2)
Majuro(IRE) hasn't quite hit the same heights for Chris Wall as he did for Kevin Ryan, but there'll be races in him if kept to this level, the fact he's clearly effective over this longer trip also increasing options. (op 8-1 tchd 6-1)
Sohcahtoa(IRE) regularly runs to a pretty useful level, but he hasn't won since his juvenile days and he could only keep on at one pace. (tchd 8-1)
Charlie Cool, like a few from the yard, isn't quite in the form he was in mid-summer, as he'd have taken some beating here if he was, but this was at least a slight step up on recent efforts. (op 5-1)
Wiseman's Diamond(USA) had a bit to do at these weights and ran creditably without ever threatening.
Sunnyside Tom(IRE) was going for a five-timer, but his wins had all come over shorter and he patently failed to stay after going freely in the lead. He'll remain a major force at this level back over shorter. Official explanation: jockey said gelding ran too free (tchd 10-3 and 4-1)
Trip The Light found this trip on the sharp side. He's another who almost certainly remains in form. (op 7-1)

5787 PRESS FAMILY RACEDAY STKS (H'CAP) 6f

3:45 (3:45) (Class 2) (0-100,98) 3-Y-O+ **£11,656** (£3,468; £1,733; £865) **Stalls** Centre

Form RPR

0006 **1** **Hitchens (IRE)**[22] 5095 5-9-5 **96** GrahamGibbons 16 107+
(T D Barron) *hld up towards rr: gd hdwy over 2f out: rdn over 1f out: chal ins fnl f: drvn and kpt on to ld nr fin* **4/1**[1]

0222 **2** *nk* **Secret Witness**[15] 5285 4-8-10 **87** (b) TomMcLaughlin 13 97
(R A Harris) *a.p: cl up 2f out: rdn over 1f out: led and hung lft ins fnl f: drvn: hdd and no ex nr fin* **14/1**

2224 **3** *1* **Misplaced Fortune**[15] 5302 5-8-9 **89** Louis-PhilippeBeuzelin(3) 4 96
(N Tinkler) *in tch: hdwy 2f out: rdn over 1f out: drvn ins fnl f: kpt on* **10/1**

3510 **4** *3/4* **Joseph Henry**[15] 5302 8-8-12 **89** AdrianNicholls 1 94
(D Nicholls) *sn led: rdn and qcknd wl over 1f out: drvn ins fnl f: sn edgd lft and hdd: hld whn sltly hmpd towards fin* **16/1**

-050 **5** *nk* **Tombi (USA)**[43] 4391 6-9-3 **94** PaulMulrennan 11 98
(J Howard Johnson) *prom: rdn along 2f out: drvn over 1f out: one pce ins fnl f* **28/1**

113 **6** *3/4* **Piazza San Pietro**[15] 5302 4-8-9 **86** RyanMoore 8 87+
(A B Haynes) *hld up: hdwy over 1f out: styng on whn nt clr ent fnl f: sn swtchd lft and rdn: kpt on: nrst fin* **6/1**[2]

0050 **7** *1/2* **Thebes**[15] 5292 5-9-0 **91** GregFairley 2 91
(M Johnston) *chsd ldr: rdn 2f out: drvn over 1f out and grad wknd* **12/1**

0005 **8** *nk* **Valery Borzov (IRE)**[29] 4832 6-8-11 **88** PaulHanagan 9 87+
(R A Fahey) *in rr: hdwy 2f out: rdn over 1f out: kpt on u.p ins fnl f: nrst fin* **17/2**[3]

6004 **9** *1/2* **Abraham Lincoln (IRE)**[5] 5632 6-8-9 **86** (b[1]) FrannyNorton 7 86
(R A Harris) *dwlt: t.k.h and hld up in rr: hdwy whn nt clr run 2f out and again over 1f out: rdn and kpt on ins fnl f: hung lft: nrst fin* **16/1**

2426 **10** *3/4* **Discanti (IRE)**[15] 5302 5-8-9 **86** (t) DavidAllan 12 81
(T D Easterby) *towards rr: sme hdwy 2f out: sn rdn and hung lft: no imp* **16/1**

0330 **11** *1* **Esoterica (IRE)**[51] 4085 7-8-13 **90** (v) WilliamBuick 15 81
(J S Goldie) *dwlt and in rr: rdn along and hung lft 2f out: sme late hdwy* **16/1**

050 **12** *3/4* **Shifting Star (IRE)**[37] 4551 5-8-8 **90** (p) JohnFahy(5) 14 79
(W R Swinburn) *hld up towards rr: effrt and sme hdwy 2f out: sn rdn and n.d* **10/1**

0610 **13** *2 ¼* **Flipando (IRE)**[70] 3489 9-9-7 **98**.............................. SilvestreDeSousa 18 80
(T D Barron) *prom on wd outside: rdn 2f out: drvn and wknd over 1f out* **20/1**

1620 **14** *1* **Five Star Junior (USA)**[15] 5308 4-9-3 **94**........................... TomEaves 5 73
(Mrs L Stubbs) *hld up in tch: effrt 2f out: sn swtchd lft and rdn: n.d* **20/1**

0003 **15** *1 ¾* **Lowdown (IRE)**[10] 5442 3-9-5 **98**... JoeFanning 3 71
(M Johnston) *chsd ldrs: rdn along over 2f out: grad wknd* **18/1**

0205 **16** *6* **Ghostwing**[27] 4904 3-8-11 **90**.. HayleyTurner 17 44
(J Gallagher) *prom: rdn along over 2f out: sn wknd and eased* **28/1**

1m 10.48s (-1.42) **Going Correction** 0.0s/f (Good)
WFA 3 from 4yo+ 2lb **16** Ran SP% **122.6**
Speed ratings (Par 109): **109,108,107,106,105 104,104,103,103,102 100,99,96,95,93 85**
toteswingers:1&2:£8.50, 1&3:£7.30, 2&3:£10.30 CSF £57.72 CT £552.69 TOTE £4.50: £1.70, £3.40, £2.20, £3.00; EX 73.10 Trifecta £534.60 Pool: £1220.99 - 1.69 winning units..
Owner Laurence O'Kane **Bred** Curragh Bloodstock Agency Ltd **Trained** Maunby, N Yorks

FOCUS
A useful and competitive affair. As so often in sprint races on this course it paid to race fairly handily. The second and third set the standard.

NOTEBOOK
Hitchens(IRE) is fresher than most sprint handicappers at this time of year and built on an encouraging effort in the Great St Wilfrid and was always travelling like the winner, though the runner-up made him pull out all the stops. The penalty he picks up for this should ensure he gets in the Ayr Gold Cup. (op 9-2)
Secret Witness continues in a rich vein of form and deserves to go one better before long, though he'll edge up a little further in the weights for this. (op 16-1)
Misplaced Fortune is similar to the runner-up in that she is a most consistent sprinter, but has gone up steadily in the ratings as a result. It could be that she'll continue to find the odd one too good.
Joseph Henry bounced back to the form he showed at Goodwood, sticking on having been in the firing line throughout. (op 12-1)
Tombi(USA) is well treated if able to recapture the pick of his form. (op 25-1)
Piazza San Pietro has enjoyed a cracking time this summer, but this is a sign that the handicapper may have finally caught up with him. (tchd 11-2)
Valery Borzov(IRE) has come down to a really attractive mark and was better than the result, keeping on having been set plenty to do. Give in the ground suits him ideally and he's a horse to bear in mind when the rain arrives. One of the Ayr Gold Cup consolation races is a likely target. (op 11-1)
Abraham Lincoln(IRE)'s overall record suggests he certainly isn't one to be going overboard about but he was better than the result in first-time blinkers, short of room at a vital stage and not knocked about. Official explanation: jockey said horse hung left (op 20-1)
Discanti(IRE) Official explanation: jockey said gelding hung left throughout
Esoterica(IRE) Official explanation: jockey said gelding hung left
Shifting Star(IRE) had been much better than the result in first-time cheekpieces last time, but failed to build on it here. Official explanation: trainer said gelding was unsuited by the good to firm ground (op 12-1)

5788 WATT FENCES STKS (H'CAP) 2m 88y
4:20 (4:20) (Class 4) (0-85,85) 3-Y-0+ **£6,540** (£1,946; £972; £485) **Stalls** Low

Form RPR

2231 **1** **Simonside**[18] 5200 7-9-0 **71**.. DavidAllan 13 81
(B Ellison) *mid-div: hdwy to chse ldrs 12f out: chal over 2f out: styd on to ld last 75yds* **16/1**

1200 **2** *1* **The Last Alzao (IRE)**[16] 5278 4-9-7 **78**......................... PaulHanagan 11 87
(R A Fahey) *chsd ldrs: led 3f out: hdd and no ex ins fnl f* **11/1**

1253 **3** *3* **Rare Ruby (IRE)**[24] 4983 6-9-1 **72**................................ JoeFanning 14 77
(Jennie Candlish) *prom: effrt over 3f out: kpt on to take n.d 3rd nr fin* **16/1**

0362 **4** *nk* **Aurorian (IRE)**[26] 4933 4-10-0 **85**.. RyanMoore 7 90
(R Hannon) *hld up in rr: hdwy over 3f out: upsides over 1f out: kpt on same pce* **12/1**

6410 **5** *2* **Theola (IRE)**[39] 4467 4-9-4 **80**.................................... AshleyMorgan(5) 9 82
(M H Tompkins) *in rr: hdwy 7f out: drvn over 4f out: kpt on fnl f* **8/1**[3]

6-11 **6** *2 ¼* **Beat The Shower**[30] 4785 4-8-9 **66**.................................. FrannyNorton 2 66
(P D Niven) *mid-div: hdwy over 3f out: kpt on: nvr rchd ldrs* **7/1**[2]

441 **7** *3* **Arab League (IRE)**[24] 5011 5-9-9 **80**.......................... WilliamCarson 5 76
(R J Price) *mid-div: effrt over 3f out: nvr nr ldrs* **16/1**

-110 **8** *hd* **Markington**[39] 4467 7-9-8 **79**...............................(b) RobertWinston 12 75
(P Bowen) *s.i.s: hdwy to chse ldrs 12f out: drvn 7f out: outpcd over 3f out: no threat after* **8/1**[3]

2213 **9** *1 ¾* **Ceoil An Aith (IRE)**[10] 5444 4-9-4 **75**.................................. GregFairley 1 69
(M Johnston) *prom: drvn along 6f out: styd far side in st: wknd over 1f out* **16/1**

2611 **10** *1* **Bergonzi (IRE)**[33] 4671 6-9-10 **81**.................................. PaulMulrennan 3 73
(J Howard Johnson) *trckd ldrs: chal over 3f out: wknd over 2f out* **16/1**

0431 **11** *10* **Hawridge King**[43] 4386 8-9-2 **76**.............................. JamesMillman(3) 10 56
(W S Kittow) *hld up in rr: drvn and sme hdwy 3f out: nvr a factor: eased fnl f* **20/1**

312 **12** *5* **Wicked Daze (IRE)**[16] 5278 7-9-13 **84**.................................. TomEaves 8 58
(Miss L A Perratt) *led tl hdd & wknd 3f out* **13/2**[1]

4100 **13** *2 ½* **Callisto Moon**[11] 4405 6-10-0 **85**...............................(p) GrahamGibbons 4 56
(F J Brennan) *chsd ldrs: lost pl over 3f out* **25/1**

3336 **14** *14* **Abayaan**[30] 4785 4-9-3 **74**...(p) TomMcLaughlin 15 29
(Jane Chapple-Hyam) *chsd ldrs: lost pl over 3f out: sn bhd: t.o* **18/1**

3001 **15** *16* **Satwa Gold (USA)**[20] 5144 4-9-10 **81**.................................. SebSanders 6 16
(Stef Higgins) *mid-div: racd far side in st: hdwy to chse ldrs over 3f out: wknd 2f out: sn eased: t.o* **7/1**[2]

3m 34.36s (-0.14) **Going Correction** +0.075s/f (Good) **15** Ran SP% **119.9**
Speed ratings (Par 105): **103,102,101,100,99 98,97,97,96,95 90,88,87,80,72**
toteswingers:1&2:£54.50, 1&3:£28.30, 2&3:£45.30 CSF £180.06 CT £2865.15 TOTE £18.90: £4.30, £4.10, £4.50; EX 381.60 TRIFECTA Not won..
Owner Racing Management & Training Ltd **Bred** Keith Richardson **Trained** Norton, N Yorks

FOCUS
A fairly useful staying event which was run at a sound pace with the form likely to prove solid. The second and third set the standard.
Satwa Gold(USA) Official explanation: trainer had no explanation for the poor form shown

5789 COUNTRYWIDE FREIGHT STKS (H'CAP) 7f
4:50 (4:52) (Class 4) (0-80,80) 3-Y-0+ **£6,540** (£1,946; £972; £485) **Stalls** Low

Form RPR

4633 **1** **Rough Rock (IRE)**[7] 5561 5-8-5 **66**......................... AdamBeschizza(5) 7 75
(C A Dwyer) *towards rr: pushed along 1/2-way: hdwy on outer over 2f out: drvn over 1f out: styd on u.p fnl f to ld nr line* **20/1**

2623 **2** *hd* **Fishforcompliments**[3] 5685 6-9-5 **80**.........................(p) LeeTopliss(5) 14 88
(R A Fahey) *trckd ldrs: hdwy wl over 2f out: rdn to chal over 1f out: drvn to ld jst ins fnl f: sn hung lft: hdd nr line* **11/2**[1]

403 **3** *1 ¼* **Slikback Jack (IRE)**[33] 4670 3-8-11 **71**......................... PJMcDonald 17 74
(J A Glover) *prom: hdwy to chse ldr 3f out: rdn wl over 1f out: drvn and ch ent fnl f: kpt on same pce* **20/1**

0014 **4** *nk* **Mujaadel (USA)**[8] 5533 5-9-6 **76**.................................. PaulMulrennan 13 80+
(D Nicholls) *midfield: wd st: hdwy over 2f out: rdn over 1f out: swtchd lft and drvn ins fnl f: kpt on* **12/1**

504 **5** *¾* **Billy Dane (IRE)**[2] 5737 6-9-1 **76**...............................(v) IanBrennan(5) 16 78
(F P Murtagh) *led: clr 1/2-way: rdn 2f out: drvn and hdd jst ins fnl f: kpt on same pce* **12/1**

5151 **6** *½* **Commando Scott (IRE)**[9] 5499 9-8-5 **68**......................... NeilFarley(7) 9 69
(D Carroll) *in tch: hdwy over 2f out: rdn to chse ldrs over 1f out: drvn and kpt on same pce fnl f* **9/1**[3]

1136 **7** *1* **King Of Eden (IRE)**[9] 5480 4-9-8 **78**.................................. DavidAllan 5 76+
(E J Alston) *dwlt and towards rr: wd st: hdwy 2f out: sn rdn and kpt on fnl f: nrst fin* **7/1**[2]

001 **8** *1* **Shotley Mac**[8] 5510 6-9-10 **80**.....................................(b) FrannyNorton 12 76
(N Bycroft) *prom: rdn along 2f out: drvn and wknd ent fnl f* **16/1**

5002 **9** *½* **Summer Dancer (IRE)**[8] 5510 6-9-10 **80**......................... MickyFenton 2 74
(P T Midgley) *bhd tl sme late hdwy* **20/1**

4226 **9** *dht* **Standpoint**[36] 4603 4-9-10 **80**...................................... GrahamGibbons 15 74
(R Hollinshead) *prom: rdn along 2f out: drvn over 1f out and grad wknd* **11/1**

3261 **11** *shd* **Tevez**[12] 5386 5-8-6 **67**...(p) SophieDoyle(5) 18 61
(D Donovan) *s.i.s and in rr: wd st: hdwy over 2f out: rdn wl over 1f out: n.d* **12/1**

4153 **12** *nk* **River Falcon**[10] 5435 10-9-8 **78**.. WilliamBuick 8 71
(J S Goldie) *hld up: a in rr* **10/1**

4500 **13** *1 ½* **Istiqdaam**[8] 5510 5-8-11 **70**...(b) JamesSullivan(3) 3 59
(M W Easterby) *a in rr* **22/1**

5104 **14** *6* **Step In Time (IRE)**[29] 4850 3-8-13 **73**.............................. JoeFanning 4 46
(M Johnston) *chsd ldrs on inner: rdn along 3f out: wknd over 2f out* **18/1**

6303 **15** *8* **Elusive Sue (USA)**[18] 5199 3-9-3 **77**............................ PaulHanagan 10 28
(R A Fahey) *in tch: rdn along over 2f out: sn wknd* **10/1**

5146 **16** *9* **Sarah's Art (IRE)**[108] 2247 7-9-9 **79**...............................(t) SebSanders 11 —
(Stef Higgins) *in tch: rdn along wl over 2f out: sn wknd* **12/1**

1m 24.19s (-1.11) **Going Correction** 0.0s/f (Good)
WFA 3 from 4yo+ 4lb **16** Ran SP% **124.9**
Speed ratings (Par 105): **106,105,104,104,103 102,101,100,99,99 99,99,97,90,81 71**
toteswingers:1&2:£30.20, 1&3:£41.00, 2&3:£40.70 CSF £123.27 CT £2374.56 TOTE £24.60: £5.70, £1.80, £5.70, £3.30; EX 302.20 TRIFECTA Not won..
Owner M M Foulger **Bred** Mrs B Stroomer **Trained** Burrough Green, Cambs
■ Stewards' Enquiry : Adam Beschizza caution: used whip down the shoulder in the forehand position

FOCUS
A fair handicap. A good pace and a big field means the form is sure to hold up, though it's not a race in which any stand out as being well ahead of their marks. A surprise personal best from the winner.
Shotley Mac Official explanation: jockey said gelding had no more to give

5790 FUTURE CLEANING SERVICES APPRENTICE STKS (H'CAP) 1m 4f
5:20 (5:21) (Class 4) (0-80,80) 4-Y-0+ **£6,540** (£1,946; £972; £485) **Stalls** Centre

Form RPR

2550 **1** **Antigua Sunrise (IRE)**[18] 5217 4-9-0 **76**......................... LeeTopliss(3) 15 85
(R A Fahey) *mid-div: hdwy 3f out: edgd lft 1f out: sn led: edgd rt last 75yds: hld on towards fin* **9/1**[3]

4603 **2** *½* **Royal Straight**[13] 5355 5-8-6 **68**.................................. IanBrennan(3) 11 76
(Miss L A Perratt) *hld up in rr: hdwy to chse ldrs over 2f out: nt clr run and swtchd rt over 1f out: styd on to take 2nd last 75yds: carried rt and no ex* **33/1**

6002 **3** *1 ¾* **Dazzling Light (UAE)**[18] 5217 5-9-0 **80**......................... PaulNorton(7) 14 85
(J S Goldie) *swtchd lft after s: hld up in rr: stdy hdwy over 3f out: chsng ldrs whn nt clr run jst ins fnl f: styd on same pce last 75yds* **6/1**[2]

2544 **4** *1 ½* **Bollin Greta**[24] 4983 5-8-7 **69**...(t) JohnFahy(3) 12 72
(T D Easterby) *s.s: swtchd lft after s: hld up in rr: hdwy and swtchd ins 4f out: upsides over 1f out: one pce* **16/1**

2301 **5** *shd* **Oriental Cavalier**[58] 3860 4-9-5 **78**...........................(v) RussKennemore 3 81+
(Mark Buckley) *chsd ldrs: upsides over 1f out: kpt on same pce* **16/1**

0423 **6** *2* **Royal Trooper (IRE)**[15] 5296 4-8-11 **73**............... MichaelO'Connell(3) 5 72+
(J G Given) *led: edgd rt 1f out: sn hdd: wknd fnl 75yds* **11/1**

606 **7** *5* **Sedgwick**[8] 5529 8-8-10 **72**... DeclanCannon(3) 4 63
(S A Harris) *t.k.h: trckd ldrs: wknd over 1f out* **16/1**

1313 **8** *hd* **Peintre D'Argent (IRE)**[36] 4597 4-8-6 **70**.................... HarryBentley(5) 7 61+
(W J Knight) *chsd ldr: wknd over 1f out* **6/1**[2]

4-00 **9** *3 ¼* **Robby Bobby**[13] 5355 5-9-1 **74**.. AmyRyan 9 60
(M Johnston) *mid-div: effrt and hung lft over 2f out: wknd over 1f out* **14/1**

1421 **10** *1 ¼* **Maneki Neko (IRE)**[23] 5019 8-9-1 **74**............................ JamesSullivan 13 58
(E W Tuer) *in tch: effrt over 3f out: wknd over 2f out* **16/1**

-415 **11** *hd* **Silent Applause**[52] 4055 7-8-10 **69**.................. Louis-PhilippeBeuzelin 2 53
(Dr J D Scargill) *wnt rt s: sn drvn along: reminders and hdwy over 4f out: lost pl over 1f out* **20/1**

-044 **12** *1 ¼* **Yossi (IRE)**[14] 5333 6-8-2 **68** oh1 ow2.........................(p) SeanPalmer(7) 10 50
(R C Guest) *chsd ldrs: wknd over 2f out* **33/1**

4350 **13** *4* **Palomar (USA)**[16] 5278 8-8-13 **77**.................................... DaleSwift(5) 6 52
(B Ellison) *trckd ldrs: t.k.h: wknd over 3f out* **10/1**

0131 **14** *1 ¼* **Mistoffelees**[22] 5071 4-8-12 **78**................................... TalibHussain(7) 1 51
(L M Cumani) *bmpd s: sn chsng ldrs: drvn over 3f out: lost pl over 2f out* **3/1**[1]

2m 34.21s (1.01) **Going Correction** +0.075s/f (Good) **14** Ran SP% **121.8**
Speed ratings (Par 105): **99,98,97,96,96 95,91,91,89,88 88,87,85,84**
toteswingers:1&2:£46.10, 1&3:£11.90, 2&3:£28.40. totesuper7: Win: Not won, Place: £670.60 CSF £285.77 CT £1925.42 TOTE £9.00: £3.00, £10.00, £2.40; EX 313.30 Trifecta £532.60 Part won. Place 6 £721.06; Place 5 £157.55.
Owner David And Jackie Knaggs **Bred** Michael Morrin **Trained** Musley Bank, N Yorks
■ Stewards' Enquiry : Lee Topliss three-day ban: careless riding (Sep 19-21)

FOCUS
Another competitive handicap, this time for apprentices, with the gallop a sound one. The first four were the last four turning in. Sound form with the winner back to her best.
Dazzling Light(UAE) Official explanation: jockey said mare was denied a clear run
Silent Applause Official explanation: jockey said gelding was never travelling
Palomar(USA) Official explanation: trainer said gelding scoped badly post race
Mistoffelees Official explanation: trainer had no explanation for the poor form shown
T/Jkpt: Not won. T/Plt: £2,505.20 to a £1 stake. Pool:£124,060.49 - 36.15 winning tickets T/Qpdt: £217.40 to a £1 stake. Pool:£9,313.69 - 31.70 winning tickets WG

5791 - 5798a (Foreign Racing) - See Raceform Interactive

5672 LONGCHAMP (R-H)

Sunday, September 5

OFFICIAL GOING: Turf: good

5799a PRIX LA ROCHETTE (GROUP 3) (2YO) (TURF) 7f

12:35 (12:00) 2-Y-O **£35,398** (£14,159; £10,619; £7,079; £3,539)

RPR

1 **My Name Is Bond (FR)**35 2-8-11 0 ChristopheSoumillon 6 111+
(J-C Rouget, France) *bkmarker fr s: travelling easily: swtchd outside to chal 1 1/2f out: cruised to chal ldrs 1f out: swept to ld 100 yds out: sn clr: winning comf* **7/2**2

2 1 1/2 **Hung Parliament (FR)**21 5133 2-8-11 0 DavyBonilla 1 107
(Tom Dascombe) *racd in 2nd sn after s: rdn to chal ldr over 1 1/2f out: led briefly 1f out: sn chal and hdd 150yds out: r.o wl to keep 2nd on line* **7/1**

3 hd **Maiguri (IRE)**53 4036 2-8-11 0 JohanVictoire 4 107
(C Baillet, France) *racd in 5th: travelling smoothly: rdn to chal for ld 1 1/2f out: u.p fnl 100yds: no ex clsng stages* **6/4**1

4 2 1/2 **Al Hazim (CAN)**33 2-8-11 0 AnthonyCrastus 5 101
(J-L Pelletan, France) *led: stl in front 2f out: hdd 1 1/2fout: r.o* **9/2**3

5 2 1/2 **King David (FR)**21 5133 2-8-11 0 GeraldMosse 3 94
(M Boutin, France) *racd in 4th on rail: rdn 2f out: no ex fnl f* **20/1**

6 3/4 **The Long Game**37 4538 2-8-11 0 MartinDwyer 2 92
(B J Meehan) *racd in 3rd on settling: rdn at 1/2-way: u.p 2f out: fnd no ex: fdd fnl f* **5/1**

1m 20.5s (-0.20) **Going Correction** +0.20s/f (Good) **6** Ran SP% **114.3**
Speed ratings: **109,107,107,104,101 100**
WIN (incl. 1 euro stake): 4.10. PLACES: 2.30, 3.80. SF: 28.40.
Owner Daniel-Yves Treves **Bred** Lord Huntingdon **Trained** Pau, France

FOCUS
This race is usually strong for the grade and the form is rated positively.

NOTEBOOK
My Name Is Bond(FR) won this in facile style. His trainer reckons he is one of the best 2-y-os in his stable and he will next be seen out in the Jean-Luc Lagardere.
Hung Parliament(FR) ran a brave race hand his trainer was delighted, as he says the colt is still immature. He will now be put away with next season in mind.
The Long Game had every possible chance but failed to pick up early in the straight when put under pressure.

5800a PRIX DE LUTECE (GROUP 3) (3YO) (TURF) 1m 7f

1:35 (12:00) 3-Y-O **£35,398** (£14,159; £10,619; £7,079; £3,539)

RPR

1 **Brigantin (USA)**49 4186 3-8-9 0 Pierre-CharlesBoudot 2 98
(A Fabre, France) *racd in last: 2f out: swtchd to wd outside: qcknd wl: chal for ld 1f out: r.o wl to take ld 100yds out: comf* **5/1**3

2 3/4 **Shamanova (IRE)**24 5138 3-8-8 0 Christophe-PatriceLemaire 4 96
(A De Royer-Dupre, France) *racd in 5th: rdn to go 3rd arnd fnl turn: qcknd wl to grab ld 1f out: hdd 100yds oiut: r.o wl* **11/8**1

3 4 **Permit**82 3-8-9 0 (b) MaximeGuyon 1 92
(A Fabre, France) *racd in 3rd: dropped bk to 5th early in st: u.p 2f out: hrd rdn fnl f: r.o to go 3rd fnl strides* **4/1**2

4 snk **Le Larron (IRE)**21 5136 3-8-11 0 GeraldMosse 5 94
(A De Royer-Dupre, France) *racd 2nd for first 6f then sent to ld: stl in front u.p 2f out: sn hdd: styd on: lost 3rd fnl strides* **4/1**2

5 4 **Amarak**21 5136 3-8-9 0 (b) OlivierPeslier 6 87
(F Head, France) *led: hdd after 6f: racd in 2nd: rdn 2f out: began to weaken 1f out: fdd* **16/1**

6 dist **Monterrey (IRE)**31 3-8-9 0 MickaelBarzalona 3 —
(A Fabre, France) *racd in 4th: hrd rdn early in st: wknd* **12/1**

3m 10.22s (-5.78) **6** Ran SP% **112.3**
WIN (incl. 1 euro stake): 3.20 (Brigantin combined with Permit and Monterrey). PLACES: 3.20, 1.40. SF: 22.90.
Owner Mme Andre Fabre **Bred** Team Valor, Mme A Fabre & Denali Stud & Partners **Trained** Chantilly, France

NOTEBOOK
Brigantin(USA) had been disqualified after passing the post first in a Listed race at Vichy on his previous start, after it was discovered he carried the wrong weight. The Swiss Derby winner was given a patient ride before hitting the front at the furlong marker. He looks almost certain to turn out for the Group 2 Prix Chaudenay at the Arc meeting.
Shamanova(IRE) has been second in her last three races now, but she was meeting colts for the first time. She will now take her chance against the winner in the Chaudenay.

5801a PRIX DU MOULIN DE LONGCHAMP (GROUP 1) (3YO+) (TURF) 1m

2:43 (12:00) 3-Y-O+ **£227,548** (£91,035; £45,517; £22,738; £11,389)

RPR

1 **Fuisse (FR)**21 5134 4-9-2 0 StephanePasquier 4 120+
(Mme C Head-Maarek, France) *(hld up s after getting loose for considerable time) bkmarker fr s: hrd rdn early in st: split horses 1 1/2f out: qcknd wl u.p 1f out: r.o strly to ld fnl strides* **14/1**

2 hd **Rio De La Plata (USA)**16 5274 5-9-2 0 MickaelBarzalona 1 119
(Saeed Bin Suroor) *racd in 2nd: chal for ld 1f out: tk ld 100yds out: hdd on line* **16/1**

3 hd **Siyouni (FR)**63 3719 3-8-11 0 Christophe-PatriceLemaire 2 118
(A De Royer-Dupre, France) *led: qcknd wl ent fnl f: hdd 100yds out: r.o wl* **7/1**3

4 1 1/2 **Paco Boy (IRE)**21 5134 5-9-2 0 RichardHughes 5 116+
(R Hannon) *racd in 3rd: no room to chal between horses 1f out: swtchd towards rail to make chal 150yds out: stdd after finding no room 100yds out: r.o again clsng stages* **10/11**1

5 1 **Lope De Vega (IRE)**63 3719 3-8-11 0 MaximeGuyon 3 112
(A Fabre, France) *settled in 5th: rdn 1 1/2f out: no ex fnl f* **5/2**2

6 2 **Via Medici (IRE)**24 5139 3-8-8 0 Francois-XavierBertras 6 105
(F Rohaut, France) *racd in 4th: on outside: rdn 2f out: r.o one pce fnl f* **25/1**

1m 37.83s (97.83) **Going Correction** +0.20s/f (Good)
WFA 3 from 4yo+ 5lb **6** Ran SP% **109.9**
Speed ratings: **110,109,109,108,107 105**
WIN (incl. 1 euro stake): 10.90. PLACES: 4.40, 4.90. SF: 91.80.
Owner Haras Du Quesnay **Bred** Alec & Ghislaine Head **Trained** Chantilly, France

FOCUS
First run in 1957, the list of previous winners of the Prix du Moulin contains some of the greatest milers to have graced the turf during that time such as Miesque, Soviet Star, Polish Precedent, Rock Of Gibraltar and Goldikova, to name but a few. This year's renewal may not have been the strongest, however, with only one European Classic winner in the line-up and no Goldikova this time. The early pace was modest to boot. The third sets the standard and Fuisse is progressive.

NOTEBOOK
Fuisse(FR), who was very much on his toes, got loose going to post after having twice unshipped Stephane Pasquier and delayed the race by 15 minutes. It's hard to know how much the delay would have affected these horses but, despite causing all the trouble, Fuisse himself somehow managed to go and win. He had proved himself a progressive colt in lesser Pattern company earlier in the season, but had 6l to find with Paco Boy on Jacques le Marois running. However, once under way he travelled kindly in last place and once asked for his effort starting up the home straight, produced a smart turn of foot to floor the placed horses in the dying strides. He is obviously a classy colt, but how much his quirks will affect his career from now on remains to be seen. He has options but may well come over to Newmarket for the Champion Stakes.
Rio De La Plata(USA) won the Lagardere here as a two-year-old and was runner-up in the Poulains at three, but his form over the last couple of seasons - including his game success over Rainbow Peak in the Strensall at York last month - left him with plenty to find against rivals of this calibre. However, he ran a blinder and much of that was due to him always being in a brilliant position in a steadily run race. He tried very hard to get past the leader over the last 2f, but no sooner had he achieved it well inside the last furlong than he was mugged by the winner. This was a fine effort, but it remains to be seen if he can still produce it at this level in a truly run race. As he likes the track, connections may have a race such as the Prix Daniel Wildenstein in mind for him at the Arc meeting.
Siyouni(FR) hasn't reached the heights this year that seemed likely when he took the Lagardere last autumn, and he was beaten fair and square by Dick Turpin in the Prix Jean Prat last time. However, he was given a fine front-running ride here by Lemaire, who was able to set the pace he wanted. He kept on pulling out more when challenged, but was finally swamped by the front pair around 50 yards from the line.
Paco Boy(IRE) has been in the form of his life this year, winning the Lockinge and losing little in defeat in both the Queen Anne, when beaten a neck by Goldikova, and in the Jacques le Marois, where the very soft ground made it just too much of a test. He didn't have the French mare to worry about this time and the good ground was more suitable, so the decision to send him here rather than contest Saturday's Betfred Sprint Cup looked the right one, but even the best-laid plans can go horribly wrong. He travelled extremely well behind the two leaders throughout, but was trapped in a pocket starting up the home straight as his jockey started to ask him for maximum effort. Having been unable to find a gap, his rider made one last desperate attempt to get up the inside of Siyouni around a furlong out, but that route soon slammed shut and, having been hampered, he had to settle for fourth. He would obviously have been much closer with a clear run, though it's far from certain that he would have won.
Lope De Vega(IRE) looked a special colt when completing the Poulains-Jockey Club double earlier in the season, which made his flop in the Jean Prat (over 8l behind Siyouni) so hard to take, though he can get edgy and nervous before his races. He seemed to take the delay well enough, if perhaps getting a little warm, but he pulled too hard once the race began and when asked for an effort the response was limited. He still has it all to prove.
Via Medici(IRE) is a progressive filly, but this was a totally different test compared to winning a three-year-old fillies' Group 3 at Deauville last month and, although she tried to put in an effort down the wide outside after turning in, it was never enough.

5802a PRIX DU PIN (GROUP 3) (3YO+) (TURF) 7f

3:15 (12:00) 3-Y-O+ **£35,398** (£14,159; £10,619; £7,079; £3,539)

RPR

1 **Sahpresa (USA)**81 3067 5-8-11 0 ChristopheSoumillon 6 113
(Rod Collet, France) *settled in 5th along rail: qcknd wl 1 1/2f out whn swtchd to centre of trck: swept into ld 100yds out: comf* **6/1**

2 1 1/2 **Dalghar (FR)**40 4457 4-9-5 0 Christophe-PatriceLemaire 7 117
(A De Royer-Dupre, France) *led: qcknd wl in st and stl in front tl ct 100yds out: r.o wl* **7/4**1

3 1 **Evaporation (FR)**35 4639 3-8-8 0 OlivierPeslier 3 105
(C Laffon-Parias, France) *racd in 3rd: r.o wl in st: styd on wl u.p fnl f* **5/1**3

4 2 1/2 **Colonial (IRE)**92 2778 3-8-11 0 MaximeGuyon 2 102
(A Fabre, France) *racd midfield on rail: rdn 1 1/2f out: r.o wl fnl f* **20/1**

5 1 1/2 **Desert Ocean (IRE)**15 6-9-1 0 ThierryThulliez 5 100
(G Collet, France) *w.w in rr: rdn early in st: r.o wl fnl f* **18/1**

6 shd **Flash Dance (IRE)**28 4885 4-8-11 0 (p) JohanVictoire 9 95
(H-A Pantall, France) *racd in 2nd fr s: pulling freely: hrd rdn to chal for ld 1 1/2f out: no ex ins fnl f* **12/1**

7 2 **Sweet Hearth (USA)**15 4-8-11 0 GeraldMosse 8 90
(A De Royer-Dupre, France) *bkmarker fr s: rdn early in st: no threat fnl f* **9/2**2

8 20 **Charming Woman (IRE)**120 1944 3-8-13 0 MircoDemuro 4 40
(Vittorio Caruso, Italy) *racd in 6th fr s: failed to qckn in st* **16/1**

1m 19.67s (-1.03) **Going Correction** +0.20s/f (Good)
WFA 3 from 4yo+ 4lb **8** Ran SP% **109.1**
Speed ratings: **113,111,110,107,105 105,103,80**
WIN (incl. 1 euro stake): 6.30. PLACES: 1.80, 1.30, 2.10. DF: 6.30. SF: 19.70.
Owner Douglas Owen McIntyre **Bred** Douglas McIntyre **Trained** France

NOTEBOOK
Sahpresa(USA) impressed enormously when taking this trial for the Prix de la Foret, as she swept past long-time leader Dalghar at the furlong marker and went on to win effortlessly. She had not been seen out since running down the field in the Windsor Forest Stakes at Royal Ascot, after which she had a lung infection, but was clearly back to her best. She could go for the Foret now or try and win the Sun Chariot for a second time, there is also the Prix Daniel Wildenstein to be taken into consideration. A lot will depend on the ground as she must have good going to show her best.
Dalghar(FR) put up a good performance from the front as he was giving 8lb to the winner. It is now likely that he will go on to the Foret.

5781 VELIEFENDI

Sunday, September 5

OFFICIAL GOING: Turf: soft

5803a INTERNATIONAL TOPKAPI TROPHY (GROUP 2) (3YO+) (TURF) 1m

1:30 (12:00) 3-Y-O+ **£238,938** (£95,575; £47,787; £23,893)

RPR

1 **Pressing (IRE)**24 5009 7-9-6 0 NeilCallan 1 119
(M A Jarvis) *broke wl: pushed along to keep position and racd 3rd on heels of ldrs: wnt 2nd st: rdn 2f out: led u.p 1f out: swvd rt: r.o wl* **13/20**1

2 1/2 **Dream Eater (IRE)**24 5009 5-9-6 0 (t) JimmyFortune 9 118
(A M Balding) *hld up towards rr: 10th st (over 2f out): short of room but rdn and r.o ins fnl f: swtchd ins 1f out: fin wl: jst failed* **51/20**2

3 1 ½ **Mabait**42 4412 4-9-6 0 KierenFallon 8 115
(L M Cumani) *outpcd early: settled towards rr: 7th 3f out: sn pushed along: 4th 2f out: r.o u.p* **107/20**

4 hd **Silverside (USA)**14 4-9-6 0 JulienGrosjean 3 114
(M Delcher-Sanchez, Spain) *led: rdn 2f out: hdd 1f out: no ex* **107/10**

5 1 **Invincible Son (IRE)**42 4-9-6 0 OzcanYildirim 4 112
(E Sogutlu, Turkey) *racd in 4th: pushed along 2 1/2f out: rdn 2f out: kpt on at one pce* **69/10**

6 2 ½ **Invisible Man**37 4537 4-9-6 0 (b) TedDurcan 7 106
(Saeed Bin Suroor) *hld up: 9th st: rdn 2f out: no imp* **51/10**

7 3 ½ **Kurtiniadis (IRE)**21 7-9-6 0 (b) SelimKaya 2 98
(S Kulak, Turkey) *in rr: last turning for home: sn rdn : styd on past btn horses fnl f* **51/20**2

8 1 ½ **Deha (TUR)**21 4-9-6 0 HalisKaratas 6 95
(E Sengel, Turkey) *racd in midfield: 8th 3f out: pushed along st: rdn 2f out: n.d* **23/5**3

9 3 **Frozen Power (IRE)**28 4888 3-8-13 0 (p) AhmedAjtebi 10 86
(Mahmood Al Zarooni) *settled in middle of pack: 7th 3f out: rdn st: nt qckn* **51/10**

10 2 **Hayri Baba (TUR)**21 4-9-6 0 (b) NurettinSen 5 83
(E Sengel, Turkey) *pushed along fr s to run 5th: rdn 2 1/2f out: wknd fnl f* **128/10**

11 2 ½ **Starfist (TUR)**32 4-9-6 0 (b) SadettinBoyraz 11 77
(E Yilmaz, Turkey) *pressed ldr: rdn over 2f out: dropped out fnl 300yds* **14/1**

1m 36.04s (0.71)
WFA 3 from 4yo+ 5lb 11 Ran SP% **218.5**
PARI-MUTUEL (all including 1Turkish lira stakes): WIN: 1.65; PLACE (first two): 1.45, 1.95; DF 3.60; SF 5.80.
Owner Gary A Tanaka **Bred** Agricola Del Parco **Trained** Newmarket, Suffolk

NOTEBOOK
Pressing(IRE) completed a hat-trick in this race, leading home a British-trained 1-2-3 with a hugely popular victory in the richly endowed Group 2 event. His success sparked scenes of jubilation among an enthusiastic Istanbul crowd, who have taken him to their hearts after four successive visits to the nation's showpiece racing occasion. Settled just off the pace in perfect stalking position by Callan, he was asked for his effort just after turning for home and took a couple of lengths out of his rivals at the furlong marker in what was the decisive move, before idling in the closing stages. Unless he gets a position as a stallion there's no reason why he won't come back again.
Dream Eater(IRE), runner-up to Pressing in this last season, repeated the feat. He missed the kick and was dropped in towards the rear before moving quickly through the field after turning for home. However, his closing effort was unavailing as he was always being held by his old rival.
Mabait looks set for a winter stint at the Dubai Carnival after a solid effort. He was been beaten only by two much more experienced horses who are well used to travelling and is still improving. He looks just the sort of horse for Dubai as he has a great turn of foot. The ground here was a bit loose for him.
Invisible Man was settled off the pace and failed to get into contention.
Frozen Power(IRE) settled well enough but failed to pick up under pressure.

5804a INTERNATIONAL BOSPHORUS CUP (GROUP 2) (3YO+) (TURF) 1m 4f
3:30 (12:00) 3-Y-O+ £159,292 (£63,716; £31,858; £15,929)

RPR

1 **Indian Days**40 4455 5-9-6 0 AlanMunro 4 117
(J G Given) *hld up towards rr: 7th st (jst over 2f out) and strly rdn: r.o wl on outside fr 1 1/2f out to ld fnl 110yds: styd on strly* **113/10**

2 2 ½ **Sri Putra**37 4535 4-9-6 0 PhilipRobinson 7 113
(M A Jarvis) *settled towards rr: hdwy 3f and tk 4th on fnl turn: sn u.str driving: rdn 2f out but tk time to respond: styd on ins fnl f to grab 2nd cl home* **27/20**2

3 nk **Buzzword**49 4184 3-8-10 0 (p) AhmedAjtebi 2 112
(Mahmood Al Zarooni) *a.p: wnt 2nd 2 1/2f out: rdn 2f out: r.o to ld appr fnl f: hdd 110yds out: no ex and wknd cl home* **17/20**1

4 1 ½ **Halicarnassus (IRE)**16 5274 6-9-6 0 NeilCallan 5 111
(M R Channon) *racd in midfield towards outside: wnt 3rd 3f out: sn pushed along: nt qckn fnl 2f* **7/2**

5 3 **Baschar**49 4184 3-8-10 0 JiriPalik 3 105
(M G Mintchev, Germany) *racd in midfield: lost pl 4f out and dropped to last: hdwy 2 1/2f out: styd on at one pce tl r.o ins fnl f* **134/10**

6 2 ½ **Adonise (TUR)**23 4-9-6 0 (b) SelimKaya 9 102
(Y Demir, Turkey) *racd towards rr: prog to go 5th 2 1/2f out: sn rdn and fdd* **59/20**

7 ½ **Estejo (GER)**42 6-9-6 0 KierenFallon 8 101
(R Rohne, Germany) *chsd ldr: wnt on 4f out: 4 l clr st: sn rdn: tiring and hdd appr fnl f: wknd qckly* **57/10**

8 17 ½ **Inspector (TUR)**23 6-9-6 0 (b) HalisKaratas 1 73
(A Sivgin, Turkey) *racd in 3rd: steadily lost pls fr 4f out: wknd qckly on turn for home* **27/10**3

9 31 **Doganhan (TUR)**28 4-9-6 0 (bt) DenizYildiz 6 23
(A Sivgin, Turkey) *rdn along to ld: hdd appr 4f out: wknd qckly* **27/10**3

2m 29.07s (0.27)
WFA 3 from 4yo+ 9lb 9 Ran SP% **228.2**
PARI-MUTUEL (all including 1Turkish lira stakes): WIN: 12.30; no place betting; DF 32.45; SF 64.95.
Owner D J Fish **Bred** Mrs C Regalado-Gonzalez **Trained** Willoughton, Lincs

NOTEBOOK
Indian Days provided James Given with the most lucrative victory of his career. Having tried to win a Group race in England he was always found a bit wanting, so had gone back to handicapping this season. However, he won this like an improving sort and might go to Hong Kong before Christmas if he gets invited. Official explanation: provided James Given with the most lucrative victory of his career. Having tried to win a Group race in England he was always found a bit wanting, so had gone back to handicapping this season. However, he won this like an improving sort and might go to Hong Kong before Christmas if he gets invited.
Sri Putra, whose trainer won the Topkapi Trophy with Pressing, responded well to pressure in the straight and was keeping on steadily at the finish.
Buzzword, taking on his elders, was never away but his compatriots proved too strong in the closing stages.
Halicarnassus(IRE), who won the race in 2009 under today's winning rider, finished fourth after holding every chance in the straight.

5739 BADEN-BADEN (L-H)
Sunday, September 5

OFFICIAL GOING: Turf: good

5805a PREIS DER BADEN-BADENER HOTELLERIE & GASTRONOMIE (LISTED RACE) (3YO FILLIES) (TURF) 1m 2f
3:00 (12:00) 3-Y-O £10,619 (£4,424; £1,769; £884)

RPR

1 **Indian Breeze (GER)**42 3-8-10 0 ow1 ADeVries 5 93
(J Hirschberger, Germany) **79/10**

2 nk **Hasay**42 3-8-11 0 FilipMinarik 9 93
(P Schiergen, Germany) **175/10**

3 2 **Power Eva (GER)**84 3-9-2 0 WPanov 6 94
(H J Groschel, Germany) **202/10**

4 1 ¼ **Good Hope (GER)**285 7508 3-8-9 0 IoritzMendizabal 12 85
(P Schiergen, Germany) **34/1**

5 nse **Totally Ours**25 4957 3-9-0 0 FrankieDettori 1 89
(W R Muir) *prom in 5th along rail pulling freely: smooth prog arnd fnl turn: r.o wl: wknd fnl f* **31/10**1

6 1 **Salve Aurora (GER)** 3-8-9 0 AStarke 11 82
(P Schiergen, Germany) **19/5**2

7 3 ½ **Warsaw Ballet (CAN)**35 4640 3-8-11 0 EPedroza 8 77
(A Wohler, Germany) **48/10**3

8 2 **All I Want**67 3-8-9 0 AHelfenbein 2 71
(Andreas Lowe, Germany) **193/10**

9 2 **Prem Ramya (GER)** 3-8-11 0 MSuerland 7 69
(W Figge, Germany) **187/10**

10 1 **Delia Eria (IRE)** 3-9-6 0 JulienAuge 10 76
(E J O'Neill, France) **78/10**

11 shd **Singuna (GER)**21 3-8-11 0 JBojko 4 67
(A Wohler, Germany) **223/10**

12 4 **Sailor Moon (IRE)**101 3-9-0 0 FabriceVeron 3 62
(H-A Pantall, France) **123/10**

13 2 **Intarsia (GER)**28 3-9-4 0 THellier 13 62
(M Munch, Germany) **43/5**

2m 4.70s (-0.29) 13 Ran SP% **130.3**
WIN (incl. 10 euro stake): 89. PLACES: 32, 49, 61. SF: 2,172..
Owner Gestut Schlenderhan **Bred** Gestut Schlenderhan **Trained** Germany

NOTEBOOK
Totally Ours, who has been running well at this level in Britain without threatening to win, raced too keenly early and, after threatening on the home turn, paid for her earlier exertions in the closing stages.

5806a GROSSER MERCEDES-BENZ PREIS VON BADEN (GROUP 1) (3YO+) (TURF) 1m 4f
3:40 (3:51) 3-Y-O+ £132,743 (£53,097; £22,123; £13,274)

RPR

1 **Night Magic (GER)**42 4418 4-9-3 0 FilipMinarik 7 114
(W Figge, Germany) *bkmarker fr s: qcknd wl to hit the front jst over 2f out: r.o strly to easily hold off late chals* **22/5**3

2 1 ¾ **Quijano (GER)**21 5132 8-9-6 0 AStarke 3 114
(P Schiergen, Germany) *racd in 3rd pulling freely: mde gd prog early in st: r.o wl fr 1 1/2f out: no threat to wnr* **92/10**

3 1 ¾ **Cavalryman**19 5186 4-9-6 0 FrankieDettori 6 111
(Saeed Bin Suroor) *trckd the pce fr s: hrd rdn early in st: r.o fnl f to claim 3rd on line* **13/10**1

4 nse **Northern Glory**21 7-9-6 0 MSuerland 2 111
(W Figge, Germany) *pcemaker for wnr: set str pce: r.o wl: hdd jst over 2f out: r.o wl: lost 3rd on line* **248/10**

5 2 **Allied Powers (IRE)**50 4164 5-9-6 0 IoritzMendizabal 5 108
(M L W Bell) *racd in 4th: gd prog arnd fnl turn: threatened briefly early in st: no ex fnl 2f* **8/1**

6 hd **Wiener Walzer (GER)**50 4164 4-9-6 0 ADeVries 1 108
(J Hirschberger, Germany) *prom bhd ldr: hrd rdn but no rspnse in st: fdd* **5/2**2

7 1 ½ **Russian Tango (GER)**49 4184 3-8-11 0 EPedroza 4 105
(A Wohler, Germany) *a towards rr: nvr figured* **56/10**

2m 32.73s (-0.73)
WFA 3 from 4yo+ 9lb 7 Ran SP% **130.5**
WIN (incl. 10 euro stake): 54. PLACES: 15, 20, 15. SF: 448.
Owner Stall Salzburg **Bred** Gestut Etzean **Trained** Germany

NOTEBOOK
Night Magic(GER) came from last to first land a first prize of over £130,000. A brave second to the Mark Johnston-trained Lady Jane Digby in a Group 1 at Munich on her last start, she went one better in scintillating fashion, quickening past all six of her rivals for a decisive victory. The Prix Von Europa could be next.
Quijano(GER), a veteran these days, showed he can still compete at this level despite being keen early.
Cavalryman was sent-off a warm order under Dettori, but was caught a little flat-footed as the pace quickened rounding the home turn, and could only plug on at the one pace to take third. His disappointed jockey felt the colt had performed below par.
Allied Powers(IRE) raced in midfield but was unable to land a blow in the closing stages.

5579 BATH (L-H)
Monday, September 6

OFFICIAL GOING: Good to firm (firm in places; 8.8)
Wind: Brisk behind Weather: Low cloud

5807 WESTERN DAILY PRESS NURSERY 1m 5y
2:10 (2:11) (Class 5) (0-75,74) 2-Y-O £2,201 (£655; £327; £163) Stalls Low

Form RPR

5003 1 **Dew Reward (IRE)**3 5709 2-7-12 51 oh1 CathyGannon 5 54
(Eve Johnson Houghton) *in tch: rdn over 3f out and sn outpcd: rallied u.p over 1f out: kpt on ins fnl f: led fnl 20yds* **3/1**1

023 2 ½ **Fly By White (IRE)**24 5029 2-9-3 70 PatDobbs 7 72
(R Hannon) *in tch: rdn 3f out and outpcd over 2f out: rallied u.p fnl f and fin wl to take 2nd last strides: nt pce of wnr* **7/2**2

The Form Book, Raceform Ltd, Compton, RG20 6NL

3643 **3** *shd* **Sheila's Star (IRE)**[14] 5374 2-8-11 **64** LiamKeniry 2 66
(J S Moore) *chsd ldrs: rdn 4f out: wnt 2nd 2f out: chal over 1f out and pushed rt: slt ld fnl 120yds: hdd and no ex fnl 20yds: lost 2nd last strides* **7/1**

1050 **4** *¾* **Whodathought (IRE)**[17] 5256 2-9-1 **68** (b[1]) RichardHughes 1 68
(R Hannon) *in rr: rdn and one pce fr 3f out: gd hdwy on ins fnl f: fin wl: nt rch ldng duo* **9/2**[3]

3060 **5** *¾* **Memorabilia**[11] 5452 2-9-0 **67** GregFairley 8 65
(M Johnston) *led 5 l clr 5f out: stl clr over 3f out: rdn over 2f out: edgd rt and jnd 1f out: hdd fnl 120yds: sn wknd* **12/1**

0015 **6** *2 ¾* **Water Ice**[33] 4701 2-9-7 **74** RichardKingscote 6 66
(Tom Dascombe) *sn chsng ldr: rdn and dropped to cl 3rd 2f out: one pce whn pushed rt 1f out: wknd fnl f* **7/1**

0204 **7** *¾* **Shaabek (IRE)**[28] 4911 2-8-13 **66** SamHitchcott 4 57
(M R Channon) *in rr: rdn over 3f out: styd on fnl f: nvr any threat* **9/1**

0006 **8** *6* **Cantonese Cat (IRE)**[26] 4962 2-8-1 **57**....(b[1]) Louis-PhilippeBeuzelin(3) 3 34
(B J Meehan) *s.i.s: rdn thrght and nvr travelling* **16/1**

1m 40.05s (-0.75) **Going Correction** -0.20s/f (Firm) **8** Ran SP% **114.0**
Speed ratings (Par 95): **95,94,94,93,92 90,89,83**
toteswingers:1&2:£2.90, 1&3:£4.20, 2&3:£3.20 CSF £13.50 CT £66.41 TOTE £4.10: £2.40, £1.10, £1.40; EX 14.50.
Owner Mrs R F Johnson Houghton **Bred** Tim Hyde Jnr **Trained** Blewbury, Oxon
■ Stewards' Enquiry : Liam Keniry caution: used whip with excessive frequency

FOCUS
The track had taken 3.5 mm of rain in the last 24 hours, but the forecast heavy rain had not arrived by the time of the first race. With the strong tail-wind and a willing front-runner, the time was decent in this moderate nursery. The winner did not need to replicate his Brighton improvment.

NOTEBOOK
Dew Reward(IRE) was well backed and showed that his recent much-improved third at Brighton, following a gelding operation, was no flash in the pan, displaying battling qualities to take this competitive nursery from 1lb out of the handicap. He greatly appreciated the step up to a mile and, after looking to be in trouble at the 3f pole, went bravely between horses inside the final furlong to get on top. Beaten in a seller on his penultimate outing, he's on the upgrade. (op 4-1)
Fly By White(IRE) ◆ was the main rival to the winner in the betting market. She ran a very similar race to that one, struggling for a change of gear 3f out and then staying on well late on to grab second near the line. It was her nursery debut and this half-sister to a winner over 1m 4f had no problem with the trip on this stiffish track. She should break her duck before long. (tchd 10-3)
Sheila's Star(IRE) was prominent in the chasing pack, and was closing under pressure when pushed right by the weakening leader hanging at the furlong pole. She flashed her tail under pressure, but it would be harsh to accuse her of not trying. Her consistency is admirable, but the assessor will not be easing her after another sound effort. (op 6-1)
Whodathought(IRE), in the first-time headgear, was backed late on having drifted in the early market moves. He looked like finishing nearer last when coming under pressure at halfway, but made good late headway without quite looking like reaching the leaders. This was much his best effort in a nursery, but one has a feeling that the way the race was run slightly flattered him. (op 5-1 tchd 13-2)
Memorabilia set a searching gallop and had every rival in trouble 3f out. He hung right when running out of gas, but this is more like the ability he showed earlier in the season at Doncaster. (op 11-1)
Water Ice is a gassy type, who is taken down early and led around at the start. He led the chasing group and was trying to mount a challenge when slightly hampered at the furlong pole. He needs to drop a bit in the weights if he is going to take a nursery. (op 6-1)
Shaabek(IRE) could never land a blow, and this has to go down a disappointing. (op 8-1)
Cantonese Cat(IRE) was on his toes in the stalls in his first time headgear. He was soon off the bridle and never competitive. Official explanation: jockey said colt missed the break (tchd 20-1)

5808 EVENING POST MAIDEN AUCTION STKS 5f 11y
2:40 (2:41) (Class 6) 2-Y-O **£1,554** (£462; £231; £115) **Stalls** Centre

Form RPR

03 **1** **Owain (USA)**[28] 4909 2-8-3 0 AdamBeschizza(5) 2 74+
(C A Dwyer) *rrd stalls: slowly away and lost 4 l s: sn rcvrd and in tch 3f out: hdwy on ins 2f out: chal 1f out: drvn to ld ins fnl f: styd on wl* **7/2**[1]

43 **2** *1 ¼* **Imogen Louise (IRE)**[21] 5147 2-8-7 0 CathyGannon 10 69
(D Haydn Jones) *sn chsng ldrs on outer: chal fr 2f out tl slt ld over 1f out: hdd ins fnl f: kpt on but nt pce of wnr* **4/1**[2]

002 **3** *2 ½* **Indian Shuffle (IRE)**[38] 4528 2-9-0 68 RobertWinston 5 67
(J G Portman) *led 1f: led again over 2f out: sn jnd: narrowly hdd appr fnl f: styd on same pce* **8/1**

204 **4** *1 ¼* **Royalorien**[17] 5255 2-8-12 71 JimCrowley 1 60
(W J Knight) *chsd ldrs: nt clr run and swtchd rt over 1f out: kpt on same pce ins fnl f* **7/2**[1]

026 **5** *3 ¼* **Poetically**[10] 5465 2-8-8 66 RichardKingscote 4 44
(J G Portman) *in tch: rdn and outpcd 2f out: styd on again fnl f: nvr any threat* **8/1**

0 **6** *nse* **Kingfisher Blue (IRE)**[41] 4460 2-9-3 0 FergusSweeney 8 53
(J A Osborne) *pushed rt s: in rr but in tch: nt clr run 2f out: styd on same pce* **12/1**

60 **7** *nk* **Shutupandrive**[17] 5255 2-8-3 0 DavidProbert 7 38
(M D I Usher) *wnt rt s: chsd ldrs and upsides over 2f out: wknd over 1f out* **40/1**

8 *13* **Grey Steel (IRE)**[15] 5339 2-8-9 0 ow1 PatDobbs 6 —
(Denis P Quinn, Ire) *led after 1f: hdd over 2f out: sn wknd* **20/1**

0 **9** *3 ¾* **Super Smile (IRE)**[30] 4844 2-8-7 0 RichardHughes 3 —
(R Hannon) *early spd: sn outpcd: eased whn no ch fnl f* **15/2**[3]

10 *½* **Alpha Delta Whisky** 2-8-12 0 ChrisCatlin 9 —
(J Gallagher) *pushed rt s: green and a wl bhd* **16/1**

61.03 secs (-1.47) **Going Correction** -0.275s/f (Firm) **10** Ran SP% **119.2**
Speed ratings (Par 93): **100,98,94,92,86 86,86,65,59,58**
toteswingers:1&2:£4.20, 1&3:£7.80, 2&3:£4.30 CSF £17.93 TOTE £6.20: £2.30, £1.10, £2.20; EX 21.10.
Owner R S G Jones **Bred** Susan Bunning **Trained** Burrough Green, Cambs

FOCUS
Only a modest event, but once gain the strong tail wind meant a good gallop. The second and third set the level.

NOTEBOOK
Owain(USA) was picked up by connections for only 2,000gns having gone through the sales ring for much bigger prices previously. Well backed, he recovered from as slow start (caused by rearing as the stalls opened) to get on top inside the final furlong. His US pedigree is all about artificial surfaces (already placed at Wolverhampton), so it gives more strings to his bow by proving as effective on turf. He still can improve and can be competitive in nurseries. (op 7-1)
Imogen Louise(IRE) has also progressed in her three runs and performed with great credit here, particularly as the drop in trip didn't look to be ideal. She can find a race in the near future and a step up to 7f should be ideal on pedigree. (op 3-1)
Indian Shuffle(IRE) posted his second good run at this track. He has plenty of pace and just came up against two more progressive opponents. He has enough ability for a similar race on fast ground. (op 7-1)
Royalorien came back to something like her previous Nottingham run here (possible excuses last twice). She needs a little more before winning and this trip looked too sharp.
Poetically turned in his best previous effort on the slow artificial surface at Southwell, and he has yet to show enough on turf. Official explanation: jockey said gelding hung left (op 9-1)
Kingfisher Blue(IRE) was dropped in grade after showing nothing on his debut six weeks ago. He kept on late here without ever being involved. This was a step in the right direction, but more is needed. Related to winners at 5f and 6f, he looks like a step up in trip will suit. Official explanation: jockey said colt hung left (op 20-1)
Shutupandrive showed pace, but was ultimately well beaten. An easier track may suit. (op 50-1)

5809 WEATHERBYS BLOODSTOCK INSURANCE H'CAP 5f 161y
3:10 (3:10) (Class 5) (0-75,75) 3-Y-O+ **£2,201** (£655; £327; £163) **Stalls** Centre

Form RPR

503 **1** **Barons Spy (IRE)**[59] 3850 9-9-7 **75** JamesDoyle 8 86
(R J Price) *chsd ldrs: led appr fnl 2f: styd on wl u.p fnl f* **11/2**[2]

4656 **2** *2 ¼* **Riflessione**[14] 5368 4-9-2 **70** (b) TomMcLaughlin 1 74
(R A Harris) *chsd ldrs: rdn 2f out: styd on u.p fnl f to take 2nd nr fin but no imp on wnr* **7/1**

3210 **3** *¾* **Comptonspirit**[9] 5513 6-9-6 **74** J-PGuillambert 7 76
(B P J Baugh) *in rr early: hdwy to chse ldrs over 2f out: disp 2nd ins fnl f but no imp on wnr: one pce into 3rd nr fin* **5/1**[1]

3200 **4** *hd* **Bonheurs Art (IRE)**[33] 4714 3-9-0 **70** RobertWinston 4 71
(B W Hills) *chsd ldr then chsd wnr over 2f out: stl disputing 2nd fnl f but no imp on wnr: wknd nr fin* **13/2**

2104 **5** *¾* **The Name Is Frank**[22] 5112 5-8-11 **65** (t) FergusSweeney 2 63
(Mark Gillard) *led tl hdd over 2f out: wknd fnl f* **8/1**

5054 **6** *1* **The Tatling (IRE)**[14] 5377 13-8-7 **61** ChrisCatlin 10 56
(J M Bradley) *in rr pushed along 2f out: kpt on fnl f but nvr a threat* **16/1**

6560 **7** *hd* **Ajara (IRE)**[66] 3637 4-8-7 **61** RichardKingscote 6 55
(Tom Dascombe) *chsd ldrs: one pce whn nt clr run and swtchd rt appr fnl f: one pce* **25/1**

442 **8** *½* **Gwilym (GER)**[17] 5262 7-9-4 **72** DaneO'Neill 3 65
(D Haydn Jones) *t.k.h: chsd ldrs: rdn and outpcd over 2f out: kpt on again ins fnl f* **5/1**[1]

0560 **9** *8* **Adventure Story**[17] 5262 3-9-2 **72** RichardHughes 5 38
(R Hannon) *s.i.s: in rr: sme prog on ins 1/2-way: sn wknd* **10/1**

2502 **10** *1 ½* **Yurituni**[7] 5588 3-9-3 **73** JimCrowley 9 34
(Eve Johnson Houghton) *in tch: hdwy on outside to get in tch wl over 2f out: sn hrd drvn: wknd wl over 1f out* **6/1**[3]

68.99 secs (-2.21) **Going Correction** -0.275s/f (Firm)
WFA 3 from 4yo+ 2lb **10** Ran SP% **118.8**
Speed ratings (Par 103): **103,100,99,98,97 96,96,95,84,82**
toteswingers:1&2:£9.90, 1&3:£7.90, 2&3:£13.40 CSF £44.68 CT £211.46 TOTE £8.30: £3.10, £3.80, £1.10; EX 57.40.
Owner Barry Veasey **Bred** Tally-Ho Stud **Trained** Ullingswick, H'fords

FOCUS
A competitive sprint handicap run in a quick time. The winner's best run of the year.
The Name Is Frank Official explanation: jockey said gelding hung right
Gwilym(GER) Official explanation: jockey said gelding missed the break

5810 FINDAPROPERTY.COM MAIDEN STKS 5f 161y
3:40 (3:40) (Class 5) 3-Y-O+ **£2,331** (£693; £346; £173) **Stalls** Centre

Form RPR

1 **Yes We Can** 3-8-12 0 SteveDrowne 3 67+
(J R Gask) *trckd ldrs: led jst ins fnl f: drvn and styd on wl* **12/1**

2 **2** *1 ¼* **Bushwhacker (AUS)**[9] 5514 5-9-5 70 (p) RichardHughes 5 68
(W R Muir) *hld up in rr but in tch: hdwy 2f out: rdn and hung lft fnl f: tk 2nd fnl 120yds but no imp on wnr* **7/2**[2]

3 *1 ½* **Two Ish** 3-9-3 0 PhilipRobinson 1 63+
(C G Cox) *s.i.s: sn on terms and chsng ldr: led 2f out: sn rdn: hdd jst ins fnl f: lost 2nd fnl 120yds: wknd cl home* **4/5**[1]

50 **4** *nk* **Excellent Thought**[7] 5588 3-8-12 67 J-PGuillambert 2 57
(P Howling) *t.k.h: led tl hdd 2f out: styd disputing 2nd tl 1f out: wknd fnl 120yds* **5/1**

000 **5** *15* **Wizzacus**[10] 5474 3-8-12 32 JamesDoyle 4 —
(R J Price) *in tch to 1/2-way sn lost tch* **66/1**

50 **R** **Sayyedati Storm (USA)**[73] 3407 3-8-12 0 RobertWinston 6 —
(B W Hills) *ref to r* **4/1**[3]

1m 10.29s (-0.91) **Going Correction** -0.275s/f (Firm)
WFA 3 from 5yo 2lb **6** Ran SP% **123.6**
Speed ratings (Par 103): **95,93,91,90,70** —
toteswingers:1&2:£3.20, 1&3:£4.60, 2&3:£1.40 CSF £58.44 TOTE £18.00: £9.00, £2.30; EX 48.50.
Owner The Rock & Rollers **Bred** Glebe Stud **Trained** Sutton Veny, Wilts

FOCUS
Understandably the time was slower than the previous race. A modest race with little previous form to go on.

5811 UNIVERSITY & LITERARY CLUB BRISTOL MAIDEN H'CAP 1m 5f 22y
4:10 (4:10) (Class 5) (0-70,67) 3-Y-O+ **£2,201** (£655; £327; £163) **Stalls** High

Form RPR

0032 **1** **Isobar (GER)**[19] 5208 4-10-0 **67** KierenFallon 5 81+
(L M Cumani) *hld up disputing 3rd tl qcknd to ld ins fnl 3f: c readily clr fr 2f out: v easily* **4/6**[1]

0260 **2** *2 ¾* **Jewellery (IRE)**[17] 5260 3-8-12 **61** JimCrowley 4 62
(J R Fanshawe) *hld up in rr tl drvn and hdwy over 2f out: chsd v easy wnr fnl f: nvr any ch* **13/2**[3]

0434 **3** *4 ½* **Chasse Coeur**[13] 5380 3-9-2 **65** DavidProbert 3 59
(A M Balding) *disp 3rd tl rdn and outpcd 3f out: rallied to disp 2nd 2f out and chsd v easy wnr over 1f out: wknd fnl f* **15/2**

043 **4** *¾* **Tigress Hill**[21] 5141 3-9-4 **67** PatDobbs 1 60
(Mrs A J Perrett) *mde most tl hdd ins fnl 3f: wknd 2f out* **6/1**[2]

0535 **5** *¾* **Prickles**[25] 4990 5-9-0 **53** oh8 ChrisCatlin 2 45
(Karen George) *t.k.h: pressed ldr to 3f out: wknd 2f out* **15/2**

2m 50.5s (-1.50) **Going Correction** -0.20s/f (Firm)
WFA 3 from 4yo+ 10lb **5** Ran SP% **111.1**
Speed ratings (Par 103): **96,94,91,91,90**
CSF £5.64 TOTE £1.80: £1.30, £1.90; EX 4.80.
Owner Leonidas Marinopoulos **Bred** E P Haep **Trained** Newmarket, Suffolk

FOCUS
A modest maiden handicap, but the winner is progressive and stepped forward again.

5812 WEATHERBYS PRINTING FILLIES' H'CAP 1m 3f 144y
4:40 (4:41) (Class 5) (0-70,69) 3-Y-O £2,201 (£655; £327; £163) Stalls Low

Form RPR
3142 1 **Shianda**[7] 5585 3-8-9 **57** (b) RichardHughes 4 64
(G L Moore) *hld up trcking ldrs: drvn to ld on outer 1f out: drvn out* **11/4**[2]
5115 2 1 ¾ **Celestial Girl**[20] 5172 3-9-3 **65** SteveDrowne 2 69
(H Morrison) *hld up in rr: hdwy 3f out: rdn and styd on over 1f out: chsd wnr ins fnl f but no imp* **9/4**[1]
4221 3 1 ¾ **Now What**[15] 5330 3-9-7 **69** JimCrowley 5 70
(J G Portman) *chsd ldrs: wnt 2nd 1m out: drvn to ld 2f out: hdd 1f out: sn one pce* **9/2**
0066 4 1 ¾ **Oak Leaves**[25] 4992 3-8-7 **55** oh6 DavidProbert 3 53?
(J G Portman) *in rr but in tch: rdn and hdwy 3f out: one pce 2f out: styd on again fnl f: nt trble ldrs* **14/1**
2121 5 ½ **Baoli**[20] 5173 3-9-4 **66** KirstyMilczarek 7 63
(L M Cumani) *sn led: rdn 3f out: hdd 2f out: wknd over 1f out* **4/1**[3]
-000 6 11 **Madj's Baby**[77] 3268 3-8-2 **55** oh9 SophieDoyle(5) 6 33
(H S Howe) *t.k.h: trckd ldrs: awkward bnd over 4f out: rdn and wknd 3f out* **33/1**
064 7 11 **Bedouin Princess (IRE)**[17] 5270 3-8-2 **55** oh1 AdamBeschizza(5) 8 15
(Lucinda Featherstone) *chsd ldrs: rdn and wd bnd 4f out: sn wknd* **25/1**
0-55 8 ¾ **Chichi (IRE)**[27] 4925 3-8-12 **60** RichardKingscote 1 19
(Tom Dascombe) *rdn 4f out: a bhd* **22/1**

2m 30.93s (0.33) **Going Correction** +0.05s/f (Good) 8 Ran SP% **113.4**
Speed ratings (Par 98): **100,98,97,96,96 88,81,81**
toteswingers:1&2:£2.20, 1&3:£3.10, 2&3:£3.60 CSF £9.05 CT £25.31 TOTE £3.60: £1.10, £1.20, £2.40; EX 9.20.
Owner Baraka 2 Partnership **Bred** Lakin Bloodstock And H And W Thornton **Trained** Lower Beeding, W Sussex

FOCUS
The rain which had started before the previous race was becoming heavy by now. The gallop here was only steady and the field only quickened up approaching the three-furlong pole. Ordinary form which makes sense around the front three.

5813 THISTLEBRISTOL.CO.UK H'CAP 1m 3f 144y
5:10 (5:12) (Class 6) (0-60,60) 4-Y-O+ £1,554 (£462; £231; £115) Stalls Low

Form RPR
4460 1 **Touch Of Style (IRE)**[16] 5311 6-9-1 **59** AdamBeschizza(5) 9 69
(Matthew Salaman) *chsd ldrs: rdn and styd on fr over 2f out: led 1f out: styd on strly* **11/4**[1]
-442 2 1 **Zelos Diktator**[16] 5289 4-9-2 **55** (p) GeorgeBaker 8 63
(G L Moore) *trckd ldrs: led over 2f out: sn rdn: hdd 1f out: kpt on same pce* **9/2**[3]
333 3 1 **Spinning Waters**[33] 4689 4-8-7 **46** (v[1]) FergusSweeney 12 52
(Eve Johnson Houghton) *in rr tl rdn and hdwy over 2f out: styd on to take 3rd ins fnl f but nvr trbld ldng duo* **4/1**[2]
055 4 1 ¾ **La Columbina**[132] 1591 5-8-2 **46** oh1 SophieDoyle(5) 5 49
(H J Evans) *chsd ldrs: rdn 3f out: styd wl there tl wknd fnl 120yds* **8/1**
-560 5 2 ¾ **Christophers Quest**[11] 5457 5-8-4 **50** ow1 (t) RyanClark(7) 10 49
(Miss N A Lloyd-Beavis) *in tch: rdn and hdwy to chse ldrs over 2f out: wknd over 1f out* **28/1**
4265 6 shd **Garafena**[34] 4676 7-8-11 **50** (p) JimCrowley 6 48
(R Lee) *disp ld tl led 3f out: hdd over 2f out: wknd over 1f out* **12/1**
5454 7 3 ¾ **Bussell Along (IRE)**[21] 5148 4-8-11 **50** (tp) ChrisCatlin 2 42
(Stef Higgins) *t.k.h towards rr early: hdwy to chse ldrs 5f out: wknd over 1f out* **16/1**
3214 8 ½ **Jenny Soba**[16] 5289 7-9-4 **57** NeilChalmers 1 48
(Lucinda Featherstone) *in rr: styd on fnl 2f: nvr in contention* **10/1**
0050 9 7 **Aaman (IRE)**[32] 4765 4-9-2 **55** LiamKeniry 3 34
(E F Vaughan) *disp ld to 3f out: wknd qckly over 2f out* **8/1**
/0-0 10 42 **Yab Adee**[19] 5208 6-8-12 **58** (b[1]) KatiaScallan(7) 7 —
(M P Tregoning) *a bhd: t.o* **25/1**

2m 30.69s (0.09) **Going Correction** +0.05s/f (Good) 10 Ran SP% **117.0**
Speed ratings (Par 101): **101,100,99,98,96 96,94,93,89,61**
toteswingers:1&2:£4.60, 1&3:£3.00, 2&3:£3.60 CSF £15.00 CT £49.11 TOTE £4.10: £1.10, £2.60, £1.10; EX 16.10 Place 6 £26.48; Place 5 £9.10.
Owner Michael Barden **Bred** Yeomanstown Stud **Trained** Upper Lambourn, Berks

FOCUS
A reasonable gallop here and the race was run in driving rain. Straightforward form to a modest handicap.
T/Plt: £34.60 to a £1 stake. Pool:£62,666.97 - 1,322.05 winning tickets T/Qpdt: £9.10 to a £1 stake. Pool:£3,814.90 - 307.90 winning tickets ST

5594 NEWCASTLE (L-H)
Monday, September 6

OFFICIAL GOING: 1m to 4f - good to firm; 4f to pull-up - good (good to firm in places; watered; 7.6)
Wind: Strong, half behind Weather: Sunny, blustery

5814 EUROPEAN BREEDERS' FUND MAIDEN STKS 6f
2:20 (2:20) (Class 5) 2-Y-O £3,154 (£944; £472; £236; £117) Stalls High

Form RPR
0 1 **Pearl Arch (IRE)**[48] 4221 2-9-3 0 MartinDwyer 12 79+
(B J Meehan) *dwlt: sn trcking ldrs: niggled along 3f out: rdn wl over 1f out: swtchd lft and squeezed through to chal over 1f out: led ins fnl f: edgd lft and drvn out* **4/6**[1]
622 2 nk **Calypso Magic (IRE)**[19] 5210 2-9-3 **80** PaulHanagan 9 78
(J Howard Johnson) *led: rdn wl over 1f out: drvn jst ins fnl f: sn hdd: rallied u.p towards fin* **9/2**[2]
3 ½ **Tasfeya** 2-9-3 0 TadhgO'Shea 6 77+
(M Johnston) *midfield: pushed along and outpcd 1/2-way: rdn and hdwy on outer 2f out: chsd ldrs over 1f out: ch ent fnl f: one pce towards fin* **8/1**
6 4 2 ¼ **Silk Bounty**[21] 5156 2-9-3 0 PaulMulrennan 4 70
(J G Given) *cl up: effrt wl over 1f out: rdn to chal over 1f out and ev ch tl drvn and one pce ins fnl f* **28/1**
0 5 3 ½ **Bosambo**[24] 5040 2-9-3 0 PJMcDonald 2 59
(G A Swinbank) *prom: rdn along over 2f out: grad wknd* **15/2**[3]
6 1 ¾ **Sangar** 2-8-9 0 BarryMcHugh(3) 1 52+
(Ollie Pears) *dwlt and green towards rr: pushed along 1/2-way: hdwy over 2f out: n.m.r and swtchd rt wl over 1f out: kpt on ins fnl f* **40/1**
00 7 1 ¼ **Geronimo Chief (IRE)**[9] 5531 2-9-0 0 KellyHarrison(3) 7 50
(B M R Haslam) *in tch: rdn along 3f out: sn wknd* **150/1**
60 8 nk **Chagal (IRE)**[24] 5040 2-9-3 0 JoeFanning 3 49
(K A Ryan) *prom: rdn along 1/2-way: sn wknd* **66/1**
0 9 26 **Geordie Joe**[7] 5595 2-9-3 0 DuranFentiman 8 —
(J R Weymes) *s.i.s: a outpcd and bhd fr 1/2-way* **150/1**
10 3 **Somerset Island (IRE)** 2-9-3 0 RoystonFfrench 11 —
(J Howard Johnson) *sn outpcd and bhd fr 1/2-way* **80/1**

1m 11.98s (-2.62) **Going Correction** -0.55s/f (Hard) 2y crse rec 10 Ran SP% **111.0**
Speed ratings (Par 95): **95,94,93,90,86 83,82,81,47,43**
toteswingers:1&2:£2.40, 1&3:£3.40, 2&3:£2.80 CSF £3.43 TOTE £1.60: £1.10, £1.30, £2.30; EX 4.20 Trifecta £8.90 Pool: £675.50 - 55.71 winning units..
Owner Pearl Bloodstock Ltd **Bred** E Mulhern, J Flynn & Mrs M Haughey **Trained** Manton, Wilts

FOCUS
An average maiden where a high draw was crucial. The winne rcan rate higher with the runner-up helping to set the level.

NOTEBOOK
Pearl Arch(IRE), stuck in the mud at Ffos Las on his debut, holds Group-race entries and was backed as if defeat was out of the question. Happy to take a lead he had to be asked some serious questions and at the line there was precious little to spare. He is clearly well thought of and appreciates quick ground. (tchd 8-1 and 8-11 in places)
Calypso Magic(IRE), having his third start and turned over at 1/3 at Hamilton on his previous start, set the pace and battled back well when headed. Rated 80 he can surely break his duck. (tchd 4-1)
Tasfeya ◆, closely related to the stable's Middle Park winner Awzaan, looked very inexperienced but there was much to like about the way he stuck to his task late on. He will improve a bundle and looks one to keep an eye on.
Silk Bounty, who made his debut on the AW, showed plenty of speed before weakening late on. He should improve again. (op 25-1)
Bosambo, who didn't run up to expectations on his debut here three weeks earlier, again came up short but looks the type to fare better at three. (op 9-1)

5815 LA TAXIS MAIDEN STKS 1m 3y(S)
2:50 (2:53) (Class 5) 3-Y-O+ £2,590 (£770; £385; £192) Stalls High

Form RPR
22 1 **Tarooq (USA)**[16] 5303 4-9-8 0 PaulHanagan 10 78+
(R A Fahey) *trckd ldrs: rdn to ld 2f out: edgd lft: kpt on strly fnl f* **11/10**[1]
02 2 3 ¾ **Wild Geese (IRE)**[10] 5478 3-9-3 0 JoeFanning 6 69
(M Johnston) *cl up: effrt and ev ch 2f out: edgd rt: kpt on same pce fnl f* **5/1**[3]
3 3 ¾ **No Rain (IRE)** 3-8-12 0 PJMcDonald 9 55+
(G A Swinbank) *midfield: shkn up and outpcd over 2f out: kpt on strly fnl f: nvr nrr* **10/1**
5504 4 1 **Colamandis**[24] 5041 3-8-12 **48** PatrickMathers 4 53
(H A McWilliams) *led to 2f out: sn rdn and outpcd* **66/1**
2 5 3 ½ **Apache Warrior**[7] 5603 3-9-3 0 TomEaves 7 50
(G M Moore) *t.k.h: trckd ldrs: rdn and outpcd over 2f out: no imp fr over 1f out* **4/1**[2]
60 6 1 ¼ **Cotton King**[10] 5493 3-9-3 0 (t) MickyFenton 3 47
(T B P Coles) *midfield: rdn and outpcd over 3f out: styd on fnl f: n.d* **33/1**
00 7 9 **Talent Scout (IRE)**[10] 5487 4-9-8 0 GrahamGibbons 11 26
(T D Walford) *bhd and pushed along 1/2-way: nvr rchd ldrs* **80/1**
00 8 4 ½ **The Chester Giant**[24] 5057 3-8-12 0 StephenCraine 12 11
(Patrick Morris) *towards rr: struggling 1/2-way: nvr on terms* **100/1**
00- 9 3 ½ **Original Dancer (IRE)**[353] 6047 3-9-3 0 RoystonFfrench 1 8
(M Johnston) *in tch: rdn and outpcd over 3f out: sn btn* **16/1**
5 10 2 ½ **I Spy Baileys**[17] 5270 3-8-12 0 LeeVickers 2 —
(J G Given) *t.k.h: in tch tl rdn and wknd fr 3f out* **80/1**
11 5 **Janie's Encore**[86] 5-9-0 0 PaulPickard(3) 8 —
(J M Jefferson) *missed break: bhd and pushed along: nvr on terms* **18/1**
0 12 ½ **Rukhsana**[37] 4601 3-8-7 0 DeanHeslop(5) 14 —
(C J Teague) *towards rr and sn drvn along: no ch fr 1/2-way* **150/1**
13 14 **Fight For You (IRE)** 3-9-3 0 PaulMulrennan 13 —
(J R Norton) *missed break: sn pushed along in rr: nvr on terms* **66/1**

1m 38.24s (-5.16) **Going Correction** -0.55s/f (Hard)
WFA 3 from 4yo+ 5lb 13 Ran SP% **114.6**
Speed ratings (Par 103): **103,99,95,94,91 89,80,76,72,70 65,64,50**
toteswingers:1&2:£2.10, 1&3:£3.80, 2&3:£5.00 CSF £6.15 TOTE £1.90: £1.02, £2.20, £2.30; EX 6.20 Trifecta £22.60 Pool: £559.70 - 18.31 winning units..
Owner Y Nasib **Bred** Kirsten Rausing **Trained** Musley Bank, N Yorks

FOCUS
A maiden with plenty of deadwood and they raced in one group towards the centre. The winner built on initial efforts but the fifth disappointed.
Fight For You(IRE) Official explanation: jockey said gelding was unsuited by the good to firm, good in places ground

5816 PARKLANDS GOLFCOURSE MAIDEN STKS 5f
3:20 (3:20) (Class 5) 3-Y-O+ £2,719 (£809; £404; £202) Stalls High

Form RPR
-343 1 **Ballarina**[23] 5097 4-8-13 **45** DavidAllan 11 62
(E J Alston) *racd nr stands' rail: mde all: rdn and qcknd clr appr fnl f: kpt on wl* **9/2**[3]
4232 2 2 ¼ **Mottley Crewe**[10] 5481 3-9-3 **62** PJMcDonald 4 59
(M Dods) *prom: effrt 2f out and sn rdn: drvn ent fnl f: kpt on same pce* **5/2**[1]
0500 3 2 ½ **Thewinnatakesitall**[8] 5548 3-8-12 **47** (p) AndrewElliott 1 45
(N Tinkler) *prom: rdn along wl over 1f out: drvn and one pce appr fnl f* **40/1**
0004 4 ¾ **Accamelia**[25] 4982 4-8-13 **49** PaulMulrennan 2 45
(C W Fairhurst) *t.k.h: hld up in tch: swtchd lft and hdwy on outer 1/2-way: chsd ldrs wl over 1f out: sn rdn and one pce appr fnl f* **5/1**
0-54 5 ¾ **Erfaan (USA)**[114] 2114 3-9-0 **68** BarryMcHugh(3) 9 45
(Julie Camacho) *chsd wnr on stands' rail: rdn along wl over 1f out: drvn and one pce appr fnl f* **7/1**
55 6 1 ¾ **Appleby Fair**[9] 5514 3-9-3 0 GrahamGibbons 6 38
(T D Barron) *t.k.h: trckd ldrs: effrt over 2f out: sn rdn and wknd* **25/1**
0- 7 ½ **Blues Jazz**[347] 6223 4-8-13 0 LeeTopliss(5) 5 36
(J A McShane) *dwlt: a towards rr* **25/1**
4266 8 3 ¾ **Gold Gleam (USA)**[55] 3994 3-9-3 **65** PaulHanagan 3 23
(J Noseda) *t.k.h: trckd ldrs: rdn along over 2f out: sn btn* **3/1**[2]
-000 9 2 ½ **Sue And Sue**[8] 5548 3-8-7 **20** RossAtkinson(5) 8 9
(G Woodward) *prom: rdn along over 2f out: sn wknd and bhd* **100/1**

59.23 secs (-1.87) **Going Correction** -0.55s/f (Hard)
WFA 3 from 4yo 1lb 9 Ran SP% **112.0**
Speed ratings (Par 103): **92,88,84,83,82 79,78,72,68**
toteswingers:1&2:£2.70, 1&3:£14.10, 2&3:£12.20 CSF £15.17 TOTE £4.40: £1.80, £2.20, £9.20; EX 17.30 Trifecta £244.30 Pool: £475.42 - 1.44 winning units..
Owner Mrs P O Morris **Bred** Mrs D Du Feu And Trickledown Stud **Trained** Longton, Lancs

FOCUS
A desperately weak maiden and the stands' rail was again the place to be. The form is rated around the second and third.

5817 TYNE VALLEY CYCLE CLUB H'CAP — 6f
3:50 (3:58) (Class 6) (0-55,55) 3-Y-0+ — **£1,942** (£578; £288; £144) **Stalls** High

Form — RPR

0600 **1** **Bravely (IRE)**[33] 4706 6-9-2 **55** .... DavidAllan 16 — 68
(T D Easterby) *mde all stands' rail: rdn 2f out: kpt on strly fnl f: 1st of 5 in gp* **15/2**

0341 **2** 2¼ **Red River Boy**[12] 5422 5-8-10 **52** .... KellyHarrison(3) 14 — 58
(C W Fairhurst) *in tch stands' side: effrt and chsd wnr that gp over 2f out: kpt on fnl f: 2nd of 5 in gp* **6/1**[3]

0320 **3** ¾ **Carnival Dream**[9] 5535 5-9-0 **53** .... PatrickMathers 6 — 57
(H A McWilliams) *prom centre: effrt and led that gp over 1f out: edgd lft ins fnl f: kpt on: 1st of 8 in gp* **40/1**

0003 **4** 2½ **This Ones For Eddy**[12] 5405 5-9-1 **54** .... AndrewElliott 9 — 50
(J Balding) *towards rr in centre: rdn and edgd lft over 2f out: rallied over 1f out: no imp fnl f: 2nd of 8 in gp* **12/1**

0540 **5** 3¾ **Darcy's Pride (IRE)**[29] 4869 6-8-9 **51** .... PaulPickard(3) 5 — 35
(P T Midgley) *chsd ldrs centre: rdn over 2f out: no ex over 1f out: 3rd of 8 in gp* **25/1**

6501 **6** ¾ **Fair Bunny**[24] 5044 3-9-0 **55** ....(b) SilvestreDeSousa 13 — 36
(A D Brown) *cl up stands' side: rdn over 2f out: wknd over 1f out: 3rd of 5 in gp* **9/2**[2]

3422 **7** *nk* **Needy McCredie**[10] 5482 4-8-12 **51** .... PaulHanagan 15 — 31
(J R Turner) *cl up stands' side tl rdn and wknd wl over 1f out: 4th of 5 in gp* **15/8**[1]

0204 **8** ½ **Dream Express (IRE)**[9] 5535 5-8-8 **50** .... MichaelStainton(3) 12 — 29
(D W Thompson) *midfield centre: drvn and outpcd over 2f out: n.d after: 4th of 8 in gp* **20/1**

5344 **9** 1¼ **Divine Spirit**[7] 5599 9-8-10 **52** .... PatrickDonaghy(3) 3 — 27
(M Dods) *swtchd to stands' side after 2f: hld up: struggling over 2f out: sn btn: last of 5 in gp* **25/1**

2546 **10** ½ **Elkhorn**[9] 5535 8-8-9 **48** ....(b) TomEaves 10 — 21
(Julie Camacho) *dwlt: bhd centre: shortlived effrt wl over 1f out: sn btn: 5th of 8 in gp* **12/1**

1505 **11** ½ **Red China Blues (USA)**[29] 4868 4-8-11 **53** ....(b) JamesSullivan(3) 4 — 24
(Mrs R A Carr) *led centre tl rdn and hdd over 1f out: sn btn: 6th of 8 in gp* **25/1**

0000 **12** *nk* **Piste**[25] 4982 4-9-2 **55** .... PJMcDonald 11 — 25
(Miss T Jackson) *awkward s: sn in tch centrre: rdn and wknd over 2f out: 7th of 8 in gp* **33/1**

22-0 **13** 1¾ **Magical Song**[10] 5482 5-8-7 **53** ....(b) AndrewSmith(7) 1 — 18
(J Balding) *prom centre tl wknd over 2f out: last of 8 in gp* **40/1**

1m 11.1s (-3.50) **Going Correction** -0.55s/f (Hard) — 13 Ran SP% **118.5**
WFA 3 from 4yo+ 2lb
Speed ratings (Par 101): **101,98,97,93,88 87,87,86,84,84 83,83,80**
toteswingers:1&2:£7.70,1&3:£48.10,2&3:£21.40 CSF £47.17 CT £1738.27 TOTE £11.90: £3.70, £1.20, £9.70; EX 43.80 TRIFECTA Not won..
Owner Ryedale Partners No 4 **Bred** James F Hanly **Trained** Great Habton, N Yorks
■ Exceedingly Good was withdrawn (14/1, keen to post and uns rdr). Deduct 10p in the £ under R4. New market formed.

FOCUS
A very ordinary handicap. Once more the stands' side group dominated. The winner ran his best race of the year with the runner-up rated to form.
Bravely(IRE) Official explanation: trainer had no explanation for the apparent improvement in form shown
Needy McCredie Official explanation: vet said filly was in season

5818 ALEXANDRA CARS NURSERY — 6f
4:20 (4:26) (Class 5) (0-70,66) 2-Y-0 — **£2,201** (£655; £327; £163) **Stalls** High

Form — RPR

0602 **1** **Whats For Pudding (IRE)**[7] 5602 2-7-7 **45** .... NeilFarley(7) 10 — 51
(D Carroll) *prom: effrt to chse ldr 1/2-way: rdn to ld over 2f out: drvn wl over 1f out: kpt on wl u.p fnl f* **6/1**

5022 **2** 1¼ **Ajaafa**[11] 5434 2-9-7 **66** ....(p) PaulMulrennan 13 — 68
(J G Given) *led: rdn and hdd over 2f out: drvn over 1f out: kpt on towards fin* **7/2**[1]

5000 **3** 2 **Chadford**[27] 4935 2-8-9 **54** .... GrahamGibbons 11 — 50
(T D Walford) *chsd ldrs: rdn along and sltly outpcd 2f out: sn drvn and kpt on wl fnl f* **50/1**

4610 **4** *nk* **Peppercorn Rent (IRE)**[33] 4701 2-8-7 **55** ....(e) KellyHarrison(3) 12 — 50
(T D Easterby) *in tch: lost pl and towards rr after 2f: rdn along 1/2-way: hdwy 2f out: edgd rt jst over 1f out: kpt on ins fnl f: hld whn eased nr fin* **11/1**

040 **5** *nk* **Yachtmaster (IRE)**[16] 5294 2-9-4 **63** ....(b[1]) TomEaves 7 — 57
(J J Quinn) *dwlt: sn outpcd and bhd: hdwy 2f out: sn rdn and kpt on ins fnl f: nrst fin* **33/1**

040 **6** ¾ **Cool In The Shade**[45] 4338 2-8-2 **50** .... PaulPickard(3) 5 — 42
(P T Midgley) *prom: rdn along wl over 2f out: drvn wl over 1f out: grad wknd* **33/1**

3000 **7** 1 **Peters Spirit (IRE)**[11] 5434 2-8-9 **57** ....(b[1]) BarryMcHugh(3) 2 — 46
(R A Fahey) *chsd ldrs on outer: hdwy 2f out: sn rdn and grad wknd appr fnl f* **22/1**

050 **8** 1¼ **Whipperoo (IRE)**[112] 2183 2-7-12 **46** .... JamesSullivan(3) 14 — 31
(Patrick Morris) *hmpd s and in rr: hdwy on inner 2f out: rdn and keeping on whn n.m.r and hmpd ent fnl f: no imp after* **25/1**

0323 **9** *nk* **Eilean Mor**[11] 5434 2-9-4 **63** .... PaulHanagan 6 — 47+
(J S Goldie) *midfield: effrt and hdwy over 2f out: sn rdn and n.d* **9/2**[2]

003 **10** ½ **None Sweeter**[30] 4848 2-9-0 **59** .... DavidAllan 9 — 42
(T D Easterby) *prom: rdn along over 2f out: drvn wl over 1f out and sn wknd* **5/1**[3]

0653 **11** 4 **Downtown Boy (IRE)**[24] 5021 2-9-2 **61** .... MickyFenton 3 — 32
(T P Tate) *sn outpcd and a bhd* **25/1**

4003 **12** 3¼ **Finn's Rainbow**[26] 4948 2-9-0 **59** .... SilvestreDeSousa 8 — 20
(K A Ryan) *chsd ldrs: rdn along wl over 2f out: sn wknd* **7/1**

404 **13** 1¼ **Princess Dayna**[28] 4896 2-9-2 **66** .... RossAtkinson(5) 4 — 23
(Tom Dascombe) *chsd ldrs: rdn along 1/2-way: sn wknd* **20/1**

1m 13.6s (-1.00) **Going Correction** -0.55s/f (Hard) — 13 Ran SP% **116.8**
Speed ratings (Par 95): **84,82,79,79,78 77,76,74,74,73 68,64,62**
CSF £24.17 CT £766.16 TOTE £8.60: £3.30, £1.40, £17.80; EX 34.70 Trifecta £390.00 Part won. Pool: £390.00 - 0.50 winning units..
Owner Dreams **Bred** Kenneth Greer **Trained** Sledmere, E Yorks
■ Stewards' Enquiry : Kelly Harrison one-day ban: careless riding (Sep 26)

FOCUS
A weak nursery where the stands' rail yet again played a big part in proceedings. As a result the form is rated a bit negatively.

NOTEBOOK
Whats For Pudding(IRE), with a double-figure draw, was having her ninth start. An 80/1 shot when eight lengths runner-up in a seller at Ripon a week earlier, she showed that improved effort was no fluke. Matching strides with the pace-setter towards the running rail, she scored in decisive fashion in the end. (op 8-1)
Ajaafa, drawn one off the rail, set the pace but was readily outpointed by the winner. He has already failed to justify favouritism in claiming company and the cheekpieces failed to make any real difference. (op 4-1)
Chadford, another with a favourable draw, was having his second start in a month after two months on the sidelines. (op 40-1)
Peppercorn Rent(IRE), winner in selling company at Ripon, had a double figure draw but could not lie up. She put in some solid late work and may have been a fraction unlucky not to claim third spot. (op 14-1)
Yachtmaster(IRE), in first-time blinkers, stayed on when it was all over after being given early reminders and he may be worth another try over 7f. (op 28-1)
Cool In The Shade, from a stable off the radar at present, showed plenty of pace and seems happier over this trip than seven. This was a better effort on her nursery bow. (op 40-1)
Eilean Mor, closely matched with Ajaafa on Ayr form, raced away from the favoured rail and never figured. (op 6-1)

5819 NORTH SEA LOGISTICS H'CAP — 1m 3y(S)
4:50 (4:53) (Class 6) (0-65,65) 3-Y-0+ — **£2,201** (£655; £327; £163) **Stalls** High

Form — RPR

-454 **1** **Nolecce**[10] 5479 3-8-2 **51** oh2 .... AndrewHeffernan(3) 3 — 58
(R C Guest) *hld up in midfield: effrt and rdn over 2f out: hdwy to ld ins fnl f: kpt on wl* **20/1**

0364 **2** *nk* **Scarab (IRE)**[10] 5486 5-9-5 **60** ....(p) GrahamGibbons 6 — 67
(T D Walford) *chsd ldrs: drvn over 2f out: hdwy to ld appr to ins fnl f: kpt on* **11/1**

5060 **3** ¾ **Glenmuir (IRE)**[52] 4119 7-9-5 **65** .... IanBrennan(5) 4 — 74+
(J J Quinn) *hld up: gd hdwy on ins whn no room and snatched up appr fnl f: sn swtchd lft: kpt on wl fnl f: nt rch first two* **16/1**

4005 **4** 1¼ **Lakeman (IRE)**[10] 5486 4-8-13 **59** ....(b) DaleSwift(5) 13 — 61
(B Ellison) *prom: drvn 3f out: rallied over 1f out: kpt on same pce ins fnl f* **16/1**

100 **5** *hd* **Celtic Step**[10] 5486 6-9-0 **55** .... PaulHanagan 1 — 57
(A Kirtley) *hld up in tch: effrt over 1f out: kpt on same pce fnl f* **12/1**

6325 **6** ¾ **Muftarres (IRE)**[9] 5530 5-9-7 **65** .... PaulPickard(3) 5 — 65
(P T Midgley) *hld up: hdwy and in tch over 1f out: no ex ins fnl f* **16/1**

2046 **7** ½ **Xpres Maite**[131] 1628 7-9-3 **61** ....(p) RussKennemore(3) 15 — 60
(S R Bowring) *led at decent gallop: rdn and hdd over 1f out: sn no ex* **9/2**[2]

1544 **8** 2¾ **Prime Circle**[14] 5360 4-9-7 **62** ....(p) SilvestreDeSousa 16 — 61+
(A D Brown) *towards rr: rdn 3f out: hdwy over 1f out: no imp whn hmpd ent fnl f* **5/1**[3]

1403 **9** 2 **Catawollow**[10] 5479 3-8-0 **51** oh2 ....(e) BillyCray(5) 7 — 38+
(R C Guest) *hld up: rdn 3f out: hdwy on ins whn nt clr run appr fnl f: no imp* **16/1**

000 **10** ½ **Isle Of Ellis (IRE)**[9] 5535 3-7-12 **51** oh6 .... NeilFarley(7) 9 — 37
(R E Barr) *bhd: struggling 1/2-way: sme hdwy over 1f out: nvr on terms* **100/1**

2313 **11** 3¼ **Call Of Duty (IRE)**[25] 4985 5-9-6 **64** .... TjadeCollier(3) 14 — 44
(Mrs Dianne Sayer) *w ldr tl rdn and wknd over 1f out* **2/1**[1]

00-0 **12** 7 **Sams Spirit**[18] 5244 4-8-5 **51** oh4 .... LeeTopliss(5) 12 — —
(J A McShane) *in tch: drvn and outpcd wl over 2f out: sn wknd* **50/1**

20-0 **13** 45 **Brisbane (IRE)**[15] 5337 3-9-4 **64** .... DuranFentiman 8 — —
(Mrs Dianne Sayer) *dwlt: bhd: lost tch 1/2-way: t.o* **66/1**

1m 38.78s (-4.62) **Going Correction** -0.55s/f (Hard) — 13 Ran SP% **116.9**
WFA 3 from 4yo+ 5lb
Speed ratings (Par 101): **101,100,99,98,98 97,97,94,92,92 88,81,36**
toteswingers:1&2:£13.30, 1&3:£27.70, 2&3:£23.80 CSF £217.38 CT £2173.34 TOTE £20.90: £4.30, £2.10, £6.40; EX 178.20 Trifecta £365.00 Part won. Pool: £493.32 - 0.10 winning units..
Owner Future Racing (Notts) Limited **Bred** Hedsor Stud **Trained** Stainforth, S Yorks
■ Stewards' Enquiry : Tjade Collier one-day ban: used whip when gelding was not responding (Sep 20)
Andrew Heffernan caution: used whip down the shoulder in the forehand position

FOCUS
A modest 51-65 handicap and they eventually raced in one group towards the stands' side. The two clear leaders seemed to go off a shade too fast for their own good. The form looks sound and the winner rates a 6lb personal best. The unlucky third has been rated a length winner.

5820 FREEBETTING.CO.UK H'CAP (DIV I) — 7f
5:20 (5:20) (Class 6) (0-60,60) 3-Y-0+ — **£1,619** (£481; £240; £120) **Stalls** High

Form — RPR

5546 **1** **Northern Flyer (GER)**[15] 5331 4-9-0 **55** ....(p) IanBrennan(5) 13 — 66
(J J Quinn) *trckd ldrs on inner: hdwy 2f out: swtchd lft and rdn to chal 1f out: led ins fnl f: sn drvn and kpt on* **6/1**[3]

0001 **2** ½ **Hot Rod Mamma (IRE)**[24] 5024 3-8-8 **48** .... DuranFentiman 16 — 59+
(Mrs Dianne Sayer) *in tch stands' rail: gd hdwy wl over 2f out: nt clr run over 1f out: swtchd lft and rdn to chal ent fnl f: sn drvn and ev ch: nt qckn towards fin* **16/1**

5030 **3** 1½ **Nuit Sombre (IRE)**[4] 5688 10-9-10 **60** ....(p) SilvestreDeSousa 9 — 66
(G A Harker) *sn led on stands' rail: rdn along 2f out: drvn over 1f out: hdd ins fnl f: kpt on* **20/1**

4044 **4** 1½ **No Quarter (IRE)**[2] 5758 3-8-10 **53** .... AndrewHeffernan(3) 8 — 53
(Miss Tracy Waggott) *trckd ldrs: hdwy over 2f out: rdn wl over 1f out: drvn and kpt on same pce ent fnl f* **8/1**

0442 **5** 1¼ **Peter's Gift (IRE)**[3] 5732 4-9-3 **56** ....(p) AmyRyan(3) 4 — 54
(K A Ryan) *prom: cl up 3f out: rdn along 2f out: drvn and one pce ent fnl f* **8/1**

32 **6** 1 **Morocchius (USA)**[11] 5439 5-9-4 **57** ....(p) BarryMcHugh(3) 14 — 52
(Julie Camacho) *towards rr: hdwy over 2f out: rdn to chse ldrs whn n.m.r over 1f out: sn no imp* **7/2**[1]

6306 **7** *nse* **Spavento (IRE)**[64] 3706 4-9-8 **58** ....(p) DavidAllan 15 — 53
(E J Alston) *bhd: hdwy on inner 2f out: sn rdn and kpt on ins fnl f: nrst fin* **11/2**[2]

2004 **8** 1¼ **Ursus**[12] 5424 5-9-8 **58** ....(p) RoystonFfrench 2 — 50
(C R Wilson) *prom on outer: effrt over 2f out: rdn wl over 1f out: grad wknd* **40/1**

2405 **9** *nk* **Bentley**[9] 5535 6-8-12 **48** .... PaulHanagan 12 — 39
(B P J Baugh) *nvr bttr than midfield* **12/1**

3462 **10** 4 ½ **Always Dazzling**[7] 5598 3-9-5 **59**........ JoeFanning 11 36
(M Johnston) *sn chsng ldr: cl up 1/2-way: rdn along over 2f out: sn wknd* **6/1**[3]
1006 **11** 2 ½ **Crianza**[10] 5482 4-9-0 **50**........ AndrewElliott 5 22
(N Tinkler) *s.i.s: a in rr* **80/1**
0350 **12** 1 **Lujano**[9] 5533 5-9-7 **60**........(p) JamesSullivan(3) 3 30
(Ollie Pears) *prom: rdn along 3f out: sn wknd* **16/1**
000 **13** 1 ¼ **Funky Munky**[18] 5244 5-9-0 **50**........ PJMcDonald 7 16
(A C Whillans) *a towards rr* **25/1**
-002 **14** ¾ **Second Reef**[15] 5331 8-8-3 **46** oh1........ SoniaEaton(7) 1 10
(T A K Cuthbert) *a towards rr: bhd fnl 3f* **50/1**

1m 24.67s (-4.03) **Going Correction** -0.55s/f (Hard)
WFA 3 from 4yo+ 4lb **14** Ran SP% **122.1**
Speed ratings (Par 101): **101,100,98,97,95 94,94,92,92,87 84,83,82,81**
toteswingers:1&2:£15.80, 1&3:£23.20, 2&3:£32.90 CSF £94.59 CT £1871.30 TOTE £6.60: £2.90, £7.50, £9.30; EX 108.30 TRIFECTA Not won..
Owner N Chapman **Bred** A Pereira **Trained** Settrington, N Yorks
■ Stewards' Enquiry : Barry McHugh four-day ban: struck gelding with his whip in annoyance (Sep 20-23)

FOCUS
Division one of a modest 48-60 handicap with the winner collecting just £1,619, and they again raced in one group towards the stands' side. It was a length slower than division II. The winner is rated back to his best with the fourth the best guide.

5821 FREEBETTING.CO.UK H'CAP (DIV II) 7f
5:50 (5:50) (Class 6) (0-60,60) 3-Y-O+ **£1,619** (£481; £240; £120) **Stalls** High

Form RPR
2653 **1** **Castle Myth (USA)**[95] 1995 4-9-0 **55**........ DaleSwift(5) 16 65
(B Ellison) *prom: rdn along 3f out: rallied to chse ldr over 1f out: styd on to ld cl home* **6/1**[3]
0230 **2** nk **Broctune Papa Gio**[82] 3073 3-8-3 **46**........ PaulPickard(3) 14 53+
(K G Reveley) *led: rdn and edgd lft over 1f out: kpt on fnl f: hdd cl home* **7/2**[1]
0603 **3** 3 **Ingleby King (USA)**[24] 5045 4-9-5 **55**........(b) GrahamGibbons 9 56
(T D Barron) *dwlt: hld up: rdn over 2f out: styd on fnl f: nt rch first two* **5/1**[2]
6633 **4** 1 ¼ **Hansomis (IRE)**[12] 5406 6-9-9 **59**........ PaulMulrennan 12 57
(B Mactaggart) *prom: effrt appr 2f out: sn rdn: one pce fnl f* **6/1**[3]
0-00 **5** 2 ¼ **Hartshead**[10] 5486 11-9-7 **57**........(p) AndrewMullen 8 49
(Miss Tracy Waggott) *hld up: rdn over 2f out: hdwy over 1f out: no imp fnl f* **16/1**
0505 **6** 2 ½ **Olympic Dream**[23] 5067 4-9-5 **60**........ MichaelO'Connell(5) 6 45
(M Herrington) *cl up tl rdn and wknd over 1f out* **12/1**
2565 **7** ½ **Shunkawakhan (IRE)**[12] 5406 7-8-13 **49**........ TomEaves 2 32
(Miss L A Perratt) *hld up: outpcd and edgd lft over 2f out: n.d after* **18/1**
050- **8** 5 **Igneous**[171] 5730 4-8-7 **46** oh1........(b) MichaelStainton(3) 13 16
(D W Thompson) *t.k.h early: hld up: outpcd 1/2-way: n.d after* **33/1**
0050 **9** 1 ½ **Piccolo Express**[12] 5406 4-9-1 **51**........ DavidAllan 1 17
(B P J Baugh) *cl up on outside tl rdn and wknd over 1f out* **25/1**
5/00 **10** 1 **Gee Ceffyl Bach**[8] 5545 6-8-8 **49**........ BillyCray(5) 3 12
(G Woodward) *midfield: outpcd over 2f out: sn btn* **50/1**
0363 **11** 4 **Forzarzi (IRE)**[10] 5496 6-9-0 **50**........ PatrickMathers 11 2
(H A McWilliams) *in tch: drvn over 2f out: sn wknd* **14/1**
5-00 **12** 1 ¾ **Old Firm**[7] 5596 4-8-10 **49**........(p) BarryMcHugh(3) 15 —
(J A McShane) *missed break: bhd and sn pushed along: nvr on terms* **28/1**
0552 **13** 24 **Broughtons Silk**[12] 5406 5-8-10 **46**........ PJMcDonald 5 —
(A C Whillans) *cl up tl rdn and wknd qckly over 2f out: t.o* **13/2**

1m 24.5s (-4.20) **Going Correction** -0.55s/f (Hard)
WFA 3 from 4yo+ 4lb **13** Ran SP% **118.5**
Speed ratings (Par 101): **102,101,98,96,94 91,90,85,83,82 77,75,48**
toteswingers:1&2:£6.90, 1&3:£7.80, 2&3:£7.80. totesuper7: Win: Not won, Place: £571.20 CSF £26.03 CT £118.70 TOTE £5.30: £1.40, £2.80, £2.30; EX 34.80 Trifecta £172.50 Pool: £300.77 - 1.29 winning units. Place 6 £190.41; Place 5 £151.50.
Owner Brian Ellison **Bred** Mr & Mrs Gerald J Stautberg **Trained** Norton, N Yorks
■ Stewards' Enquiry : Graham Gibbons six-day ban: two for careless riding + four deferred days (Sep 20-26)

FOCUS
The second and quicker division of the 7f handicap and they once again raced more towards the near side with the first three all on the rail. The first pair came clear and the winner is rated close to his AW debut.
Broctune Papa Gio Official explanation: trainer's rep said gelding finished distressed
Forzarzi(IRE) Official explanation: trainer's rep said gelding was unsuited by the good to firm, good in places ground
Broughtons Silk Official explanation: trainer said mare was unsuited by the good to firm, good in places ground
T/Jkpt: Not won. T/Plt: £189.80 to a £1 stake. Pool:£82,825.10 - 318.46 winning tickets T/Qpdt: £302.10 to a £1 stake. Pool:£4,736.19 - 11.60 winning tickets RY

5822 - 5827a (Foreign Racing) - See Raceform Interactive

5551 GOODWOOD (R-H)
Tuesday, September 7

OFFICIAL GOING: Good changing to good (good to soft in home straight) after race 3 (3.10)
Lower bend and straight dolled out 8yds to 2f marker up the straight. Top bend dolled out 4yds increasing distances by about 12yds.
Wind: Moderate, half against Weather: Changeable, heavy shower race 2

5828 BOLLINGER CHAMPAGNE CHALLENGE SERIES H'CAP (FOR GENTLEMAN AMATEUR RIDERS) 1m 3f
2:00 (2:00) (Class 5) (0-70,69) 4-Y-O+ **£2,498** (£774; £387; £193) **Stalls** Low

Form RPR
0504 **1** **Switched Off**[85] 3025 5-10-8 **63**........ MrJHodson(7) 8 75
(Ian Williams) *hld up: prog to 4th 1/2-way: smooth hdwy to chal 3f out: led u.p 2f out: hanging rt but styd on to draw clr fnl f* **16/1**
2442 **2** 6 **Megalala (IRE)**[9] 5552 9-10-12 **65**........ MrJackSalmon(5) 6 69
(J J Bridger) *settled bhd pair fighting it out: clsd to ld over 3f out: drvn and hdd 2f out: wknd fnl f* **6/1**[2]
/0-6 **3** 11 **Celticello (IRE)**[8] 5591 8-11-2 **69**........ MrJMQuinlan(5) 9 50
(M G Quinlan) *hld up in bhd clr ldrs: rdn to try to cl 4f out: outpcd over 2f out: kpt on to take modest 3rd over 1f out* **13/2**[3]
2306 **4** 7 **James Pollard (IRE)**[36] 4657 5-10-0 **55** oh5........(t) MrRJWilliams(7) 5 24
(B J Llewellyn) *s.s: wl in rr: sme prog to 6th over 3f out and jst in tch: sn outpcd and rdn: plodded on to take poor 4th ins fnl f* **20/1**
5461 **5** 1 ¾ **Mons Calpe (IRE)**[17] 5286 4-11-5 **67**........(p) MrSWalker 4 32
(P F I Cole) *lw: str reminders early to press ldr at str pce: drvn over 4f out: upsides over 3f out: sn wknd* **3/1**[1]
6602 **6** 7 **Eseej (USA)**[21] 5180 5-11-0 **65**........ MrPCollington(3) 3 18
(P W Hiatt) *sweating and taken to post steadily: led at str pce but pressed: hdd & wknd over 3f out* **9/1**
6553 **7** 5 **Yonder**[26] 5011 6-10-3 **56**........(bt) MrRPooles(5) 1 —
(H Morrison) *scrubbed along early: mostly in rr: toiling in last pair over 4f out* **13/2**[3]
3155 **8** 5 **Prince Golan (IRE)**[34] 4708 6-10-9 **60**........ MrMPrice(3) 2 —
(R J Price) *s.v.s: a in last pair: toiling fr over 4f out: wl bhd after* **14/1**

2m 31.24s (4.74) **Going Correction** +0.25s/f (Good) **8** Ran SP% **93.3**
Speed ratings (Par 103): **92,87,79,74,73 68,64,60**
Tote Swingers: 1&2 £9.20, 1&3 £10.40, 2&3 £3.40 CSF £70.39 CT £362.67 TOTE £12.10: £2.80, £1.90, £1.70; EX 62.30.
Owner P Nicholls **Bred** Mrs Byron Paterson **Trained** Portway, Worcs
■ Jake Hodson's first winner.

FOCUS
A moderate handicap for amatuer riders, run at a suicidal early pace. The runner-up sets the level and is rated close to recent form. Aragall (7/2) was withdrawn after proving unruly in the stalls. R4 applies, deduct 20p in the £.

5829 E B F RACING UK MAIDEN FILLIES' STKS 1m
2:35 (2:38) (Class 5) 2-Y-O **£3,238** (£963; £481; £240) **Stalls** High

Form RPR
33 **1** **Poplin**[15] 5369 2-9-0 0........ KierenFallon 12 84+
(L M Cumani) *str: lw: trckd ldr: led over 2f out gng easily: drifted lft fr over 1f out: shkn up and a wl in command* **7/4**[1]
2 1 ½ **Always The Lady** 2-9-0 0........ AdamKirby 3 81+
(C G Cox) *str: gd bodied: lw: trckd ldrs: prog and cl up over 2f out: chsd wnr over 1f out: styd on but readily hld* **6/1**[3]
3 3 ½ **Umseyat (USA)** 2-9-0 0........ TadhgO'Shea 1 73+
(J H M Gosden) *unf; on toes: dwlt: wl in rr: prog on outer fr 1/2-way: wnt 2nd over 2f out to over 1f out: rn green and outpcd after* **10/1**
4 3 **Entrance** 2-9-0 0........ TomQueally 5 66
(E A L Dunlop) *unf: settled in midfield: prog on outer over 3f out: shkn up over 2f out: nvr threatened ldrs: kpt on same pce* **20/1**
5 1 ¾ **Wild Mimosa (IRE)** 2-9-0 0........ SaleemGolam 8 63+
(J H M Gosden) *unf: scope: s.v.s: mostly in last pair: pushed along and stdy prog on inner over 2f out: nvr on terms* **16/1**
63 **6** nk **September Draw (USA)**[33] 4736 2-9-0 0........ RyanMoore 11 62
(R Hannon) *leggy: lt-f: trckd ldng pair: lost pl jst over 2f out: steadily outpcd after* **8/1**
7 nk **Song Of India** 2-9-0 0........ WilliamBuick 10 61+
(J H M Gosden) *str; bit bkwd: dwlt: rn green and wl in rr: nudged along on outer fr 3f out: kpt on: nrst fin* **9/2**[2]
60 **8** 2 ¼ **Ponte Di Rosa**[53] 4095 2-9-0 0........ DaneO'Neill 13 56
(B G Powell) *trckd ldrs: shkn up over 2f out: sn outpcd: fdd over 1f out* **18/1**
9 4 **Afaara (IRE)** 2-9-0 0........ EddieAhern 9 47
(Mrs A J Perrett) *athletic: trckd ldrs: nt qckn over 2f out and sn lost pl: steadily fdd* **22/1**
10 9 **No Refraction (IRE)** 2-9-0 0........ LiamKeniry 7 28
(M D I Usher) *w'like: cl cpld: settled in midfield on inner: shkn up 3f out: sn wknd* **100/1**
11 1 **Clarinette (IRE)** 2-8-11 0........ EJMcNamara(3) 2 25
(R M Beckett) *w'like: bit bkwd: last after 3f: struggling over 3f out: nvr a factor* **25/1**
00 **12** ¾ **One Cool Chick**[10] 5537 2-9-0 0........ NeilChalmers 14 24
(J J Bridger) *sweating: led to over 2f out: wknd v rapidly* **100/1**
0 **13** 10 **Carrauntoohil (IRE)**[80] 3222 2-9-0 0........ J-PGuillambert 6 2
(Miss Amy Weaver) *w'like: leggy: a towards rr: pushed along 1/2-way: wknd 3f out: t.o* **66/1**

1m 42.44s (2.54) **Going Correction** +0.25s/f (Good) **13** Ran SP% **116.6**
Speed ratings (Par 92): **97,95,92,89,87 86,86,84,80,71 70,69,59**
Tote Swingers: 1&2 £4.40, 1&3 £7.50, 2&3 £14.20 CSF £10.77 TOTE £2.70: £1.20, £2.80, £3.50; EX 14.70.
Owner Fittocks Stud **Bred** Fittocks Stud **Trained** Newmarket, Suffolk

FOCUS
An interesting fillies' maiden, run at an average pace. The first three dominated in the home straight, but there were some eye-catchers in behind. The winner is progressing well.

NOTEBOOK
Poplin deservedly got off the mark at the third time of asking and her previous experience was a distinct advantage here. She raced in the box seat and took it up going strongly 2f out. He had to fight to hold off her two main challengers, though, and didn't help her cause by drifting markedly left inside the final furlong. That could've been down to this different track and it was the first time she had been in front, so she is probably value for further. Her entry in the Fillies' Mile is flying too high, but she looks just the sort her trainer could do very well with over middle distances next season. (op 13-8 tchd 15-8)
Always The Lady ◆'s half-brother, the smart Class Is Class, has markedly improved as he got older but her dam was a 6f juvenile winner. She cost 100,000gns, is also entered in the Fillies' Mile, and this rates a very pleasing introduction. She ought to be winning next time. (op 7-1 tchd 11-2)
Umseyat(USA) ◆ proved by far the sharpest of the trio from her yard. She travelled up sweetly and looked a real threat to the winner, but ultimately lost out through greenness. This was a decent effort from the outside stall from this half-sister to her yard's 1m Listed winner Alwaary, and she ought to prove hard to stop on her next outing. (op 12-1 tchd 14-1)
Entrance, a lean half-sister to her yard's 7f winner Red Gulch, proved easy to back and took time to get the hang of things. She was noted doing some decent late work, though, and ought to know plenty more for the experience. (op 16-1)
Wild Mimosa(IRE) lost around five lengths at the start and was another to run green. She caught the eye keeping on against the far rail from 2f out, however, and this well-bred filly should be going closer next time out.
September Draw(USA) was restrained after pulling her way to the front early on and lacked the pace to mount a serious challenge in the home straight. She now qualifies for nurseries. (op 6-1)
Song Of India was the first string from her stable and she too proved too green to do herself full justice. She did show ability, though, and is yet another here that should get plenty closer on her next assignment. (op 6-1 tchd 4-1)

5830 GEORGE ANTHONY CELEBRATION NURSERY 1m
3:10 (3:11) (Class 4) (0-85,83) 2-Y-O **£3,238** (£963; £481; £240) **Stalls** High

Form RPR
01 **1** **Indigo Way**[38] 4568 2-9-2 **78**........ RyanMoore 2 88+
(B J Meehan) *lw: hld up in last pair: stdy prog on outer over 2f out: wnt 2nd over 1f out: sustained chal fnl f: edgd ahd last 75yds* **11/2**[3]

The Form Book, Raceform Ltd, Compton, RG20 6NL

61 **2** *nk* **Handsome Jack (IRE)**[63] 3769 2-8-11 **73**.............. RichardKingscote 4 82+
(R A Mills) *trckd ldng pair: led 2f out and kicked on: hrd pressed fnl f: r.o wl but hdd and jst hld last 75yds* **7/2**[1]

0325 **3** *8* **Sixty Roses (IRE)**[18] 5256 2-8-9 **71**.................................. EddieAhern 7 63
(J L Dunlop) *lw: hld up in tch: prog to chal 2f out: sn rdn and nt qckn: lft bhd by ldng pair after* **4/1**[2]

4140 **4** *2* **Bussa**[19] 5245 2-9-4 **83**.. RichardEvans(3) 8 70
(P D Evans) *hld up: rdn and struggling in last 3f out: passed wkng rivals fnl 2f* **25/1**

1262 **5** *4* **Shewalksinbeauty (IRE)**[27] 4955 2-9-1 **77**................ RichardHughes 6 56
(R Hannon) *trckd ldrs: pushed along 3f out: wknd fnl 2f* **10/1**

3040 **6** *1 ½* **May Be Some Time**[17] 5301 2-8-6 **68**.......................... ChrisCatlin 5 43
(W S Kittow) *led 3f: wknd over 2f out* **40/1**

0342 **7** *10* **Liberty Cap (USA)**[15] 5374 2-9-7 **83**..........................(b[1]) WilliamBuick 1 44
(J H M Gosden) *rrd in stalls bef s: dwlt: prog on outer to ld after 3f: hdd 2f out: wknd rapidly and eased: t.o* **7/2**[1]

1m 42.31s (2.41) **Going Correction** +0.25s/f (Good) 7 Ran SP% **95.2**
Speed ratings (Par 97): **97,96,88,86,82 81,71**
Tote Swingers: 1&2 £3.60, 1&3 £2.70, 2&3 £3.10 CSF £16.98 CT £43.75 TOTE £3.80: £2.40, £2.40; EX 17.40.
Owner N Attenborough,Mrs L Mann,Mrs L Way **Bred** Mrs Johnny Eddis **Trained** Manton, Wilts
■ Flodden (4/1) was withdrawn after proving unruly in the stalls. R4 applies, deduct 20p in the £.

FOCUS
Tnhe first pair came clear in what looked an open nursery and produced useful form. Both can rate higher.

NOTEBOOK
Indigo Way was given a very strong ride and just did enough to follow up his Doncaster maiden win in July. He had reportedly had a slight hiccup since then, but is clearly improving nicely and the step up a furlong proved much to his liking. A step up in class now looks firmly on the cards. (op 13-2 tchd 9-2)
Handsome Jack(IRE) ◆ was last seen getting off the mark at Wolverhampton 63 days earlier. Well backed for this nursery/turf debut, he made a bold bid to follow up and was only picked off by the winner near the finish. He deserves credit considering he raced prominently early and, while he will go up for this, can rate higher. (op 4-1)
Sixty Roses(IRE) travelled nicely into the race and held every chance, but was probably made to pay for taking time to settle. She can find an opening off this mark. (op 9-2)
Bussa found the ground turn in his favour and was down in class. Ridden to get the trip, he began to feel the pinch from the home turn and was never seriously a threat. Dropping back to 7f may help, but he does look weighted to his best. (op 20-1)
Shewalksinbeauty(IRE) proved friendless in the betting on this step up a furlong and was made to look one-paced. (op 11-2)
Liberty Cap(USA) was rather lit up by the first-time blinkers and dropped out from the two-furlong pole. (op 9-2 tchd 5-1)

5831 PETER WILLETT STKS (REGISTERED AS THE STARDOM STAKES) (LISTED RACE) 7f
3:45 (3:45) (Class 1) 2-Y-O **£13,340** (£5,057; £2,530; £1,261; £632) **Stalls** High

Form RPR

1 **1** **Titus Mills (IRE)**[46] 4318 2-9-0 0...................................... MartinDwyer 2 104+
(B J Meehan) *w'like: scope: mde all: tending to hang lft: drfted across to nr side rail fr 2f out: drvn and hrd pressed fnl f: fnd ex last 100yds* **5/6**[1]

213 **2** *½* **Big Issue (IRE)**[9] 5567 2-9-0 102.................................. RichardHughes 6 102
(R Hannon) *trckd wnr: drvn to chal jst over 1f out and drifted to nr side: almost upsides 100yds out: no ex* **5/2**[2]

2103 **3** *2 ½* **Surrey Star (IRE)**[17] 5306 2-9-0 105.............................. LiamKeniry 5 96
(R A Teal) *t.k.h: hld up last: chsd ldng pair over 2f out: rdn over 1f out: drifted lft and nt qckn: kpt on* **7/1**[3]

4216 **4** *5* **Trade Storm**[20] 5219 2-9-0 99... TadhgO'Shea 3 84
(J Gallagher) *lw: dwlt: chsd wnr to 3f out: sn rdn: steadily fdd* **9/1**

051 **5** *2* **Persian Herald**[14] 5385 2-9-0 83.................................... DaneO'Neill 4 79
(Pat Eddery) *t.k.h: cl up: pushed along 1/2-way: lost tch over 2f out* **40/1**

1m 29.36s (2.46) **Going Correction** +0.375s/f (Good) 5 Ran SP% **108.1**
Speed ratings (Par 103): **100,99,96,90,88**
CSF £2.97 TOTE £1.50: £1.10, £2.10; EX 3.20.
Owner Sangster Family **Bred** Irish National Stud **Trained** Manton, Wilts

FOCUS
A very interesting Listed event, run at an average pace. The runners came stands' side in the home straight. The winner progressed and the form looks solid.

NOTEBOOK
Titus Mills(IRE) showed himself to be a Group-race performer in the making with a ready effort, following up his Ascot debut success in July. That form is working out nicely and first-time-out winners from his stable very often prove to be above average. Indeed his yard's previous debutant winner of that same maiden was City Leader, who went on to take the Group 2 Royal Lodge back there later on, and this horse would have to be given plenty of respect if turning up there. The manner in which he pulled out more when challenged by the runner-up late on would suggest there is more to come and he probably found the ground easier than ideal. Getting 1m looks as though it will be within his range this term, but connections later hinted they wouldn't be in a hurry to run him over that far this term, which indicates they do believe he could be one for the 2,000 Guineas next year. That would mean the Group 1 Dewhurst at Newmarket next month could well be his next port of call, but he would be facing much classier opposition in that. (tchd 10-11 and evens in places)
Big Issue(IRE), second on debut here in July, was turning out fairly quickly after finishing third in a Group 3 at the Curragh on his previous outing. He emerged as a real threat to the winner inside the final furlong, but was ultimately put in his place. That rival also probably stayed the longer trip the better and this scopey colt looks well up to winning a race of this nature before the season's end. (op 11-4)
Surrey Star(IRE) kept on late making it a 1-2-3 for second-season sire Dubawi. Third in the Solario Stakes last time out, he proved free early on here, but still came there with his chance around 2f out. He couldn't go with the first pair thereafter, but this was the easiest ground he had encountered and he too looks capable of scoring in this grade. (op 6-1 tchd 11-2)
Trade Storm was running on when last seen in the Gimcrack, but he clearly failed to get home over this longer trip on such ground. There will be other days for him. (op 17-2 tchd 10-1)
Persian Herald found the ground ease in his favour, but he failed to settle on this marked step up in class and was the first beaten. (op 25-1)

5832 BUY A #10,000 RACING POST BONUS YEARLING MAIDEN STKS 1m 1f 192y
4:20 (4:21) (Class 5) 3-Y-O **£2,590** (£770; £385; £192) **Stalls** High

Form RPR

-033 **1** **Longliner**[48] 4258 3-9-3 82.. RyanMoore 4 81
(Sir Michael Stoute) *trckd ldng trio: clsd to chal over 1f out: hd quite high but narrow ld ins fnl f: styd on wl: edgd rt last 75yds* **10/11**[1]

6 **2** *1 ¼* **Sentosa**[18] 5258 3-8-12 0.. TomQueally 8 74
(H R A Cecil) *w'like: lw; trckd ldng pair: wnt 2nd over 2f out: rdn to ld over 1f out: hdd ins fnl f: no ex and edgd lft last 75yds* **12/1**

6- **3** *2 ¼* **Alubari**[316] 7050 3-9-3 0... AdamKirby 7 74+
(W R Swinburn) *w'like: scope: bit bkwd: hld up in 5th: pushed along over 2f out: wnt 4th but nt on terms over 1f out: styd on to take 3rd post: encouraging* **9/1**

2 **4** *hd* **Nerves Of Steel (IRE)**[7] 5623 3-9-3 0..........................(t) JamieSpencer 2 77+
(P F I Cole) *w'like: lengthy: attr: led: rdn and pressed 2f out: hdd over 1f out: hld whn squeezed out and snatched up 75yds out: lost 3rd post* **4/1**[2]

6 **5** *2* **Kashmiriana (IRE)**[25] 5038 3-8-12 0................................ KierenFallon 1 65
(L M Cumani) *t.k.h: trckd ldr to over 2f out: wknd over 1f out* **9/2**[3]

4-50 **6** *nk* **Seaside Sizzler**[27] 4964 3-9-0 70...............(b[1]) EJMcNamara(3) 6 69
(R M Beckett) *hld up in 7th: shkn up and nt qckn over 2f out: kpt on fnl f: sltly impeded nr fin* **25/1**

0 **7** *hd* **Regency Girl (IRE)**[18] 5265 3-8-12 0............................ MartinDwyer 5 64
(M P Tregoning) *dwlt: hld up in 6th: outpcd and shuffled along over 2f out: kpt on steadily fnl f: nt disgracd* **33/1**

00 **8** *8* **Sea Tobougie**[15] 5366 3-8-12 0..................................... TravisBlock 3 48?
(M D I Usher) *dwlt: mostly last: lost tch over 2f out* **100/1**

2m 14.86s (6.86) **Going Correction** +0.375s/f (Good) 8 Ran SP% **116.0**
Speed ratings (Par 101): **87,86,84,84,82 82,82,75**
Tote Swingers: 1&2 £3.70, 1&3 £2.60, 2&3 £9.00 CSF £14.03 TOTE £1.90: £1.10, £2.90, £2.80; EX 18.00.
Owner Rick Barnes **Bred** Grangecon Stud **Trained** Newmarket, Suffolk

FOCUS
A modest 3-y-o maiden, run at an ordinary pace and the runners again came stands' side in the home straight. The form is a bit muddling and it is doubtful if the winner had to be at his best.

5833 BETTING SHOPS BACK TURFTV STKS (H'CAP) 1m
4:55 (4:56) (Class 4) (0-80,79) 3-Y-O+ **£3,626** (£1,079; £539; £269) **Stalls** High

Form RPR

4050 **1** **Compton Blue**[10] 5540 4-9-6 **74**..................................(b) RyanMoore 11 81
(R Hannon) *hld up in last trio: looking for room over 2f out: swtchd outside sn after and prog: drvn to ld last 150yds: styd on wl* **8/1**

3321 **2** *1* **Gifted Apakay (USA)**[25] 5041 3-9-4 **77**....................... KierenFallon 9 81
(E A L Dunlop) *stdd s: hld up in last pair: nt clr run over 2f out: taken wd wl over 1f out: drvn and styd on fnl f to take 2nd nr fin* **7/2**[1]

5564 **3** *nse* **Effigy**[17] 5287 6-9-7 **75**.. DaneO'Neill 2 80
(H Candy) *trckd ldng pair: led 3f out: racd against nr side rail after: rdn 2f out and hrd pressed: hdd and one pce last 150yds* **6/1**[3]

0516 **4** *shd* **Salient**[9] 5556 6-9-10 **78**... TomQueally 14 83
(M J Attwater) *hld up in midfield: rdn and effrt over 2f out: nt qckn over 1f out: styd on same pce fnl f* **7/1**

0534 **5** *shd* **Sunarise (IRE)**[37] 4626 3-9-1 **74**............................... RichardHughes 13 78
(R Hannon) *lw: prom: chal 3f out: drvn 2f out and upsides: nt qckn over 1f out: one pce after* **8/1**

0030 **6** *2 ½* **Swift Chap**[10] 5540 4-9-7 **75**...................................... DarryllHolland 7 74
(B R Millman) *on toes: pressed ldr: rdn fr 3f out: stl chalng 2f out: wknd fnl f* **5/1**[2]

6545 **7** *½* **Meydan Dubai (IRE)**[22] 5146 5-8-8 **67**............................ KierenFox(5) 4 65
(J R Best) *lw: dwlt: hld up in last pair: nt clr run briefly over 2f out: drvn and kpt on fr over 1f out: nt pce to threaten* **14/1**

2405 **8** *1 ¾* **You've Been Mowed**[14] 5386 4-9-2 **70**......................... WilliamCarson 8 64
(R J Price) *t.k.h: pressed ldrs: lost pl over 2f out against rail: steadily fdd* **10/1**

5100 **9** *hd* **Very Well Red**[17] 5287 7-9-6 **74**.................................. ChrisCatlin 3 67
(P W Hiatt) *led to 3f out: sn lost pl and btn* **25/1**

2046 **10** *5* **Cookie Crumbles (IRE)**[23] 5122 3-9-1 **74**.................... AlanMunro 12 55
(C F Wall) *t.k.h: trckd ldrs: nt qckn over 2f out: lost pl sn after: wknd over 1f out* **16/1**

1235 **11** *10* **Jewelled**[19] 5237 4-9-5 **73**.......................................(v) JamieSpencer 6 32
(J W Hills) *on toes: trckd ldrs: rdn over 2f out: losing pl whn short of room over 1f out: wknd and eased* **14/1**

1m 41.81s (1.91) **Going Correction** +0.375s/f (Good)
WFA 3 from 4yo+ 5lb 11 Ran SP% **120.0**
Speed ratings (Par 105): **105,104,103,103,103 101,100,99,98,93 83**
Tote Swingers: 1&2 £7.10, 1&3 £10.70, 2&3 £4.80 CSF £36.90 CT £189.49 TOTE £10.80: £3.50, £2.40, £1.70; EX 49.40.
Owner Godfrey Wilson **Bred** Caroline Wilson **Trained** East Everleigh, Wilts

FOCUS
A modest handicap, run at a sound pace and once more the runners shunned the far side in the home straight. There was a blanket finish for the places and the form looks straightforward.

5834 GOODWOOD FREEPHONE 08000 188 191 STKS (H'CAP) 7f
5:25 (5:25) (Class 4) (0-85,85) 3-Y-O+ **£3,626** (£1,079; £539; £269) **Stalls** High

Form RPR

4150 **1** **My Kingdom (IRE)**[42] 4459 4-9-8 **83**............................(t) WilliamBuick 2 91+
(H Morrison) *hld up in last pair: gng wl but plenty to do whn plld out wd wl over 1f out: drvn and r.o after: led last strides* **9/4**[1]

3011 **2** *hd* **Hi Shinko**[7] 5627 4-9-7 **82** 6ex.. DarryllHolland 6 89
(B R Millman) *lw: led at gd pce: hrd pressed over 2f out: beat off rival over 1f out: styd on gamely: hdd last strides* **11/4**[2]

3350 **3** *1* **Kurtanella**[14] 5383 3-8-13 **78**...................................... RichardHughes 8 80
(R Hannon) *chsd ldrs: rdn and no prog over 2f out: styd on u.p fnl f to take 3rd nr fin* **10/1**

030 **4** *½* **Sunshine Always (IRE)**[11] 5495 4-8-5 **71** oh1..............(p) KierenFox(5) 7 74
(T D McCarthy) *chsd ldr: chal and upsides over 2f out: to over 1f out: one pce after* **8/1**

0040 **5** *2 ¾* **Arachnophobia (IRE)**[22] 5142 4-9-2 **77**........................... DaneO'Neill 1 73
(Pat Eddery) *chsd ldrs: rdn wl over 2f out: no prog after: fdd* **8/1**

033 **6** *1 ¾* **Jeninsky (USA)**[13] 5416 5-9-10 **85**................................... AlanMunro 4 76
(Rae Guest) *hld up in last pair: effrt on outer over 2f out: wnt 3rd briefly over 1f out: wknd fnl f* **7/1**

-061 **7** *2* **Avertis**[54] 4057 5-9-4 **79**...(tp) TomQueally 5 64
(Stef Higgins) *chsd ldr to 3f out: wknd 2f out* **6/1**[3]

1m 28.78s (1.88) **Going Correction** +0.375s/f (Good)
WFA 3 from 4yo+ 4lb 7 Ran SP% **115.5**
Speed ratings (Par 105): **104,103,102,102,98 96,94**
Tote Swingers: 1&2 £2.60, 1&3 £5.50, 2&3 £4.00 CSF £8.84 CT £49.46 TOTE £3.60: £2.00, £1.30; EX 8.50 Place 6: £18.71 Place 5: £5.13. .
Owner Wood Street Syndicate V **Bred** Irish National Stud **Trained** East Ilsley, Berks

FOCUS
A modest handicap. It was yet another race where the runners came stands' side in the home straight and there was a good pace on. The winner is probably still on the upgrade.
My Kingdom(IRE) Official explanation: one-day ban: used whip with excessive frequency (Sep 21)
T/Jkpt: £36,082.30 to a £1 stake. Pool:£127,050 - 2.50 winning tickets T/Plt: £25.80 to a £1 stake. Pool:£83,827 - 2,371.48 winning tickets T/Qpdt: £7.70 to a £1 stake. Pool:£6,248 - 594.20 winning tickets JN

5724 LINGFIELD (L-H)

Tuesday, September 7

OFFICIAL GOING: Turf course: good to firm (good in places) changing to good to soft after race 2 (2.45) all weather course: standard

Wind: modest, half behind Weather: cloudy, showers threatening

5835 LINGFIELDPARK.CO.UK MEDIAN AUCTION MAIDEN STKS (DIV I) 6f
2:10 (2:13) (Class 5) 2-Y-O £2,115 (£624; £312) **Stalls** High

Form				RPR
40	1		**Basilica**[27] 4954 2-9-0 0 JamesMillman(3) 9 (B R Millman) *mde all on stands' rail: rdn clr ent fnl f: styd on strly: comf* 9/1	75+
06	2	4 ½	**Morermaloke**[10] 5537 2-9-3 0 JimmyFortune 6 (B J Meehan) *chsd wnr thrght: rdn and pressed wnr wl over 1f out: btn ent fnl f: eased towards fin* 7/2[2]	62
4	3	1 ½	**Jinky**[12] 5453 2-9-3 0 SamHitchcott 11 (M R Channon) *wnt lft s and s.i.s: sn pushed along and rcvrerd to chse ldrs: rdn and outpcd by ldng pair wl over 1f out: plugged on same pce fnl f* 9/4[1]	57+
5	4	¾	**Camache Queen (IRE)**[90] 2867 2-8-12 0 CathyGannon 5 (D J Coakley) *racd off the pce in midfield: rdn ent fnl 2f: styd on steadily fnl f: nvr trbld ldrs* 9/1	53+
04	5	2 ½	**Abadejo**[24] 5085 2-9-3 0 IanMongan 7 (J R Jenkins) *t.k.h: chsd ldrs: rdn ent fnl 2f: btn over 1f out: wknd fnl f* 25/1	47
60	6	¾	**Sleeping Wolf**[7] 5629 2-9-3 0 PatDobbs 10 (R Hannon) *hld up in tch in midfield: rdn and fnd little 2f out: drvn and wl btn over 1f out* 5/1[3]	45
	7	¾	**My Delirium** 2-8-12 0 JimCrowley 8 (R M Beckett) *s.i.s: sn pushed along: a towards rr: pushed along and struggling over 3f out: modest hdwy fnl f: n.d* 8/1	38
024	8	1 ¼	**Summer Jasmine**[39] 4528 2-8-12 60 LukeMorris 4 (H J L Dunlop) *s.i.s: sn rdn along in midfield: lost pl u.p 1/2-way: wl btn fnl 2f* 16/1	34
0	9	2 ½	**Century Dancer**[55] 4029 2-8-12 0 FergusSweeney 2 (Miss Tor Sturgis) *s.i.s and swtchd rt s: a in rr: struggling u.p 1/2-way: wl bhd fnl 2f* 100/1	27
00	10	6	**Pipit Nest (IRE)**[7] 5626 2-8-7 0 SophieDoyle(5) 1 (T B P Coles) *chsd ldrs on outer: rdn and wknd qckly over 2f out: wl bhd over 1f out* 200/1	9
	11	4	**Pleasant Humor (USA)** 2-9-3 0 PatCosgrave 3 (R M H Cowell) *v.s.a: rn green and a wl detached in last* 20/1	2

1m 12.0s (0.80) **Going Correction** +0.05s/f (Good) 11 Ran SP% 116.7

Speed ratings (Par 95): **96,90,88,87,83 82,81,80,76,68 63**

Tote Swingers: 1&2 £12.10, 1&3 £9.20, 2&3 £4.40 CSF £39.38 TOTE £16.70: £5.90, £1.80, £1.10; EX 63.50 Trifecta £242.80 Pool: £426.57 - 1.30 winning units..

Owner N W Lake **Bred** B Minty **Trained** Kentisbeare, Devon

FOCUS

Lingfield's efforts to negate the draw bias by moving the stands' rail inwards didn't seem to have much effect judging by this race. The winner impressed but had the run of the race against the fence. The second ran close to form.

NOTEBOOK

Basilica broke well, soon bagged the fence, and made just about all. He had shown plenty of promise on his debut before disappointing second time, but he eventually won this with plenty of authority. The question is how much this performance was down to a track bias, but he should have a future in nurseries. (op 12-1)

Morermaloke faced a stiff task against previous winners in a soft-ground novice event last time and market support suggested better expected here. He pressed the winner from the start, but was blown away by his rival from over a furlong out. He now qualifies for nurseries, but may be worth dropping to the minimum as he seems to possess plenty of early speed. (op 5-1 tchd 3-1)

Jinky had the rails draw, but didn't break well enough to utilise it. As on his debut on the Polytrack here last month, he was inclined to race in snatches and ran green, only getting going when it was too late. He may well come on again for this and looks worth a try over 7f. (op 5-2 tchd 11-4)

Camache Queen(IRE) ◆, not seen since showing some promise on her Kempton debut in June, wasn't travelling that well early but stayed on late and was the only one to make any significant inroads from off the pace. She can improve again from this. (tchd 10-1)

Abadejo didn't help himself by pulling hard behind the leaders early and found little off the bridle. He will have more options now that he can be handicapped. (op 16-1)

Sleeping Wolf, who didn't get home over 7f in soft ground last time, made no impression back down in trip but also now gets a mark. (op 6-1)

Pleasant Humor(USA) Official explanation: jockey said colt was slowly away

5836 LINGFIELDPARK.CO.UK MEDIAN AUCTION MAIDEN STKS (DIV II) 6f
2:45 (2:46) (Class 5) 2-Y-O £2,115 (£624; £312) **Stalls** High

Form				RPR
53	1		**Thomas Tompion (IRE)**[21] 5170 2-9-3 0 GeorgeBaker 9 (G L Moore) *mde all against stands' rail: pushed clr ent fnl f: in command fnl f: eased ins fnl f* 11/8[1]	79+
0	2	4	**Monsieur Jamie**[10] 5523 2-9-3 0 JimCrowley 4 (J R Jenkins) *chsd wnr thrght: drvn wl over 1f out: btn 1f out: no ch w wnr but kpt on to hold modest 2nd fnl f* 9/1	63
302	3	½	**Looksmart**[77] 3295 2-8-12 76 SteveDrowne 5 (R Hannon) *dwlt: sn chsng ldrs: rdn and effrt 2f out: no ch w wnr 1f out: kpt on same pce fnl f* 2/1[2]	57
6	4	½	**Madame Solitaire**[45] 4384 2-8-12 0 PatDobbs 10 (R Hannon) *wnt lft s: sn rcvrd and chsng ldrs: rdn and outpcd by wnr wl over 1f out: kpt on same pce fnl f* 7/1[3]	55
	5	8	**Hot Spice** 2-9-3 0 JimmyFortune 8 (J L Dunlop) *s.i.s: pushed along early: in tch in rr: hmpd after 1f: rn green and edgd lft 2f out: sn wl outpcd* 12/1	36+
	6	6	**Sue's Dream** 2-8-9 0 MatthewDavies(3) 7 (A P Jarvis) *s.i.s: rn green and sn rdn along in detached last: nvr on terms* 33/1	13
	7	3	**Oh So Kool** 2-9-3 0 WilliamCarson 1 (S C Williams) *s.i.s: sn in tch in midfield: rdn and btn over 2f out: wl bhd and eased ins fnl f* 33/1	15+
0	8	6	**Soviet Suspect (IRE)**[16] 5328 2-8-10 0 LauraPike(7) 3 (Miss Amy Weaver) *in tch tl over 2f out: sn wknd and wl bhd over 1f out* 50/1	—

1m 12.27s (1.07) **Going Correction** +0.05s/f (Good) 8 Ran SP% 113.5

Speed ratings (Par 95): **94,88,87,87,76 68,64,56**

Tote Swingers: 1&2 £3.40, 1&3 £1.50, 2&3 £3.70 CSF £14.56 TOTE £2.20: £1.10, £2.70, £1.10; EX 10.60 Trifecta £81.00 Pool: £479.68 - 4.38 winning units..

Owner R A Green **Bred** Mrs M Gittins **Trained** Lower Beeding, W Sussex

FOCUS

The winning time was 0.27 seconds slower than division one, though the rain may have had an effect. As was the case in the opener, the winner was the horse that bagged the stands' rail in front after breaking from the stalls. The form may not prove too solid. The favourites flip-flopped beforehand and the market was proved right.

NOTEBOOK

Thomas Tompion(IRE) had shown plenty of ability in his first two starts and his rider exuded confidence throughout this contest. Having made all, he stretched right away inside the last furlong and, being by Captain Rio, would have appreciated any easing of the ground. He could be interesting in autumn nurseries. (op 7-4)

Monsieur Jamie, well beaten on his Newmarket debut, was a springer in the market and ran much better here, pressing the winner throughout and keeping on well for second after the favourite had broken clear. He has a small race in him. (op 16-1)

Looksmart, possibly unlucky not to do even better when second of 15 in a Newbury maiden when last seen in June, set the standard with a mark of 76 but although close enough from the off, found disappointingly little off the bridle. She is starting to look exposed. (op 6-4)

Madame Solitaire, who finished behind three subsequent winners when sixth of seven on her Salisbury debut, didn't break well enough to make full use of the stands'-rail draw and still looked green. She may well have still needed the experience and is worth another chance. (tchd 8-1)

Hot Spice needs both time and a much greater test of stamina. (op 9-1)

5837 TEENOSO NURSERY 7f
3:20 (3:21) (Class 5) (0-75,75) 2-Y-O £3,238 (£963; £481; £240) **Stalls** High

Form				RPR
0602	1		**Red Oleander**[7] 5644 2-7-12 52 oh2 (b) SilvestreDeSousa 11 (Sir Mark Prescott) *mde all: aganst stands' rail: rdn and drew readily clr ent fnl f: eased wl ins fnl f: comf* 5/4[1]	61+
3305	2	3	**Silken Thoughts**[17] 5310 2-8-11 65 MickyFenton 5 (John Berry) *sn crossed to chse wnr towards stands' rail: rdn 2f out: drvn and btn 1f out: plugged on to hold 2nd ins fnl f* 11/1	66
630	3	2	**Ivan Vasilevich (IRE)**[22] 5156 2-8-13 67 TomMcLaughlin 3 (Jane Chapple-Hyam) *chsd ldrs on outer: drvn to chse ldng trio over 1f out: no ch w wnr fnl f but kpt on to go 3rd fnl 150yds* 20/1	63+
3101	4	1 ¾	**Captain Loui (IRE)**[18] 5269 2-8-9 63 PatDobbs 4 (D Burchell) *chsd ldng pair: rdn and unable qck wl over 1f out: drvn and btn ent fnl f: lost 3rd fnl 150yds* 25/1	54
613	5	½	**Majestic Dream (IRE)**[22] 5140 2-9-7 75 ShaneKelly 7 (W R Swinburn) *hld up in tch in midfield: swtchd lft ent fnl 2f: rdn and effrt wl over 1f out: sn btn: plugged on same pce fnl f* 8/1	65
054	6	2 ¾	**Empress Charlotte**[43] 4421 2-8-7 61 HayleyTurner 10 (M L W Bell) *wl in tch: rdn and unable qck ent fnl 2f: rdn and btn over 1f out* 7/1[3]	44
0000	7	¾	**King Bling (IRE)**[6] 5659 2-7-13 53 NickyMackay 8 (S Kirk) *in tch towards rr: effrt u.p ent fnl 2f: no prog and wl btn over 1f out* 25/1	34
000	8	nk	**Folly Drove**[53] 4095 2-9-0 68 (t) SamHitchcott 6 (J G Portman) *stdd s: hld up in tch in rr: pushed along and nt clr run ent fnl 2f tl over 1f out: nvr trbld ldrs* 40/1	48
633	9	9	**Bearheart (IRE)**[22] 5156 2-9-4 72 JimmyFortune 13 (E A L Dunlop) *chsd ldrs on stands' rail: rdn and btn wl over 1f out: wknd qckly over 1f out: eased ins fnl f* 9/2[2]	30
050	10	2 ¾	**Aquilifer (IRE)**[10] 5523 2-8-3 57 CathyGannon 12 (W Jarvis) *hld up in tch towards rr: effrt and hanging rt over 2f out: sn struggling and wl btn over 1f out: eased ins fnl f* 14/1	8
3140	11	2	**Sir Lunchalott**[21] 5187 2-9-5 73 (p) LukeMorris 1 (J S Moore) *in tch towards rr on outer: rdn and struggling over 2f out: wl bhd and eased ins fnl f* 25/1	19+
01	12	17	**History Repeating**[27] 4967 2-8-6 60 DavidProbert 9 (M D I Usher) *s.i.s: bhd and sn pushed along: hmpd 4f out: lost tch over 2f out: wl bhd and eased fnl f* 20/1	—

1m 25.05s (1.75) **Going Correction** +0.20s/f (Good) 12 Ran SP% 124.7

Speed ratings (Par 95): **98,94,92,90,89 86,85,85,75,71 69,50**

Tote Swingers: 1&2 £5.80, 1&3 £12.40, 2&3 £27.40 CSF £15.73 CT £212.76 TOTE £2.00: £1.10, £3.20, £6.90; EX 20.60 Trifecta £377.80 Pool: £561.71 - 1.10 winning units..

Owner Cheveley Park Stud **Bred** Cheveley Park Stud Ltd **Trained** Newmarket, Suffolk

FOCUS

Following another downpour the ground was changed to good to soft. Despite the going change, the way the race panned out was strangely familiar as once again the winner soon grabbed the stands' rail in front. The runner-up helps with the level.

NOTEBOOK

Red Oleander finished well clear of the third when runner-up in a Fibresand nursery seven days earlier when blinkered for the first time, which showed that she could handle a testing surface. She did swerve away to her left exiting the gates, but still showed enough speed to get to the rail in the lead and from then on it was just a case of keeping her up to her work to stay in front. She may be a little flattered by this, but she was 2lb wrong and can surely find more opportunities during the autumn on turf or sand. (op 7-4, tchd 2-1 in places)

Silken Thoughts, not disgraced in better-class nurseries the last twice, did well to take a handy position from her lowish draw and although no match for the winner, stayed on well enough for second. She doesn't have much scope, but should be up to winning a routine nursery. (op 10-1)

Ivan Vasilevich(IRE) ◆, making his nursery debut after showing some ability in three maidens, may be the one to take from the race. Not only was he drawn low, he was also forced to make his effort widest of all so did well to get so close. He is worth keeping in mind. (op 18-1 tchd 25-1)

Captain Loui(IRE), making his nursery debut on his first start for the yard after winning a seller and a claimer for Kevin Ryan, raced widest of the three leaders until weakening under pressure from over a furlong out, but this was still a fair effort under the circumstances.

Majestic Dream(IRE), stepping up in trip, didn't seem to be beaten through lack of stamina but he could never get on terms with the leaders. The easing of the ground may not have helped him. (tchd 7-1 and 10-1)

Empress Charlotte, making her nursery debut and 9lb better off for a near 5l beating by Majestic Dream at Windsor last time, raced handily enough but didn't find a great deal once off the bridle. Her rider reported that she had lost her right front shoe. Official explanation: vet said filly lost a right fore shoe (op 15-2 tchd 6-1)

5838 PARTHIA H'CAP 7f
3:55 (3:55) (Class 4) (0-80,80) 3-Y-O+ £4,533 (£1,348; £674; £336) **Stalls** High

Form				RPR
5212	1		**Another Try (IRE)**[19] 5238 5-8-12 72 HarryBentley(7) 5 (A P Jarvis) *chsd ldrs on outer: wnt 2nd over 2f out: pushed to ld and hung rt fr 2f out: rdn over 1f out: in command and idled ins fnl f: rdn out* 10/1	83
6332	2	1 ¾	**Fantasy Gladiator**[9] 5561 4-9-2 69 (p) PatCosgrave 8 (R M H Cowell) *in tch in midfield: stmbld 3f out: sn rdn: hdwy u.p over 1f out: drvn and styd on to chse wnr fnl 75yds: nvr able to chal* 3/1[1]	75

The Form Book, Raceform Ltd, Compton, RG20 6NL

-210 **3** ½ **Duster**[74] 3401 3-9-9 80 JimCrowley 11 83
(H Morrison) *broke fast to ld and cross to r against stands' rail: rdn and hdd 2f out: keeping on same pce and btn whn n.m.r jst ins fnl f: lost 2nd fnl 75yds* **5/1**[3]

-006 **4** ¾ **Zebrano**[9] 5561 4-9-7 74 (b) StevieDonohoe 4 77
(A B Haynes) *bhd: last and struggling 3f out: switching lft and hdwy over 1f out: styd on wl ins fnl f: nt rch ldrs* **40/1**

0200 **5** 2¾ **My Learned Friend (IRE)**[68] 3579 6-9-2 76 ThomasBrown(7) 14 72
(A M Balding) *s.i.s: bhd on stands' rail swtchd lft and racd on outer fr 3f out: pushed along and hdwy to chse ldrs wl over 1f out: wknd ins fnl f* **14/1**

0223 **6** ½ **Yes Chef**[24] 5086 3-9-2 73 HayleyTurner 12 65
(J Gallagher) *taken down early: chsd ldr tl over 2f out: hanging lft u.p whn n.m.r over 1f out: wknd fnl f* **4/1**[2]

2013 **7** 3½ **Red Yarn**[27] 4956 3-9-3 74 (b) GeorgeBaker 9 57
(G L Moore) *sn rdn along to chse ldrs: rdn wl over 1f out: hung rt and wknd qckly jst over 1f out* **12/1**

6035 **8** 6 **Hobson**[54] 4065 5-9-2 72 PatrickHills(3) 6 41
(Eve Johnson Houghton) *stdd s: hld up in tch in rr on outer: pushed lft 3f out: rdn over 2f out: wl btn over 1f out* **25/1**

-545 **9** 6 **Hand Painted**[32] 4777 4-9-5 72 FergusSweeney 13 24
(P J Makin) *hld up wl in tch: rdn 2f out: btn over 1f out: eased fnl f* **15/2**

6411 **10** ¾ **Fault**[16] 5325 4-9-10 77 (t) SebSanders 16 27
(Stef Higgins) *chsd ldrs: rdn and struggling over 2f out: wl bhd and eased ins fnl f* **8/1**

5050 **11** 5 **Exceedingly Bold**[10] 5524 3-9-4 80 (t) AdamBeschizza(5) 3 15
(Miss Gay Kelleway) *wnt lft s and s.i.s: sn rdn along and rcvrd to r in midfield: wknd over 2f out: wl bhd and eased ins fnl f* **33/1**

1m 24.78s (1.48) **Going Correction** +0.35s/f (Good)
WFA 3 from 4yo+ 4lb **11** Ran SP% **117.2**
Speed ratings (Par 105): **105,103,102,101,98 97,93,87,80,79 73**
Tote Swingers: 1&2 £7.50, 1&3 £12.00, 2&3 £4.80 CSF £39.34 CT £172.60 TOTE £11.40: £3.20, £1.10, £2.80; EX 50.40 Trifecta £353.00 Pool: £615.38 - 1.29 winning units..
Owner The Twyford Partnership **Bred** Jarvis Associates **Trained** Twyford, Bucks

FOCUS
A reduced field with five non-runners, including those drawn one and two, but the way the race panned out bucked the earlier trend of needing to lead early against the stands' rail. Ordinary form, with a personal best from the winner.
Yes Chef Official explanation: jockey said colt hung left
Red Yarn Official explanation: jockey said filly hung badly right under pressure

5839 APRIL THE FIFTH MAIDEN STKS 7f
4:30 (4:34) (Class 5) 3-Y-O+ **£2,729** (£806; £403) **Stalls** High

Form RPR

3-P0 **1** **En Fuego**[11] 5493 3-9-3 75 JackMitchell 1 78
(P W Chapple-Hyam) *chsd ldr and crossed to r nr stands' rail: led ent fnl 3f: clr w runner-up wl over 1f out: kpt on gamely u.p ins fnl f* **9/1**

3- **2** ¾ **Hajjaan (USA)**[312] 7145 3-9-3 0 RichardHills 5 76+
(J L Dunlop) *chsd ldr: drew clr w wnr wl over 1f out: upsides and gng wl over 1f out: rdn and edgd rt ins fnl f: nt qckn and btn towards fin* **6/4**[1]

0 **3** 3½ **Maid To Dream**[27] 4966 3-8-12 0 (p) NickyMackay 7 62
(J H M Gosden) *trckd ldrs: rdn and outpcd by ldng pair wl over 1f out: plugged on same pce fnl f* **8/1**

0 **4** 3¾ **Fair Breeze**[18] 5265 3-8-12 0 FergusSweeney 6 51
(R T Phillips) *stdd s: t.k.h: hld up in tch in midfield: rdn and wl outpcd by ldng trio 2f out: wl hld whn hung lft 1f out* **50/1**

35 **5** 1¼ **Pedantic**[50] 4205 3-9-3 0 KirstyMilczarek 4 53
(L M Cumani) *sn niggled along towards rr on outer: no ch w ldrs fnl 2f: plugged on fnl f* **7/2**[2]

50 **6** 1½ **Red Flash (IRE)**[11] 5493 3-8-12 0 MarkCoumbe(5) 8 49
(P Leech) *stdd s: hld up in tch in rr: rdn and wl outpcd over 2f out: modest hdwy u.p over 1f out: nvr trbld ldrs* **33/1**

7 5 **Prince Blue** 3-9-3 0 SebSanders 3 36
(G G Margarson) *uns rdr bef s: wnt lft s and v.s.a: rn green in rr: lost tch over 2f out* **20/1**

00-5 **8** 12 **Eclipsed (USA)**[197] 655 3-9-3 0 SteveDrowne 10 3
(J R Best) *hung lft thrght: led tl 3f out: sn hung bdly lft towards centre and btn: wl bhd and eased ins fnl f* **20/1**

4240 **9** 1¼ **Khajaaly (IRE)**[15] 5367 3-8-12 65 (p) AdamBeschizza(5) 9 —
(Miss J Feilden) *dwlt: sn bustled along and rcvrd to trck ldrs: carried bdly lft fr 3f out: wl btn 2f out: no ch whn hung rt u.p ent fnl f: eased ins fnl f* **9/2**[3]

00 **10** 19 **She's Untouchable**[15] 5366 3-8-5 0 NoelGarbutt(7) 2 —
(P Leech) *v awkward leaving stalls and slowly away: a wl bhd: t.o and eased fr over 1f out* **100/1**

1m 25.56s (2.26) **Going Correction** +0.35s/f (Good) **10** Ran SP% **116.9**
Speed ratings (Par 103): **101,100,96,91,90 88,83,69,67,46**
Tote Swingers: 1&2 £3.90, 1&3 £9.00, 2&3 £4.80 CSF £22.07 TOTE £11.40: £2.70, £1.50, £2.30; EX 31.30 Trifecta £285.90 Pool: £517.81 - 1.34 winning units..
Owner Michael Daffey & Robert Markwick **Bred** Bearstone Stud **Trained** Newmarket, Suffolk
■ Stewards' Enquiry : Jack Mitchell one-say ban: used whip with excessive frequency (Sep 21)

FOCUS
A maiden lacking strength in depth and the front pair came clear. The form is rated around them. The winning time was 0.78 seconds slower than the preceding handicap.
Fair Breeze Official explanation: jockey said that the filly hung left
Red Flash(IRE) Official explanation: jockey said that the colt lost his right hind shoe
Eclipsed(USA) Official explanation: jockey said gelding hung left

5840 MID-DAY SUN (S) STKS 1m 2f (P)
5:05 (5:05) (Class 6) 3-Y-O+ **£2,047** (£604; £302) **Stalls** Low

Form RPR

556 **1** **Starburst**[46] 4329 5-8-8 58 AdamBeschizza(5) 4 52+
(Miss Gay Kelleway) *in tch in midfield: gng wl but nt clr run over 2f out: rdn and hdwy between horses jst over 1f out: led fnl 75yds: rdn out* **11/1**

0514 **2** nk **Dream Of Fortune (IRE)**[15] 5367 6-9-9 64 (t) PatCosgrave 8 62+
(P D Evans) *hld up towards rr: stl plenty to do bhd a wall of horses over 2f out: rdn and gd hdwy 2f out: str run to ld ins fnl f: hdd fnl 75yds: no ex* **7/2**[2]

0300 **3** ¾ **Pedasus (USA)**[7] 5631 4-9-4 63 (b) StevieDonohoe 13 55
(T Keddy) *s.i.s: sn bustled along and racd in midfield: rdn 6f out: gd hdwy on outer to chse ldrs 3f out: nt qckn u.p and sltly outpcd over 1f out: styd on again ins fnl f: nt rch ldrs* **33/1**

0400 **4** ¾ **Coiled Spring**[32] 4804 4-9-4 60 PatDobbs 5 54
(Mrs A J Perrett) *sn chsng ldr: led 3f out: drvn ent fnl 2f: hdd ins fnl f: one pce fnl 75yds* **8/1**

3060 **5** ¾ **Generous Lad (IRE)**[24] 5072 7-8-13 47 (b) AmyBaker(5) 10 52
(A B Haynes) *t.k.h: in tch on outer: effrt and rdn to chse ldrs jst over 2f out: kpt on same pce fnl f* **50/1**

0-06 **6** 1¼ **Given A Choice (IRE)**[7] 5635 8-9-4 63 (p) MickyFenton 7 50
(J Pearce) *s.i.s: hld up in rr: hdwy on outer over 2f out: plugged on ins fnl f: nvr gng pce to rch ldrs* **18/1**

2560 **7** 1 **Mister Frosty (IRE)**[76] 3324 4-8-11 50 CharlotteKerton(7) 6 48
(G Prodromou) *t.k.h: hld up wl in tch: rdn and unable qck over 1f out: wknd ins fnl f* **33/1**

5060 **8** ½ **Bolanderi (USA)**[17] 4227 5-9-4 66 JimCrowley 9 47
(Andrew Turnell) *chsd ldrs: wnt 2nd 3f out: upsides ldrs and rdn wl over 1f out: fnd little and btn whn short of room 1f out* **10/1**

00/5 **9** 1 **Vintage Quest**[173] 923 8-8-8 45 SimonPearce(5) 3 40
(D Burchell) *in tch in midfield: shuffled bk on inner and towards rr over 2f out: rdn and hdwy 2f out: no imp fr jst over 1f out* **25/1**

10 7 **Nobbys Girl**[264] 5-8-8 0 AmyScott(5) 11 26
(M S Tuck) *v.s.a and sn pushed along in last: clsd and in tch 7f out: rdn and wknd over 2f out: wl btn over 1f out* **100/1**

5306 **11** ½ **Zero Cool (USA)**[5] 5680 6-9-9 60 (p) GeorgeBaker 2 35
(G L Moore) *broke wl: sn stdd to trck ldrs: rdn and unable qck over 2f out: wl btn over 1f out* **9/2**[3]

0/12 **12** 1 **Domino Dancer (IRE)**[26] 4132 6-9-9 79 (b) SteveDrowne 1 33
(Jim Best) *sn led: rdn and hdd 3f out: sn dropped out: wl bhd fr over 1f out* **15/8**[1]

2m 8.67s (2.07) **Going Correction** +0.125s/f (Slow)
WFA 3 from 4yo+ 7lb **12** Ran SP% **121.7**
Speed ratings (Par 101): **96,95,95,94,93 92,92,91,90,85 84,84**
Tote Swingers: 1&2 £11.30, 1&3 £25.20, 2&3 £11.60 CSF £49.18 TOTE £12.40: £2.70, £1.40, £4.60; EX 80.40 TRIFECTA Not won..There was no bid for the winner.
Owner Winterbeck Manor Stud **Bred** Winterbeck Manor Stud **Trained** Exning, Suffolk

FOCUS
A moderate Polytrack seller containing more than a few characters and not form to get too excited about, with the form horses not at their best.
Dream Of Fortune(IRE) Official explanation: jockey said that the gelding stopped quickly
Domino Dancer(IRE) Official explanation: jockey said gelding stopped quickly

5841 EUROPEAN BREEDERS' FUND MAIDEN FILLIES' STKS 7f (P)
5:40 (5:41) (Class 5) 2-Y-O **£3,367** (£1,002; £500; £250) **Stalls** Low

Form RPR

2 **1** **Secret Love (IRE)**[25] 5029 2-9-0 0 GeorgeBaker 1 82
(M A Magnusson) *mde all: rdn and qcknd clr over 1f out: in command fnl f: comf* **2/1**[2]

2 2¾ **Submission** 2-9-0 0 KirstyMilczarek 12 75+
(L M Cumani) *t.k.h: hld up in tch: sltly hmpd and lost pl bnd 2f out: rdn and rallied ent fnl f: kpt on wl to snatch 2nd on post: no ch w wnr* **40/1**

3 shd **Sally Friday (IRE)** 2-9-0 0 IanMongan 8 75
(P Winkworth) *chsd ldrs: rdn over 2f out: chsd clr wnr over 1f out: kpt on wl u.p but no imp on wnr: lost 2nd on post* **16/1**

20 **4** hd **Pencarrow**[60] 3861 2-9-0 0 RoystonFfrench 11 74
(Mahmood Al Zarooni) *racd keenly: chsd wnr: rdn and unable qck ent fnl 2f: drvn and outpcd by wnr over 1f out: styd on same pce fnl f* **12/1**

6 **5** nse **Traffic Sister (USA)**[25] 5033 2-9-0 0 JimmyFortune 9 74
(J S Moore) *chsd ldrs: hung rt and lost pl bnd 2f out: rallied u.p fnl f: styd on wl but no ch w wnr* **15/2**[3]

6 1½ **Undulant Way** 2-9-0 0 PatDobbs 3 70
(Mrs A J Perrett) *in tch in midfield: rdn and unable qck jst over 2f out: kpt on again ins fnl f: no threat to wnr* **100/1**

0 **7** ½ **Be Amazing (IRE)**[25] 5047 2-9-0 0 TedDurcan 2 69
(D R Lanigan) *chsd ldrs: rdn and effrt ent fnl 2f: disputing 2nd but nt pce of wnr over 1f out: wknd ins fnl f* **40/1**

8 shd **Coin Box** 2-8-7 0 AntiocoMurgia(7) 10 69+
(Mahmood Al Zarooni) *racd in midfield on outer: wnt v wd and lost pl bnd 2f out: rdn and kpt on fnl f: nvr trbld ldrs* **16/1**

04 **9** 2 **Hello Tomorrow (USA)**[16] 5324 2-9-0 0 RichardMullen 5 64
(D R Lanigan) *s.i.s: hld up towards rr: rdn and effrt on inner wl over 1f out: no real prog and nvr trbld ldrs* **25/1**

10 5 **Croce Rossa (IRE)** 2-9-0 0 PatCosgrave 7 51
(J R Boyle) *rn green and alway towards rr: rdn and struggling over 2f out: wl btn whn edgd lft ent fnl f* **100/1**

32 **11** ¾ **Sahafh (USA)**[55] 4021 2-9-0 0 FrankieDettori 6 59+
(Saeed Bin Suroor) *rrd as stalls opened and lost many l s: clsd and swtchd rt wl over 2f out: no prog over 1f out: nvr able to chal* **5/4**[1]

6 **12** 1¾ **Gainsboroughs Best (IRE)**[9] 5558 2-9-0 0 RichardHills 13 45
(W J Haggas) *swtchd sharply lft after s: a in rr: rdn and lost tch over 2f out* **33/1**

0 **13** 10 **Rio Belle (IRE)**[4] 5719 2-8-11 0 JamesDoyle(3) 4 20
(Andrew Reid) *dropped towards rr over 4f out: last and struggling whn sltly hmpd wl over 2f out: sn lost tch* **100/1**

1m 25.82s (1.02) **Going Correction** +0.125s/f (Slow) **13** Ran SP% **123.6**
Speed ratings (Par 92): **99,95,95,95,95 93,93,93,90,85 84,82,70**
Tote Swingers: 1&2 £17.00, 1&3 £12.70, 2&3 £54.10 CSF £94.77 TOTE £3.00: £1.02, £18.00, £11.90; EX 115.60 TRIFECTA Not won..
Owner Eastwind Racing Ltd And Martha Trussell **Bred** Rathbarry Stud **Trained** Upper Lambourn, Berks

FOCUS
A fairly decent maiden for the track and grade which looked a two-horse race according to the market. It was weakened by the favourite's slow start and the winner and fourth set the level.

NOTEBOOK
Secret Love(IRE) ◆ was soon in front and although it was by no means an uncontested lead, she travelled nicely and once shaking off her nearest rival over 3f from home, pulled right away for a convincing success. Clear of the rest when runner-up to a Godolphin odds-on favourite on her Kempton debut, she holds a Fillies' Mile entry and looks a nice prospect. (op 13-8)
Submission ◆, out of a three-time winner at up to 1m4f, stayed on again after seeming to get outpaced at halfway and there are races to be won with her. (op 50-1)
Sally Friday(IRE) ◆, out of a winner at up to 1m4f, was never far away and she kept battling right to the line. This was a decent debut and she also looks to have a bright future over further. (op 25-1)
Pencarrow, a very disappointing favourite at Newbury last time after going down narrowly on her Kempton debut, came back to form and disputed the lead with the winner for a long way until her rival powered away from her off the home bend. She now gets a nursery mark. (op 16-1)
Traffic Sister(USA), a fair sixth of 11 on her Newbury debut, was never too far away but she lost ground by racing very wide off the home bend, but for which she would probably have finished second. She continues to progress. (op 11-1 tchd 12-1)
Undulant Way, a half-sister to three winners including the useful Midas Way, made some late progress and is going to appreciate further in time.

Be Amazing(IRE) ◆, beaten over 30l on her Newmarket debut, ran much better here and showed up for a long way before weakening inside the last furlong against the usually unfavoured inside rail. She will be interesting when handicapped after her next run. (op 66-1)
Coin Box, out of a 1m winner as a juvenile, raced wide off the pace and hung badly off the final bend, ending up closer to the stands' rail before running on. She looks sure to do better in due course. (op 14-1)
Sahafh(USA) reared up as the stalls opened and lost an enormous amount of ground. Her rider then looked after her rather than riding her hard to get into contention, so a line can be drawn through this. Official explanation: jockey said that the filly reared up as the stalls opened and was slowly away losing many lengths (op 6-4)

5842 TULYAR MEDIAN AUCTION MAIDEN STKS — 1m (P)

6:10 (6:13) (Class 6) 3-4-Y-O — **£2,047** (£604; £302) **Stalls** High

Form				RPR
2052	**1**		**Blitzed**[15] 5367 3-9-3 73 .... GeorgeBaker 10	73+
			(G L Moore) *sn chsng ldr: led over 3f out: mde rest: rdn over 1f out: edgd rt u.p but kpt on wl fnl f* **11/8**[1]	
	2	*1 ½*	**Commerce**[84] 3-8-12 0 .... HayleyTurner 7	65
			(S Dow) *chsd ldrs: hdwy to trck wnr jst over 2f out: rdn and effrt over 1f out: kpt on same pce and no imp fnl f* **7/1**	
0	**3**	*2*	**Launchpad**[11] 5493 3-9-3 0 .... KirstyMilczarek 5	65+
			(L M Cumani) *in tch in midfield: hdwy to chse ldrs over 2f out: pushed along and outpcd by ldng pair over 1f out: rallied ins fnl f: gng on fin* **20/1**	
0	**4**	*2*	**Mister Bit (IRE)**[15] 5376 3-9-3 0 .... TedDurcan 4	60
			(J R Best) *towards rr: pushed along over 4f out: hdwy on outer ent fnl 3f: chsd ldrs and pushed along 2f out: rn green and outpcd over 1f out: kpt on one pce fnl f* **50/1**	
60	**5**	*9*	**Equine Science**[22] 5150 3-8-12 0 .... SophieDoyle(5) 2	40
			(G D Blake) *chsd ldrs: sltly hmpd and wnt rt bnd 5f out: rdn and hung rt bnd ent fnl 2f: sn wknd* **40/1**	
4	**6**	*2 ½*	**Ela Gonda Mou**[32] 4805 3-8-12 0 .... SebSanders 6	29
			(P Charalambous) *sn led and grad crossed over to rail: hdd over 3f out: wknd qckly over 1f out: eased ins fnl f* **7/2**[2]	
5	**7**	*½*	**Annuity (IRE)**[11] 5493 3-9-3 0 .... JimCrowley 9	33
			(W J Knight) *s.i.s: sn rdn along towards rr: reminders over 4f out: lost tch over 2f out* **5/1**[3]	
	8	*2 ¼*	**Best Catch (USA)** 3-9-3 0 .... SteveDrowne 3	28
			(J R Best) *s.i.s: a towards rr: lost tch wl over 2f out* **25/1**	
	9	*5*	**Topaz Way (GR)** 3-9-3 0 .... DavidProbert 8	16
			(P R Chamings) *s.i.s: a struggling and sn pushed along in rr: lost tch wl over 2f out* **14/1**	
5	**10**	*20*	**Fluter Phil**[28] 4926 3-9-3 0 .... SamHitchcott 1	—
			(R Ingram) *s.i.s: sn rdn along and rcvrd to chse ldrs: lost pl qckly and bhd wl over 2f out: sn lost tch: t.o over 1f out* **80/1**	

1m 38.93s (0.73) **Going Correction** +0.125s/f (Slow) **10** Ran SP% **114.4**
Speed ratings (Par 101): **101,99,97,95,86 84,83,81,76,56**
Tote Swingers: 1&2 £2.80, 2&3 £7.20 CSF £10.80 TOTE £2.00: £1.10, £1.20, £7.70; EX 11.80 Trifecta £110.20 Pool: £248.73 - 1.67 winning units. Place 6: £23.95 Place 5: £15.50..
Owner Golden Prospect **Bred** Sir Eric Parker **Trained** Lower Beeding, W Sussex

FOCUS
A modest maiden. It is doubtful if the winner had to match her latest handicap run.
T/Plt: £19.80 to a £1 stake. Pool:£59,896 - 2,199.56 winning tickets T/Qpdt: £11.90 to a £1 stake. Pool:£4,375 - 269.96 winning tickets SP

5843 - 5848a (Foreign Racing) - See Raceform Interactive

5064 DONCASTER (L-H)

Wednesday, September 8

OFFICIAL GOING: Good to soft (good in places) changing to good (good to soft in places) after race 1 (2:00)
Round course rail moved out from Rose Hill to the straight increasing races of 10f, 12f and 14f by 12yds.
Wind: Virtually nil Weather: Overcast

5849 ARENA STRUCTURES NURSERY — 7f

2:00 (2:01) (Class 2) 2-Y-O — **£9,714** (£2,890; £1,444; £721) **Stalls** High

Form				RPR
2212	**1**		**Whisper Louise (IRE)**[31] 4872 2-9-3 **85** .... MickyFenton 11	91
			(Mrs P Sly) *hmpd s and in rr: hdwy on wd outside 2f out: rdn over 1f out: styd on ins fnl f: chal whn n.m.r and hmpd on inner last 100yds: kpt on gamely to ld nr line* **25/1**	
213	**2**	*nk*	**Byronic (IRE)**[11] 5525 2-9-4 **86** ....(p) AdamKirby 13	91
			(C G Cox) *mde most: rdn and hung rt 1f out: drvn and hung bdly rt ins fnl f: hdd and nt qckn nr fin* **10/1**	
41	**3**	*nk*	**Catalyze**[27] 5006 2-9-3 **85** ....(t) JimmyFortune 5	90
			(A M Balding) *cl up: effrt 2f out: sn ev ch: drvn ent fnl f: nt qckn towards fin* **10/1**	
313	**4**	*shd*	**Rerouted (USA)**[61] 3872 2-9-7 **89** .... MichaelHills 4	93
			(B W Hills) *slipped and dwlt s: hdwy and cl up after 1f: rdn 2f out and ev ch tl drvn ins fnl f and no ex towards fin* **15/2**	
561	**5**	*shd*	**Fred Willetts (IRE)**[9] 5602 2-8-5 **73** 6ex........(b) SilvestreDeSousa 7	77
			(P D Evans) *midfield: pushed along 3f out: rdn 2f out: drvn over 1f out: styd on strly fnl f* **8/1**	
0506	**6**	*shd*	**Planet Waves (IRE)**[11] 5525 2-8-8 **76** ....(b[1]) AdrianNicholls 8	80
			(C E Brittain) *t.k.h: hld up in rr: hdwy and n.m.r wl over 1f out: rdn and styd on strly fnl f* **80/1**	
01	**7**	*nk*	**Mariachi Man**[25] 5092 2-9-0 **82** .... DavidAllan 2	85
			(T D Easterby) *cl up on outer: rdn 2f out: drvn over 1f out: kpt on same pce fnl f* **5/1**[2]	
1	**8**	*1*	**My Freedom (IRE)**[26] 5053 2-9-4 **86** .... FrankieDettori 10	87
			(Saeed Bin Suroor) *wnt rt s: t.k.h: trckd ldrs: effrt and hdwy over 2f out: rdn and edgd lft wl over 1f out: sn drvn and one pce* **3/1**[1]	
1	**9**	*½*	**Bridle Belle**[47] 4338 2-9-0 **82** .... PaulHanagan 9	81
			(R A Fahey) *trckd ldrs: effrt whn nt clr run and hmpd wl over 1f out: swtchd lft and kpt on u.p same pce fnl f* **7/1**[3]	
4111	**10**	*4 ½*	**Orientalist**[3] 5784 2-9-2 **89** 6ex........ AdamBeschizza(5) 1	77
			(Eve Johnson Houghton) *t.k.h: chsd ldrs: rdn along over 2f out: sn wknd* **14/1**	
235	**11**	*5*	**Bowermaster (USA)**[34] 4755 2-8-9 **77** .... WilliamBuick 3	53
			(Mahmood Al Zarooni) *t.k.h: hld up towards rr: swtchd lft and rdn 2f out: sn no imp* **14/1**	
036	**12**	*nk*	**King Kurt (IRE)**[35] 4709 2-8-3 **71** .... FrannyNorton 6	50
			(K A Ryan) *chsd ldrs: rdn along 3f out: sn wknd* **50/1**	
1046	**13**	*1 ¼*	**Reginald Claude**[12] 5472 2-8-5 **73** .... LukeMorris 12	45
			(M D I Usher) *hmpd s: midfield on outer: rdn along wl over 2f out: sn wknd* **50/1**	

1m 25.46s (-0.84) **Going Correction** -0.175s/f (Firm) **13** Ran SP% **117.6**
Speed ratings (Par 101): **97,96,96,96,96 95,95,94,93,88 83,82,81**
toteswingers:1&2:£23.00, 1&3:£41.90, 2&3:£17.50 CSF £250.11 CT £2749.62 TOTE £28.40: £5.80, £3.10, £4.00; EX 164.30 TRIFECTA Not won..
Owner G A Libson **Bred** Tom Twomey **Trained** Thorney, Cambs

FOCUS
Rain the previous day had eased the ground but, after a dry morning, it was officially Good to soft, good in places before racing. The jockeys in the first reported it was good or slightly on the slow side. A decent nursery featuring mostly in-form horses and including several unexposed types. The field started off racing up the centre of the track but ended up closer to the stands' rail, and it produced a blanket finish, with the first nine covered by less than three lengths. The time was good and the form might be decent.

NOTEBOOK
Whisper Louise(IRE), a winner over 6f on fast ground, is a consistent type but was stepping up in trip and encountering cut in the ground for the first time. Held up at the back, she began to make headway from the quarter-mile pole then really picked up under pressure, and was brave in squeezing through a narrow gap against the rail to hit the front near the line. Connections will now look for a Listed race with her next. (op 20/1 tchd 16/1)
Byronic(IRE) got the better of three next-time-out winners on his second start, but had been beaten when upped to this trip on easy ground on his last outing. Wearing first-time cheekpieces, he made most of the running and looked like holding on entering the last furlong. However, he drifted right under pressure as he began to tire, and gave away the advantage as his rider corrected him from squeezing out the runner-up in the last 50yds. A sounder surface at this trip might enable him to last home. (op 17/2 tchd 8/1)
Catalyze built on a promising debut on Polytrack, when winning his maiden in clear-cut fashion upped to this trip on fast ground. He ran well on this easier surface, being in the firing line throughout and only losing out narrowly to those nearer the stands' side. (op 12/1)
Rerouted(USA), a 6f winner on fast ground who put up a good effort over this trip last time, was 2lb higher but ran his race. He recovered from a tardy start to soon race handily, and had every chance over a furlong out before his effort flattened out. Defying top weight on this easier surface just proved too much for him. (op 9/1)
Fred Willetts(IRE), the runaway winner of a 6f seller in blinkers for the first time at the end of last month, had a bit to find with Reginald Claude on previous form and was 6lb worse off under a penalty. Nevertheless, he reversed those placings and stayed on well having been one of the first under pressure, only to narrowly miss out on a place in the frame. The blinkers have brought about a fair amount of improvement. (op 20/1)
Planet Waves(IRE) ◆ was aimed high after winning his maiden over 6f on fast ground, and had been well held under similar conditions on his nursery debut on his previous start. Blinkered for the first time, he was held up before finishing strongly, and could be worth keeping in mind if the headgear works as well again. (op 66/1)
Mariachi Man stepped up considerably on his debut to win a 6f maiden on easy ground last month from two subsequent winners, and on breeding this trip presented no problem. He was never far away but raced on the outside of his field and, although he kept trying, was always being held. (op 9/2 tchd 11/2)
My Freedom(IRE) cost 260,000euros and was making his handicap debut having won a modest 6f maiden on his debut. However, he was quite keen under restraint and tended to over-race, so that when he was asked for his effort the response was limited. He was not beaten far though and might settle better in front in future. (tchd 100/30 and 7/2)
Bridle Belle ran green but beat three subsequent winners on her debut over 7f on fast ground. However, after being held up she struggled to pick up on this easier surface, although her relative inexperience might have been against her. (op 13/2 tchd 15/2 and 8/1)
Orientalist had been progressive in nurseries over 6f on fast ground of late but, up in grade and 6lb higher, he was unable to respond to pressure on this easier surface. (op 10/1)

5850 A J WEBB & SON FRESH PRODUCE SUPPLIERS CONDITIONS STKS — 6f

2:35 (2:35) (Class 2) 2-Y-O
£10,904 (£3,265; £1,632; £817; £407; £204) **Stalls** High

Form				RPR
1	**1**		**Barefoot Lady (IRE)**[27] 4981 2-8-8 85 .... PaulHanagan 3	92
			(R A Fahey) *trckd ldrs: hdwy over 2f out: rdn to ld over 1f out: drvn ins fnl f and kpt on wl* **3/1**[2]	
125	**2**	*1 ¼*	**Katell (IRE)**[22] 5184 2-8-11 86 .... SilvestreDeSousa 5	91
			(Mrs L Stubbs) *hld up: hdwy 2f out: swtchd lft and effrt to chal over 1f out: sn rdn and edgd lft: drvn and ev ch ins fnl f: sn hung lft and no ex* **7/1**	
1516	**3**	*nk*	**Belle Bayardo (IRE)**[30] 4903 2-9-1 99 .... TomMcLaughlin 4	94
			(R A Harris) *led: rdn along 2f out: hdd over 1f out: sn drvn: edgd rt and one pce ins fnl f* **16/1**	
1200	**4**	*nse*	**Dubawi Gold**[21] 5219 2-8-13 94 .... TomEaves 7	92
			(M Dods) *cl up on stands' rail: rdn along 2f out: drvn over 1f out: one pce fnl f* **4/1**[3]	
5353	**5**	*2 ½*	**Choose Wisely (IRE)**[8] 5639 2-8-11 100 .... JamieSpencer 6	82
			(K A Ryan) *trckd ldrs: effrt over 2f out: sn rdn and wknd* **11/8**[1]	
3144	**6**	*1 ½*	**Lady Royale**[33] 4797 2-8-6 81 ....(b) DavidAllan 1	73
			(G R Oldroyd) *trckd ldrs: hdwy on outer over 2f out: rdn and ch over 1f out: sn drvn and wknd* **20/1**	

1m 12.38s (-1.22) **Going Correction** -0.175s/f (Firm) **6** Ran SP% **110.2**
Speed ratings (Par 101): **101,99,98,98,95 93**
toteswingers:1&2:£2.80, 1&3:£7.20, 2&3:£6.30 CSF £22.44 TOTE £3.50: £2.40, £4.00; EX 21.30.
Owner Mrs H Steel **Bred** Arbawny Ventures 2000uc **Trained** Musley Bank, N Yorks

FOCUS
The going was changed to good, good to soft in places before this contest. A trappy conditions race, with the higher-rated runners looking vulnerable to the less-exposed sorts, and it was one who fitted into the latter category that came out on top. The favourite was below par and this is not the most robust form.

NOTEBOOK
Barefoot Lady(IRE) stayed on well for pressure to make it 2-2. Easy winner of a moderate 5f Beverley maiden on debut (runner-up well beaten in a seller next time), she clearly improved for the extra yardage here, seeing it out really well having taking over approaching the final furlong. It remains to be seen what she achieved, with the form horses appearing not to run to their best, but she's a likeable sort who will presumably go in pursuit of black type now. (op 9/4)
Katell(IRE), comfortably held in the Group 3 Acomb Stakes latest, had earlier finished second to a smart sort over this trip at Nottingham and he returned to his best to chase home the winner, staying on well once switched left without quite being good enough. (op 11/1 tchd 13/2)
Belle Bayardo(IRE), just 1lb off the top-rated Choose Wisely, had won three of his last five starts, but stopped quickly at Windsor latest, and he looked vulnerable here conceding weight all round. It was therefore a surprise to see him run so well, keeping on again once headed to just lose out on third. (tchd 18/1)
Dubawi Gold has kept good company since making a winning debut and this looked a more realistic assignment, but he raced too freely against the stands' rail, and the fact he managed to keep on to just miss third, having looked set to drop out on a couple of occasions, said a lot about the advantage there is in racing against that rail. He needs to learn to settle better before he can fulfil his potential. (op 100/30 tchd 3/1 and 9/2)

Choose Wisely(IRE), the top-rated having been placed in the Group 3 Molecomb Stakes earlier in the season, was a bit disappointing when beaten at odds of 4-7 last week, and he ran well below par on this first try at 6f, being under pressure and beaten with 2f to run. (op 15/8 tchd 2/1)
Lady Royale had a bit to find with several of these and, challenging widest of all, she could find no extra from over 1f out. (op 18/1)

5851 SCARBROUGH STKS (LISTED RACE) 5f
3:10 (3:10) (Class 1) 2-Y-O+ **£23,704** (£8,964; £4,480; £2,240) **Stalls** High

Form RPR
4312 **1** **Prohibit**[11] 5512 5-9-9 105 (p) JamieSpencer 2 112+
(R M H Cowell) *trckd ldrs: hdwy over 1f out: swtchd rt and rdn ent fnl f: qckd wl to ld last 100yds* **9/2**[2]
2615 **2** ¾ **Rose Blossom**[19] 5276 3-9-8 104 (p) PaulHanagan 3 109
(R A Fahey) *led: rdn over 1f out: drvn ins fnl f: hdd and nt qckn last 100yds* **5/1**[3]
-122 **3** ½ **Group Therapy**[41] 4505 5-9-9 108 FrankieDettori 12 107
(J Noseda) *hld up on outer: effrt 2f out: rdn over 1f out: kpt on ins fnl f* **15/8**[1]
0053 **4** nk **Captain Dunne (IRE)**[11] 5512 5-9-9 105 DavidAllan 10 106
(T D Easterby) *dwlt and towards rr: hdwy wl over 1f out: rdn and styd on ins fnl f: nrst fin* **6/1**
3441 **5** 1 ¼ **Star Rover (IRE)**[8] 5632 3-9-8 94 CathyGannon 8 102?
(P D Evans) *chsd ldrs: rdn wl over 1f out: drvn whn n.m.r and hmpd ent fnl f: one pce after* **22/1**
3600 **6** nk **Moorhouse Lad**[10] 5569 7-9-9 100 TomEaves 1 101
(B Smart) *cl up on outer: effrt and cl up 2f out: rdn and ev ch tl drvn and wknd ins fnl f* **14/1**
0006 **7** ½ **Look Busy (IRE)**[11] 5512 5-9-4 93 PhilipRobinson 6 94
(A Berry) *cl up: rdn along wl over 1f out: drvn and hld whn n.m.r and hmpd ent fnl f:* **9/1**
0040 **8** 8 **Impressible**[81] 3197 4-9-4 85 GrahamGibbons 9 65
(S C Williams) *prom: rdn along 2f out: sn wknd* **66/1**
-211 **9** 8 **Burning Thread (IRE)**[88] 2972 3-9-11 97 WilliamBuick 5 44
(T J Etherington) *j. awkwardly: sn swtchd lft: outpcd and bhd bef 1/2-way* **25/1**

58.09 secs (-2.41) **Going Correction** -0.175s/f (Firm) **9** Ran SP% **110.3**
Speed ratings: **112,110,110,109,107 107,106,93,80**
toteswingers:1&2:£3.90, 1&3:£2.20, 2&3:£2.60 CSF £25.03 TOTE £4.30: £1.60, £2.00, £1.30; EX 24.10 Trifecta £34.80 Pool: £1,163.32 - 24.69 winning units..
Owner Dasmal, Rix, Barr, Morley, Mrs Penney **Bred** Juddmonte Farms Ltd **Trained** Six Mile Bottom, Cambs

FOCUS
A competitive-looking Listed sprint in which the stands' rail was again shunned, the field electing to race more down the middle. The late defection of likely favourite Tax Free further opened things up. The fifth was closer than expected and the form is not the most solid, but the winner rates a small personal best.

NOTEBOOK
Prohibit ◆ came into this bang in-form and came out on top, coming through under a well-timed ride by Spencer and settling it with a tidy turn of foot inside the final furlong. Narrowly denied at Beverley last time, having earlier gained a much-deserved success at Ascot, the 5-y-o seems to be improving all the time and will surely be allowed to take his chance in the Abbaye next month, a race that should suit him well. (op 6/1 tchd 7/1)
Rose Blossom, fresh from her fifth in the Nunthorpe, swapped the visor for cheekpieces this time, which made little difference, and she appeared to run right up to her best. It would be no surprise to see her make the trip to Longchamp also. (op 9/2)
Group Therapy, who arguably recorded a career-best when second in a Group 2 at Goodwood latest, had the rails draw, but elected to move away from it under Dettori and he couldn't stay on as strongly as the winner inside the final furlong, possibly finding the ground a touch dead. (op 9/4)
Captain Dunne(IRE), another out-and-out speedball, was perfectly drawn to blaze away against the rail, but he was quick to move left and David Allan wanted a lead. He had only just finished behind the winner at Beverley last time, and despite picking up well to challenge 1f out, his run petered out in the final 50 yards. (tchd 11/2)
Star Rover(IRE), last week's Leicester winner, again ran his heart out back up in grade, keeping on well despite having been briefly squeezed 1f out. (op 18/1)
Moorhouse Lad showed early pace to track the speed before slowly fading. (op 10/1 tchd 9/1)
Look Busy(IRE), who hasn't won since May, was another who could not sustain her early speed. (op 11/1 tchd 12/1)
Impressible was comfortably held on this first start since June, but she will find easier opportunities. (op 50/1)
Burning Thread(IRE), a winner in this grade at Sandown latest, was soon in last place having jumped awkwardly, and never went a yard, suggesting something may well have been amiss. Official explanation: trainer said gelding was found to have twisted its back (op 14/1)

5852 FUDGE AND SMUDGE LEGER LEGENDS CLASSIFIED STKS 1m (S)
3:45 (3:47) (Class 5) 3-Y-O+ **£6,476** (£1,927; £963; £481) **Stalls** High

Form RPR
1131 **1** **Miami Gator (IRE)**[16] 5353 3-11-2 70 (v) CharlieSwan 5 79
(Mrs K Burke) *mde all: clr after 2f: rdn wl over 1f out: kpt on strly fnl f* **9/2**[2]
6031 **2** 1 ¾ **Legal Legacy**[4] 5756 4-11-13 70 DaleGibson 13 81
(M Dods) *t.k.h early: in tch: effrt over 2f out: rdn wl over 1f out: chsd wnr ins fnl f: no imp towards fin* **9/2**[1]
4302 **3** nk **Aflaam (IRE)**[8] 5634 5-11-7 70 (t) GrahamBradley 14 74
(R A Harris) *a.p: effrt 3f out: rdn 2f out and sn chsng wnr: drvn over 1f out and kpt on same pce* **8/1**[2]
0032 **4** 3 ¼ **Cape Kimberley**[15] 5388 3-11-2 68 ErnieJohnson 10 67
(A G Newcombe) *trckd ldrs: hdwy 3f out: rdn to chse wnr 2f out: drvn and one pce appr fnl f* **25/1**
42-6 **5** ¾ **Plenty O'Toole**[15] 5384 3-11-2 70 KevinDarley 17 65
(Mrs D J Sanderson) *hld up: hdwy over 2f out: rdn to chse ldrs wl over 1f out: kpt on same pce ent fnl f* **20/1**
4241 **6** 1 **Grand Diamond (IRE)**[13] 5436 6-11-7 69 (p) TonyDobbin 9 63
(J S Goldie) *hld up in rr: hdwy 2f out: rdn wl over 1f out: kpt on ins fnl f: nrst fin* **8/1**[2]
5550 **7** nk **Archie Rice (USA)**[18] 5311 4-11-7 70 JohnFrancome 12 62
(T Keddy) *chsd ldrs: rdn along over 2f out: drvn wl over 1f out and grad wknd* **20/1**
3143 **8** 3 **Daring Dream (GER)**[14] 5407 5-11-7 70 AlexGreaves 16 55
(J S Goldie) *hld up: hdwy 3f out: rdn to chse ldrs 2f out: wknd appr fnl f* **9/1**[3]
0006 **9** ½ **Dark Moment**[12] 5486 4-11-7 68 GeorgeDuffield 8 54
(Ollie Pears) *hld up in tch: hdwy over 2f out: rdn wl over 1f out: no imp* **20/1**
0005 **10** 3 ½ **Nevada Desert (IRE)**[10] 5545 10-11-7 69 JohnReid 7 46
(R M Whitaker) *hld up in rr: sme hdwy over 2f out: sn rdn and n.d* **20/1**
0012 **11** 1 ¾ **Rising Kheleyf (IRE)**[12] 5486 4-11-7 67 GaryBardwell 18 42
(John A Harris) *in tch: rdn along over 3f out: sn outpcd* **25/1**
-000 **12** 1 ½ **Kinsya**[89] 2937 7-11-7 68 SteveSmith-Eccles 6 39
(M H Tompkins) *midfield: rdn along wl over 2f out: sn wknd* **9/1**[3]
0/00 **13** 2 ¾ **Jackson (BRZ)**[53] 4154 8-11-7 68 GrahamThorner 11 32
(R C Guest) *dwlt in rr: rdn over 3f out: sn bhd* **100/1**
0546 **14** 6 **Master Of Dance (IRE)**[18] 5304 3-11-2 70 PatEddery 19 18
(J G Given) *in tch on wd outside: effrt 3f out: rdn 2f out and sn wknd* **10/1**
1066 **15** 6 **Eastern Gift**[15] 5391 5-11-7 69 GayKelleway 4 5
(Miss Gay Kelleway) *hld up in rr: hdwy 3f out: rdn over 2f out and sn btn* **33/1**
0210 **16** 5 **Army Of Stars (IRE)**[37] 4662 4-11-7 70 (p) JamieOsborne 1 —
(J A Osborne) *hld up towards rr: hdwy on wd outside over 3f out: chsd ldrs over 2f out: sn rdn: wknd and eased wl over 1f out* **20/1**

1m 39.55s (0.25) **Going Correction** -0.175s/f (Firm)
WFA 3 from 4yo+ 5lb **16** Ran SP% **123.1**
Speed ratings (Par 103): **91,89,88,85,84 83,83,80,80,76 74,73,70,64,58 53**
toteswingers:1&2:£3.20, 1&3:£9.20, 2&3:£7.90 CSF £18.93 TOTE £4.90: £1.90, £2.60, £3.10; EX 28.90 Trifecta £91.40 Pool: £749.04 - 6.06 winning units..
Owner Mrs Elaine M Burke **Bred** Newlands House Stud **Trained** Middleham Moor, North Yorks

FOCUS
A new departure with a charity race under rules featuring retired jockeys who had between them won the majority of big races in the world, both on the Flat and over the jumps, including the Derby, Arc, Champion Hurdle, Gold Cup and Grand National. Being a classified stakes the runners were tightly matched judged on official ratings, which meant the skill and more importantly, fitness of their riders, was always likely to prove paramount. In the event, nothing was able to come from off the pace. The winner is rated to the best view of his recent claiming wins.

5853 WILSON FIELD NEUROCARE CONDITIONS STKS 1m 2f 60y
4:20 (4:20) (Class 2) 3-5-Y-O
£15,577 (£4,665; £2,332; £1,167; £582; £292) **Stalls** Low

Form RPR
4010 **1** **Myplacelater**[41] 4507 3-8-8 99 PaulHanagan 2 110
(D R C Elsworth) *hld up: hdwy over 2f out: rdn wl over 1f out: swtchd rt and drvn ins fnl f: styd on strly to ld on line* **22/1**
3112 **2** shd **Wigmore Hall (IRE)**[18] 5319 3-8-11 112 JamieSpencer 6 113+
(M L W Bell) *hld up: swtchd outside and hdwy over 2f out: rdn to ld ent fnl f: sn edgd lft: hdd on line* **9/4**[2]
3-06 **3** ¾ **Al Zir (USA)**[95] 2746 3-8-9 110 FrankieDettori 4 110
(Saeed Bin Suroor) *t.k.h: chsd ldr and bit slipped through mouth after 1f: hdwy 4f out: pushed along and sltly outpcd over 2f out: rdn to chal and ev ch over 1f out: drvn ins fnl f: no ex last 100yds* **6/5**[1]
0153 **4** 1 **Black Spirit (USA)**[24] 5135 3-8-9 109 (t) LukeMorris 5 108
(C G Cox) *trckd ldng pair: hdwy over 3f out: rdn to ld wl over 1f out: drvn and hdd ent fnl f: one pce* **8/1**[3]
6240 **5** 1 ¼ **Prizefighting (USA)**[62] 3822 3-8-9 105 WilliamBuick 1 105
(J H M Gosden) *hld up in rr: rdn and hung lft fr wl over 2f out: kpt on ins fnl f* **20/1**
-024 **6** ½ **Chock A Block (IRE)**[18] 5291 4-9-2 105 TedDurcan 3 104
(Saeed Bin Suroor) *set str pce: rdn over 2f out: sn hdd & wknd* **12/1**
2/5- **7** ½ **Taameer**[502] 1485 4-9-2 104 RichardHills 7 103
(M P Tregoning) *trckd ldrs: hdwy over 3f out: cl up over 2f out: sn rdn and wknd over 1f out* **12/1**

2m 7.90s (-1.50) **Going Correction** -0.025s/f (Good)
WFA 3 from 4yo 7lb **7** Ran SP% **111.8**
Speed ratings (Par 109): **105,104,104,103,102 102,101**
toteswingers:1&2:£5.20, 1&3:£5.10, 2&3:£1.20 CSF £68.48 TOTE £15.30: £4.40, £2.20; EX 63.10.
Owner A J Thompson **Bred** Mrs N A Ward **Trained** Newmarket, Suffolk

FOCUS
A very good conditions race, with Group 1 form represented, and as expected the classic generation dominated. Chock A Block ensured the pace was a good one and it was certainly a dramatic finish. The form looks pretty sound with a 6lb personal best from the winner.

NOTEBOOK
Myplacelater, who still had five ahead of her racing into the final furlong, got up on the line under a determined drive. Officially rated at least 5lb inferior to all her rivals, she had shown smart form earlier in the season, and her latest effort over 1m6f at Goodwood was safely ignored, as she got worked up beforehand and reportedly lost her action. She still looked an unlikely winner against some potentially high-class males, however, so she deserves plenty of credit and is clearly still progressing. It's probable that will be it for the season now, though, with David Elsworth anticipating further improvement from three to four. (op 16/1 tchd 14/1)
Wigmore Hall(IRE), winner of the John Smith's Cup earlier in the season, found only one too good in the Grade 1 Secretariat Stakes at Arlington last month and his useful turn of pace was again seen to good effect when sweeping to the lead over 1f out here. However, he's a horse who doesn't always do much in front, but would have held on had Spencer maintained vigorous riding all the way to the line. The rider in mitigation said that he had put down his whip to avoid interfering with the third on his inside, and explanation that was noted. Despite this defeat, he remains a candidate for Group honours, and perhaps he will end up in the Champion Stakes at Newmarket, a race last year's winner of this Twice Over went on to collect. (op 2/1 tchd 5/2)
Al Zir(USA) is a magnificent specimen of a horse who showed smart form earlier in the season despite still looking too weak to do himself justice, finishing ninth in the 2000 Guineas and a very creditable sixth in the Derby. He looked certain to have returned from his 96-day break an improved horse, but he took a keen grip early with the bit slipping through his mouth and then couldn't quicken for pressure, but still keeping on to not be beaten far. Both his American breeding and long, raking stride point to him being a much better horse on artificial surfaces, something which he has yet to encounter, and don't be surprised if it takes him another year or so to fulfil his potential. He could really shine in the desert early next year, so also don't be surprised if he one day develops into a World Cup horse. (op 6/4 tchd 11/10 and 13/8)
Black Spirit(USA) has twice shown good form in Group 2 company in France since winning a handicap off 97 at Sandown, so this looked very winnable for him with the tongue tie back on. He ran well, coming to hold every chance, but couldn't quicken on inside the final 150 yards. (tchd 9/1)
Prizefighting(USA), who ran poorly in first-time blinkers latest, never got close enough to challenge having hung under pressure in the last 3f. He did keep on late though, and will find easier opportunities at this level. (op 16/1)
Chock A Block(IRE) had run creditably at Chester last time and he fulfilled his role as pacemaker. (tchd 14/1)

Taameer, although ending up last, showed definite promise considering he hadn't run since being a beaten favourite in the 2009 Sandown Classic Trial. This was only his fourth start in all and he should come on plenty. (op 20/1 tchd 25/1)

5854 CRABBIE'S ALCOHOLIC GINGER BEER H'CAP — 7f

4:50 (4:52) (Class 2) (0-100,98) 3-Y-O

£12,462 (£3,732; £1,866; £934; £466; £234) **Stalls** High

Form				RPR
1004	**1**		**Navajo Chief**[20] 5247 3-9-7 **98** ... TedDurcan 6 (A P Jarvis) *trckd ldrs: hdwy 2f out: rdn to ld over 1f out: drvn and edgd lft ins fnl f: hld on wl* **7/1**[3]	108
1-06	**2**	*nk*	**Leviathan**[11] 5524 3-8-10 **87** ... MickyFenton 8 (T P Tate) *hld up and bhd: hdwy over 2f out: swtchd rt and rdn over 1f out: str run ent fnl f: sn edgd lft: jst failed* **8/1**	96+
5021	**3**	*¾*	**Colepeper**[14] 5416 3-9-6 **97** ... FrankieDettori 3 (M Johnston) *trckd ldrs: hdwy on outer over 2f out: rdn to chal over 1f out and ev ch tl drvn and nt qckn wl ins fnl f* **4/1**[1]	104
1130	**4**	*1 ¼*	**Rasselas (IRE)**[24] 5121 3-8-7 **84** oh2 ... AdrianNicholls 2 (D Nicholls) *hld up and bhd: hdwy wl over 1f out: sn rdn and kpt on ins fnl f: nrst fin* **20/1**	88
-244	**5**	*nk*	**Mass Rally (IRE)**[23] 5143 3-9-3 **94** ... WilliamBuick 1 (J H M Gosden) *hld up towards rr: swtchd outside and hdwy over 2f out: rdn to chal over 1f out: drvn and ev ch ins fnl f: edgd lft and wknd last 100yds* **5/1**[2]	97
6042	**6**	*1 ½*	**Layla's Hero (IRE)**[14] 5416 3-9-3 **94** ... JamieSpencer 12 (D M Simcock) *hld up and bhd: hdwy over 2f out: swtchd rt and rdn to chse ldrs over 1f out: n.m.r and swtchd rt ent fnl f: styd on: nrst fin* **7/1**[3]	93
3000	**7**	*¾*	**Carnaby Street (IRE)**[19] 5275 3-9-6 **97** ... JimmyFortune 11 (R Hannon) *prom: effrt over 2f out: sn rdn: drvn and wknd appr fnl f* **16/1**	94
1004	**8**	*shd*	**Sunraider (IRE)**[13] 5442 3-9-3 **94** ... MichaelHills 10 (B W Hills) *chsd ldrs: rdn along 2f out: grad wknd* **9/1**	91
2036	**9**	*2 ½*	**White Devil**[28] 4956 3-8-7 **84** oh9 ... (v[1]) FrannyNorton 7 (A M Balding) *prom: pushed along 3f out: rdn and wknd over 2f out* **22/1**	74
0000	**10**	*1 ¼*	**Quarrel (USA)**[23] 5143 3-9-1 **92** ... PhilipRobinson 13 (W J Haggas) *prom: rdn along wl over 2f out: sn wknd* **25/1**	79
210-	**11**	*3*	**Flying Statesman (USA)**[449] 2993 3-8-13 **90** ... PaulHanagan 4 (R A Fahey) *chsd ldrs: hdwy and cl up 1/2-way: rdn over 2f out and sn wknd* **9/1**	68
2016	**12**	*5*	**Waveband**[15] 5393 3-9-0 **91** ... JoeFanning 5 (M Johnston) *led: rdn along 2f out: drvn over 1f out: hdd over 1f out and wknd qckly* **25/1**	56

1m 23.76s (-2.54) **Going Correction** -0.175s/f (Firm) **12** Ran SP% **115.5**

Speed ratings (Par 107): **107,106,105,104,104 102,101,101,98,97 93,87**

toteswingers:1&2:£7.30, 1&3:£6.40, 2&3:£9.50 CSF £56.70 CT £255.41 TOTE £8.60: £2.80, £2.50, £1.80; EX 53.60 Trifecta £434.20 Pool: £733.58 - 1.25 winning units..

Owner Geoffrey Bishop **Bred** Eurostrait Ltd **Trained** Twyford, Bucks

FOCUS

A good 3-y-o handicap in which they raced up the centre and went a good pace, and the time was considerably faster than the opening nursery. The winner is rated better than ever.

NOTEBOOK

Navajo Chief, a 7f winner on easy ground and fourth in a valuable handicap off this mark last time after being bumped over 1f out, gained a deserved success in game style. After tracking the leaders, he came through to hit the front but looked likely to be headed by both the market leaders over a furlong out. Having fought them off, he then found the runner-up sweeping down the outside, but he found more and held him off. He likes a race run at a good pace and will go for a heritage handicap next. (tchd 15/2)

Leviathan ◆, a C&D winner last October but absent after that until August this year, had been well held on both starts but is suited by cut in the ground. Held up at the back, he swept past all bar one of his rivals in the last 2f, only to find the winner refusing to be denied. He can gain compensation on his favoured soft surface. (op 15/2 tchd 7/1)

Colepeper, a 7f winner on soft with Layla's Hero (4lb better off) behind, was settled early and looked the likely winner when delivering his challenge. However, he had nothing more to give inside the last furlong and might be best suited by a sharp, undulating track. (op 9/2)

Rasselas(IRE) ◆ is effective at 6f-1m but was racing off 8lb above his last winning mark, including being 2lb out of the handicap. He stayed on well to make the frame and could well find another race over an extra furlong before the end of the season.

Mass Rally(IRE), a dual winner on at this trip on Polytrack, has form on turf but had yet to encounter cut in the ground. He came to have every chance over a furlong out, but appeared to be lugging left in the closing stages and backed out of contention, losing fourth place near the line. He did not look straightforward here. (op 4/1)

Layla's Hero(IRE) closely matched with Colepeper on their last run, had gained his last four wins over 6f on flat tracks, including when there was cut in the ground. He made progress from the back over 2f out, but could make no impression on the leaders. (op 8/1)

Carnaby Street(IRE), a dual winner on a soft surface last autumn, including a Group 3, had been held since but was back on a fair mark. He had his chance in the last 2f but wandered under pressure and faded.

5855 2010 LAUNCH STRATSTONE LAND ROVER DONCASTER H'CAP — 5f

5:20 (5:23) (Class 4) (0-85,85) 3-Y-O+ **£6,799** (£2,023; £1,011; £505) **Stalls** High

Form				RPR
2343	**1**		**Hazelrigg (IRE)**[11] 5513 5-8-9 **73** ... (be) DavidAllan 5 (T D Easterby) *trckd ldrs: hdwy 2f out: rdn to ld 1f out and sn hung rt: drvn and hung bdly rt ins fnl f: kpt on* **8/1**[3]	85
0354	**2**	*1 ¼*	**Grissom (IRE)**[69] 3584 4-8-10 **74** ... (t) DuranFentiman 6 (T D Easterby) *trckd ldrs: hdwy 2f out: rdn over 1f out: drvn ins fnl f: kpt on* **10/1**	81
0050	**3**	*¾*	**Indian Trail**[18] 5290 10-9-2 **80** ... (v) AdrianNicholls 7 (D Nicholls) *in tch on outer: hdwy 2f out: rdn to chse ldrs over 1f out: drvn and kpt on ins fnl f* **16/1**	84
3220	**4**	*shd*	**Noodles Blue Boy**[45] 4413 4-9-4 **82** ... FrannyNorton 21 (Ollie Pears) *trckd ldrs on inner: hdwy 2f out: rdn over 1f out: drvn and ev ch ins fnl f tl hmpd and no ex last 50yds* **14/1**	86
1112	**5**	*¾*	**Captain Coke (IRE)**[18] 5309 3-9-6 **85** ... PhilipRobinson 18 (M A Jarvis) *trckd ldrs: hdwy 2f out: rdn over 1f out: drvn and one pce ins fnl f* **11/4**[1]	86
3555	**6**	*shd*	**Invincible Lad (IRE)**[18] 5308 6-9-4 **82** ... PaulHanagan 11 (E J Alston) *hld up: hdwy 2f out: chse ldrs wl over 1f out: n.m.r and swtchd lft ent fnl f: sn rdn and kpt on same pce* **8/1**[3]	83
0006	**7**	*¾*	**Oldjoesaid**[9] 5589 6-9-5 **83** ... (t) JamieSpencer 12 (K A Ryan) *hld up and bhd: hdwy 2f out: swtchd rt over 1f out: rdn and styd on ins fnl f: nrst fin* **11/2**[2]	81+
5/06	**8**	*½*	**Marvellous Value (IRE)**[46] 4372 5-9-5 **83** ... TomEaves 19 (M Dods) *towards rr: hdwy 2f out: swtchd lft and rdn over 1f out: styd on wl fnl f* **20/1**	79
20	**9**	*nse*	**La Capriosa**[16] 5356 4-8-7 **71** oh1 ... PJMcDonald 3 (J A Glover) *led: rdn 2f out: sn drvn: hdd 1f out and wknd ins fnl f* **28/1**	67
1204	**10**	*1*	**Ajjaadd (USA)**[16] 5368 4-8-7 **71** ... TedDurcan 13 (T E Powell) *hld up towards rr: hdwy and in tch 1/2-way: rdn along wl over 1f out and grad wknd* **25/1**	64
1000	**11**	*¾*	**Frognal (IRE)**[18] 5290 4-8-9 **76** ... (b) JamesSullivan(3) 20 (Mrs R A Carr) *nvr bttr than midfield* **20/1**	66
10	**12**	*shd*	**Luscivious**[18] 5290 6-9-2 **80** ... (b) RichardMullen 9 (J A Glover) *a midfield* **14/1**	70
4000	**13**	*nk*	**Pawan (IRE)**[9] 5601 10-8-11 **80** ... (b) AnnStokell(5) 15 (Miss A Stokell) *in rr tl sme late hdwy* **66/1**	69
5030	**14**	*½*	**Hypnosis**[49] 4243 7-8-4 **73** ... DeanHeslop(5) 10 (N Wilson) *chsd ldr: rdn along 2f out: sn drvn and wknd* **22/1**	60
005	**15**	*nk*	**Danum Dancer**[9] 5599 6-8-7 **71** oh14 ... PaulQuinn 16 (N Bycroft) *a towards rr* **80/1**	57
0601	**16**	*¾*	**Italian Tom (IRE)**[18] 5309 3-8-13 **78** ... LukeMorris 14 (R A Harris) *a towards rr* **16/1**	61
2300	**17**	*¾*	**Nubar Boy**[47] 4325 3-8-6 **71** oh1 ... JoeFanning 8 (P D Evans) *awkward s and sn swtchd lft: in tch on outer: rdn along 2f out and sn wknd* **33/1**	51

58.32 secs (-2.18) **Going Correction** -0.175s/f (Firm)

WFA 3 from 4yo+ 1lb **17** Ran SP% **125.3**

Speed ratings (Par 105): **110,108,106,106,105 105,104,103,103,101 100,100,99,98,98 97,96**

toteswingers:1&2:£15.20, 1&3:£20.60, 2&3:£12.00 CSF £78.89 CT £827.42 TOTE £10.00: £2.30, £2.40, £3.60, £3.30; EX 83.00 Trifecta £627.80 Part won. Pool: £848.45 - 0.65 winning units. Place 6 £328.13; Place 5 £42.02.

Owner The Senators **Bred** Rathbarry Stud **Trained** Great Habton, N Yorks

FOCUS

A typically open, big-field sprint handicap. The field raced up the centre and prominent runners dominated. Straightforward form.

T/Jkpt: Not won. T/Plt: £220.20 to a £1 stake. Pool:£120,356.68 - 398.83 winning tickets T/Qpdt: £6.30 to a £1 stake. Pool:£9,967.24 - 1,159.76 winning tickets JR

5675 EPSOM (L-H)

Wednesday, September 8

OFFICIAL GOING: Good (good to soft in places; 7.7; home straight: stands' side 7.9; far side 7.4)

Rail dolled out up to 8yds from 1m to 7f and from 5f to winning post adding about 12yds to distances.

Wind: virtualy nil Weather: cloudy

5856 NIGHTINGALL NURSERY — 6f

2:10 (2:10) (Class 4) (0-85,89) 2-Y-O **£4,533** (£1,348; £674; £336) **Stalls** High

Form				RPR
2101	**1**		**Krypton Factor**[10] 5547 2-9-13 **89** 6ex ... (b) SebSanders 1 (Sir Mark Prescott) *mde all: pushed along and readily drew clr 2f out: pushed out fnl f: comf* **5/2**[1]	96+
4302	**2**	*2 ½*	**Top Care (USA)**[12] 5476 2-9-1 **77** ... KierenFallon 5 (M Johnston) *hmpd s and s.i.s: racd in last trio: swtchd lft and effrt over 2f out: kpt on wl fnl f to go 2nd fnl 75yds: no ch w wnr* **10/3**[2]	79+
650	**3**	*¾*	**Jolah**[39] 4595 2-8-6 **68** ... ChrisCatlin 2 (C E Brittain) *t.k.h: chsd wnr: rdn over 2f out: nt pce of wnr 2f out: no ch w wnr fnl f: lost 2nd fnl 75yds* **8/1**	65
530	**4**	*shd*	**Barista (IRE)**[4] 5745 2-8-5 **67** ... SamHitchcott 9 (M R Channon) *in tch in midfield: rdn and unable qck wl over 2f out: wanting to hang lft and no ch w wnr over 1f out: kpt on ins fnl f* **5/1**[3]	64
5135	**5**	*¾*	**Rosina Grey**[12] 5472 2-8-13 **78** ... JamesMillman(3) 7 (B R Millman) *stdd and wnt lft s: in rr: rdn and effrt on outer whn sltly hmpd over 2f out: edgd rt 2f out: no hdwy tl styd on wl ins fnl f: nvr trbld ldrs* **10/1**	75+
2130	**6**	*1*	**Goodwood Treasure**[39] 4578 2-8-13 **75** ... EddieAhern 4 (J L Dunlop) *rrd s and s.i.s: racd in last trio: hdwy into midfield 4f out: rdn and no prog 2f out: one pce and wl hld fnl f* **12/1**	67+
0330	**7**	*1 ½*	**Magic Stella**[22] 5187 2-9-1 **77** ... NeilCallan 3 (A P Jarvis) *chsd ldng pair: rdn and unable qck wl over 2f out: outpcd by wnr 2f out: wknd jst over 1f out* **14/1**	64
1500	**8**	*2 ¼*	**Believe It Or Not (IRE)**[18] 5301 2-8-13 **75** ... LiamKeniry 8 (J S Moore) *in tch in midfield: pushed along and lost pl over 2f out: bhd and edging lft u.p over 1f out* **13/2**	55

1m 11.18s (1.78) **Going Correction** +0.375s/f (Good) **8** Ran SP% **116.2**

Speed ratings (Par 97): **103,99,98,98,97 96,94,91**

toteswingers:1&2:£1.40, 1&3:£4.90, 2&3:£7.40 CSF £11.10 CT £57.61 TOTE £3.90: £1.30, £1.10, £3.80; EX 6.80.

Owner Lady Fairhaven & The Hon C & H Broughton **Bred** Lady Fairhaven **Trained** Newmarket, Suffolk

FOCUS

The rail was dolled out up to 8yds from 1m to 7f out and from 5f to the winning post, adding about 12yds to race distances. The going was officially good, good to soft in places, but the jockeys decided to take the trusted passage on soft ground and came to the stands' side where the rail is historically the place to be. The winner made all against the rail and was flattered to an extent.

NOTEBOOK

Krypton Factor was able to secure the rail thanks to a forceful ride that clearly showed no doubts about his stamina in moving up 1f after winning over the minimum ten days earlier at Beverley. He has been moved up 8lb for that 1¾l win, was 2lb better in here under a 6lb penalty, and won with enough authority to suggest he'll be winning again soon. He does hold an entry for a 5f conditions race at Sandown on Saturday, where an adjusted figure for this ready win would leave him only just shy of the top-rated entrants. (op 11/4 tchd 3/1)

Top Care(USA) had finished ahead of the winner when they were well beaten at Redcar in August, but despite being 4lb better off and running with credit since, he has not made the same amount of improvement as Krypton Factor. He stayed on well and might be worth a try over a bit further or a stiffer 6f than this. He is certainly well capable of winning a nursery or any average maiden. (op 11/4)

Jolah ran a creditable nursery debut despite dropping down a furlong to this sharp 6f and will be suited by a move back. With a greater test, she should be able to win off this mark which shouldn't alter much. (op 10/1)

Barista(IRE) was on the stands' rail and didn't have the pace to maximise it, but stayed on well enough. He managed to reverse Chepstow running in August with Rosina Grey on 6lb better terms for just over a 4l beating, but the handicapper seems to have him. (op 13/2)

Rosina Grey, 2lb lower than when disappointing last time but 7lb higher than when successful, didn't handle the track particularly well and was on the possibly unfavoured outside up the home straight. (op 8/1 tchd 15/2)

Goodwood Treasure, who lost any realistic chance at the stalls, in the circumstances didn't do too badly and this was better than her previous effort 39 days earlier. Official explanation: jockey said filly reared on leaving stalls and was slowly away (op 11/1)

5857 EUROPEAN BREEDERS' FUND MAIDEN STKS 1m 114y
2:45 (2:46) (Class 4) 2-Y-O £4,533 (£1,348; £674; £336) Stalls Low

Form RPR
032 1 **Enabling (IRE)**14 5413 2-9-3 76 RyanMoore 6 76
(R Hannon) chsd ldr after 1f: pushed along to ld and c stands' side over 3f out: clr and in command over 1f out: pushed out: easily **4/7**1
053 2 3 1/4 **Ihavenotime (IRE)**8 5633 2-8-12 0 SamHitchcott 4 64
(M R Channon) hld up in tch: rdn and c stands' side over 3f out: drvn over 2f out: wnt 2nd ent fnl f: kpt on u.p but no ch w wnr **10/1**
6 3 2 1/2 **Alajmal (USA)**42 4477 2-9-3 0 TadhgO'Shea 7 65+
(M Johnston) led and set stdy gallop tl hdd and c stands' side over 3f out: sn rdn: btn wl over 1f out: lost 2nd ent fnl f **6/1**2
000 4 1 **Prince Freddie**19 5263 2-9-0 67 RussKennemore(3) 2 64+
(P A Kirby) stdd s: hld up in tch: c stands' side and chsd ldng trio over 3f out: effrt and rdn wl over 2f out: pressing for 2nd but no ch w wnr fnl 2f: wknd ins fnl f **8/1**3
06 5 6 **Anton Dolin (IRE)**31 4856 2-9-3 0 EddieAhern 5 55+
(J L Dunlop) s.i.s: hld up in last pair: styd far side over 3f out: led far side trio and rdn 3f out: no hdwy and hanging lft 2f out: wl btn over 1f out **11/1**
5 6 11 **Embezzle**13 5440 2-9-3 0 SteveDrowne 1 26+
(R Charlton) a bhd: styd far side over 3f out: sn lost tch: wl bhd fnl 2f **25/1**
004 7 9 **Will Barrow**48 4293 2-9-3 49 PatCosgrave 3 7+
(J R Boyle) restless in stalls: chsd ldr for 1f: chsd ldng pair after tl styd far side and struggling over 3f out: wl bhd fr over 2f out: t.o **100/1**

1m 51.46s (5.36) **Going Correction** +0.375s/f (Good) 7 Ran SP% 111.3
Speed ratings (Par 97): **91,88,85,85,79 69,61**
toteswingers:1&2:£2.50, 1&3:£1.50, 2&3:£3.30 CSF £6.92 TOTE £1.40: £1.20, £2.30; EX 5.00.
Owner Ben CM Wong **Bred** Dr D Harron **Trained** East Everleigh, Wilts

FOCUS
The four who elected to come over to the stands' side had the race to themselves. The winner was the form pick but also benefited from the course bias, and a cautious view has been taken of the form.

NOTEBOOK
Enabling(IRE), the highest-rated runner in the race, won with plenty of authority. On paper it looked an easy task as he was able to dominate in the style that had suited him when second to the smart Profondo Rosso over approximately this trip at Brighton 14 days earlier, where the winner has subsequently been rated 82. It will be interesting to see how the handicapper tries to bring the pair together when this winner is reassessed. (op 4/5 tchd 10/11)
Ihavenotime(IRE) was flattered when just over 1½l third to a long odds-on winner Midnight Caller eight days earlier and although this was her fourth run, connections have not yet asked for a mark. Again she faced a hopeless task, but had the advantage of being close to the stands rail. She should be competitive off a mid-60s rating. (op 13/2)
Alajmal(USA) had more use made of him this time than on debut and that, plus a move up 2f, seemed to suit him. He's still learning and needs another run to get a mark. (op 9/2 tchd 13/2)
Prince Freddie was rated 9lb inferior to the winner and raced further off the stands' rail, but despite moving up 1f after showing promise at Sandown 19 days earlier, was never going to be a contender. On this showing his rating looks tough. (op 9/1 tchd 10/1)
Anton Dolin(IRE) was the first home of the trio that went far side, but never had a prayer and looked ill-at-ease on the camber. There's a long way to go. (op 14/1 tchd 16/1)
Embezzle was another to go far side, but was ill-suited to the track for most of the way and still looks very immature. (op 16/1)
Will Barrow is rated a modest 49 and got his chin over the stalls shortly before they opened. That didn't help a task that was made impossible by staying far side.

5858 ASHTEAD H'CAP 1m 4f 10y
3:20 (3:22) (Class 4) (0-85,80) 3-Y-O £5,828 (£1,734; £866; £432) Stalls Centre

Form RPR
1011 1 **Epic (IRE)**21 5215 3-9-4 80 (b) KierenFallon 4 89+
(M Johnston) chsd ldrs: wnt 2nd over 4f out: pushed along to ld and r against stands' rail over 3f out: racd idly and rdn along wl over 1f out: drew clr ins fnl f: eased nr fin: comf **7/2**3
3331 2 1 1/4 **First Fandango**24 5116 3-9-0 76 EddieAhern 6 81
(J W Hills) stdd s: hld up in tch in rr: nt clr run and switching lft 2f out: swtchd further lft and hdwy u.p over 1f out: wnt 2nd fnl 100yds: no threat to wnr **10/1**
6-33 3 1 **Argaum (IRE)**39 4571 3-8-6 73 JohnFahy(5) 5 76
(W R Swinburn) led: hdd over 3f out: rdn and unable qck ent fnl 2f: styd on same pce after and btn jst ins fnl f: lost 2nd fnl 100yds **10/3**2
3313 4 1/2 **Heart Of Hearts**46 4360 3-9-3 79 TomQueally 7 82
(H R A Cecil) in tch: hdwy to chse ldrs over 3f out: chsd ldng pair but n.m.r ent fnl 2f: drvn over 1f out: styd on same pce fnl f **9/4**1
1116 5 7 **Goldtrek (USA)**27 5008 3-9-3 79 SteveDrowne 2 70
(R Charlton) chsd ldr tl over 4f out: rdn and unable qck 3f out: wknd over 1f out **7/1**
1305 6 1/2 **Eltheeb**19 5266 3-8-11 73 TadhgO'Shea 3 64
(J L Dunlop) hld up in tch towards rr: rdn and no prog ent 3f out: wl btn wl over 1f out **12/1**
2145 7 shd **Lauberhorn**50 4230 3-8-10 72 SebSanders 1 62
(Eve Johnson Houghton) in tch in midfield: rdn and unable qck ent fnl 3f: drvn and wknd 2f out **16/1**

2m 42.8s (3.90) **Going Correction** +0.375s/f (Good) 7 Ran SP% 111.2
Speed ratings (Par 103): **102,101,100,100,95 95,95**
toteswingers:1&2:£3.20, 1&3:£1.90, 2&3:£8.10 CSF £34.85 TOTE £4.40: £1.20, £4.60; EX 26.50.
Owner Racegoers Club Owners Group **Bred** P D Savill **Trained** Middleham Moor, N Yorks

FOCUS
A fair handicap. The winner, who grabbed the stands' rail, continues on the upgrade and rates a 4lb personal best.

5859 GOLF COURSE H'CAP 1m 2f 18y
3:55 (3:56) (Class 4) (0-85,82) 3-Y-O+ £4,533 (£1,348; £674; £336) Stalls Low

Form RPR
0303 1 **Ramona Chase**9 5592 5-9-6 75 (t) NeilCallan 6 85
(M J Attwater) chsd ldng trio: swtchd lft and rdn ent fnl 3f: chsd ldr ent fnl 2f: chal jst over 1f out: kpt on wl to ld fnl 75yds: rdn out **9/2**2
0123 2 3/4 **North Cape (USA)**25 5091 4-9-4 78 AmyScott(5) 7 87
(H Candy) dwlt: sn pushed along: hdwy to ld over 7f out: rdn ent fnl 3f: clr w wnr over 1f out: hdd and no ex fnl 75yds **7/2**1
3216 3 5 **Licence To Till (USA)**25 5098 3-9-6 82 KierenFallon 4 81
(M Johnston) t.k.h: hld up in tch: rdn and effrt to chse ldng trio 3f out: no imp and drvn over 1f out: no ch w ldng pair fnl f: wnt 3rd fnl 100yds **9/2**2
1212 4 1 1/4 **Urban Space**16 5375 4-9-3 77 KierenFox(5) 2 73
(J L Flint) led tl over 7f out: chsd ldng pair after: rdn and chsd ldr 3f out tl ent fnl 2f: wknd u.p over 1f out: lost 3rd fnl 100yds **7/2**1
3361 5 nk **Potentiale (IRE)**6 5680 6-8-10 72 (p) HollyHall(7) 8 67
(J W Hills) stdd s: hld up wl off the pce in last: stl plenty to do and swtchd lft over 1f out: rdn and kpt on ins fnl f: nvr threatened ldrs **7/2**1
4-00 6 3 3/4 **Royal Defence (IRE)**91 2865 4-9-12 81 J-PGuillambert 5 69
(N P Littmoden) hld up in last trio: rdn and effrt ent fnl 3f: no prog and btn wl over 1f out **33/1**
-120 7 3 **Danger Mulally**18 5286 3-9-1 77 (t) DavidProbert 9 59
(A M Balding) t.k.h: chsd ldr: rdn to press ldr over 3f out: unable qck and struggling 3f out: wknd and hanging fr 2f out **18/1**3
0-60 8 3 3/4 **Mut'Ab (USA)**97 2683 5-9-5 74 PatDobbs 1 48
(G L Moore) hld up off the pce in last pair: rdn and lost tch 3f out **33/1**

2m 11.97s (2.27) **Going Correction** +0.375s/f (Good)
WFA 3 from 4yo+ 7lb 8 Ran SP% 114.2
Speed ratings (Par 105): **105,104,100,99,99 96,93,90**
toteswingers:1&2:£4.30, 1&3:£2.70, 2&3:£3.90 CSF £20.57 CT £72.88 TOTE £5.20: £1.70, £1.90, £1.20; EX 19.40.
Owner Bagden Wood Building Services Limited **Bred** Ridgecourt Stud **Trained** Epsom, Surrey

FOCUS
A very tight handicap. The first pair finished clear and the winner did not need to match this year's best.
Danger Mulally Official explanation: jockey said gelding hung left-handed

5860 WALTON DOWNS MAIDEN STKS 1m 2f 18y
4:30 (4:33) (Class 5) 3-Y-O+ £2,590 (£770; £385; £192) Stalls Low

Form RPR
24 1 **Music City (IRE)**32 4845 3-9-3 0 KierenFallon 2 81
(M Johnston) chsd ldrs: rdn to ld and racd against stands' rail over 3f out: clr w runner-up fnl 2f: kpt on wl fnl f **11/4**2
0-35 2 3/4 **Alfonso The Wise (IRE)**135 1581 3-9-3 79 RyanMoore 3 79
(J Noseda) hld up in last pair: hdwy 4f out: rdn to chal wl over 2f out: clr w wnr fnl 2f: hrd drvn fnl f: no ex and btn fnl 50yds **4/7**1
00 3 3 3/4 **Crystal Celebre (IRE)**30 4893 4-9-5 0 AmyScott(5) 1 72
(H Candy) chsd ldrs: lost pl on downhill run and dropped to rr 5f out: pushed along and effrt wl over 2f out: chsd ldng pair over 1f out: kpt on same pce fnl f **100/1**
0/0 4 6 **Four Star General (IRE)**39 4572 4-9-10 74 TomQueally 6 60
(H R A Cecil) taken down early: led tl hdd 7f out: chsd ldr after tl wknd u.p 2f out: lost 3rd and wl btn over 1f out **16/1**
4233 5 12 **Sensationally**24 5116 3-8-12 70 JimCrowley 4 31
(R M Beckett) sn bustled along to chse ldr: led 7f out: hdd and rdn over 3f out: sn dropped out: lost tch ent fnl 2f **17/2**3
6 8 **Violet Flame (IRE)**339 6518 4-9-5 0 EddieCreighton 7 —
(E J Creighton) stdd s: hld up in last: rdn and struggling whn nt clr run and swtchd lft jst over 2f out: sn wl bhd **100/1**

2m 12.76s (3.06) **Going Correction** +0.375s/f (Good)
WFA 3 from 4yo 7lb 6 Ran SP% 108.7
Speed ratings (Par 103): **102,101,98,93,84 77**
toteswingers:1&2:£1.10, 1&3:£6.80, 2&3:£6.60 CSF £4.32 TOTE £3.80: £1.10, £1.50; EX 4.80.
Owner Sheikh Hamdan Bin Mohammed Al Maktoum **Bred** Grangecon Stud **Trained** Middleham Moor, N Yorks

FOCUS
A fair maiden. The winner raced on the rail and is rated up 5lb.
Sensationally Official explanation: jockey said filly ran too freely

5861 CROYDON H'CAP 7f
5:00 (5:01) (Class 4) (0-85,85) 3-Y-O £4,533 (£1,348; £674; £336) Stalls Low

Form RPR
1200 1 **Sailorman (IRE)**26 5043 3-9-7 85 KierenFallon 6 92+
(M Johnston) mde all: gng best ent fnl 2f: pushed clr ent fnl f: r.o wl: comf **11/4**2
5334 2 3 **Wise Up**7 5661 3-8-7 71 oh1 (p) EddieCreighton 1 67
(C A Dwyer) chsd ldr: rdn over 2f out: eding rt and lft u.p and unable qck over 1f out: one pce and no ch w wnr ins fnl f **20/1**
6002 3 1 **Mark Twain (IRE)**33 4784 3-9-0 78 RyanMoore 2 71
(D M Simcock) hld up in last pair: swtchd lft and effrt u.p wl over 1f out: styd on same pce fnl f: nvr gng pce to trble wnr **13/8**1
1540 4 1 1/2 **Yabtree (IRE)**25 5086 3-8-2 71 oh1 (b1) JohnFahy(5) 4 60
(R Charlton) s.i.s: hld up in last: swtchd lft and effrt over 2f out: swtchd bk rt over 1f out: styd on same pce: nvr trbld wnr **5/1**
3456 5 shd **Burghley**35 4699 3-9-2 80 HayleyTurner 5 69
(M L W Bell) chsd ldng pair: effrt to dispute 2nd and rdn 3f out: edgd lft u.p: unable qck and btn over 1f out: lost 2 pls ins fnl f **7/2**3

1m 25.73s (2.43) **Going Correction** +0.375s/f (Good) 5 Ran SP% 108.4
Speed ratings (Par 103): **101,97,96,94,94**
CSF £39.88 TOTE £3.70: £2.20, £5.70; EX 43.80 Place 6 £49.23; Place 5 £31.81.
Owner Sheikh Hamdan Bin Mohammed Al Maktoum **Bred** 6c Racing Ltd **Trained** Middleham Moor, N Yorks

FOCUS
The winner dictated in this weakish handicap. It is doubtfuil if this was the improved effort from the winner it might look.
T/Plt: £27.60 to a £1 stake. Pool:£55,804.51 - 1,474.13 winning tickets T/Qpdt: £14.20 to a £1 stake. Pool:£3,610.80 - 186.90 winning tickets SP

5748 KEMPTON (A.W) (R-H)
Wednesday, September 8

OFFICIAL GOING: Standard
Wind: Almost Nil Weather: Fine but cloudy

5862 BOOK ON LINE AT KEMPTON.CO.UK NURSERY (DIV I) 5f (P)
5:50 (5:56) (Class 5) (0-70,70) 2-Y-O £1,944 (£574; £287) Stalls High

Form RPR
6006 1 **Brave Tiger (IRE)**9 5581 2-7-12 47 oh2 (t) DavidProbert 10 56
(S C Williams) mde all: kicked clr 2f out: in n.d after **7/2**2
506 2 2 1/2 **Rylee Mooch**20 5239 2-8-8 57 PaulEddery 9 57
(R C Guest) towards rr: outpcd 1/2-way: poor 5th jst over 1f out: rdn and r.o to take 2nd last 50yds **11/1**
4045 3 1 1/4 **Mini Bon Bon**13 5434 2-7-13 55 (v) JessicaSteven(7) 1 50
(A Bailey) nudgeed by rival s: chsd wnr after 1f to wl over 1f out: nudged along and kpt on same pce after **12/1**

4434 **4** *nse* **Till Dawn (IRE)**[9] 5581 2-8-0 **54** ow1 .... KierenFox(5) 8 49
(A W Carroll) *prom: rdn to chse wnr wl over 1f out: hanging and nt qckn: lost 2 pls last 50yds* **7/4**[1]

5605 **5** *½* **Sarandjam**[9] 5581 2-8-0 **49** .... FrankieMcDonald 4 42
(M R Channon) *awkward s: racd wd in rr: outpcd 1/2-way: pushed along over 1f out: styd on fnl f: nrst fin* **12/1**

0355 **6** *1* **Comrade Bond**[54] 4111 2-9-1 **64** .... PatCosgrave 5 53
(M H Tompkins) *chsd wnr 1f: awkward bnd sn after and dropped to 4th: one pce after: lost pls ins fnl f* **11/2**[3]

2361 **7** *1 ¼* **Upark Flyer**[17] 5334 2-8-12 **66** .... IanBrennan(5) 6 51
(Patrick Morris) *s.i.s: settled in last: outpcd 1/2-way: brief effrt 2f out: sn no prog and wl btn* **15/2**

2300 **8** *4* **Henrys Air**[13] 5453 2-8-13 **65** .... PatrickHills(3) 3 36
(D G Bridgwater) *racd v wd: a in rr: outpcd 1/2-way: n.d after* **16/1**

60.53 secs (0.03) **Going Correction** -0.125s/f (Stan) 8 Ran SP% **115.3**
Speed ratings (Par 95): **94,90,88,87,87 85,83,77**
toteswingers:1&2:£5.10, 1&3:£7.50, 2&3:£8.00 CSF £41.33 CT £419.39 TOTE £5.80: £1.20, £4.40, £3.20; EX 33.80.
Owner T Clifford & D Adams **Bred** Joe Osborne **Trained** Newmarket, Suffolk
■ Je Suis Unrockstar (8/1, unruly & uns rdr at s) was withdrawn. Deduct 10p in the £ under R4. New market formed.

FOCUS
Division one of a weak nursery but the winner turned in a much-improved display. The gallop was sound and the winner raced close to the inside rail throughout.

NOTEBOOK
Brave Tiger(IRE) ◆, who attracted plenty of support, had the run of the race from the best draw against the inside rail and turned in his best effort to reverse recent placings with Till Dawn on this all-weather debut. Given he was out of the handicap and due to drop to 40 from the weekend, he'll be no worse off under a penalty from Saturday until he's reassessed and he appeals strongly as the type to follow up. (op 15/2)
Rylee Mooch, from a yard among the winners, ran creditably on this all-weather and nursery debut, despite leaving the impression that 5f around here was an insufficient test of stamina. The return to 6f will suit and he is capable of picking up a similar event. (tchd 12/1)
Mini Bon Bon has had plenty of chances but she had the run of the race and she looks a reasonable guide to the worth of this form. She's vulnerable to an improver or a well-handicapped sort but should continue to give it her best shot. (op 10/1)
Till Dawn(IRE) had finished three lengths ahead of the winner on her latest start but, although well supported, failed to confirm those placings returned to Polytrack from her decent draw and she didn't really impress with the way she hung towards the inside rail under pressure. She's clearly limited but remains capable of picking up a small race. (tchd 15/8 and 2/1 in a place)
Sarandjam, who will be 2lb lower in future, wasn't disgraced on this all-weather debut and shaped as though the return to 6f would suit. However, he's had plenty of chances and looks the type that will need things to slot perfectly into place if he is to win a race. (op 20/1)
Comrade Bond disappointed on his nursery debut on easy ground and again had his limitations exposed after racing with the choke out over this shorter trip returned to Polytrack. He'll have to show a fair bit more before he's a solid betting proposition. (op 11/2 tchd 9/2)
Henrys Air Official explanation: jockey said gelding hung badly left-handed

5863 BOOK ON LINE AT KEMPTON.CO.UK NURSERY (DIV II) 5f (P)
6:20 (6:20) (Class 5) (0-70,69) 2-Y-O **£1,944** (£574; £287) **Stalls** High

Form RPR

4065 **1** **Sacrosanctus**[16] 5354 2-9-7 **69** .... IanMongan 6 73
(J A Glover) *chsd ldr after 1f: drvn 2f out: looked hld over 1f out: styd on fnl f to ld last strides* **11/2**

0225 **2** *½* **Johnny Hancocks (IRE)**[16] 5365 2-8-11 **62** .... MartinLane(3) 4 64
(P D Evans) *led: drvn over a l clr 1f out: kpt on: hdd last strides* **9/2**[3]

3352 **3** *1 ½* **Kokojo (IRE)**[16] 5365 2-9-3 **65** .... FergusSweeney 9 62
(B G Powell) *chsd ldr 1f: styd cl up: clr of rest over 1f out: one pce fnl f* **9/4**[1]

0450 **4** *7* **Fairy Tales**[14] 5412 2-7-8 **49** oh1 ow3 .... RyanPowell(7) 1 20
(J J Bridger) *racd wd: chsd ldrs: rdn and outpcd over 2f out: tk remote 4th nr fin* **100/1**

40 **5** *nk* **Chestival (IRE)**[27] 5000 2-8-2 **55** ow2 .... IanBrennan(5) 8 25
(Patrick Morris) *rdn in 6th after 2f: tk modest 4th over 1f out tl nr fin* **40/1**

400 **6** *nk* **Palindromic (IRE)**[58] 3964 2-8-13 **61** ....(b[1]) SteveDrowne 10 30
(J R Gask) *chsd ldng trio: rdn 1/2-way: no rspnse and sn outpcd: no ch over 1f out* **5/2**[2]

516 **7** *1 ½* **Miss Dutee**[36] 4677 2-9-2 **64** .... RichardHughes 7 28
(R Hannon) *sn pushed along in last: wl outpcd fr 1/2-way: no ch after* **5/1**

0320 **8** *½* **Bendigedig**[16] 5365 2-8-5 **53** .... ChrisCatlin 2 15
(S Kirk) *dwlt: racd wd early: a wl in rr: outpcd fr 1/2-way* **40/1**

60.56 secs (0.06) **Going Correction** -0.125s/f (Stan) 8 Ran SP% **115.4**
Speed ratings (Par 95): **94,93,90,79,79 78,76,75**
toteswingers:1&2:£3.80, 1&3:£3.60, 2&3:£3.20 CSF £30.38 CT £72.00 TOTE £3.50: £1.10, £2.60, £1.10; EX 31.60.
Owner Paul J Dixon **Bred** Worksop Manor Stud **Trained** Babworth, Notts

FOCUS
Another modest nursery but, although the gallop was sound (time nearly identical to first race), those held up were again at a disadvantage. The action unfolded close to the inside rail and the first three pulled clear. The runner-up helps with the form.

NOTEBOOK
Sacrosanctus, down in the weights and returned to Polytrack, was always well placed in a race that favoured those up with the pace and showed a good attitude to maintain his unbeaten record on Polytrack. He is worth another chance to show himself equally effective over 6f and he can win again on this surface. (tchd 6/1)
Johnny Hancocks(IRE) is a reliable sort who broke much quicker than on his last run here and ran right up to his best over a course-and-distance that favours front-runners. He's a good guide to this form and, although he'll be up in the weights for a run where everything panned out perfectly, he should continue to go well. (tchd 4/1and 6/1)
Kokojo(IRE) is a consistent sort who had the run of the race and ran creditably from her favourable draw. She pulled clear of the remainder, remains worth a try over 6f and this lightly raced type is capable of picking up a similar event on Polytrack or on turf. (tchd 5/2)
Fairy Tales is probably a bit better than the bare facts after racing wide from her low draw back on Polytrack. The return to 6f should suit but she'll have to show a higher level of form before she is a solid betting proposition. (op 80/1)
Chestival(IRE)'s form has a very patchy look to it and she showed no improvement for the switch to Polytrack for the first time. (op 33/1)
Palindromic(IRE) attracted support on this nursery debut in the first-time blinkers back over 5f but he again had his limitations firmly exposed. He is only lightly raced but has been well beaten since his debut is another that will have to show a bit more before he's worth a bet. (op 7/2)

5864 DAY TIME, NIGHT TIME, GREAT TIME CLASSIFIED STKS 1m 2f (P)
6:50 (6:50) (Class 6) 3-Y-O+ **£1,637** (£483; £241) **Stalls** High

Form RPR

0023 **1** **Big Sur**[19] 5271 4-9-4 55 .... StevieDonohoe 5 61
(T Keddy) *sn trckd ldr: led over 3f out: hrd rdn over 1f out: styd on wl* **2/1**[1]

0066 **2** *1 ¼* **Trecase**[15] 5379 3-8-11 52 .... NeilCallan 4 58
(A W Carroll) *trckd ldng trio: chsd wnr 3f out: rdn to try to chal over 1f out: styd on but no imp* **10/1**

355 **3** *3 ¼* **Best Of Broadway (IRE)**[50] 4235 3-8-11 53 ....(b) TadhgO'Shea 11 52
(D R Lanigan) *chsd ldrs in 5th: rdn over 2f out: wnt 3rd over 1f out: no imp* **3/1**[2]

4060 **4** *2* **Petsas Pleasure**[26] 5051 4-9-4 54 ....(p) ChrisCatlin 12 48+
(Ollie Pears) *racd wd: hld up in 10th: poor 8th 3f out: nt hrd rdn fnl 2f but styd on strikingly: nrst fin* **20/1**

-040 **5** *1 ¾* **Straight And Level (CAN)**[39] 4591 5-9-4 53 ....(v) FergusSweeney 2 44
(Miss Jo Crowley) *chsd ldrs in 6th: rdn and prog to chse ldng pair wl over 2f out to over 1f out: fdd* **12/1**

0000 **6** *1* **Eastern Hills**[68] 3610 5-9-4 55 ....(p) JamesDoyle 6 42
(A J McCabe) *hld up: 7th 1/2-way: gng bttr than many over 3f out: rdn over 2f out: one pce and no imp on ldrs* **8/1**

0000 **7** *8* **Medici Brave**[15] 5379 3-8-11 49 .... PatDobbs 7 26
(Mrs A J Perrett) *reminders in rr after 3f: hrd rdn and no prog 4f out* **50/1**

0260 **8** *½* **Blackstone Vegas**[7] 5663 4-8-13 55 ....(v) LeeTopliss(5) 9 25
(D Shaw) *scrubbed along in last early: nvr gng wl: bhd fnl 3f* **9/2**[3]

-000 **9** *1 ¾* **Lily Eva**[31] 4874 4-8-13 45 .... SophieDoyle(5) 10 22
(D Donovan) *led to over 3f out: wknd rapidly* **50/1**

0040 **10** *nk* **Sir Tom**[19] 5254 5-9-4 48 .... NeilChalmers 13 21
(J J Bridger) *chsd ldrs tl rdn and lost pl 1/2-way: struggling after* **28/1**

000 **11** *61* **Southwark Newsman**[15] 5380 3-8-11 45 ....(p) DavidProbert 14 —
(Mrs C A Dunnett) *prom to 1/2-way: wknd v rapidly: wl t.o* **66/1**

2m 7.35s (-0.65) **Going Correction** -0.125s/f (Stan)
WFA 3 from 4yo+ 7lb 11 Ran SP% **118.0**
Speed ratings (Par 101): **97,96,93,91,90 89,83,82,81,81 32**
toteswingers:1&2:£5.30, 1&3:£1.90, 2&3:£5.70 CSF £22.52 TOTE £3.60: £1.50, £1.10, £1.80; EX 28.40.
Owner Andrew Duffield **Bred** Sarah J Leigh And Robin S Leigh **Trained** Newmarket, Suffolk

FOCUS
Not much of future interest in this low-grade classified event. Although the gallop was a reasonable one, those held up never figured and the winner raced close to the inside rail in the straight. The form is not rated positively.

5865 DIGIBET.COM MAIDEN AUCTION STKS 6f (P)
7:20 (7:20) (Class 5) 2-Y-O **£2,797** (£826; £413) **Stalls** High

Form RPR

4223 **1** **Chevise (IRE)**[25] 5099 2-8-2 74 ....(t) MartinLane(3) 12 74
(R M Beckett) *mde all: drvn over 1f out: styd on wl enough* **10/3**[1]

4344 **2** *1* **Mother Jones**[11] 5525 2-8-7 74 .... LiamKeniry 5 74+
(D H Brown) *n.m.r and snatched up over 4f out: sn trckd ldrs: squeezed though to take 3rd over 1f out: styd on to chse wnr last 100yds* **9/2**[3]

3 **3** *1* **Whitecrest**[12] 5465 2-8-4 0 .... SamHitchcott 8 67+
(J L Spearing) *settled in midfield: drvn over 2f out: prog over 1f out: styd on wl to take 3rd nr fin* **20/1**

503 **4** *½* **Jonelha**[13] 5453 2-8-8 73 .... RichardHughes 3 70
(P W D'Arcy) *trckd wnr: rdn 2f out: no imp over 1f out: lost 2 pls last 100yds* **5/1**

20 **5** *1* **Bahri Sheen (IRE)**[19] 5277 2-8-7 0 .... KierenFox(5) 2 71+
(J R Best) *awkward and stdd s: hld up in detached last pair: rousted along over 2f out: styd on wl fnl f: nrst fin* **10/1**

03 **6** *hd* **Shes Rosie**[12] 5466 2-8-4 0 .... CathyGannon 10 62
(J G M O'Shea) *chsd ldng pair after 2f: drvn over 2f out: grad fdd* **16/1**

0 **7** *1* **Neytiri**[19] 5255 2-8-4 0 .... HayleyTurner 9 59+
(R M Beckett) *dwlt: hld up in 9th: shuffled along fr 2f out: kpt on steadily fnl f: nrst fin* **33/1**

452 **8** *shd* **Laugh Or Cry**[12] 5465 2-8-9 78 .... SebSanders 11 64
(P J Makin) *wl in tch on inner: lost pl over 2f out: drvn and effrt over 1f out: wknd fnl f* **7/2**[2]

362 **9** *shd* **Hard Bargain (IRE)**[27] 4999 2-8-12 72 .... EddieAhern 1 67
(D J Coakley) *racd wd thrght: trckd ldrs: lost pl over 2f out: rdn and n.d whn sltly hmpd over 1f out* **8/1**

10 *¾* **Burst Of Applause (IRE)** 2-8-8 0 .... WilliamCarson 6 60
(M G Quinlan) *dwlt: a in rr: rdn and no prog over 2f out* **50/1**

05 **11** *2* **Dances With Words (IRE)**[39] 4587 2-8-10 0 .... FergusSweeney 7 56
(R A Farrant) *chsd ldng pair 2f: rdn over 2f out: wknd fr over 1f out* **100/1**

12 *5* **Theavonfilly** 2-8-4 0 .... LiamJones 4 35
(R A Teal) *a struggling in last pair* **100/1**

1m 13.11s (0.01) **Going Correction** -0.125s/f (Stan) 12 Ran SP% **117.9**
Speed ratings (Par 95): **94,92,91,90,89 89,87,87,87,86 83,77**
toteswingers:1&2:£4.50, 1&3:£15.00, 2&3:£25.40 CSF £17.79 TOTE £4.50: £1.60, £2.20, £6.60; EX 16.40.
Owner R Roberts **Bred** Paul And Mrs Jenny Green **Trained** Whitsbury, Hants

FOCUS
A handful of fair performers in an ordinary maiden. The gallop was fair and the winner raced centre to far side in the closing stages. Once again those held up were at a disadvantage. Straightforward form.

NOTEBOOK
Chevise(IRE) hadn't been at her best on easy ground at Ripon on her previous start but didn't have to better previous efforts from a good draw to score on her all-weather debut in the first-time tongue-tie. Life will be tougher from now on but she's a consistent sort who should continue to give a good account. (tchd 3/1 and 7/2)
Mother Jones has been running consistently well and turned in another sound effort, despite racing with the choke out, on her all-weather debut. She has had a few chances but is capable of picking up an uncompetitive event, especially if settling better than she did here. (op 7/2 tchd 5/1)
Whitecresthad shown a modicum of ability in soft ground on her debut and she bettered that form to reverse placings with Laugh Or Cry on her first all-weather start. Run-of-the-mill nurseries will be the way forward with her.
Jonelha had the run of the race and wasn't disgraced on her first outing at this course. However, she is likely to remain vulnerable to better types in this grade. (op 11/2)
Bahri Sheen(IRE) fared the best of those to come from the back of the field on his all-weather debut from a low draw. He's now qualified for a mark, is well worth another try over 7F. He's one to keep an eye on in similar company.
Shes Rosie had the run of the race from a double-figure draw and wasn't disgraced upped slightly in trip on her all-weather debut. Ordinary handicaps will be the way forward with her. Official explanation: jockey said filly hung right-handed
Neytiri, making her all-weather debut, caught the eye without being knocked about. She remains capable of better in ordinary handicaps in due course.

Laugh Or Cry was well drawn on his return to Polytrack but failed to match his improved Bath run last time and was the disappointment. He is likely to remain vulnerable in this grade and his current mark of 78 means he'll have to improve to win a nursery. (tchd 4/1)

5866 DIGIBET H'CAP 1m (P)

7:50 (7:50) (Class 5) (0-75,75) 3-Y-0+ **£2,286** (£675; £337) **Stalls** High

Form RPR

2610 **1** **Tevez**[3] 5789 5-9-3 **67**......(p) CathyGannon 13 79
(D Donovan) *dwlt: settled wl in rr: nt clr run briefly over 2f out: gd prog after: wnt 2nd ins fnl f: drvn and r.o to ld last 75yds* **5/1**[2]

52-5 **2** ¾ **Dancing Queen (IRE)**[20] 5238 3-9-2 **71**...... GeorgeBaker 9 80+
(M A Magnusson) *chsd ldr: clsd over 2f out: led over 1f out: idled and drvn: hdd and one pce last 75yds* **9/2**[1]

0010 **3** ½ **Black N Brew (USA)**[19] 5264 4-9-5 **74**...... KierenFox(5) 10 83
(J R Best) *hld up in 8th: prog over 2f out: clsd to go 3rd ins fnl f: nt quite pce to chal* **8/1**

1155 **4** 2 ¼ **Kipchak (IRE)**[23] 5157 5-8-10 **67**......(p) FrancisHayes(7) 6 71
(C R Dore) *taken down early: led at str pce: clr 1/2-way: hdd over 1f out: wknd ins fnl f but stl clr of rest* **14/1**

3420 **5** 2 ½ **Pebblesonthebeach**[19] 5254 3-9-3 **72**...... RichardHughes 3 69+
(J W Hills) *hld up wl in rr: in last trio whn short of room 2f out: prog over 1f out: rchd 5th ins fnl f but no ch: eased nr fin* **8/1**

2300 **6** ¾ **Saturn Way (GR)**[51] 4206 4-9-6 **70**...... JimCrowley 5 66
(P R Chamings) *t.k.h: hld up wl in rr: nt clr run over 2f out: sme prog over 1f out: nvr on terms* **15/2**[3]

3600 **7** 1 ¼ **Green Earth (IRE)**[13] 5456 3-9-6 **75**...... NeilCallan 14 67
(Mrs A J Perrett) *chsd ldng pair: rdn over 2f out: steadily wknd* **22/1**

060 **8** *nk* **Calahonda**[15] 5391 4-9-8 **72**...... TonyCulhane 12 65
(P W D'Arcy) *chsd ldrs in 7th: pushed along bef 1/2-way: struggling fnl 3f* **11/1**

4434 **9** 2 ¼ **Dichoh**[31] 4870 7-9-9 **73**......(v) EddieAhern 8 61
(M Madgwick) *hld up in rr: rdn on outer over 2f out: nvr on terms w ldrs* **16/1**

4004 **10** ¾ **Dinner Date**[23] 5142 8-9-10 **74**...... LiamKeniry 4 60
(T Keddy) *dwlt: hld up in last: rdn over 2f out: v modest late hdwy* **10/1**

/56- **11** 1 ½ **La Verte Rue (USA)**[9] 4-8-12 **67**...... SophieDoyle(5) 7 49
(Mrs A Malzard, Jersey) *chsd ldrs in 5th: rdn after 3f: wknd over 2f out* **33/1**

0100 **12** 5 **Kilburn**[18] 5287 6-9-10 **74**......(p) SteveDrowne 2 45
(A J Lidderdale) *chsd ldng trio: wknd u.p 3f out: eased fnl f* **12/1**

5-00 **13** 1 ¼ **Kai Mook**[11] 5541 3-8-13 **73**...... AdamBeschizza(5) 1 40
(Miss Olivia Maylam) *chsd ldrs in 6th: drvn over 3f out: wknd over 2f out* **50/1**

1m 37.57s (-2.23) **Going Correction** -0.125s/f (Stan)
WFA 3 from 4yo+ 5lb **13** Ran SP% **115.8**
Speed ratings (Par 103): **106,105,104,102,100 99,98,97,95,94 93,88,86**
toteswingers:1&2:£3.40, 1&3:£8.50, 2&3:£12.60 CSF £26.25 CT £153.65 TOTE £6.10: £2.60, £2.30, £3.60; EX 28.40.
Owner River Racing **Bred** P A And Mrs D G Sakal **Trained** Newmarket, Suffolk

FOCUS
Mainly exposed performers in an ordinary handicap. The pace was reasonable and the winner came down the centre in the straight. He is rated back to his best.

5867 DIGIBET CLASSIFIED CLAIMING STKS 1m (P)

8:20 (8:20) (Class 6) 3-Y-0+ **£1,637** (£483; £241) **Stalls** High

Form RPR

4030 **1** **Having A Ball**[23] 5142 6-8-8 65...... ChrisCatlin 12 66
(P D Cundell) *dwlt: hld up in rr: rdn and prog fr over 2f out on outer: clsd to ld jst ins fnl f: sn clr* **9/2**[2]

5406 **2** 1 ½ **Daniel Thomas (IRE)**[72] 3508 8-8-6 65......(p) SamHitchcott 3 60
(Mrs A L M King) *dwlt: wl in rr: prog on outer fr 2f out: drvn and styd on fnl f to take 2nd last 75yds* **16/1**

20-4 **3** *hd* **Mataram (USA)**[135] 1587 7-8-12 70...... AlanMunro 7 66
(W Jarvis) *hld up but sn in midfield: rdn to cl on ldrs fr 2f out: kpt on same pce fnl f to take 3rd nr fin* **7/2**[1]

6056 **4** *hd* **War And Peace (IRE)**[19] 5254 6-8-1 62...... AdamBeschizza(5) 9 59
(P D Evans) *s.v.s: mostly in last trio: drvn on wd outside over 2f out: styd on wl fnl f: nrst fin* **8/1**

5340 **5** ½ **Musashi (IRE)**[88] 2967 5-9-0 58......(b) IanMongan 6 66
(Mrs L J Mongan) *dwlt: t.k.h: hld up wl in rr: gd prog fr 2f out: clsd on ldrs 1f out: effrt petered out last 150yds* **16/1**

0005 **6** ½ **Beauchamp Wizard**[10] 5559 5-8-11 58...... HayleyTurner 10 62
(G A Butler) *led after 2f at str pce: clr over 2f out: hdd & wknd jst ins fnl f* **50/1**

4405 **7** 2 ¼ **King's Sabre**[12] 5499 4-8-11 62......(e) MarkCoumbe(5) 4 62
(R C Guest) *stdd s: hld up wl in rr: prog and darted to inner over 2f out: threatened to cl on ldrs over 1f out: fdd fnl f* **33/1**

6223 **8** *nk* **Flying Valentino**[28] 4949 6-8-3 61...... JohnFahy(5) 5 53
(Ian Williams) *prom: chsd ldr over 2f out to over 1f out: wknd fnl f* **7/1**

1500 **9** ½ **Unlimited**[23] 5159 8-8-12 63...... NeilCallan 11 56
(A W Carroll) *hld up in midfield: hmpd over 5f out: rdn and prog 2f out: tried to cl on ldrs 1f out: wknd* **16/1**

0305 **10** 10 **Gra Adhmhar (IRE)**[25] 5073 3-8-1 63......(p) CathyGannon 8 26
(D J Coakley) *prom: chsd ldng pair over 5f out: wknd over 2f out* **25/1**

0406 **11** 2 ¾ **Affordable (IRE)**[71] 3530 3-8-8 59...... RobertLButler(3) 2 30
(Miss Sheena West) *plld hrd: chsd ldr over 5f out to over 2f out: wknd rapidly* **100/1**

4535 **12** 1 ¾ **Alqaahir (USA)**[19] 5254 8-8-11 69...... KaseyLoftus(7) 13 29
(P Butler) *hmpd in midfield over 5f out and dropped to rr: hmpd again on inner over 2f out: no ch after* **8/1**

3634 **13** 12 **Rain On The Wind (IRE)**[8] 5648 3-8-11 65......(t) WilliamCarson 14 —
(S C Williams) *led 2f: stmbld bdly sn after: lost pl fr 5f out: eased whn no ch over 1f out* **11/2**[3]

0000 **14** 35 **Red Suede Shoes**[63] 3782 4-9-6 69......(p) SebSanders 1 —
(J Pearce) *chsd ldrs over 4f: wknd rapidly: t.o and virtually p.u fnl f* **25/1**

1m 38.8s (-1.00) **Going Correction** -0.125s/f (Stan)
WFA 3 from 4yo+ 5lb **14** Ran SP% **121.7**
Speed ratings (Par 101): **100,98,98,98,97 97,94,94,94,84 81,79,67,32**
toteswingers:1&2:£8.10, 1&3:£7.00, 2&3:£8.00 CSF £71.87 TOTE £6.80: £2.10, £4.00, £1.10; EX 93.40.Daniel Thomas was claimed by Miss M. Bryant for £5,000.
Owner Miss M C Fraser **Bred** R G Percival **Trained** Compton, Berks

FOCUS
A modest but competitive classified claiming stakes in which the gallop was ordinary and the first six finished in a bit of a heap. The winner came down the centre in the straight and did not need to match his best.
Mataram(USA) Official explanation: vet said gelding lost a shoe
War And Peace(IRE) Official explanation: vet said gelding lost a shoe

5868 J20 WHITE BLEND SUMMER SERIES H'CAP 1m 4f (P)

8:50 (8:50) (Class 4) (0-80,80) 3-Y-0+ **£3,885** (£1,156; £577; £288) **Stalls** Centre

Form RPR

1114 **1** **Home Advantage**[46] 4380 3-9-3 **77**...... RichardHughes 2 89+
(R Charlton) *prom: settled into 5th after 4f: smooth prog to chal 2f out: led 1f out: shkn up and in command after* **5/1**[3]

-034 **2** 1 ¼ **Green Wadi**[6] 5679 5-9-5 **70**...... GeorgeBaker 6 80+
(G L Moore) *hld up last: gd prog and threaded through fr 2f out: r.o to snatch 2nd nr fin* **7/1**

1352 **3** *nse* **Kerchak (USA)**[25] 5084 3-9-1 **75**...... PatDobbs 10 85
(W Jarvis) *hld up wl in rr: drvn and gd prog on outer fr 2f out: styd on wl fnl f to take 3rd nr fin* **20/1**

0511 **4** ½ **Lyric Poet (USA)**[13] 5456 3-9-4 **78**......(t) WilliamCarson 11 87
(G C Bravery) *hld up early: prog on outer fr 1/2-way to join ldrs 4f out: drvn to ld over 2f out: hdd and one pce 1f out* **4/1**[2]

5316 **5** 3 **Rowan Tiger**[25] 5091 4-9-12 **77**...... PatCosgrave 9 81
(J R Boyle) *trckd ldrs in 6th: lost pl on inner fr 4f out as others mde prog: effrt again 2f out: one pce fnl f* **33/1**

112 **6** 1 ½ **Amazing King (IRE)**[20] 5243 6-9-2 **70**...... RussKennemore(3) 12 72
(P A Kirby) *prom: trckd ldng trio after 4f: rdn on inner over 2f out: one pce after* **14/1**

-062 **7** *nk* **Fantastic Strike (IRE)**[10] 5549 3-8-8 **68**...... GregFairley 4 69
(M Johnston) *prom: led after 4f: hdd over 2f out: fdd* **3/1**[1]

3436 **8** *nse* **Quarante Deux (USA)**[36] 4686 4-9-10 **75**...... NickyMackay 1 76
(G A Butler) *prom: trckd ldng pair after 4f: drvn to chal 3f out: lost pl fr over 2f out* **16/1**

2003 **9** 2 **Trachonitis (IRE)**[49] 4252 6-9-9 **74**...... EddieAhern 14 72
(J R Jenkins) *hld up in rr on inner: nudged along over 2f out: nvr nr ldrs* **40/1**

45 **10** *nk* **Missionaire (USA)**[27] 5002 3-9-3 **77**...... ShaneKelly 8 74
(W J Knight) *led 4f: prom tl wknd over 2f out* **20/1**

0044 **11** 1 **Jeer (IRE)**[55] 4051 6-9-12 **77**......(b) SebSanders 7 73
(M W Easterby) *hld up in last pair: rapid prog on wd outside bnd 4f out to 3f out: wknd over 2f out* **16/1**

0-11 **12** *nse* **Cosimo de Medici**[236] 183 3-9-6 **80**...... TravisBlock 3 76
(H Morrison) *hld up in rr: effrt on outer over 3f out: no prog over 2f out: wknd over 1f out* **16/1**

-133 **13** 2 ½ **Mecox Bay (IRE)**[48] 4304 3-9-1 **75**...... LiamKeniry 5 67
(A M Balding) *hld up in midfield: rdn and cl enough 3f out: wknd 2f out* **16/1**

00 **14** 20 **Bull Market (IRE)**[30] 4910 7-9-3 **68**...... StevieDonohoe 13 28
(M S Tuck) *hld up: a in last gp: wknd 3f out: t.o* **33/1**

2m 32.6s (-1.90) **Going Correction** -0.125s/f (Stan)
WFA 3 from 4yo+ 9lb **14** Ran SP% **122.2**
Speed ratings (Par 105): **101,100,100,99,97 96,96,96,95,95 94,94,92,79**
toteswingers:1&2:£10.00, 1&3:£14.40, 2&3:£16.50 CSF £37.89 CT £660.83 TOTE £4.90: £2.50, £2.80, £5.90; EX 45.50.
Owner K Abdulla **Bred** Juddmonte Farms Ltd **Trained** Beckhampton, Wilts

FOCUS
A competitive handicap in which the gallop steadied after about 3f. The winner raced towards the centre in the straight. The form is rated on the positive side.
Bull Market(IRE) Official explanation: jockey said gelding was keen to post

5869 BOOK KEMPTON TICKETS ON 0844 579 3008 H'CAP 1m 3f (P)

9:20 (9:22) (Class 6) (0-65,65) 3-Y-O **£1,637** (£483; £241) **Stalls** High

Form RPR

0006 **1** **Adoyen Spice**[42] 4479 3-8-4 **51** oh4...... MartinLane(3) 9 65
(Mike Murphy) *stdd s: hld up in detached last: cruised arnd rest of field on wd outside fr 3f out to ld 2f out: sn clr: hung rt fnl f but wnt further away* **50/1**

2103 **2** 7 **D'Urberville**[29] 4931 3-9-2 **60**...... RichardHughes 6 64
(J R Jenkins) *trckd ldrs: gng easily over 2f out: tried to chal sn after: r.o but vain pursuit of wnr* **4/1**[2]

0002 **3** 1 **Motirani**[23] 5161 3-8-9 **58**...... SimonPearce(5) 3 58
(J Pearce) *trckd ldng pair: led briefly over 2f out: outpcd over 1f out: kpt on* **20/1**

036 **4** 1 ¼ **Beat Route**[22] 5180 3-8-13 **62**...... JemmaMarshall(5) 2 60
(M J Attwater) *racd wd: hld up in rr: prog on outer over 2f: rdn to chal 2f out: disp 2nd over 1f out: fdd fnl f* **8/1**

5456 **5** 1 ¾ **Stoical (IRE)**[11] 5536 3-9-7 **65**...... SebSanders 5 60
(W Jarvis) *hld up midfield: prog on wd outside to press ldrs 3f out: shkn up and outpcd fr 2f out* **5/1**[3]

-245 **6** ½ **Privy Speech (IRE)**[25] 5072 3-9-2 **60**...... DavidProbert 8 54
(Rae Guest) *hld up in rr: effrt on inner over 2f out: sn outpcd and no ch w ldrs* **10/3**[1]

5323 **7** 5 **Rose Aurora**[17] 5330 3-8-7 **51** oh2...... HayleyTurner 10 36
(M P Tregoning) *trckd ldng pair on inner: gng wl enough 3f out: rdn to chal over 2f out: wknd rapidly over 1f out* **5/1**[3]

5000 **8** 6 **Kitty Koo (IRE)**[27] 4992 3-8-2 **51** oh2...... KierenFox(5) 11 25
(A W Carroll) *towards rr: u.p 4f out: sn struggling* **20/1**

545- **9** ½ **Noverre Over There (IRE)**[314] 7139 3-9-4 **62**...... GeorgeBaker 4 35
(Miss Olivia Maylam) *sn trckd ldr: rdn and nt qckn over 2f out: sn btn and lost pl* **33/1**

005 **10** 2 ¼ **Hedonist (IRE)**[18] 5303 3-9-5 **63**...... SteveDrowne 1 32
(J R Gask) *sn led and crossed fr wd draw: hdd & wknd over 2f out* **16/1**

006 **11** ¾ **Red Storm Rising**[18] 5303 3-9-4 **62**...... PatCosgrave 7 30
(K A Morgan) *trckd ldrs: drvn 3f out: sn wknd* **10/1**

2m 19.29s (-2.61) **Going Correction** -0.125s/f (Stan) **11** Ran SP% **116.9**
Speed ratings (Par 99): **104,98,98,97,96 95,92,87,87,85 85**
toteswingers:1&2:£40.40, 1&3:£92.00, 2&3:£11.10 CSF £233.43 CT £4195.34 TOTE £101.00: £18.80, £1.50, £5.70; EX 588.70 Place 6 £32.49; Place 5 £7.54..
Owner Ronald Bright **Bred** Thorsten Feddern And Mike Murphy **Trained** Westoning, Beds

FOCUS
A modest handicap in which the pace was steady but one that saw a much-improved effort from the winner, although by how much is debtable. The winner edged into the centre in the closing stages.
Beat Route Official explanation: trainer said colt lost a front and back shoe
T/Plt: £140.60 to a £1 stake. Pool:£67,381.13 - 349.65 winning tickets T/Qpdt: £16.20 to a £1 stake. Pool:£10,036.28 - 456.14 winning tickets JN

5870 - (Foreign Racing) - See Raceform Interactive

5807 BATH (L-H)

Thursday, September 9

OFFICIAL GOING: Good (good to firm in places; 7.8)

Wind: Mild breeze half across Weather: Sunny

5871 E.B.F./BRAINS SMOOTH MAIDEN STKS 1m 5y

2:15 (2:15) (Class 5) 2-Y-O **£3,238** (£963; £481; £240) **Stalls** Low

Form				RPR
42	1		**Dux Scholar**[16] 5392 2-9-3 0 RichardMullen 8 (Sir Michael Stoute) *trckd ldrs: rdn over 2f out: led jst over 1f out: r.o wl: eased nr fin* **1/3**[1]	84+
35	2	2 ½	**Another Laugh**[8] 5657 2-9-3 0 RobertWinston 10 (B W Hills) *trckd ldr: rdn to ld over 2f out: hdd jst over 1f out: kpt on but readily hld by wnr sn after* **6/1**[2]	76
0	3	6	**Plea**[124] 1905 2-9-3 0 (b[1]) NickyMackay 9 (J H M Gosden) *s.i.s: towards rr: rdn and hdwy fr over 2f out: wnt cl 3rd over 1f out: styd on same pce fnl f* **20/1**	63
05	4	2	**Holy Mackerel (IRE)**[10] 5582 2-9-3 0 CathyGannon 1 (M R Channon) *mid-div: rdn over 2f out: styd on same pce: nvr trbld ldrs* **50/1**	58
6	5	½	**Go**[46] 4396 2-9-3 0 PatDobbs 2 (R Hannon) *led tl over 2f out: sn rdn: wknd ent fnl f* **14/1**	57
06	6	5	**Young Sahib (USA)**[31] 4899 2-9-3 0 LiamKeniry 5 (B J Meehan) *t.k.h trcking ldrs: rdn over 2f out: sn wknd* **25/1**	46
5430	7	1 ¾	**Lady Excellentia (IRE)**[115] 2163 2-8-12 61 SteveDrowne 7 (A B Haynes) *t.k.h in tch: rdn over 2f out: grad fdd* **33/1**	37
00	8	7	**Wet Your Whistle**[10] 5582 2-9-3 0 (t) EddieCreighton 3 (B J Meehan) *s.i.s: a towards rr* **100/1**	27
	9	2 ½	**Jadhwah** 2-8-12 0 TedDurcan 4 (M P Tregoning) *s.i.s: a bhd: hung rt fr 2f out* **7/1**[3]	17

1m 42.11s (1.31) **Going Correction** 0.0s/f (Good) 9 Ran SP% **123.0**

Speed ratings (Par 95): **93,90,84,82,82 77,75,68,65**

toteswingers: 1&2 £1.20, 1&3 £6.20, 2&3 £14.00. CSF £3.07 TOTE £1.30: £1.20, £1.50, £5.80; EX 3.40.

Owner K Abdulla **Bred** Juddmonte Farms Ltd **Trained** Newmarket, Suffolk

FOCUS

A middling juvenile maiden with little depth. The winner did not need to match his Yarmouth level.

NOTEBOOK

Dux Scholar, beaten just a head in a novice stakes at Yarmouth last time out, was heavily backed to get off the mark in this lower grade. He scored comprehensively, too, although he needed to be hard ridden to get to the front approaching the final furlong. Once ahead, however, he stretched his advantage decisively and was going away at the finish. He should stay further and may be better suited to a more level track. (op 2/5 tchd 1/2)

Another Laugh had disappointed on the all-weather on his most recent outing, but ran a good deal better here. Always close up, he led turning for home and briefly appeared to have the odds-on favourite in trouble. When passed, though, he could not respond.

Plea, making his first appearance since May and gelded in the interim, stepped up on his debut run at Haydock. He was slowly away, but had found his feet before halfway and plugged on gamely in the closing stages.

Holy Mackerel(IRE) seems to be improving with racing and, as he now qualifies for nurseries, may have something to offer in future betting terms. He is no superstar, but his mark ought to reflect that.

Go had shown a hint of ability at Ascot on his only previous run, but did not progress nearly enough to suggest he has the talent to take an average maiden. He led early on and stayed prominent to halfway, but dropped away tamely in the closing stages.

Young Sahib(USA), slowly away on both previous runs, was keen early here. He too qualifies for nurseries now and should find life easier in those.

Jadhwah, a first-time-out half-sister to 2,000 Guineas winner Makfi, was easy in the market and slow to start. She will need to make massive progress in order to match her sibling's achievements. (tchd 8/1)

5872 BRAINS SA MAIDEN FILLIES' STKS 1m 5y

2:50 (2:50) (Class 5) 3-Y-O **£2,590** (£770; £385; £192) **Stalls** Low

Form				RPR
4-	1		**Perfect Note**[313] 7183 3-9-0 0 TedDurcan 1 (Saeed Bin Suroor) *trckd ldrs: rdn over 2f out: swtchd rt over 1f out: r.o to ld fnl 100yds: rdn out* **6/4**[1]	78
33	2	1 ½	**Bianca De Medici**[31] 4906 3-9-0 0 SteveDrowne 5 (H Morrison) *led: rdn 2f out: kpt on but no exta whn hdd fnl 100yds* **9/1**	75
02	3	1 ¼	**Land And Sea**[13] 5474 3-9-0 0 RobertWinston 4 (B W Hills) *trckd ldr: rdn to chal 2f out: no ex ins fnl f* **7/1**	72
6253	4	3 ½	**Easy Terms**[27] 5038 3-8-11 70 JamesMillman(3) 3 (B R Millman) *in tch: sn nudged along: rdn 3f out: wnt 4th ins fnl f: nt pce to get on terms* **5/1**[3]	64
2220	5	2 ¼	**Scorn (USA)**[55] 4115 3-9-0 78 NickyMackay 6 (J H M Gosden) *trckd ldrs: rdn over 2f out: wknd ins fnl f* **11/4**[2]	59
	6	4 ½	**Supatov (USA)** 3-9-0 0 TravisBlock 7 (H Morrison) *wnt rt s: s.i.s: in rr: nvr gng pce to get involved* **50/1**	48
3	7	3 ¾	**Xeralda (IRE)**[24] 5153 3-9-0 0 LiamKeniry 2 (C G Cox) *s.i.s: in rr: nvr gng pce to get involved* **66/1**	40

1m 40.46s (-0.34) **Going Correction** 0.0s/f (Good) 7 Ran SP% **109.3**

Speed ratings (Par 98): **101,99,98,94,92 88,84**

toteswingers: 1&2 £4.90, 1&3 £1.70, 2&3 £7.50. CSF £14.62 TOTE £2.20: £1.30, £4.70; EX 14.50.

Owner Godolphin **Bred** Darley **Trained** Newmarket, Suffolk

FOCUS

A run-of-the-mill fillies' maiden, staged on ground that, following the opener, had officially quickened to good, good to firm in places. Improvement from the first three and the winner can rate higher.

5873 BRAINS SA GOLD H'CAP 1m 2f 46y

3:25 (3:25) (Class 6) (0-60,64) 3-Y-O+ **£1,619** (£481; £240; £120) **Stalls** Low

Form				RPR
0421	1		**Oriental Girl**[10] 5585 5-10-4 64 6ex (p) LiamKeniry 6 (J S Moore) *hld up in tch: trckd ldrs 3f out: led ent fnl f: sn rdn: drifted lft: styd on strly* **2/1**[1]	75+
3334	2	2 ½	**Corrib (IRE)**[7] 5704 7-8-13 50 (p) DeclanCannon(5) 5 (B Palling) *little slowly away: towards rr: hdwy on outside of bnd 5f out: rdn over 2f out: led over 1f out: hdd ent fnl f: nt pce of wnr* **10/3**[2]	55
6500	3	¾	**Mid Wicket (USA)**[71] 2230 4-9-2 48 TravisBlock 8 (Mouse Hamilton-Fairley) *led tl rdn wl over 1f out: ev ch ent fnl f: kpt on same pce* **50/1**	51
5520	4	½	**Rodrigo De Freitas (IRE)**[8] 5664 3-9-7 60 (b) JackMitchell 3 (J R Boyle) *trckd ldr: rdn wl over 2f out: led over 1f out: rdr sn dropped whip and hdd: no ex* **6/1**[3]	62
606	5	½	**Court Wing (IRE)**[35] 4765 4-8-6 45 HarryBentley(7) 9 (R J Price) *trckd ldrs: rdn whn squeezed out and horse hit on nose by whip over 1f out: swtchd rt: styd on same pce* **8/1**	46
0540	6	1	**Lucas Pitt**[28] 4987 3-8-13 52 EddieCreighton 2 (M J Scudamore) *hld up in tch tl dropped to last pair 4f out: sn rdn: styng on whn short of room ins fnl f: no further imp* **14/1**	51
3205	7	nse	**Foxtrot Bravo (IRE)**[13] 5468 4-8-8 45 (b) AmyBaker(5) 7 (Miss S L Davison) *hld up: rdn over 2f out: styd on same pce* **12/1**	44
4123	8	nk	**Le Corvee (IRE)**[35] 4731 8-9-4 53 AndrewHeffernan(3) 1 (A W Carroll) *trckd ldrs: chal 2f out: rdn over 2f out: sn one pce* **7/1**	51
5240	9	36	**Green Community (USA)**[26] 5072 3-9-7 60 SteveDrowne 4 (E F Vaughan) *hld up in tch tl lost pl on bnd 4f out: sn rdn: in tch whn lost action and eased ent fnl f* **14/1**	—

2m 11.28s (0.28) **Going Correction** 0.0s/f (Good)

WFA 3 from 4yo+ 7lb 9 Ran SP% **117.3**

Speed ratings (Par 101): **98,96,95,95,94 93,93,93,64**

toteswingers: 1&2 £2.50, 1&3 £19.70, 2&3 £49.70. CSF £8.72 CT £246.16 TOTE £3.50: £1.70, £1.10, £15.60; EX 8.10.

Owner Kimpton Down Partnership **Bred** Aston Mullins Stud And D J Erwin **Trained** Upper Lambourn, Berks

FOCUS

A low-grade handicap, with the top weight rated 64. The form is rated a round the winner, with a personal best from the winner.

Green Community(USA) Official explanation: jockey said filly lost its action

5874 DIGIBET.COM NURSERY 5f 161y

4:00 (4:01) (Class 5) (0-75,75) 2-Y-O **£2,914** (£867; £433; £216) **Stalls** Centre

Form				RPR
0121	1		**Indian Ballad (IRE)**[17] 5354 2-9-6 74 StevieDonohoe 8 (E S McMahon) *trckd ldr: chal 2f out: rdn to ld ent fnl f: r.o wl* **5/1**	80+
6313	2	1 ¾	**Diamond Vine (IRE)**[25] 5111 2-9-1 69 DavidProbert 3 (R A Harris) *chsd ldrs: sn pushed along: rdn wl over 2f out: r.o ins fnl f: no ch w wnr* **9/1**	69
563	3	¾	**Sugar Beet**[30] 4921 2-8-8 62 SteveDrowne 6 (R Charlton) *unsettled in stalls: led: rdn whn pressed 2f out: hdd ent fnl f: no ex* **4/1**[2]	60+
0101	4	3	**Veil Of Night**[13] 5472 2-8-11 72 HarryBentley(7) 2 (D Haydn Jones) *outpcd in rr early: hdwy over 1f out: kpt on: nvr on terms* **7/1**	60
31	5	3	**Hammer Home (USA)**[47] 4379 2-9-7 75 LiamKeniry 9 (B J Meehan) *hld up in tch: rdn after coming wdst over 3f out but no imp on ldrs* **11/4**[1]	53
2143	6	hd	**Fantasy Fry**[17] 5354 2-9-2 70 NickyMackay 7 (H Morrison) *hld up: rdn over 2f out: nvr gng pce to chal* **9/2**[3]	47
0440	7	1 ½	**Local Diktator**[10] 5581 2-7-11 54 oh7 ow2 AndrewHeffernan(3) 5 (R A Harris) *hld up: rdn over 2f out: nvr gng pce to get on terms* **50/1**	26
5044	8	7	**Sarangoo**[66] 3721 2-8-7 61 LiamJones 10 (M S Saunders) *trckd ldr: rdn to chal wl over 2f out: wknd over 1f out* **11/1**	10

1m 12.13s (0.93) **Going Correction** +0.075s/f (Good) 8 Ran SP% **114.3**

Speed ratings (Par 95): **96,93,92,88,84 84,82,73**

toteswingers: 1&2 £8.00, 1&3 £2.70, 1&3 £9.00. CSF £48.53 CT £198.20 TOTE £3.60: £1.10, £4.70, £1.60; EX 41.90.

Owner R L Bedding **Bred** J M Beever **Trained** Lichfield, Staffs

FOCUS

Just an average nursery. The form is sound enough and the winner is the type to rate a bit higher again.

NOTEBOOK

Indian Ballad(IRE) had been raised 3lb since taking one of these at Carlisle 17 days earlier, but shrugged off that rise to notch a cosy win. Second from the start, he joined the pace-setting third 2f out and eased past inside the last. He will surely face another rise for this victory and, as this was not the strongest of races, that will make his task markedly harder. He has a good attitude, though, and is on an upward curve. (op 4/1 tchd 11/2)

Diamond Vine(IRE), third off this mark in a C&D nursery on his latest outing, looks the obvious marker for the form. Never far off the pace, he finished strongly, just snatching second in the shadow of the past. (tchd 8/1)

Sugar Beet, making her handicap debut after finishing third behind a smart rival on her latest run of three maiden runs, was restless in the stalls. She broke well, though, and was soon at the head of affairs, travelling nicely. She could not quicken when the winner came past, however, and tired in the closing stages. (op 5/1)

Veil Of Night was up 4lb since scoring in this grade at Ffos Las in August and, on this evidence, that rise has found her out. Off the pace in the early stages, she was never in a challenging position. (op 8/1)

Hammer Home(USA), twice raced previously but successful in a Newmarket maiden last time out, was disappointing, even allowing for the fact that his rating of 75 looks flattering. He was being pushed along from an early stage but, in mitigation, it has to be recorded that he did not look entirely at home on the track. (op 3/1 tchd 5/2)

Fantasy Fry, third off this mark in a Carlisle nursery last time, was another to run below par. She has already won on this course, so its eccentricities cannot really be an explanation. (op 13/2)

5875 BRAINS BLACK H'CAP 5f 161y

4:35 (4:35) (Class 6) (0-65,65) 3-Y-O+ **£1,942** (£578; £288; £144) **Stalls** Centre

Form				RPR
420	1		**Sermons Mount (USA)**[21] 5238 4-9-4 62 TravisBlock 1 (Mouse Hamilton-Fairley) *trckd ldrs: pushed along 2f out: led ent fnl f: r.o wl: rdn out* **6/1**[2]	73
0-0	2	1 ½	**The Happy Hammer (IRE)**[55] 4108 4-8-9 58 SimonPearce(5) 10 (Eugene Stanford) *s.i.s: sn pushed along in rr: hdwy fr 2f out: chsd wnr jst ins fnl f: no further imp* **14/1**	64
2053	3	nk	**Cwmni**[20] 5267 4-9-0 58 DavidProbert 13 (B Palling) *mid-div: pushed along and hdwy over 2f out: edgd lft over 1f out: kpt on ins fnl f* **6/1**[2]	63
2005	4	shd	**Pherousa**[13] 5470 3-9-0 60 LiamJones 6 (M Blanshard) *mid-div: hdwy 2f out: swtchd rt over 1f out: kpt on ins fnl f* **18/1**	65
0052	5	1 ½	**Convince (USA)**[10] 5580 9-8-10 57 (p) RussKennemore(3) 7 (J L Flint) *hld up towards rr: rdn and hdwy fr over 2f out: kpt on ins fnl f: nvr trbld ldrs* **8/1**[3]	56
1045	6	½	**The Name Is Frank**[3] 5809 5-9-2 65 (t) AmyBaker(5) 9 (Mark Gillard) *chsd ldrs: rdn over 2f out: kpt on same pce fnl f* **6/1**[2]	63
2214	7	½	**Stamford Blue**[6] 5714 9-8-8 57 (b) RossAtkinson(5) 11 (R A Harris) *prom: led over 2f out: rdn and hdd ent fnl f: no ex* **4/1**[1]	53
4546	8	3 ¼	**Kyllachy Storm**[25] 5112 6-9-7 65 RichardKingscote 15 (R J Hodges) *chsd ldrs tl wknd over 1f out* **10/1**	50

The Form Book, Raceform Ltd, Compton, RG20 6NL

446 **9** *1* **Cruise Control**[92] 2874 4-8-4 **51** oh1.................. AndrewHeffernan(3) 14 33
(R J Price) *hld up towards rr: rdn and hdwy over 2f out: wknd fnl f* **14/1**
6020 **10** *2 ½* **White Shift (IRE)**[17] 5377 4-9-7 **65**............................(p) J-PGuillambert 4 38
(P Howling) *prom: rdn over 2f out: wknd fnl f* **28/1**
0000 **11** *nse* **Ghost Dancer**[30] 4936 6-8-13 **57**.....................................(p) LiamKeniry 8 30
(J M Bradley) *trckd ldrs: rdn 2f out: wknd fnl f* **33/1**
0030 **12** *1 ¾* **Candyfloss Girl**[28] 5010 3-9-2 **62**............................ JackMitchell 16 29
(H J L Dunlop) *prom on outer early tl lost pl 3f out: nvr bk on terms* **25/1**
0224 **13** *½* **Hart Of Gold**[10] 5586 6-8-8 **55**....................................(b) RobertLButler(3) 3 20
(R A Harris) *led tl over 2f out: grad fdd* **16/1**
6600 **14** *1 ¼* **Boxer Shorts**[108] 2378 4-8-1 **52** oh1 ow1................(t) JosephYoung(7) 12 13
(M Mullineaux) *a outpcd in rr* **66/1**

1m 11.76s (0.56) **Going Correction** +0.075s/f (Good)
WFA 3 from 4yo+ 2lb **14** Ran SP% **119.3**
Speed ratings (Par 101): **99,97,96,96,94 93,93,88,87,84 84,81,81,79**
toteswingers: 1&2 £21.60, 1&3 £8.40, 2&3 £15.70. CSF £83.48 CT £546.88 TOTE £7.00: £2.70, £5.60, £1.70; EX 126.40.
Owner Fairley Risky **Bred** Sherman Family Tbs Llc **Trained** Bramshill, Hants

FOCUS
A modest handicap, but it looked competitive on paper. Sound form rated around the second and third.
Pherousa Official explanation: jockey said filly was denied a clear run
Convince(USA) Official explanation: jockey said gelding hung right-handed
White Shift(IRE) Official explanation: jockey said filly had no more to give

5876 REV JAMES H'CAP 5f 11y
5:05 (5:06) (Class 6) (0-65,65) 3-Y-O+ **£1,942** (£578; £288; £144) **Stalls** Centre

Form RPR
521 **1** **Kinigi (IRE)**[6] 5715 4-8-6 **53** 6ex..........................(b) AndrewHeffernan(3) 9 64
(R A Harris) *prom: led over 1f out: sn rdn and edgd lft: all out* **2/1**[1]
0201 **2** *nk* **Namir (IRE)**[13] 5471 8-9-7 **65**..(vt) DavidProbert 6 74
(H J Evans) *hld up in tch: rdn over 1f out: r.o wl fnl 100yds: nt quite rch wnr* **10/1**
135 **3** *1 ¼* **Imaginary Diva**[11] 5562 4-8-4 **53**................................ SimonPearce(5) 10 58
(G G Margarson) *hld up: hdwy over 2f out: sn rdn: kpt on fnl f* **9/1**
0034 **4** *¾* **Nepotism**[13] 5470 3-9-6 **65**... LiamJones 1 67
(M S Saunders) *chsd ldrs: rdn over 2f out: ch over 1f out: no ex fnl 100yds* **9/1**
6562 **5** *hd* **The Jobber (IRE)**[7] 5695 9-9-4 **62**.................................. JackMitchell 2 63
(M Blanshard) *prom: rdn and ev ch fr over 2f out: no ex ent fnl f* **8/1**[3]
6506 **6** *¾* **Green Lagonda (AUS)**[23] 5176 8-9-0 **58**......................... CathyGannon 3 56
(P D Evans) *hld up: nt clr run fr over 1f out tl jst ins fnl f: rdn and r.o but nvr any ch after* **20/1**
0113 **7** *hd* **Gracie's Games**[13] 5473 4-8-4 **55**...........................(v) HarryBentley(7) 11 53
(R J Price) *towards rr: rdn over 2f out: styd on fnl f: nvr trbld ldrs* **9/2**[2]
1602 **8** *3 ½* **Sweet Avon**[13] 5470 3-9-4 **63**.. J-PGuillambert 7 48
(Matthew Salaman) *chsd ldrs: rdn over 2f out: wknd ent fnl f* **10/1**
0000 **9** *1* **Mythical Blue (IRE)**[30] 4938 4-9-6 **64**..............................(t) LiamKeniry 8 45
(J M Bradley) *led tl rdn over 1f out: wknd fnl f* **14/1**
0024 **10** *1 ¼* **Francis Albert**[13] 5502 4-8-1 **52** ow1.......................(b) JosephYoung(7) 4 29
(M Mullineaux) *squeezed out s: sn trcking ldrs: rdn over 2f out: wknd fnl f* **14/1**
0201 **11** *37* **Boga (IRE)**[101] 2584 3-8-9 **54**.. RichardKingscote 5 —
(R J Hodges) *prom tl over 2f out: sn wknd* **33/1**

62.64 secs (0.14) **Going Correction** +0.075s/f (Good)
WFA 3 from 4yo+ 1lb **11** Ran SP% **121.8**
Speed ratings (Par 101): **101,100,98,97,97 95,95,89,88,86 27**
toteswingers: 1&2 £4.40, 1&3 £6.30, 2&3 £19.30. CSF £24.42 CT £156.17 TOTE £3.20: £1.10, £3.40, £6.10; EX 25.10.
Owner Brian Hicks **Bred** Corduff Stud **Trained** Earlswood, Monmouths

FOCUS
Another low-level handicap, with the top weight rated 65. The winner showed she was not flattered by her Brighton win.
Boga(IRE) Official explanation: jockey said filly hung left

5877 BRAINS BEER H'CAP 1m 5y
5:35 (5:35) (Class 6) (0-65,65) 3-Y-O+ **£1,942** (£578; £288; £144) **Stalls** Low

Form RPR
6452 **1** **Lutine Charlie (IRE)**[7] 5689 3-8-12 **61**................(p) RussKennemore(3) 7 73
(J L Flint) *trckd ldrs: led over 2f out: sn rdn: narrowly hdd ins fnl f: rallied gamely: led towards fin* **9/4**[1]
2341 **2** *nk* **Catchanova (IRE)**[7] 5689 3-8-13 **59**................................ JackMitchell 6 70
(Eve Johnson Houghton) *mid-div: hdwy over 2f out: sn rdn: chal over 1f out: narrow ld ins fnl f: hdd towards fin* **5/2**[2]
0660 **3** *1 ½* **Just Jimmy (IRE)**[37] 4681 5-9-2 **57**................................ CathyGannon 8 65
(P D Evans) *mid-div: rdn over 2f out: hdwy over 1f out: swtchd rt fnl 75yds: styd on* **16/1**
3400 **4** *2 ½* **Chateau Zara**[93] 2844 3-8-11 **57**.. J-PGuillambert 4 58
(C G Cox) *trckd ldrs: rdn over 2f out: kpt on same pce fnl f* **10/1**
2033 **5** *2* **Eye Of Eternity**[8] 5664 3-8-3 **54**................................ SimonPearce(5) 3 51
(Rae Guest) *hld up towards rr: pushed along whn swtchd rt off rails wl over 1f out: sn rdn: styd on fnl f* **6/1**[3]
4650 **6** *½* **Aggbag**[5] 5767 6-8-10 **51** oh5.................................(p) RichardKingscote 11 47
(A W Carroll) *in tch: rdn wl over 2f out: styd on same pce* **16/1**
100- **7** *hd* **Sir Ike (IRE)**[331] 6755 5-9-10 **65**..(t) LiamJones 10 61
(W S Kittow) *awkward leaving stalls: towards rr: swtchd to centre and hdwy over 2f out: sn rdn: kpt on same pce fr over 1f out* **40/1**
0340 **8** *2 ¼* **Musical Script (USA)**[21] 5237 7-9-2 **57**.....................(b) TravisBlock 2 48
(Mouse Hamilton-Fairley) *restrained s: rdn 2f out: a towards rr* **25/1**
0046 **9** *2 ¾* **Superstitious Me (IRE)**[7] 5700 4-8-10 **51** oh6............... DavidProbert 1 36
(B Palling) *in tch: rdn wl over 2f out: wknd over 1f out* **33/1**
460 **10** *7* **Lordship (IRE)**[15] 5407 6-8-11 **59**.. JakePayne(7) 9 27
(A W Carroll) *led tl rdn over 2f out: wknd over 1f out* **25/1**
00-2 **11** *6* **Meer Und Wind (GER)**[32] 4870 3-9-1 **64**............... RobertLButler(3) 12 18
(P R Webber) *a towards rr* **8/1**

1m 40.54s (-0.26) **Going Correction** 0.0s/f (Good)
WFA 3 from 4yo+ 5lb **11** Ran SP% **118.7**
Speed ratings (Par 101): **101,100,99,96,94 94,94,91,89,82 76**
toteswingers: 1&2 £1.20, 1&3 £7.80, 2&3 £7.20. totesuper7: WIN: Not won. PLACE: £327.60. CSF £7.67 CT £71.59 TOTE £3.30: £1.20, £2.00, £1.60; EX 9.20 Place 6: £47.27, Place 5: £39.72..
Owner Jason Tucker **Bred** Patrice O'Connell **Trained** Kenfig Hill, Bridgend

FOCUS
A moderate finale containing several out-of-form runners. The first two were well-in though and the form looks pretty solid.
T/Plt: £45.60 to a £1 winning stake. Pool: £55,817.01 - 892.69 winning units. T/Qpdt: £30.00 to a £1 winning stake. Pool: £3,971.16 - 97.90 winning units. TM

5849 DONCASTER (L-H)
Thursday, September 9

OFFICIAL GOING: Good (straight course 7.9; round course 8.1)
Round course rail moved out from Rose Hill to the straight increasing races of 10f, 12f and 14f by 12yds.
Wind: Moderate 1/2 against Weather: Fine and sunny

5878 E B F CROWNHOTEL-BAWTRY.COM MAIDEN STKS 1m (S)
2:00 (2:01) (Class 3) 2-Y-O **£6,799** (£2,023; £1,011; £505) **Stalls** High

Form RPR
1 **Picture Editor** 2-9-3 0.. TomQueally 13 92+
(H R A Cecil) *w'like: athletic: hld up in midfield: stdy hdwy over 2f out: swtchd rt 1f out: r.o to ld fnl strides* **10/1**
2 **2** *shd* **Nathaniel (IRE)**[27] 5049 2-9-3 0.................................. WilliamBuick 11 92+
(J H M Gosden) *edgy: on toes: trckd ldrs: led 1f out: no ex and hdd nr fin* **5/6**[1]
3 **3** *1 ¼* **Genius Beast (USA)**[27] 5049 2-9-3 0............................ FrankieDettori 15 89+
(Mahmood Al Zarooni) *hld up towards rr: hdwy over 2f out: chsng ldrs 1f out: styd on same pce* **4/1**[2]
0 **4** *¾* **Audacious**[34] 4803 2-9-3 0.. RyanMoore 12 87+
(Sir Michael Stoute) *w'like: scope: chsd ldrs: drvn to ld over 2f out: hdd 1f out: kpt on same pce* **13/2**[3]
5 *1 ¼* **Musnad (USA)** 2-9-3 0.. RichardHills 8 85+
(B W Hills) *w'like: bit bkwd: wnt lft s: hld up in rr: stdy hdwy over 2f out: trcking ldrs 1f out: kpt on same pce: will improve* **20/1**
44 **6** *5* **Tarantella Lady**[112] 2239 2-8-12 0.................................. PJMcDonald 4 69+
(G M Moore) *w'like: chsd ldrs: wknd over 1f out* **20/1**
0 **7** *shd* **Lejaam**[34] 4803 2-9-3 0.. TadhgO'Shea 3 73
(J L Dunlop) *w'like: mid-div: hdwy 3f out: sn chsng ldrs: effrt over 2f out: hung rt: wknd fnl f* **50/1**
6 **8** *2 ¾* **Oasis Storm**[52] 4187 2-9-3 0.. PhillipMakin 17 67
(M Dods) *w'like: hld up towards rr: effrt over 2f out: nvr nr ldrs* **100/1**
9 *½* **Indian Jack (IRE)** 2-9-3 0.. FrannyNorton 9 66
(A Bailey) *unf: scope: hld up in rr: sme hdwy over 2f out: wknd over 1f out* **40/1**
0 **10** *2 ½* **Spartan King (IRE)**[20] 5263 2-9-3 0.................................. EddieAhern 5 61
(H J L Dunlop) *leggy: t.k.h: led: hdd over 2f out: sn wknd* **66/1**
11 *2* **Silverware (USA)** 2-9-3 0.. RichardHughes 2 56
(R Hannon) *str: s.s: in rr: sme hdwy over 2f out: sn wknd* **25/1**
00 **12** *nse* **Lady Chloe**[12] 5509 2-8-12 0.. LeeVickers 14 51
(P A Kirby) *w'like: a towards rr* **100/1**
13 *hd* **Smart George (IRE)** 2-9-3 0.. PhilipRobinson 1 56
(C G Cox) *w'like: swtg: in rr: hdwy 4f out: rdn and lost pl over 2f out* **40/1**
14 *5* **Tiger's Pride** 2-9-0 0.. MartinLane(3) 16 45
(J Gallagher) *w'like: bit bkwd: s.s: a towards rr* **100/1**
00 **15** *6* **Henry Chettle (IRE)**[11] 5546 2-9-3 0................................ DaneO'Neill 7 32
(D C Griffiths) *neat: chsd ldr: lost pl 3f out* **150/1**

1m 38.28s (-1.02) **Going Correction** -0.175s/f (Firm) **15** Ran SP% **122.3**
Speed ratings (Par 99): **98,97,96,95,94 89,89,86,86,83 81,81,81,76,70**
toteswingers: 1&2 £3.70, 1&3 £8.20, 2&3 £1.70. CSF £17.74 TOTE £14.80: £3.30, £1.10, £1.70; EX 26.80 Trifecta £68.80 Pool: £1,107.04 - 11.90 winning units..
Owner K Abdulla **Bred** Juddmonte Farms Ltd **Trained** Newmarket, Suffolk

FOCUS
Usually a very informative maiden and one that is usually won by a good horse - the very useful Coordinated Cut took it last year, while the two renewals before that went to the Park Hill winner The Miniver Rose and the St Leger runner-up Kite Wood - and this year's running looks no exception with several of the field holding Group 1 entries either this year or next. The pace looked just a fair one after a steady first quarter mile, and it probably reflects credit on the first five that they managed to pull clear in the circumstances. The winner can make an impact in Listed races at least.

NOTEBOOK
Picture Editor ◆ is bred to be at least useful, being by Dansili out of a mare that has already produced two smart winners in Multiplex (7f/1m) and Memorise (at 1m2f/1m6f). In getting the better of one that had shown a decent level of form on its debut and was sent off at odds on, he seems likely to uphold the family tradition, not least since he is a May foal and so open to plenty of improvement. The winning margin might only have been narrow, but he looked to win with more in hand than that suggests after showing clear signs of greenness when asked to improve his position with 2f to run. That inexperience meant the eventual second got first run on him to the tune of around two lengths just inside the last, but he quickly cut down that deficit with a sharp turn of foot under hand riding, and was tidily on top close home. Quotes of 33-1 were flying around afterwards for the 2011 Derby, but as yet he doesn't hold an entry in that race.
Nathaniel(IRE) had made a very promising debut at Newmarket in a 7f maiden won by one of Picture Editor's stable companions Frankel (for whom there was also support for the 2011 Derby earlier in the day), and he once again impressed as a sure-fire maiden winner. Soon in a handy position, he had the leaders covered from some way out but though he briefly showed ahead, he never threatened to pull clear and was beaten by a horse with a better turn of foot under the conditions. As a strong-galloping type, this trip is probably a minimum for him now, and looking at the way he moves he won't mind a wet autumn. (op 10/11 tchd Evens)
Genius Beast(USA) had finished five lengths behind Nathaniel at Newmarket but cut back that gap significantly and showed enough to suggest that he too can win a maiden before the season is out, although he never really threatened to finish any closer. Out of a mare that won the Prix Vermeille and Irish Oaks, he looks sure to be suited by 1m2f before too long.
Audacious didn't show much on his debut at Newmarket but that race has turned out to be a rich source of winners, and he did enough to suggest he will soon join that number, showing a good turn of speed to get to the front and not given anything like a hard time late on as he was headed, leaving the impression he possibly still needed the race. He could improve significantly again next time and is bred to come into his own at middle-distances next year. (op 7/1)
Musnad(USA) left the impression that he could have finished closer as his rider wasn't as hard on him as others might have been, given his position running into the final 2f. That said, it was his first start and he'd done well anyway to recover from a poor start and get into a challenging position. Out of a 1m2f winning sister to the top miler Intikhab, he doesn't have any fancy entries but clearly has a high level of natural ability, and looks another likely improver and maiden winner. (tchd 16/1)
Tarantella Lady, who'd shown some fair form in 5f/6f maidens when last seen in May, travelled smoothly for a long way before lack of ability as well as a recent run found her out. This performance might not have done her nursery mark much good, but she once again left the impression she'll be seen to better advantage on softer ground.
Lejaam had finished behind Audacious at Newmarket and did so again. He at least showed a fair level of form on this occasion and wasn't given a hard time, but his entries in the Royal Lodge and Racing Post Trophy look highly optimistic.
Oasis Storm hinted at better to come and will find easier opportunities than this in the north.
Indian Jack(IRE) Official explanation: jockey said colt ran too freely

Spartan King(IRE) might have a Derby entry but was a little disappointing given that he had experience, yet still dropped away having been allowed an easy early lead.

5879 DFS H'CAP 1m 2f 60y
2:35 (2:35) (Class 2) (0-110,102) 3-Y-O+£16,190 (£4,817; £2,407; £1,202) Stalls Low

Form				RPR
5002	1		**Royal Destination (IRE)**[23] 5188 5-9-8 98 RyanMoore 5 (J Noseda) *hld up in tch: hdwy over 3f out: chsd ldr 2f out: led wl over 1f out: rdn clr appr fnl f: styd on strly* **4/1**[2]	109+
2501	2	3 ½	**Sweet Lightning**[23] 5188 5-9-12 102 RichardHughes 4 (M Dods) *lw: hld up: hdwy on outer 3f out: trckd ldrs over 2f out: effrt to chse wnr ent fnl f: sn rdn: edgd lft and no imp towards fin* **4/1**[2]	106
0101	3	1 ¼	**Spanish Duke (IRE)**[33] 4841 3-9-0 97 EddieAhern 1 (J L Dunlop) *lw: hld up towards rr: hdwy over 3f out: effrt and nt clr run over 2f out: swtchd rt and rdn to chse ldng pair over 1f out: drvn and one pce fnl f* **3/1**[1]	99+
-300	4	2	**Rashaad (USA)**[84] 3105 3-9-0 97 RichardHills 9 (B W Hills) *hld up in rr: hdwy on inner wl over 2f out: chsd ldrs over 1f out: sn rdn and kpt on same pce* **7/1**	95
5	5	1 ¾	**Ella**[16] 5387 6-8-12 88 PJMcDonald 7 (G A Swinbank) *chsd clr ldr: tk clsr order over 4f out: led over 3f out: rdn over 2f out: drvn and hdd wl over 1f out: grad wknd* **12/1**	83
3000	6	2 ½	**Greyfriarschorista**[21] 5247 3-9-3 100 JoeFanning 6 (M Johnston) *swtg: trckd ldrs: effrt 3f out: sn rdn along and wknd over 1f out* **16/1**	90
0000	7	13	**Tartan Gigha (IRE)**[21] 5247 5-9-11 101 KierenFallon 10 (M Johnston) *trckd ldrs: hdwy 3f out: rdn along and hld whn n.m.r and wknd wl over 1f out* **16/1**	66
0-46	8	11	**Sirvino**[23] 5188 5-9-9 99 PhillipMakin 2 (T D Barron) *lw: hld up in rr: effrt 3f out: sn rdn along and nvr a factor* **11/2**[3]	43
5304	9	23	**Cloudy Start**[17] 5370 4-9-11 101 (p) FergusSweeney 3 (J A Osborne) *t.k.h: led and sn clr: rdn along over 4f out: hdd over 3f out: sn wknd and bhd whn eased appr fnl f* **33/1**	—

2m 6.74s (-2.66) **Going Correction** -0.025s/f (Good)
WFA 3 from 4yo+ 7lb **9** Ran SP% **115.3**
Speed ratings (Par 109): **109,106,105,103,102 100,89,81,62**
toteswingers: 1&2 £2.40, 1&3 £2.90, 2&3 £3.00. CSF £20.38 CT £53.97 TOTE £4.30: £1.90, £1.20, £2.10; EX 13.90 Trifecta £23.90 Pool: £949.61 - 29.29 winning units..
Owner Vimal Khosla **Bred** Miss Deirdre Barry **Trained** Newmarket, Suffolk
■ Stewards' Enquiry : Eddie Ahern one day ban: careless riding (23 Sept)

FOCUS
This decent handicap was run at a solid pace thanks to the front-running Cloudy Start and the form makes sense through the second. The winner is rated better than ever.

NOTEBOOK
Royal Destination(IRE) readily reversed last-time-out form with Sweet Lightning and was given a copybook ride by the champion jockey. He was 5lb higher than when narrowly losing out to his old rival at York last month, and thus 2lb better off. Settled in midfield, the race was run to suit and Moore kicked him on for home with perfect timing. He probably wasn't doing a great deal out in front and this was a clear personal-best display. Another rise is forthcoming, but he could still have a little more to offer and fully deserves another crack at the valuable Dubai Duty Free Heritage Handicap at Newbury later this month, although the penalty he now picks up for that would make him nearly top weight.. It may also be that connections now opt to keep him for another go at the Cambridgeshire, though, and he would turn up full of confidence there. Bookmakers were divided, with Ladbrokes being most impressed, and slashed his odds for that to 12/1, which makes him a co-favourite for the race. However, he could still be backed as big as 25/1 with others. (op5/1)
Sweet Lightning went up 7lb for beating the winner at York 23 days earlier and had Richard Hughes taking over from Tom Eaves. He found the winner getting first run and was never going to reel him in. Perhaps the handicapper now has his measure, but he too could re-oppose his old rival at Newbury or in the Cambridgeshire. (op 5/1)
Spanish Duke(IRE) was up 9lb for scoring on easy ground at Newmarket yet still proved popular in this tougher company. He travelled nicely, but was held in by both the winner, and then the runner-up at crucial stages in the home straight. Looking at the way he flattened out towards the finish, however, it made no major difference to the overall result. He now has to prove he is not in the handicapper's grip, but has time on his side and is bred to get further, so looks well worth a go over 1m4f. (tchd 7/2)
Rashaad(USA), who has presumably had his problems, was returning from an 84-day break. Patiently ridden, he was moved to the inside for his effort from 3f out and didn't get the best of passages as a result. He is therefore a little better than the bare form, and this is a run he could build on back down in grade. (op 8/1)
Ella was made to look one-paced on ground that had turned quicker than she really cares for and over a trip short of her best. She remains on a long losing run. (op 9/1)
Greyfriarschorista failed to last home over this longer trip and needs some respite in the weights. He may get it after this, though. (op 18/1 tchd 20/1)
Tartan Gigha(IRE) turned in a laboured effort and is struggling for form at present. (tchd 20/1)
Sirvino looked a shadow of his progressive self of last season. (op 9/2 tchd 6/1)

5880 WEATHERBYS INSURANCE £300,000 2-Y-O STKS 6f 110y
3:10 (3:12) (Class 2) 2-Y-O
£193,267 (£77,322; £38,661; £19,311; £9,655; £9,655) Stalls High

Form				RPR
111	1		**Wootton Bassett**[21] 5245 2-8-9 108 PaulHanagan 4 (R A Fahey) *lw: w ldrs: led over 2f out: narrowly and briefly hdd jst ins fnl f: styd on strly fnl 75yds* **2/1**[1]	109+
1022	2	1	**Galtymore Lad**[21] 5245 2-8-6 109 KierenFallon 12 (M R Channon) *hld up in mid-div: hdwy over 2f out: chal over 1f out: slt ld jst ins fnl f: styd on same pce last 75yds* **11/2**[3]	103
3135	3	1 ½	**Premier Clarets (IRE)**[22] 5219 2-8-3 101 JimmyQuinn 2 (R A Fahey) *lw: chsd ldrs: rdn and hung rt over 1f out: styd on same pce* **28/1**	96
5612	4	nse	**Slim Shadey**[26] 5079 2-8-3 97 LukeMorris 14 (J S Moore) *lw: reluctant to go bhd stalls: chsd ldrs: sn drvn along: edgd lft over 2f out: sn outpcd: kpt on wl ins fnl f* **33/1**	96
2133	5	½	**Sir Reginald**[22] 5219 2-8-9 102 RichardHughes 15 (R A Fahey) *lw: hld up towards rr: t.k.h: effrt over 2f out: styd on wl fnl f* **14/1**	100
1412	6	¾	**Alaskan Spirit (IRE)**[12] 5532 2-8-6 92 SilvestreDeSousa 1 (Mrs A Duffield) *chsd ldrs: kpt on same pce fnl 2f* **100/1**	95
4425	7	1 ¾	**Chilworth Lad**[10] 5604 2-8-3 98 ChrisCatlin 3 (M R Channon) *sn chsng ldrs: one pce fnl 2f* **40/1**	88
601	8	½	**Nasharra (IRE)**[40] 4580 2-8-9 80 RyanMoore 13 (K A Ryan) *hld up: hdwy to chse ldrs over 2f out: kpt on same pce* **80/1**	92
11	9	hd	**Murbeh (IRE)**[19] 5301 2-8-6 89 RichardHills 21 (B J Meehan) *lw: hld up in mid-div: effrt over 2f out: kpt on: nvr trbld ldrs* **9/2**[2]	89
121	10	hd	**Forjatt (IRE)**[30] 4934 2-8-9 102 FrankieDettori 11 (M A Jarvis) *on toes: in rr: styd on fnl 2f: nt clr run over 1f out and ins fnl f: nvr nr ldrs* **9/2**[2]	91
2013	11	½	**Chiswick Bey (IRE)**[21] 5245 2-8-6 93 PaulMulrennan 7 (R A Fahey) *prom: effrt over 2f out: one pce* **50/1**	87
3042	12	hd	**Button Moon (IRE)**[12] 5527 2-8-4 74 (p) MartinLane 19 (I A Wood) *led tl over 2f out: wknd over 1f out* **50/1**	84
2113	13	½	**Madany (IRE)**[23] 5187 2-8-1 90 TadhgO'Shea 5 (B W Hills) *prom: effrt over 2f out: wknd over 1f out* **25/1**	80
1030	14	1 ¼	**Move In Time**[22] 5219 2-8-3 92 RoystonFfrench 10 (B Smart) *hld up in mid-div: effrt over 2f out: n.m.r over 1f out: nvr a factor* **80/1**	78
1345	15	1 ¾	**Imperialistic Diva (IRE)**[21] 5246 2-8-1 99 FrannyNorton 20 (T D Easterby) *towards rr: nvr a factor* **20/1**	72
2001	16	½	**El Viento (FR)**[4] 5785 2-8-9 74 (b) BarryMcHugh 18 (R A Fahey) *chsd ldrs: lost pl 2f out* **50/1**	78
0344	17	2	**Opera Dancer**[17] 5369 2-7-12 77 DuranFentiman 17 (S Kirk) *a towards rr* **100/1**	62
31	18	¾	**Cocohatchee**[18] 5328 2-8-3 77 FrankieMcDonald 9 (P M Phelan) *chsd ldrs: wkng whn hmpd over 2f out* **100/1**	65
1140	19	2 ½	**Bahceli (IRE)**[21] 5245 2-8-6 93 AdrianNicholls 22 (R Hannon) *in rr: rdn and hung lft over 2f out* **50/1**	61
0310	20	hd	**Elkmait**[33] 4842 2-7-12 84 JamieMackay 16 (C E Brittain) *rrd s: a in rr* **100/1**	52
4100	21	3 ¾	**Geesala (IRE)**[12] 5525 2-8-4 82 JoeFanning 8 (K A Ryan) *w ldrs: nt clr run over 2f out: lost pl over 1f out* **100/1**	48

1m 17.99s (-1.91) **Going Correction** -0.175s/f (Firm) **21** Ran SP% **124.4**
Speed ratings (Par 101): **103,101,100,100,99 98,96,96,95,95 95,94,94,92,90 90,87,87,84,84 79**
toteswingers: 1&2 £1.20, 1&3 £10.90, 2&3 £55.10. CSF £11.15 TOTE £2.70: £1.50, £1.90, £7.60; EX 11.70 Trifecta £188.60 Pool: £2,087.70 - 8.19 winning units..
Owner Frank Brady & The Cosmic Cases **Bred** Laundry Cottage Stud Farm **Trained** Musley Bank, N Yorks

FOCUS
A wide range of abilities on show as tends to be the case in these handsomely endowed sales races but the finish was fought out by the two with the highest official ratings, in a virtual repeat of the DBS Premier Yearling Sales race at the York Ebor meeting. The first two are better than the result suggests relative to the rest after dashing clear in the penultimate furlong, and the winning performance is almost certainly as good as has ever been put up in this race. The third ran to his Gimcrack level and the eighth and twelfth offer some perspective on the form. The field kept to the centre.

NOTEBOOK
Wootton Bassett was once again the focus of strong market support despite being 8lb worse off at the weights with old rival Galtymore Lad, and though he was made to work hard for his win, he might have had to work harder still had the eventual second not been produced so early and from as far back. He ultimately left the impression he was the best horse in the race, battling back under a cool ride having been headed briefly approaching the last. The further he went the better he looked, and on this evidence if he is to have a crack at a 6f Group race this year the Mill Reef over Newbury's more testing track will suit him better than the Middle Park. He'll have to improve again to win either of those races, and it wouldn't come as any surprise if 7f was to suit him better before long. (tchd 9/4)
Galtymore Lad ran an excellent race in defeat and probably emerges with more credit than the result suggests. In the pack early, he had to show a decent turn of foot to come through and challenge the winner, and though he sustained that well enough to just edge ahead briefly, the impression ultimately left was that he'd shot his bolt too soon. He's in the Royal Lodge but might be best at 6f/7f for now. (op 13/2 tchd 5/1)
Premier Clarets(IRE) was always to the fore racing nearest the far rail and held just about every chance 2f out but couldn't match the first two when they kicked, in the end a bit flattered to get as close as he did. All the same, this was a creditable effort considering that 7f had looked on the sharp side for him at Ascot two runs back. (tchd 33/1)
Slim Shadey had been tried early at 7f in the Chesham Stakes on just his second start and ran here as though he is in need of a return to that trip. Like the eventual third, he wasn't able to match the pace of the first two as they kicked on, but really started to motor in the closing yards and was never nearer than at the finish. This rates as a personal best.
Sir Reginald hadn't been seen until late in the day in the Gimcrack, when two places in front of Premier Clarets, and was once again given a very patient ride. He started to devour the ground late on and looks to be crying out for a step up to 7f, at which trip he might prove good enough to land a weakish Listed race. (tchd 16/1)
Alaskan Spirit(IRE) had disappointed at Redcar last time but ran respectably considering his chance at the weights without really suggesting, as he seemed to do last time, that a drop back to 6f is what he requires. He might not be easy to place as he's likely to be vulnerable in nurseries and will probably struggle in novice/conditions events. (tchd 80/1)
Chilworth Lad has had his limitations exposed in decent company lately but probably wasn't far off running his race, and is another likely to be hard to place before the season is out. (op 33/1)
Nasharra(IRE) turned in a much-improved effort considering he had only an official rating of 80, and that despite finding conditions plenty sharp enough as the race was run. (op 100/1)
Murbeh(IRE) was sent off surprisingly short in the market considering the form he had shown so far, and though he may have been slightly inconvenienced by getting a bit far back early on in the near-side group, ultimately he didn't look good enough in this stronger company. A Mill Reef entry suggests he's held in good regard, though, and a mark of 89 means it shouldn't be difficult finding him a nursery. (op 6/1)
Forjatt(IRE) was a disappointment on the face of things but he seemed to get knocked back towards the rear early on, and was in the process of trying to improve his position when running into trouble as the first two came clear. He's better than this and was entitled to be in the places on an earlier line of form with the eventual winner. Official explanation: jockey said colt suffered interference in running
Move In Time Official explanation: jockey said colt was denied a clear run
Imperialistic Diva(IRE) was another that didn't run her race but her rider had a look down twice early on and perhaps all wasn't well. (tchd 16/1)
Cocohatchee Official explanation: trainer said colt was denied a clear run

5881 DFS PARK HILL STKS (GROUP 2) (F&M) 1m 6f 132y
3:45 (3:46) (Class 1) 3-Y-O+
£56,770 (£21,520; £10,770; £5,370; £2,690; £1,350) Stalls Low

Form				RPR
0114	1		**Eastern Aria (UAE)**[26] 5108 4-9-4 108 FrankieDettori 4 (M Johnston) *lw: trckd ldrs: hdwy 3f out: rdn to ld 2f out: hdd over 1f out: drvn and rallied to ld again ins fnl f: edgd rt and kpt on gamely towards fin* **5/1**[2]	114
1043	2	1	**Rumoush (USA)**[40] 4612 3-8-6 104 RichardHills 9 (M P Tregoning) *hld up in midfield: swtchd rt and hdwy 3f out: cl up 2f out: rdn to ld over 1f out: drvn and hdd ins fnl f: no ex last 100yds* **15/2**	112
1244	3	1 ¾	**Meeznah (USA)**[21] 5248 3-8-6 113 KierenFallon 2 (D R Lanigan) *lw: hld up in tch: hdwy 3f out: effrt and n.m.r wl over 1f out: sn rdn and kpt on same pce fnl f* **2/1**[1]	110

2220 **4** *3* **Polly's Mark (IRE)**[26] 5108 4-9-4 108 RichardHughes 3 106
(C G Cox) *trckd ldng pair on inner: hdwy 3f out: rdn and ev ch 2f out: drvn and one pce appr fnl f* **12/1**

-316 **5** *½* **Ship's Biscuit**[42] 4507 3-8-7 95 ow1 RyanMoore 1 106
(Sir Michael Stoute) *lw: hld up towards rr: hdwy 4f out: effrt over 2f out: rdn wl over 1f out: kpt on same pce* **16/1**

2-13 **6** *2* **Roses For The Lady (IRE)**[19] 5314 4-9-4 108 FMBerry 11 103
(John M Oxx, Ire) *led: pushed along over 3f out: rdn and hdd 2f out: drvn: edgd rt and wknd over 1f out* **7/1**[3]

-215 **7** *1 ½* **Warling (IRE)**[11] 5553 3-8-6 78 PaulHanagan 7 101
(J Noseda) *hld up and bhd: hdwy on outer 3f out: rdn over 2f out: n.d* **28/1**

1161 **8** *1* **Brushing**[21] 5249 4-9-4 102 DarryllHolland 6 99
(M H Tompkins) *hld up and bhd: hdwy whn n.m.r over 3f out: swtchd lft and styng on whn n.m.r wl over 1f out: sn rdn and no imp* **33/1**

0205 **9** *11* **Snoqualmie Girl (IRE)**[21] 5249 4-9-4 100 DaneO'Neill 8 85
(D R C Elsworth) *hld up: a towards rr* **50/1**

2253 **10** *1 ¼* **Middle Club**[28] 5138 3-8-6 108 EddieAhern 10 83
(R Hannon) *midfield: effrt and sme hdwy 5f out: rdn along 4f out: sn btn* **16/1**

-132 **11** *1* **Shimmering Surf (IRE)**[39] 4624 3-8-6 101 JimCrowley 5 82
(P Winkworth) *lw: in tch: hmpd after 3f: pushed along 1/2-way: rdn along 5f out and sn wknd* **9/1**

5-01 **12** *6* **Dyna Waltz**[124] 1909 3-8-6 104 WilliamBuick 12 74
(J H M Gosden) *trckd ldr: hdwy 4f out: cl up wl over 2f out: sn rdn and wknd* **10/1**

3m 2.00s (-5.40) **Going Correction** -0.025s/f (Good) course record
WFA 3 from 4yo 12lb **12** Ran SP% **121.2**
Speed ratings (Par 115): **113,112,111,109,109 108,107,107,101,100 100,97**
toteswingers: 1&2 £8.30, 1&3 £3.70, 2&3 £4.40. CSF £42.81 TOTE £5.20: £2.40, £2.30, £1.40; EX 33.40 Trifecta £70.30 Pool: £6,680.14 - 70.27 winning units..
Owner Sheikh Hamdan Bin Mohammed Al Maktoum **Bred** Darley **Trained** Middleham Moor, N Yorks
■ Stewards' Enquiry : Richard Hills two-day ban: careless riding (23-24 sep)

FOCUS
A decent bunch of fillies lined up this year for what is always a fascinating test. It was run at a sound tempo and there were plenty of chances 3f out, but the first pair eventually drew clear. The form looks good for the grade with a small personal best from the winner. Seven of the past ten runnings of this event had gone to 3-y-os.

NOTEBOOK
Eastern Aria(UAE) ran out a gutsy winner to strike a blow for the older fillies. The winner had beaten a few of these at Glorious Goodwood, a track she loves, in July and was not at all disgraced on ground that went against her in France on her most recent outing. She moved sweetly into contention around 3f out and was asked for everything in between the final 2f. The runner-up, to whom she was conceding 12lb, made her pull out all the stops but once more she dug deep, and her greater stamina kicked in near the end. She has sprung back to life of late, this being a third success from her last four outings, and it has to rate as another personal-best. She finished fourth in the E.P Taylor Stakes in Canada last term, and a crack against the boys in the Woodbine International at the same meeting, over an extra 2f, is reportedly her big target this year. Looking further ahead, though, she does have an entry in the Melbourne Cup, and that test would appeal as being right up her street, so perhaps this display could sway her connections towards an audacious bid down under in November. (tchd 11/2)
Rumoush(USA) was the only one to give the winner a serious race, and she too looked to post a career-best in defeat. She ultimately got outstayed by that rival, but was a clear second-best and readily reversed her previous Oaks form with the third over this stiffer test. There is surely a Group race in her before the season's end, and she could be the type to prosper if kept in training next year. (op 7/1 tchd 8/1 and 17/2)
Meeznah(USA) was dropping down from Group 1 company and her running style gave hope of her lasting out this longer distance. Very well backed, she lacked a change of gear when it mattered, and was staying on too late inside the final furlong after meeting a little trouble. Perhaps a more positive ride would've helped as she got the trip, but she too ought to be found a deserved opening in Group company before long and isn't one to abandon. (op 3/1)
Polly's Mark(IRE) had finished behind the winner the last twice and was beaten further this time, despite travelling nicely in the home straight. A drop in grade looks on the cards. (op 11/1 tchd 10/1)
Ship's Biscuit caught the eye behind Eastern Aria at Glorious Goodwood last time out, on what was just her fourth career start. She is bred to relish this sort of test, being a half-sister to the 2007 winner of this race Hi Calypso, and surely a more prominent ride would've seen her finish closer here. Strictly on the book she ran right up to form, but there is more to come from this late-maturing filly, especially if she is kept on the go next term.
Roses For The Lady(IRE) is a proven stayer and set out to make this a test from the front. She had no more to give when challenged in the home straight, but this was more like it again from her and she gives the form a good look. (op 8/1)
Warling(IRE) ran a fair race in what was by far her most challenging task to date, but didn't get home over the much longer trip. She is one to look out for when reverting to a sharper test back down in class. (op 25/1)
Brushing was ridden to get the longer trip and was held up in her run more than once in the home straight, so rates a bit better than the bare result. (op 25/1)
Shimmering Surf(IRE) Official explanation: jockey said filly suffered interference shortly after start
Dyna Waltz, who was having her first run since getting injured when winning the Lingfield Oaks Trial in May, dropped out as though the race was much needed but does now have something to prove. (op 11/1 tchd 14/1)

5882 EUROPEAN BREEDERS' FUND CARRIE RED FILLIES' NURSERY (H'CAP) 6f 110y

4:20 (4:22) (Class 2) 2-Y-O **£25,904** (£7,708; £3,852; £1,924) **Stalls** High

Form RPR

1311 **1** **Eucharist (IRE)**[40] 4578 2-9-3 **88** RichardHughes 1 98+
(R Hannon) *stdd and swtchd rt s: in rr: effrt and nt clr run 2f out: swtchd lft over 1f out: edgd rt and led wl ins fnl f: r.o* **9/2**[2]

4106 **2** *shd* **Mortitia**[7] 5693 2-9-0 **85** PaulMulrennan 12 95+
(B J Meehan) *hld up in mid-div: effrt over 2f out: chsng ldrs whn hung bdly lft ins fnl f: keeping on whn hmpd nr fin: fin 3rd, 1/2l, shd: plcd 2nd* **20/1**

221 **3** *½* **Ragsah (IRE)**[27] 5029 2-8-13 **84** FrankieDettori 6 91+
(Saeed Bin Suroor) *trckd ldrs: led over 1f out: rdn and edgd rt fnl f: hdd and no ex clsng stages: fin 2nd, 1/2l: disqualified & plcd 3rd* **7/2**[1]

2212 **4** *1 ½* **No Poppy (IRE)**[9] 5637 2-8-3 **74** (b) DuranFentiman 10 77
(T D Easterby) *chsd ldrs: led over 2f out: hung lft and hdd over 1f out: kpt on same pce* **16/1**

522 **5** *¾* **Bakoura**[49] 4299 2-8-1 **72** JimmyQuinn 8 73
(J L Dunlop) *chsd ldrs: styng on same pce whn hmpd wl ins fnl f* **15/2**[3]

2521 **6** *1 ¾* **Azzurra Du Caprio (IRE)**[13] 5476 2-8-8 **79** PJMcDonald 15 75
(B M R Haslam) *chsd ldrs: one pce appr fnl f* **14/1**

130 **7** *nk* **Child Bride**[12] 5527 2-8-0 **76** IanBrennan(5) 4 72
(P F I Cole) *s.i.s: t.k.h: hdwy over 2f out: edgd lft over 1f out: kpt on fnl f* **25/1**

100 **8** *hd* **Honeymead (IRE)**[23] 5187 2-8-11 **82** PaulHanagan 7 77
(R A Fahey) *chsd ldrs: kpt on same pce appr fnl f* **16/1**

2221 **9** *nse* **Intrusion**[14] 5433 2-8-3 **74** RoystonFfrench 2 71+
(R A Fahey) *in rr: hdwy over 2f out: hmpd over 1f out: kpt on: nvr nr ldrs* **25/1**

0010 **10** *½* **Rafella (IRE)**[14] 5452 2-8-0 **74** ow3 (b[1]) MartinLane(3) 17 67
(R M Beckett) *hld up in rr: effrt over 2f out: kpt on fnl f: nvr a factor* **40/1**

433 **11** *2* **Layla Jamil (IRE)**[26] 5078 2-8-4 **75** ChrisCatlin 18 63
(M R Channon) *lw: in tch: effrt over 2f out: wknd appr fnl f* **10/1**

1550 **12** *hd* **Lizzie (IRE)**[19] 5301 2-7-11 **71** ow2 (p) JamesSullivan(3) 16 58
(T D Easterby) *in rr: sme hdwy whn nt clr run over 1f out: nvr on terms* **14/1**

2111 **13** *½* **Belle Royale (IRE)**[19] 5293 2-9-7 **92** FrannyNorton 19 78
(W M Brisbourne) *in rr: sn drvn along: nvr on terms* **16/1**

3241 **14** *hd* **Fifth Ave**[24] 5140 2-8-13 **84** FergusSweeney 3 69
(J A Osborne) *chsd ldrs: wkng whn n.m.r over 1f out* **66/1**

1010 **15** *4* **Bay Of Fires (IRE)**[40] 4592 2-8-6 **77** SilvestreDeSousa 14 51
(D O'Meara) *mid-div: sn drvn along: hung lft and wknd 2f out* **20/1**

0400 **16** *1 ¾* **Climaxfortackle (IRE)**[8] 5660 2-7-5 **69** oh6 NeilFarley(7) 13 39
(D Shaw) *s.i.s: sn drvn along: hung bdly rt fnl 2f* **100/1**

0521 **17** *¾* **Penny's Pearl (IRE)**[19] 5284 2-9-5 **90** RyanMoore 5 62
(R Hannon) *lw: mid-div: hdwy to chse ldrs over 2f out: hung lft and lost pl over 1f out: eased clsng stages* **16/1**

061 **18** *15* **Luv U Too**[14] 5441 2-8-5 **76** ow2 GrahamGibbons 9 —
(F J Brennan) *led: hdd over 2f out: sn lost pl: bhd whn eased ins fnl f* **25/1**

1m 19.11s (-0.79) **Going Correction** -0.175s/f (Firm) **18** Ran SP% **124.1**
Speed ratings (Par 98): **97,96,96,94,93 91,91,91,91,90 88,88,87,87,82 80,79,62**
toteswingers: 1&2 £26.00, 1&3 £2.70, 2&3 £26.00. CSF £99.80 CT £370.34 TOTE £4.70: £1.80, £7.00, £1.40, £3.70; EX 126.30 Trifecta £312.50 Pool: £1,055.91 - 2.50 winning units..
Owner Mrs J Wood **Bred** M Kelly **Trained** East Everleigh, Wilts
■ Stewards' Enquiry : Frankie Dettori three-day ban: careless riding (Sep 23, 24, 26)

FOCUS
The usual big field for this race but perhaps not the strength in depth that there has sometimes been, with the majority of the field having an official rating below 80. Nonetheless, the form horses came to the fore and the first five all have plenty going for them going forwards in similar events. The winner goes from strength to strength and the form is solid. The field again shunned either rail, and the winning time was 1.12 secs slower the earlier sales race.

NOTEBOOK
Eucharist(IRE) ◆ had done well to overcome ill luck in running at Goodwood last time, and she once again overcame circumstance to record another personal best, looking increasingly as the race went on as though she had been set too much to do but still managing to get her head in front in plenty of time. The 5lb she had been raised for her recent win was clearly lenient, and with the handicapper unlikely to penalise her too much more here on account of the bunched finish, she can go in again, with 7f unlikely to prove a problem. (op 11-2)
Mortitia is still in the Cheveley Park but for all that looks optimistic, she showed enough here to think she can win another nursery if she can stay focussed, as she tended to carry her head awkwardly and perhaps has a bit more ability than she has cared to show so far. Subsequently awarded second place, she might now be ready for a step back up to 7f, having started off at that trip. (op 16-1)
Ragsah(IRE) was a shade unfortunate to run into such a well-handicapped and progressive rival, as for a long way she looked the most likely winner. The burst of speed she showed to break out of the pack and go clear was impressive, but she didn't do much once in front except drift to her right (was later demoted a place for impeding the original third) and she left the impression that, for now, she might prove best held on to for longer back at 6f. Easier ground might not come amiss either, looking at the way she moves. (op 9-2 tchd 11-2)
No Poppy(IRE) fared the better of the two that cut out the running but doesn't need her effort upgrading in that respect given that the gallop early was just fair, but this was a better race than she's been contesting of late and if anything she still seems to be improving with experience. (tchd 14-1)
Bakoura was in the process of running a creditable race when squeezed out badly close home, and can be rated two lengths better than the bare result indicates. She's steadily going the right way and didn't have any problem with the easiest ground she has encountered so far. (op 7-1 tchd 6-1 and 8-1)
Azzurra Du Caprio(IRE) might be slightly better at 6f but she's been largely reliable this year and came here in good form, so rates a reliable benchmark for the form. (op 12-1)
Child Bride was stepping up from 6f but stamina didn't seem to be an issue it's likely that this company was a bit too warm off her current mark.
Layla Jamil(IRE) had shown promise on her second start but hadn't improved last time out and was soon struggling on her nursery debut. She needs to progress to defy a stiffish-looking mark of 75. (op 12-1)
Lizzie(IRE) ran much better than her position suggests after being denied a run on several occasions. She might be interesting in a more modest affair after a drop in the weights, with 7f looking within grasp. Official explanation: jockey said filly was denied a clear run (op 25-1)
Penny's Pearl(IRE) Official explanation: jockey said filly had no more to give

5883 JAPAN RACING ASSOCIATION SCEPTRE STKS (LISTED RACE) (F&M) 7f

4:55 (4:57) (Class 1) 3-Y-O+ **£23,704** (£8,964; £4,480; £2,240) **Stalls** High

Form RPR

1312 **1** **Dever Dream**[25] 5120 3-8-10 98 EddieAhern 10 110+
(W J Haggas) *lw: hld up: hdwy wl over 2f out: rdn to chse ldr over 1f out: drvn and kpt on ins fnl f to ld last 100yds* **4/1**[1]

1-22 **2** *1 ¾* **Mosqueras Romance**[159] 1084 4-9-0 97 DarryllHolland 7 107
(M Botti) *prom on outer: hdwy to ld over 2f out: rdn over 1f out: drvn ins fnl f: hdd and one pce last 100yds* **33/1**

0044 **3** *nk* **Blue Angel (IRE)**[19] 5305 3-8-10 102 (b[1]) RichardHughes 9 104
(R Hannon) *hld up in rr: hdwy over 2f out: rdn over 1f out: styd on ins fnl f: nrst fin* **12/1**

2605 **4** *¾* **Carioca (IRE)**[25] 5114 3-8-13 104 RyanMoore 6 105
(M Botti) *trckd ldrs: hdwy 3f out: rdn to chse ldrs wl over 1f out: drvn ent fnl f and kpt on same pce* **12/1**

-505 **5** *hd* **Electric Feel**[25] 5120 3-8-10 95 FrankieDettori 13 102
(M Botti) *hld up towards rr: hdwy over 2f out: rdn to chse ldrs over 1f out: edgd lft ins fnl f and kpt on same pce* **20/1**

-405 **6** *4* **Sent From Heaven (IRE)**[71] 3571 3-8-10 107 MichaelHills 2 91
(B W Hills) *led: rdn along wl over 2f out: sn hdd: drvn over 1f out: wknd ent fnl f* **11/2**[2]

U004 **7** *1 ¼* **Sea Of Leaves (USA)**[25] 5120 4-9-0 90 KierenFallon 1 89
(J S Goldie) *in tch: pushed along and hdwy to chse ldrs wl over 2f out: rdn wl over 1f out and sn one pce* **16/1**

1001 **8** *nse* **Miss Zooter (IRE)**[47] 4378 3-8-10 97 JimCrowley 3 87
(R M Beckett) *dwlt and towards rr: sme hdwy wl over 2f out: sn rdn and wknd* **8/1**

1 **9** *3 ¾* **Queen Of Mean**[29] 4966 3-8-10 0 WilliamBuick 11 77
(J H M Gosden) *unf: chsd ldrs: rdn along wl over 2f out: sn wknd* **10/1**

-063 **10** *3 ¼* **Summer Fete (IRE)**[12] 5518 4-9-0 100 RoystonFfrench 12 70
(B Smart) *prom: rdn along 3f out: wknd over 2f out* **25/1**

0-20 **11** *½* **Habaayib**[130] 1726 3-8-10 107 RichardHills 8 67
(E A L Dunlop) *lw: hld up: a towards rr* **7/1**[3]

-042 **12** *13* **Za Za Zoom (IRE)**[10] 5609 3-8-10 98 PaulHanagan 5 32
(B W Hills) *lw: chsd ldrs: rdn along 1/2-way: sn wknd* **25/1**

1463 **13** *3 ½* **Flora Trevelyan**[19] 5305 4-9-0 100 AdamKirby 4 25
(W R Swinburn) *lw: chsd ldng pair: rdn along wl over 2f out: sn wknd* **7/1**[3]

1m 24.07s (-2.23) **Going Correction** -0.175s/f (Firm)
WFA 3 from 4yo 4lb **13** Ran SP% **117.2**
Speed ratings (Par 111): **105,103,102,101,101 97,95,95,91,87 86,72,68**
toteswingers: 1&2 £16.00, 1&3 £9.90, 2&3 £39.70. CSF £152.67 TOTE £4.50: £1.70, £10.80, £4.10; EX 202.10 TRIFECTA Not won..
Owner Pearl Bloodstock Ltd **Bred** F C T Wilson **Trained** Newmarket, Suffolk

FOCUS
A wide-open Listed contest for fillies. Once again the runners raced towards the centre, but ended up nearer the stands' side from 2f out. There was a good pace on. The form is fair for the grade with the third to fifth setting the standard.

NOTEBOOK
Dever Dream relished this step up a furlong and ran out a convincing winner. Held up early, she travelled beautifully into the race but needed a few smacks nearing the furlong pole. She responded most positively, however, and was well on top at the finish. This highly progressive filly has had a great season, this was her best run yet and she looks a Group performer in the making. Future options remain fluid, with the Ayr Gold Cup probably coming too soon, and she is more likely to head for Ascot's QE II meeting later this month. She was promoted to 9/1 favourite with the sponsors for the totesport Challenge Cup and picks up a penalty for that, but also has the option of stepping up for the Diadem Stakes there too. (tchd 7-2)
Mosqueras Romance, the oldest of the Marco Botti trio, came out on top. This daughter of Rock Of Gibraltar was the least fancied of the three on her return from a 159-day layoff, but she was never far away and made a bold bid. It was only her second outing on turf, but the drying ground proved to her liking, and she looks well up to winning in this class back over 1m. (op 25-1)
Blue Angel(IRE), equipped with first-time blinkers, was very patiently ridden on this drop back a furlong and stayed on strongly inside the final furlong. She rates a sound benchmark. (op 14-1)
Carioca(IRE) ran a solid race in defeat and this was a step back in the right direction. (op 20-1)
Electric Feel ran close to her last-time-out form with the winner over this longer trip. She probably found the ground quicker than she cares for, though, and looks capable of winning another Listed race before the season's end.
Sent From Heaven(IRE) was down in grade and had a very similar profile to that of her stable's last winner of this race Royal Confidence. She was given an aggressive ride, though, and paid the price before the final furlong. (op 6-1 tchd 13-2)
Sea Of Leaves(USA), not for the first time, left the impression she finds this trip too demanding. (op 14-1)
Miss Zooter(IRE), who runs in the same ownership as the winner, made a tardy start on this step back up in class and lacked a change of gear when it mattered most. (op 7-1 tchd 13-2)
Summer Fete(IRE) Official explanation: jockey said filly had no more to give
Habaayib was disappointing on her return to action and retirement may well beckon for her now. (op 8-1)
Flora Trevelyan Official explanation: jockey said filly lost its action

5884 MEADOWHALL FASHION H'CAP 6f
5:25 (5:29) (Class 3) (0-90,89) 3-Y-O+ **£9,714** (£2,890; £1,444; £721) **Stalls** High

Form RPR

6625 **1** **Baby Strange**[7] 5702 6-9-7 89 FrannyNorton 4 98
(D Shaw) *dwlt: hld up in rr: hdwy and nt clr run over 2f out: swtchd lft: chal 1f out: styd on to ld nr fin* **14/1**

2222 **2** *shd* **Secret Witness**[4] 5787 4-9-5 87 (b) TomMcLaughlin 21 96
(R A Harris) *chsd ldrs: led jst ins fnl f: hdd fnl strides* **6/1**[1]

2145 **3** *½* **Ancient Cross**[27] 5043 6-9-2 84 (t) GrahamGibbons 8 91
(M W Easterby) *s.i.s: hdwy over 2f out: chsng ldrs 1f out: no ex clsng stages* **17/2**

4000 **4** *shd* **Sunrise Safari (IRE)**[41] 4536 7-9-0 82 (v) PaulHanagan 13 89
(R A Fahey) *lw: mid-div: hdwy over 1f out: edgd lft and styd on wl last 150yds* **20/1**

4231 **5** *1 ½* **R Woody**[13] 5495 3-9-5 89 AlanMunro 14 91
(D K Ivory) *lw: dwlt: in rr: hdwy 2f out: kpt on ins fnl f* **9/1**

0000 **6** *½* **Cornus**[13] 5495 8-8-13 81 (be) JamesDoyle 15 82
(A J McCabe) *mid-div: hdwy over 1f out: keeping on at fin* **66/1**

1002 **7** *½* **Mac's Power (IRE)**[16] 5393 4-9-4 86 (t) AdamKirby 2 85
(J R Fanshawe) *trckd ldrs: t.k.h: led over 1f out: wnt rt: hdd jst ins fnl f: fdd* **13/2**[2]

2515 **8** *¾* **Lujeanie**[34] 4806 4-9-0 82 (p) TomQueally 1 79
(D K Ivory) *chsd ldrs: one pce over 1f out* **18/1**

10-0 **9** *shd* **Mister Laurel**[19] 5297 4-8-6 79 (b) LeeTopliss(5) 12 75
(R A Fahey) *lw: chsd ldrs: kpt on one pce over 1f out* **66/1**

0052 **10** *1* **Roker Park (IRE)**[19] 5290 5-9-2 84 (p) DarryllHolland 17 77
(K A Ryan) *lost pl and drvn after 1f: sme hdwy over 1f out: nvr a factor* **7/1**[3]

3-14 **11** *1* **Boogie Diva**[22] 5205 3-8-10 80 IvaMilickova 6 70
(Jane Chapple-Hyam) *chsd ldrs: wknd 1f out* **22/1**

6100 **12** *nk* **Stevie Gee (IRE)**[13] 5495 6-8-3 76 (b) IanBrennan(5) 7 65
(Ian Williams) *w ldrs: wknd over 1f out* **22/1**

0035 **13** *1* **Spitfire**[11] 5551 5-9-4 86 (p) KierenFallon 10 72
(J R Jenkins) *dwlt: hld up in rr: n.m.r 2f out: nvr a factor* **14/1**

0040 **14** *3 ¼* **Abraham Lincoln (IRE)**[4] 5787 6-9-4 86 (b) JoeFanning 11 61+
(R A Harris) *w ldrs: led over 2f out: hdd over 1f out: wkng whn hmpd jst ins fnl f: eased* **16/1**

0-31 **15** *1 ¾* **Rash Judgement**[27] 5048 5-9-5 87 DavidAllan 9 57
(E J Alston) *led tl over 2f out: sn wknd* **18/1**

2010 **16** *nk* **Tabaret**[19] 5308 7-9-3 88 MichaelStainton(3) 3 57
(R M Whitaker) *chsd ldrs: wknd over 1f out* **33/1**

0000 **17** *¾* **Everymanforhimself (IRE)**[19] 5292 6-9-3 85 (b) SilvestreDeSousa 18 51
(K A Ryan) *in rr and sn drvn along: nvr on terms* **8/1**

1601 **18** *3* **La Zamora**[48] 4345 4-9-0 82 RyanMoore 5 39
(T D Barron) *chsd ldrs: wknd over 1f out: eased last 100yds* **20/1**

3050 **U** **Red Cape (FR)**[19] 5302 7-8-11 82 JamesSullivan(3) 20 —
(Mrs R A Carr) *stmbld s: sn uns rdr* **40/1**

1m 11.37s (-2.23) **Going Correction** -0.175s/f (Firm)
WFA 3 from 4yo+ 2lb **19** Ran SP% **128.1**
Speed ratings (Par 107): **107,106,106,106,104 103,102,101,101,100 98,98,97,92,90 90,89,85,—**
toteswingers: 1&2 £45.70, 1&3 £65.10, 2&3 £25.50. CSF £89.68 CT £802.28 TOTE £21.50: £3.90, £2.30, £2.70, £6.30; EX 201.20 TRIFECTA Not won. Place 6: £15.07, Place 5: £12.41..
Owner Market Avenue Racing Club Ltd **Bred** Michael John Williamson **Trained** Sproxton, Leics

FOCUS
A competitive and open handicap contested largely by horses that have been in good form on at least one of their last two starts, but in the end, for all that many of them hold entries in the Ayr Gold Cup next week, it looked more a trial overall for the Silver Cup. The field spread across the near half of the track with no advantage apparent anywhere. Ordinary if sound form for the grade.

NOTEBOOK
Baby Strange is best at this trip and, back at the scene of his most recent win, just got the best of a tight finish after finding trouble in running just at the point the race was really developing in earnest nearer the stands' rail. That caused him to be waited with then switched to the wide outside, so the fact that he could run down, albeit narrowly, one that had got first run in such a short space of time reflects well on his effort. He's probably up to defying a slightly higher mark, not least when there is a bit more give in the ground.
Secret Witness has been in cracking form in recent races and filled the runner-up spot for the fifth time in succession, on this occasion after travelling strongly and looking as if he'd just got first run. He'll probably go up again in the weights for this, but he's in the form of his life right now and deserves to get his head in front again soon. (op 7-1)
Ancient Cross had been running as if he would appreciate a drop to this trip and ran very well, just bumping into two better-handicapped rivals. That said, even softer ground would have been in his favour, and this first run for a month should have just put him right for Ayr next week. (op 12-1)
Sunrise Safari(IRE) ran better than of late after taking some time to hit full stride, but most of his efforts have left something to be desired since making a winning reappearance and he's not the type to bank on repeating this next time.
R Woody has an admirable profile but a 7lb rise for his Newmarket win made him look vulnerable if the ground wasn't as soft, and that's pretty much how it turned out after holding every chance throughout. (op 8-1)
Cornus is suited by a well-run race at this trip and ran respectably without ever threatening to finish any nearer. He's dropping in the weights now and ought to be eligible for 0-80s after this, for which he would make more appeal.
Mac's Power(IRE) ◆ is unexposed at 6f and in good hands for a sprinter. He travelled strongly as usual as well as showing his trademark turn of foot to briefly dispute the lead, but he was always seeing too much daylight and faded out of things late after drifting right. Covered up more and waited with for longer, he has a good prize in him at this trip. (op 15-2 tchd 6-1)
Lujeanie travelled strongly but didn't find quite what looked likely while carrying his head awkwardly. (op 16-1)
Mister Laurel tends to blow hot and cold but this was a fair effort, spoiled only by a tendency to veer off a straight line late on.
Roker Park(IRE) ran below form and was reported never to have travelled. Official explanation: jockey said gelding never travelled (tchd 6-1)
Spitfire Official explanation: jockey said gelding was denied a clear run
Abraham Lincoln(IRE) was just beginning to drop out when badly hampered. (op 14-1)
Everymanforhimself(IRE) was the subject of good market support at long odds ridden by Silvestre De Sousa for the first time, but looks to have a mind of his own these days and is best treated with caution. (op 22-1)
T/Jkpt: Not won. T/Plt: £10.60 to a £1 winning stake. Pool: £154,354.92 - 10,600 winning tickets. T/Qpdt: £8.70 to a £1 winning stake. Pool: £6,776.76 - 572.10 winning tickets. WG

5856 EPSOM (L-H)
Thursday, September 9

OFFICIAL GOING: Good (good to soft in places) changing to good to soft (good in places) after race 3 (3.35)
Rail dolled out up to 8yds from 1m to 7f adding about 5yds to distances.
Wind: Modest, across Weather: Bright spells, showers threatening

5885 CHALK LANE MEDIAN AUCTION MAIDEN FILLIES' STKS 6f
2:25 (2:26) (Class 5) 2-Y-O **£3,238** (£963; £481; £240) **Stalls** High

Form RPR

43 **1** **Night Carnation**[19] 5294 2-9-0 0 JimmyFortune 2 80+
(A M Balding) *wnt lft s: sn led and mde rest: pushed along and qcknd clr ent fnl f: r.o wl: easily* **6/5**[1]

52 **2** *1 ¼* **Piece Of Mind**[10] 5608 2-8-11 0 PatrickHills(3) 5 73
(R Hannon) *chsd wnr: rdn and effrt ent fnl 2f: drvn and unable qck 1f out: styd on same pce and wl hld fnl f* **9/1**[3]

52 **3** *3 ¾* **Candys Girl**[22] 5196 2-9-0 0 HayleyTurner 6 62
(M L W Bell) *stdd after s: hld up wl in tch in last: rdn and effrt 2f out: outpcd by ldng pair and btn over 1f out: plugged on to go 3rd ins fnl f* **11/8**[2]

0262 **4** *1 ¾* **Silca Conegliano (IRE)**[13] 5466 2-9-0 67 SamHitchcott 4 57
(M R Channon) *t.k.h early: hld up wl in tch: hdwy to press ldrs over 2f out: rdn and fnd little 2f out: wl btn ent fnl f* **14/1**

6 **5** *6* **Imperial Pirouette**[30] 4921 2-8-11 0 MatthewDavies(3) 7 39
(M R Channon) *in tch: effrt to press ldrs and rdn over 2f out: wknd qckly wl over 1f out: wl btn fnl f* **50/1**

006 **6** *3 ½* **Royal Classy Cleo**[20] 5268 2-9-0 0 PatCosgrave 3 28
(P D Evans) *chsd ldrs: pushed along and unable qck 3f out: wknd u.p 2f out: wl bhd over 1f out* **100/1**

1m 12.94s (3.54) **Going Correction** +0.325s/f (Good) **6** Ran SP% **107.2**
Speed ratings (Par 92): **89,87,82,80,72 67**
toteswingers: 1&2 £1.40, 1&3 £1.30, 2&3 £2.00. CSF £11.37 TOTE £2.00: £1.30, £3.70; EX 11.10.
Owner George Strawbridge **Bred** George Strawbridge **Trained** Kingsclere, Hants

FOCUS
The rail was dolled out up to 8yds from 1m to 7f markers, thereafter racing on the innermost (Derby) configuration, adding approximately 5yds to race distances. A dry night and warm day and Hayley Turner, who rode at the course on Wednesday, confirmed the ground was quicker than the previous day. Very little depth to this ordinary fillies' maiden and unlike yesterday, the runners raced in the centre of the track turning for home. The gallop was an ordinary one for a sprint but the first two pulled clear. The winner may rate in the high 80s in time.

NOTEBOOK
Night Carnation, allowed an easy lead dropped to this trip for the first time, showed improved form to win with more in hand than the official margin suggested. Her task was undoubtedly simplified by the below-par showing of her main market rival but her record is one of steady improvement and she looks the type to progress again in handicap company. Her rider felt she would be equally effective over 5f. (op 13/8 tchd 11/10)
Piece Of Mind was always well placed given the way things unfolded and, although flattered by her proximity to the eased-down winner, ran creditably dropped in distance. The switch to nurseries and the return to that longer trip should enable her to get off the mark away from progressive sorts in ordinary company. (op 7/1 tchd 10/1)
Candys Girl looked to have solid claims considering how well her Carlisle form worked out but she failed to find anywhere near as much as anticipated when asked for an effort and this has to go down as disappointing. While capable of picking up an ordinary maiden, she lacks much in the way of physical scope and may not be one to take too short a price about. (op 6/5 tchd 6/4)
Silca Conegliano(IRE) has largely been a reliable sort but she has had plenty of chances and once again had her limitations firmly exposed back over this longer trip. She is likely to remain vulnerable in this type of event. (op 10/1)

Imperial Pirouette was again soundly beaten and is going to have to show considerably more before she is of any interest. (op 66/1)

Royal Classy Cleo was again soundly beaten and is going to remain vulnerable in this grade.

5886 EUROPEAN BREEDERS' FUND MEDIAN AUCTION MAIDEN STKS 7f

3:00 (3:01) (Class 4) 2-Y-O **£4,533** (£1,348; £674; £336) **Stalls** Low

Form RPR

54 **1** **Hawdyerwheesht**[19] 5294 2-9-3 0 GregFairley 1 80
(M Johnston) *mde all: rdn and wnt clr ent fnl 2f: styd on wl: in command whn hung rt u.p ins fnl f* **11/1**

23 **2** 2 ¼ **Escholido (IRE)**[31] 4902 2-9-3 0 MartinDwyer 3 74
(B W Hills) *chsd wnr: rdn ent fnl 3f: drvn and outpcd 2f out: kpt on same pce and no imp fr over 1f out* **10/11**[1]

0 **3** 2 **Perfect Mission**[20] 5263 2-9-3 0 NeilCallan 4 69
(A M Balding) *hld up wl in tch: rdn and outpcd ent fnl 2f: kpt on again ins fnl f to go 3rd fnl 50yds: no threat to wnr* **9/1**[3]

02 **4** ½ **Fists And Stones**[29] 4954 2-9-3 0 SamHitchcott 2 68
(M R Channon) *hld up in tch: rdn and effrt to dispute 2nd ent fnl 2f: sn outpcd by wnr: wknd ins fnl f* **5/2**[2]

04 **5** 6 **Brave Battle**[13] 5465 2-9-3 0 JimmyFortune 6 53
(R Hannon) *hld up in tch: c towards centre over 3f out: rdn and outpcd ent fnl 2f: wl btn whn hung lft 1f out* **9/1**[3]

1m 26.1s (2.80) **Going Correction** +0.325s/f (Good) **5** Ran SP% **109.3**
Speed ratings (Par 97): **97,94,92,91,84**
toteswinger: 1&2 £7.80. CSF £21.67 TOTE £12.00: £4.10, £1.10; EX 21.20.
Owner J S Morrison **Bred** Baldernock Bloodstock Ltd **Trained** Middleham Moor, N Yorks

FOCUS
A shower after the first had petered out by the time this race started. A couple of fair sorts but not a competitive race for the money. The gallop was an ordinary one and once again the riders shunned both rails. A much-improved effort fom the winner but the runner-up was a bit below form.

NOTEBOOK
Hawdyerwheesht ◆ had shown modest form at best on his first two starts (finished six lengths behind the meeting's opening winner Night Carnation at Chester last time), but turned in a much-improved display under an astute front-running ride, despite looking less than happy on the track. He'll stay at least 1m, has plenty of scope, is open to further progress and appeals as the type to win in nursery company. (op 9/1)
Escholido(IRE) had shown fair form on his first two starts over 6f but, although far from disgraced against a progressive sort, failed to build on those efforts upped to this trip for the first time. However, he should stay 1m in due course and remains capable of picking up an ordinary maiden. (tchd 11/10)
Perfect Mission attracted support at double-figure odds and duly bettered the form of his debut effort at Sandown. There's every chance he'll prove effective over 1m judging on this effort and his pedigree, and he may do better in nurseries. (op 14/1)
Fists And Stones, who is bred to stay this trip, looked to have solid claims on his second placing to Big Issue (since shown smart form in Listed and in Group 3 company) but he failed to improve for the step up to 7f - even in a race that did not really place the emphasis on stamina. However, he will be worth another chance in ordinary company back on a more conventional track. (tchd 2/1 and 11/4)
Brave Battle had shown improved form in soft ground on his previous start but failed to match that at this idiosyncratic track after racing on the wide outside. He may do better returned to a flatter track in ordinary nurseries. (op 8/1)

5887 BETFAIR H'CAP 1m 114y

3:35 (3:35) (Class 5) (0-75,75) 3-Y-O **£3,885** (£1,156; £577; £288) **Stalls** Low

Form RPR

3221 **1** **Rare Tern (IRE)**[21] 5236 3-9-7 75 SebSanders 1 91+
(Sir Mark Prescott) *mde all: rdn and wnt clr 2f out: in n.d after: r.o wl: rdn out* **4/5**[1]

3522 **2** 6 **Plutocraft**[34] 4779 3-9-2 70 PatCosgrave 6 72
(J R Fanshawe) *stdd s: hld up wl in tch: towards rr: pushed along and effrt ent fnl 3f: 4th and no ch w wnr 1f out: kpt on u.p* **10/1**

3535 **3** nse **Whiepa Snappa (IRE)**[41] 4532 3-8-2 61 oh1 KierenFox(5) 5 63
(P M Phelan) *hld up wl in tch: pushed along downhill 5f out: outpcd 3f out: 7th and no hdwy over 1f out: r.o wl ins fnl f to snatch 3rd nr fin: no ch w wnr* **15/2**[3]

3563 **4** nk **Treasure Way**[28] 4997 3-8-11 65 NeilCallan 10 66
(P R Chamings) *sn chsng wnr: rdn and nt pce of wnr ent fnl 2f: wl hld after but kpt battling on tl lost 2 pls nr fin* **12/1**

4306 **5** 1 ¼ **Blue Lyric**[16] 5396 3-9-1 69 KirstyMilczarek 4 67
(L M Cumani) *t.k.h: chsd ldng pair: rdn to dispute 2nd ent fnl 2f: drvn and no ch w wnr fr over 1f out: n.m.r and wknd wl ins fnl f* **33/1**

2416 **6** nk **Dutiful**[21] 5238 3-9-3 71 GeorgeBaker 8 69
(M R Channon) *s.i.s: sn t.k.h in midfield: rdn and unable qck over 2f out: no ch w wnr and hung lft over 1f out* **8/1**

4225 **7** 1 **My Sister**[12] 5541 3-8-9 63 HayleyTurner 3 58
(M D I Usher) *dwlt: sn bustled along and in tch in midfield: rdn and outpcd 3f out: rallied and plugged on fr over 1f out: no ch w wnr* **14/1**

5140 **8** 10 **Ajool (USA)**[12] 5541 3-9-1 69 TonyCulhane 7 41
(P W D'Arcy) *stdd s: t.k.h: hld up in last pair: lost tch 3f out: wl bhd and eased ins fnl f* **33/1**

6403 **9** nk **Bin Shamardal (IRE)**[19] 5304 3-9-5 73 MartinDwyer 9 45
(B W Hills) *chsd ldrs tl wknd qckly ent fnl 2f: wl bhd and eased ins fnl f* **13/2**[2]

5000 **10** 20 **Tell Halaf**[12] 5540 3-8-12 66 MickyFenton 2 —
(M G Quinlan) *t.k.h: hld up in last pair: lost tch 3f out: wl bhd and eased ins fnl f: t.o* **50/1**

1m 47.36s (1.26) **Going Correction** +0.325s/f (Good) **10** Ran SP% **123.1**
Speed ratings (Par 101): **107,101,101,101,100 99,99,90,89,72**
toteswingers: 1&2 £3.30, 1&3 £3.10, 2&3 £7.30. CSF £10.92 CT £44.72 TOTE £2.10: £1.60, £2.00, £2.40; EX 8.90.
Owner Sir Edmund Loder **Bred** Sir E J Loder **Trained** Newmarket, Suffolk

FOCUS
The rain again came down before this race. The majority of these were exposed, the exception being the winner, who posted a career-best and was the third winner from as many races on this card to make all. The gallop was no more than fair and the field raced more towards the far rail than in the two earlier races.

5888 TOMPKINS & MAY PARTNERSHIP JUMP JOCKEYS DERBY H'CAP (TO BE RIDDEN BY NATIONAL HUNT JOCKEYS) 1m 4f 10y

4:10 (4:10) (Class 4) (0-80,77) 4-Y-O+ **£5,828** (£1,734; £866; £432) **Stalls** Centre

Form RPR

3213 **1** **Kings Troop**[26] 5084 4-11-8 75 JimmyMcCarthy 4 87
(A King) *hld up wl in tch in last pair: gd hdwy to join ldrs ent fnl 3f: led 2f out: sn rdn clr: in command fnl f: styd on wl* **4/1**[2]

-232 **2** 3 ¼ **Mohanad (IRE)**[39] 3348 4-10-11 64 JamieGoldstein 11 71
(Miss Sheena West) *in tch on outer: hdwy to join ldrs over 3f out: ev ch over 2f out: nt pce of wnr over 1f out: wnt 2nd ins fnl f: no imp* **3/1**[1]

1125 **3** 2 ¼ **Bramalea**[10] 5591 5-11-7 74 PaulMoloney 2 77
(B W Duke) *t.k.h: sn chsng ldr: led over 4f out: jnd ent fnl 3f: rdn and hdd 2f out: outpcd by wnr over 1f out: lost 2nd jst ins fnl f: wknd fnl 100yds* **5/1**[3]

1650 **4** 2 ½ **Penang Cinta**[35] 4737 7-11-3 70 LeeStephens 10 69
(P D Evans) *chsd ldrs: rdn to chse ldr 4f out tl ent fnl 3f: unable qck u.p whn n.m.r and swtchd lft 2f out: drvn and sn outpcd: wl hld fnl f* **20/1**

5325 **5** 2 ½ **Hel's Angel (IRE)**[23] 5181 4-11-10 77 JamieMoore 1 72
(Mrs A Duffield) *hld up wl in tch: rdn and outpcd wl over 2f out: no ch fr wl over 1f out* **11/1**

0050 **6** 3 ¼ **Bon Spiel**[21] 5084 6-10-13 66 (vt) ColinBolger 3 56
(C Gordon) *in tch: pushed along over 3f out: drvn and wl outpcd over 2f out: wl btn after* **16/1**

4242 **7** 8 **Hurlingham**[9] 5631 6-11-0 67 (b) DenisO'Regan 9 44
(M W Easterby) *taken down early: hld up wl in tch in last pair: pushed along and struggling on downhill run 5f out: lost tch over 3f out* **5/1**[3]

3315 **8** 15 **Maslak (IRE)**[17] 5363 6-11-4 71 NickScholfield 5 24
(P W Hiatt) *led tl over 4f out: rdn and lost pl qckly over 3f out: wl bhd fnl 2f: eased ins fnl f: t.o* **12/1**

3110 **9** 7 **Rosco Flyer (IRE)**[35] 4758 4-11-8 75 PaddyBrennan 7 17
(R A Teal) *wl in tch in midfield tl lost pl qckly on downhill run over 4f out: wl bhd and drvn 3f out: sn lost tch: eased ins fnl f: t.o* **13/2**

2m 44.73s (5.83) **Going Correction** +0.325s/f (Good) **9** Ran SP% **118.3**
Speed ratings (Par 105): **93,90,89,87,86 83,78,68,63**
toteswingers: 1&2 £4.20, 1&3 £6.80, 2&3 £4.40. CSF £16.91 CT £61.79 TOTE £5.30: £2.20, £1.10, £1.40; EX 23.90.
Owner W H Ponsonby **Bred** Wickfield Stud And Hartshill Stud **Trained** Barbury Castle, Wilts

FOCUS
The ground was changed after the previous race to 'good to soft, good in places'. An ordinary handicap for jump jockeys but, although the gallop seemed just no more than fair, the field finished fairly well strung out. The bulk of the field raced in the centre.
Bramalea Official explanation: jockey said mare hung right-handed

5889 RICHMOND H'CAP 7f

4:45 (4:47) (Class 5) (0-75,75) 3-Y-O+ **£3,885** (£1,156; £577; £288) **Stalls** Low

Form RPR

4140 **1** **Amber Sunset**[13] 5499 4-8-11 67 AdamBeschizza(5) 1 78
(D Morris) *t.k.h: w ldr tl led 4f out: rdn ent fnl 2f: 2 l clr and hung rt u.p ins fnl f: hld on cl home* **7/2**[2]

1025 **2** hd **Maze (IRE)**[13] 5480 5-9-9 74 NeilCallan 4 84
(A W Carroll) *chsd ldrs: hdwy to trck wnr over 2f out: rdn and unable qck over 1f out: swtchd lft and rallied ins fnl f: r.o: jst hld* **6/1**

3322 **3** 4 ½ **Rondeau (GR)**[50] 4260 5-9-8 73 GeorgeBaker 7 71
(P R Chamings) *hld up in tch in midfield: effrt to chse ldng pair jst over 2f out: rdn and edgd lft over 1f out: sn outpcd and btn fnl f* **15/2**

1631 **4** 3 **Leelu**[11] 5555 4-8-10 60 6ex HayleyTurner 3 51
(D W P Arbuthnot) *racd keenly: led tl 4f out: rdn and lost pl qckly ent fnl 3f: no ch w ldrs fnl 2f* **3/1**[1]

00-3 **5** 3 **Slugger O'Toole**[154] 1185 5-9-10 75 WilliamCarson 8 57
(S C Williams) *stdd and dropped in after s: pushed along and effrt 3f out: hung lft and no real prog after: nvr trbld ldrs* **9/2**[3]

3531 **6** 1 ¼ **Phluke**[8] 5655 9-8-7 61 oh3 (v) Louis-PhilippeBeuzelin(3) 2 39
(Eve Johnson Houghton) *chsd ldrs: rdn and outpcd over 3f out: drvn and btn ent fnl 2f: wl bhd fnl f* **6/1**

5055 **7** hd **Memphis Man**[13] 5473 7-8-12 63 PatCosgrave 5 41
(P D Evans) *stdd s: hld up in midfield: effrt over 2f: rdn 2f out: sn btn* **20/1**

1652 **8** 9 **Universal Circus**[6] 5712 3-9-6 75 SamHitchcott 6 28
(M R Channon) *a towards rr: rdn and struggling 4f out: lost tch 3f out* **25/1**

1m 24.98s (1.68) **Going Correction** +0.325s/f (Good)
WFA 3 from 4yo+ 4lb **8** Ran SP% **114.3**
Speed ratings (Par 103): **103,102,97,94,90 89,89,78**
toteswingers: 1&2 £5.70, 1&3 £6.00, 2&3 £6.70. CSF £24.74 CT £147.60 TOTE £5.70: £1.80, £3.40, £2.30; EX 31.20.
Owner David J Orchard **Bred** Southill Stud **Trained** Baxter's Green, Suffolk

FOCUS
A couple of previous winners in an ordinary handicap. The gallop was fair and the runners again raced in the centre turning for home.

5890 ST HELIER H'CAP 6f

5:15 (5:16) (Class 5) (0-75,74) 3-Y-O **£3,885** (£1,156; £577; £288) **Stalls** High

Form RPR

1323 **1** **Starwatch**[15] 5417 3-8-13 66 NeilChalmers 7 74
(J J Bridger) *chsd ldr: rdn 2f out: ev ch over 1f out: led ins fnl f: r.o wl* **13/2**

4122 **2** 1 **Flouncing (IRE)**[27] 5037 3-9-7 74 TonyCulhane 6 79
(W J Haggas) *chsd ldrs: led ent fnl 2f: rdn over 1f out: hdd and no ex ins fnl f* **11/2**[3]

641 **3** 1 ¼ **The Human League**[11] 5557 3-8-9 62 SamHitchcott 9 63
(M R Channon) *chsd ldrs: rdn to chse ldng pair wl over 1f out: hung lft u.p and one pce fnl f* **3/1**[2]

5001 **4** 1 ¾ **Kate Skate**[7] 5686 3-8-2 59 6ex AdamBeschizza(5) 4 55
(Miss Gay Kelleway) *v awkward s and slowly away: wl bhd: rdn 2f out: hdwy over 1f out: kpt on wl fnl f: nvr able to chal* **8/1**

2433 **5** 2 **Caramelita**[11] 5562 3-9-0 67 GregFairley 1 56
(J R Jenkins) *wl off the pce in last trio: hdwy and rdn over 2f out: drvn and no imp fr over 1f out* **8/1**

6311 **6** 1 ½ **Micky P**[28] 4998 3-9-0 67 WilliamCarson 5 51
(S C Williams) *s.i.s: wl off the pce and pushed along in last trio: rdn over 2f out: sme hdwy but edging lft over 1f out: no imp ins fnl f* **5/2**[1]

0006 **7** 16 **Goodwood Maestro**[28] 5005 3-8-8 64 (b[1]) Louis-PhilippeBeuzelin(3) 2 —
(J L Dunlop) *broke wl: sn off the pce in midfield: short-lived effrt u.p over 2f out: wl bhd and eased ins fnl f* **16/1**

6243 **8** ½ **Dancing Freddy (IRE)**[10] 5600 3-9-5 72 (b) SebSanders 8 3
(J G Given) *led and set fast gallop: hdd ent fnl 2f: sn wknd: wl bhd and eased ins fnl f* **12/1**

0606 **9** 5 **Private Olley**[23] 5182 3-8-9 62 ow2 MickyFenton 3 —
(J Akehurst) *racd in midfield: racing awkwardly and struggling downhill over 4f out: bhd and hung bdly lft 3f out: sn lost tch* **33/1**

1m 11.06s (1.66) **Going Correction** +0.325s/f (Good) **9** Ran SP% **121.0**
Speed ratings (Par 101): **101,99,98,95,93 91,69,69,62**
toteswingers: 1&2 £4.60, 1&3 £5.00, 2&3 £3.90. CSF £44.22 CT £132.29 TOTE £8.00: £2.80, £2.50, £1.10; EX 35.70 Place 6: £27.09, Place 5: £14.87..
Owner J J Bridger **Bred** Mrs J A Chapman **Trained** Liphook, Hants

FOCUS
Three last-time-out winners and a couple of other in-form types in an ordinary handicap but one in which the market leader disappointed. Although the pace was sound those up with the pace held the edge and the field again raced in the centre.
Goodwood Maestro Official explanation: jockey said gelding never travelled
Private Olley Official explanation: jockey said colt was unsuited by the track
T/Plt: £27.90 to a £1 winning stake. Pool: £52,032.99 - 1,357.90 winning units. T/Qpdt: £6.50 to a £1 winning stake. Pool: £3,971.33 - 448.80 winning units. SP

5862 KEMPTON (A.W) (R-H)
Thursday, September 9

OFFICIAL GOING: Standard
Wind: Virtually nil Weather: Bright getting dark

5891 BET PREMIER LEAGUE FOOTBALL - BETDAQ APPRENTICE H'CAP 1m (P)
5:45 (5:45) (Class 5) (0-70,70) 3-Y-O £2,286 (£675; £337) Stalls High

Form RPR
00-1 **1** **True To Form (IRE)**[6] 5729 3-8-4 **56** 6ex RosieJessop(3) 6 67
(Sir Mark Prescott) *trckd ldrs: wnt 2nd over 2f out: pushed along and qcknd to ld fnl 100yds: edgd lft cl home: a jst doing enough* **4/9**[1]
042 **2** *nk* **Abhar (USA)**[16] 5384 3-9-7 **70** KierenFox 7 80
(J R Best) *led: pushed along 2f out: hdd fnl 100yds: kpt on but a jst hld* **9/2**[2]
0424 **3** *6* **Osgood**[8] 5664 3-9-3 **69** RyanClark(3) 1 66
(M R Channon) *in rr: hdwy over 1f out: r.o fnl f to take mod 3rd last strides* **9/1**
500 **4** *shd* **Confrontation**[90] 2925 3-9-2 **65** SophieDoyle 2 61
(D M Simcock) *t.k.h: chsd ldr tl rdn and lost 2nd over 2f out: wknd ins fnl f and lost mod 3rd last strides* **40/1**
6534 **5** *1 ½* **Al Jaadi**[16] 5384 3-9-5 **68** AshleyMorgan 4 61
(W Jarvis) *in rr but in tch: hdwy over 3f out: nvr quite rchd ldrs and styd on same pce fnl 2f* **8/1**[3]
00 **6** *2 ¾* **Yorksters Prince (IRE)**[84] 3113 3-8-3 **59** RichardOld(7) 5 46
(G Prodromou) *t.k.h: in tch: rdn over 2f out: wknd wl over 1f out* **66/1**
0460 **7** *½* **Imperial Warrior**[40] 4589 3-8-4 **58** (bt[1]) NoraLooby(5) 8 43
(H Morrison) *s.i.s: rcvrd and in tch 1/2-way: wknd 2f out* **16/1**
0043 **8** *nk* **Ishtar Gate (USA)**[48] 4335 3-9-1 **67** DuilioDaSilva(3) 3 52
(P F I Cole) *sn bhd* **20/1**

1m 39.45s (-0.35) **Going Correction** -0.025s/f (Stan) 8 Ran SP% **123.1**
Speed ratings (Par 101): **100,99,93,93,92 89,88,88**
toteswingers: 1&2 £1.50, 1&3 £2.40, 2&3 £3.50. CSF £3.27 CT £10.17 TOTE £1.80: £1.30, £1.60, £1.20; EX 4.10.
Owner G Moore - Osborne House **Bred** Sir E J Loder **Trained** Newmarket, Suffolk

FOCUS
A run of the mill 56-70 handicap.
Osgood Official explanation: jockey said colt hung right-handed

5892 BET CHAMPIONS LEAGUE FOOTBALL - BETDAQ MAIDEN STKS (DIV I) 7f (P)
6:15 (6:18) (Class 5) 2-Y-O £1,944 (£574; £287) Stalls High

Form RPR
42 **1** **Custom House (IRE)**[54] 4142 2-9-3 0 PatDobbs 6 80
(R Hannon) *chsd ldrs: chal over 1f out: led and hung lft ins fnl f: in command whn veered lft again last strides* **11/4**[2]
33 **2** *1* **Buckland (IRE)**[27] 5032 2-9-3 0 MartinDwyer 5 78
(B J Meehan) *chsd ldrs: rdn along 3f out: chal 2f out: slt ld over 1f out: hdd ins fnl f: hld whn carried lft last strides* **4/5**[1]
3 *nk* **Male Model** 2-9-3 0 RichardMullen 2 77+
(Mahmood Al Zarooni) *in tch: hdwy fr 2f out: drvn and styd on thrght fnl f and clsng for 2nd last strides* **15/2**[3]
0 **4** *nk* **Malacca Straits**[33] 4844 2-8-12 0 RobertWinston 3 72+
(B W Hills) *s.i.s: drvn to chse ldrs: rdn and styng on whn hmpd ins fnl f: styd on again fnl 75yds but nt rcvr* **14/1**
06 **5** *½* **Alshazah**[28] 5006 2-9-3 0 IanMongan 7 75
(B R Millman) *led: rdn over 2f out: narrowly hdd over 1f out: styd chalng tl outpcd fnl 120yds* **66/1**
0 **6** *1 ½* **Muhandis (IRE)**[34] 4803 2-9-3 0 GeorgeBaker 4 71
(E A L Dunlop) *s.i.s: in rr: hdwy fr 3f out: chsd ldrs over 1f out: pushed along fnl f: fdd fnl 120yds* **8/1**
7 *3* **Allumeuse (USA)** 2-8-12 0 JimmyFortune 1 59
(A M Balding) *relucatant to enter stalls: slowly away: in rr: t.k.h: hdwy on outside 3f out: styd on fnl 2f but nvr a threat* **28/1**
00 **8** *8* **Al Furat (USA)**[58] 3991 2-9-3 0 TedDurcan 9 44
(D R Lanigan) *unruly in stalls: towards rr most of way* **50/1**
9 *3 ¼* **Labore** 2-9-3 0 NeilCallan 11 35
(M Botti) *unruly in stalls: a towards rr* **33/1**
00 **10** *1* **Reach Out**[9] 5629 2-9-0 0 EJMcNamara(3) 12 33
(B G Powell) *chsd ldrs 4f* **100/1**

1m 26.59s (0.59) **Going Correction** -0.025s/f (Stan) 10 Ran SP% **122.6**
Speed ratings (Par 95): **95,93,93,93,92 90,87,78,74,73**
toteswingers: 1&2 £1.10, 1&3 £3.70. 2&3 £3.10. CSF £5.48 TOTE £2.30: £1.10, £1.10, £3.00; EX 6.70.
Owner H Robin Heffer **Bred** John O'Brien **Trained** East Everleigh, Wilts
■ Stewards' Enquiry : Pat Dobbs one day ban: careless riding (Sep 23)

FOCUS
Division one of a very ordinary maiden which lacked strength in depth. It was run at a sound gallop and the first five home were covered by a couple of lengths.

NOTEBOOK
Custom House(IRE) managed to lose his maiden tag at the third attempt. Having his first start at 7f, he drifted left under pressure and might be hard to place in the future. (op 9-4)
Buckland(IRE), also having his third start, was hampered by the winner close home but could not be called unlucky. This was his first try on this surface and, with his stable going well, a similar contest should be his for the taking. (op 10-11 tchd Evens in places)
Male Model did the best of the newcomers and can also make a mark at this time of year. (op 10-1)
Malacca Straits ◆ was coming with a strong run inside the final furlong until getting badly hampered close home. She can gain compensation shortly. (op 25-1)
Allumeuse(USA), who took a long time to enter the stalls, was very slowly away and will learn a lot from this experience. (op 25-1 tchd 33-1)

5893 BET CHAMPIONS LEAGUE FOOTBALL - BETDAQ MAIDEN STKS (DIV II) 7f (P)
6:45 (6:48) (Class 5) 2-Y-O £1,944 (£574; £287) Stalls High

Form RPR
1 **Tazahum (USA)** 2-9-3 0 RichardMullen 7 86+
(Sir Michael Stoute) *in tch: hdwy and swtchd rt to rail over 2f out: drvn to ld over 1f out: c clr ins fnl f: comf* **11/1**
23 **2** *2 ¼* **Mujrayaat (IRE)**[102] 2561 2-9-3 0 TadhgO'Shea 9 78
(M A Jarvis) *led: drvn and narrowly hdd over 2f out: styd pressing ldrs and kpt on to retake 2nd nr fin but nvr any ch w wnr* **11/4**[2]
3 **3** *nk* **Double Dealer**[13] 5491 2-9-3 0 NeilCallan 8 77
(Mahmood Al Zarooni) *sn trcking ldr: slt ld over 2f out: rdn and hdd over 1f out: outpcd by wnr fnl f and lost 2nd nr fin* **9/4**[1]
4 *hd* **Dimension** 2-9-3 0 GeorgeBaker 2 77+
(J R Fanshawe) *s.i.s: in rr: hdwy on outside over 2f out: styd on wl fnl f and gng on cl home but nvr any ch w wnr* **16/1**
0 **5** *2 ½* **L'Astre De Choisir (IRE)**[17] 5372 2-9-3 0 ShaneKelly 6 71
(W R Swinburn) *chsd ldrs: rdn and btn whn hung rt fr over 1f out* **66/1**
4 **6** *hd* **Glanusk**[29] 4954 2-9-0 0 EJMcNamara(3) 5 70
(R M Beckett) *in tch: hdwy towards outside to chse ldrs over 2f out: sn one pce* **9/2**[3]
7 *5* **Come On The Irons (USA)** 2-9-0 0 Louis-PhilippeBeuzelin(3) 3 58+
(B J Meehan) *in rr and sn drvn along: stl plenty to do over 2f out: styd on fnl f but nvr a threat* **50/1**
00 **8** *1 ½* **Touch Of Red (USA)**[12] 5537 2-9-3 0 PatDobbs 4 54
(R Hannon) *s.i.s: in rr: rdn over 3f out: sme prog fnl f* **50/1**
5 **9** *2* **Proenza (USA)**[24] 5156 2-8-12 0 MartinDwyer 11 44
(B J Meehan) *chsng ldrs whn hmpd on rail ins fnl 4f: nt rcvr* **9/2**[3]
10 *2 ¾* **Kuala Limper (IRE)** 2-9-3 0 HayleyTurner 1 42
(D R C Elsworth) *s.i.s: sn chsng ldrs: wknd fr 3f out* **33/1**
11 *15* **Cross The Creek (IRE)** 2-9-3 0 TedDurcan 10 4
(D R Lanigan) *slowly away: green and a wl bhd* **25/1**

1m 25.99s (-0.01) **Going Correction** -0.025s/f (Stan) 11 Ran SP% **120.2**
Speed ratings (Par 95): **99,96,96,95,93 92,87,85,83,79 62**
toteswingers: 1&2 £4.80, 1&3 £4.00, 2&3 £1.70. CSF £41.27 TOTE £20.10: £6.10, £1.10, £1.10; EX 27.60.
Owner Hamdan Al Maktoum **Bred** Shadwell Australia Ltd **Trained** Newmarket, Suffolk

FOCUS
Division two of this 7f maiden and it looked a stronger than the first one. It was run at an even pace.

NOTEBOOK
Tazahum(USA) put up a very nice performance. Coming from a top yard, he was easy to back beforehand but he travelled well throughout and can certainly go on from this taking effort. (op 12-1 tchd 14-1)
Mujrayaat(IRE), having his first start since the end of May, was a little keen in the early part of the race. He can go one better in similar company shortly. (op 2-1)
Double Dealer, third on his debut at Newmarket, again showed ability here and will also be able to lose his maiden tag in the coming weeks. (op 10-3)
Dimension, a half-brother to the yard's useful Spacious, also showed plenty of promise on his debut. He looked like he would come on plenty for this kind of introduction and has clearly got ability. (tchd 20-1)
L'Astre De Choisir(IRE) had come on plenty from his debut and looks an ideal nursery type after another run.

5894 BETDAQ THE BETTING EXCHANGE CLAIMING STKS 7f (P)
7:15 (7:17) (Class 6) 2-Y-O £1,637 (£483; £241) Stalls High

Form RPR
5102 **1** **Daas Rite (IRE)**[7] 5701 2-9-5 70 NeilCallan 1 70+
(K A Ryan) *chsd ldrs: rdn to ld over 1f out: drvn and styd on wl fnl f* **6/1**[2]
6560 **2** *1 ¼* **Falkland Flyer (IRE)**[9] 5637 2-9-3 74 SamHitchcott 6 65
(M R Channon) *led tl hdd over 1f out: styd pressing wnr tl no ex fnl 100yds: jst hld on for 2nd* **11/4**[1]
2053 **3** *hd* **Jambo Bibi (IRE)**[15] 5412 2-8-12 73 RichardHughes 3 59
(R Hannon) *chsd ldrs: nt clr run and swtchd lft over 2f out: drvn and qcknd to chse ldrs fnl f: kpt on to press for 2nd cl home but no imp on wnr* **11/4**[1]
000 **4** *3 ½* **Run Daisy Run**[48] 4338 2-8-12 55 (b[1]) MartinDwyer 5 51
(B J Meehan) *s.i.s: mid-div: pushed along and hdwy over 2f out: styd on to take one pce 4th ins fnl f* **14/1**
00 **5** *¾* **Nutley Copse**[9] 5630 2-8-8 0 (v) NeilChalmers 7 45
(A M Balding) *s.i.s: in rr: pushed along over 2f out: mod prog fnl f* **25/1**
46 **6** *1* **Silver Age (IRE)**[16] 5381 2-8-11 0 RyanPowell(7) 9 52
(J S Moore) *chsd ldrs: rdn over 2f out: sn one pce and wknd fnl f* **11/4**[1]
00 **7** *6* **Ivanov (IRE)**[9] 5630 2-9-1 0 StevieDonohoe 8 34
(W J Musson) *s.i.s: outpcd* **50/1**
056 **8** *2 ¾* **Indiracer (IRE)**[17] 5373 2-8-10 63 (p) RobertWinston 4 22
(A Bailey) *t.k.h: chsd ldrs: rdn and wknd wl over 2f out* **11/1**[3]
5000 **P** **Helen Of Toy**[6] 5718 2-8-2 42 (t) SophieDoyle(5) 2 —
(B G Powell) *sn chsng ldr: rdn 3f out: wknd qckly over 2f out and p.u over 1f out: lame* **100/1**

1m 27.04s (1.04) **Going Correction** -0.025s/f (Stan) 9 Ran SP% **116.1**
Speed ratings (Par 93): **93,91,91,87,86 85,78,75,—**
toteswingers: 1&2 £3.70, 1&3 £4.40, 2&3 £1.40. CSF £22.83 TOTE £5.20: £1.30, £1.10, £1.10; EX 21.40.
Owner Miss Deirdre McGuire & Mrs J Ryan **Bred** Mark & Pippa Hackett **Trained** Hambleton, N Yorks
■ Stewards' Enquiry : Sam Hitchcott caution: use of whip

FOCUS
A run-of-the-mill claimer which was run at a sound pace. It proved hard to make ground off the pace.

NOTEBOOK
Daas Rite(IRE), rated 70 and a winner of a 6f seller in May, travelled well throughout. He doesn't do a lot when hitting the front, but this is his grade and he should remain competitive in it. (op 4-1)
Falkland Flyer(IRE), rated 74, has been struggling in nurseries of late and proved here that he is still a few pounds too high in the weights. He got very warm beforehand, but also can continue to pay his way at this time of year. (op 4-1)
Jambo Bibi(IRE) is now still a maiden after eight starts. She is not one to take a short price about. (op 5-2 tchd 3-1)

Run Daisy Run, rated 55, had work to do at the weights but ran respectably in her first-time headgear and there should be plenty of opportunities at this time of the year. Modest handicaps might be the way forward for her. (tchd 16-1)

5895 E B F BETDAQ MAIDEN STKS 6f (P)
7:45 (7:46) (Class 5) 2-Y-O **£3,076** (£915; £457; £228) **Stalls** High

Form RPR
24 1 **Hokoumah (USA)**59 3961 2-9-3 0 TedDurcan 6 79+
(Saeed Bin Suroor) *sn chsng ldr: rdn and styd on fr 2f out: led fnl 120yds: drvn out* 5/2[2]
4 2 ¾ **Silver Ocean (USA)**16 5381 2-9-3 0 JimCrowley 7 77
(R M Beckett) *t.k.h: sn led: drvn along fr 2f out: strly pressed fr 1f out: hdd fnl 120yds: no ex* 5/4[1]
3 3 1¾ **State Of Mind**12 5523 2-9-3 0 JimmyFortune 5 72
(P F I Cole) *plld hrd: chsd ldrs: styd on: edgd rt and tk 3rd and edgd lft 1f out but no imp on ldng duo ins fnl f* 3/1[3]
64 4 2¼ **Countess Ellen (IRE)**100 2616 2-8-12 0 SteveDrowne 8 60
(J R Gask) *chsd ldrs in 3rd: rdn over 2f out and sn one pce: lost 3rd 1f out and sn wknd* 8/1
06 5 7 **Coedmor Boy**31 4909 2-8-12 0 DeclanCannon(5) 9 44
(B Palling) *in tch: rdn and hung rt over 2f out: sn wknd* 100/1
6 2¾ **Senor Tibor (USA)** 2-9-3 0 EddieCreighton 4 36
(E J Creighton) *s.i.s: green and a bhd* 50/1
7 hd **Lisselton Cross** 2-9-3 0 GeorgeBaker 3 35+
(M R Bosley) *veered lft s: green and a bhd* 100/1

1m 13.76s (0.66) **Going Correction** -0.025s/f (Stan) 7 Ran SP% **113.1**
Speed ratings (Par 95): **94,93,90,87,78 74,74**
toteswingers: 1&2 £1.30, 1&3 £1.10, 2&3 £1.50. CSF £5.88 TOTE £3.00: £1.60, £1.10; EX 5.80.
Owner Godolphin **Bred** Darley **Trained** Newmarket, Suffolk

FOCUS
Little strength-in-depth in this maiden and again it helped to race up with the pace. The first three home are the ones to concentrate on for the future.

NOTEBOOK
Hokoumah(USA), sent off favourite on both previous starts, travelled well throughout and showed a good attitude close home. Not the biggest, a lot will depend on what mark the handicapper gives him. (tchd 2-1 and 11-4)
Silver Ocean(USA) had caught the eye on debut over C&D and was well backed here. A little keen early in the race, a similar contest will be his for the taking. (op 11-8 tchd 6-4)
State Of Mind was also keen early before staying on. He looks like he has more size and scope than some of these, so he should continue to progress. (op 5-2)
Lisselton Cross was always playing catch-up after a very slow start. Official explanation: jockey said colt missed the break (op 80-1)

5896 BET TRI NATIONS RUGBY - BETDAQ FILLIES' H'CAP 7f (P)
8:15 (8:15) (Class 4) (0-80,78) 3-Y-O+ **£3,885** (£1,156; £577; £288) **Stalls** High

Form RPR
5132 1 **Avon Lady**16 5396 3-9-6 74 PatCosgrave 11 81
(J R Fanshawe) *in tch: drvn and hdwy over 1f out: swtchd lft and str run ins fnl f to ld fnl 25yds* 10/3[2]
4606 2 hd **Breathless Kiss (USA)**15 5421 3-9-8 76 (v) NeilCallan 6 82
(K A Ryan) *s.i.s: in rr: hdwy and hung rt over 1f out: swtchd lft and r.o strly ins fnl f to take 2nd cl home but nt rch wnr* 33/1
2214 3 ½ **Valencha**27 5037 3-9-3 71 SteveDrowne 7 76
(H Morrison) *in rr: hdwy on outside fr 2f out: str run ins fnl f to take 3rd cl home: nt rch ldng duo* 14/1
044 4 ½ **Hulcote Rose (IRE)**6 5713 3-9-7 75 LiamKeniry 8 79
(S Kirk) *in tch: rapid hdwy to ld 1f out: styd on wl tl hdd fnl 25yds and lost 3 pls cl home* 16/1
3-21 5 1 **Hamloola**16 5395 3-9-10 78 TadhgO'Shea 1 79
(W J Haggas) *led after 2f: rdn and edgd rt to far rail over 2f out: hdd 1f out: wknd ins fnl f* 10/11[1]
0020 6 1¼ **Posy Fossil (USA)**27 5054 3-8-9 63 (b[1]) WilliamCarson 2 61
(S C Williams) *in rr: stl plenty to do over 2f out whn rdn and r.o fr over 1f out: styd on wl fnl f but nvr a threat* 50/1
105 7 nk **Copper Penny**33 4850 3-9-9 77 TedDurcan 5 74
(D R Lanigan) *chsd ldrs: rdn and styng on same pce whn n.m.r ins fnl f* 14/1
1100 8 ½ **Kingston Acacia**77 3375 3-9-9 77 (v) JimmyFortune 3 73
(A M Balding) *t.k.h: chsd ldrs: hung rt over 1f out: styng on whn hmpd ins fnl f: nt rcvr* 10/1[3]
1320 9 2 **Excellent Day (IRE)**16 5383 3-9-2 70 GeorgeBaker 10 60
(M R Channon) *in rr: hdwy on ins over 2f out: styng on whn nt clr run over 1f out and jst ins fnl f: nt rcvr* 20/1
1253 10 hd **Lenkiewicz**24 5145 3-9-4 75 JamesMillman(3) 9 65
(B R Millman) *chsd ldrs: wkng whn hmpd ins fnl 2f and over 1f out* 20/1
1265 11 6 **Pose (IRE)**28 5005 3-9-6 74 RichardHughes 4 47
(R Hannon) *led 2f: styd trcking ldr: drvn and swtchd rt to ins 2f out: hmpd and snatched up sn after: nt rcvr and eased whn no ch ins fnl f* 10/1[3]

1m 25.83s (-0.17) **Going Correction** -0.025s/f (Stan) 11 Ran SP% **127.3**
Speed ratings (Par 102): **99,98,98,97,96 95,94,94,91,91 84**
toteswingers: 1&2 £65.80, 1&3 £7.20, 2&3 £162.50. CSF £123.07 CT £1447.90 TOTE £2.60: £1.10, £6.20, £5.60; EX 101.80.
Owner Helena Springfield Ltd **Bred** Meon Valley Stud **Trained** Newmarket, Suffolk
■ Stewards' Enquiry : Pat Cosgrave two-day ban: careless riding (23 -24 sep)

FOCUS
A competitive 66-80 fillies' 3-y-o handicap run at an even pace and luck in running was crucial.
Pose(IRE) Official explanation: jockey said filly was denied a clear run

5897 BET ST LEGER - BETDAQ H'CAP 7f (P)
8:45 (8:45) (Class 6) (0-65,65) 3-Y-O+ **£1,637** (£483; £241) **Stalls** High

Form RPR
2332 1 **Harting Hill**11 5559 5-9-8 63 RichardHughes 9 72
(M P Tregoning) *trckd ldrs: drvn to ld jst ins fnl f: narrowly hdd fnl 120yds: led again sn after and kpt on wl* 7/4[1]
5001 2 nk **Fitz**16 5379 4-9-4 59 TedDurcan 11 67
(Matthew Salaman) *chsd ldrs: rdn to chal ins fnl f: narrow ld fnl 120yds: hdd sn after and one pce* 5/1[2]
50-4 3 ¾ **Lend A Grand (IRE)**36 4700 6-9-5 60 IanMongan 7 66
(Miss Jo Crowley) *in rr: hdwy fr 2f out: str run to chse ldng duo ins fnl f: no ex nr fin* 10/1
0316 4 ¾ **Scottish Glen**17 5377 4-9-9 64 LiamKeniry 10 68
(P R Chamings) *t.k.h: early: in rr but in tch: hdwy fr 2f out: drvn and kpt on wl fnl f: gng on cl home* 8/1
1000 5 shd **Lord Of The Dance (IRE)**26 5077 4-9-6 61 LukeMorris 1 65
(W M Brisbourne) *in rr: rdn over 2f out: styd on u.p fnl f: gng on cl home* 50/1
6331 6 2¼ **Anjomarba (IRE)**26 5075 3-9-0 62 EJMcNamara(3) 5 58
(B R Johnson) *chsd ldrs: rdn over 2f out: wknd ins fnl f* 20/1
0010 7 ½ **Sovereignty (JPN)**20 5254 8-9-2 62 SophieDoyle(5) 13 58
(D K Ivory) *t.k.h: led: rdn over 2f out: hdd jst ins fnl f: sn btn* 11/1
4400 8 ½ **Song Of Praise**6 5711 4-9-2 57 ShaneKelly 4 52
(M Blanshard) *s.i.s: in rr tl styd on fr over 1f out* 50/1
0003 9 ½ **Resplendent Alpha**18 5326 6-9-4 59 JimmyQuinn 14 53
(P Howling) *chsd ldrs: rdn and wl there 2f out: wknd fnl f* 16/1
3003 10 2 **Forward Feline (IRE)**31 4910 4-9-5 65 DeclanCannon(5) 2 53
(B Palling) *in tch on outside: rdn over 2f out: sn btn* 14/1
4100 11 hd **Bob Stock (IRE)**20 5271 4-9-5 60 TonyCulhane 6 48
(W J Musson) *t.k.h: hld up in rr tl r.o ins fnl f* 16/1
0000 12 nk **Bishopbriggs (USA)**34 4789 5-9-2 57 MickyFenton 8 44
(M G Quinlan) *s.i.s: bhd most of way* 40/1
6205 13 1 **Trip Switch**155 1170 4-8-13 59 KierenFox(5) 3 43
(G Prodromou) *s.i.s: a towards rr* 25/1
00 14 3¼ **Fernando Torres**57 4024 4-9-9 64 (b[1]) J-PGuillambert 12 39
(N P Littmoden) *t.k.h: chsd ldrs: wknd and hung rt over 2f out* 15/2[3]

1m 26.38s (0.38) **Going Correction** -0.025s/f (Stan)
WFA 3 from 4yo+ 4lb 14 Ran SP% **126.7**
Speed ratings (Par 101): **96,95,94,93,93 91,90,90,89,87 87,86,85,81**
toteswingers: 1&2 £2.20, 1&3 £7.50, 2&3 £10.00. CSF £9.81 CT £73.93 TOTE £3.60: £1.10, £1.10, £5.40; EX 15.50.
Owner Miss S Sharp **Bred** Stanley J Sharp **Trained** Lambourn, Berks

FOCUS
Seven previous course winners in the line-up made this a competitive 51-65 handicap. It was run at a solid pace and the form should stand up.

5898 BETDAQ.COM H'CAP 6f (P)
9:15 (9:15) (Class 6) (0-60,60) 3-Y-O **£1,637** (£483; £241) **Stalls** High

Form RPR
6333 1 **Tislaam (IRE)**57 4018 3-9-0 58 (p) DeclanCannon(5) 8 67+
(A J McCabe) *chsd ldrs: led ins fnl 2f: drvn out fnl f* 4/1[1]
0000 2 2¼ **Avow (USA)**11 5557 3-9-7 60 (b) NeilChalmers 4 62
(J J Bridger) *wnt rt s: in rr: drvn and hdwy on outside fr over 2f out: str run fnl f to take 2nd cl home but no ch w wnr* 50/1
0463 3 hd **Itsthursdayalready**14 5438 3-9-2 55 TomMcLaughlin 3 57
(W M Brisbourne) *in rr: hdwy 2f out: styd on wl to press for 2nd cl home but no ch w wnr* 20/1
0433 4 hd **Miss Polly Plum**68 3682 3-8-11 50 JimmyQuinn 1 51
(C A Dwyer) *rapid hdwy to ld after 2f: hdd ins fnl 2f: wknd fnl f* 8/1[2]
0453 5 1¾ **Lordsbury Pride (USA)**8 5670 3-9-1 59 KierenFox(5) 10 54
(J R Best) *chsd ldrs: rdn 2f out: wknd ins fnl f* 10/1[3]
U040 6 1½ **Music Lover**8 5668 3-9-7 60 (b[1]) LukeMorris 5 51
(R A Harris) *plunged stalls and slowly away: in rr tl styd on fr over 1f out: kpt on cl home* 33/1
4231 7 hd **Vilnius**13 5481 3-9-7 60 SamHitchcott 9 50
(M R Channon) *chsd ldrs: riddn and n.m.r 2f out: n.d after* 4/1[1]
2150 8 nse **Thalia Grace**28 5010 3-9-3 59 JamesMillman(3) 2 49
(L Montague Hall) *in rr: styd on fr over 1f out: nt rch ldrs* 20/1
5604 9 shd **Bidruma**8 5670 3-9-4 57 RichardMullen 12 46
(Mike Murphy) *led 2f: wknd over 1f out* 8/1[2]
0043 10 shd **Freedom Pass (USA)**22 5206 3-9-3 56 (t) RichardHughes 11 45
(J A R Toller) *in tch: pushed along 2f out: styd in tch tl wknd ins fnl f: eased whn no ch* 4/1[1]
20-6 11 ½ **Cane Cat (IRE)**6 5715 3-8-13 52 SebSanders 7 40
(A W Carroll) *a in rr* 25/1
3442 12 11 **Bathwick Xaara**28 4989 3-9-2 60 AdamBeschizza(5) 6 12
(J G Portman) *rrd in stalls: a in rr* 8/1[2]

1m 12.72s (-0.38) **Going Correction** -0.025s/f (Stan) 12 Ran SP% **120.7**
Speed ratings (Par 99): **101,98,97,97,95 93,92,92,92,92 91,77**
toteswingers: 1&2 £151.90, 1&3 £81.60, 2&3 £164.10. CSF £260.42 CT £3639.62 TOTE £3.50: £1.40, £17.70, £7.00; EX 246.00 Place 6: £8.91, Place 5: £7.68..
Owner Mrs Z Wentworth **Bred** Airlie Stud **Trained** Averham Park, Notts

FOCUS
An ordinary 46-60 handicap run at a furious pace.
T/Plt: £5.30 to a £1 winning stake. Pool: £62,572.30 - 8,565.16 winning tickets. T/Qpdt: £5.40 to a £1 winning stake. Pool: £8,181.49 - 1,119.42 winning tickets. ST

5799 LONGCHAMP (R-H)
Thursday, September 9

OFFICIAL GOING: Turf: soft

5899a PRIX D'AUMALE (GROUP 3) (2YO FILLIES) (TURF) 1m
1:40 (12:00) 2-Y-O **£35,398** (£14,159; £10,619; £7,079)

RPR
1 **Helleborine**40 4611 2-8-9 0 StephanePasquier 4 107+
(Mme C Head-Maarek, France) *bkmarker tl st: rdn 2f out: qcknd wl on outside to grab ld 1 1/2f out: sn clr: easily* 2/5[1]
2 5 **Immortal Verse (IRE)**19 2-8-9 0 ChristopheSoumillon 1 94
(Robert Collet, France) *racd in 3rd initially: wnt 2nd bef st: rdn 2f out: styd on wl fnl f: tk 2nd 50yds out* 14/5[2]
3 ½ **Nitza (FR)**19 5323 2-8-9 0 JohanVictoire 3 93
(Mme C Head-Maarek, France) *led: stl in front 1 1/2f whn hdd by eventual wnr: hrd rdn fnl f: styd on: lost 2nd 50yds out* 73/10[3]
4 ¾ **Split Trois (FR)**25 5133 2-8-9 0 Pierre-CharlesBoudot 2 91
(Y De Nicolay, France) *racd in 2nd initially: dropped bk to 3rd after 3f: rdn early in st: no ex fnl f: styd on* 9/1

1m 47.9s (9.50) 4 Ran SP% **119.8**
WIN (incl. 1 euro stake): 1.40. PLACES: 1.10, 1.20. SF: 2.50.
Owner K Abdulla **Bred** Juddmonte Farms Ltd **Trained** Chantilly, France

NOTEBOOK
Helleborine, unbeaten in two starts, including a Listed race at Deauville last time, settled at the back of the field before making her move on the outside 2f out. She easily stretched away from her rivals, and she will now go for the Marcel Boussac. She has been quoted as short as 8/1 for the 1000 Guineas.

[5290]CHESTER (L-H)

Friday, September 10

OFFICIAL GOING: Good to soft (soft in places between 6f & 4f; 6.6)

No false rail but rail realignment between 6f and 3f increased distances by about 12yds.

Wind: moderate across Weather: cloudy

5900 BETDAQ THE BETTING EXCHANGE E B F MAIDEN STKS (C&G) 7f 122y

2:30 (2:31) (Class 4) 2-Y-O £5,180 (£1,541; £770; £384) Stalls Low

Form RPR

32 **1** **Captain Bertie (IRE)**[41] 4577 2-9-0 0 RobertWinston 4 79
(B W Hills) *mde all: jnd 4f out: pushed along 2f out: rdn over 1f out: plld out more and r.o fnl 100yds* **8/15**[1]

05 **2** *1 ¾* **Barwick**[20] 5294 2-9-0 0 PatCosgrave 6 75
(M H Tompkins) *chsd wnr: moved upsides fr 4f out: rdn over 1f out: no ex fnl 100yds* **10/1**

5 **3** *3 ½* **Riot Police (USA)**[83] 3219 2-9-0 0 SaleemGolam 9 67+
(J H M Gosden) *hld up: hdwy u.p 2f out: hung lft and chsd front pair wl over 1f out: kpt on no imp* **15/2**[3]

0 **4** *2 ¼* **Sisindu (IRE)**[35] 4803 2-9-0 0 EddieAhern 8 61
(B J Meehan) *trckd ldrs: outpcd over 2f out: n.d after* **4/1**[2]

5 *1 ¾* **Whipphound** 2-9-0 0 TomMcLaughlin 2 57
(W M Brisbourne) *racd keenly: hld up: nt clr run 2f out: swtchd rt whn outpcd over 1f out: nvr able to chal* **66/1**

0606 **6** *5* **Suave Character**[26] 5111 2-9-0 46 FergusSweeney 1 46
(M Blanshard) *trckd ldrs: pushed along over 2f out: wknd over 1f out* **100/1**

7 *7* **Barry Crockett (IRE)**[70] 3651 2-8-9 0 IanBrennan(5) 5 29
(Mrs L Williamson) *in tch: pushed along 3f out: wknd 2f out* **40/1**

8 *40* **Steel Rain** 2-9-0 0 StevieDonohoe 7 —
(Mrs N S Evans) *missed break: a wl bhd and u.p: nvr on terms: eased ins fnl f: t.o* **66/1**

1m 39.21s (5.41) **Going Correction** +0.55s/f (Yiel) 8 Ran SP% **112.5**

Speed ratings (Par 97): **94,92,88,86,84 79,72,32**

toteswingers:1&2 £7.40, 2&3 £18.10, 1&3 £3.10 CSF £6.76 TOTE £1.50: £1.10, £2.60, £1.60; EX 7.50.

Owner A L R Morton **Bred** Glending Bloodstock **Trained** Lambourn, Berks

FOCUS

After 5mm of rain overnight and in the morning, the going was officially changed to good to soft, soft in places.

NOTEBOOK

Captain Bertie(IRE) set a clear standard on his third to subsequent Group 3 Acomb winner Waiter's Dream on debut and a close second behind a useful Richard Hannon-trained newcomer in a 7f Goodwood maiden last time. He had to work hard under a positive ride to fight off a persistent challenger, but showed a good attitude and the slow ground posed no problem for the son of Captain Rio. It is hard to rate the value of the form of a race run at over seven seconds slower than standard, but he is a scopey colt who is out of a half-sister to Sueboog and could go on to better things. (op 4-7 after early 4-5 in places and 5-6 in a place, tchd 1-2)

Barwick had plenty to find with the favourite but put in a feisty display under a prominent ride and finished clear of the third. This run will have a detrimental effect on his future nursery mark but it does represent a significant step forward on his two previous efforts and he could be open to further progress. (op 9-1 tchd 11-1 and 8-1 in places)

Riot Police(USA) was never involved behind the first two who dominated, but did some good late work on return from 83 days off. There should be more to come from this $190,000 son of Street Cry, who is closely related to some classy performers in the US, including Lisa M, a multiple winner at around 1m on dirt. (op 13-2)

Sisindu(IRE) was never dangerous at 25-1 Newmarket on debut. He was prominent in the market this time but forced wide for a long way and couldn't find an effective finishing effort when the pace quickened. (tchd 9-2)

Whipphound, a £1,000 gelded half-brother to a 6f 2-y-o winner, looked inexperienced but showed a bit of ability staying on late from some way back on debut.

Barry Crockett(IRE) Official explanation: trainer said that the gelding had a breathing problem

5901 AXON RESOURCING NURSERY 7f 2y

3:05 (3:06) (Class 3) (0-95,92) 2-Y-O £8,418 (£2,505; £1,251; £625) Stalls Low

Form RPR

1 **1** **Magic Casement**[85] 3118 2-9-3 88 AdrianNicholls 3 102+
(D Nicholls) *mde all: clr 2f out: r.o wl and a in command* **5/1**[3]

615 **2** *7* **Fred Willetts (IRE)**[2] 5849 2-8-2 73 6ex (b) CathyGannon 7 70
(P D Evans) *wnt rt s: chsd ldr: pushed along over 4f out: rdn and outpcd by wnr over 2f out: no ch after* **6/1**

3222 **3** *3 ¼* **So Is She (IRE)**[15] 5433 2-7-6 70 (v) JessicaSteven(7) 6 60+
(A Bailey) *wnt rt s: racd keenly: towards rr: kpt on over 1f out: nt gng pce to chal* **10/1**

415 **4** *½* **Whaileyy (IRE)**[13] 5525 2-9-0 85 EddieAhern 4 72
(Sir Michael Stoute) *midfield: rdn 3f out: nvr able to get on terms w ldr* **11/2**

021 **5** *8* **Hoot (IRE)**[17] 5381 2-9-1 86 TedDurcan 1 53
(Saeed Bin Suroor) *chsd ldrs: effrt over 2f out: sn outpcd: wknd ins fnl f* **4/1**[1]

3441 **6** *3 ½* **Il Battista**[10] 5644 2-8-0 76 6ex (p) DeclanCannon(5) 9 34
(A J McCabe) *bmpd s: in tch: effrt 3f out: rdn and wknd over 2f out* **9/2**[2]

1110 **7** *4* **Belle Royale (IRE)**[1] 5882 2-9-7 92 LiamJones 8 40
(W M Brisbourne) *bmpd s: towards rr: u.p 3f out: nvr on terms* **12/1**

01 **8** *12* **The Mellor Fella**[37] 4709 2-8-10 81 RoystonFfrench 5 —
(R A Fahey) *s.i.s: pushed along and a bhd* **11/1**

1m 30.36s (3.86) **Going Correction** +0.55s/f (Yiel) 8 Ran SP% **109.6**

Speed ratings (Par 99): **99,91,87,86,77 73,69,55**

toteswingers:1&2 £6.60, 2&3 £10.90, 1&3 £8.50 CSF £31.87 CT £265.06 TOTE £5.90: £2.00, £2.20, £2.70; EX 35.40.

Owner Middleham Park Racing XXXVII **Bred** Fifehead Farms M C Denning **Trained** Sessay, N Yorks

FOCUS

This looked a hot nursery, which involved four last-time-out winners, but the least exposed runner in the field hammered his opponents under a front-running ride.

NOTEBOOK

Magic Casement beat a subsequent winner when making a successful debut at 10-1 in a 6f Ripon maiden in June. He had an absence to shrug off over a longer trip on this nursery debut, but put in a smooth trailblazing performance to run his rivals into complete submission. A big rise will follow after this win but he is an exciting prospect with scope for plenty of further improvement and his sights could be raised significantly after this demolition job. (op 9-2 tchd 11-2)

Fred Willetts(IRE) had a good chance on paper, with his future mark set to be 6lb higher after a storming win in a Ripon seller before a close fifth in a Doncaster nursery two days earlier. He ran another creditable race to finish clear of the rest, but could not land a blow on the impressive winner. (op 4-1)

So Is She(IRE) ran respectably, plugging on into a remote third, but she is an eight-race maiden who is not really improving. (tchd 9-1, 11-1 and 12-1 in a place)

Whaileyy(IRE) failed to find the expected improvement in a nursery on good to soft at Newmarket after his 7f Yarmouth maiden win. It was interesting that he was well backed in the morning, but he put in another laboured run. Some questions are mounting up, but it is still early days and a return to fast ground could inspire a more dynamic effort. (op 6-1)

Hoot(IRE), a comfortable winner of a 6f Kempton maiden late last month, tried to get to the winner approaching the final turn but it was a vain pursuit and he weakened quite quickly stepped up to 7f on slow ground. A return to a sharper test and quicker ground should suit. Official explanation: tainer's representative was unable to offer any explanation for the poor performance shown (tchd 7-2 and 9-2)

Il Battista attracted support but was in trouble out wide before the final turn. This has to rate as a bit disappointing from a horse who was effectively 3lb ahead of the assessor under a penalty for a 7f Southwell nursery win. (op 6-1)

The Mellor Fella Official explanation: jockey said that the colt was never travelling

5902 WORSHIPFUL COMPANY OF DISTILLERS MAIDEN FILLIES' STKS 1m 2f 75y

3:40 (3:40) (Class 5) 3-Y-O+ £4,047 (£1,204; £601; £300) Stalls High

Form RPR

6332 **1** **Effervesce (IRE)**[40] 4618 3-8-12 76 EddieAhern 2 74
(Sir Michael Stoute) *s.i.s: hld up in tch: hdwy over 2f out: led over 1f out: r.o wl* **1/1**[1]

2646 **2** *1 ½* **Zenarinda**[13] 5541 3-8-12 64 PatCosgrave 1 71
(M H Tompkins) *trckd ldrs: pushed along and sltly hmpd 3f out: nt qckn over 1f out: kpt on to take 2nd wl ins fnl f: no imp on wnr* **5/1**[3]

4 **3** *2 ¾* **Dazzle The Crowd (IRE)**[47] 4397 3-8-12 0 SaleemGolam 7 66
(J H M Gosden) *hld up: pushed along and hdwy 3f out: outpcd 2f out: kpt on to take 3rd towards fin: nt trble front two* **5/2**[2]

4 **4** *1* **Star Hill**[18] 5366 3-8-12 0 FergusSweeney 4 64
(A King) *racd keenly: cl up: effrt 3f out: led over 2f out: hdd over 1f out: wknd ins fnl f* **12/1**

00 **5** *4 ½* **Starshine**[92] 2890 3-8-12 0 RichardKingscote 6 55
(R Charlton) *hld up in rr: u.p over 2f out: nvr on terms* **14/1**

05 **6** *7* **Jubilant Lady (USA)**[17] 5380 3-8-12 0 (v) RoystonFfrench 3 41
(B Smart) *racd keenly: led: hdd over 2f out: rdn and wknd over 1f out* **40/1**

00 **7** *dist* **Topaze Star**[56] 4114 3-8-12 0 StevieDonohoe 5 —
(Jane Chapple-Hyam) *prom: pushed along over 4f out: wknd over 2f out: t.o* **50/1**

2m 18.76s (6.56) **Going Correction** +0.70s/f (Yiel) 7 Ran SP% **114.0**

Speed ratings (Par 100): **101,99,97,96,93 87,—**

CSF £6.59 TOTE £1.80: £1.10, £2.40.

Owner Cheveley Park Stud **Bred** Mulhime Ltd **Trained** Newmarket, Suffolk

FOCUS

A fair maiden run at a steady pace. The time was over nine seconds slower than standard.

Jubilant Lady(USA) Official explanation: jockey said that the filly ran too free and hung right-handed throughout

5903 HAWKER BEECHCRAFT H'CAP 7f 2y

4:15 (4:16) (Class 3) (0-95,93) 3-Y-O £8,831 (£2,643; £1,321; £660; £329) Stalls Low

Form RPR

6000 **1** **Captain Ramius (IRE)**[25] 5154 4-9-6 87 RobertWinston 6 97
(K A Ryan) *bhd: pushed along over 3f out: swtchd rt and c on wd outside wl over 1f out: prog sn after: carried hd to one side: r.o ins fnl f to ld cl home* **18/1**

5142 **2** *nk* **Kyllachy Star**[12] 5571 4-9-10 91 StevieDonohoe 5 100
(R A Fahey) *hld up: rdn and hdwy over 1f out: r.o to ld wl ins fnl f: hdd cl home* **2/1**[1]

-021 **3** *1 ¾* **Greensward**[25] 5157 4-9-4 85 EddieAhern 2 89
(B J Meehan) *racd keenly in tch: rdn over 1f out: effrt to chal briefly ins fnl f: nt qckn fnl 100yds* **9/2**[3]

1000 **4** *1 ½* **Below Zero (IRE)**[20] 5292 3-9-8 93 AdrianNicholls 8 91
(M Johnston) *led and showed gd pce to switch lft sn after s: rdn over 1f out: hdd wl ins fnl f: no ex towards fin* **10/1**

1-01 **5** *1 ¾* **Great Charm (IRE)**[20] 5290 5-9-0 81 PatCosgrave 1 77
(E J Alston) *racd keenly: chsd ldrs: wnt 2nd 2f out tl rdn and no imp on ldr 1f out: wknd fnl 100yds* **4/1**[2]

3663 **6** *8* **Excellerator (IRE)**[25] 5154 4-9-6 90 (t) MatthewDavies(3) 4 64
(George Baker) *niggled along in rr: rdn over 1f out: nvr able to get on terms* **14/1**

4231 **7** *1 ¼* **Zomerlust**[15] 5435 8-9-0 86 (v) IanBrennan(5) 3 57
(J J Quinn) *in tch: rdn over 2f out: no imp: bhd over 1f out* **6/1**

0154 **8** *1 ¼* **Guilded Warrior**[29] 4995 7-9-8 89 FergusSweeney 7 56
(W S Kittow) *chsd ldr: rdn and lost 2nd 2f out: wknd over 1f out* **16/1**

1m 30.6s (4.10) **Going Correction** +0.70s/f (Yiel)

WFA 3 from 4yo+ 4lb 8 Ran SP% **112.7**

Speed ratings (Par 107): **104,103,101,99,97 88,87,85**

toteswingers:1&2 £7.00, 2&3 £2.90, 1&3 £9.30 CSF £52.88 CT £198.40 TOTE £19.60: £4.60, £1.40, £1.60; EX 60.50.

Owner Mrs Clodagh McStay **Bred** P G Lyons **Trained** Hambleton, N Yorks

■ Stewards' Enquiry : Adrian Nicholls one-day ban: careless riding (24 sept)

FOCUS

A useful handicap, involving three last-time-out winners and two others who were placed on their latest run. The pace was decent and it was a race of changing fortunes.

NOTEBOOK

Captain Ramius(IRE) had been generally disappointing in just six runs since kicking off with three 7f Polytrack wins in 2008 and a revival looked unlikely when he was last turning for home in this contest, but he produced a storming run out wide to take advantage of a declining mark on the step back up to 7f with headgear removed. He should not go up much for this win and will remain well treated on his best 2-y-o runs but he does not look the easiest of rides and there is a bit of doubt whether he will repeat the form next time. (op 20-1 tchd 16-1)

Kyllachy Star arrived here after a second behind a subsequent winner in the Irish Cambridgeshire. Due to go up 3lb on Saturday, he looked well treated and gave it a valiant try but was just reeled in by a faster finisher. He is a very reliable 7f-1m handicapper who has a decent strike-rate, and a record of 2142 at this track. (tchd 7-4)

Greensward belatedly added to his Newmarket juvenile success when winning in good style at Wolverhampton last time. He came up a bit short off 6lb higher but put in a creditable effort behind two well-handicapped rivals. (op 11-2)

Below Zero(IRE), the subject of a late market move, showed signs of a revival under a forcing ride back at the scene of his C&D win in June. (op 14-1)

Great Charm(IRE) was always well positioned but couldn't raise his game when things got serious in a bid to make it three wins from four starts since joining Eric Alston. (tchd 7-2 and 9-2)

The Form Book, Raceform Ltd, Compton, RG20 6NL

Zomerlust went a bit in snatches and finished well beaten in an attempt to add to his 7f win off 4lb lower at Ayr last time. These tight turns probably didn't suit him and he could bounce back on a more galloping track next time. (op 5-1)
Guilded Warrior Official explanation: jockey said that the gelding lost its action

5904 TRY BETDAQ FOR AN EXCHANGE H'CAP — 1m 2f 75y

4:45 (4:46) (Class 3) (0-90,86) 3-Y-O **£8,831** (£2,643; £1,321; £660; £329) **Stalls** High

Form / RPR

-220 **1** **Rigidity**[43] 4504 3-9-7 **86** .... EddieAhern 2 102+
(H R A Cecil) *a.p: led over 1f out: sn edgd rt: r.o wl: pushed out whn in command fnl 100yds* **6/4**[1]

6212 **2** 3 ½ **Lord Raglan (IRE)**[20] 5300 3-8-13 **78** .... AndrewElliott 4 85
(Mrs K Burke) *led: rdn and hdd over 1f out: nt pce of wnr fnl 100yds* **13/2**[3]

3122 **3** 1 ½ **Dolphin Rock**[36] 4750 3-9-4 **83** .... GrahamGibbons 1 87
(T D Barron) *trckd ldrs: outpcd 3f out: hdwy over 1f out: sn chsd ldrs u.p: kpt on: nt gng pce to mount serious chal ins fnl f* **9/2**[2]

2010 **4** ½ **Syrian**[13] 5511 3-9-0 **79** .... PatCosgrave 3 82
(Ian Williams) *s.i.s: in rr and racd keenly: pushed along 2f out: rdn over 1f out: styd on ins fnl f: unable to trble ldrs* **20/1**

000 **5** ¾ **Tipperary Boutique (IRE)**[24] 5188 3-9-1 **80** .... RobertWinston 6 82
(B W Hills) *hld up: effrt 2f out: chsd ldrs over 1f out: one pce ins fnl f* **12/1**

12-4 **6** 2 ¼ **Guest Book (IRE)**[13] 5510 3-9-4 **83** .... AdrianNicholls 8 80
(M Johnston) *racd keenly: hld up: pushed along and hdwy 3f out: rdn 2f out: nt qckn over 1f out: wknd wl ins fnl f* **9/1**

1542 **7** 2 ¾ **Qanoon (USA)**[26] 5121 3-9-6 **85** .... LiamJones 5 77
(W J Haggas) *midfield: sn niggled along: pushed along 4f out: effrt 2f out: wknd ins fnl f* **8/1**

3330 **8** 11 **Layla's Dancer**[13] 5511 3-8-11 **76** ....(b[1]) StevieDonohoe 7 46
(R A Fahey) *racd keenly: prom: rdn over 2f out: wknd wl over 1f out* **9/1**

2m 17.78s (5.58) **Going Correction** +0.70s/f (Yiel) **8** Ran SP% **115.1**
Speed ratings (Par 105): **105,102,101,100,100 98,96,87**
toteswingers:1&2 £3.60, 2&3 £3.70, 1&3 £2.70 CSF £11.81 CT £36.10 TOTE £2.50: £1.10, £2.00, £1.10; EX 10.80.
Owner Thomas Barr **Bred** Miss K Rausing **Trained** Newmarket, Suffolk

FOCUS
A decent handicap run at a stop-start gallop. Plenty had chances turning in but the favourite surged clear.

NOTEBOOK
Rigidity was just nailed close home off 7lb lower at York in May and may not have handled the undulations when disappointing at Goodwood last time. He was the subject of a landslide of support in his bid to bounce back and did the job in emphatic style. A half-brother to Derby runner-up Dragon Dancer, he is back on an upward curve and his versatility regarding ground should be a useful asset. He could have quite a bit more to offer at this trip, and beyond, and should win more races. (op 11-4)
Lord Raglan(IRE) got an easy lead in a steadily run race but still emerges with credit for his second consecutive runner-up effort since dominating over C&D in July. (op 15-2)
Dolphin Rock stuck to his task well against the far rail. He has risen 16lb in the weights this season but has had two near-misses and this third since a win at Haydock in June and may be able to strike again before reaching dead-lock with the handicapper. (tchd 4-1 and 5-2 in a place)
Syrian was keen early on but did well to stay on out wide from an unpromising position on her second run since being acquired for £12,000 after cruising clear in a 1m all-weather claimer. She has some quirks but is a smooth traveller who is potentially well treated and could be a force in a more strongly run race next time. (op 14-1)
Tipperary Boutique(IRE) looked a potential threat around the final bend but her effort flattened out and she probably paid the price for taking a strong hold in the early stages. (tchd 14-1)
Guest Book(IRE), a promising fourth from the worst draw in a 7f Beverley handicap on recent reappearance, loomed up on the outside around the final bend but he had to work quite hard to get there and paid the price for those exertions. (op 8-1 tchd 7-1)
Qanoon(USA) was a big drifter and put in a very lacklustre effort. He probably didn't handle the track, or the ground, or possibly both. (op 9-2)

5905 BOLLINGER CHAMPAGNE CHALLENGE SERIES H'CAP (FOR GENTLEMAN AMATEUR RIDERS) (DIV I) — 7f 2y

5:20 (5:21) (Class 5) (0-70,68) 3-Y-O+ **£3,591** (£1,113; £556; £278) **Stalls** Low

Form / RPR

4301 **1** **Clumber Place**[11] 5598 4-10-11 **58** 6ex........ MrSWalker 6 73
(R C Guest) *chsd ldr to over 5f out and again 2f out: led jst over 1f out: r.o wl and drvn clr w tail flashing ins fnl f* **11/4**[1]

413 **2** 3 ½ **The Human League**[1] 5890 3-10-4 **62**........ MrCBishop[(7)] 1 65
(M R Channon) *led: hdd jst over 1f out: outpcd and no ch w wnr ins fnl f* **7/2**[2]

2265 **3** ½ **Silly Gilly (IRE)**[11] 5598 6-10-3 **55**........ MrJMQuinlan[(5)] 9 59
(R E Barr) *chsd ldrs: pushed along 3f out: styd on same pce u.p fr over 1f out* **9/1**

5531 **4** ¾ **Red Dagger (IRE)**[48] 4374 4-10-6 **56**........ MrMPrice[(3)] 8 58
(R J Price) *hld up in midfield: rdn and hdwy 2f out: chsd ldrs over 1f out: kpt on towards fin: no real imp* **12/1**

6610 **5** 2 ¼ **Postman**[7] 5737 4-11-2 **68**........(p) MrJNewman[(5)] 3 64
(B Smart) *in tch: pushed along and outpcd over 3f out: kpt on ins fnl f: no imp* **7/1**

1030 **6** 7 **Two Turtle Doves (IRE)**[11] 5614 4-11-1 **65**........ MrPCollington[(3)] 7 42
(M Mullineaux) *in tch: rdn and hdwy 2f out: sn chsd ldrs: wknd ins fnl f* **20/1**

2000 **7** ½ **Takajan (IRE)**[11] 5614 3-10-9 **58** ow5........ MrBenBrisbourne[(3)] 11 37
(W M Brisbourne) *hld up: a long way bk over 2f out: sn pushed along: nvr able to get on terms* **33/1**

-050 **8** 1 **Bewdley**[48] 4366 5-10-2 **54** oh8........(v[1]) MrLRPayter[(5)] 12 27
(R E Peacock) *chsd ldrs: racd in 2nd pl over 5f out tl 2f out: wknd over 1f out* **66/1**

000 **9** hd **The Midshipmaid**[12] 5548 3-9-12 **54** oh9........ MrJPFeatherstone[(5)] 10 24
(Lucinda Featherstone) *towards rr: rdn and wl bhd 4f out: nvr on terms* **66/1**

6042 **10** 6 **King Columbo (IRE)**[11] 5593 5-10-13 **63**........ MrRBirkett[(3)] 5 19
(Miss J Feilden) *midfield: pushed along over 3f out: outpcd and toiling after* **4/1**[3]

0044 **11** ½ **Mountain Pass (USA)**[29] 4986 8-10-0 **54** oh3......(tp) MrRJWilliams[(7)] 2 9
(B J Llewellyn) *s.s: bhd: u.p over 3f out: nvr on terms* **16/1**

1m 32.67s (6.17) **Going Correction** +0.85s/f (Soft)
WFA 3 from 4yo+ 4lb **11** Ran SP% **115.7**
Speed ratings (Par 103): **98,94,93,92,90 82,81,80,80,73 72**
toteswingers:1&2 £3.50, 2&3 £7.80, 1&3 £6.20 CSF £11.62 CT £75.36 TOTE £3.60: £1.30, £1.80, £2.70; EX 10.60.
Owner The Clumber Park Syndicate **Bred** Worksop Manor Stud **Trained** Stainforth, S Yorks
■ Stewards' Enquiry : Mr J P Featherstone eight-day ban: used whip with excessive force (TBA)

FOCUS
An ordinary handicap for amateur riders. It was fast and furious and they were well strung out at an early stage.

5906 BOLLINGER CHAMPAGNE CHALLENGE SERIES H'CAP (FOR GENTLEMAN AMATEUR RIDERS) (DIV II) — 7f 2y

5:50 (5:52) (Class 5) (0-70,67) 3-Y-O+ **£3,591** (£1,113; £556; £278) **Stalls** Low

Form / RPR

6662 **1** **Mr Udagawa**[29] 4985 4-10-6 **59**........(p) MrRJWilliams[(7)] 4 68
(B J Llewellyn) *racd keenly: prom: led over 5f out: qcknd clr over 1f out: styd on on wl* **11/2**

6333 **2** 1 ¾ **Dazeen**[3] 5636 3-10-12 **62**........ MrSWalker 11 64+
(P T Midgley) *racd keenly: hld up: pushed along over 2f out: hdwy whn nt clr run and swtchd rt ins fnl f: styd on towards fin: nt rch wnr* **15/2**

0342 **3** ½ **Downhill Skier (IRE)**[11] 5614 6-10-8 **57** ow1........ MrBenBrisbourne[(3)] 6 60
(W M Brisbourne) *midfield: hdwy 2f out: rdn over 1f out: kpt on u.p ins fnl f* **5/1**[3]

0030 **4** hd **Avoncreek**[11] 5579 6-10-2 **53** oh7........ MrOGarner[(5)] 7 55
(B P J Baugh) *racd keenly: a.p: chal 3f out: nt qckn over 1f out: kpt on u.p ins fnl f: one pce fnl strides* **33/1**

-332 **5** shd **Diggeratt (USA)**[18] 5357 4-11-5 **65**........ MrMSeston 3 67
(R A Fahey) *prom: lost pl over 3f out: outpcd 2f out: rallied ins fnl f: styd on towards fin* **2/1**[1]

4135 **6** 2 **Gemma's Delight (IRE)**[29] 4988 3-10-1 **58**........(p) MrJHodson[(7)] 1 53
(J W Unett) *racd keenly: a.p: rdn and nt qckn over 1f out: keeping on same pce whn n.m.r wl ins fnl f* **4/1**[2]

00 **7** 3 **Boy The Bell**[8] 5697 3-10-6 **59**........ MrPCollington[(3)] 5 46
(M Mullineaux) *racd keenly: prom tl rdn and wknd over 2f out* **28/1**

0000 **8** ¾ **Commander Wish**[44] 4478 7-10-0 **53** oh7........ MrWFeatherstone[(7)] 10 40
(Lucinda Featherstone) *swtchd lft sn after s: hld up: rdn 4f out: nvr able to get on terms* **66/1**

0030 **9** 2 **Bahamian Kid**[32] 4910 5-11-4 **67**........(v) MrStephenHarrison[(3)] 9 48
(R Hollinshead) *racd keenly: in tch: rdn and wknd over 1f out* **14/1**

0616 **10** 9 **Timber Treasure (USA)**[23] 5198 6-10-13 **59**........(b) MrDHDunsdon 8 16
(Paul Green) *restless in stalls: hld up in tch: rdn and wknd over 1f out* **14/1**

1m 34.3s (7.80) **Going Correction** +0.85s/f (Soft)
WFA 3 from 4yo+ 4lb **10** Ran SP% **118.4**
Speed ratings (Par 103): **89,87,86,86,86 83,80,79,77,66**
toteswingers:1&2 £7.30, 2&3 £6.80, 1&3 £7.00. totesuper7: Win: Not won. Place: £90.30. CSF £46.39 CT £226.88 TOTE £7.60: £2.50, £3.40, £1.70; EX 57.70 Place 6: £11.15 Place 5: £9.01.
Owner B J Llewellyn **Bred** Richard C J Manning **Trained** Fochriw, Caerphilly
■ A first winner for 16-year-old Rob Williams, grandson of the winning owner/trainer.
■ Stewards' Enquiry : Mr Stephen Harrison caution: careless riding
Mr M Seston caution: careless riding

FOCUS
The second division of a handicap for amateur riders. The pace was steady and not many got into it.
T/Plt: £15.70 to a £1 stake. Pool of £60,176.62 - 2,791.86 winning tickets. T/Qpdt: £4.30 to a £1 stake. Pool of £4,403.93 - 755.76 winning tickets. DO

5878 DONCASTER (L-H)

Friday, September 10

OFFICIAL GOING: Good (round 8.3 stands' side 8.2 centre 8.5 far side 8.5)
Round course rail moved out from Rose Hill to the straight increasing races of 10f, 12f and 14f by 12yds.
Wind: Moderate against Weather: Sunny periods and showers

5907 POLYPIPE FLYING CHILDERS STKS (GROUP 2) — 5f

1:35 (1:35) (Class 1) 2-Y-O
£45,416 (£17,216; £8,616; £4,296; £2,152; £1,080) **Stalls** High

Form / RPR

5111 **1** **Zebedee**[13] 5527 2-9-0 103........ RichardHughes 2 108
(R Hannon) *swtchd rt after s and hld up towards stands' side: hdwy and n.m.r over 1f out: swtchd lft and qcknd through to chal ins fnl f: led last 100yds: cleverly* **10/3**[1]

1160 **2** nk **Dinkum Diamond (IRE)**[21] 5276 2-9-0 106........ DaneO'Neill 11 107
(H Candy) *swtg: hld up: swtchd lft and hdwy wl over 1f out: cl up whn rdn and sltly outpcd ent fnl f: kpt on wl u.p towards fin* **6/1**

11 **3** ¾ **New Planet (IRE)**[23] 5221 2-9-0 106........ RyanMoore 10 104
(J J Quinn) *lw: in tch towards stands' side: pushed along 1/2-way: hdwy wl over 1f out: rdn to chal and ev ch whn edgd lft ent fnl f: sn drvn and edgd rt: nt qckn last 100yds* **7/2**[2]

0203 **4** hd **Black Moth (IRE)**[11] 5604 2-9-0 97........ MartinDwyer 13 103
(B J Meehan) *hld up in tch: effrt and edgd lft wl over 1f out: rdn and squeezed through ins fnl f: kpt on* **66/1**

2223 **5** ¾ **The Thrill Is Gone**[28] 5036 2-8-11 95........ FrankieDettori 1 98
(M R Channon) *prom centre: rdn to ld over 1f out: sn drvn and hdd jst ins fnl f: one pce* **33/1**

10 **6** shd **Keratiya (FR)**[19] 5347 2-8-11 0........ Christophe-PatriceLemaire 5 97
(J-C Rouget, France) *str: trckd ldrs centre: smooth hdwy wl over 1f out: rdn and led briefly ins fnl f: sn hung lft: hdd & wknd last 100yds* **13/2**

2111 **7** nk **Electric Waves (IRE)**[28] 5036 2-8-11 101........ RichardMullen 12 96
(E S McMahon) *swtg: trckd ldrs stands' rail: hdwy wl over 1f out: rdn and ev ch ent fnl f: sn drvn and one pce* **11/1**

1110 **8** 1 ¾ **Face The Problem (IRE)**[23] 5221 2-9-0 106........ MichaelHills 4 93
(B W Hills) *chsd ldrs centre: effrt and cl up 2f out: sn rdn and wknd over 1f out* **14/1**

216 **9** 1 **Arctic Feeling (IRE)**[23] 5221 2-9-0 96........ PaulMulrennan 9 89
(R A Fahey) *cl up stands' side: rdn wl over 1f out: grad wknd* **80/1**

0341 **10** 1 ¼ **Bathwick Bear (IRE)**[11] 5604 2-9-0 96........ RichardEvans 6 85
(P D Evans) *cl up stands' side: chal 2f out: sn rdn and wknd over 1f out* **66/1**

11 1 **Ladie's Choice (IRE)**[20] 5313 2-8-11 0........ BACurtis 3 78
(M J Tynan, Ire) *w'like: swtg: prom centre: rdn along 2f out: sn wknd* **25/1**

2 **12** 9 **Meow (IRE)**[20] 5313 2-8-11 0........(t) JMurtagh 7 46
(David Wachman, Ire) *swtg: overall ldr stands' rail: rdn along 2f out: hdd over 1f out: wknd qckly and eased* **11/2**[3]

59.42 secs (-1.08) **Going Correction** -0.025s/f (Good) **12** Ran SP% **114.3**
Speed ratings (Par 107): **107,106,105,105,103 103,103,100,98,96 95,80**
toteswingers:1&2 £6.30, 2&3 £5.80, 1&3 £3.20 CSF £21.88 TOTE £4.10: £1.30, £3.20, £2.10; EX 23.40 Trifecta £116.00 Pool: £3274.21 - 20.86 winning units..
Owner Mrs J Wood **Bred** Hascombe & Valiant Studs **Trained** East Everleigh, Wilts

FOCUS

The 2007 winner Fleeting Spirit excepted, recent winners of the Flying Childers have not really enhanced their reputations later in their careers, but this looked a decent edition of this Group 2 and the winner is a smart colt. The form looks solid but is hard to rate any higher, with the winner the sort to only do enough. Fillies had won half the previous 18 runnings, including each of the last three, but were eclipsed by the colts this time.

NOTEBOOK

Zebedee came out of stall 2 and the horses drawn around him stayed in the centre of the track, but his rider knows him well and sensibly switched him to the stands' side to get some cover. The grey quickened up smartly to lead and although the runner-up was reducing his lead late on he still scored cosily, taking his record to six wins in seven starts. He proved at Newmarket last time that he is just as effective at 6f, and the Mille Reef Stakes was mentioned, but the Cornwallis at Ascot looks his likely next target. (op 7-2)

Dinkum Diamond(IRE) ran a creditable race against his elders in the Nunthorpe, where he was hampered early on, and confirmed that he is a smart sprinting 2yo. The favourite came past him travelling the better but he was coming back at him late on, reinforcing the impression that he will be worth trying over 6f. His trainer is inclined to aim him next at the Cornwallis Stakes at Ascot, where the relatively stiff 5f should suit.The yard won that race two years ago with Amour Propre. (op 7-1 tchd 15-2)

New Planet(IRE), the sole unbeaten candidate, had four of these opponents behind when taking the Listed Rous Stakes at the Ebor meeting and he cemented his superiority over that quartet. He found himself a little isolated on the outside of the main group as he edged to his left in the latter stages, but was keeping on at the end. This was only his third run and it is reasonable to expect a little more improvement. A re-match with the winner and runner-up could be on the cards in the Cornwallis. (op 11-2)

Black Moth(IRE) has been found wanting in lesser company than this but he ran on well from the back of the field to post perhaps his best effort so far.

The Thrill Is Gone showed bright pace down the centre out of the number one stall and was not beaten far in fifth. She was only a little further behind Zebedee than she had been in a Sandown Listed race earlier in the season.

Keratiya(FR) beat subsequent Prix Robert Papin winner Irish Field when landing a Chantilly Group 3, before disappointing against the colts in the Prix Morny. A first 2yo runner in this country for Jean-Claude Rouget, she travelled well and was in front briefly before she was swallowed up inside the last. This was a decent effort given that she raced on the less favoured part of the track where she lacked company. (op 6-1)

Electric Waves(IRE), taking another step up in class, was a little edgy in the preliminaries and one of the first under pressure in the race, but she did keep on in the latter stages. She does not mind easier ground and Ayr's Firth of Clyde Stakes over 6f could be a suitable option for her. (op 8-1)

Face The Problem(IRE)'s winning run came to a halt in New Planet's York race and he was again found wanting in this better grade after racing down the centre. He carried his head a little high.

Bathwick Bear(IRE) is a tough juvenile who is being kept busy, as his trainer feels he may struggle as a 3yo.

Meow(IRE) was the top rated on adjusted BHA ratings and her trainer felt she was sure to come on for her run at the Curragh last month, where she beat Ladie's Choice despite blowing up. Murtagh got her across to the rail and she was soon in front, but she stopped very quickly indeed when tackled and something may well have been amiss with her. She did become upset in the stalls but this was not her running. Official explanation: jockey said that the filly lost her action (op 5-1)

5908 LADBROKES MALLARD STKS (H'CAP) 1m 6f 132y

2:05 (2:07) (Class 2) (0-110,100) 3-Y-O **£38,856** (£11,562; £5,778; £2,886) **Stalls** Low

Form				RPR
-065	**1**		**Precision Break (USA)**[20] 5291 5-9-7 **93**..................(t) JamieSpencer 7 (P F I Cole) *hld up in midfield: hdwy 3f out: rdn to chse ldr ent fnl f: drvn to ld last 100yds* **20/1**	103
1423	**2**	*1*	**Jedi**[20] 5291 4-9-7 **93**.................. RyanMoore 9 (Sir Michael Stoute) *lw: trckd ldrs: hdwy 3f out: led wl over 1f out: rdn and edgd rt ins fnl f: hdd and no ex last 100yds* **9/1[3]**	102
2105	**3**	*1 1/4*	**Chilly Filly (IRE)**[6] 5743 4-9-3 **89**.................. SilvestreDeSousa 2 (M Johnston) *trckd ldr: led 3f out: rdn 2f out: drvn and hdd over 1f out: kpt on same pce ins fnl f* **14/1**	96
4410	**4**	*1 1/4*	**Lady Eclair (IRE)**[6] 5743 4-9-11 **97**.................. JoeFanning 12 (M Johnston) *trckd ldrs on outer: hdwy over 2f out: rdn and sltly outpcd over 1f out: drvn and kpt on ins fnl f* **20/1**	102
1022	**5**	*nk*	**Tactician**[21] 5273 3-8-7 **94**.................. MartinLane(3) 14 (M L W Bell) *dwlt and hld up in rr: hdwy over 3f out: rdn 2f out: styd on ins fnl f: nrst fin* **10/1**	99+
1014	**6**	*nse*	**Zuider Zee (GER)**[21] 5273 3-8-6 **90** ow1.................. WilliamBuick 5 (J H M Gosden) *on toes: lw: hld up in rr: stdy hdwy on inner fr wl over 2f out: rdn to chse ldrs over 1f out: one pce ins fnl f* **6/1[1]**	95
6416	**7**	*nk*	**La Vecchia Scuola (IRE)**[20] 5291 6-9-5 **94**.................. GaryBartley(3) 16 (J S Goldie) *hld up in rr: effrt on outer 3f out and sn rdn along: drvn over 1f out: styd on ins fnl f: nrst fin* **33/1**	99+
1151	**8**	*3/4*	**Mount Athos (IRE)**[21] 5273 3-8-11 **95**.................. MichaelHills 10 (J W Hills) *hld up in midfield: effrt on outer over 3f out: rdn 2f out: sn drvn and no imp* **6/1[1]**	99
5-00	**9**	*1 1/2*	**The Betchworth Kid**[23] 5220 5-9-9 **100**.................. DaleSwift(5) 15 (A King) *hld up in rr: hdwy 1/2-way: rdn along wl over 2f out: n.d* **40/1**	102
2601	**10**	*3 1/4*	**Crocus Rose**[27] 5070 4-8-10 **82** oh2.................. FrankieDettori 3 (H J L Dunlop) *trckd ldrs: effrt wl over 2f out: sn rdn and btn* **25/1**	79
-010	**11**	*2*	**Fortuni (IRE)**[23] 5220 4-9-9 **95**.................. SebSanders 13 (Sir Mark Prescott) *lw: trckd ldng pair: hdwy to chse ldr 3f out: rdn 2f out: sn drvn and wknd* **9/1[3]**	90
4232	**12**	*1 1/4*	**Plymouth Rock (IRE)**[14] 5492 4-9-7 **93**..................(v) RichardHughes 11 (J Noseda) *s.i.s: a in rr* **14/1**	86
2100	**13**	*2 1/2*	**Chiberta King**[62] 3922 4-10-0 **100**.................. JimmyFortune 6 (A M Balding) *lw: led: rdn along and hdd 3f out: sn wknd* **33/1**	90
-636	**14**	*nk*	**Desert Sea (IRE)**[23] 5220 7-9-7 **93**.................. JMurtagh 8 (D W P Arbuthnot) *t.k.h: hld up in midfield: pushed along 4f out: rdn 3f out and nvr a factor* **14/1**	83
1361	**15**	*2*	**Maxim Gorky (IRE)**[14] 5492 3-8-6 **90**.................. JimmyQuinn 4 (Sir Michael Stoute) *swtg; in tch on inner: effrt 3f out: rdn along over 2f out: sn wknd* **17/2[2]**	77
1012	**16**	*14*	**Hanoverian Baron**[20] 5307 5-9-6 **92**.................. SteveDrowne 1 (A G Newcombe) *trckd ldrs: effrt 3f out: sn rdn and wknd* **9/1[3]**	61

3m 8.00s (0.60) **Going Correction** +0.025s/f (Good)
WFA 3 from 4yo+ 12lb **16** Ran SP% **119.9**
Speed ratings (Par 109): **99,98,97,97,96 96,96,96,95,93 92,92,90,90,89 82**
toteswingers:1&2 £21.50, 2&3 £27.20, 1&3 £69.80 CSF £175.53 CT £2618.21 TOTE £24.70: £3.70, £1.60, £3.60, £4.30; EX 165.50 TRIFECTA Not won..
Owner Mrs Fitri Hay **Bred** Gainesway Thoroughbreds Ltd **Trained** Whatcombe, Oxon

FOCUS

A mini-Ebor, with three of these having contested the York feature whilst another three ran in the 3-y-o equivalent, the Melrose. This was a typically competitive handicap that had been won by a 3-y-o six times in the past ten runnings, but only a quarter of this field represented the classic generation. The early pace set by Chiberta King looked solid, if by no means breakneck, and the jockeys spurned the inside rail after turning for home.

NOTEBOOK

Precision Break(USA), who has suffered with some niggling problems, had finished unplaced in three starts since his belated reappearance in July, but he had shown a bit more in his most recent start at Chester when tongue-tied for the first time and was closely matched with three of today's rivals on that running, whilst he was also now 1lb lower than when winning at this meeting 12 months ago. Having been tucked away in the middle of the field in the early stages, he made his ground smoothly coming to the last 3f and maintained his progress to hit the front well inside the last furlong. The Cesarewitch is now an option. (op 18-1 tchd 16-1)

Jedi finished in front of Precision Break at Chester last time when both were beaten by Lady Eclair, but he has been running to a consistent level of form all season whereas Precision Break was gradually stepping up with each outing. Never far away, he was ridden to the front over a furlong out and battled on gamely to the line, but the winner had the greater finishing impetus. (tchd 10-1 in a place)

Chilly Filly(IRE), 2-2 at Doncaster (over 1m4f) before this, hadn't been totally disgraced though unplaced in both starts off this mark since winning off 9lb lower at Nottingham last month and ran she a fine race here, hitting the front over 2f out but having little left when headed by the runner-up a furlong later. She is due to go up another 2lb which won't help, but she looks a tough sort and that will continue to stand her in good stead. (op 16-1)

Lady Eclair(IRE), who was unraced before March but had won half of her 14 previous outings this term, had three of today's rivals behind her when winning at Chester last month, but she had put in tame effort in the Old Borough Cup at Haydock in the meantime. Another to race handily, she had every chance and this was certainly a step up from that last effort six days earlier, but she will need to find a bit more to win off this mark.

Tactician, whose trainer has twice supplied the winner of this race since 2003, was put up 8lb after running Mount Athos to half a length in the Melrose and was possibly flattered by the winning margin, but he was still 3lb better off with the winner. He managed to turn the York form around but, having come off the bridle at the back of the field over half a mile from home, he finished well but all too late. (op 14-1)

Zuider Zee(GER), consistent since making his racecourse debut in March, was beaten around 7l by Mount Athos and Tactician in the Melrose, but he was considerably better off in the weights with both. Carrying 1lb overweight, he made a brief effort towards the inside coming to the last 2f, but could then only plug on at one pace. (op 15-2)

La Vecchia Scuola(IRE) ◆ was a real eye-catcher here. She was right at the back of the field when switched right in order to see daylight over 2f from home, but although she had no chance of winning she finished with a real flourish. She is on a career-high mark now, but is worth keeping an eye on.

Mount Athos(IRE) was bumped up 11lb after edging out Tactician in the Melrose where he won despite hanging badly. Free enough in the early stages, he ran on down the outside over the last 2f, but again hung about under pressure and is obviously not straightforward. (op 7-1 tchd 15-2)

Fortuni(IRE), who may not have been ridden to best effect when down the field in the Ebor, raced up with the pace early but had nothing more to offer once under pressure over 2f out. He is still 10lb higher than when winning at Epsom on Derby day. (op 10-1)

Plymouth Rock(IRE) walked out of the stalls and gave away more ground than is advisable at this sort of level. (op 12-1)

Desert Sea(IRE) did his chances no good by pulling far too hard early.

Maxim Gorky(IRE) Official explanation: trainer was unable to offer any explanation for the poor performance shown

5909 DONCASTER CUP (GROUP 2) 2m 2f

2:40 (2:40) (Class 1) 3-Y-O+

£56,770 (£21,520; £10,770; £5,370; £2,690; £1,350) **Stalls** Low

Form				RPR
2/42	**1**		**Samuel**[23] 5218 6-9-1 112.................. WilliamBuick 6 (J H M Gosden) *lw: trckd ldrs: smooth hdwy 4f out: led over 2f out: rdn and wandered over 1f out: drvn ent fnl f: styd on* **5/1[3]**	116+
0206	**2**	*1 1/4*	**Tastahil (IRE)**[23] 5218 6-9-1 110.................. RichardHills 8 (B W Hills) *lw: sn trcking ldr: hdwy to ld wl over 3f out: rdn and hdd over 2f out: sn drvn and kpt on ins fnl f* **22/1**	114
1113	**3**	*hd*	**Motrice**[43] 4507 3-7-12 101.................. SilvestreDeSousa 9 (Sir Mark Prescott) *swtg: hld up and bhd: hdwy over 3f out: chsd ldrs over 2f out and sn rdn: edgd lft and drvn over 1f out: edgd rt and wandered ins fnl f: kpt on: nrst fin* **4/1[2]**	112+
3131	**4**	*3 1/2*	**Opinion Poll (IRE)**[23] 5218 4-9-4 114.................. PhilipRobinson 4 (M A Jarvis) *lw: hld up towards rr: hdwy on inner 4f out: chsd ldng pair over 2f out: rdn wl over 1f out and sn one pce* **3/1[1]**	113
1-11	**5**	*hd*	**Dirar (IRE)**[23] 5220 5-9-1 108.................. JamieSpencer 3 (Gordon Elliott, Ire) *trckd ldrs: hdwy over 3f out: rdn over 2f out: sn drvn and one pce* **8/1**	110
-300	**6**	*5*	**Darley Sun (IRE)**[23] 5220 4-9-1 104.................. FrankieDettori 10 (Saeed Bin Suroor) *hld up towards rr: hdwy on outer over 3f out: rdn over 2f out: sn drvn: edgd rt and no imp* **12/1**	104
56-0	**7**	*6*	**Askar Tau (FR)**[135] 1615 5-9-1 110..................(b[1]) RyanMoore 7 (M P Tregoning) *trckd ldng pair: pushed along over 3f out: rdn wl over 2f out and sn btn* **12/1**	98
20-5	**8**	*24*	**Pointilliste (USA)**[57] 4081 7-9-1 110.................. RichardHughes 5 (Noel Meade, Ire) *hld up in midfield: pushed along over 6f out: outpcd and bhd fnl 3f* **33/1**	71
1433	**9**	*1 1/2*	**Dayia (IRE)**[48] 4393 6-8-12 91..................(v[1]) JimmyFortune 2 (J Pearce) *a in rr: bhd fnl 3f* **40/1**	67
-324	**10**	*12*	**Electrolyser (IRE)**[23] 5218 5-9-1 112.................. TomQueally 1 (C G Cox) *led: rdn along and hdd wl over 2f out: sn wknd* **5/1[3]**	57

3m 52.99s (-2.01) **Going Correction** +0.025s/f (Good)
WFA 3 from 4yo+ 14lb **10** Ran SP% **114.6**
Speed ratings (Par 115): **105,104,104,102,102 100,97,87,86,81**
toteswingers:1&2 £18.10, 2&3 £12.70, 1&3 £4.60 CSF £107.68 TOTE £7.10: £2.70, £3.70, £1.90; EX 94.10 Trifecta £1078.80 Pool of £5284.53 - 3.60 winning units..
Owner Normandie Stud Ltd **Bred** Normandie Stud Ltd **Trained** Newmarket, Suffolk

FOCUS

No more than a fair renewal of his historic stayers' race, but a tight race on official figures. Sound form with Samuel rated back to his best and the runer-up rated to his best too. The pace appeared reasonable and the time was a second inside the standard. The runners came down the centre of the track in the home straight. Again the Lonsdale Cup at York proved to be the key trial for this event.

NOTEBOOK

Samuel was always well positioned and he struck the front moving well before seeing his race out strongly. Runner-up to Opinion Poll in the Lonsdale Cup but 3lb better off, this big, strong gelding appreciated the greater test of stamina here. This was only the second win of his life - the first came at York in 2008 for John Dunlop - but a tendon injury did cost him two years of his career. He could go for the Prix du Cadran at the Arc meeting as long as the ground isn't bottomless, and the 2m4f there ought to suit. (op 11-2)

Tastahil(IRE), never far from the pace, could not repel the winner after going on but did battle most willingly to hold second. Sixth in the York race, he was suited by this longer trip and put up an improved performance. He could run in the Jockey Club Cup at Newmarket next month but the drop back to 2m may not be in his favour. (op 20-1)

Motrice's profile bore similarities to that of her trainer's 2001 winner Alleluia, another 3yo filly who had progressed fast in handicaps. This one arrived here officially rated 101, having won a Yarmouth handicap off 59 just three months ago. Upped in trip by half a mile, she was held up in last place and was faced with quite a bit of ground to make up when the pace lifted in the straight. Although she stayed on relentlessly the line was always going to beat her, but in fairness she did not appear to be helping her rider, who also had to switch her a couple of times. If she runs again this year it is likely to be in the Jockey Club Cup, although she is also in the Cesarewitch the same day. (op 7-2 tchd 9-2 in a place)

Opinion Poll(IRE) was conceding a 3lb penalty for his win at this level in last month's Lonsdale Cup, where he had today's winner and second behind. Permitted to take his chance even though the ground was quicker than ideal, he ran creditably but could not quicken up when required. This trip might be a little further than ideal. (tchd 7-2)

Dirar(IRE) ran creditably on this step up in class but was always in a similar place and just lacked the pace to get involved. He has won hurdles at 2m4f but had not tackled this far on the Flat, and he stayed it well enough. (op 9-1)

Darley Sun(IRE) was runner-up to Askar Tau 12 months ago before landing the Cesarewitch for David Simcock. He has proved difficult to place since Godolphin acquired him, finishing unplaced in the Gold Cup and the Ebor on his latest two starts, and while he was not disgraced here he was again found wanting. (op 14-1 tchd 16-1)

Askar Tau(FR), the winner of this last season, had been off the track since picking up an injury on his seasonal reappearance back in April. Unpenalised this time round, he raced a shade keenly in the first-time blinkers (replacing the visor) and faded away after tracking the pace. (op 10-1 tchd 9-1)

Pointilliste(USA) was one of the first in trouble and is likely to switch to hurdling before long. Official explanation: jockey said that the horse had no more to give (op 28-1)

Dayia(IRE) was reported to have hung left. Official explanation: jockey said that the mare hung left in the straight (tchd 50-1)

Electrolyser(IRE) made the running, a role he has adopted before in his career, before dropping away disappointingly once tackled. (op 7-1)

5910 KEEPMOAT "DELIVERING COMMUNITY REGENERATION" MAY HILL STKS (GROUP 2) (FILLIES) — 1m (S)

3:15 (3:17) (Class 1) 2-Y-O

£45,416 (£17,216; £8,616; £4,296; £2,152; £1,080) **Stalls** High

Form				RPR
11	**1**		**White Moonstone (USA)**[34] 4842 2-8-12 106 ... FrankieDettori 7 (Saeed Bin Suroor) *lw: hld up in rr: smooth hdwy on outer wl over 2f out: shkn up to ld wl over 1f out: clr ent fnl f: easily* **8/11**[1]	110+
1040	**2**	5	**Al Madina (IRE)**[22] 5245 2-8-12 94 ... TomEaves 3 (B Smart) *lw: trckd ldrs: effrt over 2f out: sn rdn and edgd lft: swtchd rt and drvn ins fnl f: kpt on to take 2nd last 100yds* **66/1**	95
15	**3**	1 1/4	**Musharakaat (IRE)**[34] 4842 2-8-12 92 ... RichardHills 1 (E A L Dunlop) *cl up: led after 3f: rdn along and hdd wl over 1f out: sn one pce* **16/1**	92
2120	**4**	nk	**Sonning Rose (IRE)**[13] 5519 2-8-12 98 ... RyanMoore 6 (M R Channon) *lw: hld up in rr: hdwy 3f out: rdn to chse ldrs 2f out: sn drvn and kpt on same pce* **12/1**	91
2514	**5**	nk	**Lily Again**[33] 4879 2-8-12 98 ... JamieSpencer 4 (P F I Cole) *lw: led 3f: cl up tl rdn over 2f out and grad wknd* **13/2**[3]	91
33	**6**	2 1/2	**Fenella Fudge**[43] 4508 2-8-12 0 ... PaulMulrennan 5 (J G Given) *in tch: rdn along and outpcd over 2f out: n.d* **50/1**	85
21	**7**	6	**Midnight Caller**[10] 5633 2-8-12 0 ... WilliamBuick 2 (J H M Gosden) *w'like: lw: trckd ldrs: hdwy 3f out: rdn along wl over 1f out and sn wknd* **3/1**[2]	71

1m 38.73s (-0.57) **Going Correction** -0.025s/f (Good) **7** Ran SP% **113.3**

Speed ratings (Par 104): **101,96,94,94,94 91,85**

toteswingers:1&2 £7.40, 2&3 £18.10, 1&3 £3.10 CSF £55.23 TOTE £1.90: £1.50, £5.50; EX 24.90.

Owner Godolphin **Bred** Stonerside Stable **Trained** Newmarket, Suffolk

FOCUS

There was only one previous Group winner and one Listed winner amongst the seven fillies and whilst eight of the previous ten winners of this had been successful in their previous starts, only two of these matched that criteria, including White Moonstone. She was impressive and looks a Guineas candidate now.

NOTEBOOK

White Moonstone(USA) was the only unbeaten filly in the field having won her two previous outings including a convincing success in the Sweet Solera at Newmarket last month, when she had two of today's rivals behind her. Settled at the back of the field towards the nearside early, she travelled into the race smoothly and, once taking it up over a furlong out, simply destroyed the opposition with her turn of foot and she powered right away. Visually she was impressive, but with the second-favourite running so poorly and a 66-1 shot in second, it remains to be seen what she achieved. She was immediately quoted a best-price 12-1 for next year's 1,000 Guineas and she should have little difficulty getting the trip, whilst connections suggested that 1m2f will probably be her limit next year. She is likely to stepped up into Group 1 company next, probably in the Fillies' Mile. (tchd 8-13)

Al Madina(IRE), over 5l behind White Moonstone in the Sweet Solera before getting outpaced back down to 6f at York, ran almost to the pound with the winner and she did well to run on again into second after getting outpaced inside the last 2f. She may go for the Oh So Sharp Stakes at the start of next month. (op 50-1)

Musharakaat(IRE), behind White Moonstone and Al Madina in the Sweet Solera, again ran almost to the pound on that form and helped force the pace until over a furlong from home. That may be it for the season, but if she runs again it may be in a sales race at Newmarket. (op 20-1 tchd 25-1)

Sonning Rose(IRE), disappointing on the soft ground when last of seven in the Prestige Stakes at Goodwood last time, made some late progress from the back of the field but she never looked like winning. (tchd 14-1)

Lily Again, a well-held fourth in the Group 2 Debutante Stakes at the Curragh last time after making all to win a Sandown Listed event, was given another positive ride but she was given little peace by the third horse and was done with over a furlong from home. (op 9-1 tchd 10-1)

Fenella Fudge, beaten less than a length in maidens here and at Goodwood, was under pressure a long way out and found this company too hot at this stage of her career. (op 40-1)

Midnight Caller, stepping up in class after justifying long odds-on in a soft-ground Leicester maiden over a similar trip to this, was sent off a strong second-favourite but her rider was sending out distress signals a good 3f from home and she eventually dropped right out. This was too bad to be true. Official explanation: jockey said the filly was unsuited by the Good ground (tchd 7-2)

5911 BRAKES FRESH IDEAS H'CAP — 6f 110y

3:50 (3:51) (Class 2) (0-105,104) 3-Y-O+ **£12,952** (£3,854; £1,926; £962) **Stalls** High

Form				RPR
0606	**1**		**Irish Heartbeat (IRE)**[12] 5571 5-8-10 91 ... LeeTopliss(5) 11 (R A Fahey) *in tch: hdwy 2f out: rdn to chse ldrs over 1f out: led ent fnl f: sn drvn and kpt on* **7/1**[3]	102+
035	**2**	3/4	**Imperial Guest**[17] 5393 4-9-2 92 ... DaneO'Neill 7 (G G Margarson) *midfield: hdwy 2f out: rdn over 1f out: chal ent fnl f and ev ch tl drvn and nt qckn last 75yds* **16/1**	101
0040	**3**	3/4	**Sea Of Leaves (USA)**[1] 5883 4-9-0 90 ... TomQueally 14 (J S Goldie) *hld up in rr: swtchd lft and hdwy 2f out: rdn to chse ldrs over 1f out: drvn and ev ch ins fnl f: nt qckn towards fin* **20/1**	97
0060	**4**	nk	**Damien (IRE)**[24] 5183 4-9-9 99 ... JimmyFortune 13 (B W Hills) *hld up in rr: hdwy over 1f out: n.m.r and swtchd lft appr fnl f: sn rdn and ch ins fnl f: sn drvn and one pce* **16/1**	105
6100	**5**	nse	**Swilly Ferry (USA)**[65] 3791 3-9-8 102 ... MichaelHills 17 (B W Hills) *towards rr: hdwy on outer 2f out: rdn and edgd lft over 1f out: drvn and kpt on ins fnl f: nrst fin* **14/1**	106
-341	**6**	1 1/2	**Citrus Star (USA)**[43] 4509 3-9-8 102 ... GeorgeBaker 8 (C F Wall) *t.k.h: chsd ldrs: effrt 2f out: sn rdn and ch over 1f out: drvn and one pce ins fnl f* **6/1**[1]	101
0544	**7**	nse	**Take Ten**[13] 5524 3-8-6 86 ... SilvestreDeSousa 12 (M Johnston) *chsd ldrs: hdwy 2f out: rdn and ev ch ent fnl f: grad wknd* **7/1**[3]	85
0106	**8**	hd	**Fireback**[34] 4819 3-8-10 90 ... DavidProbert 16 (A M Balding) *cl up: rdn to ld 2f out: sn drvn: hdd ent fnl f: grad wknd* **20/1**	88
0400	**9**	hd	**Pastoral Player**[42] 4536 3-9-0 94 ... SteveDrowne 15 (H Morrison) *in tch: rdn along 2f out: drvn over 1f out and kpt on same pce* **12/1**	92
1052	**10**	1/2	**Medicean Man**[8] 5702 4-9-5 95 ... (v[1]) LukeMorris 4 (J R Gask) *lw: hld up in tch: swtchd lft and hdwy over 2f out: rdn to chse ldrs wl over 1f out: no imp ins fnl f* **13/2**[2]	93
14-6	**11**	1 1/4	**Mr David (USA)**[21] 5275 3-9-10 104 ... JamieSpencer 18 (B J Meehan) *in tch on outer: rdn along over 2f out: hld whn n.m.r over 1f out* **20/1**	97
6100	**12**	1 1/4	**Flipando (IRE)**[5] 5787 9-9-8 98 ... PhillipMakin 6 (T D Barron) *nvr bttr than midfield* **28/1**	89
1400	**13**	shd	**Kaptain Kirkup (IRE)**[55] 4126 3-9-8 102 ... RyanMoore 2 (M Dods) *chsd ldrs: rdn along 2f out: sn drvn and grad wknd* **14/1**	91
500-	**14**	nse	**Lowther**[322] 6994 5-8-9 92 ... NatashaEaton(7) 9 (A Bailey) *sn led: rdn along and hdd 2f out: sn wknd* **33/1**	82
2031	**15**	1 1/2	**Damika (IRE)**[27] 5095 7-9-5 98 ... MichaelStainton(3) 3 (R M Whitaker) *a in rr* **16/1**	84
0240	**16**	1/2	**Enderby Spirit (GR)**[56] 4085 4-9-3 93 ... (v) TomEaves 10 (B Smart) *chsd ldrs: rdn along 2f out: sn wknd* **40/1**	77
350	**17**	1 3/4	**Nasri**[84] 3146 4-9-6 96 ... WilliamBuick 5 (D M Simcock) *chsd ldrs: rdn along over 2f out: sn wknd* **25/1**	75
1050	**18**	6	**Hoof It**[22] 5250 3-8-12 92 ... PaulMulrennan 1 (M W Easterby) *chsd ldrs on outer: rdn along 1/2-way: sn wknd* **14/1**	51

1m 19.06s (-0.84) **Going Correction** -0.025s/f (Good)

WFA 3 from 4yo+ 2lb **18** Ran SP% **124.9**

Speed ratings (Par 109): **103,102,101,100,100 99,99,98,98,98 96,95,95,95,93 92,90,83**

toteswingers:1&2 £24.80, 2&3 £54.10, 1&3 £39.20 CSF £104.23 CT £2229.60 TOTE £6.80: £1.90, £3.70, £4.70, £4.60; EX 119.50 Trifecta £964.80 Part won. Pool of £1303.85 - 0.84 winning units..

Owner M A Leatham & G H Leatham **Bred** P D Savill **Trained** Musley Bank, N Yorks

■ Stewards' Enquiry : David Probert one-day ban: used whip with excessive frequency and without giving time to respond (24 Sep)

FOCUS

The second running of this handicap, which takes place over an intermediate trip. The pace was sound despite the absent of obvious front-runners in the field, and the form should hold up. The field raced down the centre of the track initially before spreading out.

NOTEBOOK

Irish Heartbeat(IRE), who was 2lb well in here, won the Spring Mile at this track back in March but had been unable to build on that. He had plenty of form at sprint distances when trained in Ireland, though, and travelled well on this drop back in trip before quickening up for a comfortable win. His aim all season has been the Ayr Gold Cup, and the penalty he picks up for this win should help him make the cut there. He would not mind easier ground in Scotland. (op 15-2 tchd 8-1 in a place)

Imperial Guest is well suited by large fields and he improved from the back of the pack to hold every chance. He is pretty consistent, and although he had been eased a pound in the weights before this, he remains 7lb higher than his last winning mark.

Sea Of Leaves(USA) had been well beaten in a Listed race here the day before but she could not get cover that time and this bigger field helped in that respect. She had dropped to her last winning mark and came home well from the rear. (op 28-1)

Damien(IRE) delivered his run late but the effort was just flattening out near the end. He remains winless since his 2yo debut, but did go down narrowly in the big sales race over C&D two years ago and seems to like it here. (tchd 20-1)

Swilly Ferry(USA) ran a solid race nearest the stands' rail here and was only run out of the frame in the dying strides. A two-month break looks to have freshened him up. (op 20-1)

Citrus Star(USA), raised 3lb for his win at Glorious Goodwood, was keen early on before keeping on nicely at the end, suggesting a return to 7f is desirable. This was his first run against older horses. (op 5-1)

Take Ten was never far from the pace but could not sustain his effort late on. He has edged down the weights this year but remains 13lb higher than his last winning mark from over a year ago. (op 17-2)

Fireback ran a fair race but remains held by the handicapper off 6lb higher than when winning at the Newmarket July festival, when he had Take Ten back in fourth. (op 25-1)

Pastoral Player got down in the stalls for a short time and, while he ran creditably, he remains one to tread warily with given the problems he sometimes has at the start. (op 11-1 tchd 10-1)

Medicean Man, visored for the first time, had 4lb in hand of the handicapper and it was disappointing that he could not run better than he did on this return to turf. (op 8-1)

Kaptain Kirkup(IRE), who went to post early, was held off an 8lb higher mark than when last in a handicap. (tchd 12-1)

Damika(IRE) could never get involved and was reported to have been unsuited by the ground. Official explanation: trainer said that the gelding was unsuited by the Good ground (op 14-1)

Hoof It Official explanation: jockey said that the gelding ran too free

5912 FRANK WHITTLE PARTNERSHIP CONDITIONS STKS — 7f

4:25 (4:26) (Class 2) 2-Y-O **£10,904** (£3,265; £1,632) **Stalls** High

Form				RPR
1	**1**		**Frankel**[28] 5049 2-9-2 0 ... TomQueally 4 (H R A Cecil) *lw: trckd ldr: smooth hdwy to ld wl over 1f out: sn qcknd clr: styd on strly: impressive* **1/2**[1]	115+
	2	13	**Rainbow Springs** 2-8-4 0 ... NickyMackay 2 (J H M Gosden) *w'like: scope: hld up: pushed along 3f out: rdn and hdwy over 2f out: styd on to take 2nd ins fnl f: no ch w wnr* **16/1**[3]	71+
0126	**3**	4	**Diamond Geezah (IRE)**[22] 5245 2-9-0 90 ... MichaelHills 1 (B W Hills) *led: rdn along over 2f out: drvn and hdd over 1f out: sn one pce* **14/1**[2]	71

1m 24.83s (-1.47) **Going Correction** -0.025s/f (Good) **3** Ran SP% **79.2**

Speed ratings (Par 101): **107,92,87**

CSF £2.28 TOTE £1.10; EX 2.40.

Owner K Abdulla **Bred** Juddmonte Farms Ltd **Trained** Newmarket, Suffolk

FOCUS
This had looked a fascinating conditions event on paper, featuring two highly promising colts that had been successful in their only previous starts, something they shared in common with four of the previous five winners of this race (the other was a newcomer). However, it proved something of an anti-climax after one of the pair, Farhh, was withdrawn after getting into a state in the stalls (9/4, deduct 30p in the £). They raced in Indian file down the centre of the track for most of the way. Frankel was very impressive and looks a genuine Classic prospect for next year, but the third seems to have run a long way below par.

NOTEBOOK
Frankel ◆ had a simple task and he duly completed it, but even so he was extremely impressive and the fact that he slammed a horse rated 90 by 17l giving him 2lb puts the performance into perspective. He had won with plenty more in hand than the half-length margin would suggest when landing a 1m soft-ground maiden on his Newmarket debut last month and was in a totally different league to his two rivals here, completely blowing them apart after leading over 1f from home. The son of Galileo is clearly held in high regard by his trainer and he was soon cut to a top-price 16-1 for the 2,000 Guineas and 20-1 for the Derby, but whilst his dam never won beyond 7f, she was out of a Rainbow Quest mare so there must be every chance that he will stay 1m4f. He is likely to step right up in grade now and could run in both the Royal Lodge Stakes and the Racing Post Trophy. (op 4-6)

Rainbow Springs, a half-sister to the useful Ridge Dance, was getting upwards of 10lb from the two colts, but this was still a demanding task on her racecourse debut. Settled in last of the trio, she took a long time to respond when coming under pressure over 2f from home, but the penny eventually dropped and she ran on to finish a clear second, if never in the same parish as the winner. This performance is probably best measured through the 90-rated third rather than how far she finished behind the winner, which suggests that she can win races. (op 20-1)

Diamond Geezah(IRE), back up to a more suitable trip, set the early pace but merely set the race up for two unexposed and promising rivals. He may not be the easiest to place from now on. (op 12-1 tchd 11-1)

5913 UNIVERSAL RECYCLING CLASSIFIED STKS — 1m 2f 60y
4:55 (4:55) (Class 3) 3-Y-O+
£9,346 (£2,799; £1,399; £700; £349; £175) Stalls Low

Form | | | | RPR
6-1 **1** **Willing Foe (USA)**[41] 4572 3-8-11 85 .... FrankieDettori 5 102+
(Saeed Bin Suroor) *w'like: str: hld up in tch: smooth hdwy on outer over 2f out: rdn to ld jst ins fnl f: styd on strly* **7/2**[1]

4123 **2** 2 1/4 **Opera Gal (IRE)**[34] 4815 3-8-8 85 .... DavidProbert 10 92
(A M Balding) *trckd ldr: hdwy to ld over 3f out: rdn along wl over 1f out: drvn and hdd jst ins fnl f: kpt on same pce* **9/2**[2]

1210 **3** 1/2 **Tepmokea (IRE)**[23] 5217 4-9-4 85 .... PaulMulrennan 12 94
(R A Fahey) *trckd ldrs: hdwy over 2f out: rdn and ev ch over 1f out: drvn ent fnl f and kpt on same pce* **6/1**[3]

2602 **4** nk **Abergavenny**[20] 5286 3-8-11 84 .... SilvestreDeSousa 13 93+
(M Johnston) *hld up in rr: hdwy over 2f out: rdn wl over 1f out: drvn and styd on ins fnl f: nrst fin* **12/1**

0043 **5** hd **The Which Doctor**[47] 4399 5-9-4 83 .... RyanMoore 3 93
(J Noseda) *s.i.s and bhd: hdwy over 3f out: rdn to chse ldrs 2f out: sn drvn and one pce appr fnl f* **6/1**[3]

211 **6** 1 1/4 **Pendragon (USA)**[47] 4399 7-8-13 85 .... DaleSwift(5) 4 91
(B Ellison) *hld up towards rr: hdwy 3f out: rdn to chse ldrs 2f out: drvn over 1f out: n.m.r and no imp ins fnl f* **8/1**

0204 **7** 1 **Ellemujie**[6] 5753 5-8-13 85 .... JamesO'Reilly(5) 1 89
(D K Ivory) *trckd ldrs: hdwy on inner 3f out: rdn 2f out: drvn and ch over 1f out: wknd ent fnl f* **25/1**

0222 **8** 2 **Bonfire Knight**[13] 5511 3-8-11 85 .... TomEaves 2 85
(J J Quinn) *trckd ldrs: effrt over 3f out: rdn along 2f out: grad wknd* **6/1**[3]

2140 **9** 1 1/2 **Scamperdale**[33] 4859 8-9-4 83 .... TomQueally 11 82
(B P J Baugh) *hld up in rr: sme hdwy 3f out: rdn over 2f out and sn wknd* **33/1**

3550 **10** 4 **Follow The Flag (IRE)**[30] 4943 6-9-4 85 .... (p) LeeVickers 8 75
(A J McCabe) *in tch on outer: rdn along 4f out: sn wknd* **33/1**

1214 **11** nk **Umverti**[28] 5019 5-9-1 77 .... FrannyNorton 6 71
(N Bycroft) *led: rdn along 4f out: hdd over 3f out: sn drvn and wknd over 2f out* **50/1**

2m 7.69s (-1.71) **Going Correction** +0.025s/f (Good)
WFA 3 from 4yo+ 7lb **11** Ran SP% **113.8**
Speed ratings (Par 107): **107,105,104,104,104 103,102,101,99,96 96**
toteswingers:1&2 £4.70, 2&3 £6.50, 1&3 £5.50 CSF £17.56 TOTE £4.60: £1.90, £1.60, £2.30; EX 22.00 Trifecta £164.80 Pool of £1357.04 - 6.09 winning units. Place 6: £97.35 Place 5: £65.88.

Owner Godolphin **Bred** Stonerside Stable **Trained** Newmarket, Suffolk

FOCUS
The pace was sound and again the action took place down the centre of the track.

NOTEBOOK
Willing Foe(USA) travelled well through the race and cleared away in nice style when Dettori pressed the button inside the last. He looks better than his current rating of 85 and has more to offer as he gains experience. Connections will keep him to this trip for the time being but 1m4f should be within his compass further down the line. (op 9-2 tchd 10-3)

Opera Gal(IRE) was officially 3lb best in and she ran her usual honest race up with the pace. A return to 1m4f will not bother her and she deserves to pick up another race before the end of the season. (tchd 6-1)

Tepmokea(IRE), back down in trip, was never far from the pace and kept on wilingly for third. He is proving a consistent sort. (op 13-2 tchd 5-1)

Abergavenny ◆ ran on nicely from the back of the field and will be strongly suited by a return to further on this evidence. He could be interesting when tackling the full 1m4f. (op 11-1 tchd 10-1)

The Which Doctor was slow to find his stride but stayed on for pressure from the rear. He turned around Ascot running from last time out with Pendragon. (op 11-2)

Pendragon(USA)'s recent progressive streak in handicaps was halted, but who gave the impression he is ready to tackle further again. (op 9-1 tchd 15-2)

Ellemujie ran respectably but his strike rate remains very modest. (op 20-1)

Bonfire Knight had finished second in handicaps over this trip on his last three starts, behind the progressive Aattash latest, but he was found wanting this time. Official explanation: trainer was unable to offer any explanation for the poor performance shown

T/Jkpt: Not won. T/Plt: £202.70 to a £1 stake. Pool:£161,049.44 - 579.80 winning tickets. T/Qpdt: £22.40 to a £1 stake. Pool:£9,551.27 - 314.44 winning tickets. JR

5305 SANDOWN (R-H)
Friday, September 10

OFFICIAL GOING: Good (good to firm in places on round course) changing to good after race 4 (4.00)
Wind: Moderate, against Weather: Fine but cloudy

5914 EUROPEAN BREEDERS' FUND SPRINT MAIDEN STKS — 5f 6y
2:15 (2:15) (Class 4) 2-Y-O
£4,533 (£1,348; £674; £336) Stalls High

Form | | | | RPR
3 **1** **Carrignavar (USA)**[15] 5441 2-8-12 0 .... JimCrowley 9 88+
(R M Beckett) *trckd ldrs: plld out and rdn to chse ldr over 1f out: styd on wl ins fnl f to ld last 100yds* **11/4**[2]

3 **2** 3/4 **Supercharged (IRE)**[60] 3959 2-8-12 0 .... AlanMunro 6 85+
(C F Wall) *w ldr: led after 2f: shkn up over 1f out: styd on wl: hdd last 100yds* **6/4**[1]

000 **3** 10 **Shostakovich (IRE)**[14] 5465 2-9-3 0 .... LiamKeniry 5 54
(S Kirk) *trckd ldrs: pushed along 1/2-way: wl outpcd over 1f out: plugged on u.p to take remote 3rd nr fin* **66/1**

440 **4** 1/2 **Plenty Power**[13] 5531 2-9-3 74 .... (v[1]) SamHitchcott 10 53
(M R Channon) *led 2f: hrd rdn and lft bhd by ldng pair over 1f out: lost remote 3rd nr fin* **13/2**[3]

04 **5** 1/2 **Classic Voice (IRE)**[9] 5651 2-9-3 0 .... PatDobbs 4 54+
(R Hannon) *settled in 7th: pushed along 1/2-way: prog ins fnl f: styng on and likely to fin 3rd tl out of room last 100yds* **12/1**

03 **6** nk **Tees And Cees (IRE)**[9] 5657 2-9-3 0 .... NeilCallan 2 50
(R Hannon) *chsd ldrs on outer: u.p fr 1/2-way: wl outpcd fr over 1f out: plugged on* **8/1**

50 **7** 1/2 **Swaninstockwell (IRE)**[18] 5372 2-9-3 0 .... IanMongan 8 48
(P M Phelan) *s.s: hld up in last pair: pushed along 2f out: kpt on ins fnl f: nvr involved* **33/1**

54 **8** 3 1/4 **Milldown Magic**[120] 2048 2-9-0 0 .... JamesMillman(3) 1 36
(B R Millman) *dwlt: sn chsd ldrs in 6th: rdn 1/2-way: wknd over 1f out* **16/1**

9 shd **Hey Mambo** 2-8-12 0 .... JackMitchell 3 31
(R Ingram) *hld up in 8th: pushed along 1/2-way: no prog* **66/1**

10 7 **Cara Carmela** 2-8-12 0 .... WilliamCarson 7 —
(S C Williams) *s.s: hld up: a in last pair: wknd over 1f out* **40/1**

63.08 secs (1.48) **Going Correction** +0.375s/f (Good) **10** Ran SP% **113.1**
Speed ratings (Par 97): **103,101,85,85,84 83,82,77,77,66**
toteswingers:1&2 £1.60, 2&3 £20.60, 1&3 £27.60 CSF £6.83 TOTE £3.40: £1.40, £1.10, £9.80; EX 5.00.
Owner S E Construction (Kent) Ltd **Bred** Sun Valley Farm **Trained** Whitsbury, Hants

FOCUS
An ordinary maiden run at a decent pace against a strong headwind with the front two, who drew well clear of the remainder, looking promising types.

NOTEBOOK
Carrignavar(USA) knuckled down well to her task to come out on top after travelling sweetly for much of the way. She was probably a little unlucky on her debut when running very green, but that experience had done her the power of good and looks a decent type who can only build on this. (op 5-2 tchd 3-1 in a place)

Supercharged(IRE) ◆ raced up with the pace, albeit a little too freely, which eventually proved to be her undoing when collared by the winner in the latter stages. A good effort nonetheless, and she should be going one better sooner rather than later. Quite well regarded, she holds an entry in the Cheveley Park. (op 13-8 tchd 7-4 and 2-1 in a place)

Shostakovich(IRE) had shown little in three starts to date but showed good speed here to sit just behind the leaders and kept on well enough without having the pace to go with the principals. This was a step in the right direction and it will remain to be seen if he can build on this.

Plenty Power had come in for support after reportedly working well in a visor at home. He was right up with the pace but could'nt match the front pair when they kicked and he looks a better option for nurseries. (op 7-1 tchd 6-1)

Classic Voice(IRE) had been dropped back in trip and might well have finished third had he not met trouble in running entering the final furlong. He looks as though he could make his presence felt now qualified for a mark over this trip. Official explanation: jockey said that the colt was denied a clear run (op 14-1 tchd 16-1)

Swaninstockwell(IRE) missed the break and could never get involved but has shown some promise and now qualifies for a mark. (tchd 40-1)

5915 WEYBRIDGE H'CAP — 5f 6y
2:50 (2:53) (Class 5) (0-75,76) 3-Y-O+
£3,238 (£963; £481; £240) Stalls High

Form | | | | RPR
0000 **1** **Zowington**[27] 5087 8-8-11 65 .... (v) WilliamCarson 12 76
(S C Williams) *racd against rail: hld up towards rr: prog wl over 1f out: r.o ins fnl f to ld last 75yds* **12/1**

4364 **2** 3/4 **Wanchai Whisper**[23] 5207 3-8-6 64 .... (p) AndrewHeffernan(3) 3 72+
(P R Hedger) *hld up in last pair: gd prog on wd outside fr 2f out: drvn to ld ins fnl f: hdd and hld last 75yds* **25/1**

0050 **3** 1 1/2 **Triple Dream**[10] 5628 5-9-5 73 .... (p) LiamKeniry 14 76
(J M Bradley) *racd against rail hroughout: led 2f: rdn over 2f out and nt qckn: kpt on ins fnl f* **16/1**

4121 **4** nk **Matterofact (IRE)**[8] 5695 7-9-8 76 6ex .... JimCrowley 11 78
(M S Saunders) *w ldrs and racd jst off rail: rdn in 2nd over 1f out: one pce ins fnl f* **15/2**[2]

1304 **5** 1/2 **Make My Dream**[37] 4693 7-9-3 71 .... TadhgO'Shea 10 71
(J Gallagher) *settled towards rr: rdn and nt qckn 2f out: styd on wl fnl f: nrst fin* **11/1**

0043 **6** nk **Even Bolder**[21] 5262 7-8-13 72 .... KierenFox(5) 6 71
(E A Wheeler) *racd towards outer: led after 2f: drvn over 1f out and edgd lft: hdd and fdd ins fnl f* **12/1**

4420 **7** 1 3/4 **Gwilym (GER)**[4] 5809 7-9-4 72 .... AdamKirby 15 64
(D Haydn Jones) *racd against rail: trckd ldrs: rdn 2f out: nt qckn over 1f out: fdd ins fnl f* **9/2**[1]

2613 **8** 3/4 **Maryolini**[24] 5176 5-8-4 61 oh3 .... Louis-PhilippeBeuzelin(3) 7 51
(T Keddy) *hld up in last trio: nt clr run briefly 2f out: kpt on fnl f: n.d* **25/1**

0403 **9** nk **Master Lightfoot**[25] 5151 4-9-7 75 .... ShaneKelly 9 64
(W R Swinburn) *hld up towards rr: pushed along 2f out: swtchd to rail fnl f: shkn up and kpt on: nvr nr ldrs* **9/1**[3]

1054 **10** 1 **Brandywell Boy (IRE)**[20] 5285 7-9-1 74 .... BillyCray(5) 5 59+
(D J S Ffrench Davis) *hld up in last trio: looking for room 1/2-way: shkn up and no prog 2f out: kpt on ins fnl f* **12/1**

3600 **11** 3 3/4 **Silvanus (IRE)**[13] 5513 5-8-13 67 .... MickyFenton 8 38
(P T Midgley) *prom towards outer for 3f: sn wknd* **20/1**

6260 **12** *nk* **Colorus (IRE)**[31] 4938 7-8-11 **65**....................(p) NeilCallan 1 35
(W J H Ratcliffe) *racd wdst of all: chsd ldrs: u.p 1/2-way: sn struggling* **40/1**

4142 **13** *¾* **Luminous Gold**[23] 5207 5-9-6 **74**.................... AlanMunro 13 42
(C F Wall) *tk three minutes to load into stalls: chsd ldrs: u.p 1/2-way: wknd over 1f out* **9/2**[1]

1346 **14** *6* **Grudge**[10] 5647 5-9-1 **72**....................(be) EJMcNamara[(3)] 4 18
(C R Dore) *chsd ldrs tl wknd rapidly 2f out* **14/1**

63.06 secs (1.46) **Going Correction** +0.375s/f (Good)
WFA 3 from 4yo+ 1lb **14** Ran SP% **117.0**
Speed ratings (Par 103): **103,101,99,98,98 97,94,93,93,91 85,85,83,74**
toteswingers:1&2 £36.00, 2&3 £88.70, 1&3 £45.20 CSF £285.58 CT £4840.58 TOTE £13.40: £5.00, £8.40, £6.70; EX 276.70.
Owner O Pointing **Bred** O Pointing **Trained** Newmarket, Suffolk

FOCUS
A very competitive sprint handicap run at a good pace.
Zowington Official explanation: trainer said, regarding the apparent improvement in form, that the gelding had been poorly drawn on his last two runs on ground that now appears to have been too soft
Grudge Official explanation: jockey said the gelding had stopped quickly

5916 PKF E B F MAIDEN STKS 1m 14y
3:25 (3:27) (Class 4) 2-Y-O **£4,533** (£1,348; £674; £336) **Stalls** High

Form RPR

1 **Shooting Gallery** 2-8-10 0.................... AntiocoMurgia[(7)] 3 82
(Mahmood Al Zarooni) *in tch in 5th: prog on outer over 2f out: led over 1f out: urged along and drew clr ins fnl f* **16/1**

4 **2** *3 ¾* **Musawama (IRE)**[28] 5032 2-9-3 0.................... TadhgO'Shea 6 74+
(J H M Gosden) *led: shkn up 2f out: hdd over 1f out: kpt on: no ch w wnr* **7/2**[3]

3 *nk* **Unex Renoir** 2-9-3 0.................... NeilCallan 5 73+
(J H M Gosden) *chsd ldrs in 6th: shkn up and no prog over 2f out: same pl 1f out: styd on wl after: nrly snatched 2nd* **20/1**

0 **4** *½* **Violet Ray (USA)**[21] 5263 2-9-3 0.................... JimCrowley 2 72
(R M Beckett) *sn off the pce in 7th: shkn up 3f out: no prog tl rdn and styd on wl ins fnl f: nrst fin* **66/1**

2 **5** *shd* **General Synod**[28] 5033 2-9-3 0.................... PatDobbs 7 72
(R Hannon) *chsd ldr: pushed along fr 3f out: tried to chal wl over 1f out: sn outpcd* **6/4**[1]

0 **6** *2 ¾* **Adone (IRE)**[14] 5491 2-9-0 0.................... Louis-PhilippeBeuzelin[(3)] 9 66
(Sir Michael Stoute) *chsd ldr: cl enough 2f out: nt qckn over 1f out: wknd ins fnl f* **12/1**

53 **7** *¾* **Arc Light (IRE)**[21] 5263 2-9-3 0.................... AlanMunro 8 64
(Mahmood Al Zarooni) *trckd ldng trio: pushed up to go 2nd briefly 2f out: nt qckn after: wknd ins fnl f* **11/4**[2]

0 **8** *10* **Phoenix Fantasy (IRE)**[11] 5582 2-9-3 0.................... TonyCulhane 1 42+
(J G Portman) *a same pl and sn bhd: nvr a factor* **100/1**

9 *19* **Camberley Two** 2-9-3 0.................... J-PGuillambert 4 —
(R Charlton) *a in last and sn wl bhd: t.o* **40/1**

1m 45.38s (2.08) **Going Correction** +0.075s/f (Good) **9** Ran SP% **112.1**
Speed ratings (Par 97): **92,88,87,87,87 84,83,73,54**
toteswingers:1&2 £7.90, 2&3 £7.10, 1&3 £14.40 CSF £67.93 TOTE £20.50: £5.10, £1.10, £6.10; EX 79.00.
Owner Godolphin **Bred** Kilcarn Stud **Trained** Newmarket, Suffolk

FOCUS
An interesting mile maiden run at a sound pace.

NOTEBOOK
Shooting Gallery ◆, an 80,000euros yearling who holds an Irish Group 2 entry and is a half-brother to the useful Leningrad, made a very encouraging debut. Pulling wide to make his challenge, he was soon in command, only having to be pushed out to draw clear. He got into a good rhythm turning in and, although, drifting to his right when hitting the front, he left a very favourable impression. A promising type who should be competitive when upped in class, as the yard's 2-y-os seem to improve with a run under their belt. (op 20-1)
Musawama(IRE) looked as though the step up in trip would suit after an encouraging debut over 7f, and was ridden positively from the front. He kept on well after getting headed just inside the final furlong and saw out the trip well enough. He should be getting off the mark before long. (tchd 3-1 and 4-1 in places)
Unex Renoir caught the eye after staying on well in the latter stages on this his debut. He is related to a few middle-distance winners and shaped as though he will be of interest next season when stepping up to that trip. He looks a nice sort who is entitled to come on a bundle for the experience and in the right hands. (op 14-1)
Violet Ray(USA) left his debut run far behind with a much-improved display that saw him turn the tables on Arc Light, who was 17l ahead of him that day. He stayed on well in the final furlong and should be capable of progressing if reproducing this effort.
General Synod was well-supported to open his account after a promising debut. He had his chance form over 1f out but ultimately could only stay on at the same pace. The form of his Newbury debut looked solid, so he possibly rates as a fair benchmark for this race if he ran up to that level.\n\x\x \bAdone\p ran respectably and is improving for experience.\n\x\x \bArc Light\p was a shade disappointing, as he was the more fancied of the pair from Mahmood Al Zarooni stable. He had his chances but might want to be dropped back in trip after fading inside the final furlong. (op 7-4)
Adone(IRE) ran respectably and is improving for experience. (op 10-1 tchd 14-1)
Arc Light(IRE) was a shade disappointing, as he was the more fancied of the pair from Mahmood Al Zarooni stable. He had his chances but might want to be dropped back in trip after fading inside the final furlong. (op 3-1 tchd 5-2 and 10-3 in places)

5917 SUNGARD SECURITIES H'CAP 1m 14y
4:00 (4:00) (Class 3) (0-90,88) 3-Y-O **£6,476** (£1,927; £963; £481) **Stalls** High

Form RPR

2221 **1** **Give Your Verdict (USA)**[43] 4521 3-9-0 **84**.. Louis-PhilippeBeuzelin[(3)] 3 93
(Sir Michael Stoute) *in tch: rousted along on outer fr 3f out: prog fr 2f out: drvn ahd ins fnl f: edgd rt: styd on* **12/1**

4-15 **2** *1* **Julienas (IRE)**[21] 5264 3-9-2 **83**.................... AdamKirby 9 90
(W R Swinburn) *led: shkn up and hdd over 2f out: kpt on u.p fr over 1f out: tk 2nd again last stride* **4/1**[2]

5241 **3** *shd* **Gojeri (IRE)**[33] 4860 3-8-13 **80**.................... NeilCallan 1 86
(M A Jarvis) *trckd ldng pair: chal over 2f out: led over 1f out: hdd and one pce ins fnl f* **13/2**

310 **4** *nk* **Space War**[65] 3796 3-9-4 **85**.................... TadhgO'Shea 5 91+
(J H M Gosden) *hld up last: effrt 2f out: tight for room ent fnl f: styd on wl nr fin* **14/1**

3315 **5** *½* **Linnens Star (IRE)**[28] 5030 3-9-6 **87**.................... JimCrowley 2 92
(R M Beckett) *hld up in last trio: prog on outer fr wl over 2f out: rdn and kpt on fnl 2f: nvr quite gng pce to chal* **16/1**

1563 **6** *¾* **Highland Knight (IRE)**[36] 4750 3-9-6 **87**....................(t) LiamKeniry 10 90+
(A M Balding) *trckd ldng pair: looking for room 2f out: none appeared: lost pl and then bdly hmpd 1f out: swtchd to outer and kpt on: no ch to rcvr: appeared to fin w plenty lft* **15/2**

1-40 **7** *nk* **Kings Bayonet**[17] 5383 3-8-13 **80**.................... IanMongan 7 82
(H R A Cecil) *trckd ldr: led over 2f out: drvn and hdd over 1f out: wknd ins fnl f* **16/1**

-403 **8** *nk* **Aerodynamic (IRE)**[75] 3481 3-9-0 **81**.................... ChrisCatlin 6 83+
(Pat Eddery) *trckd ldrs: nt clr run 2f out: pushed along and towards rr whn hmpd jst ins fnl f: styd on nr fin* **28/1**

110 **9** *1 ¼* **Rock N Roll Ransom**[41] 4573 3-9-7 **88**.................... J-PGuillambert 11 87+
(L M Cumani) *hld up in midfield on inner: pushed along over 2f out: keeping on: no real ch whn short of room ins fnl f* **7/2**[1]

4011 **10** *8* **Nelson's Bounty**[17] 5394 3-9-0 **81**.................... TonyCulhane 4 61+
(P W D'Arcy) *hld up in last trio: effrt over 2f out: trying to cl whn bdly hmpd jst over 1f out: nt rcvr and eased* **9/2**[3]

1m 44.44s (1.14) **Going Correction** +0.075s/f (Good) **10** Ran SP% **115.1**
Speed ratings (Par 105): **97,96,95,95,95 94,94,93,92,84**
CSF £58.81 CT £351.41 TOTE £12.40: £3.40, £2.10, £3.20; EX 77.40.
Owner Saeed Suhail **Bred** Hot Pepper Farm **Trained** Newmarket, Suffolk
■ Stewards' Enquiry : Louis-Philippe Beuzelin four-day ban: careless (24, 26, 27, 28 Sep)

FOCUS
A decent handicap, but a bit of a messy race with any number of the runners getting hampered in the latter stages.

NOTEBOOK
Give Your Verdict(USA) got off the mark at the fifth attempt in a maiden last time and began life in handicaps off a mark of 84. He was under pressure a fair way out but got the gaps to come through to lead in the closing stages to win with a little in hand. His confidence must be on a high now he has scored the last twice and looks a good, tough sort. He ought to be capable of handling a little rise in the ratings as he seems to be on an upward curve at present. (op 14-1)
Julienas(IRE) still looked rather green on handicap debut last time, but had reportedly learnt from the outing and this was a solid effort in defeat. He looked as though he would get swallowed up when headed but, to his credit, stuck to his task well and looks as though he can continue to progress with experience. (op 9-2)
Gojeri(IRE) took a keen hold early on, but hit the front at the furlong pole only to get run out of it in the closing stages. This was a better race than he has been contesting and a respectable effort. (op 6-1)
Space War was held up at the rear, but when staying on from over a furlong out, was dogged with a bad run and never got a chance to make his challenge. He can make his presence felt next time. (op 12-1 tchd 11-1)
Linnens Star(IRE) ran respectably but could never quite find the pace to challenge after making his move over 2f out. (tchd 12-1)
Highland Knight(IRE) was close enough but failed to get any clear passage before being badly hampered 1f out. He looked to have plenty left in the tank but his chance had gone. (op 7-1 tchd 8-1)
Aerodynamic(IRE) was badly hampered 1f out and could never deliver a serious effort so this run is best forgotten. Official explanation: jockey said that the gelding was denied a clear run (op 25-1)
Rock N Roll Ransom was also badly hampered 1f out and is another for whom this run is best forgotten. (op 4-1 tchd 9-2 in places)
Nelson's Bounty was eased after being badly hampered 1f out. Official explanation: jockey said that the gelding suffered interference in running (op 11-2)

5918 HWFA WILLIAMS H'CAP 1m 2f 7y
4:35 (4:36) (Class 4) (0-85,84) 3-Y-O **£4,533** (£1,348; £674; £336) **Stalls** High

Form RPR

21 **1** **Dhaamer (IRE)**[34] 4840 3-9-6 **83**.................... TadhgO'Shea 2 94+
(J H M Gosden) *hld up in 8th: prog on outer over 2f out: shkn up over 1f out: r.o to ld last 150yds: pushed clr: readily* **8/1**

2202 **2** *1 ¼* **Valiant Knight (FR)**[30] 4964 3-9-3 **80**.................... PatDobbs 6 87
(R Hannon) *trckd ldrs: moved up to chal 2f out: pushed into ld jst over 1f out: rdn and hdd last 150yds: no match for wnr* **8/1**

U121 **3** *½* **First Post (IRE)**[21] 5264 3-9-2 **79**.................... AdamKirby 7 86+
(D Haydn Jones) *trckd ldng pair: rdn over 2f out: lost pl over 1f out: rallying whn short of room and snatched up 150yds out: styd on nr fin* **9/2**[1]

12-5 **4** *1 ¼* **Realisation (USA)**[133] 1657 3-9-2 **79**.................... GregFairley 9 82
(M Johnston) *pressed ldr: rdn to ld over 2f out: drvn and hdd jst over 1f out: one pce* **8/1**

320 **5** *¾* **Pink Palace (USA)**[34] 4845 3-8-9 **75**.......... Louis-PhilippeBeuzelin[(3)] 3 77
(Sir Michael Stoute) *hld up in last pair: pushed along over 3f out: prog on inner 2f out: shkn up and styd on steadily fnl f: nrst fin* **16/1**

3331 **6** *1 ¾* **Best Intent**[23] 5209 3-8-12 **75**.................... NeilCallan 4 73
(M A Jarvis) *hld up in midfield: rdn over 2f out: no imp on ldrs over 1f out* **14/1**

4210 **7** *2 ½* **Flying Destination**[29] 4996 3-9-7 **84**.................... ShaneKelly 8 77
(W J Knight) *hld up in midfield: shkn up and no prog over 2f out: wknd ins fnl f* **6/1**[3]

3630 **8** *hd* **Hidden Glory**[18] 5375 3-9-2 **79**.................... ChrisCatlin 10 72
(Pat Eddery) *led but pressed: hdd over 2f out: styd on terms tl wknd rapidly jst over 1f out* **16/1**

-540 **9** *1* **Dynamic Drive (IRE)**[109] 2386 3-8-10 **73**.................... JimCrowley 1 64
(W R Swinburn) *hld up last: rdn wl over 2f out: no ch sn after: plugged on fnl f* **25/1**

6521 **10** *3 ½* **Saint Thomas (IRE)**[30] 4944 3-8-4 **72**.................... BillyCray[(5)] 11 56
(J A Mackie) *trckd ldng pair: rdn over 2f out: sn wknd* **11/2**[2]

2214 **11** *2 ¾* **Dashing Doc (IRE)**[27] 5084 3-8-12 **75**.................... AlanMunro 5 53
(D R C Elsworth) *hld up in last trio: rdn 3f out: sn dropped to last and btn* **8/1**

2m 10.33s (-0.17) **Going Correction** +0.075s/f (Good) **11** Ran SP% **114.6**
Speed ratings (Par 103): **103,102,101,100,100 98,96,96,95,92 90**
toteswingers:1&2 £12.50, 2&3 £9.10, 1&2 £5.90 CSF £68.68 CT £323.88 TOTE £8.90: £2.10, £1.70, £2.20; EX 69.00.
Owner Hamdan Al Maktoum **Bred** Shadwell Estate Company Limited **Trained** Newmarket, Suffolk

FOCUS
A competitive middle-distance handicap run at a good gallop.
First Post(IRE) Official explanation: jockey said that the gelding was denied a clear run
Saint Thomas(IRE) Official explanation: jockey said that the gelding hung left

5919 CHESSINGTON H'CAP 1m 14y
5:05 (5:07) (Class 4) (0-80,80) 3-Y-O+ **£3,885** (£1,156; £577; £288) **Stalls** High

Form RPR

4002 **1** **Rock Anthem (IRE)**[7] 5716 6-8-13 **72**.................... RussKennemore[(3)] 2 83
(Mike Murphy) *hld up in last pair: stdy prog gng easily fr 2f out: squeezed through ins fnl f to ld last 75yds: decisively* **9/2**[1]

5512 **2** ¾ **Beaumont's Party (IRE)**[28] 5050 3-8-13 **74** PatDobbs 3 82
(R Hannon) *trckd ldrs: shkn up over 2f out: prog over 1f out: rdn to ld ins fnl f: hdd and outpcd last 75yds* **6/1**[2]

2021 **3** *nk* **Honest Broker (IRE)**[18] 5360 3-9-0 **75** GregFairley 10 83
(M Johnston) *settled midfield: pushed along over 3f out: prog and drvn over 1f out: chal ins fnl f: stdy on same pce* **13/2**[3]

-020 **4** 2 **Qalahari (IRE)**[13] 5529 4-9-10 **80** TadhgO'Shea 7 84
(D J Coakley) *hld up towards rr: effrt on outer over 2f out: looked to be hanging and nt qckn over 1f out: styd on ins fnl f* **11/1**

-143 **5** 2 ¼ **Rockabilly Rebel**[56] 4104 3-8-10 **71** ChrisCatlin 4 69
(B W Hills) *trckd ldr: chal and upsides 2f out: wknd ins fnl f* **9/1**

1420 **6** ¾ **Dr Wintringham (IRE)**[26] 5114 4-9-8 **78** ShaneKelly 8 75
(Karen George) *s.i.s: hld up in last pair: prog on inner over 2f out: tried to squeeze through against rail to mount chal over 1f out: sn outpcd* **20/1**

4060 **7** ½ **Halsion Chancer**[21] 5264 6-8-10 **71** KierenFox(5) 6 67
(J R Best) *t.k.h: trckd ldrs: drvn and prog to ld wl over 1f out: hdd & wknd ins fnl f* **15/2**

0402 **8** *hd* **Exit Smiling**[11] 5605 8-9-9 **79** MickyFenton 9 74
(P T Midgley) *trckd ldrs: pushed along whn n.m.r over 2f out: sn lost pl and btn* **8/1**

6-00 **9** ½ **Willow Dancer (IRE)**[118] 2124 6-9-8 **78** (p) AdamKirby 14 72
(W R Swinburn) *trckd ldng pair: effrt against rail to chal and upsides 2f out: nt qckn over 1f out: wknd ins fnl f* **10/1**

0245 **10** ¾ **Habshan (USA)**[32] 4905 10-9-10 **80** AlanMunro 12 73
(C F Wall) *t.k.h: hld up in last trio: shkn up and no prog over 2f out* **16/1**

1000 **11** 4 ½ **Kilburn**[2] 5866 6-9-4 **74** (p) NeilCallan 13 56
(A J Lidderdale) *led to wl over 1f out: wknd qckly* **25/1**

1-00 **12** 7 **Burma Rock (IRE)**[20] 5311 4-9-6 **76** J-PGuillambert 11 42
(L M Cumani) *plld hrd early: hld up towards rr: rdn and no prog over 2f out: wknd qckly* **20/1**

1m 44.15s (0.85) **Going Correction** +0.075s/f (Good)
WFA 3 from 4yo+ 5lb **12** Ran SP% **115.4**
Speed ratings (Par 105): **98,97,96,94,92 91,91,91,90,90 85,78**
toteswingers:1&2 £8.20, 2&3 £5.40, 1&3 £6.40 CSF £28.51 CT £177.08 TOTE £4.20: £1.50, £1.70, £1.70; EX 32.80 Place 6: £546.58 Place 5: £403.48.
Owner Ronald Bright **Bred** Mervyn Stewkesbury **Trained** Westoning, Beds

T/Plt: £939.20 to a £1 stake. Pool of £59,702.12 - 46.40 winning tickets. T/Qpdt: £30.60 to a £1 stake. Pool of £5,575.44 - 134.60 winning tickets. JN

5763 WOLVERHAMPTON (A.W) (L-H)

Friday, September 10

OFFICIAL GOING: Standard
Wind: Light behind Weather: Light rain

5920 PLAY VEGAS GAMES AT WILLIAMHILLVEGAS.COM H'CAP 5f 216y(P)
5:30 (5:30) (Class 5) (0-70,70) 3-Y-O+ **£2,729** (£806; £403) **Stalls** Low

Form RPR

4321 **1** **Fantasy Fighter (IRE)**[6] 5764 5-9-0 **68** 6ex AdamBeschizza(5) 7 83
(J J Quinn) *hld up in tch: rdn to ld ins fnl f: r.o* **3/1**[1]

2441 **2** *nk* **Cavitie**[21] 5267 4-8-10 **59** JamesDoyle 3 73
(Andrew Reid) *chsd ldrs: led over 1f out: rdn and hdd ins fnl f: r.o* **3/1**[1]

6231 **3** 3 ½ **Forever's Girl**[13] 5535 4-9-3 **66** JimmyQuinn 4 69
(G R Oldroyd) *prom: rdn over 1f out: edgd lft and no ex ins fnl f* **11/2**[2]

2240 **4** ¾ **Albero Di Giuda (IRE)**[32] 4895 5-8-3 **57** (bt) SophieDoyle(5) 1 58
(F Sheridan) *chsd ldrs: rdn and swtchd lft over 1f out: no ex ins fnl f* **10/1**

6500 **5** *nk* **Charles Parnell (IRE)**[51] 4244 7-8-9 **65** NoraLooby(7) 8 65+
(S P Griffiths) *s.i.s: hld up: r.o ins fnl f: nrst fin* **40/1**

0200 **6** *shd* **Methaaly (IRE)**[14] 5500 7-9-0 **70** (be) JosephYoung(7) 9 69
(M Mullineaux) *hld up: r.o ins fnl f: nvr nrr* **22/1**

6000 **7** *nk* **Argentine (IRE)**[7] 5734 6-9-2 **70** MichaelO'Connell(5) 10 68
(J A McShane) *hld up: hdwy whn hmpd over 1f out: r.o ins fnl f: nvr able to chal* **33/1**

1-26 **8** 3 ½ **Diamond Blade**[139] 1524 4-9-3 **66** (p) DuranFentiman 11 53
(T D Easterby) *led: rdn and hdd over 1f out: wknd ins fnl f* **17/2**

1000 **9** 1 **Athaakeel (IRE)**[8] 5698 4-9-4 **67** LukeMorris 2 51+
(R A Harris) *s.s: hdwy and nt clr run over 1f out: sn lost pl: swtchd rt ins fnl f: n.d* **33/1**

0000 **10** 1 **Ghost Dancer**[1] 5875 6-8-5 **57** (p) MartinLane(3) 6 38
(J M Bradley) *mid-div: hdwy over 1f out: rdn and wknd ins fnl f* **40/1**

5044 **11** ½ **Nacho Libre**[27] 5067 5-8-12 **64** (b) JamesSullivan(3) 13 43
(M W Easterby) *w ldr: rdn and ev ch over 2f out: wknd fnl f* **8/1**[3]

1005 **12** 3 ¼ **Loyal Royal (IRE)**[6] 5764 7-9-1 **64** (bt) RichardHughes 12 33
(J M Bradley) *hld up: rdn over 2f out: sn wknd* **20/1**

1m 14.55s (-0.45) **Going Correction** +0.025s/f (Slow) **12** Ran SP% **116.0**
Speed ratings (Par 103): **104,103,98,97,97 97,97,92,91,89 89,84**
toteswingers:1&2 £1.60, 2&3 £4.80, 1&3 £4.50 CSF £9.89 CT £45.38 TOTE £3.00: £1.10, £1.10, £3.50; EX 10.70.
Owner The Fantasy Fellowship F **Bred** T C Clarke **Trained** Settrington, N Yorks
■ Stewards' Enquiry : Sophie Doyle three-day ban: careless riding (Sep 24, 26, 27)

FOCUS
An ordinary handicap in which the gallop was sound but those held up could never get competitive. The two market leaders, who pulled clear, raced centre to far side in the closing stages.

5921 FREE BETTING WITH FREEBETTING.CO.UK CLAIMING STKS 5f 216y(P)
6:00 (6:03) (Class 5) 2-Y-O **£2,729** (£806; £403) **Stalls** Low

Form RPR

2100 **1** **Bilko Pak (IRE)**[24] 5187 2-9-0 85 RichardHughes 11 81+
(R Hannon) *hld up: hdwy over 1f out: rdn to ld ins fnl f: edgd rt: r.o* **9/4**[2]

4214 **2** 1 ¼ **Hortensia (IRE)**[10] 5639 2-8-8 82 (v) SamHitchcott 4 72+
(M R Channon) *chsd ldrs: swtchd lft over 1f out: sn rdn and ev ch: styd on same pce towards fin* **13/8**[1]

1342 **3** 1 ½ **My Lord**[46] 4436 2-8-5 65 SophieDoyle(5) 12 69
(W G M Turner) *sn chsng ldr: rdn to ld over 1f out: hdd and unable qck ins fnl f* **16/1**

3310 **4** 1 **Scommettitrice (IRE)**[29] 5000 2-8-5 73 LukeMorris 5 61
(R A Harris) *hld up in tch: rdn over 1f out: styd on* **11/1**

3654 **5** 2 **Silly Billy (IRE)**[18] 5365 2-8-9 65 JamesDoyle 9 59
(S Kirk) *led 1f: chsd ldrs: rdn over 1f out: hung lft and no ex ins fnl f* **16/1**

5430 **6** 2 ¼ **Bachelor Knight (IRE)**[11] 5602 2-8-7 64 RoystonFfrench 13 50
(R A Fahey) *hld up: rdn over 2f out: nvr trbld ldrs* **25/1**

4144 **7** 1 **Second Encore**[7] 5725 2-7-12 74 RyanPowell(7) 2 45
(J S Moore) *led 5f out: rdn and hdd over 1f out: wknd ins fnl f* **7/1**[3]

8 2 **Mijanou** 2-7-13 0 DeclanCannon(5) 3 38
(A J McCabe) *s.i.s: rdn and hung lft over 1f out: n.d* **66/1**

9 ¾ **Winding Hill** 2-8-4 0 JamesSullivan(3) 6 42+
(M W Easterby) *s.i.s: outpcd: sme late hdwy* **66/1**

10 **10** *hd* **Mayfair Princess**[28] 5036 2-8-1 72 ow2 JohnFahy(5) 7 37
(P S McEntee) *prom: rdn 1/2-way: wknd over 1f out* **33/1**

065 **11** ½ **The Best Mode (IRE)**[38] 4678 2-8-8 60 CathyGannon 10 38
(P D Evans) *hld up: rdn 1/2-way: wknd over 2f out* **66/1**

4636 **12** 4 **Press Release**[53] 4195 2-8-8 65 (t) RichardKingscote 1 26
(Tom Dascombe) *s.i.s: hdwy 5f out: rdn and wknd over 1f out* **33/1**

13 10 **Emperorsnewclothes (IRE)** 2-8-7 0 DaraghO'Donohoe 8 —
(George Baker) *s.i.s: outpcd* **50/1**

1m 15.34s (0.34) **Going Correction** +0.025s/f (Slow) **13** Ran SP% **117.6**
Speed ratings (Par 95): **98,96,94,93,90 87,86,83,82,82 81,76,62**
toteswingers:1&2 £1.60, 2&3 £8.00, 1&3 £10.20 CSF £5.79 TOTE £3.70: £1.10, £1.10, £6.00; EX 6.20.
Owner Middleham Park Racing XLIII **Bred** Stuart Weld **Trained** East Everleigh, Wilts

FOCUS
A wide range of ability on show but a race in which the two highest-rated horses and market leaders came to the fore in the closing stages. The gallop was sound and the winner raced just off the inside rail.

NOTEBOOK
Bilko Pak(IRE) looked to have a fine chance at the weights dropped markedly in grade and he didn't have to better his early season form to maintain his unbeaten record on Polytrack, despite being off the bridle at a fairly early stage. Life will be tougher back in nurseries from his current 85 mark but he should stay 7f and can win again in this grade. (op 10-3 tchd 7-2 and 2-1)
Hortensia(IRE), who looks flattered by her proximity at Ripon on her previous start, had a good chance at the weights and ran creditably to chase home her main market rival, despite looking less than straightforward under pressure. Life will be tougher in nurseries but she's capable of winning in this grade. (op 2-1 tchd 5-2 after 9-4 in places)
My Lord was well placed throughout and ran creditably on this all-weather debut against a couple of rivals who would have been conceding him a fair amount of weight in a handicap. There will be easier opportunities than this one in this grade and he may be capable of winning an ordinary handicap unless the handicapper overreacts. Official explanation: jockey said that the gelding hung right-handed (op 12-1 tchd 20-1)
Scommettitrice(IRE), who had a good chance strictly on official ratings, had the run of the race and wasn't disgraced on this all-weather debut and first run over 6f. She should be able to pick up a low-grade event on artificial surfaces at some point. (tchd 10-1 and 14-1)
Silly Billy(IRE) didn't have an obvious chance at the weights and was far from disgraced back over this more suitable trip. The return to ordinary handicaps will be the way forward with him but consistency hasn't been his strongest suit. (op 12-1)
Second Encore had a good chance at the weights but dropped out fairly tamely once taken on for the lead back over this longer trip. She hasn't had too many chances, though, and is probably worth another chance in a lesser event. (op 6-1 tchd 9-2)

5922 £150 NEW CASINO BONUS AT WILLIAMHILL.COM H'CAP 1m 5f 194y(P)
6:30 (6:30) (Class 4) (0-85,87) 3-Y-O+ **£4,533** (£1,348; £674; £336) **Stalls** Low

Form RPR

4110 **1** **Fantino**[28] 5035 4-8-13 **70** JimmyQuinn 3 79
(J Mackie) *a.p: chsd ldr 4f out: led over 2f out: rdn out* **22/1**

2600 **2** 2 **Quinsman**[47] 4400 4-9-5 **76** LukeMorris 7 82
(J S Moore) *hld up: hdwy over 3f out: rdn and edgd lft over 1f out: styd on to go 2nd nr fin: nt rch wnr* **33/1**

4124 **3** *nk* **Reality Show (IRE)**[41] 4571 3-9-1 **83** RoystonFfrench 2 89
(Mahmood Al Zarooni) *hld up: hdwy over 3f out: chsd wnr over 2f out: sn rdn: styd on: lost 2nd nr fin* **15/2**[3]

-311 **4** ½ **Baralaka**[8] 5679 3-9-5 **87** 6ex SebSanders 6 92
(Sir Mark Prescott) *hld up: hdwy over 2f out: rdn and edgd lft over 1f out: styd on u.p: nt rch ldrs* **4/6**[1]

0144 **5** 15 **Calculating (IRE)**[15] 5443 6-9-1 **77** LeeNewnes(5) 4 61
(M D I Usher) *hld up: hdwy 6f out: rdn over 4f out: wknd over 3f out* **28/1**

2246 **6** 3 **Cloudy City (USA)**[19] 5333 3-8-4 **72** (b) HayleyTurner 9 52
(M Johnston) *chsd ldr tl led over 5f out: rdn and hdd over 2f out: sn wknd* **7/1**[2]

550- **7** 9 **Hendersyde (USA)**[349] 6273 5-9-9 **85** JohnFahy(5) 1 53
(W R Swinburn) *chsd ldrs tl rdn and wknd over 2f out* **10/1**

0232 **8** 36 **Akbabend**[27] 5070 4-9-11 **82** (b) JoeFanning 8 —
(M Johnston) *sn led: hdd & wknd over 5f out: t.o* **17/2**

3m 3.28s (-2.72) **Going Correction** +0.025s/f (Slow)
WFA 3 from 4yo+ 11lb **8** Ran SP% **114.6**
Speed ratings (Par 105): **108,106,106,106,97 96,90,70**
toteswingers:1&2 £48.70, 2&3 £14.90, 1&3 £13.20 CSF £528.75 CT £5821.62 TOTE £37.70: £5.20, £11.40, £1.70; EX 643.60.
Owner Norman A Blyth **Bred** Norman A Blyth **Trained** Church Broughton , Derbys

FOCUS
The best quality race on the card. The gallop was an ordinary one and the winner raced centre to far side in the straight. The first four finished clear.

5923 LATE NIGHT LIVE CASINO AT WILLIAMHILL.COM H'CAP 1m 4f 50y(P)
7:00 (7:00) (Class 6) (0-55,55) 3-Y-O **£1,774** (£523; £262) **Stalls** Low

Form RPR

4643 **1** **Straversjoy**[12] 5550 3-8-12 **51** GrahamGibbons 3 62
(R Hollinshead) *hld up: hdwy 1/2-way: rdn to ld ins fnl f: r.o wl* **9/1**

1030 **2** 2 ½ **Firehawk**[42] 4545 3-9-0 **53** CathyGannon 4 60
(P D Evans) *chsd ldrs: rdn over 1f out: styd on* **20/1**

-235 **3** ¾ **Consult**[53] 4200 3-8-12 **51** (b[1]) SebSanders 9 57
(Sir Mark Prescott) *s.i.s: hld up: plld hrd: hdwy and hung lft over 3f out: rdn and hmpd over 2f out: led 1f out: sn hung lft and hdd: no ex* **3/1**[1]

3032 **4** 2 ½ **Il Portico**[13] 5534 3-9-1 **54** SamHitchcott 5 56
(M R Channon) *chsd ldrs: led 3f out: rdn and hdd 1f out: no ex* **5/1**[3]

2442 **5** 3 ¼ **Aegean Destiny**[27] 5093 3-8-9 **53** DeclanCannon(5) 7 50
(J Mackie) *hld up: hdwy 6f out: swtchd rt over 2f out: sn rdn: hung lft and wknd ins fnl f* **5/1**[3]

0000 **6** 1 ¾ **Asterales**[55] 4134 3-9-2 **55** JimmyQuinn 6 49
(W J Musson) *s.i.s: hld up: nt clr run and swtchd rt over 1f out: styd on: nt rch ldrs* **10/1**

0103 **7** 1 ½ **Sternian**[37] 4718 3-8-11 **55** (b) AdamBeschizza(5) 11 46
(M E Rimmer) *hld up: hdwy u.p and hung lft over 1f out: wknd ins fnl f* **40/1**

5122 **8** 1 ¾ **Always Dixie (IRE)**[9] 5653 3-8-12 **51** JoeFanning 12 40
(M Johnston) *chsd ldr tl led over 3f out: sn hdd: wknd ins fnl f* **7/2**[2]

0564 **9** 7 **Tom Wade (IRE)**[10] 5636 3-8-13 **55** (p) GaryBartley(3) 8 32
(John A Harris) *led over 3f out: wknd over 2f out* **40/1**

0001 **10** 2 ½ **Royal Holiday (IRE)**[10] 5648 3-8-10 **54** TobyAtkinson(5) 10 27
(B Ellison) *hld up: hdwy 6f out: hmpd over 3f out: sn rdn and wknd* **14/1**

0036 **11** *17* **Blue Zealot (IRE)**[16] 5414 3-9-0 **53** ...... HayleyTurner 2 —
(M L W Bell) *prom: lost pl 6f out: wknd 3f out: t.o* **16/1**
4400 **12** *80* **Mister Pleau (USA)**[113] 2248 3-9-1 **54** ...... LukeMorris 1 —
(J R Best) *chsd ldrs: rdn over 4f out: wknd 3f out: t.o* **40/1**
2m 42.02s (0.92) **Going Correction** +0.025s/f (Slow) 12 Ran SP% **124.3**
Speed ratings (Par 99): **97,95,94,93,91 89,88,87,83,81 70,16**
toteswingers:1&2 £21.20, 2&3 £11.90, 1&3 £7.50 CSF £183.47 CT £672.68 TOTE £16.20: £8.80, £13.80, £1.50; EX 198.30.
Owner E Bennion **Bred** Eric Bennion **Trained** Upper Longdon, Staffs
FOCUS
A low-grade handicap run at an ordinary gallop. The winner came down the centre in the straight.
Tom Wade(IRE) Official explanation: jockey said that the gelding hung right-handed

5924 LATE NIGHT LIVE CASINO AT WILLIAMHILL.COM MEDIAN AUCTION MAIDEN STKS 1m 141y(P)
7:30 (7:33) (Class 5) 2-Y-O **£2,729** (£806; £403) **Stalls** Low

Form RPR
2 **1** **Makeynn**[24] 5170 2-9-3 0 ...... TedDurcan 11 82+
(Saeed Bin Suroor) *trckd ldrs: led 2f out: shkn up and c clr ins fnl f: readily* **1/4**[1]
0 **2** *4 ½* **Retreat Content (IRE)**[56] 4110 2-9-3 0 ...... FergusSweeney 9 67
(J A Osborne) *prom: chsd ldr over 6f out: led over 3f out: rdn and hdd 2f out: no ex fnl f* **25/1**
060 **3** *1 ¼* **High Kickin**[97] 2740 2-8-7 50 ......(p) DeclanCannon(5) 2 59
(A J McCabe) *hld up: hdwy 2f out: hung lft and r.o ins fnl f: nt trble ldrs* **33/1**
56 **4** *½* **Itzakindamagic (IRE)**[23] 5196 2-8-12 0 ...... JoeFanning 6 58
(M Johnston) *trckd ldrs: rdn over 1f out: styd on* **8/1**[2]
5 *nk* **Arctic Myth (USA)** 2-9-3 0 ...... JamesDoyle 5 62
(B W Duke) *drvn along early to chse ldrs: rdn and edgd lft over 1f out: no ex ins fnl f* **20/1**
0 **6** *7* **All In A Paddy**[25] 5156 2-9-3 0 ...... GrahamGibbons 13 48
(E S McMahon) *hld up: rdn over 1f out: nvr nrr* **20/1**
06 **7** *1* **Droxford (USA)**[16] 5413 2-8-12 0 ...... SophieDoyle(5) 8 46
(J A Osborne) *led over 5f: rdn and wknd over 1f out* **50/1**
02 **8** *½* **Lindo Erro**[21] 5269 2-8-12 0 ...... SebSanders 7 39
(J Mackie) *hld up in tch: rdn over 2f out: wknd ins fnl f* **10/1**[3]
9 *¾* **Blade** 2-9-3 0 ...... TomMcLaughlin 4 43
(W M Brisbourne) *dwlt: a in rr: wknd over 2f out* **28/1**
0 **10** *1 ¼* **One Of Twins**[14] 5498 2-9-0 0 ...... JamesSullivan(3) 12 40
(M W Easterby) *hld up: a in rr: wknd over 2f out* **66/1**
1m 51.58s (1.08) **Going Correction** +0.025s/f (Slow) 10 Ran SP% **123.4**
Speed ratings (Par 95): **96,92,90,90,90 83,83,82,81,80**
toteswingers:1&2 £4.10, 2&3 £21.40, 1&3 £7.90 CSF £15.66 TOTE £1.20: £1.02, £5.50, £9.60; EX 12.70.
Owner Godolphin **Bred** Darley **Trained** Newmarket, Suffolk
FOCUS
A very one-sided maiden. The gallop was no more than fair and the winner came down the centre in the straight.
NOTEBOOK
Makeynn, who showed fair form when clear of a subsequent winner at Brighton on his debut, didn't have to improve to beat inferior rivals with a good deal in hand over this longer trip. While this told us nothing new about him he should be able to make his mark in ordinary handicap company from a mark likely to be somewhere in the mid-to-high 70s. (op 3-10)
Retreat Content(IRE) didn't show much behind subsequent French Group 1 winner Dream Ahead on his debut over 6f on easy ground but had the run of the race and fared a good deal better over this longer trip on this first run on Polytrack. Modest handicaps will see him in his best light in due course.
High Kickin, from a yard in good form, wasn't disgraced over this longer trip on this all-weather debut in the first-time cheekpieces. She too will be suited by the switch into low-grade nurseries.
Itzakindamagic(IRE) is now qualified for a mark and who is in very good hands. Her dam ran one of her better races over 2m and a much stiffer test of stamina should suit in due course. (op 9-1)
Arctic Myth(USA) wasn't totally disgraced on this debut but, while he can be expected to improve for this run, he is likely to remain vulnerable in this type of event. (op 18-1)

5925 THE BLACK COUNTRY'S ONLY RACECOURSE MAIDEN STKS 1m 141y(P)
8:00 (8:01) (Class 5) 3-Y-O+ **£2,456** (£725; £362) **Stalls** Low

Form RPR
3 **1** **Fun Affair (USA)**[17] 5395 3-8-10 0 ...... WilliamBuick 12 85+
(J H M Gosden) *led: hdd 6f out: chsd ldr: rdn to ld and hung lft over 1f out: styd on wl* **15/8**[1]
204 **2** *2 ¼* **Captivator**[37] 4697 3-8-10 71 ...... HayleyTurner 1 77
(J R Fanshawe) *trckd ldrs: rdn to chse wnr fnl f: styd on same pce* **15/8**[1]
0604 **3** *3 ¼* **Music Maestro (IRE)**[32] 4910 3-9-1 68 ...... RobertWinston 9 75
(B W Hills) *chsd ldr tl led 6f out: rdn and hdd over 1f out: no ex ins fnl f* **7/1**[3]
0624 **4** *3 ¼* **Caracal**[41] 4585 3-9-1 68 ...... JimmyQuinn 2 67
(Gordon Elliott, Ire) *chsd ldrs: rdn over 2f out: wknd over 1f out* **5/1**[2]
55 **5** *9* **Alioonagh (USA)**[17] 5395 3-8-10 0 ...... J-PGuillambert 8 41
(N P Littmoden) *s.i.s: hld up: styd on appr fnl f: nvr nr to chal* **8/1**
00 **6** *4 ½* **Alnaseem (USA)**[79] 3333 3-8-3 0 ...... DavidSimmonson(7) 4 31
(M W Easterby) *prom: rdn over 2f out: wknd sn after* **100/1**
7 *3 ¼* **Feuergott (GER)**[82] 4-9-7 0 ...... SaleemGolam 3 29
(Ian Williams) *mid-div: rdn over 3f out: sn wknd* **66/1**
0-0 **8** *½* **Blues Jazz**[4] 5816 4-9-2 0 ...... MichaelO'Connell(5) 10 27
(J A McShane) *hld up: a in rr: wknd over 3f out* **100/1**
0 **9** *2 ¾* **Strong Aim**[20] 5303 3-8-7 0 ...... JamesSullivan(3) 11 16
(M W Easterby) *hld up: a in rr: wknd over 3f out* **100/1**
00- **10** *hd* **Ring Of Fire**[268] 7764 3-9-1 0 ...... SamHitchcott 5 21
(J L Spearing) *s.i.s: sn mid-div: rdn and wknd over 3f out* **100/1**
00 **11** *½* **Opera Cat (USA)**[14] 5487 3-9-1 0 ...... JoeFanning 6 19
(M Johnston) *trckd ldrs: racd keenly: rdn over 3f out: wknd over 2f out* **33/1**
00 **12** *9* **Shut Up Shapiro (IRE)**[102] 2603 3-9-1 0 ...... DaraghO'Donohoe 7 —
(George Baker) *hld up: drvn along 1/2-way: sn wknd: t.o* **100/1**
1m 50.42s (-0.08) **Going Correction** +0.025s/f (Slow)
WFA 3 from 4yo 6lb 12 Ran SP% **119.2**
Speed ratings (Par 103): **101,99,96,93,85 81,78,77,75,75 74,66**
toteswingers:1&2 £1.90, 2&3 £3.20, 1&3 £6.50 CSF £5.05 TOTE £4.60: £1.10, £1.10, £3.90; EX 6.00.
Owner H R H Princess Haya Of Jordan **Bred** Hermitage Farm LLC **Trained** Newmarket, Suffolk
FOCUS
No more than a fair maiden but the winner, who came down the centre, is a progressive type who won with something in hand. The gallop was an ordinary one.
Strong Aim Official explanation: jockey said that the filly hung right-handed

5926 PLAY ROULETTE AT WILLIAMHILL.COM H'CAP (DIV I) 7f 32y(P)
8:30 (8:31) (Class 6) (0-55,58) 3-Y-O+ **£1,433** (£423; £211) **Stalls** High

Form RPR
0161 **1** **Emiratesdotcom**[11] 5586 4-9-8 **58** 6ex ...... LiamKeniry 6 67
(J M Bradley) *hld up: hdwy 2f out: rdn to ld ins fnl f: jst hld on* **11/2**[2]
006 **2** *nk* **Know No Fear**[14] 5471 5-9-5 **55** ......(p) JamesDoyle 7 63
(A J Lidderdale) *hld up: hdwy over 1f out: hung lft and r.o wl ins fnl f: jst failed* **7/1**[3]
0205 **3** *1* **Gilderoy**[9] 5650 3-8-7 **50** ...... AshleyHamblett(3) 4 53
(D J S Ffrench Davis) *chsd ldrs: rdn over 2f out: r.o* **14/1**
0402 **4** *½* **Ayam Zainah**[7] 5730 3-8-9 **49** ......(v) SamHitchcott 1 51
(M R Channon) *led: rdn and hung lft over 1f out: hdd and unable qck ins fnl f* **9/4**[1]
0320 **5** *nk* **Rigid**[7] 5730 3-8-11 **51** ...... SebSanders 10 52
(A W Carroll) *prom: jnd ldr 6f out: rdn and ev ch fr over 1f out: sn hung lft: led briefly ins fnl f: no ex towards fin* **8/1**
0005 **6** *3* **Springwell Giant (IRE)**[59] 3972 3-8-2 **47** ...... DeclanCannon(5) 9 40
(A J McCabe) *chsd ldrs: rdn 1/2-way: styd on same pce appr fnl f* **25/1**
6420 **7** *2 ¾* **Guildenstern (IRE)**[46] 4428 8-9-4 **54** ...... JimmyQuinn 8 42
(P Howling) *hld up: shkn up over 2f out: nvr nr to chal* **8/1**
4453 **8** *1 ½* **Coolella (IRE)**[19] 5337 3-8-12 **52** ...... LukeMorris 2 34
(J R Weymes) *chsd ldrs: rdn over 2f out: hung lft and wknd ins fnl f* **11/2**[2]
0000 **9** *2 ¾* **Royal Patriot (IRE)**[16] 5424 3-8-9 **52** ...... JamesSullivan(3) 12 26
(Paul Green) *hld up: rdn over 2f out: sn wknd* **40/1**
-000 **10** *nse* **Joyeaux**[14] 5485 8-9-2 **52** ...... DuranFentiman 5 28
(Ollie Pears) *hld up: a in rr: wknd over 2f out* **25/1**
0050 **11** *nk* **Tanley**[13] 5535 5-9-0 **50** ...... RoystonFfrench 11 25
(I W McInnes) *s.i.s: hld up: a in rr: wknd over 2f out* **33/1**
0000 **12** *3* **Stonecrabstomorrow (IRE)**[17] 5388 7-8-12 **53** ......(p) MarkCoumbe(5) 3 20
(John A Harris) *mid-div: rdn 1/2-way: wknd over 2f out* **33/1**
1m 30.0s (0.40) **Going Correction** +0.025s/f (Slow)
WFA 3 from 4yo+ 4lb 12 Ran SP% **118.9**
Speed ratings (Par 101): **98,97,96,95,95 92,89,87,84,84 83,80**
toteswingers:1&2 £8.80, 2&3 £38.30, 1&3 £30.60 CSF £41.31 CT £518.76 TOTE £6.20: £1.60, £4.00, £7.20; EX 64.80.
Owner Ms S Howell **Bred** Newsells Park Stud Limited **Trained** Sedbury, Gloucs
FOCUS
Division one of a moderate handicap. The gallop was a reasonable one and the winner raced against the far rail in the straight.

5927 PLAY ROULETTE AT WILLIAMHILL.COM H'CAP (DIV II) 7f 32y(P)
9:00 (9:00) (Class 6) (0-55,55) 3-Y-O+ **£1,433** (£423; £211) **Stalls** High

Form RPR
6512 **1** **Pipers Piping (IRE)**[7] 5711 4-9-1 **54** ......(p) MichaelStainton(3) 5 66
(P Howling) *hld up in tch: led and hung lft ins fnl f: r.o* **7/4**[1]
6000 **2** *½* **Dancing Welcome**[8] 5704 4-9-3 **53** ......(b) LiamKeniry 11 64
(J M Bradley) *hld up: hdwy over 1f out: hung lft and r.o wl ins fnl f: nt rch wnr* **9/1**
0/0- **3** *3 ½* **Thistimesforgood (IRE)**[16] 5430 7-9-2 **52** ......(t) JimmyQuinn 4 53
(Gordon Elliott, Ire) *led: rdn over 1f out: hdd and no ex ins fnl f* **10/3**[2]
003 **4** *nk* **Force To Spend**[50] 4281 3-8-10 **50** ...... StevieDonohoe 8 48
(N P Littmoden) *hld up in tch: rdn over 1f out: no ex ins fnl f* **16/1**
0-66 **5** *1 ½* **Norcroft**[41] 4586 8-8-12 **48** ......(p) JamesDoyle 6 44
(Mrs C A Dunnett) *hld up: hdwy and nt clr run over 1f out: r.o ins fnl f: nvr nrr* **33/1**
0500 **6** *1* **It's A Mans World**[11] 5579 4-9-0 **55** ......(p) IanBrennan(5) 3 49
(Ian Williams) *sn pushed along in rr: hdwy u.p over 1f out: n.d* **16/1**
5304 **7** *¾* **Emperor's Well**[6] 5767 11-8-7 **46** ...... JamesSullivan(3) 1 38
(M W Easterby) *chsd ldrs: rdn 1/2-way: no ex ins fnl f* **8/1**[3]
0026 **8** *2 ¼* **Bring Sweets (IRE)**[18] 5361 3-8-4 **49** ......(p) TobyAtkinson(5) 2 33
(B Ellison) *hld up: rdn over 1f out: nvr trbld ldrs* **10/1**
5500 **9** *½* **Come On Buckers (IRE)**[80] 3292 4-8-13 **49** ......(b) EddieCreighton 10 33
(E J Creighton) *chsd ldrs: rdn 2f out: wknd ins fnl f* **50/1**
0536 **10** *½* **Charlietoo**[11] 5579 4-8-4 **47** ......(b[1]) RyanClark(7) 9 30
(E G Bevan) *chsd ldrs: rdn and ev ch over 2f out: hung lft over 1f out: wknd ins fnl f* **16/1**
0000 **11** *7* **Royal Applord**[29] 4985 5-9-0 **50** ......(b[1]) J-PGuillambert 7 14
(N Tinkler) *chsd ldr: rdn and ev ch over 2f out: hung lft over 1f out: wknd ins fnl f* **20/1**
1m 29.92s (0.32) **Going Correction** +0.025s/f (Slow)
WFA 3 from 4yo+ 4lb 11 Ran SP% **117.0**
Speed ratings (Par 101): **99,98,94,94,92 91,90,87,87,86 78**
toteswingers:1&2 £3.80, 2&3:£8.50, 1&3 £2.50 CSF £18.01 CT £50.56 TOTE £2.90: £1.10, £4.50, £1.50; EX 21.40 Place 6: £33.76 Place 5: £26.76 .
Owner C N Wright **Bred** Drumhass Stud **Trained** Newmarket, Suffolk
FOCUS
Another moderate handicap in which the gallop was reasonable. The winner edged from the centre towards the far side in the closing stages.
T/Plt: £90.10 to a £1 strike. Pool of £68,748.28 - 556.55 winning tickets. T/Qpdt: £43.40 to a £1 stake. Pool of £8,206.60 - 139.70 winning tickets. CR

5900 CHESTER (L-H)
Saturday, September 11

OFFICIAL GOING: Soft (good to soft in places; 6.1)
Rail out fr 6f to top of str with false rail (7yds out) at top of str increasing 5 and 5.5f races by 20yds, 7-10.5f by 27yds, 12f by 42yds, 2m by 50yds.
Wind: Breezy, across. Weather: Fine

5936 POMMERY CHAMPAGNE 1539 MAIDEN STKS 7f 2y
2:35 (2:35) (Class 4) 2-Y-O **£5,116** (£1,522; £760; £379) **Stalls** Low

Form RPR
53 **1** **Ibsaar**[12] 5594 2-9-3 0 ...... LiamJones 1 76
(W J Haggas) *led: rdn along over 2f out: hdd narrowly 1f out: continued to press ldr: r.o to regain ld towards fin* **7/2**[2]
25 **2** *shd* **Edmaaj (IRE)**[22] 5277 2-9-3 0 ...... MichaelHills 6 76
(B W Hills) *a.p: moved upsides 3f out: rdn to nose into ld 1f out: a hrd pressed: hdd towards fin* **5/6**[1]
5 **3** *5* **Marked Card (IRE)**[85] 3169 2-9-3 0 ...... RichardMullen 3 65+
(P W Chapple-Hyam) *dwlt: hld up: checked whn nt clr run 2f out: sn u.p: kpt on to take mod 3rd wl ins fnl f: nt trble front pair* **8/1**

20 **4** *1 ¾* **Ventura Sands (IRE)**[15] 5498 2-9-3 0 .... TomEaves 2 59+
(R A Fahey) *dwlt: racd keenly: trckd ldrs: pushed along 2f out: outpcd by front pair and hung rt over 1f out: lost 3rd and wl btn wl ins fnl f* **9/2**[3]

63 **5** *9* **Babich Bay (IRE)**[19] 5372 2-9-3 0 .... CathyGannon 7 36
(F J Brennan) *hld up: pushed along 4f out: outpcd over 2f out: toiling and bhd after* **20/1**

1m 36.65s (10.15) **Going Correction** +1.025s/f (Soft) 5 Ran SP% **110.8**
Speed ratings (Par 97): **83,82,77,75,64**
CSF £6.96 TOTE £4.50: £2.00, £1.10; EX 4.80.
Owner Hamdan Al Maktoum **Bred** Newsells Park Stud Limited **Trained** Newmarket, Suffolk

FOCUS
Probably form to view in a positive light so far as the leading pair are concerned, both having shaped with promise previously, and they pulled a long way clear. The form makes sense.

NOTEBOOK
Ibsaar has improved with each start and is very much the type to keep on progressing for a while yet. He carries his head a shade high but there's nothing wrong with his attitude, pulling out more after the runner-up briefly looked likely to take his measure early in the straight. He's raced only on good going or softer so far. (tchd 4-1 in a place)
Edmaaj(IRE) found the winner pulling out more after arguably going better than him entering the straight but this represents another sound effort from this son of Intikhab, who looks sure to go one better before much longer. He's seemingly pretty versatile regards ground, too, having raced on a firmer surface before this. (tchd 10-11 and evens in places)
Marked Card(IRE), who'd been given a break after finishing well beaten on his debut in June, was no match for the leading pair but showed clear ability by the finish and appeals as the type to progress with racing, one more run now needed to get him a handicap mark. (op 15-2)
Ventura Sands(IRE) is one it's too early to be writing off, but he has been disappointing on both starts since his debut second, the fact that effort came on an easy surface suggesting the ground can't be used as an excuse. (op 11-2)
Babich Bay(IRE)'s Windsor third doesn't amount to a great deal and he was the first beaten. He is at least now eligible for handicaps. (op 22-1 tchd 25-1)

5937 EVE H'CAP — 7f 122y
3:05 (3:05) (Class 3) (0-90,87) 3-Y-O+ **£7,771** (£2,312; £1,155; £577) **Stalls** Low

Form RPR

1100 **1** **Glenridding**[15] 5499 6-8-13 **76** .... (p) PatCosgrave 5 89
(J G Given) *mde all: rdn abt 4l clr over 1f out: kpt on wl to the line* **16/1**

4241 **2** *2 ¼* **Sir George (IRE)**[28] 5098 5-9-6 **86** .... BarryMcHugh(3) 8 93
(Ollie Pears) *midfield: nt clr run briefly whn hdwy 2f out: styd on to take 2nd ins fnl f: nt rch wnr* **7/1**[3]

-020 **3** *1* **Captain Dancer (IRE)**[93] 2885 4-9-0 **77** .... MichaelHills 11 82+
(B W Hills) *hld up: rdn over 3f out: hdwy over 1f out: edgd lft whn styng on ins fnl f: gng on at fin* **15/2**

1111 **4** *1 ½* **One Scoop Or Two**[21] 5287 4-8-8 **74** .... RussKennemore(3) 3 75
(R Hollinshead) *trckd ldrs: rdn to take 2nd jst over 2f out: nt qckn wl over 1f out: styd on same pce but lost 2nd ins fnl f: no ex towards fin* **9/2**[2]

0433 **5** *½* **Suffolk Punch (IRE)**[23] 5236 3-9-0 **82** .... LiamKeniry 16 81
(A M Balding) *trckd ldrs: rdn over 2f out: wanted to lug lft fr over 1f out: styd on same pce* **8/1**

1-04 **6** *nk* **Rock 'N' Royal**[105] 2542 3-8-12 **80** .... CathyGannon 10 78
(R A Fahey) *midfield: hdwy over 2f out: rdn over 1f out: kpt on tl one pce cl home* **22/1**

0600 **7** *2* **Deadly Encounter (IRE)**[23] 5242 4-8-13 **76** .... (p) TomEaves 15 70
(R A Fahey) *towards rr: rdn along 4f out: kpt on u.p fr over 1f out: no imp on ldrs* **40/1**

0260 **8** *shd* **My Gacho (IRE)**[7] 5754 8-9-3 **80** .... (v) RobertWinston 4 74
(M Johnston) *towards rr: pushed along 4f out: rdn over 1f out: nvr able to get on terms* **10/1**

543 **9** *nk* **Internationaldebut (IRE)**[7] 5754 5-9-5 **85** .... PaulPickard(3) 1 78
(P T Midgley) *in tch: n.m.r and hmpd 5f out: sn lost pl: u.p over 1f out: no imp on ldrs* **4/1**[1]

4420 **10** *3* **Lucky Dan (IRE)**[21] 5290 4-9-0 **77** .... FrannyNorton 7 63
(Paul Green) *racd keenly: trckd ldrs: rdn and wknd wl over 1f out: eased whn btn ins fnl f* **11/1**

4260 **11** *1* **Turn Me On (IRE)**[42] 4603 7-8-12 **82** .... LukeStrong(7) 14 65
(T D Walford) *prom: rdn over 2f out: wknd over 1f out* **25/1**

0204 **12** *14* **Game Lad**[16] 5435 8-9-3 **80** .... (tp) DuranFentiman 9 28
(T D Easterby) *a bhd: u.p 3f out: nvr on terms: eased whn wl btn fnl f* **16/1**

1424 **13** *1 ¼* **Arabian Pearl (IRE)**[15] 5495 4-8-12 **75** .... (b) RichardMullen 6 20
(P W Chapple-Hyam) *midfield: rdn and wknd over 2f out: eased whn wl btn ins fnl f* **12/1**

1m 42.24s (8.44) **Going Correction** +1.025s/f (Soft)
WFA 3 from 4yo+ 5lb 13 Ran SP% **121.1**
Speed ratings (Par 107): **98,95,94,93,92 92,90,90,90,87 86,72,70**
Tote Swingers: 1&2 £19.80, 1&3 £9.80, 2&3 £8.30 CSF £123.24 CT £957.75 TOTE £21.10: £5.00, £2.50, £3.00; EX 157.60.
Owner Tremousser Partnership **Bred** Bolton Grange **Trained** Willoughton, Lincs

FOCUS
As is so often the case round here it paid to race handily, very few ever threatening a serious blow, the winner taking full advantage of a good draw.

NOTEBOOK
Glenridding's run style is ideally suited to this venue and a second C&D success rarely looked in doubt after he'd got out sharply to grab the lead. He'll be off a career-high mark after this bit will remain one to bear in mind when it looks as if he'll be able to dominate. Official explanation: trainers rep said regarding apparent improvement in form gelding missed the break on his last start and benefited today from making the running
Sir George(IRE) has enjoyed an excellent season and will continue to be of interest, better than the bare result here as he got shuffled back a bit further than ideal before finishing strongly without having a hope with the winner. He's a real credit to connections. (op 6-1)
Captain Dancer(IRE) has had a bit of a stop-start career so far, struggling to string good efforts togther, but there's no doubt this was an eyecatching display and he definitely has the ability to win a race from this mark, ending up way too far back here, doing well to finish as close as he did. (op 8-1 tchd 17-2)
One Scoop Or Two ran a sound race on his attempt for the five-timer but had no excuses after obtaining a good early position, and it's an effort which suggests the handicapper may have finally caught up with him for the time being. Official explanation: vet said gelding had been struck into behind
Suffolk Punch(IRE) is consistent but there's no obvious sign he's in any way a progressive 3-y-o.
Rock 'N' Royal was caught a bit wider than ideal and he is lightly enough raced to suggest he may yet have more to offer. (op 25-1 tchd 20-1)
Deadly Encounter(IRE), like his stable companion was caught a bit wider than ideal and can be marked up slightly.
My Gacho(IRE) is often a front runner but ended up too far back on this occasion and shouldn't be judged on this. (op 12-1)
Internationaldebut(IRE) was back at the scene of his eye-catching effort a couple of starts back but failed to continue his run of good form. He's useful on his day but hasn't proved easy to win with in recent times. (op 11-2)
Game Lad often goes well with give in the ground but was caught too far back here. Official explanation: jockey said gelding never travelled
Arabian Pearl(IRE) is normally reliable and this can probably be regarded as a one-off for the time being. (op 11-1)

5938 FREEBETS.CO.UK STAND CUP (LISTED RACE) — 1m 4f 66y
3:35 (3:38) (Class 1) 3-Y-O+ **£21,926** (£8,291; £4,144; £2,072) **Stalls** Low

Form RPR

2120 **1** **Harris Tweed**[25] 5185 3-8-6 105 .... LiamJones 7 117
(W J Haggas) *mde all: rdn clr over 2f out: r.o wl and in command after* **7/2**[2]

1456 **2** *10* **Les Fazzani (IRE)**[7] 5749 6-9-1 108 .... PJMcDonald 4 102
(K A Ryan) *trckd ldrs: chsd wnr 4f out: rdn and outpcd over 2f out: n.d after* **9/4**[1]

3054 **3** *1 ½* **Wajir (FR)**[14] 5517 4-9-1 105 .... RichardMullen 8 100+
(Saeed Bin Suroor) *in rr: effrt and hdwy to chse ldrs over 2f out: sn no imp: plugged on at one pce fnl f* **11/2**[3]

51P4 **4** *11* **Paquerettza (FR)**[13] 5553 4-8-10 90 .... RobertWinston 3 78
(D H Brown) *hld up: pushed along 4f out: dropped away wl over 2f out: n.d after* **16/1**

0045 **5** *hd* **Golden Sword**[14] 5517 4-9-1 106 .... PatCosgrave 5 83
(Jane Chapple-Hyam) *chsd wnr: lost pl 4f out: sn hrd rdn: wknd over 2f out* **9/1**

6254 **6** *8* **Bikini Babe (IRE)**[14] 5538 3-8-1 105 .... AdrianNicholls 2 66
(M Johnston) *midfield: effrt over 3f out: no imp: wknd wl over 2f out* **11/2**[3]

2100 **7** *10* **Acquainted**[50] 4347 3-8-1 95 .... PaulEddery 1 51
(B W Hills) *hld up: pushed along over 4f out: wl bhd over 3f out: eased whn wl btn fnl f: t.o* **25/1**

2m 48.75s (8.85) **Going Correction** +1.025s/f (Soft)
WFA 3 from 4yo+ 9lb 7 Ran SP% **103.5**
Speed ratings (Par 111): **111,104,103,96,95 90,83**
Tote Swingers:1&2:£1.70, 2&3:£3.60, 1&3:£3.30 CSF £9.62 TOTE £4.30: £2.20, £1.90; EX 8.80 Trifecta £31.50 Pool: £319.83 - 7.50 winning units..
Owner B Haggas **Bred** J B Haggas **Trained** Newmarket, Suffolk
■ Nezhenka (15/2) was withdrawn after refusing to enter the stalls. R4 applies, deduct 10p in the £.

FOCUS
Hard to believe the runner-up was at her very best here, but this still represents a smart performance.

NOTEBOOK
Harris Tweed galloped his rivals into the ground, the field strung out like 3m chasers. The winner's run of progressive form came to a halt in the Great Voltigeur but he wasted little time showing he's still very much on the up, clearly relishing the softer conditions as he made all with ease. He's still got very few miles on the clock, and he'll be winning Group races before long on this evidence. Official explanation: trainer said regarding apparent improvement in form that colt benefited from a uncontested lead (op 9-2 tchd 5-1 in a place)
Les Fazzani(IRE) usually revels in the mud but wasn't at the very top of her game, struggling to keep tabs on the winner from the turn. (op 7-2)
Wajir(FR) continues a fair way below his French form, keeping on without threatening a serious blow. (op 5-1)
Paquerettza(FR) isn't up this level and was beaten a long way out over a trip she probably doesn't stay in any case.
Golden Sword dropped out pretty tamely and seems to be going the wrong way. (op 7-1 tchd 6-1)
Bikini Babe(IRE) is normally reliable but was clearly nowhere near her best. (op 9-2)
Acquainted's Cheshire Oaks second is looking a bit of a standout as she's come nowhere near reproducing it back up in class on her last three starts. (op 20-1 tchd 18-1)

5939 CHESHIRE LIFE NURSERY — 5f 110y
4:10 (4:10) (Class 3) (0-95,90) 2-Y-O **£8,200** (£2,454; £1,227; £613; £305) **Stalls** Low

Form RPR

5610 **1** **Foghorn Leghorn**[24] 5221 2-9-2 **85** .... RichardMullen 1 90
(P W Chapple-Hyam) *mde all: rdn over 1f out: r.o: in command cl home* **5/1**

3043 **2** *1 ½* **Jamesway (IRE)**[21] 5295 2-9-3 **89** .... BarryMcHugh(3) 2 89
(R A Fahey) *trckd ldrs: rdn to take 2nd over 1f out and tried to chal: nt qckn ins fnl f: no imp on wnr cl home* **3/1**[2]

5311 **3** *½* **Loki's Revenge**[12] 5613 2-8-9 **78** .... PJMcDonald 5 76+
(W Jarvis) *towards rr: hdwy 2f out: chsd ldrs over 1f out: kpt on ins fnl f: nt quite pce of ldrs towards fin* **9/4**[1]

4105 **4** *3 ¾* **First Class Favour (IRE)**[13] 5547 2-8-4 **73** .... DuranFentiman 7 59
(T D Easterby) *racd keenly: chsd ldrs: effrt on wd outer over 2f out: one pce fr over 1f out* **16/1**

3221 **5** *½* **Lexi's Hero (IRE)**[27] 5117 2-9-7 **90** .... TomEaves 4 74
(K A Ryan) *w ldr: rdn and lost 2nd over 1f out: chsd ldrs tl wknd fnl 100yds* **4/1**[3]

15 **6** *1 ¼* **Snow Bear (IRE)**[51] 4278 2-7-13 **68** .... AndrewMullen 9 48+
(J J Quinn) *bhd: pushed along whn nt clr run briefly wl over 1f out: nvr on terms* **16/1**

4004 **7** *nk* **Meandmyshadow**[15] 5476 2-8-5 **74** .... FrannyNorton 8 53+
(A D Brown) *hld up: pushed along over 2f out: nvr able to get on terms: eased whn wl btn wl ins fnl f* **12/1**

600 **8** *2 ¼* **Style And Panache (IRE)**[42] 4578 2-8-8 **77** .... CathyGannon 3 48
(P D Evans) *racd keenly: trckd ldrs: pushed along 3f out: rdn and wknd 2f out* **12/1**

1m 13.09s (5.79) **Going Correction** +1.025s/f (Soft) 8 Ran SP% **119.6**
Speed ratings (Par 99): **102,100,99,94,93 92,91,88**
Tote Swingers:1&2:£2.80, 2&3:£2.60, 1&3:£3.20 CSF £21.46 CT £44.22 TOTE £5.20: £1.80, £1.50, £1.10; EX 17.20.
Owner The Comic Strip Heroes **Bred** Cheveley Park Stud Ltd **Trained** Newmarket, Suffolk

FOCUS
A fairly useful nursery, if one devoid of obviously progressive types. The winner was favoured by the card's pace bias so this is not form to get carried away with.

NOTEBOOK
Foghorn Leghorn wasn't up to Listed class last time but got back on track with his sights lowered, clearly well suited by soft ground, but he did have the run of things from the front so perhaps wouldn't be an obvious one to defy a rise in the weights. (op 9-2 tchd 4-1)
Jamesway(IRE) put a below-par effort here last time and there's no knocking his consistency overall, but he's not obviously any better than this. (op 7-2)
Loki's Revenge couldn't complete the hat-trick but this shows he's still on a fair mark, particularly as he was caught a little further back than ideal. (op 7-2)
First Class Favour(IRE) has found life tough since last month's Catterick win, though she was always wider than ideal on this occasion.
Lexi's Hero(IRE) will need to improve to defy this opening mark and faded from prominence inside the final 1f. Official explanation: trainer's rep said gelding was unsuited by the soft (good to soft places) ground (op 7-2)

The Form Book, Raceform Ltd, Compton, RG20 6NL

Snow Bear(IRE) always found things happening too quickly for her round here after a break, being also messed around a bit towards the inner, and the overall impression is that she shouldn't be judged too harshly.

5940 GROSVENOR SHOPPING CENTRE H'CAP — 1m 7f 195y
4:45 (4:45) (Class 3) (0-95,92) 3-Y-O+ — **£6,476** (£1,927; £963; £481) **Stalls** Low

Form — RPR

5014 **1** **Topolski (IRE)**[18] 5387 4-9-8 **86**......(p) LiamKeniry 3 — 94
(A M Balding) *hld up: hdwy 4f out: led 2f out: rdn over 1f out: edgd rt briefly ins fnl f: styd on dourly* **12/1**

4216 **2** 2 ¼ **Rangefinder**[7] 5743 6-9-13 **91**...... PJMcDonald 4 — 96
(Jane Chapple-Hyam) *hld up: hdwy 9f out: led 4f out: hdd 2f out: sn rdn: tried to rally ins fnl f: one pce and no further imp cl home* **15/8**[1]

0222 **3** 2 ½ **Omokoroa (IRE)**[21] 5296 4-9-2 **80**......(p) PatCosgrave 1 — 82
(M H Tompkins) *in tch: effrt to chse ldrs over 3f out: edgd rt briefly ins fnl f: one pce fnl 100yds* **3/1**[2]

0623 **4** 1 **Rawnaq (IRE)**[15] 5497 3-8-1 **78** ow1...... AdrianNicholls 10 — 79
(M Johnston) *chsd ldrs: wnt 2nd 9f out: rdn and lost 2nd 3f out: outpcd after: kpt on ins fnl f but no real imp on ldrs* **4/1**[3]

3212 **5** nk **Blazing Desert**[15] 5497 6-8-11 **75**...... FrannyNorton 8 — 75+
(J J Quinn) *racd keenly: hld up: rdn over 3f out: kpt on ins fnl f: nvr able to chal* **8/1**

0004 **6** 8 **Mith Hill**[22] 5278 9-8-4 **75** oh1......(v) RyanPowell(7) 5 — 66
(Ian Williams) *chsd ldr to 9f out: remained handy: rdn 5f out: wknd 3f out* **8/1**

0-05 **7** 13 **Wells Lyrical (IRE)**[15] 5492 5-9-8 **86**......(v[1]) TomEaves 2 — 61
(B Smart) *racd keenly: led: hdd 4f out: rdn over 3f out: sn wknd* **16/1**

200- **8** 72 **Diktalina**[165] 6917 4-8-9 **76** oh25 ow1...... RussKennemore(3) 9 — —
(Mrs A M Thorpe) *in tch: rdn along and lost pl wl over 7f out: bhd after: t.o over 4f out* **33/1**

3m 48.75s (20.75) **Going Correction** +1.20s/f (Soft)
WFA 3 from 4yo+ 13lb — **8 Ran SP% 118.5**
Speed ratings (Par 107): **96,94,93,93,92 88,82,46**
Tote Swingers:1&2:£4.30, 2&3:£2.00, 1&3:£7.90 CSF £36.31 CT £89.68 TOTE £12.10: £3.40, £1.10, £2.00; EX 40.00.
Owner Kennet Valley Thoroughbreds V **Bred** C H Wacker Iii **Trained** Kingsclere, Hants

FOCUS
A fair staying event. The gallop looked steady for a long way, not quickening to any great extent until the final 5f, but they still finished well strung out under the testing conditions.

NOTEBOOK
Topolski(IRE) made it two wins from his last three starts and is still relatively unexposed at staying trips, also leaving the impression he was idling a bit in front, so there's reason to believe he'll be competitive once reassessed. (op 10-1)
Rangefinder was in a less competitive race than last time and matched the form he showed when winning over C&D last month, but he's always likely to be vulnerable from this mark. (op 5-2 after early 3-1 in places)
Omokoroa(IRE) is consistent, placed for the fourth time running here, but has also had plenty of chances from similar marks, the first-time cheekpieces not enabling him to pull out any more. (op 4-1)
Rawnaq(IRE) is another who seems pretty reliable but there's no obvious indication he's going to improve like so many from the yard do. (op 13-2)
Blazing Desert was caught a bit further back than ideal when the pace increased and perhaps deserves another chance as he'd progressed steadily before this, conditions also softer than he'd faced previously on the Flat. (op 6-1)
Mith Hill didn't come close to repeating last year's success in this. (op 6-1)

5941 CHESHIRE JETS H'CAP — 5f 16y
5:20 (5:20) (Class 4) (0-85,85) 3-Y-O+ — **£5,180** (£1,541; £770; £384) **Stalls** Low

Form — RPR

-120 **1** **Foxy Music**[49] 4372 6-9-5 **83**...... PatCosgrave 2 — 94
(E J Alston) *mde all: rdn over 1f out: r.o ins fnl f: a in control* **7/1**

3041 **2** 2 ¼ **Legal Eagle (IRE)**[15] 5480 5-9-2 **80**......(p) FrannyNorton 7 — 83
(Paul Green) *in tch: rdn 2f out: impr over 1f out: wnt 2nd ins fnl f: no imp on wnr* **10/3**[2]

3300 **3** 1 **Lost In Paris (IRE)**[36] 4798 4-9-1 **79**......(v) DuranFentiman 10 — 78
(T D Easterby) *pressed ldrs: chsd wnr 3f out: rdn and nt qckn over 1f out: lost 2nd ins fnl f: styd on same pce* **20/1**

2110 **4** ½ **Mey Blossom**[14] 5512 5-8-13 **80**...... MichaelStainton(3) 8 — 78
(R M Whitaker) *towards rr: dropped to last 1/2-way: hdwy 1f out: kpt on ins fnl f: nt pce to mount serious chal* **12/1**

1261 **5** 1 ¾ **Mr Wolf**[17] 5424 9-8-12 **79**......(p) BarryMcHugh(3) 4 — 70
(J J Quinn) *w wnr for 1f: remained prom: rdn over 1f out: no ex ins fnl f* **6/1**[3]

2136 **6** 1 ¼ **Vhujon (IRE)**[16] 5454 5-9-2 **80**...... CathyGannon 5 — 67
(P D Evans) *pushed along and outpcd: rdn over 1f out: no imp on ldrs* **11/1**

6420 **7** nse **Doctor Parkes**[8] 5734 4-9-7 **85**...... RobertWinston 1 — 72
(E J Alston) *chsd ldrs: rdn over 1f out: wknd ent fnl f* **2/1**[1]

0422 **8** 1 **Tasmeem (IRE)**[12] 5606 3-8-13 **78**......(b) AdrianNicholls 6 — 61
(R A Fahey) *outpcd and bhd: brief effrt wl over 1f out: no imp: eased whn btn ins fnl f* **8/1**

66.32 secs (5.32) **Going Correction** +1.20s/f (Soft)
WFA 3 from 4yo+ 1lb — **8 Ran SP% 115.1**
Speed ratings (Par 105): **105,101,99,99,96 94,94,92**
Tote Swingers:1&2:£5.80, 2&3:£12.20, 1&3:£12.60 CSF £30.81 CT £449.95 TOTE £6.80: £1.80, £1.70, £4.40; EX 45.50.
Owner G M & Mrs C Baillie **Bred** G M & C Baillie & Springs Equestrian **Trained** Longton, Lancs

FOCUS
No hanging around here, but it still paid to race handily.
Doctor Parkes Official explanation: trainer said gelding was unsuited by the soft (good to soft places) ground

5942 CRUISE NIGHTSPOT H'CAP — 1m 2f 75y
5:55 (5:56) (Class 5) (0-75,74) 3-Y-O — **£4,047** (£1,204; £601; £300) **Stalls** High

Form — RPR

-241 **1** **The Caped Crusader (IRE)**[21] 5300 3-9-1 **71**...... BarryMcHugh(3) 9 — 82
(Ollie Pears) *hld up in midfield: n.m.r 2f out: hdwy sn after: led over 1f out: edgd lft ins fnl f: r.o: wl on top at fin* **4/1**[1]

503 **2** 2 ¼ **Kingdom Of Munster (IRE)**[32] 4925 3-8-7 **60** oh1...(v) AdrianNicholls 3 — 67
(R A Fahey) *bustled along to chse ldrs and n.m.r early: rdn 2f out: chalng over 1f out: nt qckn and hld by wnr fnl 100yds* **8/1**

0665 **3** 1 ¾ **Muwalla**[21] 5300 3-9-1 **68**...... PatCosgrave 7 — 71
(J D Bethell) *s.s: hld up in rr: hdwy on outer 2f out: rdn to chse ldrs over 1f out and ch: no ex fnl 100yds* **14/1**

1340 **4** 1 ½ **Law To Himself (IRE)**[27] 5121 3-9-6 **73**...... PJMcDonald 1 — 73
(G A Swinbank) *hld up: hdwy on inner 2f out: chsd ldrs and one pce ins fnl f* **4/1**[1]

3243 **5** 6 **Dazakhee**[78] 3390 3-8-9 **62**...... TonyCulhane 2 — 50
(P T Midgley) *n.m.r early: sn led: rdn 3f out: hdd over 1f out: sn wknd* **9/2**[2]

006 **6** 3 ¼ **Epernay**[26] 5150 3-8-7 **60**...... LiamKeniry 6 — 42
(Ian Williams) *prom: chalng over 2f out: rdn and wknd over 1f out* **4/1**[1]

4154 **7** 3 **Elmfield Giant (USA)**[11] 5641 3-9-7 **74**...... TomEaves 4 — 50
(R A Fahey) *hld up: checked whn nt clr run 2f out: sn rdn and no imp* **9/1**

-543 **8** 10 **Child Of Our Time (IRE)**[18] 5391 3-9-1 **68**...... FrannyNorton 8 — 24
(P W Chapple-Hyam) *racd keenly: prom: losing pl whn n.m.r and hmpd 2f out: sn bhd: eased ins fnl f* **13/2**[3]

2m 26.22s (14.02) **Going Correction** +1.20s/f (Soft) — **8 Ran SP% 119.3**
Speed ratings (Par 101): **91,89,87,86,81 79,76,68**
toteswingers: 1&2 £4.30, 1&3 £9.50, 2&3 £18.50. CSF £37.92 CT £414.61 TOTE £3.80: £1.40, £2.90, £3.80; EX 48.90 Place 6: £36.28, Place 5: £30.74..
Owner David Silversides **Bred** Ballylinch Stud **Trained** Norton, N Yorks
■ Stewards' Enquiry : Barry McHugh one day ban; careless riding (26th Sept)

FOCUS
A fair contest. The gallop looked no more than a fair one for the most part.
T/Plt: £75.00 to a £1 stake. Pool £72,140.10. 701.77 winning tickets. T/Qpdt: £17.70 to a £1 stake. Pool £3,976.62. 166.20 winning tickets. DO

5907 DONCASTER (L-H)
Saturday, September 11

OFFICIAL GOING: Good (round 8.0, straight: stands' side 8.2, centre 8.6, far side 8.5)
All dolling removed and distances as advertised.
Wind: Moderate, half-against. Weather: overcast, changeable, heavy shower race 2

5943 NEPTUNE INVESTMENT MANAGEMENT CHAMPAGNE STKS (GROUP 2) — 7f
2:10 (2:11) (Class 1) 2-Y-O
£67,385 (£25,544; £12,783; £6,374; £3,193; £1,602) **Stalls** High

Form — RPR

1 **1** **Saamidd**[29] 5032 2-8-12 **103**...... FrankieDettori 3 — 114+
(Saeed Bin Suroor) *w'like: scope: lw: hld up: smooth hdwy over 3f out: shkn up and qcknd to ld over 1f out: pushed out: eased nr fin* **5/6**[1]

1431 **2** 2 ¼ **Approve (IRE)**[24] 5219 2-9-1 **113**...... EddieAhern 6 — 110
(W J Haggas) *lw: trckd ldrs: t.k.h: effrt and upsides over 2f out: styd on to take 2nd last 100yds* **9/2**[3]

6211 **3** ½ **Waiter's Dream**[25] 5184 2-8-12 **106**...... KierenFallon 2 — 106
(B J Meehan) *swtg: led: swtchd rt to stands' side rails after 1f: qcknd over 3f out: edgd lft and hdd over 1f out: kpt on same pce* **9/4**[2]

1 **4** nse **Karam Albaari (IRE)**[10] 5657 2-8-12 **78**...... JimmyQuinn 5 — 106+
(J R Jenkins) *str: lw: hld up in rr: effrt over 2f out: styd on wl ins fnl f* **50/1**

0 **5** 18 **Castlemorris King**[29] 5049 2-8-12 **0**...... MarkCoumbe 4 — 59
(M C Chapman) *str: dwlt: mid-div: drvn over 3f out: sn bhd* **150/1**

1155 **6** 1 **Waltz Darling (IRE)**[21] 5306 2-8-12 **95**...... PaulHanagan 1 — 56
(R A Fahey) *w ldr: rdn and wknd 2f out: sn bhd* **25/1**

1m 26.32s (0.02) **Going Correction** +0.125s/f (Good) — **6 Ran SP% 110.0**
Speed ratings (Par 107): **104,101,100,100,80 79**
Tote Swingers: 1&2 £1.40, 1&3 £1.10, 2&3 £1.20 CSF £4.86 TOTE £1.80: £1.10, £2.00; EX 5.20.

Owner Godolphin **Bred** Darley **Trained** Newmarket, Suffolk

FOCUS
There was a lack of strength in depth to this Group 2, with half the field not looking up to it, but Saamidd ran out a tidy winner. The race is rated around the second and third.

NOTEBOOK
Saamidd had a buzz surrounding him following his deeply impressive debut at Newbury and he readily made a successful debut at Group level. Strong in the market, he readily made headway widest of all, having been dropped in from the start, and quickly settled it with a fine turn of foot well over a furlong out. The winning margin was eaten into a little late on, but Frankie Dettori was merely nursing him home, no doubt with one eye on the future, and it will be fascinating to see how he fares upped in grade again in the Dewhurst, his next intended target. He would need to be supplemented for that. (op 10-11 tchd 4-5)
Approve(IRE), the Gimcrack winner who had also landed the Norfolk stakes over 5f at Royal Ascot, was having to concede 3lb to his rivals on this first try at 7f, and Eddie Ahern felt after the race that he should have finished a little closer, the rider having held on to him for too long with stamina concerns in mind. He would struggle to reverse form the winner, even at level weights and under a more positive ride, but at least connections now know he stays the trip and it's likely he will head to Longchamp for the Group 1 Jean-Luc Lagardere on Arc day. (tchd 5-1)
Waiter's Dream, winner of the Acomb Stakes, bounced out and was soon bossing the pace against the rail, but he was facing two much classier rivals than last time and simply wasn't up to it, just holding third. (tchd 5-2)
Karam Albaari(IRE), whose 33-1 maiden win on debut at Kempton just ten days earlier earned him an official rating of just 78, promised to be well suited by the extra furlong and he duly showed much-improved form, keeping on well inside the final furlong to just miss third. This will go some way to ruining what was clearly a decent mark, but at least connections know they have a horse with some quality.
Castlemorris King, well beaten when 100-1 for his debut at Newmarket, struggled as expected.
Waltz Darling(IRE), though comfortably held the last twice in Group contests, should have done a lot better. Something may well have been amiss. (op 20-1)

5944 LADBROKES PORTLAND (HERITAGE H'CAP) — 5f 140y
2:45 (2:48) (Class 2) 3-Y-O+
£49,848 (£14,928; £7,464; £3,736; £1,864; £936) **Stalls** High

Form — RPR

5201 **1** **Poet's Place (USA)**[35] 4832 5-9-4 **96**...... PhillipMakin 7 — 107
(T D Barron) *dwlt: hld up in mid-div: hdwy over 1f out: r.o strly: led nr fin* **4/1**[1]

2321 **2** ½ **Bajan Tryst (USA)**[27] 5127 4-9-4 **96**...... RyanMoore 6 — 105
(K A Ryan) *chsd ldrs: led 100yds out: hdd fnl strides* **25/1**

1022 **3** 1 ½ **Deacon Blues**[28] 5088 3-9-1 **95**...... FrankieDettori 16 — 99+
(J R Fanshawe) *hld up towards rr: effrt over 2f out: nt clr run over 1f out: styd on wl fnl f* **13/2**[3]

0440 **4** hd **Tiddliwinks**[28] 5095 4-9-2 **94**...... DarryllHolland 8 — 98
(K A Ryan) *w ldr: led over 2f out: hdd last 100yds: no ex* **6/1**[2]

1-10 **5** nse **Bay Knight (IRE)**[7] 5774 4-9-5 **97**...... CO'Donoghue 2 — 101
(K J Condon, Ire) *hld up towards rr: hdwy over 2f out: styd on wl fnl f* **28/1**

0605 **6** ½ **Arganil (USA)**[27] 5127 5-9-4 **96**....(b) PaulMulrennan 5 98
(K A Ryan) *hld up in rr: hdwy over 2f out: kpt on wl* **40/1**

411 **7** ½ **Masamah (IRE)**[41] 4616 4-9-10 **102**.... JamieSpencer 13 102+
(K A Ryan) *mid-div: effrt over 2f out: styd on fnl f* **14/1**

4220 **8** ½ **Striking Spirit**[42] 4576 5-9-2 **99**.... MichaelO'Connell(5) 11 98
(D Nicholls) *chsd ldrs: kpt on same pce fnl f* **20/1**

2201 **9** ¾ **Confessional**[7] 5742 3-8-13 **93**....(e) DavidAllan 9 89
(T D Easterby) *w ldrs: fdd fnl f* **25/1**

4603 **10** *nk* **Signor Peltro**[28] 5095 7-9-8 **100**.... TonyCulhane 21 95+
(H Candy) *lw: in rr: hdwy and nt clr run over 1f out: kpt on: nt rch ldrs* **14/1**

0000 **11** 1½ **Johannes (IRE)**[28] 5095 7-8-13 **96**.... LeeTopliss(5) 24 86
(R A Fahey) *towards rr: kpt on fnl 2f: nvr a factor* **16/1**

3443 **12** *shd* **Duchess Dora (IRE)**[23] 5250 3-8-9 **94**.... IanBrennan(5) 4 84
(J J Quinn) *mid-div: effrt over 2f out: one pce* **20/1**

5253 **13** ½ **Quest For Success (IRE)**[25] 5183 5-9-8 **100**.... PaulHanagan 14 88
(R A Fahey) *lw: mid-div: effrt over 2f out: nvr nr ldrs* **9/1**

2051 **14** ½ **Monsieur Joe (IRE)**[23] 5250 3-9-7 **101**.... EddieAhern 12 96+
(W R Swinburn) *mid-div: hdwy to chse ldrs over 2f out: edgd rt over 1f out: wkng whn hmpd ins fnl f* **20/1**

0043 **15** 1 **Singeur (IRE)**[11] 5632 3-9-3 **97**....(b) SilvestreDeSousa 20 80
(R Bastiman) *towards rr: nvr on terms* **20/1**

-630 **16** ½ **Noble Storm (USA)**[14] 5512 4-9-7 **99**.... GrahamGibbons 10 81
(E S McMahon) *swtg: led tl over 2f out: wknd over 1f out* **25/1**

6010 **17** *nse* **Hotham**[25] 5183 7-9-0 **95**.... GaryBartley(3) 18 76
(N Wilson) *lw: reluctant to load: a towards rr* **50/1**

0220 **18** 1½ **Judge 'n Jury**[13] 5569 6-9-7 **99**.... TomMcLaughlin 15 76
(R A Harris) *a towards rr* **25/1**

5350 **19** *nk* **Tawaabb**[23] 5250 3-9-1 **95**....(v) GeorgeBaker 17 71
(M R Channon) *lw: a towards rr* **40/1**

5000 **20** 1¼ **Fol Hollow (IRE)**[14] 5512 5-8-12 **95**.... BillyCray(5) 1 66
(D Nicholls) *chsd ldrs: wkng whn sltly hmpd over 1f out* **50/1**

00-0 **21** *21* **Hogmaneigh (IRE)**[98] 2759 7-9-2 **94**.... KierenFallon 22 —
(J S Goldie) *s.i.s: sn bhd and pushed along: eased fnl f: t.o* **10/1**

1102 **22** *156* **Jack My Boy (IRE)**[16] 5442 3-8-12 **95**....(b) MartinLane(3) 23 —
(P D Evans) *lw: s.s: a detached in last: t.o and virtually p.u 2f out: lame* **22/1**

67.79 secs (-0.71) **Going Correction** +0.125s/f (Good)
WFA 3 from 4yo+ 2lb **22** Ran SP% **137.0**
Speed ratings (Par 109): **109,108,106,106,106 105,104,104,103,102 100,100,99,99,97 97,97,95,94,93 65,—**
Tote Swingers: 1&2 £31.90, 1&3 £4.10, 2&3 £31.80 CSF £116.02 CT £691.20 TOTE £4.90: £1.80, £6.10, £1.60, £1.70; EX 130.00 Trifecta £1629.30 Pool: £40,799.72 - 18.53 winning units..
Owner Mrs Elaine Russell **Bred** Burning Daylight Farms **Trained** Maunby, N Yorks
■ Stewards' Enquiry : Paul Mulrennan two-day ban: used whip with excessive frequency (Sep 26-27)

FOCUS
All the winners of this valuable handicap since 2001 had been officially rated 91 or higher, indeed, six of the last seven won off a mark of at least 95, a trend this year's victor maintained. Prior to the off, a heavy but reasonably quick shower of rain hit the course, which possibly eased the ground a bit. The effect of the draw over the years had been slightly inconclusive, but in this renewal it was a positive to be drawn towards the far-side of the course, where most of the pace seemed to be.

NOTEBOOK
Poet's Place(USA) ◆, raised 10lb after beating subsequent winner Harry Patch at Haydock, looked to have plenty of improvement still to come when considering his lack of experience, and he delivered again in good style, staying on strongly inside the final furlong to get on top close to the line. He doesn't look the sort who will be a 5f type, as his record and this race shows, so it makes perfect sense for him to head to the Ayr Gold Cup next weekend, although it's not difficult to argue that a crack at Group company should be considered if a sensible target can be found. (op 5-1)
Bajan Tryst(USA), raised 7lb for success at Dundalk on his previous outing, coped with this change of surface admirably, and was mugged in the final strides. (op 22-1)
Deacon Blues, who raced down the middle of the course, kept on well once in the clear but was never going to get there. Connections indicated that he will head to a conditions or Listed contest next. (op 10-1)
Tiddliwinks, a fair seventh in the Great St Wilfred, was the subject of a lot of market support during the day and ran another respectable race after being prominent throughout. (op 8-1)
Bay Knight(IRE), down over 1f in trip, sat along side the winner about 2f out and ran a very similar race to him without quite having the same finishing kick. (op 25-1)
Arganil(USA), who finished behind his stablemate Bajan Tryst in Ireland, could be seen making late progress on ground that probably doesn't suit him. (op 50-1)
Masamah(IRE) ran really well under top weight coming down the centre of the course but did not quite get home. (op 16-1)
Signor Peltro ◆, whose only other run at this course (7f) had yielded a success, was starting to make ground when running into a wall of horses over 1f out. He may have been fairly close to Deacon Blues with a clear passage.
Quest For Success(IRE) had a two from three record at this course but ran a rare modest race after a good spell of form. (op 10-1)
Noble Storm(USA) was too keen and weakened. (op 20-1)
Hogmaneigh(IRE), the winner of this in 2008 off an official mark of 100, which was his last victory, certainly looked of interest with Kieren Fallon booked, despite it being his first outing since early June. However, his supporters soon knew their fate, as was struggling in rear before the 3f marker. Official explanation: jockey said gelding ran flat
Jack My Boy(IRE) Official explanation: jockey said gelding finished lame

5945 LADBROKES ST LEGER STKS (GROUP 1) 1m 6f 132y
3:20 (3:24) (Class 1) 3-Y-O

£283,850 (£107,600; £53,850; £26,850; £13,450; £6,750) **Stalls** Low

Form RPR

3123 **1** **Arctic Cosmos (USA)**[46] 4456 3-9-0 111....(b[1]) WilliamBuick 8 122
(J H M Gosden) *lw: chsd ldrs: effrt over 2f out: rdn to ld over 1f out: styd on wl* **12/1**

1522 **2** 1¾ **Midas Touch**[25] 5185 3-9-0 118.... CO'Donoghue 5 119
(A P O'Brien, Ire) *chsd ldrs: effrt over 2f out: upsides over 1f out: styd on to take 2nd nr fin* **13/2**[2]

3415 **3** *nse* **Corsica (IRE)**[46] 4456 3-9-0 110.... JoeFanning 6 119
(M Johnston) *led: qcknd 4f out: hdd over 1f out: styd on same pce* **40/1**

1112 **4** 1¼ **Snow Fairy (IRE)**[23] 5248 3-8-11 119.... EddieAhern 4 115+
(E A L Dunlop) *hld up towards rr: stdy hdwy over 2f out: kpt on fnl f: nvr nr to chal* **8/1**

1-3 **5** 2¾ **Joshua Tree (IRE)**[25] 5185 3-9-0 113.... JamieSpencer 2 114+
(A P O'Brien, Ire) *lw: hld up in rr: effrt on outside over 2f out: edgd lft over 1f out: nvr rchd ldrs* **9/1**

2131 **6** ¾ **Rewilding**[25] 5185 3-9-0 121.... FrankieDettori 7 113
(Mahmood Al Zarooni) *hld up towards rr: hdwy over 3f out: chsd ldrs over 1f out: sn fdd* **1/1**[1]

4126 **7** 1½ **Theology**[46] 4456 3-9-0 110.... PaulHanagan 1 111
(J Noseda) *hld up in rr: effrt and swtchd rt 4f out: kpt on fnl 2f: nvr a factor* **40/1**

1112 **8** ½ **Dandino**[46] 4456 3-9-0 113.... PaulMulrennan 10 110
(J G Given) *swtg: hld up in mid-div: drvn 3f out: nvr nr ldrs* **7/1**[3]

4130 **9** *22* **Total Command**[25] 5185 3-9-0 107.... RyanMoore 9 81
(Sir Michael Stoute) *swtg: trckd ldrs: t.k.h: drvn over 3f out: lost pl 2f out: eased whn bhd ins fnl f* **40/1**

-104 **10** *6* **Ted Spread**[25] 5185 3-9-0 104.... DarryllHolland 3 72
(M H Tompkins) *chsd ldrs: drvn 4f out: lost pl over 2f out: eased whn bhd ins fnl f* **33/1**

3m 3.12s (-4.28) **Going Correction** -0.025s/f (Good) **10** Ran SP% **114.9**
Speed ratings (Par 115): **110,109,109,108,106 106,105,105,93,90**
Tote Swingers:1&2:£9.00, 2&3:£33.50, 1&3:£26.60 CSF £83.86 CT £2984.09 TOTE £15.20: £3.30, £2.20, £7.40; EX 132.10 Trifecta £2956.60 Pool: £27,968.62 - 7.00 winning units..
Owner Rachel Hood and Robin Geffen **Bred** Sheridan & Iadora Farm **Trained** Newmarket, Suffolk
■ William Buick's first Classic winner.

FOCUS
A stronger-looking field than last season assembled for the year's final Classic, although that's probably not saying much. The form of the key trials was well represented, with the first four from the Great Voltigeur, as well as the placed runners from the Gordon Stakes, all making the line-up. In fact Snow Fairy was the only runner not to have been prepped for this in either of those races. The race was strongly run. Arctic Cosmos stepped up by 8lb on his previous best and is rated in line with most recent Leger winners. Midas Touch and Joshua Tree were close to their York form, with improvement from Corsica. The form is weakened by the warm favourite Rewilding's below-par effort, 11lb off his best.

NOTEBOOK
Arctic Cosmos(USA) found the necessary improvement in the first-time blinkers to provide his handler with win number three in the race, following the successes of Shantou in 1996 and Lucarno in 2007. Beaten off a mark of 78 at Newbury back in May, his improvement since has been remarkable, easily defying that mark next time and then finishing second just over a week later in the Group 2 King Edward VII Stakes at Royal Ascot. His Gordon Stakes third was all the more credible considering he didn't handle the track, and there was little doubt about him seeing out this longer trip, so it looked ominous for the opposition when Buick was sat in behind the leaders waiting to pounce as they raced past the three-furlong marker. Asked to go on and win the race inside the final two furlongs, he immediately picked up to take the lead and then stayed on strongly for pressure to maintain a comfy advantage all the way to the line. It will be fascinating to see how he gets on in the headgear back at 1m4f, with Gosden mooting a possible trip to the US for the Breeders' Cup Turf later in the season, but it remains to be seen whether he's capable of mixing it with the elite performers at that distance. Bizarrely, it had been decided before the race that he will embark on a hurdling career one day (probably at the end of next year), with connections hoping he will, in time, jump a fence, so there is plenty to look forward to. (op 10-1)
Midas Touch was comfortably held when second to Rewilding at York, but it's notoriously hard to win that race with a penalty, and the longer trip here offered strong hope he would reverse form, which he did. However, despite appearing to travel almost as well as the winner, he lacked a change of pace once coming under pressure, which has been his problem all season, and was always being held from over a furlong out, just shading the verdict for second. He will prove suited by 2m next season, and maybe even further, so connections will no doubt be hopeful he can develop into a cup horse. (op 7-1 tchd 15-2)
Corsica(IRE) was there to make the pace for Rewilding but was running on his own merits. In typical fashion of a Johnston runner, he didn't know when to give in and very nearly held on to second. Like the winner, he was contesting handicap off marks in the 70's earlier in the season, but struck a first blow at Group level when winning the Bahrain Trophy, and there was no disgrace in his Gordon Stakes fifth considering he was saddled with a 3lb penalty. A galloping track suits him best, but he may not be the easiest to place unless finding further improvement. (op 33-1)
Snow Fairy(IRE), bidding to become the first filly since User Friendly in 1992 to win this having already collected the English and Irish Oaks, was the sole Group 1 winner in the field, and there was no disgrace in her Yorkshire Oaks defeat by Midday, so a good run looked assured. She fared best of the hold-up horses, closing readily enough, but for all that she appeared to see the trip out, she couldn't stay on as strongly as the front three and would probably have been seen to better effect had the ground been livelier. The Prix de L'Opera on Arc day may be her next target, with the Champion Stakes also coming under consideration. (op 9-1)
Joshua Tree(IRE) caught the eye of many when third in the Voltigeur on his belated reappearance, but his claims were not as obvious as those of his stablemate, and for all that he again shaped promisingly, he never got close enough to ever be thought of as the winner. This was only his fifth start and he could develop into a smart older horse back at 1m4f. (tchd 10-1)
Rewilding came into this off the back of a stunning performance in the Voltigeur, but he arrived at that race fresh, having not run since Epsom, and there was a doubt as to whether this light-framed sort, who was reportedly carrying zero condition in the paddock, would reproduce that form after just a 25-day break. Whereas at York he travelled like a class act, Dettori was already beginning to squeeze at him turning in and he just never picked up, keeping on steadily at the one pace having been switched more towards the inside. Both the manner of his last-time-out win and earlier French form pointed to him becoming a top-notch middle-distance performer, indeed connections were talking about next year's Arc after the Voltigeur, and now it's clear he needs a good break between races, there's still a chance he could reach that sort of level. Dettori later reported he ran flat. It's unlikely he will run again this season. Official explanation: jockey said colt ran flat (op 5-4)
Theology, who only just lost out in the Queen's Vase over 2m (ahead of Corsica), couldn't cope with the return to 1m4f when sixth in the Gordon Stakes, and he was again made to look shy of pace, even over this longer trip. He will appeal to many prospective jumps buyers as a smart hurdling prospect. (op 33-1)
Dandino, a rapid improver in handicaps this year prior to finishing one place ahead of the winner at Goodwood, never got into the race and connections were reported as saying the rain-softened ground affected his chance. Despite this setback, there's nothing to say he can't still improve, although the next step for him is a far from an obvious one. He stays in training next year. (op 15-2 tchd 11-2)
Total Command ran a shocker in the Voltigeur and again ended up well held having taken a keen grip early. He hasn't progressed as expected. (op 33-1)
Ted Spread, the Voltigeur fourth, needed significant rain to boost his chance, but even so he should have run better than he did, dropping right away to finish stone last. (op 22-1)

5946 EDDIE STOBART PARK STKS (GROUP 2) 7f
3:55 (3:56) (Class 1) 3-Y-O+

£90,832 (£34,432; £17,232; £8,592; £4,304; £2,160) **Stalls** High

Form RPR

-005 **1** **Balthazaar's Gift (IRE)**[46] 4457 7-9-4 112.... PhilipRobinson 8 118
(C G Cox) *swtg: dwlt: in rr: nt clr run over 1f out and swtchd to stands' side: r.o wl to ld nr fin* **16/1**

0113 **2** ½ **Premio Loco (USA)**[45] 4469 6-9-4 119.... GeorgeBaker 11 117
(C F Wall) *hld up towards rr: hdwy and edgd lft over 1f out: styd on wl ins fnl f: no ex nr fin* **7/2**[1]

2343 **3** *nse* **Himalya (IRE)**[13] 5554 4-9-4 109.... TomQueally 6 117
(J Noseda) *hld up in rr: hdwy over 2f out: swtchd lft over 1f out: chsd ldrs ins fnl f: no ex nr fin* **20/1**

2026 **4** *nk* **Duff (IRE)**[34] 4882 7-9-4 110....(b) EddieAhern 3 116
(Edward Lynam, Ire) *led: wnt clr after 2f: jnd over 2f out: hdd and no ex nr fin* **20/1**

1023 **5** 2 **High Standing (USA)**[34] 4885 5-9-4 110 RyanMoore 5 110
(W J Haggas) *dwlt: hld up in rr: hdwy 2f out: kpt on fnl f: nvr rchd ldrs* **13/2**[3]
4022 **6** 3/4 **Cat Junior (USA)**[28] 5081 5-9-4 113 (vt) JamieSpencer 13 108
(B J Meehan) *hld up in rr: hdwy 2f out: kpt on: nvr rchd ldrs* **7/1**
2043 **7** nk **Ouqba**[28] 5081 4-9-4 115 (b) RichardHills 10 107
(B W Hills) *chsd ldrs: edgd lft and one pce fnl f* **11/1**
2135 **8** 1/2 **Rainfall (IRE)**[41] 4639 3-8-11 112 KierenFallon 2 101
(M Johnston) *chsd ldrs: drvn over 3f out: one pce fnl 2f: eased towards fin* **5/1**[2]
-200 **9** 1 3/4 **Serious Attitude (IRE)**[64] 3870 4-9-1 105 DavidProbert 1 98
(Rae Guest) *mid-div: hdwy to chse ldrs over 2f out: wknd over 1f out: hmpd ins fnl f* **22/1**
1651 **10** nse **Shakespearean (IRE)**[28] 5081 3-9-0 116 (t) FrankieDettori 9 99
(Saeed Bin Suroor) *lw: trckd ldrs: drvn and wknd over 2f out: wknd 1f out* **5/1**[2]
0136 **11** 1 1/4 **Harrison George (IRE)**[22] 5274 5-9-4 113 PaulHanagan 4 98
(R A Fahey) *chsd ldrs: drvn over 2f out: lost pl over 1f out* **20/1**
1-60 **12** 4 **Arabian Gleam**[34] 4885 6-9-4 113 (p) DarryllHolland 7 87
(J Noseda) *chsd ldrs: wknd over 1f out: eased ins fnl f* **20/1**

1m 24.3s (-2.00) **Going Correction** +0.125s/f (Good)
WFA 3 from 4yo+ 4lb **12** Ran SP% **119.0**
Speed ratings (Par 115): **116,115,115,115,112 111,111,110,108,108 107,102**
Tote Swingers: 1&2 £16.80, 1&3 £46.60, 2&3 £18.30 CSF £65.40 TOTE £24.70: £5.20, £2.00, £7.30; EX 115.90 Trifecta £1842.70 Part won. Pool: £2,490.22 - 0.69 winning units..
Owner H E Sheikh Sultan Bin Khalifa Al Nahyan **Bred** Pat Beirne **Trained** Lambourn, Berks

FOCUS
A good-quality contest over what is usually a specialist distance, and the first four home in 2009 all took each other on again. Plenty of these have clashed this season and before, so whether this is strong or reliable form is debateable.

NOTEBOOK
Balthazaar's Gift(IRE) has been running respectably this season and gained a well-deserved success after a couple of unlucky efforts. Held up, his jockey made a move just over 1f out and the combination found plenty to get to the front and stay there. He doesn't win very often but rarely fails to run up to his best. (op 12-1)
Premio Loco(USA) has always been a decent performer but had looked improved this season, as a fine third to Canford Cliffs and Rip Van Winkle in the Sussex Stakes proved. About a length in front of the winner 1f out, he took a while to hit top stride, which appeared to confirm his trainer's suspicion that the trip would be a bit sharp for him, on ground that was a little slower than ideal. (op 9-2)
Himalya(IRE), who was ponied to the start, came home well home towards the other side of the course and was making good ground in the final 50 yards. (op 18-1)
Duff(IRE), last year's winner, set off at a good pace and at one stage looked to have gained an advantage sufficient enough to allow him to hang on. It must have been agony for punters who backed him each-way, as he was passed by Himalya for third yards from the winning line.
High Standing(USA) looked almost sure to place at least when making his run, but found his effort peter out. It appeared that he didn't get home but he should be allowed another try at this trip before too many conclusions are drawn. (op 5-1)
Cat Junior(USA) looks a tricky ride, who probably needs to get as far as he can on the bridle. (op 9-1 tchd 10-1)
Ouqba had every chance as the final furlong loomed but made no ground under pressure. (tchd 12-1)
Rainfall(IRE) made a rapid rise from her debut, and contested Group 1s on her last two starts. Given a break since her fair effort in the Prix Rothschild (she was due to contest the Haydock Park Sprint but missed that due to coughing in the morning of that contest), it seemed as though she was always finding the pace a stride too quick from the halfway point, and never really got involved. (tchd 11-2)
Serious Attitude(IRE), given a break since finishing last in the July Cup, was staying on when slightly impeded. It made little difference to her final position, however. (op 25-1)
Shakespearean(IRE) was disappointing, as he proved to be one paced for much of the final 2f. He had won the Hungerford Stakes on his previous start, but failed by a long way to back it up. (op 11-2)
Arabian Gleam, winner of this race in 2007 and 2008, and third last year, wasn't disgraced in a Group 1 last time in France but, after racing handily from the outset, dropped right away in this. His jockey eased off when it was clear he was going to play no part in the finish. (op 16-1)

5947 POWELL ENGINEERING NURSERY 1m (S)
4:25 (4:29) (Class 2) 2-Y-O **£8,095** (£2,408; £1,203; £601) **Stalls** High

Form RPR
21 **1** **Buthelezi (USA)**[18] 5392 2-9-7 88 WilliamBuick 6 94
(J H M Gosden) *lw: trckd ldrs: effrt over 2f out: hung lft: styd on to ld post* **11/8**[1]
6143 **2** nse **Arabian Star (IRE)**[12] 5597 2-8-6 73 ChrisCatlin 8 79
(M R Channon) *in rr: nt clr run and swtchd rt over 1f out: gd hdwy to ld last 50yds: hdd fnl stride* **22/1**
604 **3** 1/2 **Early Applause**[50] 4346 2-8-6 73 DavidProbert 3 78
(B W Hills) *lw: trckd ldrs: led 2f out: narrowly hdd ins fnl f: no ex* **16/1**
5611 **4** 1 1/4 **My Single Malt (IRE)**[12] 5597 2-8-10 77 JamieSpencer 7 79
(T P Tate) *s.i.s: hld up in rr: swtchd lft over 2f out: sn trcking ldrs: slt ld ins fnl f: hdd last 50yds: wknd* **9/2**[2]
4462 **5** 3/4 **El Torbellino (IRE)**[6] 5784 2-7-13 66 SilvestreDeSousa 9 66
(D O'Meara) *chsd ldrs: outpcd over 2f out: kpt on last 150yds* **10/1**
6440 **6** 1 1/4 **Golden Blaze**[12] 5597 2-7-5 65 oh8 NeilFarley[(7)] 2 63
(James Moffatt) *led tl 2f out: one pce appr fnl f* **100/1**
205 **7** 4 **Ollon (USA)**[7] 5761 2-8-8 75 PaulMulrennan 5 64
(R A Fahey) *chsd ldrs: wkng whn n.m.r over 1f out* **33/1**
3442 **8** 2 **Nicola's Dream**[38] 4701 2-8-1 68 PaulHanagan 12 52
(R A Fahey) *hld up: effrt over 2f out: hung lft and lost pl over 1f out* **12/1**
16 **9** hd **Borug (USA)**[22] 5257 2-9-4 85 FrankieDettori 10 69
(Saeed Bin Suroor) *trckd ldrs: effrt over 2f out: rdn and lost pl over 1f out* **9/1**
5610 **10** 2 1/2 **Kalkan Bay**[12] 5597 2-8-2 72 PatrickDonaghy[(3)] 4 51
(Jedd O'Keeffe) *uns rdr gng to s: mid-div: hdwy to chse ldrs over 2f out: wkng whn edgd lft over 1f out* **66/1**
413 **11** 6 **Last Destination (IRE)**[58] 4049 2-8-4 74 Louis-PhilippeBeuzelin[(3)] 1 39
(N Tinkler) *chsd ldrs: lost pl 2f out* **40/1**
01 **12** 55 **Colour Vision (FR)**[15] 5498 2-9-2 83 JoeFanning 11 —
(M Johnston) *gave problems in stalls: dwlt: drvn over 3f out: lost pl over 2f out: sn bhd: eased over 1f out: t.o* **13/2**[3]

1m 40.38s (1.08) **Going Correction** +0.125s/f (Good) **12** Ran SP% **118.5**
Speed ratings (Par 101): **99,98,98,97,96 95,91,89,89,86 80,25**
Tote Swingers:1&2:£8.40, 2&3:£24.40, 1&3:£7.20 CSF £42.16 CT £370.19 TOTE £2.30: £1.30, £4.90, £4.20; EX 40.40 Trifecta £412.90 Pool: £1,706.46 - 3.05 winning units..
Owner H R H Princess Haya Of Jordan **Bred** Dr John A Chandler **Trained** Newmarket, Suffolk
■ Stewards' Enquiry : Chris Catlin one day ban; used whip with excessive frequency (26th Sept)

FOCUS
An ordinary nursery.

NOTEBOOK
Buthelezi(USA) looked the potential class act beforehand and, despite the colt doing his best to throw it away by continually wanting to hang left, William Buick managed to get his nose in front on the line. Very well backed beforehand, he beat a subsequent winner when shedding his maiden tag at Yarmouth (also hung left), and wanted to be winning this if his Royal Lodge/Racing Post Trophy entries were anything to go by. He was value for more than the official margin and should do better on quicker ground, but he's reportedly a wayward sort mentally, so may not be one to get carried away with. (op 9-4 tchd 5-2 in a place)
Arabian Star(IRE), running on late behind My Single Malt at Newcastle latest, didn't get the best of runs, but picked up well to lead deep inside the final furlong, only to be claimed in the last stride. He is clearly progressing and is another for whom better ground may suit. (op 16-1)
Early Applause struck on two furlongs out, but that may have been too soon on this first try at 1m and he couldn't quite last.
My Single Malt(IRE), raised 3lb for his Newcastle success, failed to confirm form with Arabian Star, although not by much, just emptying in the final 50 yards. (tchd 5-1)
El Torbellino(IRE) showed his York second was no fluke with another reasonable effort. (op 17-2)
Golden Blaze, racing from 8lb 'wrong', still registered easily his best effort to date, belying odds of 100-1.
Ollon(USA) went well to a point on this handicap debut. (op 20-1)
Colour Vision(FR) got worked up in the stalls and deserves another chance. (tchd 6-1 and 7-1)

5948 AGRIARGO UK TRACTOR CHALLENGE H'CAP 1m (S)
5:00 (5:02) (Class 2) (0-110,110) 3-Y-O+ **£12,952** (£3,854; £1,926; £962) **Stalls** High

Form RPR
1100 **1** **Capponi (IRE)**[23] 5247 3-8-9 100 SilvestreDeSousa 10 111
(M Johnston) *led one other towards centre: drvn over 2f out: styd on wl to ld overall last 100yds* **9/2**[1]
4006 **2** 1 **Stoic (IRE)**[23] 5247 4-9-2 102 RyanMoore 7 111
(J Noseda) *lw: trckd ldrs: led over 1f out: hung rt: hdd and no ex ins fnl f* **9/2**[1]
5430 **3** 2 1/2 **Webbow (IRE)**[12] 5605 8-8-7 96 oh6 (p) Louis-PhilippeBeuzelin[(3)] 11 99
(N Tinkler) *trckd one other towards centre: rdn 2f out: edgd lft over 1f out: styd on same pce fnl f* **25/1**
2401 **4** hd **Our Joe Mac (IRE)**[35] 4828 3-8-5 96 oh2 PaulHanagan 2 98+
(R A Fahey) *trckd ldrs: effrt over 2f out: outpcd over 1f out: styd on ins fnl f* **7/1**
0021 **5** 1 1/4 **Al Khaleej (IRE)**[35] 4843 6-8-13 102 MartinLane[(3)] 8 102
(D M Simcock) *s.i.s: t.k.h: swtchd lft to r far side after 1f: hdwy2f out: kpt on same pce* **7/1**
2666 **6** 2 1/2 **Ordnance Row**[7] 5741 7-9-2 102 PhilipRobinson 1 96
(M A Jarvis) *trckd ldr: effrt 2f out: wknd 1f out* **16/1**
3200 **7** 3 **Balcarce Nov (ARG)**[23] 5247 5-9-2 102 JamieSpencer 5 89
(T P Tate) *lw: overall ldr far side: hdd over 1f out: wknd jst ins fnl f* **12/1**
3252 **8** nk **Swop (IRE)**[190] 818 7-9-2 102 KierenFallon 3 89
(L M Cumani) *lw: s.i.s: effrt over 2f out: wkng whn hmpd over 1f out* **13/2**[3]
11-3 **9** shd **Harald Bluetooth (IRE)**[42] 4596 5-8-10 96 oh2 WilliamBuick 9 82
(D M Simcock) *s.s: swtchd lft after 1f to r far side: sme hdwy over 2f out: wknd 1f out* **16/1**
1210 **10** 7 **Balducci**[86] 3103 3-8-5 96 DavidProbert 6 65
(A M Balding) *trckd ldrs: hung lft and wknd over 1f out: heavily eased ins fnl f* **11/2**[2]

1m 38.95s (-0.35) **Going Correction** +0.125s/f (Good)
WFA 3 from 4yo+ 5lb **10** Ran SP% **113.4**
Speed ratings (Par 109): **106,105,102,102,101 98,95,95,95,88**
Tote Swingers:1&2:£3.40, 2&3:£28.10, 1&3:£24.60 CSF £23.45 CT £447.85 TOTE £5.40: £1.90, £1.80, £5.90; EX 26.30 Trifecta £443.80 Pool: £1,763.21 - 2.94 winning units.
Owner Sheikh Hamdan Bin Mohammed Al Maktoum **Bred** Darley **Trained** Middleham Moor, N Yorks
■ Stewards' Enquiry : David Probert two day ban; careless riding (26th-27th Sept)

FOCUS
A good-quality 1m handicap.

NOTEBOOK
Capponi(IRE) got back on track following reverses at both Goodwood and York. He had excuses for those defeats, though, and the return to more aggressive tactics suited this strong-galloping type well. Racing down the centre, tracked by Webbow, he really responded well when asked to up the ante and in the end stayed on too well for Stoic, who had taken the lead off him over 1f out. The Cambridgeshire looks the race now, and the extra furlong there should prove right up his street. (op 5-1 tchd 11-2 and 4-1)
Stoic(IRE), several places ahead of the winner at York, was soon tracking the pace on the far side and struck on over 1f out, but his reign in front wasn't to last. He remains capable of better, perhaps ridden with more restraint, and is another likely Cambridgeshire contender. (op 11-2 tchd 4-1)
Webbow(IRE), racing from 6lb out of the handicap, couldn't stay with the winner when he kicked for home, but he did run on well late in the day to just grab third. (op 20-1)
Our Joe Mac(IRE) ◆, 2lb 'wrong', was unable to quicken initially, but did stay on again and, as last month's Haydock win suggested, he looks worth another try at 1m2f. (op 8-1)
Al Khaleej(IRE), raised 7lb for last month's 7f Newmarket victory, kept on all too late. (op 9-2)
Swop(IRE) was reported to have been denied a clear run. Official explanation: jockey said gelding was denied a clear run (op 8-1 tchd 6-1)
Balducci had looked a potential Group performer earlier in the season, but ran no race at all on this return from an 86-day absence. David Probert reported he hung left. Official explanation: jockey said colt hung left-handed (op 7-1 tchd 8-1)

5949 DONCASTER PREMIER INN AND TABLE TABLE H'CAP 1m 4f
5:35 (5:35) (Class 2) (0-105,103) 3-Y-O+**£16,190** (£4,817; £2,407; £1,202) **Stalls** Low

Form RPR
1031 **1** **Senate**[18] 5387 3-8-9 95 WilliamBuick 5 108+
(J H M Gosden) *lw: led 2f: trckd ldrs: led over 2f out: styd on wl fnl f: readily* **11/4**[1]
5144 **2** 1 1/2 **Times Up**[24] 5217 4-9-4 95 EddieAhern 13 103+
(J L Dunlop) *swtchd lft after s: hld up in rr: hdwy 3f out: styd on wl fnl f: tk 2nd nr fin* **11/2**[2]
1306 **3** 3/4 **Thin Red Line (IRE)**[24] 5217 4-9-2 93 RyanMoore 10 100
(M Dods) *trckd ldrs: effrt over 2f out: styd on same pce fnl f* **11/2**[2]
-600 **4** hd **Blizzard Blues (USA)**[28] 5080 4-9-7 98 (b) TomQueally 16 104
(H R A Cecil) *lw: hld up towards rr: hdwy 7f out: nt clr run 2f out: sn chsng wnr: kpt on same pce* **20/1**
0512 **5** 1/2 **Magicalmysterytour (IRE)**[18] 5387 7-8-13 90 ChrisCatlin 8 96
(W J Musson) *t.k.h in rr: hdwy over 2f out: kpt on wl ins fnl f* **12/1**
1520 **6** 1 3/4 **Emerging Artist (FR)**[21] 5291 4-9-4 95 JoeFanning 7 98
(M Johnston) *lw: sn chsng ldrs: rdn over 2f out: one pce* **10/1**[3]
1320 **7** 3/4 **Admission**[27] 5136 3-9-0 100 (t) JamieSpencer 1 102
(M L W Bell) *lw: s.i.s: in rr: hdwy over 2f out: kpt on same pce: nvr trbld ldrs* **14/1**

4 **8** *nk* **Siberian Tiger (IRE)**[91] 2976 5-9-2 **93**......................(p) DarryllHolland 15 94+
(M Wigham) *swtchd lft after s: hld up in rr: nt clr run 2f out: kpt on: nvr a factor* **25/1**

1040 **9** *nk* **Red Jade**[25] 5188 5-8-12 **89** oh4.. PaulHanagan 2 90
(R A Fahey) *lw: mid-div: hdwy to chse ldrs over 2f out: one pce* **16/1**

-546 **10** *¾* **Hatton Flight**[35] 4818 6-8-13 **90**....................................(v) DavidProbert 9 90
(A M Balding) *s.i.s: reminders after s: in rr: sme hdwy 2f out: nvr on terms* **40/1**

-300 **11** *½* **Sopranist**[24] 5220 4-9-8 **99**.. RichardHills 6 98
(Saeed Bin Suroor) *mid-div: nt clr run over 2f out: swtchd lft over 1f out: nvr nr ldrs* **11/1**

0140 **12** *hd* **Porgy**[7] 5743 5-8-7 **89** oh2.. LeeTopliss(5) 12 87
(R A Fahey) *chsd ldrs: lost pl 2f out* **33/1**

0110 **13** *7* **Yorgunnabelucky (USA)**[24] 5217 4-9-2 **93**...............(p) KierenFallon 11 80
(M Johnston) *led after 2f: hdd over 2f out: lost pl over 1f out: eased towards fin* **11/1**

21-5 **14** *1 ½* **Libel Law**[28] 5090 4-9-12 **103**.. FrankieDettori 4 88
(Saeed Bin Suroor) *trckd ldrs: t.k.h: chal over 2f out: wknd over 1f out: eased towards fin* **10/1**[3]

2m 31.72s (-3.18) **Going Correction** -0.025s/f (Good)
WFA 3 from 4yo+ 9lb **14** Ran SP% **126.5**
Speed ratings (Par 109): **109,108,107,107,107 105,105,105,104,104 104,104,99,98**
Tote Swingers: 1&2 £4.90, 1&3 £4.40, 2&3 £6.40 CSF £16.91 CT £83.46 TOTE £4.10: £1.80, £2.70, £2.30; EX 18.50 Trifecta £67.40 Pool: £1,415.28 - 15.52 winning units. Place 6: £136.89, Place 5: £92.00..
Owner H R H Princess Haya Of Jordan **Bred** Watership Down Stud **Trained** Newmarket, Suffolk

FOCUS
A strong-looking field lined up for this, and plenty of them could be given a chance if running up to their best. The pace set by Yorgunnabelucky looked ordinary, and racing prominently certainly appeared to help the winner.

NOTEBOOK
Senate ◆, raised 8lb for winning on his previous start, was one of the least exposed in the line-up but took this in taking fashion despite still looking a bit inexperienced once in command. He has an entry in a heritage handicap at Newbury next weekend, and would be of obvious interest if taking in that contest but, ultimately, it appears that he will be aimed towards the November Handicap. (op 7-2)
Times Up has been running consistently and added another fine effort to his profile. This trip looks ideal but it might be worth another try over further again. (op 5-1 tchd 9-2)
Thin Red Line(IRE) ran well at York (where he looked a bit unlucky) and again here. He possibly saw too much daylight earlier than his rider would have wanted, although his attitude could not be faulted under pressure. (op 8-1)
Blizzard Blues(USA), making his handicap debut, looked distinctly quirky under pressure and may not be one to trust implicitly if he ever got into a battle, although his ability is undeniably still evident. (op 18-1)
Magicalmysterytour(IRE), the winner of this race is 2008 off a pound higher mark, produced another good performance. However, the turnabout in weights with the winner on their Leicester clash should have seen him reverse that form.
Emerging Artist(FR), disappointing at Chester last time, ran as though he was in the handicappers grip. (op 12-1 tchd 14-1)
Admission, who was tried over 1m7f on his previous outing, had a tongue-tie fitted for the first time but didn't help his cause with a slow start. He never got into contention. (op 10-1)
Siberian Tiger(IRE), absent since running in the Queen Mother's Cup for amateur riders in June, travelled strongly in rear and suggested that races can be won with him. (op 20-1)
Sopranist, dropping 2f in trip after a good run in the Ebor, was forced to switch a couple of times as horses weakened and ran a bit better than his final position suggests. (op 16-1)
Porgy raced too freely.
Libel Law, given a short break since a poor effort in Newmarket conditions event, his first start for 371 days, was trying 1m4f for the first time and faded disappointingly after coming into contention over 2f out. (op 8-1 tchd 11-1)
T/Jkpt: Not won. T/Plt: £237.70 to a £1 stake. Pool £212,082.94. 651.15 winning tickets. T/Qpdt: £109.80 to a £1 stake. Pool £9,222.90. 62.14 winning tickets. WG

5828 GOODWOOD (R-H)

Saturday, September 11

OFFICIAL GOING: Good to soft (good in places) changing to soft (good to soft in places) after race 2 (3.00).
Wind: Moderate, half against Weather: Overcast, heavy rain between races 1-2; showers after

5950 BLUEBAY H'CAP (PREVIOUSLY KNOWN AS THE SHELL HOUSE STKS) 7f

2:25 (2:25) (Class 2) (0-100,98) 3-Y-O+

£9,346 (£2,799; £1,399; £700; £349; £175) **Stalls** High

Form RPR

0001 **1** **Hajoum (IRE)**[9] 5702 4-9-5 **93**.. GregFairley 14 102
(M Johnston) *mde all: kicked 3 l clr over 2f out and stvd towards inner: same ld 1f out: v tired last 100yds: jst hld on* **10/1**

0301 **2** *nk* **Fathsta (IRE)**[21] 5297 5-9-1 **89**.. HayleyTurner 5 97+
(D M Simcock) *taken down early: hld up in 11th: prog towards inner over 2f out: chsd clr wnr over 1f out: clsd fnl f: gaining rapidly fin* **16/1**

0365 **3** *½* **Light From Mars**[23] 5247 5-9-6 **97**.......................... JamesMillman(3) 13 104
(B R Millman) *trckd ldng pair: wnt 2nd over 2f out to over 1f out: clsd on faltering wnr w pack fnl f* **5/1**[2]

0000 **4** *nse* **Carnaby Street (IRE)**[3] 5854 3-9-5 **97**...................... RichardHughes 11 102
(R Hannon) *trckd ldng quartet: reminder 1/2-way: lost pl and struggling over 2f out: styd on wl again fnl f: gaining fin* **8/1**[3]

6552 **5** *hd* **Desert Creek (IRE)**[14] 5516 4-9-3 **91**......................... JimmyFortune 10 97
(Sir Michael Stoute) *trckd ldrs in 6th: rdn on outer over 2f out: styd on and clsd grad fnl f: a hld* **11/4**[1]

0606 **6** *½* **Gallagher**[14] 5516 4-9-10 **98**.. MartinDwyer 12 103
(B J Meehan) *dwlt: sn chsd ldrs in 7th: rdn on outer over 2f out: no prog tl styd on wl fnl f: nrst fin* **16/1**

0221 **7** *1 ¾* **Woodcote Place**[30] 4995 7-8-12 **86**........................ RichardKingscote 8 86
(P R Chamings) *hld up in 9th: rdn and prog to chse ldrs over 1f out: one pce and no imp fnl f* **16/1**

6061 **8** *¾* **Bullwhip (IRE)**[14] 5524 3-9-5 **97**.. NickyMackay 4 93
(J H M Gosden) *hld up in 8th: pushed along 3f out: no prog and wl hld 2f out: kpt on fnl f* **5/1**[2]

0003 **9** *nk* **Spirit Of Sharjah (IRE)**[28] 5068 5-9-5 **98**............... AdamBeschizza(5) 1 95
(Miss J Feilden) *hld up in 12th: prog towards inner over 2f out: drvn and no imp over 1f out: fdd ins fnl f* **16/1**

0400 **10** *4* **Marajaa (IRE)**[35] 4816 8-9-5 **93**.. JamieMackay 2 79
(W J Musson) *hld up in 10th: shkn up and no prog over 2f out: btn after* **20/1**

6200 **11** *¾* **Aspectus (IRE)**[35] 4816 7-9-4 **97**..............................(p) SophieDoyle(5) 6 81
(J A Osborne) *trckd ldng trio: rdn and fnd nil over 2f out: sn wknd* **40/1**

500 **12** *3 ¾* **Coasting**[45] 4473 5-9-5 **93**... IanMongan 3 67
(Mrs A J Perrett) *hld up in last: shkn up and no prog 3f out: sn bhd* **25/1**

1130 **13** *6* **Elna Bright**[175] 944 5-9-3 **91**.. AdamKirby 7 49
(B R Johnson) *chsd wnr to over 2f out: wknd rapidly* **50/1**

1m 28.5s (1.60) **Going Correction** +0.475s/f (Yiel)
WFA 3 from 4yo+ 4lb **13** Ran SP% **116.7**
Speed ratings (Par 109): **109,108,108,108,107 107,105,104,104,99 98,94,87**
toteswingers: 1&2 £31.20, 1&3 £12.20, 2&3 £19.80. CSF £149.48 CT £923.17 TOTE £11.20: £3.50, £5.10, £2.10; EX 258.70 Trifecta £692.70 Pool: £936.17 - 1.00 winning units..
Owner Sheikh Hamdan Bin Mohammed Al Maktoum **Bred** Darley **Trained** Middleham Moor, N Yorks

■ Stewards' Enquiry : Hayley Turner three day ban; used whip in an incorrect place (26-28th Sept)

FOCUS
A competitive handicap. It was run at an ordinary early pace, which disadvantaged the hold-up horses, and that resulted in a blanket finish for the places. The majority of runners went more mid-track down the home straight, but the first pair raced towards the far side.

NOTEBOOK
Hajoum(IRE) made all in typically game fashion for one from his stable and followed up his narrow win at Wolverhampton nine days earlier from a 5lb higher mark. Drawn highest of all, being out in front was clearly to his liking and he had little trouble with this soft ground, which was of some concern beforehand. The handicapper will now have his say again, but this 4-y-o is obviously thriving. (op 9-1 tchd 8-1)
Fathsta(IRE), who went down early to post, fared best of those given waiting rides and rates better than the bare form. He, too, was up 5lb for winning on his previous outing at Chester and is clearly still on a decent mark, but he will go up again a few pounds for this.
Light From Mars, well backed, took time to pick up for pressure and would've enjoyed more of a test. He deserves to find another winning turn and helps to set the standard here. (op 7-1)
Carnaby Street(IRE) ◆ stayed on well inside the closing stages and this was his best effort of the campaign, so the easier ground has to go down as having helped. He could build on this next time. (op 12-1)
Desert Creek(IRE) proved popular to gain compensation for his near-miss over C&D a fortnight previously. He was 2lb higher and had his chance, but did prove a bit laboured under maximum pressure. That was most likely down to the lack of real early pace, as his last two wins came over 1m. (tchd 9-4)
Gallagher ran well and gave his all but continues his battle with the handicapper. (op 12-1)
Woodcote Place was another who could have done with a better pace. (op 14-1)
Bullwhip(IRE) was never seriously in the hunt and, while he may have enjoyed more of a test, has to rate as somewhat disappointing. (op 9-2 tchd 11-2)

5951 WHITELEY CLINIC SELECT STKS (GROUP 3) 1m 1f 192y

3:00 (3:01) (Class 1) 3-Y-O+

£32,358 (£12,266; £6,138; £3,060; £1,533; £769) **Stalls** High

Form RPR

4201 **1** **Red Badge (IRE)**[56] 4139 3-8-7 110............................ RichardHughes 3 118
(R Hannon) *trckd ldng pair: effrt 3f out: led narrowly 2f out: edgd lft fnl f: styd on gamely* **7/2**[3]

2111 **2** *1 ¼* **Mirror Lake**[13] 5553 3-8-4 104... MartinDwyer 7 113
(Mrs A J Perrett) *mostly trckd ldng trio: gng strly 3f out: plld out and drvn over 1f out: edgd lft but kpt trying: no imp last 150yds* **3/1**[2]

0631 **3** *nk* **Poet**[35] 4829 5-9-3 114.. AdamKirby 6 118
(C G Cox) *pressed ldr: led 3f out: sn drvn: hdd 2f out: kpt on but a hld fnl f* **2/1**[1]

4261 **4** *7* **Prince Siegfried (FR)**[12] 5590 4-9-0 110........................... TedDurcan 1 101
(Saeed Bin Suroor) *led at mod pce: rdn and hdd 3f out: styd cl up tl wknd qckly over 1f out* **4/1**

51-6 **5** *¾* **Mac Love**[45] 4469 9-9-0 116.. MickyFenton 2 99
(Stef Higgins) *t.k.h: hld up in last pair: shkn up 3f out: tried to cl on ldrs 2f out: sn wknd* **16/1**

0060 **6** *2 ¾* **Mont Agel**[42] 4574 3-8-7 97.. HayleyTurner 5 94
(M L W Bell) *hld up in 5th: rdn 3f out: no imp on ldrs 2f out: sn wknd qckly* **33/1**

420- **7** *8* **Moyenne Corniche**[314] 7208 5-9-0 104........................ JimmyFortune 4 78
(M L W Bell) *t.k.h: hld up in last pair: struggling fr 4f out: sn bhd* **33/1**

2m 11.14s (3.14) **Going Correction** +0.475s/f (Yiel)
WFA 3 from 4yo+ 7lb **7** Ran SP% **112.3**
Speed ratings (Par 113): **106,105,104,99,98 96,89**
toteswingers: 1&2 £1.70, 1&3 £1.80, 2&3 £1.50. CSF £13.89 TOTE £5.70: £3.10, £2.90; EX 12.50.
Owner Michael Pescod **Bred** Thomas Foy **Trained** East Everleigh, Wilts

FOCUS
Not the strongest contest for the class, but it was competitive and another race in which it paid to race handily, with the first three dominating.

NOTEBOOK
Red Badge(IRE) gamely followed up his Newbury success 56 days earlier on ground that evidently suits very well. The form of his previous Listed race has worked out nicely and he was racing on identical terms with Poet here. Another step up in class now beckons, and there could well be more to come. Connections later said the St Simon Stakes back at Newbury could be next up for him. (tchd 4-1)
Mirror Lake ◆ came here full of confidence, having won her last three races, the last two over this C&D. She didn't get the clearest of runs initially in the home straight, but still held every chance when switched towards the centre and this does rate another improved run in defeat. She will be kept in training next term, is well up to scoring in this grade and her trainer later added she believed it was the ground that did for her. (tchd 5-2)
Poet had his ground and ran a brave race in defeat, but his penalty was enough to anchor him towards the business end. He rates a solid benchmark. (op 5-2 tchd 11-4)
Prince Siegfried(FR), back to winning ways at Epsom last time, is not straightforward and had to be mounted out of the parade ring. He set out to make all, but wasn't given an easy lead and eventually dropped right out when the principals kicked for home. The ground was softer than he ideally cares for. (op 9-2)
Mac Love took this last season and shaped as though a return to further was what he needs when reappearing in the Sussex Stakes 45 days earlier. This wasn't a race where being held up helped though, and he, too, found the ground softer than he cares for. (op 11-1)
Mont Agel lacked the stamina for this trip on such ground, but was outclassed. (op 25-1)

The Form Book, Raceform Ltd, Compton, RG20 6NL

Moyenne Corniche was making his belated seasonal return and proved too free for his own good out the back early on. He wants dropping in class. (op 28-1 tchd 40-1)

5952 RUK STARLIT STKS (LISTED RACE) 6f
3:30 (3:31) (Class 1) 3-Y-0+

£19,869 (£7,532; £3,769; £1,879; £941; £472) **Stalls** Low

Form RPR

1001 **1** **Definightly**[13] 5551 4-9-0 96 (b) JimmyFortune 6 113
(R Charlton) *mde all: pushed along and drew rt away fnl f: impressive* **7/2**[2]

-202 **2** 6 **Lui Rei (ITY)**[42] 4569 4-9-0 102 TobyAtkinson 8 94
(M Botti) *s.i.s: hld up in 6th and off the pce: prog over 2f out: chsd wnr over 1f out: sn lft bhd* **13/2**

2151 **3** nk **Arabian Mirage**[26] 5154 4-8-9 97 MartinDwyer 5 88
(B J Meehan) *hld up in tch: rdn and effrt 2f out: disp 2nd over 1f out: kpt on but wl outpcd* **4/1**[3]

5455 **4** 1 **Georgebernardshaw (IRE)**[13] 5554 5-9-0 100 AdamKirby 7 90
(D M Simcock) *hld up in tch: rdn and effrt 2f out: kpt on but wl outpcd fnl f* **7/1**

1441 **5** 2 ¼ **Bounty Box**[27] 5120 4-8-13 103 TedDurcan 1 81
(C F Wall) *chsd wnr to 1/2-way: sn rdn: fdd over 1f out* **2/1**[1]

405 **6** 2 ½ **Requisite**[16] 5454 5-8-9 73 (v) JamesSullivan 3 69
(I A Wood) *s.v.s: a bhd: brief effrt over 2f out: wknd wl over 1f out* **66/1**

211 **7** ¾ **Poppy Seed**[54] 4204 3-8-7 86 RichardHughes 2 67
(R Hannon) *prom: chsd wnr 1/2-way to over 1f out: wknd rapidly* **12/1**

1m 13.23s (1.03) **Going Correction** +0.475s/f (Yiel)
WFA 3 from 4yo+ 2lb **7** Ran SP% **110.6**
Speed ratings (Par 111): **112,104,103,102,99 95,94**
toteswingers: 1&2 £4.00, 1&3 £2.70, 2&3 £3.80. CSF £24.28 TOTE £4.40: £2.80, £2.90; EX 21.70.
Owner S Emmet And Miss R Emmet **Bred** S Emmet And Miss R Emmet **Trained** Beckhampton, Wilts

FOCUS
Another average contest for the class, and most of these struggled on the demanding surface, but the winner still impressed. They raced right down the middle of the track.

NOTEBOOK
Definightly ◆ did the business impressively and extended his course record to 3-3. His ability to handle the ground was a massive advantage, but he is obviously peaking now and the recent application of blinkers has done the trick. A bold bid for the hat-trick should be expected if he turns up as expected at Ayr's Gold Cup meeting next week. He will look well treated under an 8lb penalty for his two recent wins and should get into that race, but there are always the valuable consolation events if he doesn't. (op 4-1 tchd 9-2)
Lui Rei(ITY), back from a 42-day break, was firmly put in his place when the winner asserted. This ground was probably against him though and he is worth another chance when reverting to a sounder surface. (op 5-1 tchd 9-2)
Arabian Mirage was a clear-cut winner on Polytrack last time, but this taxing surface blunted her finishing kick. (op 11-2 tchd 13-2)
Georgebernardshaw(IRE) was ridden more patiently again on this drop in trip, but he, too, lacked a change of pace on the soft ground. He remains on a losing run. (op 15-2 tchd 6-1)
Bounty Box arrived here in top form but clearly failed to go on the ground and her run is best forgiven. (op 15-8)
Requisite Official explanation: jockey said mare missed the break

5953 HOLT'S AUCTIONEERS STKS (H'CAP) 1m 4f
4:05 (4:05) (Class 4) (0-80,80) 3-Y-0 **£3,885** (£1,156; £577; £288) **Stalls** High

Form RPR

0011 **1** **Kathleen Frances**[31] 4972 3-8-9 73 AshleyMorgan(5) 1 84+
(M H Tompkins) *hld up in midfield: stdy prog on outer to press ldrs 3f out: led 2f out: hrd pressed fnl f: hld on* **6/1**[2]

6036 **2** nk **Paintball (IRE)**[22] 5266 3-9-2 75 MartinDwyer 2 84
(W R Muir) *t.k.h: hld up: last 1/2-way: gd prog on outer over 3f out: drvn 2f out: chsd wnr fnl f: kpt on but a jst hld* **8/1**

4214 **3** 1 **Higgy's Ragazzo (FR)**[16] 5456 3-9-5 78 RichardHughes 6 85
(R Hannon) *hld up and last to 1/2-way: gd prog 4f out to join ldrs 3f out: rdn and nt qckn over 2f out: styd on ins fnl f* **7/1**[3]

6304 **4** nk **Issabella Gem (IRE)**[22] 5259 3-9-2 75 AdamKirby 8 82
(C G Cox) *sn stdd into 5th: prog to ld 3f out to 2f out: pressed wnr tl no ex fnl f* **6/1**[2]

0402 **5** ½ **Marie De Guise (IRE)**[12] 5611 3-9-7 80 (v[1]) JimmyFortune 10 86
(Sir Michael Stoute) *hld up in rr: rdn 3f out: limited prog and sn u.str.p: styd on fnl f: nrst fin* **3/1**[1]

1543 **6** 1 ½ **Judiciary (IRE)**[65] 3807 3-8-12 78 AntiocoMurgia(7) 9 82
(Mahmood Al Zarooni) *hld up: dropped to rr 1/2-way: in last pair and rdn 3f out: kpt on fnl 2f: nvr on terms* **17/2**

2223 **7** 5 **Dolphina (USA)**[19] 5366 3-9-1 74 IanMongan 12 70
(H R A Cecil) *hld up in midfield: rdn 3f out: one pce and no imp on ldrs 2f out: fdd fnl f* **15/2**

0130 **8** 8 **Killusty Fancy (IRE)**[15] 5467 3-8-8 67 GregFairley 5 50
(D J S Ffrench Davis) *mde most to 1/2-way: rdn over 3f out: wknd over 2f out* **25/1**

042 **9** 2 ¼ **Warlu Way**[22] 5258 3-9-0 73 TedDurcan 4 52
(J L Dunlop) *prom tl wknd qckly over 2f out* **11/1**

120 **10** 4 ½ **High On A Hill (IRE)**[112] 2323 3-9-4 77 TravisBlock 7 49
(S Kirk) *pressed ldng pair tl wknd rapidly over 3f out* **28/1**

5 **11** 16 **Time Square (FR)**[35] 4827 3-9-3 79 (t) MichaelGeran(3) 3 26
(A W Carroll) *sweating: t.k.h: pressed ldr: led 1/2-way: hdd & wknd rapidly 3f out: t.o* **50/1**

2m 45.57s (7.17) **Going Correction** +0.475s/f (Yiel) **11** Ran SP% **117.1**
Speed ratings (Par 103): **95,94,94,93,93 92,89,83,82,79 68**
toteswingers: 1&2 £11.50, 1&3 £1.20, 2&3 £13.00. CSF £52.11 CT £346.02 TOTE £4.50: £2.40, £2.70, £2.00; EX 44.70.
Owner Russell Trew Ltd **Bred** Russell Trew Ltd **Trained** Newmarket, Suffolk

FOCUS
A fair 3-y-o middle-distance handicap. There was a steady early pace on and again the action developed down the middle of the home straight.
Warlu Way Official explanation: trainer's rep said colt was unsuited by the soft (good to soft places) ground

5954 E B F BUY A £10,000 RACING POST BONUS YEARLING MAIDEN STKS 1m
4:40 (4:40) (Class 4) 2-Y-0 **£3,885** (£1,156; £577; £288) **Stalls** High

Form RPR

1 **Vanguard Dream** 2-9-3 0 RichardHughes 2 85
(R Hannon) *mde all: set mod pce: shkn up 2f out: asserted over 1f out: styd on wl* **4/1**[2]

2 2 ¼ **Weapon Of Choice (IRE)** 2-9-3 0 NickyMackay 3 80
(D M Simcock) *trckd wnr: shkn up 2f out: kpt on same pce and no imp over 1f out* **8/1**

62 **3** 3 ½ **Yair Hill (IRE)**[29] 5032 2-9-3 0 TedDurcan 1 72
(J L Dunlop) *hld up in 4th: moved up to chal jst over 2f out: sn rdn and nt qckn: wknd ins fnl f* **8/13**[1]

04 **4** 2 ¼ **Kyllachy Spirit**[37] 4755 2-9-3 0 (p) AdamKirby 7 67
(B R Johnson) *chsd ldng pair to over 2f out: steadily wknd* **7/1**[3]

0 **5** 5 **Fire Crystal**[28] 5078 2-8-12 0 EddieCreighton 6 51
(M R Channon) *a same pl: pushed along 1/2-way: steadily lost tch fr over 2f out* **33/1**

6 **6** 10 **Already Basking (CAN)**[13] 5546 2-9-3 0 (b[1]) GregFairley 5 34
(P F I Cole) *sn last and many reminders: a toiling* **33/1**

1m 45.22s (5.32) **Going Correction** +0.475s/f (Yiel) **6** Ran SP% **111.4**
Speed ratings (Par 97): **92,89,86,84,79 69**
toteswingers: 1&2 £1.70, 1&3 £1.10, 2&3 £1.30. CSF £33.31 TOTE £4.80: £2.00, £3.40; EX 27.50.
Owner Malih L Al Basti **Bred** Malih L Al Basti **Trained** East Everleigh, Wilts

FOCUS
A modest juvenile maiden, run at an uneven pace and all the runners took time to settle.

NOTEBOOK
Vanguard Dream made all and ran out a ready debut winner, handing his yard yet another 2-y-o success at the track this term. He was sure to act on the ground on his breeding and did so without fuss. While he got the run of things, he looks a very useful performer in the making. (tchd 9-2)
Weapon Of Choice(IRE) ◆, a half-brother to fair 7f winner Eager To Bow, raced just off the winner and had every chance. He couldn't quicken as well as that one on this ground, but it was a nice introduction and he is clearly well up to winning races. (op 9-1 tchd 10-1)
Yair Hill(IRE) had run with promise in two maidens previously that had been won by subsequent Group winners Native Khan and Saamidd. He got warm beforehand, though, and after looking a threat on the outside 2f out, found little for pressure. He raced awkwardly inside the final furlong, perhaps not handling the track and going on the contrasting ground, so is worth another chance to prove himself. He also now qualifies for a mark. Official explanation: trainer's rep said colt was unsuited by the soft (good to soft places) ground (op 8-11)
Kyllachy Spirit dropped out from the 2f pole and failed to raise his game for first-time cheekpieces. It was his first run away from a sound surface, however, and he, too, now has the option of nurseries. (op 11-2 tchd 5-1)
Fire Crystal took a strong early hold and was beaten 4f out. (op 25-1)
Already Basking(CAN) posted a mulish effort in first-time blinkers. (op 28-1 tchd 40-1)

5955 TERRY & GERALDINE EARLE STKS (H'CAP) 1m 1f
5:15 (5:15) (Class 2) (0-100,95) 3-Y-0+

£8,723 (£2,612; £1,306; £653; £326; £163) **Stalls** High

Form RPR

221 **1** **Nationalism**[51] 4307 3-9-6 95 NickyMackay 9 108+
(J H M Gosden) *a cl up: waited bhd ldrs tl delivered to ld over 1f out: forged clr* **2/1**[1]

-130 **2** 3 **Shavansky**[87] 3069 6-9-7 93 JamesMillman(3) 3 99
(B R Millman) *dwlt: hld up in rr: prog to trck ldrs 4f out: gng wl enough whn chalng over 1f out: chsd wnr after: fnd little and sn btn* **33/1**

1331 **3** 1 **Pintura**[13] 5552 3-8-0 80 (p) SophieDoyle(5) 8 84
(D M Simcock) *trckd ldr 3f: styd cl up: rdn to chal 2f out: nt qckn over 1f out: one pce after* **16/1**

6065 **4** 2 ½ **Tartan Gunna**[12] 5592 4-9-5 88 (v) GregFairley 6 86
(M Johnston) *dwlt: t.k.h and rcvrd to press ldr after 3f: led over 2f out to over 1f out: fdd* **11/1**

6025 **5** 1 ½ **Moynahan (USA)**[14] 5529 5-9-7 90 (p) JimmyFortune 5 85
(P F I Cole) *hld up in last pair: shkn up and no prog on outer over 2f out: plugged on over 1f out* **6/1**[3]

3663 **6** 1 ¾ **South Cape**[13] 5556 7-9-2 85 RichardHughes 1 76
(G L Moore) *chsd ldrs: hrd rdn over 2f out: steadily fdd* **9/1**

1 **7** 2 ¼ **Itlaaq**[94] 2865 4-9-8 91 MartinDwyer 7 77
(J L Dunlop) *hld up towards rr: rdn and no prog over 2f out: wknd over 1f out* **3/1**[2]

1-2 **8** 3 **Sowaylm**[141] 1500 3-9-3 92 (t) TedDurcan 10 72
(Saeed Bin Suroor) *led to over 2f out: sn wknd* **13/2**

2-06 **9** 1 **The Cayterers**[32] 4924 8-9-3 89 MichaelGeran(3) 4 66
(A W Carroll) *s.i.s: hld up and sn last: rdn wl over 2f out: no prog* **33/1**

2m 0.92s (4.62) **Going Correction** +0.475s/f (Yiel)
WFA 3 from 4yo+ 6lb **9** Ran SP% **116.1**
Speed ratings (Par 109): **98,95,94,92,90 89,87,84,83**
toteswingers: 1&2 £27.80, 1&3 £7.80, 2&3 £8.70. CSF £73.53 CT £834.11 TOTE £3.60: £1.30, £6.00, £4.10; EX 106.70.
Owner George Strawbridge **Bred** George Strawbridge **Trained** Newmarket, Suffolk

FOCUS
A good handicap, run at a fair pace on such ground.

NOTEBOOK
Nationalism ◆ came home a taking winner on his handicap debut and rates value for a little further, as he had to wait for his challenge from 3f out. His three previous outings had been on quick ground, but he is bred to act on a soft surface and actually looked better suited by it, quickening nicely when asked to win the race. His stable continues in fine form and he could well turn out to be a Pattern-class performer. This display later saw him promoted into a clear favourite for the Cambridgeshire. (op 3-1)
Shavansky, whose last run was at Royal Ascot in June, was moved up to join issue turning for home and made a bold bid more towards the centre of the track. This was a decent effort under top weight and time will probably tell he faced an impossible task conceding weight to the winner.
Pintura was a ready winner over C&D on his previous outing and handles some cut, so he rates a good benchmark for the form. He was 6lb higher here and showed himself still to be nicely handicapped, so can find lesser assignments in the coming weeks. (op 14-1 tchd 12-1)
Tartan Gunna had slipped to the same mark as when successful in this event last year. He had his chance, but this ground wasn't really for him and he couldn't quicken when it mattered. He could go in again when returned to better ground. (op 17-2 tchd 8-1)
Moynahan(USA) lacked the pace to get seriously involved and is another for whom the ground was probably too soft, but he is hard to get right all the same. Official explanation: jockey said gelding hung right-handed (op 13-2 tchd 7-1)
Itlaaq was up 8lb for winning when last seen 94 days earlier and attracted support. He didn't get the best of runs from off the pace, but still flattened out when in the clear and ultimately the run looked as though it would bring him on. He has evidently had his problems, though. (tchd 7-2)
Sowaylm dropped out tamely on this return from a 141-day absence and may not have acted on this contrasting ground, but does now have something to prove. (op 6-1 tchd 9-2)

The Cayterers Official explanation: trainer's rep said colt was unsuited by the soft (good to soft places) ground

5956 COUNTRYSIDE ALLIANCE STKS (H'CAP) 5f
5:50 (5:50) (Class 5) (0-75,77) 3-Y-O **£3,238** (£963; £481; £240) **Stalls** Low

Form RPR

-641 **1** **Galatian**[34] 4861 3-9-4 **75**........ JamesMillman(3) 8 83
(B R Millman) *racd centre: pressed ldrs: rdn and on terms 2f out: kpt on fnl f to ld nr fin* **9/4**[2]

1221 **2** *hd* **Bronze Beau**[12] 5600 3-9-6 **77**........(t) JamesSullivan(3) 4 84
(Mrs L Stubbs) *racd towards nr side: disp ld: slt advantage over 1f out: urged along fnl f: hdd nr fin* **2/1**[1]

6220 **3** *nk* **Superior Edge**[21] 5309 3-9-4 **72**........ JimmyFortune 5 78
(B Palling) *racd centre: disp ld to over 1f out: kpt on ins fnl f: a jst hld* **13/2**

4534 **4** *1 ¾* **Texas Queen**[12] 5600 3-9-2 **70**........ EddieCreighton 7 70
(M R Channon) *s.i.s: t.k.h: racd centre: hld up in tch: rdn and nt qckn over 1f out: one pce after* **8/1**

-315 **5** *shd* **Star Twilight**[33] 4892 3-8-12 **66**........(v[1]) AdamKirby 2 65
(D Shaw) *racd nr side: chsd ldrs: rdn and nt qckn wl over 1f out: one pce after* **10/1**

3221 **6** *½* **Silvee**[12] 5588 3-8-7 **61** oh4........ NeilChalmers 6 58
(J J Bridger) *racd centre: hld up in tch: effrt and on terms 2f out: wknd fnl f* **6/1**[3]

61.01 secs (2.61) **Going Correction** +0.475s/f (Yiel) **6** Ran SP% **111.9**
Speed ratings (Par 101): **98,97,97,94,94 93**
toteswingers: 1&2 £1.10, 1&3 £4.00, 2&3 £3.50. CSF £7.13 CT £22.61 TOTE £3.50: £1.80, £1.90; EX 8.00 Place 6: £445.14, Place 5: £144.33..
Owner Tarka Racing **Bred** Mrs B A Matthews **Trained** Kentisbeare, Devon

FOCUS
A moderate 3-y-o sprint handicap was hit by non-runners. The field spread across the track and all had a chance of sorts, so there was no real bias.
T/Plt: £680.10 to a £1 stake. Pool of £85,487.69 - 91.75 winning tickets. T/Qpdt: £56.60 to a £1 stake. Pool of £4,203.08 - 54.95 winning tickets. JN

5891 KEMPTON (A.W) (R-H)
Saturday, September 11

OFFICIAL GOING: Standard
Wind: Virtually nil. Weather: light cloud, brighter spells

5957 KEMPTON.CO.UK H'CAP 5f (P)
5:30 (5:30) (Class 6) (0-60,60) 3-Y-O **£1,637** (£483; £241) **Stalls** High

Form RPR

0062 **1** **Pavement Games**[16] 5438 3-8-2 **49**........ KierenFox(5) 5 54
(R C Guest) *s.i.s: hld up towards rr: hdwy 2f out: rdn to chse ldrs over 1f out: sustained run u.p fnl f to ld towards fin* **7/1**

6012 **2** *nk* **Madam Isshe**[8] 5715 3-9-2 **58**........ AndreaAtzeni 10 62
(M S Saunders) *chsd ldr: rdn wl over 1f out: drvn ent fnl f: kpt on wl to ld fnl 50yds: sn hdd and no ex towards fin* **5/1**[3]

3002 **3** *nk* **Flaxen Lake**[26] 5152 3-9-4 **60**........(tp) RichardKingscote 6 63
(J M Bradley) *led: rdn over 1f out: kpt on gamely u.p fnl f tl hdd and lost 2 pls fnl 50yds* **15/2**

5362 **4** *¾* **Duke Of Rainford**[13] 5548 3-8-10 **52**........ SteveDrowne 8 52
(M Herrington) *stdd s: hld up in rr: effrt and swtchd lft over 1f out: rdn and gd hdwy ent fnl f: no imp fnl 100yds* **4/1**[2]

0000 **5** *½* **Trelicia**[8] 5729 3-8-8 **50**........ WilliamCarson 4 49
(S C Williams) *dwlt: racd in midfield: rdn and hdwy wl over 1f out: hanging lft ent fnl f: styd on same pce fnl 150yds* **25/1**

4663 **6** *2 ¼* **Tartufo Dolce (IRE)**[17] 5410 3-9-3 **59**........ MickyFenton 11 49
(J G Given) *chsd ldrs: rdn and unable qck wl over 1f out: wknd ins fnl f* **3/1**[1]

5000 **7** *nk* **My Meteor**[30] 4989 3-8-10 **52**........ FergusSweeney 1 41
(A G Newcombe) *wnt lft and stdd s: t.k.h: hld up in rr: hdwy on outer over 1f out: styd on same pce and no imp ins fnl f* **16/1**

5266 **8** *¾* **True Red (IRE)**[99] 2688 3-8-5 **50**........(b) AndrewHeffernan(3) 7 37
(Mrs N S Evans) *chsd ldrs: rdn and unable qck over 1f out: wknd u.p ent fnl f* **25/1**

-000 **9** *3* **Outshine**[30] 4989 3-8-8 **55**........(p) AdamBeschizza(5) 9 31
(Karen George) *dwlt: sn in midfield: nt clr run: lost pl and dropped to rr wl over 1f out: nt rcvr and wl btn fnl f* **8/1**

6000 **10** *14* **Rightcar Marian**[26] 5152 3-7-13 **46** oh1........ SimonPearce(5) 12 —
(Peter Grayson) *racd keenly: chsd ldrs tl wknd qckly wl over 1f out: wl bhd and eased ins fnl f* **50/1**

60.87 secs (0.37) **Going Correction** -0.05s/f (Stan) **10** Ran SP% **112.6**
Speed ratings (Par 99): **95,94,94,92,92 88,87,86,81,59**
Tote Swingers:1&2:£5.80, 2&3:£4.70, 1&3:£5.90 CSF £39.58 CT £274.93 TOTE £7.60: £2.50, £1.80, £2.20; EX 39.40.
Owner S Hussey **Bred** Mrs J M Russell **Trained** Stainforth, S Yorks
■ Stewards' Enquiry : Andrea Atzeni one day ban; excessive use of whip (26th Sept)

FOCUS
A moderate handicap run at a decent gallop. The winner raced centre to far side in the straight.

5958 JAGUAR XF H'CAP (DIV I) 1m 2f (P)
6:00 (6:01) (Class 5) (0-70,70) 3-Y-O+ **£1,944** (£574; £287) **Stalls** High

Form RPR

0051 **1** **Classically (IRE)**[19] 5367 4-9-12 **70**........ SteveDrowne 7 84
(H Morrison) *chsd ldng trio: rdn and effrt to chse ldr over 1f out: led ins fnl f: r.o strly* **7/2**[2]

3313 **2** *2* **Josr's Magic (IRE)**[10] 5663 6-9-2 **60**........ JimmyQuinn 2 70
(P R Hedger) *chsd ldr over 8f out: pushed into ld ent fnl 2f: rdn over 1f out: hdd ins fnl f: no ex* **3/1**[1]

5505 **3** *1 ¼* **Opera Prince**[11] 5635 5-9-6 **64**........(b[1]) SebSanders 1 72
(Lady Herries) *stdd s: hld up in last: stl last but gng wl 3f out: swtchd to outer 2f out: rdn and hdwy to dispute 3rd ent fnl f: styd on but nvr able to chal* **9/2**[3]

5-30 **4** *nk* **Penangdouble O One**[66] 3781 3-9-4 **69**........(t) RichardKingscote 6 76
(R M Beckett) *in tch in midfield: rdn and effrt 2f out: disputing 3rd ent fnl f: styd on u.p but nvr gng pce to rch ldng pair* **8/1**

3256 **5** *6* **Muftarres (IRE)**[5] 5819 5-9-7 **65**........ MickyFenton 3 60
(P T Midgley) *hld up towards rr: hdwy over 2f out: rdn wl over 1f out: chsd clr ldng pair over 1f out tl jst ins fnl f: wknd qckly fnl 100yds* **15/2**

1-60 **6** *5* **Levitation (IRE)**[9] 5689 4-9-8 **66**........ IanMongan 10 51
(W S Kittow) *led tl rdn and hdd ent fnl 2f: outpcd by ldng pair over 1f out: fdd fnl f* **16/1**

3005 **7** *1 ½* **Watchmaker**[19] 5367 7-9-4 **62**........ FergusSweeney 9 44
(Miss Tor Sturgis) *awkward leaving stalls: sn bustled along and in tch in midfield: rdn and outpcd wl over 1f out: wl btn after* **11/1**

6-04 **8** *2 ¾* **Montelissima (IRE)**[18] 5391 3-8-13 **64**........ TomMcLaughlin 5 40
(E A L Dunlop) *wnt lft s: a towards rr: rdn and lost tch ent fnl 2f: wl bhd fnl f* **9/1**

030 **9** *1* **Distant Waters**[19] 5366 3-8-4 **62**........ HarryBentley(7) 4 36
(A P Jarvis) *hmpd s and s.i.s: hld up towards rr: rdn and btn 2f out: wl bhd fnl f* **16/1**

5050 **10** *¾* **Baibars (USA)**[53] 4230 3-9-2 **67**........(b) SamHitchcott 11 40
(G A Butler) *chsd ldrs tl lost pl qckly u.p ent fnl 2f: wl bhd over 1f out* **40/1**

2m 5.86s (-2.14) **Going Correction** -0.05s/f (Stan)
WFA 3 from 4yo+ 7lb **10** Ran SP% **120.8**
Speed ratings (Par 103): **106,104,103,103,98 94,93,90,90,89**
Tote Swingers:1&2:£3.60, 2&3:£4.50, 1&3:£5.10. CSF £15.06 CT £49.21 TOTE £3.20: £1.02, £2.80, £1.40; EX 10.40.
Owner Ben Arbib **Bred** Bridgewater Equine Ltd **Trained** East Ilsley, Berks

FOCUS
A modest handicap in which an ordinary gallop made it difficult to make ground from off the pace. The winner raced towards the inside rail in the straight.

5959 JAGUAR XF H'CAP (DIV II) 1m 2f (P)
6:30 (6:30) (Class 5) (0-70,69) 3-Y-O+ **£1,944** (£574; £287) **Stalls** High

Form RPR

4531 **1** **Aurora Sky (IRE)**[16] 5457 4-9-5 **62**........ RichardHughes 11 73
(J Akehurst) *chsd ldrs: wnt 2nd 1/2-way: rdn to ld wl over 1f out: kpt on wl u.p fnl f: drvn out* **3/1**[2]

/5-3 **2** *1* **Ateeb**[19] 5367 4-9-12 **69**........ TomMcLaughlin 1 78
(E A L Dunlop) *chsd ldr tl 1/2-way: drvn to chse wnr over 1f out: kpt on trying but hld by wnr fnl 100yds* **15/8**[1]

3043 **3** *hd* **Cape Quarter (USA)**[29] 5039 4-9-2 **62**........(t) GilmarPereira(3) 10 71
(W J Haggas) *stdd s: hld up in last trio: hdwy over 4f out: rdn to chse ldrs wl over 1f out: wnt 3rd 1f out: kpt on u.p ins fnl f: pressing for 2nd nr fin* **13/2**[3]

0500 **4** *6* **Sounds Of Thunder**[61] 3954 3-8-9 **66**........(b[1]) RichardRowe(7) 5 63
(H J L Dunlop) *dwlt: sn bustled along to r in midfield: hdwy to chse ldrs over 4f out: rdn and nt qckn 2f out: sn swtchd lft: plugged on same pce and n.d after* **25/1**

0-00 **5** *1 ¼* **Allanit (GER)**[25] 5180 6-9-3 **60**........ MickyFenton 4 54
(B J Curley) *racd keenly: led: hdd wl over 1f out: sn hung rt and btn: wknd fnl f* **16/1**

0-06 **6** *16* **Royal Box**[15] 5470 3-8-9 **59**........ SamHitchcott 7 21
(D Burchell) *broke wl: t.k.h: prom early: grad stdd bk in to midfield: rdn and btn over 2f out: wl bhd and eased ins fnl f* **33/1**

520- **7** *2 ½* **Aphrodite's Rock**[394] 4943 4-9-3 **65**........ AdamBeschizza(5) 3 22
(G D Blake) *awkward leaving stalls and v.s.a: bhd: stdy hdwy 7f out: midfield and rdn wl over 2f out: sn struggling: wl bhd and eased ins fnl f* **22/1**

220/ **8** *17* **Acknowledgement**[189] 1526 8-8-13 **59** ow1........ JackDean(3) 9 —
(J L Spearing) *v.s.a: racd wl off the pce in last pair: rdn and toiling 5f out: sn lost tch and t.o fnl 3f: eased fnl f* **12/1**

5210 **9** *20* **Sandy Shaw**[27] 5115 3-9-5 **69**........ SebSanders 8 —
(J W Hills) *chsd ldrs tl pushed along and lost pl qckly over 3f out: virtually p.u fnl 2f: t.o* **7/1**

00/ **10** *7* **Rosenblatt (GER)**[101] 8-9-5 **65**........ RobertLButler(3) 2 —
(M S Tuck) *s.i.s: a last: lost tch 1/2-way: t.o fnl 4f* **40/1**

2m 6.60s (-1.40) **Going Correction** -0.05s/f (Stan)
WFA 3 from 4yo+ 7lb **10** Ran SP% **112.8**
Speed ratings (Par 103): **103,102,102,97,96 83,81,67,51,46**
Tote Swingers:1&2:£3.60, 2&3:£4.50, 1&3:£5.10 CSF £8.24 CT £31.54 TOTE £6.50: £2.20, £1.10, £3.10; EX 10.00.
Owner M Chandler **Bred** Roland Alder & Morton Bloodstock **Trained** Epsom, Surrey

FOCUS
Another ordinary handicap and one in which the gallop was steadied after a couple of furlongs, returning a time just slower than the first division. The winner raced towards the inside rail in the straight and the three market leaders pulled clear.

5960 HATS GROUP MAIDEN FILLIES' STKS 6f (P)
7:00 (7:03) (Class 5) 3-Y-O+ **£2,286** (£675; £337) **Stalls** High

Form RPR

1 **My Girl Anna (IRE)**[20] 5338 3-8-12 0........ SebSanders 8 76
(Muredach Kelly, Ire) *mde all: pushed along and qcknd clr 2f out: edgd lft under hands and heels fnl f: a gng to hold on* **8/11**[1]

50 **2** *½* **Wallis**[57] 4107 3-8-12 0........ KirstyMilczarek 4 74+
(L M Cumani) *wnt lft s: hld up in rr: sltly hmpd and stl plenty to do over 1f out: hdwy 2f out: modest 4th over 1f out: chsd clr wnr fnl 150yds: r.o wl: nvr quite getting to wnr* **16/1**

0-03 **3** *3 ¾* **Aalsmeer**[52] 4251 3-8-12 80........(p) TedDurcan 2 62
(Karen George) *chsd wnr: rdn and nt pce of wnr 2f out: one pce and wl hld after: lost 2nd fnl 150yds* **5/1**[2]

0443 **4** *2 ½* **Lady Berta**[51] 4297 3-8-12 65........ RichardHughes 6 54
(R Hannon) *chsd ldrs: rdn and unable qck over 2f out: one pce and no ch w wnr fr over 1f out* **11/2**[3]

5 **5** *2 ¼* **Speedy Xaara (IRE)**[10] 5668 3-8-12 0........ DaneO'Neill 5 47
(H Candy) *s.i.s: a towards rr: rdn over 3f out: wknd u.p jst over 2f out: wl btn over 1f out* **9/1**

0003 **6** *1 ¾* **Romancea (USA)**[9] 5686 3-8-12 60........(b) NeilCallan 7 41
(E F Vaughan) *dwlt: sn bustled along to chse ldrs: drvn and nt qckn over 2f out: wl btn over 1f out* **14/1**

0046 **7** *1* **Nativity**[28] 5065 4-9-0 52........ SamHitchcott 1 38
(J L Spearing) *stdd and dropped in bhd after s: hld up in rr: rdn and effrt over 2f out: sn struggling and wl btn over 1f out* **25/1**

1m 11.97s (-1.13) **Going Correction** -0.05s/f (Stan)
WFA 3 from 4yo 2lb **7** Ran SP% **116.4**
Speed ratings (Par 100): **105,104,99,96,93 90,89**
Tote Swingers:1&2:£4.70, 2&3:£9.40, 1&3:£1.10 CSF £15.68 TOTE £1.40: £1.10, £18.00; EX 25.90.
Owner Sergio Artico **Bred** Trevor Dazell **Trained** Ballinasloe, Co. Galway

FOCUS
A modest fillies' event. The gallop was reasonable and the winner raced in the centre in the straight.

Wallis ◆ Official explanation: jockey said filly lost a right-fore shoe

5961 BUZZ ASIA FILLIES' NURSERY — 1m (P)
7:30 (7:31) (Class 4) (0-85,80) 2-Y-O — **£3,238** (£963; £481; £240) **Stalls** High

Form — RPR

21 **1** **Najoum (USA)**[34] 4862 2-9-7 **80** .... TedDurcan 7 — 84
(Saeed Bin Suroor) *trckd ldrs: rdn and qcknd to ld on inner wl over 1f out: clr ent fnl f: r.o wl: rdn out* **8/11**[1]

004 **2** 1 1/4 **Barathea Dancer (IRE)**[12] 5587 2-8-13 **72** .... RichardHughes 4 — 74+
(R A Teal) *stdd after s: hld up in tch: effrt ent fnl 2f: nt clr run over 1f out: squeezed between horses ent fnl f: sn chsng wnr: r.o wl but nvr able to chal* **12/1**

005 **3** 2 1/2 **Bint Mazyouna**[16] 5441 2-8-9 **68** .... SamHitchcott 2 — 63
(M R Channon) *chsd ldr: rdn ent fnl 2f: drvn and nt pce of wnr over 1f out: styd on same pce and wl hld fnl f* **33/1**

5301 **4** 1 1/4 **Rosa Midnight (USA)**[10] 5660 2-8-4 **63** .... HayleyTurner 5 — 56
(M L W Bell) *stdd after s: hld up wl in tch: pushed along over 3f out: rdn and effrt over 2f out: styd on same pce u.p fr over 1f out* **3/1**[2]

0350 **5** nk **Dubai Glory**[22] 5256 2-8-7 **66** .... AndreaAtzeni 6 — 58
(E A L Dunlop) *led: rdn ent fnl 2f: hdd wl over 1f out: nt pce of wnr and edgd lft u.p over 1f out: wknd ins fnl f* **8/1**[3]

053 **6** 2 **Levantera (IRE)**[14] 5520 2-8-7 **71** .... JohnFahy(5) 3 — 58
(C G Cox) *dwlt: sn bustled along: hdwy to chse ldrs on outer after 2f: rdn 3f out: unable qck and drvn jst over 2f out: wknd jst over 1f out* **12/1**

1m 40.83s (1.03) **Going Correction** -0.05s/f (Stan) — **6** Ran SP% **112.3**
Speed ratings (Par 94): **92,90,88,87,86 84**
Tote Swingers:1&2:£1.50, 2&3:£13.00, 1&3:£8.30 CSF £11.11 TOTE £1.50: £1.10, £7.70; EX 9.10.
Owner Godolphin **Bred** Stoneside Stable **Trained** Newmarket, Suffolk

FOCUS
Not the most competitive of nurseries. The gallop was a modest one and the well-backed winner raced towards the inside rail throughout.

NOTEBOOK
Najoum(USA) is a steadily progressive sort who had the run of the race and turned in an improved effort to justify the market support. This wasn't the strongest of nurseries but she could do no more than win in comfortable fashion and she may be able to progress further on Polytrack. (tchd 4-5 in places)
Barathea Dancer(IRE) ◆ had shown ability at a modest level in maidens and ran creditably in this muddling event on this all-weather debut after taking a good hold in the first half of the race and after being briefly short of room. Unlike the majority of these, she has a bit of size and scope and she should be able to win in ordinary company from her current mark granted a stiffer test of stamina. (op 10-1)
Bint Mazyouna had hinted at ability on turf and wasn't disgraced upped 2f in distance on this nursery and all-weather debut in a race that didn't really place the emphasis on stamina. A stronger gallop may have suited better but she'll have to improve to win from this mark. (op 22-1)
Rosa Midnight(USA) was found out from this 6lb higher mark in this stronger grade in a race that didn't really play to her strengths. There will be easier opportunities than this one and she isn't one to write off yet.
Dubai Glory had the run of the race but was again well beaten in a nursery back on Polytrack and she has something to prove at present. (op 16-1 tchd 15-2)
Levantera(IRE), who has a progressive profile on turf, was nibbled at in the market on this nursery and all-weather debut but proved a disappointment after a tardy start in a race that wasn't really run to suit. She will be worth another chance returned to turf. (tchd 10-1)

5962 KISMAT RADIO H'CAP — 1m (P)
8:00 (8:01) (Class 6) (0-55,59) 3-Y-O+ — **£1,637** (£483; £241) **Stalls** High

Form — RPR

0-11 **1** **True To Form (IRE)**[2] 5891 3-9-4 **59** .... SebSanders 13 — 76+
(Sir Mark Prescott) *mde all: rdn and fnd ex 2f out: clr over 1f out: styd on wl fnl f* **2/5**[1]

2001 **2** 1 3/4 **Signora Frasi (IRE)**[8] 5711 5-8-13 **56** .... DavidKenny(7) 8 — 67
(A G Newcombe) *chsd ldrs: rdn and nt pce of wnr 2f out: hdwy u.p to chse wnr jst ins fnl f: r.o but no threat to wnr* **9/1**[3]

001 **3** 1 3/4 **Woolston Ferry (IRE)**[7] 5767 4-9-3 **58** .... AdamBeschizza(5) 3 — 65+
(David Pinder) *in tch in midfield on outer: wd and lost pl bnd 3f out: rallied u.p over 1f out: styd on wl u.p to go 3rd fnl 50yds: no threat to wnr* **20/1**

2360 **4** nk **Join Up**[9] 5704 4-8-9 **50** .... KierenFox(5) 11 — 56
(W M Brisbourne) *racd keenly: chsd wnr tl hdwy to press wnr 4f out: rdn and nt pce of wnr 2f out: drvn and one pce after: lost 2 pls ins fnl f* **8/1**[2]

1300 **5** 2 1/4 **Inquisitress**[38] 4690 6-9-3 **53** .... NeilChalmers 5 — 54
(J J Bridger) *rrd s: hld up towards rr: hdwy on inner over 2f out: rdn to chse ldng trio and swtchd lft over 1f out: no imp and wl hld fnl f* **33/1**

0300 **6** nk **Binnion Bay (IRE)**[41] 4621 9-9-5 **55** .... (b) RichardHughes 9 — 55
(J J Bridger) *t.k.h: hld up towards rr: hdwy into midfield 5f out: rdn and unable qck over 2f out: wl hld and plugged on same pce fr over 1f out* **25/1**

155 **7** 6 **Tallawalla (IRE)**[15] 5469 3-9-0 **55** .... SamHitchcott 12 — 41
(M R Channon) *chsd ldrs tl drvn and wknd over 2f out: no ch fr over 1f out* **20/1**

6000 **8** 3/4 **Blue Charm**[20] 5331 6-9-4 **54** .... JimCrowley 1 — 39
(I W McInnes) *stdd and dropped in bhd after s: hld up in rr: rdn and effrt over 2f out: n.d* **28/1**

600 **9** 1 **Grand Honour (IRE)**[13] 5545 4-9-3 **53** .... JimmyQuinn 10 — 36
(P Howling) *hld up in last trio: rdn and effrt on inner over 2f out: no hdwy and wl btn over 1f out* **33/1**

-000 **10** 3 **Melting Bob (USA)**[53] 4237 4-9-0 **50** .... LukeMorris 4 — 26
(Dr J D Scargill) *t.k.h: hld up wl in tch: rdn over 2f out: sn wknd* **66/1**

-405 **11** 10 **Musical Delight**[10] 5661 3-9-1 **56** .... TedDurcan 6 — —
(A P Jarvis) *chsd ldrs: drvn and wknd over 2f out: wl bhd and eased ins fnl f* **33/1**

002- **12** 2 1/4 **Daily Double**[171] 3257 4-9-5 **55** .... GeorgeBaker 14 — —
(M R Bosley) *hld up towards rr: rdn struggling ent fnl 3f: wl bhd fnl 2f* **40/1**

1m 39.62s (-0.18) **Going Correction** -0.05s/f (Stan)
WFA 3 from 4yo+ 5lb — **12** Ran SP% **122.1**
Speed ratings (Par 101): **98,96,94,94,91 91,85,84,83,80 70,68**
Tote Swingers:1&2:£1.90, 2&3:£11.20, 1&3:£4.00 CSF £3.67 CT £41.21 TOTE £1.20: £1.02, £1.50, £5.60; EX 6.90.
Owner G Moore - Osborne House **Bred** Sir E J Loder **Trained** Newmarket, Suffolk

FOCUS
An uncompetitive handicap in which the market leader probably didn't have to improve too much to extend his winning sequence. The gallop was an ordinary one and the winner raced close to the inside rail throughout.

Inquisitress Official explanation: jockey said mare reared on leaving stalls

5963 SUNRISE RADIO H'CAP — 2m (P)
8:30 (8:31) (Class 6) (0-65,65) 3-Y-O+ — **£1,637** (£483; £241) **Stalls** High

Form — RPR

-505 **1** **Dubai Phantom (USA)**[26] 5164 3-8-11 **61** .... NeilCallan 9 — 70
(D M Simcock) *hld up in tch towards rr: hdwy over 3f out: nt clr run on inner over 2f out: rdn to chse ldrs wl over 1f out: led jst over 1f out: styd on wl fnl f* **9/1**

0032 **2** 2 **Marcus Antonius**[13] 5564 3-8-0 **50** .... NickyMackay 13 — 57
(J R Boyle) *hld up in tch in midfield: rdn and effrt to chse ldrs wl over 1f out: kpt on same pce u.p fnl f: wnt 2nd nr fin* **9/2**[2]

-542 **3** hd **Viviani (IRE)**[14] 5522 3-8-12 **62** .... (t) PatDobbs 11 — 68
(Mrs A J Perrett) *hld up in tch in midfield: hdwy to chse ldrs wl over 2f out: drvn to chse wnr jst ins fnl f: kpt on same pce after: lost 2nd nr fin* **7/2**[1]

0033 **4** 1/2 **Jennerous Blue**[29] 5058 3-7-12 **48** .... (p) PaulQuinn 7 — 54
(D K Ivory) *in tch in midfield: reminders and dropped towards rr: hdwy u.p over 2f out: chsd ldrs 1f out: kpt on wl u.p but no threat to wnr* **10/1**

5460 **5** 1 1/2 **Honorable Endeavor**[8] 5722 4-8-11 **48** oh2 .... (v) JimCrowley 3 — 52
(E F Vaughan) *sn bustled along to chse ldr: led over 3f out: rdn wl over 1f out: drvn and hdd jst over 1f out: styd on same pce ins fnl f* **33/1**

5036 **6** 1 1/4 **Royal Dalakhani (IRE)**[37] 4751 3-8-13 **63** .... LiamJones 6 — 66
(P W D'Arcy) *t.k.h: chsd ldrs: wnt 3rd ent fnl 3f: rdn and hanging rt ent fnl 2f: keeping on same pce and btn whn short of room jst ins fnl f* **17/2**

5-00 **7** 4 1/2 **Kokkokila**[22] 5260 6-9-2 **53** .... (t) KirstyMilczarek 8 — 50
(Lady Herries) *stdd s: hld up in rr: rdn and effrt wl over 2f out: hdwy 2f out: nvr threatened ldrs* **25/1**

6046 **8** 1 3/4 **Juwireya**[14] 5522 3-8-11 **61** .... (v[1]) WilliamCarson 12 — 56
(P W Hiatt) *in tch in midfield: rdn and nt qckn over 2f out: wknd wl over 1f out* **22/1**

3332 **9** 16 **Lastroseofsummer (IRE)**[11] 5646 4-9-9 **65** .... AdamBeschizza(5) 10 — 41
(Rae Guest) *led tl over 3f out: wknd u.p over 2f out: wl bhd and eased ins fnl f* **11/2**[3]

6433 **10** hd **Snowberry Hill (USA)**[24] 5203 7-8-12 **49** .... TedDurcan 2 — 25
(Lucinda Featherstone) *hld up towards rr: rdn and shortlived effrt over 2f out: wl btn fnl 2f: eased ins fnl f* **8/1**

-000 **11** 2 1/4 **Steely Bird**[39] 4676 3-7-11 **52** .... SimonPearce(5) 5 — 25
(Miss Jo Crowley) *t.k.h early: hld up in midfield on outer: rdn and struggling over 3f out: wd bnd and dropped to rr 3f out: sn lost tch: eased ins fnl f* **50/1**

0000 **12** 1 **Zuwaar**[10] 5666 5-8-12 **52** ow2 .... (tp) RobertLButler(3) 4 — 24
(P Butler) *s.i.s: hld up in rr: rdn and lost tch wl over 2f out: wl bhd and eased ins fnl f* **50/1**

0234 **13** 9 **Miniyamba (IRE)**[14] 5522 3-8-12 **62** .... (b) JimmyQuinn 1 — 23
(J L Dunlop) *chsd ldrs: rdn and wknd qckly over 2f out: wl bhd and eased ins fnl f* **12/1**

060 **14** 19 **Aughcarra (IRE)**[11] 5625 5-8-11 **48** oh3 .... NeilChalmers 14 — —
(Harry Chisman) *chsd ldrs tl over 4f out: sn lost pl: wl bhd 3f out: t.o and eased fnl 2f* **100/1**

3m 28.04s (-2.06) **Going Correction** -0.05s/f (Stan)
WFA 3 from 4yo+ 13lb — **14** Ran SP% **120.3**
Speed ratings (Par 101): **103,102,101,101,100 100,98,97,89,89 87,87,82,73**
Tote Swingers:1&2:£8.10, 2&3:£2.60, 1&3:£9.20. CSF £46.61 CT £173.64 TOTE £14.70: £4.80, £3.10, £1.10; EX 84.30.
Owner Ahmad Al Shaikh **Bred** Dr John A Chandler **Trained** Newmarket, Suffolk

FOCUS
A modest handicap in which the gallop was ordinary to the home turn. The winner raced in the centre in the straight.

Aughcarra(IRE) Official explanation: jockey said gelding stopped quickly

5964 SUNRISE TV H'CAP — 7f (P)
9:00 (9:03) (Class 4) (0-80,80) 3-Y-O+ — **£3,885** (£1,156; £577; £288) **Stalls** High

Form — RPR

04 **1** **Hazzard County (USA)**[8] 5716 6-9-3 **78** .... LauraPike(7) 3 — 88
(D M Simcock) *hld up in rr: pushed along and effrt to chse ldrs over 1f out: str run fnl f to ld fnl 75yds: idling towards fin: pushed out* **10/1**

2223 **2** 1/2 **Hellbender (IRE)**[8] 5711 4-9-2 **70** .... (t) RichardHughes 10 — 79
(S Kirk) *hld up in tch: rdn and effrt 2f out: swtchd rt and drvn to chal ent fnl f: led ins fnl f tl hdd and one pce fnl 75yds* **7/2**[2]

6250 **3** 1/2 **Swiss Cross**[7] 5750 3-9-5 **77** .... (bt) NeilCallan 12 — 83
(G A Butler) *chsd ldrs: rdn to ld wl over 1f out: edgd lft u.p over 1f out: hdd ins fnl f: nt qckn and styd on same pce after* **6/1**[3]

-212 **4** nk **Barq (IRE)**[11] 5627 3-9-8 **80** .... (tp) TedDurcan 13 — 85
(Saeed Bin Suroor) *trckd ldng pair: rdn and effrt to chal 2f out: carried lft fr over 1f out: nt qckn and styd on same pce ins fnl f* **7/4**[1]

2610 **5** 4 **Kiss A Prince**[26] 5142 4-9-5 **73** .... (b) JimCrowley 4 — 69
(D K Ivory) *dwlt: sn in midfield: rdn and unable qck over 2f out: no ch w ldrs fr over 1f out* **8/1**

0-00 **6** 2 3/4 **Abriachan**[14] 5524 3-8-12 **70** .... WilliamCarson 9 — 57
(M G Quinlan) *s.i.s: towards rr: rdn and effrt on inner over 2f out: nvr trbld ldrs* **50/1**

0010 **7** 1 3/4 **Spanish Island (USA)**[18] 5383 3-9-6 **78** .... GeorgeBaker 7 — 60
(M A Magnusson) *dwlt and sn pushed along: in midfield whn carried lft and lost pl over 5f out: rcvrd and in tch 1/2-way: rdn and btn over 2f out* **16/1**

1300 **8** nk **Best Trip (IRE)**[117] 2170 3-9-2 **74** .... JimmyQuinn 14 — 55
(R C Guest) *taken down early: racd freely: chsd ldr tl wl over 1f out: sn wknd* **25/1**

442- **9** 3/4 **Tuxedo**[304] 7327 5-9-4 **72** .... LukeMorris 2 — 53
(P W Hiatt) *stdd and swtchd rt after s: a bhd: rdn and no rspnse over 2f out* **20/1**

3414 **10** 5 **Polish World (USA)**[23] 5242 6-9-7 **75** .... MickyFenton 11 — 43
(P T Midgley) *led tl wl over 1f out: sn hanging rt and wknd rapidly: eased ins fnl f* **15/2**

1000 **11** 2 1/4 **Jonnie Skull (IRE)**[135] 1633 4-8-12 **66** .... NickyMackay 1 — 27
(M D Squance) *stdd and dropped in bhd after s: a bhd* **66/1**

-010 **P** **Polar Annie**[30] 4988 5-8-13 **67** .... LiamJones 6 — —
(M S Saunders) *chsd ldrs tl sddle slipped and plld sharply lft over 5f out: t.o after tl eventually p.u and dismntd over 1f out* **33/1**

1m 25.03s (-0.97) **Going Correction** -0.05s/f (Stan)
WFA 3 from 4yo+ 4lb — **12** Ran SP% **125.7**
Speed ratings (Par 105): **103,102,101,101,96 93,91,91,90,84 82,—**
Tote Swingers:1&2:£8.10, 2&3:£5.30, 1&3:£8.90 CSF £45.83 CT £243.91 TOTE £15.90: £4.30, £1.10, £2.30; EX 69.30 Place 6 £6.72, Place 5 £2.06..
Owner Khalifa Dasmal **Bred** Cho, Llc **Trained** Newmarket, Suffolk
■ Stewards' Enquiry : Neil Callan caution; careless riding

FOCUS
A fair handicap run at a decent gallop in which the first four finished clear. The winner came down the centre in the straight.
Kiss A Prince Official explanation: jockey said gelding hung left-handed throughout
T/Plt: £8.10 to a £1 stake. Pool £47,361.91. 4,241.08 winning tickets. T/Qpdt: £2.30 to a £1 stake. Pool £6,939.41. 2,229.73 winning tickets. SP

5914 SANDOWN (R-H)

Saturday, September 11

OFFICIAL GOING: Good (sprint course 8.1; round course 8.4)
Wind: Mild against Weather: Sunny

5965 PROVIDEO CONDITIONS STKS 5f 6y
1:45 (1:45) (Class 3) 2-Y-O £6,476 (£1,927; £963; £481) **Stalls** High

Form RPR
1011 **1** **Krypton Factor**[3] 5856 2-9-0 91 (b) SebSanders 5 99+
(Sir Mark Prescott) *dwlt: sn trcking ldrs: led 3f out: sn in command: r.o strly: readily* **8/13**[1]
100 **2** *3* **Ladyanne (IRE)**[9] 5693 2-8-11 85 SteveDrowne 3 85
(S Kirk) *chsd ldrs: outpcd over 2f out: sn wandered u.p: r.o ent fnl f: veered rt: no ch w wnr* **16/1**
162 **3** *3* **Admirable Spirit**[21] 5293 2-8-13 89 PatDobbs 6 76
(R Hannon) *w ldr tl rdn to chse wnr over 2f out: kpt on same pce fnl f* **4/1**[2]
5163 **4** *2 ¾* **Belle Bayardo (IRE)**[3] 5850 2-9-8 99 LukeMorris 4 75
(R A Harris) *led tl 3f out: sn rdn to chse wnr: hung lft and wknd ent fnl f* **12/1**
0100 **5** *½* **Remotelinx (IRE)**[23] 5245 2-9-4 90 DaneO'Neill 1 70
(J W Hills) *chsd ldrs: rdn to dispute 2nd over 2f out: sn edgd rt: wknd jst over 1f out* **6/1**[3]

62.32 secs (0.72) **Going Correction** +0.15s/f (Good) 5 Ran SP% **109.8**
Speed ratings (Par 99): **100,95,90,86,85**
toteswinger: 1&2 £8.90. CSF £11.56 TOTE £1.60: £1.10, £5.50; EX 12.60.
Owner Lady Fairhaven & The Hon C & H Broughton **Bred** Lady Fairhaven **Trained** Newmarket, Suffolk

FOCUS
A useful conditions race won in clear cut style by a fast-improving horse, though his two closest pursuers are both probably better over further.

NOTEBOOK
Krypton Factor was arguably the form pick even before his improved performance and ready win at Epsom three days earlier and he made light of blowing the start to power clear from halfway, never in any danger thereafter. 5f or 6f seem to come alike to him and he'll be entitled to a shot at a Listed race after this. (op 4-6 tchd 4-7)
Ladyanne(IRE) had struggled in better races than this since making a winning debut but seemed to find the drop back to 5f as much as anything else catching her out, staying on well despite hanging badly right inside the last. She'll be suited by a return to 6f. (op 20-1 tchd 25-1)
Admirable Spirit was another that almost certainly found the trip too sharp, having been raced at 6f/7f only until now, having no answer once the winner upped the tempo at halfway. It's usually a tip worth taking when his yard bring one back to the minimum trip but it's unlikely she'll be persevered with at it. (op 10-3)
Belle Bayardo(IRE) looks flattered by his official rating and though he probably had a bit on conceding weight all round, he's not going to be easy to place either in minor events or nurseries at 5f or 6f in the near future. Official explanation: jockey said gelding swerved left leaving stalls (op 16-1)
Remotelinx(IRE) might have had something troubling him as he tended to carry his head on one side and didn't finish with his usual zest after looking threatening at halfway. Official explanation: jockey said colt hung right-handed (op 7-1 tchd 15-2)

5966 BERRYLANDS H'CAP (DIV I) 5f 6y
2:15 (2:18) (Class 3) (0-90,90) 3-Y-O+ £6,152 (£1,830; £914; £456) **Stalls** High

Form RPR
1404 **1** **Joe Packet**[18] 5390 3-9-5 88 JimCrowley 11 103
(J G Portman) *mid-div: hdwy 2f out: swtchd to farside rail ent fnl f: sn led: r.o strly to draw clr: readily* **10/1**
065 **2** *3* **Cheveton**[14] 5528 6-9-2 84 WilliamCarson 12 93+
(R J Price) *s.i.s: towards rr: making prog whn nt clr run on rail fr wl over 1f out: rdn and r.o wl whn clr run ins fnl f but no ch w wnr* **7/1**
6400 **3** *nk* **Piscean (USA)**[7] 5742 5-9-1 83 (p) RoystonFfrench 5 86
(T Keddy) *s.i.s: sn pushed along in detached last: hdwy over 1f out: r.o wl ins fnl f: nrst fin* **16/1**
132 **4** *½* **Addictive Dream (IRE)**[34] 4858 3-9-4 87 ShaneKelly 8 88
(W R Swinburn) *trckd ldrs: rdn over 1f out: led briefly jst ins fnl f: no ex fnl 100yds* **10/3**[1]
32 **5** *nk* **Avertor**[15] 5495 4-9-0 82 SteveDrowne 6 82
(R Charlton) *chsd ldr: rdn over 2f out: kpt on same pce fnl f* **7/2**[2]
3211 **6** *¾* **Cape Royal**[12] 5589 10-8-13 81 (bt) DaneO'Neill 9 79
(J M Bradley) *broke wl: led: rdn 2f out: hdd jst ins fnl f: no ex* **13/2**[3]
1110 **7** *1 ½* **Caledonia Princess**[14] 5526 4-8-5 78 RossAtkinson(5) 7 70
(F J Brennan) *mid-div: rdn wl over 2f out: no imp* **20/1**
6430 **8** *2 ¼* **Rapid Water**[48] 4401 4-8-6 79 SimonPearce(5) 1 63
(A M Balding) *sn pushed along: a towards rr* **16/1**
3200 **9** *¾* **Matsunosuke**[32] 4937 8-9-7 89 LukeMorris 10 70
(R A Harris) *chsd ldrs: rdn 3f out: wknd jst over 1f out* **16/1**
0006 **10** *3 ¼* **Duplicity**[16] 5442 3-9-3 89 (b[1]) PatrickHills(3) 4 59
(R Hannon) *s.i.s: a towards rr* **33/1**
1105 **11** *3 ½* **Kingsgate Choice (IRE)**[23] 5250 3-9-7 90 SebSanders 2 47
(J R Best) *chsd ldrs: rdn over 2f out: wknd ent fnl f* **10/1**
2300 **12** *¾* **Osiris Way**[44] 4510 8-9-5 87 NeilCallan 3 41
(P R Chamings) *chsd ldrs: rdn over 2f out: wknd over 1f out* **25/1**

61.46 secs (-0.14) **Going Correction** +0.15s/f (Good)
WFA 3 from 4yo+ 1lb 12 Ran SP% **118.5**
Speed ratings (Par 107): **107,102,101,100,100 99,96,93,92,86 81,80**
toteswingers: 1&2 £6.30, 1&3 £19.40, 2&3 £27.10. CSF £76.49 CT £1142.20 TOTE £11.50: £4.00, £2.60, £4.00; EX 57.10.
Owner Stuart McPhee **Bred** Stuart McPhee Bloodstock Ltd **Trained** Compton, Berks

FOCUS
A fairly useful handicap run at a decent pace and in which the complexion changed completely in the last furlong. The time was easily the fastest of the three on the straight track.

NOTEBOOK
Joe Packet had appeared to be slightly off the boil since his midsummer three-timer but he looked of interest dropped to 5f for the first time from his high draw and won with a good degree of authority after having to wait for a clear run. The strong pace suited him ideally, and he'll be of interest if kept to this trip with a valuable handicap at Ascot later this month an obvious target. (op 12-1)
Cheveton probably wouldn't have beaten the winner even with a clear run but he'd have finished a much closer second and finished with enough of a flourish to suggest the race hadn't got anywhere near the bottom of him. He'll be of interest in the coming weeks and is the sort to win another race or two when the ground softens. (op 11-2 tchd 5-1)
Piscean(USA) ran a typical race, blowing the start only to cut through the pack late, but he'd got too far back and was never nearer than at the finish. Official explanation: jockey said gelding missed the break
Addictive Dream(IRE) had been progressive earlier in the season but might just be finding his progress stalling now. He looked like taking more of a hand than he did eventually when hitting the front briefly inside the last, but he'd travelled strongly enough until then to suggest the drop down to 5f wasn't a problem. It might be that despite his fairly even surface record so far, Polytrack suits him best. (op 13-2)
Avertor raced close to the strong pace but perhaps can't put that forward as an excuse seeing as he didn't overhaul the leader Cape Royal until very late on. All the same, this was a good effort. (op 10-3 tchd 3-1)
Cape Royal is suited by forcing the pace next to a right hand rail, but he possibly did too much too soon here off his highest mark for over two years and couldn't sustain his run late after racing clear for much of the way. He remains in cracking form. (op 6-1)
Matsunosuke looked an interesting runner back in this grade from a high draw but was being hard driven from halfway and clearly ran below his best. His new yard haven't had him long, and he's not one to write off just yet. (tchd 14-1)
Duplicity Official explanation: jockey said gelding missed the break

5967 BERRYLANDS H'CAP (DIV II) 5f 6y
2:50 (2:52) (Class 3) (0-90,90) 3-Y-O+ £6,152 (£1,830; £914; £456) **Stalls** High

Form RPR
4241 **1** **Kanaf (IRE)**[32] 4930 3-9-1 84 NeilCallan 10 96+
(E A L Dunlop) *s.i.s: sn trcking ldrs: travelling wl whn nt clr run ent fnl f: swtchd lft: qcknd up wl to ld fnl 100yds: comf* **4/1**[1]
6321 **2** *1* **Secret Millionaire (IRE)**[8] 5734 3-9-6 89 StephenCraine 12 97
(Patrick Morris) *disp ld: rdn and outrt ldr over 1f out: wandered whn hdd ins fnl f: no ex* **9/2**[2]
0001 **3** *1* **Sohraab**[21] 5308 6-9-7 89 JimCrowley 8 93
(H Morrison) *in tch: rdn 2f out: kpt on ins fnl f* **4/1**[1]
4131 **4** *¾* **Drift And Dream**[37] 4754 3-8-13 82 SebSanders 2 93+
(C F Wall) *hld up towards rr: hdwy on rail 2f out: cl 4th whn nt clr run thrght fnl 120yds: looked to have plenty lft in the tank: unlucky* **8/1**[3]
0150 **5** *2* **Solemn**[12] 5589 5-9-1 83 (b) DaneO'Neill 6 78
(J M Bradley) *hld up towards rr: rdn over 2f out: styd on: nvr trbld ldrs* **8/1**[3]
-035 **6** *shd* **Red Avalanche (IRE)**[11] 5632 3-8-7 83 (t) DuilioDaSilva(7) 1 77
(P F I Cole) *outpcd in last: styd on fr over 1f out: nvr a factor* **40/1**
0160 **7** *1 ¼* **Bertoliver**[12] 5589 6-9-5 87 JackMitchell 4 77
(S C Williams) *sn pushed into prom position: led 2f out: sn rdn and hdd: wknd fnl f* **16/1**
-103 **8** *1 ½* **Whozthecat (IRE)**[114] 2260 3-9-7 90 DavidNolan 3 74
(D Carroll) *trckd ldrs: rdn over 2f out: wknd jst over 1f out* **16/1**
1000 **9** *1 ¼* **Palisades Park**[13] 5551 3-9-2 85 PatDobbs 9 65
(R Hannon) *trckd ldrs: short of room whn lost pl over 1f out: no ch after* **25/1**
0000 **10** *1 ¼* **Hoh Hoh Hoh**[48] 4401 8-8-6 77 (tp) AndrewHeffernan(3) 11 52
(R J Price) *led tl 2f out: sn wknd* **8/1**[3]
0503 **11** *1* **Drawnfromthepast (IRE)**[21] 5308 5-9-4 86 FergusSweeney 5 58
(J A Osborne) *mid-div: rdn 2f out: wknd fnl f* **10/1**
3-15 **12** *3 ¾* **Noble Greek (USA)**[26] 5151 3-8-6 80 KierenFox(5) 7 38
(J R Best) *a towards rr* **33/1**

62.38 secs (0.78) **Going Correction** +0.15s/f (Good)
WFA 3 from 5yo+ 1lb 12 Ran SP% **121.6**
Speed ratings (Par 107): **99,97,95,94,91 91,89,86,84,82 81,75**
toteswingers: 1&2 £4.60, 1&3 £5.50, 2&3 £5.80. CSF £21.94 CT £78.79 TOTE £5.10: £1.10, £2.60, £2.20; EX 25.80.
Owner Hamdan Al Maktoum **Bred** Catcher Equine Ltd **Trained** Newmarket, Suffolk

FOCUS
Possibly the slightly weaker of the two divisions but plenty of in-form sprinters in opposition and the right horses came to the fore to give the result a very solid look despite a steadier pace than the previous race.

NOTEBOOK
Kanaf(IRE) ◆ looks to be really getting his act together and managed to follow up his Lingfield win with some ease despite a slow start, soon slotting in nicely on the rail before going to the front readily inside the last. He didn't do a tap once there, leaving the impression he was the best horse in the race by quite some way, and given that he looked to have got away lightly with a 3lb rise for his Lingfield win anyway given its circumstances, he will almost certainly remain ahead of the handicapper after another rise in the weights. He could turn out to be useful. (op 6-1)
Secret Millionaire(IRE) looked to hold sound claims and tried to make the best of what was a good draw next to the rail, always up with the pace and perhaps showing ahead briefly. He's in a good vein of form but is as yet unproven on ground softer than good, so he'll have a bit to prove if we get a wet autumn. (op 4-1)
Sohraab possibly didn't quite make the best use of his high draw but arguably looked fourth best on the day anyway. He's always done his winning in the first half of the year and a wet autumn won't be in his favour. (op 10-3)
Drift And Dream ◆ goes well here and was unlucky not to finish a clear second taking on her elders for the first time. She was sensibly switched to the inside rail from her low draw and travelled strongly as usual but never had any room when she needed it. She can do better again. Official explanation: jockey said filly was denied a clear run
Solemn didn't have a great draw again and that was possibly the reason for a rather laboured effort, never threatening to finish any nearer. Official explanation: jockey said gelding suffered interference shortly after start (op 9-1)
Red Avalanche(IRE) was another never closer than at the finish, soon detached after a slow start then ending up widest on the track
Bertoliver didn't seem to have to go off too hard to dispute the lead, for all this track is stiffer than he prefers ideally, and he continues a bit below his best. (op 14-1)
Palisades Park Official explanation: jockey said colt was denied a clear run
Drawnfromthepast(IRE) was backed at long odds, possibly on account of a decent pull in the weights with Sohraab from last time, but he raced a bit wider than ideal and then dropped out rather tamely. His profile is a very inconsistent one. (op 14-1)

5968 WALTON H'CAP 7f 16y
3:25 (3:29) (Class 4) (0-80,82) 3-Y-O £5,180 (£1,541; £770; £384) **Stalls** High

Form RPR
4102 **1** **Master Mylo (IRE)**[18] 5383 3-8-13 75 JimCrowley 4 84
(D K Ivory) *hld up towards rr: c wdst ent st: hdwy over 2f out: sn rdn: styd on gamely: led fnl 40yds: drvn out* **16/1**
1-3 **2** *nk* **Bramshaw (USA)**[10] 5662 3-9-6 82 NeilCallan 5 90
(Mrs A J Perrett) *trckd ldrs: rdn into narrow advantage 2f out: kpt on gamely u.str.p: hdd fnl 40yds* **13/8**[1]

0360 **3** 3/4 **Sir Frank Wappat**11 5641 3-8-11 73 RoystonFfrench 3 79
(M Johnston) *s.i.s: towards rr: swtchd lft 3f out: sn rdn: no imp tl styd on wl fnl f: nrst fin* **20/1**

1243 **4** 3/4 **Love Match**24 5205 3-9-4 80 SteveDrowne 11 84
(R Charlton) *s.i.s: towards rr: hdwy over 2f out: rdn over 1f out: styd on fnl f: nrst fin* **8/1**

4145 **5** 1 1/2 **Cuthbert (IRE)**52 4260 3-8-9 74 EJMcNamara(3) 6 74
(W Jarvis) *sn w ldr: rdn and ev ch fr over 2f out: no ex and lost 3 pls ins fnl f* **16/1**

5625 **6** 1 3/4 **Fawley Green**24 5205 3-8-10 72 FergusSweeney 7 67
(W R Muir) *mid-div: rdn over 2f out: kpt on same pce* **20/1**

0424 **7** nk **Our Boy Barrington (IRE)**31 4956 3-8-11 73 PatDobbs 8 67
(R Hannon) *hld up towards rr: swtchd lft 2f out: sn rdn: bmpd over 1f out: sme late prog: n.d* **5/1**2

1-0 **8** 1/2 **Marrayah**90 3001 3-8-10 72 JackMitchell 10 65
(M A Jarvis) *trckd ldrs: rdn over 2f out: kpt on same pce* **12/1**

6140 **9** 1 3/4 **Another Magic Man (USA)**58 4057 3-8-3 70 KierenFox(5) 9 58
(J R Best) *sn led: rdn and hdd 2f out: sn wknd* **7/1**3

5320 **10** 4 **Orsett Lad (USA)**8 5730 3-8-4 66 oh12 LukeMorris 12 43
(J R Best) *mid-div: rdn wl over 2f out: wknd over 1f out* **66/1**

104 **11** 1 1/4 **Zakiy**29 5030 3-9-3 79 (t) ShaneKelly 2 53
(W J Haggas) *in tch: rdn over 2f out: wknd over 1f out* **8/1**

1m 29.58s (0.08) **Going Correction** +0.05s/f (Good) 11 Ran SP% **120.0**
Speed ratings (Par 103): **101,100,99,98,97 95,94,94,92,87 86**
toteswingers: 1&2 £6.30, 1&3 £37.00, 2&3 £19.60. CSF £42.36 CT £504.97 TOTE £17.10: £4.00, £1.10, £4.90; EX 70.40.
Owner K Quinn/ C Benham/ I Saunders **Bred** David Eiffe **Trained** Radlett, Herts

FOCUS
A tight-looking handicap. Three of the first four places went to in-form horses and the result promises to prove reliable.
Another Magic Man(USA) Official explanation: vet said colt lost a left-fore shoe

5969 DANIEL GERARD MCCARTHY 1ST BIRTHDAY NURSERY 1m 14y
4:00 (4:01) (Class 4) (0-85,81) 2-Y-O **£5,180** (£1,541; £770; £384) **Stalls** High

Form RPR

0510 **1** **Star Surprise**36 4801 2-9-7 81 SebSanders 1 85+
(M L W Bell) *mde all: kpt on gamely: rdn out* **9/1**

0300 **2** 1 1/2 **May's Boy**10 5659 2-7-6 59 HarryBentley(7) 5 58
(M D I Usher) *trckd wnr thrght: rdn over 2f out: kpt on but a being hld fnl f* **40/1**

21 **3** 1 **Marzante (USA)**16 5440 2-9-5 79 SteveDrowne 2 76
(R Charlton) *hld up in tch: swtchd lft and stdy prog u.p fr 2f out: wnt 3rd over 1f out: kpt on same pce fnl f* **11/8**1

5311 **4** 3 1/4 **Sky Falcon (USA)**38 4701 2-9-4 78 RoystonFfrench 6 67
(M Johnston) *t.k.h early: trckd wnr tl rdn 3f out: one pce fnl 2f* **9/2**3

3222 **5** 2 1/4 **Nothing To Hide (IRE)**41 4623 2-9-2 76 JimCrowley 4 60
(D J S Ffrench Davis) *in tch: rdn wl over 2f out: sn one pce: fdd ins fnl f* **4/1**2

0003 **6** 5 **Futurism**10 5659 2-8-4 64 LukeMorris 8 37
(R Hannon) *s.i.s: last but in tch: sn pushed along: nvr any imp on ldrs* **15/2**

1341 **7** 4 1/2 **Spartic**16 5452 2-8-13 73 JamesDoyle 7 37
(A J McCabe) *in tch: rdn over 3f out: wknd over 1f out* **12/1**

1m 44.95s (1.65) **Going Correction** +0.05s/f (Good) 7 Ran SP% **112.2**
Speed ratings (Par 97): **93,91,90,87,85 80,75**
toteswingers: 1&2 £30.30, 1&3 £7.40, 2&3 £6.40. CSF £237.43 CT £786.82 TOTE £12.90: £6.60, £8.50; EX 373.70.
Owner Dr Ali Ridha **Bred** Rabbah Bloodstock Limited **Trained** Newmarket, Suffolk

FOCUS
Little better than a fair nursery and one that was run at no more than a steady pace either, with the winner able to dictate.

NOTEBOOK
Star Surprise had disappointed ridden with restraint up at this trip last time, but he clearly relishes going from the front and back at the scene of his only win, made all again. He might have been at an advantage ridden from the front, but he still looked comfortably in charge from 2f out and it's unlikely he is flattered by the result. That said, this was a weakish race for a 0-85, and things are likely to be tougher next time. (op 12-1)
May's Boy had an unconvincing profile overall but a return to a more positive ride clearly benefited him and he ran his best race yet. He really ought to be competitive in 0-65 nurseries (as he ran in last time) on this showing. (op 50-1)
Marzante(USA) was arguably well-handicapped on his debut form but he possibly hadn't beaten much of note at Ffos Las last time and looked to have no excuses here, produced in plenty of time if good enough but unable to seriously threaten the first two. He looks fair at best. (op 15-8)
Sky Falcon(USA) still looks a bit inexperienced for all he has two wins under his belt already and might have been better ridden more forcefully, too, given that he looked short of pace when the leader upped the tempo. (op 4-1 tchd 5-1)
Nothing To Hide(IRE) had been running well in nurseries but possibly didn't see out the last furlong as well as might have been expected beforehand and looked also to be carrying his head a shade awkwardly. (op 9-2)
Futurism was soon struggling and probably needs dropping down again in grade. (op 13-2)
Spartic had a similar chance as Futurism on one line of form and was also struggling from early in the straight. (op 8-1 tchd 15-2)

5970 SURREY FOOD FESTIVAL H'CAP 1m 2f 7y
4:30 (4:35) (Class 2) (0-100,100) 3-Y-O+
£12,462 (£3,732; £1,866; £934; £466; £234) **Stalls** High

Form RPR

-120 **1** **Psychic Ability (USA)**14 5511 3-8-11 92 (v1) DaraghO'Donohoe 2 101
(Saeed Bin Suroor) *mde all: rdn whn hrd pressed fr over 2f out: styd on gamely to assert nr fin: all out* **10/1**

000 **2** 1/2 **Kings Destiny**21 5307 4-9-12 100 NeilCallan 1 108
(M A Jarvis) *w wnr thrght: looked to be travelling best 2f out: sn rdn: ev ch fnl f: hld nr fin* **7/1**3

0533 **3** hd **Sandor**21 5307 4-9-4 92 SteveDrowne 8 100
(P J Makin) *hld up towards rr: hdwy over 2f out: sn rdn: styd on wl ins fnl f: drifted sltly rt: nrst fin* **3/1**2

14 **4** 1 1/4 **Fox Hunt (IRE)**8 5736 3-8-10 91 RoystonFfrench 10 100+
(M Johnston) *trckd ldrs tl lost pl over 4f out: rdn and clsng steadily whn hmpd on rails over 1f out: fin strly* **11/4**1

1305 **5** 1/2 **Huygens**56 4144 3-8-9 90 ShaneKelly 5 95
(D J Coakley) *in tch tl lost pl after 3f: towards rr: hdwy over 3f out: sn rdn: wnt 3rd wl over 1f out: styng on but hld whn squeezed up nring fin* **16/1**

0404 **6** 3/4 **Safari Sunup (IRE)**35 4818 5-9-0 88 LukeMorris 9 91
(P Winkworth) *trckd ldrs: rdn over 2f out: swtchd rt over 1f out: styd on same pce* **12/1**

5006 **7** 1/2 **Reve De Nuit (USA)**11 5638 4-8-7 86 DeclanCannon(5) 6 88
(A J McCabe) *sme late prog: mainly towards rr* **14/1**

3136 **8** 6 **Ouster (GER)**48 4400 4-8-12 86 DaneO'Neill 4 76
(D R C Elsworth) *trckd ldrs: rdn over 2f out: edgd rt and bmpd over 1f out: wknd fnl f* **8/1**

213- **9** 21 **Funday**344 6452 4-8-12 86 PatDobbs 7 34
(G L Moore) *s.i.s: a towards rr: eased fnl f* **20/1**

652- **10** dist **Dr Livingstone (IRE)**173 7035 5-9-2 90 JimCrowley 11 —
(C R Egerton) *trckd ldrs untl wknd over 2f out: virtually p.u* **16/1**

2m 8.65s (-1.85) **Going Correction** +0.05s/f (Good)
WFA 3 from 4yo+ 7lb 10 Ran SP% **115.3**
Speed ratings (Par 109): **109,108,108,107,107 106,106,101,84,—**
toteswingers: 1&2 £9.90, 1&3 £9.20, 2&3 £3.30. CSF £77.27 CT £263.26 TOTE £13.10: £3.40, £2.70, £1.10; EX 57.40.
Owner Godolphin **Bred** Flaxman Holdings Ltd **Trained** Newmarket, Suffolk

FOCUS
A useful handicap, for all that one or two had a bit to prove, but it was steadily run and the first two had things between themselves for much of the straight.

NOTEBOOK
Psychic Ability(USA) had failed to settle in cheekpieces at Beverley last time and had questions to answer tried visored but back on ground that is probably ideal he wasn't subjected to much pressure in front and pretty much had things his own way. He had to fight off a sustained challenge from the runner-up in the straight and having the rail on his right was probably a help in that respect, but things might not have fallen quite so kindly on another day and he'll need to improve again as he climbs back up the weights. (tchd 12-1)
Kings Destiny was back to his last winning mark but a good position through the race counted for more in so far as his performance was concerned. He was close enough up from a long way out if good enough, but the winner was always just finding that bit more and he ended what chance he had late on by drifting to his right. He'll be interesting again when able to get to the front more easily in a small field. (op 6-1 tchd 5-1)
Sandor had looked unlucky in the big handicap won by Forte Dei Marmi here last time, hitting the front too soon after coming virtually from last to first in a strongly-run race, but the tempo of this race was totally different and it didn't suit him so well. He's undoubtedly well handicapped but is perhaps a bit over reliant on things needing to drop right. (tchd 11-4 and 10-3 in a place)
Fox Hunt(IRE) ◆ remains an interesting sort for handicaps, and could turn out to be very well treated indeed when things drop into place. Inexperience caught him out here, flat footed 3f out when the pace increased and then running into trouble on the rail, but he picked up very smartly inside the last half furlong and was really motoring late on. A strong pace at this trip, or a step up to 1m4f, will bring about plenty of improvement, and he can land a good prize. Official explanation: jockey said gelding was denied a clear run (op 7-2 tchd 4-1 and 9-2 in a place)
Huygens ran creditably and would have finished a length closer had his rider not had to snatch up very close to the line when hampered by the third, after which he was eased slightly and passed by the fourth. He seemed to stay the longer trip without any trouble, but the race didn't really test his stamina and it might be he's still better coming off a stronger pace at 1m.
Safari Sunup(IRE) is on a much more favourable mark now than he was in the spring and turned in a respectable effort. His yard are in good form and he's worth watching given his record in the autumn if kept to this trip. (tchd 14-1)
Reve De Nuit(USA) is more than capable off this mark but he didn't find the leaders coming back in time. (op 16-1 tchd 12-1)
Ouster(GER) Official explanation: jockey said colt hung right-handed
Dr Livingstone(IRE) Official explanation: jockey said gelding stopped very quickly

5971 STOKE D'ABERNON MAIDEN STKS 1m 1f
5:05 (5:06) (Class 5) 3-Y-O **£3,238** (£963; £481; £240) **Stalls** High

Form RPR

- **1** **Conduct (IRE)** 3-9-3 0 SebSanders 4 91+
(Sir Michael Stoute) *s.i.s: towards rr: hdwy over 2f out: shkn up to ld ent fnl f: drifted rt: styd on strly: comf* **8/1**

03 **2** 3 **Shallow Bay**19 5376 3-9-3 0 ShaneKelly 14 79
(W R Swinburn) *in tch: led gng wl 2f out: sn rdn: hdd ent fnl f: kpt on but nt pce of wnr* **4/1**2

44 **3** 1/2 **Piano**29 5038 3-8-12 0 NeilCallan 8 73+
(J H M Gosden) *mid-div: hdwy over 2f out: sn rdn: nt pce to chal: styd on fnl f* **7/2**1

0-2 **4** 1 1/2 **Gift Of Love (IRE)**33 4906 3-8-12 0 DaneO'Neill 2 70
(D R C Elsworth) *hld up towards rr: hdwy over 2f out: sn rdn to chse ldrs: styd on same pce fnl f* **11/2**3

6 **5** nk **Mashatu**93 2899 3-9-3 0 JackMitchell 3 74
(J R Fanshawe) *mid-div: rdn over 2f out: no imp tl styd on fnl f* **12/1**

23 **6** 3 **Magic Jack**21 5288 3-9-3 0 PatDobbs 11 68
(R Hannon) *trckd ldrs: rdn and ev ch 2f out: styd on same pce fnl f* **11/2**3

05 **7** 5 **Zawadi**19 5376 3-8-12 0 JimCrowley 9 52
(R M Beckett) *t.k.h in tch: rdn and wknd jst over 1f out* **25/1**

03 **8** 3 1/2 **Lalika**22 5265 3-8-12 0 LukeMorris 1 44
(C G Cox) *t.k.h w ldrs: rdn and ev ch 2f out: wknd over 1f out* **33/1**

24 **9** 3/4 **Invincibility (IRE)**11 5623 3-9-3 0 HayleyTurner 16 47
(S Dow) *led tl rdn 2f out: sn wknd* **13/2**

10 1 1/2 **Justazippy** 3-8-12 0 JamesDoyle 6 39
(A J McCabe) *s.i.s: a towards rr* **50/1**

0 **11** 2 1/4 **Ice Road Trucker (IRE)**10 5658 3-9-3 0 StephenCraine 12 39
(J R Boyle) *w ldrs tl over 3f out: sn rdn: wknd over 1f out* **66/1**

0 **12** 2 1/4 **Rhythm Stick**29 5026 3-9-3 0 RoystonFfrench 5 34
(John Berry) *a towards rr* **40/1**

60 **13** 9 **Penshurst Lad (IRE)**54 4205 3-9-0 0 EJMcNamara(3) 10 14
(R T Phillips) *s.i.s: a towards rr* **100/1**

06 **14** hd **Falcun**19 5376 3-9-3 0 J-PGuillambert 7 14
(L M Cumani) *hld up towards rr: sme prog over 3f out: sn rdn: wknd 2f out* **66/1**

15 dist **Arco Felice (USA)** 3-9-0 0 PatrickHills(3) 15 —
(W K Goldsworthy) *in tch: rdn over 3f out: wknd over 2f out: eased* **20/1**

1m 55.52s (-0.18) **Going Correction** +0.05s/f (Good) 15 Ran SP% **125.1**
Speed ratings (Par 101): **102,99,98,97,97 94,90,87,86,85 83,81,73,72,—**
toteswingers: 1&2 £8.10, 1&3 £7.10, 2&3 £3.10. CSF £39.05 TOTE £7.50: £2.50, £2.10, £1.30; EX 42.60.
Owner Highclere Thoroughbred Racing Royal Pal **Bred** The Lavington Stud **Trained** Newmarket, Suffolk

FOCUS
A fair maiden contested by plenty of unexposed types and likely decent form for the time of year. The pace was just steady, so the winner deserves plenty of credit for coming as far clear as he did.

5972 HERSHAM FILLIES' H'CAP 1m 1f
5:40 (5:40) (Class 4) (0-80,80) 3-Y-O+ **£5,180** (£1,541; £770; £384) **Stalls** High

Form RPR

2123 **1** **Babycakes (IRE)**95 2843 3-9-4 79 HayleyTurner 3 91
(M L W Bell) *mid-div: pushed along and hdwy over 2f out: sn rdn: chal ent fnl f: styd on to ld fnl 75yds: drvn out* **11/2**2

2624 **2** *1 1/4* **Dylanesque**[24] 5199 3-9-5 **80** .... NeilCallan 6 89
(M A Jarvis) *in tch: tk clsr order 3f out: rdn to ld jst over 1f out: kpt on but no ex whn hdd fnl 75yds* **7/1**

231 **3** *1 1/2* **Calipatria**[22] 5265 3-9-2 **77** .... SaleemGolam 2 83
(J H M Gosden) *trckd ldrs: led jst ins 2f out: sn rdn: hdd jst over 1f out: kpt on same pce* **7/2**[1]

-115 **4** *1 1/4* **Hidden Fire**[28] 5083 3-9-1 **76** .... RoystonFfrench 1 79+
(D R C Elsworth) *hld up towards rr: stmbld whn sltly hmpd 3f out: sn rdn and hdwy: wandered u.p: styd on wl fnl f* **10/1**

3-31 **5** *nk* **Red Intrigue (IRE)**[29] 5038 3-9-0 **75** .... JimCrowley 5 77
(Mrs A J Perrett) *hld up towards rr: hdwy 3f out: sn rdn: styd on same pce fnl f* **13/2**[3]

0304 **6** *4 1/2* **It's Dubai Dolly**[12] 5611 4-9-0 **69** .... JamesDoyle 8 61
(A J Lidderdale) *trckd ldr: led over 2f out: sn rdn: hdd wl over 1f out: wknd fnl f* **16/1**

2531 **7** *2 1/4* **Aquarius Star (IRE)**[22] 5266 3-9-3 **78** .... DaneO'Neill 12 65
(Pat Eddery) *trckd ldrs: rdn and one pce fnl 2f* **7/1**

-050 **8** *2 1/2* **Suzhou**[18] 5384 3-8-0 **66** oh3 ow1 .... (t) DeclanCannon(5) 11 48
(D J Coakley) *in tch: rdn over 2f out: wknd over 1f out* **20/1**

-000 **9** *nse* **Club Tahiti**[26] 5149 4-9-10 **79** .... (p) J-PGuillambert 4 61
(A W Carroll) *a towards rr* **10/1**

305 **10** *1 1/2* **Circus Girl (IRE)**[52] 4265 3-9-0 **78** .... EJMcNamara(3) 13 57
(R M Beckett) *led: rdn and hdd 2f out: wknd ent fnl f* **11/1**

0-33 **11** *12* **Swish Dish (CAN)**[135] 1644 3-8-12 **73** .... PatDobbs 7 25
(R Hannon) *a towards rr* **33/1**

51-5 **12** *3* **Maristar (USA)**[149] 1317 3-9-0 **75** .... (p) ShaneKelly 9 21
(G A Butler) *mid-div: rdn 3f out: sn btn* **20/1**

1m 54.57s (-1.13) **Going Correction** +0.05s/f (Good)
WFA 3 from 4yo 6lb **12** Ran SP% **120.8**
Speed ratings (Par 102): **107,105,104,103,103 99,97,94,94,93 82,80**
toteswingers: 1&2 £4.30, 1&3 £3.70, 2&3 £6.90. CSF £43.54 CT £156.98 TOTE £6.00: £1.90, £2.20, £1.20; EX 34.40 Place 6: £1,272.87, Place 5: £860.42..
Owner J Acheson **Bred** Alan Dargan **Trained** Newmarket, Suffolk

FOCUS
A competitive finale and probably reliable enough form for that reason despite the gallop being on the steady side until the straight.
T/Plt: £848.60 to a £1 stake. Pool of £47,908.68 - 41.21 winning tickets. T/Qpdt: £174.40 to a £1 stake. Pool of £3,394.99 - 14.40 winning tickets. TM

5973 - 5974a (Foreign Racing) - See Raceform Interactive

5566 CURRAGH (R-H)

Saturday, September 11

OFFICIAL GOING: Straight course - yielding to soft; round course - yielding both changing to soft after race 1 (2.10pm)

5975a BOYLESPORTS.COM VINCENT O'BRIEN NATIONAL (GROUP 1) 7f
3:10 (3:13) 2-Y-O

£102,654 (£33,628; £15,929; £5,309; £3,539; £1,769)

RPR

1 **Pathfork (USA)**[21] 5316 2-9-1 .... FMBerry 8 119+
(Mrs John Harrington, Ire) *settled 3rd: 2nd 1/2-way: led 2f out: 1 l advantage ent fnl f: styd on wl u.p: strly pressed cl home: all out* **2/1**[2]

2 *hd* **Casamento (IRE)**[16] 5459 2-9-1 .... DPMcDonogh 4 119+
(M Halford, Ire) *sn led: hdd 2f out: 2nd and rdn over 1f out: styd on wl u.p last 100yds: jst failed* **11/1**

3 *5* **Zoffany (IRE)**[34] 4880 2-9-1 115 .... JMurtagh 9 106
(A P O'Brien, Ire) *trckd ldrs: 5th 1/2-way: 4th and rdn 2f out: no imp: tk mod 3rd fnl f* **6/4**[1]

4 *1/2* **Samuel Morse (IRE)**[21] 5316 2-9-1 108 .... JAHeffernan 2 105
(A P O'Brien, Ire) *hld up: 7th 1/2-way: 5th and prog 2f out: tk mod 4th and no imp fnl f* **14/1**

5 *5 1/2* **Glor Na Mara (IRE)**[13] 5567 2-9-1 113 .... KJManning 6 91
(J S Bolger, Ire) *hld up in tch: hdwy into 3rd 2f out: sn rdn and no imp: wknd fnl f* **13/2**[3]

6 *2 1/2* **High Ruler (USA)**[21] 5316 2-9-1 107 .... (b1) JPO'Brien 1 85
(A P O'Brien, Ire) *chsd ldrs: 4th u.p 3f out: sn no ex and wknd* **33/1**

7 *1 1/4* **Rudolf Valentino**[21] 5316 2-9-1 104 .... (b1) SMLevey 7 82
(A P O'Brien, Ire) *sn chsd ldrs: 3rd u.p 1/2-way: lost pl over 2f out: no ex* **50/1**

8 *4* **Janood (IRE)**[28] 5079 2-9-1 .... AlanMunro 3 72
(Saeed Bin Suroor) *hld up towards rr: effrt and no imp over 2f out: eased fnl f* **8/1**

9 *8* **A Word Apart (IRE)**[7] 5777 2-9-1 100 .... PJSmullen 5 67
(D K Weld, Ire) *trckd ldrs: 6th 1/2-way: wknd over 2f out: eased fr 1 1/2f out* **16/1**

1m 27.95s (-2.85) **Going Correction** -0.15s/f (Firm) **9** Ran SP% **123.6**
Speed ratings: **110,109,104,103,97 94,92,88,79**
CSF £26.89 TOTE £2.80: £1.30, £2.20, £1.20; DF 37.20.
Owner Silverton Hill Partnership **Bred** Flaxman Holdings Limited **Trained** Moone, Co Kildare

FOCUS
A first win at Group 1 level for trainer Jessica Harrington and jockey Fran Berry with Pathfork retaining his unbeaten record and following up his win in the Group 2 Futurity Stakes over course and trip last month with a game victory on very different ground to last time. The official description was changed to soft after the first race. The first two finished clear.

NOTEBOOK
Pathfork(USA) went to the front just over 2f out and, while the runner-up came back at him in the closing stages, he stuck to his task and held on in a photo-finish. With conditions less than ideal for him, he remains an exciting prospect for next year and a genuine contender for the 2,000 Guineas, for which he is now 10-1 with Ladbrokes and William Hill, from 14 and 12 respectively. He remains 12-1 with Paddy Power for the Newmarket Classic. In the immediate aftermath of the race Harrington was uncertain whether the winner, who fully justified the decision to supplement him at a cost of Euro 20,000, will run again this season, while Berry reported that the colt "never enjoyed the soft ground at any stage". (op 5/2)
Casamento(IRE), a two-and-a-half length winner of a a maiden over a fractionally longer trip on fast ground at Tipperary on his only previous start, ran a big race, making the running until over 2f out and remaining the only threat to the winner from over 1f out. With the rail to guide him, he battled back well and was closing on the winner with every stride towards the finish.Described by trainer Michael Halford as still "a big raw colt but one with a lot of ability", where he goes next will be of considerable interest when it comes to working out the form value of this race. No other horse who ran in the maiden he won has raced since. Allowing for the ground conditions, which were probably against most of the runners, the first two did pull five lengths clear of the rest. (op 12/1)
Zoffany(IRE), winner of the Group 1 Phoenix Stakes over 6f last month, had twice won over this trip. This was his seventh start and whether his disappointing effort was all down to the ground, or not, it was obvious that he was struggling in vain pursuit of the first two from almost 2f out. Johnny Murtagh reported that he was "never really happy", while Aidan O'Brien seemed convinced that the ground, softer than anything the colt had raced on previously, was to blame. (op 11/8 tchd 13/8)
Samuel Morse(IRE), running in his eighth race, hasn't won since scoring landing the Listed Marble Hill Stakes over 5f here in May. Beaten four lengths by Pathfork in the Futurity Stakes here last month, he was just over a length and a half further adrift of the winner this time. Driven along soon after halfway, he kept on without ever posing any sort of threat. (op 25/1)
Glor Na Mara(IRE), the only maiden in the line-up, was runner-up to Zoffany in the Phoenix Stakes and to Pathfork in the Futurity before again running second in a 6f Group 3 event here last time. Held up in rear, he made headway in the centre of the track after halfway and went third 2f out before finding no extra for pressure. (op 7/1 tchd 6/1)
Janood(IRE), a supplementary entry and the winner of both his previous starts, was held up in rear and was never able to get into contention. Jockey Alan Munro reported: "I'd give him the benefit of the doubt as he couldn't handle the ground. He's a big, heavy colt and he just kept getting too far into it." (op 7/1)

5976a THE IRISH FIELD ST. LEGER (GROUP 1) 1m 6f
3:45 (3:45) 3-Y-O+

£123,362 (£40,530; £19,292; £6,548; £4,424; £2,300)

RPR

1 **Sans Frontieres (IRE)**[28] 5080 4-9-11 .... (tp) OlivierPeslier 3 118+
(J Noseda) *hld up in 7th: prog on outer early st: 2nd over 1f out: sn chal: led 100yds out: styd on wl: comf* **13/8**[1]

2 *3/4* **Profound Beauty (IRE)**[37] 4769 6-9-8 115 .... PJSmullen 6 112
(D K Weld, Ire) *trckd ldrs in 5th: impr into 3rd travelling wl ent st: led 1 1/2f out: strly pressed fnl f: hdd 100yds out: kpt on u.p wout threatening wnr* **5/2**[2]

3 *1 3/4* **Flying Cross (IRE)**[16] 5464 3-9-0 96 .... JMurtagh 7 113
(A P O'Brien, Ire) *hld up in 6th: 5th and prog early st: 2nd briefly 1 1/2f out: 3rd and kpt on ins fnl f* **7/1**[3]

4 *1 1/2* **Rajik (IRE)**[12] 5619 5-9-11 107 .... (t) DPMcDonogh 8 111
(C F Swan, Ire) *prom: 3rd fr 1/2-way: 4th and drvn along appr st: 5th under 1 1/2f out: kpt on* **16/1**

5 *7* **Lady Lupus (IRE)**[55] 4178 3-8-11 105 .... (p) JPO'Brien 2 98
(A P O'Brien, Ire) *led: jnd 4f out: regained slt advantage st: hdd 1 1/2f out: sn no ex and wknd* **25/1**

6 *3* **Tactic**[44] 4506 4-9-11 .... TadhgO'Shea 5 97
(J L Dunlop) *cl up in 2nd: disp ld 4f out: rdn and hdd early st: dropped to 6th and no ex over 1f out* **8/1**

7 *8* **Kite Wood (IRE)**[28] 5080 4-9-11 .... AlanMunro 4 86
(Saeed Bin Suroor) *prom: 4th 1/2-way: 6th st: sn no ex: eased fnl f* **7/1**[3]

8 *27* **Pop Rock (JPN)**[43] 4564 9-9-11 107 .... FMBerry 1 48
(Takashi Kodama, Ire) *hld up in rr: eased ent st: t.o* **20/1**

3m 10.36s (3.36) **Going Correction** +0.05s/f (Good)
WFA 3 from 4yo+ 11lb **8** Ran SP% **117.3**
Speed ratings: **103,102,101,100,96 95,90,75**
CSF £5.96 TOTE £2.60: £1.02, £1.02, £2.30; DF 5.80.
Owner Sir Robert Ogden **Bred** The Lavington Stud **Trained** Newmarket, Suffolk

FOCUS
They went very steady early and the time was slower than the handicap. The form has its limits and Sans Frontieres did not need to be at his best.

NOTEBOOK
Sans Frontieres(IRE) ◆ showed his class and picked up best on the ground. Held up off a pace that was a bit stop-start, he didn't pick up immediately in the straight and being switched towards the outside seemed to help. He did change gear well over a furlong out and ran on strongly inside the last without his jockey having to really get serious. He won snugly and would have to be seen as a horse very much on the upgrade, but it is a pertinent question as to how he would cope with the runner-up should they meet on better ground, which they may do at Melbourne in November. However he has been given a 2kg penalty for the Melbourne Cup which may persuade connections to miss the race. (op 15/8)
Profound Beauty(IRE) ◆ ran a blinder. She travelled much better this time on ground that wasn't quite so testing, travelling strongly to challenge and lead a furlong and a half out but she didn't quite stride out on it under pressure. It was an ideal trial for Melbourne. (op 11/4)
Flying Cross(IRE) ◆ ran tremendously well. Held up off the pace, he came under pressure early in the straight and all he did from there was stay. He doesn't hold an entry in the Melbourne Cup, which is a pity, but he'll have little difficulty stepping up in trip and could well be a Cup horse for next year. (op 8/1)
Rajik(IRE) fully justified the decision to supplement him for this race as he continued his rate of improvement. Never far from the pace on the inside rail, he just kept galloping in the straight without quite being good enough. However, being beaten four lengths in a Classic is a long way from where he was before winning a handicap at Galway a month and a half ago. (op 14/1)
Lady Lupus(IRE) helped set the pace until weakening in the straight.
Tactic shouldn't have been inconvenienced by the surface, racing prominently most of the way and leading into the straight, but he dropped away disappointingly under pressure. (op 7/1)
Kite Wood(IRE), runner-up in the Doncaster version a year ago, came under pressure half a mile out and dropped away early in the straight.
Pop Rock(JPN) was last throughout. The Japanese raider picked up a tendon injury and has been retired. (op 25/1)

5977 - 5980a (Foreign Racing) - See Raceform Interactive

TOULOUSE

Saturday, September 11

OFFICIAL GOING: Turf: good

5981a PRIX OCCITANIE (LISTED RACE) (3YO FILLIES) (TURF) 1m 2f
5:00 (12:00) 3-Y-O **£24,336** (£9,734; £7,300; £4,867; £2,433)

RPR

1 **Timepecker (IRE)**[21] 3-8-11 0 .... PhilippeSogorb 3 89
(M Delzangles, France) **11/1**

2 *hd* **Buffering**[32] 3-8-11 0 .... MaximeGuyon 2 89
(A Fabre, France) **2/1**[1]

3 *nk* **Khelwa (FR)**[30] 5139 3-8-11 0 .... GeraldMosse 5 88
(R Gibson, France) **17/2**

4 *1/2* **Fork Lightning (USA)**[30] 4997 3-8-11 0 .... Jean-BernardEyquem 9 87
(Sir Mark Prescott) *broke wl: racd in 6th on outside: prog u.p bef st: hrd rdn and r.o wl fnl f: nrest at fin* **10/1**

5 *3/4* **Roche Ambeau (FR)**[59] 4037 3-8-11 0 .... AnthonyCrastus 8 86
(E Lellouche, France) **78/10**

6 *1 1/2* **Vertana (IRE)**[23] 5253 3-8-11 0 .... FabriceVeron 10 83
(H-A Pantall, France) **68/10**[3]

7 ½ **Deep And Blue (USA)**[404] 3-8-11 0 IoritzMendizabal 4 82
(J-C Rouget, France) **12/1**
8 1 **Sound Of Summer (USA)**[105] 3-8-11 0 ChristopheSoumillon 6 80
(J-C Rouget, France) **19/5**[2]
9 ¾ **Turn Around (FR)**[126] 3-8-11 0 MlleGloriaMaderoParayre 1 78
(C Alonso Pena, Spain) **51/1**

2m 2.31s (122.31) **9** Ran SP% **115.9**
WIN (incl. 1 euro stake): 12.30. PLACES: 2.60, 1.50, 2.40. DF: 14.20. SF: 32.30.
Owner Marquesa De Moratalla **Bred** Childwick Bury Stud Management **Trained** France

NOTEBOOK
Fork Lightning(USA) raced on the outside for much of the way, but was outpaced early in the straight before putting in her best work inside the final furlong. She ran on well in the final stages to take fourth place, finishing a neck outside the placings and less than a length behind the winner.

5982 - 5984a (Foreign Racing) - See Raceform Interactive

5472 FFOS LAS (L-H)

Sunday, September 12

OFFICIAL GOING: Good (good to soft in the back straight)
Wind: Fresh across Weather: Cloudy with sunny periods

5985 E.B.F./FELINFOEL BREWERY DAY MAIDEN STKS 1m (R)

2:10 (2:11) (Class 4) 2-Y-O £4,533 (£1,348; £674; £336) Stalls Low

Form				RPR
	1		**Matula (IRE)** 2-8-12 0 JimCrowley 10 (R M Beckett) *hld up in last pair: smooth hdwy fr 2f out: led ins fnl f: r.o wl: easily* **7/2**[2]	77+
02	2	1 ¼	**Strictly Rhythm**[15] 5520 2-8-12 0 SteveDrowne 9 (R Hannon) *racd keenly: trckd ldrs: rdn to ld ent fnl f: sn hdd: kpt on but nt pce of wnr* **3/1**[1]	70
	3	1 ¼	**Ajeeb (USA)** 2-9-3 0 EddieCreighton 8 (D M Simcock) *mid-div: rdn 3f out: styd on ent fnl f: wnt 3rd towards fin* **33/1**	72
5	4	½	**Charles Camoin (IRE)**[30] 5033 2-9-3 0 LiamKeniry 7 (S Kirk) *w ldr: rdn over 2f out: styd on same pce fnl f* **11/2**	71
	5	1 ¼	**Private Cowboy (IRE)** 2-9-3 0 WilliamCarson 4 (M G Quinlan) *led: rdn over 2f out: hdd ent fnl f: no ex* **6/1**	68
03	6	nk	**Colebrooke**[8] 5762 2-9-3 0 GregFairley 2 (M Johnston) *trckd ldrs: rdn over 2f out: kpt on same pce* **6/1**	68
	7	¾	**Census (IRE)** 2-9-3 0 PatDobbs 3 (R Hannon) *s.i.s: in last pair: rdn over 2f out: sme late prog: nvr trbld ldrs* **9/2**[3]	66+
	8	½	**Rosairlie (IRE)** 2-8-12 0 LukeMorris 6 (H J L Dunlop) *trckd ldrs: rdn over 2f out: hung lft and wknd ins fnl f* **33/1**	60
	9	1	**Lady Deanie (IRE)** 2-8-12 0 CathyGannon 1 (B Palling) *s.i.s: mid-div: rdn 3f out: wknd fnl f* **50/1**	60+
0	10	2 ¾	**Tidal Run**[10] 5691 2-8-12 0 ChrisCatlin 11 (M R Channon) *mid-div: rdn over 2f out: wknd over 1f out* **14/1**	52

1m 43.88s (3.38) **Going Correction** 0.0s/f (Good) **10** Ran SP% **123.9**
Speed ratings (Par 97): **83,81,80,80,78 78,77,77,76,73**
toteswingers: 1&2 £4.30, 1&3 £28.30, 2&3 £9.40. CSF £15.34 TOTE £3.60: £1.10, £1.10, £13.90; EX 15.10.
Owner R A Pegum **Bred** D Johnson **Trained** Whitsbury, Hants

FOCUS
An ordinary looking maiden, despite the fair standard set by the Hannon runner-up. The pace did not look strong.

NOTEBOOK
Matula(IRE) ◆, the first foal of a 7f winner, came in for a lot of market support, which proved to be well placed. Held up at the rear, she won comfortably after travelling strongly into contention, quickening in the style of a useful performer. She looks destined for better things, despite holding no significant entries. Connections mentioned the Listed Montrose Stakes over 1m at Newmarket as a possible target, a race won by Timepiece last season. (op 11-2 tchd 3-1)
Strictly Rhythm was a clear second and had the rest nicely held, but met a decent sort. (op 7-2)
Ajeeb(USA), the tenth foal of an unraced dam in the States, and a half-brother to three winners out there, was under pressure with three furlongs to go but stayed on nicely in the latter stages.
Charles Camoin(IRE) had made a satisfactory debut at Newbury and proved that he had not regressed with another good performance. (op 7-1)
Private Cowboy(IRE), a half-brother to the top-class Carry On Katie among others, was handed an easy lead and gave the impression he will improve for the outing. (op 5-1)
Colebrooke didn't significantly improve for the step up in trip. (tchd 11-2)
Census(IRE), a 50,000gns son of an unraced mare, sat alongside the winner at the back of the field for much of the contest, but looked a little green when asked for maximum effort. (op 7-2 tchd 5-1)
Lady Deanie(IRE) Official explanation: jockey said that the filly hung left
Tidal Run Official explanation: vet said filly finished lame

5986 DOUBLE DRAGON NATIONAL ALE OF WALES MAIDEN FILLIES' STKS 1m (R)

2:45 (2:47) (Class 4) 3-Y-O+ £4,533 (£1,348; £674; £336) Stalls Low

Form				RPR
	1		**Gypsy Carnival** 3-8-12 0 JimCrowley 2 (R M Beckett) *s.i.s: hld up: smooth hdwy over 3f out: led over 1f out: pushed clr: v easily* **11/2**[3]	80+
-040	2	3 ¾	**Quality Mover (USA)**[11] 5654 3-8-12 65 EddieCreighton 5 (D M Simcock) *s.i.s: racd green in last pair: hdwy 3f out: sn rdn: styd on: wnt 2nd ins fnl f: no ch w wnr* **10/1**	68
66	3	1 ½	**Citadella**[19] 5395 3-8-12 0 LiamKeniry 6 (D M Simcock) *in tch: effrt over 2f out: sn no ch w wnr: kpt on same pce fnl f* **22/1**	65
2534	4	½	**Easy Terms**[3] 5872 3-8-10 70 ow1 (p) JamesMillman(3) 7 (B R Millman) *led: rdn over 2f out: hdd over 1f out: sn no ch w wnr: one pce fnl f* **7/2**[2]	64
	5	6	**La Kalam** 3-8-12 0 PhilipRobinson 8 (M A Jarvis) *racd keenly w ldrs: rdn over 2f out: wknd over 1f out* **5/4**[1]	50
043	6	nk	**Present Story**[16] 5493 3-8-7 70 MarkCoumbe(5) 9 (P Leech) *prom: rdn and ev ch 2f out: wknd ent fnl f* **6/1**	49
	7	2 ¼	**River Of Silence (IRE)** 3-8-12 0 (t) PatDobbs 3 (P J Makin) *s.i.s: in last pair: rdn over 2f out: wknd over 1f out* **12/1**	44

1m 40.71s (0.21) **Going Correction** 0.0s/f (Good) **7** Ran SP% **117.5**
Speed ratings (Par 102): **98,94,92,92,86 85,83**
toteswingers: 1&2 £6.80, 1&3 £8.90, 2&3 £17.70. CSF £58.91 TOTE £5.40: £9.90, £8.60; EX 68.20.
Owner Delamere Cottage Racing Partners (1996) **Bred** L A C Ashby Newhall Estate Farm **Trained** Whitsbury, Hants

FOCUS
None of those that had racecourse experience looked difficult to beat, so it was not surprising to see a newcomer take this.

5987 CELTIC GOLD LAGER - WALES' PREMIUM LAGER NURSERY 5f

3:20 (3:20) (Class 4) (0-85,81) 2-Y-O £3,885 (£1,156; £577; £288) Stalls High

Form				RPR
2252	1		**Johnny Hancocks (IRE)**[4] 5863 2-8-2 62 CathyGannon 4 (P D Evans) *sn swtchd to nrside rail: mde all: r.o strly: comf* **5/2**[1]	75+
4404	2	4	**Novabridge**[13] 5613 2-7-13 64 (b) AmyBaker(5) 5 (A B Haynes) *chsd wnr: rdn whn hung bdly lft 2f out: kpt on but sn hld by wnr* **7/1**	63
110	3	2	**Jollywood (IRE)**[78] 3453 2-9-7 81 PatDobbs 1 (R Hannon) *cl up: rdn 2f out: nvr chal: kpt on same pce* **11/4**[2]	72
2300	4	½	**Master Macho (IRE)**[14] 5547 2-8-8 68 ChrisCatlin 8 (M R Channon) *squeezed up sn after s: cl up: rdn over 2f out: nt pce to chal* **8/1**	58
0013	5	1 ¼	**Roman Dancer (IRE)**[36] 4831 2-9-1 75 JimCrowley 2 (J Gallagher) *chsd ldrs: rdn 2f out: wknd ins fnl f* **3/1**[3]	60
3104	6	½	**Scommettitrice (IRE)**[2] 5921 2-8-13 73 LukeMorris 6 (R A Harris) *sltly hmpd sn after s: chsd ldrs: sn pushed along: rdn over 2f out: wknd ent fnl f* **17/2**	56

58.05 secs (0.65) **Going Correction** +0.075s/f (Good) **6** Ran SP% **114.4**
Speed ratings (Par 97): **97,90,87,86,84 83**
toteswingers: 1&2 £4.90, 1&3 £2.20, 2&3 £5.40. CSF £20.54 CT £50.48 TOTE £3.00: £3.40, £5.70; EX 25.60.
Owner Shropshire Wolves 3 **Bred** Mountarmstrong Stud **Trained** Pandy, Monmouths

FOCUS
Not many of these held any secrets already from the handicapper, so the form should be reliable for the level.

NOTEBOOK
Johnny Hancocks(IRE), back on turf, had plenty of experience on his side and flew down the stands' rail after switching on to it soon after leaving the stalls. He seems best when able to dominate. (op 11-4 tchd 3-1)
Novabridge, who only ran because there was significant rain, raced keenly under restraint and wandered noticeably under pressure. However, he was still good enough to claim second. (op 8-1)
Jollywood(IRE), having her first outing since the 6f Listed Empress Stakes back in June, probably ran well considering how much weight she gave to the first two, although she never threatened to get involved. (tchd 5-2)
Master Macho(IRE) was ahead of Jollywood heading into the final furlong, but was steadily worn down for third.
Roman Dancer(IRE) travelled nicely towards the middle of the course but couldn't pick up. He has a bit of scope and should have more to come. (op 5-2)
Scommettitrice(IRE) is finding life difficult in handicap company. (op 8-1 tchd 10-1)

5988 FELINFOEL BREWERY CAMBRIAN BEST BITTER FILLIES' H'CAP 1m 2f (R)

3:55 (3:55) (Class 4) (0-80,79) 3-Y-O+ £3,885 (£1,156; £577; £288) Stalls Low

Form				RPR
0331	1		**Ashkalara**[31] 4988 3-8-7 62 CathyGannon 6 (H S Howe) *hld up: swtchd rt over 2f out: rdn to ld over 1f out: styd on wl: comf* **2/1**[2]	71+
6561	2	2	**Balatoma (IRE)**[23] 5258 3-9-1 70 (b) JimCrowley 3 (M P Tregoning) *trckd ldr: led over 3f out tl veered lft u.p over 2f out: styd on same pce* **4/1**[3]	74
2-22	3	nk	**Three Ducks**[32] 4958 4-9-12 74 SteveDrowne 1 (R Hannon) *trckd ldrs: rdn over 2f out: styd on same pce* **13/8**[1]	77
1-00	4	1 ¾	**Mirabella (IRE)**[20] 5375 3-9-10 79 PatDobbs 4 (R Hannon) *led tl over 3f out: rdn to regain ld bef being bmpd 2f out: hdd over 1f out: fdd fnl 75yds* **14/1**	79
3354	5	7	**Night Sky**[13] 5584 3-8-11 66 (p) ChrisCatlin 5 (P J Makin) *trckd ldrs: rdn over 2f out: wknd ent fnl f* **11/2**	52

2m 11.97s (3.57) **Going Correction** 0.0s/f (Good)
WFA 3 from 4yo 7lb **5** Ran SP% **113.5**
Speed ratings (Par 102): **85,83,83,81,76**
toteswinger: 1&2 £6.70. CSF £10.60 TOTE £3.10: £2.20, £1.50; EX 7.70.
Owner Roly Roper **Bred** R G Levin **Trained** Oakford, Devon

FOCUS
Just a fair handicap, run at a modest pace.

5989 FELINFOEL BREWERY DRAGON STOUT H'CAP 1m 4f (R)

4:30 (4:30) (Class 3) (0-95,95) 3-Y-O+ £6,308 (£1,888; £944; £472; £235) Stalls Low

Form				RPR
1	1		**Ferdoos**[30] 5026 3-8-9 87 PhilipRobinson 4 (M A Jarvis) *hld up: swtchd rt and smooth hdwy over 3f out: led 2f out: pushed clr: quite impressive* **1/1**[1]	107+
1110	2	6	**Sea Of Heartbreak (IRE)**[46] 4470 3-9-0 92 SteveDrowne 3 (R Charlton) *trckd ldrs: ev ch 2f out: sn rdn: kpt on for 2nd but no ch w wnr sn after* **4/1**[2]	102
3-21	3	1	**Ashbrittle**[59] 4062 3-8-11 89 JimCrowley 2 (R M Beckett) *prom: rdn over 3f out: kpt pressing ldrs tl wl over 1f out: styd on same pce* **4/1**[2]	97
0200	4	1 ¾	**Lethal Glaze (IRE)**[16] 5492 4-9-7 90 PatDobbs 6 (R Hannon) *prom: rdn wl over 2f out: styd on same pce* **12/1**	96
0130	5	9	**Spirit Is Needed (IRE)**[36] 4818 4-9-10 93 (b) GregFairley 1 (M Johnston) *sn led: rdn and hdd 2f out: wknd over 1f out* **7/1**[3]	84
/4-0	6	22	**Numide (FR)**[22] 5291 7-9-9 95 JamesMillman(3) 5 (B R Millman) *a last: rdn over 3f out: wknd 2f out* **33/1**	51

2m 34.56s (-2.24) **Going Correction** 0.0s/f (Good)
WFA 3 from 4yo+ 9lb **6** Ran SP% **113.1**
Speed ratings (Par 107): **107,103,102,101,95 80**
toteswingers: 1&2 £2.20, 1&3 £1.80, 2&3 £1.90. CSF £5.44 TOTE £1.70: £1.10, £4.70; EX 6.10.
Owner Sheikh Ahmed Al Maktoum **Bred** Miss A Shaykhutdinova **Trained** Newmarket, Suffolk

FOCUS
The early pace was not strong, so all those in the bunch that pulled away from Numide looked to have a chance two furlongs from home.

NOTEBOOK
Ferdoos ◆ was in a different class to her rivals. Settled in behind, she only really caught the eye halfway up the home straight, but once Phillip Robinson asked her to quicken, the response was immediate and she came well clear. The maiden the winner picked up on debut at Kempton had already produced two winners, and she seems sure to hold her own at a higher level if given a realistic target. Her Rock Of Gibraltar half-brother Brusco has won in easy ground at up to 1m7f (he was also third in the German St Leger on this day), so one would imagine she'll stay further without too much of a problem. (op 5-4 tchd 6-4 in places)
Sea Of Heartbreak(IRE) shaped nicely on her return from a break to suggest that she can add to her three successes already this season. She travelled strongly but couldn't go with Ferdoos when she went on. The slight ease in the ground may not have suited her considering her victories early in the year, and it's still open to debate whether this distance suits.

Ashbrittle, a non-runner the previous day at Doncaster, was making his handicap debut like the winner, but he didn't have the speed the first two showed. He is still a nice handicapper in the making, however.
Lethal Glaze(IRE) had run badly on his last two starts, so this was a little better without suggesting he is about to win. (op 17-2 tchd 14-1)
Spirit Is Needed(IRE) surrendered the lead over a furlong out and had no more to give. His best runs have come on better ground. (op 6-1)

5990 FELINFOEL BREWERY - CHAMPION BREWERS H'CAP 5f
5:05 (5:05) (Class 6) (0-60,66) 3-Y-0+ £2,047 (£604; £302) Stalls High

Form				RPR
3523	1		**The Jailer**[16] 5471 7-8-10 **56**............(p) RyanPowell(7) 2 (J G M O'Shea) *a.p: rdn 2f out: led ent fnl f: kpt on: all out* **6/1**	64
434	2	nk	**Best One**[26] 5176 6-9-0 **53**............(b) LukeMorris 8 (R A Harris) *chsd ldrs: rdn whn swtchd lft 2f out: r.o to chal ins fnl f: kpt on* **8/1**	60
2-	3	2 1/4	**Ability N Delivery**[18] 5426 5-9-7 **60**............(p) JimCrowley 4 (Michael J Browne, Ire) *led: rdn 2f out: hdd ent fnl f: no ex* **15/8**[1]	59
0631	4	nk	**Mushy Peas (IRE)**[11] 5650 3-8-9 **49**............ CathyGannon 7 (P D Evans) *prom tl outpcd 3f out: nvr bk on terms: styd on fnl f* **5/2**[2]	47
1130	5	1 3/4	**Gracie's Games**[3] 5876 4-8-9 **55**............(v) JamesRogers(7) 10 (R J Price) *hld up: rdn over 2f out: drifted lft ent fnl f: nvr any imp* **4/1**[3]	46
0004	6	1/2	**Croeso Ynol**[16] 5473 4-8-3 **47**............ SophieDoyle(5) 3 (H J Evans) *in tch on outer: rdn over 2f out: fdd fnl f* **14/1**	37
60-0	7	3 1/4	**Ariel Bender**[18] 5423 3-8-6 **46** oh1............ ChrisCatlin 6 (Peter Grayson) *s.i.s: sn pushed along in last pair: wknd over 1f out* **25/1**	24

58.79 secs (1.39) **Going Correction** +0.075s/f (Good)
WFA 3 from 4yo+ 1lb 7 Ran SP% **119.3**
Speed ratings (Par 101): **91,90,86,86,83 82,77**
toteswingers: 1&2 £4.70, 1&3 £3.60, 2&3 £4.00. CSF £54.43 CT £125.43 TOTE £8.10: £2.50, £4.10; EX 38.40 Place 6: £545.14, Place 5: £272.25..
Owner N G H Ayliffe **Bred** D R Tucker **Trained** Elton, Gloucs

FOCUS
Two horses chasing hat-tricks came out during the morning, which obviously made this less competitive than it had looked. As with the other sprint on the card, it seemed best to be close to the stands' side.
T/Plt: £464.30 to a £1 stake. Pool £62,604.01 - 98.41 winning tickets. T/Qpdt: £35.90 to a £1 stake. Pool £4,674.50 - 96.10 winning tickets. TM

5950 GOODWOOD (R-H)
Sunday, September 12

OFFICIAL GOING: Soft (good to soft in places on round course)
Fresh ground on lower and top bends.
Wind: Moderate, half against Weather: Fine

5991 TOTESWINGER BONUS STKS (H'CAP) 1m 4f
2:00 (2:00) (Class 4) (0-85,83) 3-Y-0+ £3,885 (£1,156; £577; £288) Stalls Low

Form				RPR
1-	1		**Powerful Melody (USA)**[302] 7400 3-9-2 **80**............(p) TedDurcan 6 (Saeed Bin Suroor) *w'like: scope: lw: hld up in 7th: prog 3f out: chsd ldr 2f out: sn drvn: styd on wl fnl f to ld last 100yds* **5/2**[1]	90+
3235	2	1 1/2	**Satwa Moon (USA)**[25] 5217 4-10-0 **83**............ RichardHughes 10 (E A L Dunlop) *lw: settled in 6th: rdn over 2f out: prog and n.m.r wl over 1f out: styd on fnl f to take 2nd last stride* **5/2**[1]	91
1-55	3	shd	**Zahoo (IRE)**[122] 2047 3-8-10 **74**............ TadhgO'Shea 3 (J L Dunlop) *trckd ldng trio: smooth prog to ld over 2f out: drvn over 1f out: hdd and fdd last 100yds: lost 2nd post* **11/2**[2]	82+
-062	4	1 1/2	**Clear Reef**[20] 5378 6-8-13 **75**............(p) LewisWalsh(7) 2 (Jane Chapple-Hyam) *dwlt: hld up in last pair: stdy prog on wd outside fr 3f out: u.p over 1f out: kpt on same pce after* **16/1**	80
0545	5	1/2	**Veloso (FR)**[22] 5296 8-9-11 **80**............ DarryllHolland 9 (J A Glover) *trckd ldng pair: pushed along over 2f out: trapped bhd wkng rival after and lost grnd: drvn and styd on fnl f: no ch to rcvr* **20/1**	85
0610	6	3 1/4	**Foxhaven**[13] 5591 8-9-9 **78**............(v) GeorgeBaker 4 (P R Chamings) *trckd ldrs in 5th: rdn and nt qckn over 2f out: sn outpcd: kpt on fnl f* **10/1**[3]	77
3005	7	3 1/2	**Buddy Holly**[13] 5611 5-9-7 **76**............ DaneO'Neill 1 (Pat Eddery) *led to over 2f out: wknd over 1f out* **20/1**	70
0030	8	5	**Trachonitis (IRE)**[4] 5868 6-9-5 **74**............ ShaneKelly 7 (J R Jenkins) *s.s: hld up in last: rdn and no prog over 2f out: sn no ch* **33/1**	60
5316	9	4	**Incendo**[30] 5035 4-9-13 **82**............(vt) AdamKirby 8 (J R Fanshawe) *lw: hld up in 8th: rdn and no prog over 2f out: wknd over 1f out* **12/1**	61
0042	10	nk	**Dove Cottage (IRE)**[12] 5625 8-8-9 **64** oh9............ FergusSweeney 5 (W S Kittow) *chsd ldr to wl over 2f out: wknd over 1f out: heavily eased* **25/1**	43

2m 40.63s (2.23) **Going Correction** +0.30s/f (Good)
WFA 3 from 4yo+ 9lb 10 Ran SP% **111.5**
Speed ratings (Par 105): **104,103,102,101,101 99,97,93,91,90**
toteswingers: 1&2 £2.00, 1&3 £3.00, 2&3 £2.90. CSF £7.12 CT £28.49 TOTE £4.10: £1.50, £1.10, £2.10; EX 9.30.
Owner Godolphin **Bred** B P Walden, P Madden, L Taylor Et Al **Trained** Newmarket, Suffolk
■ Stewards' Enquiry : Richard Hughes caution: used whip with excessive frequency

FOCUS
The right horses dominated the finish of this ordinary handicap.
Incendo Official explanation: jockey said gelding was unsuited by the going
Dove Cottage(IRE) Official explanation: jockey said gelding had no more left to give

5992 NICK BROOKS STKS (NURSERY) 7f
2:35 (2:35) (Class 4) (0-85,84) 2-Y-0 £3,885 (£1,156; £577; £288) Stalls High

Form				RPR
2302	1		**Bunce (IRE)**[7] 5785 2-9-1 **78**............ RichardHughes 3 (R Hannon) *mde all: allowed untrbld ld: wound it up fr over 2f out: drvn and pressed 1f out: styd on* **11/4**[3]	79
6433	2	1/2	**Tipsy Girl**[22] 5293 2-9-1 **78**............ ShaneKelly 6 (D J Coakley) *trckd wnr: pushed along to cl 2f out: rdn over 1f out: styd on nr fin but a hld* **5/1**	78
3220	3	nk	**Point Du Jour (FR)**[8] 5745 2-9-2 **79**............(t) GeorgeBaker 5 (I A Wood) *stdd s: hld up in 3rd: clsd on ldng pair 2f out: sn rdn: edgd lft and nt qckn over 1f out: kpt on nr fin* **5/2**[2]	78
4331	4	7	**Diamond Charlie (IRE)**[38] 4743 2-9-0 **77**............ SebSanders 1 (S Dow) *lw: plld hrd early: hld up in last: shkn up over 2f out: hanging and nt qckn: wknd fnl f* **15/8**[1]	59

1m 29.71s (2.81) **Going Correction** +0.30s/f (Good) 4 Ran SP% **106.7**
Speed ratings (Par 97): **95,94,94,86**
toteswinger: 1&2 £5.90. CSF £14.40 TOTE £3.20; EX 7.90.
Owner Raymond Tooth **Bred** John Doyle **Trained** East Everleigh, Wilts

FOCUS
Three of the seven runners originally declared were taken out, so this wasn't as competitive as it could have been, but there was still little between the front three at the line.

NOTEBOOK
Bunce(IRE), under a canny front-running ride from Richard Hughes, stayed on well enough to provide Richard Hannon with yet another juvenile scorer. Runner-up over 5f last time, and never previously tried beyond 6f, he saw the trip out well, having taken them along at a fair tempo, and should remain competitive in handicaps. (op 15-8)
Tipsy Girl looked ready for this trip when third over 6f at Chester last time and she stayed on well having come to hold every chance from 2f out, but not quite well enough to beat the winner. (op 4-1 tchd 11-2)
Point Du Jour(FR), proven in the ground and a certain stayer, moved up going well under George Baker, but it took him a while to get organised on the track once coming under pressure, and by the time he really found his stride close home the race was over. He's still a maiden, but should find a race at some stage. (op 7-2)
Diamond Charlie(IRE) was dropped out on this first try at 7f, but he refused to settle and never gave himself a chance of victory. Official explanation: jockey said colt ran too free (op 9-4 tchd 7-4)

5993 GOODWOOD.COM BONUS STKS (H'CAP) 1m
3:10 (3:10) (Class 4) (0-85,85) 3-Y-0+ £3,885 (£1,156; £577; £288) Stalls High

Form				RPR
0304	1		**Mujood**[18] 5416 7-10-0 **85**............(v) FergusSweeney 3 (Eve Johnson Houghton) *swtg: led 1f: chsd ldr: rdn fr 3f out: clsd fnl f: drvn ahd last 75yds: gamely* **16/1**	94
0066	2	nk	**Docofthebay (IRE)**[35] 4859 6-9-13 **84**............(p) DarryllHolland 4 (J A Glover) *dwlt: rcvrd to ld after 1f: 2 l clr over 2f out and had rest in trble: drvn over 1f out: tired fnl f: hdd last 75yds* **12/1**	92
6024	3	nk	**Finest Reserve (IRE)**[22] 5300 3-9-5 **81**............(v) TedDurcan 6 (M R Channon) *lw: s.s: tk little interest in last: rdn and hanging 3f out: consented to run on over 1f out: clsd on ldng pair 100yds out: nt qckn after* **9/2**[2]	89
2-1	4	2 3/4	**Call To Reason (IRE)**[16] 5493 3-9-7 **83**............ RichardHughes 1 (J Noseda) *lw: racd on outer: in tch: rdn wl over 2f out: wnt 3rd over 1f out but no imp: one pce after* **4/9**[1]	84
-500	5	1 1/4	**Flipping**[22] 5300 3-8-4 **66** oh3............ FrankieMcDonald 7 (W S Kittow) *chsd ldng pair: rdn 3f out: no imp over 1f out: fdd* **40/1**	64
5164	6	7	**Salient**[5] 5833 6-9-6 **77**............ NeilCallan 5 (M J Attwater) *in tch: rdn fr 1/2-way: no prog 2f out: wknd over 1f out* **8/1**[3]	59

1m 41.18s (1.28) **Going Correction** +0.30s/f (Good)
WFA 3 from 4yo+ 5lb 6 Ran SP% **114.6**
Speed ratings (Par 105): **105,104,104,101,100 93**
toteswingers: 1&2 £4.70, 1&3 £5.00, 2&3 £3.80. CSF £173.85 CT £1012.16 TOTE £11.20: £3.90, £5.60; EX 62.30.
Owner Eden Racing **Bred** Bloomsbury Stud & The Hon Sir David Sieff **Trained** Blewbury, Oxon
■ Mujood picked up the £14,400 ROA Speed Bonus for recording the card's fastest time relative to standard.
■ Stewards' Enquiry : Fergus Sweeney one-day ban: careless riding (Sep 26)

FOCUS
Probably not form to get carried away with, the red-hot favourite disappointing back in fourth and the front three being separated by a couple of necks.
Finest Reserve(IRE) Official explanation: jockey said colt hung right throughout

5994 TURFTV BONUS STKS (H'CAP) 1m 1f 192y
3:45 (3:47) (Class 4) (0-85,82) 3-Y-0+ £3,885 (£1,156; £577; £288) Stalls High

Form				RPR
32-0	1		**Harlestone Times (IRE)**[52] 4306 3-8-11 **72**............ TedDurcan 3 (J L Dunlop) *hld up in 7th: prog and nt clrest of runs fr 3f out: rdn over 2f out: wnt 3rd over 1f out: styd on strly fnl f to ld nr fin* **10/1**	84+
-530	2	1/2	**Fanditha (IRE)**[15] 5529 4-9-11 **79**............(p) J-PGuillambert 4 (L M Cumani) *led: drvn and kpt on wl fr 2f out: hdd nr fin* **4/1**[2]	90
1425	3	1/2	**Kindest**[36] 4841 4-9-12 **80**............ GeorgeBaker 8 (C F Wall) *lw: trckd ldrs: smooth prog to take 2nd 2f out: rdn and nt qckn over 1f out: hld after and lost 2nd last 100yds* **7/2**[1]	90+
0616	4	2 1/2	**Kavachi (IRE)**[15] 5540 7-10-0 **82**............ RichardHughes 7 (G L Moore) *hld up in 6th: rdn and no prog over 2f out: kpt on fnl f to take 4th nr fin: n.d* **8/1**	87
3515	5	1/2	**Jubail (IRE)**[32] 4956 3-8-11 **72**............ FergusSweeney 2 (A King) *lw: trckd ldng pair after 4f: chsd ldr 3f out gng wl: lost 2nd and rdn 2f out: wknd fnl f* **6/1**[3]	76
0332	6	1	**Veroon (IRE)**[17] 5436 4-9-6 **74**............(p) SebSanders 1 (J G Given) *hld up in last trio: prog on outer fr 3f out: rdn and nt qckn wl over 1f out: fdd ins fnl f* **7/1**	76
2153	7	shd	**Choral Festival**[15] 5536 4-8-9 **63** oh1............(v) NeilChalmers 6 (J J Bridger) *hld up in last trio: shkn up and no prog over 2f out: hanging over 1f out: modest late hdwy* **20/1**	65
-035	8	3 1/4	**Spensley (IRE)**[22] 5311 4-9-1 **69**............ AdamKirby 5 (J R Fanshawe) *swtg: nt that wl away but sn pushed up to chse ldr: lost 2nd and rdn 3f out: sn btn* **7/1**	64
-600	9	18	**Trailblazing**[16] 5499 3-9-0 **75**............ RoystonFfrench 10 (M Johnston) *trckd ldrs: pushed along over 4f out: sn lost pl: wknd 3f out: t.o* **25/1**	34
643-	10	6	**Beau Fighter**[230] 7020 5-9-3 **71**............ NeilCallan 9 (G L Moore) *bit bkwd: hld up in last trio: rdn and wknd 3f out: t.o* **16/1**	18

2m 9.69s (1.69) **Going Correction** +0.30s/f (Good)
WFA 3 from 4yo+ 7lb 10 Ran SP% **116.2**
Speed ratings (Par 105): **105,104,104,102,101 101,100,98,83,79**
toteswingers: 1&2 £9.30, 1&3 £7.60, 2&3 £4.60. CSF £49.66 CT £170.93 TOTE £13.00: £4.60, £1.40, £1.60; EX 57.30.
Owner J L Dunlop **Bred** J L Dunlop **Trained** Arundel, W Sussex

FOCUS
This was just an ordinary handicap.

The Form Book, Raceform Ltd, Compton, RG20 6NL

Spensley(IRE) Official explanation: jockey said the gelding was unsuited by the soft, good to soft in places ground

5995 GOODWOOD REVIVAL 17-19TH SEPTEMBER BONUS STKS (H'CAP) 6f

4:20 (4:20) (Class 4) (0-85,83) 3-Y-0+

£3,738 (£1,119; £559; £280; £139; £70) **Stalls** Low

Form RPR

0313 **1** **Tagula Night (IRE)**[15] 5528 4-9-2 **80**..........................(vt) JohnFahy(5) 13 93
(W R Swinburn) *trckd ldrs: plld out wd over 2f out: sn rdn and prog: led 1f out: forged clr* **7/2**[1]

031 **2** 2½ **Barons Spy (IRE)**[6] 5809 9-9-8 **81** 6ex.......................... JamesDoyle 14 86
(R J Price) *pressed ldng pair: led over 2f out: drvn and hdd 1f out: no ch w wnr* **8/1**

0642 **3** ¾ **Desert Icon (IRE)**[16] 5473 4-8-4 **70**..........................(v) HarryBentley(7) 8 73+
(W J Knight) *lw: dwlt: hld up in 7th and racd against rail: urged along over 2f out: nt clr run over 1f out and dropped to last: r.o fnl f to take 3rd nr fin* **9/2**[2]

200 **4** ¾ **Perfect Flight**[15] 5521 5-9-7 **80**..................................(b[1]) DaneO'Neill 11 80
(M Blanshard) *hld up in last trio: prog on outer 2f out: nvr rchd ldrs: disp 3rd ins fnl f: one pce* **10/1**

5002 **5** ¾ **Rocker**[12] 5628 6-9-2 **75**.. GeorgeBaker 9 73
(G L Moore) *stdd s: hld up last: prog over 2f out: rdn to go 3rd jst over 1f out: no imp: wknd last 100yds* **16/1**

62-0 **6** nk **Al Gillani (IRE)**[33] 4930 5-9-1 **74**.................................... PatCosgrave 10 71
(J R Boyle) *awkward s: trckd ldrs: shoved along over 2f out: effrt to dispute 3rd briefly ins fnl f: fdd* **14/1**

0065 **7** 2¼ **Macdillon**[91] 2997 4-9-8 **81**.. NeilCallan 2 71
(W S Kittow) *chsd ldrs and racd against rail: drvn and no prog 2f out: sn outpcd and n.d* **9/1**

1345 **8** 4 **Sutton Veny (IRE)**[29] 5087 4-9-10 **83**................................ AdamKirby 6 60
(J R Gask) *lw: w ldr: stl upsides 2f out: wknd over 1f out* **5/1**[3]

4465 **9** 2¾ **Victorian Bounty**[22] 5290 5-9-4 **77**.................................. MickyFenton 4 45
(Stef Higgins) *led and racd against rail: hdd over 2f out: hanging and wknd* **15/2**

0203 **10** 1¾ **Speak The Truth (IRE)**[13] 5614 4-7-12 **64**..........(v[1]) NathanAlison(7) 12 26
(J R Boyle) *s.i.s: sn prom: jnd ldrs on outer 1/2-way: upsides 2f out: wknd* **10/1**

1m 13.32s (1.12) **Going Correction** +0.30s/f (Good)
WFA 3 from 4yo+ 2lb **10** Ran SP% **120.7**
Speed ratings (Par 105): **104,100,99,98,97 97,94,88,85,82**
toteswingers: 1&2 £4.70, 1&3 £4.00, 2&3 £7.60. CSF £33.25 CT £133.78 TOTE £4.40: £2.10, £3.90, £1.60; EX 22.70.
Owner Hufford, Moss & Papworth **Bred** Carpet Lady Partnership **Trained** Aldbury, Herts

FOCUS

This sprint handicap had cut up a bit, but it was still competitive.

5996 RACING UK ON SKY 432 BONUS STKS (H'CAP) 2m

4:55 (4:56) (Class 4) (0-85,81) 3-Y-0+ **£3,885** (£1,156; £577; £288) **Stalls** High

Form RPR

-042 **1** **Regal Park (IRE)**[93] 2924 3-9-0 **80**.............................. RichardHughes 6 92+
(J Noseda) *hld up in midfield: taken to outer and prog to go 2nd 2f out: shkn up to ld 1f out: drvn after: jst hld on* **4/1**[1]

40-1 **2** shd **Hawridge Star (IRE)**[164] 1077 8-9-3 **70**.......................... GeorgeBaker 9 80+
(W S Kittow) *lw: hld up towards rr: lookintg for room fr 3f out: rdn and prog 2f out: wnt 2nd last 100yds: clsd on wnr: needed one more stride* **11/1**

3365 **3** 2½ **Boston Blue**[8] 5747 3-9-1 **81**...(v[1]) ShaneKelly 3 88
(W J Knight) *lw: mde most: kicked on over 4f out: drvn and kpt on 2f out: hdd and one pce 1f out* **5/1**[2]

2521 **4** 1¾ **Head Hunted**[27] 5164 3-8-1 **70**.. MartinLane(3) 2 75
(D M Simcock) *lw: hld up wl in rr: rdn on outer over 3f out: prog over 2f out: wnt 4th ins fnl f: no imp after* **5/1**[2]

2212 **5** 4 **Saute**[19] 5382 4-9-7 **74**...(p) AdamKirby 7 74
(W R Swinburn) *swtg: prom: chsd ldr 3f out to 2f out: wknd rapidly jst over 1f out* **16/1**

6362 **6** hd **Alnwick**[27] 5144 6-9-6 **73**... DaneO'Neill 8 73
(P D Cundell) *settled midfield: sltly impeded by wkng 6f out: dropped to rr and struggling 3f out: kpt on again over 1f out* **14/1**

5115 **7** hd **Yemeni Princess (IRE)**[30] 5035 4-9-5 **75**............ RussKennemore(3) 1 75
(B G Powell) *hld up in last pair: pushed along at bk of main gp 3f out: rdn 2f out: one pce and no prog after* **10/1**

10-3 **8** nk **Dulcie**[93] 2938 4-9-6 **78**.. AshleyMorgan(5) 14 77
(M H Tompkins) *lw: dwlt: hld up in midfield: effrt 3f out: no prog u.p 2f out: fdd over 1f out* **11/2**[3]

2621 **9** nse **Act Of Kalanisi (IRE)**[13] 5612 4-9-11 **78**.................... RoystonFfrench 5 77
(M Johnston) *trckd ldrs: rdn 3f out: no prog 2f out: fdd wl over 1f out* **9/1**

0120 **10** 4½ **Outrageous Request**[36] 4846 4-9-9 **81**........................ SimonPearce(5) 13 75
(Pat Eddery) *prom: rdn 3f out: wknd rapidly over 1f out* **25/1**

0115 **11** 11 **Saborido (USA)**[13] 5612 4-9-4 **71**.................................... NeilCallan 12 52
(Mrs A J Perrett) *chsd ldr 5f and 7f out to 3f out: wknd qckly* **25/1**

515- **12** 14 **Crossbow Creek**[335] 6734 12-9-10 **77**.............................. JamieMoore 11 41
(M G Rimell) *bit bkwd: s.s: a wl in rr: wknd 3f out: t.o* **50/1**

55/0 **13** 94 **Rock Soleil**[34] 4891 6-9-9 **76**.......................................(b[1]) IvaMilickova 10 —
(Jane Chapple-Hyam) *bit bkwd: t.k.h: hld up tl plld way through to chse ldr 11f out to 7f out: wknd rapidly and sn wl t.o* **50/1**

3m 31.41s (2.41) **Going Correction** +0.30s/f (Good)
WFA 3 from 4yo+ 13lb **13** Ran SP% **120.3**
Speed ratings (Par 105): **105,104,103,102,100 100,100,100,100,98 92,85,38**
toteswingers: 1&2 £11.50, 1&3 £4.00, 2&3 £14.10. CSF £47.88 CT £227.35 TOTE £3.90: £2.00, £3.50, £1.80; EX 69.20.
Owner Ms Frances Noseda **Bred** Lodge Park Stud **Trained** Newmarket, Suffolk

FOCUS

An interesting staying event. It was no surprise to see it go to one of the three-year-olds, although 'old boy' Hawridge Star did his best to deny the younger generation.

Hawridge Star(IRE) Official explanation: jockey said at the gelding was denied a clear run

5997 TURFTV FOR BETTING SHOPS BONUS STKS (H'CAP) 7f

5:30 (5:30) (Class 4) (0-85,91) 3-Y-0+ **£3,885** (£1,156; £577; £288) **Stalls** High

Form RPR

2113 **1** **Space Station**[52] 4296 4-9-11 **80**....................................(b) SebSanders 4 88+
(S Dow) *lw: hld up in 4th: prog on outer 2f out: rdn to ld narrowly ent fnl f: styd on wl nr fin* **3/1**[1]

1023 **2** ½ **L'Hirondelle (IRE)**[8] 5750 6-9-7 **76**.................................... NeilCallan 1 83
(M J Attwater) *lw: trckd ldr: rdn to ld over 1f out: hdd ent fnl f: battled on but hld last 75yds* **5/1**

3042 **3** hd **Thunderball**[9] 5737 4-9-13 **82**..................................(p) DarryllHolland 11 88+
(J A Glover) *b: lw: trckd ldng pair: looking for room on inner 2f out: got through jst over 1f out: hrd rdn and styd on: nrly snatched 2nd* **9/2**[3]

4000 **4** 2 **Cape Rock**[23] 5264 5-10-0 **83**.. ShaneKelly 5 84
(W J Knight) *hld up in 5th: rdn and nt qckn over 2f out: tried to cl on ldrs over 1f out: no imp fnl f* **3/1**[1]

0354 **5** 2¼ **Michael's Nook**[16] 5469 3-8-5 **64** oh10.................. FrankieMcDonald 10 57
(W S Kittow) *s.s: mostly last: rdn and no prog over 2f out: sn btn* **20/1**

2001 **6** 2¾ **Sailorman (IRE)**[4] 5861 3-10-4 **91** 6ex........................ RoystonFfrench 2 76
(M Johnston) *led at decent pce: drvn over 2f out: hdd over 1f out: wknd rapidly* **7/2**[2]

1m 29.15s (2.25) **Going Correction** +0.30s/f (Good)
WFA 3 from 4yo+ 4lb **6** Ran SP% **111.8**
Speed ratings (Par 105): **99,98,98,95,93 90**
toteswingers: 1&2 £2.30, 1&3 £4.10, 2&3 £3.80. totesuper7: WIN: Not won. PLACE: £893.20. CSF £17.99 CT £64.01 TOTE £4.80: £2.30, £2.90; EX 24.10 Place 6: £598.09, Place 5: £504.21..

Owner Mr & Mrs Chua, Moore & Jurd **Bred** Juddmonte Farms Ltd **Trained** Epsom, Surrey

FOCUS

A modest 7f handicap.

L'Hirondelle(IRE) Official explanation: jockey said that the gelding lost a front shoe

Michael's Nook Official explanation: jockey said that the gelding hung left

Sailorman(IRE) Official explanation: jockey said that the at the colt hit his head leaving the stalls

T/Jkpt: Not won. T/Plt: £421.60 to a £1 stake. Pool £83,492.43 - 144.54 winning tickets. T/Qpdt: £92.80 to a £1 stake. Pool £5,271.38 - 42.00 winning tickets. JN

5814 NEWCASTLE (L-H)

Sunday, September 12

OFFICIAL GOING: Soft (4.9)

Wind: Virtually Nil Weather: Bright and sunny

5998 DELIFRESH FILLIES' NURSERY 6f

2:25 (2:25) (Class 4) (0-85,78) 2-Y-0 **£4,037** (£1,208; £604; £302; £150) **Stalls** Low

Form RPR

0055 **1** **Black Annis Bower**[18] 5418 2-8-2 **62**........................ JamesSullivan(3) 8 67
(M W Easterby) *chsd ldrs: rdn to ld over 1f out: drvn and kpt on wl ins fnl f* **14/1**

4611 **2** ¾ **Maggie Mey (IRE)**[12] 5637 2-8-8 **65**............................ DuranFentiman 2 68
(D O'Meara) *w ldr: rdn over 2f out: drvn and kpt on wl ins fnl f* **13/2**

3402 **3** 1¾ **Tro Nesa (IRE)**[20] 5354 2-9-2 **73**................................ PaulMulrennan 6 71
(Mrs A Duffield) *hld up: rdn 3f out: hdwy on outer to chse ldrs 2f out: kpt on same pce ins fnl f* **6/1**[3]

4014 **4** shd **Ingleby Exceed (IRE)**[16] 5483 2-8-10 **67** ow1............... PhillipMakin 11 64
(T D Barron) *midfield: rdn over 2f out: kpt on ins fnl f* **20/1**

31 **5** 1¼ **Biaraafa (IRE)**[27] 5160 2-9-2 **73**...................................... HayleyTurner 7 67
(M L W Bell) *s.i.s and sn chsd along in rr: rcvrd to trck ldrs towards inner 3f out: drvn 2f out: sn one pce* **5/2**[1]

4533 **6** 3¾ **Lady Platinum Club**[25] 5196 2-8-13 **70**..........................(p) TomEaves 5 52
(G R Oldroyd) *hmpd s: hld up: rdn over 2f out: sn no imp* **9/1**

006 **7** 1¼ **The Oboist (IRE)**[29] 5092 2-8-4 **61**................................ JoeFanning 1 40
(M Johnston) *led narrowly: rdn whn hdd over 1f out: sn wknd* **3/1**[2]

060 **8** 1¾ **Auburn Lady**[15] 5509 2-8-6 **63** ow1.............................. AndrewElliott 3 36
(A D Brown) *in tch: rdn wl over 2f out: sn wknd* **66/1**

433 **9** 14 **Paper Dreams (IRE)**[82] 3281 2-8-7 **64**......................... PJMcDonald 10 —
(K A Ryan) *prom tl wknd over 2f out: eased ins fnl f* **10/1**

1m 20.47s (5.87) **Going Correction** +0.675s/f (Yiel) **9** Ran SP% **113.2**
Speed ratings (Par 94): **87,86,83,83,81 76,75,72,54**
toteswingers: 1&2 £10.00, 1&3 £13.70, 2&3 £4.30. CSF £99.68 CT £613.64 TOTE £16.30: £3.50, £1.50, £1.40; EX 59.10 TRIFECTA Not won..
Owner Mrs A Jarvis **Bred** Mrs A Jarvis **Trained** Sheriff Hutton, N Yorks

FOCUS

All races were on the straight, with no dolling and all distances as advertised. It was dry overnight at the course, but the ground was still officially soft. There was a very strong bias towards the stands' side rail at the previous meeting here last week, but on this more testing surface the runners in the opener raced on the far side. Thr runner-up sets the level.

NOTEBOOK

Black Annis Bower found this ground right up her street and opened her account at the fifth attempt. She caught the eye staying on late over 5f last time so not that surprisingly the stick here was much better for her and she has evidently begun life in nurseries on a good mark. Official explanation: trainer's rep said, regarding the apparent improvement in form shown, filly had been steadily improving and got a better start today (op 11-1)

Maggie Mey(IRE) was 3lb higher and posted a brave effort on this more demanding surface. She remains fairly treated and may not have finished winning yet when reverting to a slightly better ground. (op 9-2 tchd 4-1)

Tro Nesa(IRE) showed a liking for such ground when narrowly denied on her previous outing and wasn't disgraced on this return to 6f. She helps to set the level. (op 13-2 tchd 7-1 and 5-1)

Ingleby Exceed(IRE) proved very easy to back on this different surface and, with her rider putting up 1lb overweight, posted a fair effort in defeat. (tchd 18-1)

Biaraafa(IRE) ◆ looked fairly treated for this nursery debut and proved popular. She took an age to get going, but was travelling strongly 2f out having made up ground on the inside. She failed to see it out in the end, but is one to respect when returned to a sounder surface. (tchd 11-4 and 3-1 in places)

The Oboist(IRE) was given a positive ride on this switch to a nursery, but weakened tamely after the race got serious around 2f out. Better was evidently expected and perhaps the ground wasn't for her. (op 13-2 tchd 11-4)

5999 KRYSTOFER FRATER CLAIMING STKS 5f

3:00 (3:00) (Class 6) 3-Y-0+ **£1,942** (£578; £288; £144) **Stalls** Low

Form RPR

2200 **1** **Northern Bolt**[13] 5601 5-8-13 73...........................(b) PatrickMathers 8 79
(I W McInnes) *prom: rdn over 2f out: drvn to ld fnl 100yds: kpt on* **8/1**

0210 **2** 1½ **Captain Royale (IRE)**[13] 5599 5-8-9 60....................(p) AndrewMullen 6 70
(Miss Tracy Waggott) *led: rdn over 2f out: hdd and no ex fnl 100yds* **9/1**

2430 **3** ½ **Bonnie Prince Blue**[13] 5601 7-8-9 74........................(b) DaleSwift(5) 4 73
(B Ellison) *sn outpcd in rr: hdwy u.p 2f out: swtchd rt 1f out: kpt on ins fnl f: nrst fin* **9/2**[3]

4606 **4** 1¼ **Le Toreador**[9] 5734 5-9-1 81..................................(tp) JulieBurke(7) 1 76
(K A Ryan) *trckd ldrs: rdn over 1f out: kpt on tl no ex ins fnl f* **4/1**[2]

5140 **5** 1¾ **Drumpellier (IRE)**[13] 5599 3-8-0 59............................ PaulPickard(3) 2 52
(S G West) *trckd ldrs: racd keenly: rdn 2f out: edgd rt over 1f out: wknd ins fnl f* **33/1**

0002 **6** 1¼ **Atlantic Beach**[9] 5735 5-9-0 73...................................... DuranFentiman 7 58
(D O'Meara) *prom: rdn over 2f out: wknd appr fnl f* **9/2**[3]

4525 7 8 **Rowayton**[10] 5684 4-8-10 75 ow1 PhillipMakin 5 25
(J D Bethell) *s.i.s: hld up: brief hdwy 2f out: sn no imp: eased ins fnl f* 11/4[1]

-060 8 1 1/4 **Monalini (IRE)**[59] 4063 3-8-7 57 PaulQuinn 3 18
(D Nicholls) *hld up: rdn over 2f out: sn no imp* 40/1

000 9 18 **The Nifty Belle**[29] 5097 4-8-3 18 ow3 (p) DeanHeslop(5) 11 —
(N Wilson) *chsd ldrs tl lost pl qckly 3f out: sn bhd* 150/1

64.19 secs (3.09) **Going Correction** +0.675s/f (Yiel)
WFA 3 from 4yo+ 1lb 9 Ran SP% **110.2**
Speed ratings (Par 101): **102,99,98,96,94 92,79,77,48**
toteswingers: 1&2 £11.60, 1&3 £7.90, 2&3 £2.10. CSF £70.86 TOTE £12.10: £1.80, £3.50, £2.50; EX 85.70 TRIFECTA Not won..
Owner Keith Brown Properties (hull) Ltd **Bred** Mrs C Regalado-Gonzalez **Trained** Catwick, E Yorks

FOCUS
Not a bad claimer. There was a solid pace on considering the ground, and again they raced on the far side.
Rowayton Official explanation: jockey said filly hung right handed when under pressure

6000 EMILY GRADY MEMORIAL H'CAP 6f
3:35 (3:35) (Class 3) (0-95,92) 3-Y-O

£6,386 (£1,912; £956; £478; £238; £119) **Stalls** Low

Form RPR

6025 1 **Flaneur**[13] 5606 3-8-7 78 (b) DavidAllan 8 84
(T D Easterby) *prom on outer: hdwy to ld 2f out: drvn and kpt on ins fnl f: jst hld on* 9/2[2]

2045 2 nk **Coolminx (IRE)**[29] 5088 3-8-10 86 LeeTopliss(5) 2 96+
(R A Fahey) *trckd ldrs towards inner: short of room fr over 2f out: shuffled towards rr over 1f out: hdwy 1f out: swtchd ins fnl f: r.o strly: unlucky* 9/2[2]

0531 3 3/4 **Basle**[19] 5388 3-8-2 78 oh5 AdamBeschizza(5) 3 81
(Miss Gay Kelleway) *trckd ldrs: hdwy to chse ldr over 1f out: kpt on ins fnl f: lost 2nd nr fin* 11/2[3]

2000 4 2 3/4 **Midnight Martini**[29] 5095 3-9-6 91 (t) DuranFentiman 5 85
(T D Easterby) *hld up: hdwy to chse ldrs over 1f out: kpt on tl no ex ins fnl f* 20/1

2-60 5 4 **Paradise Spectre**[15] 5524 3-8-7 78 AndrewElliott 9 59
(Mrs K Burke) *hld up: rdn over 2f out: sn no imp* 7/1

5101 6 4 1/2 **Hairspray**[26] 5182 3-9-1 86 SamHitchcott 11 53
(M R Channon) *in tch: hdwy to chse ldrs over 1f out: sn drvn: wknd ins fnl f* 10/1

5-54 7 6 **Amitola (IRE)**[29] 5088 3-9-0 85 PhillipMakin 7 32
(T D Barron) *w ldrs: drvn over 2f out: wknd over 1f out* 5/2[1]

1010 8 shd **Beat Baby (IRE)**[24] 5250 3-9-2 87 PaulMulrennan 6 34
(J Howard Johnson) *led narrowly: hdd 2f out: sn wknd* 20/1

1m 19.2s (4.60) **Going Correction** +0.675s/f (Yiel) 8 Ran SP% **111.4**
Speed ratings (Par 105): **96,95,94,90,85 79,71,71**
toteswingers: 1&2 £4.30, 1&3 £4.10, 2&3 £4.40. CSF £23.68 CT £110.13 TOTE £4.30: £1.40, £1.10, £1.90; EX 23.10 Trifecta £68.80 Pool: £316.37 - 3.40 winning units..
Owner Jeremy Gompertz **Bred** C R Mason **Trained** Great Habton, N Yorks
■ Stewards' Enquiry : Lee Topliss caution: careless riding

FOCUS
This was a good-quality sprint handicap, but the taxing ground definitely played its part. The first three dominated.

NOTEBOOK
Flaneur, with the blinkers back on, just did enough to hold off the fast-finishing Coolminx and resume winning ways. He moved nicely before quickening clear and showed guts under pressure near the business end. He is now 2-3 over C&D and obviously appreciates some cut underfoot, but his profile suggests he will struggle to follow up. (op 5-1)
Coolminx(IRE) ◆ also travelled sweetly, but she was on the inside and didn't get the breaks when the winner went for home. She finished with gusto when switched out, but the line came that bit too soon. She certainly deserves to go one better again. (op 7-2)
Basle, well backed, won a claimer on her previous outing and her rider's claim negated her being 5lb out of the handicap here. She posted an improved effort in defeat, finishing clear of the remainder, and was not beaten far. He looks well up to winning a handicap off this sort of mark while in his current mood, but the handicapper will raise him for this. (op 7-1 tchd 5-1)
Midnight Martini got a positive ride and never seriously threatened, but still turned in a fair performance under top weight. (op 10-1)
Amitola(IRE) disappointed. Looking at the way she came under pressure a long way out something may have gone amiss with her. Official explanation: jockey said the filly was unsuited by the soft ground (op 3-1 tchd 10-3)

6001 FORD CENTENARY CLASSIC MAIDEN AUCTION STKS 1m 3y(S)
4:10 (4:10) (Class 5) 2-Y-O **£2,590** (£770; £385; £192) **Stalls** Low

Form RPR

60 1 **The Nought Man (FR)**[34] 4896 2-8-4 0 LeeTopliss(5) 12 75
(R A Fahey) *pressed ldr: chal fr over 2f out: rdn to ld jst ins fnl f: kpt on to go clr fnl 100yds* 15/8[1]

0524 2 5 **Regimental (IRE)**[13] 5597 2-8-7 61 SamHitchcott 3 62
(Mrs A Duffield) *led: clr w wnr over 2f out: drvn whn hdd jst ins fnl f: sn no ex: all out to hold 2nd* 15/8[1]

0 3 nk **Blake Dean**[8] 5762 2-8-11 0 PhillipMakin 5 65+
(B M R Haslam) *hld up: hdwy to go 3rd over 2f out: styd on wl ins fnl f: only jst failed to get 2nd* 50/1

0 4 6 **Subramaniam**[18] 5404 2-9-0 0 PaulMulrennan 6 55
(J G Given) *midfield: rdn and outpcd over 3f out: kpt on ins fnl 2f: nvr nr ldrs* 50/1

5 4 1/2 **See The Smile (USA)** 2-8-9 0 HayleyTurner 7 40
(M L W Bell) *hld up: rdn and outpcd over 3f out: kpt on one pce fnl 2f: nvr nr ldrs* 9/2[2]

005 6 2 **Willow's Wish**[49] 4402 2-8-2 45 DuranFentiman 2 29
(G M Moore) *hld up: outpcd over 3f out: kpt on fnl 2f: n.d* 66/1

00 7 1/2 **Good Faith**[88] 3087 2-8-7 0 PJMcDonald 11 33
(G M Moore) *trckd ldrs: wknd over 2f out* 66/1

6 8 2 **Rainbows Reach**[19] 5385 2-7-13 0 DeclanCannon(5) 4 25
(Miss Gay Kelleway) *trckd ldrs: wknd over 2f out* 14/1

9 6 **Fearless Poet (IRE)** 2-8-11 0 TomEaves 8 19
(B Smart) *trckd ldrs: rdn over 2f out: wknd over 1f out* 8/1[3]

10 9 **Vodka Red (IRE)** 2-8-7 0 PatrickMathers 9 —
(R Johnson) *dwlt and wnt rt s: sn rdn in rr: hdwy into midfield bef 1/2-way: wknd over 2f out* 50/1

1m 50.43s (7.03) **Going Correction** +0.675s/f (Yiel) 10 Ran SP% **114.4**
Speed ratings (Par 95): **91,86,85,79,75 73,72,70,64,55**
toteswingers: 1&2 £1.70, 1&3 £8.30, 2&3 £12.60. CSF £4.97 TOTE £2.70: £1.40, £1.02, £8.60; EX 6.50 Trifecta £213.30 Part won. Pool: £288.35 - 0.74 winning units..
Owner Mrs Jane Dwyer **Bred** Elevage Haras De Bourgeauville **Trained** Musley Bank, N Yorks
■ Stewards' Enquiry : Declan Cannon two-day ban: careless riding (Sep 26-27)

FOCUS
A weak maiden which would have presented a decent stamina test for these juveniles, and most were in trouble before the two-furlong marker.

NOTEBOOK
The Nought Man(FR) came good at the third time of asking with a ready effort. The winner had shown little in two previous outings and the fact he was backed almost to the exclusion of the others really sums up the strength of this event. Stepping up in trip was always likely to help according to his breeding, though, and he is clearly a middle-distance performer in the making. He should win his share of handicaps as a 3-y-o. (op 7-2 tchd 13-8)
Regimental(IRE) was always on the front-end and was the only one to give the winner a real race, but was ultimately outstayed by that rival. He deserves a change of fortune, but is clearly vulnerable in maiden company. (tchd 7-4, 9-4 and 5-2 in a place)
Blake Dean, moving up a furlong, stayed on dourly from off the pace to finish a clear third and this represents a step forward from his debut form eight days earlier. He needs one more run for a mark. (op 40-1)
Subramaniam showed more on this switch to soft ground and is another that will be eligible for nurseries after his next outing.
See The Smile(USA) proved easy to back for this racecourse debut and the experience looked needed. He showed an action that suggests cut underfoot suits and, while he looks only modest, is entitled to improve for the run. (op 4-1 tchd 7-2)

6002 NEWCASTLE INTERNATIONAL 75TH ANNIVERSARY H'CAP 7f
4:45 (4:45) (Class 3) (0-95,92) 3-Y-O

£6,386 (£1,912; £956; £478; £238; £119) **Stalls** Low

Form RPR

5564 1 **Little Scotland**[19] 5396 3-8-6 80 (p) BarryMcHugh(3) 6 93
(R A Fahey) *in tch: hdwy to chse ldr 3f out: led 2f out: rdn over 1f out: kpt on to go clr fnl f* 11/2[3]

5620 2 6 **Mistic Magic (IRE)**[15] 5521 3-9-7 92 HayleyTurner 1 89
(P F I Cole) *trckd ldrs on inner: rdn over 2f out: sn one pce: tk 2nd fnl 75yds: no ch w wnr* 33/1

411 3 1 3/4 **Kalk Bay (IRE)**[29] 5086 3-8-12 83 LiamJones 8 75
(W J Haggas) *s.i.s: hld up: hdwy 3f out: rdn to chse ldr wl over 1f out: sn no imp: wknd and lost 2nd fnl 75yds* 11/10[1]

1630 4 4 1/2 **Tres Coronas (IRE)**[8] 5759 3-8-10 81 ow1 (b) PhillipMakin 2 61
(T D Barron) *led: hdd 2f out: sn wknd* 6/1

-200 5 7 **Unshakable Will (IRE)**[71] 3696 3-8-10 81 TomEaves 4 42
(B Smart) *prom: lost pl over 3f out: sn wknd* 16/1

1-36 6 7 **Bowmaker**[149] 1352 3-9-1 86 AndrewElliott 5 28
(M Johnston) *hld up: rdn and lost pl wl over 3f out: sn bhd* 9/2[2]

0030 7 9 **Al Farahidi (USA)**[9] 5731 3-9-4 89 (b) JoeFanning 7 7
(M Johnston) *trckd ldrs: wknd qckly 3f out* 12/1

1m 33.61s (4.91) **Going Correction** +0.675s/f (Yiel) 7 Ran SP% **112.0**
Speed ratings (Par 105): **98,91,89,84,76 68,57**
toteswingers: 1&2 £11.40, 1&3 £2.50, 2&3 £4.30. CSF £133.85 CT £334.46 TOTE £5.10: £2.20, £10.70; EX 102.70 Trifecta £99.80 Pool: £311.77 - 2.31 winning units..
Owner David W Armstrong **Bred** Sir Eric Parker **Trained** Musley Bank, N Yorks
■ Stewards' Enquiry : Phillip Makin three-day ban: struck horse with whip whilst in the stalls (Sep 26-28)

FOCUS
A fair 3-y-o handicap, run at a sound pace and again underfoot conditions played a part.

NOTEBOOK
Little Scotland relished the taxing surface and came home a taking winner. He travelled beautifully into contention and knuckled down when asked for an effort 2f out. This surface may flatter his winning margin a little, but the first-time cheekpieces worked the oracle and he obviously stays well now. His connections will probably look for something under a penalty as he will be high on confidence. (op 7-1)
Mistic Magic(IRE) held every chance and, although no match for the winner from the furlong marker, this was much better again back up in trip with the blinkers left off. (op 25-1)
Kalk Bay(IRE) was bidding for a third win from four career starts having been raised 9lb for his latest success. He was very well backed earlier in the day, but proved a drifter on course and ultimately this ground proved too much for him. He isn't one to abandon on the back of this. (op 5-6 tchd 4-5)
Tres Coronas(IRE), whose rider carried 1lb overweight, got a positive ride but was treading water from the two-furlong marker. (op 17-2 tchd 11-2)
Bowmaker attracted support, but he was the first beaten and surely the ground did for him. (op 13-2 tchd 7-1 and 4-1)

6003 HILTON NEWCASTLE GATESHEAD FILLIES' H'CAP 1m 3y(S)
5:20 (5:20) (Class 4) (0-85,80) 3-Y-O+ **£4,274** (£1,271; £635; £317) **Stalls** Low

Form RPR

4222 1 **Marjury Daw (IRE)**[18] 5408 4-9-10 80 PaulMulrennan 4 90
(J G Given) *led: rdn over 1f out: drvn and hld on wl ins fnl f* 6/1

1031 2 1 1/4 **Shesells Seashells**[19] 5391 3-8-13 74 HayleyTurner 7 80+
(M L W Bell) *swtchd lft to ins at s: midfield: smooth hdwy to trck ldr over 2f out: drvn over 1f out: kpt on ins fnl f* 5/2[1]

3400 3 1 1/2 **She's In The Money**[15] 5510 4-9-5 80 LeeTopliss(5) 5 84+
(R A Fahey) *s.i.s: hld up: swtchd lft to inner 3f out: gd hdwy to chse ldr over 1f out: kpt on tl no ex fnl 75yds* 11/2

0510 4 9 **Dolly Royal (IRE)**[13] 5598 5-8-7 66 oh5 KellyHarrison(3) 2 49
(R Johnson) *hld up: rdn over 3f out: kpt on ins fnl f: nvr threatened ldrs* 66/1

2410 5 1 3/4 **Amethyst Dawn (IRE)**[15] 5510 4-9-7 77 DavidAllan 3 56
(T D Easterby) *in tch: rdn to chse ldr over 2f out: wknd over 1f out* 9/2[2]

0-15 6 13 **Bear Tobouggie**[139] 1571 3-8-11 72 PJMcDonald 9 20
(G A Swinbank) *in tch: rdn over 4f out: sn lost pl and bhd* 8/1

0361 7 2 1/2 **Cherry Bee**[8] 5758 3-8-10 71 JoeFanning 1 13
(M Johnston) *trckd ldr: rdn over 3f out: wknd over 2f out* 5/1[3]

1311 8 23 **Whispering Spirit (IRE)**[34] 4910 4-9-3 73 (v) PhillipMakin 6 —
(Mrs A Duffield) *prom: rdn and lost pl over 3f out: sn bhd: eased fnl f* 12/1

1m 48.29s (4.89) **Going Correction** +0.675s/f (Yiel)
WFA 3 from 4yo+ 5lb 8 Ran SP% **113.4**
Speed ratings (Par 102): **102,100,99,90,88 75,73,50**
toteswingers: 1&2 £3.10, 1&3 £4.30, 2&3 £3.90. CSF £21.03 CT £86.56 TOTE £5.80: £1.50, £1.40, £2.30; EX 15.80 Trifecta £140.10 Pool: £518.84 - 2.74 winning units. Place 6: £337.15, Place 5: £101.59..
Owner Danethorpe Racing Partnership **Bred** Mulhime Ltd Marston Stud & D Bonnycastle **Trained** Willoughton, Lincs

FOCUS
An ordinary fillies' handicap in which the first three came clear.
T/Plt: £381.50 to a £1 stake. Pool £71,827.99 - 137.41 winning tickets. T/Qpdt: £31.70 to a £1 stake. Pool £5,819.82 - 135.50 winning tickets. AS

5973CURRAGH (R-H)

Sunday, September 12

OFFICIAL GOING: Soft

6005a FLAME OF TARA EUROPEAN BREEDERS FUND STKS (LISTED RACE) (FILLIES) 1m

2:45 (2:45) 2-Y-O **£36,814** (£10,761; £5,097; £1,699)

RPR

1 **Chrysanthemum (IRE)** 2-8-12 .... FMBerry 9 95+
(David Wachman, Ire) *hld up towards rr: prog on far rail 1/2-way: 5th 2f out: sn rdn: led 1f out: r.o wl: comf* **25/1**

2 2 1/2 **Cambina (IRE)**[26] 5190 2-8-12 78.......... WMLordan 7 89
(T Stack, Ire) *hld up towards rr: 7th u.p 2f out: styd on fr over 1f out to go mod 2nd nr fin* **14/1**

3 shd **Aris (IRE)**[14] 5566 2-8-12 .... CDHayes 3 89+
(P J Prendergast, Ire) *hld up: 6th and sme prog 2f out: 4th 1f out: kpt on* **50/1**

4 1/2 **Peahen**[28] 5125 2-8-12 .... KLatham 1 88
(G M Lyons, Ire) *trckd ldrs: prog on outer 1/2-way: 4th over 2f out: rdn to ld 1 1/2f out: hdd 1f out: kpt on same pce* **10/1**

5 shd **Banimpire (IRE)**[22] 5315 2-8-12 .... KJManning 2 88
(J S Bolger, Ire) *prom: 3rd 1/2-way: led 2f out: hdd 1 1/2f out: kpt on same pce u.p fnl f* **4/1**[2]

6 1 1/4 **Gemstone (IRE)**[35] 4879 2-8-12 83.......... CO'Donoghue 10 85
(A P O'Brien, Ire) *hld up: last 1/2-way: rdn over 2f out: kpt on ins fnl f* **20/1**

7 2 1/2 **Luxurious (IRE)**[16] 5505 2-8-12 92.......... JAHeffernan 4 80
(A P O'Brien, Ire) *chsd ldrs in 4th: lost pl 3f out: kpt on same pce fr 1 1/2f out* **8/1**[3]

8 nk **Juliet Capulet (IRE)**[8] 5771 2-8-12 88..........(b) JPO'Brien 6 79
(A P O'Brien, Ire) *led: rdn and hdd 2f out: steadily wknd* **10/1**

9 8 **Praise Be (IRE)**[25] 5223 2-8-12 86.......... DMGrant 8 61
(John Joseph Murphy, Ire) *trckd ldrs in 3rd: 2nd and chal 2 1/2f out: wknd fr 2f out: eased fnl f* **18/1**

10 11 **Spin (IRE)**[35] 4876 2-8-12 .... JMurtagh 5 37
(A P O'Brien, Ire) *trckd ldr in 2nd: rdn and wknd qckly 3f out: eased fr 2f out* **4/5**[1]

1m 42.12s (-3.88) **Going Correction** -0.25s/f (Firm) **10** Ran SP% **127.3**
Speed ratings: **109,106,106,105,105 104,102,101,93,82**
CSF £354.95 TOTE £19.90: £3.00, £3.20, £8.20; DF 329.70.
Owner Michael Tabor **Bred** Pegasus Breeding Ltd **Trained** Goolds Cross, Co Tipperary

FOCUS
Eight of the ten runners for this Listed event were previous winners but they were upstaged by a newcomer.

NOTEBOOK
Chrysanthemum(IRE) ◆, a newcomer, came from well off the pace to hit the front 1f out before being ridden clear for a decisive victory. It was a taking debut performance and a step up to Group race level before the end of the season is likely.
Cambina(IRE), winner of an ordinary maiden and a five- runner nursery, both over 1m at Killarney, and with a rating of 78, was out the back with the winner in the early stages.Having her first run on slow ground, she began to stay on 2f out and kept on quite well to just shade the verdict for second place.
Aris(IRE) ◆, closely related to dual Group 1 winner Again and out of an unraced half-sister to Montjeu, gained valuable black type having finished in mid-division over 6f here on her only previous start last month. Held up, she closed from 2f out and stayed on over the final furlong, just losing out on second spot.She should be winning before the season ends.
Peahen, successful over the trip at Dundalk last month, tracked the leaders and took closer order after half-way.She got to the front one and a half furlongs out but after being headed 1f out she could find no extra under pressure. (op 8/1)
Banimpire(IRE), a course-and-distance winner on quick ground last month on her second start, raced close up and was vying for the lead under 2f out.She kept on under pressure. (op 7/2)
Juliet Capulet(IRE) had come good at her seventh attempt when making all over the trip on good to firm at Leopardstown eight days previously.She again made the running but was done with once headed 2f out. (op 8/1)
Spin(IRE), a four and a half length winner over 1m here last month, tracked the leader but was being pushed along after half-way and weakened quickly soon afterwards.She was slightly hampered as she began to drop out and was eased and virtually pulled up when all hope had gone. Official explanation: jockey said filly weakened quickly when running short of room at halfway (op 11/10)

6006a O'BRIEN'S WINES SUPPORTING JACK & JILL SOLONAWAY STKS (GROUP 3) 1m

3:15 (3:15) 3-Y-O+ **£34,513** (£10,088; £4,778; £1,592)

RPR

1 **Steinbeck (IRE)**[26] 5192 3-9-1 114.......... JMurtagh 8 109+
(A P O'Brien, Ire) *hld up in 5th: hdwy over 2f out: led 1 1/2f out: kpt on wl u.p fnl f* **11/8**[1]

2 3/4 **Wade Giles (IRE)**[26] 5192 3-9-1 106.......... KLatham 7 107
(G M Lyons, Ire) *hld up in rr: prog on outer early st: 4th under 1 1/2f out: 3rd 1f out: styd on wl* **4/1**[2]

3 1/2 **Across The Rhine (USA)**[113] 2351 4-9-6 105.......... MCHussey 1 107
(Tracey Collins, Ire) *hld up in 6th: 5th and rdn early st: impr into 2nd over 1f out: kpt on u.p* **14/1**

4 5 1/2 **Arazan (IRE)**[728] 5946 4-9-6 110.......... FMBerry 9 94
(John M Oxx, Ire) *settled 3rd: mod 2nd early st: rdn over 2f out: 4th and no ex fr over 1f out* **11/2**[3]

5 3/4 **Pollen (IRE)**[113] 2355 5-9-6 100.......... WJLee 4 93
(T Stack, Ire) *trckd ldrs: 4th 1/2-way: effrt early st: 5th and no imp fr 1 1/2f out* **10/1**

6 4 1/2 **Jumbajukiba**[154] 1246 7-9-6 109..........(b) KJManning 5 82
(Mrs John Harrington, Ire) *led: clr 1/2-way: rdn st: hdd 1 1/2f out: wknd fr over 1f out* **7/1**

7 3/4 **Maybe Grace (IRE)**[32] 4977 4-9-3 96..........(p) CDHayes 10 78
(Mrs John Harrington, Ire) *hld up towards rr: rdn and no imp st: eased fnl f* **16/1**

8 1 1/2 **Zafisio (IRE)**[302] 7406 4-9-6 .... GrahamGibbons 2 77
(F J Brennan) *prom: mod 2nd 1/2-way: wknd early st: eased fnl f* **7/1**

1m 40.83s (-5.17) **Going Correction** -0.25s/f (Firm)
WFA 3 from 4yo+ 5lb **8** Ran SP% **124.1**
Speed ratings: **115,114,113,108,107 103,102,100**
CSF £7.85 TOTE £2.10: £1.02, £1.50, £5.10; DF 7.70.
Owner Michael Tabor **Bred** Dr D Harron **Trained** Ballydoyle, Co Tipperary

FOCUS
The form is rated around the third and the time.

NOTEBOOK
Steinbeck(IRE) produced further evidence that he might yet live to the reputation connections created for him and make the grade at a higher level. He was following up on a Listed win over 1m at Killarney last month and had very different ground conditions to contend with here. Held up, he was ridden to close from 2f out and went to the front under pressure over 1f out. He never flinched and kept on well. The Queen Elizabeth II Stakes will be considered, although trainer Aidan O'Brien also has Rip Van Winkle and Beethoven as possibles for that Ascot event. O'Brien said: "A better race, with a better pace, on better ground will suit him a lot better. We've learned that he likes to be dropped in and, in fairness to him, after being quite fresh early in the race, he found plenty for pressure." (op 2/1 tchd 5/4)
Wade Giles(IRE), the winner of his first two starts before finishing almost three lengths behind Steinbeck at Killarney, got closer to the winner on this occasion. Held up in rear, he began to make headway on the outside 2f out and went third early in the final furlong, running on well without quite getting to the winner. He is progressive and trainer Ger Lyons is adamant that the best of him won't be seen until next season. (op 9/2)
Across The Rhine(USA), rated 105 and a three-time handicap winner running in his first Group race, acquitted himself well. Sixth into the straight, he soon moved into contention and was second with every chance entering the final furlong. He could raise no extra at a vital stage but kept on.
Arazan(IRE), a Group 2 winner at two but off the track since September 2008 due to serious chest infections, was far from disgraced considering his long absence. Soon third, he was second into the straight and could make no impression from 2f out having been ridden along soon after turning for home. "He ran like a horse who had been a long time off but, to be honest, I was afraid he would run less well than he did. We'll see how he comes out of the race and if he progresses before deciding if he will run again," trainer John Oxx said. (op 5/1)
Pollen(IRE), all of whose three wins, including last year's Irish Lincolnshire and the Group 3 Park Express Stakes early this season, have been at this track, relishes testing ground. Off the track since April, she made a satisfactory return. Fourth into the straight and ridden over 2f out, she could make no impression one and a half furlongs out before plugging on.
Jumbajukiba, winner of this race in 2007 and 2008 and a proven Curragh and soft-ground performer, was having his first run since April. He set off in front, as usual, and was four lengths clear into the straight before weakening and being headed well over 1f out.

6007a WWW.THETOTE.COM BLANDFORD STKS (GROUP 2) (F&M) 1m 2f

3:45 (3:46) 3-Y-O+ **£57,522** (£16,814; £7,964; £2,654)

RPR

1 **Eleanora Duse (IRE)**[24] 5248 3-8-12 .... RyanMoore 6 106
(Sir Michael Stoute) *trckd ldrs in 5th: swtchd lft and hdwy 2f out: 2nd and chal ent fnl f: sn led: kpt on u.p cl home: all out* **3/1**[1]

2 shd **She's Our Mark**[42] 4631 6-9-5 106.......... DMGrant 10 106+
(Patrick J Flynn, Ire) *trckd ldrs in 6th: dropped to 8th appr st: rdn over 2f out: 6th and hdwy under 1f out: r.o strly cl home: jst failed* **6/1**

3 hd **Choose Me (IRE)**[35] 4877 4-9-5 102.......... DPMcDonogh 5 106
(Kevin Prendergast, Ire) *s.i.s and hld up towards rr: 9th st: rdn under 2f out: r.o wl ins fnl f* **20/1**

4 3/4 **Lush Lashes**[14] 5568 5-9-5 108.......... KJManning 4 104
(J S Bolger, Ire) *trckd ldrs in 3rd: impr to ld 2f out: hdd wl ins fnl f: no ex cl home* **10/1**

5 1 1/4 **Aviate**[100] 2711 3-8-12 .... EddieAhern 2 102
(H R A Cecil) *trckd ldrs: 6th into st: sltly checked 2f out: sn rdn and no imp: kpt on again last 100yds* **10/3**[2]

6 1/2 **Precious Gem (IRE)**[35] 4877 4-9-5 103..........(b) PJSmullen 8 101
(D K Weld, Ire) *trckd ldrs: 6th on inner 1/2-way: 4th st: 3rd under 2f out: sn no ex and one pce* **16/1**

7 hd **Obama Rule (IRE)**[14] 5568 3-8-12 102.......... WMLordan 1 100
(Ms Joanna Morgan, Ire) *hld up in rr: sme prog under 2f out: no imp ins fnl f* **5/1**[3]

8 1 1/2 **Alsace Lorraine (IRE)**[32] 4957 5-9-5 .... JAHeffernan 9 97
(J R Fanshawe) *led and disp: hdd 2f out: sn no ex* **8/1**

9 4 1/2 **Devoted To You (IRE)**[133] 1726 3-8-12 104.......... JMurtagh 7 88
(A P O'Brien, Ire) *sn disp ld: hdd 2f out: no ex whn eased early fnl f* **10/1**

10 hd **Duchess Of Foxland (IRE)**[32] 4977 3-8-12 101.......... EJMcNamara 3 88
(Mark L Fagan, Ire) *hld up in tch: 7th on outer ent st: wknd fr 2f out* **20/1**

2m 10.6s (-2.00) **Going Correction** +0.10s/f (Good)
WFA 3 from 4yo+ 7lb **10** Ran SP% **123.7**
Speed ratings: **112,111,111,111,110 109,109,108,104,104**
CSF £22.99 TOTE £3.40: £1.80, £2.00, £4.70; DF 30.80.
Owner Ballymacoll Stud **Bred** Ballymacoll Stud Farm Ltd **Trained** Newmarket, Suffolk

FOCUS
The form is rated around the runner-up, sixth and seventh.

NOTEBOOK
Eleanora Duse(IRE), the Yorkshire Oaks third, was dropping back to the distance over which she achieved a Listed race win at Newbury in June.She was also encountering slow ground for the first time and after hitting the front early in the final furlong, she was all out to hold on by inches in a three-way photo finish. In a race run a quite an ordinary pace, the winner was switched right 2f out to begin her challenge and she battled on well under pressure. Ryan Moore reported that the lack of pace and the tacky ground did not suit the filly and he also told connections that she was "more a 1m4f filly". (op 3/1 tchd 10/3)
She's Our Mark is an eight-time winner with two Group 3 victories to her credit. She lost her place when the pace increased starting the final bend but she came back well from over 1f out and stayed on strongly, just failing to get up.
Choose Me(IRE), whose four wins include one at Listed level, had been far from disgraced when fourth behind Fame And Glory in the Royal Whip Stakes over the course and trip on her previous start. Another who appreciates ease, she was last away and was held up in rear. She had only one rival behind her into the straight and made good headway from one and a half furlongs out, running on well in the closing stages.
Lush Lashes ◆, without the tongue-tie she wore when fourth in a 1m1f Group 3 event on her return from a 14-month absence here last month, went to the front 2f out. Headed just under 1f out, she kept on without really quickening. A triple Group 1 winner two seasons back, she may not be the force she was, but allowing for the unsuitable ground conditions, she is worth another chance. (op 8/1)
Aviate, having her first run since the Investec Oaks for which she started favourite and finished seventh, had been unbeaten in three starts before Epsom and had won the Musidora Stakes over this trip in May. She was sixth into the straight and while she appeared to be slightly hampered 2f out, it appeared to make little difference.Unable to make any impression over 1f out, she kept on towards the finish. Official explanation: jockey said filly dropped back after slight interference (op 10/3 tchd 3/1)
Devoted To You(IRE) Official explanation: jockey said filly hung in straight

6009a MICHAEL KINANE RENAISSANCE STKS (GROUP 3) 6f

4:50 (4:50) 3-Y-O+ **£34,513** (£10,088; £4,778; £1,592)

RPR

1 **Bewitched (IRE)**[35] 4882 3-8-12 105..........(t) JMurtagh 1 106+
(Charles O'Brien, Ire) *hld up towards rr: hdwy under 2f out: 5th 1f out: r.o strly to ld cl home* **3/1**[1]

2 nk **Croisultan (IRE)**35 4882 4-9-3 106 BACurtis 8 108
(Liam McAteer, Ire) *sn led: rdn and strly pressed fr under 2f out: kpt on wl u.p: hdd cl home* **14/1**
3 3/4 **Snaefell (IRE)**35 4882 6-9-6 108 (b) PJSmullen 5 109
(M Halford, Ire) *hld up in tch: prog 1 1/2f out: 2nd and chal fnl f: 3rd and no ex cl home* **7/2**2
4 2 **Wrong Answer**35 4882 3-8-12 96 CDHayes 6 96
(Kevin Prendergast, Ire) *hld up in tch: prog 1/2-way: 3rd and chal under 1 1/2f out: 4th and no ex wl ins fnl f* **33/1**
5 shd **Santo Padre (IRE)**14 5569 6-9-3 105 CO'Donoghue 7 99
(David Marnane, Ire) *hld up in rr: hdwy under 2f out: 6th ins fnl f: kpt on u.p* **8/1**3
6 3 **Air Chief Marshal (IRE)**47 4457 3-9-4 110 JAHeffernan 9 92
(A P O'Brien, Ire) *prom: 2nd 1/2-way: chal under 2f out: no ex ent fnl f* **10/1**
7 3/4 **Walk On Bye (IRE)**135 1676 3-8-12 100 WMLordan 3 84
(T Stack, Ire) *hld up towards rr: sme prog 1 1/2f out: no imp ins fnl f* **7/2**2
8 1 1/4 **Rayeni (IRE)**57 4160 4-9-3 107 FMBerry 2 83
(John M Oxx, Ire) *trckd ldrs on stand's rail: 3rd after 1/2-way: wknd fr 1 1/2f out* **7/2**2
9 1/2 **Kargali (IRE)**47 4463 5-9-6 107 (t) MHarley 10 84
(Luke Comer, Ire) *chsd ldrs on outer: 4th u.p 1/2-way: wknd fr over 1 1/2f out* **20/1**
10 7 **Zorija Rose (IRE)**53 4269 5-9-0 97 WJLee 4 56
(T Stack, Ire) *cl up to 1/2-way: sn wknd: eased fnl f* **25/1**

1m 14.3s (-0.70) **Going Correction** +0.175s/f (Good)
WFA 3 from 4yo+ 2lb **10** Ran SP% **130.1**
Speed ratings: **111,110,109,106,106 102,101,100,99,90**
CSF £51.82 TOTE £3.70: £1.50, £3.10, £1.70; DF 88.50.
Owner Mrs John Magnier **Bred** Monsieur J C Coude **Trained** Straffan, Co Kildare

FOCUS
The form is rated around the first two.

NOTEBOOK
Bewitched(IRE) was drawn 1 and could have encountered traffic problems as had been the case when she ran third in a similar event over the course and trip on her previous start when she was also drawn low. However, eveything worked out for her and she was produced with her effort inside the final furlong and ran on well to lead close home. A winner over 5f, this was her fourth win at this trip and she seems adaptable in terms of ground. (op 4/1)
Croisultan(IRE) loves it soft and was back to form here with conditions to suit. He made most and his brave effort almost paid effort as it was only very late on that he gave best. (op 16/1)
Snaefell(IRE), bidding for a third course and trip win at this level, is a game and consistent performer and one who is well-suited by plenty of cut. He won the race in which Bewitched ran third here last month and a follow-up looked a possibility when he arrived to go second inside the final furlong. He had every chance but failed to raise any extra late on. (op 4/1)
Wrong Answer, both of whose wins were over 5f, handles ease well. Seventh in the race Snaefell won her last month, she came there with her chance under 2f out but was well held through the final furlong.
Santo Padre(IRE), last year's Portland Handicap winner, had run good races to be placed on his two previous starts, more recently when third to Astrophysical Jet in a 5f Group 3 here last month. Held up in rear, he was switched right to begin his run over 1f out and ran on well. (op 6/1)
Walk On Bye(IRE) ◆, a Group 3 winner here last season, was having her first start since April and, although never posing a threat, she ran well enough to suggest there will be better to come from her next time. (op 4/1)
Rayeni(IRE), a Listed winner over the trip last season, relishes testing ground but is probably best suited by 7f. He raced prominently but was unable to raise his effort from one and a half furlongs out. Official explanation: jockey said colt suffered slight interference 1 1/2f out (op 9/2 tchd 5/1)

6008 - 6010a (Foreign Racing) - See Raceform Interactive

3251 DORTMUND (R-H)
Sunday, September 12

OFFICIAL GOING: Turf: good

6011a GROSSER PREIS VON DSW21 (DEUTSCHES ST LEGER) (GROUP 3) (3YO+) (TURF) 1m 6f
4:15 (4:36) 3-Y-0+
£28,318 (£9,734; £4,867; £2,654; £1,769; £1,327)

RPR
1 **Val Mondo (GER)**28 3-8-9 0 AHelfenbein 1 102
(Uwe Ostmann, Germany) *settled 5th early: sn travelling wl on heels of ldrs: wnt 3rd 4f out: smooth hdwy to ld turning into st 2 1/2f out: styd on strly u.p* **4/1**3
2 1/2 **Burma Gold (IRE)**57 4164 3-8-9 0 JiriPalik 3 101
(P Schiergen, Germany) *racd in midfield: 5th 4f out: pushed along and outpcd 3f out: strly rdn in st and nt qckn: styd on wl appr fnl f: tk 2nd ins fnl 50yds* **156/10**
3 1 **Brusco**28 4-9-6 0 EPedroza 6 100
(A Wohler, Germany) *settled in midfield: wnt 2nd 4f out: wnt on w ldr (a hd bhd) turning for home: 2nd and ev ch st (2 1/2f out): sn rdn and styd on at same pce: lost 2nd ins fnl 50yds* **21/10**1
4 1/2 **Saldennahe (GER)**42 4640 3-8-6 0 SHellyn 9 96
(P Schiergen, Germany) *racd in fnl 3rd: hdwy 4f out to go 5th st: kpt on u.str.p: nt qckn fnl f* **29/1**
5 1 1/4 **Sworn Pro (GER)**28 4-9-3 0 MickaelForest 11 95
(Mario Hofer, Germany) *bhd: hdwy 3f out: 6th st: styd on at one pce* **48/1**
6 1 **Codoor (GER)**15 5543 3-8-9 0 AStarke 8 96
(P Schiergen, Germany) *hld up: hdwy 3f out: midfield turning for home: kpt on one pce* **39/10**2
7 5 **Caudillo (GER)**61 4012 7-9-6 0 HenkGrewe 4 89
(Dr A Bolte, Germany) *bhd: hdwy towards st: styd on wout being able to qckn* **148/10**
8 hd **Tarkheena Prince (USA)**44 4566 5-9-6 0 MSuerland 7 89
(C Von Der Recke, Germany) *chsd ldrs: pushed along 4f out and lost pl: last st: styd on u.p 2f out: no ex fnl f* **33/1**
9 6 **Egon (IRE)**28 4-9-6 0 (b1) APietsch 10 80
(W Hickst, Germany) *trckd ldrs: grad lost pl fr 3f out* **149/10**
10 1 3/4 **Lamool (GER)**56 4184 3-8-10 0 ow1 DaraghO'Donohoe 5 79
(Mario Hofer, Germany) *led tl hdd w abt 10f to run: styd prom tl lost pl 3f out: wknd u.p in st* **123/10**
11 10 **Amare**21 5345 3-8-6 0 GaetanMasure 12 61
(T Mundry, Germany) *nvr in contention: eased fnl f* **144/10**
12 5 **Next Vision (IRE)**112 2374 4-9-6 0 ADeVries 2 57
(J Hirschberger, Germany) *racd in 2nd: led w 10f to go: hdd appr st: wknd qckly and eased whn bhd fnl f* **22/5**

3m 4.53s (-0.97)
WFA 3 from 4yo+ 11lb **12** Ran SP% **132.2**
WIN (incl. 10 euro stake): 50. PLACES: 18, 35, 13. SF: 1,457..
Owner Stall Dipoli **Bred** Gestut Auenquelle **Trained** Germany

5899 LONGCHAMP (R-H)
Sunday, September 12

OFFICIAL GOING: Turf: soft

6012a QATAR PRIX DU PETIT COUVERT (GROUP 3) (3YO+) (TURF) 5f (S)
1:35 (12:00) 3-Y-0+ **£35,398** (£14,159; £10,619; £7,079; £3,539)

RPR
1 **Swiss Diva**14 5576 4-8-13 0 IoritzMendizabal 1 114
(D R C Elsworth) *settled towards rr on rail: smooth hdwy on rail to ld over 2f out: r.o strly: nvr in danger fnl f* **5/2**1
2 2 **Bluster (FR)**38 4773 4-8-13 0 WilliamBuick 2 107
(Robert Collet, France) *bhd early: hdwy on rail to press ldr 3f out: led briefly over 2f out: sn hdd: 2nd and strly rdn if out: hld on wl for 2nd* **16/1**
3 hd **Mar Adentro (FR)**22 4-8-13 0 (p) ChristopheSoumillon 7 106
(R Chotard, France) *chsd ldrs gng wl: pushed along and wnt 3rd over 1f out: kpt on wl u.p* **18/1**
4 snk **War Artist (AUS)**35 4885 7-9-4 0 MaximeGuyon 11 111
(A De Royer-Dupre, France) *settled towards rr: rdn over 2f out: styd on u.p: nrest at fin* **9/2**3
5 shd **Tiza (SAF)**14 5576 8-8-13 0 (p) GeraldMosse 5 105
(A De Royer-Dupre, France) *racd in midfield: rdn 2f out: styd on wl ins fnl 150yds: nvr nrr* **14/1**
6 snk **Poppet's Treasure**38 4773 3-8-8 0 StephanePasquier 14 101
(R Pritchard-Gordon, France) *chsd ldrs: 5th 1f out: kpt on u.p: no ex fnl 50yds* **14/1**
7 3/4 **Fred Lalloupet**25 3-8-11 0 Christophe-PatriceLemaire 3 101
(D Smaga, France) *trckd ldrs: 4th 1/2-way: pressed ldr 2f out: sn rdn but no ex: wknd fnl 100yds* **16/1**
8 3/4 **Dam D'Augy (FR)**57 4165 5-8-9 0 (b) ThierryJarnet 9 95
(Mlle S-V Tarrou, France) *hld up: rdn 2f out: mde sme late prog: n.d* **20/1**
9 3/4 **Marchand D'Or (FR)**65 3870 7-9-2 0 DavyBonilla 12 100
(M Delzangles, France) *hld up on outside in midfield: tk clsr order over 2f out: sn rdn and one pce* **4/1**2
10 3/4 **Top Music**14 5576 3-8-11 0 OlivierPeslier 6 93
(A Fabre, France) *towards rr tl mde sme late hdwy: nvr threatened ldrs* **20/1**
11 3/4 **Skyteam (FR)**11 6-8-13 0 (p) JohanVictoire 8 91
(Mme C Head-Maarek, France) *hld up: pushed along 2f out: no imp* **20/1**
12 1 1/2 **Delvita (FR)**57 4165 6-8-9 0 ThierryThulliez 10 82
(J-V Toux, France) *led: hdd over 3f out but remained prom: rdn and wknd ins fnl 300yds* **25/1**
13 8 **Chopouest (FR)**35 4885 3-8-11 0 FredericSpanu 4 56
(A Spanu, France) *broke wl and trckd ldrs: led over 3f out: hdd over 2f out: wknd qckly* **16/1**
14 3 **Pisa No Varon (JPN)**127 4-8-13 0 YutakaTake 13 46
(Katsuhiko Sumii, Japan) *gd early spd to chse ldr: wknd qckly fr 1/2-way* **20/1**

57.50 secs (1.20) **Going Correction** +0.525s/f (Yiel)
WFA 3 from 4yo+ 1lb **14** Ran SP% **125.9**
Speed ratings: **111,107,107,107,107 106,105,104,103,102 100,98,85,80**
WIN (incl. 1 euro stake): 2.30; PLACE 1.30, 7.70, 2.60; DF 47.40; SF 47.70.
Owner Lordship Stud **Bred** Lordship Stud **Trained** Newmarket, Suffolk

NOTEBOOK
Swiss Diva ◆ landed the hat-trick in impressive style after finding her way up the near-side rail. She now heads to the Prix de l'Abbaye with a leading chance.
Bluster(FR) is a fairly consistent French sprinter and did enough to claim a brave second.
Mar Adentro(FR), the winner of a Deauville handicap on his previous start, has improved his form since cheekpeices were fitted. This was by far his best performance on RPRs.
War Artist(AUS), the winner of this race last year when trained by James Eustace, is generally better over further, and wasn't making any significant ground here until it was too late.
Marchand D'Or(FR) made a move at halfway but could not quicken. This was a poor effort by his standards.

6013a QATAR PRIX VERMEILLE (GROUP 1) (3YO+ FILLIES & MARES) (TURF) 1m 4f
2:40 (12:00) 3-Y-0+ **£176,982** (£70,805; £35,402; £17,685; £8,858)

RPR
1 **Midday**24 5248 4-9-3 0 TomQueally 6 114+
(H R A Cecil) *racd in 4th: moved smoothly into 3rd 2f out: rdn 1 1/2f out: qcknd wl to chal for ld 1f out: r.o wl to take ld 100yds out: styd on wl* **9/4**1
2 3/4 **Plumania**77 3494 4-9-3 0 OlivierPeslier 9 113
(A Fabre, France) *racd in 2nd: qcknd into ld 1 1/2f out: hdd 1f out: r.o wl* **8/1**
3 1/2 **Sarafina (FR)**91 3015 3-8-8 0 Christophe-PatriceLemaire 12 112+
(A De Royer-Dupre, France) *w.w in midfield: swtchd to outside to launch chal over 1f out: r.o wl fnl f to take 3rd on line* **5/2**2
4 shd **Ashiyla (FR)**73 3-8-8 0 ThierryJarnet 2 112
(A De Royer-Dupre, France) *led fr s: set pce for Sarafina: hdd by 1 1/2f out: styd on gamely fnl f: lost 3rd on line* **100/1**
5 hd **Sarah Lynx (IRE)**31 5138 3-8-8 0 GeraldMosse 8 112
(J E Hammond, France) *towards rr: qcknd wl towards rail 1 1/2f out: fin strly fnl f: nrest at fin* **50/1**
6 2 1/2 **Dariole (FR)**112 2373 3-8-8 0 YutakaTake 5 108
(P Bary, France) *bkmarker fr s: mde gd prog in st wout threatening ldrs* **33/1**
7 1 **Peinture Rare (IRE)**29 5108 4-9-3 0 AnthonyCrastus 10 106
(E Lellouche, France) *racd in 6th: rdn 2f out: styd on* **16/1**
8 snk **High Heeled (IRE)**29 5108 4-9-3 0 WilliamBuick 4 106
(J H M Gosden) *racd in 5th tl fnl turn: rdn and no ex fnl 2f: fdd* **10/1**
9 6 **Never Forget (FR)**21 5346 3-8-8 0 JohanVictoire 1 96
(E Lellouche, France) *settled towards rr: rdn but hmpd 2f out: no ex: fdd* **33/1**

10 1 1/2 **Lady's Purse**[77] 3493 3-8-8 0 MaximeGuyon 11 94
(H-A Pantall, France) *racd in 3rd and stl prom 2f out: rdn and sn fdd* **33/1**

11 10 **Enora (GER)**[42] 4640 3-8-8 0 ChristopheSoumillon 3 78
(T Mundry, Germany) *nvr figured* **16/1**

R **Sariska**[24] 5248 4-9-3 0 JamieSpencer 7 —
(M L W Bell) *ref to r* **7/2**[3]

2m 32.4s (2.00) **Going Correction** +0.525s/f (Yiel)
WFA 3 from 4yo 9lb 12 Ran SP% **125.3**
Speed ratings: **114,113,113,113,112 111,110,110,106,105 98,—**
WIN (incl. 1 euro stake): 3.80. PLACES: 1.30, 1.70, 1.30. DF: 14.00. SF: 26.60.
Owner K Abdulla **Bred** Juddmonte Farms Ltd **Trained** Newmarket, Suffolk

FOCUS
A high-class renewal of the Prix Vermeille on paper, but weakened by Sariska's non-particpation. The form is rated through the seventh and none of the leading protagonists are rated at their best.

NOTEBOOK
Midday heads to the US to defend her Breeders' Cup crown on the back of this third successive Group 1 victory. The pace was honest and, once she was stoked up to challenge, after initially taking a stride or two to get going, she picked up takingly and surged to the lead before idling in the closing stages. The Arc has been ruled out, as the owner has Workforce for that race. "She was a little bit lazy when she hit the front. They did not go fast and she would probably have been suited by a quicker pace but she won well and it is lovely to win another Group 1 race with her." She crossed the line clear of Plumania to give her trainer Henry Cecil his first success in the race and become the first British-trained runner to win since Leggera in 1998. (op 5/2)
Plumania, returning from a break since June when she won the Grand Prix de Saint-Cloud , was never far away and kicked over 1f out but the winner proved too strong. This was a decent effort and she looks on course for the Arc with the Opera the alternative.
Sarafina(FR) came into the race unbeaten in three starts having beaten Rosanara in the Prix de Diane on her last start in the middle of June and was stepped up to 1m4f for the first time. She was held up towards the back of the field in the early stages and was still around ten lengths behind her pacemaker when the runners turned into the straight before finishing well. Her trainer reported that she did not have a hard race and that the Arc is still the aim, although she could drop back in trip for the Opera and has the Champion Stakes as an alternative.
Ashiyla(FR) was clearly in the line-up employed in pacemaking duties for Sarafina, and the fact that she finished so close does throw a little doubt over the value of the form. She was headed over 2f out but was not done with and kept on quite well in the closing stages.
Sarah Lynx(IRE) was another who looked to have plenty to do on form and was held up towards the rear. She enjoyed a dream run through on the far rail in the closing stages and ran on in a manner which suggests there are other races for her.
Dariole(FR) was held up early and made some progress in the straight, but could keep on only at one pace in the closing stages.
Peinture Rare(IRE) had won a Group 2 at Deauville on her last start but could stay on only at the one pace in the closing stages after tracking the leaders and she may need easier ground to show her best. (op 14/1)
High Heeled(IRE) was close enough turning in but dropped away in the straight. She is better at a slightly lower level and the Prix de Royallieu or a second St Simon Stakes could be on the agenda next.
Enora(GER) had won the German Oaks on her last start but was another not to figure after being held up.
Sariska refused to race for the second time in a row, resulting in connections immediately announcing her retirement. It is a great shame that her career should end in such an inglorious way but, like her relation Gull Wing, she has taken an aversion to the stalls. She had just started to get a bit fidgety prior to going in the stalls and, as at York, would not move when the others jumped out.

6014a QATAR PRIX NIEL (GROUP 2) (3YO COLTS & FILLIES) (TURF) 1m 4f
3:15 (12:00) 3-Y-O £65,575 (£25,309; £12,079; £8,053; £4,026)

RPR

1 **Behkabad (FR)**[60] 4039 3-9-2 0 Christophe-PatriceLemaire 2 127+
(J-C Rouget, France) *racd in 3rd: accelerated 2f out: hrd rdn fnl f to get up on line* **11/8**[1]

2 hd **Planteur (IRE)**[60] 4039 3-9-2 0 AnthonyCrastus 6 126
(E Lellouche, France) *pursued pcemaker: qckly grabbed ld early in st: qcknd wl 2f out: r.o strly: ct and hdd fnl strides* **7/4**[2]

3 4 **Kidnapping (IRE)**[91] 3-9-2 0 ChristopheSoumillon 7 119
(S Botti, Italy) *racd in 4th: lost grnd on ldrs early in st: qcknd wl 2f out and styd on wl fnl f* **25/1**

4 4 **Victoire Pisa (JPN)**[105] 3-9-2 0 YutakaTake 3 113
(Katsuhiko Sumii, Japan) *w.w: rdn and qcknd 2f out to go 3rd 1f out: no ex* **6/1**[3]

5 3 **Shamalgan (FR)**[49] 4420 3-9-2 0 IoritzMendizabal 5 108
(A Savujev, Czech Republic) *bkmarker fr s: rdn 2f out: no ex: fdd* **25/1**

6 dist **Apres Vous (IRE)**[45] 3-9-2 0 MaximeGuyon 4 —
(A Fabre, France) *settled towards rr: qcknd arnd fnl turn: briefly threatened early in st but sn wknd* **6/1**[3]

7 6 **Vivre Libre**[60] 4039 3-9-2 0 (b) SamuelFargeat 1 —
(E Lellouche, France) *set pce for Planteur and led tl fnl turn: wknd qckly* **200/1**

2m 30.8s (0.40) **Going Correction** +0.525s/f (Yiel) 7 Ran SP% **115.2**
Speed ratings: **119,118,116,113,111 —,—**
WIN (incl. 1 euro stake): 2.80. PLACES: 1.40, 1.30. SF: 4.50.
Owner H H Aga Khan **Bred** H H The Aga Khan's Studs S C **Trained** Pau, France

FOCUS
A race that has proved an informative Prix de l'Arc de Triomphe trial in the recent past with winners Rail Link (2006), Hurricane Run (2005), Dalakhani (2003) and Sinndar (2000) returning to take the jewel in the Longchamp crown, and Bago (third in 2004) also successful. The pace was sound which helped Behkabad post the highest RPR recorded by a Prix Niel winner. He also secured his position as the leading French 3yo.

NOTEBOOK
Behkabad(FR) came through his trial for the Arc well enough but did not hit the front until the final yards. He was already a leading contender for the end-of-season spectacular but his victory in this contest will do much to boost confidence. Not only is the Niel an important Arc trial and indicator of form, Behkabad's owner, the Aga Khan, has seen his last two winners of this race - Sinndar in 2000 and Dalakhani in 2003 - go on to win the main event come October. His trainer reckons he will be spot on for the Arc and bookmakers responded by making him joint-favourite. However, an on-song Fame And Glory would prove a tough nut to crack. (tchd 5/4)
Planteur(IRE) had finished runner-up in the Prix du Jockey Club and Grand Prix de Paris since beating Rewilding on his reappearance here in April, and put in another solid effort. He attempted to win it from the front, with only stablemate Vivre Libre, the pacemaker, initially in advance. His rider got the jump on his main rival in the straight and he very nearly hung on. He will renew rivalry in the Arc. (op 15/8)
Kidnapping(IRE), a three-time Listed winner in Italy, was up in grade and ran about as well as could be expected, although no match for the principals.
Victoire Pisa(JPN) won the Japanese Guineas before finishing third in their Derby. He came from dead last under a patient ride and between the two pole and the furlong marker appeared a real threat, but faded when the front pair got serious. He hardly looks an Arc candidate. (op 13/2)
Shamalgan(FR) was out of his depth and just plugged on after never being in the hunt.
Apres Vous(IRE) raced in close fourth for much of the way but was another found wanting at the business end and needs to be dropped in class to add to his success in a maiden at Clairefontaine in July.

6015a QATAR PRIX FOY (GROUP 2) (4YO+) (TURF) 1m 4f
3:45 (12:00) 4-Y-O+ £65,575 (£25,309; £12,079; £8,053; £4,026)

RPR

1 **Duncan**[44] 4535 5-9-2 0 WilliamBuick 3 116
(J H M Gosden) *sent to ld on wd outside after 1f: hdd 2f out: rallied gamely to regain ld 100yds out: r.o wl whn chal cl home* **10/1**

2 3/4 **Nakayama Festa (JPN)**[77] 4-9-2 0 MasayoshiEbina 1 115
(Yoshitaka Ninomiya, Japan) *racd in 3rd: qcknd wl 2f out: chal for ld 1f out: no ex fnl 50yds* **9/2**[3]

3 1 **Timos (GER)**[98] 2803 5-9-2 0 ChristopheSoumillon 2 113
(T Doumen, France) *racd in 2nd: rdn to ld 2f out: hdd 100yds out: no ex: styd on* **16/1**

4 nk **Byword**[26] 5186 4-9-2 0 MaximeGuyon 5 113
(A Fabre, France) *racd in 4th: proged early in st: threatened briefly 1f out: no ex: styd on* **11/10**[1]

5 2 1/2 **Daryakana (FR)**[50] 4359 4-8-13 0 Christophe-PatriceLemaire 4 106
(A De Royer-Dupre, France) *bkmarker fr s: rdn early in st: styd on but no threat to ldrs fnl f* **7/2**[2]

6 1 1/2 **Chinchon (IRE)**[71] 5-9-2 0 OlivierPeslier 6 106
(C Laffon-Parias, France) *racd in 5th: rdn early in st: no ex fr 2f out* **10/1**

2m 35.9s (5.50) **Going Correction** +0.525s/f (Yiel) 6 Ran SP% **112.1**
Speed ratings: **102,101,100,100,98 97**
WIN (incl. 1 euro stake): 13.80. PLACES: 4.50, 4.40. SF: 83.90.
Owner Normandie Stud Ltd **Bred** Normandie Stud Ltd **Trained** Newmarket, Suffolk

FOCUS
This trial has had little bearing on the outcome of the Prix de l'Arc de Triomphe in recent times and this year's renewal doesn't look likely to provide a main contender this time.

NOTEBOOK
Duncan, whose trainer can do nothing wrong at present, stepped on his previous efforts this term for the all-conquering stable. He had finished runner-up to Harbinger in the Hardwicke Stakes at Royal Ascot, which would have given him claims, and a change of tactics proved the key on this occasion. He had been held up in the past but, with no obvious pace in the race, Buick took his mount the front and stepped up the tempo with half a mile to travel. He was headed over a furlong out but found a renewed effort to lead inside the final furlong and kept on bravely. He could run with credit if connections elect to return for the Arc, but at this stage of his career he hardly looks the type to improve on this.
Nakayama Festa(JPN) fared better than the Japanese runner in the Prix Neil and came out of the race with a lot of credit. He had won the Grade 1 Takaranzuka Kinen in his native country at the end of June and was having his first outing since. He jumped smartly out of the stalls, settled in third place and went in pursuit of the winner in the final 2f. He kept on well to take the runner-up spot close home and can progress further with this outing under his belt.
Timos(GER) was another to get away quite smartly but was asked to track the eventual winner when he was sent on. He looked a big danger when leading over a furlong out but was just outstayed in the final half-furlong. He had finished runner-up to Allied Powers in a Group 2 event at Chantilly in June and, as good as this effort was, that hardly strikes as form good enough to win an Arc.
Byword, winner of the Group 1 Prince of Wales's Stakes at Royal Ascot and third to Rip Van Winkle in the Juddmonte International, was the major disappointment of the race. He was held up to get the trip but appeared to be hanging in the straight and, when asked for his finishing effort, picked up without ever looking likely to get there. The trip didn't look entirely responsible for his defeat, and he may well have still been feeling the effects of two hard races in mid-summer, although 1m2f is clearly his optimum distance. His Arc plans are on hold.
Daryakana(FR) was held up in last place and hasn't rediscovered her brilliant form of last year, when her unbeaten run culminated in a victory in the Hong Kong Vase. She kept on at only the same pace in the closing stages and, at her best, would have eaten these.
Chinchon(IRE) had looked unlucky when finishing behind Timos at Chantilly but, despite winning a Grade 1 at Monmouth Park when last seen out at the beginning of July, never really threatened.

6016a QATAR PRIX GLADIATEUR (GROUP 3) (4YO+) (TURF) 1m 7f 110y
4:20 (12:00) 4-Y-O+ £35,398 (£14,159; £10,619; £7,079; £3,539)

RPR

1 **Gentoo (FR)**[29] 5109 6-8-11 0 (p) GeraldMosse 1 105
(A Lyon, France) *settled towards rr: forced to r wd in st: qcknd wl on wd outside to take ld 150yds out: r.o strly to win easily* **20/1**

2 2 **Watar (IRE)**[21] 5349 5-8-11 0 DavyBonilla 8 103
(F Head, France) *racd in rr: proged to chal towards outside 2f out: drifted off st line causing interference to runners on his ins: r.o wl fnl f* **11/1**

3 3/4 **Kimble (FR)**[29] 5109 8-8-11 0 ArnaudBourgeais 4 102
(N Leenders, France) *racd in 5th: jnd ldrs early in st: led 1 1/2f out: hdd 150yds out: r.o wl* **25/1**

4 snk **Lifting Cloud**[39] 4-8-11 0 MaximeGuyon 7 102
(A Fabre, France) *led at modest pce: stl in front 2f out: hdd 1 1/2f out: styd on wl* **11/2**[3]

5 snk **Kasbah Bliss (FR)**[87] 3102 8-9-2 0 ThierryThulliez 6 107+
(F Doumen, France) *racd towards rr: making prog whn hmpd 2f out: short of room ins fnl f: unlucky* **11/8**[1]

6 1 1/2 **Green Tango (FR)**[21] 5349 7-9-0 0 RonanThomas 3 103
(P Van De Poele, France) *chsd ldr: rdn 2f out: short of room fr 1 1/2f out: styd on* **16/1**

7 1/2 **Bannaby (FR)**[28] 7-8-11 0 ChristopheSoumillon 2 100
(M Delcher-Sanchez, Spain) *racd in 3rd: rdn to chal 2f out: no ex fnl f* **2/1**[2]

8 1/2 **Winter Dream (IRE)**[14] 5575 6-8-11 0 IoritzMendizabal 5 99
(Robert Collet, France) *racd in 4th: short of room 2f out: rdn but no ex fnl 1 1/2f* **20/1**

3m 34.1s (12.60) **Going Correction** +0.525s/f (Yiel) 8 Ran SP% **118.4**
Speed ratings: **89,88,87,87,87 86,86,86**
WIN (incl. 1 euro stake): 8.10. PLACES: 2.40, 3.10, 4.90. DF: 33.10. SF: 65.70.
Owner Serge Tripier-Mondancin **Bred** Jean-Claude Seroul **Trained** France

NOTEBOOK
Gentoo(FR) created a slight surprise when he easily took this long-distance event by two lengths for his trainer Alain Lyon. The six-year-old was winning the first Group race of his career but was always travelling well on the rail near the back of the field before coming from last to first. Winner of his only other start over this distance, he had previously been bought out of a claimer in 2007 for €23,900. He will now take his chance in the Cadran.
Watar(IRE) won the Prix Chaudenay over this trip at the Arc meeting in 2009. He delivered his challenge in the straight but wandered and interefered with the challengers nearer the rail.
Kimble(FR) was stepping back up in trip and taking a rise in grade but ran creditably, only being seen off in the last furlong.
Kasbah Bliss(FR), bidding for a third successive win in this race, never got a clear run having been boxed in twice during the race. He was reportedly still on the bit passing the line, and connections viewed the defeat positively, expecting the gelding to be in perfect shape for the Cadran after this.

Bannaby(FR), runner-up in this two years ago, ran slightly free early on and faded in the straight. (op 9/4)

2637 TABY (R-H)

Sunday, September 12

OFFICIAL GOING: Turf: good

6017a STOCKHOLM CUP INTERNATIONAL (GROUP 3) (3YO+) (TURF) 1m 4f

4:05 (12:00) 3-Y-O+ £86,580 (£30,303; £10,389; £6,926; £4,329)

RPR

1 **Mores Wells**[29] 5107 6-9-4 0.....................................(b) SebastienMaillot 5 95
(R Gibson, France) *hld up towards rr: hdwy fnl turn: pushed along and 8th 2f out: r.o wl u.p to ld fnl 50yds* **63/10**[3]

2 ½ **Theatrical Award (NOR)**[21] 5350 5-9-0 0..................... CarlosLopez 10 90
(Michael Taylor, Norway) *settled towards rr: hdwy 2 1/2f out: 9th st (2f out): r.o wl to ld 100yds fr home: hdd last 50yds: no ex* **92/10**

3 1 **Appel Au Maitre (FR)**[28] 5132 6-9-4 0..................... JimmyFortune 1 92
(Wido Neuroth, Norway) *led early but hdd after 1f and settled on ldr's quarters: led appr st (jst over 2f out): styd on wl u.p: hdd fnl 100yds: one pce* **8/5**[1]

4 5 **Non Stop**[40] 4-9-4 0.. FabienLefebvre 3 84
(M Le Forestier, France) *racd freely first 3f but sn settled on rail disputing 3rd: cl 4th and ev ch st: short of room and hmpd 1 1/2f out: kpt on but unable qck* **43/1**

5 ½ **Peas And Carrots (DEN)**[21] 5350 7-9-4 0..................... RafaelSchistl 2 84
(Lennart Reuterskiold Jr, Sweden) *wl away and disp 3rd for much of the r: ev ch turning for home: one pce fnl 300yds* **121/10**

6 nk **Theocritus (USA)**[228] 314 5-9-4 0..................................... ManuelSantos 8 83
(Claes Bjorling, Sweden) *hld up towards rr: sme late hdwy: n.d* **103/10**

7 1 **Touch Of Hawk (FR)**[21] 5350 4-9-4 0.......... LennartHammer-Hansen 9 82
(Wido Neuroth, Norway) *dwlt: sn rcvrd and moved up on outside to run a cl 5th: rdn 2f out: grad fdd* **5/2**[2]

8 1 ½ **Volo Cat (FR)**[21] 5350 6-9-4 0....................................... JacobJohansen 4 79
(Bent Olsen, Denmark) *racd in midfield: rdn and wknd fnl 2 1/2f* **47/1**

9 ½ **Walzertraum (USA)**[62] 5-9-4 0...........................(b) Per-AndersGraberg 6 78
(Fredrik Reuterskiold, Sweden) *nvr bttr than midfield* **27/1**

10 hd **Condor (DEN)**[42] 4641 5-9-4 0.. KimAndersen 11 78
(Soren Jensen, Denmark) *a bhd* **82/1**

11 9 **Quality Guitar (BRZ)** 4-9-4 0.. BReis 7 64
(Givanildo Duarte, Sweden) *rushed up to ld after 1f: pushed along and hdd appr st: wknd u.p fnl 300yds* **19/2**

2m 31.6s (2.40) **11 Ran SP% 125.7**

PARI-MUTUEL (all including 1sek stake): WIN 7.32; PLACE 2.25, 3.34, 1.31; DF 71.25.

Owner Mrs Catherine O'Flynn **Bred** Cliveden Stud Ltd And Ocean Bloodstock **Trained** Lamorlaye, France

5709 BRIGHTON (L-H)

Monday, September 13

OFFICIAL GOING: Good (good to firm in places; 7.5)

Wind: Fresh, across Weather: Cloudy, steady rain from race 6

6018 BRIGHTON WEDDING EXHIBITION HERE 19TH SEPTEMBER H'CAP 5f 59y

2:00 (2:01) (Class 6) (0-65,65) 3-Y-O+ £1,942 (£578; £288; £144) Stalls Low

Form RPR

000 1 **Bouncy Bouncy (IRE)**[20] 5395 3-8-6 51 oh1................(t) HayleyTurner 7 58+
(M L W Bell) *bhd: hrd rdn and hdwy over 1f out: r.o to ld nr fin* **9/1**

0602 2 nk **Guto**[15] 5562 7-9-0 58... TravisBlock 6 64
(W J H Ratcliffe) *chsd ldrs: led over 1f out: hrd rdn and kpt on fnl f: hdd nr fin* **10/1**

0344 3 2 ¼ **Nepotism**[4] 5876 3-9-6 65.. TomMcLaughlin 8 63
(M S Saunders) *in tch disputing 4th: drvn to press ldrs over 1f out: edgd lft: cl 3rd and hld whn n.m.r ins fnl f* **4/1**[2]

0342 4 1 ¾ **Nadinska**[10] 5726 3-8-12 57.. ChrisCatlin 5 49
(M R Channon) *towards rr: rdn and hdwy fr over 1f out: nvr nrr* **13/2**[3]

56 5 nk **Step It Up (IRE)**[13] 5628 6-8-11 62........................ NathanAlison[(7)] 4 53
(J R Boyle) *in tch disputing 4th: rdn to chse ldrs 2f out: no ex 1f out* **15/2**

1106 6 nk **Replicator**[15] 5562 5-9-3 64................................(e) AshleyHamblett[(3)] 3 54
(P L Gilligan) *chsd ldr: led 3f out tl over 1f out: wknd fnl f* **14/1**

0004 7 4 ½ **Spring Horizon (IRE)**[10] 5715 4-8-7 51 oh6............ KirstyMilczarek 1 25
(Miss Z C Davison) *towards rr: effrt over 2f out: hrd rdn and wknd over 1f out* **100/1**

0000 8 nk **Captain Kallis (IRE)**[21] 5377 4-8-9 53..........................(t) CathyGannon 9 26
(D J S Ffrench Davis) *stdd s: hld up in rr: hrd rdn 2f out: nvr trbld ldrs* **15/2**

2012 9 4 ½ **Namir (IRE)**[4] 5876 8-9-7 65....................................(vt) RichardHughes 10 22
(H J Evans) *mid-div on outer: drvn along 1/2-way: sn wknd: eased whn no ch fnl f* **5/2**[1]

0400 10 6 **Hatman Jack (IRE)**[17] 5471 4-8-2 51 oh6................(p) SophieDoyle[(5)] 2 —
(B G Powell) *led 2f: prom tl wknd over 1f out* **100/1**

63.04 secs (0.74) **Going Correction** +0.20s/f (Good)

WFA 3 from 4yo+ 1lb **10 Ran SP% 113.2**

Speed ratings (Par 101): **102,101,97,95,94 94,86,86,79,69**

toteswingers:1&2:£19.40, 1&3:£7.80, 2&3:£7.70 CSF £92.43 CT £415.09 TOTE £9.40: £3.50, £2.10, £1.80; EX 79.40 Trifecta £183.70 Part won. Pool: £248.27 - 0.51 winning units..

Owner Mrs A Scotney Mrs D Asplin A Symonds **Bred** Ms Adelaide Foley & Roger O'Callaghan **Trained** Newmarket, Suffolk

FOCUS

A very moderate sprint handicap which was run at a solid tempo and the runners were spread across the straight, but they shunned either rail. The form is rated around the second and third. The main action developed in the centre.

Bouncy Bouncy(IRE) Official explanation: trainer said filly was suited by dropping to five furlongs and the fitting of a tongue strap

Namir(IRE) Official explanation: jockey said gelding hung right

6019 EUROPEAN BREEDERS' FUND MEDIAN AUCTION MAIDEN STKS 6f 209y

2:30 (2:30) (Class 6) 2-Y-O £2,590 (£770; £385; £192) Stalls Low

Form RPR

00 1 **Ebony Song (USA)**[18] 5453 2-9-3 0.................................. RyanMoore 6 72
(J Noseda) *chsd ldr: led over 1f out: drvn out* **5/4**[1]

6020 2 1 ½ **Maggie's Treasure (IRE)**[14] 5613 2-9-3 67..................... TadhgO'Shea 2 68
(J Gallagher) *led tl over 1f out: nt qckn fnl f* **13/2**[3]

3 1 **Blue Deer (IRE)** 2-9-3 0... ChrisCatlin 5 66+
(M R Channon) *hld up in 5th: rdn to chse ldrs 2f out: one pce fnl f* **7/2**[2]

4 ½ **Dare It And Smile (USA)** 2-8-12 0.................................... LiamKeniry 7 59+
(D M Simcock) *t.k.h in 4th: effrt over 2f out: 4th and no imp whn hung lft over 1f out: styd on same pce* **7/2**[2]

6 5 1 **Skeleton (IRE)**[26] 5204 2-8-9 0............................ GilmarPereira[(3)] 4 57
(W J Haggas) *dwlt: hld up and bhd: rdn over 2f out: nvr able to chal* **14/1**

04 6 3 ½ **Callie's Angel**[20] 5385 2-9-3 0.. LukeMorris 1 53
(B Palling) *disp 2nd pl tl drvn along and wknd over 2f out* **14/1**

1m 25.9s (2.80) **Going Correction** +0.20s/f (Good) **6 Ran SP% 115.6**

Speed ratings (Par 93): **92,90,89,88,87 83**

toteswingers:1&2:£4.10, 1&3:£1.10, 2&3:£2.70 CSF £10.68 TOTE £2.40: £1.90, £3.10; EX 11.30.

Owner Bluehills Racing Limited **Bred** Gulf Coast Farms LLC **Trained** Newmarket, Suffolk

FOCUS

Pretty weak maiden form, rated around the second.

NOTEBOOK

Ebony Song(USA) had run well below expectations in his two previous outings, but his yard has a cracking record at this track and he further enhanced it with a workmanlike display. The non-runner dictated he was sent off a short price and he raced more professionally this time, but still proved very hard work for the champion jockey. He was always doing enough and probably has more ability than he is yet showing, but obviously his Group1 entry is far too ambitious. (op 11-8 tchd 6-4 and 13-8 in a place)

Maggie's Treasure(IRE), rated 67, set out to make all over this stiffer test and made the winner work for his prize. This was much more like it from him again returned to quicker ground and he fully deserves to go one better. (op 5-1)

Blue Deer(IRE)'s sire is a speed influence yet his dam is from a good middle-distance family. He looked a threat 2f out, but found only the one pace when it mattered and already appears in need of a stiffer test. He has scope and should be winning before the season's end. (op 11-2)

Dare It And Smile(USA) races in the same ownership as the third and is from another yard with a good record at the track. She wasn't unfancied, but showed her inexperience and was held before she looked uncomfortable on the track late on. (op 5-1)

Skeleton(IRE), hampered when sixth on debut last month, lacked the pace to land a telling blow and she looks more of a long-term project. (op 12-1)

Callie's Angel ran below his recent level on this quicker ground and was eased off inside the final half furlong. He is now eligible for nurseries. (op 12-1)

6020 BETFAIR RACING EXCELLENCE APPRENTICE SERIES H'CAP 1m 1f 209y

3:00 (3:01) (Class 6) (0-65,63) 3-Y-O £1,942 (£578; £288; £144) Stalls High

Form RPR

0533 1 **Finch Flyer (IRE)**[19] 5414 3-8-10 52..............................(p) HarryBentley 2 62+
(G L Moore) *hld up in midfield: hdwy 3f out: led and hung rt over 2f out: rdn 3 l clr 1f out: readily* **9/4**[1]

U435 2 3 **Little Meadow (IRE)**[27] 5171 3-8-7 49 oh4.................. AdamBeschizza 6 53
(Miss J Feilden) *in tch in 5th: drvn to chse wnr 2f out: no imp* **11/2**[3]

0305 3 3 **Lovely Eyes (IRE)**[12] 5654 3-8-13 62.......................... AliceHaynes[(7)] 11 62+
(D M Simcock) *s.s: bhd: swtchd to ins and sme hdwy 5f out: wnt 3rd and sddle slipping 2f out: styd on same pce* **7/1**

0060 4 1 ¼ **Half Sister (IRE)**[31] 5050 3-9-3 62.......................(b[1]) NathanAlison[(3)] 12 58
(M E Rimmer) *s.s: bhd: hdwy and hung lft 2f out: nrst fin* **50/1**

6000 5 1 ¾ **Bubbly Braveheart (IRE)**[25] 4439 3-9-3 62.............. NatashaEaton[(3)] 7 54
(A Bailey) *mid-div: rdn and carried rt over 2f out: styd on fnl f* **25/1**

4436 6 2 ½ **Affirmable**[12] 5653 3-8-9 54...(p) HollyHall[(3)] 3 41
(J W Hills) *hld up in midfield: shkn up and hung rt over 2f out: no imp* **10/1**

5353 7 shd **Whiepa Snappa (IRE)**[4] 5887 3-9-4 60................................. AmyScott 1 47
(P M Phelan) *hld up towards rr: rdn and sme hdwy in midfield whn carried lft 2f out: nvr able to chal* **3/1**[2]

0040 8 1 ¼ **Rio Prince**[16] 5536 3-8-2 49 oh2.......................... MatthewCosham[(5)] 8 33
(J J Bridger) *prom tl hrd rdn and wknd 2f out* **16/1**

5064 9 6 **Mororless**[10] 5712 3-8-4 49 oh1.................................. RichardRowe[(3)] 4 21
(Miss Z C Davison) *a bhd* **66/1**

4060 10 2 ¾ **Sunset Place**[17] 5469 3-9-0 63.................................. ThomasDyer[(7)] 9 30
(C G Cox) *chsd ldrs tl hrd rdn and wknd over 2f out* **14/1**

6450 11 26 **Roar Talent (USA)**[12] 5656 3-8-9 58..................... ElizabethNorris[(7)] 10 —
(J R Best) *pressed ldr 4f: lost pl 4f out: sn bhd* **66/1**

0-06 12 5 **Magneto (IRE)**[41] 4669 3-8-8 50.................................... CharlesEddery 5 —
(E J Creighton) *led tl hung rt and wknd over 2f out* **66/1**

2m 5.78s (2.18) **Going Correction** +0.20s/f (Good) **12 Ran SP% 115.6**

Speed ratings (Par 99): **99,96,94,93,91 89,89,88,83,81 60,56**

toteswingers:1&2:£2.20, 1&3:£4.90, 2&3:£8.70 CSF £14.02 CT £72.46 TOTE £3.20: £1.60, £1.70, £1.90; EX 10.40 Trifecta £111.10 Pool: £279.26 - 1.86 winning units..

Owner Prix Mature Racing **Bred** Irish National Stud **Trained** Lower Beeding, W Sussex

FOCUS

A moderate handicap confined to apprentice riders. The winner is rated to his latest form and the runner-up to her best.

Lovely Eyes(IRE) Official explanation: jockey said saddle slipped

6021 HOLD YOUR WEDDING AT BRIGHTON RACECOURSE H'CAP (DIV I) 1m 3f 196y

3:30 (3:32) (Class 6) (0-60,60) 3-Y-O+ £1,619 (£481; £240; £120) Stalls High

Form RPR

4143 1 **Noah Jameel**[15] 5552 8-9-3 51.. FergusSweeney 5 59
(A G Newcombe) *in tch: effrt over 2f out: edgd lft and styd on to chal ins fnl f: drvn to take narrow ld fnl 75yds* **7/1**[3]

4422 2 hd **Zelos Diktator**[7] 5813 4-9-7 55..(p) RyanMoore 8 63
(G L Moore) *prom: disp ld 2f out: drvn to ld 1f out: kpt on u.p: narrowly hdd fnl 75yds* **13/8**[1]

0-22 3 1 **Dancing Storm**[17] 5468 7-9-12 60.. IanMongan 2 67+
(W S Kittow) *dwlt: hld up towards rr: promising hdwy whn nt clr run over 2f out: switched rt: edgd lft and styd on wl fr over 1f out* **9/2**[2]

044- 4 ¾ **Dot's Delight**[121] 5246 6-8-13 47...................................... LiamKeniry 10 52
(M G Rimell) *bhd: rdn over 2f out: styd on wl fnl f: nrst fin* **22/1**

3-20 5 nk **Home**[158] 1193 5-9-4 52...(vt) AdamKirby 9 57
(C Gordon) *in tch: disp ld 2f out tl 1f out: one pce* **33/1**

0320 6 6 **Mayfair's Future**[39] 4765 5-9-3 51...................................... NeilCallan 6 46
(J R Jenkins) *led tl 2f out: hrd rdn and wknd 1f out* **9/2**[2]

326 7 1 ½ **Rosy Dawn**[30] 5072 5-8-12 46 oh1.................................. RichardHughes 4 39
(L A Dace) *chsd ldrs: rdn 3f out: sltly hmpd and wknd over 1f out* **12/1**

4006 8 2 ½ **Carnival Time (IRE)**[17] 5467 3-8-6 49.............................(p) LukeMorris 3 38
(C G Cox) *chsd ldr tl hrd rdn and wknd 2f out* **20/1**

1230 **9** 1 ¼ **Ubiquitous**[12] 5654 5-9-1 **54**........(t) SimonPearce(5) 1 41
(S Dow) *towards rr: hdwy on ins 5f out: hrd rdn and wknd over 1f out* **14/1**

2m 37.09s (4.39) **Going Correction** +0.20s/f (Good)
WFA 3 from 4yo+ 9lb **9** Ran SP% **113.4**
Speed ratings (Par 101): **93,92,92,91,91 87,86,84,84**
toteswingers:1&2:£1.70, 2&3:£2.90, 1&3:£5.10 CSF £17.97 CT £56.89 TOTE £5.70: £1.10, £1.20, £1.40; EX 21.30 Trifecta £35.60 Pool: £184.51 - 3.83 winning units..
Owner A G Newcombe **Bred** Michael Ng **Trained** Yarnscombe, Devon
■ Stewards' Enquiry : Fergus Sweeney caution; excessive use of whip

FOCUS
A low-grade handicap, run at an average pace and in a similar time to division II. The form is taken at face value.

6022 HOLD YOUR WEDDING AT BRIGHTON RACECOURSE H'CAP (DIV II) 1m 3f 196y
4:00 (4:00) (Class 6) (0-60,60) 3-Y-O+ **£1,619** (£481; £240; £120) **Stalls** High

Form RPR
5443 **1** **New Code**[12] 5653 3-9-0 **56**........ NeilCallan 2 66
(W R Muir) *chsd ldrs: led wl over 1f out: drvn out* **11/4**[2]
1024 **2** ½ **Mediterranean Sea (IRE)**[15] 5564 4-9-8 **55**........ RyanMoore 1 64+
(J R Jenkins) *hld up in 5th: gng wl whn nt clr run 3f out: plenty of room and hrd rdn 2f out: r.o to press wnr fnl 50yds: a hld* **5/2**[1]
3035 **3** 3 **Filun**[23] 5289 5-8-5 **45**........ RichardRowe(7) 6 49
(A Middleton) *stdd s: t.k.h in rr: hdwy over 2f out: chsd wnr over 1f out tl ins fnl f: hung lft: one pce* **12/1**
55 **4** 2 ¼ **Sanctum**[95] 2902 4-9-2 **52**........ Louis-PhilippeBeuzelin(3) 7 53
(Dr J D Scargill) *sn towards rr: last and struggling 3f out: styd on wl fnl f* **14/1**
0135 **5** 1 **Lady Lam**[35] 4913 4-9-12 **59**........(t) RichardHughes 5 58
(S Kirk) *stdd in rr s: t.k.h in midfield after 3f: hdwy to ld over 2f out: hdd wl over 1f out: sn wknd* **15/2**
035 **6** 1 ½ **Suor Angelica (IRE)**[32] 4991 5-8-9 **45**........ MatthewDavies(3) 8 42
(George Baker) *led 2f: rdn 4f out: btn 2f out* **20/1**
0403 **7** 1 **Barbirolli**[13] 5625 8-8-12 **45**........ ChrisCatlin 3 40
(W B Stone) *bhd: rdn 3f out: n.d* **16/1**
004 **8** hd **Voysey (IRE)**[32] 5001 3-9-4 **60**........(t) JimCrowley 9 55
(Mrs A J Perrett) *led after 2f tl over 2f out: wknd over 1f out* **16/1**
3535 **9** 1 ¾ **Zaif (IRE)**[32] 5011 7-9-2 **54**........(b) SophieDoyle(5) 4 46
(D J S Ffrench Davis) *bhd: hdwy on ins 5f out: wknd over 2f out* **13/2**[3]
0065 **10** 21 **Massachusetts**[8] 4281 3-8-3 **45**........(p) CathyGannon 10 —
(B G Powell) *prom: rdn 4f out: wknd wl over 2f out: bhd and eased over 1f out* **40/1**

2m 37.2s (4.50) **Going Correction** +0.20s/f (Good)
WFA 3 from 4yo+ 9lb **10** Ran SP% **113.7**
Speed ratings (Par 101): **93,92,90,89,88 87,86,86,85,71**
toteswingers:1&2:£2.30, 1&3:£8.30, 2&3:£5.20 CSF £9.73 CT £67.11 TOTE £4.30: £2.10, £1.10, £4.70; EX 10.70 Trifecta £86.40 Pool: £342.16 - 2.93 winning units..
Owner Mrs D Edginton **Bred** Foursome Thoroughbreds **Trained** Lambourn, Berks

FOCUS
The second division of the 1m4f handicap, run in a similar time, and another moderate affair. There were a host of chances, but eventually two came clear. The form is best judged around the front pair.
Massachusetts Official explanation: jockey said gelding hung right

6023 HARDINGS CATERING SERVICES H'CAP 7f 214y
4:30 (4:30) (Class 5) (0-70,70) 3-Y-O+ **£2,331** (£693; £346; £173) **Stalls** Low

Form RPR
4302 **1** **Recalcitrant**[18] 5457 7-8-12 **63**........ SimonPearce(5) 11 72
(S Dow) *chsd ldrs: led 3f out: hld on wl u.p fnl 2f* **8/1**
5120 **2** nk **Bidable**[14] 5584 6-9-7 **67**........ LukeMorris 10 75
(B Palling) *hld up in midfield: hdwy 2f out: drvn to press wnr fnl f: jst hld fnl 50yds* **25/1**
5002 **3** 1 ½ **Ivory Lace**[10] 5713 9-9-8 **68**........ IanMongan 12 73
(S Woodman) *hld up in rr of midfield: rdn over 2f out: hdwy over 1f out: r.o u.p: nrst fin* **16/1**
1122 **4** ½ **Eager To Bow (IRE)**[15] 5555 4-9-6 **66**........ JimCrowley 3 70
(P R Chamings) *hld up in rr: hdwy to chse ldrs 2f out: hrd rdn and nt qckn fnl f* **3/1**[1]
0625 **5** 2 ¾ **Swift Return**[10] 5710 3-8-11 **62**........(b[1]) NeilCallan 8 58
(S C Williams) *in tch abt 6th: rdn to chse ldrs 2f out: one pce appr fnl f* **5/1**[3]
416 **6** nk **Croeso Cusan**[32] 4988 5-9-1 **66**........ SophieDoyle(5) 13 63
(J L Spearing) *stdd s: hld up in rr: hrd rdn and hdwy towards stands' rail whn hung lft fr over 1f out: nt rch ldrs* **8/1**
01-5 **7** 1 **Skyflight**[44] 4588 3-9-1 **66**........ CathyGannon 2 59
(Eve Johnson Houghton) *led tl 3f out: wknd wl over 1f out* **25/1**
3000 **8** 1 ¾ **Goodbye Cash (IRE)**[30] 5077 6-8-7 **58**........ KierenFox(5) 6 48
(R J Smith) *chsd ldrs tl hrd rdn and wknd 2f out* **16/1**
0020 **9** 1 **Beck's Bolero (IRE)**[12] 5664 4-9-1 **61**........ FergusSweeney 14 49
(J A Osborne) *pressed ldr: rdn 3f out: sn btn* **50/1**
0624 **10** 13 **Dirakh Shan**[11] 5700 3-9-3 **68**........ J-PGuillambert 1 25
(L M Cumani) *prom tl hrd rdn and wknd 2f out* **14/1**
2204 **11** ¾ **Oh So Spicy**[39] 4760 3-8-11 **62**........ JackMitchell 5 17
(C F Wall) *a in rr gp: no ch fr 2f out: eased 1f out* **12/1**
3404 **12** 4 ½ **Ocean Countess (IRE)**[19] 5415 4-9-3 **68**........ AdamBeschizza(5) 9 14
(Miss J Feilden) *s.s: bhd: styd far side st: hrd rdn and n.d 2f out: eased whn no ch 1f out* **9/2**[2]

1m 37.48s (1.48) **Going Correction** +0.20s/f (Good)
WFA 3 from 4yo+ 5lb **12** Ran SP% **117.8**
Speed ratings (Par 103): **100,99,98,97,94 94,93,91,90,77 77,72**
toteswingers:1&2:£27.90, 1&3:£13.30, 2&3:£24.60 CSF £193.86 CT £3098.38 TOTE £7.30: £1.80, £6.50, £4.40; EX 212.20 TRIFECTA Not won..
Owner T Staplehurst **Bred** T Staplehurst **Trained** Epsom, Surrey

FOCUS
A tight handicap. It was sound run and the form looks straightforward. Improvement for the first two.
Skyflight Official explanation: jockey said filly hung right

6024 BOOK YOUR CHRISTMAS ROYALE PARTY NOW H'CAP 6f 209y
5:00 (5:00) (Class 6) (0-65,64) 3-Y-O+ **£1,942** (£578; £288; £144) **Stalls** Low

Form RPR
0053 **1** **Grand Vizier (IRE)**[15] 5555 6-9-10 **63**........ JackMitchell 11 74
(C F Wall) *rdn along towards rr: gd hdwy to ld 2f out: rdn out* **11/4**[1]
0506 **2** 1 ¼ **Abhainn (IRE)**[30] 5077 4-8-11 **50**........ CathyGannon 12 58
(B Palling) *towards rr: rdn 3f out: styd on wl on stands' rail fr over 1f out: clsng at fin but a hld* **14/1**
0511 **3** nk **Foxtrot Alpha (IRE)**[22] 5326 4-9-8 **61**........ LukeMorris 4 68
(P Winkworth) *prom: drvn to chse wnr 2f out: kpt on same pce* **9/2**[3]
0505 **4** 3 **Whisper Wind**[15] 5555 3-9-3 **60**........(b) PatDobbs 1 57
(G L Moore) *in tch: effrt and hrd rdn 2f out: one pce* **18/1**
0630 **5** nk **Ganache (IRE)**[49] 4428 8-8-11 **50**........ LiamKeniry 8 48
(P R Chamings) *in tch: hrd rdn 2f out: one pce* **25/1**
0000 **6** 1 ¼ **Blue Charm**[2] 5962 6-8-12 **54**........ KellyHarrison(3) 2 49
(I W McInnes) *s.s: bhd: hdwy towards far side 2f out: no further prog over 1f out* **18/1**
4003 **7** ½ **Giulietta Da Vinci**[10] 5712 3-8-12 **60**........ AdamBeschizza(5) 6 52
(S Woodman) *mid-div: effrt and drvn along 2f out: no imp* **20/1**
5043 **8** 1 ½ **Mandhooma**[10] 5714 4-9-5 **58**........ ChrisCatlin 15 48
(P W Hiatt) *bhd: rdn 3f out: nvr rchd ldrs* **16/1**
065 **9** nse **Orangeleg**[30] 5077 4-9-4 **57**........ WilliamCarson 9 46
(S C Williams) *mid-div: rdn 3f out: sn btn* **4/1**[2]
-534 **10** ½ **Gundaroo**[105] 2588 3-9-7 **64**........ RyanMoore 7 50
(J L Dunlop) *t.k.h towards rr: sme hdwy towards far side 2f out: no imp over 1f out: eased whn wl hld ins fnl f* **8/1**
6406 **11** ½ **Joss Stick**[15] 5557 5-8-5 **49** oh4........(t[1]) SimonPearce(5) 10 36
(L A Dace) *led tl 2f out: 8th and wkng whn n.m.r 1f out* **80/1**
30-1 **12** 9 **Stellarina (IRE)**[26] 5214 4-9-10 **63**........ JimCrowley 3 25
(W J Knight) *prom: hrd rdn 2f out: wknd qckly over 1f out* **16/1**
6060 **13** ½ **On The Cusp (IRE)**[12] 5664 3-8-8 **58**........(b[1]) NathanAlison(7) 5 17
(P Butler) *in tch 3f: sn struggling: bhd fnl 2f* **33/1**
4060 **14** 10 **Affordable (IRE)**[5] 5867 3-8-13 **59**........ RobertLButler(3) 14 —
(Miss Sheena West) *prom tl hrd rdn and wknd qckly over 2f out* **50/1**

1m 24.69s (1.59) **Going Correction** +0.20s/f (Good)
WFA 3 from 4yo+ 4lb **14** Ran SP% **119.7**
Speed ratings (Par 101): **98,96,96,92,92 91,90,88,88,88 87,77,76,65**
toteswingers:1&2:£13.90, 1&3:£6.10, 2&3:£10.70 CSF £41.40 CT £177.99 TOTE £3.60: £2.00, £5.70, £1.70; EX 57.60 TRIFECTA Not won..
Owner Hintlesham SP Partners **Bred** Yeomanstown Stud **Trained** Newmarket, Suffolk

FOCUS
Another moderate handicap. The well-handicapped winner is value for further and is getting back to something like his old form.

6025 GEOFF MILLER SPORTING DINNER NOVEMBER 18TH H'CAP 5f 213y
5:30 (5:30) (Class 6) (0-55,55) 3-Y-O+ **£1,942** (£578; £288; £144) **Stalls** Low

Form RPR
3033 **1** **Dreamacha**[12] 5650 3-8-10 **51**........ WilliamCarson 5 64
(S C Williams) *towards rr: hdwy over 2f out: led over 1f out: rdn out* **4/1**[1]
5000 **2** 3 **Come On Buckers (IRE)**[3] 5927 4-8-10 **49**........(b) EddieCreighton 1 52
(E J Creighton) *led tl 2f out: remained prom: one pce fnl f* **25/1**
325 **3** shd **Shakespeare's Son**[14] 5579 5-8-10 **49**........(p) RichardHughes 6 52
(H J Evans) *mid-div: hdwy over 1f out: r.o to dispute 2nd ins fnl f* **9/2**[2]
6220 **4** 1 **Commandingpresence (USA)**[10] 5714 4-9-2 **55**........ NeilChalmers 2 55
(J J Bridger) *in tch on ins rail: effrt and hung rt to stands' side fr 2f out: kpt on* **22/1**
2404 **5** 1 **Albero Di Giuda (IRE)**[3] 5920 5-8-10 **54**........(bt) SophieDoyle(5) 13 51
(F Sheridan) *led after 1f tl over 2f out: wknd fnl f* **5/1**[3]
0500 **6** ½ **Dancing Again**[14] 5580 4-8-2 **46** oh1........ KierenFox(5) 9 41
(E A Wheeler) *prom: led over 2f out tl over 1f out: wknd fnl f* **66/1**
2344 **7** nk **Rosiliant (IRE)**[12] 5650 3-8-13 **54**........(b) AdamKirby 12 48
(C G Cox) *mid-div: hrd rdn over 2f out: styd on same pce* **11/1**
0046 **8** nk **Croeso Ynol**[1] 5990 4-8-3 **47**........ AdamBeschizza(5) 15 40
(H J Evans) *sn rdn along towards rr: sme hdwy and hung lft over 1f out: nvr able to chal* **40/1**
003 **9** ¾ **D'Allziance (IRE)**[31] 5055 4-8-13 **52**........ HayleyTurner 8 43
(Jonjo O'Neill) *s.s: bhd: hrd rdn over 2f out: sme late hdwy* **14/1**
0062 **10** hd **Know No Fear**[3] 5926 5-8-9 **55**........(p) KatiaScallan(7) 4 45
(A J Lidderdale) *in tch: outpcd 1/2-way: sn btn* **9/1**
0-53 **11** nk **Contemplate**[79] 3458 4-8-5 **47**........(b) Louis-PhilippeBeuzelin(3) 3 36
(Dr J D Scargill) *bhd: drvn along over 2f out: n.d* **28/1**
5022 **12** 1 **Avonlini**[14] 5586 4-8-11 **50**........ JackMitchell 7 36
(B P J Baugh) *prom over 3f* **8/1**
0004 **13** 1 ½ **Marjolly (IRE)**[40] 4692 3-8-13 **54**........ TadhgO'Shea 11 35
(J Gallagher) *a bhd* **40/1**
3500 **14** 1 **Mount Acclaim (IRE)**[20] 5379 4-8-12 **51**........ FergusSweeney 10 29
(J A Osborne) *trckd ldrs: rdn over 2f out: sn btn* **50/1**
0106 **15** 2 ¼ **Only A Game (IRE)**[14] 5614 5-9-2 **55**........(vt) JimCrowley 16 26
(I W McInnes) *a bhd* **14/1**
0056 **16** 2 ½ **Super Frank (IRE)**[22] 5327 7-8-13 **52**........(p) J-PGuillambert 14 15
(J Akehurst) *chsd ldrs 3f: sn rdn and lost pl: eased whn no ch fnl f* **14/1**

1m 11.76s (1.56) **Going Correction** +0.20s/f (Good)
WFA 3 from 4yo+ 2lb **16** Ran SP% **124.3**
Speed ratings (Par 101): **97,93,92,91,90 89,89,88,87,87 87,85,83,82,79 76**
toteswingers:1&2:£18.20, 1&3:£3.90, 2&3:£28.80 CSF £113.59 CT £395.14 TOTE £6.20: £1.30, £7.50, £1.10, £5.50; EX 200.60 TRIFECTA Not won. Place 6 £133.70; Place 5 £30.54.
Owner Essex Racing Club (Dreamacha) **Bred** Barry Root **Trained** Newmarket, Suffolk

FOCUS
There was a good pace on in this very moderate handicap and it threw up a clear-cut winner in the unexposed Dreamacha. Limited form.
T/Jkpt: £69,191.50 to a £1 stake. Pool:£146,179.41 - 1.50 winning tickets T/Plt: £79.40 to a £1 stake. Pool:£77,702.09 - 714.36 winning tickets T/Qpdt: £18.50 to a £1 stake. Pool:£6,288.43 - 250.84 winning tickets LM

5732 MUSSELBURGH (R-H)
Monday, September 13

OFFICIAL GOING: Good (good to soft in places; 6.7)
Wind: Light across Weather: Cloudy and showers

6026 TOTEPLACEPOT H'CAP 7f 30y
2:20 (2:20) (Class 6) (0-65,65) 3-Y-O+ **£1,942** (£578; £288; £144) **Stalls** High

Form RPR
0250 **1** **Salerosa (IRE)**[26] 5199 5-9-10 **65**........(p) PaulMulrennan 14 73
(Mrs A Duffield) *trckd ldrs on inner: smooth hdwy to trck ldr 2f out: swtchd lft and rdn over 1f out: led jst ins fnl f: drvn and kpt on wl towards fin* **8/1**
0020 **2** nk **Second Reef**[7] 5820 8-8-3 **51** oh6........ SoniaEaton(7) 6 58
(T A K Cuthbert) *hld up: hdwy over 2f out: rdn over 1f out: styd on wl fnl f: jst hld* **80/1**

4000 **3** ½ **Zabeel Tower**[19] 5406 7-8-12 **53**................................ RoystonFfrench 13 58
(R Allan) *trckd ldrs on inner: hdwy to ld over 3f out: rdn 2f out: drvn and hdd jst ins fnl f: one pce towards fin* **14/1**

6453 **4** ½ **Klynch**[11] 5688 4-9-2 **60**.................................(b) JamesSullivan(3) 8 64
(Mrs R A Carr) *midfield: hdwy to chse ldrs wl over 2f out: rdn 1f out: drvn ent fnl f: kpt on same pce towards fin* **9/1**

4344 **5** ½ **Kings Point (IRE)**[17] 5499 9-9-4 **62**.............................. MichaelGeran(3) 5 65
(D Nicholls) *chsd ldrs: hdwy 3f out: rdn and cl up 2f out: drvn over 1f out: sn wknd* **13/2**[3]

5014 **6** ½ **Cold Quest (USA)**[10] 5732 6-8-9 **55**.................................... BillyCray(5) 2 63+
(Miss L A Perratt) *stdd s: hld up and bhd: hdwy over 2f out: chsd ldrs over 1f out: n.m.r and swtchd rt to inner ins fnl f: styng on and ch whn hmpd last 100yds: nt rcvr* **7/1**

5650 **7** 1 **Shunkawakhan (IRE)**[7] 5821 7-8-10 **51** oh2...................... DavidAllan 1 50+
(Miss L A Perratt) *trckd ldrs whn carried wd home turn: hdwy over 2f out: rdn to chse ldrs wl over 1f out: sn wknd* **18/1**

3251 **8** ½ **Mrs Mogg**[12] 5670 3-9-6 **65**....................................... RichardKingscote 11 60
(Tom Dascombe) *trckd ldrs: hdwy 1/2-way: chsd wnr 3f out: rdn along over 2f out: grad wknd* **11/1**

0520 **9** 1½ **All Moving Parts (USA)**[80] 2633 3-8-13 **58**...............(p) JamesDoyle 12 49
(A J McCabe) *bustled along sn after s: sn keen in midfield: sme hdwy 3f out: rdn over 2f out and sn wknd* **5/1**[2]

1224 **10** ¾ **Luv U Noo**[14] 5598 3-8-13 **63**.. DaleSwift(5) 4 52
(B Ellison) *sn pushed along in midfield: effrt to chse ldrs 3f out: rdn along over 2f out: drvn and edgd rt over 1f out: sn wknd* **4/1**[1]

045 **11** 6 **Charity Fair**[37] 4822 3-7-13 **51** oh6.............................. VictorSantos(7) 9 24
(A Berry) *a in rr* **80/1**

5540 **12** 11 **Mr Lu**[19] 5405 5-9-6 **61**.. JoeFanning 3 —+
(J S Goldie) *cl up on outer: carried wd home turn: sn rdn along and wknd over 2f out* **14/1**

0466 **13** 3 **Going French (IRE)**[26] 5206 3-9-1 **60**........................ GrahamGibbons 7 —
(F J Brennan) *t.k.h: led tl rn wd and hdd home turn: sn rdn along and wknd wl over 2f out* **40/1**

1m 30.6s (1.60) **Going Correction** +0.15s/f (Good)
WFA 3 from 4yo+ 4lb **13** Ran SP% **115.4**
Speed ratings (Par 101): **96,95,95,94,93 93,92,91,89,89 82,69,66**
toteswingers:1&2:£165.60, 1&3:£28.60, 2&3:£118.40 CSF £522.67 CT £8694.00 TOTE £7.60: £3.00, £13.90, £3.50; EX 945.90.
Owner David K Barker & Phil White **Bred** Pedro Rosas **Trained** Constable Burton, N Yorks

FOCUS
Five previous course winners in this 51-65 handicap, made it an interesting contest and very open. It was run at a sound gallop. The runner-up is the doubt over the form.
Cold Quest(USA) Official explanation: jockey said gelding was denied a clear run
Going French(IRE) Official explanation: jockey said gelding hung left entering straight

6027 TURFTV (S) STKS — 7f 30y
2:50 (2:50) (Class 6) 2-Y-O £1,942 (£578; £288; £144) **Stalls** High

Form RPR

222 **1** **Janet's Pearl (IRE)**[11] 5699 2-8-6 71...................... SilvestreDeSousa 12 63+
(Mrs A Duffield) *t.k.h: trckd ldrs on inner: pushed along and sltly outpcd over 3f out: hdwy to chal over 2f out: sn led: rdn and hung rt over 1f out: drvn clr ent fnl f* **4/9**[1]

025 **2** 2 **Baby Driver**[54] 4240 2-8-11 59.. PaulMulrennan 3 60
(J Howard Johnson) *prom: hdwy to chal wl over 2f out: sn ev ch: rdn and chsd wnr wl over 1f out: drvn and kpt on same pce fnl f* **12/1**[3]

0021 **3** hd **Saxonette**[12] 5667 2-8-6 60.. LeeTopliss(5) 4 60
(Miss L A Perratt) *towards rr: hdwy 1/2-way: rdn to chse ldrs over 2f out: drvn wl over 1f out: kpt on same pce fnl f* **7/2**[2]

0 **4** 3¼ **Lough Corrib (USA)**[49] 4437 2-8-11 0.............................. JoeFanning 5 52+
(K A Ryan) *in tch: hdwy to chse ldrs on inner 3f out: rdn along over 2f out: sn drvn and no imp* **25/1**

050 **5** 1¼ **Indian Dip**[14] 5581 2-8-6 50... GrahamGibbons 10 44
(F J Brennan) *led: rdn along 3f out: hdd 2f out: sn drvn and grad wknd* **25/1**

0000 **6** 7 **Kings Arms**[13] 5630 2-8-8 36 ow2...................................... DaleSwift(5) 6 33
(M W Easterby) *in tch: hdwy to chse ldrs 3f out: rdn along wl over 2f out and sn outpcd* **100/1**

0 **7** 4½ **Red Ears**[14] 5602 2-8-11 0.. LNewman 11 20
(D O'Meara) *chsd ldrs: rdn along 3f out: sn wknd* **33/1**

8 3 **Likeable Lad** 2-8-8 0... JamesSullivan(3) 9 12
(Mrs R A Carr) *s.i.s: a in rr* **50/1**

060 **9** 9 **Tom Bowler**[42] 4645 2-8-11 25...............................(v[1]) RoystonFfrench 2 —
(Mrs A Duffield) *s.i.s: a towards rr* **100/1**

0 **10** 5 **Red Snapper (IRE)**[132] 1806 2-8-8 0........................ PatrickDonaghy(3) 1 —
(J R Weymes) *s.i.s and hung lft bnd after 2f: a bhd* **25/1**

1m 30.96s (1.96) **Going Correction** +0.15s/f (Good) **10** Ran SP% **117.6**
Speed ratings (Par 93): **94,91,91,87,86 78,73,69,59,53**
toteswingers:1&2:£2.40, 1&3:£1.20, 2&3:£2.80 CSF £6.83 TOTE £1.60: £1.10, £1.30, £1.60; EX 7.70.There was no bid for winner.
Owner Middleham Park Racing XL **Bred** Roundhill Stud & Gleadhill House Stud Ltd **Trained** Constable Burton, N Yorks

FOCUS
No strength-in-depth to this seller and it proved very difficult to make ground from off the pace. It was run at a sound pace. The form is limited but solid enough for the grade.

NOTEBOOK
Janet's Pearl(IRE), after a string of second places, went one better. Rated 71 she will find life tougher back in nurseries but should remain a very strong force in this grade. (op 8-15 tchd 4-7 in places)
Baby Driver, coming back from a break and well supported, ran well. He is only rated 59, so will find life easier in a small nursery. (op 10-1)
Saxonette was having her first start since being claimed from Mick Channon's yard and ran okay without jumping out as a winner waiting to happen. (op 10-3 tchd 3-1)
Lough Corrib(USA), dropped in grade on only his second start, stayed on well inside the final furlong and a small race can come his way in due course, possibly over a little further. (tchd 33-1)

6028 WEATHERBYS BANK H'CAP — 1m 6f
3:20 (3:20) (Class 5) (0-75,71) 3-Y-O+ £2,914 (£867; £433; £216) **Stalls** High

Form RPR

0110 **1** **Cat O' Nine Tails**[9] 5747 3-9-6 **71**.. JoeFanning 4 82+
(M Johnston) *trckd ldrs: hdwy to trck ldr 6f out: chal over 2f out: rdn to ld 1 1/2f out: clr ins fnl f: styd on* **5/2**[1]

0534 **2** 2½ **Red Kestrel (USA)**[15] 5549 5-9-5 **66**.................................... JulieBurke(7) 7 71
(K A Ryan) *led: pushed along and hdd over 5f out: rdn along and sltly outpcd over 2f out: drvn and rallied ins fnl f: styd on to take 2nd on line* **7/1**[3]

52-0 **3** shd **Sonara (IRE)**[115] 2295 6-10-0 **68**.................................... PaulMulrennan 1 73
(J Howard Johnson) *trckd ldr: led over 5f out: rdn along and jnd over 2f out: drvn and hdd 1 1/2f out: one pce ins fnl f: lost 2nd on line* **33/1**

2233 **4** 9 **Park's Prodigy**[22] 5333 6-9-11 **65**............................ SilvestreDeSousa 3 57
(G A Harker) *hld up in tch: hdwy to chse ldng pair over 3f out: rdn over 2f out: drvn wl over 1f out and sn wknd* **6/1**[2]

040 **5** 1¾ **Corky Dancer**[29] 5122 5-9-0 **59**... DaleSwift(5) 8 49
(P Monteith) *chsd ldrs: pushed along and lost pl 1/2-way: bhd fnl 3f* **10/1**

6222 **6** hd **Zefooha (FR)**[11] 5687 6-9-7 **61**..................................(p) GrahamGibbons 6 51
(T D Walford) *trckd ldrs on inner: pushed along over 5f out: rdn over 3f out and sn wknd* **5/2**[1]

513- **7** 3 **Toshi (USA)**[367] 4462 8-8-13 **56**....................................... GaryBartley(3) 5 41
(J S Goldie) *hld up in rr: hdwy 5f out: pushed along and in tch 3f out: rdn over 2f out and sn btn* **15/2**

310- **8** 30 **Proficiency**[113] 4498 5-9-4 **58**...................................(v) RoystonFfrench 2 —
(Mrs S C Bradburne) *a in rr: outpcd and bhd fnl 4f* **28/1**

3m 4.63s (-0.67) **Going Correction** +0.15s/f (Good)
WFA 3 from 5yo+ 11lb **8** Ran SP% **111.2**
Speed ratings (Par 103): **107,105,105,100,99 99,97,80**
toteswingers:1&2:£6.50, 1&3:£5.60, 2&3:£17.00 CSF £19.76 CT £435.58 TOTE £4.60: £2.00, £3.50, £6.10; EX 25.70.
Owner S And D Richards, N Browne And M Broke **Bred** The Duke Of Devonshire & Floors Farming **Trained** Middleham Moor, N Yorks
■ Stewards' Enquiry : Paul Mulrennan one day ban; careless riding (28th Sept)

FOCUS
A staying handicap for horses rated 56-75, but the top weight was 7lb below the ceiling rating. It was run at an even pace. The winner continues on the upgrade.

6029 SUBSCRIBE ONLINE AT RACINGUK.COM CLAIMING STKS — 1m 1f
3:50 (3:51) (Class 6) 3-Y-O+ £1,942 (£578; £288; £144) **Stalls** High

Form RPR

1132 **1** **Fremen (USA)**[15] 5545 10-9-3 85................................ MichaelGeran(3) 6 75
(D Nicholls) *trckd ldrs: hdwy 3f out: rdn to ld wl over 1f out: sn edgd lft and kpt on fnl f* **7/4**[1]

5003 **2** 1½ **King Of The Moors (USA)**[18] 5436 7-8-13 64..(b) AndrewHeffernan(3) 2 68
(R C Guest) *trckd ldrs: hdwy over 3f out: rdn and carried hd high over 2f out: sn ev ch tl drvn and one pce fnl f* **13/2**

3150 **3** hd **Baltimore Jack (IRE)**[23] 4522 6-9-2 71..................(p) GrahamGibbons 1 68
(T D Walford) *sn led: rdn along over 2f out: drvn and hdd wl over 1f out: kpt on u.p fnl f* **11/2**[3]

0054 **4** ¾ **Lakeman (IRE)**[7] 5819 4-8-9 59.....................................(b) DaleSwift(5) 3 64
(B Ellison) *trckd ldrs on outer: hdwy 3f out: rdn over 2f out: drvn over 1f out: kpt on same pce fnl f* **18/1**

6200 **5** ½ **Finsbury**[10] 5737 7-9-0 63.. LNewman 5 63
(Miss L A Perratt) *towards rr: hdwy over 2f out: rdn wl over 1f out: styd on ins fnl f: nrst fin* **14/1**

2346 **6** 3¾ **Bolodenka (IRE)**[14] 5596 8-8-13 74...........................(p) LeeTopliss(5) 12 59+
(R A Fahey) *s.i.s and bhd: rdn along and hdwy over 2f out: drvn over 1f out: kpt on ins fnl f: nt rch ldrs* **11/4**[2]

200 **7** 1½ **Catcher Of Dreams (IRE)**[40] 4707 4-8-11 48........... JamesSullivan(3) 4 52
(A G Foster) *prom on inner: rdn along over 3f out: drvn over 2f out and grad wknd* **100/1**

0-00 **8** 7 **Captain Peachey**[10] 5732 4-9-1 43......................... PatrickDonaghy(3) 10 41
(P Monteith) *a towards rr* **150/1**

1-55 **9** 4 **Intersky Charm (USA)**[157] 1199 6-9-2 65...............(t) RoystonFfrench 7 31
(Mrs S C Bradburne) *in tch: rdn along 4f out: sn outpcd* **100/1**

0000 **10** 1¾ **Power Desert (IRE)**[11] 5681 5-8-11 42..............(p) SilvestreDeSousa 11 22
(G A Harker) *a towards rr: rdn along 1/2-way: sn outpcd and bhd fnl 2f* **16/1**

11 23 **Murphys Future**[18] 5-8-8 0.. MarkCoumbe(5) 8 —
(A Berry) *s.i.s: a bhd* **200/1**

0-50 **12** 15 **Newtons Cradle (IRE)**[89] 3073 3-8-10 56........................ PaulMulrennan 9 —
(J Howard Johnson) *midfield: rdn along over 3f out: sn lost pl and bhd: eased fnl 2f* **100/1**

1m 54.27s (0.37) **Going Correction** +0.15s/f (Good)
WFA 3 from 4yo+ 6lb **12** Ran SP% **113.7**
Speed ratings (Par 101): **104,102,102,101,101 98,96,90,86,85 64,51**
toteswingers:1&2:£3.50, 1&3:£3.70, 2&3:£5.50 CSF £13.33 TOTE £2.30: £1.10, £3.70, £1.30; EX 13.10.
Owner Middleham Park Racing XXXV C King A Seed **Bred** Flaxman Holdings Ltd **Trained** Sessay, N Yorks

FOCUS
Very few could get competitive in this fair claimer. It was a bit muddling and the form horses were not at their best.
Newtons Cradle(IRE) Official explanation: jockey said gelding lost his action

6030 WEATHERBYS BLOODSTOCK INSURANCE NURSERY — 5f
4:20 (4:20) (Class 3) (0-90,84) 2-Y-O £5,677 (£1,699; £849; £424; £211) **Stalls** Low

Form RPR

2213 **1** **Earl Wild (IRE)**[38] 4797 2-9-2 **79**.................................... PaulMulrennan 9 83
(J Howard Johnson) *a.p: effrt and cl up 2f out: rdn to ld wl over 1f out: drvn and hdd ins fnl f: rallied wl to ld last 50yds* **5/1**[2]

610 **2** nk **Coconut Ice**[58] 4124 2-8-7 **70**.................................. RichardKingscote 6 73
(Tom Dascombe) *chsd ldrs: swtchd rt and hdwy over 1f out: rdn to ld ins fnl f: sn drvn: hdd and no ex last 50yds* **22/1**

5326 **3** 1¼ **Lady Kildare (IRE)**[35] 4896 2-8-4 **70**........................ PatrickDonaghy(3) 5 68
(Jedd O'Keeffe) *in tch: hdwy to chse ldrs 2f out: rdn over 1f out: drvn ins fnl f and kpt on wl towards fin* **28/1**

2441 **4** hd **Boundaries**[10] 5733 2-9-1 **78**..(v[1]) DavidAllan 1 76
(T D Easterby) *chsd ldrs: hdwy wl over 1f out: drvn ins fnl f: kpt on towards fin* **13/2**

5215 **5** hd **Crimson Knot (IRE)**[13] 5639 2-8-8 **76**.......................... MarkCoumbe(5) 4 73
(A Berry) *trckd ldrs: hdwy wl over 1f out and sn rdn: drvn and one pce ins fnl f* **11/1**

064 **6** ½ **Rothesay Chancer**[25] 5239 2-8-2 **65**.................................... JoeFanning 2 60
(J S Goldie) *towards rr: swtchd rt and hdwy over 1f out: sn rdn and kpt on ins fnl f: nrst fin* **20/1**

1332 **7** ¾ **Orchid Street (USA)**[31] 5021 2-9-2 **79**............................ RoystonFfrench 7 71
(Mrs A Duffield) *towards rr: hdwy on wd outside wl over 1f out: rdn to chse ldrs ent fnl f: sn drvn and no imp* **11/2**[3]

2214 **8** 2 **Major Muscari (IRE)**[23] 5295 2-9-7 **84**.................................. JamesDoyle 8 69
(A J McCabe) *qckly away and sn swtchd to stands' rail: led for 1 1/2f: cl up tl rdn wl over 1f out and grad wknd* **8/1**

3031 **9** ½ **Abzolutely (IRE)**[13] 5640 2-8-7 **70**.............................. SilvestreDeSousa 10 53
(D O'Meara) *wnt rt s: sn prom: led after 1 1/2f: rdn 2f out and sn hdd: drvn and wknd appr fnl f* **7/2**[1]

0410 **10** 2 ½ **Thirteen Shivers**[27] 5187 2-8-8 **74** .... JamesSullivan(3) 3 51
(M W Easterby) *a in rr* **11/2**[3]

61.21 secs (0.81) **Going Correction** +0.15s/f (Good) **10** Ran SP% **115.0**
Speed ratings (Par 99): **99,98,96,96,95 95,93,90,89,85**
toteswingers:1&2:£18.70, 1&3:£27.80, 2&3:£34.70 CSF £109.55 CT £2761.66 TOTE £6.50: £3.50, £6.50, £5.80; EX 128.40.
Owner J Howard Johnson & Exors of W M G Black **Bred** Tally-Ho Stud **Trained** Billy Row, Co Durham
■ Stewards' Enquiry : James Doyle five day ban; careless riding (27th Sept - 4th Oct)

FOCUS
A nursery for horses rated 0-90 and, although the top weight was 6lb below the ceiling rating, it was run at a furious pace and had a competitive look to it. Once again it paid to race up with the pace. The form is straightforward.

NOTEBOOK
Earl Wild(IRE), having only his fifth career start and coming back from a break, benefited from a positive ride and showed a good attitude close home. He doesn't lack for size and can go on from this.
Coconut Ice, who is all speed, put up a much better effort. (op 20-1)
Lady Kildare(IRE) ran bang up to form on her first start in over a month and she can lose her maiden tag shortly. (op 40-1)
Boundaries stayed on well and, back up to 6f, can win again. (op 6-1)
Orchid Street(USA) was always forced to race wide which didn't help her cause. (op 6-1 tchd 13-2)
Abzolutely(IRE) showed plenty of early speed before hanging to the right and weakening. Official explanation: jockey said saddle slipped (op 9-2)
Thirteen Shivers was always outpaced and never got competitive. (tchd 5-1)

6031 WATCH RACING UK ONLINE AT RACINGUK.COM H'CAP 5f
4:50 (4:51) (Class 5) (0-70,69) 3-Y-O+ **£2,590** (£770; £385; £192) **Stalls** Low

Form RPR
4434 **1** **Sandwith**[25] 5240 7-8-7 **55** ....(v) GaryBartley(3) 4 68
(A G Foster) *hld up: smooth hdwy 2f out: rdn to ld ent fnl f: kpt on strly* **7/1**[3]

0230 **2** 2 ¼ **Highland Warrior**[16] 5528 11-9-3 **65** .... PaulPickard(3) 9 70
(P T Midgley) *dwlt and sltly hmpd s: sn rdn along and bhd: swtchd rt and gd hdwy on outer wl over 1f out: styd on ins fnl f: nrst fin* **14/1**

2600 **3** nk **We'll Deal Again**[40] 4714 3-9-2 **62** .... GrahamGibbons 12 66
(M W Easterby) *trckd ldrs: hdwy on outer 2f out: rdn to chal ent fnl f: sn drvn and one pce* **25/1**

0211 **4** ¾ **Cayman Fox**[14] 5599 5-9-10 **69** .... DavidAllan 2 70+
(Miss L A Perratt) *dwlt: hld up towards rr: hdwy and nt clr run over 1f out: rdn and styd on ins fnl f: nrst fin* **13/8**[1]

4263 **5** nk **Secret Venue**[17] 5502 4-9-7 **66** ....(v) PaulMulrennan 11 66
(Jedd O'Keeffe) *sn led: rdn along wl over 1f out: drvn and hdd ent fnl f: sn wknd* **14/1**

0000 **6** nk **Argentine (IRE)**[3] 5920 6-9-4 **68** ....(b) LeeTopliss(5) 10 67
(J A McShane) *hmpd s and towards rr: hdwy over 2f out: rdn over 1f out: kpt on ins fnl f: nrst fin* **25/1**

5500 **7** 1 ¾ **Tamarind Hill (IRE)**[9] 5764 3-9-0 **60** ....(b) JamesDoyle 6 53
(A J McCabe) *trckd ldrs: swtchd lft and hdwy wl over 1f out: rdn ent fnl f and sn btn* **33/1**

3540 **8** nk **Wicked Wilma (IRE)**[16] 5513 6-8-13 **65** .... VictorSantos(7) 8 57
(A Berry) *wnt rt s: trckd ldrs: hdwy and cl up 1/2-way: rdn over 1f out: grad wknd* **14/1**

4600 **9** 1 ¼ **Mandurah (IRE)**[38] 4798 6-9-7 **69** .... JamesSullivan(3) 7 56
(Mrs R A Carr) *a towards rr* **20/1**

0030 **10** nk **Spirit Of Coniston**[14] 5599 7-8-8 **53** .... RoystonFfrench 1 39
(P T Midgley) *chsd ldrs: rdn along wl over 1f out and sn btn* **22/1**

14 **11** 1 **Lees Anthem**[15] 5548 3-8-13 **64** .... DaleSwift(5) 3 47
(C J Teague) *prom: rdn along 2f out: sn drvn and wknd* **7/1**[3]

1051 **12** 25 **Arriva La Diva**[10] 5735 4-9-6 **65** .... LNewman 5 —
(Miss L A Perratt) *prom: rdn along 2f out: sn wknd: bhd and eased ins fnl f* **6/1**[2]

60.95 secs (0.55) **Going Correction** +0.15s/f (Good)
WFA 3 from 4yo+ 1lb **12** Ran SP% **117.1**
Speed ratings (Par 103): **101,97,96,95,95 94,91,91,89,89 87,47**
toteswingers:1&2:£10.60, 1&3:£24.30, 2&3:£39.20 CSF £90.17 CT £2333.73 TOTE £7.90: £2.30, £5.40, £10.00; EX 62.00.
Owner ownaracehorse.co.uk (Foster) **Bred** R R Whitton **Trained** Haddington, East Lothian

FOCUS
A run-of-the-mill 51-70 sprint handicap run at a furious pace. The winner ran his best race this year, with the next two matching their recent best.
Cayman Fox Official explanation: jockey said mare missed the break
Secret Venue Official explanation: jockey said gelding hung left
Arriva La Diva Official explanation: jockey said filly bled from the nose

6032 SCOTTISH RACING YOUR BETTER BET H'CAP (DIV I) 1m 4f 100y
5:20 (5:20) (Class 6) (0-65,64) 3-Y-O+ **£1,619** (£481; £240; £120) **Stalls** High

Form RPR
0604 **1** **Oddsmaker (IRE)**[22] 5336 9-9-3 **58** ....(t) AndrewHeffernan(3) 11 67
(M A Barnes) *mde all: rdn over 2f out: edgd lft over 1f out: drvn and edgd rt appr fnl f: kpt on gamely* **11/4**[1]

6600 **2** 2 ¼ **Hong Kong Island (IRE)**[19] 5411 3-8-10 **57** .... PaulMulrennan 1 62
(N G Richards) *in tch: hdwy 3f out: rdn 2f out: kpt on u.p fnl f to take 2nd nr fin* **15/2**

0500 **3** nk **Edas**[16] 5530 8-9-12 **64** .... JoeFanning 5 69
(T A K Cuthbert) *trckd ldrs: hdwy over 3f out: rdn to chse wnr over 2f out: drvn and ch on inner whn n.m.r 1f out: one pce and lost 2nd nr fin* **17/2**

50-0 **4** 6 **Whaston (IRE)**[18] 5439 5-8-8 **51** .... DaleSwift(5) 3 46
(Miss P Robson) *trckd ldrs: hdwy over 3f out: rdn along wl over 2f out: sn one pce* **6/1**

050 **5** 3 **Tifoso (FR)**[30] 4582 5-8-12 **50** oh5 ....(v) GrahamGibbons 2 41
(R C Guest) *midfield: hdwy over 3f out: sn rdn and n.d* **14/1**

3111 **6** 5 **Eijaaz (IRE)**[41] 4673 9-9-11 **63** ....(p) SilvestreDeSousa 9 46
(G A Harker) *hld up towards rr: effrt and hdwy 3f out: rdn over 2f out: sn drvn and n.d* **9/2**[2]

0434 **7** 3 ½ **Roman History (IRE)**[20] 5216 7-8-12 **50** oh5 ....(p) DavidAllan 8 27
(Miss Tracy Waggott) *a towards rr* **10/1**

1062 **8** 11 **Balwearie (IRE)**[22] 5336 9-9-2 **54** .... LNewman 10 13
(Miss L A Perratt) *chsd wnr: rdn along over 3f out: drvn and wknd over 2f out* **5/1**[3]

-000 **9** 2 **Top Jaro (FR)**[35] 4897 7-8-9 **50** oh5 .... JamesSullivan(3) 4 6
(Mrs R A Carr) *chsd ldng pair: rdn along over 3f out: sn wknd* **66/1**

40-6 **10** 3 ½ **Safin (GER)**[102] 2672 10-9-3 **55** ....(t) RoystonFfrench 6 6
(Mrs S C Bradburne) *a in rr* **66/1**

0560 **11** ½ **Quitao (GER)**[18] 5437 3-8-3 **53** oh5 ow3 .... PatrickDonaghy(3) 7 3
(P Monteith) *a towards rr* **100/1**

2m 43.32s (1.32) **Going Correction** +0.15s/f (Good)
WFA 3 from 5yo+ 9lb **11** Ran SP% **117.8**
Speed ratings (Par 101): **101,99,99,95,93 89,87,80,78,76 76**
toteswingers:1&2:£7.20, 1&3:£7.90, 2&3:£10.90 CSF £24.15 CT £157.78 TOTE £4.20: £1.10, £5.10, £4.50; EX 25.20.
Owner D Maloney **Bred** Margaret Conlon **Trained** Farlam, Cumbria

FOCUS
Not for the first time this afternoon, course form stood up again. The well handicapped winner did not need to match this year's form.
Eijaaz(IRE) Official explanation: jockey said gelding lost his action inside the final furlong

6033 SCOTTISH RACING YOUR BETTER BET H'CAP (DIV II) 1m 4f 100y
5:50 (5:50) (Class 6) (0-65,64) 3-Y-O+ **£1,619** (£481; £240; £120) **Stalls** High

Form RPR
6-04 **1** **Lady Bluesky**[18] 5437 7-9-2 **53** .... PaulMulrennan 8 66
(A C Whillans) *trckd ldrs on inner: hdwy to ld 3f out: rdn over 2f out: drvn clr ent fnl f: kpt on strly* **7/4**[1]

2404 **2** 3 **Tilos Gem (IRE)**[21] 5364 4-9-7 **58** .... JoeFanning 5 66
(M Johnston) *a.p: effrt to chse wnr wl over 2f out: drvn over 1f out: edgd rt and no imp fnl f* **4/1**[2]

430 **3** 7 **La Bacouetteuse (FR)**[23] 5303 5-9-12 **63** .... LNewman 7 60
(A G Foster) *hld up in tch: hdwy on inner 3f out: rdn 2f out: kpt on u.p fnl f: n.d* **10/1**

0005 **4** 1 **Carnac (IRE)**[9] 5770 4-9-4 **55** ....(b) JamesDoyle 2 50
(A J McCabe) *prom: swtchd wd and cl up after 4f: rdn 3f out: drvn and one pce fnl 2f* **5/1**[3]

000 **5** 1 **Sri Kuantan (IRE)**[18] 5437 6-8-9 **49** oh4 ....(t) AndrewHeffernan(3) 3 43
(R C Guest) *led: rdn along over 4f out: hdd 3f out and grad wknd* **20/1**

0/0 **6** 2 ¼ **Tiger King (GER)**[6] 2859 9-8-9 **49** .... PatrickDonaghy(3) 9 39
(P Monteith) *bhd: sme hdwy over 2f out: sn rdn along and n.d* **28/1**

4335 **7** ¾ **Maid Of Meft**[18] 5437 3-9-4 **64** .... DavidAllan 6 53
(Miss L A Perratt) *trckd ldrs: rdn along 4f out: wknd 3f out* **6/1**

4330 **8** 1 ¾ **Dimashq**[21] 5364 8-8-12 **49** oh4 .... RoystonFfrench 1 35
(P T Midgley) *trckd ldrs: pushed along over 3f out: rdn wl over 2f out and sn wknd* **22/1**

9 9 **Balance On Time (IRE)**[293] 5820 4-8-7 **49** oh2 .... LeeTopliss(5) 4 21
(Miss L A Perratt) *hld up towards rr: hdwy and in tch over 3f out: rdn along wl over 2f out and sn wknd* **50/1**

0450 **10** 1 ¼ **Roydmore**[33] 4946 3-8-0 **49** oh2 .... JamesSullivan(3) 10 19
(R A Fahey) *a bhd* **20/1**

2m 44.52s (2.52) **Going Correction** +0.15s/f (Good)
WFA 3 from 4yo+ 9lb **10** Ran SP% **115.7**
Speed ratings (Par 101): **97,95,90,89,89 87,87,85,79,79**
toteswingers:1&2:£3.10, 1&3:£5.80, 2&3:£6.10. totesuper7: WIN: Not won. PLACE: £667.10. CSF £7.74 CT £53.17 TOTE £2.70: £1.90, £1.30, £1.60; EX 10.70 Place 6 £655.21; Place 5 £77.78.
Owner Mrs S Harrow Mrs L M Whillans **Bred** C E Whiteley **Trained** Newmill-On-Slitrig, Borders

FOCUS
Division two of the 51-65 handicap didn't look as strong as the first and was run in a slower time. It was run at an even pace and the first two pulled well clear. The winner translated her good bumper form to the Flat.
T/Plt: £683.00 to a £1 stake. Pool:£60,395.22 - 64.55 winning tickets T/Qpdt: £70.90 to a £1 stake. Pool:£6,057.75 - 63.16 winning tickets JR

5681 REDCAR (L-H)
Monday, September 13

OFFICIAL GOING: Good to firm (firm in places) changing to good after race 2 (2:40) changing to good to soft after race 4 (3:40)
Wind: Fairly strong, behind Weather: Wet and windy

6034 EUROPEAN BREEDERS' FUND MAIDEN FILLIES' STKS 6f
2:10 (2:12) (Class 5) 2-Y-O **£2,978** (£886; £442; £221) **Stalls** High

Form RPR
2 **1** **Nawaashi**[96] 2855 2-9-0 0 .... RichardHills 1 75+
(M Johnston) *dwlt: sn rcvrd to r promly: rdn to ld wl over 1f out: hdd narrowly ins fnl f: rallied u.p to ld again post* **1/1**[1]

5 **2** shd **Mon Visage**[63] 3961 2-9-0 0 .... WilliamBuick 8 74
(C F Wall) *trckd ldrs: rdn over 1f out: drvn to ld ins fnl f: kpt on but ct post* **3/1**[2]

3 hd **Lady Paris (IRE)** 2-9-0 0 .... TomEaves 7 74+
(B Smart) *trckd ldrs: rdn over 2f out: kpt on wl ins fnl f* **25/1**

4 **4** 2 ¼ **Jade**[23] 5298 2-9-0 0 .... TomQueally 9 67
(Ollie Pears) *chsd ldrs: rdn over 2f out: kpt on one pce* **4/1**[3]

5 2 ¾ **Simayill** 2-9-0 0 .... SteveDrowne 2 59
(C E Brittain) *green: hld up: chsd along over 3f out: kpt on wl ins fnl f: nrst fin* **22/1**

6 nk **Strictly Pink (IRE)** 2-9-0 0 .... SamHitchcott 4 58
(A Bailey) *prom: rdn and stl ev ch over 1f out: no ex ins fnl f* **50/1**

0003 **7** 1 ¼ **Ever Roses**[17] 5483 2-9-0 50 .... MickyFenton 10 54
(P T Midgley) *midfield: rdn over 2f out: sn no imp* **50/1**

054 **8** nse **Royal Hush**[36] 4862 2-9-0 74 .... FrannyNorton 5 54
(K A Ryan) *midfield: chsd along 1/2-way: nvr on terms* **10/1**

00 **9** shd **Ice Girl**[8] 5785 2-9-0 0 .... LeeVickers 3 54
(M W Easterby) *led: rdn whn hdd wl over 1f out: grad wknd* **50/1**

0223 **10** 1 ½ **Indian Giver**[14] 5595 2-9-0 64 .... PatrickMathers 11 49
(H A McWilliams) *dwlt: a towards rr* **33/1**

0 **11** 21 **Tea And Sympathy**[19] 5418 2-9-0 0 .... NickyMackay 6 —
(J R Holt) *hld up: a bhd: eased ins fnl f* **50/1**

1m 11.9s (0.10) **Going Correction** -0.275s/f (Firm) **11** Ran SP% **123.1**
Speed ratings (Par 92): **88,87,87,84,80 80,78,78,78,76 48**
toteswingers:1&2:£1.60, 1&3:£7.60, 2&3:£17.00 CSF £4.05 TOTE £1.90: £1.20, £1.80, £6.90; EX 4.80.
Owner Hamdan Al Maktoum **Bred** Shadwell Estate Company Limited **Trained** Middleham Moor, N Yorks

FOCUS
A dry night saw the ground change to good to firm, firm in places, but after prolonged rainfall before the first race, the riders reported the ground to be a fair bit easier (one even describing it as "soft") than the official. A fairly strong tailwind enabled the runners to register a time nearly 1.5secs above RP standard. The gallop was no more than reasonable. Limited form with the winner only needing to reproduce her debut effort.

NOTEBOOK
Nawaashi, who finished third to subsequent Group 3 Princess Margaret winner Soraaya on her debut in June, hadn't been seen since but attracted plenty of support and showed a good attitude to get off the mark. She should prove equally effective over 7f, is open to further improvement and, although this bare form is nothing special, she may do better in nurseries. (op 5-4 tchd 10-11)
Mon Visage had shaped well on her debut in a race that threw up several winners and she duly bettered that effort. She too should prove equally effective over 7f and is more than capable of picking up a run-of the-mill-maiden. (op 5-2 tchd 7-2)
Lady Paris(IRE) ◆ was easy in the market on this racecourse debut, but shaped pleasingly against a couple of rivals that had previously showed ability. She should have no problems with an extra furlong, is entitled to improve for this experience and is sure to win an ordinary event. (op 20-1)
Jade, a half-sister to a triple 1m2f winner, again showed promise. Although likely to remain vulnerable to the better types in this grade, she'll be one to keep an eye on granted a stiffer test when qualified for a handicap mark.
Simayill was allowed to start at a big price on this racecourse debut but she hinted at ability without being unduly knocked about. 7f or 1m will see her in a better light in due course and she too should fare best once qualified for a mark. (tchd 25-1)
Strictly Pink(IRE) wasn't disgraced on her racecourse debut and is entitled to improve for the experience. Ordinary nurseries will be the way forward with her in due course.
Ice Girl showed up well for a long way and will be one to keep an eye on in very ordinary nursery company.

6035 WEDDING RECEPTIONS @ REDCAR RACECOURSE NURSERY 5f
2:40 (2:42) (Class 6) (0-65,65) 2-Y-O £1,619 (£481; £240; £120) Stalls High

Form RPR
544 1 **Empress Royal**[58] 4149 2-9-2 60 PhillipMakin 4 66
(M Dods) *cl up: rdn to ld over 1f out: drvn ins fnl f: all out* 6/1[3]
5255 2 shd **Wild Hysteria (IRE)**[17] 5483 2-8-12 56 MickyFenton 2 62
(T P Tate) *in tch: rdn wl over 2f out: hdwy over 1f out: drvn and kpt on wl ins fnl f: jst failed* 9/1
6006 3 nse **Miss Toldyaso (IRE)**[19] 5412 2-8-1 45 NickyMackay 6 50
(M G Quinlan) *chsd ldrs: rdn over 2f out: drvn and kpt on wl ins fnl f* 22/1
5163 4 1 ½ **Nellie Ellis (IRE)**[15] 5547 2-9-3 64 AmyRyan(3) 8 64
(K A Ryan) *led: rdn whn hdd over 1f out: remained w ev ch tl no ex fnl 100yds* 17/2
0604 5 7 **Key To The Motion (IRE)**[31] 5042 2-8-6 50 ow1 PJMcDonald 3 25
(P T Midgley) *slowly away: hld up: rdn over 2f out: kpt on wl ins fnl f: nrst fin* 25/1
0061 6 2 ¾ **Brave Tiger (IRE)**[5] 5862 2-8-4 51 6ex (t) MartinLane(3) 9 16
(S C Williams) *prom: rdn over 2f out: wknd over 1f out* 7/2[1]
055 7 ¾ **Saucy Buck (IRE)**[10] 5725 2-9-7 65 SamHitchcott 11 27
(M R Channon) *sn chsd along towards rr: drvn over 2f out: little imp* 4/1[2]
005 8 nk **Wandering Lad**[16] 5531 2-9-7 65 DavidNolan 7 26
(D Carroll) *chsd ldrs: rdn over 2f out: wknd over 1f out* 10/1
0453 9 ½ **Mini Bon Bon**[5] 5862 2-8-4 55 (v) HobieGill(7) 13 14
(A Bailey) *slowly away: towards rr tl mod late hdwy* 12/1
0002 10 1 ½ **Bonjour Bongee**[12] 5667 2-9-1 59 (b) TomQueally 10 13
(A J McCabe) *hld up: a towards rr* 12/1
3000 11 2 **Shy Bird**[18] 5434 2-8-9 53 FrannyNorton 5 —
(J A Glover) *chsd ldrs: rdn over 2f out: wknd wl over 1f out* 40/1
030 12 1 ¼ **Je Suis Unrockstar**[23] 5298 2-9-2 60 DuranFentiman 15 —
(J A Glover) *prom tl wknd over 1f out* 20/1
500 13 2 ½ **Tancred Spirit**[19] 5418 2-8-12 56 TomEaves 14 —
(P T Midgley) *prom tl wknd over 1f out* 50/1
U335 14 ½ **Novalist**[29] 5117 2-9-2 63 BarryMcHugh(3) 12 —
(R Bastiman) *a towards rr* 12/1

58.09 secs (-0.51) **Going Correction** -0.275s/f (Firm) 14 Ran SP% 126.6
Speed ratings (Par 93): **93,92,92,90,79 74,73,73,72,69 66,64,60,59**
toteswingers:1&2:£9.10, 1&3:£36.90, 2&3:£72.30 CSF £58.65 CT £794.91 TOTE £4.60: £1.50, £1.70, £10.10; EX 73.20.
Owner Dennis Yardy/Eric Birks/Brian Webb **Bred** D A Yardy **Trained** Denton, Co Durham

FOCUS
A modest nursery in which the gallop was sound. The field raced centre to stands' side and the first four pulled clear in a race where those held up were at a disadvantage. Sound form with improved efforts from the first three.

NOTEBOOK
Empress Royal, who showed ability in maidens, including in a race that has worked out really well at Ripon last time, turned in her best effort and showed a good attitude on this nursery debut for a yard that is back amongst the winners. She won't be going up too much for this and may be able to step up again. (op 13-2)
Wild Hysteria(IRE)'s form has a patchy look to it but she put a couple of below-par efforts on easy ground firmly behind her. Her two best pieces of form have been over this C&D, but while worth another try at 6f, her record suggests she wouldn't be one to go in head-down for next time. (op 7-1)
Miss Toldyaso(IRE) hadn't achieved much in four previous starts but turned in a much more encouraging display dropped to 5f. The return to a bit further won't inconvenience and she is capable of picking up a small race if able to build on this. (op 25-1)
Nellie Ellis(IRE) showed plenty of foot back on this flatter track and ran as well as she has done in nursery company. The rain may have blunted her speed and she should be able to win again in low-grade company. (op 8-1 tchd 9-1)
Key To The Motion(IRE) fared best of those to come from the back of the field, but she was beaten a fair way and will have to show a fair bit more before she is a solid betting proposition. (op 22-1)
Brave Tiger(IRE), who showed much-improved form at Kempton last week, looked interesting under his penalty, but failed by a long chalk to reproduce that effort over this straight 5f on rain-soaked ground. He'll be worth another chance back on Polytrack. (op 11-4)
Saucy Buck(IRE) was well supported down in the weights and in grade returned to turf but proved a disappointment. He's better than this but looks fully exposed. Official explanation: jockey said colt was never travelling (op 11-2)

6036 EUROPEAN BREEDERS' FUND - DOUBLE TRIGGER MAIDEN STKS (FOR THE DOUBLE TRIGGER TROPHY) 1m 1f
3:10 (3:10) (Class 5) 2-Y-O £2,978 (£886; £442; £221) Stalls Low

Form RPR
54 1 **Abjer (FR)**[37] 4838 2-9-3 0 TomQueally 8 78
(C E Brittain) *hld up towards inner: swtchd rt over 4f out: gd hdwy to chal 3f out: rdn to ld wl over 1f out: drvn and styd on wl ins fnl f* 7/2[2]
2 2 **Badeel (USA)** 2-9-3 0 FrankieDettori 7 74
(Saeed Bin Suroor) *trckd ldrs: hdwy to ld 3f out: sn rdn: hdd wl over 1f out: remained w ev ch tl no ex ins fnl f* 5/6[1]
4 3 4 ½ **Defence Of Duress (IRE)**[31] 5040 2-9-3 0 MickyFenton 2 65
(T P Tate) *trckd ldrs: rdn wl over 2f out: kpt on one pce* 11/2[3]
4 2 ¼ **Ullswater (IRE)** 2-9-3 0 GregFairley 5 61
(M Johnston) *prom: rdn to ld over 3f out: hdd 3f out: sn one pce* 8/1
4 5 2 ¼ **Mojolika**[17] 5498 2-9-3 0 DavidNolan 4 57
(T D Easterby) *midfield: rdn and outpcd over 3f out: kpt on fr over 1f out* 10/1
00 6 13 **Smart Violetta (IRE)**[9] 5762 2-8-12 0 FrannyNorton 9 25
(Mrs A Duffield) *hld up: a wl bhd* 50/1
00 7 2 ½ **Santorino**[51] 4368 2-9-3 0 PJMcDonald 3 25
(P T Midgley) *led: rdn whn hdd over 3f out: sn wknd* 50/1
8 4 **Xenophon** 2-9-3 0 SteveDrowne 6 17
(G D Blake) *s.i.s: hld up: a towards rr* 50/1
0000 9 10 **Be My Spy**[30] 5066 2-8-7 42 TobyAtkinson(5) 10 —
(P Salmon) *hld up: rdn along over 5f out: a bhd* 66/1
0400 10 2 **Logans Rose**[34] 4935 2-9-3 46 TomEaves 1 —
(A D Brown) *midfield: wknd over 4f out* 66/1

1m 55.5s (2.50) **Going Correction** +0.125s/f (Good) 10 Ran SP% 121.2
Speed ratings (Par 95): **93,91,87,85,83 71,69,65,57,55**
toteswingers:1&2:£1.70, 1&3:£3.10, 2&3:£2.80 CSF £7.02 TOTE £2.70: £1.10, £1.10, £2.30; EX 8.10.
Owner Mohammed Al Shafar **Bred** Malcolm Parrish **Trained** Newmarket, Suffolk

FOCUS
Further rain saw the ground change to "good" before the start of this race. A fair maiden for the track in which the gallop was a reasonable one and the two market leaders had the race to themselves in the last 2f. Straightforward form, rated conservatively around the third.

NOTEBOOK
Abjer(FR), who had shown fair form in two starts on turf and Polytrack, turned in a career-best effort over this longer trip to justify market support, despite edging off a true line under pressure. He should be suited by 1m4f in due course, is open to further improvement and appeals as the type to win more races granted a suitable test. (op 11-2)
Badeel(USA), a well-touted brother to a couple of 7f winners, proved uneasy in the market on this rain-soaked ground just before the off but showed more than enough on this racecourse debut, despite carrying his head a shade high when asked for an effort, to suggest a similar event can be found. He is entitled to improve for this experience and should prove equally effective back over 1m. (op 4-6 tchd 10-11 and evens in a place)
Defence Of Duress(IRE) bettered the form of his racecourse debut over this longer trip. He wasn't knocked about, has a bit of size and scope and will be of more interest in ordinary handicaps over middle distances with another winter on his back. (op 5-1 tchd 4-1)
Ullswater(IRE), from a yard that won this in 2002 and 2003, was fairly easy to back, but was far from disgraced on this racecourse debut. While open to improvement this term, he too should fare a good deal better granted a stiffer test of stamina in ordinary handicaps next season. (op 15-2)
Mojolika again showed ability without being given an unduly hard time. He'll be very well suited by the step up to 1m4f and appeals as the type to win races in due course. (op 9-1)

6037 SUBSCRIBE TO RACING UK (S) STKS 1m 2f
3:40 (3:40) (Class 6) 3-5-Y-O £1,706 (£503; £252) Stalls Low

Form RPR
0000 1 **Princess Aliuska**[16] 5515 5-8-12 42 GregFairley 11 57
(C Smith) *hld up: hdwy over 3f out: drvn to ld wl over 1f out: sn clr* 16/1
0640 2 4 **Melkatant**[36] 4863 4-8-12 43 FrannyNorton 2 49
(N Bycroft) *led: rdn whn hdd wl over 1f out: no ex* 12/1
440 3 4 **Ra Junior (USA)**[25] 5244 4-9-3 67 MickyFenton 14 46
(P T Midgley) *midfield: rdn over 3f out: kpt on to take 3rd ins fnl f: nvr trbld ldrs* 3/1[2]
0160 4 3 **Media Stars**[11] 5681 5-9-3 53 (t) TomEaves 5 40
(R Johnson) *hld up: hdwy to chse ldrs 3f out: sn rdn: wknd ins fnl f* 11/1
360 5 1 ¾ **Applaude**[18] 5436 5-9-8 62 (b) PaulEddery 8 42
(R C Guest) *hld up: hdwy to trck ldrs over 3f out: rdn over 2f out: wknd ins fnl f* 9/4[1]
5064 6 2 ¾ **Mojeerr**[32] 4985 4-9-3 45 (v) TomQueally 7 31
(A J McCabe) *midfield: rdn over 2f out: wknd over 1f out* 9/2[3]
-005 7 1 ¼ **Napoletano (ITY)**[41] 4669 4-9-3 32 DuranFentiman 3 29
(R Johnson) *prom: rdn over 2f out: hung lft and wknd over 1f out* 50/1
5000 8 shd **Karate Queen**[15] 5545 5-8-9 40 BarryMcHugh(3) 1 23
(R E Barr) *trckd ldrs: wknd 3f out* 33/1
0-04 9 27 **Phantom Serenade (IRE)**[36] 4863 5-9-3 54 PhillipMakin 12 —
(M Dods) *trckd ldrs: rdn over 3f out: wknd qckly 2f out: eased* 11/2
50-0 10 12 **Igneous**[7] 5821 4-9-0 45 (b) MichaelStainton(3) 9 —
(D W Thompson) *hld up: bhd fr over 4f out* 33/1

2m 9.70s (2.60) **Going Correction** +0.125s/f (Good) 10 Ran SP% 119.1
Speed ratings (Par 101): **94,90,87,85,83 81,80,80,58,49**
toteswingers:1&2:£14.70, 1&3:£11.80, 2&3:£7.00 CSF £192.85 TOTE £28.20: £6.50, £4.40, £2.10; EX 241.20.There was no bid for the winner.
Owner R M Jeffs & J Potter **Bred** R M Jeffs And J Potter **Trained** Temple Bruer, Lincs

FOCUS
A low-grade seller and one in which several of the market leaders disappointed. The form amounts to little and the gallop was an ordinary one. The winner is rated up 4lb.
Princess Aliuska Official explanation: trainer said regarding apparent improvement in form mare was suited by slower going
Phantom Serenade(IRE) Official explanation: jockey said gelding had no more to give

6038 MARKET CROSS JEWELLERS H'CAP 1m 6f 19y
4:10 (4:11) (Class 5) (0-70,69) 3-Y-O £2,072 (£616; £308; £153) Stalls Low

Form RPR
6166 1 **Dubara Reef (IRE)**[19] 5420 3-8-11 59 (p) SteveDrowne 5 65
(Paul Green) *trckd ldrs: rdn to chal 3f out: led over 1f out: drvn and kpt on wl ins fnl f* 7/1
1454 2 1 ¼ **Light The City (IRE)**[13] 5642 3-8-7 55 TomEaves 6 59
(Mrs R A Carr) *midfield: smooth hdwy to ld 3f out: drvn whn hdd over 1f out: kpt on* 8/1
6634 3 shd **Pobs Trophy**[11] 5687 3-8-2 50 oh5 (p) PaulEddery 4 54
(R C Guest) *s.i.s: hld up: hdwy over 4f out to chse ldrs: rdn over 2f out: ev ch over 1f out: kpt on ins fnl f* 10/1
6346 4 nse **Trojan Gift (USA)**[101] 2704 3-8-7 58 BarryMcHugh(3) 8 62
(Julie Camacho) *trckd ldrs: rdn and lost pl over 5f out: rcvrd to chal 3f out: kpt on* 20/1
2513 5 2 **Dubawi King**[10] 5738 3-8-12 60 (v) FrannyNorton 3 64+
(N Tinkler) *s.i.s: hld up: hdwy to chse ldrs over 3f out: sn rdn: kpt on same pce* 6/1
3520 6 8 **Pena Dorada (IRE)**[16] 5534 3-9-4 66 (p) AndrewElliott 2 56
(Mrs K Burke) *prom: led wl over 3f out: hdd 3f out: wknd over 1f out* 4/1[2]
0556 7 2 ¾ **Nephele (IRE)**[15] 5550 3-8-4 52 DuranFentiman 9 38
(T D Easterby) *s.i.s: hld up: rn wd on bnd over 5f out: nvr on terms* 33/1
0000 8 nk **I Got Music**[105] 2606 3-8-2 50 oh5 AndrewMullen 11 36
(K G Reveley) *hld up: rdn over 4f out: nvr on terms* 50/1
5612 9 5 **Robbie Burnett**[50] 4408 3-9-7 69 PJMcDonald 10 48
(G A Swinbank) *hld up: drvn wl over 3f out: sn no imp* 3/1[1]
3011 10 15 **Cheyenne Chant**[10] 5738 3-8-3 56 (t) JohnFahy(5) 1 14
(D O'Meara) *led: hdd wl over 3f out: sn wknd* 11/2[3]

The Form Book, Raceform Ltd, Compton, RG20 6NL

3240 11 68 **Yankee Bright (USA)**[19] 5420 3-9-7 **69** LeeVickers 7 —
(J G Given) *trckd ldrs: wknd qckly over 4f out* **16/1**
3m 5.85s (1.15) **Going Correction** +0.125s/f (Good) **11** Ran SP% **122.9**
Speed ratings (Par 101): **101,100,100,100,99 94,92,92,89,81 42**
toteswingers:1&2:£9.20, 1&3:£7.80, 2&3:£10.20 CSF £63.72 CT £573.31 TOTE £6.80: £2.10, £3.40, £4.90; EX 86.90.
Owner The Four Aces **Bred** M Duffy **Trained** Lydiate, Merseyside

FOCUS
The ground was changed again to "good-to-soft" before this race. Another modest handicap featuring mainly exposed types. The gallop was fairly sound and the market leader disappointed. The form is best judged around the winner.
Robbie Burnett Official explanation: vet said gelding finished distressed
Cheyenne Chant Official explanation: jockey said filly had a breathing problem

6039 CHRISTMAS PARTIES @ REDCAR RACECOURSE MAIDEN STKS 7f
4:40 (4:43) (Class 5) 3-Y-0+ **£2,072** (£616; £308; £153) **Stalls** High

Form RPR
433 1 **Tariq Too**[56] 4207 3-9-0 71 MartinLane(3) 5 80
(D M Simcock) *trckd ldrs: rdn over 2f out: led wl over 1f out: kpt on wl ins fnl f* **5/2**[2]
63 2 3 ½ **Silvery Moon (IRE)**[96] 2852 3-9-3 0 DuranFentiman 7 71
(T D Easterby) *hld up: rdn over 3f out: hdwy over 2f out: chsd wnr over 1f out: kpt on ins fnl f* **9/2**[3]
2- 3 7 **Tomodachi (IRE)**[328] 6921 3-8-12 0 WilliamBuick 8 47
(M Botti) *sn prom: led over 2f out: drvn whn hdd wl over 1f out: wknd ins fnl f* **5/4**[1]
000 4 1 ¾ **Kookie**[36] 4864 3-8-9 43 BarryMcHugh(3) 1 42
(R E Barr) *w ldr: rdn over 2f out: wknd over 1f out* **50/1**
002 5 6 **Chaqueta**[20] 5395 3-8-12 62 TomEaves 10 26
(C F Wall) *hld up: rdn over 3f out: no imp* **11/2**
6055 6 nse **Kirkby's Gem**[31] 5041 3-8-12 35 AndrewMullen 4 26
(A Berry) *led: hdd over 2f out: sn wknd* **50/1**
5400 7 11 **Briary Mac**[17] 5501 3-8-12 55 FrannyNorton 9 —
(N Bycroft) *w ldr tl wknd qckly 3f out* **25/1**
0 R **No Thank You**[14] 5603 3-9-3 0 PJMcDonald 6 —
(K A Ryan) *veered violently lft s: ref to r* **50/1**
1m 26.31s (1.81) **Going Correction** +0.125s/f (Good) **8** Ran SP% **116.3**
Speed ratings (Par 103): **94,90,82,80,73 73,60,—**
toteswingers:1&2:£2.40, 1&3:£1.70, 2&3:£2.10 CSF £14.04 TOTE £4.40: £1.10, £2.40, £1.10; EX 17.90.
Owner Saleh Al Homaizi & Imad Al Sagar **Bred** D R Botterill **Trained** Newmarket, Suffolk

FOCUS
An uncompetitive maiden which took less winning than seemed likely, with the market leader disappointing and the proximity of the 43-rated fourth holding down the overall form. The winner is the best guide. The gallop was a modest one.

6040 FOLLOW REDCAR RACING ON FACEBOOK APPRENTICE H'CAP 6f
5:10 (5:11) (Class 5) (0-70,70) 3-Y-0+ **£2,072** (£616; £308; £153) **Stalls** High

Form RPR
0260 1 **Ryedane (IRE)**[19] 5424 8-9-7 **69** (b) NeilFarley 4 78
(T D Easterby) *chsd ldrs: rdn over 2f out: kpt on wl ins fnl f: led nr fin* **12/1**
3513 2 nk **Mata Hari Blue**[15] 5557 4-8-11 **62** JamesRogers(3) 6 70
(J R Holt) *hld up: hdwy over 2f out: rdn to ld over 1f out: kpt on ins fnl f: hdd nr fin* **8/1**
0000 3 2 **Earlsmedic**[31] 5048 5-9-5 **67** (v) RyanClark 9 69
(S C Williams) *prom: led over 2f out: rdn whn hdd over 1f out: no ex ins fnl f* **5/2**[1]
0146 4 ¾ **Arch Walker (IRE)**[19] 5422 3-8-7 **64** EleanorMcGowan(7) 5 63
(Jedd O'Keeffe) *chsd ldrs: rdn over 2f out: kpt on* **16/1**
3156 5 nk **Foreign Rhythm (IRE)**[9] 5760 5-8-8 **61** ShaneBKelly(5) 10 59
(R E Barr) *in tch: sn chsd along: kpt on ins fnl f* **14/1**
4150 6 ½ **Sea Salt**[11] 5688 7-9-0 **62** GarryWhillans 8 59
(R E Barr) *prom: rdn over 2f out: no ex ins fnl f* **16/1**
2404 7 ¾ **Bahamian Jazz (IRE)**[26] 5214 3-8-6 **63** JohnLawson(7) 3 57
(R Bastiman) *led: hdd over 2f out: wknd over 1f out* **25/1**
3412 8 1 ½ **Red River Boy**[7] 5817 5-8-7 **55** oh3 RyanPowell 7 44
(C W Fairhurst) *hld up: rdn over 2f out: sn no imp* **9/2**[3]
6160 9 ¾ **Timber Treasure (USA)**[3] 5906 6-8-6 **59** (b) JordanDodd(5) 2 46
(Paul Green) *slowly away: in rr: nvr on terms* **16/1**
1000 10 hd **Hitches Dubai (BRZ)**[29] 5123 5-9-0 **62** DuilioDaSilva 1 48
(G A Harker) *sn chsd along towards rr: nvr threatened* **25/1**
5613 11 8 **Chushka**[19] 5409 3-9-6 **70** (v) AdamCarter 11 31
(B Smart) *prom: rdn over 2f out: wknd over 1f out* **10/3**[2]
2560 12 16 **Just Sam (IRE)**[11] 5684 5-8-12 **65** DavidSimmonson(5) 12 —
(R E Barr) *chsd ldrs: lost pl 1/2-way: sn bhd* **16/1**
1m 12.1s (0.30) **Going Correction** +0.125s/f (Good)
WFA 3 from 4yo+ 2lb **12** Ran SP% **126.5**
Speed ratings (Par 103): **103,102,99,98,98 97,96,94,93,93 82,61**
toteswingers:1&2:£13.70, 1&3:£14.00, 2&3:£8.90 CSF £111.83 CT £328.66 TOTE £18.60: £5.20, £2.90, £2.60; EX 162.50 Place 6 £110.55; Place 5 £80.49.
Owner Ryedale Partners No 5 **Bred** Tally-Ho Stud **Trained** Great Habton, N Yorks

FOCUS
An ordinary handicap and one run at a decent gallop. The winner's best run since he was a 3yo at face value.
Ryedane(IRE) Official explanation: trainer was unable to offer any explanation regarding apparant improvement in form
Chushka Official explanation: jockey said filly was never travelling
T/Plt: £104.70 to a £1 stake. Pool:£54,961.27 - 382.85 winning tickets T/Qpdt: £16.00 to a £1 stake. Pool:£4,182.77 - 193.40 winning tickets AS

6041 - 6043a (Foreign Racing) - See Raceform Interactive

4419 MAISONS-LAFFITTE (R-H)
Monday, September 13

OFFICIAL GOING: Turf: good to soft

6044a PRIX D'ARENBERG (GROUP 3) (2YO) (TURF) 5f 110y
1:40 (12:00) 2-Y-0 **£35,398** (£14,159; £10,619; £7,079; £3,539)

RPR
1 **Broox (IRE)**[22] 5347 2-8-11 0 OlivierPeslier 4 111+
(E J O'Neill, France) *broke smartly: led: shkn up 1 1/2f out: sn clr: easily* **9/10**[1]
2 2 ½ **Chinese Wall (IRE)**[26] 5226 2-8-8 0 ThierryJarnet 8 100
(D Guillemin, France) *bkmarker fr s: gd prog on wd outside 2f out: r.o wl fnl f: no threat to wnr* **3/1**[2]
3 1 ½ **Boccalino (GER)**[26] 5226 2-8-11 0 GeraldMosse 3 98
(H-A Pantall, France) *racd in 4th towards outside fr s: rdn 2f out: r.o wl fnl f* **17/2**
4 2 **Miss Liberty (FR)**[71] 3718 2-8-8 0 MaximeGuyon 5 88
(Mme Pia Brandt, France) *towards rr fr s: proged 1 1/2f out on outside: r.o fnl f* **9/1**
5 2 **Bulliciosa (USA)**[10] 2-8-8 0 FranckBlondel 1 82
(M Pimbonnet, France) *racd in 3rd on stands' rail: rdn 1 1/2f out: no ex fnl f* **29/1**
6 ½ **Lone Cat (FR)**[71] 3718 2-8-8 0 StephanePasquier 6 80
(Y De Nicolay, France) *racd towards rr fr s: u.p 2f out: no ex fnl f: fdd* **15/2**[3]
7 2 **Magic Potion (FR)**[26] 5226 2-8-8 0 Christophe-PatriceLemaire 7 73
(P Bary, France) *racd in 2nd on outside: rdn 1 1/2 out: no ex: sn wknd* **21/1**
63.60 secs (-3.70) **7** Ran SP% **117.8**
WIN (incl. 1 euro stake): 1.90. PLACES: 1.10, 1.30, 1.50. DF: 2.70. SF: 3.80..
Owner G Lucas & Mme H Marsh **Bred** Canary Thoroughbreds **Trained** France

NOTEBOOK
Broox(IRE), fourth in the Prix Morny last time out, was quickly away and proceeded to make every yard, eventually coming home nicely clear. He might run in the Middle Park, but is more likely to be put away for the year, and his trainer sees him as a sprinter for next year.

5741 HAYDOCK (L-H)
Tuesday, September 14

OFFICIAL GOING: Good to soft (heavy in places in home straight on 1m 4f course) changing to soft (heavy in places in home straight on 1m 4f course) after race 1 (2.00)
Inner Sprint track used. Races over 12f around inner part of bend into the outer home straight reducing advertised distances by 52yds.
Wind: fresh 1/2 against Weather: fine

6045 E B F RACING UK £20 PER MONTH MAIDEN STKS 5f
2:00 (2:01) (Class 5) 2-Y-0 **£3,626** (£1,079; £539; £269) **Stalls** Centre

Form RPR
62 1 **Scantily Clad (IRE)**[47] 4517 2-8-12 0 RichardMullen 3 76+
(E S McMahon) *mde all: shkn up over 1f out: styd on wl: pushed out* **8/11**[1]
05 2 2 ¼ **Rowan Spirit (IRE)**[140] 1603 2-9-3 0 GrahamGibbons 9 73
(W M Brisbourne) *trckd ldrs: chsd wnr fnl 2f: edgd lft: no imp* **8/1**[3]
3 shd **Captain Kolo (IRE)** 2-9-3 0 DavidAllan 6 73+
(T D Easterby) *trckd ldrs: effrt and swtchd lft 2f out: kpt on same pce ins fnl f* **11/4**[2]
4 6 **Even Stevens** 2-9-3 0 PJMcDonald 8 52+
(J A Glover) *chsd ldrs: hung lft and wknd ins fnl f* **12/1**
0 5 6 **Taverners Jubilee**[18] 5465 2-9-3 0 StephenCraine 4 29
(Patrick Morris) *chsd ldrs: wknd over 1f out* **66/1**
00 6 1 ½ **Christine's Gold (IRE)**[9] 5785 2-8-12 0 TomEaves 2 19
(E J Alston) *trckd ldrs: lost pl over 1f out* **22/1**
7 4 **Ime Not Bitter** 2-8-12 0 BillyCray(5) 1 10
(C W Moore) *sn drvn along and outpcd: bhd after 2f* **50/1**
8 1 ½ **Ivy And Gold** 2-8-10 0 VictorSantos(7) 10 4
(A Berry) *s.s: a bhd* **50/1**
64.93 secs (3.93) **Going Correction** +0.65s/f (Yiel) **8** Ran SP% **113.1**
Speed ratings (Par 95): **94,90,90,80,71 68,62,59**
toteswingers:1&2 £2.30, 2&3 £2.40, 1&3 £1.70 CSF £7.24 TOTE £1.50: £1.10, £1.20, £1.90; EX 5.70.
Owner J C Fretwell **Bred** Rathbarry Stud **Trained** Lichfield, Staffs

FOCUS
No more than a modest juvenile sprint maiden but the time was not bad for the conditions and the form is rated a few lengths higher than it might have been.

NOTEBOOK
Scantily Clad(IRE) had shown enough in two previous attempts (both 6f) to suggest she could win a race such as this and she had little trouble taking care of the opposition, coping just fine with the ground. There should be more to come at this distance in nurseries. (tchd 4-5)
Rowan Spirit(IRE) improved on his first two efforts and was clearly suited by the soft ground. He'll be of interest when sent handicapping. (op 9-1)
Captain Kolo(IRE) has plenty of speed in his pedigree and is bred to cope with this sort of ground, so it was no surprise to see him run well on this racecourse debut. He should improve and can win an ordinary maiden, with 6f likely to suit. (op 3-1)
Even Stevens, from a yard whose juveniles often need a run, showed enough to suggest he has a future.

6046 E B F NORTHERN RACING CLUB 30TH YEAR MAIDEN STKS (DIV I) 6f
2:30 (2:33) (Class 5) 2-Y-0 **£3,626** (£1,079; £539; £269) **Stalls** Centre

Form RPR
624 1 **Cruiser**[17] 5527 2-9-3 77 MartinDwyer 3 85+
(W R Muir) *chsd ldrs: sn pushed along: styd on to ld 1f out: forged clr* **4/7**[1]
2 7 **Karate (IRE)** 2-9-3 0 GregFairley 11 67+
(M Johnston) *w ldrs: led 3f out: hdd 1f out: wknd last 100yds* **6/1**[2]
5 3 3 **Mr Dream Maker (IRE)**[15] 5608 2-9-3 0 TomEaves 7 55
(Ian Williams) *in rr: hdwy over 2f out: tk 3rd 1f out* **18/1**
0 4 1 **Wolds Agent**[17] 5531 2-9-3 0 DavidAllan 6 52
(T D Easterby) *sn outpcd in rr: kpt on fnl 2f: nvr nr ldrs* **80/1**
0 5 ½ **Ballinargh Boy**[24] 5298 2-9-3 0 AndrewElliott 5 51
(R D Wylie) *w ldrs: edgd lft over 1f out: sn wknd* **100/1**
6 2 **Adaria** 2-8-12 0 PaulMulrennan 10 40
(D C Griffiths) *unruly s: in rr: nvr on terms* **100/1**
04 7 1 **Face The Future**[15] 5595 2-9-3 0 PhillipMakin 1 42
(M Dods) *s.i.s: sn trcking ldrs: edgd rt 2f out: sn lost pl* **10/1**
640 8 2 **Secret Tycoon (IRE)**[20] 5418 2-9-3 68 StephenCraine 2 36
(Patrick Morris) *hld up: effrt 3f out: hung lft and sn wknd* **20/1**
5 9 8 **Thatstheone**[40] 4748 2-8-7 0 BillyCray(5) 8 7
(C W Moore) *led tl 3f out: wknd 2f out* **66/1**
10 2 ¾ **Loose Quality (USA)** 2-9-3 0 MickyFenton 9 —
(T P Tate) *sn trcking ldrs: lost pl over 2f out: eased whn bhd ins fnl f* **13/2**[3]
1m 19.08s (5.58) **Going Correction** +0.80s/f (Soft) **10** Ran SP% **115.1**
Speed ratings (Par 95): **94,84,80,79,78 76,74,72,61,57**
toteswingers:1&2 £2.60, 2&3 £2.70, 1&3 £4.70 CSF £4.16 TOTE £1.50: £1.10, £1.90, £3.90; EX 5.20.

Owner C L A Edginton **Bred** The Hill Stud **Trained** Lambourn, Berks

FOCUS
The first division of an ordinary 6f juvenile maiden, run in tough conditions. The time was 0.19secs slower than the second division. The winner is capable of rating higher.

NOTEBOOK
Cruiser very much won in the manner of a horse with a bright future. Fourth behind Zebedee in a valuable sales contest at Newmarket latest, he is held in the highest regard by his trainer, who believes he may develop into a classy sprinter one day, and better ground will suit in future. He may have one more run before being put away for the year. (op 8-13 tchd 8-15)
Karate(IRE), whose sales price increased to 90,000gns, went on with 3f to run, but it was clear from 2f out that the winner had his move covered. This was a promising start and he will be suited by better ground. (op 9-2)
Mr Dream Maker(IRE) shaped encouragingly over 7f on debut and there were again positives to take from this effort. He'll be one for handicaps. (op 16-1 tchd 20-1)
Wolds Agent improved markedly on his debut effort and will be interesting once handicapped. (op 100-1)
Ballinargh Boy offered a lot more than he had done on debut, despite the ground. (op 125-1)
Adaria fared well considering she threw her rider off at the start and was misbehaving in the stalls.
Face The Future never got into it following a sluggish start. (op 16-1)
Thatstheone was reportedly unsuited by the ground. Official explanation: trainer said filly was unsuited by the soft ground
Loose Quality(USA), related to several useful performers, dropped away tamely and was presumably unsuited by the ground. (tchd 7-1)

6047 E B F NORTHERN RACING CLUB 30TH YEAR MAIDEN STKS (DIV II) 6f
3:00 (3:01) (Class 5) 2-Y-O £3,626 (£1,079; £539; £269) **Stalls** Centre

Form | | | | RPR
42 **1** **Gentle Lord**[24] 5301 2-9-3 0 .... RichardKingscote 6 79
(Tom Dascombe) *mde all: edgd rt ins fnl f: hld on wl* **1/1**[1]
42 **2** ¾ **Chokidar (IRE)**[17] 5531 2-9-3 0 .... SilvestreDeSousa 9 77
(J A Glover) *chsd ldrs: sn drvn along: upsides 2f out: crowded 1f out: kpt on same pce ins fnl f* **11/4**[2]
3 3 **Shamdarley (IRE)** 2-9-3 0 .... PhillipMakin 5 68+
(M Dods) *trckd ldrs: effrt over 2f out: styd on same pce appr fnl f* **9/1**
003 **4** 1 **Major Return (IRE)**[32] 5053 2-9-3 58 .... JamesDoyle 11 65
(A J McCabe) *hld up: hdwy over 2f out: kpt on same pce appr fnl f* **50/1**
5 4 **Louis The Pious** 2-9-3 0 .... PaulHanagan 3 53+
(K A Ryan) *s.i.s: sme hdwy 3f out: lost pl over 1f out* **8/1**[3]
06 **6** ½ **Vetvey (IRE)**[31] 5099 2-9-3 0 .... GregFairley 8 51
(M Johnston) *chsd ldrs: hmpd 3f out: wknd over 1f out* **18/1**
06 **7** 3 **Silver Tigress**[40] 4748 2-8-9 0 .... KellyHarrison(3) 10 37
(C W Thornton) *in rr: sme hdwy over 2f out: nvr a factor* **66/1**
8 nse **Cool Luke** 2-9-3 0 .... PJMcDonald 7 42
(G A Swinbank) *s.s: nvr on terms* **14/1**
9 1½ **Auto Mac** 2-9-3 0 .... FrannyNorton 4 38
(N Bycroft) *chsd ldrs: drvn over 3f out: sn lost pl* **50/1**
6 **10** 21 **Stilettoesinthemud (IRE)**[17] 5531 2-8-12 0 .... PaulMulrennan 1 —
(J G Given) *chsd ldrs on outside: rdn and lost pl over 3f out: sn bhd: t.o* **20/1**

1m 18.89s (5.39) **Going Correction** +0.80s/f (Soft) **10** Ran SP% **119.9**
Speed ratings (Par 95): **96,95,91,89,84 83,79,79,77,49**
toteswingers:1&2 £1.20, 2&3 £5.70, 1&3 £3.80 CSF £3.75 TOTE £2.20: £1.10, £1.30, £3.30; EX 4.40.
Owner K P Trowbridge **Bred** R Phillips And Tweenhills Farm And Stud **Trained** Malpas, Cheshire

FOCUS
The winning time of this second division was 0.19secs quicker than the first division. Straightforward form rated around the front pair.

NOTEBOOK
Gentle Lord, although making hard work of it, probably put up a fair effort in making all against a headwind. He didn't look entirely happy on the ground, either, and his trainer now intends to put him away until next season, when he's hoping he will develop into a Listed performer at up to 1m. (tchd 10-11, 6-5 and 5-4 in a place)
Chokidar(IRE) threw down a strong challenge inside the final 2f, but always just seemed to be coming off second-best. He should be winning an ordinary contest before long. (op 7-2 tchd 4-1)
Shamdarley(IRE), the first foal of a US winner whose sales price increased to 90,000gns, shaped encouragingly back in third and looks a ready-made maiden winner once upped to 7f. (op 17-2)
Major Return(IRE) ran well above expectations and will make some appeal off his lowly mark in handicaps.
Louis The Pious, whose dam was placed up to 1m6f in France, never featured and is sure to do better in time. (op 10-1 tchd 11-1)
Vetvey(IRE) is one for handicaps. (op 16-1 tchd 20-1)
Silver Tigress should do better in handicaps. (op 50-1)
Stilettoesinthemud(IRE) was reported to have lost her action. Official explanation: jockey said filly lost its action (op 18-1)

6048 RACING UK HOME OF FLAT RACING H'CAP 6f
3:30 (3:31) (Class 4) (0-85,85) 3-Y-O+ £4,533 (£1,348; £674; £336) **Stalls** Centre

Form | | | | RPR
0362 **1** **Esprit De Midas**[27] 5197 4-9-7 85 .... TomEaves 12 96+
(K A Ryan) *hld up: nt clr run on stands' side over 2f out tl 1f out: str run to ld last 50yds* **16/1**
4233 **2** 1¼ **Lochan Mor**[21] 5386 4-9-1 79 .... HayleyTurner 2 86
(M L W Bell) *w ldrs: led over 1f out: edgd rt: hdd and no ex clsng stages* **11/4**[1]
0100 **3** ½ **Feeling Fresh (IRE)**[20] 5424 5-8-9 73 .... SilvestreDeSousa 14 78
(Paul Green) *hld up towards rr: hdwy over 2f out: upsides jst ins fnl f: kpt on same pce last 75yds* **13/2**[3]
0340 **4** 1½ **Transmit (IRE)**[20] 5421 3-8-5 71 oh1 .... (b) DuranFentiman 15 72
(T D Easterby) *chsd ldrs stands' side: edgd lft 1f out: kpt on same pce* **20/1**
0100 **5** 1¼ **Rio Cobolo (IRE)**[24] 5297 4-8-10 74 .... (v) PhillipMakin 8 71
(Paul Green) *chsd ldrs: chal over 2f out: kpt on same pce* **8/1**
000 **6** hd **Pravda Street**[90] 3083 5-8-8 79 .... DuilioDaSilva(7) 9 75
(P F I Cole) *chsd ldrs: edgd lft and one pce ins fnl f* **17/2**
0223 **7** ½ **Solar Spirit (IRE)**[20] 5424 5-8-5 74 .... IanBrennan(5) 7 68
(J J Quinn) *chsd ldrs: rdn over 2f out: nt clr run over 1f out: fdd ins fnl f* **5/1**[2]
001 **8** ¾ **Falasteen (IRE)**[12] 5678 3-9-5 85 .... PaulHanagan 11 77
(R A Fahey) *led tl over 1f out: wknd fnl 150yds* **8/1**
4400 **9** 3¾ **Sunnandaeg**[39] 4784 3-8-11 77 .... (v[1]) AndrewMullen 4 57
(V P Donoghue) *chsd ldrs on outside: edgd rt lost pl over 1f out* **14/1**
2160 **10** 13 **Lewyn**[26] 5250 3-9-2 82 .... PaulMulrennan 13 20
(K A Ryan) *dwlt: hdwy 3f out: lost pl over 1f out: bhd whn eased clsng stages* **50/1**
0432 **11** hd **Beckermet (IRE)**[18] 5496 8-8-5 72 .... JamesSullivan(3) 6 10
(Mrs R A Carr) *towards rr on outer: effrt over 2f out: hung rt and lost pl over 1f out* **11/1**

1m 18.28s (4.78) **Going Correction** +0.95s/f (Soft)
WFA 3 from 4yo+ 2lb **11** Ran SP% **117.0**
Speed ratings (Par 105): **106,104,103,101,100 99,99,98,93,75 75**
toteswingers:1&2 £6.90, 2&3 £8.30, 1&3 £15.70 CSF £59.55 CT £333.15 TOTE £17.10: £5.10, £1.20, £1.90; EX 101.10.
Owner Joseph Ogden, J Hanson, John Ogden **Bred** Jeremy Green And Sons **Trained** Hambleton, N Yorks
■ Stewards' Enquiry : Phillip Makin caution: used whip down shoulder in the forehand.

FOCUS
A competitive 6f handicap. The ground played a part but the form seems sound, with a sizeable personal bedst from the winner.

6049 E B F GRIFFITHS & ARMOUR CLASSIFIED STKS 6f
4:00 (4:03) (Class 3) 3-Y-O+ £9,066 (£2,697; £1,348; £673) **Stalls** Centre

Form | | | | RPR
-131 **1** **Horseradish**[131] 1836 3-8-11 90 .... HayleyTurner 6 98+
(M L W Bell) *trckd ldrs: rdn to ld over 1f out: edgd lft fnl f: all out* **11/8**[1]
3012 **2** shd **Fathsta (IRE)**[3] 5950 5-8-13 89 .... SilvestreDeSousa 5 98
(D M Simcock) *chsd ldrs: upsides ins fnl f: carried lft: jst failed* **9/4**[2]
2000 **3** 1 **We Have A Dream**[36] 4904 5-8-13 87 .... MartinDwyer 2 95
(W R Muir) *taken to r alone towards far side: w ldrs: pushed along 3f out: kpt on same pce last 100yds* **25/1**
1050 **4** 3¼ **Lucky Numbers (IRE)**[10] 5742 4-8-13 88 .... FrannyNorton 3 84
(Paul Green) *chsd ldrs: wknd ins fnl f* **14/1**
4500 **5** 3 **Novellen Lad (IRE)**[31] 5095 5-8-13 90 .... DavidAllan 1 75
(E J Alston) *dwlt: in rr: effrt over 2f out: wknd ins fnl f* **6/1**[3]
3066 **6** 5 **Skylla**[26] 5250 3-8-8 90 .... PaulHanagan 4 56
(R A Fahey) *led: hdd over 1f out: sn wknd* **6/1**[3]

1m 18.12s (4.62) **Going Correction** +0.95s/f (Soft)
WFA 3 from 4yo+ 2lb **6** Ran SP% **112.0**
Speed ratings (Par 107): **107,106,105,101,97 90**
toteswingers:1&2 £1.10, 2&3 £5.50, 1&3 £6.40 CSF £4.64 TOTE £1.90: £1.10, £1.30; EX 3.30.
Owner Mrs G Rowland-Clark **Bred** Mrs F A Veasey **Trained** Newmarket, Suffolk
■ Stewards' Enquiry : Hayley Turner two-day ban: used whip with excessive frequency (Sep 29-30)

FOCUS
A decent little classified stakes that produced a close finish. The first three basically ran to form.

NOTEBOOK
Horseradish, purposely kept off since winning at Chester in May, in anticipation of the ground going against him mid-summer, he was reported by his rider afterwards to have been a bit ring-rusty and likely to come on plenty. Equally effective over 7f, he will now head for the Totesport.com Challenge Cup at Ascot's QEII meeting later this month, a race for which the sponsors cut him to 14-1 from 25-1. (tchd 7-4)
Fathsta(IRE), reappearing just three days after a fast-finishing second at Goodwood, goes just as well at this trip and challenged the winner hard inside the final furlong, but couldn't quite get up. He's a tough sort who can continue to give a good account. (op 2-1 tchd 15-8)
We Have A Dream ran a solo on the far side and briefly looked to be on terms with the front two, but it emerged late on that he wasn't quite. It's hard to say whether or not he was disadvantaged, but one thing we do know is that he remains tough to win with. (tchd 20-1)
Lucky Numbers(IRE) didn't get home having chased the early speed. (op 16-1 tchd 10-1)
Novellen Lad(IRE) never threatened to get into it having been held up. (op 17-2)
Skylla wasn't without claims on her recent efforts, so it was disappointing to see her stop so quickly having towed them along to just over 1f out. (op 8-1)

6050 KING'S REGIMENT CUP H'CAP 1m 3f 200y
4:30 (4:31) (Class 4) (0-85,82) 3-Y-O+ £4,533 (£1,348; £674; £336) **Stalls** Centre

Form | | | | RPR
2655 **1** **Music Of The Moor (IRE)**[43] 4652 3-9-0 77 .... MickyFenton 4 86+
(T P Tate) *hld up in rr: stdy hdwy stands' side over 3f out: nt clr run: swtchd lft over 1f out: sn led: edgd rt: pushed clr* **5/1**[3]
4156 **2** 2¼ **Ubi Ace**[15] 5611 4-9-4 72 .... GrahamGibbons 1 77
(T D Walford) *trckd ldrs: led over 1f out: sn hdd: swtchd lft and kpt on same pce ins fnl f* **6/1**
0222 **3** 1¼ **Amazing Blue Sky**[22] 5355 4-9-4 75 .... JamesSullivan(3) 8 78
(Mrs R A Carr) *led: hdd over 1f out: swtchd lft ins fnl f and styd on same pce* **9/2**[2]
6600 **4** 2 **Amanda Carter**[36] 4891 6-9-7 75 .... PaulHanagan 9 75
(R A Fahey) *trckd ldrs: effrt over 3f out: kpt on same pce fnl 2f: styng on fin* **10/1**
004 **5** hd **Persian Peril**[22] 5355 6-9-7 75 .... PJMcDonald 3 74
(G A Swinbank) *hld up in rr: hdwy over 3f out: hung rt and one pce fnl 2f* **13/2**
300 **6** ¾ **Molon Labe (IRE)**[43] 4656 3-8-3 66 oh1 .... AndrewMullen 5 64
(T P Tate) *trckd ldrs: shkn up over 6f out: outpcd over 2f out* **14/1**
3160 **7** 2¾ **Green Lightning (IRE)**[10] 5757 3-9-5 82 .... (v[1]) GregFairley 10 76
(M Johnston) *sn trcking ldr: effrt over 3f out: wknd wl over 1f out* **5/2**[1]
0000 **8** 10 **Prince Apollo**[15] 5611 5-9-7 75 .... TomEaves 7 53
(Ian Williams) *hld up in tch: drvn 3f out: lost pl wl over 1f out: eased towards fin* **18/1**

2m 40.45s (6.45) **Going Correction** +0.675s/f (Yiel)
WFA 3 from 4yo+ 9lb **8** Ran SP% **112.1**
Speed ratings (Par 105): **105,103,102,101,101 100,98,92**
toteswingers:1&2 £5.10, 2&3 £3.60, 1&3 £4.60 CSF £33.38 CT £142.26 TOTE £4.40: £1.30, £1.40, £1.30; EX 40.40.
Owner The Ivy Syndicate **Bred** Snig Elevage **Trained** Tadcaster, N Yorks
■ Stewards' Enquiry : James Sullivan two-day ban: careless riding (Sep 28-29)
Micky Fenton caution: careless riding.

FOCUS
They came stands' side in the straight for what was an ordinary handicap. The favourite was again below form but the winner produced a clear personal best.

6051 TURFTV.CO.UK H'CAP (FOR GENTLEMAN AMATEUR RIDERS) 1m 3f 200y
5:00 (5:01) (Class 5) (0-70,69) 4-Y-O+ £2,498 (£774; £387; £193) **Stalls** Centre

Form | | | | RPR
5041 **1** **Switched Off**[7] 5828 5-11-3 69 6ex .... MrJHodson(5) 14 79+
(Ian Williams) *s.i.s: stdy hdwy 4f out: wnt 2nd over 1f out: edgd rt and led ins fnl f: all out* **9/4**[1]
0-60 **2** ½ **Follow The Sun (IRE)**[17] 5530 6-10-0 52 .... MrJBanks(5) 6 61
(Ronald O'Leary, Ire) *led 2f: led over 4f out: crowded and hdd ins fnl f: no ex nr fin* **16/1**
043 **3** 5 **Red Fama**[30] 5118 6-11-2 68 .... MrSebSpencer(5) 15 69
(N Bycroft) *s.i.s: sn prom: lost pl 7f out: hdwy over 3f out: styd on same pce fnl 2f* **4/1**[2]

4-00 **4** *8* **Feeling (IRE)**[17] 5536 6-9-9 **49** oh4 MrLLewis-Salter[(7)] 7 37+
(D Burchell) *sn w ldrs: sddle slipped and rdr lost iron 5f out: wknd over 1f out* **66/1**

/50- **5** *3 3/4* **Converti**[8] 4092 6-9-12 **50** MrPPrince[(5)] 9 32
(S C Burrough) *in rr: t.o 6f out: kpt on fnl 3f: nvr a factor* **16/1**

4052 **6** *shd* **Magnitude**[22] 5363 5-10-4 **56** MrOGarner[(5)] 13 38
(B P J Baugh) *chsd ldrs: wnt 2nd over 2f out: wknd over 1f out* **17/2**

1105 **7** *1 1/4* **Shy**[12] 5679 5-11-0 **66** MrPMillman[(5)] 5 46
(B R Millman) *in rr div: kpt on fnl 3f: nvr on terms* **5/1**[3]

0300 **8** *1/2* **Black Coffee**[19] 5437 5-10-13 **63** MrBenBrisbourne[(3)] 11 42
(W M Brisbourne) *in tch: wknd 2f out* **14/1**

0420 **9** *5* **Holiday Cocktail**[24] 4708 8-10-13 **60** (p) MrSWalker 8 31
(J J Quinn) *in rr div: drvn 8f out: nvr a factor* **7/1**

2140 **10** *2* **Jenny Soba**[8] 5813 7-10-3 **55** MrJPFeatherstone[(5)] 16 23
(Lucinda Featherstone) *s.i.s: sn chsng ldrs: lost pl over 2f out* **12/1**

-600 **11** *8* **Grethel (IRE)**[15] 4454 6-9-9 **49** oh4 MrTGarner[(7)] 12 4
(A Berry) *sn chsng ldrs: lost pl over 3f out* **66/1**

0-40 **12** *34* **Richo**[17] 4985 4-10-8 **60** (p) MrCAHarris[(5)] 4 —
(S A Harris) *led after 2f: hdd over 4f out: reign broke over 2f out: sn lost pl and bhd: t.o* **40/1**

0/00 **13** *7* **Real Dandy**[14] 5631 4-9-9 **49** oh4 MrWFeatherstone[(7)] 10 —
(Lucinda Featherstone) *chsd ldrs: lost pl after 3f: sn bhd: t.o and eased 2f out* **100/1**

2m 43.48s (9.48) **Going Correction** +0.675s/f (Yiel) **13** Ran SP% **123.0**
Speed ratings (Par 103): **95,94,91,86,83 83,82,82,78,77 72,49,44**
toteswingers:1&2 £10.10, 2&3 £19.70, 1&3 £3.70 CSF £44.65 CT £145.35 TOTE £3.20: £1.10, £6.70, £2.30; EX 79.30 Place 6: £4.88 Place 5 £4.55.
Owner P Nicholls **Bred** Mrs Byron Paterson **Trained** Portway, Worcs

FOCUS
A low-grade handicap for amateur riders that didn't make for pretty viewing. The winner confirmed his Goodwood improvement and the second sets the standard.
Feeling(IRE) Official explanation: jockey said saddle slipped
Richo Official explanation: jockey said rein snapped
T/Plt: £4.40 to a £1 stake. Pool of £59,940.42 - 9,783.14 winning tickets. T/Qpdt: £3.90 to a £1 stake. Pool of £3,457.86 - 641.68 winning tickets. WG

5835 LINGFIELD (L-H)
Tuesday, September 14

OFFICIAL GOING: Standard
Wind: Strong, half behind Weather: Overcast

6052 BREEDERS' CUP LIVE ON AT THE RACES NURSERY 6f (P)
2:20 (2:22) (Class 5) (0-70,69) 2-Y-O **£3,238** (£963; £481; £240) **Stalls** Low

Form RPR

5633 **1** **Sugar Beet**[5] 5874 2-9-3 **65** SteveDrowne 8 73+
(R Charlton) *mde all: gng easily 2f out: pushed along and wl in command ins fnl f* **4/1**[2]

6545 **2** *2* **Silly Billy (IRE)**[4] 5921 2-9-3 **65** LiamKeniry 6 67
(S Kirk) *trckd ldng trio: rdn to chse wnr over 1f out: styd on wl enough: no threat* **8/1**

0044 **3** *1 1/2* **Country Waltz**[20] 5412 2-8-6 **54** ChrisCatlin 2 52
(M R Channon) *chsd ldng pair: rdn to dispute 2nd wl over 1f out: styd on: n.d ins fnl f* **12/1**

2201 **4** *3* **Ruby Alexander (IRE)**[15] 5581 2-9-1 **63** (b) JimCrowley 1 52
(R M Beckett) *trckd ldrs on inner: shkn up 2f out: sn outpcd: kpt on* **6/1**

3435 **5** *2* **Out Of The Storm**[19] 5452 2-9-3 **65** SebSanders 5 48+
(S Dow) *hld up in midfield: effrt 2f out: reminders over 1f out: outpcd after* **5/2**[1]

5600 **6** *1/2* **Alfraamsey**[18] 5483 2-9-3 **65** RyanMoore 3 46
(M R Channon) *dwlt: mostly last and struggling to stay in tch: reminders 1/2-way: kpt on fr over 1f out: n.d* **9/2**[3]

5000 **7** *3* **Token Gift**[50] 4436 2-8-9 **57** (b[1]) PatCosgrave 9 29
(P D Evans) *chsd wnr to wl over 1f out: wknd* **66/1**

0630 **8** *1 1/4* **Atia**[37] 4872 2-9-4 **66** DaneO'Neill 10 34
(J G Portman) *racd wd: hld up in rr: shkn up and no prog 2f out* **25/1**

1006 **9** *5* **Miss Moneypenni**[12] 5675 2-9-1 **63** J-PGuillambert 7 16
(N P Littmoden) *dwlt: a towards rr: shkn up 2f out: wknd* **12/1**

0065 **10** *4 1/2* **Manchester Stanley**[62] 4020 2-8-8 **56** FergusSweeney 12 —
(J A Osborne) *racd wd: chsd ldng trio to over 2f out: wknd rapidly* **20/1**

1m 11.7s (-0.20) **Going Correction** +0.025s/f (Slow) **10** Ran SP% **117.6**
Speed ratings (Par 95): **102,99,97,93,90 90,86,84,77,71**
toteswingers:1&2 £3.90, 2&3 £13.30, 1&3 £3.80 CSF £35.55 CT £364.03 TOTE £6.40: £1.20, £3.40, £5.20; EX 27.50.
Owner Nicholas Jones **Bred** Coln Valley Stud **Trained** Beckhampton, Wilts

FOCUS
A routine maiden, but won by a progressive filly at a modest level. Pace dominated and the field finished strung out. The winner built on her minor debut promise.

NOTEBOOK
Sugar Beet, sweating on a cool afternoon, repeated the front-tactics tried in her previous race, at Bath, and this time they never looked like failing. Jockey Steve Drowne had expected this sharper track to suit her style of running better and, handling the surface well on this first experience of Polytrack, she did not let him down. (op 10-3 tchd 3-1 and 9-2)
Silly Billy(IRE), more suited by the return to nursery company, ran one of his better races but the relatively unexposed winner was far too good. He is developing into a reliable AW performer (tchd 13-2)
Country Waltz, making a respectable AW debut, has run with credit in both her nurseries. She should find a race in due course (op 10-1 tchd 14-1)
Ruby Alexander(IRE), greatly improving on one poor previous attempt at 6f, is probably still best at 5f, but the distance was not the only problem this time. She had been raised 5lb for her win last time, and is now on a stiff mark. (op 9-2)
Out Of The Storm has some ability but the hold-up tactics that have been employed to date suggest she is not the easiest of rides. She has been beaten too far in her two nurseries to suggest she can win off this mark. (op 3-1 tchd 10-3)
Alfraamsey has lost his form since notching his only victory, and has been gelded since his last race. A slow start gave him too much to do, but there were minor signs of a possible revival. (op 8-1)

6053 E. B. F. AT THE RACES SKY 415 MAIDEN STKS 7f (P)
2:50 (2:51) (Class 5) 2-Y-O **£3,561** (£1,059; £529; £264) **Stalls** Low

Form RPR

2 **1** **Blue Tiger's Eye (IRE)**[17] 5523 2-9-3 0 TedDurcan 4 85+
(Saeed Bin Suroor) *mde virtually all: drifted bdly rt fr over 1f out: r.o wl: comf* **15/8**[2]

22 **2** *3 3/4* **Johnny Castle**[40] 4755 2-9-3 0 WilliamBuick 9 76
(J H M Gosden) *racd wd: chsd ldrs: wnt 3rd 3f out: rdn 2f out: chsd wnr jst over 1f out: nt qckn and no imp* **4/5**[1]

0 **3** *1* **Twice Bitten**[32] 5047 2-9-3 0 RichardHughes 5 73
(J A R Toller) *s.s: sn wl in tch: shkn up 3f out: effrt to dispute 2nd jst over 1f out: one pce after* **50/1**

03 **4** *1 1/2* **Dubarshi**[38] 4838 2-9-3 0 DaneO'Neill 8 69+
(Miss Jo Crowley) *chsd ldrs: shkn up in 5th over 2f out: kpt on: nt gng pce to threaten* **28/1**

0253 **5** *2 1/4* **Tagansky**[11] 5718 2-9-3 73 (b[1]) SebSanders 6 64
(S Dow) *chsd wnr: upsides 1/2-way to 2f out: wknd rapidly jst over 1f out* **25/1**

3 **6** *3/4* **Old Possum (USA)**[32] 5040 2-9-3 0 AhmedAjtebi 11 62+
(Mahmood Al Zarooni) *a towards rr: pushed along 1/2-way: outpcd over 2f out: nvr on terms after* **10/1**[3]

7 *3 1/4* **Switchback** 2-9-3 0 RyanMoore 2 54
(Sir Michael Stoute) *rn green in midfield and sn pushed along: in tch over 2f out: sn wl outpcd* **12/1**

8 *3/4* **Hayaku (USA)** 2-8-12 0 JimCrowley 3 47
(R M Beckett) *settled towards rr: wl outpcd fr 3f out: no prog after tl styd on fnl 150yds* **16/1**

60 **9** *9* **Lemon Drop Red (USA)**[32] 5049 2-9-3 0 SteveDrowne 12 29
(E A L Dunlop) *dwlt: mostly in last pair and sn struggling: t.o 3f out* **66/1**

00 **10** *11* **Caledonia Prince**[21] 5385 2-9-3 0 J-PGuillambert 7 —
(F J Brennan) *dwlt: a in last trio and struggling: t.o over 2f out* **100/1**

0 **11** *1 3/4* **Striking Willow**[15] 5582 2-9-0 0 JamesMillman[(3)] 13 —
(B R Millman) *chsd ldng pair to 3f out: wknd v rapidly: t.o* **100/1**

12 *41* **Street Cred (IRE)** 2-8-12 0 LiamKeniry 1 —
(P Burgoyne) *s.s: a in last trio: wl t.o fr 1/2-way* **100/1**

1m 25.12s (0.32) **Going Correction** +0.025s/f (Slow) **12** Ran SP% **126.7**
Speed ratings (Par 95): **99,94,93,91,89 88,84,83,73,61 59,12**
toteswingers:1&2 £1.10, 2&3 £24.60, 1&3 £19.00 CSF £3.88 TOTE £2.80: £1.30, £1.10, £22.30; EX 4.50.
Owner Godolphin **Bred** Rabbah Bloodstock Limited **Trained** Newmarket, Suffolk

FOCUS
Probably an above-average AW maiden, with the first two having previously done well at decent tracks. However, there are mixed messages in the result because the third had been beaten a long way in his only previous races. The winner still stepped up on his debut form. The pace was ordinary.

NOTEBOOK
Blue Tiger's Eye(IRE) adopted front-running tactics this time, in contrast to his promising debut, and he was always in control despite hanging right-handed in the straight. This slightly quirky gelding, who looked the part in the paddock, is learning with experience and is now likely to step up in grade and distance. (tchd 9-4 and 7-4 in places)
Johnny Castle, dropped back to 7f from 1m, was making his AW debut and finished as if a return to the longer trip would be in his favour. He still looks capable of winning a maiden on turf or sand. (op 5-4)
Twice Bitten ran a much more positive race than first time out. This Beat Hollow colt is probably good enough to win a maiden but there will be other options as he matures.
Dubarshi, third at 1m last time, lacked the speed to win in this company over this shorter distance. However, he is running well enough to find a race before long, with nurseries now an option. (op 25-1)
Tagansky, blinkered for the first time, did not run any better in them. He has some ability but looks more of a nursery type. (op 12-1)
Old Possum(USA) had run better on turf on his debut and it remains to be seen if this will be his surface, but he does run as if 1m should suit. (tchd 15-2)

6054 BREEDERS' CUP LIVE ON AT THE RACES CLAIMING STKS 1m 2f (P)
3:20 (3:20) (Class 6) 3-Y-O+ **£2,047** (£604; £302) **Stalls** Low

Form RPR

0231 **1** **Lang Shining (IRE)**[19] 5455 6-9-4 81 SophieDoyle[(5)] 8 81
(J A Osborne) *hld up in midfield: prog on outer 3f out: rdn 2f out: wanting to hang lft over 1f out: led ins fnl f: styd on* **5/1**[3]

0234 **2** *1 1/4* **Orchard Supreme**[26] 5233 7-9-4 86 RichardHughes 1 74
(R Hannon) *trckd ldrs: rousted along 3f out: prog 2f out: drvn to ld 1f out: sn hdd and nt qckn* **3/1**[1]

4606 **3** *1 1/4* **Layla's Lexi**[13] 5654 3-8-8 68 ShaneKelly 2 68
(Ian Williams) *hld up towards rr: prog on inner 2f out: drvn and styd on to take 3rd ins fnl f* **12/1**

1300 **4** *1/2* **Samarinda (USA)**[10] 5750 7-9-6 84 AdamKirby 3 72
(Mrs P Sly) *led 1f: pressed ldr: led over 3f out: kicked 2 l clr 2f out: hdd & wknd 1f out* **7/2**[2]

4050 **5** *2 1/4* **Bentley**[8] 5820 6-8-5 57 HarryBentley[(7)] 6 60?
(B P J Baugh) *led after 1f to over 3f out: stl cl up over 1f out: wknd qckly* **33/1**

3500 **6** *3/4* **Charpoy Cobra**[34] 4969 3-8-2 50 JoeFanning 4 55
(J A R Toller) *chsd ldrs: rdn 3f out: sn lost pl: n.d over 1f out* **25/1**

13-0 **7** *1* **Art Man**[9] 1736 7-9-2 79 (b) DaneO'Neill 11 60
(J D Frost) *s.i.s and pushed along early: mostly in rr: rdn and no prog over 2f out* **8/1**

2300 **8** *3/4* **Lucky Punt**[11] 5723 4-9-12 89 FergusSweeney 7 69
(B G Powell) *prom: rdn and lost pl over 3f out: struggling over 2f out* **8/1**

0000 **9** *3 3/4* **Chat De Soie (IRE)**[20] 5414 3-8-1 47 (b) FrankieMcDonald 10 43
(J S Moore) *racd wd: in tch: prog to chse ldr 3f out to 2f out: wknd v rapidly* **66/1**

5142 **10** *nk* **Dream Of Fortune (IRE)**[7] 5840 6-9-0 64 (t) PatCosgrave 9 48
(P D Evans) *s.i.s and pushed along early: a in rr: struggling whn short of room over 2f out* **6/1**

6205 **11** *20* **Accountable**[13] 5670 3-8-7 57 WilliamBuick 12 8
(B G Powell) *sn last: wl bhd fr 4f out: t.o* **25/1**

2m 7.61s (1.01) **Going Correction** +0.025s/f (Slow)
WFA 3 from 4yo+ 7lb **11** Ran SP% **120.2**
Speed ratings (Par 101): **96,95,94,93,91 91,90,89,86,86 70**
toteswingers:1&2 £3.40, 2&3 £8.80, 1&3 £26.40 CSF £20.20 TOTE £6.30: £1.10, £2.50, £2.90; EX 17.60.
Owner A Taylor **Bred** Ballymacoll Stud Farm Ltd **Trained** Upper Lambourn, Berks

FOCUS
The pace was modest, but the first three home had all been ridden patiently. This was a fair claimer on paper but the form is muddling.

6055 AT THE RACES 534 H'CAP 1m 4f (P)
3:50 (3:50) (Class 5) (0-75,75) 3-Y-O+ **£3,070** (£906; £453) **Stalls** Low

Form RPR

035 **1** **Sea Change (IRE)**[38] 4845 3-9-0 **72** RyanMoore 11 88+
(J Noseda) *dwlt: rousted along early to go prom: trckd ldr after 3f: led 3f out and sn kicked on: drew clr over 1f out: rdn out* **11/4**[1]

1324 **2** 4½ **Peace Corps**[22] 5375 4-9-12 **75**..............................(vt) RichardHughes 10 81
(J R Boyle) *trckd ldng trio: moved up to chal 3f out: qcknd w wnr over 2f out: rdn and wl outpcd over 1f out: hld on for 2nd* **9/1**

6232 **3** *nk* **Wulfrida (IRE)**[29] 5141 3-9-3 **75**.. PatCosgrave 3 81
(J R Fanshawe) *settled in midfield: rdn and prog over 2f out: nt on terms: styd on to take 3rd ins fnl f* **12/1**

4315 **4** ¾ **Minikin (IRE)**[18] 5467 3-9-2 **74**.. SteveDrowne 8 78+
(H Morrison) *trckd ldrs: rdn and effrt over 2f out: disp 3rd over 1f out: outpcd: kpt on* **9/2**[3]

003 **5** ¾ **Sarwin (USA)**[97] 2859 7-8-6 **62**.. HarryBentley[(7)] 4 65
(W J Knight) *dwlt: hld up wl in rr: stl plenty to do over 2f out: prog and shkn up over 1f out: styd on: no ch* **20/1**

0035 **6** 5 **Beaubrav**[19] 5457 4-9-8 **71**..(p) ChrisCatlin 12 66
(M Madgwick) *dwlt: sn in midfield: outpcd over 2f out: no ch after* **16/1**

1000 **7** ¾ **Marju King (IRE)**[25] 5260 4-9-4 **67**.............................. FergusSweeney 7 61
(W S Kittow) *stdd s: hld up in rr: gng wl enough over 2f out: sn outpcd: shkn up and no prog over 1f out* **40/1**

6000 **8** ½ **Manshoor (IRE)**[15] 5611 5-9-2 **65**....................................(b) DaneO'Neill 1 58
(Mrs L Wadham) *dwlt: hld up in rr on inner: outpcd over 2f out: no ch after* **20/1**

0411 **9** 1 **Librettista (AUS)**[16] 5563 4-9-10 **75**........................... KirstyMilczarek 6 65
(L M Cumani) *trckd ldrs on inner: rdn over 2f out: wknd rapidly over 1f out* **7/2**[2]

5246 **10** 1 **Ghufa (IRE)**[36] 4907 6-9-4 **72**.. SimonPearce[(5)] 2 62
(J Pearce) *hld up last: shkn up and no prog over 3f out: sn lft bhd* **28/1**

-260 **11** 4 **Taste The Wine (IRE)**[31] 5084 4-9-2 **65**.......................... LiamKeniry 13 49
(J S Moore) *led after 2f to 3f out: wknd rapidly 2f out* **33/1**

5050 **12** 1¼ **Brooklyn Spirit**[59] 4141 4-9-1 **64**..................................(p) AdamKirby 9 46
(C G Cox) *led 2f: first one u.p 4f out: wknd rapidly 3f out* **16/1**

446 **13** 7 **My Galway Man (IRE)**[13] 5665 3-9-0 **72**........................... JoeFanning 5 42
(M Johnston) *wl in tch tl wknd over 3f out: sn wl bhd* **12/1**

2m 32.11s (-0.89) **Going Correction** +0.025s/f (Slow)
WFA 3 from 4yo+ 9lb **13** Ran SP% **122.6**
Speed ratings (Par 103): **103,100,99,99,98 95,94,94,93,93 90,89,85**
CSF £27.06 CT £267.06 TOTE £3.30: £1.10, £3.40, £3.10; EX 25.90.
Owner Sir Robert Ogden **Bred** Lynch Bages Ltd **Trained** Newmarket, Suffolk

FOCUS
There was just a medium pace at best, but the winner quickened up well and would have won whatever the tempo. A fair handicap with the winner capable of better.

6056 BREEDERS' CUP LIVE ON AT THE RACES MAIDEN STKS 7f (P)
4:20 (4:20) (Class 5) 3-Y-O+ **£2,729** (£806; £403) **Stalls** Low

Form RPR

0 **1** **Saint Pierre (USA)**[41] 4697 3-9-1 0.......................... J-PGuillambert 10 82+
(L M Cumani) *mde virtually all: drvn and edgd rt fr over 1f out: hrd pressed ins fnl f: hld on wl* **8/1**

0- **2** *nk* **Zip Lock (IRE)**[499] 1703 4-9-5 0.. RyanMoore 7 83+
(J Noseda) *chsd wnr over 5f out: styd cl up: wnt 2nd again wl over 1f out: str chal ins fnl f: nt qckn nr fin* **9/2**[3]

2205 **3** 2 **Streets Of War (USA)**[29] 5150 3-8-12 **74**..................... PatrickHills[(3)] 2 76
(P W Chapple-Hyam) *hld up towards rr: prog over 2f out: styd on to take 3rd ins fnl f: nvr able to chal* **7/2**[2]

2222 **4** 1 **Engulf (IRE)**[20] 5419 3-9-1 **75**..................................(b[1]) RichardHughes 4 73
(W J Haggas) *stdd s: hld up: stdy prog gng wl fr 1/2-way: rousted along over 1f out: limited rspnse and no imp on ldrs* **2/1**[1]

003 **5** ¾ **Norville (IRE)**[15] 5603 3-9-1 **70**.. PatCosgrave 1 71
(P D Evans) *chsd ldng pair: rdn over 2f out: stl 3rd but wl hld ent fnl f: fdd* **25/1**

6 2¾ **Sunset Kitty (USA)** 3-8-10 0.. ShaneKelly 5 59+
(W R Swinburn) *a towards rr: outpcd fr over 2f out* **20/1**

04 **7** ½ **Mister Bit (IRE)**[7] 5842 3-8-10 0.. KierenFox[(5)] 6 63+
(J R Best) *hld up last: stl there 2f out: shuffled along and passed wkng rivals after: nvr nr ldrs* **33/1**

4636 **8** 1½ **Hooligan Sean**[12] 5677 3-8-10 **75**.. AmyScott[(5)] 3 58
(H Candy) *a towards rr: outpcd fr over 2f out* **10/1**

9 6 **Fact** 3-8-10 0.. PatDobbs 8 37
(Mrs A J Perrett) *dwlt: racd wd: a towards rr: wl btn 2f out* **25/1**

0-2 **10** 2 **Curlew (IRE)**[115] 2334 4-9-2 0.. JamesMillman[(3)] 9 50
(C J Down) *chsd wnr over 5f out to wl over 1f out: wknd v rapidly* **11/2**

1m 24.59s (-0.21) **Going Correction** +0.025s/f (Slow)
WFA 3 from 4yo 4lb **10** Ran SP% **124.7**
Speed ratings (Par 103): **102,101,99,98,97 94,93,91,85,82**
toteswingers:1&2 £7.80, 2&3 £6.60, 1&3 £5.80 CSF £45.01 TOTE £11.40: £3.40, £1.50, £1.60; EX 33.90.
Owner J Barton & C Pizarro **Bred** Gallaghers Stud Inc **Trained** Newmarket, Suffolk

FOCUS
The first two are unexposed and should improve again, making them by far the most interesting runners in this maiden. The form is rated around the third.
Curlew(IRE) Official explanation: jockey said gelding lost its action in straight

6057 ATTHERACES.COM/BREEDERSCUP H'CAP 6f (P)
4:50 (4:51) (Class 5) (0-75,75) 3-Y-O+ **£2,729** (£806; £403) **Stalls** Low

Form RPR

010 **1** **Vintage (IRE)**[169] 1044 6-9-7 **75**.. IanMongan 12 82
(J Akehurst) *prom: chsd ldr wl over 1f out: hrd rdn to chal ins fnl f: styd on to ld post* **10/1**

-443 **2** *shd* **Pan American**[12] 5677 3-9-2 **72**.. FergusSweeney 7 79
(P J Makin) *mde most: drvn over 1f out: hrd pressed ins fnl f: hdd post* **13/2**[3]

6256 **3** *nk* **Fawley Green**[3] 5968 3-9-2 **72**..(p) JimCrowley 5 78+
(W R Muir) *hld up towards rr: effrt on outer 2f out: r.o wl ins fnl f to take 3rd last strides* **15/2**

6602 **4** *nk* **Hatta Stream (IRE)**[12] 5698 4-8-13 **72**.......................... SimonPearce[(5)] 8 77
(J Pearce) *racd wd thrght: chsd ldrs: lost grnd bnd 2f out: styd on wl again ins fnl f* **4/1**[2]

020 **5** 1 **Whiskey Junction**[43] 4662 6-9-6 **74**.. SebSanders 10 76
(M Quinn) *prom on inner: rdn and effrt over 1f out: cl enough ent fnl f: one pce last 100yds* **14/1**

5234 **6** *nk* **Lay Claim (USA)**[10] 5769 3-9-4 **74**..................................(p) RichardHughes 4 75+
(A J McCabe) *hld up in last pair: rdn and effrt on outer 2f out: styd on ins fnl f: nvr rchd ldrs* **7/2**[1]

3033 **7** ½ **Little Edward**[22] 5368 12-9-0 **68**.. LiamKeniry 1 67
(R J Hodges) *chsd ldrs on inner: cl enough over 1f out: nt qckn and sn btn* **11/1**

4555 **8** 2¾ **Sherjawy (IRE)**[115] 2331 6-9-3 **71**.......................... KirstyMilczarek 6 61
(Miss Z C Davison) *towards rr on inner: no prog 2f out: steadily fdd* **50/1**

6236 **9** ¾ **Key Light (IRE)**[32] 5037 3-9-3 **73**..................................(t) WilliamBuick 2 61
(J W Hills) *hld up towards rr: effrt 2f out: chsd ldrs wl over 1f out: wknd* **16/1**

5004 **10** ¾ **Water Gipsy**[29] 5145 3-9-4 **74**..................................(p) RyanMoore 3 60
(G L Moore) *a wl in rr: shkn up and no prog 2f out* **16/1**

5135 **11** 1¼ **Ace Of Spies (IRE)**[14] 5647 5-9-5 **73**.......................... ShaneKelly 11 55
(C R Dore) *rapid prog on wd outside to press ldr 4f out: wknd jst as rapidly wl over 1f out* **11/1**

1460 **12** 1¼ **Athwaab**[13] 5652 3-9-2 **72**.. AdamKirby 9 50
(M G Quinlan) *racd wd: hld up in rr: brief effrt over 2f out: sn wknd* **16/1**

1m 12.02s (0.12) **Going Correction** +0.025s/f (Slow)
WFA 3 from 4yo+ 2lb **12** Ran SP% **119.4**
Speed ratings (Par 103): **100,99,99,99,97 97,96,93,92,91 89,87**
toteswingers:1&2 £7.80, 2&3 £6.60, 1&3 £5.80 CSF £74.18 CT £532.67 TOTE £16.90: £5.20, £1.20, £4.90; EX 88.10 Place 6: £92.02 Place 5: £31.53.
Owner Taylor And Sheldon Partners **Bred** Mountarmstrong Stud **Trained** Epsom, Surrey

FOCUS
A competitive sprint which went to a course specialist. It didn't look strong run. The winner was close to his old form.
T/Jkpt: Not won. T/Plt: £157.00 to a £1 stake. Pool of £70,161.68 - 326.03 winning tickets. T/Qpdt: £68.10 to a £1 stake. Pool of £5,314.17 - 57.70 winning tickets. JN

5558 YARMOUTH (L-H)
Tuesday, September 14

OFFICIAL GOING: Good to soft (soft in places) changing to soft after race 7 (4.40)
Wind: fresh, half against Weather: overcast, breezy

6058 EUROPEAN BREEDERS' FUND MAIDEN FILLIES' STKS 6f 3y
1:40 (1:42) (Class 5) 2-Y-O **£3,343** (£1,000; £500; £250; £124) **Stalls** High

Form RPR

222 **1** **Mama Lulu (USA)**[57] 4203 2-9-0 76..........................(v[1]) FrankieDettori 7 77
(M L W Bell) *hmpd and short of room s: hld up towards rr: hdwy to trck ldrs ent fnl 2f: swtchd lft and effrt 1f out: drvn to chal ins fnl f: kpt on u.p to ld towards fin:* **9/4**[2]

66 **2** *nk* **Miss Exhibitionist**[32] 5047 2-9-0 0.. JackMitchell 10 76
(P W Chapple-Hyam) *t.k.h: chsd ldrs tl led after 1f: rdn wl over 1f out: edgd lft u.p ins fnl f: kpt on tl hdd and no ex towards fin* **7/2**[3]

3 2¼ **Mosaicist (IRE)** 2-8-11 0.. MartinLane[(3)] 11 69+
(J R Fanshawe) *in tch: hdwy to chse ldrs 1/2-way: chsd ldr ent fnl 2f: rdn and pressing ldr over 1f out tl no ex and btn fnl 75yds: wknd towards fin* **50/1**

6 **4** *nk* **Panoptic**[60] 4103 2-9-0 0.. TomQueally 8 68+
(H R A Cecil) *awkward leaving stalls: t.k.h: hld up in tch: hdwy to chse ldng trio ent fnl 2f: rdn and fnd little over 1f out: styd on same pce ins fnl f* **10/11**[1]

6 **5** 4 **Cat Island**[40] 4759 2-8-9 0.. AshleyMorgan[(5)] 5 56
(M H Tompkins) *chsd ldr for 1f and 3f out tl ent fnl 2f: sn rdn: btn jst over 1f out: wknd ins fnl f* **40/1**

6 4 **Petrichor** 2-9-0 0.. TonyCulhane 9 44
(E F Vaughan) *stdd s: t.k.h: hld up in rr: pushed along and wl outpcd over 2f out: plugged on past btn horses over 1f out: nvr trbld ldrs* **100/1**

03 **7** 6 **Icelady**[16] 5558 2-9-0 0.. EddieAhern 12 26
(R M H Cowell) *stdd s: hld up in tch in rr: rdn and lost tch over 2f out: wl bhd over 1f out* **80/1**

8 1 **Escala** 2-9-0 0.. MarcHalford 2 23
(M D Squance) *v.s.a: rcvrd and in tch after 1f: rdn and struggling 1/2-way: wl bhd fnl 2f* **150/1**

0 **9** 8 **Champagne Princess**[11] 5717 2-9-0 0.......................... TomMcLaughlin 4 —
(P S McEntee) *uns rdr on way to s: racd keenly: led for 1f: chsd ldr tl 1/2-way: sn struggling: wl bhd over 1f out* **150/1**

10 5 **Harlequin Girl** 2-8-7 0.. JessicaSteven[(7)] 6 —
(T T Clement) *in tch tl pushed along and struggling 1/2-way: sn wl bhd: t.o over 1f out* **250/1**

000 **11** 55 **Huckle Duckle (IRE)**[152] 1324 2-8-7 38..........................(t) LeonnaMayor[(7)] 3 —
(P S McEntee) *restless in stalls: chsd ldrs tl rdn and lost pl qckly 1/2-way: wl t.o and virtually p.u fr wl over 1f out* **250/1**

1m 17.34s (2.94) **Going Correction** +0.375s/f (Good) **11** Ran SP% **114.1**
Speed ratings (Par 92): **95,94,91,91,85 80,72,71,60,53** —
toteswingers:1&2 £2.00, 2&3 £9.80, 1&3 £8.70 CSF £10.27 TOTE £2.80: £1.10, £1.10, £4.50; EX 10.20 Trifecta £42.50 Pool: £706.86 - 12.30 winning units..
Owner My Meadowview LLC **Bred** My Meadowview Farms Llc **Trained** Newmarket, Suffolk

FOCUS
This was a modest fillies' maiden. It was run at just an ordinary pace and the field stuck more towards the stands' side, with the rail looking to be an advantage. The form has been given a chance and is rated at face value.

NOTEBOOK
Mama Lulu(USA), visored for the first time, just edged the verdict. She had found one too good on her three previous outings, but set the standard and the headgear did the trick on this return from a break. She rates a little better than the bare form as she was done no favours at the start and possesses a useful level of ability. However, the worry now is whether the visor will continue to have a positive effect, and she doesn't have all that much scope. (tchd 5-2)
Miss Exhibitionist went down fighting and finished a clear second-best. This was by far her best effort to date back down in trip, she now qualifies for nurseries and fully deserves to find an opening. (op 9-2, tchd 5-1 in places)
Mosaicist(IRE) ◆ hails from a decent sprinting family. She proved distinctly green in the preliminaries and the market strongly suggested the run would be needed, but she ultimately held every chance before tiring late on. She looks the one to take out of the race and could be very useful. (op 40-1)
Panoptic has now been a beaten odds-on favourite on both her racecourse outings and is disappointing. She didn't get a great passage through the race and almost certainly wasn't helped by having to come wide with her effort, but she wasn't in anyway unlucky. Perhaps returning to quicker ground will help, but she does have a fair bit to prove after this. (op Evens)
Cat Island, who proved edgy down at the start, was faced with easier ground and ran a similar race to that of her debut over C&D last month. She needs one more run for a mark. (op 33-1)

The Form Book, Raceform Ltd, Compton, RG20 6NL

Petrichor cost 15,000gns and comes from a yard yet to have a juvenile winner this term. She wasn't a serious factor at any stage, but caught the eye staying on and should really get closer next time out. (op 150-1)

6059 MOULTON NURSERIES NURSERY (FOR THE JACK LEADER CHALLENGE TROPHY) 1m 3y

2:10 (2:10) (Class 4) (0-85,79) 2-Y-0 **£3,154** (£944; £472; £236; £117) **Stalls** High

Form RPR

612 **1** **Handsome Jack (IRE)**[7] 5830 2-9-1 **73** EddieAhern 2 81+
(R A Mills) *t.k.h: chsd ldrs: rdn to ld over 1f out: flashed tail u.p ent fnl f: pushed along hands and heels and drew clr ins fnl f: comf* **10/11**[1]

000 **2** *2½* **Bouggatti**[17] 5523 2-8-0 **63** ow3 JohnFahy[(5)] 1 65+
(W Jarvis) *s.i.s: bustled along early: hdwy to chse ldrs 5f out: rdn ent fnl 2f: chsd wnr over 1f out: nt gng pce of wnr and btn ins fnl f* **7/1**

14 **3** *1½* **Fifth Dimension (IRE)**[12] 5699 2-9-3 **75** TomQueally 5 73
(J A Osborne) *t.k.h: hld up wl in tch: n.m.r ent fnl 2f: rdn and hdwy to chse ldng pair jst over 1f out: no imp ins fnl f* **16/1**

404 **4** *1* **Ice Magic**[28] 5178 2-8-5 **63** (b[1]) JimmyQuinn 6 59
(M H Tompkins) *stdd s: t.k.h: hld up in tch: nt clr run ent fnl 2f tl swtchd lft and rdn ent fnl f: kpt on ins fnl f: nvr gng pce to threaten ldrs* **16/1**

3231 **5** *5* **Regal Kiss**[12] 5682 2-9-5 **77** RoystonFfrench 8 62
(M Johnston) *chsd ldr tl over 1f out: wknd u.p ent fnl f* **11/2**[2]

055 **6** *½* **Al Rannan**[21] 5385 2-8-0 **65** IanBurns[(7)] 4 49
(M L W Bell) *in tch: rdn and unable qck over 2f out: wknd u.p wl over 1f out* **22/1**

0030 **7** *1* **Better Offer (IRE)**[12] 5675 2-8-7 **68** (v[1]) MartinLane[(3)] 7 50
(Miss Amy Weaver) *led tl rdn and hdd over 1f out: wknd qckly* **66/1**

2203 **8** *18* **Point Du Jour (FR)**[2] 5992 2-9-7 **79** (t) GeorgeBaker 3 21
(I A Wood) *stood stl as stalls opened and v.s.a: wl bhd: grad clsd and in tch 1/2-way: wknd qckly ent fnl 2f: wl bhd and eased ins fnl f* **6/1**[3]

1m 44.08s (3.48) **Going Correction** +0.375s/f (Good) 8 Ran SP% **112.2**
Speed ratings (Par 97): **97,94,93,92,87 86,85,67**
toteswingers:1&2 £2.40, 2&3 £16.40, 1&3 £3.20 CSF £7.50 CT £58.79 TOTE £1.70: £1.10, £1.40, £4.60; EX 7.40 Trifecta £43.80 Pool: £514.04 - 8.67.
Owner Exors Of The Late T G Mills **Bred** Louis A Walshe **Trained** Headley, Surrey

FOCUS
A modest nursery. The field again stuck towards the nearside and there was just an average pace on. The winner is rated close to

NOTEBOOK
Handsome Jack(IRE) gained compensation for his near-miss at Goodwood off this mark a week earlier and ultimately ran out a very ready winner. The ground on his previous outing was a little easier than advertised so this surface was of no real concern, although looking at his performance here it's a fair bet he will prove happiest when getting back on quicker ground. There was a lot to like about the way he battled to shake off the unexposed runner-up, to whom he was conceding 13lb, and he actually quickened again when in the clear late on. The handicapper will now have his say (already due a 5lb rise), but this son of Iffraaj remains one to follow. (op 11-10 tchd 6-5 and 5-4 in places)
Bouggatti ◆, up in trip, was making his nursery debut off a mark of 60 and has clearly begun life in this sphere on a good mark. He pushed the winner in between the final 2f, looking suited by the cut underfoot, and won't always bump into one like that rival in this sort of company. He has scope and should be off the mark before too long. (op 8-1)
Fifth Dimension(IRE) was having just his third outing and making his turf/nursery debut. He lacked the pace to land a telling blow, but kept on gamely for pressure and could prove more effective on less demanding ground on turf.
Ice Magic, another nursery debutant, was equipped with first-time blinkers and proved a bit free early on. He already looks in need of a stiffer test. (op 14-1)
Regal Kiss scored with something left in hand on her nursery debut last time out and was up 4lb. She didn't look to handle this different ground when asked for an effort, though, and wasn't given a hard time when it became apparent she was held. Don't write her off when returning to a quicker surface. (op 7-2)
Point Du Jour(FR) turned in a solid effort on soft ground at Goodwood two days earlier and met support here. However, he stood still as the gates flew back, losing around 10 lengths, and that was the end of his chances. This leaves him with a deal to prove. Official explanation: jockey said colt missed the break (op 13-2 tchd 7-1)

6060 THOMAS PRIOR MEMORIAL MAIDEN STKS 6f 3y

2:40 (3:15) (Class 5) 3-Y-0+ **£2,590** (£770; £385; £192) **Stalls** High

Form RPR

4 **1** **Arctic Lynx (IRE)**[181] 900 3-9-3 0 GeorgeBaker 4 70+
(J R Best) *chsd ldrs: hdwy to trck ldr 2f out: rdn and ev ch over 1f out: kpt on u.p to ld wl ins fnl f* **7/2**[2]

4 **2** *hd* **Meia Noite**[34] 4966 3-8-12 0 JackMitchell 11 64+
(C F Wall) *chsd ldrs: rdn to ld narrowly over 1f out: rn green u.p ins fnl f: kpt on tl hdd and no ex wl ins fnl f* **12/1**

3 *nk* **Junket** 3-8-9 0 Louis-PhilippeBeuzelin[(3)] 9 63+
(Dr J D Scargill) *s.i.s: sn rdn along in midfield: rdn over 2f out: chsd ldrs over 1f out: no prog tl r.o wl fnl 75yds: gng on fin and wnt 3rd last strides* **15/2**

2320 **4** *nk* **Faithful Duchess (IRE)**[25] 5267 3-8-12 60 EddieAhern 5 62
(E A L Dunlop) *hld up in tch: hdwy to chse ldrs over 1f out: rdn to chse ldng pair ent fnl f: nt qckn and no imp tl kpt on fnl 75yds: nvr quite gng pce to rch ldrs* **11/2**

55 **5** *6* **Miss Blink**[12] 5686 3-8-6 0 ow1 JohnLawson[(7)] 13 44
(R Bastiman) *towards rr on stands' side: rdn and hung lft ent fnl 2f: plugged on ins fnl f: nvr trbld ldrs* **100/1**

0-46 **6** *2¼* **Rose Bed (IRE)**[13] 5650 3-8-12 45 WilliamCarson 14 36
(M G Quinlan) *racd on stands' side: midfield and off the pce: styd on same pce u.p fnl 2f: nvr trbld ldrs* **50/1**

4552 **7** *2¼* **Via Aurelia (IRE)**[13] 5650 3-8-12 57 (v) TomQueally 8 29
(J R Fanshawe) *in tch in midfield: effrt and fnd little ent fnl 2f: stl plenty to do and no prog whn nt clr run and hmpd over 1f out: rdn and no hdwy 1f out* **5/2**[1]

5320 **8** *½* **Gessabelle**[29] 5162 3-8-12 49 (t) TomMcLaughlin 7 27
(P S McEntee) *led tl rdn and hdd over 2f out: sn struggling u.p: wl btn over 1f out* **50/1**

9 *1* **Itum** 3-9-3 0 MarcHalford 1 29
(Mrs C A Dunnett) *chsd ldr tl led over 2f out: rdn and hdd over 1f out: wknd qckly ent fnl f* **100/1**

06 **10** *3½* **Fastinthestraight (IRE)**[13] 5658 3-9-3 0 NickyMackay 10 18
(J R Boyle) *bmpd s and slowly away: a outpcd in rr* **100/1**

6 **11** *hd* **Jo Boy**[173] 980 3-9-3 0 RoystonFfrench 2 17
(D M Simcock) *s.i.s: sn pushed along and a outpcd in rr* **4/1**[3]

40 **12** *31* **Prince Of Nama (IRE)**[36] 4908 3-9-0 0 AshleyHamblett[(3)] 12 —
(P L Gilligan) *in tch in midfield: rdn and dropped out 1/2-way: t.o fnl 2f* **66/1**

1m 17.1s (2.70) **Going Correction** +0.375s/f (Good)
WFA 3 from 4yo 2lb 12 Ran SP% **114.0**
Speed ratings (Par 103): **97,96,96,95,87 84,81,81,79,75 75,33**
toteswingers:1&2 £10.10, 2&3 £9.80, 1&3 £7.30 CSF £41.82 TOTE £4.20: £1.30, £3.40, £2.80; EX 35.70 TRIFECTA Not won..
Owner Heading For The Rocks Partnership **Bred** Derek Veitch And Saleh Ali Hammadi **Trained** Hucking, Kent
■ Stewards' Enquiry : Nicky Mackay caution: used whip when out of contention.

FOCUS
There was a delay of around half an hour before this race due to Kentish rearing in the stalls and badly injuring his jockey, who lay there until the ambulance could move her safely. That dictated all races for the remainder of the card were put back 30 minutes. There was a difference of opinion early on as to where the best ground was, but the main action was down the centre of the track and the first four dominated. Modest maiden form but the first three can do better.
Prince Of Nama(IRE) Official explanation: jockey said colt stopped quickly; vet said colt finished distressed

6061 PREMIER RACING SERVICES H'CAP (DIV I) 1m 3y

3:10 (3:41) (Class 6) (0-60,60) 3-Y-0+ **£1,813** (£539; £269; £134) **Stalls** High

Form RPR

004 **1** **Destiny Blue (IRE)**[11] 5710 3-9-2 **56** EddieAhern 8 78+
(J A Osborne) *a travelling wl: hld up wl in tch: led wl over 1f out: qcknd clr ent fnl f: r.o wl: v easily* **5/1**[3]

541 **2** *3½* **Nolecce**[8] 5819 3-8-12 **55** 6ex AndrewHeffernan[(3)] 7 65
(R C Guest) *t.k.h: hld up in tch: n.m.r ent fnl 2f: rdn and hdwy between horses to press wnr over 1f out: outpcd and no ch w wnr 1f out: kpt on for 2nd* **5/2**[1]

-406 **3** *1½* **Final Drive (IRE)**[16] 5560 4-9-7 **56** TomMcLaughlin 1 63
(J Ryan) *hld up in tch: hdwy on bit to press ldrs ent fnl 2f: rdn and nt gng pce of wnr over 1f out: kpt on same pce ins fnl f* **14/1**

3623 **4** *1* **Al Rayanah**[12] 5704 7-9-0 **49** (p) WilliamCarson 5 54
(G Prodromou) *stdd s: hld up in tch in rr: rdn and effrt wl over 1f out: chsd ldng trio ent fnl f: plugged on but no ch w wnr* **11/4**[2]

000 **5** *2½* **My Jeanie (IRE)**[15] 5585 6-8-5 **45** AdamBeschizza[(5)] 6 44
(J C Fox) *in tch in midfield: rdn and unable qck ent fnl 3f: no ch w ldrs: plugged on u.p fr over 1f out* **8/1**

0600 **6** *9* **Athboy Auction**[25] 5271 5-8-11 **46** (v[1]) JimmyQuinn 9 24
(H J Collingridge) *t.k.h early: hld up wl in tch in last pair: rdn over 2f out: sn edging lft and btn* **16/1**

500 **7** *shd* **Fear Factor (IRE)**[15] 5603 3-8-1 **46** (t) JohnFahy[(5)] 2 24
(G A Butler) *dwlt: sn rcvrd to chsd ldrs: rdn over 2f out: wknd rapidly over 1f out* **10/1**

00-4 **8** *4½* **Yanbu (USA)**[38] 4835 5-8-5 **45** TobyAtkinson[(5)] 4 13
(T T Clement) *led: rdn and hdd wl over 1f out: sn wknd* **40/1**

0046 **9** *½* **Miss Kitty Grey (IRE)**[13] 5670 3-9-6 **60** NickyMackay 3 27
(J R Boyle) *racd keenly: chsd ldrs: rdn and ev ch ent fnl 2f: wknd qckly over 1f out: eased ins fnl f* **14/1**

4010 **10** *11* **Zeffirelli**[141] 1585 5-9-10 **59** TomQueally 10 —
(M Quinn) *chsd ldr tl hung lft u.p ent fnl 2f: sn wknd: wl bhd and eased ins fnl f* **10/1**

1m 43.4s (2.80) **Going Correction** +0.375s/f (Good)
WFA 3 from 4yo+ 5lb 10 Ran SP% **122.9**
Speed ratings (Par 101): **101,97,96,95,92 83,83,78,78,67**
toteswingers:1&2 £5.00, 2&3 £9.30, 1&3 £16.00 CSF £18.96 CT £176.25 TOTE £4.60: £1.50, £1.90, £5.20; EX 21.40 TRIFECTA Not won..
Owner Mr & Mrs Ian Bendelow & Mrs F Walwyn **Bred** Barronstown Stud **Trained** Upper Lambourn, Berks

FOCUS
A very weak handicap. There wasn't much of an early pace on and, while they raced more towards the stands' side, the near rail was shunned by most. It was the quicker division and the improved winner is value for a bit extra.
Yanbu(USA) Official explanation: trainer said mare was unsuited by the good to soft (soft in places) ground

6062 PREMIER RACING SERVICES H'CAP (DIV II) 1m 3y

3:40 (4:10) (Class 6) (0-60,58) 3-Y-0+ **£1,813** (£539; £269; £134) **Stalls** High

Form RPR

0500 **1** **Astrodonna**[21] 5391 5-9-5 **58** AshleyMorgan[(5)] 8 67
(M H Tompkins) *stdd s: hld up wl in tch in last trio: hdwy on bit to ld over 1f out: rdn and qcknd clr ent fnl f: r.o wl: eased towards fin* **7/2**[2]

2230 **2** *2* **Libre**[89] 3128 10-9-0 **48** TomQueally 4 53
(F Jordan) *stdd s: hld up wl in tch in last trio: shkn up 2f out: rdn and hdwy over 1f out: kpt on u.p to go 2nd fnl 75yds: no ch w wnr* **9/2**[3]

0501 **3** *nk* **Exopuntia**[16] 5560 4-9-2 **50** TonyCulhane 10 54
(Miss J Feilden) *chsd ldr tl led ent fnl 3f: rdn 2f out: hdd and drvn over 1f out: sn outpcd by wnr and one pce ins fnl f: lost 2nd fnl 75yds* **6/1**

502 **4** *2* **Lady Brickhouse**[14] 5645 3-8-10 **49** SaleemGolam 7 47
(M D Squance) *chsd ldrs: rdn and unable qck over 2f out: rallied u.p over 1f out: styd on same pce ins fnl f* **14/1**

000 **5** *1* **Hilltop Artistry**[40] 4763 4-9-7 **55** EddieAhern 6 52
(J R Jenkins) *chsd ldrs: rdn and pressed ldrs over 1f out: sn outpcd by wnr: wknd ins fnl f* **13/2**

/000 **6** *1* **Gee Ceffyl Bach**[8] 5821 6-8-9 **46** AndrewHeffernan[(3)] 5 41
(G Woodward) *t.k.h: stdd s: hld up wl in tch in last trio: swtchd rt and effrt ent fnl 2f: no prog over 1f out: plugged on same pce ins fnl f* **33/1**

0244 **7** *nk* **Hellenio**[16] 5560 3-8-11 **55** (tp) AdamBeschizza[(5)] 9 48
(M G Quinlan) *wl in tch in midfield: effrt u.p 2f out: outpcd wl over 1f out: one pce and wl hld ins fnl f* **3/1**[1]

5606 **8** *½* **Red Eddie**[11] 5729 3-8-1 **45** JohnFahy[(5)] 1 37
(S Dow) *sn led: hdd over 4f out: styd prom: rdn 3f out: wknd u.p over 1f out* **12/1**

0040 **9** *15* **Kings On The Roof**[12] 5680 4-8-4 **45** NoelGarbutt[(7)] 2 —
(P Leech) *s.i.s: sn rcvrd to chse ldrs: led over 4f out tl ent fnl 3f: wknd qckly wl over 1f out* **50/1**

1m 45.67s (5.07) **Going Correction** +0.375s/f (Good)
WFA 3 from 4yo+ 5lb 9 Ran SP% **112.3**
Speed ratings (Par 101): **89,87,86,84,83 82,82,81,66**
toteswingers:1&2 £4.90, 2&3 £4.50, 1&3 £4.30 CSF £18.93 CT £89.32 TOTE £4.10: £1.10, £3.30, £2.90; EX 18.40 Trifecta £85.40 Pool: £238.98 - 2.07 winning units..
Owner Mystic Meg Limited **Bred** Mystic Meg Limited **Trained** Newmarket, Suffolk

FOCUS
The second and slower division of the 1m handicap. They all raced down the middle this time. Modest, limited form, the winner not needing to match this year's best.

Astrodonna Official explanation: trainer said, regarding apparent improvement in form, that the mare benefited from a less competitive race

6063 ATTHERACES CONDITIONS STKS 6f 3y
4:10 (4:40) (Class 3) 3-Y-O+

£5,607 (£1,679; £839; £420; £209; £105) Stalls High

Form RPR

03-0 **1** **Brave Prospector**[123] 2100 5-8-9 104 TomQueally 2 101
(P W Chapple-Hyam) *t.k.h early: chsd ldr: rdn to ld ent fnl f: hrd pressed and drvn ins fnl f: hld on wl* **15/2**

2213 **2** 1/2 **Dafeef**[17] 5526 3-8-7 106 (p) FrankieDettori 1 100
(Saeed Bin Suroor) *stdd s: t.k.h: hld up wl in tch: rdn and effrt 2f out: drvn and ev ch ins fnl f: unable qck and hld towards fin* **11/8**[1]

500 **3** 1/2 **Desert Phantom (USA)**[95] 2940 4-8-6 89 MartinLane(3) 5 98
(D M Simcock) *led at stdy gallop: qcknd and pushed along 2f out: rdn and hdd ent fnl f: styd on same pce fnl 100yds* **16/1**

0000 **4** 3/4 **Iver Bridge Lad**[10] 5744 3-8-7 100 (b) MarcHalford 6 96
(J Ryan) *hld up wl in tch: rdn and effrt to chse ldrs over 1f out: styd on same pce u.p ins fnl f* **13/2**[3]

4045 **5** 6 **Tomintoul Singer (IRE)**[35] 4937 3-8-2 85 JimmyQuinn 7 71
(H R A Cecil) *t.k.h: chsd ldrs: rdn and effrt 2f out: wknd u.p 1f out* **22/1**

410- **6** nse **Royal Rock**[315] 7232 6-9-2 109 GeorgeBaker 4 83
(C F Wall) *stdd s: hld up wl in tch: rdn wl over 1f out: unable qck and wl btn 1f out* **9/4**[2]

6036 **7** 3 1/2 **Sairaam (IRE)**[12] 5688 4-8-0 63 ow1 (b[1]) JohnFahy(5) 3 61
(C Smith) *t.k.h early: hld up in tch: rdn ent fnl 2f: sn btn* **100/1**

1m 15.8s (1.40) **Going Correction** +0.375s/f (Good)
WFA 3 from 4yo+ 2lb 7 Ran SP% **109.2**
Speed ratings (Par 107): **105,104,103,102,94 94,89**
toteswingers:1&2 £2.60, 2&3 £5.30, 1&3 £8.90 CSF £16.65 TOTE £8.90: £4.40, £1.10; EX 15.20.
Owner Saleh Al Homaizi & Imad Al Sagar **Bred** Times Of Wigan Ltd **Trained** Newmarket, Suffolk

FOCUS
An interesting little conditions event, run at a muddling sort of pace. Muddling form too with the winner not needing to match his best.

NOTEBOOK
Brave Prospector, who has suffered a life-threatening colic since running below-par on his seasonal debut in May, was easy to back with his trainer indicating beforehand he would need the run. However, he ran out a gutsy winner under a positive ride and is clearly back in decent heart. He does handle cut in the ground and there's a strong chance he will improve a deal for the run, so should be respected when going back up in class as he is a fresh horse. Another crack at the Group 3 Willmott Dixon Bengough Memorial Stakes at Ascot next month, in which he was third last term, could well be on the cards. (op 8-1)

Dafeef had a great chance to resume winning ways at the weights and is proven on such ground. He went down only narrowly, but at no stage did he help his rider and his quirks are there for all to see. (op 11-10)

Desert Phantom(USA)'s proximity clouds this form. He is flattered to have been on the front-end, though, and it was the first time this year he had got his ground. His official mark may well now suffer as a result of this run and connections may well look to run again before the handicapper can reassess him. The bounce factor would be of some worry if he does turn out quickly. (tchd 18-1)

Iver Bridge Lad ran another solid race in defeat and does deserve a change of luck, but continues to be hard to place successfully. (op 9-1 tchd 6-1)

Tomintoul Singer(IRE) wasn't disgraced on this, the softest ground she had encountered to date. However, she is another tricky horse to place. (op 25-1 tchd 20-1)

Royal Rock had won first time up for the last two years and proved solid in the betting for this belated seasonal return. His trainer said beforehand this 6-y-o had been very sick earlier in the spring, though, and ultimately the run did look needed so he shouldn't be judged harshly. Official explanation: jockey said gelding lost its action

Sairaam(IRE), rated just 63, was predictably outclassed. (op 150-1)

6064 VISIT SOUTHDOWNSBETTING.CO.UK H'CAP 5f 43y
4:40 (5:11) (Class 4) (0-85,85) 3-Y-O+ £3,500 (£1,047; £523; £261; £130) Stalls High

Form RPR

5314 **1** **Magical Speedfit (IRE)**[14] 5628 5-8-0 71 oh1 RyanPowell(7) 3 80
(G G Margarson) *hld up off the pce in last trio: stl plenty to do and effrt over 1f out: str run ins fnl f to ld last stride* **14/1**

1505 **2** shd **Solemn**[3] 5967 5-9-2 83 (b) MartinLane(3) 6 92
(J M Bradley) *in tch in midfield: hdwy 1/2-way: rdn to chse ldr over 1f out: drvn to ld jst ins fnl f: kpt on u.p tl hdd last stride* **7/2**[1]

5004 **3** 1/2 **Doric Lady**[21] 5393 5-8-12 76 LiamJones 8 83
(J A R Toller) *hld up in rr: rdn and hdwy wl over 1f out: kpt on wl to press ldrs fnl 100yds: unable qck towards fin* **10/1**

0400 **4** 1 3/4 **Equuleus Pictor**[17] 5528 6-8-11 75 DarryllHolland 4 76
(J L Spearing) *led: rdn wl over 1f out: hdd jst ins fnl f: wknd fnl 100yds* **9/2**[2]

2600 **5** 3/4 **Colorus (IRE)**[4] 5915 7-8-2 71 oh6 (v) AdamBeschizza(5) 9 69
(W J H Ratcliffe) *chsd ldrs: wnt 2nd 1/2-way tl over 1f out: wknd u.p jst ins fnl f* **28/1**

2116 **6** 3 **Cape Royal**[3] 5966 10-9-3 81 (bt) NickyMackay 1 68
(J M Bradley) *in tch in midfield: rdn and effrt ent fnl 2f: wknd u.p over 1f out* **9/2**[2]

00 **7** 1 **Luscivious**[6] 5855 6-8-11 80 (b) JohnFahy(5) 10 64
(J A Glover) *chsd ldrs: rdn 1/2-way: wknd u.p wl over 1f out* **15/2**

5500 **8** nk **Canadian Danehill (IRE)**[31] 5069 8-9-0 78 (p) FrankieDettori 5 61
(R M H Cowell) *chsd ldr tl 1/2-way: sn rdn: wknd u.p over 1f out* **16/1**

4412 **9** 1/2 **Angus Newz**[14] 5632 7-9-7 85 (v) TomQueally 2 66
(M Quinn) *sn pushed along and nvr gng wl in rr: bhd fr wl over 1f out* **11/2**[3]

1446 **10** 5 **Special Quality (USA)**[24] 5309 3-8-6 71 EddieAhern 7 34
(R M H Cowell) *a towards rr: rdn and btn ent fnl 2f: wl bhd ins fnl f* **12/1**

66.84 secs (4.14) **Going Correction** +0.975s/f (Soft)
WFA 3 from 5yo+ 1lb 10 Ran SP% **118.5**
Speed ratings (Par 105): **105,104,104,101,100 95,93,93,92,84**
toteswingers:1&2 £17.20, 2&3 £11.10, 1&3 £24.30 CSF £63.72 CT £541.22 TOTE £16.80: £4.40, £1.60, £6.00; EX 79.30 Trifecta £110.10 Part won. Pool £148.80 - 0.50 winning units..
Owner Exors of the Late John Guest **Bred** John Malone **Trained** Newmarket, Suffolk
■ Stewards' Enquiry : Martin Lane one-day ban: used whip with excessive frequency (Sep 28)

FOCUS
An open-looking sprint handicap and not a bad contest for the class. The race was run in driving rain and it was a proper test thanks to the strong early tempo. A small personal best from the winner.

Angus Newz Official explanation: jockey said mare never travelled

6065 CUSTOM KITCHENS HAVE MOVED TO HAMILTON HOUSE H'CAP 1m 3f 101y
5:10 (5:40) (Class 5) (0-70,68) 3-Y-O+ £2,590 (£770; £385; £192) Stalls Low

Form RPR

0443 **1** **Extremely So**[12] 5681 4-8-12 54 oh2 JackMitchell 13 68+
(P J McBride) *mde all: drew clr 5f out: wl clr and in n.d fnl 3f: eased ins fnl f* **10/1**

6001 **2** 7 **Sancho Panza**[17] 5536 3-7-11 54 oh2 JessicaSteven(7) 9 54
(Miss J Feilden) *chsd ldrs: chsd clr wnr 3f out: sn puished along: kpt on: no imp* **16/1**

0403 **3** 8 **Aalya (IRE)**[12] 5679 3-8-6 61 JohnFahy(5) 11 49
(P W Chapple-Hyam) *in tch in midfield: rdn 4f out: no ch w wnr after but kpt plugging on u.p to go modest 3rd ins fnl f* **9/1**

0316 **4** 2 1/2 **Wood Fair**[20] 5411 3-8-0 57 NeilFarley(7) 8 41
(Mrs K Burke) *dwlt: hld up towards rr: stdy hdwy 7f out: disp modest 2nd 3f out: sn rdn and no prog: wknd wl over 1f out* **4/1**[2]

5105 **5** 4 1/2 **Knotgarden (IRE)**[16] 5563 4-9-9 68 MartinLane(3) 14 46
(J R Fanshawe) *stdd s: hld up in rr: rdn 4f out: 7th and no ch 2f out: plugged on past btn horses ins fnl f: n.d* **25/1**

0440 **6** 2 1/2 **Yossi (IRE)**[9] 5790 6-9-9 65 (p) DarryllHolland 7 39
(R C Guest) *chsd wnr: rdn and struggling ent fnl 4f: no ch w wnr whn lost modest 2nd 3f out: wknd after* **16/1**

3260 **7** 1 3/4 **Outland (IRE)**[12] 5679 4-8-9 58 DannyBrock(7) 10 29
(J R Jenkins) *in tch in midfield: rdn and no hdwy 4f out: plugged on same pce and wl btn after* **12/1**

04-1 **8** 11 **Jinto**[40] 4764 3-8-11 66 AdamBeschizza(5) 3 21
(R M H Cowell) *in tch: rdn and struggling over 4f out: wl btn fnl 3f* **7/2**[1]

3-01 **9** 3 1/4 **Karky Schultz (GER)**[137] 1262 5-9-5 61 TomMcLaughlin 6 11
(J M P Eustace) *stdd s: hld up wl in rr: lost tch over 4f out: nvr on terms: t.o* **16/1**

4554 **10** 12 **Belle Boleyn**[13] 5653 3-8-6 56 LiamJones 12 —
(C F Wall) *chsd ldrs tl rdn and btn over 4f out: wl bhd fnl 3f: t.o and eased ins fnl f* **13/2**[3]

-000 **11** 31 **Nizhoni Dancer**[38] 4847 4-9-9 65 GeorgeBaker 1 —
(C F Wall) *in tch in midfield tl rdn and dropped out qckly over 4f out: wl t.o and virtually p.u fnl 2f* **28/1**

-465 **12** 7 **Forgotten Army (IRE)**[19] 5456 3-8-10 65 AshleyMorgan(5) 5 —
(M H Tompkins) *racd in midfield: rdn and no rspnse 6f out: wl t.o and virtually p.u fnl 2f* **11/1**

2155 **13** 3/4 **Rocky's Pride (IRE)**[63] 3995 4-9-9 65 TonyCulhane 2 —
(W J Musson) *stdd s: hld up in rr: lost tch over 4f out: wl t.o and virtually p.u fnl 2f* **25/1**

-050 **14** 19 **Stagecoach Emerald**[167] 1071 8-8-7 54 oh1 TobyAtkinson(5) 4 —
(T T Clement) *sn rdn and nvr gng wl in rr: t.o fr 1/2-way: stopped to a walk wl ins fnl f* **80/1**

2m 39.07s (10.37) **Going Correction** +1.025s/f (Soft)
WFA 3 from 4yo+ 8lb 14 Ran SP% **120.7**
Speed ratings (Par 103): **103,97,92,90,87 85,83,75,73,64 42,37,36,22**
toteswingers:1&2 £15.80, 2&3 £21.50, 1&3 £12.00. totesuper7: Win: Not won. Place: £208.10. CSF £154.86 CT £1503.73 TOTE £6.90: £1.60, £5.20, £3.50; EX 171.00 Trifecta £241.00 Part won. Pool £325.68 - 0.30 winning units. Place 6: £54.20 Place 5: £24.75.
Owner N Davies **Bred** Kirtlington Stud And Gilridge Bloodstock **Trained** Newmarket, Suffolk

FOCUS
A moderate middle-distance handicap and it was another wide-open affair. The race was run at a decent early gallop, but few managed to land a blow from off the pace as they were strung out from the start. The easy winner had previously looked exposed so his effort has not been rated too positively.

Wood Fair Official explanation: jockey said filly lost a right front shoe
Nizhoni Dancer Official explanation: jockey said gelding had no more to give
Forgotten Army(IRE) Official explanation: trainer said colt was unsuited by the soft ground
Rocky's Pride(IRE) Official explanation: jockey said gelding had no more to give
T/Plt: £49.00 to a £1 stake. Pool of £64,199.92 - 956.28 winning tickets. T/Qpdt: £19.20 to a £1 stake. Pool of £5,464.94 - 210.43 winning tickets. SP

6066 - 6069a (Foreign Racing) - See Raceform Interactive

5545 BEVERLEY (R-H)
Wednesday, September 15

OFFICIAL GOING: Good (7.7)
Wind: fresh, blustery 1/2 against Weather: overcast and very breezy, showers

6070 IRISH THOROUGHBRED MARKETING MAIDEN AUCTION STKS 7f 100y
2:00 (2:02) (Class 5) 2-Y-O £3,011 (£896; £447; £223) Stalls High

Form RPR

650 **1** **Bonita Star**[23] 5369 2-8-10 73 SamHitchcott 2 80
(M R Channon) *mde all: rdn wl over 1f out: styd on strly ins fnl f* **12/1**

323 **2** 4 **King Of The Celts (IRE)**[54] 4346 2-9-1 76 DavidAllan 11 76
(T D Easterby) *in tch: pushed along after 2f: awkward bnd after: hdwy 2f out: swtchd outside and rdn appr fnl f: kpt on to take 2nd nr fin: no ch w wnr* **2/1**[1]

2023 **3** hd **Kissing Clara (IRE)**[28] 5204 2-8-4 68 (p) FrankieMcDonald 13 64
(J S Moore) *chsd wnr: rdn along over 2f out: drvn over 1f out: kpt on same pce: lost 2nd nr fin* **11/1**

5 **4** 1/2 **History Girl (IRE)**[24] 5332 2-8-6 0 JoeFanning 14 65
(M Johnston) *dwlt: in tch: swtchd lft and hdwy over 2f out: rdn over 1f out: kpt on ins fnl f* **20/1**

03 **5** 2 1/4 **Number Theory**[15] 5629 2-8-11 0 GrahamGibbons 8 65
(J R Holt) *trckd ldrs: hdwy over 2f out: swtchd rt and rdn 1 1/2f out: sn drvn and one pce* **11/2**[3]

43 **6** 1/2 **Zamina (IRE)**[51] 4437 2-8-6 0 PaulHanagan 9 58
(S Kirk) *trckd ldng pair: hdwy and cl up 3f out: rdn 2f out: drvn appr fnl f: wknd* **5/1**[2]

0 **7** 4 **Memimajic**[92] 3058 2-8-4 0 PaulQuinn 6 47
(C W Fairhurst) *in rr tl sme late hdwy* **100/1**

0 **8** 3/4 **Battery Power**[39] 4844 2-8-6 0 SaleemGolam 12 47
(M H Tompkins) *dwlt: a towards rr* **33/1**

00 **9** 3 **Twennyshortkid**[53] 4368 2-8-11 0 TonyCulhane 7 45
(P T Midgley) *trckd ldrs: hdwy and cl up 1/2-way: rdn over 2f out: drvn and wknd over 1f out* **100/1**

04 **10** 1 **Kodicil (IRE)**[11] 5762 2-8-9 0 DanielTudhope 16 45
(T D Walford) *trckd ldrs on inner: effrt over 2f out: rdn along whn hmpd 1 1/2f out: nt rcvr* **66/1**

00 **11** 1 3/4 **Hartforth**[43] 4668 2-9-1 0 SilvestreDeSousa 3 43
(J D Bethell) *a towards rr* **100/1**

000 **12** *nse* **Pinotage**[28] 5196 2-8-8 36....................(v[1]) MichaelStainton(3) 4 39
(R M Whitaker) *a in rr* **100/1**

13 *4* **Kian's Delight** 2-8-13 0.................... TomEaves 5 31
(Jedd O'Keeffe) *s.i.s: a bhd* **100/1**

1m 36.11s (2.31) **Going Correction** +0.225s/f (Good) **13** Ran SP% **95.6**
Speed ratings (Par 95): **95,90,90,89,87 86,81,81,77,76 74,74,69**
toteswingers:1&2 £4.60, 2&3 £5.30, 1&3 £13.00 CSF £23.14 TOTE £11.10: £2.70, £1.10, £2.50; EX 32.60.
Owner B P York **Bred** Miss K Rausing **Trained** West Ilsley, Berks
■ Stewards' Enquiry : Graham Gibbons three-day ban: careless riding (Sep 29-30,Oct 4)
Michael Stainton caution: used whip when out of contention.

FOCUS
An ordinary maiden auction, weakened further by the late withdrawal of the fancied Copper Canyon, who misbehaved at the start. Those that raced prominently were at an advantage and the front six came clear. Improved form from the winner.

NOTEBOOK
Bonita Star had been taking on the likes of Frankel in her first three starts, but had nothing of that calibre against her here. Her rider did well to get her across from her wide draw in front and, once there, it was just a case of seeing her race out. She had the contest in safe-keeping passing the furlong pole, and much will depend on what the handicapper does with her now. Currently rated 73, she will probably go up for this but she still has scope and connections believe she will make a better 3-y-o.
King Of The Celts(IRE) was on and off the bridle in the first half of the contest and, as a result, was forced to switch out very wide in order to see daylight. He finished well up the hill to grab second close to the line, but the winner had gone beyond recall. He can win a race like this, and would probably be competitive in nurseries off a mark of 76. (op 5-2 tchd 11-4)
Kissing Clara(IRE), placed in six of her last seven starts and rated 68, was always close to the pace and kept on to make the frame once again, but she is totally exposed and had already been well beaten in a nursery. (op 9-1)
History Girl(IRE), who fluffed the start on her debut, ran on from the middle of the field to take fourth and her pedigree suggests that middle-distance handicaps will be her forte next year.
Number Theory, a good third in a decent Leicester maiden on softer ground last time, ran well for a long way and would be interesting back on an easier surface now that he gets a mark.
Zamina(IRE), in the frame in her first two starts, didn't really improve on those efforts but she also now qualifies for nurseries. (op 9-2)
Kodicil(IRE) showed up for a long way and still wasn't totally out of it when badly hampered against the inside rail entering the last 2f. (op 50-1)

6071 EUROPEAN BREEDERS' FUND MAIDEN FILLIES' STKS 7f 100y
2:35 (2:36) (Class 5) 2-Y-O £3,561 (£1,059; £529; £264) **Stalls** High

Form RPR
62 **1** **The Shrew**[18] 5509 2-9-0 0.................... PaulHanagan 9 80+
(J H M Gosden) *chsd ldr: led over 2f out: drvn out* **4/5[1]**

5 **2** *2 ½* **Mazagee (FR)**[24] 5324 2-9-0 0.................... FrannyNorton 7 74+
(D R Lanigan) *chsd ldrs: wnt 2nd 1f out: kpt on: no imp* **12/1**

40 **3** *2* **Set To Music (IRE)**[23] 5369 2-9-0 0.................... TomQueally 12 69
(M L W Bell) *led tl over 2f out: kpt on same pce* **5/1[3]**

40 **4** *4 ½* **Phoenix Flame**[32] 5066 2-9-0 0.................... GrahamGibbons 6 59
(A J McCabe) *chsd ldrs: drvn 5f out: wknd over 1f out* **50/1**

5 *½* **Eaves Lane (IRE)** 2-8-11 0.................... BarryMcHugh(3) 11 58
(R A Fahey) *s.s: reminders and hdwy over 2f out: kpt on: nvr nr ldrs* **20/1**

025 **6** *1 ¾* **Silver Show (IRE)**[58] 4203 2-9-0 66.................... SamHitchcott 2 54
(M R Channon) *in tch: drvn over 4f out: wknd over 1f out* **20/1**

7 *1 ¼* **Kaua'i Girl** 2-9-0 0.................... SilvestreDeSousa 10 51+
(Mrs A Duffield) *rrd s: hdwy over 2f out: nvr nr ldrs* **25/1**

0 **8** *5* **Cool Wind (IRE)**[23] 5369 2-9-0 0.................... JoeFanning 8 39
(Mahmood Al Zarooni) *chsd ldrs: hung lft over 2f out: wknd over 1f out: eased ins fnl f* **4/1[2]**

4425 **9** *4 ½* **Alensgrove (IRE)**[15] 5644 2-9-0 67.................... TonyCulhane 1 28
(P T Midgley) *hld up in rr: effrt on outer over 2f out: sn wknd* **33/1**

0 **10** *2* **Detailedassessment**[55] 4286 2-9-0 0.................... TomEaves 5 24
(B Smart) *in rr div: effrt over 2f out: sn lost pl* **100/1**

11 *60* **Efrosini** 2-8-7 0.................... NoraLooby(7) 3 —
(A J McCabe) *s.i.s: sn bhd: t.o 4f out* **100/1**

1m 35.95s (2.15) **Going Correction** +0.225s/f (Good) **11** Ran SP% **120.2**
Speed ratings (Par 92): **96,93,90,85,85 83,81,76,70,68** —
toteswingers:1&2 £4.50, 2&3 £7.40, 1&3 £1.80 CSF £11.83 TOTE £1.80: £1.10, £3.50, £1.80; EX 14.80.
Owner W J Gredley **Bred** Middle Park Stud Ltd **Trained** Newmarket, Suffolk

FOCUS
A fair fillies' maiden and once again it paid to race handily. The winning time was 0.16 seconds quicker than the opener. The form makes sense around the third and fourth.

NOTEBOOK
The Shrew, beaten a neck in an identical race over C&D last month, was the only one punters wanted to know. Always travelling powerfully up with the pace, she was in little danger after taking it up over 2f from home, and she is entitled to improve again from this. It will be interesting to see what handicap mark she gets. (op 8-11 tchd 4-6 and 10-11 in a place)
Mazagee(FR), not disgraced at a huge price on her Folkestone debut, improved plenty from that and stayed on well over the last 2f to finish a clear second, despite still showing signs of greenness. She looks the type to improve with racing. (tchd 14-1)
Set To Music(IRE), disappointing on Polytrack following a promising Newmarket debut, set the pace until collared by the winner coming to the last 2f and she now gets a mark. (op 7-1)
Phoenix Flame didn't fare badly considering she was full of herself before the start, and she is another that now qualifies for a nursery mark. (op 40-1)
Eaves Lane(IRE) ◆'s prospects of making a winning debut didn't look bright considering stable jockey Paul Hanagan had deserted her in favour of the winner, but this 30,000gns first foal of the useful Cape Columbine ran a promising race, especially considering she was very slowly away. (tchd 25-1)
Silver Show(IRE), upped in trip and rated 66, was being ridden along some way out and never figured.
Kaua'i Girl ◆, a 14,000gns filly out of a half-sister to seven winners, was by no means disgraced on this debut as she lost a huge amount of ground by walking out of the stalls.
Cool Wind(IRE), very green on her Kempton debut, was up there early but she gradually faded and looked most unhappy on the track. (op 9-2 tchd 5-1)

6072 BEVERLEY ANNUAL BADGEHOLDERS (S) NURSERY 5f
3:10 (3:11) (Class 6) (0-65,63) 2-Y-O £2,729 (£806; £403) **Stalls** High

Form RPR
0303 **1** **One Cool Bex**[16] 5581 2-9-1 57....................(e) TomQueally 6 64
(P J McBride) *hld up towards rr: smooth hdwy 1/2-way: swtchd lft and effrt over 1f out: rdn and str run ent fnl f: sn edgd rt: led last 50yds* **4/1[2]**

3640 **2** *1* **Crazy In Love**[34] 5000 2-8-2 51....................(b) RyanClark(7) 13 54
(W G M Turner) *trckd ldrs: hdwy 2f out: rdn to ld 1f out: sn drvn: hdd and no ex last 50yds* **25/1**

0020 **3** *1* **Bonjour Bongee**[2] 6035 2-8-12 59....................(b) IanBrennan(5) 1 58
(A J McCabe) *hld up towards rr: hdwy wl over 1f out: rdn ent fnl f: nrst fin* **20/1**

0300 **4** *1* **Je Suis Unrockstar**[2] 6035 2-9-4 60....................(p) DavidAllan 4 56
(J A Glover) *t.k.h: hld up in rr: swtchd outside and hdwy wl over 1f out: rdn and styd on ins fnl f: nrst fin* **16/1**

3040 **5** *1* **Glenns Princess**[15] 5630 2-8-13 55....................(b[1]) PaulHanagan 17 47
(R A Fahey) *led: rdn along 2f out: drvn and hdd appr fnl f: wknd* **9/1**

004 **6** *½* **Millies Dancer (IRE)**[17] 5558 2-8-0 45.................... JamesSullivan(3) 14 35
(M G Quinlan) *cl up: pushed along and ev ch whn edgd rt over 1f out: sn rdn and one pce* **8/1**

400 **7** *¾* **Vienna Woods (IRE)**[96] 2939 2-9-4 60.................... PhillipMakin 16 48
(B M R Haslam) *cl up: rdn and ev ch over 1f out: drvn ent fnl f: one pce* **25/1**

6055 **8** *¾* **Sarandjam**[7] 5862 2-8-5 47.................... SamHitchcott 10 32
(M R Channon) *chsd ldrs: rdn along 2f out: drvn wl over 1f out: sn one pce* **6/1[3]**

0303 **9** *nk* **Ignore The Advice (IRE)**[14] 5667 2-8-12 54.......... FrankieMcDonald 5 39
(J S Moore) *dwlt and swtchd rt s to ins rail: hdwy 2f out: rdn and n.m.r over 1f out: sn one pce* **28/1**

5236 **10** *½* **Never Can Stop**[12] 5720 2-9-7 63.................... TonyCulhane 15 47
(J G Portman) *in tch on inner: effrt and hdwy 2f out: sn nt clr run and swtchd lft over 1f out: rdn and n.m.r appr fnl f: sn no imp* **10/3[1]**

3200 **11** *2* **Bendigedig**[7] 5863 2-8-11 53.................... SilvestreDeSousa 9 29
(S Kirk) *midfield: rdn along to chse ldrs over 2f out: drvn and n.m.r over 1f out: sn wknd* **20/1**

0000 **12** *1 ¼* **Shy Bird**[2] 6035 2-8-11 53.................... FrannyNorton 8 23
(J A Glover) *chsd ldrs: rdn along 2f out: grad wknd* **40/1**

0050 **13** *1 ¾* **Running Water**[18] 5531 2-8-10 52.................... PatrickMathers 3 16
(H A McWilliams) *a in rr* **50/1**

046 **14** *1 ¼* **Moving Picture**[99] 2836 2-9-1 57.................... TomEaves 11 17
(B M R Haslam) *sltly hmpd s: a towards rr* **40/1**

3556 **15** *2 ¾* **Comrade Bond**[7] 5862 2-9-5 61....................(b[1]) SaleemGolam 7 11
(M H Tompkins) *dwlt: a in rr* **18/1**

0600 **16** *2* **Muse To Use**[15] 5630 2-8-3 45.................... DuranFentiman 12 —
(I W McInnes) *wnt lft s: a in rr* **28/1**

0403 **17** *2 ¼* **Venus Empress**[26] 5268 2-9-1 57....................(b[1]) GrahamGibbons 2 —
(E S McMahon) *midfield: rdn along bef 1/2-way: sn wknd* **12/1**

66.51 secs (3.01) **Going Correction** +0.325s/f (Good) **17** Ran SP% **128.3**
Speed ratings (Par 93): **88,86,84,83,81 80,79,78,77,77 73,71,69,67,62 59,55**
toteswingers:1&2 £36.60, 2&3 £98.90, 1&3 £8.00 CSF £112.43 CT £1913.56 TOTE £4.50: £1.60, £5.30, £4.20, £4.90; EX 126.10.The winner was bought in 6,500gns.
Owner J Burns **Bred** Belgrave Bloodstock Ltd **Trained** Newmarket, Suffolk

FOCUS
A competitive selling nursery, but by definition a poor race. The form makes sense but this is not a race to dewll on.

NOTEBOOK
One Cool Bex was 1lb higher than when third in a non-selling nursery at Bath last time, and was a market mover earlier in the day. Ridden with plenty of confidence from his lowish draw, he was given plenty to do but he picked up willingly down the outside and maintained his run to lead well inside the last furlong. Bought in for 6,500gns, he can probably find another modest contest. (tchd 7-2)
Crazy In Love, in the frame three times in selling company before this, had the blinkers back on and burst through with what looked possibly a race-winning move before the winner pounced. She is exposed, but can find a modest race in due course. (op 33-1)
Bonjour Bongee ran by far his best race before now on Polytrack, but this effort shows that he can perform on turf too. Drawn lowest of all, he was forced to race very wide but ran on well inside the last furlong despite hanging right. He may be worth another try on an easier surface over this sort of trip.
Je Suis Unrockstar, whose best effort to date came on Fibresand, was tried in cheekpieces. Despite missing the break, pulling hard at the back of the field and then hanging, he ran on down the wide outside to snatch fourth and seems to have some ability as well as quirks.
Glenns Princess, who seems to be going the wrong way, had blinkers on for the first time and showed good speed from the rails draw, but she was given little peace by Vienna Woods and was swamped inside the last furlong. (op 7-1)
Sarandjam has run creditably in a couple of non-selling nurseries recently and attracted good market support, but having been up there early he was going nowhere 2f from home. (op 10-1)
Ignore The Advice(IRE) Official explanation: jockey said gelding was slow away
Never Can Stop raced close to the pace on the inside, but she had little room to play with inside the last furlong and could never land a blow. Official explanation: jockey said filly was denied a clear run (op 3-1 tchd 7-2)

6073 PONY RACING HERE ON 3 OCTOBER H'CAP 5f
3:45 (3:46) (Class 5) (0-75,72) 3-Y-O+ £3,238 (£963; £481; £240) **Stalls** High

Form RPR
5423 **1** **Select Committee**[11] 5760 5-8-9 65....................(v) IanBrennan(5) 1 80
(J J Quinn) *towards rr: hdwy on outer over 1f out: str run to ld last 75yds* **7/1[3]**

0103 **2** *1 ¼* **Captain Scooby**[28] 5198 4-9-0 68.................... MichaelStainton(3) 3 79
(R M Whitaker) *in rr: hdwy on outer over 1f out: styd on to take 2nd clsng stages* **12/1**

232- **3** *¾* **Bedloe's Island (IRE)**[357] 6220 5-9-2 67.................... FrannyNorton 8 75
(N Bycroft) *mid-div: hdwy over 1f out: kpt on wl ins fnl f: tk 3rd nr fin* **13/2[2]**

1050 **4** *1* **Miss Daawe**[18] 5513 6-8-8 59.................... PaulHanagan 7 63
(B Ellison) *mid-div: hdwy 2f out: one pce ins fnl f* **9/1**

4511 **5** *½* **Verinco**[23] 5356 4-9-0 72....................(v) AdamCarter(7) 9 74
(B Smart) *swtchd rt and led after 1f: 3 l clr over 1f out: wknd and hdd last 75yds* **7/2[1]**

5000 **6** *nk* **Tyrannosaurus Rex (IRE)**[36] 4938 6-8-9 63............... GaryBartley(3) 6 64+
(D Shaw) *in rr: nt clr run over 1f out: swtchd lft: kpt on wl ins fnl f: nt rch ldrs* **20/1**

3356 **7** *2 ½* **Bossy Kitty**[42] 4703 3-9-1 67.................... SilvestreDeSousa 5 59
(N Tinkler) *towards rr: hdwy and swtchd lft over 1f out: nvr nr ldrs* **20/1**

000 **8** *¾* **Azygous**[18] 5513 7-8-4 58 oh9.................... JamesSullivan(3) 13 48
(G P Kelly) *mid-div: nvr trbld ldrs* **66/1**

3500 **9** *nk* **Electioneer (USA)**[19] 5484 3-9-6 72....................(e[1]) LeeVickers 11 61+
(M W Easterby) *hld up towards rr: stdy hdwy whn nt clr run over 1f out: nt rcvr* **16/1**

006 **10** *nk* **Time Medicean**[88] 3205 4-8-9 60.................... TonyCulhane 15 47
(P T Midgley) *towards rr: hdwy ins over 1f out: nt clr run and swtchd lft: nvr a factor* **10/1**

5100 **11** *½* **Bahamian Ballet**[23] 5356 8-9-7 72.................... GrahamGibbons 14 58
(E S McMahon) *led 1f: chsd ldrs: wknd over 1f out* **9/1**

3520 **12** *¾* **Liberty Ship**[21] 5422 5-9-0 65....................(bt) PhilipRobinson 12 48
(J D Bethell) *chsd ldrs: lost pl over 1f out* **11/1**

200 **13** *3* **La Capriosa**[7] 5855 4-9-0 **70** ...... DaleSwift(5) 10 42
(J A Glover) *chsd ldrs: checked after 1f: wknd over 1f out* **13/2**[2]

050 **14** *2 ½* **Dispol Grand (IRE)**[23] 5356 4-8-12 **63** ...... JoeFanning 2 26
(P T Midgley) *dwlt: sn chsng ldrs on outer: lost pl over 1f out: eased whn bhd ins fnl f* **50/1**

64.65 secs (1.15) **Going Correction** +0.325s/f (Good)
WFA 3 from 4yo+ 1lb **14** Ran SP% **125.4**
Speed ratings (Par 103): **103,101,99,98,97 96,92,91,91,90 89,88,83,79**
toteswingers:1&2 £12.00, 2&3 £10.10, 1&3 £3.90 CSF £88.85 CT £605.00 TOTE £5.40: £1.60, £3.70, £2.90; EX 74.00.
Owner Which Bits Mine Syndicate **Bred** Llety Stud **Trained** Settrington, N Yorks
■ Stewards' Enquiry : Lee Vickers Fine: £140, failed to report reason for poor performance.

FOCUS
A fascinating and strong run sprint handicap which played into the hands of those that were held up out the back early. The form is rated around the first two.
Tyrannosaurus Rex(IRE) ◆ Official explanation: jockey said gelding was denied a clear run
Electioneer(USA) ◆ Official explanation: jockey said, regarding running and riding, that his orders were to get a handy position, adding that having been slightly outpaced early he was denied a run on several occasions.

6074 GEORGE KILBURN MEMORIAL H'CAP 1m 4f 16y
4:20 (4:20) (Class 3) (0-90,88) 3-Y-O **£5,828** (£1,734; £866; £432) **Stalls** High

Form RPR

-310 **1** **Blissful Moment (USA)**[31] 5118 3-9-5 **86** ...... TomEaves 4 96+
(Sir Michael Stoute) *chsd ldrs: pushed along 1/2-way: rdn 3f out: drvn wl over 1f out: styd on u.p ins fnl f to ld nr line* **9/1**

2111 **2** *hd* **Allannah Abu**[55] 4301 3-8-9 **81** ...... RosieJessop(5) 3 91
(Sir Mark Prescott) *led: pushed along wl over 2f out: rdn over 1f out: drvn ent fnl f: hdd and no ex nr line* **7/1**[3]

1251 **3** *1 ½* **Leader Of The Land (IRE)**[17] 5549 3-9-0 **81** ...... DaraghO'Donohoe 7 88+
(D R Lanigan) *hld up and bhd: hdwy on inner wl over 2f out: rdn to chse ldrs over 1f out: swtchd lft and drvn ent fnl f: kpt on: nrst fin* **6/1**[2]

4312 **4** *¾* **Meetings Man (IRE)**[21] 4944 3-8-3 **70** ...... SilvestreDeSousa 8 76
(Micky Hammond) *hld up towards rr: hdwy over 2f out: rdn to chse ldrs over 1f out: drvn and kpt on ins fnl f* **16/1**

2122 **5** *½* **Shimmering Moment (USA)**[46] 4573 3-9-7 **88** ...... TomQueally 2 93
(H R A Cecil) *trckd ldr: hdwy and cl up 3f out: rdn to chal 2f out: ev ch tl drvn and one pce ent fnl f* **9/4**[1]

2322 **6** *2 ¾* **Park View**[26] 5266 3-8-13 **80** ...... FrannyNorton 6 81
(B W Hills) *trckd ldrs: effrt 3f out: rdn over 2f out: drvn and wknd appr fnl f* **10/1**

0111 **7** *8* **Epic (IRE)**[7] 5858 3-9-5 **86** 6ex ...... (b) JoeFanning 10 74
(M Johnston) *midfield: effrt and sme hdwy 3f out: sn rdn along and btn wl over 1f out* **6/1**[2]

0100 **8** *4 ½* **Monkton Vale (IRE)**[21] 5408 3-8-8 **75** ...... PaulHanagan 1 56
(R A Fahey) *trckd ldrs: hdwy to chse ldng pair 1/2-way: rdn to chal 3f out: drvn wl over 1f out and sn wknd* **25/1**

2040 **9** *1 ½* **Hail Tiberius**[38] 4867 3-8-6 **73** ow1 ...... GrahamGibbons 9 51
(T D Walford) *in tch: rdn along 3f out: sn wknd* **25/1**

2110 **10** *13* **Yashrid (USA)**[39] 4815 3-9-5 **86** ...... PhilipRobinson 5 44
(M A Jarvis) *hld up in rr: hdwy on outer 3f out: rdn along wl over 1f out: sn wknd* **15/2**

2m 39.74s (-0.06) **Going Correction** +0.225s/f (Good) **10** Ran SP% **116.3**
Speed ratings (Par 105): **109,108,107,107,107 105,99,96,95,87**
toteswingers:1&2 £13.40, 2&3 £7.40, 1&3 £12.40 CSF £70.37 CT £407.45 TOTE £16.80: £4.40, £1.30, £2.30; EX 88.50.
Owner Saeed Suhail **Bred** Greenwood Farm Inc **Trained** Newmarket, Suffolk
■ Stewards' Enquiry : Rosie Jessop three-day ban: used whip with excessive freaquency (Sep 29-30,Oct 4)

FOCUS
A decent handicap full of in-form horses including two that were bidding for four-timers. The pace was good too and this is strong form, run in a standout time for the card. There should be more to come from the winner.

NOTEBOOK
Blissful Moment(USA) ◆, a disappointing favourite on his handicap debut at Pontefract last time, looked an unlikely winner for a long way here as he ran in snatches throughout the contest, but he is obviously not short of stamina and kept on responding to pressure to snatch the race right on the line. This was only his fifth start, so there is every reason to believe that there is plenty more to come from him over middle distances. He could be even an even better horse next year. (op 11-1 tchd 12-1)
Allannah Abu, whose stable won this last year with a similarly progressive 3-y-o, was 9lb higher in her bid for a four-timer. Given her usual positive ride, she set a decent pace and it looked for most of the home straight as though she would see it out, but she was mugged in almost the last stride. It would be dangerous to assume that the handicapper has got hold of her yet. (tchd 15-2)
Leader Of The Land(IRE), 3-3 over C&D coming into this and 6lb higher than for last month's success, ran a strange race. He dropped the bridle in the early stages and may have overdone it as he was in a detached last turning in, but he stayed on up the inside rail over the last 2f to snatch the minor placing. (op 11-2 tchd 5-1)
Meetings Man(IRE), very consistent on the Flat and over hurdles this year, stayed on to finish a very respectable fourth given that this was better company than he usually keeps. (op 14-1)
Shimmering Moment(USA), taking another step up in trip and 5lb higher than when runner-up at Glorious Goodwood, was always close to the pace and had every chance, but she finished like a non-stayer, at least on a stiff track like this. (op 11-4 tchd 3-1 in a place)
Park View, consistent in handicaps since winning a Thirsk maiden on her reappearance, probably ran too freely in the early stages and didn't have enough left for the business end. (op 17-2)
Epic(IRE) was carrying a 6lb penalty in his bid for a four-timer but was still 1lb well in compared to his revised mark. This was disappointing, even allowing for his inflated mark. (tchd 5-1)

6075 WATCH RACING UK ON SKY CHANNEL 432 MAIDEN STKS 5f
4:50 (4:51) (Class 5) 2-Y-O **£2,914** (£867; £433; £216) **Stalls** High

Form RPR

3203 **1** **Indieslad**[18] 5531 2-9-3 82 ...... PaulHanagan 12 79
(Mrs A Duffield) *stmbld s: chsd ldrs: led on ins 1f out: drvn out* **5/6**[1]

2 *1 ¾* **Pantella (IRE)** 2-8-12 0 ...... PhillipMakin 11 68
(K A Ryan) *dwlt: sn trcking ldrs: chal jst ins fnl f: no ex* **25/1**

003 **3** *2* **Breezolini**[15] 5640 2-8-9 53 ...... MichaelStainton(3) 15 60+
(R M Whitaker) *mid-div: hdwy on outer over 1f out: styd on to take 3rd post* **22/1**

260 **4** *shd* **Piccoluck**[42] 4702 2-9-3 65 ...... (t) SilvestreDeSousa 7 65
(Mrs D J Sanderson) *hmpd s: chsd ldrs: led over 1f out: sn hdd: kpt on same pce* **12/1**

0 **5** *hd* **I Got You Babe (IRE)**[42] 4702 2-8-12 0 ...... FrannyNorton 14 59
(R C Guest) *mid-div: styd on ins fnl f* **28/1**

6 *4* **Manoori (IRE)** 2-8-12 0 ...... GrahamGibbons 6 45+
(C F Wall) *chsd ldrs: wknd appr fnl f* **6/1**[3]

4 **7** *shd* **Prince Titus (IRE)**[53] 4363 2-9-3 0 ...... TomEaves 9 50
(Mrs L Stubbs) *led tl hdd & wknd over 1f out* **9/2**[2]

04 **8** *1 ¾* **Gunalt Joy**[15] 5640 2-8-9 0 ...... (t) JamesSullivan(3) 3 38
(M W Easterby) *in rr: nvr a factor* **66/1**

40 **9** *hd* **Cottam Stella**[10] 5785 2-8-12 0 ...... DavidAllan 2 38
(M Brittain) *in rr on outer: sme hdwy over 1f out: nvr on terms* **66/1**

404 **10** *1* **Mr Optimistic**[90] 3118 2-8-12 68 ...... LeeTopliss(5) 8 39
(R A Fahey) *swvd lft s: chsd ldrs: wknd over 1f out* **20/1**

06 **11** *1 ½* **Rum Sun N Sand (USA)**[111] 2474 2-8-12 0 ...... TomQueally 1 29
(J W Hills) *wnt lft s: in rr: sn swtchd rr: nvr on terms* **33/1**

00 **12** *1 ½* **Illawalla**[99] 2832 2-9-3 0 ...... PatrickMathers 16 28
(H A McWilliams) *s.i.s: a towards rr* **100/1**

13 *6* **The Datai** 2-8-12 0 ow3 ...... GaryBartley(3) 10 5
(I W McInnes) *s.s: a detached in last* **100/1**

65.19 secs (1.69) **Going Correction** +0.325s/f (Good) **13** Ran SP% **119.0**
Speed ratings (Par 95): **99,96,93,92,92 86,85,83,82,81 78,76,66**
toteswingers:1&2 £7.00, 2&3 £31.40, 1&3 £7.40 CSF £34.11 TOTE £1.80: £1.10, £5.10, £4.80; EX 22.00.
Owner Trevor Wilson **Bred** W H R John And Partners **Trained** Constable Burton, N Yorks

FOCUS
An uncompetitive juvenile maiden according to the betting market, and a straightforward success for the favourite in a time that compared favourably with the earlier older-horse handicap. The winner is rated to his mark but the form is limited.

NOTEBOOK
Indieslad, in the frame in three of his four previous starts and rated 82, therefore had a fair amount in hand over the others with ratings. He got a good lead early before coming through to score decisively, and should go on to better things with his yard going well now. (op 10-11 after early evens in places tchd 4-5)
Pantella(IRE), a 16,000euros filly out of a winning miler in Germany, ran well on this debut and was the only one with any chance against the winner in the closing stages. She should pick up a similar contest soon if going on from this.
Breezolini, rated just 53, finished well from off the pace to snatch the minor placing on the line, and will be of interest in a nursery, as she is improving with racing. (op 20-1)
Piccoluck, rated 65 and down to the minimum trip for the first time, was tried in a first-time tongue tie. He ran better and was unlucky to lose out on a place in the frame. (op 14-1)
I Got You Babe(IRE), beaten a long way on her Newcastle debut, improved considerably on that and will be of interest once qualified for handicaps after another run. (tchd 25-1)
Manoori(IRE), a 40,000euros filly out of a useful sprinter in Italy and a Cheveley Park entry, missed her intended debut at Haydock the previous day due to the softening ground. She ran promisingly under a sympathetic ride and should be able to build on this next time. (op 11-2)
Prince Titus(IRE), an eye-catching fourth on his Lingfield debut in July, went off too fast here and paid for it in the last furlong and a half. (op 4-1 tchd 5-1)

6076 BETFAIR RACING EXCELLENCE APPRENTICE TRAINING SERIES CLASSIFIED STKS (DIV I) 1m 100y
5:20 (5:22) (Class 6) 3-Y-O+ **£1,706** (£503; £252) **Stalls** High

Form RPR

6044 **1** **Youm Al Mizayin**[12] 5729 3-8-9 52 ...... AmyScott 7 61
(M R Channon) *in tch: hdwy to trck ldrs 3f out: swtchd lft and effrt over 1f out: rdn to ld ins fnl f: kpt on wl* **7/1**[3]

0443 **2** *2* **Chichen Daawe**[24] 5331 4-9-0 51 ...... DaleSwift 11 56
(B Ellison) *trckd ldrs: hdwy over 2f out: rdn to chse ldr and edgd rt over 1f out: led briefly jst fnl f: sn hdd and one pce* **2/1**[1]

004 **3** *2* **Carragold**[42] 4707 4-9-0 49 ...... (b[1]) JohnCavanagh 8 51
(M Brittain) *prom: led after 3f: rdn along and hdd 3f out: drvn wl over 1f out: swtchd rt ins fnl f: kpt on* **7/1**[3]

4000 **4** *4 ½* **Sophie's Beau (USA)**[44] 4651 3-8-4 55 ...... LeonnaMayor(5) 10 41
(M C Chapman) *prom: hdwy to ld 3f out: rdn clr wl over 1f out: hdd jst ins fnl f and wknd qckly* **20/1**

-006 **5** *2 ¾* **Jetta Joy (IRE)**[11] 5765 5-9-0 50 ...... RosieJessop 4 35
(Mrs A Duffield) *in tch: hdwy over 2f out: rdn wl over 1f out: no imp* **20/1**

6060 **6** *1 ¼* **Haka Dancer (USA)**[31] 3496 7-8-7 42 ...... VictorSantos(7) 6 32
(P A Kirby) *dwlt and towards rr: sme hdwy over 2f out: sn rdn and n.d* **14/1**

4040 **7** *½* **Eeny Mac (IRE)**[37] 4898 3-8-2 47 ...... TerenceFury(7) 1 31
(N Bycroft) *s.i.s and bhd tl sme late hdwy* **14/1**

6052 **8** *3* **Castlebury (IRE)**[38] 4863 5-8-11 54 ...... (b) SophieSilvester(3) 3 24
(Mrs R A Carr) *a in rr* **5/1**[2]

0000 **9** *1* **Isle Of Ellis (IRE)**[9] 5819 3-8-9 40 ...... LeeTopliss 13 22
(R E Barr) *in tch: rdn along 3f out: sn wknd* **33/1**

0005 **10** *2 ¼* **Marsh's Gift**[17] 5550 3-8-5 44 ow1 ...... PeterSword(5) 12 17
(Michael Smith) *dwlt: a in rr* **8/1**

0600 **11** *6* **Singing Scott (IRE)**[17] 5550 3-8-2 38 ...... JohnLawson(7) 2 3
(R Bastiman) *s.i.s: a bhd* **100/1**

-040 **12** *8* **Drubinca**[161] 1163 3-8-9 52 ...... (v) RyanClark 9 —
(S C Williams) *led 3f: rdn along 1/2-way: sn wknd* **8/1**

1m 49.65s (2.05) **Going Correction** +0.225s/f (Good)
WFA 3 from 4yo+ 5lb **12** Ran SP% **124.0**
Speed ratings (Par 101): **98,96,94,89,86 85,85,82,81,78 72,64**
toteswingers:1&2 £4.20, 2&3 £5.80, 1&3 £6.50 CSF £21.56 TOTE £8.20: £2.30, £1.10, £4.00; EX 23.60.
Owner Jaber Abdullah **Bred** Darley **Trained** West Ilsley, Berks

FOCUS
A dire contest for this first leg of the apprentice classified stakes, a banded race in all but name. They went a good gallop from the start and very few got into it. The winner is rated up 8lb.
Drubinca Official explanation: jockey said gelding hung right throughout

6077 BETFAIR RACING EXCELLENCE APPRENTICE TRAINING SERIES CLASSIFIED STKS (DIV II) 1m 100y
5:50 (5:50) (Class 6) 3-Y-O+ **£1,706** (£503; £252) **Stalls** High

Form RPR

0006 **1** **Eastern Hills**[7] 5864 5-9-0 55 ...... (p) NeilFarley 2 64
(A J McCabe) *w ldr: led over 4f out: drew clr ins fnl f* **2/1**[2]

4-00 **2** *4 ½* **Hedgerow (IRE)**[114] 2380 3-8-9 52 ...... LeeTopliss 5 53
(M Dods) *s.s: hdwy to chse ldrs over 4f out: rdn over 2f out: styd on to take 2nd last 100yds* **13/2**[3]

0-02 **3** *1 ½* **Isabella Romee (IRE)**[14] 5655 4-8-9 53 ...... LewisWalsh(5) 3 50
(Jane Chapple-Hyam) *hld up in rr: hdwy over 3f out: kpt on to take 3rd nr fin* **15/8**[1]

0500 **4** *¾* **Kheskianto (IRE)**[35] 4939 4-9-0 50 ...... CharlesEddery 8 48
(M C Chapman) *trckd ldrs: t.k.h: wnt 2nd over 3f out: wknd rapidly fnl 100yds* **9/1**

0000 **5** *2 ½* **Karate Queen**[2] 6037 5-9-0 40 ...... DaleSwift 10 43
(R E Barr) *mid-div: hdwy 3f out: nvr nr ldrs* **25/1**

0-04 **6** 1/2 **Roman Sioux (IRE)**[16] 5603 3-8-2 53........................ JohnLawson(7) 11 41
(R Bastiman) *hld up in rr: sme hdwy over 2f out: hung lft over 1f out: nvr nr ldrs* **14/1**

064 **7** 1 **Anna's Boy**[74] 3666 3-8-2 43.. VictorSantos(7) 1 38
(A Berry) *sn chsng ldrs: hung lft and c stands' side alone over 3f out: one pce fnl 2f* **40/1**

-066 **8** 2 1/4 **Mujada**[69] 3804 5-8-9 37.. ShaneBKelly(5) 12 34
(D O'Meara) *hld up towards rr: nvr a factor* **22/1**

044 **9** 2 1/4 **Plenilune (IRE)**[202] 705 5-9-0 47.................................. JohnCavanagh 6 29
(M Brittain) *in rr: sme hdwy 3f out: nvr a factor* **10/1**

0000 **10** 13 **Chardonnay Star (IRE)**[23] 5361 3-8-9 39....................(v1) AdamCarter 4 —
(C J Teague) *mde most tl over 4f out: sn drvn and lost pl: bhd fnl 3f* **100/1**

0506 **11** 54 **Future Regime (IRE)**[12] 5711 3-8-6 43..............(v1) SophieSilvester(3) 7 —
(Patrick Morris) *s.s: detached in last: t.o 7f out: eventually completed* **50/1**

1m 50.83s (3.23) **Going Correction** +0.225s/f (Good)
WFA 3 from 4yo+ 5lb **11** Ran SP% **120.8**
Speed ratings (Par 101): **92,87,86,85,82 82,81,79,76,63 9**
toteswingers:1&2 £4.10, 2&3 £4.50, 1&3 £1.80 CSF £15.36 TOTE £2.50: £1.10, £5.00, £1.10; EX 20.80 Place 6: £131.85 Place 5: £72.38.
Owner Charles Wentworth **Bred** Azienda Agricola Patrizia **Trained** Averham Park, Notts
■ Stewards' Enquiry : John Cavanagh caution: careless riding.

FOCUS
This second division of the classified race was run at a more sedate gallop, and the time was 1.18secs slower than the first in a contest dominated by the market leaders. Pretty weak form but winner was back towards his late 2009 level.
Plenilune(IRE) Official explanation: jockey said gelding lost a front shoe
T/Plt: £75.70 to a £1 stake. Pool of £55,126.61 - 531.45 winning tickets. T/Qpdt: £40.80 to a £1 stake. Pool of £3,536.49 - 64.00 winning tickets. JR

5957 KEMPTON (A.W) (R-H)
Wednesday, September 15

OFFICIAL GOING: Standard
Wind: Fresh, half against Weather: Overcast

6078 DAY TIME, NIGHT TIME, GREAT TIME CLASSIFIED CLAIMING STKS 6f (P)
5:40 (5:41) (Class 5) 3-Y-0+ **£2,286** (£675; £337) **Stalls** High

Form RPR

0000 **1** **Charlie Delta**[26] 5267 7-8-2 54..............................(b) AndrewHeffernan(3) 5 65
(R A Harris) *settled in tch: prog to take 3rd over 1f out and urged along: drvn and styd on fnl f to ld last 75yds* **33/1**

6026 **2** 3/4 **Maoi Chinn Tire (IRE)**[33] 5027 3-8-7 68..........................(p) LiamKeniry 3 67
(J S Moore) *in tch: rdn and no prog 2f out: styd on fnl f and tk 2nd nr fin* **9/1**

1250 **3** 1/2 **Dvinsky (USA)**[11] 5768 9-8-2 70....................................(b) JohnFahy(5) 4 63
(P Howling) *prom: chsd ldr 1/2-way: carried rt whn chalng over 1f out: drvn to ld jst ins fnl f: hdd and nt qckn last 75yds* **5/2**[1]

0345 **4** 1/2 **Faited To Pretend (IRE)**[51] 4430 3-8-8 68................ TobyAtkinson(5) 6 69
(M Botti) *led: clr w one rival 2f out: edgd rt over 1f out: hdd and nt qckn jst ins fnl f* **12/1**

6033 **5** 3/4 **Lodi (IRE)**[24] 5325 5-8-5 65..(tp) HayleyTurner 7 57
(J Akehurst) *chsd ldrs: u.p and struggling over 2f out: kpt on ins fnl f: no real danger* **5/2**[1]

3341 **6** 1 **Apache Ridge (IRE)**[25] 5299 4-8-12 67.........................(p) AmyRyan(3) 2 64
(K A Ryan) *dwlt: pushed along and detached in last: sme prog 2f out: kpt on same pce ins fnl f* **6/1**[2]

010 **7** 2 1/4 **C'Mon You Irons (IRE)**[22] 5388 5-8-10 75...................(v) KierenFox(5) 1 57
(M R Hoad) *disp 2nd pl tl 1/2-way: sn lost pl u.p* **6/1**[2]

5231 **8** 7 **The Jailer**[3] 5990 7-7-12 53..(p) RyanPowell(7) 8 24
(J G M O'Shea) *chsd ldr to over 3f out: wknd 2f out* **8/1**[3]

1m 12.26s (-0.84) **Going Correction** -0.10s/f (Stan)
WFA 3 from 4yo+ 2lb **8** Ran SP% **117.5**
Speed ratings (Par 103): **101,100,99,98,97 96,93,84**
toteswingers:1&2 £16.60, 2&3 £7.80, 1&3 £18.80 CSF £304.23 TOTE £57.10: £10.50, £5.50, £1.10; EX 75.80.Maoi Chinn Tire was claimed by Ms Jennie Candlish for £7000.
Owner Robert & Nina Bailey **Bred** P K Gardner **Trained** Earlswood, Monmouths
■ Stewards' Enquiry : Toby Atkinson two-day ban; careless riding (Sep 29-30)

FOCUS
A shock result to this opening claimer. The winner is rated back to his best and is the most likely guide to the form.

6079 PANORAMIC BAR & RESTAURANT MEDIAN AUCTION MAIDEN STKS 1m 4f (P)
6:10 (6:10) (Class 6) 3-4-Y-0 **£1,637** (£483; £241) **Stalls** High

Form RPR

52 **1** **Kristalette (IRE)**[23] 5366 3-8-12 0.. AdamKirby 5 89+
(W R Swinburn) *chsd ldr: led over 3f out: shkn up and drew away over 2f out: eased ins fnl f* **10/11**[1]

3222 **2** 7 **Astral Flower**[22] 5380 3-8-12 73...................................... RichardMullen 3 74
(Sir Michael Stoute) *trckd ldng pair: rdn to chse wnr over 3f out: lft bhd over 2f out* **2/1**[2]

54 **3** 11 **Ahaazeeg**[16] 5610 3-9-3 0... RichardHills 4 61
(J L Dunlop) *t.k.h: hld up in last pair: prog to dispute 2nd over 3f out: rdn over 2f out and btn: wknd over 1f out* **14/1**

3403 **4** 2 1/4 **Corres (IRE)**[89] 3170 3-9-3 70.. DaneO'Neill 2 58
(D R C Elsworth) *in tch: rdn in 5th pl over 3f out: racd really awkwardly fnl 3f and wl btn* **6/1**[3]

4562 **5** 6 **Santa Margherita**[23] 5376 3-8-12 65........................... RichardHughes 1 43
(H J L Dunlop) *racd wd 1st 2f: led at decent pce: hdd over 3f out: immediately btn* **25/1**

0 **6** 33 **Hecton Lad (USA)**[15] 5623 3-8-12 0................................ KierenFox(5) 7 —
(J R Best) *sn off the bridle in last pair: lost tch over 4f out: wl t.o* **100/1**

6034 **7** 23 **Polebrook**[47] 4552 3-9-3 47.. SebSanders 6 —
(J R Jenkins) *chsd ldrs: rdn sn after 1/2-way: wknd 4f out: sn wl t.o* **100/1**

2m 32.39s (-2.11) **Going Correction** -0.10s/f (Stan) **7** Ran SP% **112.5**
Speed ratings (Par 101): **103,98,91,89,85 63,48**
toteswingers:1&2 £1.30, 2&3 £3.50, 1&3 £2.50 CSF £2.79 TOTE £2.50: £1.30, £1.10; EX 3.20.
Owner P W Harris **Bred** Pendley Farm **Trained** Aldbury, Herts

FOCUS
A fair maiden. The runner-up provides a reliable guide to the form with the winner up 5lb.

6080 DIGIBET.COM H'CAP 1m 4f (P)
6:40 (6:41) (Class 6) (0-60,60) 3-Y-0 **£1,637** (£483; £241) **Stalls** High

Form RPR

0003 **1** **Kayaan**[14] 5656 3-9-6 59... MickyFenton 3 67+
(Mrs P Sly) *stdd s: hld up last: prog on outer wl over 2f out: shkn up and r.o to ld ent fnl f: sn clr* **7/1**

0023 **2** 2 1/4 **Motirani**[7] 5869 3-9-0 58... SimonPearce(5) 6 62
(J Pearce) *hld up in midfield: prog over 2f out: hrd rdn to ld over 1f out: hdd and outpcd ent fnl f* **16/1**

0004 **3** hd **Storm Hawk (IRE)**[14] 5663 3-8-12 58.....................(p) JamesRogers(7) 5 62
(Pat Eddery) *hld up wl in rr: gd prog 2f out gng strly: pressed ldrs over 1f out: styd on: could nt find necessary ex pce* **14/1**

5031 **4** 1 **Akamon**[17] 5550 3-9-7 60... JimCrowley 13 62
(E A L Dunlop) *hld up towards rr on inner: gd prog over 2f out to press ldrs over 1f out: nt qckn sn after on inner: one pce ins fnl f* **13/2**[3]

0460 **5** nse **Nom De La Rosa (IRE)**[14] 5663 3-8-9 55..............(p) HarryBentley(7) 11 57
(Miss Sheena West) *trckd ldrs: prog and drvn to ld 2f out: hdd over 1f out: fdd ins fnl f* **40/1**

0061 **6** hd **Adoyen Spice**[7] 5869 3-8-11 53 6ex.............................. MartinLane(3) 12 55
(Mike Murphy) *stdd s: hld up in last trio: prog on outer over 2f out: hanging and nt looking keen fr over 1f out: one pce* **5/4**[1]

0-50 **7** 1 3/4 **Dongola (IRE)**[23] 5366 3-8-11 50.. DaneO'Neill 14 49
(P Winkworth) *mostly in midfield: rdn wl over 2f out: in tch but one pce and no imp on ldrs fnl 2f* **33/1**

0031 **8** 1 1/4 **Larkrise Star**[65] 3960 3-9-4 57.. RichardHughes 10 54
(D K Ivory) *hld up in midfield: prog over 2f out to chal wl over 1f out: wknd qckly ins fnl f* **5/1**[2]

-005 **9** 3 3/4 **Pursestrings**[27] 5233 3-8-13 52.. IanMongan 9 43
(Mrs L J Mongan) *prom: drvn to ld over 2f out to 2f out: sn wknd* **66/1**

0406 **10** 2 3/4 **Footsie (IRE)**[21] 5423 3-8-11 50...................................... PaulMulrennan 2 37
(J G Given) *chsd ldr to 7f out: prom tl wknd over 2f out* **16/1**

0-50 **11** 5 **Forethought**[41] 4764 3-9-3 56...................................... RichardMullen 7 35
(P Howling) *wl in tch tl wknd over 2f out* **100/1**

006 **12** nk **Kargarann (IRE)**[34] 5007 3-9-0 53...................................... SebSanders 4 31
(Stef Higgins) *hld up in last trio: c wdst of all bnd 3f out: no prog* **25/1**

6-04 **13** 2 1/2 **Expensive Legacy**[197] 760 3-8-13 52................................. ChrisCatlin 8 26
(Miss N A Lloyd-Beavis) *trckd ldr 7f out: drvn to chal 3f out: upsides over 2f out: sn wknd* **100/1**

5000 **14** 2 1/4 **Naseby (USA)**[26] 5271 3-8-13 52.................................(b1) HayleyTurner 1 23
(Miss S L Davison) *taken down early: led and sn clr: hdd & wknd rapidly over 2f out* **66/1**

2m 35.09s (0.59) **Going Correction** -0.10s/f (Stan) **14** Ran SP% **119.6**
Speed ratings (Par 99): **94,92,92,91,91 91,90,89,87,85 81,81,80,78**
toteswingers:1&2 £8.60, 2&3 £28.20, 1&3 £14.30 CSF £107.92 CT £1531.00 TOTE £4.90: £1.20, £4.60, £5.80; EX 186.20.
Owner David L Bayliss **Bred** Shadwell Estate Company Limited **Trained** Thorney, Cambs

FOCUS
Just a low-grade handicap, but the pace was reasonable enough. The form looks sound and the winner is unexposed.
Motirani Official explanation: jockey said gelding lost left-fore shoe

6081 DIGIBET CASINO NURSERY (DIV I) 1m (P)
7:10 (7:10) (Class 6) (0-65,64) 2-Y-0 **£1,364** (£403; £201) **Stalls** High

Form RPR

031 **1** **Ninfea (IRE)**[12] 5709 2-9-6 63...................................... JamesDoyle 10 70
(S Kirk) *urged along in last trio early: hrd rdn and last over 2f out: rapid prog on outer over 1f out as ldrs sed to falter: styd on wl to ld nr fin* **6/1**[2]

6060 **2** 1/2 **Whitby Jet (IRE)**[14] 5659 2-8-8 54................................ MartinLane(3) 4 60
(E F Vaughan) *s.i.s and pushed along early: u.p in rr over 2f out: gd prog on outer as others faltered: led jst ins fnl f: collared nr fin* **33/1**

0002 **3** 2 1/2 **Highcliffe**[14] 5660 2-8-12 55...................................... RichardHughes 2 55
(R Hannon) *racd wd: trckd ldrs: shkn up and clsd fr 2f out: led briefly 1f out: sn lft bhd* **10/1**

5405 **4** 1 1/4 **Blaze On By**[23] 5373 2-8-9 52.. PatDobbs 6 49
(R Hannon) *pressed ldrs: rdn to chal fr 2f out: stl trying and cl enough 1f out: sn lft bhd* **50/1**

5304 **5** 3/4 **Barista (IRE)**[7] 5856 2-9-7 64.. ChrisCatlin 9 59
(M R Channon) *hld up in midfield: snatched up over 6f out: rdn over 2f out: kpt on bttr than sme wkng rivals: nvr a threat* **13/2**[3]

000 **6** nk **Dolcezza (IRE)**[13] 5691 2-9-2 59...................................... MartinDwyer 8 54
(B J Meehan) *pushed along in midfield at various times: lost pl over 2f out: jst nudged along and one pce ins fnl f: could do bttr* **25/1**

0530 **7** 1 **Bouzy**[20] 5452 2-9-5 62.. JimCrowley 1 54
(P Winkworth) *prom in strly run r: wnt 2nd 2f out: drvn to ld jst over 1f out: sn hdd & wknd* **66/1**

6021 **8** shd **Red Oleander**[8] 5837 2-9-4 61 6ex..............................(b) SebSanders 7 53
(Sir Mark Prescott) *led at fair pce but pressed thrght: hdd & wknd jst over 1f out* **11/10**[1]

0053 **9** 2 1/2 **Mediplomat**[26] 5256 2-9-0 62.........................(t) TobyAtkinson(5) 11 48
(M Botti) *hld up in rr on inner: rdn and no prog over 2f out* **8/1**

065 **10** 2 1/4 **Indian Wish (USA)**[14] 5651 2-9-3 60................................ HayleyTurner 3 41
(M L W Bell) *mostly in last trio: u.p and no prog over 2f out* **9/1**

6433 **11** 3 1/2 **Sheila's Star (IRE)**[9] 5807 2-9-7 64.............................(p) LiamKeniry 12 37
(J S Moore) *chsd ldrs on inner: drvn over 2f out: wknd over 1f out* **14/1**

0064 **12** 5 **Seas Of Sorrow (IRE)**[14] 5660 2-8-8 56.................... SophieDoyle(5) 5 18
(B W Duke) *pressed ldr to 2f out: wknd v rapidly* **50/1**

1m 40.04s (0.24) **Going Correction** -0.10s/f (Stan) **12** Ran SP% **124.3**
Speed ratings (Par 93): **94,93,91,89,89 88,87,87,85,82 79,74**
toteswingers:1&2 £24.20, 2&3 £53.10, 1&3 £18.30 CSF £200.47 CT £2006.91 TOTE £7.30: £3.90, £18.30, £4.00; EX 324.20.
Owner Miss A Jones **Bred** Kilco Builders **Trained** Upper Lambourn, Berks

FOCUS
The first division of a low-grade nursery. The form is rated around the third and the winner's maiden win.

NOTEBOOK
Ninfea(IRE) had clearly got in on a decent mark and she finished strongly, having been held up in rear alongside the runner-up early on, to get up in the final strides. Her half-brother was a 1m2f winner, so there's every chance she'll improve for a stiffer test, and it's likely there'll be more to come. (tchd 13-2 and 15-2 in places)
Whitby Jet(IRE), never involved from a poor draw on his recent nursery debut over C&D, had to be rousted following a slow start, which led to him racing keenly, but that didn't stop him sweeping through to lead inside the final furlong, only to be worn down close home. He's clearly modest, but can win races.

Highcliffe has now run well on both starts over this C&D since sent handicapping and looks more than good enough to win a modest race. (op 11-1)
Blaze On By, who was held in a seller latest, travelled well on this AW debut but was below her best in defeat. (tchd 66-1)
Barista(IRE), racing beyond 6f for the first time, didn't get the best of runs but was staying on late suggesting she got the trip. (op 6-1)
Dolcezza(IRE), although keeping on late under a considerate ride, doesn't look the most straightforward, as is the case with many of her sires progeny. A stiffer test will undoubtedly suit, however, and she is very lowly weighted, so a race may fall her way at some stage. (tchd 20-1)
Bouzy ran well for a long way and can find a small race back at 7f.
Red Oleander, who had the advantage of the stands' rail when winning over 7f at Lingfield latest, looked to have more on here off 9lb higher (including the penalty), especially in a competitive race, and she didn't get home having set a decent early gallop. (op 6-4)
Seas Of Sorrow(IRE) Official explanation: jockey said filly lost its action

6082 DIGIBET CASINO NURSERY (DIV II) 1m (P)
7:40 (7:40) (Class 6) (0-65,64) 2-Y-O **£1,364** (£403; £201) **Stalls** High

Form RPR
0032 **1** **Ree's Rascal (IRE)**[14] 5659 2-8-10 **53**............ PatCosgrave 7 63+
(J R Boyle) *trckd ldrs: burst through to ld over 1f out: sn rdn clr: comf* **9/4**[1]
0444 **2** 4 ½ **Ivan's A Star (IRE)**[14] 5659 2-8-12 **55**............(p) LiamKeniry 11 55
(J S Moore) *settled in rr: 9th 3f out: rdn and prog fr 2f out: styd on fnl f to take 2nd last stride* **16/1**
0643 **3** shd **Papas Fritas**[14] 5660 2-9-6 **63**............ MartinDwyer 8 62
(B J Meehan) *mde most: rdn 2f out: hdd and outpcd over 1f out: lost 2nd last stride* **5/1**[2]
3550 **4** 3 **Paco Belle (IRE)**[12] 5720 2-9-6 **63**............ RichardHughes 6 56
(R Hannon) *prom: shkn up over 2f out: no prog and outpcd over 1f out: fdd* **11/1**[3]
6350 **5** ½ **Spirit Of Oakdale (IRE)**[14] 5660 2-8-9 **57**............ JohnFahy(5) 1 48
(W R Swinburn) *trckd ldrs: effrt over 2f out: outpcd over 1f out: fdd* **20/1**
0000 **6** nse **Thank You Joy**[14] 5660 2-7-13 **49**............ DannyBrock(7) 2 40
(J R Jenkins) *in tch in rr but sn pushed along: struggling over 2f out: kpt on ins fnl f* **100/1**
2123 **7** 1 ¼ **Chilworth Lass (IRE)**[16] 5602 2-8-12 **55**............(v) ChrisCatlin 5 43
(M R Channon) *settled towards rr: gng bttr than most over 2f out: rdn and only one pce fnl 2f* **12/1**
500 **8** 8 **Sir Rocky (IRE)**[18] 5520 2-9-5 **62**............(b[1]) PatDobbs 3 32
(R Hannon) *pressed ldr after 3f to 2f out: wknd qckly* **33/1**
3621 **9** ¾ **Countrywide Flame**[14] 5659 2-9-2 **59**............ PaulMulrennan 10 27
(K A Ryan) *trckd ldr 3f: cl up on inner over 2f out: sn wknd qckly* **9/4**[1]
035 **10** 17 **Freehand (USA)**[21] 5413 2-9-5 **62**............(t) AhmedAjtebi 9 —
(Mahmood Al Zarooni) *immediately drvn in detached last and wouldn't r properly: t.o fnl 2f* **16/1**
505 **11** 5 **Rural Pursuits**[12] 5721 2-8-12 **60**............ TobyAtkinson(5) 12 —
(Mrs C A Dunnett) *lost pl on inner and snatched up over 4f out: detached after: t.o fnl 2f* **50/1**

1m 39.77s (-0.03) **Going Correction** -0.10s/f (Stan) **11** Ran SP% **116.6**
Speed ratings (Par 93): **96,91,91,88,87 87,86,78,77,60 55**
toteswingers:1&2 £7.90, 2&3 £5.10, 1&3 £3.90 CSF £43.10 CT £167.29 TOTE £2.00: £1.10, £5.80, £3.20; EX 54.70.
Owner Walter Hayford **Bred** Pier House Stud **Trained** Epsom, Surrey
■ Stewards' Enquiry : Danny Brock two-day ban; careless riding (Sep 29-30)

FOCUS
This may have marginally been the weaker division, although there wasn't much in it. The form looks solid enough, the winner backing up recent C/D improvement.

NOTEBOOK
Ree's Rascal(IRE), fancied by many to reverse recent C&D form with Countrywide Flame, having allowed that one first run, did so in some style, bursting through to lead and quickly going clear. This was his first win and there should be more to come given the manner of this success. (tchd 2-1 and 11-4 in places)
Ivan's A Star(IRE) is well exposed, but ran right up to form with the winner on last-time-out form. (tchd 14-1 in places)
Papas Fritas, raised 2lb having finished third on his nursery debut over C&D, again ran well but doesn't appear to have anything in hand on the assessor. (tchd 11-2)
Paco Belle(IRE), never involved over 6f on her recent nursery debut, seemed more at home over this trip, but may benefit from a more restrained ride next time. (op 12-1)
Spirit Of Oakdale(IRE) fared a lot better than last time, but was still well held. (op 25-1 tchd 28-1)
Thank You Joy never got into it having been held up in rear.
Sir Rocky(IRE) stopped quickly in the first-time blinkers.
Countrywide Flame very much had the run of things when winning over C&D last time, and for all that it was no surprise he failed to confirm form with Ree's Rascal, he was expected to finish a lot closer. The way he stopped suggests something may have been amiss. (op 2-1)

6083 DIGIBET CONDITIONS STKS 7f (P)
8:10 (8:10) (Class 3) 2-Y-O **£3,571** (£3,571; £818) **Stalls** High

Form RPR
1 **1** **Pausanias**[46] 4577 2-9-0 84............ RichardHughes 5 99
(R Hannon) *led 1f: sn settled in 3rd: rdn to chal 2f out: upsides fnl f: narrow ld nr fin: jnd on the nod* **5/6**[1]
3334 **1** dht **Roayh (USA)**[25] 5306 2-9-0 104............ FrankieDettori 2 99
(Saeed Bin Suroor) *racd wd early: led after 1f: rdn and pressed 2f out: narrowly hdd nr fin: forced dead-heat post* **2/1**[2]
1 **3** 1 ¼ **Zenella**[32] 5099 2-8-6 90............ MatthewDavies(3) 1 91
(Mrs A Duffield) *trckd ldr over 5f out to over 2f out: rdn and outpcd: kpt on fnl f: nvr able to chal* **4/1**[3]

1m 25.29s (-0.71) **Going Correction** -0.10s/f (Stan) **3** Ran SP% **107.9**
Speed ratings (Par 99): **100,100,98**
WIN: Pausanias £0.90, Roayh £1.20 EX: P/R £5.60, R/P £4.50 CSF: P/R £1.39, R/P £2.06.
Owner Godolphin **Bred** Overbrook Farm **Trained** Newmarket, Suffolk
Owner Sir Alex Ferguson & Sotirios Hassiakos **Bred** Granham Farm And P Hearson Bloodstock **Trained** East Everleigh, Wilts

FOCUS
This was still an interesting conditions race, despite the field being halved by non-runners. The form is good and Pausanias looks up to Listed company, while fellow dead-heater Roayh was 7lb off his Coventry effort.

NOTEBOOK
Pausanias has a big reputation and made a winning debut at Goodwood despite not being ready. This represented a step up against a higher level of opponent and, despite having looked to be coming off second-best for much of the last 2f, he managed to get up to share the prize. He clearly needed this longer trip and remains capable of better, being such a big horse, but doesn't yet look capable of winning at pattern-level. (tchd 9-4)
Roayh(USA) found plenty when challenged to take a share of the spoils. He set the standard, having finished third in the Coventry earlier in the season, and despite not really matching that form since, he was always going to take the beating in a race where he could dominate. This is as far as he wants to go and it's not clear where he heads from here. (tchd 9-4)
Zenella, a tidy winner at Ripon on debut, shaped well against the colts, staying on again having been outpaced, but a rating of 90 doesn't provide her with many opportunities. (op 9-2 tchd 5-1)

6084 JUMP RACING ON SUNDAY 17TH OCTOBER H'CAP 2m (P)
8:40 (8:41) (Class 5) (0-75,74) 3-Y-O **£2,286** (£675; £337) **Stalls** High

Form RPR
5253 **1** **Old Hundred (IRE)**[17] 5549 3-9-7 **74**............(v) PatCosgrave 3 87+
(J R Fanshawe) *trckd ldng pair: wnt 2nd 3f out: rdn to cl and led jst over 1f out: styd on wl and sn clr* **11/4**[2]
2223 **2** 3 ¾ **Saggiatore**[20] 5443 3-9-7 **74**............ JimCrowley 1 82
(E A L Dunlop) *trckd ldr: led over 3f out and kicked clr: hdd jst over 1f out: no ex* **3/1**[3]
0434 **3** 11 **Tigress Hill**[9] 5811 3-8-9 **67**............ JohnFahy(5) 5 62
(Mrs A J Perrett) *early reminders: in tch in 5th: drvn 3f out: sn hopelessly outpcd: kpt on to take modest 3rd last strides* **16/1**
3134 **4** nk **Spice Fair**[22] 5382 3-9-4 **71**............ RichardHughes 7 65
(M D I Usher) *hld up in detached last: pushed along 4f out: prog to chse clr ldng pair over 2f out: no imp: wknd and lost 3rd last strides* **5/2**[1]
0422 **5** 6 **Fine Lace (IRE)**[14] 5666 3-8-8 **61**............(v[1]) JamesDoyle 4 48
(D J S Ffrench Davis) *in tch in 5th: wknd over 2f out* **9/2**
00-0 **6** 27 **Laid Bare**[22] 5380 3-7-11 **55** oh10............ SophieDoyle(5) 2 —
(Mrs P N Dutfield) *chsd ldng trio: pushed along 5f out: wknd 3f out: t.o* **50/1**
0420 **7** 5 **Sheikhtothemusic**[20] 5437 3-8-8 **61**............ PaulMulrennan 6 —
(J G Given) *led to over 3f out: wknd rapidly: t.o* **12/1**

3m 29.16s (-0.94) **Going Correction** -0.10s/f (Stan) **7** Ran SP% **114.0**
Speed ratings (Par 101): **98,96,90,90,87 73,71**
toteswingers:1&2:£2.50, 2&3:£7.00, 1&3:£8.30 CSF £11.38 CT £106.74 TOTE £3.70: £2.30, £2.10; EX 15.40.
Owner Lael Stable **Bred** Lael Stables **Trained** Newmarket, Suffolk

FOCUS
The front two came well clear in what was a modest staying handicap. The form is rated around them.
Spice Fair Official explanation: jockey said gelding hung badly right

6085 KEMPTON.CO.UK H'CAP 7f (P)
9:10 (9:12) (Class 5) (0-75,75) 3-Y-O+ **£2,286** (£675; £337) **Stalls** High

Form RPR
3603 **1** **Chief Exec**[20] 5454 8-9-6 **71**............ AdamKirby 4 80
(J R Gask) *stdd s: hld up in last pair: prog over 2f out: swtchd to inner and clsd on ldrs fnl f: led last 50yds* **12/1**
2100 **2** nk **Army Of Stars (IRE)**[7] 5852 4-9-3 **73**............(p) SophieDoyle(5) 2 81
(J A Osborne) *trckd ldr: rdn to chal 2f out: led narrowly 1f out: hdd and nt qckn last 50yds* **10/1**
0565 **3** 1 ¾ **Flapper (IRE)**[13] 5689 4-9-1 **66**............(p) RichardHughes 6 69
(J W Hills) *trckd ldrs: rdn to chal 2f out: upsides 1f out: one pce after* **6/1**[2]
-015 **4** 2 ¼ **Hazytoo**[70] 3777 6-9-4 **69**............ SebSanders 8 66
(P J Makin) *led at decent pce: hdd & wknd 1f out* **8/1**[3]
6333 **5** hd **Copperwood**[15] 5634 5-9-5 **70**............ DaneO'Neill 10 67
(M Blanshard) *awkward s: wl in rr: rdn over 2f out: kpt on fr over 1f out: nt gng pce to threaten* **6/1**[2]
2005 **6** 1 ¼ **Marosh (FR)**[11] 5769 3-9-3 **72**............ JimCrowley 13 63
(R M H Cowell) *hld up in last: stl in last pair over 2f out: rdn and prog on outer over 1f out: nvr gng to get involved* **10/1**
2203 **7** hd **Gazboolou**[49] 4488 6-9-7 **72**............ FergusSweeney 3 67
(David Pinder) *trckd ldrs: rdn over 2f out: wl hld in 5th ent fnl f: eased w jockey looking down last 100yds* **12/1**
3601 **8** nk **George Thisby**[19] 5473 4-9-0 **68**............ JamesMillman(3) 9 60
(B R Millman) *nvr beyond midfield: u.p and no prog over 2f out* **16/1**
324 **9** 4 ½ **Buxton**[14] 5652 6-9-7 **72**............(t) JackMitchell 7 52+
(R Ingram) *a in midfield: rdn and no prog over 2f out: wl btn whn hmpd over 1f out* **11/1**
2000 **10** shd **Torres Del Paine**[33] 5031 3-8-11 **66**............ PatDobbs 11 44
(J C Fox) *chsd ldrs: rdn 2f out: swtchd lft and no prog over 1f out: wknd* **25/1**
2264 **11** 4 ½ **Pippbrook Ministar**[16] 5588 3-9-1 **70**............ HayleyTurner 1 36
(J R Boyle) *prom: lost pl over 2f out: wl btn whn sltly hmpd over 1f out* **25/1**
0031 **12** nk **Cut The Cackle (IRE)**[70] 3777 4-9-10 **75**............ StephenCraine 5 42
(D Flood) *racd wd in midfield: struggling u.p wl over 2f out: sn no ch* **7/2**[1]
0500 **13** nk **Shaded Edge**[35] 4959 6-9-1 **66**............(p) JamesDoyle 12 32
(D W P Arbuthnot) *dropped to last u.p over 4f out: a struggling after* **16/1**

1m 25.44s (-0.56) **Going Correction** -0.10s/f (Stan)
WFA 3 from 4yo+ 4lb **13** Ran SP% **123.3**
Speed ratings (Par 103): **99,98,96,94,93 92,92,91,86,86 81,81,80**
toteswingers:1&2:£37.50, 2&3:£17.00, 1&3:£15.50 CSF £130.87 CT £802.04 TOTE £21.30: £6.20, £3.40, £3.50; EX 216.60 Place 6: £196.81 Place 5: £64.79.
Owner Stuart Dobb & Miss Kate Dobb **Bred** C A Cyzer **Trained** Sutton Veny, Wilts

FOCUS
A competitive and well run handicap. The winner is rated back to his best.
Gazboolou Official explanation: jockey said gelding lost its action
Shaded Edge Official explanation: jockey said gelding never travelled
T/Plt: £175.80 to a £1 stake. Pool £53,995.19 - 224.10 winning tickets. T/Qpdt: £32.50 to a £1 stake. Pool of £7,204.68 - 163.60 winning tickets. JN

5965 SANDOWN (R-H)
Wednesday, September 15

OFFICIAL GOING: Good (good to soft in places; sprint 7.8, round 7.9)
Sprint course at full width. Round course at mid configuration around bend with drop in at 2f pole, increasing distances by about 5yds.
Wind: quite strong against Weather: dry

6086 SEPTEMBER NURSERY 5f 6y
2:20 (2:22) (Class 5) (0-75,75) 2-Y-O **£2,590** (£770; £385; £192) **Stalls** High

Form RPR
431 **1** **Jack Smudge**[21] 5418 2-9-5 **73**............ PaulMulrennan 6 78
(J G Given) *trckd ldrs: swtchd lft and hdwy over 1f out: chsd ldr ins fnl f and edgd rt: qckn to ld fnl 50yds: readily* **7/2**[2]
2540 **2** 1 **Pick A Little**[43] 4677 2-9-4 **72**............ DaneO'Neill 11 73
(B W Duke) *chsd ldrs: rdn 2f out: wnt 2nd over 1f out: one pce ins fnl f and edgd lft: rallied to chse wnr cl home: a readily hld* **50/1**

The Form Book, Raceform Ltd, Compton, RG20 6NL

2542 **3** ½ **Perfect Pastime**16 5613 2-9-7 **75** .... AdamKirby 10 74
(W R Swinburn) *led: rdn over 2f out: styd on wl tl hdd and outpcd fnl 50yds: lost 2nd cl home* **2/1**1

0223 **4** hd **Barking (IRE)**22 5381 2-9-4 **72** .... RichardHughes 1 71
(R Hannon) *stdd s: in rr: hdwy over 1f out: styng on whn n.m.r ins fnl f: r.o to press fr 3rd cl home* **15/2**

0553 **5** 2 **Buddy Miracle**16 5613 2-9-5 **73** .... JimmyFortune 5 64
(A M Balding) *hld up in rr: swtchd lft to outside and styd on u.p fnl f: nvr gng pce to get into contention* **6/1**3

660 **6** shd **Cinderkamp**18 5523 2-8-8 **62** .... LiamKeniry 8 56
(E F Vaughan) *s.i.s: t.k.h early: gng wl but nt clr run fr over 1f out: swtchd lft and edgd lft whn hdwy ins fnl f: kpt on cl home* **10/1**

5142 **7** 1 ¾ **Volcanic Dust (IRE)**17 5547 2-9-0 **68** .... JimCrowley 3 53
(E A L Dunlop) *t.k.h: chsd ldrs and wnt 2nd 2f out: rdn sn after: lost 2nd over 1f out: wkng whn hmpd ins fnl f* **9/1**

3523 **8** 3 ¼ **Kokojo (IRE)**7 5863 2-8-11 **65** .... FergusSweeney 7 38
(B G Powell) *chsd ldrs: rdn 2f out: wknd appr fnl f* **12/1**

2400 **9** 1 ¼ **Kyncraighe (IRE)**16 5613 2-9-2 **70** ....(t) SebSanders 9 38
(Eve Johnson Houghton) *chsd ldr 3f: sn btn* **25/1**

64.05 secs (2.45) **Going Correction** +0.375s/f (Good) **9** Ran SP% **114.2**
Speed ratings (Par 95): **95,93,92,92,89 88,86,80,78**
toteswingers:1&2 £13.70, 2&3 £15.30, 1&3 £2.90 CSF £144.56 CT £439.20 TOTE £4.90: £1.90, £10.70, £1.40; EX 187.10.
Owner Danethorpe Racing Partnership **Bred** P And Mrs A G Venner **Trained** Willoughton, Lincs

FOCUS
Following 3mm of rain overnight, the going was described as good, good to soft in places (from good), and there was quite a stiff headwind in the straight. The GoingStick read 7.6 on the far side and 7.8 on the stands' side. They went quick enough early in this nursery and that suited the winner. Solid, straightforward form.

NOTEBOOK
Jack Smudge, who took a while to get on top at Catterick last time, got a little outpaced here before running on strongly. He appreciated the good gallop and the stiff finish helped, but he looks to be crying out for a step up to 6f. (op 5-1)
Pick A Little, one of the most exposed horses in the line-up, had the best draw and tracked the leader on the far rail. He ran a sound race off a stiff enough mark. (tchd 40-1)
Perfect Pastime tried to make the most of his draw and led on the far rail. The half-furlong drop back in trip probably didn't suit him ideally, but it was a solid effort. (op 5-2 tchd 11-4)
Barking(IRE) had the worst of the draw so the front-running tactics employed on his last two starts had to be ditched this time. Held up in last, he didn't get the clearest of runs through, and all things considered he's probably a bit better than this performance suggests. Official explanation: jockey said colt suffered interference in running (op 5-1)
Buddy Miracle, another who has raced prominently in the past but was ridden with more restraint this time, was stuck wider than ideal most of the way, and never really looked to have the necessary pace back in trip. (op 7-1 tchd 8-1)
Cinderkamp ◆, running in a handicap for the first time, showed his inexperience before the start. Denied a clear run until it was too late, he shaped a fair bit better than his finishing position suggests, and is one to keep in mind for a similar race. Official explanation: jockey said colt was denied a clear run (op 14-1 tchd 9-1)

6087 EUROPEAN BREEDERS' FUND MAIDEN STKS 1m 14y
2:55 (2:56) (Class 4) 2-Y-O **£4,209** (£1,252; £625; £312) **Stalls** High

Form RPR

1 **Masked Marvel** 2-9-3 0 .... WilliamBuick 3 83+
(J H M Gosden) *wnt 2nd 5f out: pushed along as ldr qcknd over 2f out: drvn and styd on wl to ld fnl 120yds: won gng away* **13/8**1

5 **2** 2 **Mutayaser**15 5629 2-9-3 0 .... RichardHills 8 77
(Sir Michael Stoute) *led: pushed and qcknd over 2f out: hdd fnl 120yds: kpt on: nt gng pce of wnr* **7/4**2

3 2 ¼ **Discoteca** 2-9-3 0 .... JimmyFortune 4 72+
(A M Balding) *in tch: hdwy to chse ldrs 3f out: styd on to go 2nd over 1f out: kpt on: no ch w ldng duo fnl f* **14/1**

4 1 ¾ **Miss Diagnosis (IRE)** 2-8-12 0 .... JimCrowley 1 63+
(R M Beckett) *in rr and stl last 3f out: stdy prog on outside fr over 2f out: kpt on wl ins fnl f: nvr quite gng pce to get into contention* **22/1**

05 **5** 1 **Acute (IRE)**12 5717 2-9-3 0 .... MartinDwyer 7 66
(B J Meehan) *chsd ldrs: pushed along fr ins fnl 3f: wknd over 1f out* **33/1**

6 1 ¼ **Shooting Line (IRE)** 2-9-3 0 .... AdamKirby 10 63+
(W R Swinburn) *towards rr: hdwy 3f out: drvn and in tch over 2f out: wknd wl over 1f out* **22/1**

7 2 ¼ **Dark And Dangerous (IRE)** 2-9-3 0 .... DaneO'Neill 9 58
(P Winkworth) *sn towards rr: pushed along and sme prog ins fnl 3f: wknd 2f out* **50/1**

8 ½ **Strength And Stay (IRE)** 2-9-3 0 .... SebSanders 5 57
(Eve Johnson Houghton) *s.i.s: in rr: sme prog ins fnl 3f: wknd over 2f out* **66/1**

4 **9** 7 **Aloneinthestreet (USA)**12 5717 2-9-3 0 .... GregFairley 2 41
(M Johnston) *chsd ldrs: rdn 4f out: wknd over 3f out* **11/2**3

1m 50.36s (7.06) **Going Correction** +0.225s/f (Good) **9** Ran SP% **111.6**
Speed ratings (Par 97): **73,71,68,67,66 64,62,62,55**
toteswingers:1&2 £1.10, 2&3 £6.70, 1&3 £10.60 CSF £4.20 TOTE £2.70: £1.20, £1.30, £3.30; EX 5.20.
Owner B E Nielsen **Bred** Newsells Park Stud **Trained** Newmarket, Suffolk

FOCUS
Four of the last eight winners of this race have gone on to gain black type. Not an easy race to put figures on, but the winner looks potentially smart.

NOTEBOOK
Masked Marvel, who holds some nice entries, including the Dewhurst and Racing Post Trophy, made a pleasing racecourse debut and could well be competing at a higher level pretty soon. A 260,000euro son of Montjeu, he took a while to get the better of his main market rival, who had the benefit of previous racecourse experience, but he was nicely on top at the finish, having not been given a hard race. Green beforehand, he can only improve for this and looks a nice long-term middle-distance prospect. (op 2-1 tchd 9-4 in a place)
Mutayaser had the benefit of having had an outing already, and his jockey tried to make the most of it, making the running and briefly looking as though he'd stolen a march on the winner when quickening early in the straight. He's likely to remain vulnerable to smart rivals but there is a race to be won with him before the season is out. (op 11-8)
Discoteca, a big sort, ran a promising race for one bred to be much better over a trip next year. Improvement looks guaranteed. (tchd 12-1)
Miss Diagnosis(IRE) ◆ was given a considerate ride on her debut and is another who should come on plenty for the outing. Held up in last, she travelled up strongly on the outside early in the straight before staying on under mostly hands-and-heels riding. (op 16-1 tchd 25-1)
Acute(IRE) is now eligible for nurseries and might do better in that sphere. (op 18-1)
Shooting Line(IRE) showed his inexperience once coming under pressure, but he's a half-brother to Fairmile and should improve. (op 20-1 tchd 25-1)
Aloneinthestreet(USA) was under pressure before the top of the straight and perhaps the ground wasn't in his favour. (op 10-1)

6088 FUTURITY NOVICE STKS 7f 16y
3:30 (3:30) (Class 3) 2-Y-O **£4,984** (£1,492; £746; £373; £186) **Stalls** High

Form RPR

1 **1** **Treasury Devil (USA)**33 5033 2-9-3 87 .... WilliamBuick 4 96+
(J H M Gosden) *sn disputing cl 3rd: shkn up and qcknd to trck ldr 2f out: led appr fnl f: styd on strly and forged clr fnl 120yds: comf* **8/11**1

2312 **2** 2 ½ **Introvert (IRE)**25 5310 2-9-0 84 .... FrankieDettori 5 87
(Mahmood Al Zarooni) *trckd ldr tl led travelling wl appr fnl 2f: drvn and hdd appr fnl f: sn outpcd by wnr: stl wl clr of 3rd* **5/2**2

54 **3** 5 **Claret'N'Blue (USA)**11 5746 2-8-12 0 .... RichardHills 2 72
(B J Meehan) *stdd in rr: shkn up and hdwy fr 2f out: wnt n.d 3rd ins fnl f* **20/1**

6120 **4** 1 ¾ **Colorado Gold**31 5133 2-9-0 88 .... JimmyFortune 3 70
(P F I Cole) *led tl hdd appr fnl 2f: wknd over 1f out and lost 3rd ins fnl f* **8/1**3

5 2 ¾ **My Vindication (USA)** 2-8-12 0 .... RichardHughes 1 61+
(R Hannon) *disp 3rd to 3f out: wknd over 2f out* **16/1**

1m 33.99s (4.49) **Going Correction** +0.225s/f (Good) **5** Ran SP% **108.2**
Speed ratings (Par 99): **83,80,74,72,69**
CSF £2.61 TOTE £1.80: £1.10, £1.50; EX 2.90.
Owner Lord Lloyd-Webber **Bred** Watership Down Stud **Trained** Newmarket, Suffolk

FOCUS
A good race for favourites in recent years and Treasury Devil continued the trend with an authoritative win. The form is rated around the second and the winner has more to offer.

NOTEBOOK
Treasury Devil(USA) won well, and this should pave the way for him to step up to conditions or pattern company next time. A taking winner at Newbury first time up, he gave weight all round here and the further he went the better he looked. He'll have no trouble getting a mile this term if connections decide to go that way, but there are lots of options at this trip as well, and he looks to have plenty of potential. (tchd 4-6, 8-13 and 4-5 in a place and 10-11 in places)
Introvert(IRE), who has an official mark of 84, wasn't in the same class as the winner, but he ran a solid race and a return to quicker ground will probably help this son of Iffraaj. (tchd 11-4)
Claret'N'Blue(USA), who got a bit warm in the prelims, stayed on from the back of the field to take third and looks up to winning an ordinary race, but as a result of not being E.B.F eligible he's been pretty highly tried so far. (op 16-1)
Colorado Gold, who found conditions too testing in Deauville last time, made the running but was easily seen off early in the straight. This ground was again perhaps easier than he likes, but 7f seems to stretch him anyway. (op 17-2 tchd 10-1)
My Vindication(USA), a leggy sort, faced a stiff task on his debut. Not knocked about, he should come on for it, and as a half-brother to US Grade 1 winning juvenile Dublin, who also finished seventh in this year's Kentucky Derby, he's certainly bred to go a bit. (tchd 20-1)

6089 FORTUNE STKS (LISTED RACE) 1m 14y
4:05 (4:06) (Class 1) 3-Y-O+
£19,869 (£7,532; £3,769; £1,879; £941; £472) **Stalls** High

Form RPR

2-10 **1** **Penitent**103 2707 4-9-4 109 .... RichardHughes 3 116+
(W J Haggas) *wnt lft s: trckd ldrs: kpt wd: rdn to ld briefly 2f out: rallied wl: drifted rt ins fnl f: led fnl 75yds: drvn out* **9/2**2

5332 **2** ½ **Skysurfers**26 5275 4-9-4 113 .... FrankieDettori 4 115
(Saeed Bin Suroor) *trckd ldrs: racd off rails: led wl over 1f out: sn rdn: kpt on but no ex whn hdd fnl 75yds* **9/4**1

140- **3** 4 ½ **Bronze Cannon (USA)**353 6324 5-9-4 118 .... GeorgeBaker 7 105+
(G L Moore) *trckd ldr: kpt on rails: rdn and ev ch 2f out: kpt on: nt gng pce of front pair* **16/1**

-326 **4** 1 **Riggins (IRE)**50 4457 6-9-4 108 .... JimmyFortune 1 102
(A M Balding) *s.i.s: racd off rails: hld up in last pair: rdn 2f out: styd on fnl 100yds: snatched 4th line: nvr threatened ldrs* **9/4**1

302 **5** shd **Dunn'o (IRE)**17 5556 5-9-4 94 .... AdamKirby 5 102?
(C G Cox) *led: kpt on rails: rdn and hdd 2f out: kpt on same pce: lost 4th line* **17/2**

1032 **6** 3 ½ **Dandy Boy (ITY)**34 5016 4-9-4 106 .... CO'Donoghue 2 94
(David Marnane, Ire) *s.i.s: in last pair: kpt on rails: swtchd lft and rdn 2f out: nvr able to get on terms* **11/2**3

1m 44.49s (1.19) **Going Correction** +0.225s/f (Good)
WFA 3 from 4yo+ 5lb **6** Ran SP% **111.5**
Speed ratings (Par 111): **103,102,98,97,96 93**
toteswingers:1&2 £1.40, 2&3 £5.30, 1&3 £9.90 CSF £14.84 TOTE £5.50: £2.50, £1.10; EX 14.20.
Owner Cheveley Park Stud **Bred** Cheveley Park Stud Ltd **Trained** Newmarket, Suffolk

FOCUS
A few could be given a chance in this Listed race but in the end two came clear inside the last. The form is a little and limited by the fifth to an extent.

NOTEBOOK
Penitent saw the trip out the best. The son of Kyllachy had been off the track for 103 days but showed when winning the Lincoln that he can go well fresh, and, with the overnight rain having eased the ground slightly, conditions had come in his favour. Relatively lightly raced and still open to improvement, he'll be fresher than most this backend, and connections will no doubt be planning to step him back up to Group company now, and hoping for a wet autumn. (op 4-1 tchd 5-1)
Skysurfers, for whom this stiff mile was a concern, was suited by the fairly ordinary early pace and came to have every chance inside the last. He finished well clear of the rest and can win in this grade, although genuine soft ground is an unknown with him. (tchd 11-4)
Bronze Cannon(USA) has left John Gosden and was having his first outing for his new stable. Although best in at the weights, he'd been off the track for almost a year and was fully entitled to need this, especially as his best form has come over 1m4f. This was a perfectly satisfactory return and hopefully he can build on it. (op 14-1)
Riggins(IRE) found 7f too short in a Group 2 at Goodwood last time out and promised to be suited by the return to 1m, but he struggled to land a blow from off the pace. A stronger all-round gallop would have suited him better, as would quicker ground. (op 11-4 tchd 2-1)
Dunn'o(IRE) enjoyed the run of things out in front but this was a higher class of race than he normally competes in, and he simply wasn't good enough to take full advantage. (op 12-1 tchd 8-1)
Dandy Boy(ITY) could have done without the overnight rain as he prefers a fast surface to run on. Like Riggins, another who has made his name in big-field handicaps, he failed to get involved from off the pace. (op 5-1 tchd 4-1)

6090 HARRY THE HAT IS LOOKING FOR FILLIES' H'CAP 1m 14y
4:40 (4:40) (Class 4) (0-85,85) 3-Y-O **£3,885** (£1,156; £577; £288) **Stalls** High

Form RPR

105 **1** **Law Of The Range**22 5394 3-8-12 **76** ow1 .... AdamKirby 4 88
(M Botti) *mde all: kpt on gamely: drvn out* **33/1**

1125 **2** ¾ **Sooraah**[28] 5222 3-9-5 **83**............ GeorgeBaker 1 93+
(W J Haggas) *s.i.s: last: nt best of runs 2f out: squeezed through gap and gd hdwy sn after: r.o ins fnl f: nt rch wnr* **8/1**

2211 **3** ½ **Rare Tern (IRE)**[6] 5887 3-9-3 **81** 6ex............ SebSanders 6 90
(Sir Mark Prescott) *trckd ldrs: rdn to chse wnr fr over 2f out: nvr quite able to chal: kpt on: lost 2nd nr fin* **15/8**[1]

1053 **4** 2¾ **Veni Vedi Veci (IRE)**[16] 5593 3-8-11 **75**............ JimmyFortune 7 78
(A M Balding) *trckd wnr: rdn over 2f out: styd on same pce* **25/1**

1223 **5** shd **Anacopa (USA)**[24] 5329 3-9-7 **85**............ FrankieDettori 9 87
(Mahmood Al Zarooni) *hld up towards rr: hdwy whn nt best of runs 2f out: sn rdn: wnt 4th briefly jst over 1f out: no ex* **9/1**

1312 **6** 1 **Miss Antonia (IRE)**[14] 5662 3-9-4 **82**............ EddieAhern 2 82
(H R A Cecil) *hld up towards rr: rdn wl over 2f out: no imp tl styd on ins fnl f* **5/1**[3]

01 **7** shd **Fleeting Glance (IRE)**[75] 3620 3-8-8 **72**............ MartinDwyer 3 72
(B J Meehan) *mid-div: rdn over 2f out: styd on same pce* **7/2**[2]

5345 **8** hd **Sunarise (IRE)**[8] 5833 3-8-10 **74**............(b[1]) RichardHughes 5 73
(R Hannon) *racd keenly in mid-div: rdn over 2f out: kpt on same pce* **14/1**

0530 **9** 8 **Flip Flop (IRE)**[22] 5383 3-9-0 **78**............ WilliamBuick 11 59
(B W Hills) *t.k.h: trckd ldrs: rdn over 2f out: wknd over 1f out* **20/1**

2151 **10** 8 **Belgique (IRE)**[33] 5031 3-9-1 **82**............ PatrickHills(3) 10 45
(R Hannon) *trckd ldrs: rdn whn edgd rt 2f out: wknd over 1f out* **33/1**

0314 **11** 3¾ **Ishraaqat**[24] 5329 3-8-12 **76**............ RichardHills 8 30
(M P Tregoning) *s.i.s: sn mid-div: rdn over 2f out: sn wknd* **20/1**

1m 45.08s (1.78) **Going Correction** +0.225s/f (Good) **11** Ran SP% **120.7**
Speed ratings (Par 100): **100,99,98,96,95 94,94,94,86,78 74**
toteswingers:1&2 £45.00, 2&3 £5.40, 1&3 £17.60 CSF £267.92 CT £768.24 TOTE £56.10: £8.80, £2.90, £1.10; EX 503.10.
Owner Christopher McHale **Bred** Brookside Breeders Club **Trained** Newmarket, Suffolk

FOCUS
This looked more competitive than the betting suggested as there were plenty of in-form fillies in attendance. Sound form with the well-in winner improving by 6lb.
Sooraah Official explanation: jockey said filly was denied a clear run
Belgique(IRE) Official explanation: jockey said filly was unsuited by the good (good to soft places) ground

6091 WATCH RACING UK ON SKY CHANNEL 432 H'CAP 1m 2f 7y
5:10 (5:12) (Class 4) (0-80,80) 3-Y-O+ **£3,885** (£1,156; £577; £288) **Stalls** High

Form RPR

1 **Alazan (IRE)**[26] 4964 4-9-6 **74**............ FrankieDettori 7 87+
(P J Hobbs) *trckd ldrs: swtchd to stands' side over 3f out: short of room over 2f out: led over 1f out: rdn clr: comf* **7/4**[1]

6550 **2** 2½ **Whistleinthewind (IRE)**[20] 5456 3-8-9 **70**............(b) WilliamBuick 13 78
(G L Moore) *trckd ldrs: late switch to stands' side 3f out: sn led and rdn: edgd rt: hdd over 1f out: styd on: sn hld* **14/1**

31 **3** ½ **Status Symbol (IRE)**[13] 5700 5-9-10 **78**............ WilliamCarson 6 85
(G C Bravery) *mid-div: swtchd to stands' side over 3f out: hdwy 2f out: sn rdn: swtchd rt: styd on ins fnl f* **17/2**

3512 **4** 3¾ **Wiggy Smith**[34] 4996 11-9-11 **79**............ DaneO'Neill 4 79
(H Candy) *hld up towards rr: swtchd to stands' side over 3f out: rdn and hdwy over 2f out: styd on same pce ins fnl f* **12/1**

1050 **5** 1¼ **Agapanthus (GER)**[17] 5563 5-9-4 **72**............ MickyFenton 14 69
(B J Curley) *s.i.s: towards rr: rdn whn swtchd to stands' side over 3f out: styd on wl fr over 1f out: nt rch ldrs* **25/1**

2660 **6** 1¼ **Penchesco (IRE)**[55] 4306 5-9-6 **74**............ PatDobbs 9 69
(Mrs A J Perrett) *mid-div: swtchd to stands' side over 3f out: hdwy over 2f out: sn rdn: wknd ins fnl f* **16/1**

0012 **7** 11 **Negotiation (IRE)**[14] 5664 4-9-2 **70**............ MartinDwyer 8 43
(M Quinn) *led: remained far side and racd alone fr over 3f out: sn rdn: hdd over 2f out: wknd* **20/1**

0556 **8** shd **Tiger Star**[17] 5563 3-8-9 **70**............ RichardHughes 10 42
(J M P Eustace) *trckd ldrs: swtchd to stands' side over 3f out: rdn over 2f out: wknd over 1f out* **11/2**[3]

0102 **9** 8 **Sagredo (USA)**[49] 4476 6-9-7 **75**............ GeorgeBaker 5 31
(Jonjo O'Neill) *stdd s: swtchd to stands' side over 3f out: a towards rr* **25/1**

3/0- **10** 4½ **Bee Sting**[496] 1798 6-9-12 **80**............ JimCrowley 12 27
(Mrs L Williamson) *swtchd to stands' side over 3f out: a towards rr* **50/1**

45-6 **11** ½ **Etruscan (IRE)**[121] 2181 5-9-5 **73**............(p) ChrisCatlin 15 19
(C Gordon) *s.i.s: sn mid-div: struggling whn swtchd to stands' side over 3f out: sn wknd* **50/1**

1125 **12** 1¼ **Aestival**[41] 4737 4-9-10 **78**............(b[1]) SebSanders 1 22
(Sir Mark Prescott) *trckd ldr: led switch to stands' side over 3f out: sn hdd: wknd 2f out: eased* **4/1**[2]

1450 **13** 5 **Charlie Smirke (USA)**[103] 2714 4-8-13 **67**............ FergusSweeney 11 —
(G L Moore) *mid-div: swtchd to stands' side over 3f out: wknd 2f out* **33/1**

2m 11.28s (0.78) **Going Correction** +0.225s/f (Good)
WFA 3 from 4yo+ 7lb **13** Ran SP% **121.8**
Speed ratings (Par 105): **105,103,102,99,98 97,88,88,82,78 78,77,73**
toteswingers:1&2 £7.50, 2&3 £21.40, 1&3 £6.30 CSF £27.88 CT £174.90 TOTE £2.60: £1.10, £5.30, £2.00; EX 30.40 Place 6: £7.20 Place 5: £4.63.
Owner Mrs Caren Walsh & R J Budge **Bred** D G Iceton **Trained** Withycombe, Somerset

FOCUS
There was a difference of opinion here as they came into the straight, and while Martin Dwyer stayed on the far side on Negotiation, Seb Sanders made a beeline for the stands' rail on Aestival and the rest chose to follow him, even William Buick, who made a late call having initially been happy to stay far side. Fair form for the grade with a clear personal best from the winner.
T/Plt: £9.60 to a £1 stake. Pool of £59,415.36 - 4,481.27 winning tickets. T/Qpdt: £7.60 to a £1 stake. Pool of £4,420.01 - 428.95 winning tickets. TM

6058 YARMOUTH (L-H)
Wednesday, September 15

OFFICIAL GOING: Soft (5.3)
Wind: strong, across Weather: cloudy, windy

6092 EUROPEAN BREEDERS' FUND MAIDEN STKS 7f 3y
2:10 (2:11) (Class 5) 2-Y-O **£3,532** (£1,057; £528; £264; £131) **Stalls** High

Form RPR

5 **1** **Utley (USA)**[19] 5491 2-9-3 0............ NickyMackay 8 83+
(J H M Gosden) *a gng wl: chsd ldr tl led on bit over 1f out: shkn up ent fnl f: rdn and kpt on wl fnl 150yds* **15/8**[1]

2 ½ **Nordic Sky (USA)** 2-9-3 0............ ShaneKelly 6 82+
(W J Haggas) *hld up in tch: pushed along and hdwy wl over 1f out: rdn to chse wnr jst over 1f out: kpt on wl: a hld* **40/1**

3 2½ **Unex Dali** 2-9-3 0............ DarryllHolland 15 76+
(J H M Gosden) *in tch in midfield: pushed along and hdwy whn sltly hmpd wl over 1f out: rdn to chse ldng pair jst over 1f out: styd on same pce ins fnl f* **15/2**[3]

4 1 **Shelovestobouggie** 2-8-12 0............ IanMongan 11 68+
(H R A Cecil) *in tch: effrt to chse ldng trio over 1f out: kpt on same pce ins fnl f* **18/1**

0 **5** 6 **Franciscan**[40] 4803 2-9-3 0............ KirstyMilczarek 14 58
(L M Cumani) *in tch in midfield: rdn and outpcd over 1f out: plugged on same pce and wl hld ins fnl f* **40/1**

23 **6** 1¼ **Grand Duchy**[19] 5498 2-9-3 0............ AhmedAjtebi 9 55
(Mahmood Al Zarooni) *led: rdn and wandered over 1f out: sn hdd: wknd qckly ent fnl f* **8/1**

0 **7** 2½ **Chillie Peppar**[12] 5717 2-9-3 0............ LiamJones 13 49
(G Prodromou) *in tch in midfield: outpcd and hung lft wl over 1f out: wl btn ins fnl f* **125/1**

8 1¾ **Levitate** 2-9-0 0............ Louis-PhilippeBeuzelin(3) 5 44+
(Sir Michael Stoute) *in tch in midfield: rdn along and lost pl 4f out: no ch w ldrs after: kpt on steadily ins fnl f* **14/1**

9 4 **First Battalion (IRE)** 2-9-3 0............ RyanMoore 1 34
(Sir Michael Stoute) *s.i.s: a towards rr: struggling 1/2-way: n.d* **8/1**

5 **10** ½ **Dubawi Dancer**[19] 5488 2-8-12 0............ SimonWhitworth 16 28
(W J Haggas) *s.i.s: a bhd: struggling and rdn 1/2-way: no ch fnl 2f* **80/1**

11 1 **Cairanne** 2-8-12 0............ JimmyQuinn 12 26
(T Keddy) *chsd ldrs tl wknd qckly over 2f out: wl btn ins fnl f* **150/1**

30 **12** ½ **Annalika**[103] 2701 2-8-9 0............ KellyHarrison(3) 10 24
(W J H Ratcliffe) *t.k.h: chsd ldrs tl wknd qckly over 2f out: wl bhd ins fnl f* **200/1**

03 **13** nk **Chinook Wind (IRE)**[13] 5692 2-8-12 0............ MichaelHills 4 24
(B W Hills) *chsd ldrs: rdn over 2f out: wknd qckly 2f out: wl bhd ins fnl f* **10/3**[2]

14 1¾ **Coastal Bequest (IRE)** 2-9-3 0............ RichardMullen 3 24
(Sir Michael Stoute) *in tch in midfield: rdn and dropped in rr 4f out: bhd fnl 3f* **28/1**

15 3¾ **Guards Chapel** 2-9-3 0............ J-PGuillambert 2 15
(L M Cumani) *s.i.s: a in rr: toiling fr 1/2-way* **20/1**

16 9 **If What And Maybe** 2-9-3 0............ MarcHalford 7 —
(J Ryan) *v.s.a: a bhd* **150/1**

1m 31.11s (4.51) **Going Correction** +0.50s/f (Yiel) **16** Ran SP% **120.7**
Speed ratings (Par 95): **94,93,90,89,82 81,78,76,71,71 70,69,69,67,62 52**
toteswingers:1&2 £17.00, 2&3 £85.20, 1&3 £5.90 CSF £104.09 TOTE £2.50: £1.40, £8.00, £2.80; EX 100.10 Trifecta £304.30 Part won. Pool: £411.30 - 0.64 winning units..
Owner George Strawbridge **Bred** Augustin Stable **Trained** Newmarket, Suffolk

FOCUS
Probably a good-quality race of its type, with many top stables represented by these unexposed maidens. It is likely that several of those who finished down the field will come on a good deal as they sharpen up. The easy winner could rate as much as 10lb+ higher next time.

NOTEBOOK
Utley(USA) had benefited from his debut, and the fact that he had to battle to hold off the runner-up will have taught him even more. A strong traveller, this Group 1 entry has plenty of potential and looks a decent sort for next year, with faster ground likely to suit him at least as well as soft. (op 2-1 tchd 7-4 and 9-4 in places)
Nordic Sky(USA), by Arch out of a winning sprinter, already stays further than his dam. The family is not precocious, but he gave the winner a tough going-over on this first attempt and the best is yet to come. (op 50-1 tchd 33-1)
Unex Dali, fit enough for this debut, is a stablemate of the winner and trainer John Gosden rates him as a nice colt. Entered for three Group 1 races, this half-brother to the smart Champions Gallery can improve greatly on this promising debut (op 9-1, tchd 10-1 in places)
Shelovestobouggie, by Tobougg out of a decent family, looked likely to handle the soft ground on breeding and shaped well on this initital outing. Seen home with hands and heels when fourth place was guaranteed, she has plenty of improvement in her. (op 14-1)
Franciscan still looked green on entering the paddock. He improved significantly on his debut but looks more of a long-term prospect for next season.
Grand Duchy did not run as well as he had in his first two races, which had been on fast ground. He does not look to be a stable star but should make a middling handicapper now he is qualified. (tchd 15-2)
First Battalion(IRE), a Sadler's Wells newcomer from a fine family at 1m and beyond, was beaten a fair way but there looks to be plenty of improvement in him as he matures. (op 9-1)
Chinook Wind(IRE) Official explanation: jockey said filly stopped quickly

6093 BENNETTS CLAIMING STKS 1m 3y
2:45 (2:45) (Class 6) 3-Y-O **£1,683** (£501; £250; £125) **Stalls** High

Form RPR

2452 **1** **Indian Valley (USA)**[15] 5648 3-8-11 **72**............ MartinLane(3) 2 80
(Rae Guest) *hld up in tch: jnd ldrs on bit ent fnl 2f: pushed ahd over 1f out: in command and pushed out hands and heels ins fnl f* **7/2**[2]

1554 **2** 2½ **Strike A Deal (IRE)**[13] 5689 3-8-4 **67**............ LiamJones 8 64
(C F Wall) *hld up in tch towards rr: hdwy 3f out: rdn to ld 2f out: hdd over 1f out: drvn and kpt on same pce ins fnl f* **7/4**[1]

6340 **3** 3½ **Rain On The Wind (IRE)**[7] 5867 3-8-9 **64**............(t) TomMcLaughlin 7 61
(S C Williams) *led: hdd and rdn 2f out: kpt pressing ldrs tl btn jst over 1f out: wknd ins fnl f* **9/1**

-200 **4** 7 **Hayek**[36] 4931 3-8-9 **64**............ PJMcDonald 11 45
(W Jarvis) *t.k.h: chsd ldrs: rdn over 2f out: wknd qckly and sn wl btn* **13/2**

0000 **5** ½ **Penderyn**[17] 5550 3-7-5 **38**............ IanBurns(7) 5 33
(C Smith) *chsd ldr tl over 2f out: hung rt u.p and wknd 2f out* **100/1**

5403 **6** 4½ **Fonterutoli (IRE)**[14] 5661 3-9-0 **71**............ AndreaAtzeni 9 39
(M Botti) *chsd ldrs: drvn and edgd lft ent fnl 2f: sn wknd and wl btn over 1f out* **9/2**[3]

0 **7** nk **Mouchez**[42] 4697 3-8-2 0............ AdamBeschizza(5) 3 31
(D K Ivory) *hld up in tch towards rr: rdn and btn over 2f out* **40/1**

0 **8** 3½ **Upset**[108] 2564 3-9-7 0............ DarryllHolland 10 37
(P J O'Gorman) *s.i.s: a in rr: rdn and rn green over 3f out: sn wknd: wl btn fnl 2f* **50/1**

000 **9** hd **Shut Up Shapiro (IRE)**[5] 5925 3-8-7 0 ow2............ TedDurcan 1 22
(George Baker) *s.i.s: rn in snatches: in tch tl wknd u.p 3f out: sn bhd* **40/1**

6000 **10** 5 **Midnight M**[19] 5469 3-8-4 **38**............(t) NickyMackay 4 —
(Rae Guest) *hld up in last pair: pushed along and btn over 2f out: sn wl bhd* **66/1**

-000 **11** 3¾ **Donair**[92] 3055 3-8-3 **51**............(bt[1]) JimmyQuinn 6 —
(P F I Cole) *in tch towards rr: rdn and btn over 2f out: wl bhd fnl 2f* **16/1**

1m 44.08s (3.48) **Going Correction** +0.50s/f (Yiel) **11** Ran SP% **115.3**
Speed ratings (Par 99): **102,99,96,89,88 84,83,80,80,75 71**
toteswingers:1&2 £2.30, 2&3 £3.40, 1&3 £6.60 CSF £9.60 TOTE £3.40: £1.10, £1.50, £2.20; EX 10.90 Trifecta £46.30 Pool: £355.03 - 5.67 winning units..
Owner Triple R Racing **Bred** T Holmes, Dr & Mrs W Zent & S Caldwell **Trained** Newmarket, Suffolk

The Form Book, Raceform Ltd, Compton, RG20 6NL

FOCUS
A routine claimer on the whole, but the winner is a fair sort for the grade. Few of the others showed their form in this ground and the form is not that solid.

6094 DANNY WRIGHT MEMORIAL (S) STKS — 1m 2f 21y
3:20 (3:20) (Class 6) 3-4-Y-O — **£1,554** (£462; £231; £115) **Stalls** Low

Form — RPR

4553 **1** — **Kenyan Cat**[11] 5770 3-8-7 58 — TedDurcan 5 — 61
(George Baker) *hld up towards rr: hdwy on inner to chse clr ldr jst over 4f out: jnd ldr 3f out: rdn to ld wl over 1f out: in command ins fnl f: rdn out* **5/4**[1]

5600 **2** 2 3/4 **Mister Frosty (IRE)**[8] 5840 4-9-5 48 — KirstyMilczarek 12 — 60
(G Prodromou) *led clr over 4f out: jnd by wnr but wl clr of field 3f out: drvn and hdd wl over 1f out: btn 1f out: kpt on same pce after* **12/1**

4405 **3** 14 **Marafong**[21] 5414 3-8-7 48 — AdamBeschizza(5) 4 — 32
(Miss J Feilden) *in tch: nt clr run over 4f out: sn rdn to dispute modest 3rd fr wl over 3f out: no imp on ldrs and wl btn over 2f out: wnt 3rd over 1f out* **8/1**

04 **4** 6 **Seriy Tzarina**[40] 4780 4-9-0 55 — RobertWinston 10 — 15
(Miss Gay Kelleway) *hmpd after 1f: in tch towards rr: rdn and effrt 5f out: chsd clr ldng pair 4f out: no imp and wl btn over 2f out: lost 3rd over 1f out* **11/2**[2]

0056 **5** 15 **Suzi's Challenger**[81] 3442 3-8-7 42 — LiamJones 13 — —
(T T Clement) *dwlt: hdwy to chse ldrs after 2f: rdn and btn ent fnl 4f: wl bhd fnl 3f: t.o* **33/1**

0000 **6** 7 **Telescopic**[33] 5051 3-8-7 49 — PJMcDonald 6 — —
(W Jarvis) *bustled along early: chsd ldrs tl rdn and struggling 5f out: lost tch 4f out: t.o fnl 3f* **7/1**[3]

0000 **7** 9 **Southwark Newsman**[7] 5864 3-8-12 45 — (t) MarcHalford 11 — —
(Mrs C A Dunnett) *dwlt: sn rcvrd to chse ldr after 1f tl over 4f out: sn wknd u.p: t.o fnl 3f* **66/1**

506 **8** 7 **Converre**[12] 5738 3-8-7 46 — (b[1]) NickyMackay 9 — —
(G A Butler) *sn bhd and rdn along: lost tch over 4f out: t.o fnl 3f: eased wl ins fnl f* **14/1**

4000 **9** 26 **Power Of Dreams (IRE)**[15] 5636 3-8-12 57 — (b[1]) PatCosgrave 1 — —
(M H Tompkins) *chsd ldrs tl lost pl and dropped to rr 6f out: lost tch over 4f out: t.o fnl 3f: eased ins fnl f* **8/1**

2m 15.58s (5.08) **Going Correction** +0.575s/f (Yiel)
WFA 3 from 4yo 7lb — **9** Ran SP% **113.3**
Speed ratings (Par 101): **102,99,88,83,71 66,59,53,32**
toteswingers:1&2 £3.20, 2&3 £9.70, 1&3 £3.10 CSF £17.76 TOTE £2.20: £1.10, £3.20, £2.60; EX 19.90 Trifecta £93.10 Pool: £378.37 - 3.01 winning units..The winner was bought in for 5,200gns.
Owner David Botterill & John Guest **Bred** D R Botterill **Trained** Moreton Morrell, Warwicks

FOCUS
A decent gallop made this weakly contested race a good test of stamina for the trip, and there were only two left with a chance in the final 2f. It is hard to know how literally to take the form and the winner;s effort could rate up to 6lb higher.

6095 E B F ATTHERACES.COM JOHN MUSKER FILLIES' STKS (LISTED RACE) — 1m 2f 21y
3:55 (3:55) (Class 1) 3-Y-O+ — **£19,628** (£7,472; £3,741; £1,869; £934; £469) **Stalls** Low

Form — RPR

-311 **1** — **Nouriya**[54] 4347 3-8-13 101 — RyanMoore 5 — 104
(Sir Michael Stoute) *hld up in tch towards rr: effrt on outer over 2f out: rdn and hdwy over 1f out: r.o wl u.p ins fnl f ld fnl 100yds* **11/4**[2]

3-30 **2** 1 1/4 **Clarietta**[17] 5553 3-8-9 91 — ShaneKelly 10 — 97
(J L Dunlop) *in tch: chsd ldrs on inner over 2f out: chsd ldr over 1f out: rdn to ld 1f out: hdd and nt gng pce of wnr fnl 100yds* **20/1**

3044 **3** 1/2 **Silver Grey (IRE)**[24] 5346 3-8-9 108 — (p) PatCosgrave 7 — 96
(R Ingram) *chsd ldrs: rdn and effrt over 2f out: pressed ldrs over 1f out: drvn and kpt on same pce ins fnl f* **18/1**

4012 **4** nse **Starkat**[17] 5563 4-9-2 74 — DarryllHolland 8 — 96
(Jane Chapple-Hyam) *hld up in tch in rr: hdwy towards inner 3f out: swtchd and drvn over 1f out: r.o u.p ins fnl f* **50/1**

/46- **5** 3/4 **Montbretia**[16] 5619 5-9-2 92 — LiamJones 12 — 94
(Edward P Harty, Ire) *sn chsng ldr: led narrowly 3f out: sn rdn: hdd 2f out: kpt on gamely: one pce u.p fnl 2f* **33/1**

23-1 **6** 1 1/4 **Cheetah**[23] 5366 3-8-9 85 — KirstyMilczarek 11 — 92
(L M Cumani) *broke wl: stdd and sn chsng ldng pair: rdn to ld 2f out: drvn and hdd 1f out: wknd fnl 100yds* **10/1**

2553 **7** hd **Flying Cloud (IRE)**[18] 5539 4-9-2 109 — (t) TedDurcan 1 — 92
(Saeed Bin Suroor) *bustled along early: failed to hold pl on rail: towards rr: switching rt to outer 3f out: rdn and effrt over 2f out: no real prog: kpt on same pce ins fnl f* **15/8**[1]

-516 **8** 2 1/2 **Some Sunny Day**[84] 3319 4-9-2 78 — SteveDrowne 13 — 87
(H Morrison) *sn led: hdd and rdn 3f out: stl pressing ldrs tl btn ent fnl f: wknd* **50/1**

3112 **9** 1/2 **Resentful Angel**[19] 5475 5-9-2 87 — RobertWinston 4 — 86
(Pat Eddery) *in tch in midfield: rdn and stmbld ent fnl 2f: keeping on same pce whn swtchd lft ent fnl f: nvr able to chal* **28/1**

5131 **10** 1 1/4 **Mujdeya**[20] 5444 3-8-9 95 — TadhgO'Shea 3 — 83
(J H M Gosden) *in tch in midfield: switching rt to outer and effrt wl over 2f out: rdn and no hdwy 2f out: wl hld ins fnl f* **11/2**[3]

6344 **11** 2 **Honimiere (IRE)**[27] 5249 4-9-2 100 — PJMcDonald 2 — 79
(G A Swinbank) *hld up in last pair: rdn and no hdwy 3f out: bhd fnl 2f* **9/1**

6000 **12** 4 1/2 **Victoria Sponge (IRE)**[17] 5553 4-9-2 80 — RoystonFfrench 6 — 70
(S C Williams) *hmpd and dropped in rr sn after s: hdwy into midfield 7f out: rdn and lost pl qckly wl over 2f out: bhd fnl 2f* **66/1**

2m 15.49s (4.99) **Going Correction** +0.575s/f (Yiel)
WFA 3 from 4yo+ 7lb — **12** Ran SP% **117.8**
Speed ratings (Par 108): **103,102,101,101,100 99,99,97,97,96 94,91**
toteswingers:1&2 £32.00, 2&3 £42.80, 1&3 £19.30 CSF £63.86 TOTE £3.80: £1.70, £6.40, £3.70; EX 77.20 TRIFECTA Not won..
Owner Saleh Al Homaizi & Imad Al Sagar **Bred** Saleh Al Homaizi **Trained** Newmarket, Suffolk

FOCUS
There was an interesting mix of established and unexposed runners for this valuable prize. A solid pace that was fair to all set up a tight finish between the front-runners and hold-up performers. The favourite disappointed and the winner probably didn't need to improve in the circumstances.

NOTEBOOK
Nouriya continues on an upward curve following this likeable staying-on performance which suggests she could stay 1m4f. Connections were concerned about the ground, but she handled it well and there is plenty of ammunition left for the future. (tchd 3-1)
Clarietta had two attempts at getting through on the inside rail, and on succeeding the second time it looked as if she might win. She has been lightly campaigned this season, but this was a much better performance than last time and she can find a race at Listed level. (op 16-1)
Silver Grey(IRE), who had done well in two Group 3 races in France since racing with credit in Dubai early in the year, showed those races were an accurate reflection of her ability. She gets this 1m2f well and should stay further, particularly on better ground. (op 16-1 tchd 20-1)
Starkat's official rating of 74 meant she had a tough task in this company, but she had good recent form on soft ground and that was a big help. However, the handicapper will have noted this excellent effort.
Montbretia has been lightly raced during the last two seasons, though her last two appearances have been more encouraging. This was a creditable performance, but she has yet to prove that she is quite good enough to win at this level. (op 25-1)
Cheetah had handled easy ground last season, but this was quite holding. Connections were hoping for a place at best, and she was not beaten far, so she deserves another chance to show what she can do outside maiden company. (op 14-1)
Flying Cloud(IRE) Official explanation: jockey said filly never travelled
Some Sunny Day Official explanation: jockey said filly hung right
Mujdeya, winner of a soft-ground handicap last time, failed to make the step into Listed grade. (op 7-1 tchd 5-1)
Honimiere(IRE) Official explanation: trainer's rep said filly was unsuited by the soft ground

6096 EVENTGUARD GUMMI H'CAP (FOR THE GOLDEN JUBILEE TROPHY) — 1m 2f 21y
4:30 (4:30) (Class 3) (0-90,88) 3-Y-O+ — **£5,607** (£1,679; £839; £420; £209; £105) **Stalls** Low

Form — RPR

4156 **1** — **High Office**[23] 5355 4-8-13 75 — JimmyQuinn 2 — 90
(R A Fahey) *chsd ldng pair tl wnt 2nd 5f out: jnd ldr gng wl 3f out: pushed ahd over 2f out: rdn and in command fr over 1f out: rdn out* **8/1**

612 **2** 7 **Hear The Roar (IRE)**[69] 3813 3-8-12 81 — PatCosgrave 7 — 84
(J R Boyle) *in tch: rdn and effrt to chse wnr 2f out: drvn and no imp over 1f out: wl hld and eased wl ins fnl f* **9/2**[3]

1-52 **3** 4 **Revered**[74] 3697 3-9-3 86 — RyanMoore 5 — 79
(Sir Michael Stoute) *dwlt: stmbld sn after s and racd in last: rdn and effrt 3f out: no hdwy and wl btn 2f out: wnt modest 3rd ins fnl f* **6/4**[1]

0120 **4** 3 **Geneva Geyser (GER)**[25] 5307 4-9-12 88 — TomMcLaughlin 4 — 75
(J M P Eustace) *sn bustled along: led after 1f: jnd and rdn 3f out: hdd over 2f out: wknd u.p over 1f out* **16/1**

3101 **5** 9 **Autumn Riches**[18] 5540 3-9-4 87 — RoystonFfrench 3 — 56
(M Johnston) *led for 1f: chsd ldr after tl 5f out: sn rdn: wknd over 2f out: wl btn fnl 2f* **5/2**[2]

1030 **6** 1/2 **Oneofapear (IRE)**[52] 4405 4-9-11 87 — PJMcDonald 6 — 55
(G A Swinbank) *hld up in last pair: pushed along and lost tch over 2f out* **14/1**

2m 14.49s (3.99) **Going Correction** +0.575s/f (Yiel)
WFA 3 from 4yo 7lb — **6** Ran SP% **110.4**
Speed ratings (Par 107): **107,101,98,95,88 88**
CSF £41.30 CT £78.33 TOTE £11.30: £4.80, £3.50; EX 49.10 Trifecta £105.70 Pool: £410.99 - 2.87 winning units..
Owner R A Fahey **Bred** Genesis Green Stud Ltd **Trained** Musley Bank, N Yorks

FOCUS
A stiff gallop in these conditions put the emphasis on stamina, with the field soon strung out by 12-15 lengths. It was quicker than the Listed race but there are doubts over the form.

NOTEBOOK
High Office is a strong traveller, and the lively pace played into his hands because it gave him no chance to pull his way out of contention as he had done in his previous race. He has handled soft ground before, and in the end it was no contest. (op 10-1 tchd 11-1)
Hear The Roar(IRE), having just his fourth race, has now run well in his two handicaps. The first one was on fast ground, but he made a brave attempt in these softer conditions and looks set to win his fair share. (op 5-2)
Revered had run respectably in the soft on her juvenile debut, but her effort from the rear was laboured and she deserves another chance on better ground. Official explanation: jockey said filly stumbled shortly after start (op 9-4)
Geneva Geyser(GER) is dangerous when leading, even at a searching tempo like this, but the testing ground made it hard for him to last home. (op 12-1)
Autumn Riches appeared to find this trip too far in the stamina-sapping conditions. (op 11-4 tchd 9-4)
Oneofapear(IRE) Official explanation: trainer's rep said filly was unsuited by the soft ground

6097 SEA-DEER H'CAP — 1m 3y
5:00 (5:00) (Class 4) (0-85,83) 3-Y-O+ **£3,784** (£1,132; £566; £283; £141) **Stalls** Low

Form — RPR

0060 **1** — **Credit Swap**[35] 4943 5-9-10 83 — DarryllHolland 1 — 93
(M Wigham) *stdd and dropped in bhd after s: hld up in rr: smooth hdwy over 2f out: rdn chse ldr over 1f out: short of room and swtchd rt ins fnl f: r.o wl to ld nr fin* **15/2**[3]

0000 **2** nk **Marvo**[39] 4828 6-8-13 77 — AshleyMorgan(5) 2 — 86
(M H Tompkins) *pushed lft s: hld up in last trio: smooth hdwy to ld on bit 2f out: rdn and edgd lft fr over 1f out: hdd and no ex nr fin* **7/1**[2]

0313 **3** 3 3/4 **Oh So Saucy**[18] 5541 6-9-0 73 — JackMitchell 5 — 74
(C F Wall) *hld up in tch: rdn and effrt ent fnl 2f: pressed ldrs and drvn over 1f out: wknd ins fnl f* **8/1**

023 **4** 1/2 **Mark Twain (IRE)**[7] 5861 3-9-0 78 — RyanMoore 3 — 77
(D M Simcock) *chsd ldrs: effrt u.p to press ldrs 2f out: drvn over 1f out: wknd ins fnl f* **4/1**[1]

6331 **5** 4 **Rough Rock (IRE)**[10] 5789 5-8-7 71 6ex — AdamBeschizza(5) 6 — 61
(C A Dwyer) *hld up in tch: nt clr run over 2f out tl 2f out: sn rdn and no hdwy: wl btn 1f out* **10/1**

3201 **6** 2 1/2 **Moody Tunes**[16] 5596 7-9-2 80 — MichaelO'Connell(5) 9 — 65
(Mrs K Burke) *led tl over 3f out: sn rdn: wknd u.p wl over 1f out: wl btn 1f out* **11/1**

0505 **7** 4 1/2 **General Eliott (IRE)**[17] 5556 5-9-9 82 — (p) ShaneKelly 8 — 56
(P F I Cole) *hld up in tch towards rr: rdn over 2f out: sn btn* **10/1**

0201 **8** 11 **Youm Jamil (USA)**[25] 5288 3-8-9 76 — Louis-PhilippeBeuzelin(3) 7 — 24
(B J Meehan) *chsd ldrs tl led over 3f out tl 2f out: sn wknd: wl bhd and eased ins fnl f* **4/1**[1]

4231 **9** 3 1/2 **Sennockian Storm (USA)**[19] 5474 3-8-11 75 — J-PGuillambert 4 — 15
(M Johnston) *chsd ldr tl 3f out: sn drvn and struggling: wl bhd over 1f out* **7/1**[2]

1m 43.46s (2.86) **Going Correction** +0.50s/f (Yiel)
WFA 3 from 5yo+ 5lb — **9** Ran SP% **114.4**
Speed ratings (Par 105): **105,104,100,100,96 93,89,78,74**
toteswingers:1&2 £9.00, 2&3 £13.00, 1&3 £10.60 CSF £58.28 CT £434.09 TOTE £10.10: £2.70, £3.50, £2.30; EX 60.90 Trifecta £303.80 Part won. Pool: £410.60 - 0.10 winning units..
Owner Your Golf Travel Ltd **Bred** Jeremy Green And Sons **Trained** Newmarket, Suffolk

FOCUS
The pace was sound, and the finish was fought out by the only two runners still on the bridle entering the last 2f. The race is rated around the runner-up.

6098 VAUXHALL HOLIDAY PARK H'CAP — 7f 3y
5:30 (5:31) (Class 6) (0-60,60) 3-Y-0+ £1,813 (£539; £269; £134) Stalls High

Form RPR

0130 **1** **Batgirl**[16] 5614 3-9-5 59 TomMcLaughlin 14 71
(John Berry) *s.i.s: hld up in rr: rdn and hdwy ent fnl 2f: led over 1f out: hung bdly lft after: styd on wl to draw clr fnl 75yds* **5/1**

1136 **2** 2 ¾ **Yankee Storm**[11] 5754 5-9-8 58 (v) JimmyQuinn 8 65
(H J Collingridge) *stdd s: hld up in rr: smooth hdwy to chse ldrs ent fnl 2f: ev ch and rdn over 1f out: carried lft 1f out: btn ins fnl f: wknd fnl 75yds* **4/1**[2]

060 **3** 2 ¼ **Chief Storm Eagle (IRE)**[21] 5414 3-8-7 47 (t) AndreaAtzeni 5 46
(M Botti) *racd keenly: chsd ldr tl led gng wl 2f out: rdn and hdd over 1f out: btn whn short of room jst ins fnl f: sn wknd* **8/1**

6424 **4** 2 ½ **Billberry**[17] 5557 5-9-10 60 (vt) RyanMoore 12 54+
(S C Williams) *stdd s: t.k.h: hld up towards rr: rdn and effrt 2f out: stl plenty to do whn nt clr run over 1f out tl 1f out: styd on to go 4th ins fnl f: nvr trbld ldrs* **3/1**[1]

-665 **5** 1 ¼ **Norcroft**[5] 5927 8-8-5 46 oh1 (p) AshleyMorgan(5) 6 37
(Mrs C A Dunnett) *in tch towards rr: hdwy 3f out: rdn and wknd wl over 1f out* **16/1**

000 **6** ½ **Noble Attitude**[34] 4986 4-8-10 46 oh1 J-PGuillambert 15 35
(N Tinkler) *chsd ldrs towards stands' side: wknd u.p wl over 1f out* **33/1**

4300 **7** ½ **Easy Wonder (GER)**[14] 5655 5-8-3 46 oh1 (v) AntiocoMurgia(7) 10 34
(I A Wood) *in tch: rdn and struggling 2f out: wknd and wl btn whn edgd lft and short of room over 1f out* **14/1**

4534 **8** nse **Fathey (IRE)**[24] 5326 4-9-5 55 RobertWinston 13 43
(C Smith) *chsd ldrs tl wknd u.p wl over 1f out: wl btn fnl f* **9/2**[3]

0404 **9** 1 ¼ **Scruffy Skip (IRE)**[15] 5647 5-9-8 58 (p) MarcHalford 11 43
(Mrs C A Dunnett) *led tl rdn and hdd 2f out: sn wknd* **16/1**

0600 **10** nk **On The Cusp (IRE)**[2] 6024 3-9-1 58 RobertLButler(3) 7 40
(P Butler) *a bhd* **20/1**

000 **11** 8 **Dovedon Diva**[22] 5379 3-8-5 48 (b[1]) Louis-PhilippeBeuzelin(3) 4 —
(T Keddy) *in tch in midfield: rdn over 4f out: lost pl and bhd fnl 2f* **50/1**

1m 31.63s (5.03) **Going Correction** +0.50s/f (Yiel)
WFA 3 from 4yo+ 4lb 11 Ran SP% **119.1**
Speed ratings (Par 101): **91,87,85,82,81 80,79,79,78,78 68**
toteswingers:1&2 £6.20, 2&3 £12.00, 1&3 £9.10. totesuper7: Win: Not won. Place: Not won. CSF £25.20 CT £163.33 TOTE £8.80: £2.30, £1.10, £4.70; EX 44.10 TRIFECTA Not won. Place 6: £230.51 Place 5: £132.77.
Owner Tony Fordham **Bred** Mrs M L Parry & P M Steele-Mortimer **Trained** Newmarket, Suffolk
■ Stewards' Enquiry : Tom McLaughlin three-day ban: careless riding (Sep 29-30, Oct 4)

FOCUS
The final race, like most of the others, was dominated by a handful of runners who were home in the sticky conditions. The winner is rated in line with her Nottingham form in July.
Billberry Official explanation: jockey said gelding suffered interference in running
Dovedon Diva Official explanation: jockey said filly hung right
T/Jkpt: Not won. T/Plt: £222.60 to a £1 stake. Pool of £66,769.00 - 218.94 winning tickets. T/Qpdt: £46.00 to a £1 stake. Pool of £6,076.00 - 97.55 winning tickets. SP

6099 - 6101a (Foreign Racing) - See Raceform Interactive

5433 AYR (L-H)
Thursday, September 16

OFFICIAL GOING: Good (good to soft in places; 8.7, sprint course: far side 9.5, centre 9.1, stands' side 9.3)
Wind: Fairly strong, half-against. Weather: Cloudy, bright

6102 POLYFLOR MAIDEN AUCTION STKS — 6f
2:20 (2:22) (Class 5) 2-Y-0 £3,238 (£963; £481; £240) Stalls High

Form RPR

50 **1** **Another Citizen (IRE)**[54] 4368 2-8-13 0 DavidAllan 1 76
(T D Easterby) *towards rr: rdn and hdwy 2f out: led ins fnl f: kpt on wl* **18/1**

0 **2** 1 **Macho's Magic (IRE)**[51] 4460 2-9-2 0 AdrianNicholls 9 76
(D Nicholls) *t.k.h: led: rdn and hung lft 2f out: hdd ins fnl f: kpt on* **9/2**[3]

5 **3** 2 ¾ **Shadow Catcher**[38] 4899 2-8-13 0 PhillipMakin 3 65+
(M Dods) *hld up: outpcd and rdn 1/2-way: no imp tl styd on wl fnl f: tk 3rd cl home* **33/1**

03 **4** hd **Ted's Brother (IRE)**[29] 5210 2-8-6 0 AndrewHeffernan(3) 2 60
(R C Guest) *hld up bhd ldrs: effrt and chsd ldr briefly over 1f out: kpt on same pce fnl f: lost 3rd cl home* **16/1**

606 **5** ¾ **Granny Anne (IRE)**[19] 5523 2-7-11 59 NatashaEaton(7) 5 53
(A Bailey) *chsd ldng gp: n.m.r over 3f out: effrt and edgd lft over 1f out: no imp* **50/1**

2223 **6** 1 ¾ **So Is She (IRE)**[6] 5901 2-8-6 70 (v) GrahamGibbons 4 50
(A Bailey) *cl up tl rdn and wknd over 1f out* **2/1**[2]

3 **7** 7 **New Springs**[26] 5298 2-8-11 0 PaulHanagan 6 34
(R A Fahey) *unruly bef s: cl up tl wknd wl over 1f out: eased whn no ch* **1/1**[1]

8 13 **Joe Le Taxi (IRE)** 2-9-2 0 JoeFanning 8 —
(M Johnston) *t.k.h: cl up tl wknd 2f out: eased whn btn* **14/1**

9 23 **Librettela** 2-8-9 0 AndrewElliott 7 —
(A P Jarvis) *s.i.s and wnt rt s: a bhd: lost tch fr 1/2-way* **100/1**

1m 14.15s (0.55) **Going Correction** 0.0s/f (Good) 9 Ran SP% **125.2**
Speed ratings (Par 95): **96,94,91,90,89 87,78,60,30**
toteswingers:1&2:£11.40, 1&3:£26.10, 2&3:£25.20 CSF £104.40 TOTE £35.90: £4.70, £1.60, £7.80; EX 128.30.
Owner Middleham Park Racing V **Bred** Sandro Garavelli **Trained** Great Habton, N Yorks

FOCUS
Modest form with the front two in the betting, who themselves looked no better than fair, running below expectations. They all raced towards the stands' side, with the near rail looking advantageous. Limited but sound form, best viewed around the fifth, with improvement from the front pair.

NOTEBOOK
Another Citizen(IRE) failed to build on debut promise when a beaten favourite over 7f on his second start, but he'd clearly benefited from a 54-day break and coped with the drop back in trip. However, he may have been favoured by racing against the stands' rail in the closing stages, and this is weak form. (op 16-1 tchd 25-1)
Macho's Magic(IRE) shaped nicely on debut in a hot Goodwood maiden 51 days earlier and this was a respectable effort. Having shown speed from the off, he didn't help himself by edging away from the rail in the second half of the contest, but he was entitled to need this both fitness-wise and mentally. (op 6-1)
Shadow Catcher, well beaten over 7f on debut, finished strongly from a fair way off the pace on this drop in trip. A return to further should suit and he ought to find his level once handicapped. (tchd 40-1)
Ted's Brother(IRE) travelled better than most but raced away from the possibly favoured near rail and found little for pressure. He probably wants dropping back to 5f and might find a low-grade nursery. (op 25-1)
Granny Anne(IRE) is only moderate but shaped as though she'll be capable of a little better under a stronger rider. (op 40-1)
So Is She(IRE) broke on terms this time but didn't run on for pressure and looks one to avoid. (op 3-1 tchd 10-3)
New Springs got wound up before the start, unseating Paul Hanagan and proving reluctant to go into the stalls until the blindfold was fitted. Although away on terms, she was beaten by about halfway and failed to confirm debut promise. Official explanation: jockey said filly became upset at start (op 11-10 tchd 10-11 and 5-4 in places)
Joe Le Taxi(IRE) appeared to be hanging left for much of the way. (op 10-1)

6103 BREWIN DOLPHIN INVESTMENT MANAGEMENT H'CAP — 5f
2:50 (2:52) (Class 5) (0-70,70) 3-Y-0+ £3,238 (£963; £481; £240) Stalls High

Form RPR

-202 **1** **Mango Music**[17] 5601 7-9-6 69 PaulHanagan 18 84
(R A Fahey) *cl up stands' side: effrt over 1f out: led ins fnl f: rdn clr: 1st of 10 in gp* **7/2**[1]

0006 **2** 2 ¼ **Argentine (IRE)**[3] 6031 6-9-5 68 SebSanders 19 75
(J A McShane) *hld up stands' side: hdwy over 1f out: chsd wnr ins fnl f: kpt on: 2nd of 10 in gp* **12/1**

6001 **3** 1 ¼ **Bravely (IRE)**[10] 5817 6-8-12 61 6ex DavidAllan 16 63
(T D Easterby) *led stands' side tl rdn and hdd ins fnl f: kpt on same pce: 3rd of 10 in gp* **11/1**

0202 **4** 1 ¾ **Dispol Kylie (IRE)**[17] 5599 4-9-2 65 PhillipMakin 6 61+
(Mrs K Walton) *chsd ldrs far side: effrt and hdwy over 1f out: led that gp ins fnl f: kpt on: nt rch stands' side: 1st of 9 in gp* **11/1**

4341 **5** nk **Sandwith**[3] 6031 7-8-12 61 6ex (v) LNewman 12 56
(A G Foster) *racd on outside of stands' side gp: rdn and drifted to centre fr 2f out: kpt on fnl f: 4th of 10 in gp* **15/2**[3]

6126 **6** nse **Dies Solis**[59] 4193 3-8-12 62 AndrewMullen 11 57
(V P Donoghue) *cl up stands' side: drvn over 2f out: one pce fnl f: 5th of 10 in gp* **12/1**

1440 **7** ¾ **Poppy's Rose**[19] 5513 6-9-4 70 RobertLButler(3) 14 62
(T J Etherington) *hld up in tch stands' side: effrt and rdn 2f out: no imp fnl f: 6th of 10 in gp* **33/1**

0000 **8** 2 ¼ **Burnwynd Boy**[13] 5734 5-9-2 70 (b) LeeTopliss(5) 9 54
(J A McShane) *cl up far side: rdn over 2f out: kpt on same pce over 1f out: 2nd of 9 in gp* **40/1**

0316 **9** ½ **Pelmanism**[20] 5501 3-8-10 60 (b) RichardKingscote 13 42
(K A Ryan) *towards rr stands' side: drvn over 2f out: styd on fnl f: no imp: 7th of 10 in gp* **8/1**

0660 **10** hd **Classlin**[22] 5410 3-7-13 56 oh11 NeilFarley(7) 15 38
(J S Goldie) *bhd and rdn stands' side: sme late hdwy: nvr rchd ldrs: 8th of 10 in gp* **80/1**

5400 **11** ½ **Wicked Wilma (IRE)**[3] 6031 6-9-2 65 AdrianNicholls 3 45
(A Berry) *cl up far side: led that gp over 1f out to ins fnl f: no ex: 3rd of 9 in gp* **14/1**

0665 **12** ¾ **Rothesay Dancer**[20] 5477 7-8-9 61 GaryBartley(3) 17 38
(J S Goldie) *hld up stands' side: effrt on outside of that gp 2f out: no imp: 9th of 10 in gp* **16/1**

4223 **13** shd **Monte Mayor One**[20] 5481 3-8-9 62 PatrickDonaghy(3) 5 39
(P Monteith) *midfield far side: drvn over 2f out: nvr able to chal: 4th of 9 in gp* **20/1**

54-0 **14** ½ **Blown It (USA)**[20] 5480 4-9-7 70 AndrewElliott 2 45
(J S Goldie) *hld up far side: effrt 2f out: no imp fnl f: 5th of 9 in gp* **25/1**

0050 **15** ¾ **Distant Sun (USA)**[20] 5480 6-9-0 68 BillyCray(5) 4 40
(Miss L A Perratt) *hmpd s: bhd and pushed along far side: nvr rchd ldrs: 6th of 9 in gp* **33/1**

3220 **16** 1 ¾ **Ridley Didley (IRE)**[49] 4513 5-9-5 68 GrahamGibbons 1 34
(N Wilson) *led far side to over 1f out: sn btn: 7th of 9 in gp* **13/2**[2]

0205 **17** 3 **Areeg (IRE)**[17] 5600 3-7-13 56 oh8 VictorSantos(7) 8 11
(A Berry) *prom far side tl rdn and wknd over 1f out: 8th of 9 in gp* **100/1**

040 **18** nk **Six Wives**[22] 5410 3-8-11 61 (b[1]) PJMcDonald 7 15
(J A Glover) *in tch far side tl rdn and wknd fr 2f out: last of 9 in gp* **66/1**

1056 **19** 9 **Ya Boy Sir (IRE)**[20] 5481 3-8-10 60 (p) JoeFanning 10 —
(N Wilson) *in tch stands' side tl rdn and edgd lft 2f out: sn wknd: last of 10 in gp* **50/1**

59.69 secs (-0.41) **Going Correction** 0.0s/f (Good)
WFA 3 from 4yo+ 1lb 19 Ran SP% **125.6**
Speed ratings (Par 103): **103,99,97,94,94 94,92,89,88,88 87,86,85,85,83 81,76,75,61**
toteswingers:1&2:£13.40, 1&3:£6.60, 2&3:£26.50 CSF £43.04 CT £338.09 TOTE £3.70: £1.30, £3.90, £3.20, £3.50; EX 40.10.
Owner Northumbria Leisure Ltd **Bred** A G Antoniades **Trained** Musley Bank, N Yorks

FOCUS
They soon split into two groups and those on the stands' side readily held sway over those on the far side, being responsible for the first three finishers. Modest form which is rated at face value. The winner was back to something like her best.
Poppy's Rose Official explanation: jockey said mare hung left final 3f

6104 E B F / FARRANS CONSTRUCTION NOVICE STKS — 1m
3:20 (3:21) (Class 4) 2-Y-0 £4,533 (£1,348; £674; £336) Stalls Low

Form RPR

134 **1** **Cafe Elektric**[37] 4928 2-9-5 91 SebSanders 3 92
(Sir Mark Prescott) *mde all: pushed along over 2f out: styd on strly fnl f* **2/1**[2]

31 **2** 2 **Goldenveil (IRE)**[59] 4187 2-9-0 80 PaulHanagan 4 83
(R A Fahey) *chsd wnr: effrt and ev ch over 2f out: edgd lft u.p over 1f out: kpt on same pce fnl f* **1/1**[1]

01 **3** nk **Red Presence (IRE)**[19] 5532 2-9-2 89 RichardKingscote 1 84
(Tom Dascombe) *trckd ldrs: effrt over 2f out: edgd lft: kpt on same pce fnl f* **7/2**[3]

4 32 **A Southside Boy (GER)** 2-9-0 0 JoeFanning 5 12
(J S Goldie) *dwlt and wnt rt s: in tch tl rdn and wknd fr 3f out* **25/1**

1m 43.62s (-0.18) **Going Correction** -0.05s/f (Good) 4 Ran SP% **109.4**
Speed ratings (Par 97): **98,96,95,63**
CSF £4.47 TOTE £3.30; EX 3.70.
Owner Cheveley Park Stud **Bred** Cheveley Park Stud Ltd **Trained** Newmarket, Suffolk

FOCUS
A reasonable novice event. The form is rated around the second and third.

NOTEBOOK

Cafe Elektric, a non-runner at Kempton the previous evening, ran to a pretty useful level, although he had to work reasonably hard. He had excuses for his two defeats since his debut success, but this step up in trip, as well as the switch to a galloping track, clearly suited. He's from a stable whose runners often progress. (op 13-8)

Goldenveil(IRE), off the track since her wide-margin success in a maiden over 7f here in July, didn't knuckle down under pressure, carrying her head slightly awkwardly and wandering a bit. Strictly on the figures she ran a good race - she had 6lb to find with the winner - but she was given a hard ride in defeat and might be best watched next time. (op 5-4)

Red Presence(IRE), whose maiden win came over 7f on quick ground, didn't stay this longer trip and seemed to run below his rating of 89. (tchd 4-1)

A Southside Boy(GER) faced a stiff task on debut and showed little. (op 20-1)

6105 ISLE OF SKYE BLENDED SCOTCH WHISKY H'CAP 1m
3:50 (3:50) (Class 4) (0-85,85) 3-Y-0+ **£5,180** (£1,541; £770; £384) **Stalls** Low

Form			Horse	RPR
2003	1		**Harriet's Girl**[19] 5533 4-9-0 **75**... AndrewElliott 8 (Mrs K Burke) *t.k.h: in tch: effrt over 1f out: styd on to ld nr fin* **7/1**[3]	86+
0031	2	½	**Arabian Spirit**[22] 5407 5-9-6 **81**... PaulHanagan 11 (R A Fahey) *prom: hdwy over 2f out: led over 1f out: kpt on fnl f: hdd nr fin* **3/1**[1]	89
4452	3	1 ½	**Veiled Applause**[45] 4652 7-9-1 **76**... DavidAllan 7 (J J Quinn) *midfield: effrt over 2f out: drvn and kpt on fnl f: nt rch first two* **16/1**	81
2053	4	hd	**Keys Of Cyprus**[17] 5605 8-9-7 **82**... AdrianNicholls 12 (D Nicholls) *prom: smooth hdwy 3f out: chal over 1f out: no ex ins fnl f* **17/2**	87
0503	5	3	**Wigwam Willie (IRE)**[17] 5596 8-8-10 **71** oh1...(tp) JamieSpencer 6 (K A Ryan) *hld up: rdn over 2f out: styd on fnl f: nvr able to chal* **22/1**	69+
0121	6	nk	**Barren Brook**[39] 4865 3-9-5 **84**... GrahamGibbons 1 (M W Easterby) *t.k.h in midfield: effrt and rdn over 2f out: no imp fnl f* **12/1**	80
2-25	7	¾	**Huntingfortreasure**[112] 2466 3-8-11 **79**... PatrickDonaghy(3) 2 (M Dods) *t.k.h: hld up: rdn over 2f out: kpt on fnl f: nvr able to chal* **50/1**	73
1232	8	½	**Celtic Change (IRE)**[51] 4450 6-9-10 **85**...(bt) PhillipMakin 3 (M Dods) *cl up: ev ch over 2f out to 1f out: rdn and sn btn* **7/1**[3]	79
1540	9	¾	**Snow Bay**[46] 4617 4-9-5 **83**... MichaelGeran(3) 13 (D Nicholls) *led tl rdn and hdd over 1f out: sn btn* **20/1**	75
4433	10	nk	**Faithful Ruler (USA)**[13] 5736 6-9-5 **85**... LeeTopliss(5) 4 (R A Fahey) *hld up ins: effrt over 2f out: btn fnl f* **13/2**[2]	77
3050	11	¾	**Espero (IRE)**[13] 5737 4-8-10 **74**... AndrewHeffernan(3) 9 (Miss L A Perratt) *midfield: drvn over 2f out: wknd over 1f out* **16/1**	64
6402	12	¾	**Antoniola (IRE)**[45] 4647 3-8-11 **76**...(t) PJMcDonald 10 (T D Easterby) *hld up: rdn and edgd lft 2f out: sn btn* **8/1**	63
0206	13	10	**Wise Dennis**[69] 3846 8-9-5 **80**... SebSanders 5 (A P Jarvis) *s.i.s: rdn in rr 3f out: sn btn* **16/1**	45
3603	R		**Sir Frank Wappat**[5] 5968 3-8-8 **73**... JoeFanning 14 (M Johnston) *ref to r* **18/1**	—

1m 42.36s (-1.44) **Going Correction** -0.05s/f (Good)
WFA 3 from 4yo+ 4lb 14 Ran SP% **126.6**
Speed ratings (Par 105): **105,104,103,102,99 99,98,98,97,97 96,95,85,—**
toteswingers:1&2:£7.80, 1&3:£30.70, 2&3:£14.00 CSF £29.05 CT £344.63 TOTE £11.90: £3.60, £1.30, £6.20; EX 53.30.
Owner Ray Bailey **Bred** J Sankey **Trained** Middleham Moor, North Yorks

FOCUS
A fair handicap and sound form judged around the third and fourth. The winner is rated a bit better than the bare form.

6106 WILLIAMHILL.COM/BONUS25 H'CAP (FOR THE KILKERRAN CUP) 1m 2f
4:20 (4:20) (Class 2) (0-100,92) 3-Y-0+ **£11,656** (£3,468; £1,733; £865) **Stalls** Low

Form			Horse	RPR
2116	1		**Pendragon (USA)**[6] 5913 7-9-4 **85**... PhillipMakin 8 (B Ellison) *in tch: effrt and shkn up over 1f out: styd on wl fnl f: led last stride* **9/2**[2]	95
2111	2	shd	**Northside Prince (IRE)**[22] 5408 4-9-2 **83**... PJMcDonald 4 (G A Swinbank) *prom: rdn to ld ent fnl f: kpt on: hdd last stride* **13/2**	93
6001	3	2 ¼	**Plaisterer**[17] 5592 5-9-8 **89**... SebSanders 2 (C F Wall) *dwlt: sn chsng ldrs: effrt and edgd lft 2f out: kpt on ins fnl f* **9/2**[2]	94
1200	4	nk	**Caldercruix (USA)**[30] 5188 3-9-3 **90**... JamieSpencer 1 (T P Tate) *chsd ldr: led over 2f out to ent fnl f: kpt on same pce* **8/1**	95
1043	5	½	**Jutland**[20] 5475 3-9-5 **92**... JoeFanning 7 (M Johnston) *led: rdn and hdd over 2f out: rallied: no ex ins fnl f* **7/2**[1]	96
0510	6	¾	**Bencoolen (IRE)**[19] 5529 5-9-6 **90**... MichaelGeran(3) 3 (D Nicholls) *hld up in tch on ins: rdn over 2f out: no imp fnl f* **16/1**	92
06-0	7	¾	**European Dream (IRE)**[159] 205 7-9-6 **87**... PaulHanagan 5 (R A Fahey) *hld up: rdn and outpcd 2f out: plugged on fnl f: nvr able to chal* **13/2**	88
0000	8	6	**Mirrored**[16] 5638 4-9-9 **90**... DavidAllan 6 (T D Easterby) *plld hrd: hld up: hdwy on outside 3f out: wknd fr 2f out* **6/1**[3]	79

2m 10.8s (-1.20) **Going Correction** -0.05s/f (Good)
WFA 3 from 4yo+ 6lb 8 Ran SP% **116.5**
Speed ratings (Par 109): **102,101,100,99,99 98,98,93**
toteswingers:1&2:£1.60, 1&3:£2.80, 2&3:£1.90 CSF £34.31 CT £139.63 TOTE £7.00: £2.70, £1.60, £2.60; EX 47.40.
Owner Dan Gilbert & Kristian Strangeway **Bred** Flaxman Holdings Ltd **Trained** Norton, N Yorks

FOCUS
A decent handicap rated around the third, fourth and fifth. The first two continue to progress.

NOTEBOOK

Pendragon(USA) built on the form he showed on his first run since July at Doncaster six days earlier, picking up nicely from off the pace to get up on the line. He could well be up to defying a rise and, relatively fresh for the time of year, will be of interest back at Southwell, where he rattled up a hat-trick last winter. Whatever the case, he could go for the Cambridgeshire if he makes the cut, and he's picked up a 4lb penalty. (op 15-2 tchd 8-1)

Northside Prince(IRE), winner of his last three starts, two over C&D, was up a further 5lb and was just denied the four-timer. He ought to remain progressive. (op 4-1)

Plaisterer, 1lb lower than when runner-up in this last year, having been raised 4lb for her recent Epsom win, seemed to have her chance. (op 11-2)

Caldercruix(USA) has yet to conclusively prove his stamina for this trip. (tchd 10-1)

Jutland might prefer quicker ground. (op 5-1)

Mirrored Official explanation: jockey said gelding ran too free

6107 IRISH THOROUGHBRED MARKETING H'CAP (DIV I) 7f 50y
4:50 (4:50) (Class 5) (0-75,75) 3-Y-0+ **£2,914** (£867; £433; £216) **Stalls** High

Form			Horse	RPR
0013	1		**Revue Princess (IRE)**[17] 5601 5-9-1 **69**...(b) DavidAllan 10 (T D Easterby) *t.k.h: trckd ldrs: rdn over 2f out: styd on wl fnl f: led nr fin* **12/1**	79
013	2	nk	**George Benjamin**[45] 4646 3-9-1 **72**... AdrianNicholls 11 (D Nicholls) *cl up: led and rdn wl over 1f out: kpt on fnl f: hdd nr fin* **12/1**	79
1516	3	1 ¾	**Commando Scott (IRE)**[11] 5789 9-8-7 **68**... NeilFarley(7) 8 (D Carroll) *prom: n.m.r over 2f out: kpt on fnl f: nt rch first two* **9/2**[3]	75+
0312	4	½	**Legal Legacy**[8] 5852 4-9-7 **75**... PhillipMakin 9 (M Dods) *in tch: effrt and cl up over 1f out: kpt on same pce fnl f* **7/2**[1]	78
0400	5	1 ¾	**Deadly Secret (USA)**[21] 5435 4-9-2 **70**... PaulHanagan 3 (R A Fahey) *t.k.h: w ldr: led 1/2-way to wl over 1f out: sn no ex* **16/1**	68
2056	6	shd	**Botham (USA)**[22] 5406 6-8-7 **61** oh2... LNewman 5 (J S Goldie) *towards rr: rdn and hdwy over 1f out: kpt on fnl f: nvr able to chal* **22/1**	59
4010	7	nk	**Scrapper Smith (IRE)**[13] 5737 4-9-1 **74**... LeeTopliss(5) 4 (A C Whillans) *hld up: rdn over 2f out: styd on fnl f: n.d* **15/2**	71
1526	8	1	**Fujin Dancer (FR)**[18] 5545 5-9-4 **72**...(p) JamieSpencer 2 (K A Ryan) *hld up: nt clr run over 2f out: rdn over 1f out: no imp* **6/1**	66
0446	9	½	**Stellite**[13] 5732 10-8-11 **65**... SebSanders 6 (J S Goldie) *hld up: short-lived effrt on outside wl over 1f out: sn btn* **22/1**	58
033	10	nk	**Slikback Jack (IRE)**[11] 5789 3-9-0 **71**... PJMcDonald 1 (J A Glover) *t.k.h: led to over 3f out: wknd 2f out* **4/1**[2]	61

1m 31.65s (-1.75) **Going Correction** -0.05s/f (Good)
WFA 3 from 4yo+ 3lb 10 Ran SP% **116.4**
Speed ratings (Par 103): **108,107,105,105,103 102,102,101,100,100**
toteswingers:1&2:£10.20, 1&3:£11.10, 2&3:£13.00 CSF £146.37 CT £567.52 TOTE £14.70: £4.60, £4.70, £1.80; EX 78.70.
Owner S A Heley **Bred** Raymond Shanahan **Trained** Great Habton, N Yorks

FOCUS
The time was 0.38 seconds quicker than the second division, which was won by Lord Aeryn. The winner improved to the tune of 6lb over this longer trip, with the second up 4lb.

6108 IRISH THOROUGHBRED MARKETING H'CAP (DIV II) 7f 50y
5:20 (5:20) (Class 5) (0-75,74) 3-Y-0+ **£2,914** (£867; £433; £216) **Stalls** High

Form			Horse	RPR
01-5	1		**Lord Aeryn (IRE)**[45] 4647 3-9-1 **71**... PaulHanagan 10 (R A Fahey) *hld up on outside: hdwy over 2f out: edgd lft and rdn to ld appr fnl f: r.o* **7/2**[1]	84+
1430	2	¾	**Daring Dream (GER)**[8] 5852 5-9-0 **70**... GaryBartley(3) 7 (J S Goldie) *chsd ldng gp: effrt on ins whn hung lft and n.m.r appr fnl f: swtchd rt and styd on fnl f* **9/2**[2]	78+
614	3	1 ¾	**Cara's Request (AUS)**[16] 5634 5-9-5 **72**... AdrianNicholls 1 (D Nicholls) *t.k.h: led: clr 1/2-way: hdd appr fnl f: n.m.r briefly ins fnl f: kpt on same pce* **5/1**[3]	75
4005	4	nk	**Euston Square**[19] 5510 4-9-7 **74**...(p) AndrewMullen 11 (D Nicholls) *chsd ldr: effrt and drvn over 2f out: kpt on same pce fnl f* **12/1**	76
0033	5	1 ½	**Berbice (IRE)**[13] 5732 5-9-2 **69**... LNewman 3 (Miss L A Perratt) *t.k.h: prom: effrt whn hung lft and n.m.r over 1f out: no ex fnl f* **9/1**	67
6053	6	¾	**Geojimali**[20] 5486 8-8-7 **60** oh2...(p) PJMcDonald 9 (J S Goldie) *bhd and detached: hdwy over 1f out: nvr rchd ldrs* **12/1**	56
6334	7	hd	**Hansomis (IRE)**[10] 5821 6-8-7 **60** oh1... DavidAllan 5 (B Mactaggart) *in tch: rdn over 2f out: btn fnl f* **12/1**	56
1566	8	2 ¾	**Glenluji**[13] 5737 5-8-11 **64**... JamieSpencer 2 (J S Goldie) *dwlt: sn prom: rdn over 2f out: wknd over 1f out: eased whn btn ins fnl f* **9/2**[2]	56
0050	9	9	**The Hermitage (IRE)**[23] 5396 3-9-4 **74**... JoeFanning 8 (M Johnston) *t.k.h: hld up in tch: rdn over 2f out: wknd over 1f out* **20/1**	37
00-0	10	49	**Dubai Legend**[17] 5598 4-9-2 **69**... SebSanders 6 (N Wilson) *t.k.h: prom tl wknd over 2f out: eased whn no ch* **40/1**	—

1m 32.03s (-1.37) **Going Correction** -0.05s/f (Good)
WFA 3 from 4yo+ 3lb 10 Ran SP% **115.5**
Speed ratings (Par 103): **105,104,102,101,100 99,99,95,85,29**
toteswingers:1&2:£3.30, 1&3:£4.70, 2&3:£6.80 CSF £18.79 CT £79.69 TOTE £4.10: £1.80, £1.80, £2.40; EX 27.40.
Owner Mrs H Steel **Bred** Woodhouse Syndicate **Trained** Musley Bank, N Yorks

FOCUS
A sound pace, but the time was 0.38 seconds slower than the first division, won by Revue Princess. A clear best from the winner who was value a bit extra.

6109 AYRSHIRE HOSPICE CARING FOR THE COMMUNITY H'CAP 1m 5f 13y
5:50 (5:50) (Class 5) (0-70,70) 3-Y-0+ **£3,238** (£963; £481; £240) **Stalls** Low

Form			Horse	RPR
0021	1		**Pertemps Networks**[12] 5770 6-9-7 **65**... GrahamGibbons 8 (M W Easterby) *in tch: hdwy to ld over 2f out: edgd lft: kpt on wl fnl f* **3/1**[1]	79+
6336	2	1	**Puy D'Arnac (FR)**[26] 5296 7-9-11 **69**... PJMcDonald 16 (G A Swinbank) *hld up: hdwy over 3f out: chsd wnr 1f out: r.o* **12/1**	77
3641	3	3	**Bollin Judith**[14] 5681 4-9-12 **70**...(t) DavidAllan 4 (T D Easterby) *hld up: hdwy over 3f out: rdn and kpt on fr 2f out: nt rch first two* **9/2**[2]	74
6041	4	¾	**Oddsmaker (IRE)**[3] 6032 9-9-3 **64** 6ex...(t) AndrewHeffernan(3) 13 (M A Barnes) *led to over 2f out: kpt on same pce fr over 1f out* **16/1**	66
2150	5	1 ½	**Drop The Hammer**[40] 4854 4-8-9 **56** oh1...(v[1]) PatrickDonaghy(3) 6 (D O'Meara) *midfield: effrt on outside over 2f out: edgd lft: sn no imp* **28/1**	56
6502	6	4 ½	**Chocolate Caramel (USA)**[21] 5437 8-9-5 **63**... PaulHanagan 14 (R A Fahey) *hld up: rdn and effrt 3f out: outpcd fnl 2f* **14/1**	56
2614	7	1 ¾	**Silent Lucidity (IRE)**[40] 4825 6-8-13 **57**...(p) AndrewElliott 15 (P D Niven) *prom: rdn over 3f out: edgd lft and wknd fr 2f out* **16/1**	48
2232	8	¾	**Vittachi**[13] 5738 3-8-7 **60**... PatrickMathers 2 (A C Whillans) *cl up tl rdn and wknd over 2f out* **20/1**	50
43-6	9	9	**Dramatic Jewel (USA)**[21] 5437 4-9-5 **63**... RichardKingscote 9 (Miss Lucinda V Russell) *midfield: drvn over 4f out: wknd over 2f out* **66/1**	39
3341	10	3 ½	**Mohawk Ridge**[21] 5437 4-9-8 **66**...(p) PhillipMakin 17 (M Dods) *prom: rdn 4f out: wknd over 2f out* **16/1**	37
4142	11	5	**Houston Dynimo (IRE)**[174] 996 5-9-6 **69**... LeeTopliss(5) 12 (N G Richards) *s.i.s: bhd: rdn over 4f out: nvr on terms* **28/1**	32
6032	12	1 ¼	**Royal Straight**[11] 5790 5-9-5 **68**... BillyCray(5) 10 (Miss L A Perratt) *hld up: drvn over 4f out: shortlived effrt over 2f out: sn btn* **9/1**	30

40 **13** *12* **Hunters Belt (IRE)**[41] 4781 6-9-7 **65** .... SebSanders 1 9
(N Wilson) *midfield: drvn over 4f out: wknd over 2f out: eased whn btn* **12/1**

0225 **14** *3/4* **Lombok**[13] 5722 4-9-9 **67** .... JamieSpencer 3 9
(M L W Bell) *hld up in tch: rdn over 3f out: sn btn* **6/1**[3]

0103 **15** *nk* **Northern Acres**[31] 5161 4-9-11 **69** .... AdrianNicholls 7 11
(D Nicholls) *prom tl rdn and wknd fr 4f out* **25/1**

100- **16** *1* **Pokfulham (IRE)**[211] 6997 4-9-2 **60** .... JoeFanning 11 —
(J S Goldie) *bhd: drvn and struggling over 5f out: eased whn no ch* **50/1**

3350 **17** *5* **Maid Of Meft**[3] 6033 3-8-11 **64** .... LNewman 5 —
(Miss L A Perratt) *bhd: rdn over 5f out: nvr on terms* **50/1**

2m 53.07s (-0.93) **Going Correction** -0.05s/f (Good)
WFA 3 from 4yo+ 9lb **17** Ran SP% **128.1**
Speed ratings (Par 103): **100,99,97,97,96 93,92,91,86,84 81,80,72,72,72 71,68**
toteswingers:1&2:£10.60, 1&3:£5.50, 2&3:£8.10. totesuper7: Win: Not won. Place: £1,099.00. CSF £39.40 CT £171.31 TOTE £4.00: £2.30, £2.60, £2.00, £5.90; EX 57.50 Place 6 £518.91; Place 5 £102.96.
Owner E A Brook **Bred** H G Llewellyn **Trained** Sheriff Hutton, N Yorks

FOCUS
Plenty of runners, but no more than a fair staying handicap. The winner is rated back to his best.
T/Plt: £980.30 to a £1 stake. Pool:£75,544.47 - 56.25 winning tickets T/Qpdt: £93.50 to a £1 stake. Pool:£5,471.83 - 43.27 winning tickets RY

5117 PONTEFRACT (L-H)

Thursday, September 16

OFFICIAL GOING: Good (good to firm in places; 7.8)
Wind: Moderate, half-against. Weather: fine

6110 PONTEFRACT APPRENTICE H'CAP 6f
2:30 (2:30) (Class 5) (0-70,69) 3-Y-0+ **£2,590** (£770; £385; £192) **Stalls** Low

Form RPR

3331 **1** **Tislaam (IRE)**[7] 5898 3-9-0 **64** 6ex .... (p) NathanAlison 1 72
(A J McCabe) *trckd ldng pair on inner: hdwy and cl up 2f out: rdn to chal over 1f out: kpt on ins fnl f to ld nr fin* **7/2**[1]

0405 **2** *hd* **Kensington (IRE)**[16] 5634 9-8-11 **64** .... NoraLooby(5) 6 71
(A J McCabe) *led: rdn wl over 1f out: drvn and hdd ins fnl f: ev ch tl no ex towards fin* **25/1**

0604 **3** *shd* **Bid For Gold**[20] 5482 6-8-0 **55** .... (p) EleanorMcGowan(7) 2 62
(Jedd O'Keeffe) *hld up: gd hdwy on inner 2f out: rdn to chal 1f out: drvn to ld briefly ins fnl f: hdd and no ex towards fin* **8/1**[3]

4534 **4** *2 1/4* **Klynch**[3] 6026 4-8-12 **60** .... (b) SophieSilvester 7 59
(Mrs R A Carr) *dwlt and towards rr: hdwy over 2f out: rdn to chse ldrs over 1f out: swtchd lft ent fnl f: kpt on: nrst fin* **9/1**

5405 **5** *hd* **Darcy's Pride (IRE)**[10] 5817 6-8-2 **55** oh4 .... ShaneBKelly(5) 13 54
(P T Midgley) *blindfold removed late: stdd and swtchd lft s: hld up in rr: hdwy on inner wl over 1f out: sn rdn and kpt on ins fnl f: nrst fin* **33/1**

0600 **6** *1/2* **Bel Cantor**[19] 5528 7-9-0 **67** .... (p) MatthewCosham(5) 9 64
(W J H Ratcliffe) *prom: rdn along 2f out: drvn over 1f out: wknd ent fnl f* **14/1**

0020 **7** *1 1/4* **First Blade**[16] 5634 4-8-10 **63** .... (b) IanBurns(5) 4 56
(S R Bowring) *chsd ldrs: rdn wl over 1f out: drvn ent fnl f and sn wknd* **18/1**

4230 **8** *1 1/2* **Lindoro**[24] 5357 5-8-13 **68** .... TerenceFury(7) 10 56
(K M Prendergast) *in tch: hdwy and hung rt wl over 1f out: n.d* **20/1**

103 **9** *nse* **Rainy Night**[14] 5698 4-9-0 **67** .... (p) NicolaJackson(5) 11 55
(R Hollinshead) *chsd ldrs: rdn along 2f out: sn drvn and wknd* **8/1**[3]

4131 **10** *hd* **Angaric (IRE)**[20] 5482 7-8-7 **60** .... DavidSimmonson(5) 5 48
(B Smart) *cl up: effrt 2f out: sn rdn and ev ch tl wknd ent fnl f* **8/1**[3]

5242 **11** *1* **Young Gladiator (IRE)**[147] 1492 5-9-5 **67** .... (b) JamesRogers 14 51
(Julie Camacho) *wnt rt s: a towards rr* **11/1**

150 **12** *1 1/2* **Dickie Le Davoir**[28] 5242 6-9-4 **69** .... (b) SeanPalmer(3) 3 49
(R C Guest) *dwlt: in rr whn hmpd 1/2-way: nvr a factor* **15/2**[2]

050 **13** *nk* **Straboe (USA)**[17] 5614 4-8-7 **60** .... (v) NoelGarbutt(5) 12 39
(S C Williams) *in tch on outer: effrt 2f out: sn carried rt and rdn: n.d* **22/1**

3-05 **P** **Zarilan (IRE)**[50] 4487 5-8-10 **63** .... PeterSword(5) 8 —
(Michael Smith) *awkward s: towards rr whn lost acftion and p.u 1/2-way: fatally injured* **20/1**

1m 16.27s (-0.63) **Going Correction** -0.075s/f (Good)
WFA 3 from 4yo+ 2lb **14** Ran SP% **119.4**
Speed ratings (Par 103): **101,100,100,97,97 96,95,93,92,92 91,89,88,—**
toteswingers:1&2:£28.60, 1&3:£9.80, 2&3:£84.30 CSF £107.69 CT £667.94 TOTE £4.50: £1.50, £6.70, £2.40; EX 136.20.
Owner Mrs Z Wentworth **Bred** Airlie Stud **Trained** Averham Park, Notts
■ Stewards' Enquiry : Eleanor McGowan three-day ban: used whip with excessive frequency without giving gelding time to respond (Sep 30,Oct4-5)
Nathan Alison two-day ban: used whip with excessive frequency (Sep 30,Oct 4)

FOCUS
A modest apprentice handicap, run at a fair pace, and those that raced handily were at an advantage. It provided a one-two for trainer Alan McCabe. The winner is rated a step closer to his 2yo form.
Darcy's Pride(IRE) Official explanation: jockey said mare dipped its head and he could not remove blindfold at first attempt

6111 ROGER TRANTER APPRECIATION MEDIAN AUCTION MAIDEN STKS 5f
3:00 (3:03) (Class 5) 2-Y-0 **£3,238** (£963; £481; £240) **Stalls** Low

Form RPR

23 **1** **Old Master Expert**[115] 2389 2-9-3 0 .... JimmyFortune 1 74
(M L W Bell) *trckd ldrs: chsd ld over 1f out: kpt on to ld last 75yds: all out* **1/1**[1]

2 *nk* **Hygrove Gal** 2-8-12 0 .... TomEaves 2 68+
(B Smart) *w ldrs: led over 2f out: hdd fnl 75yds: no ex towards fin* **14/1**

600 **3** *2 1/4* **Another Wise Kid (IRE)**[75] 3658 2-9-3 60 .... MickyFenton 3 65
(P T Midgley) *chsd ldrs: kpt on same pce fnl f* **50/1**

0 **4** *1/2* **Barnet Fair**[26] 5298 2-9-3 0 .... FrannyNorton 4 63
(R C Guest) *s.i.s: in rr: hdwy over 1f out: kpt on same pce ins fnl f* **80/1**

23 **5** *1 3/4* **Valerius Maximus**[11] 5785 2-9-3 0 .... SilvestreDeSousa 8 57
(P F I Cole) *swtchd lft after s: chsd ldrs: sn drvn along: hung rt and one pce appr fnl f* **7/4**[2]

6 *5* **Rapturous Applause** 2-9-3 0 .... PhilipRobinson 5 39
(Micky Hammond) *gave problems s: in tch: outpcd and lost pl over 2f out* **12/1**[3]

65 **7** *1 1/4* **Be A Good Lady**[150] 1421 2-8-9 0 .... PaulPickard(3) 7 29
(P T Midgley) *t.k.h: led tl over 2f out: hung lft and wknd over 1f out* **66/1**

50 **8** *2 3/4* **Finnker (IRE)**[89] 3222 2-8-12 0 .... IanBrennan(5) 6 25
(J J Quinn) *s.i.s: sn drvn along and outpcd in rr* **14/1**

00 **9** *5* **Jay Jays Joy**[12] 5763 2-9-3 0 .... DuranFentiman 10 —
(T D Barron) *s.i.s: a outpcd: bhd fnl 2f* **50/1**

10 *1 1/4* **Kwik Time** 2-9-3 0 .... RichardMullen 9 —
(R Bastiman) *dwlt: nvr on terms* **80/1**

63.07 secs (-0.23) **Going Correction** -0.075s/f (Good) **10** Ran SP% **115.3**
Speed ratings (Par 95): **98,97,93,93,90 82,80,75,67,65**
toteswingers:1&2:£2.80, 1&3:£9.10, 2&3:£20.70 CSF £17.13 TOTE £1.90: £1.10, £3.20, £6.60; EX 17.20.
Owner R A Green **Bred** Worksop Manor Stud **Trained** Newmarket, Suffolk

FOCUS
An ordinary maiden run at a fair pace and dominated by low-drawn horses. The market suggested it was a two-horse race, but one was strong and one was weak, and the betting proved spot-on. The third and fourth help with the form.

NOTEBOOK
Old Master Expert was racing for the first time since twice making the frame in better-class maidens in May, but the market suggested he was considered ready. Content to track the leaders against the inside rail, he found himself up against a very determined rival when brought out to challenge over a furlong out, but he showed a good attitude to score. The form may not be anything special, however, so his future may be as a handicapper rather than anything too classy. (op 13-8)
Hygrove Gal ◆, retained for £15,000 as a yearling, is a sister to a couple of winning sprinters including the useful Fratellino. One of three to dispute the early pace, she fought off her two nearest challengers and made the favourite fight very hard to get the better of her. She should be winning before too long. (op 12-1 tchd 16-1)
Another Wise Kid(IRE), unplaced in his first three starts, raced widest of the three early leaders and didn't drop away as might have been expected. His official rating of 60 gives a guide to the level of the form.
Barnet Fair ◆, beaten a long way when 100-1 for his Ripon debut, ran much better here and stayed on steadily from the rear of the field. He looks one for nurseries after one more run. (op 100-1)
Valerius Maximus was very weak in the market and was under pressure before reaching halfway. He then appeared to hang in the home straight and, having been placed in his first two starts, this was a step backwards. (op Evens)

6112 RIFLES CHALLENGE H'CAP 1m 4y
3:30 (3:30) (Class 4) (0-80,79) 3-Y-0+ **£4,533** (£1,348; £674; £336) **Stalls** Low

Form RPR

0002 **1** **Daaweitza**[19] 5533 7-9-2 **76** .... DaleSwift(5) 6 87
(B Ellison) *a cl up: pushed along 3f out: rdn to chse ldr over 2f out: kpt on to ld ent fnl f: drvn out* **8/1**

6342 **2** *2* **Raleigh Quay (IRE)**[29] 5213 3-9-2 **75** .... PhilipRobinson 2 82
(Micky Hammond) *trckd ldrs on inner: pushed along 2f out: swtchd rt and rdn over 1f out: styd on to chse wnr ins fnl f: no imp towards fin* **5/1**[2]

1313 **3** *nk* **Dabbers Ridge (IRE)**[19] 5510 8-8-9 **77** .... DanielTudhope 9 83+
(I W McInnes) *hld up in tch: swtchd rt and hdwy 2f out: rdn to chse ldrs ent fnl f: sn drvn and kpt on same pce* **11/1**

041 **4** *1* **Chief Red Cloud (USA)**[16] 5641 4-8-13 **71** .... BarryMcHugh(3) 5 75
(Mrs K Burke) *cl up on inner: effrt to ld 3f out: rdn wl over 1f out: drvn and hdd ent fnl f: grad wknd* **7/2**[1]

26-0 **5** *nk* **Grazeon Gold Blend**[36] 4943 7-9-5 **74** .... TomEaves 11 77
(J J Quinn) *hld up and bhd: hdwy over 2f out: rdn over 1f out: styd on ins fnl f: nrst fin* **20/1**

0213 **6** *1/2* **Honest Broker (IRE)**[6] 5919 3-9-2 **75** .... GregFairley 7 77
(M Johnston) *midfield: hdwy to chse ldrs over 3f out: rdn 2f out: drvn and one pce appr fnl f* **6/1**[3]

0010 **7** *1 1/4* **West End Lad**[23] 5386 7-9-5 **79** .... (b) RussKennemore(3) 15 78
(S R Bowring) *chsd ldrs: rdn along over 2f out: sn drvn and grad wknd* **25/1**

4000 **8** *1 3/4* **Moheebb (IRE)**[22] 5407 6-9-10 **79** .... SilvestreDeSousa 12 74
(Mrs R A Carr) *hld up in rr: hdwy on outer over 2f out: sn rdn and no imp* **12/1**

0402 **9** *1/2* **Rosbay (IRE)**[12] 5756 6-8-12 **72** .... LanceBetts(5) 8 66
(T D Easterby) *slt ld: rdn along and hdd 3f out: drvn over 2f out and sn wknd* **9/1**

2105 **10** *4* **Flying Silks (IRE)**[26] 5287 4-9-2 **71** .... (v) WilliamBuick 13 56
(J R Gask) *in tch on outer: effrt over 2f out: sn rdn and hung rt wl over 1f out: sn wknd* **7/1**

-510 **11** *30* **Midwestern (USA)**[22] 5407 3-9-4 **77** .... (p) RichardMullen 1 —
(B Smart) *midfield on inner: pushed along and lost pl bef 1/2-way: sn bhd and eased fnl 2f* **11/1**

1m 44.06s (-1.84) **Going Correction** -0.075s/f (Good)
WFA 3 from 4yo+ 4lb **11** Ran SP% **119.8**
Speed ratings (Par 105): **106,104,103,102,102 101,100,98,98,94 64**
toteswingers:1&2:£9.30, 1&3:£12.60, 2&3:£7.30 CSF £48.69 CT £458.28 TOTE £12.00: £3.50, £2.70, £3.60; EX 68.60.
Owner Mrs Andrea M Mallinson **Bred** C Mallinson **Trained** Norton, N Yorks
■ Stewards' Enquiry : Philip Robinson caution: careless riding.

FOCUS
A fair handicap and a decent pace with three vying for the advantage for much of the way. Sound form, with the winner's best effort since this time last year.
Honest Broker(IRE) Official explanation: trainer had no explanation for the poor form shown
Midwestern(USA) Official explanation: trainer's rep said gelding finished distressed

6113 PONTEFRACT PARK FILLIES' H'CAP 6f
4:00 (4:02) (Class 3) (0-90,90) 3-Y-0+
£9,346 (£2,799; £1,399; £700; £349; £175) **Stalls** Low

Form RPR

0151 **1** **Who's Shirl**[14] 5684 4-8-11 **78** .... KellyHarrison(3) 14 89
(C W Fairhurst) *in tch: effrt over 2f out: edgd rt 1f out: styd on to ld post* **33/1**

2433 **2** *nse* **Pepper Lane**[17] 5606 3-8-4 **70** .... SilvestreDeSousa 8 81
(D O'Meara) *mid-div: drvn over 2f out: styd on to ld last 50yds: hdd post* **20/1**

5142 **3** *1 3/4* **Poppet's Lovein**[40] 4850 4-9-4 **82** .... SteveDrowne 15 87+
(A B Haynes) *mid-div on outside: hdwy over 2f out: styd on ins fnl f* **16/1**

0-20 **4** *3/4* **Sioux Rising (IRE)**[26] 5302 4-9-2 **83** .... BarryMcHugh(3) 12 86
(R A Fahey) *in tch: hdwy over 2f out: led 1f out: hdd last 50yds: one pce* **11/2**[3]

2-42 **5** *1/2* **Gouray Girl (IRE)**[19] 5521 3-9-10 **90** .... EddieAhern 9 91+
(W R Swinburn) *hld up in rr: hdwy and swtchd outside over 1f out: fin wl* **9/2**[2]

1145 **6** *3/4* **Rio Mist**[19] 5521 3-9-9 **89** .... JimmyFortune 2 88
(R Hannon) *hld up in rr: hdwy over 2f out: nt clr run over 1f out: hung lft: kpt on fnl f* **17/2**

2060 **7** *2* **Filligree (IRE)**[69] 3845 5-9-1 **84** ..... DeclanCannon(5) 4 76
(Rae Guest) *chsd ldrs: fdd fnl f* **50/1**

3143 **8** *1* **Offspring**[20] 5501 3-8-3 **69** ..... DuranFentiman 1 58+
(T D Easterby) *stdd and sn hld up towards rr: hdwy and nt clr run over 1f out: styd on clsng stages: nvr rchd ldrs* **25/1**

01 **9** *1 1/2* **Ardent**[33] 5065 3-9-2 **82** ..... WilliamBuick 6 74+
(J H M Gosden) *hdwy to ld after 1f: hdd 1f out: wknd and eased* **6/4**[1]

-000 **10** *2 1/4* **Ishe Mac**[40] 4850 4-8-8 **72** ..... FrannyNorton 7 49
(N Bycroft) *led 1f: w ldrs: wknd fnl f* **33/1**

1050 **11** *1/2* **Dametime (IRE)**[11] 5791 4-8-12 **76** ..... AndreaAtzeni 11 52
(Daniel Mark Loughnane, Ire) *w ldrs: wknd over 1f out* **50/1**

4213 **12** *1 3/4* **Russian Rave**[13] 5713 4-8-8 **72** ..... RichardMullen 3 42+
(J G Portman) *hld up in rr: hmpd after 100yds: nt clr run over 2f out and over 1f out: nvr nr ldrs* **16/1**

3004 **13** *1 1/4* **Ishiadancer**[17] 5609 5-9-0 **85** ..... RyanPowell(7) 10 51
(E J Alston) *chsd ldrs effrt over 2f out: hung rt and lost pl wl over 1f out* **40/1**

4300 **14** *3/4* **Capercaillie (USA)**[14] 5694 3-9-6 **86** ..... GregFairley 13 50
(M Johnston) *in rr: effrt over 2f out: sn lost pl* **20/1**

5231 **15** *nk* **Esuvia (IRE)**[77] 3599 3-9-6 **86** ..... TomEaves 5 49
(B Smart) *trckd ldrs on inner: wkng whn hmpd over 1f out: eased towards fin* **16/1**

1m 15.69s (-1.21) **Going Correction** -0.075s/f (Good)
WFA 3 from 4yo+ 2lb 15 Ran SP% **127.4**
Speed ratings (Par 104): **105,104,102,101,100 99,97,95,93,90 90,87,86,85,84**
toteswingers:1&2:£60.70, 1&3:£58.00, 2&3:£42.20 CSF £573.21 CT £10730.51 TOTE £62.60: £11.60, £6.30, £6.90; EX 723.60.
Owner Mrs Shirley France **Bred** Mrs S France **Trained** Middleham Moor, N Yorks
■ Stewards' Enquiry : Declan Cannon two-day ban: careless riding (Sep 30,Oct 4)

FOCUS
A very decent fillies' handicap run at a strong pace and on this occasion those drawn high held the advantage. It got a little messy but the form is rated on the positive side.

NOTEBOOK
Who's Shirl had won two of her last three starts and was shoved up 8lb for her Redcar success earlier this month, which may help explain her large starting price. Settled in midfield early, she was in front a furlong out and battled back well when it looked as though the runner-up might nail her inside the last 50 yards. She may be aimed at the Coral Sprint Handicap at York next month.
Pepper Lane ◆ has run consistently well since winning off a stone lower at Redcar in June and this was another cracking effort in defeat. She was off the bridle in the middle of the pack at halfway, but she responded to the pressure and looked as though she might get up well inside the last furlong, but she was just run out of it. She deserves compensation.
Poppet's Lovein ◆, trying her shortest trip to date in her 13th outing, was tucked in from the outside stall early and finished strongly down the wide outside. A return to further will help, but she can win over a stiff 6f when drawn better. (tchd 20-1)
Sioux Rising(IRE), running well since her return from a year off last month, was 2-2 over C&D coming into this and she had every chance, having tracked the pace from the start. (op 13-2 tchd 7-1)
Gouray Girl(IRE) ◆, lightly raced and progressive, was put up 3lb after an unlucky narrow defeat at Goodwood last month and things didn't work out for her here either. Held up well off the pace, she had to be taken out very wide to see daylight once into the straight and by the time she got into gear it was too late. Despite this defeat, she remains capable of winning a race like this. (op 6-1)
Rio Mist, still 8lb higher than when winning at Goodwood in June, ran on in the home straight despite not having much room to play with a furlong out, but she had work to do to reverse recent Goodwood running with Gouray Girl so probably ran her race. (op 12-1)
Offspring ◆, still 4lb above her winning mark, can be rated much closer as she got no sort of run after turning into the home straight. She only made her racecourse debut in April so remains capable of further improvement. Official explanation: jockey said filly was denied a run
Ardent, making her handicap debut after thrashing a subsequent winner by 4l in a Doncaster maiden, tried to make most but was swamped passing the furlong pole. This effort suggests she has been put in on a stiff mark. Official explanation: jockey said filly lost its action; trainer said fuilly scoped dirty on return (op 15-8 tchd 2-1 in places)
Russian Rave Official explanation: jockey said filly was denied a run

6114 PONTEFRACT STAYERS CHAMPIONSHIP H'CAP (ROUND 6) 2m 1f 22y
4:30 (4:33) (Class 5) (0-75,72) 3-Y-0+ **£2,914** (£867; £433; £216) **Stalls** Low

Form RPR

2135 **1** **Ultimate Quest (IRE)**[71] 3780 5-9-8 **66** ..... SilvestreDeSousa 3 75
(Sir Mark Prescott) *trckd ldng pair: hdwy over 4f out: tk clsr order 3f out: chsd ldr 2f out and sn rdn: drvn to chal over 1f out: styd on wl u.p to ld last 100yds* **15/8**[1]

260 **2** *2* **Dan Buoy (FR)**[52] 4433 7-9-7 **65** .....(b) GregFairley 9 72
(R C Guest) *led and set str pce: rdn along over 2f out: drvn and jnd over 1f out: hdd and no ex last 100yds* **9/1**

0/15 **3** *3 1/2* **Fair Spin**[32] 5119 10-8-3 **54** oh4 .....(v) JamesRogers(7) 7 57
(Micky Hammond) *s.i.s: hld up in rr: hdwy on outer 4f out: rdn 2f out: styd on ins fnl f: nrst fin* **14/1**

0602 **4** *1/2* **Finellas Fortune**[14] 5681 5-8-13 **57** ..... FrannyNorton 6 59
(G M Moore) *hld up towards rr: hdwy over 4f out: swtchd rt and rdn to chse ldrs over 2f out: drvn over 1f out: kpt on ins fnl f: nrst fin* **14/1**

36/0 **5** *4* **Osolomio (IRE)**[9] 5278 7-9-9 **72** .....(e) DaleSwift(5) 4 70
(Jennie Candlish) *chsd ldr: hdwy and cl up 5f out: rdn along over 3f out: drvn over 2f out and sn wknd* **40/1**

2533 **6** *2 1/4* **Rare Ruby (IRE)**[11] 5788 6-10-0 **72** ..... JimmyFortune 10 68
(Jennie Candlish) *hld up in midfield: hdwy over 4f out: rdn to chse ldrs over 2f out: drvn wl over 1f out and sn no imp* **9/2**[2]

2536 **7** *2* **French Hollow**[35] 4983 5-9-3 **64** ..... BarryMcHugh(3) 5 57
(T J Fitzgerald) *in tch: hdwy to chse ldng trio 4f out: rdn along over 2f out: sn drvn and wknd* **14/1**

4000 **8** *1 3/4* **Smugglers Bay (IRE)**[16] 5642 6-8-10 **54** oh2 .....(b) TomEaves 2 45
(T D Easterby) *hld up towards rr: hdwy over 4f out: rdn to chse ldrs on inner 3f out: drvn over 2f out and sn btn* **12/1**

0333 **9** *1/2* **Capable Guest (IRE)**[16] 5642 8-9-4 **62** ..... EddieAhern 11 53
(G M Moore) *hld up towards rr: sme hdwy over 4f out: rdn along 3f out: nvr a factor* **8/1**[3]

6033 **10** *3 1/2* **They All Laughed**[22] 5420 7-8-6 **55** .....(p) IanBrennan(5) 8 42
(Mrs Marjorie Fife) *hld up in tch: hdwy over 4f out: rdn along 3f out: drvn and wknd 2f out* **16/1**

4026 **11** *9* **Winged Farasi**[14] 5687 6-8-7 **54** oh1 ..... KellyHarrison(3) 13 31
(Miss J E Foster) *hld up in rr: a bhd* **25/1**

4030 **12** *dist* **Almutaham (USA)**[21] 5437 3-7-12 **54** oh3 ..... DuranFentiman 12 —
(James Moffatt) *hld up: a in rr: bhd fnl 3f: virtually p.u fnl 2f* **20/1**

0/-0 **13** *dist* **Noddies Way**[31] 5144 7-8-10 **54** ..... MickyFenton 1 —
(J F Panvert) *chsd ldrs: pushed along 1/2-way: rdn and lost pl 5f out: sn bhd and virtually p.u fnl 2f* **33/1**

3m 45.34s (0.74) **Going Correction** -0.075s/f (Good)
WFA 3 from 5yo+ 12lb 13 Ran SP% **121.6**
Speed ratings (Par 103): **95,94,92,92,90 89,88,87,87,85 81,67,53**
toteswingers:1&2:£6.90, 1&3:£7.90, 2&3:£15.10 CSF £18.73 CT £194.43 TOTE £2.80: £1.20, £3.50, £4.90; EX 20.50.
Owner Syndicate 2006 **Bred** T W Bloodstock Ltd **Trained** Newmarket, Suffolk

FOCUS
An ordinary staying handicap, but a true test of stamina with Dan Buoy and Osolomio soon scampering clear of the others, and the field was quickly spread out. The form is rated around the third and fourth.
Capable Guest(IRE) Official explanation: jockey said gelding never travelled
Winged Farasi Official explanation: jockey said gelding ran flat

6115 BOOK YOUR 18TH OCTOBER TOTESPORT PACKAGE MAIDEN STKS 1m 2f 6y
5:00 (5:01) (Class 5) 3-Y-0+ **£2,914** (£867; £433; £216) **Stalls** Low

Form RPR

2 **1** **Dark Promise**[34] 5038 3-8-12 0 ..... PhilipRobinson 12 86+
(M A Jarvis) *trckd ldrs: styd on to ld 1f out: drvn clr* **8/13**[1]

3036 **2** *2 3/4* **Weathervane**[36] 4964 3-9-3 75 ..... WilliamBuick 8 85
(J H M Gosden) *in rr: hdwy on outer over 2f out: edgd lft over 1f out: styd on to take 2nd last 75yds* **9/1**[3]

- **3** *1 3/4* **Highland Park (IRE)** 3-9-3 0 ..... RichardMullen 3 82+
(Sir Michael Stoute) *chsd ldrs: drvn over 2f out: styd on to take 3rd nr fin: bttr for experience* **11/1**

03 **4** *3/4* **Aneel**[17] 5610 3-9-3 0 ..... ShaneKelly 11 80
(J Noseda) *trckd ldrs: led over 1f out: sn hdd: hung lft and kpt on same pce* **20/1**

4-44 **5** *1* **Palio Square (USA)**[15] 5665 3-9-3 77 ..... EddieAhern 7 78
(H R A Cecil) *mid-div: effrt to chse ldrs 3f out: keeping on one pce whn hmpd 1f out* **9/2**[2]

0 **6** *1* **Herostatus**[47] 4572 3-9-3 0 ..... GregFairley 4 76+
(M Johnston) *mid-div: drvn and outpcd 5f out: styd on fnl 2f: will improve* **40/1**

526 **7** *1/2* **Dance Tempo**[55] 4330 3-9-3 81 ..... SteveDrowne 5 75
(H Morrison) *led 1f: led over 3f out: hdd over 1f out: wknd ins fnl f* **14/1**

8 *10* **Neptune Equester**[105] 7-9-4 0 ..... DaleSwift(5) 15 55
(B Ellison) *s.i.s: hdwy 6f out: sn chsng ldrs: lost pl over 2f out* **28/1**

00 **9** *2* **Admiral Rodney**[120] 2231 3-9-3 0 ..... MickyFenton 2 51?
(Mrs P Sly) *trckd ldrs: lost pl 3f out* **150/1**

3-6 **10** *20* **Mexican Jay (USA)**[53] 4407 4-9-4 0 ..... TomEaves 13 —
(B Smart) *in rr: reminders 6f out: bhd fnl 3f: eased: t.o* **100/1**

11 *9* **Fama Mac** 3-9-3 0 ..... FrannyNorton 1 —
(N Bycroft) *t.k.h: led after 1f: hdd over 3f out: wkng whn hmpd over 2f out: sn bhd: t.o: eased* **125/1**

12 *18* **Kiss N Kick** 4-9-6 0 ..... RussKennemore(3) 10 —
(Lucinda Featherstone) *s.i.s: drvn over 4f out: t.o 2f out: eased* **100/1**

2m 12.54s (-1.16) **Going Correction** -0.075s/f (Good)
WFA 3 from 4yo+ 6lb 12 Ran SP% **119.2**
Speed ratings (Par 103): **101,98,97,96,96 95,94,86,85,69 62,47**
toteswingers:1&2:£2.80, 1&3:£3.30, 2&3:£8.50 CSF £6.91 TOTE £1.90: £1.30, £2.90, £4.50; EX 5.90.
Owner Lordship Stud **Bred** Lordship Stud **Trained** Newmarket, Suffolk

FOCUS
Probably a fair maiden for the time of year and a couple of these are likely to make their marks. The race is rated around the fourth and fifth.

6116 BOOK YOUR CHRISTMAS PARTY HERE ON 0113 2876387 H'CAP (DIV I) 1m 4y
5:30 (5:30) (Class 5) (0-70,70) 3-Y-0+ **£2,590** (£770; £385; £192) **Stalls** Low

Form RPR

6016 **1** **Aussie Blue (IRE)**[12] 5767 6-8-11 **60** ..... MichaelStainton(3) 4 73+
(R M Whitaker) *prom: cl up 1/2-way: led 3f out: rdn clr wl over 1f out: styd on* **14/1**

2141 **2** *3 3/4* **Sharakti (IRE)**[17] 5607 3-8-12 **67** .....(p) DeclanCannon(5) 7 69
(A J McCabe) *in tch: hdwy on outer 3f out: sn chsng wnr and rdn wl over 1f out: drvn ins fnl f: no imp* **5/1**[3]

3060 **3** *3/4* **Spavento (IRE)**[10] 5820 4-8-12 **58** .....(p) FrannyNorton 2 62+
(E J Alston) *trckd ldrs on inner: effrt and nt clr run 2f out: swtchd rt and n.m.r over 1f out: rdn and kpt on ins fnl f: tk 3rd nr line* **9/1**

0460 **4** *hd* **Xpres Maite**[10] 5819 7-8-12 **61** .....(v) RussKennemore(3) 8 61
(S R Bowring) *led: rdn along and hdd 3f out: drvn wl over 1f out and grad wknd* **7/1**

1044 **5** *3/4* **Carlitos Spirit (IRE)**[18] 5545 6-9-7 **70** .....(v) BarryMcHugh(3) 11 68
(I W McInnes) *s.i.s and bhd: hdwy on inner wl over 1f out: rdn and kpt on ins fnl f: nrst fin* **25/1**

0006 **6** *1/2* **Twisted**[61] 4151 4-8-12 **58** ..... LeeVickers 3 55+
(M W Easterby) *hld up towards rr: pushed along and sltly outpcd over 2f out: swtchd rt and rdn wl over 1f out: edgd lft and kpt on fnl f* **7/2**[2]

330 **7** *1 1/4* **Forever Hope**[40] 4853 3-9-6 **70** ..... DanielTudhope 5 64
(T D Walford) *chsd ldrs: hdwy over 2f out: rdn wl over 1f out: sn drvn and wknd* **40/1**

0323 **8** *nk* **Elijah Pepper (USA)**[13] 5737 5-9-8 **68** ..... JimmyFortune 1 62+
(T D Barron) *dwlt and towards rr: hdwy over 2f out: in tch wl over 1f out: sn rdn and btn* **10/3**[1]

3-36 **9** *2 3/4* **Ykikamoocow**[90] 3180 4-9-7 **67** ..... SilvestreDeSousa 6 54
(G A Harker) *hld up towards rr: swtchd rt and sme hdwy wl over 1f out: sn rdn: sltly hmpd and swtchd lft ent fnl f: n.d* **16/1**

3665 **10** *2 1/4* **Wiseman's Diamond (USA)**[11] 5786 5-9-2 **65** ..... PaulPickard(3) 12 47
(P T Midgley) *cl up: rdn along over 2f out: sn wknd* **11/1**

0060 **11** *1/2* **Alsahil (USA)**[16] 5638 4-9-6 **66** ..... PhilipRobinson 13 47
(Micky Hammond) *chsd ldrs on outer: rdn along over 2f out: sn wknd* **11/1**

2005 **12** *nk* **Betteras Bertie**[16] 5641 7-9-0 **60** ..... TomEaves 10 40
(M Brittain) *dwlt: a towards rr* **40/1**

1m 44.3s (-1.60) **Going Correction** -0.075s/f (Good)
WFA 3 from 4yo+ 4lb 12 Ran SP% **122.4**
Speed ratings (Par 103): **105,101,100,100,99 99,97,97,94,92 92,91**
toteswingers:1&2:£17.10, 1&3:£19.40, 2&3:£8.80 CSF £84.21 CT £691.24 TOTE £17.50: £3.90, £1.90, £4.30; EX 123.80.
Owner G F Pemberton **Bred** T L Adams & G F Pemberton **Trained** Scarcroft, W Yorks

FOCUS
An ordinary handicap run at an average pace, in a slightly quicker time than division II. The form is rated in line with the winner's recent best.

Carlitos Spirit(IRE) ◆ Official explanation: jockey said gelding was slowly away

6117 BOOK YOUR CHRISTMAS PARTY HERE ON 0113 2876387 H'CAP (DIV II) 1m 4y

6:05 (6:05) (Class 5) (0-70,70) 3-Y-O+ **£2,590** (£770; £385; £192) **Stalls** Low

Form RPR

4526 1 **Mason Hindmarsh**[26] 5300 3-9-0 **62**................................ GregFairley 7 72
(Karen McLintock) *led 1f: w ldrs: led over 2f out: drvn clr 1f out: kpt on wl* **4/1**[2]

2500 2 2 **Bold Marc (IRE)**[24] 5357 8-8-12 **61**................................(p) DaleSwift(5) 2 66+
(Mrs K Burke) *hld up towards rr: stdy hdwy over 2f out: nt clr run over 1f out: styd on wl to take 2nd jst ins fnl f: nt rch wnr* **5/1**[3]

0603 3 2 **Glenmuir (IRE)**[10] 5819 7-9-2 **65**................................ IanBrennan(5) 1 66+
(J J Quinn) *chsd ldrs: nt clr run over 1f out: kpt on same pce* **7/2**[1]

3642 4 ½ **Scarab (IRE)**[10] 5819 5-9-2 **60**................................(p) DuranFentiman 8 60
(T D Walford) *chsd ldrs: effrt 2f out: styd on fnl 150yds* **6/1**

60-0 5 1½ **Dialogue**[24] 5357 4-9-10 **68**................................ SilvestreDeSousa 4 64+
(G A Harker) *dwlt: hld up in rr: hdwy over 2f out: nt clr run over 1f out: hung rt and styd on fnl 150yds* **16/1**

430 6 ¾ **Desert Hunter (IRE)**[14] 5688 7-8-12 **59**.................... KellyHarrison(3) 10 53
(Micky Hammond) *trckd ldrs: t.k.h: effrt over 2f out: one pce fnl f* **11/1**

6105 7 1½ **Postman**[6] 5905 4-9-3 **68**................................(p) AdamCarter(7) 5 59
(B Smart) *chsd ldrs: nt clr run 1f out: kpt on ins fnl f* **12/1**

2020 8 *hd* **Rowan Lodge (IRE)**[19] 5530 8-9-5 **66**..................(b) BarryMcHugh(3) 11 57
(Ollie Pears) *trckd ldrs: t.k.h: effrt over 2f out: fdd appr fnl f* **20/1**

1603 9 ½ **Seldom (IRE)**[12] 5756 4-9-4 **62**................................ TomEaves 3 51
(M Brittain) *led after 1f: hdd over 2f out: wknd fnl 150yds* **12/1**

0050 10 1½ **Nevada Desert (IRE)**[8] 5852 10-9-9 **67**.................. DaraghO'Donohoe 9 53
(R M Whitaker) *hld up in rr: effrt over 2f out: nvr a factor* **33/1**

-460 11 7 **Times Ahead (USA)**[57] 4260 3-9-8 **70**................................ JimmyFortune 6 40
(P W Chapple-Hyam) *mid-div: drvn 3f out: lost pl 1f out: eased towards fin* **25/1**

5440 12 3¾ **Prime Circle**[10] 5819 4-9-4 **62**................................(p) SteveDrowne 12 23
(A D Brown) *chsd ldrs: drvn 3f out: lost pl over 1f out: eased towards fin* **20/1**

1m 44.74s (-1.16) **Going Correction** -0.075s/f (Good)
WFA 3 from 4yo+ 4lb **12** Ran SP% **119.1**
Speed ratings (Par 103): **102,100,98,97,96 95,93,93,93,91 84,80**
toteswingers:1&2:£3.50, 1&3:£5.60, 2&3:£4.90 CSF £23.09 TOTE £5.40: £2.50, £1.10, £2.50; EX 31.40 Place 6 £678.70; Place 5 £250.61.
Owner I R Clements **Bred** Newsells Park Stud **Trained** Ingoe, Northumberland

FOCUS
The winning time was 0.44 seconds slower than the first division. This was a messy race with several getting in each others' way around a furlong from home. The form is rated around the winner to the best view of his previous form.
Dialogue Official explanation: jockey said gelding hung right
T/Jkpt: Not won. T/Plt: £517.50 to a £1 stake. Pool:£56,236.40 - 79.33 winning tickets T/Qpdt: £93.90 to a £1 stake. Pool:£4,471.05 - 35.20 winning tickets JR

5920 WOLVERHAMPTON (A.W) (L-H)
Thursday, September 16

OFFICIAL GOING: Standard
Wind: Fresh, across. Weather: Cloudy with sunny spells

6118 BREEDERS' CUP LIVE ON AT THE RACES MEDIAN AUCTION MAIDEN STKS 7f 32y(P)

5:25 (5:26) (Class 5) 2-Y-O **£2,590** (£770; £385; £192) **Stalls** High

Form RPR

0 1 **Kelinni (IRE)**[13] 5724 2-9-3 0................................ JimCrowley 4 75+
(Mrs A J Perrett) *chsd ldrs: led over 1f out: edgd rt: rdn out* **4/1**[3]

0 2 1¾ **Endaxi Mana Mou**[47] 4587 2-8-9 0................................ SophieDoyle(3) 9 66
(M G Quinlan) *hld up: hdwy over 2f out: r.o: wnt 2nd towards fin: nt rch wnr* **66/1**

00 3 *nk* **Be Amazing (IRE)**[9] 5841 2-8-12 0................................ TedDurcan 2 65
(D R Lanigan) *mid-div: drvn along thrght: hdwy 2f out: chsd wnr fnl f: styd on same pce: lost 2nd towards fin* **5/2**[2]

6 4 3 **Magic Of The Sea (IRE)**[16] 5633 2-8-12 0.................... ChrisCatlin 12 58
(M Botti) *s.i.s: hld up: edgd lft and r.o ins fnl f: nvr nr to chal* **25/1**

43 5 6 **Winged Valkyrie (IRE)**[17] 5587 2-8-12 0.................... MichaelHills 1 43
(B W Hills) *led: rdn and hdd wl over 1f out: wknd fnl f* **4/5**[1]

0 6 *nse* **Pleasant Humor (USA)**[9] 5835 2-8-12 0.................... JohnFahy(5) 8 48
(R M H Cowell) *chsd ldrs: rdn over 2f out: wknd over 1f out* **100/1**

0 7 1¼ **Juarla (IRE)**[35] 4999 2-9-3 0................................ TomMcLaughlin 3 45
(R A Harris) *chsd ldr: rdn and hung rt over 2f out: led wl over 1f out: sn hdd: wknd fnl f* **40/1**

06 8 *nk* **Classic Gem (IRE)**[117] 2347 2-8-7 0.................... RossAtkinson(5) 6 39
(Tom Dascombe) *s.i.s: a in rr* **66/1**

60 9 1½ **Jack's Revenge (IRE)**[57] 4254 2-9-3 0.................... TonyCulhane 10 40
(George Baker) *hld up: pushed along 1/2-way: a in rr* **40/1**

00 10 1¼ **Talking Back**[16] 5629 2-9-3 0................................ LiamKeniry 5 37
(S Kirk) *sn prom: rdn and wknd over 2f out* **100/1**

11 13 **Act Of Faith (IRE)** 2-8-12 0................................ FergusSweeney 11 —
(J A Osborne) *hld up in tch: rdn and wknd 2f out* **33/1**

1m 30.24s (0.64) **Going Correction** -0.025s/f (Stan) **11** Ran SP% **120.8**
Speed ratings (Par 95): **95,93,92,89,82 82,80,80,78,77 62**
Tote Swingers: 1&2 £25.30, 1&3 £3.20, 2&3 £45.00 CSF £225.05 TOTE £6.80: £2.10, £32.80, £1.30; EX 601.50.
Owner Lady Clague **Bred** Newberry Stud Farm Ltd **Trained** Pulborough, W Sussex

FOCUS
A modest juvenile maiden, run at a solid pace. There is more to come from the winner.

NOTEBOOK
Kelinni(IRE), a market mover earlier in the day, caught the eye on debut over 1m at Lingfield 13 days earlier and he ran out a ready winner on this drop back a furlong. He travelled stylishly through the race and Jim Crowley looked very confident as he delayed his challenge until the top of the home straight. He soon quickened to the front, but was hardly doing a tap out in front and showed distinct greenness. That allowed the placed horse a brief chance to close, but he was always in command and rates value for a good bit further. He becomes the first of his dam's five progeny that have raced so far to win as a juvenile and he could make up into a very useful handicapper at around 10f next term. (op 10-3)
Endaxi Mana Mou was doing her best work towards the finish and showed much-improved form on this second start. She's related to some decent Polytrack performers so it's unsurprising the surface suited and she is evidently going the right way. She is open to further improvement and may be able to find an ordinary maiden before going into nurseries, and ought to get 1m this year. (tchd 50-1 and 80-1)
Be Amazing(IRE), well backed, was having her third outing yet still looked very inexperienced and had to be ridden from the off. She kept responding and may benefit for a switch to nurseries, for which is now eligible for. However, some form of headgear may be required. (op 7-2 tchd 9-2)
Magic Of The Sea(IRE) caught the eye staying on from off the pace late in the day. It's not hard to see why she was tried over 1m on debut and this was a definite step in the right direction. (op 22-1)
Winged Valkyrie(IRE) went off significantly shorter in the on-course betting ring than she was available at on the exchanges. She did too much early on as a result of being taken on, though, and is better judged on the level of her two previous runs. Official explanation: trainer's rep had no explanation for the poor form shown (op Evens tchd 11-10 and 8-11)
Act Of Faith(IRE), bred to make her mark at around this distance, wasn't helped by having to race wide from the outside stall. She tired off the home turn, but showed ability and better can be expected now she has this run under her belt.

6119 AT THE RACES SKY 415 H'CAP 5f 216y(P)

5:55 (5:55) (Class 7) (0-50,55) 3-Y-O+ **£1,364** (£403; £201) **Stalls** Low

Form RPR

002 1 **Dancing Welcome**[6] 5927 4-9-1 **50**................................(b) LiamKeniry 7 62
(J M Bradley) *hld up: rdn over 2f out: swtchd rt and hdwy over 1f out: edgd lft and r.o to ld wl ins fnl f* **5/2**[1]

3253 2 ½ **Shakespeare's Son**[3] 6025 5-8-9 **49**................................(p) JohnFahy(5) 13 59
(H J Evans) *hld up: racd keenly: hdwy over 2f out: rdn and ev ch ins fnl f: styd on* **11/4**[2]

0054 3 2½ **Almaty Express**[24] 5362 8-9-0 **49**................................(b) RichardHughes 12 51
(J R Weymes) *chsd ldr: rdn to ld over 1f out: hdd and no ex wl ins fnl f* **9/2**[3]

4630 4 3¼ **Monsieur Harvey**[20] 5485 4-9-0 **49**................................ JimCrowley 6 41
(B Smart) *chsd ldrs: rdn over 1f out: wknd fnl f* **16/1**

0002 5 ½ **Come On Buckers (IRE)**[3] 6025 4-9-0 **49**..............(b) EddieCreighton 8 39
(E J Creighton) *led: rdn and hdd over 1f out: wknd ins fnl f* **8/1**

2030 6 1½ **Shannon Golden**[33] 5067 4-9-1 **50**................................(b) FergusSweeney 1 35
(S R Bowring) *mid-div: rdn over 2f out: wknd ins fnl f* **14/1**

200- 7 ½ **Afton View (IRE)**[555] 792 5-8-8 **50**................................(t) LeonnaMayor(7) 10 34
(P S McEntee) *s.i.s: rdn over 1f out: n.d* **40/1**

5006 8 *nk* **Wotatomboy**[34] 5024 4-8-12 **50**................................ AmyRyan(3) 3 33
(R M Whitaker) *s.i.s: sn pushed along in rr: rdn over 1f out: nvr on terms* **10/1**

650- 9 1¾ **Blakeshall Diamond**[368] 5911 5-8-9 **49**................................ MarkCoumbe(5) 4 26
(D Bourton) *chsd ldrs: rdn over 2f out: wknd over 1f out* **16/1**

-500 10 13 **Albaher**[183] 899 4-9-0 **49**................................(b) FrankieMcDonald 11 —
(Peter Grayson) *s.i.s: a in rr: bhd fnl 2f* **66/1**

1m 14.51s (-0.49) **Going Correction** -0.025s/f (Stan)
WFA 3 from 4yo+ 2lb **10** Ran SP% **116.0**
Speed ratings (Par 97): **102,101,98,93,93 91,90,89,87,70**
Tote Swingers:1&2:£2.20, 2&3:£4.10, 1&3:£3.50 CSF £9.40 CT £29.30 TOTE £2.90: £1.80, £1.60, £1.60; EX 8.10.
Owner J M Bradley **Bred** The Hon Mrs E J Wills **Trained** Sedbury, Gloucs

FOCUS
A bottom-drawer sprint handicap, run at a strong pace and the form makes sense.
Come On Buckers(IRE) Official explanation: jockey said gelding hung right-handed
Albaher Official explanation: jockey said gelding hung right-handed

6120 SPORTS BETTING AT SPORTSBETTING.CO.UK H'CAP (DIV I) 1m 5f 194y(P)

6:25 (6:25) (Class 6) (0-60,58) 3-Y-O+ **£1,433** (£423; £211) **Stalls** Low

Form RPR

6050 1 **Leyte Gulf (USA)**[38] 4915 7-9-12 **56**................................ MichaelHills 7 64+
(C C Bealby) *dwlt: hld up: hdwy 2f out: rdn to ld wl ins fnl f: comf* **6/1**[3]

4306 2 ½ **Motarjm (USA)**[12] 5770 6-9-10 **54**................................(t) ChrisCatlin 3 61
(J Pearce) *s.i.s: hld up: hdwy to ld 4f out: clr 3f out: rdn and hdd wl ins fnl f* **9/4**[1]

3120 3 1¼ **Bedarra Boy**[17] 3267 4-9-7 **51**................................ LiamKeniry 5 56
(D W P Arbuthnot) *prom: chsd ldr over 9f out to over 4f out: rdn to chse wnr over 3f out: styd on u.p* **7/1**

0006 4 2¼ **Whitley Bay (USA)**[16] 5625 3-8-3 **46**................................ AmyRyan(3) 4 48
(J R Best) *chsd ldr over 4f: remained handy: rdn over 3f out: sn outpcd: rallied over 1f out: no ex ins fnl f* **8/1**

0400 5 1¼ **Wee Ziggy**[15] 1984 7-8-12 **49**................................ JosephYoung(7) 8 49
(M Mullineaux) *plld hrd and prom: styd on same pce fnl 2f* **33/1**

3400 6 3¼ **Location**[14] 5704 4-9-6 **50**................................ JimCrowley 9 46
(Ian Williams) *hld up: rdn over 1f out: nvr on terms* **10/1**

231- 7 2¾ **Dansilver**[602] 252 6-10-0 **58**................................ RichardHughes 10 50
(A W Carroll) *hld up: rdn over 2f out: sn wknd* **10/3**[2]

0020 8 13 **Chateauneuf (IRE)**[18] 5564 4-9-1 **45**................................ TomMcLaughlin 2 19
(W M Brisbourne) *prom: rdn over 4f out: wknd 3f out* **20/1**

32/0 9 14 **Devilfishpoker Com**[17] 3496 6-9-1 **45**................................ IanMongan 1 —
(S A Harris) *led 10f: wknd wl over 2f out* **25/1**

3m 7.81s (1.81) **Going Correction** -0.025s/f (Stan)
WFA 3 from 4yo+ 10lb **9** Ran SP% **112.4**
Speed ratings (Par 101): **93,92,92,90,90 88,86,79,71**
Tote Swingers:1&2:£4.20, 2&3:£2.50, 1&3:£5.40 CSF £18.85 CT £95.15 TOTE £9.10: £4.00, £1.10, £2.90; EX 23.80.
Owner Robert Jenkinson **Bred** Paradigm Thoroughbred Inc **Trained** Barrowby, Lincs

FOCUS
A weak staying handicap, run at a stop-start pace and a bit slower than division II. The winner will remain well treated on his best form.
Leyte Gulf(USA) Official explanation: trainer had no explanation for the apparent improvement in form

6121 SPORTS BETTING AT SPORTSBETTING.CO.UK H'CAP (DIV II) 1m 5f 194y(P)

6:55 (6:55) (Class 6) (0-60,58) 3-Y-O+ **£1,433** (£423; £211) **Stalls** Low

Form RPR

0110 1 **Bute Street**[16] 5625 5-10-0 **58**................................ GeorgeBaker 8 67
(R J Hodges) *chsd ldr tl led over 2f out: rdn and hung lft 1f out: hdd wl ins fnl f: rallied to ld nr fin* **9/4**[1]

4350 2 *hd* **Resplendent Ace (IRE)**[12] 5770 6-9-11 **55**................................ IanMongan 4 64
(P Howling) *chsd ldrs: rdn over 1f out: led wl ins fnl f: hdd nr fin* **6/1**

4214 3 2 **Bright Sparky (GER)**[129] 1984 7-8-12 **49**......(vt) DavidSimmonson(7) 10 55
(M W Easterby) *hld up: hdwy 1/2-way: rdn and nt clr run 1f out: styd on same pce* **5/1**[2]

0605 4 1 **Generous Lad (IRE)**[9] 5840 7-8-12 **47**................................(v[1]) AmyBaker(5) 3 52
(A B Haynes) *s.i.s: hld up: hdwy over 1f out: sn rdn: one pce ins fnl f* **9/1**

4000 5 ¾ **Paint The Town Red**[12] 5770 5-9-9 **53**................................ RobertWinston 1 57
(H J Collingridge) *hld up: hdwy over 2f out: rdn over 1f out: no imp fnl f* **8/1**

0050 6 3¼ **Mandate**[15] 5653 3-8-13 **53**................................ LiamKeniry 5 52
(J A R Toller) *s.i.s: hld up: rdn and hung lft 2f out: nvr on terms* **8/1**

The Form Book, Raceform Ltd, Compton, RG20 6NL

4050 **7** *1 ¾* **Swords**[44] 4683 8-9-6 **50**.................................... RichardHughes 2 47
(R E Peacock) *set stdy pce tl qcknd 6f out: rdn and hdd over 2f out: wknd fnl f* **11/2**[3]

4000 **8** *68* **Mister Pleau (USA)**[6] 5923 3-9-0 **54**.................................(t) TedDurcan 7 —
(J R Best) *chsd ldrs: pushed along over 5f out: wknd over 2f out: eased: t.o* **40/1**

3m 7.25s (1.25) **Going Correction** -0.025s/f (Stan)
WFA 3 from 4yo+ 10lb 8 Ran SP% **111.8**
Speed ratings (Par 101): **95,94,93,93,92 90,89,51**
Tote Swingers:1&2:£3.80, 2&3:£7.20, 1&3:£1.90 CSF £15.20 CT £58.67 TOTE £2.30: £1.10, £3.20, £1.10; EX 21.40.
Owner J W Mursell **Bred** J W Mursell **Trained** Charlton Mackrell, Somerset

FOCUS
This second division of the weak staying handicap was run at more of an even pace, though they still didn't go much of a gallop. It was slightly quicker than division I and the form is taken at face value.

6122 NFU MUTUAL CENTENARY H'CAP 1m 1f 103y(P)
7:25 (7:25) (Class 5) (0-75,75) 3-Y-O **£2,456** (£725; £362) **Stalls Low**

Form RPR

5336 **1** **Flag Of Glory**[43] 4710 3-9-2 **70**.................................. GeorgeBaker 7 79
(C F Wall) *sn led: rdn over 1f out: hung lft ins fnl f: r.o* **14/1**

3454 **2** *nk* **Tamtara**[32] 5115 3-8-12 **71**.. JohnFahy(5) 6 79
(Mrs A J Perrett) *chsd ldrs: rdn and ev ch fr over 1f out: r.o* **7/2**[1]

1500 **3** *1 ½* **Bakongo (IRE)**[34] 5056 3-9-3 **71**.............................. ChrisCatlin 5 76
(M L W Bell) *hld up: hdwy over 1f out: sn rdn: r.o* **20/1**

344 **4** *hd* **Astound**[21] 5445 3-8-11 **65**.......................................(v[1]) TomMcLaughlin 4 70
(P D Evans) *s.i.s: hld up: racd keenly: rdn over 3f out: hung rt and r.o wl ins fnl f: nrst fin* **20/1**

003- **5** *½* **Moobeyn**[314] 7276 3-9-3 **71**......................................(b[1]) RichardHughes 10 75
(M P Tregoning) *s.i.s: sn prom: chsd wnr 6f out: rdn over 3f out: ev ch 2f out: no ex ins fnl f* **11/2**[3]

3200 **6** *1 ¼* **Lingfield Bound (IRE)**[57] 4260 3-9-3 **71**.......................... TedDurcan 11 72
(J R Best) *sn pushed along in rr: r.o ins fnl f: nvr nrr* **25/1**

4522 **7** *nk* **Southern Cape (IRE)**[21] 5456 3-8-13 **67**........................ ShaneKelly 3 67
(D J Coakley) *chsd ldrs: rdn over 3f out: hung lft over 1f out: no ex fnl f* **9/2**[2]

4000 **8** *½* **Beneath**[12] 5747 3-8-13 **70**...(p) AmyRyan(3) 2 69
(K A Ryan) *hld up: rdn over 2f out: r.o ins fnl f: nvr nrr* **7/1**

1211 **9** *1 ¾* **Mr Harmoosh (IRE)**[17] 5593 3-9-7 **75**........................... AndreaAtzeni 1 71
(E F Vaughan) *led early: chsd ldrs: rdn over 2f out: wknd fnl f* **7/2**[1]

5545 **10** *3* **Brooklands Bay (IRE)**[13] 5738 3-9-4 **72**......................(v[1]) JimCrowley 9 61
(J R Weymes) *hld up: rdn over 2f out: sn wknd* **33/1**

5510 **11** *½* **Fame Is The Spur**[35] 4996 3-9-4 **72**................................ MichaelHills 8 60
(J W Hills) *prom: rdn 3f out: wknd fnl f* **11/1**

2m 0.91s (-0.79) **Going Correction** -0.025s/f (Stan) 11 Ran SP% **121.8**
Speed ratings (Par 101): **102,101,100,100,99 98,98,97,96,93 93**
Tote Swingers:1&2:£12.30, 2&3:£18.40, 1&3:£39.10 CSF £61.97 CT £1017.59 TOTE £21.60: £6.60, £1.10, £10.40; EX 101.80.
Owner Follow The Flag Partnership **Bred** Follow The Flag Partnership **Trained** Newmarket, Suffolk

FOCUS
A moderate, but competitive enough 3-y-o handicap for the class. It was run at a sound enough pace and the form looks fair. The winner showed something of a return to form.

6123 WOLVERHAMPTON-RACECOURSE.CO.UK CONDITIONS STKS 1m 141y(P)
7:55 (7:55) (Class 3) 3-Y-O+ **£6,623** (£1,982; £991; £495; £246) **Stalls Low**

Form RPR

230- **1** **Atlantis Star**[348] 6478 3-8-9 106.................................. TedDurcan 7 108
(Saeed Bin Suroor) *wnt rt s: sn prom: rdn to ld over 1f out: rdr dropped reins and hdd ins fnl f: rallied to ld post* **5/1**

2140 **2** *hd* **Alrasm (IRE)**[91] 3104 3-8-9 102.................................. TadhgO'Shea 4 107
(M A Jarvis) *trckd ldrs: led over 6f out: rdn and hdd over 1f out: led again ins fnl f: hdd post* **4/1**[2]

2501 **3** *1 ¼* **Beauchamp Viceroy**[166] 1085 6-9-3 105..................(b) RichardHughes 6 107
(G A Butler) *led: hdd over 6f out: rdn and ev ch fr over 1f out: unable qck wl ins fnl f* **11/4**[1]

3040 **4** *2 ¼* **Cloudy Start**[7] 5879 4-9-0 106....................................(t) FergusSweeney 3 99
(J A Osborne) *trckd ldrs: rdn over 2f out: edgd lft and no ex fnl f* **11/1**

1200 **5** *8* **Mahadee (IRE)**[28] 5247 5-9-0 106...................................(b) JimCrowley 5 81
(R M Beckett) *prom: rdn over 3f out: wknd over 1f out* **9/2**[3]

1600 **6** *4 ½* **Mister New York (USA)**[17] 5611 5-9-3 95..................(b) GeorgeBaker 1 73
(Noel T Chance) *s.s: drvn along and looked reluctant early: a bhd* **25/1**

-350 **7** *8* **Calvados Blues (FR)**[173] 1025 4-8-13 110............... AntiocoMurgia(7) 2 58
(Mahmood Al Zarooni) *hld up: a in rr: bhd fnl 3f* **9/2**[3]

1m 48.43s (-2.07) **Going Correction** -0.025s/f (Stan)
WFA 3 from 4yo+ 5lb 7 Ran SP% **111.9**
Speed ratings (Par 107): **108,107,106,104,97 93,86**
Tote Swingers:1&2:£3.50, 2&3:£2.40, 1&3:£1.80 CSF £24.03 TOTE £4.90: £2.60, £3.10; EX 22.70.
Owner Godolphin **Bred** Highclere Stud **Trained** Newmarket, Suffolk

FOCUS
A good conditions event, run at a fair pace, and decent form. An improved effort from the winner.

NOTEBOOK
Atlantis Star ran out a gutsy winner on this AW debut. This son of Cape Cross was a very useful juvenile and he clearly goes well fresh, having been a clear-cut winner on debut last year. He did well to get back up after his rider momentarily lost his reins near the finish, and this obviously rates a promising comeback. (op 11-2 tchd 6-1)
Alrasm(IRE) ♦, another AW debutant, was having his first outing since failing to fire at Royal Ascot in June. This trip is a bare minimum for him and it wasn't surprising to see him make it a real test. He only just lost out and this was more like it again, so he looks one to side with when reverting to further. (op 9-2 tchd 5-1)
Beauchamp Viceroy, a three-time course winner, proved solid in the betting on this return from a 173-day break and held every chance. He just tired out of it near the finish and ought to come on nicely for the run, but will likely have to keep to conditions races in order to resume winning ways. (op 9-4)
Cloudy Start couldn't dominate as he likes to due to the frantic early pace. He is happiest on this surface, but not at all simple to place. (op 12-1)
Mahadee(IRE) got the strong pace he enjoys on this return to Polytrack, but was laboured from three furlongs out and has yet to hit form for current connections. (tchd 11-2)
Mister New York(USA) was back on his favoured surface and had a stiff task at the weights, but he didn't help his cause with a very messy start. Official explanation: jockey said gelding was slowly away (op 22-1)
Calvados Blues(FR) was the first-string for Godolphin according to the market, but he ran a lifeless race on his British debut. (op 5-1)

6124 BREEDERS' CUP LIVE ON AT THE RACES MAIDEN STKS 1m 141y(P)
8:25 (8:26) (Class 5) 3-Y-O+ **£2,456** (£725; £362) **Stalls Low**

Form RPR

5 **1** **Qamar**[16] 5623 3-9-3 0.. TedDurcan 9 87+
(Saeed Bin Suroor) *s.i.s: hdwy over 5f out: chsd ldr over 2f out: led over 1f out: rdn and hung lft ins fnl f: r.o* **7/4**[1]

3 **2** *1 ¾* **Holiday Snap**[20] 5474 4-9-3 0....................................... GeorgeBaker 2 75
(Mrs Mary Hambro) *led: clr over 6f out to over 2f out: rdn and hdd over 1f out: no ex ins fnl f* **11/1**

4002 **3** *6* **Lean Machine**[15] 5661 3-9-3 70............................(p) TomMcLaughlin 11 66
(R A Harris) *chsd ldrs: rdn over 3f out: styd on same pce fnl 2f* **20/1**

3- **4** *nse* **Mr Emirati (USA)**[328] 6982 3-9-3 0.............................. RichardMullen 4 66
(B Smart) *prom: lost pl over 5f out: hdwy over 2f out: sn rdn: styd on same pce* **11/1**

4505 **5** *4* **Ruby Dazzler**[43] 4710 3-8-12 60....................................(t) JimCrowley 8 52
(S Lycett) *sn outpcd: styd on appr fnl f: nt trble ldrs* **50/1**

3332 **6** *hd* **Danehill Sunset (IRE)**[26] 5288 3-9-3 72....................... MichaelHills 12 56
(B W Hills) *hld up: hdwy over 6f out: chsd clr ldr over 4f out tl rdn over 2f out: wknd over 1f out* **5/1**[3]

7 *7* **Wingate Street** 3-9-3 0... RobertWinston 1 40
(P D Evans) *sn outpcd* **66/1**

0 **8** *15* **Millie Mops**[17] 5610 3-8-12 0..(v[1]) ShaneKelly 3 —
(Ian Williams) *prom tl rdn and wknd over 3f out: t.o* **80/1**

0 **9** *28* **Best Catch (USA)**[9] 5842 3-9-3 0................................... AndreaAtzeni 5 —
(J R Best) *sn outpcd: t.o* **100/1**

10 *9* **Intiqaal (IRE)** 3-9-3 0.. TadhgO'Shea 6 —
(E A L Dunlop) *s.s: rn green and a bhd: t.o* **12/1**

34 **11** *6* **Waheed**[26] 5303 3-9-3 0..(b[1]) RichardHughes 7 —
(M P Tregoning) *chsd ldr 4f: rdn and wknd over 3f out: t.o* **11/4**[2]

1m 49.28s (-1.22) **Going Correction** -0.025s/f (Stan)
WFA 3 from 4yo+ 5lb 11 Ran SP% **114.5**
Speed ratings (Par 103): **104,102,97,97,93 93,87,73,48,40 35**
Tote Swingers:1&2:£4.70, 2&3:£19.10, 1&3:£18.60. CSF £21.42 TOTE £2.00: £1.10, £6.20, £7.00; EX 27.40.
Owner Godolphin **Bred** Ptarmigan Bloodstock Ltd **Trained** Newmarket, Suffolk

FOCUS
A moderate maiden, run at a sound pace. The winner is rated up a stone with the second setting the standard.
Intiqaal(IRE) Official explanation: jockey said gelding lost its action
Waheed Official explanation: trainer's rep said gelding lost its action but was sound when trotted up on return

6125 AT THE RACES VIRGIN 534 H'CAP 1m 141y(P)
8:55 (8:56) (Class 6) (0-55,55) 3-Y-O+ **£1,774** (£523; £262) **Stalls Low**

Form RPR

5500 **1** **Nicholas Pocock (IRE)**[12] 5770 4-8-11 **52**...................... JohnFahy(5) 5 67+
(B Ellison) *hld up: hdwy 2f out: rdn to ld and hung lft 1f out: r.o wl* **8/1**

2165 **2** *3* **Belle Park**[12] 5766 3-9-0 **55**... ChrisCatlin 10 61
(Karen George) *hld up: hdwy over 1f out: r.o wl: nt rch wnr* **16/1**

5325 **3** *½* **Tres Froide (FR)**[14] 5704 5-9-1 **51**..............................(p) AndreaAtzeni 6 56
(N Tinkler) *a.p: drvn along 1/2-way: styd on same pce ins fnl f* **4/1**[2]

4636 **4** *½* **Lunar River (FR)**[14] 5704 7-9-5 **55**............................(tp) FergusSweeney 9 59
(David Pinder) *s.i.s: hld up: r.o wl ins fnl f: nrst fin* **6/1**[3]

6654 **5** *1* **Desert Falls**[20] 5496 4-9-1 **54**....................................... AmyRyan(3) 13 56
(R M Whitaker) *prom: chsd ldr over 2f out: rdn to ld over 1f out: sn hdd: no ex ins fnl f* **16/1**

6033 **6** *1 ½* **Ingleby King (USA)**[10] 5821 4-9-5 **55**...........................(b) JimCrowley 1 53
(T D Barron) *hld up: rdn over 1f out: styd on: nt trble ldrs* **7/1**

0056 **7** *nk* **Beauchamp Wizard**[8] 5867 5-9-4 **54**.........................(p) RichardHughes 3 51
(G A Butler) *trckd ldrs: racd keenly: rdn over 2f out: wknd ins fnl f* **8/1**

5006 **8** *nk* **It's A Mans World**[6] 5927 4-8-11 **54**............................. RyanPowell(7) 8 51
(Ian Williams) *chsd ldr tl rdn over 2f out: wknd ins fnl f* **16/1**

0-00 **9** *shd* **Mister Fantastic**[31] 5158 4-9-5 **55**................................ ShaneKelly 4 51
(N J Vaughan) *led: rdn and hdd over 1f out: wknd ins fnl f* **20/1**

/013 **10** *1* **Colinca's Lad (IRE)**[36] 4969 8-9-2 **52**........................ RobertWinston 12 46
(P Charalambous) *s.i.s: hdwy over 5f out: rdn and hung lft 2f out: wknd fnl f* **3/1**[1]

0060 **11** *3* **Kingsmaite**[16] 5634 9-8-10 **53**.....................................(b) RyanClark(7) 11 40
(S R Bowring) *mid-div: rdn over 3f out: wknd 2f out* **66/1**

6500 **12** *11* **Goose Green (IRE)**[26] 5115 6-9-3 **53**............................ GeorgeBaker 7 15
(R J Hodges) *hld up: a in rr: rdn and wknd over 2f out* **33/1**

020- **13** *2 ¼* **Moment Of Clarity**[579] 554 8-9-0 **50**............................. LiamKeniry 2 7
(S A Harris) *chsd ldrs: rdn over 3f out: wknd over 2f out* **40/1**

1m 49.65s (-0.85) **Going Correction** -0.025s/f (Stan)
WFA 3 from 4yo+ 5lb 13 Ran SP% **123.3**
Speed ratings (Par 101): **102,99,98,98,97 96,95,95,95,94 92,82,80**
Tote Swingers:1&2:£17.10, 2&3:£23.70, 1&3:£7.10 CSF £128.64 CT £598.57 TOTE £9.90: £3.30, £5.00, £1.70; EX 111.00 Place 6 £58.86, Place 5 £20.22..
Owner Koo's Racing Club **Bred** Ballymacoll Stud Farm Ltd **Trained** Norton, N Yorks

FOCUS
Moderate stuff and more like a classified event than a handicap, but sound form. The race was run at a sound pace.
T/Plt: £109.70 to a £1 stake. Pool £65,520.54. 435.63 winning tickets. T/Qpdt: £26.40 to a £1 stake. Pool £10,252.90. 287.20 winning tickets. CR

6092 YARMOUTH (L-H)
Thursday, September 16

OFFICIAL GOING: Soft (5.3)
Wind: Moderate, across. Weather: cloudy

6126 EUROPEAN BREEDERS' FUND SPRINT MAIDEN STKS 6f 3y
2:10 (2:11) (Class 5) 2-Y-O **£3,406** (£1,019; £509; £254; £126) **Stalls High**

Form RPR

1 **Speculate** 2-9-3 0... RyanMoore 4 75+
(W J Haggas) *t.k.h: trckd ldr: rdn to ld jst over 1f out: kpt on wl fnl 100yds: rdn out* **9/4**[2]

2 *½* **Calaf** 2-9-3 0.. DarryllHolland 1 74+
(Jane Chapple-Hyam) *in tch: rdn along to chse ldng pair ent fnl 2f: no hdwy tl drvn and chsd wnr ins fnl f: kpt on wl* **14/1**

3 1 3/4 **New Latin (IRE)** 2-9-3 0 .... RoystonFfrench 3 68+
(M Johnston) *dwlt: plld hrd early and hld up towards rr: rdn and rn green over 2f out: chsd ldrs but no real prog over 1f out: styd on u.p fnl 100yds to go 3rd nr fin: nt rch ldrs* **15/8**[1]

4 nk **Rambo Will** 2-9-3 0 .... JimmyQuinn 6 67+
(J R Jenkins) *s.i.s and wnt bdly rt s: sn detached in last: clsd and in tch 1/2-way: pushed along and hdwy to chse ldrs over 1f out: rdn 1f out: kpt on same pce ins fnl f* **40/1**

0306 5 nse **Uncle Dermot (IRE)**[64] 4020 2-9-3 67 .... TomQueally 9 67
(B G Powell) *led: rdn wl over 1f out: hdd jst over 1f out: drvn ins fnl f: wknd and lost 3 pls fnl 150yds* **6/1**[3]

6 14 **Varlak** 2-9-3 0 .... LiamJones 7 25
(D Donovan) *in tch: pushed along 3f out: sn struggling: wknd 2f out and sn wl btn* **100/1**

7 1/2 **Spin Cast** 2-9-3 0 .... AdamKirby 2 24
(W R Swinburn) *s.i.s: rn v green and sn rdn along in rr: lost tch over 2f out* **8/1**

5 8 1/2 **Gekko (IRE)**[53] 4396 2-9-3 0 .... StephenCraine 5 22
(Patrick Morris) *stdd s: plld hrd: hld up in tch: hdwy to chse ldrs 4f out tl over 2f out: sn wknd: wl bhd over 1f out* **9/1**

1m 17.49s (3.09) **Going Correction** +0.40s/f (Good) **8** Ran SP% **111.0**
Speed ratings (Par 95): **95,94,92,91,91 72,72,71**
toteswingers:1&2:£5.80, 1&3:£1.40, 2&3:£8.00 CSF £31.14 TOTE £3.00: £1.10, £4.20, £1.40; EX 32.30 Trifecta £68.70 Pool £395.06 - 4.25 winning units..
Owner Ian and Christine Beard **Bred** D E And Mrs J Cash **Trained** Newmarket, Suffolk
■ Stewards' Enquiry : Darryll Holland one-day ban: used whip in incorrect place (Sep 30)

FOCUS
The ground was soft with a GoingStick reading of 5.3 for the final day of the meeting. Just an ordinary juvenile sprint maiden, run at a steady pace. The first three may leave the bare form behind.

NOTEBOOK
Speculate, despite being bred to need more time, was solid in the market on this racecourse debut. He knew his job well enough and ran out a workmanlike winner. His future will be in handicaps. (op 5-2 tchd 11-4)
Calaf, whose dam was a winner at up to 1m6f, comes from a yard capable of getting 2-y-o talent and he ran a race full of promise. Sure to come on for the experience, he looks capable of winning an ordinary maiden. (op 12-1)
New Latin(IRE), half-brother to useful French sprinter Irish Cat, very much looked in need of the experience, as is often the case with juveniles from the yard. He did enough to make him the one to take from the race and will no doubt have his supporters next time. (op 7-4 tchd 2-1)
Rambo Will, the first foal of an 18-race maiden, shaped surprisingly well given his market weakness. Slowly away and diving right coming out the stalls, he stayed on well inside the final furlong and the experience shouldn't be lost on him. Official explanation: jockey said colt missed the break (op 33-1)
Uncle Dermot(IRE), one of only two with experience in the field, tried to put it to use by setting off in front, but he was always likely to prove vulnerable at the business end. (op 7-1 tchd 11-2)
Spin Cast looked very inexperienced having been slowly away. It all proved too much for him, but there are sure to be other days. (tchd 7-1)
Gekko(IRE) failed to build on his initial effort and looks more a handicap prospect. (op 8-1)

6127 EUROPEAN BREEDERS' FUND MAIDEN STKS (DIV I) 1m 3y
2:40 (2:41) (Class 5) 2-Y-O **£3,090** (£925; £462; £231; £115) **Stalls** High

Form RPR

1 **Seelo (USA)** 2-9-3 0 .... NickyMackay 4 77+
(J H M Gosden) *awkward s and s.i.s: sn t.k.h: chsd ldrs 2f out tl rdn and ev ch wl over 1f out: kpt on wl to ld nr fin* **7/2**[3]

6 2 1/2 **Cadore (IRE)**[48] 4550 2-9-3 0 .... RyanMoore 10 76+
(P W Chapple-Hyam) *trckd ldrs against stands' rail: chsd ldr 2f out: rdn to ld wl over 1f out: rn green u.p over 1f out: kpt on tl hdd and no ex nr fin* **9/4**[1]

0 3 3 **Palitana (USA)**[33] 5066 2-8-12 0 .... SaleemGolam 11 64+
(J H M Gosden) *stdd and dropped in bhd after s: t.k.h: hld up in tch: rdn and sltly outpcd 2f out: styd on again ins fnl f: wnt 3rd nr fin: nt pce to chal ldng pair* **8/1**

4 nk **Specific Gravity (FR)** 2-9-3 0 .... TomQueally 7 68
(H R A Cecil) *t.k.h: hld up wl in tch: effrt to press ldrs 2f out: rn v green and hung lft after: wknd jst ins fnl f: lost 3rd nr fin* **5/2**[2]

0 5 4 1/2 **Breton Star**[34] 5049 2-9-0 0 .... MartinLane(3) 1 58
(D M Simcock) *wnt lft s and s.i.s: sn wl in tch: pushed along 5f out: rdn 1/2-way: styd in tch tl wknd wl over 1f out* **66/1**

0 6 nk **Govenor General (IRE)**[43] 4695 2-9-3 0 .... AdamKirby 2 57
(J Noseda) *led: rdn ent fnl 2f: hdd wl over 1f out: drvn and btn over 1f out: wknd fnl f* **28/1**

0 7 3/4 **Tanjung Agas (IRE)**[20] 5491 2-9-3 0 ....(b[1]) JackMitchell 9 56
(M A Jarvis) *plld hrd: chsd ldr tl 5f out: rdn and wknd ent fnl 2f: wl btn over 1f out* **10/1**

8 1 **Mokalif** 2-9-3 0 .... HayleyTurner 8 53
(M L W Bell) *t.k.h: hld up wl in tch in rr: rdn and struggling ent fnl 2f: wl btn over 1f out* **20/1**

9 11 **Oceans Destination** 2-9-3 0 .... MarcHalford 5 28
(J Ryan) *s.i.s: sn rcvrd and wl in tch: rdn and wknd ent fnl 2f: sn bhd* **100/1**

1m 44.74s (4.14) **Going Correction** +0.40s/f (Good) **9** Ran SP% **112.5**
Speed ratings (Par 95): **95,94,91,91,86 86,85,84,73**
toteswingers:1&2:£2.60, 1&3:£3.50, 2&3:£4.00 CSF £11.12 TOTE £5.70: £2.90, £1.10, £2.10; EX 13.40 Trifecta £45.40 Pool £394.03 - 6.41 winning units..
Owner George Strawbridge **Bred** George Strawbridge Jr **Trained** Newmarket, Suffolk

FOCUS
The first division of what looks sure to be an informative maiden. The winning time was 0.23secs quicker than the second division despite a steady pace. The first two came clear but the bare form is limited.

NOTEBOOK
Seelo(USA)'s trainer, who can do little wrong at present, won this with smart middle-distance performer Alwaary in 2008. A son of Dynaformer whose dam is a half-sister to Selkirk, he proved good enough to make a winning debut. Entered in the Racing Post Trophy, he recovered from a sluggish start to chase the speed and, although taking a while to master the favourite, always looked to be coming out on top. It will be interesting to see where he goes next. (op 9-2 tchd 10-3)
Cadore(IRE) showed enough in a novice stakes at Newmarket on debut to suggest he's up to winning a maiden, but he still looked a bit inexperienced and was eventually worn down by a useful-looking newcomer. He shouldn't be long in going one better. (op 7-2 tchd 2-1)
Palitana(USA) ran well below expectations on her debut at Doncaster, and the ground here looked far from ideal, but she managed to take a sizeable step forward and wouldn't need to improve much again to win an ordinary fillies' maiden. (op 4-1)
Specific Gravity(FR), a half-brother to numerous winners, including the smart Linda's Lad, is entered in the Derby and he shaped nicely, just getting a little tired late on in the ground. He should learn plenty from this and looks another ready-made maiden winner. (op 11-4 tchd 10-3)
Breton Star stepped up markedly on his debut effort and may be one for handicaps,
Govenor General(IRE) stopped quickly once headed, but clearly has ability. (op 18-1)
Tanjung Agas(IRE) had been well beaten on debut and suffered the same fate here, the blinkers doing little to help. (op 9-1 tchd 17-2)

6128 EUROPEAN BREEDERS' FUND MAIDEN STKS (DIV II) 1m 3y
3:10 (3:13) (Class 5) 2-Y-O **£3,090** (£925; £462; £231; £115) **Stalls** High

Form RPR

0 1 **Man Of God (IRE)**[34] 5049 2-9-3 0 .... RyanMoore 3 73+
(J H M Gosden) *dwlt: sn rcvrd and led after 1f: mde rest: rdn clr w rival 2f out: forged ahd fnl 100yds: styd on wl: drvn out* **11/8**[1]

2 3/4 **Parlour Games** 2-9-3 0 .... AhmedAjtebi 4 71
(Mahmood Al Zarooni) *w ldrs: rdn and clr w wnr 2f out: ev ch tl no ex and btn fnl 100yds* **11/2**

3 shd **Ryton Runner (IRE)** 2-9-3 0 .... NickyMackay 8 71+
(J H M Gosden) *in tch: rdn and sltly outpcd 2f out: chsd clr ldng pair wl over 1f out: styd on wl fnl 100yds* **7/2**[2]

0 4 1 **Star Commander**[108] 2594 2-8-12 0 .... AshleyMorgan(5) 6 69
(M H Tompkins) *in tch: rdn and effrt ent fnl 2f: disputing 3rd and drvn over 1f out: kpt on ins fnl f* **33/1**

5 2 1/4 **Trend (IRE)** 2-9-3 0 .... HayleyTurner 10 64+
(M L W Bell) *stdd s: rn green and hld up in tch in last: rdn and effrt ent fnl 2f: styd on same pce and no imp fr over 1f out* **14/1**

0 6 7 **Elysian Heights (IRE)**[17] 5594 2-9-3 0 .... DarryllHolland 7 49
(J Noseda) *stdd s: t.k.h early: hld up in tch in last trio: rdn and effrt ent fnl 2f: sn edgd lft and outpcd: wknd over 1f out* **5/1**[3]

7 3/4 **Makyaal (IRE)** 2-9-3 0 .... RichardHills 5 51+
(J L Dunlop) *s.i.s: rn green and in tch in midfield: rdn and outpcd ent fnl 2f: wknd wl over 1f out* **8/1**

8 1 1/4 **Diamond City (IRE)** 2-9-3 0 .... PaulMulrennan 2 44
(Mrs D J Sanderson) *led for 1f: chsd wnr tl 3f out: rdn and struggling ent fnl 2f: wknd over 1f out* **50/1**

9 49 **Trojan Touch (USA)** 2-9-3 0 .... LiamJones 1 —
(C A Dwyer) *stdd s: sn rcvrd and chsd ldrs: lost pl rapidly over 2f out: wl t.o over 1f out* **100/1**

1m 44.97s (4.37) **Going Correction** +0.40s/f (Good) **9** Ran SP% **120.0**
Speed ratings (Par 95): **94,93,93,92,89 82,82,80,31**
toteswingers:1&2:£2.40, 1&3:£2.50, 2&3:£5.40 CSF £10.01 TOTE £2.70: £1.20, £1.50, £1.60; EX 11.60 Trifecta £35.40 Pool £414.58 - 8.65 winning units..
Owner B E Nielsen **Bred** Premier Bloodstock **Trained** Newmarket, Suffolk

FOCUS
This looked like it may have been the stronger of the two divisions, on paper at least, although the time was 0.23secs slower than the previous race. Due to the steady pace it is hard to rate the bare form much higher.

NOTEBOOK
Man Of God(IRE), whose yard also won the first division, slugged it out best under a strong ride from Ryan Moore. A well-beaten eighth at Newmarket behind Frankel on debut, this brother to the likes of Yesterday and Quarter Moon was always likely to improve with that experience behind him, and having set off in front he found plenty when challenged from over 2f out, looking a strong middle-distance stayer in the making. He doesn't look good enough to take up his Racing Post Trophy engagement, but rates a decent prospect for next season. Soft ground looks a must. (op 13-8 tchd 7-4)
Parlour Games, whose dam won the Irish Oaks, is going to relish 1m2f and more next season, so it was no surprise to see him go close in a race where stamina was always going to be important. He may well have won with a previous outing under his belt, but it surely won't be long before he goes one better. (op 13-2 tchd 7-1)
Ryton Runner(IRE), the other Gosden representative, a brother to six winners, including Gypsy King, was a big mover in the market, but his inexperience was there for all to see. He did stay on well inside the final half furlong, though, and is yet another likely to be winning an end-of-season maiden. (op 6-1 tchd 13-2)
Star Commander, up 2f in trip, improved markedly on his debut effort to finish on the heels of the principals. He will be qualified for handicaps following one more run and clearly has a future at a sensible level. (tchd 40-1)
Trend(IRE), a 60,000gns son of Marju who is already gelded, kept on late having run green and should improve. (op 9-1)
Elysian Heights(IRE) disappointingly didn't step up more on his debut effort, although conditions were possibly against him. He should come good once handicapping. (op 6-1)
Makyaal(IRE), whose sales price ended up being 250,000gns, looked lost in the ground and should be seen to much better effect next time. (op 11-2)

6129 BARTHOLOMEW'S AND TILLETTS JEWELLERS (S) NURSERY 1m 3y
3:40 (3:43) (Class 6) (0-65,65) 2-Y-O **£1,554** (£462; £231; £115) **Stalls** High

Form RPR

4006 1 **Salvationist**[15] 5659 2-8-4 **51** .... MartinLane(3) 1 56
(J L Dunlop) *chsd ldrs: wnt 2nd over 2f out: drvn and ev ch over 1f out: hung rt u.p and led ins fnl f: all out* **10/1**

0463 2 shd **Sabratha (IRE)**[16] 5644 2-8-11 **55** .... TomQueally 10 60
(B J Curley) *sn led: rdn and clr w wnr over 1f out: hdd ins fnl f: hrd drvn and rallied towards fin: jst hld* **11/2**[3]

060 3 2 3/4 **Munro's Dragon**[19] 5523 2-8-2 **51** .... AshleyMorgan(5) 12 50
(M H Tompkins) *hld up in tch towards rr: rdn and effrt over 2f out: kpt on u.p fnl f to go 3rd nr fin: nvr gng pce to rch ldng pair* **4/1**[2]

10 4 1/2 **Mary Boyle**[15] 5659 2-8-7 **56** .... TobyAtkinson(5) 3 56+
(A J McCabe) *stdd s: hld up in rr: hdwy and rdn ent fnl 2f: n.m.r wl over 1f out: styd on u.p fnl f: nt rch ldrs* **12/1**

0355 5 nk **Loch Ordie**[23] 5389 2-8-12 **61** .... AdamBeschizza(5) 7 58
(M G Quinlan) *hld up in tch in midfield: effrt u.p to chse ldng pair ent fnl 2f: styd on same pce fnl f: lost 2 pls nr fin* **7/2**[1]

0530 6 3/4 **Jealousy Defined (IRE)**[17] 5602 2-8-8 **55**(p) Louis-PhilippeBeuzelin(3) 13 50
(N Tinkler) *sn pushed along towards rr: styd on fr over 1f out: plugged on fnl f nvr gng pce to threaten ldrs* **33/1**

0040 7 1 3/4 **Captain Sharpe**[15] 5659 2-8-13 **57** ....(v[1]) AdamKirby 9 48
(H J L Dunlop) *chsd ldr tl over 2f out: wknd u.p over 1f out* **16/1**

605 8 6 **A Little Bit Dusty**[14] 5701 2-9-4 **65** .... JackDean(3) 5 43
(W G M Turner) *in tch towards rr: rdn and dropped to rr 1/2-way: no ch but plugged on past btn horses fnl f* **16/1**

6003 9 1 1/2 **Bajan Bullet**[16] 5630 2-9-1 **59** .... JamesDoyle 4 34
(P D Evans) *in tch in midfield: effrt and drvn over 2f out: sn wknd: wl btn 1f out* **20/1**

0500 10 nk **Aquilifer (IRE)**[9] 5837 2-8-13 **57** ....(p) WilliamCarson 6 31
(W Jarvis) *short of room and hmpd s: t.k.h and hld up in tch towards rr: hdwy 1/2-way: rdn and wknd ent fnl 2f* **16/1**

0000 11 nk **King Bling (IRE)**[9] 5837 2-8-6 **50** .... SaleemGolam 11 24
(S Kirk) *t.k.h: chsd ldrs: rdn and struggling 1/2-way: wl btn fnl 2f* **12/1**

034 12 1 1/4 **Red Jacaranda**[16] 5630 2-8-6 **50** .... LiamJones 16 21
(C A Dwyer) *in tch: rdn and toiling over 2f out: wl btn fnl 2f* **9/1**

The Form Book, Raceform Ltd, Compton, RG20 6NL

6040 **13** *nk* **Livinadream**[16] 5630 2-8-8 **52** .... KirstyMilczarek 2 22
(N Tinkler) *in tch in midfield: rdn and effrt over 2f out: sn wl btn* **50/1**

000 **14** *8* **Blade Pirate**[24] 5365 2-8-11 **55** .... MarcHalford 15 8
(J Ryan) *chsd ldrs tl 1/2-way: sn lost pl: wl bhd over 1f out* **80/1**

2305 **15** *7* **Pigeon Hollow**[14] 5676 2-9-5 **63** .... SamHitchcott 8 —
(M R Channon) *chsd ldrs tl rdn 1/2-way: wknd wl over 2f out: wl bhd over 1f out: eased ins fnl f: t.o* **14/1**

1m 43.77s (3.17) **Going Correction** +0.40s/f (Good) **15** Ran SP% **127.3**
Speed ratings (Par 93): **100,99,97,96,96 95,93,87,86,86 85,84,84,76,69**
toteswingers:1&2:£14.20, 1&3:£7.40, 2&3:£8.90 CSF £65.76 CT £273.84 TOTE £15.20: £5.80, £1.60, £1.10; EX 85.30 Trifecta £161.10 Part won. Pool £217.77 - 0.73 winning units..There was no bid for the winner. Sabratha was claimed by Miss L. A. Perratt For £5,000.
Owner J L Dunlop **Bred** Coln Valley Stud **Trained** Arundel, W Sussex

FOCUS
A competitive selling nursery, run in a time quicker than both the earlier maidens at the distance. Limited form, rated around the principals.

NOTEBOOK
Salvationist, outpaced over this trip on the AW latest, was experiencing this sort of ground for the first time and he seemed quite at home, moving well through the race and just edging out the runner-up. He clearly stays this trip well and can continue to give a good account at a moderate level. (op 12-1)
Sabratha(IRE), a well-beaten third over 7f at Southwell on his handicap debut, really pressed on under an aggressive ride on this first try at 1m, and briefly looked like winning, but despite rallying once headed, she couldn't quite get back up. (tchd 5-1 and 7-1)
Munro's Dragon was always likely to improve once handicapping and he may benefit from a more positive ride in future. There's a race in him at this sort of level. (op 8-1 tchd 7-2)
Mary Boyle, well held in the same Kempton race as the winner last time, got going all too late and should have been closer, marking her down as one to be interested in next time. (op 10-1)
Loch Ordie, who ran well off 4lb higher at Leicester on his recent nursery debut, got going too late that day, and it was much the same story here. (op 9-2 tchd 5-1)
Jealousy Defined(IRE) was yet another doing her best work inside the final furlong. (op 22-1)
Red Jacaranda failed to make an impact on this nursery debut.
Livinadream Official explanation: jockey said filly hung right-handed throughout

6130 ATTHERACES NURSERY 7f 3y
4:10 (4:11) (Class 4) (0-80,79) 2-Y-O **£3,027** (£906; £453; £226; £112) **Stalls** High

Form RPR

0021 **1** **Cometh**[14] 5675 2-8-2 **63** .... MartinLane(3) 5 70
(N P Littmoden) *mde all: rdn clr 2f out: in command after: rdn out hands and heels fnl f: kpt on* **4/1**[2]

0505 **2** *2 1/2* **My Mate Jake (IRE)**[17] 5597 2-8-12 **70** .... PaulMulrennan 2 71
(J G Given) *chsd ldrs: wnt 2nd 1/2-way: rdn and outpcd by wnr 2f out: no imp and edgd rt u.p 1f out: kpt on towards fin* **7/1**

5304 **3** *1* **Jibaal (IRE)**[16] 5637 2-8-10 **68** .... RichardHills 3 66
(M Johnston) *awkward leaving stalls: sn chsng ldr: rdn and lost 2nd 1/2-way: edgd rt u.p and outpcd by wnr 2f out: no ch w wnr but kpt on fnl f* **5/4**[1]

435 **4** *hd* **Cornish Quest**[16] 5626 2-8-6 **69** .... AshleyMorgan(5) 9 67
(M H Tompkins) *in tch in rr: rdn and effrt 3f out: outpcd by wnr 2f out: no threat to wnr and styd on same pce u.p fr over 1f out* **8/1**

0222 **5** *13* **Ajaafa**[10] 5818 2-8-9 **67** ow1 ....(p) TomQueally 6 32
(J G Given) *in tch: rdn and lost pl qckly over 2f out: wl btn over 1f out* **5/1**[3]

2100 **6** *nse* **Joyously**[12] 5745 2-9-1 **78** .... AdamBeschizza(5) 4 43
(P D Evans) *in tch: rdn 1/2-way: wknd over 2f out: wl btn over 1f out* **22/1**

1m 29.56s (2.96) **Going Correction** +0.40s/f (Good) **6** Ran SP% **109.1**
Speed ratings (Par 97): **99,96,95,94,79 79**
toteswingers:1&2:£3.20, 1&3:£1.30, 2&3:£2.50 CSF £28.79 CT £47.65 TOTE £3.70: £1.50, £2.80; EX 25.80 Trifecta £55.70 Pool £259.97 - 3.45 winning units..
Owner Larry Stratton **Bred** Larry Stratton **Trained** Newmarket, Suffolk
■ Stewards' Enquiry : Adam Beschizza two-day ban: failed to ride out for 5th (tbn)

FOCUS
A modest nursery. The runner-up and fourth set the level.

NOTEBOOK
Cometh led throughout for a second straight win since sent handicapping. Successful from 6lb lower at Epsom, when she also made all, the softer ground here was clearly not a bother to the daughter of Iceman and, although a further rise will follow, she could be up to defying it. (tchd 9-2)
My Mate Jake(IRE), a running-on fifth over 1m on his nursery debut at Newcastle, again ran well, but it was no surprise to see him find the 7f trip too short. He's clearly got a small race in him off this sort of mark. (tchd 13-2 and 15-2)
Jibaal(IRE) looked unlucky off this mark over 6f latest, but not for the first time didn't get the best of starts, and he never looked completely happy in the ground. He should defy this mark eventually, but looks to need better ground. (op 11-8 tchd 6-4 and 6-5)
Cornish Quest kept on again having been outpaced. (tchd 6-1)
Ajaafa probably didn't like the ground. (op 11-2 tchd 6-1 and 9-2)

6131 SEAJACKS - SHE'S GOT LEGS H'CAP 1m 6f 17y
4:40 (4:40) (Class 2) (0-100,98) 3-Y-O+
£8,598 (£2,575; £1,287; £644; £321; £161) **Stalls** High

Form RPR

2351 **1** **Activate**[12] 5747 3-8-5 **85** .... HayleyTurner 2 97+
(M L W Bell) *mde all: jnd 4f out: drew clr w rival but stl on bit 2f out: rdn hands and heels to assert ins fnl f: r.o wl: comf* **6/4**[1]

5140 **2** *3/4* **Cotillion**[12] 5743 4-9-2 **86** .... PaulMulrennan 5 94
(Ian Williams) *chsd wnr after 1f: jnd ldr 4f out: shkn up and drew clr w wnr 2f out: drvn over 1f out: nt pce of wnr and btn fnl 100yds* **5/2**[2]

5304 **3** *6* **Hevelius**[20] 5492 5-9-2 **86** .... AdamKirby 4 86
(W R Swinburn) *hld up in tch in last pair: effrt on inner over 3f out: drvn and btn 2f out: no ch w ldrs after: wnt modest 3rd 1f out* **5/1**[3]

50 **4** *1 3/4* **Hollow Green (IRE)**[21] 5444 4-8-6 **79** ....(v) Louis-PhilippeBeuzelin(3) 3 76
(P D Evans) *hld up in last: rdn and outpcd by ldng pair ent fnl 2f: no ch w ldrs after: styd on u.p fnl 100yds to snatch 4th last strides* **33/1**

/2-0 **5** *hd* **Cool Judgement (IRE)**[23] 5387 5-9-10 **94** .... JackMitchell 1 91
(M A Jarvis) *t.k.h: chsd wnr for 1f: chsd ldng pair after: rdn and outpcd jst over 2f out: wl btn after: lost 2 pls fnl f* **5/1**[3]

4463 **6** *nk* **Swiss Act**[124] 2126 6-9-4 **88** .... RoystonFfrench 8 84
(M Johnston) *in tch: rdn over 4f out: outpcd by ldng pair jst over 2f out: one pce and no ch w ldrs fnl 2f* **10/1**

3m 16.03s (8.43) **Going Correction** +0.575s/f (Yiel)
WFA 3 from 4yo+ 10lb **6** Ran SP% **113.9**
Speed ratings (Par 109): **98,97,94,93,93 92**
toteswingers:1&2:£1.60, 1&3:£2.80, 2&3:£1.90 CSF £5.63 CT £13.56 TOTE £2.40: £1.10, £2.00; EX 6.00 Trifecta £13.60 Pool £204.77 - 11.09 winning units..
Owner Highclere Thoroughbred Racing Tudor Min **Bred** Card Bloodstock **Trained** Newmarket, Suffolk

FOCUS
The front pair came clear in what looked just a fair handicap. It is hard to assess how much the cosy winner had in hand.

NOTEBOOK
Activate, the sole 3-y-o who had scored over this trip off 7lb lower earlier in the month, wasn't at his best on similar ground to this the time before, but he coped just fine on this occasion and Hayley Turner always seemed confident she had enough left in reserve, just nudging him out to win. Clearly a progressive young stayer, he will surely be forced into a better race now, but it would be unwise to rule out a hat-trick. (tchd 11-8 and 13-8)
Cotillion was never far from the winner, but he always looked to be coming off second-best, keeping on well but not proving good enough. He is worth another go at 2m and remains capable of better. A few of the jumping boys are sure to be interested in him. (op 10-3 tchd 7-2)
Hevelius kept on for third, albeit he was well held, and he remains a bit below his best. (op 13-2 tchd 7-1)
Hollow Green(IRE) showed considerably more in the visor. (op 28-1)
Cool Judgement(IRE), well held on his return, still looked in need of it. (op 9-2 tchd 11-2)

6132 IRISH THOROUGHBRED MARKETING H'CAP 2m
5:10 (5:14) (Class 5) (0-70,70) 3-Y-O+ **£2,590** (£770; £385; £192) **Stalls** High

Form RPR

1332 **1** **Petella**[16] 5642 4-8-9 **52** .... AdamBeschizza(5) 14 63+
(C W Thornton) *s.i.s: wl bhd in last: stl last over 4f out and swtchd rt: rdn and relentless hdwy after: chsd ldr over 1f out: led 1f out: sn clr: r.o wl: eased towards fin* **9/2**[1]

2101 **2** *6* **Any Given Moment (IRE)**[58] 4223 4-9-8 **63** ....(b) MartinLane(3) 1 67
(D M Simcock) *led: pushed clr over 2f out: rdn over 1f out: hdd 1f out: no ch w wnr after: tiring towards fin* **7/1**[3]

0603 **3** *1 3/4* **Sparkaway**[18] 5564 4-8-13 **51** ....(b[1]) JamieMackay 8 56+
(W J Musson) *s.i.s: towards rr: hdwy over 3f out: nt clr run 3f out tl jst over 2f out: styd on steadily u.p after: wnt 3rd towards fin* **9/1**

-244 **4** *nk* **Sir Walter Raleigh**[16] 5646 3-9-4 **68** ....(t) RyanMoore 3 70
(Sir Michael Stoute) *in tch: drvn to chse clr ldr 3f out: no imp: lost 2nd over 1f out: wl hld and plugged on same pce u.p: lost 3rd towards fin* **8/1**

0611 **5** *4* **Bravo Bravo**[15] 5666 3-8-8 **58** .... SamHitchcott 11 55
(M R Channon) *stdd s: hld up in last trio: rdn and hdwy on outer over 4f out: chsd ldrs and edging lft u.p over 3f out: ended up on far rail and 4th 2f out: no hdwy and wknd over 1f out: tired fnl f* **7/1**[3]

0643 **6** *hd* **Go Amwell**[15] 5666 7-8-3 **48** .... DannyBrock(7) 12 45
(J R Jenkins) *s.i.s: hld up in last trio: hdwy over 4f out: 5th and plugged on same pce fr wl over 1f out* **33/1**

-604 **7** *9* **Akula (IRE)**[16] 5631 3-8-12 **62** .... LiamJones 4 48
(M H Tompkins) *hld up in midfield: effrt and nt clr run ent 4f out: no threat to ldrs after: styd on past btn horses fnl 2f* **33/1**

4011 **8** *4* **Fuzzypeg (IRE)**[18] 5564 3-8-8 **58** .... HayleyTurner 5 39
(J R Fanshawe) *in tch in midfield: effrt on inner ent fnl 3f: nt clr run and hmpd over 2f out: rdn and no hdwy 2f out: wl btn and tired fnl f* **9/2**[1]

3006 **9** *24* **Hidden**[15] 5666 4-9-5 **60** ....(b) Louis-PhilippeBeuzelin(3) 7 —
(B J Meehan) *s.i.s: sn in midfield: rdn and wknd over 3f out: wl bhd and virtually p.u fr wl over 1f out: t.o* **33/1**

6212 **10** *20* **Albeed**[17] 5612 3-9-6 **70** .... JimmyQuinn 13 —
(J L Dunlop) *in tch in midfield: rdn and effrt over 4f out: chsd ldrs and drvn over 2f out: wknd qckly 2f out: virtually p.u fr over 1f out: t.o* **5/1**[2]

4010 **11** *1* **Sunny Spells**[15] 5666 5-9-7 **59** .... AdamKirby 2 —
(S C Williams) *led tl 4f out: wknd u.p over 3f out: t.o and virtually p.u fnl 2f* **50/1**

/1-0 **12** *23* **Warne's Way (IRE)**[152] 1012 7-10-0 **66** .... RichardHills 15 —
(B G Powell) *a towards rr: lost tch u.p 4f out: t.o and virtually p.u fnl 2f* **33/1**

50/6 **13** *7* **Zabeel Palace**[147] 1493 8-10-0 **66** .... TomQueally 6 —
(B J Curley) *t.k.h: chsd ldrs tl rdn and wknd qckly over 4f out: wl t.o and virtually p.u fr over 2f out* **33/1**

033 **14** *8* **Mighty Mambo**[19] 5522 3-9-6 **70** ....(p) DarryllHolland 9 —
(Jane Chapple-Hyam) *chsd ldrs tl wknd qckly u.p 3f out: t.o and virtually p.u fnl 2f* **11/1**

3m 42.38s (7.78) **Going Correction** +0.575s/f (Yiel)
WFA 3 from 4yo+ 12lb **14** Ran SP% **124.1**
Speed ratings (Par 103): **103,100,99,98,96 96,92,90,78,68 67,56,52,48**
toteswingers:1&2:£7.50, 1&3:£11.10, 2&3:£13.20 CSF £35.04 CT £282.40 TOTE £4.50: £1.30, £3.20, £4.40; EX 42.20 Trifecta £346.30 Pool £594.36 - 1.27 winning units..
Owner A Crute & Partners **Bred** C And Mrs Wilson **Trained** Middleham Moor, N Yorks
■ Stewards' Enquiry : Sam Hitchcott one-day ban: careless riding (Sep 30)

FOCUS
A low-grade staying handicap where the testing ground sorted them out. The form is rated through the third.
Akula(IRE) Official explanation: jockey said colt was hampered on bend
Albeed Official explanation: jockey said filly had no more to give
Mighty Mambo Official explanation: trainer said colt made a noise

6133 PREMIER RACING SERVICES H'CAP 6f 3y
5:40 (5:43) (Class 6) (0-60,60) 3-Y-O+ **£1,748** (£520; £260; £129) **Stalls** High

Form RPR

054 **1** **Double Carpet (IRE)**[14] 5697 7-8-13 **52** .... KirstyMilczarek 12 65
(G Woodward) *chsd ldng pair tl led over 2f out: rdn clr over 1f out: in command fnl f: rdn out: comf* **14/1**

00 **2** *3 1/2* **Big Boom**[23] 5386 5-9-0 **56** ....(b[1]) MartinLane(3) 2 58
(M Quinn) *sn rdn along: hdwy to join ldr after 1f: drvn 1/2-way: chsd wnr fr over 2f out: outpcd and wl hld fr over 1f out: edgd rt u.p ins fnl f: hld on for 2nd nr fin* **12/1**

6603 **3** *hd* **Just Jimmy (IRE)**[7] 5877 5-9-4 **57** .... JamesDoyle 1 58
(P D Evans) *in tch in midfield: rdn and unable qck ent fnl 2f: hdwy u.p over 1f out: swtchd lft ins fnl f: styd on to press for 2nd nr fin: no ch w wnr* **4/1**[1]

0543 **4** *1/2* **If Only**[13] 5715 4-8-5 **49** ....(t) AdamBeschizza(5) 11 49
(D Morris) *racd in midfield: rdn and effrt 2f out: no ch w wnr but kpt on u.p fnl f* **5/1**[2]

0223 **5** *2 3/4* **Rebecca Romero**[20] 5470 3-8-10 **51** .... JimmyQuinn 13 42
(D J Coakley) *hld up towards rr: hdwy ent fnl 2f: no threat to wnr but disputing 2nd jst over 1f out: wknd qckly ins fnl f: eased towards fin* **15/2**

-604 **6** *nk* **Stargazing (IRE)**[23] 5395 4-9-4 **60** ....(b) Louis-PhilippeBeuzelin(3) 7 50
(B J Meehan) *s.i.s: in tch towards rr: rdn and effrt 2f out: sn hung rt u.p and no prog* **17/2**

2310 **7** *1 1/2* **Vilnius**[7] 5898 3-9-5 **60** .... SamHitchcott 5 45
(M R Channon) *chsd ldrs: rdn over 2f out: outpcd and drvn wl over 1f out: sn wknd* **8/1**

1353 **8** *8* **Imaginary Diva**[7] 5876 4-8-8 **52** .... SimonPearce(5) 16 11
(G G Margarson) *hld up towards rr: rdn and short-lived effrt over 2f out: wl bhd fr wl over 1f out* **6/1**[3]

000- **9** 2 ½ **Final Rhapsody**[469] 2632 4-8-12 51 .... JamieMackay 4 —
(W J Musson) *in tch: rdn and struggling whn n.m.r jst over 2f out: wl bhd fr wl over 1f out* **17/2**

500- **10** 8 **Croft Bridge**[348] 6494 3-8-10 51 ....(p) LiamJones 3 —
(P A Kirby) *led tl over 2f out: sn dropped out: wl bhd fr wl over 1f out* **33/1**

6003 **11** ¾ **Captain Bluebird (IRE)**[14] 5697 3-9-0 55 ....(b) DarryllHolland 15 —
(D Donovan) *s.i.s: a in rr: rdn and lost tch over 2f out* **16/1**

1m 16.57s (2.17) **Going Correction** +0.40s/f (Good)
WFA 3 from 4yo+ 2lb **11** Ran SP% **118.1**
Speed ratings (Par 101): **101,96,96,95,91 91,89,78,75,64 63**
toteswingers:1&2:£31.50, 1&3:£15.10, 2&3:£12.40 CSF £171.70 CT £820.32 TOTE £21.60: £6.00, £4.80, £2.30; EX 281.90 TRIFECTA Not won. Place 6 £24.68; Place 5 £17.54.
Owner Mr & Mrs Bloom **Bred** Dr John Waldron **Trained** Maltby, S Yorks

FOCUS
An open but weak sprint handicap run in bad ground and not form to be positive about.
Stargazing(IRE) Official explanation: jockey said filly missed the break
Captain Bluebird(IRE) Official explanation: jockey said gelding was fractious when stalls opened and couldn't grasp blind in time
T/Plt: £22.40 to a £1 stake. Pool:£63,184.30 - 2,056.90 winning tickets T/Qpdt: £15.10 to a £1 stake. Pool:£4,556.89 - 223.00 winning tickets SP

6134 - 6137a (Foreign Racing) - See Raceform Interactive

6102 AYR (L-H)

Friday, September 17

OFFICIAL GOING: Good (9.0, sprint course: far side 9.3, centre 9.5, stands' side 10.1)
Wind: Fairly strong, half against Weather: Cloudy, bright

6138 E B F / WEST SOUND AND WEST FM MAIDEN STKS 7f 50y
2:10 (2:11) (Class 4) 2-Y-O **£4,533** (£1,348; £674; £336) **Stalls** High

Form RPR

1 **Well Sharp** 2-9-3 0 .... TomEaves 12 81+
(M Dods) *dwlt: sn rcvrd and w ldr: led over 3f out: rdn clr fr over 1f out* **9/1**

20 **2** 3 ¼ **Sinadinou**[48] 4577 2-9-3 0 .... AdrianNicholls 1 73
(D Nicholls) *led 1f: chsd ldrs: effrt and wnt 2nd over 1f out: kpt on fnl f: nt gng pce of wnr* **4/1**[3]

6653 **3** 2 ½ **Dazzling Valentine**[15] 5699 2-8-12 68 .... GrahamGibbons 6 62
(A Bailey) *led after 1f to over 3f out: rdn and kpt on same pce fr 2f out* **8/1**

0 **4** 1 ¼ **Chilledtothebone**[46] 4645 2-9-3 0 ....(v[1]) DavidAllan 10 64
(Mrs L Stubbs) *prom: drvn over 2f out: sn one pce* **33/1**

5 nk **Way Chief (FR)** 2-9-3 0 .... PaulHanagan 5 63
(R A Fahey) *prom: drvn along over 2f out: kpt on same pce over 1f out* **7/2**[2]

05 **6** nse **Marc De Savoie (IRE)**[13] 5762 2-9-3 0 .... AndrewMullen 14 63+
(K A Ryan) *hld up in midfield: rdn and hung lft over 2f out: kpt on ins fnl f: nrst fin* **33/1**

60 **7** ¾ **Katiesister**[12] 5785 2-8-9 0 .... GaryBartley(3) 13 56+
(J S Goldie) *towards rr: pushed along over 2f out: sme late hdwy: nvr rchd ldrs* **66/1**

23 **8** hd **Uptown Guy (USA)**[62] 4123 2-9-3 0 .... PhillipMakin 9 61
(M Dods) *midfield: drvn over 2f out: no imp fr over 1f out* **9/4**[1]

54 **9** hd **Deep Applause**[18] 5594 2-9-0 0 .... PatrickDonaghy(3) 8 60
(M Dods) *hld up: pushed along over 2f out: n.m.r and swtchd rt ins fnl f: n.d* **18/1**

10 3 ½ **Zoom In** 2-9-0 0 .... JamesSullivan(3) 3 52
(Mrs L Stubbs) *bhd: pushed along over 3f out: nvr on terms* **66/1**

11 1 **Lightning Cloud (IRE)** 2-9-3 0 .... FrannyNorton 7 49
(K A Ryan) *trckd ldrs: effrt over 2f out: wknd over 1f out* **14/1**

12 ¾ **William Wainwright (IRE)** 2-9-3 0 .... SilvestreDeSousa 11 47
(Mrs A Duffield) *midfield: rdn 1/2-way: effrt on outside over 2f out: wknd over 1f out* **50/1**

13 13 **Face East (USA)** 2-8-12 0 .... MarkCoumbe(5) 4 15
(A Berry) *s.i.s: a outpcd and bhd* **100/1**

1m 32.02s (-1.38) **Going Correction** -0.275s/f (Firm) **13** Ran SP% **117.9**
Speed ratings (Par 97): **96,92,89,88,87 87,86,86,86,82 81,80,65**
CSF £43.13 TOTE £12.90: £3.20, £1.70, £2.50; EX 49.60.
Owner Andrew Tinkler **Bred** Equibreed S R L **Trained** Denton, Co Durham

FOCUS
This opening juvenile maiden was a moderate affair, but it was a true test and there should be winners coming out of the race. The form is rated conservatively around principals.

NOTEBOOK
Well Sharp ◆ was the stable's second-string according to the betting, but he ran out a decisive winner under a positive ride. He wasn't helped by being housed wide and showed his inexperience through the first furlong. He responded to make his way to the lead, though, and showed a lovely attitude in the home straight. A colt with plenty of scope, he will appreciate stepping up in trip as he matures and connections look to have a useful prospect on their hands. He could now be put away for the winter. (op 7-1)
Sinadinou returned to the sort of form that saw him finish second to a stablemate of the winner over 6f here on debut two runs back and was a clear second-best. He now qualifies for nurseries and should find a race in that sphere before long. (op 13-2)
Dazzling Valentine, dropping back down a furlong, was the most experienced of these and it told as she was always on the front-end. She lacked any sort of gear change, but helps to set the standard with a mark of 68 and deserves to get her head in front. (tchd 7-1)
Chilledtothebone had a first-time visor replacing blinkers for this second outing and showed improved form, without looking at all straightforward. She has some ability and will find things easier when qualified for a mark after her next outing. (op 16-1)
Way Chief(FR) was prominent in the betting for this racecourse debut and ran a fair race. He too is bred to appreciate a stiffer test down the line and ought to improve for this experience. (op 4-1 tchd 9-2 in places)
Marc De Savoie(IRE) wasn't disgraced from his outside stall and this was just about his best effort to date. Nurseries are now an option for him. (op 20-1)
Katiesister was still green, but caught the eye a little by keeping on late from off the pace and can be ridden more positively over this longer trip in the future. She is one to look out for in nurseries, for which she is now qualified. (op 50-1)
Uptown Guy(USA) has to rate as disappointing. He again proved free and found very little when asked for an effort. He's in danger of becoming a very expensive acquisition, but could need more time and is at least eligible for nurseries now. (op 11-4 tchd 3-1 in places)
Deep Applause was the third in attendance from his stable and very much the outsider according to the betting. He got going late in the day over this stiffer test and is another to keep an eye on now he can enter nurseries. (op 16-1 tchd 20-1)

6139 SBS AYRSHIRE LTD NURSERY 6f
2:45 (2:45) (Class 3) (0-95,91) 2-Y-O **£6,476** (£1,927; £963; £481) **Stalls** High

Form RPR

1 **1** **Alben Star (IRE)**[81] 3498 2-9-0 84 .... PaulHanagan 4 95+
(R A Fahey) *in tch on outside: hdwy to ld over 1f out: sn drvn: hrd pressed ins fnl f: hld on wl* **1/1**[1]

1205 **2** nk **Drawing Board**[39] 4903 2-9-7 91 ....(b[1]) PhillipMakin 11 101
(K A Ryan) *hld up: hdwy over 1f out: ev ch and drvn fnl f: kpt on: hld towards fin* **33/1**

3214 **3** 3 **Malgoof (IRE)**[34] 5094 2-8-11 81 .... TomEaves 12 82
(B Smart) *trckd ldrs: effrt and led briefly over 1f out: kpt on same pce ins fnl f* **12/1**

0646 **4** 3 ¼ **Rothesay Chancer**[4] 6030 2-7-5 68 oh3 .... NeilFarley(7) 6 59
(J S Goldie) *hld up: rdn over 2f out: hdwy over 1f out: nvr rchd ldrs* **40/1**

1 **5** hd **Robert The Painter (IRE)**[20] 5531 2-8-7 82 .... LeeTopliss(5) 1 74
(R A Fahey) *sn pushed along in rr: nt clr run over 2f out: styd on ins fnl f: n.d* **7/1**[3]

1626 **6** 1 ½ **Blaze Of Thunder (IRE)**[17] 5637 2-8-9 79 .... AndrewElliott 7 65
(G A Swinbank) *in tch: hmpd and lost pl over 2f out: rallied appr fnl f: nvr able to chal* **25/1**

1532 **7** ¾ **Berberana (IRE)**[13] 5745 2-8-8 78 .... DavidAllan 2 62
(T D Easterby) *cl up: ev ch over 2f out: wknd appr fnl f* **11/4**[2]

6065 **8** 2 **Granny Anne (IRE)**[1] 6102 2-7-12 68 oh9 .... SilvestreDeSousa 3 46
(A Bailey) *dwlt: sn rdn in rr: hung lft 2f out: n.d* **50/1**

1333 **9** 1 ¼ **Madam Markievicz (IRE)**[26] 5334 2-7-13 69 ....(p) PaulQuinn 5 44
(M Dods) *towards rr: rdn whn nt clr run over 2f out: n.d* **50/1**

6004 **10** 1 ½ **Serena's Pride**[35] 5036 2-9-6 90 .... SebSanders 9 60
(A P Jarvis) *cl up: rdn over 2f out: wknd over 1f out* **16/1**

5012 **11** 9 **Bellemere**[21] 5483 2-7-13 72 .... JamesSullivan(3) 8 15
(M W Easterby) *cl up tl rdn and wknd 2f out* **50/1**

1000 **12** 1 ½ **Boundless Spirit**[41] 4831 2-8-12 82 .... AdrianNicholls 10 20
(D Nicholls) *led tl hdd and hmpd over 1f out: sn lost pl* **33/1**

1m 11.98s (-1.62) **Going Correction** -0.15s/f (Firm) **12** Ran SP% **120.8**
Speed ratings (Par 99): **104,103,99,95,95 93,92,89,87,85 73,71**
toteswingers:1&2 £13.00, 2&3 £42.20, 1&3 £6.40 CSF £53.18 CT £279.56 TOTE £2.30: £1.20, £6.80, £3.80; EX 39.70.
Owner J K Shannon & M A Scaife **Bred** Rathasker Stud **Trained** Musley Bank, N Yorks
■ Stewards' Enquiry : David Allan caution: careless riding.

FOCUS
This was a fair nursery and there was no hanging about, with the field coming stands' side. The first pair eventually came clear of the decent benchmark in third. The winner will not be out of place in Listed races.

NOTEBOOK
Alben Star(IRE) was having his first outing since justifying support on debut in a Musselburgh maiden in June that has worked out well. Sent off a warm order for this nursery debut, he was made to work hard to maintain his unbeaten record, but still emerges with a decent reputation. He wasn't helped by having to race without cover and displayed a very game attitude to fend off the runner-up. This was also a much stiffer test over the extra furlong here and he left the impression he would learn a bundle for this added experience. He came into this with a very similar profile to that of his stable's previous winner of this race, the ill-fated Utmost Respect, who later went on to win Group races for connections. Indeed he could well make up into a Pattern performer himself down the line and connections later said they may now put him away for the year. (tchd 10-11 and 11-10 in places)
Drawing Board went down fighting and finished nicely clear of the remainder. He travelled sweetly in mid-field and held every chance after coming through horses around 2f out. The first-time blinkers have to go down as having held the desired effect. (op 20-1)
Malgoof(IRE) had his chance against the stands' rail and gives the form a good look. He's a likeable colt and can find less competitive assignments. (op 11-1 tchd 10-1)
Rothesay Chancer, 3lb out of the handicap, was doing her best work late in the day and this was much her best form to date. She can certainly be found easier opportunities. (tchd 50-1)
Robert The Painter(IRE) came into this on the back of a debut maiden success, in his case over 6f at Redcar last month. He ran a good bit better than the bare form, not getting a good passage through the contest, and is definitely one to take from the race. (op 11-1 tchd 12-1)
Blaze Of Thunder(IRE), a former stablemate of the winner, lacked a change of pace and looks to need some respite from the handicapper. Official explanation: jockey said colt was denied a clear run (op 20-1)
Berberana(IRE) was cooked from the 2f marker and presumably something went amiss with her. (op 7-2)
Madam Markievicz(IRE) Official explanation: jockey said filly suffered interference in running
Boundless Spirit Official explanation: jockey said colt ran too free and hung left throughout

6140 BAM PROPERTIES H'CAP 5f
3:20 (3:21) (Class 4) (0-85,84) 3-Y-0+ **£5,180** (£1,541; £770; £384) **Stalls** Centre

Form RPR

3431 **1** **Hazelrigg (IRE)**[9] 5855 5-9-3 79 6ex ....(be) DavidAllan 16 96
(T D Easterby) *trckd ldrs: led jst ins fnl f: hung rt and wnt clr: eased nr fin* **10/3**[1]

0026 **2** 2 ¼ **Atlantic Beach**[5] 5999 5-8-11 73 ....(b) SilvestreDeSousa 13 82
(D O'Meara) *chsd ldrs: chal over 1f out: styd on to take 2nd jst ins fnl f: no ch w wnr* **9/1**

2021 **3** ½ **Mango Music**[1] 6103 7-8-8 75 6ex .... LeeTopliss(5) 17 82
(R A Fahey) *in tch: hdwy u.p 2f out: styd on to take 3rd ins fnl f* **7/2**[2]

6-01 **4** 1 ¼ **Silaah**[30] 5197 6-9-7 83 ....(p) AdrianNicholls 2 86+
(D Nicholls) *racd centre: trckd ldr: t.k.h: led that gp over 1f out: edgd rt and kpt on same pce* **8/1**[3]

6064 **5** shd **Le Toreador**[5] 5999 5-9-5 81 ....(bt) FrannyNorton 11 83
(K A Ryan) *overall ldr racing towards' stands' side: hdd jst ins fnl f: kpt on same pce* **10/1**

0503 **6** ¾ **Indian Trail**[9] 5855 10-9-1 80 ....(v) MichaelGeran(3) 9 80
(D Nicholls) *mid-div: hdwy over 1f out: kpt on: nvr trbld ldrs* **11/1**

0200 **7** 1 ¼ **Titus Andronicus (IRE)**[14] 5734 4-9-4 80 .... PaulHanagan 10 75
(R A Fahey) *trckd ldrs: effrt over 1f out: kpt on same pce* **14/1**

4-00 **8** hd **Blown It (USA)**[1] 6103 4-8-8 70 .... GregFairley 14 64
(J S Goldie) *towards rr: effrt over 2f out: kpt on: nvr nr ldrs* **33/1**

1654 **9** 1 **Galpin Junior (USA)**[20] 5513 4-8-9 71 .... PaulQuinn 1 62
(D Nicholls) *wnt rt s: racd centre: in rr: effrt 2f out: kpt on: nvr nr ldrs* **11/1**

1065 **10** hd **Ryan Style (IRE)**[27] 5297 4-9-3 79 .... TomEaves 4 69
(Mrs L Williamson) *dwlt: racd centre: in tch: effrt over 2f out: nvr rchd ldrs* **33/1**

0500 **11** ½ **Distant Sun (USA)**[1] 6103 6-8-6 71 oh1 ow2 .... BarryMcHugh(3) 5 59
(Miss L A Perratt) *s.s: swtchd rt after s: nvr on terms* **66/1**

00-0 **12** *shd* **Magic Cat**[20] 5528 4-9-6 **82** AndrewElliott 8 70
(Mrs K Burke) *towards rr: swtchd lft over 1f out: edgd lft: nvr nr ldrs* **33/1**
5240 **13** *1* **The Bear**[14] 5734 7-8-6 **71** JamesSullivan(3) 6 55
(Miss L A Perratt) *swvd lft s: led 5 others in centre: edgd rt and hdd that gp over 1f out: wknd ins fnl f* **28/1**
5015 **14** *2 3/4* **Lesley's Choice**[26] 5335 4-9-1 **77** (b) LNewman 12 51
(Miss L A Perratt) *chsd ldrs: lost pl over 1f out* **25/1**
0020 **15** *3/4* **Magical Macey (USA)**[29] 5250 3-9-7 **84** (b) PhillipMakin 7 56
(T D Barron) *racd centre: chsd ldrs: effrt over 2f out: edgd rt: wknd appr fnl f* **25/1**
0120 **16** *2 1/2* **Sir Geoffrey (IRE)**[14] 5734 4-8-11 **78** (b) DaleSwift(5) 15 41
(J A Glover) *chsd ldrs: lost pl over 1f out* **16/1**
3026 **17** *4 1/2* **Stolt (IRE)**[104] 2756 6-8-12 **74** ow1 SebSanders 3 21
(N Wilson) *w ldr centre: wknd over 1f out: eased* **50/1**

58.70 secs (-1.40) **Going Correction** -0.15s/f (Firm)
WFA 3 from 4yo+ 1lb **17** Ran SP% **128.1**
Speed ratings (Par 105): **105,101,100,98,98 97,95,94,93,93 92,92,90,86,84 80,73**
toteswingers:1&2 £11.10, 2&3 £13.50, 1&3 £3.50 CSF £32.32 CT £112.76 TOTE £4.30: £1.60, £3.20, £1.10, £2.90.
Owner The Senators **Bred** Rathbarry Stud **Trained** Great Habton, N Yorks

FOCUS
A competitive sprint for the class. The stalls were in the centre, but very much in keeping with the bias here the previous day those drawn high were at a real advantage. In the end stall 16, beat stalls 17, 13 and 2.The form is rated on the positive side with another clear personal best from the winner.
The Bear Official explanation: jockey said gelding hung right
Magical Macey(USA) Official explanation: jockey said gelding hung right

6141 ZENITH LTD REFURBISHMENT SPECIALISTS HARRY ROSEBERY STKS (SOUTH AYRSHIRE CUP) (LISTED RACE) 5f

3:55 (3:56) (Class 1) 2-Y-O

£15,327 (£5,810; £2,907; £1,449; £726; £364) **Stalls** High

Form RPR
160 **1** **Arctic Feeling (IRE)**[7] 5907 2-9-3 96 PaulHanagan 6 99
(R A Fahey) *in tch: hdwy over 1f out: led and hung lft ins fnl f: hld on wl u.p* **8/1**
0111 **2** *nk* **Krypton Factor**[6] 5965 2-9-3 91 (b) SebSanders 2 98
(Sir Mark Prescott) *sn prom: rdn along 1/2-way: effrt and ev ch ins fnl f: kpt on: hld cl home* **7/4**[1]
2235 **3** *1 1/2* **The Thrill Is Gone**[7] 5907 2-8-12 95 PhillipMakin 8 88
(M R Channon) *t.k.h: trckd ldrs: ev ch and rdn over 1f out: edgd lft: one pce ins fnl f* **5/2**[2]
0300 **4** *nk* **Move In Time**[8] 5880 2-9-3 92 TomEaves 5 91
(B Smart) *hld up: effrt on outside over 1f out: edgd rt: kpt on ins fnl f: nt gng pce to chal* **33/1**
2401 **5** *3/4* **Mappin Time (IRE)**[17] 5639 2-9-3 90 (b) DavidAllan 7 90
(T D Easterby) *sn drvn towards rr: nt clr run briefly 1/2-way: rdn and kpt on ins fnl f: no imp* **14/1**
0110 **6** *1/2* **Marlinka**[35] 5036 2-9-1 92 AdrianNicholls 9 85
(R Charlton) *led: rdn and hung lft over 1f out: hdd ins fnl f: sn btn* **7/1**[3]
0432 **7** *1/2* **Jamesway (IRE)**[6] 5939 2-9-3 89 BarryMcHugh 3 85
(R A Fahey) *hld up stands' rail: nt clr run over 2f out to over 1f out: no imp ins fnl f* **20/1**
1120 **8** *1 1/4* **Bold Bidder**[52] 4458 2-8-12 87 FrannyNorton 10 76
(K A Ryan) *prom tl rdn and wknd over 1f out* **18/1**
0413 **9** *5* **Julius Geezer (IRE)**[30] 5221 2-9-3 98 RichardKingscote 1 63
(Tom Dascombe) *trckd ldrs: drvn over 2f out: wknd wl over 1f out* **10/1**

59.35 secs (-0.75) **Going Correction** -0.15s/f (Firm) **9** Ran SP% **117.3**
Speed ratings (Par 103): **100,99,97,96,95 94,93,91,83**
toteswingers:1&2 £4.60, 2&3 £1.80, 1&3 £9.90 CSF £22.76 TOTE £8.70: £2.40, £1.10, £1.90.
Owner Percy/Green Racing 2 **Bred** John McEnery **Trained** Musley Bank, N Yorks

FOCUS
This wasn't a strong Listed event. There wasn't much between the field on official figures and, as expected, it was run at a frantic early pace. Despite the previous bias towards the nearside, the main action developed more towards the middle of the track. The race rather fell apart in front of the winner and the form is rated around the fourth and fifth.

NOTEBOOK
Arctic Feeling(IRE) got a strong ride from Paul Hanagan and handed another winner to his in-form stable. He met support on this drop down from Group company and enjoyed the way the race was run. He didn't help his cause by drifting markedly out towards his left under pressure, but was always just holding the runner-up at the business end. This has to rate as a career-best effort and he has developed into a likeable 2-y-o. (op 12-1)
Krypton Factor, making his debut in this grade, has been given a typically aggressive campaign by his trainer, and came into this having won five of his eight career starts. He was taken off his feet early on and came under pressure a fair way out, but kept responding to his rider's urgings. He only narrowly lost out and could nick one of these before the year is out. (op 15-8 tchd 2-1)
The Thrill Is Gone posted her best effort yet when a close fifth in the Flying Childers a week earlier and was well backed here. She held every chance, but ultimately paid for doing a bit too much through the early parts off the frantic gallop. She seems the best guide for the form. (op 7-2 tchd 9-4)
Move In Time, back down in trip, had to race wide with his challenge and this was a step back in the right direction, but he is not simple to place.
Mappin Time(IRE) hit a flat spot in between the final 2f before keeping on without posting a threat. (op 18-1)
Marlinka paid for her early exertions and really wants a sharper 5f. Official explanation: jockey said filly hung left-handed throughout (op 6-1 tchd 11-2)
Julius Geezer(IRE) put in a lifeless effort. Official explanation: jockey said colt ran too freely (op 15-2)

6142 WILLIAM HILL (AYR) BRONZE CUP (H'CAP) 6f

4:30 (4:30) (Class 2) 3-Y-O+

£15,577 (£4,665; £2,332; £1,167; £582; £292) **Stalls** Centre

Form RPR
652 **1** **Cheveton**[6] 5966 6-9-1 **85** DaleSwift(5) 25 101
(R J Price) *cl up stands' side: led wl over 1f out: edgd lft: hrd pressed ins fnl f: hld on wl: 1st of 14 in gp* **11/1**
0403 **2** *hd* **Courageous (IRE)**[13] 5742 4-9-2 **86** BillyCray(5) 22 101
(D Nicholls) *midfield stands' side: effrt over 1f out: edgd lft and chal ins fnl f: kpt on: jst hld: 2nd of 14 in gp* **13/2**[2]
0-00 **3** *1 1/2* **Mastership (IRE)**[27] 5302 6-8-12 **82** (p) IanBrennan(5) 12 92+
(J J Quinn) *bhd stands' side: nt clr run briefly over 2f out: hdwy over 1f out: styd on fnl f: nt rch first two: 3rd of 14 in gp* **20/1**
0000 **4** *1 3/4* **Everymanforhimself (IRE)**[8] 5884 6-9-6 **85** (b) AndrewMullen 26 90
(K A Ryan) *trckd stands' side ldrs: effrt over 2f out: kpt on u.p ins fnl f: 4th of 14 in gp* **33/1**
1453 **5** *1/2* **Ancient Cross**[8] 5884 6-9-5 **84** (t) GrahamGibbons 1 87+
(M W Easterby) *in tch gng wl far side: shkn up to ld that gp ins fnl f: kpt on: nt rch stands' side ldrs: 1st of 13 in gp* **18/1**
-400 **6** *shd* **Eton Rifles (IRE)**[41] 4843 5-9-8 **87** TomEaves 10 90
(J Howard Johnson) *cl up far side: led that gp over 2f out to ins fnl f: kpt on u.p: 2nd of 13 in gp* **40/1**
1204 **7** *hd* **Beat The Bell**[14] 5734 5-9-5 **84** PhillipMakin 8 86
(T D Barron) *trckd far side ldrs: effrt and ev ch that gp ins fnl f: r.o: 3rd of 13 in gp* **25/1**
1001 **8** *1 1/2* **Northern Fling**[35] 5043 6-9-4 **86** GaryBartley(3) 16 83
(J S Goldie) *dwlt: bhd stands' side: gd hdwy over 1f out: nrst fin: 5th of 14 in gp* **28/1**
-015 **9** *hd* **Great Charm (IRE)**[7] 5903 5-9-2 **81** AndrewElliott 27 78
(E J Alston) *led stands' side to wl over 1f out: kpt on same pce: 6th of 14 in gp* **20/1**
0333 **10** *1/2* **The Nifty Fox**[14] 5734 6-9-6 **85** DavidAllan 3 80
(T D Easterby) *trckd far side ldrs: effrt and rdn over 1f out: kpt on same pce ins fnl f: 4th of 13 in gp* **33/1**
2144 **11** *nse* **Tyfos**[15] 5678 5-9-5 **84** PaulQuinn 2 79
(B P J Baugh) *trckd far side ldrs: rdn over 2f out: kpt on same pce ins fnl f: 5th of 13 in gp* **66/1**
0452 **12** *3/4* **Coolminx (IRE)**[5] 6000 3-9-5 **86** PaulHanagan 23 78
(R A Fahey) *trckd stands' side ldrs: drvn over 2f out: sn outpcd: no imp fnl f: 7th of 14 in gp* **6/1**[1]
4640 **13** *nse* **Medici Time**[13] 5742 5-9-5 **84** (v) DavidNolan 24 76
(T D Easterby) *bhd stands' side: drvn over 2f out: sme late hdwy: nvr rchd ldrs: 8th of 14 in gp* **25/1**
/060 **14** *hd* **Marvellous Value (IRE)**[9] 5855 5-9-1 **83** PatrickDonaghy(3) 18 75
(M Dods) *midfield stands' side: rdn whn n.m.r over 2f out: edgd lft over 1f out: nvr able to chal: 9th of 14 in gp* **25/1**
0520 **15** *shd* **Roker Park (IRE)**[8] 5884 5-9-2 **84** (p) AmyRyan(3) 14 75
(K A Ryan) *swtchd to far side gp after 1f: bhd tl hdwy over 1f out: nrst fin: 6th of 13 in gp* **33/1**
430 **16** *1/2* **Internationaldebut (IRE)**[6] 5937 5-9-1 **85** DeclanCannon(5) 5 75
(P T Midgley) *dwlt: bhd far side: hdwy over 2f out: kpt on same pce ins fnl f: 7th of 13 in gp* **33/1**
0000 **17** *nk* **Saucy Brown (IRE)**[20] 5510 4-9-3 **82** FrannyNorton 20 71
(D Nicholls) *in tch stands' side: rdn over 2f out: no ex over 1f out: 10th of 14 in gp* **28/1**
4345 **18** *hd* **Haajes**[13] 5742 6-9-4 **86** PaulPickard(3) 17 74
(P T Midgley) *hld up stands' side: effrt over 2f out: sn no imp: 11th of 14 in gp* **33/1**
0004 **19** *hd* **Sunrise Safari (IRE)**[8] 5884 7-9-3 **82** (v) DanielTudhope 6 69
(R A Fahey) *midfield far side: rdn over 2f out: wknd over 1f out: 8th of 13 in gp* **40/1**
1216 **20** *1 1/4* **Barren Brook**[1] 6105 3-9-0 **84** JamesSullivan(3) 15 67
(M W Easterby) *racd on outside of stands' side gp: towards rr: struggling over 2f out: sn btn: 12th of 14 in gp* **40/1**
0060 **21** *2 3/4* **Oldjoesaid**[9] 5855 6-9-4 **83** (t) SilvestreDeSousa 13 58
(K A Ryan) *swtchd to far side sn after s: hld up: rdn over 2f out: nvr able to chal: 9th of 13 in gp* **16/1**
22 *3/4* **Empirico (FR)**[67] 3997 4-9-5 **84** GregFairley 7 56
(David Marnane, Ire) *t.k.h: led far side to over 2f out: wknd over 1f out: 10th of 13 in gp* **14/1**
0003 **23** *nk* **Baldemar**[46] 4653 5-9-6 **88** BarryMcHugh(3) 19 59
(R A Fahey) *racd on outside of stands' side gp: towards rr: struggling over 2f out: sn btn: 13th of 14 in gp* **10/1**[3]
0050 **24** *nk* **Valery Borzov (IRE)**[12] 5787 6-9-2 **88** NeilFarley(7) 9 58
(R A Fahey) *towards rr far side: drvn and struggling over 2f out: sn btn: 11th of 13 in gp* **20/1**
1201 **25** *1* **Jeannie Galloway (IRE)**[29] 5242 3-9-2 **88** LeeTopliss(5) 4 55
(R A Fahey) *cl up far side tl rdn and wknd fr 2f out: 12th of 13 in gp* **16/1**
5111 **26** *1/2* **Amenable (IRE)**[18] 5606 3-9-8 **89** 5ex AdrianNicholls 21 55
(D Nicholls) *cl up stands' side tl rdn and wknd over 1f out: last of 14 in gp* **14/1**
6631 **27** *1* **Ginger Ted (IRE)**[18] 5601 3-9-0 **84** 5ex (p) AndrewHeffernan(3) 11 46
(R C Guest) *swtchd to r far side sn after s: bhd: drvn over 2f out: sn btn: last of 13 in gp* **28/1**

1m 11.41s (-2.19) **Going Correction** -0.15s/f (Firm)
WFA 3 from 4yo+ 2lb **27** Ran SP% **135.1**
Speed ratings (Par 109): **108,107,105,103,102 102,102,100,100,99 99,98,98,98,97 97,96,96,96,94 90,89,89,89,87 87,85**
toteswingers:1&2 £5.80, 2&3 £100.00, 1&3 £153.80 CSF £64.55 CT £1487.40 TOTE £12.70: £3.40, £2.40, £7.50, £12.70; EX 70.10.
Owner Mrs K Oseman **Bred** Miss K Rausing **Trained** Ullingswick, H'fords

FOCUS
The second running of the consolation race for those that failed to make the cut for the Silver Cup, which is obviously the first consolation race for the Gold Cup. With the strong bias on the stands' side in previous sprints here this week, those drawn high were expected to come out on top, in total contrast to last year's race. It played out so, as the first four raced on the nearside despite the far side group going off at a strong pace, and the first two came clear in a tight finish. The winner ran his best race since late last year, and overall the form could have been rated higher.

NOTEBOOK
Cheveton belatedly opened his account for the year and completed the task in tenacious fashion. He has often seemed happiest over the minimum trip, but the way he finished over that distance when second on his previous outing strongly suggested stepping back up here would be to his liking. The ground was just easy enough for him and there was a lot to like about his attitude when pressed by the runner-up. It was his tenth outing of the season and he raced off a mark 12lb lower than when resuming this year, so he will still look fairly treated after being reassessed. (op 12-1 tchd 10-1)
Courageous(IRE) warmed up for this with a promising effort off this mark over 5f on his previous outing, and looked sure to enjoy this greater test. He didn't get the breaks when trying to improve from off the pace, though, and the winner got first run on him. He closed quickly on that rival when out in the clear and still had his chance, but Cheveton pulled out that bit more where it mattered. With a clearer passage, however, he would've likely won and, while he will go up for this, he deserves another chance. (tchd 6-1)
Mastership(IRE) finished close up in the Silver Cup last year. He enjoyed the decent pace on and posted his best effort of the season. He showed his customary high head-carriage when under pressure and isn't an easy horse to win with, but is well handicapped if consenting to build on this. (tchd 22-1 and 25-1 in a place)
Everymanforhimself(IRE) was the subject of a sizeable gamble when disappointing at Doncaster the previous week. This was a lot more like it from him, however, and he looks well worth another try at 7f.
Ancient Cross travelled strongly and just edged it on the far-side group. He remains in decent heart. (op 20-1)
Eton Rifles(IRE) was always to the fore and this was a definite return to form, so he is one to bear in mind next time out.

Beat The Bell was the other close up on the far side and posted a solid effort back over this stiffer test. He could still be weighted to go in when reverting to a slightly sharper test. (op 33-1)
Coolminx(IRE) came into this in decent form and was an unfortunate loser at Newcastle on testing ground five days earlier. She came under pressure a long way out, however, and presumably found it coming too soon. (op 8-1)
Baldemar was reported to have run flat. Official explanation: jockey said gelding ran flat (op 11-1 tchd 12-1)
Amenable(IRE) was chasing a four-timer under a penalty and dropped right out from the 2f marker. He was later reported to have hung right. Official explanation: jockey said gelding hung right (tchd 12-1)

6143 INVESTEC STRUCTURED PRODUCTS H'CAP (FOR THE EGLINTON & WINTON CHALLENGE CUP) 2m 1f 105y

5:05 (5:05) (Class 4) (0-85,82) 4-Y-O+ **£5,180** (£1,541; £770; £384) **Stalls** Low

Form RPR

0261 **1** **Descaro (USA)**[17] 5642 4-8-2 **63** SilvestreDeSousa 4 77+
(D O'Meara) *hld up in rr: smooth hdwy to trck ldrs over 2f out: led on bit appr fnl f: v cheekily* **6/4**[1]

2544 **2** *3/4* **Tillietudlem (FR)**[21] 5497 4-8-6 **67** PaulHanagan 6 74
(J S Goldie) *trckd ldr: chal 7f out: led over 4f out: hdd appr fnl f: no match* **10/3**[2]

66-3 **3** *1 3/4* **Summer Soul (IRE)**[81] 3496 8-8-0 **64** (p) JamesSullivan(3) 2 69
(Miss Lucinda V Russell) *chsd ldrs: sn drvn along: kpt on same pce appr fnl f* **7/1**

3235 **4** *2* **Forrest Flyer (IRE)**[28] 5278 6-8-11 **72** LNewman 5 75
(J S Goldie) *hld up in rr: effrt over 4f out: one pce fnl 2f* **8/1**

120 **5** *21* **Wicked Daze (IRE)**[12] 5788 7-9-7 **82** PhillipMakin 3 62
(Miss L A Perratt) *led: hdd 4f out: wknd 2f out: eased towards fin* **9/2**[3]

500/ **6** *40* **Whispering Death**[338] 4439 8-9-5 **80** TomEaves 1 16
(J Howard Johnson) *trckd ldrs: drvn over 3f out: hung lft and sn lost pl: t.o: virtually p.u* **25/1**

3m 53.54s (-6.96) **Going Correction** -0.275s/f (Firm) **6 Ran SP% 108.7**
Speed ratings (Par 105): **105,104,103,102,93 74**
CSF £6.17 TOTE £2.50: £1.40, £2.60; EX 4.40.
Owner R Fell & K Everitt **Bred** Langley House Stud **Trained** Nawton, N Yorks

FOCUS
A fair staying handicap, run at an even pace despite the small field size. The winner looked to have plenty in hand and looks one to follow in the short term.

6144 JOHN SMITH'S H'CAP 1m

5:40 (5:40) (Class 5) (0-70,76) 3-Y-O **£3,238** (£963; £481; £240) **Stalls** Low

Form RPR

5204 **1** **Opening Nite (IRE)**[24] 5394 3-9-3 **66** (b[1]) PaulHanagan 1 75
(R A Fahey) *in tch: effrt over 2f out: edgd lft over 1f out: styd on wl ins fnl f: led post* **15/2**

6640 **2** *nse* **Hades (IRE)**[21] 5479 3-8-10 **59** DavidAllan 12 68
(T D Easterby) *cl up: rdn to ld over 1f out: edgd lft ins fnl f: kpt on wl: hdd post* **13/2**[3]

3355 **3** *4* **North Central (USA)**[21] 5479 3-9-0 **63** LNewman 14 63
(J S Goldie) *prom: drvn over 2f out: kpt on ins fnl f: nt rch first two* **20/1**

2215 **4** *hd* **Viking Warrior (IRE)**[21] 5484 3-9-5 **68** PhillipMakin 7 67+
(M Dods) *hld up: hmpd after 2f: rdn and hdwy over 1f out: nrst fin* **14/1**

4454 **5** *2 1/2* **Spread Boy (IRE)**[26] 5337 3-9-0 **63** DanielTudhope 9 56
(A Berry) *cl up tl rdn and wknd over 1f out* **22/1**

4023 **6** *1* **Blue Moon**[13] 5766 3-8-12 **61** FrannyNorton 3 52
(K A Ryan) *towards rr: hmpd after 2f: effrt over 1f out: nvr able to chal* **4/1**[2]

1311 **7** *3/4* **Miami Gator (IRE)**[9] 5852 3-9-13 **76** 6ex (v) AndrewElliott 6 65
(Mrs K Burke) *led tl hdd over 1f out: sn btn* **3/1**[1]

4053 **8** *hd* **Petrocelli**[13] 5758 3-8-8 **60** JamesSullivan(3) 11 49
(W Storey) *in tch tl rdn and wknd over 1f out* **25/1**

4205 **9** *3 3/4* **Tribal Myth (IRE)**[39] 4898 3-8-11 **63** AmyRyan(3) 10 43
(K A Ryan) *t.k.h: prom: rdn over 2f out: wknd over 1f out* **11/1**

5523 **10** *hd* **Leitzu (IRE)**[18] 5598 3-8-13 **62** TomEaves 4 42
(M R Channon) *trckd ldrs tl rdn and wknd wl over 1f out* **10/1**

640 **11** *2 3/4* **Wolf Rock**[27] 5303 3-8-10 **59** GrahamGibbons 13 33
(T D Barron) *bhd: rdn over 2f out: nvr on terms* **20/1**

4350 **12** *3 3/4* **Big Wave Bay (IRE)**[16] 5656 3-9-0 **63** GregFairley 2 28
(A P Jarvis) *bhd and sn pushed along: nvr on terms* **16/1**

0460 **13** *15* **Jibrrya**[29] 5241 3-9-2 **65** AdrianNicholls 8 —
(D Nicholls) *dwlt: hld up: effrt on outside over 2f out: no imp over 1f out* **20/1**

660- **14** *3 1/2* **Lofthouse**[308] 7363 3-8-7 **59** BarryMcHugh(3) 5 —
(A C Whillans) *midfield: outpcd over 2f out: sn btn* **66/1**

1m 40.99s (-2.81) **Going Correction** -0.275s/f (Firm) **14 Ran SP% 124.0**
Speed ratings (Par 101): **103,102,98,98,96 95,94,94,90,90 87,83,68,65**
toteswingers:1&2 £7.40, 2&3 £41.10, 1&3 £26.20. totesuper7: Win: Not won. Place: Not won. CSF £51.67 CT £987.23 TOTE £10.40: £2.90, £2.30, £6.80; EX 76.00 Place 6: £28.44 Place 5: £7.20.
Owner Peter O'Callaghan **Bred** Conor Murphy & Rathmore Stud **Trained** Musley Bank, N Yorks
■ Stewards' Enquiry : L Newman three-day ban: careless riding (Oct 4-6)
David Allan two-day ban: used whip with excessive frequency (Oct 4-5)

FOCUS
This moderate handicap was run at a solid pace and the first pair came clear in a desperately tight finish. The first two are on the upgrade, with the next two setting the standard.
Jibrrya Official explanation: jockey said gelding hung right-handed throughout
T/Jkpt: Not won. T/Plt: £86.90 to a £1 stake. Pool of £83,160.97 - 697.91 winning tickets. T/Qpdt: £13.30 to a £1 stake. Pool of £7,654.39 - 425.75 winning tickets. RY

5078 NEWBURY (L-H)

Friday, September 17

OFFICIAL GOING: Good (good to firm in places)
Rail realignment increased distances on round course by about 12metres.
Wind: Virtually nil Weather: Cloudy

6145 MALONE ROOFING E B F MAIDEN STKS (DIV I) 6f 8y

1:30 (1:30) (Class 4) 2-Y-O **£4,857** (£1,445; £722; £360) **Stalls** Centre

Form RPR

1 **Dark Secret** 2-9-3 0 LukeMorris 1 78+
(J R Gask) *s.i.s: in rr: rdn and green ins fnl 3f: drvn and styd on over 1f out: str run ins fnl f to ld fnl 50yds: won gng away* **40/1**

02 **2** *3/4* **Enlightening (IRE)**[16] 5651 2-9-3 0 PatDobbs 3 76+
(R Hannon) *led: pushed along ins fnl 2f: strly chal ins fnl f: hdd and outpcd fnl 50yds* **15/8**[1]

3 *1 1/4* **Poppy** 2-8-12 0 JimmyFortune 2 67+
(R Hannon) *s.i.s: sn in tch: pushed along: hung lft and green fr 2f out: stl green: kpt on wl to take 3rd wl ins fnl f* **10/1**

540 **4** *nk* **Proper Charlie**[25] 5372 2-9-3 72 NeilCallan 4 71
(W J Knight) *chsd ldr: drvn and str chal fr jst ins fnl f and stl upsides fnl 100yds: wknd and lost two pls fnl 50yds* **7/1**[3]

5 *1 3/4* **Khaleeji** 2-9-3 0 RichardHills 7 66
(J W Hills) *stdd in rr s: hdwy and hung lft over 1f out: kpt on and hung lft again wl ins fnl f: kpt on cl home* **25/1**

0 **6** *2 1/4* **Tony Hollis**[63] 4096 2-9-3 0 IanMongan 5 59
(B R Millman) *plld hrd and chsd ldrs tl stdd after 2f: styd in tch: rdn 2f out: sn one pce* **100/1**

0 **7** *hd* **Mister Ben Vereen**[16] 5657 2-9-3 0 RichardMullen 10 59
(Eve Johnson Houghton) *t.k.h: sn stdd off pce: in tch: pushed along 2f out: kpt on fnl f: nvr gng pce to get into contention* **16/1**

8 *1/2* **Commended** 2-9-3 0 MichaelHills 8 57+
(B W Hills) *in rr: pushed along over 2f out: sme prog ins fnl f* **7/2**[2]

9 *1 3/4* **Captain Noble (IRE)** 2-9-3 0 FergusSweeney 12 52
(P J Makin) *s.i.s: sn chsng ldrs: rdn over 2f out: wknd appr fnl f* **14/1**

0 **10** *2 3/4* **Silbury (IRE)**[35] 5029 2-8-12 0 SteveDrowne 6 39
(R Charlton) *plld hrd: chsd ldrs 4f* **10/1**

11 *1* **Fire N'Brimstone** 2-9-3 0 TravisBlock 9 41
(Mouse Hamilton-Fairley) *outpcd most of way* **100/1**

12 *7* **Spirit Of Gondree (IRE)** 2-9-3 0 TedDurcan 11 20
(J L Dunlop) *in rr and v green thrght* **16/1**

1m 15.27s (2.27) **Going Correction** +0.125s/f (Good) **12 Ran SP% 114.4**
Speed ratings (Par 97): **89,88,86,85,83 80,80,79,77,73 72,63**
toteswingers:1&2 £28.50, 2&3 £2.60, 1&3 £63.30 CSF £110.33 TOTE £41.00: £8.70, £1.10, £3.10; EX 158.80 TRIFECTA Not won. .
Owner Carmel Stud **Bred** Carmel Stud **Trained** Sutton Veny, Wilts

FOCUS
Conditions were drying out and the official going description was amended from good all over before racing. Some riders felt that the ground was on the fast side of good. Probably just a modest maiden for the track, this was run at a very steady pace and a number pulled for their heads in the first half of the race. The time was almost four seconds outside the standard and the form may be worth treating with a little caution. The field raced down the centre and, interestingly, the first four home came from the four lowest stalls.

NOTEBOOK
Dark Secret's yard has had very little success with juveniles and this one, who is already gelded, has a modest pedigree, so it was no surprise he went off the price he did. Green early on, after standing still as the stalls opened, he was being ridden along by halfway but came with a strong run down the outer inside the last to win going away. He looked to have a bit up his sleeve in the end and this was a decent effort considering the lack of pace in the race. (op 50-1)
Enlightening(IRE)'s trainer won a division of this in 2007 with Paco Boy, the best recent winner of this event. Dropped in trip after being worn down over 7f at Brighton, the favourite set a sedate pace in front and saw off a couple of challengers before the winner went past him late on. His sheepskin noseband slipped out of position early in the race but it did not seem to affect him unduly. His dam is a half-sister to the very speedy sprinter Morinqua and he might be worth a try over the minimum trip. (op 13-8 tchd 2-1 in a place)
Poppy, the runner-up's stablemate, was another to dwell in the stalls. She carried her head to one side but was keeping on quite nicely at the end. She is sprint bred and best kept to this sort of trip. (op 8-1 tchd 11-1)
Proper Charlie was the most experienced in the field and looks the best guide to the level of the form. With the tongue tie discarded and back on a sound surface, he had every chance and showed a game attitude in defeat, but he may remain vulnerable to less exposed opponents. (op 15-2 tchd 8-1)
Khaleeji, a half-brother to a couple of modest winners, shaped with promise and should come on for this sympathetic introduction. (op 22-1)
Tony Hollis showed more than he had on his previous racecourse visits, down the field behind Waiter's Dream over 7f here and withdrawn when breaking out of the stalls at Windsor. However, he may have been flattered by the slowly-run nature of this race.
Mister Ben Vereen became fractious beforehand. He could never make an impact, but confirmed the impression of his debut that he has ability. (op 12-1)
Commended, a half-brother to useful miler Perfect Star who holds a Middle Park Stakes entry, will have to show more. (op 3-1 tchd 11-4)

6146 MALONE ROOFING E B F MAIDEN STKS (DIV II) 6f 8y

2:00 (2:02) (Class 4) 2-Y-O **£4,857** (£1,445; £722; £360) **Stalls** Centre

Form RPR

22 **1** **Enthusing (IRE)**[35] 5053 2-9-3 74 DaneO'Neill 1 77
(D R C Elsworth) *chsd ldrs: drvn to chal ins fnl f: slt ld fnl 120yds: hung rt u.p cl home: jst hld on* **3/1**[2]

43 **2** *nse* **Jinky**[10] 5835 2-9-3 0 SamHitchcott 7 77
(M R Channon) *sn led: jnd 1f out: kpt on u.p: narrowly hdd fnl 120yds: rallied gamely cl home: nt quite get up* **12/1**

3 *1* **Expose** 2-9-3 0 ShaneKelly 9 74+
(W J Haggas) *t.k.h: hld up towards rr: in tch: gd prog fr 2f out: qcknd to chal 1f out and styd upsides fnl 120yds tl fdd and squeezed out cl home* **9/2**[3]

3 **4** *2 1/4* **Apollo D'Negro (IRE)**[54] 4396 2-8-12 0 JohnFahy(5) 8 67
(C G Cox) *awkward leaving stalls: sn chsng ldrs: drvn fr over 2f out and kpt in fnl f: nvr gng pce of ldng trio* **11/4**[1]

0 **5** *hd* **Danceyourselfdizzy (IRE)**[37] 4954 2-9-3 0 JimmyFortune 10 67
(R Hannon) *chsd ldrs: rdn over 2f out: styd on same pce ins fnl f* **18/1**

6 *1/2* **Dazzling Diamond** 2-9-3 0 MichaelHills 6 65+
(B W Hills) *s.i.s: t.k.h and green in rr: stl plenty to do over 2f out: hung lft and hdwy over 1f out: kpt on wl ins fnl f: nvr a threat* **16/1**

0 **7** *3/4* **Special Endeavour (IRE)**[25] 5372 2-9-3 0 RichardMullen 4 63
(W R Muir) *chsd ldrs: rdn over 2f out: wknd 1f out* **100/1**

8 *1/2* **Conducting** 2-9-3 0 MartinDwyer 11 61
(B J Meehan) *unruly stalls: in rr: green and hung lft over 2f out: shkn up and kpt on ins fnl f* **14/1**

9 *nk* **Piccolete** 2-8-12 0 PatDobbs 2 55+
(R Hannon) *rrd stalls: bhd: hdwy fr 2f out: styd on same pce ins fnl f* **18/1**

10 *1 3/4* **Redvers (IRE)** 2-9-3 0 GeorgeBaker 12 55+
(R M Beckett) *in rr: rdn and green whn sme hdwy over 2f out: sn outpcd* **6/1**

11 *3/4* **Wong Again** 2-8-12 0 RichardHills 3 48
(J W Hills) *chsd ldrs: pushed along and green 1/2-way: wknd over 1f out* **33/1**

65 **12** ¾ **Paris Is Burning**[107] 2642 2-8-12 0.................................... LukeMorris 5 46
(J S Moore) *chsd ldrs 4f* **40/1**

1m 14.94s (1.94) **Going Correction** +0.125s/f (Good) **12** Ran SP% **121.3**
Speed ratings (Par 97): **92,91,90,87,87 86,85,85,84,82 81,80**
toteswingers:1&2 £5.60, 2&3 £18.30, 1&3 £3.90 CSF £39.96 TOTE £3.00: £1.10, £4.20, £2.60; EX 31.20 Trifecta £138.20 Pool: £276.53 - 1.48 winning units..
Owner Ben CM Wong **Bred** Paul Kavanagh **Trained** Newmarket, Suffolk

FOCUS
The quicker and probably the better of the two divisions, but still not form as strong as you might expect for the track. The first three finished clear and the winner is rated to his mark.

NOTEBOOK
Enthusing(IRE), who had finished second on each of his first three outings, got off the mark by the skin of his teeth. Racing from stall 1, like the winner of the opener, he took a narrow lead late on but edged right and the runner-up was rallying in the last strides. A nursery type with a BHA rating of 74 before this, he clearly handles fast ground but again gave the impression that he might appreciate easier conditions. (tchd 11-4)
Jinky broke a lot better this time and seemed to appreciate being able to bowl along in front. After being headed inside the last, he nearly pulled the race out of the fire late on. He should find a winning opportunity, either at this trip or 7f. (tchd 11-1)
Expose, a half-brother to several winning sprinters from the family of Sussex Stakes winner Court Masterpiece, made a very pleasing debut. After making smooth progress, he looked set to win at one stage but was just held when he was squeezed out between the first two late on. A maiden should come his way. (op 5-1 tchd 4-1)
Apollo D'Negro(IRE) ran respectably without really building on what he had shown on his debut at Ascot in July. It could be that he is not entirely straightforward. (op 10-3 tchd 4-1)
Danceyourselfdizzy(IRE) showed more than he had behind stablemate Big Issue on his Salisbury debut but did not convince that he wanted this drop in trip. (op 20-1)
Dazzling Diamond ◆ was keeping on nicely from the back and should benefit from the run. (op 14-1)
Special Endeavour(IRE) travelled quite well on this second start before dropping away.
Piccolete, a half-sister to smart sprinter Edge Closer out of an unbeaten 2-y-o, could never get into it after rearing as the stalls opened. (tchd 20-1)
Redvers(IRE), a half-brother to both Listed 2-y-o scorer Sir Xaar and Chester Cup winner Mamlook, was not well drawn for this debut and ran as if in need of the experience. (op 7-1 tchd 15-2)

6147 DUBAI DUTY FREE CUP (LISTED RACE) 7f (S)
2:35 (2:35) (Class 1) 3-Y-O+

£19,869 (£7,532; £3,769; £1,879; £941; £472) **Stalls** Centre

Form RPR
135- **1** **Delegator**[314] 7308 4-9-2 121.................................... TedDurcan 3 116+
(Saeed Bin Suroor) *hld up in rr: stdy hdwy on outside fr 3f out: drvn to ld ins fnl f: r.o gamely whn 2nd attempted to bite cl home* **3/1**[2]
0060 **2** *nk* **Sir Gerry (USA)**[13] 5744 5-9-2 103.................................... GeorgeBaker 2 115
(C A Dwyer) *plld hrd and hld up in rr: stdy hdwy on outside fr 2f out: rdn and qcknd fnl 100yds: upsides whn tried to bite wnr cl home: jst failed* **33/1**
1-03 **3** *shd* **Awzaan**[13] 5741 3-8-13 112.................................... RichardHills 4 114
(M Johnston) *in rr tl hdwy fr 3f out: chsd ldrs over 1f out: edgd rt and styd on strly ins fnl f: gng on cl to home to press fr 2nd: nt quite gng pce of wnr* **7/2**[3]
520- **4** 2¼ **Huntdown (USA)**[349] 6487 4-9-2 111.................................... JamieSpencer 8 109
(Saeed Bin Suroor) *led tl hdd ins fnl f: wknd fnl 120yds* **16/1**
-000 **5** 1½ **Finjaan**[34] 5081 4-9-2 112.................................... TadhgO'Shea 7 105
(M P Tregoning) *s.i.s: in rr: hdwy over 2f out: styd on ins fnl f: nvr gng pce to get into contention* **16/1**
-641 **6** 1½ **Ashram (IRE)**[18] 5609 4-9-2 110..........................(v) DaraghO'Donohoe 12 101
(Saeed Bin Suroor) *chsd ldrs: rdn over 2f out: wknd appr fnl f* **14/1**
3020 **7** 3 **Dunelight (IRE)**[52] 4457 7-9-2 105....................................(v) LukeMorris 9 93+
(C G Cox) *slowly away and lost 6 l s: sn latched on to main gp: stl last 2f out: rdn and styd on sn after and kpt on ins fnl f: nvr any ch* **20/1**
204 **8** *nk* **Palace Moon**[26] 5275 5-9-2 109....................................(t) ShaneKelly 13 100+
(W J Knight) *in rr: hdwy and in tch 1/2-way: styng on whn hmpd over 1f out: keeping on again whn v bdly hmpd ins fnl f: nt rcvr* **12/1**
9 *hd* **Code Of War (USA)**[34] 4-9-2 93.................................... JimmyFortune 10 91
(A De Royer-Dupre, France) *plld hrd: chsd ldrs: rdn and hld whn hmpd over 1f out: wknd ins fnl f* **25/1**
0300 **10** *shd* **Mon Cadeaux**[20] 5526 3-8-13 95.................................(v^1) MartinDwyer 11 90
(A M Balding) *plld hrd: chsd ldrs tl wknd over 1f out* **66/1**
-006 **11** *hd* **Prince Of Dance**[19] 5554 4-9-2 102....................................(t) SteveDrowne 6 91
(J R Gask) *chsd ldrs: chal fr 3f out tl wknd insde fnl 2f* **28/1**
2141 **12** 5 **Yaa Wayl (IRE)**[28] 5275 3-8-13 115.................................... NeilCallan 1 76
(M A Jarvis) *chsd ldrs: rdn over 2f out: wkng whn hmpd over 1f out: no ch whn hung rt ins fnl f* **11/4**[1]
250/ **13** *nk* **Alhaban (IRE)**[719] 6317 4-9-2 100.................................... TomMcLaughlin 15 76
(R A Harris) *chsd ldrs 5f* **100/1**
0324 **14** 7 **Aldovrandi (IRE)**[19] 5554 3-8-13 105.................................... MircoDemuro 14 56
(M Botti) *plld hrd: chsd ldrs over 4f* **16/1**

1m 24.2s (-1.50) **Going Correction** +0.125s/f (Good)
WFA 3 from 4yo+ 3lb **14** Ran SP% **123.4**
Speed ratings (Par 111): **113,112,112,109,108 106,103,102,102,102 102,96,96,88**
toteswingers:1&2 £32.40, 2&3 £34.70, 1&3 £3.60 CSF £115.28 TOTE £4.00: £1.50, £6.20, £2.20; EX 143.10 Trifecta £667.80 Part won. Pool of £902.52 - 0.10 winning units..
Owner Godolphin **Bred** Mrs P Good **Trained** Newmarket, Suffolk

FOCUS
A competitive Listed race, and while there were no runners with a Group-race penalty this looks strong form for the grade. the winner is rated 7lb off his 3yo best. The pace was sound. The first three were all drawn low and came from the rear of the field down the outside.

NOTEBOOK
Delegator had not run since last autumn's Breeders' Cup, sore shins and a troublesome wart keeping him off the track this year. Dropped back in trip after running over a mile for the whole of last season, he travelled nicely off the pace before coming through for a narrow win. Although he was entitled to win being 6lb clear on official ratings, this was a decent performance as he was reported likely to come on for the run. The Group 2 Challenge Stakes over this trip at Newmarket next month looks a suitable target, and if that goes well then he has options at the Breeders' Cup and in Hong Kong later in the year. He could drop back to 6f but his days of racing over a mile look to be over. (op 10-3 tchd 7-2)
Sir Gerry(USA) ran in the Haydock Sprint Cup as if worth another try at this trip. After taking a pull he was finishing strongly from the back, and things might have been interesting had he not paused to aim a bite at the winner late on. His trainer has a race at Ascot in mind for him.
Awzaan was third over 1m in this grade on his return to action at Haydock and he improved for the run, holding every chance and going down fighting. This dispels any lingering suspicions that he had not trained on and he will be a force for the rest of the season over this trip or 1m. (op 4-1 tchd 3-1)
Huntdown(USA), the winner's stablemate, ran well on this belated return to action and was not given a hard time once headed. He seems to like Newbury in September as he was runner-up in this event 12 months ago and gained his only win to date in the 6f maiden on this card as a 2-y-o. (op 18-1 tchd 20-1)
Finjaan was never close enough to get in a blow, but this rates a step up on his recent efforts.
Ashram(IRE) came here with a win in a Warwick minor race under his belt. He beat stablemate Huntdown in this event last year but that was a considerably weaker edition and he never looked like following up.
Dunelight(IRE) lost his chance with a very tardy start but was passing beaten rivals late on. Official explanation: jockey said horse reared on leaving stalls (op 16-1)
Palace Moon was attempting to stay on when he was hampered by the weakening Yaa Wayl, whom he had finished behind at York. (op 11-1)
Code Of War(USA) Official explanation: jockey said colt ran too free
Yaa Wayl(IRE), winner of the City Of York Stakes in this grade last time, did not find much under pressure and quickly dropped away. (op 7-2)

6148 DUBAI DUTY FREE ARC TRIAL (GROUP 3) 1m 3f 5y
3:10 (3:10) (Class 1) 3-Y-O+

£32,358 (£12,266; £6,138; £3,060; £1,533; £769) **Stalls** Low

Form RPR
6610 **1** **Dangerous Midge (USA)**[30] 5220 4-9-3 108.................. MartinDwyer 9 121
(B J Meehan) *chsd ldrs: wnt 2nd over 2f out: drvn to ld wl over 1f: rdn clr ins fnl f* **9/2**[3]
-212 **2** 4 **Rainbow Peak (IRE)**[28] 5274 4-9-3 115.................................... NeilCallan 6 114
(M A Jarvis) *trckd ldrs: rdn and styd on fr over 1f out to chse wnr ins fnl f: no imp* **8/11**[1]
4311 **3** 2 **Campanologist (USA)**[33] 5132 5-9-10 116.......................... TedDurcan 5 117
(Saeed Bin Suroor) *chsd ldr tl over 6f out: styd front rnk: rdn 3f out: outpcd by ldng duo fr over 1f out but styd on for 3rd ins fnl f* **4/1**[2]
12/5 **4** *hd* **Bauer (IRE)**[15] 5696 7-9-3 100.. J-PGuillambert 1 110
(L M Cumani) *in rr: in tch: rdn 3f out and styd on to chse ldrs over 2f out: kpt on same pce ins fnl f* **66/1**
3-06 **5** *nse* **Monitor Closely (IRE)**[19] 5575 4-9-3 113...................... JimmyFortune 7 110
(M L W Bell) *sn led: rdn over 2f out: hdd wl over 1f out: wknd ins fnl f* **6/1**
4030 **6** ½ **Saphira's Fire (IRE)**[29] 5249 5-9-0 100.......................... RichardMullen 4 106
(W R Muir) *in rr: drvn along over 3f out: styd on fr over 1f out: nvr gng pce to get into contention* **80/1**
0004 **7** 4½ **Halicarnassus (IRE)**[12] 5804 6-9-3 105.......................... SamHitchcott 8 101
(M R Channon) *rdn on outside over 3f out: a towards rr* **50/1**

2m 19.45s (-1.75) **Going Correction** -0.175s/f (Firm)
WFA 3 from 4yo+ 7lb **7** Ran SP% **115.1**
Speed ratings (Par 113): **99,96,94,94,94 94,90**
toteswingers:1&2 £2.20, 2&3 £1.30, 1&3 £3.30 CSF £8.35 TOTE £5.70: £2.90, £1.50; EX 10.50 Trifecta £49.30 Pool: £820.10 - 12.30 winning units..
Owner Iraj Parvizi **Bred** Tony Holmes & Dr Walter Zent **Trained** Manton, Wilts

FOCUS
A reasonable Group 3 run at just a modest pace, with a consequent slight doubt over how solid the form will prove. That said, the first two are progressive types with more to offer. The time was 2.45 seconds outside the standard.\n

NOTEBOOK
Dangerous Midge(USA) was always well placed and he quickened up well to lead before drawing clear for an emphatic win. Back in trip after failing to stay 1m6f in the Ebor, he was tackling pattern company for the first time and is clearly still improving. His trainer is keen on a crack at the Breeders' Cup Turf at Churchill Downs, and while the 4yo needs to improve on this bare form he definitely has more to offer. The yard won that race with Red Rocks in 2006. (op 6-1)
Rainbow Peak(IRE), whose York conqueror Rio De La Plata went on to boost the form in France, was expected to improve again for this step up in trip but the fairly steady pace did not see him in his best light. He would not have beaten the winner in any case, but still finished clear of the third and remains on an upward curve. (op 4-6 tchd 4-5 in places)
Campanologist(USA), also third in this a year ago, has won a pair of Group 1s in Germany this summer which saw him saddled with a 7lb penalty here. He was momentarily outpaced when the pace lifted but stuck on stoutly to reclaim third and remains in good heart. He is set to head to Australia for a crack at the Melbourne Cup. (op 9-2 tchd 5-1)
Bauer(IRE) had been well beaten on his return from injury at Salisbury recently and this was a very pleasing step up on that, as he would have been more inconvenienced than most by the modest tempo of the race. (op 50-1)
Monitor Closely(IRE) set the steady pace and stuck on as best he could when headed. He is still operating below last season's level. (op 7-1)
Saphira's Fire(IRE) could never quite get to the leaders on her first start against males this year. (op 100-1)
Halicarnassus(IRE) won this event in 2007 but has been unplaced in the last three runnings now. He was unsuited by the way this race panned out.

6149 30TH HAYNES, HANSON & CLARK CONDITIONS STKS 1m (S)
3:45 (3:46) (Class 2) 2-Y-O

£11,215 (£3,358; £1,679; £840; £419; £210) **Stalls** Centre

Form RPR
021 **1** **Moriarty (IRE)**[28] 5277 2-9-2 91.................................... PatDobbs 7 93
(R Hannon) *trckd ldr tl led appr fnl 2f: drvn and hung lft whn chal ins fnl f: kpt on strly and asserted nr fin* **3/1**[1]
1 **2** *nk* **Seattle Drive (IRE)**[21] 5491 2-9-2 0.................................... DaneO'Neill 5 92
(D R C Elsworth) *t.k.h: stdd in tch: hdwy over 2f out: chsd wnr ins fnl f and edgd lft: str chal fnl 120yds tl outpcd by wnr nr fin* **3/1**[1]
0321 **3** 1 **Enabling (IRE)**[9] 5857 2-9-2 76.................................... SteveDrowne 8 90
(R Hannon) *hld up towards rr: hdwy fr 2f out: drvn and styd on wl to take 3rd fnl 120yds: gng on cl home* **28/1**
1 **4** 1 **Cloud Rock**[30] 5204 2-8-12 85.................................... JimmyFortune 6 84
(P W Chapple-Hyam) *t.k.h: in tch: drvn and hdwy fr 2f out: styd on u.p to press for 3rd ins fnl f: one pce into 4th fnl 120yds* **4/1**[2]
1 **5** *nse* **Sergeant Ablett (IRE)**[18] 5595 2-9-2 0.................................... JoeFanning 4 88
(M Johnston) *chsd ldrs: wnt 2nd 2f out but sn rt pce of wnr: dropped to cl 3rd ins fnl f and kpt on same pce ins fnl 120yds* **4/1**[2]
3 **6** 4 **Aerial Acclaim (IRE)**[48] 4577 2-8-12 0.................................... LukeMorris 10 74
(C G Cox) *in rr: stl last whn pushed along 2f out: rdn and styd on ins fnl f: nvr any ch* **8/1**[3]
0 **7** *nk* **Zahraan (IRE)**[24] 5381 2-8-12 0.................................... MartinDwyer 9 74
(M P Tregoning) *in rr: in tch: rdn: hung lft and green over 2f out: sme prog over 1f out: nvr any ch* **22/1**
8 2½ **Argocat (IRE)** 2-8-12 0.................................... JamieSpencer 2 68
(P F I Cole) *s.i.s: sn chsng ldrs: rdn over 2f out: wknd over 1f out* **33/1**
5 **9** 2½ **Arctic Myth (USA)**[7] 5924 2-8-12 0.................................... IanMongan 1 62
(B W Duke) *led: rdn along 3f out: hdd appr fnl 2f: wknd sn after* **100/1**

10 *nk* **Evergreen Forest (IRE)** 2-8-12 0 FergusSweeney 3 62
(A J Lidderdale) *s.i.s: in rr tl in tch 1/2-way: sn bhd* **150/1**
1m 40.02s (0.32) **Going Correction** +0.125s/f (Good) **10** Ran SP% **113.5**
Speed ratings (Par 101): **103,102,101,100,100 96,96,93,91,91**
toteswingers:1&2 £2.00, 2&3 £13.40, 1&3 £6.60 CSF £11.20 TOTE £4.20: £1.70, £1.40, £4.10; EX 12.50 Trifecta £106.80 Pool: £826.03 -5.72 winning units..
Owner Justin Dowley & Michael Pescod **Bred** Rathasker Stud **Trained** East Everleigh, Wilts

FOCUS
Traditionally a very warm conditions race, with Authorized, third in 2006, the latest of a long string of luminaries to come out of it. This year's race had five last-time-out winners in attendance but looked below the level the race can produce. The form still has a sound feel to it. The pace was fair and the runners came down the centre of the track.

NOTEBOOK
Moriarty(IRE) has improved with each run and he followed up his win in York's Racing Post Convivial maiden. He travelled strongly up with the pace, if carrying his head a shade high, and knuckled down well when let down to win a shade more easily than the narrow margin might suggest. He saw out the mile well and won't mind easier underfoot conditions. (tchd 5-2)
Seattle Drive(IRE) came through to have every chance and was just held after drifting over to the far side. He had no problem with the extra frulong and different ground and remains a useful prospect. (op 7-2 tchd 11-4)
Enabling(IRE), the winner's stablemate, stayed on strongly inside the last, as befits a horse with a win over half a furlong longer than this to his name, and would appear to still be improving. (op 18-1)
Cloud Rock won only a Folkestone maiden auction first time but he confirmed himself a useful colt. He ran an honest race and appeared to have no excuses. (op 9-2)
Sergeant Ablett(IRE)'s trainer had won this race three times in the past decade, most recently when Teslin accounted for Authorized in 2006. This Newcastle winner was greener than most but stuck on willingly for fourth. He will not mind a return to softer ground and still has strengthening to do. (tchd 7-2)
Aerial Acclaim(IRE), upped in trip, did not really build on his third to a pair of subsequent winners at Glorious Goodwood. (op 9-1 tchd 10-1)
Zahraan(IRE), from another yard with a good record in this race, was tackling a quarter of a mile further than on his Polytrack debut. He still showed signs of inexperience and is worth keeping on the right side. (op 20-1)
Arctic Myth(USA) made the running and will have learnt from this. A maiden at one of the lesser tracks should be within his compass.

6150 DUBAI DUTY FREE FULL OF SURPRISES E B F FILLIES' CONDITIONS STKS 7f (S)
4:20 (4:21) (Class 2) 2-Y-O
£11,215 (£3,358; £1,679; £840; £419; £210) **Stalls** Centre

Form RPR
6 **1** **Sister Red (IRE)**[15] 5692 2-8-12 0 TedDurcan 7 85
(R Hannon) *set modest early pce: drvn and qcknd fr 2f out: styd on gamely whn chal ins fnl f: forged clr fnl 75yds* **10/1**
2 **2** *2* **Zing Wing**[14] 5721 2-8-12 0 NeilCallan 4 80
(P F I Cole) *t.k.h: chsd wnr thrght: drvn and styd on fr 2f out: chal ins fnl f: no ex and outpcd fnl 75yds: jst hld on for 2nd* **5/1**[2]
3 *nk* **Parvana (IRE)** 2-8-12 0 JamieSpencer 5 79+
(W J Haggas) *crossed and stdd s: in rr: stl plenty to do 2f out: grad edgd rt to stands' side over 1f out: str run ins fnl f and fin fast to press for 3rd: should improve* **5/1**[2]
3 **4** *1* **Question Times**[20] 5509 2-8-12 0 JimmyFortune 1 77+
(P W Chapple-Hyam) *t.k.h: chsd ldrs: rdn and styd on to take 3rd ins fnl f: sn one pce* **10/11**[1]
5 *hd* **Daffydowndilly** 2-8-12 0 SteveDrowne 8 76+
(H Morrison) *hld up in rr: hdwy fr 2f out to disp 3rd 1f out: nvr nr wnr and no ex fnl 120yds* **16/1**
6 *hd* **Crystal Etoile** 2-8-12 0 RichardMullen 2 78+
(Sir Michael Stoute) *t.k.h: hld up towards rr: sme hdwy whn hmpd over 3f out: sn rcvrd and styd on to dispute 3rd 1 l out: sn one pce and fdd fnl 75yds* **9/1**[3]
7 *13* **Red Soles (IRE)** 2-8-12 0 MichaelHills 10 42
(B W Hills) *chsd ldrs 3f: rdn over 2f out: green: hung lft and wknd qckly* **33/1**
65 **P** **Imperial Pirouette**[8] 5885 2-8-12 0 DaneO'Neill 6 —
(M R Channon) *chsd ldrs tl lost action and p.u 3f out* **100/1**
1m 27.99s (2.29) **Going Correction** +0.125s/f (Good) **8** Ran SP% **114.6**
Speed ratings (Par 98): **91,88,88,87,87 86,71,—**
toteswingers:1&2 £5.50, 2&3 £4.20, 1&3 £5.20 CSF £59.22 TOTE £15.00: £2.70, £1.50, £2.10; EX 34.40 Trifecta £439.70 Part won. Pool of £594.25 - 42 winning units..
Owner Michael Pescod **Bred** Thomas Foy **Trained** East Everleigh, Wilts

FOCUS
A fair conditions event but maybe not the strongest form for the grade. It was steadily run and the front pair were 1-2 throughout.

NOTEBOOK
Sister Red(IRE) dictated the pace, quickened things up with two to run and ran on strongly to see off the challenge of the runner-up. The only Hannon runner after paper favourite Attracted To You was taken out, she built on her debut effort at Salisbury. Her half-brother Red Badge landed a Group 3 earlier this month. (op 9-1)
Zing Wing, also runner-up on her Kempton debut, was again keen early on. She was in second place all the way, but could not prevent the winner from pulling away in the last half-furlong. This looks her trip for now. (op 7-2)
Parvana(IRE) ◆ is a 140,000euros half-sister to My One Weakness, a winning juvenile over 6f-7f. Held up, she was being niggled along by halfway and still had five in front of her entering the final furlong, but ran on strongly from there and would have been second in another couple of strides. A daughter of Galileo, she will get further than this and looks one to keep an eye on. (op 12-1)
Question Times was well enough placed, but failed to find a quickening touch when one was required and has to rate a little disappointing. (op Evens tchd 5-6 and 11-10 in places)
Daffydowndilly is a daughter of Oasis Dream out of a Listed winner over 1m6f. She improved from the back to challenge for the places before her effort flattened out. (op 14-1)
Crystal Etoile ◆ can learn from this debut experience and there should be races to be won with her. She is a half-sister to her connections' tough and very smart filly Crystal Capella (by Cape Cross), who stayed 1m4f. (op 8-1 tchd 10-1 in places)
Imperial Pirouette pulled up with what appeared a serious injury.

6151 DUBAI DUTY FREE FINEST SURPRISE STKS (H'CAP) 1m 2f 6y
4:55 (4:55) (Class 4) (0-85,85) 3-Y-O+ **£4,209** (£1,252; £625; £312) **Stalls** Low

Form RPR
2442 **1** **Sharaayeen**[20] 5529 3-8-11 **78** RichardHills 15 101+
(B W Hills) *stdd s and hld up in rr tl smooth hdwy over 2f out and sn trcking ldr: led 1f out: sn qcknd clr: easily* **9/4**[1]
2413 **2** *5* **Scottish Boogie (IRE)**[22] 5456 3-8-2 **74** JohnFahy(5) 14 87
(S Kirk) *t.k.h in rr on outside: stl t.k.h whn hdwy to ld ins fnl 3f: rdn fr 2f out: hdd 1f out: sn no ch w wnr: kpt on wl for clr 2nd* **8/1**
21-6 **3** *4 1/2* **Dahaam**[34] 5086 3-9-0 **81** JamieSpencer 3 85
(B J Meehan) *in tch: swtchd rt off rails to outside 3f out then rdn and hung rt: styd on u.p fr over 1f out to take wl hld 3rd ins fnl f* **8/1**
00S3 **4** *1 1/4* **Truly Asia (IRE)**[17] 5624 4-8-10 **71** oh1 SteveDrowne 1 73
(R Charlton) *t.k.h and hld up in rr: swtchd rt to outside 3f out: sn hrd drvn: styd on same pce into wl hld 4th ins fnl f* **14/1**
0154 **5** *hd* **Munsarim (IRE)**[34] 5091 3-9-1 **82** TedDurcan 4 83
(J L Dunlop) *sn led: hdd ins fnl 3f: styd chsng ldr tl ins fnl 2f: wknd appr fnl f* **9/1**
1-14 **6** *2 1/2* **Nazreef**[97] 2969 3-9-1 **82** (t) TravisBlock 7 78
(H Morrison) *plld hrd: chsd ldrs tl wknd qckly 2f out* **3/1**[2]
3311 **7** *5* **Eastern Paramour (IRE)**[34] 5084 5-9-4 **79** JoeFanning 2 65
(B R Millman) *in tch: hdwy to chse ldrs on ins 4f out: rdn 3f out: sn btn* **7/1**[3]
446- **8** *2 1/4* **Stan's Cool Cat (IRE)**[295] 7540 4-9-0 **82** DuilioDaSilva(7) 12 64
(P F I Cole) *towards rr most of way* **33/1**
1/52 **9** *13* **Top Mark**[29] 5235 8-8-12 **73** FergusSweeney 8 29
(A King) *sn chsng ldr tl over 3f out: sn wknd* **16/1**
2m 5.73s (-3.07) **Going Correction** -0.175s/f (Firm)
WFA 3 from 4yo+ 6lb **9** Ran SP% **116.0**
Speed ratings (Par 105): **105,101,97,96,96 94,90,88,78**
toteswingers:1&2 £5.40, 2&3 £8.80, 1&3 £4.80 CSF £21.20 CT £123.52 TOTE £2.60: £1.40, £2.40, £2.90; EX 34.60 Trifecta £182.50 Pool of £444.06 - 1.80 winning units..
Owner Hamdan Al Maktoum **Bred** D D And Mrs Jean P Clee **Trained** Lambourn, Berks

FOCUS
A fair handicap run at a decent pace. They finished well strung out and the form should prove solid. The winner rates a clear personal best.

6152 BURGES SALMON H'CAP 1m 4f 5y
5:30 (5:32) (Class 4) (0-85,81) 3-Y-O+ **£4,209** (£1,252; £625; £312) **Stalls** Low

Form RPR
143/ **1** **Oldrik (GER)**[182] 6243 7-9-1 **70** (p) JamieSpencer 3 81+
(P J Hobbs) *s.i.s and lost 5 l s: rcvrd to get in tch w main gp over 6f out: hdwy on outside over 2f out: tendency to hang lft: drvn to ld over 1f out: sn hanging lft: styd strly u.p* **11/4**[2]
4262 **2** *2 1/2* **Valid Reason**[28] 5259 3-9-3 **80** PatDobbs 6 87
(Mrs A J Perrett) *chsd ldr tl rdn and outpcd ins fnl 3f: rallied to take slt ld ins fnl 2f: hdd over 1f out: no ch w wnr ins fnl f: hld on wl for 2nd* **5/2**[1]
455 **3** *nk* **Roanstar**[95] 3038 3-8-2 **70** SimonPearce(5) 8 77
(A M Balding) *stdd in tch: hdwy over 2f out: str chal fr ins fnl 2f tl over 1f out: kpt on ins fnl f: no ch w wnr* **20/1**
024 **4** *1 1/2* **Pool Of Knowledge (FR)**[18] 5591 4-9-7 **76** MartinDwyer 5 81
(Miss Venetia Williams) *t.k.h: chsd ldrs: drvn and styd on to chal fr ins fnl 2f: wknd ins fnl f* **10/1**
0650 **5** *nk* **Street Entertainer (IRE)**[48] 4573 3-8-8 **71** NeilCallan 11 75
(Mrs A J Perrett) *s.i.s: towards rr: hdwy on outside fr 3f out: chsd ldrs u.p 2f out: wknd ins fnl f* **7/1**
6603 **6** *1* **Sohcahtoa (IRE)**[12] 5786 4-9-12 **81** (b) JimmyFortune 7 85
(R Hannon) *hld up in rr: hdwy to trck ldrs 3f out: n.m.r on ins over 2f out: wknd ins fnl f* **12/1**
1143 **7** *1 3/4* **Dolcetto (IRE)**[18] 5611 5-9-7 **76** FergusSweeney 9 76
(A King) *in rr: hdwy to chse ldrs and n.m.r over 2f out: sn rdn: wknd over 1f out* **10/1**
3/2- **8** *1* **Silvador**[485] 2181 4-9-3 **72** DaneO'Neill 1 70
(W R Muir) *led: kpt on whn chal fr 3f out tl hdd ins fnl 2f: sn btn* **18/1**
3012 **9** *2 1/4* **Raktiman (IRE)**[21] 5467 3-8-6 **69** (p) RichardMullen 4 67
(Tom Dascombe) *chsd ldrs: chal 3f out tl wknd ins fnl 2f* **20/1**
2300 **10** *10* **Grey Bunting**[28] 5273 3-9-4 **81** MichaelHills 10 60
(B W Hills) *chsd ldrs tl wknd qckly 3f out* **6/1**[3]
2m 34.71s (-0.79) **Going Correction** -0.175s/f (Firm)
WFA 3 from 4yo+ 8lb **10** Ran SP% **122.7**
Speed ratings (Par 105): **95,93,93,92,91 91,90,89,87,81**
toteswingers:1&2 £2.50, 2&3 £15.30, 1&3 £16.40 CSF £10.72 CT £113.35 TOTE £3.30: £1.10, £1.80, £6.30; EX 12.70 Trifecta £307.80 Part won. Pool of £416.06 - 0.74 winning units. Place 6: £56.83 Place 5: £25.37 .
Owner D J Jones **Bred** H Feldt **Trained** Withycombe, Somerset

FOCUS
A fair handicap and sound form, with the runner-up setting the standard. It was well run but most of them held some sort of chance at the two pole.
T/Plt: £27.50 to a £1 stake. Pool of £55,317.81 - 1,463.25 winning tickets. T/Qpdt: £10.70 to a £1 stake. Pool of £4,881.39 - 334.75 winning tickets. ST

5523 NEWMARKET (Rowley Mile) (R-H)
Friday, September 17

OFFICIAL GOING: Good (6.7)
Far side of Rowley Mile track used.
Wind: fresh, behind Weather: cloudy, brighter spells

6153 EXPRESS COFFEE CARS MEDIAN AUCTION MAIDEN STKS 6f
1:50 (1:53) (Class 4) 2-Y-O **£3,885** (£1,156; £577; £288) **Stalls** Low

Form RPR
33 **1** **State Of Mind**[8] 5895 2-9-3 0 KierenFallon 15 79
(P F I Cole) *str: gd bodied: lw: chsd ldng pair: rdn and ev ch over 1f out: led ent fnl f: styd on wl* **11/4**[1]
2 *1/2* **White Frost (IRE)** 2-9-3 0 RobertWinston 2 78+
(B W Hills) *leggy: scope: bit bkwd: hld up wl in tch: chsd ldrs and swtchd rt ent fnl f: r.o wl to chse wnr fnl 100yds: hld towards fin* **16/1**
6 **3** *1 1/4* **Cultural Desert**[28] 5255 2-9-3 0 JimCrowley 9 74
(R M Beckett) *w'like: tall: scope: lw: chsd ldr: ev ch ent fnl 2f: rdn over 1f out: no ex and btn fnl 100yds* **6/1**
4 *1 1/4* **Soweto Star (IRE)** 2-9-3 0 JimmyQuinn 1 70+
(J R Best) *w'like: dwlt: in tch towards rr: pushed along 1/2-way: stmbld bdly wl over 1f out: hdwy and switching rt ent fnl f: r.o strly and gng on wl fin: nt rch ldrs* **20/1**
5 *nk* **Suddenly Susan (IRE)** 2-8-12 0 RyanMoore 5 64+
(J Noseda) *unf: scope: tall: in tch in midfield: rdn 2f out: no prog tl styd on ins fnl f: keeping on wl fin: nt rch ldrs* **4/1**[2]
6 *1/2* **Puttingonthestyle (IRE)** 2-9-3 0 RichardHughes 17 68+
(R Hannon) *lengthy: in tch: effrt and rdn to chse ldrs over 1f out: unable qck and sltly hmpd 1f out: wknd ins fnl f* **5/1**[3]
7 *nk* **King Ferdinand** 2-9-3 0 LiamKeniry 8 67+
(A M Balding) *athletic: attr: bit bkwd: dwlt: sn rdn along and hdwy into midfield: swtchd rt to outer and rdn 2f out: styd on steadily ins fnl f: nvr gng pce to rch ldrs* **25/1**

64 **8** *shd* **Silk Bounty**[11] 5814 2-9-3 0 PaulMulrennan 4 66
(J G Given) *w'like: lw: broke v fast and led: rdn and hrd pressed 2f out: hdd ent fnl f: sn wknd* **12/1**

9 *2* **Sim Sala Bim** 2-9-3 0 JackMitchell 16 60+
(S C Williams) *unf: bit bkwd: dwlt: towards rr: rdn and rn green 2f out: sme hdwy over 1f out: kpt on steadily ins fnl f: nvr trbld ldrs* **100/1**

10 *shd* **Wom** 2-9-3 0 LiamJones 12 60
(W J Haggas) *lengthy: angular: bit bkwd: dwlt: sn in midfield: rdn and effrt 2f out: kpt on same pce and no imp fr over 1f out* **16/1**

11 *nk* **Stirling Bridge** 2-9-3 0 TomQueally 10 59
(W Jarvis) *w'like: tall: bit bkwd: in tch in midfield: rdn over 2f out: kpt on same pce and no prog fr wl over 1f out: nvr trbld ldrs* **25/1**

12 *½* **Acclamatory** 2-8-12 0 WilliamCarson 7 59+
(S C Williams) *w'like: cl cpld: bit bkwd: towards rr: pushed along over 2f out: kpt on: nvr gng pce to trble ldrs* **66/1**

13 *1* **Midnight Trader (IRE)** 2-9-3 0 TonyCulhane 13 55+
(P W D'Arcy) *w'like: str: edgy: v.s.a: rn green in rr: swvd rt after 1f: rdn and sme hdwy over 1f out: styd steadily on ins fnl f: n.d* **66/1**

14 *shd* **Arctic Maiden** 2-8-12 0 JamieMackay 6 49
(W J Musson) *w'like: t.k.h: stdd bk towards rr sn after s: rdn and no real prog 2f out: n.d* **100/1**

15 *¾* **Orthodox Lad** 2-9-3 0 EddieAhern 14 52
(J R Best) *leggy: scope: edgy: racd towards rr on outer: rdn and no prog ent fnl 2f: n.d* **50/1**

0000 **16** *3½* **Complicate**[16] 5660 2-8-9 48 RussKennemore(3) 11 37
(Andrew Reid) *chsd ldrs: rdn 1/2-way: wknd qckly u.p wl over 1f out* **100/1**

17 *½* **Ferruccio (IRE)** 2-9-3 0 HayleyTurner 3 40
(J R Fanshawe) *w'like: bit bkwd: s.i.s: a bhd: rdn and no prog 2f out* **25/1**

1m 12.83s (0.63) **Going Correction** -0.025s/f (Good) **17** Ran SP% **121.3**
Speed ratings (Par 97): **94,93,91,90,89 88,88,88,85,85 85,84,83,83,82 77,76**
toteswingers:1&2 £8.30, 2&3 £19.60, 1&3 £3.90 CSF £45.92 TOTE £3.70: £1.60, £5.10, £2.40; EX 44.30.
Owner C Shiacolas **Bred** Thierry De La Herroniere **Trained** Whatcombe, Oxon

FOCUS
Rarely that hot a maiden by Newmarket's standards, but plenty of powerful connections were represented in this latest running and the race should produce some winners. Just a minor step forward from State Of Mind. The action unfolded towards the stands' rail, and a low draw was probably a help.

NOTEBOOK
State Of Mind did well to overcome stall 15, racing enthusiastically on the pace after gradually edging over towards the stands' side, although his experience was an obvious advantage against a field largely made up of newcomers. A colt with size, Kieren Fallon reported him to still be on the weak side, and he should make a useful sprinter next year. (op 7-2)
White Frost(IRE) could be considered a little unlucky as he only got in the clear once switched off the rail shortly after passing the furlong pole, but he was always being held by the winner late on. Whatever, this 52,000euros purchase, a half-brother to a number of winners, can surely make his mark. (tchd 20-1)
Cultural Desert stepped up a fair bit on the form he showed on debut at Salisbury and should continue to progress. (tchd 5-1)
Soweto Star(IRE) ◆, a half-brother to a 5f 2-y-o winner in France and a winning juvenile in the US, very much caught the eye. He didn't handle the dip, stumbling badly just inside the final 2f, and at no stage was he given a hard ride, but he still finished in taking fashion. He could be very useful in time.
Suddenly Susan(IRE), a 23,000gns purchase out of a 3-y-o winner in the US, hit a flat spot when first under pressure before keeping on. One of only four fillies in the line up, this was a respectable debut and she can improve. (op 9-2)
Puttingonthestyle(IRE) ◆ was poorly drawn and, lacking the sharpness of some of these late on, wasn't given a hard time once held. He can do better. (op 9-2)
King Ferdinand started slowly and was niggled along a fair way out, but he ran on quite nicely after being switched wide. This £40,000 purchase, who's a half-brother to smart sprint handicapper Spanish Bounty, should improve plenty. (op 20-1)
Silk Bounty looks all speed and is probably a 5f horse for the time being, with handicaps now an option. (tchd 16-1)
Sim Sala Bim is bred to want further and this was a pleasing debut, keeping on after running green. He's open to significant improvement in the long term.
Complicate Official explanation: jockey said filly lost its action

6154 E B F PIE EMPORIUM MAIDEN FILLIES' STKS (DIV I) 1m
2:25 (2:26) (Class 4) 2-Y-O **£4,209** (£1,252; £625; £312) **Stalls** Low

Form RPR

2 **1** **Khawlah (IRE)**[15] 5692 2-9-0 0 KierenFallon 7 80+
(Saeed Bin Suroor) *lw: t.k.h: chsd ldr: rdn to ld over 1f out: r.o wl fnl f: eased towards fin* **4/6**[1]

2 *1* **Elas Diamond** 2-9-0 0 RyanMoore 9 78+
(J Noseda) *unf: scope: chsd ldrs: rdn along 3f out: drvn to chse wnr over 1f out: r.o wl: a hld fnl f* **28/1**

3 *4½* **Matilda's Waltz** 2-9-0 0 JimCrowley 8 67
(R M Beckett) *unf: scope: tall: lw: in tch in midfield: rdn along and effrt 3f out: outpcd by ldrs wl over 1f out: chsd clr ldng pair u.p 1f out: no imp after* **50/1**

652 **4** *2* **Choral**[25] 5369 2-9-0 79 RichardHughes 12 65
(R Hannon) *str: lw: hld up in midfield: sn outpcd by ldrs over 2f out: kpt on u.p over 1f out: wnt 4th ins fnl f: no threat to ldng pair* **9/1**[3]

02 **5** *2* **Grecian Goddess (IRE)**[21] 5488 2-9-0 0 MarcHalford 4 58
(J Ryan) *led tl rdn and hdd over 1f out: sn outpcd: wknd ins fnl f* **33/1**

6 *1¼* **Alfouzy** 2-9-0 0 PhilipRobinson 5 55
(M A Jarvis) *w'like: scope: bit bkwd: restless in stalls: awkward s and s.i.s: sn rcvrd and in tch: rdn and unable qck over 2f out: wknd 2f out* **25/1**

7 *½* **Palm Pilot (IRE)** 2-9-0 0 HayleyTurner 2 54
(E A L Dunlop) *athletic: bit bkwd: lw: in tch: rn green and pushed along 1/2-way: rdn and outpcd rdn fnl 2f: wl btn after* **66/1**

0 **8** *nse* **Chesnut Coffee**[34] 5066 2-9-0 0 LiamKeniry 16 54
(D M Simcock) *str: towards rr: rdn and effrt on outer over 2f out: sn outpcd and no ch w ldrs: kpt on again ins fnl f* **100/1**

9 *1¼* **Dragonera** 2-9-0 0 EddieAhern 11 51
(E A L Dunlop) *leggy: weak: s.i.s: hdwy into midfield 6f out: rdn and outpcd over 2f out: wknd 2f out* **100/1**

10 *shd* **Galivant (IRE)** 2-9-0 0 RobertWinston 15 51+
(J W Hills) *leggy: bit bkwd: s.i.s: rn green in rr: rdn and edgd rt 3f out: n.d* **100/1**

11 *nse* **Astromagick** 2-8-9 0 AshleyMorgan(5) 14 51
(M H Tompkins) *lengthy: angular: a towards rr: rdn and struggling 1/2-way: no ch fnl 2f* **100/1**

06 **12** *hd* **Merrjanah**[118] 2312 2-9-0 0 ChrisCatlin 3 50
(C E Brittain) *w'like: t.k.h: chsd ldrs tl wknd qckly 2f out* **100/1**

13 *nk* **Highest** 2-9-0 0 WilliamBuick 10 50
(J H M Gosden) *w'like: str: gd bodied: scope: lw: a towards rr: pushed along and struggling 1/2-way: n.d after* **11/4**[2]

14 *4* **Mujarah (IRE)** 2-9-0 0 TomQueally 1 40
(J L Dunlop) *leggy: a bhd: hung rt and lost tch 3f out* **66/1**

15 *nk* **Sforza (IRE)** 2-8-11 0 Louis-PhilippeBeuzelin(3) 13 40
(B J Meehan) *w'like: cl cpld: a towards rr: struggling 1/2-way: wl bhd fnl 2f* **100/1**

1m 38.84s (0.24) **Going Correction** -0.025s/f (Good) **15** Ran SP% **117.8**
Speed ratings (Par 94): **97,96,91,89,87 86,85,85,84,84 84,84,83,79,79**
toteswingers:1&2 £6.00, 2&3 £29.40, 1&3 £11.60 CSF £32.07 TOTE £1.70: £1.10, £5.10, £7.10; EX 21.50.
Owner Godolphin **Bred** Darley **Trained** Newmarket, Suffolk
■ Godolphin's 1,000th winner in Britain. The first was in 1994.

FOCUS
This fillies' maiden has produced some really smart types in recent years, but Henry Cecil, who won the race with Light Shift in 2006 and Midday in '08, as well as sending out Timepiece to take second last year, was not represented in either division. It remains to be seen whether there was much strength in depth, with the field finishing strung out, and the time 0.46 slower than the second division, won by Beatrice Aurore. The winner is rated pretty much to her debut form. They all raced towards the stands' side.

NOTEBOOK
Khawlah(IRE) had no trouble confirming the promise she showed when runner-up over 7f on debut, breaking much better this time and finding plenty for pressure, despite having raced keenly early on. It's hard to know how good she may be, but Kieren Fallon reportedly thinks she could be smart next year. She can be expected to stay at least 1m2f next year and it's probably fair to say her connections will be disappointed if she's not pattern class. (op 10-11 tchd evens in places)
Elas Diamond ◆, a 150,000gns purchase out of Lancashire Oaks winner Ela Athena, fared best of the newcomers, ultimately no match for the winner but nicely clear of the remainder. She could be decent in time, particularly over a little further next year. (tchd 33-1)
Matilda's Waltz, a 55,000gns half-sister to 1m4f winner Wadnaan out of a 1m2f scorer in Germany, showed plenty of ability but lacked the pace of the front two in the closing stages. She's going to want further.
Choral didn't handle the dip all that well and, somewhat surprisingly for the most experienced runner in the line up, still looked immature. (op 8-1)
Grecian Goddess(IRE) displayed plenty of early speed but was readily left behind the closing stages, showing a knee action and basically looking a bit ungainly on this undulating track. She probably needs more time and can do better over further next year (plenty of stamina in pedigree), probably with a bit of give underfoot.
Alfouzy, who's out of a 1m3f winner, completely missed the break after getting a little wound up in the stalls, but showed ability.
Palm Pilot(IRE) didn't handle the dip and can do better with the benefit of this experience. (op 100-1)
Highest, a big, scopey filly, really took the eye in the paddock and was well fancied, but she ran poorly, looking absolutely clueless. Surely this performance cannot be explained simply by greenness, but whatever, she's evidently thought capable of much better. (op 15-8)

6155 E B F PIE EMPORIUM MAIDEN FILLIES' STKS (DIV II) 1m
3:00 (3:01) (Class 4) 2-Y-O **£4,209** (£1,252; £625; £312) **Stalls** Low

Form RPR

0 **1** **Beatrice Aurore (IRE)**[15] 5691 2-9-0 0 TomQueally 5 82+
(J L Dunlop) *in tch on stands' side: chsd wnr 4f out: gng wl ent fnl 2f: rdn to ld over 1f out: r.o wl ins fnl f* **16/1**

2 *2* **Mohedian Lady (IRE)** 2-9-0 0 HayleyTurner 10 77+
(M L W Bell) *w'like: tall: lw: s.i.s: hld up in centre tl gps merged 1/2-way: swtchd rt to outer and hdwy wl over 1f out: rdn to chse wnr 1f out: kpt on: no imp ins fnl f* **10/1**

3 *shd* **Polygon (USA)** 2-9-0 0 WilliamBuick 12 77+
(J H M Gosden) *w'like: rangy: scope: lw: racd in centre tl gps merged 1/2-way: chsd ldrs: rdn and unable qck over 2f out: rallied u.p over 1f out: chsd ldng pair jst ins fnl f: kpt on wl: nt gng pce to trble wnr* **5/1**[2]

4 *1* **Fortunateencounter (FR)** 2-9-0 0 NickyMackay 16 75+
(J H M Gosden) *unf: scope: hmpd s and s.i.s: racd in centre tl gps merged 1/2-way: bhd: rdn over 2f out: hdwy over 1f out: styd on wl ins fnl f: nt rch ldrs* **20/1**

06 **5** *nk* **Spade**[15] 5691 2-9-0 0 JimCrowley 7 74+
(D R C Elsworth) *on toes: s.i.s: towards rr on stands' side: hdwy and switching rt fr wl over 1f out: r.o wl ins fnl f: nt rch ldrs* **10/1**

5 **6** *¾* **Scented**[21] 5489 2-9-0 0 LiamJones 2 72
(W J Haggas) *w'like: tall: scope: racd on stands' side: overall ldr: rdn 2f out: hdd over 1f out: lost 2nd 1f out: wknd ins fnl f* **25/1**

7 *1* **Marhaba** 2-9-0 0 PhilipRobinson 14 70
(M A Jarvis) *lengthy: bit bkwd: racd in centre: led that gp and prom overall: rdn and merged w rivals 2f out: wknd ent fnl f* **12/1**

8 *nk* **Lady Bridget** 2-9-0 0 RobertWinston 11 69
(B W Hills) *w'like str: racd in centre tl gps merged 1/2-way: midfield: rdn and edging rt fr 2f out: one pce and no imp ins fnl f* **100/1**

04 **9** *nk* **Azlaa**[17] 5633 2-9-0 0 RichardHughes 1 69
(R Hannon) *racd stands' side: chsd overall ldr tl 1/2-way: wknd u.p jst over 1f out* **12/1**

10 *½* **Rumh (GER)** 2-9-0 0 TonyCulhane 4 74+
(Saeed Bin Suroor) *unf: scope: tall: rrd s and s.i.s: bhd on stands' side: effrt and nt clr run ent fnl 2f tl ins fnl f: nvr able to chal* **10/1**

3 **11** *nk* **Abergeldie (USA)**[21] 5488 2-9-0 0 RyanMoore 8 67+
(Sir Michael Stoute) *w'like: scope: tall: racd stands' side: in tch in midfield: rdn and effrt over 2f out: unable qck u.p and n.m.r wl over 1f out: one pce and no prog after* **6/1**[3]

2 **12** *1½* **Mia Madonna**[21] 5489 2-8-11 0 Louis-PhilippeBeuzelin(3) 3 63
(B J Meehan) *w'like: cl cpld: chsd ldrs on stands' side tl wknd u.p 2f out: wl btn ent fnl f* **13/2**

13 *2¾* **Cinta** 2-9-0 0 JackMitchell 15 57
(M Botti) *w'like: wnt rt s: racd in centre tl gps merged 1/2-way: in tch: chsd ldrs and rdn ent fnl 2f: wknd over 1f out: fdd ins fnl f* **66/1**

14 *4½* **Illandrane (IRE)** 2-9-0 0 KierenFallon 13 51+
(E A L Dunlop) *w'like str: racd in centre tl gps merged 1/2-way: rdn and wknd qckly ent fnl 2f: bhd and eased ins fnl f* **4/1**[1]

0 **15** *8* **Generous Genella**[43] 4747 2-8-9 0 AdamBeschizza(5) 9 28
(Miss J Feilden) *leggy: s.i.s: a bhd on satnds' side: lost tch over 2f out* **66/1**

16 *6* **Classical Air** 2-9-0 0 EddieAhern 6 15
(J L Dunlop) *str: bkwd: s.i.s: a wl bhd on stands' side* **66/1**

1m 38.38s (-0.22) **Going Correction** -0.025s/f (Good) **16** Ran SP% **126.9**
Speed ratings (Par 94): **100,98,97,96,96 95,94,94,94,93 93,91,89,84,76 70**
toteswingers:1&2 £51.50, 2&3 £17.80, 1&3 £20.20 CSF £167.87 TOTE £24.20: £5.60, £4.30, £2.70.

Owner Benny Andersson **Bred** Chess Racing Ab **Trained** Arundel, W Sussex

FOCUS

Often a good race and the time was decent, being 0.46 seconds quicker than the first division, won by Khawlah. They split into two groups early on, but the majority of the seven runners who started off up the middle of the track gradually joined up the others towards the near rail in the latter stages. The field finished quite impressed.

NOTEBOOK

Beatrice Aurore(IRE), an Irish Oaks entrant, stepped up a good deal on the form she showed on debut over 7f at Salisbury, finding plenty after travelling with ease. She could be pattern class. (op 22-1)

Mohedian Lady(IRE), a 240,000gns half-sister to smart 7f-1m2f winner Distant Memories out of a useful triple 1m1f-1m2f scorer in France, made her move extremely wide but still ran well. She clearly has plenty of ability and could be decent over middle-distances next term. (op 14-1)

Polygon(USA), who is out of a smart 7f-1m2f winner, shaped with plenty of encouragement and ought to have little trouble winning a maiden before stepping up in class. (op 7-1)

Fortunateencounter(FR) was short of room on leaving the stalls and then covered plenty of ground, starting off up the centre before switching to the nearside, and then being taken out widest of all with her challenge. All in all she did well to get so close on debut and looks decent. (op 33-1)

Spade ◆, who looked tucked up in the paddock, had today's winner behind at Salisbury last time, but that one has obviously made the greater progress. That said, the Elsworth filly was an eyecatcher and is better than she showed. Having missed the break, she was left with too much to do and ran on without being subjected to a hard ride. She can now switch to handicaps if connections so choose, and may stay further in due course. (op 20-1)

Scented didn't see her race out after setting a good pace against the near rail. She's going to want further next year.

Marhaba ◆, a 160,000gns purchase as a foal out of a French Oaks winner, led the bunch up the middle of the track through the early stages, but was left on her own for a period when the other runners joined to make one big group in the latter stages. She can do better, especially over middle-distances in 2011. (op 9-1)

Rumh(GER) ◆, a 300,000gns half-sister to 3-y-o 1m winners in Germany Rahad and Rahada, has been given a Derby entry and is significantly better than she showed on debut. Having got upset in the stalls and then missed the break, she was left with an awful lot to do, but still looked to have plenty to offer when continually denied a clear run towards the near rail in the closing stages. She should have finished a good deal closer and is a filly to get on side. Official explanation: jockey said filly was denied a clear run (op 15-2 tchd 11-1)

Abergeldie(USA) failed to build on the form she showed over 7f on a soft surface first time up. (op 7-2)

Mia Madonna showed ability on debut over a furlong shorter on an easy surface but disappointed this time. (op 7-1 tchd 15-2)

Illandrane(IRE) had apparently been given an entry in an Italian Group 3 and she was well fancied on debut, but is seems something was amiss. Official explanation: jockey said filly had no more to give (op 5-1 tchd 11-2 and 6-1 in places)

6156 EXPRESS CAFES NURSERY 7f

3:35 (3:35) (Class 3) (0-95,87) 2-Y-O **£7,123** (£2,119; £1,059; £529) **Stalls** Low

Form				RPR
431	1		**Azrael**[40] 4856 2-9-3 **83** ... JamesDoyle 3 (A J McCabe) *on toes: chsd ldrs tl wnt 2nd 5f out: rdn clr w ldr and ev ch fr 2f out: drvn over 1f out: battle on wl to ld wl ins fnl f: jst hld on* **8/1**[3]	88
211	2	shd	**Ardour (IRE)**[29] 5234 2-9-7 **87** ... RichardHughes 1 (R Hannon) *t.k.h: chsd ldr for 2f: chsd ldrs after: rdn and outpcd by ldng pair 2f out: edging rt u.p over 1f out: no hdwy tl styd on wl fnl 100yds: string chal nr fin: jst failed* **9/4**[1]	92
51	3	nk	**Song Of The Siren**[17] 5626 2-8-8 **74** ... WilliamBuick 4 (A M Balding) *lw: led: rdn clr w wnr 2f out: kpt on gamely u.p tl hdd and no ex wl ins fnl f* **8/1**[3]	78
002	4	3	**One Lucky Lady**[43] 4741 2-8-3 **69** ... JimmyQuinn 8 (B W Hills) *in tch towards rr: rdn and struggling over 3f out: no threat to ldrs fr wl over 1f out: kpt on u.p to go 4th ins fnl f* **16/1**	66
1633	5	1 ¼	**Mayhab**[20] 5527 2-9-1 **81** ... RyanMoore 5 (C E Brittain) *lw: in tch: rdn and outpcd ent fnl 2f: styd on same pce and no imp u.p fr over 1f out* **11/2**[2]	74
044	6	1	**Right Said Fred (IRE)**[62] 4142 2-8-7 **73** ... JimCrowley 6 (R M Beckett) *on toes: chsd ldrs: rdn 3f out: outpcd and drvn ent fnl 2f: one pce and no threat to ldrs after* **18/1**	64
1	7	hd	**Azameera (IRE)**[15] 5691 2-8-12 **78** ... PhilipRobinson 2 (C G Cox) *lw: s.i.s: in tch towards rr: rdn and outpcd over 2f out: one pce and n.d after* **9/4**[1]	68
0440	8	1 ¼	**Saskia's Dream**[12] 5784 2-8-8 **74** ... HayleyTurner 7 (Jane Chapple-Hyam) *stdd and dropped in bhd after s: hld up in rr: effrt: stl plenty to do whn nt clr run ent fnl 2f: edging lft and no prog after* **18/1**	63

1m 25.24s (-0.16) **Going Correction** -0.025s/f (Good) **8** Ran SP% **115.6**

Speed ratings (Par 99): **99,98,98,95,93 92,92,90**

toteswingers:1&2 £4.50, 2&3 £4.60, 1&3 £8.30 CSF £26.72 CT £151.63 TOTE £8.20: £2.20, £1.10, £2.70.

Owner The Cor Blimey Partnership **Bred** Ian Neville Marks **Trained** Averham Park, Notts

■ Stewards' Enquiry : William Buick caution: used whip down shoulder in the forehand

FOCUS

The fourth running of this nursery, won last year by the smart Audacity Of Hope. Racing stands' side, they went a good pace (time 0.50 seconds quicker than later maiden winner Up In Time), but few got into it. Fair form, the winner building on his maiden win.

NOTEBOOK

Azrael, making his nursery debut after getting the better of a couple of subsequent winners in a maiden last time, was content to sit on the shoulder of the leader. It took him a long time to wear down Song Of The Siren, and no sooner had he achieved it than the runner-up arrived on his outside, but he held on under a strong ride. Already due to go up another 1lb, there is some stamina on the dam's side of his pedigree so he may have a bit more to offer over an extra furlong. According to connections his target in the Group 3 Somerville Tattersall Stakes back over C&D on September 30. (op 6-1 tchd 11-2)

Ardour(IRE), bidding for a hat-trick off a 4lb higher mark than when winning a four-runner Epsom nursery, was free to post and keen enough early, and took too long to respond when coming off the bridle over 2f from home, but he really took off up the final climb and would have got there in another stride. There are more races to be won with him, though his pedigree suggests he wouldn't get much further than this. (op 5-2 tchd 11-4)

Song Of The Siren, making her nursery debut after making all to win a Folkestone maiden, attempted the same tactics and wasn't worn down until very late. She can continue to progress. (op 15-2 tchd 13-2)

One Lucky Lady saw plenty of daylight on the wide outside but plugged on for fourth having been given reminders before reaching halfway. (tchd 14-1)

Mayhab, who was raised 6lb for finishing third behind Zebedee in a sales race on the July Course last month, made no impression after coming under pressure 3f from home and is already due to go up another 3lb, which won't help. (op 15-2 tchd 5-1)

Right Said Fred(IRE), making his nursery debut over a longer trip after showing some ability in three maidens, showed up early but found nothing for pressure and didn't stay. (op 14-1)

Azameera(IRE), another in a nursery for the first time after beating 16 rivals on her Salisbury debut earlier this month, was disappointing, even allowing for a slow start. Official explanation: jockey said filly hung left throughout (op 3-1)

Saskia's Dream never saw much daylight and looked ungainly on the track. (op 16-1 tchd 20-1)

6157 £100,000 TATTERSALLS MILLIONS FILLIES' AUCTION STKS 6f

4:10 (4:10) (Class 2) 2-Y-O

£55,769 (£25,341; £10,142; £5,066; £3,047; £2,028) **Stalls** Low

Form				RPR
213	1		**Khor Sheed**[41] 4842 2-9-1 98 ... KierenFallon 8 (L M Cumani) *b.hind: lw: racd in midfield: pushed along and hdwy ent fnl 2f: rdn to chal jst over 1f out: drvn to ld ins fnl f: hld on u.p cl home* **7/2**[3]	102
15	2	shd	**Tale Untold (USA)**[15] 5693 2-8-9 97 ... RichardHughes 11 (R Hannon) *b.hind: sn pushed along to chse ldrs: led gng strly wl over 1f out: rdn and clr w wnr ent fnl f: drvn and hdd ins fnl f: rallied gamely towards fin* **11/4**[2]	96+
1024	3	3	**Masaya**[20] 5519 2-9-1 94 ... ChrisCatlin 2 (C E Brittain) *towards rr: hdwy and hanging rt 2f out: chsd ldng pair jst over 1f out: styd on same pce and wl hld ins fnl f* **20/1**	93
0660	4	2 ¾	**Queen Of Spain (IRE)**[6] 5974 2-9-1 94 ... (v[1]) JMurtagh 7 (A P O'Brien, Ire) *s.i.s: sn rdn along and outpcd towards rr: hdwy and wandered u.p over 1f out: kpt on u.p to go modest 4th ins fnl f: nvr trbld ldrs* **12/1**	85
013	5	1 ¼	**Kalahaag (IRE)**[21] 5490 2-8-11 82 ... RyanMoore 1 (R Hannon) *lw: s.i.s: sn wl outpcd and detached in last: edgd rt fr over 2f out: styd on past btn horse ins fnl f: nvr trbld ldrs* **12/1**	77
5	6	½	**Simayill**[4] 6034 2-8-9 0 ... WilliamBuick 4 (C E Brittain) *unf: scope: t.k.h early: towards rr: rdn: rn green and hanging rt over 2f out: no threat to ldrs and kpt on same pce fr over 1f out* **66/1**	74
05	7	2 ½	**Queen O'The Desert (IRE)**[20] 5527 2-8-9 0 ... LiamKeniry 5 (A M Balding) *chsd ldrs: rdn over 2f out: wknd over 1f out* **50/1**	66
	8	4	**Pizzarra** 2-8-7 0 ... PaulMulrennan 9 (J G Given) *str: towards rr: rdn and struggling over 2f out: wl btn over 1f out* **66/1**	52
0420	9	1	**Button Moon (IRE)**[8] 5880 2-8-7 74 ... (p) MartinLane 10 (I A Wood) *on toes: pressed ldr tl rdn and hdd wl over 1f out: wknd qckly over 1f out* **25/1**	49
1	10	5	**Warm Breeze**[50] 4517 2-8-13 0 ... PhilipRobinson 6 (M A Jarvis) *w'like: str: lw: mde most tl rdn and hdd wl over 1f out: sn dropped out: wl bhd ins fnl f: burst blood vessel* **7/4**[1]	40+

1m 11.51s (-0.69) **Going Correction** -0.025s/f (Good) **10** Ran SP% **114.2**

Speed ratings (Par 98): **103,102,98,95,93 92,89,84,82,76**

toteswingers:1&2 £3.00, 2&3 £8.40, 1&3 £6.70 CSF £12.64 TOTE £4.00: £1.10, £2.90, £5.10; EX 16.70.

Owner Sheikh Mohammed Obaid Al Maktoum **Bred** Card Bloodstock **Trained** Newmarket, Suffolk

FOCUS

A decent fillies' sales race, and a smart performance from Khor Sheed, who was conceding weight to seven of her nine rivals, including 6lb to the 97-rated runner-up. They raced stands' side and the pace was strong. Improved form from the winner.

NOTEBOOK

Khor Sheed was unsuited by a modest pace when third behind the potentially high-class White Moonstone over 7f on easy ground at Group 3 level last time, but had previously won a Listed race over this distance on a fast surface, and the race was run to suit on her return to 6f. Kieren Fallon reportedly felt he got there too soon, and that the filly was idling, and that supports the visual impression that she was always holding the runner-up. Khor Sheed should have no problem getting further in time, provided she has a decent pace to chase to help her settle, but her connections suggested afterwards she'll be kept to 6f for now, and they'll look for suitable Group races. She's in the Cheveley Park and, having proven herself over the C&D, it wouldn't surprise to see her line up. (op 3-1)

Tale Untold(USA) proved she wasn't flattered by her close fifth in a Salisbury Listed race last time, but she might not be easy to place from now on. (op 3-1 tchd 7-2)

Masaya made her move out wide and didn't help herself by hanging right. She still ran to a useful level, though. (op 25-1)

Queen Of Spain(IRE), despite having a visor on for the first time, blew the start and didn't travel with any fluency, before not really handling the dip. (op 10-1)

Kalahaag(IRE) was totally unsuited by the drop in trip, racing in a detached last for much of the contest after missing the break, but having handled the dip better than most, she finished closer than appeared likely at halfway. She needs at least 7f. (op 14-1 tchd 16-1)

Simayill stepped up on her debut performance despite running green and going out to her right under pressure. She can improve a fair bit again. (op 100-1)

Warm Breeze looked potentially smart when a wide-margin winner over this trip on debut, but she hadn't been seen for the best part of two months and, after being hassled for the lead on her return, she burst a blood vessel. Official explanation: trainer's rep said filly bled from the nose (op 2-1 tchd 13-8 and 9-4 in places)

6158 WARRENS OF WARWICK MAIDEN AUCTION STKS 7f

4:45 (4:48) (Class 5) 2-Y-O **£3,885** (£1,156; £577; £288) **Stalls** Low

Form				RPR
0	1		**Up In Time**[16] 5657 2-8-9 0 ... WilliamBuick 20 (W J Knight) *w'like: athletic: chsd ldrs: wnt 2nd ent fnl 3f: pushed into ld over 1f out: sn stormed clr: r.o strly* **15/2**	88+
3	2	7	**Songsmith**[24] 5385 2-8-12 0 ... JimCrowley 5 (Mrs L Wadham) *str: chsd ldrs: rdn and effrt ent fnl 2f: 3rd and no ch w wnr jst over 1f out: kpt on u.p to go 2nd nr fin* **6/1**[3]	73
04	3	½	**Cross Culture (IRE)**[17] 5629 2-9-0 0 ... LiamKeniry 10 (A M Balding) *lw: led: rdn ent fnl 2f: hdd over 1f out: sn outpcd by wnr and wl btn 1f out: plugged on same pce and lost 2nd nr fin* **4/1**[2]	74
	4	1 ¼	**Show Rainbow** 2-8-6 0 ... ChrisCatlin 2 (M R Channon) *str: chsd ldrs: rdn over 2f out: outpcd and no ch w wnr fr over 1f out: styd on same pce ins fnl f* **33/1**	62+
	5	shd	**Mattoral** 2-8-9 0 ... MartinLane[(3)] 6 (P J Makin) *w'like: str: s.i.s: towards rr: hdwy and edging rt whn nt clr run ent fnl 2f: no ch w wnr fr over 1f out: r.o wl ins fnl f: gng on fin* **33/1**	68+
	6	½	**Chill (IRE)** 2-8-13 0 ... KierenFallon 19 (L M Cumani) *w'like: gd bodied: scope: bit bkwd: in tch: rdn and unable qck wl over 2f out: no ch w wnr and styd on same pce fr over 1f out* **8/1**	68+
0	7	3 ½	**Saint Helena (IRE)**[15] 5691 2-8-5 0 ... HayleyTurner 17 (H J L Dunlop) *chsd ldrs on outer: rdn and unable qck over 2f out: wl btn over 1f out* **16/1**	51
	8	hd	**Kalendar Girl (IRE)** 2-8-7 0 ... JamieMackay 8 (W J Musson) *w'like: cl cpld: stdd s: t.k.h: hld up towards rr: no ch w wnr: hdwy on inner whn n.m.r 1f out: kpt on: nvr trbld ldrs* **100/1**	53+
	9	¾	**Ministry** 2-8-12 0 ... JimmyQuinn 1 (J R Best) *unf: stdd s: t.k.h: hld up in tch in midfield: n.m.r and outpcd ent fnl 2f: no prog and wl btn after* **40/1**	56+
65	10	½	**Go**[8] 5871 2-8-12 0 ... RyanMoore 4 (R Hannon) *chsd ldr tl ent fnl 3f: wknd u.p wl over 1f out: wl btn and eased ins fnl f* **12/1**	57

00 **11** *nse* **Shutterbug**[106] 2680 2-8-6 0 NeilChalmers 18 48
(S C Williams) *in tch tl wknd u.p 2f out: wl btn ins fnl f* **100/1**

12 *nse* **Warden Bond** 2-8-2 0 RyanClark(7) 9 51
(S C Williams) *leggy: on toes: s.i.s: bhd and reminders after 1f: hanging rt and hdwy into midfield 3f out: sn rdn and no hdwy over 2f out* **100/1**

13 *hd* **Face Value** 2-8-10 0 Louis-PhilippeBeuzelin(3) 7 54
(B J Meehan) *w'like: s.i.s: towards rr: rdn and effrt whn n.m.r jst over 2f out: rdn and kpt on same pce fr over 1f out* **33/1**

6 **14** *1 1/2* **If You Whisper (IRE)**[14] 5717 2-8-9 0 TonyCulhane 15 49+
(Mike Murphy) *str: scope: b.hind: racd in midfield tl lost pl over 4f out: towards rr after: rdn and no hdwy whn hmpd 2f out: wl btn after* **14/1**

15 *1* **Seeking Glory** 2-8-13 0 EddieAhern 13 50+
(E A L Dunlop) *unf: tall: lw: s.i.s: bhd: pushed along and sme hdwy 2f out: nvr on terms: eased wl ins fnl f* **14/1**

0 **16** *1 3/4* **Colzium**[32] 5160 2-8-4 0 AshleyMorgan(5) 16 39
(M H Tompkins) *w'like: scope: edgy: in tch: rdn and struggling wl over 2f out: wl btn over 1f out: wknd ins fnl f* **100/1**

65 **17** *2 1/4* **Skeleton (IRE)**[4] 6019 2-8-6 0 GilmarPereira(3) 3 33
(W J Haggas) *w'like: lw: s.i.s: towards rr early: hdwy into midfield: rdn and wkng whn edgd rt ent fnl 2f: wl bhd ins fnl f* **33/1**

18 *nk* **Nella Sofia** 2-8-7 0 ow1 PaulMulrennan 11 31
(J G Given) *leggy: scope: free to post: s.i.s: a wl outpcd in rr* **100/1**

19 *7* **Tidal Star** 2-8-13 0 RichardHughes 14 22
(Miss Gay Kelleway) *lengthy: str: gd bodied: lw: s.i.s: hdwy and in midfield on outer over 4f out: rdn and struggling over 2f out: wl btn over 1f out: eased ins fnl f* **7/2**[1]

00 **20** *7* **Rio Belle (IRE)**[10] 5841 2-8-1 0 (v[1]) SophieDoyle(3) 12 —
(Andrew Reid) *neat: s.i.s: nvr gng and sn rdn in detached last: wl bhd fr 1/2-way: t.o* **150/1**

1m 25.74s (0.34) **Going Correction** -0.025s/f (Good) **20** Ran SP% **126.1**
Speed ratings (Par 95): **97,89,88,87,86 86,82,82,81,80 80,80,80,78,77 75,72,72,64,56**
toteswingers:1&2 £8.80, 2&3 £7.00, 1&3 £9.30 CSF £50.22 TOTE £10.40: £3.30, £2.20, £2.20; EX 60.40.
Owner Mrs N Welby **Bred** Larry Stratton **Trained** Patching, W Sussex

FOCUS
An impressive winner, but the front three had all recorded RPRs in the 60s on their previous starts, and the time was 0.50 seconds slower than the earlier nursery won by the 83-rated Azrael. All things considered, this is not form to get carried away with. They raced towards the near rail.

NOTEBOOK
Up In Time wasn't beaten far over 6f on debut and showed significantly improved form on this step up in trip, a particularly good effort considering she was drawn out widest in stall 20. She didn't have to be given a particularly hard time, and has to be worth a shot in better company, but while she's clearly useful, on the day her rivals most certainly were not. Her next run should tell us more. (op 8-1)
Songsmith didn't seem to improve on the form he showed on a soft surface first time up. (op 11-2 tchd 5-1)
Cross Culture(IRE) had his chance under a positive ride but again ran to only a modest level. Handicaps are now an option. (op 6-1)
Show Rainbow, a £13,000 half-sister to 1m winner Flag Of Glory, out of a winner over 1m21/2f, is a good walker and fared best of the newcomers but didn't achieve a great deal. (op 66-1)
Mattoral, an £18,000 purchase, kept on nicely in the latter stages despite not getting the clearest of runs, and gave the impression he'll improve a good deal, especially over further. (op 20-1)
Chill(IRE) was weak in the market on course and needed the run. (op 5-1)
Ministry was coltish in the paddock. (op 33-1)
If You Whisper(IRE) Official explanation: jockey said gelding was denied a clear run
Tidal Star was well backed but showed nothing. (op 5-1 tchd 11-2 in places)

6159 MC SEAFOOD MEDIAN AUCTION MAIDEN STKS 1m
5:20 (5:29) (Class 4) 2-Y-O **£3,885** (£1,156; £577; £288) **Stalls** Low

Form RPR

0 **1** **Rain Mac**[44] 4695 2-9-3 0 WilliamBuick 12 84
(J H M Gosden) *unf: scope: lw: in tch on outer: rdn and outpcd 3f out: sltly hmpd and edgd rt over 2f out: rdn and rallied over 1f out: ev ch 1f out: led ins fnl f: styd on wl* **4/1**[2]

3 **2** *3/4* **Halfsin (IRE)**[14] 5717 2-9-3 0 RyanMoore 18 82
(M Botti) *athletic: lw: chsd ldrs: rdn and unable qck 3f out: chsd clr ldr wl over 2f out: edgd lft u.p ent fnl f: drvn to chal 1f out: styd on same pce fnl 100yds* **5/1**[3]

2 **3** *hd* **Fulgur**[21] 5491 2-9-3 0 KierenFallon 9 82
(L M Cumani) *str: lw: racd keenly: led: pushed along and clr over 2f out: rdn over 1f out: hrd pressed ent fnl f: hdd and one pce ins fnl f* **10/11**[1]

4 *7* **Circus Star (USA)** 2-9-0 0 Louis-PhilippeBeuzelin(3) 1 66+
(B J Meehan) *lengthy: scope: racd off the pce in midfield: rdn and effrt on stands' rail over 2f out: no ch w ldng trio fnl 2f: wnt modest 4th 1f out* **66/1**

2 **5** *6* **Charles Fosterkane**[14] 5724 2-9-3 0 JimmyQuinn 8 52
(J R Best) *w'like: cl cpld: plld hrd: hld up wl in tch: rdn and outpcd over 2f out: wl btn and hung bdly rt fnl 2f* **14/1**

00 **6** *1* **Diplomasi**[116] 2389 2-9-3 0 JamieMackay 6 50
(C E Brittain) *unf: scope: tall: chsd ldrs: rdn and nt gng pce of ldr wl over 2f out: sn struggling: wl btn over 1f out* **100/1**

0 **7** *1* **Hollow Tree**[18] 5582 2-9-3 0 NeilChalmers 3 47
(A M Balding) *w'like: racd in midfield: rdn and outpcd ent fnl 3f: no ch w ldrs fnl 2f* **100/1**

06 **8** *nk* **Illustrious Forest**[21] 5498 2-9-0 0 RussKennemore(3) 11 47
(J Mackie) *in tch: pushed along 4f out: rdn and wl outpcd 3f out: wl btn fnl 2f* **100/1**

0 **9** *1/2* **Grumeti**[17] 5629 2-9-3 0 HayleyTurner 15 45
(M L W Bell) *w'like: scope: s.i.s: rdn and hanging rt over 3f out: plugged on past btn horses fr over 1f out: nvr trbld ldrs* **25/1**

0 **10** *1 1/2* **Bumbling Bertie**[18] 5582 2-9-3 0 LiamKeniry 5 42
(A M Balding) *unf: scope: bit bkwd: racd in midfield: rdn and struggling over 3f out: wl btn fnl 2f* **100/1**

11 *nk* **Rasam Aldaar** 2-9-3 0 ChrisCatlin 13 41+
(M R Channon) *str: lw: bhd: rdn and struggling over 3f out: no ch fnl 2f: n.m.r and swtchd lft ins fnl f* **66/1**

0 **12** *3 1/4* **Odin (IRE)**[21] 5491 2-9-3 0 JimCrowley 2 34
(D R C Elsworth) *unf: scope: lengthy: lw: a towards rr: rdn and wl btn over 2f out* **16/1**

13 *hd* **Malanos (IRE)** 2-9-3 0 PhilipRobinson 16 33
(D R C Elsworth) *str: bit bkwd: s.i.s: a towards rr: hung rt and wl btn 4f out* **40/1**

06 **14** *1 1/4* **Reachforthebucks**[105] 2715 2-9-0 0 SophieDoyle(3) 10 31
(G D Blake) *chsd ldr tl wl over 2f out: sn hung bdly rt and struggling: wl btn over 1f out: fdd ins fnl f* **125/1**

0 **15** *3* **My Mate Les (IRE)**[21] 5491 2-9-0 0 MartinLane(3) 17 24
(J R Best) *w'like: str: racd in midfield: rdn and struggling over 3f out: sn wknd: no ch fr wl over 2f out* **100/1**

16 *4 1/2* **Mrs Lovely** 2-8-12 0 TonyCulhane 4 8
(P W D'Arcy) *unf scope: taken down early: s.i.s: hld up in rr: nvr on terms* **80/1**

17 *7* **Captain Bellamy (USA)** 2-9-3 0 RichardHughes 7 —
(H Morrison) *w'like: scope: s.i.s: a bhd: t.o* **33/1**

18 *3/4* **Black Iceman** 2-9-3 0 MarcHalford 14 —
(J Pearce) *w'like leggy: s.i.s: a bhd: t.o* **100/1**

1m 38.62s (0.02) **Going Correction** -0.025s/f (Good) **18** Ran SP% **121.8**
Speed ratings (Par 97): **98,97,97,90,84 83,82,81,81,79 79,76,76,74,71 67,60,59**
toteswingers:1&2 £4.70, 2&3 £2.30, 1&3 £2.30 CSF £23.08 TOTE £5.20: £1.50, £1.70, £1.40.
Owner K Abdulla **Bred** Juddmonte Farms Ltd **Trained** Newmarket, Suffolk

FOCUS
A few of these proved tricky to load, resulting in the race being delayed by almost ten minutes; not ideal for inexperienced juveniles. There was a long gap back to the fourth, who was in turn well clear of the remainder, suggesting a lack of strength in depth to this maiden, but the front three all look at least useful. The time was similar to both divisions of the earlier fillies' maidens, and they raced stands' side.

NOTEBOOK
Rain Mac did not face the kickback on debut over 7f at Kempton according to his trainer, and was a different proposition with that experience behind him and upped in trip. He deserves extra credit considering he was caught wide without cover for much of the way, with stall 12 not ideal. (op 7-2 tchd 9-2)
Halfsin(IRE) probably improved a little on the form he showed on Polytrack first time up. He can find easier races. (tchd 9-2)
Fulgur, a Racing Post Trophy entrant, failed to find as much improvement as one might have expected from his promising debut over 7f on soft ground. He looked all over the winner when in a clear lead inside the final 3f, but he had been keen enough early on and, having not handled the dip all that well, he was soon one paced. He also failed to settle first time up and is unlikely to progress until learning to relax. (op Evens tchd 6-5 and 5-4 in places)
Circus Star(USA) hails from a stable whose juveniles often improve significantly for a run.
Charles Fosterkane, just as on debut, carried his head high despite the fitting of a sheepskin noseband, and he also hung right this time. He clearly didn't appreciate the track, but while there's no denying he has the ability to win races, he already looks best avoided, with his attitude a little suspect. (op 12-1 tchd 10-1)

6160 NORFOLK COUNTY ICE CREAM & THAI STREET CAFE NURSERY 1m 1f
5:55 (6:02) (Class 4) (0-85,84) 2-Y-O **£5,180** (£1,541; £770; £384) **Stalls** Low

Form RPR

3420 **1** **Liberty Cap (USA)**[10] 5830 2-9-6 **83** (b) WilliamBuick 6 85
(J H M Gosden) *hld up wl in tch in rr: effrt on outer over 2f out: chsd ldr jst over 1f out: edging lft: rdn to ld ins fnl f: kpt on* **20/1**

642 **2** *1/2* **El Mansour (USA)**[18] 5582 2-8-12 **75** PhilipRobinson 1 76
(C G Cox) *trckd ldrs on stands' rail: nt clr run and switching rt 2f out: drvn to chse ldrs over 1f out: kpt on ins fnl f to snatch 2nd on post* **12/1**

2413 **3** *nse* **Jehanbux (USA)**[27] 5310 2-9-7 **84** RichardHughes 9 85
(R Hannon) *led: stdd gallop 6f out: rdn and qcknd wl over 2f out: drvn over 1f out: hdd and no ex ins fnl f: lost 2nd on post* **10/3**[2]

1 **4** *1 1/2* **Suzy Wong**[36] 4993 2-9-0 **77** RyanMoore 8 76
(J Akehurst) *hld up in tch towards rr: rdn and sltly outpcd 3f out: rallied to chse ldrs 2f out: styd on same pce ins fnl f: btn whn n.m.r nr fin* **7/4**[1]

021 **5** *2 1/4* **Time To Work (IRE)**[15] 5676 2-9-4 **81** LiamKeniry 2 74
(A M Balding) *wnt rt s: hld up in tch: rdn and effrt 3f out: styd on same pce u.p fr over 1f out* **11/2**[3]

1 **6** *10* **Devoted (IRE)**[20] 5520 2-8-13 **76** JimCrowley 7 49
(R M Beckett) *stdd and awkward leaving stalls: in tch: rdn 3f out: wknd qckly ent fnl 2f: wl bhd ins fnl f* **9/1**

006 **7** *2 1/4* **Orange Ketchup (IRE)**[14] 5718 2-8-6 **69** HayleyTurner 4 38
(P F I Cole) *t.k.h: chsd ldr tl ent fnl 3f: sn lost pl: wl bhd fr over 1f out* **20/1**

51 **8** *1 1/4* **Bawaab (USA)**[31] 5178 2-8-13 **76** (t) KierenFallon 3 42+
(Saeed Bin Suroor) *s.i.s: towards rr early: hdwy to chse ldrs 6f out: wnt 2nd ent fnl 3f out: wknd qckly jst over 1f out: eased ins fnl f* **7/1**

1m 52.21s (0.51) **Going Correction** -0.025s/f (Good) **8** Ran SP% **114.5**
Speed ratings (Par 97): **96,95,95,94,92 83,81,80**
toteswingers:1&2 £13.40, 2&3 £5.90, 1&3 £6.50 CSF £231.71 CT £1008.15 TOTE £21.70: £6.00, £2.90, £1.10; EX 140.80 Place 6: £79.68 Place 5: £42.07.
Owner H R H Princess Haya Of Jordan **Bred** Randy Bloch Et Al **Trained** Newmarket, Suffolk

FOCUS
An ordinary nursery for the class. Straightforward form, rated around the principals.

NOTEBOOK
Liberty Cap(USA) responded better to the blinkers than he had at Goodwood last time and proved suited by the slight step up in trip. He'll make no appeal as one to back to follow up. (op 12-1)
El Mansour(USA) had to switch off the rail to get a clear run but took an age to pick up and wasn't unlucky. Despite his pedigree suggesting otherwise, he'll probably stay 1m2f this year. (op 9-1 tchd 7-1)
Jehanbux(USA) was given every chance from the front but was outstayed. He found 7f too short last time and 1m is probably his trip. (op 7-2 tchd 4-1)
Suzy Wong ran okay without building on the form she showed when a 33-1 winner on easy ground first time up. (op 5-2 tchd 3-1)
Time To Work(IRE) had been progressing nicely, but he failed to build on his Epsom maiden win and was disappointing. (op 4-1 tchd 7-2)
Bawaab(USA) lost his action in the dip and then hung badly left. He was in the process of running of a creditable race, but probably wouldn't have won. Official explanation: jockey said colt lost its action (tchd 8-1)
T/Plt: £87.00 to a £1 stake. Pool of £57,793.24 - 484.63 winning tickets. T/Qpdt: £22.90 to a £1 stake. Pool of £3,799.80 - 122.45 winning tickets SP

6118 WOLVERHAMPTON (A.W) (L-H)
Friday, September 17

OFFICIAL GOING: Standard
Wind: Fesh across Weather: Coudy with sunny spells

6161 £400 POKER BONUS AT WILLIAMHILL.COM MEDIAN AUCTION MAIDEN FILLIES' STKS 5f 216y(P)
5:50 (5:51) (Class 5) 2-Y-O **£3,561** (£1,059; £529; £264) **Stalls** Low

Form RPR

54 **1** **Camache Queen (IRE)**[10] 5835 2-9-0 0 CathyGannon 10 73
(D J Coakley) *broke wl: sn stdd and hld up in tch: rdn over 1f out: r.o to ld post* **12/1**

22 **2** *shd* **Celtic Sixpence (IRE)**[19] 5558 2-9-0 0 WilliamCarson 9 73
(M G Quinlan) *chsd ldr tl led over 2f out: rdn and hung rt over 1f out: hung lft wl ins fnl f: hdd post* **10/11**[1]

3 1 1/2 **Heart In Motion (IRE)** 2-9-0 0.. MickyFenton 2 69+
(M R Channon) *sn chsng ldrs: rdn over 1f out: styng on same pce whn hmpd wl ins fnl f* **25/1**

33 4 4 1/2 **Whitecrest**[9] 5865 2-9-0 0.. AdamKirby 12 55
(J L Spearing) *chsd ldrs: rdn and hung rt over 1f out: hung lft and wknd ins fnl f* **7/1**[3]

0 5 1/2 **Melbury**[14] 5719 2-8-11 0.. MichaelStainton(3) 8 54
(P Howling) *hld up: shkn up over 1f out: r.o ins fnl f: nvr nr to chal* **28/1**

00 6 shd **Formidable Girl (USA)**[50] 4508 2-9-0 0........................ DarryllHolland 4 54
(K A Ryan) *s.i.s and sn pushed along into mid-div: rdn over 1f out: nvr on terms* **3/1**[2]

7 3 1/4 **Ashgrove Nell (IRE)**[44] 4721 2-9-0 0........................ AndreaAtzeni 7 43
(Daniel Mark Loughnane, Ire) *led: rdn and hdd over 2f out: wknd over 1f out* **14/1**

00 8 nk **Lady Ellice**[14] 5721 2-9-0 0.. RoystonFfrench 6 43
(P S McEntee) *mid-div: hmpd 5f out: wknd over 2f out* **100/1**

9 8 **Bella Nemica** 2-9-0 0.. EddieCreighton 5 19
(E J Creighton) *dwlt: sn drvn along and a in rr* **100/1**

0 10 1 1/4 **Croce Rossa (IRE)**[10] 5841 2-9-0 0........................ StephenCraine 1 15
(J R Boyle) *s.i.s: sn prom: rdn and wknd over 2f out* **50/1**

1m 14.89s (-0.11) **Going Correction** -0.125s/f (Stan) **10** Ran SP% **115.5**
Speed ratings (Par 92): **95,94,92,86,86 86,81,81,70,69**
toteswingers:1&2 £3.40, 2&3 £5.50, 1&3 £17.80 CSF £22.87 TOTE £17.40: £5.20, £1.02, £6.90; EX 33.00.

Owner Keeper's 12 **Bred** Yeomanstown Stud **Trained** West Ilsley, Berks

■ Stewards' Enquiry : William Carson one-day ban: careless riding (Oct 4)

FOCUS
An ordinary fillies' maiden auction. It was run at a decent pace and the first three pulled clear of the rest. The form looks pretty solid.

NOTEBOOK
Camache Queen(IRE) had quite a bit to find but produced a surging run against the far rail to get up in the dying strides. This was a much improved effort switched to Polytrack by the filly who is out of a triple 6f-7f winner and shapes like a stiffer test could encourage further progress in nurseries. (op 10-1 tchd 9-1)
Celtic Sixpence(IRE) had leading form claims on her clear second behind a heavily backed Godolphin newcomer in a 6f soft-ground Yarmouth maiden on her second run. She travelled well up with the pace but couldn't shake off the pursuers and was just caught. (op 8-11)
Heart In Motion(IRE) attracted a bit of support at big prices and showed plenty of promise on her debut. An 11,000gns half-sister to a dual 7f-1m winner in Italy, she should have learned from this initial experience and should be able to win a similar race. (op 33-1)
Whitecrest, third at big prices in a pair of maidens at Bath and Kempton, was never far away but veered right around the final turn before fading behind the breakaway trio. Official explanation: jockey said filly hung right-handed (op 5-1)
Melbury did some late work from a long way back and has probably stepped up a bit from her low-key 100-1 debut. She cost just £1,600 but could be a quietly progressive type and it is encouraging that seven of her dam's eight previous foals have won. (op 25-1)
Formidable Girl(USA) was a springer in the market but was never involved and did not look the easiest of rides. She was rated highly enough to hold a Lowther entry at one point but has not shown a great deal in three starts so far. Official explanation: jockey said filly missed the break (op 13-2)
Ashgrove Nell(IRE) Official explanation: jockey said filly had no more to give

6162 REAL DEALERS AT WILLIAMHILL.COM LIVE CASINO NURSERY (DIV I) 7f 32y(P)
6:20 (6:21) (Class 5) (0-70,69) 2-Y-O **£2,914** (£867; £433; £216) **Stalls** High

Form RPR

354 1 **Hawk Moth (IRE)**[40] 4871 2-9-1 **63**........................ CathyGannon 8 68
(J L Spearing) *s.i.s: hld up: hdwy over 2f out: rdn over 1f out: r.o u.p to ld wl ins fnl f* **12/1**

603 2 1 1/2 **Polar Auroras**[14] 5719 2-9-3 **65**........................ RobertWinston 12 66
(Pat Eddery) *s.i.s: hld up: hdwy over 2f out: rdn over 1f out: hung lft and r.o wl ins fnl f* **7/1**

340 3 nk **Mega Mount (IRE)**[67] 3961 2-9-1 **63**........................(b[1]) JackMitchell 5 64
(R M Beckett) *hld up in tch: rdn over 2f out: led over 1f out: hdd wl ins fnl f* **8/1**

4243 4 3/4 **Prophet In A Dream**[31] 5177 2-8-13 **61**........................ SamHitchcott 4 60
(M R Channon) *trckd ldrs: plld hrd: rdn and hung lft over 1f out: styd on* **12/1**

0350 5 1 **Apazine (USA)**[70] 3871 2-9-6 **68**........................(b) NickyMackay 2 64
(J H M Gosden) *chsd ldrs: led over 4f out: rdn and hdd over 1f out: no ex ins fnl f* **11/4**[1]

630 6 1 1/2 **Book Keeper**[36] 4993 2-9-6 **68**........................ AhmedAjtebi 3 61
(Mahmood Al Zarooni) *led: hdd over 5f out: chsd ldrs: rdn over 1f out: no ex ins fnl f* **4/1**[2]

043 7 2 1/2 **Royal Reverie**[18] 5608 2-9-7 **69**........................ AdamKirby 1 56
(W R Swinburn) *chsd ldr: led over 5f out: hdd over 4f out: chsd ldr: rdn over 1f out: wknd ins fnl f* **9/2**[3]

0430 8 4 1/2 **All The Evil (IRE)**[15] 5675 2-9-5 **67**........................ EddieCreighton 9 42
(B J Meehan) *hld up in tch: rdn 4f out: wknd 3f out* **20/1**

000 9 1 1/2 **Appyjack**[21] 5465 2-8-7 **62**........................(b[1]) RyanPowell(7) 11 34
(J S Moore) *chsd ldrs tl rdn and wknd over 2f out* **100/1**

350 10 1 1/2 **King Of The Desert (IRE)**[22] 5453 2-9-2 **64**........................ TadhgO'Shea 6 32
(E A L Dunlop) *mid-div: lost pl over 5f out: wknd 3f out* **8/1**

1m 29.86s (0.26) **Going Correction** -0.125s/f (Stan) **10** Ran SP% **120.7**
Speed ratings (Par 95): **93,91,90,90,88 87,84,79,77,75**
CSF £96.66 CT £742.88 TOTE £14.80: £3.10, £4.90, £3.60; EX 52.30.

Owner Kinnersley Partnership **Bred** Dr D Harron **Trained** Kinnersley, Worcs

FOCUS
A nursery involving plenty of unexposed types. There were a number of different leaders in a race of changing fortunes. Modest form rated around the second and sixth.

NOTEBOOK
Hawk Moth(IRE) was slowly away but found a power-packed run out wide to get off the mark in good style. He is a scopey son of Hawk Wing who is related to a number of winners and should be capable of further success. (op 11-1 tchd 9-1)
Polar Auroras stayed on well from some back to post an encouraging effort stepped up to 7f on her nursery debut. She is getting better with practice and is a half-sister to smart J M W Turner who was a very progressive multiple sprint winner at two. (op 6-1 tchd 11-2 and 8-1)
Mega Mount(IRE) gave it a good try up in trip in first-time blinkers. He has made stilted progress but this was an encouraging nursery/AW debut and there should be more to come if the headgear continues to work. (op 10-1 tchd 15-2)
Prophet In A Dream continued his trend of finishing in the frame in nurseries but the 5f Brighton maiden winner seems to have reached the top-end of his ability after ten runs. (op 11-1)
Apazine(USA) was heavily backed and things looked to be going well under enterprising tactics for a long way before her effort petered. This expensive filly has an unconvincing profile but is in good hands and could go close back at 6f next time. (op 15-2)
Book Keeper was very disappointing when hot favourite on the third of his three maiden runs at Epsom. He was prominent in the betting again but didn't find a great deal switched to nursery company. (op 3-1 tchd 9-2)
Royal Reverie was always well placed but didn't pick up when things got serious on his first skirmish in nursery company. (op 5-1 tchd 6-1)

6163 REAL DEALERS AT WILLIAMHILL.COM LIVE CASINO NURSERY (DIV II) 7f 32y(P)
6:50 (6:54) (Class 5) (0-70,69) 2-Y-O **£2,914** (£867; £433; £216) **Stalls** High

Form RPR

4440 1 **Tamareen (IRE)**[14] 5720 2-9-3 **65**........................(t) TadhgO'Shea 4 68
(E A L Dunlop) *hld up: hdwy over 1f out: rdn to ld wl ins fnl f: r.o* **12/1**

4450 2 1 **Restless Bay (IRE)**[17] 5629 2-9-6 **68**........................(p) AdamKirby 1 69
(R Hollinshead) *hld up: hdwy over 2f out: rdn and ev ch fr over 1f out: unable qck nr fin* **8/1**[3]

530 3 nk **Green Pearl (IRE)**[21] 5465 2-9-7 **69**........................ GeorgeBaker 9 69
(R M Beckett) *sn chsng ldrs: led over 1f out: rdn and hdd wl ins fnl f* **7/2**[1]

5215 4 shd **Magic Cross**[18] 5613 2-8-7 **55**........................(t[1]) NickyMackay 8 55
(P J McBride) *s.i.s: hld up: hdwy over 2f out: rdn and ev ch ins fnl f: unable qck nr fin* **10/1**

6054 5 3/4 **Blackleyf (IRE)**[14] 5720 2-9-4 **66**........................(b) RobertWinston 5 65
(Tom Dascombe) *s.s: hld up: hdwy over 1f out: hrd rdn ins fnl f: eased whn hld nr fin* **11/1**

4440 6 1 1/4 **Dunmore Boy (IRE)**[25] 5354 2-9-0 **62**........................ JamesDoyle 2 57
(R A Fahey) *led early: prom: rdn over 2f out: styd on same pce ins fnl f* **15/2**[2]

0030 7 3 1/2 **None Sweeter**[11] 5818 2-8-11 **59**........................ DuranFentiman 6 46
(T D Easterby) *sn led: hdd 6f out: chsd ldrs: rdn over 2f out: wknd ins fnl f* **40/1**

0605 8 3/4 **Memorabilia**[11] 5807 2-9-5 **67**........................ RoystonFfrench 10 52
(M Johnston) *prom: jnd ldrs 6f out: rdn and ev ch 2f out: wknd ins fnl f* **14/1**

3052 9 3/4 **Silken Thoughts**[10] 5837 2-9-1 **63**........................ MickyFenton 7 46
(John Berry) *chsd ldrs: led over 5f out: rdn and hdd over 1f out: wknd ins fnl f* **7/2**[1]

403 10 1 **Silver Shine (IRE)**[99] 2895 2-8-11 **59**........................ LiamJones 3 39
(W J Haggas) *s.i.s: hld up: rdn over 2f out: a in rr* **8/1**[3]

533 11 26 **Norwegian Liberty (IRE)**[25] 5358 2-9-1 **63**........................(p) CathyGannon 11 —
(B M R Haslam) *prom: led 6f out: sn hdd: rdn and wknd over 2f out* **33/1**

1m 29.9s (0.30) **Going Correction** -0.125s/f (Stan) **11** Ran SP% **115.6**
Speed ratings (Par 95): **93,91,91,90 89,85,84,83,82 52**
toteswingers:1&2 £17.50, 2&3 £10.10, 1&3 £12.20 CSF £102.84 CT £418.26 TOTE £19.00: £6.90, £5.10, £1.10; EX 76.10.

Owner Hamdan Al Maktoum **Bred** Mcdonnell Cbs Bloodstock **Trained** Newmarket, Suffolk

FOCUS
This second division of the nursery was run at a fast pace which played into the hands of the hold-up performers. Modest form, rated around the principals.

NOTEBOOK
Tamareen(IRE) had not really progressed in maidens and was beaten over 7l on his nursery debut at Kempton but he found plenty of spark to win with a bit in hand stepped up to 7f for the first time. This first success should boost his confidence and there could be more improvement to come. (op 10-1)
Restless Bay(IRE) stayed on steadily with cheekpieces applied on this nursery debut. He has looked unruly at times and has an uneven profile since a 50-1 debut second but this was a definite move back in the right direction and the headgear could prompt another step forward next time. (op 14-1)
Green Pearl(IRE) was well backed and moved smoothly for a long way but couldn't fight off the pair who came from further back off the strong pace. However, this was a very promising AW/nursery debut from a half-brother to the yard's triple 1m2f-1m4f Polytrack winner Keenes Royale, particularly as he was reported to have been struck into. Official explanation: trainer said colt was struck into (op 5-1)
Magic Cross put in a decent effort stepped up in trip with the combination of eyeshields and a tongue-tie. She was a 6f Bath winner last month and could be up to defying this 7lb higher mark. (op 17-2 tchd 7-1 and 11-1)
Blackleyf(IRE) did really well to latch on to the leading pack after missing the break. The brutal pace helped him get as close as he did but he could be a major player in a similar race if getting away on terms next time. (op 10-1 tchd 8-1)
Silken Thoughts, second in a 7f nursery on good to soft at Lingfield last time, was a bit disappointing but probably paid the price for getting involved in a damaging battle for the lead with Memorabilia. (tchd 10-3 and 4-1)
Norwegian Liberty(IRE) Official explanation: jockey said filly hung right-handed on bend

6164 RINGSIDE CONFERENCE SUITE - 700 THEATRE STYLE CLASSIFIED CLAIMING STKS 7f 32y(P)
7:20 (7:21) (Class 5) 3-Y-O+ **£2,729** (£806; £403) **Stalls** High

Form RPR

6241 1 **Sabatini (IRE)**[16] 5661 3-8-6 70........................ RoystonFfrench 2 72
(J Pearce) *pushed along early and prom: hmpd and lost pl over 6f out: hld up: hdwy over 1f out: rdn to ld ins fnl f: r.o* **6/1**[3]

3045 2 1/2 **Lady Kent (IRE)**[14] 5713 4-8-5 69........................ SamHitchcott 4 68
(J R Boyle) *trckd ldrs: racd keenly: rdn over 2f out: ev ch ins fnl f: styd on* **7/1**

3003 3 1 3/4 **Law Of Attraction (IRE)**[13] 5769 3-8-4 70........................ LukeMorris 7 64
(J R Gask) *hld up: plld hrd: hdwy over 1f out: sn rdn and hung lft: rdr dropped reins ins fnl f: r.o* **9/2**[2]

5004 4 hd **Hierarch (IRE)**[21] 5494 3-8-2 67........................ CharlesEddery(7) 5 70+
(R Hannon) *hld up: hdwy and hmpd over 1f out: r.o: nt rch ldrs* **16/1**

2230 5 1/2 **Piddie's Power**[17] 5634 3-8-9 69........................ DarryllHolland 10 67
(E S McMahon) *led over 5f out: rdn: hung rt and hdd ins fnl f: no ex* **4/1**[1]

3200 6 3 **Excellent Day (IRE)**[8] 5896 3-8-4 70........................ LiamJones 3 54
(M R Channon) *hld up: hdwy over 2f out: sn rdn: no ex ins fnl f* **17/2**

2503 7 3/4 **Dvinsky (USA)**[2] 6078 9-8-3 70........................(b) WilliamCarson 11 49
(P Howling) *led: hdd wl over 5f out: trckd ldrs: racd keenly: rdn over 1f out: wknd ins fnl f* **8/1**

1060 8 1/2 **Hustle (IRE)**[18] 5235 5-8-4 67........................ AdamBeschizza(5) 12 54
(Miss Gay Kelleway) *s.i.s: hdwy over 5f out: rdn over 2f out: wknd over 1f out* **9/1**

0300 9 6 **Bahamian Kid**[7] 5906 5-8-7 67........................(v) RichardKingscote 6 35
(R Hollinshead) *chsd ldr over 5f out tl rdn and wknd over 1f out* **20/1**

3200 10 8 **Rubenstar (IRE)**[67] 3970 7-8-4 70........................ SaleemGolam 1 —
(Patrick Morris) *s.s: a bhd* **12/1**

1250 **11** 1/2 **Panpiper**18 5588 3-8-12 68 TomMcLaughlin 8 —
(G L Moore) *chsd ldrs: rdn 1/2-way: wknd wl over 2f out* **33/1**

1m 28.32s (-1.28) **Going Correction** -0.125s/f (Stan)
WFA 3 from 4yo+ 3lb **11** Ran SP% **117.9**
Speed ratings (Par 103): **102,101,99,99,98 95,94,93,86,77 77**
toteswingers:1&2 £3.90, 2&3 £6.00, 1&3 £5.70 CSF £47.82 TOTE £6.00: £1.10, £3.40, £3.30; EX 40.90.
Owner A Watford, D Leech, M Prince **Bred** O Bourke **Trained** Newmarket, Suffolk

FOCUS
All the runners in this tight claimer had BHA ratings between 67 and 70. The pace was decent and the first five finished clear of the rest. There were doubts over a few and the form is not rated too positively.

6165 FREE BETTING WITH FREEBETTING.CO.UK H'CAP 1m 1f 103y(P)
7:50 (7:50) (Class 6) (0-65,65) 3-Y-O+ **£1,774** (£523; £262) **Stalls** Low

Form RPR

-111 **1** **True To Form (IRE)**6 5962 3-9-5 65 6ex SebSanders 6 81+
(Sir Mark Prescott) *led over 8f out: shkn up over 2f out: rdn clr ins fnl f* **4/6**1

00 **2** 3 1/2 **Marrimeclaire (IRE)**105 2725 3-9-1 61 JackMitchell 12 68
(B J McMath) *hld up: rdn over 1f out: r.o ins fnl f: wnt 2nd nr fin: no ch w wnr* **50/1**

0-00 **3** 3/4 **New Beginning (IRE)**207 666 6-9-6 61 RoystonFfrench 8 66+
(J Mackie) *led 1f: chsd wnr: rdn over 2f out: styd on same pce fnl f: lost 2nd nr fin* **11/1**3

056- **4** 1 1/4 **Forbidden (IRE)**37 4978 7-9-9 64 (t) AndreaAtzeni 3 67
(Daniel Mark Loughnane, Ire) *mid-div: hdwy u.p over 2f out: styd on: nt trble ldrs* **33/1**

4062 **5** hd **Daniel Thomas (IRE)**9 5867 8-9-7 65 (p) RobertLButler(3) 2 67
(P Butler) *s.i.s: hld up: hmpd over 2f out: r.o ins fnl f: nrst fin* **33/1**

4353 **6** 1 1/2 **Vertigo On Course (IRE)**20 5530 5-9-5 60 PaulMulrennan 5 59
(R A Fahey) *chsd ldrs: rdn over 2f out: sn outpcd* **9/2**2

3540 **7** 3/4 **Faith Jicaro (IRE)**33 5115 3-9-5 65 DarryllHolland 7 63
(N J Vaughan) *hld up: rdn over 3f out: styd on: nt trble ldrs* **33/1**

1420 **8** nse **Dream Of Fortune (IRE)**3 6054 6-9-6 64 (bt) RichardEvans(3) 10 62
(P D Evans) *hld up: rdn over 1f out: r.o ins fnl f: nvr nrr* **20/1**

0120 **9** 4 **Provost**39 4897 6-9-6 61 (b) SamHitchcott 1 50
(M W Easterby) *hld up in tch: nt clr run and lost pl wl over 2f out: nt rcvr* **12/1**

-036 **10** 1/2 **Anaya**103 2792 3-8-9 60 MarkCoumbe(5) 11 48
(D Bourton) *prom: rdn over 3f out: wknd 2f out* **50/1**

0000 **11** 8 **Hilbre Court (USA)**13 5767 5-9-3 58 RobertWinston 9 29
(B P J Baugh) *hld up: rdn over 2f out: a in rr* **33/1**

0033 **12** 10 **Full Victory (IRE)**18 5584 8-9-5 60 AdamKirby 4 10
(R A Farrant) *chsd ldrs: rdn over 3f out: wknd wl over 2f out: t.o* **16/1**

203 **13** 7 **Markhesa**16 5655 4-9-4 59 GeorgeBaker 13 —
(J R Boyle) *hld up: rdn and wknd 3f out: t.o* **16/1**

1m 59.21s (-2.49) **Going Correction** -0.125s/f (Stan)
WFA 3 from 4yo+ 5lb **13** Ran SP% **126.4**
Speed ratings (Par 101): **106,102,102,101,100 99,98,98,95,94 87,78,72**
toteswingers:1&2 £20.70, 2&3 £172.90, 1&3 £3.80 CSF £70.64 CT £265.09 TOTE £1.70: £2.00, £18.50, £3.90; EX 48.70.
Owner G Moore - Osborne House **Bred** Sir E J Loder **Trained** Newmarket, Suffolk

FOCUS
An ordinary handicap won in emphatic style by the hot favourite, who probably ran another personal best. The pace was sound.
Vertigo On Course(IRE) Official explanation: jockey said mare hung left and right
Full Victory(IRE) Official explanation: jockey said gelding moved poorly

6166 GET BEST ODDS GUARANTEED AT WILLIAMHILL.COM H'CAP 1m 4f 50y(P)
8:20 (8:20) (Class 5) (0-75,72) 3-Y-O **£2,914** (£867; £433; £216) **Stalls** Low

Form RPR

432 **1** **Affinity**59 4229 3-9-2 67 TomQueally 3 75+
(H R A Cecil) *a.p: shkn up to ld over 1f out: r.o: comf* **10/3**1

0243 **2** 1/2 **Egmarey (IRE)**18 5607 3-9-2 67 (b) ChrisCatlin 1 74
(D R Lanigan) *hld up in tch: pushed along over 3f out: rdn over 1f out: hung lft ins fnl f: r.o* **6/1**

0-46 **3** 1/2 **Ertiyaad**63 4115 3-9-7 72 TadhgO'Shea 6 78
(Sir Michael Stoute) *chsd ldr after 1f: rdn to ld over 2f out: edgd rt and hdd over 1f out: r.o* **8/1**

-161 **4** 1 1/4 **Dhan Dhana (IRE)**16 5654 3-9-7 72 LiamJones 5 76
(W J Haggas) *hld up: rdn over 1f out: r.o: nt rch ldrs* **7/2**2

2141 **5** 1/2 **Sula Two**21 5467 3-9-5 70 GeorgeBaker 2 73
(R J Hodges) *chsd ldrs: rdn whn nt clr run wl over 1f out: styd on same pce ins fnl f* **11/2**3

5431 **6** 3 **Bondage (IRE)**17 5631 3-9-6 71 AdamKirby 4 69
(J R Fanshawe) *sn led at stdy pce: qcknd over 3f out: rdn and hdd over 2f out: no ex ins fnl f* **7/2**2

2m 44.27s (3.17) **Going Correction** -0.125s/f (Stan) **6** Ran SP% **108.3**
Speed ratings (Par 101): **84,83,83,82,82 80**
toteswingers:1&2 £7.20, 2&3 £10.40, 1&3 £8.00 CSF £21.30 TOTE £4.60: £2.40, £5.40; EX 26.50.
Owner Elite Racing Club **Bred** Elite Racing Club **Trained** Newmarket, Suffolk

FOCUS
There were not many runners but this handicap involved three last-time-out winners and a couple of other potential improvers. The pace was only steady but the winner produced a very likeable display and looks on the upgrade. This is probably not form to take too literally though.

6167 MOBILE.WILLIAMHILL.COM - LATEST ODDS ON YOUR IPHONE H'CAP 7f 32y(P)
8:50 (8:51) (Class 4) (0-85,85) 3-Y-O+ **£4,533** (£1,348; £674; £336) **Stalls** High

Form RPR

133 **1** **Regeneration (IRE)**64 4057 4-9-1 79 JamieSpencer 6 88
(M L W Bell) *prom: chsd ldr 6f out: rdn over 2f out: led ins fnl f: styd on u.p* **10/3**1

2214 **2** nk **Cheers For Thea (IRE)**18 5605 5-9-7 85 (bt) DuranFentiman 9 93
(T D Easterby) *hld up: hdwy over 1f out: sn rdn: r.o* **5/1**

54 **3** 3/4 **Caprio (IRE)**35 5027 5-9-2 80 NickyMackay 8 86+
(J R Boyle) *hld up: r.o wl ins fnl f: nrst fin* **28/1**

2260 **4** nk **Standpoint**12 5789 4-9-2 80 AdamKirby 1 85
(R Hollinshead) *chsd ldr 1f: remained handy: rdn over 2f out: r.o* **5/1**

542 **5** nse **Mambo Spirit (IRE)**13 5754 6-9-2 80 TomQueally 4 85
(Stef Higgins) *led: rdn over 2f out: edgd rt and hdd ins fnl f: styd on u.p* **9/2**3

2000 **6** nse **Battlemaiden (IRE)**30 5199 3-8-9 76 RoystonFfrench 5 80
(M Johnston) *a.p: rdn over 1f out: r.o* **33/1**

2-00 **7** shd **Conry (IRE)**27 5290 4-8-11 75 StephenCraine 10 80
(Patrick Morris) *hld up: rdn over 1f out: r.o ins fnl f: nt rch ldrs* **33/1**

4145 **8** 1 1/4 **Brannagh (USA)**41 4849 3-9-3 84 (t) DarryllHolland 11 84
(J Noseda) *s.i.s: nt clr run and swtchd rt ins fnl f: r.o: nt trble ldrs* **7/1**

3211 **9** hd **Fantasy Fighter (IRE)**7 5920 5-8-3 72 6ex AdamBeschizza(5) 2 73
(J J Quinn) *chsd ldrs: rdn over 1f out: styd on same pce ins fnl f* **4/1**2

0-04 **10** 6 **Iasia (GR)**41 4849 4-9-7 85 TomMcLaughlin 7 70
(Jane Chapple-Hyam) *chsd ldrs: rdn over 2f out: hung lft and wknd over 1f out* **18/1**

1m 27.69s (-1.91) **Going Correction** -0.125s/f (Stan)
WFA 3 from 4yo+ 3lb **10** Ran SP% **121.7**
Speed ratings (Par 105): **105,104,103,103,103 103,103,101,101,94**
toteswingers:1&2 £5.10, 2&3 £11.20, 1&3 £22.70 CSF £20.92 CT £403.53 TOTE £3.60: £1.10, £1.60, £6.80; EX 25.70.
Owner Tamdown Group Limited **Bred** Tally-Ho Stud **Trained** Newmarket, Suffolk

FOCUS
A fair handicap. It was run at a solid pace but they finished in a bit of a bunch.

6168 LATE NIGHT LIVE CASINO AT WILLIAMHILL.COM H'CAP 7f 32y(P)
9:20 (9:21) (Class 6) (0-65,65) 3-Y-O **£1,774** (£523; £262) **Stalls** High

Form RPR

2310 **1** **Fleetwoodsands (IRE)**66 3975 3-9-7 65 (t) TomQueally 1 74+
(Ollie Pears) *s.i.s: hld up: hdwy over 1f out: r.o to ld wl ins fnl f* **3/1**1

5500 **2** 1 1/4 **Ice Cool Lady (IRE)**16 5669 3-8-11 60 (b1) RosieJessop(5) 5 64
(W R Swinburn) *s.i.s: hld up: hdwy over 1f out: rdr dropped whip 1f out: r.o* **8/1**

6000 **3** hd **Quaestor (IRE)**36 4989 3-9-2 60 RichardKingscote 4 63
(Tom Dascombe) *chsd ldr: led 5f out: rdn over 1f out: hdd and unable qck wl ins fnl f* **20/1**

3555 **4** 3/4 **Chinese Democracy (USA)**35 5037 3-9-1 59 (v) CathyGannon 11 60
(P D Evans) *hld up: rdn over 1f out: hung lft and r.o ins fnl f: nrst fin* **9/1**

60-5 **5** 1 1/4 **George Baker (IRE)**58 4248 3-9-5 63 (t) TonyCulhane 10 61
(George Baker) *chsd ldrs: rdn over 1f out: no ex ins fnl f* **3/1**1

0-04 **6** 1/2 **Far View (IRE)**16 5658 3-9-2 60 SebSanders 2 57+
(J W Hills) *hld up: plld hrd: nt clr run fr over 1f out: tl r.o wl ins fnl f: nt trble ldrs* **13/2**2

0500 **7** nk **Verluga (IRE)**13 5758 3-9-2 60 DuranFentiman 3 56
(T D Easterby) *chsd ldrs: rdn 1/2-way: no ex ins fnl f* **7/1**3

8 3/4 **Jumbo Vision (USA)**32 5167 3-9-5 63 (t) AndreaAtzeni 6 57
(Daniel Mark Loughnane, Ire) *hld up: hdwy over 2f out: rdn and hung lft over 1f out: one pce* **33/1**

0000 **9** 1 1/4 **Takajan (IRE)**7 5905 3-9-4 62 LiamJones 8 53
(W M Brisbourne) *chsd ldrs: rdn over 2f out: wknd ins fnl f* **33/1**

434 **10** 2 3/4 **Angel Of Fashion (IRE)**23 5417 3-9-2 60 RobertWinston 9 43
(P Charalambous) *sn led: hdd 5f out: chsd ldr: rdn over 1f out: wknd ins fnl f* **9/1**

1m 28.81s (-0.79) **Going Correction** -0.125s/f (Stan) **10** Ran SP% **117.6**
Speed ratings (Par 99): **99,97,97,96,95 94,94,93,91,88**
toteswingers:1&2 £8.10, 2&3 £25.30, 1&3 £14.00 CSF £27.86 CT £404.35 TOTE £3.90: £1.10, £3.80, £7.70; EX 25.00 Place 6: £148.82 Place 5: £87.09.
Owner P Wilkinson **Bred** Gary O'Reilly **Trained** Norton, N Yorks
■ Stewards' Enquiry : Tom Queally one-day ban: careless riding (Oct 4)

FOCUS
An ordinary handicap run at a reasonable pace. The time was decent but there were doubts over several of these, with the fourth perhaps the best guide.
Jumbo Vision(USA) Official explanation: jockey said gelding hung left-handed
T/Plt: £151.60 to a £1 stake. Pool of £77,909.75 - 375.07 winning tickets. T/Qpdt: £28.50 to a £1 stake. Pool of £10,170.42 - 263.30 winning tickets. CR

6169 - 6173a (Foreign Racing) - See Raceform Interactive

6138 AYR (L-H)
Saturday, September 18

OFFICIAL GOING: Good (good to firm in places; 9.2; sprint course: far side 9.6, centre 9.8, stands' side 10.2)
Home bend moved out 2m from inner line to give fresh ground increasing distances on Round course by about 6yds.
Wind: Fresh, half against Weather: Cloudy

6174 NIGEL ANGUS MEMORIAL NURSERY 1m
1:40 (1:40) (Class 2) 2-Y-O
£11,215 (£3,358; £1,679; £840; £419; £210) **Stalls** High

Form RPR

10 **1** **Bridle Belle**10 5849 2-8-12 81 LeeTopliss(5) 2 86
(R A Fahey) *dwlt: sn prom: hdwy to trck ldrs over 2f out: styd on to ld jst ins fnl f: hld on towards fin* **7/2**2

4406 **2** nk **Golden Blaze**7 5947 2-7-5 62 oh2 NoelGarbutt(7) 8 66
(James Moffatt) *w ldr: led over 3f out: edgd rt and hdd jst ins fnl f: kpt on: no ex towards fin* **33/1**

1021 **3** nk **Daas Rite (IRE)**9 5894 2-8-7 74 AmyRyan(3) 5 77
(K A Ryan) *sn chsng ldrs: edgd rt 2f out: styd on same pce last 100yds* **25/1**

4212 **4** 1 **Diamond Penny (IRE)**16 5690 2-9-7 85 JamieSpencer 3 86
(P F I Cole) *swvd lft s: hld up in rr: effrt on outside over 2f out: hrd rdn and styd on fnl f: nt rch ldrs* **9/2**

1 **5** 1 **Raucous Behaviour (USA)**17 5651 2-9-1 79 SilvestreDeSousa 7 78
(M Johnston) *sn drvn along: chsd ldrs: outpcd over 2f out: styd on ins fnl f* **15/8**1

406 **6** shd **Purkab**27 5332 2-7-5 62 oh2 NeilFarley(7) 1 60
(J S Goldie) *in rr: drvn 3f out: styng on whn hmpd 2f out: nvr trbld ldrs* **33/1**

1 **7** 3/4 **Cosmic Moon**28 5294 2-8-11 75 PaulHanagan 6 72
(R A Fahey) *hld up in midfield: effrt over 3f out: chsng ldrs over 1f out: wknd fnl 150yds* **4/1**3

2332 **8** 1/2 **Residence And Spa (IRE)**44 4747 2-8-11 75 (b1) DavidAllan 4 71
(T D Easterby) *mde most: hdd over 3f out: wknd ins fnl f* **11/1**

1m 41.52s (-2.28) **Going Correction** -0.325s/f (Firm) **8** Ran SP% **113.2**
Speed ratings (Par 101): **98,97,97,96,95 95,94,94**
toteswingers:1&2 £33.60, 2&3 £37.30, 1&3 £13.60 CSF £106.11 CT £2457.15 TOTE £4.00: £1.10, £7.40, £3.50; EX 166.60.
Owner Mrs H Steel **Bred** Mrs C R Philipson & Mrs H G Lascelles **Trained** Musley Bank, N Yorks

FOCUS
The two unbeaten runners, one of whom was the well-fancied favourite, both disappointed, and with the top weight rated only 85, the form is ordinary for the level. The field finished compressed, and the form is limited but compressed.

NOTEBOOK

Bridle Belle, upped in trip, was solid in the market, despite Paul Hanagan riding the other Richard Fahey runner, and she fully justified in the support, finding enough after travelling as well as any. She's now won two of her three starts, with her sole defeat easily excused, but as mentioned, this form is below the usual standard for a Class 2 event. (op 4-1 tchd 3-1 and 9-2 in a place)

Golden Blaze ran well from 2lb out of the handicap, a particularly creditable effort considering he was hassled up front by Residence And Spa. He will probably go up in the weights for this, but can still contest lesser races. (op 28-1)

Daas Rite(IRE) found this tougher than the Polytrack claimer he won last time but had every chance and ran well. (op 12-1)

Diamond Penny(IRE) didn't travel that well early and was laboured under pressure when taken to the outside in the straight. (op 5-1 tchd 11-2)

Raucous Behaviour(USA) looked a very useful prospect when overcoming greenness to win on debut over 7f at Brighton, and seemed sure to progress over this longer trip, but he proved most disappointing, never travelling at any stage. Being a big colt with a bit of knee action, perhaps this ground was quicker than he can for, and he may yet fulfil that initial promise under more suitable conditions as he strengthens up. Official explanation: jockey said colt never travelled (op 5-2)

Cosmic Moon, the winner of a Chester maiden on debut, appeared to choice of Hanagan, but she was weak in the market. She's bred to have been well suited by this step up from 7f, but was a bit keen early and found little for pressure, looking another who may need more time. (op 7-2)

Residence And Spa(IRE) was too free in first-time blinkers. (tchd 12-1)

6175 WILLIAM HILL (AYR) SILVER CUP H'CAP — 6f

2:15 (2:16) (Class 2) 3-Y-0+

£31,155 (£9,330; £4,665; £2,335; £1,165; £585) **Stalls** Centre

Form				RPR
0021	1		**Colonel Mak**[25] 5390 3-9-4 **93** 5ex ..... PhillipMakin 7 (T D Barron) *prom far side: effrt over 1f out: led that gp ins fnl f: r.o wl: 1st of 10 in gp* **33/1**	106
0000	2	¾	**Sonny Red (IRE)**[28] 5302 6-8-13 **89** ..... MichaelGeran(3) 8 (D Nicholls) *missed break: towards rr far side: hdwy 2f out: chsd wnr ins fnl f: r.o: 2nd of 10 in gp* **25/1**	99+
2243	3	2	**Misplaced Fortune**[13] 5787 5-8-11 **89** ..... (v) DaleSwift(5) 25 (N Tinkler) *cl up stands' side: led that gp over 1f out to ins fnl f: rallied to regain ld that gp nr fin: nt rch far side ldrs: 1st of 14 in gp* **12/1**	93
0002	4	nse	**Advanced**[21] 5526 7-9-5 **95** ..... AmyRyan(3) 6 (K A Ryan) *cl up far side: effrt over 2f out: kpt on same pce ins fnl f: 3rd of 10 in gp* **14/1**	99
6061	5	nse	**Irish Heartbeat (IRE)**[8] 5911 5-9-4 **96** 5ex ..... LeeTopliss(5) 20 (R A Fahey) *hld up in midfield stands' side: smooth hdwy over 2f out: led that gp ins fnl f to nr fin: 2nd of 14 in gp* **8/1**[3]	100+
4230	6	1	**Manassas (IRE)**[21] 5516 5-9-9 **96** ..... (v[1]) TadhgO'Shea 9 (B J Meehan) *led far side tl hdd ins fnl f: kpt on same pce: 4th of 10 in gp* **33/1**	96
4120	7	½	**Gap Princess (IRE)**[28] 5302 6-9-3 **90** ..... SilvestreDeSousa 10 (G A Harker) *hld up in tch far side: effrt 2f out: no imp ins fnl f: 5th of 10 in gp* **40/1**	89
0050	8	hd	**Able Master (IRE)**[91] 3193 4-9-8 **95** ..... AdamKirby 22 (J R Gask) *towards rr stands' side: hdwy u.p over 1f out: kpt on: nvr able to chal: 3rd of 14 in gp* **33/1**	93
5104	9	nk	**Joseph Henry**[13] 5787 8-9-2 **89** ..... AdrianNicholls 27 (D Nicholls) *led stands' side tl hung lft and hdd over 1f out: kpt on same pce: 4th of 14 in gp* **16/1**	86
0403	10	hd	**Sea Of Leaves (USA)**[8] 5911 4-9-3 **90** ..... TedDurcan 4 (J S Goldie) *hld up far side: effrt over 2f out: kpt on ins fnl f: no imp: 6th of 10 in gp* **22/1**	87
00-0	11	dht	**Lowther**[8] 5911 5-9-5 **92** ..... RobertWinston 21 (A Bailey) *in tch stands' side: rdn over 2f out: rallied: kpt on same pce ins fnl f: 5th of 14 in gp* **16/1**	89
0030	12	¾	**Lowdown (IRE)**[13] 5787 3-9-9 **98** ..... PaulMulrennan 16 (M Johnston) *hld up stands' side: effrt over 1f out: styng on whn hmpd ins fnl f: nt rcvr: 6th of 14 in gp* **50/1**	96+
0100	13	nk	**Hotham**[7] 5944 7-9-5 **95** ..... BarryMcHugh(3) 19 (N Wilson) *dwlt: towards rr and sn pushed along stands' side: effrt over 1f out: nvr able to chal: 7th of 14 in gp* **50/1**	88
1015	14	hd	**Rasaman (IRE)**[15] 5734 6-9-0 **90** 5ex ..... GaryBartley(3) 15 (J S Goldie) *bhd stands' side: drvn along 1/2-way: sme late hdwy: n.d: 8th of 14 in gp* **50/1**	83
0011	15	nse	**Hajoum (IRE)**[7] 5950 4-9-9 **96** 8ex ..... PJMcDonald 17 (M Johnston) *in tch on outside of stands' side gp: effrt over 2f out: edgd lft: no ex over 1f out: 9th of 14 in gp* **12/1**	88
0011	16	hd	**Definightly**[7] 5952 4-9-4 **96** 8ex ..... (b) AdamBeschizza(5) 13 (R Charlton) *racd alone centre: rdn along over 2f out: sn no imp* **9/2**[2]	88
4404	17	nse	**Tiddliwinks**[7] 5944 4-9-7 **94** ..... JamieSpencer 24 (K A Ryan) *hld up stands' side: no room fr over 2f out tl wl ins fnl f: nt rcvr: 10th of 14 in gp* **4/1**[1]	86+
3030	18	hd	**Bonnie Charlie**[35] 5068 4-9-8 **95** ..... (v[1]) TonyCulhane 5 (W J Haggas) *trckd far side ldrs: rdn over 2f out: no ex over 1f out: 7th of 10 in gp* **28/1**	86
1000	19	1 ¼	**Kellys Eye (IRE)**[47] 4653 3-9-5 **94** ..... SteveDrowne 26 (D H Brown) *trckd stands' side ldrs: rdn over 2f out: wknd over 1f out: 11th of 14 in gp* **16/1**	81
6251	20	½	**Baby Strange**[9] 5884 6-9-7 **94** 5ex ..... PaulHanagan 18 (D Shaw) *hld up stands' side: rdn over 2f out: nvr able to chal: 12th of 14 in gp* **20/1**	79
0100	21	1 ½	**Something (IRE)**[28] 5292 8-9-1 **93** ..... BillyCray(5) 11 (D Nicholls) *hld up on outside of far side gp: rdn over 2f out: no imp over 1f out: 8th of 10 in gp* **40/1**	74
1106	22	1 ½	**Favourite Girl (IRE)**[14] 5742 4-9-5 **92** ..... (v) DavidAllan 12 (T D Easterby) *prom on outside of stands' side gp: rdn over 2f out: wknd over 1f out: 13th of 14 in gp* **40/1**	68
0004	23	5	**Below Zero (IRE)**[8] 5903 3-9-4 **93** ..... ChrisCatlin 1 (M Johnston) *trckd far side ldrs tl rdn and wknd fr 2f out: 9th of 10 in gp* **66/1**	53
0-00	24	1 ¼	**Hogmaneigh (IRE)**[7] 5944 7-9-7 **94** ..... SebSanders 3 (J S Goldie) *hld up far side: rdn over 2f out: sn btn: last of 10 in gp* **33/1**	50
0200	25	1 ¼	**Pavershooz**[28] 5308 5-9-2 **89** ..... AndrewElliott 23 (N Wilson) *cl up stands' side tl rdn and wknd qckly over 1f out: last of 14 in gp* **25/1**	41

1m 10.97s (-2.63) **Going Correction** -0.20s/f (Firm)

WFA 3 from 4yo+ 2lb — **25** Ran SP% **135.7**

Speed ratings (Par 109): **109,108,105,105,105 103,103,102,102,102 102,101,100,100,100 100,100,99,98,97 95,93,86,85,83**

toteswingers:1&2 not won, 2&3 £155.20, 1&3 £73.90 CSF £714.76 CT £10122.84 TOTE £70.80: £11.90, £5.60, £3.30, £3.60; EX 2882.80 TRIFECTA Not won..

Owner Norton Common Farm Racing **Bred** Peter Baldwin **Trained** Maunby, N Yorks

FOCUS

The previous day's Bronze Cup and a couple of other large-field sprints strongly suggested that unless you were drawn high, it was going to be very difficult to win this, but 24 hours is a long time in racing and any bias that was perceived to be in place was nullified. The field split into two main packs, although the well-fancied Definightly stayed towards the middle of the course. Another clear best from the winner, with the scond possibly unlucky.

NOTEBOOK

Colonel Mak ◆'s connections can start dreaming of better things to come, as the 3-y-os that have taken this contest usually go on to be decent (Utmost Respect in 2007 and Eisteddfod in 2004). Raised 5lb for his Leicester success at the end of last month, a race that has worked out well, he came with a strong late burst on the far side to claim his biggest success.

Sonny Red(IRE), who caught the eye behind his stable companion Tajneed last time, didn't start that quickly but was soon back on terms in the far-side bunch. He came home well but the winner had his measure. (op 28-1)

Misplaced Fortune, whose record in a visor is 4-9, ran a blinder after getting to the stands'-side rail about 2f out.

Advanced, the 2007 Ayr Gold Cup winner, is fairly treated and kept on resolutely after being prominent on his side of the course. (op 20-1)

Irish Heartbeat(IRE), raised 5lb for his win at Doncaster, hadn't won over this distance but looked to be travelling well just over a furlong out. He kept on but wasn't able to win the race on his side. (op 9-1)

Manassas(IRE), visored for the first time, is on a fair mark and showed good pace until steadily weakening.

Gap Princess(IRE) is on her highest ever mark, but stayed on well down the far side and is still performing to her best. (op 50-1)

Able Master(IRE) ◆, off the track since finishing well behind Laddies Poker Two in the Wokingham Handicap, looked a little unlucky as he met trouble in running on at least a couple of occasions.

Joseph Henry, 16th in this race last season, seemed to be the stable's first string judged on jockey bookings and set the pace on his side until joined. His jockey reported afterwards that his mount hung left throughout. Official explanation: jockey said gelding hung left throughout (op 12-1)

Lowther didn't run too badly on his return to action recently and appeared to have every chance in this despite being a little short of room about a furlong out. (op 18-1 tchd 20-1)

Definightly, a winner in Listed company last time, stayed in the centre of the course. (op 5-1)

Tiddliwinks ◆, who shaped nicely in the Portland, could be spotted going really well behind horses on his side but found plenty of traffic problems. Every gap Jamie Spencer went for closed, and the combination passed the post still on the bridle. Official explanation: jockey said gelding weas denied a clear run (op 6-1)

Bonnie Charlie, visored for the first time, was said to have got on his toes leaving the paddock and probably boiled over.

Something(IRE) looked to have sweated up and probably didn't run up to his best.

Pavershooz looked to have a few positives coming into this but dropped out quickly once starting to hang. He reportedly finished distressed. Official explanation: jockey said gelding finished distressed

6176 LAUNDRY COTTAGE STUD FIRTH OF CLYDE STKS (GROUP 3) (FILLIES) — 6f

2:45 (2:47) (Class 1) 2-Y-O

£34,062 (£12,912; £6,462; £3,222; £1,614; £810) **Stalls** Centre

Form				RPR
01	1		**Majestic Dubawi**[22] 5465 2-8-12 78 ..... ChrisCatlin 4 (M R Channon) *wnt lft s: w ldr: led 2f out: styd on wl* **22/1**	101
2212	2	1	**Ragsah (IRE)**[9] 5882 2-8-12 88 ..... FrankieDettori 10 (Saeed Bin Suroor) *hld up towards rr: hdwy whn nt clr run over 1f out: r.o strly ins fnl f: nt rch wnr* **10/3**[2]	98
11	3	hd	**Barefoot Lady (IRE)**[10] 5850 2-8-12 92 ..... PaulHanagan 7 (R A Fahey) *mid-div: effrt over 2f out: styd on ins fnl f* **6/1**[3]	97
1063	4	¾	**Mortitia**[9] 5882 2-8-12 95 ..... PaulMulrennan 1 (B J Meehan) *swvd lft s: sn chsng ldrs: kpt on same pce ins fnl f* **14/1**	95
2600	5	1 ¼	**Shoshoni Wind**[30] 5245 2-8-12 90 ..... RobertWinston 2 (K A Ryan) *led: t.k.h: drvn and hdd 2f out: kpt on one pce* **33/1**	91
11	6	½	**Tallahasse (IRE)**[44] 4748 2-8-12 88 ..... PJMcDonald 5 (G A Swinbank) *sn trcking ldrs: drvn over 2f out: kpt on one pce* **16/1**	90
132	7	¾	**Rimth**[16] 5693 2-8-12 102 ..... JamieSpencer 6 (P F I Cole) *hld up towards rr: effrt over 2f out: nt clr run over 1f out: keeping on same pce whn eased fnl 50yds* **11/8**[1]	88
6	8	1 ¼	**Strictly Pink (IRE)**[5] 6034 2-8-12 0 ..... SteveDrowne 9 (A Bailey) *hld up in rr: effrt over 2f out: nvr a factor* **80/1**	84
01	9	1	**Days Of Summer (IRE)**[23] 5453 2-8-12 80 ..... SilvestreDeSousa 11 (R M Beckett) *hld up in rr: effrt over 2f out: nvr a factor* **20/1**	81
1	10	shd	**Finoon (IRE)**[20] 5558 2-8-12 0 ..... TedDurcan 3 (Saeed Bin Suroor) *wnt rt s: chsd ldrs: styd on and 2nd whn wnt bdly wrong and heavily eased 75yds out: fatally injured* **12/1**	91

1m 12.01s (-1.59) **Going Correction** -0.20s/f (Firm) — **10** Ran SP% **113.0**

Speed ratings (Par 102): **102,100,100,99,97 97,96,94,93,92**

toteswingers:1&2 £28.70, 2&3 £4.30, 1&3 £39.80 CSF £88.99 TOTE £38.60: £7.60, £1.60, £2.70; EX 162.70 TRIFECTA Not won..

Owner Jaber Abdullah **Bred** P A Mason **Trained** West Ilsley, Berks

FOCUS

Not always that strong a race, but it has been contested by some smart types in recent times, including Airwave, who was successful in 2002, and Astrophysical Jet, third last year. It's hard to be confident about the level of this season's contest (winner and runner-up had to step up significantly on previous efforts), but it looked of reasonable quality. The form is rated around the fourth and fifth.

NOTEBOOK

Majestic Dubawi achieved an official rating of 78 when winning a Bath maiden last time, but she's clearly improving rapidly. She's an uncomplicated filly with a good attitude, finding plenty after being well placed, and at this stage it's impossible to know how far she'll progress. Her pedigree suggests she'll stay further (she holds an entry in the Irish Oaks, as well as the Irish Guineas), but she's obviously not short of speed and her connections will no doubt be tempted to supplement her for the Cheveley Park at a cost of £15,000. Should she be stepped up in trip, the obvious target is the Rockfel, an event her trainer won last year with Music Show, who was beaten in this race. (op 16-1)

Ragsah(IRE) went to the front too soon when second to the promising Eucharist in a nursery at Doncaster, but was set too much to do this time, for all that she didn't look an unlucky loser. A filly who possesses an impressive but short burst of speed, she was dropped in at the start but didn't get the best of runs, eventually finishing well when in the clear, but too late. She should prove suited by a return to further in due course, provided waiting tactics are employed, and the Rockfel could be a suitable target. (op 11-2)

Barefoot Lady(IRE), the winner of her first two starts in lesser company, took a while to pick up and may be worth a try over 7f. (op 5-1 tchd 9-2)

Mortitia was closely matched with Ragsah on recent Doncaster form, but that one has found the greater improvement. (op 10-1)

Shoshoni Wind has struggled since taking second behind subsequent sales race winner Khor Sheed in a Listed contest in June, but although again well held, this was better than of late. (op 25-1)

Tallahasse(IRE) is now in the Highclere colours, but her first two wins came in relatively ordinary company and this was much tougher. (op 12-1)
Rimth couldn't confirm Salisbury Listed race placings with Mortitia, but she wasn't given a particularly good ride and is easily excused. She had little room to make her move in the latter stages, being kept in by Barefoot Lady while stuck behind Tallahasse, and had insufficient momentum when switched backed inside with less than a furlong to run, eventually being heavily eased near the line. (op 13-8)
Finoon(IRE), who won a Yarmouth maiden on soft first time up, was keeping on in second, but looking held by the winner, when unfortunately going wrong inside the final furlong. It turned out she had shattered a pastern, and sadly she had to be put down. (op 10-1)

6177 WILLIAM HILL (AYR) GOLD CUP (HERITAGE H'CAP) 6f

3:20 (3:23) (Class 2) 3-Y-0+

£93,465 (£27,990; £13,995; £7,005; £3,495; £1,755) **Stalls** Centre

Form RPR

003 **1** **Redford (IRE)**[28] 5292 5-9-2 **97** .... FrankieDettori 17 115+
(D Nicholls) *hld up and bhd stands' side gp: weaved through fr over 1f out to ld ins fnl f: rdn and r.o strly: 1st of 10 in gp* **14/1**

-112 **2** 2 1/4 **Victoire De Lyphar (IRE)**[50] 4536 3-9-4 **101** .... AdrianNicholls 24 112
(D Nicholls) *cl up stands' side: rdn over 2f out: kpt on ins fnl f: nt gng pce of wnr: 2nd of 10 in gp* **8/1**[3]

0061 **3** 1/2 **Hitchens (IRE)**[13] 5787 5-9-6 **101** 5ex .... SilvestreDeSousa 8 110
(T D Barron) *in tch far side: rdn to ld that gp appr fnl f: kpt on: nt gng pce of stands' side wnr: 1st of 16 in gp* **25/1**

6103 **4** shd **Genki (IRE)**[14] 5744 6-9-8 **103** .... (v) SteveDrowne 11 112+
(R Charlton) *hld up on outside of far side gp: gd hdwy over 1f out: styd on ins fnl f: 2nd of 16 in gp* **8/1**[3]

2212 **5** 1 **Jonny Mudball**[49] 4576 4-9-9 **104** .... (t) SebSanders 25 110
(Tom Dascombe) *cl up stands' side: rdn over 1f out: kpt on same pce ins fnl f: 3rd of 10 in gp* **13/2**[1]

4400 **6** shd **Knot In Wood (IRE)**[35] 5095 8-9-7 **102** .... PaulHanagan 13 107
(R A Fahey) *prom far side: led over 2f out to appr fnl f: kpt on same pce: 3rd of 16 in gp* **20/1**

3020 **7** 1/2 **Kaldoun Kingdom (IRE)**[49] 4576 5-9-5 **105** .... AdamBeschizza(5) 9 109
(R A Fahey) *hld up far side: hdwy over 2f out: kpt on same pce ins fnl f: 4th of 16 in gp* **33/1**

6030 **8** 3/4 **Signor Peltro**[7] 5944 7-9-5 **100** .... TonyCulhane 22 101
(H Candy) *hld up stands' side: rdn over 2f out: kpt on fnl f: nvr rchd ldrs: 4th of 10 in gp* **20/1**

0244 **9** hd **Rileyskeepingfaith**[35] 5095 4-9-7 **102** .... (v) ChrisCatlin 5 103
(M R Channon) *hld up in midfield far side: effrt 2f out: no imp over 1f out: 5th of 16 in gp* **12/1**

2011 **10** hd **Poet's Place (USA)**[7] 5944 5-9-6 **101** 5ex .... PhillipMakin 12 101
(T D Barron) *dwlt far side: towards rr: rdn and hdwy over 1f out: nvr able to chal: 6th of 16 in gp* **15/2**[2]

0604 **11** dht **Damien (IRE)**[8] 5911 4-9-4 **99** .... RobertWinston 19 99
(B W Hills) *towards rr stands' side gp: rdn over 2f out: plugged on ins fnl f: n.d: 5th of 10 in gp* **40/1**

0400 **12** nse **Jimmy Styles**[49] 4576 6-9-8 **103** .... (b) AdamKirby 14 103
(C G Cox) *in tch far side: effrt over 2f out: wknd over 1f out: 7th of 16 in gp* **33/1**

2530 **13** hd **Quest For Success (IRE)**[7] 5944 5-9-5 **100** .... DavidAllan 23 99
(R A Fahey) *cl up stands' side: rdn over 2f out: wknd ent fnl f: 6th of 10 in gp* **25/1**

0010 **14** shd **Prime Exhibit**[49] 4576 5-8-11 **97** .... LeeTopliss(5) 3 96
(R A Fahey) *midfield far side: drvn over 2f out: no ex over 1f out: 8th of 16 in gp* **33/1**

2301 **15** nk **Hawkeyethenoo (IRE)**[56] 4391 4-9-2 **97** .... TedDurcan 16 95
(J S Goldie) *hld up on outside of far side gp: rdn over 2f out: nt gng pce to chal: 9th of 16 in gp* **8/1**[3]

2200 **16** 1/2 **Striking Spirit**[7] 5944 5-9-4 **99** .... TadhgO'Shea 27 95
(D Nicholls) *led stands' side tl hdd ins fnl f: sn wknd: 7th of 10 in gp* **25/1**

3100 **17** 3/4 **Castles In The Air**[29] 5275 5-9-5 **103** .... BarryMcHugh(3) 10 97
(R A Fahey) *in tch far side: rdn over 2f out: wknd over 1f out: 10th of 16 in gp* **50/1**

0001 **18** hd **Evens And Odds (IRE)**[49] 4576 6-9-4 **104** .... BillyCray(5) 21 97
(D Nicholls) *bhd stands' side: drvn along 1/2-way: no imp: 8th of 10 in gp* **22/1**

0000 **19** shd **Johannes (IRE)**[7] 5944 7-9-1 **96** .... PaulMulrennan 1 89
(R A Fahey) *trckd far side ldrs tl wknd fr 2f out: 11th of 16 in gp* **33/1**

1000 **20** nk **Barney McGrew (IRE)**[14] 5744 7-9-5 **105** .... DaleSwift(5) 7 97
(M Dods) *cl up far side tl rdn and wknd over 1f out: 12th of 16 in gp* **40/1**

1000 **21** hd **Flipando (IRE)**[8] 5911 9-9-3 **98** .... LNewman 26 89
(T D Barron) *towards rr stands' side: drvn over 2f out: nvr able to chal: 9th of 10 in gp* **66/1**

/1-4 **22** 1/2 **Partner (IRE)**[41] 4881 4-8-13 **97** .... (b) EJMcNamara(3) 6 87
(David Marnane, Ire) *midfield far side: rdn over 2f out: wknd over 1f out: 13th of 16 in gp* **25/1**

0310 **23** 3/4 **Damika (IRE)**[8] 5911 7-9-0 **98** .... MichaelStainton(3) 15 85
(R M Whitaker) *prom far side tl rdn and wknd over 1f out: 14th of 16 in gp* **66/1**

1302 **24** 3 1/2 **Parisian Pyramid (IRE)**[28] 5302 4-9-4 **99** .... JamieSpencer 4 75
(K A Ryan) *led far side to over 2f out: wknd over 1f out: 15th of 16 in gp* **22/1**

6056 **25** 1 1/2 **Arganil (USA)**[7] 5944 5-9-1 **96** .... (b) PJMcDonald 2 67
(K A Ryan) *rrd s: bhd far side: nvr on terms: last of 16 in gp* **33/1**

3105 **26** 6 **Noverre To Go (IRE)**[49] 4576 4-8-11 **97** .... (t) RossAtkinson(5) 20 49
(Tom Dascombe) *prom stands' side tl rdn and wknd 2f out: last of 10 in gp* **16/1**

1m 10.26s (-3.34) **Going Correction** -0.20s/f (Firm)
WFA 3 from 4yo+ 2lb **26** Ran SP% **136.8**
Speed ratings (Par 109): **114,111,110,110,108 108,108,107,106,106 106,106,106,106,105 105,104,103,103,103 102,102,101,96**
toteswingers:1&2 £17.70, 2&3 £187.60, 1&3 £78.70 CSF £101.99 CT £2875.10 TOTE £11.20: £2.60, £2.80, £9.70, £2.50; EX 87.40 Trifecta £13504.70 Part won. Pool: £18,249.62 - 0.40 winning units..
Owner Dr Marwan Koukash **Bred** T J Rooney **Trained** Sessay, N Yorks
■ A sixth Ayr Gold Cup for David Nicholls, who had the 1-2.

FOCUS
A red-hot contest as one would expect for the money on offer, which included a horse placed in Group 1 company on its previous start. The first four in 2009 reopposed, and the winners of many big sprint handicaps during the season also lined up. The Silver Cup earlier on the card appeared to suggest that low numbers might have the advantage, but it swung back in the favour of the near side, although whichever part of the track the winner had come down, there is a fair chance he would have prevailed. Strong, solid handicap form, run in a good time compared with the Silver Cup. A bit of drama unfolded even beforehand, as Tajneed (33/1) broke through his stall and was withdrawn.

NOTEBOOK
Redford(IRE) ◆ finally delivered on the big stage, something he has looked capable of doing on quite a few occasions in the past. He had caught the eye at Chester on his previous start from off the pace over 7.5f and could be spotted tanking away behind runners here. It was a fine ride by Dettori, as he failed to panic in the final stages, and whilst being strong in the saddle, he didn't seem to resort to his whip that much, if at all. The plan is head to Ascot next Saturday for the 7f heritage handicap.

Victoire De Lyphar(IRE) ◆ had improved a lot this season and looked to hold good claims. Indeed, he kept on strongly after hitting the front and is probably a Group-class sprinter in the making. He still looks capable of physical improvement given his stature, and can make into a decent 4yo. Connections indicated that he is finished now for the year. (op 10-1)

Hitchens(IRE) had been threatening a return to form throughout the season, and duly gained a deserved success at York on his previous outing. Raised 5lb for that win, he was well placed down his side of the track on ground that had come right for him, and just managed to hang on to be the winner of those drawn low. (tchd 40-1 in a place)

Genki(IRE) finished third to Markab in the Group 1 Sprint Cup last time (Barney McGrew behind there as well), so came in with obvious credentials to take the big pot, despite his big weight. Proven in big fields, he came home strongly on his side after being held up, and once again proved he is a classy type. (op 11-1, after 12-1 in places early)

Jonny Mudball, not seen since a good second in the Stewards' Cup, has been progressive throughout the season and looked to have been produced at the right time here after tracking the pace. However, the fact that he wasn't able to get past the runner-up after travelling on the bridle for longer suggests that the handicapper has him just about right now. That probably doesn't matter, as he looks set to go into Listed and better company from now on. (op 15-2)

Knot In Wood(IRE), third off a 6lb higher mark last year, hadn't been threatening recently but bounced back to something resembling his best with another fine effort in this contest.

Kaldoun Kingdom(IRE), last year's Silver Cup winner, was ridden with restraint and kept on well, albeit at the one pace, when the gap opened up for him on the far-side.

Signor Peltro, beaten just over 5l in this last season, had been noted as returning to form recently and kept on in this after appearing to get outpaced over 1f out.

Rileyskeepingfaith, behind three he met here in the Great St Wilfrid on his previous start, ran another solid race in a big handicap and is sure to be a runner in these types of events for a while. (tchd 14-1)

Poet's Place(USA) came into this contest with a consistent stream of improvement. His Portland victory was gained by getting on top in the latter stages, so this step back up in trip looked sure to suit. He didn't have lots of room whilst being held up, but he appeared to have every chance from 1f out before merely staying on at the one pace. (op 7-1)

Jimmy Styles, last year's winner off a 3lb lower mark, battled his way into a good position, after racing freely, but couldn't raise his game under pressure.

Hawkeyethenoo(IRE) beat plenty of these on his last start in the Sky Bet Dash at York back in July, for which he was 6lb higher here, but failed to quicken when asked to catch the leaders.

Noverre To Go(IRE), off since his fifth in the Stewards' Cup, looked to have every chance coming to the 2f marker, but dropped away quite quickly once under pressure. It transpired his tongue strap had come off. Official explanation: trainer said tongue strap came undone during race

6178 JOHN CONNOR MEMORIAL H'CAP 7f 50y

3:55 (3:55) (Class 3) (0-95,91) 3-Y-0+

£9,346 (£2,799; £1,399; £700; £349; £175) **Stalls** High

Form RPR

0662 **1** **Docofthebay (IRE)**[6] 5993 6-9-0 **84** .... PJMcDonald 3 97
(J A Glover) *mid-div: effrt 3f out: styd on to ld jst ins fnl f: edgd lft: hld on towards fin* **12/1**

0115 **2** nk **Zero Money (IRE)**[39] 4924 4-9-2 **86** .... SteveDrowne 9 98
(R Charlton) *trckd clr ldr: led 1f out: sn hdd: no ex clsng stages* **6/1**[3]

1003 **3** 2 1/2 **Celtic Sultan (IRE)**[16] 5702 6-9-6 **90** .... (b) MickyFenton 4 95
(T P Tate) *led: set str pce: clr after 2f: hdd 1f out: kpt on same pce* **20/1**

6021 **4** nk **Justonefortheroad**[15] 5737 4-8-13 **83** .... PaulHanagan 8 88
(R A Fahey) *trckd ldrs: t.k.h: effrt over 2f out: styd on same pce appr fnl f* **9/4**[1]

0001 **5** 1/2 **Captain Ramius (IRE)**[8] 5903 4-9-7 **91** .... RobertWinston 5 94
(K A Ryan) *t.k.h: sn trcking ldrs: drvn 3f out: edgd rt over 1f out: kpt on one pce* **16/1**

2006 **6** nk **Collateral Damage (IRE)**[19] 5605 7-9-5 **89** .... (t) DavidAllan 12 91
(T D Easterby) *trckd ldrs: drvn over 3f out: one pce fnl 2f* **4/1**[2]

0020 **7** 1 1/2 **The Osteopath (IRE)**[56] 4370 7-9-5 **89** .... PhillipMakin 10 87
(M Dods) *in rr div: effrt 3f out: nvr nr ldrs* **40/1**

1050 **8** 1/2 **Kiwi Bay**[49] 4570 5-9-1 **90** .... DaleSwift(5) 11 87
(M Dods) *hld up towards rr: effrt 3f out: n.m.r 1f out: nvr a factor* **16/1**

3300 **9** hd **Esoterica (IRE)**[13] 5787 7-9-1 **88** .... (v) GaryBartley(3) 2 85
(J S Goldie) *mid-div: effrt 3f out: nvr a factor* **7/1**

2255 **10** 3/4 **Academy Blues (USA)**[40] 4894 5-9-4 **88** .... AdrianNicholls 7 83
(D Nicholls) *s.s: sme hdwy on outside over 2f out: nvr on terms* **14/1**

640 **11** 3 3/4 **Fullandby (IRE)**[35] 5095 8-9-6 **90** .... JamieSpencer 6 74
(T J Etherington) *s.i.s: bhd and sn pushed along: nvr on terms: eased towards fin* **12/1**

1m 29.03s (-4.37) **Going Correction** -0.325s/f (Firm) **11** Ran SP% **118.6**
Speed ratings (Par 107): **111,110,107,107,106 106,104,104,104,103 98**
toteswingers:1&2 £32.00, 2&3 £16.40, 1&3 £19.60 CSF £83.06 CT £1475.15 TOTE £13.60: £3.30, £2.40, £4.10; EX 85.80.
Owner Paul J Dixon **Bred** G And Mrs Middlebrook **Trained** Babworth, Notts

FOCUS
Just an ordinary handicap for the class, but the pace was strong. Not many got involved and the form is rated around the winner.

NOTEBOOK
Docofthebay(IRE) ◆, without the cheekpieces and returned to waiting tactics, built on his recent second at Goodwood to end a losing run stretching back over three years. This may well boost his confidence and, well handicapped on old form (once rated 107), he should not be opposed lightly next time. (op 10-1 tchd 14-1)

Zero Money(IRE) has gained his two wins this year from the front, but he proved himself fully effective under slightly more patient tactics with a solid effort. (op 8-1 tchd 11-2)

Celtic Sultan(IRE), as is often the case, set a good pace in a clear lead, racing freely, but he found a couple too strong in the closing stages. (op 14-1)

Justonefortheroad was found out by a 5lb higher mark than when winning over 1m at Musselburgh on his previous start. (op 4-1)

Captain Ramius(IRE) couldn't defy a 4lb rise for his recent Chester victory, with the ground perhaps quicker than ideal. (op 9-1)

Collateral Damage(IRE) lacked the pace for 7f on quick ground and can be given another chance when there is slightly more emphasis on stamina. Official explanation: jockey said gelding hung left (op 6-1)

6179 WILLIAMHILL.COM DOONSIDE CUP STKS (LISTED RACE) 1m 2f

4:30 (4:30) (Class 1) 3-Y-O+

£28,385 (£10,760; £5,385; £2,685; £1,345; £675) **Stalls** High

Form RPR

0214 **1** **Vesuve (IRE)**29 5274 4-9-0 110 .... FrankieDettori 2 116
(Saeed Bin Suroor) *prom: effrt over 2f out: led over 1f out: rdn out* **2/1**2

5223 **2** *nk* **Kings Gambit (SAF)**29 5274 6-9-0 111 .... JamieSpencer 8 115
(T P Tate) *led: qcknd over 2f out: rdn and hdd over 1f out: kpt on u.p towards fin* **15/8**1

5105 **3** *1* **Circumvent**34 5135 3-8-8 107 .... PaulHanagan 1 113
(P F I Cole) *hld up: rdn and hdwy over 1f out: kpt on ins fnl f: nrst fin* **9/1**

110- **4** *hd* **Kirklees (IRE)**336 6871 6-9-0 116 .... TedDurcan 7 113+
(Saeed Bin Suroor) *hld up: hdwy and ev ch over 1f out: sn rdn: kpt on same pce ins fnl f* **7/2**3

6503 **5** *2 1/4* **Nanton (USA)**14 5772 8-9-0 105 .... PhillipMakin 3 108
(J S Goldie) *prom: outpcd over 2f out: rallied fnl f: nt rch ldrs* **20/1**

002 **6** *5* **Kings Destiny**7 5970 4-9-0 100 .... SteveDrowne 5 98
(M A Jarvis) *trckd ldrs: drvn and outpcd over 2f out: sn btn* **12/1**

2254 **7** *1 3/4* **Suits Me**141 1664 7-9-0 105 .... MickyFenton 4 95
(T P Tate) *plld hrd: cl up tl rdn and wknd fr 2f out* **28/1**

2m 6.20s (-5.80) **Going Correction** -0.325s/f (Firm)
WFA 3 from 4yo+ 6lb **7** Ran SP% **116.2**
Speed ratings (Par 111): **110,109,108,108,107 103,101**
toteswingers:1&2 £1.40, 2&3 £3.40, 1&3 £4.10 CSF £6.39 TOTE £3.10: £2.00, £1.70; EX 6.50.
Owner Godolphin **Bred** Dayton Investments Ltd **Trained** Newmarket, Suffolk

FOCUS
A reasonable Listed race and up-to-scratch form for the grade. It was sound run.

NOTEBOOK
Vesuve(IRE) came under pressure at the top of the straight but kept responding and was always doing just enough, reversing York placings from August 20 with Kings Gambit. Frankie Dettori reportedly felt the ground was quick enough for the winner, so he might be capable of a little better. (tchd 15-8)
Kings Gambit(SAF) took them along at a good pace, resulting in a time 1.30 seconds under standard. He stuck on when headed, and briefly looked as though he might get back up, but he couldn't go by. (op 5-2)
Circumvent ran well, appreciating the drop in class, but wasn't good enough. (op 8-1)
Kirklees(IRE), having his first start since finishing a close-up seventh in last year's Caulfield Cup, travelled well but soon got tired in the straight and shaped as though in need of the run. (op 4-1 tchd 5-1)
Nanton(USA) had something to find at the weights with the four who finished ahead of him. (op 16-1)
Kings Destiny had little chance at the weights. (op 11-1)
Suits Me hadn't been seen for 141 days and this should help ready him ready for a winter campaign on his favoured Polytrack. (op 20-1)

6180 WILLIAMHILL.COM AYRSHIRE H'CAP 1m

5:00 (5:00) (Class 2) (0-105,105) 3-Y-O+

£21,808 (£6,531; £3,265; £1,634; £815; £409) **Stalls** High

Form RPR

0400 **1** **Tiger Reigns**19 5605 4-9-5 97 .... PhillipMakin 1 108
(M Dods) *in tch: smooth hdwy over 2f out: led over 1f out: rdn out ins fnl f* **14/1**

0213 **2** *2* **Colepeper**10 5854 3-9-2 98 .... FrankieDettori 7 104
(M Johnston) *hld up: hdwy on outside over 1f out: chsd wnr ins fnl f: r.o* **9/2**2

3060 **3** *hd* **Dream Lodge (IRE)**42 4830 6-9-8 100 .... SebSanders 5 106
(R A Fahey) *trckd ldrs: drvn over 2f out: rallied: kpt on same pce ins fnl f* **11/1**

4014 **4** *1/2* **Our Joe Mac (IRE)**7 5948 3-8-12 94 .... PaulHanagan 3 98
(R A Fahey) *in tch: rdn and outpcd over 2f out: rallied over 1f out: kpt on ins fnl f* **7/2**1

/-00 **5** *1 3/4* **Rain Rush (IRE)**14 5774 7-9-1 93 .... SteveDrowne 9 93
(David Marnane, Ire) *dwlt: t.k.h in rr: hdwy u.p over 1f out: nvr able to chal* **12/1**

0401 **6** *shd* **Osteopathic Remedy (IRE)**19 5605 6-9-0 92 .... PJMcDonald 14 92
(M Dods) *w ldr: led over 2f out to over 1f out: no ex ins fnl f* **9/1**

1110 **7** *hd* **Camerooney**28 5292 7-8-7 90 .... DaleSwift(5) 6 90
(B Ellison) *led to over 2f out: kpt on same pce fr over 1f out* **10/1**

0051 **8** *nse* **Dhaular Dhar (IRE)**15 5736 8-8-9 90 .... GaryBartley(3) 12 90
(J S Goldie) *hld up: rdn and hdwy over 1f out: nvr able to chal* **10/1**

0000 **9** *1 3/4* **Extraterrestrial**30 5247 6-8-13 91 .... PaulMulrennan 13 87
(R A Fahey) *hld up: rdn over 2f out: sn no imp* **15/2**

2000 **10** *3 3/4* **Balcarce Nov (ARG)**7 5948 5-9-7 99 .... JamieSpencer 2 93
(T P Tate) *hld up: rdn over 1f out: sn btn: eased whn no ch ins fnl f* **5/1**3

1m 39.3s (-4.50) **Going Correction** -0.325s/f (Firm)
WFA 3 from 4yo+ 4lb **10** Ran SP% **119.7**
Speed ratings (Par 109): **109,107,106,106,104 104,104,104,102,98**
toteswingers:1&2 £14.90, 2&3 £9.30, 1&3 £22.60 CSF £78.06 CT £755.29 TOTE £17.90: £5.10, £1.70, £4.30; EX 95.90.
Owner Joe Buzzeo **Bred** Richard Green And New England Stud **Trained** Denton, Co Durham

FOCUS
Another ordinary handicap for the class, with a few of these finding the ground too fast. A clear personal best from the winner at face value.

NOTEBOOK
Tiger Reigns, one of the few who handled the conditions well, readily defied a mark 4lb higher than when only fourth in this last year. He's hard to fancy for the Cambridgeshire, for which he's picked up a 4lb penalty.
Colepeper, back up to 1m, was forced to make his challenge wider than the winner and was readily held by that one. He might have found this ground quicker than ideal. (op 5-1)
Dream Lodge(IRE) had to be driven along to get going through the opening stages, not appreciating the drop back to 1m on quick ground, but he plugged out dourly in the straight. (op 12-1)
Our Joe Mac(IRE) travelled well but was one-paced under pressure. This was a respectable effort on ground that may have been quicker than ideal. (op 4-1)
Rain Rush(IRE), another who may have found conditions quicker than he cares for, was set a lot to do and, although sticking on, never threatened.
Extraterrestrial was 4lb lower than when winning the race last year but disappointed. (op 7-1 tchd 8-1)
Balcarce Nov(ARG) Official explanation: jockey said horse had no more to give

6181 ASHLEIGH CONSTRUCTION H'CAP 1m 5f 13y

5:35 (5:35) (Class 3) (0-90,85) 3-Y-O+ **£7,771** (£2,312; £1,155; £577) **Stalls** Low

Form RPR

4400 **1** **Cosmic Sun**19 5591 4-9-11 82 .... (p) PaulHanagan 3 92
(R A Fahey) *mde all at stdy gallop: qcknd over 2f out: edgd lft u.p ins fnl f: hld on wl* **4/1**2

210 **2** *1 3/4* **Royal Swain (IRE)**105 2761 4-9-1 72 .... PJMcDonald 4 79+
(G A Swinbank) *in tch: effrt over 2f out: chsd wnr over 1f out: r.o fin* **9/1**

6530 **3** *1 3/4* **Becausewecan (USA)**14 5743 4-10-0 85 .... SilvestreDeSousa 5 90
(M Johnston) *pressed wnr: rdn over 2f out: kpt on same pce over 1f out* **4/1**2

-050 **4** *1* **Camps Bay (USA)**129 2031 6-9-6 82 .... DaleSwift(5) 9 85+
(B Ellison) *hld up: hdwy over 2f out: no imp fr over 1f out* **16/1**

4615 **5** *1/2* **Bollin Felix**42 4846 6-10-0 85 .... (v) DavidAllan 1 88
(T D Easterby) *trckd ldrs: drvn over 2f out: no ex over 1f out* **13/2**

0023 **6** *3/4* **Dazzling Light (UAE)**13 5790 5-9-4 80 .... AdamBeschizza(5) 11 81
(J S Goldie) *hld up: rdn over 2f out: nvr able to chal* **7/2**1

3202 **7** *shd* **Lady Luachmhar (IRE)**14 5757 4-9-9 85 .... LeeTopliss(5) 6 86
(R A Fahey) *t.k.h: hld up in tch: rdn over 2f out: sn outpcd: n.d after* **8/1**

5120 **8** *hd* **Strathcal**36 5035 4-9-9 80 .... SteveDrowne 7 81
(H Morrison) *prom: drvn over 2f out: sn btn* **6/1**3

-003 **9** *7* **Best Prospect (IRE)**58 4290 8-9-2 73 .... (t) PhillipMakin 2 63
(M Dods) *hld up: shkn up wl over 1f out: sn btn* **20/1**

2m 54.82s (0.82) **Going Correction** -0.325s/f (Firm) **9** Ran SP% **121.6**
Speed ratings (Par 107): **84,82,81,81,80 80,80,80,75**
toteswingers:1&2 £7.20, 2&3 £7.40, 1&3 £2.00 CSF £42.06 CT £157.26 TOTE £5.40: £1.90, £3.80, £1.90; EX 55.80 Place 6: £905.36 Place 5: £218.26 .
Owner The Cosmic Cases **Bred** M Wassall **Trained** Musley Bank, N Yorks

FOCUS
No early pace makes this form to be wary of in the future, as not many held a serious chance of victory after being held up.

NOTEBOOK
Cosmic Sun dictated a pace to suit and then quickened it at the right time to secure enough of an advantage to hang on. Fairly handicapped on his winning form, the first-time cheekpieces may have had a positive effect, but he had the run of the race and it cannot be sure that they did. Official explanation: trainer said, regarding apparent improvement in form, that the gelding benefited from the application of first time cheekpieces. (op 9-2 tchd 5-1)
Royal Swain(IRE) took a strong hold early but showed that his last effort back in June was all wrong with a solid performance. His trainer has done well with this type before, so he should have more to come. (op 10-1 tchd 11-1)
Becausewecan(USA) tracked the leader\winner from the outset but was one paced when his rider asked for maximum effort. He could do with edging down the weights a bit more. (op 9-2)
Camps Bay(USA), another to look keen early, ran with promise on his first start for this trainer after a lengthy break. He hasn't won for a while and will need to build on this before he becomes of serious interest. (op 20-1 tchd 14-1)
Bollin Felix, with a visor back on, was never far away but didn't possess a turn of pace when the tempo lifted. He would have preferred a stiffer test. (op 6-1)
Dazzling Light(UAE) posed no threat once the sprint started and needs to come down the handicap a bit more before being really interesting. (op 9-2)
Lady Luachmhar(IRE), the stable's second string on jockey bookings, was much too keen under restraint and had no change of gear.
Strathcal ran his second modest race in a row and is probably too high in the weights. (op 7-1)
T/Jkpt: Not won. T/Plt: £2,375.50 to a £1 stake. Pool of £161,407.62 - 49.60 winning tickets. T/Qpdt: £56.00 to a £1 stake. Pool of £12,687.55 167.58 winning tickets. RY

5418 CATTERICK (L-H)

Saturday, September 18

OFFICIAL GOING: Good to firm (firm in places)

6182 EUROPEAN BREEDERS' FUND MAIDEN STKS 5f 212y

2:05 (2:06) (Class 5) 2-Y-O **£2,978** (£886; £442; £221) **Stalls** Low

Form RPR

220 **1** **Nine Before Ten (IRE)**21 5531 2-8-12 69 .... GregFairley 1 75
(Mrs D J Sanderson) *mde all: rdn and qcknd 2f out: clr ent fnl f: kpt on wl* **4/1**3

32 **2** *3* **Insolenceofoffice (IRE)**16 5683 2-9-3 0 .... DaraghO'Donohoe 5 71
(Mrs A Duffield) *a chsng wnr: rdn along 2f out: drvn ent fnl f: no imp* **11/4**2

6332 **3** *1 1/2* **Hortensis**52 4480 2-8-9 65 .... KellyHarrison(3) 9 62
(T D Easterby) *trckd ldng pair: effrt over 2f out: rdn wl over 1f out: sn hung lft: drvn and one pce ent fnl f* **8/1**

4 *nse* **Silver Turn** 2-8-12 0 .... TomEaves 4 61+
(B Smart) *dwlt: sn pushed along and in tch on inner after 1f: effrt and hdwy over 2f out: sn rdn to chse ldrs: kpt on same pce appr fnl f: fin 5th: plcd 4th* **9/4**1

604 **5** *1/2* **Clever Man**44 4743 2-9-3 67 .... EddieCreighton 12 65
(M R Channon) *in tch: hdwy on outer to chse ldrs over 2f out: sn rdn and one pce: fin 6th: plcd 5th* **16/1**

6305 **6** *3 1/4* **Paragons Folly (IRE)**19 5602 2-8-12 66 .... (b1) IanBrennan(5) 2 55
(J J Quinn) *chsd ldrs on inner: rdn along over 2f out: sn wknd: fin 7th: plcd 6th* **18/1**

0 **7** *8* **Maunby Rumba (IRE)**18 5640 2-8-12 0 .... LeeVickers 11 26+
(B M R Haslam) *dwlt: a towards rr: fin 8th: plcd 7th* **150/1**

3 **8** *1 3/4* **Like A Charm (IRE)**45 4709 2-8-12 0 .... JohnEgan 6 21
(J Howard Johnson) *chsd ldrs: rdn along 1/2-way: drvn over 2f out and sn wknd: fin 9th: plcd 8th* **20/1**

00 **9** *1/2* **Kwik Lightening**14 5755 2-9-0 0 .... PatrickDonaghy(3) 10 24
(B M R Haslam) *s.i.s: a bhd: fin 9th: plcd 10th* **150/1**

10 *16* **Tinzo (IRE)** 2-9-3 0 .... DanielTudhope 7 —
(A Berry) *s.i.s: a in rr: fin 11th: plcd 10th* **125/1**

20 **D** *nk* **Podgies Boy (IRE)**21 5531 2-9-0 0 .... JamesSullivan(3) 8 66+
(R A Fahey) *t.k.h early: midfield: hdwy on outer over 2f out: rdn over 1f out: styd on ins fnl f: tk 4th nr fin: fin 4th, 3l, 11/2l, nk: disq: jockey failed to weigh in* **15/2**

1m 11.89s (-1.71) **Going Correction** -0.35s/f (Firm) **11** Ran SP% **118.3**
Speed ratings (Par 95): **97,93,91,90,89 85,74,72,71,50 90**
toteswingers:1&2 £2.40, 2&3 £3.40, 1&3 £2.50 CSF £15.40 TOTE £4.80: £1.80, £1.90, £2.00; EX 19.10.
Owner R J Budge **Bred** Deerpark Stud **Trained** Sturton le Steeple, Notts
■ Stewards' Enquiry : James Sullivan six-day ban: failed to weigh in (Oct 2, 4-8)

FOCUS
The going had been changed to good to firm, good in places after a dry spell for this open-looking maiden run at a decent pace in a time a shade under the RP standard. It rates improved form from the winner, but she did get the run of things.

NOTEBOOK
Nine Before Ten(IRE) had to bounce back after a disappoining effort at Redcar last time but she did so with a fine front running display. She set the standard with a mark of 69 and probably ran to that level but, it will be of no surprise if she can progress a little further as this was a very likeable performance. (tchd 7-2 and 9-2)
Insolenceofoffice(IRE) recorded another decent performance stepped up to 6f but could never find the pace to challenge the winner after chasing him throughout. He remains progressive and his turn will come now qualifying for a mark. (op 10-3 tchd 4-1)
Hortensis had come in for some good support after a two-month break and travelled well behind the leaders but could not up his tempo to challenge when asked. He has a mark of 65, which looks realistic, and he should find an opportunity sent back handicapping. (op 11-2)
Silver Turn is a nice scopey sort who is related to a couple of winners. She missed the break and could never get involved off the strong pace, although staying on inside the final furlong. She can only build on this. (op 3-1, tchd10-3 in places)
Clever Man had only shown a modest level of form in three maidens. He made an effort over 2f out but ultimately could stay on only at the same pace. (op 14-1 tchd 12-1)
Like A Charm(IRE) Official explanation: jockey said filly was unsuited by the good to firm (firm in places) ground
Kwik Lightening Official explanation: jockey said gelding reared in stalls and missed the break
Podgies Boy(IRE) failed to build on initial promise last time but this was a step back in the right direction although never finding the pace to get involved. He was subsequently disqualified from 4th after the jockey failed to weigh in. (op 8-1 tchd 13-2)

6183 YORKSHIRE4X4.COM ADVENTURE ACTIVITIES (S) STKS 1m 5f 175y
2:35 (2:36) (Class 6) 3-Y-O **£1,706** (£503; £252) **Stalls** Low

Form RPR
1220 **1** **Always Dixie (IRE)**[8] 5923 3-8-11 51 ... GregFairley 5 59+
(M Johnston) *mde all: pushed along 3f out: rdn 2f out: clr over 1f out: styd on* **5/2**[2]
4643 **2** *6* **Miss Whippy**[24] 5423 3-8-2 49 ... KellyHarrison(3) 6 43
(P Howling) *trckd wnr: effrt 3f out: rdn 2f out: drvn: flashed tail repeatedly and no imp ins fnl f* **7/2**[3]
6006 **3** *nse* **Barra Raider**[27] 5336 3-8-5 50 ... IanBrennan(5) 2 48
(R F Fisher) *trckd ldrs on inner: hdwy 3f out: rdn along over 2f out: drvn wl over 1f out and kpt on same pce* **28/1**
0260 **4** *nk* **Bring Sweets (IRE)**[8] 5927 3-8-10 47 ... LeeVickers 7 47
(B Ellison) *s.i.s: hld up and bhd: hdwy wl over 2f out: rdn over 1f out: styd on ins fnl f: n.m.r towards fin* **10/1**
-004 **5** *1 3/4* **Miss Wendy**[37] 4980 3-8-0 47 ... AshleyMorgan(5) 9 40
(M H Tompkins) *trckd ldng pair: effrt 3f out: rdn along over 2f out: drvn wl over 1f out and grad wknd* **6/1**
0-60 **6** *4 1/2* **Green Army**[19] 5603 3-8-10 46 ... EddieCreighton 4 38
(M R Channon) *in tch: rdn along over 4f out: drvn 3f out: sn outpcd and bhd* **33/1**
-156 **7** *4 1/2* **Bear Tobougie**[6] 6003 3-8-11 72 ... TomEaves 3 33
(G A Swinbank) *trckd ldrs: pushed along 1/2-way: rdn over 4f out: sn lost pl and bhd fnl 2f* **9/4**[1]
0-00 **8** *16* **Destiny Rules**[17] 5665 3-8-5 40 ... PaulQuinn 8 —
(John Berry) *trckd ldrs: pushed along 1/2-way: rdn over 4f out: sn lost pl and bhd fnl 2f* **33/1**

3m 2.65s (-0.95) **Going Correction** -0.225s/f (Firm) **8** Ran SP% **114.3**
Speed ratings (Par 99): **93,89,89,89,88 85,83,74**
CSF £11.49 TOTE £3.10: £1.50, £1.10, £4.20; EX 11.30.There was no bid for the winner.
Owner Always Trying Partnership VII **Bred** Mark Johnston Racing Ltd **Trained** Middleham Moor, N Yorks

FOCUS
A weak seller run at an ordinary pace. The favourite was again way off his maiden form and the winner looks the best guide.
Bear Tobouggie Official explanation: jockey said filly never travelled

6184 CATTERICKBRIDGE.CO.UK NURSERY 7f
3:10 (3:11) (Class 4) (0-85,82) 2-Y-O **£3,238** (£963; £481; £240) **Stalls** Low

Form RPR
1054 **1** **First Class Favour (IRE)**[7] 5939 2-8-6 72 ow1 ... LanceBetts(5) 6 75
(T D Easterby) *mde all: rdn wl over 1f out: kpt on strly ins fnl f* **14/1**
006 **2** *1 1/4* **The Bells O Peover**[19] 5594 2-8-6 67 ... GregFairley 11 67
(M Johnston) *trckd ldng pair: hdwy to chse wnr 3f out: rdn to chal wl over 1f out: drvn and kpt on same pce ins fnl f* **4/1**[1]
3215 **3** *1 1/2* **Cathedral Spires**[28] 5301 2-9-4 79 ... JohnEgan 1 75
(J Howard Johnson) *chsd wnr: rdn along over 2f out: drvn over 1f out: kpt on same pce ins fnl f* **4/1**[1]
6205 **4** *2 1/4* **Cotton Spirit**[24] 5404 2-8-2 68 ... IanBrennan(5) 3 58
(R A Fahey) *in tch: hdwy on inner wl over 2f out: rdn to chse ldrs over 1f out: drvn and one pce ins fnl f* **8/1**
01 **5** *nk* **Fairlie Dinkum**[27] 5332 2-8-13 74 ... TomEaves 2 63
(B Smart) *trckd ldrs: hdwy 3f out: rdn over 2f out: drvn and edgd rt over 1f out: sn one pce* **7/1**[3]
4503 **6** *2 1/4* **Roman Ruler (IRE)**[14] 5755 2-8-1 62 ... PaulQuinn 4 45
(C W Fairhurst) *t.k.h: chsd ldng pair: rdn along 1/2-way: drvn over 2f out and grad wknd* **40/1**
5602 **7** *3 1/4* **Falkland Flyer (IRE)**[9] 5894 2-8-8 69 ... EddieCreighton 7 44
(M R Channon) *in tch: hdwy to chse ldrs wl over 2f out: sn rdn and wknd over 1f out* **10/1**
14 **8** *4 1/2* **Clipthorne**[78] 3611 2-8-13 77 ... JamesSullivan(3) 5 40+
(Ollie Pears) *dwlt: awkward bnd after 3f: a towards rr* **16/1**
01 **9** *5* **Layali Al Arab (IRE)**[33] 5156 2-9-7 82 ... DaraghO'Donohoe 10 32+
(Saeed Bin Suroor) *towards rr: rdn along: awkward bnd after 3f: nvr a factor* **9/2**[2]
0030 **10** *1 3/4* **Market Maker (IRE)**[45] 4701 2-7-13 63 ... KellyHarrison(3) 8 9+
(T D Easterby) *a towards rr* **25/1**
1350 **11** *2 1/4* **King Of Aquitaine (IRE)**[14] 5745 2-8-11 79 ... JulieBurke(7) 9 19+
(K A Ryan) *s.i.s: a bhd* **20/1**

1m 24.52s (-2.48) **Going Correction** -0.35s/f (Firm) **11** Ran SP% **114.5**
Speed ratings (Par 97): **100,98,96,94,93 91,87,82,76,74 72**
toteswingers:1&2 £25.50, 2&3 £5.50, 1&3 £19.00 CSF £66.04 CT £274.86 TOTE £14.10: £4.40, £2.10, £1.60; EX 93.10.
Owner S A Heley **Bred** Oghill House Stud **Trained** Great Habton, N Yorks

FOCUS
A lively betting market for this nursery which was run at a good clip with only a few managing to get involved. The winner is rated back to his best and this is low-impact form.

NOTEBOOK
First Class Favour(IRE) made all the running under a positive ride to run out a very gutsy winner. She set a searching pace and found enough when being challenged to assert in the final furlong. She has plenty of speed and clearly likes it around here as she has now won over 5f, 6f, 7f now at the course. The Tim Easterby yard are in fine form and she should be capable of handling a small rise. (op 20-1)
The Bells O Peover has a Derby entry and was beginning his nursery career off a mark of 67. He got within striking distance of the winner but was eventually outstayed in the final furlong. This was a fair effort on nursery debut and with his connections he ought to be capable of finding an opening before long. (op 5-1)
Cathedral Spires got off the mark over 5f in July and had run respectably in defeat since. He could never quite lay down a serious challenge to the winner but kept on well enough on this step up in trip and remains on a reasonable mark. (op 9-2)
Cotton Spirit had the benefit of a good claimer and with the 4lb drop in the weights had plenty going for him. He was soon struggling to go the pace and apart from looking as though he would be in the mix over two furlongs out, his effort soon flattened out. (op 10-1 tchd 11-1)
Fairlie Dinkum stepped up considerably on debut when getting off the mark last time and was starting off on a mark of 74 for nurseries. She had her chance but could only stay on at the same pace from 2f out. (tchd 15-2)
Roman Ruler(IRE) looks to be struggling to cope with a harsh new mark.
Layali Al Arab(IRE), who won in a manner of a promising type on AW last time, was very disappointing. He clearly has some ability but was beaten a long way out and has it all to prove again now. Official explanation: jockey said colt never travelled (op 10-3)

6185 CONSTANT SECURITY SEPTEMBER STKS (H'CAP) 1m 3f 214y
3:45 (3:45) (Class 3) (0-90,88) 3-Y-O+ **£5,828** (£1,734; £866; £432) **Stalls** Low

Form RPR
6305 **1** **Arizona John (IRE)**[18] 5638 5-9-0 **81** ... DeclanCannon(5) 6 90
(J Mackie) *hld up in tch: hdwy 3f out: chsd ldrs 2f out: rdn to ld over 1f out: edgd lft ins fnl f: drvn out* **15/2**[3]
6024 **2** *1 1/4* **Abergavenny**[8] 5913 3-9-0 **84** ... GregFairley 9 91
(M Johnston) *trckd ldr: hdwy 3f out: chsd ldrs 2f out: drvn to chal over 1f out and ev ch tl one pce ins fnl f* **6/5**[1]
3210 **3** *nk* **Destinys Dream (IRE)**[30] 5249 5-9-7 **86** ... KellyHarrison(3) 8 92
(Miss Tracy Waggott) *hld up in rr: hdwy over 2f out: swtchd ins and effrt over 1f out: styng on and ch whn hmpd 1f out: swtchd rt and rdn ins fnl f: kpt on* **6/1**[2]
3000 **4** *nk* **Record Breaker (IRE)**[15] 5723 6-9-9 **85** ... (b) JohnEgan 5 91
(M Johnston) *trckd ldng pair: pushed along 1/2-way: rdn wl over 2f out: drvn over 1f out: swtchd rt ent fnl f: kpt on u.p towards fin* **15/2**[3]
10-0 **5** *4* **Burnett (IRE)**[25] 5387 3-8-11 **81** ... (v[1]) DaraghO'Donohoe 4 81
(Saeed Bin Suroor) *led: rdn along 2f out: drvn: hung bdly lft and hdd appr fnl f: sn wknd* **14/1**
3103 **6** *1 1/4* **Granston (IRE)**[18] 5638 9-9-9 **88** ... JamesSullivan(3) 7 86
(J D Bethell) *trckd ldrs: hdwy over 3f out: rdn 2f out: hld whn n.m.r ins fnl f* **10/1**
0-54 **7** *3 3/4* **Folk Tune (IRE)**[34] 5118 7-8-10 **77** ... IanBrennan(5) 3 69
(J J Quinn) *midfield: effrt over 3f out: sn rdn along and n.d* **16/1**
0260 **8** *1/2* **Sir Royal (USA)**[18] 5638 5-9-1 **77** ... TomEaves 2 68
(G A Swinbank) *hld up towards rr: swtchd outside and hdwy over 3f out: rdn over 2f out and sn btn* **12/1**
6610 **9** *4* **Ahlawy (IRE)**[15] 5736 7-9-3 **79** ... (t) LeeVickers 1 63
(F Sheridan) *hld up: a in rr* **28/1**

2m 33.96s (-4.94) **Going Correction** -0.225s/f (Firm)
WFA 3 from 5yo+ 8lb **9** Ran SP% **116.1**
Speed ratings (Par 107): **107,106,105,105,103 102,99,99,96**
toteswingers:1&2 £2.40, 2&3 £5.00, 1&3 £14.60 CSF £16.97 CT £59.62 TOTE £6.60: £1.60, £1.10, £2.90; EX 34.20.
Owner Derbyshire Racing **Bred** Abergwaun Farms **Trained** Church Broughton , Derbys

FOCUS
A fair gallop for this decent little handicap but the front-runners possibly overdid it. The form is rated though the third and fourth.

NOTEBOOK
Arizona John(IRE) proved suited by the step up in trip. It had been a little disappointing he had not added to his tally since winning in June but he shaped a little bit better the than bare form suggested last time. There are no immediate plans for him and, if he reproduces this effort, he can remain competitive when reassessed. (op 9-1)
Abergavenny was all the rage in the market and was backed in to 6-5 favourite after a decent effort when fourth in decent contest at Doncaster last time. He had his chance entering the final furlong but could not match the winner's late surge. A solid effort nonetheless. (op 7-4, tchd 15-8 in a place)
Destinys Dream(IRE) struggled upped to Listed class last time and was worse off at the weights with Granston when the pair last met in May but proved she is still effective in this grade and can continue to pay her way.
Record Breaker(IRE) looks a hard ride and owes a lot to his finishing position to the persistence of John Egan, who was at work from a long way out. He is racing off a handy mark at present. (op 17-2 tchd 7-1)
Burnett(IRE) was trying a visor for the first time after a disappointing return to action coming back from a break. He was a little too keen as he dictated the pace and soon tired when headed. (op 16-1)
Granston(IRE) was beginning to feel the pinch when hampered over a furlong out after chasing the leaders for most of the way. (op 7-1)

6186 BOOK NOW FOR SATURDAY 16TH OCTOBER MAIDEN STKS 7f
4:20 (4:21) (Class 5) 3-4-Y-O **£2,201** (£655; £327; £163) **Stalls** Low

Form RPR
044 **1** **Khandaq (USA)**[79] 3586 3-9-3 78 ... TomEaves 2 65+
(V P Donoghue) *mde all: rdn wl over 1f out: drvn ins fnl f and kpt on* **11/10**[1]
3402 **2** *2* **Uddy Mac**[16] 5686 3-8-9 56 ... KellyHarrison(3) 7 55
(N Bycroft) *trckd ldng pair: hdwy on inner 2f out: rdn over 1f out: drvn to chse wnr ins fnl f: no imp towards fin* **10/3**[2]
504 **3** *nk* **Excellent Thought**[12] 5810 3-8-12 64 ... GregFairley 4 54
(P Howling) *chsd wnr: rdn along 2f out: drvn ent fnl f: kpt on same pce* **7/2**[3]
4 *1 1/2* **Reset To Fit** 3-9-0 0 ... JamesSullivan(3) 10 55+
(E J Alston) *hld up in rr: pushed along wl over 1f out: swtchd rt and rdn over 1f out: styd on ins fnl f: nrst fin* **12/1**
0556 **5** *1/2* **Kirkby's Gem**[5] 6039 3-8-9 35 ... PaulPickard(3) 6 49
(A Berry) *towards rr: rdn along 1/2-way: drvn 2f out: plugged on appr fnl f* **100/1**
55 **6** *1 1/4* **Deferto Delphi**[22] 5487 3-8-12 0 ... IanBrennan(5) 1 50
(F P Murtagh) *in tch on inner: rdn along 1/2-way: drvn 2f out and n.d* **12/1**
0000 **7** *2 1/2* **Trading Nation (USA)**[14] 5766 4-9-3 47 ... (b) RobertLButler(3) 9 44
(P W Hiatt) *chsd ldrs: rdn along 2f out: drvn over 1f out and sn wknd* **20/1**

6066 **P** **Clare Harrier (IRE)**[24] 5419 3-9-3 **50**.................................... JohnEgan 5 —
(A Berry) *s.i.s and bhd whn p.u after 2f* **50/1**

1m 25.78s (-1.22) **Going Correction** -0.35s/f (Firm)
WFA 3 from 4yo 3lb 8 Ran SP% **116.0**
Speed ratings (Par 103): **92,89,89,87,87 85,82,—**
CSF £4.99 TOTE £1.50: £1.02, £1.10, £2.40; EX 4.40.
Owner Gordon McDowall **Bred** Shadwell Farm LLC **Trained** Carluke, South Lanarkshire

FOCUS
A weak maiden run in a slow time. The winner did not need to match his best.
Clare Harrier(IRE) Official explanation: jockey said gerlding lost its action

6187 EDWARD COOKE FIT AT FIFTY H'CAP — 1m 5f 175y
4:55 (4:56) (Class 6) (0-65,63) 3-Y-0+ — **£2,047** (£604; £302) **Stalls** Low

Form RPR

5344 **1** **Danceintothelight**[21] 5534 3-8-8 **56**............................ KellyHarrison(3) 5 69
(Micky Hammond) *trckd ldng pair: hdwy 3f out: led wl over 2f out: rdn clr over 1f out: kpt on strly* **12/1**

3466 **2** *4* **Locum**[31] 5208 5-9-5 **59**.. AshleyMorgan(5) 8 66
(M H Tompkins) *trckd ldrs: hdwy to chse wnr wl over 2f out: drvn over 1f out: no imp ins fnl f* **14/1**

6-02 **3** *3/4* **Rosewin (IRE)**[31] 5200 4-9-8 **60**.............................. JamesSullivan(3) 12 66
(Ollie Pears) *led 1f: trckd ldrs: hdwy on inner to chse ldng pair over 2f out: swtchd rt and rdn over 1f out: drvn and edgd lft ins fnl f: kpt on* **12/1**

3143 **4** *1 3/4* **Simple Jim (FR)**[16] 5687 6-10-0 **63**............................ AndrewMullen 2 67+
(D O'Meara) *hld up towards rr: hdwy wl over 3f out: effrt to chse ldrs wl over 1f out: sn rdn and kpt on same pce ins fnl f* **3/1**[1]

4042 **5** *2 1/2* **Tilos Gem (IRE)**[5] 6033 4-9-9 **58**................................. GregFairley 3 58
(M Johnston) *hld up: hdwy on inner 3f out: rdn to chse ldrs over 1f out: sn drvn and no imp* **7/2**[2]

4536 **6** *5* **Madamlily (IRE)**[64] 4117 4-9-6 **60**................................ IanBrennan(5) 10 53+
(J J Quinn) *hld up: sme hdwy 3f out: rdn 2f out: nvr nr ldrs* **15/2**[3]

5320 **7** *4* **Leaving Alone (USA)**[21] 5530 3-9-3 **62**............................ JohnEgan 4 50
(E W Tuer) *hld up: a towards rr* **12/1**

4060 **8** *2* **Aegean King**[31] 5208 4-9-8 **57**...................................... EddieCreighton 1 42
(M Wigham) *hld up: a towards rr* **20/1**

2330 **9** *2 1/2* **Strikemaster (IRE)**[18] 5642 4-9-11 **60**............................ LeeVickers 15 42
(B Ellison) *a towards rr* **18/1**

5630 **10** *1 1/2* **The Mighty Mod (USA)**[17] 5666 3-8-0 **48**.................(b) PaulPickard(3) 7 27
(M Johnston) *a towards rr* **14/1**

2013 **11** *1 1/4* **Golden Future**[21] 5336 7-9-7 **56**................................... PatrickMathers 13 34
(P D Niven) *nvr bttr than midfield* **16/1**

0325 **12** *1* **Harcas (IRE)**[16] 5681 8-8-13 **48**...................................(b) TomEaves 9 24
(M Todhunter) *prom: rdn along over 3f out: wknd wl over 2f out* **22/1**

3 **13** *3/4* **Authentic Act (IRE)**[11] 1801 6-9-11 **63**..............(p) CampbellGillies(3) 11 38
(M Todhunter) *a towards rr* **50/1**

0000 **14** *2 1/2* **Cigalas**[23] 5437 5-8-12 **50**.. PatrickDonaghy(3) 14 22
(Mrs J C McGregor) *prom: led after 1f: rdn along over 3f out: hdd wl over 2f out: sn drvn and wknd* **50/1**

2m 59.02s (-4.58) **Going Correction** -0.225s/f (Firm)
WFA 3 from 4yo+ 10lb 14 Ran SP% **119.6**
Speed ratings (Par 101): **104,101,101,100,98 96,93,92,91,90 89,89,88,87**
toteswingers:1&2 £35.30, 2&3 £35.30, 1&3 £4.50 CSF £162.27 CT £2059.49 TOTE £14.40: £9.60, £9.50, £8.70; EX 168.00.
Owner Roland Roper **Bred** Mrs David Low **Trained** Middleham Moor, N Yorks

FOCUS
A competitive but ordinary staying handicap. It was run at a decent pace with little getting into it with the principals always to the fore. The winner is rated back to something like his best 2yo form.
Madamlily(IRE) Official explanation: jockey said filly clipped heels causing him to lose his irons

6188 RACINGUK.COM H'CAP (DIV I) — 7f
5:30 (5:30) (Class 6) (0-60,64) 3-Y-0+ — **£1,706** (£503; £252) **Stalls** Low

Form RPR

5000 **1** **Not My Choice (IRE)**[29] 5267 5-9-3 **56**..........................(t) JohnEgan 13 74
(D C Griffiths) *qckly away and sn led: rdn clr wl over 1f out: styd on strly* **20/1**

0603 **2** *4 1/2* **Spavento (IRE)**[2] 6116 4-8-11 **55**............................(p) LanceBetts(5) 12 61+
(E J Alston) *hld up: hdwy and in tch over 2f out: swtchd outside and rdn over 1f out: styd on ins fnl f* **5/1**[2]

5002 **3** *nk* **Real Diamond**[24] 5424 4-9-1 **57**................................... KellyHarrison(3) 1 62
(Ollie Pears) *trckd ldrs on inner: hdwy 2f out: swtchd rt and rdn to chse ldr over 1f out: sn drvn and no imp* **11/2**[3]

0444 **4** *hd* **No Quarter (IRE)**[12] 5820 3-8-13 **55**............................. AndrewMullen 9 59
(Miss Tracy Waggott) *midfield: hdwy 3f out: rdn to chse ldrs wl over 1f out: drvn and kpt on ins fnl f* **13/2**

0600 **5** *2* **Taborcillo**[24] 5410 3-8-10 **57**......................................(b) DeanHeslop(5) 6 55
(T D Barron) *prom: rdn along wl over 2f out: drvn over 1f out and sn one pce* **33/1**

0500 **6** *3 1/2* **Piccolo Express**[12] 5821 4-8-10 **49**................................. SaleemGolam 4 39
(B P J Baugh) *prom: rdn along wl over 2f out: drvn wl over 1f out and grad wknd* **20/1**

5060 **7** *1 1/2* **Dhhamaan (IRE)**[15] 5732 5-9-0 **56**.....................(b) JamesSullivan(3) 14 42
(Mrs R A Carr) *chsd wnr: rdn along wl over 2f out: drvn wl over 1f out and sn wknd* **9/1**

5206 **8** *1* **Safari Guide**[27] 5325 4-9-4 **60**................................ PatrickDonaghy(3) 11 43
(K M Prendergast) *towards rr: rdn and sme hdwy on wd outside wl over 2f out: drvn wl over 1f out and n.d* **14/1**

0540 **9** *1 1/4* **Stoic Leader (IRE)**[141] 1673 10-8-10 **54**........................ IanBrennan(5) 10 34
(R F Fisher) *a towards rr* **28/1**

5003 **10** *nk* **Hi Spec (IRE)**[20] 5560 7-8-8 **50** ow3.........................(p) RobertLButler(3) 2 29
(Miss M E Rowland) *midfield: effrt and in tch wl over 2f out: sn rdn and wknd* **20/1**

5056 **11** *2* **Olympic Dream**[12] 5821 4-9-5 **58**.. LeeVickers 8 31
(M Herrington) *t.k.h early: a in rr* **20/1**

4220 **12** *1 1/4* **Needy McCredie**[12] 5817 4-8-5 **51**............................. ShaneBKelly(7) 5 21
(J R Turner) *dwlt and towards rr: sme hdwy on inner wl over 2f out: sn rdn and wknd* **5/2**[1]

00-0 **13** *2 3/4* **Drinking Buddy**[155] 1362 3-8-3 **52** ow3...................(b[1]) DuilioDaSilva(7) 7 —
(D W Thompson) *dwlt: a in rr* **33/1**

0020 **14** *4 1/2* **Tombellini (IRE)**[22] 5484 3-9-4 **60**................................. TomEaves 3 —
(D Nicholls) *a in rr* **14/1**

1m 24.24s (-2.76) **Going Correction** -0.35s/f (Firm)
WFA 3 from 4yo+ 3lb 14 Ran SP% **125.7**
Speed ratings (Par 101): **101,95,95,95,93 89,87,86,84,84 82,80,77,72**
toteswingers:1&2 £27.20, 2&3 £2.20, 1&3 £2.30 CSF £113.26 CT £662.15 TOTE £39.40: £8.80, £1.60, £3.00; EX 225.70.
Owner D Kilpatrick W McKay **Bred** Alan Dargan **Trained** Bawtry, S Yorks
■ Stewards' Enquiry : Duilio Da Silva one-day ban: used whip when out of contention (Oct 4)

FOCUS
Division one of the low-grade 46-60 handicap. Front-runners were doing well on the card and there are doubts over the winner's effort. It was the pick of the four C/D times though and the winner is rated to last year's best.
Real Diamond Official explanation: jockey said filly was unsuited by the good to firm (firm in places) ground
Olympic Dream Official explanation: jockey said gelding hung right-handed and was denied a clear run
Needy McCredie Official explanation: jockey said filly became upset in stalls
Tombellini(IRE) Official explanation: jockey said gelding moved poorly throughout

6189 RACINGUK.COM H'CAP (DIV II) — 7f
6:00 (6:00) (Class 6) (0-60,60) 3-Y-0+ — **£1,706** (£503; £252) **Stalls** Low

Form RPR

5461 **1** **Northern Flyer (GER)**[12] 5820 4-9-1 **59**......................(p) IanBrennan(5) 6 69+
(J J Quinn) *hld up towards rr: nt clr run and swtchd rt 2f out: str run to ld last 50yds* **2/1**[1]

4425 **2** *1 1/4* **Peter's Gift (IRE)**[12] 5820 4-8-11 **57**.............................(b) JulieBurke(7) 5 64
(K A Ryan) *trckd ldrs: led wl over 1f out: hdd: edgd lft and no ex clsng stages* **4/1**[2]

3-04 **3** *1 1/2* **Chookie Avon**[76] 3710 3-9-1 **57**... TomEaves 2 59
(V P Donoghue) *chsd ldrs: styd on same pce appr fnl f* **16/1**

3000 **4** *1* **Fuzzy Cat**[58] 4285 4-9-0 **58**.. DeanHeslop(5) 3 58
(T D Barron) *w ldrs: sn drvn along: kpt on same pce appr fnl f* **10/1**

5122 **5** *1/2* **Mr Chocolate Drop (IRE)**[14] 5767 6-8-13 **55**........(t) RobertLButler(3) 10 54+
(Miss M E Rowland) *hld up towards rr: effrt and n.m.r 2f out: kpt on appr fnl f: nvr nr ldrs* **7/1**[3]

0304 **6** *hd* **Avoncreek**[8] 5906 6-8-6 **50**.. JemmaMarshall(5) 13 48+
(B P J Baugh) *s.i.s: bhd: effrt and swtchd outside over 1f out: kpt on: nvr nr ldrs* **20/1**

0000 **7** *1* **Barton Bounty**[14] 5758 3-8-2 **47**................................... JamesSullivan(3) 4 42
(P D Niven) *s.i.s: bhd tl kpt on fnl 2f: nvr a factor* **50/1**

0600 **8** *3/4* **Cutting Comments**[58] 4285 4-9-7 **60**.................................. GregFairley 7 54
(P F Holmes) *led: edgd rt and hdd wl over 1f out: sn wknd* **20/1**

0556 **9** *3 1/4* **My One Weakness (IRE)**[14] 5758 3-9-3 **59**......................... LeeVickers 9 43
(B Ellison) *s.i.s: bhd: sme hdwy over 2f out: nvr nr ldrs: eased fnl f* **15/2**

0040 **10** *7* **Ursus**[12] 5820 5-9-0 **56**..(p) KellyHarrison(3) 14 22
(C R Wilson) *mid-div on outside: effrt over 3f out: lost pl over 1f out* **10/1**

0000 **11** *1 1/4* **Piste**[12] 5817 4-8-13 **52**.. PatrickMathers 11 15
(Miss T Jackson) *t.k.h in mid-div: effrt on outer over 3f out: wknd over 1f out: eased* **33/1**

0500 **12** *13* **Tanley**[8] 5926 5-8-10 **49**... JohnEgan 15 —
(I W McInnes) *mid-div: wkng whn hmpd 2f out: sn heavily eased and bhd* **40/1**

1m 25.23s (-1.77) **Going Correction** -0.35s/f (Firm)
WFA 3 from 4yo+ 3lb 12 Ran SP% **118.5**
Speed ratings (Par 101): **96,94,92,91,91 90,89,88,85,77 75,60**
toteswingers:1&2 £2.20, 2&3 £31.30, 1&3 £11.90 CSF £8.75 CT £100.78 TOTE £2.60: £1.30, £1.10, £7.60; EX 10.40 Place 6: £56.73 Place £28.69 .
Owner N Chapman **Bred** A Pereira **Trained** Settrington, N Yorks
■ Stewards' Enquiry : Tom Eaves two-day ban: careless riding (Oct 4-5)

FOCUS
The second division of the 46-60 handicap run in a time a second slower than the first division with a similar fair pace being set. The winner is rated back to his best but this doesn't look strong form.
Tanley Official explanation: jockey said gelding had a breathing problem
T/Plt: £61.00 to a £1 stake. Pool of £44,685.42 - 534.62 winning tickets. T/Qpdt: £25.70 to a £1 stake. Pool of £3,079.34 - 88.60 winning tickets. JR

6145 NEWBURY (L-H)
Saturday, September 18

OFFICIAL GOING: Good to firm (good in places; 8.7)
Rail realignment increased distances on round course by about 18metres.
Wind: Virtually nil Weather: Sunny spells

6190 BATHWICK TYRES E B F MAIDEN STKS (DIV I) — 7f (S)
1:30 (1:32) (Class 4) 2-Y-O — **£4,533** (£1,348; £674; £336) **Stalls** Centre

Form RPR

1 **Baptist (USA)** 2-9-3 0.. JimmyFortune 10 82+
(A M Balding) *in tch: hdwy 2f out: rdn and str run to ld ins fnl f: hld on wl* **16/1**

02 **2** *hd* **Chain Lightning**[65] 4054 2-9-3 0................................... RichardHughes 8 81
(R Hannon) *led: rdn and hung rt over 1f out: hdd ins fnl f: kpt on wl but a jst hld* **7/2**[2]

3 *2 1/4* **Colombian (IRE)** 2-9-3 0.. WilliamBuick 5 79+
(J H M Gosden) *hld up in rr: nt clr run over 2f out tl swtchd rt and hdwy over 1f out fin strly and gaining on ldng duo cl home* **5/2**[1]

0 **4** *3 1/4* **Deny**[22] 5491 2-9-3 0.. RyanMoore 7 67
(Sir Michael Stoute) *chsd ldrs: pushed along and wl there over 1f out: outpcd ins fnl f* **11/2**[3]

5 *nk* **Discovery Bay** 2-9-3 0... FergusSweeney 9 66+
(R Charlton) *in rr: nt clr run 2f out: green: hdwy and swtchd lft over 1f out: styd on fnl f* **33/1**

6 *hd* **Musical Flight** 2-9-3 0.. FrannyNorton 11 65
(B W Hills) *chsd ldrs: pushed along over 2f out: fdd ins fnl f* **12/1**

7 *3/4* **L'Hermitage (IRE)** 2-9-3 0.. MartinDwyer 13 63+
(B J Meehan) *in rr: pushed along over 2f out: styd on ins fnl f: nt rch ldrs* **20/1**

0 **8** *1 3/4* **Toucan Tango (IRE)**[119] 2319 2-9-3 0............................... JackMitchell 15 59
(P W Chapple-Hyam) *chsd ldrs: rdn along 3f out: stl green and hung lft over 1f out: styd on same pce* **40/1**

9 *hd* **Rastaban** 2-9-3 0.. KierenFallon 1 58
(W J Haggas) *in tch: rdn and styd on over 2f out: nvr quite rchd ldrs and fdd ins fnl f* **12/1**

10 *hd* **Royal Reason** 2-8-12 0.. SamHitchcott 6 53
(M R Channon) *chsd ldrs: rdn over 2f out: hanging lft fr over 1f out and sn wknd* **50/1**

11 *1/2* **Red Lover** 2-9-3 0.. NeilCallan 3 57+
(E A L Dunlop) *in rr tl hdwy fr 3f out to chse ldrs 2f out: wknd fnl f* **8/1**

12 *1/2* **Misk Khitaam (USA)** 2-9-3 0... RichardHills 14 55
(J L Dunlop) *chsd ldrs tl green and wknd qckly 2f out* **20/1**

13 *1 3/4* **Court Applause (IRE)** 2-9-3 0...................................... RichardMullen 2 51
(W R Muir) *nvr beyond mid-div* **80/1**

14 2 1/4 **Spartan Spirit (IRE)** 2-9-3 0 .... TravisBlock 12 45
(H Morrison) *chsd ldrs tl shkn up: green and wknd 2f out* **50/1**

1m 27.08s (1.38) **Going Correction** 0.0s/f (Good) **14** Ran SP% **118.6**
Speed ratings (Par 97): **92,91,89,85,85 84,84,82,81,81 81,80,78,75**
toteswingers:1&2:£11.00, 1&3:£12.70, 2&3:£1.70 CSF £66.43 TOTE £19.90: £4.00, £1.90, £1.80; EX 81.40 Trifecta £173.30 Pool: £632.63 - 2.70 winning units..
Owner Highclere Thoroughbred Racing (Tapit) **Bred** B P Walden & J Willard **Trained** Kingsclere, Hants

FOCUS
With only three having previous experience, this contest is likely to throw up a number of future winners. This maiden has been run in two divisions since 2005 and has produced the subsequent Listed winner Critical Moment, as well as the good handicappers Capricorn Run and Proponent.

NOTEBOOK
Baptist(USA), a £42,000 breeze-up buy who is related to winners in the USA at 5-7f, was wearing the second colours of his owners. Held up at the back early, he got a clear run towards the stands' side when asked for his effort and, after hitting the front, found extra to repel the renewed challenge of the more experienced runner-up. (op 12-1)
Chain Lightning improved from his debut, when he started slowly, to finish runner-up in a fair 7f maiden at Epsom in July. He set a fair standard and his rider tried to make his experience count by jumping him out and dictating the gallop. He could not hold off the winner's challenge but battled back under pressure and should not have to wait too long to get off the mark. (op 5-2)
Colombian(IRE) ◆, a 170,000euros half-brother to the Poule d'Essai des Poulains winner Clodovil, was sent off favourite for this debut and was a big eyecatcher. Held up at the back with the winner, he started his run later than his rival as his rider struggled for a clear passage. He finished strongly but by that time the first two had gone beyond recall. He was not given a hard race and a similar maiden should be a formality. (op 10-3)
Deny, a 150,000gns son of Marcel Boussac winner Sulk, had been well beaten on his debut on soft. Wearing his owner's first colours ahead of the eventual winner, he was never far away but lacked a change of gear in the closing stages. He is likely to appreciate longer trips on this evidence. (op 5-1 tchd 4-1)
Discovery Bay, the first foal of a winning half-sister to Film Script, made a promising debut, running on steadily despite looking in need of the experience. He is the type to come into his own over middle distances next season.
Musical Flight, the first foal of a lightly raced maiden from the family of Brian Boru and Workforce, is not very big but was another to give encouragement for the future. She will appreciate trips of 1m-plus in the future. (op 33-1)
L'Hermitage(IRE), a half-brother to a miler out of a smart sprinter, looked in need of the experience and should come on a good deal for the outing. (op 28-1)
Red Lover, a 45,000gns second foal from the family of Love Divine, was another to make a promising start. (op 12-1)

6191 THE DUBAI DUTY FREE NURSERY 6f 8y
2:00 (2:04) (Class 3) 2-Y-O

£7,477 (£2,239; £1,119; £560; £279; £140) **Stalls** Centre

Form			Horse	RPR
21	**1**		**Invincible Ridge (IRE)**[26] 5372 2-8-11 **85** .... RichardHughes 10 (R Hannon) *trckd ldrs: wnt 2nd over 1f out: pushed along and chal ins fnl f: led fnl 120yds: readily* **7/2**[2]	95+
4054	**2**	1 1/2	**Twist Of Silver (USA)**[29] 5261 2-8-8 **82** .... EddieAhern 9 (J Noseda) *hld up in rr: nt clr run fr 2f out tl swtchd rt 1f out: str run ins fnl f and fin fast to take 2nd last strides: nt rch wnr* **25/1**	88
2121	**3**	nk	**Easy Ticket (IRE)**[14] 5745 2-9-4 **92** .... RichardMullen 6 (D H Brown) *led: rdn and hung lft ins fnl f: hdd and outpcd fnl 120yds: lost 2nd last strides* **13/8**[1]	97
210	**4**	1 3/4	**Gold Pearl (USA)**[31] 5219 2-8-11 **85** .... RyanMoore 12 (S C Williams) *in tch: rdn over 2f out: styd on ins fnl f to take 4th but nt trble ldng trio* **6/1**	85
156	**5**	1 3/4	**Satin Love (USA)**[32] 5184 2-9-7 **95** .... RoystonFfrench 7 (M Johnston) *chsd ldrs: drvn along fr over 2f out: styd on same pce fnl f* **33/1**	90
310	**6**	nse	**Cocohatchee**[9] 5880 2-8-2 **76** .... LukeMorris 13 (P M Phelan) *s.i.s: sn in tch: rdn and hung lft fr 2f out: styd on fnl f but nvr any ch* **50/1**	70
2160	**7**	nse	**Capaill Liath (IRE)**[30] 5245 2-8-10 **84** .... WilliamBuick 14 (B W Hills) *chsd ldrs: rdn and wl there 2f out: wknd ins fnl f* **20/1**	78
2522	**8**	2 1/4	**Captain Dimitrios**[22] 5472 2-8-1 **75** .... CathyGannon 8 (P D Evans) *disp ld: rdn 3f out: wknd ins fnl f* **22/1**	62
2005	**9**	1 1/2	**Silence Is Bliss (IRE)**[39] 4928 2-7-11 **78** .... RyanPowell(7) 4 (J S Moore) *chsd ldrs: rdn over 2f out: wknd ins fnl f* **50/1**	61
004	**10**	3/4	**Velvet Underground (IRE)**[75] 3735 2-8-5 **79** ow1 .... MartinDwyer 15 (B J Meehan) *chsd ldrs tl wknd over 1f out* **20/1**	60
1100	**11**	nk	**Major Conquest (IRE)**[14] 5745 2-8-10 **84** .... (t) RichardHills 1 (J W Hills) *chsd ldrs: rdn 2f out: wknd wl over 1f out* **50/1**	64
0460	**12**	1/2	**Reginald Claude**[10] 5849 2-7-12 **72** oh1 .... (p) JamieMackay 16 (M D I Usher) *s.i.s: outpcd most of way* **66/1**	50
1014	**13**	6	**Veil Of Night**[9] 5874 2-7-12 **72** .... AndreaAtzeni 2 (D Haydn Jones) *chsd ldrs tl wknd qckly 2f out* **50/1**	32
214	**L**		**Regal Approval**[32] 5187 2-8-7 **81** .... KierenFallon 11 (H Morrison) *unruly in stalls and rdr nt in sddle whn stalls opened: lft at s* **5/1**[3]	—

1m 12.83s (-0.17) **Going Correction** 0.0s/f (Good) **14** Ran SP% **121.3**
Speed ratings (Par 99): **101,99,98,96,93 93,93,90,88,87 87,86,78,—**
toteswingers:1&2:£21.50, 1&3:£1.70, 2&3:£8.00 CSF £92.20 CT £196.81 TOTE £4.10: £1.70, £7.90, £1.10; EX 118.00 Trifecta £308.10 Pool: £895.40 - 2.15 winning units..
Owner Con Harrington **Bred** Con Harrington **Trained** East Everleigh, Wilts

FOCUS
A decent nursery that looked pretty competitive but the betting suggested otherwise, with the market going 20-1 bar four. Some of the interest was lost when Regal Approval played up in the stalls and was left when the gates opened, while Fifth Ave was withdrawn for the same reason.

NOTEBOOK
Invincible Ridge(IRE), runner-up in a Windsor 6f maiden on fast ground before winning over the same C&D on easy going next time, was making his handicap debut. Travelling well up the centre throughout, once delivered to challenge he always looked stronger than the favourite and eventually won with something in hand. He should go on again from this. (op 5-1)
Twist Of Silver(USA), back up in trip, was settled off the pace virtually alongside the winner early on. However, her rider failed to get an opening when he needed one and, although she finished strongly once in the clear, the winner had gone beyond recall. (op 16-1)
Easy Ticket(IRE), a speedy sort who had won two of his four starts, all at this trip on fast ground, had been raised 11lb for his last success. He made the running as usual but had nothing in reserve when the winner ranged alongside. (op 15-8 tchd 2-1 and 9-4 in a place)
Gold Pearl(USA) beat Invincible Ridge by a neck at Windsor on his second start and was meeting that rival on the same terms. Well beaten in the Gimcrack last time, this was more his grade but he has not improved as much as the winner. (op 17-2)
Satin Love(USA), the winner of a small race on his debut but held in Group company subsequently, was making his handicap debut off 95. He showed pace early before fading and might be better suited by easier ground. (op 25-1 tchd 40-1)
Cocohatchee stayed on when the race was over.
Capaill Liath(IRE), a Windsor fast-ground maiden winner in June but out the back in a sales race last time, showed up towards the nearside but could not get involved in the latter stages. (tchd 25-1)
Regal Approval could not be deemed a non-runner, but some firms refunded punters who had backed him. (tchd 11-2)

6192 DUBAI DUTY FREE MILL REEF STKS (GROUP 2) 6f 8y
2:30 (2:33) (Class 1) 2-Y-O

£37,468 (£14,203; £7,108; £3,544; £1,775; £891) **Stalls** Centre

Form			Horse	RPR
114	**1**		**Temple Meads**[31] 5219 2-9-1 102 .... RichardMullen 2 (E S McMahon) *stdd s: t.k.h and hld up in rr tl stdy hdwy 2f out to ld appr fnl f: sn drvn clr: comf* **4/1**[3]	115
3116	**2**	1 3/4	**Formosina (IRE)**[71] 3868 2-9-4 106 .... RyanMoore 7 (J Noseda) *in rr: pushed along and hung lft fr 2f out: styd on u.p fnl f to take 2nd cl home but nvr any ch w wnr* **8/1**	113
1162	**3**	1/2	**Crown Prosecutor (IRE)**[31] 5219 2-9-1 108 .... (t) MartinDwyer 5 (B J Meehan) *chsd ldr: hrd rdn to chse wnr ins fnl f but no imp: ct for 2nd cl home* **3/1**[2]	108
212	**4**	1/2	**The Paddyman (IRE)**[50] 4538 2-9-1 107 .... KierenFallon 4 (W J Haggas) *in tch: pushed along 3f out: outpcd over 2f out: rdn: hung lft and styd on fnl f but nvr gng pce to be competitive* **9/2**	107
1116	**5**	nk	**Libranno**[27] 5347 2-9-4 113 .... RichardHughes 3 (R Hannon) *led: rdn ins fnl 2f: hdd appr fnl f wknd fnl 120yds* **5/2**[1]	109
1412	**6**	2 1/2	**Mayson**[19] 5604 2-9-1 100 .... NeilCallan 1 (R A Fahey) *chsd ldrs: rdn and ev ch over 1f out: wknd fnl f* **28/1**	98
2	**7**	3 1/2	**Desert Law (IRE)**[25] 5381 2-9-1 0 .... JimmyFortune 6 (A M Balding) *v keen: chsd ldrs: pushed along 2f out: wknd over 1f out* **14/1**	88

1m 11.73s (-1.27) **Going Correction** 0.0s/f (Good) **7** Ran SP% **113.0**
Speed ratings (Par 107): **108,105,105,104,103 100,95**
toteswingers:1&2:£10.50, 1&3:£3.10, 2&3:£4.70 CSF £34.11 TOTE £7.30: £3.40, £3.40; EX 47.10.
Owner J C Fretwell **Bred** Whitsbury Manor Stud **Trained** Lichfield, Staffs

FOCUS
In recent years this Group 2 has produced subsequent Group 1 winners Firebreak, Zafeen, Dark Angel, Lord Shanakill and Awzaan. This looked a decent renewal, with a number having previous form at a similar level.

NOTEBOOK
Temple Meads ◆, a winner on his debut who did well to take the Super Sprint over 5f here from a low draw, ran pretty well in the Gimcrack next time on his first try in Group company and over 6f, despite running too free. He settled better here dropped out with his usual jockey back on board and came to challenge still on the bridle before a change of gear took him clear. He proved he is well up to this level and the Middle Park looks the obvious target. His trainer is concerned that race may come too soon, though. (tchd 5-1)
Formosina(IRE), dropping back in trip, was held up before running on late to grab the runner-up spot. He is worth another chance against the winner, especially if ridden closer to the pace. (op 7-1 tchd 10-1)
Crown Prosecutor(IRE) won his first two starts but finished behind King Torus on his third run, when he was hampered and finished distressed. He put up a better effort when runner-up in the Gimcrack back at this trip next time, with Temple Meads behind. He appeared to have every chance but was a little keen early and failed to pick up under pressure. (tchd 5-2)
The Paddyman(IRE) improved to run well against Libranno in the Richmond and was meeting him on the same terms here. He struggled to pick up under pressure before running on at the end and gives the impression he needs further now, as his breeding suggests. (op 8-1)
Libranno had won the Group 2 July Stakes and Richmond Stakes but disappointed in the Prix Morny on his previous start. Dropped back in grade, he made the running as usual but could not sustain the effort and it could be his development has flattened out for the moment. (op 9-4 tchd 2-1 and 11-4 in places)
Mayson had run well in Listed and Group races previously but was trying his highest level so far. He put up a bold effort and was only seen off entering the final furlong. He can win a Listed race at least on this evidence. (op 16-1)
Desert Law(IRE), the first foal of Listed winner Speed Cop, had posted a promising effort on his debut in a 6f Polytrack maiden. This was a big step up on his turf debut and he found it all too much, although he did not help himself by being too keen early on. He will do better in time. Official explanation: jockey said colt ran too free early (op 12-1 tchd 10-1)

6193 DUBAI DUTY FREE STKS (HERITAGE H'CAP) 1m 2f 6y
3:05 (3:05) (Class 2) (0-105,103) 3-Y-O+

£62,310 (£18,660; £9,330; £4,670; £2,330; £1,170) **Stalls** Low

Form			Horse	RPR
4101	**1**		**Forte Dei Marmi**[28] 5307 4-9-10 **102** .... KierenFallon 13 (L M Cumani) *pushed along in rr early: hdwy on ins fr 3f out: gng wl but nt clr run fr over 2f out: stl full of running whn swtchd lft and squeezed through 1f out: str run to ld fnl 30yds: won gng away* **4/1**[1]	116+
4015	**2**	nk	**Elliptical (USA)**[28] 5307 4-9-1 **93** .... DaneO'Neill 8 (G A Butler) *in rr: stl plenty to do whn swtchd rt to outside 2f out: str run to ld ins fnl f: hdd and outpcd fnl 30yds* **18/1**	104
2103	**3**	2 1/2	**Tepmokea (IRE)**[8] 5913 4-8-7 **85** .... EddieAhern 4 (R A Fahey) *chsd ldrs: rdn to ld ins fnl 2f: hdd and outpcd ins fnl f* **14/1**	91
4230	**4**	hd	**Demolition**[31] 5220 6-9-1 **93** .... JimmyFortune 20 (R A Fahey) *in tch: rdn and hdwy on outside fr 2f out: kpt on u.p fnl f but nvr gng pce to rch ldng trio* **20/1**	99
1220	**5**	shd	**Breakheart (IRE)**[42] 4830 3-8-7 **91** .... FrannyNorton 19 (A M Balding) *chsd ldrs: drvn and ev ch 2f out tl over 1f out: styd on one pce* **7/1**[2]	96
3022	**6**	hd	**Magaling (IRE)**[42] 4830 4-8-10 **88** .... GrahamGibbons 15 (M W Easterby) *s.i.s: chsd ldrs 7f out: hrd rdn fr 2f out and rt there 1f out: styd on same pce* **16/1**	93
1440	**7**	1/2	**Cumulus Nimbus**[21] 5529 3-8-9 **93** .... RichardHughes 14 (R Hannon) *s.i.s: nt clr run fr 3f out and swtchd rt 2f out: styd on u.p ins fnl f: nt rch ldrs* **16/1**	97+
0030	**8**	nk	**Submariner (USA)**[28] 5307 4-8-9 **87** .... RoystonFfrench 18 (M Johnston) *in rr: rdn and hdwy on outside fr over 2f out: kpt on fnl f but nvr a threat* **33/1**	90
420	**9**	1/2	**Changing The Guard**[28] 5307 4-8-8 **86** .... CathyGannon 10 (R A Fahey) *mid-div: hdwy fr 3f out: nt clr run 2f out: kpt on fnl f* **33/1**	88+
3312	**10**	1/2	**Resurge (IRE)**[19] 5592 5-8-9 **87** .... FergusSweeney 6 (W S Kittow) *s.i.s: in rr: hdwy over 2f out: nt clr run over 1f out: styd on fnl f* **33/1**	88+
0021	**11**	1/2	**Royal Destination (IRE)**[9] 5879 5-9-11 **103** 5ex .... RyanMoore 11 (J Noseda) *chsd ldrs: rdn over 2f out: n.m.r sn after: styd on tl fdd ins fnl f* **8/1**[3]	103
0000	**12**	nk	**Tartan Gigha (IRE)**[9] 5879 5-9-9 **101** .... NeilCallan 5 (M Johnston) *chsd ldrs: rdn 3f out: wknd ins fnl f* **66/1**	101

0600 **13** ½ **Red Merlin (IRE)**[55] 4400 5-9-0 **92**....................(v) LukeMorris 7 91
(C G Cox) *hmpd after 1f: in rr: swtchd rt and effrt fr 2f out: nvr rchd ldrs* **33/1**

0-0 **14** 1½ **The Only Key**[21] 5529 4-8-10 **88**.................... AndreaAtzeni 16 84
(S W James) *s.i.s: sn chsng ldrs: wknd over 2f out* **100/1**

5440 **15** 2¾ **Almiqdaad**[32] 5188 4-9-6 **98**.................... RichardHills 1 88+
(M A Jarvis) *hmpd after 1f and in tch: chsng ldrs whn n.m.r and pushed rt over 1f out: wknd fnl f* **10/1**

3063 **16** ¾ **Thin Red Line (IRE)**[7] 5949 4-8-12 **93**.................... MartinLane(3) 3 82
(M Dods) *chsd ldrs: rdn and ev ch 2f out: wknd and edgd lft over 1f out* **22/1**

0311 **17** 4 **Senate**[7] 5949 3-8-10 **94** 7ex.................... WilliamBuick 17 75
(J H M Gosden) *chsd ldr 7f out: led over 2f out: hdd sn after: wkng whn hmpd 1f out* **4/1**[1]

1511 **18** 5 **Aattash (IRE)**[21] 5511 3-9-2 **100** 5ex.................... SamHitchcott 9 71
(M R Channon) *led tl hdd over 2f out: btn whn bdly hmpd on rail 1f out* **12/1**

2m 4.52s (-4.28) **Going Correction** -0.20s/f (Firm)
WFA 3 from 4yo+ 6lb **18** Ran SP% **127.4**
Speed ratings (Par 109): **109,108,106,106,106 106,105,105,105,104 104,104,103,102,100 99,96,92**
toteswingers:1&2:£23.50, 1&3:£23.20, 2&3:£77.50 CSF £78.63 CT £958.82 TOTE £4.40: £2.30, £3.90, £3.10, £3.20; EX 75.80 Trifecta £888.80 Pool: £1,681.59 - 1.40 winning units..
Owner Fittocks Stud **Bred** Fittocks Stud **Trained** Newmarket, Suffolk
■ Stewards' Enquiry : Martin Lane three-day ban: careless riding (Oct 4-6)

FOCUS
This high-class, ultra-competitive handicap has been seen as something of a trial for the Cambridgeshire but represents a worthwhile target in its own right. It was quite a messy race but the form makes a fair bit of sense at face value. The winner progressed again and is looking a Listed/Group horse.

NOTEBOOK
Forte Dei Marmi ◆ improved his trainer's good record under a brave man's ride from Kieren Fallon. A three-time winner over this trip this season, including over C&D, and effective in big-field handicaps, he was held up right at the back and had a wall of horses ahead of him halfway up the straight. However, his rider stuck more towards the inside and the gaps opened enough for him to squeeze through. Once there, he was always going to score and in the end won a little cosily. He looks a Group performer in the making and apparently will not be taking his chance in the Cambridgeshire. (op 5-1)
Elliptical(USA) ◆ had finished behind Forte Dei Marmi on his previous start but was 4lb better off for a length and three-quarters and closely matched with Tartan Gigha on previous form. Given a good waiting ride, he swept down the outside and looked set to score until the winner got through. He looks well up to taking a good race. (op 11-1)
Tepmokea(IRE), a dual winner at around this trip, was 3lb above his last winning mark and posted a personal-best against a couple of improving sorts. He lost little in defeat and can win again providing the rains stay away. (op 16-1 tchd 18-1)
Demolition, a winner at up to 1m4f, had not scored since this time last year and was 10lb higher than for his last success. He is well used to big-field handicaps, having finished runner-up in the Old Newton Cup and third in the John Smith's Cup, and ran another good race.
Breakheart(IRE) ◆, a dual winner at 1m who stays this trip, had finished behind Magaling on his previous start but ran well for a stable going well at present. He is in the Cambridgeshire and could well figure if allowed to take his chance. Longer term, he looks the sort to put in the notebook for next season. (op 9-1 tchd 13-2)
Magaling(IRE), effective on soft ground, had run well when upped to this trip against a progressive type on his previous start. Never far away, he did not get a clear passage at one point but stayed on to just miss a place in the frame. (op 14-1 tchd 12-1)
Cumulus Nimbus was 4lb better off with Forte Dei Marmi for one and a half lengths compared with previous form. Switched off right out the back from his high draw, he had to come wide to get a run and was doing his best work at the finish.
Submariner(USA) was progressive in the late spring but has been busy since and generally held in similar handicaps. He ran reasonably without troubling the principals.
Royal Destination(IRE), raised 5lb for winning a similar handicap at Doncaster the previous week, came into this in good form but did not get the best of runs and failed to get involved. (op 9-1)
Tartan Gigha(IRE), a dual winner at up to 1m1f in the late spring, both times under Fallon, had struggled off similar marks since. He ran better this time and the test offered by the Cambridgeshire will suit him.
Almiqdaad won this in 2009 and was attempting to repeat the feat off a 5lb higher mark. However, he had not built on a good start this season and the blinkers he wore on his last three starts were left off. He made some ground from the rear, hampering the fading Aattash in the process, before fading. (op 14-1)
Senate had won three of his six starts at 1m2f-1m4f but had a 7lb penalty for his last success. He appeared to do too much early running in order to negate his high draw and dropped away in the straight. (op 9-2)

6194 DUBAI AIRPORT WORLD TROPHY (GROUP 3) 5f 34y
3:40 (3:40) (Class 1) 3-Y-O+
£34,062 (£12,912; £6,462; £3,222; £1,614; £405) **Stalls** Centre

Form RPR

6131 **1** **Astrophysical Jet**[20] 5569 3-8-13 **110**.................... GrahamGibbons 14 113+
(E S McMahon) *hld up in tch: rdn and hdwy over 1f out: str run to chal ins fnl f: kpt on strly to ld fnl 50yds* **3/1**[1]

0022 **2** ½ **Golden Destiny (IRE)**[14] 5742 4-8-11 **99**..........(b) FergusSweeney 10 108
(P J Makin) *led: rdn and kpt on fr over 1f out: jnd ins fnl f: hdd and no ex fnl 50yds* **40/1**

3121 **3** ½ **Prohibit**[10] 5851 5-9-0 **108**....................(p) WilliamBuick 12 109
(R M H Cowell) *in tch: pushed along 2f out: styd on wl fnl f to take 3rd cl home: no imp on ldng duo* **7/1**[3]

4614 **4** hd **Hamish McGonagall**[20] 5569 5-9-0 **109**.................... KierenFallon 9 108
(T D Easterby) *chsd ldrs: rdn over 2 out: ev ch fnl f: one pce fnl 100yds* **7/1**[3]

4165 **5** ¾ **Inxile (IRE)**[112] 2536 5-9-0 **107**.................... FrannyNorton 11 106
(D Nicholls) *chsd ldrs: rdn 2f out: wknd fnl 100yds* **28/1**

1303 **6** shd **Gilt Edge Girl**[20] 5573 4-9-0 **105**.................... LukeMorris 2 105
(C G Cox) *chsd ldrs: rdn 2f out: ev ch fnl f: wknd fnl 100yds* **33/1**

6500 **6** dht **Total Gallery (IRE)**[91] 3192 4-9-0 **112**.................... RichardHughes 13 105+
(J S Moore) *hld up in rr: hdwy over 1f out: pushed along and styd on wl thrght ins fnl f: gng on cl home* **10/1**

1223 **8** nk **Group Therapy**[10] 5851 5-9-0 **106**.................... RyanMoore 6 104+
(J Noseda) *bdly hmpd sn after s: in rr: hdwy and nt clr run over 1f out: swtchd lft and r.o on fnl f but nvr a threat* **7/2**[2]

0401 **9** ½ **Mister Hughie (IRE)**[21] 5512 3-8-13 **106**.................... SamHitchcott 4 103+
(M R Channon) *bdly hmpd sn after s: drvn and hdwy whn bdly hmpd again 1/2-way: swtchd rt to outside and styd on again fnl f: nt rcvr* **14/1**

110 **10** nk **Masamah (IRE)**[7] 5944 4-9-0 **102**.................... DaneO'Neill 8 101
(K A Ryan) *chsd ldrs: rdn and wl there over 1f out: wknd fnl 120yds* **20/1**

01U5 **11** nk **Triple Aspect (IRE)**[20] 5569 4-9-3 **110**.................... LiamJones 15 103
(W J Haggas) *outpcd tl styd on fnl f* **8/1**

5500 **12** shd **Spin Cycle (IRE)**[21] 5512 4-9-0 **104**....................(v) RichardMullen 7 100
(B Smart) *hmpd sn after s: sn chsng ldrs: wknd over 1f out* **25/1**

-120 **13** 1¼ **Beyond Desire**[34] 5120 3-8-10 **98**.................... NeilCallan 5 93
(M A Jarvis) *bdly hmpd s: sn mid-div: hdwy 2f out: wknd over 1f out* **20/1**

5363 **14** nk **Secret Asset (IRE)**[42] 4814 5-9-0 **97**.................... EddieAhern 3 94
(Jane Chapple-Hyam) *bdly hmpd sn after s: in rr: hdwy: hanging lft and nt clr run wl over 1f out: n.d after* **33/1**

0044 **15** 3½ **Anglezarke (IRE)**[14] 5742 4-8-11 **95**....................(p) JimmyFortune 1 79
(R A Fahey) *chsd ldrs 3f* **66/1**

60.07 secs (-1.33) **Going Correction** 0.0s/f (Good)
WFA 3 from 4yo+ 1lb **15** Ran SP% **125.7**
Speed ratings (Par 113): **110,109,108,108,106 106,106,106,105,104 104,104,102,101,96**
toteswingers:1&2:£23.20, 1&3:£2.80, 2&3:£78.70 CSF £145.29 TOTE £3.40: £1.90, £14.20, £2.00; EX 111.90 Trifecta £2609.20 Pool: £4,936.42 - 1.40 winning units..
Owner Ladas **Bred** Grangecon Stud **Trained** Lichfield, Staffs

FOCUS
A good Group 3 sprint featuring several progressive and in-form types taking on some established performers with something to prove. The former group came out on top. The runner-up is a slight doubt over the form and the winner probably did not need to improve, though she is capable of doing so.

NOTEBOOK
Astrophysical Jet ◆ has been progressive of late, having beaten several of these in a Group 3 at the Curragh last time. She came through to lead inside the last and battled on, running pretty much to the pound with the fourth compared with their meeting in Ireland. She has now finished for the year, but looks the sort to take high rank among the sprinters next season. (op 7-2 tchd 5-2)
Golden Destiny(IRE) ◆, a progressive sort last season, had not been beaten far by Prohibit at Ascot in August but was up in grade. She managed to reverse that form despite being only a pound better off and looks up to winning a Listed race at least.
Prohibit has improved this season, winning a good handicap and a Listed race of late. He did not arrive on the scene until too late this time, but clearly remains in good heart and a stiffer track might suit him better. (op 6-1 tchd 11-2)
Hamish McGonagall, a smart handicapper who is well suited by 5f on a flat track, had a bit to find with Astrophysical Jet and Triple Aspect on recent form but ran really well, only being squeezed out of the places on the line. He is a reliable sort. (op 15-2 tchd 8-1)
Inxile(IRE), a multiple Listed winner having his first start since May, showed plenty of early pace and was only run out of it in the last furlong. He is best suited by cut in the ground and can win a race before the end of the season, providing the rains come. (op 25-1 tchd 33-1)
Total Gallery(IRE) won the Prix de l'Abbaye last year but has been below par this season. Reported beforehand by his trainer to be on the way back, he travelled much better and was not beaten far. A repeat win in France is not out of the question with this behind him. (op 11-1 tchd 12-1)
Gilt Edge Girl ran her race and is another who helps set the level of the form. (op 11-1 tchd 12-1)
Group Therapy, racing over his ideal trip, he had a bit to find with Prohibit and Triple Aspect on earlier form but was involved in some scrimmaging early and never got involved. Official explanation: vet said gelding cut its left-fore fetlock (op 7-1)
Mister Hughie(IRE), who had beaten Prohibit in a Listed race on his previous start, was the worst sufferer in some bunching just after the start and could not get back into contention. (op 12-1)

6195 DUBAI DUTY FREE CONDITIONS STKS 1m 1f
4:15 (4:15) (Class 3) 3-Y-O+ **£6,231** (£1,866; £933; £467; £233) **Stalls** Low

Form RPR

2333 **1** **Tazeez (USA)**[28] 5321 6-8-11 **118**....................(p) RichardHills 3 115+
(J H M Gosden) *wnt lft s: mde all: shkn up and c clr wl over 1f out: unchal* **5/6**[1]

5044 **2** 1¾ **Steele Tango (USA)**[63] 4139 5-8-11 **103**.................... EddieAhern 5 111
(R A Teal) *chsd wnr 3f: styd wl there tl rdn to go 2nd again 2f out: nvr any ch w wnr but kpt on* **13/2**[3]

0024 **3** 2 **Fair Trade**[37] 5009 3-8-8 **110**.................... RichardHughes 1 109
(D R C Elsworth) *stdd s and hld up off pce in rr: hdwy over 2f out and sn rdn: styd on: wl hld in 3rd ins fnl f* **5/2**[2]

0-45 **4** 2½ **Layali Al Andalus**[19] 5590 3-8-6 **101**....................(vt[1]) WilliamBuick 4 102
(Saeed Bin Suroor) *in tch: hdwy on outer to dispute 2nd over 2f out: sn rdn: fnd nil and sn wknd* **20/1**

1150 **5** 5 **Green Moon (IRE)**[42] 4829 3-9-3 **106**.................... RyanMoore 2 102
(H J L Dunlop) *bmpd s: chsd wnr 6f out tl 2f out: wknd qckly* **8/1**

1m 54.13s (-1.37) **Going Correction** -0.20s/f (Firm)
WFA 3 from 5yo+ 5lb **5** Ran SP% **112.3**
Speed ratings (Par 107): **98,96,94,92,88**
CSF £7.16 TOTE £1.80: £1.10, £4.20; EX 6.80.
Owner Hamdan Al Maktoum **Bred** Clovelly Farms **Trained** Newmarket, Suffolk

FOCUS
A small field for this conditions stakes, which was at least up to Listed grade judged by the official ratings of the runners. Muddling form and the winner did not need to be at his best.

NOTEBOOK
Tazeez(USA) was clear top on official ratings and duly made all to score in cosy fashion. He has been running consistently in Group races this season, including third place in the Arlington Million on his previous start, and this first success for nearly 18 months should help restore confidence. He will now be aimed at the Prix Dollar at the Arc meeting early next month. (op 8-11 tchd 10-11)
Steele Tango(USA), who won the Darley Stakes last season, ran another creditable race over what appears his optimum trip. He will presumably head for that race at Newmarket once again. (op 8-1)
Fair Trade was quite keen under restraint early on but stayed on in the straight. He has plenty of size about him and looks as though he will be a better horse, and capable of competing at Pattern level, next season. (op 7-2)
Layali Al Andalus was Group 2-placed as a juvenile but has not really gone on for his new yard this season. Fitted with a visor for the first time, he appeared to have a chance halfway up the straight before fading. (op 16-1)
Green Moon(IRE) was progressive in the spring but has not sustained the improvement and, in this better than average conditions race, he again failed to make an impact. (tchd 15-2 and 9-1)

6196 BATHWICK TYRES E B F MAIDEN STKS (DIV II) 7f (S)
4:50 (4:51) (Class 4) 2-Y-O **£4,533** (£1,348; £674; £336) **Stalls** Centre

Form RPR

1 **Fury** 2-9-3 0.................... KierenFallon 7 80+
(W J Haggas) *trckd ldrs: led 2f out: styng on strly whn rdn and edgd rt cl home* **15/8**[1]

2 1½ **Yojimbo (IRE)** 2-9-3 0.................... SamHitchcott 8 74
(M R Channon) *chsd ldrs: wnt 2nd over 1f out and pressed wnr ins fnl f: hld whn carried rt cl home* **33/1**

3 2 **No Heretic** 2-9-3 0.................... RyanMoore 1 69+
(P F I Cole) *in tch: pushed along over 2f out: styd on wl to take 3rd cl home but nt trble ldng duo* **9/4**[2]

4 ¾ **Novel Dancer** 2-9-3 0.................... RichardHughes 5 67+
(R Hannon) *in tch: pushed along over 2f out: styd on fnl f to take 4th nr fin but nvr a threat* **15/2**[3]

5 nk **Maraheb** 2-9-3 0 RichardHills 9 66
(J L Dunlop) *s.i.s: t.k.h and in rr: hdwy and hung lft over 2f out: kpt on fnl f but nvr a threat* 8/1

6 nk **Red Inca** 2-9-3 0 MartinDwyer 14 65
(B J Meehan) *in tch: pushed along and hdwy fr 2f out: kpt on fnl f but nvr a danger* 10/1

0 7 shd **Ceffyl Gwell**[41] 4871 2-9-0 0 PatrickHills(3) 6 65
(R Hannon) *chsd ldrs: ev ch over 1f out and stl disputing 2nd ins fnl f: wknd fnl 120yds* 20/1

8 shd **Abbakhan (IRE)** 2-9-3 0 EddieAhern 10 67+
(J L Dunlop) *s.i.s: t.k.h and hld up in rr: stdy hdwy fr over 1f out: shkn up and styd on wl fnl f: gng on cl home* 40/1

0 9 1 1/4 **Cunning Act**[19] 5582 2-9-3 0 NeilChalmers 15 62
(J G Portman) *in rr: pushed along over 2f out: kpt on fnl f but nvr a danger* 80/1

0 10 1/2 **No Larking (IRE)**[18] 5629 2-9-3 0 DaneO'Neill 2 60
(H Candy) *led tl hdd 2f out: wknd qckly fnl f* 33/1

11 1 1/4 **Angelic Upstart (IRE)** 2-9-3 0 JimmyFortune 3 60+
(A M Balding) *s.i.s: towards rr most way* 16/1

0 12 1 1/2 **Valley Tiger**[19] 5587 2-9-3 0 RichardMullen 12 53
(W R Muir) *chsd ldrs: wkng whn hmpd 1f out* 33/1

13 23 **Major Dance** 2-9-3 0 FrannyNorton 13 —
(B W Hills) *in tch: bmpd 1/2-way: sn pushed along and green: wknd qckly 2f out: eased* 40/1

1m 26.81s (1.11) **Going Correction** 0.0s/f (Good) 13 Ran SP% 123.1
Speed ratings (Par 97): **93,91,89,88,87 87,87,87,85,85 83,82,55**
toteswingers:1&2:£15.10, 1&3:£1.80, 2&3:£25.70 CSF £80.25 TOTE £2.90: £1.10, £7.00, £1.30; EX 157.10 TRIFECTA Not won..
Owner Cheveley Park Stud **Bred** Cheveley Park Stud Ltd **Trained** Newmarket, Suffolk

FOCUS
The second division of this juvenile maiden was run 0.27sec faster than the first leg.

NOTEBOOK
Fury, a half-brother to five winners from the family of Cassandra Go and Verglas, was sent off a warm favourite for this debut and duly scored under a straightforward ride. He looked a little green inside the final furlong but still found extra for pressure. He is entered in a valuable sales race at Newmarket next month and that could be the target. (op 11-4 tchd 3-1)
Yojimbo(IRE) ◆, a half-brother to a 6f debut winner, had clearly inherited his sibling's precocity and was the only one to trouble the winner in the closing stages. He looks more than capable of winning a similar contest before long. (op 22-1)
No Heretic ◆, a 260,000gns first foal of a half-sister to Aussie Rules, tracked the leaders and stayed on in the closing stages. He should come on a lot for the outing, looks to have plenty of scope and, with entries in the Royal Lodge, Dewhurst and Racing Post Trophy, is obviously highly regarded. (op 11-4 tchd 3-1 in a place)
Novel Dancer, a half-brother to Quadrille from the family of the Queen's high-class mare Phantom Gold, ran a nice race, doing his best work in the final furlong. He will be better for the experience and will appreciate a little further in time. (op 11-2 tchd 8-1)
Maraheb, a half-brother to several winners at 7f-1m1f out of a half-sister to Muqbil, was slowly into stride on this debut and was being pushed along at halfway. He was another doing his best work in the closing stages and should be more streetwise next time. (op 15-2)
Red Inca, an £80,000 half-brother to a 7f winner from the family of Agnes World, is from a yard whose juveniles usually improve for a run, and that should be the case with him. (op 14-1)
Ceffyl Gwell, a beaten favourite on his debut, had clearly improved for the run and showed up until fading inside the last furlong. (op 16-1 tchd 14-1)
Abbakhan(IRE), a half-brother to four winners out of a high-class sprinter, was out the back for much of the race but was keeping on at the end, once he got the hang of things. (op 25-1)

6197 HEATHERWOLD STUD H'CAP 7f (S)
5:25 (5:27) (Class 4) (0-80,79) 3-Y-O £4,209 (£1,252; £625; £312) Stalls Centre

Form RPR

2446 1 **Red Gulch**[25] 5383 3-9-0 75 DaneO'Neill 14 89+
(E A L Dunlop) *s.i.s: in rr tl rdn and gd hdwy over 2f out: str run fnl f to ld fnl 50yds* 16/1

2-1 2 3/4 **Xilerator (IRE)**[185] 911 3-9-4 79 FrannyNorton 2 91+
(D Nicholls) *led: rdn 2f out: narrowly hdd 1f out: rallied gamely to ld again fnl 120yds: hdd and no ex fnl 50yds* 14/1

1550 3 2 3/4 **Illustrious Prince (IRE)**[39] 4929 3-9-3 78 (v1) RyanMoore 3 83
(J Noseda) *chsd ldrs: rdn and slt ld 1f out: hdd fnl 120yds and sn wknd* 8/1[3]

2401 4 1 **Spa's Dancer (IRE)**[17] 5658 3-9-4 79 RichardHills 12 84+
(J W Hills) *s.i.s: hld up in rr and t.k.h: hdwy and hmpd 2f out: styng on whn hmpd again 1f out: kpt on ins fnl f but nt rch ldrs* 10/1

3051 5 2 1/2 **Walcot Square (IRE)**[14] 5769 3-9-0 75 (b1) NeilCallan 6 70
(R Charlton) *in rr: hdwy 2f out: styng on whn edgd rt 1f out: kpt on fnl f: nvr in contention* 7/1[2]

1313 6 1/2 **Merchant Of Medici**[38] 4963 3-9-0 75 KierenFallon 1 69
(W R Muir) *in tch: hrd rdn and styd on fr 2f out: nvr in contention and one pce fnl f* 7/1[2]

5-10 7 1 1/2 **He's Invincible**[108] 2644 3-8-13 74 (b) MartinDwyer 11 64
(B J Meehan) *chsd ldrs: rdn over 2f out: wknd over 1f out* 25/1

0421 8 hd **Chat De La Burg (USA)**[16] 5677 3-8-11 77 KierenFox(5) 15 66
(J R Best) *in tch: rdn and outpcd over 2f out: kpt on again u.p fnl f* 12/1

4141 9 2 **Aleqa**[31] 5205 3-8-12 73 WilliamBuick 4 57
(C F Wall) *in tch: hdwy to chse ldrs 2f out: sn rdn: wknd wl over 1f out* 9/1

460 10 4 1/2 **Byrd In Hand (IRE)**[40] 4905 3-8-4 65 oh3 NeilChalmers 8 37
(J J Bridger) *chsd ldrs over 4f* 50/1

-200 11 1 1/4 **Sasheen**[25] 5384 3-8-6 67 RichardMullen 10 35
(J R Boyle) *chsd ldrs over 4f* 50/1

0441 12 14 **Rosedale**[20] 5561 3-8-6 67 LiamJones 5 —
(J A R Toller) *chsd ldrs: rdn 1/2-way: sn btn* 16/1

-P01 13 2 3/4 **En Fuego**[11] 5839 3-9-3 78 JackMitchell 13 1
(P W Chapple-Hyam) *nvr beyond mid-div* 16/1

4221 14 9 **Red Scintilla**[22] 5484 3-8-11 72 EddieAhern 16 —
(N Tinkler) *bhd most of way* 16/1

120 R **Stefanki (IRE)**[51] 4509 3-9-0 78 MatthewDavies(3) 7 —
(George Baker) *ref to r and lft in stalls* 5/2[1]

1m 25.03s (-0.67) **Going Correction** 0.0s/f (Good) 15 Ran SP% 129.4
Speed ratings (Par 103): **103,102,99,97,95 94,92,92,90,85 83,67,64,54,—**
toteswingers:1&2:£54.20, 1&3:£30.50, 2&3:£28.80 CSF £235.81 CT £1994.14 TOTE £21.50: £6.60, £5.30, £3.40; EX 343.20 TRIFECTA Not won. Place 6: £58.93 Place 5: £41.40.
Owner R J Arculli **Bred** Cheveley Park Stud Ltd **Trained** Newmarket, Suffolk

FOCUS
This fair handicap has been won by some decent performers, the best in recent times being subsequent Group winner Premio Loco. The time was 1.78sec faster than the quickest of the two divisions of the juvenile maiden. A clear personal best from the winner, with the runner-up also improving.
T/Plt: £74.20 to a £1 stake. Pool:£120,469.83 - 1,183.85 winning tickets T/Qpdt: £37.00 to a £1 stake. Pool:£5,635.79 - 112.50 winning tickets ST

6153
NEWMARKET (Rowley Mile) (R-H)
Saturday, September 18

OFFICIAL GOING: Good (6.6)
Far side of Rowley Mile track used.
Wind: modest, behind Weather: light cloud, bright spells

6198 BLOODSTOCK SOUTH AFRICA H'CAP 6f
1:45 (1:46) (Class 4) (0-85,84) 3-Y-O+ £5,180 (£1,541; £770; £384) Stalls High

Form RPR

1-11 1 **Kuanyao (IRE)**[70] 3914 4-9-7 84 GeorgeBaker 11 97+
(P J Makin) *led for 1f: chsd ldr after: rdn to ld again 1f out: styd on wl and in command fnl 100yds* 3/1[1]

2503 2 1 3/4 **Swiss Cross**[7] 5964 3-8-12 77 (bt) PhilipRobinson 4 84
(G A Butler) *chsd ldrs: hdwy to press ldr over 3f out: rdn and ev ch ent fnl 2f: styd on same pce u.p fnl f* 13/2[2]

1511 3 nk **Divertimenti (IRE)**[14] 5760 6-8-9 75 (b) RussKennemore(3) 1 81
(S R Bowring) *broke wl and crossed to r towards far rail: led after 1f: rdn over 1f out: hdd 1f out: styd on same pce fnl f* 8/1[3]

000 4 3/4 **Excellent Guest**[54] 4440 3-8-10 80 SimonPearce(5) 7 84
(G G Margarson) *hld up wl in tch towards rr: hdwy over 3f out: chsd ldrs and rdn wl over 1f out: kpt on u.p fnl f but nt pce to rch ldrs* 16/1

-600 5 3/4 **Soap Wars**[15] 5731 5-9-7 84 PatCosgrave 17 85+
(J A Osborne) *hld up in tch in midfield: effrt whn nt clr run and swtchd lft over 1f out: styd on wl ins fnl f: unable to chal* 66/1

36U1 6 hd **Liberty Lady (IRE)**[27] 5327 3-8-12 77 DarryllHolland 12 78+
(D Donovan) *in tch in midfield: effrt on outer and rdn ent fnl 2f: hung rt u.p and styd on same pce fr over 1f out* 22/1

4-10 7 1/2 **Curtains**[106] 2712 3-9-4 83 HayleyTurner 10 82
(S Dow) *chsd ldrs: drvn and unable qck over 1f out: styd on same pce fnl f* 20/1

0023 8 3/4 **New Leyf (IRE)**[22] 5495 4-9-2 79 (v1) LiamKeniry 15 76
(J R Gask) *in tch towards rr: rdn and effrt whn nt clr run over 1f out: sn swtchd lft: kpt on ins fnl f: nvr gng pce to rch ldrs* 13/2[2]

4530 9 1/2 **Danny's Choice**[61] 4204 3-9-1 80 JimCrowley 18 75
(R M Beckett) *chsd ldrs: rdn and unable qck ent fnl 2f: wknd u.p jst over 1f out* 25/1

1300 10 nse **Last Sovereign**[28] 5297 6-8-13 81 JamesO'Reilly(5) 13 76
(J O'Reilly) *in tch towards rr on far rail: rdn and effrt ent fnl 2f: styd on but no real imp fr over 1f out: nvr able to chal* 20/1

0006 11 hd **Cornus**[9] 5884 8-9-4 81 (be) JamesDoyle 8 75
(A J McCabe) *s.i.s: sn niggled along in rr: hdwy jst over 1f out: styd on wl ins fnl f: nvr trbld ldrs* 16/1

2155 12 1 1/2 **Kings 'n Dreams**[22] 5495 3-8-8 73 (b) PatDobbs 14 62
(D K Ivory) *hld up in tch towards rr: stl plenty to do whn sltly hmpd over 1f out: sn rdn and no prog: nvr trbld ldrs* 14/1

-140 13 1/2 **Boogie Diva**[9] 5884 3-9-0 79 JimmyQuinn 6 67
(Jane Chapple-Hyam) *v.s.a: wl bhd and sn pushed along: styd on fnl f: nvr trbld ldrs* 14/1

143 14 1 3/4 **Pin Cushion**[36] 5037 3-8-9 77 Louis-PhilippeBeuzelin(3) 2 59
(B J Meehan) *taken down early and ponied to s: chsd ldrs: rdn and wknd over 1f out: fdd fnl f: burst blood vessel* 20/1

0001 15 1 1/2 **Zowington**[8] 5915 8-8-7 70 (v) WilliamCarson 3 47
(S C Williams) *s.i.s: a bhd* 12/1

50-1 16 3/4 **Elusive Hawk (IRE)**[45] 4717 6-8-10 73 TomQueally 9 48
(B J Curley) *a towards rr: rdn and struggling 1/2-way: wl btn over 1f out* 9/1

1500 17 shd **Neduardo**[25] 5386 3-8-7 72 JoeFanning 16 47
(P W Chapple-Hyam) *in tch in midfield: rdn and struggling ent fnl 2f: wkng and towards rr whn sltly hmpd over 1f out: fdd fnl f* 33/1

1m 11.04s (-1.16) **Going Correction** -0.125s/f (Firm)
WFA 3 from 4yo+ 2lb 17 Ran SP% 132.5
Speed ratings (Par 105): **102,99,99,98,97 97,96,95,94,94 94,92,91,89,87 86,86**
toteswingers:1&2:£4.20, 1&3:£6.20, 2&3:£7.00 CSF £20.49 CT £160.72 TOTE £3.90: £1.50, £1.80, £2.50, £5.00; EX 25.50.
Owner D M Ahier **Bred** Newlands House Stud **Trained** Ogbourne Maisey, Wilts

FOCUS
The winning jockey described it as "lively, good ground". This was an ordinary handicap which was dominated by those who raced up with the pace. The winner continues on the up and the runner-up is rated back to his best. The time was 0.86 outside the standard.
Liberty Lady(IRE) Official explanation: jockey said filly hung right
Boogie Diva Official explanation: jockey said filly was slow into its stride
Pin Cushion Official explanation: trainer said filly bled from the nose

6199 CAPE PREMIER YEARLING SALE E B F FILLIES' H'CAP 1m 4f
2:20 (2:21) (Class 3) (0-95,90) 3-Y-O+ £9,066 (£2,697; £1,348; £673) Stalls Centre

Form RPR

1226 1 **Calatrava Cape (IRE)**[14] 5747 3-9-8 84 TomQueally 3 97+
(J L Dunlop) *stdd s: hld up towards rr: hdwy over 4f out: trckd ldrs and stl on bit wl over 1f out: pushed into ld 1f out: clr fnl 100yds: idling towards fin: rdn out* 3/1[1]

1315 2 1 **Roxy Flyer (IRE)**[34] 5118 3-9-12 88 JimmyQuinn 8 96
(Mrs A J Perrett) *in tch in midfield: rdn and outpcd over 2f out: rallied u.p over 1f out: styd on wl u.p fnl f to go 2nd nr fin* 11/1

-221 3 1/2 **Western Pearl**[23] 5445 3-9-9 85 ShaneKelly 11 92
(W J Knight) *chsd ldrs wnt 2nd 9f out tl 3f out: rdn and sltly outpcd over 2f out: rallied u.p over 1f out: nt clr run and swtchd lft ent fnl f: kpt on to go 3rd nr fin* 16/1

4322 4 nse **Nafura**[27] 5329 3-9-11 87 (p) AhmedAjtebi 10 94
(Saeed Bin Suroor) *t.k.h: chsd ldr tl 9f out: rdn to chse ldr again 3f out: drvn over 1f out: chsd wnr ins fnl f: kpt on same pce after and wl hld after: lost 2 pls nr fin* 8/1

6116 5 2 **Critical Path (IRE)**[20] 5553 4-9-9 82 SimonPearce(5) 13 86
(A M Balding) *hld in tch in midfield: rdn and unable qck over 2f out: rallied u.p and chsng ldrs whn nt clr run: hmpd and swtchd rt 1f out: kpt on same pce after* 11/1

4100 6 1 3/4 **Desert Sage**[29] 5273 3-10-0 90 JimCrowley 5 91
(R M Beckett) *led: rdn ent fnl 2f: drvn wl over 1f out: hdd 1f out: wknd qckly ins fnl f* 16/1

4221 7 8 **Marywell**[19] 5610 3-9-11 87 NickyMackay 4 75
(J H M Gosden) *in tch: rdn and unable qck over 3f out: drvn 3f out: wknd 2f out: wl btn fnl f* 4/1[2]

1131 **8** *nk* **Aktia (IRE)**[37] 5008 3-9-11 **87** KirstyMilczarek 7 75
(L M Cumani) *t.k.h: hld up towards rr: rdn and effrt over 3f out: no prog over 2f out: wl btn fnl f* **5/1**[3]

6120 **9** *hd* **Granite Girl**[21] 5511 3-9-2 **78** PatCosgrave 6 66
(P J McBride) *stdd s: hld up towards rr: rdn ent fnl 3f: wknd over 2f out: wl btn fnl f* **33/1**

5431 **10** *4* **Ethics Girl (IRE)**[14] 5757 4-9-5 **73** HayleyTurner 9 54
(John Berry) *chsd ldrs: rdn and unable qck over 2f out: wknd qckly wl over 1f out: wl bhd fnl f* **22/1**

3401 **11** *1* **Spiritual Art**[14] 5753 4-9-1 **69** PatDobbs 2 49
(L A Dace) *sltly hmpd s: hld up towards rr: rdn and struggling ent fnl 3f: wl bhd over 1f out* **22/1**

1262 **12** *8* **Akhmatova**[15] 5727 3-9-3 **79** (t) CDHayes 1 46
(G A Butler) *taken down early and ponied to s: hld up in midfield: rdn and struggling over 2f out: wknd qckly 2f out: virtually p.u ins fnl f* **12/1**

2m 28.74s (-3.26) **Going Correction** -0.125s/f (Firm)
WFA 3 from 4yo 8lb **12** Ran SP% **120.5**
Speed ratings (Par 104): **110,109,109,108,107 106,101,100,100,98 97,92**
toteswingers:1&2:£8.90, 1&3:£13.10, 2&3:£23.00 CSF £37.08 CT £467.02 TOTE £4.30: £1.50, £5.40, £5.00; EX 43.40.
Owner Windflower Overseas Holdings Inc **Bred** Windflower Overseas **Trained** Arundel, W Sussex

FOCUS
A reasonable fillies' handicap, run at a sound pace. The first six finished clear and the form looks good for the grade, with the first four all 3yos on the up. The winner is value for more than the bare form.

NOTEBOOK
Calatrava Cape(IRE) travelled really well under restraint before scything her way through the field to lead. She did not win by as far as she had promised to, idling a little as the placed fillies closed, but was value for a greater margin of victory. The 1m6f did for her at Haydock but she resumed her upward curve here. (op 7-2 tchd 4-1)
Roxy Flyer(IRE) has had a good season and she stayed on willingly for second, suggesting that she is well worth keeping to this sort of trip. (op 10-1)
Western Pearl, a Ffos Las maiden winner last time, tracked the pace throughout and was staying on stoutly near the finish. This was a good effort on her handicap debut. (tchd 18-1)
Nafura did not reach the front this time but was always chasing the pace and stuck on in her usual fashion over this longer trip. She is hard work for her jockeys but essentially is pretty consistent. (op 9-1)
Critical Path(IRE) is worth continuing with over this trip but the handicapper looks in charge of her now. (op 9-1 tchd 17-2)
Desert Sage, whose stable won this event 12 months ago, set a good gallop. She could not fend off the winner but was still in second place passing the furlong pole before weakening. (op 14-1)
Marywell, off the mark in a Warwick maiden last time, was eased when beaten a furlong or so out, accentuating her margin of defeat. (op 11-2 tchd 7-2)
Aktia(IRE) had won three of her last four, including a last-gasp defeat of Calatrava Cape last time, but she could never get into the race off this 7lb higher mark. (tchd 10-1 and 14-1)
Akhmatova was very disappointing in the first-time tongue-tie. (tchd 10-1 and 14-1)

6200 £200,000 TATTERSALLS MILLIONS AUCTION TROPHY 7f
2:55 (2:56) (Class 2) 2-Y-O
£111,538 (£50,682; £20,285; £10,132; £6,095; £4,057) **Stalls** High

Form RPR

1 **I Love Me** 2-8-2 0 KirstyMilczarek 16 90+
(A M Balding) *chsd ldr tl led over 2f out: clr over 1f out: kpt edging lft u.p fnl f: kpt on wl* **50/1**

1335 **2** *1 ½* **Sir Reginald**[9] 5880 2-8-13 105 DPMcDonough 3 97
(R A Fahey) *stdd s: hld up towards rr: swtchd lft: rdn and effrt ent fnl 2f: stl plenty to do and drvn ent fnl f: kpt on wl u.p to go 2nd wl ins fnl f: nvr gng to rch wnr* **11/4**[1]

4320 **3** *¾* **Shafgaan**[21] 5527 2-8-5 83 AhmedAjtebi 13 87
(C E Brittain) *t.k.h: chsd ldrs: rdn and hanging rt over 2f out: outpcd 2f out: kpt on u.p to chse clr wnr 1f out: kpt on but nvr gng pce to chal wnr: lost 2nd wl ins fnl f* **33/1**

3 **4** *1* **Madawi**[43] 4803 2-8-13 0 TomQueally 6 93+
(C E Brittain) *s.i.s: towards rr: rdn and hanging rt ent fnl 2f: switching lft and stl plenty to do over 1f out: styd on strly fnl f to go 4th last strides: nvr any threat to wnr* **4/1**[2]

6602 **5** *nk* **Masonic Lady (IRE)**[15] 5709 2-8-0 65 (b) NickyMackay 11 79?
(W J Haggas) *led tl over 2f out: sn rdn and outpcd by wnr wl over 1f out: lost 2nd 1f out: styd on same pce and lost 2 pls fnl 100yds* **100/1**

14 **6** *shd* **Auld Burns**[56] 4355 2-9-1 98 PatDobbs 12 94
(R Hannon) *chsd ldrs: rdn and unable qck 3f out: swtchd lft and bmpd rival wl over 1f out: kpt on same pce u.p fnl f* **6/1**

1 **7** *½* **Roman Eagle (IRE)**[78] 3631 2-8-13 86 PhilipRobinson 10 90
(M A Jarvis) *in tch in midfield: rdn and effrt over 2f out: styd on same pce u.p fr over 1f out: nvr gng pce to threaten ldrs* **5/1**[3]

10 **8** *2* **Malthouse (GER)**[21] 5527 2-9-1 85 J-PGuillambert 2 87
(M Johnston) *chsd ldrs: rdn 3f out: drvn wl over 1f out: wknd ent fnl f* **25/1**

5106 **9** *1 ¼* **Kojak (IRE)**[39] 4934 2-8-9 80 HayleyTurner 5 78
(R Hannon) *chsd ldrs: rdn and unable qck whn hung rt and bumping match ent fnl 2f: wknd wl over 1f out* **40/1**

2 **10** *1 ¼* **Oracle (IRE)**[7] 5979 2-9-3 0 JMurtagh 1 83
(A P O'Brien, Ire) *in tch in midfield: rdn and unable qck 3f out: one pce and no hdwy whn short of room ent fnl 2f: wl btn over 1f out* **12/1**

51 **11** *1 ¾* **Mubtadi**[32] 5170 2-8-7 83 LiamKeniry 14 69
(D M Simcock) *hld up in tch: rdn and unable qck whn n.m.r jst over 2f out: wknd 2f out* **13/2**

5 **12** *hd* **Barney Rebel (IRE)**[53] 4460 2-8-7 0 MichaelHills 7 68
(B W Hills) *stdd s: hld up towards rr: rdn and effrt over 2f out: no real prog: nvr trbld ldrs* **16/1**

0 **13** *2 ¼* **Control Chief**[78] 3631 2-8-7 0 JimCrowley 8 63
(R M Beckett) *stdd s: hld up towards rr: rdn and btn over 2f out* **66/1**

222 **14** *11* **Dubawi Gulf**[27] 5324 2-8-0 79 JimmyQuinn 4 28
(E A L Dunlop) *in tch: rdn and wknd qckly 2f out: sn bhd* **20/1**

1226 **15** *18* **Stentorian (IRE)**[28] 5306 2-9-1 100 JoeFanning 9 —
(M Johnston) *s.i.s: towards rr: lost tch qckly 4f out: virtually p.u fnl 2f: t.o* **25/1**

16 *54* **Little Black Book (IRE)** 2-8-13 0 CDHayes 15 —
(G A Butler) *s.i.s: sn struggling: t.o and virtually p.u fr 1/2-way* **80/1**

1m 23.95s (-1.45) **Going Correction** -0.125s/f (Firm) **16** Ran SP% **128.0**
Speed ratings (Par 101): **103,101,100,99,98 98,98,95,94,93 91,90,88,75,55** —
toteswingers:1&2:£53.60, 1&3:£272.40, 2&3:£23.10 CSF £184.76 TOTE £70.40: £12.60, £1.30, £9.50; EX 537.10.
Owner N Botica **Bred** S R Hope **Trained** Kingsclere, Hants

FOCUS
This newly instituted sales event was the richest race of the day in Britain. It was run at a sound pace and the form should prove solid, although the proximity of the fifth lends doubts. A fine effort from I Love Me on her debut, with Sir Reginald rated 8lb off.

NOTEBOOK
I Love Me ran out a shock winner. Drawn against the rail and showing bright pace, the filly came clear over a furlong out but showed her greenness when edging to her left and momentarily looking as if she might throw it away, a threat quickly averted when her rider pulled her whip through. Out of a winning half-sister to Fillies' Mile winner Glorosia, she had been taken out of a Newbury conditions race the day before when the good ground was deemed unsuitable. She will return to this track at the beginning of next month for a similar sales race for fillies, and there could be another nice pay-day in the offing. (tchd 40-1)
Sir Reginald was 7lb clear on adjusted official figures and he beat all those with previous experience, only to be undone by a newcomer. The Gimcrack third, who had been fifth in another sales race at the Leger meeting, he had promised to be suited by the step up to 7f. Held up again and a little keen early on, he then had to be switched out and took time to pick up. He came home in good style, seeing out the trip well, but once more his finishing effort came too late. (op 10-3 tchd 7-2 in a place)
Shafgaan was never far away near the far rail and he was only run out of second close home. A very useful maiden, he got the 7f well enough. (op 25-1)
Madawi ◆, representing the same connections as the third, had subsequent winners all around him on his debut in a newcomers' race on the July course. Held up and not looking entirely comfortable on the track, he was only in 11th place passing the furlong pole but ate up the ground from there. Entered in the Racing Post Trophy, he is a smart prospect who will be suited by a step up to a mile. (op 8-1)
Masonic Lady(IRE), runner-up in a Brighton auction maiden last time, had the lowest official rating but ran a good race up with the pace on this drop in trip.
Auld Burns disappointed connections at Ascot on his second start and could have done with a drop of rain here. He ran a reasonable race but seemed held when veering to his left under pressure. (op 15-2)
Roman Eagle(IRE) has been given time to grow since his winning debut at Sandown in July. He ran respectably but won't be living up to his big-race entries on this evidence. (op 9-2)
Malthouse(GER)'s debut win has not worked out and his limitations were again exposed. (op 20-1)
Oracle(IRE) got off the mark in soft ground at the Curragh a week earlier but was well held in this better company and looks to be a good way down the pecking order at Ballydoyle. (tchd 10-1)
Mubtadi was found out on this rise in grade. (op 17-2)
Little Black Book(IRE) Official explanation: jockey said gelding moved poorly and hung left

6201 INVESTEC CESAREWITCH TRIAL (H'CAP) 2m 2f
3:30 (3:35) (Class 2) (0-105,100) 3-Y-O+**£22,666** (£6,744; £3,370; £1,683) **Stalls** Centre

Form RPR

4105 **1** **Theola (IRE)**[13] 5788 4-8-2 78 (v[1]) JimmyQuinn 3 87
(M H Tompkins) *hld up towards rr: nt clr run and swtchd rt over 2f out: sn rdn: hdwy whn nt clr run and swtchd lft over 1f out: str run u.p to ld ins fnl f: sn clr: r.o strly* **7/1**[3]

422 **2** *2 ¼* **Red Cadeaux**[14] 5743 4-9-8 98 JMurtagh 10 105
(E A L Dunlop) *hld up in tch in midfield: n.m.r ent fnl 3f: rdn and hdwy jst over 2f out: led ent fnl f: hdd and nt pce of wnr ins fnl f: kpt on to hold 2nd* **11/4**[1]

5463 **3** *½* **Ocean's Minstrel**[22] 5492 4-8-9 85 MichaelHills 7 91+
(J Ryan) *hld up in tch in rr: nt clr run on rail over 2f out: grad swtchd lft to outer but stl 9th 1f out: r.o wl to go 3rd wl ins fnl f: nvr able to chal* **20/1**

2311 **4** *1 ½* **Simonside**[13] 5788 7-8-0 76 ow1 CDHayes 9 80
(B Ellison) *in tch: rdn 4f out: ev ch and drvn over 2f out: led wl over 1f out tl hdd 1f out: styd on same pce after* **11/1**

1153 **5** *1 ¾* **Montparnasse (IRE)**[14] 5747 3-7-12 90 oh2 ow3 Louis-PhilippeBeuzelin[(3)] 8 92+
(B J Meehan) *stdd s: hld up in rr: swtchd lft to outer and effrt ent fnl 3f: hdwy to press ldrs 2f out: no ex ent fnl 1f: wknd fnl 150yds* **5/1**[2]

-050 **6** *shd* **Ajaan**[14] 5743 6-9-10 100 (b) TomQueally 1 102
(H R A Cecil) *towards rr: rdn 4f out: little rspnse tl hdwy but hanging rt ent fnl 2f: plugged on u.p fnl f: nvr threatened ldrs* **5/1**[2]

240 **7** *1 ½* **Epsom Salts**[71] 3843 5-7-11 76 AndrewHeffernan[(3)] 15 78
(P M Phelan) *t.k.h: hld up wl in tch: stl travelling wl whn hmpd and snatched up ent 3f out: effrt u.p on inner 2f out: no prog and btn over 1f out* **25/1**

4446 **8** *1 ½* **Simenon (IRE)**[32] 5185 3-8-6 95 LiamKeniry 2 94+
(A M Balding) *travelled wl: trckd ldrs tl led gng wl over 2f out: rdn and hdd wl over 1f out: wknd 1f out: wl btn and eased ins fnl f* **16/1**

156- **9** *3 ¾* **Kayf Aramis**[149] 2994 8-8-7 83 JimCrowley 12 78
(N A Twiston-Davies) *chsd ldrs: rdn 5f out: effrt u.p and ev ch 3f out tl 2f out: wknd qckly ent fnl f* **11/1**

20-0 **10** *23* **Nemo Spirit (IRE)**[136] 1821 5-8-12 88 RichardKingscote 4 58
(Tom Dascombe) *chsd ldr tl led ent fnl 3f: hdd over 2f out: wknd qckly ent fnl 2f: wl bhd and eased ins fnl f: t.o* **40/1**

410 **11** *5* **Arab League (IRE)**[13] 5788 5-8-2 78 WilliamCarson 14 42
(R J Price) *led: rdn over 4f out: hdd 3f out: sn struggling: bhd 2f out: eased ins fnl f: t.o* **33/1**

P/60 **12** *7* **Shipmaster**[14] 5743 7-9-5 95 IanMongan 6 51
(A King) *in tch in midfield: rdn and effrt over 3f out: pressed ldrs briefly but hanging rt over 2f out: wknd qckly and continued to hang rt and eased ent fnl f: t.o* **50/1**

1020 **13** *1* **Dazinski**[29] 5278 4-8-11 87 PatCosgrave 11 42
(M H Tompkins) *hld up in tch in midfield: rdn and striggling over 3f out: sn bhd: eased ins fnl f: t.o* **20/1**

14-0 **14** *21* **Veiled**[42] 4846 4-8-3 84 SimonPearce[(5)] 5 16
(J Pearce) *hld up in rr: lost tch 5f out: t.o fnl 4f* **50/1**

3m 48.31s (-8.49) **Going Correction** -0.125s/f (Firm)
WFA 3 from 4yo+ 13lb **14** Ran SP% **117.7**
Speed ratings (Par 109): **109,108,107,107,106 106,105,104,103,93 90,87,87,77**
CSF £22.88 CT £326.44 TOTE £8.90: £2.40, £1.70, £7.60; EX 31.80 Trifecta £419.60 Part won. Pool: £567.09 - 0.93 winning units..
Owner E Buddle **Bred** Richard Klay And Dr M Klay **Trained** Newmarket, Suffolk
■ Stewards' Enquiry : C D Hayes three-day ban: careless riding (Oct 4-6)

FOCUS
A valuable and suitably competitive staying handicap, and probably sound form. The pace was strong but they were still well bunched with two or three furlongs left and things became rather messy. The form looks sound though with the front pair posting small steps up.

NOTEBOOK
Theola(IRE) travelled well off the pace but was briefly outpaced by the leaders before bursting through to win well. A thorough stayer, she was galvanised by the first-time visor and is now unbeaten in three for Jimmy Quinn. She picks up a 4lb penalty for the Cesarewitch and may run if she gets in, but she would not want it soft. (op 13-2 tchd 15-2)
Red Cadeaux, who was well backed, was one of those who had to wait for a run, but he was through in plenty of time. After coming to win his race, no sooner was he in front than the filly swept past him. This was a solid effort which proved his stamina for this marathon trip. (op 11-2)
Ocean's Minstrel has reportedly been gelded since his last outing. He travelled strongly towards the rear but his path was blocked when he first tried to improve. When in the clear he came home well, and the Cesarewitch would seem a suitable target for him. (op 16-1)
Simonside, racing from a career-high mark on this hat-trick quest, worked his way to the front but could not fight off the challengers. He remains in fine heart. (op 10-1)

The Form Book, Raceform Ltd, Compton, RG20 6NL

Montparnasse(IRE) avoided the trouble when coming with his run down the outside but his stamina for this longer trip was just waning late on. The 3yo was 2lb out of the weights, with his rider unable to draw his claim too, and this was a commendable effort. (op 11-2 tchd 9-2 and 6-1 in a place)
Ajaan, who never looked entirely happy but eventually stayed on from the back, was fifth in the Cesarewitch itself last autumn and no doubt that race will be on the agenda again. (op 8-1 tchd 9-2)
Epsom Salts, third in this race last year, might have been closer this time round had he not met trouble near the rail. That said, he did appear to carry his head rather high. (op 40-1)
Simenon(IRE) ◆ travelled really strongly on this handicap debut and took it up looking sure to win if he got home, but he patently didn't. A classy 3yo who has been running in Group company, he looks one to follow dropped back to around 2m. (op 14-1)
Kayf Aramis, a smart hurdler and a rare Flat runner for the yard, ran a satisfactory race on this first appearance since April. (op 17-2)
Shipmaster Official explanation: jockey said gelding pulled up lame
Veiled Official explanation: jockey said filly lost its action

6202 BETTING WORLD CLAIMING STKS 1m 4f
4:05 (4:11) (Class 4) 3-5-Y-O £5,180 (£1,541; £770; £384) **Stalls** Centre

Form RPR
1305 **1** **Spirit Is Needed (IRE)**[6] 5989 4-9-4 93 (b) JoeFanning 8 89+
(M Johnston) *mde all: pushed clr 2f out: in n.d over 1f out: pushed out: easily* **15/8**[1]
3400 **2** *4* **Dance The Star (USA)**[15] 5723 5-8-13 87 JMurtagh 7 75
(E A L Dunlop) *travelled wl: hld up in tch: rdn and nt pce of wnr ent fnl 2f: drvn and chsd clr wnr over 1f out: no imp* **7/2**[2]
5500 **3** *1* **Archie Rice (USA)**[10] 5852 4-8-13 69 TomQueally 2 73
(T Keddy) *s.i.s: hld up in rr: rdn and hdwy 2f out: nt clr run and swtchd lft jst over 1f out: drvn and styd on to go 3rd ins fnl f: no ch w wnr* **33/1**
4360 **4** *3/4* **Quarante Deux (USA)**[10] 5868 4-8-11 72 (tp) CDHayes 5 70
(G A Butler) *hld up in tch: rdn and unable qck ent fnl 3f: u.p and swtchd lft wl over 1f out: kpt on fnl f: no ch w wnr* **16/1**
0330 **5** *3/4* **Cool Strike (UAE)**[19] 5591 4-9-4 85 (v) LiamKeniry 6 76
(A M Balding) *w ldr tl rdn and outpcd ent fnl 2f: no ch w wnr after: lost 2nd over 1f out: plugged on same pce after* **13/2**
4236 **6** *hd* **Relative Strength (IRE)**[19] 5612 5-8-11 72 (v) HayleyTurner 4 68
(A M Balding) *in tch: rdn and nt qckn ent fnl 2f: no ch w wnr and plugged on same pce u.p fr over 1f out* **5/1**[3]
0255 **7** *1 3/4* **Resplendent Light**[15] 5727 5-8-11 78 JimCrowley 3 65
(W R Muir) *hld up in tch towards rr: effrt and rdn 3f out: outpcd by wnr and drvn ent fnl 2f: wknd 1f out* **13/2**
0440 **8** *nk* **Essexbridge**[21] 5529 3-8-5 74 (b[1]) FrankieMcDonald 1 67
(R Hannon) *hld up in last pair: rdn and no rspnse wl over 2f out: nvr trbld ldrs* **16/1**

2m 30.37s (-1.63) **Going Correction** -0.125s/f (Firm)
WFA 3 from 4yo+ 8lb 8 Ran SP% **115.0**
Speed ratings (Par 105): **105,102,101,101,100 100,99,99**
CSF £8.52 TOTE £3.10: £2.10, £2.10, £5.80; EX 6.90.
Owner Mrs Joan Keaney **Bred** Mrs Joan Keaney **Trained** Middleham Moor, N Yorks

FOCUS
A fair claimer on paper, but there were doubts over several and it was something of a falsely run and unsatisfactory race. the winner was well on top but the form does not look that solid.

6203 PHUMELELA GOLD ENTERPRISES H'CAP 1m 2f
4:40 (4:43) (Class 2) (0-100,98) 3-Y-O £10,361 (£3,083; £1,540; £769) **Stalls** High

Form RPR
4115 **1** **Spoken**[21] 5511 3-9-1 92 (p) JimCrowley 14 103+
(R Charlton) *mde all and styd on far rail: rdn 2f out: kpt edging lft u.p but kpt on wl fr over 1f out: drvn out* **20/1**
1122 **2** *1* **Snoqualmie Star**[14] 5753 3-8-10 87 (b) PatDobbs 10 94+
(D R C Elsworth) *hld up towards rr of centre gp: hdwy and swtchd rt ent fnl 2f: drvn ent fnl f: chsd clr wnr fnl 100yds: kpt on but nvr gng to rch wnr* **22/1**
3063 **3** *1/2* **Contract Caterer (IRE)**[52] 4470 3-9-0 91 DarryllHolland 4 97
(A M Balding) *led centre gp: rdn over 2f out: drvn over 1f out: kpt on fnl f: nvr quite pce to rch wnr* **9/2**[2]
3134 **4** *1 1/2* **Gritstone**[21] 5511 3-8-7 84 oh2 DPMcDonogh 1 87
(R A Fahey) *chsd ldrs in centre gp: rdn 3f out: kpt on u.p fr over 1f out: nvr quite gng pce to chal wnr* **14/1**
4000 **5** *nse* **Classic Colori (IRE)**[30] 5247 3-9-6 97 RichardKingscote 13 100
(Tom Dascombe) *taken down early: chsd wnr and racd on far rail: rdn 2f out: kpt on same pce and no imp: lost 3 pls ins fnl f* **33/1**
0423 **6** *1/2* **Life And Soul (IRE)**[31] 5217 3-8-13 90 PhilipRobinson 5 92
(Mrs A J Perrett) *t.k.h: chsd ldrs in centre gp: rdn over 2f out: hrd rdn and styd on same pce fr over 1f out: nvr gng pce to rch ldrs* **7/2**[1]
2201 **7** *2 1/4* **Rigidity**[8] 5904 3-9-4 95 TomQueally 8 92
(H R A Cecil) *hld up in rr in centre gp: rdn and hdwy over 2f out: hanging rt u.p and no real prog ent fnl 2f: nvr trbld ldrs* **5/1**[3]
4030 **8** *3* **Togiak (IRE)**[15] 5723 3-9-3 94 JMurtagh 12 85
(E A L Dunlop) *hld up in last of far rail trio: rdn and hung lft 2f out: no prog and btn over 1f out* **50/1**
-120 **9** *4 1/2* **Sour Mash (IRE)**[52] 4470 3-9-1 92 J-PGuillambert 7 74
(L M Cumani) *dwlt: hld up in rr of centre gp: rdn and no rspnse 4f out: hanging rt over 2f wl btn fnl 2f* **10/1**
4-20 **10** *1 1/2* **Pallantes Cross**[21] 5511 3-9-4 95 JoeFanning 6 74
(M Johnston) *chsd ldr in centre gp: rdn 3f out: wknd qckly over 1f out: fdd fnl f* **50/1**
031 **11** *6* **Oriental Scot**[14] 5759 3-8-13 90 IanMongan 11 57
(W Jarvis) *t.k.h: hld up in midfield in centre gp: rdn and no reponse 3f out: wknd 2f out: wl btn and eased ins fnl f* **12/1**
2324 **12** *1 1/4* **Power Series (USA)**[105] 2742 3-8-13 90 NickyMackay 2 55
(J H M Gosden) *stdd s: hld up in rr of centre gp: hdwy into midfield and rdn 4f out: wknd qckly over 2f out: wl btn and heavily eased towards fin* **5/1**[3]
-110 **13** *1 1/4* **Uphold**[19] 5605 3-9-0 91 MichaelHills 9 53
(B W Hills) *chsd ldrs in centre gp: rdn and struggling 5f out: wl bhd fnl 2f: eased ins fnl f* **33/1**
3200 **14** *30* **Admission**[7] 5949 3-9-7 98 (t) HayleyTurner 3 —
(M L W Bell) *stdd s: hld up towards rr in centre gp: rdn and btn 3f out: wl bhd and eased fr wl over 2f out: t.o* **20/1**

2m 2.59s (-3.21) **Going Correction** -0.125s/f (Firm) 14 Ran SP% **120.9**
Speed ratings (Par 107): **107,106,105,104,104 104,102,99,96,95 90,89,88,64**
toteswingers:1&2:£34.60, 1&3:£18.90, 2&3:£14.40 CSF £379.32 CT £2329.61 TOTE £29.60: £6.50, £4.50, £2.40; EX 307.50.
Owner Beckhampton Stables Ltd **Bred** The Rt Hon Lord Rothschild **Trained** Beckhampton, Wilts

FOCUS
A good 3yo handicap containing a number of progressive types. The form may not prove entirely solid as three of the field, including the winner, raced down the far side where the ground looked to be riding faster, while the remainder came down the centre. The winner seemed to set only an ordinary pace.

NOTEBOOK
Spoken enjoys bowling along in front on a sound surface and he made it three wins from his last four starts, having been unable to adopt his favoured tactics at Beverley last time. He edged away from the far side under pressure and was probably out on his own long enough, but was always going to hold on.
Snoqualmie Star stayed on well from the rear of the centre-course bunch. She was up another 5lb to a mark 15lb higher than when last winning, but continues to go the right way. (op 25-1)
Contract Caterer(IRE) has left Pat Eddery since his last appearance at the big Goodwood meeting. Making the running down the centre, he ran another solid race, and seems equally at home at this trip and 1m4f. (op 5-1 tchd 4-1 and 11-2 in a place)
Gritstone ran well again despite being 2lb out of the weights, and there could be a race for him before the end of the season. (op 12-1 tchd 16-1)
Classic Colori(IRE) has faced some stiff tasks and this was a decent effort in this more suitable grade. Upped in trip, he stuck to the far rail and was still in second place overall inside the final furlong. (op 25-1)
Life And Soul(IRE) ran his race again but the drop back from 1m4f did not look ideal. He has risen 11lb in the handicap since the spring without winning. (op 5-1 tchd 11-2)
Rigidity, a comfortable winner at Chester, was never a threat off a 9lb higher mark. He was hanging as he was at Goodwood two runs back and does not look the most reliable. (op 9-2)
Oriental Scot disappointed off a 7lb higher mark and may have found this coming too soon after his Thirsk win. (op 17-2 tchd 8-1)
Power Series(USA), who had been off the track since a decent effort at Epsom on Derby day, failed to make an impact. (op 8-1)
Admission Official explanation: jockey said gelding lost its action

6204 RACING SOUTH AFRICA H'CAP (DIV I) 1m
5:15 (5:15) (Class 3) (0-90,89) 3-Y-O+ £6,152 (£1,830; £914; £456) **Stalls** High

Form RPR
4253 **1** **Kindest**[6] 5994 4-9-1 80 GeorgeBaker 13 92+
(C F Wall) *trckd ldrs: gng wl and nt clr run ent fnl 2f: rdn and qcknd through gap to ld 1f out: clr ins fnl f: rdn out* **9/2**[1]
0261 **2** *1/2* **Chapter And Verse (IRE)**[14] 5750 4-9-3 85 RussKennemore(3) 10 94
(Mike Murphy) *hld up towards rr: hdwy and nt clr run 2f out tl swtchd lft and followed wnr through gap 1f out: edgd lft u.p but r.o wl to chse wnr fnl 100yds: gng on fin* **12/1**
2202 **3** *3/4* **Directorship**[29] 5264 4-9-7 86 JimCrowley 11 93
(P R Chamings) *in tch: rdn and effrt over 2f out: kpt on u.p to chse wnr jst ins fnl f tl fnl 100yds: kpt on same pce after* **7/1**[3]
4120 **4** *2* **Watch Amigo (IRE)**[19] 5605 4-9-7 86 ShaneKelly 9 88
(W R Swinburn) *trckd ldrs: rdn and ev ch 2f out tl nt pce of wnr 1f out: no ex and btn ins fnl f: wknd towards fin* **9/2**[1]
2104 **5** *1/2* **Clockmaker (IRE)**[14] 5750 4-9-10 89 NickyMackay 6 90
(J H M Gosden) *in tch in midfield: rdn and unable qck over 2f out: kpt on u.p ins fnl f: styng on steadily fin* **11/2**[2]
460 **6** *1/2* **Huzzah (IRE)**[53] 4459 5-9-5 84 MichaelHills 4 84+
(B W Hills) *restless stalls: hld up in tch towards rr: rdn and effrt ent fnl 2f: drvn and kpt on same pce ent fnl f* **8/1**
3104 **7** *nk* **Kay Gee Be (IRE)**[29] 5264 6-9-7 86 IanMongan 8 85
(W Jarvis) *led: rdn over 2f out: drvn and hdd 1f out: wknd and short of room ins fnl f* **11/1**
5000 **8** *2 1/4* **Jarrow (IRE)**[19] 5606 3-8-11 80 JoeFanning 3 74+
(M Johnston) *hld up in rr: swtchd to outer and effrt wl over 2f out: keeping on but stl plenty to do whn sltly hmpd over 1f out: plugged on but nvr gng pce to rch ldrs* **33/1**
2320 **9** *1/2* **Ithinkbest**[48] 4617 4-9-6 88 Louis-PhilippeBeuzelin(3) 1 81+
(Sir Michael Stoute) *in tch in midfield: effrt u.p over 2f out: keeping on same pce whn hung lft u.p over 1f out: no prog and btn fnl f* **10/1**
3212 **10** *2 3/4* **Gifted Apakay (USA)**[11] 5833 3-8-10 79 TomQueally 12 66
(E A L Dunlop) *w ldr tl rdn and unable qck wl over 1f out: wknd qckly over 1f out* **15/2**
401- **11** *6* **Ultimate**[187] 6946 4-9-3 82 CDHayes 7 55
(B Ellison) *chsd ldrs: rdn and struggling over 2f out: wknd wl over 1f out: wl btn and eased ins fnl f* **12/1**
4000 **12** *hd* **Bravo Echo**[15] 5731 4-9-9 88 PatCosgrave 2 61
(M J Attwater) *stdd and swtchd rt after s: hld up in rr: rdn and no prog 3f out: n.d* **40/1**
6-10 **13** *nk* **Highland Quaich**[175] 1018 3-8-12 81 HayleyTurner 5 53
(D R C Elsworth) *stdd s: t.k.h and sn hld up in midfield: lost pl and bhd 2f out* **33/1**

1m 36.27s (-2.33) **Going Correction** -0.125s/f (Firm)
WFA 3 from 4yo+ 4lb 13 Ran SP% **128.3**
Speed ratings (Par 107): **106,105,104,102,102 101,101,99,98,95 89,89,89**
toteswingers:1&2:£18.20, 1&3:£10.50, 2&3:£12.80 CSF £63.97 CT £309.97 TOTE £6.10: £2.70, £3.10, £2.20; EX 106.80.
Owner Peter Botham **Bred** Gainsborough Stud Management Ltd **Trained** Newmarket, Suffolk
■ Stewards' Enquiry : Louis-Philippe Beuzelin caution: careless riding.

FOCUS
A fair handicap run in a time slightly quicker than the second division. The whole field raced on the far side, shunning the centre of the course, although they did spread across the track late on. The first three were all drawn high and the winner posted a personal best.

NOTEBOOK
Kindest had travelled well but failed to get home over 1m2f in soft ground at Goodwood last Sunday. Again moving easily on this quick reappearance, she quickened up smartly to assert. She will be well treated on her best form even after a rise for this. (op 7-1 tchd 15-2)
Chapter And Verse(IRE) ◆ was able to race off a mark 2lb lower than when winning on the Kempton Polytrack last time but was still 5lb above his most recent turf mark. Confirming himself to be in fine heart, he came home strongly, and things might have been a bit different had the winner not taken first run on him. (op 8-1)
Directorship is proving difficult to win with but he is performing well in defeat and this was a solid effort off a career-high mark. (op 8-1)
Watch Amigo(IRE) had every chance but this trip on this stiff track was finding him out late on. (op 8-1)
Clockmaker(IRE), fourth to Chapter And Verse in the Kempton race, stayed on well when it was all too late. The extra furlong of the Cambridgeshire would suit him but he might not get in the race. (tchd 8-1)
Huzzah(IRE), who is 9lb below his last winning mark, back in May 2008, was staying on from the back out wide.

Kay Gee Be(IRE) ran a fair race from the front but his strike rate in recent seasons is uninspiring. (op 9-1)

6205 RACING SOUTH AFRICA H'CAP (DIV II) 1m
5:50 (5:50) (Class 3) (0-90,89) 3-Y-0+ **£6,152** (£1,830; £914; £456) **Stalls** High

Form RPR

1611 **1** **Parvaaz (IRE)**[14] 5754 3-9-4 **87** PhilipRobinson 11 98+
(M A Jarvis) *stdd s: t.k.h: hld up wl in tch: hdwy to join ldrs ent fnl 3f: drvn ahd ent fnl f: styd on wl* **5/1**[2]

-600 **2** 1 ¾ **Decent Fella (IRE)**[35] 5068 4-9-5 **84** (v[1]) LiamKeniry 8 91
(A M Balding) *t.k.h: chsd ldrs: led over 2f out: clr w wnr over 1f out: hdd ent fnl f: kpt on same pce ins fnl f* **6/1**[3]

3225 **3** nk **First Cat**[38] 4963 3-9-2 **85** FrankieMcDonald 10 91+
(R Hannon) *hld up bhd: effrt and edging rt wl over 1f out: rdn and hdwy over 1f out: r.o fnl f: nvr gng pce to rch wnr* **12/1**

0060 **4** 1 ¾ **Reve De Nuit (USA)**[7] 5970 4-9-6 **85** TomQueally 4 89+
(A J McCabe) *hld up towards rr: nt clr run and hmpd 2f out: swtchd lft over 1f out: styd on wl fnl f: nt rch ldrs* **7/1**

6005 **5** nk **Viva Vettori**[26] 5370 6-9-8 **87** JimCrowley 13 89
(D R C Elsworth) *t.k.h: stdd after s: hld up in tch: hdwy to chse ldrs ent fnl 2f: rdn wl over 1f out: no ex and btn 1f out* **6/1**[3]

1203 **6** 1 ¼ **Major Phil (IRE)**[29] 5264 4-9-10 **89** J-PGuillambert 2 88
(L M Cumani) *t.k.h: broke wl but sn stdd to chse ldrs: rdn over 2f out: kpt on same pce fr over 1f out* **4/1**[1]

3040 **7** 2 ¼ **Gaily Noble (IRE)**[19] 5605 4-9-2 **88** AntiocoMurgia(7) 9 82
(A B Haynes) *hld up in midfield: effrt and rdn ent fnl 2f: edgd lft u.p over 1f out: wknd ent fnl f* **20/1**

-114 **8** nse **Seasonal Cross**[52] 4472 5-8-11 **76** HayleyTurner 6 69
(S Dow) *stdd s: hld up in rr: swtchd to outer and effrt 2f out: kpt on same pce and no imp over 1f out* **12/1**

-010 **9** 3 ½ **King's Colour**[56] 4354 5-9-7 **86** GeorgeBaker 3 71
(B R Johnson) *stdd after s: hld up in tch in midfield: rdn and hdwy jst over 2f out: wkng whn short of room and squeezed out over 1f out* **20/1**

0100 **10** ½ **West End Lad**[2] 6112 7-8-11 **79** (b) RussKennemore(3) 5 63
(S R Bowring) *sn bustled along to ld: hdd and rdn over 2f out: wknd qckly 2f out* **33/1**

016 **11** 1 **Dajen**[24] 5415 4-9-0 **86** LauraPike(7) 12 68
(D M Simcock) *hld up in tch: rdn along and lost pl ent fnl 2f: wl btn over 1f out* **33/1**

0600 **12** 2 ½ **Karaka Jack**[42] 4828 3-8-12 **81** (b[1]) JoeFanning 7 57+
(M Johnston) *chsd ldrs: rdn and struggling over 2f out: wkng and btn whn squeezed for room and eased over 1f out* **16/1**

1355 **P** **Squall**[21] 5533 3-8-8 **77** ow1 (v[1]) DarryllHolland 1 —
(J Noseda) *dwlt: racd freely and sn chsng ldrs: rdn and dropped out qckly ent fnl 3f: t.o whn p.u over 1f out* **12/1**

1m 36.46s (-2.14) **Going Correction** -0.125s/f (Firm)
WFA 3 from 4yo+ 4lb **13** Ran SP% **122.1**
Speed ratings (Par 107): **105,103,102,101,100 99,97,97,93,93 92,89,**—
toteswingers:1&2:£7.90, 1&3:£6.90, 2&3:£22.10 CSF £34.19 CT £347.16 TOTE £5.00: £2.60, £2.40, £3.70; EX 46.30 Place 6: £161.62 Place 5: £72.48 .
Owner Sheikh Ahmed Al Maktoum **Bred** Darley **Trained** Newmarket, Suffolk

FOCUS
Division two was run in a time slightly slower than the first part. They raced a little way off the far rail. The winner was well drawn and continues on the upgrade. The form is rated around the runner-up.

NOTEBOOK
Parvaaz(IRE) shrugged off a 6lb rise to notch his fourth win in his last five starts. He was not as keen as he had been on his previous try at 1m and was certainly not stopping at the end. This was only his sixth race and it is not unreasonable to assume that he can step up further. (op 4-1)
Decent Fella(IRE), beaten favourite on his last two starts, ran well in the first-time visor, pushing the pace all the way and confirming the good impression he made on his British debut at this track back in the spring. He saw out the longer trip well enough. (op 8-1)
First Cat ran another creditable race on this return to 1m, but remains one to oppose for win purposes.
Reve De Nuit(USA) encountered traffic problems before staying on strongly inside the last. He is 1lb lower than when last winning and could add to his tally if things go his way. (op 11-1 tchd 12-1 in a place)
Viva Vettori, who is still without a win on turf, lost a couple of places late on. (op 7-1 tchd 8-1)
Major Phil(IRE) looks held off his current mark but a return to 1m2f should help his cause. (tchd 5-1)
Squall, equipped with a first-time visor, dropped away rapidly and was pulled up with something apparently amiss. Official explanation: trainer's rep said gelding bled from the nose (tchd 10-1 and 14-1)
T/Plt: £159.10 to a £1 stake. Pool:£81,267.16 - 372.70 winning tickets T/Qpdt: £21.60 to a£1 stake. Pool:£3,729.99 - 127.54 winning tickets SP

6161 WOLVERHAMPTON (A.W) (L-H)
Saturday, September 18

OFFICIAL GOING: Standard changing to standard to fast after race 2 (6:20)
Wind: Light half-behind Weather: Light rain

6206 CLAIRE HASLUM 30TH BIRTHDAY CELEBRATION H'CAP 5f 20y(P)
5:45 (5:46) (Class 6) (0-55,54) 3-Y-0+ **£1,774** (£523; £262) **Stalls** Low

Form RPR

0543 **1** **Almaty Express**[2] 6119 8-8-9 **49** (b) MartinLane(3) 4 59
(J R Weymes) *chsd ldrs: led over 1f out: rdn out* **9/4**[1]

6366 **2** ½ **Desert Strike**[16] 5697 4-8-8 **52** (p) NoraLooby(7) 6 60
(A J McCabe) *hld up: hdwy 2f out: rdn to chse wnr ins fnl f: r.o* **16/1**

5635 **3** 1 ¼ **Luisa Tetrazzini (IRE)**[165] 1142 4-8-12 **54** MarkCoumbe(5) 13 58
(D Bourton) *dwlt: hld up: rdn over 1f out: r.o wl ins fnl f: nt rch ldrs* **40/1**

1436 **4** nk **Mansii**[19] 5586 5-9-2 **53** (t) JamesDoyle 3 56
(P J McBride) *chsd ldrs: rdn over 1f out: styd on same pce ins fnl f* **5/2**[2]

0000 **5** 1 ¼ **Pinball (IRE)**[19] 5580 4-8-13 **50** (b[1]) RoystonFfrench 7 48
(Mrs L Williamson) *sn pushed along in rr: hdwy u.p over 1f out: nt rch ldrs* **33/1**

621 **6** 1 **Pavement Games**[7] 5957 3-8-6 **51** HarryBentley(7) 8 46
(R C Guest) *hld up: hdwy u.p fr over 1f out: nrst fin* **14/1**

0240 **7** nse **Francis Albert**[9] 5876 4-8-6 **50** (b) JosephYoung(7) 11 44
(M Mullineaux) *chsd ldrs: rdn over 1f out: no ex insde fnl f* **33/1**

4120 **8** 1 **Red River Boy**[5] 6040 5-8-9 **53** RyanPowell(7) 5 44
(C W Fairhurst) *in rr: rdn 1/2-way: nvr on terms* **8/1**

000 **9** nk **Noisy Noverre (IRE)**[17] 5658 3-8-13 **51** ow1 TomMcLaughlin 9 41
(George Baker) *mid-div: rdn over 2f out: styd on same pce appr fnl f* **50/1**

0555 **10** ¾ **Lithaam (IRE)**[16] 5697 6-8-8 **52** (p) RyanClark(7) 10 39
(J M Bradley) *mid-div: rdn 1/2-way: n.d* **10/1**

4125 **11** ¾ **Annia Galeria (IRE)**[15] 5715 3-9-2 **54** (b) CathyGannon 1 38
(C A Dwyer) *led 1f: chsd ldr: rdn over 1f out: wknd ins fnl f* **15/2**[3]

0050 **12** ¾ **Mazzola**[16] 5697 4-8-12 **49** (v[1]) KirstyMilczarek 2 31
(J M Bradley) *led 4f out: rdn and hdd over 1f out: wknd ins fnl f* **16/1**

6005 **13** 14 **Helping Hand (IRE)**[19] 5580 5-8-11 **48** AndreaAtzeni 12 —
(R Hollinshead) *prom: rdn 1/2-way: sn wknd* **20/1**

61.19 secs (-1.11) **Going Correction** -0.125s/f (Stan)
WFA 3 from 4yo+ 1lb **13** Ran SP% **124.8**
Speed ratings (Par 101): **103,102,100,99,97 96,96,94,93,92 91,90,67**
toteswingers:1&2:£15.20, 1&3:£33.10, 2&3:£62.80 CSF £40.22 CT £1232.73 TOTE £3.90: £1.80, £11.10, £5.80; EX 70.40.
Owner Highmoor Racing & Miss K Buckle **Bred** P G Airey **Trained** Middleham Moor, N Yorks

FOCUS
Conditions were overcast and light rain started to fall an hour before this poor opener. Mazzola, Francis Albert and Annia Galeria set a strong pace, for which all three duly paid up the straight. The winner ran his best race since last year.
Helping Hand(IRE) Official explanation: jockey said gelding lost its action

6207 GOT THE FEELING, GET TO LADBROKES H'CAP (DIV I) 5f 216y(P)
6:20 (6:20) (Class 5) (0-75,73) 3-Y-0+ **£2,115** (£624; £312) **Stalls** Low

Form RPR

4502 **1** **Defector (IRE)**[36] 5027 4-9-1 **72** MarkCoumbe(5) 10 82
(D Bourton) *sn led: racd keenly: rdn ins fnl f: jst hld on* **14/1**

623 **2** ½ **Stratton Banker (IRE)**[19] 5588 3-8-5 **59** WilliamCarson 3 67+
(S C Williams) *hld up: hdwy over 2f out: rdn and r.o wl: nt rch wnr* **11/8**[1]

0062 **3** 1 ¼ **Catherines Call (IRE)**[14] 5769 3-9-5 **73** LukeMorris 8 77
(D Donovan) *led early: chsd wnr: rdn over 1f out: styd on* **9/2**[2]

056 **4** nk **Requisite**[7] 5952 5-9-4 **73** (v) MartinLane(3) 2 76
(I A Wood) *dwlt: hld up: hdwy over 1f out: sn rdn: r.o* **7/1**[3]

2000 **5** 1 ¼ **Silver Wind**[47] 4662 5-9-4 **70** (v) CathyGannon 6 69
(P D Evans) *chsd ldrs: sn pushed along: rdn over 2f out: styd on same pce fnl f* **8/1**

2006 **6** 2 ¼ **Methaaly (IRE)**[8] 5920 7-8-10 **69** (be) JosephYoung(7) 1 61
(M Mullineaux) *hld up: nt clr run over 1f out: nvr trbld ldrs* **20/1**

0050 **7** 1 **Loyal Royal (IRE)**[8] 5920 7-8-5 **60** (bt) AndrewHeffernan(3) 4 49
(J M Bradley) *plld hrd and prom: rdn over 1f out: no ex* **33/1**

000 **8** 9 **Princess Valerina**[199] 767 6-9-3 **69** AndreaAtzeni 9 29
(D Haydn Jones) *s.i.s: sn chsng ldrs: rdn and wknd over 1f out* **7/1**[3]

211 **9** 3 ½ **Bubbly Bellini (IRE)**[37] 5014 3-9-0 **68** RoystonFfrench 7 17
(Lee Smyth, Ire) *hld up: a in rr: wknd 2f out* **25/1**

1m 13.71s (-1.29) **Going Correction** -0.125s/f (Stan)
WFA 3 from 4yo+ 2lb **9** Ran SP% **114.6**
Speed ratings (Par 103): **103,102,100,100,98 95,94,82,77**
toteswingers:1&2:£2.50, 1&3:£7.70, 2&3:£1.60 CSF £32.86 CT £106.32 TOTE £19.10: £4.60, £1.10, £1.40; EX 40.00.
Owner Ian O'Connor Construction Ltd **Bred** Grenane House Stud, Steve Hillen & Sean Graham **Trained** Wolverhampton, W Midlands

FOCUS
Another race run at a very solid pace, and clerk of the course Fergus Cameron changed the going to standard to fast afterwards from standard. It was a length faster than division II and the form seems sound.

6208 GOT THE FEELING, GET TO LADBROKES H'CAP (DIV II) 5f 216y(P)
6:50 (6:51) (Class 5) (0-75,73) 3-Y-0+ **£2,115** (£624; £312) **Stalls** Low

Form RPR

0644 **1** **Sweet Gale (IRE)**[27] 5327 6-8-7 **58** JimmyQuinn 9 70+
(Mike Murphy) *dwlt: hld up: hdwy over 1f out: shkn up to ld ins fnl f: r.o* **13/2**

2601 **2** 1 **Ryedane (IRE)**[5] 6040 8-9-4 **69** (b) DavidNolan 2 78
(T D Easterby) *chsd ldrs: led over 1f out: rdn and hdd ins fnl f: styd on* **7/2**[2]

5044 **3** 1 ½ **Cape Melody**[14] 5768 4-9-7 **72** TravisBlock 6 76
(H Morrison) *chsd ldrs: rdn over 1f out: styd on same pce ins fnl f* **8/1**

1400 **4** 2 ½ **Knightfire (IRE)**[23] 5454 3-9-5 **72** (t) RichardHughes 3 68
(W R Swinburn) *trckd ldrs: rdn over 1f out: no ex ins fnl f* **9/4**[1]

0434 **5** 1 ½ **Sheer Force (IRE)**[23] 5454 3-8-13 **73** (v) HarryBentley(7) 7 64
(W J Knight) *hld up: rdn over 1f out: nvr trbld ldrs* **5/1**[3]

4350 **6** ½ **Perlachy**[16] 5698 6-9-3 **68** (v) LukeMorris 5 58
(D Shaw) *hld up: rdn over 1f out: n.d* **20/1**

2500 **7** 1 ½ **Ginobili (IRE)**[26] 5377 4-8-11 **62** (e[1]) JamesDoyle 4 47
(Andrew Reid) *chsd ldr tl rdn over 1f out: hung lft and wknd fnl f* **33/1**

4-06 **8** 6 **Devil You Know (IRE)**[106] 2696 4-9-7 **72** (t) GrahamGibbons 1 38
(M W Easterby) *led: rdn and hdd over 1f out: wknd fnl f* **12/1**

1m 13.89s (-1.11) **Going Correction** -0.125s/f (Stan)
WFA 3 from 4yo+ 2lb **8** Ran SP% **109.5**
Speed ratings (Par 103): **102,100,98,95,93 92,90,82**
toteswingers:1&2:£4.70, 1&3:£4.30, 2&3:£4.10 CSF £26.94 CT £168.93 TOTE £5.10: £1.40, £2.40, £2.50; EX 29.10.
Owner Ms L M Bartlett **Bred** Rozelle Bloodstock **Trained** Westoning, Beds

FOCUS
The slower of the two legs of the 0-75 handicap and the field was reduced by one instantly when Danzoe burst through the stalls and was withdrawn. Similar form to division I, with the winner getting closer to her old form.

6209 THE BLACK COUNTRY'S ONLY RACECOURSE (S) STKS 7f 32y(P)
7:20 (7:21) (Class 6) 2-Y-O **£1,774** (£523; £262) **Stalls** High

Form RPR

1400 **1** **Sir Lunchalott**[11] 5837 2-9-3 70 (b[1]) RichardHughes 10 68
(J S Moore) *trckd ldrs: rdn ins fnl f: r.o to ld nr fin* **11/4**[2]

0030 **2** nk **Better Self**[16] 5682 2-8-6 67 JimmyQuinn 5 56
(Mrs A Duffield) *led: hdd over 5f out: chsd ldr tl led again over 2f out: rdn fnl f: hdd nr fin* **13/8**[1]

02 **3** ¾ **Green With Envy (IRE)**[18] 5630 2-8-11 0 (p) KirstyMilczarek 2 59
(George Baker) *hld up: hdwy over 1f out: swtchd lft ins fnl f: r.o* **9/1**

4606 **4** 1 ½ **Moorland Boy**[17] 5667 2-8-11 58 FergusSweeney 3 56
(J A Osborne) *hld up in tch: plld hrd: n.m.r over 6f out: rdn over 1f out: r.o* **25/1**

6060 **5** ½ **Amber Mist**[16] 5675 2-7-13 51 HarryBentley(7) 11 50
(David Pinder) *chsd ldrs: led over 5f out: rdn and hdd over 2f out: no ex ins fnl f* **50/1**

00 **6** ¾ **Century Dancer**[11] 5835 2-8-3 0 SophieDoyle(3) 4 48
(Miss Tor Sturgis) *chsd ldrs: rdn over 2f out: no ex fnl f* **66/1**

05 **7** ½ **Fire Crystal**[7] 5954 2-8-6 0 LukeMorris 6 46
(M R Channon) *s.i.s: hdwy u.p over 1f out: styd on same pce ins fnl f* **12/1**

The Form Book, Raceform Ltd, Compton, RG20 6NL

00 **8** 1 1/2 **Senor Sassi (USA)**[26] 5373 2-8-4 0 RyanPowell(7) 1 48
(J S Moore) *hld up: rdn over 1f out: nvr on terms* **50/1**

5 **9** 1/2 **Simmons**[17] 5667 2-8-1 0 SimonPearce(5) 7 42
(Matthew Salaman) *hld up: racd keenly: n.d* **8/1**[3]

500 **10** *shd* **Regal Rocket (IRE)**[68] 3959 2-8-3 50 (t) MartinLane(3) 9 41
(J R Weymes) *hld up in tch: racd keenly: rdn over 1f out: wknd fnl f* **40/1**

64 **11** 2 1/2 **Bathwick Scanno (IRE)**[16] 5701 2-8-11 0 CathyGannon 12 40
(P D Evans) *hld up: hdwy 4f out: rdn over 2f out: sn wknd* **12/1**

0055 **12** 4 1/2 **Silver Angel (IRE)**[18] 5640 2-8-6 50 SamHitchcott 8 24
(M R Channon) *s.i.s: hdwy 4f out: rdn over 2f out: wknd over 1f out* **40/1**

1m 30.44s (0.84) **Going Correction** -0.125s/f (Stan) **12** Ran SP% **115.4**
Speed ratings (Par 93): **90,89,88,87,86 85,85,83,82,82 79,74**
toteswingers:1&2:£2.10, 1&3:£3.60, 2&3:£2.80 CSF £6.94 TOTE £3.70: £1.10, £1.20, £1.20; EX 8.60.There was no bid for the winner. Better Self was claimed by P. D. Evans for £6,000
Owner Richard J Lilley & A J Speyer **Bred** The National Stud Blakeney Club **Trained** Upper Lambourn, Berks

FOCUS
Few featured in an ordinary juvenile seller.

NOTEBOOK
Sir Lunchalott, dropped to this level and acquiring blinkers both for the first time, received a perfectly judged ride from Richard Hughes, kept close to the action throughout but not hitting the front until close home. Admittedly something of a character and a bridle horse, according to connections, they also regard a bad handicap mark as having prevented him from going on since his maiden victory in May. He was retained without a bid. (op 7-2 tchd 4-1)
Better Self ◆ emerges with plenty of credit on her all-weather debut, especially as the fight with the free-running Amber Mist for the outright lead wasn't finally resolved in her favour until the turn in. She was claimed by David Evans afterwards. (op 2-1)
Green With Envy(IRE) took another step in the right direction. An extra furlong probably wouldn't go amiss on this surface, though. (op 6-1 tchd 10-1)
Moorland Boy's refusal to settle was once again evident and that did his chances far more harm than the crowding he experienced after a furlong. He can only be watched until consenting to help his riders more. (op 16-1)
Fire Crystal didn't look any less short of gears for this change to an artificial surface. (op 16-1)
Simmons, just ahead of Moorland Boy in this company at Lingfield last time, was another to race too wastefully. A big filly, she still looks to need a bit of time to grow fully into her frame in any event. (op 7-1)

6210 BEST ODDS GUARANTEED AT LADBROKES.COM H'CAP 7f 32y(P)
7:50 (7:50) (Class 6) (0-65,65) 3-Y-0+ **£1,774** (£523; £262) **Stalls** High

Form RPR

0523 **1** **Perfect Friend**[34] 5113 4-9-7 **65** RichardHughes 6 76
(S Kirk) *chsd ldrs: led over 1f out: rdn and edgd lft ins fnl f: r.o* **9/2**[2]

0462 **2** 3/4 **Just Timmy Marcus**[14] 5766 4-9-5 **63** (b) GrahamGibbons 3 72
(B P J Baugh) *dwlt: hld up: hdwy over 2f out: rdn and hung lft ins fnl f: r.o* **3/1**[1]

0005 **3** *nk* **Lord Of The Dance (IRE)**[9] 5897 4-9-3 **61** LukeMorris 1 69
(W M Brisbourne) *a.p: rdn over 1f out: edgd lft ins fnl f: r.o* **22/1**

0030 **4** 1 1/4 **Forward Feline (IRE)**[9] 5897 4-9-1 **64** DeclanCannon(5) 2 69
(B Palling) *hld up: hdwy over 2f out: rdn over 1f out: r.o* **16/1**

1340 **5** 3 1/2 **Gracie's Gift (IRE)**[18] 5647 8-9-1 **64** KierenFox(5) 5 59
(R C Guest) *prom: rdn 1/2-way: styd on same pce appr fnl f* **10/1**

0012 **6** 2 1/4 **Fitz**[9] 5897 4-9-3 **61** KirstyMilczarek 12 50
(Matthew Salaman) *stdd s: hld up: nt clr run over 1f out: nvr on terms* **7/1**

0466 **7** *shd* **First Service (IRE)**[42] 4839 4-9-4 **62** FergusSweeney 11 51
(M J Attwater) *hld up: rdn over 2f out: n.d* **11/1**

546 **8** 3/4 **Miss Bounty**[36] 5039 5-9-1 **59** (p) DaraghO'Donohoe 7 46
(George Baker) *hld up: nvr on terms* **18/1**

2411 **9** *nse* **Towy Boy (IRE)**[16] 5697 5-8-13 **60** (bt) MartinLane(3) 8 47
(I A Wood) *w ldr: racd keenly: led 4f out: rdn and hdd over 1f out: wknd ins fnl f* **6/1**[3]

0040 **10** 5 **Shaws Diamond (USA)**[21] 5533 4-9-5 **63** (v) JimmyQuinn 9 36
(D Shaw) *chsd ldrs: rdn and wknd 2f out* **12/1**

0000 **11** 11 **Grand Stitch (USA)**[46] 4670 4-9-5 **63** (v[1]) DavidNolan 4 7
(D Carroll) *led 3f: chsd ldr: rdn over 2f out: wknd over 1f out* **33/1**

0564 **P** **War And Peace (IRE)**[10] 5867 6-9-3 **61** CathyGannon 10 —
(P D Evans) *s.i.s: a in rr: p.u wl over 1f out: lame* **12/1**

1m 27.59s (-2.01) **Going Correction** -0.125s/f (Stan) **12** Ran SP% **121.2**
Speed ratings (Par 101): **106,105,104,103,99 96,96,95,95,90 77,—**
toteswingers:1&2:£2.60, 1&3:£20.00, 2&3:£19.90 CSF £18.80 CT £280.57 TOTE £8.90: £3.90, £1.40, £3.50; EX 20.30.
Owner Lady Davis **Bred** Speedlith Group **Trained** Upper Lambourn, Berks

FOCUS
The faster of the two 7f races on the card by nearly three seconds, and the first four finished clear. The form looks pretty solid.
Fitz Official explanation: jockey said gelding was denied a clear run

6211 EUROPEAN BREEDERS' FUND MAIDEN STKS 1m 141y(P)
8:20 (8:21) (Class 5) 2-Y-0 **£3,561** (£1,059; £529; £264) **Stalls** Low

Form RPR

3 **1** **Biographical (USA)**[19] 5582 2-9-3 0 WilliamBuick 3 77+
(J H M Gosden) *chsd ldr over 1f: remained handy: shkn up over 3f out: wnt 2nd again over 2f out: rdn and hung lft fr over 1f out: led ins fnl f: jst hld on* **4/11**[1]

2 *nse* **Jaridh (USA)** 2-9-3 0 DaraghO'Donohoe 1 77+
(Saeed Bin Suroor) *hld up: pushed along over 3f out: hdwy over 2f out: rdn over 1f out: r.o strly towards fin: jst failed* **3/1**[2]

06 **3** 1 **Cuban Piece (IRE)**[16] 5676 2-9-3 0 RichardKingscote 5 71
(Tom Dascombe) *led: rdn over 1f out: hdd ins fnl f: lost 2nd nr fin* **12/1**[3]

0 **4** 3 **Jelyvator**[73] 3785 2-9-3 0 JimmyQuinn 4 65
(A M Hales) *s.i.s: hld up: hdwy over 1f out: styd on same pce ins fnl f* **66/1**

005 **5** 7 **Lettering**[39] 4921 2-8-12 45 AndreaAtzeni 6 45
(D Haydn Jones) *prom: rdn over 3f out: wknd over 1f out* **50/1**

0 **6** 3/4 **Bournefree (IRE)**[127] 2078 2-8-12 0 LiamKeniry 8 43
(S Kirk) *s.i.s: hld up: nvr on terms* **66/1**

0 **7** 5 **Punt Road (IRE)**[8] 5929 2-9-3 0 (p) RoystonFfrench 7 38
(Lee Smyth, Ire) *chsd ldr 7f out to over 2f out: sn rdn and wknd* **66/1**

1m 53.18s (2.68) **Going Correction** -0.125s/f (Stan) **7** Ran SP% **112.4**
Speed ratings (Par 95): **83,82,82,79,73 72,68**
toteswingers:1&2:£1.10, 1&3:£1.80, 2&3:£2.10 CSF £1.65 TOTE £1.10: £1.02, £3.00; EX 1.40.
Owner H R H Princess Haya Of Jordan **Bred** Claiborne Farm **Trained** Newmarket, Suffolk

FOCUS
It was 12-1 bar two in this juvenile maiden, and those market leaders duly served up the closest finish of the evening.

NOTEBOOK
Biographical(USA) had posted a pleasing racecourse debut over this trip at Bath, which suggested there would be more to come second time out, and this artificial surface should have rated another plus on breeding. Already in receipt of several shakes of the reins before leaving the back straight, however, he made very hard work of passing the longtime leader, and would have been run out of victory in another few strides. In mitigation, he may still be learning what the job of racing fully entails, as further evinced by his attempt to hang when asked to seize the lead. He holds no fancy entries at present. (op 4-9)
Jaridh(USA) ◆, conversely, seemed to grasp what was required of him as soon as he was first pushed along turning in, and absolutely flew home to run the winner to a nose. Going one better in an identical contest should prove a formality, and there may be something a little better to be won with him later this autumn if his half-brother and dam (both winners of October minor conditions events over 1m2f and 1m respectively) are any guide. (op 9-4)
Cuban Piece(IRE) didn't curl up entirely once headed, keeping on creditably to record his best effort so far. His Derby entry looks very fanciful on the evidence to date, not least as his worst performance has come at Epsom. Nevertheless, the best of him is still probably to be seen, given that none of his five siblings to win races in this country did so until their third year. (op 20-1)
Jelyvator did make a little late progress and offered more than on debut.

6212 BET IN-PLAY AT LADBROKES.COM H'CAP 1m 141y(P)
8:50 (8:50) (Class 5) (0-70,70) 3-Y-0 **£2,456** (£725; £362) **Stalls** Low

Form RPR

363 **1** **Snow Magic (IRE)**[18] 5623 3-9-5 **68** PatCosgrave 2 77+
(J R Fanshawe) *a.p: rdn to ld ins fnl f: r.o* **9/2**[2]

2214 **2** 1/2 **Madame Excelerate**[14] 5758 3-9-6 **69** TomMcLaughlin 1 77
(W M Brisbourne) *led: shkn up over 2f out: rdn and hdd ins fnl f: r.o* **6/1**[3]

4243 **3** 1 3/4 **Osgood**[9] 5891 3-9-5 **68** SamHitchcott 13 72
(M R Channon) *hld up: hdwy over 1f out: rdn and hung lft ins fnl f: r.o* **10/1**

3530 **4** 1 1/4 **Bizarrely (IRE)**[17] 5656 3-9-1 **64** LiamKeniry 5 65
(J Pearce) *dwlt: hld up: hdwy over 1f out: r.o u.p ins fnl f: nt rch ldrs* **6/1**[3]

562 **5** 1 3/4 **Tasza (USA)**[36] 5057 3-9-0 **63** JamesDoyle 4 60
(A J McCabe) *chsd ldr: rdn and hung rt over 1f out: no ex ins fnl f* **8/1**

0460 **6** 2 3/4 **Aldo**[26] 5367 3-9-3 **69** (t) SophieDoyle(3) 3 60
(A J Lidderdale) *chsd ldrs: rdn over 1f out: wkng whn hung lft and hit rail ins fnl f* **25/1**

0100 **7** *hd* **Zubova**[15] 5716 3-9-2 **70** SimonPearce(5) 10 60
(D Shaw) *s.i.s: hld up: rdn over 1f out: nvr on terms* **16/1**

3003 **8** 1 **South African Gold (USA)**[17] 5669 3-9-0 **63** LukeMorris 6 51
(J M P Eustace) *chsd ldrs: rdn over 2f out: hung lft and wknd over 1f out* **9/1**

6106 **9** 3 1/4 **Perfect Ch'I (IRE)**[14] 5769 3-9-4 **70** MartinLane(3) 12 50
(I A Wood) *hld up: hdwy over 2f out: rdn and wknd over 1f out* **25/1**

1632 **10** 3/4 **Angelena Ballerina (IRE)**[14] 5768 3-8-10 **59** (v) RichardHughes 11 38
(Karen George) *hld up in tch: rdn 2f out: wkng whn hmpd over 1f out* **4/1**[1]

0520 **11** 2 1/2 **Laverre (IRE)**[44] 4752 3-9-1 **64** DavidNolan 7 37
(T D Easterby) *prom: lost pl over 5f out: sn pushed along: wknd over 2f out* **11/1**

1m 49.35s (-1.15) **Going Correction** -0.125s/f (Stan) **11** Ran SP% **118.9**
Speed ratings (Par 101): **100,99,98,96,95 92,92,91,88,88 86**
toteswingers:1&2:£1.10, 1&3:£1.80, 2&3:£2.10 CSF £32.14 CT £260.04 TOTE £3.30: £1.02, £1.40, £4.30; EX 31.20.
Owner Nigel & Carolyn Elwes **Bred** Aylesfield Farms Stud Ltd **Trained** Newmarket, Suffolk

FOCUS
A 3-y-o handicap run in driving rain. Muddling form but the winner was at least unexposed.
South African Gold(USA) Official explanation: jockey said colt ran too free
Laverre(IRE) Official explanation: trainer's rep said filly bled from the nose

6213 PLAY POKER AT LADBROKES.COM H'CAP 1m 4f 50y(P)
9:20 (9:21) (Class 6) (0-65,63) 3-Y-0+ **£1,774** (£523; £262) **Stalls** Low

Form RPR

6431 **1** **Straversjoy**[8] 5923 3-8-10 **55** LiamKeniry 1 67+
(R Hollinshead) *hld up: hdwy over 2f out: led over 1f out: rdn out* **15/8**[1]

0366 **2** 3 1/4 **Hallstatt (IRE)**[20] 5549 4-9-11 **62** (p) PatCosgrave 6 69
(J Mackie) *hld up in tch: rdn to ld over 1f out: hdd 1f out: styd on same pce* **8/1**[3]

30-0 **3** 1 1/4 **Dubburg (USA)**[54] 4433 5-9-7 **58** TonyCulhane 4 63
(W J Musson) *s.i.s: hld up: hdwy over 1f out: r.o: nt rch ldrs* **25/1**

1450 **4** 1 1/2 **Dunaskin (IRE)**[23] 4891 10-9-5 **61** (b) KierenFox(5) 3 64
(R C Guest) *hld up: r.o ins fnl f: nrst fin* **12/1**

0/5- **5** 1/2 **Thief**[481] 2338 4-9-11 **62** (t) LukeMorris 5 64
(W R Swinburn) *prom: lost pl over 5f out: styd on u.p fr over 1f out* **16/1**

2544 **6** 1/2 **Dazzling Begum**[22] 5468 5-9-0 **56** SimonPearce(5) 10 57
(J Pearce) *sn pushed along in rr: hdwy over 5f out: rdn and ev ch over 1f out: wknd ins fnl f* **16/1**

5002 **7** 1/2 **Gearbox (IRE)**[17] 5663 4-9-6 **57** JimmyQuinn 11 57
(H J L Dunlop) *prom: chsd ldr over 6f out: led over 3f out: rdn and hdd over 1f out: wknd ins fnl f* **8/1**[3]

2100 **8** 2 1/4 **Astronomical (IRE)**[20] 5549 8-9-11 **62** (p) GrahamGibbons 2 59
(R Hollinshead) *chsd ldrs: rdn over 1f out: wknd and eased ins fnl f* **22/1**

4431 **9** 4 **Extremely So**[4] 6065 4-9-7 **58** 6ex RichardHughes 7 48
(P J McBride) *led 4f: chsd ldrs: rdn over 2f out: wknd over 1f out* **11/4**[2]

0000 **10** 15 **Portrush Storm**[40] 4914 5-8-12 **49** oh3 FergusSweeney 8 15
(R E Peacock) *hld up: sme hdwy over 2f out: sn wknd* **66/1**

3000 **11** 6 **Black Coffee**[4] 6051 5-9-12 **63** TomMcLaughlin 9 20
(W M Brisbourne) *chsd ldr: led 8f out: rdn and hdd over 3f out: wknd over 2f out: t.o* **25/1**

4360 **12** 8 **King's Jester (IRE)**[61] 4188 8-8-13 **50** (b) RoystonFfrench 12 —
(Lee Smyth, Ire) *chsd ldrs: rdn 4f out: wknd 3f out: t.o* **80/1**

2m 38.35s (-2.75) **Going Correction** -0.125s/f (Stan)
WFA 3 from 4yo+ 8lb **12** Ran SP% **117.9**
Speed ratings (Par 101): **104,101,101,100,99 99,99,97,94,84 80,75**
toteswingers:1&2:£4.30, 1&3:£9.30, 2&3:£23.30 CSF £16.57 CT £289.36 TOTE £2.90: £1.10, £3.40, £12.10; EX 22.20 Place 6 £15.45; Place 5 £5.58.
Owner E Bennion **Bred** Eric Bennion **Trained** Upper Longdon, Staffs

FOCUS
A good early pace was steadied right down entering the back straight the final time. Sound form, rated around the third.
Dubburg(USA) Official explanation: jockey said gelding was denied a clear run final bend
Portrush Storm Official explanation: jockey said mare ran too free
T/Plt: £14.60 to a £1 stake. Pool:£85,978.80 - 4,275.54 winning tickets T/Qpdt: £3.80 to a £1 stake. Pool:£9,281.88 - 1,797.54 winning tickets CR

6214 - 6217a (Foreign Racing) - See Raceform Interactive

6012 LONGCHAMP (R-H)

Saturday, September 18

OFFICIAL GOING: Turf: good to soft

6218a PRIX DES CHENES (GROUP 3) (2YO) (TURF) 1m

1:35 (12:00) 2-Y-O **£35,398** (£14,159; £10,619; £7,079)

RPR

1 **French Navy**[19] 2-9-2 0 MaximeGuyon 3 108
(A Fabre, France) *settled in 2nd: rdn to chal ldr 1 1/2f out: tk ld 1f out: qcknd wl whn chal 100yds out: comf* **7/10**[1]

2 ¾ **Havane Smoker**[43] 2-9-2 0 ChristopheSoumillon 2 106
(J-C Rouget, France) *settled in 3rd: followed eventual wnr ent fnl f: swtchd and hrd rdn to chal 100yds out: no ex fnl 50yds: nt hrd rdn fnl 25yds* **9/5**[2]

3 5 **Surfrider (IRE)**[34] 2-9-2 0 OlivierPeslier 1 95
(E Libaud, France) *bkmarker fr s: r.o fnl f* **58/10**[3]

4 1 ½ **King David (FR)**[13] 5799 2-9-2 0 IoritzMendizabal 4 92
(M Boutin, France) *led fr s: chal 1 1/2f out: hdd 1f out and fdd* **9/1**

1m 46.4s (8.00) **4 Ran SP% 119.2**
WIN (incl. 1 euro stake): 1.70. PLACES: 1.10, 1.10. SF: 3.00.
Owner Godolphin SNC **Bred** Darley Stud Management Co Ltd **Trained** Chantilly, France

NOTEBOOK
French Navy quickened up when asked and was always comfortably holding off the runner-up. A progressive and improving colt, the Criterium International at Saint-Cloud is likely to his next target.

6219a PRIX DU PRINCE D'ORANGE (GROUP 3) (3YO) (TURF) 1m 2f

2:45 (12:00) 3-Y-O **£35,398** (£14,159; £10,619; £7,079; £3,539)

RPR

1 **Prince Bishop (IRE)**[36] 3-9-2 0 MaximeGuyon 1 105
(A Fabre, France) *settled in 2nd: outpcd 1 1/2f out: rdn 1f out: qcknd wl: fnd split 100yds out: fin strly to get up on line* **10/1**

2 snk **Wealthy (IRE)**[34] 5135 3-9-2 0 Pierre-CharlesBoudot 4 105
(A Fabre, France) *racd in 3rd fr s: rdn to chal 1 1/2f out: tk ld 1f out: r.o wl: hdd fnl strides* **5/2**[1]

3 nse **Rajsaman (FR)**[125] 2159 3-9-2 0 Christophe-PatriceLemaire 5 105
(A De Royer-Dupre, France) *racd in 6th: prog 1 1/2f out: qcknd wl fnl f: r.o strly fnl 50yds* **73/10**

4 hd **Lancelot (FR)**[54] 4446 3-9-2 0 ThierryThulliez 6 105
(J-M Beguigne, France) *racd in midfield: qcknd wl 1 1/2f out: threatened ldrs 1f out: no ex fnl 100yds* **6/1**[3]

5 1 ½ **Vertiformer (USA)**[30] 5253 3-9-2 0 ChristopheSoumillon 8 102
(J-C Rouget, France) *towards the rr tl st: r.o wl fnl f wout threatening ldrs* **4/1**[2]

6 snk **Black Spirit (USA)**[10] 5853 3-9-2 0 IoritzMendizabal 3 101
(C G Cox) *prom fr s: rdn 1 1/2f out: r.o wl fnl f* **78/10**

7 1 **Arasin (IRE)**[20] 5574 3-9-2 0 GeraldMosse 2 99
(P Bary, France) *sn prom: rdn 1 1/2f out: r.o wl fnl f wout threatening ldrs* **12/1**

8 1 ½ **Lumineux**[34] 5135 3-9-2 0 OlivierPeslier 7 96
(A Fabre, France) *towards rr fr s: rdn but nvr threatened in st: styd on* **14/1**

9 hd **Foreteller**[20] 5574 3-9-2 0 (b) StephanePasquier 9 96
(D Smaga, France) *towards rr fr s: nvr threatened in st: styd on* **31/1**

10 hd **Neatico (GER)**[17] 5671 3-9-2 0 GaetanMasure 10 95
(P Schiergen, Germany) *led fr s: hdd 1 1/2f out: no ex fnl f* **21/1**

2m 9.60s (5.60) **10 Ran SP% 117.4**
WIN (incl. 1 euro stake): 2.70 (Prince Bishop coupled with Wealthy). PLACES: 4.10, 1.60, 2.40. DF: 13.40. SF: 19.30.
Owner Godolphin SNC **Bred** Thurso Limited **Trained** Chantilly, France

NOTEBOOK
Prince Bishop(IRE) completed a hat-trick on this step up in class. Although first under pressure in the straight, he picked up well and finished best of all to shade a four-way photo. The Prix du Conseil de Paris (1m4f) at Longchamp next month is likely to be his next target.
Black Spirit(USA) could have done with a stronger all-round gallop. He finished his race off well enough but could not get involved in the finish.

5476 HAMILTON (R-H)

Sunday, September 19

OFFICIAL GOING: Good to soft (good in places; rnd 7.8, str 8.6)
Fresh ground on far side of straight course.
Wind: Breezy, half behind Weather: Cloudy, bright

6220 TOTEPLACEPOT NURSERY 6f 5y

2:10 (2:12) (Class 5) (0-75,70) 2-Y-O **£2,914** (£867; £433; £216) **Stalls** Low

Form RPR

546 1 **Reason To Believe (IRE)**[50] 4599 2-8-6 **60** IanBrennan(5) 3 67
(B M R Haslam) *in tch: hdwy to ld over 1f out: rdn out fnl f* **8/1**[3]

3230 2 ¾ **Eilean Mor**[13] 5818 2-8-11 **63** GaryBartley(3) 7 68
(J S Goldie) *bhd and sn pushed along: gd hdwy over 1f out: chsd wnr and edgd lft ins fnl f: r.o* **20/1**

4644 3 2 ¼ **Cathcart Castle**[17] 5675 2-8-11 **60** RichardHughes 6 58
(M R Channon) *wnt rt and bmpd s: bhd and pushed along over 3f out: hdwy over 1f out: n.m.r briefly ins fnl f: r.o* **5/2**[1]

6021 4 ½ **Whats For Pudding (IRE)**[13] 5818 2-7-13 **55** NeilFarley(7) 2 52
(D Carroll) *prom: ev ch 2f out to 1f out: edgd rt: one pce fnl f* **18/1**

0144 5 hd **Ingleby Exceed (IRE)**[7] 5998 2-9-3 **66** GrahamGibbons 1 64+
(T D Barron) *cl up: effrt over 2f out: one pce whn n.m.r ins fnl f* **18/1**

0213 6 hd **Saxonette**[6] 6027 2-8-8 **60** BarryMcHugh(3) 9 56
(Miss L A Perratt) *cl up: rdn and ev ch over 1f out: kpt on same pce fnl f* **9/1**

0661 7 ¾ **Fleet Captain**[24] 5434 2-9-3 **69** MartinLane(3) 10 62
(K A Ryan) *cl up tl rdn and no ex fr over 1f out* **8/1**[3]

054 8 4 ½ **Rocky Coast**[27] 5352 2-8-8 **57** TomEaves 8 37
(B Smart) *led tl rdn and hdd over 1f out: sn wknd* **25/1**

1036 9 1 ½ **Las Verglas Star (IRE)**[29] 5310 2-9-7 **70** PaulHanagan 5 45
(R A Fahey) *in tch: drvn over 2f out: wknd wl over 1f out* **9/1**

4430 10 3 **Trading**[20] 5602 2-9-2 **65** PaulMulrennan 11 31
(T D Easterby) *cl up: struggling over 2f out: sn btn* **12/1**

064 11 4 **Reachtothestars (USA)**[35] 5117 2-9-4 **67** PhillipMakin 4 21
(M Dods) *half-rrd s: bhd and outpcd: nvr on terms* **11/2**[2]

1m 13.39s (1.19) **Going Correction** +0.05s/f (Good) **11 Ran SP% 113.0**
Speed ratings (Par 95): **94,93,90,89,89 88,87,81,79,75 70**
toteswingers: 1&2 £31.70, 1&3 £5.20, 2&3 £10.90 CSF £149.38 CT £511.78 TOTE £11.00: £3.50, £6.90, £1.10; EX 164.50 TRIFECTA Not won..
Owner Mrs Carol Aldridge **Bred** Yeomanstown Stud **Trained** Middleham Moor, N Yorks

FOCUS
Fresh ground on far side of straight course and all distances as advertised. Overnight rain of 6.2mm had fallen and the ground was officially described as good to soft, good in places. The GoingStick readings were 8.6 on the straight course and 7.8 on the loop. A modest nursery in which very few looked generously handicapped.

NOTEBOOK
Reason To Believe(IRE), making his handicap debut after three runs in maidens, broke his duck with a little in hand. Backed at each-way odds beforehand, he was never too far off the pace and had worked his way into third by the 2f marker. Driven thereafter, he stayed on well and may handle further in time. He should not go up too much for this and ought to remain competitive after being reassessed. Connections expect him to make a better three-year-old, perhaps over as far as a mile. (op 9-1)
Eilean Mor, placed previously off his current mark of 63, looks a reasonable guide to the form. He has already shown he handles some cut in the ground and this distance on a stiff course looks ideal for him. (op 16-1 tchd 14-1)
Cathcart Castle, dropped in trip after fading over 7f at Epsom last time out, was well-backed prior to the off. He was not the quickest away, though, and seemed to be outpaced in the early stages. He was making ground late on, but was short of room inside the final furlong and unable to launch a serious challenge. On this evidence, he may require a return to longer distances. (op 4-1 tchd 9-2)
Whats For Pudding(IRE), up 10lb since taking a Newcastle nursery 13 days previously, did her best to overcome that hike. After figuring prominently at halfway, however, she could not maintain her momentum in the closing stages. (tchd 20-1)
Ingleby Exceed(IRE) had been dropped 1lb since finishing fourth in a similar event at Newcastle a week earlier but, after chasing the pace from the start, was treading water in the final furlong. She probably needs more help with her rating. (op 12-1)
Saxonette, winner of a Lingfield seller at the start of the month and a solid third at that level since, was simply not good enough. She was never far off the pace, but lacked the necessary zip to make a more significant impact. (tchd 8-1)
Rocky Coast Official explanation: jockey said colt hung right throughout

6221 TOTEPOOL.COM E B F FLOWER OF SCOTLAND FILLIES' H'CAP 6f 5y

2:40 (2:40) (Class 3) (0-95,95) 3-Y-O+ **£9,066** (£2,697; £1,348; £673) **Stalls** Centre

Form RPR

6010 1 **La Zamora**[10] 5884 4-8-11 **82** GrahamGibbons 9 91
(T D Barron) *cl up: led over 1f out: drvn and hld on wl fnl f* **12/1**[3]

0160 2 nk **Waveband**[11] 5854 3-9-3 **90** JoeFanning 7 98
(M Johnston) *led to over 1f out: kpt on fnl f: hld towards fin* **14/1**

P021 3 nse **Ming Meng (IRE)**[27] 5359 3-8-3 **76** oh1 HayleyTurner 2 84+
(M L W Bell) *prom: rdn over 2f out: effrt and swtchd lft over 1f out: styd on towards fin* **3/1**[2]

0016 4 2 ¼ **Ursula (IRE)**[29] 5290 4-8-9 **80** AndrewElliott 1 81
(Mrs K Burke) *t.k.h: trckd ldrs: rdn and outpcd 2f out: kpt on ins fnl f* **3/1**[2]

1600 5 3 ¼ **Lewyn**[5] 6048 3-8-9 **82** RichardHughes 10 72
(K A Ryan) *hld up: effrt and hdwy over 1f out: no imp fnl f* **50/1**

3340 6 1 ¼ **Hansomis (IRE)**[3] 6108 6-8-3 **79** oh18 ow3 (b[1]) IanBrennan(5) 4 65?
(B Mactaggart) *t.k.h: prom: outpcd and hung rt over 2f out: n.d after* **50/1**

5641 7 ¾ **Little Scotland**[7] 6002 3-8-13 **86** 6ex (p) PaulHanagan 3 70
(R A Fahey) *cl up: rdn 1/2-way: wknd over 1f out* **15/8**[1]

3604 8 3 ¼ **Eternal Instinct**[25] 5409 3-7-10 **76** oh2 NeilFarley(7) 6 49
(J S Goldie) *s.i.s: hld up: effrt over 2f out: wknd over 1f out* **16/1**

1m 12.32s (0.12) **Going Correction** +0.05s/f (Good)
WFA 3 from 4yo+ 2lb **8 Ran SP% 108.9**
Speed ratings (Par 104): **101,100,100,97,93 91,90,86**
toteswingers: 1&2 £6.60, 1&3 £6.10, 2&3 £4.90 CSF £146.84 CT £583.51 TOTE £17.20: £3.80, £3.60, £1.10; EX 82.90 TRIFECTA Not won..
Owner J G Brown **Bred** Miss S J Smith **Trained** Maunby, N Yorks

FOCUS
A decent fillies' handicap, even though three were racing from above their correct weight, and it resulted in a thrilling finish. The winner and second are rated to the best view of their previous form.

NOTEBOOK
La Zamora was 5lb higher than when scoring at York in July and, although she is not the most consistent filly, had a decent chance on the best of her form. She was always travelling kindly here, racing on the far right of the field throughout, and held on bravely when challenged. Given her inconsistency, though, it remains to be seen how she will fare when the handicapper has another say.\n Official explanation: trainer said, regarding apparent improvement in form, that the filly was better suited by the small field. (op 10-1)
Waveband, who made all from a 4lb lower mark at Leicester in August, was always prominent and led 2f out. She was overhauled by the winner at the furlong pole, but fought back tigerishly and was closing at the line. This was a commendable effort. (op 11-1)
Ming Meng(IRE) was making her handicap debut from 1lb out of the weights, having taken a maiden here by seven lengths on her most recent start, and had evidently been given a mark from which she is competitive. Held up early on, she made good progress through the final furlong and was clawing back the first two in the dying strides. She might be worth a try at a slightly longer trip. (op 11-4)
Ursula(IRE), disadvantaged by a wide draw at Chester, had a better starting position this time but could not take advantage. She was always in about the same place and lacked the pace to make a serious challenge. (op 7-2 tchd 4-1 in a place)
Lewyn, seemingly out of form on turf recently, showed up better than for some time. Held up early on, she made some late progress.
Hansomis(IRE) did remarkably well, considering she was well out of the handicap and her jockey was putting up overweight. First-time blinkers appear to have helped her. (op 40-1 tchd 66-1)
Little Scotland was carrying a 6lb penalty for winning over 7f at Newcastle a week earlier. That rise, plus perhaps the exertions required to notch that victory, seemed to count against her here. She led early on, but was under pressure 2f out and faded when push came to shove. Connections reported that she lost a shoe. Official explanation: jockey said filly finished sore having lost near-fore shoe (op 2-1)

6222 EUROPEAN BREEDERS' FUND MAIDEN STKS 1m 65y

3:10 (3:10) (Class 5) 2-Y-O **£3,626** (£1,079; £539; £269) **Stalls** High

Form RPR

1 **State Opera** 2-9-3 0 JoeFanning 8 89+
(M Johnston) *mde all: qcknd 3f out: rdn and edgd lft over 1f out: styd on strly: promising* **2/1**[2]

0 2 3 ¼ **Spey Song (IRE)**[30] 5277 2-8-12 0 PaulHanagan 1 77+
(J D Bethell) *prom: rdn 3f out: chsd wnr and edgd rt over 1f out: sn no imp* **11/1**

4332 **3** *5* **Galloping Queen (IRE)**[20] 5583 2-8-12 77 RichardHughes 2 66
(M R Channon) *trckd ldrs: rdn over 2f out: wknd ins fnl f* **13/8**[1]

446 **4** *1* **Tarantella Lady**[10] 5878 2-8-12 78 TomEaves 3 64
(G M Moore) *trckd wnr: rdn over 3f out: wknd over 1f out* **9/2**[3]

55 **5** *1 1/4* **Miss Villefranche**[19] 5633 2-8-12 0 HayleyTurner 7 61
(M L W Bell) *hld up in tch: effrt and shkn up over 2f out: outpcd wl over 1f out* **10/1**

6 *5* **Operateur (IRE)** 2-9-3 0 PhillipMakin 6 55
(B M R Haslam) *hld up: outpcd and shkn up 3f out: no imp after* **66/1**

7 *10* **Geminus (IRE)** 2-9-3 0 PaulMulrennan 5 33
(Jedd O'Keeffe) *dwlt: bhd: struggling after 4f: nvr on terms* **80/1**

8 *7* **Nay Secret** 2-9-0 0 GaryBartley[(3)] 4 18
(J S Goldie) *s.i.s: bhd: struggling over 5f out: nvr on terms* **50/1**

1m 48.38s (-0.02) **Going Correction** +0.05s/f (Good) **8** Ran SP% **111.7**
Speed ratings (Par 95): **102,98,93,92,91 86,76,69**
toteswingers: 1&2 £4.50, 1&3 £1.70, 2&3 £3.60 CSF £22.53 TOTE £3.20: £1.10, £3.70, £1.10; EX 24.40 Trifecta £75.30 Pool: £472.36 - 4.64 winning units..
Owner Sheikh Hamdan Bin Mohammed Al Maktoum **Bred** Genesis Green Stud Ltd **Trained** Middleham Moor, N Yorks

FOCUS
Only a fair juvenile maiden, judged on the form of those that had run, but enlivened by the presence of a clutch of well-bred newcomers.

NOTEBOOK
State Opera, a 75,000gns newcomer from a decent family and with plenty of scope for improvement, notched a very taking first success. He was always in front and quickened impressively in the home straight. The rest never threatened to catch him and he seems sure go on to better things. His pedigree suggests he will stay at least 1m2f next season. (tchd 5-2 in a place)
Spey Song(IRE) had hinted that she has ability when 12th of 17 in a York maiden first time out and underlined that impression here. She raced in fourth for much of the journey and stayed on well enough in the closing stages to improve her position with all bar the winner. Her maiden win should not be too long delayed. (op 14-1)
Galloping Queen(IRE), making her sixth appearance and officially rated 77, almost certainly ran below that level, as she was eased once the first two had drawn clear of her. She is becoming a little frustrating, especially as she has a Listed-race fourth on her CV, and now looks decidedly vulnerable against less exposed opposition. (op 6-4 tchd 11-8)
Tarantella Lady, sixth in a smart 1m Doncaster maiden last time out and officially rated 78, might be better off dropped back in trip. Her best form seems to have been posted over 6f and she did not have a great deal left at the finish. (op 11-2)
Miss Villefranche had shown only moderate form in two previous starts and the fact that she was not far behind the third and fourth indicates some caution might be wise in assessing the overall standard achieved here. Her future looks to be in minor nurseries, for which she is now qualified. (op 15-2)
Operateur(IRE), a first-time-out half-brother to useful middle-distance winners, was not disgraced. He never threatened to take a hand in the finish, but plugged on in the closing stages and should benefit from this experience. (op 80-1 tchd 100-1)

6223 TOTEEXACTA FLEXI BETTING CLAIMING STKS — 1m 1f 36y
3:40 (3:40) (Class 4) 3-5-Y-O **£3,885** (£1,156; £577; £288) **Stalls** High

Form RPR

5260 **1** **Fujin Dancer (FR)**[3] 6107 5-9-2 72 (p) RichardHughes 1 75
(K A Ryan) *hld up last but in tch: smooth hdwy 2f out: shkn up ins fnl f: styd on to ld towards fin* **7/2**[3]

2064 **2** *nk* **Bullet Man (USA)**[24] 5436 5-9-9 79 PaulHanagan 5 81
(R A Fahey) *cl up: rdn over 2f out: led over 1f out: edgd rt: kpt on fnl f: hdd towards fin* **11/10**[1]

0300 **3** *3* **Cool Baranca (GER)**[43] 4823 4-8-13 68 PaulMulrennan 4 65
(P Monteith) *prom on ins: n.m.r fr over 2f out tl swtchd lft ent fnl f: styd on: nt rch first two* **12/1**

2606 **4** *5* **Templetuohy Max (IRE)**[16] 5736 5-9-2 76 (v) GrahamGibbons 2 58
(J D Bethell) *led: rdn and hdd over 1f out: sn btn* **5/2**[2]

6600 **5** *6* **Kumbeshwar**[22] 5524 3-9-2 74 CathyGannon 3 50
(P D Evans) *plld hrd: cl up: rdn over 3f out: edgd rt and wknd fr 2f out* **33/1**

1m 59.13s (-0.57) **Going Correction** +0.05s/f (Good)
WFA 3 from 4yo+ 5lb **5** Ran SP% **109.0**
Speed ratings (Par 105): **104,103,101,96,91**
CSF £7.68 TOTE £4.40: £4.50, £1.10; EX 8.10.
Owner John Duddy **Bred** Loughtown Stud Ltd **Trained** Hambleton, N Yorks

FOCUS
Not a bad contest by claiming standards. The form is probably best judged around the front pair.

6224 TOTESUPER7 H'CAP — 1m 5f 9y
4:10 (4:11) (Class 4) (0-80,79) 3-Y-O+ **£3,885** (£1,156; £577; £288) **Stalls** High

Form RPR

4236 **1** **Royal Trooper (IRE)**[14] 5790 4-9-6 70 PaulMulrennan 9 80
(J G Given) *mde all: rdn whn jnd over 1f out: styd on strly fnl f* **6/1**[3]

2244 **2** *2 3/4* **Mykingdomforahorse**[20] 5612 4-9-6 70 (v) RichardHughes 13 76
(M R Channon) *hld up in midfield: smooth hdwy to chal over 1f out: sn rdn: fnd little* **9/2**[2]

2621 **3** *shd* **Graceful Descent (FR)**[27] 5363 5-9-11 75 GregFairley 11 81
(J S Goldie) *trckd ldrs: drvn and outpcd 3f out: rallied 2f out: kpt on fnl f* **10/1**

220- **4** *3/4* **Taikoo**[463] 2932 5-10-0 78 PaulHanagan 8 83+
(H Morrison) *t.k.h: in tch: rdn and outpcd over 3f out: rallying whn n.m.r over 2f out: hmpd over 1f out: styd on wl fnl f* **16/1**

5-04 **5** *shd* **Chookie Hamilton**[92] 3198 6-9-7 71 PhillipMakin 3 75
(V P Donoghue) *hld up: hdwy over 2f out: kpt on u.p ins fnl f* **20/1**

5444 **6** *1/2* **Bollin Greta**[14] 5790 5-9-3 67 (t) DavidAllan 2 71
(T D Easterby) *t.k.h: in tch: effrt over 3f out: hung rt and one pce over 1f out* **9/2**[2]

0221 **7** *1 1/4* **Bosamcliff (IRE)**[198] 719 5-9-13 77 CathyGannon 12 79
(P D Evans) *hld up: drvn and outpcd over 3f out: hdwy over 1f out: nvr rchd ldrs* **40/1**

-401 **8** *1/2* **Terenzium (IRE)**[27] 5364 8-8-2 59 oh3 (p) NeilFarley[(7)] 5 60
(Micky Hammond) *dwlt: bhd: drvn over 4f out: sme late hdwy: nvr on terms* **28/1**

-420 **9** *shd* **Elite Land**[21] 5549 7-8-11 66 DaleSwift[(5)] 6 67
(B Ellison) *hld up: outpcd 5f out: hdwy wl over 1f out: nvr nr ldrs* **16/1**

4205 **10** *2 1/2* **Regent's Secret (USA)**[27] 5364 10-8-9 59 LNewman 1 56
(J S Goldie) *s.i.s: hld up: hdwy over 3f out: wknd fr 2f out* **66/1**

1101 **11** *8* **Cat O' Nine Tails**[6] 6028 3-9-3 76 6ex JoeFanning 10 61
(M Johnston) *cl up: rdn 3f out: wknd 2f out* **9/4**[1]

106 **12** *6* **Stags Leap (IRE)**[25] 5408 3-9-6 79 TomEaves 7 55
(P Monteith) *cl up tl rdn and wknd fr 2f out* **50/1**

0-56 **13** *4* **Louisa (GER)**[27] 5364 6-8-6 59 oh14 JamesSullivan[(3)] 4 29
(P Monteith) *midfield: drvn and outpcd over 4f out: sn struggling* **125/1**

2m 54.31s (0.41) **Going Correction** +0.05s/f (Good)
WFA 3 from 4yo+ 9lb **13** Ran SP% **117.2**
Speed ratings (Par 105): **100,98,98,97,97 97,96,96,96,94 89,86,83**
toteswingers: 1&2 £6.70, 1&3 £6.80, 2&3 £6.20 CSF £30.83 CT £268.55 TOTE £6.40: £2.00, £1.70, £3.20; EX 33.30 Trifecta £147.10 Pool: £518.97 - 2.61 winning units..
Owner J Barson **Bred** Western Bloodstock **Trained** Willoughton, Lincs

FOCUS
A competitive handicap, in which few could be confidently discounted. The fully exposed winner is probably the best guide to the form, which looks fairly sound.

6225 TOTESWINGER FLEXI BETTING H'CAP — 1m 3f 16y
4:40 (4:40) (Class 5) (0-70,68) 3-Y-O **£2,590** (£770; £385; £192) **Stalls** High

Form RPR

0561 **1** **Tobernea (IRE)**[25] 5411 3-9-0 61 JoeFanning 10 75+
(M Johnston) *mde all: rdn and hrd pressed fr 2f out: styd on gamely fnl f* **3/1**[2]

6601 **2** *hd* **Plan A (IRE)**[25] 5414 3-9-0 61 WilliamCarson 8 75+
(M G Quinlan) *hld up: rdn 3f out: hdwy and edgd lft 2f out: kpt on wl fnl f: jst hld* **6/1**[3]

-524 **3** *3/4* **Palawi (IRE)**[116] 2439 3-9-7 68 PhillipMakin 5 81
(J J Quinn) *t.k.h: in tch: hdwy and ev ch 1f out: rdn and flicked tail: one pce wl ins fnl f* **25/1**

124 **4** *1* **Rockweiller**[20] 5585 3-9-3 64 (v) CathyGannon 4 75
(P D Evans) *cl up: rdn and ev ch 2f out: one pce ins fnl f* **14/1**

5011 **5** *3 1/2* **Emerald Glade (IRE)**[36] 5093 3-9-6 67 DavidAllan 6 72+
(T D Easterby) *hld up and bhd: rdn and hdwy on outside over 2f out: nvr able to chal* **5/2**[1]

4134 **6** *2* **Frontline Phantom (IRE)**[20] 5607 3-9-0 61 AndrewElliott 11 62
(Mrs K Burke) *trckd ldrs tl rdn and outpcd fr 2f out* **17/2**

3646 **7** *1 1/4* **Swiftly Done (IRE)**[23] 5487 3-9-4 65 DavidNolan 3 64
(D Carroll) *hld up: drvn and effrt over 2f out: no imp fr wl over 1f out* **25/1**

2325 **8** *5* **Ice Viking (IRE)**[19] 5631 3-9-3 64 PaulMulrennan 7 54
(J G Given) *midfield: drvn over 3f out: wknd wl over 1f out* **10/1**

4440 **9** *2* **Kathlatino**[42] 4867 3-9-4 65 TomEaves 1 51
(Micky Hammond) *towards rr: rdn over 4f out: btn fnl 2f* **50/1**

2656 **10** *nse* **Sheiling (IRE)**[22] 5534 3-8-13 60 PaulHanagan 9 46
(R A Fahey) *midfield: drvn and outpcd over 3f out: sn btn* **12/1**

264 **11** *3* **Widow Bird (IRE)**[42] 4874 3-9-5 66 RichardHughes 2 47
(H Morrison) *prom tl rdn and wknd over 2f out* **12/1**

2m 25.61s (0.01) **Going Correction** +0.05s/f (Good) **11** Ran SP% **119.2**
Speed ratings (Par 101): **101,100,100,99,97 95,94,91,89,89 87**
toteswingers: 1&2 £5.20, 1&3 £20.30, 2&3 £29.50 CSF £21.43 CT £385.09 TOTE £5.50: £2.50, £1.90, £6.90; EX 21.50 Trifecta £158.50 Part won. Pool: £214.19 - 0.30 winning units..
Owner Mrs Joan Keaney **Bred** Mrs Joan Keaney **Trained** Middleham Moor, N Yorks
■ Stewards' Enquiry : Joe Fanning one-day ban: used whip with excessive frequency (Oct 4)

FOCUS
A moderate handicap, with the top weight rated just 68, but it looked wide open on paper. The form is fair for the grade and is rated around the third and fourth.
Emerald Glade(IRE) Official explanation: jockey said filly ran too free early

6226 TOTETRIFECTA FLEXI BETTING H'CAP — 6f 5y
5:10 (5:16) (Class 5) (0-70,70) 3-Y-O **£2,590** (£770; £385; £192) **Stalls** Centre

Form RPR

01 **1** **Ritual (IRE)**[60] 4251 3-9-7 70 PaulHanagan 5 83+
(J Noseda) *plld hrd: cl up: led 2f out: rdn out fnl f* **8/13**[1]

5554 **2** *1 3/4* **Chinese Democracy (USA)**[2] 6168 3-8-10 59 (v) CathyGannon 1 66
(P D Evans) *hld up: hdwy to chse wnr appr fnl f: kpt on ins fnl f* **33/1**

0000 **3** *2 1/2* **Steed**[53] 4479 3-8-6 62 JulieBurke[(7)] 13 61
(K A Ryan) *bhd: hdwy on outside over 1f out: kpt on fnl f: nvr able to chal* **50/1**

0000 **4** *shd* **Belinsky (IRE)**[42] 4865 3-9-2 70 DaleSwift[(5)] 9 69
(N Tinkler) *dwlt: sn prom: rdn and hung rt 2f out: r.o fnl f* **50/1**

5016 **5** *3/4* **Spinning Spirit (IRE)**[25] 5409 3-9-1 64 PaulMulrennan 3 60
(J G Given) *hld up: hdwy over 1f out: edgd rt: no imp ins fnl f* **33/1**

1300 **6** *1 1/2* **Sir Louis**[45] 4749 3-8-8 60 BarryMcHugh[(3)] 7 51
(R A Fahey) *cl up: rdn over 2f out: edgd rt over 1f out: nt qckn* **12/1**

2322 **7** *1 1/2* **Mottley Crewe**[13] 5816 3-8-12 61 PhillipMakin 11 48
(M Dods) *chsd ldng gp: rdn over 2f out: wknd over 1f out* **5/1**[2]

3404 **8** *3/4* **Transmit (IRE)**[5] 6048 3-9-7 70 (b) DavidAllan 12 54
(T D Easterby) *cl up tl rdn and wknd appr fnl f* **6/1**[3]

2230 **9** *6* **Monte Mayor One**[3] 6103 3-8-10 62 (p) JamesSullivan[(3)] 4 27
(P Monteith) *in tch: rdn over 2f out: wknd over 1f out* **33/1**

00-0 **10** *1 1/2* **Sumay Buoy (IRE)**[24] 5438 3-8-0 56 oh5 NeilFarley[(7)] 6 16
(Mrs J C McGregor) *led to 2f out: sn rdn and wknd* **100/1**

0000 **11** *3* **Reach For The Sky (IRE)**[23] 5481 3-8-0 56 oh4 VictorSantos[(7)] 10 7
(A Berry) *missed break: a outpcd* **100/1**

1m 12.83s (0.63) **Going Correction** +0.05s/f (Good) **11** Ran SP% **115.3**
Speed ratings (Par 101): **97,94,91,91,90 88,86,85,77,75 71**
toteswingers: 1&2 £6.00, 1&3 £13.20, 2&3 £83.30. totesuper7: Win: Not won. Place: £118.40. CSF £34.73 CT £562.76 TOTE £1.50: £1.10, £3.70, £8.50; EX 18.10 Trifecta £291.40 Pool: £649.83 - 1.65 winning units. Place 6 £56.62, Place 5 £30.87.
Owner Highclere Thoroughbred Racing Churchill **Bred** Agricola Del Parco **Trained** Newmarket, Suffolk

FOCUS
Not the classiest finale, with the top weight rated 70, and several looked out of their depth. The form is not that solid with the runner-up the best guide.
T/Plt: £81.30 to a £1 stake. Pool: £72,605.78. 651.23 winning tickets. T/Qpdt: £12.00 to a £1 stake. Pool: £5,720.47. 351.96 winning tickets. RY

6227 - 6229a (Foreign Racing) - See Raceform Interactive

3926 FAIRYHOUSE (R-H)
Sunday, September 19

OFFICIAL GOING: Soft

6230a TATTERSALLS IRELAND SUPER AUCTION SALE STKS — 7f
3:45 (3:48) 2-Y-O
£65,486 (£25,663; £16,814; £7,964; £3,539; £884)

RPR

1 **Stand To Attention (IRE)**[8] 5979 2-8-11 CDHayes 12 89
(P D Deegan, Ire) *in rr of mid-div: 15th early st: gd hdwy fr 2f out: wnt 2nd u.p 1f out: led ins fnl f: kpt on wl to draw clr* **16/1**

2 3 **The Four Masters (IRE)**[20] 5618 2-8-13 77.................... WMLordan 13 83
(David Wachman, Ire) *mid-div: 9th 2f out: hdwy u.p into 5th 1f out: kpt on wl ins fnl f: no ch w wnr* **12/1**

3 shd **Bathwick Bear (IRE)**[9] 5907 2-9-4 .... RichardEvans 1 88
(P D Evans) *a.p: 2nd 1/2-way: rdn to ld over 2f out: strly pressed and hdd ins fnl f: no ex and kpt on same pce* **10/1**

4 ½ **Rudegirl (IRE)**[20] 5594 2-8-6 .... SilvestreDeSousa 7 75
(N Tinkler) *chsd ldrs: 8th 1/2-way: drvn along fr 2f out: 3rd 1f out: no imp ins fnl f* **20/1**

5 1 ¾ **Mama Sox (IRE)**[9] 5929 2-7-13 .... SHJames(7) 4 70
(John C McConnell, Ire) *mid-div on outer: drvn along early in st: 11th over 1f out: kpt on u.p ins fnl f: nrest at fin* **50/1**

6 ¾ **Moonlit Garden (IRE)**[21] 5567 2-8-10 96......................(b) KJManning 14 72+
(D K Weld, Ire) *mid-div: hdwy on inner early st: 6th under 2f out: no imp fr over 1f out: kpt on one pce* **11/2**[2]

7 1 **Chin'n Tonic (IRE)**[20] 5597 2-8-13 .... PJMcDonald 15 73
(G A Swinbank) *in rr of mid-div: sme hdwy early st: kpt on fr over 1f out* **10/1**

8 hd **Long Time Coming (IRE)**[7] 6010 2-8-11 79........................... WJLee 2 73+
(Michael Mulvany, Ire) *mid-div on outer: 10th 1/2-way: rdn fr 2f out: no ex fr over 1f out* **25/1**

9 ½ **Act Of Love (IRE)**[20] 5618 2-8-8 80.........................(b[1]) CO'Donoghue 17 66
(David Marnane, Ire) *mid-div on outer: sme hdwy u.p fr 2f out: kpt on one pce* **7/1**[3]

10 ¾ **Going Gaga (IRE)**[9] 5930 2-8-11 69..................................... BACurtis 20 67
(Michael Mulvany, Ire) *mid-div best: kpt on one pce u.p in st* **50/1**

11 ¾ **Dereenatra (IRE)**[59] 2-8-13 .... JMurtagh 22 —
(E J O'Neill, France) *chsd ldrs: 5th 1/2-way: drvn along fr 2f out: no ex u.p fr over 1f out* **2/1**[1]

12 ¾ **Catalpa Sail (IRE)**[9] 5928 2-8-11 82.................................. SMGorey 11 63
(D K Weld, Ire) *nvr bttr than mid-div: no imp and kpt on one pce fr over 1f out* **33/1**

13 nk **Gold Post**[5] 6066 2-8-11 79.. RPCleary 8 63
(P D Deegan, Ire) *trckd ldrs: 3rd 1/2-way: rdn and no ex fr under 2f out* **12/1**

14 12 **Glendaragh (IRE)**[5] 6066 2-9-3 ....(b[1]) CPGeoghegan 6 39
(Kevin Prendergast, Ire) *chsd ldrs: 9th appr st: no ex fr under 2f out* **20/1**

15 nk **Up The Dubs**[7] 2-8-11 ....(p) NGMcCullagh 10 32
(E J O'Neill, France) *led: hdd over 2f out: sn no ex* **50/1**

16 nk **Tell The Wind (IRE)**[15] 5771 2-8-12 .... DPMcDonogh 9 32
(Kevin Prendergast, Ire) *chsd ldrs: 6th ent st: rdn and no imp over 1f out: kpt on one pce* **11/1**

17 2 **The Reaper (IRE)**[14] 5793 2-9-1 76..................................(b) KLatham 19 30
(G M Lyons, Ire) *trckd ldrs: 4th 1/2-way: rdn and no ex fr early st* **10/1**

18 nk **Master Melody (IRE)**[113] 2550 2-8-11 80...................(b[1]) MCHussey 16 25
(Kevin Prendergast, Ire) *a towards rr* **33/1**

19 1 **Safari Team (IRE)**[16] 5724 2-9-3 .... JAHeffernan 18 29
(P Winkworth) *nvr a factor* **18/1**

20 11 **Adorable Choice (IRE)**[16] 5721 2-8-12 .... RichardKingscote 3 —
(Tom Dascombe) *a towards rr* **25/1**

21 5 ½ **The Munster Maori (IRE)**[29] 5312 2-8-11 75.................... GFCarroll 21 —
(M Halford, Ire) *chsd ldrs: 7th appr st: no ex fr 2f out: wknd* **33/1**

22 1 **Retreat Content (IRE)**[9] 5924 2-8-13 .... FergusSweeney 5 —
(J A Osborne) *a bhd* **40/1**

1m 34.05s (3.55) **22** Ran SP% **157.7**
CSF £222.12 TOTE £19.80: £3.50, £7.40, £4.00; DF 316.90.
Owner YITBA Racing Club **Bred** Mr Thomas Cahalan & Kye Fassnidge **Trained** The Curragh, Co Kildare

■ Stewards' Enquiry : K J Manning advise: careless riidng

FOCUS
The Four Masters finishing second in this race off a mark of 77 does put the level of the form in to some sort of perspective.

NOTEBOOK
Stand To Attention(IRE) showed the requisite improvement to go and win this race. Held up off the pace and racing towards the outside, he was asked to improve his position early in the straight and, once he picked up, he quickened and really sustained his effort to the line. It was quite an impressive performance and, while one can always question the quality of the opposition, he was visually good and looks ready to step up in class. (op 20/1)
The Four Masters(IRE) had the race run to suit and he took advantage by passing tired horses for second. The winner is better than him, but he was able to make the most of horses weakening in front of him to be nearest at the finish.
Bathwick Bear(IRE) was able to tack across and take close order. His rider went for home early in the straight, without any reservations about his mount's stamina, but the four-length lead he opened up over a furlong out was whittled away quickly inside the last. He patently didn't get home. (op 14/1 tchd 9/1)
Rudegirl(IRE) raced handily and managed to make her way across towards the inside, but despite her effort flattening out inside the last she still ran well.
Mama Sox(IRE) ran a cracker and came home well inside the final furlong from mid-division without making an impression.
Moonlit Garden(IRE)'s rider held on to her as much as possible and she did make some reasonable ground to have half a chance inside the last, but she couldn't sustain it. She probably doesn't stay 7f, especially on this ground. (op 9/2 tchd 6/1)
Act Of Love(IRE) Official explanation: jockey said filly checked early due to general bunching

6231 - 6234a (Foreign Racing) - See Raceform Interactive

4889

WOODBINE (R-H)

Sunday, September 19

OFFICIAL GOING: Turf: good (7.30pm race); firm (9.34pm & 10.42pm races)

6235a CANADIAN STKS (GRADE 2) (3YO+ FILLIES & MARES) (TURF) 1m 1f
7:30 (12:00) 3-Y-O+

£105,882 (£35,294; £19,411; £10,588; £5,294; £235)

RPR

1 **Miss Keller (IRE)**[22] 4-8-3 0 ow2.................................... JJCastellano 3 110
(Roger L Attfield, Canada) *pressed ldr (disp ld for a while) til settled in 4th after 2f: cl 4th st and sn swtchd ins: qcknd to chal ldr fnl f and led fnl 160yds: styd on strly to win gng away* **8/5**[1]

2 1 ¾ **Latin Love (IRE)**[63] 4177 4-8-3 0 ow2............................. GKGomez 6 107
(David Wachman, Ire) *racd on heels of ldrs (4th then 3rd fr 4f out): clsd up 2 1/2f out: in line of three at top of st: led jst ins fnl 2f: r.o wl but hdd fnl 160yds: kpt on wl* **9/5**[2]

3 5 **Magic Broomstick (USA)**[63] 4-8-1 0...................... ChantalSutherland 5 94
(Mark Frostad, Canada) *a.p: wnt 2nd after 3f: pressed ldr: pushed along 3f out: one of three in line at top of st: led briefly 2f out: sn hdd and rdn: no ex fnl 300yds* **7/1**

4 nse **Points Of Grace (USA)**[63] 5-8-7 0.................................... PHusbands 2 100
(Malcolm Pierce, Canada) *sn led (disp ld for part of first 2f): pressed fr 5f out: disp ld w two others st: hdd 2f out: kpt on u.p til wknd fnl f* **53/20**[3]

5 1 **Lemon Twirl (USA)**[435] 6-8-4 0 ow3.................................. JMcAleney 1 95
(John Mattine, Canada) *settled towards rr: last st: sn rdn and plld wd 2f out: kpt on at one pce: n.d* **33/1**

6 1 **Jenny's So Great (CAN)**[22] 3-8-3 0 ow7.......................... VEspinoza 4 97
(Gregory De Gannes, Canada) *racd towards rr: 5th st: rdn 2f out: wknd fnl f* **226/10**

1m 45.84s (105.84)
WFA 3 from 4yo+ 5lb **6** Ran SP% **121.3**
PARI-MUTUEL (all including $2 stake): WIN 5.20; PLACE (1-2) 2.60, 3.10; SHOW (1-2-3) 2.10, 2.20, 2.80; SF 13.00.
Owner Three Chimneys Racing LLC **Bred** Hascombe & Valiant Studs **Trained** Canada

NOTEBOOK
Latin Love(IRE), racing on Lasix for the first time, travelled well but came a little wide into the straight and didn't see her race out as well as the winner.

6236a NORTHERN DANCER TURF STKS (GRADE 1) (3YO+) (TURF) 1m 4f (T)
9:34 (12:00) 3-Y-O+

£229,411 (£76,470; £42,058; £22,941; £11,470; £235)

RPR

1 **Redwood**[21] 5575 4-8-7 0.. MichaelHills 5 113
(B W Hills) *dwlt and settled in rr: smooth hdwy on rail bk st to trck ldrs gng wl: disp 2nd turning for home: sn shkn up and r.o along ins rail to ld ins fnl f: styd on strly* **19/10**[1]

2 ½ **Fifty Proof (CAN)** 4-8-5 0.. JStein 6 110
(Ian Black, Canada) *broke wl and led: pressed bk st and fnl bnd: hdd ins fnl f: kpt on gamely u.p: no ex fnl 50yds* **29/1**

3 1 ¼ **Windward Islands (USA)**[28] 6-8-9 0..................(b) ChantalSutherland 2 112
(Mark Frostad, Canada) *a.p: cl 3rd and ev ch 2f out: sn rdn: styd on wout qckning fnl f* **191/10**

4 2 ½ **Spice Route**[77] 6-8-7 0..(b) MESmith 8 106
(Roger L Attfield, Canada) *hld up towards rr: hdwy on outside 1/2-way: cl 5th and gng wl appr st: rdn 2f out: unable qck and no ex fnl f* **19/5**[3]

5 4 **Memorial Maniac (USA)**[29] 5-8-7 0...........................(b) JamesGraham 4 100
(Larry Demeritte, U.S.A) *racd in last most of the way: sme hdwy through btn rivals fnl 2f: n.d* **226/10**

6 ½ **Guipago (CAN)**[13] 4-8-5 0.. JRosario 9 97
(Analisa M Delmas, U.S.A) *prom early stages: sn racd in fnl 3rd: 7th over 2f out: no imp* **68/1**

7 ¾ **Perfect Shower (CAN)**[29] 4-8-5 0...............................(b) JJCastellano 7 96
(Roger L Attfield, Canada) *rn freely in 4th early stages: rn wd first bnd and lost grnd: moved up to 3rd on outside bk st: pushed along 3f out: c wd fnl turn into st: grad wknd* **213/10**

8 ½ **Marsh Side (USA)**[28] 7-8-9 0... EPrado 1 99
(Neil Drysdale, U.S.A) *broke wl and settled in 2nd: pressed ldr on bk st: 2nd fnl turn: rdn st: hung rt 2f out: grad wknd* **43/20**[2]

9 9 ¾ **Expansion (USA)**[36] 5-8-7 0... GKGomez 3 81
(Steven Asmussen, U.S.A) *racd in midfield: brief effrt 3f out: sn rdn and btn: n.d* **11/2**

2m 28.97s (-0.63) **9** Ran SP% **120.9**
PARI-MUTUEL (all including $2 stake): WIN 5.80; PLACE (1-2) 4.10, 15.80; SHOW (1-2-3) 2.90, 8.00, 6.40; SF 123.30.
Owner K Abdulla **Bred** Juddmonte Farms Ltd **Trained** Lambourn, Berks

NOTEBOOK
Redwood, the only runner not using Lasix, benefited from one of the finest rides of Michael Hills's career. Typically for a British runner in North America, he missed the break, meaning he was immediately last of all, but he was soon taken towards the inside rail and stayed there throughout. Travelling enthusiastically, he made steady progress, with Hills always doing enough to ensure the gap didn't close, and then gradually squeezed through a narrow opening towards the inside of the runner-up from early in the straight. He was nicely on top at the line, despite edging right. The Canadian International back over C&D on October 16 is the obvious target, and more realistic than the Breeders' Cup Turf, although it's not out of the question he could take in both races.

6237a WOODBINE MILE STKS (GRADE 1) (3YO+) (TURF) 1m (T)
10:42 (12:00) 3-Y-O+

£352,941 (£117,647; £64,705; £35,294; £17,647; £235)

RPR

1 **Court Vision (USA)**[106] 5-8-12 0.................................(b) RAlbarado 4 122
(Richard Dutrow Jr, U.S.A) **73/10**

2 1 ¼ **The Usual Q. T. (USA)**[21] 5577 4-8-12 0.......................... VEspinoza 11 119
(James Cassidy, U.S.A) **16/5**[2]

3 1 ½ **Woodbourne (CAN)**[36] 6-8-5 0.......................... ChantalSutherland 10 109
(Robert Tiller, Canada) **52/1**

4 nse **Crowded House**[21] 5577 4-8-5 0.....................................(b) JRosario 1 108
(B Cecil, U.S.A) **167/20**

5 nk **Zifzaf (USA)**[49] 4-8-5 0... JRLeparoux 3 108
(James J Toner, U.S.A) **225/10**

6 3 ¼ **Smokey Fire (CAN)**[21] 5-8-9 0.. JCJones 6 104
(Sid Attard, Canada) **157/10**

7 nk **Famous Name**[15] 5775 5-8-7 0.. PJSmullen 12 102
(D K Weld, Ire) **29/10**[1]

8 ½ **Grand Adventure (USA)**[57] 4-8-9 0.............................. PHusbands 13 102
(Mark Frostad, Canada) **81/10**

9 nk **Victor's Cry (USA)**[56] 4417 5-8-12 0................................ CNakatani 2 105
(Eoin Harty, U.S.A) **67/10**[3]

10 1 ¾ **Riviera Cocktail (USA)**[238] 4-8-5 0..................................(b) EPrado 9 94
(Neil Drysdale, U.S.A) **29/1**

11 nse **Auteur (USA)**[287] 4-8-7 0 ow2.......................................(b) MESmith 8 96
(Barbara J Minshall, Canada) **60/1**

12 2 **Signature Red (USA)**[21] 4-8-9 0............................ ERosaDaSilva 7 93
(Sid Attard, Canada) **56/1**

13 1 ½ **Straight Story (USA)**[31] 4-8-5 0... RMaragh 5 86
(Alan E Goldberg, U.S.A) **166/10**

1m 34.62s (94.62) **13** Ran SP% **120.7**
PARI-MUTUEL (all including $2 stake): WIN 16.60; PLACE (1-2) 7.60, 4.50; SHOW (1-2-3) 5.40, 4.50, 14.50; SF 77.40.
Owner IEAH Stables & Resolute Group Stables **Bred** W S Farish & Kilroy Thoroughbred Partnership **Trained** USA

NOTEBOOK
Court Vision(USA) was suited by the strong pace and stayed on well for a convincing success. He was only fourth in last year's Breeders' Cup Mile, but looks a better horse now.
Famous Name, racing on Lasix for the first time, missed the break and, although quickly rushed up to try and recover, lacked the required speed, with 1m on quickish ground an insufficent test of stamina. He kept on in the straight, but posed no threat.

3495 SAN SIRO (R-H)
Sunday, September 19

OFFICIAL GOING: Turf: very soft

6238a PREMIO CANCELLI (LISTED RACE) (3YO+) (TURF) 5f
3:10 (12:00) 3-Y-O+ **£24,778** (£10,902; £5,946; £2,973)

RPR
1 **Farrel (IRE)**98 5-8-6 0 DVargiu 6 102
(B Grizzetti, Italy) **25/4**
2 1 **Jakor (ITY)**155 4-8-6 0 SSulas 7 99
(M Marcialis, Italy) **37/10**2
3 ½ **Above Limits (IRE)**31 5250 3-8-2 0 APolli 10 94
(D M Simcock) *broke wl to share ld after 1f: hdd ent fnl f: kpt on to hold 3rd fnl strides* **106/10**
4 shd **Ekin**98 5-8-9 0 GMarcelli 4 100
(P Riccioni, Italy) **167/20**
5 1 ¼ **Jiroft (ITY)**98 3-8-5 0 PierantonioConvertino 3 92
(M Marcialis, Italy) **29/20**1
6 1 ¼ **At First Sight (GER)**383 3-8-2 0 FilipMinarik 8 85
(Frau E Mader, Germany) **151/10**
7 nse **Dagda Mor (ITY)**63 4185 3-8-5 0 FabioBranca 1 87
(S Botti, Italy) **9/1**
8 snk **Shellder (IRE)**154 1419 3-8-2 0 CDemuro 5 84
(L Riccardi, Italy) **46/1**
9 nse **Rebecca Rolfe**63 4185 4-8-6 0 MircoDemuro 2 87
(M Gasparini, Italy) **41/10**3

58.00 secs (-1.20)
WFA 3 from 4yo+ 1lb 9 Ran SP% **133.1**
WIN (incl. 1 euro stake): 7.24. PLACES: 2.39, 2.02, 3.45. DF: 16.55.
Owner Scuderia Arvenig **Bred** Allevamento Dei Sei Srl **Trained** Italy

NOTEBOOK
Above Limits(IRE), close up throughout, took a narrow lead from halfway to just over a furlong from home and kept on under pressure on the testing going to just hold on to third place near the finish, securing further valuable black type in the process.

6239a PREMIO FEDERICO TESIO (GROUP 3) (3YO+) (TURF) 1m 3f
3:45 (12:00) 3-Y-O+ **£44,247** (£19,469; £10,619; £5,309)

RPR
1 **Voila Ici (IRE)**98 3019 5-8-11 0 MircoDemuro 3 112
(Vittorio Caruso, Italy) *stdd nr rr: prog to move 4th ent st: gd hdwy to ld 3f out: a holding runner-up: comf* **7/8**1
2 1 ¼ **Cima De Triomphe (IRE)**14 5-8-11 0 CColombi 1 110
(B Grizzetti, Italy) *settled in midfield for 6f: moved into 2nd ent fnl 3f: hrd rdn fnl 2f: styd on wl for 2nd* **63/20**2
3 1 ¾ **Nicea (GER)**49 4640 3-8-2 0 FilipMinarik 6 105
(P Schiergen, Germany) *hld up in rr: prog to move 4th ent fnl 3f: hrd rdn fnl 2f: styd on* **89/20**3
4 3 **Baschar**14 5804 3-8-5 0 MEsposito 7 103
(M G Mintchev, Germany) *hld up nr rr for 4f: hdwy to go 3rd after 6f: ct for pce ent fnl 3f: styd on fnl 2f* **76/10**
5 hd **Camill (IRE)**42 4886 6-8-11 0 GHind 2 101
(P Kalas, Slovakia) *mid-div tl ent st: effrt 3 1/2f out: hrd rdn to stay in tch fnl 2 1/2f: styd on* **31/1**
6 5 **Apprimus (IRE)**14 4-8-11 0 NPinna 4 92
(S Botti, Italy) *broke wl to ld: passed ent fnl 3f: hrd rdn and no imp fnl 2f: eased fnl 100yds* **243/10**
7 dist **Il Fenomeno (ITY)**134 1943 4-8-11 0 DVargiu 5 —
(B Grizzetti, Italy) *broke wl to trck ldr: rdn 4f out: sn btn: eased fnl 2f* **21/4**

2m 18.1s (-0.50)
WFA 3 from 4yo+ 7lb 7 Ran SP% **130.5**
WIN (incl. 1 euro stake): 1.88. PLACES: 1.40, 1.60. SF: 3.00.
Owner Incolinx **Bred** Soc Finanza Locale Consulting Srl **Trained** Italy

6220 HAMILTON (R-H)
Monday, September 20

OFFICIAL GOING: Good to soft (good in places; rnd 7.7; str 8.3)
Wind: Fresh, across Weather: Sunny

6240 EUROPEAN BREEDERS' FUND MAIDEN STKS 6f 5y
2:10 (2:12) (Class 5) 2-Y-O **£3,238** (£963; £481; £240) **Stalls** Low

Form RPR
1 **Present Danger** 2-8-12 0 RichardKingscote 3 74+
(Tom Dascombe) *dwlt: hld up in tch: smooth hdwy over 1f out: led and flashed tail ins fnl f: sn clr: comf* **5/4**1
00 2 3 ½ **Marina Belle**84 3498 2-8-12 0 JoeFanning 9 61
(M Johnston) *led 2f: cl up: led over 1f out to ins fnl f: kpt on same pce* **11/1**
33 3 nse **Inside**28 5352 2-8-12 0 PaulHanagan 4 61
(R A Fahey) *prom: rdn over 2f out: sn outpcd: styd on u.p fnl f* **2/1**2
0 4 ¾ **Magnini (IRE)**70 3945 2-9-3 0 PJMcDonald 7 64
(K A Ryan) *t.k.h: led after 2f to over 1f out: kpt on same pce fnl f* **7/1**3
04 5 4 ½ **Lough Corrib (USA)**7 6027 2-9-3 0 StephenCraine 6 50+
(K A Ryan) *s.i.s: bhd and rdn 1/2-way: sme hdwy over 1f out: n.d* **25/1**
6 6 **Crabbies Gold (IRE)** 2-9-3 0 TomEaves 1 32
(Mrs L Williamson) *prom tl rdn: hung rt and wknd fr 2f out* **66/1**
7 4 ½ **Meniscus** 2-8-12 0 PhillipMakin 8 14
(V P Donoghue) *reluctant to enter stalls: bhd: struggling over 3f out: nvr on terms* **33/1**
45 8 6 **Hollyhocks (IRE)**125 2210 2-8-12 0 PaulMulrennan 2 —
(V P Donoghue) *dwlt: bhd: outpcd and hung rt over 3f out: sn btn* **40/1**

1m 14.56s (2.36) **Going Correction** +0.40s/f (Good) **8** Ran SP% **109.3**
Speed ratings (Par 95): **100,95,95,94,88 80,74,66**
Tote Swingers: 1&2 £4.90, 1&3 £1.60, 2&3 £3.70 CSF £14.21 TOTE £2.00: £1.10, £2.50, £1.20; EX 21.10.
Owner A Black & M Owen **Bred** Watership Down Stud **Trained** Malpas, Cheshire

FOCUS
No depth to this maiden.

NOTEBOOK
Present Danger justified the strength behind her in the market with ease, leading on the bridle and not hard pressed to come clear. A well-bred daughter of Cadeax Genereux, she'll stay at least 7f (dam 1m winner) and is sure to leave the bare form of this promising start behind. (op 2-1)
Marina Belle had been well beaten on her two previous outings but proved a different proposition after a 12-week break. This form is nothing out of the ordinary but she's in excellent hands and it would be no surprise if she went on again from this. (op 10-1 tchd 12-1)
Inside has finished third on all three starts but doesn't appear to be progressing, somewhat laboured in the way she went about things here, but it's clearly still early days and she is bred to be suited by longer trips. (op 13-8)
Magnini(IRE), who'd been gelded since his debut ten weeks earlier, offered more on this occasion, showing speed as he travelled comfortably in the lead for a long way. He appeals as the type to progress with racing, particularly once qualified for handicaps. (op 13-2 tchd 11-2)
Lough Corrib(USA) hasn't achieved a great deal, only fourth in a seller last week, but can't get much of a mark and it would be no surprise if he did better now eligible for nurseries. (op 18-1)

6241 TOTESPORT.COM CONDITIONS STKS 6f 5y
2:40 (2:40) (Class 2) 3-Y-O+ **£8,723** (£2,612; £1,306; £653) **Stalls** Centre

Form RPR
5300 1 **Quest For Success (IRE)**2 6177 5-8-9 99 PaulMulrennan 7 99
(R A Fahey) *prom: smooth hdwy to ld over 1f out: rdn out fnl f* **7/4**2
-310 2 ¾ **Rash Judgement**11 5884 5-8-9 87 DavidAllan 6 97
(E J Alston) *cl up: effrt and ev ch over 1f out: kpt on u.p ins fnl f but a hld* **14/1**
1600 3 ½ **Global City (IRE)**50 4616 4-8-9 102 (t) TedDurcan 4 95
(Saeed Bin Suroor) *trckd ldrs: effrt and rdn over 1f out: kpt on ins fnl f: hld towards fin* **15/2**3
4006 4 1 **Knot In Wood (IRE)**2 6177 8-9-2 102 PaulHanagan 5 99
(R A Fahey) *led tl rdn and hdd over 1f out: rallied ins fnl f: no ex last 50yds* **4/5**1

1m 13.35s (1.15) **Going Correction** +0.40s/f (Good) **4** Ran SP% **110.4**
Speed ratings (Par 109): **108,107,106,105**
CSF £18.45 TOTE £2.30; EX 19.60.
Owner Morebrooke Ltd **Bred** Desmond Monaghan **Trained** Musley Bank, N Yorks

FOCUS
A useful condtions event. Given the size of the field it wasn't a surprise the pace wasn't that strong, all four of the runners still holding every chance inside the final furlong. Muddling form.

NOTEBOOK
Quest For Success(IRE) had been behind stable-companion Knot In Wood in the Ayr Gold Cup two days earlier but a 5lb swing in the weights saw him turn the tables, and he is now 2-2 at the track. He was always travelling well and knuckled down gamely when his rider asked for maximum effort. He's likely to have more on his plate wherever we see him next, but his ability to handle testing conditions should hold him in good stead this autumn. (op 5-2)
Rash Judgement seemed to show a fair bit of improvement on just his second start for Eric Alston and that's not out of the question given his yard's record with sprinters. However, he's sure to be hit by the handicapper for splitting some higher-rated rivals, and his best chance of success near to hand may be turned out before reassessed for this (has until Friday week). (op 11-1 tchd 10-1)
Global City(IRE) put two below-par efforts behind him after a seven-week break, showing his ability to handle testing conditions into the bargain. (op 5-1 tchd 8-1)
Knot In Wood(IRE) had a bit more on his plate than the market implied conceding 7lb all round, but clearly wasn't in quite the same form as when sixth in the Ayr Gold Cup on Saturday, presumably not fully recovered from those exertions. (op 10-11 tchd Evens)

6242 PLAY BINGO AT TOTESPORT.COM APPRENTICE H'CAP (FINAL OF HAMILTON PARK APPRENTICE SERIES) 1m 3f 16y
3:10 (3:11) (Class 6) (0-65,65) 3-Y-O+ **£1,942** (£578; £288; £144) **Stalls** High

Form RPR
3331 1 **Sharp Sovereign (USA)**33 5216 4-9-6 59 NeilFarley 10 72
(T D Barron) *mde all: hrd pressed over 1f out: hld on gamely fnl f* **15/8**1
000- 2 1 **Prince Rhyddarch**236 7354 5-8-9 51 oh1 PaulNorton(3) 1 62
(M Dods) *in tch: stdy hdwy 3f out: rdn and ev ch over 1f out: no ex ins fnl f* **7/2**3
3-60 3 7 **Dramatic Jewel (USA)**4 6109 4-9-10 63 GarryWhillans 8 62
(Miss Lucinda V Russell) *midfield: hdwy 3f out: chsd clr ldng pair over 1f out: no imp* **20/1**
2-16 4 11 **Sovento (GER)**27 5403 6-9-7 60 DaleSwift 2 39
(Shaun Harley, Ire) *t.k.h: hld up towards rr: rdn 4f out: sn no imp* **2/1**2
0620 5 5 **Balwearie (IRE)**7 6032 9-9-1 54 IanBrennan 5 24
(Miss L A Perratt) *bhd: drvn over 5f out: nvr able to chal* **10/1**
-550 6 6 **Intersky Charm (USA)**7 6029 6-9-7 65 (t) LukeStrong(5) 7 24
(Mrs S C Bradburne) *trckd ldrs tl rdn and wknd over 2f out* **50/1**
0-00 7 1 ¾ **Sams Spirit**14 5819 4-8-12 51 oh6 (b1) AdamCarter 6 —
(J A McShane) *pressed wnr tl rdn and wknd fr 3f out* **66/1**
0 8 9 **Balance On Time (IRE)**7 6033 4-8-7 51 oh4 ShaneBKelly(5) 4 —
(Miss L A Perratt) *bhd: drvn 1/2-way: struggling fnl 3f* **50/1**
-000 9 8 **Shanavaz**18 5681 4-8-7 51 oh6 (p) DavidSimmonson(5) 3 —
(C J Teague) *s.i.s: sn in tch: struggling 1/2-way: sn btn* **80/1**
10 8 **Chaotic (IRE)**47 4725 4-9-2 55 (tp) RosieJessop 9 —
(T Hogan, Ire) *towards rr: rdn and hung lft 4f out: sn btn* **25/1**

2m 28.7s (3.10) **Going Correction** +0.40s/f (Good) **10** Ran SP% **114.7**
Speed ratings (Par 101): **104,103,98,90,86 82,80,74,68,62**
Tote Swingers: 1&2 £2.60, 1&3 £4.60, 2&3 £8.60 CSF £8.14 CT £95.18 TOTE £2.60: £1.40, £2.20, £3.20; EX 9.50.
Owner Raymond Miquel **Bred** James Sumter Carter **Trained** Maunby, N Yorks

FOCUS
A race which lacked depth overall but still form to view positively from the leading pair, who came home well clear, the winner making all in a race in which few ever threatened to get competitive.

6243 PLAY BLACKJACK AT TOTESPORT.COM H'CAP 1m 1f 36y
3:40 (3:41) (Class 5) (0-70,69) 3-Y-O+ **£2,590** (£770; £385; £192) **Stalls** High

Form RPR
0404 1 **Casino Night**32 5244 5-8-7 55 DaleSwift(5) 12 66
(Miss L A Perratt) *t.k.h: chsd ldr: rdn to ld over 1f out: styd on wl fnl f* **9/2**2
0653 2 ¾ **Formulation (IRE)**94 3155 3-9-7 69 PaulHanagan 14 78
(H Morrison) *prom: effrt over 2f out: chsd wnr and edgd rt 1f out: r.o: hld towards fin* **11/8**1

0566 **3** *2* **Botham (USA)**[4] 6107 6-8-10 **60** ow1 .... PaulNorton(7) 5 65
(J S Goldie) *hld up: rdn and hdwy 2f out: styd on fnl f: nt pce of first two* **22/1**

2-65 **4** *2* **Plenty O'Toole**[12] 5852 3-9-6 **68** .... SilvestreDeSousa 16 70
(Mrs D J Sanderson) *led to over 1f out: kpt on same pce fnl f* **5/1**[3]

2355 **5** *shd* **Zaplamation (IRE)**[103] 2859 5-9-5 **67** .... IanBrennan(5) 10 68
(J J Quinn) *hld up in tch: effrt over 2f out: no imp over 1f out* **13/2**

0500 **6** *1* **Nevada Desert (IRE)**[4] 6117 10-9-4 **64** .... MichaelStainton(3) 9 62
(R M Whitaker) *hld up: hdwy over 2f out: no ex fnl f* **16/1**

5460 **7** *13* **Diamondgeezer Luke (IRE)**[31] 5271 3-8-3 **58** .... NeilFarley(7) 11 30
(Patrick Morris) *plld hrd: in tch: struggling over 3f out: sn btn* **28/1**

5120 **8** *nk* **Bed Fellow (IRE)**[17] 5737 6-9-3 **63** .... PatrickDonaghy(3) 3 34
(P Monteith) *hld up in tch: effrt over 2f out: wknd over 1f out* **40/1**

2005 **9** *2 ¾* **Finsbury**[7] 6029 7-9-6 **63** .... PhillipMakin 1 28
(Miss L A Perratt) *s.s: bhd: rdn 3f out: sn btn* **25/1**

-000 **10** *¾* **Celestial Tryst**[97] 3062 3-9-3 **65** .... PJMcDonald 7 29
(G M Moore) *trckd ldrs: drvn 3f out: wknd 2f out* **50/1**

2m 2.18s (2.48) **Going Correction** +0.40s/f (Good)
WFA 3 from 4yo+ 5lb **10** Ran SP% **112.2**
Speed ratings (Par 103): **104,103,101,99,99 98,87,86,84,83**
Tote Swingers: 1&2 £2.60, 1&3 £6.60, 2&3 £8.30 CSF £9.99 CT £116.47 TOTE £5.20: £1.10, £1.70, £3.60; EX 11.80.
Owner Barry Robson **Bred** Kingsmead Breeders **Trained** East Kilbride, S Lanarks

FOCUS
A fair handicap. The pace looked sound and there's no reason why the form won't hold up. The winner has slipped to a good mark and the third sets the standard.
Finsbury Official explanation: jockey said gelding missed the break

6244 PLAY ROULETTE AT TOTESPORT.COM MAIDEN STKS 1m 1f 36y
4:10 (4:10) (Class 5) 3-4-Y-O **£2,590** (£770; £385; £192) **Stalls** High

Form RPR

3226 **1** **Broadway Dancer**[21] 5607 3-8-12 69 .... PaulHanagan 5 64
(R A Fahey) *trckd ldrs: hdwy to ld over 2f out: edgd lft u.p ins fnl f: hld on gamely* **7/2**[2]

6-43 **2** *hd* **Tayacoba (CAN)**[24] 5478 3-9-0 0 .... GaryBartley(3) 9 69
(J S Goldie) *trckd ldrs: effrt over 2f out: edgd rt and ev ch over 1f out: blkd ins fnl f: r.o* **8/1**

44 **3** *1 ¾* **Crimson Empire (USA)**[36] 5122 3-8-12 0 .... TomEaves 8 60
(B Smart) *led 1f: cl up: led over 3f out to over 2f out: rallied: one pce ins fnl f* **9/2**[3]

4 *11* **Machir Bay** 3-9-3 0 .... PaulMulrennan 2 42
(V P Donoghue) *hld up in tch: rdn and outpcd over 3f out: n.d after* **50/1**

43 **5** *½* **Pearl Huntsman (USA)**[63] 4205 3-9-3 0 .... PhillipMakin 3 41
(J Noseda) *plld hrd: in tch: rdn: carried hd high and hung lft over 2f out: sn btn* **4/5**[1]

0 **6** *10* **Harsh But Fair**[30] 5303 4-9-5 0 .... JamesSullivan(3) 10 20
(M W Easterby) *missed break: bhd: rdn over 4f out: sn struggling* **33/1**

00 **7** *3 ¼* **Strong Aim**[10] 5925 3-8-5 0 .... DavidSimmonson(7) 1 8
(M W Easterby) *wnt lft and s.s: bhd: struggling fr 4f out* **150/1**

5 **8** *¾* **Psalm Twentythree**[24] 5478 4-9-8 0 .... DavidAllan 6 12
(J A McShane) *led after 1f to over 3f out: wknd over 2f out* **66/1**

2m 2.74s (3.04) **Going Correction** +0.40s/f (Good)
WFA 3 from 4yo 5lb **8** Ran SP% **114.1**
Speed ratings (Par 103): **102,101,100,90,90 81,78,77**
Tote Swingers: 1&2 £3.80, 1&3 £2.80, 2&3 £3.30 CSF £29.68 TOTE £4.20: £1.30, £1.50, £2.10; EX 29.60.
Owner Philip F Myerscough **Bred** Darley **Trained** Musley Bank, N Yorks

FOCUS
Back-end maidens for older horses are seldom strong and this looks no exception, the form no better than fair. The winner probably only had to match her previous turf form.
Pearl Huntsman(USA) Official explanation: jockey said colt was unsuited by the good to soft (good in places) ground
Harsh But Fair Official explanation: jockey said gelding missed the break

6245 PLAY SLOTS AT TOTESPORT.COM H'CAP 5f 4y
4:40 (4:42) (Class 4) (0-80,79) 3-Y-0+ **£3,885** (£1,156; £577; £288) **Stalls** Centre

Form RPR

1032 **1** **Captain Scooby**[5] 6073 4-8-10 **68** .... MichaelStainton(3) 12 79
(R M Whitaker) *bhd and sn pushed along: hdwy 2f out: led ins fnl f: hld on wl* **4/1**[2]

0514 **2** *1 ¼* **Night Trade (IRE)**[26] 5421 3-9-8 **78** .... (p) SilvestreDeSousa 5 85
(Mrs D J Sanderson) *midfield: drvn and outpcd over 2f out: rallied over 1f out: chsd wnr ins fnl f: r.o* **13/2**

0062 **3** *hd* **Argentine (IRE)**[4] 6103 6-8-12 **67** .... PaulMulrennan 4 73
(J A McShane) *hld up: hdwy over 1f out: sn rdn: kpt on fnl f* **7/2**[1]

3003 **4** *¾* **Lost In Paris (IRE)**[9] 5941 4-9-10 **79** .... (v) DavidAllan 9 82
(T D Easterby) *led at decent gallop: rdn 2f out: hdd ins fnl f: one pce* **5/1**

2212 **5** *4 ½* **Bronze Beau**[9] 5956 3-9-5 **78** .... (t) JamesSullivan(3) 10 65
(Mrs L Stubbs) *w ldr to over 1f out: rdn and wknd ins fnl f* **8/1**

40-0 **6** *1 ½* **Sloop Johnb**[29] 5335 4-9-7 **76** .... PaulHanagan 2 57
(R A Fahey) *bhd and sn pushed along: hdwy over 1f out: nvr able to chal* **16/1**

2114 **7** *¾* **Cayman Fox**[7] 6031 5-9-0 **69** .... PJMcDonald 7 48
(Miss L A Perratt) *trckd ldrs tl rdn and wknd over 1f out* **9/2**[3]

0000 **8** *hd* **Burnwynd Boy**[4] 6103 5-8-10 **70** .... (b) DaleSwift(5) 1 48
(J A McShane) *s.i.s: bhd and pushed along: nvr rchd ldrs* **33/1**

0150 **9** *1 ¼* **Lesley's Choice**[3] 6140 4-9-3 **77** .... (b) IanBrennan(5) 13 51
(Miss L A Perratt) *trckd ldrs: rdn over 2f out: wknd wl over 1f out* **11/1**

61.63 secs (1.63) **Going Correction** +0.40s/f (Good)
WFA 3 from 4yo+ 1lb **9** Ran SP% **113.0**
Speed ratings (Par 105): **102,100,99,98,91 88,87,87,85**
Tote Swingers: 1&2 £9.10, 1&3 £4.60, 2&3 £10.00 CSF £49.53 CT £182.88 TOTE £7.20: £1.80, £3.30, £3.00; EX 48.70.
Owner Paul Davies (H'gte) **Bred** Hellwood Stud Farm & Paul Davies (h'Gate) **Trained** Scarcroft, W Yorks

FOCUS
A few confirmed front runners in opposition here and they went hard under the conditions, setting it up for those coming from behind. The form looks sound, the winner rated to his latest.
Cayman Fox Official explanation: jockey said mare was unsuited by the good to soft (good in places) ground

6246 FREE RACING POST FORM AT TOTESPORT.COM H'CAP 5f 4y
5:10 (5:10) (Class 6) (0-65,65) 3-Y-0+ **£1,942** (£578; £288; £144) **Stalls** Centre

Form RPR

6650 **1** **Rothesay Dancer**[4] 6103 7-8-11 **61** .... PaulNorton(7) 2 75
(J S Goldie) *hld up: hdwy over 1f out: led ins fnl f: r.o* **7/1**

0046 **2** *2* **Sharp Bullet (IRE)**[21] 5599 4-9-2 **59** .... (b) SilvestreDeSousa 6 66
(Bruce Hellier) *led: swtchd to stands' rail over 3f out: rdn 2f out: hdd ins fnl f: kpt on same pce* **7/2**[1]

2420 **3** *¾* **Rio Sands**[23] 5513 5-8-10 **56** .... MichaelStainton(3) 11 60
(R M Whitaker) *midfield: drvn over 2f out: rallied over 1f out: no imp fnl f* **5/1**[2]

3431 **4** *hd* **Ballarina**[14] 5816 4-9-0 **57** .... DavidAllan 3 60
(E J Alston) *chsd ldr: effrt over 2f out: kpt on same pce fnl f* **5/1**[2]

3466 **5** *¾* **Dower Glen**[94] 3167 3-8-2 **53** .... ShirleyTeasdale(7) 1 54
(V P Donoghue) *midfield: edgd rt 1/2-way: hdwy over 1f out: nvr rchd ldrs* **50/1**

6 *1 ¼* **Lovestoned (IRE)**[13] 5843 4-9-3 **60** .... (bt) JoeFanning 5 56
(T Hogan, Ire) *prom: rdn over 2f out: edgd lft and no ex over 1f out* **8/1**

0044 **7** *shd* **Accamelia**[14] 5816 4-8-7 **50** oh2 .... PaulMulrennan 13 46
(C W Fairhurst) *hld up in tch: rdn and hung rt 1/2-way: nvr rchd ldrs* **13/2**[3]

-644 **8** *1 ¾* **Billionaire Boy (IRE)**[25] 5438 3-8-6 **50** .... PaulHanagan 4 39
(Patrick Morris) *in tch: rdn over 2f out: wknd appr fnl f* **9/1**

-010 **9** *nse* **Prince James**[20] 5647 3-9-4 **65** .... JamesSullivan(3) 9 54
(M W Easterby) *bhd and sn pushed along: nvr on terms* **14/1**

0050 **10** *4 ½* **Miacarla**[24] 5502 7-8-9 **52** oh5 ow2 .... (p) TomEaves 12 25
(H A McWilliams) *in tch: rdn 1/2-way: wknd wl over 1f out* **33/1**

62.04 secs (2.04) **Going Correction** +0.40s/f (Good)
WFA 3 from 4yo+ 1lb **10** Ran SP% **114.1**
Speed ratings (Par 101): **99,95,94,94,93 91,90,88,88,80**
Tote Swingers: 1&2 £6.80, 1&3 £5.70, 2&3 £5.20 CSF £30.98 CT £137.31 TOTE £9.20: £3.30, £3.50, £2.70; EX 50.50 Place 6: £30.58 Place 5: £26.41..
Owner Highland Racing **Bred** Frank Brady **Trained** Uplawmoor, E Renfrews
■ Melundy (13/2) was withdrawn (rider injured). Deduct 10p in the £ under R4, new market formed.

FOCUS
Run-of-the-mill fare run at a strong pace. The winner took advantage of a slide in the weights.
Lovestoned(IRE) Official explanation: jockey said gelding hung left from halfway
T/Jkpt: £3,000.80 to a £1 stake. Pool of £147,928.00 - 35 winning tickets. T/Plt: £54.20 to a £1 stake. Pool of £79,549 - 1,070.12 winning tickets. T/Qpdt: £9.70 to a £1 stake. Pool of £4,894 - 371.85 winning tickets. RY

6078 KEMPTON (A.W) (R-H)
Monday, September 20

OFFICIAL GOING: Standard
Wind: virtually nil Weather: cloudy, mild

6247 CRN RACE DAY E.B.F MAIDEN FILLIES' STKS (DIV I) 7f (P)
2:30 (2:32) (Class 4) 2-Y-O **£3,950** (£1,175; £587; £293) **Stalls** High

Form RPR

22 **1** **Zing Wing**[3] 6150 2-9-0 0 .... NeilCallan 13 75
(P F I Cole) *mde all: rdn and hung lft ent fnl 2f: styd on wl u.p fnl f* **9/4**[2]

2 *1 ¼* **Cross Examination (USA)** 2-9-0 0 .... AhmedAjtebi 9 72
(Mahmood Al Zarooni) *chsd wnr: carried lft ent fnl 2f: sn rdn and hung lft: lost 2nd 1f out: racing on stands' rail and rallied ins fnl f: wnt 2nd again nr fin* **25/1**

05 **3** *½* **Magical Flower**[28] 5369 2-9-0 0 .... JimCrowley 8 71
(W J Knight) *in tch: rdn and effrt over 2f out: drvn and chsd wnr 1f out: styd on same pce fnl f: lost 2nd nr fin* **8/1**

4 **4** *¾* **Entrance**[13] 5829 2-9-0 0 .... KierenFallon 4 69
(E A L Dunlop) *in tch in midfield: swtchd lft and effrt over 2f out: swtchd rt and hdwy u.p over 1f out: styd on same pce ins fnl f* **9/2**[3]

0 **5** *hd* **Isolate**[18] 5692 2-9-0 0 .... SteveDrowne 11 68
(H Morrison) *chsd ldrs: rdn ent fnl 2f: pressed ldrs over 1f out: no ex and styd on same pce fnl 150yds* **16/1**

0 **6** *nk* **Emperor's Princess (FR)**[18] 5692 2-9-0 0 .... RyanMoore 6 68
(R Hannon) *chsd ldrs: rdn and unable qck over 2f out: lost pl 2f out: rallied u.p ent fnl f: kpt on wl* **9/4**[1]

6 **7** *2* **Corvette**[24] 5489 2-9-0 0 .... JimmyQuinn 2 63+
(J R Jenkins) *s.i.s: towards rr: hdwy and rdn ent fnl 2f: kpt on u.p fnl f: nt pce to rch ldrs* **100/1**

8 *½* **Aristeia** 2-9-0 0 .... PatDobbs 3 61+
(R Hannon) *v.s.a: bhd: rdn and sme hdwy 2f out: kpt on fnl f but nvr threatened ldrs* **50/1**

9 *½* **Make A Dance (USA)** 2-9-0 0 .... MichaelHills 5 60+
(B W Hills) *v.s.a: bhd: rdn and hdwy on inner 2f out: kpt on fnl f: nvr trbld ldrs* **11/1**

0 **10** *½* **Sandtail (IRE)**[18] 5692 2-9-0 0 .... SebSanders 12 59+
(J W Hills) *dwlt: hld up in midfield: rdn and effrt jst over 2f out: no imp over 1f out: wknd ins fnl f* **100/1**

11 *3 ¼* **Misefi** 2-9-0 0 .... LiamKeniry 1 51+
(M R Bosley) *stdd after s: t.k.h: hld up in rr: rdn and no prog wl over 2f out: bhd fnl 2f* **100/1**

12 *3* **Farmer's Wife** 2-9-0 0 .... JamieSpencer 10 43+
(W J Haggas) *s.i.s: a bhd: n.d* **20/1**

0 **13** *4 ½* **Night Witch (IRE)**[161] 1256 2-9-0 0 .... EddieCreighton 7 32
(E J Creighton) *dwlt: sn t.k.h in midfield: hung rt and struggling over 2f out: bhd fr wl over 1f out* **100/1**

1m 27.85s (1.85) **Going Correction** +0.025s/f (Slow) **13** Ran SP% **119.6**
Speed ratings (Par 94): **90,88,88,87,86 86,84,83,83,82 78,75,70**
Tote Swingers: 1&2 £5.50, 1&3 £5.30, 2&3 £30.20 CSF £70.69 TOTE £4.10: £1.60, £5.10, £1.70; EX 38.70.
Owner The Fairy Story Partnership **Bred** Deepwood Farm Stud **Trained** Whatcombe, Oxon

FOCUS
A fair fillies' maiden, but the pace was just modest and few got involved. Despite that, the time was 0.33 seconds quicker than the second division, won by Submission.

NOTEBOOK
Zing Wing, a runner-up in two conditions races, first up over C&D and then on turf just three days prior to this, put her experience to good use. Well drawn, she was a bit keen under restraint early on, but was able to set just a modest tempo and, despite edging left late on, won well. She's clearly useful but will need to continue to progress, with things set to get tougher from now on. (op 13-8, tchd 5-2 in a place)
Cross Examination(USA), the first foal of a French 6f Listed winner, had a cross noseband fitted. She edged left in the straight, ending up towards the near rail, but was probably intimidated by the winner, who was also going in that direction. This was a fair start. (tchd 28-1)
Magical Flower, dropped in trip, kept much straighter than the front two but made no impression on the winner. This looks about as good as she is for now, and handicaps are an option. (op 6-1 tchd 9-1)
Entrance was unsuited by a steadily run race on this drop in trip and didn't improve much on her debut performance. She looks limited, but it's early days. (op 5-1 tchd 11-2)

Isolate, better than the bare form on debut, had her chance and ran respectably. She's likely to be suited by further (dam 1m4f winner). (op 14-1 tchd 20-1)
Emperor's Princess(FR) was well backed on course but still looked in need of the experience and never looking like picking up sufficiently. (op 5-1)
Make A Dance(USA) reportedly got upset before the saddle was fitted. In the race itself, she missed the break before racing keenly and made little impression in the straight. (op 12-1 tchd 14-1)

6248 CRN RACE DAY E.B.F MAIDEN FILLIES' STKS (DIV II) 7f (P)
3:00 (3:01) (Class 4) 2-Y-O **£3,950** (£1,175; £587; £293) **Stalls** High

Form RPR
2 **1** **Submission**[13] 5841 2-9-0 0 .... KierenFallon 1 78+
(L M Cumani) *trckd ldr and a travelling wl: rdn to ld 2f out: clr and in command 1f out: r.o wl under hands and heels riding fnl f: comf* **7/4**[1]
2 1 ¾ **Complexion** 2-9-0 0 .... RyanMoore 12 71+
(Sir Michael Stoute) *dwlt: towards rr: effrt in centre 2f out: str run ent fnl f: chsd wnr fnl 100yds: r.o wl but no ch w wnr* **2/1**[2]
0 **3** 1 ¼ **Etarre (IRE)**[37] 5078 2-9-0 0 .... LiamKeniry 8 68+
(Mrs P Sly) *dwlt: sn t.k.h and hld up in midfield: rdn ent fnl 2f: styd on wl ins fnl f to go 3rd last strides: no ch w wnr* **25/1**
0 **4** *hd* **Ayaarah (IRE)**[51] 4595 2-9-0 0 .... FrankieDettori 6 68
(M A Jarvis) *chsd ldrs: rdn and unable qck over 2f out: kpt on again u.p ins fnl f: no threat to wnr* **9/1**
0 **5** ¾ **Jahanara (IRE)**[59] 4317 2-9-0 0 .... PatDobbs 4 66
(R Hannon) *led: hdd and rdn 2f out: sn outpcd and no ch w wnr 1f out: lost 2nd fnl 100yds: wknd towards fin* **11/2**[3]
0 **6** ½ **Abeer (USA)**[18] 5692 2-9-0 0 .... RichardHills 9 64
(E A L Dunlop) *hld up wl in tch: rdn and effrt on inner ent fnl 2f: outpcd and no ch w wnr over 1f out: styd on same pce after* **14/1**
7 2 **Lucky Legs (IRE)** 2-9-0 0 .... MichaelHills 13 59
(B W Hills) *dwlt: t.k.h and sn chsng ldrs: rdn and outpcd ent fnl 2f: wknd u.p 1f out* **40/1**
8 1 ¾ **Delphi Dream** 2-9-0 0 .... SteveDrowne 5 55+
(H Morrison) *dwlt: rn green and sn pushed along towards rr: rdn over 2f out: kpt on same pce fr over 1f out: nvr trbld ldrs* **66/1**
60 **9** 3 **Sukhothai (USA)**[82] 3562 2-9-0 0 .... TomQueally 3 47
(H R A Cecil) *s.i.s: sn pushed along towards rr: rdn and struggling 3f out: wl btn over 2f out* **40/1**
0 **10** 2 **Melancholy Hill (IRE)**[18] 5692 2-9-0 0 .... JamieSpencer 2 42
(P F I Cole) *v.s.a: a bhd: n.d* **66/1**
50 **11** 1 ½ **Dubawi Dancer**[5] 6092 2-9-0 0 .... SimonWhitworth 7 38
(W J Haggas) *stdd after s: hld up in last trio: pushed along and outpcd over 2f out: wl btn fnl 2f* **66/1**
25 **12** 9 **Kilk**[24] 5466 2-9-0 0 .... FergusSweeney 11 14
(A G Newcombe) *in tch in midfield: rdn and lost pl qckly wl over 2f out: wl bhd fnl f* **66/1**

1m 28.18s (2.18) **Going Correction** +0.025s/f (Slow) **12** Ran SP% **116.4**
Speed ratings (Par 94): **88,86,84,84,83 82,80,78,75,72 71,60**
Tote Swingers: 1&2 £1.10, 1&3 £8.70, 2&3 £8.90 CSF £5.00 TOTE £3.20: £1.60, £1.30, £5.60; EX 5.90.
Owner Fittocks Stud **Bred** Fittocks Stud Ltd **Trained** Newmarket, Suffolk

FOCUS
The time was 0.33 seconds slower than the modestly run first division, suggesting the bare form is no better than fair.

NOTEBOOK
Submission, runner-up on debut over this trip on Lingfield's Polytrack, was always well placed and did not required anything like maximum pressure to assert and, along with the eyecatching runner-up, looks better than the bare form. She should be suited by further in due course and is potentially very useful. (op 6-4 tchd 5-4)
Complexion, a half-sister to occasional high-class miler Zacinto, took a while to pick up before finishing strongly. She can leave the bare form behind with this experience behind her. (op 11-4 tchd 7-4)
Etarre(IRE) showed ability over 6f on debut at Newbury and confirmed that promise behind two very useful-looking fillies. (op 16-1)
Ayaarah(IRE), off the track since showing little 51 days earlier, lacked the required pace and still looked in need of the experience. (tchd 12-1)
Jahanara(IRE) showed ability on debut but had been off for two months. She displayed early speed but was left behind in the straight, and being a half-sister to Cavalryman, out of a 1m4f winner, she probably needs more time and distance. (op 8-1)
Abeer(USA) was well held after racing a little keenly. (op 11-1 tchd 20-1)

6249 STELJES, TECHNOLOGY WITH PURPOSE E B F MAIDEN STKS 1m (P)
3:30 (3:31) (Class 4) 2-Y-O **£4,274** (£1,271; £635; £317) **Stalls** High

Form RPR
0440 **1** **Aciano (IRE)**[21] 5587 2-9-3 75 .... ShaneKelly 6 85
(B J Meehan) *chsd ldr: pushed along to join ldr jst over 2f out: rdn along hands and heels after: led wl ins fnl f: pushed out* **16/1**
0 **2** ½ **Terdaad (IRE)**[31] 5277 2-9-3 0 .... FrankieDettori 9 84
(Saeed Bin Suroor) *led: rdn and jnd jst over 2f out: hrd drvn over 1f out: hdd and no ex wl ins fnl f* **4/9**[1]
0 **3** 7 **Plattsburgh (USA)**[21] 5582 2-9-3 0 .... AhmedAjtebi 11 68
(Mahmood Al Zarooni) *dwlt: sn pushed along and hdwy on inner to chse ldng pair after 1f: rdn and outpcd jst over 2f out: 3rd and wl btn over 1f out* **25/1**
5 **4** 1 ¾ **Divine Rule (IRE)**[17] 5718 2-9-3 0 .... SteveDrowne 5 65
(H Morrison) *t.k.h: hld up in tch on outer: hdwy 4f out: rdn and sltly hmpd over 2f out: 4th and no ch w ldrs whn edgd rt over 1f out* **12/1**[3]
5 2 ¾ **Royal Talisman** 2-9-3 0 .... LiamKeniry 7 57
(Matthew Salaman) *t.k.h: hld up in midfield: pushed along and outpcd over 2f out: one pce and wl hld fnl 2f* **66/1**
024 **6** 1 ¼ **Flodden (USA)**[31] 5277 2-9-3 76 .... JamieSpencer 10 55
(P F I Cole) *dwlt: sn rcvrd and in tch: hmpd and dropped to rr of main gp after 1f out: rdn and btn over 2f out* **10/3**[2]
7 1 ½ **Swift Blade (IRE)** 2-9-3 0 .... JimCrowley 12 51
(W J Knight) *hld up in tch in midfield: pushed along and outpcd over 2f out: nt clr run and sltly hmpd ent fnl 2f: wl btn after* **50/1**
00 **8** ¾ **Invigilator**[58] 4384 2-9-3 0 .... DaneO'Neill 1 49
(H J L Dunlop) *t.k.h: chsd ldrs: rdn and edging lft over 2f out: sn outpcd: wl btn over 1f out* **66/1**
9 2 ½ **Salaamie** 2-9-3 0 .... KierenFallon 8 44
(E A L Dunlop) *chsd ldrs: sltly hmpd after 1f: rdn and hanging rt over 2f out: sn wknd* **33/1**
0 **10** 6 **Laafhd**[27] 5385 2-8-12 0 .... FergusSweeney 3 25
(A G Newcombe) *s.i.s: bhd: clsd and in tch over 3f out: rdn and wl btn over 2f out* **80/1**
0 **11** 9 **Windsor Knights**[86] 3459 2-9-3 0 .... GregFairley 4 —
(A J Lidderdale) *s.i.s: sn struggling bdly in rr: lost tch 1/2-way: t.o* **80/1**

1m 39.64s (-0.16) **Going Correction** +0.025s/f (Slow) **11** Ran SP% **120.1**
Speed ratings (Par 97): **101,100,93,91,89 87,86,85,83,77 68**
Tote Swingers: 1&2 £5.60, 1&3 £40.20, 2&3 £6.70 CSF £24.02 TOTE £12.40: £1.80, £1.30, £4.90; EX 46.70.
Owner Mrs Sheila Tucker **Bred** Miss Sarah Thompson **Trained** Manton, Wilts

FOCUS
Just a fair maiden, with the winner coming into this officially rated 75. The pace seemed to slow at about halfway.

NOTEBOOK
Aciano(IRE), upped in trip, switched to Polytrack, returned to a galloping track, and with the blinkers removed, battled on well to get the better of a protracted dual with the runner-up, yet wasn't hit with the whip at any stage. These conditions clearly suited and maybe he'll go on from this. (op 14-1 tchd 20-1)
Terdaad(IRE), who raced on the wrong side of the track on debut over 7f at York, when reported to have been unsuited by ground on the fast side, showed improved form. He had the run of the race, seeming to slow the pace down in front by about halfway, and pulled clear of all bar the winner in the straight. There's some size about him and he may do better again. (op 4-7, tchd 4-6 and 8-13 in a place)
Plattsburgh(USA) achieved an RPR of just 43 on debut and, although this was better, he was beaten a long way. (op 33-1)
Divine Rule(IRE) raced wider than ideal and was below the form he showed over C&D on debut.
Royal Talisman made a respectable introduction.
Flodden(USA) had today's runner-up well behind at York on his previous start, but things didn't go his way this time. Having missed the break, he was soon rushed up to try and recover, but quickly became short of room and lost his position. He never recovered. (op 3-1 tchd 7-2)

6250 MICRO-P 30TH ANNIVERSARY MAIDEN FILLIES' STKS 1m 4f (P)
4:00 (4:00) (Class 4) 3-4-Y-O **£3,885** (£1,156; £577; £288) **Stalls** High

Form RPR
4-33 **1** **Giants Play (USA)**[59] 4341 3-8-12 81 .... RyanMoore 3 84+
(Sir Michael Stoute) *chsd ldrs: rdn and qcknd to ld over 2f out: clr and in command fr wl over 1f out: rdn out* **5/6**[1]
43 **2** 2 ¾ **Dazzle The Crowd (IRE)**[10] 5902 3-8-12 0 .... WilliamBuick 8 79+
(J H M Gosden) *in tch: chsd ldng pair over 5f out: rdn over 2f out: chsd clr wnr fr wl over 1f out: kpt on same pce and no imp* **7/2**[2]
5-32 **3** 4 **Strictly Lambada**[25] 5445 3-8-12 75 .... FrankieDettori 6 73
(J H M Gosden) *led tl over 10f out: lft in ld again 8f out: rdn and hdd 2f out: sn btn: 3rd and no ch fr over 1f out* **11/2**[3]
0 **4** 1 ¼ **Gakalina (IRE)**[157] 1356 3-8-12 0 .... TomQueally 7 71
(J Noseda) *in tch in midfield: nudged along 5f out: rdn and outpcd over 2f out: wnt 4th but wl btn 1f out* **20/1**
4 **5** 3 ¾ **Hibba (USA)**[36] 5116 3-8-12 0 .... RichardHills 9 65
(M P Tregoning) *hld up in tch in midfield: rdn and outpcd jst over 2f out: 4th and wl btn over 1f out* **12/1**
30 **6** 4 ½ **Pursuit Of Reason**[19] 5665 3-8-12 0 .... PatDobbs 2 58
(G L Moore) *hmpd s and s.i.s: hld up in last trio: rdn and lost tch over 2f out* **80/1**
0 **7** 7 **Precious Spring (IRE)**[102] 2890 3-8-12 0 .... KierenFallon 5 47
(E A L Dunlop) *rn green in last trio: taken wd 8f out: lost tch over 2f out* **33/1**
0- **8** ¾ **Velvet Nayef**[423] 4270 4-9-1 0 .... SimonPearce(5) 1 45
(J Pearce) *wnt bdly rt s and s.i.s: a last: rdn and lost tch over 2f out* **100/1**
5 **9** 2 ¼ **Moonlight Mischief (IRE)**[28] 5366 3-8-12 0 .... ShaneKelly 4 42
(B J Meehan) *taken down early and ponied to s: t.k.h: chsd ldr tl led over 10f out: rn green and hdd bnd 8f out: chsd ldr after tl wknd rapidly over 2f out* **16/1**

2m 33.31s (-1.19) **Going Correction** +0.025s/f (Slow)
WFA 3 from 4yo 8lb **9** Ran SP% **115.7**
Speed ratings (Par 102): **104,102,99,98,96 93,88,88,86**
Tote Swingers: 1&2 £2.30, 1&3 £2.30, 2&3 £3.20 CSF £3.75 TOTE £1.90: £1.40, £1.50, £1.20; EX 5.10.
Owner Mrs R J Jacobs **Bred** Swettenham Stud **Trained** Newmarket, Suffolk

FOCUS
A reasonable older-horse maiden for the time of year, but they finished strung out. The pace seemed just modest through the opening stages, but the time was a respectable 0.57 seconds slower than the following Class 3 handicap won by the progressive Home Advantage. The winner and third were close to form with the runner-up posting a 9lb personal best.
Strictly Lambada Official explanation: jockey said bit pulled through
Moonlight Mischief(IRE) Official explanation: jockey said bit pulled through

6251 BROTHER 141 H'CAP 1m 4f (P)
4:30 (4:31) (Class 3) (0-95,90) 3-Y-O **£6,281** (£1,869; £934; £466) **Stalls** High

Form RPR
1141 **1** **Home Advantage**[12] 5868 3-8-12 **81** .... SteveDrowne 5 92+
(R Charlton) *t.k.h early: hld up in tch: rdn and effrt to ld over 1f out: r.o wl fnl f: rdn out* **6/4**[1]
1460 **2** 1 **Into Wain (USA)**[30] 5291 3-9-7 **90** .... NeilCallan 6 99
(D M Simcock) *led: rdn and hung lft ent fnl 2f: hdd over 1f out: kpt battling on u.p tl no ex and btn fnl 100yds* **16/1**
215 **3** 1 ¼ **Sagamore**[28] 5371 3-9-5 **88** .... WilliamBuick 7 95
(J H M Gosden) *chsd ldng pair: rdn ent fnl 2f: stl pressing ldrs whn short of room and squeezed out wl over 1f out: styd on same pce fnl f* **10/3**[2]
6114 **4** ¾ **Nave (USA)**[17] 5727 3-9-5 **88** .... GregFairley 1 94
(M Johnston) *dwlt: in tch in last pair: rdn and effrt on outer over 2f out: styd on same pce u.p fr over 1f out* **8/1**
3214 **5** 6 **Chelsea Morning (USA)**[25] 5444 3-8-7 **76** oh1 .... KierenFallon 3 72
(B W Hills) *chsd ldr: rdn 3f out: drvn and lost 2nd whn short of room and swtchd rt 2f out: wknd over 1f out: eased wl ins fnl f* **14/1**
1-54 **6** 14 **Hymnsheet**[17] 5723 3-9-5 **88** .... (t) RyanMoore 4 71
(Sir Michael Stoute) *awkward s and s.i.s: in tch in last pair: rdn and effrt on inner jst over 2f out: btn over 1f out: eased heavily ins fnl f* **7/2**[3]

2m 32.74s (-1.76) **Going Correction** +0.025s/f (Slow) **6** Ran SP% **109.0**
Speed ratings (Par 105): **106,105,104,104,100 90**
Tote Swingers: 1&2 £4.00, 1&3 £1.90, 2&3 £6.20 CSF £24.60 TOTE £2.10: £1.20, £1.90; EX 22.80.
Owner K Abdulla **Bred** Juddmonte Farms Ltd **Trained** Beckhampton, Wilts
■ Stewards' Enquiry : Neil Callan two-day ban: careless riding (Oct 4-5)

FOCUS
A decent enough handicap and the pace seemed fair. The form is rated on the positive side with the winner continuing his progress.

NOTEBOOK

Home Advantage, 4lb higher than when winning over C&D last time, ground out his fifth success from his last six starts, finding plenty having briefly looked in trouble around the turn into the straight, and his effort is all the more creditable considering he apparently lost a shoe. He's now likely to be put away until next year, when he can be expected to continue his progression. (op 5-4 tchd 6-5)

Into Wain(USA), the winner of two of his three previous starts on Polytrack, didn't help himself by hanging left in the straight but stuck on well behind the improving winner. (op 12-1)

Sagamore was keeping on, upsides the winner and in with every chance, when short of room over 1f out. He has more to offer. (op 9-2)

Nave(USA) ran creditably, but he's yet to prove himself fully effective on Polytrack. (op 15-2)

Chelsea Morning(USA) looked held when short of room inside the final 2f. (tchd 16-1)

Hymnsheet ran as if there was seemingly something amiss. (op 4-1)

6252 COMPUTING.CO.UK H'CAP — 1m (P)

5:00 (5:02) (Class 4) (0-85,85) 3-Y-0+ — £3,885 (£1,156; £577; £288) Stalls High

Form — RPR

6215 **1** **Night Lily (IRE)**[35] 5149 4-9-4 82 .... JohnFahy(5) 8 — 91
(P W D'Arcy) *hld up in midfield: effrt whn pushed rt and nt clr run 2f out: sn swtchd lft and gd hdwy over 1f out: str run to ld ins fnl f: sn clr: readily* — 10/1

2600 **2** 2 ¼ **Prince Of Thebes (IRE)**[16] 5750 9-9-2 75 .... NeilCallan 11 — 79
(M J Attwater) *hld up in tch: rdn and swtchd rt over 1f out: nt pce of wnr ins fnl f but kpt on wl to take 2nd wl towards fin* — 25/1

054 **3** nk **Nezami (IRE)**[20] 5627 5-9-6 79 .... DaneO'Neill 1 — 82
(J Akehurst) *chsd ldr: rdn and qcknd to ld 2f out: clr and drvn over 1f out: hdd and nt pce of wnr ins fnl f: lost 2nd towards fin* — 40/1

-000 **4** 2 **Burma Rock (IRE)**[10] 5919 4-9-3 76 .... KierenFallon 7 — 75
(L M Cumani) *in tch: sltly hmpd bnd 5f out: rdn and effrt whn edgd rt ent fnl 2f: sn outpcd: rallied and kpt on ins fnl f* — 16/1

6660 **5** 1 ¼ **Getcarter**[16] 5750 4-9-5 78 .... RyanMoore 5 — 79+
(R Hannon) *stdd after s: hld up in rr: effrt and nt clr run whn swtchd lft 2f out: hdwy ent fnl f: nt clr run and swtchd lft again 1f out: r.o wl: nvr able to chal* — 15/2[3]

0600 **6** nk **Halsion Chancer**[10] 5919 6-9-4 77 .... JohnEgan 3 — 72
(J R Best) *in tch in midfield: rdn over 3f out: no prog tl swtchd lft over 1f out: kpt on u.p fnl f: nvr gng pce to rch ldrs* — 33/1

11- **7** ½ **Eolith**[381] 5639 3-9-7 84 .... JimCrowley 10 — 78
(W J Knight) *chsd ldrs: rdn and unable qck jst over 2f out: wknd ent fnl f* — 11/4[1]

0520 **8** 1 ¼ **Rule Breaker (IRE)**[31] 5264 3-9-8 85 .... GregFairley 13 — 76
(M Johnston) *led tl rdn and outpcd 2f out: lost 2nd 1f out: wknd fnl f* — 8/1

2401 **9** 1 ½ **My Best Bet**[17] 5716 4-9-8 81 .... TomQueally 2 — 68
(Stef Higgins) *stdd after s: hld up towards rr: hdwy but stl plenty to do over 1f out: nt clr run and swtchd lft jst ins fnl f: nvr trbld ldrs* — 14/1

000 **10** ¾ **Hurricane Hymnbook (USA)**[35] 5142 5-9-6 79 .... TonyCulhane 9 — 65
(W J Musson) *stdd after s: hld up in last pair: rdn and no prog wl over 1f out: swtchd lft and past btn horses wl ins fnl f: n.d* — 20/1

0-05 **11** 4 ½ **Cool Hand Jake**[17] 5716 4-9-5 78 .... FergusSweeney 14 — 53
(P J Makin) *chsd ldrs: rdn over 2f out: wknd u.p 2f out: wl btn and eased wl ins fnl f* — 12/1

5500 **12** ½ **Follow The Flag (IRE)**[10] 5913 6-9-10 83 ....(p) SebSanders 6 — 57
(A J McCabe) *hld up in last pair: n.d* — 20/1

0400 **13** 1 **Highly Regal (IRE)**[16] 5750 5-9-9 82 ....(b) LiamKeniry 12 — 54
(R A Teal) *in tch in midfield: rdn and unable qck over 2f out: wknd wl over 1f out* — 10/1

-210 **14** 6 **Point Out (USA)**[74] 3824 3-9-8 85 .... WilliamBuick 4 — 43
(J H M Gosden) *s.i.s: in rr tl hdwy on outer 5f out: chsd ldrs 5f out: rdn and unable qck whn pushed rt and hmpd 2f out: sn btn: bhd and eased ins fnl f* — 9/2[2]

1m 38.62s (-1.18) **Going Correction** +0.025s/f (Slow)
WFA 3 from 4yo+ 4lb — 14 Ran SP% **124.9**
Speed ratings (Par 105): **106,103,103,101,100 99,99,98,96,95 91,90,89,83**
Tote Swingers: 1&2 £65.40, 1&3 £26.90, 2&3 £44.60 CSF £251.40 CT £9457.75 TOTE £7.40: £2.60, £7.30, £10.00; EX 241.00.
Owner K Snell **Bred** Keith Wills **Trained** Newmarket, Suffolk
■ Stewards' Enquiry : Kieren Fallon caution: careless riding
William Buick one-day ban: careless riding (Oct 4)

FOCUS
This looked a fair, competitive handicap. It was well run and the winner was rated better than ever.
Getcarter Official explanation: jockey said colt was denied a clear run

6253 CRN BUSINESS CLUB H'CAP — 6f (P)

5:30 (5:31) (Class 4) (0-85,85) 3-Y-0 — £3,885 (£1,156; £577; £288) Stalls High

Form — RPR

2124 **1** **Barq (IRE)**[9] 5964 3-9-2 80 ....(tp) FrankieDettori 5 — 93+
(Saeed Bin Suroor) *led for 1f: chsd ldr after: rdn 2f out: hung rt and led ins fnl f: rdn out* — 9/2[3]

0004 **2** ¾ **Edinburgh Knight (IRE)**[27] 5383 3-9-7 85 .... TonyCulhane 3 — 96+
(P W D'Arcy) *stdd after s: hld up in rr: gd hdwy to chal jst over 1f out: rdn to ld jst ins fnl f: sn hdd and styd on same pce towards fin* — 5/2[2]

0211 **3** 1 ¼ **Dubai Media (CAN)**[25] 5454 3-9-6 84 .... KierenFallon 8 — 95+
(E A L Dunlop) *hld up in midfield on outer: hdwy and nt clr run over 1f out: chsd ldng trio 1f out: running on whn squeezed out and snatched up ins fnl f: swtchd lft and r.o fnl 100yds: unable to chal* — 9/4[1]

4022 **4** 1 **Freddie's Girl (USA)**[25] 5454 3-8-12 76 .... SebSanders 12 — 80
(Stef Higgins) *chsd ldrs: rdn to chal jst over 2f out: led wl over 1f out: drvn and hdd jst ins fnl f: keeping on same pce whn sltly hmpd fnl 150yds* — 14/1

3360 **5** ¾ **Edgewater (IRE)**[16] 5754 3-9-2 80 .... DaneO'Neill 6 — 81
(J Akehurst) *in tch in midfield early: grad lost pl and in last pair over 2f out: hdwy on outer over 1f out: styd on wl u.p: nt rch ldrs* — 25/1

2404 **6** nk **Rule Of Nature**[40] 4963 3-9-4 82 .... RyanMoore 1 — 85+
(Sir Michael Stoute) *hld up in last pair: n.m.r and stl plenty to do 2f out: swtchd lft over 1f out: r.o wl u.p fnl f: nt gng pce to rch ldrs* — 7/1

1050 **7** 1 ½ **Clifton Bridge**[50] 4625 3-9-1 79 ....(b) JimCrowley 2 — 75
(R M Beckett) *in tch towards rr: effrt and rdn towards inner 2f out: kpt on fnl f: nvr gng pce to trble ldrs* — 40/1

0356 **8** nk **Red Avalanche (IRE)**[9] 5967 3-9-4 82 .... TomQueally 9 — 77
(P F I Cole) *t.k.h: hld up in tch in midfield: n.m.r and hanging rt over 2f out: lost pl and towards rr 2f out: hdwy 1f out: kpt on fnl f: no threat to ldrs* — 33/1

2046 **9** 1 ¼ **The Strig**[18] 5678 3-8-11 75 .... WilliamCarson 10 — 66
(S C Williams) *dwlt: hld up towards rr: rdn and effrt on inner 2f out: no prog and btn 1f out* — 66/1

6660 **10** ½ **Haadeeth**[41] 4930 3-9-4 82 ....(b1) RichardHills 11 — 71
(M P Tregoning) *dwlt: sn dashed up to ld after 1f: rdn and hdd wl over 1f out: wknd qckly jst over 1f out* — 10/1

0014 **11** 2 ½ **Crown (IRE)**[34] 5182 3-9-6 84 .... IanMongan 4 — 65
(Miss Jo Crowley) *chsd ldrs on outer: wknd u.p over 1f out: wl btn fnl f* — 33/1

155- **12** 1 ¼ **Arabian Pride**[367] 6063 3-9-3 81 ....(b1) NeilCallan 7 — 58
(D M Simcock) *dwlt and pushed along early: sn rcvrd and in tch in midfield: rdn over 2f out: wknd qckly wl over 1f out: bhd fnl f* — 50/1

1m 12.28s (-0.82) **Going Correction** +0.025s/f (Slow) — 12 Ran SP% **121.4**
Speed ratings (Par 103): **106,105,103,102,101 100,98,98,96,95 92,90**
Tote Swingers: 1&2 £4.20, 1&3 £3.20, 2&3 £3.00 CSF £15.77 CT £33.22 TOTE £7.30: £2.90, £1.50, £1.10; EX 21.50 Place 6: £67.68 Place 5: £31.40..
Owner Godolphin **Bred** Darley **Trained** Newmarket, Suffolk

FOCUS
A decent sprint handicap with the first three all progressive or lightly raced. The fourth is a solid guide.
T/Plt: £164.70 to a £1 stake. Pool of £66,664 - 295.47 winning tickets. T/Qpdt: £135.70 to a £1 stake. Pool of £3,798 - 20.70 winning tickets. SP

5629 LEICESTER (R-H)

Monday, September 20

OFFICIAL GOING: Good (good to firm in places on round course; good to soft in places on straight course)
Wind: Light half-behind Weather: Overcast

6254 E B F KEGWORTH NOVICE STKS — 7f 9y

2:20 (2:21) (Class 4) 2-Y-0 — £4,533 (£1,348; £674; £336) Stalls Low

Form — RPR

1 **1** **Vanguard Dream**[9] 5954 2-9-3 0 .... JimmyFortune 4 — 89+
(R Hannon) *mde all: rdn over 1f out: edgd rt: r.o* — 4/9[1]

1 **2** 2 **Try The Chance**[52] 4528 2-9-0 72 .... ChrisCatlin 1 — 79
(M R Channon) *chsd ldrs: rdn and hung rt fr over 2f out: wnt 2nd ins fnl f: styd on same pce* — 8/1[3]

6210 **3** ½ **Tinkertown (IRE)**[24] 5490 2-9-3 83 .... EddieAhern 2 — 81
(P F I Cole) *chsd wnr: rdn over 1f out: edgd rt and styd on same pce ins fnl f* — 11/1

4 3 ¼ **Dean Swift** 2-8-12 0 .... MartinDwyer 3 — 67+
(B J Meehan) *pushed along in last pl but in tch: rdn over 1f out: no ex fnl f* — 9/2[2]

1m 25.14s (-1.06) **Going Correction** -0.125s/f (Firm) — 4 Ran SP% **106.9**
Speed ratings (Par 97): **101,98,98,94**
CSF £4.37 TOTE £1.30; EX 2.80.
Owner Malih L Al Basti **Bred** Malih L Al Basti **Trained** East Everleigh, Wilts

FOCUS
A decent little novice stakes, despite the small field.

NOTEBOOK

Vanguard Dream made it 2-2 with a workmanlike success. Making all, as he had done over 1m at Goodwood on his debut, he always seemed to be doing enough from over 1f out. He holds no notable entries, but is a likable sort. (op 1-2 tchd 2-5)

Try The Chance, an Irish 2,000 Guineas entry who won over 5.5f on his debut at Bath, didn't make things easy for his rider by hanging under pressure, but he was never going to beat the winner anyway. There's not a lot of him and he can expect a busy end to his campaign. (op 13-2)

Tinkertown(IRE), disappointing on soft ground in a Newmarket nursery latest, looked vulnerable to these and ran about as well as could have been expected. (op 9-1 tchd 12-1)

Dean Swift, who is entered in the Dewhurst and Racing Post Trophy, was expected to need this and he did. He showed distinct signs of inexperience and, like many runners from this yard, should come on a ton. (op 11-2 tchd 7-1)

6255 GOLDEN HAND (S) STKS — 7f 9y

2:50 (2:50) (Class 6) 3-Y-0 — £1,942 (£578; £288; £144) Stalls Low

Form — RPR

6500 **1** **Scooby Dee**[49] 4651 3-8-6 43 ....(p) DaraghO'Donohoe 18 — 50
(R M Whitaker) *sn outpcd: hdwy u.p over 1f out: styd on to ld wl ins fnl f* — 25/1

020 **2** nk **Katmai River (IRE)**[19] 5658 3-8-11 48 .... MartinDwyer 16 — 54
(M D I Usher) *a.p: rdn to ld over 1f out: sn hung lft: hdd wl ins fnl f* — 22/1

00-0 **3** 1 ¼ **Dudley**[39] 4989 3-8-11 46 ....(p) CathyGannon 17 — 51
(J G Portman) *s.i.s: sn prom: rdn over 1f out: styd on same pce ins fnl f* — 66/1

1046 **4** 2 ¼ **Thaliwarru**[30] 5299 3-9-2 65 ....(p) AdamKirby 14 — 50
(J R Gask) *prom: rdn and hung lft over 1f out: nt run on* — 11/4[2]

1040 **5** hd **Cereal Killer (IRE)**[56] 4426 3-9-2 66 ....(b) JimmyFortune 12 — 49
(R Hannon) *mid-div: pushed along and hdwy 1/2-way: rdn over 1f out: no ex ins fnl f* — 9/4[1]

0100 **6** 1 ½ **Ellen Vannin (IRE)**[21] 5580 3-8-6 56 ....(b1) AmyScott(5) 15 — 40
(Eve Johnson Houghton) *chsd ldrs: rdn over 1f out: no ex ins fnl f* — 16/1

5600 **7** 2 ½ **Sandy Toes**[49] 4651 3-8-13 42 .... AndrewHeffernan(3) 5 — 38
(J A Glover) *hld up: rdn over 2f out: hdwy over 1f out: nt trble ldrs* — 100/1

0460 **8** hd **Truly Magic**[35] 5158 3-8-4 48 .... RichardRowe(7) 4 — 33
(H J L Dunlop) *sn outpcd: styd on fnl f: nvr nrr* — 18/1

0546 **9** hd **Zelos Spirit**[22] 5559 3-8-3 42 .... MartinLane(3) 11 — 27
(Rae Guest) *chsd ldrs: rdn over 2f out: wknd over 1f out* — 25/1

0406 **10** ½ **Music Lover**[11] 5898 3-8-11 58 .... LukeMorris 9 — 31
(R A Harris) *chsd ldr: led 1/2-way: rdn and hdd over 1f out: wknd ins fnl f* — 16/1

5003 **11** 2 ¾ **Thewinnatakesitall**[14] 5816 3-8-6 47 ....(p) AndrewElliott 7 — 19
(N Tinkler) *prom: racd keenly: rdn and wknd over 1f out* — 20/1

6300 **12** 3 ¼ **Thoughtful (IRE)**[17] 5730 3-8-6 44 .... FrannyNorton 3 — 10
(J W Hills) *s.i.s: hld up: rdn 1/2-way: sme hdwy fnl f: sn eased* — 25/1

451 **13** 2 ¼ **Frequency**[24] 5494 3-9-2 67 .... J-PGuillambert 8 — 14
(P Howling) *led to 1/2-way: rdn and wknd over 1f out* — 6/1[3]

-000 **14** 3 ¾ **Battleship Grey**[19] 5668 3-8-11 0 .... ChrisCatlin 1 — —
(D K Ivory) *s.i.s: bhd fr 1/2-way* — 80/1

5600 **15** 5 **Deely Plaza**[28] 5357 3-8-11 58 ....(b1) RobertWinston 6 — —
(J A Glover) *prom: wknd and eased fr over 1f out* — 22/1

05 **16** 26 **Mr Shammie**[20] 5645 3-8-11 0 .... MickyFenton 2 — —
(M G Quinlan) *s.i.s: sn prom: lost pl over 4f out: sn wl bhd: t.o* — 100/1

1m 26.08s (-0.12) **Going Correction** -0.125s/f (Firm) — 16 Ran SP% **118.5**
Speed ratings (Par 99): **95,94,93,90,90 88,85,85,85,84 81,77,75,71,65 35**
Tote Swingers: 1&2 £40.30, 1&3 £161.90, 2&3 £78.40 CSF £460.71 TOTE £32.30: £6.70, £6.20, £15.00; EX 623.80 TRIFECTA Not won..There was no bid for the winner.
Owner Paul Davies (H'gte) **Bred** Hellwood Stud Farm & Paul Davies (h'Gate) **Trained** Scarcroft, W Yorks

The Form Book, Raceform Ltd, Compton, RG20 6NL

FOCUS
Those with a high draw, hence racing more down the centre of the track, came to the fore in this big-field seller. Weak and dubious form, rated around the winner.
Scooby Dee Official explanation: trainer had no explanation regarding the apparent improvement in form
Frequency Official explanation: trainer said gelding returned distressed
Deely Plaza Official explanation: jockey said gelding hung right-handed

6256 HARRY SPOONER 100TH BIRTHDAY H'CAP — 5f 2y
3:20 (3:22) (Class 3) (0-95,91) 3-Y-0+ **£5,828** (£1,734; £866; £432) **Stalls** Low

Form RPR
2204 **1** **Noodles Blue Boy**[12] 5855 4-8-12 **82** FrannyNorton 8 92
(Ollie Pears) *led: hdd over 3f out: led again 2f out: sn rdn: hdd 1f out: rallied to ld ins fnl f: r.o gamely* **14/1**
003 **2** *hd* **Desert Phantom (USA)**[6] 6063 4-9-2 **89** MartinLane(3) 11 98
(D M Simcock) *chsd ldrs: rdn and ev ch ins fnl f: r.o* **3/1**[1]
0005 **3** *1 ½* **Fathom Five (IRE)**[21] 5589 6-9-7 **91** GeorgeBaker 13 95
(C F Wall) *chsd ldrs: led 1f out: hdd ins fnl f: no ex nr fin* **8/1**
1040 **4** *2 ½* **Olynard (IRE)**[17] 5731 4-9-3 **90** EJMcNamara(3) 12 85
(R M Beckett) *hld up in tch: rdn over 1f out: edgd rt and styd on same pce fnl f* **9/2**[3]
0060 **5** *hd* **Cornus**[2] 6198 8-8-6 **81** (be) AdamBeschizza(5) 7 75
(A J McCabe) *hld up: rdn over 1f out: r.o ins fnl f: nt rch ldrs* **16/1**
0312 **6** *1 ¼* **Barons Spy (IRE)**[8] 5995 9-8-10 **80** JamesDoyle 10 70
(R J Price) *mid-div: hdwy 1/2-way: rdn over 1f out: styd on same pce* **12/1**
0020 **7** *1 ¾* **Coleorton Choice**[24] 5495 4-8-7 **77** (p) HayleyTurner 3 60
(R Hollinshead) *prom: rdn over 1f out: wknd fnl f* **20/1**
4003 **8** *1 ¼* **Piscean (USA)**[9] 5966 5-8-13 **83** (p) StevieDonohoe 2 62
(T Keddy) *s.i.s: outpcd: nvr nrr* **14/1**
1122 **9** *nse* **La Fortunata**[21] 5589 3-8-12 **83** AndreaAtzeni 5 62
(Mike Murphy) *w wnr: led over 3f out: rdn and hdd 2f out: wknd fnl f* **4/1**[2]
5310 **10** *2 ¼* **Walvis Bay (IRE)**[34] 5183 3-9-1 **86** MickyFenton 1 57
(T P Tate) *chsd ldrs: pushed along and hung rt fr 1/2-way: wknd over 1f out* **7/1**
3401 **11** *1 ½* **Evelyn May (IRE)**[66] 4090 4-8-0 **77** oh2 DanielHarris(7) 4 42
(B W Hills) *hld up: nt clr run and swtchd lft 1/2-way: sn bhd* **25/1**
4040 **12** *7* **Tourist**[176] 1032 5-8-10 **80** RobertWinston 6 20
(D Shaw) *prom tl rdn and wknd wl over 1f out* **33/1**

58.79 secs (-1.21) **Going Correction** -0.125s/f (Firm)
WFA 3 from 4yo+ 1lb 12 Ran SP% **125.3**
Speed ratings (Par 107): **104,103,101,97,96 94,92,90,90,86 84,72**
Tote Swingers: 1&2 £15.30, 1&3 £18.30, 2&3 £5.00 CSF £57.82 CT £381.40 TOTE £15.00: £4.50, £1.50, £4.10; EX 69.50 Trifecta £248.20 Part won. Pool: £335.46 - 0.10 winning units..
Owner Keith Taylor & Keith West **Bred** Fifehead Farms M C Denning **Trained** Norton, N Yorks

FOCUS
A good-quality sprint handicap. Those racing centre-to-far side were once again at an advantage. A length personal best from the winner.

NOTEBOOK
Noodles Blue Boy, not beaten far off this mark behind a subsequent winner at Doncaster last time, has been running well pretty much all season and he showed a gritty attitude to get back up close home. He will be targeted toward the Portland next season, with the unique distance of that race (5.5f) said to be ideal. (op 12-1 tchd 11-1)
Desert Phantom(USA), third in a conditions race at Yarmouth last week, was soon prominent and had his chance, but couldn't repel the winner close home. He looks to have returned an improved performer. (op 5-1)
Fathom Five(IRE) ran a fine race under top weight, quickening well to lead 1f out but in the end not staying on as strongly as the front two. (op 6-1)
Olynard(IRE) is more effective over 6f and he lacked the pace on this return to the minimum trip. (op 15-2 tchd 8-1)
Cornus, making a quick reappearance, was another staying on late. (op 18-1 tchd 20-1)
Barons Spy(IRE) had been in good form but was never really going here. (tchd 11-1)
La Fortunata is all about speed and she failed to run her race on this slow surface. Official explanation: jockey said filly had no more to give (op 13-2)
Walvis Bay(IRE) hasn't gone on from his Ripon success and probably needs a faster surface. (op 8-1)

6257 HENRY ALKEN CLAIMING STKS — 1m 1f 218y
3:50 (3:50) (Class 6) 3-4-Y-0 **£1,942** (£578; £288; £144) **Stalls** High

Form RPR
4400 **1** **Essexbridge**[2] 6202 3-9-4 74 (b) JimmyFortune 3 78+
(R Hannon) *sn led: rdn clr over 1f out: eased last strides* **4/1**[3]
6063 **2** *2 ¼* **Layla's Lexi**[6] 6054 3-8-10 68 EddieAhern 4 64
(Ian Williams) *hld up in tch: rdn to chse wnr over 1f out: sn hung rt: styd on* **9/4**[2]
5006 **3** *7* **Second Brook (IRE)**[20] 5631 3-8-9 48 LukeMorris 5 49
(R Hollinshead) *s.i.s: hld up: hdwy u.p over 3f out: no imp fnl 2f* **40/1**
4053 **4** *5* **Marafong**[5] 6094 3-8-2 48 AdamBeschizza(5) 2 37
(Miss J Feilden) *chsd ldrs: rdn over 3f out: wknd 2f out* **33/1**
3242 **5** *1 ½* **Peace Corps**[6] 6055 4-9-9 75 (vt) PatCosgrave 6 44
(J R Boyle) *led early: chsd wnr tl rdn over 1f out: sn hung rt and wknd* **10/11**[1]
0650 **6** *3 ¾* **Massachusetts**[7] 6022 3-8-7 45 (b) CathyGannon 7 27
(B G Powell) *chsd ldrs: rdn over 4f out: wknd over 3f out* **66/1**
6-00 **7** *17* **Le Petit Vigier**[67] 1922 4-9-2 42 (tp) AndrewElliott 1 —
(P F Holmes) *s.i.s: sn in tch: wknd 4f out: t.o* **100/1**

2m 6.06s (-1.84) **Going Correction** -0.125s/f (Firm)
WFA 3 from 4yo 6lb 7 Ran SP% **111.0**
Speed ratings (Par 101): **102,100,94,90,89 86,72**
Tote Swingers: 1&2 £1.80, 1&3 £6.30, 2&3 £7.50 CSF £12.54 TOTE £5.90: £2.40, £2.30; EX 14.40.
Owner Morecombe Elsom Notley Burnham **Bred** Whatton Manor Stud **Trained** East Everleigh, Wilts

FOCUS
Only three of these mattered, and two of them, though not the favourite, drew well clear. It is doubtful if the winner had to match his recent best.
Peace Corps Official explanation: jockey said regarding easing inside final furlong that the gelding was choking and had no more to give.

6258 ASTON FLAMVILLE FILLIES' NURSERY (DIV I) — 5f 218y
4:20 (4:24) (Class 5) (0-75,74) 2-Y-0 **£1,942** (£578; £288; £144) **Stalls** Low

Form RPR
0443 **1** **Country Waltz**[6] 6052 2-8-1 **54** CathyGannon 6 61
(M R Channon) *mde all: rdn over 1f out: edgd rt ins fnl f: r.o* **4/1**[3]
2250 **2** *1 ¾* **Russian Ice**[73] 3864 2-8-8 **61** SamHitchcott 10 63
(D K Ivory) *chsd ldrs: rdn over 3f out: r.o to go 2nd wl ins fnl f: nt trble wnr* **28/1**
1300 **3** *½* **Child Bride**[11] 5882 2-9-0 **74** DuilioDaSilva(7) 8 75
(P F I Cole) *chsd wnr: rdn over 1f out: styd on same pce ins fnl f* **10/3**[2]
036 **4** *1* **Shes Rosie**[12] 5865 2-8-11 **64** LukeMorris 2 62
(J G M O'Shea) *plld hrd and prom: rdn over 1f out: styd on same pce* **10/1**
523 **5** *11* **Park Ballet (IRE)**[31] 5255 2-9-5 **72** RobertWinston 7 37+
(J G Portman) *awkward leaving stalls: hdwy over 3f out: rdn and wknd over 1f out* **15/8**[1]
600 **6** *2 ¼* **Shutupandrive**[14] 5808 2-7-5 **51** oh3 HarryBentley(7) 9 9
(M D I Usher) *chsd ldrs: rdn 1/2-way: wknd over 1f out* **33/1**
0060 **7** *70* **Miss Moneypenni**[6] 6052 2-8-7 **63** MartinLane(3) 1 —
(N P Littmoden) *unruly bhd stalls: prom tl wknd over 2f out: eased: t.o* **25/1**

1m 12.8s (-0.20) **Going Correction** -0.125s/f (Firm) 7 Ran SP% **97.2**
Speed ratings (Par 92): **96,93,93,91,77 74,—**
Tote Swingers: 1&2 £7.20, 1&3 £2.20, 2&3 £5.70 CSF £69.52 CT £236.70 TOTE £4.10: £2.20, £10.60; EX 44.60 Trifecta £128.10 Part won. Pool: £173.12 - 0.42 winning units..
Owner Ridgeway Downs Racing **Bred** Mike Channon Bloodstock Ltd **Trained** West Ilsley, Berks
■ Jambo Bibi (5/1) was withdrawn after refusing to enter the stalls. Deduct 15p in the £ under R4.

FOCUS
The first division of a moderate nursery.

NOTEBOOK
Country Waltz ran creditably off this mark at Lingfield last week and the more forceful ride here worked in her favour. The slow ground was clearly not a bother and she's expected to improve for 7f. (op 7-2 tchd 3-1 and 9-2)
Russian Ice has been struggling in sellers the last twice, but seemed much better suited by slower ground here and recorded an improved effort. (op 16-1 tchd 33-1)
Child Bride ran well off top weight and will probably benefit from a faster surface. (op 3-1 tchd 11-4 and 7-2)
Shes Rosie showed improved form on this nursery debut, despite not settling. (op 15-2 tchd 12-1)
Park Ballet(IRE), well backed beforehand, was very awkward at the gate, costing her vital ground, and despite making a swift forward move, it left its mark at the business end. Official explanation: jockey said filly lost its action (op 4-1)
Miss Moneypenni Official explanation: jockey said filly never travelled

6259 ASTON FLAMVILLE FILLIES' NURSERY (DIV II) — 5f 218y
4:50 (4:53) (Class 5) (0-75,74) 2-Y-0 **£1,942** (£578; £288; £144) **Stalls** Low

Form RPR
015 **1** **Speedfit Girl (IRE)**[23] 5537 2-9-1 **68** PhilipRobinson 6 75
(G G Margarson) *led 1f: swtchd towards centre over 4f out: chsd ldrs: rdn to ld ins fnl f: r.o* **7/2**[2]
0002 **2** *2* **Three Scoops**[26] 5412 2-7-9 **51** oh3 (t) SophieDoyle(3) 10 52
(D J S Ffrench Davis) *chsd ldr in centre to over 4f out: remained handy: rdn over 1f out: styd on same pce ins fnl f* **10/1**
432 **3** *¾* **Imogen Louise (IRE)**[14] 5808 2-9-3 **70** CathyGannon 7 69
(D Haydn Jones) *hld up in tch: swtchd centre over 4f out: rdn over 2f out: led over 1f out: sn hdd: styd on same pce ins fnl f* **3/1**[1]
2014 **4** *shd* **Ruby Alexander (IRE)**[6] 6052 2-8-7 **63** (b) EJMcNamara(3) 8 61
(R M Beckett) *chsd ldrs: swtchd centre over 4f out: rdn over 1f out: styd on same pce ins fnl f* **14/1**
13 **5** *2 ¼* **Fluvial (IRE)**[17] 5721 2-9-0 **74** AntiocoMurgia(7) 3 66
(Mahmood Al Zarooni) *hld up: swtchd centre over 4f out: styd on ins fnl f: nvr nrr* **7/2**[2]
2020 **6** *1 ¾* **Delira (IRE)**[17] 5720 2-8-11 **64** RobertWinston 9 50
(J G Portman) *led centre: rdn over 2f out: hdd over 1f out: wknd ins fnl f* **11/1**
1440 **7** *½* **Wotsthehurry**[25] 5452 2-8-13 **66** ChrisCatlin 1 51
(M R Channon) *prom: swtchd centre over 4f out: rdn over 1f out: wknd ins fnl f* **20/1**
566 **8** *1 ½* **Illmindu (IRE)**[16] 5763 2-8-0 **53** NickyMackay 4 33
(B R Millman) *hld up: swtchd centre over 4f out: rdn over 1f out: wknd ins fnl f* **18/1**
000 **9** *4* **Tweenie (IRE)**[31] 5255 2-8-1 **54** FrankieMcDonald 2 22
(R Hannon) *prom: swtchd centre over 4f out: rdn over 2f out: wknd over 1f out* **40/1**
0030 **U** **Red Lite (IRE)**[17] 5720 2-8-10 **63** MartinDwyer 5 64+
(B J Meehan) *chsd ldrs: swtchd centre over 4f out: rdn to ld 1f out: sn hdd: stl ev ch whn swvd lft and uns rdr 40yds fr the line* **7/1**[3]

1m 13.05s (0.05) **Going Correction** -0.125s/f (Firm) 10 Ran SP% **118.5**
Speed ratings (Par 92): **94,91,90,90,87 84,84,82,76,—**
Tote Swingers: 1&2 £9.30, 1&3 £4.90, 2&3 £6.30 CSF £39.26 CT £118.32 TOTE £4.40: £1.90, £5.60, £2.30; EX 52.40 Trifecta £159.40 Part won. Pool: £215.46 - 0.42 winning units..
Owner Exors of the Late John Guest **Bred** John Cullinan **Trained** Newmarket, Suffolk
■ Martin Dwyer will miss the rest of the turf season after this fall.

FOCUS
There was a dramatic finish to the second division, with Red Lite, who was still in with every chance, swerving left and unseating Martin Dwyer, leaving the path clear for Speedfit Girl to make a winning nursery debut.

NOTEBOOK
Speedfit Girl(IRE) made a winning nursery debut. A mark of 68 seemed very fair indeed judged on last month's August win and, having chased the early speed, she came with a strong challenged before being left clear late on. There should be more to come and she shapes as though 7f will be within range. (op 7-1)
Three Scoops ran a fine race from 3lb 'wrong', keeping on well and marking herself down as a likely future winner, albeit at a very lowly level. (op 9-1 tchd 12-1)
Imogen Louise(IRE), making her nursery debut, came through to lead approaching the final furlong, but her finishing effort wasn't the strongest. (op 4-1 tchd 5-2)
Ruby Alexander(IRE) again ran creditably without suggesting she's up to winning off this mark. (op 8-1)
Fluvial(IRE) was never going on this nursery debut and probably disliked the cut in the ground, keeping on late. (op 3-1 tchd 5-2)
Delira(IRE) didn't last home having made the running. (op 12-1 tchd 14-1)
Red Lite(IRE), well held off 3lb higher on her nursery debut, was in the process of showing much-improved form and looked set to be involved in a close finish until swerving left and unseating her rider. She's clearly up to winning off this mark, but looks one to tread carefully with. (op 9-1 tchd 10-1)

6260 ADRENALIN TATTOOS, LUTON 10TH ANNIVERSARY H'CAP — 1m 60y
5:20 (5:59) (Class 5) (0-75,75) 3-Y-0+ **£2,266** (£674; £337; £168) **Stalls** High

Form RPR
6101 **1** **Tevez**[12] 5866 5-9-6 **71** (p) CathyGannon 14 81+
(D Donovan) *hld up: swtchd lft and hdwy over 1f out: rdn ins fnl f: str run to ld last strides* **6/1**[3]

-000 **2** *nk* **Willow Dancer (IRE)**[10] 5919 6-9-8 **73**..........................(p) AdamKirby 13 82
(W R Swinburn) *a.p: rdn to ld 2f out: hdd last strides* **17/2**
5552 **3** *hd* **Song To The Moon (IRE)**[24] 5469 3-9-0 **69**.............(v) JimmyFortune 4 78
(A M Balding) *hld up: hdwy over 2f out: rdn and edgd rt over 1f out: edgd rt and ev ch ins fnl f: r.o* **16/1**
20 **4** *1 3/4* **Supa Seeker (USA)**[21] 5609 4-9-7 **72**............................ JamesDoyle 10 77
(A W Carroll) *prom: rdn over 2f out: swtchd rt ins fnl f: styd on* **33/1**
0030 **5** *1 1/2* **Bold Cross (IRE)**[15] 5786 7-9-6 **71**............................. PaulFitzsimons 3 73
(E G Bevan) *prom: rdn over 2f out: styd on same pce ins fnl f* **40/1**
0312 **6** *shd* **Shesells Seashells**[8] 6003 3-9-5 **74**................................ HayleyTurner 8 75
(M L W Bell) *hld up: hdwy over 5f out: nt clr run over 2f out: rdn over 1f out: styd on* **10/3**[1]
6060 **7** *3/4* **Mcconnell (USA)**[157] 1346 5-9-5 **70**.......................... GeorgeBaker 12 70
(G L Moore) *chsd ldr: rdn and ev ch over 1f out: no ex ins fnl f* **4/1**[2]
4315 **8** *1/2* **Lastkingofscotland (IRE)**[23] 5540 4-9-7 **75**..........(v) EJMcNamara(3) 6 73
(C R Dore) *hld up: rdn over 2f out: styd on: nt trble ldrs* **18/1**
4050 **9** *1 1/2* **You've Been Mowed**[13] 5833 4-8-11 **67**................ AdamBeschizza(5) 7 62
(R J Price) *led: rdn and hdd 2f out: wknd fnl f* **25/1**
3023 **10** *3 1/4* **Aflaam (IRE)**[12] 5852 5-9-5 **73**...............................(t) AndrewHeffernan(3) 9 60
(R A Harris) *hld up: racd keenly: hmpd after 1f: hdwy over 2f out: rdn and wknd over 1f out* **8/1**
0000 **11** *hd* **Striding Edge (IRE)**[17] 5716 4-9-0 **72**........................ JamesRogers(7) 2 59
(W R Muir) *hld up: nvr on terms* **33/1**
0306 **12** *6* **Swift Chap**[13] 5833 4-9-8 **73**..(p) DarryllHolland 11 46
(B R Millman) *chsd ldrs: rdn over 3f out: wknd over 1f* **7/1**
000 **13** *1/2* **Mountain Cat (IRE)**[35] 5157 6-9-10 **75**..................... RobertWinston 1 47
(W J Knight) *in rr: pushed along 1/2-way: nvr on terms* **40/1**
1000 **14** *nse* **Very Well Red**[13] 5833 7-9-8 **73**... ChrisCatlin 5 45
(P W Hiatt) *chsd ldrs: rdn over 2f out: wknd over 1f out* **66/1**

1m 43.2s (-1.90) **Going Correction** -0.125s/f (Firm)
WFA 3 from 4yo+ 4lb **14** Ran SP% **118.7**
Speed ratings (Par 103): **104,103,103,101,100 100,99,98,97,94 93,87,87,87**
Tote Swingers: 1&2 £14.20, 1&3 £11.80, 2&3 £31.50 CSF £52.11 CT £805.72 TOTE £5.40: £2.60, £3.70, £5.90; EX 78.90 TRIFECTA Not won..
Owner River Racing **Bred** P A And Mrs D G Sakal **Trained** Newmarket, Suffolk

FOCUS
A moderate handicap, but it was well run and the form is sound. The winner is rated better than ever.

6261 RACING EXCELLENCE "HANDS AND HEELS" APPRENTICE SERIES H'CAP 7f 9y

5:50 (6:22) (Class 5) (0-70,70) 3-Y-0+ **£2,266** (£674; £337; £168) **Stalls** Low

Form RPR
4132 **1** **The Human League**[10] 5905 3-8-13 **65**................................ JulieBurke 5 74+
(M R Channon) *hld up: hdwy 1/2-way: shkn up to ld ins fnl f: r.o* **8/1**[3]
2261 **2** *3/4* **Nisaal (IRE)**[20] 5634 5-9-7 **70**..................................... RyanPowell 10 78+
(A W Carroll) *hld up: hdwy over 2f out: sn pushed along: r.o* **11/2**[1]
5121 **3** *1/2* **Pipers Piping (IRE)**[10] 5927 4-8-8 **60**...................(p) LeonnaMayor(3) 17 67
(P Howling) *hld up: hdwy over 1f out: r.o: nt rch ldrs* **8/1**[3]
5604 **4** *shd* **Spinning Bailiwick**[32] 5238 4-9-6 **69**............................... HarryBentley 8 75
(G L Moore) *prom: pushed along 1/2-way: styd on* **11/1**
0360 **5** *1 1/4* **Sairaam (IRE)**[6] 6063 4-8-11 **63**.......................................(b) IanBurns(3) 14 66
(C Smith) *prom: swtchd to r alone on far rail over 4f out: led over 2f out: shkn up and edgd lft over 1f out: hdd and unable qck ins fnl f* **6/1**[2]
5132 **6** *1* **Mata Hari Blue**[7] 6040 4-8-13 **62**.................................... JamesRogers 7 62
(J R Holt) *prom: ev ch over 2f out: no ex ins fnl f* **6/1**[2]
0525 **7** *nk* **Convince (USA)**[11] 5875 9-8-6 **58**........................(p) MatthewCosham(3) 2 57
(J L Flint) *hld up: pushed along 1/2-way: hung rt fr over 1f out: styd on: nt trble ldrs* **22/1**
5316 **8** *1 1/4* **Phluke**[11] 5889 9-8-6 **60**..(v) DanielBlackett(5) 15 56
(Eve Johnson Houghton) *led over 4f: styd on same pce appr fnl f* **18/1**
5314 **9** *hd* **Red Dagger (IRE)**[10] 5905 4-8-7 **56**.............................. NathanAlison 11 52
(R J Price) *chsd ldrs: pushed along over 2f out: styd on same pce appr fnl f* **20/1**
-300 **10** *shd* **Perfect Secret**[214] 593 4-8-7 **59**................................. FrancisHayes(3) 3 54
(A M Balding) *mid-div: lost pl 3f out: n.d after* **16/1**
3400 **11** *1/2* **Hettie Hubble**[51] 4581 4-8-4 **56** oh11............................... NoraLooby(3) 4 50
(D W Thompson) *s.i.s: hdwy 1/2-way: styd on same pce fr over 1f out* **100/1**
1356 **12** *hd* **Gemma's Delight (IRE)**[10] 5906 3-8-5 **57**..................(p) AlexEdwards 9 49
(J W Unett) *prom: pushed along over 2f out: no ex fnl f* **16/1**
U043 **13** *nk* **Toby Tyler**[28] 5357 4-8-13 **62**.. RichardRowe 18 55
(P T Midgley) *hld up: hdwy over 1f out: wknd ins fnl f* **17/2**
0004 **14** *1 1/2* **Ten To The Dozen**[21] 5596 7-8-7 **56** oh10.................. AntiocoMurgia 16 45
(D W Thompson) *chsd ldrs tl wknd over 1f out* **66/1**
0420 **15** *1* **King Columbo (IRE)**[10] 5905 5-9-1 **64**........................ AdamBeschizza 6 50
(Miss J Feilden) *prom: pushed along 1/2-way: wknd over 1f out* **12/1**
600 **16** *3/4* **Lordship (IRE)**[11] 5877 6-8-4 **56**.................................... JakePayne(3) 12 40
(A W Carroll) *plld hrd and prom: wknd over 1f out* **25/1**

1m 25.96s (-0.24) **Going Correction** -0.125s/f (Firm)
WFA 3 from 4yo+ 3lb **16** Ran SP% **125.2**
Speed ratings (Par 103): **96,95,94,94,93 91,91,90,89,89 89,88,88,86,85 84**
Tote Swingers: 1&2 £12.20, 1&3 £10.80, 2&3 £9.50. totesuper7: Win: Not won. Place: Not won. CSF £50.26 CT £392.34 TOTE £10.40: £2.40, £2.60, £3.50, £3.60; EX 71.80 TRIFECTA Not won. Place 6: £2,567.48 Place 5: £1,745.61..
Owner M Channon **Bred** C J Murfitt **Trained** West Ilsley, Berks

FOCUS
A competitive apprentice handicap. The form horses came to the fore and the race is rated around the second and third.
Convince(USA) Official explanation: jockey said gelding hung right-handed
T/Plt: £11,673.10 to a £1 stake. Pool of £55,807 - 3.49 winning tickets. T/Qpdt: £46.90 to a £1 stake. Pool of £6,221 - 98 winning tickets. CR

6070 BEVERLEY (R-H)

Tuesday, September 21

OFFICIAL GOING: Good (8.2)
Wind: Light across Weather: Fine and dry

6262 SEASON FINALE (S) STKS 1m 4f 16y

2:00 (2:02) (Class 5) 3-4-Y-0 **£2,590** (£770; £385; £192) **Stalls** High

Form RPR
0045 **1** **Miss Wendy**[3] 6183 3-8-2 47 ow4.......... totesupper7: AshleyMorgan(5) 9 58
(M H Tompkins) *cl up: led over 6f out: rdn along wl over 1f out: drvn ins fnl f: hld on gamely* **20/1**
0060 **2** *hd* **Without Equal**[19] 5681 4-8-11 40.. PJMcDonald 1 54
(N Wilson) *hld up in tch: pushed along and reminder over 4f out: swtchd outside and rdn 2f out: styd on to chal ent fnl f: sn hung rt and ev ch tl drvn and no ex nr fin* **66/1**
6450 **3** *2* **Maybeme**[19] 5681 4-8-8 54.. KellyHarrison(3) 7 50
(N Bycroft) *dwlt and sltly hmpd s: in rr tl sme hdwy on inner 3f out: rdn to chse ldrs over 1f out: sn drvn and one pce* **11/2**
2201 **4** *6* **Always Dixie (IRE)**[3] 6183 3-8-8 51..................................... JoeFanning 10 46
(M Johnston) *led: hdd 6f out: cl up whn n.m.r on inner and hmpd 4f out: rdn and rallied to chse wnr wl over 1f out: sn drvn and wknd ins fnl f* **13/8**[1]
0000 **5** *nk* **Liszt (IRE)**[45] 4846 4-9-2 85.. PaulHanagan 8 45
(Ian Williams) *unruly stalls and wnt lft s: trckd ldrs: hdwy over 3f out: rdn and ch 2f out: sn drvn and wknd over 1f out* **9/4**[2]
6 *2 3/4* **Jolly Roger (IRE)** 3-8-9 0 ow1.. RobertWinston 2 42
(N Bycroft) *in tch: hdwy 3f out: rdn to chse ldrs 2f out: sn drvn and wknd* **16/1**
2456 **7** *12* **Privy Speech (IRE)**[13] 5869 3-7-12 57...................... DeclanCannon(5) 5 17
(Rae Guest) *trckd ldng pair: hdwy 4f out: cl up 3f out: effrt and ev ch over 2f out: sn rdn: hung rt and wknd* **5/1**[3]
560 **8** *28* **Just Nod (IRE)**[21] 5636 4-8-8 0................................ JamesSullivan(3) 3 —
(Mrs R A Carr) *sn rdn along in rr: lost pl after 3f: t.o fnl 4f* **100/1**

2m 42.94s (3.14) **Going Correction** +0.275s/f (Good)
WFA 3 from 4yo 8lb **8** Ran SP% **114.0**
Speed ratings (Par 103): **100,99,98,94,94 92,84,65**
toteswingers:1&2:£34.20, 1&3:£10.20, 2&3:£26.10 CSF £685.41 TOTE £18.10: £3.50, £14.90, £1.50; EX 649.80.There was no bid for winner. Always Dixie was claimed by A Crook for £6,000.
Owner Miss Clare Hollest **Bred** Dullingham Park **Trained** Newmarket, Suffolk
■ Stewards' Enquiry : Ashley Morgan four-day ban: used whip with excessive frequency without giving filly time to respond (Oct 5-8)

FOCUS
A poor seller run at a very steady pace and a shock result. Dubious and unconvincing form.

6263 THANKS FOR YOUR SUPPORT IN 2010 MAIDEN AUCTION STKS (DIV I) 5f

2:30 (2:30) (Class 4) 2-Y-O **£3,561** (£1,059; £529; £264) **Stalls** High

Form RPR
42 **1** **Kinlochrannoch**[21] 5640 2-8-7 0.. PaulHanagan 3 79+
(B M R Haslam) *qckly away: mde all: clr wl over 1f out: rdn out* **10/1**
5 **2** *5* **Shesastar**[52] 4599 2-8-7 0.. SilvestreDeSousa 7 61
(T D Barron) *trckd ldrs: hdwy 1/2-way: rdn and edgd rt wl over 1f out: sn chsng wnr: drvn and no imp fnl f* **11/4**[2]
022 **3** *5* **Moral Issue**[31] 5298 2-8-11 76.. PatrickDonaghy(3) 6 51
(Jedd O'Keeffe) *chsd ldrs on inner: rdn along over 2f out: drvn and outpcd whn edgd lft over 1f out: n.d* **5/4**[1]
040 **4** *1 1/4* **Gunalt Joy**[6] 6075 2-8-3 0..(t) JamesSullivan(3) 5 38
(M W Easterby) *chsd wnr: rdn along over 2f out: hld whn n.m.r and sltly hmpd over 1f out* **66/1**
3 **5** *nk* **Whitstable Native**[30] 5328 2-8-12 0.. TedDurcan 9 42
(J R Best) *in tch: rdn along over 2f out: sn wknd* **10/3**[3]
6 *nk* **Ellikan (IRE)** 2-8-9 0.. J-PGuillambert 1 38
(N P Littmoden) *in tch: hdwy to chse ldrs 1/2-way: sn rdn and wknd wl over 1f out* **22/1**
0 **7** *4* **Mujapiste (IRE)**[27] 5418 2-8-6 0.. HayleyTurner 10 21
(L A Mullaney) *chsd ldrs on inner: rdn along 1/2-way: sn wknd* **33/1**
00 **8** *2 1/4* **Red Snapper (IRE)**[8] 6027 2-8-12 0.. DuranFentiman 8 19
(J R Weymes) *dwlt: a outpcd in rr* **50/1**

64.85 secs (1.35) **Going Correction** +0.20s/f (Good) **8** Ran SP% **114.0**
Speed ratings (Par 97): **97,89,81,79,78 78,71,68**
toteswingers:1&2:£3.50, 1&3:£2.90, 2&3:£1.50 CSF £36.69 TOTE £12.20: £2.30, £1.30, £1.10; EX 36.00.
Owner Mrs Carol Aldridge **Bred** Mrs S L Gibson Fleming **Trained** Middleham Moor, N Yorks

FOCUS
A weak maiden auction event and the first two in the betting both seriously under-performed. Solid but limited form.

NOTEBOOK
Kinlochrannoch improved a good deal on her 4l second behind an exposed type on her second start at Ripon. She secured the far-side rail position after the first furlong and came clear, being kept right up to her work. With the third already rated 76, she can hardly expect a lenient nursery mark. (tchd 8-1)
Shesastar, a staying-on fifth first time at Thirsk, went in pursuit of the winner but was never going to get anywhere near her. She should be able to find a modest maiden event. (op 3-1 tchd 10-3)
Moral Issue, rated 76, was dropping back to five after finishing runner-up over 6f at Ripon on his third start. After jumping off first, he was being run off his feet at the halfway mark. (op 13-8)
Gunalt Joy, less than 4l behind the winner when they finished second and fourth respectively at Ripon two outings ago, stayed on when it was all over and will need at least 6f in nursery company.
Whitstable Native, from a stable without a juvenile success this time, failed hopelessly to build on his strong finishing third first time at Folkestone. (op 5-2)
Ellikan(IRE), bred exclusively for speed, showed a glimmer of ability and was by no means knocked about on her racecourse bow. (op 16-1)

6264 THANKS FOR YOUR SUPPORT IN 2010 MAIDEN AUCTION STKS (DIV II) 5f

3:00 (3:01) (Class 4) 2-Y-O **£3,561** (£1,059; £529; £264) **Stalls** High

Form RPR
0033 **1** **Breezolini**[6] 6075 2-8-3 53.. AmyRyan(3) 10 72
(R M Whitaker) *chsd ldrs: effrt on inner and n.m.r over 1f out: sn swtchd lft and rdn: styd on strly ins fnl f to ld last 75yds* **9/2**[2]
2 *1 1/2* **Norton Girl** 2-8-6 0.. JoeFanning 4 67+
(J J Quinn) *trckd ldrs: swtchd lft and hdwy on outer 2f out: rdn to chal over 1f out: drvn to ld briefly ins fnl f: sn hdd and one pce towards fin* **33/1**
3 **3** *1* **Elusive Prince**[26] 5433 2-9-0 0.. PhillipMakin 3 71
(T D Barron) *chsd ldrs: hdwy 2f out: rdn over 1f out: ev ch tl drvn and one pce ins fnl f* **15/2**
5034 **4** *1 1/4* **Jonelha**[13] 5865 2-8-9 71.. KierenFallon 8 62
(P W D'Arcy) *led: rdn 2f out: drvn over 1f out: hdd & wknd ins fnl f* **5/4**[1]
5004 **5** *2 3/4* **Guinea Seeker**[17] 5755 2-8-11 60.. DavidAllan 7 54
(T D Easterby) *chsd ldrs: hdwy wl over 1f out: rdn and ch over 1f out: sn drvn and wknd ins fnl f* **10/1**
0034 **6** *3 3/4* **Major Return (IRE)**[7] 6047 2-8-12 56.. JamesDoyle 1 41
(A J McCabe) *cl up on outer: effrt and ev ch 2f out: sn rdn and wknd 1f out* **7/1**
000 **7** *3/4* **Ice Girl**[8] 6034 2-8-5 0.. JamesSullivan(3) 5 34
(M W Easterby) *cl up: rdn 2f out: grad wknd* **33/1**

054 **8** *8* **Deva Le Deva (IRE)**[61] 4286 2-8-9 63 .... HayleyTurner 9 —
(Tom Dascombe) *dwlt: in tch on inner: rdn along 2f out and sn wknd* **6/1**[3]
9 *½* **Cannon Bolt (IRE)** 2-8-12 0 .... SilvestreDeSousa 6 —
(R Bastiman) *s.i.s and a bhd* **66/1**
06 **10** *1 ½* **Countess Cheval (IRE)**[83] 3550 2-8-9 0 .... PaulHanagan 2 —
(B M R Haslam) *towards rr: rdn along 2f out: sn edgd rt and outpcd* **33/1**

64.78 secs (1.28) **Going Correction** +0.20s/f (Good) **10** Ran SP% **120.6**
Speed ratings (Par 97): **97,94,93,91,86 80,79,66,65,63**
toteswingers:1&2:£16.50, 1&3:£5.00, 2&3:£14.00 CSF £147.00 TOTE £5.40: £1.10, £11.00, £3.50; EX 163.20.
Owner Nice Day Out Partnership **Bred** Hellwood Stud Farm **Trained** Scarcroft, W Yorks

FOCUS
Part two and another weak event, and the winner's time was very similar to division one. There were five almost in a line just inside the final furlong. Limited but sound form.

NOTEBOOK
Breezolini, having her fifth start, was raised 7lb to a new mark of 60 after her improved run to finish third here last week. She made her effort one off the far side and scored decisively in the end. She is clearly going the right way.
Norton Girl, unconsidered on her debut, made her effort widest of all and deserves credit for this. (op 25-1)
Elusive Prince stepped up on his third of four first time at Ayr and should progress further. (op 9-1 tchd 7-1)
Jonelha, rated 71, was dropping back to five so it was disappointing to see her flatten out after making the running. (op 6-4 tchd 7-4)
Guinea Seeker, rated 60 after five previous starts, looks all speed and will be suited by a less stiff track. (op 9-1 tchd 17-2)
Major Return(IRE), who showed improvement when fourth over 6f at Haydock, was taken to post early and did not run up to his best from stall one. (op 13-2 tchd 6-1)
Deva Le Deva(IRE), who ran over seven last time, was already getting outpaced when she stumbled badly just before halfway. She was then eased right off. Official explanation: jockey said filly hung left and clipped heels approx 3f out (op 7-1 tchd 15-2)

6265 VIOLET AND EDDIE SMITH MEMORIAL CONDITIONS STKS 5f
3:30 (3:31) (Class 3) 3-Y-0+
£6,231 (£1,866; £933; £467; £233; £117) **Stalls** High

Form RPR
1014 **1** **Tangerine Trees**[77] 3753 5-8-9 81 .... (v) TomEaves 1 108
(B Smart) *qckly away: mde all: rdn over 1f out: kpt on strly fnl f* **33/1**
0534 **2** *2 ¼* **Captain Dunne (IRE)**[13] 5851 5-8-9 105 .... DavidAllan 3 100
(T D Easterby) *trckd ldng pair: effrt to chse wnr wl over 1f out: rdn ent fnl f: sn drvn and no imp* **13/8**[2]
532 **3** *½* **Tax Free (IRE)**[23] 5569 8-8-9 107 .... AdrianNicholls 8 98
(D Nicholls) *cl up: pushed along 2f out: rdn wl over 1f out: sn drvn and one pce* **5/4**[1]
0440 **4** *nk* **Anglezarke (IRE)**[3] 6194 4-8-4 95 .... (b) PaulHanagan 6 92
(R A Fahey) *chsd ldrs: rdn along 2f out: drvn over 1f out: kpt on towards fin* **8/1**[3]
-600 **5** *1 ¾* **Our Jonathan**[17] 5744 3-8-8 100 .... PaulMulrennan 7 91
(K A Ryan) *chsd ldrs on inner: rdn along 2f out: sn drvn and wknd over 1f out* **10/1**
6200 **6** *1 ¾* **Five Star Junior (USA)**[16] 5787 4-8-9 93 .... KierenFallon 5 84
(Mrs L Stubbs) *in tch: effrt over 2f out: sn rdn and btn* **12/1**
0060 **7** *4* **Look Busy (IRE)**[13] 5851 5-9-2 93 .... PatrickMathers 4 77
(A Berry) *dwlt: a in rr* **25/1**
0000 **8** *9* **Pawan (IRE)**[13] 5855 10-8-11 75 ow7 .... (b) AnnStokell(5) 2 45
(Miss A Stokell) *towards rr: rdn along 1/2-way: sn outpcd and bhd* **100/1**

62.82 secs (-0.68) **Going Correction** +0.20s/f (Good)
WFA 3 from 4yo+ 1lb **8** Ran SP% **118.2**
Speed ratings (Par 107): **113,109,108,108,105 102,96,81**
toteswingers:1&2:£9.20, 1&3:£7.30, 2&3:£1.40 CSF £89.51 TOTE £27.30: £4.70, £1.50, £1.10; EX 121.10.
Owner Tangerine Trees Partnership **Bred** Mrs B A Matthews **Trained** Hambleton, N Yorks

FOCUS
A well contested Class 3 sprint and on paper it looked a match between last year's winner Captain Dunne and Tax Free but punters were in for a shock. These races are often unreliable and it is doubtful how much improvement the winner actually showed, but it was certainly a clear personal best.

NOTEBOOK
Tangerine Trees, who won first time out this year at Pontefract from a mark of 69, was back after an 11-week break and wore a visor for the first time since his 3-y-o days. He had over a stone and a half to find with the two market leaders, but from stall one he made all the running and won going away in the end. He has developed nicely at five and this was his eighth career success but it remains to be seen if he can reproduce this seemingly vastly improved effort. Whether he can or cannot, he is a fine advertisement for his trainer. Official explanation: trainer had no explanation for the apparent improvement in form (op 50-1)
Captain Dunne(IRE) was inclined to run a bit freely. He got to the winner's quarters but was very much second best in the end. He is better than ever at five and a model of consistency. (op 9-4)
Tax Free(IRE), 2lb best-in on official figures, had finished runner-up behind Astrophysical Jet at the Curragh. He hunted up the winner but was possibly not at his very best on this dead ground. (op 10-11 tchd 11-8 and 6-4 in a place)
Anglezarke(IRE) is running better this back-end with the headgear on but in truth she never really threatened. (op 11-1)
Our Jonathan, who ended his juvenile career with two Group victories, has struggled this time round but this was a better effort. Connections will be hoping he bounces back at four. (op 9-1)
Five Star Junior(USA) had plenty to find and is another better suited by quicker ground than he encountered here. (tchd 14-1)
Look Busy(IRE), under her penalty, never figured and continues off the boil.
Pawan(IRE) was running in this race for the fifth time but after a tardy start was always occupying his rightful last place.

6266 BEVERLEY ANNUAL BADGEHOLDERS H'CAP 1m 100y
4:00 (4:00) (Class 5) (0-75,75) 3-Y-O **£3,238** (£963; £481; £240) **Stalls** High

Form RPR
3131 **1** **Hail Bold Chief (USA)**[25] 5479 3-9-4 72 .... PJMcDonald 2 79
(G A Swinbank) *trckd ldrs on outer: hdwy over 2f out: rdn over 1f out: styd on entering fnl f to ld last 100yds: drvn towards fin and jst hld on* **17/2**
0622 **2** *nse* **Dream On Buddy (IRE)**[17] 5758 3-9-5 73 .... RobertWinston 5 80+
(B W Hills) *hld up in rr: hdwy 2f out: rdn over 1f out: drvn and str run ent fnl f: jst failed* **4/1**[2]
501 **3** *nk* **First In The Queue (IRE)**[20] 5664 3-9-2 70 .... TravisBlock 8 76
(S Kirk) *led: rdn and qcknd clr over 1f out: drvn and hung lft ins fnl f: hdd and no ex last 100yds* **8/1**
-652 **4** *2* **Ella Grace (USA)**[23] 5550 3-8-7 61 oh2 .... PaulHanagan 6 63
(R A Fahey) *t.k.h early: chsd ldrs: hdwy over 2f out: rdn wl over 1f out and ch tl drvn and one pce ent fnl f* **5/1**[3]
2554 **5** *hd* **Queen's Scholar (USA)**[20] 5654 3-8-8 62 .... JoeFanning 4 63
(M Johnston) *in tch: hdwy on outer 3f out: chsd ldrs 2f out: drvn and ev ch ent fnl f: kpt on same pce* **14/1**
2240 **6** *3 ½* **Luv U Noo**[8] 6026 3-8-9 63 .... TomEaves 10 56
(B Ellison) *s.i.s: hld up in rr: swtchd wd and hdwy over 2f out: rdn wl over 1f out: sn no imp* **14/1**
1223 **7** *1 ¼* **Jupiter Fidius**[25] 5484 3-8-7 66 .... DaleSwift(5) 9 56
(Mrs K Walton) *trckd ldrs on inner: rdn along over 2f out: drvn wl over 1f out and sn wknd* **7/2**[1]
2451 **8** *1 ¼* **Tamarillo Grove (IRE)**[25] 5478 3-9-5 73 .... RichardMullen 3 60
(B Smart) *cl up: rdn along over 2f out: drvn and wknd over 1f out* **4/1**[2]
050 **9** *3 ¾* **Copper Penny**[12] 5896 3-9-7 75 .... TedDurcan 7 54
(D R Lanigan) *hld up towards rr: hdwy on inner over 2f out: rdn wl over 1f out: sn wknd* **7/1**

1m 48.92s (1.32) **Going Correction** +0.275s/f (Good) **9** Ran SP% **126.4**
Speed ratings (Par 101): **104,103,103,101,101 97,96,95,91**
toteswingers:1&2:£5.70, 1&3:£8.60, 2&3:£8.40 CSF £46.67 CT £298.56 TOTE £12.00: £4.10, £2.30, £1.40; EX 41.30.
Owner Solway Stayers **Bred** Tracy Farmer **Trained** Melsonby, N Yorks
■ Stewards' Enquiry : Travis Block one-day ban: used whip above shoulder height (Oct 5)

FOCUS
A competitive 61-75 3-y-os only handicap but the pace was very steady. Improved form from the first two.

6267 PONY RACING HERE ON 3 OCTOBER H'CAP 7f 100y
4:30 (4:30) (Class 5) (0-75,72) 3-Y-0+ **£3,238** (£963; £481; £240) **Stalls** High

Form RPR
0422 **1** **Ours (IRE)**[21] 5641 7-9-1 71 .... (p) BillyCray(5) 7 79
(John A Harris) *dwlt: sn pushed along and bhd: detached and rdn over 3f out: hdwy wl over 1f out: drvn and str run ent fnl f to ld on line* **9/2**[2]
3130 **2** *hd* **Call Of Duty (IRE)**[15] 5819 5-8-13 64 .... DuranFentiman 3 72+
(Mrs Dianne Sayer) *led: rdn 2f out: drvn 1f out: kpt on ins fnl f: hdd nr line* **7/2**[1]
0000 **3** *½* **Steel Stockholder**[25] 5499 4-9-1 66 .... RobertWinston 9 72
(M Brittain) *hld up towards rr: hdwy on wd outside over 2f out: rdn over 1f out: drvn and ev ch ent fnl f: kpt on* **7/1**
0445 **4** *1 ¼* **Carlitos Spirit (IRE)**[5] 6116 6-9-0 70 .... (v) DaleSwift(5) 8 73
(I W McInnes) *cl up on inner: effrt over 2f out and ev ch tl drvn and one pce ins fnl furlon g* **6/1**
6531 **5** *1* **Castle Myth (USA)**[15] 5821 4-8-9 60 .... PaulHanagan 1 61
(B Ellison) *chsd ldrs: rdn along over 2f out: drvn over 1f out: kpt on same pce* **8/1**
2065 **6** *2 ¼* **Mister Jingles**[19] 5688 7-8-4 58 oh2 .... (v) AmyRyan(3) 4 53
(R M Whitaker) *in tch: hdwy to chse ldrs 3f out: rdn over 2f out: drvn wl over 1f out and sn one pce* **12/1**
-400 **7** *½* **White Deer (USA)**[41] 4939 6-9-7 72 .... (p) SilvestreDeSousa 10 66
(G A Harker) *chsd ldrs on inner: hdwy 3f out: rdn over 2f out: drvn wl over 1f out and sn one pce* **16/1**
3041 **8** *4 ½* **Piquante**[19] 5688 4-8-13 67 .... Louis-PhilippeBeuzelin(3) 6 50
(N Tinkler) *in tch: hdwy on inner over 2f out: rdn to chse ldrs over 1f out: sn drvn and wknd* **11/2**[3]
0201 **9** *nk* **Cavendish Road (IRE)**[18] 5710 4-9-7 72 .... (t) HayleyTurner 5 54
(N J Vaughan) *chsd ldng pair: hdwy over 2f out: sn rdn and wknd wl over 1f out* **12/1**
2630 **10** *1 ½* **Mandalay King (IRE)**[19] 5684 5-8-13 67 .... RobertLButler(3) 2 45
(Mrs Marjorie Fife) *dwlt: a in rr* **22/1**

1m 35.55s (1.75) **Going Correction** +0.275s/f (Good) **10** Ran SP% **119.3**
Speed ratings (Par 103): **101,100,100,98,97 95,94,89,89,87**
toteswingers:1&2:£5.20, 1&3:£7.30, 2&3:£7.50 CSF £21.19 CT £113.33 TOTE £5.90: £1.30, £1.90, £3.00; EX 23.40.
Owner Peter Smith P C Coaches Limited **Bred** David John Brown **Trained** Eastwell, Leics
■ Stewards' Enquiry : Duran Fentiman one-day ban: used whip with excessive frequency (Oct 5)

FOCUS
A 58-72 handicap and the early pace was not strong, but it soon picked up. A small turf best from the winner.
Castle Myth(USA) Official explanation: trainer said gelding failed to handle the track

6268 MARTIN CAMPBELL SORRY YOU'RE LEAVING E B F MAIDEN STKS 7f 100y
5:00 (5:00) (Class 5) 2-Y-0 **£3,412** (£1,007; £504) **Stalls** High

Form RPR
2 **1** **Corsicanrun (IRE)**[17] 5762 2-9-3 0 .... PaulHanagan 2 75+
(R A Fahey) *cl up: effrt over 2f out: rdn wl over 1f out: led appr fnl f: drvn and kpt on towards fin* **1/1**[1]
2 *nk* **Jalors (IRE)** 2-9-3 0 .... JoeFanning 8 74+
(M Johnston) *in tch on inner: swtchd lft over 2f out and sn rdn: drvn over 1f out: styd on wl fnl f* **11/2**[3]
2036 **3** *½* **Rojo Boy**[16] 5785 2-9-3 78 .... (b[1]) KierenFallon 11 73
(D R C Elsworth) *hld up towards rr: hdwy over 2f out: rdn wl over 1f out: drvn and styd on wl fnl f* **9/4**[2]
0 **4** *1 ¼* **Kaua'i Girl**[6] 6071 2-8-12 0 .... SilvestreDeSousa 9 65
(Mrs A Duffield) *led: rdn along over 2f out: drvn and hdd over 1f out: rallied u.p ins fnl f: one pce towards fin* **12/1**
5 *4* **Sobea Star (IRE)** 2-8-12 0 .... MickyFenton 5 56
(Mrs P Sly) *dwlt and in rr: hdwy over 2f out: rdn wl over 1f out: kpt on ins fnl f: nrst fin* **40/1**
03 **6** *hd* **Blake Dean**[9] 6001 2-9-3 0 .... PhillipMakin 4 60
(B M R Haslam) *in tch: rdn along wl over 2f out: kpt on same pce* **16/1**
00 **7** *¾* **Coracle**[27] 5404 2-9-3 0 .... (t) PJMcDonald 7 58
(J A Glover) *chsd ldng pair on inner: swtchd and hdwy wl over 2f out: rdn to chal over 1f out and ev ch tl hung lft ent fnl f and sn wknd* **66/1**
60 **8** *1 ¼* **Izzet**[48] 4716 2-8-12 0 .... AshleyMorgan(5) 6 55
(M H Tompkins) *hld up: a towards rr* **33/1**
0 **9** *¾* **Blade**[11] 5924 2-9-3 0 .... TomMcLaughlin 1 54
(W M Brisbourne) *chsd ldrs: rdn along over 3f out: grad wknd fnl 2f* **66/1**
10 *12* **Kieron's Dream (IRE)** 2-9-0 0 .... PatrickDonaghy(3) 10 26
(Jedd O'Keeffe) *s.i.s: a in rr* **50/1**
0 **11** *nse* **Our Mate Joe (IRE)**[17] 5762 2-8-12 0 .... MichaelO'Connell(5) 3 25
(G A Harker) *a towards rr: outpcd fnl 3f* **50/1**

1m 37.24s (3.44) **Going Correction** +0.275s/f (Good) **11** Ran SP% **122.0**
Speed ratings (Par 95): **91,90,90,88,84 83,83,81,80,67 66**
toteswingers:1&2:£3.10, 1&3:£1.30, 2&3:£3.20 CSF £7.41 TOTE £2.30: £1.10, £1.40, £2.00; EX 10.20.
Owner Mrs H Steel **Bred** Dr D Harron **Trained** Musley Bank, N Yorks

FOCUS
A fair juvenile maiden with one or two likely improvers. The third governs the level somewhat.

NOTEBOOK

Corsicanrun(IRE), quite an expensive purchase, is a real good-looker. Very inexperienced, after a sluggish start when runner-up first time at Thirsk, he was very keen in the early stages and made very hard work of going one better. He is well related and sure to make a better 3-y-o. (tchd 6-5)

Jalors(IRE), out of an Irish Listed-race winner, has plenty of size and scope. He finished with a rattle and looks a certain future winner. (op 6-1 tchd 13-2)

Rojo Boy, edgy beforehand in first-time blinkers, was having his eighth start and has an official rating of 78. Stepping up in trip, he was off the pace and hard at work turning in. Persuaded to put his best foot forward, he was staying on in good style at the death but is clearly not straightforward. (op 2-1 tchd 5-2)

Kaua'i Girl, expected to step up on her debut effort here last week, was soon taking them along and made the winner work hard to get the better of her. She will improve again and should find a race. Official explanation: jockey said filly hung right (op 14-1 tchd 16-1)

Sobea Star(IRE) stayed on in her own time late on after a tardy start. She looks unfurnished as yet and should do better over further at three.

Blake Dean looks a slow learner but showed ability on his third start and is now qualified for a nursery mark. (tchd 18-1)

Coracle, well beaten on his first two starts, hung in the home straight and ended up under the stands'-side rail. He is not without ability but is not straightforward either. Official explanation: jockey said gelding hung left

Kieron's Dream(IRE) Official explanation: jockey said colt was slowly away

6269 BRIAN AND JASON MERRINGTON MEMORIAL AMATEUR RIDERS' H'CAP — 1m 1f 207y

5:30 (5:31) (Class 6) (0-60,60) 3-Y-0+ **£2,186** (£677; £338; £169) **Stalls** High

Form				RPR
2165	1		**Dean Iarracht (IRE)**[52] 4582 4-10-8 54 ... MrSWalker 3 (Miss Tracy Waggott) *midfield: hdwy over 4f out: chsd ldrs over 2f out: rdn over 1f out: drvn ent fnl f: styd on to ld last 100yds* 10/3[1]	65
61	2	2 ½	**Tropical Duke (IRE)**[24] 5530 4-10-8 59 ... MissVBarr(5) 9 (R E Barr) *hld up towards rr: hdwy on outer over 3f out: led over 2f out: rdn over 1f out: edgd rt ent fnl f hdd and no ex last 100yds* 11/2[3]	65
-600	3	½	**Bold Indian (IRE)**[65] 4170 6-10-1 52 ... MrJNewman(5) 7 (M E Sowersby) *hld up towards rr: hdwy on outer over 3f out: rdn to chse ldrs over 1f out: kpt on ins fnl f* 50/1	57
4602	4	4 ½	**Masterofceremonies**[19] 5704 7-10-1 54 ...(v) MissALMurphy(7) 8 (W M Brisbourne) *s.i.s and in rr: hdwy 4f out: effrt to chse ldrs over 2f out: rdn and no imp fnl f* 25/1	50
2653	5	3 ½	**Silly Gilly (IRE)**[11] 5905 6-10-3 54 ... MrJMQuinlan(5) 5 (R E Barr) *chsd ldrs: rdn along over 2f out: drvn over 1f out: kpt on same pce* 12/1	43
00-0	6	shd	**Monfils Monfils (USA)**[17] 1028 8-10-5 58 ... MissLucyBell(7) 14 (P A Kirby) *towards rr: hdwy over 2f out: rdn wl over 1f out: kpt on ins fnl f* 33/1	47
1204	7	3 ¼	**Hurricane Thomas (IRE)**[24] 5530 6-10-9 60 ... MissPhillipaTutty(5) 4 (R A Fahey) *chsd ldrs: rdn along and outpcd 3f out: styd on appr fnl f* 11/1	42
3130	8	1 ½	**Strike Force**[24] 5530 6-10-7 58 ...(t) MissALHutchinson(5) 13 (Miss Olivia Maylam) *s.i.s and bhd: hdwy on outer over 2f out: styd on appr fnl f: n.d* 14/1	37
1450	9	4 ½	**Kyle Of Bute**[24] 5530 4-10-13 59 ... MissSBrotherton 17 (B P J Baugh) *prom: rdn along over 3f out: grad wknd fnl 2f* 7/1	29
0544	10	1 ¼	**Lakeman (IRE)**[8] 6029 4-10-7 58 ...(b) MrDCottle(5) 16 (B Ellison) *led: rdn along and hdd over 3f out: drvn over 2f out and grad wknd* 12/1	26
-005	11	nse	**Hartshead**[15] 5821 11-10-2 55 ... MissStephanieBowey(7) 2 (Miss Tracy Waggott) *trckd ldrs: hdwy over 3f out: cl up over 2f out: sn rdn and wknd over 1f out* 40/1	23
500-	12	5	**Bishop Rock (USA)**[459] 3099 4-10-6 52 ...(t) MissEJJones 15 (N Tinkler) *in tch on inner: rdn along 3f out: sn wknd* 50/1	10
-023	13	2 ½	**Isabella Romee (IRE)**[6] 6077 4-10-0 53 ... MissAZetterholm(7) 6 (Jane Chapple-Hyam) *towards rr: effrt and sme hdwy on inner over 2f out: sn wknd* 14/1	6
5032	14	1	**Kingdom Of Munster (IRE)**[10] 5942 3-10-3 60 ...(v) MrsVFahey(5) 10 (R A Fahey) *cl up: led over 3f out: rdn and hdd over 2f out: sn wknd* 7/2[2]	11
-504	15	19	**Mister Fizzbomb (IRE)**[99] 2694 7-10-10 56 ...(v) MrSDobson 12 (J S Wainwright) *in tch: rdn along over 4f out: sn wknd* 25/1	—
0000	16	1 ¼	**King Of Rhythm (IRE)**[186] 757 7-9-12 51 ... MissCLWhitehead(7) 1 (D Carroll) *chsd ldng pair on outer: rdn along 4f out: sn wknd* 33/1	—

2m 10.35s (3.35) **Going Correction** +0.275s/f (Good)

WFA 3 from 4yo+ 6lb **16** Ran SP% **130.2**

Speed ratings (Par 101): **97,95,94,91,88 88,85,84,80,79 79,75,73,72,57 56**

toteswingers:1&2:£5.80, 1&3:£44.80, 2&3:£35.60. totesuper7: Win: Not won. Place: £406.00. CSF £21.99 CT £821.60 TOTE £4.80: £1.70, £1.50, £10.70, £6.20; EX 27.80 Place 6 £230.07; Place 5 £30.41.

Owner Michael Howarth **Bred** Ken Carroll **Trained** Spennymoor, Co Durham

■ Stewards' Enquiry : Miss C L Whitehead two-day ban: careless riding (tbn)
Miss A L Murphy three-day ban: used whip with excessive frequency (tbn)
Mr D Cottle caution: careless riding.

FOCUS

A low-grade amateur riders' handicap run at a strong pace and the field was soon well spread out. The winner's best effort of the year.

Silly Gilly(IRE) Official explanation: jockey said mare suffered interference in running

T/Plt: £325.30 to a £1 stake. Pool:£59,385.16 - 133.25 winning tickets T/Qpdt: £12.70 to a £1 stake. Pool:£5,059.19 - 292.90 winning tickets JR

5623 FOLKESTONE (R-H)

Tuesday, September 21

OFFICIAL GOING: Good to firm (8.2)

Wind: virtually nil Weather: sunny, beautiful

6270 LADBROKES.COM H'CAP — 5f

2:20 (2:20) (Class 6) (0-60,60) 3-Y-0+ **£2,047** (£604; £302) **Stalls** Low

Form				RPR
232	1		**Stratton Banker (IRE)**[3] 6207 3-9-5 59 ... WilliamCarson 8 (S C Williams) *t.k.h: stdd after s and hld up towards rr: hdwy on outer 2f out: rdn to ld jst ins fnl f: r.o strly and sn in command: comf* 13/8[1]	75+
342	2	2 ¼	**Best One**[9] 5990 6-9-0 53 ...(b) LukeMorris 3 (R A Harris) *chsd ldrs: wnt 2nd over 3f out: rdn to ld over 1f out: drvn and hdd jst ins fnl f: no ch w wnr after but kpt on for 2nd* 8/1	59
6022	3	¾	**Guto**[8] 6018 7-9-0 58 ... AdamBeschizza(5) 2 (W J H Ratcliffe) *chsd ldrs: rdn along over 3f out: lost pl ent fnl 2f: rallied ins fnl f: kpt on to 3rd nr fin* 11/4[2]	61+
4334	4	nk	**Miss Polly Plum**[12] 5898 3-8-10 50 ... JimmyQuinn 4 (C A Dwyer) *stdd s: t.k.h: hld up in tch: rdn and unable qck wl over 1f out: drvn ent fnl f: kpt on fnl 100yds but nvr gng pce to threaten ldrs* 15/2[3]	52
0-66	5	shd	**Jimmy Ryan (IRE)**[75] 3818 9-9-5 58 ...(t) SebSanders 9 (T D McCarthy) *taken down early and led to s: stdd and dropped in bhd after s: hld up in last: swtchd rt and hdwy jst over 1f out: kpt on ins fnl f: no ch w wnr* 33/1	60
2260	6	¾	**Pocket's Pick (IRE)**[35] 5176 4-9-7 60 ...(b) SteveDrowne 7 (Jim Best) *taken down early: broke fast: led and grad crossed to r on stands' rail: rdn and hdd over 1f out: btn whn nt clr run and eased wl ins fnl f* 25/1	59
5066	7	nk	**Green Lagonda (AUS)**[12] 5876 8-9-1 57 ow1 ... RichardEvans(3) 6 (P D Evans) *taken down early: chsd ldr tl over 3f out: styd handy: rdn to chal wl over 1f out: btn jst ins fnl f: wknd ins fnl f* 16/1	55
0305	8	¾	**Mr Skipiton (IRE)**[52] 4589 5-8-12 58 ... RoryHanley(7) 1 (B J McMath) *hld up in tch on stands' rail: rdn whn jinked at rail and lost pl wl over 1f out: rdn 1f out: keeping on same pce whn nt clr run fnl 100yds: nvr able to chal* 9/1	53+
0000	9	shd	**Captain Kallis (IRE)**[8] 6018 4-8-11 53 ...(t) AshleyHamblett(3) 10 (D J S Ffrench Davis) *towards rr: rdn and effrt on outer ent fnl 2f: drvn and btn jst over 1f out: wknd ins fnl f* 33/1	48

59.00 secs (-1.00) **Going Correction** -0.175s/f (Firm)

WFA 3 from 4yo+ 1lb **9** Ran SP% **113.2**

Speed ratings (Par 101): **101,97,96,95,95 94,93,92,92**

toteswingers:1&2:£3.90, 1&3:£1.90, 2&3:£3.20 CSF £14.84 CT £32.90 TOTE £2.80: £1.10, £2.10, £2.00; EX 16.70 Trifecta £36.60 Pool: £352.24 - 7.11 winning units..

Owner James & Sarah **Bred** Pat Grogan **Trained** Newmarket, Suffolk

FOCUS

An ordinary sprint handicap, run at a brisk early pace. The runner-up is a fair guide to the form.

Pocket's Pick(IRE) Official explanation: jockey said gelding was denied a clear run last 100yds

6271 LADBROKESPOKER.COM NURSERY — 5f

2:50 (2:50) (Class 5) (0-70,72) 2-Y-0 **£3,070** (£906; £453) **Stalls** Low

Form				RPR
6331	1		**Sugar Beet**[7] 6052 2-9-5 68 6ex ... SteveDrowne 8 (R Charlton) *restless stalls: mde all: grad crossed to r on stands' rail: rdn over 1f out: r.o wl u.p fnl f* 3/1[1]	77+
2521	2	1	**Johnny Hancocks (IRE)**[9] 5987 2-9-4 72 6ex ... AdamBeschizza(5) 10 (P D Evans) *chsd wnr thrght: rdn and drew clr w wnr over 1f out: drvn ent fnl f: kpt on same pce fnl 100yds* 4/1[2]	78+
0003	3	3	**Shostakovich (IRE)**[11] 5914 2-8-7 56 ... LiamKeniry 9 (S Kirk) *towards rr: nt clr run 2f out tl over 1f out: no ch w ldng pair but r.o wl fnl f to snatch 3rd on post* 14/1	51
01	4	nse	**Secret Gold (IRE)**[17] 5763 2-9-5 68 ... PatCosgrave 4 (B J Meehan) *awkward leaving stalls and s.i.s: t.k.h: chsd ldrs after 1f: rdn and outpcd by ldng pair over 1f out: wl hld and styd on same pce u.p after: lost 3rd on post* 4/1[2]	63
0002	5	hd	**Regal Bullet (IRE)**[22] 5581 2-8-7 56 ... WilliamCarson 6 (D K Ivory) *in tch: rdn ent fnl 2f: drvn and outpcd by ldng pair over 1f out: kpt on same pce ins fnl f* 12/1	50
3004	6	1 ¼	**Master Macho (IRE)**[9] 5987 2-9-5 68 ...(v[1]) SamHitchcott 11 (M R Channon) *in tch towards rr: nt clr run ent fnl 2f: rdn along and hdwy over 1f out: no ch w ldng pair but pressing for 3rd 1f out tl wknd fnl 75yds* 11/1	58
0023	7	hd	**Indian Shuffle (IRE)**[15] 5808 2-9-6 69 ... TonyCulhane 3 (J G Portman) *chsd ldrs on stands' rail: rdn and unable qck wl over 1f out: wl hld fnl f* 11/1	58
1404	8	1 ¼	**Instructress**[38] 5089 2-9-7 70 ...(p) EddieAhern 1 (R M H Cowell) *hld up in tch towards rr on stands' rail: nt clr run and switching rt ent fnl 2f: no prog fr wl over 1f out: n.d* 10/1[3]	54
6066	9	¾	**Suave Character**[11] 5900 2-7-12 47 oh1 ... CathyGannon 7 (M Blanshard) *sn outpcd and rdn along in last: switching rt and sme hdwy u.p over 1f out: nvr trbld ldrs* 100/1	29
5600	10	3 ¼	**Melodize**[22] 5581 2-8-9 58 ...(b[1]) JimmyQuinn 2 (W R Muir) *outpcd in last pair: n.d* 28/1	28
4265	11	1 ½	**Avalon Bay**[18] 5720 2-8-5 61 ... JamesRogers(7) 14 (Pat Eddery) *in tch on outer: rdn and effrt ent fnl 2f: wknd wl over 1f out: bhd fnl f* 14/1	26
4000	12	6	**Kyncraighe (IRE)**[6] 6086 2-9-7 70 ...(bt[1]) SebSanders 13 (Eve Johnson Houghton) *in tch: rdn 1/2-way: drvn and struggling ent fnl 2f: wknd and wl btn 1f out* 66/1	13

59.35 secs (-0.65) **Going Correction** -0.175s/f (Firm) **12** Ran SP% **117.7**

Speed ratings (Par 95): **98,96,91,91,91 89,88,86,85,80 78,68**

toteswingers:1&2:£2.50, 1&3:£12.90, 2&3:£14.20 CSF £14.29 CT £145.89 TOTE £4.90: £2.60, £1.70, £6.10; EX 14.20 Trifecta £105.80 Pool: £263.18 - 1.84 winning units..

Owner Nicholas Jones **Bred** Coln Valley Stud **Trained** Beckhampton, Wilts

FOCUS

There was a solid early pace on and the first pair, both penalised, came clear. They showed decent nursery form.

NOTEBOOK

Sugar Beet followed up her clear-cut success at Lingfield over 6f a week earlier, and did the job gamely under a penalty. Her early pace was a decent asset here as she made her way across to the favoured near rail, and knuckled down well when pressed by the runner-up from the furlong marker. Despite being bred to want further she is obviously all about speed, and it's not that hard to see her rating a bit higher, so it will be interesting to see how she copes from her new mark (already due to race off 5lb higher). (op 9-4)

Johnny Hancocks(IRE) made a bold bid to follow up his Ffos Las win nine days earlier, and this was a decent effort under top weight. He is a likeable sprinter and can probably find another opening before the season's end. (op 9-2)

Shostakovich(IRE) ◆ is better than the bare form. He didn't get the breaks when trying to improve from midfield, and this was no doubt his most encouraging effort to date. A stiffer test could be what he really wants and his turn could be nearing. (op 20-1)

Secret Gold(IRE) lacked the pace to land a telling blow on this nursery debut, but wasn't disgraced and looks worth another chance back on a more conventional track. (op 11-2)

Regal Bullet(IRE), 2lb higher, had his chance this time and is another that may now appreciate a bit further.

Instructress would have likely been better off under a more prominent ride. (op 9-1 tchd 17-2)

6272 LADBROKESBINGO.COM H'CAP (DIV I) — 1m 7f 92y

3:20 (3:20) (Class 6) (0-60,60) 3-Y-0+ **£1,706** (£503; £252) **Stalls** Low

Form				RPR
0443	1		**Princess Flame (GER)**[30] 4991 8-9-0 46 oh1 ... SebSanders 6 (B G Powell) *t.k.h: hld up in last trio: rdn and hdwy over 2f out: chsd ldng trio 2f out: kpt on to ld ins fnl f: sn clr: r.o wl* 16/1	54

4020 **2** 2 1/4 **Mymateeric**[19] 5687 4-8-11 **48** SimonPearce(5) 4 54
(J Pearce) *in tch: rdn to chse ldng pair jst over 2f out: keeping on steadily whn nt clr run and swtchd lft jst ins fnl f: kpt on to go 2nd nr fin* **9/2**[2]

-404 **3** *nk* **Astrovenus**[35] 5173 3-8-7 **50** JimmyQuinn 1 55
(M H Tompkins) *t.k.h: chsd ldrs: rdn to chse ldr 3f out: drvn and ev ch over 1f out: led jst ins fnl f: hdd and no ex ins fnl f: lost 2nd nr fin* **40/1**

6115 **4** 1 1/2 **Bravo Bravo**[5] 6132 3-9-1 **58** SamHitchcott 9 61+
(M R Channon) *s.i.s: pushed along briefly after: bhd: pushed along 7f out: swtchd to outer and effrt 3f out: stl only 7th and edging rt u.p 2f out: kpt on ins fnl f: nvr rchd ldrs* **9/4**[1]

4330 **5** 3/4 **Snowberry Hill (USA)**[10] 5963 7-8-11 **46** oh1....(p) RussKennemore(3) 7 48
(Lucinda Featherstone) *t.k.h: chsd ldr tl led 4f out: rdn over 2f out: drvn and hdd jst ins fnl f: wknd fnl 100yds* **11/1**

0356 **6** 3 **Suor Angelica (IRE)**[8] 6022 5-8-11 **46** oh1 MatthewDavies(3) 3 44
(George Baker) *hld up in last pair: rdn and no hdwy over 2f out: wl hld and plugged on same pce fr over 1f out* **12/1**

0064 **7** 9 **Whitley Bay (USA)**[5] 6120 3-8-3 **46** LukeMorris 2 32
(J R Best) *in tch: rdn to chse ldng trio 7f out: drvn 3f out: wknd u.p 2f out* **8/1**[3]

5350 **8** 5 **Zaif (IRE)**[8] 6022 7-9-5 **54** (be) SophieDoyle(3) 5 34
(D J S Ffrench Davis) *t.k.h: hld up in midfield: rdn and effrt on outer over 3f out: lost pl qckly and dropped to last 3f out: lost tch over 2f out: eased fr over 1f out* **14/1**

333 **9** *nk* **Spinning Waters**[15] 5813 4-9-0 **46** (v) FergusSweeney 8 26
(Eve Johnson Houghton) *hld up in midfield: rdn and nt qckn over 2f out: wknd ent fnl 2f: wl bhd and eased ins fnl f* **9/2**[2]

110- **10** 27 **Starstruck Peter (IRE)**[17] 3927 6-10-0 **60** (b) SteveDrowne 10 —
(Jim Best) *led tl 4f out: sn lost pl: wl bhd and eased fr over 1f out: t.o* **12/1**

3m 28.22s (-1.48) **Going Correction** -0.025s/f (Good)
WFA 3 from 4yo+ 11lb 10 Ran SP% **116.9**
Speed ratings (Par 101): **102,100,100,99,99 97,93,90,90,75**
toteswingers:1&2:£15.30, 1&3:£19.00, 2&3:£27.20 CSF £86.94 CT £2854.23 TOTE £13.30: £3.80, £1.10, £8.00; EX 100.30 TRIFECTA Not won..
Owner B G Powell **Bred** V Kaufling **Trained** Upper Lambourn, Berks

FOCUS
A weak staying handicap, run at a fair pace and a bit quicker than division II. The first two did not need to improve on this year's best.

6273 LADBROKESBINGO.COM H'CAP (DIV II) 1m 7f 92y
3:50 (3:50) (Class 6) (0-60,59) 3-Y-0+ **£1,706** (£503; £252) **Stalls** Low

Form RPR

322 **1** **Marcus Antonius**[10] 5963 3-8-9 **51** PatCosgrave 9 62+
(J R Boyle) *trckd ldrs: nt clr run and swtchd lft over 3f out: sn chsng ldr: rdn to ld ent fnl 2f: sn drvn clr: heavily eased wl ins fnl f* **15/8**[1]

0060 **2** 2 1/4 **Mixing**[99] 3040 8-8-9 **45** KierenFox(5) 3 48
(M J Attwater) *bhd: rdn and hdwy over 2f out: no ch w wnr fnl 2f: kpt on u.p to chse wnr jst ins fnl f: clsd on heavily eased wnr fnl 75yds* **50/1**

0334 **3** *nk* **Jennerous Blue**[10] 5963 3-8-6 **48** (p) PaulQuinn 5 51+
(D K Ivory) *hld up in rr: stl wl bhd and swtchd wd 3f out: hmpd bnd over 2f out: rdn and styd on wl fr over 1f out: wnt 3rd towards fin: nvr trbld wnr* **7/2**[2]

2254 **4** 1 1/4 **The Composer**[20] 5666 8-9-2 **47** JimmyQuinn 7 48
(M Blanshard) *dwlt: towards rr: rdn 5f out: hdwy u.p but no ch w wnr over 1f out: wnt 2nd 1f out tl ins fnl f: styd on one pce after* **7/1**

000 **5** 4 1/2 **The Midshipmaid**[11] 5905 3-8-3 **45** CathyGannon 6 41
(Lucinda Featherstone) *t.k.h: hld up in tch in midfield: rdn 6f out: struggling and press whn hung lft bnd over 2f out: wl hld and plugged on same pce after* **40/1**

-063 **6** *nk* **Ned Ludd (IRE)**[138] 1849 7-10-0 **59** (v) StephenCraine 10 54
(J G Portman) *hld up in tch towards rr: hdwy 6f out: chsd ldng pair over 2f out: rdn and fnd little 2f out: no ch w wnr after: wknd fnl f* **11/2**[3]

3646 **7** 4 **Free Falling**[23] 5564 4-8-9 **45** (b) AdamBeschizza(5) 4 35
(Miss Gay Kelleway) *s.i.s: steadily rcvrd and led after 2f: rdn and hdd 2f out: sn no ch w wnr: lost 2nd 1f out: fdd fnl f* **8/1**

5003 **8** 11 **Mid Wicket (USA)**[12] 5873 4-9-2 **47** JimCrowley 1 23
(Mouse Hamilton-Fairley) *styd away fr rivals for 4f: chsd ldr tl 3f out: sn struggling u.p: wl btn fnl 2f* **12/1**

260 **9** 1 1/4 **Rosy Dawn**[8] 6021 5-9-0 **45** PatDobbs 8 19
(L A Dace) *led for 2f: chsd ldrs tl rdn and wknd over 2f out: wl bhd over 1f out* **14/1**

3m 28.73s (-0.97) **Going Correction** -0.025s/f (Good)
WFA 3 from 4yo+ 11lb 9 Ran SP% **114.8**
Speed ratings (Par 101): **101,99,99,98,96 96,94,88,87**
toteswingers:1&2:£13.10, 1&3:£2.90, 2&3:£20.40 CSF £103.83 CT £312.33 TOTE £3.00: £1.40, £7.50, £1.10; EX 93.40 Trifecta £207.20 Part won. Pool: £280.09 - 0.84 winning units..
Owner Mrs J Dye **Bred** Mrs J J Dye **Trained** Epsom, Surrey

FOCUS
The second and slower division of the 1m7f handicap and another weak race. Like the first division it was run at a sound enough gallop. The winner was much improved but there are doubts over the form with the runner-up 5lb wrong.

6274 LADBROKES.COM ON YOUR MOBILE H'CAP 7f (S)
4:20 (4:20) (Class 4) (0-85,80) 3-Y-0+ **£4,857** (£1,445; £722; £360) **Stalls** Low

Form RPR

3315 **1** **Rough Rock (IRE)**[6] 6097 5-8-6 **70** AdamBeschizza(5) 8 77
(C A Dwyer) *hld up in tch in last trio: effrt on outer 2f out: rdn and ev ch ent fnl f: led fnl 100yds: r.o wl* **7/1**

-400 **2** 3/4 **Kings Bayonet**[11] 5917 3-9-2 **78** TomQueally 2 85+
(H R A Cecil) *hld up in rr: hdwy to trck ldrs but nt clr run ent fnl 2f tl fnlly gap opened fnl 100yds: rdn and r.o to go 2nd towards fin: unable to chal* **9/4**[1]

2103 **3** 1/2 **Duster**[14] 5838 3-9-4 **80** SteveDrowne 4 83
(H Morrison) *w ldrs: ev ch and rdn wl over 1f out: led jst ins fnl f tl hdd fnl 100yds: no ex: lost 2nd towards fin* **5/2**[2]

0005 **4** *shd* **Silver Wind**[3] 6207 5-9-0 **73** (v) CathyGannon 7 77
(P D Evans) *chsd ldrs: rdn 1/2-way: drvn and ev ch ent fnl f: styd on same pce fnl 100yds* **12/1**

0-14 **5** 3 1/2 **Realt Na Mara (IRE)**[43] 4894 7-9-2 **75** JimCrowley 3 69
(H Morrison) *w ldrs tl led 4f out: rdn wl over 1f out: hdd jst ins fnl f: btn fnl 100yds: eased towards fin* **6/1**[3]

5614 **6** 3 1/4 **Tewin Wood**[111] 2644 3-9-1 **77** ChrisCatlin 5 62
(A Bailey) *t.k.h: hld up in tch: lost pl ent fnl 3f: rdn and btn 2f out* **11/1**

1401 **7** 3 **Amber Sunset**[12] 5889 4-8-13 **72** WilliamCarson 9 49
(D Morris) *broke wl and led tl 4f out: styd pressing ldrs tl wknd u.p wl over 1f out* **9/1**

1m 26.22s (-1.08) **Going Correction** -0.175s/f (Firm)
WFA 3 from 4yo+ 3lb 7 Ran SP% **112.2**
Speed ratings (Par 105): **99,98,97,97,93 89,86**
toteswingers:1&2:£3.80, 1&3:£3.60, 2&3:£2.40 CSF £22.26 CT £49.66 TOTE £6.00: £3.40, £2.90; EX 27.90 Trifecta £57.70 Pool: £332.73 - 4.26 winning units..
Owner M M Foulger **Bred** Mrs B Stroomer **Trained** Burrough Green, Cambs
■ Stewards' Enquiry : Cathy Gannon two-day ban: used whip with excessive frequency (Oct 5-6)

FOCUS
A modest handicap, run at a decent early pace, but somewhat muddling form. The runner-up has been rated a narrow winner .
Kings Bayonet ◆ Official explanation: jockey said gelding was denied a clear run

6275 MOBILE.LADBROKES.COM MAIDEN STKS 1m 1f 149y
4:50 (4:50) (Class 5) 3-Y-0+ **£2,729** (£806; £403) **Stalls** Centre

Form RPR

1 **Modun (IRE)** 3-9-3 0 RyanMoore 9 79+
(Sir Michael Stoute) *s.i.s: rn green and pushed along at times in last pair: 6th and plenty to do 3f out: rdn along mainly hands and heels and clsd fr wl over 1f out: styd on relentlessly fnl f to ld fnl 50yds* **8/11**[1]

24 **2** 1/2 **Nerves Of Steel (IRE)**[14] 5832 3-9-3 0 JamieSpencer 3 78
(P F I Cole) *led tl over 7f out: chsd ldr after: rdn over 2f out: drvn to ld 1f out: hdd and no ex fnl 50yds* **4/1**[3]

0050 **3** 1 **Silent Oasis**[24] 5541 4-9-4 65 FergusSweeney 5 71
(B G Powell) *in tch: rdn and effrt over 2f out: styd on u.p to chse ldrs 1f out: kpt on same pce fnl 100yds* **14/1**

4 1 1/4 **Vezere (USA)**[98] 3-8-12 70 SebSanders 2 69?
(S Dow) *t.k.h: chsd ldr after 1f: led 7f out and sn clr: rdn ent fnl 2f: drvn and hdd 1f out: styd on same pce ins fnl f* **28/1**

62 **5** 2 1/4 **Sentosa**[14] 5832 3-8-12 0 TomQueally 7 64
(H R A Cecil) *trckd ldrs: rdn and effrt ent fnl 2f: nt qckn u.p and no imp fr over 1f out* **11/4**[2]

0 **6** 17 **Wingate Street**[5] 6124 3-9-1 0 ow1 RichardEvans(3) 4 36
(P D Evans) *chsd ldrs for 2f: steadily lost pl: bhd and rdn over 3f out: lost tch over 2f out* **66/1**

5605 **7** 6 **Christophers Quest**[15] 5813 5-9-9 46 (t) PaulFitzsimons 1 23
(Miss N A Lloyd-Beavis) *t.k.h: chsd ldrs: rdn 4f out: wknd 3f out: wl bhd fnl 2f* **80/1**

8 63 **You Mug** 3-9-3 0 LiamKeniry 6 —
(S Curran) *sn dropped to last: rn green: rdn and lost tch 5f out: wl t.o fnl 2f* **50/1**

2m 4.39s (-0.51) **Going Correction** -0.025s/f (Good)
WFA 3 from 4yo+ 6lb 8 Ran SP% **119.4**
Speed ratings (Par 103): **101,100,99,98,97 83,78,28**
toteswingers:1&2:£1.60, 1&3:£2.80, 2&3:£4.20 CSF £4.38 TOTE £1.60: £1.02, £1.10, £3.50; EX 4.50 Trifecta £20.70 Pool: £472.63 - 16.87 winning units..
Owner Ballymacoll Stud **Bred** Ballymacoll Stud Farm Ltd **Trained** Newmarket, Suffolk

FOCUS
This maiden was run at a sound pace and the form looks straightforward enough. A nice start frrom the winner with more to come.

6276 LADBROKESGAMES.COM H'CAP 1m 1f 149y
5:20 (5:20) (Class 4) (0-80,78) 3-Y-0+ **£4,857** (£1,445; £722; £360) **Stalls** Centre

Form RPR

2341 **1** **City Ground (USA)**[32] 5270 3-9-4 **78** PhilipRobinson 1 86
(M A Jarvis) *sn led: mde rest: rdn over 1f out: edgd lft and flashed tail u.p 1f out: hld on wl fnl f: drvn out* **11/4**[2]

53 **2** 3/4 **Monte Cavallo (SAF)**[31] 5311 5-9-10 **78** StephenCraine 2 84+
(M Wigham) *chsd ldrs: rdn and effrt ent fnl 2f: swtchd rt over 1f out: drvn to chse wnr ent fnl f: styd on same pce and hld fnl 100yds* **9/4**[1]

5634 **3** 1 1/2 **Mingun Bell (USA)**[24] 5540 3-9-1 **75** TomQueally 3 78
(H R A Cecil) *led: sn hdd: pressed wnr after: rdn ent fnl 2f: drvn and lost 2nd ent fnl f: keeping on same pce whn sltly hmpd 1f out: btn fnl 100yds* **11/4**[2]

2640 **4** 3/4 **Addwaitya**[17] 5311 5-9-10 **78** IanMongan 5 80
(Mrs L J Mongan) *detached in last and nudged along for 2f: clsd and in tch 7f out: c towards centre and effrt 2f out: kpt on ins fnl f but nvr gng pce to rch ldrs* **11/2**[3]

010 **5** 3 1/4 **Boom And Bust (IRE)**[20] 5662 3-8-12 **72** PatDobbs 4 67
(M P Tregoning) *chsd ldrs: hmpd 8f out: rdn and outpcd over 2f out: kpt on same pce fnl 2f* **8/1**

2m 3.70s (-1.20) **Going Correction** -0.025s/f (Good)
WFA 3 from 5yo 6lb 5 Ran SP% **110.6**
Speed ratings (Par 105): **103,102,101,100,98**
CSF £9.38 TOTE £3.20: £1.20, £2.60; EX 10.40 Place 6 £28.72; Place 5 £22.35.
Owner R J Baines **Bred** Mrs E Scott Jr & Mrs L Macelree **Trained** Newmarket, Suffolk

FOCUS
A fair little handicap. They didn't hang about, but the winner set something of an uneven pace. The form is worth taking at face value.
T/Jkpt: Not won. T/Plt: £56.10 to a £1 stake. Pool:£67,651.82 - 878.84 winning tickets T/Qpdt: £25.80 to a £1 stake. Pool:£4,491.49 - 128.70 winning tickets SP

5991 GOODWOOD (R-H)
Wednesday, September 22

OFFICIAL GOING: Good to firm (good in places on straight course)
Wind: Virtually nil Weather: Sunny

6278 ELECTROLUX PROFESSIONAL E B F MAIDEN STKS 7f
2:00 (2:03) (Class 5) 2-Y-O **£2,914** (£867; £433; £216) **Stalls** High

Form RPR

1 **Dominant (IRE)** 2-9-3 0 PhilipRobinson 5 77+
(M A Jarvis) *trckd ldrs: pushed along: green and styd on to chal over 1f out: led ins fnl f: asserted cl home and won gng away* **7/2**[3]

53 **2** 1 **Riot Police (USA)**[12] 5900 2-9-3 0 WilliamBuick 7 74
(J H M Gosden) *sn trcking ldr: pushed along to chal over 1f out: sn stl upsides and rdn ins fnl f: kpt on to take 2nd cl home but nvr gng pce of wnr* **11/4**[2]

3 *hd* **Mariners Lodge (USA)** 2-9-3 0 FrankieDettori 10 74
(Mahmood Al Zarooni) *led: pushed along 2f out jnd over 1f out: hdd ins fnl f: kpt on tl no ex and lost 2nd cl home* **9/4**[1]

0 **4** *3* **Silverware (USA)**[13] 5878 2-9-3 0 .... RichardHughes 9 66
(R Hannon) *chsd ldrs: puhed along over 2f out: outpcd by ldng trio fnl f* **8/1**

6 **5** *4 ½* **Iron Green (FR)**[49] 4695 2-9-3 0 .... EddieAhern 13 54
(Mrs H S Main) *s.i.s: sn rcvrd and in tch: rdn ins fnl 3f: wknd fr 2f out* **50/1**

6 *hd* **Namibian (IRE)** 2-9-3 0 .... KierenFallon 1 54+
(M Johnston) *broke wl: sn pushed along: green and bhd: sme prog on outside fr over 3f out: nvr in contention and sn btn* **7/1**

6 **7** *1* **Amazon Twilight**[26] 5488 2-8-9 0 .... EJMcNamara(3) 12 46
(B R Johnson) *chsd ldrs: keen early: chsd ldrs: rdn 3f out: btn over 2f out* **100/1**

8 *2 ½* **Cool Water Oasis** 2-8-12 0 .... PatDobbs 3 40
(G L Moore) *s.i.s: mid-div and wknd over 2f out* **66/1**

4000 **9** *1* **Welsh Dancer**[18] 5745 2-9-3 77 .... RyanMoore 4 42
(R Hannon) *a towards rr* **16/1**

5 **10** *nse* **Hot Spice**[15] 5836 2-9-3 0 .... JimmyFortune 11 42+
(J L Dunlop) *in tch early: green and sn towards rr* **40/1**

00 **11** *3 ¾* **Iwantobreakfree**[53] 4599 2-9-3 0 .... CathyGannon 6 32
(P D Evans) *rdn over 3f out: a wl bhd* **100/1**

1m 28.14s (1.24) **Going Correction** +0.025s/f (Good) 11 Ran SP% **117.0**
Speed ratings (Par 95): **93,91,91,88,83 82,81,78,77,77 73**
Tote Swingers: 1&2 £3.20, 1&3 £3.30, 2&3 £2.40 CSF £13.37 TOTE £4.80: £1.20, £1.50, £1.50; EX 14.40 Trifecta £64.80 Pool: £299.75 - 3.42 winning units..
Owner Highclere Thoroughbred Racing(Isinglass) **Bred** Newhall Ltd **Trained** Newmarket, Suffolk

FOCUS

A fair juvenile maiden, rated around the third. The winner should improve on this nice start.

NOTEBOOK

Dominant(IRE) got his career off to a perfect start with a ready success. He sported a cross-noseband and took a hold on the way to post, but settled well enough through the early parts of the race in a handy position. He proved a little green until being asked for his effort from the furlong marker, but responded positively and was always just doing enough to repel the placed horses where it mattered. This was his first-season sire's debut winner, who was himself top-class at around 10f, and his dam also got that trip so it's likely to prove this colt's optimum distance next term. He was the only one of these to hold any fancy entries this year, with the Racing Post Trophy the most notable at this stage, and he should improve a good deal for this initial experience. (op 11-4)

Riot Police(USA) ◆ was having his third outing and rates the benchmark. This was certainly his best effort to date, he appreciated getting back on some quick ground, and shouldn't be long in winning. Nurseries are an option now for him. (op 3-1)

Mariners Lodge(USA) ◆ cost $350,000 and, like the winner, is also entered in next year's Derby. He knew his job and was soon dictating out in front. He only gave way near the finish and this was a very pleasing introduction, so he too will likely be on the score sheet in the coming weeks. (op 3-1)

Silverware(USA) attracted support and stepped up nicely on his debut form. It's not hard to see why he started off over 1m and, with plenty of physical improvement on the cards, he can find an opening when reverting to a stiffer test. (op 12-1)

Iron Green(FR) is one to keep an eye on. Sixth on debut at Kempton last month, he still showed some inexperience here, but was noted keeping on nicely from off the pace and looks capable of rating higher in due course as he is a good-looking horse.

Namibian(IRE), easy to back, proved far too green to do himself justice. He is bred to want a stiffer test next year and he should prove a lot sharper for this experience. (op 13-2 tchd 6-1)

Amazon Twilight was one her toes.

Hot Spice was on his toes in the paddock.

6279 R H HALL E B F MAIDEN STKS 1m 1f

2:35 (2:36) (Class 4) 2-Y-O £4,533 (£1,348; £674; £336) **Stalls** High

Form RPR

1 **Dordogne (IRE)** 2-9-3 0 .... KierenFallon 11 91+
(M Johnston) *in tch: pushed along and hdwy over 2f out: str run to ld appr fnl f: c steadily clr: easily* **10/1**[3]

2 **2** *4 ½* **Sud Pacifique (IRE)**[23] 5595 2-9-3 0 .... RyanMoore 8 80
(J Noseda) *trckd ldrs: chsd ldr ins fnl 3f: led appr fnl 2f: rdn and hdd appr fnl f: sn no ch w wnr but kpt on for 2nd* **4/7**[1]

022 **3** *1 ¼* **Strictly Rhythm**[10] 5985 2-8-12 0 .... RichardHughes 6 73
(R Hannon) *trckd ldrs tl led ins fnl 3f: hdd appr fnl 2f: styd disputing wl hld 2nd ins fnl f tl no ex fnl 75yds* **7/2**[2]

06 **4** *4* **Major Domo (FR)**[19] 5724 2-9-3 0 .... DaneO'Neill 1 70+
(H J L Dunlop) *sn chsng ldrs: rdn over 2f out and sn outpcd* **33/1**

0 **5** *3 ¾* **Canaveral**[22] 5629 2-9-3 0 .... ShaneKelly 7 62
(B J Meehan) *hld up in rr: pushed along and mod prog fnl 2f* **20/1**

03 **6** *shd* **Plea**[13] 5871 2-9-3 0 .... (b) WilliamBuick 9 62
(J H M Gosden) *t.k.h: in tch: pushed along to chse ldrs ins fnl 3f: nvr on terms and wknd ins fnl 2f* **12/1**

55 **7** *2* **Mountain Range (IRE)**[25] 5520 2-9-3 0 .... EddieAhern 4 61
(J L Dunlop) *in rr pushed along and hung lft over 2f out: nvr in contention* **16/1**

06 **8** *½* **Drummer Boy**[23] 5582 2-9-3 0 .... LukeMorris 5 57
(P Winkworth) *mid-div: wd bnd over 4f out and over 3f out: sn wknd* **100/1**

56 **9** *7* **Embezzle**[14] 5857 2-9-3 0 .... (b[1]) JimmyFortune 2 43
(R Charlton) *sn led: hdd ins fnl 3f: wkng whn hung rt over 2f out* **66/1**

50 **10** *5* **Beautiful Lando (FR)**[22] 5626 2-9-3 0 .... ChrisCatlin 10 33
(Mrs H S Main) *a towards rr* **100/1**

0 **11** *1 ¼* **Dust Cloud (IRE)**[23] 5582 2-9-3 0 .... JimCrowley 3 30
(P Winkworth) *chsd ldr 7f out tl over 3f out: sn wknd* **100/1**

1m 56.27s (-0.03) **Going Correction** +0.025s/f (Good) 11 Ran SP% **120.7**
Speed ratings (Par 97): **101,97,95,92,89 88,87,86,80,76 74**
Tote Swingers: 1&2 £3.60, 1&3 £3.40, 2&3 £1.10 CSF £16.41 TOTE £8.00: £1.80, £1.20, £1.20; EX 24.10 Trifecta £101.20 Pool: £691.16 - 5.05 winning units..
Owner Sheikh Hamdan Bin Mohammed Al Maktoum **Bred** Mr & Mrs G Middlebrook **Trained** Middleham Moor, N Yorks

FOCUS

An average maiden and an impressive winner, a potentially decent 3yo in the making. The form looks solid rated around the placed horses.

NOTEBOOK

Dordogne(IRE) ◆ was the only newcomer in attendance and he bolted up. He hails from a stable whose juvenile this term have mainly needed their debuts, and that was again well advertised with stablemate Namibian in the preceding maiden. The manner in which he went about his business was impressive, though, and Kieran Fallon was able to ease off him near the finish. He is certainly bred to take a high ranking at three, being by Singspiel and out of a dam that was smart for the same yard (also went well at this track) that has already produced a 1m Listed winner. Indeed she has also thrown up two that have scored over as a far as 1m6f and this scopey colt ought to have no trouble getting 1m4f next year. He could very well be smart. (op 11-1)

Sud Pacifique(IRE), up in trip, raced more professionally than he did on debut and looked a likely winner 2f out. He had no answer when the winner asserted for home, but probably improved in defeat and should have little trouble in going one better before the season is out. His Racing Post Trophy entry is surely too fanciful at this stage, however. (op 4-6 tchd 8-11 in places)

Strictly Rhythm, having her fourth outing, travelled sweetly but she too was made to look one paced when the winner hit top gear. She probably found this slightly longer trip just stretching her, but gives the form a sound look and she too can find a maiden before going handicapping. (tchd 4-1)

Major Domo(FR) took time to settle and lacked the pace to get seriously involved, but this was his most encouraging run to date. He is now eligible for a mark.

Plea, on his toes in the paddock, has ability, but also real temperament issues. He is at least now qualified for nurseries. (op 11-1 tchd 14-1)

6280 3663 FIRST FOR FOOD SERVICE STKS (H'CAP) 6f

3:10 (3:10) (Class 4) (0-80,80) 3-Y-O+ **£3,626** (£1,079; £539; £269) **Stalls** Low

Form RPR

1221 **1** **Humidor (IRE)**[28] 5417 3-9-0 78 .... MatthewDavies(3) 5 88
(George Baker) *trckd ldrs: slt ld but strly pressed fr 3f out: rdn 2f out: styd on wl u.p fnl f* **13/2**[2]

5450 **2** *½* **Hand Painted**[15] 5838 4-8-11 70 .... SebSanders 3 78
(P J Makin) *s.i.s: sn in tch: rdn and styd on fr 2f out: kpt on u.p fnl f to dispute 2nd fnl 120yds: chse wnr cl home but a hld* **13/2**[2]

6423 **3** *nk* **Desert Icon (IRE)**[10] 5995 4-8-4 70 .... (v) HarryBentley(7) 10 77
(W J Knight) *t.k.h: in tch: hdwy 2f out: rdn and styd on to dispute 2nd fnl 120yds: no imp and one pce into cl 3rd nr fin* **3/1**[1]

0540 **4** *1 ½* **Brandywell Boy (IRE)**[12] 5915 7-8-13 72 .... JamesDoyle 8 74
(D J S Ffrench Davis) *chsd ldrs: drvn to chal fr 3f out: stl disputing 2nd u.p fnl f: wknd fnl 75yds* **8/1**

0403 **5** *nk* **Seamus Shindig**[24] 5551 8-8-13 77 .... AmyScott(5) 1 78
(H Candy) *in rr: swtchd rt fr 2f out: shkn up and kpt on fnl f: gng on clse home but nvr a threat* **13/2**[2]

0440 **6** *½* **Fivefold (USA)**[26] 5495 3-8-13 74 .... J-PGuillambert 4 74
(J Akehurst) *led after 1f: hdd 3f out: rdn and hung rt over 2f out: outpcd appr fnl f: kpt on again nr fin* **13/2**[2]

0065 **7** *1 ¼* **Safari Mischief**[22] 5627 7-8-13 77 .... AshleyMorgan(5) 12 73
(P Winkworth) *chsd ldrs: chal fr 3f out tl ins fnl 2f: wknd fnl f* **7/1**[3]

-140 **8** *4* **Fayre Bella**[129] 2140 3-8-12 73 .... ChrisCatlin 6 56
(J Gallagher) *s.i.s: in rr: rdn 1/2-way and nvr gng pce to get into contention* **33/1**

4200 **9** *2 ¾* **Gwilym (GER)**[12] 5915 7-8-12 71 .... NeilCallan 2 45
(D Haydn Jones) *led 1f: rdn and hung rt over 2f out sn btn* **16/1**

16 **10** *7* **Miss Hollybell**[90] 3373 4-9-0 73 .... FergusSweeney 7 25
(J Gallagher) *rdn over 3f out: a outpcd* **25/1**

1m 11.78s (-0.42) **Going Correction** +0.025s/f (Good)
WFA 3 from 4yo+ 2lb 10 Ran SP% **114.6**
Speed ratings (Par 105): **103,102,101,99,99 98,97,91,88,78**
Tote Swingers: 1&2 £8.10, 1&3 £2.40, 2&3 £5.00 CSF £47.49 CT £155.67 TOTE £5.80: £2.20, £2.40, £1.10; EX 57.30 Trifecta £346.00 Pool: £509.72 - 1.09 winning units..
Owner M Khan X2 **Bred** Yeomanstown Stud **Trained** Moreton Morrell, Warwicks

FOCUS

A modest sprint handicap. They went a fair pace and raced more towards the stands' side. Not much got in the race. The winner rates a clear personal best.

6281 MOUTON CADET CLASSIC FOUNDATION STKS (LISTED RACE) 1m 1f 192y

3:45 (3:45) (Class 1) 3-Y-O+ **£19,869** (£7,532; £3,769; £1,879; £941) **Stalls** High

Form RPR

-152 **1** **Holberg (UAE)**[18] 5749 4-9-0 115 .... FrankieDettori 4 113
(Saeed Bin Suroor) *sn led: pushed along over 2f out: jnd ins fnl f and narrowly hdd fnl 50yds: styd chalng and led again last stride* **11/10**[1]

4200 **2** *shd* **Pink Symphony**[42] 4957 3-8-3 100 .... ChrisCatlin 3 108
(P F I Cole) *chsd ldrs: rdn to go 2nd 2f out: upsides u.p ins fnl f nosed ahd of wnr fnl 50yds: hdd last stride* **33/1**

3430 **3** *4* **Heliodor (USA)**[18] 5749 4-9-0 104 .... RichardHughes 1 105
(R Hannon) *hld up in rr off pce tl rdn and hdwy over 2f out: nvr gng pce to trble ldng duo but styd on for one pce 3rd fnl f* **22/1**

0512 **4** *¾* **Hot Prospect**[25] 5539 3-8-8 110 .... PhilipRobinson 2 103
(M A Jarvis) *chsd ldrs: rdn along fr 3f out and sme hdwy to cl on ldng duo over 2f out: nvr on terms w ldng duo and disp one pce 3rd tl wknd into 4th ins fnl f* **6/4**[2]

1065 **5** *2 ½* **Bullet Train**[25] 5538 3-8-11 109 .... TomQueally 5 101
(H R A Cecil) *chsd wnr tl rdn and hung rt fr 3f out: btn over 2f out* **5/1**[3]

2m 5.06s (-2.94) **Going Correction** +0.025s/f (Good)
WFA 3 from 4yo 6lb 5 Ran SP% **111.6**
Speed ratings (Par 111): **112,111,108,108,106**
CSF £29.48 TOTE £1.90: £1.10, £6.70; EX 39.60.
Owner Godolphin **Bred** Darley **Trained** Newmarket, Suffolk

■ Stewards' Enquiry : Chris Catlin one-day ban: used whip with excessive frequency (Oct 6)

FOCUS

An interesting race and, despite the lack of runners, it was a fair field for the class. It was run at a sound enough pace and the first two pulled clear in a battling finish. Ordinary form for the grade and the winner did not need to be at his best.

NOTEBOOK

Holberg(UAE) made it 2-2 at the track with a last-gasp success and enhanced his stable's excellent record in the race. His best form had been over 1m4f-plus, indeed he had never run over this distance, but the money came pouring in for him late on. He had to be ridden to get to the front, which was expected beforehand, and always looked to be going that stride quicker than Frankie Dettori wanted. He looked vulnerable when challenged by the runner-up nearing the furlong marker and was headed, but Dettori was at his strongest and he gamely just got back up at the line. He is a fairly fresh horse and is now due to go into quarantine for a trip down under for the Melbourne Cup in November. His trainer later said that he is the likely mount of Dettori there, rather than Campanologist, and the test of that prestigious handicap could be right up his street. (op 2-1 tchd 9-4 in places)

Pink Symphony had faced some stiff tasks since winning her maiden earlier in the year, but had been particularly disappointing the last twice and this event looked beyond her. Despite running somewhat in snatches early on, it looked very much as though she would cause an upset when hitting the front late on. The winner's superior stamina kicked in, however, and she was mugged right on the line. It must rate as a career-best from her, though, and she deserves to win one of these before the year is out. (op 25-1 tchd 20-1)

Heliodor(USA) is a difficult horse to place successfully but ran his race here and rates the most sensible guide for the form. (op 16-1)

Hot Prospect confirmed his last-time-out form with Bullet Train, but never looked that happy on this quicker ground and was beaten 3f out. (op 11-8 tchd 5-4 and 13-8 in a place)

Bullet Train, whose trainer had won the last two renewals of this event, was back on quicker ground but the signs were not good for him beforehand as he got warm and edgy. He took time to settle and proved laboured shortly after being asked for an effort around 3f out. This leaves him with plenty to prove. (op 7-2)

6282 PIPER CHAMPAGNE STKS (H'CAP) 1m 3f
4:20 (4:20) (Class 4) (0-85,85) 3-Y-O £3,626 (£1,079; £539; £269) **Stalls** Low

Form RPR

51 **1** **Doon Kalal (IRE)**[22] 5623 3-9-4 **82**........(b) PatDobbs 4 92+
(M P Tregoning) trckd ldrs: drvn to ld jst ins fnl f: r.o strly **10/1**

3134 **2** *1 1/2* **Heart Of Hearts**[14] 5858 3-9-1 **79**........ TomQueally 1 86
(H R A Cecil) trckd ldr: rdn to ld over 1f out: hdd jst ins fnl f: btn whn hung rt sn after and one pce **11/2**

0351 **3** *nk* **Sea Change (IRE)**[8] 6055 3-9-0 **78** 6ex........ RyanMoore 8 84
(J Noseda) pushed along in rr over 3f out: drvn and styd on fr 2f out: kpt on fnl f to cl on 2nd nr fin but nvr any ch w wnr **11/8**[1]

2424 **4** *3/4* **Shelfah (IRE)**[89] 3414 3-8-12 **76**........ FrankieDettori 5 81
(M A Jarvis) chsd ldrs: rdn over 2f out: styd on same pce fnl f **4/1**[2]

-231 **5** *2 1/4* **Exemplary**[151] 1518 3-9-7 **85**........ KierenFallon 7 91+
(M Johnston) sn led: rdn over 2f out: hdd over 1f out: btn whn hmpd ins fnl f **9/2**[3]

0256 **6** *hd* **Meglio Ancora**[53] 4573 3-8-10 **74**........ FergusSweeney 2 75
(J G Portman) pushed along fr 3f out: a towards rr **14/1**

2m 27.46s (0.96) **Going Correction** +0.025s/f (Good) **6** Ran SP% **111.4**
Speed ratings (Par 103): **97,95,95,95,93 93**
Tote Swingers: 1&2 £4.30, 2&3 £2.90 CSF £60.54 CT £119.82 TOTE £10.70: £5.10, £1.90; EX 41.10 Trifecta £205.30 Pool: £519.02 - 1.87 winning units..
Owner Sheikh Ahmed Al Maktoum **Bred** Shadwell Estate Company Limited **Trained** Lambourn, Berks

■ Stewards' Enquiry : Tom Queally two-day ban: careless riding (Oct 6-7)

FOCUS
What was a good little 3-y-o handicap was somewhat spoilt by a stop-start pace, and the form should be treated with a bit of caution. The winner continues on the upgrade with the second and fourth setting the standard.

6283 DISCOVERY FOODS STKS (H'CAP) 1m 4f
4:55 (4:56) (Class 3) (0-90,90) 3-Y-O+ £5,828 (£1,734; £866; £432) **Stalls** Low

Form RPR

1232 **1** **North Cape (USA)**[14] 5859 4-8-11 **80**........ AmyScott(5) 2 90
(H Candy) slowly away and lost 5 l: sn rcvrd off modest pce to ld after 1 1/2f and 12 l clr 1m out: pushed along and stl clr over 2f out: styd on fnl f and a holding on fnl 120yds **10/1**

2131 **2** *1* **Kings Troop**[13] 5888 4-9-4 **82**........ FergusSweeney 11 90+
(A King) in tch: rdn and hdwy 3f out: styd on to chse wnr over 1f out: kpt on ins fnl f but a hld **9/2**[2]

4236 **3** *4* **Dromore (IRE)**[30] 5371 3-8-0 **77**........ SimonPearce(5) 3 79
(A M Balding) chsd ldrs: disp 2nd 6f out tl chsd wnr 3f out: hung rt and dropped bk to 3rd fr over 1f out: wknd fnl f **7/1**[3]

-352 **4** *2 1/4* **Alfonso The Wise (IRE)**[14] 5860 3-8-7 **79** ow1........ RyanMoore 4 77
(J Noseda) led 1 1/2f: styd on chsng wnr and disp 2nd fr 6f out tl drvn along 3f out: fnd little and btn ins fnl 2f **10/11**[1]

5515 **5** *15* **Mabuya (UAE)**[27] 5443 4-9-3 **81**........ SebSanders 7 55
(P J Makin) in rr: sme hdwy and rdn 3f out: no imp on ldrs and wknd qckly over 2f out **10/1**

2004 **6** *25* **Lethal Glaze (IRE)**[10] 5989 4-9-12 **90**........(b[1]) KierenFallon 1 24
(R Hannon) in rr and rdn 7f out: nvr travelling and sn t.o **10/1**

2m 38.93s (0.53) **Going Correction** +0.025s/f (Good)
WFA 3 from 4yo+ 8lb **6** Ran SP% **110.3**
Speed ratings (Par 107): **99,98,95,94,84 67**
Tote Swingers: 1&2 £3.30, 1&3 £3.60, 2&3 £4.00 CSF £51.25 CT £319.29 TOTE £9.70: £3.10, £1.80; EX 25.00 Trifecta £262.80 Pool: £522.17 - 1.47 winning units..
Owner Henry Candy **Bred** W S Farish **Trained** Kingston Warren, Oxon

FOCUS
A handicap decimated by non-runners and the winner was gifted a very easy lead. It is unlikely this form will prove sound.

NOTEBOOK
North Cape(USA) fell out of the stalls, but the pace was so steady he was able to get to the front and he had soon opened up a clear advantage. Indeed he was still well clear turning for home and, although tiring near the business end, it was enough to see him last home in front. It was his first win beyond 1m2f and he is a likeable enough handicapper, but really he was gifted this. (op 6-1)
Kings Troop had been raised 7lb for his Epsom success over this trip 13 days earlier. He was closing on the winner all the way to the line, but the bird had flown. Providing the handicapper doesn't raise him for this, he is clearly still weighted to find another race. (tchd 5-1)
Dromore(IRE) shaped better, but probably paid late on for running freely through the early parts and is a happier horse on the AW. (tchd 13-2 and 15-2)
Alfonso The Wise(IRE), who went down narrowly at Epsom on his previous outing, looked fairly treated for this handicap debut and was very popular. He is also bred to enjoy this longer trip, but Ryan Moore didn't look too happy with him at the top of the home straight and he was soon under the pump. He dropped out from the furlong pole and this completed a frustrating afternoon for both his trainer and rider. (op 6-5 tchd 5-4 and 11-8 in a place)
Mabuya(UAE) weakened tamely after making up his ground in the home straight. (op 9-1 tchd 11-1)
Lethal Glaze(IRE) never went a yard in first-time blinkers. Official explanation: jockey said gelding never travelled (op 8-1)

6284 MERBURY 20TH ANNIVERSARY APPRENTICE STKS (H'CAP) 5f
5:30 (5:30) (Class 5) (0-70,69) 3-Y-O+ £2,590 (£770; £385; £192) **Stalls** Low

Form RPR

6005 **1** **Colorus (IRE)**[8] 6064 7-8-8 **62**........(v) MatthewCosham(7) 9 71
(W J H Ratcliffe) pressed ldr: chal fr over 2f out tl slt ld ins fnl f: styd on wl u.p whn strly chal fnl 120yds **11/2**[2]

2213 **2** *hd* **Admirable Duchess**[41] 4998 3-9-3 **68**........ BillyCray(3) 2 76
(D J S Ffrench Davis) led: jnd fr over 2f out: narrowly hdd ins fnl f: kpt on gamely but no ex nr fin **7/1**[3]

002 **3** *1 1/4* **Elhamri**[36] 5176 6-9-6 **67**........ EJMcNamara 10 71
(S Kirk) chsd ldng duo: rdn over 2f out: kpt on same pce ins fnl f **10/1**

0660 **4** *shd* **Green Lagonda (AUS)**[1] 6270 8-8-9 **56**........ Louis-PhilippeBeuzelin 4 59
(P D Evans) chsd ldrs: rdn over 2f out: styd on fnl f but nvr gng pce to chal **25/1**

3642 **5** *nse* **Wanchai Whisper**[12] 5915 3-9-5 **67**........(p) AndrewHeffernan 11 70+
(P R Hedger) s.i.s: in rr tl hdwy 1/2-way: rdn an styd on thrght fnl f: nt rch ldrs **9/2**[1]

2266 **6** *1* **Tiger Trail (GER)**[85] 3527 6-8-6 **56**........ JohnFahy(3) 5 56+
(Mrs N Smith) s.i.s: hld up in rr: hdwy over 1f out: kpt on ins fnl f nt rch ldrs **8/1**

4253 **7** *1 1/2* **Miss Firefly**[23] 5580 5-8-9 **59**........ SimonPearce(3) 3 53
(R J Hodges) plld hrd: in tch: hdwy and edgd rt ins fnl f: nt rch ldrs **16/1**

3000 **8** *nk* **Nubar Boy**[14] 5855 3-9-6 **68**........ RichardEvans 8 61
(P D Evans) chsd ldrs: rdn and styng on same pce whn hmpd ins fnl f: sn btn **25/1**

0312 **9** *1 1/4* **Witchry**[24] 5557 8-9-2 **63**........ RussKennemore 1 52
(A G Newcombe) in rr: pushed along 2f out: a outpcd **9/2**[1]

4022 **10** *nk* **Mrs Boss**[18] 5764 3-9-3 **65**........ JamesMillman 12 53
(B R Millman) uns rdr to s but sn ct: s.i.s: sme hdwy on outside 1/2-way: sn wknd **11/1**

5344 **11** *1 1/4* **Texas Queen**[11] 5956 3-9-2 **69**........ MatthewLawson(5) 6 52
(M R Channon) chsd ldrs: rdn 1/2-way: sn hung lft and wknd **10/1**

58.05 secs (-0.35) **Going Correction** +0.025s/f (Good)
WFA 3 from 4yo+ 1lb **11** Ran SP% **115.4**
Speed ratings (Par 103): **103,102,100,100,100 98,96,95,93,93 91**
Tote Swingers: 1&2 £12.40, 1&3 £13.90, 2&3 £11.20 CSF £39.32 CT £284.71 TOTE £7.70: £2.80, £1.30, £5.00; EX 55.30 TRIFECTA Not won. Place 6: £119.96 Place 5:£98.85.
Owner J Sheard & W J S Ratcliffe **Bred** M Ervine **Trained** Newmarket, Suffolk

FOCUS
A moderate sprint handicap, confined to apprentice riders. It was run at a decent tempo and, as was the case in the earlier 6f handicap, they raced towards the stands' side. The principals were always prominent and the winner ran to his summer form.
Texas Queen Official explanation: vet said filly was struck into
T/Plt: £55.30 to a £1 stake. Pool:£67,747 - 894.10 winning tickets T/Qpdt: £22.70 to a £1 stake. Pool:£3,556 - 115.80 winning tickets ST

6247 KEMPTON (A.W) (R-H)
Wednesday, September 22

OFFICIAL GOING: Standard
Wind: Light, half behind Weather: Fine, warm

6285 CBS NATIONAL BOND MEDIAN AUCTION MAIDEN STKS 5f (P)
5:50 (5:50) (Class 6) 3-4-Y-O £1,637 (£483; £241) **Stalls** High

Form RPR

0306 **1** **Speedyfix**[47] 4789 3-8-12 48........(v) KierenFox(5) 7 69
(Mrs C A Dunnett) sn off the pce: 9th after 2f: rapid prog arnd field after: led over 1f out: sn clr **10/1**

4-5 **2** *3 3/4* **Little Rufus**[19] 5726 3-9-3 0........ AndreaAtzeni 9 56
(K A Morgan) pressed ldr: upsides over 1f out: sn outpcd by wnr: jst hung on for 2nd **9/1**

3424 **3** *shd* **Nadinska**[9] 6018 3-8-12 60........ ChrisCatlin 12 50
(M R Channon) chsd ldng pair: no ch after wnr sped past over 1f out: kpt on and nrly snatched 2nd **11/4**[2]

3200 **4** *1 1/4* **Gessabelle**[8] 6060 3-8-12 49........(t) TomMcLaughlin 6 46
(P S McEntee) mounted on crse and taken down early: chsd ldng quartet: no imp over 1f out: kpt on **33/1**

46 **5** *2* **Laser Ruby**[91] 3333 3-8-12 0........ JimmyFortune 2 38
(A M Balding) s.i.s: rcvrd to chse ldng pair: nt qckn wl over 1f out: btn after **2/1**[1]

4543 **6** *1/2* **Ruler's Honour (IRE)**[25] 5514 3-9-3 56........(p) LeeVickers 4 42
(T J Etherington) settled in midfield: rdn and no prog over 1f out: one pce after **8/1**

6033 **7** *1/2* **Papageno**[19] 5726 3-9-3 60........ RichardHughes 1 40
(J R Jenkins) fast away fr wdst draw: led to over 1f out: wknd fnl f: fin lame **15/2**[3]

0040 **8** *3 1/4* **Spring Horizon (IRE)**[9] 6018 4-8-13 44........ KirstyMilczarek 11 23
(Miss Z C Davison) plld hrd early: hld up in rr: no prog fnl 2f **25/1**

0-00 **9** *8* **Diamond Affair (IRE)**[19] 5726 3-8-12 42........(p) WilliamCarson 5 —
(M G Quinlan) s.s: a in rr: wknd 2f out **66/1**

0004 **10** *1 1/2* **Avec Moi**[22] 5645 3-8-12 38........(b[1]) MarcHalford 10 —
(Mrs C A Dunnett) t.k.h early and n.m.r after 1f: swtchd and wd bnd sn after: toiling in rr fr 1/2-way **33/1**

0-00 **11** *13* **Starstreamer (IRE)**[21] 5668 3-8-12 40........(b[1]) TedDurcan 8 —
(M P Tregoning) s.s: sn t.o **16/1**

59.95 secs (-0.55) **Going Correction** -0.10s/f (Stan)
WFA 3 from 4yo 1lb **11** Ran SP% **119.1**
Speed ratings (Par 101): **100,94,93,91,88 87,87,81,69,66 45**
Tote Swingers: 1&2 £12.30, 1&3 £5.00, 2&3 £3.70 CSF £94.57 TOTE £19.40: £5.70, £7.10, £1.02; EX 102.30.
Owner Mark Riley **Bred** Mrs Christine Dunnett **Trained** Hingham, Norfolk

FOCUS
A weak maiden auction, won by an 18-race maiden with a BHA rating of 48. Not a race to be too positive about.
Laser Ruby Official explanation: jockey said filly did not handle the bend
Ruler's Honour(IRE) Official explanation: jockey said gelding hung left on bend
Papageno Official explanation: vet said gelding returned lame behind
Avec Moi Official explanation: jockey said filly did not face the first-time blinkers

6286 KIA SPORTAGE MAIDEN STKS 5f (P)
6:20 (6:20) (Class 5) 2-Y-O £2,286 (£675; £337) **Stalls** High

Form RPR

24 **1** **Latin Lashes (USA)**[39] 5074 2-8-12 0........ RichardHughes 10 72
(R Hannon) mde all: rdn over 1f out: kpt on wl enough and in command fnl f **11/4**[2]

3033 **2** *1 3/4* **My Love Fajer (IRE)**[19] 5720 2-8-12 69........ KierenFox(5) 3 71
(G Prodromou) chsd wnr: rdn over 1f out: kpt on but no imp **14/1**

0 **3** *1/2* **Barbieri (IRE)**[51] 4658 2-8-12 0........ SteveDrowne 5 64
(J R Gask) prom: chsd ldng pair 1/2-way: rdn to dispute 2nd over 1f out: nt qckn fnl f **33/1**

222 **4** *hd* **Florestans Match**[43] 4921 2-8-12 84........ JimCrowley 6 63+
(R M Beckett) sn rdn and detached in 7th: hd to one side and no interest tl r.o over 1f out: nrly snatched 3rd **4/9**[1]

5 **5** *3 3/4* **Ma Quillet**[42] 4960 2-8-12 0........ DaneO'Neill 7 50
(H Candy) chsd ldrs: wnt 4th over 2f out: rdn and fnd nil over 1f out: wknd **8/1**[3]

2624 **6** *1 3/4* **Silca Conegliano (IRE)**[13] 5885 2-8-12 66........ ChrisCatlin 2 43
(M R Channon) jst in tch in 6th: outpcd fr 2f out: no ch after **25/1**

00 **7** *hd* **Urban Kode (IRE)**[53] 4599 2-8-12 0........ AdamBeschizza(5) 4 48
(P D Evans) bdly outpcd in last pair and pushed along: virtually t.o 1/2-way: kpt on fnl f **66/1**

66 **8** *hd* **Duquesa (IRE)**[27] 5441 2-8-12 0........ CathyGannon 8 42
(P D Evans) bdly outpcd in last pair and pushed along: virtually t.o 1/2-way: kpt on fnl f **50/1**

305 **9** *3* **Sirens**[39] 5089 2-8-12 56 .... TomMcLaughlin 11 31
(P S McEntee) *sn rdn: prom to 1/2-way: wknd rapidly* **50/1**
60.44 secs (-0.06) **Going Correction** -0.10s/f (Stan) **9** Ran SP% **125.9**
Speed ratings (Par 95): **96,93,92,92,86 83,82,82,77**
Tote Swingers: 1&2 £4.10, 1&3 £14.90, 2&3 £13.40 CSF £39.17 TOTE £3.20: £1.60, £2.10, £9.30; EX 35.30.

Owner EHR Partnership **Bred** Bridlewood Farm **Trained** East Everleigh, Wilts

FOCUS

The odds-on favourite was disappointing in this maiden and the 69-rated runner-up puts the form in context. The first two set the level.

NOTEBOOK

Latin Lashes(USA) looked the main form danger to the odds-on favourite. A disappointment at Lingfield last time blurred the picture, but she bounced back with a professional front-running performance to get off the mark on the third attempt. Out of a half-sister to a Breeders' Cup Mile winner, she still has some scope for physical development and could make an impact in nurseries for the Hannon team. (op 3-1)

My Love Fajer(IRE) put in a fair effort back at 5f and probably ran near his current mark of 69. He seems to be quietly progressing and may be able to pick up a small race. (op 16-1)

Barbieri(IRE) found plenty of improvement on her second run. She still needs to learn to settle better, but is a half-sister to useful Irish sprinter Leitra and could be capable of quite a bit of further progress.

Florestans Match had finished runner-up as favourite on her last three starts and set a clear standard on form. The 84-rated filly was sent off a hot favourite, but she was run off her feet almost immediately before staying on when it was all over. The drop back to 5f was probably a major reason for her downfall, but this still has to rate as a very laboured effort by a runner who chased home a subsequent May Hill winner at Ascot in July. Official explanation: vet said filly was in season (op 1-2 tchd 8-15 and 4-7 in places)

Ma Quillet seemed to be travelling well in the chasing group around the final turn, but she didn't pick up. She did not really build on her debut fifth at Sandown, but should do better with time and distance. (op 7-1)

6287 DIGIBET.COM H'CAP 1m 2f (P)
6:50 (6:51) (Class 6) (0-60,60) 3-Y-O **£1,637** (£483; £241) **Stalls** High

Form RPR

1032 **1** **D'Urberville**[14] 5869 3-9-7 **60** .... RichardHughes 11 68
(J R Jenkins) *t.k.h: mde all: drvn fnl f: kpt finding enough* **3/1**[1]

6405 **2** *1¼* **Shoot The Pot (IRE)**[21] 5656 3-9-4 **57** .... JimmyQuinn 6 62
(J Mackie) *hld up in midfield on outer: prog fr 4f out to chse ldrs over 2f out: drvn over 1f out: kpt on to take 2nd last 75yds: a hld* **8/1**

3500 **3** *shd* **Wasara**[28] 5411 3-9-3 **56** .... DaneO'Neill 4 61
(Miss Amy Weaver) *settled in last trio: prog on outer fr 3f out: drvn and styd on fr over 1f out: nrly tk 2nd* **16/1**

0662 **4** *½* **Trecase**[14] 5864 3-9-2 **55** .... NeilCallan 7 59
(A W Carroll) *prom: drvn to chse wnr over 1f out: cl enough but nt qckn ent fnl f: lost 2 pls last 75yds* **10/3**[2]

030 **5** *1* **Lalika**[11] 5971 3-9-3 **56** .... LukeMorris 10 58
(C G Cox) *t.k.h early: chsd ldrs: pushed along over 4f out: nvr gng pce to trble ldrs: kpt on* **16/1**

4605 **6** *1¾* **Nom De La Rosa (IRE)**[7] 6080 3-8-9 **55** ....(p) HarryBentley(7) 9 53
(Miss Sheena West) *chsd ldr to over 1f out: fdd* **17/2**

3424 **7** *½* **Sheila's Bond**[62] 4301 3-9-5 **58** .... LiamKeniry 14 55
(J S Moore) *in tch in midfield: rdn over 2f out: one pce and no imp over 1f out* **6/1**[3]

0400 **8** *¾* **Pictures (IRE)**[20] 5689 3-8-11 **55** .... KierenFox(5) 13 51
(J J Bridger) *a nrr last than first: rdn 3f out: no prog: plugged on* **33/1**

3500 **9** *nk* **Mary Helen**[28] 5411 3-9-4 **57** .... LiamJones 3 52
(W M Brisbourne) *settled in last: rdn in 10th 3f out: struggling after: kpt on fnl f* **50/1**

5200 **10** *¾* **All Moving Parts (USA)**[9] 6026 3-9-5 **58** ....(p) JamesDoyle 12 52
(A J McCabe) *chsd ldng pair: rdn 3f out: steadily lost pl on inner fr over 1f out* **10/1**

5430 **11** *1¼* **River Tease**[28] 5414 3-9-6 **59** ....(p) CathyGannon 8 50
(J S Moore) *sn pushed along in last trio: detached in last pair over 3f out: plugged on* **33/1**

006 **12** *7* **Yorksters Prince (IRE)**[13] 5891 3-8-9 **55** .... RichardOld(7) 2 32
(G Prodromou) *a towards rr: dropped to last pair and detached over 3f out: t.o* **66/1**

45-0 **P** **Noverre Over There (IRE)**[14] 5869 3-9-5 **58** .... GeorgeBaker 1 —
(Miss Olivia Maylam) *sn prom: 5th whn p.u 1/2-way: dismntd* **33/1**

2m 7.67s (-0.33) **Going Correction** -0.10s/f (Stan) **13** Ran SP% **117.1**
Speed ratings (Par 99): **97,96,95,95,94 93,92,92,92,91 90,84,—**
Tote Swingers: 1&2 £6.60, 1&3 £16.50, 2&3 £27.60 CSF £25.74 CT £332.56 TOTE £3.60: £1.10, £1.50, £7.00; EX 28.60.

Owner Smart K Syndicate **Bred** Llety Stud **Trained** Royston, Herts

FOCUS

A low-grade handicap in which the winner set a fairly steady pace. Modest form.

Noverre Over There(IRE) Official explanation: jockey said gelding moved poorly

6288 DIGIBET H'CAP (DIV I) 1m 2f (P)
7:20 (7:20) (Class 5) (0-75,75) 3-Y-O+ **£1,944** (£574; £287) **Stalls** High

Form RPR

-062 **1** **Tenessee**[21] 5658 3-9-4 **75** .... LukeMorris 9 85+
(C G Cox) *pressed ldr: pushed up to ld 3f out: hrd rdn over 1f out: jnd last 75yds: hld on wl* **5/1**[2]

1232 **2** *hd* **Sunley Spinalonga**[21] 5656 3-9-2 **73** .... RichardHughes 3 83+
(D R C Elsworth) *hld up in last: pushed along 3f out: prog 2f out: drvn to go 2nd last 150yds: clsd and looked likely wnr: wouldn't go by last 75yds* **5/2**[1]

10-0 **3** *2½* **Silverglas (IRE)**[158] 1388 4-9-10 **75** .... JimCrowley 7 80+
(W J Knight) *trckd ldng pair: wnt 2nd 2f out: rdn and nt qckn over 1f out: lost 2nd last 150yds: wknd* **7/1**

1364 **4** *1* **Ballinteni**[18] 5756 8-8-9 **65** .... AdamBeschizza(5) 2 68
(Miss Gay Kelleway) *s.i.s and pushed along early: sn in 4th: rdn and nt qckn over 2f out: one pce after* **11/2**[3]

1425 **5** *1* **Chain Of Events**[39] 5091 3-9-4 **75** .... JackMitchell 5 76
(N B King) *chsd ldrs in 5th: rdn and effrt 3f out: tried to squeeze through over 1f out: sn wknd* **17/2**

0112 **6** *2¾* **Gross Prophet**[22] 5624 5-9-4 **72** .... SophieDoyle(3) 10 68
(A J Lidderdale) *led to 3f out: grad wknd* **15/2**

0625 **7** *nse* **Daniel Thomas (IRE)**[5] 6165 8-8-9 **63** ....(p) RobertLButler(3) 8 58
(P Butler) *s.s: mostly in last pair: in tch 2f out: sn btn* **25/1**

046 **8** *1* **At Wits End**[30] 5375 4-9-5 **70** .... KirstyMilczarek 4 63
(J A R Toller) *settled in 6th: rdn and dropped to last on outer over 2f out: no ch after* **11/2**[3]

2m 6.36s (-1.64) **Going Correction** -0.10s/f (Stan)
WFA 3 from 4yo+ 6lb **8** Ran SP% **114.6**
Speed ratings (Par 103): **102,101,99,99,98 96,96,95**
Tote Swingers: 1&2 £5.50, 1&3 £10.20, 2&3 £1.70 CSF £17.99 CT £86.90 TOTE £11.10: £3.20, £1.10, £4.20; EX 18.20.

Owner Ms Liza Judd **Bred** Mrs Liza Judd **Trained** Lambourn, Berks

FOCUS

A fairly competitive handicap. There was an exciting finish and the first two forged clear. It was the slower division but the form looks fairly interesting with the winner finally fulfilling his 2yo debut promise.

6289 DIGIBET H'CAP (DIV II) 1m 2f (P)
7:50 (7:50) (Class 5) (0-75,75) 3-Y-O+ **£1,944** (£574; £287) **Stalls** High

Form RPR

3132 **1** **Josr's Magic (IRE)**[11] 5958 6-8-11 **62** .... JimmyQuinn 7 72
(P R Hedger) *t.k.h: restrained towards rr after 3f: prog 3f out: rdn and styd on wl fr over 1f out: led last 75yds* **4/1**[2]

3325 **2** *1* **Diggeratt (USA)**[12] 5906 4-9-0 **65** .... TedDurcan 4 73
(R A Fahey) *wl in tch: prog to trck ldng pair over 2f out: wnt 2nd over 1f out: clsd on ldr fnl f but wnr wnt past* **4/1**[2]

1542 **3** *½* **Diamond Twister (USA)**[20] 5680 4-8-9 **65** .... KierenFox(5) 1 72
(J R Best) *rapid prog on outer to go 2nd over 5f out rousted along to ld over 2f out: hdd and no ex last 75yds* **10/1**

1200 **4** *7* **Danger Mulally**[14] 5859 3-9-4 **75** ....(t) JimmyFortune 6 68
(A M Balding) *led 3f: settled to trck ldrs after: rdn to dispute 3rd over 2f out: wknd over 1f out* **11/1**

0165 **5** *shd* **Aviso (GER)**[24] 5561 6-9-5 **70** .... TomQueally 3 63
(B J Curley) *prog to ld at str pce 6f out: hdd and pushed along over 2f out: wkng whn rdn over 1f out* **12/1**

0006 **6** *½* **Wind Star**[23] 5592 7-9-3 **68** .... SamHitchcott 2 60
(M F Harris) *settled in rr: rdn 3f out: no prog 2f out* **33/1**

3165 **7** *1¾* **Rowan Tiger**[14] 5868 4-9-10 **75** .... PatCosgrave 5 63
(J R Boyle) *t.k.h early: hld up in tch: stmbld after 3f: effrt on outer 3f out: no prog 2f out* **6/1**[3]

5602 **8** *2¼* **Expensive Problem**[19] 5716 7-9-3 **71** .... AndrewHeffernan(3) 8 55
(R J Smith) *awkward s: hld up last: gng wl enough 3f out: pushed along and limited prog fnl 2f: nvr remotely involved* **20/1**

1404 **9** *5* **Midfielder (USA)**[110] 2717 3-9-4 **75** ....(b[1]) WilliamBuick 10 49
(J H M Gosden) *pressed ldrs on inner: restrained after 2f: nt gng wl fr 1/2-way: u.p and no prog 3f out: eased over 1f out* **11/4**[1]

4416 **10** *28* **Heading To First**[83] 3594 3-8-11 **71** ....(p) RobertLButler(3) 9 —
(P Butler) *led 7f out to 6f out: prom tl wknd rapidly 3f out: t.o* **33/1**

2m 5.83s (-2.17) **Going Correction** -0.10s/f (Stan)
WFA 3 from 4yo+ 6lb **10** Ran SP% **116.7**
Speed ratings (Par 103): **104,103,102,97,97 96,95,93,89,67**
Tote Swingers: 1&2 £3.60, 1&3 £4.00, 2&3 £6.50 CSF £19.97 CT £146.90 TOTE £3.10: £1.10, £2.30, £4.60; EX 17.60.

Owner Ken Tyre & Lee Tyre **Bred** Bryan Ryan **Trained** Dogmersfield, Hampshire

FOCUS

The second division of this handicap was run at a decent pace. The lead changed hands several times in the early stages and the first three eventually pulled a long way clear of the rest. Sound form, rated around the third.

6290 DIGIBET SPORTS BETTING H'CAP 1m 4f (P)
8:20 (8:22) (Class 5) (0-70,70) 3-Y-O **£2,286** (£675; £337) **Stalls** Centre

Form RPR

0023 **1** **Iron Condor**[37] 5164 3-9-4 **67** .... LukeMorris 10 80
(J M P Eustace) *dwlt: hld up but sn in tch on inner: gd prog over 2f out: drvn to cl on ldrs over 1f out: led last 150yds: edgd lft but hld on wl* **17/2**

1152 **2** *hd* **Celestial Girl**[16] 5812 3-9-2 **65** .... SteveDrowne 13 78+
(H Morrison) *trckd ldrs: nt clr run wl over 2f out: more to do whn in the clr and rdn: gd prog on outer over 1f out: pressed wnr last 100yds: jst hld* **13/2**[3]

40-0 **3** *2¼* **Loden**[20] 5689 3-9-3 **66** .... J-PGuillambert 14 75+
(L M Cumani) *sddle slipped no later than 8f out: rapid prog on outer to ld over 4f out: stl 2 l clr 2f out: hdd last 150yds* **12/1**

3222 **4** *¾* **Azaday (IRE)**[21] 5654 3-9-6 **69** .... TedDurcan 3 77
(C F Wall) *prom: chsd ldr wl over 2f out: clsd to chal 1f out and nrly upsides: wknd last 100yds* **3/1**[1]

5554 **5** *2* **Mavalenta (IRE)**[24] 5552 3-9-5 **68** .... RichardHughes 5 74
(J W Hills) *hld up in last quartet: swtchd lft wl over 2f out: drvn and prog over 1f out: rchd 5th jst ins fnl f: no ch and nt pushed after* **12/1**

2400 **6** *2¼* **Musical Mark**[54] 4545 3-9-4 **67** .... LiamKeniry 1 68
(Mrs P Sly) *sn prom: drvn into 3rd briefly over 2f out: wknd over 1f out* **66/1**

2213 **7** *1½* **Now What**[16] 5812 3-9-4 **67** .... JimCrowley 12 66
(J G Portman) *mostly in midfield: lost pl sltly on inner 4f out: nt clr run wl over 2f out: prog sn after: effrt petered out over 1f out and wknd* **14/1**

0-00 **8** *nse* **Danvilla**[30] 5366 3-9-0 **63** .... WilliamCarson 7 62
(P R Webber) *dwlt: nt gng wl in last quartet: hrd rdn and no prog over 3f out: styd on fr 2f out: swtchd rt 1f out: nvr nrr* **33/1**

5631 **9** *3¾* **Halyard (IRE)**[21] 5656 3-9-1 **69** ....(v) JohnFahy(5) 9 62
(W R Swinburn) *nvr beyond midfield: rdn and no imp on ldrs over 2f out* **13/2**[3]

4650 **10** *17* **Forgotten Army (IRE)**[8] 6065 3-9-2 **65** .... PatCosgrave 2 31
(M H Tompkins) *sn pushed up to press ldr to 1/2-way: drvn and wknd over 2f out: t.o* **33/1**

11 *½* **Fearchar (IRE)**[48] 4770 3-8-13 **62** ....(tp) PBBeggy 11 27
(Paul W Flynn, Ire) *a wl in rr and nvr gng wl: t.o* **5/1**[2]

1640 **12** *1½* **Dream Spinner**[20] 5679 3-9-7 **70** ....(b[1]) EddieAhern 4 33
(J L Dunlop) *led to over 4f out: wknd rapidly over 2f out: eased and t.o* **20/1**

6-06 **13** *13* **Sir William Orpen**[34] 5236 3-9-0 **63** .... IanMongan 8 —
(P M Phelan) *hld up in last quartet: no prog 4f out: hung to nr side rail over 2f out: t.o* **66/1**

0-00 **14** *22* **Ildiko (USA)**[42] 4972 3-9-0 **63** ....(t) SebSanders 6 —
(Sir Mark Prescott) *drvn in last after 3f: nvr gng: t.o* **9/1**

2m 32.33s (-2.17) **Going Correction** -0.10s/f (Stan) **14** Ran SP% **124.5**
Speed ratings (Par 101): **103,102,101,100,99 98,97,97,94,83 82,81,73,58**
Tote Swingers: 1&2 £17.70, 1&3 £26.30, 2&3 £14.60 CSF £62.61 CT £680.65 TOTE £13.30: £4.30, £1.20, £6.90; EX 101.00.

Owner Harold Nass **Bred** Rockville Pike Partnership **Trained** Newmarket, Suffolk

The Form Book, Raceform Ltd, Compton, RG20 6NL

FOCUS
There were quite a few in-form runners involved in this middle-distance handicap which was run at a decent pace. Sound form.
Loden Official explanation: jockey said saddle slipped
Halyard(IRE) Official explanation: jockey said gelding never travelled
Dream Spinner Official explanation: jockey said gelding ran too free
Sir William Orpen Official explanation: jockey said gelding hung left-handed

6291 BOOK KEMPTON TICKETS ON 0844 579 3008 FILLIES' H'CAP 7f (P)
8:50 (8:53) (Class 4) (0-85,83) 3-Y-0+ **£3,885** (£1,156; £577; £288) **Stalls** High

Form RPR
0304 **1** **Sakhee's Pearl**39 5087 4-9-1 **75**........(b) TomQueally 4 84
(Miss Gay Kelleway) *t.k.h: hld up in tch: rdn and sustained prog on outer fr 2f out to ld 1f out: styd on wl* **13/2**
1510 **2** 1 3/4 **Belgique (IRE)**7 6090 3-9-5 **82**........ RichardHughes 3 85
(R Hannon) *trckd ldr to over 4f out: styd cl up: rdn and nt qckn wl over 1f out: styd on fnl f to take 2nd last strides* **10/1**
-165 **3** hd **Mainstay**29 5396 4-9-7 **81**........ WilliamBuick 5 84
(J H M Gosden) *prog on wd outside to trck ldr over 4f out: drvn 2f out: cl enough over 1f out: outpcd by wnr fnl f: lost 2nd last strides* **8/1**
2214 **4** 1 **Touch Tone**21 5662 3-9-1 **78**........ MichaelHills 1 78+
(B W Hills) *hld up in last pair: looking to angle to outer over 2f out but hemmed in: lost grnd and no ch after: shkn up and styd on fr over 1f out* **5/1**3
502 **5** 1 **Wallis**11 5960 3-8-12 **75**........ KirstyMilczarek 8 72
(L M Cumani) *fractious bef ent stalls: plld hrd early: prom: nt qckn over 1f out: fdd* **5/2**1
1000 **6** 1 1/2 **Kingston Acacia**13 5896 3-8-12 **75**........(v) JimmyFortune 6 68
(A M Balding) *led: kicked on over 2f out: hdd & wknd 1f out* **10/1**
0444 **7** shd **Hulcote Rose (IRE)**13 5896 3-8-12 **75**........ LiamKeniry 2 68
(S Kirk) *hld up in last pair: outpcd fr over 2f out: n.d after* **12/1**
-130 **8** 2 **Miss Mittagong (USA)**98 3071 3-9-6 **83**........(v) JimCrowley 7 70
(R M Beckett) *t.k.h: hld up on inner: rousted along over 2f out: wknd tamely over 1f out* **9/2**2

1m 25.34s (-0.66) **Going Correction** -0.10s/f (Stan)
WFA 3 from 4yo 3lb **8** Ran SP% **113.7**
Speed ratings (Par 102): **99,97,96,95,94 92,92,90**
Tote Swingers: 1&2 £11.70, 1&3 £11.30, 2&3 £3.50 CSF £67.38 CT £525.12 TOTE £10.60: £3.10, £1.10, £2.40; EX 66.20.
Owner The Peregrina Partnership **Bred** Andrea Wilkinson Gay Kelleway **Trained** Exning, Suffolk

FOCUS
An interesting fillies' handicap but the pace was fairly steady and a few disappointed, so it is hard to know what to make of the form. The winner was back to her spring form.

6292 PANORAMIC H'CAP 6f (P)
9:20 (9:21) (Class 6) (0-65,65) 3-Y-0+ **£1,637** (£483; £241) **Stalls** High

Form RPR
6441 **1** **Sweet Gale (IRE)**4 6208 6-9-6 **64** 6ex........ JimmyQuinn 9 76+
(Mike Murphy) *hld up in 6th: smooth prog on inner 2f out: led over 1f out whn stl gng wl: 1 l up fnl f: drvn and jst lasted nr fin* **11/4**2
11 **2** 1/2 **Tislaam (IRE)**6 6110 3-9-4 **64**........(p) JamesDoyle 4 73+
(A J McCabe) *chsd ldng trio: forced to check wd 2f out: drvn and prog to take 2nd jst over 1f out: looked hld tl clsd on tiring wnr fin* **2/1**1
0050 **3** 1 3/4 **Fromsong (IRE)**30 5377 12-9-3 **61**........ SamHitchcott 6 64
(D K Ivory) *chsd ldng pair: clsd to ld 2f out: hdd over 1f out: one pce* **33/1**
1354 **4** 1/2 **Cativo Cavallino**24 5561 7-9-0 **61**........ NataliaGemelova(3) 8 63
(J E Long) *racd v wd in last trio: struggling over 2f out: r.o fr over 1f out: nrst fin* **8/1**
3164 **5** hd **Scottish Glen**13 5897 4-9-6 **64**........ LiamKeniry 12 65
(P R Chamings) *sn off the pce in 7th: drvn over 2f out: kpt on fr over 1f out u.p: nrst fin* **6/1**3
5625 **6** 2 3/4 **The Jobber (IRE)**13 5876 9-9-4 **62**........ DaneO'Neill 11 54
(M Blanshard) *chsd ldrs in 5th: rdn and no imp 2f out: grad fdd* **16/1**
1066 **7** 1 **Replicator**9 6018 5-9-3 **64**........(e) AshleyHamblett(3) 3 53
(P L Gilligan) *chsd ldr: upsides 2f out: wknd over 1f out* **25/1**
0500 **8** 6 **Footstepsofspring (FR)**47 4806 3-9-5 **65**........ TonyCulhane 10 35
(W J Musson) *racd wd towards rr: nvr gng the pce to be involved* **25/1**
6344 **9** nse **Decency (IRE)**21 5669 3-9-4 **64**........ RichardHughes 7 34
(H J L Dunlop) *stdd s: hld up in last pair and wl off the pce: brief effrt on inner over 2f out: sn no prog and eased* **8/1**
0000 **10** nk **Tell Halaf**13 5887 3-9-2 **62**........ GeorgeBaker 5 31
(M G Quinlan) *mostly in last pair and sn struggling* **33/1**
1060 **11** 1 1/4 **Silver Prelude**49 4717 9-9-0 **65**........ RyanClark(7) 2 30
(S C Williams) *blasted off in front fr wd draw: clr over 3f out: hdd & wknd rapidly 2f out* **50/1**

1m 12.17s (-0.93) **Going Correction** -0.10s/f (Stan)
WFA 3 from 4yo+ 2lb **11** Ran SP% **117.9**
Speed ratings (Par 101): **102,101,99,98,98 94,93,85,85,84 82**
Tote Swingers: 1&2 £8.40, 1&3 £6.50, 2&3 £9.20 CSF £8.16 CT £147.61 TOTE £5.80: £2.00, £1.90, £10.30; EX 11.90 Place 6: £204.83 Place 5: £90.64. .
Owner Ms L M Bartlett **Bred** Rozelle Bloodstock **Trained** Westoning, Beds

FOCUS
A modest handicap run at a good pace. The two market leaders filled the first two positions and the form should be reliable. the winner looks a bit better than the bare form.
Decency(IRE) Official explanation: jockey said filly never travelled
T/Plt: £179.30 to a £1 stake. Pool:£60,314.60 - 245.48 winning tickets T/Qpdt: £20.40 to a £1 stake. Pool:£9,030 - 326.80 winning tickets JN

6034 REDCAR (L-H)
Wednesday, September 22

OFFICIAL GOING: Good to firm (9.4)
Wind: light 1/2 behind Weather: fine, becoming overcast, light rain last 2

6293 EUROPEAN BREEDERS' FUND MAIDEN STKS 7f
2:15 (2:16) (Class 5) 2-Y-0 **£3,043** (£905; £452; £226) **Stalls** High

Form RPR
3 **1** **Male Model**13 5892 2-9-3 0........ AhmedAjtebi 4 83+
(Mahmood Al Zarooni) *cl up: led after 1f: rdn wl over 1f out: styd on* **6/4**1
04 **2** 1 1/4 **Baileys Moneypenny**18 5761 2-8-12 0........ PaulMulrennan 2 75
(J G Given) *led 1f: cl up: rdn 2f out: ev ch tl drvn and nt qckn ins fnl f* **16/1**
0 **3** 1 1/2 **Ashva (USA)**33 5277 2-9-3 0........ PhillipMakin 8 76
(M Dods) *cl up: rdn 2f out and ev ch tl drvn and one pce ent fnl f* **9/4**2
4 9 **Newby Lodge (IRE)** 2-8-12 0........ TomEaves 12 47+
(B Smart) *midfield: hdwy 3f out: chsd ldrs over 2f out: rdn and kpt on appr fnl f: nrst fin* **22/1**
05 **5** 3/4 **Homeboy (IRE)**33 5255 2-9-3 0........ PaulHanagan 15 51
(M P Tregoning) *in tch: hdwy to chse ldrs 3f out: rdn wl over 2f out: sn hung lft and one pce* **11/2**3
00 **6** 4 **One Of Twins**12 5924 2-9-0 0........ JamesSullivan(3) 10 40
(M W Easterby) *towards rr and reminders after 2f: pushed along 1/2-way: rdn and hdwy over 2f out: sn edgd lft: kpt on fnl f: nvr nr ldrs* **66/1**
0 **7** 1 3/4 **Fearless Poet (IRE)**10 6001 2-9-3 0........ DavidAllan 3 36
(B Smart) *chsd ldrs: rdn along over 2f out: sn one pce* **50/1**
8 hd **Oakwell (IRE)** 2-9-0 0........ MichaelStainton(3) 1 35
(Miss S E Hall) *midfield: hdwy on outer and in tch over 2f out: sn rdn and kpt on same pce* **66/1**
0 **9** 3 3/4 **Hobbesian War**68 4089 2-9-3 0........ MickyFenton 14 25
(T P Tate) *chsd ldrs: pushed along over 3f out: sn wknd* **28/1**
0 **10** 2 **Karens Legacy (IRE)**18 5761 2-8-9 0........(t) GaryBartley(3) 5 15
(I W McInnes) *chsd ldrs: rdn along 3f out: grad wknd* **66/1**
0000 **11** 7 **Be My Spy**9 6036 2-8-12 42........ GregFairley 6 —
(P Salmon) *sltly hmpd s: a towards rr* **66/1**
12 1 3/4 **Inca Blue** 2-8-12 0........ LanceBetts(5) 18 —
(T D Easterby) *s.i.s: a bhd* **66/1**
13 1 1/4 **Vizean (IRE)** 2-8-12 0........ PJMcDonald 17 —
(G A Swinbank) *s.i.s: a in rr* **20/1**
14 4 1/2 **Colonel Percy (IRE)** 2-9-3 0........ JoeFanning 13 —
(M Johnston) *chsd ldrs: pushed along 1/2-way: sn outpcd* **12/1**
0 **15** 27 **Barry Crockett (IRE)**12 5900 2-9-3 0........(t) RoystonFfrench 7 —
(Mrs L Williamson) *chsd ldrs: rdn along and wknd qckly 1/2-way: sn bhd and eased over 1f out* **66/1**

1m 22.0s (-2.50) **Going Correction** -0.35s/f (Firm) **15** Ran SP% **123.2**
Speed ratings (Par 95): **100,98,96,86,85 81,79,78,74,72 64,62,60,55,24**
Tote Swingers: 1&2 £6.20, 1&3 £1.80, 2&3 £8.80 CSF £27.63 TOTE £2.10: £1.10, £4.20, £1.20; EX 24.50.
Owner Godolphin **Bred** Whitsbury Manor Stud And Mrs M E Slade **Trained** Newmarket, Suffolk

FOCUS
An ordinary maiden in which few were ever involved, with the front three, who finished well clear, dominating from an early stage. The winner stepped up.

NOTEBOOK
Male Model confirmed the promise of his debut third on Polytrack, keeping on strongly after showing speed to record a straightforward success. While his stable have plenty of better juveniles, he is useful. (op 13-8 tchd 11-8)
Baileys Moneypenny is an improving filly. She may find a similarly ordinary maiden, but also now has the option of handicaps. (tchd 14-1)
Ashva(USA), who got a bit warm, travelled strongly (went odds on in running) but didn't see his race out, just as on debut in a good York maiden over the same trip, albeit this was an improvement. He may gain more stamina as he strengthens up, but for now at least he looks a sprinter. (op 3-1 tchd 10-3 and 7-2 in a place)
Newby Lodge(IRE), in the same ownership as the third, though sporting the second colours, attracted little market interest and was beaten a long way, but she did fare best of the newcomers. This 60,000gns purchase may improve. (op 20-1)
Homeboy(IRE) did not improve for the step up to 7f and looks limited. Perhaps he'll find his level now he's qualified for a mark. (op 5-1)
One Of Twins was under pressure early. He one could be of interest in Fibresand handicaps (sire unbeaten in three runs at Southwell)
Oakwell(IRE), already gelded, looked backward in the paddock, so this was a respectable introduction.
Inca Blue was another who looked backward and completely blew the start.
Vizean(IRE), weak in the market, showed little after being keen to post. (op 14-1)
Colonel Percy(IRE), easy to back, was outpaced before halfway and looks to need more time and distance. (op 11-1)

6294 HOLD YOUR CHRISTMAS PARTY HERE NURSERY (DIV I) 1m
2:50 (2:50) (Class 6) (0-65,66) 2-Y-0 **£1,295** (£385; £192; £96) **Stalls** High

Form RPR
5242 **1** **Regimental (IRE)**10 6001 2-9-3 **61**........ PhillipMakin 1 70+
(Mrs A Duffield) *dwlt: hld up in rr: smooth hdwy 4f out: led on bit over 2f out: rdn clr jst ins fnl f: eased towards fin* **15/8**1
4300 **2** 2 1/2 **Bigalo's Laura B (IRE)**23 5602 2-8-2 **51**........(e) DeclanCannon(5) 5 53
(L A Mullaney) *chsd ldrs: kpt on to take 2nd ins fnl f: no imp* **28/1**
605 **3** 1 **Syncopated Lady (IRE)**18 5755 2-8-9 **53**........ SilvestreDeSousa 7 53
(D O'Meara) *hld up towards rr: hdwy 4f out: chsd wnr 2f out: edgd rt and styd on same pce fnl f* **9/2**2
5001 **4** 3/4 **Sky Diamond (IRE)**22 5630 2-9-7 **65**........ PaulMulrennan 11 63
(J G Given) *towards rr: hdwy over 2f out: chsng ldrs whn hung lft over 1f out: kpt on same pce* **7/1**3
5060 **5** 1 1/4 **Grazeon Again (IRE)**17 5784 2-9-6 **64**........ RobertWinston 3 59
(J J Quinn) *in rr: effrt over 2f out: one pce* **10/1**
004 **6** 5 **Arashone**31 5332 2-8-9 **53**........ DuranFentiman 2 37
(J R Weymes) *chsd ldrs: wkng whn hmpd over 1f out* **22/1**
0006 **7** 2 1/4 **Kings Arms**9 6027 2-7-12 **45**........ JamesSullivan(3) 8 23
(M W Easterby) *mid-div: effrt over 2f out: nvr nr ldrs* **50/1**
000 **8** 4 1/2 **Carver County (IRE)**63 4240 2-8-1 **45**........(b1) FrannyNorton 14 13
(K A Ryan) *chsd ldrs: lost pl over 1f out: eased ins fnl f* **8/1**
6005 **9** nk **Louis Girl**40 5020 2-8-4 **48**........(p) PaulHanagan 12 15
(R A Fahey) *w ldrs: wknd 2f out* **9/1**
000 **10** nk **Sea The Flames (IRE)**44 4902 2-8-12 **56**........(b1) JoeFanning 10 23
(M P Tregoning) *s.i.s: a bhd: hung lft and nt keen* **10/1**
0600 **11** 7 **Auburn Lady**10 5998 2-8-13 **62**........ DaleSwift(5) 15 13
(A D Brown) *led tl over 2f out: hung lft and sn lost pl* **20/1**

1m 37.38s (-0.62) **Going Correction** -0.35s/f (Firm) **11** Ran SP% **119.3**
Speed ratings (Par 93): **89,86,85,84,83 78,76,71,71,71 64**
Tote Swingers: 1&2 £11.30, 1&3 £2.60, 2&3 £21.80 CSF £72.02 CT £220.57 TOTE £2.30: £1.10, £8.90, £1.60; EX 73.00.
Owner I Farrington & R Chapman **Bred** Deer Forest Stud **Trained** Constable Burton, N Yorks

FOCUS
A very moderate nursery run for really poor prize money. The time was 0.23 seconds quicker than the second division, won by Tapis Libre. The winner did it well but the opposition was very limited.

NOTEBOOK
Regimental(IRE), back on quick ground, was a notch above his rivals. Having travelled best, he was probably in front sooner than ideal but still found plenty, ultimately being eased down and looking value for at least another length. He can be competitive in a higher grade. (op 2-1 tchd 9-4)
Bigalo's Laura B(IRE), without the blinkers this time, proved suited by the step up in trip but was no match at all for the winner. (op 25-1)
Syncopated Lady(IRE), upped in trip on nursery debut, plugged on without threatening. She is due to be eased 2lb. (op 7-1)

Sky Diamond(IRE)'s recent selling win came over 7f on soft ground and these quicker conditions were no use to him. He did well to get fourth after coming under pressure a fair way out. Official explanation: jockey said gelding was unsuited by the good to firm ground (tchd 11-2)
Grazeon Again(IRE), eased 3lb and dropped in grade, finished clear of the rest. (tchd 11-1)

6295 SUBSCRIBE TO RACING UK H'CAP 6f
3:25 (3:26) (Class 6) (0-65,65) 3-Y-0+ **£1,706** (£503; £252) **Stalls** High

Form RPR

1506 **1** **Sea Salt**[9] 6040 7-9-1 **62** MichaelStainton(3) 8 72
(R E Barr) *led: swtchd to r alone far rail and hdd after 1 1/2f: a.p: rdn to ld ins fnl f: kpt on* **28/1**

2313 **2** *hd* **Forever's Girl**[12] 5920 4-8-13 **57** PaulMulrennan 13 66
(G R Oldroyd) *cl up: led after 1f: rdn over 1f out: drvn and hdd ins fnl f: kpt on* **11/2**[2]

4605 **3** *2 1/2* **Tawzeea (IRE)**[49] 4706 5-9-6 **64** PhillipMakin 5 65
(M Dods) *midfield: hdwy over 2f out: rdn wl over 1f out: kpt on ins fnl f* **5/1**[1]

5024 **4** *1/2* **Secret City (IRE)**[18] 5760 4-9-1 **59** (b) SilvestreDeSousa 3 58
(R Bastiman) *prom: rdn along over 2f out: drvn over 1f out: kpt on same pce* **7/1**

4342 **5** *1/2* **Bateleur**[19] 5714 6-9-1 **59** RobertWinston 2 57
(M R Channon) *hld up: hdwy over 2f out: rdn wl over 1f out: styd on ins fnl f: nrst fin* **9/1**

1565 **6** *hd* **Foreign Rhythm (IRE)**[9] 6040 5-8-10 **61** GarryWhillans(7) 10 58
(R E Barr) *trckd ldrs: hdwy 1/2-way: cl up and ev ch 2f out: sn rdn and wknd appr fnl f* **25/1**

-000 **7** *1* **Ubenkor (IRE)**[24] 5545 5-9-4 **62** PJMcDonald 4 56
(M Herrington) *hld up in rr: swtchd lft and hdwy over 2f out: rdn over 1f out: kpt on ins fnl f: nrst fin* **50/1**

2 **8** *3* **The Happy Hammer (IRE)**[13] 5875 4-9-1 **59** JoeFanning 14 43
(Eugene Stanford) *chsd ldrs: rdn along 2f out: drvn and wknd over 1f out* **14/1**

2204 **9** *3/4* **Micky Mac (IRE)**[20] 5684 6-9-2 **65** DaleSwift(5) 9 47
(C J Teague) *prom: rdn along wl over 2f out: drvn wl over 1f out and grad wknd* **33/1**

0060 **10** *nk* **Dark Moment**[14] 5852 4-9-2 **65** (p) IanBrennan(5) 1 46
(Ollie Pears) *hld up: effrt over 2f out: sn rdn and n.d* **6/1**[3]

110 **11** *1/2* **Clerical (USA)**[24] 5557 4-9-0 **58** (p) AdrianNicholls 16 37
(R M H Cowell) *towards rr and reminders after 1f: nvr a factor* **14/1**

1464 **12** *1/2* **Arch Walker (IRE)**[9] 6040 3-8-13 **64** MichaelO'Connell(5) 12 42
(Jedd O'Keeffe) *chsd ldrs: rdn along over 2f out: sn drvn and grad wknd* **16/1**

0054 **13** *hd* **Espy**[18] 5764 5-9-1 **59** (v[1]) PatrickMathers 7 36
(I W McInnes) *s.i.s: a in rr* **25/1**

1004 **14** *1* **Thinking**[40] 5046 3-8-12 **58** DavidAllan 11 32
(T D Easterby) *a towards rr* **40/1**

1266 **15** *1* **Dies Solis**[6] 6103 3-9-2 **62** TomEaves 18 33
(V P Donoghue) *prom: rdn along wl over 2f out: sn wknd: struck into* **12/1**

6000 **16** *1/2* **Cutting Comments**[4] 6189 4-9-2 **60** AndrewElliott 19 29
(P F Holmes) *chsd ldrs on wd outside: rdn along wl over 2f out: sn wknd* **20/1**

2636 **17** *1/2* **Minturno (USA)**[20] 5684 4-9-2 **60** (p) RoystonFfrench 20 28
(Mrs A Duffield) *hld up: a towards rr* **20/1**

5104 **18** *1 1/2* **Tabiet**[28] 5410 3-9-0 **60** PaulHanagan 17 23
(James Moffatt) *cl up: rdn along 1/2-way: sn wknd* **25/1**

69.50 secs (-2.30) **Going Correction** -0.35s/f (Firm)
WFA 3 from 4yo+ 2lb **18** Ran SP% **127.6**
Speed ratings (Par 101): **101,100,97,96,96 95,94,90,89,89 88,87,87,86,84 84,83,81**
Tote Swingers: 1&2 £40.00, 1&3 £46.30, 2&3 £8.10 CSF £164.78 CT £957.50 TOTE £36.70: £5.40, £1.90, £1.80, £2.30; EX 329.70.
Owner R E Barr **Bred** D R Tucker **Trained** Seamer, N Yorks

FOCUS
A moderate handicap in which Sea Salt, taken to race alone against the far rail after a furlong or so, while the others stayed up the middle, recorded a narrow success. A tricky race to rate and the main pack could be rated 6-7lb higher.
Espy Official explanation: jockey said gelding failed to face the visor
Dies Solis Official explanation: trainer's rep said colt was struck into

6296 FOLLOW REDCAR RACING ON FACEBOOK CLAIMING STKS 1m
4:00 (4:01) (Class 4) 3-Y-0+ **£3,626** (£1,079; £539; £269) **Stalls** High

Form RPR

1321 **1** **Fremen (USA)**[9] 6029 10-9-3 85 AdrianNicholls 9 78
(D Nicholls) *trckd ldrs: effrt 2f out: led jst ins fnl f: styd on strly* **6/1**

4050 **2** *2 1/2* **King's Sabre**[14] 5867 4-8-6 60 (e) MarkCoumbe(5) 11 66
(R C Guest) *s.i.s: mid-div: effrt over 2f out: hrd rdn over 1f out: styd on to take 2nd nr fin* **66/1**

0004 **3** *1/2* **Charlie Cool**[17] 5786 7-9-4 90 (b) JamesSullivan(3) 3 75
(Mrs R A Carr) *wnt lft s: trckd ldrs: rdr dropped whip over 1f out: styd on same pce* **9/4**[2]

1116 **4** *shd* **Sunnyside Tom (IRE)**[17] 5786 6-9-7 89 PaulHanagan 4 75
(R A Fahey) *trckd ldrs: led after 2f: hdd jst ins fnl f: no ex* **7/4**[1]

010 **5** *1 1/2* **Shotley Mac**[17] 5789 6-10-0 80 (b) FrannyNorton 13 78
(N Bycroft) *w ldrs: one pce fnl 2f* **11/1**

0000 **6** *1/2* **Dubai Dynamo**[23] 5605 5-9-11 90 (b) AndrewElliott 7 74
(Mrs R A Carr) *towards rr: effrt over 2f out: kpt on ins fnl f* **11/2**[3]

000 **7** *1/2* **Talent Scout (IRE)**[16] 5815 4-9-1 44 DanielTudhope 8 63
(T D Walford) *towards rr: reminders 3f out: hdwy: nt clr run and swtchd rt over 1f out: nvr trbld ldrs* **66/1**

624 **8** *hd* **Crocodile Bay (IRE)**[27] 5439 7-8-6 57 IanBrennan(5) 12 58
(R C Guest) *t.k.h: led 2f: chsd ldrs: hung rt and wknd over 1f out* **50/1**

2110 **9** *5* **Island Chief**[25] 5530 4-8-13 75 PaulMulrennan 10 49
(M W Easterby) *in rr: bhd fnl 2f* **20/1**

6500 **10** *nk* **French Applause (IRE)**[28] 5408 4-8-11 56 MickyFenton 2 46
(T P Tate) *carried lft s: sn trcking ldrs: lost pl over 1f out* **50/1**

3040 **11** *12* **Emperor's Well**[12] 5927 11-8-4 44 DavidSimmonson(7) 5 19
(M W Easterby) *in rr: lost pl over 3f out: sn wl bhd* **66/1**

006 **12** *35* **Shamo Hill Theatre**[30] 5360 3-8-4 40 ow2 (p) DeanHeslop(5) 1 —
(C J Teague) *wnt lft s: sn pushed along: rdn and lost pl over 3f out: hung rt and sn bhd: t.o fnl 2f* **66/1**

1m 34.77s (-3.23) **Going Correction** -0.35s/f (Firm)
WFA 3 from 4yo+ 4lb **12** Ran SP% **119.8**
Speed ratings (Par 105): **102,99,99,98,97 96,96,96,91,90 78,43**
Tote Swingers: 1&2 £45.80, 1&3 £5.10, 2&3 £52.30 CSF £349.12 TOTE £8.50: £1.50, £18.50, £1.20; EX 198.30.
Owner Middleham Park Racing XXXV C King A Seed **Bred** Flaxman Holdings Ltd **Trained** Sessay, N Yorks

■ Stewards' Enquiry : Mark Coumbe one-day ban: used whip with excessive frequency (Oct 6)

FOCUS
A good claimer, although those with lofty ratings probably didn't run to their best judged on the proximity of the likes of 60-rated runner-up and the 44-rated seventh. The form could be rated a length higher on time.

6297 WIN A VIP DAY OUT @ REDCARRACING.CO.UK H'CAP 1m 2f
4:35 (4:36) (Class 5) (0-70,70) 3-Y-0+ **£2,072** (£616; £308; £153) **Stalls** Low

Form RPR

041 **1** **Destiny Blue (IRE)**[8] 6061 3-8-10 **62** 6ex PaulMulrennan 1 77+
(J A Osborne) *trckd ldrs: smooth hdwy on inner to ld wl over 2f out: clr over 1f out: pushed out* **9/4**[1]

01- **2** *2 1/4* **Kiama Bay (IRE)**[462] 3018 4-8-9 **60** IanBrennan(5) 6 68
(J J Quinn) *trckd ldng pair: pushed along and outpcd over 3f out: rdn 2f out: styd on u.p to chse wnr ins fnl f: no imp* **8/1**

1116 **3** *2 1/4* **Eijaaz (IRE)**[9] 6032 9-9-3 **63** (p) SilvestreDeSousa 9 67
(G A Harker) *hld up towards rr: hdwy over 4f out: effrt and nt clr run over 2f out: rdn and styd on same pce ent fnl f* **12/1**

6304 **4** *1 1/2* **Sir Mark (IRE)**[134] 1996 6-9-4 **64** DanielTudhope 7 65
(M A Peill) *led: rdn along 4f out: hdd wl over 2f out: sn drvn and kpt on same pce* **33/1**

32 **5** *nse* **Dandarrell**[26] 5479 3-8-4 **56** PaulHanagan 8 56
(Julie Camacho) *t.k.h: chsd ldr: effrt and cl up 4f out: rdn along over 2f out: sn drvn and one pce* **13/2**

022 **6** *1/2* **Avitus**[25] 5515 4-8-11 **57** ow1 PhillipMakin 5 56
(Micky Hammond) *trckd ldrs: hdwy on outer over 3f out: rdn over 2f out: sn drvn and one pce* **9/2**[2]

-000 **7** *1/2* **Robby Bobby**[17] 5790 5-9-10 **70** GregFairley 4 68
(M Johnston) *in tch: pushed along over 4f out: rdn and sme hdwy on inner over 3f out: drvn 2f out and sn wknd* **6/1**[3]

5620 **8** *9* **Knight's Victory (IRE)**[38] 5118 4-9-2 **65** (p) MichaelStainton(3) 2 45
(Michael Smith) *s.i.s: a bhd* **9/1**

2330 **9** *9* **Blue Spinnaker (IRE)**[82] 3613 11-9-6 **69** JamesSullivan(3) 3 31
(M W Easterby) *s.i.s and reminders after s: a bhd* **16/1**

2m 4.84s (-2.26) **Going Correction** -0.15s/f (Firm)
WFA 3 from 4yo+ 6lb **9** Ran SP% **114.2**
Speed ratings (Par 103): **103,101,99,98,98 97,97,90,82**
Tote Swingers: 1&2 £4.50, 1&3 £7.70, 2&3 £13.70 CSF £20.72 CT £175.82 TOTE £2.90: £1.10, £4.00, £1.80; EX 25.60.
Owner Mr & Mrs Ian Bendelow & Mrs F Walwyn **Bred** Barronstown Stud **Trained** Upper Lambourn, Berks

FOCUS
A good race for the grade - the winner is clearly better than a Class 5 handicapper, and the runner-up is also open to improvement. Sound form. The time was 1.40 seconds quicker than the following seller won by the 70-rated Prince Apollo, although that one didn't run to his mark.

6298 WEDDING RECEPTIONS AT REDCAR RACECOURSE (S) STKS 1m 2f
5:10 (5:13) (Class 6) 3-5-Y-0 **£1,706** (£503; £252) **Stalls** Low

Form RPR

0000 **1** **Prince Apollo**[8] 6050 5-9-1 75 PaulHanagan 8 61
(Ian Williams) *hld up in midfield: hdwy to chse ldrs over 3f out: styd on to ld last 100yds* **9/2**[3]

2405 **2** *1 1/4* **Free As A Lark**[21] 5664 3-8-4 67 NickyMackay 1 53
(C F Wall) *trckd ldrs: edgd rt 4f out: led 1f out: edgd lft: hdd and no ex ins fnl f* **9/4**[2]

6435 **3** *2* **Guga (IRE)**[22] 5636 4-9-7 59 (p) SilvestreDeSousa 11 60
(G A Harker) *chsd ldrs: sn pushed along: n.m.r over 2f out: kpt on fnl f* **9/1**

5402 **4** *shd* **Chantilly Pearl (USA)**[22] 5636 4-8-10 58 PaulMulrennan 10 53+
(J G Given) *trckd ldrs: led over 2f out: edgd lft: hdd 1f out: one pce whn n.m.r last 75yds* **2/1**[1]

0050 **5** *1* **Napoletano (ITY)**[9] 6037 4-8-12 32 JamesSullivan(3) 3 52?
(R Johnson) *led: hdd over 2f out: one pce* **66/1**

1604 **6** *6* **Media Stars**[9] 6037 5-9-2 53 LeeTopliss(5) 13 46
(R Johnson) *s.i.s: hld up in midfield: effrt over 3f out: nvr a factor* **40/1**

5036 **7** *1/2* **Joinedupwriting**[59] 4411 5-8-12 58 MichaelStainton(3) 7 39
(R M Whitaker) *dwlt: hld up in rr: hdwy over 4f out: nvr nr ldrs* **11/1**

605 **8** *3/4* **Applaude**[9] 6037 5-9-2 62 (b) MarkCoumbe(5) 4 44
(R C Guest) *dwlt: hld up in rr: t.k.h: sme hdwy 3f out: nvr on terms* **20/1**

0520 **9** *3 1/2* **Castlebury (IRE)**[7] 6076 5-9-1 54 (b) PJMcDonald 6 31
(Mrs R A Carr) *s.i.s: hld up in rr: nvr on terms* **33/1**

60 **10** *14* **Good Bye Day**[32] 5303 3-8-4 0 DuranFentiman 5 —
(T D Easterby) *sn in tch: lost pl 3f out: sn bhd* **66/1**

4500 **11** *6* **Roydmore**[9] 6033 3-8-9 47 TomEaves 9 —
(R A Fahey) *s.i.s: sn chsng ldrs: lost pl 3f out: sn bhd* **66/1**

12 *73* **Danrose** 3-8-1 0 KellyHarrison(3) 12 —
(R Craggs) *slowly away: in rr: rn wd bnd over 5f out: t.o whn hung rt 3f out: virtually p.u* **50/1**

2m 6.24s (-0.86) **Going Correction** -0.15s/f (Firm)
WFA 3 from 4yo+ 6lb **12** Ran SP% **117.2**
Speed ratings (Par 101): **97,96,94,94,93 88,88,87,84,73 68,10**
Tote Swingers: 1&2 £4.20, 1&3 £6.70, 2&3 £5.10 CSF £14.17 TOTE £5.70: £2.80, £1.70, £1.60; EX 21.80.The winner was bought in for £8,500. Guga was claimed by John Mackie for £6,000. Free As A Lark claimed by R E R Williams for £6,000.
Owner Dr Marwan Koukash **Bred** Juddmonte Farms Ltd **Trained** Portway, Worcs

FOCUS
A reasonable seller, though the proximity of the 59-rated third and 32-rated fifth limit the form, and the time was 1.40 seconds slower than the previous Class 5 handicap won by the rapidly improving Destiny Blue.
Applaude Official explanation: jockey said gelding ran too free and lost a front shoe

6299 BUY YOUR TICKETS ONLINE @ REDCARRACING.CO.UK H'CAP 5f
5:40 (5:43) (Class 5) (0-70,71) 3-Y-0+ **£2,072** (£616; £308; £153) **Stalls** High

Form RPR

4231 **1** **Select Committee**[7] 6073 5-9-5 **71** 6ex (v) IanBrennan(5) 3 79
(J J Quinn) *trckd ldrs: hdwy on outer 2f out: rdn to chal and hung rt jst over 1f out: led ins fnl f: drvn out* **9/4**[1]

2635 **2** *3/4* **Secret Venue**[9] 6031 4-9-0 **66** (v) MichaelO'Connell(5) 6 71
(Jedd O'Keeffe) *prom: effrt to chse ldr 2f out: sn rdn and hung lft: kpt on u.p fnl f* **11/2**[3]

3155 **3** *1 1/4* **Star Twilight**[11] 5956 3-9-3 **65** (v) RobertWinston 1 66
(D Shaw) *led: rdn wl over 1f out: drvn and edgd lft ent fnl f: sn hdd and one pce* **10/1**

4132 **4** *hd* **Angelo Poliziano**[26] 5477 4-9-5 **66** (v) PaulHanagan 9 68+
(Mrs A Duffield) *trckd ldrs: nt clr run and swtchd lft wl over 1f out: effrt and ch whn hmpd jst over 1f out: rdn and kpt on ins fnl f* **10/3**[2]

5112 **5** 1 **Rio's Girl**28 5410 3-8-12 **60** PaulQuinn 8 56
(R M Whitaker) *chsd ldrs: hdwy 2f out: rdn over 1f out: sn one pce* **11/2**3
1066 **6** shd **Tournedos (IRE)**30 5362 8-8-9 **56** (b) PJMcDonald 5 52
(Mrs R A Carr) *chsd ldrs: rdn wl over 1f out: drvn ent fnl f and sn one pce* **20/1**
3400 **7** 3/4 **Greek Secret**38 5123 7-8-10 **62** ow5 (b) JamesO'Reilly(5) 10 55
(J O'Reilly) *towards rr: rdn along 1/2-way: styd on ins fnl f: n.d* **33/1**
505U **8** hd **Lucky Art (USA)**26 5502 4-8-13 **63** JamesSullivan(3) 2 55
(Mrs R A Carr) *chsd ldr: hdwy 2f out: sn rdn and wknd over 1f out* **16/1**
200 **9** 4 1/2 **Durham Express (IRE)**83 3599 3-9-7 **69** (p) PhillipMakin 7 45
(M Dods) *stmbld and hmpd s: a in rr* **20/1**
6000 **10** 1/2 **Silvanus (IRE)**12 5915 5-9-3 **64** MickyFenton 11 38
(P T Midgley) *s.i.s: a in rr* **22/1**

57.52 secs (-1.08) **Going Correction** -0.35s/f (Firm)
WFA 3 from 4yo+ 1lb **10** Ran SP% **116.4**
Speed ratings (Par 103): **94,92,90,90,88 88,87,87,80,79**
Tote Swingers: 1&2 £5.00, 1&3 £6.10, 2&3 £9.80 CSF £13.90 CT £103.13 TOTE £3.20: £1.10, £1.60, £1.70; EX 18.80.
Owner Which Bits Mine Syndicate **Bred** Llety Stud **Trained** Settrington, N Yorks
■ Stewards' Enquiry : Ian Brennan three-day ban: careless riding (Oct 6-8)
Michael O'Connell three-day ban: used whip with excessive frequency down shoulder in the forehand (Oct 6-8)

FOCUS
An ordinary sprint handicap and sound enough form.

6300 HOLD YOUR CHRISTMAS PARTY HERE NURSERY (DIV II OF THE 2.50) 1m
6:10 (6:11) (Class 6) (0-65,65) 2-Y-O £1,295 (£385; £192; £96) Stalls High

Form RPR
0564 **1** **Tapis Libre**17 5784 2-9-1 **62** JamesSullivan(3) 13 65
(M W Easterby) *mid-div: effrt over 2f out: chsng ldrs over 1f out: styd on to ld nr fin* **10/1**
0003 **2** hd **Chadford**16 5818 2-8-10 **54** DuranFentiman 7 57
(T D Walford) *in rr: hdwy over 2f out: led over 1f out: hdd: edgd rt and no ex cl home* **25/1**
504 **3** 1 1/4 **Ad Value (IRE)**23 5602 2-8-8 **52** PJMcDonald 4 52
(G A Swinbank) *dwlt: in rr: hdwy over 2f out: styd on fnl f* **6/1**3
5266 **4** 2 1/4 **Unknown Rebel (IRE)**49 4701 2-9-5 **63** TomEaves 3 57
(K A Ryan) *hld up: hdwy over 3f out: sn chsng ldrs: one pce fnl f* **12/1**
0430 **5** hd **Eduardo**29 5389 2-8-11 **60** MichaelO'Connell(5) 10 54
(Jedd O'Keeffe) *led: hdd over 1f out: edgd lft and kpt on same pce* **14/1**
0040 **6** nk **Bright Dictator (IRE)**22 5644 2-8-5 **49** RoystonFfrench 1 42
(J G Given) *chsd ldrs: edgd rt and one pce fnl f* **50/1**
0060 **7** 2 **Rainbows Son**23 5597 2-8-1 **48** ow3 (p) PaulPickard(3) 6 37
(P T Midgley) *chsd ldrs: rdn over 2f out: one pce whn n.m.r and eased last 100yds* **40/1**
000 **8** 1 1/4 **Tigerino (IRE)**32 5298 2-8-0 **47** ow2 KellyHarrison(3) 5 33
(C W Thornton) *chsd ldrs: wknd fnl f* **50/1**
21 **9** 4 1/2 **Rather Cool**30 5373 2-8-12 **56** StevieDonohoe 15 32
(A B Haynes) *in rr: drvn 3f out: nvr on terms* **11/2**2
6006 **10** 1/2 **Alfraamsey**8 6052 2-9-7 **65** RobertWinston 14 39
(M R Channon) *hld up in rr: sme hdwy over 2f out: lost pl over 1f out* **10/1**
4250 **11** 1 1/2 **Dark Dune (IRE)**23 5597 2-9-7 **65** DavidNolan 12 36
(T D Easterby) *in rr: effrt over 2f out: sn btn* **12/1**
560 **12** hd **Hal Of A Lover**39 5099 2-9-4 **62** PaulHanagan 8 32
(R A Fahey) *t.k.h: sn w ldr: rdn and wknd over 2f out* **2/1**1
600 **13** 2 3/4 **Playful Girl (IRE)**50 4668 2-8-9 **53** (b1) DavidAllan 11 17
(T D Easterby) *w ldr: lost pl over 2f out: sn bhd* **33/1**

1m 37.61s (-0.39) **Going Correction** -0.35s/f (Firm) **13** Ran SP% **116.4**
Speed ratings (Par 93): **87,86,85,83,83 82,80,79,75,74 73,72,70**
Tote Swingers: 1&2 £17.10, 1&3 £11.50, 2&3 £18.80. Totesuper7: Win: Not won. Place: £177.60. CSF £241.63 CT £1683.80 TOTE £14.30: £2.90, £8.60, £3.50; EX 149.60 Place 6: £38.61 Place 5:£29.48.
Owner Bamford Trading Ltd **Bred** Sedgecroft Stud **Trained** Sheriff Hutton, N Yorks

FOCUS
Again poor prize money, even for a really moderate race. The time was 0.23 seconds slower than the first division, won by Regimental. Not a race to be positive about.

NOTEBOOK
Tapis Libre proved suited by the step up in trip and drop in grade, and ran on gamely after making his move more towards the stands' rail than most of these. (op 9-1)
Chadford, upped from 6f, plugged on having been well placed throughout and seemed to get the trip okay. (op 28-1 tchd 33-1)
Ad Value(IRE), beaten a long way in sprint sellers the last twice, seemed better suited by this longer trip, keeping on after a sluggish start, but the form doesn't amount to much. (op 7-1 tchd 15-2)
Unknown Rebel(IRE) ran respectably on this step up in trip after a 49-day break. (op 18-1 tchd 22-1)
Rather Cool Official explanation: jockey said filly never travelled
Hal Of A Lover failed to improve as many were anticipating for the step up in trip on his nursery debut, ruining his chance by refusing to settle when racing on the pace without cover. Official explanation: jockey said colt ran too free (op 7-4 tchd 6-4)
T/Jkpt: Not won. T/Plt: £32 to a £1 stake. Pool:£58,611 - 1,334.22 winning tickets T/Qpdt: £14.30 to a £1 stake. Pool:£4,020 - 207.20 winning tickets JR

6110 PONTEFRACT (L-H)
Thursday, September 23

OFFICIAL GOING: Good to firm (good in places; 8.0)
Wind: Virtually nil Weather: Cloudy with sunny periods

6301 EUROPEAN BREEDERS' FUND SHEILA JACK 50TH BIRTHDAY MAIDEN STKS 6f
2:30 (2:31) (Class 4) 2-Y-O £4,533 (£1,348; £674; £336) Stalls Low

Form RPR
44 **1** **Jade**10 6034 2-8-12 0 KierenFallon 12 75
(Ollie Pears) *racd wd: in tch: gd hdwy 2f out: led wl over 1f out: rdn clr ent fnl f: kpt on* **7/1**3
30 **2** nk **Lowawatha**30 5385 2-9-3 0 JimCrowley 1 79
(R M Beckett) *trckd ldrs on inner: swtchd rt and hdwy wl over 1f out: rdn to chse wnr ins fnl f: kpt on u.p towards fin* **7/1**3
5 **3** 3 **Sovereign Street**26 5509 2-8-12 0 SilvestreDeSousa 2 65
(Mrs A Duffield) *t.k.h: led: rdn along 2f out: hdd wl over 1f out: drvn and kpt on same pce fnl f* **15/2**
0 **4** 2 1/4 **Bertiewhittle**45 4896 2-9-3 0 PhillipMakin 10 63+
(T D Barron) *t.k.h: hld up in midfield: pushed along and hdwy 2f out: swtchd lft and rdn over 1f out: kpt on ins fnl f: nrst fin* **100/1**
42 **5** nk **Fityaan**28 5453 2-9-3 0 TadhgO'Shea 9 65+
(B W Hills) *trckd ldrs: swtchd lft and rdn along wl over 2f out: swtchd rt and drvn over 1f out: kpt on same pce* **10/3**2
6 **6** 3/4 **Rapturous Applause**7 6111 2-9-3 0 TomEaves 3 60
(Micky Hammond) *chsd ldrs: rdn 2f out: drvn wl over 1f out: kpt on same pce* **40/1**
33 **7** 2 1/4 **Double Dealer**14 5893 2-9-3 0 AhmedAjtebi 5 53
(Mahmood Al Zarooni) *cl up: effrt 2f out: sn rdn and wknd over 1f out* **5/4**1
00 **8** 1/2 **West Leake Melody**27 5465 2-9-3 0 MichaelHills 13 52
(B W Hills) *hld up towards rr: hdwy on outer 2f out: swtchd lft and rdn appr fnl f: n.d* **66/1**
9 3 3/4 **Scottish Lake** 2-8-12 0 MichaelO'Connell(5) 4 41
(Jedd O'Keeffe) *midfield: rdn along on inner 1/2-way: sn outpcd* **100/1**
00 **10** 3 **Dreamweaving (IRE)**33 5298 2-8-9 56 KellyHarrison(3) 7 27
(N Tinkler) *chsd ldrs: rdn along 1/2-way: edgd lft and wknd wl over 1f out* **50/1**
4 **11** 3/4 **Susiesstaying**114 2623 2-8-12 0 MickyFenton 8 24
(P T Midgley) *t.k.h: hld up: a in rr* **50/1**
12 15 **Rattleyurjewellery** 2-8-12 0 PaulHanagan 11 —
(D H Brown) *s.i.s and sn rdn along: a outpcd and bhd* **33/1**

1m 17.81s (0.91) **Going Correction** 0.0s/f (Good) **12** Ran SP% **117.1**
Speed ratings (Par 97): **93,92,88,85,85 84,81,80,75,71 70,50**
toteswingers:1&2:£7.20, 1&3:£7.20, 2&3:£7.90 CSF £52.87 TOTE £6.90: £2.00, £3.80, £1.50; EX 51.20 Trifecta £428.20 Pool: £653.92 - 1.13 winning units..
Owner L C Sigsworth **Bred** Brook Stud Bloodstock Ltd **Trained** Norton, N Yorks

FOCUS
Following 2.5mm of rain overnight the going was changed to good to firm, good in places (from good to firm). No more than a fair maiden, but tyhe first two finished clear and showed improved form.

NOTEBOOK
Jade deserves extra credit as she overcame an outside draw and racing wide throughout to keep on strongly and hold off Lowawatha close home. A step up to 7f looks sure to suit her and she could well win a nursery before the season is out. (op 6-1)
Lowawatha, in contrast to the winner, was drawn best of all and went the shortest way round. Back in trip and on better ground, this was a return to form, and she can now go the handicap route. (op 8-1 tchd 9-1)
Sovereign Street, another well drawn, showed ability on her debut and again here, despite being taken on in front and racing a shade keenly. (tchd 7-1 and 8-1)
Bertiewhittle, never a factor on his debut over 5f at Thirsk, showed more here over an extra furlong, while still looking green, and looks the type to do better once eligible for handicaps. (op 66-1)
Fityaan was disappointing, although he wasn't knocked about on this third run, and handicaps might offer more opportunities for him. (op 5-2)
Double Dealer looked likely to be suited by this stiff 6f, but having disputed the lead he weakened tamely in the straight and was below the form that saw him finish third on his first two starts. (op 15-8, after early 2-1 in places)

6302 BEST HORSE RACING SKY CHANNEL 432 FILLIES' NURSERY 1m 4y
3:00 (3:00) (Class 4) (0-85,78) 2-Y-O £3,238 (£963; £481; £240) Stalls Low

Form RPR
564 **1** **Itzakindamagic (IRE)**13 5924 2-8-7 **64** KierenFallon 3 68+
(M Johnston) *cl up: led 3f out: rdn clr appr fnl f: kpt on* **4/1**3
0060 **2** 2 1/2 **Amistress**22 5660 2-7-12 **55** oh10 SilvestreDeSousa 6 52
(Eve Johnson Houghton) *in rr and pushed along 1/2-way: hdwy on outer 2f out: rdn over 1f out: styd on wl fnl f* **25/1**
620 **3** 1/2 **Lady Amakhala**26 5509 2-9-1 **72** PJMcDonald 1 68+
(G M Moore) *dwlt: trckd ldrs on inner: rdn along and outpcd 1/2-way: swtchd outside and drvn wl over 1f out: styd on strly ins fnl f: nrst fin* **7/1**
01 **4** hd **Geordie Iris (IRE)**21 5699 2-9-4 **75** JimCrowley 5 71
(R Hannon) *trckd ldrs: hdwy and cl up 2f out: sn rdn: drvn and wknd ent fnl f* **9/2**
0532 **5** 2 1/2 **Ihavenotime (IRE)**15 5857 2-8-11 **68** SamHitchcott 7 58
(M R Channon) *dwlt: hld up: hdwy over 2f out: rdn to chse ldrs and hung lft over 1f out: sn one pce* **7/2**2
006 **6** 2 1/2 **Memory Lane**31 5369 2-9-1 **72** SebSanders 2 56
(Sir Mark Prescott) *led: pushed along and hdd 3f out: sn rdn and wknd* **15/8**1

1m 46.97s (1.07) **Going Correction** 0.0s/f (Good) **6** Ran SP% **111.5**
Speed ratings (Par 94): **94,91,91,90,88 85**
toteswingers:1&2:£6.80, 1&3:£2.80, 2&3:£16.20 CSF £76.19 TOTE £5.10: £3.40, £16.20; EX 67.00.
Owner Mrs Sabina Kelly **Bred** Waterford Hall Stud **Trained** Middleham Moor, N Yorks

FOCUS
Kieren Fallon boasts an impressive strike-rate when teaming up with Mark Johnston and improved that statistic here. The form is solid and the winner was value for a little further.

NOTEBOOK
Itzakindamagic(IRE) provided the pair with another winner, staying on strongly from the turn in to win by a clear margin. This was a step up on her maiden form, there could be more improvement in her, and she'll stay further than this in time, too. (op 9-2 tchd 5-1)
Amistress's performance puts a bit of a question mark over the form as she'd shown little in four previous starts and was competing here from 10lb out of the handicap. The stiff finish suited this filly, who's bred to stay much further next year. (tchd 33-1)
Lady Amakhala, whose dam won over 1m5f, promised to be suited by the step up to 1m, and she did stay on late to take third, but she was never a real danger. (op 15-2)
Geordie Iris(IRE) travelled well to the turn in but she was seen off by the winner and then lost second and third place inside the last. An easier mile will probably suit her better. (op 7-2)
Ihavenotime(IRE) was below her best and perhaps she needs a bit of give to be seen at her best. (op 4-1)
Memory Lane, running on turf for the first time following three outings on the Kempton Polytrack, was given a positive ride early but was unable to hold her position and was beaten before the turn in. She is surely capable of better than this. (op 2-1 tchd 9-4 in places)

6303 TOTEPOOL A BETTER WAY TO BET H'CAP 5f
3:30 (3:31) (Class 5) (0-75,75) 3-Y-O+ £2,914 (£867; £433; £216) Stalls Low

Form RPR
5020 **1** **Yurituni**17 5809 3-9-6 **75** (b1) KierenFallon 8 84
(Eve Johnson Houghton) *mde all: rdn and qcknd clr wl over 1f out: drvn and edgd rt ins fnl f: hung lft nr fin* **14/1**
102 **2** 1/2 **Littlemisssunshine (IRE)**36 5207 5-8-11 **68** (t) SophieDoyle(3) 4 75
(T B P Coles) *trckd ldrs: swtchd rt and hdwy to chse wnr over 1f out: drvn and styd on wl fnl f* **16/1**

6540 **3** *nk* **Galpin Junior (USA)**[6] 6140 4-9-0 **71**........................ MichaelGeran(3) 1 77+
(D Nicholls) *s.i.s and bhd: hdwy 2f out: rdn over 1f out: styd on ins fnl f: swtchd lft and fining wl whn hmpd nr line* **13/8**[1]

4403 **4** *3* **Di Stefano**[47] 4837 3-9-6 **75**.. AdrianNicholls 12 70
(D Nicholls) *dwlt: sn in tch on wd outside: rdn along 2f out: drvn over 1f out: kpt on same pce fnl f* **14/1**

0006 **5** *1* **Tyrannosaurus Rex (IRE)**[8] 6073 6-8-9 **66** ow3........... GaryBartley(3) 2 58+
(D Shaw) *sn outpcd and pushed along in rr: hdwy 2f out: rdn and n.m.r over 1f out: kpt on ins fnl f: nrst fin* **11/2**[2]

4400 **6** *1 1/4* **Poppy's Rose**[7] 6103 6-8-11 **70**.. DaleSwift(5) 5 57
(T J Etherington) *towards rr: effrt on inner 2f out: sn rdn and no imp fnl f* **10/1**

2403 **7** *1 1/4* **Sir Nod**[21] 5684 8-9-6 **74**.. PaulHanagan 9 57
(Julie Camacho) *cl up: rdn 2f out: drvn wl over 1f out and sn wknd* **13/2**[3]

0401 **8** *1* **Bosun Breese**[39] 5123 5-9-2 **75**.. DeanHeslop(5) 7 54
(T D Barron) *trckd ldrs: effrt over 2f out: sn rdn and wknd over 1f out* **17/2**

1146 **9** *2 1/4* **Musical Bridge**[91] 3356 4-9-2 **70**....................................(b) TomEaves 11 41
(Mrs L Williamson) *chsd ldrs: rdn along 2f out: sn drvn and wknd* **16/1**

6400 **10** *hd* **Incomparable**[98] 3114 5-9-6 **74**...................................(bt) IanMongan 10 44
(J A Glover) *racd wd: in tch: rdn along 1/2-way: sn in rr* **18/1**

62.81 secs (-0.49) **Going Correction** 0.0s/f (Good)
WFA 3 from 4yo+ 1lb **10** Ran SP% **116.8**
Speed ratings (Par 103): **103,102,101,96,95 93,91,89,86,85**
toteswingers:1&2:£14.00, 1&3:£7.20, 2&3:£8.30 CSF £216.25 CT £573.93 TOTE £13.00: £3.90, £3.90, £1.30; EX 100.70 Trifecta £292.30 Pool: £723.09 - 1.83 winning units..
Owner Mrs R F Johnson Houghton **Bred** Jeremy Green And Sons **Trained** Blewbury, Oxon
■ Stewards' Enquiry : Michael Geran three-day ban: weighed in 2lb heavy (Oct 7-9)
Kieren Fallon two-day ban: careless riding (Oct7-8)

FOCUS
A modest handicap. The winner returned to her best under a good ride, with the second also rated to her best.

6304 SIMON SCROPE DALBY SCREW-DRIVER H'CAP 1m 2f 6y
4:00 (4:00) (Class 2) (0-100,93) 3-Y-0+
£12,462 (£3,732; £1,866; £934; £466; £234) **Stalls** Low

Form RPR

2163 **1** **Licence To Till (USA)**[15] 5859 3-8-6 **81**.................. SilvestreDeSousa 3 92
(M Johnston) *prom: cl up after 2f: rdn to chal wl over 1f out: drvn to ld jst ins fnl f: kpt on* **12/1**

460 **2** *1* **Sirvino**[14] 5879 5-9-10 **93**.. PhillipMakin 2 102
(T D Barron) *trckd ldrs on inner: swtchd rt and hdwy wl over 2f out: rdn wl over 1f out: drvn to chse wnr ins fnl f: kpt on* **5/1**[3]

0042 **3** *1 1/4* **Fastnet Storm (IRE)**[23] 5638 4-9-4 **87**................................. NeilCallan 6 93
(T P Tate) *led: rdn along 3f out: drvn over 1f out: hdd jst ins fnl f: kpt on same pce* **8/1**

1561 **4** *hd* **High Office**[8] 6096 4-8-12 **81** 6ex....................................... PaulHanagan 7 87
(R A Fahey) *hld up in tch: hdwy over 3f out: rdn and outpcd 2f out: drvn over 1f out and kpt on ins fnl f* **10/3**[2]

060 **5** *nk* **Just Lille (IRE)**[56] 4507 7-9-9 **92**...............................(p) PaulMulrennan 5 97
(Mrs A Duffield) *hld up in rr: hdwy and nt clr run on inner wl over 1f out: sn swtchd rt and effrt whn n.m.r and swtchd lft ins fnl f: styng on whn n.m.r nr fin* **18/1**

0300 **6** *2 1/4* **Submariner (USA)**[5] 6193 4-9-3 **86**.................................... KierenFallon 4 87
(M Johnston) *trckd ldrs: hdwy on outer and cl up 3f out: rdn wl over 1f out: wknd appr fnl f* **6/4**[1]

5300 **7** *2* **Take It To The Max**[26] 5511 3-8-8 **83**................................... TomEaves 1 80
(G M Moore) *t.k.h: trckd ldng pair: effrt 3f out: rdn along 2f out: sn wknd* **18/1**

1400 **8** *3 3/4* **Porgy**[12] 5949 5-8-13 **82**.. JamieSpencer 8 71
(R A Fahey) *swvd bdly rt s: a in rr* **8/1**

2m 11.28s (-2.42) **Going Correction** 0.0s/f (Good)
WFA 3 from 4yo+ 6lb **8** Ran SP% **120.2**
Speed ratings (Par 109): **109,108,107,107,106 105,103,100**
toteswingers:1&2:£8.60, 1&3:£4.60, 2&3:£5.50 CSF £74.18 CT £522.73 TOTE £13.50: £3.80, £2.90, £2.40; EX 93.10 Trifecta £377.30 Part won. Pool: £509.87 - 0.43 winning units..
Owner The Vine Accord **Bred** John Hettinger **Trained** Middleham Moor, N Yorks

FOCUS
Quite a competitive little heat, although the top-weight weighed in 7lb below the ceiling for the race. A clear personal best from the winner, with the third helping with the standard.

NOTEBOOK
Licence To Till(USA) has been consistent for most of the year and, back on decent ground, settled better than at Epsom last time and saw this trip out surprisingly well having mastered Fastnet Storm. Given his pedigree and previous form, he looks the type who will relish going back on sand over the winter. (op 14-1)
Sirvino, whose connections were hoping for some rain after the gelding had failed to let himself down on the ground at Doncaster last time, kept on steadily from off the pace to post a solid enough effort. He's fairly handicapped now, being 1lb higher than when a clear-cut winner of the John Smith's Cup last summer. (op 7-1 tchd 8-1)
Fastnet Storm(IRE) made a bold bid to make all at a track where he had been successful in two of his previous three starts, but he was eventually outbattled. It was a good effort but he has little in hand of the handicapper. (op 7-1)
High Office, 4lb well in under the penalty he picked up for his runaway Yarmouth win, had different ground conditions to deal with here and struggled to land a blow. (op 3-1 tchd 7-2)
Just Lille(IRE) was outclassed in a Group 3 last time and her current mark leaves her vulnerable in handicaps. She is hard to place on the level but is bound for a hurdling campaign this winter anyway. (op 16-1)
Submariner(USA) probably found this coming too soon after his outing in a tough Newbury handicap five days earlier. He really should be competitive off his current mark, though. (op 2-1)

6305 EUROPEAN BREEDERS' FUND FRIER WOOD MAIDEN STKS 1m 4y
4:30 (4:30) (Class 4) 2-Y-0 **£4,857** (£1,445; £722; £360) **Stalls** Low

Form RPR

0 **1** **Pink Diva (IRE)**[24] 5594 2-8-12 0.................................... JamieSpencer 3 74
(T P Tate) *cl up: rdn to ld 2f out: drvn and hung rt over 1f out: wandered and hdd wl ins fnl f: kpt on u.str.p to ld nr line* **14/1**

22 **2** *hd* **Tiger Webb**[21] 5676 2-9-3 0... IanMongan 1 79
(H R A Cecil) *t.k.h early: trckd ldrs: effrt over 2f out and sn rdn along: hdwy over 1f out: styd on to chal 1f out: drvn to ld wl ins fnl f: hdd nr fin* **11/10**[1]

6 **3** *4 1/2* **Oversteer (USA)**[34] 5263 2-9-3 0...................................... WilliamBuick 5 69+
(J H M Gosden) *dwlt: sn trcking ldrs: effrt over 2f out: rdn along and outpcd wl over 1f out: kpt on u.p fnl f* **6/5**[2]

0 **4** *1/2* **Sam Nombulist**[29] 5404 2-9-0 0.................................... MichaelStainton(3) 2 68
(R M Whitaker) *s.i.s: hld up in rr: hdwy 2f out and sn rdn: kpt on same pce appr fnl f* **80/1**

44 **5** *1* **My Little Star (IRE)**[28] 5441 2-8-12 0................................ MichaelHills 7 60
(B W Hills) *led: rdn along 3f out: hdd 2f out and sn drvn: wknd over 1f out* **11/1**[3]

05 **6** *8* **Castlemorris King**[12] 5943 2-9-0 0............................. RobertLButler(3) 6 47
(M C Chapman) *plld hrd early: hld up in rr: sme hdwy 2f out: sn rdn and wknd* **100/1**

1m 48.41s (2.51) **Going Correction** 0.0s/f (Good) **6** Ran SP% **110.3**
Speed ratings (Par 97): **87,86,82,81,80 72**
toteswingers:1&2:£1.90, 1&3:£2.70, 2&3:£1.10 CSF £29.25 TOTE £13.90: £5.10, £1.10; EX 16.60.
Owner Mrs Fitri Hay **Bred** J Joyce **Trained** Tadcaster, N Yorks

FOCUS
There was a steady early pace to this maiden and the first two in the betting raced keenly. Good efforts from the front pair to pulle clear, and the form has a solid feel despite the slow tempo.

NOTEBOOK
Pink Diva(IRE), a daughter of Irish 1000 Guineas winner Saoire who cost 475,000euros at the sales, was too green to do herself justice on her debut but knew a lot more this time and, having tracked the leader for much of the race, was sent on turning in. Soon taken on by the favourite, she was briefly headed by him, but rallied back well to be in front again on the line. She has plenty of size about her and looks sure to make a better 3-y-o. (op 12-1 tchd 10-1)
Tiger Webb had to settle for second for the third time, but did little wrong. A stronger early gallop would no doubt have suited him as he raced keenly, but although he came to have his chance in the straight it was more as a result of the winner running green in front. (tchd 10-11 and 6-5)
Oversteer(USA), who holds a Racing Post Trophy entry, didn't get cover on the outside and was another who could have done with a stronger pace. He ran on nicely at the finish but won't be going to Doncaster on this evidence. (op 11-8 tchd 13-8)
Sam Nombulist, who carried his head high and still looked green, should do better once eligible for handicaps. (op 66-1 tchd 100-1)
My Little Star(IRE) was up 2f in distance, which should have suited her on pedigree, but having led the field to the turn in she didn't get home. (tchd 10-1 and 14-1)

6306 PONTEFRACT APPRENTICE H'CAP 1m 4f 8y
5:00 (5:00) (Class 5) (0-75,73) 3-Y-0+ **£2,590** (£770; £385; £192) **Stalls** Low

Form RPR

0600 **1** **Alsahil (USA)**[7] 6116 4-9-6 **66**.................................... JamesRogers(3) 5 76
(Micky Hammond) *mde all: rdn clr wl over 1f out: styd on strly* **8/1**[2]

/33- **2** *7* **Tricky Situation**[469] 2843 4-9-13 **70**................................ GarryWhillans 3 69
(D H Brown) *t.k.h early: trckd ldrs: hdwy 3f out: rdn to chse wnr wl over 1f out: sn one pce* **11/4**[1]

3200 **3** *5* **Leaving Alone (USA)**[5] 6187 3-8-11 **62**........................(p) AdamCarter 2 53
(E W Tuer) *prom: trckd wnr after 2f: effrt 3f out: rdn 2f out: sn drvn and wknd over 1f out* **11/4**[1]

504 **4** *3/4* **Royal Premier (IRE)**[72] 3996 7-8-13 **56** oh4........................ AmyScott 7 46
(H J Collingridge) *hld up: hdwy to chse ldrs over 3f out: rdn 2f out: sn outpcd* **8/1**[2]

3506 **5** *5* **Amir Pasha (UAE)**[21] 5681 5-8-13 **63**......................(p) KatieDowson(7) 4 45
(Micky Hammond) *plld hrd: chsd ldrs on outer: pushed along over 3f out: wknd over 2f out* **11/4**[1]

5000 **6** *4 1/2* **Grey Command (USA)**[26] 5515 5-8-13 **56** oh7........... JohnCavanagh 1 30
(M Brittain) *hld up in rr: effrt 4f out: rdn along 3f out: nvr a factor* **9/1**[3]

2m 41.14s (0.34) **Going Correction** 0.0s/f (Good)
WFA 3 from 4yo+ 8lb **6** Ran SP% **112.2**
Speed ratings (Par 103): **98,93,90,89,86 83**
toteswingers:1&2:£4.20, 1&3:£3.10, 2&3:£2.40 CSF £30.10 TOTE £6.70: £4.50, £2.50; EX 32.80 Place 6 £586.99; Place 5 £167.30.
Owner R D Bickenson **Bred** Shadwell Farm LLC **Trained** Middleham Moor, N Yorks

FOCUS
A weak apprentice handicap in which the winner achieved an easy lead. He's rated back to his 3yo form.
Alsahil(USA) Official explanation: trainer said, regarding apparent improvement in form, that the colt was suited by a step up in trip and being able to dominate.
T/Jkpt: Not won. T/Plt: £601.10 to a £1 stake. Pool:£71,021.70 - 86.25 winning tickets T/Qpdt: £27.20 to a £1 stake. Pool:£6,085.67 - 165.47 winning tickets JR

6206 WOLVERHAMPTON (A.W) (L-H)
Thursday, September 23

OFFICIAL GOING: Standard
Wind: Fresh behind becoming light across race 2 to race 4, then dropping to almost nil Weather: Overcast becoming thundery

6307 DAY TIME, NIGHT TIME, GREAT TIME CLAIMING STKS 7f 32y(P)
5:30 (5:32) (Class 5) 2-Y-0 **£2,729** (£806; £403) **Stalls** High

Form RPR

0263 **1** **Takeaway**[21] 5701 2-9-9 82.. RichardHughes 4 80
(R Hannon) *mid-div: pushed along and hdwy over 2f out: chsd ldr over 1f out: rdn to ld ins fnl f: hung lft: r.o* **6/4**[1]

2142 **2** *1/2* **Hortensia (IRE)**[13] 5921 2-9-4 78..........................(v) ChrisCatlin 12 74
(M R Channon) *chsd ldr tl led 5f out: rdn and edgd rt over 1f out: hdd ins fnl f: hung lft: r.o* **5/1**[3]

0156 **3** *1 1/4* **Water Ice**[17] 5807 2-9-4 74.. RichardKingscote 3 71
(Tom Dascombe) *led 2f: chsd ldr: rdn over 2f out: styd on* **3/1**[2]

02 **4** *1 1/4* **Areopagitica**[31] 5373 2-8-1 0.. JohnFahy(5) 1 55
(C G Cox) *chsd ldrs: rdn and hung lft over 1f out: styd on u.p* **12/1**

2360 **5** *1* **Never Can Stop**[8] 6072 2-7-13 63.................................... HarryBentley(7) 8 53
(J G Portman) *mid-div: hdwy over 2f out: sn rdn: styd on* **8/1**

1046 **6** *hd* **Scommettitrice (IRE)**[11] 5987 2-9-0 70.............................. LukeMorris 5 61
(R A Harris) *chsd ldrs: rdn over 2f out: no ex ins fnl f* **20/1**

00 **7** *1/2* **Beating Harmony**[41] 5047 2-8-12 0.................................... MartinLane(3) 6 60
(J R Fanshawe) *hld up: rdn over 2f out: r.o: nt trble ldrs* **33/1**

1006 **8** *1/2* **Joyously**[7] 6130 2-8-5 78..(v[1]) AdamBeschizza(5) 7 54
(P D Evans) *s.i.s: in rr: rdn and hung lft over 1f out: r.o: nvr nrr* **11/1**

00 **9** *1/2* **Gypsy Legend (IRE)**[24] 5583 2-8-8 0.................................. LiamKeniry 9 51
(S Kirk) *s.i.s: hld up: rdn over 1f out: styd on: nvr on terms* **100/1**

00 **10** *12* **Generale (IRE)**[21] 5701 2-8-11 0....................................(t) LeeVickers 2 24
(F Sheridan) *s.i.s: sn pushed along and a in rr: lost tch over 2f out* **150/1**

00 **11** *2* **Somebody Loves You**[19] 5761 2-8-1 0 ow1............... FrannyNorton 10 10
(Mrs A Duffield) *prom: racd keenly: rdn and wknd over 2f out* **100/1**

00 **12** *1 3/4* **Antipas (IRE)**[41] 5020 2-8-6 0.. AndrewElliott 11 10
(Mrs K Burke) *hld up: wknd over 2f out* **150/1**

1m 30.6s (1.00) **Going Correction** -0.05s/f (Stan) **12** Ran SP% **119.8**
Speed ratings (Par 95): **92,91,90,88,87 87,86,86,85,71 69,67**
toteswingers:1&2:£3.00, 1&3:£2.70, 2&3:£4.80 CSF £9.24 TOTE £2.50: £1.10, £2.00, £1.10; EX 11.20.Areopagitica was claimed by J. L. Flint for £6,000. Hortensia was claimed by Claes Bjorling for £12,000. Takeaway was claimed by J. R. Boyle for £12,000.

The Form Book, Raceform Ltd, Compton, RG20 6NL

Owner S Mahal, R Morecombe & D Anderson **Bred** Redhill Bloodstock Limited **Trained** East Everleigh, Wilts

FOCUS
A claimer featuring plenty of exposed juveniles. Straightforward form, rated around the principals.

NOTEBOOK
Takeaway, who won first time out on Polytrack at Kempton in March, was dropping to claiming company on his ninth start. He went in pursuit of the leader once in line for home and had to dig deep to master her near the line. (op 2-1 tchd 9-4)
Hortensia(IRE), closely matched with the winner on official ratings, made hard work of landing a similar event at Hamilton three outings ago. Fitted with a visor since she went on before halfway and went down fighting. (tchd 6-1)
Water Ice had a couple of pounds to find with the first two and probably ran close to her nursery mark of 74. (op 11-4 tchd 10-3)
Areopagitica, runner-up in a soft ground seller over a mile at Windsor, seemed to improve on that on her all-weather debut. (op 17-2)
Never Can Stop was not disgraced on her ninth start, but overall she has proved a disappointment. (op 12-1)
Scommettitrice(IRE), fourth when Hortensia was runner-up in a similar event here two outings ago, had finished last in a nursery since on his first try on turf.
Beating Harmony, who showed little in two starts in maiden company, stayed on when it was all over and might improve sufficiently to find a seller over a mile. (op 20-1)
Joyously, clear top-rated on official figures, had run well below her best in two recent starts in nurseries and a first-time visor did not revive her. (op 14-1)

6308 WILLIAMHILL.COM - SPORTS BETTING MEDIAN AUCTION MAIDEN STKS (DIV I) 5f 216y(P)
6:00 (6:02) (Class 5) 2-Y-O **£2,388** (£705; £352) **Stalls** Low

Form | | | | RPR
3 **1** **Expose**[6] 6146 2-9-3 0 RichardHughes 11 76+
(W J Haggas) hld up: hdwy over 2f out: shkn up to ld and hung lft ins fnl f: r.o wl **8/15**[1]
066 **2** 2 ½ **Vetvey (IRE)**[9] 6047 2-9-3 0 JoeFanning 5 66
(M Johnston) chsd ldr: rdn: hung lft and ev ch fr over 1f out: styd on same pce wl ins fnl f **22/1**
3 1 **Tenby Lady (USA)** 2-8-12 0 SebSanders 9 58+
(Sir Mark Prescott) sn pushed along in rr: hdwy over 1f out: hung lft and r.o ins fnl f: nrst fin **5/1**[2]
4254 **4** shd **Darwin Star**[70] 4040 2-8-12 65 SamHitchcott 4 57
(D K Ivory) led: rdn over 1f out: hdd and no ex ins fnl f **14/1**
54 **5** 1 **Scoglio**[23] 5643 2-9-3 0 LeeVickers 10 59
(F Sheridan) sn pushed along in rr: hdwy over 1f out: swtchd lft ins fnl f: r.o: nt trble ldrs **66/1**
53 **6** shd **Zalano**[23] 5643 2-9-3 0 AdamKirby 6 59
(D Haydn Jones) trckd ldrs: rdn over 1f out: no ex ins fnl f **11/1**[3]
045 **7** 1 ½ **Brave Battle**[14] 5886 2-9-3 67 RichardMullen 7 56
(R Hannon) prom: rdn over 2f out: styd on same pce appr fnl f **16/1**
8 7 **Amun Ra (USA)** 2-9-3 0 SteveDrowne 1 33
(J R Gask) s.i.s: hdwy 4f out: wknd over 2f out **20/1**
00 **9** 4 **Juarla (IRE)**[7] 6118 2-9-3 0 TomMcLaughlin 2 21
(R A Harris) chsd ldrs tl rdn and wknd over 1f out **50/1**
10 21 **River Avon** 2-9-0 0 JamesSullivan(3) 8 —
(M W Easterby) s.i.s: outpcd **80/1**
00 **11** 5 **Champagne Princess**[9] 6058 2-8-7 0 JohnFahy(5) 3 —
(P S McEntee) s.i.s: outpcd **200/1**

1m 15.02s (0.02) **Going Correction** -0.05s/f (Stan) **11** Ran SP% **117.1**
Speed ratings (Par 95): **97,93,92,92,90 90,88,79,74,46 39**
toteswingers:1&2:£4.90, 1&3:£2.10, 2&3:£7.90 CSF £22.35 TOTE £1.50: £1.10, £4.90, £1.90; EX 15.50.
Owner The Royal Ascot Racing Club **Bred** John And Susan Davis **Trained** Newmarket, Suffolk

FOCUS
A weak maiden and a very short-priced favourite. The fourth and sixth initially set the level.

NOTEBOOK
Expose, a promising third at Newbury on his debut eight days earlier, had to be put about his job once in line for home. Making his effort on the wide outside he was firmly in command at the line. He should make a useful handicapper at three. (op 4-9 tchd 2-5)
Vetvey(IRE), making his all-weather debut on his fourth career start, seemed to show much improved form, but this will have blown a possibly lenient nursery mark out of the water. A brother to the stable's Norfolk Stakes winner Russian Valour, he can surely go one better in maiden company. (op 16-1)
Tenby Lady(USA), in an unpromising position at halfway, put in some solid work once in line for home. She will improve a good deal and looks sure to open her account. (op 15-2)
Darwin Star, having her eighth start and rated 65, is the best guide to the overall merit of the form. (op 11-1 tchd 10-1)
Scoglio, whose first two outings were over five furlongs, appeared late on the scene and will be of interest in modest nursery company.
Zalano, another having his third run, travelled strongly, but did not really get home. Six furlongs might suit him better in nursery company. (op 12-1 tchd 14-1)
Brave Battle, already rated 67, was having his fourth start and may have to descend to claiming company. Official explanation: trainer's rep said colt had a breathing problem (op 14-1)

6309 WILLIAMHILL.COM - SPORTS BETTING MEDIAN AUCTION MAIDEN STKS (DIV II) 5f 216y(P)
6:30 (6:31) (Class 5) 2-Y-O **£2,388** (£705; £352) **Stalls** Low

Form | | | | RPR
235 **1** **Valerius Maximus**[7] 6111 2-9-3 0 ChrisCatlin 8 78
(P F I Cole) w ldr tl led over 2f out: rdn over 1f out: r.o **9/2**[3]
05 **2** 2 ½ **L'Astre De Choisir (IRE)**[14] 5893 2-9-3 0 ShaneKelly 4 71
(W R Swinburn) hld up in tch: rdn over 1f out: r.o to go 2nd towards fin: nt trble wnr **13/2**
3 ½ **Celestyna** 2-8-12 0 TomQueally 5 64
(H R A Cecil) trckd ldrs: rdn over 1f out: styd on **9/2**[3]
2 **4** hd **Karate (IRE)**[9] 6046 2-9-3 0 JoeFanning 3 68
(M Johnston) led over 3f: sn rdn: no ex ins fnl f: lost 2 pls towards fin **15/8**[1]
3023 **5** 1 ½ **Looksmart**[16] 5836 2-8-12 72 RichardHughes 2 59
(R Hannon) chsd ldrs: rdn over 2f out: no ex ins fnl f **4/1**[2]
000 **6** ½ **Commercial (IRE)**[27] 5465 2-9-3 0 FergusSweeney 6 62
(J A Osborne) hld up: plld hrd: hdwy over 1f out: styd on same pce fnl f **100/1**
7 4 ½ **Snow Ridge** 2-9-3 0 SebSanders 9 51+
(Sir Mark Prescott) sn pushed along in rr: hdwy 4f out: shkn up over 2f out: wkng whn n.m.r 1f out **20/1**
36 **8** 7 **Brian Sprout**[91] 3365 2-9-3 0 DarryllHolland 7 28
(J R Weymes) sn outpcd: a in rr **66/1**
500 **9** 1 ¼ **Miss Nimbus**[34] 5269 2-8-12 40 TonyCulhane 1 19
(George Baker) mid-div: lost pl 4f out: bhd fr 1/2-way **100/1**
0 **10** 1 ¼ **Belles Boudier**[42] 4981 2-8-7 0 RossAtkinson(5) 10 15
(G Woodward) sn outpcd: bhd fr 1/2-way **200/1**

1m 15.62s (0.62) **Going Correction** -0.05s/f (Stan) **10** Ran SP% **113.2**
Speed ratings (Par 95): **93,89,89,88,86 86,80,70,69,67**
toteswingers:1&2:£4.60, 1&3:£3.70, 2&3:£5.80 CSF £31.74 TOTE £5.10: £3.50, £1.80, £1.10; EX 32.00.
Owner The Fairy Story Partnership **Bred** Deepwood Farm Stud **Trained** Whatcombe, Oxon

FOCUS
Part two of the divided six furlong maiden and form probably of a similar level to the first division. The time was marginally slower. Sound, straightforward form.

NOTEBOOK
Valerius Maximus, placed at Windsor and York on his first two starts, was not at his best over 5f at Pontefract a week earlier. Always well placed, he struck for home straightening up and ran out a decisive winner in the end. Nurseries from a mark in the low 80s now beckon. (tchd 7-2)
L'Astre De Choisir(IRE), dropping in trip on his third start, stayed on in good style late on and is a likely type for a 7f nursery. (op 8-1 tchd 6-1)
Celestyna was quite keen on her debut. She kept on surprisingly well and should improve and make her mark. (tchd 11-2)
Karate(IRE), well beaten runner-up behind an odds-on shot at Haydock a week earlier, made the running but was readily cut down in the home straight. On the weak side, he will benefit from being given a little more time. (op 2-1)
Looksmart, placed in three of her previous four starts, has an official rating of 72 and already looks fully exposed. (op 7-2)
Commercial(IRE), who has already been gelded, will need to learn to settle if he is to progress. Official explanation: jockey said gelding ran too free
Snow Ridge shaped well on his debut but tired late on. He is not without some ability. (op 25-1)

6310 GET BEST ODDS GUARANTEED AT WILLIAMHILL.COM H'CAP 5f 216y(P)
7:00 (7:00) (Class 5) (0-75,78) 3-Y-O+ **£2,456** (£725; £362) **Stalls** Low

Form | | | | RPR
2650 **1** **Pose (IRE)**[14] 5896 3-9-6 74 RichardHughes 7 82
(R Hannon) a.p: chsd ldr 2f out: rdn to ld and edgd rt ins fnl f: r.o **10/1**
020- **2** ¾ **Opus Dei**[306] 7494 3-9-2 70 (p) RichardMullen 11 76+
(J A Glover) chsd ldrs: rdn over 1f out: r.o **16/1**
5021 **3** ½ **Defector (IRE)**[5] 6207 4-9-7 78 6ex MarkCoumbe(5) 3 82+
(D Bourton) chsd ldrs: n.m.r over 1f out: sn rdn: r.o **13/2**
6562 **4** ½ **Riflessione**[17] 5809 4-9-4 70 (b) TomMcLaughlin 2 72
(R A Harris) w ldr: led 4f out: rdn and hung rt fr over 1f out: hdd and unable qck ins fnl f **7/1**
22 **5** 1 ½ **Bushwhacker (AUS)**[17] 5810 5-9-7 73 (b[1]) NeilCallan 9 71
(W R Muir) mid-div: hdwy over 1f out: styd on **22/1**
2104 **6** ¾ **Kummel Excess (IRE)**[115] 2599 3-9-2 73 MatthewDavies(3) 10 68
(George Baker) hld up: rdn over 1f out: r.o: nt rch ldrs **33/1**
1301 **7** ½ **Progress (IRE)**[20] 5713 3-9-4 72 DarryllHolland 1 66
(J Noseda) sn led: hdd 4f out: chsd ldr tl rdn 2f out: no ex ins fnl f **11/2**[3]
4542 **8** 2 ¼ **Avontuur (FR)**[19] 5760 8-8-10 65 JamesSullivan(3) 4 51
(Mrs R A Carr) chsd ldrs: lost pl 5f out: n.d after **5/1**[2]
032 **9** hd **Toms Return**[22] 5668 3-8-11 70 KierenFox(5) 6 56+
(J R Best) s.i.s: last and rdn over 2f out: nvr on terms **7/2**[1]
6666 **10** 2 **Charles Darwin (IRE)**[19] 5764 7-8-10 62 (b) FrannyNorton 5 41
(M Blanshard) s.i.s: hld up: rdn over 2f out: nvr on terms **9/1**
2520 **11** 1 ¾ **Bookiesindex Boy**[23] 5647 6-9-6 72 (b) StephenCraine 8 46
(J R Jenkins) hld up in tch: wknd over 1f out **33/1**

1m 14.71s (-0.29) **Going Correction** -0.05s/f (Stan)
WFA 3 from 4yo+ 2lb **11** Ran SP% **115.3**
Speed ratings (Par 103): **99,98,97,96,94 93,93,90,89,87 84**
toteswingers:1&2:£27.80, 1&3:£9.10, 2&3:£23.30 CSF £151.22 CT £1134.23 TOTE £9.70: £3.50, £5.30, £3.10; EX 138.80.
Owner Highclere Thoroughbred Racing(Childers)1 **Bred** Rathbarry Stud **Trained** East Everleigh, Wilts

FOCUS
A wide open 62-78 sprint handicap. The winner and fourth are the best guides to this ordinary form.

6311 VIRTUAL HORSES & HOUNDS AT WILLIAMHILL.COM NURSERY 5f 216y(P)
7:30 (7:31) (Class 5) (0-70,70) 2-Y-O **£2,729** (£806; £403) **Stalls** Low

Form | | | | RPR
4502 **1** **Restless Bay (IRE)**[6] 6163 2-9-5 68 (p) AdamKirby 8 73
(R Hollinshead) s.i.s: sn pushed along in rr: hdwy over 1f out: r.o u.p to ld post **10/1**
2414 **2** nse **Brave Dream**[19] 5745 2-9-5 68 NeilCallan 2 73
(K A Ryan) chsd ldrs: rdn to ld ins fnl f: edgd lft: hdd post **4/1**[1]
3326 **3** 2 **Misscomplacent**[24] 5602 2-8-13 62 SebSanders 13 61
(Mrs A Duffield) mid-div: sn pushed along: hdwy over 2f out: rdn and hung lft fr over 1f out: styd on same pce ins fnl f **16/1**
663 **4** 1 **Crucis Abbey (IRE)**[19] 5763 2-9-7 70 AdrianNicholls 7 66
(J W Unett) mid-div: sn drvn along: hdwy u.p over 1f out: r.o: edgd lft wl ins fnl f: nt rch ldrs **7/1**
3635 **5** hd **Not So Bright (USA)**[22] 5659 2-8-11 60 PaulMulrennan 5 55
(J G Given) prom: rdn over 2f out: styd on **7/1**
045 **6** 1 **Classic Voice (IRE)**[13] 5914 2-9-5 68 RichardHughes 9 60
(R Hannon) hld up: rdn over 1f out: r.o ins fnl f: nt clr run towards fin: nvr nrr **9/2**[2]
5451 **7** nse **Spennymoor (IRE)**[29] 5412 2-9-5 68 AhmedAjtebi 10 60
(Mahmood Al Zarooni) prom: led over 2f out: hdd and no ex ins fnl f **8/1**
4006 **8** 1 ¾ **Palindromic (IRE)**[15] 5863 2-8-10 59 (b) SteveDrowne 12 46
(J R Gask) hld up: hdwy over 2f out: sn rdn: edgd lft and no imp fnl f **33/1**
006 **9** 3 ¾ **On Wings Of Love (IRE)**[27] 5490 2-9-1 64 SamHitchcott 4 40
(A Bailey) s.i.s: nt clr run over 1f out: n.d **25/1**
5452 **10** shd **Silly Billy (IRE)**[9] 6052 2-9-2 65 LiamKeniry 1 40
(S Kirk) chsd ldrs: rdn whn hmpd over 2f out: hmpd again and wknd wl over 1f out **5/1**[3]
2600 **11** 4 **Jamaica Grande**[47] 4851 2-8-11 60 ChrisCatlin 6 23
(T T Clement) hld up: a in rr **80/1**
100 **12** 4 **Mayfair Princess**[13] 5921 2-8-13 67 (bt[1]) JohnFahy(5) 11 18
(P S McEntee) led: hdd over 3f out: wknd wl over 1f out **66/1**
3610 **13** 11 **Upark Flyer**[15] 5862 2-8-12 64 (v[1]) JamesSullivan(3) 3 —
(Patrick Morris) chsd ldr: led over 3f out: hdd over 2f out: sn wknd **40/1**

1m 15.16s (0.16) **Going Correction** -0.05s/f (Stan) **13** Ran SP% **117.9**
Speed ratings (Par 95): **96,95,93,91,91 90,90,87,82,82 77,72,57**
toteswingers:1&2:£7.20, 1&3:£16.10, 2&3:£10.40 CSF £47.59 CT £668.20 TOTE £14.10: £5.60, £1.10, £6.10; EX 58.10.
Owner John L Marriott **Bred** Grangemore Stud **Trained** Upper Longdon, Staffs

FOCUS
This modest nursery was run with thunder and lightning ringing round Dunstall Park.

NOTEBOOK

Restless Bay(IRE), runner-up on his nursery debut here in first-time cheekpieces a week earlier, was dropping back a furlong in trip. He came with a sustained run after a tardy start to put his head in front right on the line.

Brave Dream, making his all-weather debut, capitalised on his favourable draw only to miss out in the final stride. (tchd 9-2)

Misscomplacent, a springer in the market, did well from her outside draw on her first try on the all-weather. A step up to seven might bring further improvement. (op 40-1)

Crucis Abbey(IRE), stepping up to six on his nursery debut, did well from what looked a very stiff mark. (op 13-2 tchd 6-1)

Not So Bright(USA), tried over a mile at Kempton on his previous start, never got competitive and this trip looks too sharp. (op 11-1)

Classic Voice(IRE), another drawn in double figures, was making his all-weather and nursery debut. He appeared very late on the scene without enjoying the clearest of passages and will be suited by a return to 7f. Official explanation: jockey said colt was denied a clear run (tchd 4-1 and 5-1)

Spennymoor(IRE), very weak in the market, was 4lb higher than his Brighton success and came up well short in the end from his outside draw after showing ahead briefly going into the final turn.

Silly Billy(IRE) Official explanation: jockey said colt was denied a clear run

Upark Flyer Official explanation: jockey said filly ran too free

6312 BET IN-PLAY AT WILLIAMHILL.COM H'CAP 1m 141y(P)

8:00 (8:01) (Class 3) (0-95,94) 3-Y-O+ **£6,623** (£1,982; £991; £495; £246) **Stalls** Low

Form RPR

2003 **1** **High Twelve (IRE)**[41] 5030 3-9-3 **92** .... WilliamBuick 4 106
(J H M Gosden) *sn led: hdd over 7f out: chsd ldr tl led again over 2f out: rdn over 1f out: styd on wl* **3/1**[1]

0520 **2** *3* **Audemar (IRE)**[111] 2708 4-9-4 **88** .... RichardHughes 13 95
(E F Vaughan) *s.i.s: hld up: hdwy over 1f out: rdn to chse wnr ins fnl f: no imp* **14/1**

4206 **3** *2 ¾* **Brouhaha**[19] 5757 6-8-12 **82** .... RichardKingscote 8 83+
(Tom Dascombe) *hld up in tch: rdn over 2f out: hmpd over 1f out: styd on same pce* **20/1**

0525 **4** *1 ¼* **Satwa Laird**[29] 5415 4-9-3 **87** .... PaulHanagan 3 85
(E A L Dunlop) *hld up in tch: rdn over 1f out: no ex fnl f* **6/1**[2]

0006 **5** *¾* **Dubai Dynamo**[1] 6296 5-9-6 **90** ....(b) AndrewElliott 10 86
(Mrs R A Carr) *chsd ldrs: rdn over 2f out: hung lft over 1f out: no ex* **33/1**

3004 **6** *hd* **Dubai Miracle (USA)**[56] 4500 3-8-11 **89** ....(b) MartinLane(3) 11 85
(D M Simcock) *hld up: hdwy u.p and hung lft over 1f out: nt rch ldrs* **33/1**

045 **7** *nse* **Flowing Cape (IRE)**[21] 5703 5-9-3 **87** .... AdamKirby 6 83
(R Hollinshead) *hld up: hdwy over 2f out: rdn over 1f out: styd on same pce* **20/1**

0202 **8** *¾* **Layline (IRE)**[21] 5703 3-9-4 **93** ....(b) JimCrowley 7 87
(R M Beckett) *hld up: r.o ins fnl f: nvr nrr* **10/1**

0022 **9** *1 ¾* **Red Somerset (USA)**[19] 5750 7-9-3 **90** .... EJMcNamara(3) 9 80
(Mike Murphy) *hld up: rdn over 2f out: nvr on terms* **6/1**[2]

4201 **10** *¾* **Secretive**[29] 5415 3-9-2 **91** ....(b) JoeFanning 5 79
(M Johnston) *chsd ldrs: rdn over 3f out: wknd fnl f* **8/1**

6465 **11** *2 ¼* **Good Again**[20] 5736 4-9-0 **89** .... AdamBeschizza(5) 2 72
(G A Butler) *prom: rdn over 3f out: wknd 2f out* **13/2**[3]

2000 **12** *4 ½* **Aspectus (IRE)**[12] 5950 7-9-10 **94** .... FergusSweeney 12 67
(J A Osborne) *led over 7f out: rdn and hdd over 2f out: wknd wl over 1f out* **50/1**

0504 **13** *13* **Titan Triumph**[21] 5703 6-9-1 **85** ....(t) GeorgeBaker 1 28
(W J Knight) *hld up: hmpd over 5f out: rdn and wknd over 2f out* **18/1**

1m 47.94s (-2.56) **Going Correction** -0.05s/f (Stan)
WFA 3 from 4yo+ 5lb **13** Ran SP% **116.4**
Speed ratings (Par 107): **109,106,103,102,102 101,101,101,99,99 97,93,81**
toteswingers:1&2:£6.90, 1&3:£36.30, 2&3:£21.40 CSF £43.74 CT £739.74 TOTE £2.80: £1.10, £7.30, £4.30; EX 49.10.
Owner Thomas Barr **Bred** Grangecon Stud **Trained** Newmarket, Suffolk

FOCUS

There had been heavy rain after the previous race but it had cleared before this highly competitive 82-94 handicap. The winner got back towards his smart 2yo form.

NOTEBOOK

High Twelve(IRE), third on his all-weather debut at Kempton, justified market confidence, travelling strongly and having this in the bag once in line for home. He should be able to follow up. (op 5-2)

Audemar(IRE), worst drawn, put a poor effort at Epsom behind him. All of his four wins have been on Polytrack and he finished clear second behind a relatively unexposed winner here. (op 20-1)

Brouhaha, down in trip and happy to be back on Polytrack, is now just 2lb higher than his last all-weather success here a year and a half ago now.

Satwa Laird, another to come in for good market support, had reportedly finished lame when fifth behind Secretive at Brighton in August. He has won just once in the last two years, yet is still 4lb higher than that success on turf at Chepstow in May. (op 9-1 tchd 11-2)

Dubai Dynamo was having his second outing in two days having finished sixth in a claimer at Redcar the previous day.

Dubai Miracle(USA), who has slipped to a lenient mark, ran his best race for some time from a double-figure draw. (op 40-1)

Flowing Cape(IRE), suited by Polytrack, has yet to win beyond 7f. (tchd 22-1, 25-1 in a place)

Red Somerset(USA) seemed to lay well out of his ground and never figured. (tchd 11-2 and 13-2)

Secretive couldn't dominate and seemed to throw in the towel. (op 15-2)

Good Again, 2lb below her last success on turf almost a year ago, continues to underperform. (tchd 7-1)

Titan Triumph Official explanation: vet said gelding finished lame left-hind

6313 FREE BETTING WITH FREEBETTING.CO.UK MAIDEN STKS 1m 4f 50y(P)

8:30 (8:34) (Class 5) 3-Y-O+ **£2,456** (£725; £362) **Stalls** Low

Form RPR

-445 **1** **Palio Square (USA)**[7] 6115 3-9-2 77 .... TomQueally 9 89
(H R A Cecil) *hld up in tch: rdn over 2f out: led ins fnl f: styd on wl* **7/1**

06 **2** *1 ½* **Herostatus**[7] 6115 3-9-2 0 .... JoeFanning 7 87
(M Johnston) *hld up: hdwy over 3f out: rdn: hung lft and ev ch fr over 1f out tl no ex wl ins fnl f* **7/1**

05 **3** *nk* **Honest Strike (USA)**[62] 4330 3-9-2 0 .... IanMongan 2 86
(H R A Cecil) *sn chsng ldr: led over 5f out: rdn over 2f out: rdr dropped whip over 1f out: hdd and unable qck ins fnl f* **17/2**

4 **4** *10* **Almarmooq (USA)**[34] 5258 3-9-2 0 .... TadhgO'Shea 5 70
(J H M Gosden) *hld up in tch: pushed along 5f out: outpcd fr over 3f out* **15/8**[1]

3323 **5** *5* **Mutanaker**[22] 5665 3-9-2 77 .... RichardMullen 11 62
(Sir Michael Stoute) *prom: chsd ldr 4f out: rdn whn hmpd over 2f out: wknd over 1f out* **11/2**[3]

06 **6** *12* **Harsh But Fair**[3] 6244 4-9-3 0 .... DavidSimmonson(7) 6 43
(M W Easterby) *s.i.s: hld up: wknd 3f out* **125/1**

65 **7** *4 ½* **Kashmiriana (IRE)**[16] 5832 3-8-11 0 .... KierenFallon 10 31
(L M Cumani) *unruly to post: s.i.s: hld up: rdn 3f out: sn wknd: t.o* **7/2**[2]

4 **8** *1 ½* **Blackmore**[126] 2244 3-8-11 0 .... AdamBeschizza(5) 3 33
(Miss J Feilden) *s.i.s: sn drvn along in rr: hmpd after 1f: wknd over 4f out: t.o* **40/1**

00 **9** *¾* **Best Catch (USA)**[7] 6124 3-8-11 0 .... KierenFox(5) 1 32
(J R Best) *chsd ldrs: rdn over 4f out: wknd 3f out: t.o* **40/1**

54 **10** *25* **Missionary**[54] 4572 3-9-2 0 .... RichardHughes 8 —
(W J Haggas) *led: hdd over 5f out: rdn and wknd over 3f out: t.o* **10/1**

000 **11** *1 ¼* **Strong Aim**[3] 6244 3-8-8 0 .... JamesSullivan(3) 12 —
(M W Easterby) *hld up: a in rr: bhd fnl 4f: t.o* **200/1**

0 **P** **Dalanoni (IRE)**[31] 5376 3-8-13 0 .... MartinLane(3) 4 —
(J R Fanshawe) *prom: rdn over 6f out: wknd 4f out: t.o whn p.u over 1f out* **80/1**

2m 38.61s (-2.49) **Going Correction** -0.05s/f (Stan)
WFA 3 from 4yo 8lb **12** Ran SP% **124.4**
Speed ratings (Par 103): **106,105,104,98,94 86,83,82,82,65 64,—**
toteswingers:1&2:£11.10, 2&3:£12.60, 1&3:£8.60 CSF £57.72 TOTE £6.50: £2.90, £3.40, £3.50; EX 59.50.
Owner Mogeely Stud & Mrs Maura Gittins **Bred** Steven Nicholson & Brandy Nicholson **Trained** Newmarket, Suffolk

FOCUS

A fair maiden but in the event only three showed their form. Their efforts have a sound look to them.

Dalanoni(IRE) Official explanation: jockey said gelding lost its action

6314 MOBILE.WILLIAMHILL.COM - NEW IPHONE APP H'CAP 1m 4f 50y(P)

9:00 (9:00) (Class 6) (0-60,62) 3-Y-O+ **£1,774** (£523; £262) **Stalls** Low

Form RPR

606 **1** **Cotton King**[17] 5815 3-9-2 **60** ....(vt[1]) TomMcLaughlin 7 68
(T B P Coles) *s.i.s: hld up: hdwy u.p over 2f out: r.o to ld post* **20/1**

0-03 **2** *nk* **Dubburg (USA)**[5] 6213 5-9-8 **58** .... TonyCulhane 12 66
(W J Musson) *hld up: hdwy over 1f out: rdn to ld wl ins fnl f: hdd post* **5/1**[3]

512 **3** *hd* **Carlton Scroop (FR)**[19] 5770 7-9-5 **60** ....(b) KierenFox(5) 2 68
(A W Carroll) *prom: pushed along 5f out: rdn to ld 1f out: hdd wl ins fnl f* **3/1**[2]

4311 **4** *nk* **Straversjoy**[5] 6213 3-9-3 **61** 6ex .... LiamKeniry 6 68
(R Hollinshead) *hld up in tch: rdn and ev ch over 1f out: edgd lft ins fnl f: styd on* **2/1**[1]

3062 **5** *2 ½* **Motarjm (USA)**[7] 6120 6-9-4 **54** ....(t) ChrisCatlin 3 57
(J Pearce) *hld up: hdwy over 2f out: rdn over 1f out: styd on same pce ins fnl f* **8/1**

4431 **6** *2 ¾* **New Code**[10] 6022 3-9-4 **62** 6ex .... NeilCallan 4 61
(W R Muir) *chsd ldrs: rdn to ld over 1f out: sn hdd: no ex ins fnl f* **13/2**

6054 **7** *1 ½* **Generous Lad (IRE)**[7] 6121 7-9-4 **54** ....(b) TomQueally 9 50
(A B Haynes) *chsd ldr tl led 3f out: rdn and hdd over 1f out: wknd fnl f* **40/1**

561 **8** *7* **Starburst**[16] 5840 5-9-3 **58** .... AdamBeschizza(5) 5 43
(Miss Gay Kelleway) *chsd ldrs: rdn over 2f out: wknd over 1f out* **28/1**

450- **9** *7* **Troubletimestwo (FR)**[158] 1811 4-9-10 **60** .... MickyFenton 8 34
(A W Carroll) *hld up: a in rr: wknd over 3f out* **12/1**

0-10 **10** *20* **Abulharith**[22] 5011 4-9-7 **57** .... RichardHughes 10 —
(M J Scudamore) *led: rdn and hdd 3f out: sn wknd: t.o* **33/1**

2m 40.28s (-0.82) **Going Correction** -0.05s/f (Stan)
WFA 3 from 4yo+ 8lb **10** Ran SP% **120.7**
Speed ratings (Par 101): **100,99,99,99,97 95,94,90,85,72**
toteswingers:1&2:£18.40, 1&3:£21.20, 2&3:£5.00 CSF £117.42 CT £397.60 TOTE £44.80: £8.10, £1.10, £1.10; EX 259.70 Place 6 £137.65; Place 5 £116.40.
Owner Mrs Sarah Hamilton **Bred** Meon Valley Stud **Trained** Newmarket, Suffolk
■ Stewards' Enquiry : Tom McLaughlin one-day ban: used whip with excessive frequency (Oct 8)

FOCUS

A low-grade handicap and four in a line inside the final furlong. The form looks sound if rather ordinary.

Cotton King Official explanation: trainer said, regarding apparent improvement in form, that the gelding appeared to benefit from the all-weather surface, first time visor and a half mile further than previous.

Abulharith Official explanation: jockey said gelding had no more to give

T/Plt: £86.50 to a £1 stake. Pool:£101,914.67 - 859.68 winning tickets T/Qpdt: £117.00 to a £1 stake. Pool:£8,384.41 - 53.00 winning tickets CR

4814 ASCOT (R-H)

Friday, September 24

OFFICIAL GOING: Good to soft (soft in places on round course) (stands' side 8.3; far side 8.5; centre 9.0; round 7.1)

6317 FRED COWLEY MBE FILLIES' NURSERY 6f 110y

2:00 (2:01) (Class 2) 2-Y-O

£9,346 (£2,799; £1,399; £700; £349; £175) **Stalls** Centre

Form RPR

51 **1** **Winter's Night (IRE)**[43] 4999 2-8-3 **72** .... LukeMorris 11 85+
(C G Cox) *hld up wl in tch: effrt and rdn to chse ldr 2f out: drvn to ld 1f out: styd on strly: drew clr fnl 100yds* **10/1**

21 **2** *2 ½* **Darajaat (USA)**[21] 5719 2-8-10 **79** .... TadhgO'Shea 9 85
(M P Tregoning) *led: pushed along 2f out: rdn and hdd 1f out: no ex and btn fnl 100yds: eased towards fin* **3/1**[1]

233 **3** *1 ¾* **Sylvestris (IRE)**[22] 5691 2-8-7 **76** .... JimCrowley 6 77
(R M Beckett) *awkward s: in tch in midfield: rdn and effrt over 2f out: chsd ldng trio and drvn over 1f out: styd on same pce and no imp after* **7/1**[2]

3331 **4** *hd* **Golden Tempest (IRE)**[21] 5720 2-8-4 **78** .... JohnFahy(5) 8 79
(W R Swinburn) *in tch in midfield: rdn and no prog over 2f out: styd on u.p fr over 1f out: no ch w ldng pair but kpt on to press for 3rd nr fin* **10/1**

1002 **5** *1 ¼* **Ladyanne (IRE)**[13] 5965 2-9-5 **88** .... LiamKeniry 5 85
(S Kirk) *swtchd rt after s: hld up towards rr: rdn and effrt over 2f out: no imp on ldrs tl styd on fr over 1f out: edgd lft u.p 1f out: kpt on fnl f: nvr trbld ldrs* **33/1**

01 **6** *3* **Picabo (IRE)**[20] 5755 2-7-12 **67** .... JimmyQuinn 4 56
(Mrs L Wadham) *hld up towards rr: rdn and effrt ent fnl 2f: no imp and wl hld fr over 1f out* **12/1**

431 **7** *2* **Apace (IRE)**[33] 5324 2-8-11 **80** .... RyanMoore 10 64
(Sir Michael Stoute) *dwlt: sn pushed along and rcvrd to chse ldrs: swtchd rt and drvn to chse ldrs jst over 2f out: btn over 1f out: wknd fnl f* **8/1**[3]

310 **8** *2* **Lenjawi Pride**[121] 2436 2-8-9 **78** RichardKingscote 1 56
(Tom Dascombe) *rrd as stalls opened and s.i.s: hld up in rr: rdn and effrt over 2f out: no prog 2f out: n.d* **40/1**

0211 **9** *3 ¾* **Cometh**[8] 6130 2-8-0 **69** 6ex AndreaAtzeni 13 37
(N P Littmoden) *w ldr tl jst over 2f out: wknd u.p wl over 1f out: fdd fnl f* **8/1**[3]

4100 **10** *6* **Idiom (IRE)**[77] 3872 2-8-12 **88** AntiocoMurgia(7) 12 39
(Mahmood Al Zarooni) *s.i.s: sn pushed along: hdwy into midfield 4f out: rdn and btn over 2f out: wl bhd fnl f* **50/1**

5535 **11** *¾* **Buddy Miracle**[9] 6086 2-8-4 **73** ChrisCatlin 2 22
(A M Balding) *awkward s and s.i.s: a towards rr: rdn and btn over 2f out: wl bhd fnl f* **33/1**

4111 **12** *4 ½* **Byrony (IRE)**[38] 5177 2-9-7 **90** RichardHughes 7 27
(R Hannon) *s.i.s: sn pushed along towards rr: sme prog u.p ent fnl 2f: no hdwy and wl btn over 1f out: eased fnl f* **10/1**

01 **13** *11* **Miss Sinatra (IRE)**[50] 4729 2-8-9 **78** KierenFallon 3 —
(B J Meehan) *chsd ldrs tl 3f out: sn lost pl: wl bhd and eased fnl f: t.o* **8/1**[3]

1m 23.19s (1.99) **Going Correction** +0.25s/f (Good) **13** Ran SP% **116.1**
Speed ratings (Par 98): **98,95,93,92,91 88,85,83,79,72 71,66,53**
Tote Swingers: 1&2 £9.90, 1&3 £18.60, 2&3 £3.60 CSF £37.87 CT £228.97 TOTE £13.40: £3.40, £2.00, £2.10; EX 44.70 Trifecta £383.80 Pool: £710.57 - 1.37 winning units..
Owner J T Thomas **Bred** J T And Mrs Thomas **Trained** Lambourn, Berks

FOCUS
In the region of 6mm of rain since the previous night eased the ground, which had been advertised as "good" all over. It appeared to be riding slow and Richard Hughes described conditions as "soft" with Kieren Fallon opting for "just on the soft side". This decent fillies' nursery filled the slot left by the discontinued Watership Down Stud sales race, which was also run over this intermediate distance. There were two groups early on but they quickly merged to race down the centre. Solid form, with the winner promising better to come.

NOTEBOOK
Winter's Night(IRE) followed up her Goodwood maiden win with a taking performance on this nursery debut. Racing on the far side of the bunch and cutting down the leader at the furlong pole, she was not stopping at the end of this longer trip and may well have further improvement in her when she tackles 7f. (op 16-1)
Darajaat(USA) made a lot of running but could not hold off the winner. She beat the rest well enough, but in contrast to the winner it could be that she is most effective over the bare 6f. Her Cheveley Park entry is unlikely to come to anything. (tchd 11-4, 10-3 and 7-2 in places)
Sylvestris(IRE) finished two places in front of today's winner when they made their respective debuts at Newbury, but was 4lb worse off now. She ran a solid race in this first nursery but has now been placed in each of her four starts without picking up a win. A return to further may suit. (op 10-1)
Golden Tempest(IRE) was a clear winner of a Kempton nursery on her last start, recording a faster time than Darajaat had on the same card, but was hit with a 12lb rise. She took a bit of time to pick up on this markedly different surface but was staying on determinedly at the end. (op 8-1)
Ladyanne(IRE), running on quite well over this longer trip, flashed her tail a couple of times to confirm that she has her quirks.
Picabo(IRE), another to come out of the aforementioned Newbury maiden, won a weak race second time up at Thirsk. After travelling well on this nursery debut she lacked a change of pace when the race developed, but did best of a group of four low-drawn fillies who raced separately from the rest early on. A drop back in trip will suit. (op 14-1)
Apace(IRE) faded out of things in the final furlong, and it could be that she needs to return to a bit further on better ground. (op 11-2)
Cometh had ground conditions to suit and was officially a pound well in, but her hat-trick bid came unstuck. Racing on her own initially, she set the pace but wasn't given any peace up front and was beaten some way out. Official explanation: jockey said filly had no more to give (op 11-1)
Byrony(IRE) Official explanation: jockey said filly was unsuited by the good to soft ground

6318 E B F RATCLIFFES SYNDICATION CLASSIFIED STKS 1m 2f
2:35 (2:35) (Class 3) 3-Y-0+

£9,346 (£2,799; £1,399; £700; £349; £175) **Stalls** High

Form RPR

1100 **1** **Rock N Roll Ransom**[14] 5917 3-8-10 88 KierenFallon 4 100+
(L M Cumani) *chsd ldr: rdn to ld 2f out: pressed over 1f out: styd on strly to assert ins fnl f: eased towards fin* **7/4**[1]

-230 **2** *2 ¼* **Splinter Cell (USA)**[38] 5188 4-9-2 90 WilliamBuick 3 95
(M Botti) *t.k.h: chsd ldng trio: rdn and effrt over 2f out: pressed wnr over 1f out: no ex and btn ins fnl f: hld on for 2nd towards fin* **6/1**[3]

0604 **3** *½* **Reve De Nuit (USA)**[6] 6205 4-8-11 85 JohnFahy(5) 1 94
(A J McCabe) *hld up wl in tch in last trio: rdn and hdwy 2f out: chsd ldng pair over 1f out: kpt on fnl f but no threat to wnr* **11/1**

1110 **4** *2 ¼* **Don't Call Me (IRE)**[27] 5511 3-8-10 90 (t) RichardMullen 2 90
(B Smart) *stdd and dropped in bhd after s: hld up in tch in last: rdn over 3f out: drvn and hanging rt 2f out: kpt on to go 4th ins fnl f: nvr trbld ldrs* **6/1**[3]

0260 **5** *1* **Right Step**[38] 5188 3-8-10 89 TedDurcan 6 88
(A P Jarvis) *stdd s: hld up wl in tch in midfield: rdn and unable qck over 2f out: one pce and no ch w ldrs over 1f out* **12/1**

0255 **6** *2 ½* **Moynahan (USA)**[13] 5955 5-9-2 89 (p) NeilCallan 9 83
(P F I Cole) *t.k.h: chsd ldng pair: rdn and effrt ent fnl 2f: drvn and btn over 1f out* **9/1**

4206 **7** *2 ¾* **Hypnotized (USA)**[42] 5030 3-8-10 90 (p) JamieSpencer 5 77
(M L W Bell) *sn led: rdn and edgd lft u.p jst over 2f out: hdd 2f out: wknd over 1f out* **11/2**[2]

8 *6* **L Frank Baum (IRE)**[132] 3-8-10 90 MichaelHills 8 65
(Miss Gay Kelleway) *stdd s: hld up in last pair: rdn and no prog over 2f out: wknd wl over 1f out* **20/1**

2m 11.35s (4.35) **Going Correction** +0.50s/f (Yiel)
WFA 3 from 4yo+ 6lb **8** Ran SP% **111.1**
Speed ratings (Par 107): **102,100,99,98,97 95,93,88**
Tote Swingers: 1&2 £2.90, 1&3 £4.60, 2&3 £10.40 CSF £11.61 TOTE £2.60: £1.10, £1.70, £3.20; EX 11.00 Trifecta £75.40 Pool: £927.64 - 9.10 winning units..
Owner Castle Down Racing **Bred** Meon Valley Stud **Trained** Newmarket, Suffolk

FOCUS
An interesting classified event run at a sound pace. It was won last year by the smart Rainbow Peak, and Rock N Roll Ransom is potentially smart too.

NOTEBOOK
Rock N Roll Ransom ◆ put recent frustrations behind him and will stay in training next year, when he may have Group-race aspirations, like last year's winner Rainbow Peak. Sitting on the shoulder of the leader before pressing for home, he quickly saw off the runner-up and forged clear to win in good style. This scopey individual was having only his fifth race and there is plenty more improvement to come at this trip or a little further. He likes this sort of ground and could run again this year. (op 2-1 tchd 9-4 in places and 5-2 in a place)
Splinter Cell(USA) was sharper for his return at the Ebor meeting and he ran a solid race, but came up against an unexposed rival. He is going to be fresher than most at this stage of the year and has the option of switching back to Polytrack. (op 5-1 tchd 9-2)
Reve De Nuit(USA) was comfortably worst off at the weights but he ran another creditable race and remains capable of further success when things fall his way. A solid pace suits him. (op 8-1)
Don't Call Me(IRE) has now been found wanting twice from this mark since compiling a July hat-trick over shorter. He did not appear to stay this trip at Beverley but was staying on quite well from the back here. (op 7-1 tchd 8-1)
Right Step has gone off the boil of late, although he may have finished a little closer had he not been slightly squeezed out over a furlong out. (tchd 16-1)
Moynahan(USA) raced more prominently than usual but could not sustain his effort. (op 17-2 tchd 10-1)
Hypnotized(USA), who was allowed to bowl along over this longer trip, did not seem to get home. (op 5-1 tchd 6-1)
L Frank Baum(IRE) showed quite useful form in Italy in the spring but was always in the last pair on this British debut. He is well regarded by his trainer, who has next year's Melbourne Cup as a long term objective, and it could pay to give him another chance over further. (op 16-1)

6319 DJP INTERNATIONAL H'CAP 6f
3:10 (3:11) (Class 2) (0-100,100) 3-Y-O

£9,969 (£2,985; £1,492; £747; £372; £187) **Stalls** Centre

Form RPR

2203 **1** **Little Garcon (USA)**[21] 5731 3-8-11 **90** WilliamBuick 10 102
(M Botti) *stdd s: hld up in last trio: stl plenty to do and switching rt wl over 1f out: str run fnl f to ld nr fin* **20/1**

1321 **2** *nk* **Dungannon**[50] 4742 3-8-2 **86** oh4 SimonPearce(5) 12 97
(A M Balding) *t.k.h: hld up wl in tch: rdn and effrt to chse ldr over 1f out: led ent fnl f: kpt on u.p fnl f tl hdd and no ex nr fin* **16/1**

0004 **3** *1 ¼* **Iver Bridge Lad**[10] 6063 3-9-7 **100** (b) MichaelHills 13 107
(J Ryan) *hld up in tch towards rr: rdn and effrt wl over 1f out: hdwy u.p ent fnl f: chsd ldng pair fnl 75yds: kpt on wl* **16/1**

0000 **4** *1 ¼* **Kellys Eye (IRE)**[6] 6175 3-9-1 **94** JamieSpencer 15 97+
(D H Brown) *stdd s: hld up in last trio: rdn and hanging rt wl over 1f out: stl plenty to do and swtchd lft jst ins fnl f: r.o wl to snatch 4th last strides: nvr trbld ldrs* **14/1**

4041 **5** *nk* **Joe Packet**[13] 5966 3-9-2 **95** JimCrowley 4 97
(J G Portman) *chsd ldrs: rdn to chse ldr briefly over 1f out: carried lft fr over 1f out and n.m.r ent fnl f: kpt on same pce fnl 150yds* **12/1**

1456 **6** *½* **Rio Mist**[8] 6113 3-8-10 **89** JimmyFortune 1 89
(R Hannon) *in tch in midfield: effrt and drvn over 1f out: kpt on same pce ins fnl f* **25/1**

4415 **7** *shd* **Star Rover (IRE)**[16] 5851 3-9-2 **95** RichardMullen 2 95
(P D Evans) *chsd ldr: rdn ent fnl 2f: lost 2nd over 1f out: btn and kpt on same pce fnl f* **25/1**

3241 **8** *nk* **Oil Strike**[21] 5731 3-8-13 **92** IanMongan 16 91
(P Winkworth) *chsd ldrs: rdn to ld wl over 1f out: edgd lft u.p fr over 1f out: hdd 1f out: wknd fnl 100yds* **12/1**

-425 **9** *½* **Gouray Girl (IRE)**[8] 6113 3-8-11 **90** ShaneKelly 5 88+
(W R Swinburn) *s.i.s: sn in tch in midfield: n.m.r and lost pl wl over 1f out: rallied u.p ent fnl f: no imp fnl 150yds* **12/1**

6112 **10** *½* **Slip Sliding Away (IRE)**[26] 5551 3-8-2 **86** oh4 JohnFahy(5) 14 82
(P R Hedger) *in tch: effrt u.p to press ldrs 2f out: btn ent fnl f: wknd fnl 150yds* **25/1**

0223 **11** *1 ½* **Deacon Blues**[13] 5944 3-9-2 **95** KierenFallon 3 86
(J R Fanshawe) *hld up in tch in midfield: rdn and effrt 2f out: n.m.r wl over 1f out: keeping on but nt threatening ldrs whn nt clr run and snatched up fnl 100yds: eased after* **3/1**[1]

1201 **12** *1 ¼* **Cansili Star**[29] 5442 3-9-3 **96** PhilipRobinson 7 83
(M A Jarvis) *led: rdn and hdd wl over 1f out: wknd over 1f out* **10/1**

4351 **13** *4 ½* **Alice Alleyne (IRE)**[27] 5521 3-8-7 **86** RyanMoore 6 59
(Sir Michael Stoute) *chsd ldrs: rdn ent fnl 2f: wknd u.p over 1f out: bhd fnl f* **15/2**[3]

2411 **14** *nse* **Kanaf (IRE)**[13] 5967 3-8-12 **91** TadhgO'Shea 9 64
(E A L Dunlop) *taken down early: hld up towards rr: rdn and no prog 2f out: nvr trbld ldrs* **7/1**[2]

5053 **15** *1* **Yer Woman (IRE)**[27] 5521 3-8-11 **90** RichardHughes 8 59
(R Hannon) *stdd s: hld up in last trio: rdn and no prog 2f out: wl btn over 1f out* **28/1**

1016 **16** *2 ¼* **Hairspray**[12] 6000 3-8-7 **86** ChrisCatlin 11 48
(M R Channon) *taken down early: chsd ldrs: rdn and wkng whn n.m.r wl over 1f out: bhd fnl f* **66/1**

1m 16.01s (1.61) **Going Correction** +0.50s/f (Yiel) **16** Ran SP% **121.1**
Speed ratings (Par 107): **109,108,106,105,104 104,104,103,103,102 100,98,92,92,91 88**
Tote Swingers: 1&2 £40.90, 1&3 £53.70, 2&3 £77.60 CSF £289.21 CT £5174.04 TOTE £26.30: £4.90, £4.50, £3.20, £4.00; EX 406.30 TRIFECTA Not won..
Owner Joseph Barton **Bred** Castleton Lyons **Trained** Newmarket, Suffolk

FOCUS
A competitive handicap which features Genki and Laddies Poker Two on the roll of recent winners, both of whom progresed to better things. They raced in one bunch and three of the first four came from the rear. A positive view has been taken of the form, with the winner a biggish improver and the fourth better than the bare form.

NOTEBOOK
Little Garcon(USA) was last at one stage but picked up well down the outside. He deserved this first turf victory, having been pretty consistent in defeat since his Lingfield win in April. (op 16-1)
Dungannon raced more prominently than the others in the frame and he showed in front before the winner pounced. He is tough and progressive but was 4lb out of the weights which will not help his mark. (tchd 20-1)
Iver Bridge Lad has been hard to place in his second season, but he was finishing to good effect from the back. He was due for a 2lb ease in his rating before this.
Kellys Eye(IRE) has been held in some warm handicaps since his Ripon hat-trick. After taking time to gather full momentum he was flashing home on the near-side of the bunch. (op 20-1 tchd 25-1)
Joe Packet had Ayr Bronze Cup winner Cheveton behind when winning at Sandown and, although 7lb higher here, was officially 2lb well in. He ran well back up in trip, and encountered a few traffic problems in the latter stages, which might have cost him a place. (op 8-1)
Rio Mist ran a decent race from the lowest draw and, while the handicapper looks in charge, an imminent pound ease in her rating can only help her cause.
Star Rover(IRE) did nothing wrong, but all six of his career wins have been over 5f or thereabouts and he is yet to strike in a handicap.
Oil Strike had Little Garcon in third when winning at Lingfield, for which a 4lb rise saw him on a career-high mark. He showed ahead briefly before forfeiting his chance when edging to his left, and could be worth trying in some headgear.
Gouray Girl(IRE), tackling male opposition again, was running on after being slightly hampered and remains in decent nick.
Slip Sliding Away(IRE) was not discredited from 4lb out of the handicap but could not maintain his upward curve. (op 20-1)
Deacon Blues was starting to run on when a door was shut in his face inside the last. He had been short of room earlier too and is probably worth another chance. (op 11-4 tchd 5-2)
Cansili Star Official explanation: jockey said gelding was unsuited by the good to soft ground
Kanaf(IRE) was disappointing on this hat-trick bid. He was another 7lb higher and the ground may well have been softer than ideal. (op 8-1 tchd 5-1)

Yer Woman(IRE) Official explanation: jockey said filly was unsuited by the good to soft ground

6320 PRINCESS ROYAL TRANSFORMERS AND RECTIFIERS E B F HARVEST STKS (LISTED RACE) (F&M) 1m 4f

3:45 (3:45) (Class 1) 3-Y-0+

£25,546 (£9,684; £4,846; £2,416; £1,210; £607) **Stalls** High

Form RPR

2204 **1** **Polly's Mark (IRE)**[15] 5881 4-9-3 105 RichardHughes 9 107
(C G Cox) *in tch: effrt to chse ldrs and barging match w rival over 2f out: drvn to chal over 1f out: led jst ins fnl f: edgd rt u.p and kpt on gamely ins fnl f: jst hld on* **5/2**[2]

11 **2** *nse* **Ferdoos**[12] 5989 3-8-9 87 PhilipRobinson 10 107+
(M A Jarvis) *in tch towards rr: rdn over 2f out: stl 7th and plenty to do 2f out: hdwy to chse ldng trio ent fnl f: hung lft u.p ins fnl f: stened and r.o strly fnl 75yds: jst failed* **2/1**[1]

2050 **3** *1 ¾* **Snoqualmie Girl (IRE)**[15] 5881 4-9-3 97 (p) JamieSpencer 4 104
(D R C Elsworth) *chsd ldr after 1f: rdn to ld over 2f out: hrd pressed and drvn over 1f out: hdd jst ins fnl f: no ex and btn fnl 100yds* **33/1**

-010 **4** *1 ¾* **Dyna Waltz**[15] 5881 3-8-12 104 WilliamBuick 12 104
(J H M Gosden) *led for 1f: trckd ldng pair after: effrt and barging match w wnr over 2f out tl swtchd ins 2f out: styd on same pce u.p fr over 1f out* **11/1**

1610 **5** *½* **Brushing**[15] 5881 4-9-6 102 KierenFallon 11 104
(M H Tompkins) *hld up in rr: rdn and effrt on outer over 2f out: kpt on steadily fr over 1f out: nvr gng pce to rch ldrs* **10/1**

111 **6** *4 ½* **Sparkling Smile (IRE)**[21] 5727 3-8-9 92 TedDurcan 14 93
(D R Lanigan) *in tch in midfield: rdn and unable qck over 2f out: swtchd lft and no prog fr wl over 1f out* **8/1**[3]

2150 **7** *½* **Warling (IRE)**[15] 5881 3-8-9 90 TomQueally 1 93
(J Noseda) *t.k.h: hld up towards rr: hdwy into midfield 4f out: rdn and no prog over 2f out: wl btn over 1f out* **14/1**

2336 **8** *2* **Lady Artemisia (IRE)**[54] 4624 4-9-3 100 RyanMoore 5 89
(M Botti) *chsd ldr tl crossed to rail and led after 1f: rdn and hdd over 2f out: wknd u.p wl over 1f out: wl bhd fnl f* **25/1**

5160 **9** *15* **Some Sunny Day**[9] 6095 4-9-3 78 SteveDrowne 7 65
(H Morrison) *swtchd rt and dropped in bhd after s: a in rr: effrt and sme hdwy over 2f out: wknd 2f out: wl bhd and eased fnl f* **66/1**

1320 **10** *45* **Shimmering Surf (IRE)**[15] 5881 3-8-9 101 LukeMorris 6 —
(P Winkworth) *in tch: rdn and struggling 4f out: bhd and eased fr over 2f out: t.o* **12/1**

2m 36.58s (4.08) **Going Correction** +0.50s/f (Yiel)
WFA 3 from 4yo+ 8lb **10** Ran SP% **113.1**
Speed ratings (Par 111): **106,105,104,103,103 100,99,98,88,58**
Tote Swingers: 1&2 £2.30, 1&3 £15.10, 2&3 £12.60 CSF £7.45 TOTE £3.50: £1.40, £1.40, £5.00; EX 7.10 Trifecta £175.80 Pool: £1,656.41 - 6.97 winning units..
Owner Wickham Stud **Bred** Glashare House Stud **Trained** Lambourn, Berks

FOCUS

A decent Listed event run at sound pace. The form has been rated around the third, fourth and fifth and looks fairly solid, although the winner did not quite match her best form.

NOTEBOOK

Polly's Mark(IRE) had been running well all season in Group company and was the form pick after a string of solid efforts in defeat. She travelled well before going on, but lightning nearly struck twice, as a year ago she had been caught on the line in this by Spirit Of Dubai, when she carried a penalty, and she would have lost the race in another stride this time too. Fourth in the Park Hill over an extended 1m6f last time, she confirmed the form with four fillies who finished behind her that day, with the rain-eased ground in her favour. She may stay in training next season. (op 2-1)

Ferdoos ◆ only made her debut last month and came here unbeaten in a Kempton maiden and a Ffos Las handicap. She so nearly made it three, but after picking up ground off the home turn and running on down the outside she hung badly left inside the last, losing momentum. Once her rider switched his stick she ran on again, but the line came too soon. The Group 2 Pride Stakes at Newmarket next month would seem to be a suitable target. (tchd 15-8 tchd 9-4 in places)

Snoqualmie Girl(IRE), who was only sixth in this a year ago, had been below her best in most starts this season but ran a better race in the first-time cheekpieces. (op 22-1)

Dyna Waltz was hemmed in by the winner when looking to pull out at the two pole and her rider had to angle inside again. This was a respectable effort on her second run back from injury. (tchd 12-1)

Brushing, carrying a 3lb penalty for her win in the Listed Galtres Stakes at York, stayed on from the back without troubling the principals. (op 11-1 tchd 12-1)

Sparkling Smile(IRE) has been one of the season's success stories, winning five consecutive handicaps, but she was found out on this rise in grade. (op 10-1)

Warling(IRE) promised to be suited by this intermediate trip, but she took a hold when trapped wide through the early parts and could make no progress once into the straight. (op 18-1)

Lady Artemisia(IRE) got over to lead but could not fend off the challengers once in line for home. (op 20-1)

Some Sunny Day Official explanation: jockey said filly hung right

Shimmering Surf(IRE), who sweated up and went to post early, was the first beaten. (op 16-1 tchd 18-1 and 20-1 in places)

6321 TRANSFORMERS & RECTIFIERS H'CAP 7f

4:20 (4:21) (Class 3) (0-95,93) 3-Y-0 **£7,771** (£2,312; £1,155; £577) **Stalls** Centre

Form RPR

004 **1** **Excellent Guest**[6] 6198 3-8-3 80 SimonPearce(5) 10 93
(G G Margarson) *chsd ldrs and a travelling wl: led 2f out: sn rdn clr: edging lft and idling u.p ins fnl f: a doing enough* **14/1**

2445 **2** *¾* **Mass Rally (IRE)**[16] 5854 3-9-7 93 (v[1]) WilliamBuick 6 104+
(J H M Gosden) *stdd after s: hld up towards rr: pushed along and hdwy 2f out: rdn to chse clr wnr over 1f out: edgd lft and rt u.p ins fnl f: kpt on reluctantly and nvr gng to rch wnr* **7/1**

2-01 **3** *¾* **Brick Red**[31] 5383 3-8-13 85 JimmyFortune 1 94
(A M Balding) *chsd ldrs: rdn to chse clr wnr wl over 1f out tl over 1f out: kpt on ins fnl f but nvr gng pce to threaten wnr* **4/1**[1]

3123 **4** *5* **Ertikaan**[47] 4858 3-9-0 86 TadhgO'Shea 13 81
(M A Jarvis) *hld up in midfield: hdwy to chse ldng trio ent 2f out: sn rdn and unable qck: wl hld whn hung lft ins fnl f* **12/1**

0426 **5** *¾* **Layla's Hero (IRE)**[16] 5854 3-9-7 93 GeorgeBaker 12 86
(D M Simcock) *stdd s: hld up in rr: sme hdwy u.p over 1f out: nvr trbld ldrs* **10/1**

1200 **6** *nk* **Venutius**[25] 5605 3-9-4 90 RichardMullen 4 83
(E S McMahon) *led tl 2f out: sn rdn and outpcd by wnr: wknd and wl btn ent fnl f* **9/1**

1450 **7** *hd* **Brannagh (USA)**[7] 6167 3-8-12 84 (t) JamieSpencer 3 76
(J Noseda) *s.i.s: hld up in rr: rdn and effrt ent fnl 2f: sn hung rt u.p and no real prog tl kpt on past btn horses fnl f: nvr trbld ldrs* **25/1**

1-32 **8** *6* **Bramshaw (USA)**[13] 5968 3-8-13 85 NeilCallan 5 61
(Mrs A J Perrett) *t.k.h: hld up wl in tch: rdn and unable qck ent fnl 2f: wknd and wl btn over 1f out* **9/2**[2]

-000 **9** *4 ½* **Rum King (USA)**[39] 5143 3-8-13 88 PatrickHills(3) 2 52
(R Hannon) *chsd ldrs: rdn and struggling 3f out: dropping to rr and edgd lft u.p ent fnl 2f: wl bhd over 1f out* **66/1**

3500 **10** *4 ½* **Tawaabb**[13] 5944 3-9-6 92 (v) RyanMoore 16 44
(M R Channon) *stdd after s: hld up towards rr: effrt u.p ent fnl 2f: sn no hdwy and wl btn over 1f out: eased ins fnl f* **25/1**

0016 **11** *4 ½* **Sailorman (IRE)**[12] 5997 3-9-5 91 JoeFanning 9 30
(M Johnston) *sn pressing ldr: rdn and wknd ent fnl 2f: wl bhd over 1f out: eased ins fnl f* **25/1**

3016 **12** *hd* **Whirly Dancer**[44] 4963 3-8-13 85 TomQueally 7 24
(H R A Cecil) *sn pushed along towards rr: in tch tl wknd u.p jst over 2f out: wl btn and eased ins fnl f* **16/1**

0000 **13** *18* **Quarrel (USA)**[16] 5854 3-9-3 89 PhilipRobinson 15 —
(W J Haggas) *t.k.h: hld up in rr: wknd over 2f out: wl bhd and eased fr over 1f out: t.o* **33/1**

1- **14** *3 ¾* **Bronze Prince**[315] 7376 3-9-4 90 (t) TedDurcan 8 —
(Saeed Bin Suroor) *in tch in midfield: rdn and btn 2f out: no ch and heavily eased fnl f: t.o* **11/2**[3]

1m 30.04s (2.04) **Going Correction** +0.50s/f (Yiel) **14** Ran SP% **121.4**
Speed ratings (Par 105): **108,107,106,100,99 99,99,92,87,82 76,76,56,51**
Tote Swingers: 1&2 £26.20, 1&3 £22.80, 2&3 £10.00 CSF £104.20 CT £488.90 TOTE £18.80: £5.30, £2.00, £2.40; EX 168.30 TRIFECTA Not won..
Owner Exors of the Late John Guest **Bred** John Guest Racing Ltd **Trained** Newmarket, Suffolk

FOCUS

A competitive handicap run on ground that was becoming cut up. The first three finished clear, with the remainder well strung out. Not many showed their form, but there were small personal bests from the winner and the third.

NOTEBOOK

Excellent Guest, at the foot of the weights, led going well and went a couple of lengths to the good, but wandered as he perhaps began to idle and did not win as comfortably as he had looked set to. He had shown something of a return to form at Newmarket last time and was unexposed over this longer trip. (tchd 16-1)

Mass Rally(IRE), racing on the opposite side of the pack to the winner, stayed on well through the final furlong but was never quite going to reach his rival. He is not straightforward, and had a visor on for the first time, but is a useful colt when on song. (tchd 15-2)

Brick Red, for whom there was money, came under pressure not long after halfway but was staying on at the end. Raised 3lb for his win at Kempton a month ago, he is fully effective on turf too and continues on the upgrade. (op 7-1)

Ertikaan, who tracked the winner, ran reasonably well without shaping as if the 7f in softish ground was ideal. He carried his head a little high and is not without his quirks. (op 9-1 tchd 14-1)

Layla's Hero(IRE) came home well from the back but finished further behind Mass Rally than he had at Doncaster. (tchd 12-1)

Venutius was backed at big prices and he ran respectably from the front on ground that was going against him. (op 10-1)

Brannagh(USA) merely made late progress past beaten rivals. (tchd 33-1)

Bramshaw(USA) was well held in the end after racing a shade keenly just off the pace. Reported by his trainer to have not handled the ground, he is not one to write off yet. Official explanation: trainer said colt was unsuited by the good to soft ground (tchd 7-2 and 5-1 in places)

Sailorman(IRE) was on his toes in the paddock. (op 20-1)

Quarrel(USA) Official explanation: jockey said gelding was un suited by the good to soft ground

Bronze Prince Official explanation: jockey said colt was unsuited by the good to soft ground

6322 BOLLINGER CHAMPAGNE CHALLENGE SERIES FINAL H'CAP (GENTLEMAN AMATEURS IN ASSOC WITH DAILY TELEGRAPH) 1m 4f

4:55 (4:55) (Class 4) (0-80,77) 4-Y-0+

£6,002 (£1,875; £937; £469; £234; £118) **Stalls** High

Form RPR

1253 **1** **Bramalea**[15] 5888 5-10-13 73 MrTGarner(7) 6 91
(B W Duke) *taken down early: t.k.h: chsd ldrs tl wnt 2nd 9f out: clr w ldr 7f out: led over 5f out: rdn wl clr ent fnl 2f: eased ins fnl f: easily* **20/1**

0411 **2** *13* **Switched Off**[10] 6051 5-11-4 76 6ex MrJHodson(5) 3 73
(Ian Williams) *s.i.s: wl bhd in rr: hdwy 3f out: swtchd lft ent fnl 2f: hanging rt after but kpt on to go 2nd ins fnl f: no ch w wnr* **6/1**[2]

-351 **3** *1 ¾* **Talenti (IRE)**[39] 5148 7-10-12 70 (t) MrTJCannon(5) 12 64
(Mrs Lawney Hill) *sn rdn along towards rr and nt gng wl: stl wl bhd whn switching lft and barging match w rival over 2f out tl 2f out: kpt on to go 3rd ins fnl f: nvr trbld ldrs* **14/1**

2442 **4** *2* **Mykingdomforahorse**[5] 6224 4-10-10 70 (v) MrCBishop(7) 1 61
(M R Channon) *hld up in tch: outpcd by ldng pair 6f out: effrt on inner whn hmpd bnd fnl 3f: no ch w wnr and rdn ent fnl 2f: wnt modest 2nd and no prog over 1f out: lost 2 pls ins fnl f* **9/2**[1]

01/ **5** *1 ¼* **Striking Force (IRE)**[19] 5798 8-10-13 66 MrSWalker 10 55
(V C Ward, Ire) *sn towards rr and nt gng wl: rdn over 7f out: sme hdwy u.p over 2f out: kpt on fnl f: nvr trbld ldrs* **7/1**[3]

015 **6** *1 ¾* **Oriental Cavalier**[19] 5790 4-11-10 77 (v) MrMSeston 5 63
(Mark Buckley) *in tch in midfield: hdwy to chse clr wnr and drvn over 2f out: no imp: lost 2nd over 1f out: wknd ins fnl f* **14/1**

4622 **7** *3 ¼* **Arashi**[25] 5591 4-10-12 68 (v) MrPCollington(3) 14 49
(Lucinda Featherstone) *wl bhd: rdn and sme hdwy whn barging match w rival over 2f out tl 2f out: no prog after: n.d* **8/1**

4422 **8** *3 ½* **Megalala (IRE)**[17] 5828 9-10-7 65 MrJackSalmon(5) 2 41
(J J Bridger) *led: clr w wnr 7f out: hdd over 5f out: lost 2nd and wl btn over 2f out: wknd* **22/1**

064/ **9** *5* **Gtaab**[722] 6423 4-10-6 64 MrPPrince(5) 8 32
(P R Webber) *in tch: outpcd by ldrs 6f out: wknd u.p wl over 2f out* **20/1**

0500 **10** *3* **Wing Play (IRE)**[25] 5591 5-11-3 75 MrRPooles(5) 4 38
(H Morrison) *styd on outer in midfield: rdn and wl btn over 2f out: hung rt fnl 2f* **25/1**

54- **11** *5* **Safari Journey (USA)**[161] 3247 6-10-10 68 MrJMQuinlan(5) 13 23
(P J Hobbs) *racd off the pce in midfield: pushed along 8f out: bhd and rdn wl over 2f out: wl bhd fnl 2f: eased ins fnl f: t.o* **7/1**[3]

/20- **12** *¾* **Benfleet Boy**[169] 7036 6-11-3 70 MrSDobson 9 24
(B G Powell) *chsd ldrs early: steadily lost pl: rdn and wl btn over 2f out: eased fnl f: t.o* **7/1**[3]

4601 **13** *11* **Touch Of Style (IRE)**[18] 5813 6-10-5 63 oh2 MrRJWilliams(5) 7 —
(Matthew Salaman) *t.k.h: chsd ldrs: wkng u.p whn squeezed ent fnl 3f: wl bhd fnl 2f: t.o fnl f* **18/1**

2230 **14** *13* **Bavarica**[25] 5591 8-11-5 75 MrRBirkett(3) 15 —
(Miss J Feilden) *stdd s: a bhd: lost tch 3f out: t.o* **25/1**

The Form Book, Raceform Ltd, Compton, RG20 6NL

20-0 **15** *23* **Ramora (USA)**21 5722 4-10-9 **67** ...... MrCMartin(5) 11 —
(Miss Olivia Maylam) *racd in midfield: struggling and losing pl 7f out: t.o and eased fnl 2f* **33/1**

2m 40.67s (8.17) **Going Correction** +0.50s/f (Yiel) **15** Ran SP% **124.2**
Speed ratings (Par 105): **92,83,82,80,80 78,76,74,71,69 65,65,57,49,33**
Tote Swingers: 1&2 £24.70, 1&3 £30.70, 2&3 £11.60 CSF £128.69 CT £1779.47 TOTE £21.60: £5.30, £2.90, £2.80; EX 172.20 Trifecta £520.90 Part won. Pool: £704.04 - 0.20 winning units. Place 6: £201.88 Place 5: £106.93..
Owner P J Cave **Bred** P J Cave **Trained** Lambourn, Berks
■ Tom Garner's first winner. Only fifth in this final round, Simon Walker was winning the Bollinger Championship for a fifth time.

FOCUS
Not the strongest of amateur riders' handicaps for the track, but it was run at a strong pace and the field was soon strung out. The form could have been rated higher, but is probably best treated with a degree of caution.
Safari Journey(USA) Official explanation: jockey said horse was unsuited by the good to soft ground
Ramora(USA) Official explanation: jockey said filly was unsuited by the good to soft ground
T/Jkpt: Not won. T/Plt: £558 to a £1 stake. Pool:£133,414 - 174.53 winning tickets T/Qpdt: £198.90 to a £1 stake. Pool:£8,846 - 32.90 winning tickets SP

6045 HAYDOCK (L-H)

Friday, September 24

OFFICIAL GOING: Soft (heavy in places in straight for races of one mile and upwards) (5f & 6f 7.4; 1m+ 5.5)
Inner Sprint track used. For races of 1m plus back straight and bend out of back straight on inner line leading to outer home straight.
Wind: moderate across Weather: fine

6323 E B F VALE UK MAIDEN FILLIES' STKS 6f
2:10 (2:10) (Class 5) 2-Y-O **£3,238** (£963; £481; £240) **Stalls** Centre

Form RPR
3 **1** **Lady Paris (IRE)**11 6034 2-9-0 0 ...... TomEaves 8 79
(B Smart) *mde all: styd on wl to forge clr ins fnl f* **7/4**1
522 **2** *2* **Piece Of Mind**15 5885 2-9-0 72 ...... PatDobbs 7 73
(R Hannon) *w wnr: drvn 3f out: kpt on same pce fnl f* **9/4**2
3 *5* **Waltzing Cat (USA)** 2-8-10 0 ...... SebSanders 5 54+
(Sir Mark Prescott) *s.s: last and drvn 3f out: kpt on to take modest 3rd last 100yds* **7/1**
400 **4** *4* **Cerejeira (IRE)**100 3070 2-9-0 52 ...... DavidAllan 6 46
(E J Alston) *trckd ldrs: drvn over 2f out: wknd over 1f out* **20/1**
5 *5* **Queen's Choice (IRE)** 2-8-9 0 ow2 ...... RussKennemore(3) 2 29
(Mrs A L M King) *dwlt: sn drvn along: lost pl 2f out* **50/1**
6 *3* **Stravsambition** 2-8-10 0 ...... FergusSweeney 3 18
(R Hollinshead) *wnt rt s: hdwy over 3f out: hung lft and lost pl over 1f out* **16/1**
6 **P** **Muroona (IRE)**20 5761 2-9-0 0 ...... GregFairley 1 —
(M Johnston) *p.u and dismntd after 100yds: lame bhd* **5/1**3

1m 18.33s (4.83) **Going Correction** +0.425s/f (Yiel) **7** Ran SP% **108.9**
Speed ratings (Par 92): **84,81,74,69,62 58,—**
Tote Swingers: 1&2 £1.10, 1&3 £2.50, 2&3 £2.70 CSF £5.23 TOTE £2.50: £1.10, £2.90; EX 4.20.

Owner R C Bond **Bred** D Cantillon **Trained** Hambleton, N Yorks

FOCUS
Probably not much strength in depth in just a fair maiden and experience came to the fore in testing conditions. The winner's debut form is working out well.

NOTEBOOK
Lady Paris(IRE) had shaped well on her debut at Redcar when ahead of Thursday's Pontefract winner Jade and eventually got the better of her market rival after a sustained battle as the first two pulled clear. This was a good test of stamina at the trip and she will have no problems staying 7f or making further progress. (op 9-4)
Piece Of Mind had been improving gradually but that progress might well have come to an end now, for all that she pulled clear of the remainder. She's not really up to winning a maiden, and ought to have better prospects in nurseries, with a switch to the AW possibly her best option of finding a race. (op 15-8)
Waltzing Cat(USA) is an American-bred filly by More Than Ready from the family of the St Leger winner Toulon. She was very green early on after a slow start but began to stay on encouragingly late, for all that she never threatened. She's sure to improve and might do significantly better if upped in trip and switched to artificial surfaces. (tchd 6-1)
Cerejeira(IRE) was having her first run since finishing down the field in the Queen Mary and stayed prominent to just past halfway until lack of a recent run found her out. She's another that will do better in nurseries. (op 16-1 tchd 25-1)
Queen's Choice(IRE) is a half-sister to the 5f/7f winner Rocket Rob but she looked some way off the finished article and won't be of interest for another run at least. (op 40-1)
Stravsambition is a half-sister to the fairly useful Stravara and ran better than her finishing position suggests, as she was slowly away then dropped out as if badly in need of the run. She should last longer next time. (op 12-1)
Muroona(IRE)'s rider was looking down almost on exiting the stalls and something was clearly amiss. (op 13-2 tchd 7-1)

6324 E B F VALE UK MAIDEN STKS (C&G) 6f
2:45 (2:45) (Class 5) 2-Y-O **£3,238** (£963; £481; £240) **Stalls** Centre

Form RPR
3025 **1** **Squires Gate (IRE)**53 4650 2-9-0 78 ...... RobertWinston 1 79
(B W Hills) *t.k.h: mde all: wnt 4 l clr over 3f out: 2 l clr 100yds out: lasted home* **9/4**2
3 **2** *1* **New Latin (IRE)**8 6126 2-9-0 0 ...... GregFairley 6 76
(M Johnston) *trckd wnr: effrt over 2f out: hung lft and styd on fnl f* **15/8**1
3 *7* **Muffraaj** 2-9-0 0 ...... EddieAhern 4 55
(D M Simcock) *trckd ldrs: drvn 3f out: wknd fnl 2f* **9/2**3
4 *1 ½* **Lion Court (IRE)** 2-9-0 0 ...... SebSanders 3 54+
(Sir Mark Prescott) *dwlt: hld up in rr: drvn 3f out: sn wknd* **7/1**
5 *1 ½* **Gnr Steamtrain (IRE)** 2-9-0 0 ...... PaulHanagan 2 46
(R A Fahey) *sn drvn along to chse ldrs: lost pl over 3f out* **8/1**

1m 17.83s (4.33) **Going Correction** +0.425s/f (Yiel) **5** Ran SP% **107.3**
Speed ratings (Par 95): **88,86,77,75,73**
CSF £6.49 TOTE £3.70: £2.50, £1.10; EX 5.10.
Owner Mr & Mrs Jenkins & Mr & Mrs Middlebrook **Bred** Mr & Mrs G Middlebrook **Trained** Lambourn, Berks

FOCUS
No more than a fair maiden in which the two with experience dominated almost right from the stalls. The winner is rated back to form.

NOTEBOOK
Squires Gate(IRE) had the best form and, despite being uneasy in the market, put a modest run at Ripon nearly two months ago behind him with a win that owed as much to his good early speed as it did to his gritty attitude in fending off the persistent runner-up. He might be set for a decent autumn given that he clearly handles soft ground very well, with 6f looking as far as he wants for now. (op 5-2 tchd 15-8)
New Latin(IRE) had a bit to find with the winner on form and ran well considering he still looked inexperienced. He has an action that suggests this sort of ground might be ideal, and he'll win a race this autumn, with a step up to 7f also likely to be in his favour. (op 5-4)
Muffraaj, who holds a Middle Park entry and is a half-brother to a 6f Group 1 winner in Hong Kong, lost touch with the first two before halfway but still saw his race out well enough to emerge best of the newcomers. Conditions put big store by experience, and he's sure to do a lot better next time. (op 6-1 tchd 4-1)
Lion Court(IRE), a 40,000gns yearling and a half-brother to a 2-y-o 1m winner, was the subject of support at big odds but never threatened after a slow start. Nonetheless, he showed signs of ability as well as something of a round action, and ought to be sharper next time. (op 16-1)
Gnr Steamtrain(IRE) is the first foal of a maiden mare but didn't shape with any real encouragement. However, he's with a powerful yard and is entitled to improve. (op 15-2)

6325 PAUL LATHAM'S 50TH JUVENILE TO SENILE NURSERY 6f
3:20 (3:20) (Class 4) (0-80,80) 2-Y-O **£4,533** (£1,348; £674; £336) **Stalls** Centre

Form RPR
1355 **1** **Rosina Grey**16 5856 2-9-0 **76** ...... JamesMillman(3) 1 85
(B R Millman) *dwlt: mid-div: hdwy on wd outside and carried lft 2f out: led over 1f out: pushed clr ins fnl f: comf* **8/1**
2124 **2** *2 ½* **No Poppy (IRE)**15 5882 2-9-2 **75** ...... (b) DuranFentiman 7 76
(T D Easterby) *led: hdd over 1f out: hung lft ins fnl f: kpt on same pce* **4/1**2
665 **3** *1 ¼* **Icy Blue**26 5546 2-8-6 **65** ...... FrannyNorton 4 62
(R M Whitaker) *in rr: effrt over 2f out: styd on fnl f: tk n.d 3rd nr fin* **28/1**
216 **4** *½* **Riverdale (IRE)**34 5301 2-9-6 **79** ...... PhillipMakin 6 74
(Mrs A Duffield) *chsd ldrs: rdn and hung lft 2f out: kpt on same pce sltly hmpd 100yds out* **11/4**1
5220 **5** *2 ½* **Captain Dimitrios**6 6191 2-8-13 **75** ...... MartinLane(3) 8 63
(P D Evans) *w ldr: drvn 3f out: wknd appr fnl f* **6/1**
0551 **6** *1* **Black Annis Bower**12 5998 2-8-6 **68** 6ex ...... JamesSullivan(3) 3 53
(M W Easterby) *in rr: reminders and hdwy 3f out: edgd lft and wknd over 1f out* **8/1**
0214 **7** *3 ¼* **Whats For Pudding (IRE)**5 6220 2-7-5 **57** oh2 ...... NeilFarley(7) 9 32
(D Carroll) *chsd ldrs: lost pl over 1f out* **16/1**
310 **8** *2 ¼* **Cruise Tothelimit (IRE)**28 5472 2-9-7 **80** ...... StephenCraine 10 48
(Patrick Morris) *swvd rt s: sn trcking ldrs: effrt over 2f out: wknd over 1f out* **20/1**
3145 **9** *8* **Bahamian Sunset**28 5476 2-9-5 **78** ...... PaulHanagan 5 22
(R A Fahey) *dwlt: in rr: hung lft: lost pl over 2f out: eased whn bhd ins fnl f* **11/2**3

1m 16.43s (2.93) **Going Correction** +0.425s/f (Yiel) **9** Ran SP% **112.7**
Speed ratings (Par 97): **97,93,92,91,88 86,82,79,68**
Tote Swingers: 1&2 £6.10, 1&3 £44.90, 2&3 £13.50 CSF £38.88 CT £856.58 TOTE £9.50: £2.90, £1.80, £2.80; EX 46.30.
Owner P Gibbins M Daly **Bred** The Three Point Partnership **Trained** Kentisbeare, Devon

FOCUS
A fairly useful nursery that most of the runners came into in good form. The time was easily the fastest of the three on the straight track. The runner-up is the bset guide to the form.

NOTEBOOK
Rosina Grey has been holding her form well despite things arguably not having gone her way the last twice, but this softest ground that she has raced on seemed to bring out the best in her and she got to the front without her rider having to be anything like hard on her, in the end winning with more ease than the official distance suggests. She'll have to be of interest faced with similar underfoot conditions before the season is out, even off a higher mark. (tchd 9-1)
No Poppy(IRE) again gave her running while coping with the softest underfoot conditions she has yet encountered and, while her head carriage inside the last wasn't the most attractive, she didn't stop trying. (tchd 7-2)
Icy Blue looked more at home in this company than he has in maidens but he never threatened and his campaign so far suggests connections are unsure of his best trip. On this evidence it might be 7f. (op 25-1)
Riverdale(IRE) left the impression that the ground might have been softer than he is properly effective on, having looked at one point as though he was sure to be involved in the finish. (op 3-1)
Captain Dimitrios has form in softish conditions and seemed to run somewhere near his level. He's been in decent form lately and helps give the form a solid look. (op 10-1)
Black Annis Bower might have been expected to have fared better seeing as he she'd scored in similar conditions at Newcastle last time, but that win against her own sex came in a weaker race than this and she didn't seem to have any excuses under a penalty. (op 13-2)
Cruise Tothelimit(IRE) had something to find on recent form with some of these and, after seeming to travel well enough to halfway, dropped away tamely. He's not progressed since his win. (op 10-1)
Bahamian Sunset might not have been suited by the ground but has something to prove now after this second successive modest run in a nursery. (op 7-1 tchd 5-1)

6326 VALE UK (S) STKS 1m 2f 95y
3:55 (3:55) (Class 4) 3-4-Y-O **£5,828** (£1,734; £866; £432) **Stalls** Centre

Form RPR
244 **1** **Rockweiller**5 6225 3-9-1 64 ...... (v) RichardEvans(3) 5 75
(P D Evans) *trckd ldrs: drvn to ld over 3f out: narrowly hdd over 1f out: hrd rdn and styd on to ld last 75yds: jst hld on* **9/2**3
234 **2** *nse* **Mark Twain (IRE)**9 6097 3-9-0 78 ...... PaulHanagan 1 71
(D M Simcock) *trckd ldrs: t.k.h: drvn to take narrow ld over 1f out: hdd wl ins fnl f: kpt on* **8/11**1
3046 **3** *20* **Dane Cottage**24 5636 3-8-13 56 ...... (v1) CathyGannon 3 32
(P D Evans) *dwlt: t.k.h in rr: effrt over 3f out: tk modest 3rd 2f out: one pce* **33/1**
3556 **4** *4 ½* **Munaawer (USA)**41 5093 3-9-4 70 ...... (p) SebSanders 4 28
(J D Bethell) *led: hdd over 3f out: wknd 2f out: eased towards fin* **14/1**
46-0 **5** *12* **Stan's Cool Cat (IRE)**7 6151 4-9-1 82 ...... SilvestreDeSousa 6 —
(P F I Cole) *hld up in rr: drvn over 5f out: wknd over 2f out: eased whn bhd ins fnl f* **7/2**2

2m 19.9s (3.90) **Going Correction** +0.475s/f (Yiel)
WFA 3 from 4yo 6lb **5** Ran SP% **107.9**
Speed ratings (Par 105): **103,102,86,83,73**
CSF £7.98 TOTE £5.00: £2.00, £1.10.The winner was sold Steve Gollings for £10,000.
Owner W Clifford **Bred** Exors Of The Late Mrs E A Hankinson **Trained** Pandy, Monmouths
■ Stewards' Enquiry : Paul Hanagan caution: used whip with excessive frequency.
Richard Evans three-day ban: used whip with excessive frequency down shoulder in the forehand (Oct 8-10)

FOCUS
A close finish to a seller contested by horses of varying abilities. The pace was muddling and the form is probably no more than modest despite the long gap back to the third. Not a race to be positive about.

6327 FRANK FITZGERALD H'CAP — 1m 30y
4:30 (4:31) (Class 3) (0-95,90) 3-Y-0+
£7,788 (£2,332; £1,166; £583; £291; £146) Stalls Low

Form — RPR
0203 1 **Captain Dancer (IRE)**[13] 5937 4-8-11 77 .... RobertWinston 8 85
(B W Hills) *trckd ldrs: drvn over 3f out: edgd lft and styd on to ld last 75yds: all out* **6/1[3]**
0002 2 nk **Ingleby Spirit**[41] 5086 3-8-12 82 .... PaulHanagan 3 90
(R A Fahey) *chsd ldrs: drvn 3f out: nt clr run and swtchd lft ins fnl f: no ex towards fin* **5/1[2]**
0-00 3 ¾ **Unbreak My Heart (IRE)**[164] 1274 5-9-2 87 .... LeeTopliss(5) 4 93
(R A Fahey) *in rr: hdwy over 3f out: nt clr run ins fnl f: styng on wl at fin* **25/1**
6541 4 shd **Medici Pearl**[44] 4950 6-9-7 87 .... DavidAllan 10 93
(T D Easterby) *in rr: effrt over 2f out: swtchd outside 1f out: styng on wl at fin* **12/1**
1422 5 nk **Play It Sam**[27] 5540 4-9-8 88 .... EddieAhern 11 94
(W R Swinburn) *sn trcking ldr: led over 1f out: hdd ins fnl f: 3rd and hld whn hmpd and eased nr fin* **8/1**
0002 6 ¾ **Marvo**[9] 6097 6-8-6 77 .... AshleyMorgan(5) 12 80
(M H Tompkins) *hld up towards rr: effrt over 3f out: keeping on same pce whn nt clr run 1f out* **6/1[3]**
-062 7 ½ **Leviathan**[16] 5854 3-9-6 90 .... MickyFenton 7 92
(T P Tate) *hld up in rr: hdwy on outside over 2f out: chsng ldrs 1f out: fdd fnl 75yds* **6/1[3]**
1540 8 3½ **Guilded Warrior**[14] 5903 7-9-8 88 .... FergusSweeney 2 82
(W S Kittow) *led: hdd over 1f out: wknd fnl 150yds* **33/1**
4042 9 7 **Lucky Dance (BRZ)**[62] 4371 8-9-9 89 .... RobertHavlin 9 67
(T T Clement) *mid-div: effrt over 3f out: wknd 2f out: eased nr fin* **33/1**
00 10 13 **Icelandic**[48] 4832 8-9-10 90 ....(t) LeeVickers 5 38
(F Sheridan) *s.i.s: sme hdwy and nt clr run over 2f out: wknd over 1f out: eased towards fin* **50/1**
1414 11 9 **Innocuous**[26] 5556 3-9-0 87 .... MartinLane(3) 1 14
(D M Simcock) *chsd ldrs: drvn 3f out: lost pl over 2f out: heavily eased* **3/1[1]**

1m 47.07s (2.37) **Going Correction** +0.475s/f (Yiel)
WFA 3 from 4yo+ 4lb — **11** Ran SP% **115.0**
Speed ratings (Par 107): **107,106,105,105,105 104,104,100,93,80 71**
Tote Swingers: 1&2 £5.70, 1&3 £24.20, 2&3 £17.00 CSF £34.03 CT £697.04 TOTE £7.90: £2.30, £2.10, £3.60; EX 36.40.
Owner R J Arculli **Bred** King Bloodstock And Swettenham Stud **Trained** Lambourn, Berks
■ Stewards' Enquiry : Robert Winston caution: used whip with excessive frequency.

FOCUS
A keenly-contested handicap that was run at a good clip in the conditions with the two confirmed front runners taking each other on. Several horses looked to hold a winning chance at some point in the straight. The winner is rated to his best.

NOTEBOOK
Captain Dancer(IRE) had caught the eye coming from a long way back at Chester last time from a poor draw and he confirmed that that run was better than it looked with a gutsy win in which he battled on well after coming under pressure a long way out. He acts well on soft ground and, being fresher than most right now, could have a fruitful autumn if it stays wet now his yard have hit top form again. An extra 2f probably wouldn't be a problem. (op 8-1)
Ingleby Spirit stayed on resolutely after also coming under pressure a long way out without ever really looking likely to come through and win it. He's in his element in these conditions and, being eligible for 0-85s, can win something less competitive before the season is out, perhaps back up in trip. (op 6-1)
Unbreak My Heart(IRE) has a good record fresh so may not improve as much as might seem likely given that this was his first run since April. All the same, this was a good effort, though the small piece of interference he suffered late on didn't affect his finishing position. (op 20-1)
Medici Pearl has a good record in soft ground at this trip and belied market weakness with a solid effort, keeping on strongly but not looking unlucky despite having to switch to make her run. (op 8-1)
Play It Sam is best when able to dominate and didn't have that luxury with Guilded Warrior in the field, but he gave it his best shot after playing second fiddle to that one to 2f out, beaten off only late on. His new mark doesn't look beyond him. (op 9-1)
Marvo probably found this a bit more competitive than he would care for and never landed a blow. His mark is due to go up 5lb at the weekend, so his chance might have gone for now. (tchd 13-2)
Leviathan ◆ had finished a very good second at Doncaster last time and looked to hold good claims if he could reproduce that form trying this longer trip for the first time. He looked sure to take a hand when produced with his challenge only to find stamina failing him inside the last. He can win another race back at 7f. (op 9-2)
Innocuous came into this as an in-form potential improver proven in the conditions, so his no-show was a big disappointment. He was the first beaten, and something may well have been amiss. Official explanation: trainer had no explanation for the poor form shown (op 4-1)

6328 BETDAQ THE BETTING EXCHANGE APPRENTICE SERIES H'CAP — 1m 2f 95y
5:05 (5:06) (Class 5) (0-70,70) 3-Y-0+ £3,238 (£963; £481; £240) Stalls Centre

Form — RPR
0126 1 **King Zeal (IRE)**[41] 5071 6-9-9 70 .... JamesRogers(3) 5 86
(B D Leavy) *w ldr: led 4f out: drvn and styd on wl* **5/1[3]**
0-00 2 2¼ **Spring Secret**[31] 5386 4-9-2 65 .... ThomasBrown(5) 12 77
(B Palling) *chsd ldrs: wnt 2nd 3f out: kpt on: no imp* **50/1**
0602 3 3¾ **Strategic Mission (IRE)**[24] 5635 5-9-9 67 .... DuilioDaSilva 10 72
(P F I Cole) *trckd ldrs: hmpd bnd over 6f out: hdwy on ins and 4th 3f out: kpt on to take 3rd last 50yds* **4/1[1]**
5003 4 ½ **Dream Of Olwyn (IRE)**[26] 5563 5-9-7 65 .... DaleSwift 9 69
(J G Given) *prom: wnt 3rd 3f out: edgd rt and one pce fnl f* **9/2[2]**
2014 5 7 **Cherri Fosfate**[24] 5635 6-9-5 63 ....(v) NeilFarley 13 54
(D Carroll) *s.i.s: bhd and sn drvn along: kpt on fnl 3f: nvr on terms* **10/1**
6000 6 2¾ **Lordship (IRE)**[4] 6261 6-8-7 56 .... JakePayne(5) 14 41
(A W Carroll) *hld up in rr: kpt on fnl 3f: nvr on terms* **14/1**
6040 7 1 **Bagutta Sun**[74] 3960 4-9-12 70 .... AmyScott 7 54
(B D Leavy) *awkward s: bhd: kpt on fnl 3f: nvr nr ldrs* **28/1**
-066 8 2½ **Given A Choice (IRE)**[17] 5840 8-8-9 56 oh2......(p) SophieSilvester(3) 15 35
(J Pearce) *in tch: effrt on inner over 3f out: wknd over 2f out* **25/1**
6060 9 1½ **Sedgwick**[19] 5790 8-9-12 70 .... BrianToomey 3 46
(S A Harris) *stdd s: in rr: sme hdwy over 2f out: nvr on terms* **10/1**
113- 10 6 **Prairie Hawk (USA)**[455] 3346 5-8-10 61 .... TimothyAyres(7) 8 26
(B S Rothwell) *mid-div: lost pl over 2f out* **20/1**
0060 11 70 **Supercast (IRE)**[49] 4793 7-8-9 58 .... IanBurns(5) 4 —
(N J Vaughan) *led: hdd 4f out: sn lost pl and bhd: t.o* **50/1**
-423 12 4½ **Moon Lightning (IRE)**[116] 2596 4-9-4 62 .... LeeTopliss 1 —
(Miss T Jackson) *chsd ldrs: lost pl over 3f out: sn bhd: t.o* **14/1**
434 R **Rare Malt (IRE)**[27] 5536 3-9-6 70 ....(v) AdamBeschizza 16 —
(Miss Amy Weaver) *ref to r: lft at s: tk no part* **5/1[3]**

2m 20.44s (4.44) **Going Correction** +0.475s/f (Yiel)
WFA 3 from 4yo+ 6lb — **13** Ran SP% **119.0**
Speed ratings (Par 103): **101,99,96,95,90 88,87,85,84,79 23,19,—**
Tote Swingers: 1&2 £43.40, 1&3 £5.70, 2&3 £52.70. totesuper7: Win: Not won. Place: Not won. CSF £250.69 CT £1098.57 TOTE £7.50: £2.20, £13.60, £1.80; EX 287.00 Place 6: £44.18 Place 5: £33.52..
Owner Deborah Hart & Alan Jackson **Bred** Janus Bloodstock **Trained** Forsbrook, Staffs
■ Stewards' Enquiry : Jake Payne caution: used whip when out of contention.

FOCUS
Just an ordinary race for the grade, though at least it was well run and the form horses largely came to the fore. Despite the gallop, little made much headway from the rear.
Moon Lightning(IRE) Official explanation: jockey said gelding stopped quickly 3f out
T/Plt: £55.90 to a £1 stake. Pool:£51,283 - 669.42 winning tickets T/Qpdt: £39.00 to a £1 stake. Pool:£3,274 - 62 winning tickets WG

6307 WOLVERHAMPTON (A.W) (L-H)
Friday, September 24

OFFICIAL GOING: Standard
Wind: Light half-against Weather: Overcast

6329 PLAY BINGO AT WILLIAMHILLBINGO.COM H'CAP — 5f 216y(P)
5:45 (5:46) (Class 6) (0-55,61) 3-Y-0+ £1,774 (£523; £262) Stalls Low

Form — RPR
0331 1 **Dreamacha**[11] 6025 3-9-5 57 6ex .... WilliamCarson 1 69
(S C Williams) *hld up in tch: shkn up over 1f out: led wl ins fnl f: readily* **10/3[1]**
0606 2 1¼ **Equinity**[49] 4790 4-9-2 52 ....(bt[1]) AdamKirby 10 60
(J Pearce) *a.p: rdn to chse ldr 2f out: led ins fnl f: sn hdd and unable qck* **16/1**
0001 3 nk **Charlie Delta**[9] 6078 7-9-7 60 6ex ....(b) AndrewHeffernan(3) 3 67
(R A Harris) *hld up: racd keenly: hdwy over 2f out: swtchd lft over 1f out: r.o: nt rch ldrs* **20/1**
3000 4 ½ **Sweet Applause (IRE)**[66] 4234 4-9-0 55 .... KierenFox(5) 4 60
(G Prodromou) *hld up: rdn over 1f out: r.o ins fnl f: nt rch ldrs* **10/1**
0541 5 1½ **Double Carpet (IRE)**[8] 6133 7-9-11 61 6ex .... KirstyMilczarek 12 62
(G Woodward) *sn led: rdn over 1f out: hdd and no ex ins fnl f* **16/1**
002 6 ¾ **Embra (IRE)**[28] 5485 5-9-0 53 .... RobertLButler(3) 5 51
(T J Etherington) *s.i.s: outpcd: rdn over 1f out: r.o ins fnl f: nrst fin* **25/1**
4633 7 nk **Itsthursdayalready**[15] 5898 3-9-3 55 .... TomMcLaughlin 13 52
(W M Brisbourne) *trckd ldrs: racd keenly: rdn over 1f out: styd on same pce fnl f* **16/1**
0001 8 ¾ **Bouncy Bouncy (IRE)**[11] 6018 3-9-4 56 6ex.............(t) PaulMulrennan 7 51
(M L W Bell) *hld up in tch: rdn over 1f out: no ex* **4/1[2]**
4000 9 ½ **Song Of Praise**[15] 5897 4-9-4 54 .... DaneO'Neill 2 47
(M Blanshard) *s.i.s: hld up: hdwy over 2f out: sn rdn: wknd fnl f* **12/1**
1020 10 ½ **Metropolitan Chief**[130] 2184 6-9-4 54 .... LiamKeniry 8 46
(P Burgoyne) *chsd ldr tl rdn 2f out: wknd fnl f* **40/1**
3203 11 1½ **Carnival Dream**[18] 5817 5-9-2 52 .... PatrickMathers 6 39
(H A McWilliams) *hld up: rdn 1/2-way: n.d* **13/2[3]**
0 12 8 **Alana Banana (IRE)**[98] 3171 3-9-2 54 .... SimonWhitworth 11 15
(J Akehurst) *s.s: hdwy over 2f out: sn wknd* **33/1**

1m 14.5s (-0.50) **Going Correction** -0.05s/f (Stan)
WFA 3 from 4yo+ 2lb — **12** Ran SP% **104.8**
Speed ratings (Par 101): **101,99,98,98,96 95,94,93,93,92 90,79**
Tote Swingers: 1&2 £10.80, 1&3 £10.20, 2&3 £27.10 CSF £43.30 CT £672.38 TOTE £5.60: £1.90, £10.30, £2.50; EX 68.00.
Owner Essex Racing Club (Dreamacha) **Bred** Barry Root **Trained** Newmarket, Suffolk
■ Luisa Tetrazzini was withdrawn (9/1, unruly in stalls). R4 applies, deduct 10p in the £.
■ Stewards' Enquiry : Adam Kirby caution: used whip without giving filly time to respond.

FOCUS
A moderate handicap in which the gallop wasn't overly strong and those held up were at a bit of a disadvantage. The winner raced in the centre in the straight. It was run in a fair time for the grade and the form is pretty solid.
Bouncy Bouncy(IRE) Official explanation: jockey said filly ran too free
Carnival Dream Official explanation: jockey said mare suffered interference in running
Alana Banana(IRE) Official explanation: jockey said filly was slowly away

6330 ENJOY THE PARTY PACK GROUP OFFER (S) STKS — 5f 216y(P)
6:15 (6:15) (Class 6) 3-4-Y-0 £1,774 (£523; £262) Stalls Low

Form — RPR
1240 1 **Romantic Queen**[22] 5698 4-8-12 65 ....(t) MatthewDavies(3) 6 69
(George Baker) *hld up: hdwy to ld 1f out: rdn and r.o wl* **5/1[2]**
0005 2 3¼ **Coolree Star (IRE)**[30] 5409 3-8-12 63 .... DaneO'Neill 1 58
(J A Glover) *sn led: rdn and hdd 1f out: styd on same pce* **6/1[3]**
0030 3 hd **Captain Bluebird (IRE)**[8] 6133 3-8-12 55 .... JamesDoyle 7 57
(D Donovan) *broke wl and led early: chsd ldr: rdn and ev ch over 1f out: styd on same pce fnl f* **28/1**
3300 4 hd **Gone Hunting**[113] 2678 4-9-0 70 ....(t) LiamKeniry 8 56
(J Pearce) *hld up: pushed along 1/2-way: hdwy over 2f out: sn rdn: hung lft over 1f out: styd on* **7/2[1]**
0000 5 ½ **Athaakeel (IRE)**[14] 5920 4-8-12 64 .... AndrewHeffernan(3) 11 56+
(R A Harris) *dwlt: hld up: hdwy over 1f out: sn rdn: r.o: nt trble ldrs* **16/1**
4060 6 ¾ **Music Lover**[4] 6255 3-8-12 58 .... WilliamCarson 12 52
(R A Harris) *hld up in tch: rdn over 1f out: no ex ins fnl f* **20/1**
0000 7 ½ **Donair**[9] 6093 3-8-12 51 ....(bt) GregFairley 4 51
(P F I Cole) *sn outpcd: r.o ins fnl f: nrst fin* **33/1**
5600 8 hd **Ajara (IRE)**[18] 5809 4-8-9 59 .... RichardKingscote 3 45
(Tom Dascombe) *chsd ldrs: rdn and nt clr run over 1f out: styd on same pce* **7/1**
0000 9 hd **Outshine**[13] 5957 3-8-7 52 ....(tp) JamieMackay 5 44
(Karen George) *mid-div: racd keenly: hdwy over 2f out: rdn over 1f out: styd on same pce* **66/1**
0300 10 2 **Candyfloss Girl**[15] 5875 3-8-13 69 .... AdamKirby 2 44
(H J L Dunlop) *prom: rdn over 2f out: wknd over 1f out* **18/1**
1-50 11 25 **Point To Prove**[26] 5548 3-8-12 59 ....(e) AndrewElliott 10 —
(J Balding) *s.i.s: hdwy 4f out: rdn and hung rt over 2f out: sn wknd: t.o* **40/1**

1-50 **12** 2 1/4 **Skyflight**[11] 6023 3-8-7 66 CathyGannon 9 —
(Eve Johnson Houghton) *prom: pushed along 1/2-way: hung rt and wknd over 2f out: t.o* **7/2**[1]

1m 14.39s (-0.61) **Going Correction** -0.05s/f (Stan)
WFA 3 from 4yo 2lb **12** Ran SP% **114.1**
Speed ratings (Par 101): **102,97,97,97,96 95,94,94,94,91 58,55**
Tote Swingers: 1&2 £4.70, 1&3 £22.40, 2&3 £13.70 CSF £31.69 TOTE £4.30: £1.10, £4.60, £6.30; EX 34.50.There was no bid for the winner.
Owner The Betfair Radioheads **Bred** G B Turnbull Ltd **Trained** Moreton Morrell, Warwicks

FOCUS
Not many in-form types in a modest seller. The gallop was sound and the winner raced against the inside rail in the straight. The winner is the best guide to the form.
Skyflight Official explanation: jockey said filly hung badly right

6331 WILLIAMHILL.COM - SPORTS BETTING H'CAP 1m 5f 194y(P)
6:45 (6:45) (Class 4) (0-80,77) 3-Y-0+ **£4,209** (£1,252; £625; £312) **Stalls** Low

Form RPR
3210 **1** **Never Can Tell (IRE)**[34] 5296 3-9-4 **76** FergusSweeney 4 85
(J A Osborne) *a.p: led over 3f out: rdn and hung rt over 1f out: styd on wl* **16/1**
3041 **2** 1 **Country Road (IRE)**[20] 5765 4-9-5 **72** (be) KierenFox[(5)] 1 80
(A W Carroll) *plld hrd and prom: rdn over 1f out: ev ch ins fnl f: kpt on* **8/1**
5-32 **3** 1 **Ateeb**[13] 5959 4-9-10 **72** DaneO'Neill 6 79
(E A L Dunlop) *hld up: hdwy over 4f out: rdn and edgd rt over 1f out: styd on same pce wl ins fnl f* **4/1**[2]
0005 **4** 4 **Lovers Causeway (USA)**[20] 5753 3-9-5 **77** GregFairley 2 78
(M Johnston) *chsd ldr 1f: remained handy: outpcd over 2f out: styd on ins fnl f* **6/1**
3130 **5** 3/4 **Peintre D'Argent (IRE)**[19] 5790 4-9-0 **69** HarryBentley[(7)] 7 69
(W J Knight) *hld up: hdwy over 1f out: sn rdn: nt trble ldrs* **11/2**
5/00 **6** hd **Rock Soleil**[12] 5996 6-9-7 **76** LewisWalsh[(7)] 9 76
(Jane Chapple-Hyam) *chsd ldr after 1f: rdn over 1f out: wknd ins fnl f* **66/1**
6002 **7** nk **Quinsman**[14] 5922 4-10-0 **76** LukeMorris 8 75
(J S Moore) *hld up: hdwy over 4f out: rdn and wknd over 1f out* **5/1**[3]
3436 **8** 3 1/4 **Lord Theo**[27] 5530 6-9-9 **71** J-PGuillambert 5 66
(N P Littmoden) *s.i.s: hld up: racd keenly: rdn 3f out: wknd 2f out* **20/1**
-333 **9** 1/2 **Argaum (IRE)**[16] 5858 3-9-1 **73** AdamKirby 3 67
(W R Swinburn) *led: hdd over 3f out: sn rdn: wknd over 1f out* **3/1**[1]

3m 3.64s (-2.36) **Going Correction** -0.05s/f (Stan)
WFA 3 from 4yo+ 10lb **9** Ran SP% **114.6**
Speed ratings (Par 105): **104,103,102,100,100 100,99,98,97**
Tote Swingers: 1&2 £19.60, 1&3 £11.80, 2&3 £7.10 CSF £135.97 CT £616.62 TOTE £26.50: £8.00, £4.40, £1.10; EX 136.90.
Owner T Hyde **Bred** Shaanara Syndicate **Trained** Upper Lambourn, Berks

FOCUS
A fair handicap but a modest gallop that only really picked up turning for home. The first three finished clear and the winner raced towards the centre in the straight. The form looks fairly sound with a small step up from the winner.
Argaum(IRE) Official explanation: jockey said colt had no more to give

6332 CBS NATIONAL BOND MEDIAN AUCTION MAIDEN STKS 7f 32y(P)
7:15 (7:15) (Class 6) 3-5-Y-O **£1,774** (£523; £262) **Stalls** High

Form RPR
40 **1** **Personified (GER)**[42] 5038 3-8-12 0 LiamKeniry 2 77
(E F Vaughan) *trckd ldrs: swtchd lft over 1f out: rdn to ld 1f out: r.o wl* **16/1**
232 **2** 2 **Norman Orpen (IRE)**[22] 5700 3-9-3 73 DarryllHolland 10 77
(N P Littmoden) *s.i.s: hld up: hdwy over 2f out: rdn and ev ch 1f out: edgd lft: styd on same pce* **11/8**[1]
6255 **3** 3 1/2 **Swift Return**[11] 6023 3-9-3 67 SteveDrowne 11 68
(S C Williams) *hld up: hdwy 1/2-way: rdn to chse ldr over 1f out: no ex ins fnl f* **3/1**[2]
00- **4** 1 3/4 **Madame Boot (FR)**[386] 5604 3-8-12 0 FergusSweeney 9 58+
(P J Makin) *hld up: r.o ins fnl f: nrst fin* **28/1**
5044 **5** hd **Colamandis**[18] 5815 3-8-12 50 PaulHanagan 8 57
(H A McWilliams) *led: rdn and hdd 1f out: wknd ins fnl f* **20/1**
6 3/4 **My Name Is Bert** 4-9-3 0 RussKennemore[(3)] 3 61
(Lucinda Featherstone) *s.i.s: hdwy over 5f out: hmpd over 3f out: rdn over 1f out: styd on same pce* **50/1**
55 **7** 5 **Speedy Xaara (IRE)**[13] 5960 3-8-12 0 DaneO'Neill 6 42
(H Candy) *prom: rdn over 2f out: wknd wl over 1f out* **14/1**
4-3 **8** 3/4 **Spirit Of Love (IRE)**[22] 5700 3-9-3 0 StephenCraine 7 45
(M Wigham) *prom: outpcd 3f out: styd on towards fin* **4/1**[3]
0005 **9** 3/4 **Wizzacus**[18] 5810 3-8-12 32 JamesDoyle 5 38
(R J Price) *mid-div: rdn over 2f out: sn wknd* **100/1**
0000 **10** 2 **Southwark Newsman**[9] 6094 3-8-12 44 (t) KierenFox[(5)] 4 37
(Mrs C A Dunnett) *chsd ldrs: rdn over 2f out: wknd over 1f out* **100/1**
3250 **11** 2 1/4 **Blue Zephyr**[74] 3966 3-9-3 55 LeeVickers 12 31
(D C Griffiths) *hld up: rdn over 2f out: sn wknd* **40/1**
500 **12** 3 **One Cat Diesel (IRE)**[22] 5686 3-9-3 45 (b[1]) PatrickMathers 1 23
(H A McWilliams) *pushed along early: sn chsng ldrs: rdn over 2f out: wknd over 1f out* **100/1**

1m 29.58s (-0.02) **Going Correction** -0.05s/f (Stan)
WFA 3 from 4yo 3lb **12** Ran SP% **115.2**
Speed ratings (Par 101): **98,95,91,89,89 88,82,82,81,78 76,72**
Tote Swingers: 1&2 £7.30, 1&3 £7.60, 2&3 £2.40 CSF £36.36 TOTE £21.00: £5.40, £1.10, £1.30; EX 72.80.
Owner The Emerald Syndicate **Bred** Dr R Wilhelms **Trained** Newmarket, Suffolk

FOCUS
Not a strong maiden and one lacking anything in the way of strength-in-depth. The form is rated around the second and fifth. The gallop was ordinary and the winner raced centre to far side in the closing stages.

6333 GET BEST ODDS GUARANTEED AT WILLIAMHILL.COM MAIDEN STKS (DIV I) 7f 32y(P)
7:45 (7:46) (Class 4) 2-Y-O **£3,238** (£963; £481; £240) **Stalls** High

Form RPR
1 **Tahaamah** 2-9-3 0 TedDurcan 9 69+
(Saeed Bin Suroor) *hld up: hdwy over 2f out: led over 1f out: pushed out* **5/6**[1]
2 1 1/2 **In Babylon (GER)** 2-9-3 0 RichardKingscote 3 63+
(Tom Dascombe) *hld up: hdwy over 1f out: r.o to go 2nd nr fin: nt rch wnr* **10/3**[2]
3 1/2 **Materialism** 2-9-3 0 GregFairley 7 62+
(M Johnston) *chsd ldr tl led 2f out: rdn and hdd over 1f out: hung lft ins fnl f: styd on same pce: lost 2nd nr fin* **7/1**[3]
0 **4** 1/2 **Come On The Irons (USA)**[15] 5893 2-9-3 0 LiamJones 4 60
(B J Meehan) *chsd ldrs: pushed along 1/2-way: rdn over 1f out: styd on* **7/1**[3]
000 **5** 2 3/4 **Arctic Reach**[78] 3832 2-9-3 50 LiamKeniry 2 54
(G D Blake) *hld up: hdwy over 2f out: rdn whn hmpd over 1f out: nt trble ldrs* **150/1**
00 **6** nk **Spartan King (IRE)**[15] 5878 2-9-3 0 DaneO'Neill 6 54+
(H J L Dunlop) *trckd ldrs: racd keenly: nt clr run wl over 1f out: hmpd 1f out: styd on same pce* **10/1**
7 1 1/2 **Fire Fighter (IRE)** 2-9-3 0 SebSanders 10 50
(Sir Mark Prescott) *s.s: hdwy over 1f out: hmpd 1f out: n.d* **33/1**
4400 **8** 3 1/2 **Local Diktator**[15] 5874 2-9-3 41 LukeMorris 8 40
(R A Harris) *chsd ldrs: rdn and hung lft over 1f out: sn wknd* **66/1**
06 **9** 1 1/2 **Pleasant Humor (USA)**[8] 6118 2-8-12 0 JohnFahy[(5)] 5 37
(R M H Cowell) *led: rdn and hdd 2f out: wkng whn hmpd 1f out* **66/1**
10 4 **Calico Bay (IRE)** 2-9-3 0 JamesDoyle 11 27
(A J McCabe) *s.i.s: a in rr* **66/1**

1m 30.06s (0.46) **Going Correction** -0.05s/f (Stan) **10** Ran SP% **119.8**
Speed ratings (Par 97): **95,93,92,92,89 88,86,82,81,76**
Tote Swingers: 1&2 £2.00, 1&3 £2.70, 2&3 £5.40 CSF £3.88 TOTE £1.50: £1.10, £1.30, £2.50; EX 6.20.
Owner Godolphin **Bred** Darley **Trained** Newmarket, Suffolk

FOCUS
The gallop was only ordinary and the proximity of a couple who finished just behind the first four holds the form down to an extent but this looked a reasonable maiden for the track and a couple could hold their own at a higher level. The winner raced towards the centre in the straight.

NOTEBOOK
Tahaamah ◆, a half-brother to very useful Russian Society and to a couple of other winners, raced with the choke out but produced a fluent display to get off the mark at the first time of asking and to justify the market confidence. He's the type to progress further, especially over 1m and he's sure to win more races. (op 4-5 tchd 10-11)
In Babylon(GER) ◆, who has several winners in his pedigree up to 1m5f, shaped with plenty of promise (despite greenness) without being unduly knocked about to chase home the market leader on this racecourse debut. He should be suited by the step up to 1m, is open to plenty of improvement and it'll be a big surprise if he doesn't win a similar event at the very least. (op 4-1 tchd 9-2 and 3-1)
Materialism, a half-brother to smart 6f juvenile winner Cedarberg, was easy in the market but shaped with credit after enjoying the run of the race on this racecourse debut. He's certain to improve a good deal for the experience and he should be able to win a similar event. (op 11-2 tchd 5-1)
Come On The Irons(USA) had been well beaten on his debut after starting a big price but shaped with much more encouragement against a couple of promising sorts. He should be able to pick up a race either in ordinary company in this grade or in handicaps. (op 12-1)
Arctic Reach, a 50-rated performer, holds the overall form down but his best chance of success lies in ordinary handicaps. (op 125-1)
Spartan King(IRE) wasn't totally disgraced on this all-weather debut after being nibbled at in the market and should do better in ordinary handicaps. (op 12-1)
Fire Fighter(IRE) wasn't totally disgraced after a sluggish start and after meeting trouble on this racecourse debut. This half-brother to Phoenix Flight and La De Two, who won over 1m4f and beyond, will be one to keep a very close eye on in middle-distance handicaps next year.
Calico Bay(IRE) Official explanation: jockey said colt hyung left

6334 GET BEST ODDS GUARANTEED AT WILLIAMHILL.COM MAIDEN STKS (DIV II) 7f 32y(P)
8:15 (8:16) (Class 4) 2-Y-O **£3,238** (£963; £481; £240) **Stalls** High

Form RPR
4 **1** **Gentleman Is Back (USA)**[21] 5718 2-9-3 0 WilliamBuick 6 79+
(J H M Gosden) *chsd ldr: led and edgd lft over 1f out: r.o* **2/1**[2]
2 nk **Flag Officer** 2-9-3 0 TedDurcan 7 78+
(Saeed Bin Suroor) *trckd ldrs: rdn over 1f out: r.o* **7/2**[3]
3 **3** 1/2 **Tasfeya**[18] 5814 2-9-3 0 TadhgO'Shea 3 77+
(M Johnston) *sn led: rdn: hung lft and hdd over 1f out: styd on* **7/4**[1]
4 2 **Irons On Fire (USA)** 2-9-3 0 PaulHanagan 10 73+
(B J Meehan) *hld up: hdwy over 2f out: rdn over 1f out: r.o* **25/1**
5 nse **Danadana (IRE)** 2-9-3 0 J-PGuillambert 5 72+
(L M Cumani) *s.i.s: sn prom: rdn over 2f out: no ex wl ins fnl f* **11/1**
5000 **6** 2 1/4 **Echos Of Motivator**[23] 5659 2-9-3 59 LukeMorris 2 67
(R A Harris) *mid-div: sn pushed along: hdwy over 1f out: styd on same pce fnl f* **125/1**
7 1 1/2 **Invent** 2-9-3 0 SebSanders 9 63+
(Sir Mark Prescott) *in rr: rdn over 1f out: edgd lft: nvr on terms* **20/1**
5 **8** 1/2 **Whipphound**[14] 5900 2-9-3 0 TomMcLaughlin 8 63
(W M Brisbourne) *hld up: rdn and nt clr run wl over 1f out: n.d* **50/1**
9 11 **High Table (IRE)** 2-9-3 0 RichardKingscote 1 35
(Tom Dascombe) *chsd ldrs: rdn 1/2-way: wknd over 1f out* **40/1**

1m 29.74s (0.14) **Going Correction** -0.05s/f (Stan) **9** Ran SP% **114.1**
Speed ratings (Par 97): **97,96,96,93,93 91,89,88,76**
Tote Swingers: 1&2 £2.40, 1&3 £2.10, 2&3 £1.90 CSF £8.81 TOTE £3.20: £1.20, £1.40, £1.20; EX 11.20.
Owner Salman Rashed **Bred** Torros Straits Syndicate **Trained** Newmarket, Suffolk

FOCUS
No more than a fair maiden in which the gallop was ordinary. The winner raced towards the centre in the straight. The bare form is limited but several shaped with promise and are capable of better.

NOTEBOOK
Gentleman Is Back(USA), dropped in trip, raced with the choke out for much of the way but showed a good attitude to fully confirm debut promise. This wasn't a strong race but he's entitled to improve again in handicaps. (op 5-2 tchd 11-4)
Flag Officer ◆, a half-brother to an Italian Oaks runner-up, was fairly easy to back on this racecourse debut but showed more than enough to suggest a similar event can be found. He should prove equally effective over 1m and should be able to better this bare form. (op 10-3 tchd 3-1)
Tasfeya had shaped encouragingly on his debut and probably wasn't far off that level after being allowed an easy time of it in front on this first run on artificial surfaces. He saw this trip out well enough and is more than capable of picking up an uncompetitive race in this grade. (op 6-4 tchd 11-8 and 15-8)
Irons On Fire(USA), a $100,000 brother to a 1m winner in the US, ran creditably and should be all the wiser for this initial experience. There will be easier races than this one on Polytrack in the coming months.
Danadana(IRE), the first foal of a 1m4f winner, herself a sister to one-time smart Lost Soldier Three, should be all the better for this first run, should have no problems with at least 1m and is capable of making his mark in ordinary company on Polytrack. (tchd 12-1)
Echos Of Motivator, well beaten on his handicap debut over 1m, wasn't totally disgraced in the face of a stiff task dropped in trip and back in maiden company. He'll have to show this can be built on before he's a betting proposition, though. (op 100-1)

Invent, who has several winners in his pedigree, is sure to leave these bare facts behind at some point. (tchd 22-1)

6335 MOBILE.WILLIAMHILL.COM - NEW IPHONE APP H'CAP 1m 141y(P)
8:45 (8:45) (Class 6) (0-55,55) 3-Y-O+ £1,774 (£523; £262) Stalls Low

Form				RPR
5030	1		**Cross The Boss (IRE)**[119] 2503 3-9-0 **55** (t) PhillipMakin 1 (B M R Haslam) *hld up: hdwy over 2f out: swtchd rt over 1f out: led ins fnl f: r.o* **15/2**	66+
	2	1	**Philosophers Guest (IRE)**[31] 5399 4-9-0 **55** JohnFahy(5) 8 (M J Grassick, Ire) *hld up: hdwy over 2f out: rdn and swtchd lft over 1f out: r.o* **12/1**	63
0061	3	1	**Eastern Hills**[9] 6077 5-8-8 **51** (p) NeilFarley(7) 11 (A J McCabe) *chsd ldrs: led wl over 2f out: rdn clr over 1f out: hdd and unable qck ins fnl f* **9/4**[1]	57
3253	4	1 ½	**Tres Froide (FR)**[8] 6125 5-9-1 **51** (p) PaulMulrennan 10 (N Tinkler) *hld up: hdwy over 3f out: rdn over 1f out: styd on* **17/2**	54
3604	5	½	**Join Up**[13] 5962 4-8-9 **50** RossAtkinson(5) 2 (W M Brisbourne) *hld up in tch: racd keenly: nt clr run wl over 1f out: sn rdn: styd on same pce ins fnl f* **11/1**	51
5626	6	½	**Fly By Nelly**[22] 5689 4-9-5 **55** SteveDrowne 3 (H Morrison) *chsd ldrs: rdn over 1f out: no ex ins fnl f* **9/2**[2]	55
6050	7	1 ¼	**Why Nee Amy**[20] 5770 4-8-11 **50** MatthewDavies(3) 12 (Miss Olivia Maylam) *s.i.s: sn pushed along in rr: hdwy over 1f out: no ex ins fnl f* **28/1**	47
0-40	8	½	**Parisian Dream**[47] 4868 6-9-4 **54** (t) PaulHanagan 13 (T J Pitt) *hld up: styd on ins fnl f: nvr nrr* **16/1**	50
1652	9	11	**Belle Park**[8] 6125 3-9-0 **55** ChrisCatlin 7 (Karen George) *hld up in tch: shkn up over 2f out: wknd over 1f out* **7/1**[3]	26
006	10	3 ¾	**Lady Slippers (IRE)**[29] 5456 3-9-0 **55** DaneO'Neill 9 (H J L Dunlop) *chsd ldr tl led over 5f out: hdd wl over 2f out: rdn and wknd over 1f out* **25/1**	17
0/0	11	29	**Bogside Dancer**[24] 5635 8-9-2 **52** (t) SebSanders 4 (John A Harris) *pushed along to ld: hdd over 5f out: remained handy tl rdn and wknd 2f out* **50/1**	—

1m 49.61s (-0.89) **Going Correction** -0.05s/f (Stan)
WFA 3 from 4yo+ 5lb **11** Ran SP% **114.9**
Speed ratings (Par 101): **101,100,99,97,97 97,95,95,85,82 56**
Tote Swingers: 1&2 £8.30, 1&3 £4.90, 2&3 £10.20 CSF £89.65 CT £271.83 TOTE £6.60: £2.10, £5.00, £1.20; EX 74.90.
Owner Widdop Wanderers **Bred** Dermot Brennan & Associates Ltd **Trained** Middleham Moor, N Yorks

FOCUS
A moderate handicap run at a reasonable gallop. The winner came down the centre in the straight. Fair form for the grade, with the winner the type to do better.

6336 WILLIAMHILL.COM - BINGO H'CAP 1m 1f 103y(P)
9:15 (9:15) (Class 5) (0-70,70) 3-Y-O £2,729 (£806; £403) Stalls Low

Form				RPR
0513	1		**Key Breeze**[32] 5361 3-8-7 **59** (t) PaulHanagan 11 (K A Ryan) *hld up: hdwy over 1f out: rdn to ld ins fnl f: r.o wl* **8/1**	71
4166	2	3	**Dutiful**[15] 5887 3-9-4 **70** TedDurcan 10 (M R Channon) *hld up: hdwy over 1f out: styd on same pce ins fnl f* **8/1**	76
2142	3	2	**Madame Excelerate**[6] 6212 3-9-3 **69** TomMcLaughlin 13 (W M Brisbourne) *chsd ldr over 7f out: rdn and ev ch over 1f out: no ex ins fnl f* **5/1**[2]	71
	4	hd	**King Of Aran (IRE)**[27] 5128 3-9-2 **68** (p) EddieAhern 12 (M J Grassick, Ire) *mid-div: hdwy over 3f out: rdn over 1f out: one pce fnl f* **5/2**[1]	69
0063	5	¾	**Second Brook (IRE)**[4] 6257 3-8-4 **56** oh8 LukeMorris 5 (R Hollinshead) *hld up: rdn over 4f out: hdwy over 1f out: no ex ins fnl f* **16/1**	56
4565	6	hd	**Stoical (IRE)**[16] 5869 3-8-10 **62** DaneO'Neill 7 (W Jarvis) *hld up: hdwy over 2f out: styd on same pce fnl f* **6/1**[3]	61
5443	7	½	**Chicane**[28] 5467 3-8-13 **65** (b[1]) LiamJones 9 (W J Haggas) *pushed along to ld over 8f out: rdn over 1f out: edgd rt hdd and no ex ins fnl f* **10/1**	63
0-20	8	1 ½	**Meer Und Wind (GER)**[15] 5877 3-8-12 **64** ChrisCatlin 6 (P R Webber) *chsd ldrs: rdn over 3f out: wknd fnl f* **22/1**	59
-000	9	9	**Antoella (IRE)**[122] 2412 3-8-1 **58** oh9 ow2 JohnFahy(5) 8 (Ian Williams) *hld up: hdwy u.p over 2f out: sn wknd* **50/1**	34
4205	10	3	**Pebblesonthebeach**[16] 5866 3-9-3 **69** (p) SebSanders 3 (J W Hills) *prom: rdn over 3f out: nt clr run over 2f out: wknd over 1f out* **8/1**	39
5430	11	8	**Child Of Our Time (IRE)**[13] 5942 3-9-2 **68** JackMitchell 2 (P W Chapple-Hyam) *led 1f: chsd ldrs: rdn over 2f out: wknd over 1f out* **16/1**	21

2m 0.14s (-1.56) **Going Correction** -0.05s/f (Stan) **11** Ran SP% **120.0**
Speed ratings (Par 101): **104,101,99,99,98 98,98,96,88,86 78**
Tote Swingers: 1&2 £14.40, 1&3 £9.90, 2&3 £14.90 CSF £72.09 CT £358.83 TOTE £7.60: £1.50, £1.50, £3.70; EX 78.30 Place 6: £44.76 Place 5: £15.99. .
Owner Allan Kerr Peter McGivney **Bred** Farmers Hill Stud **Trained** Hambleton, N Yorks

FOCUS
A modest handicap in which an ordinary gallop picked up passing halfway. A clear pesonal best from the winner but the fifth may limit the form. The winner raced down the centre in the straight.
T/Plt: £19.00 to a £1 stake. Pool:£78,038 - 2,995.33 winning tickets T/Qpdt: £3.90 to a £1 stake. Pool:£8,165 - 1,544.54 winning tickets CR

6337 - 6343a (Foreign Racing) - See Raceform Interactive

6277 MAISONS-LAFFITTE (R-H)
Friday, September 24

OFFICIAL GOING: Turf: good to soft changing to soft after race 2 (1.25) and to very soft after race 5 (3.00)

6344a LA COUPE DE MAISONS-LAFFITTE (GROUP 3) (3YO+) (TURF) 1m 2f (S)
2:25 (12:00) 3-Y-O+ £35,398 (£14,159; £10,619; £7,079; £3,539)

			RPR
1		**Akarlina (FR)**[21] 4-8-10 0 ThierryThulliez 10 (N Clement, France) *sn led and a few l clr: shkn up 1 1/2f out: wnt further clr: eased down towards fin: comf* **84/10**	103
2	2	**Reggane**[33] 5348 4-8-10 0 GeraldMosse 6 (A De Royer-Dupre, France) *in rr fr s: qcknd 1 1/2f out: fin wl fnl f to take 2nd in fnl strides* **33/10**[1]	99
3	nk	**Hermoun (FR)**[13] 5982 4-9-0 0 GregoryBenoist 3 (X Nakkachdji, France) *racd in 3rd: rdn to cl on ldr 2f out: styd on wl fnl f: lost 2nd clsng strides* **22/1**	102
4	snk	**Russian Cross (IRE)**[23] 5674 5-9-0 0 (b[1]) MickaelBarzalona 9 (A Fabre, France) *chsd ldr fr s: rdn to cl 2f out: r.o fnl f: no ex fnl 50yds* **17/1**	102
5	shd	**Starlish (IRE)**[41] 5107 5-9-0 0 AnthonyCrastus 7 (E Lellouche, France) *racd in 4th: rdn 2f out: styd on fnl f* **48/10**[3]	102
6	1 ½	**Royal Revival**[9] 3-8-8 0 MaximeGuyon 2 (A Fabre, France) *racd towards rr: qcknd wl 1 1/2f out on stands' side: briefly threatened to figure in fin: fdd fnl 100yds* **48/10**[3]	99
7	snk	**Mr Brock (SAF)**[23] 7-9-0 0 Christophe-PatriceLemaire 4 (Mme C Head-Maarek, France) *prom fr s: rdn but failed to qckn fnl 1 1/2f* **49/1**	98
8	3	**Capitaine Courage (IRE)**[23] 5674 5-9-0 0 FranckBlondel 8 (F Doumen, France) *racd in rr: rdn 2f out: no ex* **17/1**	92
9	5	**Scolari**[27] 5542 5-9-0 0 ChristopheSoumillon 1 (T Mundry, Germany) *racd in midfield: rdn but failed to qckn fr 1 1/2f out* **7/2**[2]	82
10	snk	**World Heritage**[102] 3045 4-9-0 0 StephanePasquier 5 (P Bary, France) *racd towards rr: rdn but failed to qckn 2f out: sn fdd* **10/1**	82

2m 7.20s (4.80)
WFA 3 from 4yo+ 6lb **10** Ran SP% **117.1**
WIN (incl. 1 euro stake): 9.40. PLACES: 3.20, 1.90, 5.10. DF: 24.70. SF: 48.10.
Owner Nicolas Clement **Bred** Sarl Haras De La Faisanderie **Trained** Chantilly, France

NOTEBOOK
Akarlina(FR) made every yard to record her fourth win of the campaign, and connections, who hoped to get an invitation to race in Hong Kong, have entered her in the sales on Arc weekend.

6317 ASCOT (R-H)
Saturday, September 25

OFFICIAL GOING: Good to soft (soft in places on round course) (stands' side 8.0, centre 8.9, far side 8.2; round 6.8)
Wind: fresh, across Weather: bright, chilly

6346 DELOITTE ROSEMARY H'CAP (LISTED RACE) (F&M) 1m (S)
1:55 (1:56) (Class 1) (0-110,102) 3-Y-O+
£22,708 (£8,608; £4,308; £2,148; £1,076; £540) Stalls Centre

Form				RPR
2450	1		**Aspectoflove (IRE)**[101] 3067 4-9-10 **100** TedDurcan 6 (Saeed Bin Suroor) *hld up in tch in midfield: rdn and hdwy wl over 1f out: drvn to chse ldr ent fnl f: kpt on wl to ld on post* **20/1**	111
1041	2	nse	**Sajjhaa**[41] 5114 3-9-8 **102** (t) PhilipRobinson 8 (M A Jarvis) *taken down early: chsd ldrs: effrt to chse ldr wl over 1f out: rdn to ld and edgd lft over 1f out: kpt on u.p fnl f: hdd on post* **7/2**[1]	113
1115	3	1 ½	**I'm A Dreamer (IRE)**[64] 4319 3-9-1 **95** JMurtagh 12 (D M Simcock) *t.k.h: hld up in tch in rr: nt clr run 2f out: hdwy over 1f out: chsd ldrs ent fnl f: drvn and one pce fnl 150yds* **13/2**[3]	103+
2005	4	¾	**Bahati (IRE)**[23] 5694 3-8-9 **89** RichardKingscote 5 (J G Portman) *taken down early: hld up wl in tch: n.m.r 2f out: rdn and effrt to chse ldrs jst over 1f out: styd on same pce u.p fnl f* **33/1**	95
2163	5	1 ¾	**Forest Crown**[41] 5114 3-8-12 **92** JimCrowley 10 (R M Beckett) *stdd s: hld up in tch in rr: nt clr run ent fnl 2f: rdn and gd hdwy over 1f out: edgd rt u.p and no imp fnl f* **12/1**	94+
4316	6	1	**Perfect Silence**[23] 5694 5-8-10 **86** oh4 (b) EddieAhern 7 (C G Cox) *chsd ldr: rdn ent fnl 2f: lost 2nd wl over 1f out: styd on same pce and no threat to ldrs ins fnl f* **25/1**	86
1120	7	¾	**Fontley**[35] 5307 3-9-3 **97** TomQueally 13 (Eve Johnson Houghton) *hld up in tch in rr: nt clr run ent fnl 2f tl gd hdwy over 1f out: styd on same pce and no imp ins fnl f* **25/1**	95
1205	8	2 ½	**Bintalwaadi**[28] 5524 3-8-9 **89** RichardHills 4 (E A L Dunlop) *t.k.h: led at stdy gallop: rdn ent fnl 2f: hdd over 1f out: wknd ent fnl f* **25/1**	81
3440	9	¾	**Simla Sunset (IRE)**[13] 6008 4-8-12 **88** (t) JimmyFortune 14 (P J Prendergast, Ire) *hld up in tch towards rr: rdn and n.m.r whn swtchd lft over 1f out: sn drvn and no prog* **12/1**	78
0000	10	¾	**Victoria Sponge (IRE)**[10] 6095 4-8-10 **86** oh6 WilliamCarson 1 (S C Williams) *stdd s: hld up in tch in rr: swtchd rt and hdwy u.p 2f out: drvn and wknd over 1f out* **50/1**	75
2405	11	nk	**Please Sing**[21] 5782 4-9-6 **96** ChrisCatlin 3 (M R Channon) *hld up in tch towards rr: rdn and effrt ent fnl 2f: drvn and plugged on same pce fr over 1f out: nvr trbld ldrs* **40/1**	84
0-42	12	1 ¾	**Long Lashes (USA)**[35] 5305 3-9-8 **102** (p) FrankieDettori 9 (Saeed Bin Suroor) *taken down early: hld up wl in tch in midfield: rdn and effrt 2f out: sn struggling and btn over 1f out: wknd ent fnl f* **11/2**[2]	86
1314	13	¾	**Dance East**[41] 5114 3-9-2 **96** RyanMoore 21 (J Noseda) *t.k.h: chsd ldrs: rdn and effrt jst over 2f out: wknd over 1f out: fdd fnl f* **12/1**	78
2151	14	½	**Night Lily (IRE)**[5] 6252 4-8-10 **86** oh4 TonyCulhane 16 (P W D'Arcy) *stdd s: hld up in tch in rr: rdn and effrt ent fnl 2f: no prog and btn over 1f out: n.d* **20/1**	67
0-12	15	shd	**Thrill**[23] 5694 3-8-11 **91** RichardHughes 18 (J H M Gosden) *hld up in tch towards rr: hdwy 1/2-way: rdn to chse ldrs 2f out: btn over 1f out: wknd and eased wl ins fnl f* **13/2**[3]	72
1522	16	13	**Gobama**[38] 5222 3-8-10 **90** SebSanders 17 (J W Hills) *t.k.h: hld up in tch towards rr: hdwy into midfield 1/2-way: rdn and unable qck ent fnl 2f: btn over 1f out: eased fnl f* **25/1**	41
6202	17	6	**Mistic Magic (IRE)**[13] 6002 3-8-11 **91** KierenFallon 20 (P F I Cole) *chsd ldrs: rdn over 2f out: wknd qckly wl over 1f out: wl btn and eased ins fnl f* **25/1**	28

1m 42.55s (1.95) **Going Correction** +0.40s/f (Good)
WFA 3 from 4yo+ 4lb **17** Ran SP% **123.4**
Speed ratings (Par 111): **106,105,104,103,101 100,100,97,96,96 95,94,93,92,92 79,73**
Tote Swingers: 1&2 £43.60, 1&3 £200.80, 2&3 £3.10 CSF £80.64 CT £531.28 TOTE £28.80: £6.80, £1.50, £1.80, £8.10; EX 149.50 TRIFECTA Not won..
Owner Godolphin **Bred** Patrick Cassidy **Trained** Newmarket, Suffolk
■ Stewards' Enquiry : Ted Durcan two-day ban: used whip with excessive frequency (Oct 9-10)

The Form Book, Raceform Ltd, Compton, RG20 6NL

FOCUS

The going was given as good to soft, and on the round course good to soft, soft in places. The GoingStick readings were 8.0 on the stands' side, 8.9 in the centre and 8.2 on the far side, while on the round course it was 6.8. This was a rough race last season so sensibly it was transferred from the round course to the straight track this year. A competitive affair on paper, but the early pace wasn't hectic. They raced centre to stands' side. The form is up to scratch for the grade with the winner back to her best.

NOTEBOOK

Aspectoflove(IRE) was the Godolphin second string based on jockey bookings, but she held a solid chance on her best form, which came in Dubai in the spring when twice narrowly beaten in Group 3 company. She'd been below that level in three outings in Britain since, but had been freshened up by a 101-day break and returned to her best this time. Having tracked the pace, she launched her bid nearest the stands' side rail, picked up in good style when asked, and finally hit the front right on the line. It appears that she's the type who needs delivering as late as possible. (op 18-1)

Sajjhaa ◆ returned from a break to win nicely at Bath last time in a first-time tongue tie, and with the breathing aid on again she was a popular choice. Never far away, she quickened up well to take the lead and was only run down right on the line. This is clearly her trip and, given that this was only her fifth ever start and she's to be kept in training, there should be plenty more to come from her. (tchd 4-1 in places)

I'm A Dreamer(IRE) ◆ could have done with a stronger early gallop as she tried to challenge form well off the pace. She finished well but the front two, who had raced more prominently, were not for catching. She's another who remains relatively unexposed and open to further improvement. (op 15-2)

Bahati(IRE) only has a maiden win to her name but she was second in a Listed race in June and she at least ran up to that form on her first try on easy ground. She is going to remain hard to place, though.

Forest Crown, who had a 10lb pull with Sajjhaa compared with when they met at Bath, was staying on quite nicely at the finish, but was another who could have done with a stronger all-round pace. She looked warm before the off.

Perfect Silence, who was running over 1m for the first time and was 4lb wrong at the weights, was probably helped by being prominent in a race not run at a strong early gallop. (op 28-1 tchd 33-1 in places)

Fontley, who had an excuse last time as she was in season, is a confirmed hold-up performer who is at her best coming late from off a strong pace. She didn't get that here. (tchd 28-1 and 33-1 in a place)

Bintalwaadi, who likes to make the running but is quite a keen sort, took them along at quite a steady pace until headed shortly after passing the 2f pole. (tchd 22-1)

Simla Sunset(IRE) took a while to pick up and gave the impression that she might be worth a try over a bit further. (op 14-1)

Long Lashes(USA) found little under pressure and might not have been at home on this ground. (op 13-2 tchd 5-1)

Dance East had done most of her previous racing on a quick surface. (op 14-1)

Thrill's stamina seemed to give out on this step up in trip. (op 7-1 tchd 15-2 in a place)

6347 JUDDMONTE ROYAL LODGE STKS (GROUP 2) (C&G) 1m (R)

2:30 (2:31) (Class 1) 2-Y-O £70,962 (£26,900; £13,462; £6,712; £3,362) Stalls High

Form RPR

11 **1** **Frankel**[15] 5912 2-8-12 0 ... TomQueally 2 124+
(H R A Cecil) *t.k.h: hld up in last: swtchd lft and gd hdwy on bit to ld ent fnl 3f: shkn up and readily qcknd clr over 2f out: wl clr and nudged along after: v impressive* **30/100**[1]

1532 **2** *10* **Klammer**[35] 5323 2-8-12 99 ... KierenFallon 3 102
(Jane Chapple-Hyam) *t.k.h: trckd ldrs: rdn and outpcd by wnr over 2f out: chsd clr wnr and hung rt u.p over 1f out: kpt on but no ch w wnr* **11/1**[3]

3 *¾* **Treasure Beach**[12] 6043 2-8-12 0 ... JMurtagh 4 102
(A P O'Brien, Ire) *t.k.h: trckd ldrs: rdn and n.m.r wl over 2f out: sn rdn and nt pce of wnr: pressing for modest 2nd whn hmpd and swtchd lft over 1f out: kpt on same pce after* **11/2**[2]

0 **4** *1 ¼* **Eskimo (IRE)**[98] 3190 2-8-12 0 ...(t) RyanMoore 5 98
(A P O'Brien, Ire) *led and set stdy gallop: hdd and rdn ent fnl 3f: nt pce of wnr and btn 2f out: lost 2nd and squeezed against rail over 1f out: wl btn and styd on same pce after* **20/1**

6124 **5** *2 ¾* **Slim Shadey**[16] 5880 2-8-12 101 ... LiamKeniry 6 92
(J S Moore) *pressed ldr tl rdn and dropped to rr wl over 2f out: outpcd and wl btn ent fnl 2f* **16/1**

1m 41.73s (1.03) **Going Correction** +0.40s/f (Good) 5 Ran SP% **111.3**

Speed ratings (Par 107): **110,100,99,98,95**

CSF £4.80 TOTE £1.30: £1.10, £3.20; EX 4.10 Trifecta £1197.40 Pool: £67,159.76 - 41.50 winning units..

Owner K Abdulla **Bred** Juddmonte Farms Ltd **Trained** Newmarket, Suffolk

■ Stewards' Enquiry : Kieren Fallon two-day ban: careless riding (Oct 9-10)

FOCUS

The winning time was 1.02secs quicker than the Fillies' Mile, but 1.97secs slower than the time recorded by older horses in the QEII. This year's edition looked deeply uncompetitive and the steady early pace threatened to turn it into a farce, but Frankel produced a quite breathtaking performance to maintain his 100 per cent record. The form has a solid feel and he gave the runner-up a beating of more than 20lb, so he looks odds-on to end the season champion 2-y-o.

NOTEBOOK

Frankel ◆ produced a quite breathtaking performance to maintain his 100 per cent record and cement his position at the head of next year's 2,000 Guineas and Derby markets. Although Tom Queally managed to get him settled early, it was clear he wanted to go faster, and having allowed the horse an inch of rein, he swept past the field on the home bend before quickening clear under hands and heels riding, a move that marked him down as a colt right out of the top drawer. He had beaten just two rivals at Doncaster the time before and the opposition again wasn't that taxing, but Henry Cecil believes him to be his best 2-y-o since Wollow, who went on to win the Guineas, back in the mid-70s, and he's done little to suggest otherwise. As seen with St Nicholas Abbey this year, there's never a guarantee they'll train on and maintain their brilliance, and he's got one more run to get out of the way yet, probably in the Dewhurst, which would be the favoured option given his abundant pace, or perhaps in the Racing Post Trophy, but he certainly looks a worthy favourite for the Guineas, for which he is best-priced 5-2. As for the Derby (best-priced 9-2), it's far from certain he'll stay the 1m4f distance, but that's a long way off, and connections' priority will lie primarily with ensuring the son of Galileo ends the year unbeaten. (op 1-3 tchd 4-11 and 2-5 in places)

Klammer improved for this trip when being awarded a Listed contest at Deauville in similar conditions last time, and he ran his race, but the winner was in a different league. It remains to be seen whether he'd have held on for second had he not hampered the third, and is probably up to winning another ordinary Listed prize. (op 12-1 tchd 10-1 and 14-1 in places)

Treasure Beach, who like his trainer's winner of the race last year, Joshua Tree, had been beaten in a nursery on his previous outing, was boxing on best he could when hampered. It may well have cost him second and he can be seen to better effect in a more truly-run race at this distance. (tchd 6-1 in places)

Eskimo(IRE), off since finishing well beaten in the Chesham, tried a first-time tongue-tie here and was responsible for the steady gallop. He too was impeded, but it didn't affect his finishing position. (tchd 16-1 and 25-1 in places)

Slim Shadey has twice shown useful form in defeat of late, but he couldn't handle this first try at Group level.

6348 MEON VALLEY STUD FILLIES' MILE (GROUP 1) 1m (R)

3:05 (3:05) (Class 1) 2-Y-O £123,758 (£46,913; £23,478; £11,706; £5,864) Stalls High

Form RPR

111 **1** **White Moonstone (USA)**[15] 5910 2-8-12 111 ... FrankieDettori 1 112+
(Saeed Bin Suroor) *hld up in last: rdn and effrt on outer jst over 2f out: chsd ldr over 1f out: ev ch and flashed tail u.p 1f out: edgd rt and led ins fnl f: kpt on wl* **4/5**[1]

134 **2** *nk* **Together (IRE)**[27] 5570 2-8-12 0 ... JMurtagh 4 111
(A P O'Brien, Ire) *t.k.h: hld up wl in tch: rdn and effrt over 2f out: chsd wnr fnl 75yds: kpt on wl towards fin* **5/1**[3]

011 **3** *1 ¼* **Theyskens' Theory (USA)**[28] 5519 2-8-12 103 ... RyanMoore 3 109
(B J Meehan) *chsd ldr tl rdn to ld ent fnl 2f: drvn and hdd ins fnl f: lost 2nd fnl 75yds: wknd towards fin* **9/4**[2]

403 **4** *7* **Fork Handles**[35] 5322 2-8-12 98 ... ChrisCatlin 5 93
(M R Channon) *led: rdn and hdd ent fnl 2f: sn outpcd by wnr: lost 2nd and wknd u.p over 1f out* **25/1**

65 **5** *1* **Traffic Sister (USA)**[18] 5841 2-8-12 0 ... JamieSpencer 6 91
(J S Moore) *chsd ldrs: rdn and lost pl over 2f out: sn outpcd and wl btn fr wl over 1f out* **50/1**

1m 42.75s (2.05) **Going Correction** +0.40s/f (Good) 5 Ran SP% **108.8**

Speed ratings (Par 106): **105,104,103,96,95**

CSF £5.21 TOTE £1.80: £1.10, £2.20; EX 4.20 Trifecta £516.00 Pool: £13,836.55 - 19.84 winnnig units..

Owner Godolphin **Bred** Stoneside Stable **Trained** Newmarket, Suffolk

FOCUS

The winning time was 1.02secs slower than the Royal Lodge and 2.99secs slower than the QEII. Although lacking strength in depth, the race was all about whether White Moonstone could maintain her unbeaten record, up to Group 1 level for the first time. It would be hard to rate the winner any higher than at Doncaster, but she could well rate higher off a stronger pace. The second improved significantly.

NOTEBOOK

White Moonstone(USA) failed to travel as powerfully as she did on a quicker surface at Doncaster when winning the May Hill in such impressive fashion. Despite this, Dettori always looked confident she would pull out enough, only picking up his stick inside the final furlong, and she was just punched out hands and heels in the final 50 yards. It's safe to rate her better than the bare form, as this probably came a bit quick after Doncaster, and like Frankel, she will no doubt appeal to many as the sort of filly who could go on and win at both Newmarket and Epsom next season (best-priced 8-1 and 10-1 respectively), but whether she'll come back from Dubai next spring the same filly remains to be seen, as Godolphin's record in getting them to reproduce their best in the first half of the season at three has been pretty poor in recent years. A light-framed sort, that's her done for the season now. (tchd 5-6 and 10-11 in places)

Together(IRE) looked a definite player, having finished a close fourth in the Moyglare last time. Always likely to be suited by the extra furlong, as a daughter of Galileo who's closely related to Jan Vermeer, she was under pressure straightening for home, but did respond to what was a very strong ride by Murtagh, closing on the winner right the way to the line. She paid a nice compliment to stablemate Misty For Me, who beat her in the Moyglare, and it would come as no surprise to see her take her chance in the Breeders' Cup Juvenile Fillies' Turf. (op 13-2)

Theyskens' Theory(USA) handled similar conditions well when winning the Prestige Stakes and she was nicely positioned to kick turning in, but the front two were soon after her and she backed out of it inside the final 150 yards. A fine, big sort, she is almost certain to improve for a faster surface, on which she'll see this trip out stronger. Given both her connections and breeding (half-sister to Breeders' Cup Juvenile winner Stevie Wonderboy), it would come as no surprise to see her shipped to the US at some point. (op 2-1)

Fork Handles, well behind the winner in the Sweet Solera and only third in a Listed race at Deauville last time, was quickly swept aside in the straight and isn't up to Group level. (op 22-1 tchd 20-1)

Traffic Sister(USA) had been unplaced in a couple of maidens prior to this and was just here for a day out and some easy prize-money. (tchd 33-1)

6349 TOTESPORT.COM CHALLENGE CUP (HERITAGE H'CAP) 7f

3:40 (3:41) (Class 2) 3-Y-O+

£93,465 (£27,990; £13,995; £7,005; £3,495; £1,755) Stalls Centre

Form RPR

0031 **1** **Redford (IRE)**[7] 6177 5-9-7 103 6ex ... FrankieDettori 28 117+
(D Nicholls) *racd far side: hld up in rr: sltly hmpd 3f out: smooth hdwy over 1f out: chsd ldrs ent fnl f: rdn to ld fnl 100yds: sn in command: readily* **7/1**[1]

5131 **2** *1 ¾* **Side Glance**[35] 5292 3-9-3 102 ... DavidProbert 27 112
(A M Balding) *racd far side: hld up in tch: rdn and effrt 2f out: led jst over 1f out tl jst ins fnl f: stl ev ch tl nt pce of wnr fnl 100yds: kpt on: 2nd of 19 in gp* **15/2**[2]

352 **3** *1* **Imperial Guest**[15] 5911 4-8-10 92 ... SebSanders 26 98
(G G Margarson) *racd far side: hld up in midfield: rdn and hdwy 2f out: ev ch jst over 1f out: drvn to ld jst ins fnl f: hdd and one pce fnl 100yds: 3rd of 19 in gp* **16/1**

0053 **4** *1 ¼* **Golden Desert (IRE)**[91] 3461 6-9-3 99 ... EddieAhern 9 102+
(R A Mills) *racd far side: hld up towards rr: rdn and effrt whn nt clr run over 1f out tl ent fnl f: styd on wl fnl 150yds: nt rch ldrs: 4th of 19 in gp* **33/1**

0602 **5** *hd* **Swift Gift**[42] 5068 5-9-2 98 ... RyanMoore 14 100+
(B J Meehan) *racd far side: hld up in rr: effrt but nt clr run fr wl over 1f out tl swtchd lft jst ins fnl f: r.o wl fnl 100yds: gng on strly at fin: 5th of 19 in gp* **16/1**

1000 **6** *hd* **Castles In The Air**[7] 6177 5-9-7 103 ... RichardHughes 6 105+
(R A Fahey) *stdd after s and swtchd sharply rt to r on far side: hld up in rr: gd hdwy over 1f out: styd on wl ins fnl f: nt rch ldrs: 6th of 19 in gp* **25/1**

0202 **7** *1 ¼* **Acrostic**[37] 5247 5-9-10 106 ... J-PGuillambert 3 104+
(L M Cumani) *racd in centre: in tch and midfield overall: effrt and rdn jst over 2f out: kpt on same pce and no threat to ldrs fnl f: 1st of 6 in gp* **20/1**

1422 **8** *½* **Kyllachy Star**[15] 5903 4-8-12 94 ... JimmyQuinn 5 91+
(R A Fahey) *racd in centre: chsd gp ldrs and in tch overall: rdn to ld centre gp 2f out: styd on one pce and no threat to ldrs fnl f: 2nd of 6 in gp* **25/1**

4000 **9** *shd* **Jimmy Styles**[7] 6177 6-9-2 103 ... JohnFahy(5) 13 100
(C G Cox) *racd far side: hld up in midfield: rdn and hdwy jst over 2f out: drvn and styd on same pce ent fnl f: 7th of 19 in gp* **33/1**

003 **10** *¾* **Wannabe King**[26] 5609 4-9-6 102 ...(p) ChrisCatlin 2 97+
(D R Lanigan) *racd in centre: chsd ldrs in centre: rdn and effrt to press gp ldrs 2f out: styd on same pce and no threat to ldrs fnl f: 3rd of 6 in gp* **20/1**

0024 **11** *1 ¼* **Advanced**[7] 6175 7-9-0 99 ... AmyRyan(3) 20 90
(K A Ryan) *racd far side: led and overall ldr: hdd and rdn 2f out: wknd u.p ent fnl f: 8th of 19 in gp* **25/1**

1111 **12** ¾ **Kakatosi**[40] 5143 3-9-4 **103** JimmyFortune 18 93
(A M Balding) *racd far side: hld up in tch: rdn and effrt ent fnl 2f: unable qck u.p over 1f out: wkng whn n.m.r ent fnl f: 9th of 19 in gp* **16/1**

2132 **13** 1 ¼ **Colepeper**[7] 6180 3-8-12 **97** ChristopheSoumillon 24 84
(M Johnston) *racd far side: chsd ldrs: wnt 2nd 3f out: rdn to ld 2f out: hdd jst over 1f out: wknd fnl f: 10th of 19 in gp* **20/1**

4021 **14** *hd* **Rulesn'regulations**[59] 4473 4-9-5 **101** RobertWinston 12 86
(Matthew Salaman) *racd far side: in tch: rdn and effrt ent fnl 2f: wknd u.p over 1f out: 11th of 19 in gp* **28/1**

0300 **15** *nk* **Lowdown (IRE)**[7] 6175 3-8-13 **98** PhilipRobinson 19 83
(M Johnston) *racd far side: chsd ldrs: rdn ent fnl 2f: wknd over 1f out: 12th of 19 in gp* **50/1**

4602 **16** 1 ½ **Noble Citizen (USA)**[63] 4358 5-8-10 **95** (be) MartinLane(3) 29 75
(D M Simcock) *racd far side: chsd ldrs: rdn and unable qck ent fnl 2f: wknd u.p over 1f out: 13th of 19 in gp* **22/1**

4000 **17** *hd* **Marajaa (IRE)**[14] 5950 8-8-11 **93** JamieMackay 23 73
(W J Musson) *racd far side: hld up in rr: edging rt looking for run 2f out: rdn and no prog over 1f out: nvr trbld ldrs: 14th of 19 in gp* **50/1**

0051 **18** *nk* **Axiom**[28] 5516 6-9-7 **103** KierenFallon 16 82
(L M Cumani) *racd far side: hld up towards rr: rdn and edging rt looking for run over 2f out: hdwy u.p wl over 1f out: no prog and btn 1f out: 15th of 19 in gp* **10/1**3

6066 **19** ½ **Gallagher**[14] 5950 4-9-2 **98** EddieCreighton 11 76
(B J Meehan) *racd far side: hmpd s: hld up in rr: rdn ent fnl 2f: sn hung lft and no hdwy: n.d: 16th of 19 in gp* **33/1**

2315 **20** *hd* **St Moritz (IRE)**[55] 4630 4-9-6 **102** RichardHills 21 79
(M Johnston) *racd far side: chsd overall ldr tl 3f out: wknd u.p wl over 1f out: 17th of 19 in gp* **16/1**

0041 **21** 2 **Navajo Chief**[17] 5854 3-9-5 **104** 6ex TedDurcan 15 77
(A P Jarvis) *racd far side: in tch: rdn and unable qck over 2f out: wknd wl over 1f out: wl btn fnl f: 18th of 19 in gp* **33/1**

2200 **22** ½ **Mia's Boy**[101] 3069 6-9-2 **103** AdamBeschizza(5) 4 73
(C A Dwyer) *racd in centre: hld up in tch: rdn and effrt to press gp ldrs 2f out: wknd over 1f out: wl bhd fnl f:4th of 6 in gp* **20/1**

121 **23** ½ **Sarasota Sunshine**[23] 5694 4-8-11 **93** (v) JMurtagh 25 62
(J Noseda) *racd far side: in tch: rdn and unable qck ent fnl 2f: sn struggling: wl btn ent fnl f: 19th of 19 in gp* **12/1**

3416 **24** 2 ¾ **Citrus Star (USA)**[15] 5911 3-9-3 **102** GeorgeBaker 7 65
(C F Wall) *racd in centre: chsd ldrs tl rdn and wknd wl over 1f out: wl btn and eased ins fnl f: 5th of 6 in gp* **25/1**

3653 **25** 15 **Light From Mars**[14] 5950 5-8-12 **97** JamesMillman(3) 8 18
(B R Millman) *racd in centre: led gp and in tch overall: rdn and wknd qckly 2f out: wl bhd and eased ins fnl f: 6th of 6 in gp* **33/1**

0300 **26** 1 **Bonnie Charlie**[7] 6175 4-8-13 **95** (v) TonyCulhane 1 13
(W J Haggas) *racd along on stands' rail: prom overall tl edgd rt and wknd qckly 2f out: wl bhd and eased ins fnl f:* **33/1**

353 **P** **Suruor (IRE)**[28] 5516 4-9-4 **100** TomQueally 22 —
(D M Simcock) *racd far side: hld up in rr tl lost action and p.u 3f out: dismntd* **14/1**

2110 **P** **Gramercy (IRE)**[42] 5088 3-9-0 **99** JamieSpencer 10 —
(M L W Bell) *racd far side: stdd and swtchd sharply rt after s: hld up in rr: bdly hmpd and lost tch 3f out: eased and p.u 2f out* **25/1**

1m 28.26s (0.26) **Going Correction** +0.40s/f (Good)
WFA 3 from 4yo+ 3lb **28** Ran SP% **138.9**
Speed ratings (Par 109): **114,112,110,109,109 108,107,106,106,106 104,103,102,102,101 100,99,99,98,98 96,95,95,92,74 73**
Tote Swingers: 1&2 £17.20, 1&3 £23.70, 2&3 £21.90 CSF £44.41 CT £588.10 TOTE £5.60: £2.40, £2.60, £3.70, £11.30; EX 41.70 Trifecta £1197.40 Pool: £67,159.76 - 41.50 winning units..
Owner Dr Marwan Koukash **Bred** T J Rooney **Trained** Sessay, N Yorks

FOCUS
A typically competitive looking heat on paper, but the field split into two groups early on, with the majority heading to the far side. It was from that group that the first six came, and the first three were all drawn in the top four boxes, even though the GoingStick report suggesting that the centre would be favoured over both flanks. The market got it spot on, with the favourite beating the well-backed second-favourite, and it was another big handicap success for David Nicholls. Strong handicap form.

NOTEBOOK
Redford(IRE) followed up last week's Ayr Gold Cup success in similar style. Although shouldering a 6lb penalty, the gelding was officially 3lb well in, and after travelling in his customary strong fashion, he quickened up strongly between horses inside the last to win well. Clearly just as effective over 7f as 6f given the right circumstances, he's going to have to have his sights raised to Listed level and above now. The Challenge Stakes is in connections' thoughts, as well as the Hong Kong Mile towards the end of the year, but it remains to be seen if he can replicate this level of form in races that usually have smaller fields and are often more tactical. (tchd 13-2)
Side Glance, a C&D winner earlier in the campaign, had Redford behind him when successful at Chester last time, and was well supported to confirm the form despite being 2lb worse off at the weights. He ran a fine race in defeat and remains firmly on the up, but he's sure to go up again for this. (op 9-1 tchd 7-1)
Imperial Guest, third in the Buckingham Palace Stakes and first home on the wrong side in a heritage handicap, both over this C&D, earlier this season, again showed his liking for the track, albeit with the benefit this time of a favourable draw. His wins have all come over 6f, but he stays 7f all right.
Golden Desert(IRE) raced more towards the outer of the far-side group, which may have been a relative disadvantage. Fifth in the Wokingham earlier this year, he rarely runs a bad race at this track and also showed he can go well fresh following a three-month break. (tchd 50-1 in a place)
Swift Gift, winner of the Victoria Cup last season, is another course specialist, and he improved two places on his seventh in this race last year despite having the door shut in his face 1f out and having to be switched. He finished well once in the clear. (op 22-1)
Castles In The Air, despite being drawn in single figures, tacked over to race with the far-side group, and came through late to take sixth. It was a fair effort in the circumstances, especially given his current mark. (op 28-1)
Acrostic won his race on the stands' side from six others. He's done most of his racing over a mile so this was probably a bit on the short side for him, but unsurprisingly he finished his race off well. He could be a Cambridgeshire type, but will again likely be up against one or two with more in hand of the handicapper. (op 25-1)
Kyllachy Star, who appreciates a bit of give in the ground, was second home on the stands' side. He had a career-high mark to overcome here so didn't run badly. (op 33-1)
Jimmy Styles, better known as a 6f sprinter, didn't quite see this trip out. (op 40-1)
Wannabe King, third home from the stands' side group, currently looks handicapped up to the hilt. (op 25-1)
Advanced, winner of this race last year off the same mark, probably had a bit too much use made of him for he was there to be shot at from 2f out.
Kakatosi was very weak in the market, especially in comparison to his stablemate, and despite coming here on the back of a four-timer and being entered for the Group 2 Challenge Stakes next month, he couldn't really muster a challenge having raced close to the pace on the far side for much of the way. Perhaps he needs quicker ground. (tchd 20-1 in a place)
Colepeper led briefly inside the final 2f but didn't see his race out. His two wins have come when dominating small fields. (tchd 28-1 in a place)
Rulesn'regulations, who raced on the outer of the far-side group, was another who had a career-high mark to defy and wasn't up to it. (op 25-1)
Axiom, runner-up in this race last year, won a shade comfortably at Goodwood last time but as a result of that success he returned here on a 3lb higher mark than last season. The ground looked to be in his favour but he was under pressure some way out and failed to land a blow. (op 9-1)
Gallagher Official explanation: jockey said colt hung left
St Moritz(IRE), the Bunbury Cup winner, has shown all his best form on quick ground and perhaps this surface wasn't to his liking. (op 20-1)
Sarasota Sunshine is by Oasis Dream and her recent improvement has come on good to firm ground. Official explanation: jockey said filly suffered interference in running (tchd 11-1)
Bonnie Charlie Official explanation: jockey said colt hung right
Suruor(IRE) sustained a serious leg injury and subsequently had to be put down.
Gramercy(IRE) was badly hampered when Suruor was pulled up quickly, so his run can be safely ignored. Official explanation: jockey said colt was hampered 3f out

6350 QUEEN ELIZABETH II STKS (SPONSORED BY SONY) (GROUP 1) 1m (R)
4:15 (4:20) (Class 1) 3-Y-O+

£151,859 (£57,566; £28,809; £14,364; £7,195; £3,611) **Stalls** High

Form RPR

0021 **1** **Poet's Voice**[28] 5518 3-8-13 115 (t) FrankieDettori 2 123+
(Saeed Bin Suroor) *stdd s: hld up in last: effrt on outer over 2f out: rdn to chse ldrs jst over 1f out: drvn to ld wl ins fnl f: hld on cl home: all out* **9/2**3

6212 **2** *nse* **Rip Van Winkle (IRE)**[21] 5775 4-9-3 126 JMurtagh 1 123
(A P O'Brien, Ire) *chsd ldr and clr of field: rdn to ld and edgd rt over 1f out: drvn and hrd pressed 1f out: hdd wl ins fnl f: kpt on v gamely and rallied nr fin: jst hld* **11/4**2

2205 **3** ½ **Red Jazz (USA)**[36] 5275 3-8-13 113 MichaelHills 4 122
(B W Hills) *chsd clr ldng pair: rdn to chse ldr over 1f out: ev ch ins fnl f: no ex and kpt on same pce fnl 100yds* **40/1**

6414 **4** 1 ¾ **Beethoven (IRE)**[21] 5775 3-8-13 117 (v) RyanMoore 7 118+
(A P O'Brien, Ire) *racd off the pce in midfield: rdn over 2f out: effrt u.p whn squeezed between horses over 1f out: kpt on u.p to go 4th fnl 75yds: nvr quite pce to rch ldrs* **14/1**

1101 **5** ¾ **Makfi**[41] 5134 3-8-13 129 ChristopheSoumillon 3 116
(M Delzangles, France) *hld up off the pce in midfield: rdn and effrt over 2f out: sme hdwy u.p but hanging rt over 1f out: switching lft and kpt on same pce ins fnl f* **1/1**1

0345 **6** 2 ½ **Hearts Of Fire**[44] 5009 3-8-13 117 RobertWinston 8 111
(Pat Eddery) *hld up wl off the pce in last trio: rdn and unable qck over 2f out: wl hld and edging lft u.p over 1f out: nvr trbld ldrs* **14/1**

1120 **7** 1 **Bushman**[39] 5186 6-9-3 110 TomQueally 6 108
(D M Simcock) *hld up wl off the pce in last trio: rdn and no prog over 2f out: wl hld and edging rt u.p over 1f out: nvr trble ldrs* **40/1**

0106 **8** 18 **Air Chief Marshal (IRE)**[13] 6009 3-8-13 110 JamieSpencer 5 67
(A P O'Brien, Ire) *led tl rdn and hdd over 1f out: sn n.m.r and wknd qckly: eased ins fnl f* **66/1**

1m 39.76s (-0.94) **Going Correction** +0.40s/f (Good)
WFA 3 from 4yo+ 4lb **8** Ran SP% **114.6**
Speed ratings (Par 117): **120,119,119,117,116 114,113,95**
Tote Swingers: 1&2 £2.00, 1&3 £16.60, 2&3 £14.90 CSF £17.22 TOTE £5.60: £2.00, £1.30, £8.50; EX 14.00 Trifecta £516.00 Pool: £13,836.55 - 19.84 winning units..
Owner Godolphin **Bred** Darley **Trained** Newmarket, Suffolk
■ A fifth win in the race for both Frankie Dettori and Saeed Bin Suroor.

FOCUS
Canford Cliffs was an absentee due to an unsatisfactory scope. The Ballydoyle pacemaker Air Chief Marshal ensured there was no hiding place, making it a good test at the distance, but the fact Red Jazz, only fifth in a Listed contest at York last time, was so close as they crossed the line does raise questions over the merit of the form. The winning time, somewhat surprisingly given the ground description, was 0.44secs quicker than RP standard. The form has been rated around the fourth, with the second and fifth not at their best and the third improving around 7lb.

NOTEBOOK
Poet's Voice was a classy 2-y-o but struggled badly for form in the spring. Hold up tactics and the reapplication of a tongue-tie brought him back to life at Salisbury, and an easy last-time-out win in the Celebration Mile at Goodwood suggested he was well on his way to fulfilling his early potential. With conditions seemingly ideal, he looked content settled in last through the early stages, and despite having plenty of ground to make up as Rip Van Winkle kicked for home, he was more than up to the task, responding well when Dettori went for the stick and just shading it in a desperately close finish. Progressing all the time, he has the potential to be an even better 4-y-o, and his telling turn of foot will continue to be an asset when utilised properly. He could easily run a big race in the Breeders' Cup Mile, his next intended target. (op 6-1 tchd 13-2 in a place)
Rip Van Winkle(IRE) has been slogging it out with the best 1m2f horses around of late and attempted to put his proven stamina to full use on this return to 1m. Having chased his pacemaker, he was driven to lead 2f out and tried to kick away, but was unable to shake Red Jazz, let alone anything else, and despite a spirited effort, he couldn't quite hang on. A high-class galloper who tends to be a bit one-paced regardless of the trip he's running over, there was no disgrace in just losing out to a member of the younger generation, and he may well return to America now for another crack at the Breeders' Cup. The Champion Stakes is the other option. (tchd 3-1)
Red Jazz(USA), on his toes in the paddock, has still to win at Group level and it was a major surprise to see him run so well, although he had finished eighth, beaten 4l, behind Makfi in the Guineas on his one previous try at the distance. Considering he chased the early pace it would have been no surprise to see him fade inside the final furlong, but he stuck on pluckily and was only half a length away from causing a major upset. Evidence suggests that this could be his trip now, and connections will surely want to get a first Group win under his belt.
Beethoven(IRE) has been running creditably all season, including when one place ahead of Makfi at Royal Ascot and when fourth in the Irish Champion latest. This represented another stiff task, but he again acquitted himself well, keeping on as though a return to 1m2f will suit. He's a probable contender for the Champion Stakes. (op 16-1)
Makfi had much expected of him after bouncing back from a below-par effort in the St James's Palace Stakes to beat the great Goldikova in the Jacques Le Marois, but his trainer had said that this was being used as a stepping stone toward the Breeders' Cup Mile and that he wouldn't be fully wound up. Add to that the fact he was disappointing on his previous visit to the course and there were good grounds for opposing him, indeed after he had trailed in fifth Christophe Soumillon reported that he disliked the course and had got fractious at the start. Despite travelling well enough into the straight, it was clear from over 2f he wasn't going to be winning, but he was by no means given a hard time and this should put him straight for the trip to America, although whether he can confirm form with Goldikova on likely better ground, or indeed reverse form with Poet's Voice, remains to be seen. (op 10-11 tchd 11-10 and 6-5 in places)
Hearts Of Fire, a beaten favourite behind Poet's Voice at Salisbury, had conditions in his favour, but couldn't quicken sufficiently to get himself in the mix and ended up well held. (tchd 12-1)
Bushman, a well-beaten last when 66-1 for the Juddmonte International behind Rip Van Winkle, never threatened to get involved and isn't up to this level. (op 50-1 tchd 33-1)

Air Chief Marshal(IRE) performed his task admirably. Official explanation: jockey said, regarding easing, that having made the running, the colt began to tire, he was short of room approaching final furlong and that it had no more to give.

6351 MILES & MORRISON OCTOBER STKS (LISTED RACE) 7f
4:50 (4:56) (Class 1) 3-Y-O+

£22,708 (£8,608; £4,308; £2,148; £1,076; £540) Stalls Centre

Form RPR

1350 **1** **Rainfall (IRE)**[14] 5946 3-9-2 112 FrankieDettori 7 116+
(M Johnston) *hld up in tch in midfield: rdn and effrt wl over 1f out: led jst ins fnl f: styd on strly: rdn out* **7/4**[1]

0443 **2** *2* **Blue Angel (IRE)**[16] 5883 3-8-10 100 (b) RichardHughes 3 105
(R Hannon) *hmpd s: hld up in rr: stl plenty to do and nt clr run 2f out: edging rt and hdwy over 1f out: styd on wl u.p to go 2nd wl ins fnl f: no threat to wnr* **15/2**[3]

5055 **3** *1* **Electric Feel**[16] 5883 3-8-10 97 JamieSpencer 9 102+
(M Botti) *racd towards far side tl merged w field 4f out: chsd ldrs: rdn and pressing ldrs 2f out: edgd rt and styd on same pce fnl f* **14/1**

0102 **4** *3/4* **First City**[27] 5554 4-8-13 101 TomQueally 10 101
(D M Simcock) *swtchd lft sn after s: hld up in tch: rdn and hdwy 2f out: drvn to ld over 1f out: hdd and edgd rt u.p fnl 150yds: wknd fnl 75yds* **10/1**

-106 **5** *2* **Puff (IRE)**[57] 4540 3-9-2 107 JimCrowley 6 101
(R M Beckett) *chsd ldrs: hdwy to chse ldr 3f out: rdn and ev ch ent fnl 2f: unable qck and btn jst ins fnl f* **14/1**

1031 **6** *1 1/4* **Fleeting Echo**[42] 5082 3-8-10 93 KierenFallon 2 91
(R Hannon) *wnt rt s: chsd ldrs tl led wl over 2f out: rdn ent fnl 2f: hdd and edgd rt u.p over 1f out: wknd fnl f* **12/1**

-222 **7** *1 3/4* **Mosqueras Romance**[16] 5883 4-8-13 100 JMurtagh 1 87
(M Botti) *chsd ldr tl rdn wl over 2f out: drvn and btn over 1f out* **4/1**[2]

0010 **8** *nse* **Miss Zooter (IRE)**[16] 5883 3-8-10 97 RichardKingscote 12 86
(R M Beckett) *racd in far side pair tl merged w field 4f out: in tch in midfield after: rdn and unable qck ent fnl 2f: wknd over 1f out* **33/1**

-111 **9** *nk* **Wake Up Call**[32] 5396 4-9-0 90 ow1 GeorgeBaker 8 86
(C F Wall) *stdd s: hld up in rr: nt clr run ent 2f out tl over 1f out: no prog and wl hld fnl f* **9/1**

-200 **10** *hd* **Habaayib**[16] 5883 3-8-10 105 RichardHills 13 85
(E A L Dunlop) *stdd and swtchd lft after s: hld up towards rr: rdn and short-lived effrt wl over 1f out: wl btn ent fnl f* **20/1**

2530 **11** *3 1/2* **Lenkiewicz**[16] 5896 3-8-10 74 SebSanders 4 76
(B R Millman) *hmpd and stdd s: hld up in rr: stl plenty to do whn swtchd rt and rdn wl over 1f out: no prog: n.d* **100/1**

6054 **12** *6* **Carioca (IRE)**[16] 5883 3-8-13 102 AndreaAtzeni 5 62
(M Botti) *led tl 3f out: rdn and wknd qckly 2f out: bhd fnl f* **20/1**

1m 29.21s (1.21) **Going Correction** +0.40s/f (Good)
WFA 3 from 4yo 3lb **12** Ran SP% **121.7**
Speed ratings (Par 111): **109,106,105,104,102 101,99,98,98,98 94,87**
Tote Swingers: 1&2 £4.50, 1&3 £7.70, 2&3 £16.40 CSF £15.08 TOTE £2.80: £1.40, £2.80, £4.30; EX 19.60 Trifecta £212.00 Pool: £1,936.62 - 6.75 winning units..
Owner Sheikh Hamdan Bin Mohammed Al Maktoum **Bred** Barouche Stud Ireland Ltd **Trained** Middleham Moor, N Yorks
■ A 217/1 four-timer for Frankie Dettori, 14 years on from his 'Magnificent Seven'.

FOCUS
Not a particularly competitive Listed race but the form makes sense. It was a small personal best from the winner, with the second and third to their Doncaster form.

NOTEBOOK
Rainfall(IRE) was head and shoulders above her rivals on the pick of her form and duly ran out a ready winner, getting to the front just inside the final furlong and staying on strongly under her 3lb penalty. Winner of the Jersey Stakes over C&D before twice not being beaten far in Group 1s, she's a thoroughly likable filly, who is versatile with regards to ground and trip, and looks sure to gain more black-type, with a return to Group level likely. (op 2-1 tchd 9-4 in a place)
Blue Angel(IRE) has been running well of late, including in the first-time blinkers at Doncaster latest, and she did well here considering she got behind having been hampered at the start and then had a troubled run through. This wasn't the first time she's run as though worth a try at 1m2f. (op 9-1)
Electric Feel, towards the far side early, had finished ahead of the below-par winner at Doncaster latest and she again ran well, just not seeing it out as strongly as the front pair having come to hold every chance. (op 12-1 tchd 16-1)
First City fared best of the older horses, closing to lead over 1f out, only to fade late on. (op 8-1 tchd 7-1)
Puff(IRE) faced a tough task under her 3lb penalty and ran about as well as expected. (op 12-1)
Fleeting Echo, winner of a Newbury handicap, didn't get home under a positive ride. (op 16-1)
Mosqueras Romance had a few of these, including the winner, behind when finishing second at Doncaster, but she couldn't repeat the form on this softer surface. (op 6-1 tchd 13-2)
Wake Up Call was trying to stay on when denied a run and failed to pick up afterwards. (op 8-1 tchd 7-1)
Habaayib travelled well until tiring in the ground. (op 18-1 tchd 25-1)

6352 TABAC GORDON CARTER H'CAP 2m
5:25 (5:25) (Class 3) (0-95,95) 3-Y-O+ £6,799 (£2,023; £1,011; £505) Stalls High

Form RPR

-110 **1** **Ermyn Lodge**[99] 3159 4-8-12 79 (v) IanMongan 7 87
(P M Phelan) *mde all: rdn ent fnl 2f: drvn over 1f out: styd on gamely fnl f: eased nr fin* **7/1**

1640 **2** *1/2* **Desert Recluse (IRE)**[36] 5273 3-8-11 90 RobertWinston 8 98
(Pat Eddery) *t.k.h: hld up in midfield: effrt on outer and rdn over 2f out: edgd rt u.p and chsng ldrs over 1f out: kpt on to go 2nd wl ins fnl f: nvr quite getting to wnr* **16/1**

3020 **3** *1/2* **Aaim To Prosper (IRE)**[42] 5080 6-9-6 87 FrankieDettori 10 94
(B J Meehan) *chsd ldng pair: rdn and chsd wnr jst over 2f out: drvn and unable qck over 1f out: styd on same pce and a hld after: lost 2nd wl ins fnl f* **11/4**[1]

2223 **4** *1 3/4* **Omokoroa (IRE)**[14] 5940 4-8-12 79 (v[1]) JimmyQuinn 1 84
(M H Tompkins) *hld up in midfield: effrt on inner over 2f out: chsd ldng pair and drvn jst over 1f out: plugged on same pce fnl f* **13/2**[3]

1320 **5** *2 1/2* **Atlantic Tiger (IRE)**[49] 4815 3-8-8 87 RichardHills 6 89
(M Johnston) *chsd wnr: rdn to press wnr 3f out: lost 2nd jst over 2f out: wknd u.p over 1f out* **4/1**[2]

0206 **6** *2 1/2* **Bow To No One (IRE)**[49] 4817 4-8-11 85 HarryBentley[(7)] 2 84
(A P Jarvis) *stdd and dropped in bhd after s: hld up in last: hdwy on outer and rdn ent fnl 2f: edging rt and no hdwy over 1f out* **10/1**

1420 **7** *1 3/4* **Woolfall Treasure**[21] 5743 5-10-0 95 (v) RyanMoore 5 92
(G L Moore) *hld up in last trio: rdn along over 3f out: c wd and drvn over 2f out: no prog and carried rt 2f out: swtchd lft and styd on same pce u.p after* **13/2**[3]

0060 **8** *10* **Perfect Shot (IRE)**[21] 5743 4-9-7 88 (p) EddieAhern 4 73
(J L Dunlop) *t.k.h: trckd ldrs gng wl: rdn and fnd nil over 2f out: wl btn over 1f out* **12/1**

001 **9** *2* **Keenes Day (FR)**[44] 4983 5-9-7 88 KierenFallon 3 70
(M Johnston) *a last trio: rdn and struggling ent fnl 3f: lost tch 2f out* **13/2**[3]

3m 33.54s (4.54) **Going Correction** +0.40s/f (Good)
WFA 3 from 4yo+ 12lb **9** Ran SP% **121.8**
Speed ratings (Par 107): **104,103,103,102,101 100,99,94,93**
Tote Swingers: 1&2 £22.10, 1&3 £6.30, 2&3 £13.00 CSF £116.10 CT £388.04 TOTE £10.10: £2.70, £4.70, £1.90; EX 158.00 TRIFECTA Not won. Place 6: £29.81, Place 5: £14.49..
Owner Ermyn Lodge Stud & Heatherwold Stud **Bred** Horizon Bloodstock Limited **Trained** Epsom, Surrey

FOCUS
This looked quite an open race on paper. It was a small personal best from the winner, who may yet rate a bit higher still, and the runner-up ran as well as ever.

NOTEBOOK
Ermyn Lodge had a few of these behind him when successful over this C&D back in May, and if one was prepared to forgive a tame effort at Goodwood when he was unable to lead, then he was entitled to plenty of respect off just a 2lb higher mark, especially as he had shown more than once in the past that he goes well fresh, so a three-month absence was, if anything, a plus. Soon in front, he dominated throughout and bravely fought off each of his challengers. As a proven Polytrack performer he could well switch surfaces if conditions deteriorate on turf, so there might be more to come from him. (op 9-1)
Desert Recluse(IRE) tended to edge right under pressure in the closing stages but kept on well to take second. It's been a busy campaign for him, having been on the go for 11 months now, but he's largely held his form. (tchd 20-1)
Aaim To Prosper(IRE) was a big gamble as Dettori went for a five-timer. Yet to run a bad race in five starts at this track, he had his chance in the straight but couldn't quite muster the pace to get by the winner. (op 9-4 tchd 3-1)
Omokoroa(IRE), wearing a visor instead of cheekpieces this time, is consistent enough but struggles to win races. He could probably do with being dropped a pound or two. (op 9-1)
Atlantic Tiger(IRE) looked a potential improver at the foot of the weights and was well backed beforehand. He'd shaped on more than one occasion as though he would be suited by this step up to 2m, but in the event he was seen off from the turn in. Perhaps a return to Polytrack will suit him. (op 5-1)
Bow To No One(IRE) was unable to get at the leaders, who quickened things up from the front turning in, and she probably needs quicker ground to be at her best, too. (op 9-1 tchd 11-1)
Woolfall Treasure remains weighted up to the hilt. (op 9-1)
Perfect Shot(IRE) was a little keen in the first-time cheekpieces and didn't get home. (op 11-1 tchd 14-1)
Keenes Day(FR) never got close enough to throw down a challenge. Perhaps the ground was against him - his best form on turf is on good to firm. (op 6-1 tchd 11-2)
T/Plt: £40.70 to a £1 stake. Pool:£169,520.17 - 3,034.61 winning tickets T/Qpdt: £17.40 to a £1 stake. Pool:£7,311.91 - 309.35 winning tickets SP

5936 CHESTER (L-H)
Saturday, September 25

OFFICIAL GOING: Good to soft (soft in places; 6.2)
Rail realignment increased 5.5f races by 17yds, 6f and 7f by 19yds, 1m2f 75yds by 21yds and extended 1m6f race by 38yds.
Wind: light 1/2 against Weather: fine and sunny

6353 CONTRACT SERVICES MAIDEN FILLIES' STKS 7f 2y
2:25 (2:25) (Class 3) 2-Y-O £5,180 (£1,541; £770; £384) Stalls Low

Form RPR

022 **1** **Humdrum**[30] 5441 2-9-0 70 PatDobbs 4 77
(R Hannon) *trckd ldrs: n.m.r over 1f out: r.o fnl f: led nr fin* **5/2**[1]

4 **2** *1/2* **Show Rainbow**[8] 6158 2-9-0 0 SamHitchcott 2 76
(M R Channon) *led: hdd and no ex towards fin* **7/2**[2]

04 **3** *2 1/4* **Malacca Straits**[16] 5892 2-9-0 0 FrannyNorton 6 70
(B W Hills) *drvn along to sn chse ldrs: styd on same pce fnl f* **5/2**[1]

4 *3/4* **Distinguish (IRE)** 2-9-0 0 JoeFanning 5 68+
(M Johnston) *chsd ldrs: chal over 1f out: kpt on same pce* **6/1**[3]

5 *11* **Decadence** 2-9-0 0 TomEaves 1 41
(E J Alston) *dwlt: sn chsng ldrs: drvn 3f out: lost pl over 1f out* **14/1**

P **Moonlight Rhapsody (IRE)** 2-9-0 0 RobertHavlin 3 —
(B W Hills) *s.s: detached: lost action and eased after 1f: sn p.u and dismntd* **17/2**

1m 33.82s (7.32) **Going Correction** +0.725s/f (Yiel) **6** Ran SP% **110.8**
Speed ratings (Par 96): **87,86,83,83,70** —
Tote Swingers: 1&2 £2.00, 1&3 £1.70, 2&3 £2.20 CSF £11.17 TOTE £2.90: £1.30, £2.60; EX 11.60.
Owner The Queen **Bred** The Queen **Trained** East Everleigh, Wilts

FOCUS
A fair maiden. The trio with experience filled the first three places in a race in which the pace increased approaching the straight. Trciky form to pin down but the winner apparently showed improvement.

NOTEBOOK
Humdrum looked to set the standard on her two earlier seconds at 6f, not least in the expectation that this step back up in trip was what was needed, and though the winning margin wasn't large, she always looked in control. She'll have to take her chance in nurseries now, with a further step up in trip likely to bring about more progress. (op 9-4)
Show Rainbow stepped up on her debut run but didn't have any excuses as the race was run, able to dictate the tempo on the inside then also having the advantage of the rail in the straight. She will be vulnerable in similar company next time, but promises to prove just as effective at 1m. (op 11-2)
Malacca Straits had looked unlucky at Kempton last time when a place behind a subsequent winner, but she never really threatened to get really competitive here despite a handy position entering the straight. She might not have been suited by the softish ground here. (op 11-4 tchd 3-1 in a place)
Distinguish(IRE) is a half-sister to a couple of 2yo 6f winners and she ran well for a long way, second into the straight but running green then just losing third late on. She'll improve a fair bit if taking after most of the youngsters her yard has run this year. (op 11-2 tchd 5-1)
Decadence, by Singspiel and a sister to the useful 2yo C&D winner Prompter, and with something of a round action, comes from a stable still looking for its first 2yo winner this season and is entitled to improve, dropping away as if in need of the race.

Moonlight Rhapsody(IRE), by Danehill Dancer and bought for 50,000 guineas as a yearling, started slowly and was soon detached with her rider giving the impression something had gone amiss. Official explanation: jockey said filly lost its action (op 7-1 tchd 9-1)

6354 CORBETT'S ON BESTBETTING.COM NURSERY 5f 110y

2:55 (2:56) (Class 2) 2-Y-O **£7,123** (£2,119; £1,059; £529) **Stalls** Low

Form				RPR
4414	**1**		**Boundaries**[12] 6030 2-8-8 **77**........(v) TomEaves 1 (T D Easterby) *mde all: sn drvn along: styd on strly fnl 2f* **5/2**[1]	82
155	**2**	2 1/4	**Crimson Knot (IRE)**[12] 6030 2-8-6 **75**........ PatrickMathers 3 (A Berry) *drvn to chse ldrs: styd on to chse wnr fnl f: no imp* **14/1**	73
4023	**3**	3/4	**Tro Nesa (IRE)**[13] 5998 2-7-12 **72**........ RosieJessop(5) 5 (Mrs A Duffield) *dwlt: drvn along: hdwy and n.m.r over 1f out: styd on same pce fnl 150yds* **8/1**	67
3320	**4**	3/4	**Orchid Street (USA)**[12] 6030 2-8-8 **77**........(p) JackMitchell 2 (Mrs A Duffield) *chsd ldrs: drvn over 2f out: kpt on same pce appr fnl f* **9/2**[2]	70
6101	**5**	5	**Foghorn Leghorn**[14] 5939 2-9-7 **90**........ RichardMullen 8 (P W Chapple-Hyam) *chsd ldrs: drvn over 2f out: lost pl over 1f out* **5/2**[1]	66
0220	**6**	1	**West Leake Bridge (IRE)**[35] 5301 2-8-4 **73**........ JoeFanning 4 (B W Hills) *chsd ldrs: lost pl over 1f out* **11/2**[3]	46

1m 11.1s (3.80) **Going Correction** +0.725s/f (Yiel) **6** Ran SP% **108.5**
Speed ratings (Par 101): **103,100,99,98,91 90**
Tote Swingers: 1&2 £3.80, 1&3 £3.80, 2&3 £10.40 CSF £34.08 CT £213.43 TOTE £3.20: £1.80, £4.20; EX 28.50.
Owner T G & Mrs M E Holdcroft **Bred** Bearstone Stud **Trained** Great Habton, N Yorks

FOCUS

Something of a lopsided nursery with the top weight conceding upwards of 13lb all round. The pace was a decent one but the winner was still able to make all. A good effort from him, but it is probably dangerous to take this at face value.

NOTEBOOK

Boundaries had made all when finally shedding his maiden tag two runs back and once again made the best use of that early speed, soon in front and never looking likely to get caught. He was tried over as far as 7f earlier in the year but looks best at around 5f and moves like a horse that will not be inconvenienced by even softer ground. (op 11-4 tchd 3-1)

Crimson Knot(IRE) had a bit to prove off a stiffish-looking mark with this softer ground also an unknown, but with the benefit of the inside rail she probably reproduced the best of her previous form for all she never really worried the winner. She's largely reliable. (op 12-1 tchd 11-1)

Tro Nesa(IRE) has been knocking at the door lately and again ran well after getting switched to the rail following a sluggish start. 5f or 6f seems to suit her equally well. (op 13-2 tchd 11-2)

Orchid Street(USA) was tried in cheekpieces here after a lack lustre effort last time but she dropped away mid race only to start to stay on again near the finish. She doesn't look the most straightforward ride but, that said, will be suited by a return to 6f. (tchd 4-1)

Foghorn Leghorn was the disappointment of the race up 5lb after his all-the-way C&D win last time, even allowing for things not dropping anywhere as kindly here. He had to switch wide entering but looked beaten at the time anyway and presumably wasn't right. Official explanation: jockey said colt never travelled (tchd 9-4 and 11-4)

West Leake Bridge(IRE) dropped away with no excuses and looks too high in the weights on the balance of his form. (op 13-2 tchd 5-1 and 7-1 in a place)

6355 RAYMOND & KATHLEEN CORBETT MEMORIAL H'CAP 1m 2f 75y

3:30 (3:30) (Class 2) (0-105,102) 3-Y-O

£19,066 (£5,709; £2,854; £1,429; £712; £358) **Stalls** High

Form				RPR
1232	**1**		**Opera Gal (IRE)**[15] 5913 3-8-4 **85**........ FrannyNorton 14 (A M Balding) *led after 1f: racd freely: drvn 3 l clr appr fnl f: jst hld on* **13/2**[3]	101
144	**2**	shd	**Fox Hunt (IRE)**[14] 5970 3-8-10 **91**........ JoeFanning 12 (M Johnston) *in rr: hdwy 4f out: chsd wnr 1f out: styd on towards fin: jst hld* **4/1**[2]	107+
3313	**3**	6	**Pintura**[14] 5955 3-7-10 **80**........(p) SophieDoyle(3) 10 (D M Simcock) *chsd ldrs: chsd wnr over 2f out: styd on same pce appr fnl f* **8/1**	85
5600	**4**	3	**Cracking Lass (IRE)**[93] 3368 3-8-7 **93**........ LeeTopliss(5) 2 (R A Fahey) *s.i.s: in rr: effrt and nt clr run over 2f out: hdwy over 1f out: kpt on* **16/1**	92+
0335	**5**	8	**Arlequin**[39] 5188 3-8-9 **90**........ SilvestreDeSousa 9 (J D Bethell) *trckd ldrs: t.k.h: wknd over 1f out* **9/1**	74
5110	**6**	1	**Aattash (IRE)**[7] 6193 3-9-6 **101**........ SamHitchcott 8 (M R Channon) *led 1f: chsd ldrs: wknd over 1f out* **12/1**	83
3300	**7**	2 1/4	**Layla's Dancer**[15] 5904 3-7-5 **79** oh4........ RyanPowell(7) 6 (R A Fahey) *s.i.s: hdwy over 3f out: kpt on fnl f: nvr nr ldrs* **25/1**	57
1402	**8**	3/4	**Alrasm (IRE)**[9] 6123 3-9-7 **102**........ TadhgO'Shea 13 (M A Jarvis) *trckd ldrs: lost pl 2f out* **10/1**	78
4444	**9**	2 1/2	**Ejteyaaz**[41] 5121 3-7-12 **79**........ DuranFentiman 3 (R A Fahey) *mid-div: lost pl over 2f out* **14/1**	50
0-30	**10**	1/2	**Spying**[43] 5030 3-8-7 **88**........ TomEaves 11 (Mrs A Duffield) *t.k.h: sn w ldrs: lost pl over 1f out* **33/1**	59
0435	**11**	1	**Jutland**[9] 6106 3-8-11 **92**........ RoystonFfrench 1 (M Johnston) *prom: hmpd after 1f: lost pl over 2f out* **14/1**	61
2122	**12**	1	**Lord Raglan (IRE)**[15] 5904 3-7-5 **79** oh1........ NeilFarley(7) 4 (Mrs K Burke) *hld up in mid-div: rdn and lost pl 3f out* **7/2**[1]	46

2m 17.69s (5.49) **Going Correction** +0.725s/f (Yiel) **12** Ran SP% **119.5**
Speed ratings (Par 107): **107,106,102,99,93 92,90,90,88,87 86,86**
Tote Swingers: 1&2 £4.60, 1&3 £5.10, 2&3 £6.30 CSF £32.88 CT £215.99 TOTE £7.10: £2.40, £2.10, £2.60; EX 32.00 Trifecta £105.70 Pool: £740.09 - 5.18 winning units..
Owner J C Smith **Bred** Littleton Stud **Trained** Kingsclere, Hants

FOCUS

A valuable handicap contested by plenty of in-form horses but it was one run at a muddling pace and the winner was able to dictate. Probably unreliable form overall, for all the first two would have finished clear however the race was run. It is worth taking a positive view of the front pair.

NOTEBOOK

Opera Gal(IRE) is clearly thriving and despite the strong finish of the runner-up looked to win a shade cosily. The other runners might have allowed her an easy time of it in front, but she was clearly travelling best turning for home and her rider didn't have to get serious as she and the second pulled clear. She possesses enough speed to think this trip might suit her better than 1m4f, and she's probably entitled to a crack at something like the Listed Severals Stakes at Newmarket after this. (op 7-1 tchd 15-2)

Fox Hunt(IRE) ◆ is a very progressive handicapper sure to win a good handicap this autumn. The sharp track didn't play to his strengths and he found himself with more to do than ideal as the race went, and wide too, but he got a nice run through into the straight and finished with plenty of gusto. A more galloping track at this trip or a step up to 1m4f will see him improve further, with the November Handicap appealing as a likely target. (op 9-2 tchd 7-2 and 5-1 in a place)

Pintura had conditions in his favour and ran another good race in cheekpieces, travelling smoothly to the straight and losing nothing in defeat to two-well handicapped rivals. (op 7-1)

Cracking Lass(IRE) was running in her first handicap after some stiff assignments lately in Listed/Group races. She was soon in a poor position towards the rear of the field but stayed on through beaten horses late to think her current mark doesn't make her uncompetitive. (op 14-1)

Arlequin had been below form the only time before on softer than good and he was readily left behind once the tempo increased entering the straight.

Aattash(IRE) went to post very freely and those exertions might have told late in the race so far back did he drop having been well placed (if not adopting his usual position at the head of affairs) for the most part. This was his first run on a soft surface. (op 11-1 tchd 14-1)

Ejteyaaz looked interesting given his potential for improvement but he was forced to come wide entering the straight after which he dropped away tamely. A return to 1m looks in order. (op 12-1 tchd 16-1)

Lord Raglan(IRE)'s recent form figures here read 12 but he couldn't get to the front on this occasion and seemed to find a steadily run race up steeply in grade against him. He'll be of more interest next time back at a lower level Official explanation: trainer said gelding was unable to dominate (op 5-1 tchd 6-1 in a place)

6356 BET AT CORBETTSPORTS.COM MAIDEN STKS 1m 2f 75y

4:05 (4:05) (Class 3) 3-Y-O+ **£5,828** (£1,734; £866; £432) **Stalls** High

Form				RPR
4	**1**		**Sense Of Pride**[33] 5376 3-8-12 0........ RobertHavlin 1 (J H M Gosden) *hld up in rr: hdwy 7f out: effrt over 2f out: hung lft and styd on wl appr fnl f: led last 75yds: won gng rt away* **5/1**[3]	85+
6462	**2**	3 1/4	**Zenarinda**[15] 5902 3-8-7 67........ AshleyMorgan(5) 3 (M H Tompkins) *led early: stdd and hld up in rr: hdwy 5f out: led over 2f out: hdd and no ex wl ins fnl f* **9/2**[2]	74
6-3	**3**	1 1/2	**Alubari**[18] 5832 3-9-3 0........ AdamKirby 8 (W R Swinburn) *swtchd lft after s: hld up in rr: hdwy 4f out: chal over 1f out: kpt on same pce* **5/1**[3]	76+
0	**4**	10	**Mutasareb (USA)**[66] 4257 3-9-3 0........(v[1]) TadhgO'Shea 5 (Saeed Bin Suroor) *t.k.h: sn led: hdd over 2f out: wknd over 1f out* **12/1**	57
03	**5**	31	**Maroon**[43] 5022 3-8-12 0........ FrannyNorton 2 (B W Hills) *chsd ldrs: lost pl over 2f out: sn bhd: t.o* **6/1**	—
0	**6**	nk	**Judicious**[114] 2684 3-9-3 0........ RichardMullen 6 (Sir Michael Stoute) *t.k.h: trckd ldrs: drvn over 3f out: lost pl over 2f out: sn bhd: eased: t.o: b.b.v* **9/4**[1]	—
00-	**7**	1/2	**Bollin Julie**[325] 7243 3-8-12 0........ RoystonFfrench 4 (T D Easterby) *dwlt: sn prom: reminders 8f out: lost pl over 3f out: sn bhd: t.o* **33/1**	—
002	**8**	14	**Fifty Moore**[29] 5487 3-9-3 74........ TomEaves 7 (Jedd O'Keeffe) *chsd ldrs: rdn over 5f out: lost pl 3f out: sn bhd: virtually p.u: wl t.o* **16/1**	—

2m 22.74s (10.54) **Going Correction** +1.075s/f (Soft) **8** Ran SP% **113.1**
Speed ratings (Par 107): **100,97,96,88,63 63,62,51**
Tote Swingers: 1&2 £4.10, 1&3 £4.10, 2&3 £3.30 CSF £27.06 TOTE £4.80: £1.90, £1.70, £2.30; EX 29.80.
Owner K Abdulla **Bred** Juddmonte Farms Ltd **Trained** Newmarket, Suffolk

FOCUS

A maiden lacking strength in depth in which the softish conditions likely played their part in a couple of disappointing performances. The pace was no more than fair and this is muddling form, rated around the runner-up.

NOTEBOOK

Sense Of Pride ◆, whose full brother Day Flight won the Ormonde Stakes here in softish ground, landed this despite tending to carry her head high, presumably still because of inexperience. This track will have taught her plenty and the manner in which she surged clear in the straight suggests there is a good deal more improvement to come, not least under these conditions at 1m4f. She can't be assessed too highly in handicaps and will be tough to beat next time in that sphere (op 9-2 tchd 11-2 and 6-1 in a place)

Zenarinda has been running well in maidens/handicaps, including here, but, rated just 67 officially, not surprisingly found only an unexposed one too good. She's a poor mover who looks like she will handle heavy ground. (op 5-1)

Alubari again shaped nicely without being given a hard time and is now eligible for handicaps, in which he's likely to do a fair bit better. (op 11-2 tchd 4-1 and 6-1 in places)

Mutasareb(USA) ran a better race for the application of a visor but was readily outpointed once into the straight. He's clearly limited, and looks more of a galloper than anything else. (tchd 14-1)

Maroon was another with the form to figure but she was having her first run on soft ground and it seemed that, rather than the drop back in trip, that was responsible for a poor effort. (op 13-2 tchd 15-2)

Judicious found disappointingly little once into the straight and couldn't build on his promising debut. He was reported to have bled from the nose. Official explanation: vet said colt bled from the nose (tchd 2-1 and 5-2 in a place)

6357 INNOSPEC H'CAP 7f 2y

4:40 (4:41) (Class 3) (0-95,91) 3-Y-O+ **£12,952** (£3,854; £1,926; £962) **Stalls** Low

Form				RPR
1501	**1**		**My Kingdom (IRE)**[18] 5834 4-9-2 **86**........(t) TadhgO'Shea 6 (H Morrison) *hld up in rr: effrt over 2f out: str run on outside over 1f out: led towards fin* **9/1**	98+
0122	**2**	1/2	**Fathsta (IRE)**[11] 6049 5-9-6 **90**........ RichardMullen 10 (D M Simcock) *t.k.h: trckd ldrs: hung lft and styd on to ld last 50yds: hdd and no ex nr fin* **7/1**[3]	101
0040	**3**	2 1/4	**Below Zero (IRE)**[7] 6175 3-9-3 **90**........ SilvestreDeSousa 11 (M Johnston) *swtchd lft after s: led: hdd last 50yds: kpt on same pce* **12/1**	96
2550	**4**	1	**Academy Blues (USA)**[7] 6178 5-8-12 **87**........ MichaelO'Connell(5) 4 (D Nicholls) *in tch: effrt over 2f out: kpt on same pce fnl f* **8/1**	89
0103	**5**	3/4	**Golden Shaheen (IRE)**[23] 5703 3-9-1 **88**........(b) JoeFanning 2 (M Johnston) *dwlt: in rr: hdwy and swtchd outside over 1f out: styd on:* **10/1**	89+
6621	**6**	nk	**Docofthebay (IRE)**[7] 6178 6-9-6 **90**........ PJMcDonald 12 (J A Glover) *dwlt: hdwy on outside to chse ldrs after 2f: one pce appr fnl f* **9/1**	89
0015	**7**	1/2	**Captain Ramius (IRE)**[7] 6178 4-9-7 **91**........ StephenCraine 7 (K A Ryan) *in rr: hdwy and nt clr run over 1f out: kpt on: nvr rchd ldrs* **11/1**	89+
2560	**8**	3 3/4	**Horatio Carter**[35] 5302 5-9-1 **85**........(p) RoystonFfrench 3 (Michael Smith) *sn chsng ldrs: chal over 2f out: wknd appr fnl f* **25/1**	73
6232	**9**	nse	**Fishforcompliments**[20] 5789 6-8-8 **83**........(p) LeeTopliss(5) 8 (R A Fahey) *rrd s: in rr: hdwy over 3f out: chsng ldrs 2f out: sn wknd* **10/1**	71
5-1	**10**	nk	**Soccerjackpot (USA)**[114] 196 6-9-7 **91**........ AdamKirby 9 (A E Jones) *a in rr* **50/1**	78
0-00	**11**	nk	**Lowther**[7] 6175 5-9-5 **89**........(v[1]) FrannyNorton 5 (A Bailey) *chsd ldrs: drvn 3f out: wkng whn sltly hmpd over 1f out* **4/1**[1]	75

The Form Book, Raceform Ltd, Compton, RG20 6NL

3621 **12** *nk* **Esprit De Midas**[11] 6048 4-9-6 **90** TomEaves 1 75
(K A Ryan) *hld up in midfield: effrt over 2f out: wknd over 1f out* **6/1**[2]

1m 32.8s (6.30) **Going Correction** +1.075s/f (Soft)
WFA 3 from 4yo+ 3lb **12** Ran SP% **117.9**
Speed ratings (Par 107): **107,106,103,102,101 101,100,96,96,96 95,95**
Tote Swingers: 1&2 £10.70, 1&3 £30.80, 2&3 £21.40 CSF £70.34 CT £779.11 TOTE £11.00: £3.40, £2.20, £4.90; EX 109.70.
Owner Wood Street Syndicate V **Bred** Irish National Stud **Trained** East Ilsley, Berks

FOCUS
A competitive handicap contested by three last-time-out winners as well as some in-form course specialists. The advantage was with those ridden prominently and the winner needs his effort marking up considering the steady pace. The runner-up is rated back to his best.

NOTEBOOK
My Kingdom(IRE), just as he had when winning at Goodwood in June, needs this run upgrading as he was poorly placed entering the straight but still showed a good turn of foot to cut down rivals that looked to have got first run. He's just as effective in a strongly run 6f and will remain ahead of the handicapper after being reassessed. Still relatively lightly raced, there might well be a good handicap in him this autumn. (op 8-1 tchd 10-1)
Fathsta(IRE) came into this in excellent form and extended his good course record with another creditable run. (op 6-1 tchd 11-2)
Below Zero(IRE) had made all when allowed to dictate here in the summer and looked to have pulled off the same stroke again, only to get reeled in late. He had the run of the race and can have no excuses. (op 11-1)
Academy Blues(USA) hasn't had much racing since the spring but this was a more encouraging effort than of late, but he still leaves the impression that off his current mark he is vulnerable to better-treated rivals. (op 10-1)
Golden Shaheen(IRE) isn't the most predictable but he ran better than the result suggests considering his position entering the straight. He doesn't look the most straightforward, but once again left the impression he's worth a try at 1m. (op 9-1)
Docofthebay(IRE) had looked resurgent coming into this but probably paid for making his move round the outside in the middle of the race. He's still on a good mark on his old form, and might well prove that back on a more conventional track next time. (op 8-1)
Lowther was well supported in a first-time visor but was beaten even before he was hampered early in the straight. He was later reported to have been unsuited by the ground. Official explanation: jockey said horse was unsuited by the good to soft (soft in places) ground (op 6-1 tchd 13-2 and 7-1 in a place)
Esprit De Midas Official explanation: trainer had no explanation for the poor form shown

6358 ADVANCED INSULATION PLC H'CAP — 6f 18y
5:15 (5:15) (Class 4) (0-85,85) 3-Y-O+ **£5,180** (£1,541; £770; £384) **Stalls** Low

Form RPR
2053 **1** **Green Park (IRE)**[35] 5297 7-9-0 **76** (b) DavidNolan 2 88
(D Carroll) *trckd ldrs: shkn up to ld jst ins fnl f: drvn clr* **13/2**[3]
0-06 **2** *2 1/2* **Cape Vale (IRE)**[34] 5340 5-9-2 **83** MichaelO'Connell(5) 4 87
(D Nicholls) *led: hdd jst ins fnl f: no ex* **16/1**
3542 **3** *3/4* **Grissom (IRE)**[17] 5855 4-9-0 **76** (t) DuranFentiman 3 84+
(T D Easterby) *chsd ldrs: hmpd over 2f out: styd on same pce fnl f* **11/4**[1]
4220 **4** *hd* **Tasmeem (IRE)**[14] 5941 3-8-9 **78** (b) LeeTopliss(5) 6 79
(R A Fahey) *hld up: hdwy over 3f out: chsng ldrs over 1f out: kpt on same pce ins fnl f* **25/1**
0605 **5** *nk* **Cornus**[5] 6256 8-9-2 **78** (be) JamesDoyle 5 78
(A J McCabe) *mid-div: hdwy over 1f out: kpt on: nvr rchd ldrs* **20/1**
0150 **6** *2 1/4* **Great Charm (IRE)**[8] 6142 5-9-4 **80** JackMitchell 10 73
(E J Alston) *chsd ldrs: one pce fnl 2f* **13/2**[3]
4200 **7** *1/2* **Lucky Dan (IRE)**[14] 5937 4-9-0 **76** FrannyNorton 7 67
(Paul Green) *mid-div: edgd rt and kpt on fnl f: nvr nr ldrs* **8/1**
1440 **8** *3 1/2* **Tyfos**[8] 6142 5-9-7 **83** TomMcLaughlin 12 63
(B P J Baugh) *chsd ldr: wknd over 1f out* **20/1**
13- **9** *3/4* **Nadeen (IRE)**[481] 2547 3-9-3 **81** SilvestreDeSousa 11 59
(Michael Smith) *in rr on outer: nvr a factor* **28/1**
0412 **10** *1* **Legal Eagle (IRE)**[14] 5941 5-8-11 **80** (p) DuilioDaSilva(7) 1 54
(Paul Green) *chsd ldrs: hmpd over 2f out: lost pl appr fnl f* **4/1**[2]
0060 **11** *2* **Duplicity**[14] 5966 3-9-7 **85** (b) PatDobbs 8 53
(R Hannon) *a in rr* **33/1**
5556 **12** *nk* **Invincible Lad (IRE)**[17] 5855 6-9-5 **81** TomEaves 13 48
(E J Alston) *mid-div: lost pl 2f out* **20/1**
0200 **13** *77* **Coleorton Choice**[5] 6256 4-9-1 **77** (p) TadhgO'Shea 9 —
(R Hollinshead) *in rr: eased over 1f out: heavily eased: virtually p.u: wl t.o* **16/1**

1m 20.04s (6.24) **Going Correction** +1.075s/f (Soft)
WFA 3 from 4yo+ 2lb **13** Ran SP% **120.7**
Speed ratings (Par 105): **101,97,96,96,96 93,92,87,86,85 82,82,—**
Tote Swingers: 1&2 £25.30, 1&3 £6.00, 2&3 £15.10 CSF £93.35 CT £308.74 TOTE £7.40: £2.30, £4.60, £1.50; EX 136.20.
Owner G A Fixings Ltd **Bred** James Burns And A Moynan **Trained** Sledmere, E Yorks

FOCUS
Perhaps not as competitive as the numbers suggest with plenty coming into some way off top form. Once again, the advantage was with those up with the pace. It is doubtful if the winner suddenly improved.
Coleorton Choice Official explanation: jockey said colt lost its action

6359 FREE £15 BET AT CORBETTSPORTS.COM H'CAP — 1m 6f 91y
5:45 (5:45) (Class 4) (0-85,85) 3-Y-O **£5,180** (£1,541; £770; £384) **Stalls** Low

Form RPR
1661 **1** **Dubara Reef (IRE)**[12] 6038 3-8-2 **66** oh3 (p) SilvestreDeSousa 7 71
(Paul Green) *led early: trckd ldr: led 3f out: styd on gamely fnl f* **8/1**
2442 **2** *1* **Bombadero (IRE)**[24] 5665 3-9-0 **78** (b[1]) TadhgO'Shea 4 82
(J L Dunlop) *trckd ldrs gng wl: nt clr run over 2f out: effrt to chse wnr over 1f out: fnd little* **6/1**[3]
0320 **3** *2* **Kingdom Of Munster (IRE)**[4] 6269 3-8-2 **66** oh6 DuranFentiman 2 67
(R A Fahey) *s.i.s: hld up: drvn over 4f out: kpt on same pce appr fnl f* **14/1**
3213 **4** *2 1/4* **Joseph Lister**[36] 5259 3-9-3 **81** RichardMullen 6 79
(J H M Gosden) *trckd ldrs: effrt over 2f out: one pce over 1f out* **2/1**[2]
1-1 **5** *6* **Powerful Melody (USA)**[13] 5991 3-9-7 **85** (p) DaraghO'Donohoe 1 75
(Saeed Bin Suroor) *dwlt: hld up in rr: drvn 7f out: hdwy over 4f out: chsng ldrs 2f out: hung lft and wknd appr fnl f* **6/4**[1]
006 **6** *2 1/2* **Molon Labe (IRE)**[11] 6050 3-8-2 **66** oh4 AndrewMullen 5 52
(T P Tate) *sn led: hdd 3f out: sn outpcd: lost pl wl over 1f out* **22/1**
200 **7** *1 3/4* **High On A Hill (IRE)**[14] 5953 3-8-11 **75** PatDobbs 3 59
(S Kirk) *in tch: reminders after 4f: effrt over 3f out: sn chsng ldrs: lost pl 2f out* **20/1**

3m 26.43s (19.43) **Going Correction** +1.075s/f (Soft) **7** Ran SP% **114.5**
Speed ratings (Par 103): **87,86,85,84,80 79,78**
Tote Swingers: 1&2 £3.50, 1&3 £5.60, 2&3 £6.40 CSF £54.29 TOTE £9.50: £3.10, £3.20; EX 46.60 Place 6: £126.15, Place 5: £61.57..
Owner The Four Aces **Bred** M Duffy **Trained** Lydiate, Merseyside

FOCUS
A fair staying handicap to end the card and competitive for all that three were out of the weights, although the form is not that strong for the grade. The pace looked on the steady side initially.
Powerful Melody(USA) Official explanation: jockey said colt never travelled
T/Plt: £97.70 to a £1 stake. Pool:£66,675 - 498.10 winning tickets T/Qpdt: £19.90 to a £1 stake. Pool:£4,094 - 151.92 winning tickets WG

6323 HAYDOCK (L-H)
Saturday, September 25

OFFICIAL GOING: Soft (heavy in places in straight for races of one mile and upwards) (5f & 6f 7.5; 1m+ 6.5)
Inner Sprint track used. For races of 1m plus back straight and bend out of back straight on inner line leading to outer home straight.
Wind: Light across Weather: Sunny and cold

6360 E B F CHESS TELECOM MAIDEN FILLIES' STKS — 1m 30y
1:30 (1:31) (Class 5) 2-Y-O **£3,238** (£963; £481; £240) **Stalls** Low

Form RPR
3 **1** **Umseyat (USA)**[18] 5829 2-9-0 0 TadhgO'Shea 6 84+
(J H M Gosden) *trckd ldrs: smooth hdwy 3f out: cl up 2f out: led on bit wl over 1f out: sn pushed clr: easily* **10/11**[1]
2 *2 1/4* **Moonsail** 2-9-0 0 AhmedAjtebi 3 75+
(Mahmood Al Zarooni) *trckd ldrs: pushed along 3f out: swtchd rt and rdn 2f out: styd on to chse wnr ins fnl f: sn no imp* **3/1**[2]
6 **3** *2 3/4* **Pandorica**[26] 5583 2-9-0 0 LukeMorris 4 69
(C G Cox) *trckd ldr: cl up 1/2-way: rdn to ld jst over 2f out: hdd wl over 1f out and sn drvn: one pce appr fnl f* **14/1**
5 **4** *1 1/4* **Eaves Lane (IRE)**[10] 6071 2-9-0 0 PaulHanagan 1 66
(R A Fahey) *dwlt: sn trcking ldrs on inner: hdwy 3f out: rdn 2f out: sn one pce* **9/2**[3]
00 **5** *4* **Milly Filly**[65] 4286 2-9-0 0 DaneO'Neill 2 57
(Miss Amy Weaver) *led: rdn along over 3f out: hdd jst over 2f out and sn wknd* **66/1**
6 *4* **She's Got The Luck (IRE)** 2-9-0 0 RoystonFfrench 5 48
(G M Moore) *in rr: rdn along 4f out: swtchd rt and sme hdwy 2f out: nvr a factor* **20/1**
7 *1 3/4* **Alluring Star** 2-8-11 0 JamesSullivan(3) 7 45
(M W Easterby) *a in rr* **66/1**
06 **8** *3/4* **Nippy Nikki**[25] 5630 2-9-0 0 AdrianNicholls 8 43
(J R Norton) *chsd ldrs on outer: rdn along 1/2-way: wknd fnl 3f* **66/1**
9 *1 1/4* **Shirocco Vice (IRE)** 2-8-11 0 BarryMcHugh(3) 10 40
(R A Fahey) *a towards rr: rdn along and bhd fnl 2f* **25/1**
0 **10** *30* **Winding Hill**[15] 5921 2-8-7 0 DavidSimmonson(7) 9 —
(M W Easterby) *s.i.s and a in rr: outpcd and wl bhd fnl 3f* **100/1**

1m 46.96s (2.26) **Going Correction** +0.10s/f (Good) **10** Ran SP% **116.3**
Speed ratings (Par 92): **92,89,87,85,81 77,76,75,74,44**
Tote Swingers: 1&2 £1.80, 1&3 £4.20, 2&3 £5.70 CSF £3.51 TOTE £2.00: £1.02, £1.60, £3.40; EX 3.90.
Owner Hamdan Al Maktoum **Bred** Shadwell Farm LLC **Trained** Newmarket, Suffolk

FOCUS
Juat a fair-looking maiden with questionable depth, but the winner impressed and was value for extra.

NOTEBOOK
Umseyat(USA) ◆ had shaped well when third on her debut at Goodwood earlier in the month and confirmed that promise with the minimum of fuss, not hard pressed to pull clear in the final two furlongs. She's a useful performer in the making for a yard which continues in excellent form. (op Evens tchd 11-10)
Moonsail ◆ has an excellent pedigree being a daughter of 1,000 Guineas/Oaks heroine Kazzia and a half-sister to the very smart Eastern Anthem, and she made a promising start, being no match for the winner but keeping on well at the finish having run green when first under pressure. Improvement looks assured and she'll have good claims of going one better in similar company next time. (op 11-4)
Pandorica's yard has banged in a few winners in recent days and this daughter of Indesatchel duly improved on last month's debut, though she'll need to step up again to win a similar event near to hand. (op 12-1 tchd 16-1)
Eaves Lane(IRE) has shown ability on both starts, but she probably won't really come into her own until qualified for handicaps. (op 6-1)
Milly Filly offered a bit more faced with more testing conditions than previously and is now eligible for nurseries.
She's Got The Luck(IRE) was green on debut but hinted at ability by the finish and should do better with this behind her. (op 16-1)
Alluring Star left the impression this initial experience will do her some good.

6361 EUROPEAN BREEDERS' FUND "REPROCOLOR" FILLIES' H'CAP — 1m 2f 95y
2:05 (2:06) (Class 3) (0-90,90) 3-Y-O+ **£12,952** (£3,854; £1,926; £962) **Stalls** High

Form RPR
043 **1** **All Annalena (IRE)**[32] 5387 4-9-0 **80** DaneO'Neill 15 94
(Mrs L Wadham) *trckd ldrs: hdwy to ld 3f out: pushed clr 2f out: rdn over 1f out: kpt on strly fnl f* **20/1**
3044 **2** *3 1/4* **Issabella Gem (IRE)**[14] 5953 3-8-4 **76** oh1 LukeMorris 5 84
(C G Cox) *hld up towards rr: hdwy 1/2-way: effrt and swtchd lft 2f out: sn rdn and chsd wnr ins fnl f: no imp* **9/1**
5501 **3** *1 1/4* **Antigua Sunrise (IRE)**[20] 5790 4-9-0 **80** PaulHanagan 11 85
(R A Fahey) *in tch: hdwy to trck ldrs 1/2-way: hdwy 3f out: rdn to chse ldng pair 2f out: sn drvn and no imp fnl f* **7/1**[2]
421U **4** *2 1/4* **Bahamian Music (IRE)**[28] 5529 3-8-5 **80** BarryMcHugh(3) 8 81
(R A Fahey) *midfield: hdwy 1/2-way: chsd ldrs 3f out: rdn over 2f out: drvn and kpt on same pce appr fnl f* **20/1**
-315 **5** *8* **Red Intrigue (IRE)**[14] 5972 3-8-4 **76** oh1 AdrianNicholls 6 62
(Mrs A J Perrett) *awkward s: sn in tch: hdwy 4f out: rdn along to chse ldrs whn n.m.r and sltly hmpd 2f out: sn drvn and kpt on same pce* **16/1**
1231 **6** *2 3/4* **Babycakes (IRE)**[14] 5972 3-8-13 **85** HayleyTurner 1 66
(M L W Bell) *in tch on inner: hdwy 4f out: rdn to chse ldrs 3f out: drvn over 2f out and sn one pce* **7/1**[2]
3321 **7** *3/4* **Effervesce (IRE)**[15] 5902 3-8-1 **76** Louis-PhilippeBeuzelin(3) 14 55
(Sir Michael Stoute) *s.i.s and towards rr: rdn along and hdwy on inner over 3f out: swtchd rt and drvn 2f out: nvr nr ldrs* **12/1**
1251 **8** *4 1/2* **On Khee**[61] 4426 3-8-5 **77** NickyMackay 7 48
(H Morrison) *prom: hdwy 4f out: chal over 3f out: sn rdn and wknd over 2f out* **8/1**
1341 **9** *6* **Ailsa Craig (IRE)**[25] 5638 4-8-9 **78** JamesSullivan(3) 17 37
(E W Tuer) *chsd ldr: rdn along over 4f out: sn wknd* **25/1**

3126 **10** 3 ½ **Miss Antonia (IRE)**[10] 6090 3-8-10 **82**.............................. NeilCallan 16 35
(H R A Cecil) *midfield: hdwy on outer 1/2-way: rdn along over 3f out: sn wknd* **14/1**

0341 **11** 3 **Madhaaq (IRE)**[71] 4098 3-8-11 **83**.................................. TadhgO'Shea 2 30
(J L Dunlop) *hld up in midfield: effrt and sme hdwy 4f out: rdn along 3f out and sn wknd* **11/2**[1]

3311 **12** 2 ¾ **Ashkalara**[13] 5988 3-8-4 **76** oh9....................................... CathyGannon 3 18
(H S Howe) *s.i.s: a in rr* **33/1**

-000 **13** 15 **Leceile (USA)**[86] 3585 4-9-2 **82**.. ShaneKelly 13 —
(W J Haggas) *led: rdn along 4f out: hdd 3f out: sn wknd and bhd whn eased fnl f* **50/1**

2313 **14** ¾ **Calipatria**[14] 5972 3-8-5 **77**... WilliamBuick 12 —
(J H M Gosden) *towards rr and reminders after 2f: rdn along bef 1/2-way: nvr a factor* **15/2**[3]

0124 **15** 4 ½ **Starkat**[10] 6095 4-9-10 **90**... DarryllHolland 10 —
(Jane Chapple-Hyam) *a towards rr: rdn along and bhd fr 1/2-way: eased fnl 2f* **16/1**

2221 **16** 14 **Marjury Daw (IRE)**[13] 6003 4-9-5 **85**.................................... PaulMulrennan 4 —
(J G Given) *chsd ldrs: rdn along over 4f out: wknd qckly 3f out: sn bhd and eased over 1f out* **14/1**

2m 15.78s (-0.22) **Going Correction** +0.10s/f (Good)
WFA 3 from 4yo 6lb **16** Ran SP% **124.3**
Speed ratings (Par 104): **104,101,100,98,92 90,89,85,81,78 75,73,61,61,57 46**
Tote Swingers: 1&2 £77.60, 1&3 £59.90, 2&3 £7.10 CSF £184.49 CT £1414.04 TOTE £36.60: £6.60, £3.00, £1.80, £5.30; EX 338.90 TRIFECTA Not won..
Owner Mr And Mrs A E Pakenham **Bred** Ashbrittle Stud **Trained** Newmarket, Suffolk

FOCUS
Probably not quite the race it looked like being beforehand, with none of the less-exposed types running up to expectations. They finished well strung out on the ground too and perhaps this is not form to be too positive about. It has been rated around the second and third.

NOTEBOOK
All Annalena(IRE) had this sewn up a long way out. She's taken a bit of time to find her feet in this country but had useful form to her name in Germany last time and has undoubtedly recaptured that level here. The winner would be a potentially smart hurdling prospect if her largely jumps-orientated yard opted to go down that route with her.
Issabella Gem(IRE) hails from a stable in form and probably stepped up a little on her recent in-frame efforts, though never looking like getting to the winner. Testing conditions clearly suit her well and she'd be a good thing dropped back to a maiden if connections wanted to get a win to her name. (op 12-1)
Antigua Sunrise(IRE) has yet to win off a mark this high but had proven herself in the mud last year and ran every bit as well as when successful at York last time without having any excuses. (op 17-2 tchd 6-1)
Bahamian Music(IRE) is enjoying a good season and gave her running again, but it does serve to confirm that improvement will be needed if she's to defy this mark.
Red Intrigue(IRE) turned around Sandown form with a couple of these but wasn't anywhere near her best in a remote fifth. Official explanation: jockey said filly was denied a clear run
Babycakes(IRE) looked a filly on the up when returning from a break to win at Sandown recently, but failed to confirm it here, with these more testing conditions presumably not in her favour. She deserves another chance. (tchd 6-1)
Effervesce(IRE) had finally got off the mark at Chester last time but found things a lot tougher back in a handicap. (op 16-1)
On Khee hadn't been seen since an impressive win at Windsor in July. She travelled well for a long way but faded right out of it the end under more testing conditions than she'd faced previously. Official explanation: jockey said filly had no more to give (op 17-2 tchd 9-1)
Madhaaq(IRE) had created a really good impression when scoring on her handicap debut at Newbury in July but hadn't been seen since and, after showing a bit of reluctance at the stalls, the writing was on the wall a long way out. Official explanation: trainer's rep said filly was unsuited by the soft (heavy in home straight) ground (op 6-1 tchd 5-1 and 13-2 in a place)
Calipatria had been been progressive prior to this but never went a yard on this much softer ground. She's another who probably deserves another chance. Official explanation: trainer's rep said filly was unsuited by the soft (heavy in home straight) ground (tchd 7-1 and 8-1)
Marjury Daw(IRE) had been a model of consistency prior to this, but she clearly had an off-day. (op 12-1 tchd 11-1)

6362 J20 WHITE BLEND H'CAP — 1m 6f
2:35 (2:35) (Class 2) (0-100,98) 3-Y-O+ **£16,190** (£4,817; £2,407; £1,202) **Stalls** Low

Form RPR

511 **1** **Herculean**[29] 5475 3-8-11 **91**.. ShaneKelly 7 102
(W J Haggas) *hld up in rr: pushed along 4f out: hdwy 2f out: swtchd rt and rdn over 1f out: styd on strly ent fnl f to ld last 75yds* **11/2**[2]

6155 **2** 1 ½ **Bollin Felix**[7] 6181 6-9-1 **85**...(v) DavidAllan 4 94
(T D Easterby) *led: jnd and rdn along 3f out: drvn and hdd 1 1/2f out: rallied u.p to ld again ins fnl f: hdd and no ex last 75yds* **11/2**[2]

-000 **3** 2 ¾ **The Betchworth Kid**[15] 5908 5-9-6 **95**.............................. DaleSwift(5) 10 100
(A King) *hld up in tch: hdwy to trck ldrs over 4f out: rdn to ld and hung lft over 1f out: drvn and hdd ins fnl f: one pce* **11/2**[2]

0316 **4** ¾ **Proud Times (USA)**[22] 5723 4-9-3 **87**.................................. PJMcDonald 9 91
(G A Swinbank) *trckd ldrs: hdwy 3f out: rdn to chal and ev ch whn hmpd 1 1/2f out: sn drvn and one pce* **16/1**

5303 **5** ½ **Becausewecan (USA)**[7] 6181 4-9-0 **84**.............................. GregFairley 1 87
(M Johnston) *trckd ldr: effrt over 4f out: rdn to chal 3f out and ev ch tl drvn and wknd over 1f out* **8/1**

013 **6** *shd* **Sunny Game**[126] 2315 3-8-2 **82**.. HayleyTurner 8 85
(M L W Bell) *hld up towards rr: hdwy over 4f out: effrt to chse ldrs over 2f out: swtchd lft and rdn wl over 1f out: sn drvn and one pce* **11/4**[1]

2162 **7** *nk* **Rangefinder**[14] 5940 6-9-9 **93**.. StevieDonohoe 11 96
(Jane Chapple-Hyam) *trckd ldrs: rdn along over 4f out: drvn wl over 2f out and kpt on same pce* **6/1**[3]

3004 **8** 24 **Crackentorp**[21] 5743 5-9-6 **90**.. PaulMulrennan 2 59
(T D Easterby) *trckd ldng pair on inner: rdn along 4f out: sn wknd and bhd whn eased fnl 2f* **10/1**

000/ **9** 1 ¼ **Pippa Greene**[707] 6817 6-8-13 **90**................................ DuilioDaSilva(7) 3 57
(P F I Cole) *hld up: a bhd* **28/1**

3m 6.32s (5.12) **Going Correction** +0.10s/f (Good)
WFA 3 from 4yo+ 10lb **9** Ran SP% **116.6**
Speed ratings (Par 109): **89,88,86,86,85 85,85,71,71**
Tote Swingers: 1&2 £6.70, 1&3 £3.90, 2&3 £4.30 CSF £36.16 CT £175.40 TOTE £5.90: £1.30, £2.00, £2.00; EX 39.40 Trifecta £314.50 Pool: £544.03 - 1.28 winning units..
Owner Highclere Thoroughbred Racing Tudor Min **Bred** Meon Valley Stud **Trained** Newmarket, Suffolk

FOCUS
A useful handicap and a sound pace under the conditions means it was a thorough test at the trip. The form is rated arouind the placed horses.

NOTEBOOK
Herculean ◆ is a 3yo very much on the up and defied a 7lb rise for Ffos Las with something to spare by the finish. That looked unlikely when he was chased along at the back of the field at the top of the straight, but he picked up really well in the end, clearly being well suited by the longer trip. He's a smart performer in the making and is very much one to keep on side. (op 9-2)
Bollin Felix ◆ goes really well in the mud and emerges with plenty of credit, pulling out more in front but having no answer to the winner's late surge. He won't always run into one as progressive as the winner and will continue to be of interest when faced with conditions as testing as these. (op 7-1 tchd 15-2 in a place)
The Betchworth Kid had his ground for the first time this term and duly fared better. He'll presumably go back hurdling at some stage but is on a fair mark in this sphere and will always be one to bear in mind when the ground rides testing. (op 15-2 tchd 5-1)
Proud Times(USA) is still relatively unexposed on soft ground and certainly travelled well enough for a long way to suggest this mark may not be beyond him another day, with his stamina probably just stretched in the end (both wins have come at 1m4f). (op 14-1)
Becausewecan(USA) is well treated on the form he showed earlier in the season, but there's no real indication he's about to take advantage. (op 10-1)
Sunny Game isn't one to be giving up on just yet. He'd been off since a promising third on his handicap bow at Chester in May and is entitled to come on for this, getting on to the heels of the leaders before a combination of fitness/lack of stamina began to tell. (tchd 3-1)
Rangefinder had gone up another 2lb and looks held by the handicapper for now. (tchd 11-2)
Crackentorp Official explanation: trainer said gelding was unsuited by the soft (heavy in home straight) ground
Pippa Greene gave no immediate cause for encouragement after a near two-year absence. (op 22-1)

6363 J R TAYLOR H'CAP — 6f
3:10 (3:11) (Class 2) (0-100,98) 3-Y-O+ **£11,333** (£3,372; £1,685; £841) **Stalls** Centre

Form RPR

-250 **1** **Summerinthecity (IRE)**[40] 5154 3-8-8 **87** ow1............. DarryllHolland 5 98
(J Noseda) *in tch: hdwy 2f out: rdn over 1f out: styd on ent fnl f: drvn to ld last 100yds and edgd rt: kpt on* **16/1**

2222 **2** ½ **Secret Witness**[16] 5884 4-8-13 **90**..........................(b) TomMcLaughlin 10 99
(R A Harris) *hld up: hdwy over 2f out: rdn to chse ldrs over 1f out: swtchd lft and drvn ins fnl f: kpt on* **10/1**

1311 **3** *nk* **Horseradish**[11] 6049 3-8-12 **91**....................................... HayleyTurner 8 99+
(M L W Bell) *cl up: rdn to ld wl over 1f out: drvn ent fnl f: hdd and nt qckn last 100yds* **10/3**[1]

10-0 **4** *nk* **Flying Statesman (USA)**[17] 5854 3-8-9 **88** ow1.......... MickyFenton 14 95
(R A Fahey) *t.k.h early: hld up in rr: hdwy over 2f out: swtchd lft and rdn over 1f out: styd on strly ins fnl f* **50/1**

0003 **5** 1 **We Have A Dream**[11] 6049 5-8-10 **87**............................ PhillipMakin 12 91
(W R Muir) *cl up: rdn along 2f out and ev ch tl drvn and one pce ent fnl f* **20/1**

0110 **6** *nse* **Hajoum (IRE)**[7] 6175 4-9-4 **95**.. GregFairley 3 99+
(M Johnston) *prom towards far side: effrt and cl up 1/2-way: rdn over 2f out and ch tl drvn and one pce ent fnl f* **10/1**

0004 **7** ½ **Everymanforhimself (IRE)**[8] 6142 6-8-7 **84** oh1........(v) CathyGannon 6 86
(K A Ryan) *chsd ldrs: hdwy 2f out: sn rdn and ev ch tl drvn ent fnl f and kpt on same pce* **16/1**

6400 **8** *shd* **Fullandby (IRE)**[7] 6178 8-8-11 **88**.................................... NeilCallan 17 90
(T J Etherington) *s.i.s and in rr: hdwy 2f out: rdn wl over 1f out: kpt on ins fnl f: nrst fin* **14/1**

3100 **9** 1 **Damika (IRE)**[7] 6177 7-9-3 **97**............................... MichaelStainton(3) 9 96
(R M Whitaker) *chsd ldrs: hdwy and cl up 2f out: sn rdn and hld whn n.m.r and hmpd ins fnl f: one pce after* **16/1**

0500 **10** 2 ¼ **Valery Borzov (IRE)**[8] 6142 6-8-8 **85**............................. PaulHanagan 7 76
(R A Fahey) *chsd ldrs: effrt and ch 2f out: sn rdn and wknd ent fnl f* **6/1**[2]

1602 **11** ½ **Waveband**[6] 6221 3-8-11 **90**.. AdrianNicholls 16 80
(M Johnston) *led on stands' rail: rdn along over 2f out: drvn and hdd wl over 1f out: wknd ent fnl f* **25/1**

4040 **12** 2 ½ **Invincible Force (IRE)**[104] 2992 6-9-1 **92**................(b) PaulMulrennan 4 74
(Paul Green) *racd towards far side: prom: swtchd rt and chsd ldrs 1/2-way: sn rdn and wknd 2f out* **33/1**

0040 **13** 1 ¾ **Sunraider (IRE)**[17] 5854 3-9-0 **93**..............................(p) DaneO'Neill 15 69
(B W Hills) *chsd ldrs stands' rail: rdn along wl over 2f out: sn wknd* **9/1**

0002 **14** *shd* **Sonny Red (IRE)**[7] 6175 6-9-0 **94**............................ MichaelGeran(3) 2 70
(D Nicholls) *s.i.s: racd towards far side: outpcd and bhd fr 1/2-way* **8/1**[3]

0260 **15** 1 **Brae Hill (IRE)**[21] 5774 4-9-1 **95**................................ BarryMcHugh(3) 1 68
(R A Fahey) *prom towards far side: swtchd rt after 2f: sn outpcd and bhd* **16/1**

4554 **16** 2 ½ **Georgebernardshaw (IRE)**[14] 5952 5-9-7 **98**............. WilliamBuick 13 63
(D M Simcock) *midfield: rdn along and wknd 1/2-way: sn bhd* **20/1**

1m 14.93s (1.43) **Going Correction** +0.325s/f (Good)
WFA 3 from 4yo+ 2lb **16** Ran SP% **125.1**
Speed ratings (Par 109): **103,102,101,101,100 100,99,99,98,95 94,91,88,88,87 83**
Tote Swingers: 1&2 £15.50, 1&3 £19.50, 2&3 £8.60 CSF £161.48 CT £677.82 TOTE £24.90: £4.90, £2.50, £1.60, £10.20; EX 347.10 Trifecta £510.60 Part won. Pool: £690.03 - 0.10 winning units..
Owner Mrs Susan Roy **Bred** J Costello **Trained** Newmarket, Suffolk
■ Stewards' Enquiry : Tom McLaughlin two-day ban: careless riding (Oct 9-10)

FOCUS
A few unexposed sorts and a really good yardstick in the runner-up came to the fore here, so no reason to doubt the merit of this form. The field threatened to split to begin with, with the winner one of those who raced more towards the far side initially, but they ended up merging centre to stands' side. The winner probably has more to offer.

NOTEBOOK
Summerinthecity(IRE) has had a somewhat truncated campaign, but he finally showed his true worth, bursting through inside the final furlong. He's yet to prove he can string good efforts together, but this was just his sixth start and it'd be a surprise if we've seen the best of him yet, while testing conditions clearly suit him well. (op 20-1)
Secret Witness has to be considered one of the most unlucky horses in training, finishing runner-up for the seventh time in his last eight starts. This proves he's versatile as regards ground, and it goes without saying that he should continue to give a good account. (op 9-1)
Horseradish couldn't complete the hat-trick, but showed he's still very much on the up, travelling powerfully for a long way up with the pace. He's well worth a try at 5f on this evidence. (op 7-2 tchd 4-1 in a place)
Flying Statesman(USA) ◆ got back on track on his second outing back after an absence, finishing well. He's worth another crack at 7f and certainly goes into the rest of the campaign fresher than most.
We Have A Dream was twice runner-up off 1lb higher earlier in the term and showed he can still be competitive, but more will be needed if he's to win one of these. (tchd 25-1 in a place)
Hajoum(IRE) has found himself a little wide of where the main action unfolded on his last two starts and is still very much at the top of his game. He certainly has the speed for sprinting. (op 9-1)
Everymanforhimself(IRE) is back in a bit better form, but there's no real indication he's ready to take advantage of a potentially good mark. (op 20-1)

Fullandby(IRE) really found his form around this time last year and there was a hint in this that he might be about to do the same again, keeping on at the finish. He's certainly well treated if he does recapture anything like his best. (tchd 16-1)
Valery Borzov(IRE) had his ground on this occasion, but is one of few Richard Fahey hasn't managed to get the best out of so far.
Sunraider(IRE) ran poorly in first-time cheekpieces. (op 8-1)
Sonny Red(IRE) wasn't in anything like the form which saw him finish second at Ayr last week, and that not a big surprise given his overall profile. (op 17-2)

6364 TAYLORMADE BETTING LESTER PIGGOTT "START TO FINISH" H'CAP 5f

3:45 (3:49) (Class 2) (0-100,95) 3-Y-O+ **£16,190** (£4,817; £2,407; £1,202) **Stalls** Centre

Form RPR

521 **1** **Cheveton**[8] 6142 6-8-13 **92** .... DaleSwift(5) 7 104
(R J Price) *dwlt and sltly hmpd s: hld up: hdwy 2f out: trckd ldrs and nt clr run over 1f out: swtchd rt and rdn ent fnl f: drvn to chal and edgd lft last 100yds: led on line* **4/1**[1]

0500 **2** *shd* **Hoof It**[15] 5911 3-9-1 **90** .... NeilCallan 3 102
(M W Easterby) *in tch: smooth hdwy to trck ldrs wl over 1f out: rdn to ld ins fnl f: sn drvn and hdd on line* **20/1**

4311 **3** *1 ½* **Hazelrigg (IRE)**[8] 6140 5-9-0 **88** .... (be) DavidAllan 15 94
(T D Easterby) *hld up in tch: gd hdwy over 1f out: rdn ent fnl f: sn hung lft and kpt on wl towards fin* **11/2**[3]

0000 **4** *1* **Fol Hollow (IRE)**[14] 5944 5-9-2 **93** .... MichaelGeran(3) 11 96
(D Nicholls) *led: rdn 2f out: drvn over 1f out: hdd jst ins fnl f: one pce* **28/1**

3450 **5** *shd* **Haajes**[8] 6142 6-8-7 **84** .... PaulPickard(3) 6 86
(P T Midgley) *rt s and in rr: pushed along 1/2-way: swtchd lft and rdn wl over 1f out: styd on strly ins fnl f: nrst fin* **10/1**

0030 **6** *1 ¼* **Strike Up The Band**[21] 5742 7-8-13 **87** .... AdrianNicholls 2 85
(D Nicholls) *cl up: rdn 2f out and ev ch tl drvn ent fnl f and grad wknd* **14/1**

0504 **7** *shd* **Lucky Numbers (IRE)**[11] 6049 4-8-10 **87** .... JamesSullivan(3) 13 84
(Paul Green) *chsd ldrs: rdn along and sltly outpcd wl over 1f out: drvn and kpt on ins fnl f* **20/1**

6300 **8** *nse* **Noble Storm (USA)**[14] 5944 4-9-7 **95** .... StevieDonohoe 12 92
(E S McMahon) *prom: rdn along wl over 1f out: wknd ent fnl f* **14/1**

1040 **9** *¾* **Archers Road (IRE)**[21] 5742 3-9-5 **94** .... PhillipMakin 4 89
(T D Barron) *chsd ldrs: rdn along and edgd lft wl over 1f out: grad wknd* **28/1**

032 **10** *1 ¼* **Desert Phantom (USA)**[5] 6256 4-9-2 **90** .... WilliamBuick 8 80
(D M Simcock) *awkward and sltly hmpd s: rdn along in rr 1/2-way: nvr a factor* **9/2**[2]

5052 **11** *½* **Solemn**[11] 6064 5-8-11 **85** .... (b) DaneO'Neill 5 73
(J M Bradley) *chsd ldrs: rdn along wl over 1f out: sn one pce* **25/1**

4430 **12** *½* **Duchess Dora (IRE)**[14] 5944 3-9-0 **92** .... IanBrennan(3) 14 78
(J J Quinn) *dwlt: a towards rr* **16/1**

1201 **13** *¾* **Foxy Music**[14] 5941 6-9-0 **88** .... PatCosgrave 17 72
(E J Alston) *chsd ldrs: rdn along 2f out: grad wknd* **9/1**

3100 **14** *nk* **Walvis Bay (IRE)**[5] 6256 3-8-11 **86** .... MickyFenton 10 69
(T P Tate) *chsd ldrs: rdn along bef 1/2-way: sn wknd* **16/1**

0010 **15** *½* **Falasteen (IRE)**[11] 6048 3-8-10 **85** .... PaulHanagan 9 66
(R A Fahey) *a towards rr* **16/1**

1030 **16** *3 ½* **Whozthecat (IRE)**[14] 5967 3-8-13 **88** .... DavidNolan 16 56
(D Carroll) *chsd ldrs on wd outside: rdn along over 2f out and sn wknd* **33/1**

61.48 secs (0.48) **Going Correction** +0.325s/f (Good)
WFA 3 from 4yo+ 1lb **16** Ran SP% **126.8**
Speed ratings (Par 109): **109,108,106,104,104 102,102,102,101,99 98,97,96,95,95 89**
Tote Swingers: 1&2 £38.40, 1&3 £4.30, 2&3 £39.80 CSF £93.90 CT £479.43 TOTE £5.70: £2.10, £4.50, £2.00, £11.50; EX 160.00 TRIFECTA Not won..
Owner Mrs K Oseman **Bred** Miss K Rausing **Trained** Ullingswick, H'fords

FOCUS
Another useful sprint. There was predictably plenty of pace on, with the main action unfolding up the centre. Solid handicap form.

NOTEBOOK
Cheveton ◆ had gone up 7lb for Ayr but it still left him just 1lb above the mark he won off here 12 months ago, and he followed up with conditions very much in his favour, getting up on the line. He can't go up much for this and is sure to continue to be of interest, with the Coral Sprint, a race he was second in last year, the obvious next target. (op 11-2)
Hoof It quickly put Doncaster behind him, with the drop back to 5f very much in this speedy sort's favour. He's clearly equally as effective on testing ground and there's got to be the possibility of more to come given he's only three and is still relatively lightly raced as sprinters go. (tchd 18-1)
Hazelrigg(IRE)'s winning run came to an end, but this another good effort, arguably a little better than the bare result too as he found himself a bit wide of where the main action unfolded. He should continue to give a good account. (tchd 6-1)
Fol Hollow(IRE) ran his best race since finishing runner-up to Flipando on Derby day at Epsom, showing all his customary speed.
Haajes should be able to find weaker races than this from his current mark. (op 14-1)
Strike Up The Band wasn't discredited, but he couldn't be relied upon to build on this these days.
Noble Storm(USA) has been a bit disappointing this year given how promising he'd looked at three. (op 12-1)
Desert Phantom(USA) was entitled to be bang there given how well he'd run at Leicester earlier in the week, and perhaps he simply found a third run in quick succession since returning from a break too much as he was never going after a slowish start. Official explanation: trainer had no explanation for the poor form shown (tchd 7-2)
Foxy Music had dominated round the turns of Chester a couple of weeks ago but was always going to find this a different test and weakened out of it in the end. Official explanation: jockey said gelding hung left (op 8-1 tchd 10-1)

6365 E B F PREMIER STEEL STOCKHOLDING MAIDEN STKS 1m 30y

4:20 (4:21) (Class 5) 2-Y-O **£3,238** (£963; £481; £240) **Stalls** Low

Form RPR

33 **1** **Genius Beast (USA)**[16] 5878 2-9-0 0 .... AhmedAjtebi 1 89
(Mahmood Al Zarooni) *led 2f: cl up: hdwy to ld over 3f out: jnd and rdn 2f out: drvn over 1f out: kpt on gamely ins fnl f* **10/11**[1]

0 **2** *1* **Purification (IRE)**[106] 2932 2-9-0 0 .... WilliamBuick 6 87+
(J H M Gosden) *dwlt and towards rr: hdwy to trck ldrs over 4f out: rdn over 2f out: chsd wnr over 1f out: drvn to chal ins fnl f and ev ch tl no ex last 50yds* **6/1**[3]

3 *6* **Sadler's Risk (IRE)** 2-9-0 0 .... GregFairley 2 74+
(M Johnston) *towards rr: hdwy over 3f out: rdn along over 2f out: drvn over 1f out: kpt on ins fnl f: nrst fin* **11/1**

4 *3 ¼* **Indian Emperor (IRE)** 2-9-0 0 .... NeilCallan 10 67
(M A Jarvis) *trckd ldrs: hdwy 3f out: chal 2f out: sn rdn and ev ch tl wknd appr fnl f* **6/1**[3]

06 **5** *8* **Elysian Heights (IRE)**[9] 6128 2-9-0 0 .... DarryllHolland 5 49
(J Noseda) *in rr: hdwy over 3f out: green and rdn along 2f out: kpt on same pce* **28/1**

5534 **6** *2 ½* **Red Marling (IRE)**[29] 5472 2-9-0 75 .... PaulHanagan 8 44+
(B W Hills) *prom: rdn along 3f out: drvn over 2f out and grad wknd* **9/2**[2]

0 **7** *8* **William Wainwright (IRE)**[8] 6138 2-9-0 0 .... PatCosgrave 9 26
(Mrs A Duffield) *s.i.s: a in rr* **66/1**

05 **8** *12* **Ballinargh Boy**[11] 6046 2-9-0 0 .... AdrianNicholls 7 —
(R D Wylie) *t.k.h: hld up in tch tl rapid hdwy on outer to ld after 2f: rdn along and hdd over 3f out: sn drvn and wknd* **50/1**

0 **9** *3 ¼* **Inca Chief**[81] 3767 2-9-0 0 .... PaulMulrennan 3 —
(Mrs A Duffield) *a in rr: outpcd and bhd fnl 3f* **33/1**

0 **10** *1 ¼* **Ime Not Bitter**[11] 6045 2-8-7 0 .... MatthewMcGhee(7) 4 —
(C W Moore) *plld hrd: chsd ldrs: rdn along 1/2-way: sn wknd* **66/1**

1m 46.7s (2.00) **Going Correction** +0.10s/f (Good) **10** Ran SP% **118.8**
Speed ratings (Par 95): **94,93,87,83,75 73,65,53,50,48**
Tote Swingers: 1&2 £3.10, 1&3 £3.80, 2&3 £5.60 CSF £6.86 TOTE £1.90: £1.10, £2.20, £2.80; EX 6.60.
Owner Godolphin **Bred** Darley **Trained** Newmarket, Suffolk
■ Stewards' Enquiry : Ahmed Ajtebi one-day ban: used whip in incorrect place (Oct 9)

FOCUS
A fair-looking maiden run in bad ground. The winner matched his good pre-race form.

NOTEBOOK
Genius Beast(USA) had contested two of the hottest maidens this season prior to this and duly got off the mark at the third time of asking, though he did have to dig pretty deep to see off the runner-up. The winner's bred to be suited by further next year (dam Irish Oaks winner) and should continue to progress. (op Evens tchd 11-10 in places)
Purification(IRE) was well beaten on his debut back in June but proved a totally different proposition here, with his yard in much better form now. He still showed inexperience early on (missed break) but kept on to pull well clear of the remainder. The level of form he's shown here will be good enough to win most maidens, while there's clearly the prospect of even more to come after just two starts. (op 7-1 tchd 11-2)
Sadler's Risk(IRE), a Sadler's Wells colt, was green on debut but showed clear promise by the finish and, in excellent hands, can surely only go on from this. (op 12-1 tchd 14-1)
Indian Emperor(IRE), a gelded son of Araafa, was much better than the result on his debut, with this stamina test clearly too much for him at this stage of his career, having looked like posing the biggest threat to the winner over a furlong out. A drop to 7f will suit and he could leave this bare form well behind next time. (op 5-1 tchd 13-2)
Elysian Heights(IRE), held up, wasn't given an unduly hard time on his third start and it'll be surprise if he doesn't prove capable of better now being eligible for handicaps.
Red Marling(IRE) patently failed to stay the two-furlong longer trip and is better judged on earlier efforts. Official explanation: trainer's rep said colt was unsuited by the soft (heavy in home straight) ground (tchd 4-1 and 5-1)
Ballinargh Boy Official explanation: jockey said colt ran too free

6366 NEALES WASTE MANAGEMENT H'CAP (DIV I) 1m 30y

4:55 (4:56) (Class 4) (0-80,80) 3-Y-O+ **£4,533** (£1,348; £674; £336) **Stalls** Low

Form RPR

43/3 **1** **Amazing Star (IRE)**[29] 5500 5-8-8 **71** .... NeilFarley(7) 8 81+
(D Carroll) *hld up towards rr: hdwy over 3f out: trckd ldrs over 2f out: swtchd rt and rdn to ld over 1f out: drvn and edgd lft ins fnl f: kpt on wl towards fin* **11/2**[3]

0064 **2** *¾* **Zebrano**[18] 5838 4-9-2 **72** .... (b) StevieDonohoe 10 80
(A B Haynes) *hld up in rr: hdwy on outer over 2f out: rdn to chse ldrs over 1f out: drvn to chal ins fnl f: no ex last 75yds* **16/1**

0054 **3** *2 ¼* **Euston Square**[9] 6108 4-9-3 **73** .... (p) AdrianNicholls 4 76
(D Nicholls) *hld up: hdwy on outer 3f out: chal over 2f out: rdn to ld briefly over 1f out: sn hdd and edgd lft: one pce fnl f* **11/1**

0000 **4** *4* **Quanah Parker (IRE)**[30] 5435 4-9-2 **75** .... MichaelStainton(3) 6 69
(R M Whitaker) *trckd ldrs: hdwy over 3f out: rdn to ld briefly over 2f out: drvn and hdd wl over 1f out: grad wknd* **11/1**

3133 **5** *2* **Dabbers Ridge (IRE)**[9] 6112 8-9-4 **77** .... GaryBartley(3) 5 66
(I W McInnes) *dwlt and in rr: pushed along over 3f out: rdn and hdwy over 2f out: drvn and hung lft over 1f out: nvr rchd ldrs* **15/2**

0032 **6** *1 ¼* **Aquarian Spirit**[21] 5759 3-9-2 **76** .... PaulHanagan 7 62
(R A Fahey) *led: rdn along and hdd over 3f out: sn drvn and grad wknd* **3/1**[1]

4651 **7** *½* **William Van Gogh**[25] 5645 3-9-3 **77** .... (p) WilliamBuick 12 62
(J H M Gosden) *trckd ldrs: effrt on outer 3f out: rdn along wl over 2f out: grad wknd* **4/1**[2]

2040 **8** *5* **Game Lad**[14] 5937 8-9-10 **80** .... (tp) DavidAllan 3 54
(T D Easterby) *hld up in midfield: rdn along over 4f out: nvr a factor* **16/1**

030 **9** *2 ¼* **Miss Glitters (IRE)**[27] 5553 5-9-4 **74** .... TravisBlock 11 42
(H Morrison) *cl up: effrt to ld jst over 3f out: rdn and hdd over 2f out: sn drvn and wknd wl over 1f out* **9/1**

1003 **10** *3 ½* **Feeling Fresh (IRE)**[11] 6048 5-9-3 **73** .... PaulMulrennan 9 33
(Paul Green) *hld up: a towards rr* **16/1**

6030 **11** *11* **Arrivederla (IRE)**[22] 5739 4-9-10 **80** .... NeilCallan 2 15
(H J L Dunlop) *chsd ldrs on inner: rdn along over 3f out: sn wknd* **20/1**

1m 47.11s (2.41) **Going Correction** +0.10s/f (Good)
WFA 3 from 4yo+ 4lb **11** Ran SP% **121.2**
Speed ratings (Par 105): **91,90,88,84,82 80,80,75,73,69 58**
Tote Swingers: 1&2 £18.60, 1&3 £8.90, 2&3 £16.40 CSF £92.69 CT £969.75 TOTE £7.90: £2.50, £5.30, £3.80; EX 192.10.
Owner Kevin McConnell **Bred** Glending Bloodstock **Trained** Sledmere, E Yorks

FOCUS
A fair handicap which was run at a sound pace, but the time was slow compared to division I. The form is rated around the second and third.
William Van Gogh Official explanation: trainer's rep said colt was unsuited by the soft (heavy in home straight) ground
Feeling Fresh(IRE) Official explanation: trainer's rep said horse was unsuited by the soft (heavy in home straight) ground

6367 PRINCE'S TRUST H'CAP (DIV II OF 4.55) 1m 30y

5:30 (5:37) (Class 4) (0-80,80) 3-Y-O+ **£4,533** (£1,348; £674; £336) **Stalls** Low

Form RPR

0100 **1** **Scrapper Smith (IRE)**[9] 6107 4-8-9 **72** .... GarryWhillans(7) 10 85
(A C Whillans) *hld up and bhd: hdwy over 3f out: trckd ldng pair over 1f out: swtchd rt and rdn ent fnl f: styd on strly to ld last 50yds* **16/1**

4105 **2** *1 ½* **Amethyst Dawn (IRE)**[13] 6003 4-9-6 **76** .... DavidAllan 9 86
(T D Easterby) *trckd ldrs: hdwy on wd outside to ld 3f out: rdn and hdd wl over 1f out: drvn and rallied to ld again ins fnl f: hdd and no ex last 50yds* **14/1**

331 **3** *1 ½* **Tariq Too**[12] 6039 3-9-1 **75** .... WilliamBuick 4 82+
(D M Simcock) *dwlt and towards rr: smooth hdwy 3f out: rdn to ld over 1f out: drvn and hdd ins fnl f: one pce* **4/1**[1]

1262	4	4	**Miss Bootylishes**[28] 5541 5-9-0 75 ... AmyBaker(5) 8 (A B Haynes) *trckd ldrs: hdwy and cl up over 3f out: rdn and ev ch over 2f out: drvn and one pce appr fnl f* **10/1**	72
121	5	2 1/4	**Frontline Girl (IRE)**[29] 5486 4-9-3 73 ... AndrewElliott 12 (Mrs K Burke) *hld up: hdwy 4f out: rdn to chse ldrs over 2f out: sn drvn and no imp appr fnl f* **7/1**[2]	65
4020	6	3	**Exit Smiling**[15] 5919 8-9-7 80 ... PaulPickard(3) 6 (P T Midgley) *trckd ldrs on inner: rdn along 3f out: sn drvn and wknd 2f out* **7/1**[2]	65
1606	7	2 1/2	**Trans Sonic**[29] 5500 7-8-11 72 ... DaleSwift(5) 7 (D O'Meara) *chsd ldrs: led after 2f: rdn along and hdd 3f out: sn drvn and grad wknd* **10/1**	52
0005	8	3	**Bond City (IRE)**[26] 5601 8-9-5 78 ... BarryMcHugh(3) 3 (G R Oldroyd) *a towards rr* **20/1**	51
1114	9	14	**One Scoop Or Two**[14] 5937 4-9-1 74 ... RussKennemore(3) 2 (R Hollinshead) *led 2f: cl up on inner: rdn along 3f out: sn wknd* **4/1**[1]	14
5035	10	3 1/4	**Wigwam Willie (IRE)**[9] 6105 8-9-0 70 ...(tp) PaulMulrennan 11 (K A Ryan) *hld up towards rr: hdwy and in tch 3f out: rdn over 2f out and sn wknd* **9/1**[3]	—
1005	11	5	**Rio Cobolo (IRE)**[11] 6048 4-9-3 73 ...(v) PaulHanagan 5 (Paul Green) *a towards rr: effrt over 3f out: sn rdn along and outpcd: bhd fnl 2f* **16/1**	—
0000	12	1 1/4	**Jack Dawkins (USA)**[25] 5638 5-9-2 72 ... AdrianNicholls 1 (D Nicholls) *a in rr* **16/1**	—

1m 45.89s (1.19) **Going Correction** +0.10s/f (Good)
WFA 3 from 4yo+ 4lb 12 Ran SP% **122.3**
Speed ratings (Par 105): **98,96,95,91,88 85,83,80,66,63 58,56**
Tote Swingers: 1&2 £48.90, 1&3 £18.00, 2&3 £14.80 CSF £228.98 CT £1097.30 TOTE £20.60: £4.50, £5.60, £1.50; EX 284.90 Place 6: £85.79, Place 5: £68.50..
Owner A C Whillans **Bred** John Costello **Trained** Newmill-On-Slitrig, Borders

FOCUS
The second division of this handicap was very much set up for those coming from off the pace, with the leaders going hard under the conditions. The time compared favourably with the first division and the form looks sound.
One Scoop Or Two Official explanation: trainer's rep said gelding was unsuited by the soft (heavy in home straight) ground
T/Jkpt: Not won. T/Plt: £79.30 to a £1 stake. Pool:£104,037 - 956.65 winning tickets T/Qpdt: £8.60 to a £1 stake. Pool:£5,042 - 433.45 winning tickets JR

6329 WOLVERHAMPTON (A.W) (L-H)
Saturday, September 25

OFFICIAL GOING: Standard changing to standard to fast after race 3 (6.35)
Wind: Fresh across, becoming lighter race 3 onwards Weather: Cloudy with sunny spells

6368 BREEDERS' CUP LIVE ONLY ON ATR CLAIMING STKS — 5f 20y(P)
5:35 (5:39) (Class 5) 3-Y-0+ £2,456 (£725; £362) Stalls Low

Form				RPR
1440	1		**Six Diamonds**[33] 5356 3-8-4 77 ... NickyMackay 1 (H Morrison) *sn led: rdn ins fnl f: jst hld on* **11/4**[2]	75
023	2	hd	**Elhamri**[3] 6284 6-8-8 67 ... LiamKeniry 5 (S Kirk) *chsd wnr: rdn over 1f out: r.o* **13/2**	77
0046	3	3/4	**Green Manalishi**[35] 5297 9-9-10 93 ...(tp) PhillipMakin 6 (K A Ryan) *chsd ldrs: rdn over 1f out: r.o* **5/1**[3]	90
0400	4	2 1/4	**Abraham Lincoln (IRE)**[16] 5884 6-8-10 82 ...(p) LukeMorris 3 (R A Harris) *chsd ldrs: rdn over 1f out: no ex ins fnl f* **15/8**[1]	68
0330	5	1	**Little Edward**[11] 6057 12-8-8 67 ... SamHitchcott 2 (R J Hodges) *s.i.s: hld up: rdn 1/2-way: nvr on terms* **9/1**	63
040-	6	2 1/2	**Excelling (IRE)**[365] 6241 3-8-4 83 ...(p) CathyGannon 8 (P J Makin) *dwlt: rdn 1/2-way: a in rr* **9/1**	51

60.65 secs (-1.65) **Going Correction** -0.175s/f (Stan)
WFA 3 from 5yo+ 1lb 6 Ran SP% **111.4**
Speed ratings (Par 103): **106,105,104,100,99 95**
toteswingers: 1&2 £4.60, 1&3 £3.00, 2&3 £5.90. CSF £19.99 TOTE £3.60: £1.70, £4.20; EX 24.00.
Owner A J Struthers And Mrs Julia Scott **Bred** Mrs S F Dibben **Trained** East Ilsley, Berks

FOCUS
Not a bad claimer, but the form is unreliable with the first pair always 1-2. The race is rated around the winner.
Excelling(IRE) Official explanation: jockey said filly never travelled

6369 ATTHERACES.COM/BREEDERSCUP MEDIAN AUCTION MAIDEN STKS — 5f 20y(P)
6:05 (6:09) (Class 6) 2-Y-0 £2,047 (£604; £302) Stalls Low

Form				RPR
634	1		**Key Lago (IRE)**[31] 5418 2-9-3 72 ...(p) PhillipMakin 4 (M Dods) *s.i.s: hdwy 1/2-way: rdn to ld and edgd lft wl ins fnl f* **9/4**[2]	75
322	2	shd	**Insolenceofoffice (IRE)**[7] 6182 2-9-0 72 ... MatthewDavies(3) 11 (Mrs A Duffield) *chsd ldrs: rdn 1/2-way: led over 1f out: hung lft and hdd wl ins fnl f* **7/2**[3]	74
0	3	5	**Arabella Fenella**[29] 5466 2-8-12 0 ... HayleyTurner 10 (R M H Cowell) *hld up: hdwy 1/2-way: rdn over 1f out: styd on same pce fnl f: wnt 3rd towards fin* **20/1**	51
50	4	nk	**Majestic Ridge (IRE)**[53] 4678 2-9-3 0 ... LukeMorris 1 (R A Harris) *chsd ldr: rdn over 2f out: no ex fnl f* **100/1**	55
2000	5	nk	**Bendigedig**[10] 6072 2-8-12 49 ... LiamKeniry 9 (S Kirk) *led: rdn and hdd over 1f out: no ex fnl f* **66/1**	49
06	6	shd	**Kingfisher Blue (IRE)**[19] 5808 2-9-0 0 ... SophieDoyle(3) 2 (J A Osborne) *chsd ldrs: rdn over 1f out: styd on same pce* **18/1**	54+
50	7	5	**Thatstheone**[11] 6046 2-8-7 0 ... BillyCray(5) 6 (C W Moore) *in rr: rdn over 1f out: n.d* **100/1**	31
3	8	1	**Heart In Motion (IRE)**[8] 6161 2-8-12 0 ... SamHitchcott 8 (M R Channon) *sn outpcd: hdwy 1/2-way: rdn and wknd over 1f out* **15/8**[1]	27
	9	4 1/2	**Tough Customer** 2-9-3 0 ... VinceSlattery 5 (G Brown) *s.s: outpcd* **66/1**	16
0	10	2	**Grey Steel (IRE)**[19] 5808 2-9-0 0 ... EJMcNamara(3) 3 (Denis P Quinn, Ire) *trckd ldrs: plld hrd: hung rt over 3f out: sn wknd* **50/1**	9
0	11	3 1/2	**Maureens Litlun (IRE)**[24] 5657 2-8-12 0 ... NickyMackay 12 (M Wigham) *prom: carried rt and lost pl over 3f out: sn bhd* **100/1**	—

61.97 secs (-0.33) **Going Correction** -0.175s/f (Stan) 11 Ran SP% **105.7**
Speed ratings (Par 93): **95,94,86,86,85 85,77,76,68,65 60**
toteswingers: 1&2 £1.70, 1&3 £7.40, 2&3 £7.30. CSF £7.89 TOTE £2.70: £1.10, £1.10, £4.90; EX 11.40.
Owner Andrew Tinkler **Bred** Victor Stud Bloodstock Ltd **Trained** Denton, Co Durham
■ Sailing North (9/2) was withdrawn after proving unruly in the stalls. R4 applies.

FOCUS
A moderate juvenile maiden in which the first two pulled clear, producing decent efforts.
NOTEBOOK
Key Lago(IRE) hadn't found much for pressure when beaten at Catterick (form which has worked out very well), but, with the assistance of cheekpieces this time, he found enough having travelled strongly to get up close home and nab Insolenceofoffice. (op 11-4 tchd 3-1)
Insolenceofoffice(IRE) looked like he was going to make it fourth time lucky entering the final furlong but was collared late on. The drop back to 5f proved no problem and, having pulled five lengths clear of the remainder, he shouldn't be long in getting off the mark. (op 3-1 tchd 4-1)
Arabella Fenella stepped up on her debut effort and kept on in a manner which suggests she'll be seen to better effect when upped in trip. (op 16-1)
Majestic Ridge(IRE) posted a career-best effort on this AW debut and is now eligible for a mark.
Heart In Motion(IRE) was well backed to build on a promising first run over 6f. However, the drop back to 5f proved her undoing as she was always struggling to go the gallop and dropped away having been forced wide. It's probably best to forgive her this. (op 5-2)
Grey Steel(IRE) Official explanation: jockey said gelding hung right
Maureens Litlun(IRE) Official explanation: jockey said filly hung right

6370 TICANCHILLED.CO.UK H'CAP (DIV I) — 7f 32y(P)
6:35 (6:36) (Class 5) (0-70,69) 3-Y-0+ £2,115 (£624; £312) Stalls High

Form				RPR
0001	1		**Not My Choice (IRE)**[7] 6188 5-9-3 65 ...(t) JohnEgan 2 (D C Griffiths) *mde all: rdn over 1f out: styd on wl* **13/2**	76
5231	2	2	**Perfect Friend**[7] 6210 4-9-7 69 ... RichardHughes 9 (S Kirk) *a.p: chsd wnr over 2f out: rdn over 1f out: no imp ins fnl f* **11/4**[1]	75
6033	3	1	**Just Jimmy (IRE)**[9] 6133 5-8-9 62 ... AdamBeschizza(5) 7 (P D Evans) *chsd wnr tl rdn over 2f out: styd on same pce ins fnl f* **7/1**	65
5000	4	nse	**Unlimited**[17] 5867 8-8-8 61 ... KierenFox(5) 5 (A W Carroll) *chsd ldrs: rdn over 2f out: styd on* **16/1**	64
5005	5	1 1/2	**Charles Parnell (IRE)**[15] 5920 7-8-13 64 ... MichaelStainton(3) 6 (S P Griffiths) *hld up: hdwy u.p over 1f out: nt rch ldrs* **16/1**	63
4622	6	1 1/2	**Just Timmy Marcus**[7] 6210 4-9-3 65 ...(b) CathyGannon 1 (B P J Baugh) *s.i.s: hld up: rdn over 1f out: nvr nrr* **7/2**[2]	60
2000	7	nse	**Rubenstar (IRE)**[8] 6164 7-9-6 68 ... StephenCraine 8 (Patrick Morris) *hld up in tch: rdn fnl f: no rspnse* **50/1**	63
53	8	shd	**One Hit Wonder**[99] 3154 3-8-10 61 ... DaneO'Neill 10 (Mouse Hamilton-Fairley) *s.i.s: hld up: rdn over 2f out: nrst fin* **6/1**[3]	55
-006	9	nk	**Abriachan**[14] 5964 3-9-2 67 ... WilliamCarson 3 (M G Quinlan) *hld up: rdn over 2f out: hung lft over 1f out: n.d* **16/1**	60
6650	10	1/2	**Fazza**[21] 5769 3-9-4 69 ... LiamKeniry 12 (D W P Arbuthnot) *hld up in tch: rdn over 2f out: wknd fnl f* **22/1**	61
5000	11	2 3/4	**Istiqdaam**[20] 5789 5-8-12 67 ...(b) DavidSimmonson(7) 11 (M W Easterby) *s.i.s: a in rr* **14/1**	52

1m 28.05s (-1.55) **Going Correction** -0.175s/f (Stan)
WFA 3 from 4yo+ 3lb 11 Ran SP% **119.6**
Speed ratings (Par 103): **101,98,97,97,95 94,94,93,93,93 89**
toteswingers: 1&2 £3.80, 1&3 £8.10, 2&3 £7.40. CSF £25.11 CT £134.89 TOTE £17.10: £3.20, £1.10, £2.80; EX 20.40.
Owner D Kilpatrick W McKay **Bred** Alan Dargan **Trained** Bawtry, S Yorks

FOCUS
An ordinary handicap and another race where it paid to race handily, with the front pair always 1-2. It was run in a quicker time than division II and the winner showed his best form since he was a 3yo.

6371 TICANCHILLED.CO.UK H'CAP (DIV II) — 7f 32y(P)
7:05 (7:06) (Class 5) (0-70,68) 3-Y-0+ £2,115 (£624; £312) Stalls High

Form				RPR
3553	1		**Smart Endeavour (USA)**[22] 5710 4-9-4 65 ...(v) AdamKirby 2 (W R Swinburn) *chsd ldrs: rdn to ld ins fnl f: r.o* **5/2**[1]	76+
1213	2	2 1/2	**Pipers Piping (IRE)**[5] 6261 4-8-10 60 ...(p) MichaelStainton(3) 6 (P Howling) *hld up: hdwy over 1f out: swtchd rt ins fnl f: r.o to go 2nd post: nt rch wnr* **3/1**[2]	64
R-0	3	shd	**The Winged Assasin (USA)**[26] 5584 4-9-5 66 ... NickyMackay 5 (M Wigham) *prom: rdn over 1f out: styd on same pce ins fnl f: lost 2nd post* **14/1**	70
0521	4	1/2	**Darcey**[23] 5698 4-9-4 68 ... IanBrennan(3) 11 (Miss Amy Weaver) *hld up: hung lft and r.o ins fnl f: nrst fin* **15/2**	71+
1200	5	3/4	**Annes Rocket (IRE)**[48] 4870 5-8-13 60 ... RichardHughes 4 (J C Fox) *s.s: hld up: swtchd lft and r.o ins fnl f: nt trble ldrs* **7/1**[3]	61+
0303	6	shd	**Liberty Trail (IRE)**[21] 5764 4-8-11 58 ... CathyGannon 8 (P D Evans) *led early: chsd ldr: rdn to ld over 1f out: hdd and no ex ins fnl f* **12/1**	58
1426	7	2	**Cawdor (IRE)**[71] 4084 4-9-4 68 ... JamesSullivan(3) 9 (Mrs L Stubbs) *chsd ldrs: rdn over 1f out: styd on same pce* **25/1**	63
0200	8	1/2	**Adam De Beaulieu (USA)**[127] 2274 3-9-3 67 ...(t) PhillipMakin 10 (B M R Haslam) *hld up: rdn over 1f out: styd on ins fnl f: nvr nrr* **12/1**	61
0406	9	3/4	**Fol Liam**[21] 5768 4-9-3 64 ...(p) JamesDoyle 7 (A J McCabe) *hld up: hdwy 2f out: sn rdn: styd on same pce* **14/1**	56
-000	10	shd	**Kai Mook**[17] 5866 3-9-4 68 ... SteveDrowne 1 (Miss Olivia Maylam) *sn led: rdn and hdd over 1f out: wknd ins fnl f* **40/1**	59
3000	11	nk	**Whipma Whopma Gate (IRE)**[20] 5786 5-8-8 62 ...(v) NeilFarley(7) 3 (D Carroll) *mid-div: rdn over 2f out: hdwy over 1f out: wknd ins fnl f* **12/1**	53
0440	12	3 1/2	**Nacho Libre**[15] 5920 5-8-9 63 ...(b) DavidSimmonson(7) 12 (M W Easterby) *hld up: hdwy 3f out: rdn and wknd over 1f out* **20/1**	44

1m 28.54s (-1.06) **Going Correction** -0.175s/f (Stan)
WFA 3 from 4yo+ 3lb 12 Ran SP% **125.3**
Speed ratings (Par 103): **99,96,96,95,94 94,92,91,90,90 90,86**
toteswingers: 1&2 £2.20, 1&3 £14.80, 2&3 £4.90. CSF £10.21 CT £92.77 TOTE £4.20: £2.20, £1.50, £4.60; EX 7.80.
Owner The Lamplighters **Bred** Silverleaf Farms Inc **Trained** Aldbury, Herts
■ Stewards' Enquiry : Adam Kirby caution: careless riding.

FOCUS
The second division of the 7f handicap was another modest affair and it was slower than the first. The runner-up is a pretty solid guide.

6372 TICAN 10TH ANNIVERSARY CELEBRATION H'CAP — 1m 141y(P)
7:35 (7:36) (Class 5) (0-75,75) 3-Y-0+ £2,456 (£725; £362) Stalls Low

Form				RPR
-216	1		**Mazamorra (USA)**[71] 4098 3-9-3 73 ... ChrisCatlin 1 (M Botti) *a.p: chsd ldr over 2f out: led over 1f out: styd on wl* **15/2**	87
3110	2	3 1/4	**Whispering Spirit (IRE)**[13] 6003 4-9-8 73 ...(v) PhillipMakin 11 (Mrs A Duffield) *prom: rdn and ev ch fr over 1f out tl no ex wl ins fnl f* **16/1**	80
-052	3	2	**Becuille (IRE)**[43] 5039 5-9-4 69 ...(b) RichardHughes 7 (B J Meehan) *prom: rdn and lost pl 1/2-way: rallied over 1f out: styd on* **15/2**	71

416/ **4** 2 3/4 **Prairie Tiger (GER)**[1065] 6474 6-9-9 **74** RichardKingscote 4 70
(Tom Dascombe) *s.i.s: pushed along and hdwy into mid-div over 6f out: rdn over 2f out: styd on: nt trble ldrs* **9/2**[2]

1001 **5** 1 1/4 **Glenridding**[14] 5937 6-9-10 **75** (p) PaulMulrennan 9 68
(J G Given) *led: clr 3f out: rdn and hdd over 1f out: wknd ins fnl f* **15/2**

5026 **6** nk **Rascal In The Mix (USA)**[21] 5756 4-8-12 **66** (p) AmyRyan(3) 3 58
(R M Whitaker) *hld up: hdwy over 2f out: no imp fr over 1f out* **14/1**

0506 **7** 2 **Justcallmehandsome**[24] 5655 8-9-0 **70** (v) BillyCray(5) 8 57
(D J S Ffrench Davis) *hld up: rdn over 1f out: nvr on terms* **18/1**

464 **8** 1 1/2 **Marsh Warbler**[23] 5680 3-9-0 **73** MartinLane(3) 6 57
(D M Simcock) *sn pushed along and a in rr* **7/1**[3]

1554 **9** 5 **Kipchak (IRE)**[17] 5866 5-9-1 **66** (p) LiamKeniry 5 38
(C R Dore) *prom: chsd ldr over 6f out to over 3f out: wknd 2f out* **10/1**

-541 **10** 3/4 **Mr Money Maker**[26] 5584 3-9-0 **73** RussKennemore(3) 10 44
(J L Flint) *chsd ldr to over 6f out: wnt 2nd again over 3f out to over 2f out: wknd over 1f out* **7/2**[1]

00-0 **11** 10 **Addikt (IRE)**[43] 5039 5-9-0 **65** LeeVickers 13 13
(H J Evans) *s.i.s: a in rr* **66/1**

-000 **12** 1 1/2 **Alpen Glen**[26] 5611 4-9-5 **70** JohnEgan 12 14
(John Berry) *mid-div: rdn over 4f out: wknd wl over 2f out* **25/1**

600 **13** 11 **Calahonda**[17] 5866 4-9-0 **70** (e) JohnFahy(5) 2 —
(P W D'Arcy) *rdr removed hood sltly late and missed break: a in rr: lost tch fr over 3f out: t.o* **9/1**

1m 47.74s (-2.76) **Going Correction** -0.175s/f (Stan)
WFA 3 from 4yo+ 5lb 13 Ran SP% **130.4**
Speed ratings (Par 103): **105,102,100,97,96 96,94,93,88,88 79,78,68**
toteswingers: 1&2 £39.60, 1&3 £17.00, 2&3 £19.20. CSF £133.11 CT £989.60 TOTE £6.40: £1.70, £10.80, £2.10; EX 211.30.
Owner J Barton & C Pizarro **Bred** Sarah S Farish **Trained** Newmarket, Suffolk
■ Stewards' Enquiry : John Egan one-day ban: careless riding (Oct 9)

FOCUS
A strong-run handicap though again pace held up well. Fair form for the grade with a clear personal best from the winner.
Mr Money Maker Official explanation: jockey said gelding hung right throughout
Calahonda Official explanation: jockey said filly lost its noseband

6373 BREEDERS' CUP LIVE ONLY ON ATR H'CAP 2m 119y(P)
8:05 (8:06) (Class 6) (0-65,65) 3-Y-0+ **£1,774** (£523; £262) **Stalls** Low

Form RPR

3305 **1** **Snowberry Hill (USA)**[4] 6272 7-8-8 **48** ow1 RussKennemore(3) 7 60
(Lucinda Featherstone) *hood removed late and slowly away: hld up: hdwy over 2f out: rdn to ld over 1f out: styd on wl* **8/1**[3]

1051 **2** 2 **Al Shababiya (IRE)**[24] 5653 3-8-13 **65** MartinLane(3) 4 75
(D M Simcock) *hld up: hdwy over 5f out: rdn to chse wnr and hung lft ins fnl f: styd on* **4/1**[1]

1101 **3** 4 1/2 **Bute Street**[9] 6121 5-9-10 **61** GeorgeBaker 13 65
(R J Hodges) *chsd ldrs: led 1/2-way: rdn and hdd over 1f out: sn hung rt: no ex fnl f* **4/1**[1]

0054 **4** nse **Carnac (IRE)**[12] 6033 4-9-1 **52** JamesDoyle 2 56
(A J McCabe) *hld up in tch: chsd ldr 5f out: rdn over 3f out: styng on same pce whn hmpd over 1f out* **10/1**

2143 **5** 1 1/4 **Bright Sparky (GER)**[9] 6121 7-8-9 **49** (bt) JamesSullivan(3) 6 52
(M W Easterby) *hld up: rdn 5f out: hdwy over 2f out: styd on same pce* **14/1**

5114 **6** 3 **Ballade De La Mer**[38] 5202 4-8-12 **49** (p) LNewman 9 48
(A G Foster) *chsd ldrs: pushed along 7f out: wknd over 1f out* **25/1**

3-5 **7** nk **Torina (IRE)**[32] 5403 5-10-0 **65** RichardHughes 5 64
(M J Grassick, Ire) *s.i.s: hld up: rdn and edgd lft over 1f out: nvr on terms* **11/2**[2]

4343 **8** 4 **Tigress Hill**[10] 6084 3-9-0 **63** PatDobbs 12 57
(Mrs A J Perrett) *w ldr to 1/2-way: remained handy: rdn and wknd over 2f out* **16/1**

5230 **9** hd **Pearl (IRE)**[121] 2476 6-8-10 **47** (t) JimmyQuinn 11 41
(Mrs A M Thorpe) *s.i.s: hld up and a in rr* **16/1**

2602 **10** nk **Jewellery (IRE)**[19] 5811 3-8-11 **60** PatCosgrave 3 53
(J R Fanshawe) *chsd ldrs tl rdn and wknd 3f out* **8/1**[3]

1203 **11** 2 3/4 **Bedarra Boy**[9] 6120 4-9-0 **51** LiamKeniry 1 41
(D W P Arbuthnot) *chsd ldrs: rdn over 3f out: wknd over 2f out* **16/1**

0641 **12** 22 **Deejan (IRE)**[29] 5468 5-9-4 **60** DeclanCannon(5) 8 24
(B Palling) *led to 1/2-way: wknd 4f out: t.o* **8/1**[3]

3m 39.22s (-2.58) **Going Correction** -0.175s/f (Stan)
WFA 3 from 4yo+ 12lb 12 Ran SP% **126.0**
Speed ratings (Par 101): **99,98,95,95,95 93,93,91,91,91 90,80**
toteswingers: 1&2 £12.50, 1&3 £6.20, 2&3 £5.10. CSF £42.61 CT £154.40 TOTE £21.30: £6.90, £1.10, £1.20; EX 89.20.
Owner J Roundtree **Bred** Russell S Fisher And Joe Sagginario **Trained** Atlow, Derbyshire

FOCUS
A moderate handicap, run at a fair pace. The winner is rated back to his form of this time last year.
Bute Street Official explanation: jockey said gelding hung right
Carnac(IRE) Official explanation: jockey said gelding hung left
Torina(IRE) Official explanation: jockey said mare hung left
Deejan(IRE) Official explanation: jockey said mare hung left

6374 CORAL TV H'CAP 5f 20y(P)
8:35 (8:37) (Class 4) (0-85,85) 3-Y-0+ **£4,209** (£1,252; £625; £312) **Stalls** Low

Form RPR

5030 **1** **Drawnfromthepast (IRE)**[14] 5967 5-9-4 **85** SophieDoyle(3) 13 94
(J A Osborne) *a.p: rdn to ld wl ins fnl f: r.o* **10/1**

0503 **2** 1/2 **Triple Dream**[15] 5915 5-8-8 **72** (p) LiamKeniry 11 79
(J M Bradley) *chsd ldrs: rdn and ev ch 1f out: edgd lft: r.o* **14/1**

-110 **3** 3/4 **Fair Passion**[165] 1281 3-8-10 **75** JimmyQuinn 5 80+
(D Shaw) *mid-div: hdwy over 1f out: r.o: wnt 3rd post: nt rch ldrs* **10/1**

000- **4** nse **Toms Laughter**[271] 7862 6-9-7 **85** (t) CathyGannon 10 89+
(D H Brown) *s.i.s: hld up: hdwy over 1f out: r.o: nt rch ldrs* **16/1**

0600 **5** hd **Rievaulx World**[35] 5297 4-8-11 **75** StephenCraine 6 79
(K A Ryan) *trckd ldrs: rdn to ld 1f out: hdd and unable qck wl ins fnl f* **14/1**

2110 **6** 1 1/2 **Fantasy Fighter (IRE)**[8] 6167 5-8-4 **73** AdamBeschizza(5) 2 71
(J J Quinn) *s.i.s: hld up: r.o ins fnl f: nrst fin* **7/2**[1]

1200 **7** 3/4 **Sir Geoffrey (IRE)**[8] 6140 4-8-12 **76** (b) ChrisCatlin 4 72
(J A Glover) *led: clr 2f out: hung rt over 1f out: sn hdd and no ex* **12/1**

0310 **8** 1/2 **Cut The Cackle (IRE)**[10] 6085 4-8-11 **75** (be[1]) RichardHughes 3 69
(D Flood) *mid-div: sn drvn along: nvr trbld ldrs* **9/1**

0006 **9** nk **Wigram's Turn (USA)**[22] 5716 5-8-11 **78** JamesSullivan(3) 9 71
(M W Easterby) *s.i.s: hld up: nvr on terms* **6/1**[3]

5000 **10** nk **Canadian Danehill (IRE)**[11] 6064 8-8-9 **73** (p) HayleyTurner 12 65
(R M H Cowell) *hld up: rdn over 1f out: n.d* **25/1**

0604 **11** hd **Ivory Silk**[22] 5731 5-9-4 **82** (b) SteveDrowne 7 73
(J R Gask) *sn pushed along and a in rr* **4/1**[2]

0000 **12** 6 **Hoh Hoh Hoh**[14] 5967 8-8-5 **72** (vt[1]) AndrewHeffernan(3) 1 41
(R J Price) *chsd ldr tl rdn 2f out: wknd over 1f out* **10/1**

60.84 secs (-1.46) **Going Correction** -0.175s/f (Stan)
WFA 3 from 4yo+ 1lb 12 Ran SP% **124.5**
Speed ratings (Par 105): **104,103,102,101,101 99,98,97,96,96 95,86**
toteswingers: 1&2 £32.60, 1&3 £31.00, 2&3 £16.40. CSF £149.17 CT £1479.87 TOTE £12.00: £3.40, £5.20, £2.70; EX 314.70.
Owner H R H Prince of Saxe-Weimar **Bred** D And Mrs D Veitch **Trained** Upper Lambourn, Berks
■ Stewards' Enquiry : Chris Catlin two-day ban: careless riding (Oct 9-10)

FOCUS
A fair handicap, run at a strong pace, and there was a bunched finish. The winner matched his best post-2yo form.
Cut The Cackle(IRE) Official explanation: vet said filly was struck into

6375 DINE IN THE HORIZONS H'CAP 1m 1f 103y(P)
9:05 (9:06) (Class 6) (0-60,60) 3-Y-0+ **£1,774** (£523; £262) **Stalls** Low

Form RPR

1350 **1** **Highland Love**[28] 5515 5-9-5 **57** TonyCulhane 11 62
(Jedd O'Keeffe) *chsd ldr: rdn over 1f out: edgd lft and led wl ins fnl f: r.o* **25/1**

0505 **2** 1/2 **Bentley**[11] 6054 6-8-12 **57** NeilFarley(7) 9 61
(B P J Baugh) *led: pushed along over 1f out: hdd wl ins fnl f* **25/1**

0360 **3** 1 **Joinedupwriting**[3] 6298 5-9-6 **58** PaulMulrennan 5 60
(R M Whitaker) *chsd ldrs: rdn over 1f out: r.o* **20/1**

6364 **4** 1 **Lunar River (FR)**[9] 6125 7-8-11 **54** (t) KierenFox(5) 2 54+
(David Pinder) *broke wl: n.m.r and lost pl after 1f: hdwy over 3f out: rdn over 1f out: r.o* **8/1**

1431 **5** hd **Pattern Mark**[23] 5704 4-9-1 **56** (p) BarryMcHugh(3) 7 55+
(Ollie Pears) *hld up: hdwy u.p over 1f out: nt rch ldrs* **2/1**[1]

3263 **6** 2 1/4 **Gallego**[23] 5689 8-9-2 **54** GeorgeBaker 13 49
(R J Price) *s.s: swtchd lft sn after s: hld up: plld hrd: hdwy over 1f out: nvr trbld ldrs* **7/1**[3]

5002 **7** shd **Bold Marc (IRE)**[9] 6117 8-9-2 **59** (p) DaleSwift(5) 12 54
(Mrs K Burke) *hld up: racd keenly: r.o ins fnl f: nrst fin* **8/1**

-000 **8** nk **Lunar Limelight**[107] 2894 5-9-5 **57** RichardHughes 1 51
(P J Makin) *mid-div: hdwy over 2f out: sn rdn: no ex fnl f* **3/1**[2]

5-0 **9** 1 3/4 **Zagarock**[26] 5584 3-9-2 **59** (v[1]) LukeMorris 8 49
(B Palling) *s.i.s: hld up: rdn over 3f out: a in rr* **40/1**

5106 **10** 3/4 **Tomintoul Star**[21] 5766 4-9-2 **57** JamesSullivan(3) 3 46
(Mrs R A Carr) *mid-div: hdwy over 5f out: rdn and wknd over 1f out* **14/1**

6-61 **11** 2 **Ptolomeos**[27] 5565 7-9-0 **59** IanBurns(7) 6 43
(S Regan) *hld up: hdwy over 2f out: wkng whn rdr dropped reins over 1f out* **14/1**

03-0 **12** 30 **Richelieu**[18] 5843 8-9-8 **60** (bt[1]) JohnEgan 4 —
(J J Lambe, Ire) *chsd ldrs tl wknd over 2f out: virtually p.u ins fnl f* **33/1**

2m 1.44s (-0.26) **Going Correction** -0.175s/f (Stan)
WFA 3 from 4yo+ 5lb 12 Ran SP% **124.2**
Speed ratings (Par 101): **94,93,92,91,91 89,89,89,87,87 85,58**
toteswingers: 1&2 £123.20, 1&3 £72.90, 2&3 £118.30. CSF £537.15 CT £12036.58 TOTE £59.30: £11.30, £13.80, £8.90; EX 791.40 Place 6: £120.70, Place 5: £48.47..
Owner John & Susan Robertson **Bred** Farmers Hill Stud **Trained** Middleham Moor, N Yorks

FOCUS
A weak handicap, run at a modest pace. The front pair were always 1-2 and the form is rated around the winner.
Richelieu Official explanation: vet said gelding finished distressed
T/Plt: £91.60 to a £1 stake. Pool:£62,815.11 - 500.25 winning tickets. T/Qpdt: £17.40 to a £1 stake. Pool:£10,165.10 - 431.40 winning tickets. CR

6376 - 6378a (Foreign Racing) - See Raceform Interactive

4973 GOWRAN PARK (R-H)
Saturday, September 25

OFFICIAL GOING: Yielding

6379a DENNY CORDELL LAVARACK & LANWADES STUD FILLIES STKS (GROUP 3) 1m 1f 100y
3:50 (3:51) 3-Y-0+ **£46,017** (£13,451; £6,371; £2,123)

RPR

1 **Shareen (IRE)**[27] 5568 3-8-11 100 NGMcCullagh 4 103
(John M Oxx, Ire) *led: hdd 4f out: disp ld ent st: rdn to ld 1 1/2f out: strly pressed cl home: all out* **9/1**

2 shd **She's Our Mark**[13] 6007 6-9-5 107 DMGrant 10 106+
(Patrick J Flynn, Ire) *chsd ldrs: 4th ent st: sn rdn: wnt 3rd 1f out: styd on wl fnl f: jst failed* **7/4**[1]

3 2 **Miss Laa Di Da**[27] 5568 3-8-11 100 (t) KJManning 11 99
(Noel Meade, Ire) *prom: led 4f out: jnd ent st: sn rdn: hdd 1 1/2f out: no ex and dropped to 3rd fnl f* **14/1**

4 nk **Devoted To You (IRE)**[13] 6007 3-8-11 103 JAHeffernan 5 98
(A P O'Brien, Ire) *in rr of mid-div: hdwy and rdn ent st: kpt on wout threatening fr 2f out* **10/1**

5 1 1/4 **Lady Lupus (IRE)**[14] 5976 3-8-11 103 (b[1]) JPO'Brien 7 96
(A P O'Brien, Ire) *prom: 3rd 4f out: rdn st: no imp fr 2f out* **9/1**

6 3/4 **Choose Me (IRE)**[13] 6007 4-9-2 106 DPMcDonogh 12 94
(Kevin Prendergast, Ire) *in rr: rdn st: kpt on one pce* **4/1**[2]

7 4 **You'll Be Mine (USA)**[27] 5568 3-8-11 102 CO'Donoghue 2 86
(A P O'Brien, Ire) *hld up early: prog on outer bef 1/2-way: 4th 4f out: sn rdn and no imp* **16/1**

8 4 **New Magic (IRE)**[34] 5341 3-8-11 96 BACurtis 3 78
(Mrs John Harrington, Ire) *mid-div on outer: rdn and no imp st* **14/1**

9 1 **Indiana Gal (IRE)**[21] 5772 5-9-2 99 (p) PBBeggy 13 76
(Patrick Martin, Ire) *a towards rr: no imp st* **20/1**

10 1 1/4 **Romie's Kastett (GER)**[27] 5568 3-8-11 90 (b[1]) WMLordan 9 73
(John M Oxx, Ire) *towards rr: 9th 4f out: sn rdn and no imp* **16/1**

11 1 3/4 **Dazzling Day**[66] 4271 3-8-11 93 CDHayes 8 70
(Kevin Prendergast, Ire) *a bhd* **28/1**

12 7 **Obama Rule (IRE)**[13] 6007 3-9-0 103 PJSmullen 6 58
(Ms Joanna Morgan, Ire) *chsd ldrs: 5th 4f out: sn rdn and wknd* **6/1**[3]

2m 5.73s (-1.27)
WFA 3 from 4yo+ 5lb 12 Ran SP% **133.0**
CSF £28.17 TOTE £9.60: £1.50, £1.40, £2.60; DF 37.60.
Owner H H Aga Khan **Bred** His Highness The Aga Khan's Stud S C **Trained** Currabeg, Co Kildare

FOCUS
The winner is gradually progressive and the runner-up ran to par.
NOTEBOOK
Shareen(IRE) has been gradually progressive this season and has clearly come on plenty since finishing an unplaced favourite here in August. She was always up there and travelled well into the straight. Niall McCullagh brought her into the centre of the track and, despite it looking at one stage as though she would give way, she showed guts to hold off the favourite. She should have no problem going further than this and seemed to cope well with the yielding ground, which connections admitted was a worry. (op 8/1)
She's Our Mark did what she always does and ran a cracking race. She had a lovely position throughout and was poised to challenge turning in. She seemed to hit a flat spot, before finding her stride over a furlong out. Just as at the Curragh last time, she just failed. She is a remarkably reliable sort at this level. (op 9/4)
Miss Laa Di Da had finished just behind Shareen at The Curragh last time and ran an excellent race from the front. She was no match for the first two but battled on and has now been placed in two Group 3s.
Devoted To You(IRE) was running on well at the finish and would have appreciated the ease in the ground. This is her level. (op 8/1)
Lady Lupus(IRE) broke well and ultimately had every chance. She looks to be better over further and is probably better than this. (op 9/1 tchd 8/1)
Choose Me(IRE) was a shade disappointing. She was settled in rear and may have been a bit inconvenienced by how the race was run, as she was still travelling well as they turned in. She passed plenty of horses and is better than the bare form. Nothing else ever got into it. (op 9/2)

6380 - 6385a (Foreign Racing) - See Raceform Interactive

6346 ASCOT (R-H)
Sunday, September 26

OFFICIAL GOING: Good to soft (soft in places on round course) (straight: far side 8.6, centre 9.5, stands' side, 8.5; round 7.4)
Wind: Fresh, across Weather: Dull, chilly

6386 ABF SOLDIERS' CHARITY NURSERY 7f
2:25 (2:25) (Class 3) 2-Y-O

£6,231 (£1,866; £933; £467; £233; £117) **Stalls** Centre

Form				RPR
1600	**1**		**Capaill Liath (IRE)**[8] 6191 2-9-2 **82**........(p) MichaelHills 4 (B W Hills) *stdd s: t.k.h: hld up towards rr: rdn and hdwy over 1f out: drvn to chse ldrs ent fnl f: kpt on wl to ld nr fin* **12/1**[3]	87
4062	**2**	*hd*	**Golden Blaze**[8] 6174 2-7-5 **64**........ NoelGarbutt(7) 10 (James Moffatt) *led: rdn wl over 1f out: clr ent fnl f: kpt on tl worn down and hdd nr fin* **12/1**[3]	69
332	**3**	¾	**Buckland (IRE)**[17] 5892 2-9-1 **81**........(b[1]) JimmyFortune 5 (B J Meehan) *stdd s: hld up in rr: stl last 2f out: rdn and hdwy over 1f out: drvn ent fnl f: chsd ldng pair fnl 150yds: kpt on: nt rch ldrs* **7/1**[2]	84
6135	**4**	¾	**Majestic Dream (IRE)**[19] 5837 2-8-7 **73**........(v[1]) ShaneKelly 11 (W R Swinburn) *stdd s: hld up towards rr: swtchd rt and effrt u.p wl over 1f out: kpt on u.p ins fnl f: nt rch ldrs* **25/1**	74
321	**5**	½	**Tick Tock Lover**[23] 5717 2-9-3 **83**........ IanMongan 1 (Miss Jo Crowley) *chsd ldrs: rdn 2f out: chsd clr ldr over 1f out: no imp and lost 2nd ent fnl f: edgd rt and styd on same pce fnl f* **9/2**[1]	83
531	**6**	2 ¼	**Ibsaar**[15] 5936 2-8-13 **79**........ RichardHills 8 (W J Haggas) *chsd ldrs: rdn and unable qck ent fnl 2f: wknd u.p ent fnl f* **9/2**[1]	73
5153	**7**	¾	**Buzz Law (IRE)**[21] 5784 2-8-7 **73** ow7........ Christophe-PatriceLemaire 2 (Mrs K Burke) *hld up in tch in midfield: shuffled bk towards rr 4f out: rdn over 3f out: kpt on u.p but no threat to ldrs fr over 1f out* **12/1**[3]	65
0515	**8**	*hd*	**Persian Herald**[19] 5831 2-9-3 **83**........ DaneO'Neill 3 (Pat Eddery) *chsd ldr: rdn ent fnl 2f: lost 2nd over 1f out: wknd u.p jst over 1f out* **20/1**	75
1110	**9**	3 ¼	**Orientalist**[18] 5849 2-9-7 **87**........ SebSanders 7 (Eve Johnson Houghton) *in tch in midfield: rdn and unable qck over 2f out: drvn and btn wl over 1f out* **14/1**	70
0040	**10**	*1*	**Velvet Underground (IRE)**[8] 6191 2-8-11 **77**........(b[1]) RyanMoore 6 (B J Meehan) *hld up in rr: rdn and no prog wl over 1f out: nvr trbld ldrs* **25/1**	58
421	**11**	1 ½	**Custom House (IRE)**[17] 5892 2-9-3 **83**........ RichardHughes 12 (R Hannon) *wnt bdly rt s: sn rcvrd and chsd ldrs: rdn ent fnl 2f: wknd over 1f out: wl btn 1f out: eased ins fnl f* **7/1**[2]	65
004	**12**	*2*	**Aldwick Bay (IRE)**[27] 5608 2-8-3 **69**........ FrankieMcDonald 9 (R Hannon) *dwlt: in tch towards rr: nudged along and hdwy into midfield 1/2-way: rdn and wknd qckly wl over 1f out* **7/1**[2]	41

1m 30.06s (2.06) **Going Correction** +0.35s/f (Good) 12 Ran SP% 116.1
Speed ratings (Par 99): **102,101,100,100,99 96,96,95,92,90 89,86**
toteswingers: 1&2 £36.30, 1&3 £30.60, 2&3 £19.50 CSF £140.85 CT £1097.17 TOTE £18.10: £5.70, £3.60, £2.80; EX 208.30 TRIFECTA Not won..
Owner D Hanafin **Bred** Stanley Estate & Stud Co & Mount Coote Stud **Trained** Lambourn, Berks

FOCUS
Following a dry night the ground remained good to soft on the straight course and good to soft, soft in places on the round course. There were some interesting handicap debutants in this line-up, but in the end a couple of the most experienced colts in the race fought out the finish. The time was decent and the winner produced a good effort, but this is not form to go overboard about.
NOTEBOOK
Capaill Liath(IRE) had looked to be a little high in the weights following his maiden win at Windsor back in June, but he had been eased slightly recently and, more importantly, the step up to 7f coupled with the fitting of first-time cheekpieces brought about improvement, contrary to what his pedigree had forecast. With a seemingly exposed rival in second the form might not be all that, though, and one wonders if the headgear will continue to have a positive effect. (op 20-1)
Golden Blaze was dropping back from a mile and was given a positive ride. He took some passing, only being caught close home, and similar tactics on a turning track could well see him get off the mark. (op 14-1)
Buckland(IRE), a beaten short-priced favourite in his previous two starts in maidens, had blinkers on for the first time back on turf. He tracked the winner through on the stands' side of the bunch but could never quite peg him back, and it's questionable whether he improved a great deal here. (op 5-1)
Majestic Dream(IRE), another wearing headgear for the first time, in his case a visor, was ridden patiently and ran a better race than at Lingfield last time, but quicker ground will probably suit him ideally. (op 22-1 tchd 20-1)
Tick Tock Lover was never too far off the pace and had every chance. The drop back from 1m didn't prove a huge plus, though. (op 13-2)
Ibsaar was denied his own way in front this time and gradually faded in the closing stages. A return to a sharper 7f might be more to his liking. (op 11-2 tchd 7-2)
Buzz Law(IRE) was due to be ridden by Silvestre de Sousa, but he was unwell and Christophe Lemaire was a late replacement. He put up 7lb overweight, and in such a tightly knit handicap that did for any chance the colt had. (op 16-1 tchd 10-1)
Custom House(IRE), who beat the third in a maiden at Kempton last time out, was drawn widest of all and veered badly right exiting the stalls. He gave away significant ground with that manoeuvre. (op 13-2 tchd 15-2)
Aldwick Bay(IRE), who was well backed in the morning but drifted close to the off, lacked the pace to get seriously involved and might be suited by a step up to 1m - there's plenty of stamina on his dam's side. Official explanation: jockey said colt had no more to give (op 5-1 tchd 9-2)

6387 PWC H'CAP 1m 4f
3:00 (3:00) (Class 2) (0-105,102) 3-Y-O+

£9,969 (£2,985; £1,492; £747; £372; £187) **Stalls** High

Form				RPR
4236	**1**		**Life And Soul (IRE)**[8] 6203 3-8-11 **90**........ NeilCallan 2 (Mrs A J Perrett) *hld up in last trio: hdwy over 4f out: lft 4th and sltly hmpd over 2f out: hanging lft u.p fr 2f out: swtchd lft and drvn over 1f out: kpt on wl to ld fnl 75yds: all out* **4/1**[2]	98
2053	**2**	¾	**Prompter**[27] 5590 3-9-9 **102**........ JamieSpencer 1 (M L W Bell) *stdd and dropped in bhd after s: hld up in last: stl last whn sltly hmpd and pushed lft over 2f out: 6th and stl plenty do and drvn over 1f out: hdwy 1f out: styd on wl to go 2nd nr fin: nt quite rch wnr* **16/1**	109
2101	**3**	*hd*	**The Fonz**[39] 5217 4-9-7 **92**........ RyanMoore 6 (Sir Michael Stoute) *hld up in midfield: hdwy to trck ldrs over 3f out: lft 3rd over 2f out: drvn to ld over 1f out: edgd rt u.p ent fnl f: hdd fnl 75yds: no ex and lost 2nd nr fin* **7/2**[1]	98
1210	**4**	¾	**Bay Willow (IRE)**[37] 5273 3-9-9 **102**........ RichardHills 4 (M Johnston) *chsd ldr after 1f: rdn to ld over 2f out: drvn and hdd over 1f out: kpt on gamely but one pce ins fnl f* **13/2**[3]	107
5125	**5**	*nk*	**Magicalmysterytour (IRE)**[15] 5949 7-9-4 **89**........ RichardHughes 3 (W J Musson) *hld up in last trio: rdn 3f out: hmpd and pushed lft over 2f out: hdwy u.p over 1f out: chsng ldrs and keeping on whn nt clr run wl ins fnl f* **4/1**[2]	94+
0500	**6**	4 ½	**Bowdler's Magic**[22] 5747 3-8-10 **89**........ KierenFallon 9 (M Johnston) *sn pushed up to ld: rdn ent fnl 3f: hdd over 2f out: wknd ent fnl f* **9/1**	87
1000	**7**	3 ¾	**Chiberta King**[16] 5908 4-9-12 **97**........ JimmyFortune 8 (A M Balding) *t.k.h: chsd ldr for 1f: stdd and chsd ldrs after: rdn and effrt whn hmpd over 2f out: sn rdn and wl btn after* **22/1**	89
2106	**8**	*8*	**Final Victory**[85] 3672 4-9-6 **91**........ LiamKeniry 7 (A M Balding) *in tch in midfield: rdn 5f out: lost pl and dropped to rr whn hmpd over 2f out: wl btn after* **10/1**	70
5100	**U**		**Anhar (USA)**[39] 5217 3-9-5 **98**........(t) TedDurcan 5 (Saeed Bin Suroor) *s.i.s: t.k.h: sn chsng ldng pair tl lost action: stmbld bdly and uns rdr over 2f out: fatally injured* **8/1**	—

2m 33.79s (1.29) **Going Correction** +0.35s/f (Good)
WFA 3 from 4yo+ 8lb 9 Ran SP% **116.0**
Speed ratings (Par 109): **109,108,108,107,107 104,102,96,—**
toteswingers: 1&2 £9.20, 1&3 £3.80, 2&3 £7.10 CSF £65.21 CT £245.70 TOTE £4.50: £2.00, £2.80, £1.40; EX 80.20 Trifecta £449.00 Pool: £958.67 - 1.58 winning units..
Owner A D Spence **Bred** Kildaragh Stud **Trained** Pulborough, W Sussex

FOCUS
This good-quality handicap had a wide open look about it. There was a sound gallop on and the first five were closely covered at the finish. The form is rated slightly positively. The race was marred by Anhar going wrong off the home turn.
NOTEBOOK
Life And Soul(IRE) relished stepping back up to this distance and scored under a well-judged ride. He has run well in defeat this season since winning on his return in May, but wasn't suited by the drop to 1m2f on his previous outing and this was much more up his street. It was a career-best effort from him and he appeals as the sort to rate even higher as a four-year-old. (op 5-1 tchd 11-2)
Prompter was having his first outing over this far and was ridden accordingly. He stayed on stoutly without ever quite looking like hitting the front and this was a pleasing effort. He can be ridden more prominently now connections know he stays. (op 14-1)
The Fonz, 5lb higher, made his move nearing the home turn and held every chance. He remains in decent heart but perhaps the handicapper now has his measure. (op 4-1)
Bay Willow(IRE), a winner over course and distance on his last visit to the track, showed his true colours again and proved his lifeless effort at York 37 days earlier to be all wrong. He is another that now looks to be in the handicapper's grip. (op 6-1 tchd 7-1)
Magicalmysterytour(IRE), well backed once again, stayed on all too late having been set a fair bit to do. It is surprising connections continually opt for patient tactics with him as he does stay very well, and surely more positive handling is what he needs. (op 5-1)

6388 SIS LIVE FENWOLF STKS (LISTED RACE) 2m
3:35 (3:35) (Class 1) 3-Y-O+

£22,708 (£8,608; £4,308; £2,148; £1,076; £540) **Stalls** High

Form				RPR
	1		**Fictional Account (IRE)**[16] 5932 5-8-12 96........ WilliamBuick 5 (V C Ward, Ire) *rrd s: hld up in last: hdwy to trck ldrs gng wl ent fnl 2f: pushed along to ld 1f out: in command fnl 150yds: eased towards fin* **16/1**	106+
141	**2**	1 ½	**Free Agent**[24] 5696 4-9-6 107........ RyanMoore 2 (R Hannon) *t.k.h: hld up in tch in last trio: rdn and effrt 3f out: swtchd ins and drvn over 1f out: kpt on u.p to go 2nd last strides: no threat to wnr* **9/2**[3]	112
0153	**3**	*hd*	**Pompeyano (IRE)**[29] 5538 5-9-3 107........ KierenFallon 4 (Saeed Bin Suroor) *hld up wl in tch: swtchd rt and rdn to chal ent fnl 2f: led jst over 1f out tl 1f out: one pce and btn fnl 150yds: lost 2nd last strides* **7/2**[2]	109
2062	**4**	*nse*	**Tastahil (IRE)**[16] 5909 6-9-3 111........ RichardHills 3 (B W Hills) *led: jnd over 3f out: rdn over 2f out: kpt on u.p tl hdd 1f out: styd on same pce after* **13/8**[1]	109
3110	**5**	*6*	**Martyr**[39] 5220 5-9-3 105........ RichardHughes 1 (R Hannon) *chsd ldr: jnd ldr on bit over 3f out: rdn and unable qck 2f out: btn jst ins fnl f: wknd fnl 100yds* **11/2**	102+
1004	**6**	*14*	**On Terms (USA)**[41] 5144 4-8-12 75........ SebSanders 6 (S Dow) *chsd ldrs: rdn 4f out: wknd qckly wl over 2f out: wl bhd fnl 2f* **50/1**	80
6004	**7**	*5*	**Blizzard Blues (USA)**[15] 5949 4-9-3 98........(b) TomQueally 9 (H R A Cecil) *awkward s: t.k.h: hld up in tch in last trio: shkn up and effrt to chse ldrs 3f out: rdn and wknd qckly jst over 2f out: wl btn and hung lft over 1f out* **8/1**	79

3m 32.86s (3.86) **Going Correction** +0.35s/f (Good)
WFA 3 from 4yo+ 12lb 7 Ran SP% **112.8**
Speed ratings (Par 111): **104,103,103,103,100 93,90**
toteswingers: 1&2 £5.90, 1&3 £7.80, 2&3 £3.70 CSF £83.13 TOTE £15.30: £4.70, £3.20; EX 83.70 Trifecta £508.50 Pool: £927.67 - 1.35 winning units..
Owner Cill Choca Syndicate **Bred** Moyglare Stud Farm Ltd **Trained** Kilcock, Co Meath

The Form Book, Raceform Ltd, Compton, RG20 6NL

FOCUS
The early pace wasn't particularly strong here but Richard Hills gradually wound things up from the front on Tastahil, which eventually found out the smooth-travelling Martyr, who came there swinging early in the straight but found little off the bridle and was eventually outstayed by four others. Ordinary form for the grade, with the winner a surprise improver.

NOTEBOOK
Fictional Account(IRE) reared as the stalls opened and lost several lengths but the modest early gallop meant no great harm was done. Held up in last for much of the race, she swept by her rivals approaching the final furlong and won a shade comfortably. With a mark of 96 she had a bit to find with the market principals strictly on ratings, but her stamina was proven. She came into this race on the back of a comfortable success at Down Royal and confirmed here that she's right at the top of her game. Her connections, who brought her over here for better ground rather than run in the Cesarewitch at the Curragh, will no doubt thrilled to have secured valuable black type for her.
Free Agent didn't have an easy task conceding weight all round and kept on nicely enough to take second close home, but quicker ground probably suits him best. (tchd 5-1)
Pompeyano(IRE) began to be pushed along some way out, although he came to have every chance in the straight. A stronger all-round gallop would probably have been more to his advantage. (tchd 4-1)
Tastahil(IRE) enjoyed the run of things out in front and can have few excuses. For a horse rated 111, three wins from 22 starts is not a great return. (op 2-1)
Martyr settled well during the early part of the race despite the ordinary gallop and his turn of foot threatened to be a valuable asset. However, the pace increased up front from far enough out to ensure it was a proper test over the trip and this ground was undoubtedly softer than he would like. He travelled strongly into the straight but found nothing under pressure and could be worth dropping back in trip. (op 9-2 tchd 4-1)
On Terms(USA) had a mountain to climb on the ratings.
Blizzard Blues(USA) comprehensively failed the stamina test on this 4f step up in trip. (op 10-1)

6389 GROSVENOR CASINOS CUMBERLAND LODGE STKS (GROUP 3) 1m 4f
4:10 (4:10) (Class 1) 3-Y-O+

£36,900 (£13,988; £7,000; £3,490; £1,748; £877) **Stalls** High

Form RPR
2121 **1** **Laaheb**[22] 5749 4-9-3 114 RichardHills 3 118
(M A Jarvis) *chsd ldr: rdn to chal jst over 2f out: carried lft wl over 1f out: led 1f out: edgd rt u.p fnl f: kpt on gamely* **5/6**[1]
4201 **2** *nse* **Whispering Gallery**[29] 5538 4-9-0 110 KierenFallon 7 115
(Saeed Bin Suroor) *led: rdn over 2f out: jnd and edgd lft u.p wl over 1f out: narrowly hdd 1f out: carried rt and battled on wl fnl f: a jst hld* **3/1**[2]
-065 **3** *10* **Monitor Closely (IRE)**[9] 6148 4-9-0 112 JamieSpencer 1 99
(M L W Bell) *stdd ldrs tl rdn and struggling over 2f out: wl btn fnl 2f* **13/2**[3]
0040 **4** *1 ¼* **Halicarnassus (IRE)**[9] 6148 6-9-0 102 NeilCallan 2 97
(M R Channon) *hld up in last pair: rdn 4f out: drvn and no ch w ldng pair fr over 2f out: plugged on ins fnl f to snatch 4th last stride* **40/1**
2-31 **5** *shd* **Mikhail Glinka (IRE)**[42] 3-8-9 110 RyanMoore 6 100
(G L Moore) *chsd ldrs: rdn 3f out: sn drvn and struggling: 4th and no ch w ldng pair fnl 2f: hung bdly lft and lost 4th last stride* **13/2**[3]
-436 **6** *64* **Shahwardi (FR)**[73] 4081 4-9-0 103 WilliamBuick 5 —
(J R Gask) *taken down early: t.k.h: hld up in last pair: rdn and lost tch over 2f out: virtually p.u fr over 1f out: t.o* **25/1**

2m 34.32s (1.82) **Going Correction** +0.35s/f (Good)
WFA 3 from 4yo+ 8lb **6 Ran SP% 112.5**
Speed ratings (Par 113): **107,106,100,99,99 56**
toteswingers: 1&2 £1.20, 1&3 £1.90, 2&3 £2.30 CSF £3.58 TOTE £2.10: £1.70, £2.00; EX 4.90.
Owner Hamdan Al Maktoum **Bred** Darley **Trained** Newmarket, Suffolk

FOCUS
It's a shame that Patkai didn't turn up, but this was still an interesting Group 3. The race has been something of a nightmare for bookmakers in the past decade and Laaheb continued the trend of winning favourites, prevailing in a thrilling finish from Whispering Gallery. There were doubts over most of these and the form is rated around the front pair.

NOTEBOOK
Laaheb is a model of consistency and his clear-cut success at Kempton 22 days earlier was given a boost when the runner-up that day, Holberg, went one better at Goodwood on his next outing. He was entitled to win at these weights, despite his penalty, but he was made to work hard to follow up due to the persistence of the runner-up. He certainly wasn't helped by that rival leaning into him throughout the home straight, though, and there was an awful lot to like about his attitude under maximum pressure. This likeable four-year-old is capable of stepping up to Group 2 company and finding further success. He could be even better next year as he doesn't have too many miles on the clock. (op 8-11 tchd 10-11 and 1-1 in places)
Whispering Gallery was a game winner on soft ground at Windsor last month and so nearly went in again. He was able to dictate, but came under pressure a fair way out and he too showed a very willing attitude for his rider's urgings, despite drifting left. He too could improve if kept in training next year as he is another relatively lightly raced four-year-old, and it wouldn't be surprising to see him develop into more of a stayer. (op 7-2 tchd 5-2)
Monitor Closely(IRE) has struggled to find his best form since resuming from injury this term. (tchd 6-1 and 7-1)
Halicarnassus(IRE) remains out of form. (op 33-1)
Mikhail Glinka(IRE) was having his first run for Gary Moore and his first at this venue since gamely winning the Queen's Vase at the Royal meeting in June. He unsurprisingly looked to find this too sharp, but remains a horse of potential and is one to be more interested in again when reverting to a stiffer test. (op 10-1)
Shahwardi(FR) had plenty to find on this return from a 73-day break and never figured. (op 28-1)

6390 JOHN GUEST DIADEM STKS (GROUP 2) 6f
4:45 (4:45) (Class 1) 3-Y-O+

£61,396 (£23,273; £11,647; £5,807; £2,909; £1,460) **Stalls** Centre

Form RPR
3662 **1** **Lady Of The Desert (USA)**[22] 5744 3-8-9 111 RichardHughes 5 121
(B J Meehan) *ponied to s: hld up in tch: hdwy to trck ldrs and looking for run wl over 1f out: swtchd ins and qcknd to chal 1f out: led ins fnl f: r.o strly: readily* **4/1**[2]
1532 **2** *2 ¼* **Dalghar (FR)**[21] 5802 4-9-0 117 Christophe-PatriceLemaire 7 117
(A De Royer-Dupre, France) *led: rdn wl over 1f out: clr w wnr 1f out: hdd ins fnl f: no ch w wnr after but kpt on for clr 2nd* **9/4**[1]
6404 **3** *3 ¾* **Kingsgate Native (IRE)**[22] 5744 5-9-4 116 RyanMoore 1 109
(Sir Michael Stoute) *in tch in midfield: swtchd rt and effrt u.p over 1f out: chsd clr ldng pair ent fnl f: no imp and wl hld* **5/1**[3]
3433 **4** *½* **Himalya (IRE)**[15] 5946 4-9-0 111 TomQueally 4 103+
(J Noseda) *ponied to s: stdd s: t.k.h: hld up towards rr: hdwy and switching rt over 1f out: immediately swtchd bk lft and nt clr run: no ch after: kpt on to go 4th fnl 100yds* **8/1**
2000 **5** *1* **Serious Attitude (IRE)**[15] 5946 4-8-11 105 JimmyFortune 10 97
(Rae Guest) *stdd s: swtchd rt to r against stands' rail: t.k.h: hld up in rr: swtchd rt and nt clr run wl over 1f out: drvn and kpt on same pce fr jst over 1f out: nvr trbld ldrs* **16/1**
4415 **6** *1 ½* **Bounty Box**[15] 5952 4-8-11 103 NeilCallan 12 92
(C F Wall) *chsd ldrs: rdn to chse ldr 2f out tl over 1f out: btn ent fnl f: wknd ins fnl f* **33/1**
2440 **7** *2 ¼* **Rileyskeepingfaith**[8] 6177 4-9-0 102 (v) DarryllHolland 6 88
(M R Channon) *stdd s: hld up in rr: rdn and effrt ent fnl 2f: no real prog: wl hld whn edgd rt u.p ins fnl f* **14/1**
1260 **8** *3 ¾* **Tropical Treat**[28] 5569 3-8-9 102 JimCrowley 3 73
(R M Beckett) *stdd s: hld up in midfield: rdn and struggling ent fnl 2f: wknd and wl btn 1f out* **25/1**
1-00 **9** *3 ¾* **Sayif (IRE)**[99] 3192 4-9-0 114 RichardHills 2 64
(Sir Michael Stoute) *chsd ldr tl 2f out: sn rdn and wknd: wl bhd fnl f* **11/1**
2022 **10** *1 ¾* **Lui Rei (ITY)**[15] 5952 4-9-0 100 WilliamBuick 9 59
(M Botti) *stdd s: hld up in rr: rdn and no hdwy whn pushed rt 2f out: wl bhd fnl f* **33/1**
4035 **11** *1* **Santo Padre (IRE)**[14] 6009 6-9-0 105 JamieSpencer 8 55
(David Marnane, Ire) *sn nudged along towards rr: edgd rt u.p 2f out: wknd over 1f out: eased wl ins fnl f* **16/1**

1m 14.13s (-0.27) **Going Correction** +0.35s/f (Good)
WFA 3 from 4yo+ 2lb **11 Ran SP% 115.0**
Speed ratings (Par 115): **115,112,107,106,105 103,100,95,90,87 86**
toteswingers: 1&2 £2.70, 1&3 £3.80, 2&3 £2.70 CSF £12.75 TOTE £4.40: £1.70, £1.30, £1.50; EX 12.50 Trifecta £50.70 Pool: £6,101.34 - 88.98 winning units..
Owner Jaber Abdullah **Bred** Rabbah Bloodstock Llc **Trained** Manton, Wilts

FOCUS
A good race, well up to its Group 2 status. The winner has claims to be rated top sprinter after this. The second is rated to form but the rest were 10lb+ off.

NOTEBOOK
Lady Of The Desert(USA), who gained compensation for being drawn on the wrong side at Haydock last time. One of the best sprinting fillies around as a two-year-old (she won the Princess Margaret over this course and distance), the attempt to get her to stay the Guineas trip failed. However, a summer's rest and being brought back to sprints has seen her return to form with a bang. This performance suggests she's now one of the best over 6f. Richard Hughes stalked the favourite throughout, went for a brave run between him and the stands' rail a furlong out, and the filly quickened up right away inside the last to win in emphatic style. Fresher than most at the moment, it's a shame for her that further opportunities this year are thin on the ground. However, while connections later said plans were undecided, they did not rule out supplementing her for the Prix de l'Abbeye next weekend and also have one eye on the Breeder's Cup. If they do opt to keep her in training she's one to look forward to next season. (tchd 9-2)
Dalghar(FR) promised to be suited by the drop back to sprinting having shown plenty of pace over 7f on his last two starts. Sent to the front immediately, he pulled well clear of the third in the closing stages but had no answer to the winner's impressive turn of foot. There was no shame in being beaten by a top-class filly. (tchd 5-2)
Kingsgate Native(IRE) had no easy task giving weight all round and the first two stretched clear of him from a furlong out, but it wasn't a bad effort considering the ground had more give in it than he ideally prefers. (op 6-1 tchd 9-2)
Himalya(IRE) runs well at this track (placed in two big-field handicaps earlier this season) but 7f suits him better than 6f and, although clearly smart, remains a difficult horse to win with.
Serious Attitude(IRE), poorly away from the stalls, was dropped in last early. Switched to the inside rail, she made some late progress without worrying the principals, but this was still probably her best effort of the campaign.
Bounty Box, who found the ground too soft at Goodwood last time, was up against it in this company. She tried to keep tabs on the leader for a long way and probably paid the price for that as she weakened in the closing stages. (op 25-1 tchd 20-1)
Rileyskeepingfaith, who has run well in some of the big handicaps this term, stayed on past some beaten horses but was never a threat. (op 16-1 tchd 11-1)
Tropical Treat, who has done her winning over 5f, was a bit keen early and dropped right out. (op 33-1)
Sayif(IRE) won this race last year but he hasn't been in anywhere near as good form this season and, after being switched to a new trainer, he was having his first outing for three months here. He showed pace to 2f out but weakened quickly from there. (op 16-1)
Santo Padre(IRE), last year's Portland winner, never looked like getting seriously involved. (op 9-1)

6391 GCASINO.COM H'CAP 1m (S)
5:20 (5:21) (Class 2) (0-100,94) 3-Y-O+

£9,969 (£2,985; £1,492; £747; £372; £187) **Stalls** Centre

Form RPR
-013 **1** **Brick Red**[2] 6321 3-8-11 85 JimmyFortune 8 93+
(A M Balding) *in tch in midfield: hdwy to chse ldr jst over 2f out: rdn to ld over 1f out: wandered u.p ins fnl f: hrd drvn and hld on towards fin* **3/1**[1]
6636 **2** *hd* **South Cape**[15] 5955 7-9-0 84 RyanMoore 7 92
(G L Moore) *hld up towards rr: rdn and hdwy 2f out: drvn to chse wnr over 1f out: ev ch ins fnl f: kpt on but a jst hld* **12/1**
0601 **3** *hd* **Credit Swap**[11] 6097 5-9-5 89 DarryllHolland 13 97+
(M Wigham) *stdd and dropped in bhd after s: hld up in rr: swtchd lft over 1f out: gd hdwy jst ins fnl f: hanging rt and swtchd lft again ins fnl f: r.o strly fnl 75yds: nt quite rch ldng pair* **5/1**[2]
2253 **4** *½* **First Cat**[8] 6205 3-8-11 85 FrankieMcDonald 4 91
(R Hannon) *stdd s: t.k.h: hld up towards rr: effrt and looking for run ent fnl 2f: nt clr run tl swtchd lft over 1f out: chsd ldrs and hanging rt u.p 1f out: kpt on but nvr quite gng pce to rch ldrs* **16/1**
2434 **5** *2* **Oratory (IRE)**[50] 4843 4-9-10 94 (t) RichardHughes 12 96
(R Hannon) *stdd and dropped in bhd after s: hld up in rr: rdn and hdwy wl over 1f out: chsd ldrs and drvn ent fnl f: no imp and hld fnl 100yds* **8/1**
1103 **6** *1 ¼* **Ginger Jack**[22] 5759 3-9-4 92 RichardHills 1 91
(M Johnston) *chsd ldrs: rdn and effrt 2f out: edgd rt and one pce u.p fnl f* **14/1**
4303 **7** *2 ½* **Webbow (IRE)**[15] 5948 8-9-9 93 (p) EddieAhern 5 86
(N Tinkler) *t.k.h: chsd ldrs: rdn and effrt wl over 1f out: btn 1f out: nt pushed whn wl hld ins fnl f* **10/1**
020- **8** *¾* **The Fifth Member (IRE)**[303] 7560 6-9-4 88 PatCosgrave 11 79
(J R Boyle) *led: drvn and hdd over 1f out: wknd u.p ent fnl f* **40/1**
1426 **9** *9* **King Of Windsor (IRE)**[25] 5662 3-9-1 89 JimCrowley 10 60
(R M Beckett) *in tch: rdn 1/2-way: drvn and wknd over 2f out: wl bhd fr over 1f out* **15/2**[3]
2143 **10** *1* **Benandonner (USA)**[50] 4816 7-9-6 90 TonyCulhane 3 58
(Mike Murphy) *pressed ldr tl jst over 2f out: wknd u.p wl over 1f out* **8/1**
0000 **11** *1 ¾* **Sarah Park (IRE)**[71] 4137 5-9-1 85 WilliamBuick 6 49
(B J Meehan) *chsd ldrs tl wknd u.p 2f out: wl bhd fnl f* **25/1**
0330 **12** *9* **Opus Maximus (IRE)**[43] 5068 5-9-3 87 KierenFallon 9 31
(M Johnston) *chsd ldrs: rdn along 5f out: wknd over 2f out: wl bhd fr over 1f out: eased ins fnl f* **16/1**

1302 **13** *45* **Shavansky**[15] 5955 6-9-6 **93** JamesMillman(3) 2 —
(B R Millman) *rrd s and v.s.a: a bhd: lost tch 2f out: virtually p.u fnl f: t.o: dismntd immediately after fin* **12/1**

1m 43.82s (3.22) **Going Correction** +0.35s/f (Good)
WFA 3 from 4yo+ 4lb 13 Ran SP% **124.8**
Speed ratings (Par 109): **97,96,96,96,94 92,90,89,80,79 77,68,23**
toteswingers: 1&2 £11.40, 1&3 £5.90, 2&3 £28.40 CSF £42.99 CT £190.10 TOTE £3.70: £1.80, £3.50, £2.90; EX 58.20 Trifecta £366.60 Pool: £1,253.50 - 2.53 winning units. Place 6 £109.14, Place 5 £18.96.
Owner Brick Racing **Bred** Raimon Bloodstock **Trained** Kingsclere, Hants

FOCUS
This wasn't the strongest of handicaps for the class. The main action developed down the centre of the track and there was little covering the first four at the finish. The winner probably only has to repeat his form from two days earlier, with the runner-up limiting things.

NOTEBOOK
Brick Red, third over 7f here two days previously, was well backed and resumed winning ways with a game display. He moved sweetly through the race and was perfectly positioned when things got really serious. He did appear vulnerable near the finish, but kept responding to pressure and just did enough to hold on at the business end. This lightly raced son of Dubawi is just the sort his trainer tends to do well with and he remains open to improvement over this trip. Connections hope he will develop into a Cambridgeshire horse next year. (op 9-2 tchd 5-1)
South Cape was given every chance by Ryan Moore and went down fighting. This was more like it again from him and he knows all about this track, so rates a solid benchmark. (tchd 14-1)
Credit Swap was raised 6lb for a narrow success at Yarmouth 11 days earlier and would have likely followed that up had he been more positively ridden here. He remains weighted to win and is one to side with next time out. (op 7-1)
First Cat got going late on and had his chance. A drop in grade could see him deservedly back to winning ways. (op 12-1)
Oratory(IRE), another returning from a 50-day break, was equipped with a first-time tongue-tie and back up in trip. He never seriously threatened, but ran close to his mark again and is another that helps to set the level.
Ginger Jack ran another sound race in defeat and not for the first time left the impression stepping up to 1m2f could further help his cause. (op 10-1)
Shavansky Official explanation: jockey said gelding reared in stalls
T/Jkpt: Not won. T/Plt: £208.90 to a £1 stake. Pool: £141,402.31 493.98 winning tickets. T/Qpdt: £21.00 to a £1 stake. Pool: £9,610.80. 338.05 winning tickets. SP

6026 MUSSELBURGH (R-H)
Sunday, September 26

OFFICIAL GOING: Straight course - good to soft (good in places); round course - good (6.4)
Rails on both bends and along back straight moved out 2-3 yards to provide fresh ground.
Wind: Light, across Weather: Cloudy

6392 ROYAL SCOTS H'CAP 5f
2:15 (2:16) (Class 6) (0-65,65) 3-Y-O £2,590 (£770; £385; £192) Stalls Low

Form RPR
2021 **1** **Red Roar (IRE)**[29] 5514 3-9-0 **58** FrannyNorton 2 68
(A Berry) *trckd ldrs on inner: swtchd rt and rdn over 1f out: qcknd to ld jst ins fnl f: rdn out* **9/2[2]**
2151 **2** *1* **Oondiri (IRE)**[28] 5548 3-9-3 **61** PJMcDonald 6 67
(T D Easterby) *led: shkn up 1f out: sn rdn and hdd ins fnl f: kpt on same pce* **5/2[1]**
1405 **3** *1 ½* **Drumpellier (IRE)**[14] 5999 3-8-11 **58** PaulPickard(3) 9 59
(S G West) *cl up: rdn to chal over 1f out and ev ch tl drvn and one pce ins fnl f* **9/1**
3624 **4** *½* **Duke Of Rainford**[15] 5957 3-8-6 **50** PaulHanagan 7 49
(M Herrington) *chsd ldrs: rdn wl over 1f out: swtchd rt ent fnl f: sn drvn and kpt on same pce* **9/2[2]**
0-00 **5** *2 ½* **Sumay Buoy (IRE)**[7] 6226 3-8-7 **51** AndrewMullen 1 41
(Mrs J C McGregor) *dwlt and in rr tl styd on appr fnl f* **40/1**
4665 **6** *½* **Dower Glen**[6] 6246 3-8-2 **53** ShirleyTeasdale(7) 4 41
(V P Donoghue) *towards rr: rdn along 1/2-way: drvn and kpt on appr fnl f* **11/1**
00-0 **7** *4 ½* **Croft Bridge**[10] 6133 3-8-1 **48** ow2 (p) AndrewHeffernan(3) 11 20
(P A Kirby) *in tch: rdn along 2f out: sn wknd* **16/1**
4120 **8** *½* **Philosophers Stone (FR)**[87] 3599 3-9-7 **65** GrahamGibbons 10 35
(T D Barron) *prom: rdn along wl over 1f out: sn drvn and wknd* **11/2[3]**
30R **9** *½* **Kristen Jane (USA)**[32] 5410 3-8-0 **47** JamesSullivan(3) 5 15
(Miss L A Perratt) *rrd s: a in rr* **25/1**
0-00 **10** *8* **Ariel Bender**[14] 5990 3-8-4 **48** oh1 ow2 PatrickMathers 8 —
(Peter Grayson) *a in rr: rdn along 1/2-way: sn bhd* **100/1**

60.93 secs (0.53) **Going Correction** +0.075s/f (Good) 10 Ran SP% **111.8**
Speed ratings (Par 99): **98,96,94,93,89 88,81,80,79,66**
toteswingers: 1&2 £1.50, 1&3 £8.10, 2&3 £5.90 CSF £15.20 CT £96.28 TOTE £6.50: £2.70, £1.02, £2.00; EX 12.30.
Owner Sporting Kings **Bred** Tally-Ho Stud **Trained** Cockerham, Lancs
■ Stewards' Enquiry : Paul Pickard caution: used whip with excessive frequency.

FOCUS
A modest 46-65 three-year-olds' sprint. The runner-up looks the best guide.
Kristen Jane(USA) Official explanation: jockey said filly reared as stalls opened

6393 RACING UK (S) STKS 1m 4f 100y
2:50 (2:50) (Class 6) 3-Y-0+ £1,942 (£578; £288; £144) Stalls High

Form RPR
6002 **1** **Hong Kong Island (IRE)**[13] 6032 3-8-10 57 PaulHanagan 7 74
(N G Richards) *chsd clr ldr: tk clsr order over 4f out: chal over 3f out: rdn to ld wl over 2f out: drvn and edgd rt over 1f out: clr fnl f* **11/4[2]**
0320 **2** *10* **Royal Straight**[10] 6109 5-9-7 69 IanBrennan(3) 5 66
(Miss L A Perratt) *trckd ldrs: hdwy on inner 3f out: rdn to chse wnr wl over 1f out: sn drvn and one pce* **7/2[3]**
0414 **3** *3 ¼* **Oddsmaker (IRE)**[10] 6109 9-9-7 62 (t) AndrewHeffernan(3) 8 59
(M A Barnes) *led and sn clr: pushed along over 4f out: rdn 3f out: sn hdd and drvn: wknd fnl 2f* **9/4[1]**
550 **4** *½* **Kames Park (IRE)**[22] 5757 8-9-10 72 AndrewElliott 3 58
(R C Guest) *hld up in rr: effrt and sme hdwy on outer over 2f out: sn rdn and hung bdly rt over 1f out: n.d* **9/2**
3553 **5** *10* **North Central (USA)**[9] 6144 3-8-10 63 LNewman 6 36
(J S Goldie) *chsd ldng pair: rdn along over 3f out: sn drvn and wknd* **7/1**
/000 **6** *3 ¼* **Emirate Isle**[115] 2670 6-9-4 55 (p) PJMcDonald 2 31
(B Storey) *chsd ldrs: rdn along over 4f out: sn outpcd and bhd fnl 3f* **80/1**

2m 42.07s (0.07) **Going Correction** -0.05s/f (Good)
WFA 3 from 5yo+ 8lb 6 Ran SP% **111.6**
Speed ratings (Par 101): **97,90,88,87,81 79**
toteswingers: 1&2 £2.60, 1&3 £2.70, 2&3 £1.10 CSF £12.57 TOTE £4.50: £2.10, £1.80; EX 14.40.The winner sold to A G Foster for £11,000.
Owner Mrs J Penman **Bred** The Goldsmith Bloodstock Partnership **Trained** Greystoke, Cumbria

FOCUS
A seller run at a furious pace but in the end an eased-down, wide-margin winner. He showed improved form but it appeared to be no fluke.

6394 RSP CONSULTING ENGINEERS H'CAP 7f 30y
3:25 (3:25) (Class 4) (0-80,80) 3-Y-0+ £5,180 (£1,541; £770; £384) Stalls High

Form RPR
6143 **1** **Cara's Request (AUS)**[10] 6108 5-8-8 **72** ow1 MichaelO'Connell(5) 6 84
(D Nicholls) *qckly away: mde all: rdn along over 2f out: drvn over 1f out: kpt on gamely fnl f* **11/1**
0132 **2** *1* **George Benjamin**[10] 6107 3-8-12 **74** AdrianNicholls 10 82
(D Nicholls) *trckd ldrs on inner: hdwy over 2f out: rdn to chse wnr wl over 1f out: drvn ins fnl f: no imp towards fin* **4/1[1]**
0335 **3** *3 ½* **Berbice (IRE)**[10] 6108 5-8-7 **69** JamesSullivan(3) 11 69
(Miss L A Perratt) *hld up: hdwy and in tch 1/2-way: effrt on inner to chse ldng pair wl over 1f out: drvn and one pce ent fnl f* **20/1**
5163 **4** *1* **Commando Scott (IRE)**[10] 6107 9-8-2 **68** NeilFarley(7) 5 65+
(D Carroll) *hld up towards rr: hdwy 3f out: rdn to chse ldrs wl over 1f out: kpt on ins fnl f: nrst fin* **8/1[3]**
0131 **5** *2 ¼* **Revue Princess (IRE)**[10] 6107 5-9-0 **73** (b) DavidAllan 1 64
(T D Easterby) *chsd ldrs: rdn along 3f out: drvn wl over 1f out and sn one pce* **11/1**
1530 **6** *½* **River Falcon**[21] 5789 10-8-12 **78** PaulNorton(7) 9 68
(J S Goldie) *hld up and bhd: hdwy on wd outside over 2f out: rdn wl over 1f out: kpt on ins fnl f: nrst fin* **8/1[3]**
4332 **7** *nk* **Pepper Lane**[10] 6113 3-8-12 **74** GrahamGibbons 7 62
(D O'Meara) *midfield: hdwy on inner wl over 2f out: rdn wl over 1f out and sn no imp* **6/1[2]**
2600 **8** *1 ¼* **Turn Me On (IRE)**[15] 5937 7-9-0 **80** LukeStrong(7) 12 66
(T D Walford) *hld up and bhd: hdwy over 2f out: hung rt over 1f out: kpt on ins fnl f* **33/1**
5156 **9** *2 ¾* **Nufoudh (IRE)**[30] 5499 6-8-11 **70** AndrewMullen 14 48
(Miss Tracy Waggott) *dwlt: sn chsng wnr: rdn 3f out: drvn over 2f out and sn wknd* **9/1**
1040 **10** *1 ¾* **Step In Time (IRE)**[21] 5789 3-8-10 **72** GregFairley 8 44
(M Johnston) *in tch: rdn along 3f out: sn wknd* **14/1**
0441 **11** *1 ¼* **Khandaq (USA)**[8] 6186 3-9-2 **78** TomEaves 4 47
(V P Donoghue) *chsd ldng pair: rdn along 3f out: drvn over 2f out and sn wknd* **20/1**
6000 **12** *2 ½* **Deadly Encounter (IRE)**[15] 5937 4-9-1 **74** (b[1]) PaulHanagan 2 37
(R A Fahey) *a towards rr* **11/1**
2600 **13** *1 ¾* **My Gacho (IRE)**[15] 5937 8-9-5 **78** (v) J-PGuillambert 13 37
(M Johnston) *a towards rr* **14/1**
0-20 **14** *2* **Toledo Gold (IRE)**[163] 1361 4-9-0 **73** PJMcDonald 3 26
(E J Alston) *midfield: hdwy and in tch 3f out: sn rdn and wknd fnl 2f* **22/1**

1m 28.19s (-0.81) **Going Correction** -0.05s/f (Good)
WFA 3 from 4yo+ 3lb 14 Ran SP% **121.7**
Speed ratings (Par 105): **102,100,96,95,93 92,92,90,87,85 84,81,79,77**
toteswingers: 1&2 £11.60, 1&3 £51.00, 2&3 £22.00 CSF £52.30 CT £896.76 TOTE £13.40: £4.10, £2.10, £7.00; EX 38.30.
Owner Stewart Aitken **Bred** S Aitken **Trained** Sessay, N Yorks

FOCUS
A competitive 68-80 handicap run at a strong pace. The winner is rated back to his best.
My Gacho(IRE) Official explanation: jockey said gelding suffered interference in running

6395 EUROPEAN BREEDERS' FUND FILLIES' H'CAP 1m
4:00 (4:00) (Class 3) (0-90,87) 3-Y-0+
£8,100 (£2,425; £1,212; £607; £302; £152) Stalls High

Form RPR
215 **1** **Hamloola**[17] 5896 3-8-12 **77** TomEaves 9 89+
(W J Haggas) *trckd ldrs on inner: swtchd lft and smooth hdwy to chal over 2f out: led wl over 1f out: rdn and hung rt ent fnl f: drvn out* **3/1[1]**
5154 **2** *1* **Path Of Peace**[39] 5222 3-8-10 **75** GrahamGibbons 6 83
(J D Bethell) *hld up in tch: hdwy 3f out: pushed along and sltly outpcd over 2f out: sn rdn: styd on to chse wnr ins fnl f: kpt on* **5/1**
0311 **3** *2 ¼* **Social Rhythm**[23] 5732 6-8-7 **68** oh1 PJMcDonald 8 71
(A C Whillans) *dwlt: hld up in rr: hdwy on outer wl over 2f out: rdn wl over 1f out: kpt on ins fnl f* **10/1**
0031 **4** *2 ½* **Harriet's Girl**[10] 6105 4-9-4 **79** AndrewElliott 7 76
(Mrs K Burke) *t.k.h: trckd ldrs: effrt over 2f out: sn rdn and ch tl drvn: edgd rt and one pce appr fnl f* **7/2[2]**
1000 **5** *1 ¾* **Zubova**[8] 6212 3-8-3 **75** (t) NeilFarley(7) 4 68
(D Shaw) *trckd ldrs on outer: effrt and cl up 3f out: rdn over 2f out: drvn and wknd over 1f out* **50/1**
3610 **6** *1* **Cherry Bee**[14] 6003 3-8-6 **71** GregFairley 1 62
(M Johnston) *led: rdn along 3f out: jnd and drvn 2f out: sn hdd & wknd* **16/1**
4003 **7** *3 ¼* **She's In The Money**[14] 6003 4-9-5 **80** PaulHanagan 5 63
(R A Fahey) *t.k.h: trckd ldrs: effrt over 2f out: sn rdn and btn* **6/1**
-400 **8** *8* **Tatiana Romanova (USA)**[27] 5598 3-8-2 **70** JamesSullivan(3) 2 35
(R A Fahey) *rrd s: a in rr* **40/1**
2142 **P** **Cheers For Thea (IRE)**[9] 6167 5-9-12 **87** (bt) DavidAllan 3 —
(T D Easterby) *in tch: hdwy 3f out: rdn 2f out: wknd qckly and eased: bhd whn p.u ins fnl f* **9/2[3]**

1m 40.11s (-1.09) **Going Correction** -0.05s/f (Good)
WFA 3 from 4yo+ 4lb 9 Ran SP% **115.7**
Speed ratings (Par 104): **103,102,99,97,95 94,91,83,—**
toteswingers: 1&2 £5.60, 1&3 £6.00, 2&3 £10.30 CSF £18.37 CT £132.40 TOTE £4.50: £2.70, £3.80, £3.10; EX 26.80.
Owner Hamdan Al Maktoum **Bred** Floors Farming And Dominic Burke **Trained** Newmarket, Suffolk

FOCUS
A competitive 70-87 fillies' handicap run at a strong pace. The form looks sound and the winner was value for further.

NOTEBOOK
Hamloola, who created a good impression when a wide-margin winner of a maiden at Yarmouth in August on her third start, had the outside draw and raced too keenly when fifth on her handicap bow on the all-weather at Kempton. Free early, she was skilfully settled thanks to the generous gallop. Her inexperience showed for a few strides before she put her stamp on the race and in the end ran out a convincing winner. She will improve again and can follow up. (op 5-2 tchd 10-3 in places)
Path Of Peace, who met traffic problems when fourth at York five weeks earlier, stayed on after struggling to keep up. Relatively unexposed she will be suited by a stiffer test. (op 8-1)
Social Rhythm, hoisted 11lb after her Ayr success, was able to follow up here without a penalty. She stayed on in willing fashion from the rear but has plenty on her plate now. (tchd 12-1)
Harriet's Girl, who came late to score from a 4lb lower mark at Ayr, jumped too well, raced far too keenly and saw far too much daylight. There will be another day. (op 9-2 tchd 10-3)
Zubova, another who raced keenly, ended up on the wide outside. Her two wins this year came in claiming company.
Cherry Bee, who took them along at a good pace, was 4lb higher than her two career wins and she prefers proper quick ground. (op 14-1)
Cheers For Thea(IRE), racing from a career high mark, had to race wide early on from her outside draw. She dropped right out and, eventually, pulled up, something had clearly gone amiss. Official explanation: jockey said mare lost its action (tchd 4-1 and 5-1)

6396 SCOTTISH RACING CLAIMING STKS — 1m 1f
4:35 (4:35) (Class 6) 4-Y-O+ — **£1,942** (£578; £288; £144) Stalls High

Form — RPR
5106 **1** **Bencoolen (IRE)**[10] 6106 5-9-4 89 ... MichaelO'Connell(5) 5 — 93
(D Nicholls) *trckd ldrs: effrt 3f out: rdn to chal 2f out: led over 1f out: drvn and styd on strly fnl f* **9/4**[2]
400 **2** *4* **Red Jade**[15] 5949 5-9-13 85 ... PaulHanagan 10 — 89
(R A Fahey) *trckd ldrs: effrt 3f out: rdn and ch 2f out: drvn and one pce appr fnl f* **1/1**[1]
0032 **3** *2 1/4* **King Of The Moors (USA)**[13] 6029 7-8-8 64 ... (b) GrahamGibbons 3 — 65
(R C Guest) *cl up: effrt to ld 3f out: rdn along and hdd 2f out: drvn over 1f out: sn one pce* **9/2**[3]
403 **4** *nk* **Ra Junior (USA)**[13] 6037 4-8-6 65 ... PaulPickard(3) 4 — 65
(P T Midgley) *trckd ldrs: effrt on outer 3f out: rdn 2f out: drvn over 1f out: kpt on same pce* **25/1**
0050 **5** *8* **Finsbury**[6] 6243 7-8-6 62 ... IanBrennan(3) 6 — 49
(Miss L A Perratt) *hld up in rr: sme hdwy 3f out: rdn 2f out and n.d* **20/1**
3445 **6** *11* **Kings Point (IRE)**[13] 6026 9-8-13 60 ... AdrianNicholls 1 — 40
(D Nicholls) *led: rdn along and hdd 3f out: sn wknd* **12/1**
6000 **7** *12* **Sendreni (FR)**[31] 5439 6-8-7 44 ... (p) AndrewMullen 2 — —
(Mrs J C McGregor) *a in rr: bhd fnl 2f* **100/1**
/-00 **8** *27* **Billy One Punch**[57] 4585 8-8-7 54 ... AndrewElliott 8 — —
(A G Foster) *a in rr: bhd fnl 2f* **66/1**

1m 52.77s (-1.13) **Going Correction** -0.05s/f (Good) — **8** Ran SP% **117.7**
Speed ratings (Par 101): **103,99,97,97,90 80,69,45**
toteswingers: 1&2 £1.40, 1&3 £3.20, 2&3 £2.40 CSF £4.90 TOTE £3.20: £1.10, £1.40, £1.70; EX 6.20.
Owner Eamon Maher **Bred** Darley **Trained** Sessay, N Yorks

FOCUS
An uncompetitive claimer. The first two were standouts for the grade and the winner was close to his recent handicap form.
Kings Point(IRE) Official explanation: jockey said horse lost its action

6397 ROYAL SCOTS CLUB H'CAP — 1m 6f
5:10 (5:10) (Class 4) (0-80,78) 3-Y-O+ — **£5,180** (£1,541; £770; £384) Stalls High

Form — RPR
-045 **1** **Chookie Hamilton**[7] 6224 6-9-10 71 ... TomEaves 9 — 83
(V P Donoghue) *trckd ldrs: smooth hdwy 3f out: chal over 2f out: rdn to ld wl over 1f out: drvn ins fnl f and kpt on gamely* **14/1**
-116 **2** *1/2* **Beat The Shower**[21] 5788 4-9-4 65 ... DavidAllan 8 — 76
(P D Niven) *hld up in tch: hdwy on inner over 3f out: swtchd lft and rdn over 2f out: drvn to chal appr fnl f: ev ch tl no ex last 75yds* **9/2**[3]
6210 **3** *2 1/4* **Act Of Kalanisi (IRE)**[14] 5996 4-10-0 75 ... GregFairley 5 — 83
(M Johnston) *led: rdn along over 3f out: drvn and hdd wl over 1f out: kpt on same pce fnl f* **6/1**
-041 **4** *hd* **Lady Bluesky**[13] 6033 7-8-10 60 ... IanBrennan(3) 7 — 68
(A C Whillans) *hld up and bhd: stdy hdwy 3f out: rdn to chse ldrs 2f out: drvn and ch ent fnl f: kpt on same pce* **3/1**[1]
4303 **5** *5* **La Bacouetteuse (FR)**[13] 6033 5-8-13 60 ... LNewman 6 — 61
(A G Foster) *hld up towards rr: hdwy 3f out: rdn over 2f out: sn drvn and no imp appr fnl f* **33/1**
0405 **6** *11* **Corky Dancer**[13] 6028 5-8-8 58 ... JamesSullivan(3) 3 — 43
(P Monteith) *chsd ldrs: rdn along 4f out: wknd over 3f out* **40/1**
6004 **7** *1 3/4* **Amanda Carter**[12] 6050 6-9-11 72 ... PaulHanagan 1 — 55
(R A Fahey) *trckd ldrs: effrt 3f out: sn rdn: drvn over 2f out and sn wknd* **15/2**
2354 **8** *3/4* **Forrest Flyer (IRE)**[9] 6143 6-9-2 70 ... PaulNorton(7) 2 — 52
(J S Goldie) *disp ld: rdn along over 3f out: sn wknd* **9/1**
-212 **9** *3 1/2* **Fourth Generation (IRE)**[34] 5371 3-9-7 78 ... PJMcDonald 4 — 55
(G A Swinbank) *hld up in rr: effrt over 3f out: sn rdn and nvr a factor* **10/3**[2]

3m 2.76s (-2.54) **Going Correction** -0.05s/f (Good)
WFA 3 from 4yo+ 10lb — **9** Ran SP% **114.4**
Speed ratings (Par 105): **105,104,103,103,100 94,93,92,90**
toteswingers: 1&2 £15.80, 1&3 £13.40, 2&3 £5.50 CSF £75.16 CT £424.98 TOTE £13.00: £3.40, £1.40, £2.30; EX 93.50.
Owner Hamilton Park Members Syndicate **Bred** D And J Raeburn **Trained** Carluke, South Lanarkshire

FOCUS
A competitive 58-75 stayers' handicap run at a sound pace. The winner rates a small personal best on turf.
Corky Dancer Official explanation: vet said gelding returned lame right-fore
Fourth Generation(IRE) Official explanation: trainer had no explanation for the poor form shown

6398 ROYAL REGIMENT OF SCOTLAND H'CAP — 5f
5:40 (5:40) (Class 6) (0-65,65) 4-Y-O+ — **£2,590** (£770; £385; £192) Stalls Low

Form — RPR
2302 **1** **Highland Warrior**[13] 6031 11-9-4 65 ... PaulPickard(3) 2 — 75
(P T Midgley) *in rr: hdwy 2f out: swtchd rt and rdn over 1f out: str run ent fnl f to ld last 100yds* **6/1**
3415 **2** *1 1/4* **Sandwith**[10] 6103 7-9-3 61 ... (v) LNewman 4 — 66
(A G Foster) *chsd ldrs: hdwy wl over 1f out: rdn and kpt on ins fnl f: tk 2nd nr fin* **9/2**[2]
4000 **3** *1/2* **Wicked Wilma (IRE)**[10] 6103 6-9-5 63 ... AdrianNicholls 7 — 66
(A Berry) *trckd ldng pair: hdwy 1/2-way: led over 1f out: rdn ins fnl f: hdd & wknd last 100yds* **12/1**
0462 **4** *3/4* **Sharp Bullet (IRE)**[6] 6246 4-9-1 59 ... (b) GregFairley 1 — 60
(Bruce Hellier) *qckly away and led: jnd 2f out and sn rdn: hdd over 1f out: wknd ent fnl f* **7/2**[1]
1005 **5** *5* **Cross Of Lorraine (IRE)**[22] 5760 7-9-4 62 ... (b) PaulHanagan 6 — 45
(C Grant) *chsd ldrs: rdn along 2f out: sn wknd* **6/1**
0013 **6** *3 3/4* **Bravely (IRE)**[10] 6103 6-9-3 61 ... DavidAllan 3 — 30
(T D Easterby) *chsd ldr: rdn along wl over 2f out: sn drvn and wknd appr fnl f* **7/2**[1]
0004 **7** *1 3/4* **Fuzzy Cat**[8] 6189 4-8-13 57 ... (b) GrahamGibbons 5 — 20
(T D Barron) *sn rdn along and a in rr* **11/2**[3]

60.57 secs (0.17) **Going Correction** +0.075s/f (Good) — **7** Ran SP% **114.3**
Speed ratings (Par 101): **101,99,98,97,89 83,80**
toteswingers: 1&2 £4.40, 1&3 £14.60, 2&3 £22.20 CSF £32.77 TOTE £8.00: £3.70, £2.40; EX 31.10 Place 6 £59.77, Place 5 £41.92.
Owner R Wardlaw **Bred** Rowcliffe Stud **Trained** Westow, N Yorks

FOCUS
Plenty of course regulars in this modest finale. It was strongly run. the winner was back to his early-season form.
Bravely(IRE) Official explanation: jockey said gelding never travelled
T/Plt: £70.80 to a £1 stake. Pool: £55,093.62. 567.91 winning units. T/Qpdt: £17.70 to a £1 stake. Pool: £3,845.55. 160.20 winning units. JR

6399 - 6400a (Foreign Racing) - See Raceform Interactive

6004 CURRAGH (R-H)
Sunday, September 26

OFFICIAL GOING: Yielding to soft

6401a C.L. WELD PARK STKS (GROUP 3) (FILLIES) — 7f
3:15 (3:19) 2-Y-O — **£34,513** (£10,088; £4,778; £1,592)

RPR
1 **Chrysanthemum (IRE)**[14] 6005 2-8-12 ... WMLordan 7 — 104+
(David Wachman, Ire) *hld up early: impr into 5th 2 1/2f out: rdn and hdwy under 2f out: chal ins fnl f: styd on to ld cl home* **7/2**[2]
2 *hd* **Wild Wind (GER)**[28] 5570 2-8-12 97 ... JMurtagh 2 — 104
(A P O'Brien, Ire) *uns rdr bef s: hld up in rr: hdwy into 6th under 2f out: 3rd and chal ins fnl f: ev ch last 100yds: jst hld* **11/4**[1]
3 *hd* **Bible Belt (IRE)**[20] 5822 2-8-12 90 ... FMBerry 1 — 103
(Mrs John Harrington, Ire) *prom: 4th 1/2-way: 3rd and rdn under 2f out: led under 1f out: sn strly pressed: kpt on u.p: hdd cl home* **5/1**[3]
4 *1 1/4* **Quiet Oasis (IRE)**[23] 5721 2-8-12 ... CO'Donoghue 11 — 100
(B J Meehan) *trckd ldrs: 5th and rdn 2f out: 3rd 1 1/2f out: 4th and kpt on ins fnl f* **6/1**
5 *7* **Katla (IRE)**[15] 5974 2-8-12 101 ... WJLee 5 — 86+
(J F Grogan, Ire) *mod 2nd: smooth hdwy 2 1/2f out: led under 2f out: hdd under 1f out: sn 4th and no ex whn eased cl home* **8/1**
6 *nk* **Hope Of An Angel (IRE)**[27] 5618 2-8-12 80 ... (p) GFCarroll 4 — 82
(Niall Moran, Ire) *chsd ldrs in 5th: drvn along 1/2-way: no imp fr 2f out* **33/1**
7 *nk* **Banimpire (IRE)**[14] 6005 2-8-12 95 ... KJManning 10 — 81
(J S Bolger, Ire) *hld up towards rr: no imp fr over 2f out: one pce* **12/1**
8 *3* **Peahen**[14] 6005 2-8-12 89 ... KLatham 6 — 73
(G M Lyons, Ire) *hld up: rdn and no imp fr over 2f out* **12/1**
9 *hd* **Eirnin (IRE)**[22] 5771 2-8-12 ... JPO'Brien 8 — 73
(A P O'Brien, Ire) *mid-div: wknd fr over 2f out* **50/1**
10 *1 3/4* **Sonning Rose (IRE)**[16] 5910 2-8-12 ... DPMcDonogh 3 — 69
(M R Channon) *mod 3rd: rdn after 1/2-way: sn wknd* **10/1**
11 *1/2* **Juliet Capulet (IRE)**[14] 6005 2-8-12 86 ... (b) JAHeffernan 9 — 67
(A P O'Brien, Ire) *led: clr 1/2-way: rdn 2 1/2f out: hdd under 2f out: sn wknd* **25/1**

1m 28.96s (-1.84) **Going Correction** -0.05s/f (Good) — **11** Ran SP% **124.2**
Speed ratings: **108,107,107,106,98 97,97,94,93,91 91**
CSF £14.23 TOTE £4.10: £1.40, £1.60, £2.00; DF 17.70.
Owner Michael Tabor **Bred** Pegasus Breeding Ltd **Trained** Goolds Cross, Co Tipperary

FOCUS
The sixth is an anchor to the form and the winner has been rated 9lb off the current top fillies, but she should improve for a step up to 1m.

NOTEBOOK
Chrysanthemum(IRE) made it two wins from as many outings and completed the task in tenacious fashion over this sharper trip. She still looked green here and does have that touch of class about her. It is unlikely that she will run again this season, although the Rockfel at Newmarket next month appeals as a viable target should connections pull her out again, but she looks a promising prospect for next season at 1m and maybe a bit further. (op 5/2)
Wild Wind(GER), beaten almost seven lengths by stablemate Misty For Me in the Group 1 Moyglare Stud Stakes, had beaten the Moyglare runner-up Laughing Lashes in a maiden over this C&D in June. Racing on slow ground for the first time here, she unseated her rider before the start and was held up in rear until beginning her run over 2f out. She drew level with Chrysanthemum inside the last 100 yards and stayed on although the winner was edging ahead near the finish. (op 3/1)
Bible Belt(IRE), a 5l winner of a maiden over this trip on soft to heavy ground at Roscommon on her second start this month, closed early in the straight and challenged to lead inside the final furlong. She kept on under pressure when headed and could bag herself a race of this class when ridden with a little more restraint. (op 11/2)
Quiet Oasis(IRE), a winner over the trip on the AW at Kempton on the second of her two previous starts, went third under 2f out and had every chance before failing to raise her effort entering the final furlong. This was still a decent run. (op 8/1)
Katla(IRE), winner of a 6f maiden on good ground at Cork, had lost out by only a short head at Listed level here 15 days previously. She was tackling this distance for the first time and after racing prominently she went to the front under 2f out before being headed and weakening quickly inside the final furlong. (op 7/1)

6403a JUDDMONTE BERESFORD STKS (GROUP 2) — 1m
4:25 (4:27) 2-Y-O — **£57,522** (£16,814; £7,964; £2,654)

RPR
1 **Casamento (IRE)**[15] 5975 2-9-1 ... PJSmullen 6 — 109+
(M Halford, Ire) *racd in 2nd: impr to ld under 1 1/2f out: rdn clr fnl f: easily* **4/6**[1]
2 *4* **Mawaakef (IRE)**[37] 5279 2-9-1 91 ... DPMcDonogh 3 — 101
(Kevin Prendergast, Ire) *trckd ldrs in 3rd: pushed along ent st: kpt on u.p to go mod 2nd ins fnl f* **7/2**[2]
3 *2 1/2* **Robin Hood (IRE)**[22] 5746 2-9-1 92 ... JAHeffernan 1 — 95
(A P O'Brien, Ire) *led: rdn 2f out: sn strly pressed: hdd under 1 1/2f out: 3rd and no ex ins fnl f* **12/1**

4 *hd* **Factum (USA)**[21] 5792 2-9-1 90.. JMurtagh 7 95
(A P O'Brien, Ire) *trckd ldrs in 4th: 5th and outpcd early st: kpt on fr over 1f out* **7/1**[3]
5 *2 ½* **Rossvoss**[15] 5979 2-9-1 .... WMLordan 2 89
(T M Walsh, Ire) *hld up towards rr: 6th and rdn early st: no imp: one pce* **40/1**
6 *nk* **Music In The Rain (IRE)**[67] 4270 2-9-1 ....(t) KJManning 4 88
(J S Bolger, Ire) *trckd ldrs in 5th: 4th and rdn ent st: no ex fr 2f out* **9/1**
7 *2 ½* **Hold The Aces**[12] 6067 2-9-1 .... DMGrant 5 83
(John Joseph Murphy, Ire) *hld up in rr: effrt and no imp early st: no ex whn eased ins fnl f* **40/1**

1m 43.52s (-2.48) **Going Correction** -0.05s/f (Good) 7 Ran SP% **117.3**
Speed ratings: **110,106,103,103,100 100,98**
CSF £3.49 TOTE £1.50: £1.40, £1.60; DF 3.30.
Owner Sheikh Mohammed **Bred** D And J Cantillon & C & K Canning **Trained** Doneany, Co Kildare

FOCUS
The winner has been rated 10lb below his National Stakes form despite coming clear in the closing stages.

NOTEBOOK
Casamento(IRE), supplemented for this at a cost of 10,000euros earlier in the week, ran out a decisive winner, paying a compliment to Jessica Harrington's unbeaten Pathfork, and advertising his own potential as a Classic contender by drawing clear of his rivals over the final furlong of this Group 2 event. It may not have been a vintage renewal of a race which numbers Alamshar, Azamour, Sea The Stars and St Nicholas Abbey among its winners over the past decade, but, after taking time to reach full stretch, the winner, who went to the front over 1f out, stayed on well despite appearing to idle in front. He was cut to 16-1(from 20-1) by Ladbrokes for the 2000 Guineas. (op 1/2)
Mawaakef(IRE), winner of a maiden over the trip at Killarney last month, stayed on best of the rest over the last 1½f without ever posing a threat to the winner. (op 5/1)
Robin Hood(IRE), well beaten on his two starts since winning a 7f maiden at the Galway festival in July, led after about 1f and stuck to his task untilt the winner took his measure over 1f out. (op 12/1 tchd 10/1)
Factum(USA), beaten a neck by Mawaakef at Killarney before scoring a narrow win over 7f at Dundalk, was held up in touch and kept on from over 1f out without ever being in serious contention.

6402 - 6405a (Foreign Racing) - See Raceform Interactive

5132 COLOGNE (R-H)
Sunday, September 26

OFFICIAL GOING: Turf: soft

6406a ILSE UND HEINZ RAMM ERINNERUNGSRENNEN (LISTED RACE) (TURF) 5f
1:00 (12:00) 3-Y-0+ **£11,504** (£3,539; £1,769; £442; £442)

RPR
1 **Calrissian (GER)**[14] 6-9-1 0... AStarke 9 92
(Fredrik Reuterskiold, Sweden) **22/5**
2 *shd* **Govinda (USA)**[72] 4122 3-9-4 0.. EPedroza 7 96
(A Wohler, Germany) **2/1**[1]
3 *2* **Walero (GER)**[28] 5573 4-8-13 0... AHelfenbein 2 83
(Uwe Ostmann, Germany) **33/10**[2]
4 *½* **Saldenaera (GER)** 3-9-1 0.. ADeVries 1 84
(Uwe Ostmann, Germany) **155/10**
4 *dht* **Ardha (USA)**[13] 3-8-8 0... DominiqueBoeuf 5 77
(H-A Pantall, France) **74/10**
6 *shd* **Love And Devotion**[108] 3-8-10 0.. JohanVictoire 4 79
(H-A Pantall, France) **214/10**
7 *hd* **Impressible**[18] 5851 4-8-9 0... MickyFenton 3 76
(S C Williams) *broke fast to ld initially: then settled in 2nd: chal for ld ent st: r.o u.p: fafed fnl f* **27/1**
8 *1 ½* **Pareia (GER)**[338] 6-8-9 0... APietsch 8 71
(Uwe Ostmann, Germany) **39/10**[3]
9 *hd* **Lady Areia (GER)**[23] 5739 4-8-11 0... VSchulepov 6 72
(H J Groschel, Germany) **101/10**

56.54 secs (-0.39)
WFA 3 from 4yo+ 1lb 9 Ran SP% **130.5**
WIN (incl 10 euro stake); 54. PLACES: 18, 13, 14. SF: 187.
Owner Fredrik Reuterskiold **Bred** Graf & Grfin Von Stauffenberg **Trained** Sweden

NOTEBOOK
Impressible is an 85-rated handicapper who hasn't won for over a year, and her quest for black type came up short.

6407a PREIS DES UNION GESTUTS (LISTED RACE) (TURF) 7f 110y
1:30 (12:00) 2-Y-0 **£26,548** (£8,849; £4,867; £2,654; £1,327)

RPR
1 **Jardina (GER)** 2-8-11 0... AStarke 7 95
(P Schiergen, Germany) **13/2**
2 *2* **Taleia (GER)** 2-8-11 0... EPedroza 8 91
(A Wohler, Germany) **154/10**
3 *nk* **Night Of Dubai (IRE)**[23] 5740 2-9-2 0... THellier 1 95
(Mario Hofer, Germany) **33/10**[2]
4 *1 ½* **Fanny May**[57] 4611 2-9-2 0.. JohanVictoire 6 91
(D J Coakley) *racd in midfield: unsuited by slow pce and nvr settled: moved into 2nd at end of bk st: r.o wl to the line* **48/10**[3]
5 *8* **Alajana (GER)** 2-8-11 0.. ThierryThulliez 2 68
(J-P Carvalho, Germany) **232/10**
6 *2 ½* **Selkis (GER)** 2-9-2 0.. ADeVries 5 67
(J Hirschberger, Germany) **9/10**[1]
7 *¾* **Shy Fairy (GER)** 2-9-2 0.. VSchulepov 4 65
(H J Groschel, Germany) **12/1**
8 *9* **Master Shade (ITY)** 2-9-2 0.. FilipMinarik 9 44
(P Schiergen, Germany) **112/10**

1m 33.46s (93.46) 8 Ran SP% **132.6**
WIN (incl 10 euro stake): 75. PLACES: 22, 33, 20. SF: 769.
Owner Stall Nizza **Bred** J Imm **Trained** Germany

NOTEBOOK
Fanny May stayed on at the finish but couldn't quite make the places. Her pedigree suggests she'll appreciate a step up to 1m and make a better 3-y-o.

6408a GROSSE EUROPA MEILE DER STALL ASTERBLUTE GMBH UND DER ROWER & RUB GMBH (GROUP 2) (3YO+) (TURF) 1m
3:05 (12:00) 3-Y-0+ **£35,398** (£13,716; £5,752; £3,539; £2,212; £1,327)

RPR
1 **Alianthus (GER)**[28] 5-9-2 0.. ADeVries 7 110
(J Hirschberger, Germany) *broke wl to ld: set gd pce: r.o wl in st: extended ld: won comf* **33/10**[2]
2 *3* **Noble Alpha (IRE)**[63] 4418 3-8-11 0.. THellier 9 102
(Mario Hofer, Germany) *settled in midfield: sn to chal early in st: gd move 1 1/2f out and r.o wl to claim 2nd ins fnl f* **107/10**
3 *1 ¾* **Win For Sure (GER)**[26] 5649 5-9-2 0...................................... EPedroza 5 99
(A Wohler, Germany) *prom fr s: pursuing ldr: r.o wl in st but no ex fnl f and ct ins fnl f for 2nd* **17/5**[3]
4 *5* **Freminius (GER)**[49] 4888 6-9-2 0................................ DominiqueBoeuf 8 87
(W Baltromei, Germany) *settled in 5th: r.o wl in st but nvr threatened ldrs* **42/10**
5 *1 ¾* **Le Big (GER)**[26] 5649 6-9-2 0... FilipMinarik 3 83
(U Stoltefuss, Germany) *broke poorly and settled towards rr: appearing rel to r: mde move towards end of bk st: styd on in st but no threat* **208/10**
6 *hd* **Beagle Boy (IRE)**[39] 3-8-11 0.. JBojko 1 82
(A Wohler, Germany) *broke slowly and settled towards rr: briefly threatned early in st but then fdd* **57/10**
7 *4* **Fabiana**[26] 5649 4-8-13 0.. AStarke 2 71
(Andreas Lowe, Germany) *settled in 4th: rdn early in st: no ex: fdd bdly fnl f* **11/5**[1]
8 *3* **Santino (GER)**[12] 3-8-11 0... ThierryThulliez 4 66
(J-P Carvalho, Germany) *racd in 3rd: moved to 2nd in bk st: briefly threatened early in st but sn btn* **149/10**

1m 38.01s (-0.38)
WFA 3 from 4yo+ 4lb 8 Ran SP% **130.8**
WIN (incl 10 euro stake): 43. PLACES: 20, 27, 18. SF: 388.
Owner Baron G Von Ullmann **Bred** Gestut Karlshof **Trained** Germany

6409a PREIS DER SPIELBANK BAD NEUENAHR (LISTED RACE) (F&M) (TURF) 1m
3:40 (12:00) 3-Y-0+ **£11,504** (£3,539; £1,769; £884)

RPR
1 **Reine Heureuse (GER)**[14] 3-9-1 0... DPorcu 10 101
(Uwe Ostmann, Germany) **29/10**[2]
2 *1 ¼* **Flash Dance (IRE)**[21] 5802 4-9-3 0..................................... JohanVictoire 1 96
(H-A Pantall, France) **5/2**[1]
3 *3* **Diatribe**[112] 3-8-8 0.. ThierryThulliez 6 84
(W Baltromei, Germany) **239/10**
4 *3* **Glady Romana (GER)**[56] 4640 3-8-8 0........................... DominiqueBoeuf 11 77
(W Baltromei, Germany) **17/2**
5 *½* **Kameruka**[26] 4-9-3 0.. RonanThomas 4 81
(R Pritchard-Gordon, France) **73/10**
6 *1 ½* **Amazing Beauty (GER)**[23] 5739 3-8-10 0.................................... EPedroza 5 75
(A Wohler, Germany) **92/10**
7 *3* **Singuna (GER)**[21] 5805 3-8-8 0.. JBojko 7 66
(A Wohler, Germany) **27/1**
8 *1* **Adorna (GER)** 3-8-8 0.. SHellyn 9 63
(J Hirschberger, Germany) **48/10**[3]
9 *hd* **Ronja (USA)**[148] 1715 3-9-1 0... APietsch 2 70
(W Hickst, Germany) **61/10**
10 *nk* **Qalahari (IRE)**[16] 5919 4-8-13 0.. MickyFenton 3 63
(D J Coakley) *settled in midfield: grad dropped bk: nvr figured in st* **185/10**

1m 39.82s (1.43)
WFA 3 from 4yo 4lb 10 Ran SP% **130.6**
WIN (incl 10 euro stake): 39. PLACES: 16, 15, 33. SF: 102.
Owner Gestut Auenquelle **Bred** Gestut Auenquelle **Trained** Germany

NOTEBOOK
Qalahari(IRE), who is rated 79 on turf, faced a stiff task in this company and never got competitive.

6410a PREIS VON EUROPA (GROUP 1) (3YO+) (TURF) 1m 4f
4:15 (12:00) 3-Y-0+ **£88,495** (£29,203; £13,274; £6,194)

RPR
1 **Scalo**[42] 5135 3-8-13 0... OlivierPeslier 5 117
(A Wohler, Germany) *broke wl: settled in 5th: then dropped bk to the rr: mde gd prog arnd fnl turn: swtchd wd to make chal in st: qcknd wl to take ld 1 1/2f out: drew clr fnl f* **11/5**[2]
2 *1 ¾* **Night Magic (GER)**[21] 5806 4-9-3 0.. KKerekes 9 110
(W Figge, Germany) *broke wl but plld hrd fr the s: racd bhd ldrs on rail: full of running ent st: gd move on ins to chse wnr home* **8/5**[1]
3 *1 ½* **Quijano (GER)**[21] 5806 8-9-6 0.. AStarke 6 111
(P Schiergen, Germany) *settled in midfield: mde move early in st: r.o wl fnl f to win battle for 3rd clsng stages* **42/10**[3]
4 *½* **Soberania (GER)**[43] 5108 4-9-3 0... EPedroza 4 107
(A Wohler, Germany) *broke wl: settled in 3rd bhd ldr: moved to 2nd at end of bk st: qcknd to chal early in st: tk ld 2f out: no ex fnl f: fdd* **17/1**
5 *4 ½* **Tres Rock Danon (FR)**[35] 5349 4-9-6 0............................ DominiqueBoeuf 8 103
(W Hickst, Germany) *settled in 5th: rdn but no ex in st: styd on at one pce* **63/10**
6 *3 ½* **Mulan (GER)**[25] 5671 3-8-13 0.. APietsch 2 98
(W Hickst, Germany) *broke wl: a.p: no ex in st: wknd* **227/10**
7 *¾* **Allied Powers (IRE)**[21] 5806 5-9-6 0.. MickyFenton 7 96
(M L W Bell) *settled towards rr fr s: nvr figured in st* **59/10**
8 *12* **Northern Glory**[21] 5806 7-9-6 0... MSuerland 3 77
(W Figge, Germany) *led fr s: setting gd pce for favourite (Night Magic): led into st: r.o u.p but sn fdd* **26/1**

2m 34.53s (1.63)
WFA 3 from 4yo+ 8lb 8 Ran SP% **130.6**
WIN (incl 10 euro stake): 32. PLACES: 11, 11, 13. SF: 81.
Owner Gestut Ittlingen **Bred** Gestut Hof Ittlingen **Trained** Germany

NOTEBOOK

Scalo showed a bright turn of pace in the closing stages to record his first win at Group 1 level and stamp himself Germany's top 3-y-o. The Canadian International could well be on his agenda now, while it was also confirmed that he will stay in training as a 4-y-o.

Allied Powers(IRE), who has come up short since stepping up to Group 1 company, never threatened to land a blow on this occasion, with his rider reporting that he slipped on the first bend and lost his action.

5871 BATH (L-H)

Monday, September 27

OFFICIAL GOING: Good to firm (9.1)

Last two races abandoned due to fog.

Wind: Moderate across Weather: Fog, poor visibility

6411 JOHN SISK NURSERY (DIV I) 1m 5y

2:00 (2:01) (Class 5) (0-70,70) 2-Y-O **£1,748** (£520; £260; £129) Stalls Low

Form RPR

0504 **1** **Whodathought (IRE)**[21] 5807 2-9-5 **68**.........................(b) RyanMoore 7 71
(R Hannon) *trckd ldr: drvn to take slt ld 2f out: strly chal fr over 1f out and ins fnl f: asserted u.p fnl 120yds* **7/2**[1]

5333 **2** 1 **Zakon (IRE)**[46] 4993 2-9-7 **70**.. EddieAhern 6 71
(D J Coakley) *in tch: hmpd ins fnl 2f: styd on fr over 1f out and r.o ins fnl f to take 2nd nr fin but no imp on wnr* **4/1**[2]

054 **3** 3/4 **Holy Mackerel (IRE)**[18] 5871 2-8-12 **61**.......................... SamHitchcott 2 60
(M R Channon) *sn led: rdn and narrowly hdd 2f out: styd pressing wnr tl outpcd fnl 120yds: lost 2nd cl home* **7/1**

0031 **4** nk **Dew Reward (IRE)**[21] 5807 2-9-0 **63**........................... CathyGannon 1 62
(Eve Johnson Houghton) *chsd ldrs: rdn along 3f out: styd on fnl f but nvr gng pce to chal* **8/1**

000 **5** 1 1/4 **Focail Maith**[45] 5047 2-9-2 **65**...................................... StevieDonohoe 3 61
(J Ryan) *in tch: rdn 3f out: kpt on ins fnl f but nvr gng pce to trble ldrs* **7/1**

3002 **6** 1 **May's Boy**[16] 5969 2-8-6 **60**...............................(p) AdamBeschizza(5) 5 53
(M D I Usher) *chsd ldrs: rdn over 3f out: styd on same pce fnl 2f* **11/2**[3]

005 **7** 2 1/4 **Beach Babe**[28] 5583 2-9-2 **65**... TravisBlock 11 53
(J G Portman) *towards rr: styd on fnl 2f but nvr a threat* **33/1**

5550 **8** 1 1/2 **Minus Tolerance**[28] 5581 2-8-0 **49** oh2 ow2............ FrankieMcDonald 4 34
(Miss S L Davison) *chsd ldrs: n.m.r and rdn 2f out: sn wknd* **100/1**

060 **9** 2 3/4 **Droxford (USA)**[17] 5924 2-8-7 **56** ow1...................(b) FergusSweeney 12 34
(J A Osborne) *chsd ldrs: rdn 3f out: wknd fr 2f out* **25/1**

4306 **10** 1 1/4 **Stacey**[26] 5660 2-8-7 **56**.. NeilChalmers 10 32
(M Blanshard) *a towards rr* **40/1**

050 **11** 12 **Sodashy (IRE)**[32] 5452 2-9-3 **66**................................. J-PGuillambert 8 14
(Miss Amy Weaver) *racd on outer: a in rr* **18/1**

0006 **12** 4 **Dolcezza (IRE)**[12] 6081 2-8-8 **57**................................ EddieCreighton 9 —
(B J Meehan) *chsd ldrs over 5f* **12/1**

1m 41.72s (0.92) **Going Correction** -0.10s/f (Good) **12** Ran SP% **116.9**

Speed ratings (Par 95): **91,90,89,88,87 86,84,82,80,78 66,62**

toteswingers:1&2:£2.30, 1&3:£11.20, 2&3:£9.30 CSF £16.49 CT £94.75 TOTE £3.80: £1.30, £1.50, £3.50; EX 16.70 Trifecta £50.70 Pool: £192.69 - 2.81 winning units..

Owner Mrs Philip Snow **Bred** Meadowlands Stud **Trained** East Everleigh, Wilts

FOCUS

Thick mist obscured most of the first half of the race but the action in the home straight could be pieced together from television pictures. Those who raced near the front did best.

NOTEBOOK

Whodathought(IRE) had shown he was competitive off this mark last time but this was still a step up on previous nursery form. Despite being one of the most experienced in the field, he is still improving but these middling events will remain his level. (op 4-1)

Zakon(IRE) ◆ made a good impression on this first outing in handicap company, doing by far the best of the hold-up runners. He needs this trip to bring out the best in him and should win a similar race as long as there is a good gallop. (op 7-2)

Holy Mackerel(IRE) was supported at longish odds to make a winning nursery debut. Though run out of it late on, he ran much better than he had in maidens and has prospects in similar company, with these more positive tactics appearing to suit him. (op 14-1 tchd 13-2)

Dew Reward(IRE) was 12lb higher than when winning over C&D last time, and the turnaround in the weights with the winner proved to be crucial. (op 13-2)

Focail Maith had shown some ability in his second and third maidens, and the step up to 1m helped him get even closer. His handicap mark looks reasonable, so he is one to consider for a similar event as he continues to come on. (tchd 13-2)

May's Boy is inconsistent and did not live up to the promise of his Sandown performance despite wearing first-time cheekpieces. (op 6-1 tchd 13-2)

Sodashy(IRE) Official explanation: jockey said filly lost its action

6412 JOHN SISK NURSERY (DIV II) 1m 5y

2:30 (2:32) (Class 5) (0-70,68) 2-Y-O **£1,748** (£520; £260; £129) Stalls Low

Form RPR

0602 **1** **Amistress**[4] 6302 2-7-12 **45**... CathyGannon 11 52
(Eve Johnson Houghton) *trckd ldr: drvn to ld over 2f out: styd on strly fnl f* **8/1**

3045 **2** 3 **Barista (IRE)**[12] 6081 2-9-4 **65**.. SamHitchcott 3 65
(M R Channon) *in tch: rdn 3f out and hdwy over 2f out: styd on u.p to take 2nd fnl 100yds but no imp on wnr* **13/2**

6433 **3** 1 **Papas Fritas**[12] 6082 2-9-2 **63**...................................(b[1]) EddieCreighton 8 61
(B J Meehan) *unruly stalls: plld hrd and led: hdd over 2f out: no ch w wnr over 1f out: one pce and dropped to 3rd fnl 100yds* **11/1**

6303 **4** 2 **Ivan Vasilevich (IRE)**[20] 5837 2-9-4 **65**........................ TomMcLaughlin 5 58
(Jane Chapple-Hyam) *chsd ldrs: rdn 3f out: one pce fnl 2f* **4/1**[2]

0233 **5** 1 1/4 **Kissing Clara (IRE)**[12] 6070 2-9-5 **66**......................(b[1]) StevieDonohoe 6 56
(J S Moore) *t.k.h: chsd ldrs: rdn over 2f out: wknd fnl f and no ch whn eased fnl 50yds* **14/1**

0311 **6** 2 1/2 **Ninfea (IRE)**[12] 6081 2-9-2 **68**............................. AdamBeschizza(5) 12 52
(S Kirk) *sn trcking ldrs: awkward on bnd ins fnl 5f and lost position: sme prog u.p over 2f out: nvr a threat and wknd fnl f* **11/4**[1]

523 **7** 3 **Mark Harbour (IRE)**[32] 5440 2-9-6 **67**................................ RyanMoore 9 45
(R Hannon) *in rr: wd bnd over 3f out and hrd drvn: mod prog fr over 1f out* **9/2**[3]

0400 **8** 1 **Gower Rules (IRE)**[34] 5389 2-8-9 **56**........................ FergusSweeney 4 31
(M D I Usher) *in rr hrd drvn 3f out and no imp fnl 2f* **50/1**

005 **9** 1/2 **Nutley Copse**[18] 5894 2-8-4 **51** ow1...........................(v) NeilChalmers 10 25
(A M Balding) *v.s.a: in rr: mod prog fnl 2f* **14/1**

010 **10** 12 **History Repeating**[20] 5837 2-8-13 **60**................................ TravisBlock 2 7
(M D I Usher) *a towards rr* **50/1**

0640 **11** 1 **Seas Of Sorrow (IRE)**[12] 6081 2-8-9 **59** ow3........(b[1]) RobertLButler(3) 7 3
(B W Duke) *chsd ldrs 5f* **100/1**

1m 41.34s (0.54) **Going Correction** -0.10s/f (Good) **11** Ran SP% **115.9**

Speed ratings (Par 95): **93,90,89,87,85 83,80,79,78,66 65**

toteswingers:1&2:£12.20, 1&3:£12.50, 2&3:£13.00 CSF £58.07 CT £584.49 TOTE £7.60: £2.00, £1.30, £3.30; EX 69.70 TRIFECTA Not won..

Owner Mrs P Robeson **Bred** Southcourt Stud **Trained** Blewbury, Oxon

FOCUS

Though far from perfect, the visibility was slightly better than it had been for the first. They went a decent gallop and the field was soon strung out.

NOTEBOOK

Amistress has improved significantly in her last two races and this was due reward for an excellent run from out of the handicap last time. She is capable of handling a 6-7lb rise in the weights but her mark will still be a low one so it would make sense not to get over-excited.

Barista(IRE) has been running well regularly in nurseries off this sort of mark, and this was a typically gallant effort. Once again he appeared to be a few pounds too high, but that was exaggerated by the well-handicapped winner. (op 8-1 tchd 6-1)

Papas Fritas was over-keen wearing blinkers for the first time but he just ran a similar race to his previous two, both of which had been on Polytrack. He is consistent enough and should get his chance if he is dropped a little in the handicap. (op 17-2)

Ivan Vasilevich(IRE) ran another fair race in handicap company. While his mark looks to be a testing one, he stayed 1m and is worth another try at this trip. (tchd 7-2 and 9-2)

Kissing Clara(IRE) ran better than she had in her only previous nursery, but the first-time blinkers could not disguise the fact that she has too much weight in these events. Official explanation: jockey said filly lost its action closing stages (tchd 12-1)

Ninfea(IRE) was on a tough mark following her Polytrack win last time, but this was still disappointing. (op 7-2)

Mark Harbour(IRE) took far too long to get going, setting himself too much to do on this first run in handicap company. He will have to do much better than this to justify his mark. (tchd 5-1 in places)

Nutley Copse Official explanation: jockey said filly missed the break

6413 SISK RAIL "HANDS AND HEELS" APPRENTICE SERIES H'CAP (PART OF THE RACING EXCELLENCE INITIATIVE) 1m 5y

3:00 (3:00) (Class 5) (0-70,69) 3-Y-O **£2,007** (£597; £298; £149) Stalls Low

Form RPR

4521 **1** **Lutine Charlie (IRE)**[18] 5877 3-9-1 **66**................(p) MatthewCosham(3) 8 72
(J L Flint) *mde all: drvn along fr over 2f out: styd on gamely fnl f* **9/4**[1]

0044 **2** 3/4 **Hierarch (IRE)**[10] 6164 3-9-7 **69**....................................... RyanPowell 4 73
(R Hannon) *hld up in tch: hdwy over 2f out: ev ch 1f out: styd on to take 2nd ins fnl f but no imp on wnr* **11/1**

0054 **3** 3/4 **Collect Art (IRE)**[37] 5299 3-8-12 **63**......................... LucyBarry(3) 6 66
(A B Haynes) *in rr: improving whn nt clr run over 2f out: styd on fr over 1f out and kpt on fnl 120yds to take 3rd cl home but nvr a threat* **20/1**

6043 **4** nk **Music Maestro (IRE)**[17] 5925 3-8-8 **61**..................... DanielHarris(5) 5 63
(B W Hills) *trckd wnr: wnt wd on bnd ins fnl 5f: pushed along and ev ch appr fnl f: kpt on same pce* **11/1**

3412 **5** 1/2 **Catchanova (IRE)**[18] 5877 3-9-2 **64**............................... NathanAlison 1 65
(Eve Johnson Houghton) *chsd ldrs: drvn to chal over 1f out: wknd fnl 50yds* **3/1**[2]

6460 **6** 2 3/4 **Swiftly Done (IRE)**[8] 6225 3-9-3 **65**....................................... NeilFarley 7 60
(D Carroll) *in rr: drvn and sme hdwy over 2f out: styd on same pce fnl f* **11/2**[3]

0441 **7** 1 1/4 **Youm Al Mizayin**[12] 6076 3-8-8 **56**............................ MatthewLawson 2 48
(M R Channon) *chsd ldrs: rdn over 2f out: wknd over 1f out* **13/2**

2400 **8** 8 **Magenta Strait**[23] 5767 3-8-2 **54**.................................. JackDuern(5) 9 28
(R Hollinshead) *s.i.s: in tch: chsd ldrs and rdn 3f out: wknd wl over 1f out* **33/1**

0430 **9** 26 **Ishtar Gate (USA)**[18] 5891 3-9-5 **67**........................... AdamBeschizza 3 —
(P F I Cole) *s.i.s: rdn and in tch 3f out: sn wknd* **16/1**

1m 41.1s (0.30) **Going Correction** -0.10s/f (Good) **9** Ran SP% **114.7**

Speed ratings (Par 101): **94,93,92,92,91 88,87,79,53**

toteswingers:1&2:£8.20, 1&3:£17.50, 2&3:£51.90 CSF £28.23 CT £395.98 TOTE £3.30: £1.10, £3.30, £4.00; EX 32.10 Trifecta £280.70 Pool: £402.14 - 1.06 winning units..

Owner Jason Tucker **Bred** Patrice O'Connell **Trained** Kenfig Hill, Bridgend

FOCUS

The gallop was just a medium one, resulting in an ordinary time, which helped the front-running winner. The form looks a bit muddling.

6414 E B F & PARKGARDENCENTRES.CO.UK MAIDEN STKS 1m 2f 46y

3:30 (3:32) (Class 5) 2-Y-O **£3,238** (£963; £481; £240) Stalls Low

Form RPR

1 **Marhaba Malyoon (IRE)** 2-9-3 0.. WilliamBuick 3 74
(D M Simcock) *in tch: drvn along 4f out: rdn 3f out: hdwy over 1f out: str run u.p fnl 100yds: led last stride* **7/1**

4 **2** shd **Ullswater (IRE)**[14] 6036 2-9-3 0.. JoeFanning 2 74
(M Johnston) *w ldr 6f out: slt ld 3f out but a strly chal: rdn fr over 2f out: kpt slt advantage ins fnl f: ct last stride* **6/1**[3]

6422 **3** nse **El Mansour (USA)**[10] 6160 2-9-3 77.................................. EddieAhern 11 74
(C G Cox) *led tl narrowly hdd 3f out: styd pressing ldr and upsides and rdn ins fnl f: stl chalng last strides: jst failed* **6/4**[1]

4 **4** nse **Kinyras (IRE)**[68] 4263 2-9-3 0.. RyanMoore 8 74
(Sir Michael Stoute) *chsd ldrs: drvn along fr 3f out: styd on wl thrght fnl f and clsng to chal last strides: nt quite get up* **2/1**[2]

5000 **5** 10 **Sir Rocky (IRE)**[12] 6082 2-9-3 55.................................. RobertWinston 6 56
(R Hannon) *in rr: rdn and hanging bdly lft fr 3f out: no imp on ldrs and tk modest 5th over 1f out* **66/1**

6 1/2 **Round Turn (IRE)** 2-9-3 0.. RichardMullen 4 55
(E S McMahon) *in rr tl hdwy to get in tch over 3f out: sn pushed along and outpcd: lost mod 5th over 1f out* **25/1**

0 **7** 6 **Glenavon**[109] 2887 2-9-3 0.. SebSanders 9 44
(Mrs A J Perrett) *chsd ldrs: rdn over 2f out: hung bdly lft and wknd sn after* **40/1**

0 **8** nk **Xenophon**[14] 6036 2-9-3 0.. FergusSweeney 1 44
(G D Blake) *chsd ldrs 6f* **100/1**

0 **9** 1 1/4 **Looney Les (IRE)**[35] 5372 2-9-3 0.................................. KevinGhunowa 10 41
(F J Brennan) *rdn over 4f out: a bhd* **100/1**

00 **10** hd **Boogie Star**[46] 5006 2-9-3 0... CathyGannon 7 41
(J S Moore) *a in rr* **50/1**

2m 13.09s (2.09) **Going Correction** -0.10s/f (Good) **10** Ran SP% **111.8**

Speed ratings (Par 95): **87,86,86,86,78 78,73,73,72,72**

toteswingers:1&2:£6.40, 1&3:£5.90, 2&3:£2.80 CSF £43.74 TOTE £4.90: £1.40, £2.50, £1.10; EX 39.00 Trifecta £196.70 Pool: £366.86 - 1.38 winning units..

Owner Ahmad Al Shaikh **Bred** Mrs Clodagh McStay **Trained** Newmarket, Suffolk

FOCUS
They went a fair gallop, making it a good test for these juveniles. The four involved in the photo-finish were all handy throughout, but the betting indicates that they were by far the best four in the race anyway.

NOTEBOOK
Marhaba Malyoon(IRE), a 40,000gns Irish Derby entry, just got there in time to make a winning debut. There is plenty of stamina on his dam's side and that should set the scene for a staying campaign next year. (op 13-2)

Ullswater(IRE), who had the advantage of a previous race, only just came off second best. Stamina is his strength and he should remain competitive in long-distance juvenile events. (op 7-1 tchd 15-2)

El Mansour(USA), more experienced that the first two, looked comfortable in front for a long way. Though not quite able to see it out to victory, he was still battling away at the finish and already gets 1m2f well (tchd 5-4 and 13-8 in places)

Kinyras(IRE) ◆, stepping up from the 7f of his debut, gave the impression that he needs at least this trip even at this stage of his career. He should stay 1m4f-plus next season and ought to win races. (tchd 7-4)

Sir Rocky(IRE) is bred for stamina but he was outclassed by the first four.

Round Turn(IRE), a £28,000 Oratorio half-brother to a 1m2f winner, was making his debut over a trip which suggests that he needs a test of stamina.

Looney Les(IRE) Official explanation: jockey said gelding hung left-handed

6415 E B F / PARK & GARDEN CENTRES FRIENDS & FAMILY MAIDEN FILLIES' STKS — 1m 2f 46y
4:00 (4:02) (Class 5) 3-Y-O+ — **£3,302** (£982; £491; £245) **Stalls** Low

Form				RPR
2230	1		**Dolphina (USA)**[16] 5953 3-8-12 72 ... EddieAhern 1 (H R A Cecil) *chsng ldr 4f out and stl 2nd whn bk into view over 2f out: slt ld whn bk into view again ins fnl f: styd on wl* **9/2**[3]	80
342	2	1 ¼	**Mascarene (USA)**[67] 4294 3-8-12 75 ... RyanMoore 11 (Sir Michael Stoute) *chsng ldrs 4f out: in slt ld whn bk into view over 2f out: narrowly hdd whn bk into view again ins fnl f* **11/8**[1]	78
4222	3	1 ¾	**Fascination (IRE)**[40] 5209 3-8-7 73 ... AdamBeschizza(5) 8 (M L W Bell) *chsng ldrs 4f out: stl chsng ldrs in 3rd whn bk into view over 2f out and stl styling on same pce whn bk into view again ins fnl f* **4/1**[2]	74
2205	4	3 ¾	**Scorn (USA)**[18] 5872 3-8-12 75 ...(p) WilliamBuick 7 (J H M Gosden) *chsng ldrs 4f out: rdn and styng on same pce whn bk into view over 2f out and again whn bk into view fnl f* **5/1**	67
00	5	1	**Three Bay Leaves**[28] 5603 3-8-12 0 ... JoeFanning 12 (M Johnston) *in tch 4f out: u.p whn bk into view over 2f out: styng on same pce whn bk into view ins fnl f* **66/1**	65
00	6	7	**Regency Girl (IRE)**[20] 5832 3-8-12 0 ... RichardMullen 3 (M P Tregoning) *chsng ldrs 4f out: wkng whn bk into view over 2f out* **33/1**	51
0-	7	2	**Morning Drive**[371] 6163 3-8-12 0 ... SebSanders 9 (W R Swinburn) *towards rr 4 out: rdn and no prog whn bk into view over 2f out* **20/1**	47
	8	10	**Arakette (IRE)** 3-8-12 0 ... RobertHavlin 10 (A B Haynes) *in rr fr 4f out* **100/1**	27
	9	nk	**Bathwick Quest (IRE)**[284] 6-9-4 0 ... FergusSweeney 4 (B G Powell) *in ld 4f out: hdd and btn whn bk into view over 2f out* **40/1**	26
0640	10	6	**Bedouin Princess (IRE)**[21] 5812 3-8-12 49 ... CathyGannon 2 (Lucinda Featherstone) *bhd fr 4f out* **100/1**	14
000	11	1	**Belvidera**[77] 3960 4-9-4 30 ... LiamJones 5 (A W Carroll) *losing pl 4f out* **150/1**	12

2m 10.26s (-0.74) **Going Correction** -0.10s/f (Good)
WFA 3 from 4yo+ 6lb — 11 Ran SP% **111.2**
Speed ratings (Par 100): **98,97,95,92,91 86,84,76,76,71 70**
toteswingers:1&2:£2.60, 1&3:£3.80, 2&3:£2.60 CSF £10.08 TOTE £4.00: £1.60, £1.10, £1.70; EX 13.10 Trifecta £27.30 Pool: £693.99 - 18.76 winning units..
Owner Niarchos Family **Bred** Flaxman Holdings Ltd **Trained** Newmarket, Suffolk

FOCUS
An ordinary fillies' maiden.

6416 LECHLADE GARDEN CENTRE H'CAP — 2m 1f 34y
4:30 (4:37) (Class 5) (0-75,75) 3-Y-O+ — **£2,072** (£616; £308; £153) **Stalls** Centre

Form				RPR
1150	1		**Saborido (USA)**[15] 5996 4-9-8 **69** ... RyanMoore 5 (Mrs A J Perrett) *in rr: u.p whn styng on whn bk into view 4f out: styng on to chse ldr whn bk into view again over 2f out: wl clr whn bk into view ins fnl f* **5/1**[3]	83
5423	2	13	**Viviani (IRE)**[16] 5963 3-8-4 **63** ...(t) LiamJones 7 (Mrs A J Perrett) *prom whn in view early: chsng ldrs whn bk into view 4f out: led whn in view again over 2f out: 2nd and wl btn whn bk into view again ins fnl f* **6/1**	63
1351	3	1	**Ultimate Quest (IRE)**[11] 6114 5-9-9 **70** ... SebSanders 10 (Sir Mark Prescott) *prom whn in view early: in ld whn c bk into view 4f out: hdd and wkng whn c bk into view again over 2f out* **6/4**[1]	69
-331	4	3	**Sir Freddie**[34] 5382 4-9-11 **72** ... RobertWinston 8 (Lady Herries) *disputing ld early: chsng ldr u.p whn bk into view 4f out: wkng whn bk into view over 2f out* **3/1**[2]	68
2544	5	12	**The Composer**[6] 6273 8-8-9 **56** oh10 ... FergusSweeney 6 (M Blanshard) *in rr whnvr in view and no ch fr 4f out* **40/1**	38
1400	6	6	**Jenny Soba**[13] 6051 7-8-4 **56** oh4 ... AdamBeschizza(5) 9 (Lucinda Featherstone) *prom whn in view early: wkng whn bk in view 4f out* **66/1**	32
4205	7	11	**Spiritonthemount (USA)**[26] 5666 5-8-9 **56** oh11 ...(b) RichardMullen 1 (P W Hiatt) *disputing ld whn in view early: t.o whn bk in view 4f out* **40/1**	20
3625	8	2 ¼	**Party Palace**[56] 4045 6-8-9 **56** oh9 ... CathyGannon 4 (H S Howe) *in tch whn in view early: t.o whn bk in view 4f out* **40/1**	17
2466	9	30	**Cloudy City (USA)**[17] 5922 3-8-10 **69** ...(b) JoeFanning 3 (M Johnston) *chsd ldrs whn in view early: wkng and easing down whn bk in view 4f out* **10/1**	—

3m 48.72s (-3.18) **Going Correction** -0.10s/f (Good)
WFA 3 from 4yo+ 12lb — 9 Ran SP% **113.9**
Speed ratings (Par 103): **103,96,96,95,89 86,81,80,66**
toteswingers:1&2:£5.10, 1&3:£2.30, 2&3:£3.40 CSF £33.39 CT £65.25 TOTE £6.70: £2.00, £2.20, £1.50; EX 36.60 Trifecta £286.50 Pool: £487.86 - 1.26 winning units. Place 6 £28.83; Place 5 £17.70.
Owner Tracey, Cotton, James, Slade **Bred** R D Hubbard And R Masterson **Trained** Pulborough, W Sussex

FOCUS
After some deliberation because of poor visibility, the race was eventually allowed to start seven minutes late. However, it was impossible to see most of it and the winner appeared to show much-improved form.

6417 CHEDDAR GARDEN CENTRE H'CAP (DIV I) — 5f 11y
() (Class 6) (0-60,) 3-Y-O+ £

6418 CHEDDAR GARDEN CENTRE H'CAP (DIV II) — 5f 11y
() (Class 6) (0-60,) 3-Y-O+ £

T/Plt: £44.30 to a £1 stake. Pool:£67,370.34 - 1,109.26 winning tickets T/Qpdt: £5.30 to a £1 stake. Pool:£5,211.48 - 719.40 winning tickets ST

5985 FFOS LAS (L-H)
Monday, September 27

OFFICIAL GOING: Good to firm (8.5)
Wind: mild breeze across Weather: overcast

6419 AUDI MAIDEN STKS — 5f
2:20 (2:22) (Class 5) 2-Y-O — **£2,914** (£867; £433; £216) **Stalls** High

Form				RPR
	1		**Yellow Dandy (IRE)**[15] 6010 2-8-12 0 ... AndreaAtzeni 7 (Liam McAteer, Ire) *a.p: led over 2f out: drifted rt ins fnl f: r.o wl: pushed out* **7/1**[3]	72
32	2	2	**Supercharged (IRE)**[17] 5914 2-8-12 0 ... RichardHughes 5 (C F Wall) *s.i.s: sn trcking ldrs: rdn whn swtchd rt over 1f out: kpt on to go 2nd towards fin: nt pce to chal* **2/5**[1]	65
6034	3	½	**Forty Proof (IRE)**[22] 5785 2-9-3 72 ... ShaneKelly 2 (W J Knight) *prom: rdn and ev ch fr over 2f out: kpt on but no ex fnl f: lost 2nd towards fin* **12/1**	68
0544	4	hd	**Partout Le Magasin**[52] 4787 2-9-3 67 ...(p) LukeMorris 8 (J S Moore) *trckd ldrs: rdn 2f out: kpt on fnl f: nt pce to chal* **40/1**	67
645	5	2	**Swendab (IRE)**[31] 5465 2-9-3 65 ... WilliamCarson 1 (J G M O'Shea) *wnt lft s: chsd ldrs: rdn wl over 2f out: one pce fr over 1f out* **40/1**	60
540	6	hd	**Milldown Magic**[17] 5914 2-9-0 74 ... JamesMillman(3) 3 (B R Millman) *wnt to s early: rdn along in last trio fr over 3f out: kpt on ins fnl f: nvr gng pce to get on terms* **50/1**	59
4200	7	½	**Button Moon (IRE)**[10] 6157 2-8-9 82 ...(p) MartinLane(3) 6 (I A Wood) *led tl rdn over 2f out: kpt chsng ldrs tl fdd fnl 100yds* **6/1**[2]	53
0	8	8	**Deveze (IRE)**[31] 5466 2-8-12 0 ... TomQueally 10 (J W Hills) *towards rr: effrt over 2f out: wknd over 1f out* **50/1**	24
4	9	3 ¼	**Shugar Rhi (IRE)**[31] 5466 2-8-12 0 ... JimCrowley 9 (B Palling) *towards rr: rdn 3f out: wknd 2f out* **25/1**	12

57.32 secs (-0.08) **Going Correction** -0.025s/f (Good) — 9 Ran SP% **118.6**
Speed ratings (Par 95): **99,95,95,94,91 91,90,77,72**
toteswingers:1&2:£1.80, 1&3:£3.80, 2&3:£2.40 CSF £10.35 TOTE £9.30: £2.10, £1.02, £2.50; EX 13.20.
Owner Frank Cosgrove **Bred** Mrs Brid Cosgrove **Trained** Navan, Co Meath

FOCUS
An average juvenile maiden, run at a brisk early pace. The runner-up was well below par and the form looks limited.

NOTEBOOK
Yellow Dandy(IRE), who got wound up in the paddock, found this drop back a furlong and return to quicker ground right up her street and opened her account at the fifth attempt with a ready effort. She travelled best of all through the race and knuckled down well when asked to win the race. She is probably best kept to this trip for the time being and, with her confidence now boosted, should make her mark in nurseries. (op 8-1 tchd 9-1 and 13-2)

Supercharged(IRE) was all the rage on her third outing, but proved disappointing. She began to feel the pinch a fair way out and, although responding to pressure from the furlong marker, the winner was not for catching. It could be that another furlong is now what she wants and Richard Hughes later reported that the bit had slipped through her mouth, so don't be surprised if she makes amends next time. Official explanation: jockey said bit slipped through filly's mouth (tchd 4-9 and 1-2 in places)

Forty Proof(IRE), who got himself warm beforehand, proved somewhat free on the front end through the early parts and lacked a change of gear when it mattered. He was coming back late in the day, but is struggling to find his ideal trip and a mark of 72 looks beyond him at this stage

Partout Le Magasin, returning from a 52-day break, failed to land a serious blow but this was a step back in the right direction from him. With an official mark of 67 he looks a sensible guide for the form.

Button Moon(IRE) was taking a marked drop in grade and returning to 5f looked a good move. She backed out of things tamely when things got serious, though, and now has it to prove. (tchd 7-1)

6420 CASTELL HOWELL FOODS MEDIAN AUCTION MAIDEN STKS — 6f
2:50 (2:50) (Class 6) 3-5-Y-O — **£2,266** (£674; £337; £168) **Stalls** High

Form				RPR
236	1		**Magic Jack**[16] 5971 3-9-3 74 ... RichardHughes 7 (R Hannon) *led for 2f: prom: rdn 2f out: led fnl 100yds: kpt on wl: rdn out* **8/13**[1]	73
4243	2	1	**Nadinska**[5] 6285 3-8-12 56 ... LukeMorris 4 (M R Channon) *prom: led over 2f out: rdn over 1f out: hdd fnl 100yds: kpt on but no ex* **11/1**[3]	65
42	3	1	**Meia Noite**[13] 6060 3-8-12 0 ... TomQueally 2 (C F Wall) *wnt sltly lft s: prom: rdn wl over 2f out: ev ch ent fnl f: no ex fnl 75yds* **5/2**[2]	62
	4	5	**Griffin Point (IRE)** 3-8-12 0 ... JimCrowley 6 (W R Muir) *hld up bhd ldrs: swtchd lft for effrt over 2f out: wknd ins fnl f* **16/1**	46
-466	5	4	**Rose Bed (IRE)**[13] 6060 3-8-12 45 ...(p) WilliamCarson 3 (M G Quinlan) *prom: led 4f out tl over 2f out: sn wknd* **50/1**	33
0600	6	23	**Little Buddy**[55] 4679 3-9-0 30 ... RussKennemore(3) 1 (R J Price) *carried sltly lft s: trckd ldrs: rdn over 2f out: sn wknd: eased* **100/1**	—

69.69 secs (-0.01) **Going Correction** -0.025s/f (Good) — 6 Ran SP% **107.7**
Speed ratings (Par 101): **99,97,96,89,84 53**
toteswingers:1&2:£1.80, 1&3:£1.10, 2&3:£1.70 CSF £7.98 TOTE £1.50: £1.10, £3.30; EX 5.50.
Owner Carmel Stud **Bred** Carmel Stud **Trained** East Everleigh, Wilts

FOCUS
A modest maiden with a time to match. The runner-up provides a guide to the form.

Little Buddy Official explanation: jockey said gelding lost its action

6421 SCARLETS AND WRW H'CAP — 6f
3:20 (3:23) (Class 5) (0-70,69) 3-Y-0+ — **£2,866** (£846; £423) **Stalls** High

Form — RPR

0003 **1** **Earlsmedic**[14] 6040 5-9-5 **67**......(v) WilliamCarson 2 — 76
(S C Williams) *chsd ldrs: rdn wl over 1f out to chse ldr: kpt on wl to ld fnl 50yds: drvn out* **7/2**[1]

44-0 **2** 3/4 **First In Command (IRE)**[16] 5973 5-9-7 **69**......(t) AndreaAtzeni 5 — 75
(Daniel Mark Loughnane, Ire) *led: rdn over 1f out: wandered ins fnl f: no ex whn hdd fnl 50yds* **7/1**

3425 **3** 1 1/4 **Bateleur**[5] 6295 6-8-11 **59**...... LukeMorris 8 — 61+
(M R Channon) *hld up: swtchd to stands-side and hdwy 2f out: nt clr run whn swtchd lft over 1f out: sn short of room: kpt on ins fnl f* **9/1**

0456 **4** 1 **The Name Is Frank**[18] 5875 5-8-13 **64**......(t) MichaelStainton(3) 3 — 63
(Mark Gillard) *w ldr for 3f: sn rdn: kpt on same pce* **16/1**

1611 **5** nse **Emiratesdotcom**[17] 5926 4-8-11 **62**...... MartinLane(3) 11 — 61
(J M Bradley) *mid-div: rdn over 3f out: kpt on but nt pce to get on terms* **13/2**[3]

3216 **6** 3/4 **Dream Number (IRE)**[28] 5588 3-9-4 **68**...... ShaneKelly 7 — 64
(W R Muir) *prom: rdn 2f out: fdd ins fnl f* **11/1**

0054 **7** 1 1/2 **Pherousa**[18] 5875 3-8-10 **60**...... JimmyQuinn 13 — 52
(M Blanshard) *little slowly away: sn trcking ldrs: rdn over 2f out: sn one pce: fdd fnl f* **16/1**

-046 **8** nk **Far View (IRE)**[10] 6168 3-8-10 **60**...... RichardHughes 1 — 51
(J W Hills) *sn swtchd rt: chsd ldrs: rdn over 2f out: wknd ins fnl f* **5/1**[2]

6010 **9** 1 1/4 **George Thisby**[12] 6085 4-9-3 **68**...... JamesMillman(3) 4 — 55
(B R Millman) *s.i.s: mainly towards rr* **16/1**

0066 **10** 1 1/2 **Bold Argument (IRE)**[48] 4936 7-8-3 **56**...... SimonPearce(5) 6 — 38
(Mrs P N Dutfield) *a towards rr* **33/1**

4431 **11** hd **Bermondsey Bob (IRE)**[24] 5714 4-8-12 **60**...... JimCrowley 12 — 41
(J L Spearing) *prom: rdn 3f out: wknd ent fnl f* **8/1**

6020 **12** hd **Sweet Avon**[18] 5876 3-8-12 **62**...... TomQueally 9 — 43
(Matthew Salaman) *mid-div for 2f: sn rdn: in rr after* **33/1**

68.98 secs (-0.72) **Going Correction** -0.025s/f (Good)
WFA 3 from 4yo+ 2lb — 12 Ran SP% **117.7**
Speed ratings (Par 103): **103,102,100,99,98 97,95,95,93,91 91,91**
toteswingers:1&2:£5.60, 1&3:£11.20, 2&3:£13.20 CSF £27.37 CT £204.89 TOTE £5.60: £2.50, £4.30, £3.70; EX 44.40.
Owner Mad Man Plus Five **Bred** W N Greig **Trained** Newmarket, Suffolk
■ Stewards' Enquiry : William Carson caution: used whip with excessive frequency.

FOCUS
An ordinary sprint handicap. The front pair had slipped to decent marks.

6422 CAROL HARRIES ANNIVERSARY H'CAP — 1m 2f (R)
3:50 (3:51) (Class 4) (0-80,76) 3-Y-0 — **£4,209** (£1,252; £625; £312) **Stalls** Low

Form — RPR

0420 **1** **Warlu Way**[16] 5953 3-9-3 **72**...... TomQueally 6 — 81
(J L Dunlop) *hld up bhd ldrs: rdn and stdy prog fr 3f out: chal jst over 1f out: styd on: led fnl stride: all out* **4/1**[3]

0050 **2** nse **Countess Comet (IRE)**[23] 5753 3-9-6 **75**...... JimCrowley 1 — 84
(R M Beckett) *led for 2f: prom: rdn to ld wl over 1f out: hrd pressed thrght fnl f: styd on: narrowly hdd fnl stride* **5/1**

6112 **3** 5 **Rock The Stars (IRE)**[95] 3363 3-8-12 **67**...... RichardHughes 3 — 66
(J W Hills) *hld up bhd ldrs: rdn over 4f out: no imp tl styd on fnl f: no ch w ldng pair* **2/1**[1]

5210 **4** 1 **Saint Thomas (IRE)**[17] 5918 3-9-4 **73**...... JimmyQuinn 2 — 70
(J Mackie) *trckd ldrs: rdn 3f out: no ex ent fnl f* **9/2**

5410 **5** 3 3/4 **Mr Money Maker**[2] 6372 3-9-1 **73**...... RussKennemore(3) 5 — 63
(J L Flint) *led after 2f: rdn and hdd wl over 1f out: sn wknd* **7/2**[2]

2m 8.28s (-0.12) **Going Correction** +0.10s/f (Good) — 5 Ran SP% **110.4**
Speed ratings (Par 103): **104,103,99,99,96**
CSF £22.86 TOTE £7.20: £3.60, £4.20; EX 20.60.
Owner The Earl Cadogan **Bred** The Earl Cadogan **Trained** Arundel, W Sussex

FOCUS
A modest 3-y-o handicap, run at a fair enough pace despite the small field. The runner-up provides a solid guide to the form.

6423 TINOPOLIS H'CAP — 1m 6f (R)
4:20 (4:21) (Class 3) (0-90,88) 3-Y-0+ — **£7,771** (£2,312; £1,155; £577) **Stalls** Low

Form — RPR

6-04 **1** **Rugell (ARG)**[89] 3566 5-9-9 **83**...... LukeMorris 7 — 93
(C G Cox) *mde virtually all: rdn clr over 1f out: styd on strly* **8/1**

3210 **2** 2 1/4 **Plato (JPN)**[23] 5747 3-9-0 **84**...... TomQueally 6 — 90
(H R A Cecil) *trckd ldrs: rdn over 2f out: chsd wnr jst over 1f out: styd on same pce* **5/2**[1]

0200 **3** 1/2 **Dazinski**[9] 6201 4-9-7 **86**...... AshleyMorgan(5) 1 — 91
(M H Tompkins) *trckd ldrs: rdn 3f out: styd on same pce fnl 2f* **18/1**

3624 **4** 2 1/4 **Aurorian (IRE)**[22] 5788 4-9-10 **84**...... RichardHughes 2 — 86
(R Hannon) *in tch: rdn 3f out: nt best of runs jst over 1f out: styd on same pce* **11/4**[2]

015 **5** 1/2 **Cotton Mill**[52] 4805 3-9-4 **88**...... JimCrowley 4 — 89+
(W Jarvis) *mid-div: smooth hdwy over 2f out to go 2nd: sn rdn: nvr quite got on terms w wnr: fdd ins fnl f* **8/1**

1101 **6** 8 **Fantino**[17] 5922 4-9-1 **75**...... JimmyQuinn 3 — 65
(J Mackie) *led briefly early: trckd wnr: rdn to chal over 2f out: wknd over 1f out* **11/2**[3]

5/3- **7** 1/2 **Master At Arms**[352] 5706 7-8-10 **70**...... AndreaAtzeni 8 — 60
(Daniel Mark Loughnane, Ire) *a in last trio: rdn over 3f out: no imp: wknd over 1f out* **40/1**

-010 **8** 2 1/2 **Rajeh (IRE)**[52] 3159 7-9-11 **88**...... JackDean(3) 9 — 74
(J L Spearing) *hld up towards rr: rdn over 4f out: no imp: wknd over 1f out* **16/1**

1100 **9** 6 **Markington**[22] 5788 7-9-4 **78**......(b) WilliamCarson 5 — 56
(P Bowen) *a in last pair: swtchd rt u.p over 3f out: sn wknd* **8/1**

3m 3.78s (-0.02) **Going Correction** +0.10s/f (Good)
WFA 3 from 4yo+ 10lb — 9 Ran SP% **117.5**
Speed ratings (Par 107): **104,102,102,101,100 96,96,94,91**
toteswingers:1&2:£4.70, 1&3:£19.50, 2&3:£11.90 CSF £28.88 CT £358.50 TOTE £7.10: £1.90, £1.80, £5.80; EX 34.60.
Owner H E Sheikh Sultan Bin Khalifa Al Nahyan **Bred** Vacacion **Trained** Lambourn, Berks

FOCUS
A fair staying handicap and there was a sound enough pace on. A personal-best since coming to Britain form the winner. The form looks solid enough.

NOTEBOOK
Rugell(ARG) made most of the running for a ready success. He tried to dictate when held over 2m at Kempton on his previous outing back in June, but that was a much improved effort in defeat and this rates another step forward. He found this galloping track right up his street and was well on top inside the final furlong. Indeed he took a long time to pull up afterwards and probably had a lot in hand passing the line. He is entitled to come on for the run, should be high on confidence after this and so he would have to be of serious interest if taking up his engagement at Warwick on Thursday. (op 7-1)
Plato(JPN) was well backed on this second outing over the trip and ran a game race in defeat, but was never going to reel in the winner. This showed he gets the trip and the handicapper may have him where he wants him at present, but he could be the type to improve next year (op 7-2)
Dazinski wasn't a serious threat on this drop back in trip, but turned in a better effort in defeat and does help to set the level. (op 14-1)
Aurorian(IRE) was dropping back from 2m and lacked a change of gear when asked to pick up from off the pace. He remains 4lb higher than his last winning mark. (op 3-1 tchd 7-2)
Cotton Mill ◆, returning from a 52-day break, ran better than the bare form on this handicap debut. He was going very well nearing the 3f marker, but his reluctance to settle through the early parts ultimately cost him over this longer distance. A drop back to 1m4f can see this lightly raced 3-y-o back to winning ways. (op 15-2 tchd 7-1)
Fantino came into this having won three of his last four outings. Racing off a 5lb higher mark, he was the one that kept closest tabs on the winner through the race and looked to be going well turning for home. He failed to last it out, however, and may now appreciate a break. Official explanation: jockey said gelding stopped quickly (op 6-1)

6424 OWENS - PALLETFORCE LOGISTICS APPRENTICE H'CAP — 1m 4f (R)
4:50 (4:50) (Class 5) (0-75,75) 3-Y-0 — **£2,719** (£809; £404; £202) **Stalls** Low

Form — RPR

0301 **1** **Milnagavie**[91] 3513 3-9-0 **71**...... CharlesEddery(3) 3 — 78+
(R Hannon) *mde all: styd on wl: rdn out* **5/2**[2]

1650 **2** 2 1/4 **Lucky Breeze (IRE)**[41] 5181 3-9-3 **74**...... HarryBentley(3) 2 — 76
(W J Knight) *fly-leapt leaving stalls: in tch in last pair: rdn over 2f out: styd on to go 2nd ins fnl f: no ch w wnr* **7/1**

106 **3** 2 **Cornish Beau (IRE)**[38] 5266 3-9-2 **70**...... AshleyMorgan 1 — 69
(M H Tompkins) *trckd wnr: swtchd rt 3f out: sn rdn: no ex whn lost 2nd fnl 100yds: fin lame* **2/1**[1]

1450 **4** 1 1/2 **Lauberhorn**[19] 5858 3-8-9 **70**...... DanielBlackett(7) 4 — 66
(Eve Johnson Houghton) *hld up in tch in last pair: rdn 2f out: no imp* **15/2**

113P **5** 6 **Corr Point (IRE)**[23] 5752 3-9-7 **75**......(t) SimonPearce 5 — 62
(J A Osborne) *trckd wnr: rdn over 2f out: sn hld: wknd ent fnl f* **3/1**[3]

2m 37.48s (0.68) **Going Correction** +0.10s/f (Good) — 5 Ran SP% **111.2**
Speed ratings (Par 101): **101,99,98,97,93**
totesuper7: Win: Not won. Place: Not won. CSF £18.90 TOTE £3.00: £2.20, £3.50; EX 19.20 Place 6 £120.55; Place 5 £103.31.
Owner Mrs R Ablett **Bred** Darley **Trained** East Everleigh, Wilts

FOCUS
An ordinary handicap for apprentice riders, with the favourite disappointing, and there was another winner from the front.
Cornish Beau(IRE) Official explanation: vet said colt finished lame
T/Plt: £80.50 to a £1 stake. Pool:£62,969.73 - 570.50 winning tickets T/Qpdt: £34.50 to a £1 stake. Pool:£4,202.96 - 90.05 winning tickets TM

6285 KEMPTON (A.W) (R-H)
Monday, September 27

OFFICIAL GOING: Standard

6425 BET NFL - BETDAQ MAIDEN AUCTION STKS — 6f (P)
2:10 (2:11) (Class 5) 2-Y-0 — **£2,286** (£675; £337) **Stalls** High

Form — RPR

04 **1** **Chilledtothebone**[10] 6138 2-8-10 0......(v) KierenFallon 6 — 72
(Mrs L Stubbs) *chsd ldrs: outpcd and swtchd rt wl over 1f out: str run u.p ent fnl f: led fnl 100yds: in command whn hung lft towards fin* **4/1**[2]

04 **2** 1 **Soviet Spring (IRE)**[53] 4741 2-8-10 0...... LiamKeniry 12 — 69
(A M Balding) *led: rdn and qcknd clr wl over 1f out: drvn and hung lft fr 1f out: hdd and one pce fnl 100yds* **9/4**[1]

00 **3** 1 1/2 **Neytiri**[19] 5865 2-8-4 0...... NickyMackay 1 — 60+
(R M Beckett) *chsd ldr: rdn over 2f out: nt pce of ldr wl over 1f out: 3rd and styng on same pce whn carried lft fnl f: hld whn hmpd and eased nr fin* **10/1**

0 **4** hd **Captain Noble (IRE)**[10] 6145 2-9-0 0...... NeilCallan 9 — 68
(P J Makin) *v.s.a: bhd: nt clr run wl over 2f out: hdwy u.p ent fnl 2f: styd on wl fnl f and pressing for 3rd nr fin: nt rch ldrs* **5/1**[3]

5 1 1/4 **Poyle Judy** 2-8-0 0 ow1...... JohnFahy(5) 2 — 55
(R M Beckett) *s.i.s: bhd: pushed along 4f out: hdwy on outer wl over 1f out: kpt on same pce and no imp ins fnl f* **16/1**

50 **6** 1/2 **Hi Note**[27] 5626 2-8-7 0...... ChrisCatlin 8 — 56
(M R Channon) *stdd s: t.k.h: hld up in tch in midfield: rdn: effrt and edging rt over 2f out: drvn and wknd over 1f out* **50/1**

00 **7** 1 1/2 **Chillie Peppar**[12] 6092 2-8-6 0...... AshleyHamblett(3) 5 — 53
(G Prodromou) *racd wd: chsd ldrs: rdn and outpcd over 2f out: styd on same pce u.p fr wl over 1f out* **16/1**

00 **8** nk **Snow Trooper**[98] 3269 2-8-10 0...... PatCosgrave 11 — 53
(D K Ivory) *s.i.s: in tch in rr: pushed along 4f out: rdn and unable qck over 2f out: wknd ent fnl 2f* **100/1**

6 **9** 3 **Tourmaline (IRE)**[30] 5520 2-8-6 0 ow1...... JackMitchell 7 — 40
(P W Chapple-Hyam) *in tch in midfield: hmpd and lost pl over 2f out: nt rcvr and n.d after* **20/1**

0 **10** 3 1/4 **Sea Of Love (IRE)**[23] 5763 2-8-4 0...... AndrewHeffernan(3) 10 — 32
(R A Harris) *chsd ldrs tl rdn and wknd qckly jst over 2f out: wl bhd fnl f* **50/1**

1m 14.01s (0.91) **Going Correction** -0.05s/f (Stan) — 10 Ran SP% **98.0**
Speed ratings (Par 95): **91,89,87,87,85 85,83,82,78,74**
toteswingers:1&2:£2.00, 1&3:£5.00, 2&3:£4.50 CSF £9.44 TOTE £3.10: £1.10, £1.60, £2.30; EX 8.90.
Owner G & T Bloodstock **Bred** Broughton Bloodstock **Trained** Norton, N Yorks

FOCUS
A modest maiden. The form looks limited.

NOTEBOOK
Chilledtothebone improved on his debut effort when fourth over 7f at Ayr last time and, dropped back in trip, he stepped forward again. This wasn't much of a race, though, and things will be tougher now. (tchd 7-2)
Soviet Spring(IRE), dropped in trip after 53 days off, was allowed the run of the race in front, appearing to steady the gallop before the straight, and had his chance. He should find his level in ordinary handicaps. (op 5-2 tchd 3-1)

Neytiri was a bit keen on the pace through the early stages, but she still ran creditably, not least considering she had the worst of the draw. Handicaps are now an option. (op 12-1 tchd 14-1 in a place)
Captain Noble(IRE) ruined his chance with a slow start. He can do better when getting away on terms. (op 13-2)
Poyle Judy, carrying 1lb overweight, missed the break yet was still taken wide throughout. Considering how much ground she covered, this was a pleasing introduction.
Chillie Peppar Official explanation: jockey said colt hung left

6426 BET CHAMPIONS LEAGUE FOOTBALL - BETDAQ NURSERY 7f (P)
2:40 (2:41) (Class 4) (0-80,79) 2-Y-O **£3,238** (£963; £481; £240) **Stalls** High

Form RPR
4401 **1** **Tamareen (IRE)**[10] 6163 2-8-11 **69**....(t) RichardHills 1 72
(E A L Dunlop) *stdd s: hld up in last: rdn and effrt on outer 2f out: qcknd to ld ent fnl f: kpt on wl: rdn out* **7/1**[2]
1462 **2** ½ **Sceal Nua (IRE)**[25] 5675 2-9-0 **72**.... PatDobbs 5 74
(R Hannon) *chsd ldr: rdn and hung lft over 1f out: pressed wnr thrght fnl f: unable qck and a hld* **2/1**[1]
6330 **3** *nk* **Bearheart (IRE)**[20] 5837 2-8-13 **71**.... SteveDrowne 3 72
(E A L Dunlop) *hld up in rr: switching lft fr over 2f out: hdwy u.p on outer ent fnl f: styd on wl fnl f: nt quite rch ldng pair* **20/1**
664 **4** *shd* **Fimias (IRE)**[23] 5763 2-8-9 **67**.... KierenFallon 8 68
(L M Cumani) *chsd ldng trio: rdn whn short of room and sltly outpcd over 1f out: rallied but edging rt ins fnl f: swtchd lft wl ins fnl f: styng on fin* **2/1**[1]
6443 **5** *1* **Cathcart Castle**[8] 6220 2-8-3 **61** ow1.... ChrisCatlin 2 60
(M R Channon) *in tch in midfield: n.m.r briefly jst over 2f out: gd hdwy u.p over 1f out: styd on same pce ins fnl f* **14/1**[3]
2030 **6** *3 ½* **Point Du Jour (FR)**[13] 6059 2-9-6 **78**.... GeorgeBaker 9 68
(I A Wood) *stdd s: hld up towards rr: rdn and effrt on inner ent fnl 2f: no prog over 1f out* **20/1**
5210 **7** ¾ **Titus Two (IRE)**[37] 5310 2-9-7 **79**.... JackMitchell 4 67
(P W Chapple-Hyam) *towards rr: hdwy on outer over 3f out: wknd u.p wl over 1f out* **20/1**
2044 **8** *1* **Royalorien**[21] 5808 2-8-11 **69**.... NeilCallan 10 54
(W J Knight) *chsd ldrs: rdn and wknd jst over 2f out* **18/1**
0202 **9** ½ **Maggie's Treasure (IRE)**[14] 6019 2-8-9 **67**.... TadhgO'Shea 7 51
(J Gallagher) *led: rdn ent fnl 2f: hdd ent fnl f: sn fdd* **33/1**
3132 **10** *2 ¼* **Diamond Vine (IRE)**[18] 5874 2-8-13 **71**....(p) DaneO'Neill 6 50
(R A Harris) *dwlt: sn rdn along to r in midfield: rdn and n.m.r over 2f out: wknd 2f out* **14/1**[3]

1m 26.29s (0.29) **Going Correction** -0.05s/f (Stan) **10** Ran SP% **115.0**
Speed ratings (Par 97): **96,95,95,94,93 89,88,87,87,84**
toteswingers:1&2:£2.10, 1&3:£20.50, 2&3:£13.80 CSF £19.89 CT £269.93 TOTE £6.30: £2.10, £5.50; EX 24.10.
Owner Hamdan Al Maktoum **Bred** Mcdonnell Cbs Bloodstock **Trained** Newmarket, Suffolk

FOCUS
A fair enough nursery.

NOTEBOOK
Tamareen(IRE) was well ridden to defy a 4lb rise for his Wolverhampton success. Dropped in from the lowest stall, he saved ground by only switching wide once in the straight, and showed a decent change of pace. Now 2-2 since being upped to 7f, he can win again, although it remains to be seen whether his hold-up style will be quite so effective back on turf. (op 10-1)
Sceal Nua(IRE), 2lb higher than when runner-up at Epsom on her previous start, was always well placed and had her chance. (op 11-4 tchd 3-1 in a place)
Bearheart(IRE) was similarly ridden to the winner, only he was switched into the clear later than that rival and the line came too soon. (op 16-1)
Fimias(IRE) was dropped back to 5f on his qualifying run for a mark last time, but that proved less than ideal preparation for this step up to 7f, as he was keen early. Once in the straight, he got outpaced before running on, giving the impression we've yet to see the best of him. (op 9-4 tchd 15-8)
Cathcart Castle, carrying 1lb overweight, seemed to benefit from the return to 7f on his Polytrack debut and wasn't beaten far. (op 12-1 tchd 11-1)
Point Du Jour(FR), without the tongue-tie this time, raced more towards the inside than those who finished ahead of him, but he kept on steadily, looking as though he'll be worth another try over 1m. Official explanation: jockey said colt missed the break (op 14-1 tchd 25-1)
Diamond Vine(IRE) Official explanation: jockey said colt hung right

6427 BET MULTIPLES - BETDAQ H'CAP 1m 4f (P)
3:10 (3:13) (Class 5) (0-75,75) 3-Y-O+ **£2,286** (£675; £337) **Stalls** Centre

Form RPR
0350 **1** **Spensley (IRE)**[15] 5994 4-9-6 **68**.... KierenFallon 13 82+
(J R Fanshawe) *in tch in midfield: steadily lost pl and last over 3f out: stl last and switching lft fr ins to outer over 2f out: 13th and stl plenty to do over 1f out: str run to ld fnl 100yds: sn clr: eased nr fin* **15/2**[2]
5400 **2** *2* **Dynamic Drive (IRE)**[17] 5918 3-9-2 **72**.... AdamKirby 6 81
(W R Swinburn) *hld up towards rr: rdn and hdwy over 2f out: chsd ldng pair over 1f out: kpt on and pressed ldrs ins fnl f tl wnr swept past and outpcd fnl 100yds* **14/1**
630 **3** *1* **Aphrodisia**[40] 5217 6-9-7 **74**.... JohnFahy(5) 7 81
(Ian Williams) *stdd s: hld up in rr: hdwy on outer 4f out: rdn to chse clr ldr 2f out: kpt on u.p to press ldrs ins fnl f: nt pce of wnr fnl 100yds: wnt 3rd towards fin* **8/1**[3]
-026 **4** *nk* **Cast Of Stars (IRE)**[47] 4965 3-8-13 **72**....(v[1]) EJMcNamara(3) 1 79
(R M Beckett) *chsd ldr tl rdn to ld over 2f out: clr wl over 1f out: wknd u.p and hdd fnl 100yds: lost 2 pls after* **25/1**
0342 **5** *1 ½* **Green Wadi**[19] 5868 5-9-10 **72**.... GeorgeBaker 11 76+
(G L Moore) *hld up towards rr: hemmed in and nt clr run wl over 2f out tl ent fnl 2f: hdwy wl over 1f out: kpt on same pce and nvr threatened ldrs* **9/4**[1]
5311 **6** ¾ **Aurora Sky (IRE)**[16] 5959 4-9-5 **67**.... LiamKeniry 8 70+
(J Akehurst) *t.k.h: hld up in midfield: travelling wl but nt clr run over 2f out tl 2f out: sn rdn and sme hdwy: kpt on same pce and no imp fnl f* **10/1**
663 **7** *3 ¾* **Charming Man**[83] 3754 3-9-5 **75**.... AhmedAjtebi 10 72
(Mahmood Al Zarooni) *chsd ldrs tl wknd u.p ent fnl 2f* **12/1**
6026 **8** *1* **Eseej (USA)**[20] 5828 5-9-3 **65**.... DarryllHolland 14 61
(P W Hiatt) *led tl rdn and hdd over 2f out: wknd wl over 1f out* **10/1**
330- **9** *nk* **Peter Grimes (IRE)**[191] 5570 4-9-1 **63**.... SteveDrowne 2 58
(A King) *in tch in midfield: rdn 6f out: outpcd u.p wl over 1f out: wl btn over 1f out* **20/1**
0300 **10** *1 ¼* **Trachonitis (IRE)**[15] 5991 6-9-8 **70**....(t) NeilCallan 9 63
(J R Jenkins) *stdd s: hld up towards rr: rdn and no real prog over 2f out: wl btn over 1f out* **33/1**
3204 **11** *nse* **Gandalf**[24] 5722 8-9-5 **67**.... DaneO'Neill 12 60
(Miss Amy Weaver) *hld up towards rr: hdwy on outer over 3f out: struggling over 2f out: wl btn over 1f out* **16/1**
003 **12** ¾ **Crystal Celebre (IRE)**[19] 5860 4-9-5 **72**.... AmyScott(5) 5 64
(H Candy) *dwlt: sn chsng ldrs: wknd over 2f out: wl bhd fnl f* **40/1**
6131 **13** *2 ¾* **Moscow Oznick**[38] 5272 5-9-4 **66**....(v) PatCosgrave 4 53
(D Donovan) *hld up in midfield: n.m.r and shuffled bk over 2f out: drvn and no hdwy wl over 1f: wl btn fnl f* **16/1**
0000 **14** *1 ¼* **Marju King (IRE)**[13] 6055 4-9-2 **64**.... IanMongan 3 49
(W S Kittow) *in tch in midfield: hdwy 1/2-way: chsd ldrs 5f out: struggling u.p wl over 2f out: bhd wl over 1f out* **33/1**

2m 32.84s (-1.66) **Going Correction** -0.05s/f (Stan)
WFA 3 from 4yo+ 8lb **14** Ran SP% **114.9**
Speed ratings (Par 103): **103,101,101,100,99 99,96,96,95,95 95,94,92,91**
toteswingers:1&2:£22.40, 1&3:£9.30, 2&3:£25.00 CSF £95.87 CT £861.56 TOTE £9.40: £3.80, £5.90, £2.30; EX 140.30.
Owner Axom (XV) **Bred** Mount Coote Stud And M H Dixon **Trained** Newmarket, Suffolk

FOCUS
Not a particularly strong handicap, but Spensley can be considered better than the bare form, having won been poorly placed at the top of the straight. They went a fair gallop with both the front pair showing improved form.
Aphrodisia Official explanation: jockey said mare hung right

6428 BET ASIAN H'CAPS - BETDAQ HANDICAP 1m 3f (P)
3:40 (3:45) (Class 4) (0-85,85) 3-Y-O+ **£3,885** (£1,156; £577; £288) **Stalls** High

Form RPR
-646 **1** **Dubai Crest**[114] 2747 4-9-8 **79**.... NeilCallan 1 91
(Mrs A J Perrett) *chsd ldrs: rdn over 2f out: styd on u.p to chse wnr ins fnl f: hrd drvn to ld wl ins fnl f: all out* **8/1**
0321 **2** *nk* **Isobar (GER)**[21] 5811 4-9-4 **75**.... KierenFallon 6 86
(L M Cumani) *chsd ldr tl 6f out: chsd ldrs after tl rdn to ld 2f out: clr jst ins fnl f: hrd drvn fnl 100yds: hdd and no ex wl ins fnl f* **6/4**[1]
620 **3** *1* **Akhmatova**[9] 6199 3-9-1 **79**.... SteveDrowne 2 89+
(G A Butler) *stdd s: hld up in rr: rdn and effrt on outer ent fnl 2f: chsd ldrs 1f out: kpt on wl to go 3rd ins fnl f: nt rch ldrs* **8/1**
411- **4** *1* **Sulwaan (IRE)**[377] 5970 3-9-7 **85**.... RichardHills 5 93+
(M Johnston) *hld up in midfield tl rapid hdwy to chse ldr 6f out: rdn and unable qck 2f out: kpt on same pce u.p fnl f* **15/2**[3]
3164 **5** *3 ¼* **Sing Sweetly**[35] 5371 3-9-0 **83**.... JohnFahy(5) 10 85
(G A Butler) *in tch: rdn and outpcd jst over 2f out: one pce and no ch w ldrs fnl f* **9/2**[2]
0000 **6** ½ **Franco Is My Name**[91] 3512 4-9-12 **83**.... DaneO'Neill 9 84
(P R Hedger) *hld up towards rr: rdn and no prog over 2f out: hdwy over 1f out: no threat to ldrs but kpt on steadily fnl f* **40/1**
2043 **7** *1 ½* **Rumble Of Thunder (IRE)**[23] 5753 4-9-7 **78**.... LiamKeniry 8 76
(D W P Arbuthnot) *led tl rdn and hdd 2f out: wknd over 1f out* **8/1**
420 **8** ½ **Encircled**[23] 5753 6-9-11 **82**.... PatDobbs 12 80
(J R Jenkins) *hld up towards rr: rdn and sme hdwy 2f out: no prog ent fnl f: nvr trbld ldrs* **66/1**
401/ **9** *4 ½* **Tuanku (IRE)**[661] 4978 5-9-2 **73**.... PatCosgrave 4 62
(A King) *in tch in midfield: rdn and struggling over 2f out: wknd 2f out* **33/1**
0400 **10** *nk* **Prohibition (IRE)**[88] 3582 4-8-12 **69** oh2.... JackMitchell 7 58
(G L Moore) *t.k.h: hld up towards rr: sme hdwy 4f out: wknd u.p over 2f out* **50/1**
0040 **11** *10* **Stand Guard**[24] 5716 6-9-5 **83**.... LauraSimpson(7) 11 54
(P Howling) *chsd ldrs tl wknd qckly jst over 2f out: wl bhd fnl f* **80/1**
6340 **12** *29* **Free Tussy (ARG)**[164] 1348 6-9-4 **75**....(bt) GeorgeBaker 3 —
(G L Moore) *t.k.h: chsd ldrs tl wknd wl over 2f out: wl btn and eased fr over 1f out: t.o* **33/1**
410 **P** **Peadar Miguel**[177] 1086 3-8-13 **77**.... TonyCulhane 13 —
(M G Quinlan) *broke wl: t.k.h and sn stdd bk to midfield: dropped to last 5f out: lost tch 4f out: eased and p.u wl over 2f out* **50/1**

2m 20.38s (-1.52) **Going Correction** -0.05s/f (Stan)
WFA 3 from 4yo+ 7lb **13** Ran SP% **118.2**
Speed ratings (Par 105): **103,102,102,101,98 98,97,97,93,93 86,65,—**
toteswingers:1&2:£5.20, 1&3:£9.50, 2&3:£5.70 CSF £19.48 CT £104.14 TOTE £9.00: £2.80, £1.70, £2.60; EX 39.00.
Owner A D Spence **Bred** Bearstone Stud **Trained** Pulborough, W Sussex

FOCUS
A fair handicap run at an ordinary gallop. The front four were clear with the winner returning to his best back on Polytrack. Decent form.

6429 BET IN RUNNING - BETDAQ H'CAP 6f (P)
4:10 (4:14) (Class 3) (0-95,95) 3-Y-O+ **£6,281** (£1,869; £934; £466) **Stalls** High

Form RPR
0020 **1** **Mac's Power (IRE)**[18] 5884 4-8-13 **85**....(t) PatCosgrave 3 97+
(J R Fanshawe) *stdd after s: hld up in last pair: hdwy and swtchd lft jst over 1f out: rdn and qcknd to ld ins fnl f: r.o wl: rdn out* **5/1**[2]
106 **2** *1* **Arteus**[24] 5731 4-9-1 **87**....(b) TadhgO'Shea 2 96
(Jane Chapple-Hyam) *chsd ldr for 2f: chsd ldng pair after tl drvn to ld over 1f out: hdd ins fnl f: kpt on same pce after* **33/1**
2006 **3** *1 ½* **Five Star Junior (USA)**[6] 6265 4-9-7 **93**.... KierenFallon 9 97
(Mrs L Stubbs) *in tch: rdn and effrt ent fnl 2f: chsd ldr over 1f out tl ent fnl f: styd on same pce and wl hld fnl f* **11/1**
2412 **4** ½ **Bohemian Melody**[42] 5143 3-9-7 **95**.... AdamKirby 8 98
(M Botti) *hld up towards rr: rdn and hdwy over 1f out: drvn ent fnl f: kpt on u.p but nt pce to rch ldrs* **9/4**[1]
5440 **5** *nk* **Take Ten**[17] 5911 3-8-11 **85**.... RoystonFfrench 12 87
(M Johnston) *chsd ldrs: rdn and effrt on inner 2f out: styd on same pce and btn 1f out* **7/1**[3]
3450 **6** ½ **Sutton Veny (IRE)**[15] 5995 4-8-10 **82**.... SteveDrowne 10 82+
(J R Gask) *led tl rdn and hdd over 1f out: wknd fnl f* **15/2**
3212 **7** *nk* **Secret Millionaire (IRE)**[16] 5967 3-9-2 **90**.... StephenCraine 11 89
(Patrick Morris) *hld up in midfield: hdwy on bit ent fnl 2f: rdn and fnd nil ent fnl f: one pce and wl hld fnl f* **12/1**
5005 **8** *nse* **Novellen Lad (IRE)**[13] 6049 5-9-2 **88**.... PatDobbs 6 87
(E J Alston) *in tch in midfield on outer: lost pl and dropped to rr over 2f out: rallied u.p over 1f out: kpt on but no ch w ldrs* **7/1**[3]
500 **9** *1* **Shifting Star (IRE)**[22] 5787 5-8-11 **88**....(p) JohnFahy(5) 4 84
(W R Swinburn) *stdd s: hld up in last pair: rdn and effrt wl over 1f out: no real prog: nvr trbld ldrs* **16/1**
0600 **10** *1 ¾* **Filligree (IRE)**[11] 6113 5-8-7 **82**.... KierenFox(3) 5 72
(Rae Guest) *in tch in midfield: rdn wl over 2f out: drvn and wknd ent fnl 2f: wl hld fnl f* **25/1**

The Form Book, Raceform Ltd, Compton, RG20 6NL

2050 **11** *6* **Ghostwing**[22] 5787 3-9-4 **92**.......................................(b[1]) DarryllHolland 1 63
(J Gallagher) *chsd ldrs tl hdwy to join ldr 4f out: ev ch and hung rt whn rdn wl over 1f out: wknd qckly over 1f out* **20/1**

1m 11.02s (-2.08) **Going Correction** -0.05s/f (Stan)
WFA 3 from 4yo+ 2lb **11** Ran SP% **117.7**
Speed ratings (Par 107): **111,109,107,107,106 105,105,105,104,101 93**
toteswingers:1&2:£35.40, 1&3:£11.20, 2&3:£25.10 CSF £163.40 CT £1773.46 TOTE £7.00: £1.90, £11.50, £2.10; EX 189.00.
Owner Michael McDonnell **Bred** Ballyhane Stud **Trained** Newmarket, Suffolk

FOCUS
A good sprint handicap, run at a strong gallop, and the winner returned to his best. The third and fourth give the form a solid look.

NOTEBOOK
Mac's Power(IRE), well backed, confirmed the promise of his recent Doncaster effort. He's not had that many goes over 6f lately and probably has more to offer. (op 11-2 tchd 9-2)
Arteus has had relatively few starts over sprint trips and this was a decent effort in second. There may be better to come.
Five Star Junior(USA), back on Polytrack, ran creditably but his last two wins have been gained over the minimum trip. (op 10-1)
Bohemian Melody lacked the required finishing speed on this return to 6f and failed to confirm the encouragement of his recent, slightly unlucky second over 7f around here. (op 7-2 tchd 4-1 in a place)
Take Ten is not badly treated and offered some encouragement on his Polytrack debut. (op 13-2 tchd 6-1)

6430 BETDAQ ON 0870 178 1221 H'CAP 1m (P)
4:40 (4:42) (Class 4) (0-85,85) 3-Y-O+ **£3,885** (£1,156; £577; £288) **Stalls** High

Form RPR

6300 **1** **Hidden Glory**[17] 5918 3-8-10 **78**.......................... JamesRogers(7) 6 90
(Pat Eddery) *sn pushed along to chse ldr after 1f: led 5f out tl hdd wl over 2f out: rdn to ld again 2f out: kpt on wl* **8/1**

2235 **2** *2 ½* **Anacopa (USA)**[12] 6090 3-9-10 **85**.......................... AhmedAjtebi 7 91
(Mahmood Al Zarooni) *chsd ldrs: wnt 2nd 3f out: sn led: rdn and hdd 2f out: drvn and styd on same pce fr over 1f out* **10/1**

422 **3** *2* **Abhar (USA)**[18] 5891 3-8-11 **75**.......................... KierenFox(3) 8 77
(J R Best) *led tl 5f out: 3rd and drvn over 1f out: kpt on same pce and no imp fnl 2f* **6/1[3]**

1 **4** *shd* **Daboos (USA)**[81] 3816 3-9-4 **79**.......................... RichardHills 12 80+
(M P Tregoning) *dwlt: wl off the pce towards rr: rdn and effrt on inner ent fnl 2f: kpt on fnl f and pressing for 3rd nr fin: nvr trbld ldrs* **7/2[1]**

6002 **5** *¾* **Prince Of Thebes (IRE)**[7] 6252 9-9-4 **75**.......................... NeilCallan 2 75+
(M J Attwater) *hld up off the pce in midfield: rdn and effrt over 2f out: keeping on but no ch w ldrs whn nt clr run and swtchd lft ins fnl f* **11/1**

6242 **6** *nk* **Dylanesque**[16] 5972 3-9-8 **83**.......................... PhilipRobinson 11 82
(M A Jarvis) *chsd clr ldng trio: rdn over 2f out: no imp and plugged on same pce u.p fnl 2f* **5/1[2]**

4206 **7** *nk* **Dr Wintringham (IRE)**[17] 5919 4-9-6 **77**.......................... DarryllHolland 4 75
(Karen George) *racd off the pce in midfield: rdn and no prog over 2f out: kpt on u.p fnl f: nvr able to chal* **33/1**

5060 **8** *¾* **Gallantry**[24] 5716 8-8-12 **76**.......................... LauraSimpson(7) 10 73
(P Howling) *dwlt: sn pushed up into midfield: rdn and no prog over 2f out: wl btn ent fnl f* **50/1**

6000 **9** *shd* **Karaka Jack**[9] 6205 3-9-3 **78**.......................... RoystonFfrench 1 74
(M Johnston) *a towards rr: rdn along over 3f out: n.d* **16/1**

0021 **10** *nk* **Rock Anthem (IRE)**[17] 5919 6-9-2 **73**.......................... TonyCulhane 9 69
(Mike Murphy) *hld up wl off the pce towards rr: rdn and no hdwy over 2f out: n.d* **7/1**

4010 **11** *3* **My Best Bet**[7] 6252 4-9-5 **81**.......................... JohnFahy(5) 5 70
(Stef Higgins) *stdd s: hld up wl bhd: nvr on terms* **10/1**

4405 **12** *6* **Robust Wish (USA)**[109] 2892 3-9-3 **78**..........................(b) KierenFallon 3 53
(B J Meehan) *sn rdn along and dropped to rr: lost tch wl over 2f out* **20/1**

1m 37.65s (-2.15) **Going Correction** -0.05s/f (Stan)
WFA 3 from 4yo+ 4lb **12** Ran SP% **118.8**
Speed ratings (Par 105): **108,105,103,103,102 102,102,101,101,100 97,91**
toteswingers:1&2:£22.30, 1&3:£11.00, 2&3:£12.50 CSF £84.11 CT £520.28 TOTE £11.60: £3.90, £3.00, £2.10; EX 162.20 Place 6 £163.98; Place 5 £115.52.
Owner Pat Eddery Racing (Reel Buddy) **Bred** P Balding **Trained** Nether Winchendon, Bucks

FOCUS
The first three finishers filled the front three positions pretty much throughout. The time was good, though, and the form looks solid enough.
T/Jkpt: Not won. T/Plt: £327.50 to a £1 stake. Pool:£81,763.45 - 182.24 winning tickets T/Qpdt: £451.50 to a £1 stake. Pool:£4,454.89 - 7.30 winning tickets SP

6431 - 6434a (Foreign Racing) - See Raceform Interactive

6018 BRIGHTON (L-H)
Tuesday, September 28

OFFICIAL GOING: Good to firm (watered; 8.1)
Rail moved out from 6f to 3f adding 9yds to distances.
Wind: Almost nil Weather: Cloudy

6435 SMITH & WESTERN NURSERY 5f 213y
2:10 (2:11) (Class 4) (0-80,80) 2-Y-O **£4,163** (£1,246; £623; £311; £155) **Stalls** Centre

Form RPR

6503 **1** **Jolah**[20] 5856 2-8-8 **67**.......................... ChrisCatlin 13 75
(C E Brittain) *led over 1f: led 3f out: rdn and hung lft fr over 1f out: hld on narrowly* **12/1**

031 **2** *shd* **Owain (USA)**[22] 5808 2-8-11 **75**.......................... AdamBeschizza(5) 3 83+
(C A Dwyer) *bmpd s and missed break: hdwy 3f out: drvn to press wnr fnl f: clsd grad: jst failed* **11/2[2]**

2434 **3** *1 ½* **Prophet In A Dream**[11] 6162 2-7-13 **61** ow1........ AndrewHeffernan(3) 6 64
(M R Channon) *a.p: drvn along and styd on same pce fnl 2f* **18/1**

3022 **4** *1 ½* **Top Care (USA)**[20] 5856 2-9-5 **78**.......................... GregFairley 10 77
(M Johnston) *dwlt: t.k.h in rr: sme hdwy whn hmpd over 3f out: hrd rdn and styd on fnl 2f: nvr nrr* **9/1**

231 **5** *¾* **Old Master Expert**[12] 6111 2-9-7 **80**.......................... TomQueally 12 76
(M L W Bell) *t.k.h in midfield: nt clr run over 2f out: disputing 4th and styng on whn n.m.r ins fnl f* **6/1[3]**

1060 **6** *3* **Kojak (IRE)**[10] 6200 2-9-7 **80**.......................... PatDobbs 7 67
(R Hannon) *prom tl outpcd fnl 2f* **13/2**

062 **7** *nk* **Morermaloke**[21] 5835 2-8-12 **71**..........................(b[1]) RobertWinston 1 58
(B J Meehan) *prom: hrd rdn over 1f out: disputing 4th and btn whn sltly hmpd ins fnl f* **13/2**

3423 **8** *2 ¾* **My Lord**[18] 5921 2-8-12 **74**.......................... JackDean(3) 8 52
(W G M Turner) *in tch: rdn and lost pl over 2f out: eased whn wl hld fnl f* **50/1**

5402 **9** *1 ¾* **Pick A Little**[13] 6086 2-8-13 **72**.......................... SebSanders 15 45
(B W Duke) *mid-div on outer: lost pl and in rr 3f out: modest hdwy fnl f* **33/1**

1420 **10** *½* **Volcanic Dust (IRE)**[13] 6086 2-8-9 **68**.......................... DarryllHolland 11 40
(E A L Dunlop) *t.k.h in rr: effrt in centre 2f out: wknd 1f out* **25/1**

0650 **11** *1 ½* **Granny Anne (IRE)**[11] 6139 2-7-13 **58**.......................... NickyMackay 9 25
(A Bailey) *sn outpcd in rr: no ch fnl 2f* **50/1**

5212 **12** *nk* **Johnny Hancocks (IRE)**[7] 6271 2-8-11 **70**.......................... CathyGannon 2 36
(P D Evans) *dwlt: sn w ldr: led over 4f out tl 3f out: wknd 2f out* **7/2[1]**

1306 **13** *2* **Goodwood Treasure**[20] 5856 2-8-12 **71**.......................... RichardMullen 4 31
(J L Dunlop) *in tch: rdn over 2f out: sn wknd* **16/1**

0203 **14** *1* **Bonjour Bongee**[13] 6072 2-8-0 **59**..........................(b) DavidProbert 14 16
(A J McCabe) *dwlt: a rdn along in rr* **66/1**

1m 10.59s (0.39) **Going Correction** +0.10s/f (Good) **14** Ran SP% **116.3**
Speed ratings (Par 97): **101,100,98,96,95 91,91,87,85,84 82,82,79,78**
toteswingers:1&2:£15.30, 1&3:£43.20, 2&3:£23.50 CSF £71.57 CT £1224.04 TOTE £16.70: £5.20, £1.40, £8.00; EX 96.80 TRIFECTA Not won..
Owner Saeed Manana **Bred** Genesis Green Stud Ltd **Trained** Newmarket, Suffolk
■ Stewards' Enquiry : Chris Catlin caution: used whip down the shoulder in the forehand position

FOCUS
The inside rail was dolled out from between the 6f and 3f poles, adding 9yds to race distances. A competitive nursery for the track, but this looked a case of the best horse not winning. The runners all came over to the stands' rail.

NOTEBOOK
Jolah hadn't helped herself by taking a keen hold in her previous three starts and she took a good grip here, but her rider let her stride on from her wide draw. That enabled her to bag the stands' rail when the field came across and she was in front over 2f from home. Despite hanging away to her left inside the last furlong, she was always doing just enough and she still seems to be improving. (tchd 14-1)
Owain(USA) ◆ was definitely an unlucky loser. Making his nursery debut after winning an ordinary Bath maiden earlier this month despite rearing at the stalls and losing a lot of ground, he repeated the trick here but it cost him dear this time. He travelled supremely well into the race and tried his hardest to catch the winner, but he fell just short. If he can learn to break on terms there are plenty more races to be won with him. (op 7-1 tchd 5-1)
Prophet In A Dream, winless and mainly campaigned over further since winning a five-runner maiden over the minimum trip here in April, was never far away and ran on well inside the last furlong but he lacks the scope of the front pair. The 1lb overweight made no difference. (op 20-1)
Top Care(USA), hampered at the start when runner-up to the smart Krypton Factor in a similar event at Epsom earlier this month, stayed on late from off the pace and may be worth a try over 7f. (op 6-1)
Old Master Expert, making his nursery debut after narrowly winning an uncompetitive Pontefract maiden, didn't enjoy the best of trips at various stages, including when still in with a chance entering the last furlong. He is worth another chance. (op 11-2)
Morermaloke showed up for a while, but was probably a bit too keen in the first-time blinkers. (op 17-2)
Johnny Hancocks(IRE), having his 16th outing of the season, was well drawn to attack but he always going to find it hard to dominate this field. Having propped exiting the gates, he had to be ridden to gain the early advantage but was then hassled by the winner and had run his race before the 2f marker. Official explanation: jockey said gelding hung right (tchd 10-3)

6436 CONSORT FROZEN FOODS LTD MEDIAN AUCTION MAIDEN STKS 6f 209y
2:45 (2:45) (Class 5) 2-Y-O **£2,523** (£755; £377; £188; £94) **Stalls** Centre

Form RPR

53 **1** **Marked Card (IRE)**[17] 5936 2-9-3 0.......................... RichardMullen 2 78+
(P W Chapple-Hyam) *rrd sltly s: sn led: hdd 4f out: led wl over 1f out: drvn clr ent fnl f: readily* **14/1**

3 **2** *3 ¼* **Blue Deer (IRE)**[15] 6019 2-9-3 0.......................... ChrisCatlin 4 70
(M R Channon) *pressed ldr: led 4f out tl wl over 1f out: one pce* **14/1**

64 **3** *4 ½* **Madame Solitaire**[21] 5836 2-8-12 0.......................... PatDobbs 1 53
(R Hannon) *chsd ldrs: rdn to chal ent fnl 2f: no ex over 1f out* **25/1**

4 *1 ¾* **Captain Brown** 2-9-3 0.......................... SebSanders 7 54
(Sir Mark Prescott) *s.s and lost 7 l: bhd: pushed along and hdwy to chse ldrs whn n.m.r 2f out: rn green and hung bdly lft: nt rcvr* **7/1[3]**

32 **5** *¾* **Red Riverman**[34] 5404 2-9-3 0.......................... TomQueally 6 52
(W J Haggas) *t.k.h towards rr: hdwy 3f out: wknd over 1f out* **8/15[1]**

0 **6** *1 ¼* **Handicraft (IRE)**[36] 5369 2-8-12 0.......................... GregFairley 3 44
(M Johnston) *chsd ldrs: drvn along over 4f out: hung lft and outpcd fnl 3f* **33/1**

4 **7** *3 ½* **Chief Of Men**[66] 4384 2-9-3 0..........................(t) RobertWinston 5 39
(D J Coakley) *prom: rdn over 2f out: sn wknd* **9/2[2]**

00 **8** *16* **Nice Chimes (IRE)**[108] 2951 2-8-9 0.......................... RobertLButler(3) 10 —
(B W Duke) *a bhd: rdn and no ch fnl 3f* **100/1**

50 **9** *1 ¼* **Safe Haven (IRE)**[38] 5294 2-8-13 0 ow1.......................... IanMongan 8 —
(A Bailey) *mid-div to rr: wknd over 3f out: sn bhd* **80/1**

1m 24.37s (1.27) **Going Correction** +0.10s/f (Good) **9** Ran SP% **118.3**
Speed ratings (Par 95): **96,92,87,85,84 82,78,60,59**
toteswingers:1&2:£4.50, 1&3:£8.30, 2&3:£6.90 CSF £181.09 TOTE £16.80: £3.70, £1.70, £3.60; EX 60.60 Trifecta £609.10 Part won. Pool: £823.12 - 0.52 winning units..
Owner J C Fretwell **Bred** Yeomanstown Stud **Trained** Newmarket, Suffolk
■ Stewards' Enquiry : Pat Dobbs caution: careless riding

FOCUS
An ordinary maiden featuring just one newcomer, but an impressive winner. Unlike in the opener the runners stayed far side after the cutaway.

NOTEBOOK
Marked Card(IRE) had missed the break in his first two starts, but this time his rider pushed him straight into an early advantage. He responded well to pressure after the false rail ended 3f from home and he soon powered right away from his rivals. Apparently highly regarded, his jockey was of the opinion that it has just taken time for the penny to drop, and he should go on from here. (op 12-1)
Blue Deer(IRE), third of six on debut in a moderate C&D maiden earlier this month, was up with the winner from the start and ran on again after getting momentarily outpaced around 2f from home. He may appreciate stepping up to 1m. (op 11-1)
Madame Solitaire, who appeared to need the experience in each of her first two starts, was up in trip and plugged on over the last couple of furlongs. She now gets a nursery mark.
Captain Brown, a 67,000gns half-brother to three winners abroad including a couple of useful types, was backed in from as big as 20-1 earlier in the day but he gave away a lot of ground by walking out of the stalls. He managed to reach the heels of the leaders passing the 2f pole, but then ran green and was beaten when hampered against the rail inside the last furlong. He is going to need further than this on pedigree. (op 13-2)
Red Riverman, placed in his first two starts in maidens which have both produced winners, was keen in the middle of the field early but found nothing off the bridle and this was disappointing. He now gets a mark, but has questions to answer. (op 4-5)

Handicraft(IRE) was off the bridle throughout and has a lot of improving to do in order to start recouping her 120,000gns price tag.

6437 DIGIBET.COM H'CAP — 1m 3f 196y
3:20 (3:20) (Class 3) (0-95,93) 3-Y-0+

£7,165 (£2,145; £1,072; £537; £267; £134) Stalls High

Form — RPR

2-01 **1** **Harlestone Times (IRE)**[16] 5994 3-8-4 **79** oh1 .... JimmyQuinn 1 94+
(J L Dunlop) *stdd s: hld up in 6th: rdn over 4f out: eased outside and hdwy to ld 2f out: sn clr: comf* **7/2**[2]

3312 **2** 5 **First Fandango**[20] 5858 3-8-4 **79** oh1 .... ChrisCatlin 6 85
(J W Hills) *towards rr: pushed along 5f out: hdwy and hung lft over 1f out: wnt 2nd jst ins fnl f: no ch w wnr* **17/2**

3051 **3** 2 ½ **Spirit Is Needed (IRE)**[10] 6202 4-9-11 **92** .... (b) GregFairley 8 94
(M Johnston) *chsd ldrs: rdn 3f out: one pce fnl 2f* **11/1**

0004 **4** 1 ½ **Record Breaker (IRE)**[10] 6185 6-9-4 **85** .... (b) RoystonFfrench 4 85
(M Johnston) *hld up in 5th: drvn along and struggling to stay in tch 3f out: styd on same pce fr over 1f out* **13/2**

0100 **5** 3 ½ **Fortuni (IRE)**[18] 5908 4-9-12 **93** .... SebSanders 7 87
(Sir Mark Prescott) *disp ld: led 3f out tl 2f out: wknd over 1f out* **5/2**[1]

5140 **6** 3 ½ **Goodwood Starlight (IRE)**[25] 5727 5-8-12 **82** .... RobertLButler(3) 5 70
(Miss Sheena West) *stdd s: hld up in last: rdn over 3f out: n.d* **14/1**

4046 **7** ¾ **Safari Sunup (IRE)**[17] 5970 5-9-5 **86** .... (b[1]) IanMongan 3 73
(P Winkworth) *dwlt: sn prom: hrd rdn over 2f out: wknd wl over 1f out* **6/1**[3]

561 **8** 2 ¼ **Inspirina (IRE)**[40] 5235 6-9-2 **83** .... TomQueally 2 67
(R Ford) *disp ld tl 3f out: sn lost pl* **10/1**

2m 32.12s (-0.58) **Going Correction** +0.10s/f (Good)
WFA 3 from 4yo+ 8lb — **8** Ran SP% **113.0**
Speed ratings (Par 107): **105,101,100,99,96 94,93,92**
toteswingers:1&2:£4.40, 1&3:£4.70, 2&3:£7.40 CSF £32.16 CT £292.42 TOTE £4.70: £2.00, £3.20, £3.60; EX 18.40 Trifecta £37.40 Pool: £364.92 - 7.22 winning units..
Owner J L Dunlop **Bred** J L Dunlop **Trained** Arundel, W Sussex

FOCUS
A decent handicap and the pace looked solid with a contested lead. The runners once again stayed far side and the race was dominated by the two 3-y-os, both of whom were 1lb out of the weights.

NOTEBOOK
Harlestone Times(IRE) was 7lb higher than when overcoming trouble in running to win a soft-ground handicap at Goodwood earlier this month. Trying this trip for the first time, neither the quicker ground nor longer trip proved any problem at all and, once in front over 1f out, he soon quickened right away. There is more to come from him over this sort of trip and he can win again. (tchd 10-3)

First Fandango, a consistent sort, was off a 3lb higher mark than when beaten by an in-form rival at Epsom earlier this month. Given plenty to do, he stayed on from the rear of the field over the last couple of furlongs but never had a hope of catching the winner. Official explanation: jockey said colt hung left (op 10-1 tchd 8-1)

Spirit Is Needed(IRE), favoured by the weights when winning a Newmarket claimer earlier this month, came off the bridle some way out and only managed to stay on at one pace. He remains 3lb above his last winning mark in a handicap, which came in first-time blinkers. (op 17-2)

Record Breaker(IRE) made only limited late progress and doesn't look a winner waiting to happen, despite now being 11lb lower than for his last success at Ascot a year ago. (op 6-1)

Fortuni(IRE), well beaten in both the Ebor and Mallard since winning off 8lb lower over this trip at Epsom, never looked happy despite being given a positive ride. Sweaty and with his tongue hanging out, he may have resented the close attentions of Inspirina from the start of the contest, and no sooner had he seen that rival off over 2f from home than the winner was cantering all over him. He does not look an easy ride. (op 3-1 tchd 10-3)

6438 RENDEZVOUS CASINO AT BRIGHTON MARINA H'CAP — 6f 209y
3:55 (3:55) (Class 4) (0-80,80) 3-Y-O £4,415 (£1,321; £660; £330; £164) Stalls Centre

Form — RPR

-100 **1** **Curtains**[10] 6198 3-9-2 **80** .... SimonPearce(5) 5 89
(S Dow) *hld up towards rr: hdwy to ld 2f out: continually edgd rt: rdn out* **11/1**

0650 **2** 1 **Fly Silca Fly (IRE)**[33] 5442 3-9-4 **77** .... ChrisCatlin 11 83
(M R Channon) *hld up towards rr: hdwy in centre 2f out: rdn to chal over 1f out: kpt on* **28/1**

3022 **3** 2 ½ **Cat Hunter**[26] 5677 3-8-11 **70** .... TomQueally 2 69+
(H R A Cecil) *s.s: hld up in rr: hdwy and n.m.r 2f out: rdn to go 3rd 1f out: kpt on* **11/4**[1]

0000 **4** 3 **Amary (IRE)**[31] 5524 3-9-4 **77** .... (b[1]) SteveDrowne 10 68
(C E Brittain) *chsd ldrs: rdn to chal 2f out: no ex over 1f out* **33/1**

0213 **5** nse **Ming Meng (IRE)**[9] 6221 3-8-11 **75** .... AdamBeschizza(5) 13 66
(M L W Bell) *dwlt and rdn s: sn in midfield: effrt and wnt lft 2f out: drvn along and styd on same pce* **4/1**[2]

1435 **6** 4 ½ **Rockabilly Rebel**[18] 5919 3-8-11 **70** .... SebSanders 3 49
(B W Hills) *mid-div on rail: lost pl over 3f out: sn rdn and bhd: sme late hdwy* **5/1**[3]

1200 **7** 2 ¼ **If I Were A Boy (IRE)**[25] 5728 3-9-5 **78** .... RobertWinston 12 51
(D J S Ffrench Davis) *cl up: jnd ldrs 3f out: wknd 2f out* **25/1**

3231 **8** 1 **Starwatch**[19] 5890 3-8-11 **70** .... NeilChalmers 8 40
(J J Bridger) *disp ld tl 2f out: sn hrd rdn and wknd* **20/1**

0000 **9** 2 ¼ **Jarrow (IRE)**[10] 6204 3-9-4 **77** .... GregFairley 9 41
(M Johnston) *disp ld tl wknd 2f out* **8/1**

3342 **10** 14 **Wise Up**[20] 5861 3-8-11 **70** .... (p) CathyGannon 6 —
(C A Dwyer) *disp ld tl wknd qckly 2f out* **20/1**

6005 **11** 122 **Kumbeshwar**[9] 6223 3-9-1 **74** .... StevieDonohoe 7 —
(P D Evans) *mid-div tl virtually p.u 3f out* **40/1**

120R **R** **Stefanki (IRE)**[10] 6197 3-9-2 **78** .... MatthewDavies(3) 4 —
(George Baker) *ref to r* **5/1**[3]

1m 23.44s (0.34) **Going Correction** +0.10s/f (Good) — **12** Ran SP% **121.6**
Speed ratings (Par 103): **102,100,98,94,94 89,86,85,83,67 —,—**
toteswingers:1&2:£43.70, 1&3:£8.80, 2&3:£14.40 CSF £292.55 CT £1104.14 TOTE £13.50: £4.40, £4.90, £2.00; EX 200.80 Trifecta £277.30 Part won. Pool: £374.80 - 0.30 winning units..
Owner The Pull Yourself Together Partnership **Bred** Sir Eric Parker **Trained** Epsom, Surrey

■ Stewards' Enquiry : Adam Beschizza two-day ban: careless riding (Oct 13-14)

FOCUS
A wide-open handicap with three horses contesting the early advantage, none of which figured in the finish, and there were eight horses in a line across the track passing the 2f pole. The field raced centre-to-far-side after the cutaway.

Kumbeshwar Official explanation: jockey said gelding lost it's action coming down the hill

6439 BRIGHTON SQUARE "HEART OF LANES" CLAIMING STKS — 6f 209y
4:30 (4:30) (Class 6) 3-Y-O+ £1,748 (£520; £260; £129) Stalls Centre

Form — RPR

4110 **1** **Fault**[21] 5838 4-9-2 77 .... (t) SebSanders 8 71
(Stef Higgins) *hld up in rr: hdwy and hrd rdn 2f out: styd on to chal fnl 75yds: jst got up* **8/1**

5013 **2** nk **Dingaan (IRE)**[24] 5768 7-9-2 81 .... DavidProbert 3 70
(A M Balding) *trckd ldrs: effrt and edgd lft over 1f out: disp ld ins fnl f: jst tchd off* **7/4**[1]

5542 **3** nk **Chinese Democracy (USA)**[9] 6226 3-8-8 58 .... (v) CathyGannon 14 64
(P D Evans) *bhd: hdwy and hrd rdn 2f out: styd on wl fnl f: unable to get up in time* **16/1**

0066 **4** nse **Highland Harvest**[27] 5652 6-9-4 65 .... StevieDonohoe 5 71
(Jamie Poulton) *hld up in midfield: hdwy 2f out: continually hung lft: disp ld ins fnl f: nt qckn nr fin* **50/1**

2321 **5** 3 **Timeteam (IRE)**[25] 5712 4-8-9 77 .... HarryBentley(7) 4 61
(G L Moore) *chsd ldrs: hrd rdn 2f out: one pce* **8/1**

1013 **6** 2 ½ **Lady Florence**[27] 5652 5-9-2 75 .... RussKennemore(3) 6 57
(A B Coogan) *led at gd pce tl wknd ins fnl f* **4/1**[2]

6520 **7** 2 ¼ **Universal Circus**[19] 5889 3-8-8 72 .... ChrisCatlin 11 43
(M R Channon) *towards rr: hrd rdn 2f out: nt trble ldrs* **16/1**

4060 **8** 1 ¾ **Joss Stick**[15] 6024 5-8-6 42 .... (t) SimonPearce(5) 12 38
(L A Dace) *prom: jnd ldr 3f out: hrd rdn and wknd 2f out* **150/1**

3400 **9** 2 **Musical Script (USA)**[19] 5877 7-9-4 55 .... (b) AndreaAtzeni 1 40
(Mouse Hamilton-Fairley) *chsd ldrs: hrd rdn over 2f out: wknd wl over 1f out* **33/1**

1662 **10** 3 ¾ **Monashee Rock (IRE)**[48] 4939 5-8-7 62 .... (p) JimmyQuinn 2 19
(Matthew Salaman) *hld up in rr: rdn over 2f out: nvr nr ldrs* **12/1**

00 **11** 6 **Clearing House**[43] 5159 5-8-12 45 .... LiamJones 10 8
(J Ryan) *a bhd: drvn along and n.d fnl 3f* **50/1**

3302 **12** 5 **I Confess**[37] 5325 5-8-8 66 .... AdamBeschizza(5) 7 —
(G C Bravery) *prom tl wknd over 2f out* **9/2**[3]

1m 24.51s (1.41) **Going Correction** +0.10s/f (Good)
WFA 3 from 4yo+ 3lb — **12** Ran SP% **123.7**
Speed ratings (Par 101): **95,94,94,94,90 87,85,83,81,76 69,64**
toteswingers:1&2:£6.90, 2&3:£8.80, 1&3:£16.40 CSF £23.14 TOTE £9.30: £3.00, £1.20, £4.00; EX 34.50 Trifecta £337.00 Part won. Pool: £455.47 - 0.10 winning units..
Owner David Gilbert **Bred** Mrs A M Vestey **Trained** Lambourn, Berks

FOCUS
A modest claimer, but a tight contest with only around half a length covering the first four home. Again the runners stayed centre-to-far-side after the false rail ended. The winning time was 1.07 seconds slower than the preceding handicap.

6440 AMC SECURITY SYSTEMS H'CAP — 5f 59y
5:05 (5:06) (Class 5) (0-75,75) 3-Y-O+ £2,523 (£755; £377; £188; £94) Stalls Centre

Form — RPR

2040 **1** **Ajjaadd (USA)**[20] 5855 4-9-1 **69** .... SteveDrowne 2 78
(T E Powell) *t.k.h in rr: rdn and hdwy over 1f out: led ins fnl f: drvn out* **5/1**[1]

3141 **2** ¾ **Magical Speedfit (IRE)**[14] 6064 5-9-1 **74** .... SimonPearce(5) 10 80
(G G Margarson) *mid-div on outer: hrd rdn and hdwy over 1f out: r.o fnl f: nt rch wnr* **5/1**[1]

5000 **3** ¾ **Tamarind Hill (IRE)**[15] 6031 3-8-3 **61** oh3 .... (b) AndrewHeffernan(3) 7 64
(A J McCabe) *prom: rdn over 2f out: kpt on* **40/1**

3045 **4** ½ **Make My Dream**[18] 5915 7-9-2 **70** .... AndreaAtzeni 6 72
(J Gallagher) *chsd ldrs: rdn and lost pl 2f out: r.o again fnl f* **10/1**

5300 **5** ¾ **Danny's Choice**[10] 6198 3-9-3 **75** .... EJMcNamara(3) 4 74
(R M Beckett) *prom: jnd ldr over 1f out: no ex fnl f* **7/1**

0025 **6** ½ **Rocker**[16] 5995 6-9-0 **75** .... HarryBentley(7) 8 72
(G L Moore) *dwlt: sn in midfield: effrt and hrd rdn over 1f out: no imp* **13/2**[3]

6130 **7** hd **Maryolini**[18] 5915 5-8-2 **61** oh3 .... AdamBeschizza(5) 1 58
(T Keddy) *towards rr: hdwy on ins rail over 1f out: hrd rdn and no ex fnl f* **14/1**

1214 **8** nk **Matterofact (IRE)**[18] 5915 7-9-6 **74** .... RobertWinston 9 70
(M S Saunders) *pressed ldr: slt ld over 2f out tl wknd ins fnl f* **15/2**

5032 **9** 1 ¼ **Triple Dream**[3] 6374 5-9-4 **72** .... (p) ChrisCatlin 5 63
(J M Bradley) *led tl over 2f out: wknd wl over 1f out* **6/1**[2]

0436 **10** nk **Even Bolder**[18] 5915 7-9-3 **71** .... SebSanders 3 61
(E A Wheeler) *s.i.s: in rr whn checked over 4f out: n.d* **7/1**

63.48 secs (1.18) **Going Correction** +0.10s/f (Good)
WFA 3 from 4yo+ 1lb — **10** Ran SP% **115.9**
Speed ratings (Par 103): **94,92,91,90,89 88,88,88,86,85**
toteswingers:1&2:£7.90, 1&3:£31.60, 2&3:£24.00 CSF £29.29 CT £917.54 TOTE £5.00: £2.00, £1.80, £12.10; EX 46.70 TRIFECTA Not won. Place 6 £1,420.60, Place 5 £330.04.
Owner Katy & Lol Pratt **Bred** Darley **Trained** Reigate, Surrey

FOCUS
A tight little sprint handicap in which all ten runners still had some sort of chance entering the last furlong. The field tended to stay in the middle of the track following the cutaway.

Tamarind Hill(IRE) Official explanation: jockey said lost his whip inside the final furlong

T/Plt: £1,140.90 to a £1 stake. Pool:£78,119.04 - 49.98 winning tickets T/Qpdt: £30.80 to a £1 stake. Pool:£6,810.05 - 163.59 winning tickets LM

6190 NEWBURY (L-H)
Tuesday, September 28

OFFICIAL GOING: Good (good to soft in places; 7.5)
Wind: VIrtually nil Weather: Overcast

6441 LOUIS AND VALERIE FREEDMAN MAIDEN FILLIES' STKS — 6f 8y
2:00 (2:01) (Class 4) 2-Y-O £3,561 (£1,059; £529; £264) Stalls High

Form — RPR

1 **Face Reality (USA)** 2-9-0 0 .... RyanMoore 2 79+
(R Hannon) *trckd ldrs: pushed along to take slt ld 2f out: jnd fr over 1f out and strly chal thrght fnl f tl asserted fnl 50yds* **12/1**

3 **2** nk **Wiqaaya (IRE)**[95] 3411 2-9-0 0 .... RichardHills 14 78
(E A L Dunlop) *trckd ldrs: gng wl 2f out: jnd wnr and shkn up fnl f: stl upsides tl outpcd fnl 50yds* **10/3**[1]

3 2 ¾ **Super (IRE)** 2-9-0 0 .... JimmyFortune 10 70+
(R Hannon) *s.i.s: in rr: swtchd rt over 2f out and swtchd rt again 1f out to get stands' rail: r.o wl to take 3rd ins fnl f but no imp on ldng duo* **25/1**

The Form Book, Raceform Ltd, Compton, RG20 6NL

00 4 1 **Mirabile Visu**[35] 5381 2-9-0 0................................ DaneO'Neill 1 67
(Mrs H S Main) *trckd ldrs: pushed along and wl there 2f out: wknd ins fnl f* **200/1**

5 1/2 **Map Of Heaven** 2-9-0 0................................ MichaelHills 6 65+
(W J Haggas) *in rr: pushed along over 2f out: hdwy over 1f out and kpt on fnl f but nvr a threat* **9/2**[3]

6 2 1/4 **Glas Burn** 2-9-0 0................................ RichardKingscote 13 59
(J G Portman) *slowly away: in rr: pushed along and hdwy 2f out: hung lft and green over 1f out: outpcd ins fnl f* **100/1**

6 7 2 3/4 **Chokurei (IRE)**[71] 4203 2-9-0 0................................ PhilipRobinson 7 50
(C G Cox) *pressed ldrs: drvn along over 2f out: wknd over 1f out* **6/1**

8 nse **Pearl Blue (IRE)** 2-9-0 0................................ JackMitchell 3 50
(C F Wall) *in rr: pushed along and green over 2f out: styd on but nvr gng pce to get into contention* **50/1**

6 9 2 **Bird In The Wind (USA)**[25] 5719 2-9-0 0................................ JimCrowley 9 44
(R M Beckett) *slt ld tl hdd 2f out: sn btn* **16/1**

3 10 nk **Poppy**[11] 6145 2-9-0 0................................ RichardHughes 5 43
(R Hannon) *in tch: chsd ldrs 3f out: rdn: hung lft and green ins fnl 2f: sn wknd* **7/2**[2]

11 3/4 **Ride The Wind** 2-9-0 0................................ TedDurcan 4 41
(C F Wall) *s.i.s: mod prog fnl f* **25/1**

12 3/4 **Shadow Of The Sun** 2-9-0 0................................ SamHitchcott 11 39
(M R Channon) *chsd ldrs tl rdn and wknd over 2f out* **20/1**

50 13 1/2 **Proenza (USA)**[19] 5893 2-9-0 0................................(t) KierenFallon 15 37
(B J Meehan) *pressed ldr 3f: sn hung lft and wknd over 2f out* **11/1**

0 14 2 **Bella Nemica**[11] 6161 2-9-0 0................................ EddieCreighton 12 31
(E J Creighton) *mid-div and rdn 3f out: sn wknd* **250/1**

1m 13.35s (0.35) **Going Correction** -0.075s/f (Good) **14** Ran SP% **116.0**
Speed ratings (Par 94): **94,93,89,88,87 84,81,81,78,78 77,76,75,72**
toteswingers:1&2:£6.30, 1&3:£27.90, 2&3:£13.50 CSF £47.89 TOTE £14.60: £3.90, £1.70, £4.40; EX 54.50.
Owner Noel O'Callaghan **Bred** Lemons Mill Farm & Churchull B'Stock Inv **Trained** East Everleigh, Wilts

FOCUS
Some powerful connections were represented, but the proximity of 200-1 shot Mirabile Visu, who had shown little in two starts on Polytrack, suggests the form is limited.

NOTEBOOK
Face Reality(USA), a $150,000 first foal of a 7.5f-1m2f winner, was passed over by Richard Hughes, but had sufficient ability and knowhow to make a successful introduction. She showed a willing attitude, finding plenty despite being intimidated by the runner-up, and looks likely to improve. (op 9-1)
Wiqaaya(IRE), off the track since finishing third in a decent maiden on the July course 95 days earlier, travelled well but edged slightly left once under pressure and simply found one too good. She has plenty of speed and should soon win a similar race. (op 7-2)
Super(IRE), a 60,000euros purchase, raced off the pace after starting slowly but finished well once switched to the stands' rail. (op 22-1)
Mirabile Visu found improvement for the switch to turf and can now contest handicaps.
Map Of Heaven, a sister to smart sprinter Enticing, out of high-class juvenile Superstar Leo (runner-up Prix de l'Abbaye), made a sluggish start and basically wasn't as sharp as some of these. (op 5-1 tchd 6-1)
Glas Burn lost quite a bit of ground leaving the stalls and was niggled along from a fair way out, but she showed ability. (op 66-1)
Chokurei(IRE), whose pedigree is a mix of speed and stamina, lacked the finishing speed of a few of her rivals and failed to build on her debut effort. (op 7-1 tchd 11-2)
Poppy, seemingly the choice of Richard Hughes over the winner and third, proved most disappointing. She had made a pleasing debut over C&D 11 days earlier, but was hanging left and in trouble from an early stage this time. Official explanation: jockey said filly hung left-handed throughout (op 10-3 tchd 3-1)

6442 HEATON-ELLIS TRUST E B F MAIDEN STKS (DIV I) 7f (S)
2:35 (2:36) (Class 4) 2-Y-O **£3,885** (£867; £867; £288) **Stalls** High

Form RPR

0 1 **Norse Blues**[48] 4962 2-9-3 0................................ LiamKeniry 2 79+
(S Kirk) *mde virtually all: drvn and edgd lft fnl f and stl green but styd on to go clr fnl 120yds* **50/1**

3 2 3 **Above All**[24] 5751 2-9-3 0................................ RichardHills 14 71
(W J Haggas) *chsd ldrs: rdn over 1f out: styd on wl fnl f to join 2nd on line but no ch w wnr* **11/2**[2]

6 2 dht **Puttingonthestyle (IRE)**[11] 6153 2-9-3 0................................ RichardHughes 3 71
(R Hannon) *chsd ldrs: chsd wnr fnl f but no imp: one pce and jnd for 2nd on line* **9/2**[1]

4 3/4 **Encore Une Annee** 2-8-12 0................................ JimCrowley 1 64
(R M Beckett) *mid-div: hdwy and pushed along over 2f out: styd on fnl f and gng on cl home but no ch w wnr* **20/1**

0 5 hd **Aristeia**[8] 6247 2-8-12 0................................ RyanMoore 7 64
(R Hannon) *pressed wnr tl rdn 2f out: outpcd and lost 2nd 1f out: no ex fnl 100yds* **10/1**

0 6 1/2 **Mrs Greeley**[26] 5692 2-8-12 0................................ ShaneKelly 6 62
(Eve Johnson Houghton) *in tch: pushed along and hdwy fr 2f out: kpt on ins fnl f: gng on cl home* **12/1**

7 1 3/4 **Warneford** 2-9-3 0................................ KierenFallon 5 63
(B J Meehan) *chsd ldrs: drvn along 1/2-way: once pce 2f out:* **15/2**

00 8 1/2 **Night Witch (IRE)**[8] 6247 2-8-12 0................................ EddieCreighton 9 57
(E J Creighton) *pushed rt s: s.i.s: in rr: rdn and hdwy over 2f out: styd on same pce ins fnl f* **200/1**

9 4 **Heart Beat Song** 2-9-3 0................................ WilliamBuick 10 52
(E A L Dunlop) *wnt lft s: in rr: sme prog fr over 1f out* **25/1**

10 1/2 **Slumber** 2-9-3 0................................ MichaelHills 16 51
(B W Hills) *s.i.s: in rr: sme hdwy 2f out: nvr a threat* **6/1**[3]

0 11 2 1/2 **Korngold**[74] 4096 2-9-3 0................................ TedDurcan 13 44
(J L Dunlop) *in rr: pushed along 1/2-way: sme hdwy fnl f* **11/2**[2]

12 1/2 **Hoofprintinthesnow** 2-9-3 0................................ NeilCallan 11 43
(Mrs A J Perrett) *rdn 1/2-way: a towards rr* **25/1**

5440 13 3 1/4 **Beach Patrol (IRE)**[69] 4274 2-9-0 62................................ AlanCreighton(3) 4 35
(E J Creighton) *chsd ldrs: rdn over 2f out: sn wknd* **100/1**

0 14 nk **Major Dance**[10] 6196 2-9-3 0................................ DaneO'Neill 12 34
(B W Hills) *chsd ldrs to 1/2-way* **100/1**

15 3 **Ninth Parallel (USA)** 2-9-3 0................................ JimmyFortune 8 27
(B J Meehan) *nvr beyond mid-div: bhd fnl 2f* **20/1**

16 1/2 **Snow Hill** 2-9-3 0................................ GeorgeBaker 15 25
(C F Wall) *a in rr* **28/1**

1m 26.25s (0.55) **Going Correction** -0.075s/f (Good) **16** Ran SP% **116.9**
Speed ratings (Par 97): **93,89,89,88,88 87,85,85,80,80 77,76,73,72,69 68**
PL: AA £2.10, PTS £1.50 EX: NB/AA £374.70 NB/PTS £189.70 CSF: NB/AA £138.91 NB/PTS £119.03 .toteswingers: NB&AA £35.90, AA&PTS £3.90, NB&PTS £34.00. TOTE £81.10: £14.60.

Owner J C Smith **Bred** Littleton Stud **Trained** Upper Lambourn, Berks

FOCUS
The time was 0.81 seconds quicker than the second division, won by Mantoba, but it still paid to race prominently. This looked a fair maiden and the race ought to produce a few winners.

NOTEBOOK
Norse Blues raced keenly and ran green on debut 48 days earlier, but did hint at ability. A colt with size, he proved suited by a more positive ride this time, travelling strongly without overdoing it, and stayed on well for a convincing success, showing much-improved form. There's plenty of speed in his pedigree, but he might stay a little further and has the scope to keep progressing.
Above All, last of three, beaten 6l on his debut in a Polytrack conditions race, was coltish in the paddock but still ran well. He travelled nicely on the speed, but was one paced under pressure, giving the impression he'll do better in time. (op 7-2)
Puttingonthestyle(IRE), green on debut in just a reasonable 6f Newmarket maiden, showed improvement, but is far from the finished article, still looking in need of the experience. He also displayed quite a fluent action and may appreciate better ground. (op 7-2)
Encore Une Annee, a sister to a 1m3f Fibresand winner, was dropped in from the lowest stall and kept on nicely in the closing stages, without being subjected to a hard ride. She can improve, particularly when upped in trip.
Aristeia ◆, slowly away on debut, broke well this time but raced freely early on and didn't see her race out. She looks to be a sprinter and can do better. (op 14-1)
Mrs Greeley plugged on from off the pace, improving on her debut performance.
Warneford, who cost 115,000gns, was niggled along from a fair way out and needed the experience. (op 7-1 tchd 6-1)
Night Witch(IRE) Official explanation: jockey said filly hung both ways
Slumber travelled okay but found little. (op 15-2 tchd 8-1)
Korngold had been off for 74 days since showing ability on debut over C&D and offered little on his return. (tchd 5-1 and 6-1)
Ninth Parallel(USA) Official explanation: jockey said colt hung right-handed

6443 HEATON-ELLIS TRUST E B F MAIDEN STKS (DIV II) 7f (S)
3:10 (3:12) (Class 4) 2-Y-O **£3,885** (£1,156; £577; £288) **Stalls** High

Form RPR

4 1 **Mantoba**[26] 5690 2-9-3 0................................(t) KierenFallon 8 77
(B J Meehan) *disp ld tl slt ld over 2f out: drvn fr over 1f out: styd on strly to assert fnl 120yds* **11/2**[3]

2 1/2 **Sirius Prospect (USA)** 2-9-3 0................................ PhilipRobinson 13 76
(D K Ivory) *slt advantage after 1f tl hdd over 2f out: styd chalng and stl ev ch tl outpcd fnl 120yds* **25/1**

0 3 1/2 **Red Lover**[10] 6190 2-9-3 0................................ JimCrowley 6 75
(E A L Dunlop) *in tch: hdwy to trck ldrs gng wl fr 2f out: drvn and effrt ins fnl f: nvr quite in terms: no ex and one pce fnl 120yds* **9/1**

2 4 1 **Yojimbo (IRE)**[10] 6196 2-9-3 0................................ SamHitchcott 11 72
(M R Channon) *sn disputing ld: rdn over 2f out: styd on same pce fnl 120yds* **5/2**[1]

5 2 1/2 **Carrick A Rede (IRE)** 2-9-3 0................................ AdamKirby 5 66+
(C G Cox) *s.i.s: in rr: pushed along and hdwy over 2f out: kpt on fnl f but nvr a threat* **25/1**

6 2 3/4 **Omnipotent (IRE)** 2-9-3 0................................ RichardHughes 4 59
(R Hannon) *pressed ldrs: rdn 2f out: wknd over 1f out* **8/1**

7 1 1/4 **Heezararity** 2-9-3 0................................ MickyFenton 3 56
(W S Kittow) *in rr: pushed along and hdwy 2f out: edgd rt and green 1f out but kpt on* **100/1**

04 8 1 1/4 **Flinty**[26] 5676 2-9-3 0................................ RyanMoore 15 53
(R Hannon) *in rr and drvn along 3f out: styd on fnl f but nvr any ch* **40/1**

6 9 1/2 **Senor Tibor (USA)**[19] 5895 2-9-3 0................................ EddieCreighton 9 51
(E J Creighton) *s.i.s: in rr: hung lft and green fr 2f out but sme prog fnl f* **150/1**

10 nk **Teazel** 2-8-12 0................................ NeilCallan 1 46
(D J S Ffrench Davis) *pressed ldrs tl over 2f out: wknd over 1f out* **66/1**

11 1 **Making Eyes (IRE)** 2-8-12 0................................ TedDurcan 2 43
(C F Wall) *s.i.s: outpcd tl mod last prog* **40/1**

12 shd **Fennica (USA)** 2-8-12 0................................ WilliamBuick 7 43
(J H M Gosden) *nvr bttr than mid-div: bhd fr 3f* **10/3**[2]

0 13 3/4 **Pivot Bridge**[46] 5032 2-9-3 0................................ MichaelHills 14 46
(B W Hills) *chsd ldrs over 4f* **16/1**

14 2 1/2 **Boston Court (IRE)** 2-9-3 0................................ RichardHills 12 40
(B J Meehan) *in tch to 1/2-way* **40/1**

15 1 1/4 **Home Office** 2-9-3 0................................ JoeFanning 10 37
(M Johnston) *pressed ldrs tl wknd qckly over 2f out* **12/1**

1m 27.06s (1.36) **Going Correction** -0.075s/f (Good) **15** Ran SP% **119.9**
Speed ratings (Par 97): **89,88,87,86,83 80,79,77,77,76 75,75,74,71,70**
toteswingers:1&2:£33.20, 1&3:£8.20, 2&3:£44.30 CSF £142.92 TOTE £5.30: £2.00, £6.40, £2.60; EX 255.70.
Owner Manton Racing Partnership **Bred** Kirtlington Stud **Trained** Manton, Wilts

FOCUS
The time was 0.81 seconds slower than the first division, won by Norse Blues, but this still looked a fair maiden.

NOTEBOOK
Mantoba, beaten a long way when last of four in a 1m Salisbury novice event first time up, showed greatly improved form on this drop in trip with a tongue-tie fitted. He showed a good attitude, responding well to pressure, but things are set to get tougher from now on and he'll need to keep progressing. (tchd 5-1)
Sirius Prospect(USA), a 115,000gns first foal of a 2-y-o Group 3 winner over 7f in France (also won in Canada at four), was backed at big prices and justified the support with a good debut effort. He was sweating beforehand, but in the race itself he travelled strongly on the pace, before keeping on for pressure. Provided he's not the type who will always get stirred up before the off, he could be useful. (op 66-1 tchd 22-1)
Red Lover attracted market support and duly improved on what he showed over C&D on debut, but such was the ease with which he travelled through the race, even better could have been expected. He looked the winner going inside the final 2f, but although keeping on, he didn't find as much as looked likely. Perhaps he needs more time, but whatever, if he can see his race out better then he could be properly decent. (op 12-1 tchd 14-1)
Yojimbo(IRE) ran respectably without finding much improvement on the form he showed when runner-up over C&D on quick ground first time up. (op 11-4 tchd 10-3)
Carrick A Rede(IRE) a 27,000gns half-brother to a 6f juvenile winner, wasn't given a hard time and should improve. (op 33-1)
Omnipotent(IRE), a £52,000 purchase, out of a 1m winner, travelled well on the pace to a point but displayed an ungainly action under pressure, rather climbing and showing a knee action. (op 14-1)
Heezararity ◆, an already gelded first foal of a winning sprinter, kept on steadily without being given a hard time and showed ability. He can do better and could pick up a weak maiden, or will more likely find his level in handicaps. (tchd 125-1)
Senor Tibor(USA) Official explanation: vet said colt lost a near hind shoe

Fennica(USA), a half-sister to top-class miler Observatory, was niggled along over 3f out and found nothing, never looking likely to justify market confidence. (op 5-2 tchd 9-4)

6444 OPUS ENERGY H'CAP — 1m 7y(R)
3:45 (3:47) (Class 5) (0-75,75) 3-Y-0+ — **£2,590** (£770; £385; £192) **Stalls** Low

Form — RPR

3133 **1** **Oh So Saucy**[13] 6097 6-9-4 **73** .... GeorgeBaker 5 — 82+
(C F Wall) *hld up in tch: hdwy: nt clr run and swtchd lft ins fnl f: str run fnl 50yds to ld last strides* **12/1**

0002 **2** *hd* **Willow Dancer (IRE)**[8] 6260 6-9-4 **73** .... (p) AdamKirby 11 — 81
(W R Swinburn) *sn pressing ldr: led 3 out: hrd rdn and 2 l clr 1f out: kpt on u.p: ct last strides* **9/2**[2]

5643 **3** *3/4* **Effigy**[21] 5833 6-9-1 **75** .... AmyScott(5) 2 — 82+
(H Candy) *s.i.s: in rr: hdwy on ins over 2f out: pushed along and styd on wl whn n.m.r fnl 100yds: gng on cl home* **13/2**[3]

-223 **4** *1/2* **Three Ducks**[16] 5988 4-9-5 **74** .... RichardHughes 1 — 79
(R Hannon) *led tl rdn and hdd 3f out: edgd rt u.p ins fnl f: wknd fnl 100yds* **15/2**

2100 **5** *nk* **Towbaat**[111] 2863 3-9-2 **75** .... PhilipRobinson 12 — 80
(M A Jarvis) *in rr: swtchd rt to outside over 2f out: rdn and kpt on fnl f and gng on cl home: nt rch ldrs* **12/1**

1140 **6** *1/2* **Seasonal Cross**[10] 6205 5-9-6 **75** .... KierenFallon 8 — 79
(S Dow) *s.i.s and bhd: drvn and hdwy on outside fr 2f out: kpt on u.p but nt rch ldrs* **8/1**

0103 **7** *shd* **Black N Brew (USA)**[20] 5866 4-9-3 **75** .... KierenFox(3) 6 — 78
(J R Best) *towards rr and rdn over 3f out: kpt on ins fnl f but nt rch ldrs* **14/1**

0000 **8** *1* **Club Tahiti**[17] 5972 4-9-5 **74** .... NeilCallan 3 — 75
(A W Carroll) *chsd ldrs: rdn over 2f out: styd chsng ldrs u.p tl wknd fnl 120yds* **22/1**

0305 **9** *2 1/2* **Bold Cross (IRE)**[8] 6260 7-9-2 **71** .... PaulFitzsimons 4 — 66
(E G Bevan) *chsd ldrs rdn over 2f out: wknd over 1f out* **20/1**

5312 **10** *shd* **Advertise**[38] 5287 4-9-5 **74** .... JimmyFortune 9 — 69
(A M Balding) *t.k.h: chsd ldrs: rdn 2f out: wknd and eased whn n.m.r fnl f* **5/2**[1]

-223 **11** *1/2* **Patavium Prince (IRE)**[71] 4206 7-9-4 **73** .... DaneO'Neill 7 — 67
(Miss Jo Crowley) *in tch: rdn over 2f out and sn btn* **33/1**

6050 **12** *1 1/4* **King's Caprice**[81] 3863 9-8-11 **71** .... RossAtkinson(5) 10 — 62
(J C Fox) *plld hrd: chsd ldrs tl wknd over 2f out* **50/1**

1m 38.69s (98.69)
WFA 3 from 4yo+ 4lb — **12** Ran SP% **119.0**
toteswingers:1&2:£11.00, 1&3:£18.20, 2&3:£7.90 CSF £63.02 CT £396.51 TOTE £12.00: £3.00, £1.90, £2.90; EX 63.80.
Owner The Eight Of Diamonds **Bred** Mrs C J Walker **Trained** Newmarket, Suffolk

FOCUS
More like a classified event than a handicap, with just 4lb separating the entire field. A steady pace meant they were still well bunched on entering the straight, and they finished in a bit of a heap. The runner-up ran to form, with the third looking a tad unlucky not to be closer.
Willow Dancer(IRE) Official explanation: jockey said gelding had been struck into near hind
Advertise Official explanation: jockey said gelding ran too free

6445 STHREE PLC NURSERY — 5f 34y
4:20 (4:21) (Class 4) (0-85,85) 2-Y-0 — **£3,412** (£1,007; £504) **Stalls** High

Form — RPR

000 **1** **Style And Panache (IRE)**[17] 5939 2-8-11 **75** .... PatCosgrave 6 — 82
(P D Evans) *chsd ldrs: chal over 2f out tl def advantage over 1f out: hld on gamely u.p thrght fnl f: all out* **66/1**

1132 **2** *nk* **Millyluvstobouggie**[25] 5725 2-8-7 **71** .... LukeMorris 3 — 77
(C G Cox) *chsd ldrs: rdn and styd on to chse wnr fnl 120yds: hrd rdn sn after and kpt on but a jst hld* **10/1**

611 **3** *1/2* **Sadafiya**[25] 5725 2-9-4 **82** .... RichardHills 8 — 86
(E A L Dunlop) *chsd ldrs: rdn over 1f out and styd on thrght fnl f: gng on cl home but nt quite rch ldng duo* **6/1**[3]

2410 **4** *nk* **Fifth Ave**[19] 5882 2-8-11 **78** .... SophieDoyle(3) 2 — 81
(J A Osborne) *pressed ldrs: slt ld 2f out: narrowly hdd over 1f out: styd on u.p fnl f but no imp fnl 100yds* **20/1**

1304 **5** *1/2* **Phoebs**[88] 3630 2-9-7 **85** .... KierenFallon 4 — 86
(R A Mills) *towards rr but in tch: swtchd rt and hdwy ins fnl 2f: kpt on u.p thrght fnl f but nvr gng pce to chal* **20/1**

2520 **6** *2 3/4* **Whoateallthepius (IRE)**[25] 5725 2-8-13 **77** .... PhilipRobinson 7 — 68
(D K Ivory) *slt ld to 2f out wknd ins fnl f* **14/1**

2105 **7** *1/2* **Dress Up (IRE)**[73] 4138 2-9-4 **82** .... RyanMoore 10 — 72
(S Kirk) *chsd ldrs: rdn and styng on whn rdr dropped whip ins fnl 2f: kpt on same pce after* **4/1**[1]

5423 **8** *nk* **Perfect Pastime**[13] 6086 2-8-5 **74** .... JohnFahy(5) 14 — 62
(W R Swinburn) *racd alone jst off stands' rail and in rr tl jnd main gp 1/2-way: styd on fnl f but nvr any ch* **11/2**[2]

102 **9** *hd* **Coconut Ice**[15] 6030 2-8-9 **73** .... RichardKingscote 5 — 61
(Tom Dascombe) *s.i.s: in rr: swtchd lft whn crossed ins fnl 2f: nvr in contention* **16/1**

2234 **10** *2* **Barking (IRE)**[13] 6086 2-8-7 **71** .... RichardHughes 1 — 52
(R Hannon) *outpcd most of way* **6/1**[3]

4520 **11** *2 3/4* **Laugh Or Cry**[20] 5865 2-8-9 **73** .... JimCrowley 12 — 44
(P J Makin) *outpcd most of way* **12/1**

316 **12** *nk* **Native Picture (IRE)**[29] 5613 2-8-6 **70** .... FrannyNorton 11 — 40
(R Hannon) *outpcd most of way* **16/1**

401 **13** *40* **Basilica**[21] 5835 2-9-2 **83** .... JamesMillman(3) 13 — —
(B R Millman) *unruly stalls: racd alone stands' side: nvr travelling and sn wl bhd: t.o* **11/1**

61.28 secs (-0.12) **Going Correction** -0.075s/f (Good) — **13** Ran SP% **118.5**
Speed ratings (Par 97): **97,96,95,95,94 90,89,88,88,85 80,80,16**
toteswingers:1&2:£81.10, 1&3:£46.10, 2&3:£5.50 CSF £625.02 CT £4540.52 TOTE £61.00: £9.40, £2.30, £2.30; EX 941.60.
Owner Roger Ambrose,Sean Ambrose & Bill Reilly **Bred** Rathasker Stud **Trained** Pandy, Monmouths
■ Stewards' Enquiry : Sophie Doyle caution: used whip with excessive frequency

FOCUS
A fair, competitive nursery.

NOTEBOOK
Style And Panache(IRE) hadn't been in much form lately, but according to connections she got bogged down on soft ground at Chester last time, having previously not acted at Goodwood. Some of her earlier form was more than respectable (won a maiden and sixth in Windsor Castle), and she proved tremendously game this time, looking a typically tough Evans runner. Official explanation: trainer said, regarding the apparent improvement in form shown, filly was unsuited by the track at Chester last time and appeared better suited by the straight track and better ground (op 100-1)
Millyluvstobouggie reversed recent Polytrack placings with Sadafiya on 8lb better terms (for just 1/2l). Like the winner, she's a tough and honest filly. (op 9-1)
Sadafiya couldn't defy a 6lb rise for her Lingfield win, but she ran well, a particularly creditable effort considering the ground was probably easier than ideal, with her lacking size. (op 9-2)
Fifth Ave was only 1lb higher than when winning a Polytrack nursery in August and ran a good race. (op 25-1)
Phoebs, dropped in grade after three months off, took a while to pick up and was never doing enough. Perhaps this will sharpen her up, or maybe she wants 6f now.
Dress Up(IRE)'s jockey dropped his whip inside the final 2f, but the filly was in trouble at the time and did not return from her 73-day break in much form. (op 7-2)
Coconut Ice Official explanation: jockey said filly ran flat
Basilica Official explanation: jockey said colt was very restless in the stall and felt wrong in the race

6446 GBI BRITISH AND IRISH RACING WORLDWIDE H'CAP — 5f 34y
4:55 (4:55) (Class 3) (0-90,89) 3-Y-0+ — **£6,476** (£1,927; £963; £481) **Stalls** High

Form — RPR

0043 **1** **Doric Lady**[14] 6064 5-8-9 **77** .... KirstyMilczarek 5 — 89
(J A R Toller) *in rr early: hdwy 1/2-way: led over 1f out: drvn and hung lft ins fnl f: kpt on strly* **11/2**[2]

0300 **2** *1 1/4* **Whozthecat (IRE)**[3] 6364 3-9-5 **88** .... (v1) DavidNolan 4 — 95
(D Carroll) *pressed ldrs: drvn and ev ch over 1f out: hung lft ins fnl f and kpt on same pce* **16/1**

3030 **3** *1* **Russian Spirit**[99] 3261 4-9-1 **83** .... PhilipRobinson 7 — 86
(M A Jarvis) *pressed ldrs: slt ld 2f out tl hdd over 1f out: kpt on same pce ins fnl f* **7/1**

1166 **4** *hd* **Cape Royal**[14] 6064 10-8-12 **80** .... (bt) PatCosgrave 11 — 83
(J M Bradley) *led tl narrowly hdd 2f out: styd pressing ldrs tl one pce fnl f* **11/1**

5404 **5** *1* **Brandywell Boy (IRE)**[6] 6280 7-8-2 **75** oh3 .... BillyCray(5) 12 — 74
(D J S Ffrench Davis) *sn rdn along in rr: hdwy and hung lft over 1f out: kpt on fnl f but nvr any ch* **6/1**[3]

2400 **6** *nk* **Living It Large (FR)**[37] 5335 3-9-2 **85** .... (b1) NeilCallan 9 — 83
(R F Fisher) *chsd ldrs rdn over 2f out: wknd fnl f and no ch whn hmpd cl home* **14/1**

3000 **7** *2 1/2* **Osiris Way**[17] 5966 8-9-2 **84** .... GeorgeBaker 15 — 73
(P R Chamings) *chsd ldrs: pushed along and outpcd fr 1/2-way* **20/1**

0013 **8** *1 1/4* **Sohraab**[17] 5967 6-9-7 **89** .... JimCrowley 14 — 74
(H Morrison) *outpcd most of way* **9/2**[1]

1100 **9** *1 1/2* **Caledonia Princess**[17] 5966 4-8-9 **77** .... RyanMoore 3 — 56
(F J Brennan) *chsd ldrs tl wknd over 1f out* **7/1**

-010 **10** *4* **Present Alchemy**[80] 3891 4-9-5 **87** .... (t) JimmyFortune 8 — 52
(H Morrison) *s.i.s: rdn and hung lft 2f out: a struggling* **6/1**[3]

2000 **11** *3/4* **Matsunosuke**[17] 5966 8-9-5 **87** .... (p) LukeMorris 2 — 49
(R A Harris) *a outpcd* **18/1**

61.44 secs (0.04) **Going Correction** -0.075s/f (Good)
WFA 3 from 4yo+ 1lb — **11** Ran SP% **118.0**
Speed ratings (Par 107): **96,94,92,92,90 90,86,84,81,75 74**
toteswingers:1&2:£25.60, 1&3:£8.10, 2&3:£24.20 CSF £90.12 CT £628.62 TOTE £9.00: £3.10, £5.70, £1.50; EX 138.50.
Owner Buckingham Thoroughbreds I **Bred** Minster Enterprises Ltd **Trained** Newmarket, Suffolk

FOCUS
An ordinary sprint for the class and the leaders went off a bit too fast. The front pair, possibly racing on the best ground in the centre, both ran right up to their best.

NOTEBOOK
Doric Lady returned to form with a couple of solid efforts in defeat at Yarmouth recently and, with plenty in her favour this time (ease in the ground and strong pace), she stayed on well to record a sixth-career win. (op 6-1 tchd 5-1)
Whozthecat(IRE), well beaten three days earlier, responded to a first-time visor, running a good race despite sweating up. (op 14-1)
Russian Spirit, returning from 99 days off, was always up with the quick gallop and stuck on well. A good effort, and she's entitled to come on for the run. (op 11-2)
Cape Royal went off fast enough and didn't see his race out. (op 12-1)
Brandywell Boy(IRE), 3lb out of the handicap, was outpaced for most of the way before plugging on. (op 10-1 tchd 12-1)
Sohraab received reminders soon after leaving the stalls and was never going. He can be quite moody these days and, as such, is certainly not one for maximum faith. (op 4-1 tchd 5-1)

6447 HEATON-ELLIS TRUST H'CAP — 1m 2f 6y
5:30 (5:30) (Class 3) (0-90,89) 3-Y-0+ — **£6,476** (£1,927; £963; £481) **Stalls** Low

Form — RPR

-1 **1** **Conduct (IRE)**[17] 5971 3-9-0 **85** .... RyanMoore 13 — 100+
(Sir Michael Stoute) *hld up in rr: stdy hdwy over 2f out chal 1f out: sn pushed along to ld: green and hd to one side but styd on strly fnl 120yds: comf* **7/4**[1]

5302 **2** *2 3/4* **Fanditha (IRE)**[16] 5994 4-9-4 **83** .... (p) KierenFallon 12 — 92
(L M Cumani) *chsd ldrs: drvn to take narrow ld 2f out: rdn and jnd 1f out: sn hd: no ch w wnr but kpt on wl for 2nd* **9/1**

0-00 **3** *1/2* **The Only Key**[10] 6193 4-9-2 **81** .... LukeMorris 3 — 89
(S W James) *led 3f: styd chsng ldrs: rdn and one pce over 2f out: kpt on again u.p fnl f* **40/1**

1120 **4** *nk* **Resentful Angel**[13] 6095 5-9-1 **87** .... JamesRogers(7) 4 — 94
(Pat Eddery) *in rr: stdy hdwy on outside fr 2f out: styd on strly ins fnl f: gng on cl home* **25/1**

1045 **5** *1* **Clockmaker (IRE)**[10] 6204 4-9-10 **89** .... WilliamBuick 7 — 94
(J H M Gosden) *s.i.s: hld up in rr tl rdn and hdwy fr 2f out: nvr quite rchd ldrs and fnd no ex fnl f* **7/1**[2]

0342 **6** *1* **Majuro (IRE)**[23] 5786 6-9-2 **81** .... GeorgeBaker 9 — 84
(C F Wall) *t.k.h: led 7f out: narrowly hdd 3f out but styd upsides tl rdn 2f out: wknd u.p 1f out* **12/1**

5124 **7** *1/2* **Wiggy Smith**[13] 6091 11-8-13 **78** .... DaneO'Neill 1 — 80
(H Candy) *mid-div: rdn and one pce over 2f out: kpt on ins fnl f but nvr a threat* **25/1**

6032 **8** *shd* **Laudatory**[38] 5311 4-9-1 **80** .... (p) AdamKirby 2 — 82
(W R Swinburn) *in tch: rdn to chse ldrs and hung lft over 2f out: kpt on fnl f but nvr gng pce to get into contention* **16/1**

1015 **9** *2 1/2* **Autumn Riches**[13] 6096 3-9-2 **87** .... JoeFanning 10 — 84
(M Johnston) *chsd ldrs: rdn over 2f out: wknd over 1f out* **22/1**

2040 **10** *nk* **Ellemujie**[18] 5913 5-8-13 **83** .... (p) JamesO'Reilly(5) 8 — 80
(D K Ivory) *in rr: hdwy 3f out: sn rdn: styng on same pce and no ch whn hmpd ins fnl f* **28/1**

1204 **11** *nk* **Geneva Geyser (GER)**[13] 6096 4-9-7 **86** .... MickyFenton 17 — 82
(J M P Eustace) *s.i.s: sn chsng ldrs: slt ld 3f out to 2f out: sn btn* **50/1**

410 **12** *3* **Baylini**[59] 4579 6-8-9 **77** .... SophieDoyle(3) 14 — 67
(J A Osborne) *in tch: rdn 3f out: wknd over 2f out* **28/1**

2022 **13** *8* **Valiant Knight (FR)**[18] 5918 3-8-9 **80** .... (p) RichardHughes 15 — 54
(R Hannon) *in rr: hrd rdn: hung lft and little rspnse 3f out* **8/1**[3]

-110 **14** 2 1/4 **Cosimo de Medici**[20] 5868 3-8-9 80 (t) JimCrowley 5 50
(H Morrison) *a towards rr* **33/1**
3024 **15** 2 1/4 **Blues Music (IRE)**[29] 5592 3-8-9 80 (p) MichaelHills 16 45
(B W Hills) *stdd s: a in rr* **28/1**
1211 **16** 60 **Grams And Ounces**[28] 5624 3-8-5 76 KirstyMilczarek 6 —
(Miss Amy Weaver) *chsd ldrs tl wknd qckly fr 3f out: eased whn no ch fnl 2f* **9/1**
2m 6.13s (-2.67) **Going Correction** -0.075s/f (Good)
WFA 3 from 4yo+ 6lb **16** Ran SP% **123.3**
Speed ratings (Par 107): **107,104,104,104,103 102,102,102,100,99 99,97,90,89,87 39**
toteswingers:1&2:£4.00, 1&3:£21.50, 2&3:£28.60 CSF £15.07 CT £495.03 TOTE £2.70: £1.50, £2.70, £6.40, £4.00; EX 18.00.
Owner Highclere Thoroughbred Racing Royal Pal **Bred** The Lavington Stud **Trained** Newmarket, Suffolk
FOCUS
A good handicap. The form looks sound though the placed horses and the winner has plenty of potential.
NOTEBOOK
Conduct(IRE) ◆ followed up his debut success over 1m1f at Sandown with an improved performance on this handicap debut. Held up, he made good headway early in the straight, and although taking a little while to really get going once off the bridle, looking a galloper rather a quickener, he ultimately stayed on strongly. He carried his head to the right in the closing stages, but it didn't stop him and he was much the best. His dam was successful over 2m, so there will surely be better to come as he strengths up and goes over further, and he rates an exciting middle-distance/staying prospect. He could be aimed at the November Handicap, a logical target, and in the longer term he's a possible for the Dubai Carnival. (op 15-8 tchd 13-8)
Fanditha(IRE), 4lb higher than when runner-up at Goodwood last time, was always well placed and ran a good race behind the classy winner, but she seemed to finish with little left, stopping quite quickly when eased in the final strides. (op 10-1 tchd 11-1)
The Only Key, beaten only 8l by Forte Dei Marmi over C&D on her previous start, ran a strange race, looking set to drop away from her prominent position when under pressure in the straight, before running on again when the race was over. She would appear to want further. (op 50-1)
Resentful Angel ran on in a manner that suggests she needs at least 1m4f (runner-up over that trip only previous try).
Clockmaker(IRE), carrying top weight, simply didn't stay as strongly as some of these on this step up in trip.
Geneva Geyser(GER) Official explanation: vet said gelding lost a near fore shoe
Grams And Ounces Official explanation: jockey said gelding ran flat, having had a hard season

6448 EXECUTION CHARITABLE TRUST H'CAP 2m
6:00 (6:02) (Class 4) (0-85,83) 3-Y-O **£3,561** (£1,059; £529; £264) **Stalls** Low

Form RPR
0421 **1** **Regal Park (IRE)**[16] 5996 3-9-7 83 RichardHughes 3 90+
(J Noseda) *hld up in rr: swtchd rt to outside and rdn 3f out: str run over 1f out to take slt ld ins fnl f and hung lft: narrowly hdd fnl 100yds led again u.p last strides* **11/8**[1]
3653 **2** nse **Boston Blue**[16] 5996 3-9-4 80 (v) JimCrowley 5 87
(W J Knight) *t.k.h: trckd ldr tl led over 2f out: rdn and jnd 1f out: hdd sn after: rallied u.p to ld again fnl 100yds: ct last strides* **9/2**[2]
1415 **3** 1 3/4 **Sula Two**[11] 6166 3-8-7 69 RichardKingscote 1 76+
(R J Hodges) *trckd ldrs tl n.m.r and shuffled bk 3f out: hdwy over 1f out and styng on whn hmpd and swtchd rt jst ins fnl f: fin strly to take 3rd last strides but nt rcvr* **16/1**
0260 **4** 1/2 **Hayzoom**[24] 5747 3-9-4 80 JimmyFortune 4 86+
(P W Chapple-Hyam) *chsd ldrs: rdn and edgd lft fr over 2f out: styng on same pce whn hmpd jst insde fnl f: lost 3rd last strides* **9/1**
6234 **5** 2 **Rawnaq (IRE)**[17] 5940 3-9-0 76 RichardHills 7 78
(M Johnston) *led tl hdd over 2f out: wknd over 1f out* **5/1**[3]
5212 **6** 4 **The Starboard Bow**[24] 5752 3-9-2 78 LiamKeniry 8 75
(S Kirk) *in rr: rdn and sme prog on outside fr 3f out: nvr on terms and wknd 2f out* **12/1**
321 **7** 3 1/2 **Baltimore Clipper (USA)**[67] 4341 3-9-6 82 NeilCallan 6 75
(P F I Cole) *in rr tl hdwy 5f out: chsd ldrs 3f out but nvr on terms: wknd sn after* **16/1**
4210 **8** 5 **Sidney Melbourne (USA)**[24] 5747 3-9-2 78 KierenFallon 2 65
(J R Best) *chsd ldrs: rdn 3f out: sn wknd* **12/1**
3m 34.71s (2.71) **Going Correction** -0.075s/f (Good) **8** Ran SP% **114.1**
Speed ratings (Par 103): **90,89,89,88,87 85,84,81**
toteswingers:1&2:£2.10, 1&3:£6.80, 2&3:£10.70. totesuper7: Win: Not won. Place: £69.70. CSF £7.55 CT £66.08 TOTE £2.10: £1.10, £1.30, £4.50 Place 6 £744.30; Place 5 £234.88.
Owner Ms Frances Noseda **Bred** Lodge Park Stud **Trained** Newmarket, Suffolk
■ Stewards' Enquiry : Richard Hughes one-day ban: careless riding (Oct 12)
FOCUS
A fair staying handicap. The form can be rated around the runner-up, with the third snd fourth also close to form.
T/Jkpt: Not won. T/Plt: £715.20 to a £1 stake. Pool:£76,277.55 - 77.85 winning tickets T/Qpdt: £104.60 to a £1 stake. Pool:£5,728.98 - 40.50 winning tickets ST

6425 KEMPTON (A.W) (R-H)
Wednesday, September 29

OFFICIAL GOING: Standard
Wind: Light, half behind Weather: Raining heavily

6449 BOOK KEMPTON TICKETS ON 0844 579 3008 H'CAP 1m 2f (P)
5:50 (5:50) (Class 4) (0-85,85) 3-Y-O+ **£3,885** (£1,156; £577; £288) **Stalls** High

Form RPR
-152 **1** **Julienas (IRE)**[19] 5917 3-9-3 84 AdamKirby 6 99
(W R Swinburn) *mde all: stdd pce after 4f: kicked on again 3f out: hung lft and rdn fr 2f out: ended up against nr side rail but wl clr fnl f* **9/2**[2]
2100 **2** 4 1/2 **Flying Destination**[19] 5918 3-8-11 83 JohnFahy(5) 4 89
(W J Knight) *towards rr: rdn 2f out: gd prog to take 2nd last 150yds: styd on but no ch* **16/1**
4605 **3** 2 1/4 **Desert Vision**[26] 5723 6-9-10 85 (vt) JimmyQuinn 10 86+
(M W Easterby) *chsd ldrs in midfield: rdn over 2f out: styd on fnl f towards inner: tk 3rd last strides* **20/1**
1150 **4** hd **Chalice Welcome**[116] 2739 7-9-5 83 RussKennemore(3) 5 84
(N B King) *s.s: wl in rr and racd wd: prog into midfield 3f out: sn rdn: styd on to go 2nd briefly 1f out: one pce after* **66/1**
0435 **5** 3/4 **The Which Doctor**[19] 5913 5-9-9 84 RyanMoore 7 84
(J Noseda) *s.s and drvn early: wl in rr: 11th and struggling over 2f out: styd on fnl f* **9/2**[2]
0511 **6** nk **Classically (IRE)**[18] 5958 4-9-1 76 SteveDrowne 11 75
(H Morrison) *chsd ldrs: rdn to go 3rd 3f out: carried wd bnd 2f out: sn lost pl: one pce after* **9/2**[2]
0004 **7** nk **Burma Rock (IRE)**[9] 6252 4-9-1 76 KierenFallon 12 74
(L M Cumani) *settled midfield: rdn 3f out: prog to go 2nd over 1f out: no ch w wnr: fdd fnl f: eased nr fin* **11/4**[1]
1-63 **8** hd **Mustakmil (IRE)**[44] 5142 4-9-6 81 DarryllHolland 1 79
(S Dow) *hld up in midfield: prog on outer 4f out to press for 2nd 3f out: hanging and lost pl bnd 2f out: drvn and kpt on fnl f* **9/1**[3]
0-00 **9** 3/4 **Summer Winds**[39] 5311 5-9-3 78 (p) TomQueally 13 74
(R A Mills) *chsd wnr 6f out to over 1f out: grad fdd* **25/1**
0040 **10** 5 **Dinner Date**[21] 5866 8-8-7 73 SimonPearce(5) 9 59
(T Keddy) *hld up in last pair: rdn on outer 3f out: no prog* **33/1**
540 **11** 4 1/2 **Uncle Fred**[55] 4758 5-9-6 81 GeorgeBaker 2 58
(P R Chamings) *stdd s: hld up last: shkn up and no prog over 1f out: nvr nr ldrs* **25/1**
-004 **12** 1/2 **Mirabella (IRE)**[17] 5988 3-8-8 82 CharlesEddery(7) 14 58
(R Hannon) *chsd wnr 4f: rdn and wknd fr 3f out* **40/1**
2m 5.74s (-2.26) **Going Correction** -0.025s/f (Stan)
WFA 3 from 4yo+ 6lb **12** Ran SP% **116.4**
Speed ratings (Par 105): **108,104,102,102,101 101,101,101,100,96 93,92**
toteswingers:1&2:£18.00, 1&3:£15.40, 2&3:£39.00 CSF £64.30 CT £1306.86 TOTE £6.50: £2.20, £4.80, £5.00; EX 93.30.
Owner P W Harris **Bred** Pendley Farm **Trained** Aldbury, Herts
■ Stewards' Enquiry : Darryll Holland one-day ban: carless riding (Oct 13)
FOCUS
A competitive handicap on paper, run at a modest pace to halfway. The form is rated around the runner-up and fourth.
Burma Rock(IRE) Official explanation: jockey said gelding had no more to give

6450 KIA VENGA CLAIMING STKS 1m 4f (P)
6:20 (6:23) (Class 6) 3-Y-O+ **£1,637** (£483; £241) **Stalls** Centre

Form RPR
2311 **1** **Lang Shining (IRE)**[15] 6054 6-9-8 81 SophieDoyle(3) 11 86
(J A Osborne) *hld up in midfield: prog 4f out: c to chal and disp ld 2f out: nk ld fnl f: jst hld on* **9/2**[2]
4002 **2** shd **Dance The Star (USA)**[11] 6202 5-9-11 87 RyanMoore 10 86
(E A L Dunlop) *hld up in rr: prog 4f out: chal and disp ld 2f out: nt qckn and nk down fnl f: rallied last strides* **13/8**[1]
4200 **3** 9 **Dream Of Fortune (IRE)**[12] 6165 6-9-2 64 (bt) KierenFallon 12 62
(P D Evans) *t.k.h: prom: chsd ldng pair 5f out: c to chal and upsides jst over 2f out: sn wl outpcd* **14/1**
4453 **4** 5 **Stadium Of Light (IRE)**[43] 5180 3-8-12 63 (t) TravisBlock 1 58
(H Morrison) *pressed ldr: led over 3f out to over 2f out: sn wknd* **9/1**
3000 **5** 1 1/2 **Lucky Punt**[15] 6054 4-9-11 88 FergusSweeney 5 61
(B G Powell) *led to over 3f out: led again briefly over 2f out: sn wknd* **16/1**
-065 **6** 1/2 **Primera Rossa**[252] 237 4-8-10 40 (p) JimmyQuinn 9 45
(J S Moore) *wl in rr: lost tch over 3f out: no ch after* **66/1**
6 **7** 9 **Thistle Stikk**[91] 3563 3-8-13 0 SteveDrowne 3 42
(R Charlton) *stdd s: sn trckd ldrs: lost pl and pushed along over 4f out: lft bhd over 3f out* **7/1**
0 **8** 3 **Najca De Thaix (FR)**[30] 5610 9-8-13 0 AdamKirby 7 29
(J L Spearing) *dwlt: reminders in last pair after 1f: nvr a factor* **100/1**
534 **9** 9 **Acropolis (IRE)**[236] 420 9-8-10 52 GeorgeDowning(7) 8 19
(A W Carroll) *plld hrd: hld up: lft bhd fr over 3f out: t.o* **33/1**
1-2P **10** 6 **Kaleo**[48] 4996 6-9-3 79 DarryllHolland 6 9
(S Dow) *t.k.h: trckd ldng pair to 5f out: sed hanging sn after: wknd over 3f out: eased over 1f out: t.o* **5/1**[3]
0 **11** hd **Nobbys Girl**[22] 5840 5-8-8 0 AmyScott(5) 2 5
(M S Tuck) *allowed to s slowly: wl adrift tl rapid prog on wd outside to go 4th 7f out: lost pl as rapidly 6f out: t.o 4f out* **100/1**
2m 31.74s (-2.76) **Going Correction** -0.025s/f (Stan)
WFA 3 from 4yo+ 8lb **11** Ran SP% **114.4**
Speed ratings (Par 101): **108,107,101,98,97 97,91,89,83,79 79**
toteswingers:1&2:£2.50, 1&3:£11.60, 2&3:£5.00 CSF £11.71 TOTE £5.00: £1.10, £2.00, £2.10; EX 11.60.Dance The Star was claimed by Alan Swinbank for £15,000.
Owner A Taylor **Bred** Ballymacoll Stud Farm Ltd **Trained** Upper Lambourn, Berks
FOCUS
A claimer with little strength in depth. The form is rated around the third and sixth.
Kaleo Official explanation: jockey said gelding ran too freely

6451 DIGIBET MAIDEN FILLIES' STKS 7f (P)
6:50 (6:55) (Class 5) 2-Y-O **£2,286** (£675; £337) **Stalls** High

Form RPR
1 **Tuscania** 2-9-0 0 RyanMoore 14 81+
(Sir Michael Stoute) *trckd ldng pair: swift move to ld on inner wl over 1f out: sn clr: in n.d after* **3/1**[2]
2 2 3/4 **Celani** 2-8-9 0 SimonPearce(5) 13 74
(Andrew Turnell) *dwlt: sn prom: effrt over 2f out: chsd wnr over 1f out: styd on but no ch* **66/1**
3 1 3/4 **Loving Thought** 2-9-0 0 (t) TomQueally 12 69
(H R A Cecil) *in tch towards rr: prog over 2f out: disp 2nd over 1f out: one pce after* **6/1**
4 nk **Charleston Lady** 2-9-0 0 FergusSweeney 5 69+
(R M Beckett) *dwlt: rn green in last pair: pushed along 1/2-way: styd on in taking style on outer fr over 1f out: nrly snatched 3rd* **9/1**
5 2 1/2 **Viking Rose (IRE)** 2-9-0 0 DarryllHolland 8 62
(J M P Eustace) *rn green in last and wl off the pce: effrt on inner over 2f out: rdn and kpt on fr over 1f out* **33/1**
2 **6** 3/4 **Cross Examination (USA)**[9] 6247 2-9-0 0 KierenFallon 2 60
(Mahmood Al Zarooni) *led: hung bdly lft fr 2f out: sn hdd: gave up tamely* **5/2**[1]
7 shd **Hurricane Lady (IRE)** 2-8-9 0 JohnFahy(5) 11 60+
(W R Swinburn) *wl in rr and rn green: struggling fr 1/2-way: styd on quite encouragingly fnl f* **25/1**
8 nk **I Hate To Lose (USA)** 2-9-0 0 GeorgeBaker 4 59
(P J McBride) *prom: trckd ldr over 2f out and gng strly: carried lft after and edgd lft of own volition: wknd* **9/2**[3]
02 **9** nk **Endaxi Mana Mou**[13] 6118 2-9-0 0 JimmyQuinn 9 58
(M G Quinlan) *in tch in midfield: rdn over 2f out: sn outpcd and btn* **14/1**
10 3 **The Absent Mare** 2-9-0 0 LeeVickers 6 51
(F Sheridan) *dwlt: rn green and wl in rr: brief effrt over 2f out: sn btn* **66/1**
11 1/2 **Blowing Bubbles (USA)** 2-9-0 0 SteveDrowne 3 49
(B J Meehan) *dwlt: rcvrd and sn chsd ldr: wknd over 2f out* **28/1**
0 **12** 24 **Street Cred (IRE)**[15] 6053 2-9-0 0 AdamKirby 10 —
(P Burgoyne) *chsd ldrs: wknd rapidly over 2f out: t.o* **66/1**
1m 26.75s (0.75) **Going Correction** -0.025s/f (Stan) **12** Ran SP% **117.4**
Speed ratings (Par 92): **94,90,88,88,85 84,84,84,84,80 80,52**
toteswingers:1&2:£16.00, 1&3:£5.00, 2&3:£19.50 CSF £208.51 TOTE £4.50: £1.40, £23.60, £2.60; EX 156.70.

Owner K Abdulla **Bred** Juddmonte Farms Ltd **Trained** Newmarket, Suffolk

FOCUS

An interesting maiden with little public form to go on.

NOTEBOOK

Tuscania ◆, a half-sister to Confront, who won over this distance at two and was probably best around a mile and won off 116, has no late-closing entries, but clearly has a future. (tchd 11-4)

Celani is very interesting, being a daughter of the lightly raced 2002 Derby fourth Jelani out of a mare that won at two. Her predomiantely jumping yard knows what to do with a decent Flat horse and she showed a good attitude when asked to quicken after feeling the pace turning for home. (op 100-1)

Loving Thought will have learned plenty from this and won't be a maiden for long if she keeps going this year. (op 11-2 tchd 7-1)

Charleston Lady ◆ was the real eyecatcher, only picking up once the race had been put to bed by the winner. She wasn't passing beaten horses and has plenty of stamina in her page. Very interesting over a mile-plus next time. (op 10-1 tchd 11-1)

Viking Rose(IRE) is another than comes from a good family and by a sire that is doing well. Her half-brother, Rapscallion, was decent over this trip at two, winning four times, including the Horris Hill on heavy ground. She needed this experience, but kept on well enough and will know more next time. (op 25-1)

Cross Examination(USA), who had the benefit of a solid second-place on debut here nine days ago, had to use pace to get on the pace from a poor draw, but that was no excuse and her chance had gone before she hung badly left. She's better than this and the run may have simply come too soon. Official explanation: jockey said filly hung badly left (op 13-8)

Hurricane Lady(IRE) ◆ was another to catch the eye, running on from an unpromising position. She learned plenty here. (op 33-1)

I Hate To Lose(USA) was beaten before hanging up the home straight and will be better next season. (op 8-1 tchd 9-1)

Endaxi Mana Mou is now qualified for nurseries and is one to look out for next time in that category. (tchd 16-1)

Street Cred(IRE) Official explanation: jockey said filly stopped quickly

6452 DIGIBET.COM CLASSIFIED CLAIMING STKS — 1m (P)

7:20 (7:24) (Class 6) 3-4-Y-0 — **£1,637** (£483; £241) **Stalls** High

Form — RPR

5235 **1** **Blue Noodles**52 4857 4-8-5 65 AndrewHeffernan(3) 10 — 56
(Jim Best) *chsd clr ldr and clr of rest: clsd to ld over 2f out: drvn at least 2 l clr over 1f out: hld on* **7/2**1

0100 **2** ¾ **Hip Hip Hooray**28 5664 4-9-10 61 FergusSweeney 5 — 70
(L A Dace) *hld up in rr: prog over 2f out: drvn to chse wnr jst ins fnl f: styd on* **20/1**

4136 **3** ½ **Frank Street**54 4793 4-9-0 56 (t) TomQueally 9 — 59
(Eve Johnson Houghton) *chsd clr ldng pair: drvn and hanging over 2f out: clsd to take 2nd briefly 1f out: kpt on* **15/2**

0-55 **4** 1 **George Baker (IRE)**12 6168 3-8-7 61 MatthewDavies(3) 2 — 57+
(George Baker) *hld up in last pair fr wd draw: pushed along over 3f out: stl in last pair over 1f out: r.o fnl f: gaining at fin* **14/1**

6000 **5** ¾ **Tarita (IRE)**47 5027 3-8-9 65 ow1 SteveDrowne 12 — 54
(R Hannon) *mostly chsd ldng trio: rdn and no imp over 2f out: kpt on: nvr able to chal* **16/1**

456 **6** 1 ¾ **Bell's Ocean (USA)**33 5494 3-9-4 60 AdamKirby 13 — 59
(J Ryan) *pushed along in rr early: rdn and prog fr 2f out: rchd 6th ins fnl f: n.d* **33/1**

0502 **7** 1 ½ **King's Sabre**7 6296 4-8-13 60 (e) MarkCoumbe(5) 8 — 51+
(R C Guest) *hld up in last pair: gng strly but stl in last pair and looking for room over 2f out: swtchd rt and effrt over 1f out: one pce* **10/1**

3403 **8** 2 **Rain On The Wind (IRE)**14 6093 3-9-4 63 (t) WilliamCarson 11 — 51
(S C Williams) *v fast away: led and clr: hdd over 2f out: wknd over 1f out* **15/2**

5235 **9** 1 ½ **Atacama Sunrise**84 3787 4-8-9 65 CharlotteKerton(7) 14 — 41
(G Prodromou) *plld hrd in midfield: bmpd along and no prog 2f out: fdd* **16/1**

605 **10** 1 ¼ **Equine Science**22 5842 3-8-10 58 JimmyQuinn 7 — 36
(G D Blake) *racd wd in midfield: rdn and no prog over 2f out* **50/1**

2030 **11** 1 ½ **Markhesa**12 6165 4-8-7 58 (b1) NathanAlison(7) 6 — 33
(J R Boyle) *hld up in rr on inner: rdn and no prog over 2f out* **20/1**

0005 **12** ¾ **Wunder Strike (USA)**60 4586 4-8-9 65 (p) PatCosgrave 4 — 26
(J R Boyle) *racd wd and nvr bttr than midfield: struggling over 2f out* **4/1**2

506 **13** 16 **Inner Angel**37 5366 3-8-7 65 JohnFahy(5) 3 — —
(R A Teal) *chsd ldrs to 3f out: wknd rapidly: t.o* **7/1**3

1m 39.37s (-0.43) **Going Correction** -0.025s/f (Stan)
WFA 3 from 4yo 4lb — **13** Ran SP% **120.2**
Speed ratings (Par 101): **101,100,99,98,98 96,94,92,91,90 88,87,71**
toteswingers:1&2:£10.00, 1&3:£4.40, 2&3:£31.40 CSF £80.51 TOTE £5.70: £3.10, £8.90, £4.40; EX 106.30.Blue Noodles was claimed by I. W. McInnes for £3,000.
Owner Diamond Racing Ltd **Bred** P And Mrs A G Venner **Trained** Lewes, E Sussex

FOCUS

Some exposed horses in an unremarkable claimer which is best rated around the placed horses.

Bell's Ocean(USA) Official explanation: jockey said filly was slowly away

6453 DIGIBET CASINO NURSERY — 1m (P)

7:50 (7:51) (Class 4) (0-85,78) 2-Y-0 — **£3,238** (£963; £481; £240) **Stalls** High

Form — RPR

0213 **1** **Daas Rite (IRE)**11 6174 2-8-11 **75** JulieBurke(7) 2 — 79
(K A Ryan) *trckd ldng pair to over 2f out: styd cl up: rdn and kpt on fnl f to ld last strides* **8/1**3

6121 **2** nse **Handsome Jack (IRE)**15 6059 2-9-7 **78** TomQueally 6 — 82
(R A Mills) *hld up in 4th: trckd ldng pair over 2f out: drvn between rivals to ld 1f out but making hrd work of it: hdd last strides* **8/11**1

3541 **3** 1 ½ **Hawk Moth (IRE)**12 6162 2-8-10 **67** CathyGannon 1 — 68
(J L Spearing) *hld up in 5th: urged along to cl on ldrs fr 2f out: fnd little but kpt on to take 3rd post* **13/2**2

5253 **4** nse **Tokum (IRE)**41 5234 2-8-10 **67** RyanMoore 4 — 67
(J Noseda) *mde most: hdd 1f out: hld whn short of room nr fin: lost 3rd post* **13/2**2

0066 **5** 4 **Memory Lane**6 6302 2-9-1 **72** DarryllHolland 3 — 63
(Sir Mark Prescott) *mostly last: pushed along and struggling over 2f out: n.d after* **10/1**

143 **6** 1 ¼ **Fifth Dimension (IRE)**15 6059 2-9-1 **72** FergusSweeney 7 — 60
(J A Osborne) *pressed ldr: stl upsides 2f out: wknd qckly jst over 1f out* **16/1**

1m 40.57s (0.77) **Going Correction** -0.025s/f (Stan) — **6** Ran SP% **110.7**
Speed ratings (Par 97): **95,94,93,93,89 88**
toteswingers:1&2:£2.40, 1&3:£3.20, 2&3:£1.40 CSF £14.03 TOTE £6.50: £1.90, £1.20; EX 13.20.
Owner Miss Deirdre McGuire & Mrs J Ryan **Bred** Mark & Pippa Hackett **Trained** Hambleton, N Yorks
■ Stewards' Enquiry : Julie Burke one-day ban: careless riding (Oct 13)

FOCUS

A tricky nursery on paper and so it turned out.

NOTEBOOK

Daas Rite(IRE) prevailed by the narrowest margin. He was rated 70 when winning a 7f claimer here 20 days ago and was a close third off 75 in a decent Ayr nursery 9 days later and clearly needed every yard of the 1m to get home off a 1lb higher mark. Although hanging right close home, his inexperienced rider looked very competent.

Handsome Jack(IRE) confirmed form with third-home Fifth Dimension. However, he stays this trip really well and had he got rolling when his rider wanted, he may have gone beyond the winner's recall. (op 8-13)

Hawk Moth(IRE) was 4lb higher than when winning a 7f nursery at Wolverhampton 12 days ago and got third courtesy of Tokum being squeezed out close home. He stays this trip well enough, though. (op 6-1)

Tokum(IRE) was held when tightened up and it may be that a drop back to 7f helps if he is going to race on the pace. (op 8-1 tchd 9-1)

Memory Lane was never travelling with any fluency and might need a stiffer test, possibly next year. (op 12-1 tchd 14-1)

Fifth Dimension(IRE) may not have been suited by being on the pace and may need to be ridden with more restraint. (op 14-1)

6454 PANORAMIC CLASSIFIED STKS — 1m 3f (P)

8:20 (8:27) (Class 6) 3-Y-0+ — **£1,637** (£483; £241) **Stalls** High

Form — RPR

0064 **1** **Burnbrake**30 4591 5-9-4 51 (b1) JamesMillman(3) 4 — 58
(L Montague Hall) *hld up in last trio: pushed along and prog on outer fr 2f out: sustained effrt fnl f: r.o to ld last strides* **20/1**

4625 **2** ½ **Champagne Fizz (IRE)**43 5180 4-9-7 53 FergusSweeney 8 — 57
(Miss Jo Crowley) *hld up in rr: pushed along and prog over 2f out: clsd on ldrs over 1f out: led ins fnl f: styd on: hdd last strides* **5/2**1

3 1 ¾ **Storms Over (USA)**44 5167 3-8-11 50 RobertLButler(3) 2 — 54
(B W Duke) *prom: trckd ldr over 3f out: rdn to cl and led briefly 1f out: outpcd after* **66/1**

4000 **4** hd **Pictures (IRE)**7 6287 3-8-11 55 KierenFox(3) 7 — 53
(J J Bridger) *trckd ldrs: rdn and effrt over 2f out: pressed ldrs and ch 1f out: nt qckn* **10/1**

006 **5** 2 ½ **Alnaseem (USA)**19 5925 3-9-0 52 JimmyQuinn 1 — 49
(M W Easterby) *led: kicked on over 3f out: hdd and fdd 1f out* **15/2**3

-006 **6** 1 ¼ **Retrato (USA)**96 3414 3-9-0 48 (t) SebSanders 12 — 47
(Rae Guest) *trckd ldrs: rdn and effrt over 2f out: nt qckn in 5th over 1f out: fdd* **25/1**

0 **7** nk **Feuergott (GER)**19 5925 4-9-2 45 JohnFahy(5) 9 — 46
(Ian Williams) *hld up wl in rr: rdn on inner 3f out: swtchd to outer 2f out: 11th jst over 1f out: styd on* **12/1**

-506 **8** 2 ¾ **Avon Castle**45 5113 3-8-11 53 AndrewHeffernan(3) 13 — 41
(R A Harris) *fractious preliminaries: nvr bttr than midfield: no imp on ldrs 2f out: fdd* **33/1**

0060 **9** ½ **Kargarann (IRE)**14 6080 3-9-0 49 MickyFenton 10 — 40
(Stef Higgins) *s.s: hld up last: effrt on outer over 3f out: nvr on terms w ldrs* **33/1**

0600 **10** 4 ½ **Look Officer (USA)**144 1919 4-9-7 55 (b) AdamKirby 11 — 32
(Miss M E Rowland) *dwlt: towards rr on inner: rdn and no prog 3f out: sn btn* **9/1**

045- **11** 1 ½ **Blazing Buck**164 5790 4-9-0 53 GeorgeDowning(7) 3 — 30
(A W Carroll) *s.s: rapid prog arnd the rest to go 2nd 8f out: steadily wknd over 3f out* **10/1**

506 **12** hd **Red Flash (IRE)**22 5839 3-9-0 55 (b1) ChrisCatlin 14 — 29
(P Leech) *t.k.h: trckd ldr 4f: styd prom tl wknd over 2f out* **20/1**

0-60 **13** 43 **Bonamassa**36 5380 3-9-0 52 NickyMackay 5 — —
(M J Attwater) *prom tl wknd rapidly 3f out: t.o* **66/1**

050 **14** 15 **Zawadi**18 5971 3-9-0 52 JimCrowley 6 — —
(R M Beckett) *racd v wd in midfield: dropped away qckly 3f out: eased: t.o* **9/2**2

2m 22.87s (0.97) **Going Correction** -0.025s/f (Stan)
WFA 3 from 4yo+ 7lb — **14** Ran SP% **116.6**
Speed ratings (Par 101): **95,94,93,93,91 90,90,88,87,84 83,83,52,41**
toteswingers:1&2:£8.10, 1&3:£115.20, 2&3:£24.10 CSF £64.22 TOTE £23.90: £4.50, £1.90, £12.40; EX 79.50.
Owner B H Page **Bred** M E Wates **Trained** Epsom, Surrey
■ Stewards' Enquiry : Nicky Mackay two-day ban: careless riding (Oct 13-14)

FOCUS

A modest handicap and limited form, rated around the second and fourth.

Look Officer(USA) Official explanation: jockey said filly hung right

Zawadi Official explanation: jockey said filly hung left throughout

6455 SPONSOR AT KEMPTON H'CAP (DIV I) — 6f (P)

8:50 (8:54) (Class 6) (0-60,60) 3-Y-0+ — **£1,364** (£403; £201) **Stalls** High

Form — RPR

0200 **1** **White Shift (IRE)**20 5875 4-9-2 **59** KierenFox(3) 8 — 67+
(P Howling) *hld up in last pair: gd prog on inner over 2f out: clsd on ldng pair and eased off rail 1f out: nudged along and r.o to ld nr fin: cleverly* **16/1**

211 **2** ½ **Kinigi (IRE)**20 5876 4-9-3 **60** (b) AndrewHeffernan(3) 10 — 66
(R A Harris) *trckd ldng pair: wnt 2nd on inner 2f out: led jst over 1f out: 1 l clr ins fnl f: collared nr fin* **7/2**1

021 **3** nk **Dancing Welcome**13 6119 4-9-3 **57** (b) LiamKeniry 3 — 62+
(J M Bradley) *towards rr: shkn up and no prog 2f out: gd hdwy fnl f: fin wl to take 3rd post* **7/1**3

4000 **4** shd **Greek Secret**7 6299 7-8-12 **57** (b) JamesO'Reilly(5) 9 — 62
(J O'Reilly) *plld hrd: prom: urged along and nt qckn 2f out: styd on again fnl f* **16/1**

0013 **5** shd **Charlie Delta**5 6329 7-8-13 **60** (b) JakePayne(7) 1 — 65
(R A Harris) *dropped in fr wd draw and hld up last: taken out wd and effrt 2f out: clsd on ldrs 1f out: bmpd along and styd on same pce* **8/1**

4400 **6** 1 **Durgan**29 5623 4-9-3 **57** (p) RobertHavlin 5 — 58
(Mrs L C Jewell) *led to jst over 1f out: one pce and lost pls fnl f* **33/1**

4165 **7** nk **Dualagi**26 5714 6-9-2 **56** GeorgeBaker 12 — 57
(M R Bosley) *hld up on inner: trying to cl on ldrs whn nt clr run 1f out: kpt on same pce after* **7/1**3

6500 **8** nse **Bold Diva**25 5766 5-9-2 **56** (v) AdamKirby 7 — 56
(A W Carroll) *hld up in midfield: rdn 2f out: clsd on ldrs over 1f out: nt qckn ins fnl f* **9/1**

0550 **9** 1 ¾ **Memphis Man**20 5889 7-9-1 **58** RichardEvans(3) 2 — 53
(P D Evans) *dwlt: t.k.h: hld up wl in rr: nvr involved* **20/1**

5000 **10** 1 ½ **Ginobili (IRE)**11 6208 4-9-2 **59** (e) RussKennemore(3) 11 — 49+
(Andrew Reid) *dwlt: plld hrd early in midfield: nt qckn 2f out: wkng whn n.m.r 1f out* **12/1**

3204 **11** *1* **Faithful Duchess (IRE)**[15] 6060 3-9-4 **60**........................ JimCrowley 6 47
(E A L Dunlop) *chsd ldr to 2f out: wknd* **5/1**[2]

5060 **12** *1* **Figaro Flyer (IRE)**[27] 5697 7-9-3 **57**.............................. J-PGuillambert 4 48+
(P Howling) *trckd ldrs: cl up on outer over 2f out: wkng whn squeezed out 1f out* **20/1**

1m 13.47s (0.37) **Going Correction** -0.025s/f (Stan)
WFA 3 from 4yo+ 2lb **12** Ran SP% **116.9**
Speed ratings (Par 101): **96,95,94,94,94 93,92,92,90,88 87,85**
toteswingers:1&2:£17.80, 1&3:£25.20, 2&3:£5.00 CSF £68.64 CT £446.57 TOTE £29.80: £9.80, £1.50, £1.20; EX 98.70.
Owner Martin Sellars & Joanne Webster **Bred** Grange Stud **Trained** Newmarket, Suffolk

FOCUS
A modest sprint rated through the runner-up to recent turf form.
Dualagi Official explanation: jockey said mare was denied a clear run
Ginobili(IRE) Official explanation: jockey said gelding hung right throughout

6456 SPONSOR AT KEMPTON H'CAP (DIV II) 6f (P)
9:20 (9:22) (Class 6) (0-60,60) 3-Y-0+ **£1,364** (£403; £201) **Stalls** High

Form RPR

3160 **1** **Mack's Sister**[28] 5670 3-9-4 **60**.......................... RobertHavlin 2 71+
(D K Ivory) *trckd ldng pair: rdn to ld on outer over 1f out: drvn out: hld on* **14/1**

20 **2** *nk* **The Happy Hammer (IRE)**[7] 6295 4-9-5 **59**................ WilliamCarson 5 69
(Eugene Stanford) *bmpd s: hld up in last trio: prog on outer fr 2f out: r.o to take 2nd last 100yds and cl on wnr: jst hld* **7/1**[2]

0430 **3** *3/4* **Mandhooma**[16] 6024 4-9-3 **57**............................. ChrisCatlin 9 65
(P W Hiatt) *hld up in 8th: rdn 2f out: prog over 1f out: styd on fnl f to take 3rd nr fin* **16/1**

0030 **4** *shd* **Resplendent Alpha**[20] 5897 6-9-3 **57**............................... IanMongan 4 65
(P Howling) *dwlt: hld up in last pair: rdn and prog fr 2f out: disp 2nd ins fnl f: one pce after* **12/1**

3423 **5** *1 1/2* **Downhill Skier (IRE)**[19] 5906 6-9-3 **57**........................... GeorgeBaker 1 60
(W M Brisbourne) *racd wd: trckd ldrs: hanging rt and nt qckn 2f out: styd on fnl f* **9/2**[1]

1300 **6** *1/2* **Maryolini**[1] 6440 5-9-4 **58**... JimmyQuinn 7 59
(T Keddy) *trckd ldrs: rdn and prog to chal wl over 1f out: wknd ins fnl f* **7/1**[2]

0002 **7** *3* **Avow (USA)**[20] 5898 3-9-4 **60**.......................................(b) NeilChalmers 11 52
(J J Bridger) *trckd ldrs on inner: chal and upsides 2f out: wknd fnl f* **8/1**

0540 **8** *1/2* **Espy**[7] 6295 5-9-2 **59**.. MartinLane[(3)] 8 49
(I W McInnes) *dwlt: hld up in 9th: shkn up and sme prog 2f out: no hdwy fnl f: nvr nr ldrs* **9/1**

1030 **9** *3/4* **West Leake (IRE)**[99] 3299 4-9-6 **60**............................. LiamKeniry 12 48
(P Burgoyne) *trckd ldrs in 7th: effrt on inner 2f out: cl enough over 1f out: wknd* **8/1**

0606 **10** *1/2* **Music Lover**[5] 6330 3-8-13 **58**............................(b) AndrewHeffernan[(3)] 6 44
(R A Harris) *wnt lft s w blindfold stl on: rcvrd to ld after 1f: hung lft 2f out: hdd & wknd over 1f out* **25/1**

5030 **11** *nk* **Spoof Master (IRE)**[132] 2257 6-8-11 **56**.................. SimonPearce[(5)] 10 41
(J Pearce) *led 1f: chsd ldr to 2f out: wknd jst over 1f out* **15/2**[3]

2050 **12** *1* **Trip Switch**[20] 5897 4-9-0 **57**.. KierenFox[(3)] 3 39
(G Prodromou) *restless stalls: dwlt: a last: nvr a factor* **16/1**

1m 12.23s (-0.87) **Going Correction** -0.025s/f (Stan)
WFA 3 from 4yo+ 2lb **12** Ran SP% **117.1**
Speed ratings (Par 101): **104,103,102,102,100 99,95,95,94,93 93,91**
toteswingers:1&2:£27.20, 1&3:£145.70, 2&3:£32.00 CSF £107.54 CT £1619.18 TOTE £17.30: £4.90, £2.00, £7.00; EX 156.80 Place 6 £131.00; Place 5 £22.70.
Owner Recycled Products Limited **Bred** Mrs L R Burrage **Trained** Radlett, Herts

FOCUS
The second division of a modest sprint but well run and rated positively for the time being.
Trip Switch Official explanation: trainer's rep said gelding reared in stalls and cut its mouth
T/Plt: £93.00 to a £1 stake. Pool:£55,779.19 - 437.61 winning tickets T/Qpdt: £31.70 to a £1 stake. Pool:£8,031.57 - 186.92 winning tickets JN

5998 NEWCASTLE (L-H)
Wednesday, September 29

OFFICIAL GOING: Soft (heavy in places) changing to heavy after race 1 (2:10)
Wind: Light, half against Weather: Dull, raining

6457 EUROPEAN BREEDERS' FUND MAIDEN STKS 1m 3y(S)
2:10 (2:11) (Class 4) 2-Y-0 **£4,274** (£1,271; £635; £317) **Stalls** Centre

Form RPR

4625 **1** **El Torbellino (IRE)**[18] 5947 2-8-12 71........................ SilvestreDeSousa 6 78+
(D O'Meara) *mde virtually all: pushed clr over 2f out: eased ins fnl f* **5/2**[2]

303 **2** *9* **Good Boy Jackson**[38] 5332 2-9-3 67.................................. TomEaves 9 63
(K A Ryan) *t.k.h: in tch: smooth hdwy to chse wnr over 2f out: rdn and hung lft over 1f out: sn no imp* **14/1**[3]

056 **3** *7* **Willow's Wish**[17] 6001 2-8-9 38..................................... PatrickDonaghy[(3)] 7 43
(G M Moore) *sn pushed along bhd ldng gp: drvn and outpcd fr over 3f out: rallied 2f out: sn no imp* **100/1**

4 *14* **Blue Ronnie (IRE)** 2-9-3 0.. PhillipMakin 1 17
(B M R Haslam) *in tch: drvn along 1/2-way: sn struggling* **40/1**

2 **5** *16* **Parlour Games**[13] 6128 2-9-3 0.. AhmedAjtebi 2 —
(Mahmood Al Zarooni) *cl up tl rdn and wknd over 2f out: t.o* **6/4**[1]

2 **6** *18* **Jalors (IRE)**[8] 6268 2-9-3 0.. JoeFanning 4 —
(M Johnston) *pressed wnr tl wknd over 2f out: t.o* **5/2**[2]

7 *4 1/2* **Copt Hill** 2-8-12 0.. MichaelO'Connell[(5)] 10 —
(Miss Tracy Waggott) *relutcant to enter stalls: dwlt: bhd: struggling after 3f: t.o* **50/1**

000 **8** *1 1/2* **Good Faith**[17] 6001 2-9-3 37.. DavidAllan 3 —
(G M Moore) *trckd ldrs: drvn and outpcd after 3f: sn struggling* **150/1**

1m 50.95s (7.55) **Going Correction** +0.875s/f (Soft) **8** Ran SP% **109.9**
Speed ratings (Par 97): **97,88,81,67,51 33,28,27**
toteswingers:1&2:£6.00, 1&3:£61.90, 2&3:£61.90 CSF £30.90 TOTE £2.00: £1.02, £4.10, £23.60; EX 45.50 TRIFECTA Not won..
Owner Crowther, Fell & Everitt **Bred** Tally-Ho Stud **Trained** Nawton, N Yorks

FOCUS
This had looked a match between Parlour Games and Jalors, but neither appeared to handle the ground. Not form to take too literally, despite being best time on card.

NOTEBOOK
El Torbellino(IRE) ran on strongly to win with any amount in hand. Rated 71, but previously unproven on the ground, she clearly relished it and may be able to improve again returned to handicaps. (op 7-2)
Good Boy Jackson, rated 67, was another unproven in the ground, but he travelled strongly for a long way and seemed to handle it. (tchd 12-1)
Willow's Wish stayed on best of the remainder and underlines the strength of the form, being rated just 38.
Blue Ronnie(IRE), whose dam handled testing ground, was beaten a very long way. (op 66-1)
Parlour Games looked a standout pick having split two promising types in soft ground on his debut at Yarmouth, but this was a different type of testing ground and he was in trouble by halfway, dropping away tamely. Official explanation: jockey said colt was unsuited by the heavy ground (op 5-4 tchd 6-5)
Jalors(IRE), runner-up at Beverley on debut, was beaten even earlier than his market rivals and deserves another chance on a sounder surface. (op 9-4 tchd 11-4)

6458 E.B.F./PARKLANDS GOLFCOURSE MAIDEN STKS 6f
2:40 (2:41) (Class 4) 2-Y-O **£4,274** (£1,271; £635; £317) **Stalls** Centre

Form RPR

1 **Stamp Duty (IRE)** 2-8-11 0.. BarryMcHugh[(3)] 1 70+
(Ollie Pears) *hld up: hdwy over 2f out: chsd ldr over 1f out: rdn to ld wl ins fnl f: r.o* **6/1**

0 **2** *1/2* **Oh So Kool**[22] 5836 2-9-0 0.. AndrewMullen 3 69
(S C Williams) *led: rdn over 1f out: hdd wl ins fnl f: kpt on* **20/1**

53 **3** *4 1/2* **Shadow Catcher**[13] 6102 2-9-0 0.................................. TomEaves 10 55
(M Dods) *trckd ldrs tl rdn and outpcd appr fnl f* **11/4**[1]

4 *1* **Motivado** 2-9-0 0.. StevieDonohoe 2 52
(Sir Mark Prescott) *s.i.s: bhd and pushed along: hdwy over 1f out: no imp fnl f* **7/1**

5 *6* **Youhavecontrol (IRE)** 2-9-0 0.. PhillipMakin 11 34
(M Dods) *in tch tl shkn up and wknd over 1f out* **3/1**[2]

0 **6** *2 3/4* **Vodka Red (IRE)**[17] 6001 2-8-9 0.................................... LeeTopliss[(5)] 8 26
(R Johnson) *dwlt: t.k.h and sn prom: rdn and wknd over 1f out* **40/1**

5 **7** *1 3/4* **Cheylesmore (IRE)**[95] 3439 2-9-0 0.................................. SaleemGolam 6 21
(S C Williams) *plld hrd: cl up: rdn over 2f out: wknd wl over 1f out* **12/1**

4 **8** *6* **Even Stevens**[15] 6045 2-9-0 0.. PaulMulrennan 9 3
(J A Glover) *cl up tl rdn and wknd over 1f out* **11/2**[3]

000 **9** *14* **Illawalla**[14] 6075 2-9-0 40.. PatrickMathers 4 —
(H A McWilliams) *towards rr: struggling over 2f out: t.o* **100/1**

0 **10** *2* **Cottam Donny**[56] 4702 2-9-0 0.. DavidAllan 7 —
(M Brittain) *bhd: pushed along 1/2-way: sn struggling: t.o* **22/1**

1m 22.79s (8.19) **Going Correction** +1.175s/f (Soft) **10** Ran SP% **114.1**
Speed ratings (Par 97): **92,91,85,84,76 72,70,62,43,40**
toteswingers:1&2:£18.90, 1&3:£5.30, 2&3:£14.50 CSF £117.25 TOTE £7.50: £1.60, £5.20, £1.80; EX 139.00 Trifecta £57.90 Part won. Pool: £78.25 - 0.10 winning units..
Owner J J Harrison **Bred** Windymains Farm Ltd **Trained** Norton, N Yorks

FOCUS
A moderate maiden. A pleasing start from the winner, though hard to know what form is worth.

NOTEBOOK
Stamp Duty(IRE) wore down long-time leader Oh So Cool in the final strides. His stable had a juvenile winner last week, so their youngsters are clearly in decent form, and he's shown he can handle testing conditions, but much will depend on how generous the handicapper is. (tchd 11-2 and 7-1 in a place)
Oh So Kool stepped up markedly on his debut effort, soon leading and drawing clear with the winner, but proving unable to hold on. (op 22-1 tchd 18-1)
Shadow Catcher was up there throughout, but couldn't race on with the front pair. He'll do better in handicaps. (op 3-1 tchd 10-3)
Motivado, a Derby entry bred to want further, is a fine, big sort who looked clueless early, but he did keep on nicely inside the final furlong and is sure to be of interest once upped in trip. (op 17-2)
Youhavecontrol(IRE), a half-brother to multiple winner Merchant In Dubai, who handles soft ground, looked in need of the experience and should improve. (tchd 11-4 and 10-3 in a place)
Even Stevens failed to build on a promising debut effort. (op 4-1)

6459 E.B.F./CHAMPIONS LEAGUE BETTING WITH FREEBETTING.CO.UK MAIDEN FILLIES' STKS 6f
3:15 (3:15) (Class 4) 2-Y-0 **£3,885** (£1,156; £577; £288) **Stalls** Centre

Form RPR

2230 **1** **Indian Giver**[16] 6034 2-9-0 60.. PatrickMathers 4 66
(H A McWilliams) *prom: rdn to ld over 1f out: edgd lft: sn clr* **13/2**

2 *5* **Yorketa** 2-8-11 0.. PatrickDonaghy[(3)] 2 51
(M Dods) *s.i.s: t.k.h: in tch: outpcd over 2f out: swtchd rt and rallied appr fnl f: chsd wnr wl ins fnl f: no imp* **14/1**

04 **3** *2 1/4* **Kaua'i Girl**[8] 6268 2-9-0 0... SilvestreDeSousa 1 44
(Mrs A Duffield) *led tl drvn and hdd over 1f out: sn outpcd: rallied ins fnl f: no imp* **13/8**[1]

0 **4** *1/2* **Rhal (IRE)**[45] 5117 2-9-0 0.. TomEaves 8 43
(B Smart) *cl up: effrt and ev ch over 1f out: sn chsng wnr: lost 2nd and no ex wl ins fnl f* **11/1**

0 **5** *2 1/4* **Pizzarra**[12] 6157 2-9-0 0.. PaulMulrennan 7 36
(J G Given) *t.k.h: cl up: ev ch over 1f out: sn rdn and btn* **11/4**[2]

0 **6** *1 1/4* **Cootehill Lass (IRE)**[68] 4338 2-8-9 0........................ MichaelO'Connell[(5)] 9 32
(G A Harker) *chsd ldng gp: pushed along over 3f out: outpcd over 1f out* **50/1**

7 *15* **Dan's Martha** 2-9-0 0.. PhillipMakin 5 —
(B M R Haslam) *missed break: bhd: hdwy 1/2-way: wknd over 1f out: t.o* **6/1**[3]

00 **8** *45* **Porthgwidden Beach (USA)**[44] 5147 2-9-0 0...........(t) SaleemGolam 6 —
(S C Williams) *t.k.h: hld up: rdn 1/2-way: sn struggling: t.o* **33/1**

1m 22.98s (8.38) **Going Correction** +1.175s/f (Soft) **8** Ran SP% **112.3**
Speed ratings (Par 94): **91,84,81,80,77 76,56,—**
toteswingers:1&2:£10.80, 1&3:£2.40, 2&3:£3.20 CSF £86.64 TOTE £6.30: £1.10, £6.90, £1.10; EX 41.10 Trifecta £253.00 Pool: £396.69 - 1.16 winning units..
Owner J D Riches **Bred** M C Denning **Trained** Pilling, Lancs

FOCUS
A moderate sprint maiden. Improved effort from the winner, though ground played its part and everything else tired late.

NOTEBOOK
Indian Giver handled the ground best and pulled clear to win comfortably. Although failing to score in seven previous tries, he had twice finished runner-up and, despite his rating of just 60, was more than good enough. (tchd 9-2)
Yorketa, from a yard who can get one ready, stayed on nicely for second and should improve. (op 11-1)
Kaua'i Girl was readily brushed aside, but did keep on again for third and will probably need further once sent handicapping. (op 15-8 tchd 9-4)
Rhal(IRE) was never far away and improved on her debut effort. (tchd 10-1 and 12-1)

Pizzarra, faced with much easier opposition than on debut, didn't get home having raced freely. (tchd 9-4 and 3-1)

6460 FREEBETTING WITH FREEBETTING.CO.UK FILLIES' H'CAP 7f
3:50 (3:51) (Class 5) (0-70,68) 3-Y-0+ £2,007 (£597; £298; £149) Stalls Centre

Form RPR
3011 1 Clumber Place[19] 5905 4-8-13 65 .... MichaelO'Connell(5) 13 74
(R C Guest) w ldr: led over 4f out: mde rest: pushed out fnl f 3/1[1]
5104 2 3 Dolly Royal (IRE)[17] 6003 5-8-9 61 .... LeeTopliss(5) 12 62
(R Johnson) dwlt: hld up: hdwy to chse wnr 2f out: edgd lft and kpt on fnl f: no imp last 75yds 25/1
-000 3 1 1/2 House Point[29] 5631 3-8-7 57 .... SaleemGolam 14 54
(S C Williams) hld up: rdn over 2f out: hdwy over 1f out: kpt on fnl f: nrst fin 18/1
6506 4 1 1/4 Celtic Lynn (IRE)[30] 5598 5-9-7 68 .... PhillipMakin 8 62
(M Dods) hld up: rdn along over 2f out: hdwy over 1f out: nt pce to chal 7/1
0004 5 3/4 Kookie[16] 6039 3-8-4 57 oh9 ow3 .... PaulPickard(3) 6 49
(R E Barr) midfield: rdn and outpcd 3f out: rallied over 1f out: no imp fnl f 80/1
4022 6 6 Uddy Mac[11] 6186 3-8-2 55 .... KellyHarrison(3) 7 32
(N Bycroft) trckd ldrs tl rdn and wknd wl over 1f out 18/1
2406 7 5 Luv U Noo[8] 6266 3-8-12 62 .... DavidAllan 2 26
(B Ellison) hld up bhd ldng gp: pushed along over 2f out: sn btn 8/1
4252 8 11 Peter's Gift (IRE)[11] 6189 4-8-8 58 .... (b) AmyRyan(3) 4 —
(K A Ryan) prom: drvn over 3f out: wknd over 2f out 5/1[2]
-560 9 11 Cils Blancs (IRE)[36] 5379 4-8-7 54 oh2 .... (v[1]) TomEaves 9 —
(B Smart) led to over 4f out: wknd over 2f out 16/1
3003 10 nk Midnight Fantasy[29] 5627 4-9-2 68 .... DaleSwift(5) 3 —
(Rae Guest) missed break: wl bhd and rdn along: nvr on terms 6/1[3]
2501 11 3 1/2 Salerosa (IRE)[16] 6026 5-9-7 68 .... (p) PaulMulrennan 10 —
(Mrs A Duffield) in tch tl rdn and wknd over 2f out 12/1
0060 12 1 3/4 Wotatomboy[13] 6119 4-8-7 54 oh9 .... PaulQuinn 1 —
(R M Whitaker) prom tl rdn and wknd over 2f out 40/1
003 13 3 3/4 Gypsy Style[33] 5487 3-9-4 68 .... (t) AndrewMullen 11 —
(Mrs K Walton) towards rr: struggling 1/2-way: sn btn 40/1
0006 14 6 Rescent[52] 4864 3-8-4 54 oh9 .... (b) SilvestreDeSousa 5 —
(Mrs R A Carr) trckd ldrs to 1/2-way: sn lost pl: eased whn no ch fnl 2f 40/1

1m 36.61s (7.91) **Going Correction** +1.175s/f (Soft)
WFA 3 from 4yo+ 3lb 14 Ran SP% **116.1**
Speed ratings (Par 100): **101,97,95,94,93 86,81,68,55,55 51,49,45,38**
toteswingers:1&2:£22.50, 1&3:£48.90, 2&3:£33.70 CSF £88.15 CT £865.30 TOTE £4.80: £1.10, £13.60, £11.70; EX 88.40 TRIFECTA Not won..
Owner The Clumber Park Syndicate **Bred** Worksop Manor Stud **Trained** Stainforth, S Yorks
■ Stewards' Enquiry : Amy Ryan caution: careless riding.

FOCUS
A low-grade fillies' handicap with the fifth from well out of the handicap rasiign doubts about the form.
Wotatomboy Official explanation: jockey said filly lost its action

6461 SHREWD PUNTERS VISIT FREEBETTING.CO.UK H'CAP 6f
4:25 (4:25) (Class 5) (0-75,75) 3-Y-0 £2,072 (£616; £308; £153) Stalls Centre

Form RPR
2000 1 Durham Express (IRE)[7] 6299 3-9-1 69 .... (p) PhillipMakin 2 74
(M Dods) cl up: led over 1f out: sn hrd pressed: hld on gamely ins fnl f 16/1
505 2 1 1/4 Coin From Heaven (IRE)[52] 4865 3-9-2 75 .... LeeTopliss(5) 1 76
(R A Fahey) prom: effrt over 1f out: chal ins fnl f: hld towards fin 12/1
060 3 8 Pilgrim Dancer (IRE)[138] 2069 3-9-4 72 .... (b[1]) StephenCraine 3 47
(Patrick Morris) trckd ldrs tl rdn and outpcd over 1f out: n.d after 15/2
0165 4 2 1/4 Spinning Spirit (IRE)[10] 6226 3-8-10 64 .... PaulMulrennan 6 32
(J G Given) cl up: effrt and ev ch over 1f out: sn wknd 7/1
2210 5 6 Red Scintilla[11] 6197 3-8-12 71 .... DaleSwift(5) 7 20
(N Tinkler) in tch: drvn along 1/2-way: struggling fr 2f out 11/4[1]
6050 6 3 1/2 Master Leon[29] 5647 3-8-12 66 .... (v) TomEaves 8 4
(B Smart) cl up: led over 2f out to 1f out: sn btn 9/2[3]
5016 7 9 Fair Bunny[23] 5817 3-8-7 61 oh6 .... (b) SilvestreDeSousa 5 —
(A D Brown) slt ld to over 2f out: sn rdn and wknd 15/2
3321 8 42 Erebus (IRE)[30] 5614 3-9-3 71 .... AdrianNicholls 4 —
(S Kirk) cl up tl wknd over 2f out: eased whn no ch 7/2[2]

1m 22.43s (7.83) **Going Correction** +1.175s/f (Soft) 8 Ran SP% **116.7**
Speed ratings (Par 101): **94,92,81,78,70 66,54,—**
toteswingers:1&2:£14.10, 1&3:£21.20, 2&3:£13.60 CSF £190.62 CT £1098.50 TOTE £34.90: £6.10, £4.30, £5.50; EX 117.10 Trifecta £347.10 Part won. Pool: £469.16 - 0.53 winning units..
Owner M J Sedgewick **Bred** Rathbarry Stud **Trained** Denton, Co Durham
■ Stewards' Enquiry : Silvestre De Sousa one-day ban: careless riding (Oct 13)

FOCUS
This turned into a bit of a slog and the front two drew clear. They set the standard but not form to be too positive about.
Erebus(IRE) Official explanation: trainer said colt was unsuited by the heavy ground and lost a near-fore shoe

6462 HORSE RACING FREE BETS WITH FREEBETTING.CO.UK H'CAP (DIV I) 1m 3y(S)
5:00 (5:00) (Class 5) (0-70,70) 3-Y-0+ £1,683 (£501; £250; £125) Stalls Centre

Form RPR
5412 1 Nolecce[15] 6061 3-8-6 56 oh1 .... SilvestreDeSousa 6 69
(R C Guest) trckd ldrs: led over 2f out: edgd rt and styd on wl fnl f 3/1[1]
6033 2 3 3/4 Glenmuir (IRE)[13] 6117 7-9-4 67 .... IanBrennan(3) 3 71
(J J Quinn) hld up: hdwy to chse wnr over 1f out: effrt ins fnl f: no ex last 75yds 9/1
6402 3 7 Hades (IRE)[12] 6144 3-9-0 64 .... DavidAllan 9 52
(T D Easterby) cl up: led over 3f out to 2f out: outpcd by ldng pair wl over 1f out 9/2[3]
5440 4 3 Lakeman (IRE)[8] 6269 4-8-9 58 .... (b) BarryMcHugh(3) 10 39
(B Ellison) dwlt: hld up in tch: rdn and outpcd over 2f out: plugged on fnl f: no imp 5/1
4041 5 hd Casino Night[9] 6243 5-8-10 61 6ex .... DaleSwift(5) 5 42
(Miss L A Perratt) dwlt: sn pushed bhd ldng gp: hdwy and cl up 1/2-way: wknd over 2f out 10/3[2]
4454 6 5 Carlitos Spirit (IRE)[8] 6267 6-9-5 70 .... (v) LeeTopliss(5) 1 39
(I W McInnes) led to over 3f out: wknd over 2f out 16/1
005 7 1 Celtic Step[23] 5819 6-8-7 56 oh2 .... PaulPickard(3) 7 23
(A Kirtley) hld up in tch: rdn and carried hd high 2f out: edgd rt and sn btn 10/1
2060 8 57 Safari Guide[11] 6188 4-8-7 56 .... PatrickDonaghy(3) 2 —
(K M Prendergast) hld up: struggling 1/2-way: eased whn no ch fnl 2f 33/1

1m 53.74s (10.34) **Going Correction** +1.175s/f (Soft)
WFA 3 from 4yo+ 4lb 8 Ran SP% **110.8**
Speed ratings (Par 103): **95,91,84,81,81 76,75,18**
toteswingers:1&2:£4.60, 1&3:£3.60, 2&3:£6.40 CSF £28.40 CT £114.35 TOTE £4.00: £1.10, £2.40, £2.40; EX 29.20 Trifecta £144.60 Pool: £394.90 - 2.02 winning units.
Owner Future Racing (Notts) Limited **Bred** Hedsor Stud **Trained** Stainforth, S Yorks
■ Stewards' Enquiry : Dale Swift one-day ban: careless riding (Oct 13)

FOCUS
The first division of a moderate handicap with the runner-up rated close to this year's form.
Carlitos Spirit(IRE) Official explanation: jockey said gelding hung right
Safari Guide Official explanation: jockey said gelding was unsuited by the heavy ground

6463 HORSE RACING FREE BETS WITH FREEBETTING.CO.UK H'CAP (DIV II) 1m 3y(S)
5:30 (5:30) (Class 5) (0-70,69) 3-Y-0+ £1,683 (£501; £250; £125) Stalls Centre

Form RPR
5460 1 Master Of Dance (IRE)[21] 5852 3-9-8 69 .... PaulMulrennan 7 78
(J G Given) cl up: rdn to ld over 2f out: edgd lft: hld on wl fnl f 15/2[3]
0200 2 2 1/2 Tombellini (IRE)[11] 6188 3-8-10 57 .... PaulQuinn 6 60
(D Nicholls) t.k.h: hld up bhd ldng gp: effrt and hdwy over 1f out: chsd wnr ins fnl f: r.o 14/1
326 3 1 1/4 Morocchius (USA)[23] 5820 5-9-0 57 .... (p) DavidAllan 8 57
(Julie Camacho) w ldrs: ev ch tl outpcd over 1f out: rallied ins fnl f: nt pce of first two 7/2[1]
5315 4 shd Castle Myth (USA)[8] 6267 4-8-12 60 .... DaleSwift(5) 3 60
(B Ellison) cl up: rdn and outpcd over 2f out: rallied ent fnl f: r.o 4/1[2]
0530 5 2 Petrocelli[12] 6144 3-8-8 60 .... DeanHeslop(5) 9 56
(W Storey) slt ld to over 2f out: ev ch over 1f out: sn no ex 16/1
4444 6 nse No Quarter (IRE)[11] 6188 3-8-4 54 .... KellyHarrison(3) 4 49
(Miss Tracy Waggott) t.k.h: trckd ldrs: effrt 2f out: no ex fnl f 4/1[2]
-400 7 26 Baraconti (IRE)[68] 4344 3-9-2 63 .... TomEaves 2 —
(Mrs R A Carr) t.k.h: cl up tl rdn and wknd over 2f out: t.o 14/1
0200 8 10 Rowan Lodge (IRE)[13] 6117 8-9-4 64 .... (b) BarryMcHugh(3) 10 —
(Ollie Pears) t.k.h: hld up in tch: struggling 3f out: sn btn: t.o 7/2[1]

1m 55.8s (12.40) **Going Correction** +1.175s/f (Soft)
WFA 3 from 4yo+ 4lb 8 Ran SP% **115.4**
Speed ratings (Par 103): **85,82,81,81,79 79,53,43**
toteswingers:1&2:£11.80, 1&3:£4.90, 2&3:£7.30 CSF £103.89 CT £432.29 TOTE £11.80: £3.20, £2.80, £2.60; EX 73.40 TRIFECTA Not won..
Owner Peter Swann **Bred** Mick McGinn **Trained** Willoughton, Lincs

FOCUS
Like the first division, it went to a 3-y-o, who is rated to the best of this year's form.
Master Of Dance(IRE) Official explanation: trainer's rep said, regarding apparent improvement in form, that the colt was better suited bythe slower ground.
Petrocelli Official explanation: jockey said gelding hung left

6464 DIGIBET.COM H'CAP 5f
6:00 (6:00) (Class 6) (0-60,60) 3-Y-0+ £1,489 (£443; £221; £110) Stalls Centre

Form RPR
3505 1 Tenancy (IRE)[33] 5485 6-8-3 47 .... (b) BillyCray(5) 3 63
(S A Harris) mde all: drew clr fr 2f out: unchal 9/1
0440 2 8 Accamelia[9] 6246 4-8-6 48 .... (p) PatrickDonaghy(3) 7 35+
(C W Fairhurst) dwlt: bhd: hdwy 2f out: chsd wnr ins fnl f: no imp 18/1
0050 3 1 1/4 Danum Dancer[21] 5855 6-9-3 56 .... PaulQuinn 2 39
(N Bycroft) prom: effrt over 2f out: chsd wnr briefly ins fnl f: no imp 9/1
6304 4 2 1/4 Monsieur Harvey[13] 6119 4-8-2 48 .... AdamCarter(7) 8 23
(B Smart) cl up: chsd wnr over 2f out to ins fnl f: no ex 14/1
0026 5 1 3/4 Embra (IRE)[5] 6329 5-9-0 53 .... StevieDonohoe 4 21
(T J Etherington) bhd: rdn 1/2-way: hdwy over 1f out: nvr rchd ldrs 15/2[3]
0030 6 3/4 Thewinnatakesitall[9] 6255 3-8-5 47 ow1 .... BarryMcHugh(3) 12 14
(N Tinkler) towards rr: rdn along 1/2-way: styd on fnl f: n.d 25/1
5656 7 3 1/2 Foreign Rhythm (IRE)[7] 6295 5-9-2 60 .... DaleSwift(5) 14 13
(R E Barr) bhd and rdn along: hdwy over 1f out: nvr rchd ldrs 9/1
4020 8 1 1/4 Sea Crest[33] 5485 4-8-8 50 .... MichaelStainton(3) 6 —
(M Brittain) midfield: drvn along 1/2-way: no imp fr 2f out 16/1
0223 9 5 Guto[8] 6270 7-9-4 60 .... KellyHarrison(3) 5 —
(W J H Ratcliffe) sn rdn along in midfield: no imp fr 1/2-way 6/1[1]
0523 10 3/4 Gower Sophia[31] 5548 3-8-10 50 .... (v) DavidAllan 1 —
(M Brittain) racd alone far rail: prom tl wknd fr 2f out 12/1
4203 11 3 1/4 Rio Sands[9] 6246 5-9-0 56 .... AmyRyan(3) 11 —
(R M Whitaker) in tch: drvn along 1/2-way: wknd over 1f out 10/1
6400 12 4 Turf Time[32] 5535 3-8-5 48 .... (t) IanBrennan(3) 9 —
(J A Glover) midfield: rdn after 2f: sn struggling 33/1
0003 13 1 Future Gem[30] 5599 4-8-7 46 .... (p) JoeFanning 10 —
(N Wilson) chsd wnr to over 2f out: wknd over 1f out 7/1[2]
6636 14 2 3/4 Tartufo Dolce (IRE)[18] 5957 3-9-4 58 .... PaulMulrennan 13 —
(J G Given) sn drvn along in midfield: wknd fr 1/2-way 25/1
005- 15 7 Italian Dame[391] 5599 4-8-7 46 oh1 .... TomEaves 16 —
(J R Turner) a bhd: struggling fr 1/2-way 50/1
6000 16 15 Angle Of Attack (IRE)[148] 1813 5-8-13 52 .... (b) SilvestreDeSousa 15 —
(A D Brown) in tch to 1/2-way: sn rdn and wknd 25/1

66.73 secs (5.63) **Going Correction** +1.175s/f (Soft)
WFA 3 from 4yo+ 1lb 16 Ran SP% **119.6**
Speed ratings (Par 101): **101,88,86,82,79 78,73,71,63,61 56,50,48,44,33 9**
toteswingers:1&2:£34.00, 1&3:£12.20, 2&3:£36.40. totesuper7: Win: Not won. Place: Not won. CSF £148.45 CT £1508.09 TOTE £13.50: £2.80, £7.00, £3.90, £2.20; EX 197.40 TRIFECTA Not won. Place 6 £450.52; Place 5 £104.38.
Owner Ian Lindsay **Bred** G A E And J Smith Bloodstock **Trained** Carburton, Notts

FOCUS
What had looked a competitive sprint was turned into a rout but not form to take literally.
Guto Official explanation: trainer had no explanation for the poor form shown
Rio Sands Official explanation: jockey said gelding was unsuited by the heavy ground
T/Plt: £783.30 to a £1 stake. Pool:£61,972.21 - 57.75 winning tickets T/Qpdt: £72.00 to a £1 stake. Pool:£6,979.19 - 71.70 winning tickets RY

The Form Book, Raceform Ltd, Compton, RG20 6NL

5053 NOTTINGHAM (L-H)
Wednesday, September 29

OFFICIAL GOING: Good (good to firm in places back straight) changing to good to soft (good in places) after race 1 (2:20) changing to soft after race 6 (5:10)
Wind: Light against Weather: Raining

6465 E B F PHS WASHROOMS CONSUMABLES MAIDEN STKS 6f 15y
2:20 (2:22) (Class 5) 2-Y-O £3,561 (£1,059; £529; £264) **Stalls** High

Form RPR
5 **1** **Earl Of Leitrim (IRE)**[71] 4221 2-9-3 0 ShaneKelly 12 82
(B J Meehan) *racd stands' side: chsd ldrs: led over 2f out: rdn and hung lft fr over 1f out: overall ldr ins fnl f: r.o* **5/1**[3]
432 **2** *1 3/4* **Jinky**[12] 6146 2-9-3 73 SamHitchcott 5 77
(M R Channon) *racd far side: overall ldr: rdn over 1f out: hdd ins fnl f: styd on same pce: 1st of 8 in gp* **9/2**[2]
05 **3** *5* **Franciscan**[14] 6092 2-9-3 0 J-PGuillambert 11 62
(L M Cumani) *racd stands' side: hld up: hdwy over 2f out: sn rdn: styd on to go 3rd nr fin: nt trble ldrs: 2nd of 9 in gp* **25/1**
5 **4** *nk* **Louis The Pious**[15] 6047 2-9-3 0 PaulHanagan 15 61+
(K A Ryan) *racd stands' side: prom: rdn over 2f out: sn edgd lft: styd on same pce fnl f: 3rd of 9 in gp* **9/1**
0 **5** *nse* **Three Sparrows (IRE)**[33] 5491 2-9-3 0 PatDobbs 16 61
(R Hannon) *racd stands' side: s.i.s: sn prom: rdn to chse wnr over 1f out: styd on same pce: 4th of 9 in gp* **14/1**
0 **6** *hd* **Street Band (IRE)**[74] 4142 2-9-3 0 FergusSweeney 6 60
(H Candy) *racd far side: chsd ldr: rdn over 2f out: no ex fnl f: 2nd of 8 in gp* **16/1**
0324 **7** *hd* **Bajan Bear**[46] 5099 2-9-3 70 LukeMorris 7 60
(M Blanshard) *racd far side: prom: rdn over 2f out: no ex fnl f: 3rd of 8 in gp* **40/1**
46 **8** *7* **Glanusk**[20] 5893 2-9-3 0 JimCrowley 17 39
(R M Beckett) *racd stands' side: prom: rdn over 2f out: wknd wl over 1f out: 5th of 9 in gp* **4/1**[1]
00 **9** *3/4* **Silbury (IRE)**[12] 6145 2-8-12 0 SteveDrowne 8 32
(R Charlton) *racd far side: hld up: rdn over 2f out: sn wknd: 4th of 8 in gp* **40/1**
4 **10** *nk* **St Augustine (IRE)**[32] 5523 2-9-0 0 KierenFox(3) 2 36
(J R Best) *racd far side: chsd ldrs: rdn over 2f out: wknd over 1f out: 5th of 8 in gp* **12/1**
0 **11** *3 3/4* **Loose Quality (USA)**[15] 6046 2-9-3 0 MickyFenton 4 24
(T P Tate) *racd far side: prom: rdn and wknd over 2f out: 6th of 8 in gp* **28/1**
53 **12** *1/2* **Mishtaag**[100] 3274 2-9-3 0 SebSanders 14 23
(C E Brittain) *racd stands' side: led over 3f: wknd over 1f out: 6th of 9 in gp* **6/1**
6 **13** *1/2* **Bobbyow**[120] 2621 2-9-3 0 DavidProbert 10 21
(B Palling) *racd stands' side: chsd ldr: rdn and ev ch over 2f out: wknd over 1f out: 7th of 9 in gp* **50/1**
14 *3/4* **Ace Master** 2-8-10 0 RyanClark(7) 1 19
(S R Bowring) *racd far side: in tch: rdn over 3f out: wknd over 2f out: 7th of 8 in gp* **150/1**
0 **15** *8* **Sarojini**[158] 1510 2-8-12 0 RichardMullen 9 —
(J A Glover) *racd stands' side: mid-div: rdn 1/2-way: wknd over 2f out: 8th of 9 in gp* **100/1**
16 *3* **Alspritza** 2-8-12 0 JackMitchell 13 —
(C F Wall) *s.s: racd stands' side: a in rr: lost tch fr 1/2-way: last of 9 in gp* **50/1**
17 *8* **Flash Forward** 2-9-3 0 GeorgeBaker 3 —
(C F Wall) *s.s: racd far side: outpcd: last of 8 in gp* **25/1**

1m 14.69s (-0.21) **Going Correction** -0.15s/f (Firm) **17 Ran SP% 121.0**
Speed ratings (Par 95): **95,92,86,85,85 85,85,75,74,74 69,68,67,66,56 52,41**
toteswingers:1&2:£6.00, 1&3:£61.90, 2&3:£61.90 CSF £25.18 TOTE £4.70: £1.20, £2.30, £12.00; EX 22.00.
Owner Gallagher Equine Ltd **Bred** Gordon Phillips **Trained** Manton, Wilts

FOCUS
There was rain around and following this opener the ground was changed to good to soft, good in places, with general opinion amongst the jockeys that conditions were on the easy side. However, the time suggested that the going was still on the good side. The field split into two fairly even groups, with those drawn in the bottom eight stalls going far side and the others racing stands' side, and there seemed no major bias. This looked no more than a fair maiden, but the form is solid rated through the runner-up.

NOTEBOOK
Earl Of Leitrim(IRE) hadn't been seen since making an encouraging debut in a reasonable Ffos Las maiden 71 days earlier, but he showed he's gone the right way since then with a convincing success, although he did hang badly left late on. He's potentially useful, provided he's not as wayward under pressure in future, and this is probably his trip for now. (op 3-1)
Jinky convincingly fared best of those on the far side, producing another creditable performance. Although just a fair type, he may be a little better than his current official mark of 73 suggests. (op 4-1 tchd 10-3)
Franciscan ◆ was having his final qualifying run for an official mark and his breeding strongly suggested he would be unsuited by this drop in trip (half-brother to Forte Dei Marmi). He ran a noteworthy race, lacking the speed of the winner on the near side of the track, but keeping on well. Surely he'll do a lot better over further in handicaps. (tchd 20-1 and 28-1)
Louis The Pious improved on his debut showing but was still well held and is probably more of a handicap prospect. (op 14-1)
Three Sparrows(IRE) ran okay and is another for handicaps. (op 20-1)
Street Band(IRE) was second best of those on the far side. He needs one more run for a mark and should find his level in due course. (op 20-1)
Bajan Bear was third best far side, but still below his official rating of 70. (tchd 33-1)
Glanusk has not gone forward as anticipated from a pleasing debut at Salisbury and this was his least promising performance to date. Handicaps are now an option, but he won't appeal as one to back until showing a bit more. (op 11-2 tchd 6-1)
Mishtaag, for whom there was money on his turf debut, was well below the form of his previous Polytrack effort after an absence of 100 days. (op 9-1 tchd 10-1)
Flash Forward Official explanation: jockey said colt missed the break

6466 PHS PAPER PRODUCTS H'CAP 5f 13y
2:50 (2:51) (Class 5) (0-75,75) 3-Y-O £2,590 (£770; £385; £192) **Stalls** High

Form RPR
2203 **1** **Superior Edge**[18] 5956 3-9-4 72 DavidProbert 4 78
(B Palling) *chsd ldr: sn drvn along: styd on to ld nr fin* **12/1**
030 **2** *hd* **Bilash**[36] 5390 3-8-11 65 TonyCulhane 10 70
(R Hollinshead) *in rr: gd hdwy 2f out: edgd lft: led last 75yds: hdd nr fin* **33/1**
2321 **3** *shd* **Stratton Banker (IRE)**[8] 6270 3-8-13 67 6ex WilliamCarson 3 72+
(S C Williams) *in rr: hdwy to chse ldrs and nt clr run over 1f out tl ins fnl f: styd on wl fnl clsng stages* **15/8**[1]
1046 **4** *1/2* **Kummel Excess (IRE)**[6] 6310 3-9-2 73 MatthewDavies(3) 1 76
(George Baker) *towards rr: hdwy over 2f out: chsng ldrs ins fnl f: no ex* **25/1**
2430 **5** *hd* **Dancing Freddy (IRE)**[20] 5890 3-9-2 70 (b) FrankieDettori 9 72
(J G Given) *led and clr over 3f out: edgd lft over 1f out: hdd & wknd fnl 75yds* **6/1**[3]
1060 **6** *1* **Choc'A'Moca (IRE)**[47] 5024 3-8-0 61 oh11 (v) NeilFarley(7) 5 60?
(D Carroll) *stmbld s: mid-div: hdwy over 2f out: kpt on same pce fnl f* **16/1**
3560 **7** *1/2* **Bossy Kitty**[14] 6073 3-8-8 65 Louis-PhilippeBeuzelin(3) 8 62+
(N Tinkler) *in rr: hdwy and nt clr run over 1f out: nvr rchd ldrs* **25/1**
5600 **8** *nk* **Adventure Story**[23] 5809 3-9-0 68 PatDobbs 11 64
(R Hannon) *gave problems in stalls: dwlt: in rr: sme hdwy 2f out: nvr nr ldrs* **20/1**
6425 **9** *1 1/4* **Wanchai Whisper**[7] 6284 3-8-10 67 (p) AndrewHeffernan(3) 2 58
(P R Hedger) *in rr: hdwy over 2f out: wknd fnl f* **16/1**
4313 **10** *1* **Sharp Eclipse**[37] 5356 3-9-6 74 (p) PaulHanagan 6 62
(K A Ryan) *dwlt: sn chsng ldrs: wknd over 1f out* **11/2**[2]
-033 **11** *3 1/4* **Aalsmeer**[18] 5960 3-9-2 70 (p) TedDurcan 13 46
(Karen George) *racd alone stands' side: bhd fnl 2f* **16/1**
0154 **12** *3 3/4* **Mark Anthony (IRE)**[30] 5606 3-9-7 75 FrannyNorton 7 37
(K A Ryan) *chsd ldrs: lost pl over 1f out* **9/1**

60.92 secs (-0.08) **Going Correction** +0.025s/f (Good) **12 Ran SP% 115.2**
Speed ratings (Par 101): **101,100,100,99,99 97,97,96,94,92 87,81**
toteswingers:1&2:£54.70, 1&3:£6.30, 2&3:£18.80 CSF £358.52 CT £1086.77 TOTE £12.80: £5.40, £11.00, £1.10.
Owner Christopher & Annabelle Mason **Bred** Christopher J Mason **Trained** Tredodridge, Vale Of Glamorgan

FOCUS
Few of these looked particularly well treated, but it was at least competitive. The main action was up the middle of the track, and Aalsmeer, racing alone against the stands' rail, was well beaten. The time again suggested the ground was little worse than good.

6467 PHS SMART DRI HAND DRYER H'CAP 1m 75y
3:25 (3:26) (Class 4) (0-85,85) 3-Y-O £6,152 (£1,830; £914; £456) **Stalls** Centre

Form RPR
521- **1** **Quick Wit**[334] 7146 3-9-5 83 FrankieDettori 3 104+
(Saeed Bin Suroor) *mde all: pushed clr over 1f out: eased ins fnl f* **7/2**[1]
4030 **2** *3 1/4* **Aerodynamic (IRE)**[19] 5917 3-9-3 81 RobertWinston 8 89
(Pat Eddery) *a.p: rdn over 2f out: styd on: wnt 2nd nr fin: no ch w wnr* **7/1**[3]
221 **3** *hd* **Al Muthanaa**[30] 5603 3-9-0 78 RichardHills 2 86
(W J Haggas) *a.p: rdn over 2f out: chsd wnr over 1f out: no imp: lost 2nd nr fin* **12/1**
0243 **4** *hd* **Finest Reserve (IRE)**[17] 5993 3-9-3 81 (v) SamHitchcott 9 88
(M R Channon) *mid-div: sn pushed along: hdwy over 3f out: hrd rdn fr over 1f out: styd on* **11/1**
3120 **5** *1 1/4* **Purple Gallery (IRE)**[25] 5750 3-8-8 79 (p) RyanPowell(7) 10 83+
(J S Moore) *hld up: rdn over 2f out: r.o ins fnl f: nvr nrr* **28/1**
1 **6** *2* **Gypsy Carnival**[17] 5986 3-9-0 78 JimCrowley 5 78+
(R M Beckett) *hld up: hdwy 3f out: rdn over 1f out: wknd fnl f* **8/1**
0104 **7** *1/2* **Syrian**[19] 5904 3-9-0 78 TedDurcan 16 76
(Ian Williams) *s.i.s: hld up: rdn over 2f out: nt trble ldrs* **14/1**
-464 **8** *3/4* **Bonded (IRE)**[51] 4898 3-8-7 71 oh1 (b) EddieCreighton 15 68
(B J Meehan) *mid-div: pushed along 1/2-way: hdwy 3f out: rdn and wknd over 1f out* **20/1**
-250 **9** *1/2* **Huntingfortreasure**[13] 6105 3-8-13 77 ShaneKelly 14 73
(M Dods) *prom: rdn over 3f out: wknd over 1f out* **28/1**
6653 **10** *1/2* **Muwalla**[18] 5942 3-8-0 71 oh6 NeilFarley(7) 13 65
(J D Bethell) *s.s: hld up: rdn over 3f out: hdwy over 2f out: hmpd and wknd over 1f out* **14/1**
3104 **11** *hd* **Space War**[19] 5917 3-9-7 85 WilliamBuick 17 79
(J H M Gosden) *prom: rdn over 2f out: hung lft and wknd over 1f out* **5/1**[2]
0-16 **12** *nk* **Lucky Windmill**[32] 5511 3-9-4 82 PJMcDonald 4 75
(G A Swinbank) *chsd wnr tl rdn over 1f out: wknd ins fnl f* **7/1**[3]
1-20 **13** *17* **Medicinal Compound**[32] 5511 3-9-3 81 PaulHanagan 6 35
(K A Ryan) *s.i.s: hld up: wknd over 2f out* **14/1**

1m 45.5s (-0.10) **Going Correction** +0.075s/f (Good) **13 Ran SP% 122.7**
Speed ratings (Par 103): **103,99,99,99,98 96,95,94,94,93 93,93,76**
toteswingers:1&2:£7.70, 1&3:£5.20, 2&3:£11.60 CSF £27.59 CT £269.61 TOTE £4.60: £1.80, £2.40, £2.90; EX 41.40.
Owner Godolphin **Bred** Ptarmigan Bloodstock Limited **Trained** Newmarket, Suffolk

FOCUS
A reasonable contest won in impressive fashion.

6468 E B F PHS WATER SAVING MAIDEN FILLIES' STKS (DIV I) 1m 75y
4:00 (4:02) (Class 5) 2-Y-O £3,238 (£963; £481; £240) **Stalls** Centre

Form RPR
65 **1** **Istishaara (USA)**[76] 4048 2-9-0 0 TedDurcan 6 76+
(J L Dunlop) *trckd ldr: chal over 3f out: led over 2f out: all out* **8/1**
2 *shd* **Devastation** 2-9-0 0 WilliamBuick 11 76+
(J H M Gosden) *sn trcking ldr: chal over 2f out: r.o: jst hld* **7/2**[1]
3 *3 3/4* **Shuhra (IRE)** 2-9-0 0 RichardHills 1 70+
(W J Haggas) *sn mid-div: hdwy over 2f out: nt clr run and swtchd lft over 1f out: r.o to snatch 3rd on line: will improve* **9/1**
03 **4** *hd* **Miss Chicane**[55] 4755 2-9-0 0 ShaneKelly 9 67
(W R Swinburn) *trckd ldrs: effrt over 2f out: hung lft: kpt on same pce appr fnl f* **7/1**[3]
5 *1/2* **Sinnfonia (IRE)** 2-9-0 0 IanMongan 5 66+
(H R A Cecil) *drvn to r in mid-div on outer: drvn 3f out: sn outpcd: edgd lft and kpt on fnl f* **7/2**[1]
06 **6** *2 1/4* **Emperor's Princess (FR)**[9] 6247 2-9-0 0 PatDobbs 10 62
(R Hannon) *led tl over 2f out: wknd 1f out* **13/2**[2]
0 **7** *hd* **Dragonera**[12] 6154 2-9-0 0 PaulHanagan 4 61
(E A L Dunlop) *hld up in rr: outpcd over 2f out: kpt on fnl f: nvr rchd ldrs* **12/1**
8 *2 3/4* **Desert Location** 2-9-0 0 SebSanders 12 56
(M L W Bell) *trckd ldrs: effrt 3f out: wknd over 1f out* **20/1**
9 *1/2* **Promenadia** 2-9-0 0 RichardMullen 8 54
(R Charlton) *hld up in mid-div: drvn 3f out: swtchd lft over 1f out: sn wknd* **12/1**

10 *18* **Blazing Field** 2-9-0 0 .... LukeMorris 7 17
(C G Cox) *s.s: sn drvn along in last: bhd fnl 3f: t.o* **22/1**

1m 51.19s (5.59) **Going Correction** +0.40s/f (Good) 10 Ran SP% **115.9**
Speed ratings (Par 92): **88,87,84,83,83 81,81,78,77,59**
toteswingers:1&2:£7.70, 1&3:£7.00, 2&3:£6.10 CSF £35.91 TOTE £8.40: £1.70, £1.50, £2.00; EX 52.50.
Owner Hamdan Al Maktoum **Bred** Shadwell Farm LLC **Trained** Arundel, W Sussex

FOCUS
They went slow and the time was poor, being over eight seconds above standard, and 2.11 seconds off the time Tameen, representing the same owner/trainer as the winner of this, recorded in the other division. There were certainly some promising types on show.

NOTEBOOK
Istishaara(USA), upped in trip on her return from a 76-day break, was popular in the market, being sent off a shorter price than Shuhra, who was seemingly the choice of Richard Hills. The market confidence proved fully justified, with the filly travelling well under a positive ride and knuckling down under pressure, putting her experience to good use to narrowly get the better of a newcomer. It's hard to know exactly how good she is, but she seems to have a fair amount of ability.
Devastation ◆, the second foal of top-class miler Attraction (first foal won over 7f on Polytrack at two), was well placed and just failed to overhaul a more experienced rival. She has plenty of scope and John Gosden reportedly believes she'll make a "nice staying filly next year." (op 11-4 tchd 5-1)
Shuhra(IRE) is related to some decent winners, indeed her sister Oriental Fashion won this race in 1998 before being successful in Listed and Group 2 company over the same trip. She looked the choice of Richard Hills, but is unfurnished and was weak in the market. Having briefly been denied a clear run towards the inside in the closing stages, she was not given a hard time and it will be a surprise if she can't do better. (op 17-2 tchd 13-2)
Miss Chicane possibly has her share of temperament as her jockey had his feet out of the irons on the way to the start. In the race itself, she was a bit keen early and then not given a hard time in the closing stages. This was a respectable effort after a near two-month break and, likely to do better off a stronger pace, she could find her level in handicaps. (op 17-2 tchd 10-1)
Sinnfonia(IRE) ran green early, soon coming off the bridle and getting behind, and was then stuck wide in the straight. There should be a fair bit more to come. (op 10-3 tchd 3-1)
Emperor's Princess(FR) ran well for a long way ought to find her level in handicaps. Official explanation: jockey said filly hung right-handed in straight (op 17-2 tchd 6-1)
Dragonera was never competitive but made late headway and seems likely to do better over middle-distances and maybe beyond once handicapped. (op 20-1)

6469 E B F PHS WATER SAVING MAIDEN FILLIES' STKS (DIV II) 1m 75y
4:35 (4:35) (Class 5) 2-Y-O **£3,238** (£963; £481; £240) **Stalls** Centre

Form RPR
60 1 **Tameen**[27] 5692 2-9-0 0 .... RichardHills 1 75+
(J L Dunlop) *hld up in tch: led over 1f out: drvn out: eased nr fin* **9/2[2]**
20 2 *1 ½* **Mia Madonna**[12] 6155 2-9-0 0 .... ShaneKelly 5 70
(B J Meehan) *chsd ldr tl led over 2f out: rdn: edgd lft and hdd over 1f out: styd on same pce ins fnl f* **13/2[3]**
0 3 *1 ¼* **Glyn Ceiriog**[30] 5583 2-9-0 0 .... TonyCulhane 12 67
(George Baker) *a.p: rdn over 2f out: hung lft over 1f out: styd on* **66/1**
0 4 *nk* **Highest**[12] 6154 2-9-0 0 .... WilliamBuick 2 67
(J H M Gosden) *trckd ldrs: shkn up over 3f out: rdn over 1f out: styd on* **11/8[1]**
0 5 *1* **Heart Felt**[27] 5691 2-9-0 0 .... PatDobbs 4 65
(R Hannon) *sn led: rdn and hdd over 2f out: no ex fnl f* **33/1**
6 *1 ½* **Insieme (IRE)** 2-9-0 0 .... AndreaAtzeni 9 61
(M Botti) *s.i.s: hld up: rdn over 2f out: styd on ins fnl f: nvr nrr* **14/1**
03 7 *1* **Etarre (IRE)**[9] 6248 2-9-0 0 .... MickyFenton 11 59
(Mrs P Sly) *hdwy 6f out: rdn over 2f out: hmpd and wknd over 1f out* **8/1**
0 8 *2 ¼* **Palm Pilot (IRE)**[12] 6154 2-9-0 0 .... PaulHanagan 7 55
(E A L Dunlop) *prom: racd keenly: rdn over 2f out: wknd over 1f out* **8/1**
9 *hd* **Mystic Edge** 2-9-0 0 .... SebSanders 8 54
(M L W Bell) *s.i.s: hld up: rdn over 2f out: a in rr* **33/1**
10 *18* **Intombi** 2-9-0 0 .... DavidProbert 10 16
(A J McCabe) *sn pushed along in rr: wknd over 2f out* **50/1**
11 *3 ½* **Devon Delight** 2-9-0 0 .... J-PGuillambert 3 9
(R M H Cowell) *a in rr: rdn and wknd over 2f out: eased* **50/1**

1m 49.08s (3.48) **Going Correction** +0.40s/f (Good) 11 Ran SP% **113.8**
Speed ratings (Par 92): **98,96,95,94,93 92,91,89,89,71 67**
toteswingers:1&2:£6.30, 1&3:£29.40, 2&3:£27.30 CSF £31.39 TOTE £4.20: £1.40, £2.90, £9.30; EX 30.30.
Owner Hamdan Al Maktoum **Bred** Shadwell Estate Company Limited **Trained** Arundel, W Sussex

FOCUS
They went steady, but the time was still 2.11 seconds quicker than the slowly run first division, won by Istishaara, who represented the same owner/trainer. Just fair form, a bit below what's expected for race here at this time of year.

NOTEBOOK
Tameen ◆ probably improved a little on her two previous performances over 7f, clearly benefiting from this step up in trip. She has a really nice middle-distance pedigree and can be expected to leave this form behind next year. (op 4-1 tchd 5-1)
Mia Madonna was a touch keen on the pace but still ran well. She looks limited, but handicaps are now an option. (op 6-1 tchd 8-1)
Glyn Ceiriog stepped up on the form she showed on debut at Bath, plugging on despite hanging left in the closing stages. She shaped as though she'll come again for this and may want further in due course.
Highest flopped when well fancied for a better maiden on debut and this impressive-looking filly again failed to justify market support. She's clearly not living up to expectations, but she wasn't subjected to a hard ride and, being quite a big type, she'll surely be capable of better when she strengthens up and matures mentally. (op 2-1)
Heart Felt ran like a non-stayer.
Insieme(IRE) made minor late headway following a very slow start and should improve. (op 16-1)
Palm Pilot(IRE), who didn't handle the dip at Newmarket on debut, was much too keen this time. (op 10-1 tchd 7-1)
Devon Delight Official explanation: jockey said filly had no more to give

6470 PHS TREADSMART ENTRANCE MATTING MAIDEN STKS 1m 75y
5:10 (5:11) (Class 5) 3-Y-O+ **£2,590** (£770; £385; £192) **Stalls** Centre

Form RPR
33 1 **Titivation**[145] 1882 3-8-12 0 .... WilliamBuick 17 76+
(M L W Bell) *racd wd early: sn chsng ldng pair: wnt 2nd over 1f out: hung lft and styd on to ld fnl 50yds* **2/1[1]**
03 2 *½* **Launchpad**[22] 5842 3-9-3 0 .... J-PGuillambert 10 80+
(L M Cumani) *chsd clr ldr: led over 2f out: hdd and no ex wl ins fnl f* **10/1**
3 *7* **Morning Chief (IRE)** 3-9-3 0 .... PhilipRobinson 9 64+
(C G Cox) *in tch: drvn over 3f out: kpt on same pce fnl 2f* **5/1[2]**
4 *¾* **Room For A View** 3-8-12 0 .... PatDobbs 2 57+
(M P Tregoning) *mid-div: hdwy over 2f out: styd on steadily fnl f* **12/1**
5 *¾* **Myboyalfie (USA)** 3-9-3 0 .... IanMongan 7 60
(J R Jenkins) *mid-div: effrt over 3f out: kpt on fnl f* **40/1**
4/ 6 *hd* **First Coming**[881] 1741 6-9-7 0 .... ShaneKelly 8 60
(B J McMath) *trckd ldrs: effrt over 3f out: one pce* **25/1**
20 7 *3 ¼* **Silvan Stream**[95] 3437 3-8-12 0 .... PaulHanagan 5 47
(J D Bethell) *chsd ldrs: drvn and outpcd over 4f out: kpt on fnl 2f* **13/2[3]**
3-0 8 *2 ½* **Marie Cuddy (IRE)**[28] 5658 3-8-12 0 .... JamieMackay 3 42
(Karen George) *t.k.h: led and sn clr: hdd over 2f out: sn wknd* **25/1**
9 *½* **Stardust Dancer** 3-9-3 0 .... GregFairley 6 45
(Paul Green) *s.i.s: in rr: kpt on fnl 2f: nvr on terms* **22/1**
4 10 *14* **Reset To Fit**[11] 6186 3-9-3 0 .... RobertWinston 11 13
(E J Alston) *chsd ldrs: lost pl 2f out* **13/2[3]**
11 *1* **Chik's Dream** 3-9-3 0 .... NeilChalmers 1 11
(C Roberts) *s.s: a bhd* **100/1**
12 *4* **Neissa (USA)** 3-8-12 0 .... LukeMorris 13 —
(J R Best) *in rr and sn drvn along: nvr on terms* **28/1**
13 *2 ¼* **Flying Trump** 3-8-12 0 .... AndrewElliott 4 —
(R M H Cowell) *s.i.s: drvn along in rr: bhd fnl 3f* **33/1**

1m 48.58s (2.98) **Going Correction** +0.40s/f (Good)
WFA 3 from 6yo 4lb 13 Ran SP% **115.3**
Speed ratings (Par 103): **101,100,93,92,92 91,88,86,85,71 70,66,64**
toteswingers:1&2:£4.90, 1&3:£3.60, 2&3:£6.60 CSF £20.25 TOTE £3.40: £1.10, £2.50, £2.10; EX 14.10.
Owner The Duchess Of Roxburghe **Bred** Floors Farming **Trained** Newmarket, Suffolk

FOCUS
Rain continued to fall and, following this race, the ground was changed to soft. Winning jockey William Buick described conditions as almost heavy. An ordinary maiden, but the pace was quick, with Marie Cuddy much too free in a clear lead, but it still paid to race prominently in the chasing pack.

6471 PHS GROUP NURSERY 1m 2f 50y
5:40 (5:41) (Class 5) (0-75,74) 2-Y-O **£2,590** (£770; £385; £192) **Stalls** Low

Form RPR
032 1 **Slight Advantage (IRE)**[29] 5633 2-9-1 68 .... LukeMorris 8 74
(C G Cox) *led 2f: chsd ldr: rdn to ld and hung lft fr over 2f out: styd on gamely* **12/1**
0536 2 *nk* **Levantera (IRE)**[18] 5961 2-9-1 68 .... PhilipRobinson 4 73
(C G Cox) *w wnr tl led 8f out: rdn and hdd over 2f out: stl ev ch fr there: styd on gamely* **16/1**
0004 3 *2 ¾* **Prince Freddie**[21] 5857 2-9-0 67 .... TonyCulhane 1 68
(P A Kirby) *hld up: hdwy over 2f out: sn rdn: styd on* **28/1**
056 4 *1 ½* **Marc De Savoie (IRE)**[12] 6138 2-8-12 65 .... FrannyNorton 2 63
(K A Ryan) *chsd ldrs: rdn over 2f out: sn hung rt: styd on same pce fnl f* **22/1**
0425 5 *¾* **Standout**[26] 5709 2-9-1 68 .... GregFairley 5 64
(R Hannon) *s.i.s: hld up: rdn over 4f out: styd on fr over 1f out: nt trble ldrs* **20/1**
3505 6 *hd* **Dubai Glory**[18] 5961 2-8-10 63 .... RichardMullen 7 59
(E A L Dunlop) *chsd ldrs: rdn over 2f out: styd on same pce appr fnl f* **33/1**
2054 7 *½* **Cotton Spirit**[11] 6184 2-8-13 66 .... PaulHanagan 3 61
(R A Fahey) *mid-div: hdwy over 2f out: sn rdn: styd on same pce appr fnl f* **8/1[3]**
030 8 *hd* **Beer Flush (IRE)**[30] 5594 2-8-13 66 .... AndrewElliott 6 61
(Jedd O'Keeffe) *hld up: hdwy over 2f out: rdn and hung lft over 1f out: nt trble ldrs* **33/1**
0232 9 *¾* **Fly By White (IRE)**[23] 5807 2-9-5 72 .... PatDobbs 14 65
(R Hannon) *s.i.s: hld up: hdwy over 3f out: rdn over 2f out: styd on same pce appr fnl f* **17/2**
4044 10 *1 ½* **Roi Du Boeuf (IRE)**[33] 5490 2-8-6 62 .... MartinLane(3) 13 53
(D M Simcock) *hld up in tch: rdn: n.m.r and lost pl 4f out: n.d after* **3/1[1]**
0314 11 *1 ¼* **Dew Reward (IRE)**[2] 6411 2-8-10 63 .... RobertWinston 15 52
(Eve Johnson Houghton) *prom: rdn over 2f out: wknd over 1f out* **17/2**
0603 12 *4 ½* **High Kickin**[19] 5924 2-8-12 65 .... DavidProbert 11 45
(A J McCabe) *prom: lost pl 6f out: hdwy over 4f out: rdn over 2f out: sn wknd* **33/1**
055 13 *1* **Acute (IRE)**[14] 6087 2-9-3 70 .... RichardHills 16 49
(B J Meehan) *mid-div: hdwy 4f out: rdn over 2f out: wknd over 1f out* **16/1**
0060 14 *17* **Orange Ketchup (IRE)**[12] 6160 2-8-12 65 .... ShaneKelly 12 13
(P F I Cole) *hld up: hdwy over 3f out: rdn: hung lft and wknd over 2f out: t.o* **33/1**
31 15 *23* **Biographical (USA)**[11] 6211 2-9-7 74 .... WilliamBuick 10 —
(J H M Gosden) *chsd ldrs: rdn over 3f out: wknd wl over 1f out: eased: t.o* **9/2[2]**
0211 16 *2 ½* **Lord Of The Storm**[70] 4241 2-9-1 71 .... (p) JackDean(3) 9 —
(W G M Turner) *hld up: a in rr: rdn and bhd fnl 4f: t.o* **33/1**

2m 18.32s (6.62) **Going Correction** +0.55s/f (Yiel) 16 Ran SP% **122.1**
Speed ratings (Par 95): **95,94,92,91,90 90,90,90,89,88 87,83,82,69,50 48**
toteswingers:1&2:£19.80, 1&3:£20.90, 2&3:£40.00 CSF £171.07 CT £5117.90 TOTE £14.80: £4.30, £4.80, £6.70, £6.70; EX 56.20.
Owner The City & Provincial Partnership **Bred** Airlie Stud **Trained** Lambourn, Berks

FOCUS
A modest nursery and, with the pace steady, it paid to race prominently, indeed the first two were in front two pretty much throughout. The principals are all likely to make up into fair handicappers.

NOTEBOOK
Slight Advantage(IRE) had the ground in her favour (runner-up on soft last time) and proved suited by the step up in trip. She's clearly a tough filly with plenty of stamina. (tchd 10-1)
Levantera(IRE), another with soft ground form, did nothing wrong. Her pedigree is a mix of speed and stamina, but she clearly stayed well.
Prince Freddie fared best of those from off the pace and, as such, deserves credit. (op 33-1)
Marc De Savoie(IRE), upped 3f in trip on his nursery debut, was always close to the pace and had his chance. (op 16-1 tchd 25-1)
Standout needed to be ridden along early after missing the break, but he finished better than most. (op 18-1)
Roi Du Boeuf(IRE) was sent off favourite but ran nowhere near the form he showed when fourth over 1m on soft ground at Newmarket last time. He lost his place when short of room about half a mile out and that clearly didn't help. (op 4-1)
Orange Ketchup(IRE) Official explanation: trainer's rep said colt was unsuited by the soft ground
Biographical(USA) Official explanation: trainer's rep said colt was unsuited by the soft ground

6472 AJA INSURE THEIR MEMBERS H'CAP (FOR GENTLEMAN AMATEUR RIDERS) 1m 2f 50y
6:10 (6:13) (Class 5) (0-70,67) 3-Y-O+ **£2,307** (£709; £354) **Stalls** Low

Form RPR
6424 1 **Scarab (IRE)**[13] 6117 5-11-2 62 .... (p) MrMSeston 3 71+
(T D Walford) *chsd ldr tl led over 4f out: clr fr over 3f out: eased nr fin* **11/2[3]**

					RPR
064	2	2 1/4	**James Pollard (IRE)**[22] 5828 5-10-2 53 oh5..........(t) MrRJWilliams(5) 11 (B J Llewellyn) *s.i.s: hld up: hdwy over 3f out: rdn to go 2nd over 1f out: no ch w wnr* **20/1**		55
1050	3	1 1/4	**Postman**[13] 6117 4-11-2 67..............(p) MrJNewman(5) 13 (B Smart) *sn prom: chsd wnr over 2f out to over 1f out: styd on same pce* **10/1**		67
0646	4	1/2	**Mojeerr**[16] 6037 4-10-4 53 oh8.............. MrPCollington(3) 2 (A J McCabe) *hld up: hdwy 2f out: styd on: nt trble ldrs* **28/1**		52
5423	5	2 1/4	**Diamond Twister (USA)**[7] 6289 4-11-2 65.............. MrPJTolman(3) 10 (J R Best) *mid-div: sn pushed along: hmpd 1/2-way: rdn over 3f out: sn outpcd* **7/1**		60
0040	6	2	**Dragon Slayer (IRE)**[31] 5545 8-11-7 67.............. MrSDobson 1 (John A Harris) *s.s: hld up: hdwy over 2f out: n.d* **25/1**		58
530	7	hd	**Fantastic Storm**[39] 5303 3-9-10 53 oh6..........(v1) MrJBanks(5) 12 (R Bastiman) *trckd ldrs: lost pl over 5f out: n.d after* **50/1**		44
0323	8	nk	**Tivers Song (USA)**[32] 5515 6-10-2 53 oh4..........(b) MrPPrince(5) 4 (John A Harris) *hld up: rdn over 3f out: nvr on terms* **14/1**		43
3140	9	6	**Red Dagger (IRE)**[9] 6261 4-10-7 56.............. MrMPrice(3) 16 (R J Price) *prom: rdn 1/2-way: wknd over 2f out* **16/1**		35
3002	10	3/4	**Orpen Wide (IRE)**[8] 5051 8-10-8 59..........(bt) MrOGarner(5) 9 (M C Chapman) *led: hdd over 4f out: wknd over 2f out* **16/1**		36
5053	11	2	**Opera Prince**[18] 5958 5-11-4 64..........(b) MrSWalker 8 (Lady Herries) *s.i.s: hld up: hdwy over 3f out: rdn and wknd over 2f out* **7/2**[1]		37
4012	12	8	**Pennfield Pirate**[32] 5530 3-10-5 62.............. MrRPooles(5) 7 (H Morrison) *prom: rdn over 3f out: wknd over 2f out* **9/2**[2]		20
0/00	13	1 3/4	**Bogside Dancer**[5] 6335 8-10-4 53.............. MrDGPrichard(3) 6 (John A Harris) *hld up: rdn 4f out: a in rr* **40/1**		8
06-0	14	nk	**Credential**[31] 5565 8-10-2 53 oh4.............. MrTGarner(5) 15 (John A Harris) *prom: rdn whn hmpd over 5f out: wknd 4f out* **50/1**		7
0/50	15	21	**Vintage Quest**[22] 5840 8-10-0 53 oh8.............. MrLLewis-Salter(7) 14 (D Burchell) *s.i.s: hdwy 8f out: rdn over 4f out: sn wknd* **66/1**		—

2m 19.86s (8.16) **Going Correction** +0.55s/f (Yiel)
WFA 3 from 4yo+ 6lb 15 Ran SP% **115.7**
Speed ratings (Par 103): **89,87,86,85,84 82,82,82,77,76 75,68,67,66,50**
toteswingers:1&2:£26.70, 1&3:£15.20, 2&3:£42.30 CSF £113.78 CT £1070.25 TOTE £10.70: £5.30, £13.40, £6.60; EX 119.10 Place 6 £87.87; Place 5 £30.31.
Owner G Mett Racing **Bred** Gainsborough Stud Management Ltd **Trained** Sheriff Hutton, N Yorks
■ Stewards' Enquiry : Mr D G Prichard three-day ban: used whip when out of contention (Oct 25,27,Nov 17)

FOCUS
Moderate form and not a race to dwell. Once again on this card, a positive ride paid dividends.
Pennfield Pirate Official explanation: trainer's rep said gelding was unsuited by the soft ground
T/Jkpt: £71,211.90 to a £1 stake. Pool:£551,641.62 - 5.50 winning tickets T/Plt: £37.40 to a £1 stake. Pool:£67,991.44 - 1,323.59 winning tickets T/Qpdt: £11.50 to a £1 stake. Pool:£4,011.89 - 257.85 winning tickets CR

5689 SALISBURY (R-H)
Wednesday, September 29

OFFICIAL GOING: Soft
Wind: quite strong against Weather: rain, heavy at times

6473 E B F MOLSON COORS MAIDEN STKS (DIV I) 1m
2:00 (2:04) (Class 4) 2-Y-O £4,533 (£1,348; £674; £336) **Stalls High**

Form				RPR
022	1		**Chain Lightning**[11] 6190 2-9-3 83.............. RichardHughes 1 (R Hannon) *in tch: hdwy to ld jst over 2f out: sn rdn: styd on wl* **15/8**[1]	83
0	2	1 1/2	**Census (IRE)**[17] 5985 2-9-3 0.............. RyanMoore 6 (R Hannon) *s.i.s: towards rr in centre: pushed along and stdy prog over 2f out: rdn to chse wnr jst over 2f out: styd on for clr 2nd but a being hld* **11/2**[3]	80
3	3	5	**Discoteca**[14] 6087 2-9-3 0.............. JimmyFortune 13 (A M Balding) *trckd ldr: chal 3f out: sn rdn: styd on same pce fr over 1f out* **5/1**[2]	69
0	4	4	**Argocat (IRE)**[12] 6149 2-9-3 0.............. NeilCallan 4 (P F I Cole) *mid-div: swtchd rt and stdy prog over 2f out: swtchd lft over 1f out: styd on same pce* **7/1**	60
	5	hd	**Great Shot** 2-9-3 0.............. LiamKeniry 3 (S Kirk) *chsd ldrs: rdn 3f out: styd on same pce fnl 2f* **50/1**	59
	6	11	**Kadoodd (IRE)** 2-9-3 0.............. ChrisCatlin 2 (M R Channon) *s.i.s: rn green and sn pushed along in rr: styd on past btn horses fr over 1f out: nvr trbld ldrs* **33/1**	35
00	7	1 1/2	**Drumadoon (IRE)**[35] 5413 2-9-3 0.............. DaneO'Neill 11 (J L Dunlop) *trckd ldr: chal 3f out: sn rdn: wknd 2f out* **100/1**	32
66	8	nse	**Blue Dazzler (IRE)**[123] 2547 2-9-3 0.............. PatCosgrave 9 (Mrs A J Perrett) *trckd ldr: rdn and ev ch over 2f out: wknd over 1f out* **15/2**	32
04	9	8	**Violet Ray (USA)**[19] 5916 2-9-0 0.............. EJMcNamara(3) 10 (R M Beckett) *trckd ldrs: pushed along over 4f out: wknd over 2f out* **14/1**	14
0	10	1/2	**Smart George**[20] 5878 2-9-3 0.............. AdamKirby 12 (C G Cox) *mid-div tl 3f out* **25/1**	13
	11	1/2	**Sum Satisfaction** 2-9-3 0.............. TadhgO'Shea 7 (Miss Tor Sturgis) *s.i.s: a towards rr* **80/1**	12
0	12	20	**Salaamie**[9] 6249 2-9-3 0.............. KierenFallon 8 (E A L Dunlop) *led tl rdn jst over 2f out: sn wknd* **16/1**	—

1m 49.06s (5.56) **Going Correction** +0.75s/f (Yiel) 12 Ran SP% **114.6**
Speed ratings (Par 97): **102,100,95,91,91 80,78,78,70,70 69,49**
toteswingers:1&2:£4.00, 1&3:£3.00, 2&3:£4.90 CSF £11.02 TOTE £3.00: £1.10, £2.40, £1.30; EX 13.90.
Owner Michael Pescod **Bred** Ecurie I M Fares **Trained** East Everleigh, Wilts

FOCUS
Rainfall of 5mm overnight followed by more up to the start of racing resulted in the official going being changed to soft.\n\x\x This maiden has produced some fair sorts, but by far the best recent winner was subsequent Oaks heroine Look Here. The field raced up the stands' rail and the time was not surprisingly slow. The form should be fine.

NOTEBOOK
Chain Lightning set a decent standard off a mark of 83 and put his experience to good use to get off the mark in comfortable fashion. This was his first try on a soft surface and he handled it well enough. (op 2-1 tchd 9-4)
Census(IRE), a 50,000gns son of an unraced mare, improved for his debut and was the only one to give his stable companion any sort of race. He will probably appreciate a better surface but should be capable of winning one of these. (op 8-1)
Discoteca ran a promising race for one bred to be much better over further on his debut over this trip. He travelled well enough for a long way but could only keep on at the one pace. (op 4-1 tchd 11-2)
Argocat(IRE), a 105,000euros first foal from a family of middle-distance/stayers, had finished well beaten on his debut over 1m on good/fast ground. He stayed on from the rear without reaching a challenging position. (op 13-2 tchd 8-1)
Great Shot ◆, a half-brother to a 1m winner out of multiple scorer at around this trip, from one of the owner's good families, showed promise on this debut despite looking in need of the experience. He should come on a good deal for the run.
Kadoodd(IRE), a 120,000gns half-brother to four winners from the family of a Cheveley Park winner, missed the break and only stayed on past beaten rivals. He is another who should benefit from the experience. (op 50-1)
Blue Dazzler(IRE) has a middle-distance pedigree but had shown promise in the spring. Making his reappearance after four months off, he showed ability again and now qualifies for handicaps. (op 17-2)

6474 E B F MOLSON COORS MAIDEN STKS (DIV II) 1m
2:30 (2:37) (Class 4) 2-Y-O £4,533 (£1,348; £674; £336) **Stalls High**

Form				RPR
	1		**Pivotman** 2-9-3 0.............. NeilCallan 5 (Mrs A J Perrett) *travelled wl: trckd ldrs: led over 1f out: pushed clr: readily* **10/1**	82+
	2	4	**Carlton House (USA)** 2-9-3 0.............. RyanMoore 3 (Sir Michael Stoute) *hld up towards rr: hdwy 3f out: rdn 2f out: styd on to go 2nd ins fnl f: no ch w wnr* **6/1**[3]	73
3	3	2 1/2	**Zain Shamardal (IRE)**[27] 5690 2-9-3 0.............. KierenFallon 6 (B J Meehan) *led: rdn and hdd over 1f out: sn hld: no ex whn lost 2nd ins fnl f* **6/4**[1]	67
0	4	6	**Tileyf (IRE)**[30] 5582 2-8-12 0.............. JohnFahy(5) 11 (C G Cox) *prom: rdn over 3f out: hld whn edgd rt over 1f out: fdd ent fnl f* **100/1**	54
	5	1/2	**Experimentalist** 2-9-3 0.............. TravisBlock 12 (H Morrison) *mid-div: pushed along and hdwy 3f out: effrt 2f out: fdd ent fnl f* **66/1**	53
	6	3/4	**Whiplash Willie** 2-9-3 0.............. LiamKeniry 9 (A M Balding) *sn pushed along in rr: swtchd rt and styd on steadily fr over 1f out: nvr trbld ldrs* **28/1**	51+
	7	3/4	**Albert Bridge** 2-9-0 0.............. EJMcNamara(3) 10 (R M Beckett) *sn swtchd to stands' side rails: hld up towards rr: rdn over 2f out: little imp* **12/1**	50
	8	4 1/2	**Xclaim** 2-9-3 0.............. AdamKirby 8 (C G Cox) *chsd ldrs: rdn over 4f out: wknd wl over 1f out* **22/1**	40
05	9	7	**Danceyourselfdizzy (IRE)**[12] 6146 2-9-3 0.............. RichardHughes 2 (R Hannon) *trckd ldrs: rdn over 4f out: wknd wl 2f out* **8/1**	24
	10	9	**Diamond Bob** 2-9-3 0.............. DaneO'Neill 7 (E A L Dunlop) *hld up towards rr: rdn over 2f out: sn wknd* **66/1**	5
0	11	6	**Fleeting Tiger**[47] 5033 2-9-3 0.............. JimmyFortune 4 (J L Dunlop) *prom tl short of room over 3f out: sn wknd* **66/1**	—
00	12	19	**Lejaam**[20] 5878 2-9-3 0.............. TadhgO'Shea 1 (J L Dunlop) *sn trcking ldrs: rdn over 3f out: wknd over 2f out* **4/1**[2]	—

1m 49.56s (6.06) **Going Correction** +0.75s/f (Yiel) 12 Ran SP% **115.4**
Speed ratings (Par 97): **99,95,92,86,86 85,84,80,73,64 58,39**
toteswingers:1&2:£11.30, 1&3:£4.80, 2&3:£2.20 CSF £64.23 TOTE £16.10: £4.30, £1.40, £1.10; EX 103.40.
Owner John Connolly **Bred** Cheveley Park Stud Ltd **Trained** Pulborough, W Sussex

FOCUS
The second division of this maiden was run 0.50secs slower than the opener. Again they came up the stands' rail and finished well strung out, with the winner showing a good attitude to go clear and a promising start from the runner-up, although it is not easy to set the level.

NOTEBOOK
Pivotman ◆, a 190,000gns third foal of a 7f winner from a good Cheveley Park Stud family, travelled well behind the leaders and galloped on strongly once hitting the front entering the final furlong. He should improve for the run and looks the type to go on to better things, especially next season. (op 18-1)
Carlton House(USA) ◆, a half-brother to four winners at up to 1m, was another debutant to show plenty. He was not given a hard race in the conditions and this Derby entry should have no trouble winning a maiden. (op 9-2 tchd 4-1)
Zain Shamardal(IRE) had made a promising debut here on a sound surface, closing on the two leaders at the finish. He set the level but, despite making much of the running, did not look entirely happy in the conditions and tired once headed by the winner. He should do better back on a sound surface. (op 8-11)
Tileyf(IRE) started at long odds when well behind on his debut at Bath over this trip, had clearly learnt for that experience and showed up for much of the way. He can make his mark in handicaps once qualified.
Experimentalist, a 22,000gns half-brother to seven winners at up to 1m, including Ringmoor Down, ran with promise on this debut despite looking green, and has races in him. (op 50-1)
Whiplash Willie, a half-brother to a winner at 2m out of a 1m2f winner from the family of Kayf Tara, stayed on from the rear and should come into his own next season (tchd 25-1)
Albert Bridge, a 60,000gns second foal from the family of Alborada, is another who will do better with another winter over his back. (op 28-1)
Danceyourselfdizzy(IRE) had put up modest but promising efforts in maidens over 6f on good. Although up in trip, that was not the reason for his defeat, as he was struggling from halfway and did not appear to handle the conditions. (op 11-1)
Lejaam was well-backed but was another who did not appear to handle the conditions. He had improved on his debut when mid-division on his second start over 1m at Doncaster but dropped right away here. (op 11-1)

6475 EUROPEAN BREEDERS' FUND NOVICE STKS 6f 212y
3:05 (3:05) (Class 3) 2-Y-O £6,476 (£1,927) **Stalls High**

Form				RPR
2132	1		**Big Issue (IRE)**[22] 5831 2-9-3 107.............. RichardHughes 5 (R Hannon) *mde all: qckند pce 3f out: drew clr over 1f out: unchal* **1/9**[1]	102+
361	2	11	**Highlife Dancer**[72] 4208 2-9-0 78.............. CathyGannon 6 (M R Channon) *chsd wnr: rdn 3f out: nvr gng pce to get on terms: fdd fr over 1f out* **6/1**[2]	67

1m 35.06s (6.06) **Going Correction** +0.75s/f (Yiel) 2 Ran SP% **104.3**
Speed ratings (Par 99): **95,82**
TOTE £1.10.
Owner Malih L Al Basti **Bred** Tinnakill Bloodstock & P Lawlor **Trained** East Everleigh, Wilts

FOCUS
An uncompetitve novice stakes, with the winner thrashing his only rival.

NOTEBOOK
Big Issue(IRE), whose trainer had been responsible for two of the previous four winner, made all the running and had the race in safe keeping some way from home. He is likely to go for the Horris Hill next.

Highlife Dancer had scored on his previous start but his form was on fast ground and, having his first race for over ten weeks, was no match for the winner, who was rated over two stones higher.

6476 FRANCIS CLARK CHARTERED ACCOUNTANTS CLAIMING STKS 1m 1f 198y
3:40 (3:40) (Class 5) 3-4-Y-O £3,238 (£963; £481; £240) Stalls High

Form RPR
05-5 1 **State Visit**[108] 3002 3-8-4 62 ow3 (b) JamesRogers(7) 8 70
(W R Muir) *mde all: jnd 3f out: wandered u.p fr 2f out: jst hld on* 10/1
6036 2 *nse* **Sohcahtoa (IRE)**[12] 6152 4-9-8 80 (b) RichardHughes 3 75
(R Hannon) *trckd ldrs: jnd ldrs over 2f out: rdn over 1f out: lightly bmpd ent fnl f: kpt on: jst failed* 15/8[2]
4521 3 2 1/4 **Indian Valley (USA)**[14] 6093 3-8-3 74 AdamBeschizza(5) 4 62
(Rae Guest) *hld up in last trio: hdwy 3f out: effrt 2f out: styd on same pce fnl f* 5/4[1]
5344 4 1/2 **Easy Terms**[17] 5986 3-8-4 64 ChrisCatlin 7 57
(B R Millman) *hld up last: hdwy 3f out: effrt whn clr run 2f out: styd on same pce fnl f* 13/2[3]
5004 5 4 **Sounds Of Thunder**[18] 5959 3-7-9 61 (b) RichardRowe(7) 6 47
(H J L Dunlop) *hld up in last trio: hdwy over 3f out: effrt over 2f out: wknd over 1f out* 16/1
6 6 5 **Raghdaan**[30] 5610 3-8-8 0 CathyGannon 2 43
(P W Hiatt) *trckd ldr: jnd wnr 3f out: rdn and ev ch 2f out: sn wknd* 50/1
600- 7 49 **Richardlionheart (USA)**[317] 6966 4-9-1 42 LiamKeniry 1 —
(M Madgwick) *trckd ldrs: rdn over 4f out: sn btn: t.o* 100/1

2m 17.13s (7.23) **Going Correction** +0.75s/f (Yiel)
WFA 3 from 4yo 6lb 7 Ran SP% **110.5**
Speed ratings (Par 103): **101,100,99,98,95 91,52**
toteswingers:1&2:£3.60, 1&3:£3.10, 2&3:£1.40 CSF £27.26 TOTE £9.50: £2.80, £1.20; EX 33.70.State Visit was claimed by Miss A. Weaver for £8,000.
Owner The Stately Partnership **Bred** Mr & Mrs G Middlebrook **Trained** Lambourn, Berks

FOCUS
A typical claimer featuring horses of varying levels of ability and a close finish.

6477 AXA WEALTH CONDITIONS STKS 6f
4:15 (4:15) (Class 2) 2-Y-O £7,477 (£2,239) Stalls High

Form RPR
0222 1 **Galtymore Lad**[20] 5880 2-9-8 109 KierenFallon 4 103+
(M R Channon) *little slowly away: chsd ldr: led 2f out: pushed clr: comf* 8/15[1]
2152 2 12 **Avonmore Star**[51] 4903 2-9-1 94 RichardHughes 2 60+
(R Hannon) *led: rdn and hdd 2f out: sn hld: eased ent fnl f* 6/4[2]

1m 19.12s (4.32) **Going Correction** +0.75s/f (Yiel) 2 Ran SP% **105.2**
Speed ratings (Par 101): **101,85**
TOTE £1.50.
Owner M Channon **Bred** Bearstone Stud **Trained** West Ilsley, Berks

FOCUS
A conditions stakes which has been dominated in recent seasons by local yards. The winner was clearly much the best but the race told us little from a form perspective.

NOTEBOOK
Galtymore Lad was left as the odds-on favourite. He got a good lead from his sole rival and, once he gained the upper hand 2f out, he soon went clear, despite not looking altogether happy on the ground. This was a well-deserved success after finishing runner-up three times, in a Listed race and then two valuable sales races. He is likely to go for the Prix Eclipse next month. (op 1-2 tchd 4-7)
Avonmore Star, twice a winner, including over C&D, was returning from a break of just over seven weeks and had never encountered ground this soft. He made the running but had no answer when the winner went past, and was soon eased. (tchd 11-8)

6478 WOOD BMW H'CAP 6f
4:50 (4:53) (Class 4) (0-85,84) 3-Y-O+ £4,209 (£1,252; £625; £312) Stalls High

Form RPR
4514 1 **Mirza**[54] 4806 3-9-5 82 RichardHughes 10 94
(Rae Guest) *trckd ldrs in centre gp: rdn over 2f out: led fnl 100yds: r.o* 13/2[3]
1130 2 1/2 **Poppanan (USA)**[83] 3815 4-8-11 77 AdamBeschizza(5) 1 87
(S Dow) *mid-div: nrest standside of centre gp: hdwy 2f out: rdn to ld over 1f out: hdd fnl 100yds: no ex* 10/1
2130 3 2 1/4 **Russian Rave**[13] 6113 4-8-11 72 RichardKingscote 9 75
(J G Portman) *hld up towards rr of centre gp: hdwy 3f out: sn rdn: styd on fnl f: wnt 3rd towards fin* 12/1
4300 4 1 1/4 **Rapid Water**[18] 5966 4-9-1 76 (b) JimmyFortune 14 75
(A M Balding) *overall ldr on far side: rdn over 2f out: hdd over 1f out: no ex* 15/2
0650 5 1 3/4 **Macdillon**[17] 5995 4-9-4 79 (p) ChrisCatlin 3 72
(W S Kittow) *prom in centre gp: rdn 2f out: kpt on same pce* 16/1
3605 6 *shd* **Edgewater (IRE)**[9] 6253 3-9-0 77 SimonWhitworth 8 70
(J Akehurst) *wnt lft s: sn pushed along towards rr of centre gp: styd on ent fnl f: nrst fin* 20/1
000 7 3/4 **Stevie Gee (IRE)**[20] 5884 6-9-0 75 (p) CathyGannon 7 65
(Ian Williams) *queezed out s: towards rr of centre gp: rdn over 3f out: no imp tl styd on ins fnl f* 12/1
004 8 3/4 **Perfect Flight**[17] 5995 5-9-4 79 KirstyMilczarek 16 67
(M Blanshard) *restrained s: racd far side: rdn 3f out: nvr on terms* 12/1
5150 9 1 **Lujeanie**[20] 5884 4-9-6 81 (p) NeilCallan 17 66
(D K Ivory) *chsd ldrs on far side: rdn over 3f out: wknd fnl f* 12/1
2332 10 *nk* **Lochan Mor**[15] 6048 4-8-12 80 IanBurns(7) 18 64
(M L W Bell) *chsd ldrs on far side: struggling whn hung to centre gp 3f out: wknd fnl f* 10/3[1]
4500 11 1 **Spanish Bounty**[32] 5528 5-9-4 79 TadhgO'Shea 12 60
(J G Portman) *led centre gp: rdn over 2f out: hdd over 1f out: sn wknd* 16/1
0114 12 6 **Imperial Delight**[88] 3696 3-9-5 82 DaneO'Neill 6 44
(H Candy) *wnt rt s: chsd ldrs in centre tl wknd 2f out* 6/1[2]
20-0 13 2 1/4 **Romanticize**[121] 2601 4-8-11 72 LiamKeniry 11 26
(Dr J D Scargill) *chsd ldrs in centre gp tl 3f out* 25/1

1m 18.69s (3.89) **Going Correction** +0.75s/f (Yiel)
WFA 3 from 4yo+ 2lb 13 Ran SP% **122.7**
Speed ratings (Par 105): **104,103,100,98,96 96,95,94,92,92 91,83,80**
toteswingers:1&2:£12.90, 1&3:£19.70, 2&3:£22.30 CSF £72.16 CT £801.79 TOTE £6.30: £1.90, £1.80, £4.40; EX 70.70.
Owner C J Mills **Bred** C J Mills **Trained** Newmarket, Suffolk

FOCUS
A tight-looking sprint handicap that often falls to a battle-hardened sort but this time proved an exception. They ended up racing centre to far side and the time was only 0.43secs faster than the preceding juvenile match and the form is rated around the placed horses.

6479 BEGBIES TRAYNOR GROUP H'CAP 1m
5:20 (5:21) (Class 6) (0-65,65) 3-Y-O+ £2,590 (£770; £385; £192) Stalls High

Form RPR
5001 1 **Astrodonna**[15] 6062 5-8-13 62 AshleyMorgan(5) 9 73
(M H Tompkins) *hld up towards rr: smooth hdwy over 2f out: jnd ldr over 1f out: rdn ent fnl f: led fnl 100yds: kpt on wl* 12/1
2441 2 1/2 **Sweet Secret**[36] 5384 3-9-2 64 (b[1]) RichardHughes 8 74
(R Hannon) *trckd ldrs: rdn 2f out: led over 1f out: hdd fnl 100yds: kpt on but no ex* 6/1[2]
4440 3 6 **Hulcote Rose (IRE)**[7] 6291 3-9-3 65 LiamKeniry 16 61
(S Kirk) *hld up towards rr: hdwy over 2f out: sn trcking ldrs: rdn over 1f out: kpt on same pce* 7/1
6105 4 1 3/4 **Kiss A Prince**[18] 5964 4-9-7 65 (b) JimmyFortune 5 57
(D K Ivory) *s.i.s: towards rr: rdn 2f out: styd on past btn horses ins fnl f: nvr trbld ldrs* 7/1
1236 5 *nk* **Daddy's Gift (IRE)**[31] 5555 4-9-1 62 PatrickHills(3) 15 53
(R Hannon) *w ldr: rdn into narrow advantage over 2f out: hdd over 1f out: wknd fnl 120yds* 16/1
2636 6 1/2 **Gallego**[4] 6375 8-8-11 61 ow1 HollyHall(7) 1 52
(R J Price) *s.i.s: sn swtchd to far side rails: towards rr: hdwy 4f out: effrt 3f out: kpt on same pce fnl 2f* 11/2[1]
6314 7 1 1/4 **Leelu**[20] 5889 4-9-2 60 CathyGannon 4 47
(D W P Arbuthnot) *mid-div: effrt 3f out: wknd jst over 1f out* 13/2[3]
4340 8 1 **Dichoh**[21] 5866 7-9-2 60 (v) ChrisCatlin 10 45
(M Madgwick) *mid-div: rdn over 2f out: wknd ent fnl f* 14/1
5653 9 3 3/4 **Flapper (IRE)**[14] 6085 4-9-7 65 (p) PatCosgrave 3 42
(J W Hills) *mid-div: rdn over 2f out: wknd ent fnl f* 15/2
5634 10 *nk* **Treasure Way**[20] 5887 3-9-2 64 RichardKingscote 13 40
(P R Chamings) *wnt lft s: sn led: rdn and narrowly hdd over 2f out: wknd fnl f* 13/2[3]
0-00 11 32 **Doric Echo**[91] 3557 4-9-2 60 (v[1]) JamieGoldstein 12 —
(C P Morlock) *trckd ldrs tl wknd over 3f out: t.o* 28/1

1m 50.27s (6.77) **Going Correction** +0.75s/f (Yiel)
WFA 3 from 4yo+ 4lb 11 Ran SP% **116.8**
Speed ratings (Par 101): **96,95,89,87,87 86,85,84,80,80 48**
toteswingers:1&2:£2.30, 1&3:£19.20, 2&3:£10.50 CSF £81.80 CT £560.01 TOTE £16.00: £5.70, £3.00, £3.80; EX 31.70.
Owner Mystic Meg Limited **Bred** Mystic Meg Limited **Trained** Newmarket, Suffolk

FOCUS
A modest but competitive handicap and once again they raced centre to far side. The time was slower than both divisions of the juvenile maiden, suggesting the rain through the afternoon had really softened the ground. The winner is rated close to his best.
Gallego Official explanation: jockey said gelding was unsuited by the soft ground
Treasure Way Official explanation: jockey said filly was unsuited by the soft ground

6480 BOOKER CASH & CARRY H'CAP 1m 6f 21y
5:55 (5:55) (Class 5) (0-75,75) 3-Y-O+ £3,238 (£963; £481; £240) Stalls Far side

Form RPR
3/06 1 **Pocketwood**[84] 3780 8-9-8 67 RichardKingscote 13 79
(A J Lidderdale) *led for 2f: trckd ldrs: pushed along 5f out: rdn to ld over 2f out: clr ent fnl f: v easily* 20/1
2322 2 6 **Mohanad (IRE)**[20] 5888 4-9-6 65 JamieGoldstein 2 68
(Miss Sheena West) *mid-div: hdwy over 3f out: ev ch 2f out: rdn and sn no ch w wnr: styd on same pce:* 10/1
3154 3 1/2 **Minikin (IRE)**[15] 6055 3-9-4 73 TadhgO'Shea 7 75
(H Morrison) *led after 2f: rdn whn hung lft and hdd over 2f out: styd on same pce* 7/1[3]
2240 4 2 1/2 **Gaselee (USA)**[110] 2938 4-9-2 66 AdamBeschizza(5) 8 64
(Rae Guest) *t.k.h early: sn trcking ldrs: rdn 3f out: lost pl 2f out: styd on again ins fnl f* 12/1
0-12 5 *hd* **Hawridge Star (IRE)**[17] 5996 8-10-0 73 RichardHughes 12 71
(W S Kittow) *hld up towards rr: hdwy over 3f out: rdn over 2f out: wknd fnl f* 2/1[1]
6505 6 11 **Street Entertainer (IRE)**[12] 6152 3-9-1 70 NeilCallan 5 53
(Mrs A J Perrett) *mid-div: hdwy over 3f out: rdn to chse ldrs over 2f out: wknd over 1f out* 7/1[3]
0630 7 1 1/2 **King Supreme (IRE)**[27] 5679 5-9-8 70 PatrickHills(3) 11 51
(R Hannon) *hld up towards rr: pushed along 5f out: hdwy over 3f out: wknd 2f out* 25/1
4304 8 30 **Elvira Madigan**[33] 5467 3-9-0 69 (p) JimmyFortune 6 —
(A M Balding) *trckd ldrs for 6f: mid-div: rdn and hdwy over 3f out: wknd 2f out: eased* 15/2
2232 9 2 1/2 **Saggiatore**[14] 6084 3-9-6 75 DaneO'Neill 3 —
(E A L Dunlop) *mid-div: hdwy over 4f out: sn rdn: wknd 3f out: eased* 11/2[2]
-114 10 38 **Russian Music (USA)**[252] 232 5-9-7 66 ChrisCatlin 1 —
(Ian Williams) *a towards rr: lost tch qckly 5f out: virtually p.u* 12/1

3m 16.77s (9.37) **Going Correction** +0.75s/f (Yiel)
WFA 3 from 4yo+ 10lb 10 Ran SP% **118.6**
Speed ratings (Par 103): **103,99,99,97,97 91,90,73,72,50**
toteswingers:1&2:£70.70, 1&3:£49.50, 2&3:£17.60 CSF £208.74 CT £1555.30 TOTE £33.40: £7.20, £2.10, £1.80; EX 416.70 Place 6 £25.16; Place 5 £19.88.
Owner The Sw1ft Buck Partnership **Bred** M J Lewin **Trained** Eastbury, Berks

FOCUS
Another competitive event with only 7lb covering the field on official ratings in this staying contest but a surprise winner. The runner-up up to recent form is the best guide.
T/Plt: £26.80 to a £1 stake. Pool:£43,232.75 - 1,176.77 winning tickets T/Qpdt: £24.20 to a £1 stake. Pool:£2,518.75 - 76.77 winning tickets TM

6481 - 6486a (Foreign Racing) - See Raceform Interactive

6344 MAISONS-LAFFITTE (R-H)
Wednesday, September 29

OFFICIAL GOING: Turf: very soft

6487a PRIX DE THOIRY (CLAIMER) (3YO) (TURF) 6f (S)
12:20 (12:00) 3-Y-O £9,292 (£3,716; £2,787; £1,858; £929)

RPR
1 **Auendon (GER)**[141] 3-9-1 0 (b) GaetanMasure 2 73
(Uwe Ostmann, Germany) 111/10

2 8 **Mark Of Brazil (FR)**16 3-9-2 0 DominiqueBoeuf 12 48
(F Chappet, France) 9/13

3 1 **Safe Steps (FR)**126 3-8-11 0 (b1) IoritzMendizabal 5 40
(Mme Pia Brandt, France) 29/1

4 1 **Flouncing (IRE)**20 5890 3-8-11 0 DavyBonilla 4 37
(W J Haggas) *broke wl to be prom: rdn 1 1/2f out to chse ldr: nt qckn: styd on* 14/51

5 3/4 **Johnnycometomamie (FR)**28 3-8-6 0 (p) CharlesBegue(5) 16 34
(U Suter, France) 44/1

6 nk **Blue Sparkle (IRE)**42 3-8-8 0 GregoryBenoist 1 30
(Mme J Bidgood, Spain) 7/12

7 3/4 **Shine A Line (FR)**29 3-8-11 0 (b) MaximeGuyon 20 31
(U Suter, France) 14/1

8 1/2 **Paschmina (FR)**29 3-8-5 0 MorganDelalande(3) 6 26
(C Lerner, France) 22/1

9 nse **Dikta Melody (FR)**99 3-8-11 0 (p) StephanePasquier 3 29
(P Demercastel, France) 22/1

10 1 1/2 **Vianello (IRE)**42 3-8-13 0 (b) TheoBachelot(5) 9 31
(P Schiergen, Germany) 16/1

0 **Calvero (FR)**16 3-9-2 0 (p) SebastienMaillot 14 —
(Mlle Valerie Boussin, France) 78/1

0 **Whipchip (IRE)**482 3-8-11 0 MickaelBarzalona 7 —
(U Suter, France) 120/1

0 **Orestias (IRE)**16 3-9-2 0 OlivierPeslier 15 —
(C Laffon-Parias, France) 19/1

0 **Diamond Max (GER)**10 3-8-11 0 GeraldMosse 11 —
(Manfred Hofer, Germany) 23/1

0 **Basle**17 6000 3-8-3 0 AnthonyCaramanolis(5) 18 —
(Miss Gay Kelleway) *broke wl in centre of trck to be prom on far side: rdn 2f out: nt qckn: no ex fnl f: eased fnl 100yds* 20/1

0 **Diplomatic (FR)**16 3-9-4 0 (b) JohanVictoire 19 —
(Mme C Head-Maarek, France) 40/1

0 **Silver Black (USA)**16 3-9-8 0 AnthonyCrastus 10 —
(C Boutin, France) 17/1

0 **Wisterya (FR)**55 3-9-1 0 SylvainRuis 8 —
(Mlle S-V Tarrou, France) 84/1

0 **On Earth**60 3-8-8 0 (b1) Christophe-PatriceLemaire 13 —
(P Bary, France) 17/1

0 **Dessert Flower (IRE)** 3-8-11 0 (b) AurelienLemaitre(4) 17 —
(F Poulsen, France) 136/1

1m 14.0s (0.60) **20** Ran SP% **115.4**
WIN (incl. 1 euro stake): 12.10. PLACES: 3.90, 3.30, 8.00. DF: 49.00. SF: 113.80.
Owner Gestut Auenquelle **Bred** Gestut Auenquelle **Trained** Germany

NOTEBOOK
Flouncing(IRE) weakened in the soft ground and will be happier back on a sounder surface.

6174 AYR (L-H)
Thursday, September 30

OFFICIAL GOING: Good to soft (soft in places on round course)
Back straight and home bend out 4m, home straight out 6m from innermost line adding 12yds to distances on round course.
Wind: Light, half against Weather: Cloudy

6488 BEAZLEY MARINE 2010 MEDIAN AUCTION MAIDEN STKS 6f
2:20 (2:21) (Class 5) 2-Y-O £2,719 (£809; £404; £202) **Stalls** Low

Form RPR

1 **Iron Range (IRE)** 2-9-3 0 RichardMullen 7 85+
(E S McMahon) *trckd ldrs gng wl: shkn up to ld over 1f out: sn clr: readily* 4/51

325 2 5 **Maverik**31 5594 2-9-3 72 PhillipMakin 6 70
(M Dods) *w ldr: led over 3f out to over 1f out: no ch w wnr* 7/22

05 3 3 1/4 **I Got You Babe (IRE)**15 6075 2-8-9 0 KierenFox(3) 1 55
(R C Guest) *t.k.h: in tch: effrt wl over 1f out: sn no imp* 22/1

002 4 9 **Marina Belle**10 6240 2-8-12 0 JoeFanning 3 28
(M Johnston) *trckd ldrs tl rdn and wknd 2f out* 11/1

0 5 5 **Lightning Cloud (IRE)**13 6138 2-9-3 0 PaulHanagan 4 18
(K A Ryan) *led to over 3f out: sn rdn: wknd fr 2f out* 8/13

0 6 13 **Face East (USA)**13 6138 2-9-3 0 PJMcDonald 2 —
(A Berry) *missed break: bhd: struggling 3f out: sn btn* 125/1

1m 14.07s (0.47) **Going Correction** +0.10s/f (Good) **6** Ran SP% **102.4**
Speed ratings (Par 95): **100,93,89,77,70 53**
toteswingers:1&2 £1.10, 2&3 £4.90, 1&3 £3.20 CSF £2.98 TOTE £1.50: £1.10, £2.10; EX 3.40.
Owner J C Fretwell **Bred** Rathasker Stud **Trained** Lichfield, Staffs

FOCUS
After a wet week the ground was described as good to soft, soft in places on the round course. Probably just an ordinary maiden, which was weakened further with the withdrawal of Norton Girl, who had shown clear ability on her debut. That said, it was run at an even gallop.

NOTEBOOK
Iron Range(IRE), very well backed beforehand, travelled well and clearly knew his job. He can go on from this fine performance. (op 6-4, tchd 7-4 in places)
Maverik is the best guide to the form. Rated 72, he has shown ability on all four starts now and, although starting to look a little exposed, a small maiden at this time of the year can come his way. (op 4-1)
I Got You Babe(IRE) is going the right way. Coming from a yard going well, she appeals as the type to continue to progress in nurseries in due course. (op 14-1)
Marina Belle may have found this race coming too soon after her Hamilton run. (op 13-2)

6489 WISECALL CLAIMS ASSISTANCE NURSERY 5f
2:55 (2:55) (Class 5) (0-75,70) 2-Y-O £2,590 (£770; £385; £192) **Stalls** Low

Form RPR

3401 1 **Heartbreak**28 5683 2-9-7 70 PaulHanagan 2 74
(R A Fahey) *mde virtually all: rdn and styd on gamely ins fnl f* 3/12

2136 2 1 **Saxonette**11 6220 2-8-8 60 JamesSullivan(3) 9 60
(Miss L A Perratt) *trckd ldrs: effrt and ev ch over 1f out: chsd wnr ins fnl f: r.o* 16/1

621 3 1 3/4 **Scantily Clad (IRE)**16 6045 2-9-7 70 RichardMullen 8 64
(E S McMahon) *disp ld to 1f out: rdn and kpt on same pce last 100yds* 8/111

6464 4 2 1/2 **Rothesay Chancer**13 6139 2-8-11 63 GaryBartley(3) 1 48
(J S Goldie) *bhd: rdn and outpcd over 2f out: rallied ins fnl f: r.o* 7/13

4042 5 shd **Novabridge**18 5987 2-9-0 63 (b) PhillipMakin 4 48
(A B Haynes) *prom: rdn and outpcd 2f out: n.d after* 11/1

15U0 6 3/4 **Misty Morn**117 2757 2-8-9 61 IanBrennan(3) 6 43
(A D Brown) *trckd ldrs tl wandered and wknd 2f out* 40/1

6360 7 11 **Press Release**20 5921 2-9-0 63 (t) RichardKingscote 7 5
(Tom Dascombe) *dwlt: hld up bhd ldng gp: struggling over 2f out: sn btn* 40/1

61.47 secs (1.37) **Going Correction** +0.10s/f (Good) **7** Ran SP% **114.5**
Speed ratings (Par 95): **93,91,88,84,84 83,65**
toteswingers:1&2 £6.70, 2&3 £4.70, 1&3 £1.70 CSF £46.86 CT £66.09 TOTE £3.20: £1.80, £5.80; EX 41.20.
Owner T G & Mrs M E Holdcroft **Bred** Bearstone Stud **Trained** Musley Bank, N Yorks

FOCUS
A sound pace for this nursery and a taking performance by the well-bred winner. The first three pulled nicely clear.

NOTEBOOK
Heartbreak, having his first try on this ground, appeared to handle it well and there are more races to be won with him before the season is out, as the handicapper shouldn't be too harsh on him for this victory. (op 7-2 tchd 4-1)
Saxonette, a winner of a 6f seller for Mick Channon, was having her third start for current connections and this was her best effort so far. A return to 6f should see her back in the winner's enclosure in similar company. (op 14-1 tchd 18-1)
Scantily Clad(IRE), very well backed beforehand, travelled well throughout but just failed to pick up. It's possible she found the ground too testing, and she can bounce back in due course. (op 4-5 tchd 4-6 and 5-6 in places)
Rothesay Chancer, like his half-sister Rothesay Dancer, stayed on all too late. That said, he looks the type to do better over 6f and is at the right end of the handicap to lose his maiden tag. (op 8-1)
Novabridge, a winner of his maiden on heavy ground, was well held and is starting to look exposed. (op 10-1 tchd 12-1)

6490 INTECHNOLOGY CHALLENGE IN ASSOCIATION WITH GILES INSURANCE H'CAP 5f
3:30 (3:31) (Class 6) (0-58,56) 3-Y-O+ £2,047 (£604; £302) **Stalls** Low

Form RPR

600 1 **Avertuoso**26 5760 6-8-12 55 (v) AdamCarter(7) 10 73
(B Smart) *cl up: rdn to ld over 1f out: drew clr ins fnl f* 6/1

4026 2 4 1/2 **Sharp Shoes**34 5485 3-9-0 51 (p) PhillipMakin 8 53
(Mrs A Duffield) *led tl rdn and hdd over 1f out: kpt on ins fnl f: no ch w wnr* 6/1

3440 3 1 1/4 **Divine Spirit**24 5817 9-8-11 50 PatrickDonaghy(3) 7 47
(M Dods) *midfield: drvn 1/2-way: hdwy over 1f out: no imp ins fnl f* 5/12

216 4 2 1/4 **Pavement Games**12 6206 3-8-11 51 KierenFox(3) 5 40
(R C Guest) *stdd s: bhd tl hdwy appr fnl f: nvr rchd ldrs* 11/23

30R0 5 1/2 **Kristen Jane (USA)**4 6392 3-8-7 47 JamesSullivan(3) 1 34
(Miss L A Perratt) *chsd ldrs tl rdn and wknd over 1f out* 25/1

0045 6 2 **Hold On Tiger (IRE)**36 5410 3-9-5 56 PaulHanagan 12 36
(N G Richards) *prom tl rdn and wknd over 1f out* 7/21

2050 7 1 1/2 **Areeg (IRE)**14 6103 3-8-4 48 VictorSantos(7) 9 23
(A Berry) *dwlt: sn midfield: edgd lft and outpcd 2f out: n.d after* 25/1

0000 8 1 1/4 **Joyeaux**20 5926 8-8-12 48 FrannyNorton 11 18
(Ollie Pears) *towards rr and sn drvn along: no imp fr 1/2-way* 8/1

6656 9 3 1/2 **Dower Glen**4 6392 3-8-9 53 ShirleyTeasdale(7) 4 11
(V P Donoghue) *in tch tl wknd fr 1/2-way* 14/1

0-00 10 1 **The Magic Of Rio**232 477 4-8-6 45 KellyHarrison(3) 6 —
(Peter Grayson) *cl up tl rdn and wknd over 1f out* 40/1

0000 11 1/2 **Officer Mor (USA)**39 5331 4-8-9 45 DuranFentiman 3 —
(Mrs Dianne Sayer) *bhd and sn drvn along: nvr on terms* 20/1

60.43 secs (0.33) **Going Correction** +0.10s/f (Good)
WFA 3 from 4yo+ 1lb **11** Ran SP% **115.5**
Speed ratings (Par 101): **101,93,91,88,87 84,81,79,74,72 71**
toteswingers:1&2 £8.20, 2&3 £6.50, 1&3 £7.00 CSF £39.01 CT £193.78 TOTE £6.00: £2.40, £1.30, £1.70; EX 53.70.
Owner Crossfields Racing **Bred** P A Mason **Trained** Hambleton, N Yorks

FOCUS
A run-of-the-mill sprint for horses rated 46-58. It was run at a sound pace.

6491 BUD AND JOE PIERONI MEMORIAL H'CAP (DIV I) 6f
4:05 (4:05) (Class 5) (0-70,70) 3-Y-O+ £2,266 (£674; £337; £168) **Stalls** Low

Form RPR

3405 1 **Gracie's Gift (IRE)**12 6210 8-8-11 63 (v1) KierenFox(3) 6 70
(R C Guest) *cl up: rdn and led over 1f out: hld on wl ins fnl f* 6/13

4260 2 nk **Cawdor (IRE)**5 6371 4-9-4 70 JamesSullivan(3) 12 76
(Mrs L Stubbs) *prom: drvn and outpcd 2f out: styd on wl ins fnl f* 12/1

2300 3 nk **Monte Mayor One**11 6226 3-8-10 61 PaulHanagan 10 66
(P Monteith) *trckd ldrs: effrt and rdn over 1f out: kpt on u.p ins fnl f* 11/1

6053 4 1 1/4 **Tawzeea (IRE)**8 6295 5-9-1 64 PhillipMakin 9 65
(M Dods) *hld up bhd ldrs: drvn over 1f out: kpt on same pce ins fnl f* 5/21

6043 5 1 1/2 **Bid For Gold**14 6110 6-8-8 57 (p) AndrewElliott 7 53
(Jedd O'Keeffe) *prom: drvn and outpcd over 2f out: rallied over 1f out: no imp ins fnl f* 6/13

0000 6 nk **Burnwynd Boy**10 6245 5-8-13 67 LeeTopliss(5) 11 62
(J A McShane) *led to over 1f out: kpt on same pce* 20/1

6501 7 1 3/4 **Rothesay Dancer**10 6246 7-8-10 66 6ex PaulNorton(7) 8 56
(J S Goldie) *hld up: rdn over 2f out: nvr able to chal* 11/1

0000 8 2 1/2 **Ubenkor (IRE)**8 6295 5-8-13 62 PJMcDonald 1 44
(M Herrington) *prom tl rdn and wknd fr 2f out* 17/2

/40- 9 1 1/4 **Parc Aux Boules**3 6433 9-8-6 64 (t) NicolaWalsh(7) 4 42
(John C McConnell, Ire) *cl up tl rdn and wknd fr 2f out* 11/22

1m 13.92s (0.32) **Going Correction** +0.10s/f (Good)
WFA 3 from 4yo+ 2lb **9** Ran SP% **112.2**
Speed ratings (Par 103): **101,100,100,98,96 96,93,90,88**
toteswingers:1&2 £10.40, 2&3 £14.20, 1&3 £10.50 CSF £71.89 CT £769.93 TOTE £7.50: £2.40, £3.30, £3.30; EX 54.00.
Owner S Hussey **Bred** Richard O'Hara **Trained** Stainforth, S Yorks
■ Stewards' Enquiry : Kieren Fox two-day ban: used whip with excessive frequency (Oct 14-15)

FOCUS
Division 1 of a 56-70 handicap which was run at an even pace, and the race developed down the centre of the track.
Parc Aux Boules Official explanation: jockey said gelding ran flat

6492 GILES INSURANCE H'CAP (DIV II OF 4.05) 6f
4:40 (4:41) (Class 5) (0-70,70) 3-Y-O+ £2,266 (£674; £337; £168) **Stalls** Low

Form RPR

2102 1 **Captain Royale (IRE)**18 5999 5-8-10 62 (p) JamesSullivan(3) 1 82
(Miss Tracy Waggott) *mde all: drvn and kpt on strly to go clr fr over 1f out* 6/1

-020 2 5 **Dubai Hills**31 5601 4-8-10 66 AdamCarter(7) 11 70
(B Smart) *chsd wnr: rdn and kpt on same pce fr over 1f out* 9/22

2030 3 3 **Cheyenne Red (IRE)**[50] 4952 4-9-4 67.......................... PhillipMakin 12 61
(M Dods) *t.k.h: hld up: effrt and hdwy over 1f out: nvr rchd ldrs* **15/2**
1302 4 ½ **Call Of Duty (IRE)**[9] 6267 5-9-1 64.......................... DuranFentiman 10 57
(Mrs Dianne Sayer) *sn drvn towards rr: sme hdwy 2f out: nt gng pce to chal* **4/1**[1]
3631 5 3¼ **Music Festival (USA)**[36] 5409 3-8-11 62.......................... JoeFanning 9 44
(J S Goldie) *midfield: drvn along 2f out: sn outpcd* **11/2**[3]
5031 6 2½ **Schoolboy Champ**[51] 4920 3-9-1 66.......................... StephenCraine 7 40
(Patrick Morris) *trckd ldrs tl rdn and wknd over 1f out* **18/1**
1040 7 3¼ **Tabiet**[8] 6295 3-8-9 60.......................... FrannyNorton 4 24
(James Moffatt) *cl up tl rdn and wknd fr 2f out* **25/1**
0623 8 3¼ **Argentine (IRE)**[10] 6245 6-9-4 70.......................... MichaelO'Connell(3) 8 24
(J A McShane) *dwlt and n.m.r s: hld up: rdn over 2f out: n.d* **7/1**
0135 9 1¼ **Amoureuse**[32] 5548 3-8-2 56 oh9.......................... KellyHarrison(3) 2 —
(D Carroll) *prom tl rdn and wknd 2f out* **40/1**
-000 10 1½ **Blown It (USA)**[13] 6140 4-9-4 67.......................... PaulHanagan 3 —
(J S Goldie) *in tch to 1/2-way: sn rdn and wknd* **9/1**

1m 12.65s (-0.95) **Going Correction** +0.10s/f (Good)
WFA 3 from 4yo+ 2lb **10 Ran SP% 113.7**
Speed ratings (Par 103): **110,103,99,98,94 91,86,82,80,78**
toteswingers:1&2 £6.20, 2&3 £8.80, 1&3£10.80 CSF £32.26 CT £208.67 TOTE £11.00: £3.50, £1.10, £2.50; EX 31.70.
Owner H Conlon **Bred** Skymarc Farm Inc **Trained** Spennymoor, Co Durham

FOCUS
Division 2 of the 56-70 handicap looked wide open beforehand but in the end it proved anything but.

6493 GILES INSURANCE CORPORATE H'CAP 1m 5f 13y
5:15 (5:16) (Class 3) (0-95,93) 3-Y-0+ **£6,476** (£1,927; £963; £481) **Stalls** Low

Form RPR
6213 1 **Graceful Descent (FR)**[11] 6224 5-8-10 75.......................... FrannyNorton 2 84
(J S Goldie) *t.k.h early: trckd ldrs: led over 2f out: styd on strly ins fnl f* **4/1**[2]
1053 2 2¼ **Chilly Filly (IRE)**[20] 5908 4-9-12 91.......................... JoeFanning 7 97
(M Johnston) *hld up in tch: hdwy to ld briefly over 2f out: kpt on fnl f: nt gng pce of wnr* **11/4**[1]
4160 3 ¾ **La Vecchia Scuola (IRE)**[20] 5908 6-9-7 93.......................... PaulNorton(7) 6 98
(J S Goldie) *hld up last but in tch: effrt over 2f out: kpt on ins fnl f: no imp* **9/2**[3]
0-00 4 3½ **Nemo Spirit (IRE)**[12] 6201 5-9-6 85.......................... RichardKingscote 4 85
(Tom Dascombe) *prom: rdn and outpcd over 2f out: no imp fr over 1f out* **7/1**
5 1¾ **Beidh Tine Anseo (IRE)**[91] 3414 4-9-9 91.......................... CampbellGillies(3) 5 88
(Miss Lucinda V Russell) *prom: hdwy over 2f out: sn rdn: outpcd over 1f out* **12/1**
2223 6 17 **Amazing Blue Sky**[16] 6050 4-8-7 75.......................... JamesSullivan(3) 1 47
(Mrs R A Carr) *set stdy pce: rdn and hdd over 3f out: wknd over 2f out* **11/1**
4001 7 11 **Cosmic Sun**[12] 6181 4-9-7 86..........................(p) PaulHanagan 3 41
(R A Fahey) *pressed ldr: led over 3f out to over 2f out: edgd lft and sn wknd* **4/1**[2]

2m 57.96s (3.96) **Going Correction** +0.275s/f (Good) **7 Ran SP% 113.4**
Speed ratings (Par 107): **98,96,96,94,92 82,75**
toteswingers:1&2 £3.80, 2&3 £9.10, 1&3 £5.50 CSF £15.15 TOTE £4.30: £2.30, £1.80; EX 23.20.
Owner Eric Nisbet & Stan Moffat **Bred** Castleton Group **Trained** Uplawmoor, E Renfrews

FOCUS
An interesting 76-95 handicap and, although, the pace was a little stop-start, the form should prove reliable.

NOTEBOOK
Graceful Descent(FR) stayed on strongly and is still unexposed over this trip. She appears versatile regarding the ground and can win again. (op 6-1)
Chilly Filly(IRE) has enjoyed a fine season and again ran bang up to form. However, the slight worry now is that the handicapper is in charge (11lb higher than her last win). (op 5-2 tchd 3-1)
La Vecchia Scuola(IRE) remains 6lb higher than she has been successful off. (tchd 7-2 and 5-1)
Nemo Spirit(IRE) has only had a few starts for this yard. He was well backed beforehand and, although he never looked like landing the cash, it was a step in the right direction, and he is 2lb below his last winning mark. (op 16-1)
Beidh Tine Anseo(IRE), coming back from a break, showed up well, and this outing will have left him spot on for his next target which is a handicap hurdle at Cheltenham next month. (op 10-1)
Cosmic Sun, a recent C&D winner, was the disappointment of the race, being eased when beaten. Whether it was the ground or something else, only time will tell. Official explanation: jockey said gelding was unsuited by the good to soft (soft in places) ground (op 7-2 tchd 3-1)

6494 GILES INSURANCE PERSONAL LINES H'CAP 7f 50y
5:50 (5:51) (Class 6) (0-60,60) 3-Y-0+ **£2,047** (£604; £302) **Stalls** High

Form RPR
1520 1 **Emeralds Spirit (IRE)**[26] 5758 3-8-12 54.......................... PhillipMakin 11 65
(J R Weymes) *hld up: hdwy over 1f out: led ins fnl f: r.o strly* **7/1**
0536 2 2 **Geojimali**[14] 6108 8-9-2 58..........................(p) GaryBartley(3) 3 64
(J S Goldie) *hld up: hdwy over 2f out: chsd wnr ins fnl f: r.o* **9/2**[3]
-043 3 ¾ **Chookie Avon**[12] 6189 3-9-0 56.......................... PaulHanagan 8 60
(V P Donoghue) *prom: rdn over 2f out: kpt on u.p ins fnl f* **4/1**[2]
0560 4 1 **Olympic Dream**[12] 6188 4-9-1 57..........................(p) MichaelO'Connell(3) 10 58
(M Herrington) *prom: hdwy to ld over 2f out: hdd ins fnl f: kpt on same pce* **16/1**
0023 5 nse **Real Diamond**[12] 6188 4-9-4 57.......................... FrannyNorton 1 58
(Ollie Pears) *plld hrd: cl up: effrt and ev ch over 2f out: one pce ins fnl f* **7/2**[1]
5344 6 ¾ **Klynch**[14] 6110 4-9-3 59..........................(b) JamesSullivan(3) 12 58
(Mrs R A Carr) *chsd ldrs: effrt over 2f out: one pce ins fnl f* **7/1**
3046 7 2½ **Avoncreek**[12] 6189 6-8-7 49.......................... KellyHarrison(3) 9 41
(B P J Baugh) *cl up: drvn over 2f out: wknd ins fnl f* **12/1**
60-0 8 14 **Lofthouse**[13] 6144 3-8-12 54.......................... PJMcDonald 4 9
(A C Whillans) *led to over 2f out: sn rdn and wknd* **40/1**
6000 9 1½ **Olympic Ceremony**[43] 5211 3-8-13 58.......................... IanBrennan(3) 14 9
(Miss Tracy Waggott) *fly-jmpd s: bhd: rdn 3f out: nvr on terms* **33/1**
056 10 9 **Jubilant Lady (USA)**[20] 5902 3-8-11 53..........................(v) JoeFanning 2 —
(B Smart) *prom tl rdn and wknd fr 3f out* **9/1**

1m 35.42s (2.02) **Going Correction** +0.275s/f (Good)
WFA 3 from 4yo+ 3lb **10 Ran SP% 114.4**
Speed ratings (Par 101): **99,96,95,94,94 93,90,74,73,62**
toteswingers:1&2 £8.30, 2&3 £4.10, 1&3 £6.60 CSF £37.75 CT £146.86 TOTE £7.00: £1.90, £4.80, £1.30; EX 45.70.
Owner T A Scothern **Bred** Epona Bloodstock Ltd **Trained** Middleham Moor, N Yorks

FOCUS
A run of the mill 46-60 handicap which was full of horses that find winning hard. It was run at a sound pace.
Real Diamond Official explanation: jockey said filly ran too free

6495 BETFAIR RACING EXCELLENCE APPRENTICE TRAINING SERIES H'CAP 1m
6:20 (6:21) (Class 6) (0-60,61) 3-Y-0+ **£2,047** (£604; £302) **Stalls** Low

Form RPR
0415 1 **Casino Night**[1] 6462 5-9-11 61 6ex.......................... DaleSwift 3 73
(Miss L A Perratt) *dwlt: sn rdn into midfield: hdwy over 2f out: led ins fnl f: kpt on strly* **3/1**[1]
2 3 **Little Village (IRE)**[97] 3418 4-8-9 48.......................... CPHoban(3) 5 53
(John C McConnell, Ire) *dwlt: sn in tch: smooth hdwy to ld over 1f out: hdd ins fnl f: kpt on same pce* **12/1**
5663 3 ¾ **Botham (USA)**[10] 6243 6-9-5 58.......................... PaulNorton(3) 1 61
(J S Goldie) *bhd: pushed along over 2f out: hdwy over 1f out: nrst fin* **4/1**[2]
00-0 4 ¾ **Pokfulham (IRE)**[14] 6109 4-9-1 56..........................(v) NoelGarbutt(5) 10 58
(J S Goldie) *prom: rdn over 2f out: one pce over 1f out* **11/1**
5350 5 nk **Tanforan**[31] 5584 8-9-9 59.......................... GarryWhillans 7 60
(B P J Baugh) *bhd tl hdwy over 1f out: kpt on fnl f: nvr rchd ldrs* **10/1**
5020 6 1 **Indian Violet (IRE)**[68] 4374 4-9-4 54..........................(p) LeeTopliss 2 53
(D W Thompson) *led to over 1f out: sn drvn and outpcd* **40/1**
-603 7 ½ **Dramatic Jewel (USA)**[10] 6242 4-9-10 60.......................... AmyScott 13 58
(Miss Lucinda V Russell) *prom: drvn over 2f out: no ex over 1f out* **17/2**
6500 8 10 **Shunkawakhan (IRE)**[17] 6026 7-8-5 48.......................... CherylArmstrong(7) 6 23
(Miss L A Perratt) *cl up tl wknd fr 2f out* **16/1**
6200 9 ¾ **Shy Glance (USA)**[36] 5408 8-9-10 60.......................... BrianToomey 9 33
(P Monteith) *hld up: rdn and outpcd over 2f out: sn btn* **14/1**
0202 10 1¾ **Second Reef**[17] 6026 8-8-13 52.......................... SoniaEaton(3) 4 21
(T A K Cuthbert) *towards rr: rdn over 2f out: sn btn* **16/1**
643 11 1¼ **Catbells (IRE)**[65] 4453 3-9-1 58.......................... NatashaEaton(3) 14 24
(A Bailey) *prom tl rdn and wknd over 2f out* **6/1**[3]

1m 45.8s (2.00) **Going Correction** +0.275s/f (Good)
WFA 3 from 4yo+ 4lb **11 Ran SP% 115.8**
Speed ratings (Par 101): **101,98,97,96,96 95,94,84,83,82 80**
toteswingers:1&2 £12.00, 2&3 £12.70, 1&3 £3.00 CSF £39.76 CT £146.24 TOTE £2.50: £1.10, £10.50, £1.70; EX 72.30 Place 6: £152.58 Place 5: £135.92.
Owner Barry Robson **Bred** Kingsmead Breeders **Trained** East Kilbride, S Lanarks

FOCUS
A good gallop for this 46-60 handicap and rated around the first two.
T/Plt: £631.70 to a £1 stake. Pool of £46,859.43 - 54.15 winning tickets. T/Qpdt: £62.00 to a £1 stake. Pool of £4,098.68 - 48.90 winning tickets. RY

6449 KEMPTON (A.W) (R-H)
Thursday, September 30

OFFICIAL GOING: Standard
Wind: Virtually nil Weather: Overcast, getting dark

6496 OUR IDEAS YOUR HORSE MAIDEN STKS 7f (P)
5:25 (5:26) (Class 5) 3-4-Y-0 **£2,286** (£675; £337) **Stalls** High

Form RPR
0-2 1 **Zip Lock (IRE)**[16] 6056 4-9-6 0.......................... RichardHughes 6 77+
(J Noseda) *trckd ldrs: smooth prog to ld appr fnl f: pushed out fnl 100yds and a doing enough* **10/11**[1]
0 2 hd **Chris's Ridge**[45] 5150 3-9-3 0.......................... PatDobbs 11 76
(B J Meehan) *in tch: chsd ldrs over 2f out: edgd lft but styd on strly to chse wnr fnl 120yds: gng on cl home but a jst hld* **40/1**
6 3 1¼ **Sunset Kitty (USA)**[16] 6056 3-8-12 0.......................... ShaneKelly 13 68
(W R Swinburn) *rrd and burst stalls: led 1f: styd trcking ldrs: kpt on to chse wnr fnl f: no imp whn swtchd lft and lost 2nd fnl 120yds* **14/1**
03 4 3½ **Maid To Dream**[23] 5839 3-8-12 0..........................(p) NickyMackay 8 59
(J H M Gosden) *chsd ldrs: pushed along 2f out: one pce whn swtchd lft 1f out: wknd ins fnl f* **12/1**[3]
5 3¼ **Hippique** 3-8-12 0.......................... ChrisCatlin 3 50+
(A M Balding) *s.i.s: in rr tl pushed along and hdwy over 2f out: kpt on fnl f but nvr a threat* **40/1**
6 6 ¾ **Supatov (USA)**[21] 5872 3-8-12 0.......................... SteveDrowne 5 48+
(H Morrison) *in rr: hdwy and tendency to edge lft fr 2f out: styd on ins fnl f but nvr nr ldrs* **40/1**
50 7 1¼ **Sonnellino**[160] 1501 3-8-12 0.......................... GregFairley 12 44
(J R Holt) *s.i.s: in rr stl last over 2f out: styd on wl fnl f but nvr a threat* **12/1**[3]
0-0 8 2 **Wet Feet**[114] 2841 3-9-3 0.......................... LiamKeniry 9 44
(P R Chamings) *led after 1f tl 5f out: styd chsng ldrs tl wknd 2f out* **66/1**
9 hd **Clear Praise (USA)**[126] 3-9-3 0.......................... JimCrowley 1 43
(S Dow) *led 5f out: hdd & wknd appr fnl f* **33/1**
10 8 **Boldly Go** 3-9-0 0.......................... PatrickHills(3) 7 22
(R Hannon) *nvr beyond mid-div and bhd fnl 3f* **50/1**
5 11 3 **La Kalam**[18] 5986 3-8-12 0.......................... NeilCallan 14 —
(M A Jarvis) *chsd ldrs tl wknd qckly over 2f out* **3/1**[2]

1m 25.58s (-0.42) **Going Correction** -0.075s/f (Stan)
WFA 3 from 4yo 3lb **11 Ran SP% 113.6**
Speed ratings (Par 103): **99,98,97,93,89 88,87,85,84,75 72**
Tote Swingers:1&2:£16.40, 2&3:£36.80, 1&3:£5.90 CSF £59.82 TOTE £1.60: £1.02, £13.70, £4.50; EX 56.10.
Owner The Searchers **Bred** Major K R Thompson **Trained** Newmarket, Suffolk
■ Stewards' Enquiry : Neil Callan caution: used whip in incorrect place.

FOCUS
A weak maiden which was made up of largely late-maturing 3yos. It was the sole 4yo that prevailed, though, and the first three came nicely clear from the furlong marker.
Sunset Kitty(USA) Official explanation: jockey said filly reared as stalls opened
Sonnellino Official explanation: jockey said filly ran green

6497 INDESIT WE WORK, HORSE PLAY MAIDEN AUCTION STKS (DIV I) 7f (P)
6:00 (6:00) (Class 5) 2-Y-0 **£2,331** (£693; £346; £173) **Stalls** High

Form RPR
034 1 **Dubarshi**[16] 6053 2-9-1 75.......................... DaneO'Neill 1 81
(Miss Jo Crowley) *in tch: gd prog fr 2f out but sn edging rt: led jst ins fnl f and hung bdly rt sn after and strly chal fnl 100yds: wnt rt again last strides: jst hld on* **13/2**

03 **2** *shd* **Twice Bitten**[16] 6053 2-8-11 0 LiamKeniry 10 77
(J A R Toller) *chsd ldrs: drvn to ld over 1f out: hdd jst ins fnl f and edgd rt: carried rt sn after and rallying whn bmpd cl home: kpt on again: jst failed* **10/3**[3]
5 **3** *3 ½* **Suddenly Susan (IRE)**[13] 6153 2-8-10 0 RichardHughes 4 67
(J Noseda) *sn trcking ldr: pushed along over 2f out: drvn and ev ch appr fnl f: sn outpcd by ldng duo* **7/4**[1]
6025 **4** *hd* **Masonic Lady (IRE)**[12] 6200 2-8-7 75 (b) NickyMackay 5 63
(W J Haggas) *sn led: rdn and styd on over 2f out: hdd over 1f out: sn outpcd* **3/1**[2]
0 **5** *3 ¾* **Seeking Glory**[13] 6158 2-9-1 0 JimCrowley 2 61
(E A L Dunlop) *s.i.s: in rr tl styd on steadily fnl 2f: kpt on cl home but nvr a threat* **14/1**
6 *nk* **Achalas (IRE)** 2-8-13 0 IanMongan 8 59
(Mrs H S Main) *slowly into strde: in rr tl pushed along and hdwy 2f out: nvr rchd ldrs and one pce fr over 1f out* **50/1**
0 **7** *4 ½* **Court Applause (IRE)**[12] 6190 2-8-13 0 NeilCallan 7 47
(W R Muir) *chsd ldrs: rdn and wknd over 1f out* **25/1**
0 **8** *1 ¾* **No Refraction (IRE)**[23] 5829 2-8-5 0 ChrisCatlin 9 34
(M D I Usher) *a towards rr* **66/1**
0 **9** *5* **Ministry**[13] 6158 2-8-12 0 SteveDrowne 3 28
(J R Best) *chsd ldrs tl hung rt and wknd ins fnl 3f* **20/1**
00 **10** *1 ¾* **Investment World (IRE)**[31] 5587 2-8-12 0 GregFairley 6 24
(M Johnston) *chsd ldrs over 4f* **50/1**

1m 25.37s (-0.63) **Going Correction** -0.075s/f (Stan) 10 Ran SP% 118.5
Speed ratings (Par 95): **100,99,95,95,91 91,85,83,78,76**
Tote Swingers:1&2:£2.90, 2&3:£3.00, 1&3:£3.00 CSF £27.74 TOTE £4.90: £1.30, £1.50, £1.20; EX 28.40.
Owner Kilstone Limited **Bred** R G Levin **Trained** Whitcombe, Dorset

FOCUS
This ordinary juvenile maiden was run at a sound pace and the first two came clear in a driving finish.

NOTEBOOK
Dubarshi just edged the verdict and opened his account at the fourth attempt, reversing last-time-out form with the runner-up in the process. He wasn't helped by being drawn on the outside, but he was ridden confidently and made his move nearing the furlong marker. He appeared likely win well once hitting the front, but hung badly right under maximum pressure and idled near the finish. That allowed the second another chance and he did that rival no favours when bumping him. He was always just doing enough, though, and it rates a career-best effort. Whether he will be able to make his mark in nurseries off his current mark remains to be seen, but he is versatile as regards trip and will continue to pay his way. (op 8-1 tchd 6-1)
Twice Bitten moved up going strongly 2f out and, although losing out to his old rival, proved very game in defeat. He is now eligible for a mark, and he too could find a bit of improvement over another furlong. (op 4-1)
Suddenly Susan(IRE), a market drifter, failed to build on her Newmarket debut as could've been expected and paid for racing near the early pace. On this evidence, dropping back a furlong could help but she doesn't look to have all that much scope. (op 11-8 tchd 2-1)
Masonic Lady(IRE) posted her best effort yet when not beaten that far in a sales race at Newmarket 12 days earlier. She set out to make all, but was a sitting duck 2f out and is likely to prove tricky to place successfully outside of plating company. (tchd 100-30 in places)
Seeking Glory was never a serious factor from off the pace, but still showed more on this second outing and has some scope. (op 25-1)
Achalas(IRE), who has plenty of stamina on his dam's side of his pedigree, was the only newcomer in attendance and it showed. He was doing some encouraging late work, though, and should only improve for the experience. (tchd 66-1)

6498 INDESIT WE WORK, HORSE PLAY MAIDEN AUCTION STKS (DIV II) 7f (P)
6:30 (6:31) (Class 5) 2-Y-O **£2,331** (£693; £346; £173) **Stalls High**

Form RPR
52 **1** **Sagramor**[49] 5006 2-8-9 0 SteveDrowne 2 78
(H Morrison) *trckd ldrs: swtchd lft and hdwy over 2f out: drvn and qcknd to ld over 1f out: c clr: readily* **5/2**[2]
5 **2** *4* **Mattoral**[13] 6158 2-8-13 0 SebSanders 4 72
(P J Makin) *s.i.s: in rr: hdwy on outside fr 3f out: pushed along and stl green 2f out: kpt on wl to take 2nd fnl 120yds but nvr any ch w wnr* **2/1**[1]
065 **3** *1 ¼* **Alshazah**[21] 5892 2-9-1 79 IanMongan 3 70
(B R Millman) *chsd ldrs tl led over 2f out: rdn and hdd over 1f out: sn one pce: lost 2nd fnl 120yds* **7/1**[3]
0 **4** *½* **Face Value**[13] 6158 2-9-0 0 ShaneKelly 6 68+
(B J Meehan) *s.i.s: in rr: pushed along and stl green 2f out: kpt on wl fnl f: gng on cl home* **12/1**
00 **5** *3 ¼* **Special Endeavour (IRE)**[13] 6146 2-8-10 0 JimCrowley 7 56
(W R Muir) *in rr: pushed along 3f out: kpt on fnl f but nvr any ch* **18/1**
650 **6** *1 ¾* **Go**[13] 6158 2-8-13 60 DaneO'Neill 1 54
(R Hannon) *chsd ldrs: rdn over 2f out and hung rt: wknd qckly over 1f out* **20/1**
4 **7** *3 ½* **Benidorm**[32] 5546 2-8-11 0 NeilCallan 8 43
(A J McCabe) *s.i.s: sn chsng ldrs: wknd fr 2f out: no ch whn hmpd jst ins fnl f* **8/1**
0 **8** *1* **Joe Le Taxi (IRE)**[14] 6102 2-9-1 0 GregFairley 10 44
(M Johnston) *led tl hdd over 2f out: sn wknd and no ch whn veered rt jst ins fnl f* **16/1**
060 **9** *4* **Rum Sun N Sand (USA)**[15] 6075 2-8-9 48 PatDobbs 9 28
(J W Hills) *a in rr* **66/1**
0 **10** *7* **Notify**[48] 5029 2-8-5 0 ChrisCatlin 5 6
(P R Chamings) *chsd ldrs tl wknd ins fnl 3f* **40/1**

1m 25.42s (-0.58) **Going Correction** -0.075s/f (Stan) 10 Ran SP% 113.0
Speed ratings (Par 95): **100,95,94,93,89 87,83,82,78,70**
Tote Swingers:1&2:£2.40, 2&3:£3.90, 1&3:£3.30 CSF £7.43 TOTE £4.40: £1.30, £1.20, £1.70; EX 8.90.
Owner Melksham Craic **Bred** Melksham Craic **Trained** East Ilsley, Berks

FOCUS
The second division of the juvenile maiden. It was run in a fractionally slower winning time than the first and the form looks straightforward.

NOTEBOOK
Sagramor proved very easy to back, but ran out a comfortable winner to shed his maiden tag at the third time of asking. He tacked in early from his low draw and got cover. It was clear he was going easily just off the pace 2f out, and he quickened nicely when eventually asked to go about his business. He is bred to be a better 3-y-o over a stiffer test, so the fact he has shown useful form at this stage of his career bodes well and it will be interesting to see how he copes off a likely mark in the 80s in handicaps. (op 6-4 tchd 11-4)
Mattoral was a slow starter on debut at Newmarket 13 days earlier and again made a sluggish start here. He improved to have his chance in the home straight, but the ready winner got first run and he still proved too green to really do himself justice when under pressure. His starting issue will need to be ironed out, but it's a good bet he will come on again for the run and is capable of winning in this sphere. (op 11-4 tchd 13-8)
Alshazah was ridden with a bit more restraint than when finishing fifth over C&D 21 days earlier and lacked a change of gear. He helps to set the standard, but his official mark of 79 needs reassessing. (op 11-2)
Face Value finished well behind the runner-up on debut at Newmarket when also making a slow start, and he too fell out of the gates on this AW debut. He lacked the pace to recover sufficiently and was last turning for home, but he stayed on nicely when the penny dropped. He may need extra experience before coming good, but no doubt he has a future and another furlong may suit. (op 20-1)

6499 HOTPOINT 1600 SPINNIES MEDIAN AUCTION MAIDEN STKS 1m 4f (P)
7:00 (7:00) (Class 5) 3-5-Y-O **£2,286** (£675; £337) **Stalls Centre**

Form RPR
2323 **1** **Wulfrida (IRE)**[16] 6055 3-8-12 75 PatCosgrave 6 75+
(J R Fanshawe) *in tch: hdwy 3f out: drvn to ld over 1f out: hld on u.p cl home* **9/4**[2]
2 *hd* **Sarbola** 3-9-3 0 NeilCallan 9 80+
(M A Jarvis) *chsd ldrs: rdn and styd on fr over 2f out: chsd wnr appr fnl f: styd on u.p and gng on cl home but nt quite get up* **9/2**[3]
5 **3** *2 ¼* **Miss Kingwood**[52] 4906 3-8-12 0 PatDobbs 5 71+
(M P Tregoning) *t.k.h: hld up in rr: hdwy on outside fr 4f out: styd on wl to take 3rd ins fnl f and gng on cl home: edgd rt cl home but nvr a threat* **12/1**
33 **4** *5* **Sophies Trophy (IRE)**[147] 1851 5-9-11 0 IanMongan 7 68
(P M Phelan) *chsd ldrs: led over 2f out: hdd over 1f out and sn wknd* **7/1**
2222 **5** *1 ¾* **Astral Flower**[15] 6079 3-8-12 73 RichardHughes 10 60
(Sir Michael Stoute) *trckd ldr: led over 5f out: rdn 3f out: hdd over 2f out and sn btn* **13/8**[1]
5006 **6** *3 ¼* **Charpoy Cobra**[16] 6054 3-8-12 50 LiamKeniry 12 55?
(J A R Toller) *chsd ldrs tl wknd over 2f out* **33/1**
0 **7** *½* **Justazippy**[19] 5971 3-8-9 0 MartinLane(3) 3 54?
(A J McCabe) *mid-div: in tch 4f out: rdn 3f out: sn wknd* **66/1**
8 *22* **Alhudhud (USA)**[119] 4-9-11 0 (t) AndreaAtzeni 1 24
(K A Morgan) *rdn and hung rt 4f out: a in rr* **66/1**
9 *6* **Epsom Girl** 3-8-7 0 JemmaMarshall(5) 4 9
(P M Phelan) *a in rr* **66/1**
0 **10** *8* **Les Andelys**[29] 5665 4-9-4 0 (p) JessicaSteven(7) 11 2
(T T Clement) *led tl hdd over 5f out: wknd ins fnl 4f* **100/1**
50 **11** *14* **Annuity (IRE)**[23] 5842 3-9-3 0 JimCrowley 2 —
(W J Knight) *bhd fr 1/2-way: eased fnl 2f* **20/1**

2m 32.92s (-1.58) **Going Correction** -0.075s/f (Stan)
WFA 3 from 4yo+ 8lb 11 Ran SP% 120.4
Speed ratings (Par 103): **102,101,100,97,95 93,93,78,74,69 60**
Tote Swingers:1&2:£3.90, 2&3:£18.90, 1&3:£10.80 CSF £12.73 TOTE £2.40: £1.10, £1.10, £5.00; EX 17.10.
Owner Lord Halifax **Bred** Lord Halifax **Trained** Newmarket, Suffolk

FOCUS
A moderate maiden run at a fair pace.

6500 INDESIT IRELAND TRICOLOUR CLAIMING STKS 1m (P)
7:30 (7:31) (Class 6) 2-Y-O **£1,637** (£483; £241) **Stalls High**

Form RPR
0060 **1** **Joyously**[7] 6307 2-8-9 74 CathyGannon 10 62
(P D Evans) *in rr: rdn 4f out and stl plenty to do 3f out: hdwy on ins fr 2f out: str run fnl f to ld fnl 120yds: hld on wl* **10/1**
5504 **2** *½* **Paco Belle (IRE)**[15] 6082 2-8-11 60 DaneO'Neill 13 63
(R Hannon) *in rr: hdwy 2f out: str run fr over 1f out and kpt on to chse wnr nr fin but a hld* **12/1**
2631 **3** *shd* **Takeaway**[7] 6307 2-9-7 82 RichardHughes 11 73
(J R Boyle) *chsd ldrs: rdn 2f out: led over 1f out: edgd lft ins fnl f and hdd fnl 120yds: lost 2nd nr fin* **1/1**[1]
000 **4** *1 ½* **Beating Harmony**[7] 6307 2-8-12 0 PatCosgrave 8 60
(J R Fanshawe) *in tch: hdwy 4f out: str run fr over 1f out and kpt on wl fnl f but nvr gng pce to chal* **16/1**
4446 **5** *2 ¼* **Bright Applause**[30] 5626 2-9-0 68 (b[1]) NeilCallan 7 57
(G L Moore) *chsd ldrs: rdn and hung rt 1f out: hmpd sn after and wknd* **20/1**
050 **6** *1 ¾* **Cool Land (IRE)**[28] 5701 2-8-12 54 LukeMorris 4 51
(R A Harris) *chsd ldrs: led 5f out: hdd over 1f out: btn whn edgd lft and hmpd jst ins fnl f* **80/1**
0023 **7** *½* **Highcliffe**[15] 6081 2-8-11 55 PatDobbs 5 49
(R Hannon) *in rr: hdwy on outside fr 3f out: kpt on but nvr a threat* **14/1**
4001 **8** *1 ¾* **Sir Lunchalott**[12] 6209 2-9-1 70 (b) LiamKeniry 12 49
(J S Moore) *chsd ldrs: rdn 2f out: wkng whn hmpd 1f out* **7/1**[2]
0060 **9** *2 ¼* **Wanchai Minx**[29] 5660 2-8-0 52 HarryBentley(7) 14 36
(A P Jarvis) *nvr bttr than mid-div* **66/1**
06 **10** *3 ¼* **Bournefree (IRE)**[12] 6211 2-8-8 0 SteveDrowne 3 29
(S Kirk) *hung rt bnd after 3f out: a bhd* **66/1**
0004 **11** *2 ¾* **Run Daisy Run**[21] 5894 2-8-4 56 (b) ChrisCatlin 6 19
(B J Meehan) *s.i.s: t.k.h and chsd ldrs after 3f: wknd fr 2f out* **20/1**
12 *9* **He'Sahit (FR)** 2-9-0 0 IanMongan 9 8
(P R Hedger) *t.k.h: chsd ldrs after 2f: wknd 2f out* **66/1**
0 **13** *29* **Likeable Lad**[17] 6027 2-9-0 0 PaulMulrennan 1 —
(Mrs R A Carr) *t.k.h: led: hdd 5f out: wknd over 3f out* **100/1**
0545 **R** **Blackleyf (IRE)**[13] 6163 2-9-0 66 (b) JimCrowley 2 —
(Tom Dascombe) *ref to r* **9/1**[3]

1m 40.45s (0.65) **Going Correction** -0.075s/f (Stan) 14 Ran SP% 118.1
Speed ratings (Par 93): **93,92,92,90,88 86,86,84,82,79 76,67,38,—**
Tote Swingers:1&2:£22.50, 2&3:£5.40, 1&3:£3.50 CSF £116.11 TOTE £8.80: £2.10, £5.80, £1.90; EX 152.40.Beating Harmony was claimed by Mr T. Dascombe for £6,000. Joyously was claimed by Mr S. Arnold for £8,000.
Owner Nick Shutts **Bred** N Shutts **Trained** Pandy, Monmouths
■ Stewards' Enquiry : Neil Callan one-day ban: careless riding (Oct 14)

FOCUS
A typically moderate juvenile claimer, run at a solid pace.

NOTEBOOK
Joyously, with the visor abandoned, quickened up positively when taken to the inside with her effort inside the final furlong and got on top near the finish. She tended to go in snatches and was last coming into the home straight. The strong early pace helped, however, and she obviously enjoyed the longer trip. This was a marked return to form, but it was her third win of the year and she had a good chance at the weights if bouncing back. (op 9-1)
Paco Belle(IRE) has been disappointing, but this drop in grade proved much more to her liking and she wasn't beaten at all far. The more patient tactics helped and she ought to have no trouble winning a race of this class. (tchd 14-1)

Takeaway, who won the first juvenile race of the year at this venue when scoring on his debut in March, was having his first run for new connections and proved very popular. He looked to have done enough half a furlong out, but his stamina for the longer trip began to wane and he was mugged late on. More patient tactics over this trip or a drop back to 7f in this class can see him back in the winner's enclosure. (tchd 11-10)

Beating Harmony showed his first worthwhile form on this drop in grade and has evidently now found his level (tchd 14-1)

Sir Lunchalott narrowly won a seller on his previous outing and was the chief danger to the winner on that form, but he spoilt his chance by refusing to settle. Official explanation: jockey said gelding ran too free (op 8-1 tchd 11-2)

6501 HOT TO TROT H'CAP 6f (P)
8:00 (8:03) (Class 4) (0-80,79) 3-Y-0+ **£3,885** (£1,156; £577; £288) **Stalls** High

Form RPR

5503 **1** **Illustrious Prince (IRE)**[12] 6197 3-9-4 **78**.............(v) RichardHughes 12 88+
(J Noseda) *trckd ldrs: drvn to ld jst ins fnl f: rdn and kpt on wl fnl 50yds* **4/1**[2]

101 **2** *nk* **Vintage (IRE)**[16] 6057 6-9-6 **78**.......... IanMongan 6 85
(J Akehurst) *chsd ldrs: drvn to ld over 1f out: hdd jst ins fnl f: rallied and kpt on wl but a jst hld by wnr* **12/1**

3322 **3** *nk* **Fantasy Gladiator**[23] 5838 4-9-0 **72**..........(p) LiamKeniry 5 78+
(R M H Cowell) *s.i.s: in rr: hdwy and n.m.r over 2f out tl swtchd rt to ins and hdwy over 1f out: chsd ldrs ins fnl f: rallied to press for 2nd nr fin but nvr quite gng pce to trble wnr* **7/2**[1]

5065 **4** *½* **Lord Of The Reins (IRE)**[38] 5368 6-8-12 **70**.......... PaulMulrennan 9 74
(J G Given) *chsd ldrs: rdn over 2f out: kpt on ins fnl f but nvr gng pce to chal* **14/1**

0213 **5** *nk* **Defector (IRE)**[7] 6310 4-8-13 **76**.......... MarkCoumbe(5) 7 79
(D Bourton) *in rr tl drvn and hdwy over 1f out: kpt on wl fnl f: nt rch ldrs* **8/1**

0224 **6** *1 ¾* **Freddie's Girl (USA)**[10] 6253 3-9-2 **76**.......... SebSanders 4 74
(Stef Higgins) *chsd ldrs: rdn over 2f out and styd on same pce ins fnl f* **12/1**

1 **7** *1 ¾* **Yes We Can**[24] 5810 3-8-12 **72**.......... SteveDrowne 3 64
(J R Gask) *hld up in rr: rdn 3f out: kpt on fnl f but nvr a threat* **20/1**

0626 **8** *nk* **Peter Island (FR)**[74] 4171 7-9-7 **79**..........(v) ChrisCatlin 10 70
(J Gallagher) *led tl hdd & wknd over 1f out* **7/1**

1460 **9** *½* **Sarah's Art (IRE)**[25] 5789 7-9-7 **79**..........(t) PatCosgrave 1 69
(Stef Higgins) *stdd s: outpcd* **25/1**

0000 **10** *1 ¾* **Frognal (IRE)**[22] 5855 4-9-0 **72**..........(b) LukeMorris 11 56
(Mrs R A Carr) *in tch: chsd ldrs 3f out: rdn 2f out: wknd appr fnl f* **25/1**

3400 **11** *1* **Tubby Isaacs**[50] 4961 6-9-3 **75**.......... NeilCallan 8 56
(D K Ivory) *rdn along 1/2-way: a outpcd* **9/2**[3]

1m 11.96s (-1.14) **Going Correction** -0.075s/f (Stan)
WFA 3 from 4yo+ 2lb **11** Ran SP% **118.5**
Speed ratings (Par 105): **104,103,103,102,102 99,97,97,96,94 92**
Tote Swingers:1&2:£6.80, 2&3:£10.00, 1&3:£3.80 CSF £50.21 CT £186.39 TOTE £6.00: £1.50, £4.80, £1.10; EX 47.40.
Owner Saeed Suhail **Bred** Rathbarry Stud **Trained** Newmarket, Suffolk
■ Stewards' Enquiry : Richard Hughes caution: used whip without giving gelding time to respond.

FOCUS
This was a tight sprint handicap with 5lb covering the field. There was a decent pace on and the form should work out.

6502 PRIME H'CAP 2m (P)
8:30 (8:31) (Class 6) (0-65,65) 4-Y-0+ **£1,637** (£483; £241) **Stalls** High

Form RPR

/0-0 **1** **Foreign King (USA)**[11] 409 6-8-9 **51**.......... LiamKeniry 3 59
(J W Mullins) *chsd ldrs: rdn over 2f out: styd on to ld ins fnl f: hld on wl u.p* **10/1**

31-0 **2** *nk* **Dansilver**[14] 6120 6-9-0 **56**.......... NeilCallan 4 64
(A W Carroll) *in rr but in tch: rdn and hdwy over 2f out: styd on to chse wnr ins fnl f and kpt on cl home but a jst hld* **5/1**[2]

0-00 **3** *1* **Trempari**[172] 506 7-8-1 **46** oh1..........(b) MartinLane(3) 8 52
(Mike Murphy) *chsd ldr: persistently hung bdly rt fr 4f out: stl hanging whn led wl over 2f out: hdd and one pce ins fnl f* **14/1**

2600 **4** *3* **Taste The Wine (IRE)**[16] 6055 4-8-13 **62**.......... RyanPowell(7) 6 67+
(J S Moore) *chsd ldrs: nt clr run 2f out: styng on whn hmpd and swtchd lft over 1f out: one pce* **12/1**

1-40 **5** *shd* **M'Lady Rousseur (IRE)**[202] 874 4-9-1 **57**.......... DaneO'Neill 2 60
(C C Bealby) *in rr: pushed along and hdwy fr 2f out: kpt on ins fnl f but nt rch ldrs* **7/1**[3]

0400 **6** *nk* **Soundbyte**[52] 4907 5-9-9 **65**.......... RichardHughes 9 67
(J Gallagher) *chsd ldrs: pushed along over 5f out: styd wl there and rdn wl over 2f out: sn one pce: wknd ins fnl f* **11/4**[1]

4034 **7** *2 ¼* **Croix Rouge (USA)**[30] 5625 8-8-5 **50**.......... AndrewHeffernan(3) 5 50
(R J Smith) *in rr but in tch: pushed along 3f out: styd on same pce fnl 2f* **15/2**

0602 **8** *7* **Mixing**[9] 6273 8-8-4 **46** oh1.......... AndreaAtzeni 1 37
(M J Attwater) *rdn 3f out: a in rr* **8/1**

3044 **9** *7* **Sir Mark (IRE)**[8] 6297 6-9-8 **64**.......... DanielTudhope 10 47
(M A Peill) *led tl hdd & wknd qckly wl over 2f out* **8/1**

3m 31.22s (1.12) **Going Correction** -0.075s/f (Stan) **9** Ran SP% **113.3**
Speed ratings (Par 101): **94,93,93,91,91 91,90,87,83**
Tote Swingers:1&2:£9.20, 2&3:£25.20, 1&3:£20.60 CSF £58.13 CT £701.49 TOTE £10.10: £3.00, £2.60, £7.80; EX 42.80.
Owner John Collins **Bred** Jayeff 'B' Stables **Trained** Wilsford-Cum-Lake, Wilts
■ Stewards' Enquiry : Martin Lane two-day ban: careless riding (Oct 14-15)

FOCUS
A weak staying handicap, run no more than an average gallop.
Trempari Official explanation: jockey said gelding hung right-handed

6503 ULTIMATE H'CAP 7f (P)
9:00 (9:00) (Class 4) (0-85,84) 3-Y-0+ **£3,885** (£1,156; £577; £288) **Stalls** High

Form RPR

01 **1** **Saint Pierre (USA)**[16] 6056 3-9-0 **80**.......... J-PGuillambert 14 96+
(L M Cumani) *plld hrd: stdd in tch: swtchd lft over 2f out: rdn and hdwy on outside over 1f out: str run u.p and hung rt ins fnl f: led last stride* **9/2**[2]

1005 **2** *shd* **Primaeval**[26] 5754 4-9-4 **81**..........(v[1]) PatCosgrave 5 92
(J R Fanshawe) *hld up in tch: gd hdwy over 2f out: drvn to ld ins fnl f: ct last stride* **13/2**[3]

0234 **3** *¾* **Saharia (IRE)**[26] 5754 3-9-0 **80**.......... RichardHughes 1 88
(J Noseda) *hld up towards rr: stdy hdwy fr 2f out: drvn and qcknd to dispute 2nd fnl 120yds: nt qckn nr fin* **8/1**

0000 **4** *1 ½* **Inheritor (IRE)**[33] 5510 4-9-3 **80**..........(p) TomEaves 10 85
(B Smart) *disp ld and rdn to chal over 2f out tl over 1f out: no ex ins fnl f* **12/1**

1002 **5** *nk* **Army Of Stars (IRE)**[15] 6085 4-8-9 **75**..........(p) SophieDoyle(3) 9 79
(J A Osborne) *chsd ldrs: rdn over 2f out and kpt on same pce* **14/1**

3000 **6** *hd* **Last Sovereign**[12] 6198 6-8-12 **80**.......... JamesO'Reilly(5) 12 84
(J O'Reilly) *led and sn jnd: stl hrd pressed whn rdn over 2f out: asserted wl over 1f out: hdd & wknd ins fnl f* **20/1**

041 **7** *nk* **Hazzard County (USA)**[19] 5964 6-8-11 **81**.......... LauraPike(7) 7 84
(D M Simcock) *in rr: sme hdwy over 2f out: nvr rchd ldrs and styd on same pce* **8/1**

5425 **8** *2* **Mambo Spirit (IRE)**[13] 6167 6-9-3 **80**.......... SebSanders 8 77
(Stef Higgins) *in tch tl wknd 2f out* **15/2**

0252 **9** *½* **Maze (IRE)**[21] 5889 5-9-1 **78**.......... NeilCallan 13 74
(A W Carroll) *plld hrd: chsd ldrs to 2f out: wknd sn after* **20/1**

543 **10** *1 ¾* **Nezami (IRE)**[10] 6252 5-9-2 **79**.......... DaneO'Neill 11 70
(J Akehurst) *trckd ldrs on outside: wknd ins fnl 2f* **7/2**[1]

0200 **11** *3 ¾* **Lisahane Bog**[145] 1934 3-8-12 **78**.......... IanMongan 2 58
(P R Hedger) *wd into st: a towards rr* **33/1**

6031 **12** *3* **Chief Exec**[15] 6085 8-8-11 **74**.......... SteveDrowne 3 47
(J R Gask) *s.i.s: bhd most of way* **16/1**

1m 24.71s (-1.29) **Going Correction** -0.075s/f (Stan)
WFA 3 from 4yo+ 3lb **12** Ran SP% **120.4**
Speed ratings (Par 105): **104,103,103,101,100 100,100,98,97,95 91,87**
Tote Swingers:1&2:£11.00, 2&3:£12.10, 1&3:£9.20 CSF £33.57 CT £235.50 TOTE £6.40: £2.30, £2.80, £2.80; EX 48.40 Place 6 £8.90, Place 5 £5.22..
Owner J Barton & C Pizarro **Bred** Gallaghers Stud Inc **Trained** Newmarket, Suffolk

FOCUS
A fair and competitive handicap. It was run at a sound enough pace and the form is straightforward.
Chief Exec Official explanation: jockey said gelding hit its head on stalls
T/Plt: £12.90 to a £1 stake. Pool of £49,333.23 - 2,789.82 winning tickets. T/Qpdt: £6.90 to a £1 stake. Pool of £6,645.44 - 705.60 winning tickets. ST

6198 NEWMARKET (R-H)
Thursday, September 30

OFFICIAL GOING: Soft (stands' side 6.7 centre 6.6 far side 7.1)
Far side of Rowley Mile track used.
Wind: modest, half against Weather: bright, light cloud

6504 NGK SPARK PLUGS E B F MAIDEN STKS (C&G) 1m
2:00 (2:01) (Class 4) 2-Y-0 **£5,180** (£1,541; £770; £384) **Stalls** Low

Form RPR

23 **1** **Auden (USA)**[29] 5651 2-9-0 0.......... AhmedAjtebi 9 81
(Mahmood Al Zarooni) *lw: chsd ldrs: wnt 2nd wl over 2f out: rdn to ld over 1f out: kpt on u.p ins fnl f: drvn out* **13/2**

2 *1 ¼* **Academy (IRE)** 2-9-0 0.......... RyanMoore 6 79+
(Sir Michael Stoute) *lengthy: scope: bit bkwd: t.k.h: hld up in tch: hdwy 2f out: rn green and edgd rt over 1f out: styd on to chse wnr ins fnl f: kpt on same pce and no imp towards fin* **5/1**[3]

3 *½* **Trumpington Street (IRE)** 2-9-0 0.......... RobertHavlin 2 78+
(J H M Gosden) *athletic: s.i.s: hld up in rr: hdwy and n.m.r on stands' rail over 2f out: swtchd rt over 1f out: chsd wnr 1f out: kpt on same pce after: lost 2nd ins fnl f* **40/1**

5 **4** *nk* **Musnad (USA)**[21] 5878 2-9-0 0.......... RichardHills 4 77
(B W Hills) *lw: hld up in tch: swtchd rt and effrt to chse ldrs over 1f out: styd on same pce u.p ins fnl f* **4/1**[2]

5 *1 ¼* **Muqtarrib (IRE)** 2-9-0 0.......... TadhgO'Shea 13 74
(B J Meehan) *w'like: bit bkwd: s.i.s: hld up in rr: gd hdwy 3f out: chsd ldrs and rdn over 1f out: pushed along and unable qck over 1f out: btn and edgd lft 1f out* **25/1**

05 **6** *hd* **Jeeran**[47] 5085 2-9-0 0.......... ChrisCatlin 11 74
(C E Brittain) *t.k.h: pressed ldrs tl led 3f out: rdn and hdd over 1f out: wknd jst ins fnl f* **100/1**

3 **7** *nk* **Unex Renoir**[20] 5916 2-9-0 0.......... WilliamBuick 1 73
(J H M Gosden) *unf: scope: led tl 3f out: chsd ldr after tl wknd u.p ent fnl f* **9/4**[1]

8 *2* **Knightly Escapade** 2-9-0 0.......... DaneO'Neill 15 69
(J L Dunlop) *leggy: bit bkwd: wnt rt s: hung rt and rn v green early: rcvrd and in tch in midfield after 2f: pushed along 3f out: swtchd lft and outpcd wl over 1f out: plugged on same pce and no threat to ldrs fnl f* **50/1**

9 *hd* **Maharana (USA)** 2-9-0 0.......... JamieSpencer 12 68
(M L W Bell) *str: bit bkwd: v.s.a and rn v green early: bhd: stdy hdwy and chsng ldrs 1/2-way: rdn and wknd over 1f out: wl btn and eased towards fin* **9/1**

0 **10** *5* **If What And Maybe**[15] 6092 2-9-0 0.......... MarcHalford 10 57
(J Ryan) *leggy: chsd ldrs tl rdn and struggling over 2f out: wknd 2f out* **100/1**

0 **11** *½* **Warrant**[27] 5717 2-9-0 0.......... JimmyQuinn 14 56
(P Howling) *w'like: leggy: hld up in rr: rdn and struggling over 2f out: no ch w ldrs fnl 2f* **100/1**

12 *hd* **Old Boy Ted** 2-9-0 0.......... TomQueally 16 56
(M H Tompkins) *str: lw: stdd and swtchd lft after s: hld up in rr: switching rt and rdn 3f out: sn struggling: n.d fnl 2f* **28/1**

13 *6* **Lordofthehouse (IRE)** 2-9-0 0.......... KierenFallon 8 42
(W J Haggas) *lengthy: scope: s.i.s: a bhd: lost tch over 2f out* **8/1**

00 **14** *6* **Rasteau (IRE)**[26] 5761 2-9-0 0.......... NickyMackay 5 29
(T Keddy) *w ldrs tl 1/2-way: sn lost pl u.p: wl bhd over 1f out* **200/1**

0 **15** *8* **Oceans Destination**[14] 6127 2-9-0 0.......... JimmyFortune 7 12
(J Ryan) *leggy: in tch in midfield: rdn and lost pl 3f out: wl bhd over 1f out: eased ins fnl f* **100/1**

1m 42.7s (4.10) **Going Correction** +0.25s/f (Good) **15** Ran SP% **118.0**
Speed ratings (Par 97): **89,87,87,86,85 85,85,83,83,78 77,77,71,65,57**
toteswingers:1&2 £5.20, 2&3 £31.20, 1&3 £34.90 CSF £36.51 TOTE £5.60: £1.60, £2.40, £8.90; EX 41.30 Trifecta £427.90 Part won. Pool: £578.35 - 0.73 winning units..
Owner Godolphin **Bred** Darley **Trained** Newmarket, Suffolk
■ Stewards' Enquiry : Richard Hills one-day ban: careless riding (Oct 14)

FOCUS
A number of good horses have taken this in the last ten years, most notably Redwood in 2008 and Twice Over in 2007, so this winner should be kept a close eye on in the future. The early pace did not seem strong, and there was a slight tailwind down the course.

NOTEBOOK

Auden(USA) was beaten at 1-3 last time in what has proved to be an ordinary contest. However, it may have been that Brighton did not suit him, as he had sound claims on his debut effort at Newmarket's July course. Godolphin took this race last season with Fareej, who has been a little disappointing, so it remains to be seen how good this well-related sort turns out to be. (tchd 8-1)

Academy(IRE) ◆, a £90,000 yearling, who is the first foal of a dam that was successful over 1m4f winner in France, is a fine looker and seems sure to develop into a 3-y-o. A Derby entrant, he moved well under restraint and stayed on in good style despite an awkward head carriage. Only time will tell whether it was greenness or a quirk which saw that happen. (op 6-1 tchd 9-2)

Trumpington Street(IRE) ◆, whose dam is a half-sister to 1m4f Group 1 winner Zambezi Sun and two smart middle-distance performers, travelled nicely in midfield and kept on well for pressure. It was a good introduction and he should be hard to beat in any ordinary maiden next time.

Musnad(USA) seemed the one to beat on the back of his debut effort at Doncaster. He drifted in the betting before the off and was forced to make his effort really wide after tracking the pace down the rail before finding little under pressure. Given his pedigree (Mr Greeley out of a Red Ransom mare) he is worth giving another chance to on quicker ground or Polytrack. (op 9-4)

Muqtarrib(IRE) ◆, who cost £140,000 as a yearling and is a brother to 6f-1m winner Sugar Mint, seemed very green in the latter stages under pressure and was one of the biggest eyecatchers. (op 33-1)

Jeeran had been well beaten on his previous two starts, so this looked an improved performance up to 1m for the first time. It remains to be seen whether or not he holds the form back.

Unex Renoir was prominent while the fractions were modest down the stands' side but found disappointingly little when asked for maximum effort. His ears were pricked in the latter stages, so he may have still needed this. (op 11-4 tchd 3-1)

Knightly Escapade ◆, the first foal of a fair 1m6f winner, ran as though he will need a stiffer test, which isn't surprising given his pedigree. Already gelded, he looks sure to win races. (op 66-1)

Maharana(USA), a brother to useful 1m4f winner Anhar, flashed his tail shortly after leaving the stalls but was soon fairly prominent on the outside of the field. His rider was fairly hard on him, considering it was a debut run, so the horse should be sharper next time. (op 16-1)

Old Boy Ted seemed really green and had no idea what was going on. (op 40-1)

Lordofthehouse(IRE) ◆, a half-brother to the top-class but ill-fated miler George Washington, and the talented but quirky Grandera, is a late foal and didn't run as badly as his final position suggests. He looked in need of the run mentally and should improve. (op 9-1)

6505 WEATHERBYS NURSERY 1m

2:35 (2:36) (Class 3) (0-95,91) 2-Y-O **£6,476** (£1,927; £963; £481) **Stalls** Low

Form RPR

010 **1** **Mariachi Man**22 5849 2-8-12 **82** DavidAllan 7 89
(T D Easterby) *racd in centre: chsd overall ldr tl rdn to ld over 1f out: edgd rt u.p ent fnl f: hrd pressed and hld on gamely ins fnl f* **10/1**

011 **2** *nse* **Indigo Way**23 5830 2-9-0 **84** FrankieDettori 12 91
(B J Meehan) *racd in centre: stdd and dropped in bhd after s: hld up in rr: swtchd rt and effrt 2f out: drvn and ev ch thrght fnl f: kpt on wl: jst hld: 2nd of 7 in gp* **13/2**3

331 **3** *nk* **Poplin**23 5829 2-9-1 **85** KierenFallon 10 91
(L M Cumani) *lw: racd in centre: stdd s: t.k.h: hld up in last trio: hdwy 2f out: ev ch and rdn ent fnl f: hrd drvn and kpt on same pce fnl 100yds: 3rd of 7 in gp* **7/1**

101 **4** *1* **Bridle Belle**12 6174 2-9-0 **84** JimmyFortune 9 88
(R A Fahey) *lw: racd in centre: in tch in midfield: effrt u.p 2f out: drvn to chse ldng trio jst over 1f out: kpt on: nvr quite pce to rch ldrs: 4th of 7 in gp* **16/1**

6043 **5** *½* **Early Applause**19 5947 2-8-4 **74** AdrianNicholls 8 77
(B W Hills) *racd in centre: hld up in last trio: rdn and unable qck 3f out: hdwy u.p over 1f out: kpt on wl ins fnl f: styng on wl fin: nt rch ldrs: 5th of 7 in gp* **8/1**

4133 **6** *2¼* **Jehanbux (USA)**13 6160 2-9-2 **86** (b1) RichardHughes 2 84
(R Hannon) *racd on stands' side: overall ldr: rdn 2f out: hdd over 1f out: wknd ent fnl f: 1st of 5 in gp* **20/1**

421 **7** *1¾* **Profondo Rosso (IRE)**36 5413 2-8-12 **82** RyanMoore 1 76
(Sir Michael Stoute) *lw: racd stands' side: s.i.s: chsd ldrs in gp but midfield overall: rdn and struggling wl over 2f out: no ch w ldrs fr over 1f out: 2nd of 5 in gp* **5/2**1

441 **8** *1¼* **Loukoumi**31 5594 2-8-7 **77** ow1 TomEaves 6 68
(B Smart) *racd in centre: swtchd rt after s: t.k.h: chsd ldrs: rdn and unable qck 3f out: wknd over 1f out: 6th of 7 in gp* **40/1**

0202 **9** *hd* **Bradbury (IRE)**28 5682 2-7-13 **69** ow1 (b) JimmyQuinn 11 60
(J D Bethell) *racd in centre: pressed ldrs: ev ch and rdn over 2f out: wknd qckly 2f out: 7th of 7 in gp* **50/1**

661 **10** *1¼* **Kingarrick**31 5608 2-8-10 **80** TomQueally 4 68
(Eve Johnson Houghton) *racd stands' side: in tch: rdn and struggling wl over 2f out: wl btn over 1f out: 3rd of 5 in gp* **40/1**

211 **11** *½* **Buthelezi (USA)**19 5947 2-9-7 **91** (e1) WilliamBuick 3 78
(J H M Gosden) *unf: scope: swtg: racd stands' side: chsd gp ldr but midfield overall: rdn and btn wl over 1f out: 4th of 5 in gp* **7/2**2

5066 **12** *9* **Planet Waves (IRE)**22 5849 2-8-6 **76** (b) ChrisCatlin 5 43
(C E Brittain) *racd stands' side: a bhd: lost tch over 2f out: wl bhd and eased ins fnl f: 5th of 5 in gp* **25/1**

1m 39.75s (1.15) **Going Correction** +0.25s/f (Good) **12** Ran SP% **118.2**
Speed ratings (Par 99): **104,103,103,102,102 99,98,96,96,95 94,85**
toteswingers:1&2 £13.40, 2&3 £6.40, 1&3 £15.60 CSF £69.49 CT £498.24 TOTE £11.10: £3.30, £2.40, £3.20; EX 119.40 Trifecta £653.00 Pool: £882.55 - 1 winning unit..
Owner Jeremy Gompertz **Bred** Jeremy Gompertz **Trained** Great Habton, N Yorks

FOCUS

A decent nursery that produced a good finish. The field split into two groups and those racing up the middle filled the first five places. The time was 2.95sec faster than the opening maiden.

NOTEBOOK

Mariachi Man ◆ finished ahead of Bridle Belle at Doncaster and, although racing off the same mark, was 2lb better off. Stepping up in trip, he led the group racing up the centre throughout, and stuck on really gamely up the hill to hold off the late challengers. A big, rangy sort, this track played to his strengths and he looks capable of going on to make a useful handicapper next season. (op 11-1 tchd 12-1)

Indigo Way, a dual winner on good, was raised 6lb for a narrow success last time. Unraced on slower than good, he handled it well and was produced with what appeared a race-winning challenge, but could not quite get past. He continues on the upgrade. (op 5-1 tchd 9-2)

Poplin, a 1m maiden winner on good ground, was making her handicap debut and having her first race on soft. She was delivered to challenge going into the dip and kept trying all the way up the hill, but the winner proved too tough. She lost nothing in defeat. (op 6-1)

Bridle Belle, a winner at 7f and 1m but beaten in between when there was cut in the ground, was 2lb worse off with today's winner, having finished behind him at Doncaster. She ran her race though, and finished about the same distance behind that rival, giving the form a sound appearance. (tchd 20-1)

Early Applause is progressing with racing since stepping up in trip. He was not beaten far when third behind Buthelezi last time and reversed those placings. He was under pressure to improve some way from home but stayed on all the way to the line. (op 9-1)

Jehanbux(USA), a 1m maiden winner on fast ground and narrowly beaten over 1m1f here last time, was blinkered for the first time. He made the running next to the stands' rail and held off all his rivals in that group, but was well beaten by those up the centre. (tchd 16-1)

Profondo Rosso(IRE), a winner at around this trip on easy ground, had put up both his recent efforts on sharp, turning tracks. Making his handicap debut, he was one of the first under pressure and could never get involved. (op 7-2)

Buthelezi(USA), a dual winner at 1m, including on easy ground, was fitted with an eyeshield for the first time as he apparently works in one at home. He was close enough early on the near side, but was in trouble before reaching the top of the hill over 2f out. (op 10-3 tchd 4-1)

6506 NOEL MURLESS STKS (LISTED RACE) 1m 6f

3:10 (3:12) (Class 1) 3-Y-O

£19,869 (£7,532; £3,769; £1,879; £941; £472) **Stalls** Centre

Form RPR

1201 **1** **Harris Tweed**19 5938 3-9-3 112 LiamJones 6 116+
(W J Haggas) *racd keenly: mde all: pushed clr ent fnl 2f: in command fr over 1f out: eased towards fin: comf* **5/4**1

3165 **2** *3* **Ship's Biscuit**21 5881 3-8-9 100 RyanMoore 3 102
(Sir Michael Stoute) *stdd and dropped after s: hld up in last trio: rdn and effrt 4f out: no prog tl hdwy u.p wl over 1f out: wnt 3rd 1f out: kpt on u.p to go 2nd fnl 100yds: nvr a threat to wnr* **5/1**2

2213 **3** *1¾* **Western Pearl**12 6199 3-8-9 86 JamieSpencer 4 100
(W J Knight) *wnt rt and bmpd rival s: sn rcvrd and chsd ldng pair: rdn to chse wnr jst over 3f out: drvn and no imp ent fnl 2f: plugged on same pce and wl hld after: lost 2nd fnl 100yds* **8/1**3

1350 **4** *3¼* **Moose Moran (USA)**41 5273 3-9-0 99 TomQueally 5 100
(H R A Cecil) *in tch in midfield: effrt u.p ent fnl 3f: unable qck and drvn jst over 2f out: chsd ldng pair and no prog u.p over 1f out: lost 3rd 1f out* **14/1**

1222 **5** *½* **Snoqualmie Star**12 6203 3-8-9 89 (b) DaneO'Neill 7 94
(D R C Elsworth) *stdd s: hld up in last trio: effrt u.p on far rail jst over 3f out: no prog and wl btn 2f out* **10/1**

0 **6** *2* **L Frank Baum (IRE)**6 6318 3-9-0 90 MichaelHills 1 97?
(Miss Gay Kelleway) *sn chsng wnr: rdn and lost 2nd jst over 3f out: sn struggling u.p: wl btn over 1f out* **80/1**

1040 **7** *4* **Ted Spread**19 5945 3-9-5 102 KierenFallon 8 96
(M H Tompkins) *hld up in tch in midfield: rdn and effrt 4f out: no hdwy and wl btn ent fnl 2f* **5/1**2

2405 **8** *45* **Prizefighting (USA)**22 5853 3-9-0 105 (b) WilliamBuick 2 28
(J H M Gosden) *stdd s: hld up in rr: swtchd lft to r alone towards centre 6f out: rdn and btn over 3f out: wl btn and virtually p.u fr over 1f out: t.o* **16/1**

3m 0.69s (3.69) **Going Correction** +0.25s/f (Good) **8** Ran SP% **111.8**
Speed ratings (Par 109): **103,101,100,98,98 97,94,69**
toteswingers:1&2 £2.80, 2&3 £4.60, 1&3 £3.10 CSF £7.25 TOTE £2.20: £1.50, £1.40, £2.20; EX 6.40 Trifecta £33.90 Pool: £1,133.81 - 24.73 winning units..
Owner B Haggas **Bred** J B Haggas **Trained** Newmarket, Suffolk

FOCUS

A solid-looking race for the level and the form looks reasonable. Last season's winner Akmal is holding his own at a higher level now, and it seems likely that this year's will be able to do the same, although it could be argued that he stole this from the front.

NOTEBOOK

Harris Tweed ◆ has made good progress this season after a couple of moderate efforts as a 2-y-o. A ten-length winner of a Listed race on his previous outing, this was the furthest he had ever tried and the signs weren't good early in the contest for him to get home, as he took a strong grip. He was still looking to go a stride too quickly for much of the race, so the fact that he quickened away so impressively bodes well for his future. Punters who backed him for the Ebor back in August must be surely thinking how unlucky they are, as he was diverted to the Voltigeur instead of taking up that engagement in case he missed the cut. He is clearly not short of pace, which should make him one to follow next season given his apparent versatility, and his racing style means he is unlikely to be a Cup horse unless he can learn to settle. William Haggas suggested afterwards that his horse will be given a break now and return for the Ormonde Stakes next May, which makes sense considering his success at Chester last time. (op Evens)

Ship's Biscuit has been running well since stepping up to this distance (she'd been beaten by Melbourne Cup candidate Eastern Aria on her last two outings) but wasn't suited by the way this race developed. It probably would have been better for her had she raced more prominently, although there is also little doubt that she would have still finished second. (op 9-2)

Western Pearl, the lowest rated of these on official figures, lost her footing at the start but kept on well after racing prominently. She should have more to come considering her relative lack of experience. (op 12-1)

Moose Moran(USA) looked a promising stayer when a good fifth in the Queens Vase, but was beaten a whopping 93 lengths in the Melrose Stakes after a break in August. Returning from another absence, he sat towards the head of the chasing bunch but was one-paced and has something to prove now. (op 20-1 tchd 22-1)

Snoqualmie Star, trying this sort of trip for the first time, attracted some market support but never got involved. (op 14-1)

L Frank Baum(IRE) wasn't obviously suited by the step up in trip. (op 66-1)

Ted Spread, a well-beaten last in the St Leger last time, looks to have completely lost his way, as he found little after travelling kindly. (op 11-2)

Prizefighting(USA), with the blinkers back on, and stepped up in trip again, was ridden down the course to the start after unshipping his jockey once on the track - the remainder cut across the middle of the course. His rider appeared keen to keep his mount away from his rivals down the home straight, but that made little difference when push came to shove. (op 11-1)

6507 SOMERVILLE TATTERSALL STKS (GROUP 3) (C&G) 7f

3:45 (3:46) (Class 1) 2-Y-O

£28,385 (£10,760; £5,385; £2,685; £1,345; £675) **Stalls** Low

Form RPR

3134 **1** **Rerouted (USA)**22 5849 2-8-12 89 MichaelHills 7 102
(B W Hills) *lw: led: hdd and drvn over 1f out: edging lft u.p ins fnl f: battled on wl to ld again last stride: all out* **8/1**

1033 **2** *shd* **Surrey Star (IRE)**23 5831 2-8-12 104 KierenFallon 1 102
(R A Teal) *in tch in midfield: niggled along 4f out: hdwy u.p and edging rt over 1f out: drvn to ld ins fnl f: kpt on wl tl hdd last stride* **11/2**3

2111 **3** *½* **Royal Exchange**41 5257 2-8-12 99 RichardHughes 2 101
(R Hannon) *lw: stdd s: hld up in rr: rdn ent fnl 2f: hdwy u.p jst over 1f out: kpt on wl fnl 100yds to go 3rd nr fin: gng on fin: nvr quite gng pce to rch ldrs* **9/4**1

2124 **4** *¾* **The Paddyman (IRE)**12 6192 2-8-12 106 PhilipRobinson 6 99
(W J Haggas) *chsd wnr tl rdn to ld over 1f out: hdd ins fnl f: no ex and btn fnl 75yds* **11/4**2

4213 **5** *¾* **Ahlaain (USA)**41 5257 2-8-12 92 WilliamBuick 5 97
(D M Simcock) *stdd s: sn chsng ldrs: rdn and effrt ent fnl 2f: kpt on same pce u.p ins fnl f* **16/1**

212 **6** 1 3/4 **Belgian Bill**[33] 5525 2-8-12 86 TonyCulhane 8 93
(George Baker) *stdd s: hld up in tch towards rr: rdn and effrt wl over 1f out: styd on same pce and no imp fr over 1f out: nvr trbld ldrs* **10/1**

1510 **7** shd **Casual Glimpse**[43] 5219 2-8-12 101 RyanMoore 3 92
(R Hannon) *hld up in tch in rr: rdn and nt qckning whn edgd rt and hmpd over 1f out: sn swtchd rt and styd on same pce ins fnl f: nvr trbld ldrs* **15/2**

1m 26.06s (0.66) **Going Correction** +0.25s/f (Good) **7** Ran SP% **110.7**
Speed ratings (Par 105): **106,105,105,104,103 101,101**
toteswingers:1&2 £7.10, 2&3 £2.90, 1&3 £4.60 CSF £47.38 TOTE £7.30: £4.10, £3.90; EX 58.70 Trifecta £186.20 Pool: £1,021.15 - 4.05 winning units..
Owner K Abdulla **Bred** Juddmonte Farms Inc **Trained** Lambourn, Berks

FOCUS
This Group 3 has often proved a useful guide to future events, having produced subsequent Group 1 winners King Charlemagne, Where Or When, Milk It Mick and Aussie Rules in the past ten years. This looked an ordinary renewal and that impression was rather backed up by the result.

NOTEBOOK
Rerouted(USA), a 6f winner on fast ground but beaten in nursery company last twice, including when three places ahead of the earlier winner Mariachi Man at Doncaster, was up in grade and looked to have a fair amount to find. He went off in front, dictating a steady pace until about halfway but, after being headed going into the Dip, kept battling away and got back in front near the line. He could go for the Horris Hill if he comes out of this well enough. (op 17-2 tchd 9-1)
Surrey Star(IRE) had been placed in a Listed and Group race on a sound surface and, after being held up, came through to hit the front meeting the rising ground. He looked sure to score but was outbattled near the line. (op 7-1 tchd 15-2)
Royal Exchange ◆ had stepped up from nurseries to win a Listed race at Salisbury on soft. He was dropping back in trip but had won over six and 7f before that. Held up at the back, he struggled to make ground as the pace quickened in front, before staying on best of all up the hill. He would have been in front in another half-furlong and can win a race at this level before too long. (op 2-1 tchd 5-2)
The Paddyman(IRE), a 6f winner on fast ground, had put up decent efforts in the Richmond and Mill Reef since. Stepping up in trip, he came through to lead running into the Dip but could not sustain his effort on the climb to the line. (op 5-2)
Ahlaain(USA), a winner over 7f on fast ground, finished 2 1/4l third behind Royal Exchange in Listed race at Salisbury on soft ground last time. He ran his race and ended up closer to that rival over this shorter trip. (op 20-1 tchd 14-1)
Belgian Bill, a 7f winner on fast ground, was up in grade and failed to get involved having been held up. (tchd 9-1 and 11-1)
Casual Glimpse, a winner at 5f and 6f on a sound surface but held in Listed and Group 2 company, had never raced on soft ground. Held up at the back, he failed to come down the hill but has now been beaten in all three tries at Pattern level. (op 8-1)

6508 NEWSELLS PARK STUD GOLDEN BONUS ROUS STKS (LISTED RACE) 5f

4:20 (4:20) (Class 1) 3-Y-O+

£19,869 (£7,532; £3,769; £1,879; £941; £472) **Stalls** Low

Form RPR

0141 **1** **Tangerine Trees**[9] 6265 5-8-12 81 (v) TomEaves 1 108
(B Smart) *awkward s: sn led and mde rest: rdn over 1f out: drvn and hld on wl ins fnl f* **9/1**

323 **2** nk **Tax Free (IRE)**[9] 6265 8-8-12 107 AdrianNicholls 4 107
(D Nicholls) *lw: chsd wnr: rdn 1/2-way: drvn wl over 1f out: pressed wnr thrght fnl f: a hld* **9/2**[2]

3001 **3** 3/4 **Quest For Success (IRE)**[10] 6241 5-8-12 98 JimmyFortune 9 104
(R A Fahey) *in tch in midfield: effrt u.p wl over 1f out: kpt on ins fnl f: nvr quite gng pce to chal ldrs* **6/1**[3]

6144 **4** hd **Hamish McGonagall**[12] 6194 5-8-12 108 DavidAllan 10 103
(T D Easterby) *chsd ldrs: rdn and effrt over 1f out: unable qck u.p 1f out: kpt on same pce fnl 150yds* **9/4**[1]

4404 **5** hd **Anglezarke (IRE)**[9] 6265 4-8-7 94 (b) JimmyQuinn 2 98
(R A Fahey) *sn in tch in midfield: rdn wl over 1f out: drvn and kpt on same pce ins fnl f* **14/1**

0510 **6** 1/2 **Monsieur Joe (IRE)**[19] 5944 3-8-11 99 TomQueally 8 101
(W R Swinburn) *hld up in rr: effrt u.p and edging lft over 1f out: kpt on but nvr gng pce to chal ldrs* **11/1**

0415 **7** 2 3/4 **Joe Packet**[6] 6319 3-8-11 97 KierenFallon 3 91
(J G Portman) *a towards rr: pushed along 3f out: keeping on same pce and btn whn hmpd jst over 1f out* **13/2**

3630 **8** 19 **Secret Asset (IRE)**[12] 6194 5-8-12 97 JamieSpencer 6 22
(Jane Chapple-Hyam) *t.k.h: hld up in tch: eased and btn over 1f out: virtually p.u ins fnl f* **8/1**

59.24 secs (0.14) **Going Correction** +0.25s/f (Good)
WFA 3 from 4yo+ 1lb **8** Ran SP% **112.7**
Speed ratings (Par 111): **108,107,106,106,105 104,100,70**
toteswingers:1&2 £4.00, 2&3 £6.30, 1&3 £7.60 CSF £47.63 TOTE £7.70: £2.80, £1.50, £1.70; EX 27.30 Trifecta £242.40 Pool: £837.13 - 2.55 winning units..
Owner Tangerine Trees Partnership **Bred** Mrs B A Matthews **Trained** Hambleton, N Yorks

FOCUS
A recent contest at Beverley, where Tangerine Trees caused a bit of a surprise when beating Tax Free and Anglezarke, proved the key to the outcome. The form is not strong for the grade with the third and fifth the best guides.

NOTEBOOK
Tangerine Trees ◆ proved that his Beverley success was no fluke with a fine piece of front running. His jockey seemed keen to get to the lead before dictating, and quickened the pace up again to hold on. He is still improving in what has been a good year for him already, with or without the visor, and looks ready for a rise into Group company next. It is also noteworthy that this win came on a surface that he hasn't excelled on in the past. (tchd 8-1 and 10-1)
Tax Free(IRE) chased the winner throughout but wasn't able to force his way past. He often runs well at this course and did so again. (op 4-1 tchd 5-1)
Quest For Success(IRE), who ran respectably in the Portland and Ayr Gold Cup, won a small-field conditions race two days after that effort at Ayr, but didn't get going here until it was a bit too late. He finished strongly to just get the better of Hamish McGonagall in the final strides to claim third. (op 7-1)
Hamish McGonagall, who was on his toes leaving the paddock, ran yet another sound race and is consistent at whatever level he runs at. Arguably, he would have preferred quicker ground, although his trainer stated in the morning that he felt it wouldn't be an excuse. (tchd 2-1 and 5-2 in places)
Anglezarke(IRE) hasn't won for a while but she didn't run too badly here, and can be found a winning opportunity by her trainer. (op 16-1 tchd 12-1)
Monsieur Joe(IRE), down the field in the Portland Handicap last time, raced towards the rear in the early stages but stayed on under pressure. He probably needs much quicker ground to be at his best, especially as his trainer has hinted that Dubai is on the horse's agenda next year. (tchd 12-1)
Joe Packet, back down to 5f, has enjoyed a good season (mostly over 6f) but was slightly outpaced from the start, which makes sense given his best form. Official explanation: jockey said gelding lost its action coming down the hill (op 7-1 tchd 15-2)
Secret Asset(IRE) appeared to go wrong about 2f from home after racing keenly. Official explanation: jockey said gelding lost its action (op 10-1 tchd 11-1)

6509 EUROPEAN BREEDERS' FUND FILLIES' H'CAP 6f

4:55 (4:55) (Class 2) (0-100,95) 3-Y-O+

£9,969 (£2,985; £1,492; £747; £372; £187) **Stalls** Low

Form RPR

-540 **1** **Amitola (IRE)**[18] 6000 3-8-9 85 JamieSpencer 11 95
(T D Barron) *chsd ldr tl rdn to ld over 1f out: hrd drvn and hld on gamely ins fnl f: all out* **14/1**

0004 **2** nk **Midnight Martini**[18] 6000 3-8-13 89 (t) DavidAllan 12 98
(T D Easterby) *lw: t.k.h: chsd ldrs: rdn and effrt 2f out: ev ch ent fnl f: kpt on wl u.p: a jst hld ins fnl f* **12/1**

1504 **3** 1 1/2 **Pretty Bonnie**[28] 5694 5-8-7 84 NataliaGemelova(3) 8 88
(A E Price) *sn led: rdn and hdd over 1f out: styd on same pce u.p ins fnl f* **16/1**

-204 **4** 1 1/2 **Sioux Rising (IRE)**[14] 6113 4-8-8 82 JimmyQuinn 4 81
(R A Fahey) *stdd s: hld up in tch in rr: rdn and effrt ent fnl f: edging rt and flashed tail u.p over 1f out: kpt on to go 4th ins fnl f: nvr trbld ldrs* **6/1**[3]

2113 **5** 3/4 **Dubai Media (CAN)**[10] 6253 3-8-8 84 KierenFallon 10 81
(E A L Dunlop) *broke wl sn std and t.k.h towards rr: rdn and effrt whn unbalanced over 1f out: one pce and no imp ins fnl f* **7/2**[1]

1215 **6** hd **Desert Poppy (IRE)**[35] 5442 3-8-9 90 JohnFahy(5) 9 86
(W R Swinburn) *hld up in tch in midfield: effrt to chse ldrs over 1f out: hrd drvn and no prog 1f out: wknd ins fnl f* **8/1**

1252 **7** 3/4 **Sooraah**[15] 6090 3-8-11 87 MichaelHills 3 81
(W J Haggas) *lw: stdd s: hld up towards rr: c to r towards stands' side 1/2-way: rdn and no hdwy wl over 1f out: nvr trbld ldrs* **7/1**

010 **8** nk **Ardent**[14] 6113 3-8-6 82 WilliamBuick 6 75
(J H M Gosden) *stdd s: hld up in tch in rr: rdn and effrt ent fnl 2f: no real prog and wl hld ent fnl f* **5/1**[2]

6020 **9** 3 **Waveband**[5] 6363 3-9-0 90 FrankieDettori 2 73
(M Johnston) *broke wl: sn stdd to chse ldrs: c to r towards stands' side 1/2-way: wknd u.p over 1f out: wl btn ins fnl f* **8/1**

4120 **10** 1/2 **Angus Newz**[16] 6064 7-8-10 84 RyanMoore 7 66
(M Quinn) *chsd ldrs: c to r towards stands' side 1/2-way: rdn and struggling 2f out: wl btn ins fnl f* **12/1**

1m 12.68s (0.48) **Going Correction** +0.25s/f (Good)
WFA 3 from 4yo+ 2lb **10** Ran SP% **115.8**
Speed ratings (Par 96): **106,105,103,101,100 100,99,98,94,94**
toteswingers:1&2 £22.90, 2&3 £33.20, 1&3 £33.10 CSF £168.84 CT £2701.57 TOTE £20.20: £5.30, £4.30, £5.20; EX 155.70 TRIFECTA Not won..
Owner J Browne **Bred** Patrick J Monahan **Trained** Maunby, N Yorks

FOCUS
A decent fillies' sprint handicap which was slightly weakened by the withdrawal of the two top weights. As in earlier races, it proved difficult to get involved from off the pace. The placed horses are rated to form and set the level.

NOTEBOOK
Amitola(IRE), a 6f winner on fast ground, had run well on soft in recent starts. She disputed the lead throughout and found plenty for pressure to get the better of the runner-up late on. She has not had much racing and looks capable of building on this. (tchd 16-1)
Midnight Martini, a winner at 5f and 6f on fast and easy ground in August 2009, had shown mixed form this season. She tracked the winner before delivering her challenge and taking a narrow lead briefly in the Dip, but could not hold on near the line. (tchd 11-1)
Pretty Bonnie, a 6f winner on fast ground who has also won on soft, disputed the lead from the start and was only seen off on the climb to the line. She ran her race but seems ideally suited by a turning track.
Sioux Rising(IRE), a dual winner at Pontefract on a sound surface last year before rather losing her way, had been showing better form of late and ran on at the finish on her first try on soft ground. (op 8-1 tchd 11-2)
Dubai Media(CAN), another who was untried on soft ground, was never far away but failed to pick up sufficiently to deliver a challenge. (op 10-3 tchd 4-1)
Desert Poppy(IRE), whose wins have been on a sound surface, had gone up 11lb for her latest win and, as last time, was again held on this soft surface.
Ardent, a lightly raced winner over 6f on good, was another unraced on soft and never got involved, having been held up. (op 11-2 tchd 6-1)
Angus Newz was running in this for the fifth time, having won it in 2007, and the ground had come in her favour. However, she raced towards the stands' side, along with Waveband and Soorah, and the trio were out of contention from over 2f out. (op 10-1)

6510 RACING UK SKY 432 H'CAP 1m

5:30 (5:32) (Class 3) (0-95,93) 3-Y-O+

£8,723 (£2,612; £1,306; £653; £326; £163) **Stalls** Low

Form RPR

1206 **1** **Dance And Dance (IRE)**[28] 5702 4-9-10 90 JamieSpencer 7 99
(E F Vaughan) *stdd after s: hld up in rr: rdn and gd hdwy wl over 1f out: ev ch jst ins fnl f: drvn to ld fnl 75yds: all out* **33/1**

2645 **2** nse **Gunner Lindley (IRE)**[63] 4509 3-9-2 86 MichaelHills 17 95
(B W Hills) *led: rdn and hdd wl over 1f out: led again jst over 1f out: drvn fnl f: hdd fnl 75yds: kpt on gamely: jst hld* **14/1**

0312 **3** hd **Arabian Spirit**[14] 6105 5-9-4 84 TomEaves 14 92
(R A Fahey) *lw: hld up in tch: rdn and hdwy over 1f out: chsd ldrs and drvn ins fnl f: kpt on wl u.p towards fin* **16/1**

6013 **4** shd **Credit Swap**[4] 6391 5-9-9 89 JimmyFortune 2 99+
(M Wigham) *lw: stdd s: hld up in rr: hdwy over 1f out: bmpd and pushed sltly lft 1f out: str run fnl 150yds: nt quite rch ldrs* **4/1**[2]

6111 **5** 1 **Parvaaz (IRE)**[12] 6205 3-9-9 93 FrankieDettori 9 99+
(M A Jarvis) *t.k.h: hld up towards rr: hdwy whn nt clr run wl over 1f out tl wnt between horses 1f out: sn drvn and chsng ldrs: kpt on same pce fnl 100yds* **11/2**[3]

0423 **6** 1 **Thunderball**[18] 5997 4-9-2 82 DavidAllan 13 86
(J A Glover) *b: chsd ldrs: wnt 2nd 2f out: sn rdn to ld: drvn and hdd jst over 1f out: wknd u.p fnl 100yds* **22/1**

1304 **7** 1 **Rasselas (IRE)**[22] 5854 3-8-10 83 MichaelGeran(3) 12 84+
(D Nicholls) *swtg: hld up towards rr: effrt and nt clr run wl over 1f out tl swtchd lft 1f out: styd on wl ins fnl f: nvr able to chal* **20/1**

1040 **8** 1 1/2 **Kay Gee Be (IRE)**[12] 6204 6-9-0 85 JohnFahy(5) 4 83
(W Jarvis) *dwlt and bmpd s: t.k.h: hld up in tch in midfield: rdn and effrt to chse ldrs wl over 1f out: wknd jst ins fnl f* **16/1**

21-0 **9** nse **Botanist**[49] 5004 3-8-11 81 RyanMoore 11 79
(Sir Michael Stoute) *stdd s: hld up in midfield: rdn and hdwy 2f out: chsd ldrs and drvn over 1f out: wknd fnl 150yds* **9/1**

2531 **10** 1 3/4 **Kindest**[12] 6204 4-9-5 85 GeorgeBaker 6 79
(C F Wall) *trckd ldrs: rdn and unable qck wl over 1f out: btn and losing pl whn sltly hmpd and pushed lft 1f out: wknd ins fnl f* **7/2**[1]

3041 **11** ½ **Mujood**[18] 5993 7-9-7 87 (v) TomQueally 16 80
(Eve Johnson Houghton) *chsd ldr tl 2f out: sn struggling u.p: one pce and no threat to ldrs fr over 1f out* **25/1**

0534 **12** ¾ **Keys Of Cyprus**[14] 6105 8-9-2 82 AdrianNicholls 1 73
(D Nicholls) *s.i.s: hld up in rr: rdn and no prog 2f out: nvr trbld ldrs* **14/1**

0100 **13** 3½ **King's Colour**[12] 6205 5-9-2 85 EJMcNamara(3) 15 68
(B R Johnson) *b: stdd s: t.k.h: hld up towards rr: hdwy into midfield 1/2-way: rdn and wknd wl over 1f out* **20/1**

0404 **14** 3¼ **Hacienda (IRE)**[26] 5759 3-9-9 93 PhilipRobinson 5 68
(M Johnston) *swtg: chsd ldrs tl rdn and wknd qckly over 1f out: wl bhd ins fnl f* **25/1**

11-0 **15** *nk* **Eolith**[10] 6252 3-9-0 84 WilliamBuick 3 59
(W J Knight) *in tch in midfield: rdn and struggling ent fnl 2f: wknd and bhd fr wl over 1f out* **11/1**

1m 39.65s (1.05) **Going Correction** +0.25s/f (Good)
WFA 3 from 4yo+ 4lb **15** Ran SP% **125.5**
Speed ratings (Par 107): **104,103,103,103,102 101,100,99,99,97 96,96,92,89,89**
toteswingers:1&2 £79.50, 2&3 £26.90, 1&3 £52.50 CSF £422.27 CT £7665.56 TOTE £42.20: £9.10, £6.10, £3.90; EX 485.80 TRIFECTA Not won. Place 6: £2440.41 Place 5: £729.55.
Owner Mohammed Rashid **Bred** Darley **Trained** Newmarket, Suffolk

FOCUS
Earlier on the card it had looked an advantage to race up with the pace, but that angle was changed in this, as although a prominent racer finished second, all the action centred on those coming from the back. The third sets the standard.

NOTEBOOK
Dance And Dance(IRE), trying 1m again, was held up towards the rear early on before threading his way round the field to win in a close finish. It's entirely possible that Jamie Spencer is the key to this horse as he has a 32111 record on him after this victory. (op 28-1)
Gunner Lindley(IRE), having his first run since the end of July, sat towards the head of the field and rallied bravely under pressure to almost get up again. (op 12-1)
Arabian Spirit could be picked out travelling strongly in mid-pack, and kept on well under a strong drive once in the clear. (op 14-1)
Credit Swap ◆ was travelling smoothly alongside the winner in rear for much of the race but could not find an instant gap when needed. He kept on strongly once getting through, and would have probably been in front in another 50 yards. (op 9-2)
Parvaaz(IRE) ◆, 6lb higher than last time, lost his place soon after the start and then became a bit keen under restraint. His rider tried to find his way through runners but appeared to get hampered at least twice before room was found. The horse quickened when in the clear but he had no chance of catching the leading bunch quickly enough to cause them a problem. He is not one to give up on, especially as this run came on ground that was against him. Official explanation: jockey said colt was denied a clear run (op 5-1 tchd 9-2)
Thunderball, without headgear this time, helped to set the gallop but didn't get home as well as others. She needs to drop in the weights to hold an obvious winning chance. (op 20-1 tchd 25-1)
Rasselas(IRE) ◆ was another horse who had to delay his bid due to a lack of room, and can be rated a bit better than his finishing position. (op 18-1)
Botanist ◆, having his first run since mid-August, which was his first outing in 303 days, shaped like a horse in need of further. His Group 1-winning sister Red Bloom (that victory came in the Fillies' Mile as a 2-y-o) achieved her best RPRs over 1m2f. (op 8-1 tchd 10-1)
Kindest, raised 5lb for winning over C&D last time, looked sure to play a big part at the end over 2f out but steadily weakened. (op 5-1)
King's Colour was starting to weaken when his rider dropped his whip over 1f out. (op 25-1 tchd 33-1)
Eolith was backed again but is not showing anything like the form that saw her go unbeaten as a juvenile. (op 14-1)
T/Plt: £1,770.30 to a £1 stake. Pool of £85,679.60 - 35.33 winning tickets. T/Qpdt: £198.70 to a £1 stake. Pool of £6,580.25 - 24.50 winning tickets. SP

5608 WARWICK (L-H)
Thursday, September 30

OFFICIAL GOING: Soft (good to soft in places; 5.0)
Throughout the card there appeared to be an advanatage in coming wide and racing near the stands' rail in the straight, the closer the better.
Wind: Light behind Weather: Fine

6511 EUROPEAN BREEDERS' FUND MAIDEN FILLIES' STKS (DIV I) 7f 26y
2:10 (2:13) (Class 5) 2-Y-O **£3,070** (£906; £453) **Stalls** Low

Form RPR

1 **Janicellaine (IRE)** 2-9-0 0 WilliamCarson 5 72
(B W Hills) *s.s: hld up: hdwy over 2f out: r.o to ld wl ins fnl f* **25/1**

2 ¾ **Desert Shine (IRE)** 2-9-0 0 NeilCallan 2 70
(M L W Bell) *chsd ldrs: led over 1f out: rdn and hdd wl ins fnl f* **9/1**

60 **3** 1¾ **Gainsboroughs Best (IRE)**[23] 5841 2-8-11 0 GilmarPereira(3) 7 66
(W J Haggas) *led: rdn and hdd over 1f out: styd on same pce wl ins fnl f* **66/1**

4 ½ **Port Hollow** 2-9-0 0 RobertWinston 10 65
(B W Hills) *s.s: hld up: hdwy 1/2-way: rdn and hung rt fr over 1f out: no ex ins fnl f* **9/2[3]**

6 **5** ½ **Undulant Way**[23] 5841 2-9-0 0 PatDobbs 3 63
(Mrs A J Perrett) *chsd ldrs: rdn over 1f out: styd on same pce ins fnl f* **9/2[3]**

0 **6** 7 **Miss T**[31] 5595 2-9-0 0 PaulMulrennan 4 46
(J G Given) *hld up: rdn over 2f out: nvr on terms* **50/1**

3 **7** *nk* **Sally Friday (IRE)**[23] 5841 2-9-0 0 IanMongan 8 45
(P Winkworth) *chsd ldr tl rdn over 2f out: hung lft and wknd ins fnl f* **7/2[2]**

0 **8** 1¾ **Mrs Neat (IRE)**[139] 2077 2-9-0 0 DavidProbert 9 41
(S Kirk) *hld up: a in rr* **50/1**

320 **9** *13* **Sahafh (USA)**[23] 5841 2-9-0 77 (p) TedDurcan 11 8
(Saeed Bin Suroor) *chsd ldrs: rdn over 3f out: wknd over 2f out* **2/1[1]**

10 ¾ **Last Act (IRE)** 2-9-0 0 FergusSweeney 1 6
(M R Hoad) *s.s: outpcd* **66/1**

1m 29.17s (4.57) **Going Correction** +0.475s/f (Yiel) **10** Ran SP% **112.7**
Speed ratings (Par 92): **92,91,89,88,88 80,79,77,62,61**
toteswingers:1&2 £33.80, 2&3 £57.70, 1&3 £23.30 CSF £218.91 TOTE £32.20: £8.90, £3.90, £14.70; EX 290.00.
Owner Christopher Wright & Minster Stud **Bred** Ballylinch Stud **Trained** Lambourn, Berks

FOCUS
They went a fair gallop, with the placed horses coming from both ends of the field. All the runners raced in the stands' side half of the course in the straight, as is usually the case on soft ground.

NOTEBOOK
Janicellaine(IRE), a Beat Hollow filly, did well to win after missing the break, at which point her chance had looked minimal, but she got a lovely run along the favoured stands' rail. This big filly should stay 1m already and ought to get at least 1m2f next season.
Desert Shine(IRE), by Green Desert, is not likely to stay as far as the winner on breeding but made an equally encouraging debut. This looks a good trip for her at present and she has a sporting chance of winning a similar event. (op 8-1 tchd 10-1)
Gainsboroughs Best(IRE) had had got behind early on in her first two races but was sharper mentally this time. Running much better as a consequence, she might be good enough to win a maiden but nurseries now look an attractive alternative. (op 40-1)
Port Hollow, by Beat Hollow, made a satisfactory debut despite being too headstrong. The paddock pick, she will improve for the experience and should stay 1m-plus next season. (op 15-2)
Undulant Way has done reasonably well in both her maidens, and has enough ability to win races, but is effectively waiting for a handicap mark. (op 5-1)
Miss T, a Bertolini filly, has not done well enough in her first two races to suggest she is good maiden-race material, but she will not be without hope when qualified for a handicap mark. (op 40-1)
Sally Friday(IRE) had done better on Polytrack first time out and needs another race to assess her prospects. It may be that either the turf generally, or the soft ground in particular, did not suit her as well. (op 3-1 tchd 11-4)
Sahafh(USA), wearing a blanket and blindfold for stalls entry, got away on good terms this time but folded quickly off the turn. The soft ground may have been against her, but she is starting to disappoint. Official explanation: jockey said filly was unsuited by the soft (good to soft places) ground (op 15-8 tchd 9-4)

6512 EUROPEAN BREEDERS' FUND MAIDEN FILLIES' STKS (DIV II) 7f 26y
2:45 (2:47) (Class 5) 2-Y-O **£3,070** (£906; £453) **Stalls** Low

Form RPR

52 **1** **Mazagee (FR)**[15] 6071 2-9-0 0 TedDurcan 10 79
(D R Lanigan) *a.p: pushed along over 2f out: rdn and r.o to ld nr fin* **3/1[2]**

336 **2** *shd* **Fenella Fudge**[20] 5910 2-9-0 90 PaulMulrennan 3 79
(J G Given) *chsd ldr tl led over 2f out: rdn ins fnl f: hdd nr fin* **11/4[1]**

3 1¼ **Fine Threads** 2-9-0 0 RobertWinston 4 76
(B W Hills) *s.s: hdwy over 4f out: pushed along 1/2-way: styd on* **8/1**

00 **4** 2¼ **Gothic Chick**[70] 4286 2-9-0 0 JamieMackay 2 70
(Miss Amy Weaver) *led: hdd over 2f out: no ex ins fnl f* **150/1**

5 *nse* **Sacred Shield** 2-9-0 0 IanMongan 11 70
(H R A Cecil) *hld up: pushed along 1/2-way: styd on ins fnl f: nvr nrr* **3/1[2]**

60 **6** 2 **Strictly Pink (IRE)**[12] 6176 2-9-0 0 CathyGannon 9 65
(A Bailey) *chsd ldrs: lost pl over 4f out: sn pushed along: rallied and hung lft over 1f out: wknd ins fnl f* **5/1[3]**

0 **7** *11* **Farmer's Wife**[10] 6247 2-9-0 0 ShaneKelly 5 37
(W J Haggas) *dwlt: hld up: rdn over 2f out: wknd and eased over 1f out* **25/1**

0055 **8** 1¼ **Lettering**[12] 6211 2-8-11 47 (b[1]) MartinLane(3) 6 34
(D Haydn Jones) *chsd ldrs: rdn 1/2-way: wknd over 2f out* **100/1**

1m 28.92s (4.32) **Going Correction** +0.475s/f (Yiel) **8** Ran SP% **109.9**
Speed ratings (Par 92): **94,93,92,89,89 87,74,73**
toteswingers:1&2 £1.70, 2&3 £5.70, 1&3 £4.00 CSF £10.69 TOTE £3.80: £1.70, £1.10, £1.80; EX 10.10.
Owner Saif Ali & Saeed H Altayer **Bred** Jean-Philippe Dubois **Trained** Newmarket, Suffolk

FOCUS
As with division one, there was a respectable pace in the conditions, and the two times were similar.

NOTEBOOK
Mazagee(FR), who has improved steadily in three maidens, knuckled down well just off the stands' rail to snatch the race from the long-time leader, whose previous form had been good for this level. She should have no problem staying 1m. (op 11-4 tchd 5-2)
Fenella Fudge, who appreciated the drop back to maiden company and return to 7f, had the favoured stands' rail and was the winner everywhere bar the line. She is rated to win most maidens and it would be disappointing if she could not be found a suitable opportunity. (tchd 5-2 and 3-1)
Fine Threads, a Barathea sister to a Grade 2 winner, shaped nicely on this debut. The form of the first two looks sound enough at this level, so she must have a fair chance of getting off the mark soon.
Gothic Chick was ridden more positively than on her first two starts and ran by far her best race to date. Now qualified for nurseries, she would have a chance as long as her mark is not distorted by her relative proximity to the runner-up. (op 100-1)
Sacred Shield, by Beat Hollow and from a decent family, made little impact but there were more encouraging signs as the race reached its climax. She has plenty of improvement in her and is worth another chance. (tchd 4-1)
Strictly Pink(IRE), not beaten far in a Group 3 race last time, was well below that form here. The ground may not have been ideal, and maidens may still be the best option for her if her impending handicap mark is based upon her last outing. (op 8-1 tchd 4-1)

6513 EXPO ANNIVERSARY NURSERY 7f 26y
3:20 (3:21) (Class 5) (0-75,75) 2-Y-O **£2,590** (£770; £385; £192) **Stalls** Low

Form RPR

1160 **1** **Mica Mika (IRE)**[31] 5597 2-9-0 70 BarryMcHugh(3) 6 76
(R A Fahey) *a.p: rdn over 1f out: r.o to ld wl ins fnl f* **10/1**

236 **2** ¾ **Grand Duchy**[15] 6092 2-9-0 74 AntiocoMurgia(7) 2 78
(Mahmood Al Zarooni) *chsd ldrs: led over 1f out: rdn: hung rt and hdd wl ins fnl f* **8/1**

0300 **3** 5 **Alexs Rainbow (USA)**[40] 5301 2-8-12 65 FergusSweeney 3 57
(J Gallagher) *w ldr tl led over 2f out: rdn and hdd over 1f out: wknd ins fnl f* **40/1**

4400 **4** 1½ **Saskia's Dream**[13] 6156 2-8-10 70 (p) LewisWalsh(7) 1 58
(Jane Chapple-Hyam) *mid-div: hdwy 1/2-way: rdn over 1f out: wknd ins fnl f* **15/2[3]**

1 **5** *shd* **Lucy Limelites**[34] 5488 2-9-6 73 SteveDrowne 4 61
(R Charlton) *dwlt: sn pushed along in rr: styd on fr over 1f out: nvr on terms* **3/1[1]**

0432 **6** ¾ **Millies Folly**[52] 4899 2-8-10 70 NeilFarley(7) 12 56
(D Carroll) *led: hdd over 2f out: wknd fnl f* **12/1**

015 **7** 2 **Fairlie Dinkum**[12] 6184 2-9-6 73 RoystonFfrench 5 54
(B Smart) *prom: lost pl over 4f out: n.d after* **12/1**

0456 **8** 1 **Classic Voice (IRE)**[7] 6311 2-9-1 68 PatDobbs 14 46
(R Hannon) *hld up: pushed along over 2f out: nvr on terms* **14/1**

5021 **9** *hd* **Restless Bay (IRE)**[7] 6311 2-9-8 75 6ex (p) AdamKirby 7 53
(R Hollinshead) *s.i.s: hdwy 1/2-way: rdn over 2f out: wknd over 1f out: eased* **11/1**

0140 **10** 2 **Veil Of Night**[12] 6191 2-8-11 71 HarryBentley(7) 10 44
(D Haydn Jones) *prom: rdn over 2f out: sn wknd* **22/1**

0405 **11** 1 **Philharmonic Hall**[30] 5637 2-8-13 66 PaulMulrennan 11 36
(R A Fahey) *hld up: a in rr* **16/1**

3253 **12** ¾ **Sixty Roses (IRE)**[23] 5830 2-9-4 71 ShaneKelly 13 39
(J L Dunlop) *s.s: rdn over 2f out: a in rr* **11/2[2]**

1m 27.6s (3.00) **Going Correction** +0.475s/f (Yiel) **12** Ran SP% **115.4**
Speed ratings (Par 95): **101,100,94,92,92 91,89,88,88,85 84,83**
toteswingers:1&2 £12.60, 2&3 £53.20, 1&3 £15.00 CSF £85.37 CT £3041.18 TOTE £9.40: £2.10, £3.20, £15.10; EX 104.00.
Owner Mrs Una Towell **Bred** Yeomanstown Stud **Trained** Musley Bank, N Yorks

■ Stewards' Enquiry : Fergus Sweeney caution: careless riding.

FOCUS

A solid gallop gave everyone a chance, but again it looked helpful to race close to the outside rail in the straight.

NOTEBOOK

Mica Mika(IRE) had twice been beaten off a mark only a pound higher than this, but he won the race for the stands' rail and handled the ground better than most. He has already proved himself to be a tough battler, and his will-to-win did the rest. (op 14-1)

Grand Duchy, running better than he had done on soft ground in his final maiden, appears to have arrived in nurseries on a fair mark. He should be placed to win a similar race. (op 17-2 tchd 9-1)

Alexs Rainbow(USA) has handled soft ground in her two attempts on it, but she was stepping up in trip and the final furlong just stretched her a bit in the conditions. However, she excelled herself and has fair prospects in similar company. (op 33-1)

Saskia's Dream just looks on too high a mark judged on her three nurseries to date. However, she was not helped by racing in the middle of the track and her overall form suggests she has the ability to win races when she is dropped a few pounds. (op 9-1)

Lucy Limelites, who won her maiden in the soft, got going too late in the unfavoured middle of the track. She is bred to stay 1m-plus and can do better when stepped up in trip, with trainer Roger Charlton believing she may be at least as good on better ground. Official explanation: jockey said filly missed the break (op 5-2 tchd 7-2)

Millies Folly, already proven on soft, adopted her usual front-running tactics. However, she was beaten in the dash to the stands' rail and that was the end of her. (op 16-1)

Sixty Roses(IRE) Official explanation: jockey said filly reared as stalls opened

6514 EUROPEAN BREEDERS' FUND MAIDEN STKS (C&G) 7f 26y

3:55 (3:58) (Class 5) 2-Y-O £3,238 (£963; £481; £240) Stalls Low

Form				RPR
64	1		**Labarinto**[41] 5263 2-8-11 0 Louis-PhilippeBeuzelin(3) 10 (Sir Michael Stoute) *a.p: rdn to chse ldr and swtchd lft over 2f out: led over 1f out: sn clr: eased nr fin* **3/1**[2]	81+
62	2	4	**Cadore (IRE)**[14] 6127 2-9-0 0 JackMitchell 2 (P W Chapple-Hyam) *chsd ldr tl led over 5f out: rdn and hdd over 1f out: sn outpcd* **11/8**[1]	71
54	3	1	**Dressing Room (USA)**[36] 5404 2-9-0 0 SilvestreDeSousa 1 (M Johnston) *s.s: hdwy u.p over 1f out: r.o to go 3rd nr fin* **13/2**[3]	69
03	4	nse	**Perfect Mission**[21] 5886 2-9-0 0 DavidProbert 9 (A M Balding) *chsd ldrs: rdn over 2f out: no ex fnl f: lost 3rd nr fin* **10/1**	68
0	5	1 ¼	**Spirit Of Gondree (IRE)**[13] 6145 2-9-0 0 TedDurcan 5 (J L Dunlop) *hld up: hdwy over 2f out: swtchd rt over 1f out: nvr nr to chal* **40/1**	65
	6	nk	**Red Mercury (IRE)** 2-9-0 0 CathyGannon 12 (M R Channon) *hld up: hdwy over 2f out: rdn over 1f out: styd on* **33/1**	65
6	7	2	**Pasquino (USA)**[147] 1845 2-9-0 0 RoystonFfrench 3 (Mahmood Al Zarooni) *hld up in tch: rdn over 2f out: wknd over 1f out* **9/1**	60
	8	4	**Cadmium Loch** 2-8-11 0 RussKennemore(3) 4 (R Hollinshead) *s.i.s: hld up: sme hdwy 2f out: wknd over 1f out* **100/1**	50
04	9	2	**Jelyvator**[12] 6211 2-9-0 0 LukeMorris 14 (A M Hales) *prom: rdn 1/2-way: wknd 2f out* **100/1**	45
0	10	2 ½	**Ferruccio (IRE)**[13] 6153 2-9-0 0 PatCosgrave 7 (J R Fanshawe) *hld up in tch: rdn over 2f out: sn wknd* **33/1**	38
0	11	2 ¼	**Hawridge Knight**[61] 4577 2-8-12 0 ow1 JamesMillman(3) 6 (B R Millman) *hld up: rdn 3f out: sn wknd* **80/1**	34
	12	2 ¾	**Kepler's Law** 2-9-0 0 StevieDonohoe 8 (Sir Mark Prescott) *s.s: a in rr: wknd over 2f out* **33/1**	26
	13	2	**Easydoesit (IRE)** 2-9-0 0 MickyFenton 13 (D Donovan) *dwlt: a in rr: wknd over 2f out* **100/1**	21
	14	3 ½	**Cliffords Reprieve** 2-9-0 0 TravisBlock 11 (E A Wheeler) *led: hdd over 5f out: remained handy: rdn over 2f out: wkng whn hmpd over 1f out* **100/1**	12

1m 29.38s (4.78) **Going Correction** +0.475s/f (Yiel) **14** Ran SP% **116.0**

Speed ratings (Par 95): **91,86,85,85,83 83,81,76,74,71 68,65,63,59**

toteswingers:1&2 £2.00, 2&3 £3.50, 1&3 £4.20 CSF £6.81 TOTE £3.60: £1.10, £1.40, £1.30; EX 8.20.

Owner K Abdulla **Bred** Juddmonte Farms Ltd **Trained** Newmarket, Suffolk

FOCUS

The gallop was again fair enough in the ground, and the first two were the pair who made an immediate beeline for the stands' rail off the bend. Both have Group 1 entries, which gives the form a solid look.

NOTEBOOK

Labarinto was beaten to the rail by the runner-up, but he was still able to challenge just outside his rival and impressively drew clear. This progressive colt showed promise in fast-ground maidens, but he looked particularly at home in these softer conditions. (op 7-2)

Cadore(IRE) won the dash for the stands' side rail but was then left standing by the improving winner. He has now run well twice on soft ground and that should help him find a maiden this autumn unless conditions significantly dry up. (op 6-5 tchd Evens)

Dressing Room(USA), well-backed, caught the eye, coming home in the unhelpful middle of the course after a slow start. Probably capable of winning a typical maiden, with 1m likely to suit, he is now qualified for nurseries and should find a race soon whichever route he takes. (op 8-1 tchd 9-1)

Perfect Mission has done better in his second and third maidens and looks ready to make his mark in nurseries. (op 9-1)

Spirit Of Gondree(IRE) improved greatly on his debut. He is one to note when he has a handicap mark. (op 33-1)

Red Mercury(IRE), a Majestic Missile colt who has winners in the family, should come on for this satisfactory first outing.

Pasquino(USA) has not done much in two maidens but will get a rating after one more run. (op 16-1)

6515 CHAMPAGNE LANSON H'CAP 6f

4:30 (4:32) (Class 6) (0-65,65) 3-Y-O+ £1,942 (£578; £288; £144) Stalls Low

Form				RPR
6024	1		**Hatta Stream (IRE)**[16] 6057 4-9-2 65 SimonPearce(5) 13 (J Pearce) *a.p: rdn to ld over 1f out: r.o* **10/1**	75
0055	2	½	**Charles Parnell (IRE)**[5] 6370 7-8-10 57 MichaelStainton(3) 3 (S P Griffiths) *dwlt: in rr: hdwy over 1f out: sn rdn: r.o* **10/1**	65
4310	3	2 ¼	**Bermondsey Bob (IRE)**[3] 6421 4-9-2 60 CathyGannon 1 (J L Spearing) *chsd ldrs: rdn over 1f out: sn hung rt: styd on same pce ins fnl f* **15/2**[2]	61
3415	4	½	**Cardinal**[37] 5379 5-9-7 65 JackMitchell 12 (R M H Cowell) *rrd s and lost many l: hdwy and swtchd lft over 1f out: r.o: nrst fin* **8/1**[3]	64+
6006	5	nk	**Bel Cantor**[14] 6110 7-9-0 65 (v) MatthewCosham(7) 4 (W J H Ratcliffe) *hld up in tch: rdn over 1f out: no ex ins fnl f* **7/1**[1]	63
6115	6	nk	**Emiratesdotcom**[3] 6421 4-9-4 62 AdamKirby 7 (J M Bradley) *hmpd s: outpcd: r.o ins fnl f: nrst fin* **7/1**[1]	59+
3316	7	1	**Anjomarba (IRE)**[21] 5897 3-9-2 62 WilliamCarson 14 (B R Johnson) *w ldr tl rdn over 2f out: hung lft fr over 1f out: no ex* **18/1**	56
2030	8	nk	**Speak The Truth (IRE)**[18] 5995 4-9-5 63 (p) PatCosgrave 9 (J R Boyle) *led: rdn and hdd over 1f out: wknd ins fnl f* **20/1**	56
6046	9	2 ½	**Stargazing (IRE)**[14] 6133 4-8-11 58 (b) Louis-PhilippeBeuzelin(3) 10 (B J Meehan) *mid-div: hdwy over 2f out: rdn and hung lft over 1f out: wknd ins fnl f* **25/1**	43
500-	10	1 ¾	**Senate Majority**[377] 6068 3-8-12 58 PaulMulrennan 8 (T D Easterby) *hld up: hdwy 2f out: hmpd and lost pl over 1f out: n.d after* **16/1**	38
2140	11	½	**Stamford Blue**[21] 5875 9-9-1 59 (b) LukeMorris 2 (R A Harris) *chsd ldrs: outpcd over 2f out: rallied over 1f out: wknd and eased ins fnl f* **8/1**[3]	43
1326	12	1	**Mata Hari Blue**[10] 6261 4-9-7 65 KirstyMilczarek 17 (J R Holt) *prom: rdn over 2f out: wknd over 1f out* **12/1**	40
5460	13	2 ¼	**Kyllachy Storm**[21] 5875 6-9-5 63 (b) FergusSweeney 6 (R J Hodges) *hmpd s: nvr on terms* **18/1**	31
000	14	2	**Fernando Torres**[21] 5897 4-9-2 60 J-PGuillambert 5 (N P Littmoden) *wnt rt s: a in rr* **20/1**	21
0052	15	2 ¾	**Coolree Star (IRE)**[6] 6330 3-9-3 63 RobertWinston 15 (J A Glover) *chsd ldrs: rdn over 3f out: wknd over 2f out* **22/1**	15

1m 14.43s (2.63) **Going Correction** +0.475s/f (Yiel)

WFA 3 from 4yo+ 2lb **15** Ran SP% **119.0**

Speed ratings (Par 101): **101,100,97,96,96 95,94,94,90,88 87,86,83,80,77**

toteswingers:1&2 £14.80, 2&3 £11.00, 1&3 £14.30 CSF £98.23 CT £817.69 TOTE £7.80: £3.20, £3.00, £4.10; EX 91.80.

Owner Macniler Racing Partnership **Bred** T W Bloodstock Ltd **Trained** Newmarket, Suffolk

FOCUS

On this occasion high stalls were a help rather than a hindrance. The winner grabbed the favoured outside rail in the straight, but the runner-up was wider until gradually edging towards the outside in the last 200 yards.

Cardinal Official explanation: jockey said horse reared as stalls opened

Senate Majority Official explanation: jockey said gelding suffered interference in running

Fernando Torres Official explanation: vet said gelding lost its off-hind shoe

6516 IGNITE INCENTIVES H'CAP 1m 6f 213y

5:05 (5:08) (Class 4) (0-85,92) 3-Y-O+ £6,152 (£1,830; £914; £456) Stalls Low

Form				RPR
2361	1		**Royal Trooper (IRE)**[11] 6224 4-9-5 76 6ex PaulMulrennan 1 (J G Given) *mde virtually all: rdn over 1f out: styd on gamely* **9/2**[1]	83
100	2	nk	**Arab League (IRE)**[12] 6201 5-9-4 75 WilliamCarson 10 (R J Price) *hld up: hdwy over 4f out: rdn to chse wnr over 1f out: edgd rt: styd on* **9/1**	82
5455	3	¾	**Veloso (FR)**[18] 5991 8-9-3 79 SimonPearce(5) 2 (J A Glover) *a.p: chsd wnr 6f out tl rdn over 3f out: styd on* **9/1**	85
20-4	4	½	**Taikoo**[11] 6224 5-9-7 78 TravisBlock 6 (H Morrison) *hld up: hdwy over 6f out: rdn over 3f out: styng on whn nt clr run wl ins fnl f: nvr able to chal* **9/2**[1]	84+
/006	5	nk	**Rock Soleil**[6] 6331 6-8-12 69 StevieDonohoe 13 (Jane Chapple-Hyam) *a.p: chsd wnr over 3f out tl rdn over 1f out: styd on same pce ins fnl f* **25/1**	74
6413	6	½	**Bollin Judith**[14] 6109 4-8-12 69 (t) DavidNolan 7 (T D Easterby) *hld up: hdwy over 2f out: sn rdn: no ex towards fin* **6/1**[2]	73
1200	7	6	**Outrageous Request**[18] 5996 4-9-1 79 JamesRogers(7) 11 (Pat Eddery) *pushed along early: chsd wnr over 3f: remained handy: rdn over 2f out: wknd over 1f out* **18/1**	76
504	8	4 ½	**Hollow Green (IRE)**[14] 6131 4-9-6 77 (v) CathyGannon 8 (P D Evans) *hld up: rdn over 3f out: wknd over 2f out* **33/1**	68
433	9	9	**Red Fama**[16] 6051 6-8-11 68 SilvestreDeSousa 9 (N Bycroft) *sn prom: chsd wnr 11f out to 6f out: rdn over 3f out: sn wknd* **13/2**[3]	47
33-2	10	4 ½	**Tricky Situation**[7] 6306 4-8-13 70 RobertWinston 5 (D H Brown) *s.i.s: sn hld up in tch: racd keenly: lost pl over 6f out: rdn over 3f out: sn wknd* **12/1**	43

3m 27.17s (8.17) **Going Correction** +0.675s/f (Yiel) **10** Ran SP% **103.7**

Speed ratings (Par 105): **105,104,104,104,104 103,100,98,93,90**

toteswingers:1&2 £3.80, 2&3 £9.10, 1&3 £5.50 CSF £36.16 CT £251.48 TOTE £4.50: £2.00, £2.60, £2.60; EX 42.30.

Owner J Barson **Bred** Western Bloodstock **Trained** Willoughton, Lincs

FOCUS

They went a solid gallop, with the winner claiming the stands' rail off the turn and making all.

6517 WARWICK (S) STKS 1m 6f 213y

5:40 (5:41) (Class 5) 3-Y-O £2,388 (£705; £352) Stalls Low

Form				RPR
4225	1		**Fine Lace (IRE)**[15] 6084 3-8-12 60 (v) SilvestreDeSousa 9 (D J S Ffrench Davis) *hld up: rn in snatches: hdwy u.p to chse ldr over 1f out: led ins fnl f: styd on wl: comf* **7/4**[1]	57
3-02	2	2 ½	**Admiral Breese**[105] 3113 3-9-3 54 AdamKirby 8 (R Hollinshead) *hld up: hdwy over 3f out: led 2f out: sn rdn clr: hdd and unable qck ins fnl f* **8/1**	59
0000	3	9	**Kitty Koo (IRE)**[22] 5869 3-8-12 46 MickyFenton 1 (A W Carroll) *chsd ldr tl led 13f out: rdn over 4f out: hdd 2f out: sn wknd* **20/1**	42
4300	4	¾	**River Tease**[8] 6287 3-9-0 59 (p) RussKennemore(3) 4 (J S Moore) *chsd ldrs: pushed along over 7f out: wknd over 1f out* **14/1**	46
-606	5	nk	**Green Army**[12] 6183 3-8-10 42 MatthewLawson(7) 6 (M R Channon) *hld up: nt clr run wl over 3f out: nvr nrr* **40/1**	46
4343	6	6	**Chasse Coeur**[24] 5811 3-8-12 63 DavidProbert 2 (A M Balding) *led 4f: chsd ldr: rdn and ev ch over 2f out: sn hung lft: wknd over 1f out* **11/4**[2]	33
3200	7	3	**Septemberintherain**[34] 5467 3-9-3 67 (v) RobertHavlin 10 (R A Mills) *prom: racd keenly: rdn over 2f out: wkng whn nt clr run wl over 1f out* **7/2**[3]	34
0000	8	35	**Shut Up Shapiro (IRE)**[15] 6093 3-9-3 49 (b[1]) TedDurcan 7 (George Baker) *trckd ldrs tl rdn and wknd over 3f out: t.o* **28/1**	—

3m 30.31s (11.31) **Going Correction** +0.675s/f (Yiel) **8** Ran SP% **113.7**

Speed ratings (Par 101): **96,94,89,89,89 86,84,65**

.The winner was sold to E Williams for 9,000gns. Admiral Breese was claimed by R. E. R. Williams for £6,000.\n\x\x

Owner Miss A Jones **Bred** R A Major **Trained** Lambourn, Berks

The Form Book, Raceform Ltd, Compton, RG20 6NL

FOCUS
A staying seller in which only two runners had the necessary combination of stamina and speed in the soft ground.

6518 SUPPORT US AT ACE-EGYPT.ORG.UK AMATEUR RIDERS' H'CAP 1m 2f 188y
6:10 (6:12) (Class 6) (0-60,60) 3-Y-O+ **£1,717** (£532; £266; £133) **Stalls** Low

Form RPR

5531 **1** **Kenyan Cat**[15] 6094 3-10-5 58 MrSWalker 9 66+
(George Baker) *hld up: hdwy wl over 1f out: hmpd 1f out: rdn to ld wl ins fnl f* **9/4**[1]

1355 **2** *1* **Lady Lam**[17] 6022 4-10-8 57 (t) MrPCollington(3) 7 63
(S Kirk) *s.s: hld up: hdwy u.p over 1f out: r.o* **14/1**

0 **3** *nk* **Heredias (GER)**[232] 173 4-10-7 60 MissBeckyBrisbourne(7) 11 66+
(W M Brisbourne) *chsd ldrs: rdn and ev ch whn hung rt 1f out: styd on* **66/1**

0006 **4** *1* **Munich (IRE)**[39] 5326 6-10-1 54 (p) MrFTett(7) 6 58
(R Curtis) *chsd ldr tl led 9f out: hdd 3f out: led again over 1f out: sn hung lft: hdd wl ins fnl f* **40/1**

0000 **5** *3 ¾* **Black Coffee**[12] 6213 5-10-11 60 MrBenBrisbourne(3) 12 57
(W M Brisbourne) *hld up: hdwy 1/2-way: rdn over 2f out: sn ev ch: hung lft fr over 1f out: no ex ins fnl f* **33/1**

-602 **6** *½* **Follow The Sun (IRE)**[16] 6051 6-10-1 52 MrJBanks(5) 3 48
(P D Niven) *chsd ldrs: led 3f out: rdn and hdd over 1f out: wknd ins fnl f* **4/1**[2]

-000 **7** *½* **Aine's Delight (IRE)**[108] 3040 4-10-5 58 MrBJPoste(7) 13 53
(Andrew Turnell) *hld up: hdwy over 4f out: rdn over 2f out: wknd over 1f out* **25/1**

6024 **8** *½* **Masterofceremonies**[9] 6269 7-10-1 54 (v) MissALMurphy(7) 8 48
(W M Brisbourne) *s.s: hld up: hdwy over 2f out: rdn and nt clr run over 1f out: wknd ins fnl f* **25/1**

5210 **9** *¾* **Royal Composer (IRE)**[49] 4985 7-9-13 50 MissRKneller(5) 4 43
(T D Easterby) *hld up: nvr on terms* **8/1**[3]

0/0- **10** *4* **Sweet World**[11] 500 6-10-11 57 MissIsabelTompsett 1 43
(B J Llewellyn) *chsd ldrs: rdn over 4f out: sn lost pl* **8/1**[3]

0050 **11** *1 ¼* **Love In The Park**[44] 5180 5-10-1 52 MrPPrince(5) 10 36
(R Brotherton) *prom: rdn over 2f out: edgd rt and wknd over 1f out* **18/1**

0-06 **12** *1* **Monfils Monfils (USA)**[9] 6269 8-10-5 58 MissLucyBell(7) 17 40
(P A Kirby) *dwlt: hdwy over 8f out: wknd over 3f out* **33/1**

5054 **13** *1 ½* **Whisper Wind**[17] 6024 3-10-2 58 (b) MrRBirkett(3) 2 37
(G L Moore) *hld up in tch: wknd over 3f out* **10/1**

2040 **14** *1* **Hurricane Thomas (IRE)**[9] 6269 6-10-9 60 MissPhillipaTutty(5) 5 37
(R A Fahey) *led 2f: chsd ldrs: rdn and wknd over 2f out* **16/1**

0000 **15** *17* **King Of Rhythm (IRE)**[9] 6269 7-9-12 51 MissCLWhitehead(7) 15 —
(D Carroll) *hld up: plld hrd: wknd 3f out: t.o* **66/1**

2m 29.77s (8.67) **Going Correction** +0.675s/f (Yiel)
WFA 3 from 4yo+ 7lb **15 Ran SP% 118.9**
Speed ratings (Par 101): **95,94,94,93,90 90,89,89,88,86 85,84,83,82,70**
toteswingers:1&2 £6.80, 2&3 £26.60, 1&3 £14.90. totesuper7: Win: Not won. Place: Not won. CSF £33.25 CT £1631.15 TOTE £3.40: £1.40, £2.50, £13.50; EX 40.90 Place 6: £1081.22 Place 5: £72.56 .
Owner David Botterill & John Guest **Bred** D R Botterill **Trained** Moreton Morrell, Warwicks

FOCUS
A race for amateurs in which the runners covered more of the width of the track than they had in previous events on the card. However, the winner still made her run more towards the stands' rail than some of her rivals.
T/Jkpt: Not won. T/Plt: £11,513.50 to a £1 stake. Pool of £52,835.94 - 3.35 winning tickets. T/Qpdt: £121.20 to a £1 stake. Pool of £4,801.00 - 29.30 winning tickets. CR

5980 TOULOUSE
Thursday, September 30
OFFICIAL GOING: Turf: good to soft

6519a PRIX PANACEE (LISTED RACE) (3YO+ FILLIES & MARES) (TURF) 1m 4f
12:20 (12:00) 3-Y-O+ **£23,008** (£9,203; £6,902; £4,601; £2,300)

RPR

1 **Vertana (IRE)**[19] 5981 3-8-6 0 FabriceVeron 5 90
(H-A Pantall, France) **83/10**

2 *nk* **Ma Preference (FR)**[18] 4-9-0 0 Francois-XavierBertras 4 89
(F Rohaut, France) **7/1**

3 *1 ½* **Ensaya (IRE)**[33] 5543 3-8-6 0 Christophe-PatriceLemaire 7 87
(M Delzangles, France) **2/1**[1]

4 *1 ½* **Soudanaise (IRE)**[27] 3-8-6 0 AnthonyCrastus 6 85
(E Lellouche, France) **58/10**

5 *1* **Lake Palace**[67] 4-9-4 0 ThierryThulliez 1 87
(N Clement, France) **9/2**[3]

6 *nk* **Allannah Abu**[15] 6074 3-8-7 0 ow1 Jean-BernardEyquem 3 84
(Sir Mark Prescott) *broke wl to ld: stl in front ent fnlng st: rdn 2f out: hdd 1 1/2f out: failed to qckn: grad fdd* **7/2**[2]

7 *2 ½* **Cavaliere (FR)**[27] 4-9-0 0 FranckBlondel 2 79
(M Cesandri, France) **17/1**

2m 31.81s (-0.49)
WFA 3 from 4yo 8lb **7 Ran SP% 117.3**
WIN (incl. 1 euro stake): 9.30. PLACES: 4.60, 4.30. SF: 55.00.
Owner Mme Sibylle Egloff **Bred** Gestut Sohrenhof **Trained** France

NOTEBOOK
Allannah Abu, officially rated 85, didn't get home. She may have been unsuited by the easier ground, but this was a big step up in class for her.

6052 LINGFIELD (L-H)
Friday, October 1
OFFICIAL GOING: Standard
Wind: Brisk behind Weather: Rain

6520 SYNDICATES AT JOHNBESTRACING.COM MEDIAN AUCTION MAIDEN STKS 5f (P)
1:45 (1:46) (Class 6) 2-Y-O **£2,047** (£604; £302) **Stalls** High

Form RPR

402 **1** **Look Who's Kool**[27] 5763 2-9-3 71 GrahamGibbons 5 73
(E S McMahon) *led 1f: styd trcking ldrs: led over 1f out: sn rdn: styd on wl u.p cl home: jst hld on* **6/1**[3]

2 *shd* **Pearl Ice** 2-9-3 0 StevieDonohoe 8 73
(Sir Mark Prescott) *in tch: rdn 2f out: hdwy towards outer over 1f out: str run ins fnl f to take 2nd cl home and clsng on wnr: jst failed* **9/4**[2]

42 **3** *nk* **Silver Ocean (USA)**[22] 5895 2-9-3 0 JimCrowley 7 72
(R M Beckett) *towards rr: in tch: hdwy 2f out: chsd wnr 1f out: styd on to cl u.p and gng on cl home but a jst hld and edgd bk to 3rd last strides* **13/8**[1]

00 **4** *1 ¾* **Firstknight**[34] 5527 2-9-3 0 PhillipMakin 9 65
(Tom Dascombe) *in rr and racd on outside: hdwy over 1f out and qcknd to chse ldrs ins fnl f: outpcd fnl 120yds* **8/1**

3 **5** *2 ½* **Loved To Bits**[102] 3260 2-8-12 0 FergusSweeney 4 51
(P J Makin) *chsd ldrs: rdn and kpt on fr over 1f out: one pce ins fnl f* **10/1**

35 **6** *2 ¾* **Whitstable Native**[10] 6263 2-9-0 0 KierenFox(3) 10 46
(J R Best) *led after 1f: hdd over 1f out and sn wknd* **20/1**

7 *shd* **Elusive Diva (IRE)** 2-8-12 0 EddieCreighton 1 41
(E J Creighton) *in rr: hrd drvn ins fnl 2f: sme prog ins fnl f* **50/1**

8 *3 ¾* **Lucky Royale** 2-8-12 0 LiamKeniry 6 28
(S Kirk) *s.i.s: rcvrd into mid-div and rdn over 2f out: wknd wl over 1f out* **40/1**

56 **9** *¾* **Hackett (IRE)**[51] 4960 2-9-0 0 MartinLane(3) 2 30
(M Quinn) *broke wl: hmpd after 50yds: rcvrd to chse ldrs sn after: wknd u.p ins fnl 2f* **33/1**

0 **10** *6* **Hey Mambo**[21] 5914 2-8-12 0 TomQueally 3 3
(R Ingram) *t.k.h: in tch tl wknd 1/2-way* **80/1**

59.19 secs (0.39) **Going Correction** +0.05s/f (Slow) **10 Ran SP% 116.7**
Speed ratings (Par 93): **98,97,97,94,90 86,86,80,78,69**
toteswingers:1&2 £5.00, 2&3 £2.20, 1&3 £3.00 CSF £19.23 TOTE £8.60: £2.10, £1.10, £1.90; EX 33.50 Trifecta £53.60 Pool: £463.66 - 6.39 winning units..
Owner S L Edwards **Bred** S L Edwards **Trained** Lichfield, Staffs

FOCUS
A miserably wet day but the going remained standard with a strong wind behind them in the straight.

NOTEBOOK
Look Who's Kool, who had been well-supported throughout the morning after a decent effort in defeat at Wolverhampton last time, just held on to a fast diminishing advantage after racing on the pace throughout. He is a speedy gelding who has a good attitude and can make his presence felt when tackling nurseries as he remains open to further improvement. (op 9-2)
Pearl Ice ◆, a 135,000euros purchase out of a winning 2-y-o sprinter, ran with plenty of promise on debut. He raced a little green and had to be scrubbed along from a fair way out but ran on well in the straight only to be narrowly denied. He will get further than this but will come on a bundle for this experience and looks certain to go one better. (op 5-2 tchd 2-1, 3-1and 7-2 in places)
Silver Ocean(USA) ◆ looked to have been found a good opportunity after some promising efforts now dropped back to the minimum. He was a little slowly away but travelled well in the midfield and had his chance in the straight. He should be capable of picking up a similar affair before long. (op 6-4 tchd 15-8)
Firstknight showed he is capable of finding an opening after being dropped back in grade but, from his poor draw, he was always racing wide and could never land a blow. (op 9-1 tchd 10-1)
Loved To Bits ran to a similar level to that of his debut after racing up with the pace for much of the way. He shaped as though he would be of interest when tackling nurseries. (op 14-1)
Whitstable Native set a decent clip but had no more to offer when headed. (op 25-1)

6521 BEST RACING LAUNCHES NEW KINGSGATE SYNDICATES MAIDEN AUCTION FILLIES' STKS 1m (P)
2:20 (2:27) (Class 6) 2-Y-O **£2,047** (£604; £302) **Stalls** High

Form RPR

6533 **1** **Dazzling Valentine**[14] 6138 2-8-4 67 ChrisCatlin 5 68
(A Bailey) *sn trcking ldr: led 3f out: c readily clr over 1f out: easily* **3/1**[2]

4 **2** *3* **Dare It And Smile (USA)**[18] 6019 2-8-5 0 MartinLane(3) 8 65
(D M Simcock) *in tch: puhed along 3f out: drvn and hdwy fr 2f out: styd on wl to go 2nd fnl 120yds: nvr any ch w easy wnr* **10/3**[3]

00 **3** *¾* **Battery Power**[16] 6070 2-8-1 0 AshleyMorgan(5) 9 61
(M H Tompkins) *in rr: pushed along over 2f out: drvn and styd on wl fr over 1f out to take 3rd fnl 75yds: gng on cl home: nvr any ch w easy wnr* **16/1**

6 **4** *1 ¼* **Petrichor**[17] 6058 2-8-10 0 LiamKeniry 10 63
(E F Vaughan) *chsd ldrs: wnt 2nd over 2f out: sn no ch w easy wnr: wknd and lost two pls fnl 120yds* **16/1**

2220 **5** *5* **Dubawi Gulf**[13] 6200 2-8-8 77 JimCrowley 4 49
(E A L Dunlop) *chsd ldrs: hrd drvn over 2f out: no imp and wknd u.p over 1f out* **13/8**[1]

0000 **6** *nse* **Magical Star**[47] 5111 2-8-4 41 FrankieMcDonald 3 45
(R Hannon) *in tch: hrd drvn to chse ldrs over 2f out: nvr on terms and wknd wl over 1f out* **33/1**

0240 **7** *2* **Summer Jasmine**[24] 5835 2-8-1 56 (v[1]) HarryBentley(7) 7 44
(H J L Dunlop) *s.i.s: in rr: pushed along 3f out: sme prog ins fnl 2f: nvr in contention and wknd wl over 1f out* **16/1**

5050 **8** *11* **Rural Pursuits**[16] 6082 2-8-4 56 NickyMackay 2 15
(Mrs C A Dunnett) *rdn 1/2-way: a in rr* **66/1**

06 **9** *½* **Patricia's Hope**[29] 5699 2-8-3 0 KierenFox(3) 12 16
(P W D'Arcy) *sn led: hdd 3f out: wknd qckly* **33/1**

0 **10** *½* **High Fallutin (IRE)**[85] 3832 2-8-5 0 ow1 LiamJones 6 14
(Eve Johnson Houghton) *rdn 1/2-way: a towards rr* **25/1**

1m 39.95s (1.75) **Going Correction** +0.05s/f (Slow) **10 Ran SP% 115.0**
Speed ratings (Par 90): **93,90,89,88,83 82,80,69,69,68**
toteswingers:1&2 £2.30, 2&3 £19.50, 1&3 £12.00 CSF £12.81 TOTE £3.60: £1.10, £2.00, £3.10; EX 12.20 Trifecta £73.20 Pool: £500.62 - 5.06 winning units..
Owner The Glenbuccaneers **Bred** Chippenham Lodge Stud Ltd **Trained** Newmarket, Suffolk

FOCUS
A fillies' maiden that lacked a lot of strength in depth.

NOTEBOOK

Dazzling Valentine sprinted away in the straight to get off the mark at the ninth attempt. Officially rated 67, she had looked as though she would always be vulnerable to an improver but, with the well-fancied favourite running well below-par, she capitalised in fine style. It's hard to assess the performance, but she is consistent and deserved this success. (tchd 11-4 and 10-3)

Dare It And Smile(USA) had shown enough on debut to suggest she has some ability and again confirmed that initial promise stepped up in trip. She remains on an upward curve. (op 7-2 tchd 4-1)

Battery Power comes from a family that improve with time when stepped up in distance. She was doing all her best work late on and posted her best effort to date. (op 12-1)

Petrichor shaped as though a step up to 1m would suit after staying on over 6f on debut. She had come on for the experience and had a chance in the straight before fading inside the final furlong. (tchd 20-1)

Dubawi Gulf was again disappointing, as on RPRs she was rated superior to her rivals. She finished soundly beaten on her AW debut on her step up to 1m and she clearly has questions to answer at present. Official explanation: jockey said filly stopped quickly (op 7-4 tchd 11-8)

6522 C BREWER & SONS (S) STKS 7f (P)

2:55 (2:57) (Class 6) 3-Y-O £2,047 (£604; £302) Stalls Low

Form RPR

0030 1 **So Surreal (IRE)**[30] 5661 3-8-7 56....(b) LiamKeniry 3 63
(G L Moore) *s.i.s: hld up in rr: stl wl bhd whn smooth hdwy on ins wl over 1f out: drvn to ld fnl 150yds: c clr: comf* **14/1**

0006 2 3 ½ **Saigon Kitty (IRE)**[52] 4931 3-8-4 58.... KierenFox(3) 11 54
(J R Best) *in rr: drvn and hdwy towards outside over 1f out: styd on wl to chse wnr fnl 75yds: nvr any ch* **25/1**

4-06 3 nk **Rich Boy**[79] 4022 3-8-13 67 ow1.... IanMongan 8 59
(Mrs L J Mongan) *in rr: hdwy on outside fr 2f out: styd on u.p fr over 1f out to cl on 2nd fnl 75yds: nvr any ch w wnr* **4/1**[1]

0P 4 1 ½ **Premier League**[238] 433 3-8-12 0.... RobertWinston 4 54
(P Howling) *chsd ldrs: rdn over 2f out: chsd wnr over 1f out but no imp: styd on same pce ins fnl f* **33/1**

0030 5 nse **Giulietta Da Vinci**[18] 6024 3-8-7 54....(p) ChrisCatlin 14 49
(S Woodman) *chsd ldr tl led 4f out: rdn 2f out: hdd & wknd fnl 150yds* **10/1**

6530 6 nk **Reddy To Star (IRE)**[80] 3975 3-8-12 57.... PhillipMakin 10 53
(Julie Camacho) *steadid towards rr: rdn over 2f out: hdwy on outside over 1f out and kpt on ins fnl f: nvr a threat* **14/1**

5024 7 ½ **Fever Tree**[56] 4791 3-8-7 58.... FergusSweeney 13 47
(P J Makin) *chsd ldrs: wnt 2nd u.p 2f out: wknd ins fnl f* **4/1**[1]

0026 8 2 **Stef And Stelio**[30] 5661 3-8-12 65....(bt) NickyMackay 1 46
(G A Butler) *in tch: rdn over 2f out: styd on same pce* **9/2**[2]

3560 9 1 **Lou Bear (IRE)**[40] 5325 3-8-12 50.... PatDobbs 12 44
(J Akehurst) *chsd ldrs tl wknd ins fnl 2f* **33/1**

0-03 10 1 **Dudley**[11] 6255 3-8-12 46....(v[1]) JimCrowley 6 41
(J G Portman) *chsd ldrs tl wknd fr 2f out* **12/1**

0240 11 ½ **King's Approach (IRE)**[30] 5669 3-8-12 57....(p) KirstyMilczarek 7 40
(R A Harris) *sn led: hdd 4f out: wknd qckly fr 2f out* **8/1**[3]

4600 12 2 **Imperial Warrior**[22] 5891 3-8-12 55....(t) EddieCreighton 2 34
(H Morrison) *plld hrd: awkward in rr early: a bhd* **20/1**

0-50 13 shd **Eclipsed (USA)**[24] 5839 3-8-12 48....(t) LiamJones 5 34
(J R Best) *chsd ldrs tl wknd ins fnl 2f: eased whn no ch* **50/1**

0000 14 7 **Donair**[7] 6330 3-8-12 46....(t) TomQueally 9 15
(P F I Cole) *a in rr* **25/1**

1m 25.73s (0.93) **Going Correction** +0.05s/f (Slow) **14** Ran SP% **119.7**
Speed ratings (Par 99): **96,92,91,89,89 89,88,86,85,84 83,81,81,73**
toteswingers:1&2 £52.50, 2&3 £26.90, 1&3 £28.20 CSF £333.72 TOTE £11.30: £5.40, £13.70, £1.10; EX 318.10 TRIFECTA Not won..There was no bid for the winner.

Owner R Henderson **Bred** Rathasker Stud **Trained** Lower Beeding, W Sussex

FOCUS
Ten of the 14 runners were dropping into selling company for the first time with question marks surrounding all of them. The form does not look solid.

Eclipsed(USA) Official explanation: jockey said hung left throughout

6523 NATASHA MITCHELL'S NEW WORLD OF RACING H'CAP (DIV I) 6f (P)

3:30 (3:31) (Class 5) (0-75,75) 3-Y-0+ £3,070 (£906; £453) Stalls Low

Form RPR

2114 1 **Titus Gent**[29] 5698 5-9-1 69.... KirstyMilczarek 6 80
(R A Harris) *mde virtually all: rdn and styd on strly thrght fnl f* **5/1**[3]

330- 2 1 ¾ **Dear Maurice**[344] 6973 6-9-7 75....(t) IanMongan 9 80
(T B P Coles) *hld up in rr: hdwy on outside 2f out: styd on wl to chse wnr over 1f out: kpt on: a readily hld* **10/1**

5550 3 3 ½ **Sherjawy (IRE)**[17] 6057 6-9-3 71.... LiamKeniry 8 65
(Miss Z C Davison) *chsd ldrs: rdn and one pce over 2f out: hung lft over 1f out and r.o again to take 3rd ins fnl f: no ch w ldng duo* **20/1**

4432 4 1 **Pan American**[17] 6057 3-9-5 74.... FergusSweeney 11 65
(P J Makin) *chsd ldrs towards outside: chsd wnr and rdn 2f out: no imp and wknd qckly 1f out* **10/3**[1]

5600 5 ½ **Cerito**[114] 2872 4-9-7 75.... StephenCraine 7 64
(J R Boyle) *s.i.s: in rr: drvn and mod prog fr over 1f out: nvr a threat* **25/1**

4600 6 hd **Athwaab**[17] 6057 3-9-1 70.... PatDobbs 2 58
(M G Quinlan) *pressed wnr to 1/2-way: wknd jst ins fnl f* **14/1**

4025 7 1 ¼ **Steelcut**[41] 5285 6-8-11 68.... RussKennemore(3) 1 52
(Andrew Reid) *n.m.r and hit rail sn after s: chsd ldrs tl wknd ins fnl 2f* **6/1**

5415 8 1 ¼ **Bobs Dreamflight**[29] 5698 4-8-13 67.... JimCrowley 3 47
(D K Ivory) *a in rr* **4/1**[2]

205 9 2 ¼ **Whiskey Junction**[17] 6057 6-9-6 74.... TomQueally 10 47
(M Quinn) *pressed ldrs tl wknd 2f out* **8/1**

4535 10 3 **Lordsbury Pride (USA)**[22] 5898 3-8-6 61 oh3.... LiamJones 4 25
(J R Best) *rdn over 2f out: a in rr* **14/1**

1m 11.56s (-0.34) **Going Correction** +0.05s/f (Slow)
WFA 3 from 4yo+ 1lb **10** Ran SP% **116.2**
Speed ratings (Par 103): **104,101,97,95,95 94,93,91,88,84**
toteswingers:1&2 £6.40, 2&3 £29.60, 1&3 £20.80 CSF £53.90 CT £920.30 TOTE £7.30: £2.10, £3.70, £6.50; EX 73.60 TRIFECTA Not won..

Owner Alan & Adam Darlow, A Darlow Productions **Bred** Heather Raw **Trained** Earlswood, Monmouths

FOCUS
The first division of the competitive 61-75 handicap sprint with plenty of pace on with the front pair finishing clear in the marginally quicker time of the two divisions. The runner-up is rated to last year's form.

6524 NATASHA MITCHELL'S NEW WORLD OF RACING H'CAP (DIV II) 6f (P)

4:05 (4:06) (Class 5) (0-75,75) 3-Y-0+ £3,070 (£680; £680) Stalls Low

Form RPR

2124 1 **Grand Zafeen**[35] 5501 3-9-5 74.... ChrisCatlin 1 84
(M R Channon) *in rr: stl plenty to do ins fnl 2f: str run appr fnl f to ld fnl 150yds: drvn out* **10/1**

4502 2 1 **Hand Painted**[9] 6280 4-9-2 70.... FergusSweeney 2 77
(P J Makin) *in tch: hdwy 2f out: chsd ldr over 1f out: drvn to take slt ld jst ins fnl f: hdd and outpcd fnl 150yds: jnd for 2nd on line* **9/2**[1]

2563 2 dht **Fawley Green**[17] 6057 3-9-4 73....(p) JimCrowley 4 80
(W R Muir) *in rr and racd on outside thrght: hdwy over 1f out and str run ins fnl f to join 2nd on line but nt rch wnr* **9/2**[1]

-241 4 ¾ **Elsie's Orphan**[30] 5668 3-8-12 67.... LiamKeniry 3 72
(P R Chamings) *chsd ldr: rdn over 2f out: lost 2nd over 1f out and styd on same pce* **9/2**[1]

4650 5 1 ¼ **Victorian Bounty**[19] 5995 5-9-7 75....(v) TomQueally 7 76
(Stef Higgins) *sn led: rdn over 1f out and hdd jst ins fnl f: sn btn* **13/2**[3]

5030 6 2 ½ **Dvinsky (USA)**[14] 6164 9-9-1 69....(b) IanMongan 6 62
(P Howling) *chsd ldrs tl wknd fr 2f out* **12/1**

-150 7 8 **Noble Greek (USA)**[20] 5967 3-9-6 75.... RobertWinston 5 42
(J R Best) *rdn 1/2-way: a outpcd* **20/1**

0320 8 ¾ **Toms Return**[8] 6310 3-8-12 70.... KierenFox(3) 9 35
(J R Best) *outpcd* **5/1**[2]

1410 9 nk **Spanish Acclaim**[41] 5285 3-9-5 74.... NeilChalmers 8 38
(A M Balding) *spd to 1/2-way* **10/1**

1m 12.07s (0.17) **Going Correction** +0.05s/f (Slow)
WFA 3 from 4yo+ 1lb **9** Ran SP% **115.2**
TOTE £11.40: £4.00 Trifecta £40.70 27 Owner.

FOCUS
The second division of the 61-75 sprint handicap and just as tight a heat as the first with the time marginally slower. The form looks sound with the runner-up to form.

6525 BET365 H'CAP (DIV I) 1m 4f (P)

4:40 (4:41) (Class 6) (0-60,60) 3-Y-O £1,706 (£503; £252) Stalls Low

Form RPR

1444 1 **Frameit (IRE)**[12] 3960 3-9-3 56....(vt) LiamKeniry 11 64
(Tim Vaughan) *in tch: rdn fr 3f out: styd on to ld over 1f out: hrd drvn ins fnl f: hld on wl* **9/1**

5540 2 hd **Belle Boleyn**[17] 6065 3-8-13 52.... IanMongan 9 60
(C F Wall) *s.i.s: in rr tl hdwy on outer 2f out: wnt 2nd u.p ins fnl f: styd on: a jst hld by wnr* **7/1**

1421 3 1 ¾ **Shianda**[25] 5812 3-9-7 60....(b) FergusSweeney 5 65
(G L Moore) *in tch on outside hdwy 3f out: styd on but stl wd fr over 1f out: tk 3rd ins fnl f: nt pce of ldng duo* **2/1**[1]

3230 4 2 ¼ **Rose Aurora**[23] 5869 3-8-8 47....(p) PatDobbs 10 48
(M P Tregoning) *hld up in rr: stl plenty to do whn drvn wl over 1f out: r.o ins fnl f and gng on cl home: nt rch ldrs* **8/1**

2043 5 nk **Tower**[27] 5752 3-9-1 57.... KierenFox(3) 2 58
(G Prodromou) *sn led: narrowly hdd 2f out: styd wl there tl wknd ins fnl f* **8/1**

0050 6 ¾ **Hedonist (IRE)**[23] 5869 3-9-5 58.... RobertWinston 8 58
(J R Gask) *chsd ldrs: chal 4f out: slt ld 2f out: hdd over 1f out: wknd ins fnl f* **33/1**

5-00 7 1 **Danube (IRE)**[73] 4229 3-9-5 58.... TomQueally 7 56
(H R A Cecil) *in tch: rdn 3f out: styd on one pce* **6/1**[2]

0005 8 1 ½ **The Midshipmaid**[10] 6273 3-8-7 46 oh1.... LiamJones 6 42
(Lucinda Featherstone) *in rr tl mod prog fnl f* **33/1**

0043 9 ½ **Storm Hawk (IRE)**[16] 6080 3-8-13 59....(p) JamesRogers(7) 3 54
(Pat Eddery) *in tch: rdn over 2f out: sn btn* **13/2**[3]

000 10 4 **Admiral Rodney**[15] 6115 3-9-1 54.... MickyFenton 4 43
(Mrs P Sly) *sn led: rdn 3f out: narrowly hdd 2f out: styd chalng and stl upsides over 1f out: wknd rapidly fnl f* **20/1**

0-00 11 11 **Star Of Soho (IRE)**[156] 1621 3-8-4 46 oh1....(b) MartinLane(3) 1 17
(E J Creighton) *slowly into strie: a towards rr* **66/1**

2m 35.06s (2.06) **Going Correction** +0.05s/f (Slow) **11** Ran SP% **117.8**
Speed ratings (Par 99): **95,94,93,92,92 91,90,89,89,86 79**
toteswingers:1&2 £16.50, 2&3 £5.40, 1&3 £5.00 CSF £68.24 CT £177.59 TOTE £16.40: £5.30, £2.50, £1.10; EX 88.80 Trifecta £269.10 Pool: £520.11 - 1.43 winning units..

Owner M Khan X2 **Bred** Liam Butler **Trained** Aberthin, Vale of Glamorgan

FOCUS
An ordinary pace for this low-grade 1m 4f handicap. The winner is rated back to his best with the third to form.

6526 BET365 H'CAP (DIV II) 1m 4f (P)

5:15 (5:15) (Class 6) (0-60,60) 3-Y-O £1,706 (£503; £252) Stalls Low

Form RPR

0364 1 **Beat Route**[23] 5869 3-9-2 60.... JemmaMarshall(5) 11 68+
(M J Attwater) *racd on outside: wnt wd bnd after 3f and again bnd over 4f out: chal fr 2f out tl slt ld ins fnl f: kpt on wl whn pressed fnl 120yds* **8/1**[3]

0310 2 ½ **Larkrise Star**[16] 6080 3-9-2 55.... LiamKeniry 6 62
(D K Ivory) *in tch whn drvn along 3f out: hdwy and wd into st ins fnl 2f: swtchd lft and r.o to chse wnr ins fnl f: kpt on u.p: a hld* **10/1**

0-22 3 3 ½ **Honoured (IRE)**[37] 5414 3-9-4 57.... StevieDonohoe 5 59
(Sir Mark Prescott) *led: awkward bnd after 3f: hrd drvn whn chal over 3f out and narrowly hdd ins fnl 2f: styd wl there tl one pce ins fnl f: tk 3rd cl home* **1/1**[1]

6056 4 nk **Nom De La Rosa (IRE)**[9] 6287 3-8-7 53....(p) HarryBentley(7) 9 54
(Miss Sheena West) *chsd ldrs: rdn and slt ld ins fnl 2f: hdd jst ins fnl f: sn outpcd: lost 3rd cl home* **16/1**

0040 5 2 **Voysey (IRE)**[18] 6022 3-9-4 57....(bt[1]) JimCrowley 4 55
(Mrs A J Perrett) *in rr: rdn and styd on fr 2f out: hung lft over 1f out and nvr rchd ldrs* **10/1**

0664 6 8 **Oak Leaves**[25] 5812 3-8-11 50.... RobertWinston 10 35
(J G Portman) *chsd ldrs on outer: rdn 3f out: sn lost position: no ch whn wnt wd bnd ins fnl 2f* **12/1**

0604 7 1 **Half Sister (IRE)**[18] 6020 3-8-12 58....(b) NatashaEaton(7) 1 42
(M E Rimmer) *racd on outer: carried wd bnd over 4f out: styd in tch: rdn 3f out: wknd and wnt wd bnd ins fnl 2f* **33/1**

The Form Book, Raceform Ltd, Compton, RG20 6NL

3053 **8** *8* **Lovely Eyes (IRE)**[18] 6020 3-9-3 59 MartinLane(3) 8 30
(D M Simcock) *t.k.h chsd ldrs tl wknd qckly 3f out* **5/1**[2]

-500 **9** *10* **Dongola (IRE)**[16] 6080 3-8-4 48 AshleyMorgan(5) 3 3
(P Winkworth) *chsd ldrs tl wknd qckly 5f out* **33/1**

0000 **10** *30* **Hannah Hawk**[46] 5155 3-8-7 46 oh1 LiamJones 7 —
(Lucinda Featherstone) *slowly away: rapid hdwy to press ldr 5f out: wknd rapidly 4f out: t.o* **66/1**

2m 33.25s (0.25) **Going Correction** +0.05s/f (Slow) **10** Ran SP% **116.9**
Speed ratings (Par 99): **101,100,98,98,96 91,90,85,78,58**
toteswingers:1&2 £5.40, 2&3 £3.50, 1&3 £3.60 CSF £83.76 CT £148.17 TOTE £9.40: £3.40, £1.70, £1.10; EX 85.60 TRIFECTA Not won..
Owner Canisbay Bloodstock **Bred** Canisbay Bloodstock Ltd **Trained** Epsom, Surrey

FOCUS
The second division of the 46-60 handicap run at a similarly ordinary pace, but nearly two seconds quicker than the first division. The form is rated around the first two.

6527 NCYPE H'CAP 1m 2f (P)
5:50 (5:50) (Class 6) (0-65,65) 3-Y-O **£2,047** (£604; £302) **Stalls** Low

Form RPR

1522 **1** **Celestial Girl**[9] 6290 3-9-7 65 ChrisCatlin 11 74+
(H Morrison) *in rr: hdwy 3f out: slt ld 2f out: drvn 3 l clr 1f out: styd on strly* **2/1**[1]

040 **2** *1 1/2* **Mister Bit (IRE)**[17] 6056 3-9-3 64 KierenFox(3) 14 70+
(J R Best) *in rr: rdn over 2f out: styd on u.p fnl f to take 2nd cl home: no ch w wnr* **16/1**

0004 **3** *nk* **Jovial (IRE)**[40] 5330 3-8-7 51 oh3 NickyMackay 6 56
(D J Coakley) *chsd ldrs: drvn to chse wnr ins fnl f: no imp: lost 2nd cl home* **14/1**

4352 **4** *1/2* **Little Meadow (IRE)**[18] 6020 3-8-2 51 oh4 AmyBaker(5) 12 55
(Miss J Feilden) *in rr: rdn and hdwy towards outside 2f out: rdn and hung lft over 1f out: styd on ins fnl f: gng on cl home* **16/1**

0314 **5** *1* **Akamon**[16] 6080 3-9-1 59 JimCrowley 10 61
(E A L Dunlop) *in tch: chsd ldrs fr 2f out: styd on same pce u.p ins fnl f* **13/2**[3]

600 **6** *2 1/4* **Byrd In Hand (IRE)**[13] 6197 3-9-2 60 NeilChalmers 4 58
(J J Bridger) *in tch early: dropped towards rr over 4f out: hdwy fr 2f out: styng on whn n.m.r appr fnl f: one pce sn after* **25/1**

0402 **7** *1 3/4* **Quality Mover (USA)**[19] 5986 3-9-4 65 MartinLane(3) 5 59
(D M Simcock) *in rr: stl bhd 2f out: drvn and r.o fnl f but nvr a threat* **9/1**

2666 **8** *1/2* **Fire Raiser**[30] 5664 3-9-1 59 LiamKeniry 9 52
(A M Balding) *trckd ldr tl led appr fnl 3f: hdd 2f out: wknd over 1f out* **8/1**

5204 **9** *5* **Rodrigo De Freitas (IRE)**[22] 5873 3-9-0 58 (b) StephenCraine 13 41
(J R Boyle) *chsd ldrs towards outside: hmpd and wknd ins fnl 2f* **14/1**

0-05 **10** *4* **Daryainur (IRE)**[116] 2820 3-8-7 51 oh6 AdrianLayt 7 26
(F J Brennan) *bhd fr 1/2-way:* **66/1**

060- **11** *nse* **King's Realm (IRE)**[359] 6592 3-9-4 62 StevieDonohoe 2 37
(Sir Mark Prescott) *chsd ldrs: rdn and btn 3f out* **10/3**[2]

0000 **12** *30* **Glan Y Mor (IRE)**[32] 5584 3-8-7 51 oh6 LiamJones 1 —
(A W Carroll) *led tl hdd & wknd over 3f out* **25/1**

2m 6.61s (0.01) **Going Correction** +0.05s/f (Slow) **12** Ran SP% **125.1**
Speed ratings (Par 99): **101,99,99,99,98 96,95,94,90,87 87,63**
toteswingers:1&2 £7.00, 2&3:£34.20, 1&3 £6.20 totesuper7: Win: Not won. Place: £65.50 CSF £40.15 CT £384.76 TOTE £2.00: £1.10, £3.70, £6.00; EX 41.50 TRIFECTA Not won. Place 6: £94.84 Place 5: £81.65.
Owner Helena Springfield Ltd **Bred** Meon Valley Stud **Trained** East Ilsley, Berks

FOCUS
A modest handicap with the winner to form and the next three improvers, so rated slightly positively.
Glan Y Mor(IRE) Official explanation: trainer's rep said filly ran too free
T/Plt: £156.80 to a £1 stake. Pool of £48,523.01 - 225.85 winning tickets. T/Qpdt: £54.20 to a £1 stake. Pool £4,537.03 - 61.90 winning tickets. ST

6504
NEWMARKET (Rowley Mile) (R-H)
Friday, October 1

OFFICIAL GOING: Good to soft changing to soft after race 3 (2.30)
Far side of Rowley Mile track used.
Wind: strong, against Weather: windy, light rain at moment

6528 SAKHEE OH SO SHARP STKS (GROUP 3) (FILLIES) 7f
1:25 (1:25) (Class 1) 2-Y-O
£22,708 (£8,608; £4,308; £2,148; £1,076; £540) **Stalls** High

Form RPR

1 **1** **Havant**[35] 5489 2-8-12 0 RyanMoore 2 103+
(Sir Michael Stoute) *w'like: dwlt: sn bustled along and chsng ldrs: pushed along to chse ldr 2f out: led wl over 1f out: clr ent fnl f: styd on strly: readily* **11/2**[3]

2 *3 1/4* **Look At Me (IRE)**[12] 6228 2-8-12 0 JMurtagh 6 95+
(A P O'Brien, Ire) *w'like: lengthy: stdd s: t.k.h: hld up in tch tl stdd bk towards rr after 2f: effrt and n.m.r ent fnl 2f: sn rdn and hdwy over 1f out: chsd clr wnr ent fnl f: kpt on: no imp* **10/3**[1]

21 **3** *1 3/4* **Khawlah (IRE)**[14] 6154 2-8-12 88 FrankieDettori 5 91
(Saeed Bin Suroor) *lw: led for 1f: stdd bk and chsng ldrs after: rdn and effrt 2f out: nt pce of wnr over 1f out: lost 2nd ent fnl f: one pce and wl hld after* **7/2**[2]

0025 **4** *3/4* **Ladyanne (IRE)**[7] 6317 2-8-12 88 SteveDrowne 11 89
(S Kirk) *hld up towards rr: niggled along over 3f out: swtchd rt and effrt towards far side wl over 1f out: no imp and wl hld 1f out* **33/1**

5145 **5** *2 1/4* **Lily Again**[21] 5910 2-8-12 98 JamieSpencer 8 83
(P F I Cole) *chsd ldrs: rdn ent fnl 2f: hung lft u.p and wknd over 1f out: wl btn ins fnl f* **9/1**

122 **6** *shd* **Cochabamba (IRE)**[34] 5519 2-8-12 98 JackMitchell 9 83
(R A Teal) *stdd s: in tch in midfield: rdn and unable qck ent fnl 3f: wknd u.p over 1f out* **6/1**

01 **7** *shd* **Up In Time**[14] 6158 2-8-12 87 WilliamBuick 7 83
(W J Knight) *lw: chsd ldrs: wnt 2nd 4f out: led ent fnl 2f: sn rdn and hdd: wknd qckly over 1f out* **8/1**

0223 **8** *1 1/2* **Strictly Rhythm**[9] 6279 2-8-12 73 JimmyFortune 3 79
(R Hannon) *stdd s: hld up in last pair: hdwy ent fnl 2f: rdn and wknd wl over 1f out* **80/1**

3551 **9** *8* **Rosina Grey**[7] 6325 2-8-12 76 JamesMillman 10 59
(B R Millman) *stdd s: hld up in last: swtchd lft 4f out: rdn and short-lived effrt over 2f out: wknd qckly 2f out: wl bhd and eased ins fnl f* **20/1**

61 **10** *4* **Sister Red (IRE)**[14] 6150 2-8-12 83 RichardHughes 4 49
(R Hannon) *t.k.h: chsd ldr tl led after 1f: hdd ent fnl 2f: sn dropped out: wl bhd and eased ins fnl f* **16/1**

1m 28.74s (3.34) **Going Correction** +0.525s/f (Yiel) **10** Ran SP% **110.9**
Speed ratings (Par 102): **101,97,95,94,91 91,91,89,80,76**
toteswingers:1&2 £4.60, 2&3 £2.40, 1&3 £3.20 CSF £22.46 CT £38.30 TOTE £6.10: £2.70, £1.40, £1.40; EX 18.70 Trifecta £38.30 Pool: £1000.68 - 19.29 winning units..
Owner Mr & Mrs James Wigan **Bred** Mrs James Wigan & London TB Services Ltd **Trained** Newmarket, Suffolk

FOCUS
There was a strong headwind and that, combined with soft ground, made this a good test for these juveniles. Unsurprisingly, the time was slow, being over five seconds above standard, although the early pace wasn't particularly strong. There were no stars among the last ten winners of the Oh So Sharp, but this was only the fourth year that the race has held Group 3 status, upgraded from Listed class.

NOTEBOOK
Havant, a 5l winner of a slowly run maiden at the July course under similar conditions on debut, confirmed herself a smart filly with a taking success on this rise in class. She half missed the break, but travelled strongly before drawing right away for pressure, a particularly smart effort seeing as she was not hit with the whip at any stage, and still appeared green. Visually, this looked the performance of a serious 1000 Guineas candidate, for she showed plenty of pace and handled the track well. However, there are two major reservations on that front - her breeding strongly suggest she'll want middle-distances next year, and she showed a notable knee action, meaning fast ground will be a worry until she proves otherwise. She's around 12-1 for both the Guineas and Oaks. (op 4-1 tchd 6-1 in places)
Look At Me(IRE) ◆, who carried her head a bit high and looked green when winning on debut at Fairyhouse, appeared in need of this further experience. She was keen through the early stages and had little chance after not handling the Dip as well as the winner, but she kept on gradually. Out of a sister to Henrythenavigator, it's not out of the question that she could progress into a Guineas candidate, and her action suggests she'll cope with quicker ground. (op 3-1 tchd 11-4)
Khawlah(IRE) won her maiden over 1m on a decent surface at this track, and the drop in trip and switch to softish ground did not suit. In the circumstances this was a good effort. (op 4-1 tchd 9-2)
Ladyanne(IRE) has yet to look good enough for this level, but the increase in trip suited and she ran creditably in defeat. (op 40-1)
Lily Again, fifth in the May Hill on her previous start, didn't seem to handle the Dip, quickly losing her prominent position after passing the 2f pole. (op 10-1 tchd 11-1)
Cochabamba(IRE) was runner-up in the Prestige Stakes last time, but had previously finished behind Lily Again at Sandown. Even so, this was a bit disappointing. (op 11-2 tchd 13-2)
Up In Time won her maiden by a wide margin over C&D, but her rivals that day were only modest, and this was tougher. (op 10-1)
Sister Red(IRE) was much too keen.

6529 NAYEF JOEL STKS (GROUP 3) 1m
1:55 (1:55) (Class 1) 3-Y-O+
£34,062 (£12,912; £6,462; £3,222; £1,614; £810) **Stalls** High

Form RPR

-421 **1** **Cityscape**[27] 5741 4-9-0 113 SteveDrowne 3 124
(R Charlton) *lw: stdd s: hld up in tch: swtchd 3f out: rdn and gd hdwy to ld over 1f out: r.o strly and drew wl clr ins fnl f: rdn out* **4/1**[2]

-101 **2** *7* **Penitent**[16] 6089 4-9-0 114 JMurtagh 1 108
(W J Haggas) *lw: chsd ldr tl 4f out: drvn and outpcd over 1f out: no ch w wnr: plugged on u.p to go 2nd again fnl 100yds: kpt on* **7/2**[1]

0243 **3** *nse* **Fair Trade**[13] 6195 3-8-11 110 JamieSpencer 4 108
(D R C Elsworth) *swtg: stdd s: hld up in rr: effrt u.p wl over 1f out: no ch w wnr: drvn and kpt on to press for 2nd fnl 100yds* **14/1**

342 **4** *3 1/2* **Tamaathul**[41] 5292 3-8-11 105 TadhgO'Shea 2 100
(B W Hills) *led: rdn 2f out: hdd over 1f out: btn ent fnl f: fdd and lost 2 pls ins fnl 100yds* **7/1**

2023 **5** *1* **Alexandros**[68] 4418 5-9-0 112 FrankieDettori 10 97
(Saeed Bin Suroor) *stdd after s: hld up in tch towards rr: rdn and effrt 2f out: hld hd awkwardly u.p and btn over 1f out: no ch and hung lft ins fnl f* **5/1**[3]

5-35 **6** *nk* **Nideeb**[34] 5539 3-8-11 99 SebSanders 9 97
(C E Brittain) *chsd ldrs: wnt 2nd 4f out tl over 1f out: sn hung lft and wknd: wl btn whn swtchd rt jst over 1f out* **40/1**

0062 **7** *1 3/4* **Stoic (IRE)**[20] 5948 4-9-0 105 RyanMoore 5 93
(J Noseda) *hld up wl in tch: rdn and lost pl ent fnl 2f: wl btn over 1f out* **12/1**

1132 **8** *3/4* **Premio Loco (USA)**[20] 5946 6-9-5 119 GeorgeBaker 7 96
(C F Wall) *stdd s: hld up in last trio: rdn and effrt 2f out: no hdwy and wl hld whn short of room and hmpd jst over 1f out: nvr trbld ldrs* **9/1**

-033 **9** *21* **Awzaan**[14] 6147 3-8-11 114 RichardHills 8 43
(M Johnston) *chsd ldrs: pushed along wl over 2f out: wknd qckly ent fnl 2f: wl bhd and virtually p.u ins fnl f: t.o* **8/1**

1m 39.84s (1.24) **Going Correction** +0.525s/f (Yiel)
WFA 3 from 4yo+ 3lb **9** Ran SP% **109.3**
Speed ratings (Par 113): **114,107,106,103,102 102,100,99,78**
toteswingers:1&2 £2.40, 2&3 £6.70, 1&3 £7.90 CSF £16.70 TOTE £4.90: £2.30, £1.30, £3.50; EX 10.70 Trifecta £216.00 Pool: £1030.77 - 3.53 winning units..
Owner K Abdulla **Bred** Juddmonte Farms Ltd **Trained** Beckhampton, Wilts

FOCUS
Only 6lb separated seven of the nine runners on adjusted official ratings, and this looked a competitive affair on paper, but Cityscape ran out a most impressive winner and looked a class above the rest, although they are all rated below their best.

NOTEBOOK
Cityscape's connections have been patient, waiting for the bit of cut he requires to show his best, and he showed here that, given some nice bit of dig, he's a smart performer, well worth his place in even better company. Having been held up off the pace he quickened up in great style inside the final 2f before drawing further and further clear inside the last. Opportunities over the next few weeks are few; there's the Darley Stakes over 1m1f here later in the month, but Roger Charlton also mentioned the Prix Perth over 1m at Saint-Cloud, a race in which he sent out Border Patrol to finish second last year, and that looks a good target, especially as Cityscape is virtually guaranteed to get his ground there. (op 7-2 tchd 10-3)
Penitent had conditions to suit and had his chance if good enough, but the winner proved much too classy for him. He has still come a long way this season, though, remains lightly raced and looks just the type to do better again as a 5-y-o. (tchd 4-1 in places)
Fair Trade, since his debut on good ground, had done all his racing on good to firm, but he coped quite well, picking up nicely from off the pace to run on late for third. Not for the first time he gave the impression that he'll be worth another go over 1m2f. (op 18-1)
Tamaathul had the ground in his favour and, soon in front, attempted to make all. Winding things up heading to the 2f poll, it looked for a moment as though he might stretch clear and put his 1m2f stamina to good use, but he was soon reeled in by the winner and weakened inside the last. This was slightly disappointing, but he's only had the six starts in his life, and is another who could well improve as a 4-y-o. (op 15-2)

Alexandros, given a two-month break since finishing third in a German Group 1, acts in soft ground and was back down to the level he is more comfortable racing at. His form figures in races up to Group 3 level coming into this read 211142231311112, while his form figures in Group 1 and 2 races read 7737287203, but for some reason he was well below his best on this occasion. (op 4-1)

Nideeb promised to be suited by the drop back to 1m, but he had a bit to find at the weights with the main players and the soft ground was a concern to his connections beforehand. He ran about as well as could be expected.

Stoic(IRE) faced a stiff task as he was one of the worst in at the weights, and he's a son of Green Desert who had never previously run on ground softer than good. Conditions clearly proved too testing for him. (op 16-1)

Premio Loco(USA) is another who hadn't run on ground this soft before, despite having had 14 previous starts on turf, and there had been doubts about his participation beforehand. He just wasn't able to show his best on this ground. Official explanation: jockey said gelding was unsuited by the good to soft ground (tchd 10-1)

Awzaan was beaten a lot further by Cityscape than at Haydock last month, and presumably the softer ground was against him. He had shaped with promise at Newbury on his last start and deserves another chance back on a sounder surface. Official explanation: jockey said colt lost its action (tchd 9-1)

6530 ADNAMS CHEVELEY PARK STKS (GROUP 1) (FILLIES) 6f

2:30 (2:30) (Class 1) 2-Y-O

£98,439 (£37,315; £18,675; £9,311; £4,664; £2,340) **Stalls** High

Form				RPR
3611	1		**Hooray**[27] 5748 2-8-12 110 SebSanders 10 (Sir Mark Prescott) *mde all: gng best ent fnl 2f: rdn clr wl over 1f out: styd on strly ins fnl f: readily* **7/2**[1]	117
1320	2	4 1/2	**Rimth**[13] 6176 2-8-12 101 WilliamBuick 6 (P F I Cole) *lw: in tch: rdn and effrt ent fnl 2f: drvn to chse clr ldr over 1f out: kpt on u.p: no imp ins fnl f* **11/1**	103
114	3	1 1/4	**Maqaasid**[43] 5246 2-8-12 107 RichardHills 4 (J H M Gosden) *lw: stdd s: hld up in rr: stl travelling wl but plenty to do whn nt clr run 2f out tl hdwy between horses over 1f out: kpt on u.p ins fnl f: no ch w wnr* **8/1**	99
2122	4	3/4	**Ragsah (IRE)**[13] 6176 2-8-12 95 FrankieDettori 7 (Saeed Bin Suroor) *stdd s: hld up wl bhd: nt clr run and switching lft over 2f out: styd on u.p ins fnl f: no ch w wnr* **6/1**[3]	97
2223	5	hd	**Margot Did (IRE)**[29] 5693 2-8-12 108 HayleyTurner 3 (M L W Bell) *t.k.h: hld up in midfield: rdn and effrt 2f out: drvn and kpt on ins fnl f: no ch w wnr* **9/1**	96
0634	6	2	**Mortitia**[13] 6176 2-8-12 94 PaulMulrennan 2 (B J Meehan) *t.k.h: rdn and effrt over 2f out: no ch w wnr and one pce fr over 1f out* **40/1**	90
31	7	1/2	**Sharnberry**[48] 5074 2-8-12 91 RyanMoore 9 (E A L Dunlop) *lw: chsd ldrs: wnt 2nd over 3f out: rdn and outpcd by wnr wl over 1f out: wl btn and lost 2nd over 1f out: wknd ins fnl f* **15/2**	89
52	8	nk	**Wild Wind (GER)**[5] 6401 2-8-12 0 JMurtagh 11 (A P O'Brien, Ire) *racd in midfield: rdn 4f out: struggling u.p wl over 2f out: wl btn fnl 2f* **5/1**[2]	88
1524	9	7	**Sweet Cecily (IRE)**[29] 5693 2-8-12 97 RichardHughes 8 (R Hannon) *chsd ldrs: rdn and wknd over 2f out: wl bhd and eased ins fnl f* **25/1**	67
2131	10	nk	**Khor Sheed**[14] 6157 2-8-12 103 KierenFallon 1 (L M Cumani) *b: t.k.h: hld up towards rr: rdn and btn over 2f out: wl bhd and eased ins fnl f* **6/1**[3]	66
1200	11	10	**Bold Bidder**[14] 6141 2-8-12 86 JamieSpencer 5 (K A Ryan) *chsd wnr tl over 3f out: sn dropped out: wl bhd over 1f out: t.o* **100/1**	36

1m 14.09s (1.89) **Going Correction** +0.525s/f (Yiel) 11 Ran SP% **115.9**
Speed ratings (Par 106): **108,102,100,99,99 96,95,95,86,85 72**

CSF £42.33 TOTE £4.10: £1.70, £5.60, £1.90; EX 60.90 Trifecta £197.70 Pool: £5647.31 - 21.13 winning units..

Owner Cheveley Park Stud **Bred** Cheveley Park Stud Ltd **Trained** Newmarket, Suffolk

FOCUS
The ground was changed to soft all over straight after the race. This Group 1 contest has produced the subsequent 1,000 Guineas winner three times in the last eight years (Russian Rhythm, Natagora and Special Duty), but the latest running looked a weak contest for the level, and it will be a surprise if there's a domestic classic winner amongst this lot.

NOTEBOOK
Hooray, soon in front, tight against the possibly favoured far rail, she thrashed her ten rivals, and while the form in behind looks limited, she's clearly a high-class 2-y-o. She was much too keen earlier in her career, but has now won all three of her starts since being allowed to stride on, adding to her victories in the Lowther and Sirenia Stakes. The soft ground was a worry beforehand, but she clearly handled the conditions well. She's reminiscent of another classy, front-running juvenile sprinter from a few years back, Attraction, but while that one trained on extremely well, and surprisingly stayed 1m, there has to be a doubt this filly will do likewise. Some of Hooray's immediate family struggled at three, notably her dam, and her trainer doubts whether she'll make the grade next year. (op 5-1 after early 6-1 in places)

Rimth looked better than the result suggested in the Firth of Clyde last time (denied clear run), and having had every chance this time after recovering from a sluggish start, she reversed form with Ragsah and Mortitia, returning to sort of level she showed when third behind Hooray in the Lowther. She might stay slightly further, and may also appreciate a return to better ground. (op 8-1)

Maqaasid, the Queen Mary winner, seems to have just a short finishing effort once off the bridle and the soft ground was against her. Racing away from the front two in the closing stages didn't help either, with that pair getting first run, and ideally she wants a longer lead into a race. She may be capable of better when she has more in her favour, but she might not be easy to place at Group level in the early part of next year. John Gosden indicated that he'll aim her at a Guineas trial, but she looks a sprinter. (op 7-1)

Ragsah(IRE) shaped as though she'd appreciate a return to 7f when second in the Firth of Clyde on her previous start, and she could make no impression this time, ending up extremely wide without mustering the required speed. (op 13-2)

Margot Did(IRE) is a strong traveller with only a short burst off the bridle, but even so, she really should have won at least one of the pattern races she'd contested before now. The soft ground didn't suit this time, with her below the form she showed when ahead of Rimth and Maqaasid in the Lowther, and she may have missed her chance. (op 8-1)

Mortitia was below the form she showed at Ayr last time. (tchd 50-1 in places)

Sharnberry had every chance, tracking the winner against the rail, but wasn't good enough. (op 8-1)

Wild Wind(GER) put in a poor effort, failing to get near the form she showed when second in a 7f Group 3 in Ireland last time. (op 11-2 tchd 9-2, 6-1 in places)

Khor Sheed, a recent sales race winner over C&D, probably didn't appreciate the ground. (tchd 11-2)

6531 SHADWELL MIDDLE PARK STKS (GROUP 1) (ENTIRE COLTS) 6f

3:05 (3:05) (Class 1) 2-Y-O

£106,046 (£40,199; £20,118; £10,031; £5,024; £2,521) **Stalls** High

Form				RPR
11	1		**Dream Ahead (USA)**[40] 5347 2-8-12 117 WilliamBuick 4 (D M Simcock) *lengthy: scope: lw: stdd s: hld up in tch in rr: smooth hdwy over 1f out: led ent fnl f: hung lft but drew readily clr ins fnl f: impressive* **5/4**[1]	125+
113	2	9	**Strong Suit (USA)**[54] 4880 2-8-12 113 (t) RichardHughes 8 (R Hannon) *lw: stdd s: hld up in last trio: swtchd rt and hdwy on bit ent fnl 2f: pushed into ld over 1f out: rdn and hdd ent fnl f: sn outpcd by wnr: tired and edgd lft fnl 100yds: jst hld 2nd* **7/2**[2]	98
4312	3	shd	**Approve (IRE)**[20] 5943 2-8-12 113 RyanMoore 5 (W J Haggas) *pressed ldrs: ev ch and rdn jst over 2f out: outpcd and drvn over 1f out: no ch w wnr ins fnl f: kpt on to press for 2nd nr fin* **9/1**	98
215	4	3/4	**Irish Field (IRE)**[40] 5347 2-8-12 0 KierenFallon 3 (J W Hills) *chsd ldrs: effrt and ev ch ent fnl 2f: outpcd by wnr ent fnl f: no ch w wnr and kpt on same pce u.p ins fnl f* **16/1**	95
1015	5	3/4	**Foghorn Leghorn**[6] 6354 2-8-12 90 JimmyFortune 1 (P W Chapple-Hyam) *lw: broke wl: sn stdd bk towards rr: effrt whn nt clr run and swtchd rt over 1f out: no ch w wnr and kpt on one pce ins fnl f* **100/1**	93
2534	6	1 3/4	**Samuel Morse (IRE)**[20] 5975 2-8-12 0 (vt[1]) JMurtagh 2 (A P O'Brien, Ire) *w ldrs: drvn ent fnl 2f: btn and hung lft ent fnl f: wknd ins fnl f* **28/1**	88
1010	7	1/2	**Al Aasifh (IRE)**[40] 5347 2-8-12 109 (p) FrankieDettori 6 (Saeed Bin Suroor) *led tl over 2f out: wknd qckly u.p over 1f out: fdd ins fnl f* **14/1**	86
1141	8	5	**Temple Meads**[13] 6192 2-8-12 113 RichardMullen 7 (E S McMahon) *stdd s: hld up in rr: sddle slipped and swtchd rt 4f out: hdwy to press ldrs over 3f out: led over 2f out tl over 1f out: rdr unable to offer any assistance and sn btn: eased ins fnl f* **4/1**[3]	71

1m 14.28s (2.08) **Going Correction** +0.675s/f (Yiel) 8 Ran SP% **113.7**
Speed ratings (Par 109): **113,101,100,99,98 96,95,89**
toteswingers:1&2 £2.20, 2&3 £3.20, 1&3 £3.20 CSF £5.61 TOTE £2.30: £1.10, £1.20, £2.30; EX 5.40 Trifecta £16.00 Pool: £18864.73 - 868.73 winning units..

Owner Khalifa Dasmal **Bred** Darley **Trained** Newmarket, Suffolk

FOCUS
This looked a strong renewal on paper, featuring as it did the winners of the Prix Morny, Coventry, Mill Reef, Gimcrack and Prix Robert Papin. It produced a most impressive winner, and possibly a rival to Frankel in the race to be champion 2-y-o, although it has to be pointed out that the performance of the fifth suggests that the other leading candidates all ran below their best in the testing conditions.

NOTEBOOK
Dream Ahead(USA), the only unbeaten horse in the race, came here on the back of a cosy win in the Prix Morny. Held up off the pace, he cruised through the race, came there swinging 1½f out, and when Buick went for him the response was immediate. He quickened right away inside the last and, despite once again edging left in front, was so far clear it made no difference. It was a smashing performance from a very talented, classy 2-y-o, which prompted his 2000 Guineas price to be cut to 7-1 best, but with a view to that particular race there are a few question marks. Firstly, recent winners of the Middle Park have tended to develop into sprinters rather than milers at three, and while Dream Ahead shapes like he'll get further, he is out of a mare who showed her best form over 5f. Secondly, he's ground dependent. By Diktat, he has a pronounced knee action and clearly revelled in this soft ground, while the Guineas is usually run on a sound surface. Thirdly, there's the prospect of him being sold in the off-season, and his 3-y-o campaign mapping out quite differently to that forecast. All in all he looks a risky ante-post proposition. His trainer suggested that it's still possible the colt could make a quick reappearance in the Dewhurst. (tchd 6-5 tchd 11-8 in places)

Strong Suit(USA), who disappointed in the Phoenix Stakes last time out, was ridden more patiently this time and travelled well to 2f out. He did pick up, but not in the electric manner the winner did, and in the end he just held on narrowly for second place. His action suggests this ground was much softer than he would ideally like, and his pedigree gives plenty of hope that he'll stay a mile next year. Nevertheless, the bookmakers shunted him out to 25-1 for the Guineas. (op 4-1)

Approve(IRE), who has had a busy campaign, found Saamidd too good for him in the Champagne but it was questionable whether the drop back to 6f was the answer. Up there throughout, he rallied after being headed, suggesting that a return to seven will suit him. It wouldn't be a surprise to see him take his chance in the Dewhurst. (op 10-1 tchd 11-1)

Irish Field(IRE) finished 3½l behind Dream Ahead in the Morny and faced a struggle to reverse that form, especially in conditions which promised to suit David Simcock's colt even better. He ran a solid race on just his second start for the stable.

Foghorn Leghorn, another who has been on the go since the spring, was making a quick reappearance after disappointing in a nursery six days earlier. His performance, which can be rated a personal best but was on ground which he'd recorded his best previous RPR of 90, helps give a guide to the level of the form.

Samuel Morse(IRE) was dropping back from 7f and had both a tongue-tie and a visor on for the first time. Having his ninth start of the campaign and pretty exposed now, he hung right under pressure and doesn't look up to this level. (op 25-1)

Al Aasifh(IRE) finished 12l behind Dream Ahead in France and it was a similar result here, despite the application of cheekpieces for the first time. (op 20-1 tchd 25-1 in places)

Temple Meads looked a leading contender based on his Mill Reef win, although the softer ground was a big question mark. He didn't get a chance to show how good he is, though, as his saddle slipped early on in the race and his rider was largely a passenger. Official explanation: jockey said saddle slipped (op 7-2)

6532 HAAFHD EBF MAIDEN STKS 7f

3:40 (3:44) (Class 4) 2-Y-O **£5,180** (£1,541; £770; £384) **Stalls** High

Form				RPR
	1		**Loving Spirit** 2-9-3 0 RobertHavlin 19 (J A R Toller) *lengthy: hld up in tch and travelling wl: chsd ldng pair wl over 1f out: rdn to chse ldr over 1f out: led and hung lft ent fnl f: continued to hang lft but styd on strly fnl f: rdn out: readily* **10/1**	90+
2	2	5	**White Frost (IRE)**[14] 6153 2-9-3 0 MichaelHills 6 (B W Hills) *lw: led: rdn wl over 1f out: hdd ent fnl f: hung lft and wknd ins fnl f: tired but hld on for 2nd nr fin* **4/1**[2]	77
	3	1/2	**Bridgefield (USA)** 2-9-3 0 AhmedAjtebi 15 (Mahmood Al Zarooni) *w'like: scope: tall: s.i.s: sn rcvrd and in tch in midfield: rdn to chse ldrs and rn green over 1f out: outpcd and no ch wirh wnr ins fnl f: kpt on to press for 2nd towards fin* **11/1**	76
	4	1/2	**Canna (IRE)** 2-9-3 0 DarryllHolland 9 (B W Hills) *str: bit bkwd: s.i.s: in tch towards rr: rdn and hdwy over 1f out: kpt on steadily ins fnl f: no threat to wnr* **25/1**	75

0 **5** *shd* **Misk Khitaam (USA)**[13] 6190 2-9-3 0 RichardHills 1 74
(J L Dunlop) *w'like: bit bkwd: s.i.s: hld up towards rr: sltly hmpd and outpcd ent fnl 2f: modest 10th over 1f out: pushed along and styd on wl ins fnl f: gng on wl at fin: nvr able to chal* **16/1**

6 *1 3/4* **Figaro** 2-9-3 0 JMurtagh 20 70
(W J Haggas) *w'like: scope: broke wl w ldr tl ent fnl 2f: sn rdn: btn over 1f out: wknd ins fnl f* **7/1**[3]

7 *2 3/4* **Groomed (IRE)** 2-9-3 0 NeilCallan 8 63
(W J Haggas) *w'like: in tch in midfield: rdn and unable qck ent fnl 2f: wknd over 1f out* **50/1**

8 *hd* **Garde Cotiere (USA)** 2-9-3 0 RyanMoore 14 63
(J Noseda) *w'like: scope: tall: t.k.h: chsd ldrs: rdn over 3f out: wknd wl over 1f out* **3/1**[1]

9 *5* **Encore Un Fois** 2-9-3 0 SteveDrowne 11 50
(B W Hills) *w'like: leggy: s.i.s: in tch: rdn and effrt over 2f out: struggling 2f out: btn whn rn green and hung lft over 1f out: wknd fnl f* **25/1**

10 *1/2* **Quails Hollow (IRE)** 2-9-3 0 KierenFallon 10 49
(W J Haggas) *w'like: scope: chsd ldrs tl rdn and wknd over 2f out: wl btn over 1f out* **10/1**

0 **11** *10* **Kuala Limper (IRE)**[22] 5893 2-9-0 0 EJMcNamara(3) 4 24
(D R C Elsworth) *bit bkwd: awkward and wnt lft s: plld hrd: chsd ldrs tl 1/2-way: sn lost pl: wl bhd over 1f out* **66/1**

12 *1 1/4* **Any Odds (IRE)** 2-8-12 0 (t) MarcHalford 3 16
(J Ryan) *w'like: leggy: s.i.s: a bhd: struggling bdly fr 1/2-way: sn wl bhd* **100/1**

13 *2 1/2* **Greenhead High** 2-9-3 0 J-PGuillambert 18 14
(P Howling) *str: bit bkwd: chsd ldrs tl 1/2-way: wknd qckly over 2f out: wl bhd over 1f out* **100/1**

14 *1/2* **Tommy Tiger** 2-9-3 0 SaleemGolam 17 13
(S C Williams) *w'like: scope: tall: bit bkwd: s.i.s: a bhd: lost tch and wl bhd fr 1/2-way* **100/1**

15 *11* **Lady Gabrielle (IRE)** 2-8-12 0 JamieSpencer 16 —
(M L W Bell) *athletic: awkward leaving stalls and v.s.a: rn green and a wl bhd: lost tch 1/2-way: t.o fnl 2f* **25/1**

16 *1/2* **Short Takes (USA)** 2-9-3 0 WilliamBuick 12 —
(J H M Gosden) *athletic: dropped in rr and rn green after 2f: lost tch 1/2-way: t.o fnl 2f* **15/2**

17 *14* **Black Cadillac (IRE)** 2-9-3 0 JimmyFortune 7 —
(A M Balding) *w'like: leggy: bit bkwd: chsd ldrs tl ent fnl 3f: sn dropped out: wl bhd over 1f out: t.o and eased ins fnl f* **20/1**

1m 30.13s (4.73) **Going Correction** +0.675s/f (Yiel) **17** Ran SP% **124.4**
Speed ratings (Par 97): **99,93,92,92,92 90,86,86,80,80 68,67,64,64,51 50,34**
toteswingers:1&2 £13.80, 2&3 £11.10, 1&3 £28.30 CSF £46.82 TOTE £13.00: £3.60, £1.90, £3.50; EX 70.70 Trifecta £584.80 Part won. Pool: £790.26 - 0.10 winning units..
Owner P C J Dalby & R Schuster **Bred** Elsdon Farms **Trained** Newmarket, Suffolk

FOCUS
Hard to know exactly what to make of the form, with many of these probably not taking to the ground, but plenty of powerful connections were represented and the race really ought to produce a few winners. The main action was up the middle of the track, although the runner-up finished against the stands' rail.

NOTEBOOK
Loving Spirit ◆, a 42,000gns first foal of a 1m3f-1m4f winner, attracted market support and, clearly relishing the conditions, ran out a wide-margin winner on debut. This performance was all the more promising considering his breeding clearly suggests he'll want middle distances next year, and he looks a very useful prospect. He'll be worth his place in a good race next time, and the Autumn Stakes at Ascot on October 9, or the Horris Hill at Newbury on October 23 could be suitable targets, although it remains to be seen whether he'll be as effective on a quicker surface. (op 14-1 tchd 20-1 in places)
White Frost(IRE) confirmed the promise he showed when an eyecatching second over 6f here on debut, although he didn't help himself by badly hanging left in the closing stages, and he was getting tired at the line. He might appreciate a return to shorter. (op 3-1 tchd 11-4)
Bridgefield(USA), a $700,000 half-brother to a winner in the US, out of a juvenile scorer in the US, had his head a touch high when first under pressure but basically looked green and he was keeping on quite well at the finish. (op 14-1 tchd 16-1)
Canna(IRE), a 42,000euros purchase, looked quite a willing type, keeping on nicely after a slow start.
Misk Khitaam(USA) ◆, down the field on debut at Newbury, very much caught the eye. Having been denied a clear run just inside the final 3f, she initially found little once in the open, losing her place and looking set to finish out the back, perhaps not handling the Dip, and almost certainly not appreciating the ground. However, she ultimately finished in taking fashion, looking as though she had plenty left at the line. Her fluent action suggests a quicker surface will suit better and she could be one to be with next time. (op 20-1)
Figaro, who is out of the same owner and trainer's high-class 1m2f mare Chorist, ran as though in need of the outing. (op 12-1)
Garde Cotiere(USA), a 500,000euros purchase who is out of a Marcel Boussac winner, has been entered in the Racing Post Trophy and Irish Guineas. He showed up well to a point, but didn't look comfortable on the ground in the closing stages. (op 11-4 tchd 7-2)
Encore Un Fois ◆, a brother to Cockney Rebel, can do better on a faster surface with this experience behind him. (op 20-1)
Lady Gabrielle(IRE) only has one eye. (op 20-1)

6533 AQLAAM GODOLPHIN STKS (LISTED RACE) 1m 4f
4:15 (4:18) (Class 1) 3-Y-O+ **£19,869** (£7,532; £3,769; £1,879; £941) **Stalls** Centre

Form RPR
0101 **1** **Myplacelater**[23] 5853 3-8-6 110 ow1 WilliamBuick 6 111+
(D R C Elsworth) *t.k.h: trckd ldng pair: styd on far side 9f out: hdwy to trck ldr gng wl over 1f out: rdn to ld ent fnl f: styd on strly and drew clr fnl 100yds: comf* **3/1**[2]

5-15 **2** *6* **Dreamspeed (IRE)**[146] 1945 3-8-10 103 JimmyFortune 4 106
(A M Balding) *lw: led: styd on far side 9f out: rdn 2f out: hdd over 1f out: btn ins fnl f: tired fnl 100yds* **7/2**[3]

0543 **3** *1 3/4* **Wajir (FR)**[20] 5938 4-9-3 103 FrankieDettori 2 103
(Saeed Bin Suroor) *lw: stdd s: hld up in rr: c to r in centre 9f out: rdn and effrt ent fnl 2f: chsd ldng pair and edgd rt jst over 1f out: wknd jst ins fnl f* **9/4**[1]

346- **4** *6* **Alwaary (USA)**[409] 5134 4-9-3 117 RichardHills 1 93
(J H M Gosden) *t.k.h: hld up in tch in last pair: c to r in centre 9f out: rdn and wknd 2f out: wl btn and eased ins fnl f* **3/1**[2]

0504 **5** *6* **Three Moons (IRE)**[51] 4957 4-8-12 99 RichardHughes 5 79
(H J L Dunlop) *chsd ldr: styd far side 9f out: lost 2nd and wknd u.p wl over 1f out: wl bhd and eased ins fnl f* **12/1**

2m 41.35s (9.35) **Going Correction** +0.825s/f (Soft)
WFA 3 from 4yo+ 7lb **5** Ran SP% **110.7**
Speed ratings (Par 111): **106,102,100,96,92**
CSF £13.65 TOTE £4.40: £1.20, £2.50; EX 15.40.
Owner A J Thompson **Bred** Mrs N A Ward **Trained** Newmarket, Suffolk

FOCUS
A small field for this Listed event and the field split in two 9f out, with Richard Hills leading Frankie Dettori centre to stands' side, while the rest raced centre to far side, and it was from the latter group that the first two emerged. The form is rather messy and muddling.

NOTEBOOK
Myplacelater travelled quite nicely and quickened up when she hit the rising ground. She stayed on strongly, proving well suited by the step up in distance, and put to bed any concerns that she wouldn't handle the soft ground with a convincing display, despite her rider putting up 1lb overweight. She appears to be progressing fast, and it could well be worth her taking her chance in the Group 2 Pride Stakes. (tchd 10-3)
Dreamspeed(IRE) led the group towards the far side and, while the winner pulled clear in the closing stages, he kept on well to retain second place. He hadn't run since finishing fifth in an Italian Group 2 in May, is fully entitled to come on for this, and it wouldn't be a surprise to see his trainer find an opening for him before the season is out, perhaps on the continent. (tchd 4-1)
Wajir(FR) may have been at a disadvantage racing more towards the stands' side, but he remains below the form he showed in France for his previous trainer last year. (op 11-4 tchd 3-1)
Alwaary(USA) was a little keen early on his return from an absence stretching back to August last year. Although best in at the weights, he was unproven on anything softer than good and his trainer had warned that he would need the outing. It was no surprise to see him tire late on. Official explanation: jockey said colt ran too free (tchd 11-4 and 10-3)
Three Moons(IRE), who only has a maiden win to her name, has shown her best form on good to firm ground, and her stamina for this distance remains in question. (op 9-1 tchd 8-1)

6534 STANDING FOR SUCCESS H'CAP (SILVER CAMBRIDGESHIRE) 1m 1f
4:50 (4:53) (Class 2) 3-Y-O+
£24,924 (£5,598; £5,598; £1,868; £932; £468) **Stalls** High

Form RPR
1331 **1** **Sarrsar**[28] 5728 3-9-10 90 4ex FrankieDettori 15 101+
(M A Jarvis) *lw: chsd ldrs: hdwy to chse ldr 2f out: rdn to ld ent fnl f: tired fnl 75yds: jst lasted: all out* **7/2**[1]

3340 **2** *shd* **Sand Skier**[32] 5605 3-9-10 90 KierenFallon 4 98
(M Johnston) *chsd ldrs: rdn whn hmpd and swtchd rt over 1f out: rallied ent fnl f: kpt on wl u.p ins fnl f: jnd 2nd on line: jst failed* **7/1**[2]

0114 **2** *dht* **Lost In The Moment (IRE)**[28] 5728 3-9-9 89 RyanMoore 7 97
(J Noseda) *hld up towards rr: rdn and effrt 1/2-way: drvn to chse ldrs over 1f out: chsd wnr fnl 100yds: kpt on wl: jnd for 2nd on line: jst failed* **7/1**[2]

6043 **4** *hd* **Reve De Nuit (USA)**[7] 6318 4-9-10 86 JMurtagh 6 94
(A J McCabe) *chsd ldrs: rdn and sltly outpcd over 1f out: rallied u.p fnl f: kpt on wl fnl 100yds: nt quite rch ldrs* **7/1**[2]

5636 **5** *1/2* **Highland Knight (IRE)**[21] 5917 3-9-7 87 (t) JimmyFortune 12 93
(A M Balding) *lw: led: edging lft thrght: hung lft to r on stands' rail wl over 1f out: rdn and hdd ent fnl f: no ex and lost 3 pls fnl 100yds* **8/1**[3]

1205 **6** *1/2* **Tartan Trip**[27] 5750 3-8-12 83 (v) SimonPearce(5) 5 88+
(A M Balding) *stdd s: hld up in rr: hdwy and n.m.r ent fnl 2f: hdwy over 1f out: kpt on wl ins fnl f: nt rch ldrs* **25/1**

5001 **7** *1* **Nicholas Pocock (IRE)**[15] 6125 4-7-12 59 4ex JimmyQuinn 1 63+
(B Ellison) *stdd and dropped in bhd after s: hdwy 2f out: n.m.r and hmpd over 1f out: kpt on ins fnl f: unable to chal* **20/1**

5000 **8** *3 1/2* **Follow The Flag (IRE)**[11] 6252 6-9-4 85 (p) DeclanCannon(5) 9 80
(A J McCabe) *in tch: rdn and effrt ent fnl 2f: pushed rt and hmpd over 1f out: styd on same pce u.p after* **66/1**

1223 **9** *1 1/4* **Dolphin Rock**[21] 5904 3-9-3 83 JamieSpencer 8 76
(T D Barron) *chsd ldrs: rdn and hmpd wl over 1f out: sn swtchd rt and bmpd rival: wknd u.p over 1f out* **8/1**[3]

00/5 **10** *1/2* **Levera**[50] 5004 7-9-10 86 NeilCallan 3 78
(A King) *in tch in midfield: rdn and effrt over 2f out: wknd u.p over 1f out* **33/1**

-146 **11** *nk* **Nazreef**[14] 6151 3-9-2 82 (t) TravisBlock 11 73+
(H Morrison) *chsd ldr tl hmpd ent fnl 2f: rdn and trying to rally whn pushed rt and hmpd over 1f out: wl btn ent fnl f* **16/1**

0-05 **12** *2* **Global**[45] 3973 4-8-3 70 JohnFahy(5) 14 57
(B Ellison) *in tch: rdn and effrt over 2f out: keeping on same pce and no prog whn pushed rt and hmpd over 1f out: sn wknd* **20/1**

130 **13** *4* **Be Invincible (IRE)**[31] 5638 3-9-8 88 MichaelHills 2 66
(B W Hills) *in tch in midfield: rdn and unable qck 3f out: wknd 2f out* **20/1**

1240 **14** *30* **Rosko**[34] 5533 6-8-12 74 WilliamBuick 10 —
(B Ellison) *stdd s: hld up in tch: rdn and struggling jst over 3f out: wl btn and eased fr over 1f out: t.o* **33/1**

0026 **15** *9* **Marvo**[7] 6327 6-9-1 77 SebSanders 16 —
(M H Tompkins) *stdd s: hld up towards rr: rdn and struggling 3f out: wl bhd and eased fr over 1f out: t.o* **8/1**[3]

1m 57.37s (5.67) **Going Correction** +0.825s/f (Soft)
WFA 3 from 4yo+ 4lb **15** Ran SP% **124.4**
Speed ratings (Par 109): **107,106,106,106,106 105,104,101,100,100 100,98,94,68,60**PL: Sand Skier £2.20, Lost in the Moment £3.80, EX: Sarrsar/SS £14.80, S/LM £12.70 CSF: S/SS £12.57 S/LM £12.57 TRI: S/SS/LM £86.95, S/LM/SS £86.95 toteswingers:1&SS £4.60, 2&2 £10.50, 1&LM £5.70 TOTE £4.30: £1.60 Trifecta £47.80 Pool: £983.44 - 7.6027 Owner.

FOCUS
The first ever consolation race for the Cambridgeshire was a competitive contest, but the form is rank ordinary by Class 2 standards, as 90 was the highest official rating on offer, and plenty of exposed types finished close up. They started off up the middle of the track, but all ended up towards the stands' side, being led in that direction by Highland Knight. The form is rated around the four immediately behind the winner.

NOTEBOOK
Sarrsar was 5lb well in but he rather struggled in these conditions and it's to his credit he prevailed. Both his previous wins had been gained on Polytrack, and that may yet prove to be his favoured surface, but whatever, it seems likely he'll leave this form behind and continue his progression back on better going. (op 10-3 tchd 4-1)
Lost In The Moment(IRE) got much closer to Sarrsar than on the Polytrack last time, but he's not the finished article just yet. He takes a while to get going when under pressure and gives the impression he's still got some growing up to do mentally. (op 8-1)
Sand Skier, 2lb wrong, was forced to switch off the rail after Highland Knight crossed his path about 2f out, but he did not look unlucky. (op 8-1)
Reve De Nuit(USA), 1lb well in, seemed to cope with the ground okay and ran a good race. (op 9-1)
Highland Knight(IRE), as is often the case, hung left under pressure and that cost him his chance. Official explanation: jockey said colt hung left
Tartan Trip, who started slowly, had to wait for a run towards the near rail around 2f out and got going too late. (op 20-1)
Nicholas Pocock(IRE), 7lb higher than when winning on Polytrack last time, didn't get the best of runs through and is a little better than he showed. (op 22-1 tchd 25-1)
Dolphin Rock was a bit short of room inside the final 2f, but basically didn't handle the Dip and can be excused this below-par performance. (tchd 15-2)
Nazreef was badly baulked on more than one occasion in the closing stages and is much better than he showed. (tchd 20-1 in places)

Marvo Official explanation: jockey said gelding never travelled

6535 NEWMARKET CHALLENGE WHIP (A H'CAP) 1m 2f
5:25 (5:25) (Class 6) (0-85,87) 3-Y-0+ £0Stalls High

Form RPR
4132 1 **Scottish Boogie (IRE)**[14] 6151 3-8-7 **76**...................... RichardHughes 4 88
(S Kirk) *mde all: drew wl clr fr 3f out: eased fnl 100yds: easily* **5/4**[1]
0020 2 *19* **Gearbox (IRE)**[13] 6213 4-7-6 **63** oh5 ow1.................. RichardRowe(7) 3 37
(H J L Dunlop) *chsd wnr on far side: rdn and outpcd by wnr 3f out: wnt poor 2nd and wandered u.p over 2f out: no imp and wl btn after* **14/1**
1006 3 *17* **Desert Sage**[13] 6199 3-9-1 **87**...................................... EJMcNamara(3) 1 27
(R M Beckett) *lw: racd alone in centre: t.k.h: chsd wnr tl struggling ent fnl 3f: lost 2nd and wl btn over 2f out: eased ins fnl f: t.o* **7/4**[2]
4622 4 *6* **Zenarinda**[5] 6356 3-7-13 **68** ow1.. JimmyQuinn 2 —
(M H Tompkins) *t.k.h: hld up in last: lost tch qckly over 3f out: t.o and eased ent fnl f* **7/2**[3]

2m 13.56s (7.76) **Going Correction** +0.825s/f (Soft)
WFA 3 from 4yo+ 5lb 4 Ran SP% **109.7**
Speed ratings (Par 101): **101,85,72,67**
toteswingers:1&2 £4.60, 2&2 £10.50, 1&2 £5.70 CSF £14.91 TOTE £2.00; EX 12.10 Place 6: £56.84 Place 5: £47.17.
Owner J C Smith **Bred** Littleton Stud **Trained** Upper Lambourn, Berks

FOCUS
Just the four runners for a race restricted to horses owned by members of the Jockey Club, and for which there is no prize money. Despite the small field, they raced apart, with Desert Sage coming up the centre of the track, Zenarinda and Gearbox racing centre to far side and Scottish Boogie (joined 6f out by Zenarida) racing hard up against the far rail. The form looks guessy with the winner the only one to handle the ground.
T/Jkpt: Not won. T/Plt: £30.30 to a £1 stake. Pool of £120,779.16 2,900.48 winning tickets.
T/Qpdt: £17.00 to a £1 stake. Pool of £6,511.67 - 282.44 winning tickets. SP

6368 WOLVERHAMPTON (A.W) (L-H)
Friday, October 1

OFFICIAL GOING: Standard
Wind: Almost nil Weather: Rain clearing

6536 BREEDERS' CUP LIVE ONLY ON ATR H'CAP 5f 20y(P)
5:45 (5:45) (Class 6) (0-60,60) 3-Y-0+ £1,706 (£503; £252) Stalls Low

Form RPR
0000 1 **Grand Stitch (USA)**[13] 6210 4-8-12 **58**...........................(v) NeilFarley(7) 4 74
(D Carroll) *sn chsng ldr: led 3f out: rdn clr over 1f out: styd on* **16/1**
422 2 *2 ¼* **Best One**[10] 6270 6-9-1 **54**...(b) LukeMorris 5 62
(R A Harris) *s.i.s: hld up: nt clr run 1/2-way: hdwy over 1f out: sn rdn: r.o: nt trble wnr* **8/1**
4110 3 *nse* **Towy Boy (IRE)**[13] 6210 5-9-7 **60**.............................(bt) CathyGannon 13 68
(I A Wood) *sn pushed along in rr: rdn over 1f out: edgd lft and r.o ins fnl f: nrst fin* **13/2**[3]
6604 4 *shd* **Green Lagonda (AUS)**[9] 6284 8-9-1 **54**.................. SilvestreDeSousa 3 61
(P D Evans) *mid-div: sn pushed along: hdwy u.p over 1f out: r.o* **5/1**[1]
2516 5 *½* **Wooden King (IRE)**[28] 5714 5-9-3 **56**........................ WilliamCarson 12 62
(M S Saunders) *prom: rdn 1/2-way: hung lft fr over 1f out: r.o* **11/1**
0023 6 *1 ¼* **Flaxen Lake**[20] 5957 3-9-7 **60**.......................................(tp) PaulHanagan 1 61
(J M Bradley) *prom: rdn over 1f out: styd on same pce ins fnl f* **5/1**[1]
4624 7 *2* **Sharp Bullet (IRE)**[5] 6398 4-8-13 **59**....................(b) DanielleMooney(7) 8 53
(Bruce Hellier) *chsd ldrs: rdn over 1f out: wknd ins fnl f* **11/1**
004 8 *shd* **Shamarlane**[53] 4908 3-9-3 **56**.. TomEaves 9 50
(Daniel Miley, Ire) *s.i.s: sn pushed along in rr: hung lft ins fnl f: nvr nrr* **20/1**
5415 9 *1 ½* **Double Carpet (IRE)**[7] 6329 7-8-13 **57**........................ RossAtkinson(5) 6 45
(G Woodward) *sn outpcd: nvr on terms* **6/1**[2]
0122 10 *nk* **Madam Isshe**[20] 5957 3-9-6 **59**.................................... TomMcLaughlin 7 46
(M S Saunders) *led early: chsd ldrs tl rdn and wknd over 1f out* **10/1**
0-60 11 *½* **I'Lldoit**[174] 1222 3-9-5 **58**.. LeeVickers 11 43
(H J Evans) *s.i.s: outpcd* **50/1**
4640 12 *4 ½* **Morgans Choice**[35] 5470 3-9-3 **56**............................(b) SamHitchcott 2 25
(J L Spearing) *sn led: hdd 3f out: rdn and wknd over 1f out* **25/1**

61.70 secs (-0.60) **Going Correction** -0.075s/f (Stan) 12 Ran SP% **114.3**
Speed ratings (Par 101): **101,97,97,97,96 94,91,91,88,88 87,80**
toteswingers:1&2 £37.60, 2&3 £8.30, 1&3 £25.30 CSF £130.80 CT £936.70 TOTE £27.10: £7.10, £1.60, £1.60; EX 234.10.
Owner Danny Fantom **Bred** Fortress Pacific Equine Llc **Trained** Sledmere, E Yorks

FOCUS
Typical low grade fare but an impressive winner and straightforward form rated around those in the frame.

6537 BREEDERS' CUP LIVE ONLY ON ATR CLAIMING STKS 5f 216y(P)
6:15 (6:17) (Class 6) 3-Y-0+ £1,706 (£503; £252) Stalls Low

Form RPR
1130 1 **Orpenindeed (IRE)**[27] 5768 7-9-0 82.................. AndrewHeffernan(3) 1 79
(Jim Best) *sn drvn to ld: rdn over 1f out: styd on* **9/2**[2]
1366 2 *½* **Vhujon (IRE)**[20] 5941 5-9-4 78..................................... AdamBeschizza(5) 3 83
(P D Evans) *prom: rdn over 2f out: chsd wnr fnl f: r.o* **16/1**
2401 3 *shd* **Romantic Queen**[7] 6330 4-8-5 65 ow2...................(t) MatthewDavies(3) 8 68
(George Baker) *s.i.s: hld up: hdwy over 1f out: rdn and r.o wl* **7/1**
3416 4 *1 ½* **Apache Ridge (IRE)**[16] 6078 4-9-1 65.......................(b) PaulMulrennan 2 70
(K A Ryan) *chsd ldrs: rdn over 1f out: styd on* **16/1**
6000 5 *½* **Ajara (IRE)**[7] 6330 4-8-6 59...................................... RichardKingscote 10 60
(Tom Dascombe) *chsd wnr: rdn over 1f out: styd on same pce ins fnl f* **66/1**
3004 6 *2 ¾* **Gone Hunting**[7] 6330 4-8-9 70..(t) CathyGannon 5 54
(J Pearce) *s.s: outpcd: rdn and hung lft over 1f out: r.o ins fnl f: nvr nrr* **8/1**
0165 7 *2* **Melody In The Mist (FR)**[35] 5501 3-8-13 72............ GrahamGibbons 4 52
(T D Barron) *in rr and pushed along 1/2-way: styd on nr fin: nvr on terms* **12/1**
0040 8 *½* **Sunrise Safari (IRE)**[14] 6142 7-9-9 82........................(v) PaulHanagan 13 60
(R A Fahey) *prom: rdn over 2f out: wknd over 1f out* **5/1**[3]
3001 9 *nk* **King's Wonder**[35] 5496 5-9-9 82................................ AdrianNicholls 12 59
(D Nicholls) *mid-div: hdwy over 3f out: rdn over 2f out: sn hung lft: wknd over 1f out* **4/1**[1]
0344 10 *hd* **Excusez Moi (USA)**[60] 4653 8-9-6 86........................ JamesSullivan(3) 6 58
(Mrs R A Carr) *mid-div: hdwy 1/2-way: rdn over 2f out: wknd over 1f out* **13/2**

1m 14.27s (-0.73) **Going Correction** -0.075s/f (Stan)
WFA 3 from 4yo+ 1lb 10 Ran SP% **112.7**
Speed ratings (Par 101): **101,100,100,98,97 93,91,90,90,89**
toteswingers:1&2 £13.00, 2&3 £19.90, 1&3 £6.40 CSF £70.93 TOTE £6.00: £1.90, £6.80, £2.10; EX 57.70.
Owner Diamond Racing Ltd **Bred** A Pereira **Trained** Lewes, E Sussex

FOCUS
Quite a competitive claimer on paper and the placed horses set the standard.
King's Wonder Official explanation: jockey said gelding hung left-handed

6538 ATTHERACES.COM/BREEDERSCUP H'CAP 1m 5f 194y(P)
6:45 (6:46) (Class 6) (0-65,64) 3-Y-0+ £1,706 (£503; £252) Stalls Low

Form RPR
3502 1 **Resplendent Ace (IRE)**[15] 6121 6-9-7 **57**................. TomMcLaughlin 5 69
(P Howling) *s.i.s: hld up: pushed along and rapid hdwy to chse ldr over 3f out: led over 2f out: sn rdn: styd on* **14/1**
0500 2 *1 ½* **Aaman (IRE)**[25] 5813 4-9-7 **64**.. RyanClark(7) 3 74
(E F Vaughan) *trckd ldr: racd keenly: led over 9f out: rdn and hdd over 2f out: styd on* **22/1**
0501 3 *½* **Leyte Gulf (USA)**[15] 6120 7-9-10 **60**.................................... DaneO'Neill 8 69
(C C Bealby) *s.s: hld up: hung lft and hdwy over 3f out: sn rdn: hung lft ins fnl f: styd on* **8/1**[3]
3230 4 *3 ½* **Tivers Song (USA)**[2] 6472 6-8-10 **49**.........................(b) BarryMcHugh(3) 9 53
(John A Harris) *hld up: outpcd over 3f out: hdwy over 1f out: nt trble ldrs* **12/1**
1434 5 *1* **Simple Jim (FR)**[13] 6187 6-9-13 **63**......................... SilvestreDeSousa 12 66+
(D O'Meara) *hld up: dropped in rr 5f out: hdwy over 1f out: nrst fin* **9/2**[2]
1250 6 *5* **Galiotto (IRE)**[31] 5625 4-9-5 **55**....................................(b[1]) GeorgeBaker 13 51
(C F Wall) *hld up in tch: rdn and wknd over 1f out* **8/1**[3]
/5-5 7 *1 ¼* **Thief**[13] 6213 4-9-10 **60**...(t) LukeMorris 10 54
(W R Swinburn) *chsd ldrs: rdn over 6f out: hung lft and wknd over 1f out* **8/1**[3]
5446 8 *8* **Dazzling Begum**[13] 6213 5-9-4 **54**... AdamKirby 4 37
(J Pearce) *hld up: hmpd over 3f out: n.d* **10/1**
04-5 9 *5* **Criterion**[246] 330 5-9-11 **61**... PJMcDonald 11 37
(Ian Williams) *bhd and rdn 1/2-way: n.d* **25/1**
3662 10 *2 ¼* **Hallstatt (IRE)**[13] 6213 4-9-12 **62**.....................................(p) PaulHanagan 1 35
(J Mackie) *chsd ldrs tl rdn and wknd over 2f out* **4/1**[1]
4330 11 *1* **Rare Coincidence**[53] 4915 9-9-0 **50**.................................(p) TomEaves 6 22
(R F Fisher) *chsd ldrs: rdn over 4f out: hmpd and wknd over 3f out* **25/1**
056/ 12 *nk* **Stormin Heart (USA)**[364] 7368 5-8-11 **47**.......................... CathyGannon 7 18
(P D Evans) *hld up: rdn over 4f out: wknd 3f out* **50/1**
1000 13 *31* **Astronomical (IRE)**[13] 6213 8-9-10 **60**...................(p) GrahamGibbons 2 —
(R Hollinshead) *led: hdd over 9f out: chsd ldr: rdn over 6f out: wknd over 3f out: t.o* **16/1**

3m 3.80s (-2.20) **Going Correction** -0.075s/f (Stan) 13 Ran SP% **114.8**
Speed ratings (Par 101): **103,102,101,99,99 96,95,91,88,87 86,86,68**
toteswingers:1&2 £57.70, 2&3 £13.80, 1&3 £6.60 CSF £289.46 CT £2612.24 TOTE £12.90: £2.90, £11.20, £4.70; EX 219.50.
Owner Paul Howling **Bred** Newlands House Stud **Trained** Newmarket, Suffolk

FOCUS
An ordinary handicap but soundly run and rated slightly positively.
Astronomical(IRE) Official explanation: jockey said gelding never travelled

6539 BET RYDER CUP - BETDAQ H'CAP 5f 20y(P)
7:15 (7:17) (Class 4) (0-85,91) 3-Y-0+ £3,594 (£1,069; £534; £266) Stalls Low

Form RPR
0301 1 **Drawnfromthepast (IRE)**[6] 6374 5-9-10 **91** 6ex.......... SophieDoyle(3) 9 101
(J A Osborne) *chsd ldrs: led 2f out: rdn out* **11/2**[2]
56 2 *1 ¼* **Ziggy Lee**[41] 5308 4-9-7 **85**.. WilliamCarson 6 91
(S C Williams) *a.p: rdn over 1f out: hung lft and chsd wnr ins fnl f: r.o* **5/2**[1]
1103 3 *3* **Fair Passion**[6] 6374 3-8-11 **75**... DaneO'Neill 8 70
(D Shaw) *s.i.s: plld hrd and sn trcking ldrs: hung rt fr over 3f out tl rdn over 1f out: hung lft and styd on same pce ins fnl f* **6/1**[3]
3264 4 *1 ¼* **Spring Green**[77] 4090 4-8-10 **74**.....................................(t) SteveDrowne 10 64
(H Morrison) *sn led: hdd 2f out: wknd ins fnl f* **7/1**
2510 5 *¾* **Baby Strange**[13] 6175 6-9-6 **84**.. FrannyNorton 3 72
(D Shaw) *broke wl: sn outpcd: r.o ins fnl f: nt trble ldrs* **7/1**
00-4 6 *½* **Toms Laughter**[6] 6374 6-9-7 **85**..................................(t) CathyGannon 11 71
(D H Brown) *s.i.s: sn pushed along in rr: rdn over 1f out: nvr on terms* **8/1**
344 7 *¾* **High Spice (USA)**[53] 4901 3-9-2 **80**.............................(p) J-PGuillambert 1 63
(R M H Cowell) *dwlt: outpcd: rdn over 1f out: nvr on terms* **16/1**
0420 8 *2* **Our Piccadilly (IRE)**[31] 5628 5-8-8 **72**............................. SamHitchcott 7 48
(W S Kittow) *prom: rdn 1/2-way: wknd over 1f out* **20/1**
1502 9 *1 ½* **Where's Reiley (USA)**[152] 1719 4-8-13 **82**........................ DeanHeslop(5) 5 52
(T D Barron) *prom: drvn along 1/2-way: wknd wl over 1f out* **16/1**

61.05 secs (-1.25) **Going Correction** -0.075s/f (Stan) 9 Ran SP% **110.9**
Speed ratings (Par 105): **107,105,100,98,97 96,95,91,89**
toteswingers:1&2 £3.50, 2&3 £2.40, 1&3 £6.50 CSF £18.41 CT £80.30 TOTE £9.40: £2.60, £3.20, £1.80; EX 22.50.
Owner H R H Prince of Saxe-Weimar **Bred** D And Mrs D Veitch **Trained** Upper Lambourn, Berks

FOCUS
Easily the strongest race on the card and the pace held up well. The runner-up is rated in line with his best form.
Fair Passion Official explanation: jockey said filly hung badly right-handed

6540 BET SUPER LEAGUE GRAND FINAL - BETDAQ H'CAP (DIV I) 7f 32y(P)
7:45 (7:46) (Class 5) (0-70,70) 3-Y-0 £1,774 (£523; £262) Stalls High

Form RPR
332 1 **Bianca De Medici**[22] 5872 3-9-7 **70**................................. SteveDrowne 4 80
(H Morrison) *chsd ldrs: pushed along 1/2-way: rdn to ld ins fnl f: r.o* **5/1**[2]
0035 2 *1 ½* **Norville (IRE)**[17] 6056 3-9-6 **69**...................................... CathyGannon 3 75
(P D Evans) *chsd ldr: rdn to ld over 1f out: hdd and unable qck ins fnl f* **20/1**
5560 3 *shd* **Tiger Star**[16] 6091 3-9-4 **67**.. LukeMorris 1 73+
(J M P Eustace) *s.i.s and hmpd s: hdwy 5f out: rdn over 1f out: r.o* **5/1**[2]
0056 4 *2* **Marosh (FR)**[16] 6085 3-9-7 **70**....................................... GrahamGibbons 5 70
(R M H Cowell) *prom: rdn over 2f out: hung lft over 1f out: styd on same pce ins fnl f* **13/2**[3]
5131 5 *1* **Key Breeze**[7] 6336 3-9-2 **65** 6ex.................................(t) PaulHanagan 6 63
(K A Ryan) *hld up: racd keenly: hdwy over 2f out: rdn over 1f out: no ex ins fnl f* **2/1**[1]

0206 6 1 **Posy Fossil (USA)**[22] 5896 3-8-12 **61**....................(e[1]) WilliamCarson 11 56
(S C Williams) *hld up: rdn over 2f out: hdwy over 1f out: nvr trbld ldrs* **18/1**

4600 7 1 3/4 **Jibrrya**[14] 6144 3-8-11 **60**........................ AdrianNicholls 10 50
(D Nicholls) *s.i.s: rdn over 1f out: nvr on terms* **33/1**

00-2 8 1 **Mad Millie (IRE)**[108] 3062 3-8-9 **58**.................. SilvestreDeSousa 7 45
(D O'Meara) *led: rdn and hdd over 1f out: wknd ins fnl f* **13/2**[3]

6606 9 2 3/4 **Bill's Story**[30] 5669 3-8-4 **60**...................... MatthewLawson(7) 12 40
(M R Channon) *hld up: rdn over 2f out: n.d* **33/1**

5002 10 1/2 **Ice Cool Lady (IRE)**[14] 6168 3-8-6 **60**..................(b) RosieJessop(5) 2 39
(W R Swinburn) *s.i.s and wnt lft s: hld up: rdn over 2f out: sn wknd* **14/1**

3056 11 1 1/2 **Gertmegalush (IRE)**[54] 4858 3-9-4 **70**................... BarryMcHugh(3) 8 45
(John A Harris) *prom: rdn 1/2-way: wknd over 2f out* **33/1**

5455 12 2 1/4 **Roose Blox (IRE)**[58] 4705 3-9-2 **65**........................ TomEaves 9 34
(R F Fisher) *chsd ldrs tl rdn and wknd over 2f out* **33/1**

1m 28.78s (-0.82) **Going Correction** -0.075s/f (Stan) **12** Ran SP% **121.8**
Speed ratings (Par 101): **101,99,99,96,95 94,92,91,88,87 86,83**
toteswingers:1&2 £9.40, 2&3 £28.00, 1&3 £4.90 CSF £107.98 CT £413.88 TOTE £6.80: £1.80, £7.70, £3.00; EX 73.70.
Owner Lady Bland **Bred** Lady Bland **Trained** East Ilsley, Berks

FOCUS
A modest handicap but the winner is unexposed and is rated a 5lb improver.

6541 BET SUPER LEAGUE GRAND FINAL - BETDAQ H'CAP (DIV II) 7f 32y(P)
8:15 (8:15) (Class 5) (0-70,70) 3-Y-O **£1,774** (£523; £262) **Stalls** High

Form RPR
2023 1 **Sir Bruno (FR)**[57] 4732 3-9-6 **69**....................(p) DavidProbert 5 81
(B Palling) *prom: chsd ldr over 1f out: rdn to ld wl ins fnl f: jst hld on* **8/1**[3]

0236 2 nse **Blue Moon**[14] 6144 3-8-11 **60**........................ PaulHanagan 10 72
(K A Ryan) *hld up: hdwy 1/2-way: rdn over 1f out: r.o: jst failed* **8/1**[3]

5055 3 1 3/4 **Mount Juliet (IRE)**[55] 4839 3-9-3 **66**...................... AdamKirby 11 73
(M Botti) *hld up: hdwy over 1f out: rdn and r.o ins fnl f: nrst fin* **11/1**

1321 4 hd **The Human League**[11] 6261 3-8-9 **65**................... MatthewLawson(7) 9 71
(M R Channon) *chsd ldr: led wl over 2f out: rdn and hdd wl ins fnl f* **8/1**[3]

0011 5 nk **Paphos**[28] 5730 3-8-9 **58**..............................(v) WilliamCarson 1 64
(S C Williams) *chsd ldrs: rdn over 2f out: r.o* **4/1**[1]

3101 6 1 3/4 **Fleetwoodsands (IRE)**[14] 6168 3-9-4 **70**................(t) BarryMcHugh(3) 6 71
(Ollie Pears) *s.i.s: hld up: hdwy over 2f out: rdn over 1f out: no imp ins fnl f* **4/1**[1]

3662 7 1 1/4 **Powerful Pierre**[29] 5688 3-9-2 **65**........................ TomEaves 2 63
(I W McInnes) *prom: outpcd 1/2-way: styd on ins fnl f* **12/1**

5423 8 1 3/4 **Chinese Democracy (USA)**[3] 6439 3-8-9 **58**............(v) CathyGannon 8 51
(P D Evans) *hld up: rdn over 2f out: n.d* **13/2**[2]

0033 9 1 3/4 **Law Of Attraction (IRE)**[14] 6164 3-9-7 **70**...................(p) LukeMorris 7 58
(J R Gask) *s.i.s: hld up: rdn over 2f out: n.d* **12/1**

3420 10 4 **Wise Up**[3] 6438 3-9-7 **70**........................ EddieCreighton 4 47
(C A Dwyer) *led: hdd wl over 2f out: wknd over 1f out* **40/1**

043 11 4 **Excellent Thought**[13] 6186 3-8-12 **61**...................... J-PGuillambert 12 28
(P Howling) *prom: rdn and ev ch over 2f out: wknd over 1f out* **40/1**

1m 28.92s (-0.68) **Going Correction** -0.075s/f (Stan) **11** Ran SP% **115.3**
Speed ratings (Par 101): **100,99,97,97,97 95,93,91,89,85 80**
toteswingers:1&2 £8.60, 2&3 £10.00, 1&3 £20.20 CSF £69.11 CT £715.61 TOTE £5.60: £1.40, £2.80, £7.30; EX 63.70.
Owner G Deren **Bred** Sarl Elevage Du Haras De Bourgeauville **Trained** Tredodridge, Vale Of Glamorgan
■ Stewards' Enquiry : William Carson caution: used whip with excessive frequency.

FOCUS
Ordinary fare, but several of these came into this in good form. The form looks straightforward rated around the third and fifth.
Fleetwoodsands(IRE) Official explanation: jockey said gelding ran flat

6542 DINE IN THE HORIZONS RESTAURANT MAIDEN AUCTION STKS 1m 141y(P)
8:45 (8:46) (Class 5) 2-Y-O **£2,115** (£624; £312) **Stalls** Low

Form RPR
5 1 **Haylaman (IRE)**[28] 5724 2-8-11 0........................ PaulHanagan 5 73
(E A L Dunlop) *hld up in tch: rdn to ld 1f out: jst hld on* **11/8**[1]

436 2 nse **Zamina (IRE)**[16] 6070 2-8-5 64........................ DavidProbert 9 67
(S Kirk) *hld up: hdwy over 2f out: rdn and ev ch fr over 1f out: r.o: jst failed* **4/1**[2]

00 3 2 3/4 **Windsor Knights**[11] 6249 2-8-10 0....................(b[1]) JamesDoyle 10 66
(A J Lidderdale) *hld up: hdwy over 2f out: rdn and hung lft over 1f out: styd on same pce* **66/1**

6 4 3 1/2 **Operateur (IRE)**[12] 6222 2-8-12 0........................ PaulMulrennan 4 61
(B M R Haslam) *hld up: hdwy 1/2-way: running on whn hmpd over 1f out: nt rcvr* **8/1**

020 5 3/4 **Retreat Content (IRE)**[12] 6230 2-8-10 0.................. SophieDoyle(3) 6 60
(J A Osborne) *led: hdd over 5f out: chsd ldrs: rdn and styng on whn hmpd over 1f out: nt rcvr* **11/2**[3]

5 6 1 3/4 **See The Smile (USA)**[19] 6001 2-8-5 0.................. AdamBeschizza(5) 1 54
(Miss Gay Kelleway) *chsd ldrs: nt clr run over 2f out: styng on whn hmpd over 1f out: nt rcvr* **8/1**

050 7 2 1/2 **Amore Et Labore**[76] 4131 2-8-12 50........................ DaneO'Neill 7 50
(S Kirk) *prom: led over 5f out: rdn: hung lft and hdd 1f out: wknd ins fnl f* **33/1**

8 6 **Lynchpin** 2-8-10 0........................ LukeMorris 11 36
(R A Harris) *sn pushed along in rr: n.d* **33/1**

000 9 nk **Talking Back**[15] 6118 2-8-12 48........................ SteveDrowne 8 37
(S Kirk) *s.i.s: hld up: hdwy over 5f out: chsd ldr over 3f out: rdn and wknd over 1f out* **50/1**

10 3/4 **Voovoo (IRE)** 2-8-4 0........................ SilvestreDeSousa 3 27
(D O'Meara) *s.i.s: a in rr: bhd fnl 3f* **12/1**

00 P **Precious Diamond**[29] 5676 2-8-8 0........................ SamHitchcott 2 —
(M R Channon) *prom: lost pl 1/2-way: p.u over 3f out* **50/1**

1m 51.88s (1.38) **Going Correction** -0.075s/f (Stan) **11** Ran SP% **118.7**
Speed ratings (Par 95): **90,89,87,84,83 82,79,74,74,73** —
toteswingers:1&2 £2.80, 2&3 £48.30, 1&3 £16.30 CSF £6.59 TOTE £2.70: £1.20, £1.10, £28.10; EX 8.00.
Owner Abdulla Ahmad Al Shaikh **Bred** M Morrin **Trained** Newmarket, Suffolk

FOCUS
A steadily-run affair in which seven or eight were spread across the track turning for home. It is encouraging that two were able to pull clear.

NOTEBOOK
Haylaman(IRE), who was fifth in an ordinary-looking Lingfield maiden on debut, showed the benefit of that experience by putting in an improved performance, keeping on strongly to pull clear with the runner-up. It's early days, but he looks to be going the right way and two of his half-brothers won over 1m2f, so he may well get further than this. (op 6-5)
Zamina(IRE) has an official mark of 64 after three turf maidens, which helps to get a handle on what this form is worth. She saw this longer trip out well and should be going one better soon. (op 9-2)
Windsor Knights had shown nothing in two previous starts but, with blinkers on for the first time, he shaped with much more promise. Although no match for the front two, he was well clear of the rest so there is cause for optimism.
Operateur(IRE) would have finished closer but for being hampered when staying on over a furlong out. He is bred to want middle distances so this was encouraging, as was his debut, and he's one to keep an eye on as he steps up in trip. (op 9-1 tchd 10-1)

6543 BET NEWMARKET CAMBRIDGESHIRE - BETDAQ H'CAP 1m 1f 103y(P)
9:15 (9:16) (Class 5) (0-75,75) 3-Y-O+ **£2,115** (£624; £312) **Stalls** Low

Form RPR
1-50 1 **Maristar (USA)**[20] 5972 3-9-5 **73**........................ DaneO'Neill 10 82
(G A Butler) *hld up: hdwy over 2f out: rdn to ld 1f out: hung lft: jst hld on* **25/1**

3326 2 nk **Veroon (IRE)**[19] 5994 4-9-10 **74**....................(p) PaulMulrennan 2 82
(J G Given) *hld up: hdwy over 1f out: sn rdn and ev ch: r.o* **5/1**[3]

1540 3 shd **Elmfield Giant (USA)**[20] 5942 3-9-0 **68**........................ PaulHanagan 5 77+
(R A Fahey) *prom: rdn and nt clr run over 1f out: r.o: n.m.r towards fin* **9/1**

1/2- 4 1 3/4 **Beetuna (IRE)**[40] 5-9-5 **74**........................ MarkCoumbe(5) 8 78
(D Bourton) *chsd ldrs: sn pushed along: rdn to ld wl over 1f out: hdd 1f out:* **20/1**

-002 5 2 1/2 **Spring Secret**[7] 6328 4-9-1 **65**........................ LukeMorris 3 64
(B Palling) *chsd ldrs: rdn over 3f out: no ex ins fnl f* **11/1**

6532 6 nse **Formulation (IRE)**[11] 6243 3-9-1 **69**....................(b[1]) GeorgeBaker 1 68
(H Morrison) *s.i.s: hld up: rdn over 3f out: hdwy over 2f out: hung lft over 1f out: no imp ins fnl f* **5/2**[2]

503 7 1 1/2 **Baltimore Jack (IRE)**[18] 6029 6-9-6 **70**................(p) GrahamGibbons 11 66
(T D Walford) *led: rdn and hdd wl over 1f out: wknd ins fnl f* **16/1**

3-41 8 4 1/2 **Kronful**[150] 1809 3-9-7 **75**........................ PhilipRobinson 9 61
(M A Jarvis) *chsd ldr: ev ch 2f out: wknd over 1f out* **9/4**[1]

-400 9 1 1/2 **Shifting Gold (IRE)**[87] 3764 4-8-11 **64**....................(p) AmyRyan(3) 12 47
(K A Ryan) *s.i.s: a in rr* **40/1**

2010 10 4 1/2 **Cavendish Road (IRE)**[10] 6267 4-9-3 **72**............(t) AdamBeschizza(5) 6 46
(N J Vaughan) *hld up: rdn over 2f out: a in rr* **33/1**

2m 0.79s (-0.91) **Going Correction** -0.075s/f (Stan)
WFA 3 from 4yo+ 4lb **10** Ran SP% **114.2**
Speed ratings (Par 103): **101,100,100,99,96 96,95,91,90,86**
toteswingers:1&2 £18.60, 2&3 £5.20, 1&3 £50.80 CSF £131.07 CT £1071.38 TOTE £45.00: £9.10, £2.00, £3.60; EX 122.30 Place 6: £1026.82 Place 5: £232.82.
Owner M V Deegan **Bred** Barnett Enterprises **Trained** Newmarket, Suffolk
■ Stewards' Enquiry : Dane O'Neill caution: careless riding.

FOCUS
An even pace to this handicap and the hold-up performers dominated the finish. The form is ordinary with the placed horses setting the level.
T/Plt: £956.50 to a £1 stake. Pool of £77,965.19 - 59.50 winning tickets. T/Qpdt: £139.30 to a £1 stake. Pool of £10,543.47 - 56.00 winning tickets. CR

6544 - 6547a (Foreign Racing) - See Raceform Interactive

6337 DUNDALK (A.W) (L-H)
Friday, October 1

OFFICIAL GOING: Standard

6548a DIAMOND STKS (GROUP 3) 1m 2f 150y(P)
8:30 (8:32) 3-Y-O+ **£34,513** (£10,088; £4,778; £1,592)

RPR
1 **Gitano Hernando**[188] 1027 4-9-2 .... KierenFallon 1 107+
(M Botti) *trckd ldrs: 5th 1/2-way: swtchd to outer 1 1/2f out: sn drvn along: impr into 2nd and chal 1f out: r.o wl to ld cl home: comf* **9/10**[1]

2 nk **Wade Giles (IRE)**[19] 6006 3-8-11 106........................ KLatham 6 104
(G M Lyons, Ire) *hld up: 6th into st: hdwy on outer 2f out: led 1 1/2f out: strly pressed ins fnl f: hdd cl home: nt gng pce of wnr* **6/1**[3]

3 1 1/2 **Mid Mon Lady (IRE)**[27] 5776 5-8-13 99....................(b) DCByrne 3 97
(H Rogers, Ire) *hld up in rr: last travelling wl ent st: 5th and rdn 1f out: kpt on wl* **33/1**

4 1 1/2 **Northgate (IRE)**[47] 5130 5-9-2 101........................ CDHayes 4 97
(Joseph G Murphy, Ire) *trckd ldrs in 4th: impr into 2nd and chal 2f out: 3rd 1f out: sn no ex* **33/1**

5 3 **Swing Pattern (USA)**[15] 6135 3-8-11 ....(t) FMBerry 2 92?
(John M Oxx, Ire) *racd keenly: 3rd 1/2-way: wknd early st* **25/1**

6 nk **Beethoven (IRE)**[6] 6350 3-8-11 117....................(b) JPO'Brien 7 92
(A P O'Brien, Ire) *prom: 2nd 1/2-way: led 2f out: rdn and hdd 1 1/2f out: no ex fr over 1f out* **3/1**[2]

7 1 1/2 **Dansant**[27] 5781 6-9-2 ....(b[1]) PJSmullen 5 88
(G A Butler) *led: rdn and hdd 2f out: sn no ex: eased ins fnl f* **8/1**

2m 12.94s (132.94)
WFA 3 from 4yo+ 6lb **7** Ran SP% **112.8**
CSF £6.67 TOTE £1.70: £1.40, £2.80; DF 8.00.
Owner Team Valor **Bred** Newsells Park Stud Ltd **Trained** Newmarket, Suffolk

FOCUS
This Group 3 featured the return of last year's Dubai World Cup favourite Gitano Hernando, who appeared to have an arduous task on his hands trying to make a winning return from a 188-day absence with talented home pair Beethoven and Wade Giles in the line-up.

NOTEBOOK
Gitano Hernando ◆ was not fully wound up for this, which makes his performance all the more impressive and he was certainly value for more than the winning margin of a neck, as he endued a troubled passage up the home straight. When he did finally get room, he had two lengths to make up on Wade Giles but he quickened impressively to win a shade snugly at the line. Indeed, Fallon didn't even resort to using his whip. This was a promising performance and the winner will certainly come on for the run. The Champion Stakes is likely to be his next assignment and the stiff uphill finish at Newmarket should be tailor-made for his long stride. The Breeders' Cup Classic at Churchill Downs could also be on the agenda. (op 1/1 tchd 11/10)
Wade Giles(IRE) put up another cracking effort in defeat. He had plenty to find on ratings with the winner but almost spoiled the visiting party when scooting to the front down the outside a furlong and a half out. At that stage he appeared to have the measure of Gitano Hernando but the winner's class shone though inside the final furlong. Wade Giles looks well up to winning a Group 3. The extra two furlongs didn't bother him and he looks a nice prospect for next term. (op 11/2)
Mid Mon Lady(IRE) put up a career-best effort to finish third. The steady early pace allowed her to travel into the race and she was arguably travelling best of all turning for home at the back of the field. This likeable mare just lacked a change of gear when the race began in earnest but connections are sure to be delighted with this showing.
Northgate(IRE) looked like having a say in the finish for a brief spell just over a furlong out but couldn't quicken.
Swing Pattern(USA) was too keen in the early stages and weakened into fifth.

Beethoven(IRE) was a blatant non-stayer. Fresh from a cracking effort behind Poet's Voice in the Queen Elizabeth II Stakes at Ascot last week, Joseph O'Brien settled last year's Dewhurst winner just off the pace and he looked poised to mount a serious challenge turning for home. He did hit the front passing the 2f marker but the writing was on the wall at that stage and he was swallowed up. He will surely return to a mile on his next start. Official explanation: jockey said race may have come too soon after Ascot and colt ran free in the early stages (op 11/4)

Dansant made the running but he didn't appear to relish the front-running role and folded tamely in the home straight.

6549 - 6550a (Foreign Racing) - See Raceform Interactive

6315 SAINT-CLOUD (L-H)

Friday, October 1

OFFICIAL GOING: Turf: very soft

6551a PRIX CHARLES LAFFITTE (LISTED RACE) (3YO FILLIES) (TURF) 1m 2f

2:20 (12:00) 3-Y-O **£24,336** (£9,734; £7,300; £4,867; £2,433)

Pos	Dist	Horse	Jockey	RPR
1		**Baahama (IRE)**[119] 3-8-11 0 (A Fabre, France)	OlivierPeslier 9 **56/10**	98
2	nk	**Louve Rare (IRE)**[30] 5673 3-8-11 0 (E Lellouche, France)	AnthonyCrastus 11 **11/1**	97
3	1	**Valasyra (FR)**[30] 5672 3-8-11 0 (A De Royer-Dupre, France)	Christophe-PatriceLemaire 8 **5/1**[3]	95
4	snk	**Middle Club**[22] 5881 3-9-2 0 (R Hannon) *settled towards rr on outside: mde gd prog at end of bk st: qcknd wl on outside 1 1/2f out: led briefly 1f out: no ex fnl 100yds*	IoritzMendizabal 10 **7/2**[1]	100
5	1 ½	**Homepage**[30] 5672 3-8-11 0 (P Bary, France)	StephanePasquier 4 **10/1**	92
6	1 ½	**Hasay**[26] 5805 3-8-11 0 (P Schiergen, Germany)	FilipMinarik 1 **21/1**	89
7	½	**Heaven's Vault (IRE)**[8] 6316 3-9-2 0 (Robert Collet, France)	ThierryJarnet 12 **34/1**	93
8	snk	**Buffering**[20] 5981 3-8-11 0 (A Fabre, France)	MaximeGuyon 3 **19/5**[2]	87
9	2	**Khelwa (FR)**[20] 5981 3-8-11 0 (R Gibson, France)	GeraldMosse 2 **16/1**	83
10	2	**Clarietta**[16] 6095 3-8-11 0 (J L Dunlop) *broke wl to r in 2nd: chal for ld early in st: led briefly over 1 1/2f out but sn wknd*	MickaelBarzalona 5 **21/1**	79
11		**Gone Shopping (FR)**[156] 3-8-11 0 (Y De Nicolay, France)	Pierre-CharlesBoudot 6 **16/1**	79

2m 13.2s (-2.80) **11** Ran SP% **116.0**

WIN (incl. 1 euro stake): 6.60. PLACES: 2.50, 4.10, 2.20. DF: 44.00. SF: 99.80.

Owner Wertheimer & Frere **Bred** Wertheimer Et Frere **Trained** Chantilly, France

NOTEBOOK

Middle Club, prominent throughout, coped quite well with the soft ground.

5885 EPSOM (L-H)

Saturday, October 2

OFFICIAL GOING: Soft (heavy in places) changing to heavy after race 1 (2.05)

Rail dolled out up to 4yds from 6f to winning post adding about 5yds to advertised distances.

Wind: Moderate across Weather: Light rain

6552 TICKETS FOR TROOPS H'CAP 1m 2f 18y

2:05 (2:06) (Class 3) (0-95,92) 3-Y-O+ **£9,714** (£2,890; £1,444; £721) **Stalls** Low

Form	Pos	Dist	Horse	Jockey	RPR
3120	1		**Resurge (IRE)**[14] 6193 5-9-10 **89** (W S Kittow) *stdd s: hld up in rr: in tch: hdwy fr 3f out to chse ldr 2f out: sn hrd drvn and styd on wl to ld fnl 120yds: readily*	FergusSweeney 6 **11/4**[1]	98
0300	2	2 ½	**Togiak (IRE)**[14] 6203 3-9-8 **92** (E A L Dunlop) *in tch: hdwy 4f out: sn chalng and led under stands' rail ins fnl 3f: hrd drvn 2f out: hdd and no ex fnl 120yds*	DarryllHolland 5 **8/1**	96
1-56	3	4 ½	**Kithonia (FR)**[86] 3822 3-9-8 **92** (H R A Cecil) *chsd ldrs: rdn over 2f out: styd on for one pce 3rd fr over 1f out*	IanMongan 3 **4/1**[3]	87
0013	4	4	**Plaisterer**[16] 6106 5-9-10 **89** (C F Wall) *chsd ldr: rdn to take slt ld ins fnl 4f: sn jnd and hdd ins fnl 3f: wknd ins fnl 2f*	JackMitchell 7 **3/1**[2]	76
3031	5	½	**Ramona Chase**[24] 5859 5-9-3 **82** (M J Attwater) *in tch: rdn 3f out: no ch fnl 2f but kpt on again cl home*	(t) AndreaAtzeni 4 **7/1**	68
1250	6	25	**Aestival**[17] 6091 4-8-11 **76** (Sir Mark Prescott) *in rr: rdn 3f out: wknd wl over 2f out: eased whn no ch: t.o*	DavidProbert 8 **10/1**	12
-2P0	7	13	**Kaleo**[3] 6450 6-8-11 **79** (S Dow) *led tl hdd ins fnl 4f: sn wknd: t.o*	SimonPearce[(3)] 2 **16/1**	—

2m 14.86s (5.16) **Going Correction** +0.70s/f (Yiel)

WFA 3 from 4yo+ 5lb **7** Ran SP% **110.3**

Speed ratings (Par 107): **107,105,101,98,97 77,67**

Tote Swingers: 1&2 £6.60, 1&3 £4.20, 2&3 £18.60 CSF £22.98 CT £80.20 TOTE £4.30: £2.10, £4.20; EX 30.20 Trifecta £177.70 Pool: £384.35 - 1.60 winning units..

Owner Chris & David Stam **Bred** Sweetmans Bloodstock **Trained** Blackborough, Devon

■ Stewards' Enquiry : Fergus Sweeney caution: used whip with excessive frequency.

FOCUS

The ground had eased from that advertised and was soft, heavy in places. The rail was dolled out 4yds from the 6f pole to the winning post, adding around 5yds to race distances. Unsurprisingly given the conditions, the runners made straight for the stands' rail on reaching the home straight. The runner-up is the best guide to the form.

NOTEBOOK

Resurge(IRE) had bolted up off 9lb lower over C&D in August, and had a 2lb pull for a length defeat by Plaisterer back here later the same month. Dropped out at the back of the field early, he made smooth progress on reaching the home straight and maintained his effort to nail the runner-up half a furlong from home and defy a career-high mark. He may head back to Newbury for a heritage handicap in three weeks' time. (op 3-1)

Togiak(IRE) had seemed to be going the wrong way, but he was given a fine ride by Holland here, even though it was ultimately unsuccessful. Held up early, he made a quick move around the outside on reaching Tattenham Corner, which meant he was able to bag the nearside rail in front on reaching the straight. He did his best to run the finish out of his rivals, but the favourite managed to wear him down well inside the last furlong. (op 10-1)

Kithonia(FR) won her sole start at two in similar conditions, and was making her handicap debut after two unplaced efforts in Pattern company on faster ground. She may not have been in the ideal place by challenging furthest off the rail passing the 2f pole, but she was still well held by the front pair and will need to show more. (op 9-2 tchd 5-1)

Plaisterer, who proved his effectiveness here when winning off 4lb lower over C&D two starts ago, took over from the runaway leader half a mile from home but did not last there long and had nothing left over the last 2f. (op 10-3 tchd 7-2)

Ramona Chase has run some of his best races here and was winning his first race since his 2-y-o days when successful over C&D last month, but he was put up 7lb for that and was making hard work of it from some way out. (op 13-2)

Aestival has gone right off the boil since completing a fast-ground hat-trick in May/June and was still 9lb higher than for the last of those successes. This ground was also a major question mark and he did not handle the descent into the straight at all well. (op 15-2)

Kaleo, 4lb higher than when winning this race last year, did far too much too early in the conditions. (op 12-1)

6553 NIGHTSTALKER CONDITIONS STKS 1m 114y

2:35 (2:35) (Class 3) 2-Y-O **£6,231** (£1,866) **Stalls** Low

Form	Pos	Dist	Horse	Jockey	RPR
10	1		**Roman Eagle (IRE)**[14] 6200 2-8-11 92 (M A Jarvis) *racd in 2nd: pushed along 4f out: drvn to chal 3f out and led wl over 2f out: grabbed stands' rail and in command wl over 1f out: drvn out*	MartinLane[(3)] 2 **6/5**[2]	90
1341	2	2 ½	**Cafe Elektric**[16] 6104 2-9-3 91 (Sir Mark Prescott) *mde running: rdn and jnd 3f out: grabbed stands' rail: hdd wl over 2f out: sn no imp on wnr and kpt on same pce u.p*	JackMitchell 3 **8/11**[1]	88

1m 52.53s (6.43) **Going Correction** +0.75s/f (Yiel) **2** Ran SP% **103.4**

Speed ratings (Par 99): **101,98**

TOTE £2.60.

Owner A D Spence **Bred** Longueville B'Stk & H Lascelles B'Stk **Trained** Newmarket, Suffolk

FOCUS

It was disappointing that this should become a match given the prizemoney, but at least the pace set by Jack Mitchell aboard Cafe Elektric meant that it was more of a proper test than many two-horse races. However, neither colt looked totally at ease on the track, so it may be worth treating the form with some caution. Again they came stands' side.

NOTEBOOK

Roman Eagle(IRE) was disappointing in a valuable Newmarket sales event last month, considering how well the form of his Sandown debut victory has worked out, but he was 4lb well-in with his sole rival at these weights. Content to track the favourite early, he did not handle the home bend too well but he was rushed up to take the lead passing the 3f pole, and then saw his race out gamely despite not doing that much in front. He is still in the Racing Post Trophy and, although that may be aiming a bit high, he probably still has more to offer back on a more conventional track. (op 5-4 tchd Evens)

Cafe Elektric is bred to go in this sort of ground and set a fair pace, but he started to race awkwardly as he made for the stands' rail straightening up for home, which allowed the winner to wrest the lead from him, and he could never rally to any great effect. Official explanation: jockey said colt lost a right-fore shoe (op 4-6 tchd 5-6)

6554 TOMPKINS & MAY PARTNERSHIP APPRENTICES' DERBY H'CAP 1m 4f 10y

3:10 (3:14) (Class 4) (0-80,76) 3-Y-O+ **£5,180** (£1,541; £770; £384) **Stalls** Centre

Form	Pos	Dist	Horse	Jockey	RPR
450	1		**Missionaire (USA)**[24] 5868 3-8-12 **72** (W J Knight) *mde all: 2 l clr of 2nd and 8 l clr of main gp fr 7f out: pushed along and styd on strly whn packed tried to cl over 3f out: forged clr fr over 2f out: unchal*	(p) AdamBeschizza[(3)] 4 **4/1**[2]	87
0-24	2	11	**Not In The Clock (USA)**[33] 5593 3-8-2 **62** (J R Best) *chsd ldrs in 3rd but 8 l off wnr 7f out: styd on fr 3f out to go 2nd over 2f out but nvr any ch w unchal wnr*	KierenFox[(3)] 2 **5/1**	61
0050	3	5	**Buddy Holly**[20] 5991 5-9-10 **74** (F Jordan) *towards rr tl drvn and hdwy fr 4f out: styd on fr 3f out to take wl hld 3rd over 1f out*	AndreaAtzeni 3 **11/1**	65
0620	4	2 ½	**Fantastic Strike (IRE)**[24] 5868 3-9-1 **72** (M Johnston) *trckd wnr at 2 l but 6 l clr of remainder: hrd drvn and effrt over 3f out: nvr on terms and readily outpcd wl over 2f out: wknd in 3rd sn after and lost 4th wl over 1f out*	Louis-PhilippeBeuzelin 6 **9/2**[3]	59
3311	5	1 ¼	**Super Duplex**[51] 4994 3-8-10 **67** (P M Phelan) *in rr: rdn and sme prog fr 3f out: nvr any ch and wl btn over 2f out*	AndrewHeffernan 5 **5/2**[1]	52
43-0	6	10	**Beau Fighter**[20] 5994 5-8-12 **69** (G L Moore) *sn bhd: no ch fr 1/2-way*	ChelseyBanks[(7)] 7 **25/1**	39
30-6	7	5	**Squad**[171] 1303 4-9-2 **69** (S Dow) *in rr: rdn 5f out: a wl bhd*	SimonPearce[(3)] 8 **11/1**	32
6504	8	14	**Penang Cinta**[23] 5888 7-8-11 **68** (P D Evans) *s.i.s: a wl bhd*	(v) MatthewCosham[(7)] 9 **9/1**	10

2m 48.23s (9.33) **Going Correction** +0.75s/f (Yiel)

WFA 3 from 4yo+ 7lb **8** Ran SP% **113.9**

Speed ratings (Par 105): **98,90,87,85,84 78,74,65**

Tote Swingers: 1&2 £6.30, 1&3 £4.00, 2&3 £7.30 CSF £24.08 CT £201.15 TOTE £4.40: £1.50, £2.10, £1.80; EX 31.20.

Owner Bluehills Racing Limited **Bred** Mt Joy Stables **Trained** Patching, W Sussex

FOCUS

As the drizzle continued, the ground was change to heavy all round before this race and it did look hard work for these apprentices. The winner is rated to his previous best.

Beau Fighter Official explanation: trainer said gelding had a breathing problem and hung left

6555 RED PEONY NURSERY 1m 114y

3:50 (3:52) (Class 4) (0-85,85) 2-Y-O **£6,476** (£1,927; £963; £481) **Stalls** Low

Form	Pos	Dist	Horse	Jockey	RPR
0215	1		**Time To Work (IRE)**[15] 6160 2-9-2 80 (A M Balding) *chsd ldrs: drvn along over 3f out: str chal between horses fr 2f out tl slt advantage u.p jst ins fnl f: persistently pressed tl asserted fnl 50yds*	DavidProbert 3 **7/2**[2]	83
0024	2	½	**One Lucky Lady**[15] 6156 2-8-2 66 (B W Hills) *led tl hdd appr fnl 3f: rdn and styd on to chal ins fnl 2f: stl upsides u.p ins fnl f tl outpcd fnl 50yds*	PaulEddery 2 **8/1**	68
0042	3	1	**Barathea Dancer (IRE)**[21] 5961 2-8-10 74 (R A Teal) *chsd ldrs tl drvn to ld appr fnl 3f and grabbed stands' rail: kpt on but jnd again ins fnl 2f: narrowly hdd jst insde fnl f: no ex fnl 120yds*	JackMitchell 5 **11/1**	74
14	4	1 ½	**Suzy Wong**[15] 6160 2-8-10 77 (J Akehurst) *chsd ldrs: drvn and styd on to chse ldrs over 2f out: chal u.p sn after: wknd ins fnl f*	KierenFox[(3)] 1 **5/2**[1]	73
036	5	nk	**Plea**[10] 6279 2-8-0 67 (J H M Gosden) *wnt bdly lft and lost 4 l at s: in rr and t.k.h: hdwy and drvn over 2f out: hung lft 1f out but styd on fnl f: nvr any threat*	Louis-PhilippeBeuzelin[(3)] 8 **9/1**	63

21	6	1 1/2	**Makeynn**[22] 5924 2-9-7 85 DaraghO'Donohoe 6		77
			(Saeed Bin Suroor) *chsd ldrs over 5f: sn wknd*	5/1[3]	
2225	7	7	**Nothing To Hide (IRE)**[21] 5969 2-8-9 76 MartinLane(3) 7		53
			(D J S Ffrench Davis) *in tch tl rdn and wknd 3f out*	9/1	
010	8	52	**Colour Vision (FR)**[21] 5947 2-9-3 81 DarryllHolland 4		—
			(M Johnston) *in rr: rdn over 4f out: sn lost tch: eased: t.o*	12/1	

1m 53.39s (7.29) **Going Correction** +0.75s/f (Yiel) **8** Ran SP% **114.6**
Speed ratings (Par 97): **97,96,95,94,94 92,86,40**
Tote Swingers: 1&2 £5.00, 1&3 £6.00, 2&3 £7.20 CSF £31.44 CT £277.52 TOTE £4.30: £1.50, £2.90, £3.30; EX 43.60.
Owner Another Bottle Racing 2 **Bred** Scuderia San Pancrazio Sas **Trained** Kingsclere, Hants
■ Stewards' Enquiry : David Probert one-day ban: used whip with excessive frequency (Oct 17)

FOCUS
A competitive nursery and there were four in a line passing the furlong pole, but the conditions still seemed to find out a few of these.

NOTEBOOK
Time To Work(IRE) had proved his effectiveness here when winning his maiden over C&D last month, but he had twice previously had a rear view of Suzy Wong. However, these testing conditions seemed to bring out the best in him. Never far off the pace, he came off the bridle 3f from home and did not have much room to play with when trying to challenge between Suzy Wong and One Lucky Lady between the 2f and 1f poles. However, once through the gap he proved very game in a driving finish. He would be of obvious interest back under similar conditions, and the only question is whether he can show his best form away from Epsom. (op 11-2)

One Lucky Lady earns plenty of plaudits as not only was she trying this trip for the first time, she was also keen enough in front in the conditions yet battled back very gamely after being marginally headed 3f from home. There are races to be won with her. (tchd 7-1)

Barathea Dancer(IRE) has been improving with racing, but she did not look happy here two starts ago. Prominent on the outside of the field, she was able to grab the nearside rail just about in front 3f from home and kept on trying right to the line. Despite this effort, a flatter track may suit her better. (op 8-1)

Suzy Wong, who was also declared to run in the earlier conditions event, may have expended a bit too much energy early and, although she had every chance passing the 2f pole, she was racing furthest off the rail of the four battling for the advantage and did not get home. (op 3-1 tchd 9-4)

Plea, making his nursery debut after showing a little ability (and some temperament) in three maidens, again looked quirky as he swerved away to his right exiting the stalls and gave himself a lot to do. He finished well, but still has question marks against him. (op 10-1 tchd 11-1)

Makeynn, making his nursery debut after easily landing odds of 1-4 in a weak Wolverhampton maiden, seemed to handle the undulations of Brighton well enough on his debut, but the market seemed to know that this was not going to be his day. (op 3-1)

Colour Vision(FR), a 100,000gns yearling, lost his race at the start at Doncaster last time and did not handle Tattenham Corner at all here. He was reported to have lost his action and is better than his last two starts suggest. Official explanation: jockey said colt lost its action (tchd 11-1)

6556 SYLVA HONDA H'CAP 1m 114y
4:25 (4:25) (Class 3) (0-90,87) 3-Y-O **£7,771** (£2,312; £1,155; £577) **Stalls** Low

Form					RPR
3133	1		**Pintura**[7] 6355 3-8-11 **80** MartinLane(3) 4		94+
			(D M Simcock) *in rr tl hdwy 4f out: drvn and styd on to take ld and grab stands' rail wl over 2f out: pushed out and styd on wl fnl f*	5/2[1]	
2-46	2	3/4	**Guest Book (IRE)**[22] 5904 3-9-2 **82** DarryllHolland 1		93+
			(M Johnston) *sn chsng ldr: rdn and lost position over 2f out: rallied u.p to chse wnr over 1f out and kpt on u.p but a readily hld*	4/1[2]	
5-03	3	5	**Pittodrie Star (IRE)**[35] 5540 3-8-7 **73** oh2 (p) DavidProbert 2		74
			(A M Balding) *chsd ldrs tl rdn and outpcd over 3f out: styd on again to take wl hld 3rd over 1f out*	4/1[2]	
0046	4	4	**Dubai Miracle (USA)**[9] 6312 3-9-7 **87** (b) FergusSweeney 6		80
			(D M Simcock) *t.k.h: hld up in rr tl hdwy on ins to press ldrs 3f out: rdn over 2f out and wknd qckly*	10/1	
3-16	5	9	**Agony And Ecstasy**[66] 4472 3-9-5 **85** (p) JackMitchell 7		59
			(R M Beckett) *led: rdn 3f out: hdd wl over 2f out: styd chsng wnr u.p but no ch: wknd qckly over 1f out*	11/2[3]	
4115	6	2	**Conciliatory**[31] 5662 3-8-13 **79** IanMongan 3		48
			(Rae Guest) *rdn over 3f out: a in rr*	6/1	
2000	7	3	**If I Were A Boy (IRE)**[4] 6438 3-8-7 **78** (p) BillyCray(5) 5		41
			(D J S Ffrench Davis) *chsd ldrs to 1/2-way*	16/1	

1m 51.22s (5.12) **Going Correction** +0.75s/f (Yiel) **7** Ran SP% **113.2**
Speed ratings (Par 105): **107,106,101,98,90 88,85**
Tote Swingers: 1&2 £2.00, 1&3 £1.90, 2&3 £3.00 CSF £12.36 TOTE £3.00: £1.20, £3.00; EX 11.20.
Owner Dr Marwan Koukash **Bred** Dulverton Equine **Trained** Newmarket, Suffolk

FOCUS
A decent handicap and the pace seemed solid enough for the conditions. The winner is rated as having run a personal best.

NOTEBOOK
Pintura was back down to probably his ideal trip and handles soft ground. Held up off the pace early, he made a swift move on the outside rounding Tattenham Corner, and was able to grab the nearside rail in front passing the 3f pole. From then on it was just a case of keeping his only conceivable danger at bay. Given his ability to handle testing ground, there may still be more opportunities for him before the turf season ends. (tchd 9-4)

Guest Book(IRE) ◆ had the worst of the draw in both starts since returning from 11 months off in August, but had the rails pitch this time. However, he was pressing the leader when not handling the downhill run into the straight very well and losing a length or two, but he rallied once in line for home and, in view of how close he got to the winner, he may have been unlucky not to have gone even closer. He still remains open to improvement, and it would be no surprise to see him go one better in the coming weeks. (op 5-1)

Pittodrie Star(IRE), sporting first-time cheekpieces from 2lb out of the weights, made an effort coming to the last 3f but then tended to hang about under pressure and could never get to the front pair. He will appreciate a stiffer test. (op 9-2 tchd 5-1)

Dubai Miracle(USA) had failed to sparkle so far this season and the soft ground was an issue as well, but he looked dangerous when enjoying a dream run up the inside rounding the home bend, which took him right into contention. However, he came under pressure soon afterwards and there was little left. (op 12-1 tchd 14-1)

Agony And Ecstasy goes well fresh, so the absence since July was not an issue and the soft ground would not have been a problem either. She had just about made all in gaining her three previous victories, so it was no surprise that she was ridden straight into the lead, but she was struggling as soon as the winner headed her 3f from home, and she had run her race before the furlong pole. (op 5-1 tchd 6-1)

Conciliatory, thwarted in her hat-trick bid off this mark on Polytrack last time, needs a decent test at this trip but she never made any impression from off the pace. She was reported to have been unsuited by the heavy ground. Official explanation: jockey said filly was unsuited by the heavy ground (op 5-1 tchd 9-2)

If I Were A Boy(IRE) seems to have gone right off the boil lately, and she has shown her best form when able to grab the early lead. That was not possible here and she dropped right out after racing in snatches. (tchd 20-1)

6557 OCTOBER MAIDEN STKS 1m 2f 18y
5:00 (5:03) (Class 5) 3-Y-O **£3,238** (£963; £481; £240) **Stalls** Low

Form					RPR
244	1		**All Action (USA)**[127] 2507 3-9-3 82 IanMongan 3		93+
			(H R A Cecil) *trckd ldrs: drvn to ld and edgd rt over 2f out: sn clr: in n.d whn hung rt ins fnl f*	6/5[1]	
30	2	11	**Momkinzain (USA)**[46] 5185 3-9-0 0 AndrewHeffernan(3) 2		71
			(M R Channon) *chsd ldr tl rdn 3f out and veered rt over 2f out: continued to wander and hung bdly lft ins fnl f to retake poor 2nd last stride*	7/2[3]	
034	3	shd	**Aneel**[16] 6115 3-9-3 76 DarryllHolland 1		73+
			(J Noseda) *led tl bmpd: hdd and veered rt over 2f out: continued to wander and hung bdly lft but styd chsng easy wnr: vered bdly lft ins fnl f: lost poor 2nd last stride*	2/1[2]	
0436	4	18	**Present Story**[20] 5986 3-8-12 67 DaraghO'Donohoe 5		30
			(P Leech) *bhd fnl 5f*	16/1	
0	5	3	**Tristar Way (GR)**[59] 4697 3-9-3 0 NeilChalmers 7		29
			(P R Chamings) *s.i.s: bhd fnl 5f*	25/1	

2m 20.02s (10.32) **Going Correction** +0.925s/f (Soft) **5** Ran SP% **110.7**
Speed ratings (Par 101): **95,86,86,71,69**
CSF £5.87 TOTE £1.80: £1.10, £2.70; EX 4.80.
Owner K Abdulla **Bred** Juddmonte Farms Inc **Trained** Newmarket, Suffolk

FOCUS
A weak maiden that only concerned the three market leaders. It was a very messy contest as well and the form behind the winner amounts to little. The field bucked the trend of the earlier races by coming down the centre in the home straight and not a race to rate too positively.
Aneel Official explanation: jockey said colt hung badly left and was virtually unrideable final 2f.

6558 CAPISTRANO H'CAP 7f
5:35 (5:35) (Class 4) (0-85,83) 3-Y-O+ **£5,180** (£1,541; £770; £384) **Stalls** Low

Form					RPR
0015	1		**Glenridding**[7] 6372 6-9-6 **82** (p) LeeVickers 5		91
			(J G Given) *led tl hdd 3f out: rdn and hung rt wl over 1f out: swtchd lft and styd on strly to ld again fnl 120yds: hld on wl*	11/1	
4010	2	1/2	**Amber Sunset**[11] 6274 4-8-5 **72** AshleyMorgan(5) 6		80
			(D Morris) *in tch: styng on whn hmpd wl over 1f out and swtchd lft sn after: kpt on strly to press wnr fnl 120yds: no ex nr fin*	11/1	
0230	3	shd	**Aflaam (IRE)**[12] 6260 5-8-6 **71** (t) AndrewHeffernan(3) 4		78+
			(R A Harris) *in rr: rdn and hdwy fr 2f out: str run fnl f to press for 2nd last strides but nt rch wnr*	9/2[3]	
1131	4	nk	**Space Station**[20] 5997 4-9-4 **83** (b) SimonPearce(3) 10		90+
			(S Dow) *chsd ldr tl led 3f out: sn drvn: hung lft u.p fnl f: hdd and no ex fnl 120yds*	3/1[1]	
6200	5	1 1/4	**Mishrif (USA)**[28] 5754 4-9-2 **78** (v) IanMongan 1		81
			(J R Jenkins) *chsd ldrs: rdn and styd on u.p fnl 2f: no ex ins fnl f*	11/1	
0230	6	3/4	**New Leyf (IRE)**[14] 6198 4-9-2 **78** (v) DarryllHolland 2		79
			(J R Gask) *chsd ldrs: rdn fr 2f out: styd on same pce fr over 1f out*	6/1	
3000	7	1 1/4	**Seek The Fair Land**[30] 5702 4-9-7 **83** (b[1]) RobertHavlin 9		81
			(J R Boyle) *in tch: rdn and styng on whn hmpd wl over 1f out: kpt on again fnl f but nvr a threat*	18/1	
2216	8	2 3/4	**Silvee**[21] 5956 3-8-2 **69** oh12 KierenFox(3) 3		59
			(J J Bridger) *a towards rr*	25/1	
331	9	1 1/2	**Regeneration (IRE)**[15] 6167 4-9-6 **82** JackMitchell 8		68
			(M L W Bell) *chsd ldrs: outpcd fnl 3f*	4/1[2]	
0336	10	1 3/4	**Jeninsky (USA)**[25] 5834 5-9-4 **83** MartinLane(3) 7		65
			(Rae Guest) *s.i.s: a outpcd*	12/1	

1m 28.83s (5.53) **Going Correction** +0.925s/f (Soft)
WFA 3 from 4yo+ 2lb **10** Ran SP% **119.3**
Speed ratings (Par 105): **105,104,104,103,102 101,100,97,95,93**
Tote Swingers: 1&2 £33.80, 1&3 £7.90, 2&3 £7.80 CSF £128.12 CT £632.03 TOTE £10.00: £4.30, £6.20, £2.40; EX 124.40 Place 6: £112.21 Place 5: £47.55.
Owner Tremousser Partnership **Bred** Bolton Grange **Trained** Willoughton, Lincs
■ Stewards' Enquiry : Lee Vickers one-day ban: careless riding (Oct 17)

FOCUS
A fair handicap and the jockeys returned to racing up the nearside rail in the straight. The third to his recent best looks the guide to the form.
Seek The Fair Land Official explanation: jockey said gelding suffered interference 2f out
T/Plt: £256.40 to a £1 stake. Pool of £46,109.03 - 131.27 winning tickets. T/Qpdt: £35.80 to a £1 stake. Pool of £6,461.28 - 71.40 winning tickets. ST

6528 NEWMARKET (Rowley Mile) (R-H)
Saturday, October 2

OFFICIAL GOING: Soft (stands' side 6.6, centre 6.6, far side 6.7)
Far side of Rowley Mile track used.
Wind: modest, against Weather: bright, sunny

6559 £300,000 TATTERSALLS MILLIONS 2YO FILLIES' TROPHY 7f
1:55 (1:55) (Class 2) 2-Y-O
£167,338 (£68,455; £30,458; £15,198; £7,599; £3,027) **Stalls** High

Form					RPR
0243	1		**Masaya**[15] 6157 2-9-0 95 TomQueally 15		96
			(C E Brittain) *led and racd against far rail: rdn wl over 1f out: hdd jst ins fnl f: stl ev ch whn lft in ld fnl 100yds: jst hld on*	20/1	
152	2	shd	**Tale Untold (USA)**[15] 6157 2-9-0 96 RichardHughes 19		96
			(R Hannon) *in tch: rdn to chse ldng pair wl over 1f out: drvn and keeping on whn lft 2nd fnl 100yds: grad clsng on wnr after: jst hld*	9/1[3]	
1342	3	nk	**Together (IRE)**[7] 6348 2-9-0 0 JMurtagh 21		95+
			(A P O'Brien, Ire) *chsd wnr: rdn to chal jst over 1f out: led jst ins fnl f: veered bdly lft and hdd fnl 100yds: continued to hang lft and nt rcvr*	13/8[1]	
2	4	1/2	**Aneedah (IRE)**[30] 5691 2-9-0 0 WilliamBuick 13		94
			(J H M Gosden) *chsd ldrs: rdn and outpcd wl over 1f out: rallied and kpt on again ins fnl f: styng on wl at fin*	14/1	
1	5	hd	**I Love Me**[14] 6200 2-9-0 90 JimmyFortune 4		93
			(A M Balding) *racd in centre tl gps merged 1/2-way: in tch in midfield: hdwy over 2f out: rdn to chse ldng trio over 1f out: kpt on ins fnl f: nvr quite gng pce to rch ldrs*	7/1[2]	
4	6	3/4	**Blessed Biata (USA)**[29] 5719 2-9-0 0 LiamJones 14		91
			(W J Haggas) *hld up bhd: nt clr run ent fnl 2f: swtchd lft and hdwy wl over 1f out: nt clr run again briefly jst over 1f out: r.o strly fnl f: nt rch ldrs*	50/1	

153 **7** *1* **Musharakaat (IRE)**[22] 5910 2-9-0 98 .... RichardHills 16 89
(E A L Dunlop) *in tch in midfield: rdn and effrt ent fnl 2f: no imp over 1f out: kpt on ins fnl f: nvr gng pce to rch ldrs* **16/1**

1130 **8** *½* **Madany (IRE)**[23] 5880 2-9-0 90 .... TadhgO'Shea 20 88
(B W Hills) *hld up towards rr: hdwy against far rail over 2f out: styd on same pce u.p and no imp fr over 1f out* **33/1**

2 **9** *¾* **Mohedian Lady (IRE)**[15] 6155 2-9-0 0 .... KierenFallon 8 86
(M L W Bell) *stdd s: hld up towards rr: rdn and effrt over 2f out: sme hdwy wl over 1f out: kpt on ins fnl f: nvr trbld ldrs* **10/1**

0 **10** *nse* **Rumh (GER)**[15] 6155 2-9-0 0 .... FrankieDettori 18 86
(Saeed Bin Suroor) *in tch: rdn and unable qck wl over 2f out: kpt on same pce u.p fr wl over 1f out* **11/1**

21 **11** *shd* **Secret Love (IRE)**[25] 5841 2-9-0 80 .... GeorgeBaker 11 85
(M A Magnusson) *chsd ldrs: rdn and unable qck ent fnl 2f: one pce and no threat to ldrs fr over 1f out* **16/1**

6604 **12** *½* **Queen Of Spain (IRE)**[15] 6157 2-9-0 92 .... CO'Donoghue 5 84
(A P O'Brien, Ire) *racd in centre tl gps merged 1/2-way: stdd s: hld up towards rr: rdn and hdwy over 2f out: hung rt and no prog over 1f out* **50/1**

56 **13** *1 ¼* **Simayill**[15] 6157 2-9-0 0 .... PhilipRobinson 17 81
(C E Brittain) *stdd s: hld up in tch in rr: hdwy and rdn over 2f out: kpt on ins fnl f: nvr trbld ldrs* **100/1**

0135 **14** *¾* **Kalahaag (IRE)**[15] 6157 2-9-0 82 .... RichardMullen 3 79
(R Hannon) *racd in centre tl gps merged 1/2-way: hld up towards rr: rdn and no prog 3f out: kpt on same pce fr over 1f out: n.d* **66/1**

0 **15** *1 ½* **Illandrane (IRE)**[15] 6155 2-9-0 0 .... ChristopheSoumillon 1 75
(E A L Dunlop) *racd in centre tl gps merged 1/2-way: stdd s: hld up wl in rr: rdn and effrt ent fnl 2f: plugged on past btn horses fnl f: nvr trbld ldrs* **40/1**

0 **16** *½* **Vita Lika**[30] 5692 2-9-0 0 .... FMBerry 12 74
(B J Meehan) *hld up in rr: stl wl bhd whn nt clr run and swtchd rt ent fnl 2f: sme prog over 1f out: kpt on ins fnl f: nvr threatened ldrs* **100/1**

0 **17** *8* **Hayaku (USA)**[18] 6053 2-9-0 0 .... JimCrowley 9 54
(R M Beckett) *in tch in midfield: struggling u.p and losing pl ent fnl 3f: wl bhd over 1f out* **100/1**

0 **18** *3 ¼* **Lucky Legs (IRE)**[12] 6248 2-9-0 0 .... MichaelHills 6 46
(B W Hills) *chsd ldrs tl over 3f out: wknd qckly over 2f out: wl bhd over 1f out* **66/1**

5 **19** *1 ½* **Daffydowndilly**[15] 6150 2-9-0 0 .... SteveDrowne 7 42
(H Morrison) *a towards rr: struggling u.p over 2f out: wl bhd over 1f out* **50/1**

4310 **20** *2 ½* **Apace (IRE)**[8] 6317 2-9-0 77 .... RyanMoore 2 36
(Sir Michael Stoute) *racd in centre tl gps merged 1/2-way: led gp and chsd ldrs overall: rdn over 2f out: wknd wl over 1f out: wl btn and eased ins fnl f* **33/1**

1m 27.56s (2.16) **Going Correction** +0.475s/f (Yiel) **20** Ran SP% **121.4**
Speed ratings (Par 98): **106,105,105,104,104 103,102,102,101,101 101,100,99,98,96 96,86,83,81,78**
toteswingers:1&2 £49.40, 2&3 £4.70, 1&3 £13.10 CSF £177.74 TOTE £25.50: £6.20, £3.50, £1.30; EX 169.20 Trifecta £253.50 Pool: £753.77 - 2.20 winning units..
Owner Saeed Manana **Bred** S P Tindall **Trained** Newmarket, Suffolk

FOCUS
The third running of this very valuable prize for juvenile fillies. It was a very mixed bunch in attendance this year, but the form should looks sound enough with the market principals coming to the fore. They raced towards the far side and went a solid pace.

NOTEBOOK
Masaya scored in tenacious fashion against the far rail and landed her first success since winning on debut back in May. She posted her best effort in defeat when one place behind the runner-up over 6f at this course 15 days earlier, but was 6lb better off with that rival here and a change to front-running tactics over this stiffer test obviously suited. Having the rail was a big advantage when things got tough up the rising finish, and she is clearly versatile as regards going. Her trainer intends on training her for the 1000 Guineas next year and, while that looks far too ambitious, she is capable of making her mark in Pattern company. (tchd 18-1)

Tale Untold(USA) came out of the pack after the 2f marker and again went down narrowly. She got the extra furlong without much fuss, but being 6lb worse off with her old rival ultimately made the difference. A sounder surface is also what she really needs and she richly deserves to find compensation before the season's end. Connections may well take her over for the Breeders' Cup Juvenile Fillies next month. (tchd 10-1)

Together(IRE), who ran a big race in the Group 1 Fillies' Mile at Ascot a week earlier, was attempting to give her powerful connections consecutive wins in the race as they sent out subsequent dual Group 1 winner Lillie Langtry to win it in 2009. Her previous efforts made her the clear form pick and the only worry beforehand was whether the run would come too soon. She had to be ridden to gain a handy early position, but soon settled down just off the winner on the far rail. Murtagh asked her to win the race in between the final 2f and she went clear, looking to have done enough. However, she began to drift badly left under maximum pressure inside the final furlong and eventually ended up right against the stands' rail, despite Murtagh doing his best to correct her. The fact she was only just held by the first two means she really threw the race away, but it's not the track that's to blame as she previously did this when fourth in the Group 2 Debutante Stakes at the Curragh in August. The drop back a furlong wasn't ideal as it panned out, and she will fare better again when back over 1m, but she obviously is far from straightforward. (op 7-4)

Aneedah(IRE) ◆ ran with promise on debut last month and took another step forward in defeat in this much better race, doing her best work late in the day. The contrasting surface posed her with no problems and winning a maiden should prove a formality in the coming weeks. (op 12-1)

I Love Me sprang a surprise when winning a less-valuable version of this event over C&D a fortnight earlier. She was faced with slower ground and, while running a solid race in defeat here, the ground did look to somewhat blunt her finishing kick. It wouldn't be surprising to see her win in Pattern company down the line, and she is probably ready to tackle 1m. (op 8-1)

Blessed Biata(USA) ◆ was a big eye-catcher on her debut at Kempton last month and, finding a troubled passage this time, she ran a decent race in defeat on this much tougher assignment. She is another that probably wants the ground a bit better and there could be a nice prize in her next term.

Musharakaat(IRE) had been beaten by White Moonstone by identical distances in Group company on her last two outings and she gives the form a good look. She ought to enjoy going back up in trip and can find another race this year. (tchd 18-1)

6560 £500,000 TATTERSALLS MILLIONS 2YO TROPHY 7f

2:25 (2:29) (Class 2) 2-Y-0

£278,898 (£114,092; £50,764; £25,330; £12,665; £5,045) **Stalls** High

Form RPR

1 **1** **Fury**[14] 6196 2-9-3 0 .... KierenFallon 24 101+
(W J Haggas) *hld up in mid-div: hdwy over 2f out: qcknd to ld 1f out: styd on strly* **11/2**[1]

011 **2** *1 ¾* **Pisco Sour (USA)**[40] 5374 2-9-3 85 .... JimmyFortune 15 97
(H Morrison) *w ldrs: led over 2f out: edgd lft: hdd 1f out: styd on same pce* **14/1**

1162 **3** *1 ¼* **Formosina (IRE)**[14] 6192 2-9-3 112 .... RyanMoore 9 94+
(J Noseda) *s.i.s: hdwy over 2f out: chsng ldrs over 1f out: styd on same pce* **7/1**[2]

1122 **4** *½* **Measuring Time**[28] 5746 2-9-3 105 .... RichardHughes 16 92
(R Hannon) *chsd ldrs: nt clr run over 1f out: styd on ins fnl f* **10/1**[3]

1 **5** *½* **Questioning (IRE)**[56] 4838 2-9-3 81 .... FrannyNorton 18 91
(J H M Gosden) *in tch: nt clr run and swtchd rt over 1f out: styd on wl clsng stages* **40/1**

146 **6** *¾* **Auld Burns**[14] 6200 2-9-3 98 ....(p) ChristopheSoumillon 20 89
(R Hannon) *chsd ldrs: upsides 2f out: kpt on same pce ins fnl f* **22/1**

3203 **7** *½* **Shafgaan**[14] 6200 2-9-3 88 .... SteveDrowne 13 88
(C E Brittain) *in tch: effrt over 2f out: kpt on ins fnl f* **66/1**

1 **8** *hd* **Dominant (IRE)**[10] 6278 2-9-3 77 .... PhilipRobinson 8 87
(M A Jarvis) *chsd ldrs: effrt over 2f out: sn outpcd: kpt on same pce appr fnl f* **10/1**[3]

110 **9** *nk* **Janood (IRE)**[21] 5975 2-9-3 102 .... FrankieDettori 25 87
(Saeed Bin Suroor) *mid-div: effrt over 2f out: kpt on same pce* **11/1**

34 **10** *1* **Madawi**[14] 6200 2-9-3 0 .... TomQueally 4 84
(C E Brittain) *racd towards stands' side: in tch: outpcd over 2f out: styd on ins fnl f* **16/1**

20 **11** *hd* **Oracle (IRE)**[14] 6200 2-9-3 0 .... CO'Donoghue 5 84
(A P O'Brien, Ire) *led 6 others towards stands' side: edgd rt and kpt on same pce appr fnl f* **40/1**

2 **12** *¾* **Cobbs Quay**[37] 5440 2-9-3 0 .... WilliamBuick 19 82
(J H M Gosden) *in rr: kpt on fnl 2f: nvr nr ldrs* **14/1**

4 **13** *½* **Factum (USA)**[6] 6403 2-9-3 0 .... JMurtagh 21 81
(A P O'Brien, Ire) *mid-div: effrt over 2f out: kpt on ins fnl f* **25/1**

100 **14** *½* **Malthouse (GER)**[14] 6200 2-9-3 88 .... RichardHills 6 79
(M Johnston) *racd stands' side: w ldr: wknd over 1f out* **66/1**

6241 **15** *hd* **Cruiser**[18] 6046 2-9-3 83 .... RichardMullen 11 79
(W R Muir) *in tch: effrt over 2f out: sn chsng ldrs: wknd over 1f out* **33/1**

15 **16** *½* **Sergeant Ablett (IRE)**[15] 6149 2-9-3 89 .... GregFairley 3 78
(M Johnston) *racd stands' side: s.i.s: effrt over 2f out: sn lost pl* **33/1**

3 **17** *2 ¼* **Sadler's Risk (IRE)**[7] 6365 2-9-3 0 .... JimmyQuinn 12 72
(M Johnston) *mid-div: outpcd over 2f out: kpt on fnl f* **100/1**

3 **18** *3 ½* **Ryton Runner (IRE)**[16] 6128 2-9-3 0 .... NickyMackay 1 63
(J H M Gosden) *racd stands' side: prom: lost pl over 2f out* **50/1**

19 *½* **It's Freezing (IRE)**[27] 5793 2-9-3 0 .... FMBerry 10 62
(Mrs John Harrington, Ire) *mid-div: outpcd and lost pl over 2f out* **40/1**

3352 **20** *shd* **Sir Reginald**[14] 6200 2-9-3 105 .... DPMcDonogh 17 62
(R A Fahey) *chsd ldrs: nt clr run 2f out: sn wknd* **14/1**

5 **21** *¾* **Private Cowboy (IRE)**[20] 5985 2-9-3 0 .... AdamKirby 2 60
(M G Quinlan) *towards rr stands' side: nvr a factor* **100/1**

1 **22** *½* **State Opera**[13] 6222 2-9-3 94 .... JoeFanning 26 59
(M Johnston) *led tl over 2f out: lost pl over 1f out* **11/2**[1]

2534 **23** *1 ¾* **Tokum (IRE)**[3] 6453 2-9-3 67 .... MichaelHills 23 54
(J Noseda) *s.i.s: in rr: bhd fnl 2f* **100/1**

3 **24** *hd* **Shamdarley (IRE)**[18] 6047 2-9-3 0 .... PhillipMakin 27 54
(M Dods) *chsd ldrs: wknd wl over 1f out* **100/1**

5003 **25** *2* **Oliver's Gold**[30] 5675 2-9-3 65 .... JimCrowley 7 49
(Mrs A J Perrett) *racd stands' side: chsd ldrs: lost pl over 2f out: sn bhd* **100/1**

4401 **26** *3* **Aciano (IRE)**[12] 6249 2-9-3 85 .... LiamJones 22 41
(B J Meehan) *s.i.s: drvn along in rr: bhd fnl 2f* **50/1**

06 **27** *4* **Govenor General (IRE)**[16] 6127 2-9-3 0 .... GeorgeBaker 14 31
(J Noseda) *mid-div: lost pl over 2f out: sn bhd and eased* **150/1**

1m 27.43s (2.03) **Going Correction** +0.475s/f (Yiel) **27** Ran SP% **129.6**
Speed ratings (Par 101): **107,105,103,103,102 101,101,100,100,99 99,98,97,97,96 96,93,89,89,89 88,87,85,85,83 79,75**
toteswingers:1&2 £46.20, 2&3 £45.30, 1&3 £3.40 CSF £73.87 TOTE £7.70: £2.70, £5.50, £2.80; EX 184.60 TRIFECTA Not won..
Owner Cheveley Park Stud **Bred** Cheveley Park Stud Ltd **Trained** Newmarket, Suffolk

FOCUS
The third running of this sales race, the first winner of which Donativum, went on to take the Breeders' Cup Juvenile Turf. The time was 0.13secs faster than the preceding fillies' race and this was an impressive success for a potential Group-race performer.

NOTEBOOK
Fury ◆, a half-brother to five winners from the family of Cassandra Go and Verglas, was a winner on his debut over 7f on fast ground and had clearly come on a good deal for that. Held up off the pace, he made his ground smoothly from 3f out and, once in front, came away for a comfortable success. He looks sure to build on this again and was quoted at 33-1 for the 2000 Guineas in some places, although the trainer gave the impression he thought he might be more of a Jersey Stakes horse. (op 8-1 tchd 17-2)

Pisco Sour(USA), a dual winner at up to 1m, was already proven on soft ground and his rider did his best to make full use of his proven stamina, hitting the front over 2f out. He stuck on well but was outclassed by the winner, although connections will be pleased to have more than recouped the 100,000gns they paid for him at the sales. (op 16-1)

Formosina(IRE), a dual winner at 6f including a Group 2 and runner-up in Mill Reef since, was up in trip but set the standard on that form. He had never raced on soft ground but spoilt his chance by blowing the start, and then had to make his effort more towards the centre of the course. He did well to get into contention in the Dip and kept on up the hill, but even with a level start it is unlikely he would have beaten the winner. (op 11-2)

Measuring Time, a dual winner over 7f on a sound surface and runner-up in a Listed and a Group 3 since, was another bringing solid and high-class form into this. Another not previously raced on soft ground, he was in the leading group and had every chance but could only stay on at the one pace in the final furlong. (op 12-1)

Questioning(IRE) ◆, a 160,000gns yearling who was a debut winner over 1m on Polytrack, was rejected by the stable jockey in favour of Cobbs Quay. He was never far away and stayed on again up the hill, so a return to further will be in his favour, and he could be the type to make his mark in the 3-y-o sales race over 1m2f here early next season. (op 33-1)

Auld Burns, a winner over 7f on fast ground, had put up decent efforts in a Listed and sales race since. Wearing first-time cheekpieces, he was close up throughout and only backed out of things on the climb to the line. A return to a sounder surface should be in his favour. (tchd 20-1)

Shafgaan, whose trainer won the earlier fillies' sales race, had been placed in maidens and a sales race here over 7f with several of these behind. Proven on soft ground, he ran well, especially considering he raced more towards the centre of the track than most of the principals.

Dominant(IRE), a winner on his debut over 7f on fast ground, had different conditions here. He showed up throughout but tended to wander under pressure, especially in the Dip, and gave the impression this came a little soon in his career. He should have more to offer providing the experience does not set him back. (op 11-1 tchd 12-1)

Janood(IRE), a dual winner including a Listed race on easy going but beaten in a Group1 on soft last time, was dropping in grade but failed to get involved and presumably will be happier on a sounder surface. (tchd 12-1)

Madawi, in the frame in a sales race here last time, ahead of several of these, was another having his first try on soft ground. He was unfortunate to have to race in the group on the stands' side and ended up doing best of those. (tchd 18-1)

Oracle(IRE), whose only win was over 7f on soft and who had run well against Temple Meads on easy ground in the spring, ran a fine race from his low draw. He got close enough to look a threat in the Dip, but paid for his exertions on the climb to the line.
Sir Reginald, a winner over 6f and placed in the Gimcrack, finished second in a sales race here with a number of these behind. He showed up early but was a little keen and was in trouble 2f out. It might have been the soft ground, but perhaps recent hard races have caught up with him. (op 10-1)
State Opera, a debut winner on easy ground, was the stable first string on jockey bookings and had a good draw. He made the early running but, when headed by the eventual runner-up over 2f out, dropped away pretty quickly. He is another who is likely to be seen to better effect next season. Official explanation: jockey said colt hung left (op 13-2)

6561 KINGDOM OF BAHRAIN SUN CHARIOT STKS (GROUP 1) (F&M) 1m
3:00 (3:04) (Class 1) 3-Y-O+

£102,186 (£38,736; £19,386; £9,666; £4,842; £2,430) **Stalls** High

Form RPR

3-01 **1** **Sahpresa (USA)**[27] 5802 5-9-2 115 ChristopheSoumillon 3 119+
(Rod Collet, France) *stdd after s: hld up in last trio hdwy gng wl 2f out: chsd ldng trio and rdn over 1f out: led ins fnl f: r.o wl: readily* **9/2**[2]

1144 **2** 1 3/4 **Strawberrydaiquiri**[63] 4575 4-9-2 114 RyanMoore 7 115
(Sir Michael Stoute) *t.k.h: chsd ldrs: rdn to chse ldr over 2f out: drvn to ld jst ins fnl f: sn hdd and nt gng pce of wnr: kpt on same pce* **5/1**[3]

3501 **3** 1 **Rainfall (IRE)**[7] 6351 3-8-13 112 FrankieDettori 11 113+
(M Johnston) *stdd s: hld up in rr: effrt and n.m.r 2f out: swtchd rt and hdwy u.p over 1f out: kpt on wl ins fnl f: wnt 3rd nr fin* **6/1**

4123 **4** nk **Music Show (IRE)**[28] 5773 3-8-13 118 RichardHughes 5 112
(M R Channon) *hld up in tch in midfield: effrt to chse ldng pair and rdn wl over 1f out: drvn and pressed ldrs ent fnl f: no ex and btn fnl 100yds* **4/1**[1]

1105 **5** 3/4 **Aviate**[20] 6007 3-8-13 107 TomQueally 2 110
(H R A Cecil) *hld up in tch towards rr: rdn 2f out: hdwy u.p over 1f out: kpt on ins fnl f: nvr quite gng pce to rch ldrs* **12/1**

3222 **6** 1 1/4 **Spacious**[28] 5773 5-9-2 116 JMurtagh 4 107
(J R Fanshawe) *chsd ldr after 1f: rdn to ld over 2f out: drvn over 1f out: hdd jst ins fnl f: wknd fnl 100yds* **11/2**

6600 **7** 3 1/2 **Lahaleeb (IRE)**[87] 3793 4-9-2 109 JohnEgan 9 99
(P W D'Arcy) *sn niggled along: chsd ldrs: rdn 3f out: drvn and outpcd wl over 1f out: wl btn ent fnl f* **50/1**

0111 **8** 1 3/4 **Seta**[42] 5305 3-8-13 107 KierenFallon 6 95
(L M Cumani) *stdd s: t.k.h: hld up in rr: swtchd to r against far rail after 2f: nt clr run and swtchd lft ent fnl 2f: rdn and no hdwy over 1f out: wl btn after* **7/1**

314 **9** 2 1/4 **Hen Night (IRE)**[28] 5773 3-8-13 107 WMLordan 1 90
(David Wachman, Ire) *dwlt: hld up in tch towards rr: rdn and effrt wl over 2f out: struggling ent fnl 2f: wl btn over 1f out* **40/1**

4310 **10** 3 **Alsace Lorraine (IRE)**[20] 6007 5-9-2 106 WilliamBuick 8 83
(J R Fanshawe) *hld up in tch: rdn and unable qck whn sltly hmpd wl over 1f out: sn btn: wl bhd and eased ins fnl f* **40/1**

4056 **11** 11 **Sent From Heaven (IRE)**[23] 5883 3-8-13 105 MichaelHills 10 58
(B W Hills) *led tl rdn and hdd over 2f out: sn dropped out: wl bhd and eased ins fnl f* **25/1**

1m 38.8s (0.20) **Going Correction** +0.475s/f (Yiel)
WFA 3 from 4yo+ 3lb **11** Ran SP% **115.4**
Speed ratings (Par 117): **118,116,115,114,114 112,109,107,105,102 91**
toteswingers:1&2 £5.70, 2&3 £6.50, 1&3 £6.80 CSF £25.93 TOTE £2.70: £1.40, £2.20, £2.20; EX 20.10 Trifecta £75.00 Pool: £13,415.50 - 132.22 winning units..
Owner Douglas Owen McIntyre **Bred** Douglas McIntyre **Trained** France

FOCUS
This was not the strongest Sun Chariot, but it was certainly competitive. They again raced on the far side and there was a brisk early pace on, with the race really developing 3f out. Solid form rated around the placed horses and the fifth.

NOTEBOOK
Sahpresa(USA), last year's winner, defended her title with a stylish success, becoming the first back-to-back winner since Luca Cumani's Free Guest 25 years earlier, on ground softer than she cares for. She warmed up for this with when readily beating Dalgar in a Group 3 over 7f at Longchamp last month, and the only worry was the slow surface. The race was run very much to suit, though, and she went through the ground without hassle. Indeed she could've been called the winner well before the furlong marker. It was just her third outing this year, she wasn't right when reappearing in the Windsor Forest on her seasonal return at Royal Ascot, and connections will no doubt be looking to travel her again. Another trip to Japan next month is most likely. (tchd 5-1)
Strawberrydaiquiri is admirably tough, and ran another solid race in defeat in the Nassau Stakes over 1m2f on her previous outing in July, and was having her first run for a new owner. She had yet to race on ground this slow, but there was a chance she could improve for it and she turned in a sterling effort in defeat. She displayed real guts when winning the Windsor Forest in June, when well ahead of Sahpresa, and was expected to build on her fourth in this race last year behind that rival. She wasn't ridden as aggressively as has often been the case over this trip in the past, and looking at the way she was coming back towards the finish perhaps more positive tactics would've suited. It still rates a career-best in defeat, however, and she really deserves to win at the top level, with connections intending to keep her in training next year. No doubt she will remain vulnerable to a classy filly with a turn of foot, however. (op 6-1)
Rainfall(IRE) ◆ gained a confidence booster when winning in Listed company at Ascot a week earlier and didn't go unbacked on this return to a Group 1. She got ridden to get this extra distance and was motoring home late in the day, without threatening the first pair. She holds an entry in the 6f event in Canada later this month, but connections later said she is unlikely to take that up. She will stay in training as a 4-y-o, though, and would be open to improvement next year. With that in mind it wouldn't be at all surprising to see her back for another crack next season, and she ought to get the trip better then too. (op 13-2 tchd 7-1)
Music Show(IRE) had her chance, but probably just found this ground slower than she really cares for and has had a long season. (op 9-2)
Aviate was taking a drop back in trip for this second outing in a Group 1 and she wasn't disgraced. More positive tactics over this trip should see her winning again if she's dropped down a grade before the end of term.
Spacious had made the frame in this event for the past two years and went down by a whisker at Leopardstown on her previous outing, when Music Show was back in third. She wasn't able to dictate here and, looking at the way she backed out of things, the different ground may have been to blame. She now heads off for an honourable retirement. (op 13-2 tchd 5-1)
Lahaleeb(IRE), who won at this level in Canada last year, hasn't been near her best this term and was having her first run back in Britain for a new stable. She proved one paced from 3f out and this does look as good as she is these days. (op 40-1)
Seta put up a disappointing effort. She who had been patiently handled and gone unbeaten since flopping in the 1000 Guineas earlier in the year. She did get hampered on the inside around 2f out, but was beaten at the time and may not have enjoyed this ground. She could improve if kept in training next year as she still has physical scope. (op 11-2 tchd 5-1)
Hen Night(IRE) posted her best effort yet when comfortably held by Spacious last time out, but was again biting off more than she can chew and does seem happier on quicker ground.
Alsace Lorraine(IRE) was out of her depth. (op 33-1)
Sent From Heaven(IRE) paid for her early exertions from 3f out. (tchd 33-1)

6562 TOTESPORT.COM CAMBRIDGESHIRE (HERITAGE H'CAP) 1m 1f
3:40 (3:43) (Class 2) 3-Y-O+

£99,696 (£29,856; £14,928; £7,472; £3,728; £1,872) **Stalls** High

Form RPR

0134 **1** **Credit Swap**[2] 6510 5-8-7 87 4ex JimCrowley 33 99
(M Wigham) *racd far side: hld up in rr: rdn and gd hdwy wl over 1f out: drvn to ld ins fnl f: r.o wl: drvn out: 1st of 25 in gp* **14/1**

0442 **2** 3/4 **Steele Tango (USA)**[14] 6195 5-9-4 103 JohnFahy[(5)] 16 113
(R A Teal) *racd far side: hld up towards rr on outer: hdwy into midfield 4f out: rdn and effrt 2f out: chsd ldrs and drvn ent fnl f: chsd wnr ins fnl f: kpt on: 2nd of 25 in gp* **16/1**

00-5 **3** 1/2 **Pires**[21] 5978 6-8-9 89 WMLordan 21 98
(A J Martin, Ire) *racd far side: hld up in rr: stl plenty to do and swtchd lft wl over 1f out: r.o strly ins fnl f: gng on wl at fin: nt rch ldrs: 3rd of 25 in gp* **18/1**

5333 **4** 1/2 **Sandor**[21] 5970 4-8-12 92 (v[1]) SteveDrowne 14 100
(P J Makin) *racd far side: hld up wl bhd: rdn and effrt 2f out: stl plenty to do over 1f out: r.o wl u.p ins fnl f: wnt 4th towards fin: nt rch ldrs: 4th of 25 in gp* **50/1**

1100 **5** 1 **Camerooney**[14] 6180 7-8-10 90 WilliamCarson 32 96
(B Ellison) *racd far side: overall ldr: rdn ent fnl 2f: hung lft u.p and hdd over 1f out: stl ev ch tl no ex and btn fnl 100yds: 5th of 25 in gp* **100/1**

0-11 **6** 1/2 **Taqleed (IRE)**[35] 5529 3-8-11 95 RichardHills 26 100+
(J H M Gosden) *racd far side: chsd ldr: rdn 2f out: led narrowly and carried lft over 1f out: edgd lft u.p jst ins fnl f: hdd ins fnl f: wknd fnl 75yds: 6th of 25 in gp* **8/1**[2]

2061 **7** 1/2 **Jo'Burg (USA)**[27] 5786 6-8-5 90 4ex JamesO'Reilly[(5)] 8 94+
(J O'Reilly) *led stands' side and in tch overall: rdn over 2f out: chsd ldrs over 1f out: styd on same pce and btn ins fnl f: 1st of 10 in gp* **80/1**

1161 **8** 1 1/2 **Pendragon (USA)**[16] 6106 7-8-9 89 4ex RichardMullen 12 89
(B Ellison) *racd far side: in tch: rdn and effrt ent fnl 2f: chsd ldrs and drvn over 1f out: no ex and btn whn bmpd ins fnl f: 7th of 25 in gp* **80/1**

5543 **9** nk **Proponent (IRE)**[44] 5247 6-9-3 97 RyanMoore 18 97
(R Charlton) *racd far side: hld up in tch towards rr: hdwy over 2f out: chsd ldrs and drvn over 1f out: kpt on same pce and no imp fnl f: 8th of 25 in gp* **16/1**

1001 **10** nk **Capponi (IRE)**[21] 5948 3-9-6 104 4ex JMurtagh 31 103+
(M Johnston) *racd far side: in tch: rdn and effrt ent fnl 2f: drvn and pressing ldrs over 1f out: btn jst ins fnl f: wknd fnl 150yds: 9th of 25 in gp* **25/1**

0055 **11** nk **Viva Vettori**[14] 6205 6-8-2 87 DeclanCannon[(5)] 17 85
(D R C Elsworth) *racd far side: hld up towards rr: swtchd lft and effrt over 2f out: kpt on same pce and no prog fr over 1f out: 10th of 25 in gp* **66/1**

0031 **12** hd **High Twelve (IRE)**[9] 6312 3-8-12 96 4ex FrannyNorton 13 94+
(J H M Gosden) *racd far side: swtchd rt after s: in tch: rdn and effrt to chse ldrs 2f out: drvn over 1f out: wkng whn carried lft and hmpd jst ins fnl f: nt pushed and lost pls after: 11th of 25 in gp* **25/1**

-311 **13** 1 **Absinthe (IRE)**[40] 5375 4-8-12 92 AdamKirby 28 88
(W R Swinburn) *taken down early: racd far side: hld up in tch: effrt over 2f out: chsd ldrs and drvn wl over 1f out: btn ent fnl f: wknd ins fnl f: 12th of 25 in gp* **10/1**[3]

2205 **14** 1/2 **Breakheart (IRE)**[14] 6193 3-8-7 91 LiamKeniry 19 86
(A M Balding) *racd far side: chsd ldrs: rdn over 2f out: wknd u.p over 1f out: 13th of 25 in gp* **33/1**

2522 **15** 1/2 **Speed Dating**[54] 4891 4-8-9 89 (b) StevieDonohoe 23 82
(Sir Mark Prescott) *racd far side: hld up in tch towards rr: rdn and hdwy over 2f out: drvn to chse ldrs over 1f out: btn jst over 1f out: wknd qckly fnl f: 14th of 25 in gp* **25/1**

1053 **16** 3/4 **Circumvent**[14] 6179 3-9-9 107 TomQueally 35 99
(P F I Cole) *racd far side: chsd ldrs: rdn and struggling 3f out: wknd u.p wl over 1f out: 15th of 25 in gp* **25/1**

0114 **17** nk **Start Right**[34] 5571 3-8-12 96 KierenFallon 9 87+
(L M Cumani) *racd stands' side: chsd ldrs: rdn and effrt to press gp ldr ent fnl 2f: edgd rt u.p and wknd ent fnl f: eased whn wl btn ins fnl f: 2nd of 10 in gp* **14/1**

1001 **18** 2 1/4 **Ransom Note**[44] 5247 3-9-9 107 MichaelHills 22 93
(B W Hills) *racd far side: hld up in tch towards rr: rdn and effrt ent fnl 2f: no imp and btn whn eased fnl 100yds: nvr trbld ldrs: 16th of 25 in gp* **16/1**

1320 **19** 1 1/4 **Colepeper**[7] 6349 3-8-13 97 GregFairley 24 80
(M Johnston) *racd far side: chsd ldrs tl wknd u.p wl over 1f out: wl btn ins fnl f: 17th of 25 in gp* **66/1**

2023 **20** 3/4 **Directorship**[14] 6204 4-8-6 86 NickyMackay 15 68
(P R Chamings) *racd far side: in tch: rdn and unable qck 3f out: wknd wl over 1f out: 18th of 25 in gp* **100/1**

-060 **21** 1/2 **The Cayterers**[21] 5955 8-8-6 89 MichaelGeran[(3)] 34 70
(A W Carroll) *racd far side: hld up in tch towards rr: rdn and effrt jst over 2f out: no real prog: nvr trbld ldrs: 19th of 25 in gp* **100/1**

-201 **22** 1 3/4 **Set The Trend**[56] 4816 4-9-6 100 JimmyFortune 5 77+
(A M Balding) *racd stands' side: chsd gp ldrs: rdn and wl btn 2f out: eased ins fnl f: 3rd of 10 in gp* **40/1**

5012 **23** hd **Sweet Lightning**[23] 5879 5-9-8 102 RichardHughes 11 78
(M Dods) *racd far side: swtchd sharply rt afters: hld up in rr: rdn and no prog ent fnl 2f: n.d: 20th of 25 in gp* **25/1**

20P **24** 4 1/2 **Smokey Oakey (IRE)**[34] 5556 6-8-12 92 (v[1]) JimmyQuinn 30 59
(M H Tompkins) *racd far side: hld up towards rr: rdn and no hdwy over 2f out: wl btn and eased ins fnl f: 21st of 25 in gp* **40/1**

0152 **25** 3/4 **Elliptical (USA)**[14] 6193 4-8-13 93 ChristopheSoumillon 20 58
(G A Butler) *racd far side: hld up in tch in midfield: rdn and struggling ent fnl 3f: wl bhd over 1f out: eased ins fnl f: 22nd of 25 in gp* **12/1**

1006 **26** hd **Brunston**[92] 3633 4-8-9 89 HayleyTurner 25 53
(R Charlton) *racd far side: in tch in midfield: struggling u.p ent fnl 3f: wl bhd over 1f out: eased ins fnl f: 23rd of 25 in gp* **28/1**

4001 **27** 6 **Tiger Reigns**[14] 6180 4-9-8 102 4ex PhillipMakin 6 53
(M Dods) *racd stands' side: in tch tl 4f out: sn struggling: wl btn over 2f out: eased ins fnl f: 4th of 10 in gp* **50/1**

2211 **28** hd **Nationalism**[21] 5955 3-9-1 99 4ex WilliamBuick 3 50
(J H M Gosden) *racd stands' side: in tch: rdn and btn over 2f out: wl bhd fnl 2f: eased ins fnl f: 5th of 10 in gp* **7/1**[1]

0603 **29** 1 1/2 **Dream Lodge (IRE)**[14] 6180 6-9-6 100 DPMcDonogh 7 48
(R A Fahey) *racd stands' side: in tch tl 4f out: sn struggling: wl btn over 2f out: wl bhd and eased ins fnl f: 6th of 10 in gp* **100/1**

0010 **30** *hd* **Northern Fling**[15] 6142 6-7-13 **86** .... HarryBentley(7) 2 33
(J S Goldie) *racd stands' side: a towards rr: lost tch wl over 2f out: wl bhd and eased ins fnl f: 7th of 10 in gp* **100/1**

0301 **31** *2* **Emirates Dream (USA)**[34] 5556 3-8-13 **97** 4ex........... FrankieDettori 29 40
(Saeed Bin Suroor) *racd far side: in tch: rdn and struggling ent fnl 3f: wknd over 2f out: wl bhd and eased ins fnl f: 24th of 25 in gp* **12/1**

0000 **32** *4 ½* **Tartan Gigha (IRE)**[14] 6193 5-9-7 **101** .... JoeFanning 4 34
(M Johnston) *racd stands' side: chsd gp ldrs tl rdn 4f out: sn struggling: wl btn over 2f out: wl bhd and eased ins fnl f: 8th of 10 in gp* **66/1**

/5-0 **33** *1 ¾* **Taameer**[24] 5853 4-9-10 **104** .... TadhgO'Shea 1 33
(M P Tregoning) *racd stands' side: a bhd: lost tch over 3f out: wl bhd and eased ins fnl f: t.o: 9th of 10 in gp* **100/1**

0000 **34** *¾* **Mirrored**[16] 6106 4-8-10 **90** .... JohnEgan 10 17
(T D Easterby) *taken down early: racd stands' side: a bhd: lost tch 4f out: wl bhd over 2f out: eased ins fnl f: t.o:10th of 10 in gp* **80/1**

2010 **35** *9* **King Olav (UAE)**[119] 2747 5-8-11 **91** .... JamesDoyle 27 —
(A W Carroll) *racd far side: in tch: rdn and struggling wl over 3f out: wl bhd fnl 2f: eased ins fnl f: t.o: last of 25 in gp* **100/1**

1m 53.87s (2.17) **Going Correction** +0.475s/f (Yiel)
WFA 3 from 4yo+ 4lb **35** Ran SP% **133.9**
Speed ratings (Par 109): **109,108,107,107,106 106,105,104,104,103 103,103,102,102,101 100,100,98,97,96 96,94,94,90,90 8**
toteswingers:1&2 £97.60, 2&3 £73.00, 1&3 £48.10 CSF £190.17 CT £4049.63 TOTE £17.50: £3.90, £4.90, £4.30, £8.70; EX 260.80 Trifecta £15314.50 Pool: £26,903.86 - 1.30 winning units..
Owner Your Golf Travel Ltd **Bred** Jeremy Green And Sons **Trained** Newmarket, Suffolk
■ Stewards' Enquiry : Richard Hills two-day ban: careless riding (Oct 17-18)

FOCUS
This historic high-class handicap is often won by a battle-hardened handicapper but has on several occasions fallen to a progressive 3-y-o. This year there were several in the latter category in evidence but it went to one of the former group. The pace looked good as three of the first four came from well back. The form looks solid rated around the first five.

NOTEBOOK
Credit Swap had gained all his wins on soft and had appeared unlucky twice in the preceding week, being beaten narrowly here just two days previously. Again ridden with restraint, he got plenty of room towards the far rail and, hitting the front inside the last furlong, won well. Connections are likely to look for another opportunity while the ground is in his favour. (op 16-1)
Steele Tango(USA), a Group 3 winner over C&D last October, has also put up numerous good efforts in Listed and Group company. Although 8lb higher than for his last run in a handicap, he still looked fairly treated and ran a fine race, especially as he raced more towards the centre of the track than the winner. He is likely to be back here later in the month to attempt a repeat success in the Darley Stakes. (op 20-1)
Pires, who mixes Flat racing and hurdling, has not won on the Flat since 2006 but came into this in good form and, after being last of all around 3f out, finished well up the centre of the track. A return to further will be in his favour, though connections later said he is likely to go back hurdling soon and the Greatwood Hurdle at Cheltenham's Open Meeting in November is a likely target. (op 20-1)
Sandor is well suited by fast ground and had never raced on soft. However, visored for the first time, he came from well back to make the frame, so the headgear clearly worked and the conditions were no inconvenience.
Camerooney, a multiple winner on fast ground and Fibresand, had yet to prove as effective on soft turf. Racing off 5lb above his last winning mark, he ran a terrific race from the front, and kept trying all the way to the line.
Taqleed(IRE) ◆, a winner over 1m2f on the July Course last time on easy ground, was raised 10lb for that but continues to progress and ran another good race, having been in the leading group throughout. Having just his fourth start and already gelded, he looks sure to win more good races for connections. (tchd 17-2)
Jo'Burg(USA), a multiple winner at 1m2f on a sound surface, had not proved as effective on soft ground. However, having his first run for a new yard having been claimed after scoring at York, he did best of those to race in the stands'-side group and was not beaten that far in the end. He should do well for new connections. (op 66-1)
Pendragon(USA), a multiple winner on a sound surface and Fibresand, was 4lb above his last winning mark but handles soft ground, and came to have his chance 2f out before being unable to sustain his effort up the hill.
Proponent(IRE) is very useful in this grade and had gained his last three wins here. He also ran a decent race having been posted more towards the centre of the track than most. (op 20-1)
Capponi(IRE) had gained his wins at 1m on a sound surface and Polytrack and had never raced on softer than good. Raised 4lb for his last success, he came to have his chance over a furlong out but perhaps found his stamina ebbing up the hill.
Viva Vettori had gained all his wins on Polytrack and had been well held on his only tries on soft turf. He ran creditably, staying on towards the finish.
High Twelve(IRE) had never raced on soft but had run well on this track and seems to be improving, as he showed up for a long way here.
Absinthe(IRE), a dual winner at 1m2f on fast and soft ground, had been raised 9lb for that last success but had run well on this course in the past. He was always tracking the leading group but failed to find an extra gear from over a furlong out. (tchd 8-1)
Breakheart(IRE) had finished well beaten on his only run on soft and was 10lb above last winning mark. In the circumstances he ran reasonably, especially as he was quite free early on.
Speed Dating is a winner at up to 1m4f but was 15lb above his last winning turf mark and was being pushed along vigorously to keep his place before halfway. Not surprisingly he was doing his best work in the last quarter-mile. (op 33-1)
Circumvent, a Group 3 winner as a juvenile who handles any ground, was the winner of a heritage handicap on the July course earlier in the season. He showed up early before losing his place, but was running on again up the hill.
Start Right had gained his wins at 1m on fast ground and Polytrack and had never raced on soft. The biggest inconvenience though was that he was drawn on the stands' side and, despite doing his best to get competitive, could not land a blow and tired in the closing stages. He can be rated better than the bare form. (op 16-1)
Ransom Note, the winner of the Britannia and a big mile handicap at York but raised 7lb for that last success, was drawn on the right side of the track but failed to figure.
Elliptical(USA), narrowly beaten by Tartan Gigha in a similar race over C&D in May, has also won on soft ground. He was close enough early but dropped away in the closing stages and was eased. (tchd 14-1)
Nationalism, the winner of two of his four starts and runner-up in the others, was sent off favourite but was forced to race on the near side from his drawn and never got into contention. This run can be ignored. (op 15-2 tchd 8-1)
Emirates Dream(USA), a 1m winner on easy ground was raised 4lb for last success. He tracked the leaders for much of the way but dropped away and was eased as if something was amiss. (tchd 11-1)

6563 EUROPEAN BREEDERS' FUND JERSEY LILY FILLIES' NURSERY 7f
4:15 (4:18) (Class 2) 2-Y-O
£18,693 (£5,598; £2,799; £1,401; £699; £351) **Stalls** High

Form RPR

1000 **1** **Honeymead (IRE)**[23] 5882 2-8-2 **78** .... HayleyTurner 3 84
(R A Fahey) *trckd ldrs: chal over 1f out: edgd rt and led last 100yds: edgd lft and hld on towards fin* **16/1**

0221 **2** *¾* **Humdrum**[7] 6353 2-7-12 **74** .... FrankieMcDonald 11 78
(R Hannon) *prom: effrt over 2f out: styd on strly ins fnl f* **12/1**

2121 **3** *nk* **Whisper Louise (IRE)**[24] 5849 2-8-12 **88** .... MickyFenton 5 91
(Mrs P Sly) *w ldrs: led over 2f out: hdd and nt qckn last 100yds* **9/1**

3450 **4** *½* **Imperialistic Diva (IRE)**[23] 5880 2-9-7 **97** .... FrankieDettori 7 99
(T D Easterby) *in tch: hdwy over 2f out: styd on same pce ins fnl f* **9/1**

1242 **5** *shd* **No Poppy (IRE)**[8] 6325 2-8-1 **77** ....(b) DuranFentiman 13 79
(T D Easterby) *chsd ldrs: one pce ins fnl f* **20/1**

2221 **6** *1 ¼* **Mama Lulu (USA)**[18] 6058 2-7-6 **75** ....(v) IanBurns(7) 9 73
(M L W Bell) *s.s: hdwy over 2f out: kpt on one pce appr fnl f* **8/1**

3003 **7** *1 ¼* **Child Bride**[12] 6258 2-7-12 **74** oh1 .... JamieMackay 15 69
(P F I Cole) *hld up in rr div: hdwy over 2f out: nt clr run tl over 1f out: one pce fnl f* **28/1**

041 **8** *nk* **Wafeira**[40] 5369 2-8-2 **78** .... JimmyQuinn 12 73
(H R A Cecil) *hld up in mid-div: effrt over 2f out: sn outpcd: kpt on ins fnl f* **13/2**[3]

621 **9** *2 ½* **The Shrew**[17] 6071 2-8-3 **79** .... NickyMackay 8 67
(J H M Gosden) *chsd ldrs: effrt over 2f out: wknd appr fnl f: eased towards fin* **9/2**[1]

4332 **10** *2 ¾* **Tipsy Girl**[20] 5992 2-7-11 **78** .... DeclanCannon(5) 2 59
(D J Coakley) *mid-div: effrt over 2f out: wknd over 1f out* **20/1**

2210 **11** *7* **Intrusion**[23] 5882 2-7-9 **74** .... NataliaGemelova(3) 6 38
(R A Fahey) *in rr: bhd fnl 3f* **25/1**

6501 **12** *1 ¾* **Bonita Star**[17] 6070 2-8-2 **78** .... JoeFanning 16 38
(M R Channon) *chsd ldrs: lost pl over 1f out* **9/1**

513 **13** *½* **Song Of The Siren**[15] 6156 2-8-0 **76** .... FrannyNorton 14 34
(A M Balding) *w ldrs: wknd wl over 1f out: eased ins fnl f* **11/2**[2]

600 **14** *nk* **Ponte Di Rosa**[25] 5829 2-7-5 **74** oh7 .... RyanPowell(7) 4 32
(B G Powell) *s.i.s: sn outpcd in rr: bhd fnl 3f* **100/1**

3100 **15** *8* **Elkmait**[23] 5880 2-8-8 **84** .... KierenFallon 1 22
(C E Brittain) *gave problems s: racd wd: overall ldr: hdd over 2f out: lost pl and eased over 1f out* **25/1**

1m 28.4s (3.00) **Going Correction** +0.475s/f (Yiel) **15** Ran SP% **123.2**
Speed ratings (Par 98): **101,100,99,99,99 97,96,95,93,89 81,79,79,79,69**
toteswingers:1&2 £53.80, 2&3 £14.10, 1&3 £28.30 CSF £182.33 CT £1896.56 TOTE £21.00: £6.20, £3.20, £3.10; EX 259.00 TRIFECTA Not won..
Owner Mrs H Steel **Bred** London Thoroughbred Services Ltd **Trained** Musley Bank, N Yorks

FOCUS
Although it's a shame Eucharist didn't turn up, this still looked a highly competitive fillies' nursery. They went a fair pace and unsurprisingly the main action developed towards the far side.

NOTEBOOK
Honeymead(IRE), taking another slight step up in trip, bounced back to winning ways and completed the task in game fashion. This was her first outing on soft ground, but being by Pivotal there was always a good chance it would suit and she is also a half-sister to a dual winner on such a surface. She kept finding for pressure inside the final furlong and, with not many miles on the clock, is open to more improvement over this distance. (op 25-1)
Humdrum ◆, off the mark at the fourth attempt at Chester a week earlier, was finishing with real purpose after not getting a great trip through the race. She has evidently begun life in nurseries on a fair mark and shouldn't be long in winning again, but looks well worth trying over another furlong. (op 14-1)
Whisper Louise(IRE), easy to back, made a really good fist of things from the front and went down fighting. She probably remains capable of further success and may prove happier back on a less-demanding track. (op 11-2)
Imperialistic Diva(IRE) had faced some stiff tasks since getting off the mark earlier in the year and was taking a drop in class on this switch to a nursery. She got going late on and posted a respectable effort under top weight, but the handicapper looks to have got her spot on. (op 11-1)
No Poppy(IRE) was produced with every chance towards the far rail, but failed to see out the extra furlong up this rising finish. Despite having just one success to her name she has developed into a likeable sort, and looks one to be interested in again when reverting to an easier course. (op 16-1)
Mama Lulu(USA) came good under a fine ride by Dettori on similar ground at Yarmouth last month. Well backed in the second-time visor, she looked to have ruined her chance when falling out of the gates. She came there with a slight chance towards the centre of the track 1f out, though, and would've surely been involved with a better start. (op 11-1 tchd 12-1)
Child Bride was heavily restrained early on and didn't get the breaks on the inside when trying to improve around 2f out. She is capable of better and can find easier assignments. (op 25-1 tchd 33-1)
Wafeira got caught out by the drop back a furlong on this nursery debut. (op 11-2 tchd 15-2)
The Shrew didn't look so happy on this more demanding surface. (op 11-2 tchd 13-2)

6564 TOTESPORT 0800 221 221 H'CAP 7f
4:50 (4:50) (Class 2) (0-100,100) 3-Y-O+
£12,462 (£3,732; £1,866; £934; £466; £234) **Stalls** High

Form RPR

0004 **1** **Carnaby Street (IRE)**[21] 5950 3-9-4 **97** .... RichardHughes 6 105
(R Hannon) *hld up in tch midfield: hdwy and n.m.r ent fnl 2f: wnt between horses and rdn to chse ldr over 1f out: ev ch jst over 1f out: led ins fnl f: jst hld on* **11/2**[1]

0043 **2** *shd* **Iver Bridge Lad**[8] 6319 3-9-7 **100** ....(b) MichaelHills 12 108+
(J Ryan) *stdd s: hld up in rr: hdwy to chse ldrs and nt clr run over 1f out: sn swtchd lft and rdn: r.o wl to chsewnr ins fnl f: kpt on wl: jst failed* **9/1**

2600 **3** *1 ½* **Brae Hill (IRE)**[7] 6363 4-9-3 **94** .... DPMcDonogh 4 98
(R A Fahey) *led: rdn ent fnl 2f: kpt on gamely u.p tl hdd ins fnl f: one pce fnl 100yds* **18/1**

3155 **4** *1* **Linnens Star (IRE)**[22] 5917 3-8-8 **87** .... JimCrowley 1 88
(R M Beckett) *in tch on outer: rdn and effrt to press ldrs over 1f out: no ex and btn ins fnl f* **12/1**

0520 **5** *shd* **Medicean Man**[22] 5911 4-9-4 **95** ....(b[1]) SteveDrowne 11 96+
(J R Gask) *hld up in tch: hdwy to trck ldrs gng wl 2f out: rdn and ev ch ent fnl f: unable qck ins fnl f: wknd fnl 75yds* **15/2**[3]

4335 **6** *½* **Suffolk Punch (IRE)**[21] 5937 3-8-5 **84** oh3 .... FrannyNorton 9 83
(A M Balding) *in tch in midfield: effrt and rdn whn n.m.r 2f out: kpt on same pce u.p fr over 1f out* **10/1**

0610 **7** *¾* **Bullwhip (IRE)**[21] 5950 3-9-4 **97** .... WilliamBuick 13 94
(J H M Gosden) *in tch towards rr: rdn 4f out: no imp u.p fr wl over 1f out* **11/2**[1]

-422 **8** *1 ½* **Santefisio**[100] 3346 4-8-11 **88** .... JimmyFortune 5 81
(P J Makin) *s.i.s: in tch towards rr: rdn and effrt ent fnl 2f: styd on same pce and no imp over 1f out* **7/1**[2]

3000 **9** *1* **Autumn Blades (IRE)**[85] 3869 5-9-5 **96** ....(p) AdamKirby 7 87
(A Bailey) *stdd s: hld up in tch in rr: rdn and effrt on outer 2f out: edgd rt and no prog over 1f out* **40/1**

0403 **10** *4* **Below Zero (IRE)**[7] 6357 3-8-11 **90** .... JoeFanning 10 70
(M Johnston) *chsd ldrs: rdn over 2f out: wkng whn n.m.r wl over 1f out: wl btn ins fnl f* **20/1**

-130 **11** *shd* **Prescription**55 4882 5-9-6 **97**....(b1) StevieDonohoe 8 77
(Sir Mark Prescott) *chsd ldrs: rdn over 2f out: struggling and losing pl whn n.m.r 2f out: sn wknd* **8/1**

0006 **12** *3 1/2* **Pravda Street**18 6048 5-8-1 **85** oh7 ow1....(b) DuilioDaSilva(7) 2 55
(P F I Cole) *chsd ldr tl 2f out: wknd qckly u.p over 1f out: wl bhd ins fnl f* **40/1**

-000 **13** *14* **Lowther**7 6357 5-8-10 **87**....(v) KierenFallon 3 19
(A Bailey) *sn bhd: lost tch 5f out: t.o fnl 2f* **10/1**

1m 28.08s (2.68) **Going Correction** +0.475s/f (Yiel)
WFA 3 from 4yo+ 2lb **13** Ran SP% **116.9**
Speed ratings (Par 109): **103,102,101,100,99 99,98,96,95,91 90,86,70**
toteswingers:1&2 £11.00, 2&3 £46.10, 1&3 £25.00 CSF £52.06 CT £856.40 TOTE £5.70: £2.60, £3.30, £3.60; EX 62.10 Trifecta £484.70 Part on. Pool: £655.11 - 0.64 winning units..
Owner Noodles Racing **Bred** D And Mrs D Veitch **Trained** East Everleigh, Wilts

FOCUS
A good, competitive handicap in which victories in recent seasons have been split between exposed handicappers and improvers. Several were in with a chance entering the final furlong and it resulted in a desperate finish. Not form to take too literally with the fourth and sixth the best guides to the level.

NOTEBOOK
Carnaby Street(IRE), a winner over 7f on soft (Group 3) and 6f on easy ground last season, had not previously won at three but had produced a better effort last time. He tracked the leaders early before picking up to take the advantage entering the final furlong, and stuck on gamely up the hill. It got desperate near the line but he just had the advantage on the nod. He loves this ground and is likely to be out again in the next week or so. (op 5-1 tchd 9-2)
Iver Bridge Lad had also not won since his juvenile days but is suited by soft ground. He was held up early before making his ground in the second half of the race. However, he had to switch entering the final furlong to get a run before finishing well. It looked as if he might have done enough to get up on the line, but his head was up when the winner's was down and so he just lost out. He has to be considered unlucky. (op 10-1)
Brae Hill(IRE) has gained all his wins on fast ground but cut out the running here. He looked sure to be swamped when headed meeting the rising ground but stuck to his task well. (op 16-1 tchd 20-1)
Linnens Star(IRE) ◆ winner on fast ground on the July course, was dropping in trip but was unraced on soft. He ran a creditable race and more can be expected of him next season. (tchd 14-1)
Medicean Man had gained all his wins at 5-6f on good and easy ground and Polytrack. Blinkered for the first time having worn a visor last time and cheekpieces before that, he was keen under restraint early but still looked the most likely winner when arriving between rivals in the Dip. However, when asked to win his race the response was limited and he faded up the hill. The combination of longer trip, soft ground and pulling too hard probably beat him, but he looks one to treat with caution in any case. (op 8-1)
Suffolk Punch(IRE), a 7f winner on fast ground who appears to handle cut, had dropped slightly in weights and had been running fairly consistently over this trip and further. He was held up before staying on best of the rest late and seems to need a return to a mile. (op 12-1)
Bullwhip(IRE), a dual 7f winner on easy ground, including on the July course was sent off joint favourite but was being ridden along before halfway to hold his place. He stayed on in the closing stages without threatening but probably found the ground on the dead side. (op 5-1)
Santefisio is well suited by 7f and fast ground and had yet to race on softer than good, although his sire's progeny usually handle it. He made an effort 2f out but it failed to come to anything. (op 8-1)
Prescription, a multiple 6f winner who acts on any ground, was blinkered for the first time and pulled too hard to enable her to see out the trip. (tchd 9-1)
Lowther Official explanation: jockey said horse never travelled

6565 LA HOGUE FARM SHOP & CAFE H'CAP 1m 4f
5:25 (5:26) (Class 3) (0-95,94) 3-Y-O+
£8,723 (£2,612; £1,306; £653; £326; £163) **Stalls** Centre

Form RPR

0046 **1** **Lethal Glaze (IRE)**10 6283 4-9-4 **86**.... RyanMoore 2 99
(R Hannon) *stdd and bmpd s: hld up in rr: pushed along and hdwy 4f out: rdn to chse clr ldr ent fnl 2f: led over 1f out: hung lft u.p fnl f: styd on: drvn out* **25/1**

4421 **2** *2 1/4* **Sharaayeen**15 6151 3-9-2 **91**.... TadhgO'Shea 7 100+
(B W Hills) *stdd s: hld up wl in rr: stl plenty to do and swtchd rt 3f out: rdn to chse ldrs over 1f out: wnt 2nd ent fnl f: kpt on same pce fnl 100yds* **11/2**3

3035 **3** *3 3/4* **Becausewecan (USA)**7 6362 4-9-1 **83**.... JoeFanning 5 86
(M Johnston) *led: clr ent fnl 3f: rdn and hdd over 1f out: wknd ins fnl f* **12/1**

400/ **4** *3 1/2* **Samsons Son**583 6784 6-9-1 **83**.... SteveDrowne 4 81+
(A King) *hld up in tch: hdwy over 4f out: chsd clr ldr 3f out tl ent fnl 2f: sn rdn and unable qck: wknd jst over 1f out* **40/1**

52-0 **5** *1/2* **Dr Livingstone (IRE)**21 5970 5-9-5 **87**.... HayleyTurner 3 84
(C R Egerton) *stdd s: hld up in last trio: hdwy 4f out: chsd ldrs and rdn 2f out: no prog and wl btn 1f out* **33/1**

4-00 **6** *1* **Bothy**112 2976 4-8-12 **85**.... JohnFahy(5) 6 80
(B Ellison) *chsd ldrs tl wnt 2nd 6f out tl 4f out: sn lost pl: no ch w ldrs fnl 2f: no ch but kpt on again past btn horses ins fnl f* **16/1**

211 **7** *2 3/4* **Dhaamer (IRE)**22 5918 3-8-12 **87**.... RichardHills 13 78+
(J H M Gosden) *hld up in tch: hdwy to chse ldrs gng wl 3f out: rdn and fnd little over 1f out: sn btn: wknd ins fnl f* **3/1**1

2352 **8** *5* **Satwa Moon (USA)**20 5991 4-9-2 **84**....(b1) JMurtagh 12 67
(E A L Dunlop) *stdd s: hld up in tch: rdn and effrt 4f out: no prog u.p 2f: wl btn over 1f out* **9/2**2

20-0 **9** *9* **Spring Jim**150 1821 9-9-3 **85**.... WilliamBuick 11 54
(J R Fanshawe) *hld up in last trio: hdwy over 4f out: rdn and no prog ent fnl 2f: wl btn and eased ins fnl f* **14/1**

0000 **10** *2* **Macarthur**28 5743 6-8-13 **88**.... LewisWalsh(7) 10 53
(Jane Chapple-Hyam) *in tch tl lost pl over 4f out: wl bhd over 2f out* **14/1**

00/0 **11** *1/2* **Pippa Greene**7 6362 6-8-12 **87**.... DuilioDaSilva(7) 1 52
(P F I Cole) *stdd s: plld hrd: sn chsng ldrs: wnt 2nd 4f out tl over 3f out: sn wknd: eased ins fnl f* **66/1**

0141 **12** *3/4* **Topolski (IRE)**21 5940 4-9-9 **91**....(p) JimmyFortune 15 54
(A M Balding) *chsd ldrs tl 4f out: lost pl u.p 3f out: wl bhd fnl 2f: eased ins fnl f* **7/1**

1110 **13** *36* **Epic (IRE)**17 6074 3-8-11 **86**....(b) KierenFallon 16 —
(M Johnston) *in tch: chsd ldr over 3f out tl 3f out: sn wknd: wl bhd and eased fr over 1f out: t.o* **14/1**

-406 **14** *9* **Deportment**35 5517 4-9-0 **82**.... WilliamCarson 14 —
(S C Williams) *chsd ldrs: styd on far rail 10f out: lost 2nd 6f out: lost pl 4f out: wl bhd fnl 2f: eased fr over 1f out: t.o* **16/1**

2m 36.59s (4.59) **Going Correction** +0.475s/f (Yiel)
WFA 3 from 4yo+ 7lb **14** Ran SP% **121.2**
Speed ratings (Par 107): **108,106,104,101,101 100,98,95,89,88 87,87,63,57**
toteswingers:1&2 £28.80, 2&3 £13.80, 1&3 £38.10 CSF £155.81 CT £1774.90 TOTE £35.50: £7.30, £3.00, £2.80; EX 323.80 TRIFECTA Not won. Place 6: £621.68 Place 5: £394.83.
Owner Nigel Morris **Bred** B Kennedy **Trained** East Everleigh, Wilts

FOCUS
This fair middle-distance handicap had an open look about it. It was run at a fair pace and the majority raced away from the far rail. The first pair eventually came clear with the runner-up rated to Newbury form.

NOTEBOOK
Lethal Glaze(IRE), who relished the softer ground, showed his true colours again with a ready effort to score. It wasn't at all surprising to see the blinkers left off after a dismal run at Goodwood last time, for which he was dropped 4lb, and he could've been called the winner passing the furlong marker. He showed his quirky side by drifting right over to the stands' side late on, although he certainly wasn't the first horse to do that at this meeting, and rates value for a bit further. This was his first success since winning on the AW off a 6lb higher last August, and he is capable of holding his form well when in the mood. (op 20-1)
Sharaayeen bolted up at Newbury 15 days earlier and was raised 13lb in the handicap. Ridden out the back on this return to 1m4f, he made smooth headway from 3f out. He was never going to reel in the winner, but finished a clear second-best and it rates another career-best effort in defeat. (op 5-1)
Becausewecan(USA) was given a positive ride as expected and ran one of his better races in defeat. He is on a fair mark, but has had plenty of chances this term. (op 10-1)
Samsons Son ◆ travelled sweetly through the race. He couldn't find an extra gear when push came to shove, but this was his first run since he won over hurdles last February and he should come on a bundle for the run. (op 50-1)
Dr Livingstone(IRE) posted a much more encouraging display on ground he likes. He could build on this back over 1m2f.
Bothy, who has gone well fresh before, had his ground on this return from a 112-day absence and left the impression the run would do him good. He too looks worth dropping back to 1m2f in this sphere. (op 20-1)
Dhaamer(IRE), seeking a hat-trick, was 4lb higher and had her chance, but didn't stay this longer trip sufficiently on the taxing surface. (op 10-3 tchd 7-2)
Satwa Moon(USA) was very disappointing in first-time blinkers. (op 6-1)
T/Jkpt: Not won. T/Plt: £848.30 to a £1 stake. Pool of £191,661.19 - 164.92 winning tickets. T/Qpdt: £150.50 to s £1 stake. Pool of £9,579.89 - 47.10 winning tickets. SP

6293 REDCAR (L-H)
Saturday, October 2
OFFICIAL GOING: Good to soft

6566 EUROPEAN BREEDERS' FUND MAIDEN STKS (DIV I) 7f
2:10 (2:14) (Class 4) 2-Y-O
£4,533 (£1,348; £674; £336) **Stalls** High

Form RPR

1 **Zoowraa** 2-8-12 0.... NeilCallan 2 88
(M A Jarvis) *trckd ldrs: smooth hdwy and cl up over 2f out: led wl over 1f out: sn pushed clr: easily* **9/2**3

6222 **2** *5* **Calypso Magic (IRE)**26 5814 2-9-3 76.... PaulHanagan 8 81
(J Howard Johnson) *cl up: led after 2f: rdn along 2f out: drvn and hdd wl over 1f out: kpt on same pce* **15/8**1

3 *2 1/2* **Roninski (IRE)** 2-9-3 0.... TomEaves 10 74
(B Smart) *in tch: hdwy over 2f out: rdn to chse ldng pair and edgd lft over 1f out: sn no imp* **11/1**

0 **4** *6* **Kian's Delight**17 6070 2-9-0 0.... MichaelO'Connell(3) 3 59
(Jedd O'Keeffe) *chsd ldrs: rdn along 3f out: drvn and kpt on same pce fnl 2f* **100/1**

5 *2 1/2* **Yas Marina (USA)** 2-9-3 0.... AhmedAjtebi 6 53
(Mahmood Al Zarooni) *wnt rt s: t.k.h and chsd ldrs: pushed along and green 3f out: rdn over 2f out and sn btn* **11/4**2

6 *3/4* **Tahitian Princess (IRE)** 2-8-12 0.... RoystonFfrench 5 46
(Mrs A Duffield) *dwlt and in rr: hdwy wl over 2f out: rdn and kpt on fr over 1f out: n.d* **33/1**

0 **7** *3 3/4* **Inca Blue**10 6293 2-9-3 0.... GrahamGibbons 7 42
(T D Easterby) *s.i.s and in rr: hdwy 1/2-way: pushed along over 2f out: nvr nr ldrs* **80/1**

8 *shd* **Hot Toddie** 2-8-12 0.... PaulMulrennan 1 37
(J G Given) *chsd ldrs on wd outside: rdn along wl over 2f out and grad wknd* **25/1**

05 **9** *nk* **Bon Appetit**144 1986 2-8-9 0.... BarryMcHugh(3) 12 36
(N Tinkler) *led 2f: cl up tl rdn along wl over 2f out and grad wknd* **25/1**

00 **10** *3 1/2* **Maunby Rumba (IRE)**14 6182 2-8-9 0.... PatrickDonaghy(3) 14 27
(B M R Haslam) *towards rr and pushed along after 2f: sme hdwy fnl 2f: nvr a factor* **100/1**

0 **11** *8* **Zoom In**15 6138 2-9-3 0.... TedDurcan 4 12
(Mrs L Stubbs) *s.i.s and bhd: effrt and sme hdwy over 2f out: nvr a factor* **16/1**

06 **12** *3* **Sokolka**49 5066 2-8-12 0.... DavidAllan 13 —
(T D Easterby) *a towards rr* **12/1**

0 **13** *1* **Oakwell (IRE)**10 6293 2-9-0 0.... MichaelStainton(3) 16 2
(Miss S E Hall) *in tch on outer: rdn along 1/2-way: sn wknd* **50/1**

0 **14** *1 1/4* **Meniscus**12 6240 2-8-9 0.... IanBrennan(3) 9 —
(V P Donoghue) *chsd ldrs: pushed along bef 1/2-way: sn wknd* **100/1**

4 **15** *5* **A Southside Boy (GER)**16 6104 2-9-0 0.... GaryBartley(3) 15 —
(J S Goldie) *a in rr: bhd fr 1/2-way* **50/1**

16 *5* **Danbrook (IRE)** 2-9-3 0.... PJMcDonald 11 —
(C W Thornton) *s.i.s: a bhd* **100/1**

1m 25.88s (1.38) **Going Correction** +0.30s/f (Good) **16** Ran SP% **121.3**
Speed ratings (Par 97): **104,98,95,88,85 84,80,80,80,76 66,63,62,60,55 49**
toteswingers:1&2 £1.80, 2&3 £5.10, 1&3 £13.60 CSF £12.52 TOTE £6.00: £2.20, £1.10, £2.50; EX 11.40.
Owner Sheikh Ahmed Al Maktoum **Bred** Darley **Trained** Newmarket, Suffolk

FOCUS
After 8mm of rain in the last 24 hours the ground was described as good to soft all around. The stalls were situated under the stands' rail but the race developed down the centre of the track. No more than an ordinary maiden, run at a sound pace.

NOTEBOOK
Zoowraa put up an impressive performance. A filly with a lovely pedigree (the dam a specialist at this trip) she travelled well throughout and has clearly got a future. (op 3-1)
Calypso Magic(IRE), the most experienced runner in the line-up is the bench mark to the form. Not convincing in his attitude at Newcastle the time before, he ran well here and an ordinary maiden can come his way at this time of the year. Rated 76, he doesn't appear to be that well handicapped. (tchd 13-8 and 2-1)
Roninski(IRE), coming from a yard going very well, showed plenty on his debut and can win races if able to build on this pleasing debut. (op 10-1 tchd 8-1)
Kian's Delight ran a lot better than on his debut when failing to beat a rival home. He got upset at the stalls, but if able to hold everything together looks the type for modest handicaps next term.

Yas Marina(USA) was easy to back and beaten at halfway. His Derby entry looks very ambitious at this stage. (op 9-2)

6567 JOHN SMITH'S REDCAR STRAIGHT-MILE CHAMPIONSHIP FINAL (H'CAP) 1m
2:45 (2:45) (Class 2) 3-Y-0+

£15,577 (£4,665; £2,332; £1,167; £582; £292) Stalls High

Form RPR

0500 1 **Kiwi Bay**[14] 6178 5-9-10 89 PaulHanagan 1 100
(M Dods) *hld up in rr: hdwy 3f out: effrt to chse ldrs 2f out: drvn to chal jst ins fnl f: styd on u.p to ld nr fin* 5/1[1]

0043 2 ½ **Charlie Cool**[10] 6296 7-9-9 88 (b) RobertWinston 2 98
(Mrs R A Carr) *trckd ldrs: hdwy 3f out: rdn to ld 2f out: drvn ins fnl f: hdd and no ex nr fin* 10/1

0144 3 7 **Mujaadel (USA)**[27] 5789 5-8-11 76 (p) PaulMulrennan 3 70
(D Nicholls) *trckd ldrs: hdwy and cl up 3f out: rdn along and ev ch wl over 1f out: drvn and one pce ent fnl f* 10/1

-204 4 ¾ **Right Grand**[30] 5685 3-8-12 80 (b[1]) NeilCallan 7 72
(W J Haggas) *hld up: hdwy on outer 1/2-way: rdn to chse ldrs wl over 2f out: drvn and ch over 1f out: wknd ent fnl f* 7/1

4426 5 4 **Whispered Times (USA)**[30] 5685 3-8-9 77 (p) SilvestreDeSousa 5 60
(Miss Tracy Waggott) *cl up: led 3f out: rdn along and hdd 2f out: sn drvn and wknd over 1f out* 16/1

1104 6 4 ½ **Don't Call Me (IRE)**[8] 6318 3-9-8 90 (t) TomEaves 8 62
(B Smart) *trckd ldrs: rdn along wl over 2f out: sn drvn and btn* 13/2[3]

1215 7 2 **Shadowtime**[30] 5685 5-9-1 83 MichaelO'Connell(3) 4 51
(Miss Tracy Waggott) *chsd ldrs: rdn along 3f out: sn drvn and wknd* 11/1

2320 8 1 ½ **Celtic Change (IRE)**[16] 6105 6-9-1 85 (bt) LeeTopliss(5) 9 49
(M Dods) *sn led: rdn along and hdd 3f out: drvn over 2f out and sn wknd* 8/1

0021 9 12 **Daaweitza**[16] 6112 7-8-11 81 DaleSwift(5) 10 18
(B Ellison) *towards rr: rdn along after 3f: sme hdwy 1/2-way: sn drvn and wknd* 6/1[2]

2004 10 26 **Caldercruix (USA)**[16] 6106 3-9-8 90 TedDurcan 11 —
(T P Tate) *chsd ldrs: rdn along 1/2-way: sn wknd: bhd and eased fnl 2f* 5/1[1]

1m 41.33s (3.33) **Going Correction** +0.30s/f (Good)
WFA 3 from 4yo+ 3lb 10 Ran SP% **117.0**
Speed ratings (Par 109): **95,94,87,86,82 78,76,74,62,36**
toteswingers:1&2 £12.20, 2&3 £23.80, 1&3 £48.10 CSF £55.36 CT £374.81 TOTE £4.10: £1.60, £3.00, £3.30; EX 34.80 Trifecta £218.90 Part won. Pool: £295.90 - 0.60 winning units..
Owner Kiwi Racing **Bred** Templeton Stud **Trained** Denton, Co Durham
■ Stewards' Enquiry : Robert Winston caution: used whip with excessive frequency.
Paul Hanagan caution: used whip with excessive frequency.

FOCUS
Plenty with course form on offer here, as six of the ten already winners at the track for this final. A lot of exposed horses and the handicapper was in charge with many of them. The race developed centre to stands' side. The first two pulled clear and are rated basically to form.

NOTEBOOK
Kiwi Bay put up a brave performance on ground that might have been softer than ideal. His yard appear to be going better now, but it will take a career-best to follow-up once the handicapper has had his say. (op 9-2 tchd 11-2 in a place)
Charlie Cool, coming from a yard struggling for winners, did very little wrong in defeat. Beating in a claimer last time out, he is done to a mark in which he can win off, so he should remain competitive. (op 14-1)
Mujaadel(USA) stayed on without really threatening. He is 3lb higher than he has ever been successful off. (tchd 9-1)
Right Grand, lightly raced on turf, got never land a blow in his first-time headgear. (op 13-2 tchd 6-1)
Celtic Change(IRE), a stablemate to the winner, is also in the grips of the handicapper. (op 9-1)
Daaweitza Official explanation: jockey said gelding was unsuited by the good to soft ground
Caldercruix(USA) was the disappointment of the race as he was unbeaten in two previous starts at the track. Eased when beaten, it is best to forget all about this run. Official explanation: jockey said gelding was unsuited by the good to soft ground (op 13-2)

6568 TOTEPOOL TWO-YEAR-OLD TROPHY (LISTED RACE) 6f
3:20 (3:21) (Class 1) 2-Y-0

£130,003 (£49,280; £18,480; £18,480; £6,160; £3,091) Stalls High

Form RPR

13 1 **Ladies Are Forever**[108] 3070 2-7-12 105 SilvestreDeSousa 15 91
(G R Oldroyd) *trckd ldrs: hdwy over 2f out: led wl over 1f out and sn rdn: drvn and hung lft ins fnl f: kpt on wl* 3/1[1]

21 2 1 ¼ **Codemaster**[35] 5523 2-8-6 93 DaneO'Neill 20 95
(H Candy) *in tch: hdwy to chse ldrs 2f out: sn rdn and edgd lft over 1f out: styd on strly u.p ins fnl f: tk 2nd nr fin* 7/2[2]

1112 3 nk **Krypton Factor**[15] 6141 2-8-12 99 (b) SebSanders 2 100
(Sir Mark Prescott) *racd towards far rail: prom: rdn 2f out and ev ch: drvn ent fnl f and kpt on same pce* 6/1[3]

130 3 dht **Ballista (IRE)**[77] 4138 2-8-6 90 RichardKingscote 22 94
(Tom Dascombe) *racd wd: in tch: hdwy to chse ldrs over 2f out: rdn wl over 1f out and ev ch tl drvn and one pce ins fnl f* 33/1

3004 5 ¾ **Move In Time**[15] 6141 2-8-3 94 IanBrennan 14 89
(B Smart) *chsd ldrs: rdn 2f out: drvn over 1f out: kpt on same pce ins fnl f* 18/1

3131 6 1 ¼ **Dingle View (IRE)**[34] 5567 2-8-9 106 CathyGannon 3 91
(P D Evans) *led: rdn along over 2f out: hdd wl over 1f out: sn drvn and kpt on same pce* 10/1

322 7 1 ¼ **Jinky**[3] 6465 2-8-9 73 SamHitchcott 1 88
(M R Channon) *chsd ldrs: rdn over 2f out: sn drvn and one pce* 33/1

0010 8 nse **El Viento (FR)**[23] 5880 2-8-12 88 (b) BarryMcHugh 5 90
(R A Fahey) *midfield: hdwy over 2f out: sn rdn and kpt on: nt rch ldrs* 100/1

2110 9 ½ **Morache Music**[28] 5745 2-8-9 88 PatCosgrave 10 86
(P J Makin) *hmpd s: hld up: hdwy over 2f out: rdn wl over 1f out: kpt on: nt rch ldrs* 16/1

0130 10 3 ¼ **Chiswick Bey (IRE)**[23] 5880 2-8-9 93 PaulHanagan 8 76
(R A Fahey) *midfield: effrt whn n.m.r over 2f out: sn rdn and n.d* 16/1

1210 11 2 ¼ **Forjatt (IRE)**[23] 5880 2-9-0 102 NeilCallan 21 74
(M A Jarvis) *midfield: pushed along 1/2-way: rdn over 2f out: n.d* 7/1

4320 12 2 ¼ **Jamesway (IRE)**[15] 6141 2-8-12 90 TomEaves 18 66
(R A Fahey) *midfield: swtchd wd and rdn along 1/2-way: n.d* 100/1

4015 13 ½ **Mappin Time (IRE)**[15] 6141 2-8-9 92 DavidAllan 4 61
(T D Easterby) *in tch: rdn along over 2f out: grad wknd* 33/1

010 14 ¾ **Nasharra (IRE)**[23] 5880 2-9-0 95 RobertWinston 17 64
(K A Ryan) *dwlt: midfield whn n.m.r over 2f out: n.d* 100/1

21 15 ¾ **Sikeeb (IRE)**[149] 1845 2-8-12 86 ChrisCatlin 12 60
(C E Brittain) *chsd ldrs: rdn along 1/2-way: hld whn n.m.r over 2f out: sn wknd* 16/1

5320 16 nse **Berberana (IRE)**[15] 6139 2-8-7 78 GrahamGibbons 19 55
(T D Easterby) *midfield: rdn along and edgd lft over 2f out: sn wknd* 100/1

0014 17 ½ **Sky Diamond (IRE)**[10] 6294 2-8-9 65 PJMcDonald 9 55
(J G Given) *sn outpcd and a in rr* 100/1

4326 18 1 ½ **Millies Folly**[2] 6513 2-8-4 70 NeilFarley 16 46
(D Carroll) *midfeild: rdn along whn n.m.r over 2f out: sn wknd* 100/1

640 19 2 ¼ **Silk Bounty**[15] 6153 2-8-12 68 PaulMulrennan 13 47
(J G Given) *wnt lft s: a in rr* 100/1

541 20 ¾ **Hawdyerwheesht**[23] 5886 2-8-9 82 RoystonFfrench 23 42
(M Johnston) *sn rdn along and a in rr* 66/1

2005 21 14 **On The High Tops (IRE)**[28] 5745 2-8-9 81 TedDurcan 6 —
(T P Tate) *cl up: rdn along bef 1/2-way: sn wknd* 100/1

46 22 6 **Just For Leo (IRE)**[50] 5021 2-8-12 69 ShaneKelly 7 —
(P D Evans) *sn rdn along: a outpcd and bhd* 100/1

1m 12.6s (0.80) **Going Correction** +0.30s/f (Good) 22 Ran SP% **125.2**
Speed ratings (Par 103): **106,104,103,103,102 101,99,99,98,94 91,88,87,86,85 85,85,83,80,79 60,52**PL: Krypton Factor £1.50 Ballista £5.30. TRI: Ladies are Forever/Codemaster/Krypton Factor £24.00 LAF/C/Ballista £137.50 toteswingers:Krypton Factor &2 £8.00, KF&1 £2.60, Ballista&Codemaster £30.10, B&1 £30.10, 1&2 £1.02 CSF £12.32 TOTE £4.30: £1.80, £2.50;27 Owner Trifecta £R C Bond Bred Bond Thoroughbred Corporation.
■ Stewards' Enquiry : Sam Hitchcott caution: used whip with excessive force.

FOCUS
A cracking renewal for this valuable prize. There were no real surprises and the form should prove reliable.

NOTEBOOK
Ladies Are Forever had a massive chance at the weights, and she didn't disappoint, with a gutsy effort on her first start since finishing third in the Queen Mary at Royal Ascot. Rated 105, she was ridden along at halfway but showed a willing attitude. From a smart family, this was only her third start and can continue to progress. (op 4-1)
Codemaster, also having his third start, stayed on well in the final furlong. Not lacking for size, he might appreciate better ground. His trainer excels with these types and it's highly unlikely we have seen the best of him. (op 4-1)
Ballista(IRE), also coming back from a break, showed plenty of early speed, and this was a solid effort trying to give 8lb to the winner. (op 11-2 tchd 5-1)
Krypton Factor was forced to race alone for part of the race and his rider also dropped his whip. At the weights he has run with credit. (op 11-2 tchd 5-1)
Move In Time, behind Krypton Factor last time up at Ayr, is also a good benchmark to the form. From a yard going well, he appeared to run bang up to form. (op 20-1 tchd 22-1)
Dingle View(IRE), carrying a penalty for her Group 3 success at the Curragh last time out, was under pressure at halfway and had no extra inside the final furlong. (op 8-1)
Jinky, rated 73, ran way above his rating and a small maiden would be his for the taking at this time of the year.
Forjatt(IRE) was well held but might have found the ground unsuitable. (op 13-2 tchd 15-2)
Jamesway(IRE) Official explanation: jockey said colt hung right throughout

6569 EUROPEAN BREEDERS' FUND MAIDEN STKS (DIV II) 7f
4:00 (4:00) (Class 4) 2-Y-0 £4,533 (£1,348; £674; £336) Stalls High

Form RPR

63 1 **Lady Gar Gar**[85] 3874 2-8-12 0 SilvestreDeSousa 4 69
(G R Oldroyd) *dwlt: towards rr: sn pushed along: hdwy 3f out: sn chsng ldrs: styd on to ld last 50yds* 5/1[2]

0450 2 nk **Bernisdale**[30] 5682 2-8-12 57 PJMcDonald 3 68
(G M Moore) *led: hdd and no ex wl ins fnl f* 50/1

0 3 1 ½ **Labore**[23] 5892 2-9-3 0 NeilCallan 1 69
(M Botti) *trckd ldrs: t.k.h: ev ch over 1f out: styd on same pce ins fnl f* 28/1

4 4 1 **Dimension**[23] 5893 2-9-3 0 PatCosgrave 12 67
(J R Fanshawe) *hmpd s: hld up: hdwy over 2f out: sn chsng ldrs: styd on same pce ins fnl f* 5/4[1]

0 5 ½ **Caramella Brownie**[107] 3106 2-8-7 0 LanceBetts(5) 6 61
(T D Easterby) *chsd ldrs: effrt over 2f out: kpt on same pce ins fnl f* 66/1

0223 6 1 ¼ **Moral Issue**[11] 6263 2-9-0 74 PatrickDonaghy(3) 9 62
(Jedd O'Keeffe) *trckd ldrs: t.k.h: rdn over 1f out: wknd ins fnl f* 8/1

6 7 ½ **Sangar**[26] 5814 2-8-9 0 BarryMcHugh(3) 13 56
(Ollie Pears) *carried lft s: in rr: hdwy over 1f out: styng on at fin* 15/2[3]

0 8 11 **Fire Fighter (IRE)**[8] 6333 2-9-3 0 SebSanders 8 34
(Sir Mark Prescott) *s.i.s: in rr: sme hdwy 3f out: sn wknd* 10/1

9 nk **Another For Joe** 2-9-0 0 GaryBartley(3) 10 33
(J S Goldie) *dwlt: towards rr: dropped detached last after 2f* 20/1

10 1 ¼ **Uncle Bryn** 2-9-0 0 IanBrennan(3) 11 30
(J J Quinn) *dwlt and sltly hmpd s: hld up in midfield: effrt over 2f out: wknd over 1f out* 20/1

00 11 ¾ **Belles Boudier**[9] 6309 2-8-7 0 RossAtkinson(5) 7 23
(G Woodward) *a towards rr* 100/1

00 12 ¾ **William Wainwright (IRE)**[7] 6365 2-9-3 0 PaulMulrennan 5 26
(Mrs A Duffield) *trckd ldrs: effrt over 2f out: sn lost pl* 100/1

2302 13 3 ¼ **Beyaz Villas**[65] 4512 2-9-3 68 AdrianNicholls 14 18
(D Nicholls) *swvd lft s: sn given reminders: sn chsng ldrs: lost pl over 1f out: eased ins fnl f* 12/1

1m 27.34s (2.84) **Going Correction** +0.30s/f (Good) 13 Ran SP% **119.2**
Speed ratings (Par 97): **95,94,92,91,91 89,89,76,76,74 74,73,69**
toteswingers:1&2 £38.20, 2&3 £32.70, 1&3 £25.00 CSF £242.46 TOTE £4.10: £1.10, £16.70, £11.60; EX 377.60.
Owner R C Bond **Bred** R C Bond **Trained** Brawby, N Yorks

FOCUS
An ordinary maiden run at an even gallop and it proved hard to make ground off the pace.

NOTEBOOK
Lady Gar Gar, having her third start, showed a willing attitude to keep up the fine run of her stable. The handicapper shouldn't be too harsh for this effort and she can win again. This trip looks fine. (op 13-2)
Bernisdale, rated 57, was well held in a nursery over C&D last time out. It's unlikely the handicapper will let this run go unnoticed and she could be set for a rise in the weights.
Labore, having his first start on turf, showed up well and a similar contest can go his way.
Dimension never looked like winning on his first start on turf. (op 11-8 tchd 6-4 in places)
Moral Issue, rated 74, stepping up to 7f for the first time, looked a non-stayer. (op 7-1)
Sangar, who was hampered at the start, was noted doing some good late work under hands and heels riding. She can do better in due course. (op 8-1)

Uncle Bryn Official explanation: jockey said gelding had no more to give

6570 GUISBOROUGH STKS (LISTED RACE) 7f
4:35 (4:41) (Class 1) 3-Y-0+

£19,869 (£7,532; £3,769; £1,879; £941; £472) Stalls High

Form RPR

1360 1 **Harrison George (IRE)**[21] 5946 5-9-0 111 PaulHanagan 2 104
(R A Fahey) *trckd ldrs: hdwy 1/2-way: cl up over 2f out: rdn over 1f out: led ent fnl f: drvn out* **7/1**[2]

4006 2 1 **Eton Rifles (IRE)**[15] 6142 5-9-0 87 PaulMulrennan 8 101
(J Howard Johnson) *led: rdn along over 2f out: drvn over 1f out: hdd and hung lft ent fnl f: no ex last 100yds* **40/1**

1410 3 1 1/4 **Yaa Wayl (IRE)**[15] 6147 3-9-1 115 NeilCallan 11 101
(M A Jarvis) *hld up: hdwy on outer 3f out: rdn to chse ldng pair wl over 1f out: drvn and edgd lft ins fnl f: no imp towards fin* **7/1**[2]

0010 4 4 **Evens And Odds (IRE)**[14] 6177 6-9-0 104 AdrianNicholls 4 87
(D Nicholls) *chsd ldrs: rdn along and outpcd wl over 2f out: styd on appr fnl f* **12/1**

1- 5 3/4 **Kingsfort (USA)**[385] 5892 3-8-12 0 TedDurcan 10 85
(Saeed Bin Suroor) *awkward s: hld up: hdwy to chse ldrs 3f out: rdn along over 2f out: sn btn* **11/4**[1]

1-05 6 1 1/2 **Inler (IRE)**[141] 2075 3-8-12 98 ShaneKelly 3 81
(B J Meehan) *t.k.h: sn cl up: effrt over 2f out and ev ch tl rdn and wknd over 1f out* **9/1**[3]

3240 7 3/4 **Aldovrandi (IRE)**[15] 6147 3-8-12 104 SebSanders 6 79
(M Botti) *hmpd s: hld up in rr: hdwy to chse ldrs wl over 2f out: sn rdn and wknd wl over 1f out* **22/1**

0602 8 2 **Sir Gerry (USA)**[15] 6147 5-9-3 114 CathyGannon 7 76
(C A Dwyer) *a towards rr* **12/1**

5-1 9 1/2 **Arry's Orse**[241] 392 3-8-12 87 TomEaves 1 72
(B Smart) *wnt lft s: hld up in rr: hdwy on outer to chse ldrs over 3f out: sn rdn and wknd over 2f out* **28/1**

3322 10 7 **Skysurfers**[17] 6089 4-9-0 113 AhmedAjtebi 5 53
(Saeed Bin Suroor) *trckd ldrs: hdwy 3f out: rdn over 2f out: btn wl over 1f out and sn eased* **11/4**[1]

1m 25.5s (1.00) **Going Correction** +0.30s/f (Good)
WFA 3 from 4yo+ 2lb **10** Ran SP% **114.0**
Speed ratings (Par 111): **106,104,103,98,98 96,95,93,92,84**
toteswingers:1&2 £36.80, 2&3 £53.70, 1&3 £7.00 CSF £252.31 TOTE £8.70: £2.50, £12.20, £2.80; EX 262.50.
Owner P D Smith Holdings Ltd **Bred** R P Ryan **Trained** Musley Bank, N Yorks

FOCUS
It again proved hard to make ground off the pace in this Listed race, which was full of horses with questions to answer and is debatable what the form is truly worth. It was run at an even tempo. The form could be rated higher at face value.

NOTEBOOK
Harrison George(IRE) enjoyed the drop back in grade after contesting two Group races. A good servant to the yard, he is versatile regarding the ground and will always be popular in this type of contest. (tchd 13-2 and 15-2 and 8-1 in a place)
Eton Rifles(IRE), rated only 87, had major work to do with most of his rivals at the weights. After a few below-par efforts, he appears to be hitting form again. Proven on easy ground, connections will be hoping the handicapper doesn't over react. (op 33-1)
Yaa Wayl(IRE), well-backed beforehand, bounced back after a bad run last time with a solid effort. He won't be the easiest to place. (op 12-1)
Evens And Odds(IRE), normally seen over sprint distances, was well held back in fourth and also won't be easy to find opportunities for him. (op 14-1 tchd 11-1)
Kingsfort(USA) can only be watched for the time being. (op 2-1)
Inler(IRE), having his first start for current connections, was well held after his break. (op 12-1 tchd 14-1)
Skysurfers was very disappointing. Well backed beforehand, he was eased when beaten inside the final furlong. Official explanation: trainer's rep said colt was unsuited by the good to soft ground (op 7-2 tchd 5-2)

6571 MARKET CROSS JEWELLERS (S) STKS 1m 2f
5:10 (5:11) (Class 5) 3-5-Y-0 £2,914 (£867; £433; £216) Stalls Low

Form RPR

6 1 **Jolly Roger (IRE)**[11] 6262 3-8-6 0 BarryMcHugh(3) 1 74
(N Bycroft) *in rr: hdwy 3f out: r.o to ld jst ins fnl f: kpt on wl* **25/1**

2550 2 1 3/4 **Resplendent Light**[14] 6202 5-9-0 75 NeilCallan 3 70
(W R Muir) *trckd ldrs: nt clr run over 2f out: smooth hdwy to ld over 1f out: drvn and hdd jst ins fnl f: no ex* **15/8**[1]

6200 3 5 **Knight's Victory (IRE)**[10] 6297 4-8-11 63 MichaelStainton(3) 2 60
(Michael Smith) *in rr: hdwy on ins over 3f out: nt clr run over 2f out tl over 1f out: kpt on same pce* **8/1**

1100 4 3 1/2 **Island Chief**[10] 6296 4-9-6 74 PaulMulrennan 7 59
(M W Easterby) *mid-div: effrt and outpcd 3f out: kpt on appr fnl f* **14/1**

0463 5 nk **Dane Cottage**[8] 6326 3-8-10 53 (v) CathyGannon 12 53
(P D Evans) *in rr: drvn over 5f out: kpt on fnl 3f: nvr a factor* **20/1**

5106 6 8 **Kielder (IRE)**[36] 5484 3-9-1 67 GrahamGibbons 6 42
(T D Barron) *in rr: drvn over 4f out: nvr a factor* **15/2**[3]

2036 7 3 **Peaceful Rule (USA)**[59] 4705 4-8-11 63 MichaelO'Connell(3) 5 30
(D Nicholls) *led after 1f: hdd over 2f out: wknd over 1f out* **12/1**

4230 8 2 3/4 **Moon Lightning (IRE)**[8] 6328 4-9-0 60 PJMcDonald 4 25
(Miss T Jackson) *t.k.h: led 1f: trckd ldrs: led on bit over 2f out: hdd over 1f out: sn wknd* **25/1**

000 9 1 **Funky Munky**[26] 5820 5-9-0 45 RoystonFfrench 14 23
(A C Whillans) *in rr: sme hdwy over 3f out: wknd over 2f out* **40/1**

0-50 10 1 **Inside Knowledge (USA)**[60] 4683 4-8-9 47 RossAtkinson(5) 13 21
(G Woodward) *t.k.h on wd outside: trckd ldrs: lost pl over 3f out* **100/1**

-361 11 7 **Love In The West (IRE)**[47] 5158 4-8-12 62 GaryBartley(3) 9 —
(John A Harris) *hld up in mid-div: lost pl over 2f out* **8/1**

1030 12 3 **Northern Acres**[16] 6109 4-9-6 68 AdrianNicholls 8 —
(D Nicholls) *t.k.h: trckd ldrs: wknd over 2f out: heavily eased* **5/1**[2]

6530 13 25 **Miereveld**[25] 5423 3-8-9 48 PaulHanagan 10 —
(B Ellison) *mid-div on outer: rdn and lost pl over 3f out: sn bhd* **33/1**

2m 10.81s (3.71) **Going Correction** +0.45s/f (Yiel)
WFA 3 from 4yo+ 5lb **13** Ran SP% **118.6**
Speed ratings (Par 103): **103,101,97,94,94 88,85,83,82,81 76,73,53**
toteswingers:1&2 £13.00, 2&3 £3.70, 1&3 £49.10 CSF £68.15 TOTE £49.70: £13.20, £2.10, £6.10; EX 137.80.The winner was bought by J Flint for £8,000.
Owner Tony Coyle **Bred** Paget Bloodstock **Trained** Brandsby, N Yorks

FOCUS
Hard to get excited about this ordinary seller, although it was run at an even pace and there appeared no fluke about the result. The runner-up to his latest mark sets the level.

Northern Acres Official explanation: jockey said gelding was unsuited by the good to soft ground

6572 WIN A VIP DAY OUT @ REDCARRACING.CO.UK H'CAP 5f
5:45 (5:46) (Class 5) (0-75,75) 3-Y-0+ £2,914 (£867; £433; £216) Stalls High

Form RPR

2110 1 **Mayoman (IRE)**[30] 5698 5-9-7 75 (v) DavidNolan 3 88
(D Carroll) *qckly away: mde all: rdn over 1f out: kpt on wl towards fin* **10/1**

000 2 1 1/4 **La Capriosa**[17] 6073 4-9-0 68 RobertWinston 9 76
(J A Glover) *prom: rdn along wl over 1f out: drvn and kpt on ins fnl f: tk 2nd nr fin* **22/1**

5115 3 nk **Verinco**[17] 6073 4-8-11 72 (v) AdamCarter(7) 13 79
(B Smart) *prom: effrt to chse wnr 2f out: rdn and hung lft jst ins fnl f: sn drvn and one pce: lost 2nd nr fin* **8/1**[3]

0321 4 1 **Captain Scooby**[12] 6245 4-9-3 74 MichaelStainton(3) 5 77
(R M Whitaker) *midfield: hdwy to chse ldrs 1/2-way: rdn wl over 1f out: kpt on ins fnl f* **8/1**[3]

5403 5 shd **Galpin Junior (USA)**[9] 6303 4-9-4 72 AdrianNicholls 11 75
(D Nicholls) *dwlt: midfield: hdwy wl over 1f out: sn rdn and kpt on ins fnl f: nrst fin* **7/2**[1]

2001 6 1/2 **Northern Bolt**[20] 5999 5-9-5 73 (b) PatrickMathers 14 74
(I W McInnes) *sn rdn along towards rr: hdwy wl over 1f out: styd on wl u.p ins fnl f: nrst fin* **14/1**

32-3 7 2 3/4 **Bedloe's Island (IRE)**[17] 6073 5-9-1 69 SilvestreDeSousa 12 60+
(N Bycroft) *blind removed late and s.i.s: bhd tl hdwy wl over 1f out: sn rdn and kpt on ins fnl f: nrst fin* **13/2**[2]

0003 8 hd **Wicked Wilma (IRE)**[6] 6398 6-8-9 63 TedDurcan 6 54
(A Berry) *trckd ldrs: effrt wl over 1f out: sn rdn and wknd appr fnl f* **16/1**

2311 9 3/4 **Select Committee**[10] 6299 5-9-3 74 (v) IanBrennan(3) 15 62
(J J Quinn) *n.m.r and hmpd shortly after s: towards rr: sme hdwy 1/2-way: sn rdn and n.d* **9/1**

4010 10 2 1/2 **Bosun Breese**[9] 6303 5-9-6 74 GrahamGibbons 18 53
(T D Barron) *dwlt: midfield: effrt to chse ldrs 1/2-way: rdn along 2f out and sn wknd* **28/1**

-260 11 1 **Diamond Blade**[22] 5920 4-8-11 65 (p) DavidAllan 7 40
(T D Easterby) *chsd ldrs to 1/2-way: sn rdn and wknd* **16/1**

2024 12 1 1/2 **Dispol Kylie (IRE)**[16] 6103 4-8-11 65 PaulHanagan 10 35
(Mrs K Walton) *chsd ldrs: rdn along 1/2-way: sn wknd* **9/1**

5600 13 1/2 **Timeless Elegance (IRE)**[38] 5424 3-8-11 70 DaleSwift(5) 1 38
(J Howard Johnson) *blind renoved late and dwlt: sn chsng ldrs on wd outside: rdn over 2f out and sn wknd* **20/1**

0000 14 1/2 **Nubar Boy**[10] 6284 3-8-11 65 CathyGannon 8 31
(P D Evans) *a in rr* **33/1**

0065 15 3 3/4 **Tyrannosaurus Rex (IRE)**[9] 6303 6-8-9 63 TomEaves 19 16
(D Shaw) *midfield: rdn along bef 1/2-way and sn in rr* **25/1**

0260 16 1 1/4 **Stolt (IRE)**[15] 6140 6-9-1 69 (p) SebSanders 17 17
(N Wilson) *chsd ldrs: rdn along 1/2-way: sn wknd* **40/1**

59.68 secs (1.08) **Going Correction** +0.30s/f (Good) **16** Ran SP% **127.1**
Speed ratings (Par 103): **103,101,100,98,98 97,93,92,88 86,84,83,82,76 74**
toteswingers:1&2 £49.40, 2&3 £44.10, 1&3 £17.00 CSF £227.45 CT £1952.14 TOTE £10.10: £1.50, £5.30, £2.10, £2.90; EX 341.90.
Owner Tom Tuohy **Bred** James Cosgrove **Trained** Sledmere, E Yorks

FOCUS
A sprint handicap for horses rated 61-75 which was pretty competitive with three last-time-out winners in the line-up. The placed horses are rated to their best.

Bosun Breese Official explanation: jockey said gelding reared as gates opened
Stolt(IRE) Official explanation: jockey said gelding hung left

6573 FOLLOW REDCAR RACING ON FACEBOOK H'CAP 1m 2f
6:15 (6:15) (Class 5) (0-75,75) 3-Y-0+ £2,914 (£867; £433; £216) Stalls Low

Form RPR

44-1 1 **Leslingtaylor (IRE)**[175] 1012 8-9-3 75 ShaneBKelly(7) 1 85+
(J J Quinn) *hld up in mid-div: hdwy on ins over 2f out: n.m.r and squeezed through last 100yds: led fnl strides* **10/1**[3]

3555 2 hd **Zaplamation (IRE)**[12] 6243 5-8-12 66 IanBrennan(3) 13 76
(J J Quinn) *in rr: hdwy 4f out: styd on to chse ldrs over 1f out: led last 50yds: hdd nr fin* **16/1**

4241 3 1 **Scarab (IRE)**[3] 6472 5-9-3 68 6ex (p) GrahamGibbons 9 76
(T D Walford) *led: hdd and no ex wl ins fnl f* **13/2**[2]

1111 4 2 **True To Form (IRE)**[15] 6165 3-9-3 73 SebSanders 3 77
(Sir Mark Prescott) *sn trcking ldr: rdn over 2f out: one pce fnl f: wknd towards fin* **7/4**[1]

6-05 5 3 1/4 **Grazeon Gold Blend**[16] 6112 7-9-9 74 RobertWinston 2 71
(J J Quinn) *trckd ldrs: t.k.h: one pce fnl 2f* **12/1**

4020 6 3 **Rosbay (IRE)**[16] 6112 6-9-7 72 DavidNolan 14 63
(T D Easterby) *w ldr: drvn 4f out: outpcd and lost pl over 2f out* **10/1**[3]

1420 7 6 **Houston Dynimo (IRE)**[16] 6109 5-9-3 68 RoystonFfrench 11 47
(N G Richards) *hld up in rr: effrt 3f out: nvr nr ldrs* **50/1**

0433 8 5 **Cape Quarter (USA)**[21] 5959 4-8-12 63 (t) ShaneKelly 8 32
(W J Haggas) *hld up in rr: effrt over 3f out: sn btn* **14/1**

201 9 2 1/4 **Mainland (USA)**[42] 5303 4-9-10 75 PaulMulrennan 4 40
(K A Ryan) *in tch: effrt 3f out: sn wknd* **10/1**[3]

6053 10 1 **Sanctuary**[40] 5363 4-9-9 74 TomEaves 15 37
(B Smart) *chsd ldrs on outer: rdn 3f out: sn wknd* **10/1**[3]

2041 11 29 **Opening Nite (IRE)**[15] 6144 3-9-2 72 (b) PaulHanagan 7 —
(R A Fahey) *sn trcking ldrs: dropped in rr over 5f out: bhd and eased over 2f out: virtually p.u: t.o* **13/2**[2]

2m 12.12s (5.02) **Going Correction** +0.45s/f (Yiel)
WFA 3 from 4yo+ 5lb **11** Ran SP% **121.6**
Speed ratings (Par 103): **97,96,96,94,91 89,84,80,78,78 54**
toteswingers:1&2 £30.80, 2&3 £16.70, 1&3 £8.20 CSF £163.76 CT £1131.85 TOTE £12.20: £3.20, £2.20, £3.70; EX 108.40 Place 6: £201.43 Place 5: £128.76.
Owner Mrs Marie Taylor **Bred** Mrs Peggy Kelly **Trained** Settrington, N Yorks

FOCUS
A competitive 61-75 handicap run at an even pace and a good result for trainer, John Quinn who saddled the first two home. The form makes sense with the placed horses to their best.

Opening Nite(IRE) Official explanation: jockey said gelding became restless in stalls

T/Plt: £459.80 to a £1 stake. Pool of £67,251.11 - 106.75 winning tickets. T/Qpdt: £51.90 to a £1 stake. Pool of £3,555.95 - 50.70 winning tickets. JR

6536 WOLVERHAMPTON (A.W) (L-H)

Saturday, October 2

OFFICIAL GOING: Standard

Wind: Light half-against Weather: Overcast

6574 CE RISK, SAFETY & SECURITY H'CAP (DIV I) 1m 1f 103y(P)

5:30 (5:30) (Class 6) (0-55,55) 3-Y-O £1,364 (£403; £201) Stalls Low

Form RPR

5004 1 **Empress Leizu (IRE)**[47] 5155 3-8-7 **53** JulieBurke(7) 8 63
(A W Carroll) *chsd ldr tl led over 1f out: rdn and edgd lft ins fnl f: r.o* **13/2**

0043 2 ¾ **Jovial (IRE)**[1] 6527 3-8-9 **48** EddieCreighton 10 56
(D J Coakley) *trckd ldrs: racd keenly: pushed along over 3f out: rdn to chse wnr ins fnl f: r.o* **3/1**[1]

0635 3 3 ¾ **Second Brook (IRE)**[8] 6336 3-8-11 **50** LukeMorris 3 51
(R Hollinshead) *chsd ldrs: rdn and ev ch over 1f out: sn hung lft: no ex ins fnl f* **9/2**[3]

2644 4 nk **Wavertree Bounty**[52] 4971 3-8-5 **49** TobyAtkinson(5) 4 49
(J Ryan) *broke wl: sn stdd and lost pl: hdwy over 2f out: rdn over 1f out: edgd lft and styd on ins fnl f* **7/1**

5013 5 1 ¾ **Franki J**[29] 5730 3-8-13 **55** SophieDoyle(3) 2 51
(D Donovan) *sn led: rdn and hdd over 1f out: wknd ins fnl f* **4/1**[2]

0006 6 4 **Asterales**[22] 5923 3-8-13 **52** TonyCulhane 11 40
(W J Musson) *s.i.s: rn wd bnd 7f out: hdwy over 5f out: rdn over 3f out: wknd over 2f out* **7/1**

6000 7 nk **Sandy Toes**[12] 6255 3-8-4 **46** oh1 KellyHarrison(3) 6 33
(J A Glover) *hld up: hdwy over 5f out: rdn and wknd 2f out* **40/1**

5000 8 28 **Elegant Dancer (IRE)**[77] 4127 3-8-8 **47** LiamJones 9 —
(Paul Green) *hld up: hdwy over 5f out: rdn and wknd over 2f out: t.o* **16/1**

0006 9 10 **Patricks Lodge**[45] 5201 3-8-7 **46** oh1 AndrewElliott 5 —
(Mrs R A Carr) *chsd ldrs: sn pushed along: lost pl 6f out: bhd fnl 3f: t.o* **40/1**

2m 1.06s (-0.64) **Going Correction** -0.10s/f (Stan) 9 Ran SP% **112.3**
Speed ratings (Par 99): **98,97,94,93,92 88,88,63,54**
CSF £25.37 CT £95.58 TOTE £6.00: £1.20, £1.90, £1.80; EX 47.10.
Owner Dark Horse Racing Partnership Five **Bred** Lynn Lodge Stud **Trained** Cropthorne, Worcs

FOCUS
A very weak handicap in which solid recent placed winning form was all but absent. The pace looked fair for the grade.
Franki J Official explanation: jockey said filly hung badly right-handed throughout

6575 EUROPEAN BREEDERS' FUND MEDIAN AUCTION MAIDEN STKS 5f 216y(P)

6:00 (6:02) (Class 5) 2-Y-O £2,978 (£886; £442; £221) Stalls Low

Form RPR

0640 1 **Reachtothestars (USA)**[13] 6220 2-9-3 67 (t) PhillipMakin 3 73
(M Dods) *mde all: rdn over 1f out: styd on* **10/1**

34 2 1 ¼ **Apollo D'Negro (IRE)**[15] 6146 2-9-3 0 LukeMorris 8 69
(C G Cox) *s.i.s: sn drvn along in rr: hdwy over 1f out: r.o u.p to go 2nd nr fin: nt trble wnr* **5/2**[2]

426 3 nk **Cristaliyev**[31] 5657 2-9-3 72 StephenCraine 4 68
(J R Boyle) *a.p: rdn over 2f out: chsd wnr over 1f out: styd on: lost 2nd nr fin* **8/1**

4 shd **Missile Command (IRE)** 2-9-3 0 LiamJones 6 68
(W J Haggas) *chsd ldrs: rdn over 1f out: styd on* **11/8**[1]

05 5 1 ¾ **Melbury**[15] 6161 2-8-12 0 KirstyMilczarek 9 58
(P Howling) *sn outpcd: r.o fr over 1f out: nrst fin* **40/1**

0 6 2 ¾ **Escala**[18] 6058 2-8-12 0 MarcHalford 2 49
(M D Squance) *s.i.s: sn pushed along in rr: styd on appr fnl f: nvr nrr* **100/1**

0662 7 1 ¾ **Vetvey (IRE)**[9] 6308 2-9-3 66 AndrewElliott 10 49
(M Johnston) *chsd wnr tl rdn over 1f out: wknd fnl f* **9/2**[3]

8 2 ¼ **Boushra** 2-8-12 0 PatDobbs 5 37
(S Kirk) *s.s: a in rr* **50/1**

0660 9 7 **Suave Character**[11] 6271 2-9-3 46 J-PGuillambert 7 21
(M Blanshard) *prom: rdn over 3f out: wknd over 2f out* **100/1**

1m 15.14s (0.14) **Going Correction** -0.10s/f (Stan) 9 Ran SP% **115.4**
Speed ratings (Par 95): **95,93,92,92,90 86,84,81,72**
CSF £35.27 TOTE £6.90: £2.10, £3.50, £1.40; EX 37.00.
Owner Andrew Tinkler **Bred** Haymarket Farm **Trained** Denton, Co Durham

FOCUS
No more than a fair maiden and a bunch finish suggests the form is just ordinary. The pace wasn't strong and the winner was able to make all.

NOTEBOOK
Reachtothestars(USA) ◆ didn't look good enough on form he'd shown on turf, but a first-time tongue tie as well as the switch to all-weather (pedigree suggested it would suit), and possibly front running tactics too, brought about plenty of improvement. He looks to have quite a lot of scope, and might be the sort that does well in nurseries if kept on the go on this surface this winter. (op 14-1 tchd 16-1 and 8-1)
Apollo D'Negro(IRE) had probably come across weakish maidens for the track when placed at Ascot and Newbury previously, and he looked nothing out of the ordinary here, for all he didn't help his chance with a sluggish start, never nearer than at the finish after taking time to get to grips with the surface. His pedigree doesn't suggest he wants a step up to 7f. (op 7-2 tchd 9-4)
Cristaliyev looked the biggest danger to the eventual winner turning in but didn't see his race out as strongly as looked likely and, unless 5f on turf suits him better than 6f on all-weather, looks a touch flattered by his official rating of 72. (op 6-1)
Missile Command(IRE), related to a smart Group 3 7f winner, was all the rage in the betting hailing from a yard that have a good strike rate with 2-y-os here, but he held every chance for much of the straight with the penny only really dropping close home. Presumably well regarded, he should step up on this form next time. (op 6-5 tchd 11-10 and 7-4, 15-8 in a place)
Melbury ◆ needed this for a mark and shaped nicely, staying on well from a poor position. Being out of a mare that won at up to 1m4f, she will be of more interest when stepped up in trip in a low-grade nursery, particularly if there is a market move for her.
Vetvey(IRE) was disappointing considering his fair C&D effort on his most recent start and looks no more than modest on balance. (tchd 5-1)
Boushra has just an ordinary pedigree but shaped better than the result suggests, losing many lengths with a slow start but starting to make some progress when hampered on the home turn. Her yard doesn't get many first-time-out juvenile winners, and she seems likely to do better in time.

6576 CE PROPERTY SERVICES GROUP (S) STKS 5f 20y(P)

6:30 (6:31) (Class 6) 2-Y-O £1,706 (£503; £252) Stalls Low

Form RPR

1440 1 **Second Encore**[22] 5921 2-8-11 68 LiamKeniry 6 68
(J S Moore) *sn chsng ldr: led over 1f out: sn rdn: styd on* **7/1**

3330 2 nk **Madam Markievicz (IRE)**[15] 6139 2-8-11 67 (p) PhillipMakin 4 67
(M Dods) *chsd ldrs: rdn over 1f out: edgd lft: r.o* **9/2**[3]

634 3 1 ½ **Nellie Ellis (IRE)**[19] 6035 2-8-8 63 AmyRyan(3) 3 62
(K A Ryan) *hld up in tch: rdn over 1f out: r.o* **4/1**[2]

3033 4 nse **Saltergate**[30] 5683 2-8-11 66 (p) KirstyMilczarek 9 61
(N Tinkler) *mid-div: hdwy over 1f out: r.o* **20/1**

0014 5 ½ **Two Feet Of Snow (IRE)**[31] 5667 2-8-8 70 KellyHarrison(3) 2 60
(I W McInnes) *sn outpcd: hdwy and nt clr run fr over 1f out tl swtchd rt ins fnl f: r.o wl: nt rch ldrs* **5/1**

530 6 nk **Mini Bon Bon**[19] 6035 2-8-6 53 (v) AdamBeschizza(5) 7 58
(A Bailey) *s.i.s: in rr: r.o ins fnl f: nrst fin* **33/1**

4030 7 nse **Venus Empress**[17] 6072 2-8-6 53 AndrewElliott 11 53
(E S McMahon) *hld up: hdwy 1/2-way: rdn over 1f out: hung lft: r.o* **40/1**

2030 8 hd **Bonjour Bongee**[4] 6435 2-8-11 59 (b) JamesDoyle 1 58
(A J McCabe) *hld up: hdwy over 1f out: r.o* **16/1**

0110 9 1 **Tedious**[36] 5472 2-8-11 75 RichardHughes 12 54
(S Kirk) *led: hdd over 1f out: no ex ins fnl f* **5/2**[1]

0060 10 3 ½ **Molly Mylenis**[35] 5525 2-8-11 65 RichardMullen 13 41
(P D Evans) *prom: rdn 1/2-way: hung lft over 1f out: wknd fnl f* **66/1**

504 11 3 ¼ **Majestic Ridge (IRE)**[7] 6369 2-8-11 57 LukeMorris 5 30
(R A Harris) *chsd ldrs: rdn over 2f out: wknd over 1f out* **25/1**

00 12 19 **Soviet Suspect (IRE)**[25] 5836 2-8-4 0 LauraPike(7) 8 —
(Miss Amy Weaver) *free to post: dwlt: outpcd* **100/1**

62.34 secs (0.04) **Going Correction** -0.10s/f (Stan) 12 Ran SP% **118.3**
Speed ratings (Par 93): **95,94,92,92,91 90,90,90,88,83 77,47**
Tote Swingers: 1&2 £6.90, 1&3 £7.70, 2&3 £4.80 CSF £36.22 TOTE £10.30: £3.30, £1.10, £1.20; EX 42.40.There was no bid for the winner. Nellie Ellis was claimed by Mr C. J. Harper for £6,000.
Owner G V March **Bred** D A Yardy **Trained** Upper Lambourn, Berks
■ Stewards' Enquiry : Phillip Makin three-day ban: weighed in 2lb heavy (Oct 17-19)

FOCUS
A better-than-usual seller for the track, with many of the runners having form at a higher level. The result looked the right one on the day.

NOTEBOOK
Second Encore has already won in higher grade than this before and, back at 5f after a modest run in a 6f claimer here last time, did just enough for all the winning margin was being cut down towards the finish. This is probably her level nowadays. (tchd 6-1 and 15-2)
Madam Markievicz(IRE) handled the surface well on her all weather debut and, despite getting worked up beforehand, had every chance. She's been running in nurseries but is more than good enough to win another seller if tried again at this level. (op 11-2 tchd 6-1)
Nellie Ellis(IRE) continued her run of decent efforts and looks a good guide to the level of the form. (op 7-2)
Saltergate looked more tractable back in cheekpieces after his woeful effort visored last time, but didn't seem to have any excuses and is another for whom this level is probably about right nowadays. (tchd 16-1 and 25-1)
Two Feet Of Snow(IRE) looked a shade unfortunate not to have finished closer, soon poorly placed after a bit of bumping at the start and then not getting a clear run towards the finish. That said, it remains to be seen if she retains all of her ability since leaving Richard Hannon. (op 15-2 tchd 8-1)
Mini Bon Bon has a patchy record, but this was one of her better efforts albeit she was never dangerous. (op 40-1)
Venus Empress seemed to step up on her recent form, but her overall record suggests she wouldn't be sure to build on it next time. (op 33-1)
Bonjour Bongee ran about as well as could have been expected at the weights. (op 12-1)
Tedious was bounced out quickly to take up the running but never got clear and was a sitting duck from early in the straight. She doesn't possess much scope, and it's likely the best has already been seen of her. (op 11-4)

6577 GRAHAM & JANETTE ANNIVERSARY CLAIMING STKS 7f 32y(P)

7:00 (7:02) (Class 5) 3-Y-O+ £2,388 (£705; £352) Stalls High

Form RPR

3004 1 **Samarinda (USA)**[18] 6054 7-9-0 82 (p) MickyFenton 12 80
(Mrs P Sly) *mde all: rdn over 1f out: styd on gamely* **9/1**

0606 2 nk **Imprimis Tagula (IRE)**[30] 5703 6-9-5 86 (v) AdamBeschizza(5) 8 89
(A Bailey) *a.p: chsd wnr 5f out: rdn over 1f out: ev ch ins fnl f: styd on* **14/1**

0623 3 ½ **Catherines Call (IRE)**[14] 6207 3-8-9 73 LukeMorris 11 74+
(D Donovan) *hld up: hdwy over 1f out: hrd rdn ins fnl f: r.o* **9/1**

450 4 1 **Flowing Cape (IRE)**[9] 6312 5-9-2 85 RichardHughes 2 77
(R Hollinshead) *hld up in tch: rdn over 2f out: styd on same pce ins fnl f* **7/4**[1]

2411 5 2 **Sabatini (IRE)**[15] 6164 3-8-9 72 ChrisCatlin 6 66
(J Pearce) *sn prom: rdn over 2f out: no ex fnl f* **9/2**[3]

0065 6 1 ½ **Dubai Dynamo**[9] 6312 5-9-8 88 (b) AndrewElliott 1 74
(Mrs R A Carr) *hld up: nt clr run over 2f out: styd on fnl f: nvr nrr* **7/2**[2]

0000 7 1 ¼ **Stonecrabstomorrow (IRE)**[22] 5926 7-8-6 48 ow1 MarkCoumbe(5) 4 59
(D Bourton) *prom: rdn over 1f out: no ex ins fnl f* **100/1**

6001 8 ¾ **Southandwest (IRE)**[28] 5768 6-8-8 72 JimmyQuinn 5 54
(A M Hales) *s.i.s: hld up: a in rr* **10/1**

0050 9 7 **All You Need (IRE)**[53] 4936 6-8-5 46 (p) KellyHarrison(3) 10 35
(R Hollinshead) *hld up: rdn over 2f out: n.d* **100/1**

0460 10 6 **Superstitious Me (IRE)**[23] 5877 4-7-12 46 (b[1]) DeclanCannon(5) 7 14
(B Palling) *chsd wnr 2f: remained handy tl rdn and wknd 2f out* **50/1**

1m 27.87s (-1.73) **Going Correction** -0.10s/f (Stan)
WFA 3 from 4yo+ 2lb 10 Ran SP% **116.5**
Speed ratings (Par 103): **105,104,104,102,100 98,97,96,88,81**
Tote Swingers: 1&2 £13.80, 1&3 £14.70, 2&3 £23.70 CSF £125.12 TOTE £11.50: £3.90, £7.00, £5.60; EX 100.90.
Owner D Bayliss, T Davies, G Libson & P Sly **Bred** Gainsborough Farm Llc **Trained** Thorney, Cambs

FOCUS
A mixture of abilities as always in a claimer but the standard among the principals was good for all that the form itself promises to be muddling on account of an uneven gallop.

6578 CLEANEVENT H'CAP 1m 4f 50y(P)

7:30 (7:35) (Class 5) (0-70,70) 3-Y-O+ £2,388 (£705; £352) Stalls Low

Form RPR

2432 1 **Egmarey (IRE)**[15] 6166 3-9-2 **67** (b) RichardMullen 4 74
(D R Lanigan) *unruly in the stalls: s.i.s: hld up: hdwy over 3f out: sn rdn: led over 1f out: styd on u.p* **7/2**[1]

4615 2 shd **Mons Calpe (IRE)**[25] 5828 4-9-12 **70** (b) ChrisCatlin 5 77
(P F I Cole) *pushed along early: led over 10f out: rdn and hdd over 1f out: hung lft ins fnl f: styd on* **8/1**[3]

5400 3 1 ¼ **Faith Jicaro (IRE)**[15] 6165 3-8-12 **63** LukeMorris 10 68
(N J Vaughan) *hld up: hdwy over 4f out: rdn over 2f out: carried lft ins fnl f: styd on* **16/1**

03-5 **4** *hd* **Moobeyn**[16] 6122 3-9-4 **69**......(b) PatDobbs 3 74
(M P Tregoning) *a.p: chsd ldr over 2f out: rdn over 1f out: hung lft: styd on* **7/2**[1]

0523 **5** *nk* **Becuille (IRE)**[7] 6372 5-9-11 **69**......(b) RichardHughes 11 73
(B J Meehan) *hld up: hdwy u.p over 2f out: styd on wl: nt rch ldrs* **4/1**[2]

5052 **6** *3 ¾* **Bentley**[7] 6375 6-8-7 **58**...... NeilFarley[(7)] 7 56
(B P J Baugh) *chsd ldrs: rdn over 3f out: styd on same pce appr fnl f* **16/1**

-031 **7** *¾* **Venir Rouge**[28] 1207 6-9-9 **67**...... PatCosgrave 6 64
(Matthew Salaman) *hld up: rdn over 2f out: nvr on terms* **11/1**

4006 **8** *3 ½* **Musical Mark**[10] 6290 3-9-0 **65**...... MickyFenton 9 56
(Mrs P Sly) *s.i.s: a in rr* **20/1**

0/60 **9** *3 ¼* **Zabeel Palace**[16] 6132 8-9-4 **62**...... LiamKeniry 2 48
(B J Curley) *s.i.s: hld up: hdwy 3f out: wknd wl over 1f out* **16/1**

0400 **10** *13* **Bagutta Sun**[8] 6328 4-9-8 **66**...... KirstyMilczarek 1 31
(B D Leavy) *hld up: a in rr* **33/1**

0035 **11** *1* **Two Oclock John**[31] 5663 4-9-2 **60**......(b[1]) LiamJones 12 24
(T T Clement) *prom: chsd ldr over 7f out to over 2f out: sn wknd* **10/1**

010/ **12** *66* **Novestar (IRE)**[787] 4732 5-9-8 **66**...... KevinGhunowa 8 —
(G J Smith) *led: hdd over 10f out: chsd ldr to over 7f out: wknd over 4f out: t.o* **50/1**

2m 39.16s (-1.94) **Going Correction** -0.10s/f (Stan)
WFA 3 from 4yo+ 7lb 12 Ran SP% **120.3**
Speed ratings (Par 103): **102,101,101,100,100 98,97,95,93,84 83,39**
Tote Swingers: 1&2 £3.20, 1&3 £14.10, 2&3 £26.00 CSF £31.89 CT £405.10 TOTE £4.40: £1.90, £1.40, £6.70; EX 38.40.
Owner Saif Ali & Saeed H Altayer **Bred** D G Hardisty Bloodstock **Trained** Newmarket, Suffolk
■ Stewards' Enquiry : Pat Dobbs two-day ban: careless riding (Oct 17-18)

FOCUS
Just an ordinary race for the grade and not form to be getting carried away with despite the market leaders largely coming to the fore. The field was soon strung out despite the pace not looking strong.
Novestar(IRE) Official explanation: jockey said gelding had no more to give

6579 CE RISK, SAFETY & SECURITY H'CAP (DIV II) 1m 1f 103y(P)
8:00 (8:01) (Class 6) (0-55,55) 3-Y-O £1,364 (£403; £201) Stalls Low

Form RPR
6432 **1** **Miss Whippy**[14] 6183 3-8-10 **49**...... KirstyMilczarek 4 54
(P Howling) *prom: pushed along over 2f out: rdn and swished tail thrght the latter stages: r.o to ld wl ins fnl f* **9/2**[1]

1550 **2** *nk* **Tallawalla (IRE)**[21] 5962 3-9-0 **53**...... RichardHughes 7 57
(M R Channon) *hld up: hdwy on outer over 2f out: rdn over 1f out: r.o* **9/2**[1]

3205 **3** *nse* **Rigid**[22] 5926 3-8-11 **50**...... JamesDoyle 11 54
(A W Carroll) *a.p: chsd ldr over 2f out: rdn to ld over 1f out: edgd rt: hdd wl ins fnl f* **5/1**[2]

5024 **4** *nk* **Lady Brickhouse**[18] 6062 3-8-9 **48**...... SaleemGolam 9 52
(M D Squance) *chsd ldrs: rdn over 1f out: r.o* **12/1**

5001 **5** *1 ¾* **Scooby Dee**[12] 6255 3-8-7 **49**...... KellyHarrison[(3)] 2 49
(R M Whitaker) *hld up: hdwy over 1f out: r.o: nt rch ldrs* **7/1**

0060 **6** *nse* **Carnival Time (IRE)**[19] 6021 3-8-8 **47**......(p) LukeMorris 3 47
(C G Cox) *mid-div: hdwy over 5f out: rdn over 1f out: r.o* **6/1**[3]

-066 **7** *¾* **Royal Box**[21] 5959 3-9-2 **55**......(p) PatDobbs 6 53
(D Burchell) *hld up: rdn and hdd over 1f out: no ex ins fnl f* **22/1**

005 **8** *3 ¼* **Clearly Cryptonite (USA)**[38] 5419 3-8-6 **50**...... AdamBeschizza[(5)] 5 41
(T J Pitt) *s.i.s: hld up: hdwy over 2f out: shkn up and edgd lft over 1f out: nvr nr to chal* **16/1**

4530 **9** *21* **Coolella (IRE)**[22] 5926 3-8-13 **52**...... AndrewElliott 10 —
(J R Weymes) *chsd ldr tl rdn over 2f out: sn wknd* **8/1**

00-0 **10** *7* **Princess Neenee (IRE)**[69] 4408 3-8-7 **46** oh1...... ChrisCatlin 1 —
(Paul Green) *a in rr: t.o* **33/1**

0060 **11** *27* **Zamid (FR)**[45] 5201 3-8-7 **46** oh1......(p) JimmyQuinn 8 —
(R A Fahey) *hld up in tch: lost pl over 4f out: wknd over 2f out: t.o* **20/1**

2m 2.01s (0.31) **Going Correction** -0.10s/f (Stan) 11 Ran SP% **116.6**
Speed ratings (Par 99): **94,93,93,93,91 91,91,88,69,63 39**
Tote Swingers: 1&2 £3.30, 1&3 £2.80, 2&3 £3.80 CSF £23.51 CT £105.36 TOTE £3.20: £1.50, £1.10, £5.60; EX 16.20.
Owner N George **Bred** Rabbah Bloodstock Limited **Trained** Newmarket, Suffolk
■ Stewards' Enquiry : Richard Hughes one-day ban: used whip with excessive frequency (Oct 17)

FOCUS
A very weak handicap in which it was hard beforehand to argue a solid case for any of the runners. The pace was just a fair one, and the field was well bunched on the home turn.
Zamid(FR) Official explanation: jockey said filly lost its action

6580 CLEANWASTESOLUTIONS H'CAP (DIV I) 1m 141y(P)
8:30 (8:30) (Class 5) (0-75,81) 3-Y-O+ £2,047 (£604; £302) Stalls Low

Form RPR
0100 **1** **Spanish Island (USA)**[21] 5964 3-9-6 **75**...... GeorgeBaker 1 83
(M A Magnusson) *mde all: rdn over 1f out: hung lft ins fnl f: styd on gamely* **12/1**

0161 **2** *½* **Aussie Blue (IRE)**[16] 6116 6-9-0 **68**...... KellyHarrison[(3)] 10 75
(R M Whitaker) *chsd wnr: rdn and ev ch fr over 1f out: hung lft ins fnl f: styd on* **8/1**

0500 **3** *nk* **Copper Penny**[11] 6266 3-9-4 **73**...... RichardMullen 9 79
(D R Lanigan) *a.p: rdn over 2f out: swtchd lft ins fnl f: styd on* **14/1**

3631 **4** *2* **Snow Magic (IRE)**[14] 6212 3-9-2 **71**...... PatCosgrave 8 76+
(J R Fanshawe) *hld up: hdwy over 1f out: sn rdn: styng on whn n.m.r ins fnl f: bdly hmpd towards fin* **2/1**[1]

6240 **5** *3* **Dirakh Shan**[19] 6023 3-8-11 **66**...... J-PGuillambert 2 61
(L M Cumani) *chsd ldrs: rdn over 2f out: wknd fnl f* **14/1**

2053 **6** *1 ¾* **Streets Of War (USA)**[18] 6056 3-9-4 **73**...... RichardHughes 3 64
(P W Chapple-Hyam) *hld up in tch: rdn over 2f out: wknd over 1f out* **3/1**[2]

3321 **7** *nk* **Harting Hill**[23] 5897 5-9-1 **66**...... PatDobbs 6 56
(M P Tregoning) *hld up in tch: rdn over 2f out: wknd over 1f out* **9/2**[3]

0040 **8** *9* **Toga Tiger (IRE)**[31] 5662 3-8-13 **68**...... TonyCulhane 5 37
(P T Midgley) *hld up: a in rr: lost tch fr over 2f out* **25/1**

1m 49.58s (-0.92) **Going Correction** -0.10s/f (Stan)
WFA 3 from 5yo+ 4lb 8 Ran SP% **112.5**
Speed ratings (Par 103): **100,99,99,97,94 93,93,85**
Tote Swingers: 1&2 £30.60, 1&3 £7.20, 2&3 £10.10 CSF £99.32 CT £1362.29 TOTE £11.40: £5.10, £5.30, £6.00; EX 112.60.
Owner Eastwind Racing Ltd And Martha Trussell **Bred** E T Buckley, S Varney & A O'Donnell **Trained** Upper Lambourn, Berks
■ Stewards' Enquiry : Richard Mullen seven-day ban: careless riding (Oct 16-22)
George Baker one-day ban: used whip down shoulder in the forehand (Oct 17)

FOCUS
What looked a very intriguing contest was impacted severely by the withdrawal beforehand of the two most interesting runners, but it still featured three last-time out winners. The pace was no more than fair, and another winner on the night made all.
Streets Of War(USA) Official explanation: jockey said colt hung throughout

6581 CLEANWASTESOLUTIONS H'CAP (DIV II) 1m 141y(P)
9:00 (9:00) (Class 5) (0-75,74) 3-Y-O+ £2,047 (£604; £302) Stalls Low

Form RPR
1655 **1** **Aviso (GER)**[10] 6289 6-9-4 **68**...... RichardHughes 9 76
(B J Curley) *chsd ldr: rdn over 1f out: styd on u.p to ld nr fin* **3/1**[1]

330 **2** *nk* **Slikback Jack (IRE)**[16] 6107 3-9-3 **71**...... PatCosgrave 8 78+
(J A Glover) *hld up: plld hrd: hdwy over 1f out: rdn and hung lft ins fnl f: r.o* **13/2**

1140 **3** *nk* **One Scoop Or Two**[7] 6367 4-9-7 **74**...... RussKennemore[(3)] 2 80
(R Hollinshead) *led: rdn over 1f out: hdd nr fin* **7/1**

0414 **4** *2 ¾* **Chief Red Cloud (USA)**[16] 6112 4-9-4 **71**...... MichaelO'Connell[(3)] 5 71
(Mrs K Burke) *hld up: hmpd over 7f out: hdwy over 2f out: rdn over 1f out: styd on same pce ins fnl f* **7/2**[2]

0333 **5** *1 ¼* **Just Jimmy (IRE)**[7] 6370 5-8-7 **62**...... AdamBeschizza[(5)] 6 59
(P D Evans) *hld up: hdwy over 1f out: r.o: nt trble ldrs* **5/1**[3]

4063 **6** *nk* **Final Drive (IRE)**[18] 6061 4-9-1 **65**...... StevieDonohoe 10 61
(J Ryan) *s.s: hld up: pushed along over 3f out: r.o ins fnl f: nrst fin* **14/1**

3050 **7** *hd* **Bold Cross (IRE)**[4] 6444 7-9-5 **69**...... PaulFitzsimons 1 65
(E G Bevan) *chsd ldrs: rdn over 2f out: no ex fnl f* **9/1**

5-05 **8** *2* **The Grey One (IRE)**[26] 1508 7-8-11 **61**......(p) LiamKeniry 4 52
(J M Bradley) *mid-div: rdn over 2f out: wknd fnl f* **25/1**

4036 **9** *¾* **Fonterutoli (IRE)**[17] 6093 3-9-5 **73**...... ChrisCatlin 3 63
(M Botti) *chsd ldrs: rdn over 2f out: wknd fnl f* **12/1**

000- **10** *36* **April Fool**[388] 5780 6-9-3 **67**......(v) LukeMorris 7 —
(R A Harris) *chsd ldrs tl rdn and wknd over 2f out: t.o* **33/1**

1m 49.17s (-1.33) **Going Correction** -0.10s/f (Stan)
WFA 3 from 4yo+ 4lb 10 Ran SP% **120.9**
Speed ratings (Par 103): **101,100,100,98,96 96,96,94,94,62**
Tote Swingers: 1&2 £6.90, 1&3 £7.70, 2&3 £4.80 CSF £23.96 CT £133.35 TOTE £4.30: £1.10, £2.00, £1.70; EX 27.00 Place 6: £193.40 Place 5: £112.32..
Owner Curley Leisure **Bred** Gestut Schlenderhan **Trained** Newmarket, Suffolk
■ Stewards' Enquiry : Richard Hughes six-day ban: careless riding (Oct 16, 18-22)

FOCUS
A run-of-the mill handicap for the grade, run at just a fair pace with those at the head of affairs tending to be favoured again.
T/Plt: £66.40 to a £1 stake. Pool of £54,492 - 599.06 winning tickets. T/Qpdt: £18.10 to a £1 stake. Pool of £8,150 - 331.40 winning tickets. CR

2776 BELMONT PARK (L-H)
Saturday, October 2

OFFICIAL GOING: Dirt: fast; turf: yielding

6582a VOSBURGH STKS (GRADE 1) (3YO+) (DIRT) 6f (D)
8:23 (8:24) 3-Y-O+
£129,629 (£43,209; £21,604; £10,802; £6,481; £1,080)

RPR
1 **Girolamo (USA)**[28] 5779 4-8-12 0...... AGarcia 2 122+
(Saeed Bin Suroor) *smartly away but sltly hmpd in opening f and shuffled bk to 3rd: pressed ldr after 2f and jnd ldr 3f out: led st: r.o strly fnl f for clr-cut success* **21/10**[1]

2 *2 ½* **Riley Tucker (USA)**[20] 5-8-12 0......(b) RADominguez 8 113
(Steven Asmussen, U.S.A) *racd in 4th: clsd up on outside3f out to take 3rd in virtual line of three turning for home (2f out): wnt 2nd 1 1/2f out and sn on wnr's quarters: unable qck fnl f* **73/10**

3 *½* **Wildcat Brief (USA)**[27] 4-8-12 0...... GKGomez 9 112
(Ben Perkins Jr, U.S.A) *outpcd and last (8l adrift of nrest rival): hdwy 2 1/2f out and r.o along rail fnl bnd: 8th 1 1/2f out: styd on wl u.p: nrest at fin* **43/5**

4 *3* **Temecula Creek (USA)**[27] 6-8-12 0......(b) CVelasquez 5 103
(Rudy Rodriguez, U.S.A) *racd in midfield trying to keep tabs on ldng gp: unable qck fnl f and styd on at same pce* **11/1**

5 *1 ¼* **Driven By Success (USA)**[182] 5-8-12 0...... JRVelazquez 1 99
(Todd Pletcher, U.S.A) *bhd: rdn 2 1/2f out: r.o through btn horses fnl 300yds: nvr in contention* **71/20**[2]

6 *2 ¼* **Latigo Shore (USA)**[35] 3-8-10 0...... JJCastellano 4 91
(Nicholas Zito, U.S.A) *struggled to go the pce: a in rr* **236/10**

7 *½* **Golden Spikes (USA)**[84] 5-8-12 0......(b) JLezcano 3 91
(Richard Dutrow Jr, U.S.A) *a bhd and n.d* **71/1**

8 *hd* **Wall Street Wonder (USA)**[27] 4-8-12 0......(b) CHill 7 90
(John Terranova II, U.S.A) *broke wl and sn led: pressed after 2f: jnd 3f out: hdd st and wknd appr fnl f* **116/10**

9 *nse* **Snapshot (USA)**[84] 4-8-12 0......(b) KDesormeaux 6 90
(William Mott, U.S.A) *a.p: cl 4th (1l off the leder) turning for home (2f out): sn rdn and drifted rt: wknd fnl 300yds* **73/20**[3]

69.41 secs (0.21)
WFA 3 from 4yo+ 1lb 9 Ran SP% **119.9**
PARI-MUTUEL (all including $2 stakes): WIN 6.20; PLACE (1-2) 4.30, 6.90; SHOW (1-2-3) 3.10, 4.20, 4.80; SF 49.80.
Owner Godolphin Racing LLC **Bred** B P Walden, P Steinberg & Winstar Farm **Trained** Newmarket, Suffolk

NOTEBOOK
Girolamo(USA), fifth in the Forego off a ten-month break last time, his first start since blowing out in last year's Classic, proved suited by this first try over 6f and provided Godolphin with their first US Graded stakes winner of the year. Always handy, he had to battle in the straight but responded well to strong pressure to draw clear near line, ultimately winning a shade comfortably. The impression is he'll improve again off this and he looks a major player for the Breeders' Cup Sprint.

6586a JOCKEY CLUB GOLD CUP INVITATIONAL STKS (GRADE 1) (3YO+) (DIRT) 1m 2f (D)
10:48 (10:49) 3-Y-O+
£277,777 (£92,592; £46,296; £23,148; £13,888; £3,086)

RPR
1 **Haynesfield (USA)**[56] 4855 4-9-0 0...... RADominguez 4 125+
(Steven Asmussen, U.S.A) *sn led: 4l clr 3f out: grad plld further away: unchal and coasted home* **15/2**

2 *4* **Blame (USA)**[56] 4855 4-9-0 0...... GKGomez 2 118+
(Albert M Stall Jr, U.S.A) *broke wl but qckly settled in 4th: hdwy 2 1/2f out to chse ldr: r.o but no imp and nvr on terms despite cutting the defecit* **4/5**[1]

3 2 **Fly Down (USA)**[35] 5544 3-8-10 0 .... JLezcano 1 115+
(Nicholas Zito, U.S.A) *hld up: sme hdwy 2 1/2f out: kpt on at one pce st: nvr threatened* **31/10**[2]

4 6 **Hold Me Back (USA)**[34] 5577 4-9-0 0 .... RMaragh 5 103+
(William Mott, U.S.A) *hld up: nvr plcd to chal* **34/1**

5 4½ **Rail Trip (USA)**[83] 5-9-0 0 .... CVelasquez 6 95+
(Richard Dutrow Jr, U.S.A) *trckd ldr: rdn and no imp fr 2 1/2f out: no imp* **7/2**[3]

6 5½ **Tranquil Manner (USA)**[28] 5780 4-9-0 0 .... AGarcia 3 85+
(Kiaran McLaughlin, U.S.A) *hld up in last adrift of the others: remained bhd: nvr a factor* **31/1**

2m 2.48s (1.86)
WFA 3 from 4yo+ 5lb **6** Ran SP% **119.9**
PARI-MUTUEL (all including $2 stakes): WIN 17.00; PLACE (1-2) 5.10, 2.50; SHOW (1-2-3) 3.00, 2.10, 2.20; SF 37.20.
Owner Turtle Bird Stable **Bred** Barry Weisbord & Margaret Santulli **Trained** USA

6588 - (Foreign Racing) - See Raceform Interactive

6218 LONGCHAMP (R-H)
Saturday, October 2

OFFICIAL GOING: Turf: very soft

6589a PRIX HORSE RACING ABOARD (CLAIMER) (2YO) (TURF) 1m
1:00 (12:00) 2-Y-0 **£11,061** (£4,424; £3,318; £2,212; £1,106)

RPR

1 **Creyente (IRE)**[29] 2-8-9 0 .... TheoBachelot(6) 4 92
(C Delcher-Sanchez, Spain) **12/1**

2 8 **Julie's Love** 2-8-13 0 .... MaximeGuyon 10 73
(Manfred Hofer, Germany) **7/2**[1]

3 2½ **Cat Melody (FR)**[15] 2-8-8 0 ....(b[1]) AurelienLemaitre(3) 5 65
(B Dutruel, France) **30/1**

4 snk **Cresta Run (GER)** 2-9-2 0 .... GeraldMosse 3 70
(C Von Der Recke, Germany) **44/5**[3]

5 1½ **Honneur Supreme (FR)**[26] 5826 2-8-13 0 .... MorganDelalande(3) 15 66
(Y Barberot, France) **27/1**

6 ½ **The Nought Man (FR)**[20] 6001 2-9-5 0 .... StephanePasquier 9 68
(R A Fahey) *racd midfield fr break: u.p bef st: picked up 1 1/2f out on outside: styd on wl fnl f* **5/1**[2]

7 1 **Perennite (FR)**[19] 2-8-13 0 .... FlavienPrat 6 60
(P Bary, France) **14/1**

8 ½ **La Joie De Vivre (USA)**[15] 2-8-4 0 .... AlexisAchard(7) 11 57
(R Gibson, France) **16/1**

9 3 **Platine Rose (FR)**[64] 2-8-7 0 .... PaulineProd'homme(6) 7 52
(D Prod'Homme, France) **21/1**

10 5 **Urban Kiss (FR)**[54] 2-8-13 0 .... SylvainRuis 14 41
(G Botti, Italy) **22/1**

0 **Muchtar (FR)**[11] 2-9-2 0 ....(p) IoritzMendizabal 8 —
(J-L Pelletan, France) **46/1**

0 **Mister Segway (IRE)**[73] 4274 2-8-8 0 .... EddyHardouin(8) 2 —
(Robert Collet, France) **30/1**

0 **Nashi (FR)**[26] 5826 2-9-5 0 .... JulienAuge 13 —
(E J O'Neill, France) **10/1**

0 **Dellarte (FR)**[54] 2-9-2 0 ....(p) JohanVictoire 12 —
(L A Urbano-Grajales, France) **13/1**

0 **Pumpkinette (FR)**[28] 2-8-5 0 ....(p) EnzoCorallo(8) 1 —
(C Ferland, France) **10/1**

1m 46.5s (8.10) **15** Ran SP% **115.7**
WIN (incl. 1 euro stake): 12.60. PLACES: 4.10, 2.30, 6.90. DF: 33.60. SF: 90.00.
Owner Celso Mendez-Urena **Bred** Yeguada Milagro **Trained** Spain

NOTEBOOK
The Nought Man(FR), winner of a soft-ground maiden at Newcastle last time out, finished his race off strongly and is clearly not short of stamina.

6590a QATAR PRIX CHAUDENAY (GROUP 2) (3YO) (TURF) 1m 7f
2:40 (12:00) 3-Y-0 **£65,575** (£25,309; £12,079; £8,053; £4,026)

RPR

1 **Celtic Celeb (IRE)**[35] 5543 3-9-2 0 .... ThierryThulliez 3 106
(F Doumen, France) *racd in 3rd: wnt 2nd bef st: tk ld 1 1/2f out: r.o wl whn chal 100yds out: comf* **14/1**

2 1½ **Ivory Land (FR)**[35] 5543 3-9-2 0 .... GeraldMosse 4 104
(A De Royer-Dupre, France) *racd in midfield: qcknd wl 1 1/2f out on wd outside: r.o wl fnl f to take 2nd on line* **12/1**

3 hd **Le Larron (IRE)**[27] 5800 3-9-2 0 .... Christophe-PatriceLemaire 9 104
(A De Royer-Dupre, France) *racd in midfield: qcknd wl 2f out: wnt 2nd 1f out: chal for ld 100yds out: no ex: lost 2nd on line* **10/1**

4 2½ **Goldwaki (GER)**[34] 5575 3-9-2 0 .... OlivierPeslier 7 101
(A Fabre, France) *settled in rr: prog in st: no ex fr over 1f out: styd on fnl f: no threat to ldrs* **6/4**[1]

5 ¾ **Irish Song (FR)**[26] 3-8-13 0 .... IoritzMendizabal 8 97
(A Couetil, France) *prom fr s: rdn early in st: styd on* **66/1**

6 nk **Brigantin (USA)**[27] 5800 3-9-2 0 .... Pierre-CharlesBoudot 1 100
(A Fabre, France) *racd in 3rd on rail: rdn early in st: wnt 4th 1f out: no ex: fdd* **4/1**[2]

7 6 **Permit**[27] 5800 3-9-2 0 ....(b) MaximeGuyon 5 92
(A Fabre, France) *led fr s: stl in front ent st: chal 2f out: surrendered ld 1 1/2f out and qckly fdd fnl f* **10/1**

8 1½ **Caucus**[35] 5517 3-9-2 0 .... StephanePasquier 2 91
(H Morrison) *racd in 2nd: rdn early in st: no ex fr 2f out: fdd* **10/1**

9 nk **Lawspeaker**[21] 5980 3-9-2 0 .... MickaelBarzalona 6 90
(A Fabre, France) *settled towards rr: rdn but no ex in st: wknd* **6/1**[3]

3m 32.4s (212.40) **Going Correction** +1.05s/f (Soft) **9** Ran SP% **117.4**
Speed ratings: **98,97,97,95,95 95,92,91,91**
WIN (incl. 1 euro stake): 22.00. PLACES: 5.30, 4.30, 2.50. DF: 72.20. SF: 187.00.
Owner Henri De Pracomtal **Bred** Horse Breeding Corporation **Trained** Bouce, France

FOCUS
Few of these were comfortable on the testing ground and, as such, the form is weak by Group 2 standards, with Irish Song, who had looked exposed as an ordinary handicapper, finishing only around 5l away in fifth. There was competition for the lead, with Permit and Caucus taking turns up front, but they seemed to go just an even gallop.

NOTEBOOK
Celtic Celeb(IRE) is not bred for staying trips - dam best at around 1m, and likewise his siblings - but he proved himself a strong stayer, and clearly relished the ground. While it's hard to rate him particularly highly, there was much to like about this performance, with him showing a really willing attitude after coming under pressure early in the straight, and maybe he could be the next Kasbah Bliss, a terrific servant in top middle-distance/staying events over the years for the same owner and trainer. The winner could now go for either the Prix Royal-Oak, or the Prix du Conseil de Paris.
Ivory Land(FR) was just under 1l ahead of Celtic Celeb over 1m4f at Clairefontaine on his previous start, but was 5lb worse off this time. He proved suited by this increase in distance, but raced further back than the winner and failed to make a telling impression, only getting second on the line. A more positive ride would probably have helped.
Le Larron(IRE) tracked the winner through early in the straight, with his jockey looking quietly confident, but his head was ever so slightly high under pressure and he didn't totally convince that he went through with his effort. Still, he reversed recent C&D placings with Brigantin, coping with the easier going better than that rival.
Goldwaki(GER), held up well off the pace, was under pressure sooner than most and made only limited progress. This was some way below his best form, a disappointing effort even if he ideally wants a quicker surface.
Brigantin(USA) travelled well but found little when going for a run against the far rail in the straight. He thrashed the third over C&D on his previous start, but that was on ground described as good and clearly these much softer conditions did not suit.
Caucus, upped to his furthest trip to date, was a bit keen and found little for pressure.

6591a NYSE EURONEXT PRIX DE ROYALLIEU (GROUP 2) (3YO+ FILLIES & MARES) (TURF) 1m 4f 110y
3:15 (12:00) 3-Y-0+ **£65,575** (£25,309; £12,079; £8,053; £4,026)

RPR

1 **Maria Royal (IRE)**[51] 5138 3-8-7 0 .... GeraldMosse 1 107
(A De Royer-Dupre, France) *settled in rr: proged early in st: qcknd wl on ins 1f out: ct ldr 50yds out* **25/1**

2 nk **High Heeled (IRE)**[20] 6013 4-9-1 0 .... OlivierPeslier 2 107
(J H M Gosden) *racd in 2nd: qcknd to ld 1 1/2f out: r.o wl: ct fnl 50yds* **5/1**[3]

3 1 **Sarah Lynx (IRE)**[20] 6013 3-8-7 0 .... IoritzMendizabal 4 106
(J E Hammond, France) *prom fr s: rdn and qcknd wl 1 1/2f out: chal for ld 1f out: r.o wl: fin 4th: plcd 3rd* **13/2**

4 hd **Peinture Rare (IRE)**[20] 6013 4-9-7 0 .... AnthonyCrastus 3 111
(E Lellouche, France) *racd in 3rd: prom 1 1/2f out: rdn to chal 1f out: hmpd over 100yds out: fin 5th: plcd 4th* **12/1**

5 hd **La Boum (GER)**[34] 5575 7-9-1 0 .... ThierryJarnet 8 105
(Robert Collet, France) *racd in 5th: mde gd prog in st: chal for ld 1f out: r.o wl but caused interference: fin 3rd: disqualified and plcd 5th* **8/1**

6 ½ **Superstition (FR)**[24] 5870 4-9-1 0 .... StephanePasquier 7 104
(A De Royer-Dupre, France) *led fr s: hdd 1 1/2f out: r.o one pce fnl f* **20/1**

7 hd **Shamanova (IRE)**[27] 5800 3-8-7 0 .... Christophe-PatriceLemaire 6 104
(A De Royer-Dupre, France) *racd at rr: rdn early in st: no ex fnl 1 1/2f out* **7/2**[2]

8 2½ **Announce**[51] 5138 3-8-7 0 .... MaximeGuyon 5 100
(A Fabre, France) *settled towards rr: rdn to cl early in st: no ex fnl 1 1/2f* **15/8**[1]

2m 49.6s (9.70) **Going Correction** +1.05s/f (Soft)
WFA 3 from 4yo+ 7lb **8** Ran SP% **114.4**
Speed ratings: **112,111,111,110,111 110,110,108**
WIN (incl. 1 euro stake): 30.90. PLACES: 6.20, 4.00, 3.50. DF: 111.90. SF: 331.60.
Owner Slim Chiboub **Bred** Lynch-Bages Ltd **Trained** Chantilly, France

FOCUS
Form to treat with real caution for they went a steady pace, resulting in a relative sprint finish, and few of these were suited by such soft ground.

NOTEBOOK
Maria Royal(IRE), a well-beaten last of six behind Announce, Shamanova and Sarah Lynx 51 days earlier, caused an upset. The best RPR she had achieved prior to this was just 98, when winning a Listed race at Vichy on her penultimate start, but crucially the going was described as very soft on that occasion, and clearly these conditions suit best. She may now be aimed at the Prix Royal-Oak.
High Heeled(IRE) ran better than when disappointing in the Prix Vermeille, but it's still slightly disappointing that she couldn't put away a filly like Maria Royal. It can be argued the sprint finish was not ideal, but she was better placed than most, and she basically just hasn't gone on as expected from her third in the Coronation Cup on debut for this yard. According to James Wigan, racing manager to the owner, the filly is likely to go to the paddocks next year, but does still have options at Woodbine and in Italy and France later this season.
Sarah Lynx(IRE) could not match the form she showed when fifth in the Vermeille and probably didn't appreciate the ground, or the lack of pace.
Peinture Rare(IRE), second to Daryakana in this last year, had no easy task under her penalty and was unable to confirm form with High Heeled from their meeting at Deauville in August.
La Boum(GER), who produced a good effort against males on her previous start, travelled well and had every chance, running another sound race. However, she was demoted to fifth after causing interference.
Superstition(FR), a stable companion of the winner, was responsible for the modest gallop but was easily brushed aside in the straight.
Shamanova(IRE) clearly didn't act on the ground, failing to make any impression in the dash to the line.
Announce, previously unbeaten, had three of these behind, including today's winner, when successful last time. She won a Listed race on very soft on her second start, but couldn't cope with testing ground in this better company.

6592a QATAR PRIX DOLLAR (GROUP 2) (3YO+) (TURF) 1m 1f 165y
3:50 (12:00) 3-Y-0+ **£65,575** (£25,309; £12,079; £8,053; £4,026)

RPR

1 **Cirrus Des Aigles (FR)**[31] 5674 4-9-0 0 .... FranckBlondel 2 120
(Mme C Barande-Barbe, France) *broke wl: led initially then settled in 3rd on rail: cruised to ld 1f out: r.o strly: comf* **9/2**[1]

2 2 **Budai (GER)**[35] 5542 4-9-0 0 .... DominiqueBoeuf 1 116
(W Hickst, Germany) *racd in 5th tl st: qcknd wl to join ldr distant memories 1f out: r.o wl fnl f to claim 2nd in fnl strides* **5/1**[2]

3 hd **Distant Memories (IRE)**[35] 5539 4-9-0 0 .... StephanePasquier 7 116
(T P Tate) *racd in 2nd: qcknd wl early in st: grabbed ld on wd outside 1 1/2f out: no answer whn chal by wnr 1f out: r.o wl: lost 2nd fnl strides* **9/1**

4 hd **Poet**[21] 5951 5-9-0 0 .... MaximeGuyon 4 115
(C G Cox) *broke wl and sn led: hdd 1 1/2f out: r.o wl fnl f* **5/1**[2]

5 ¾ **Shimraan (FR)**[34] 5575 3-9-0 0 .... GeraldMosse 9 119
(A De Royer-Dupre, France) *racd in rr: rdn to cl early in st but outpcd: no ex fnl f: styd on* **5/1**[2]

6 3 **Shamalgan (FR)**[20] 6014 3-8-9 0 .... IoritzMendizabal 3 107
(A Savjuev, Czech Republic) *settled towards rr: rdn early in st: no ex 1 1/2f out: styd on fnl f* **12/1**

7 4 **Cima De Triomphe (IRE)**13 6239 5-9-0 0 YutakaTake 5 99
(B Grizzetti, Italy) *racd bhd ldrs fr s: rdn but no ex in st: styd on* **11/1**
8 5 **Three Bodies (IRE)**31 5674 4-9-0 0 Christophe-PatriceLemaire 6 88
(P Bary, France) *racd in 6th: failed to qckn u.p in st* **12/1**
9 4 **Zazou (GER)**48 5132 3-9-0 0 OlivierPeslier 8 85
(Mario Hofer, Germany) *a towards rr: no threat in st* **8/1**3
10 2 **The Bogberry (USA)**153 1747 5-9-0 0 GregoryBenoist 10 76
(R Tugusev, Slovakia) *a towards rr and nvr figured in st* **66/1**

2m 9.60s (6.70) **Going Correction** +1.05s/f (Soft)
WFA 3 from 4yo+ 5lb **10** Ran SP% **114.5**
Speed ratings: **115,113,113,113,112 110,106,102,99,98**
WIN (incl. 1 euro stake): 3.60. PLACES: 1.50, 2.10, 3.80. DF: 8.90. SF: 16.00.
Owner Jean-Claude-Alain Dupouy **Bred** Yvon Lelimouzin & Benoit Deschamps **Trained** France

FOCUS
Fair form for the level. It paid to race prominently and the first four finishers had this to themselves inside the final couple of furlongs.

NOTEBOOK
Cirrus Des Aigles(FR) probably needed the run when just behind Budai at Deauville on August 14, having been off for six months, and he convincingly reversed form this time, building on his recent Listed race success. He travelled really smoothly and found plenty for pressure, quite possibly producing a career best. This tough and versatile type could have even more to offer and may now go for the Prix du Conseil de Paris, a race he won last year. The Japan Cup and Hong Kong Vase (fifth last year) will also be considered.
Budai(GER), like the winner, is progressing. He came into this off the back of a comfortable win at Group 3 level in his native Germany and this was another smart performance.
Distant Memories(IRE), a Group 3 winner at Windsor on his previous start, was always well placed and had every chance, posting a good effort on this slight rise in class.
Poet struggled when challenged in the straight, but was staying on again near the finish. He had the ground to suit but his trainer is of the opinion he didn't make this enough of a test, and could well be correct.
Shimraan(FR) looked to be given a seriously ill-judged ride by Gerald Mosse. Held up well off the pace, he wasn't asked for an effort until about 2f out, at which point the first four were upwards of 5l clear. The colt ran on when finally coming under pressure, but had absolutely no chance of getting involved and this really was a poor effort from the jockey.

6593a QATAR PRIX DANIEL WILDENSTEIN (GROUP 2) (3YO+) (TURF) 1m
4:25 (12:00) 3-Y-O+
£65,575 (£25,309; £12,079; £8,053; £2,013; £2,013)

RPR
1 **Royal Bench (IRE)**48 5134 3-8-11 0 OlivierPeslier 8 114
(Robert Collet, France) *settled towards rr disputing 5th: plld outside and shkn up 2f out: r.o to ld 1 1/2f fr home: r.o strly and a in command fnl f* **8/1**
2 3 **Lochinver (USA)**18 3-8-11 0 MaximeGuyon 4 107
(A Fabre, France) *settled in last 4 l adrift of main pack: clsd up 2 1/2f out but stl last: hdwy on outside 2f out: r.o to take 2nd 150yds out: nvr threatened wnr* **17/2**
3 1 1/2 **Emerald Commander (IRE)**32 5649 3-9-0 0 MickaelBarzalona 7 107
(Saeed Bin Suroor) *trckd ldr: wnt on over 2f out: sn rdn: hdd 1 1/2f out: unable qck and lost 2nd fnl 150yds: no ex* **5/2**2
4 2 1/2 **Vertigineux (FR)**34 5574 6-9-1 0 PhilippeSogorb 5 99
(Mme C Dufreche, France) *disp 3rd: shkn up over 2f out: unable qck: one pce fnl f* **4/1**3
5 1 1/2 **Elusive Wave (IRE)**34 5574 4-8-11 0 IoritzMendizabal 1 91
(J-C Rouget, France) *broke wl and plld hrd: disp 3rd: 4th and cl up 2f out: sn rdn and nt qckn: wknd fnl f* **9/4**1
5 dht **Sweet Hearth (USA)**27 5802 4-8-11 0..(b[1]) Christophe-PatriceLemaire 3 91
(A De Royer-Dupre, France) *hld up disputing 5th: rdn fr 2f out: no imp: kpt on ins fnl 100yds* **9/1**
7 8 **Corconte (FR)**31 5-9-1 0 YutakaTake 6 77
(S Kobayashi, France) *broke wl and sn led: set a gd gallop tl hdd over 2f out: wknd qckly* **33/1**

1m 44.3s (5.90) **Going Correction** +1.05s/f (Soft)
WFA 3 from 4yo+ 3lb **7** Ran SP% **113.9**
Speed ratings: **112,109,107,105,103 103,95**
PARI-MUTUEL (all including 1 euro stakes): WIN 6.30; PLACE 2.60, 3.10, 2.80; DF 25.20; SF 35.90.
Owner R C Strauss **Bred** Kilfrush Stud **Trained** Chantilly, France

FOCUS
The race was delayed by about six minutes after Across The Rhine played up and had to be withdrawn. Several of these failed to give their true running and this is weak form for the grade. The pace was overly strong and the first two finishers had filled the last two places for the much of the way.

NOTEBOOK
Royal Bench(IRE) benefited from a well-judged ride and clearly handled the conditions better than most. He was a Listed winner earlier in the season, but looked far removed from top class when beaten 12l by Makfi in the Jacques Le Marois last time. Although this was better, he'll probably struggle back up in grade.
Lochinver(USA) didn't look up to this level, having only won a conditions race on his latest start, but he represented a trainer who had won this three times in the past. His justified his place in the line-up with a solid effort, although he was helped by being held up well off the quick gallop and is probably a bit flattered.
Emerald Commander(IRE), a German Group 2 winner last time, had the ground to suit but he over-raced through the early stages and had little chance of seeing his race out.
Vertigineux(FR) reversed recent Deauville Group 3 placings with Elusive Wave, but made no real impression and was probably found out by the combination of ground softer than ideal, and chasing the overly strong gallop.
Elusive Wave(IRE), like the fourth, probably didn't like the ground and was also close enough to the quick gallop.
Sweet Hearth(USA) had blinkers on for the first time, but the ground was against her.

6544 DUNDALK (A.W) (L-H)
Sunday, October 3
OFFICIAL GOING: Standard

6597a WWW.DUNDALKSTADIUM.COM H'CAP 7f (P)
3:30 (3:32) (70-100,96) 3-Y-O+ £12,367 (£3,615; £1,712; £570)

RPR
1 **Hajoum (IRE)**8 6363 4-9-10 95 GregFairley 12 102
(M Johnston) *settled in 2nd: led 2f out: sn edgd clr: styd on wl u.p fr over 1f out* **4/1**1
2 1 1/4 **Greatwallofchina (USA)**18 6100 5-9-3 88 (b) CO'Donoghue 9 92
(A P O'Brien, Ire) *trckd ldrs in 4th: prog early st: 2nd and styd on fnl f wout threatening wnr* **6/1**3
3 4 **Hard Rock City (USA)**21 6008 10-9-1 93 DCByrne(7) 5 86
(M J Grassick, Ire) *trckd ldrs on inner: 5th after 1/2-way: rdn st: kpt on to go mod 3rd wl ins fnl f* **20/1**
4 3/4 **Banna Boirche (IRE)**78 4159 4-8-10 88 CPHoban(7) 4 79
(M Halford, Ire) *hld up in 9th: prog into 6th over 1f out: kpt on* **7/1**
5 shd **Sean Og Coulston (IRE)**14 6233 6-9-4 89 DPMcDonogh 2 80
(John J Coleman, Ire) *trckd ldrs in 3rd: rdn st: no imp fr 1 1/2f out: no ex ins fnl f* **4/1**1
6 1 **Mountain Coral (IRE)**98 3489 6-9-4 89 DMGrant 11 77
(F Oakes, Ire) *mid-div: 8th 1/2-way: 7th and effrt early st: no imp fr over 1f out* **20/1**
7 3/4 **He's Got Rhythm (IRE)**6 6432 5-8-10 88 EDLinehan(7) 6 74
(David Marnane, Ire) *hld up: 10th travelling wl appr st: rdn 2f out: no imp: one pce* **5/1**2
8 shd **Award Ceremony (IRE)**56 4881 5-8-12 90 (bt) LFRoche(7) 10 76
(D K Weld, Ire) *hld up towards rr: 11th 1/2-way: rdn and no imp st* **9/1**
9 nk **Anam Chara (IRE)**29 5774 4-9-5 90 RPCleary 3 75
(Andrew Oliver, Ire) *rdn to ld s: strly pressed ent st: hdd 2f out: sn no ex and wknd* **20/1**
10 1 1/2 **Copper Dock (IRE)**49 5127 6-9-7 92 KLatham 1 73
(T G McCourt, Ire) *mid-div on inner: 7th 1/2-way: no ex early st* **20/1**
11 hd **Toufan Express**7 6400 8-9-1 89 EJMcNamara(3) 7 70
(Adrian McGuinness, Ire) *a towards rr* **14/1**
12 3 **Lord Kenmare (USA)**29 5778 4-9-3 91 (p) GFCarroll(3) 8 63
(M Halford, Ire) *s.i.s and a bhd* **9/1**
13 1 1/4 **Aznavour (IRE)**63 4630 3-9-2 89 NGMcCullagh 14 58
(John M Oxx, Ire) *trckd ldrs on outer: 6th 1/2-way: wknd ent st* **14/1**

1m 22.85s (82.85)
WFA 3 from 4yo+ 2lb **13** Ran SP% **135.8**
CSF £30.30 CT £452.66 TOTE £3.90: £2.70, £2.50, £8.20; DF 55.30.
Owner Sheikh Hamdan Bin Mohammed Al Maktoum **Bred** Darley **Trained** Middleham Moor, N Yorks

NOTEBOOK
Hajoum(IRE) was having his 13th run since May. Despite being drawn wide and burdened by top weight, he quickly got over to the lead and was up front alongside Anam Chara. This was by no means a soft lead (the winning time was fast) and he was slightly niggled as they hit the straight, but the four-year-old kept finding and won with considerable authority. This seems his ideal trip, though no plans were mentioned post-race. (op 7/2)
Greatwallofchina(USA) would have won this easily if no overseas horses had partook. He was initially rated 109 but ran off 88 here and was down to a good mark. He performs well on the AW and is unlucky not to have won since his only success back in May 2008. He briefly looked a threat to the winner, who found more. (op 8/1)
Hard Rock City(USA) was making his AW debut and has no issues with the surface. He was nicely positioned throughout and just emerged best of those bunched up for third. He has been a fine servant.
Banna Boirche(IRE) did best from those held up. He has been consistent but might be a shade high in the handicap still.
Sean Og Coulston(IRE) had every chance. He had no more to give when passed by the runner-up, and may be just a bit too high in the weights; against that, this was his fourth run in a month. (op 4/1 tchd 7/2)
Mountain Coral(IRE) has an excellent record here, bounced back to something like his form. He should be interesting here next time off his declining mark.

6602 - (Foreign Racing) - See Raceform Interactive

6587 HOLLYWOOD PARK (L-H)
Sunday, October 3
OFFICIAL GOING: Turf: firm; cushion track: fast

6603a LADY'S SECRET STKS (GRADE 1) (3YO+ FILLIES & MARES) (CUSHION TRACK) 1m 110y(D)
12:15 (12:18) 3-Y-O+ £92,592 (£30,864; £13,888; £13,888; £3,086)

RPR
1 **Zenyatta (USA)**56 4887 6-8-11 0 MESmith 4 114+
(John Shirreffs, U.S.A) *settled in last: hdwy 1 1/2f out: stl 2 l down ins fnl f: qcknd fnl 100yds to ld cl home* **1/10**1
2 1/2 **Switch (USA)**27 3-8-8 0 AQuinonez 1 112
(John W Sadler, U.S.A) *a cl up: jnd ldr 2 1/2f out and wnt on st: r.o gamely but ct cl home* **42/10**2
3 4 3/4 **Satans Quick Chick (USA)**344 4-8-11 0 JAlvarado 3 101
(Eric R Reed, U.S.A) *racd in 4th: rdn and nt qckn 2f out: kpt on fnl f to grab share of 3rd on line* **216/10**
3 dht **Moon De French (USA)**27 5-8-11 0 JTalamo 2 101
(Bob Baffert, U.S.A) *led: jnd 2 1/2f out: hdd st: drifted rt ins fnl f: wknd fnl 100yds: jst hld share of 3rd* **125/10**3
5 5 1/2 **Emmy Darling (USA)**78 4-8-11 0 PValenzuela 5 88
(Doug O'Neill, U.S.A) *chsd ldr: rdn and wknd fr 2f out* **25/1**

1m 42.97s (0.98)
WFA 3 from 4yo+ 3lb **5** Ran SP% **125.8**
PARI-MUTUEL (all including $2 stakes): WIN 2.20; PLACE (1-2) 2.10, 2.60; DF 3.40; SF 4.00.
Owner Mr & Mrs Jerome S Moss **Bred** Maverick Production Limited **Trained** USA

NOTEBOOK
Zenyatta(USA) gave her supporters plenty to worry about in a race run over a shorter trip than ideal and at a less-than-furious gallop, but she was delivered with her usual late challenge and just got up close home. The form is well below what she is capable of, but this will have set her up nicely for the Breeders' Cup Classic, for which she's a best price 5-1, and the only question is whether she's capable of running to her very best synthetic form on dirt, as a likely strong pace in the Classic will surely suit her down to the ground. With this 19th straight success, she equalled the consecutive win record of New Mexico mare Peppers Pride.

6604a YELLOW RIBBON STKS (GRADE 1) (3YO+ FILLIES & MARES) (TURF) 1m 2f
12:50 (12:55) 3-Y-O+ £92,592 (£30,864; £18,518; £9,259; £3,086)

RPR
1 **Hibaayeb**45 5248 3-8-8 0 RBejarano 9 108
(Saeed Bin Suroor) *dwlt: sn chsng ldrs: cl 3rd but forced wd 2f out: r.o wl st to ld fnl 150yds: r.o wl* **33/10**2
2 1 **Turning Top (IRE)**48 4-8-11 0 BBlanc 8 104
(Simon Callaghan, U.S.A) *trckd ldr: led briefly ins fnl f: hdd fnl 150yds: kpt on* **47/10**3

3 ½ **Gypsy's Warning (SAF)**[43] 5320 5-8-11 0 MESmith 3 103
(H Graham Motion, U.S.A) *led tl hdd ins fnl f: no ex* **21/10**[1]
4 1 **Sweet And Flawless (USA)**[27] 4-8-11 0 JAlvarado 7 101
(Eric R Reed, U.S.A) *settled in bk two: clsd up fr 2 1/2f out: ev ch over 1 1/2f out: unable qck* **50/1**
5 ½ **Restless Soul**[98] 6-8-11 0 PValenzuela 2 100
(B Cecil, U.S.A) *racd in bk 3rd: effrt over 2f out: one pce st* **27/1**
6 ½ **Princess Taylor**[56] 4887 6-8-11 0 VEspinoza 5 99
(Patrick Gallagher, U.S.A) *chsd ldrs: 4th and ev ch over 2f out: wknd fnl 300yds* **66/10**
7 ½ **Princess Haya (USA)**[48] 5-8-11 0 CNakatani 6 98
(Carl O'Callaghan, U.S.A) *hld up towards rr: unable qck fr 2f out* **177/10**
8 1 ¼ **Go Forth North (USA)**[27] 3-8-8 0 OBerrio 4 98
(A C Avila, U.S.A) *a bhd* **149/10**
9 2 ¼ **Lilly Fa Pootz (USA)**[27] 5-8-11 0 (b) JTalamo 1 91
(Jerry Hollendorfer, U.S.A) *racd in midfield: rdn and wknd appr 2f out* **54/10**

2m 0.44s (120.44)
WFA 3 from 4yo+ 5lb **9** Ran SP% **119.0**
PARI-MUTUEL (all including $2 stakes): WIN 8.60; PLACE (1-2) 5.00, 5.60; SHOW (1-2-3) 3.40, 3.40, 2.20; DF 28.60; SF 53.60.
Owner Godolphin Racing LLC **Bred** Rabbah Bloodstock Limited **Trained** Newmarket, Suffolk

NOTEBOOK
Hibaayeb, who was winning for the first time since taking the Ribblesdale at Royal Ascot, was on Lasix for the first time and bounced off the fast ground to put herself in the picture for the Breeders' Cup Filly & Mare Turf.

2805 HOPPEGARTEN (R-H)
Sunday, October 3
OFFICIAL GOING: Turf: good

6606a WESTMINSTER PREIS DER DEUTSCHEN EINHEIT (GROUP 3) (3YO+) (TURF) 1m 2f
3:50 (12:00) 3-Y-0+
£28,318 (£9,734; £4,867; £2,654; £1,769; £1,327)

RPR
1 **Russian Tango (GER)**[28] 5806 3-9-0 0 EPedroza 7 109
(A Wohler, Germany) *racd bhd ldr pulling freely: mde move ent st: r.o wl: tk ld 1 1/2f out: drew clr: comf* **21/10**[2]
2 1 ½ **Illo (GER)**[36] 5542 4-9-4 0 ADeVries 8 105
(J Hirschberger, Germany) *broke wl to ld: set gd pce: wnt a few l clr: r.o wl in st: hdd 1 1/2f out: battled on to chse wnr home* **31/5**[3]
3 3 ½ **Falun (GER)**[36] 5542 4-9-4 0 EFrank 5 98
(A Trybuhl, Germany) *racd in rr pulling freely: gng wl ent st: r.o wl to go 3rd fnl f: no threat to ldrs* **114/10**
4 1 **Usbeke (GER)**[35] 4-9-4 0 NeilChalmers 1 96
(J-P Carvalho, Germany) *racd in rr: r.o wl in st but no ex fnl f* **157/10**
5 5 **Schiller Danon (GER)**[14] 6234 4-9-4 0 APietsch 2 86
(W Hickst, Germany) *racd in 3rd: gng wl ent st: no ex: styd on* **103/10**
6 44 **Cutlass Bay (UAE)**[29] 5781 4-9-4 0 (b) TedDurcan 4 —
(Saeed Bin Suroor) *broke wl and settled in 4th on rail: began to struggle bef end of bkst: wknd qckly arnd fnl turn: t.o* **3/5**[1]

2m 3.70s (-3.00)
WFA 3 from 4yo 5lb **6** Ran SP% **131.5**
WIN (incl. 10 euro stake): 31. PLACES: 17, 25. SF: 213.
Owner Rennstall Darboven **Bred** Gestut Idee **Trained** Germany

NOTEBOOK
Cutlass Bay(UAE) appeared to lose his action on loose ground around the bend into the straight. He was apparently unsound straight afterwards but was better by the time he was unsaddled, so the suspicion was that he might just have tweaked a muscle.

6589 LONGCHAMP (R-H)
Sunday, October 3
OFFICIAL GOING: Turf: very soft

6607a QATAR PRIX DU CADRAN (GROUP 1) (4YO+) (TURF) 2m 4f
12:05 (12:00) 4-Y-0+ **£126,415** (£50,575; £25,287; £12,632; £6,327)

RPR
1 **Gentoo (FR)**[21] 6016 6-9-2 0 (p) GeraldMosse 2 113
(A Lyon, France) *settled in rr: rdn 2f out: swtchd to wd outside: qcknd wl 1 1/2f out: grabbed ld 1f out: r.o wl to win comf* **9/2**[2]
2 2 ½ **Winter Dream (IRE)**[21] 6016 6-9-2 0 IoritzMendizabal 6 110
(Robert Collet, France) *settled in rr and last ent st: hrd rdn and prog 1 1/2f out: r.o wl fnl f to go 2nd fnl 100yds* **33/1**
3 1 ½ **Kasbah Bliss (FR)**[21] 6016 8-9-2 0 ThierryThulliez 8 109
(F Doumen, France) *racd in 6th: qcknd wl to ld 2f out: sn chal and hdd over 1 1/2f out: no ex fnl f: styd on* **9/4**[1]
4 snk **Los Cristianos (FR)**[42] 5349 4-9-2 0 MaximeGuyon 4 108
(A Couetil, France) *racd in 5th: rdn and prog 2f out: r.o wl: jst missed 3rd* **10/1**[3]
5 3 **Askar Tau (FR)**[23] 5909 5-9-2 0 (v) RyanMoore 5 105
(M P Tregoning) *racd promly fr s and wnt cl 2nd w a circ to go: hrd rdn 2f out: no ex: styd on fnl f* **16/1**
6 6 **Brusco**[21] 6011 4-9-2 0 OlivierPeslier 7 99
(A Wohler, Germany) *prom fr s and settled in 4th: rdn early in st: no ex fnl 2f: wknd* **10/1**[3]
7 dist **Shawnee Saga (FR)**[41] 5-9-2 0 DominiqueBoeuf 1 —
(W Baltromei, Germany) *racd in 3rd: rdn early in st: no ex: wknd fnl 2f* **16/1**
8 5 **Blek (FR)**[42] 5349 5-9-2 0 AnthonyCrastus 3 —
(E Lellouche, France) *led fr s: rdn early in st: hdd and fnd no ex fnl 2f: wknd* **9/4**[1]

4m 40.8s (22.80) **Going Correction** +0.625s/f (Yiel) **8** Ran SP% **112.6**
Speed ratings: **79,78,77,77,76 73,—,—**
WIN (incl. 1 euro stake): 5.20. PLACES: 1.90, 5.40, 1.70. DF: 69.00. SF: 154.40.
Owner Serge Tripier-Mondancin **Bred** Jean-Claude Seroul **Trained** France

FOCUS
Following a dry night the going was changed slightly to read soft to very soft, and there was a strong wind behind in the straight. A poor turnout for a Group 1 race, with no previous winners at this level, and only two previous Group 2 winners, namely Askar Tau and Blek, lining up. They went quite steady early, but this was still a real test in the ground, and the principals came from well off the pace.

NOTEBOOK
Gentoo(FR), given a patient ride, tracked Kasbah Bliss through early in the straight, and stayed on strongest of all inside the final furlong. Having come through the handicapping ranks and won his previous two starts over 2m, including a messy Group 3 Prix Gladiateur last time out, he found the combination of soft ground and an even greater test of stamina just what he needed. The form doesn't look up to much, but he was clearly the best on the day.
Winter Dream(IRE) has five wins to his name and three of them came over 2m in heavy ground. These conditions were never going to faze him and, having been held up at the back of the field and got slightly outpaced heading to the turn into the straight, he finished strongly to take second. He is only a Listed winner, though, and his performance doesn't do a lot for the form.
Kasbah Bliss(FR) was narrowly beaten in this race last year, having taken the Gladiateur en route. Unlucky in running when a beaten favourite in that prep race this time around, he found the ground had gone against him here, and despite hitting the front with a furlong and a half to go, he got tired, wandered about in the closing stages and didn't see it out. Although one of the most talented dual-purpose horses of modern times, he has yet to win at the top level under either code.
Los Cristianos(FR) had every chance in the straight but didn't see it out quite as well as the first two. Nevertheless, he has had relatively few starts over staying trips and is possibly open to a bit more improvement than most in this field.
Askar Tau(FR), below his best in his previous two starts this season, ran a decent race considering conditions were all against him. He went for home turning in but was soon floundering in the ground and couldn't pick up. He'll be much happier back on a quicker surface.
Brusco, a Listed winner in Italy and Germany, didn't seem to stay on his first attempt beyond 2m.
Shawnee Saga(FR) only has two minor race wins to his name and was taking a big step up in class.
Blek(FR), winner of 11 of his previous 20 starts including a Group 2 earlier this season, and perfectly at home in soft ground, looked to have plenty in his favour, but he still had his stamina to prove over this longer trip and, having made the running to the turn in, he fell in a heap once straightening up. He can resume winning ways back over 2m.

6608a QATAR PRIX DE L'ABBAYE DE LONGCHAMP (GROUP 1) (2YO+) (TURF) 5f (S)
12:35 (12:00) 2-Y-0+ **£126,415** (£50,575; £25,287; £12,632; £6,327)

RPR
1 **Gilt Edge Girl**[15] 6194 4-9-7 0 LukeMorris 1 114
(C G Cox) *a.p: pushed along at 1/2-way and qcknd wl to ld over 1 1/2f out: r.o wl* **25/1**
2 1 **Lady Of The Desert (USA)**[7] 6390 3-9-7 0 RichardHughes 3 110
(B J Meehan) *chsd ldrs in abt 7th (on outside of wnr): n.m.r 2f out: sn rdn and r.o wl to go 2nd 75yds fr home: nvr chal wnr* **11/4**[1]
3 1 ½ **Mar Adentro (FR)**[21] 6012 4-9-11 0 (p) ChristopheSoumillon 18 109+
(R Chotard, France) *settled in midfield travelling wl: shkn up 2f out: r.o strly u.p fnl f to take 3rd cl home* **66/1**
4 ¾ **Marchand D'Or (FR)**[21] 6012 7-9-11 0 DavyBonilla 14 106+
(M Delzangles, France) *hld up in midfield: rdn appr fnl 2f: styd on 1f out: nt clr run and swtchd outside 50yds out: fin wl* **14/1**[3]
5 shd **Arctic (IRE)**[98] 3486 3-9-11 0 JAHeffernan 2 106
(Tracey Collins, Ire) *wl away and a.p: cl 4th and ev ch over 1f out: wknd ins fnl 100yds* **14/1**[3]
6 1 ½ **Prohibit**[15] 6194 5-9-11 0 (p) FrankieDettori 10 100+
(R M H Cowell) *outpcd towards rr: rdn 1/2-way: styd on wl fnl f: nvr nrr* **20/1**
7 hd **Piccadilly Filly (IRE)**[44] 5276 3-9-7 0 EddieCreighton 17 96
(E J Creighton) *rrd and uns rdr bef ent stalls: sn chsng ldrs and in first five at 1/2-way: rdn and nt qckn over 1f out: kpt on again fnl 100yds* **33/1**
8 snk **Judge 'n Jury**[22] 5944 6-9-11 0 KJManning 13 99
(R A Harris) *broke wl and pressed ldr: rdn 2f out: fdd u.p ins fnl f* **66/1**
9 snk **Moorhouse Lad**[25] 5851 7-9-11 0 (b[1]) TomEaves 7 98
(B Smart) *broke wl and sn led: pushed along 2 1/2f out: hdd appr fnl 1 1/2f: wknd fnl f* **66/1**
10 ½ **Total Gallery (IRE)**[15] 6194 4-9-11 0 JMurtagh 16 97
(J S Moore) *pushed along to keep tabs in midfield: styd on wl fnl 300yds: nvr rchd chalng position* **10/1**[2]
11 ¾ **Poppet's Treasure**[21] 6012 3-9-7 0 StephanePasquier 6 90
(R Pritchard-Gordon, France) *racd in midfield: rdn sn after 1/2-way: btn and wkng whn snatched up fnl 100yds* **50/1**
12 nk **Rose Blossom**[25] 5851 3-9-7 0 (p) PaulHanagan 12 89
(R A Fahey) *broke wl and w ldrs tl dropped away appr 2f out* **28/1**
13 ½ **Swiss Diva**[21] 6012 4-9-7 0 IoritzMendizabal 9 87
(D R C Elsworth) *settled in midfield (abt 9th): rdn 2f out: no imp* **11/4**[1]
14 nk **Blue Jack**[35] 5569 5-9-11 0 (b) RichardKingscote 15 90
(Tom Dascombe) *dwlt: nvr beyond mid-div* **40/1**
15 snk **Prime Defender**[29] 5744 6-9-11 0 RobertWinston 5 89
(B W Hills) *outpcd and rdn along fr the off: nvr beyond mid-div* **25/1**
16 1 **Bluster (FR)**[21] 6012 4-9-11 0 WilliamBuick 11 86
(Robert Collet, France) *chsd ldrs: rdn 1/2-way: wknd fnl f* **33/1**
17 nk **Planet Five (USA)**[56] 4885 4-9-11 0 Christophe-PatriceLemaire 19 85
(P Bary, France) *nvr gng pce: a towards rr* **16/1**
18 ¾ **War Artist (AUS)**[21] 6012 7-9-11 0 OlivierPeslier 21 82
(A De Royer-Dupre, France) *hld up towards rr: nvr in contention* **14/1**[3]
19 2 **Amico Fritz (GER)**[35] 5573 4-9-11 0 MaximeGuyon 20 75
(H-A Pantall, France) *racd in midfield: shkn up 2f out: unable qck* **20/1**
20 1 ½ **Mister Hughie (IRE)**[15] 6194 3-9-11 0 GeraldMosse 8 69
(M R Channon) *missed break: nvr rcvrd: a bhd* **33/1**
21 1 **Chopouest (FR)**[21] 6012 3-9-11 0 FredericSpanu 4 66
(A Spanu, France) *slowly away and a bhd* **100/1**

57.00 secs (0.70) **Going Correction** +0.575s/f (Yiel) **21** Ran SP% **127.7**
Speed ratings: **117,115,113,111,111 109,108,108,108,107 106,105,105,104,104 102,102,101,97,95 93**
PARI-MUTUEL (all including 1 euro stakes): WIN 54.30; PLACE 12.20, 3.00, 5.80; DF 159.40; SF 309.10.
Owner Wood Street Syndicate V & C J Harper **Bred** Whitsbury Manor Stud **Trained** Lambourn, Berks
■ A first Group 1 winner for both Clive Cox and Luke Morris.

FOCUS
The Abbaye is often a weak Group 1 and this latest running was no exception. Despite the biggest field in the race's 54-year history (previous record 20 in 2002), only three runners had previously been successful at the top level, and not one of them this year, with all of Europe's 2010 Group 1 winners absent. To further devalue the form, those drawn low looked to be at an advantage, and the majority of the field were no doubt uncomfortable on the testing going, meaning very few were ever involved.

NOTEBOOK

Gilt Edge Girl was only sixth in Group 3 company on quick ground last time, albeit under a penalty, and had previously finished just behind Amico Fritz over 6f in Germany, but the combination of a favourable draw, the minimum trip and testing ground resulted in a career best. She showed good speed from the off against the probably favoured near rail, only leaving the fence to get past Moorhouse Lad in the closing stages, and was always holding the runner-up late on. Everything went her way, but she's not had that much racing and will warrant respect under similar conditions if kept in training next year.

Lady Of The Desert(USA), like the winner, was favourably drawn, but even so this was still a highly creditable effort considering it was just seven days on from her success in the Diadem Stakes over 6f at Ascot, and the ground was probably softer than ideal. Provided her recent busy spell doesn't leave its mark (also second in Haydock Sprint Cup in recent weeks), she looks a filly with more to offer. If kept on the go, presumably her connections will look at the Breeders' Cup Turf Sprint and/or the Hong Kong Sprint in December. She stays in training next year.

Mar Adentro(FR) is greatly improved since being dropped to sprinting and fitted with cheekpieces (won over 1m2f last year) and comprehensively reversed recent C&D placings with Swiss Diva, a terrific effort considering he was drawn extremely wide. After racing in about mid-division, he was doing all his best work at the finish. The Hong Kong Sprint is a possibility if he is invited.

Marchand D'Or(FR), the 2008 winner of this race, raced that bit further back than the third and simply took too long to get going after having to weave his way through. He is reportedly finished for the season now.

Arctic(IRE) was well beaten on quick ground on his only previous start this year, but he had some high-class form to his name on a testing surface as a juvenile and, back after a 98-day absence, he ran a fine race. It's true he had the benefit of a low draw, but he tired near the line like a horse in need of the run, and there's more to come when he gets his ground. (op 16-1)

Prohibit finished in front of today's winner on quick ground at Newbury last time but, most unusually for him, was never going the pace under these vastly different conditions.

Piccadilly Filly(IRE) reared up beforehand and needed a blindfold for stalls entry. She has form on soft ground, but her Nunthorpe third was on really quick going.

Judge 'n Jury had the ground to suit but basically wasn't up to the level, even allowing for a less than ideal draw.

Moorhouse Lad, who got warm before, showed early speed in first-time blinkers but faded soon enough.

Total Gallery(IRE) won this last year but hasn't been in the same form in 2010. Stuck out wide and with the ground probably softer than ideal, he was never going. (op 9-1 tchd 11-1)

Rose Blossom is all speed and was probably unsuited by the conditions.

Swiss Diva was in nowhere near the form she showed when a smart winner over C&D on her previous start, a race in which she had, among others, today's third and fourth behind. Her trainer reported afterwards that, as she was coming out of the stalls, she took a bang on her left side and Ioritz Mendizabal said she was never travelling after that. (op 3-1)

Blue Jack was soon detached after missing the break.

Prime Defender couldn't take advantage of his handy draw.

Mister Hughie(IRE) lost a lot of ground at the start.

6609a TOTAL PRIX MARCEL BOUSSAC - CRITERIUM DES POULICHES (GROUP 1) (2YO FILLIES) (TURF) 1m

1:10 (12:00) 2-Y-O **£151,699** (£60,690; £30,345; £15,159; £7,592)

			RPR
1		**Misty For Me (IRE)**^{35} 5570 2-8-11 0 ... JMurtagh 1 (A P O'Brien, Ire) *racd in 2nd: rdn 1 1/2f out: briefly led 1f out: sn hdd: c bk to regain ld 100yds out: r.o wl* **3/1**^{2}	114
2	1	**Helleborine**^{24} 5899 2-8-11 0 ... StephanePasquier 5 (Mme C Head-Maarek, France) *racd in 4th on outside: qcknd wl to chal for ld 1 1/2f out: grabbed ld 1f out: r.o wl but hdd 100yds out: r.o* **10/11**^{1}	112+
3	3	**Rainbow Springs**^{23} 5912 2-8-11 0 ... WilliamBuick 3 (J H M Gosden) *racd in 3rd: outpcd 1 1/2f out but fought bk fnl f to go 3rd in clsng strides* **16/1**	105
4	hd	**Mambia**^{43} 5322 2-8-11 0 ... DavyBonilla 2 (J Boisnard, France) *led fr s: rdn 2f out: r.o wl: hdd 1 1/2f out: r.o wl fnl f but lost 3rd in fnl strides* **10/1**	105
5	1	**Galikova (FR)**^{15} 2-8-11 0 ... OlivierPeslier 8 (F Head, France) *racd in rr: wl bk in st: r.o fnl f* **5/1**^{3}	103+
6	1/2	**Danedream (GER)**^{43} 5323 2-8-11 0 ... AStarke 6 (P Schiergen, Germany) *in rr fr s: rdn 2f out: no ex: styd on fnl f* **33/1**	101
7	1 1/2	**Miss Fifty (IRE)**^{43} 5322 2-8-11 0 ... MaximeGuyon 4 (U Suter, France) *racd in midfield on rail: rdn 2f out: r.o: no ex fnl f: fdd fnl 100yds* **40/1**	98
8	10	**Nitza (FR)**^{24} 5899 2-8-11 0 ... Christophe-PatriceLemaire 7 (Mme C Head-Maarek, France) *prom fr s: rdn 2f out: wknd* **33/1**	76

1m 42.5s (4.10) **Going Correction** +0.625s/f (Yiel) **8** Ran SP% **117.3**

Speed ratings: **104,103,100,99,98 98,96,86**

WIN (incl. 1 euro stake): 5.00. PLACES: 1.60, 1.20, 2.90. DF: 3.90. SF: 9.70.

Owner M Tabor, D Smith & Mrs John Magnier **Bred** March Thoroughbreds **Trained** Ballydoyle, Co Tipperary

FOCUS

The two with the best credentials coming into the race fought out the finish and, despite the ground, the form should work out.

NOTEBOOK

Misty For Me(IRE), the Moyglare winner, was forced to skip the Fillies' Mile as a result of a bruised foot, but this was more than adequate compensation. She made the running at the Curragh, but was content to track the leader over this longer trip. Murtagh got stuck in as soon as they turned into the straight, though, keen to make use of her stamina, and she found more when tackled by Helleborine. She has admirable fighting qualities and looks the type that will improve for racing, and a longer trip next season. It was interesting that while most bookmakers shortened her to around 7-1 for the 1,000 Guineas, Ladbrokes were happy to go a standout 10-1, and one can see why, as this daughter of Galileo looks more of an Oaks prospect (14-1 with Stan James). That said, she looks sure to be campaigned with both races in mind. (op 11-4)

Helleborine came here on the back of three wins, including a Group 3 over this C&D last time out. She travelled strongly into contention and quickened up well from 2f out, but found the winner a very determined rival. She looks to have more speed than the winner, which is backed up by her pedigree, and these testing conditions were probably no help to her. Indeed, her rider confirmed the impression, later reporting that the ground was too sticky. Despite this defeat she remains a leading candidate for the Guineas (eased slightly to a best price of 9-1). (op 11-10)

Rainbow Springs, whose dam finished fourth in this race to Six Perfections in 2002, is a sister to Ridge Dance, who improved significantly in his first start on soft ground when fourth in the Royal Lodge. There was no shame in being beaten 13l by Frankel on her debut, and for her to turn up here on just her second start said much about what she has been showing her trainer at home on the gallops. She showed signs of inexperience but was running on nicely at the finish and justified her connections' faith, while her performance also gave supporters of Frankel a nice boost. Her trainer sees her as a 1m2f filly for next year, and so she could be the type to return to France for the Prix de Diane.

Mambia, a winner of her previous four starts, likes to make the running, and she got her way on her first start over 1m. She made a bold bid but the first two were just too classy for her and the effort she put in to maintain her position eventually told and she lost third close home. She shouldn't have any trouble staying this trip next year.

Galikova(FR) came here on the back of an impressive success in a newcomers' event over this C&D last month, the same race won by Zarkava in 2007 prior to success in this Group 1. Held up right out the back, she never got seriously competitive, but was hardly knocked about by Peslier, who simply nudged her out over the final 2f. Her trainer hadn't been too keen to run her, as he thought she was too immature for such a big race, but her owners decided otherwise. There is much better to come from her and, being by Galileo, she promises to stay further than her half-sister Goldikova. (op 9-2)

Danedream(GER) had more to do than when winning a Listed race (later demoted to third) at Deauville last time, and didn't help her cause by racing keenly early. She can do better at a more realistic level.

Miss Fifty(IRE), who started her campaign racing over 5f and who has yet to win a race, didn't get home and it looked like the step up in trip in this ground proved too much for her. (op 33-1)

Nitza(FR), over 5l behind Helleborine here last time, sweated up beforehand, raced with the choke out and weakened quickly from 2f out.

6610a PRIX JEAN-LUC LAGARDERE (GRAND CRITERIUM) (GROUP 1) (2YO) (TURF) 7f

1:45 (12:00) 2-Y-O **£176,982** (£53,103; £53,103; £17,685; £8,858)

			RPR
1		**Wootton Bassett**^{24} 5880 2-9-0 0 ... PaulHanagan 3 (R A Fahey) *sn led: shkn up and qcknd clr over 2 1/2f out: r.o wl u.p fnl f* **4/1**^{2}	120
2	2 1/2	**Maiguri (IRE)**^{28} 5799 2-9-0 0 ... JohanVictoire 6 (C Baillet, France) *hld up towards rr: qcknd on outside 2f out: wnt 2nd 1 1/2f out: kpt on wl: jst failed to hold 2nd outrt* **16/1**	114
2	dht	**Tin Horse (IRE)**^{42} 5347 2-9-0 0 ... ThierryJarnet 1 (D Guillemin, France) *settled in bk three: pushed along 3f out: n.m.r whn starting to stay on 2f out: nt qckn whn in clr but styd on again fnl 100yds to snatch share of 2nd* **6/1**	114
4	1	**Moonlight Cloud**^{24} 2-8-10 0 ... DavyBonilla 5 (F Head, France) *settled in 5th: shkn up 2f out: nt qckn immediately: kpt on fnl 100yds* **11/4**^{1}	107+
5	1 1/2	**Utley (USA)**^{18} 6092 2-9-0 0 ... FrankieDettori 7 (J H M Gosden) *chsd ldr: strly rdn 1 1/2f out: kpt on tl fdd ins fnl 100yds* **20/1**	108
6	4	**My Name Is Bond (FR)**^{28} 5799 2-9-0 0 ... ChristopheSoumillon 9 (J-C Rouget, France) *hld up: rdn 2f out: flattered briefly to run on: no imp* **9/2**^{3}	98
7	2 1/2	**King Torus (IRE)**^{67} 4468 2-9-0 0 ... RichardHughes 2 (R Hannon) *disp 3rd: shkn up ins fnl 2 1/2f: nt qckn and wknd fnl f* **6/1**	91
8	3/4	**Whipless (IRE)**^{43} 5312 2-9-0 0 ... KJManning 8 (J S Bolger, Ire) *disp 3rd: rdn over 2f out: sn wknd* **20/1**	89
9	4	**Treasury Devil (USA)**^{18} 6088 2-9-0 0 ... WilliamBuick 4 (J H M Gosden) *hld up: squeezed for room ins fnl 4f: nvr able to chal* **10/1**	79

1m 23.0s (2.30) **Going Correction** +0.625s/f (Yiel) **9** Ran SP% **117.9**

Speed ratings: **111,108,108,107,105 100,97,97,92**

PARI-MUTUEL (all including 1 euro stakes): WIN 6.10; PLACE 2.90, 2.60 (Tin Soldier), 3.50 (Maiguri); DF 21.40 (Maiguri), 13.40 (Tin Soldier); SF 38.70 (Maiguri), 25.20 (Tin Soldier).

Owner Frank Brady & The Cosmic Cases **Bred** Laundry Cottage Stud Farm **Trained** Musley Bank, N Yorks

■ A first Group 1 success for Richard Fahey and Paul Hanagan.

FOCUS

Of the last five horses to win this, only Rio De La Plata has won subsequently, though not at the top level. However, previous winners within the last ten years include Rock Of Gibraltar, American Post and Oratorio, all of whom were successful in Group 1 company as 3-y-os. This year's race looked weak for the level, with the likes of Aidan O'Brien (won the race seven times), Andre Fabre (three times), Saeed Bin Suroor (once) and Alain de Royer-Dupre (once) all unrepresented. The time, though, was highly respectable, being only 0.90 seconds slower than Goldikova recorded in the following Prix De La Foret.

NOTEBOOK

Wootton Bassett over-raced early on, but was probably getting away with setting just an ordinary tempo through the first couple of furlongs. He committed early in the straight, a long way from the finish considering the second winning post was in use, but that decisive move soon had his rivals in trouble and, staying on really strongly, he was never seriously challenged. He did, though, have a hard race, being hit with the whip 12 times in the closing stages (jockey fined 150 euros). Now unbeaten in five starts, having followed two minor victories with two valuable sales races, he's clearly a high-class juvenile, and particularly tough to boot. Whether he's 2,000 Guineas material, though, remains to be proven. For starters, although he has the scope to make a 3-y-o, this was not the first tough race he's had this year. Secondly, his suitability for 1m is questionable. It's not his pedigree that's the concern, it's his naturally free-going style that could compromise him. Finally, even if he does stay, the signs are he's part of a red-hot generation, and next year's Newmarket Classic winner might just have to be extra special. (op 9-2)

Maiguri(IRE) was just under 2l behind My Name Is Bond in a C&D Group 3 on good ground last time, but his RPRs show steady improvement with each run and this was another fine effort. He clearly appreciated the ground more than his old rival.

Tin Horse(IRE), trying 7f for the first time following his second to Dream Ahead in the Prix Morny, was held up towards the inside and got caught in behind King Torus in the straight. After having to be angled out for a run, he finished strongly, and though not an unlucky loser, he's probably value for outright second. A likable type who looks likely to improve on what we've seen so far, he could be one for the French Guineas.

Moonlight Cloud is extremely well regarded by Freddie Head, although in a recent interview the trainer gave the impression that the filly turning up in this race (instead of the Marcel Boussac) was more about keeping her to 7f than it was about wanting to test her against colts. She travelled well enough, but her rider took a while to get after her in the straight, presumably either misjudging how much the leader had left or not wanting to give her an overly hard race. Once finally under pressure, the filly hit a bit of flat spot before running on. Her connections may have expected better.

Utley(USA) did not see his race out after chasing the pace. His maiden win came on soft ground, but while his half-sister Rainbow View handled similar conditions, this one is a strong traveller who gives the impression a faster surface will suit better.

My Name Is Bond(FR) was keen enough early on and seemed to get bogged down on the soft surface.

King Torus(IRE) looked good when winning the Vintage Stakes by 6l, but that form is really weak by Group 2 standards, and he'd been off since. Sweating between his hind legs on his return, he ran no sort of race and did not seem to take to the ground (all previous starts on good to firm).

Whipless(IRE), a 6f maiden winner on a fast surface at the Curragh, ran poorly under these different conditions.

Treasury Devil(USA), the winner of his first two starts at Newbury and Sandown, was never going and presumably didn't handle the ground.

6611a QATAR PRIX DE LA FORET (GROUP 1) (3YO+) (TURF) 7f

2:20 (12:00) 3-Y-O+ **£126,415** (£50,575; £25,287; £12,632; £6,327)

RPR

1 **Goldikova (IRE)**[49] 5134 5-8-13 0 OlivierPeslier 1 124+
(F Head, France) *broke wl to ld: hdd 2f out: w.w: qcknd wl 1f out: r.o strly: a in control fnl 50yds* **7/4**[1]

2 ½ **Paco Boy (IRE)**[28] 5801 5-9-2 0 RichardHughes 10 125
(R Hannon) *w.w towards rr: qcknd wl 1 1/2f out on outside: r.o strly fnl f: looked threatening 100yds out: no ex fnl 50yds* **9/2**[2]

3 ½ **Dick Turpin (IRE)**[47] 5186 3-9-0 0 RyanMoore 9 122
(R Hannon) *racd in midfield: qcknd wl to chal strly 1f out: r.o wl but no ex fnl 100yds* **5/1**[3]

4 ¾ **Regal Parade**[29] 5744 6-9-2 0 AdrianNicholls 3 121
(D Nicholls) *prom fr s: chal for ld early in st: grabbed ld 2f out: wnt 2 l clr: r.o wl: hdd 1f out: styd on wl* **7/1**

5 1 **Joanna (IRE)**[56] 4885 3-8-10 0 ChristopheSoumillon 5 114
(J-C Rouget, France) *racd in midfield: rdn 1 1/2f out: no ex: styd on* **8/1**

6 1 ½ **Special Duty**[88] 3793 3-8-10 0 StephanePasquier 6 110
(Mme C Head-Maarek, France) *racd towards rr: rdn but failed to qckn 2f out: styd on fnl f* **16/1**

7 1 ½ **Siyouni (FR)**[28] 5801 3-9-0 0 Christophe-PatriceLemaire 2 110
(A De Royer-Dupre, France) *broke wl to r in 2nd: rdn 2f out: failed to qckn: styd on fnl f* **6/1**

8 6 **Mariol (FR)**[35] 5576 7-9-2 0 IoritzMendizabal 4 95
(Robert Collet, France) *racd in 5th on rail: rdn 2f out: no ex fnl f* **100/1**

9 4 **Smooth Operator (GER)**[35] 5573 4-9-2 0 MaximeGuyon 7 85
(Mario Hofer, Germany) *prom fr s: racd in 3rd on outside: rdn and no ex fr 2f out: sn wknd* **50/1**

10 20 **Kargali (IRE)**[21] 6009 5-9-2 0 KierenFallon 8 33
(Luke Comer, Ire) *racd in rr: rdn but no ex in st: sn wknd* **100/1**

1m 22.1s (1.40) **Going Correction** +0.625s/f (Yiel)
WFA 3 from 4yo+ 2lb **10** Ran SP% **118.9**
Speed ratings: **117,116,115,115,113 112,110,103,99,76**
WIN (incl. 1 euro stake): 2.30. PLACES: 1.40, 1.90, 2.10. DF: 5.90. SF: 6.60.
Owner Wertheimer & Frere **Bred** Wertheimer Et Frere **Trained** France
■ Goldikova's 11th Group or Grade 1 success, a new record for a European-trained thoroughbred.

FOCUS
Top-class form with Group 1 winners filling six of the first seven placings, the only exception being Joanna, who herself was second at the top level last time.

NOTEBOOK
Goldikova(IRE) ◆'s greatness was indisputable pre-race, and this latest victory only enhances her profile further, not just because of the record, but it was her first victory over 7f (all previous wins between 1m-1m1f), helping to erase the memory of an unsatisfactory defeat in this 12 months ago, when an unhelpful draw combined with an uninspired ride proved her undoing. Just like in last season's race, she was without the help of a pacemaker, and she was soon in front, racing plenty freely enough. However, Olivier Peslier, whether at fault or not for chasing an overly strong pace in the race last year, got it absolutely spot on this time, waiting patiently as Regal Parade came past her in the straight. That rival had gone too soon, which Peslier clearly knew full well, and when he let Goldikova go, the result was inevitable, for she soon swept back to the front and had no trouble finding extra as the Hannon closers began to emerge. The next, and possible final stop, is Churchill Downs, where she'll bid to outdo Miesque once again by landing an unprecedented third Breeders' Cup Mile. Versatile ground-wise and tactically, it's hard to see beyond her. (op 2-1)
Paco Boy(IRE), the 2008 winner of this, has now finished behind Goldikova on all four occasions that they've met. The widest draw was no help, although presumably he was going to be held up anyway, and although staying on in fine style down the outside in the straight, he never looked like getting to the winner. This is about as good as he is, but he is due to have another crack at Goldikova in the Breeders' Cup Mile before retiring to stud.
Dick Turpin(IRE), unsuited by 1m2f on a fast surface in the International Stakes on his previous start, had the ground to suit this time, but gave the impression the drop to 7f was not ideal. He tried hard and this was a terrific effort from a less than ideal draw, but ultimately he just didn't quite have the speed of the front two. He stays in training.
Regal Parade had the ground in his favour after being unsuited by a fast surface in the Haydock Sprint Cup, but he surely committed for home too soon, going to the front a good few strides before Peslier had asked long-time leader Goldikova for any kind of effort, and was inevitably worn down. Despite that, this was a fantastic run in defeat and probably not that far off the level he showed when winning the Prix Maurice De Gheest. (op 15-2)
Joanna(IRE) seemed to run slightly below the level she showed when just behind Regal Parade last time, proving unable to reverse form despite her old rival being there for the taking in the closing stages.
Special Duty pulled muscles across her pelvis in the Falmouth according to the owner's racing manager, and had been off since. Considering she was below her best behind Joanna in the Prix Imprudence on her only previous start on this sort of ground, this wasn't a bad effort after three months off. (op 14-1)
Siyouni(FR) did not improve as one might have hoped for the return to 7f and remains winless since last year's Prix Jean-Luc Lagardere.

6612a QATAR PRIX DE L'ARC DE TRIOMPHE (GROUP 1) (3YO+ COLTS, FILLIES & MARES) (TURF) 1m 4f

3:05 (12:00) 3-Y-O£2,022,654 (£809,203; £404,601; £202,123; £101,238)

RPR

1 **Workforce**[71] 4359 3-8-11 0 RyanMoore 8 130+
(Sir Michael Stoute) *settled in midfield: shuffled bk on rail at 1/2-way: hdwy on ins 3f out: chal between Planteur and Nakayama Festa 1 1/2f out: led appr fnl f: r.o strly u.p* **6/1**

2 hd **Nakayama Festa (JPN)**[21] 6015 4-9-5 0 MasayoshiEbina 10 129
(Yoshitaka Ninomiya, Japan) *hld up in midfield: cl up and snatched up 3f out: sn rcvrd and hdwy on outside to ld 1 1/2f out: hdd 1f out: r.o wl u.p* **22/1**

3 2 ½ **Sarafina (FR)**[21] 6013 3-8-8 0 GeraldMosse 3 124+
(A De Royer-Dupre, France) *hld up: hdwy into midfield and nrly b.d by wkng Midas Touch on fnl turn: plld wd 2f out and r.o wl to go 3rd fnl 100yds* **12/1**

4 1 ½ **Behkabad (FR)**[21] 6014 3-8-11 0 Christophe-PatriceLemaire 9 123+
(J-C Rouget, France) *settled bhd ldng gp: cl 8th whn tightened up and nowhere to go 2f out: swtchd ins and running on whn short of room 1 1/2f out: styd on ins fnl f: no ex fnl 50yds* **7/2**[1]

5 1 **Fame And Glory**[56] 4877 4-9-5 0 JMurtagh 1 121+
(A P O'Brien, Ire) *chsd ldrs travelling wl: cl 6th and gng wl over 3f out: 3rd st and n.m.r: rdn and hmpd 1 1/2f out: nt really rcvr* **9/2**[2]

6 1 **Marinous (FR)**[35] 5575 4-9-5 0 DavyBonilla 17 119
(F Head, France) *w.w in rr: rdn and plld wd 3f out: styng on whn rdn and drifted rt 1 1/2f out (bmpd Liang Kay): kpt on at same pce* **50/1**

7 hd **Victoire Pisa (JPN)**[21] 6014 3-8-11 0 YutakaTake 5 115
(Katsuhiko Sumii, Japan) *settled in midfield: styd on at one pce ins fnl 2f: fin 8th: plcd 7th* **40/1**

8 1 **Cavalryman**[28] 5806 4-9-5 0 (b[1]) FrankieDettori 4 113+
(Saeed Bin Suroor) *racd in midfield on rail: trcking Fame And Glory turning for home: tk gap on rail to go 4th 1 1/2f out: sn rdn and wknd ins fnl f: fin 9th: plcd 8th* **20/1**

9 4 **Liang Kay (GER)**[36] 5542 5-9-5 0 StephanePasquier 20 107+
(Uwe Ostmann, Germany) *settled towards rr: rdn and 9th 2f out: keeping on at same pce whn hmpd 1 1/2f out: no ex: fin 10th: plcd 9th* **150/1**

10 2 ½ **Youmzain (IRE)**[71] 4359 7-9-5 0 RichardHughes 12 103
(M R Channon) *hld up towards rr: last 3f out: prog up ins to be 11th 1 1/2f out: sn rdn and no ex: wknd fnl 100yds: fin 11th: plcd 10th* **12/1**

11 1 **Lope De Vega (IRE)**[28] 5801 3-8-11 0 MaximeGuyon 13 101+
(A Fabre, France) *trckd four ldrs in gp of three (outside Behkabad and Fame And Glory): clsng whn bmpd by Duncan over 3 1/2f out: disp ld st: rdn and wknd fr 2f out: fin 12th: plcd 11th* **20/1**

12 nse **Wiener Walzer (GER)**[28] 5806 4-9-5 0 TomQueally 6 101
(J Hirschberger, Germany) *a bhd and nvr plcd to chal: fin 13th: plcd 12th* **100/1**

13 5 **Cape Blanco (IRE)**[29] 5775 3-8-11 0 ChristopheSoumillon 11 93+
(A P O'Brien, Ire) *hld up in fnl 3rd: hdwy to go 7th over 3f out whn bmpd: 4th st: rdn and nt qckn fr 2f out: eased: fin 14th: plcd 13th* **11/1**

14 5 **Timos (GER)**[21] 6015 5-9-5 0 KierenFallon 14 85+
(T Doumen, France) *bhd: sme hdwy 3f out: btn whn hmpd ins fnl 2f: eased: fin 15th: plcd 14th* **66/1**

15 hd **Duncan**[21] 6015 5-9-5 0 WilliamBuick 16 85
(J H M Gosden) *a.p: plld out and bmpd Lope De Vega over 3 1/2f out: chsd ldrs tl dropped away over 2f out: fin 16th: plcd 15th* **33/1**

16 1 **Plumania**[21] 6013 4-9-2 0 OlivierPeslier 15 83
(A Fabre, France) *hld up: rdn and no imp over 2f out: eased: fin 17th: plcd 16th* **25/1**

17 8 **Midas Touch**[22] 5945 3-8-11 0 JAHeffernan 18 71
(A P O'Brien, Ire) *sn pressing ldr: wknd ins fnl 3 1/2f: fin 18th: plcd 17th* **40/1**

18 20 **Pouvoir Absolu**[35] 5575 5-9-5 0 (b) SamuelFargeat 2 —
(E Lellouche, France) *rdn to take over ld fr stablemate after nrly a f: moved off rail 3f out to let Planteur through on rail: wknd qckly: fin 19th: plcd 18th* **150/1**

D 2 **Planteur (IRE)**[21] 6014 3-8-11 0 AnthonyCrastus 7 116
(E Lellouche, France) *led early but sn settled bhd pcemaker: disp ld 3f out: chal by 1st and 2nd whn jinked lft and hit Fame And Glory 1 1/2f out then wnt rt and tightened up Cavalryman: unable qck u.p: fdd fnl 100yds: disqualifie* **11/2**[3]

2m 35.3s (4.90) **Going Correction** +0.95s/f (Soft)
WFA 3 from 4yo+ 7lb **19** Ran SP% **125.1**
Speed ratings: **121,120,119,118,117 116,115,114,112,110 109,109,106,103,102 102,96,83,115**
PARI-MUTUEL (all including 1 euro stakes): WIN 8.60; PLACE 5.80, 8.10, 5.40; DF 209.00; SF 462.00.
Owner K Abdulla **Bred** Juddmonte Farms Ltd **Trained** Newmarket, Suffolk
■ A fourth Arc win for owner Khalid Abdullah, who also bred Workforce, but a first for Sir Michael Stoute and Ryan Moore.

FOCUS
Having been spoilt the previous two years with top-class performances from Zarkava and Sea The Stars, this year's Arc looked to lack star quality beforehand. There were still 12 individual Group 1 winners in the field though, and as the betting suggested it was a highly competitive affair. The soft ground and the presence of a quality pacemaker for Planteur promised to make this a real test of stamina, but in reality the early gallop wasn't that strong, so a few raced keenly and as the field bunched up there was plenty of trouble in running. The winning time was the slowest since Sakhee won in 2001 but still over three seconds quicker than that recorded by Montjeu in heavy ground in 1999.

NOTEBOOK
Workforce, despite being drawn in stall eight, managed to bag a rail position towards the back of the pack. Ryan Moore threaded a passage through on the Derby winner and, in a final-furlong duel with the Japanese raider Nakayama Festa, proved the stronger jockey as his mount just saw it out the better to give Sir Michael Stoute his first win in the race. Although a brilliant winner of the Derby, Workforce had run an inexplicable stinker in the King George and came here with something to prove, not least his ability to handle soft ground. Despite being one of the least experienced in the line-up, he bravely quickened up between horses 2f out and then settled down to battle it out inside the last. Huge credit goes to his trainer for getting him back to his best after Ascot, and, given how lightly raced he is one would imagine that there could be even better to come from him if he is kept in training. In the meantime the Breeders' Cup Turf is a possibility.
Nakayama Festa(JPN) beat Buena Vista to take a Japanese Grade 1 race in June and shaped quite well when runner-up in a muddling Prix Foy last time out. This was a big step up on that effort, especially as his rider had to snatch up rounding the turn into the straight as things got a bit tight. He quickened up well alongside the winner, and it was arguably just strength from the saddle on Workforce that made the difference. He could well become a regular in the big international races now, with the likes of the Sheema Classic a possible target early next year, but in the short term he'll surely now be aimed at the Japan Cup.
Sarafina(FR), the Prix de Diane winner, emerges with plenty of credit, as she was keen, squeezed up early and forced to drop back in the field, then badly hampered along the false straight as the weakening Midas Touch fell back into her. With just three behind her turning in, she was switched to the outside and then stayed on really strongly to take third. There had been concerns about her stamina, but those were quashed, and in a clean race there's every reason to think that she would have given the winner plenty to do. This was only her fifth start and she has plenty more to offer. She is likely to be kept in training, and in the meantime would be an interesting contender for the Breeders' Cup Filly & Mare Turf if allowed to take her chance. (op 10-1)
Behkabad(FR) had a nice run until early in the straight, at which point he found himself behind a wall of horses with nowhere to go. Lemaire had to sit and suffer while the first two were striking for home, but it has to be said that when he saw daylight he didn't pick up instantly and didn't finish as well as Sarafina. A stronger pace might have suited him better, but more importantly, as a son of Cape Cross, he wants quicker ground than this. Hong Kong is a possibility if he is to be retired to stud, but if he stays in training he probably will not run again this year.
Fame And Glory, sixth in this race last year, had missed an intended prep race in the Irish Champion/Prix Foy, but he was still strong in the market beforehand. He turned into the straight going well in behind Planteur but didn't pick up when asked to quicken between horses, and he was badly hampered soon afterwards. He's a high-class galloper, at his best coming off a strong pace, and it was his lack of pace that caught him out here. He could get back on track in the Breeders' Cup Turf, which is looking a weak renewal unless Workforce runs. (op 11-2)
Marinous(FR), who ran a personal best to take a Group 2 at Deauville last time out, had a poor draw to overcome but on the plus side he's a soft-ground specialist. Held up at the back of the field, he came wide in the straight, edged right under pressure and bumped into Liang Kay, but basically stayed on pretty well.
Victoire Pisa(JPN), a winner of a Grade 1 over 1m2f in Japan and fourth in the Niel in his prep for this, had plenty of work to do at the top of the straight. He stayed on but never really threatened to land a blow. He goes for the Japan Cup next.

Cavalryman was third from stall 19 in this race last year when trained by Andre Fabre, and although he hadn't matched that level of form for Godolphin this year, he was back at Longchamp for the first time since, was well drawn, and was wearing blinkers for the first time, having apparently worked well in them at home. He didn't get the clearest of passages next to the rail in the straight, but in truth he lacked the pace to really lay down a challenge. Quicker ground probably suits him best. (op 18-1)
Liang Kay(GER) wasn't going anywhere when hampered.
Youmzain(IRE) was not comfortable on the ground and never looked like improving his record of three successive seconds. He now retires to stud in Normandy, the winner of six of his 32 starts and almost £3.4m, much of it in place money.
Lope De Vega(IRE) stayed calm through the preliminaries and was ridden as though stamina wouldn't be an issue, but it was. Having looked strong on the outside he was weakening when badly hampered a furlong and a half out.
Wiener Walzer(GER) hasn't quite matched the form he showed at three this year, and this ground was softer than he likes.
Cape Blanco(IRE), who loves to hear his hooves rattle, is probably at his best over 1m2f, and was coming here as a bit of an afterthought. He got trapped wide for most of the race and was also hampered, so it's easy to forgive him this.
Timos(GER) was out of his depth.
Duncan, who stole a slowly run Prix Foy last time out, found this altogether tougher. He was weakening when hampered. (op 28-1)
Plumania, drawn high, was stuck wide the whole way round. (op 20-1)
Midas Touch had a lot of use made of him early in crossing over from stall 18 to dispute the lead.
Planteur(IRE), who has a soft-ground action and was fully expected to enjoy these conditions, got a nice lead through the race from his pacemaker Pouvoir Absolu, who kindly edged off the rail for him along the false straight. He was given every chance and was simply exposed as not good enough. He was disqualified for hampering Fame And Glory. (op 6-1)

6613a NYSE EURONEXT PRIX DE L'OPERA (GROUP 1) (3YO+ FILLIES & MARES) (TURF) — 1m 2f

4:35 (12:00) 3-Y-O+ **£151,699** (£60,690; £30,345; £15,159; £7,592)

RPR

1 **Lily Of The Valley (FR)**[42] 5346 3-8-11 0 .... IoritzMendizabal 1 121
(J-C Rouget, France) *racd in 3rd on rail: patiently rdn in st: rdn ent fnl f: qcknd wl to chal ldr 1f out: tk command fnl 100yds* **7/1**[3]

2 ¾ **Stacelita (FR)**[42] 5348 4-9-2 0 .... ChristopheSoumillon 3 119
(J-C Rouget, France) *racd in 2nd: qcknd wl to take ld over 2f out: r.o wl u.p: chal 1f out and hdd fnl 100yds: r.o bravely* **6/4**[1]

3 6 **Fleur Enchantee (FR)**[14] 6234 6-9-2 0 ....(p) StephanePasquier 8 107
(P Van De Poele, France) *racd towards the rr: rdn 2f out and responded wl: r.o wl fnl f but no threat to ldrs* **40/1**

4 1 ½ **Field Day (IRE)**[52] 5139 3-8-11 0 .... KierenFallon 5 104
(B J Meehan) *racd promly fr s: hrd rdn 2f out: responded wl and styd on* **10/1**

5 ½ **Rosanara (FR)**[64] 4575 3-8-11 0 .... Christophe-PatriceLemaire 9 103
(A De Royer-Dupre, France) *racd towards rr: rdn early in st: failed to qckn and styd on* **8/1**

6 snk **Elle Shadow (IRE)**[32] 5671 3-8-11 0 .... AStarke 11 103
(P Schiergen, Germany) *w.w towards rr: prog in the st: r.o one pce fr 2f out* **25/1**

7 1 **Nouriya**[18] 6095 3-8-11 0 .... RyanMoore 10 101
(Sir Michael Stoute) *w.w in rr: threatened briefly early in st but r.o at one pce* **14/1**

8 snk **Board Meeting (IRE)**[42] 5348 4-9-2 0 .... AnthonyCrastus 6 100
(E Lellouche, France) *racd promly: rdn early in st but fnd no ex and wknd* **12/1**

9 1 **Dariole (FR)**[21] 6013 3-8-11 0 .... YutakaTake 7 98
(P Bary, France) *racd towards rr: rdn early in st but fnd no ex and wknd* **25/1**

10 20 **Lush Lashes**[21] 6007 5-9-2 0 ....(t) KJManning 2 58
(J S Bolger, Ire) *racd in 6th: rdn early in st: no ex: fdd* **16/1**

11 4 **Antara (GER)**[42] 5348 4-9-2 0 .... FrankieDettori 4 50
(Saeed Bin Suroor) *rdn to ld and stl in front ent st: sn rdn and hdd over 2f out: grad wknd* **4/1**[2]

2m 9.80s (5.80) **Going Correction** +0.95s/f (Soft)
WFA 3 from 4yo+ 5lb — **11** Ran SP% **123.1**
Speed ratings: **114,113,108,107,107 106,106,105,105,89 85**
WIN (incl. 1 euro stake): 8.00. PLACES: 2.30, 1.50, 5.70. DF: 7.90. SF: 23.10.
Owner Bernard Barsi **Bred** Dunmore Stud Limited **Trained** Pau, France

FOCUS
In the absence of Midday, this was just a reasonable fillies' Group 1, and the front two finished clear. They seemed to go an even gallop.

NOTEBOOK
Lily Of The Valley(FR) looked pretty limited when beaten on her first two outings, but she hasn't stopped improving since gaining her first success in minor company almost a year ago to the day, and has now won her last seven starts. She missed out on the Classics, basically not being up to such a standard at that stage of her career, and she only made her Group-race debut in July. However, she earned a shot at this level with back-to-back Group 3 wins, and proved herself a high-class filly with a hard-earned success, just managing to get the better of a protracted duel with her stable companion, the pair well clear. Considering her profile there's every reason to believe she could keep on progressing and, though unlikely to run again this year, she is set to stay in training. According to her trainer, next year's Arc could be the plan. (op 13-2)
Stacelita(FR), seventh in the Arc last year rather than contesting this race, came here off the back of success in an ordinary Group 1 at Deauville. Beautifully placed, she had her chance and found plenty for pressure, but the winner was just that bit stronger at the line. This is as good as she is. (op 7-4)
Fleur Enchantee(FR) ran a good race, but was further behind Stacelita than when fourth in the Prix Jean Romanet on her penultimate start.
Field Day(IRE), racing beyond 1m for the first time and debuting at the top level, ran a sound race on ground that both her fluent action, and her breeding, suggests was softer than ideal. Lightly raced, she looks a filly with more to offer.
Rosanara(FR), last year's Prix Marcel Boussac winner, ran better when well beaten in the Nassau, probably benefiting from racing in her home country (theory is she doesn't travel well), but she lacks pace these days and never looked like getting involved.
Elle Shadow(IRE), the German Oaks runner-up, came into this off the back of a Group 3 success at Baden-Baden, but she failed to prove herself up to this top level out of her home country.
Nouriya was up significantly in class after victories in a maiden and two Listed contests. She seemed to be short of room on leaving the false straight, and didn't have much room once in line for the finish either, but while she might have finished slightly closer, she didn't look unlucky.
Lush Lashes, runner-up in this in 2008, returned to racing this year following a failed mating with Sea The Stars. She had appeared to be working her way into form, but this was a major step backwards.
Antara(GER) seemed to recover from an awkward start, managing to lead for much of the way and looking comfortable in the process, but the way she weakened suggests something was amiss. She was only a head behind Stacelita last time, well in front of Fleur Enchantee.

6615 - 6616a (Foreign Racing) - See Raceform Interactive

5458 TIPPERARY (L-H)

Sunday, October 3

OFFICIAL GOING: Flat course - soft (heavy in places); jumps courses - yielding (yielding to soft in places)

6617a COOLMORE STUD HOME OF CHAMPIONS CONCORDE STKS (GROUP 3) — 7f 100y

3:15 (3:17) 3-Y-O+ **£40,265** (£11,769; £5,575; £1,858)

RPR

1 **Emulous**[52] 5016 3-8-12 103 .... PJSmullen 10 108
(D K Weld, Ire) *chsd ldrs: 5th 3f out: rdn in 2nd 1 1/2f out: led under 1f out: kpt on wl* **3/1**[2]

2 1 ¾ **Keredari (IRE)**[134] 2354 3-9-1 107 .... FMBerry 7 107
(John M Oxx, Ire) *chsd ldrs: rdn to ld under 2f out: hdd under 1f out: kpt on same pce* **13/8**[1]

3 10 **Air Chief Marshal (IRE)**[8] 6350 3-9-4 110 ....(b[1]) JPO'Brien 1 85
(A P O'Brien, Ire) *chsd ldrs: rdn in 4th ent st: no imp on ldrs fr 1 1/2f out: wnt mod 3rd ins fnl f* **10/1**

4 2 **Croisultan (IRE)**[21] 6009 4-9-3 106 .... BACurtis 2 77
(Liam McAteer, Ire) *led: rdn and jnd briefly 3f out: hdd under 2f out: no ex fr 1 1/2f out* **6/1**[3]

5 hd **Libano (IRE)**[175] 1246 4-9-3 113 .... SMGorey 9 77
(D K Weld, Ire) *prom: disp ld briefly 3f out: sn rdn: 5th 1 1/2f out: no ex* **12/1**

6 3 **Rock Jock (IRE)**[35] 5573 3-9-1 105 .... MCHussey 8 69
(Tracey Collins, Ire) *towards rr: kpt on one pce fr 3f out* **12/1**

7 3 ½ **Pollen (IRE)**[21] 6006 5-9-3 99 .... WMLordan 4 60
(T Stack, Ire) *chsd ldrs on inner: rdn and no imp fr 3f out* **11/1**

8 4 **Wrong Answer**[21] 6009 3-8-12 98 .... CDHayes 6 47
(Kevin Prendergast, Ire) *a towards rr* **16/1**

9 ¾ **Jumbajukiba**[21] 6006 7-9-3 104 .... CO'Farrell 11 48
(Mrs John Harrington, Ire) *chsd ldrs on outer: wknd fr 3f out* **11/1**

10 1 **Excelerate (IRE)**[7] 6402 7-9-3 94 ....(b[1]) BryanJCooper 3 45
(Edward Lynam, Ire) *a bhd* **33/1**

1m 37.38s (97.38)
WFA 3 from 4yo+ 2lb — **10** Ran SP% **127.3**
CSF £9.17 TOTE £4.30: £1.40, £1.40, £3.00; DF 8.70.
Owner K Abdulla **Bred** Juddmonte Farms Ltd **Trained** The Curragh, Co Kildare

FOCUS
Two lightly raced three-year-olds with proven ability on testing ground dominated here.

NOTEBOOK
Emulous ◆ got the better of Keredari under a furlong from home to win ridden out, with the pair pulling well clear of the third. The winner's only previous success was on her debut a year ago and, as this was only her fourth start of the season, trainer Dermot Weld may find another opportunity for her before the end of the year. She still has plenty of developing to do, and Weld is keen on her in training next year. (op 11/4)
Keredari(IRE), twice a winner from four previous attempts, had won a Listed event over 7f at the Curragh first time out this season. This was his first start since he finished sixth in the Irish 2000 Guineas, and with conditions in his favour he was the subject of strong market support (3-1 to 13-8). He tracked the leaders and got to the front a furlong and a half out, before failing to raise his effort sufficiently when tackled and headed by the winner. (op 5/2)
Air Chief Marshal(IRE), who was a pacemaker for Rip Van Winkle in the Queen Elizabeth II Stakes on his previous start, won a similar type of event to this over 7f at the Curragh in July. Blinkered for the first time here, he raced prominently, but failed to raise his game in the straight as the race developed into a match. (op 9/1 tchd 10/1)
Croisultan(IRE), a four-time winner including once at Listed level, has never won beyond 6f, although he has been placed at up to 1m. He made the running until a furlong and a half out and was soon done with. While he is well suited by soft ground, getting this trip on it was a bit of a struggle and it will be no suprise to see him dropped back to 6f next time. (op 6/1 tchd 13/2)
Libano(IRE), a five-time winner who scored four times in Italy, once at this level, before joining the Weld Stable. He won a 7f Listed event at Leopardstown at the end of last season and had not run since April. He relishes testing ground and can be placed to good effect in the coming weeks judged by this encouraging effort. He raced in second place until the turn in before the lack of a recent run came into play.

6301 PONTEFRACT (L-H)

Monday, October 4

OFFICIAL GOING: Soft (good to soft in places; 7.0)
Wind: Very light half against Weather: Fine and dry

6618 E B F TOTESPORT DAY ON MONDAY 18TH OCTOBER MAIDEN STKS — 1m 2f 6y

2:10 (2:11) (Class 4) 2-Y-O **£4,533** (£1,348; £674; £336) Stalls Low

Form — RPR

1 **Mahab El Shamaal** 2-9-3 0 .... JackMitchell 12 75+
(D M Simcock) *dwlt and hld up towards rr: gd hdwy on outer over 3f out: chsd ldrs 2f out: led over 1f out: sn rdn: rn green and edgd lft: kpt on wl ins fnl f* **12/1**

6 2 2 ½ **She's Got The Luck (IRE)**[9] 6360 2-8-12 0 .... PaulHanagan 3 66
(G M Moore) *in tch on inner: n.m.r 3f out: rdn and hdwy to chal over 1f out: drvn and edgd rt ins fnl f: kpt on same pce* **7/1**[3]

0 3 nse **Rasam Aldaar**[17] 6159 2-9-3 0 .... SamHitchcott 7 71
(M R Channon) *chsd ldr: effrt and cl up over 3f out: sn rdn along and sltly outpcd 2f out: styd on u.p ent fnl f: sn drvn and one pce* **14/1**

0 4 6 **Astromagick**[17] 6154 2-8-7 0 .... AshleyMorgan[(5)] 14 55
(M H Tompkins) *s.i.s and towards rr: gd hdwy on outer to trck ldrs after 4f: effrt and cl up 3f out: rdn along and ch wl over 1f out: sn drvn and one pce ent fnl f* **9/1**

42 5 ¾ **Ullswater (IRE)**[7] 6414 2-9-3 0 .... GregFairley 10 59
(M Johnston) *sn led: rdn along 3f out: drvn and hdd over 1f out: wknd ins fnl f* **5/4**[1]

45 6 1 **Mojolika**[21] 6036 2-9-3 0 .... PhillipMakin 6 57
(T D Easterby) *trckd ldrs: hdwy 3f out: rdn along 2f out: drvn over 1f out and sn wknd* **9/2**[2]

04 7 1 **Subramaniam**[22] 6001 2-9-3 0 .... PaulMulrennan 11 55
(J G Given) *hld up and bhd: pushed along and hdwy on outer 3f out: rdn wl over 1f out: kpt on ins fnl f: nrst fin* **25/1**

0 8 4 ½ **Nay Secret**[15] 6222 2-9-0 0 .... GaryBartley[(3)] 9 47
(J S Goldie) *nvr bttr than midfield* **100/1**

0000 **9** *2 ¼* **Pinotage**[19] 6070 2-9-0 36 .... MichaelStainton(3) 8 43
(R M Whitaker) *trckd ldrs: hdwy 3f out: chsd ldr 2f out: sn rdn and wknd over 1f out* **100/1**
6000 **10** *hd* **Silver Writer**[34] 5629 2-8-12 45 .... DaleSwift(5) 1 43
(M W Easterby) *midfield: rdn along 1/2-way: sn outpcd and bhd* **100/1**
0600 **11** *18* **Rainbows Son**[12] 6300 2-9-3 43 .... (p) MickyFenton 4 10
(P T Midgley) *midfield: pushed along after 4f: sn lost pl and bhd* **40/1**
12 *3 ¾* **Hurricane Guest** 2-9-0 0 .... BarryMcHugh(3) 2 —
(G G Margarson) *s.i.s: a towards rr* **14/1**
000 **13** *27* **Santorino**[21] 6036 2-9-3 40 .... PJMcDonald 5 —
(P T Midgley) *chsd ldrs on inner: rdn along over 4f out: sn wknd* **100/1**

2m 19.18s (5.48) **Going Correction** +0.45s/f (Yiel) **13** Ran SP% **116.4**
Speed ratings (Par 97): **96,94,93,89,88 87,86,83,81,81 67,64,42**
toteswingers:1&2 £9.70, 2&3 £19.00, 1&3 £18.90 CSF £89.25 TOTE £15.30: £2.90, £1.20, £6.20; EX 93.10.
Owner Saif Ali & Saeed H Altayer **Bred** M Kerr-Dineen **Trained** Newmarket, Suffolk

FOCUS
A total of 17mm of rain on Sunday saw the ground ease significantly but it was dry overnight and conditions were unseasonably hot and sunny throughout the morning and afternoon. Little strength to a maiden in which the gallop was ordinary and one that took even less winning than seemed likely beforehand with the market leader disappointing. As usual on soft ground at this course, the bulk of the field came centre to stands' side in the straight. The time was over eight seconds above standard and two riders stated the ground was "soft" and "hard work".

NOTEBOOK
Mahab El Shamaal ◆, a 27,000gns brother to 1m4f winner Domination out of a triple 1m2f scorer (herself a half-sister to high-class Hong Kong performer Salford Mill), was nibbled at in the market and created a favourable impression on debut. Although this form is nothing special, he can only improve and looks capable of picking up a decent handicap granted a sufficient test of stamina next year. (tchd 11-1)
She's Got The Luck(IRE), who hinted at ability on debut over 1m in soft ground, duly stepped up on that effort over this longer trip. While she is likely to remain vulnerable to the better types in this grade, she will be of interest once handicapped and should improve again over 1m4f. (op 6-1)
Rasam Aldaar has plenty of stamina in his pedigree and, after attracting support at big prices, fared better than on debut at Newmarket over this longer trip. He too should be seen to better effect over a bit further when qualified for a handicap mark. (op 25-1)
Astromagick is out of a dam who stayed 2m and acted on soft, and she posted an improved effort over this longer trip. She will have no problems with 1m4f and is capable of picking up a minor event at some point. (op 11-1 tchd 12-1)
Ullswater(IRE) had the run of the race but who failed to confirm the improved effort shown on much quicker ground on his previous start. His yard has been relatively quiet in recent times and he will be worth another chance back on a sounder surface. (op 6-5 tchd 11-8)
Mojolika was sweating beforehand but who finished closer to the market leader than at Redcar on his previous start. He'll have no problems with 1m4f and is open to a little improvement. (op 6-1)

6619 RON AND JOAN SENIOR - LIFETIMES IN RACING NURSERY — 6f
2:40 (2:42) (Class 5) (0-85,82) 2-Y-O **£2,914** (£867; £433; £216) **Stalls** Low

Form RPR
4311 **1** **Jack Smudge**[19] 6086 2-9-2 77 .... PaulMulrennan 6 82
(J G Given) *trckd ldrs: hdwy over 2f out: chal and sltly hmpd wl over 1f out: rdn to ld and edgd lft ent fnl f: drvn and hung lft nr fin: hld on* **6/1**[3]
15 **2** *½* **Robert The Painter (IRE)**[17] 6139 2-9-0 80 .... LeeTopliss(5) 10 84
(R A Fahey) *prom: hdwy to chal 2f out: rdn whn sltly hmpd wl over 1f out and sn ev ch: drvn to dispute ld whn hmpd ins fnl f: hld whn bmpd and no ex towards fin* **7/2**[1]
5500 **3** *3 ½* **Lizzie (IRE)**[25] 5882 2-8-8 69 .... (b) PJMcDonald 2 62
(T D Easterby) *led: rdn and hung rt wl over 1f out: drvn and hdd ent fnl f: sn hung lft and one pce* **9/1**
4142 **4** *3* **Brave Dream**[11] 6311 2-8-11 72 .... PaulHanagan 11 56
(K A Ryan) *cl up: effrt 2f out and ev ch: rdn wl over 1f out and grad wknd* **11/2**[2]
2302 **5** *1 ½* **Eilean Mor**[15] 6220 2-8-5 66 .... SilvestreDeSousa 3 46
(J S Goldie) *chsd ldrs: rdn along 2f out: drvn over 1f out and sn one pce* **6/1**[3]
034 **6** *hd* **Ted's Brother (IRE)**[18] 6102 2-8-3 67 .... IanBrennan(3) 9 46
(R C Guest) *dwlt and in rr: hdwy over 2f out: rdn wl over 1f out: kpt on ins fnl f: nt rch ldrs* **10/1**
0360 **7** *nk* **Las Verglas Star (IRE)**[15] 6220 2-8-7 68 .... (b1) GregFairley 12 46
(R A Fahey) *prom on outer: rdn along over 2f out: drvn wl over 1f out and sn wknd* **18/1**
5216 **8** *¾* **Azzurra Du Caprio (IRE)**[25] 5882 2-9-4 79 .... JimmyFortune 1 55
(B M R Haslam) *trckd ldrs: hdwy on inner and cl up 2f out: rdn wl over 1f out: wknd and eased ent fnl f* **7/1**
130 **9** *¾* **Last Destination (IRE)**[23] 5947 2-8-13 74 .... PhillipMakin 8 48
(N Tinkler) *a in rr* **40/1**
15 **10** *½* **Rhythm Of Light**[30] 5746 2-9-7 82 .... RichardKingscote 5 54
(Tom Dascombe) *in rr: effrt and rdn 1/2-way: hung rt 2f out: nvr a factor* **16/1**
140 **11** *10* **Clipthorne**[16] 6184 2-8-11 75 .... BarryMcHugh(3) 7 17
(Ollie Pears) *in tch on outer: rdn along and edgd rt 1/2-way: sn wknd* **33/1**

1m 19.97s (3.07) **Going Correction** +0.45s/f (Yiel) **11** Ran SP% **114.3**
Speed ratings (Par 95): **97,96,91,87,85 85,85,84,83,82 69**
toteswingers:1&2 £5.30, 2&3 £7.30, 1&3 £11.20 CSF £26.40 CT £190.31 TOTE £5.20: £1.40, £1.90, £3.90; EX 30.90.
Owner Danethorpe Racing Partnership **Bred** P And Mrs A G Venner **Trained** Willoughton, Lincs
■ Stewards' Enquiry : P J McDonald caution: careless riding.
Paul Mulrennan one-day ban: careless riding (Oct 18)

FOCUS
Several previous winners in a fair nursery. The gallop was a reasonable one in the conditions and the first two pulled clear. The field again raced towards the stands side in the straight.

NOTEBOOK
Jack Smudge, who was noticeably easy to back before the off, is a progressive sort who had no problems with the return to 6f or the testing ground and he turned in his best effort, despite drifting off a true line under pressure to register the three-timer. He'll be at least as effective back on better ground and he's capable of winning more races. (op 4-1 tchd 7-2)
Robert The Painter(IRE) ◆ showed he was at least as effective on soft ground as on a sounder surface, despite being carried off a true line in the closing stages (made no difference to the result). He's a progressive sort who is in very good hands, and it'll be a big surprise if he isn't able to win more races over sprint distances. (op 9-2 tchd 5-1)
Lizzie(IRE) attracted support with the blinkers back on to replace cheekpieces and bettered her previous efforts in nursery company on this first run in soft ground against a couple of progressive rivals. There will be easier opportunities than this one from her current mark and she should be able to pick up another small race. (op 12-1 tchd 8-1)
Brave Dream seems fully exposed on turf and he again had his limitations exposed against a couple of improving types. Arguably his best effort came on his previous start on Polytrack and he'll be of interest returned to that surface in the coming weeks. (op 6-1)
Eilean Mor has yet to win but wasn't totally disgraced after going up in the weights and in grade returned to a soft surface. He remains capable of winning a small race and may be worth a try on artificial surfaces at some point. (tchd 5-1)
Ted's Brother(IRE) had shown ability at an ordinary level and wasn't disgraced after losing a bit of ground at the start on this nursery debut. This brother to soft ground specialist Ginger Ted will be worth another chance in ordinary company. (op 16-1)
Azzurra Du Caprio(IRE) Official explanation: trainer said filly was unsuited by the soft (good to soft places) ground
Rhythm Of Light Official explanation: jockey said filly hung right final bend

6620 RACING UK ON SKY CHANNEL 432 H'CAP — 1m 4y
3:10 (3:10) (Class 3) (0-95,88) 3-Y-O **£6,231** (£1,866; £933; £467; £233) **Stalls** Low

Form RPR
0300 **1** **Al Farahidi (USA)**[22] 6002 3-9-7 88 .... GregFairley 3 98
(M Johnston) *mde all: qcknd clr over 2f out: rdn and hung rt ins fnl f: kpt on* **16/1**
3402 **2** *2* **Sand Skier**[3] 6534 3-9-7 88 .... SilvestreDeSousa 9 93
(M Johnston) *trckd ldng pair: effrt to chse wnr 3f out: rdn along wl over 1f out: drvn ent fnl f: kpt on same pce* **5/4**[1]
2160 **3** *3* **Barren Brook**[17] 6142 3-9-2 83 .... PhillipMakin 5 82
(M W Easterby) *t.k.h: hld up in rr: hdwy and wd st: rdn to chse ldng pair over 1f out: sn drvn and no imp* **9/1**
2413 **4** *1 ¾* **Gojeri (IRE)**[24] 5917 3-9-0 81 .... PhilipRobinson 2 75
(M A Jarvis) *sn trcking wnr: effrt 3f out: rdn 2f out: drvn and wknd over 1f out* **15/8**[2]
0020 **5** *7* **She's A Character**[47] 5222 3-8-13 80 .... PaulHanagan 1 58
(R A Fahey) *trckd ldrs: pushed along 3f out: rdn over 2f out: sn wknd* **7/1**[3]

1m 48.41s (2.51) **Going Correction** +0.45s/f (Yiel) **5** Ran SP% **107.6**
Speed ratings (Par 105): **105,103,100,98,91**
CSF £35.42 TOTE £15.30: £6.80, £1.02; EX 19.50.
Owner Sheikh Hamdan Bin Mohammed Al Maktoum **Bred** Gainsborough Farm Llc **Trained** Middleham Moor, N Yorks

FOCUS
A depleted field, but despite comprising useful types, the gallop was a modest one in the conditions and this bare form may not prove fully reliable.

NOTEBOOK
Al Farahidi(USA)'s form has been very patchy since his maiden win in March and he had been soundly beaten on his first run on testing ground on his previous start, but he was allowed an easy lead and showed himself to be fully effective in the conditions. However, the removal of the headgear may have helped, he did have the run of the race and his overall record suggests he would not be one to take too short a price about next time. Official explanation: trainer said, regarding apparent improvement in form, that the gelding had benefitted from leaving off the blinkers. (op 20-1 tchd 14-1)
Sand Skier is a reliable yardstick who was turned out quickly after a career-best effort over 1m1f at Newmarket but, while running creditably, didn't really shape as though a muddling gallop over this shorter trip fully played to his strengths. The return to 1m2f will suit better and he's capable of winning again before the season is out. (op 11-8 tchd 6-4)
Barren Brook's two wins have been on quick ground and he wasn't disgraced on this first run on soft ground against a couple of rivals that weren't stopping in the straight. A more truly run race back on a sound surface could be more to his liking and he's lightly raced enough to be open to further progress. He's well worth another chance. (tchd 8-1 and 10-1)
Gojeri(IRE), who, like several from this yard, raced with the choke out and he failed to match the pick of his AW and turf form returned to a soft surface. However, he too isn't fully exposed and will be of more interest returned to a sound surface or to Polytrack. Official explanation: trainer said gelding was unsuited by the soft (good to soft places) ground (op 7-4 tchd 9-4)
She's A Character was proven on soft ground but she isn't noted for her consistency, and was again below the form she showed in a muddling four-runner race at Hamilton in August. She has slipped to a fair mark and is in very good hands but doesn't look one to place much faith in. (op 6-1)

6621 PHIL BULL TROPHY CONDITIONS STKS — 2m 1f 216y
3:40 (3:40) (Class 3) 3-Y-O+ **£9,346** (£2,799; £1,399; £700) **Stalls** Low

Form RPR
0506 **1** **Ajaan**[16] 6201 6-9-3 99 .... IanMongan 2 90
(H R A Cecil) *hld up: hdwy over 6f out: led over 2f out: wd st and sn rdn: jnd and drvn over 1f out: kpt on gamely ins fnl f* **5/4**[2]
3006 **2** *¾* **Darley Sun (IRE)**[24] 5909 4-9-3 102 .... FrankieDettori 3 89
(Saeed Bin Suroor) *t.k.h: trckd ldrs: hdwy over 3f out: rdn to chse wnr wl over 1f out: drvn to chal appr fnl f and ev ch tl no ex last 75yds* **11/10**[1]
1012 **3** *22* **Any Given Moment (IRE)**[18] 6132 4-9-3 63 .... (b) JackMitchell 5 65
(D M Simcock) *led: pushed along 3f out: hdd over 2f out: sn drvn and plugged on same pce* **13/2**[3]
2-00 **4** *1* **Night Orbit**[10] 4511 6-9-3 57 .... GregFairley 4 64
(Miss J Feilden) *trckd ldr: rdn along 6f out: drvn and outpcd over 3f out* **50/1**

4m 13.94s (17.74) **Going Correction** +0.45s/f (Yiel) **4** Ran SP% **107.4**
Speed ratings (Par 107): **78,77,67,67**
CSF £2.93 TOTE £3.20; EX 3.60.
Owner Niarchos Family **Bred** Miss K Rausing & Course Investment Corporation **Trained** Newmarket, Suffolk

FOCUS
A most uncompetitive race for the money and one in which a steady gallop only picked up on the approach to the straight.

NOTEBOOK
Ajaan, who hasn't been disgraced in some decent handicaps, took advantage of this much easier assignment with his usual blinkers left off. He grabbed the stands' rail in the straight, and beat his only serious rivals with a little bit more in hand than the margin suggested in a race that didn't place much of an emphasis on stamina. He isn't the most straightforward, though, and life will be tougher returned to handicaps. (op 11-8)
Darley Sun(IRE), who had 3lb in hand of the winner judging by official ratings and who was bidding to give his yard its third consecutive win in this race, was far from disgraced dropped markedly in grade in a race that was not run to suit on ground that may have been plenty soft enough. A truer gallop on better ground are his requirements, but he has been essentially disappointing since posting an encouraging reappearance display (first run for this yard) in May. (op 10-11 tchd 6-5)
Any Given Moment(IRE) had no ground worries and was allowed a soft lead but he was readily brushed aside by two much higher-rated rivals once the tempo increased. The return to ordinary handicaps will see him in a much more favourable light. (op 9-1 tchd 11-2)
Night Orbit had his limitations firmly exposed switched back from a stint over fences.

6622 PONTEFRACT DISCO DINES CLAIMING STKS — 1m 4y
4:10 (4:10) (Class 4) 3-Y-O **£3,885** (£1,156; £577; £288) **Stalls** Low

Form RPR
5213 **1** **Indian Valley (USA)**[5] 6476 3-8-2 74 .... SilvestreDeSousa 3 77+
(Rae Guest) *trckd ldng pair: hdwy on inner 2f out: rdn to ld over 1f out and sn hung rt: styd on strly ins fnl f* **5/4**[1]

The Form Book, Raceform Ltd, Compton, RG20 6NL

5542 **2** 3 1/4 **Strike A Deal (IRE)**[19] 6093 3-8-2 64 PaulHanagan 2 70
(C F Wall) *dwlt: hdwy to ld after 1f: rdn along over 2f out: hdd and sltly outpcd over 1f out: drvn and kpt on ins fnl f: tk 2nd nr fin* **9/2**
1322 **3** 1 1/4 **George Benjamin**[8] 6394 3-8-9 74 PaulQuinn 6 74
(D Nicholls) *trckd ldng pair: hdwy on outer over 2f out: rdn to chal and ev ch wl over 1f out: drvn and one pce ins fnl f: lost 2nd towards fin* **3/1**[2]
5261 **4** 6 **Mason Hindmarsh**[18] 6117 3-8-12 68 GregFairley 4 63
(Karen McLintock) *led 1f: cl up: rdn along 2f out and sn wknd* **4/1**[3]
1m 48.34s (2.44) **Going Correction** +0.45s/f (Yiel) 4 Ran SP% **107.6**
Speed ratings (Par 103): **105,101,100,94**
CSF £6.89 TOTE £2.00; EX 4.60.
Owner Triple R Racing **Bred** T Holmes, Dr & Mrs W Zent & S Caldwell **Trained** Newmarket, Suffolk

FOCUS
Another race with a glut of non-runners but the winner is a fair type who relished the conditions. The gallop was a steady one and the field again avoided the far rail.

6623 DEM WINDOW SOLUTIONS H'CAP 1m 4f 8y
4:40 (4:42) (Class 5) (0-70,70) 3-Y-O £2,914 (£867; £433; £216) Stalls Low

Form RPR
6012 **1** **Plan A (IRE)**[15] 6225 3-9-2 65 PaulHanagan 11 77
(M G Quinlan) *trckd ldrs: hdwy and cl up 3f out: rdn to chal and hung rt wl over 1f out: sn led: drvn and hdd ins fnl f: rallied under press and hung rt ins fnl f: led last 50yds* **3/1**[1]
5243 **2** hd **Palawi (IRE)**[15] 6225 3-9-7 70 PhillipMakin 3 82
(J J Quinn) *trckd ldrs: hdwy 3f out: rdn to chal wl over 1f out: drvn and slt ld ins fnl f: hdd: bmpd and no ex last 50yds* **6/1**[2]
1412 **3** 2 1/4 **Sharakti (IRE)**[18] 6116 3-9-1 67 (p) MichaelO'Connell(3) 12 75+
(A J McCabe) *trckd ldrs: hdwy to ld over 2f out: styd far side st: rdn and hdd over 1f out: kpt on same pce* **12/1**
0115 **4** 2 1/2 **Emerald Glade (IRE)**[15] 6225 3-9-3 66 (e[1]) PJMcDonald 6 70
(T D Easterby) *hld up towards rr: hdwy 4f out: rdn to chse ldrs wl over 1f out: kpt on same pce* **7/1**[3]
5135 **5** 9 **Dubawi King**[21] 6038 3-8-9 58 (v) PaulMulrennan 8 48
(N Tinkler) *hld up towards rr: hdwy over 3f out: rdn over 2f out: kpt on: nt rch ldrs* **12/1**
4033 **6** nk **Aalya (IRE)**[20] 6065 3-8-6 60 JohnFahy(5) 14 50
(P W Chapple-Hyam) *hld up towards rr: hdwy on outer and in tch over 4f out: rdn along 3f out: sn no imp* **20/1**
0031 **7** 2 1/2 **Kayaan**[19] 6080 3-9-2 65 MickyFenton 1 51
(Mrs P Sly) *s.i.s: plld hrd in rr: sme hdwy on outer over 4f out: rdn 3f out and sn no imp* **10/1**
0050 **8** nk **The Midshipmaid**[3] 6525 3-8-4 56 oh11 AmyRyan(3) 9 41
(Lucinda Featherstone) *prom: rdn along 3f out: wknd fnl 2f* **66/1**
5612 **9** 8 **Balatoma (IRE)**[22] 5988 3-9-7 70 (b) RichardHills 7 42
(M P Tregoning) *s.i.s and in rr: sme hdwy over 4f out: sn rdn and n.d* **8/1**
4460 **10** 1 1/2 **My Galway Man (IRE)**[20] 6055 3-9-7 70 GregFairley 5 40
(M Johnston) *chsd ldrs: rdn along 3f out: drvn over 2f out and sn wknd* **33/1**
330 **11** 9 **Mighty Mambo**[18] 6132 3-9-6 69 (p) AndreaAtzeni 10 24
(Jane Chapple-Hyam) *led: rdn along 3f out: hdd & wknd over 2f out* **14/1**
3540 **12** 3 1/4 **Layla's Boy**[35] 5607 3-9-2 65 SilvestreDeSousa 13 15
(J Mackie) *a towards rr* **40/1**
0-60 **13** hd **Myraid**[149] 1927 3-8-10 62 BarryMcHugh(3) 4 12
(Ollie Pears) *a towards rr* **15/2**
2m 45.69s (4.89) **Going Correction** +0.45s/f (Yiel) 13 Ran SP% **117.4**
Speed ratings (Par 101): **101,100,99,97,91 91,89,89,84,83 77,75,75**
toteswingers:1&2 £4.00, 2&3 £11.80, 1&3 £11.20 CSF £18.74 CT £190.54 TOTE £6.20: £2.60, £1.30, £5.10; EX 23.90.
Owner Liam Mulryan **Bred** L Mulryan **Trained** Newmarket, Suffolk

FOCUS
A modest handicap in which the gallop was an ordinary one. The first two raced towards the stands' side while the third elected to race towards the far side in the straight. The first four finished clear and those held up could never land a blow.
Balatoma(IRE) Official explanation: trainer had no explanation for the poor form shown

6624 BUY YOUR 2011 ANNUAL BADGE TODAY MAIDEN STKS 1m 4y
5:10 (5:10) (Class 5) 3-Y-O £3,238 (£963; £481; £240) Stalls Low

Form RPR
3326 **1** **Danehill Sunset (IRE)**[18] 6124 3-9-3 72 JimmyFortune 7 78
(B W Hills) *hld up in tch: smooth hdwy on outer over 3f out: led 2f out: rdn wl over 1f out: drvn out* **13/2**
632 **2** 1 3/4 **Silvery Moon (IRE)**[21] 6039 3-9-3 0 PhillipMakin 6 74
(T D Easterby) *in tch: hdwy 3f out: rdn to chse ldrs wl over 1f out: drvn and kpt on ins fnl f: tk 2nd nr line* **6/1**[3]
65 **3** 1/2 **Mashatu**[23] 5971 3-9-3 0 JackMitchell 3 73
(J R Fanshawe) *trckd ldrs: hdwy 4f out: led wl over 2f out: hdd and rdn 2f out: drvn and ev ch over 1f out: one pce ins fnl f: lost 2nd nr line* **5/2**[1]
0 **4** 2 1/2 **Point North (IRE)**[170] 1387 3-9-3 0 PaulHanagan 1 67
(J Noseda) *in tch on inner: hdwy over 2f out: rdn wl over 1f out: sn one pce* **5/2**[1]
05 **5** 1 3/4 **Safwaan**[114] 2981 3-9-3 0 RichardHills 4 63
(W J Haggas) *trckd ldrs: effrt 3f out: cl up and rdn 2f out: wknd appr fnl f* **4/1**[2]
0 **6** 7 **Moorgate Lad**[38] 5487 3-9-3 0 GregFairley 9 47
(O Brennan) *in rr: hdwy over 2f out: kpt on appr fnl f: n.d* **100/1**
5 **7** 2 1/2 **Maxi Moo (IRE)**[89] 3776 3-9-0 0 MichaelO'Connell(3) 12 41
(G A Harker) *towards rr: sme hdwy 3f out: rdn 2f out: n.d* **50/1**
0000 **8** 3 1/4 **Hannah Hawk**[9] 6526 3-8-9 32 (p) AmyRyan(3) 2 29
(Lucinda Featherstone) *prom: rdn along over 3f out: sn wknd* **100/1**
9 1 1/4 **Pyjoma** 3-8-9 0 MichaelStainton(3) 10 26
(Miss J Feilden) *s.i.s: a in rr* **40/1**
020 **10** 1/2 **Fifty Moore**[9] 6356 3-9-3 73 AndrewElliott 13 30
(Jedd O'Keeffe) *cl up: effrt 3f out: rdn over 2f out and sn wknd* **33/1**
5 **11** 15 **Seven Sons**[35] 5603 3-9-3 0 PatrickMathers 11 —
(I W McInnes) *led: rdn along over 3f out: drvn and hdd wl over 2f out: sn wknd* **100/1**
12 30 **Pengula (IRE)** 3-8-12 0 PaulMulrennan 5 —
(R Johnson) *s.i.s: a in rr: outpcd and t.o fnl 3f* **100/1**
1m 49.36s (3.46) **Going Correction** +0.45s/f (Yiel) 12 Ran SP% **116.1**
Speed ratings (Par 101): **100,98,97,95,93 86,84,80,79,79 64,34**
toteswingers:1&2: £4.00, 2&3 £4.80, 1&3 £4.10 CSF £43.34 TOTE £6.50: £1.10, £2.60, £1.10; EX 26.30 Place 6: £155.57 Place 5: £23.73.
Owner Cavendish Investing Ltd **Bred** Atha Bloodstock **Trained** Lambourn, Berks

FOCUS
Little strength in depth to this ordinary maiden. The gallop was an ordinary one and the whole field raced towards the stands' side.

T/Plt: £510.80 to a £1 stake. Pool of £61,579.64 - 88.00 winning tickets. T/Qpdt: £16.50 to a £1 stake. Pool of £5,272.93 - 235.08 winning tickets. JR

6511 WARWICK (L-H)
Monday, October 4

OFFICIAL GOING: Heavy (3.8)
Rail on round course from 1m start to end of back straight (3f from home) moved out 2yds from meeting on Thursday September 30.
Wind: Virtually nil Weather: Sunny

6625 WARWICKRACECOURSE.CO.UK H'CAP 6f
2:20 (2:20) (Class 4) (0-85,85) 3-Y-O+ £4,209 (£1,252; £625; £312) Stalls Low

Form RPR
0531 **1** **Green Park (IRE)**[9] 6358 7-9-4 82 (b) DavidNolan 8 97
(D Carroll) *trckd ldrs: led appr fnl f: hrd drvn and styd on strly* **9/1**
6062 **2** 2 1/2 **Imprimis Tagula (IRE)**[2] 6577 6-8-4 75 (v) HobieGill(7) 2 82
(A Bailey) *disp 2nd: styd on to chse wnr ins fnl f: no imp whn hung lft fnl 120yds* **10/1**
1321 **3** 1/2 **Westwood**[34] 5647 5-8-8 72 NickyMackay 6 77
(D Haydn Jones) *led to post: led: pushed along 2f out: hdd over 1f out: one pce and lost 2nd ins fnl f* **7/2**[2]
00 **4** 1 **Icelandic**[10] 6327 8-9-7 85 (t) LeeVickers 12 87+
(F Sheridan) *in rr: racd alone centre crse over 2f out: edgd towards main gp over 1f out and kpt on ins fnl f: no imp on ldng trio* **33/1**
5423 **5** shd **Grissom (IRE)**[9] 6358 4-8-12 76 (t) DuranFentiman 5 78
(T D Easterby) *disp 2nd: rdn over 2f out: wknd ins fnl f* **9/4**[1]
0350 **6** 1/2 **Spitfire**[25] 5884 5-9-6 84 (p) KierenFallon 7 84
(J R Jenkins) *in tch but drvn along 1/2-way: kpt on ins fnl f: nvr a threat* **13/2**[3]
0040 **7** 4 1/2 **Perfect Flight**[5] 6478 5-9-1 79 SteveDrowne 1 65
(M Blanshard) *chsd ldrs: rdn ins fnl 3f: no ch fnl 2f* **14/1**
2000 **8** 4 1/2 **Coleorton Choice**[9] 6358 4-8-11 75 (p) LukeMorris 11 46
(R Hollinshead) *in tch 3f* **20/1**
4035 **9** 3/4 **Seamus Shindig**[12] 6280 8-8-7 76 AmyScott(5) 15 45
(H Candy) *bhd most of way* **14/1**
0045 **10** 1 3/4 **Protector (SAF)**[114] 2982 9-9-2 80 (t) RobertHavlin 10 43
(T T Clement) *a in rr* **20/1**
4632 **11** 1 3/4 **Imperial Djay (IRE)**[52] 5043 5-8-13 77 RobertWinston 14 35
(Mrs R A Carr) *a in rr* **16/1**
1m 14.42s (2.62) **Going Correction** +0.575s/f (Yiel)
WFA 3 from 4yo+ 1lb 11 Ran SP% **117.1**
Speed ratings (Par 105): **105,101,101,99,99 98,92,86,85,83 81**
toteswingers:1&2 £11.90, 2&3 £8.70, 1&3 £3.50 CSF £92.42 CT £378.37 TOTE £6.80: £2.30, £4.20, £1.90; EX 93.90.
Owner G A Fixings Ltd **Bred** James Burns And A Moynan **Trained** Sledmere, E Yorks

FOCUS
The course's last Flat meeting of the year and it survived an early morning inspection, with the ground officially described as heavy. The running rail on the back straight was out by a couple of yards to provide fresher ground. This opening sprint was a modest affair and, perhaps unsurprisingly on such ground, it was a race where it paid to be handy. Clerk of the course Andrew Morris's assertion beforehand that the best ground in the home straight would be towards the middle of the home straight looked correct, and the form is straightforward enough.

6626 EUROPEAN BREEDERS' FUND MAIDEN STKS 6f
2:50 (2:50) (Class 5) 2-Y-O £3,626 (£1,079; £539; £269) Stalls Low

Form RPR
6 **1** **Chill (IRE)**[17] 6158 2-9-3 0 KierenFallon 6 74
(L M Cumani) *hld up towards rr but in tch: pushed along over 2f out: swtchd lft to outer wl over 1f out and str run ins fnl f to ld cl home* **15/8**[1]
00 **2** nk **Ceffyl Gwell**[16] 6196 2-9-3 0 PatDobbs 4 73
(R Hannon) *chsd ldrs: chal over 1f out tl slt ld fnl 120yds: hdd and no ex cl home* **9/2**[3]
6 **3** 1/2 **Dazzling Diamond**[17] 6146 2-9-3 0 RobertWinston 8 72
(B W Hills) *sn chsng ldr: led over 2f out: sn rdn: jnd over 1f out: hdd fnl 120yds: styd on same pce* **4/1**[2]
4 9 **Coax** 2-9-3 0 RoystonFfrench 7 45
(M Johnston) *chsd ldrs tl rdn and green over 2f out: sn btn* **17/2**
0225 **5** 1 1/4 **His Grace (IRE)**[39] 5453 2-9-3 73 RobertHavlin 2 41
(A B Haynes) *led tl hdd over 2f out: sn btn* **6/1**
6 **6** 4 1/2 **Stravsambition**[10] 6323 2-8-9 0 RussKennemore(3) 1 22
(R Hollinshead) *in rr: sme hdwy over 2f out but sn green and wknd* **33/1**
7 shd **Glass Mountain (IRE)** 2-9-3 0 PatCosgrave 5 27
(J R Fanshawe) *in rr: sme hdwy and nt clr run wl over 2f out: sn btn* **9/1**
1m 17.32s (5.52) **Going Correction** +0.575s/f (Yiel) 7 Ran SP% **110.7**
Speed ratings (Par 95): **86,85,84,72,71 65,65**
toteswingers:1&2 £2.80, 2&3 £5.50, 1&3 £2.10 CSF £9.76 TOTE £2.70: £1.20, £2.40; EX 10.60.

Owner R J Baines **Bred** J C Bloodstock **Trained** Newmarket, Suffolk
■ Stewards' Enquiry : Kieren Fallon caution: used whip down shoulder in the forehand
Robert Havlin caution: used whip down shoulder in the forehand.

FOCUS
This modest juvenile maiden was run at a sound pace and the field came stands' side off the home turn. There was a tight three-way finish.

NOTEBOOK
Chill(IRE) ◆ was near last turning into the home straight and had work to do after improving in between the final 2f. Once Fallon pulled him off the rail at the furlong pole he really found his stride, though, and that move ultimately won him the day. This testing ground just negated the drop back a furlong, but he should be happier back over further if turned out again this term, and he is potentially very useful. (op 9-4 tchd 5-2)
Ceffyl Gwell had shown steady improvement on his two previous outings and came in for some late support. He too was dropping back in trip and his stamina came to the fore on this heavy surface as he went down narrowly. There should be a race for him back over 7f on slightly better ground before the season's end. (op 8-1 tchd 4-1)
Dazzling Diamond posted an encouraging debut at Newbury 17 days earlier and is a half-brother to a heavy ground winner. He was sent over to the stands' rail 2f out and had every chance, but that probably wasn't the best place to be as the ground was poached up from the last couple of meetings here when it was heavily used. The first pair are bred to stay better than him, though, and he looks a sure-fire winner when reverting to a sounder surface over this distance. (tchd 7-2)
Coax fared best of the newcomers. He is bred to want further in time, but his half-sister did score over this trip at two. The experience looked needed and he will know more next time. (op 13-2)
His Grace(IRE), rated 73, failed to raise his game on this return to turf but looked all at sea when asked for an effort on this testing surface. Official explanation: jockey said colt hung right (op 4-1)
Stravsambition was another that didn't prove suited by the going. (tchd 28-1)

Glass Mountain(IRE) looks to need a stiffer test. His pedigree backs that up. (tchd 10-1)

6627 TURFTV BETTING SHOP SERVICE NURSERY 6f
3:20 (3:20) (Class 3) (0-95,95) 2-Y-O £5,828 (£1,734; £866; £432) Stalls Low

Form RPR

3021 **1** **Bunce (IRE)**[22] 5992 2-8-5 **79** FrankieMcDonald 5 82
(R Hannon) *mde virtually all: rdn and asserted wl over 1f out: kpt on ins fnl f* **11/2**

13 **2** ½ **Zenella**[19] 6083 2-9-0 **91** MatthewDavies(3) 3 93
(Mrs A Duffield) *in tch: drvn and hdwy over 2f out: styd on to chse wnr wl ins fnl f: gng on cl home: a jst hld* **5/1**[3]

3113 **3** ½ **Loki's Revenge**[23] 5939 2-8-4 **78** ChrisCatlin 2 78
(W Jarvis) *hld up in tch: hdwy 2f out: drvn to chse wnr appr fnl f: styd on same pce u.p and outpcd into 3rd fnl 50yds* **9/4**[1]

1100 **4** 3 ¼ **Belle Royale (IRE)**[24] 5901 2-8-13 **87** FrannyNorton 4 77
(W M Brisbourne) *t.k.h: chsd ldrs: rdn over 2f out: wknd wl over 1f out* **7/1**

5346 **5** ¾ **Red Marling (IRE)**[9] 6365 2-8-1 **75** JimmyQuinn 6 63
(B W Hills) *pressed wnr and stl ev ch ins fnl 2f: hung rt and wknd over 1f out* **5/2**[2]

1634 **6** 2 **Belle Bayardo (IRE)**[23] 5965 2-9-7 **95** LukeMorris 7 77
(R A Harris) *chsd ldrs: rdn over 2f out and sn btn* **14/1**

1m 16.08s (4.28) **Going Correction** +0.575s/f (Yiel) 6 Ran SP% **110.6**
Speed ratings (Par 99): **94,93,92,88,87 84**
toteswingers:1&2 £2.30, 2&3 £2.80, 1&3 £2.90 CSF £31.14 TOTE £6.40: £3.40, £1.10; EX 15.80.
Owner Raymond Tooth **Bred** John Doyle **Trained** East Everleigh, Wilts

FOCUS
A decent little nursery, run at a fair pace and the first three came clear.

NOTEBOOK
Bunce(IRE) shed his maiden tag when winning off a mark of 78 in a soft-ground nursery at Goodwood 22 days earlier and, just 1lb higher here, followed up in determined fashion. His proven stamina on this drop back a furlong was a big plus and so was his clear preference for cut underfoot. There was plenty to like about the way he knuckled down inside the final furlong and there could be more to come on this sort of ground. (op 7-2)

Zenella, another eased a furlong in trip, was produced with every chance on this return to turf and lost nothing in defeat. She has few miles on the clock, but the handicapper probably has her where he wants her on a mark of 91. (op 7-2 tchd 3-1)

Loki's Revenge, a previous C&D winner, got warm and edgy beforehand but was still well backed. He had his chance and ran well, but failed to see it out like the first pair. This was his first outing over this far, and he can find another opening when reverting to less-testing ground. (op 3-1 tchd 10-3)

Belle Royale(IRE) came under pressure turning for home and, although the ground was probably too much for her, she needs further respite in the weights. (op 8-1 tchd 10-1)

Red Marling(IRE) proved a bit free under a positive ride and that would've blunted him late on, but this ground wasn't for him. (op 7-2)

Belle Bayardo(IRE), who had yet to race on soft ground, was sweating beforehand and refused to settle through the early parts. (op 11-1)

6628 TINSLETOWN CHRISTMAS PARTY NIGHTS BOOK NOW MAIDEN AUCTION STKS 7f 26y
3:50 (3:53) (Class 5) 2-Y-O £2,914 (£867; £433; £216) Stalls Low

Form RPR

046 **1** **Callie's Angel**[21] 6019 2-8-11 **61** RobertWinston 4 64
(B Palling) *chsd ldrs: rdn to go 2nd over 1f out: styd on u.p to ld fnl 100yds: kpt on strly* **7/1**

2 1 ¼ **Fonnie (IRE)** 2-8-6 **0** NickyMackay 3 56
(Rae Guest) *pushed along towards rr 1/2-way: hdwy over 2f out: drvn and styd on wl ins fnl f to take 2nd nr fin: no imp on wnr* **9/1**

0022 **3** *hd* **Three Scoops**[14] 6259 2-8-1 **51** ow2 (t) BillyCray(5) 5 55
(D J S Ffrench Davis) *trckd ldr tl drvn ahd over 2f out: sn hrd drvn: styd on wl tl hdd and no ex fnl 100yds: lost 2nd cl home* **9/2**[2]

4 1 ½ **Dancing All Night** 2-8-7 **0** ChrisCatlin 6 53
(M R Channon) *stdd s: in rr and t.k.h: drvn and styd on fr 2f out and kpt on ins fnl f and gng on cl home: nt rch ldng trio* **13/2**

6634 **5** 10 **Crucis Abbey (IRE)**[11] 6311 2-8-11 **68** SebSanders 7 32
(J W Unett) *chsd ldrs tl rdn and wknd 2f out* **2/1**[1]

6 1 **Dancing Cavalier (IRE)** 2-8-11 **0** LukeMorris 8 29
(R Hollinshead) *in tch: c to r along on stands' side over 2f out and no ch after* **6/1**[3]

0 **7** *shd* **Emperorsnewclothes (IRE)**[24] 5921 2-8-6 **0** (p) MatthewDavies(3) 2 27
(George Baker) *led tl hdd over 2f out: sn wknd* **33/1**

6 **8** 12 **Varlak**[18] 6126 2-8-9 **0** JamieMackay 9 —
(D Donovan) *a in rr* **33/1**

9 ¾ **Fully Armed (IRE)** 2-8-4 **0** FrannyNorton 1 —
(Rae Guest) *a in rr* **14/1**

1m 32.4s (7.80) **Going Correction** +0.825s/f (Soft) 9 Ran SP% **114.2**
Speed ratings (Par 95): **88,86,86,84,73 72,71,58,57**
toteswingers:1&2 £9.00, 2&3 £7.50, 1&3 £4.40 CSF £67.09 TOTE £5.90: £1.20, £2.70, £1.80; EX 87.10.
Owner Wayne Devine **Bred** Mrs F A Veasey **Trained** Tredodridge, Vale Of Glamorgan

FOCUS
A very weak maiden, run at an average pace and again the place to be was towards the centre in the home straight.

NOTEBOOK
Callie's Angel got off the mark at the fourth attempt under a strong ride. His dam was a soft-ground lover and this move to testing ground saw him come good. Winston had him perfectly placed turning for home and kept him to the centre from 2f out. This should boost his confidence for a switch to nurseries and his mark shouldn't be too affected by this win. (op 6-1)

Fonnie(IRE), green in the preliminaries, was making her belated debut over a suitable trip on breeding and ran a very pleasing race. She hails from a yard whose juveniles nearly always come on for their initial outings and obviously has a future. (op 10-1 tchd 11-1)

Three Scoops, whose claiming rider put up 2lb overweight, had finished runner-up in low-grade nurseries on her last two outings and attracted support. She was given every chance and posted another respectable effort on this softer ground. With an official mark of 51, she puts the form into perspective. (op 11-2)

Dancing All Night, whose yard won this with a newcomer last season, was a market drifter on her racecourse debut. She took a long time to get the hang of things, but still posted a fair effort and should improve a good deal for the experience. With that in mind she looks one to take from the race. (op 5-1)

Crucis Abbey(IRE) dropped out tamely and surely failed to handle this surface. (tchd 5-2)

Dancing Cavalier(IRE) is bred to need further down the line and showed some ability, despite being well beaten off. (op 10-1)

6629 KOKO'S BAR STUDENT NIGHTS - TUESDAY & THURSDAY H'CAP 1m 22y
4:20 (4:23) (Class 5) (0-75,75) 3-Y-O+ £3,561 (£1,059; £529; £264) Stalls Low

Form RPR

4606 **1** **Swiftly Done (IRE)**[7] 6413 3-7-12 **62** (v[1]) NeilFarley(7) 12 73
(D Carroll) *s.i.s: in rr: hdwy over 3f out: str run on stands' rail and squeezed through jst ins fnl 2f: chal u.p ins fnl f: led last stride* **8/1**

0231 **2** *shd* **Ken's Girl**[37] 5541 6-9-3 **71** PatCosgrave 8 82
(W S Kittow) *w ldr tl def advantage after 2f: rdn and kpt on fr 2f out: jnd ins fnl f: hdd last stride* **9/1**

1403 **3** 2 ½ **One Scoop Or Two**[2] 6581 4-9-3 **74** RussKennemore(3) 9 79
(R Hollinshead) *chsd ldrs: rdn to go 2nd 3f out: pressed ldr over 1f out: styd on same pce into 3rd ins fnl f* **7/1**[3]

5523 **4** 2 **Song To The Moon (IRE)**[14] 6260 3-8-13 **70** (v) KierenFallon 10 71
(A M Balding) *trcking ldrs and styng on towards stands' rail whn bmpd and veered lft ins fnl 2f and lost position: styd on again ins fnl f* **9/2**[1]

4221 **5** ½ **Ours (IRE)**[13] 6267 7-9-0 **73** (p) BillyCray(5) 7 73
(John A Harris) *slowly away: in rr and rdn 4f out: stl last 3f out: styd on u.p fnl 2f: nvr a threat* **12/1**

1423 **6** 2 ¼ **Madame Excelerate**[10] 6336 3-8-12 **69** FrannyNorton 4 63
(W M Brisbourne) *in rr tl drvn and hdwy ins fnl 3f: styd on same pce fnl 2f* **6/1**[2]

0006 **7** 10 **Lordship (IRE)**[10] 6328 6-8-0 **61** oh8 JakePayne(7) 3 32
(A W Carroll) *sn bhd and n.d* **12/1**

0310 **8** 1 **Wild Rockette**[49] 5149 3-9-1 **72** (b) ShaneKelly 16 41
(B J Meehan) *s.i.s: in rr: in tch 1/2-way: rdn over 2f out: wknd sn after* **14/1**

1202 **9** *hd* **Bidable**[21] 6023 6-9-2 **70** LukeMorris 2 39
(B Palling) *chsd ldrs early: rdn and towards rr fr 1/2-way* **12/1**

3106 **10** 5 **Zambuka (FR)**[35] 5593 3-8-4 **61** oh1 JimmyQuinn 6 18
(F J Brennan) *chsd ldrs tl wknd over 2f out* **16/1**

0000 **11** *shd* **Very Well Red**[14] 6260 7-9-3 **71** ChrisCatlin 1 28
(P W Hiatt) *disp ld 2f: wknd over 3f out* **33/1**

00-0 **12** ¾ **Koraleva Tectona (IRE)**[75] 4260 5-9-6 **74** RobertWinston 15 29
(Pat Eddery) *racd alone and wd: prom to 1/2-way* **40/1**

0-35 **13** 5 **Slugger O'Toole**[25] 5889 5-9-5 **73** (v[1]) AdamKirby 14 17
(S C Williams) *chsd ldrs tl wknd rapidly ins fnl 3f* **14/1**

1m 47.28s (6.28) **Going Correction** +0.825s/f (Soft)
WFA 3 from 4yo+ 3lb 13 Ran SP% **113.8**
Speed ratings (Par 103): **101,100,98,96,95 93,83,82,82,77 77,76,71**
toteswingers:1&2 £18.30, 2&3 £9.20, 1&3 £13.40 CSF £74.29 CT £527.98 TOTE £12.50: £5.30, £3.50, £1.70; EX 105.20.
Owner D Watts, Miss C King, M Syme **Bred** Joe Fogarty **Trained** Sledmere, E Yorks
■ Stewards' Enquiry : Russ Kennemore two-day ban: careless riding (Oct 18-19)

FOCUS
This moderate handicap was wide open. There was a fair pace on and the first pair fought out a battling finish.

6630 RACING UK H'CAP 1m 2f 188y
4:50 (4:50) (Class 3) (0-95,92) 3-Y-O+ £7,123 (£2,119; £1,059; £529)

Form RPR

6000 **1** **Red Merlin (IRE)**[16] 6193 5-9-8 **90** (v) AdamKirby 6 102
(C G Cox) *hld up in rr: stdy hdwy fr 3f out: rdn to go 2nd wl over 1f out: sn chalng: hrd rdn to ld fnl 100yds: hld on wl* **5/2**[1]

2-54 **2** ½ **Realisation (USA)**[24] 5918 3-8-4 **78** RoystonFfrench 4 89
(M Johnston) *trckd ldr: chal 4f out tl led jst ins fnl 3f: hrd rdn and jnd 1f out: hdd fnl 100yds and a jst hld* **5/2**[1]

-600 **3** 9 **Centennial (IRE)**[47] 5220 5-9-10 **92** (b) KierenFallon 5 88
(Jonjo O'Neill) *led: jnd and rdn 4f out: hdd ins fnl 3f and dropped to rr ins fnl 2f: styd on again past btn horses to take poor 3rd cl home* **9/2**[2]

4330 **4** 1 **Faithful Ruler (USA)**[18] 6105 6-9-2 **84** JimmyQuinn 2 78
(R A Fahey) *chsd ldrs: rdn to go 2nd 2f out: nvr quite on terms and wknd qckly over 1f out: lost poor 3rd cl home* **5/1**[3]

0420 **5** 3 **Lucky Dance (BRZ)**[10] 6327 8-9-5 **87** RobertHavlin 3 76
(T T Clement) *slowly away fr flip s: in rr: styd to r alone on far side and stl bhd wl over 2f out: no ch whn hung rt wl over 1f out* **10/1**

6 52 **Shalambar (IRE)**[222] 6885 4-9-2 **84** SteveDrowne 1 —
(A W Carroll) *chsd ldrs tl wknd rapidly over 3f out: t.o* **14/1**

2m 28.12s (7.02) **Going Correction** +0.825s/f (Soft)
WFA 3 from 4yo+ 6lb 6 Ran SP% **107.7**
Speed ratings (Par 107): **107,106,100,99,97 59**
toteswingers:1&2 £1.80, 2&3 £2.90, 1&3 £2.20 CSF £7.99 TOTE £4.20: £2.80, £1.10; EX 9.60.
Owner Reid's Allstars **Bred** Keatly Overseas Ltd **Trained** Lambourn, Berks
■ Stewards' Enquiry : Adam Kirby one-day ban: used whip without giving gelding time to respond (Oct 18)

FOCUS
There was a flip start due to difficulties getting the stalls down to the 1m3f start, and it was a fairly ragged beginning. The front-running Centennial sent out to make it a test and eventually the first pair came clear.

NOTEBOOK
Red Merlin(IRE) finally resumed winning ways under a good ride by Adam Kirby. He responded off the home turn and his rider's decision to pull him away from the stands' rail inside the final furlong proved a winning move. He was 11lb lower than resuming this term and thus 2lb lower than when registering his last success in July 2009. It should serve his confidence well and, providing he comes out of this sufficiently, he could head for a valuable handicap at Ascot on Saturday. (op 11-4 tchd 9-4 and 3-1 in places)

Realisation(USA), whose yard won this with a 3-y-o last term, came here with a little to prove, not least on the testing surface. Being by Alhaarth, though, there was every chance he would act on it and he went through it without that much fuss. He only just went down after asserting for home off the home bend, but coming right over to the stands' rail probably wasn't the wisest move by his jockey. (op 9-4 tchd 11-4)

Centennial(IRE) was in trouble at the top of the home straight over this shorter trip. He could well make the switch to hurdling soon in a bid to rekindle his enthusiasm. (op 6-1)

Faithful Ruler(USA) was produced with his chance, but failed to get home like the first pair on such ground. He can defy this mark before the end of the season. (op 9-2 tchd 11-2)

6631 JUMP SEASON IS NEXT H'CAP 1m 6f 213y
5:20 (5:21) (Class 5) (0-75,70) 3-Y-O £2,729 (£806; £403) Stalls Low

Form RPR

5611 **1** **Tobernea (IRE)**[15] 6225 3-9-3 **66** KierenFallon 9 83+
(M Johnston) *bmpd and awkward s: sn rcvrd to press ldr and led 11f out: pushed clr over 2f out: v easily* **13/8**[1]

5104 **2** *6* **Sir Pitt**[30] 5752 3-9-7 **70** RobertHavlin 1 75
(J H M Gosden) *hld up in rr: hdwy and n.m.r on ins 4f out: styd on to take 2nd wl over 1f out: nvr any ch w easy wnr: clr 2nd best* **9/1**

4321 **3** *4* **Affinity**[17] 6166 3-9-6 **69** JimmyQuinn 2 68
(H R A Cecil) *in tch: chsd ldrs fr 4f out: nvr any ch w easy wnr and one pce into 3rd wl over 1f out* **10/3**[2]

3114 **4** *2 ¾* **Straversjoy**[11] 6314 3-8-12 **61** PaulEddery 7 57
(R Hollinshead) *in rr: drvn and sme prog 3f out: c to stands' side and styd on for one pce 4th ins fnl f* **9/1**

2005 **5** *2 ¾* **Storming Redd**[34] 5625 3-8-8 **57** LukeMorris 8 49
(J M P Eustace) *wnt rt s: pressed ldrs 4f: styd front rnk tl rdn 4f out: wknd 2f out* **14/1**

4200 **6** *3 ¾* **Sheikhtothemusic**[19] 6084 3-8-11 **60** RoystonFfrench 10 46
(J G Given) *bmpd s: chsd ldrs: rdn over 4f out: wknd 3f out* **25/1**

60-6 **7** *6* **Young Firth**[152] 1830 3-8-4 **53** FrannyNorton 11 31
(J R Norton) *sn led: hdd 11f out: wknd over 3f out* **66/1**

4542 **8** *hd* **Light The City (IRE)**[21] 6038 3-8-3 **55** KellyHarrison[(3)] 3 33
(Mrs R A Carr) *chsd ldrs: rdn 4f out: wknd 3f out* **9/2**[3]

3m 34.5s (15.50) **Going Correction** +0.825s/f (Soft) **8** Ran SP% **111.4**
Speed ratings (Par 101): **91,87,85,84,82 80,77,77**
toteswingers:1&2 £4.30, 2&3 £6.00, 1&3 £2.20 CSF £16.54 CT £41.79 TOTE £2.70: £1.10, £3.30, £1.60; EX 16.20 Place 6: £174.05 Place 5: £68.87.
Owner Mrs Joan Keaney **Bred** Mrs Joan Keaney **Trained** Middleham Moor, N Yorks

FOCUS
While it's a shame the non-runners didn't turn up, this was still a fair staying 3-y-o handicap for the grade. It was run at a fair enough gallop and the form makes sense.
T/Plt: £162.70 to a £1 stake. Pool of £46,303.64 - 207.68 winning tickets. T/Qpdt: £40.30 to a £1 stake. Pool of £4,150.19 - 76.20 winning tickets. ST

5536 WINDSOR (R-H)
Monday, October 4

OFFICIAL GOING: Soft (heavy in places; 6.5)
Stands' rail dolled out 3yds at 6f and half-a-yard at winning post. Top bend dolled out 9yds adding 21yds to races of 1m and over.
Wind: virtually nil Weather: overcast

6632 CORAL.CO.UK H'CAP (DIV I) 1m 67y
2:30 (2:30) (Class 5) (0-70,70) 3-Y-O+ **£1,944** (£574; £287) **Stalls** High

Form RPR

5005 **1** **Flipping**[22] 5993 3-8-10 **62** FergusSweeney 10 72
(W S Kittow) *chsd ldrs: wnt 2nd 1/2-way: effrt to chal over 2f out: rdn to ld wl over 1f out: clr and edgd rt u.p ins fnl f: styd on wl* **8/1**

5211 **2** *2 ¾* **Lutine Charlie (IRE)**[7] 6413 3-9-0 **66** (p) HayleyTurner 8 70
(J L Flint) *chsd ldrs: effrt to chse ldng pair over 2f out: drvn and kpt on same pce fr over 1f out: wnt 2nd ins fnl f* **15/8**[1]

0001 **3** *1* **Prince Apollo**[12] 6298 5-9-7 **70** TedDurcan 1 72
(Ian Williams) *led: jnd over 2f out: rdn and hdd wl over 1f out: edgd rt u.p and btn ent fnl f: lost 2nd ins fnl f* **12/1**

6020 **4** *2 ½* **Profligate (IRE)**[41] 5391 3-9-1 **67** JimCrowley 9 63
(W Jarvis) *hld up in rr: rdn and hdwy 2f out: chsd ldng trio and drvn over 1f out: kpt on same pce and no imp after* **22/1**

1400 **5** *2 ¼* **Another Magic Man (USA)**[23] 5968 3-9-0 **69** KierenFox[(3)] 11 60
(J R Best) *t.k.h: sn chsng ldr: lost 2nd 1/2-way: wknd u.p 2f out* **10/1**

2054 **6** *¾* **Edition**[74] 4289 3-8-11 **63** LiamKeniry 7 52
(J R Gask) *hld up in tch: rdn and effrt over 2f out: no prog and wl hld fr over 1f out* **6/1**[2]

3335 **7** *½* **Just Jimmy (IRE)**[2] 6581 5-8-9 **58** CathyGannon 5 46
(P D Evans) *taken down early: t.k.h: hld up towards rr: hdwy on outer into midfield 5f out: wknd u.p over 2f out* **7/1**[3]

0266 **8** *4 ½* **Trafalgar Square**[46] 5237 8-8-2 **56** (v) JemmaMarshall[(5)] 4 34
(M J Attwater) *taken down early: s.i.s: hld up in rr: rdn and no prog over 2f out: n.d* **16/1**

40 **9** *9* **Rezwaan**[82] 4022 3-9-1 **67** EddieCreighton 12 24
(M J McGrath) *t.k.h: chsd ldrs: rdn and struggling wl over 2f out: bhd over 1f out: wl btn and eased ins fnl f* **18/1**

1400 **10** *2 ¾* **Ajool (USA)**[25] 5887 3-8-13 **65** TonyCulhane 6 16
(P W D'Arcy) *chsd ldrs tl rdn and wknd wl over 2f out: wl bhd and eased ins fnl f* **33/1**

-330 **11** *1 ¼* **Swish Dish (CAN)**[23] 5972 3-9-4 **70** RichardHughes 14 18
(R Hannon) *stdd s: hld up in tch towards rr: swtchd rt and rdn ent fnl 2f: no hdwy and wl btn over 1f out: eased ins fnl f* **16/1**

1m 49.73s (5.03) **Going Correction** +0.65s/f (Yiel)
WFA 3 from 4yo+ 3lb **11** Ran SP% **113.8**
Speed ratings (Par 103): **100,97,96,93,91 90,90,85,76,74 72**
CSF £22.44 CT £185.18 TOTE £10.10: £2.00, £1.90, £1.50; EX 42.60 Trifecta £177.80 Part won. Pool of £240.34 - 0.73 winning units..
Owner Reg Gifford **Bred** D R Tucker **Trained** Blackborough, Devon

FOCUS
There was just a medium gallop, and it proved hard to come from a long way back. As is usual on soft ground at this course, the runners went to the far side from the intersection, 3f out.
Just Jimmy(IRE) Official explanation: jockey said gelding ran too free
Swish Dish(CAN) Official explanation: jockey said filly jumped the path 1 1/2f out

6633 CORAL.CO.UK H'CAP (DIV II) 1m 67y
3:00 (3:01) (Class 5) (0-70,70) 3-Y-O+ **£1,944** (£574; £287) **Stalls** High

Form RPR

166 **1** **Croeso Cusan**[21] 6023 5-9-1 **65** SophieDoyle[(3)] 8 76
(J L Spearing) *taken down early: stdd s: hld up in rr: stl plenty to do 2f out: hdwy over 1f out: r.o wl u.p ins fnl f to ld on post* **8/1**[3]

2433 **2** *nse* **Osgood**[16] 6212 3-9-3 **67** CathyGannon 4 78
(M R Channon) *t.k.h: sn led: hrd pressed and rdn over 2f out: battled on v gamely u.p ins fnl f tl hdd on post* **8/1**[3]

0613 **3** *1* **Eastern Hills**[10] 6335 5-8-6 **56** (p) AndrewHeffernan[(3)] 3 65
(A J McCabe) *t.k.h: chsd ldr for 3f and again over 2f out: ev ch u.p wl fr over 1f out: no ex and btn fnl 75yds* **9/2**[1]

0330 **4** *1* **Full Victory (IRE)**[17] 6165 8-8-12 **59** FergusSweeney 7 65
(R A Farrant) *hld up in midfield: effrt 3f out: chsd ldrs and drvn 2f out: no ex and one pce fnl 100yds* **9/1**

530 **5** *nk* **One Hit Wonder**[9] 6370 3-8-10 **60** DaneO'Neill 2 66
(Mouse Hamilton-Fairley) *in tch in midfield on outer: hdwy to chse ldrs over 2f out: rdn ent fnl 2f: no ex and btn ins fnl f* **16/1**

3006 **6** *1 ¾* **Saturn Way (GR)**[26] 5866 4-9-7 **68** LiamKeniry 14 70
(P R Chamings) *hld up in tch in midfield: rdn and hdwy 2f out: chse ldrs over 1f out: drvn and wknd jst ins fnl f* **7/1**[2]

0352 **7** *2 ¼* **Norville (IRE)**[3] 6540 3-9-2 **69** RichardEvans[(3)] 11 66
(P D Evans) *stdd after s: hld up in last trio: rdn and effrt 2f out: styd on same pce and no prog ent fnl f* **9/1**

05 **8** *1 ¼* **Ermyn Express**[35] 5593 3-8-1 **56** JemmaMarshall[(5)] 9 50
(P M Phelan) *in tch in midfield: pushed along 4f out: styd on same pce and no hdwy u.p fr over 1f out* **16/1**

336 **9** *hd* **The Shuffler**[34] 5624 3-9-6 **70** GeorgeBaker 10 63
(G L Moore) *hld up in tch in midfield: hdwy ent fnl f: drvn and btn over 1f out* **7/1**[2]

5450 **10** *4 ½* **Meydan Dubai (IRE)**[27] 5833 5-9-4 **65** HayleyTurner 5 48
(J R Best) *hld up towards rr: rdn and effrt over 2f out: no hdwy and wl btn over 1f out: eased wl ins fnl f* **14/1**

2000 **11** *nk* **Sasheen**[16] 6197 3-8-13 **63** StephenCraine 12 45
(J R Boyle) *t.k.h: chsd ldrs: wnt 2nd 5f out tl over 2f out: sn wknd u.p* **40/1**

6000 **12** *13* **Calahonda**[9] 6372 4-9-2 **63** TonyCulhane 1 15
(P W D'Arcy) *anticipated s and broke early: sn stdd and in tch: rdn and btn ent fnl f: eased ins fnl f* **20/1**

6430 **13** *11* **Pastello**[32] 5689 3-9-2 **66** RichardHughes 13 —
(R Hannon) *in tch: rdn and struggling 3f out: wl btn wl over 1f out: eased ins fnl f* **16/1**

1m 49.21s (4.51) **Going Correction** +0.65s/f (Yiel)
WFA 3 from 4yo+ 3lb **13** Ran SP% **116.9**
Speed ratings (Par 103): **103,102,101,100,100 98,96,95,95,90 90,77,66**
toteswingers:1&2 £21.60, 2&3 £9.90, 1&3 £8.70 CSF £69.09 CT £326.13 TOTE £6.30: £3.10, £3.80, £1.10; EX 65.00 Trifecta £124.40 Part won. Pool of £168.19 - 0.40 winning units..
Owner Oxstalls Farm Stud **Bred** Richard Evans Bloodstock **Trained** Kinnersley, Worcs
■ Stewards' Enquiry : Sophie Doyle caution: used whip with excessive frequency.
Cathy Gannon three-day ban: used whip with excessive frequency without giving colt time to respond (Oct 18-20)

FOCUS
A solid gallop in the conditions enabled the patiently ridden winner to get up from last place. Although the field raced in the far side half of the course in the final 3f, the first two were more towards the centre but later races suggested that was not a factor. The time was half a second faster than division one.
Ermyn Express Official explanation: vet said filly finished lame

6634 EUROPEAN BREEDERS' FUND MAIDEN STKS (DIV I) 1m 67y
3:30 (3:31) (Class 4) 2-Y-O **£3,723** (£1,108; £553; £276) **Stalls** High

Form RPR

06 **1** **Buxfizz (USA)**[58] 4838 2-9-3 0 JimCrowley 9 79
(R A Mills) *chsd ldrs: reminder and rdn 4f out: drvn to chse ldr wl over 1f out: led ins fnl f: styd on wl: rdn out* **10/1**

6524 **2** *¾* **Choral**[17] 6154 2-8-12 74 RichardHughes 8 72
(R Hannon) *w ldr tl rdn to ld 2f out: drvn and clr w wnr ent fnl f hdd and no ex fnl 100yds* **11/4**[1]

00 **3** *5* **Cunning Act**[16] 6196 2-9-3 0 StephenCraine 1 68+
(J G Portman) *dwlt: racd in last trio: rdn over 2f out: hanging lft and no ch w ldng pair over 1f out: swtchd rt ent fnl f: plugged on to go modest 3rd ins fnl f* **33/1**

352 **4** *1* **Another Laugh**[25] 5871 2-9-3 76 MichaelHills 3 64
(B W Hills) *led tl hdd and rdn 2f out: wkng whn stmbld over 1f out: wl btn 1f out* **4/1**[2]

5 *1 ¼* **Secret Edge** 2-9-3 0 FergusSweeney 10 61
(A King) *v.s.a: bhd: rdn and hdwy on far side whn rn green and hung lft over 2f out: no ch w ldng pair and swtchd rt over 1f out: kpt on ins fnl f* **25/1**

54 **6** *1 ¼* **Divine Rule (IRE)**[14] 6249 2-9-3 0 GeorgeBaker 7 58
(H Morrison) *dwlt: sn bustled along and hdwy to chse ldr after 1f: rdn to chse ldr briefly wl over 1f out: wknd qckly jst over 1f out* **9/2**[3]

5 **7** *4* **Trend (IRE)**[18] 6128 2-9-3 0 HayleyTurner 11 50
(M L W Bell) *in tch in midfield: rdn along over 4f out: sme prog over 2f out: no prog and wl btn over 1f out* **4/1**[2]

8 *4* **Justice Walk (IRE)** 2-9-3 0 PaulFitzsimons 4 41
(Miss J R Tooth) *in tch on outer: rdn and struggling ent fnl 2f: wl btn over 1f out* **66/1**

06 **9** *1 ¾* **Waterborne**[35] 5608 2-9-3 0 TedDurcan 2 37
(R Charlton) *a towards rr: rdn and hung lft over 2f out: sn wknd* **33/1**

0 **10** *11* **Invent**[10] 6334 2-9-3 0 StevieDonohoe 5 13
(Sir Mark Prescott) *t.k.h early: in tch in midfield: rdn and dropped in rr over 3f out: lost tch 2f out* **14/1**

1m 51.27s (6.57) **Going Correction** +0.65s/f (Yiel) **10** Ran SP% **111.8**
Speed ratings (Par 97): **93,92,87,86,85 83,79,75,74,63**
toteswingers:1&2 £7.80, 2&3 £25.40, 1&3 £6.10 CSF £35.15 TOTE £20.30: £7.40, £1.10, £15.10; EX 57.80 TRIFECTA Not won..
Owner Buxted Partnership **Bred** Darley **Trained** Headley, Surrey

FOCUS
An average maiden, but there should be future winners in the line-up.

NOTEBOOK
Buxfizz(USA), meeting soft ground for the first time, produced significant improvement on his first two runs, though it is unlikely that he needs this much cut. He should hold his own in middling handicaps. (op 11-1 tchd 12-1)
Choral continues to do well in maidens on turf and Polytrack. Even though she has long since received her handicap mark, she finished clear of the third and is worth another chance in this company. (op 5-2 tchd 3-1 in a place)
Cunning Act has run with credit in his second and third maidens. He is likely to stay even further next year and will be more interesting now he qualifies for a handicap rating. (op 25-1)
Another Laugh was not helped by stumbling, though he seemed to be fighting a losing battle at the time. His maiden form is sound enough but connections also have the option of nurseries instead. Official explanation: jockey said gelding stumbled 1 1/2f out (op 3-1)
Secret Edge, a £25,000 Tobougg colt out of a 1m winner, made a fair debut and looks sure to benefit from the experience. (op 20-1)
Trend(IRE) is taking time to mature mentally, but he again showed some ability and is worth monitoring. He should be effective beyond 1m next year. (op 5-1)
Waterborne is now qualified for handicaps and is certainly worth a look when he makes the switch. (op 25-1)

6635 EUROPEAN BREEDERS' FUND MAIDEN STKS (DIV II) 1m 67y
4:00 (4:01) (Class 4) 2-Y-O **£3,723** (£1,108; £553; £276) **Stalls** High

Form RPR

232 **1** **Escholido (IRE)**[25] 5886 2-9-3 77 MichaelHills 3 77
(B W Hills) *mde all: rdn ent fnl 2f: clr w runner-up ent fnl f: kpt on wl u.p* **2/1**[1]

2 ½ **Hermes** 2-9-3 0 JimCrowley 7 76
(R M Beckett) *chsd ldrs: wnt 2nd jst over 2f out: rdn to chal and clr w wnr ent fnl f: nt qckn and hld fnl 100yds* **12/1**

0 3 3¾ **Afaara (IRE)**27 5829 2-8-12 0 DaneO'Neill 11 63
(Mrs A J Perrett) *hld up in tch towards rr: shkn up and effrt ent fnl 2f: sn hung lft and rdn: no ch w ldng pair and continued to hang lft over 1f out: swtchd rt 1f out: kpt on to go 3rd ins fnl f* **16/1**

0 4 1¼ **Sergeant Troy (IRE)**38 5491 2-9-3 0 TedDurcan 1 65
(R Charlton) *t.k.h: hld up in midfield on outer: hdwy over 2f out: rn green and outpcd by ldng pair over 1f out: wknd ent fnl f* **8/1**

04 5 1 **Star Commander**18 6128 2-9-3 0 LiamJones 4 63
(M H Tompkins) *chsd wnr tl over 2f out: wknd u.p wl over 1f out* **5/1**3

6 1½ **Conjuror's Bluff** 2-9-3 0 RichardHughes 9 59
(R Hannon) *in tch in midfield: effrt and rdn over 2f out: chsd ldng pair wl over 1f out: wknd u.p ent fnl f* **11/2**

00 7 10 **Phoenix Fantasy (IRE)**24 5916 2-9-3 0 StephenCraine 8 37
(J G Portman) *s.i.s: sn rcvrd and t.k.h in midfield: rdn and wknd qckly 2f out: wl bhd fnl f* **100/1**

8 1 **Air Of Grace (IRE)** 2-9-3 0 AhmedAjtebi 5 35
(Mahmood Al Zarooni) *s.i.s: in tch in rr tl struggling bdly and rdn over 3f out: sn wl btn* **7/2**2

0000 9 12 **Complicate**17 6153 2-8-12 48 (p) J-PGuillambert 6 4
(Andrew Reid) *t.k.h: chsd ldrs tl wknd qckly over 2f out: wl bhd over 1f out* **100/1**

10 4 **Osgoodisgood** 2-9-3 0 SaleemGolam 10 —
(S C Williams) *s.i.s: a towards rr: struggling over 3f out: rn green and lost tch over 2f out: eased ins fnl f* **33/1**

11 3¼ **Ede'Sajolygoodfelo** 2-8-12 0 JemmaMarshall(5) 2 —
(P M Phelan) *s.i.s: sn niggled along in rr: lost tch 1/2-way: t.o* **66/1**

1m 51.56s (6.86) **Going Correction** +0.65s/f (Yiel) 11 Ran SP% **118.7**
Speed ratings (Par 97): **91,90,86,85,84 83,73,72,60,56 52**
toteswingers:1&2 £7.70, 2&3 £10.70, 1&3 £22.20 CSF £28.93 TOTE £2.20: £1.10, £5.40, £7.50; EX 26.70 Trifecta £485.60 Part won. Pool of £656.32 - 0.93 winning units..
Owner S E Sangster & Mrs M Findlay **Bred** Peter J Doyle Bloodstock Ltd **Trained** Lambourn, Berks

FOCUS
Probably a similar standard to division one, and a time that was only slightly slower.

NOTEBOOK
Escholido(IRE)'s experience was helpful in these tough conditions and he put to bed any doubts about his ability to win with a game victory. Placed in maidens at 6f and 7f, he found the extra 1f playing to his strengths, and he handled the soft ground well. (op 9-4 tchd 15-8)
Hermes ◆, an Observatory newcomer whose dam won over this C&D, made a fine debut. Even though it was obvious he lacked the edge of the battle-hardened winner, he handled the soft ground well and should win a maiden. (op 10-1)
Afaara(IRE), running much better than on her debut, showed plenty of stamina and looks likely to come into her own at 1m2f-plus as she matures. (op 14-1)
Sergeant Troy(IRE) took a step forward from his debut and should be ready to strike after he gets his handicap mark. (op 10-1)
Star Commander had finished closer than this over 1m on soft ground last time, but this looked a stronger race. (op 9-2 tchd 4-1)
Conjuror's Bluff, a 45,000gns Tiger Hill debutant, made a satisfactory debut without threatening. He looks a handicap sort in the longer term. (op 5-1 tchd 6-1)
Air Of Grace(IRE), a Dalakhani colt from a good family around 1m-1m2f, changed hands for 170,000gns at the breeze-ups. He showed nothing and, while that was undoubtedly disappointing, he deserves another chance to show what he can do on better ground. (op 13-2)

6636 TIME 106.6 FM RADIO NURSERY 5f 10y
4:30 (4:30) (Class 3) (0-95,94) 2-Y-O £5,504 (£1,637; £818; £408) Stalls High

Form RPR

3045 1 **Phoebs**6 6445 2-8-12 85 JimCrowley 3 89
(R A Mills) *hld up in last pair: hdwy and rdn wl over 1f out: chal jst over 1f out: led wl ins fnl f: r.o wl* **9/1**

4104 2 hd **Fifth Ave**6 6445 2-8-2 78 SophieDoyle(3) 7 81
(J A Osborne) *chsd ldr: rdn ent fnl 2f: led over 1f out: clr w wnr ins fnl f: hdd and no ex wl ins fnl f* **11/2**

001 3 3¼ **Style And Panache (IRE)**6 6445 2-8-3 81 6ex AdamBeschizza(5) 2 73
(P D Evans) *t.k.h: sn chsng ldrs: rdn and unable qck ent fnl 2f: racd awkwardly and outpcd by ldng pair over 1f out: no ch w ldng pair: kpt on to go 3rd wl ins fnl f* **7/1**

210 4 nk **Where's Romeo (IRE)**121 2743 2-8-12 85 RichardMullen 6 76
(D H Brown) *led: rdn 2f out: hdd over 1f out: btn ent fnl f: wknd fnl 150yds* **4/1**2

1522 5 ¾ **Avonmore Star**5 6477 2-9-7 94 RichardHughes 4 82
(R Hannon) *wnt rt and stdd s: hld up in last pair: rdn and effrt 2f out: swtchd rt over 1f out: kpt on same pce and no threat to ldrs after* **5/1**3

0251 6 1¾ **Squires Gate (IRE)**10 6324 2-8-5 78 DavidProbert 1 60
(B W Hills) *chsd ldrs: rdn: unable qck and hung lft ent fnl 2f: wknd over 1f out* **2/1**1

060 7 4½ **Scarlet Rocks (IRE)**47 5226 2-8-7 80 CathyGannon 5 45
(P D Evans) *pushed rt s: in tch in rr: rdn and struggling over 2f out: wl bhd and eased ins fnl f* **12/1**

62.40 secs (2.10) **Going Correction** +0.40s/f (Good) 7 Ran SP% **115.6**
Speed ratings (Par 99): **99,98,93,93,91 89,81**
toteswingers:1&2 £7.20, 2&3 £11.50, 1&3 £6.20 CSF £57.95 TOTE £7.10: £2.40, £2.90; EX 51.70.
Owner R A Mills N Clement **Bred** Sherwoods Transport Ltd **Trained** Headley, Surrey
■ Stewards' Enquiry : Sophie Doyle one-day ban: used whip with excessive frequency (Oct 18)

FOCUS
A decent nursery, but it probably came down to the ones who were best-suited by the soft ground.

NOTEBOOK
Phoebs is admirably versatile, having done well on good and fast ground as well as Polytrack, and these conditions were no barrier to success. She was beaten in Group 3 company on her only attempt at 6f but ran here as if the extra 1f should be no problem at a lower level. (op 11-2 tchd 5-1)
Fifth Ave had to overcome a little stumble as she came to take the lead, and she only failed to hold on by inches. A likeable battler, she remains equally adept at 5f and 6f, and she coped well with the soft ground on this first experience of it. (op 6-1 tchd 13-2 and 9-2)
Style And Panache(IRE) is back in form and just about ran her race under a 6lb penalty, but the extra weight gave her a stiff task following her narrow win last time. (op 15-2 tchd 9-1)
Where's Romeo(IRE), outclassed in Listed company last time, had not previously run on soft ground. The jury is still out, even though he was reportedly unsuited by the fast ground at Epsom. (op 13-2 tchd 9-1)
Avonmore Star had a big weight to carry in these conditions, and is probably better at 6f anyway. (op 7-2 tchd 11-2)
Squires Gate(IRE) Official explanation: jockey said colt never travelled

Scarlet Rocks(IRE) Official explanation: jockey said filly jumped awkwardly leaving stalls

6637 JOIN THE ROYAL WINDSOR RACING CLUB CLAIMING STKS 1m 2f 7y
5:00 (5:00) (Class 6) 3-4-Y-O £1,706 (£503; £252) Stalls Low

Form RPR

2124 1 **Urban Space**26 5859 4-9-4 77 KierenFox(3) 9 84
(J L Flint) *in tch: hdwy to ld over 3f out: rdn over 2f out: clr over 1f out: kpt on wl: eased towards fin* **10/11**1

4001 2 3¾ **Essexbridge**14 6257 3-9-2 72 (b) RichardHughes 6 78
(R Hannon) *chsd ldr after 2f: rdn and clr w wnr over 2f out: btn over 1f out: eased whn wl btn fnl 50yds* **3/1**2

4635 3 8 **Dane Cottage**2 6571 3-8-0 53 (v) CathyGannon 2 45
(P D Evans) *s.i.s: towards rr: swtchd lft and effrt over 3f out: chsd clr ldng pair 2f out: no prog and wl hld after* **12/1**

3100 4 4 **Cut The Cackle (IRE)**9 6374 4-8-10 75 TonyCulhane 4 42
(D Flood) *stdd s: hld up towards rr: lost tch w ldrs over 3f out: wnt modest 4th over 1f out: n.d* **15/2**3

2050 5 3½ **Foxtrot Bravo (IRE)**25 5873 4-8-5 42 (b) AmyBaker(5) 7 35
(Miss S L Davison) *t.k.h: chsd ldr for 2f: styd handy tl wknd over 2f out: sn bhd* **33/1**

0000 6 6 **Belvidera**7 6415 4-8-7 30 (v1) LiamJones 5 20
(A W Carroll) *bhd: rdn and toiling bdly over 4f out: n.d* **100/1**

0300 7 1¼ **Markhesa**5 6452 4-8-4 58 SophieDoyle(3) 12 17
(J R Boyle) *hld up towards rr: rdn and btn over 2f out: wl btn after* **10/1**

55 8 ¾ **Guppy's Girl (IRE)**30 5765 3-7-12 0 SimonPearce(3) 8 15
(Miss S L Davison) *chsd ldrs: pressed ldrs briefly over 3f out: sn fdd and wl btn fnl 2f* **66/1**

600- 9 18 **Dalrymple (IRE)**300 7549 4-9-2 43 LiamKeniry 1 —
(M Madgwick) *in tch tl wknd u.p over 3f out: t.o fnl 2f: eased ins fnl f* **100/1**

00 10 9 **Mouchez**19 6093 3-8-11 0 FergusSweeney 11 —
(D K Ivory) *s.i.s: a towards rr: lost tch over 2f out: t.o and virtually p.u fnl 2f* **100/1**

000- 11 11 **Improper (USA)**361 6611 4-8-10 38 (tp) DaneO'Neill 3 —
(Mouse Hamilton-Fairley) *led tl over 3f out: sn dropped out: t.o fnl 2f* **100/1**

2m 15.3s (6.60) **Going Correction** +0.65s/f (Yiel)
WFA 3 from 4yo 5lb 11 Ran SP% **114.3**
Speed ratings (Par 101): **99,96,89,86,83 78,77,77,62,55 46**
toteswingers:1&2 £1.70, 2&3 £6.30, 1&3 £4.10 CSF £3.42 TOTE £2.50: £1.80, £1.10, £1.90; EX 4.50 Trifecta £15.20 Pool: £763.34 - 37.06 winning units..Cut The Cackle was claimed by P. Butler for £9,000. Urban Space was claimed by C. R. Dore for £15,000.
Owner Jason Tucker **Bred** Winterbeck Manor Stud **Trained** Kenfig Hill, Bridgend

FOCUS
An above-average claimer at its top end, with the winner rated 77 and the runner-up 72. The gallop was good, which sorted out the better horses from the rest.
Mouchez Official explanation: jockey said gelding had no more to give

6638 ATTHERACES.COM MAIDEN STKS 6f
5:30 (5:31) (Class 5) 3-Y-O+ £2,286 (£675; £337) Stalls High

Form RPR

3 1 **Junket**20 6060 3-8-12 0 TedDurcan 1 79
(Dr J D Scargill) *in tch: hdwy to chse ldr ent fnl 2f: rdn to ld ent fnl f: styd on strly* **7/4**1

2432 2 4½ **Nadinska**7 6420 3-8-12 56 RichardHughes 6 65
(M R Channon) *stdd after s: hld up in tch: hdwy to trck ldng pair ent fnl 2f: trckd wnr 1f out: sn rdn and fnd little: wl btn and eased fnl 50yds* **5/1**3

2346 3 1¾ **Lay Claim (USA)**20 6057 3-9-3 74 (p) RichardMullen 3 64
(A J McCabe) *chsd ldrs tl led over 2f out: rdn wl over 1f out: hdd 1f out: sn btn* **7/2**2

0 4 5 **Cloth Ears**33 5658 4-8-13 0 CathyGannon 13 43
(P S McEntee) *led tl over 2f out: sn struggling u.p: wl btn over 1f out* **66/1**

00 5 2¾ **Ice Road Trucker (IRE)**23 5971 3-9-3 0 StephenCraine 9 40
(J R Boyle) *in tch: rdn and struggling over 2f out: no ch w ldrs over 1f out* **100/1**

6 shd **Doc Hay (USA)** 3-9-3 0 JimCrowley 8 39
(P F I Cole) *pushed rt s: in tch: outpcd over 2f out: no ch w ldrs fnl 2f* **7/1**

0320 7 2½ **Acquaviva**126 2584 3-8-7 62 (p) AmyScott(5) 10 26
(Eve Johnson Houghton) *in tch in midfield: struggling u.p over 2f out: wl btn fnl 2f* **20/1**

8 1 **Old Peg** 5-8-8 0 MarkCoumbe(5) 4 23
(D Bourton) *towards rr: swtchd lft and rdn ent fnl 2f: kpt on: nvr trbld ldrs* **50/1**

2640 9 ½ **Pippbrook Ministar**19 6085 3-8-12 67 HayleyTurner 5 21
(J R Boyle) *chsd ldrs: rdn and hung rt jst over 2f out: sn wknd* **8/1**

10 1 **Hidden Destiny** 3-9-3 0 FergusSweeney 12 23+
(P J Makin) *s.i.s: bhd and rn green: nvr trbld ldrs* **33/1**

0005 11 ½ **Aldorable**107 3210 3-8-12 44 LiamKeniry 7 17
(R A Teal) *short of room s: a towards rr: rdn and no hdwy over 2f out* **66/1**

5000 12 ½ **Fear Factor (IRE)**20 6061 3-9-3 44 (tp) StevieDonohoe 11 20
(G A Butler) *chsd ldr tl 3f out: sn lost pl: wl bhd fr wl over 1f out:* **33/1**

0000 13 8 **Natalie N G**33 5668 3-8-5 25 DannyBrock(7) 2 —
(J R Jenkins) *in tch in midfield: rdn and struggling 1/2-way: wl bhd fnl 3f: t.o* **200/1**

1m 15.87s (2.87) **Going Correction** +0.40s/f (Good)
WFA 3 from 4yo+ 1lb 13 Ran SP% **115.9**
Speed ratings (Par 103): **96,90,87,81,77 77,73,72,71,70 69,69,58**
toteswingers:1&2 £3.70, 2&3 £4.60, 1&3 £2.60 CSF £9.66 TOTE £3.00: £1.10, £1.90, £1.70; EX 9.30 Trifecta £24.70 Pool of £577.40 - 17.28 winning units..
Owner Silent Partners **Bred** Cheveley Park Stud Ltd **Trained** Newmarket, Suffolk

FOCUS
A modest maiden on the whole, but with an unexposed winner, and only four having any chance in the last 2f. The first two were the only pair to head for the far rail from the intersection, though other races suggested that did not distort the result.

6639 TRAINER MAGAZINE NOW ON ITUNES H'CAP 1m 3f 135y
6:00 (6:00) (Class 5) (0-75,75) 3-Y-O+ £2,286 (£675; £337) Stalls Low

Form RPR

6106 1 **Foxhaven**22 5991 8-9-12 75 (v) GeorgeBaker 4 86
(P R Chamings) *chsd ldrs: wnt 2nd over 3f out: rdn to chal 2f out: led 1f out: drvn clr ins fnl f: eased towards fin* **5/1**2

1650 2 2 **Rowan Tiger**12 6289 4-9-11 74 StephenCraine 5 82
(J R Boyle) *led: pushed clr ent fnl 2f: rdn and jnd 2f out: hdd 1f out: one pce after* **20/1**

1530 **3** *3* **Choral Festival**[22] 5994 4-8-12 **61** .... NeilChalmers 3 64
(J J Bridger) *in tch in midfield: hdwy over 2f out: drvn to chse ldng pair over 1f out: no imp and styd on same pce after* **11/1**

2110 **4** *nk* **Where's Susie**[41] 5382 5-9-5 **68** .... (p) DaneO'Neill 14 70
(M Madgwick) *hld up towards rr: hdwy over 2f out: rdn 2f out: styd on same pce fr over 1f out* **16/1**

-223 **5** *shd* **Dancing Storm**[21] 6021 7-9-0 **63** .... FergusSweeney 10 65
(W S Kittow) *hld up in tch in midfield: effrt and rdn over 2f out: chsd ldng pair and no imp u.p over 1f out: lost 2 pls ins fnl f* **13/2**[3]

-134 **6** *1 1/2* **Love Action (IRE)**[48] 5181 3-9-5 **75** .... RichardHughes 7 75
(R Hannon) *chsd ldrs: rdn 4f out: outpcd u.p over 3f out: kpt on same pce fnl 2f* **4/1**[1]

2210 **7** *2 1/2* **Bosamcliff (IRE)**[15] 6224 5-9-9 **75** .... RichardEvans(3) 11 70
(P D Evans) *in tch in midfield: effrt and barging match w rival jst over 2f out: sn rdn: no hdwy and btn jst over 1f out* **10/1**

5-60 **8** *3/4* **Etruscan (IRE)**[19] 6091 5-9-6 **69** .... LiamKeniry 2 63
(C Gordon) *in tch in midfield: rdn and unable qck 3f out: one pce and no threat to ldrs fnl 2f* **33/1**

1050 **9** *1 1/4* **Shy**[20] 6051 5-8-12 **64** .... JamesMillman(3) 6 56
(B R Millman) *in tch: rdn and outpcd over 3f out: rallied u.p 2f out: wknd over 1f out: wl btn whn eased ins fnl f* **12/1**

2566 **10** *1 3/4* **Meglio Ancora**[12] 6282 3-9-1 **71** .... J-PGuillambert 16 60
(J G Portman) *stdd s: hld up in rr: hdwy ent fnl 2f: hung lft and no prog after: continued to hang and eased ins fnl f* **11/1**

5003 **11** *9* **Archie Rice (USA)**[16] 6202 4-9-9 **72** .... StevieDonohoe 9 46
(T Keddy) *stdd s: hld up in rr: rdn and no rspnse 3f out: wl bhd fnl 2f* **20/1**

230/ **12** *3 1/4* **No To Trident**[676] 6400 5-8-13 **65** .... (p) AndrewHeffernan(3) 8 33
(J L Flint) *chsd ldrs: rdn and lost pl over 3f out: wl bhd over 1f out* **8/1**

5041 **13** *8* **Straight Laced**[80] 4101 4-8-12 **61** .... (v) JimCrowley 12 16
(W J Knight) *chsd ldr tl over 3f out: sn dropped out: wl bhd and eased ins fnl f* **11/1**

2m 38.58s (9.08) **Going Correction** +0.65s/f (Yiel)
WFA 3 from 4yo+ 7lb **13 Ran SP% 121.2**
Speed ratings (Par 103): **95,93,91,91,91 90,88,88,87,86 80,78,72**
toteswingers:1&2 £32.30, 2&3 £42.60, 1&3 £14.00. totesuper7: Win: Not won. Place: £663.80. CSF £106.00 CT £1068.40 TOTE £6.50: £2.80, £5.20, £5.10; EX 127.20 TRIFECTA Not won. Place 6: £130.74 Place 5: £73.60.
Owner Inhurst Players **Bred** Highclere Stud Ltd **Trained** Baughurst, Hants

FOCUS
A modest pace favoured those who raced near the front.
Meglio Ancora Official explanation: jockey said gelding hung left
T/Jkpt: Not won. T/Plt: £130.30 to a £1 stake. Pool of £64,669.04 - 362.06 winning tickets. T/Qpdt: £8.70 to a £1 stake. Pool of £6,237.31 - 524.60 winning tickets. SP

6486 MAISONS-LAFFITTE (R-H)

Monday, October 4

OFFICIAL GOING: Turf: heavy

6640a PRIX DE BONNEVAL (LISTED RACE) (3YO+) (TURF) 5f 110y
12:20 (12:00) 3-Y-O+ £23,008 (£9,203; £6,902; £4,601; £2,300)

RPR

1 **Alcohuaz (CHI)**[22] 5-9-6 0 .... StephanePasquier 6 108
(Lennart Reuterskiold Jr, Sweden) **193/10**

2 *1/2* **Kachgai (IRE)**[36] 5576 7-9-2 0 .... MickaelBarzalona 13 102
(Y De Nicolay, France) **78/10**

3 *nk* **Tiza (SAF)**[22] 6012 8-9-2 0 .... (p) GeraldMosse 11 101
(A De Royer-Dupre, France) **9/1**

4 *snk* **Fred Lalloupet**[22] 6012 3-8-11 0 .... OlivierPeslier 5 97
(D Smaga, France) **21/1**

5 *1 1/2* **Spectacle Du Mars (FR)**[21] 3-8-11 0 .... GregoryBenoist 4 92
(X Nakkachdji, France) **9/2**[1]

6 *hd* **Orpen Shadow (IRE)**[79] 4165 3-8-11 0 .... ChristopheSoumillon 1 91
(J-C Rouget, France) **13/1**

7 *nse* **Nuit De Glace (FR)**[19] 6-8-8 0 .... RamuntchoMaillot 8 87
(Mlle Valerie Boussin, France) **17/1**

8 *1/2* **Desert Ocean (IRE)**[29] 5802 6-8-11 0 .... ThierryThulliez 12 88
(G Collet, France) **26/1**

9 *1/2* **Salut L'Africain (FR)**[36] 5576 5-9-2 0 .... (p) MaximeGuyon 10 91
(Robert Collet, France) **10/1**

10 *1 1/2* **Letteratura (IRE)**[36] 5576 4-8-8 0 .... Christophe-PatriceLemaire 2 78
(J-C Rouget, France) **5/1**[2]

0 **Inxile (IRE)**[16] 6194 5-9-2 0 .... AdrianNicholls 3 —
(D Nicholls) *played up in stalls: broke slowly: qckly mde up lost grnd to go 5th on stands' side: hrd rdn at 1/2-way: no ex: wknd and eased* **6/1**[3]

0 **Dam D'Augy (FR)**[22] 6012 5-8-13 0 .... (b) ThierryJarnet 7 —
(Mlle S-V Tarrou, France) **21/1**

0 **Aiboa (IRE)**[68] 4-8-8 0 .... JohanVictoire 9 —
(L A Urbano-Grajales, France) **14/1**

1m 10.0s (2.70) **13 Ran SP% 116.7**
WIN (incl. 1 euro stake): 20.30. PLACES: 5.90, 2.50, 2.70. DF: 60.00. SF: 127.00.
Owner Dr Omar Zawawi **Bred** Haras De Pirque (chile) **Trained** Sweden

6641 - 6642a (Foreign Racing) - See Raceform Interactive

6182 CATTERICK (L-H)

Tuesday, October 5

OFFICIAL GOING: Soft (good to soft in places; 7.2)
Wind: Across (light) Weather: Cloudy initially, rain between races 2 and 4, bright thereafter

6643 CATTERICKBRIDGE.CO.UK AMATEUR RIDERS' H'CAP (DIV I) 5f
2:00 (2:01) (Class 6) (0-55,61) 3-Y-O+ £1,318 (£405; £202) Stalls Low

Form RPR

6001 **1** **Avertuoso**[5] 6490 6-11-1 **61** 6ex .... (v) MrJNewman(5) 3 75
(B Smart) *chsd ldrs: rdn to ld 1f out: drvn clr* **3/1**[1]

0606 **2** *3* **Choc'A'Moca (IRE)**[6] 6466 3-10-2 **50** .... (v) MrJHarney(7) 11 54
(D Carroll) *pressed ldr: led over 1f out: hdd 1f out: kpt on but no ch w wnr* **7/1**[3]

055 **3** *1 1/4* **Attrition**[77] 4222 3-10-3 **51** .... MrAJones(7) 12 50
(Andrew Reid) *trckd ldrs: rdn over 2f out: kpt on same pce* **25/1**

0630 **4** *nk* **Best Known Secret (IRE)**[39] 5485 4-10-0 **48** .... MrMTStanley(7) 7 46
(C C Bealby) *dwlt: sn in tch: hdwy to chse ldrs 2f out: kpt on* **25/1**

4045 **5** *1/2* **Albero Di Giuda (IRE)**[22] 6025 5-10-6 **52** .... (bt) MrMOwen(5) 6 48
(F Sheridan) *rrd and s.i.s: hld up: swtchd lft and hdwy over 1f out: kpt on: nvr rch ldrs* **5/1**[2]

0000 **6** *1* **Officer Mor (USA)**[5] 6490 4-9-12 **46** oh1 .... MissRobynGray(7) 8 39
(Mrs Dianne Sayer) *chsd ldrs: rdn over 2f out: kpt on same pce* **40/1**

5051 **7** *4* **Tenancy (IRE)**[6] 6464 6-10-7 **53** 6ex .... (b) MrCAHarris(5) 2 31
(S A Harris) *led: rdn whn hdd over 1f out: sn wknd* **3/1**[1]

-005 **8** *nk* **Maragna (IRE)**[39] 5481 3-10-5 **46** oh1 .... (p) MrSWalker 9 23
(Paul Green) *wnt lft s: hld up: rdn over 2f out: sn no imp* **17/2**

0500 **9** *1 1/4* **Areeg (IRE)**[5] 6490 3-10-2 **48** .... MissWGibson(5) 1 21
(A Berry) *hld up: a bhd* **33/1**

0045 **10** *3/4* **Kookie**[6] 6460 3-10-0 **46** oh1 .... MissVBarr(5) 10 16
(R E Barr) *hld up: a towards rr* **10/1**

0030 **11** *2 3/4* **Future Gem**[6] 6464 4-10-0 **46** .... (p) MrTGarner(5) 4 6
(N Wilson) *chsd ldrs: rdn 3f out: sn wknd* **10/1**

660- **12** *80* **Wing Forward (IRE)**[400] 5512 3-9-12 **46** oh1 .... (b[1]) MrLMichael(7) 5 —
(A Berry) *virtually ref to r: t.o* **66/1**

61.12 secs (1.32) **Going Correction** +0.30s/f (Good) **12 Ran SP% 122.4**
Speed ratings (Par 101): **101,96,94,93,92 91,84,84,82,81 76,—**
Tote Swingers: 1&2 £5.40, 1&3 £12.20, 2&3 £19.20 CSF £24.45 CT £463.25 TOTE £3.30: £1.10, £4.20, £4.80; EX 28.90.
Owner Crossfields Racing **Bred** P A Mason **Trained** Hambleton, N Yorks

FOCUS
The first division of a moderate amateur riders' handicap.

6644 CATTERICKBRIDGE.CO.UK AMATEUR RIDERS' H'CAP (DIV II) 5f
2:30 (2:30) (Class 6) (0-55,54) 3-Y-O+ £1,318 (£405; £202) Stalls Low

Form RPR

1406 **1** **Fashion Icon (USA)**[39] 5502 4-10-8 **48** .... (p) MissSBrotherton 9 61
(D O'Meara) *wnt rt s: mde all: kpt on gamely whn strly chal ins fnl f* **4/1**[3]

-060 **2** *shd* **Sands Of Dee (USA)**[35] 5634 3-11-0 **54** .... MrMSeston 2 67
(J A Glover) *sn prom: chal over 1f out: kpt on wl ins fnl f: jst hld* **15/2**

0012 **3** *3* **Hot Rod Mamma (IRE)**[29] 5820 3-10-6 **51** .... MissECSayer(5) 4 53
(Mrs Dianne Sayer) *chsd ldrs: drvn to chal over 1f out: no ex ins fnl f* **11/4**[1]

1350 **4** *3* **Amoureuse**[5] 6492 3-10-0 **47** .... MrJHarney(7) 10 38
(D Carroll) *bmpd s pressed ldr: rdn over 2f out: no ex over 1f out* **11/2**

0360 **5** *1 3/4* **Lieu Day Louie (IRE)**[45] 5299 3-10-0 **45** .... MrTGarner(5) 7 30
(N Wilson) *s.i.s: sn rcvrd to chse ldrs: wknd over 1f out* **12/1**

0302 **6** *hd* **Barraland**[41] 5405 5-10-10 **50** .... (p) MrSWalker 8 34
(George Baker) *chsd ldrs: rdn over 2f out: wknd over 1f out* **7/2**[2]

/000 **7** *2 1/2* **High Window (IRE)**[54] 4986 10-10-5 **45** .... MissJCoward 6 20
(G P Kelly) *hld up: rdn 3f out: no imp* **50/1**

-000 **8** *1/2* **Neva A Mull Moment (IRE)**[69] 4487 4-10-7 **52** .... MissVBarr(5) 12 26
(R E Barr) *hld up: a towards rr* **22/1**

0300 **9** *1 3/4* **Angelofthenorth**[48] 5212 8-9-12 **45** .... MrMAllan(7) 3 12
(C J Teague) *dwlt: a outpcd in rr* **22/1**

000- **10** *1/2* **Little Pandora**[407] 5309 6-10-0 **45** .... (b[1]) MissWGibson(5) 11 10
(L R James) *hld up: a towards rr* **50/1**

0000 **11** *2 3/4* **Mr Rooney (IRE)**[43] 5362 7-9-12 **45** .... MrLMichael(7) 1 —
(A Berry) *hld up: a bhd* **40/1**

61.50 secs (1.70) **Going Correction** +0.30s/f (Good) **11 Ran SP% 118.8**
Speed ratings (Par 101): **98,97,93,88,85 85,81,80,77,76 72**
Tote Swingers: 1&2 £6.40, 1&3 £3.00, 2&3 £4.40 CSF £32.40 CT £97.78 TOTE £4.60: £1.40, £2.00, £1.10; EX 42.10.
Owner Trendy Ladies **Bred** Mr & Mrs Theodore Kuster **Trained** Nawton, N Yorks
■ Stewards' Enquiry : Miss S Brotherton six-day ban: careless riding (Oct 23,27,Nov 17,23,29,30)
Miss V Barr caution: used whip when out of contention.

FOCUS
The nearer the stands' rail the better in this second division.

6645 RACING UK NURSERY 5f
3:00 (3:01) (Class 6) (0-65,65) 2-Y-O £2,047 (£604; £302) Stalls Low

Form RPR

6606 **1** **Cinderkamp**[20] 6086 2-9-1 **59** .... SilvestreDeSousa 5 69
(E F Vaughan) *s.i.s: sn chsd ldrs: hdwy to chal over 1f out: led jst ins fnl f and sn hung lft: kpt on wl* **5/2**[1]

0045 **2** *3/4* **Guinea Seeker**[14] 6264 2-8-13 **57** .... PaulMulrennan 1 64
(T D Easterby) *prom: rdn to ld over 2f out: hdd jst ins fnl f: kpt on* **11/1**

3004 **3** *2 3/4* **Je Suis Unrockstar**[20] 6072 2-9-0 **58** .... (p) PJMcDonald 7 55
(J A Glover) *hld up: hdwy on outer over 1f out: kpt on wl ins fnl f: nrst fin* **11/1**

5062 **4** *3/4* **Rylee Mooch**[27] 5862 2-9-0 **58** .... PaulEddery 15 52
(R C Guest) *s.i.s: midfield: rdn over 2f out: drvn and kpt on wl ins fnl f* **8/1**[3]

0602 **5** *3/4* **Dotty Darroch**[32] 5733 2-8-12 **59** .... PaulPickard(3) 14 51
(R Bastiman) *towards rr: hdwy over 2f out: short of room 2f out: kpt on ins fnl f* **50/1**

6402 **6** *1* **Crazy In Love**[20] 6072 2-8-6 **53** .... (b) MatthewDavies(3) 13 41
(W G M Turner) *hld up: rdn over 2f out: short of room over 1f out: kpt on ins fnl f: nvr able to chal* **25/1**

5U06 **7** *hd* **Misty Morn**[5] 6489 2-9-3 **61** .... FrannyNorton 4 48
(A D Brown) *led: hdd over 2f out: wknd ins fnl f* **16/1**

5441 **8** *nk* **Empress Royal**[22] 6035 2-9-6 **64** .... PhillipMakin 11 50
(M Dods) *hld up: persistently short of room fr 2f out: nvr able to chal* **5/1**[2]

4300 **9** *1 1/4* **Trading**[16] 6220 2-8-13 **62** .... (b[1]) LanceBetts(5) 9 44
(T D Easterby) *midfield: rdn over 2f out: sn no imp* **20/1**

4000 **10** *1* **Vienna Woods (IRE)**[20] 6072 2-8-9 **56** .... (v[1]) KellyHarrison(3) 12 34
(B M R Haslam) *midfield: outpcd and lost pl over 2f out: n.m.r over 1f out tl ins fnl f: n.d* **33/1**

4230 **11** *1 1/2* **Chester Deelyte (IRE)**[70] 4451 2-8-5 **52** .... PatrickDonaghy(3) 2 25
(Mrs L Williamson) *chsd ldrs on outer: rdn over 2f out: wknd over 1f out* **50/1**

1000 **12** *1 1/2* **Mayfair Princess**[12] 6311 2-9-4 **62** .... (bt) DavidNolan 3 29
(P S McEntee) *cl up: rdn over 2f out: sn wknd* **22/1**

0404 **13** *2 1/2* **Gunalt Joy**[14] 6263 2-8-3 **47** .... (t) PaulHanagan 6 5
(M W Easterby) *in tch: short of room over 1f out and sn lost pl* **8/1**[3]

0000 **14** *2 1/2* **Peters Spirit (IRE)**[29] 5818 2-8-6 **53** .... (b) BarryMcHugh(3) 8 —
(R A Fahey) *sn chsd along towards rr: a bhd* **12/1**

156 **15** *3/4* **Snow Bear (IRE)**[24] 5939 2-9-4 **65** .... IanBrennan(3) 10 12
(J J Quinn) *s.i.s: hld up: a bhd* **9/1**

62.33 secs (2.53) **Going Correction** +0.30s/f (Good) **15 Ran SP% 127.5**
Speed ratings (Par 93): **91,89,85,84,83 81,81,80,78,77 74,72,68,64,63**
Tote Swingers: 1&2 £8.70, 1&3 £9.80, 2&3 £31.50 CSF £30.69 CT £280.04 TOTE £2.80: £1.80, £3.00, £7.30; EX 38.00.
Owner Ali Saeed **Bred** Baron F Von Oppenheim **Trained** Newmarket, Suffolk

FOCUS
A competitive little nursery.
NOTEBOOK
Cinderkamp, unlucky not to get closer on his nursery debut at Sandown, proved well suited by the conditions and stayed on strongly, despite hanging, to win with a bit in hand. There's probably more to come on similar going and he shapes as though 6f will suit. Official explanation: trainer's rep said, regarding apparent improvement in form, that the colt had been hampered on its previous run although not beaten far and may have been better suited by the soft ground. (op 3-1)
Guinea Seeker stepped up on previous efforts to finish second and looks capable of winning a moderate contest. (op 12-1)
Je Suis Unrockstar, declared to run again at Nottingham again today, ran well whilst suggesting he will prove suited by 6f. (op 16-1)
Rylee Mooch, runner-up off 1lb lower at Kempton on his nursery debut, didn't prove quite so effective returned to turf, but still showed enough to suggest he'll win races. (op 13-2 tchd 6-1)
Dotty Darroch stayed on in the straight from an unpromising position. Official explanation: jockey said filly was denied a clear run
Crazy In Love was another edging nearer as they crossed the line. Official explanation: jockey said filly was denied a clear run (op 22-1)
Empress Royal didn't get much of a run and but was then unable to make late ground when in the clear. Official explanation: jockey said filly was denied a clear run (op 7-2)
Vienna Woods(IRE) Official explanation: jockey said filly was denied a clear run
Gunalt Joy Official explanation: jockey said filly was denied a clear run

6646 EUROPEAN BREEDERS' FUND MAIDEN STKS — 5f
3:30 (3:30) (Class 5) 2-Y-O — **£3,626** (£1,079; £539; £269) **Stalls** Low

Form				RPR
3	**1**		**Captain Kolo (IRE)**[21] 6045 2-9-3 0 ... PaulMulrennan 2 (T D Easterby) *led: crossed over to stands' side rail over 2f out: styd on wl ins fnl f* **11/4**[2]	76
0	**2**	*1*	**Crimson Cloud**[57] 4896 2-8-9 0 ... BarryMcHugh(3) 1 (R A Fahey) *w ldrs: edgd rt over 2f out: chal over 1f out: no ex last 100yds* **9/1**	67
052	**3**	*1 3/4*	**Rowan Spirit (IRE)**[21] 6045 2-9-3 69 ... RichardKingscote 6 (W M Brisbourne) *chsd ldrs: outpcd over 2f out: hdwy on outer over 1f out: kpt on to take n.d 3rd ins fnl f* **11/2**[3]	66
2	**4**	*1/2*	**Hygrove Gal**[19] 6111 2-8-12 0 ... PaulHanagan 13 (B Smart) *w ldrs: kpt on same pce appr fnl f* **9/4**[1]	59
5	**5**	*hd*	**Oldmeldrum (IRE)**[54] 4981 2-8-12 0 ... PhillipMakin 8 (B M R Haslam) *dwlt: outpcd and in rr: hdwy stands' side whn n.m.r over 2f out: styng on at fin* **16/1**	59
20	**6**	*4 1/2*	**Red Gold And Green (IRE)**[55] 4941 2-9-0 0 ... MichaelO'Connell(3) 4 (D Nicholls) *chsd ldrs: hmpd over 2f out: wknd over 1f out* **6/1**	47
66	**7**	*hd*	**Rapturous Applause**[12] 6301 2-9-0 0 ... KellyHarrison(3) 14 (Micky Hammond) *sn outpcd and in rr: stdy hdwy over 1f out: kpt on: nvr nr ldrs* **16/1**	47
00	**8**	*7*	**Mujapiste (IRE)**[14] 6263 2-8-9 0 ... (p) IanBrennan(3) 5 (L A Mullaney) *chsd ldrs: hmpd over 2f out: edgd lft and lost pl over 1f out* **66/1**	16
0255	**9**	*nse*	**Kheya (IRE)**[109] 3163 2-8-12 68 ... PJMcDonald 9 (G M Moore) *chsd ldrs: hmpd over 2f out: wknd over 1f out* **20/1**	16
300	**10**	*6*	**Callipygos**[55] 4960 2-8-12 56 ... DavidNolan 10 (P S McEntee) *outpcd and in rr after 2f: bhd fnl 2f* **66/1**	—
	11	*nk*	**Skiddaw View** 2-8-12 0 ... SilvestreDeSousa 12 (A D Brown) *s.s: rn green and sn bhd* **33/1**	—

61.35 secs (1.55) **Going Correction** +0.30s/f (Good) **11 Ran SP% 119.6**
Speed ratings (Par 95): **99,97,94,93,93 86,85,74,74,65 64**
Tote Swingers: 1&2 £5.80, 1&3 £3.90, 2&3 £7.60 CSF £27.56 TOTE £4.30: £2.30, £4.40, £3.40; EX 29.80.
Owner Middleham Park Racing Xii **Bred** J K Grimes **Trained** Great Habton, N Yorks
■ Stewards' Enquiry : Barry McHugh three-day ban: careless riding (Oct 19,20,21)

FOCUS
A modest juvenile maiden.
NOTEBOOK
Captain Kolo(IRE), third at Haydock on debut, didn't need to have improved much to win this and he stayed on strongly for a ready success. There's more to come under these conditions and he will be an interesting sort for handicaps. (tchd 5-2)
Crimson Cloud stepped up markedly on her debut effort, improving for the slower ground as her pedigree suggested she would. (op 8-1)
Rowan Spirit(IRE), ahead of the winner at Haydock, was unable to confirm that form and clearly isn't as progressive. (op 5-1 tchd 9-2)
Hygrove Gal, runner-up at Pontefract on debut, clearly wasn't as effective in these softer conditions. (tchd 11-4)
Oldmeldrum(IRE) caught the eye in behind and will be of obvious interest once handicapping (op 25-1)
Red Gold And Green(IRE) was hampered at a critical stage and should do better handicapping. (op 13-2 tchd 7-1)

6647 EAT SLEEP DRINK AT NAGS HEAD PICKHILL NURSERY — 7f
4:00 (4:01) (Class 4) (0-85,85) 2-Y-O — **£3,238** (£963; £481; £240) **Stalls** Low

Form				RPR
4116	**1**		**Talley Close**[31] 5745 2-9-7 85 ... PaulHanagan 4 (R A Fahey) *hld up in midfield: hdwy over 2f out: chsd ldr over 1f out: drvn ent fnl f: kpt on wl to ld fnl 50yds* **7/2**[1]	89
0541	**2**	*1/2*	**First Class Favour (IRE)**[17] 6184 2-8-8 77 ... LanceBetts(5) 9 (T D Easterby) *led: drvn 2f out: kpt on: hdd fnl 50yds* **11/2**[3]	80
0100	**3**	*3/4*	**Bay Of Fires (IRE)**[26] 5882 2-8-11 75 ... SilvestreDeSousa 1 (D O'Meara) *prom: rdn over 2f out: chal over 1f out: kpt on ins fnl f* **14/1**	76
2421	**4**	*nk*	**Regimental (IRE)**[13] 6294 2-8-3 70 ... AmyRyan(3) 2 (Mrs A Duffield) *sn pushed along towards rr: hdwy over 2f out: chsd ldrs over 1f out: kpt on ins fnl f* **11/2**[3]	70
0066	**5**	*5*	**Smart Step**[30] 5784 2-8-5 69 ... GregFairley 6 (M Johnston) *trckd ldrs: rdn over 2f out: grad wknd* **5/1**[2]	57
1000	**6**	*1 1/2*	**Geesala (IRE)**[26] 5880 2-8-13 77 ... PJMcDonald 10 (K A Ryan) *sn prom on outer: rdn over 2f out: wknd over 1f out* **20/1**	61
2143	**7**	*6*	**Malgoof (IRE)**[18] 6139 2-9-2 80 ... PaulMulrennan 8 (B Smart) *in tch: rdn over 2f out: wknd over 1f out* **11/2**[3]	49
2226	**8**	*9*	**Greek Islands (IRE)**[57] 4911 2-9-3 81 ... AhmedAjtebi 5 (Mahmood Al Zarooni) *hld up: rdn over 2f out: sn no imp: eased* **10/1**	27
6240	**9**	*5*	**Damascus Symphony**[36] 5597 2-8-1 65 ow1 ... (b[1]) FrannyNorton 3 (J D Bethell) *s.i.s: a towards rr* **14/1**	—
3135	**10**	*2 1/4*	**Fabiello**[33] 5699 2-8-12 76 ... RichardKingscote 7 (Tom Dascombe) *midfield on outer: rdn along 1/2-way: wknd over 1f out: eased* **12/1**	4

1m 27.81s (0.81) **Going Correction** +0.05s/f (Good) **10 Ran SP% 119.9**
Speed ratings (Par 97): **97,96,95,95,89 87,80,70,64,62**
Tote Swingers: 1&2 £6.50, 1&3 £10.10, 2&3 £13.50 CSF £23.32 CT £250.57 TOTE £4.20: £1.80, £2.60, £6.80; EX 29.80.
Owner Skeltools Ltd **Bred** A B Phipps **Trained** Musley Bank, N Yorks

FOCUS
A tricky little nursery.
NOTEBOOK
Talley Close got a nice run through inside the final furlong to win his third race of the season. Disappointing off this mark at Haydock latest, he had earlier won off 7lb lower and produced an improved display to score under top weight, the step up to 7f definitely helping.
First Class Favour(IRE), up 5lb having won over C&D latest, had no trouble with the return to softer conditions and her busy schedule shows no signs of catching up with her. (op 6-1)
Bay Of Fires(IRE) was only worn down late on and this represented a return to her best. (op 16-1)
Regimental(IRE) was never going like a winner on this return to 7f. The 9lb rise for winning at Redcar may have proved too much. (op 13-2 tchd 7-1)
Smart Step was one of the first beaten and looks to need further. (op 7-1)
Geesala(IRE)'s stamina ebbed away over this longer trip. (op 16-1)
Malgoof(IRE) was reportedly unsuited by the ground. Official explanation: jockey said colt was unsuited by the soft (good to soft places) ground (op 4-1 tchd 7-2)
Fabiello was reportedly never going. Official explanation: jockey said colt never travelled (op 10-1 tchd 14-1)

6648 SKYRAM H'CAP (DIV I) — 1m 7f 177y
4:30 (4:30) (Class 6) (0-60,60) 3-Y-O+ — **£1,706** (£503; £252) **Stalls** Low

Form				RPR
0414	**1**		**Lady Bluesky**[9] 6397 7-10-0 60 ... PaulMulrennan 6 (A C Whillans) *trckd ldr: smooth hdwy to ld 3f out: drvn over 1f out: kpt on wl* **4/1**[2]	71
3300	**2**	*2 1/4*	**Rare Coincidence**[4] 6538 9-9-1 50 ... (p) IanBrennan(3) 11 (R F Fisher) *led: rdn whn hdd 3f out: styd far side over 2f out: kpt on* **20/1**	58
/153	**3**	*8*	**Fair Spin**[19] 6114 10-9-6 52 ... (v) PaulHanagan 14 (Micky Hammond) *midfield: rdn over 3f out: kpt on fnl 2f: nvr trbld ldrs* **6/1**	50
515	**4**	*3*	**Escape Artist**[38] 5534 3-8-9 52 ... (t) SilvestreDeSousa 10 (T D Easterby) *prom: racd keenly: rdn over 3f out: wknd over 1f out* **5/2**[1]	47
6346	**5**	*3*	**Unawatuna**[35] 5642 5-9-6 55 ... KellyHarrison(3) 2 (Mrs K Walton) *midfield: rdn wl over 3f out: kpt on same pce* **5/1**[3]	46
3300	**6**	*1 1/2*	**Strikemaster (IRE)**[17] 6187 4-9-9 58 ... PatrickDonaghy(3) 8 (B Ellison) *s.i.s: hld up: mod hdwy fnl 2f: n.d* **12/1**	47
0006	**7**	*hd*	**Emirate Isle**[9] 6393 6-9-9 55 ... (p) PJMcDonald 3 (B Storey) *midfield: reminders over 5f out: hrd drvn over 3f out: one pce* **50/1**	44
6300	**8**	*10*	**The Mighty Mod (USA)**[17] 6187 3-8-4 47 ... (v[1]) GregFairley 12 (M Johnston) *s.i.s: hld up: n.d* **12/1**	24
0330	**9**	*6*	**They All Laughed**[19] 6114 7-9-7 53 ... (p) PhillipMakin 4 (Mrs Marjorie Fife) *hld up in midfield: rdn over 4f out: sn no imp* **8/1**	23
/30-	**10**	*4*	**Pinewood Legend (IRE)**[82] 4848 8-8-11 46 oh1 (bt) BarryMcHugh(3) 13 (P D Niven) *trckd ldrs: wknd over 3f out* **22/1**	11
0000	**11**	*3 1/4*	**Shanavaz**[15] 6242 4-9-0 46 oh1 ... LeeVickers 1 (C J Teague) *hld up: a bhd* **66/1**	7
5040	**12**	*1 1/4*	**Mister Fizzbomb (IRE)**[14] 6269 7-9-8 54 ... (p) DavidNolan 7 (J S Wainwright) *trckd ldrs: rdn over 4f out: wknd 3f out* **40/1**	14
0/0-	**13**	*24*	**Amjad**[4] 2656 13-8-11 46 oh1 ... PaulPickard(3) 5 (S G West) *s.i.s: hld up: reminders bef 1/2-way: t.o fnl 6f* **66/1**	—

3m 36.26s (4.26) **Going Correction** +0.30s/f (Good)
WFA 3 from 4yo+ 11lb **13 Ran SP% 122.5**
Speed ratings (Par 101): **101,99,95,94,92 92,92,87,84,82 80,79,67**
Tote Swingers: 1&2 £20.90, 1&3 £4.70, 2&3 £26.20 CSF £90.38 CT £487.03 TOTE £4.10: £1.10, £9.20, £1.80; EX 129.20.
Owner Mrs S Harrow Mrs L M Whillans **Bred** C E Whiteley **Trained** Newmill-On-Slitrig, Borders

FOCUS
The first division of a low-grade staying handicap. The front pair drew clear.

6649 SKYRAM H'CAP (DIV II) — 1m 7f 177y
5:00 (5:00) (Class 6) (0-60,59) 3-Y-O+ — **£1,706** (£503; £252) **Stalls** Low

Form				RPR
1505	**1**		**Drop The Hammer**[19] 6109 4-9-9 54 ... (b[1]) SilvestreDeSousa 3 (D O'Meara) *led 1f: chsd ldr: led 5f out: rdn clr over 1f out: eased towards fin* **7/1**[2]	67
-023	**2**	*8*	**Rosewin (IRE)**[17] 6187 4-9-11 59 ... BarryMcHugh(3) 5 (Ollie Pears) *hld up in rr: stdy hdwy 6f out: wnt 3rd over 3f out: kpt on to chse wnr appr fnl f: hung lft: no ch w wnr* **11/4**[1]	62
0000	**3**	*2*	**I Got Music**[22] 6038 3-8-3 48 ow3 ... PaulPickard(3) 8 (K G Reveley) *in rr: hdwy and poor 6th 3f out: mod 4th over 1f out: kpt on to take 3rd nr line* **33/1**	49
0000	**4**	*1/2*	**Smugglers Bay (IRE)**[19] 6114 6-9-5 50 ... (b) PaulMulrennan 6 (T D Easterby) *hld up in rr: hdwy to chse ldrs after 5f: wnt 2nd 4f out: one pce fnl 2f* **9/1**[3]	50
6024	**5**	*22*	**Finellas Fortune**[19] 6114 5-9-11 56 ... PJMcDonald 10 (G M Moore) *in rr: sme hdwy 6f out: nvr on terms* **10/1**	30
2353	**6**	*nk*	**Consult**[25] 5923 3-8-9 51 ... (b) PaulHanagan 4 (Sir Mark Prescott) *t.k.h: led after 1f: hdd 5f out: lost pl over 3f out* **11/4**[1]	24
4503	**7**	*3/4*	**Maybeme**[14] 6262 4-9-5 53 ... KellyHarrison(3) 9 (N Bycroft) *in rr: hdwy over 5f out: nvr a factor* **12/1**	25
3566	**8**	*35*	**Suor Angelica (IRE)**[14] 6272 5-8-11 45 ... MatthewDavies(3) 12 (George Baker) *sn chsng ldrs: lost pl over 4f out: eased over 1f out: t.o* **10/1**	—
3250	**9**	*14*	**Harcas (IRE)**[17] 6187 8-9-2 47 ... PhillipMakin 7 (M Todhunter) *chsd ldrs: drvn and lost pl 8f out: wknd over 5f out: t.o 2f out: virtually p.u* **25/1**	—
-144	**10**	*2 1/2*	**Sendali (FR)**[131] 2464 6-9-8 53 ... GregFairley 2 (J D Bethell) *sn chsng ldrs: drvn and lost pl over 6f out: sn bhd: t.o 3f out: virtually p.u* **7/1**[2]	—
300-	**11**	*2 1/2*	**Art Gallery**[36] 6559 6-8-9 45 ... BillyCray(5) 1 (D W Thompson) *chsd ldrs: reminders and lost pl 8f out: sn bhd: t.o 3f out: virtually p.u* **50/1**	—

3m 37.14s (5.14) **Going Correction** +0.30s/f (Good)
WFA 3 from 4yo+ 11lb **11 Ran SP% 123.0**
Speed ratings (Par 101): **99,95,94,93,82 82,82,64,57,56 55**
Tote Swingers: 1&2 £6.20, 1&3 £32.70, 2&3 £24.60 CSF £27.46 CT £622.85 TOTE £6.20: £2.40, £3.40, £11.70; EX 33.20.
Owner A Crowther **Bred** Mrs N J Gidley Wright **Trained** Nawton, N Yorks

FOCUS
The runners came home well strung out, as had been the case in the first division.
Consult Official explanation: trainer's rep had no explanation for the poor form shown

Art Gallery Official explanation: jockey said gelding never travelled

6650 YORKSHIRE4X4.COM ADVENTURE ACTIVITIES H'CAP 1m 3f 214y
5:30 (5:30) (Class 5) (0-75,75) 3-Y-O+ £2,072 (£616; £308; £153) Stalls High

Form RPR

2102 1 **Royal Swain (IRE)**[17] 6181 4-9-11 74 PJMcDonald 1 82+
(G A Swinbank) *trckd ldrs: hdwy to ld over 1f out: drvn and kpt on wl ins fnl f* 11/4[1]

4425 2 1 3/4 **Aegean Destiny**[25] 5923 3-8-1 62 BillyCray[(5)] 9 67
(J Mackie) *hld up: rdn over 2f out: hdwy to chse ldrs over 1f out: kpt on ins fnl f* 8/1

3203 3 1 1/4 **Kingdom Of Munster (IRE)**[10] 6359 3-8-9 65 PaulHanagan 11 68
(R A Fahey) *prom: rdn to ld 3f out: drvn whn hdd over 1f out: no ex fnl 100yds* 9/2[2]

3441 4 hd **Danceintothelight**[17] 6187 3-8-3 62 KellyHarrison[(3)] 8 65
(Micky Hammond) *in tch: racd keenly: rdn and hdwy to chal 2f out: kpt on tl no ex ins fnl f* 5/1[3]

2140 5 1 3/4 **Umverti**[25] 5913 5-9-9 75 BarryMcHugh[(3)] 4 75
(N Bycroft) *led: rdn whn hdd 3f out: stl ev ch over 1f out: no ex ins fnl f* 17/2

1163 6 3 1/4 **Eijaaz (IRE)**[13] 6297 9-8-13 62 (p) SilvestreDeSousa 5 57
(G A Harker) *hld up: rdn over 2f out: n.d* 10/1

612 7 3 1/4 **Tropical Duke (IRE)**[14] 6269 4-8-9 61 oh1 MichaelStainton[(3)] 10 50
(R E Barr) *v s.i.s: hld up: rdn over 3f out: sn no imp* 11/2

114- 8 1 **Bagber**[347] 6986 4-9-8 74 IanBrennan[(3)] 2 62
(P Monteith) *midfield: racd keenly: rdn over 3f out: wknd over 1f out* 22/1

2420 9 1 **Hurlingham**[26] 5888 6-9-4 67 (b) PaulMulrennan 7 53+
(M W Easterby) *trckd ldrs: rdn whn rdr lost irons over 2f out: eased* 11/1

2m 44.58s (5.68) **Going Correction** +0.30s/f (Good)
WFA 3 from 4yo+ 7lb 9 Ran SP% **120.3**
Speed ratings (Par 103): **93,91,91,90,89 87,85,84,84**
Tote Swingers: 1&2 £8.20, 1&3 £7.70, 2&3 £3.50. totesuper7: Win: Not won. Place: £755.30. CSF £26.90 CT £99.08 TOTE £4.40: £3.20, £4.40, £3.20; EX 29.60 Place 6: £105.59 Place 5: £46.24..
Owner Andrew Sparks **Bred** Patrick Cummins **Trained** Melsonby, N Yorks

FOCUS
A modest handicap.
Tropical Duke(IRE) Official explanation: jockey said he was slow to remove blindfold on 1st attempt as it was tucked tightly underneath the bridle
Bagber Official explanation: jockey said gelding ran too free
Hurlingham Official explanation: jockey said pin broke in stirrup
T/Jkpt: £9,871.80 to a £1 stake. Pool of £83,424 - 6 winning tickets. T/Plt: £186.30 to a £1 stake. Pool of £77,081 - 301.89 winning tickets. T/Qpdt: £51.90 to a £1 stake. Pool of £4,155 - 59.20 winning tickets. AS

6254 LEICESTER (R-H)
Tuesday, October 5

OFFICIAL GOING: Heavy (soft in places; 5.3)
False rail from round course bend to the 1f marker adding 9yds to distances on round course.
Wind: Light half-behind Weather: Overcast

6651 E B F LADBROKES.COM MAIDEN FILLIES' STKS 7f 9y
2:10 (2:12) (Class 4) 2-Y-O £4,533 (£1,348; £674; £336) Stalls Low

Form RPR

05 1 **Isolate**[15] 6247 2-9-0 0 SteveDrowne 5 81
(H Morrison) *chsd ldrs: rdn to ld and hung lft fr over 1f out: styd on wl* 8/1[3]

3 2 2 1/2 **Our Gal**[88] 3871 2-9-0 0 WilliamCarson 3 75
(M G Quinlan) *racd alone stands' side and overall ldr tl rdn: hung rt and hdd over 1f out: styd on same pce ins fnl f* 3/1[1]

3 1 1/2 **Sugar Hiccup (IRE)** 2-9-0 0 LukeMorris 4 71
(C G Cox) *prom: rdn 1/2-way: styd on: wnt 3rd nr fin* 25/1

4 1 **Heatherbird** 2-9-0 0 RichardHughes 9 69
(W Jarvis) *chsd ldrs: rdn over 1f out: wknd and lost 3rd towards fin* 17/2

60 5 nk **Amazon Twilight**[13] 6278 2-8-9 0 JohnFahy[(5)] 15 68
(B R Johnson) *hld up: rdn 1/2-way: sn hung lft: hdwy over 1f out: styd on* 100/1

6 2 **Elfine (IRE)** 2-9-0 0 DaneO'Neill 12 63
(H J L Dunlop) *s.i.s: sn pushed along in rr: r.o ins fnl f: nrst fin* 100/1

7 3 1/2 **Deslaya (IRE)** 2-9-0 0 TomQueally 8 54
(H R A Cecil) *chsd ldrs: rdn over 2f out: wknd over 1f out* 7/1

0 8 1/2 **Cinta**[18] 6155 2-9-0 0 MichaelHills 14 53
(M Botti) *prom: rdn over 2f out: wknd fnl f* 7/1[2]

9 nk **Highest Bid (USA)** 2-9-0 0 PhilipRobinson 13 52
(M A Jarvis) *led main gp over 5f: wknd fnl f* 3/1[1]

10 13 **Moonlight Mystery** 2-9-0 0 TedDurcan 2 20
(C F Wall) *s.i.s: sn pushed along and a in rr: lost tch fr over 2f out* 14/1

1m 29.42s (3.22) **Going Correction** +0.35s/f (Good) 10 Ran SP% **107.7**
Speed ratings (Par 94): **95,92,90,89,88 86,82,82,81,66**
Tote Swingers: 1&2 £4.90, 1&3 £19.20, 2&3 £12.00 CSF £28.53 TOTE £7.10: £1.90, £1.10, £9.70; EX 30.60 Trifecta £288.40 Part won. Pool of £389.79 - 03.30 winning units..
Owner Gillian, Lady Howard De Walden **Bred** Avington Manor Stud **Trained** East Ilsley, Berks

FOCUS
This modest fillies' maiden would have taken some getting on the testing ground. All bar one of the runners shunned the near rail and the main group tacked over to the far side around halfway. The main action still developed middle-to-stands' side, though, as pretty much most of the straight was covered.

NOTEBOOK
Isolate travelled nicely before putting the race to bed passing the furlong marker and shed her maiden tag at the third attempt. This was her first run on such ground and it evidently suited, but her previous experience was also a definite help in getting through it. This daughter of Verglas has improved with every outing to date, and one imagines her future now lies with the handicapper, though connections may very well go off in search of some valuable black type. (op 9-1 tchd 15-2)
Our Gal was having her first outing since showing up nicely on debut over 6f at Newmarket in July and attracted support. She was taken over to the stands' rail before coming off it after the 2f marker, and had her chance. The ground was different probably more testing than she cares for over this extra distance but, while she may be able to nick a small maiden, she looks one to be more interested in when switching to nurseries. (op 11-4 tchd 7-2)
Sugar Hiccup(IRE) came under pressure around halfway, but responded and fared best of the newcomers. Her pedigree suggests a mix of speed and stamina, but she obviously stays well and should get closer next time out. (op 28-1)
Heatherbird, out of a half-sister to Fillies' Mile winner Teggiano, failed to seriously threaten on debut yet was keeping on encouragingly towards the finish. She will get further next year and has a future. (op 11-1 tchd 12-1)
Amazon Twilight kept on stoutly after coming under heavy pressure and needed this for a mark.
Elfine(IRE) ◆ took an age to get the hang of things, but was noted keeping on through horses inside the final furlong. The market strongly suggested this debut outing would be needed, she had bags of stamina on the dam's side of her pedigree and ought to know a lot more on her next assignment.
Deslaya(IRE) will want a good bit further at three looking at her dam's pedigree, but her sire is a speed influence. There is also a very good chance she wants quicker ground, and so she shouldn't be fully judged on this debut display. (tchd 17-2)
Cinta, who met support, showed little on debut at Newmarket 18 days earlier. She struggled when asked for an effort on this surface, but it was a step in the right direction. (op 15-2)
Highest Bid(USA), a half-sister to the stout stayer Amerigo, proved green in the preliminaries but knew her job from the gates and was soon up with the pace. She tired badly in between the final 2f, however, and it's a fair bet that she wants quicker ground. Official explanation: jockey said filly hung left (op 11-4)

6652 LADBROKES.COM STOAT (S) STKS 1m 1f 218y
2:40 (2:41) (Class 6) 3-Y-O £1,942 (£578; £288; £144) Stalls High

Form RPR

640 1 **Marsh Warbler**[10] 6372 3-8-11 70 TomQueally 4 75
(D M Simcock) *hld up: hdwy over 3f out: led over 2f out: sn clr: easily* 9/4[2]

643 2 11 **Flighty Frances (IRE)**[39] 5494 3-8-11 72 RichardHughes 6 53
(D R C Elsworth) *hld up: rdn over 3f out: hdwy u.p to go 2nd 1f out: nvr any ch w wnr* 11/8[1]

6040 3 1 3/4 **Half Sister (IRE)**[4] 6526 3-8-6 58 NickyMackay 3 45
(M E Rimmer) *chsd ldrs: rdn and ev ch over 2f out: wknd fnl f* 8/1

0005 4 3 **Penderyn**[20] 6093 3-8-1 38 JohnFahy[(5)] 2 39
(C Smith) *sn pushed along to chse ldr: rdn and ev ch over 2f out: wknd over 1f out* 33/1

6353 5 1 **Second Brook (IRE)**[3] 6574 3-8-11 50 (p) LukeMorris 1 42
(R Hollinshead) *led after 1f: rdn and hdd over 2f out: wknd over 1f out* 11/2[3]

6 hd **Broughtons Bandit** 3-8-11 0 AndreaAtzeni 5 41
(W J Musson) *hld up: hdwy over 3f out: rdn and wknd wl over 1f out* 16/1

5000 7 80 **Mujdy (IRE)**[83] 4027 3-8-11 40 (p) WilliamCarson 7 —
(B R Johnson) *led 1f: chsd ldrs: drvn along over 4f out: wknd over 2f out: t.o* 100/1

2m 14.34s (6.44) **Going Correction** +0.575s/f (Yiel) 7 Ran SP% **109.2**
Speed ratings (Par 99): **97,88,86,84,83 83,19**
Tote Swingers: 1&2 £1.60, 1&3 £2.90, 2&3 £2.60 CSF £5.13 TOTE £4.00: £1.20, £1.20; EX 5.90.There was no bid for the winner.
Owner Malcolm Caine **Bred** Darley **Trained** Newmarket, Suffolk

FOCUS
An uncompetitive claimer and a very easy winner.

6653 LADBROKES.COM SQUIRREL CONDITIONS STKS 1m 1f 218y
3:10 (3:10) (Class 3) 2-Y-O £5,235 (£1,567; £783) Stalls High

Form RPR

1 1 **Picture Editor**[26] 5878 2-8-13 91 TomQueally 2 97+
(H R A Cecil) *trckd ldr: led on bit over 4f out: c clr fr over 2f out: canter* 1/14[1]

50 2 30 **Arctic Myth (USA)**[18] 6149 2-8-11 0 DaneO'Neill 1 41
(B W Duke) *led: hdd over 4f out: rdn and wknd over 2f out: t.o* 11/1[2]

0 3 18 **Hurricane Guest**[1] 6618 2-8-11 0 SebSanders 3 9
(G G Margarson) *chsd ldrs: rdn over 4f out: wknd over 3f out: t.o* 40/1[3]

2m 16.28s (8.38) **Going Correction** +0.575s/f (Yiel) 3 Ran SP% **104.1**
Speed ratings (Par 99): **89,65,50**
CSF £1.26 TOTE £1.10; EX 1.40.
Owner K Abdulla **Bred** Juddmonte Farms Ltd **Trained** Newmarket, Suffolk

FOCUS
A bloodless success for the smart Picture Editor.

NOTEBOOK
Picture Editor ◆ went into many a notebook when running out a taking winner over 1m on debut at Doncaster last month, for which he was allotted an official mark of 91. That form made him impossible to oppose here, but the manner in which he went about his business was still very impressive and he clearly enjoys cut in the ground. Along with the hugely talented Frankel he rates another very promising juvenile for connections, but will no doubt stay better than his illustrious stablemate, and it's very hard to gauge at this stage just how good he may be. He has plenty of size and scope about him so ought to peak next year, and was available to back at around 20/1 for next season's Derby after this, although he is surprisingly not yet entered for that. Connections will probably look to test him in Pattern company before putting him away, but he would need to be supplemented for the Group 1 Racing Post Trophy next month, and it wouldn't be that surprising to see him head for the Zetland Stakes at Newmarket instead, although that is another conditions event. It should be remembered Henry Cecil won that with Twice Over three years ago, and wherever this son of Dansili goes next it will be eagerly anticipated. A trip to France for the Group 1 Criterium de Saint-Cloud could also be an option. (tchd 1-12 and 1-8 in a place)
Arctic Myth(USA) set out to make this a test, but was firmly put in his place by the winner as far as 4f out. He plugged on to finish a clear second-best and now has the option of nurseries. (op 14-1 tchd 9-1)
Hurricane Guest had only made his debut the previous day at Pontefract, when finishing well down the field. Unsurprisingly he was the first beat here, but bagged the best part £800 for finishing third, and this extra experience will be to his benefit. (op 20-1)

6654 LADBROKES.COM QUORN H'CAP 1m 3f 183y
3:40 (3:40) (Class 2) (0-100,97) 3-Y-O
£8,723 (£2,612; £1,306; £653; £326; £163) Stalls High

Form RPR

6004 1 **Cracking Lass (IRE)**[10] 6355 3-8-10 91 LeeTopliss[(5)] 6 100
(R A Fahey) *chsd ldrs: lost pl over 7f out: sn pushed along: hdwy over 3f out: sn rdn: styd on u.p to ld wl ins fnl f* 17/2

2043 2 1 **Averroes (IRE)**[38] 5511 3-8-9 90 JohnFahy[(5)] 3 97
(C G Cox) *chsd ldrs: led over 2f out: rdn and hdd wl ins fnl f* 5/2[1]

6551 3 5 **Music Of The Moor (IRE)**[21] 6050 3-8-7 83 oh1 AndrewMullen 7 82
(T P Tate) *hld up: hdwy 2f out: sn rdn: nt trble ldrs* 7/2[2]

1225 4 5 **Shimmering Moment (USA)**[20] 6074 3-8-12 88 TomQueally 8 79
(H R A Cecil) *led after 1f: hdd over 8f out: chsd ldr tl led again over 3f out: rdn and hdd over 2f out: wknd over 1f out* 4/1[3]

3114 5 31 **Baralaka**[25] 5922 3-8-11 87 SebSanders 1 29
(Sir Mark Prescott) *prom: led over 8f out: rdn and hdd over 3f out: wknd over 2f out: t.o* 9/2

6520 6 8 **Private Story (USA)**109 3145 3-9-7 97 RichardHughes 4 26
(R Hannon) *led 1f: chsd ldrs: rdn over 3f out: sn wknd: t.o* 10/1
2m 38.51s (4.61) **Going Correction** +0.575s/f (Yiel) 6 Ran SP% **108.6**
Speed ratings (Par 107): **107,106,103,99,79 73**
Tote Swingers: 1&2 £5.20, 1&3 £6.70, 2&3 £3.90 CSF £28.03 CT £78.80 TOTE £9.50: £8.40, £2.30; EX 37.80 Trifecta £169.40 Pool of £403.00 - 1.76 winning units..
Owner Mel Roberts and Ms Nicola Meese **Bred** Thomas Doherty **Trained** Musley Bank, N Yorks

FOCUS
A good 3-y-o handicap in which two came clear. The second sets the level.

NOTEBOOK
Cracking Lass(IRE) was the first in trouble coming out of the back straight, but she kept finding for her rider's urgings and got better the further she went. She was readily on top at the finish, her ability to handle soft ground proved a big help and it was her first success since winning her maiden last year. Indeed it was only her second outing in a handicap and she should have some more to offer over the trip, though she does have her quirks. (op 8-1 tchd 10-1)
Averroes(IRE), whose stable won this with Electrolyser in 2008, has yet to win over this trip but has no problem staying this far. He was given every chance and went down fighting, but the winner ultimately handled this deeper ground that bit better. Nicely clear of the remainder, he certainly deserves to get off the mark for the season, but his long-term future may well lie over hurdles. (op 15-8 tchd 11-4)
Music Of The Moor(IRE), another hurdling prospect, was 5lb higher than when winning over this trip on deep ground at Haydock last month. He came from behind that day, but his rider judged the pace wrong this time and he was given too much to do. There could still be another race for him before he goes jumping. (op 9-2 tchd 11-4)
Shimmering Moment(USA) looked a non-stayer over this trip on less-testing ground at Beverley on her previous outing, so it was surprising to see her ridden prominently here. She was held from the 2f marker and a drop back in trip looks on the cards. (op 5-1)
Baralaka was dropping back down in trip on this return to turf, and was another that seemed to be found out by the ground. (tchd 4-1)
Private Story(USA) was having his first outing since finishing seventh in the Queen's Vase at Royal Ascot. He had yet to race on such ground and it looked against him, but the run should bring him on a good bit. (op 11-1 tchd 12-1)

6655 LADBROKES.COM DORMOUSE MAIDEN STKS 7f 9y
4:10 (4:13) (Class 5) 3-Y-O £2,266 (£674; £337; £168) Stalls Low

Form RPR
3-2 1 **Hajjaan (USA)**28 5839 3-9-3 0 RichardHills 1 83+
(J L Dunlop) *mde virtually all: rdn over 1f out: jst hld on* 5/4[1]
03 2 shd **Divine Call**117 2903 3-9-3 0 RichardHughes 4 83+
(W J Haggas) *trckd wnr: rdn and ev ch fr over 1f out: r.o* 11/4[2]
3 3 1/2 **Asterisk** 3-8-12 0 TomMcLaughlin 13 69
(John Berry) *chsd ldrs: rdn over 2f out: edgd lft over 1f out: styd on same pce* 28/1
4 6 **Handsome King** 3-9-3 0 JimmyQuinn 12 58
(J R Jenkins) *hld up: rdn over 1f out: n.d* 40/1
2002 5 1 1/2 **Tombellini (IRE)**6 6463 3-9-3 57 PaulQuinn 8 54
(D Nicholls) *prom: rdn over 2f out: wknd over 1f out* 9/1
00 6 shd **Zarius**34 5658 3-9-3 0 GeorgeBaker 11 54
(C F Wall) *chsd ldrs: rdn over 2f out: wknd over 1f* 80/1
4 7 8 **Transeggselence**39 5493 3-8-12 0 SteveDrowne 5 28
(P Leech) *trckd ldrs: racd keenly: rdn over 2f out: wknd over 1f out* 4/1[3]
6006 8 14 **Little Buddy**8 6420 3-8-12 30 TobyAtkinson(5) 6 —
(R J Price) *s.s: hld up: plld hrd: rdn 1/2-way: sn wknd: t.o* 150/1
0 9 18 **Prince Blue**28 5839 3-9-3 0 SebSanders 2 —
(G G Margarson) *hld up: hung rt and wknd wl over 2f out: t.o* 40/1
1m 29.27s (3.07) **Going Correction** +0.35s/f (Good) 9 Ran SP% **111.3**
Speed ratings (Par 101): **96,95,91,85,83 83,74,58,37**
Tote Swingers: 1&2 £1.60, 1&3 £6.60, 2&3 £8.50 CSF £4.42 TOTE £2.70: £1.30, £1.10, £3.00; EX 5.30 Trifecta £27.10 Pool of £877.61 - 23.88 winning units..
Owner Hamdan Al Maktoum **Bred** Philip Robertson & Brenda Robertson **Trained** Arundel, W Sussex

FOCUS
The two market leaders dominated this ordinary maiden.

6656 LADBROKESCASINO.COM FILLIES' H'CAP 5f 218y
4:40 (4:41) (Class 5) (0-70,70) 3-Y-O+ £2,266 (£674; £337; £168) Stalls Low

Form RPR
4420 1 **Bathwick Xaara**26 5898 3-8-6 60 AdamBeschizza(5) 12 71
(J G Portman) *a.p: led over 2f out: rdn out* 16/1
3311 2 2 1/2 **Dreamacha**11 6329 3-9-2 65 WilliamCarson 9 68
(S C Williams) *chsd ldrs: rdn and ev ch over 1f out: styd on same pce ins fnl f* 11/2[2]
1305 3 1/2 **Gracie's Games**23 5990 4-8-2 55 oh2 (v) TobyAtkinson(5) 8 56
(R J Price) *hld up: hdwy over 2f out: rdn over 1f out: styd on* 22/1
5135 4 nk **Avonvalley**37 5557 3-9-0 63 TedDurcan 4 63
(George Baker) *hld up: hdwy over 2f out: rdn over 1f out: styd on* 10/1
6000 5 1/2 **Adventure Story**6 6466 3-9-5 68 PatDobbs 10 67
(R Hannon) *prom: rdn over 2f out: styd on* 14/1
6044 6 1/2 **Spinning Bailiwick**15 6261 4-9-7 69 GeorgeBaker 13 66
(G L Moore) *s.i.s: hld up: hdwy u.p over 1f out: nt rch ldrs* 15/2
4335 7 6 **Caramelita**26 5890 3-9-4 67 RichardHughes 3 45
(J R Jenkins) *hld up in tch: rdn over 1f out: wknd fnl f* 7/1[3]
5113 8 nk **Foxtrot Alpha (IRE)**22 6024 4-9-0 62 LukeMorris 11 39
(P Winkworth) *led: rdn and hdd over 2f out: wknd fnl f* 4/1[1]
3605 9 4 1/2 **Sairaam (IRE)**15 6261 4-8-10 63 (b) JohnFahy(5) 15 26
(C Smith) *s.i.s: hld up: sn prom: rdn and wknd over 1f out* 17/2
010P 10 shd **Polar Annie**24 5964 5-9-5 67 TomMcLaughlin 6 29
(M S Saunders) *chsd ldrs: rdn over 2f out: wknd over 1f out* 12/1
2606 11 3/4 **Midget**37 5548 3-8-1 57 NeilFarley(7) 14 17
(D Carroll) *mid-div: wknd over 2f out* 18/1
0006 12 5 **Gibraltar Lass (USA)**57 4908 3-8-6 55 oh10 (v) JimmyQuinn 7 —
(H J Collingridge) *dwlt: outpcd* 50/1
00 13 1 1/2 **Transcentral**178 1236 4-8-7 55 oh10 (b) NeilChalmers 1 —
(T Wall) *chsd ldrs: rdn and wknd over 2f out* 100/1
0-04 14 2 **Polemica (IRE)**168 1457 4-8-7 55 AndreaAtzeni 5 —
(F Sheridan) *mid-div: rdn 1/2-way: wknd over 2f out* 28/1
1400 15 3 1/4 **Fayre Bella**13 6280 3-9-7 70 JimCrowley 2 —
(J Gallagher) *chsd ldrs: rdn over 2f out: wknd and eased over 1f out* 28/1
1m 14.99s (1.99) **Going Correction** +0.35s/f (Good)
WFA 3 from 4yo+ 1lb 15 Ran SP% **119.0**
Speed ratings (Par 100): **100,96,96,95,94 94,86,85,79,79 78,72,70,67,63**
Tote Swingers: 1&2 £21.20, 1&3 £49.30, 2&3 £23.20 CSF £95.60 CT £1965.76 TOTE £23.50: £8.10, £2.30, £8.30; EX 148.40 TRIFECTA Not won..
Owner Mrs S Clifford **Bred** Charlock Farm Stud **Trained** Compton, Berks

FOCUS
A wide open fillies' handicap.
Caramelita Official explanation: jockey said filly had no more to give

6657 LADBROKES.COM APPRENTICE H'CAP 7f 9y
5:10 (5:10) (Class 5) (0-70,68) 3-Y-O+ £2,266 (£674; £337; £168) Stalls Low

Form RPR
0202 1 **Katmai River (IRE)**15 6255 3-8-5 54 oh2 AmyBaker 10 63
(M D I Usher) *mid-div: hdwy 1/2-way: led over 1f out: rdn and hung lft ins fnl f: styd on* 10/1
0060 2 1 1/2 **Lordship (IRE)**1 6629 6-8-2 54 oh1 JakePayne(5) 8 59
(A W Carroll) *chsd ldrs: rdn over 1f out: styd on to go 2nd wl ins fnl f* 10/3[2]
6621 3 nk **Mr Udagawa**25 5906 4-8-11 63 (p) MatthewCosham(5) 2 67
(B J Llewellyn) *chsd ldr tl led 1/2-way: rdn and hdd over 1f out: styd on same pce ins fnl f* 11/4[1]
0464 4 4 1/2 **Thaliwarru**15 6255 3-9-1 64 (p) AdamBeschizza 7 57
(J R Gask) *sn pushed along in rr: hdwy 1/2-way: rdn over 1f out: wknd ins fnl f* 9/1
3440 5 2 **Rosiliant (IRE)**22 6025 3-8-5 54 oh2 (b) JohnFahy 5 41
(C G Cox) *chsd ldrs: rdn over 2f out: wknd over 1f out* 5/1[3]
0 6 1 1/2 **Sapperton**136 2329 3-8-13 62 TobyAtkinson 9 45
(George Baker) *led to 1/2-way: wknd 2f out* 16/1
3000 7 4 **Perfect Secret**15 6261 4-8-10 57 DeclanCannon 6 30
(A M Balding) *hld up: rdn over 2f out: sn wknd* 11/2
064 8 11 **Young Simon**50 5162 3-8-12 61 (b[1]) RossAtkinson 3 5
(G G Margarson) *hld up: rdn and wknd over 2f out* 14/1
1m 29.92s (3.72) **Going Correction** +0.35s/f (Good)
WFA 3 from 4yo+ 2lb 8 Ran SP% **113.4**
Speed ratings (Par 103): **92,90,89,84,82 80,76,63**
Tote Swingers: 1&2 £6.80, 1&3 £2.50, 2&3 £2.70 CSF £42.67 CT £118.57 TOTE £11.70: £2.80, £3.60, £1.10; EX 68.90 Trifecta £194.90 Pool of £727.10 - 2.76 winning units. Place 6: £26.62 Place 5: £10.93..
Owner M D I Usher **Bred** Mrs S M Roy **Trained** Upper Lambourn, Berks

FOCUS
A typically moderate handicap for apprentice riders. It was run at a fair pace and the majority raced more towards the middle and far side.
Perfect Secret Official explanation: jockey said filly never travelled
Young Simon Official explanation: trainer said gelding was unsuited by the heavy (soft in places) ground
T/Plt: £17.50 to a £1 stake. Pool of £57,693 - 2,394.49 winning tickets. T/Qpdt: £7.10 to a £1 stake. Pool of £3,441 - 355.33 winning tickets. CR

5643 SOUTHWELL (L-H)
Tuesday, October 5

OFFICIAL GOING: Standard
Wind: Light across Weather: Fine and dry

6658 E B F WATCH LIVE SPORT AT LADBROKES.COM MAIDEN FILLIES' STKS 6f (F)
2:20 (2:23) (Class 4) 2-Y-O £4,435 (£1,309; £655) Stalls Low

Form RPR
2 1 **Abtasaamah (USA)**59 4844 2-9-0 0 FrankieDettori 4 85+
(Saeed Bin Suroor) *cl up on outer: smooth hdwy to ld over 2f out: sn pushed clr: v easily* 2/7[1]
2 9 **Luckbealadytonight (IRE)** 2-9-0 0 JoeFanning 1 54+
(M Johnston) *dwlt: sn cl up on inner: led 4f out: rdn and hdd over 2f out: sn drvn and kpt on same pce* 4/1[2]
03 3 hd **Arabella Fenella**10 6369 2-9-0 0 HayleyTurner 7 53
(R M H Cowell) *chsd ldrs: hdwy over 2f out: rdn wl over 1f out: kpt on same pce* 6/1[3]
0030 4 1 3/4 **Ever Roses**22 6034 2-9-0 54 TonyCulhane 9 48
(P T Midgley) *sn outpcd and wl bhd: rdn along 1/2-way: styd on on inner fnl 2f: nrst fin* 25/1
00 5 6 **Tsarina Louise**31 5763 2-9-0 0 RoystonFfrench 8 30
(J G Given) *sn rdn along and a in rr* 50/1
650 6 nk **Be A Good Lady**19 6111 2-9-0 54 MickyFenton 6 29
(P T Midgley) *s.i.s and bhd: sme hdwy 1/2-way: rdn 2f out: sn hung lft and nvr a factor* 20/1
006 7 12 **Phair Winter**121 2785 2-9-0 45 GrahamGibbons 3 —
(A D Brown) *led 2f: cl up tl rdn along 1/2-way: sn wknd* 33/1
1m 16.57s (0.07) **Going Correction** -0.125s/f (Stan) 7 Ran SP% **125.6**
Speed ratings (Par 94): **94,82,81,79,71 71,55**
Tote Swingers: 1&2 £1.10, 1&3 £1.60, 2&3 £2.10 CSF £2.28 TOTE £1.20: £1.02, £2.90; EX 2.40.
Owner Godolphin **Bred** Stonerside Stable **Trained** Newmarket, Suffolk

FOCUS
A seriously uncompetitive fillies' maiden.

NOTEBOOK
Abtasaamah(USA) ◆ won with any amount in hand. She had been off since finishing third in a decent July course maiden over 7f in August, but proved in no uncertain terms that she's gone the right way since. Her half-brother Midshipman won the Breeders' Cup Juvenile on synthetics, and this one could be a filly for the UAE Guineas and Oaks. (tchd 1-3 and 1-4 in places)
Luckbealadytonight(IRE), a 100,000euros purchase, out of a useful sprinter (5f Listed winner at two), achieved little on debut, being flattered to get so close to the winner, but she should improve.
Arabella Fenella might find her level in low-grade nurseries.
Ever Roses, rated only 54, plugged on after being badly outpaced and puts the form in context. (tchd 20-1)

6659 GOT THE FEELING! GET TO LADBROKES H'CAP 1m (F)
2:50 (2:52) (Class 2) (0-100,100) 3-Y-O £9,390 (£2,794; £1,396; £697) Stalls Low

Form RPR
4113 1 **Kalk Bay (IRE)**23 6002 3-8-7 86 oh3 WilliamBuick 3 94
(W J Haggas) *dwlt: hld up: swtchd ins and hdwy 2f out: rdn to ld over 1f out: drvn and edgd rt ins fnl f: kpt on* 10/3[2]
11- 2 nk **Sahara Kingdom (IRE)**334 7251 3-9-6 99 FrankieDettori 4 107
(Saeed Bin Suroor) *dwlt: sn trcking ldr: hdwy to ld over 2f out and sn rdn: hdd over 1f out: drvn and rallied to have ev ch ins fnl f: sn edgd lft and no ex towards fin* 11/8[1]
2010 3 2 1/2 **Secretive**12 6312 3-8-11 90 (b) JoeFanning 2 92
(M Johnston) *cl up on inner: effrt to chal over 2f out: sn rdn and hung rt: drvn and one pce ent fnl f* 10/3[2]

1106 4 3 1/4 **Aattash (IRE)**^{10} [6355] 3-9-7 **100** SamHitchcott 5 95
(M R Channon) *t.k.h: led: rdn along 3f out: hdd over 2f out: sn drvn and wknd wl over 1f out* **9/2**^{3}

1m 40.86s (-2.84) **Going Correction** -0.125s/f (Stan) 4 Ran SP% **106.4**
Speed ratings (Par 107): **109,108,106,102**
CSF £8.13 TOTE £5.40; EX 11.70.
Owner Bernard Kantor **Bred** Wentworth Racing **Trained** Newmarket, Suffolk

FOCUS
Only four runners, but this is strong 3-y-o form.

NOTEBOOK
Kalk Bay(IRE) ◆ flopped when dropped back to 7f last time (11-10, only third), but he produced a very useful performance from 3lb out of the handicap to upset the smart favourite on this step back in trip, clearly taking well to Fibresand. It's early days, but he compares favourably with stablemate Penitent who, like this one, didn't make his debut until a 3-y-o and finished runner-up over this C&D off a mark of 93 on his fifth start last October, before landing the Lincoln and a Group 3. (op 7-2 tchd 9-2)
Sahara Kingdom(IRE) ◆ looked potentially Group class when winning twice over 7f on the Lingfield Polytrack last year, but had been off since November, presumably having had his problems. This was a smart performance on his Fibresand debut off an official mark of 99, and he could belatedly make an impression at the Dubai Carnival. (op 11-10 tchd Evens and 6-4 in a place)
Secretive, a maiden winner on debut on his only previous Fibresand start, ran his race but simply bumped into two pretty decent, progressive types. (op 4-1 tchd 3-1)
Aattash(IRE) was a bit free in front and failed to prove himself on Fibresand. He doesn't look particularly well handicapped. (tchd 5-1)

6660 PLAY POKER AT LADBROKES.COM H'CAP (DIV I) 1m 4f (F)
3:20 (3:22) (Class 6) (0-55,55) 3-Y-O+ **£1,364** (£403; £201) **Stalls** Low

Form RPR
0510 1 **Short Supply (USA)**^{48} [5216] 4-9-0 **51** GrahamGibbons 2 57
(T D Walford) *led: rdn along and hdd over 2f out: drvn and rallied to chal over 1f out: led jst ins fnl f: hld on gamely* **10/1**
065 2 *hd* **Court Wing (IRE)**^{26} [5873] 4-8-6 **46** oh1 AndrewHeffernan$^{(3)}$ 6 52
(R J Price) *a.p: effrt to chal over 2f out: rdn over 1f out: drvn and ev ch ins fnl f tl no ex nr fin* **9/1**
0-04 3 1 1/4 **Whaston (IRE)**^{22} [6032] 5-8-8 **50** ow1 DaleSwift$^{(5)}$ 10 54
(Miss P Robson) *a cl up: rdn to ld over 2f out: drvn over 1f out: hdd jst ins fnl f: wknd last 100yds* **13/2**^{3}
-006 4 3/4 **St Savarin (FR)**^{71} [4433] 9-9-2 **53** StevieDonohoe 1 56
(M S Tuck) *chsd ldrs on inner: rdn along and sltly outpcd over 2f out: kpt on u.p fnl f* **7/1**
3200 5 *shd* **Davana**^{37} [5564] 4-8-11 **48** HayleyTurner 12 51
(W J H Ratcliffe) *trckd ldrs: rdn along 4f out: swtchd rt and drvn wl over 1f out: kpt on ins fnl f: nrst fin* **12/1**
0004 6 2 1/4 **Pound Lane (IRE)**^{63} [4683] 4-8-9 **46** oh1 SamHitchcott 11 45
(Miss T Spearing) *t.k.h: hld up: swtchd wd and hdwy over 2f out: sn rdn and kpt on: nrst fin* **5/1**^{2}
4105 7 4 1/2 **Black Falcon (IRE)**^{245} [377] 10-9-1 **52** RobertWinston 3 44
(John A Harris) *trckd ldrs: effrt over 3f out: rdn over 2f out and grad wknd* **33/1**
0-04 8 1/2 **Moonlight Blaze**^{67} [2792] 3-8-6 **50** RoystonFfrench 5 41
(C W Fairhurst) *hld up in tch: rdn along 4f out: sn one pce* **14/1**
1431 9 2 3/4 **Noah Jameel**^{22} [6021] 8-9-4 **55** AdamKirby 7 42
(A G Newcombe) *hld up in rr: pushed along 1/2-way: rdn 4f out and nvr a factor* **7/2**^{1}
0000 10 20 **Melinoise**^{50} [5164] 3-7-9 **46** oh1 NoelGarbutt$^{(7)}$ 8 1
(Rae Guest) *dwlt: sn pushed along and in tch on inner: rdn over 5f out and sn wknd* **66/1**

2m 40.09s (-0.91) **Going Correction** -0.125s/f (Stan)
WFA 3 from 4yo+ 7lb 10 Ran SP% **102.6**
Speed ratings (Par 101): **98,97,97,96,96 94,91,91,89,76**
CSF £76.72 CT £460.90 TOTE £8.80: £2.70, £2.20, £3.90; EX 99.30.
Owner Mrs G B Walford **Bred** Juddmonte Farms Inc **Trained** Sheriff Hutton, N Yorks

FOCUS
Moderate form. The pace was steady and it paid to race prominently.
Pound Lane(IRE) Official explanation: jockey said gelding hung right
Black Falcon(IRE) Official explanation: jockey said gelding hung left
Noah Jameel Official explanation: trainer had no explanation for the poor form shown
Melinoise Official explanation: jockey said filly never travelled

6661 BET IN-PLAY AT LADBROKES.COM MAIDEN STKS 1m 4f (F)
3:50 (3:53) (Class 5) 3-Y-O+ **£2,388** (£705; £352) **Stalls** Low

Form RPR
053 1 **Honest Strike (USA)**^{12} [6313] 3-9-3 77 IanMongan 6 88+
(H R A Cecil) *trckd ldrs: hdwy 4f out: led wl over 2f out: sn rdn and wandered over 1f out: drvn ins fnl f and kpt on* **9/4**^{2}
04 2 3/4 **Gakalina (IRE)**^{15} [6250] 3-8-12 0 DarryllHolland 9 82
(J Noseda) *hld up: hdwy on outer 1/2-way: pushed along to chse ldrs 4f out: hdwy 3f out: swtchd ins and drvn over 1f out: styd on to chal ins fnl f: no ex last 75yds* **13/2**
4422 3 7 **Bombadero (IRE)**^{10} [6359] 3-9-3 78 (b) ShaneKelly 1 76
(J L Dunlop) *led: rdn along 3f out: hdd wl over 2f out: drvn wl over 1f out and grad wknd* **5/2**^{3}
4 21 **Mashdood (USA)**^{95} 4-9-10 0 ChrisCatlin 4 42
(P W Hiatt) *chsd ldr: rdn along 5f out: sn outpcd* **33/1**
062 5 1/2 **Herostatus**^{12} [6313] 3-9-3 77 JoeFanning 3 41
(M Johnston) *dwlt: sn chsng ldng pair: rdn along over 3f out: sn wknd* **2/1**^{1}
4 6 17 **All We Know**^{168} [1447] 3-9-3 0 (p) HayleyTurner 2 14
(T T Clement) *s.i.s and sn rdn along: a bhd* **50/1**
34-0 7 25 **Spanish Cross (IRE)**^{204} [576] 5-9-5 47 KirstyMilczarek 7 —
(G Prodromou) *a in rr: bhd fnl 4f* **100/1**
8 *nse* **Surprise Us** 3-9-3 0 RoystonFfrench 5 —
(Mrs A Duffield) *in tch: rdn along 1/2-way: sn outpcd and bhd* **66/1**
9 30 **Tilly Thorpe** 5-8-13 0 ow1 AndrewYoxall$^{(7)}$ 10 —
(O Brennan) *s.i.s: a bhd: wl t.o fnl 4f* **100/1**

2m 37.12s (-3.88) **Going Correction** -0.125s/f (Stan)
WFA 3 from 4yo+ 7lb 9 Ran SP% **114.4**
Speed ratings (Par 103): **107,106,101,87,87 76,59,59,39**
Tote Swingers: 1&2 £3.20, 1&3 £2.40, 2&3 £3.10 CSF £16.51 TOTE £3.30: £1.40, £1.60, £1.40; EX 14.20.
Owner K Abdulla **Bred** Juddmonte Farms Inc **Trained** Newmarket, Suffolk

FOCUS
An uncompetitive maiden, though the time was much quicker than both divisions of the Class 6 handicap.
Herostatus Official explanation: trainer had no explanation for the poor form shown

6662 PLAY POKER AT LADBROKES.COM H'CAP (DIV II) 1m 4f (F)
4:20 (4:20) (Class 6) (0-55,55) 3-Y-O+ **£1,364** (£403; £201) **Stalls** Low

Form RPR
3-60 1 **Mexican Jay (USA)**^{19} [6115] 4-9-4 **55** RoystonFfrench 10 67
(B Smart) *trckd ldr: cl up 4f out: rdn 2f out: led appr fnl f: drvn out* **33/1**
6002 2 1 1/4 **Mister Frosty (IRE)**^{20} [6094] 4-9-1 **52** KirstyMilczarek 7 62
(G Prodromou) *led: rdn along over 2f out: drvn and hdd appr fnl f: kpt on same pce* **7/2**^{1}
3400 3 7 **Dispol Diva**^{64} [4656] 4-8-11 **48** (v) JoeFanning 5 47
(P T Midgley) *chsd ldrs on inner: effrt over 3f out: rdn over 2f out: sn drvn and kpt on same pce* **20/1**
4030 4 *nk* **Barbirolli**^{22} [6022] 8-8-4 **48** oh1 ow2 LauraPike$^{(7)}$ 6 46
(W B Stone) *hld up in rr: stdy hdwy 4f out: chsd ldrs 3f out: rdn over 2f out: sn one pce* **14/1**
0500 5 9 **Swords**^{19} [6121] 8-8-10 **47** LiamKeniry 8 31
(R E Peacock) *dwlt and towards rr: hdwy 1/2-way: rdn along 4f out: nvr nr ldrs* **7/1**^{2}
0604 6 6 **Petsas Pleasure**^{27} [5864] 4-9-0 **51** (p) ChrisCatlin 1 25
(Ollie Pears) *stdd and dropped last after s: sn swtchd wd and hdwy on outer to chse ldrs 1/2-way: cl up 4f out: rdn along over 3f out: sn wknd* **9/1**
0650 7 2 1/2 **Lis Pendens**^{38} [5522] 3-8-4 **48** HayleyTurner 3 18
(W R Muir) *chsd ldrs on inner: rdn along 1/2-way: sn wknd* **7/1**^{2}
4430 8 3 1/4 **Iguacu**^{110} [3128] 6-9-0 **51** TonyCulhane 11 16
(George Baker) *towards rr: sme hdwy on outer 1/2-way: rdn along over 4f out and sn wknd* **8/1**^{3}
0005 9 2 3/4 **Sri Kuantan (IRE)**^{22} [6033] 6-8-6 **46** oh1 (t) KierenFox$^{(3)}$ 4 7
(R C Guest) *chsd ldrs: rdn along 1/2-way: lost pl over 4f out and sn in rr* **10/1**
00 10 3/4 **Feuergott (GER)**^{6} [6454] 4-8-9 **46** oh1 ShaneKelly 2 6
(Ian Williams) *midfield: rdn along over 4f out: sn wknd* **7/2**^{1}

2m 39.77s (-1.23) **Going Correction** -0.125s/f (Stan)
WFA 3 from 4yo+ 7lb 10 Ran SP% **114.0**
Speed ratings (Par 101): **99,98,93,93,87 83,81,79,77,77**
Tote Swingers: 1&2 £21.40, 1&3 £14.60, 2&3 £8.50 CSF £142.92 CT £2414.54 TOTE £39.10: £13.20, £1.10, £8.30; EX 127.10.
Owner A Turton, P Langford & S Brown **Bred** Barry Weisbord & Bobby Flay **Trained** Hambleton, N Yorks

FOCUS
The time was 0.38 seconds quicker than the first division, but 2.65 seconds slower than the maiden won by the 77-rated Honest Strike. Again, it paid to race prominently.
Mexican Jay(USA) Official explanation: trainer said, regarding apparent improvement in form, that the filly was suited by the step up in trip and the first-time run on Fibresand.
Petsas Pleasure Official explanation: trainer said gelding was unsuited by the Fibresand surface
Feuergott(GER) Official explanation: jockey said colt never travelled

6663 DAVE MORGAN MEMORIAL CONDITIONS STKS 5f (F)
4:50 (4:50) (Class 2) 3-Y-O+ **£9,146** (£2,737; £1,368; £684; £340) **Stalls** High

Form RPR
5342 1 **Captain Dunne (IRE)**^{14} [6265] 5-9-0 104 RobertWinston 4 107
(T D Easterby) *cl up: led over 1f out: rdn ins fnl f and kpt on wl* **11/8**^{1}
3000 2 3/4 **Noble Storm (USA)**^{10} [6364] 4-9-0 93 GrahamGibbons 6 104
(E S McMahon) *led: rdn along 2f out: hdd 1f out: drvn and rallied ins fnl f: no ex last 100yds* **6/1**^{3}
1002 3 2 3/4 **Nickel Silver**^{32} [5734] 5-9-0 93 (v) RoystonFfrench 3 94
(B Smart) *cl up: effrt 2f out and ev ch tl rdn and one pce ent fnl f* **11/2**^{2}
5010 4 1/2 **Masta Plasta (IRE)**^{38} [5512] 7-9-5 101 AdrianNicholls 5 97
(D Nicholls) *cl up: rdn along 1/2-way: drvn wl over 1f out and kpt on same pce* **15/2**
203- 5 2 3/4 **Waffle (IRE)**^{346} [7015] 4-9-0 101 DarryllHolland 2 82+
(J Noseda) *sn rdn along and outpcd in rr tl sme late hdwy* **13/2**
4150 6 2 **Star Rover (IRE)**^{11} [6319] 3-9-5 94 PatCosgrave 1 80
(P D Evans) *a towards rr* **14/1**
0645 7 *nk* **Le Toreador**^{18} [6140] 5-9-0 89 (tp) ChrisCatlin 7 74
(K A Ryan) *prom: rdn along 2f out: sn edgd lft and wknd* **33/1**
000 8 1 3/4 **Luscivious**^{21} [6064] 6-9-0 93 (b) IanMongan 10 68
(J A Glover) *chsd ldrs: rdn 2f out: sn wknd* **14/1**

58.03 secs (-1.67) **Going Correction** -0.10s/f (Stan) 8 Ran SP% **113.1**
Speed ratings (Par 109): **109,107,103,102,98 95,94,91**
Tote Swingers: 1&2 £3.40, 1&3 £3.50, 2&3 £7.50 CSF £9.71 TOTE £2.70: £1.40, £1.60, £1.80; EX 11.20.
Owner Middleham Park Racing Xv **Bred** Ballybrennan Stud Ltd **Trained** Great Habton, N Yorks

FOCUS
A good conditions race.

NOTEBOOK
Captain Dunne(IRE), a comfortable winner of a C&D handicap off 83 on his only previous start on Fibresand back in 2008, confirmed himself capable of smart form on the surface with a win more decisive than the official margin suggests. Having fairly tanked along for much of the way, he found plenty for pressure and never looked in trouble. Also up to running to a similar level on turf, he's basically just a very good 5f horse. (tchd 5-4 and 6-4)
Noble Storm(USA), like the winner, travelled well and stayed on for pressure, pulling clear of the remainder. Considering he had 11lb to find with Captain Dunne on the figures, this was a return to something like his best form, and he clearly took well to Fibresand at the first attempt. (op 8-1)
Nickel Silver, like the runner-up, had quite a bit on at the weights but posted a respectable effort. He should be in for another decent AW season. (op 8-1)
Masta Plasta(IRE) ran okay, but not up to his best form on his Fibresand debut. (op 6-1 tchd 11-2)
Waffle(IRE) ran with real credit on his Fibresand debut off the back of a 346-day absence. He looks to retain plenty of his ability and should come on for the run. (op 6-1)

6664 ATTHERACES.COM/BREEDERSCUP H'CAP 7f (F)
5:20 (5:21) (Class 5) (0-75,74) 3-Y-O+ **£2,388** (£705; £352) **Stalls** Low

Form RPR
3562 1 **Elusive Warrior (USA)**^{35} [5647] 7-8-6 **65** (p) NoraLooby$^{(7)}$ 5 76
(A J McCabe) *a.p: rdn 2f out: led over 1f out: kpt on wl fnl f* **6/1**^{3}
2210 2 3/4 **El Dececy (USA)**^{32} [5732] 6-9-5 **71** (p) RobertWinston 11 80
(J Balding) *a.p: rdn along and outpcd 3f out: styd on u.p to chal over 1f out: sn drvn and ev ch tl edgd rt and no ex last 100yds* **16/1**
6000 3 1 3/4 **Trailblazing**^{23} [5994] 3-9-2 **70** (b^{1}) JoeFanning 8 73+
(M Johnston) *dwlt and bhd: rdn and hdwy 2f out: swtchd lft over 1f out: kpt on ins fnl f: nrst fin* **14/1**
0506 4 1 1/4 **Master Leon**^{6} [6461] 3-8-13 **74** (v) AdamCarter$^{(7)}$ 12 74
(B Smart) *sn led: rdn 2f out: drvn and hdd over 1f out: wknd fnl f* **16/1**

2232 **5** 1 ¼ **Hellbender (IRE)**[24] 5964 4-9-6 **72**....................(t) LiamKeniry 6 70
(S Kirk) *in tch: hdwy on inner to chse ldrs 3f out: sn rdn: drvn wl over 1f out and no imp* **3/1**[1]

5000 **6** 1 ¼ **Electioneer (USA)**[20] 6073 3-9-4 **72**....................(e) GrahamGibbons 1 65
(M W Easterby) *dwlt and bhd tl styd on fnl 2f* **12/1**

0330 **7** 3 ¾ **Law Of Attraction (IRE)**[4] 6541 3-9-2 **70**....................(p) DarryllHolland 10 53
(J R Gask) *s.i.s: sme hdwy into midfield 1/2-way: n.d* **17/2**

-145 **8** 2 ¾ **Realt Na Mara (IRE)**[14] 6274 7-9-6 **72**.................... HayleyTurner 3 49
(H Morrison) *nvr nr ldrs* **10/3**[2]

4040 **9** 3 **Scruffy Skip (IRE)**[20] 6098 5-8-11 **66**....................(p) KierenFox(3) 4 34
(Mrs C A Dunnett) *sn rdn along and a towards rr* **7/1**

0430 **10** 6 **Toby Tyler**[15] 6261 4-9-0 **66**.................... AdamKirby 2 18
(P T Midgley) *dwlt and sn rdn along on inner to chse ldrs: drvn 3f out and sn wknd* **16/1**

0000 **11** 16 **Ponting (IRE)**[134] 2378 4-8-13 **65**.................... TonyCulhane 7 —
(P T Midgley) *chsd ldrs on outer: rdn along 3f out: sn wknd* **28/1**

-060 **12** 13 **Devil You Know (IRE)**[17] 6208 4-8-9 **68**............(t) DavidSimmonson(7) 9 —
(M W Easterby) *chsd ldrs: rdn along 1/2-way and sn wknd* **33/1**

1m 29.25s (-1.05) **Going Correction** -0.125s/f (Stan)
WFA 3 from 4yo+ 2lb **12** Ran SP% **123.8**
Speed ratings (Par 103): **101,100,98,96,95 93,89,86,83,76 57,43**
Tote Swingers: 1&2 £10.80, 1&3 £19.30, 2&3 £15.80 CSF £102.60 CT £1332.19 TOTE £4.60: £1.10, £5.80, £6.60 Place 6: £91.71 Place 5: £84.05..
Owner Mrs M J McCabe **Bred** Steve Peskoff **Trained** Averham Park, Notts

FOCUS
It proved difficult to come from off the pace for most of the afternoon, and this race provided another example.
Toby Tyler Official explanation: jockey said gelding had no more to give
T/Plt: £134.40 to a £1 stake. Pool of £58,401 - 317.01 winning tickets. T/Qpdt: £47.80 to a £1 stake. Pool of £5,258 - 81.30 winning tickets. JR

6496 KEMPTON (A.W) (R-H)
Wednesday, October 6

OFFICIAL GOING: Standard
Wind: Almost Nil Weather: Fine

6665 KIA SPORTAGE H'CAP 5f (P)
5:30 (5:30) (Class 7) (0-50,53) 3-Y-O+ **£1,364** (£403; £201) **Stalls** High

Form RPR

6244 **1** **Duke Of Rainford**[10] 6392 3-9-0 **50**.................... TonyCulhane 7 56
(M Herrington) *trckd ldr after 1f: gng easily 2f out: led over 1f out: drvn over a l ahd ins fnl f: jst hld on* **11/2**[3]

2235 **2** nse **Rebecca Romero**[20] 6133 3-9-0 **50**....................(v) RichardHughes 12 55
(D J Coakley) *settled in 5th: effrt over 1f out: wnt 2nd last 100yds: r.o wl nr fin: jst failed* **10/3**[1]

5005 **3** 1 ½ **Bluebok**[124] 2721 9-8-13 **49**....................(bt) LiamKeniry 8 49
(J M Bradley) *led to over 1f out: steadily outpcd ins fnl f* **12/1**

00 **4** nk **Alana Banana (IRE)**[12] 6329 3-9-0 **50**.................... SimonWhitworth 11 49
(J Akehurst) *hld up last: shkn up over 1f out: styd on and nrly snatched 3rd: no ch* **9/1**

0-60 **5** ½ **Cane Cat (IRE)**[27] 5898 3-8-13 **49**....................(t) NeilCallan 10 46
(A W Carroll) *chsd ldr 1f: cl up tl fdd ins fnl f* **8/1**

5550 **6** ¾ **Lithaam (IRE)**[18] 6206 6-8-13 **49**....................(p) DaneO'Neill 9 43
(J M Bradley) *a in last trio: rdn and no prog over 1f out* **5/1**[2]

0005 **7** 2 **Trelicia**[25] 5957 3-8-13 **49**.................... SteveDrowne 4 36
(S C Williams) *ct between two rivals gng berserk in stalls: racd wd: in tch to 2f out: sn btn* **16/1**

60.26 secs (-0.24) **Going Correction** -0.10s/f (Stan) **7** Ran SP% **89.8**
Speed ratings (Par 97): **97,96,94,94,93 92,88**
toteswingers:1&2 £3.70, 2&3 £3.60, 1&3 £6.30 CSF £14.70 CT £90.38 TOTE £5.10: £3.00, £1.10; EX 13.80.
Owner P Ringer **Bred** Worksop Manor Stud **Trained** Cold Kirby, N Yorks

FOCUS
There were several infrequent winners in a low-grade handicap in which all the runners were rated either 50 or 49. The field saw three early defections and a further two close to the off. The gallop was just an ordinary one for a sprint and, as usual over this C&D, the action unfolded close to the inside rail.
Rebecca Romero Official explanation: jockey said he droped his whip closing stages

6666 EUROPEAN BREEDERS' FUND MAIDEN STKS 5f (P)
6:00 (6:00) (Class 5) 2-Y-O **£3,140** (£934; £467; £233) **Stalls** High

Form RPR

03 **1** **Barbieri (IRE)**[14] 6286 2-8-12 0.................... SteveDrowne 9 70
(J R Gask) *hld up in rr: gd prog jst over 1f out: shkn up and r.o wl to ld last 50yds* **7/2**[2]

6 **2** nk **Manoori (IRE)**[21] 6075 2-8-12 0.................... TedDurcan 7 69
(C F Wall) *trckd ldrs gng wl: prog over 1f out: led ent fnl f: styd on wl but hdd last 50yds* **7/2**[2]

04 **3** ¾ **Barnet Fair**[20] 6111 2-9-0 0.................... KierenFox(3) 8 71
(R C Guest) *dwlt: hld up last: gd prog jst over 1f out: styd on wl fnl f: nt quite gng pce of wnr* **9/1**

2544 **4** 2 ¼ **Darwin Star**[13] 6308 2-8-12 65.................... RichardHughes 5 58
(D K Ivory) *prom: chsd ldr 2f out: clsd and upsides 1f out: sn outpcd* **6/1**[3]

4263 **5** 1 ½ **Cristaliyev**[4] 6575 2-9-3 72.................... PatCosgrave 6 58
(J R Boyle) *chsd ldrs: drvn to try to cl over 1f out: wknd ins fnl f* **13/2**

5444 **6** 1 **Partout Le Magasin**[9] 6419 2-9-3 67....................(p) LiamKeniry 3 54
(J S Moore) *slowly away: racd awkwardly: mostly in last pair: styd on ins fnl f whn r was over* **16/1**

4400 **7** ¾ **Beach Patrol (IRE)**[8] 6442 2-9-0 62....................(v[1]) AlanCreighton(3) 4 51
(E J Creighton) *led: drvn over 1f out: hdd & wknd ent fnl f* **50/1**

24 **8** 4 **Karate (IRE)**[13] 6309 2-9-3 0.................... KierenFallon 1 37
(M Johnston) *nt wl away fr outside stall: wd bnd over 3f out: in rr after: wknd over 1f out* **3/1**[1]

050 **9** 3 **Furiosa (IRE)**[77] 4274 2-8-12 0....................(t) EddieCreighton 2 21
(E J Creighton) *t.k.h early: chsd ldr to 2f out: wknd rapidly* **66/1**

60.28 secs (-0.22) **Going Correction** -0.10s/f (Stan) **9** Ran SP% **116.4**
Speed ratings (Par 95): **97,96,95,91,89 87,86,80,75**
toteswingers:1&2 £4.20, 2&3 £5.10, 1&3 £4.40 CSF £16.36 TOTE £7.10: £1.30, £4.10, £1.10; EX 18.80.
Owner O.T.I. Racing & Associate **Bred** P G Connolly **Trained** Sutton Veny, Wilts

FOCUS
An ordinary maiden and one run at a sound pace, The first two raced towards the centre in the straight.

NOTEBOOK
Barbieri(IRE) is a progressive sort who showed a good turn of foot and posted her best effort to get off the mark at the third attempt, despite racing with the choke out early on and having to be switched for a run. She should stay 6f and may improve in handicaps as she settles better. (op 5-1)
Manoori(IRE) attracted support and duly bettered the form of her debut run on this first start on an artificial surface. While this form is nothing special, she is more than capable of winning a similar race, or a small handicap when qualified for a mark. (op 4-1 tchd 9-2)
Barnet Fair ◆ confirmed his previous turf promise on this all-weather debut. He will be suited by the step up to 6f, is now eligible for a handicap mark and will be one to keep an eye on in ordinary company granted a suitable test. (tchd 10-1)
Darwin Star, back in trip, was far from disgraced after chasing the decent gallop throughout. She is a reliable sort who remains capable of picking up a minor event, but she has had a few chances now and is is likely to remain vulnerable in this type of event. (op 11-2 tchd 5-1)
Cristaliyev had a decent chance strictly on official ratings, but was fairly easy to back and failed to match the pick of his efforts back over 5f. The return to 6f will be much more to his liking. (op 11-2 tchd 5-1)
Karate(IRE) was never travelling with any fluency from his outside draw and failed by a long way to confirm previous all-weather promise. However, he is in good hands, is now qualified for a mark and will be suited by a much stiffer test of stamina. (tchd 11-4)

6667 DIGIBET.COM NOVICE STKS 6f (P)
6:30 (6:30) (Class 5) 2-Y-O **£2,286** (£675; £337) **Stalls** High

Form RPR

013 **1** **Signs In The Sand**[32] 5748 2-9-5 94.................... FrankieDettori 7 97+
(Saeed Bin Suroor) *mde all: 2l clr and gng easily 2f out: wl in command after: pushed out* **13/8**[1]

0542 **2** 2 **Twist Of Silver (USA)**[18] 6191 2-8-11 85.................... RichardHughes 1 83
(J Noseda) *hld up in 5th: prog to chse wnr 2f out: pushed along and unavailing pursuit after* **7/4**[2]

0312 **3** 1 ¼ **Owain (USA)**[8] 6435 2-8-11 75.................... AdamBeschizza(5) 3 84
(C A Dwyer) *fluffed s bdly: latched on to bk of main gp after 2f: prog 2f out: wnt 3rd ins fnl f: styd on: no ch* **13/2**

12 **4** 4 **Jerrazzi (IRE)**[39] 5537 2-9-5 86.................... GeorgeBaker 4 75
(G L Moore) *chsd wnr to 2f out: grad wknd* **11/2**[3]

315 **5** 10 **Hammer Home (USA)**[27] 5874 2-9-5 73.................... NeilCallan 6 45
(B J Meehan) *cl up to over 2f out: sn wknd qckly* **25/1**

0 **6** 12 **Trojan Touch (USA)**[20] 6128 2-9-0 0.................... EddieCreighton 5 4
(C A Dwyer) *outpcd in last after 1f: sn t.o* **100/1**

6000 **7** 1 ¾ **Jamaica Grande**[13] 6311 2-9-0 57.................... PatCosgrave 2 —
(T T Clement) *prom 4f: wknd v rapidly: t.o* **100/1**

1m 11.44s (-1.66) **Going Correction** -0.10s/f (Stan) **7** Ran SP% **109.0**
Speed ratings (Par 95): **107,104,102,97,84 68,65**
toteswingers:1&2 £1.10, 2&3 £3.10, 1&3 £1.60 CSF £4.24 TOTE £2.10: £1.10, £3.10; EX 3.70.
Owner Godolphin **Bred** Darley **Trained** Newmarket, Suffolk

FOCUS
The two previous runnings of this race have thrown up decent types in Tishtar (useful) and this year's Royal Ascot winner Treadwell (smart) and, although this was not a competitive event, the winner is already a very useful performer. The gallop was an ordinary one and the field came down the centre in the straight.

NOTEBOOK
Signs In The Sand, who had the misfortune to come up against subsequent Cheveley Park winner Hooray over C&D last time, faced nothing of that calibre this time and confirmed himself a very useful performer on the surface under a typically well-judged, front-running ride. Although he has only raced over sprint distances, he is bred to stay further (by Cape Cross out of a UAE 1000 Guineas runner-up, who won over 1m1f) and is open to progress and it will be interesting to see if he is campaigned at the forthcoming Dubai Carnival. (op 11-8)
Twist Of Silver(USA), the only filly in the field, is a useful sort who allowed the winner to get first run, but she still showed she was fully effective on a synthetic surface on this all-weather debut. A more truly run race would have suited even better and, although she only has a debut maiden win to her name, she remains capable of adding to her tally in ordinary novice company or from her current mark of 85 in nurseries. (tchd 13-8 and 15-8)
Owain(USA) had something to find with the first two strictly on official ratings, but he ran creditably in the face of a stiffish task returned to Polytrack. His rating is due to go up to 78 in future, and this lightly raced type should be seen to better effect returned to ordinary nurseries and when stepped up to 7f. (op 15-2 tchd 10-1 in places)
Jerrazzi(IRE) had shown useful form in two turf starts, but failed to match the pick of those efforts on this all-weather debut and was disappointing. However, this was only his third run, he is in very good hands and will be well worth another chance. (tchd 6-1)
Hammer Home(USA) faced a tough task on these terms for this all-weather debut and was well beaten for the second successive run. Ordinary nurseries would see him in a better light, but he looks one to tread carefully with.

6668 DIGIBET H'CAP (DIV I) 1m 4f (P)
7:00 (7:00) (Class 6) (0-65,65) 3-Y-O+ **£1,364** (£403; £201) **Stalls** Centre

Form RPR

2250 **1** **Lombok**[20] 6109 4-9-12 **65**.................... HayleyTurner 7 77
(M L W Bell) *hld up in midfield: prog over 3f out: looking for room bhd ldrs over 2f out: led over 1f out: rdn and r.o wl* **8/1**

1550 **2** 3 **Rocky's Pride (IRE)**[22] 6065 4-9-10 **63**.................... StevieDonohoe 4 70
(W J Musson) *towards rr on outer: rdn wl over 2f out: prog to take 2nd 1f out: styd on: no ch w wnr* **25/1**

3444 **3** 2 ½ **Astound**[20] 6122 3-9-4 **64**....................(v) TomMcLaughlin 11 67
(P D Evans) *sltly hmpd s: settled in midfield: effrt over 2f out: outpcd over 1f out: styd on to take 3rd ins fnl f* **8/1**

005 **4** 1 ¾ **Starshine**[26] 5902 3-9-5 **65**.................... SteveDrowne 3 65
(R Charlton) *prom: chsd ldng pair over 3f out: rdn and fnd nil 2f out: lost pl qckly: plugged on again ins fnl f* **16/1**

100- **5** ¾ **Stormy Morning**[302] 6457 4-9-9 **62**.................... DaneO'Neill 13 61
(Mrs Lawney Hill) *cl up on inner: effrt and upsides over 1f out: chsd wnr next 100yds: wknd* **25/1**

4060 **6** nse **Shooting Party (IRE)**[55] 5011 4-9-5 **58**.................... RichardHughes 14 57
(R Hannon) *settled towards rr: pushed along over 3f out: no prog and swtchd out wd 2f out: plugged on* **11/2**[2]

3405 **7** ½ **Musashi (IRE)**[17] 5867 5-9-0 **58**.................... JemmaMarshall(5) 6 56
(Mrs L J Mongan) *s.v.s: hld up last: prog over 2f out: 9th and no ch whn nt clr run over 1f out: kpt on* **14/1**

035 **8** 1 ¾ **Sarwin (USA)**[22] 6055 7-9-4 **62**.................... AdamBeschizza(5) 10 58
(W J Knight) *s.s and urged along early: settled in last trio: prog on inner over 2f out and sn cl up: nt qckn over 1f out: sn wknd* **7/2**[1]

3061 **9** nk **Rowan Light**[50] 5180 4-9-6 **59**....................(b) PatCosgrave 12 54
(J R Boyle) *wnt lft s: trckd ldr: led over 2f out to over 1f out: wknd qckly* **6/1**[3]

4220 **10** 3 **Megalala (IRE)**[12] 6322 9-9-11 **64**.................... NeilChalmers 9 54
(J J Bridger) *led to over 2f out: wknd over 1f out* **7/1**

1400 **11** *nk* **Lyrical Intent**[107] 3278 4-9-3 **56** KirstyMilczarek 5 46
(P Howling) *hld up in midfield on outer: prog over 3f out: wknd 2f out* **33/1**

00/0 **12** *32* **Rosenblatt (GER)**[25] 5959 8-9-4 **60** RobertLButler(3) 8 —
(M S Tuck) *a in last trio: urged along and wknd 1/2-way: sn t.o* **66/1**

0233 **13** *2 1/4* **Vinces**[41] 5457 6-9-12 **65** GeorgeBaker 1 —
(T D McCarthy) *prom on outer tl wknd rapidly over 3f out: t.o and eased* **12/1**

2m 32.76s (-1.74) **Going Correction** -0.10s/f (Stan)
WFA 3 from 4yo+ 7lb 13 Ran SP% **119.0**
Speed ratings (Par 101): **101,99,97,96,95 95,95,94,93,91 91,70,68**
toteswingers:1&2 £61.10, 2&3 £51.80, 1&3 £22.40 CSF £199.08 CT £1656.46 TOTE £10.80: £3.50, £9.00, £3.30; EX 261.20.
Owner J L C Pearce **Bred** J L C Pearce **Trained** Newmarket, Suffolk

FOCUS
Division one of a modest handicap in which a couple of the market leaders disappointed. The gallop was ordinary and the first two came down the centre in the straight.
Lombok Official explanation: trainer's rep said, regarding apparent improvement in form, that the gelding appreciated the stronger pace.
Vinces Official explanation: jockey said gelding had no more to give

6669 DIGIBET H'CAP (DIV II) 1m 4f (P)
7:30 (7:31) (Class 6) (0-65,65) 3-Y-0+ **£1,364** (£403; £201) **Stalls** Centre

Form RPR

123 **1** **Carlton Scroop (FR)**[13] 6314 7-9-4 **60** (b) KierenFox(3) 8 70+
(A W Carroll) *t.k.h: hld up in midfield: smooth prog to go 2nd over 2f out: led over 1f out: bounded clr* **9/4**[1]

006 **2** *2 1/2* **Knockdolian (IRE)**[110] 3170 3-9-5 **65** SteveDrowne 1 70+
(R Charlton) *hld up in last trio: pushed along and prog over 2f out: rdn and styd on to take 2nd wl ins fnl f: too much to do* **10/1**

120 **3** *1* **Iceman George**[82] 4102 6-9-4 **62** (v) AdamBeschizza(5) 4 65
(G C Bravery) *in tch: prog to chse ldng pair over 4f out: rdn over 3f out: lost pl over 2f out: styd on again over 1f out: wnt 2nd briefly ins fnl f* **12/1**

4025 **4** *1/2* **Quince (IRE)**[55] 4980 7-9-0 **56** (v) SimonPearce(3) 5 59
(J Pearce) *racd on outer in midfield: drvn and prog over 3f out: v wd bnd sn after: kpt on fnl 2f: no ch* **16/1**

-032 **5** *1* **Dubburg (USA)**[13] 6314 5-9-5 **58** TonyCulhane 3 59
(W J Musson) *hld up in rr on outer: appeared to be hmpd bnd 3f out: urged along over 2f out: styd on late: no ch* **13/2**[3]

0616 **6** *hd* **Adoyen Spice**[21] 6080 3-9-0 **60** NeilCallan 13 61
(Mike Murphy) *hld up wl in rr: prog over 2f out: drvn to take 2nd 1f out: fnd nil and sn wknd* **11/2**[2]

4016 **7** *nk* **Rebellious Spirit**[51] 5155 7-9-11 **64** KirstyMilczarek 12 64
(S Curran) *t.k.h: hld up towards rr on inner: swtchd to outer 3f out: urged along over 2f out: kpt on: no ch* **33/1**

4004 **8** *1/2* **Coiled Spring**[29] 5840 4-9-5 **58** PatDobbs 11 57
(Mrs A J Perrett) *prom on inner: gng wl enough but lost pl fr 5f out and wl in rr 3f out: shuffled along and sme hdwy 2f out: no prog ins fnl f* **9/1**

0050 **9** *2 3/4* **Watchmaker**[25] 5958 7-9-9 **62** (p) FergusSweeney 9 57
(Miss Tor Sturgis) *led: drew 4 l clr 3f out: hdd over 1f out: wknd rapidly ins fnl f* **33/1**

0-00 **10** *7* **Ramora (USA)**[12] 6322 4-9-7 **65** KylieManser(5) 10 49
(Miss Olivia Maylam) *prom on inner: urged along over 3f out: cl enough 2f out: wknd rapidly jst over 1f out* **50/1**

3603 **11** *1 3/4* **Joinedupwriting**[11] 6375 5-9-4 **57** PaulMulrennan 7 38
(R M Whitaker) *chsd ldr to over 2f out: wknd* **16/1**

6250 **12** *2 1/4* **Daniel Thomas (IRE)**[14] 6288 8-9-7 **63** (p) RobertLButler(3) 2 40
(P Butler) *dwlt: hld up wl in rr: sme prog 3f out: no imp over 2f out: sn wknd* **50/1**

00 **13** *86* **Bull Market (IRE)**[28] 5868 7-9-12 **65** StevieDonohoe 14 —
(M S Tuck) *prom on inner tl wknd rapidly 5f out: sn wl t.o* **50/1**

5633 **14** *39* **Sunset Boulevard (IRE)**[30] 3442 7-9-4 **57** RichardHughes 6 —
(Jim Best) *hld up in rr: virtually p.u 5f out w jockey looking down: ambled home* **9/1**

2m 33.32s (-1.18) **Going Correction** -0.10s/f (Stan)
WFA 3 from 4yo+ 7lb 14 Ran SP% **119.8**
Speed ratings (Par 101): **99,97,96,96,95 95,95,95,93,88 87,85,28,2**
toteswingers:1&2 £6.60, 2&3 £42.40, 1&3 £12.70 CSF £24.64 CT £223.76 TOTE £3.10: £1.30, £4.50, £5.00; EX 34.90.
Owner S Hussain & P O'Neill **Bred** Jonathan Jay **Trained** Cropthorne, Worcs

FOCUS
Mainly exposed performers in another modest event. A moderate gallop only picked up turning for home and the winner came down the centre in the straight.
Dubburg(USA) Official explanation: jockey said gelding hung right-handed and was denied a clear run
Rebellious Spirit Official explanation: jockey said gelding hung right-handed
Joinedupwriting Official explanation: jockey said gelding hung right final 4f
Sunset Boulevard(IRE) Official explanation: jockey said he heavily eased gelding after it stumbled and lost its action

6670 DIGIBET NURSERY 1m (P)
8:00 (8:01) (Class 2) 2-Y-O
£6,916 (£2,071; £1,035; £518; £258; £129) **Stalls** High

Form RPR

160 **1** **Borug (USA)**[25] 5947 2-8-11 **82** (p) FrankieDettori 1 89
(Saeed Bin Suroor) *hld up in last trio: prog 2f out to ld over 1f out: rdn clr: decisively* **9/1**

15 **2** *2* **Raucous Behaviour (USA)**[18] 6174 2-8-8 **79** KierenFallon 6 81
(M Johnston) *racd wd in last trio: pushed along 1/2-way: drvn over 2f out: styd on fr over 1f out to take 2nd nr fin* **6/1**[3]

1 **3** *1/2* **Jaaryah (IRE)**[98] 3562 2-9-4 **89** PhilipRobinson 11 90
(M A Jarvis) *plld hrd: trckd ldng pair: chal and upsides 2f out: chsd wnr over 1f out: sn lft bhd: lost 2nd nr fin* **6/4**[1]

3314 **4** *hd* **Golden Tempest (IRE)**[12] 6317 2-8-2 **78** JohnFahy(5) 2 78
(W R Swinburn) *t.k.h: trckd ldng trio: tried to chal 2f out: outpcd over 1f out* **9/1**

1535 **5** *3/4* **Deep South**[43] 5392 2-9-7 **92** AhmedAjtebi 9 91
(Mahmood Al Zarooni) *t.k.h: trckd ldr: narrow ld over 2f out to over 1f out: fdd* **33/1**

3323 **6** *1/2* **Buckland (IRE)**[10] 6386 2-8-10 **81** (v1) ShaneKelly 7 79
(B J Meehan) *trckd ldrs: carried hd at most unattractive angle whn asked for effrt over 2f out: one pce after* **11/1**

301 **7** *shd* **Malice Or Mischief (IRE)**[34] 5701 2-8-0 **74** SophieDoyle(3) 8 71
(A W Carroll) *hld up in last trio: urged along over 2f out: one pce and no prog* **33/1**

1212 **8** *10* **Handsome Jack (IRE)**[7] 6453 2-8-7 **78** RichardKingscote 10 52
(R A Mills) *s.i.s but sn pushed up to ld: hdd over 2f out: wknd rapidly over 1f out* **3/1**[2]

1m 38.93s (-0.87) **Going Correction** -0.10s/f (Stan) 8 Ran SP% **113.5**
Speed ratings (Par 101): **100,98,97,97,96 96,95,85**
toteswingers:1&2 £4.10, 2&3 £3.00, 1&3 £4.50 CSF £60.63 CT £125.47 TOTE £15.70: £3.80, £1.30, £1.30; EX 54.80.
Owner Godolphin **Bred** Rabbah Bloodstock Llc **Trained** Newmarket, Suffolk

FOCUS
The best quality event on the card and one in which all bar one of the runners had won races. The gallop wasn't a true one, though, and the winner edged towards the inside rail in the closing stages.

NOTEBOOK
Borug(USA) had been disappointing on turf since his debut win but he confirmed himself to be bordering on very useful with a fluent display (despite edging right late on) to come off an ordinary gallop in the first-time cheekpieces on this debut on a synthetics. A better overall gallop would have suited, and he's the type to hold his own in slightly stronger company if the headgear continues to have the desired effect. (op 14-1)
Raucous Behaviour(USA) ◆ again failed to travel with any fluency on this all-weather debut but made up a fair amount of ground on the wide outside in the last quarter mile, leaving the strong impression that the step up to 1m2f would be very much to his liking. He is a lightly raced sort who is in good hands and it'll be a surprise if he doesn't win more races. Official explanation: jockey said gelding hung right-handed (op 7-1)
Jaaryah(IRE), the well-backed market leader, looked interesting on this handicap debut after a break of over three months considering how well her debut win at this course had worked out but, like several from this yard, she didn't help her chance by racing very freely in the first half of the race. However, she is also in good hands and will be well worth another chance in similar company. (op 11-8 tchd 13-8 in a place)
Golden Tempest(IRE), upped in distance for this return to Polytrack, wasn't disgraced in a race run at just an ordinary gallop. There will be easier opportunities in this grade than this one, and she will be worth another chance when it looks as though a more end-to-end gallop will be on the cards. Official explanation: jockey said filly ran too free (op 8-1 tchd 10-1)
Deep South hadn't been at his best on easy ground in cheekpieces on his previous start but fared better returned to Polytrack with that headgear left off after enjoying the run of the race. He's unlikely to be inconvenienced by the return to 7f but doesn't have much margin for error from this mark. (op 25-1)
Buckland(IRE), with a first-time visor replacing the blinkers he wore last time, wasn't disgraced on his first run over this trip. A stronger overall gallop would have suited him, but he'll have to raise his game to get off the mark in similar company, as he'll be 2lb higher in future handicaps. (op 9-1)
Handsome Jack(IRE), a steadily progressive sort who was 3lb well-in compared to future handicaps, dropped out tamely after setting just an ordinary gallop. However, he may have been feeling the exertions of four races in the space of a month and he will be worth another chance. (op 10-3 tchd 7-2)

6671 AG BARR SOFT DRINKS - AGBARR.CO.UK H'CAP 1m (P)
8:30 (8:30) (Class 6) (0-60,61) 3-Y-0+ **£1,637** (£483; £241) **Stalls** High

Form RPR

3065 **1** **Cheddar George**[56] 4968 4-9-4 **59** RichardHughes 9 69
(P W Chapple-Hyam) *t.k.h: hld up in rr: gd prog over 1f out: pressed ldr ins fnl f: hrd rdn to ld last strides* **4/1**[1]

0004 **2** *nk* **Unlimited**[11] 6370 8-9-5 **60** NeilCallan 5 69
(A W Carroll) *t.k.h: trckd ldr after 2f: gng easily over 2f out: led over 1f out: drvn and pressed ins fnl f: hdd last strides* **12/1**

2132 **3** *1* **Pipers Piping (IRE)**[11] 6371 4-9-2 **60** (p) MichaelStainton(3) 4 67
(P Howling) *hld up: rchd midfield after 3f: prog on outer wl over 1f out but wnr sn wnt by: styd on wl: nvr able to chal* **11/2**[3]

4504 **4** *1 1/4* **Al Aqabah (IRE)**[39] 5541 5-8-13 **59** JohnFahy(5) 14 63
(B Gubby) *hld up wl in rr: swtchd to inner and prog 2f out: cl enough over 1f out: kpt on same pce* **9/2**[2]

213 **4** *dht* **Dancing Welcome**[7] 6455 4-9-2 **57** (b) LiamKeniry 7 61
(J M Bradley) *chsd ldrs: rdn over 2f out: tried to mount chal over 1f out: sn outpcd* **14/1**

060- **6** *1/2* **Royal Willy (IRE)**[338] 7211 4-9-5 **60** SteveDrowne 11 63+
(W Jarvis) *hld up wl in rr: looking for room 2f out: rdn and styd on wl last 150yds: no ch to rch ldrs* **25/1**

4660 **7** *2* **First Service (IRE)**[18] 6210 4-9-5 **60** LukeMorris 8 58
(M J Attwater) *nvr gng that wl in midfield: urged along bef 1/2-way: effrt u.p to cl on ldrs 2f out: sn outpcd* **7/1**

0100 **8** *hd* **Sovereignty (JPN)**[27] 5897 8-9-2 **60** SophieDoyle(3) 6 58
(D K Ivory) *t.k.h: wl in tch on outer: nt qckn 2f out: one pce after* **20/1**

0-43 **9** *3/4* **Lend A Grand (IRE)**[27] 5897 6-9-5 **60** IanMongan 2 56
(Miss Jo Crowley) *slowest away: wl in rr: rdn over 2f out on outer: plugged on: nvr on terms* **8/1**

0500 **10** *1 1/2* **You've Been Mowed**[16] 6260 4-8-12 **58** TobyAtkinson(5) 10 51
(R J Price) *led at fair pce: hdd & wknd over 1f out* **10/1**

1000 **11** *1/2* **Bob Stock (IRE)**[27] 5897 4-9-4 **59** TonyCulhane 12 51
(W J Musson) *t.k.h: hld up in last pair: urged along in same pl over 2f out: no prog* **16/1**

013 **12** *hd* **Woolston Ferry (IRE)**[25] 5962 4-8-13 **59** AdamBeschizza(5) 1 50
(David Pinder) *prom: chsd ldng pair over 3f out to over 2f out: wknd qckly over 1f out* **14/1**

03 **13** *6* **Derby Desire (IRE)**[49] 5209 6-9-5 **60** JamesDoyle 13 37
(D Donovan) *chsd ldr tl jinked after 2f: drvn and wknd over 2f out* **66/1**

1m 38.47s (-1.33) **Going Correction** -0.10s/f (Stan)
WFA 3 from 4yo+ 3lb 13 Ran SP% **123.3**
Speed ratings (Par 101): **102,101,100,99,99 98,96,96,96,94 94,93,87**
toteswingers:1&2 £17.20, 2&3 £23.50, 1&3 £5.40 CSF £53.65 CT £274.14 TOTE £5.90: £1.70, £6.30, £1.60; EX 43.10.
Owner The Comic Strip Heroes **Bred** Cheveley Park Stud Ltd **Trained** Newmarket, Suffolk

FOCUS
A moderate and very tight handicap run at only a fair gallop. The principals came down the centre in the straight.
Royal Willy(IRE) Official explanation: jockey said gelding was denied a clear run

6672 BOOK NOW FOR JUMP RACING H'CAP 7f (P)
9:00 (9:01) (Class 6) (0-55,55) 3-Y-0+ **£1,637** (£483; £241) **Stalls** High

Form RPR

0000 **1** **Goodbye Cash (IRE)**[23] 6023 6-9-1 **55** AndrewHeffernan(3) 10 58
(R J Smith) *led: hung lft over 2f out: sn hdd and lost pl: styd on again u.p ins fnl f to ld last strides* **14/1**

2204 **2** *1/2* **Commandingpresence (USA)**[23] 6025 4-9-3 **54** NeilChalmers 12 56
(J J Bridger) *trckd ldrs: rdn to cl fr 2f out: styd on to ld last 100yds: hdd fnl strides* **16/1**

2500 **3** *3/4* **Blue Zephyr**[12] 6332 3-9-2 **55** (tp) LeeVickers 3 54
(D C Griffiths) *trckd ldng pair: wnt 2nd 3f out: led 2f out: hdd and lft in ld jst over 1f out: hdd and one pce last 100yds* **25/1**

5434 **4** *1* **If Only**[20] 6133 4-8-11 **53**........(p) AdamBeschizza(5) 13 50
(D Morris) *trckd ldrs: produced to chal 2f out: nt qckn over 1f out: one pce ins fnl f* **6/1**[2]
-060 **5** *nk* **Woodsley House (IRE)**[110] 3164 8-9-3 **54**........ RobertHavlin 14 50
(T T Clement) *hld up in midfield: prog over 2f out: drvn to chse ldrs over 1f out but nt on terms: kpt on ins fnl f* **40/1**
454 **6** *3* **Ever Cheerful**[61] 4790 9-8-12 **54**........(p) AmyBaker(5) 1 42
(A B Haynes) *mostly chsd ldr to 3f out: nt qckn and outpcd 2f out: n.d after* **16/1**
3200 **7** *2* **Orsett Lad (USA)**[25] 5968 3-9-1 **54**........ SteveDrowne 4 36
(J R Best) *dwlt: hld up in last pair: pushed along over 2f out: sme late hdwy: nvr nr ldrs* **16/1**
060 **8** *1* **Kladester (USA)**[58] 4897 4-9-2 **53**........ TonyCulhane 8 33
(M Herrington) *hld up towards rr: urged along and no imp on ldrs fnl 2f* **16/1**
6545 **9** *½* **Desert Falls**[20] 6125 4-8-13 **53**........ MichaelStainton(3) 2 32
(R M Whitaker) *prom: drvn and lost pl over 2f out: wl btn whn hmpd ent fnl f* **6/1**[2]
040 **10** *3 ¼* **Queenie's Star (IRE)**[35] 5669 3-9-2 **55**........ NeilCallan 6 24
(M J Attwater) *lost pl qckly 5f out: a towards rr after: struggling over 2f out* **40/1**
0000 **11** *7* **Ghost Dancer**[26] 5920 6-9-3 **54**........(b1) LiamKeniry 9 5
(J M Bradley) *t.k.h: hld up wl in rr: shkn up and no prog over 2f out* **33/1**
2260 **12** *9* **Lady Of Garmoran (USA)**[35] 5656 3-9-2 **55**........ TadhgO'Shea 5 —
(P F I Cole) *swtchd to r v wd sn after s: on terms to 3f out: sn bhd* **13/2**[3]
3545 **13** *2* **Michael's Nook**[24] 5997 3-9-2 **55**........ FergusSweeney 7 —
(W S Kittow) *dwlt: racd wd: a in rr: struggling over 2f out: t.o* **13/2**[3]
0650 **P** **Orangeleg**[23] 6024 4-9-4 **55**........ WilliamCarson 11 61+
(S C Williams) *hld up in midfield: stdy prog over 2f out: pushed into ld whn broke down jst over 1f out: p.u* **3/1**[1]

1m 25.82s (-0.18) **Going Correction** -0.10s/f (Stan)
WFA 3 from 4yo+ 2lb **14** Ran SP% **122.1**
Speed ratings (Par 101): **97,96,95,94,94 90,88,87,86,82 74,64,62,—**
toteswingers:1&2 £27.10, 2&3 £54.60, 1&3 £52.80 CSF £216.68 CT £5570.80 TOTE £6.50: £4.50, £5.90, £10.20; EX 135.80 Place 6: £60.23 Place 5: £37.85.
Owner Kevin Old **Bred** Mrs A C Peters **Trained** Epsom, Surrey
■ Stewards' Enquiry : Lee Vickers one-day ban: careless riding (Oct 20)

FOCUS
Another very tight handicap in which the whole field was rated from 53-55. The gallop was a reasonable one but the complexion of the race changed dramatically in the closing stages when Orangeleg broke down badly after looking the likely winner when hitting the front. The principals again came down the centre.
Kladester(USA) Official explanation: jockey said gelding hung right and suffered interference in running
Desert Falls Official explanation: jockey said gelding suffered interference in running
Queenie's Star(IRE) Official explanation: jockey said filly suffered interference in runing
Michael's Nook Official explanation: jockey said gelding suffered interference in running
T/Plt: £69.10 to a £1 stake. Pool of £63,264.37 - 667.62 winning tickets. T/Qpdt: £21.50 to a £1 stake. Pool of £8,195.64 - 281.94 winning tickets. JN

6465 NOTTINGHAM (L-H)
Wednesday, October 6

OFFICIAL GOING: Soft (heavy in places)
All races on outer course and no rail movements and all distances as advertised.
Wind: Light against Weather: Fine and dry

6673 RED BOX RECORDERS SIMPLY, SMARTER, VOICE NURSERY (DIV I) 6f 15y
2:10 (2:12) (Class 6) (0-60,60) 2-Y-O **£1,706** (£503; £252) **Stalls** High

Form RPR
4343 **1** **Prophet In A Dream**[8] 6435 2-9-7 **60**........ RichardHughes 10 69
(M R Channon) *prom: led wl over 2f out: pushed clr over 1f out: eased towards fin* **5/2**[1]
500 **2** *¾* **High Class Lady**[40] 5466 2-9-0 **58**........ JohnFahy(5) 15 65
(W R Swinburn) *hld up and bhd: smooth hdwy wl over 2f out: rdn to chse wnr over 1f out: styd on ins fnl f* **20/1**
0030 **3** *5* **Robber Stone**[44] 5365 2-9-2 **55**........ SamHitchcott 17 47
(M R Channon) *hld up on stands' rail: hdwy wl over 2f out: rdn to chse wnr wl over 1f out: sn drvn and one pce* **10/1**
000 **4** *4* **Urban Kode (IRE)**[14] 6286 2-9-0 **53**........ PaulHanagan 16 33
(P D Evans) *dwlt: hdwy to chse ldrs 1/2-way: rdn along 2f out: sn one pce* **10/1**
0033 **5** *4* **Shostakovich (IRE)**[15] 6271 2-9-1 **54**........ LiamKeniry 13 22
(S Kirk) *trckd ldrs: hdwy wl over 2f out: rdn wl over 1f out and sn one pce* **8/1**[2]
0300 **6** *3 ½* **None Sweeter**[19] 6163 2-9-3 **56**........ DavidAllan 8 13
(T D Easterby) *chsd ldrs: rdn along wl over 2f out: grad wknd* **20/1**
600 **7** *nk* **Newzflash**[61] 4782 2-9-1 **54**........ GrahamGibbons 11 10
(T D Barron) *led: pushed along 1/2-way: rdn and hdd wl over 2f out: sn wknd* **20/1**
000 **8** *hd* **High Avon**[56] 4960 2-9-3 **56**........ AdamKirby 6 12
(D K Ivory) *trckd ldrs: hdwy and cl up 1/2-way: rdn along over 2f out: grad wknd* **12/1**
4300 **9** *3 ½* **Lady Excellentia (IRE)**[27] 5871 2-9-6 **59**........ RobertHavlin 7 —
(A B Haynes) *dwlt and sltly hmpd s: a in rr* **50/1**
065 **10** *½* **Coedmor Boy**[27] 5895 2-9-1 **54**........ DavidProbert 14 —
(B Palling) *dwlt: sn cl up: rdn along 1/2-way: wknd over 2f out* **33/1**
0560 **11** *1* **Indiracer (IRE)**[27] 5894 2-9-6 **59**........ IanMongan 4 —
(A Bailey) *prom: rdn along 1/2-way: sn wknd* **40/1**
000 **12** *nk* **West Leake Melody**[13] 6301 2-9-6 **59**........ MichaelHills 2 —
(B W Hills) *in tch on outer: rdn along wl over 2f out: sn wknd* **8/1**[2]
606 **13** *3 ¾* **Sleeping Wolf**[29] 5835 2-9-3 **59**........ PatrickHills(3) 3 —
(R Hannon) *in tch towards outer: rdn along bef 1/2-way: sn outpcd and bhd* **16/1**
0650 **14** *nk* **Manchester Stanley**[22] 6052 2-8-12 **54**........(b1) SophieDoyle(3) 9 —
(J A Osborne) *in tch: rdn along 1/2-way: sn wknd* **33/1**
044 **15** *10* **King Cobra (IRE)**[45] 5328 2-9-5 **58**........ SimonWhitworth 5 —
(J W Hills) *dwlt and wnt rt s: a in rr* **17/2**[3]
020 **16** *¾* **Lindo Erro**[26] 5924 2-9-2 **55**........ SebSanders 12 —
(J Mackie) *chsd ldrs: rdn along bef 1/2-way: sn lost pl and bhd fnl 2f* **22/1**

1m 20.48s (5.58) **Going Correction** +0.875s/f (Soft) **16** Ran SP% **122.0**
Speed ratings (Par 93): **97,96,89,84,78 74,73,73,68,68 66,66,61,60,47 46**
toteswingers:1&2 £22.10, 2&3 £49.10, 1&3 £7.40 CSF £61.18 CT £467.85 TOTE £2.80: £1.30, £4.90, £2.30, £3.00; EX 48.30 Trifecta £208.90 Part won. Pool of £282.36 - 0.63 winning units..
Owner Lord Ilsley Racing (Stokes Syndicate) **Bred** Mike Channon Bloodstock Ltd **Trained** West Ilsley, Berks

FOCUS
A moderate nursery and a difficult race to work out, with plenty making their handicap debuts and nine of the 16 runners having had just the three outings. The field raced centre-to-stands' side, but those that raced down the centre had little chance and the front five came from stalls 10, 15, 17, 16 and 13.

NOTEBOOK
Prophet In A Dream ◆, the only previous winner in the field and in the frame in his last six starts, had never raced on soft ground before, but he seemed to relish it as he travelled supremely well up with the pace from the off. Set alight over 1f out, he was soon in an unassailable lead and was able to take things fairly easy in the closing stages. The winning distance understates his superiority and he can win again. (op 3-1)
High Class Lady ◆, making her nursery debut after finishing unplaced in three maidens, deserves plenty of credit as she was just about last at halfway, but she made up a lot of late ground and was the only one to get near the winner. She is a bit flattered, but still pulled clear of the rest and there are races to be won with her.
Robber Stone, disappointing on Polytrack last time, was surrounded by subsequent winners when third off this mark in a Goodwood nursery the time before, but he had never raced on soft ground before. He made up late ground against the nearside rail to finish a remote third, but he raced very awkwardly on occasions and may not have appreciated the conditions. Official explanation: vet said colt finished sore (op 12-1)
Urban Kode(IRE), making his nursery debut after finishing unplaced in three 5f maidens, ran better than his finishing position would suggest at Kempton last time, and he was the subject of good market support earlier in the day. He ran on after coming off the bridle over 2f from home, but was never a threat. (op 9-1 tchd 11-1)
Shostakovich(IRE), unlucky not to finish closer when third of 12 in a 5f Folkestone nursery last month, was 2lb lower here but, having travelled well, he didn't find as much off the bridle as had looked likely. He may need better ground and is already due to drop another 2lb. (tchd 17-2)
High Avon, making his nursery debut after finishing seventh in three starts in maidens, ran better than his finishing position would suggest as he raced up the unfavoured centre of the track. (op 14-1)
King Cobra(IRE) Official explanation: trainer's rep said colt was unsuited by the soft (heavy in places) ground

6674 RED BOX RECORDERS SIMPLY, SMARTER, VOICE NURSERY (DIV II) 6f 15y
2:40 (2:43) (Class 6) (0-60,60) 2-Y-O **£1,706** (£503; £252) **Stalls** High

Form RPR
660 **1** **Duquesa (IRE)**[14] 6286 2-9-4 **57**........ PaulHanagan 8 61
(P D Evans) *towards rr: pushed along 1/2-way: swtchd lft and gd hdwy on outer over 2f out: rdn to ld over 1f out: drvn and edgd lft ins fnl f: jst hld on* **16/1**
400 **2** *nse* **Hernando Torres**[92] 3756 2-9-1 **54**........ PaulMulrennan 12 58
(M W Easterby) *hld up: n.m.r and swtchd lft 2f out: rdn over 1f out: chsd wnr and swtchd rt ins fnl f: drvn and styd on strly towards fin: jst failed* **8/1**[3]
0025 **3** *2 ¼* **Regal Bullet (IRE)**[15] 6271 2-9-3 **56**........ WilliamCarson 7 53
(D K Ivory) *dwlt and sltly hmpd s: in rr tl gd hdwy over 2f out: rdn to chal over 1f out and ev ch tl drvn and one pce ins fnl f* **11/1**
545 **4** *1 ¾* **Scoglio**[13] 6308 2-9-7 **60**........ LeeVickers 16 52
(F Sheridan) *dwlt and bhd stands' rail: rdn along 1/2-way: sn swtchd lft to outer and chsd ldrs wl over 1f out: kpt on u.p fnl f: nrst fin* **8/1**[3]
5355 **5** *2 ¾* **Crown Ridge (IRE)**[42] 5412 2-9-1 **54**........ SamHitchcott 15 38
(M R Channon) *dwlt and towards rr: hdwy 1/2-way: rdn to chse ldrs and n.m.r 2f out: sn swtchd rt and one pce* **10/1**
2154 **6** *1* **Magic Cross**[19] 6163 2-9-2 **55**........(t) NickyMackay 3 36
(P J McBride) *dwlt: sn trcking ldrs: hdwy over 2f out: rdn to ld briefly wl over 1f out: sn hdd and grad wknd* **15/2**[2]
454 **7** *hd* **Roman Strait**[63] 4709 2-9-6 **59**........ LukeMorris 9 39
(M Blanshard) *midfield: rdn along and n.m.r 2f out: n.d* **28/1**
0043 **8** *nk* **Je Suis Unrockstar**[1] 6645 2-9-5 **58**........(p) PJMcDonald 4 37
(J A Glover) *hld up: swtchd lft and hdwy 2f out: rdn to chse ldrs over 1f out: drvn and wknd ent fnl f* **12/1**
6104 **9** *2 ¼* **Peppercorn Rent (IRE)**[30] 5818 2-8-12 **54**........(e) KellyHarrison(3) 17 26
(T D Easterby) *chsd ldrs on inner: rdn along over 2f out: sn n.m.r and wknd* **14/1**
000 **10** *½* **Slumbering Sioux**[82] 4095 2-9-6 **59**........ AdamKirby 14 30
(H J L Dunlop) *trckd ldrs: effrt and n.m.r 2f out: sn rdn and no hdwy* **22/1**
4344 **11** *1 ¼* **Till Dawn (IRE)**[28] 5862 2-9-1 **54**........ JamesDoyle 1 21
(A W Carroll) *prom on outer: hdwy and cl up 1/2-way: rdn over 2f out and sn wknd* **20/1**
4060 **12** *3 ¾* **Mirror Lad**[34] 5675 2-9-5 **58**........ RichardKingscote 6 14
(Tom Dascombe) *wnt rt s: sn cl up: rdn along and edgd rt 2f out: sn drvn and wknd* **25/1**
6600 **13** *nk* **Sleights Boy (IRE)**[32] 5755 2-9-3 **59**........(b1) GaryBartley(3) 10 14
(I W McInnes) *in rr: hdwy over 2f out: rdn along and n.m.r wl over 1f out: sn wknd* **50/1**
0540 **14** *5* **Rocky Coast**[17] 6220 2-9-2 **55**........ TomEaves 5 —
(B Smart) *prom: cl up over 2f out: sn rdn: edgd rt and wknd* **20/1**
0060 **15** *nse* **Palindromic (IRE)**[13] 6311 2-9-0 **53**........(b) HayleyTurner 2 —
(J R Gask) *prom: led after 2f: rdn along over 2f out: drvn and hdd wl over 1f out: sn wknd* **16/1**
4431 **16** *2 ¾* **Country Waltz**[16] 6258 2-9-6 **59**........ RichardHughes 13 —
(M R Channon) *trckd ldrs: effrt and nt clr run 2f out: cl up whn hmpd over 1f out: no ch and eased after* **3/1**[1]
050 **17** *¾* **Assertion**[56] 4941 2-9-4 **57**........ DavidAllan 11 —
(M Brittain) *led 2f: cl up tl rdn along and wknd over 2f out* **25/1**

1m 20.63s (5.73) **Going Correction** +0.875s/f (Soft) **17** Ran SP% **129.5**
Speed ratings (Par 93): **96,95,92,90,86 85,85,84,81,81 79,74,74,67,67 63,62**
toteswingers:1&2 £17.70, 2&3 £22.40, 1&3 £49.30 CSF £133.80 CT £1510.66 TOTE £23.00: £5.60, £3.00, £3.90, £2.50; EX 184.60 TRIFECTA Not won. Pool of £291.47 - winning units..
Owner Raymond N R Auld **Bred** R N Auld **Trained** Pandy, Monmouths

FOCUS
Like the first division, a nursery full of handicap debutants though at least three of these had tasted success before. However, on this occasion the high-drawn horses didn't dominate in the same way and in fact the first four home were all forced to make their efforts out wide. The winning time was 0.15 seconds slower.

NOTEBOOK
Duquesa(IRE) ◆, making her nursery debut after finishing unplaced in three maidens, didn't enjoy the smoothest of passages - she was bumped at the start and was then forced to switch and make her run widest of all - but she was in front over a furlong out and kept going to hang on by the skin of her teeth. She is entitled to improve further. Official explanation: trainer's rep said, regarding apparent improvement in form, that the filly appeared suited by racing over a furlong further and being dropped in class.

Hernando Torres, making his turf and nursery debuts after showing modest form in three AW maidens, was also forced to circle the field in order to get a run and he only just failed to get up. He should be able to win a race like this in similar conditions. (op 12-1)
Regal Bullet(IRE) had looked as though this step back up in trip would suit after a couple of sound efforts in 5f nurseries, and he ran his race having had every chance a furlong from home. This ground was a question mark, but he seemed to handle it well enough. (op 10-1)
Scoglio ◆, another making his nursery and turf debuts after showing ability in three Polytrack maidens, caught the eye as he was being ridden along in last place early but he made up plenty of late ground, and it looks as though he needs a stiffer test. (op 11-1)
Crown Ridge(IRE), a consistent nine-raced maiden, was down 4lb here and can be rated closer as he didn't see daylight until it was far too late, but he came home in good style. (op 14-1)
Peppercorn Rent(IRE) Official explanation: jockey said filly suffered interference
Slumbering Sioux ◆ never saw much daylight, but made up some late ground when she eventually did. (op 20-1 tchd 18-1)
Sleights Boy(IRE) Official explanation: jockey said gelding was denied a clear run
Country Waltz's performance can be completely ignored. She made her move 2f from home, but the gap she was aiming for then closed and her rider just had to sit and suffer. The combination eventually called it a day. (op 9-2)

6675 EUROPEAN BREEDERS' FUND MAIDEN STKS 6f 15y
3:10 (3:10) (Class 5) 2-Y-O £3,561 (£1,059; £529; £264) Stalls High

Form				RPR
2206	1		**West Leake Bridge (IRE)**[11] 6354 2-9-3 69 MichaelHills 9 *(B W Hills) in tch: hdwy 1/2-way: led over 2f out: pushed clr over 1f out: edgd rt ins fnl f: kpt on* 5/1[3]	75
4	2	¾	**Lion Court (IRE)**[12] 6324 2-9-3 0 SebSanders 6 *(Sir Mark Prescott) dwlt and towards rr: hdwy 1/2-way: rdn to chse wnr over 1f out: kpt on ins fnl f* 9/1	73
302	3	9	**Lowawatha**[13] 6301 2-9-3 82 JimCrowley 3 *(R M Beckett) led: rdn along and hdd over 2f out: sn drvn and one pce* 9/4[2]	46
0	4	1	**Ace Master**[7] 6465 2-9-3 0 LukeMorris 4 *(S R Bowring) chsd ldrs: rdn along over 2f out: sn one pce* 100/1	43
022	5	7	**Enlightening (IRE)**[19] 6145 2-9-3 76 RichardHughes 7 *(R Hannon) cl up: rdn along wl over 2f out: sn btn and eased* 11/10[1]	22
40	6	½	**Even Stevens**[7] 6458 2-9-3 0 PJMcDonald 2 *(J A Glover) in tch: pushed along 1/2-way: sn outpcd and bhd* 40/1	20
	7	28	**Poppet's Joy** 2-8-12 0 RobertHavlin 5 *(A B Haynes) s.i.s: a in rr: outpcd and bhd fr 1/2-way* 25/1	—

1m 20.84s (5.94) **Going Correction** +0.875s/f (Soft) 7 Ran SP% 112.3
Speed ratings (Par 95): **95,94,82,80,71 70,33**
CSF £44.08 TOTE £4.70: £1.50, £4.70; EX 44.30 Trifecta £106.20 Pool: £947.95 - 6.60 winning units..
Owner Henry Barton **Bred** J Costello **Trained** Lambourn, Berks

FOCUS
A modest maiden, even though a few of these had already shown ability. Surprisingly, given what happened in the first race, the runners spurned the nearside rail and came down the centre. They finished very well spread out and the winning time was slower than both divisions of the nursery, indicating that the form is on the weak side.

NOTEBOOK
West Leake Bridge(IRE), officially rated 69, was the most exposed in the field but had run poorly the last twice after finishing runner-up in a couple of 6f maidens. However, he was sent into the lead at halfway and never looked like being caught after that. The problem for him now is how the handicapper views this, as he put plenty of daylight between himself and a couple of much higher-rated rivals. (op 11-2)
Lion Court(IRE) ◆, a well-beaten fourth of five on his Haydock debut, again missed the break but he stayed on from off the pace in the latter stages and made sure the winner had to be kept up to his work. There should be better to come from him in due course. (tchd 10-1)
Lowawatha, rated 82 after making the frame in two 6f maidens, was beaten a long way in a 7f soft-ground maiden in between but, having had every chance, he failed to get home here. This would seem to confirm that he needs better ground. (op 2-1)
Ace Master, beaten a very long way on his debut over C&D last month, ran well but looks one for AW handicaps in due course. (op 80-1)
Enlightening(IRE), rated 76 after finishing runner-up in maidens at Brighton and Newbury, set the pace to halfway but was struggling once headed and dropped right out. The ground was a possible excuse. (op 11-8)
Poppet's Joy Official explanation: jockey said filly got upset in stalls

6676 EUROPEAN BREEDERS' FUND MAIDEN STKS 1m 75y
3:40 (3:40) (Class 4) 2-Y-O £4,533 (£1,348; £674; £336) Stalls Centre

Form				RPR
4	1		**Specific Gravity (FR)**[20] 6127 2-9-3 0 IanMongan 11 *(H R A Cecil) trckd ldr: hdwy to ld wl over 3f out: rdn clr 2f out: kpt on strly* 5/1[3]	85
	2	6	**Glencadam Gold (IRE)** 2-9-3 0 PaulHanagan 4 *(H R A Cecil) hld up towards rr: hdwy over 3f out: swtchd rt and rdn to chse ldrs 2f out: styd on ins fnl f: tk 2nd nr fin: no ch w wnr* 16/1	72
32	3	nk	**Halfsin (IRE)**[19] 6159 2-9-3 0 WilliamBuick 6 *(M Botti) trckd ldng pair on inner: effrt over 3f out: rdn along wl over 2f out: swtchd rt and drvn wl over 1f out: kpt on u.p ins fnl f* 9/4[2]	71
04	4	1	**Audacious**[27] 5878 2-9-3 0 RyanMoore 8 *(Sir Michael Stoute) trckd ldrs: hdwy 4f out: rdn to chse wnr over 2f out: drvn over 1f out: sn one pce: lost 2nd nr fin* 10/11[1]	69
000	5	3 ¼	**Night Witch (IRE)**[8] 6442 2-8-12 0 ShaneKelly 5 *(E J Creighton) chsd ldrs on inner: rdn along over 3f out: drvn over 2f out and sn one pce* 100/1	57
0	6	1	**Royal Reason**[18] 6190 2-8-12 0 SamHitchcott 12 *(M R Channon) hld up: sme hdwy on outer 3f out: rdn over 2f out and sn one pce* 50/1	55
	7	2 ½	**Greyfriars Drummer** 2-9-3 0 GregFairley 7 *(M Johnston) hld up: a in rr* 22/1	54
0	8	12	**Mokalif**[20] 6127 2-9-3 0 HayleyTurner 3 *(M L W Bell) dwlt: a in rr* 66/1	28
0	9	4 ½	**Kepler's Law**[6] 6514 2-9-3 0 SebSanders 9 *(Sir Mark Prescott) a in rr* 100/1	18
00	10	6	**Henry Bond**[77] 4247 2-8-12 0 (b[1]) DeclanCannon(5) 10 *(S A Harris) led: rdn along and hdd wl over 3f out: sn wknd* 200/1	5
0	11	nk	**Makyaal (IRE)**[20] 6128 2-9-3 0 RichardHills 13 *(J L Dunlop) trckd ldrs on outer: hdwy 4f out: rdn along 3f out: sn wknd* 28/1	4

1m 52.06s (6.46) **Going Correction** +0.70s/f (Yiel) 11 Ran SP% 119.4
Speed ratings (Par 97): **95,89,88,87,84 83,80,68,64,58 58**
toteswingers:1&2 £4.50, 2&3 £6.10, 1&3 £2.70 CSF £74.75 TOTE £5.30: £1.70, £2.70, £1.70; EX 39.20 Trifecta £206.10 Pool: £713.29 - 2.56 winning units..
Owner Niarchos Family **Bred** Suc S Niarchos **Trained** Newmarket, Suffolk

FOCUS
This maiden, or a division of it, has been won by the likes of Patkai and Mastery in recent years. A decent test in the ground and they finished very well spread out. It resulted in a one-two for Henry Cecil.

NOTEBOOK
Specific Gravity(FR) ◆ ran green yet was still promising when fourth of nine in similar ground on his Yarmouth debut last month, but judging by this performance he obviously learned plenty from that initial experience. Always up with the pace, he was sent for home over 3f out and gradually pulled further and further clear. There was a lot to like about this performance and he looks a nice prospect. (op 4-1)
Glencadam Gold(IRE) ◆, a stable-companion of the winner, was retained for 14,000gns as a yearling and is a half-brother to four winners at up to 2m, so perhaps it was no surprise that he took a while to grasp what was required, but he stayed on steadily to grab second place late on and he will win races. Official explanation: jockey said colt hung left
Halfsin(IRE), a narrowly beaten runner-up in an 18-runner Newmarket maiden last month, had every chance but couldn't quicken, and perhaps he needs better ground. (op 5-2)
Audacious, fourth of 15 in a decent Doncaster maiden last month that has since worked out very well, was always handy and was sent in pursuit of the winner over the last couple of furlongs, but could make no impression. This was a step backwards, but any horse can be excused a modest effort on this ground. (op Evens tchd 11-10)
Night Witch(IRE), unplaced in her first three starts, though not disgraced at Newbury last time, again ran better than might have been expected and she may be worth a try in a handicap off her current mark of 59.
Royal Reason, green when tenth of 14 in a Newbury maiden on debut last month, fared only a little better here and may be more of a handicap type. Official explanation: jockey said filly hung left (op 66-1)
Greyfriars Drummer, a 14,000gns half-brother to two winners including the high-class Lovelace, ran far too green on this debut but should be capable of better.

6677 STUDENT DISCOUNTS AT NOTTINGHAM RACECOURSE - NOTTINGHAMRACECOURSE.CO.UK H'CAP 1m 2f 50y
4:10 (4:10) (Class 4) (0-85,83) 3-Y-O+ £6,152 (£1,830; £914; £456) Stalls Low

Form				RPR
-156	1		**Oriental Cat**[33] 5727 3-9-8 82 WilliamBuick 4 *(J H M Gosden) dwlt and hld up in rr: hdwy on inner over 3f out: swtchd rt to wd outside and rdn over 2f out: str run to ld 1 1/2f out: sn clr* 14/1	97
2031	2	3 ½	**Captain Dancer (IRE)**[12] 6327 4-9-10 79 MichaelHills 3 *(B W Hills) trckd ldrs: hdwy 4f out: led 3f out and sn rdn clr: drvn and hdd wl over 1f out: kpt on same pce* 9/2[2]	87
6023	3	4 ½	**Strategic Mission (IRE)**[12] 6328 5-8-12 67 RyanMoore 2 *(P F I Cole) dwlt and towards rr: hdwy on inner over 3f out: rdn along to chse ldrs wl over 2f: drvn wl over 1f out and kpt on same pce* 7/1[3]	66
-561	4	1 ¼	**Tamanaco (IRE)**[61] 4786 3-9-5 79 DuranFentiman 10 *(T D Walford) hld up in rr: pushed along over 3f out: swtchd ins and rdn over 2f out: kpt on appr fnl f* 9/1	76
04	5	hd	**Supa Seeker (USA)**[16] 6260 4-9-1 70 JamesDoyle 9 *(A W Carroll) hld up towards rr: effrt 4f out: rdn along and hdwy 3f out: drvn and edgd lft over 2f out: kpt on u.p appr fnl f* 12/1	66
3255	6	¾	**Hel's Angel (IRE)**[27] 5888 4-9-6 75 JackMitchell 5 *(Mrs A Duffield) led 4f: cl up tl rdn along wl over 3f out and grad wknd* 22/1	70
1344	7	1 ½	**Gritstone**[18] 6203 3-9-9 83 PaulHanagan 8 *(R A Fahey) hld up in tch: hdwy to chse ldrs 3f out: drvn over 2f out and sn btn* 10/3[1]	75
3300	8	3	**King Fingal (IRE)**[56] 4943 5-9-10 79 TomEaves 7 *(J J Quinn) hld up towards rr: effrt 4f out: sn rdn and btn* 25/1	65
6364	9	7	**Norwegian Dancer (UAE)**[36] 5638 4-9-10 79 GrahamGibbons 6 *(E S McMahon) chsd ldng pair: rdn along over 3f out: drvn wl over 2f out and sn wknd* 8/1	51
6343	10	10	**Mingun Bell (USA)**[15] 6276 3-9-0 74 IanMongan 1 *(H R A Cecil) sn trcking ldr: led after 4f: rdn along and hdd 3f out: sn drvn and wknd* 10/1	26
0621	11	½	**Tenessee**[14] 6288 3-9-6 80 LukeMorris 11 *(C G Cox) chsd ldrs on outer: rdn along 1/2-way: wknd 4f out: sn bhd and eased fnl 2f* 7/1[3]	31

2m 17.24s (5.54) **Going Correction** +0.70s/f (Yiel)
WFA 3 from 4yo+ 5lb 11 Ran SP% 119.0
Speed ratings (Par 105): **105,102,98,97,97 96,95,93,87,79 79**
toteswingers:1&2 £15.30, 2&3 £8.90, 1&3 £14.80 CSF £76.93 CT £491.96 TOTE £22.60: £5.90, £2.20, £2.70; EX 117.30 TRIFECTA Not won..
Owner H R H Princess Haya Of Jordan **Bred** Whitley Stud **Trained** Newmarket, Suffolk
■ Stewards' Enquiry : Ian Mongan two-day ban: careless riding (Oct 20-21)

FOCUS
A decent handicap and a race of changing fortunes, run at a fair pace thanks to a disputed lead between Hel's Angel and Mingun Belle.
Tenessee Official explanation: trainer said colt was unsuited by the soft (heavy in places) ground

6678 RED BOX RECORDERS QUANTIFY VOICE RATING RELATED MAIDEN STKS 1m 2f 50y
4:40 (4:40) (Class 5) 3-Y-O+ £2,590 (£770; £385; £192) Stalls Low

Form				RPR
232	1		**Significant Move**[40] 5493 3-9-0 79 PaulHanagan 8 *(R Charlton) hld up: hdwy 3f out: swtchd lft over 2f out: rdn to ld jst over 1f out: drvn and edgd rt ins fnl f: kpt on* 2/1[1]	75
6045	2	1 ¼	**On The Feather**[37] 5584 4-9-2 51 AndreaAtzeni 2 *(B R Millman) trckd ldrs: hdwy over 3f out: led jst over 2f out: sn rdn and hdd over 1f out: drvn and kpt on ins fnl f* 66/1	69
4265	3	2 ¼	**Prince Of Dreams**[32] 5752 3-9-0 76 ShaneKelly 10 *(W J Knight) led 2f: cl up: rdn over 3f out: ch over 2f out: sn drvn and edgd lft: kpt on same pce appr fnl f* 8/1[3]	68
3524	4	1 ½	**Alfonso The Wise (IRE)**[14] 6283 3-9-0 77 (p) RyanMoore 5 *(J Noseda) in tch: effrt 4f out: rdn along to chse ldrs 3f out: drvn over 2f out and sn no imp* 2/1[1]	65
543	5	3	**Ahaazeeg**[21] 6079 3-9-0 76 RichardHills 3 *(J L Dunlop) cl up on inner: led after 2f: rdn along over 3f out: hdd over 2f out: grad wknd* 11/1	59
0006	6	20	**Sensible**[38] 5565 5-8-13 40 (v[1]) Louis-PhilippeBeuzelin(3) 7 *(H J Collingridge) dwlt: a in rr: bhd and eased wl over 1f out* 100/1	16
-000	7	11	**Star Of Soho (IRE)**[5] 6525 3-8-8 41 SophieDoyle(3) 6 *(E J Creighton) dwlt: a in rr: bhd fnl 2f* 200/1	—

542 **8** *2 ¾* **Short Break**[57] 4926 3-8-11 77 ... IanMongan 9 —
(H R A Cecil) *chsd ldng pair: rdn along over 3f out: sn wknd and bhd whn eased wl over 1f out* **7/2**[2]

2m 19.27s (7.57) **Going Correction** +0.70s/f (Yiel)
WFA 3 from 4yo+ 5lb 8 Ran SP% **111.3**
Speed ratings (Par 103): **97,96,94,93,90 74,65,63**
toteswingers:1&2 £6.70, 2&3 £11.00, 1&3 £5.20 CSF £103.89 TOTE £3.10: £1.90, £6.70, £2.60; EX 57.20 Trifecta £579.30 Part won. Pool of £782.87 - 0.44 winning units..
Owner K Abdulla **Bred** Juddmonte Farms Ltd **Trained** Beckhampton, Wilts

FOCUS
Older horses had taken the last two runnings of this, but the previous status quo was restored with the race going to a 3-y-o. The runners came down the centre of the track in the home straight. It's not hard to have serious doubts over the value of the form, however, with a few of the markets leaders running moderately and a couple of them looking most reluctant. The proximity of the 51-rated runner-up is another negative, whilst the winning time was over two seconds slower than the preceding handicap.

6679 EXTEND FRESHERS' WEEK AT NOTTINGHAM RACECOURSE APPRENTICE H'CAP 6f 15y
5:10 (5:13) (Class 5) (0-70,69) 3-Y-O+ **£2,266** (£674; £337; £168) **Stalls** High

Form RPR

000 **1** **Commander Wish**[26] 5906 7-8-0 **54** oh8 ... VictoriaFletcher(7) 3 62
(Lucinda Featherstone) *hld up: hdwy over 2f out: chsd ldrs whn sltly hmpd wl over 1f out: led ent fnl f: kpt on* **66/1**

3103 **2** *1 ¾* **Bermondsey Bob (IRE)**[6] 6515 4-8-13 **60** ... JackDean 4 62
(J L Spearing) *a.p: led 1/2-way: rdn wl over 1f out: hdd ent fnl f: kpt on same pce* **5/1**[1]

0421 **3** *¾* **Lake Chini (IRE)**[54] 5045 8-8-11 **65** ...(b) DavidSimmonson(7) 11 65
(M W Easterby) *hmpd s and towards rr: rapid hdwy after 2f out and sn prom: rdn over 2f out and ev ch tl one pce ent fnl f* **8/1**

002 **4** *½* **Big Boom**[20] 6133 5-8-9 **56** ...(b) AndreaAtzeni 10 54
(M Quinn) *led to 1/2-way: cl up tl rdn wl over 1f out and kpt on same pce ins fnl f* **10/1**

256 **5** *hd* **Super Yellow**[69] 4503 3-9-7 **69** ... SophieDoyle 13 66+
(J A Osborne) *hmpd s and again after 1f: bhd: hdwy over 1f out: styd on strly ins fnl f: nrst fin* **12/1**

2346 **6** *shd* **Residency (IRE)**[42] 5405 4-8-7 **59** ... AdamCarter(5) 1 56
(B Smart) *prom: rdn along over 2f out: drvn over 1f out and kpt on same pce* **13/2**[2]

3050 **7** *1 ¾* **Mr Skipiton (IRE)**[15] 6270 5-8-3 **57** ... IanBurns(7) 6 48
(B J McMath) *chsd ldrs: hdwy over 2f out: rdn and hung lft wl over 1f out: wknd appr fnl f* **7/1**[3]

6000 **8** *nse* **Top Bid**[60] 4833 6-9-2 **66** ... LanceBetts(3) 7 57
(T D Easterby) *nvr nr ldrs* **16/1**

0503 **9** *nse* **Danum Dancer**[7] 6464 6-8-6 **56** ... DeanHeslop(3) 5 47
(N Bycroft) *chsd ldrs: rdn along over 2f out: grad wknd* **7/1**[3]

0614 **10** *shd* **Eye For The Girls**[37] 5579 4-8-5 **57** ... MatthewLawson(5) 12 48
(M R Channon) *wnt rt and hmpd s: a in rr* **14/1**

0004 **11** *1* **Belinsky (IRE)**[17] 6226 3-9-6 **68** ... Louis-PhilippeBeuzelin 2 56
(N Tinkler) *chsd ldrs on outer: rdn along wl over 2f out: sn wknd* **25/1**

4052 **12** *hd* **Kensington (IRE)**[20] 6110 9-8-12 **66** ... NoraLooby(7) 8 53
(A J McCabe) *prom: rdn along wl over 2f out: sn wknd* **11/1**

2040 **13** *¾* **Micky Mac (IRE)**[14] 6295 6-8-12 **62** ... DaleSwift(3) 15 47
(C J Teague) *wnt bdly lft and hmpd s: a towards rr* **16/1**

1354 **14** *12* **Exceedingly Good (IRE)**[85] 3976 4-8-7 **54** oh2 ... PaulPickard 14 —
(S R Bowring) *hmpd s: swtchd lft and hdwy to chse ldrs after 1f: rdn along 1/2-way: sn wknd* **12/1**

1m 19.64s (4.74) **Going Correction** +0.875s/f (Soft)
WFA 3 from 4yo+ 1lb 14 Ran SP% **122.7**
Speed ratings (Par 103): **103,100,99,99,98 98,96,96,96,96 94,94,93,77**
toteswingers:1&2 £48.90, 2&3 £5.00, 1&3 £85.10. totesuper7: Win: Not won. Place: Not won. CSF £383.49 CT £3077.94 TOTE £91.30: £18.20, £2.20, £3.50; EX 331.00 TRIFECTA Not won.. Place 6: £514.19 Place 5: £237.27 .
Owner J Roundtree **Bred** P R Featherstone **Trained** Atlow, Derbyshire
■ A winner on her first ride for apprentice Victoria Fletcher.

FOCUS
A modest apprentice handicap and a messy start, with Micky Mac swerving left exiting the rails stall and hampering the quartet drawn closest to him.
Super Yellow ◆ Official explanation: jockey said gelding was denied a clear run
Exceedingly Good(IRE) Official explanation: jockey said filly was hampered at start and did not like the soft (heavy in places) ground
T/Plt: £788.00 to a £1 stake. Pool of £60,669.75 - 56.20 winning tickets. T/Qpdt: £72.10 to a £1 stake. Pool of £4,503.98 - 46.20 winning tickets. JR

6680 - 6687a (Foreign Racing) - See Raceform Interactive

6441 NEWBURY (L-H)
Thursday, October 7

OFFICIAL GOING: Soft
Rail out from 10f to 2.5f where there was a cut off and distances on round course increased by 16metres.
Wind: Moderate behind Weather: Sunny intervals

6688 E B F BROADBASE UK MAIDEN STKS 6f 110y
2:10 (2:11) (Class 4) 2-Y-O **£4,209** (£1,252; £625; £312) **Stalls** High

Form RPR

1 **Golden Delicious** 2-8-12 0 ... SteveDrowne 2 83+
(H Morrison) *wnt lft s and s.i.s: in rr tl pushed along and gd hdwy over 2f out: chsd ldr over 1f out: drvn to ld ins fnl f: c clr fnl 75yds: won gng away* **7/1**[3]

05 **2** *3 ¾* **Three Sparrows (IRE)**[8] 6465 2-9-3 0 ... RyanMoore 5 77
(R Hannon) *sn trcking ldr: led jst ins fnl 2f: sn drvn 3 l clr: hdd and outpcd fnl 75yds but kpt on wl for 2nd* **11/4**[2]

3 *1 ½* **Qushchi** 2-8-12 0 ... JimmyFortune 10 68
(W Jarvis) *trckd ldrs: pushed along: green and hung lft wl over 1f out: styd on wl to hold 3rd ins fnl f* **11/1**

05 **4** *1 ½* **Aristeia**[9] 6442 2-8-12 0 ... RichardHughes 11 64
(R Hannon) *s.i.s: t.k.h: and sn in tch: hdwy 2f out: pushed along and one pce ins fnl f* **15/8**[1]

5 *2 ¾* **Bint Nas (IRE)** 2-8-12 0 ... ChrisCatlin 4 56
(M R Channon) *sn in tch: pushed along 3f out: green but styd on over 1f out: nvr rchd ldrs and wknd ins fnl f* **7/1**[3]

00 **6** *2 ¼* **No Larking (IRE)**[19] 6196 2-9-3 0 ... DaneO'Neill 7 55
(H Candy) *led tl hdd 2f out: wknd over 1f out* **8/1**

7 *4* **Zartina (IRE)** 2-8-12 0 ... LiamKeniry 3 39
(S Kirk) *in tch: pushed along 3f out: wknd over 2f out* **33/1**

0 **8** *2 ¼* **Cliffords Reprieve**[7] 6514 2-9-3 0 ... FrankieMcDonald 1 38
(E A Wheeler) *chsd ldrs 4f* **66/1**

0 **9** *2 ½* **Fire N'Brimstone**[20] 6145 2-9-3 0 ... TravisBlock 9 31
(Mouse Hamilton-Fairley) *plld hrd: bhd fr 1/2-way* **66/1**

1m 23.72s (4.42) **Going Correction** +0.375s/f (Good) 9 Ran SP% **111.8**
Speed ratings (Par 97): **89,84,83,81,78 75,71,68,65**
toteswingers:1&2 £4.10, 2&3 £5.90, 1&3 £7.80 CSF £25.39 TOTE £9.10: £2.20, £1.20, £3.00; EX 38.00 Trifecta £214.00 Pool: £539.93 - 1.86 winning units..
Owner Nicholas Jones **Bred** Coln Valley Stud **Trained** East Ilsley, Berks

FOCUS
An ordinary maiden by Newbury standards, but there was a potentially useful winner. They raced towards the stands' side for most of the way, but the rail was not an advantage.

NOTEBOOK
Golden Delicious missed the break and ran green in rear through the early stages, but she produced a sustained challenge when switched wide in the closing stages, ending up in the middle of the track. Hughie Morrison likes introducing a good one at Newbury (subsequent pattern-race winners Queen's Grace and Stimulation two examples) and this half-sister to 6f-7f winner Imperial Delight could be smart. She may now be aimed at the Listed Radley Stakes back at Newbury on October 23. (op 15-2)
Three Sparrows(IRE), well backed despite Richard Hughes seemingly choosing Aristeia, travelled well on the pace (touched 1.14 in-running), but he was readily brushed aside by the winner. This was an improvement on his first two efforts and he's now qualified for an official mark. (op 3-1 tchd 5-2)
Qushchi was worked up in the paddock and briefly got loose. By the same sire as brilliant sprinter Sacred Kingdom, out of a dual 1m2f Listed winner for this trainer, she's clearly bred to be smart but she ran green throughout, noticeably so under pressure. (op 10-1)
Aristeia ◆ soon recovered from a slow start but, just as over 7f here last time, was keen early. She failed to pick up for pressure and should prove a different proposition over the bare 6f, or even 5f, on a quick surface in handicaps, for which she is now eligible. (op 9-4 tchd 5-2)
Bint Nas(IRE) showed a round action, suggesting the ground wasn't a problem, but she failed to make any impression. (op 8-1 tchd 13-2)

6689 CRUSADER CONNECT MAIDEN STKS 1m (S)
2:45 (2:48) (Class 4) 2-Y-O **£3,885** (£1,156; £577; £288) **Stalls** High

Form RPR

23 **1** **Fulgur**[20] 6159 2-9-3 0 ... J-PGuillambert 17 85+
(L M Cumani) *trckd ldr after 2f: led appr fnl 2f: drvn: edgd lft and c clr ins fnl f: easily* **15/8**[1]

2 *2 ¾* **Mijhaar** 2-9-3 0 ... PhilipRobinson 7 77
(M A Jarvis) *t.k.h and led 1f: stdd: styd in tch: drvn and one pce 2f out tl qcknd over 1f out: green: hung lft but chsd wnr fnl 120yds yds: gng on cl home: no ch* **11/1**

00 **3** *2* **Hollow Tree**[20] 6159 2-9-0 0 ... SimonPearce(3) 8 73
(A M Balding) *led after 1f: hdd over 2f out: sn one pce but rallied ins fnl f to take 3rd fnl 120yds* **100/1**

0 **4** *3* **Levitate**[22] 6092 2-9-3 0 ... RyanMoore 18 66
(Sir Michael Stoute) *in rr: green and pushed along in rr: stl pushed along and plenty to do over 2f out: styd on wl appr fnl f and styd on strly fnl 150yds: kpt on wl: nvr a danger* **8/1**

5 *hd* **Al Kazeem** 2-9-3 0 ... SteveDrowne 4 66
(R Charlton) *chsd ldrs: disp cl 2nd 2f out: wknd ins fnl f* **40/1**

5 **6** *¾* **My Vindication (USA)**[22] 6088 2-9-3 0 ... PatCosgrave 9 64
(R Hannon) *chsd ldrs: rdn over 2f out: styd on same pce* **28/1**

00 **7** *1* **Grumeti**[20] 6159 2-9-3 0 ... JamieSpencer 13 62
(M L W Bell) *stdd in tch: swtchd lft over 3f out: pushed along to dispute cl 2nd 2f out: wknd ins fnl f* **50/1**

4 **8** *½* **Novel Dancer**[19] 6196 2-9-3 0 ... RichardHughes 14 61
(R Hannon) *in tch: rdn over 2f out: nvr rchd ldrs and sn outpcd* **7/2**[2]

0 **9** *1 ¼* **Angelic Upstart (IRE)**[19] 6196 2-9-3 0 ... JimmyFortune 2 58
(A M Balding) *t.k.h: stdd in tch: hdwy over 2f out: nvr quite rchd ldrs and wknd ins fnl f* **22/1**

6 **10** *1* **Omnipotent (IRE)**[9] 6443 2-9-3 0 ... PatDobbs 15 56
(R Hannon) *s.i.s: in rr: hdwy fr 2f out: sme prog ins fnl f* **28/1**

11 *nk* **Viking Storm** 2-9-3 0 ... DaneO'Neill 5 55
(H J L Dunlop) *s.i.s: sme hdwy fnl 2f* **80/1**

0 **12** *¾* **Brezza Di Mare (IRE)**[34] 5718 2-9-0 0 ... Louis-PhilippeBeuzelin(3) 16 53
(B J Meehan) *wnt lft s: in tch: rdn and green 1/2-way: wknd over 1f out* **100/1**

13 *1* **High Samana** 2-9-3 0 ... JimCrowley 12 51
(R M Beckett) *s.i.s: towards rr most of way: mod late prog* **33/1**

0 **14** *1* **Abbakhan (IRE)**[19] 6196 2-9-3 0 ... TedDurcan 3 49
(J L Dunlop) *in tch: rdn over 2f out and sn wknd* **5/1**[3]

15 *3 ¼* **Gold Mine** 2-9-3 0 ... LiamKeniry 11 42
(A M Balding) *s.i.s: nvr beyond mid-div* **66/1**

0 **16** *4* **Captain Bellamy (USA)**[20] 6159 2-9-3 0 ... GeorgeBaker 1 33
(H Morrison) *chsd ldrs over 5f* **80/1**

17 *12* **Zaheeb** 2-9-3 0 ... ChrisCatlin 6 7
(M R Channon) *rdn and green 1/2-way: a in rr* **66/1**

1m 42.46s (2.76) **Going Correction** +0.375s/f (Good) 17 Ran SP% **119.1**
Speed ratings (Par 97): **101,98,96,93,93 92,91,90,89,88 88,87,86,85,82 78,66**
toteswingers:1&2 £5.80, 2&3 £133.70, 1&3 £33.60 CSF £21.37 TOTE £2.70: £1.10, £4.30, £31.90; EX 23.40 Trifecta £486.90 Part won. Pool: £658.04 - 0.20 winning units..
Owner Scuderia Rencati Srl **Bred** Azienda Agricola Francesca **Trained** Newmarket, Suffolk

FOCUS
Plenty of interesting types on show and a race that ought to produce a good few winners. The action unfolded up the middle of the track, and it paid to race prominently.

NOTEBOOK
Fulgur had shown plenty of ability on his first two starts, but had been keen on both occasions and also didn't handle the dip at Newmarket on good ground latest. Although again racing enthusiastically on the pace, the difference this time was that he didn't fight his jockey, and the combination of a flat track and soft ground also suited. He still looked green when first asked to stretch, carrying his head to the right, but he was soon straightened out and didn't need to be hit with the whip. He's a smart colt in the making, with there more to come when he steps up to middle-distances. (op 13-8 tchd 6-4)
Mijhaar, a half-brother to smart 1m-1m1f winner Yaddree, raced keenly without much cover through the first half of the contest. He then hit a flat spot when coming under pressure inside the final 3f, losing his place, but despite looking green when working his way back into the open, briefly carrying his head to the right and getting unbalanced, he ran on nicely. He showed a knee action, suggesting this is his sort of ground, and he could be very useful. (op 9-1)
Hollow Tree finished 15l behind Fulgur last time, so this was clearly a greatly improved performance, but he probably knew his job better than most of these. Handicaps are now an option.

Levitate ◆, well beaten on debut at Yarmouth over 7f, was badly in need of this further experience, getting soon behind and coming under pressure a fair way out. He did, though, make good late headway to fare best of those from off the pace, suggesting he's getting the idea, and further improvement seems likely. (op 12-1)
Al Kazeem ◆ is a big, leggy colt and still considered on the weak side by Roger Charlton, who expected him to tire in the ground after showing ability. That's exactly what happened. (op 50-1)
My Vindication(USA), passed over by Richard Hughes, had hinted at ability at Sandown and did so again this time. He might find a weak maiden, but is more likely a handicap prospect. (op 33-1 tchd 20-1)
Grumeti ◆ was too keen early, but showed up well when switched wide into the clear at about halfway, before unsurprisingly fading. This was promising and he'll be of interest if going handicapping next time, although his knee action suggests he won't want fast ground. (tchd 40-1)
Novel Dancer has a low, quick action and isn't bred for soft ground, so he had no hope of confirming his debut promise. (op 4-1 tchd 9-2)
Angelic Upstart(IRE) ◆ was allowed to coast home in the last half-furlong and would have been closer had he been pushed out. There's more to come. (op 16-1 tchd 25-1)
Abbakhan(IRE) wasn't far behind subsequent sales race winner Fury here on debut, but he ran poorly this time. (op 11-2 tchd 9-2 and 6-1 in places)

6690 SIR GERALD WHENT MEMORIAL NURSERY — 7f (S)
3:20 (3:21) (Class 2) 2-Y-O — **£7,123** (£2,119; £1,059; £529) **Stalls** High

Form — RPR
11 **1** **Vanguard Dream**[17] 6254 2-9-7 **89** ... RichardHughes 7 98+
(R Hannon) *mde all: rdn over 1f out: styd on gamely u.p whn chal thrght fnl f: asserted cl home* **4/1**[3]
1 **2** ½ **Unex El Greco**[37] 5629 2-8-13 **81** ... WilliamBuick 2 89+
(J H M Gosden) *stdd and hld up in rr: stdy hdwy but hanging lft fr over 2f out: pressed wnr over 1f out and ins fnl f: fnd no ex cl home* **2/1**[1]
2130 **3** 3 **Royal Opera**[47] 5301 2-8-8 **76** ... DavidProbert 1 76
(B R Millman) *t.k.h: chsd ldrs: rdn 2f out: outpcd by ldng duo fnl f: kpt on wl for 3rd* **16/1**
106 **4** ½ **Cocohatchee**[19] 6191 2-8-6 **74** ... LukeMorris 11 73
(P M Phelan) *s.i.s: in rr: hdwy but hanging lft fr over 2f out: stl hanging: kpt on ins fnl f to cl on 3rd but no ch w ldng duo* **10/1**
6020 **5** ¾ **Falkland Flyer (IRE)**[19] 6184 2-8-1 **69** ... CathyGannon 10 66
(M R Channon) *chsd ldrs: rdn and hung lft ins fnl 2f: styd on same pce* **33/1**
3612 **6** 3 ¼ **Highlife Dancer**[8] 6475 2-8-3 **78** ... MatthewLawson(7) 4 67
(M R Channon) *chsd ldrs: rdn over 2f out: wknd over 1f out* **40/1**
4153 **7** hd **Arctic Mirage**[41] 5472 2-8-7 **75** ... WilliamCarson 3 64
(M Blanshard) *plld hrd: in tch whn hmpd after 1f: in rr: swtchd rt 3f out: rdn hung lft and no imp ins fnl 2f* **20/1**
6114 **8** ½ **My Single Malt (IRE)**[26] 5947 2-8-9 **77** ... JamieSpencer 5 64
(T P Tate) *s.i.s: in rr: swtchd rt over 3f out: drvn and no imp over 2f out* **7/2**[2]
3116 **9** 1 ½ **Ninfea (IRE)**[10] 6412 2-8-0 **68** ... NickyMackay 9 52
(S Kirk) *chsd ldrs: rdn over 2f out: sn btn* **20/1**
531 **10** 9 **Thomas Tompion (IRE)**[30] 5836 2-9-1 **83** ... RyanMoore 6 44
(G L Moore) *in tch: chsd ldrs 1/2-way: sn wknd* **17/2**
0000 **11** 11 **Welsh Dancer**[15] 6278 2-8-2 **70** ... (b[1]) FrankieMcDonald 8 4
(R Hannon) *prom to 1/2-way* **50/1**

1m 27.99s (2.29) **Going Correction** +0.375s/f (Good) 11 Ran SP% **117.9**
Speed ratings (Par 101): **101,100,97,96,95 91,91,91,89,79 66**
toteswingers:1&2 £2.00, 2&3 £8.40, 1&3 £9.20 CSF £11.65 CT £118.49 TOTE £4.00: £1.10, £2.10, £3.20; EX 12.70 Trifecta £173.30 Pool: £990.66 - 4.23 winning units..
Owner Malih L Al Basti **Bred** Malih L Al Basti **Trained** East Everleigh, Wilts

FOCUS
Not much strength in depth to this nursery, but the first two both look decent and produced strong form for the grade. The early pace was not particularly strong, and they all raced up the middle of the track.

NOTEBOOK
Vanguard Dream ◆, who had previously picked up a 1m maiden and a 7f novice event, extended his unbeaten sequence with a likeable performance. He didn't settle in front, but that probably had much to do with him setting an ordinary early gallop and he stuck on well for pressure to turn away a useful type in the shape of Unex El Greco, albeit that one had also been keen. His action suggests he'll cope with quick ground and there's probably more to come. (op 5-1)
Unex El Greco ◆, the winner of an ordinary maiden under similar conditions on debut at Leicester, raced without much cover and was much too keen. He was also inclined to hang left under pressure, but still finished clear of the remainder and can do better again if settling in future. (op 7-4 tchd 9-4)
Royal Opera, back up in trip, was plenty keen enough but still ran well behind two progressive types.
Cocohatchee, who got going too late over 6f here last time, ruined his chance by continually hanging left, but still managed fourth. (op 16-1)
Falkland Flyer(IRE) found this company a bit hot and can contest lesser races off his current sort of mark. (op 40-1)
My Single Malt(IRE) started slowly and found little for pressure. He has won on good to soft ground, but maybe these even slower conditions did not suit. (op 4-1)
Welsh Dancer Official explanation: jockey said colt moved poorly

6691 INSURE WISER FILLIES' H'CAP — 1m 2f 6y
3:55 (3:55) (Class 4) (0-85,79) 3-Y-O+ — **£3,885** (£1,156; £577; £288) **Stalls** Low

Form — RPR
-331 **1** **Diamond Duchess (IRE)**[118] 2935 3-9-4 **78** ... (b) TedDurcan 8 92
(D R Lanigan) *stdd in rr s: rdn and hdwy and c towards centre of crse over 1f out: styd on wl u.p to ld fnl 100yds: rdn out* **11/2**[3]
-553 **2** ½ **Zahoo (IRE)**[25] 5991 3-9-1 **75** ... RichardHills 4 88
(J L Dunlop) *mid-div: hdwy fr 4f out: swtchd rt towards centre of crse and chsd wnr ins fnl 2f: led over 1f out: hdd and no ex fnl 100yds* **6/4**[1]
3-00 **3** 2 ¼ **Dream In Waiting**[125] 2705 4-9-3 **72** ... WilliamBuick 2 81
(B J Meehan) *in tch: swtchd rt to centre crse and racd along wl over 3f out: drvn and hdwy to ld appr fnl 2f: hdd over 1f out: one pce u.p ins fnl f* **25/1**
3501 **4** 1 ¼ **Starla Dancer (GER)**[54] 5096 4-9-5 **79** ... LeeTopliss(5) 6 85
(R A Fahey) *chsd ldrs: rdn 2f out: hung rt and wknd ins fnl f* **10/1**
3155 **5** 1 ½ **Red Intrigue (IRE)**[12] 6361 3-8-13 **73** ... PatDobbs 9 76
(Mrs A J Perrett) *stdd in rr: rdn and hdwy over 2f out: nvr rchd ldrs and one pce whn hung rt fr over 1f out: sn btn* **5/1**[2]
5625 **6** 3 ¾ **Santa Margherita**[22] 6079 3-8-5 **65** ... ChrisCatlin 3 61
(H J L Dunlop) *chsd ldr: chal 4f out tl led over 3f out: hdd: hdd appr fnl 2f: sn btn* **25/1**
1-65 **7** 4 ½ **Perfect Vision**[118] 2935 3-8-8 **68** ... LukeMorris 7 55
(C G Cox) *in rr: rdn 3f out: no imp on ldrs 2f out and sn wknd* **10/1**
1065 **8** 4 ½ **Make Amends (IRE)**[108] 3257 5-9-1 **70** ... GeorgeBaker 5 48
(R J Hodges) *in rr: rdn 3f out and sme prog over 2f out: nvr rchd ldrs and wknd sn after* **28/1**
3110 **9** 24 **Eastern Paramour (IRE)**[20] 6151 5-9-10 **79** ... SteveDrowne 1 9
(B R Millman) *led tl hdd over 3f out: wknd qckly wl over 2f out: eased* **9/1**

2m 12.12s (3.32) **Going Correction** +0.40s/f (Good)
WFA 3 from 4yo+ 5lb 9 Ran SP% **111.4**
Speed ratings (Par 102): **102,101,99,98,97 94,91,87,68**
toteswingers:1&2 £1.90, 2&3 £10.30, 1&3 £22.70 CSF £13.27 CT £179.92 TOTE £5.00: £1.80, £1.10, £6.70; EX 11.90 Trifecta £530.40 Part won. Pool of £716.82 - 0.54 winning units..
Owner Saif Ali **Bred** R N Auld **Trained** Newmarket, Suffolk

FOCUS
A fair fillies' handicap in which they raced up the middle of the track in the closing stages.

6692 NEWVOICEMEDIA H'CAP — 1m 7y(R)
4:30 (4:31) (Class 5) (0-75,75) 3-Y-O — **£2,590** (£770; £385; £192) **Stalls** Low

Form — RPR
5013 **1** **First In The Queue (IRE)**[16] 6266 3-9-2 **70** ... TravisBlock 1 83+
(S Kirk) *sn led: drvn clr over 2f out: styd on strly ins fnl f: unchal* **12/1**
0411 **2** 1 ½ **Destiny Blue (IRE)**[15] 6297 3-9-3 **71** ... GeorgeBaker 6 79
(J A Osborne) *t.k.h early and hld up in rr: hdwy over 2f out: rdn and hung lft over 1f out and sn chsng wnr: kpt on: no imp* **13/8**[1]
0534 **3** 1 ¼ **Veni Vedi Veci (IRE)**[22] 6090 3-9-7 **75** ... DavidProbert 2 80
(A M Balding) *chsd wnr: rdn over 2f out: lost 2nd over 1f out: kpt on ins fnl f* **12/1**
42 **4** 2 ¼ **Mark Twain (IRE)**[13] 6326 3-9-4 **75** ... (b[1]) MartinLane(3) 8 75
(D M Simcock) *t.k.h: hld up in rr: rdn and hdwy on outside over 2f out: hung lft and styd on ins fnl f: nt rch ldrs* **4/1**[2]
5404 **5** nk **Yabtree (IRE)**[29] 5861 3-9-1 **69** ... SteveDrowne 4 68
(R Charlton) *sn in tch: trckd ldrs over 4f out: rdn over 2 over: wknd over 1f out* **25/1**
0501 **6** ½ **Tilsworth Glenboy**[39] 5559 3-9-0 **68** ... StephenCraine 7 66
(J R Jenkins) *stdd s: towards rr: hdwy over 2f out: sn rdn: wknd and hung rt ins fnl f* **12/1**
4640 **7** 1 **Bonded (IRE)**[8] 6467 3-9-2 **70** ... (b) WilliamBuick 5 66
(B J Meehan) *in rr: rdn over 2f out and no imp on ldrs* **16/1**
6266 **8** 1 ¼ **Starry Mount**[44] 5394 3-9-2 **70** ... (p) RobertHavlin 10 63
(A B Haynes) *chsd ldrs tl wknd 2f out* **22/1**
4240 **9** 2 ¾ **Our Boy Barrington (IRE)**[26] 5968 3-9-4 **72** ... RyanMoore 12 59
(R Hannon) *rdn over 2f out: a towards rr* **11/1**
-100 **10** ¾ **He's Invincible**[19] 6197 3-9-3 **71** ... (b) JimmyFortune 3 57
(B J Meehan) *t.k.h: chse ldrs tl wknd ins fnl 2f* **20/1**
6305 **11** 4 ½ **Mountrath**[56] 4994 3-9-0 **68** ... WilliamCarson 9 44
(B R Johnson) *t.k.h: chsd ldrs over 2f out* **20/1**
1005 **12** 7 **Towbaat**[9] 6444 3-9-7 **75** ... PhilipRobinson 11 35
(M A Jarvis) *racd on outside: bhd fr 1/2-way* **10/1**[3]

1m 42.39s (102.39) 12 Ran SP% **122.2**
toteswingers:1&2 £4.90, 2&3 £5.40, 1&3 £8.00 CSF £31.04 CT £264.48 TOTE £12.60: £5.40, £1.10, £3.90; EX 49.20 Trifecta £435.10 Pool of £799.79 - 1.36 winning units..
Owner Liam Breslin **Bred** Holborn Trust Co **Trained** Upper Lambourn, Berks

FOCUS
A good race for the class.
Tilsworth Glenboy Official explanation: jockey said gelding hung right under pressure
He's Invincible Official explanation: jockey said gelding ran too freely
Towbaat Official explanation: trainer said filly was unsuited by the soft ground

6693 BE WISER APPRENTICE H'CAP — 2m
5:05 (5:06) (Class 5) (0-75,70) 4-Y-O+ — **£2,590** (£770; £385; £192) **Stalls** Low

Form — RPR
2125 **1** **Saute**[25] 5996 4-9-7 **70** ... (p) JohnFahy(3) 7 78
(W R Swinburn) *reminders paddock bnd after 1f: in tch: drvn along 4f out: styd on fr over 2f out: swtchd lft and r.o to ld fnl 120yds: all out* **15/2**
1-00 **2** ½ **Warne's Way (IRE)**[21] 6132 7-9-2 **62** ... (b) EJMcNamara 3 70
(B G Powell) *led: rdn and narrowly hdd ins fnl 2f: rallied to ld again jst ins fnl f: hdd and no ex fnl 120yds* **40/1**
0065 **3** 1 ¼ **Rock Soleil**[7] 6516 6-9-2 **69** ... LewisWalsh(7) 5 75
(Jane Chapple-Hyam) *chsd ldr to 3f out: sn drvn and one pce: hung lft u.p ins fnl f but kpt on again to take 3rd last strides* **9/1**
-245 **4** hd **Ragdollianna**[97] 3634 6-9-8 **68** ... WilliamCarson 6 74
(M J McGrath) *chsd ldrs: wnt 2nd 3f out: drvn to chal sn after and slt ld ins fnl 2f: narrowly hdd jst ins fnl f: no ex fnl 120yds and lost 3rd cl home* **16/1**
6033 **5** 1 **Sparkaway**[21] 6132 4-8-5 **51** ... (b) AndreaAtzeni 11 56
(W J Musson) *mid-div: hdwy over 2f out: styd on fnl f: nvr gng pce to rch ldrs* **9/2**[2]
0636 **6** 3 **Ned Ludd (IRE)**[16] 6273 7-8-10 **59** ... (p) LeeTopliss(3) 2 60
(J G Portman) *chsd ldrs: rdn and hung bdly lft fr 3f out and no ch after* **11/1**
3321 **7** 1 **Petella**[21] 6132 4-8-11 **60** ... AdamBeschizza(3) 9 60
(C W Thornton) *bhd and wl off pce: stl last over 2f out: styd on fr over 1f out and kpt on fnl f but nvr any ch* **7/4**[1]
2404 **8** 1 ¾ **Gaselee (USA)**[8] 6480 4-9-6 **66** ... MartinLane 1 64
(Rae Guest) *chsd ldrs to 3f out: wknd over 2f out* **11/2**[3]
5340 **9** ¾ **Naughty Naughty**[13] 5722 5-9-1 **61** ... RussKennemore 4 58
(B G Powell) *in tch 9f* **33/1**
6-00 **10** 1 ¼ **Whitcombe Spirit**[157] 1758 5-8-6 **52** ... MarcHalford 10 48
(Jamie Poulton) *in tch: rdn 4f out: wknd ins fnl 3f* **40/1**
1445 **11** shd **Calculating (IRE)**[27] 5922 6-8-13 **62** ... TobyAtkinson(3) 8 57
(M D I Usher) *a towards rr* **25/1**

3m 45.82s (13.82) **Going Correction** +0.40s/f (Good) 11 Ran SP% **117.6**
Speed ratings (Par 103): **81,80,80,80,79 78,77,76,76,75 75**
toteswingers:1&2 £39.70, 2&3 £75.40, 1&3 £9.30 CSF £278.93 CT £2709.12 TOTE £7.40: £2.10, £13.50, £4.20; EX 283.80 TRIFECTA Not won. Place 6: £124.90 Place 5: £40.40.
Owner P W Harris **Bred** Azienda Agricola Rosati Colarieti **Trained** Aldbury, Herts

FOCUS
A modest staying handicap.

T/Jkpt: Not won. T/Plt: £159.00 to a £1 stake. Pool of £55,042.02 - 252.56 winning tickets. T/Qpdt: £45.10 to a £1 stake. Pool of £5,749.02 - 94.14 winning tickets. ST

6574 WOLVERHAMPTON (A.W) (L-H)

Thursday, October 7

OFFICIAL GOING: Standard

Wind: Light, half-against Weather: Fine

6694 BETTING.COM "HOW'S YA FATHER" NURSERY (DIV I) 7f 32y(P)

5:40 (5:41) (Class 6) (0-65,65) 2-Y-O £1,364 (£403; £201) Stalls High

Form RPR

0000 1 **Folly Drove**[30] 5837 2-9-6 **64** RichardKingscote 8 68
(J G Portman) *hld up: hdwy on inner under 2f out: led 1f out: drvn out and kpt on wl towards fin* **22/1**

1014 2 ½ **Captain Loui (IRE)**[30] 5837 2-9-5 **63** (p) PaulMulrennan 4 66
(D Burchell) *sn led: rdn 2f out: hdd 1f out: kpt on u.p ins fnl f: a jst hld* **8/1**[3]

461 3 *nk* **Reason To Believe (IRE)**[18] 6220 2-9-7 **65** PaulHanagan 3 67
(B M R Haslam) *broke wl: led early: trckd ldrs: effrt to chal 2f out: ev ch over 1f out: nt qckn towards fin* **6/4**[1]

0600 4 2 ¼ **Orange Ketchup (IRE)**[8] 6471 2-9-7 **65** NeilCallan 2 62
(P F I Cole) *trckd ldrs: rdn and nt qckn over 1f out: hung lft u.p and styd on same pce ins fnl f* **12/1**

4300 5 3 **All The Evil (IRE)**[20] 6162 2-9-6 **64** ShaneKelly 5 53
(B J Meehan) *bhd: niggled along 5f out: hdwy over 1f out: kpt on one pce fnl f: no imp on ldrs* **28/1**

4406 6 2 ½ **Dunmore Boy (IRE)**[20] 6163 2-8-13 **60** BarryMcHugh(3) 7 43
(R A Fahey) *midfield: effrt and hdwy 2f out: rdn over 1f out: sn no imp on ldrs* **15/2**[2]

0060 7 *hd* **Alfraamsey**[15] 6300 2-9-2 **60** RichardHughes 1 43
(M R Channon) *midfield: effrt to chse ldrs 2f out: nvr able to mount serious chal: fdd ins fnl f* **10/1**

4330 8 1 **Paper Dreams (IRE)**[25] 5998 2-9-3 **61** DarryllHolland 11 41
(K A Ryan) *chsd ldr tl rdn 2f out: wknd over 1f out* **25/1**

0405 9 ¾ **Yachtmaster (IRE)**[31] 5818 2-9-4 **62** TomEaves 9 40
(J J Quinn) *sn in rr: struggling over 3f out: nvr able to get on terms* **12/1**

2502 10 *shd* **Russian Ice**[17] 6258 2-9-3 **61** SamHitchcott 10 39
(D K Ivory) *s.i.s: sn in midfield: lost pl 5f out: u.p sn after and n.d* **14/1**

450 11 6 **Chibchan (IRE)**[55] 5040 2-9-5 **63** RoystonFfrench 12 26
(Mahmood Al Zarooni) *sn chsd ldrs: rdn and lost pl wl over 3f out: toiling after* **16/1**

0006 12 5 **Commercial (IRE)**[14] 6309 2-9-7 **65** FergusSweeney 6 16
(J A Osborne) *hdwy after 2f: sn prom and racd keenly: rdn and wknd 2f out* **12/1**

1m 30.28s (0.68) **Going Correction** -0.075s/f (Stan) **12** Ran SP% **119.2**
Speed ratings (Par 93): **93,92,92,89,86 83,83,81,81,80 74,68**
toteswingers::1&2:£53.60, 1&3:£23.90, 2&3:£3.20 CSF £186.24 CT £438.34 TOTE £54.50: £12.80, £1.10, £1.50; EX 616.50.
Owner Mrs J Edwards-Heathcote **Bred** Mrs R Pease **Trained** Compton, Berks

FOCUS
An ordinary nursery. The pace was not particularly strong.

NOTEBOOK
Folly Drove was beaten 11l on nursery debut on good to soft at Lingfield last month. She was sent off a big price but produced a much more dynamic effort to get off the mark on her AW debut. This performance can be marked up because the placed horses raced much more prominently and this half-sister to two 7f/1m AW winners should have scope for further improvement. Official explanation: trainer's rep said, regarding apparent improvement in form, that the filly had been slow to mature and appeared to have been better suited by the polytrack surface. (tchd 20-1)
Captain Loui(IRE) gave it a good shot with cheekpieces reapplied under an attacking ride. He won a seller/claimer during the summer and could be closing in on a first nursery success. Official explanation: jockey said gelding hung right (tchd 17-2)
Reason To Believe(IRE) showed improvement and a good attitude when winning a 6f nursery at Hamilton last month. He gave it a decent try in a bid to defy a 5lb rise up in trip on Polytrack but couldn't find overdrive when he needed it and may ideally appreciate a return to slow turf. (op 7-4 tchd 15-8)
Orange Ketchup(IRE) put in a much better effort to bounce back from a couple of no-shows in nurseries on turf. (op 18-1 tchd 20-1)
All The Evil(IRE) couldn't work his way into it and finished well held. (op 25-1 tchd 33-1)
Dunmore Boy(IRE) was closer to the pace than the winner turning in but his effort flattened out quite quickly. He has been well held in three nurseries and is not progressing. (op 8-1 tchd 9-1 and 6-1)
Alfraamsey Official explanation: jockey said colt hung right
Commercial(IRE) was a market mover during the morning but he compromised his chance by racing freely and dropped away on this step up to 7f.

6695 BETTING.COM "HOW'S YA FATHER" NURSERY (DIV II) 7f 32y(P)

6:10 (6:11) (Class 6) (0-65,65) 2-Y-O £1,364 (£403; £201) Stalls High

Form RPR

040 1 **Azlaa**[20] 6155 2-9-6 **64** RichardHughes 11 72
(R Hannon) *hld up: rdn over 3f out: hdwy whn nt clr run briefly over 2f out: prog to ld ins fnl f: r.o: pushed out and on top towards fin* **11/4**[1]

2040 2 1 ¼ **Shaabek (IRE)**[31] 5807 2-9-5 **63** SamHitchcott 6 68
(M R Channon) *chsd ldrs over 5f out: chal 2f out: rdn over 1f out: stl ev ch ins fnl f: nt pce of wnr towards fin* **28/1**

030 3 1 ¼ **Educated Son**[51] 5170 2-9-3 **61** ShaneKelly 2 63
(W R Muir) *led: hdd over 5f out: chsd ldr after tl regained ld over 2f out: hdd ins fnl f: no ex fnl 75yds* **28/1**

403 4 *shd* **Mega Mount (IRE)**[20] 6162 2-9-6 **64** (v[1]) JimCrowley 10 66
(R M Beckett) *bhd: hdwy on outer 3f out: rdn to chse ldrs over 1f out: styd on ins fnl f: nt quite pce of ldrs* **13/2**[2]

0452 5 1 ¾ **Barista (IRE)**[10] 6412 2-9-7 **65** CathyGannon 5 62
(M R Channon) *midfield: u.p 2f out: hdwy on inner over 1f out to chse ldrs: nvr able to rch ldrs* **11/4**[1]

0433 6 1 ¾ **Eyes On**[35] 5682 2-9-7 **65** DaneO'Neill 1 58
(P J McBride) *chsd ldrs: pushed along 2f out: rdn over 1f out: one pce fnl f* **8/1**[3]

0006 7 ½ **C P Joe (IRE)**[62] 4783 2-9-5 **63** TomEaves 9 55
(Paul Green) *midfield: hdwy and effrt over 3f out: sn chsd ldrs: one pce fnl f* **40/1**

404 8 3 ½ **Phoenix Flame**[22] 6071 2-8-12 **61** DeclanCannon(5) 7 44
(A J McCabe) *in rr: struggling 4f out: nvr rchd chalng position* **22/1**

060 9 2 ¼ **Aramid (IRE)**[67] 4622 2-9-2 **60** RobertWinston 3 38
(B W Hills) *missed break: bhd: struggling 3f out: nvr on terms w ldrs* **12/1**

3555 10 4 ½ **Loch Ordie**[21] 6129 2-9-2 **60** (b[1]) AdamKirby 8 27
(M G Quinlan) *bustled along leaving stalls: gd hdwy to ld over 5f out: rdn and hdd over 2f out: wknd over 1f out* **12/1**

5600 11 14 **Hal Of A Lover**[15] 6300 2-9-4 **62** PaulHanagan 4 —
(R A Fahey) *broke wl: chsd ldrs: lost pl qckly over 6f out: sn in midfield: outpcd 3f out: bhd after* **11/1**

1m 29.77s (0.17) **Going Correction** -0.075s/f (Stan) **11** Ran SP% **115.2**
Speed ratings (Par 93): **96,94,93,93,91 89,88,84,81,76 60**
toteswingers:1&2:£17.90, 1&3:£8.30, 2&3:£68.40 CSF £96.78 CT £1809.60 TOTE £4.70: £1.50, £12.20, £10.20; EX 85.40.
Owner Mohammed Sultan **Bred** James Robert Mitchell **Trained** East Everleigh, Wilts

FOCUS
They went a fast and furious pace in this second division of a modest nursery.

NOTEBOOK
Azlaa ◆ had improved with each of three runs in maidens and was prominent in the betting on this nursery debut. There were severe warning signs when she looked in trouble and going nowhere before the final turn but she knuckled down well and surged through the pack to eventually score with something in hand after hitting 23-1 in-running. She is a half-sister to very smart 7f winner The Cheka and could be capable of further progress for the Hannon team, particularly back at 1m. (op 5-2 tchd 3-1)
Shaabek(IRE) did well to hang on for second after racing near the brutal pace. He has struggled to build on his second in an Ascot maiden in July but this was a better effort off a sliding mark. (tchd 33-1)
Educated Son made an enterprising move around the final bend but was reeled in. He showed mixed form in three fast-ground maidens but this was an encouraging AW/nursery debut. (op 25-1)
Mega Mount(IRE) stayed on steadily out wide but couldn't land a telling blow in a bid to justify market support. However, this was a promising run in a first-time visor by a runner who is bred to appreciate a stiffer test. (op 8-1 tchd 11-2)
Barista(IRE), a reliable 6f-1m performer, ran a decent enough race but couldn't find a decisive finishing kick. (tchd 3-1)
Eyes On moved well for a long way before her effort petered out. She may not have got home and this sister to a pair of 6f 2-y-o winners could be suited by a return to sprinting. (op 7-1 tchd 13-2)
Hal Of A Lover Official explanation: jockey said colt was unsteerable

6696 DSL BETTING FREEPHONE 0800 521924 MEDIAN AUCTION MAIDEN STKS 7f 32y(P)

6:40 (6:40) (Class 5) 3-4-Y-O £2,115 (£624; £312) Stalls High

Form RPR

434 1 **Compton Park**[136] 2393 3-9-3 76 ShaneKelly 8 68
(W J Knight) *racd keenly: chsd ldrs: led on inner over 1f out: r.o to draw clr ins fnl f: in command after: eased towards fin* **6/4**[1]

0/0- 2 4 **Tax Dodger (IRE)**[319] 7416 4-9-5 49 PaulMulrennan 4 57
(P Cluskey, Ire) *led for 1f: chsd ldr after: u.p over 1f out: no ch w wnr fnl f* **20/1**

0360 3 3 ½ **Anaya**[20] 6165 3-8-12 57 (b[1]) NeilCallan 3 43
(D Bourton) *busled along early: led after 1f: rdn and hdd over 1f out: btn after* **5/1**[3]

6 4 *nk* **My Name Is Bert**[13] 6332 4-9-5 0 CathyGannon 10 47
(Lucinda Featherstone) *dwlt: sn chsd ldrs: pushed along over 3f out: rdn over 2f out: one pce over 1f out* **20/1**

2242 5 4 ½ **Ezra Church (IRE)**[107] 3285 3-9-3 75 GrahamGibbons 11 35
(T D Barron) *midfield: u.p and outpcd 3f out: nvr able to chal* **9/4**[2]

0000 6 1 ½ **Devon Diva**[99] 3559 4-8-7 29 RichardRowe(7) 6 26
(M Hill) *in rr: sme hdwy u.p over 2f out: nvr threatened ldrs* **100/1**

6400 7 ¾ **Bedouin Princess (IRE)**[10] 6415 3-8-9 49 (p) AmyRyan(3) 5 24
(Lucinda Featherstone) *in tch: rdn over 2f out: wknd over 1f out* **50/1**

0430 8 5 **Kalahari Desert (IRE)**[39] 5548 3-9-0 55 MichaelStainton(3) 2 15
(R M Whitaker) *midfield: u.p and outpcd over 2f out: nvr on terms* **9/1**

00- 9 *nk* **Northern Champ (IRE)**[84] 4073 4-9-5 43 SilvestreDeSousa 7 14
(Patrick G Kelly, Ire) *shuffled bk after 1f: in rr after: struggling 4f out: nvr a danger* **16/1**

0 10 1 ¾ **Bigern**[54] 5065 3-8-10 0 JosephYoung(7) 1 9
(M Mullineaux) *towards rr: toiling fnl 3f* **100/1**

00 11 15 **Chateau Galliard (IRE)**[41] 5493 4-8-12 0 (p) JessicaSteven(7) 9 —
(T T Clement) *racd in rr: toiling fnl 3f* **100/1**

1m 29.05s (-0.55) **Going Correction** -0.075s/f (Stan)
WFA 3 from 4yo 2lb **11** Ran SP% **117.8**
Speed ratings (Par 103): **100,95,91,91,85 84,83,77,77,75 58**
toteswingers:1&2:£11.10, 1&3:£2.70, 2&3:£12.10 CSF £39.75 TOTE £2.20: £1.10, £16.30, £1.70; EX 56.70.
Owner Mrs P G M Jamison **Bred** David Jamison Bloodstock **Trained** Patching, W Sussex
■ Stewards' Enquiry : Jessica Steven two-day ban: careless riding (Oct 21-22)

FOCUS
There was little strength in depth in this modest auction maiden. It was run at a solid pace and they finished well strung out.
Kalahari Desert(IRE) Official explanation: jockey said gelding ran too free
Northern Champ(IRE) Official explanation: jockey said gelding suffered interference in running

6697 GTECH G2 SPORTS BETTING MEDIAN AUCTION MAIDEN STKS 5f 216y(P)

7:10 (7:11) (Class 6) 2-Y-O £1,706 (£503; £252) Stalls Low

Form RPR

52 1 **Mon Visage**[24] 6034 2-8-12 0 TedDurcan 5 74
(C F Wall) *racd keenly: trckd ldrs: effrt to chse ldr over 1f out: r.o ins fnl f to ld towards fin* **5/4**[1]

5 2 *nk* **Khaleeji**[20] 6145 2-9-3 0 DaneO'Neill 2 78
(J W Hills) *midfield: hdwy on inner over 2f out: led wl over 1f out: sn rdn: hdd towards fin* **5/1**[3]

0 3 ½ **Blowing Bubbles (USA)**[8] 6451 2-8-12 0 PaulHanagan 8 72+
(B J Meehan) *ponied to s: racd keenly in midfield: effrt and hdwy to chse ldrs wl over 1f out: r.o and gng on at fin* **8/1**

4 2 ½ **Lady Mango (IRE)** 2-8-12 0 LukeMorris 9 64
(R A Harris) *chsd ldrs: outpcd over 2f out: rallied to chse ldrs over 1f out: one pce and no further imp fnl 100yds* **18/1**

5660 5 9 **Illmindu (IRE)**[17] 6259 2-8-12 50 CathyGannon 1 37
(B R Millman) *w ldr over 4f out: rdn over 1f out: sn wknd* **33/1**

05 6 1 ¾ **Jahanara (IRE)**[17] 6248 2-8-12 0 RichardHughes 11 32
(R Hannon) *led: rdn and hdd wl over 1f out: sn wknd* **4/1**[2]

0 7 12 **My Delirium**[30] 5835 2-8-12 0 JimCrowley 10 —
(R M Beckett) *towards rr: struggling 3f out: nvr on terms* **10/1**

0 8 2 **Act Of Faith (IRE)**[21] 6118 2-8-12 0 FergusSweeney 3 —
(J A Osborne) *hld up: rdn and outpcd over 2f out: nvr on terms* **66/1**

0 9 *shd* **Primo Muscovado**[59] 4909 2-9-3 0 SamHitchcott 7 —
(M Mullineaux) *sn outpcd and bhd: nvr on terms* **100/1**

10 1 ¾ **Ladydolly** 2-8-12 0 TomEaves 6 —
(R Brotherton) *missed break: a outpcd and bhd* **66/1**

1m 15.2s (0.20) **Going Correction** -0.075s/f (Stan) **10** Ran SP% **113.5**
Speed ratings (Par 93): **95,94,93,90,78 76,60,57,57,55**
toteswingers:1&2:£2.20, 1&3:£2.70, 2&3:£8.00 CSF £7.32 TOTE £1.90: £1.10, £1.10, £6.90; EX 7.80.

Owner D S Lee **Bred** Lilac Bloodstock & Redmyre Bloodstock **Trained** Newmarket, Suffolk

FOCUS

An uncompetitive maiden. The early tempo was steady but the pace gradually quickened.

NOTEBOOK

Mon Visage set the standard on her short head defeat in a 6f Redcar maiden on her second start, form which had been franked by the third and fourth winning next time. She was a bit keen early on but gradually settled just behind the pace and showed a professional attitude to wear down the runner-up in the closing stages. She is a likeable type with scope who should have more to offer but her future will depend on what mark she receives for nurseries. (tchd 11-8)

Khaleeji made a strong move against the far rail early in the straight but he was just pegged back by the favourite. He was a keeping on fifth on 6f Newbury debut last month and built on that with this promising and fluent display under a closing ride. Another step forward looks likely next time and he should be able strike in similar company. (tchd 9-2 and 11-2)

Blowing Bubbles(USA) was beaten a long way on 7f debut at Kempton last week but she left that form well behind with a fast-finishing third after being forced to switch wide. An $80,000 filly who is a half-sister to a smart US dirt miler, she could take some stopping in a similar race next time. (op 15-2 tchd 17-2)

Lady Mango(IRE), a 6,000euros half-sister to a smart prolific winner at around 1m in US, showed a fair bit of promise on debut, particularly as she was keen early on and forced wide for most of the way. (op 33-1)

Jahanara(IRE) showed quite a bit of promise in two previous starts at Ascot and Kempton but went out very quickly under a prominent ride this time. Official explanation: jockey said filly stopped quickly (tchd 7-2)

6698 MRG MIRAGE H'CAP — 1m 4f 50y(P)

7:40 (7:42) (Class 4) (0-85,85) 3-Y-O — **£3,594** (£1,069; £534; £266) **Stalls** Low

Form				RPR
0054	1		**Lovers Causeway (USA)**[13] 6331 3-8-11 **75**.....(b) JoeFanning 6 (M Johnston) *midfield: hdwy 3f out: chalng 2f out: led over 1f out: r.o ins fnl f: wl on top cl home* **13/2**	85
5040	2	1 1/2	**Tominator**[53] 5121 3-9-7 **85**..... GrahamGibbons 3 (R Hollinshead) *racd keenly in midfield: hdwy 2f out: chsd wnr over 1f out: nt qckn and hld towards fin* **16/1**	93
1645	3	2	**Sing Sweetly**[10] 6428 3-9-5 **83**..... PaulHanagan 4 (G A Butler) *racd keenly: hld up: hdwy to chse ldrs over 3f out: rdn and nt qckn over 1f out: styd on to chse front 2 ins fnl f: no real imp* **9/2**[2]	88
4244	4	3 1/4	**Shelfah (IRE)**[15] 6282 3-8-12 **76**..... NeilCallan 8 (M A Jarvis) *prom: led 3f out: rdn and hdd over 1f out: wknd ins fnl f* **5/1**[3]	76
-463	5	2 1/2	**Ertiyaad**[20] 6166 3-8-7 **71**..... TadhgO'Shea 1 (Sir Michael Stoute) *led early: remained prom: regained ld after 4f: hdd 3f out: wknd over 1f out* **8/1**	67
5310	6	1 3/4	**Aquarius Star (IRE)**[26] 5972 3-9-0 **78**..... DaneO'Neill 2 (Pat Eddery) *bmpd s: hld up: rdn over 1f out: nvr able to chal* **16/1**	72
1410	7	4 1/2	**Line Of Duty (IRE)**[33] 5747 3-9-6 **84**..... PJMcDonald 9 (G A Swinbank) *sn led at gd pce: hdd after 4f: remained cl up: u.p 4f out: sn wknd* **15/2**	71
1342	8	shd	**Heart Of Hearts**[15] 6282 3-9-2 **80**..... IanMongan 7 (H R A Cecil) *in tch: chalng 3f out: wknd over 1f out* **4/1**[1]	67
210	9	12	**Baltimore Clipper (USA)**[9] 6448 3-9-4 **82**.....(t) RichardHughes 5 (P F I Cole) *hld up: rdn and hdwy to chse ldrs over 3f out: wknd 2f out: heavily eased ins fnl f* **15/2**	51

2m 37.96s (-3.14) **Going Correction** -0.075s/f (Stan) 9 Ran SP% 114.6

Speed ratings (Par 103): **107,106,104,102,100 99,96,96,88**

toteswingers::1&2:£30.40, 1&3:£8.90, 2&3:£13.20 CSF £101.87 CT £514.72 TOTE £9.20: £2.10, £10.60, £2.00; EX 177.50.

Owner Crone Stud Farms Ltd **Bred** Skara Glen Stables **Trained** Middleham Moor, N Yorks

FOCUS

A decent handicap run at a steady pace. The runners finished fairly strung out.

Heart Of Hearts Official explanation: jockey said filly hung left in back straight

Baltimore Clipper(USA) Official explanation: jockey said colt lost its action

6699 HOTEL & CONFERENCING AT WOLVERHAMPTON CLAIMING STKS — 1m 4f 50y(P)

8:10 (8:10) (Class 6) 3-Y-O+ — **£1,706** (£503; £252) **Stalls** Low

Form				RPR
3513	1		**Talenti (IRE)**[13] 6322 7-9-6 68.....(t) DaneO'Neill 7 (Mrs Lawney Hill) *chsd clr ldrs: rdn 3f out: abt 4 l adrift of front pair 1f out: styd on and clsd ins fnl f: got up fnl strides* **11/4**[2]	74
3400	2	1/2	**Free Tussy (ARG)**[10] 6428 6-9-12 75.....(bt) GeorgeBaker 8 (G L Moore) *hld up bhd: hdwy over 3f out: chsd ldr over 2f out: edgd lft and moved upsides to chal strly ins fnl f: outstyd by wnr and hld fnl strides* **11/1**	79
2	3	nse	**Mongoose Alert (IRE)**[199] 963 8-9-6 0..... StevieDonohoe 5 (W J Musson) *midfield: hdwy over 4f out: led over 2f out: rdn over 1f out: strly pressed and jnd ins fnl f: hdd and hld fnl strides* **13/2**	73
5006	4	12	**Nevada Desert (IRE)**[17] 6243 10-9-2 60..... MichaelStainton(3) 4 (R M Whitaker) *dwlt: hld up: u.p over 2f out: nvr able to get on terms w ldrs* **14/1**	54
4504	5	2	**Dunaskin (IRE)**[12] 6213 10-9-7 59.....(b) GrahamGibbons 2 (R C Guest) *led: clr after 3f tl over 3f out: hdd over 2f out: wknd over 1f out* **5/1**[3]	53
6620	6	1/2	**Paktolos (FR)**[67] 4619 7-9-8 84.....(p) RobertWinston 3 (John A Harris) *midfield: pushed along over 3f out: sn outpcd: toiling under 2f out* **15/8**[1]	53
030/	7	1 1/2	**Babe Maccool (IRE)**[18] 5299 8-9-2 67.....(v) GregFairley 6 (D E Pipe) *chsd clr ldr tl over 3f out: wknd 2f out* **33/1**	45
00	8	38	**Nobbys Girl**[8] 6450 5-9-0 0..... RobertLButler(3) 1 (M S Tuck) *stdd s: hld up: rdn 4f out: lost tch 3f out: t.o* **100/1**	—

2m 40.59s (-0.51) **Going Correction** -0.075s/f (Stan) 8 Ran SP% 110.4

Speed ratings (Par 101): **98,97,97,89,88 87,86,61**

toteswingers:1&2:£4.20, 1&3:£3.60, 2&3:£4.40 CSF £30.19 TOTE £3.70: £1.20, £1.30, £1.20; EX 29.60.

Owner Alan Hill **Bred** Watership Down Stud **Trained** Aston Rowant, Oxon

FOCUS

A fair claimer run at a strong pace. There was an exciting three-way-finish and a huge gap back to the rest.

Paktolos(FR) Official explanation: vet said gelding had a breathing problem

6700 SIS THE NUMBER 1 INDUSTRY SUPPLIER H'CAP — 5f 20y(P)

8:40 (8:41) (Class 5) (0-70,70) 3-Y-O+ — **£2,115** (£624; £312) **Stalls** Low

Form				RPR
24	1		**Angelo Poliziano**[15] 6299 4-9-3 **66**.....(p) SilvestreDeSousa 6 (Mrs A Duffield) *in tch: rdn over 1f out: r.o to ld ins fnl f: in command towards fin* **5/1**[2]	77
5624	2	2 1/4	**Riflessione**[14] 6310 4-9-7 **70**.....(p) JoeFanning 8 (R A Harris) *a.p: rdn and nt qckn over 1f out: styd on ins fnl f: nt pce of wnr* **12/1**	73
1000	3	3/4	**Bahamian Ballet**[22] 6073 8-9-7 **70**..... GrahamGibbons 2 (E S McMahon) *chsd ldrs: rdn over 1f out: styd on ins fnl f: gng on at fin* **14/1**	70
0312	4	nk	**Island Legend (IRE)**[45] 5368 4-9-6 **69**.....(p) LiamKeniry 5 (J M Bradley) *led: kicked abt 3 l clr over 1f out: hdd ins fnl f: no ex towards fin* **11/2**[3]	68
232	5	3/4	**Elhamri**[12] 6368 6-9-6 **69**..... RichardHughes 13 (S Kirk) *in rr: rdn over 1f out: styd on ins fnl f: nrst fin* **11/2**[3]	65
3506	6	nk	**Perlachy**[19] 6208 6-9-3 **66**.....(v) LukeMorris 1 (D Shaw) *midfield: rdn and hdwy on inner to chse ldrs over 1f out: styd on same pce ins fnl f* **20/1**	61
0002	7	nk	**La Capriosa**[5] 6572 4-9-5 **68**..... RobertWinston 4 (J A Glover) *midfield: effrt whn nt clr run jst over 1f out: nt pce to chal ins fnl f* **11/1**	62
6230	8	hd	**Argentine (IRE)**[7] 6492 6-9-7 **70**.....(b) PaulHanagan 9 (J A McShane) *midfield: rdn and outpcd over 1f out: no imp after* **12/1**	64
3132	9	nk	**Forever's Girl**[15] 6295 4-9-2 **65**..... PaulMulrennan 3 (G R Oldroyd) *in rr: trying to keep on whn swtchd lft 1f out: unable to rch ldrs* **4/1**[1]	57
0000	10	1	**Canadian Danehill (IRE)**[12] 6374 8-9-7 **70**.....(p) NeilCallan 7 (R M H Cowell) *chsd ldr to 2f out: rdn over 1f out: wknd ins fnl f* **11/1**	59
4460	11	4 1/2	**Special Quality (USA)**[23] 6064 3-9-3 **66**.....(p) ShaneKelly 11 (R M H Cowell) *a bhd* **40/1**	39
6352	12	2 1/4	**Secret Venue**[15] 6299 4-9-4 **67**.....(v) DarryllHolland 10 (Jedd O'Keeffe) *a bhd* **20/1**	32

61.55 secs (-0.75) **Going Correction** -0.075s/f (Stan) 12 Ran SP% 118.1

Speed ratings (Par 103): **103,99,98,97,96 96,95,95,94,93 85,82**

toteswingers:1&2:£17.70, 1&3:£17.10, 2&3:£29.50 CSF £61.75 CT £806.91 TOTE £4.30: £2.30, £6.20, £5.90; EX 81.20.

Owner Middleham Park Racing XXVIII **Bred** Bumble Bs, C Liesack & Mrs S Nicholls **Trained** Constable Burton, N Yorks

FOCUS

A competitive handicap, eight of the runners had finished in the frame on their previous start.

Forever's Girl Official explanation: jockey said filly missed the break

6701 MRG'S DAILY FORM H'CAP — 1m 141y(P)

9:10 (9:10) (Class 4) (0-80,84) 3-Y-O+ — **£3,594** (£1,069; £534; £266) **Stalls** Low

Form				RPR
4050	1		**Robust Wish (USA)**[10] 6430 3-9-5 **78**.....(b) NeilCallan 6 (B J Meehan) *in tch: effrt whn carried rt over 1f out: sn led: r.o ins fnl f: won gng away* **40/1**	92
203	2	3 1/4	**Akhmatova**[10] 6428 3-9-6 **79**..... RichardHughes 3 (G A Butler) *midfield: rdn and hdwy over 1f out: ev ch ent fnl f: nt pce of wnr after* **7/2**[1]	86
0022	3	shd	**Willow Dancer (IRE)**[9] 6444 6-9-5 **74**.....(p) AdamKirby 13 (W R Swinburn) *chsd ldr: rdn and chalng whn carried rt over 1f out: nt qckn ins fnl f* **7/2**[1]	81
2604	4	2	**Standpoint**[20] 6167 4-9-10 **79**..... GrahamGibbons 1 (R Hollinshead) *chsd ldrs: rdn and ev ch ent fnl f: no ex fnl 100yds* **8/1**[3]	82
4500	5	1	**Charlie Smirke (USA)**[22] 6091 4-9-8 **77**..... GeorgeBaker 12 (G L Moore) *midfield: rdn over 1f out: hung lft sltly ins fnl f: kpt on: nt pce to trble ldrs* **20/1**	77
-202	6	1 1/2	**Aultcharn (FR)**[52] 5150 3-9-5 **78**.....(b[1]) ShaneKelly 4 (B J Meehan) *led: rdn and edgd rt over 1f out: sn hdd: wknd fnl 100yds* **8/1**[3]	75
3001	7	1	**Hidden Glory**[10] 6430 3-9-4 **84** 6ex..... JamesRogers(7) 8 (Pat Eddery) *awkward s: midfield: rdn and outpcd over 2f out: kpt on ins fnl f: no imp on ldrs* **5/1**[2]	79
0000	8	3 3/4	**Stevie Gee (IRE)**[8] 6478 6-9-6 **75**.....(p) PaulHanagan 9 (Ian Williams) *chsd ldrs tl rdn and wknd over 1f out* **12/1**	62
000	9	nk	**Hurricane Hymnbook (USA)**[17] 6252 5-9-8 **77**..... StevieDonohoe 7 (W J Musson) *hld up: u.p over 2f out: nvr on terms* **40/1**	64
0500	10	1 1/4	**Exceedingly Bold**[30] 5838 3-9-2 **75**..... DarryllHolland 11 (Miss Gay Kelleway) *hld up: u.p over 2f out: nvr on terms* **50/1**	59
0050	11	3/4	**Bond City (IRE)**[12] 6367 8-9-7 **76**..... PaulMulrennan 10 (G R Oldroyd) *midfield: u.p and dropped away over 1f out: outpcd* **40/1**	59
6100	12	3 1/4	**Ahlawy (IRE)**[19] 6185 7-9-9 **78**.....(t) LeeVickers 5 (F Sheridan) *missed break: in rr: pushed along over 3f out: nvr on terms* **28/1**	54
-050	13	23	**Cool Hand Jake**[17] 6252 4-9-7 **76**..... FergusSweeney 2 (P J Makin) *a bhd: toiling over 2f out: nvr on terms* **12/1**	3

1m 49.21s (-1.29) **Going Correction** -0.075s/f (Stan)

WFA 3 from 4yo+ 4lb 13 Ran SP% 116.2

Speed ratings (Par 105): **102,99,99,97,96 95,94,90,90,89 88,85,65**

toteswingers:1&2:£17.30, 1&3:£34.30, 2&3:£2.80 CSF £164.82 CT £658.69 TOTE £31.60: £11.30, £1.70, £1.10; EX 235.80 Place 6 £66.84, Place 5 £43.93..

Owner Thomas Conway **Bred** Dinwiddie Farm **Trained** Manton, Wilts

FOCUS

A competitive handicap run at a fair pace.

Aultcharn(FR) Official explanation: jockey said gelding hung right

Ahlawy(IRE) Official explanation: jockey said gelding was slowly away

T/Plt: £235.30 to a £1 stake. Pool of £66,260.59 - 205.52 winning tickets T/Qpdt: £17.70 to a £1 stake. Pool of £10,546.39 - 440.20 winning tickets DO

6551 SAINT-CLOUD (L-H)

Thursday, October 7

OFFICIAL GOING: Turf: heavy

6702a PRIX THOMAS BRYON (GROUP 3) (2YO) (TURF) — 1m

1:40 (12:00) 2-Y-O — **£35,398** (£14,159; £10,619; £7,079; £3,539)

			RPR
1		**Maxios**[19] 2-8-11 0..... Christophe-PatriceLemaire 4 (J E Pease, France) *racd in 3rd on outside: rdn 2f out: no immediate rspnse but qcknd wl ins fnl f and chal for ld 100yds out: got up to win almost on line* **6/5**[1]	104
2	shd	**Private Jet (FR)**[20] 6173 2-8-11 0..... OlivierPeslier 1 (H-A Pantall, France) *led fr s: rdn 2f out: r.o wl fnl f: hdd almost on line* **11/2**[3]	104

3 2 ½ **Grand Vent (IRE)**[24] 2-8-11 0 .... MickaelBarzalona 3 99
(A Fabre, France) *racd in 2nd on ins: rdn 2f out: no ex: styd on fnl f: no threat to ldrs* **44/5**

4 6 **Shooting Gallery**[27] 5916 2-8-11 0 .... AhmedAjtebi 5 85
(Mahmood Al Zarooni) *racd towards rr: rdn 2f out: no ex: styd on fnl f: tk 4th in fnl strides* **44/5**

5 ¾ **Pontenuovo (FR)**[46] 5347 2-8-11 0 .... ChristopheSoumillon 6 84
(Y De Nicolay, France) *racd towards rr: followed eventual wnr in st: rdn 2f out: no ex fnl f* **7/2**[2]

1m 48.3s (0.80) 5 Ran SP% **103.5**
WIN (incl. 1 euro stake): 2.20. PLACES: 1.80, 2.40. SF: 12.60.
Owner Niarchos Family **Bred** Suc S Niarchos **Trained** Chantilly, France

NOTEBOOK
Maxios, a half-brother to 2004 Arc winner Bago, got up right on the line and has the look of a Classic contender for next year. If he has another race this season it will be in either the Criterium International over this C&D, a race Bago won in 2003, or the longer Criterium de Saint-Cloud.

6703 - (Foreign Racing) - See Raceform Interactive

6392 MUSSELBURGH (R-H)
Friday, October 8

OFFICIAL GOING: Good to soft (soft in places on straight course; 5.5)
Wind: Light behind Weather: Cloudy

6704 EUROPEAN BREEDERS' FUND MAIDEN STKS — 7f 30y
2:20 (2:21) (Class 5) 2-Y-O £3,238 (£963; £481; £240) **Stalls** High

Form				RPR
0	**1**		**Conducting**[21] 6146 2-9-3 0 .... PaulMulrennan 7 (B J Meehan) *mde all: rdn along 2f out: drvn ent fnl f: kpt on* **5/2**[1]	78
0	**2**	1 ¾	**Home Office**[10] 6443 2-9-3 0 .... JoeFanning 3 (M Johnston) *trckd wnr: cl up 1/2-way: chal over 2f out: rdn wl over 1f out and ev ch tl drvn and no ex ins fnl f* **14/1**	73
4632	**3**	3 ¼	**Sabratha (IRE)**[22] 6129 2-8-12 59 .... DavidAllan 2 (Miss L A Perratt) *dwlt: sn trcking ldrs on outer: rdn along to chse ldng pair 2f out: sn edgd rt and no imp appr fnl f* **10/1**	60
6653	**4**	nse	**Icy Blue**[14] 6325 2-9-3 64 .... FrannyNorton 6 (R M Whitaker) *chsd ldrs: hdwy 3f out: rdn over 2f out: sn no imp* **9/1**	65
62	**5**	3 ¼	**Qenaa**[72] 4471 2-8-12 0 .... TadhgO'Shea 4 (M Johnston) *in rr: pushed along 1/2-way: rdn and sme hdwy over 2f out: n.d* **11/4**[2]	52
2	**6**	3 ¾	**In Babylon (GER)**[14] 6333 2-9-3 0 .... RichardKingscote 1 (Tom Dascombe) *chsd ldrs: rdn along 3f out: sn btn* **3/1**[3]	47
	7	1 ¼	**Lady Intrigue (IRE)** 2-8-9 0 .... BarryMcHugh(3) 9 (R A Fahey) *dwlt: a towards rr* **16/1**	39
0	**8**	1 ¼	**Cannon Bolt (IRE)**[17] 6264 2-9-3 0 .... (t) PhillipMakin 8 (R Bastiman) *plld hrd: chsd ldng pair on inner: rdn along 3f out: wknd 2f out* **150/1**	41
5	**9**	3 ½	**Gnr Steamtrain (IRE)**[14] 6324 2-8-12 0 .... LeeTopliss(5) 5 (R A Fahey) *a in rr* **33/1**	32

1m 33.3s (4.30) **Going Correction** +0.375s/f (Good) 9 Ran SP% **115.5**
Speed ratings (Par 95): **90,88,84,84,80 76,74,73,69**
toteswingers:1&2:£5.30, 1&3:£8.50, 2&3:£18.10 CSF £38.78 TOTE £3.70: £1.30, £5.40, £3.10; EX 36.00.
Owner Mr & Mrs David Brown **Bred** David J Brown **Trained** Manton, Wilts

FOCUS
The ground was slightly easier than advertised and was officially good to soft, soft in places on the straight course. Few could be fancied in this maiden and a modest early pace meant those that raced handily were at an advantage, whilst a few pulled too hard. The winning time was 5.5secs outside standard, which suggests the ground was soft and that was backed up by the jockeys.

NOTEBOOK
Conducting, a rare runner at the track for the Meehan stable and well backed, was up a furlong after running green on his Newbury debut. Given a positive ride from the start, the runner-up provided the only meaningful challenge to him passing the 2f pole, but he soon saw that off and was well on top at the line. This is only ordinary form, but he should progress further. (op 3-1)
Home Office, last of 15 on his Newbury debut ten days earlier, looked the stable's second string here but he improved plenty from that first run, and ended up performing much the better of the Johnston pair. Always in about the same place despite taking a grip early, he tried his best to overhaul the winner but lacked the pace to do so. He is bred to get further and looks one for handicaps over 1m-plus in due course. (op 16-1)
Sabratha(IRE), making her debut for the yard after just getting touched off in a Yarmouth selling nursery for Barney Curley, ran creditably but her official mark of 59 does little for the form. (op 9-1 tchd 11-1)
Icy Blue, a fair third off a mark of 65 in a soft-ground Haydock nursery last time, made some late progress but he is another with less scope than a few of these. (op 11-1)
Qenaa, not seen since getting touched off in a hot fillies' maiden at Glorious Goodwood, was weak in the market and it soon became obvious why as her rider was getting after her at halfway. The absence suggests that all may not have been well with her since Goodwood, and her rider reported that she was never travelling. Official explanation: jockey said that the filly was never travelling (op 9-4 tchd 15-8 and 3-1 in places)
In Babylon(GER), runner-up to an odds-on Godolphin representative on his Wolverhampton debut, pulled hard early and then found nothing once under pressure 3f from home. This was a step backwards, though his rider reported that he wasn't suited by the ground. Official explanation: jockey that the colt was unsuited by the good to soft, soft in places going (op 10-3)
Lady Intrigue(IRE), a 50,000euros filly out of a winning half-sister to eight other winners, missed the break and looked badly in need of the experience. (op 20-1)
Cannon Bolt(IRE) Official explanation: jockey said that the colt ran too free

6705 JOHN & DEBBIE FORRESTER WEDDING DAY NURSERY — 5f
2:55 (2:55) (Class 5) (0-75,75) 2-Y-O £3,238 (£963; £481; £240) **Stalls** Low

Form				RPR
3130	**1**		**Normandy Maid**[38] 5637 2-8-11 68 .... BarryMcHugh(3) 5 (R A Fahey) *prom: cl up 1/2-way: led 1 1/2f out: rdn ins fnl f and kpt on wl* **7/1**	73
552	**2**	nk	**Crimson Knot (IRE)**[13] 6354 2-9-2 75 .... MarkCoumbe(5) 4 (A Berry) *hld up in rr: hdwy 1/2-way: trckd ldrs wl over 1f out: n.m.r ent fnl f: sn rdn to chal and ev ch tl nt qckn nr fin* **15/2**	79
222	**3**	1	**Insolenceofoffice (IRE)**[13] 6369 2-9-4 72 .... PaulMulrennan 6 (Mrs A Duffield) *a.p: effrt 2f out: sn rdn and ev ch tl drvn and one pce ins fnl f* **9/2**[3]	72
1362	**4**	½	**Saxonette**[8] 6489 2-8-7 61 ow1 .... DavidAllan 3 (Miss L A Perratt) *hld up in rr: hdwy 2f out: swtchd lft and rdn over 1f out: kpt on ins fnl f* **6/1**	60
4011	**5**	¾	**Heartbreak**[8] 6489 2-9-2 75 5ex .... LeeTopliss(5) 7 (R A Fahey) *chsd ldrs on outer: rdn along 2f out: drvn over 1f out and kpt on same pce* **4/1**[2]	71
0452	**6**	5	**Guinea Seeker**[3] 6645 2-8-0 57 .... KellyHarrison(3) 2 (T D Easterby) *chsd ldrs: rdn along 2f out: sn wknd* **11/4**[1]	35
4644	**7**	1 ½	**Rothesay Chancer**[8] 6489 2-8-9 63 .... (p) FrannyNorton 8 (J S Goldie) *wnt rt s: a in rr* **16/1**	35
050	**8**	9	**Mr Mo Jo**[44] 5418 2-8-13 67 .... PhillipMakin 1 (R Bastiman) *led: rdn along 2f out: sn hdd & wknd* **40/1**	7

62.15 secs (1.75) **Going Correction** +0.375s/f (Good) 8 Ran SP% **111.7**
Speed ratings (Par 95): **101,100,98,98,96 88,86,72**
toteswingers:1&2:£6.70, 1&3:£7.20, 2&3:£8.30 CSF £55.10 CT £257.84 TOTE £7.80: £2.80, £2.80, £1.40; EX 49.70.
Owner Mrs Sheila Oakes **Bred** Mrs Sheila Oakes **Trained** Musley Bank, N Yorks

FOCUS
An ordinary nursery.

NOTEBOOK
Normandy Maid didn't see out the sixth furlong at Ripon last time, but she had some decent form to her name prior to that and she relished this return to the minimum trip. She proved game after taking over in front around 2f out, and there should be more races to be won with her as a sprinter. (op 17-2 tchd 9-1)
Crimson Knot(IRE), running well off similar marks in nurseries since winning a C&D maiden auction in August, was appearing at this track for the seventh time in an 11-race career. Having become slightly outpaced after breaking well enough, she didn't have much room to play with when trying to get back into the contest inside the last 2f, but it did appear that the gap opened in enough time had she been good enough. (tchd 7-1 and 8-1)
Insolenceofoffice(IRE), making his nursery debut after finishing runner-up in three consecutive maidens, was always up there and had every chance but again fell just short. He doesn't seem to do much wrong. (tchd 4-1 and 5-1)
Saxonette finished well up the rail and ideally needs at least another furlong, but she is already due to go up 3lb which won't help. (op 8-1)
Heartbreak, carrying a 5lb penalty but still 1lb well-in compared with his revised mark, had three of today's rivals behind him in gaining both victories last month. He failed in his hat-trick bid having been handy from the start, though he was rather marooned on the outside of the field. (op 3-1)
Guinea Seeker, beaten under a length off this mark on similar ground over this trip at Catterick three days earlier, found little once off the bridle 2f from home. His rider reported that he ran flat. Official explanation: jockey said that the gelding ran flat (op 3-1 tchd 5-2 and 10-3 in a place)
Rothesay Chancer, who doesn't seem to be progressing and is already due to drop 2lb, had cheekpieces on for the first time but soon became badly outpaced before making some late progress and ideally he needs further. His rider reported that he was denied a clear run. Official explanation: jockey said that the colt was denied a clear run

6706 DUNDAS AND WILSON H'CAP — 5f
3:30 (3:31) (Class 2) (0-100,92) 3-Y-O+
£10,592 (£3,172; £1,586; £793; £396; £198) **Stalls** Low

Form				RPR
2040	**1**		**Beat The Bell**[21] 6142 5-8-13 84 .... PhillipMakin 4 (T D Barron) *trckd ldrs: hdwy over 1f out: nt clr run and swtchd lft ins fnl f: qcknd wl to ld nr fin* **7/2**[1]	92
0400	**2**	hd	**Archers Road (IRE)**[13] 6364 3-9-7 92 .... PaulMulrennan 1 (T D Barron) *prom: cl up 2f out: rdn to ld ent fnl f and edgd lft: sn drvn and hdd nr line* **14/1**	99
3330	**3**	hd	**The Nifty Fox**[21] 6142 6-8-13 84 .... DavidAllan 3 (T D Easterby) *hld up in rr: swtchd markedly rt to outer and hdwy 2f out: rdn to chse ldrs over 1f out: styd on to chal ins fnl f and ev ch tl drvn and nt qckn nr fin* **4/1**[2]	90
2041	**4**	1 ¾	**Noodles Blue Boy**[18] 6256 4-9-1 86 .... FrannyNorton 6 (Ollie Pears) *midfield: rdn along 1/2-way: hdwy to chse ldrs over 1f out: rdn and ch ent fnl f: sn drvn and one pce* **8/1**	86
1140	**5**	hd	**Cayman Fox**[18] 6245 5-8-0 74 oh5 ow1 .... KellyHarrison(3) 10 (Miss L A Perratt) *sn led: rdn wl over 1f out: hdd and n.m.r ent fnl f: sn wknd* **25/1**	73
0150	**6**	hd	**Rasaman (IRE)**[20] 6175 6-9-1 89 .... GaryBartley(3) 2 (J S Goldie) *triggered stall and led early: sn lost pl and outpcd in rr: bhd 1/2-way: sn rdn and styd on fnl f: nrst fin* **9/1**	88
0600	**7**	1	**Look Busy (IRE)**[17] 6265 5-9-2 92 .... SladeO'Hara(5) 8 (A Berry) *dwlt and in rr tl styd on appr fnl f* **16/1**	87
3002	**8**	nse	**Whozthecat (IRE)**[10] 6446 3-8-10 86 .... (v) NeilFarley(5) 7 (D Carroll) *prom: rdn along 2f out: sn edgd lft and wknd over 1f out* **10/1**	81
0666	**9**	1 ¼	**Skylla**[24] 6049 3-8-12 88 .... LeeTopliss(5) 5 (R A Fahey) *awkward s and a in rr* **8/1**	78
0004	**10**	1 ½	**Fol Hollow (IRE)**[13] 6364 5-9-7 92 .... AdrianNicholls 9 (D Nicholls) *chsd ldrs on outer: rdn along 2f out: sn wknd* **15/2**[3]	77

61.43 secs (1.03) **Going Correction** +0.375s/f (Good) 10 Ran SP% **111.7**
Speed ratings (Par 109): **106,105,105,102,102 101,100,100,98,95**
toteswingers:1&2:£15.80, 1&3:£3.30, 2&3:£8.50 CSF £50.72 CT £178.81 TOTE £4.00: £1.60, £4.30, £2.50; EX 40.70.
Owner D Pryde & J Cringan **Bred** D J P Turner **Trained** Maunby, N Yorks

FOCUS
A cracking sprint handicap and a race of changing fortunes. It provided a one-two for trainer David Barron and the runner-up sets the standard.

NOTEBOOK
Beat The Bell had been unlucky over C&D two starts back before finishing third on his side in the Ayr Bronze Cup, so perhaps it wasn't a surprise that he was sent off so well backed. The only anxious moment for his supporters came over a furlong out when he needed to be switched to the stands' rail in order to see daylight, but he took off once there and was always going to get up. He will probably turn out for a race at Doncaster in a few weeks' time before heading out to Dubai. (op 6-1)
Archers Road(IRE), down to a new career-low mark, had a little bit to find with Fol Hollow on recent Haydock running but he reversed the form in no uncertain terms. Always up there, he was only run down by his stablemate very late on and this was a much better effort from him.
The Nifty Fox found 6f too far last time, but has only once finished out of the first four in ten previous outings over C&D, and he maintained that sequence. He looked to have timed his effort just right, but he was racing much further off the stands' rail than the front pair and that may have just counted against him. (tchd 9-2)
Noodles Blue Boy, raised 4lb for his narrow Leicester success, was never too far away and had his chance, but he lacked a finishing kick and has gained all six career successes on stiffer tracks than this. (tchd 13-2)
Cayman Fox seemed to have gone off the boil for her new yard, but having got to the front early she set a strong pace until headed a furlong out. She was 6lb wrong including the overweight, so this was a good effort. (op 18-1)
Rasaman(IRE), 3-6 over C&D this year but still 4lb above his highest winning mark, burst the gates but even so he was soon getting outpaced at the back of the field and his late rally was nowhere near enough. (op 8-1 tchd 10-1 in a place)
Skylla, back to probably her best trip, missed the break and then found herself racing on the wide outside which was probably not ideal. Her rider reported that she had hung right throughout. Official explanation: jockey said that the filly hung right throughout (tchd 9-1)

Fol Hollow(IRE) was disappointing considering he had shown a lot more in his previous start and was down to a mark 1lb lower than when winning at Thirsk in May. Official explanation: the trainer was unable to offer any explanation for the poor performance shown (op 13-2 tchd 6-1)

6707 DONALDSON TIMBER ENGINEERING H'CAP 1m 6f

4:05 (4:06) (Class 5) (0-70,76) 3-Y-O+ **£3,238** (£963; £481; £240) **Stalls** High

Form RPR

0451 **1** **Chookie Hamilton**[12] 6397 6-10-1 **76** 6ex LeeTopliss(5) 1 88
(V P Donoghue) *in tch: hdwy 3f out: rdn to chse ldr wl over 1f out: styd on to ld ent fnl f: drvn out* **5/1[3]**

6111 **2** 1 1/4 **Tobernea (IRE)**[4] 6631 3-9-7 **72** 6ex JoeFanning 8 82
(M Johnston) *led: pushed along 3f out: rdn wl over 1f out: drvn and hdd ent fnl f: kpt on same pce* **1/1[1]**

0021 **3** 2 1/4 **Hong Kong Island (IRE)**[12] 6393 3-8-12 **63** 6ex PaulMulrennan 2 70
(A G Foster) *trckd ldr: effrt over 3f out: rdn along wl over 2f out: drvn wl over 1f out and kpt on same pce* **7/2[2]**

4143 **4** 6 **Oddsmaker (IRE)**[12] 6393 9-9-3 **62** (t) AndrewHeffernan(3) 6 61
(M A Barnes) *trckd ldrs on inner: hdwy and cl up over 4f out: rdn along wl over 2f out: drvn wl over 1f out and grad wknd* **17/2**

13-0 **5** 6 **Toshi (USA)**[25] 6028 8-8-11 **53** FrannyNorton 4 43
(J S Goldie) *t.k.h: in tch: rdn along over 3f out: n.d* **16/1**

4000 **6** 2 3/4 **Goodison Park**[51] 5216 3-7-7 **51** oh6 (p) NoelGarbutt(7) 3 37
(A G Foster) *chsd ldrs: rdn along 4f out: wknd 3f out* **50/1**

5210 **7** 3/4 **Miss Ferney**[36] 5687 6-8-13 **60** NeilFarley(5) 9 45
(A Kirtley) *hld up: a bhd* **25/1**

0450 **8** 5 **Kyber**[15] 4825 9-8-6 **51** oh6 KellyHarrison(3) 5 29
(J S Goldie) *a bhd* **40/1**

3m 7.30s (2.00) **Going Correction** +0.375s/f (Good)
WFA 3 from 4yo+ 9lb **8** Ran SP% **113.5**
Speed ratings (Par 103): **109,108,107,103,100 98,98,95**
toteswingers:1&2:£2.30, 1&3:£2.60, 2&3:£2.00 CSF £10.22 CT £19.02 TOTE £5.40: £1.80, £1.10, £1.10; EX 13.90.
Owner Hamilton Park Members Syndicate **Bred** D And J Raeburn **Trained** Carluke, South Lanarkshire
■ Stewards' Enquiry : Noel Garbutt three-day ban: careless riding (22, 25, 26 Oct)

FOCUS
A decent test in the conditions and they finished well spread out. The winner was better than ever in beating a couple of well-in 3yos.

6708 "PIPPIN, SHE'S ONLY AFTER YOUR MONEY" CLAIMING STKS 5f

4:40 (4:43) (Class 6) 3-Y-O+ **£1,942** (£578; £288; £144) **Stalls** Low

Form RPR

1500 **1** **Lesley's Choice**[18] 6245 4-9-0 73 (v) PaulMulrennan 10 80
(Miss L A Perratt) *cl up on outer: led wl over 1f out: rdn and edgd lft ent fnl f: kpt on* **16/1**

0030 **2** 2 **Wicked Wilma (IRE)**[6] 6572 6-8-7 63 (t) DavidAllan 2 66
(A Berry) *trckd ldrs: hdwy 2f out: swtchd rt and rdn to chse wnr ins fnl f: drvn and one pce towards fin* **9/1**

0016 **3** 1 3/4 **Northern Bolt**[6] 6572 5-8-9 73 ow1 (b) GaryBartley(3) 8 65
(I W McInnes) *s.i.s and bhd: hdwy over 2f out: rdn over 1f out: styd on ins fnl f: nrst fin* **4/1[2]**

00 **4** 1 3/4 **Distant Sun (USA)**[21] 6140 6-8-9 66 LNewman 7 55
(Miss L A Perratt) *in tch: hdwy on outer 2f out: rdn to chse ldrs over 1f out: sn one pce* **33/1**

3105 **5** nk **Mandarin Spirit (IRE)**[35] 5735 10-8-5 69 (b) AndrewHeffernan(3) 6 53
(Miss L A Perratt) *led: rdn along over 2f out: hdd wl over 1f out: grad wknd* **14/1**

2000 **6** 3/4 **Titus Andronicus (IRE)**[21] 6140 4-8-13 79 (p) LeeTopliss(5) 5 61
(R A Fahey) *chsd ldrs: rdn along 2f out: sn wknd* **9/2[3]**

0300 **7** 1 1/4 **Hypnosis**[30] 5855 7-8-6 71 ow2 BarryMcHugh(3) 3 47
(N Wilson) *midfield: rdn along 2f out: n.d* **8/1**

3000 **8** nk **Angelofthenorth**[3] 6644 8-8-0 45 ow1 KellyHarrison(3) 1 40
(C J Teague) *a in rr* **100/1**

0020 **9** 4 1/2 **Sonny Red (IRE)**[13] 6363 6-9-12 94 AdrianNicholls 9 47
(D Nicholls) *s.i.s: a bhd* **13/8[1]**

61.91 secs (1.51) **Going Correction** +0.375s/f (Good) **9** Ran SP% **113.9**
Speed ratings (Par 101): **102,98,96,93,92 91,89,89,81**
toteswingers:1&2:£9.70, 1&3:£7.10, 2&3:£4.40 CSF £148.80 TOTE £16.10: £3.20, £1.80, £1.10; EX 95.90.
Owner Jackton Racing Club **Bred** B C Allen **Trained** East Kilbride, S Lanarks

FOCUS
A fair claimer rendered less competitive when the favourite completely fluffed the start. The winning time was around half a second slower than the earlier Class 2 handicap. There are the usual doubts over the form, and the winner is probably the best guide.
Northern Bolt Official explanation: jockey said that the gelding missed the break
Sonny Red(IRE) Official explanation: jockey said that the gelding missed the break

6709 GORDON & HALLIDAY FLOORING H'CAP 1m

5:10 (5:10) (Class 3) (0-90,90) 3-Y-O+ **£6,476** (£1,927; £963; £481) **Stalls** High

Form RPR

1052 **1** **Amethyst Dawn (IRE)**[13] 6367 4-8-9 **78** DavidAllan 13 87
(T D Easterby) *mde all: rdn clr 2f out: drvn over 1f out: kpt on gamely ins fnl f* **4/1[1]**

1-51 **2** 1 1/4 **Lord Aeryn (IRE)**[22] 6108 3-8-5 **77** TadhgO'Shea 9 83
(R A Fahey) *prom: effrt to chse wnr 2f out: drvn and edgd rt ins fnl f: kpt on same pce* **6/1[2]**

3100 **3** shd **Cockney Class (USA)**[93] 3791 3-9-2 **88** PaulMulrennan 5 94+
(B J Meehan) *hld up towards rr: hdwy on wd outside over 2f out: rdn to chse ldng pair over 1f out: drvn and one pce ins fnl f* **18/1**

3040 **4** 1 1/4 **Rasselas (IRE)**[8] 6510 3-8-11 **83** AdrianNicholls 1 86
(D Nicholls) *chsd ldrs on wd outside: cl up 1/2-way: rdn along over 2f out: drvn wl over 1f out: kpt on same pce fnl f* **6/1[2]**

2412 **5** 3/4 **Sir George (IRE)**[27] 5937 5-9-1 **87** BarryMcHugh(3) 6 88
(Ollie Pears) *trckd ldrs: effrt over 2f out: sn rdn and sltly outpcd: kpt on ins fnl f* **4/1[1]**

0510 **6** 1 1/2 **Dhaular Dhar (IRE)**[20] 6180 8-9-0 **90** PaulNorton(7) 11 88
(J S Goldie) *hld up: hdwy on inner: hdwy to chse ldrs over 2f out: sn rdn and no imp fnl f* **9/1**

1335 **7** 1 3/4 **Avonrose**[35] 5737 3-8-5 **77** FrannyNorton 12 71
(M Johnston) *trckd ldrs on inner: hdwy 3f out: rdn along over 2f out: drvn over 1f out and sn one pce* **12/1**

0500 **8** 3/4 **Espero (IRE)**[22] 6105 4-8-4 **76** oh4 AndrewHeffernan(3) 3 68
(Miss L A Perratt) *a towards rr* **25/1**

3300 **9** 1/2 **Opus Maximus (IRE)**[12] 6391 5-9-4 **87** JoeFanning 10 78
(M Johnston) *nvr bttr than midfield* **16/1**

4410 **10** 2 3/4 **Khandaq (USA)**[12] 6394 3-7-13 **78** (t) ShirleyTeasdale(7) 7 63
(V P Donoghue) *hld up: a in rr* **50/1**

3124 **11** nk **Legal Legacy**[22] 6107 4-8-3 **77** NeilFarley(5) 2 61
(M Dods) *hld up in midfield: effrt and sme hdwy on outer over 3f out: rdn wl over 2f out: sn btn* **8/1[3]**

3-40 **12** 8 **Spinning**[209] 885 7-9-1 **84** (b) PhillipMakin 4 50
(T D Barron) *a bhd* **12/1**

1m 43.13s (1.93) **Going Correction** +0.375s/f (Good)
WFA 3 from 4yo+ 3lb **12** Ran SP% **122.0**
Speed ratings (Par 107): **105,103,103,102,101 100,98,97,97,94 94,86**
toteswingers:1&2:£7.20, 1&3:£20.00, 2&3:£26.20 CSF £28.24 CT £404.44 TOTE £4.80: £1.70, £3.70, £9.40; EX 36.20.
Owner D A West **Bred** W Kane **Trained** Great Habton, N Yorks
■ Stewards' Enquiry : Shirley Teasdale caution: usd whip when out of contention

FOCUS
A decent handicap and they went a fair pace in the conditions. The winner dictated and is rated basically to form.

NOTEBOOK
Amethyst Dawn(IRE) had been put up 2lb for her gritty performance in defeat at Haydock last month, which put her on a career-high mark, but that didn't stop her from being well backed and her rider was positive from the start. She kept on finding plenty to ward off a host of challengers down the home straight, and this was another game performance from her. She seems to handle all types of ground. (op 6-1)
Lord Aeryn(IRE), 6lb higher than when successful on his second start of the season at Ayr last month, was trying 1m for the first time and he ran well, as he was keen enough in a handy position early and came off the bridle a fair way out, but he never stopped trying. The trip didn't appear to be a problem. (tchd 13-2)
Cockney Class(USA), given a break since a couple of moderate efforts in midsummer, was another trying this trip for the first time. He was forced to make his effort very wide once into the home straight, and he deserves credit as he fared much the best of those held up.
Rasselas(IRE), still 7lb higher than for the second of two victories in July, had caught the eye in his previous two outings and he had every chance here as he raced closest to the winner for most of the way, but couldn't quicken sufficiently in the ground when asked. (op 5-1)
Sir George(IRE) is now 5lb above his highest winning mark, but he has been a model of consistency during the past year. Off the bridle over 2f from home, he had his chance but could never pick up the winner, and perhaps the handicapper now has him where he wants him. (tchd 9-2)
Dhaular Dhar(IRE) didn't pick up well enough under pressure and is still 5lb higher than when winning over a furlong further here last month. (op 11-1 tchd 12-1)

6710 SCOTTISH RACING YOUR BETTER BET H'CAP 7f 30y

5:40 (5:42) (Class 5) (0-70,69) 3-Y-O+ **£2,914** (£867; £433; £216) **Stalls** High

Form RPR

0433 **1** **Chookie Avon**[8] 6494 3-8-6 **56** (p) JoeFanning 2 64
(V P Donoghue) *hld up towards rr: gd hdwy over 2f out: rdn to ld over 1f out: drvn ins fnl f and kpt on gamely* **12/1**

5201 **2** nk **Emeralds Spirit (IRE)**[8] 6494 3-8-7 **60** 6ex KellyHarrison(3) 10 67
(J R Weymes) *hld up in rr: hdwy 3f out: rdn 2f out: chal ent fnl f and ev ch tl drvn and no ex towards fin* **8/1**

4151 **3** 1 **Casino Night**[8] 6495 5-9-1 **59** TadhgO'Shea 12 68
(Miss L A Perratt) *s.i.s and bhd: hdwy wl over 2f out: rdn over 1f out: styd on to chse ldng pair ins fnl f: drvn and no imp towards fin* **9/4[1]**

5535 **4** 1 **North Central (USA)**[12] 6393 3-8-6 **63** PaulNorton(7) 6 65
(J S Goldie) *chsd ldrs: rdn along and sltly outpcd over 2f out: kpt on u.p fnl f* **12/1**

4446 **5** hd **No Quarter (IRE)**[9] 6463 3-8-2 **55** oh1 AndrewHeffernan(3) 9 56
(Miss Tracy Waggott) *in tch: hdwy wl over 2f out: rdn wl over 1f out: kpt on ins fnl f* **11/1**

3353 **6** nk **Berbice (IRE)**[12] 6394 5-9-7 **69** PaulMulrennan 5 70
(Miss L A Perratt) *cl up on inner: led 2f out: sn rdn and hdd over 1f out: wknd fnl f* **17/2**

4005 **7** 1/2 **Deadly Secret (USA)**[22] 6107 4-9-0 **67** LeeTopliss(5) 11 67
(R A Fahey) *cl up: rdn along wl over 2f out and ev ch tl drvn wl over 1f out and grad wknd* **7/1[3]**

00 **8** 1 1/4 **Mr Lu**[25] 6026 5-8-9 **60** GaryBartley(3) 3 57
(J S Goldie) *nvr bttr then midfield* **28/1**

2020 **9** 1 **Hits Only Jude (IRE)**[137] 2392 7-8-10 **63** NeilFarley(5) 14 57
(D Carroll) *sn led: rdn along 3f out: hdd 2f out: sn drvn and wknd* **11/2[2]**

4545 **10** 1 1/2 **Spread Boy (IRE)**[21] 6144 3-8-7 **62** MarkCoumbe(5) 8 51
(A Berry) *bhd tl sme late hdwy* **14/1**

0-00 **11** 5 **Blues Jazz**[28] 5925 4-8-6 **57** oh6 ow2 (b[1]) BarryMcHugh(3) 13 33
(J A McShane) *chsd ldrs on inner: rdn along 3f out: wknd over 2f out* **50/1**

0 **12** 30 **Rosbertini**[62] 4823 4-8-9 **57** DavidAllan 7 —
(Miss L A Perratt) *a in rr* **28/1**

1m 32.81s (3.81) **Going Correction** +0.375s/f (Good)
WFA 3 from 4yo+ 2lb **12** Ran SP% **119.5**
Speed ratings (Par 103): **93,92,91,90,90 89,89,87,86,84 79,44**
toteswingers:1&2:£6.70, 1&3:£5.30, 2&3:£3.80. totesuper7: Win: Not won. Place: £845.80. CSF £103.98 CT £303.02 TOTE £14.80: £4.70, £2.10, £1.90; EX 79.30 Place 6 £97.33; Place 5 £41.17.
Owner Raeburn Brick Limited **Bred** D And J Raeburn **Trained** Carluke, South Lanarkshire

FOCUS
A modest handicap, but they went a strong pace with the first three coming from the rear. The first two both improved on what they showed at Ayr, where Emeralds Spirit came out on top.
T/Plt: £180.20 to a £1 stake. Pool of £46,439.33 - 188.12 winning tickets T/Qpdt: £17.10 to a £1 stake. Pool of £5,463.35 - 235.12 winning tickets JR

6694 WOLVERHAMPTON (A.W) (L-H)

Friday, October 8

OFFICIAL GOING: Standard
Wind: Light against Weather: Overcast

6711 TRY BETDAQ FOR AN EXCHANGE MEDIAN AUCTION MAIDEN STKS (DIV I) 7f 32y(P)

5:50 (5:50) (Class 6) 2-Y-O **£1,364** (£403; £201) **Stalls** High

Form RPR

2 **1** **Flag Officer**[14] 6334 2-9-3 0 TedDurcan 6 79
(Saeed Bin Suroor) *s.i.s: rcvrd to ld 6f out: rdn over 1f out: r.o* **8/11[1]**

42 **2** 1/2 **Show Rainbow**[13] 6353 2-8-12 0 RichardHughes 3 73
(M R Channon) *led 1f: chsd wnr: ev ch fr over 2f out: rdn over 1f out: styd on* **7/2[2]**

3 **3** 2 1/4 **Tenby Lady (USA)**[15] 6308 2-8-12 0 SebSanders 8 67
(Sir Mark Prescott) *s.i.s and sn pushed along in rr: hdwy over 2f out: r.o: nt rch ldrs* **7/1**

5 **4** 2 1/2 **Royal Talisman**[18] 6249 2-9-3 0 LiamKeniry 7 66
(Matthew Salaman) *prom: chal over 2f out: no ex fnl f* **40/1**

44 **5** 3 1/4 **Entrance**[18] 6247 2-8-12 0 WilliamBuick 2 53
(E A L Dunlop) *hld up: styd on ins fnl f: nvr nrr* **6/1**[3]

0506 **6** 3 1/2 **Cool Land (IRE)**[8] 6500 2-9-3 54 LukeMorris 4 50
(R A Harris) *trckd ldrs: plld hrd: rdn and wknd 2f out* **66/1**

605 **7** 3 **Rational Act (IRE)**[132] 2522 2-9-3 53 GrahamGibbons 5 42
(T D Easterby) *trckd ldrs: plld hrd: hung rt over 4f out: rdn and wknd 2f out* **100/1**

0 **8** 7 **Dolly Colman (IRE)**[38] 5626 2-8-12 0 RobertHavlin 11 20
(A B Haynes) *hld up: rdn and hung rt over 2f out: sn wknd* **150/1**

1m 29.78s (0.18) **Going Correction** -0.10s/f (Stan) 8 Ran SP% **112.5**
Speed ratings (Par 93): **94,93,90,88,84 80,76,68**
toteswingers:1&2:£1.90, 1&3:£2.50, 2&3:£2.30 CSF £3.36 TOTE £2.30: £1.10, £1.10, £1.40; EX 3.60.
Owner Godolphin **Bred** Floors Farming And Dominic Burke **Trained** Newmarket, Suffolk

FOCUS
Abysmal prize-money, but a fair maiden by the track's standards. The time was 0.70 seconds quicker than the modestly run second division won by Opera Dancer.

NOTEBOOK
Flag Officer confirmed the promise he showed when runner-up over C&D on debut two weeks earlier. He had to be ridden along to get to the front after half-missing the break and was then a bit keen, but he settled soon enough. Despite then carrying his head a little high under pressure, he found enough to see off the runner-up's strong challenge. He will probably have his limitations exposed in better company. (tchd 4-5)
Show Rainbow travelled that bit stronger than the winner into the straight, but even so it was a surprise to see she was matched at as low as 1.06 in-running. Although ultimately finding one too strong, she built on her first two efforts and should find a similar race.
Tenby Lady(USA), third in a weak 6f contest here on debut, was still green, missing the break and not travelling as well as the front two. She plugged on without threatening and might learn enough to win an ordinary maiden, but handicapping will probably be her game.
Royal Talisman stepped up on the form he showed over 1m at Kempton on debut. He should make an all right handicapper in due course.
Entrance was soon behind following a sluggish start and made no impression, running below the form she showed on her first two starts. Handicaps are now an option. (tchd 7-1)
Dolly Colman(IRE) Official explanation: jockey said that the filly hung right-handed

6712 TRY BETDAQ FOR AN EXCHANGE MEDIAN AUCTION MAIDEN STKS (DIV II) 7f 32y(P)
6:20 (6:21) (Class 6) 2-Y-O £1,364 (£403; £201) Stalls High

Form RPR

3440 **1** **Opera Dancer**[29] 5880 2-8-12 76 RichardHughes 5 70
(S Kirk) *chsd ldrs: led over 2f out: hung lft ins fnl f: rdn out* **13/8**[1]

2 1 **Never Never Land** 2-9-3 0 WilliamBuick 9 72
(J H M Gosden) *hld up: hdwy over 2f out: rdn to chse wnr and hung lft ins fnl f: r.o* **7/2**[2]

0 **3** 2 1/2 **Snow Ridge**[15] 6309 2-9-3 0 SebSanders 11 66
(Sir Mark Prescott) *hdwy over 5f out: rdn over 1f out: styd on same pce ins fnl f* **20/1**

0 **4** 3/4 **Wong Again**[21] 6146 2-8-12 0 DaneO'Neill 10 59
(J W Hills) *sn prom: rdn over 1f out: no ex ins fnl f* **20/1**

5 3/4 **Bill Page (USA)** 2-9-0 0 MartinLane(3) 3 62
(D M Simcock) *chsd ldrs: rdn over 1f out: styd on same pce* **13/2**[3]

0 **6** 4 1/2 **Cadmium Loch**[8] 6514 2-9-0 0 RussKennemore(3) 6 51
(R Hollinshead) *chsd ldrs: ev ch over 2f out: sn rdn: wknd fnl f* **50/1**

7 1/2 **Areef (IRE)** 2-8-12 0 HayleyTurner 2 45
(M L W Bell) *hld up: rdn over 2f out: nvr on terms* **8/1**

0 **8** 1/2 **Always De Man (IRE)**[46] 5352 2-9-3 0 RoystonFfrench 12 49
(M Johnston) *s.i.s: sn pushed along in rr: nvr on terms* **28/1**

9 nk **Holcombe Boy** 2-9-3 0 StevieDonohoe 1 48
(Mrs A Duffield) *s.i.s: hld up and a in rr* **25/1**

00 **10** nk **Ime Not Bitter**[13] 6365 2-8-10 0 MatthewMcGhee(7) 4 47
(C W Moore) *sn led: hdd over 2f out: sn rdn: wknd jst over 1f out* **100/1**

06 **11** 1/2 **All In A Paddy**[28] 5924 2-9-3 0 GrahamGibbons 7 46
(E S McMahon) *hld up: a in rr: wknd over 2f out* **20/1**

0 **12** 8 **Master Perfect**[37] 5651 2-9-3 0 (t) J-PGuillambert 8 27
(L M Cumani) *prom: pushed along over 4f out: wknd over 2f out* **22/1**

1m 30.48s (0.88) **Going Correction** -0.10s/f (Stan) 12 Ran SP% **113.6**
Speed ratings (Par 93): **90,88,86,85,84 79,78,78,77,77 76,67**
toteswingers:1&2:£2.20, 1&3:£4.30, 2&3:£7.30 CSF £5.51 TOTE £2.10: £1.10, £1.10, £5.60; EX 8.30.
Owner J C Smith **Bred** Littleton Stud **Trained** Upper Lambourn, Berks

FOCUS
An ordinary maiden run at a modest pace, and the time was 0.70 seconds slower than the first division, won by Flag Officer.

NOTEBOOK
Opera Dancer, out of her depth in a hot sales race last time, found this a lot easier and, having been well placed, stayed on strongly, despite edging left, after getting first run on the runner-up. This performance confirmed the promise of her earlier efforts in maidens, but things are set to get tougher again. (op 7-4 tchd 2-1)
Never Never Land, a £55,000 half-brother to triple 5f winner Windjammer, has already been gelded. He recovered from a slow start to travel well in mid-division and looked a danger to the winner going around the bend into the straight, but having lost momentum when forced to switch widest once in line for the finish, he got going too late. There should be better to come. (tchd 10-3 and 4-1)
Snow Ridge, well beaten over 6f here on debut, came wide into the straight and never threatened the winner. Very much like his trainer's runner in the first division (Tenby Lady), he might improve enough to win a similar race, but will surely come into his own once handicapped. (op 16-1)
Wong Again was always well placed and improved on the form she showed over 6f at Newbury first time up. She should find her level once handicapped. (tchd 22-1)
Bill Page(USA) lost his place when stuck in behind a rival going nowhere around the bend into the straight and was one-paced thereafter. (op 7-1 tchd 5-1)
All In A Paddy, on his final qualifying run for a mark, was not given a hard time. (op 16-1)

6713 BETDAQ THE BETTING EXCHANGE H'CAP 7f 32y(P)
6:50 (6:50) (Class 6) (0-65,65) 3-Y-O+ £1,706 (£503; £252) Stalls High

Form RPR

0301 **1** **So Surreal (IRE)**[7] 6522 3-9-2 62 6ex (b) GeorgeBaker 11 70
(G L Moore) *hld up: hdwy over 1f out: rdn and hung lft ins fnl f: r.o to ld nr fin* **14/1**

2005 **2** nk **Annes Rocket (IRE)**[13] 6371 5-9-2 60 PatDobbs 9 68
(J C Fox) *broke wl: sn stdd and lost pl: hld up and racd keenly: hdwy over 1f out: rdn and ev ch wl ins fnl f: r.o* **12/1**

1156 **3** 1/2 **Emiratesdotcom**[8] 6515 4-9-4 62 LiamKeniry 1 69
(J M Bradley) *chsd ldrs: rdn to ld ins fnl f: hdd nr fin* **4/1**[1]

0600 **4** 1/2 **Hustle (IRE)**[21] 6164 5-9-7 65 RichardHughes 3 70
(Miss Gay Kelleway) *sn led: hdd 4f out: rdn to ld over 1f out: hdd ins fnl f: styd on* **11/1**

6226 **5** nse **Just Timmy Marcus**[13] 6370 4-9-7 65 (b) GrahamGibbons 2 70
(B P J Baugh) *sn chsng ldrs: nt clr run wl over 1f out: sn rdn: styng on whn n.m.r wl ins fnl f* **9/2**[2]

2000 **6** 2 3/4 **Adam De Beaulieu (USA)**[13] 6371 3-9-5 65 (t) SebSanders 6 65+
(B M R Haslam) *chsd ldrs: led 4f out: rdn: hung lft and hdd over 1f out: styng on same pce whn hmpd wl ins fnl f* **6/1**[3]

3000 **7** 1 **Bahamian Kid**[21] 6164 5-9-4 62 (v) LukeMorris 5 57
(R Hollinshead) *prom: rdn 1f out: styd on same pce* **18/1**

0003 **8** 1/2 **Connor's Choice**[39] 5586 5-9-0 61 SimonPearce(3) 4 55
(Andrew Turnell) *chsd ldrs: rdn and n.m.r over 1f out: no ex ins fnl f* **12/1**

0126 **9** 1 **Fitz**[20] 6210 4-9-3 61 TedDurcan 10 52
(Matthew Salaman) *hld up: rdn over 2f out: nvr on terms* **7/1**

0534 **10** hd **Tawzeea (IRE)**[8] 6491 5-9-5 63 TomEaves 12 53
(M Dods) *hld up: rdn over 2f out: n.d* **8/1**

11 2 3/4 **Flyjack (USA)**[132] 2551 3-9-4 64 RoystonFfrench 8 46
(Mrs L Williamson) *hld up: rdn over 1f out: n.d* **33/1**

1m 28.69s (-0.91) **Going Correction** -0.10s/f (Stan)
WFA 3 from 4yo+ 2lb 11 Ran SP% **114.7**
Speed ratings (Par 101): **101,100,100,99,99 96,95,94,93,93 90**
toteswingers:1&2:£31.10, 1&3:£5.80, 2&3:£14.60 CSF £166.94 CT £813.33 TOTE £18.00: £5.20, £6.20, £2.40; EX 134.20.
Owner R Henderson **Bred** Rathasker Stud **Trained** Lower Beeding, W Sussex
■ Stewards' Enquiry : George Baker two-day ban: careless riding (Oct 22-25)

FOCUS
A moderate handicap run at an even pace.

6714 BET EURO 2012 QUALIFIERS - BETDAQ H'CAP 5f 216y(P)
7:20 (7:20) (Class 5) (0-75,73) 3-Y-O+ £2,115 (£624; £312) Stalls Low

Form RPR

5214 **1** **Darcey**[13] 6371 4-9-2 68 CathyGannon 8 76
(Miss Amy Weaver) *plld hrd and prom: rdn over 2f out: r.o to ld towards fin* **8/1**[3]

0443 **2** 3/4 **Cape Melody**[20] 6208 4-9-6 72 TravisBlock 1 78
(H Morrison) *dwlt: hld up: hdwy over 1f out: rdn and hung lft ins fnl f: r.o wl* **8/1**[3]

4-02 **3** hd **First In Command (IRE)**[11] 6421 5-9-3 69 (t) AndreaAtzeni 5 74+
(Daniel Mark Loughnane, Ire) *chsd ldrs: led over 1f out: shkn up and sn hung lft: rdn ins fnl f: hdd towards fin* **5/1**[1]

6012 **4** 2 1/2 **Ryedane (IRE)**[20] 6208 8-9-7 73 (b) RobertWinston 11 70
(T D Easterby) *mid-div: hdwy 1/2-way: rdn over 2f out: edgd lft fnl f: styd on* **14/1**

066 **5** 1 1/4 **Methaaly (IRE)**[20] 6207 7-8-9 68 (be) JosephYoung(7) 4 61
(M Mullineaux) *sn chsng ldrs: rdn over 1f out: no ex ins fnl f* **28/1**

0302 **6** 1/2 **Jigajig**[39] 5600 3-8-11 71 (p) JulieBurke(7) 7 62
(K A Ryan) *chsd ldr: led wl over 1f out: sn hung lft and hdd: no ex ins fnl f* **8/1**[3]

4411 **7** 3/4 **Sweet Gale (IRE)**[16] 6292 6-9-4 70 JimmyQuinn 13 59
(Mike Murphy) *s.s: hdwy over 2f out: rdn and nt clr run over 1f out: nvr able to chal* **8/1**[3]

2300 **8** 3/4 **Argentine (IRE)**[1] 6700 6-9-4 70 SteveDrowne 12 57
(J A McShane) *sn pushed along in rr: hdwy over 2f out: rdn over 1f out: nt trble ldrs* **20/1**

030 **9** 3/4 **Rainy Night**[22] 6110 4-9-1 67 (p) GrahamGibbons 6 54+
(R Hollinshead) *hld up: hdwy and nt clr run fr over 1f out: nvr able to chal* **8/1**[3]

4004 **10** 1 1/4 **Knightfire (IRE)**[20] 6208 3-9-4 71 (t) RichardHughes 9 51
(W R Swinburn) *hld up in tch: rdn over 1f out: wknd ins fnl f* **9/1**

510 **11** 2 1/2 **Frequency**[18] 6255 3-9-5 72 J-PGuillambert 2 44
(Miss Amy Weaver) *led: rdn and hdd wl over 1f out: wknd fnl f* **25/1**

3340 **12** 13 **Thoughtsofstardom**[74] 4435 7-8-10 67 TobyAtkinson(5) 10 —
(P S McEntee) *chsd ldrs tl wknd over 2f out* **50/1**

5632 **13** 25 **Fawley Green**[7] 6524 3-9-6 73 (p) HayleyTurner 3 —
(W R Muir) *sn outpcd: t.o fr 1/2-way* **11/2**[2]

1m 13.98s (-1.02) **Going Correction** -0.10s/f (Stan)
WFA 3 from 4yo+ 1lb 13 Ran SP% **118.3**
Speed ratings (Par 103): **102,101,100,97,95 95,94,93,92,90 87,69,36**
toteswingers:1&2:£22.30, 1&3:£8.40, 2&3:£8.50 CSF £66.89 CT £369.19 TOTE £14.50: £4.10, £2.70, £3.50; EX 106.60.
Owner Bringloe & Lennox **Bred** Raymond Cowie **Trained** Newmarket, Suffolk

FOCUS
A modest but competitive sprint handicap.
Rainy Night Official explanation: jockey said that the gelding was denied a clear run
Fawley Green Official explanation: jockey that the gelding finished lame

6715 WOLVERHAMPTON-RACECOURSE.CO.UK H'CAP 1m 5f 194y(P)
7:50 (7:50) (Class 4) (0-80,92) 3-Y-O+ £3,594 (£1,069; £534; £266) Stalls Low

Form RPR

4451 **1** **Palio Square (USA)**[15] 6313 3-9-2 80 TomQueally 6 92
(H R A Cecil) *hld up in tch: led over 3f out: rdn and hung lft over 1f out: styd on wl* **5/2**[1]

5041 **2** 2 1/4 **Bivouac (UAE)**[38] 5646 6-9-6 75 PJMcDonald 2 84
(G A Swinbank) *hld up: hdwy to chse wnr 3f out: rdn over 1f out: hung lft and no ex ins fnl f* **14/1**

605 **3** 1 1/2 **Just Lille (IRE)**[15] 6304 7-10-4 92 (p) RosieJessop(5) 7 99
(Mrs A Duffield) *led early: chsd ldrs: outpcd over 2f out: rallied over 1f out: styd on* **16/1**

0020 **4** 3/4 **Quinsman**[14] 6331 4-9-6 75 RichardHughes 11 81
(J S Moore) *dwlt: hld up: hdwy 3f out: sn rdn: styd on: nt trble ldrs* **6/1**[2]

2236 **5** 7 **My Mate Max**[59] 4933 5-9-6 75 (p) GrahamGibbons 9 71
(R Hollinshead) *hld up: hdwy 3f out: rdn and wknd over 1f out* **12/1**

2320 **6** nse **Akbabend**[28] 5922 4-9-11 80 (b) RoystonFfrench 3 76
(M Johnston) *hld up: nt clr run wl over 3f out: sn rdn: nvr on terms* **22/1**

323 **7** 4 **Royal Riviera**[62] 4845 4-9-7 76 SteveDrowne 5 66
(J R Gask) *prom tl rdn and wknd over 2f out* **7/1**[3]

142 **8** 33 **Nezhenka**[34] 5747 3-9-10 88 (b[1]) SebSanders 1 32
(Sir Mark Prescott) *s.i.s: hdwy to chse ldr after 1f: led over 5f out: rdn and hdd over 3f out: wknd over 2f out: t.o* **5/2**[1]

1000 9 23 **Callisto Moon**[12] 5788 6-9-10 **82**...(b) MartinLane(3) 12 —
(F J Brennan) *sn led: rdn and hdd over 5f out: wknd wl over 3f out: t.o* **33/1**

3m 1.81s (-4.19) **Going Correction** -0.10s/f (Stan)
WFA 3 from 4yo+ 9lb 9 Ran SP% **111.5**
Speed ratings (Par 105): **107,105,104,104,100 100,98,79,66**
toteswingers:1&2:£6.50, 1&3:£10.10, 2&3:£11.90 CSF £39.89 CT £446.63 TOTE £2.90: £1.10, £5.90, £5.60; EX 31.60.
Owner Mogeely Stud & Mrs Maura Gittins **Bred** Steven Nicholson & Brandy Nicholson **Trained** Newmarket, Suffolk

FOCUS
An ordinary staying handicap for the grade in which the leaders went off much too fast.
Nezhenka Official explanation: jockey said that the filly ran too free

6716 BREEDERS' CUP LIVE ONLY ON ATR MEDIAN AUCTION MAIDEN STKS 1m 141y(P)
8:20 (8:20) (Class 6) 3-5-Y-O £1,706 (£503; £252) Stalls Low

Form				RPR
2	1		**Commerce**[31] 5842 3-8-11 0... HayleyTurner 5 (S Dow) *a.p: led over 1f out: rdn out* **10/11**[1]	61+
5	2	½	**Sennybridge**[49] 5265 3-8-11 0... DaneO'Neill 3 (J W Hills) *hld up: hdwy over 2f out: rdn to chse wnr ins fnl f: r.o* **20/1**	59+
5200	3	3 ¼	**Noche De Reyes**[88] 3968 5-9-6 51... PatCosgrave 7 (E J Alston) *chsd ldr tl led over 2f out: rdn and hdd over 1f out: no ex ins fnl f* **20/1**	57
3	4	5	**No Rain (IRE)**[32] 5815 3-8-11 0... PJMcDonald 1 (G A Swinbank) *hld up in tch: rdn over 2f out: wknd over 1f out* **15/8**[2]	41
460	5	1 ¼	**Cruise Control**[29] 5875 4-9-6 49...(p) RobertWinston 4 (R J Price) *hld up: hdwy over 3f out: rdn and hung lft fr over 2f out: wknd over 1f out* **11/1**[3]	43
6	6	nk	**Mr Howe**[86] 4018 3-9-2 0... RoystonFfrench 13 (T J Fitzgerald) *s.i.s: swtchd lft sn after s: hld up: shkn up over 1f out: nvr on terms* **66/1**	42
0	7	1 ¾	**Arakette (IRE)**[11] 6415 3-8-11 0... RobertHavlin 9 (A B Haynes) *chsd ldrs: rdn over 3f out: wknd over 1f out* **66/1**	33
06	8	2	**Wingate Street**[17] 6275 3-9-2 0... CathyGannon 12 (P D Evans) *sn in mid-div: drvn along 1/2-way: wknd 3f out* **40/1**	33
0560	9	1 ¾	**Jubilant Lady (USA)**[8] 6494 3-8-11 53...(v) TomEaves 8 (B Smart) *sn led: rdn and hdd over 2f out: wknd over 1f out* **33/1**	24
0	10	43	**Neissa (USA)**[9] 6470 3-8-11 0... LukeMorris 11 (J R Best) *a in rr: t.o* **50/1**	—
50	11	9	**Psalm Twentythree**[18] 6244 4-9-6 0... SteveDrowne 6 (J A McShane) *prom tl eased fr over 2f out: t.o* **66/1**	—
	12	10	**Will'N'Glad** 3-9-2 0... WilliamCarson 2 (N Tinkler) *s.s: outpcd: t.o* **40/1**	—

1m 50.14s (-0.36) **Going Correction** -0.10s/f (Stan)
WFA 3 from 4yo+ 4lb 12 Ran SP% **119.3**
Speed ratings (Par 101): **97,96,93,89,88 87,86,84,82,44 36,27**
toteswingers:1&2:£6.00, 1&3:£3.70, 2&3:£35.60 CSF £27.09 TOTE £2.20: £1.10, £8.10, £2.40; EX 38.60.
Owner Two & A Half Men **Bred** Juddmonte Farms Ltd **Trained** Epsom, Surrey

FOCUS
A moderate maiden run at a strong pace. Not form to dwell on.
Cruise Control Official explanation: jockey said that the gelding hung left
Mr Howe Official explanation: jockey said that the gelding was upset in the stalls
Psalm Twentythree Official explanation: vet said gelding finished lame

6717 ATTHERACES.COM/BREEDERSCUP NURSERY 1m 141y(P)
8:50 (8:50) (Class 6) (0-65,65) 2-Y-O £1,706 (£503; £252) Stalls Low

Form				RPR
006	1		**Diplomasi**[21] 6159 2-9-3 **61**... ChrisCatlin 3 (C E Brittain) *chsd ldrs: edgd rt ins fnl f: r.o u.p to ld nr fin* **7/1**	65
0002	2	1	**Bouggatti**[24] 6059 2-9-0 **63**... JohnFahy(5) 7 (W Jarvis) *s.s: reminders sn after s: hld up: hdwy and nt clr run over 1f out: edgd lft and r.o wl: wnt 2nd nr fin: nt trble wnr* **4/1**[2]	65
4333	3	shd	**Papas Fritas**[11] 6412 2-9-5 **63**...(b) ShaneKelly 1 (B J Meehan) *chsd ldr tl led 7f out: rdn and edgd rt over 1f out: hdd nr fin* **6/1**[3]	65
2664	4	1	**Unknown Rebel (IRE)**[16] 6300 2-9-3 **61**... PaulHanagan 2 (K A Ryan) *led: hdd 7f out: chsd ldr: rdn over 2f out: styd on same pce fnl f* **14/1**	61
0556	5	1	**Al Rannan**[24] 6059 2-9-3 **61**... TomQueally 10 (E A L Dunlop) *hld up: hdwy over 2f out: sn rdn and hung lft: styd on* **25/1**	59
6030	6	1	**High Kickin**[9] 6471 2-9-2 **65**...(p) DeclanCannon(5) 5 (A J McCabe) *chsd ldrs: rdn over 2f out: no ex fnl f* **22/1**	60
0543	7	1 ¼	**Holy Mackerel (IRE)**[11] 6411 2-9-3 **61**... RichardHughes 8 (M R Channon) *mid-div: sn pushed along: hdwy u.p 3f out: no ex ins fnl f* **3/1**[1]	54
6501	8	1	**Imperial Look**[45] 5389 2-9-5 **63**... GrahamGibbons 9 (E S McMahon) *hld up: rdn over 3f out: sn outpcd: styd on ins fnl f* **6/1**[3]	54
60	9	½	**On Wings Of Love (IRE)**[15] 6311 2-9-3 **61**... SamHitchcott 12 (A Bailey) *hld up: rdn over 1f out: nvr on terms* **33/1**	51
0005	10	½	**Arctic Reach**[14] 6333 2-9-2 **60**... LiamKeniry 6 (G D Blake) *s.i.s: hld up: rdn over 2f out: styd on same pce appr fnl f* **28/1**	49
040	11	¾	**Face The Future**[24] 6046 2-9-5 **63**... TomEaves 4 (M Dods) *plld hrd and prom: rdn over 2f out: hung lft over 1f out: wknd fnl f* **18/1**	50
023	12	nse	**Green With Envy (IRE)**[20] 6209 2-9-0 **61**...(p) MatthewDavies(3) 13 (George Baker) *s.i.s: a in rr* **22/1**	48
3140	13	2 ½	**Dew Reward (IRE)**[9] 6471 2-9-5 **63**... CathyGannon 11 (Eve Johnson Houghton) *hld up: hdwy u.p over 2f out: wknd over 1f out* **22/1**	45

1m 51.35s (0.85) **Going Correction** -0.10s/f (Stan) 13 Ran SP% **121.3**
Speed ratings (Par 93): **92,91,91,90,89 88,87,86,85,85 84,84,82**
toteswingers:1&2:£13.20, 1&3:£14.00, 2&3:£3.40 CSF £32.20 CT £190.58 TOTE £15.70: £6.10, £3.90, £1.20; EX 54.60.
Owner Saeed Manana **Bred** Ercan Dogan **Trained** Newmarket, Suffolk

FOCUS
A moderate nursery in which it paid to race prominently.

NOTEBOOK
Diplomasi left his maiden form well behind to make a winning debut in handicap company, proving well suited by his first taste of Polytrack. He might be able to defy a rise in similar company. Official explanation: trainer's representative said, regarding the apparent improvement of form, that the colt had benefitted from its first run on an all-weather surface and from the tight track (op 14-1)
Bouggatti, off the same mark as when runner-up at Yarmouth on his previous start, would have come close to overcoming the bias towards those prominent had he enjoyed a better trip. He didn't help himself with a lazy start, losing ground and needing reminders to taken an interest, but he looked to be going well when having little room to make his challenge around the final bend and early in the straight. He ran on when in the clear, but too late. His attitude can be questioned, but not his ability. (op 7-2)
Papas Fritas, back on Polytrack, responded well to a positive ride and ran a solid race in defeat. (op 5-1 tchd 9-2)
Unknown Rebel(IRE) was always handy but simply wasn't good enough. (tchd 12-1)
Al Rannan, having his first start since leaving Michael Bell, was stuck wide throughout and is better than he showed, although he did seem to be hanging left in the straight. (op 20-1)
Holy Mackerel(IRE) was well backed but he ran in snatches and was hanging when under serious pressure heading into the straight. (op 9-2 tchd 5-2)
Imperial Look, a winner on soft ground on his nursery debut, never looked like following up off a 5lb higher mark back on Polytrack. (tchd 7-1)

6718 BREEDERS' CUP LIVE ONLY ON ATR H'CAP 1m 1f 103y(P)
9:20 (9:20) (Class 5) (0-70,70) 3-Y-O+ £2,115 (£624; £312) Stalls Low

Form				RPR
5003	1		**Bakongo (IRE)**[22] 6122 3-9-5 **70**... HayleyTurner 9 (M L W Bell) *hld up: hdwy over 1f out: rdn and r.o to ld wl ins fnl f* **5/1**[3]	78
2003	2	nk	**Dream Of Fortune (IRE)**[9] 6450 6-9-3 **64**...(bt) TomQueally 10 (P D Evans) *s.i.s: hld up: hdwy over 2f out: rdn to ld ins fnl f: sn hdd: styd on* **9/1**	71
4330	3	½	**Cape Quarter (USA)**[6] 6573 4-9-2 **63**...(t) ShaneKelly 2 (W J Haggas) *a.p: rdn: hung rt and ev ch ins fnl f: kpt on* **9/2**[2]	69
3252	4	hd	**Diggeratt (USA)**[16] 6289 4-9-7 **68**... PaulHanagan 11 (R A Fahey) *chsd ldrs: rdn to ld over 1f out: edgd rt and hdd ins fnl f: styd on* **7/2**[1]	74
0000	5	3 ¾	**Striding Edge (IRE)**[18] 6260 4-9-8 **69**... GeorgeBaker 1 (W R Muir) *hld up: nt clr run wl over 1f out: styd on ins fnl f: nvr nrr* **10/1**	67
0316	6	½	**Beat Up**[46] 5367 4-9-3 **64**... RichardHughes 6 (G D Blake) *hld up: hdwy over 3f out: rdn over 1f out: no ex ins fnl f* **6/1**	61
5545	7	3	**Folio (IRE)**[40] 5565 10-9-6 **67**... StevieDonohoe 3 (W J Musson) *hld up: rdn over 1f out: n.d* **25/1**	57
5060	8	½	**Justcallmehandsome**[13] 6372 8-9-0 **68**...(v) KatiaScallan(7) 12 (D J S Ffrench Davis) *prom: rdn over 1f out: wknd fnl f* **28/1**	57
0023	9	¾	**Lean Machine**[22] 6124 3-9-3 **68**...(p) LukeMorris 8 (R A Harris) *chsd ldr tl led over 2f out: rdn and hdd over 1f out: wknd ins fnl f* **16/1**	56
20-0	10	8	**Aphrodite's Rock**[27] 5959 4-9-2 **63**...(t) LiamKeniry 7 (G D Blake) *chsd ldrs: rdn over 2f out: wknd over 1f out* **50/1**	34
1405	11	5	**Bernix**[50] 5244 8-9-3 **64**...(p) J-PGuillambert 5 (N Tinkler) *hld up: racd keenly: rdn over 3f out: wknd over 2f out* **20/1**	24
0120	12	½	**Negotiation (IRE)**[23] 6091 4-9-9 **70**... PatCosgrave 13 (M Quinn) *led: hdd over 2f out: wknd over 1f out* **10/1**	29

2m 0.06s (-1.64) **Going Correction** -0.10s/f (Stan)
WFA 3 from 4yo+ 4lb 12 Ran SP% **119.4**
Speed ratings (Par 103): **103,102,102,102,98 98,95,95,94,87 83,82**
toteswingers:1&2:£12.80, 1&3:£14.90, 2&3:£13.30 CSF £47.67 CT £220.37 TOTE £4.80: £1.10, £7.10, £4.00; EX 56.80 Place 6 £24.76; Place 5 £20.56.
Owner Sheikh Marwan Al Maktoum **Bred** Darley **Trained** Newmarket, Suffolk

FOCUS
A modest but competitive handicap.
T/Plt: £36.70 to a £1 stake. Pool of £71,851.11 - 1,428.29 winning tickets T/Qpdt: £29.80 to a £1 stake. Pool of £7,266.36 - 180.20 winning tickets CR

5784 YORK (L-H)
Friday, October 8

OFFICIAL GOING: Good to soft (soft in places) changing to soft (good to soft in places) after race 4 (3:55)
Races on inside line on home bend reducing races of one mile and over by 27yds.
Wind: moderate 1/2 behind Weather: overcast, cool

6719 TSG NURSERY 6f
2:10 (2:11) (Class 3) 2-Y-O £6,540 (£1,946; £972; £485) Stalls Centre

Form				RPR
1211	1		**Indian Ballad (IRE)**[29] 5874 2-8-12 **81**... GrahamGibbons 3 (E S McMahon) *swvd lft s: hdwy over 2f out: w ldrs whn swtchd lft over 1f out: slt ld last 75yds: jst hld on* **8/1**[3]	83
0331	2	nse	**Breezolini**[17] 6264 2-8-1 **73** ow3... AmyRyan(3) 14 (R M Whitaker) *sn outpcd and in rr: hdwy 2f out: edgd lft over 1f out: led jst ins fnl f: sn hdd: rallied and jst failed* **16/1**	75
6112	3	hd	**Maggie Mey (IRE)**[26] 5998 2-7-13 **68**... SilvestreDeSousa 2 (D O'Meara) *w ldrs: no ex last 50yds* **9/1**	69
31	4	2 ¼	**Lady Paris (IRE)**[14] 6323 2-8-8 **77**... TomEaves 8 (B Smart) *bmpd s: sn w ldrs: led 3f out tl jst ins fnl f: wknd last 75yds* **7/1**[2]	72
4100	5	3 ¼	**Thirteen Shivers**[25] 6030 2-8-4 **73**... JimmyQuinn 12 (M W Easterby) *sn outpcd: hdwy over 2f out: hung lft and kpt on fnl f* **20/1**	58
11	6	1 ¼	**Alben Star (IRE)**[21] 6139 2-9-7 **90**... PaulHanagan 11 (R A Fahey) *hld up: hdwy over 2f out: chsng ldrs and rdn whn hmpd over 1f out: sn fdd* **7/4**[1]	71
2351	7	6	**Valerius Maximus**[15] 6309 2-8-4 **80**... DuilioDaSilva(7) 5 (P F I Cole) *w ldrs: wknd over 1f out* **16/1**	43
0040	8	4 ½	**Serena's Pride**[21] 6139 2-8-10 **86**... HarryBentley(7) 7 (A P Jarvis) *w ldrs: wknd 2f out* **25/1**	36
4141	9	11	**Boundaries**[13] 6354 2-9-0 **83**...(v) TomQueally 10 (T D Easterby) *led tl 3f out: lost pl over 1f out* **8/1**[3]	—
6431	10	1 ¾	**Watts Up Son**[42] 5483 2-8-10 **79**...(t) DavidNolan 6 (D Carroll) *w ldrs: lost pl 2f out* **16/1**	—
0040	11	4 ½	**Meandmyshadow**[27] 5939 2-7-9 **71**... RyanPowell(7) 1 (A D Brown) *wnt rt s: w ldrs: wknd 2f out* **33/1**	—
0145	12	3 ½	**Two Feet Of Snow (IRE)**[6] 6576 2-8-1 **70**... PatrickMathers 9 (I W McInnes) *reluctant to go to s: sn outpcd: lost pl over 2f out* **80/1**	—
6610	13	3 ¼	**Fleet Captain**[19] 6220 2-8-0 **69**...(b[1]) DavidProbert 4 (K A Ryan) *chsd ldrs: wknd 2f out* **33/1**	—
3323	14	4 ½	**Hortensis**[20] 6182 2-7-12 **67** oh2... DuranFentiman 13 (T D Easterby) *slowly away and wnt lft s: a detached in last* **40/1**	—

1m 17.66s (5.76) **Going Correction** +0.825s/f (Soft) 14 Ran SP% **116.9**
Speed ratings (Par 99): **94,93,93,90,86 84,76,70,56,53 47,43,38,32**
toteswingers:1&2:£21.20, 1&3:£6.70, 2&3:£18.60 CSF £115.15 CT £1204.97 TOTE £9.30: £2.90, £3.80, £2.50; EX 147.90 Trifecta £817.40 Part won. Pool: £1,104.67 - 0.63 winning units..
Owner R L Bedding **Bred** J M Beever **Trained** Lichfield, Staffs

FOCUS

A competitive nursery, run at a strong pace and the field elected to come down the middle. The first four dominated from the furlong marker and there was a very tight three-way finish.

NOTEBOOK

Indian Ballad(IRE) proved easy to back, but found the race run very much to suit and just did enough to register a fourth success from his last five outings. The return to this trip on a sharp track proved fine for him and he has not looked back since going into nurseries. He was 7lb higher than when scoring at Bath last time and will be going up again for this, but further improvement from this tough colt is not ruled out yet. Connections later hinted he may have done enough for the year, though. (op 15-2)

Breezolini was hiked up 17lb for winning her maiden at Beverley 17 days earlier, and things didn't look too good beforehand on this nursery debut as she got warm and proved very edgy. The stiffer trip was also of some concern for her, but Beverley is a stiff track and she too proved suited by being held up off the decent early fractions here. She only just lost out, but her rider negated her claim by carrying 3lb overweight and that made the difference between winning and losing. Another rise in the weights is now forthcoming, but she is clearly still progressing. (op 18-1)

Maggie Mey(IRE), 3lb higher, was awash with sweat. She had to be ridden from a very early stage, but kept responding and went down narrowly. She has developed into a tough performer and deserves to go in again.

Lady Paris(IRE) ◆, off the mark at Haydock a fortnight earlier, looked fairly treated for this nursery debut and so it proved as she ran a big race from the front. She paid for her exertions near the finish, but this lightly raced filly remains on an upwards curve and should be found another opening before the season's end. (tchd 13-2)

Thirteen Shivers was back up in trip after being taken off his feet over 5f last time out. He again lacked the early toe to land a serious blow, but this was more encouraging again and he will appreciate getting back on quicker ground in due course. (op 25-1)

Alben Star(IRE) was 6lb higher than when winning gamely at Ayr last month. He didn't get the best of trips through the race, but didn't look so comfortable on this easier surface and remains a horse of some promise. (tchd 2-1 in a place)

Boundaries came in for support, but after racing in the firing line he was done with passing the 2f marker, and is a good indication of how hard they went early doors. (op 11-1)

6720 GARBUTT & ELLIOTT CONDITIONS STKS 1m 2f 88y

2:45 (2:45) (Class 3) 3-Y-O+ £7,771 (£2,312; £1,155; £577) Stalls Low

Form RPR

-650 **1** **Waseet**[112] 3142 3-8-11 97 .... RichardHills 1 116
(J L Dunlop) *stdd s: hld up in rr: effrt over 2f out: rdn and hung lft over 1f out: styd on strly to ld nr fin* **18/1**

2232 **2** ¾ **Kings Gambit (SAF)**[20] 6179 6-9-4 110 .... JamieSpencer 3 116
(T P Tate) *led 1f: trckd ldrs: led over 3f out: hrd rdn and briefly hdd over 1f out: ct last 50yds* **10/3**[2]

10-4 **3** 1½ **Kirklees (IRE)**[20] 6179 6-9-2 115 .... FrankieDettori 5 111
(Saeed Bin Suroor) *sn trcking ldrs: shkn up to ld briefly over 1f out: kpt on same pce last 150yds* **6/5**[1]

2304 **4** 7 **Demolition**[20] 6193 6-9-2 93 .... PaulHanagan 4 98
(R A Fahey) *led after 1f: hdd over 3f out: wknd fnl 2f* **15/2**

0246 **5** 4 **Chock A Block (IRE)**[30] 5853 4-9-2 105 .... DarryllHolland 7 90
(Saeed Bin Suroor) *trckd ldrs: lost pl over 2f out* **14/1**

5112 **6** 1 **Jet Away**[39] 5590 3-8-11 105 .... TomQueally 2 89
(H R A Cecil) *racd keenly towards rr: effrt over 3f out: lost pl over 2f out* **6/1**[3]

-030 **7** 25 **Mystery Star (IRE)**[111] 3194 5-9-2 97 .... MichaelHills 6 41
(M H Tompkins) *chsd ldrs: lost pl 3f out: sn bhd: t.o* **40/1**

2m 15.26s (2.76) **Going Correction** +0.45s/f (Yiel)

WFA 3 from 4yo+ 5lb 7 Ran SP% **109.0**

Speed ratings (Par 107): **106,105,104,98,95 94,74**

toteswingers:1&2:£6.10, 1&3:£5.30, 2&3:£1.60 CSF £69.88 TOTE £20.70: £5.40, £1.50; EX 99.60.

Owner Hamdan Al Maktoum **Bred** Shadwell Estate Company Limited **Trained** Arundel, W Sussex

FOCUS

This decent little conditions event was run at a sound enough pace and the first three came well clear. The time was ordinary but this is pretty sound conditions form cinsidering the ground, rated through the runner-up.

NOTEBOOK

Waseet bounced right back to form and, given a patient ride, got on top late in the day to make a winning return from his 112-day layoff. Third in last season's Royal Lodge, he had disappointed in three subsequent outings since resuming as a 3-y-o. There was no obvious confidence behind him in the market for this return and he had something to prove on this contrasting surface. It was a drop in class for him, though, and being by Selkirk it cannot be considered a surprise that he improved for this soft surface. Providing he comes of out this without hitch and is given sufficient time to get over his exertions, there could well be another opportunity for him before the end of term, and he appeals as the type to show his true colours as a 4-y-o. (op 20-1)

Kings Gambit(SAF) also had something to prove on this ground, but he acted on it without much bother and again ran a big race in defeat, conceding weight all round. He probably went for home that bit too soon as, after digging deep to fend off Kirkless from 2f out, he looked to have done enough, but ultimately he teed it up for the winner. He may be finished now for the year, but will be back next season and he richly deserves to get his head back in front. (tchd 3-1)

Kirklees(IRE) was the one to be on at these weights and had won a Group 2 on his only previous outing over C&D. He moved up looking the most likely winner nearing the 2f marker, but found King's Gambit too resolute and was unable to reverse his last-time-out form with that rival. This ground was softer than he ideally cares for and, as he is still a fresh horse for the time of year, connections will presumably look to find him another opportunity this season. (tchd 11-8 in places)

Demolition faced a stiff task at these weights and was a sitting duck from the front turning for home. He is very tricky to place successfully. (op 12-1 tchd 7-1)

Chock A Block(IRE), his stable's second string, came under heavy pressure soon after straightening for home and is another difficult horse to place. (op 16-1)

Jet Away probably found the ground against him, but never looked that happy and is in danger of becoming another "twilight" horse. (op 9-2)

Mystery Star(IRE) needs better ground and shaped as though this return from a 111-day break was needed. (op 66-1)

6721 ACORN WEB OFFSET H'CAP 7f

3:20 (3:21) (Class 2) (0-100,100) 3-Y-O+ £11,656 (£3,468; £1,733; £865) Stalls Low

Form RPR

0214 **1** **Justonefortheroad**[20] 6178 4-8-7 84 oh1 .... SaleemGolam 7 95
(R A Fahey) *chsd ldrs: wnt 2nd over 1f out edgd lft and styd on to ld towards fin* **25/1**

0062 **2** ¾ **Eton Rifles (IRE)**[6] 6570 5-8-10 87 .... TomQueally 8 96
(J Howard Johnson) *trckd ldr: led over 1f out: hdd: crowded and no ex last 50yds* **5/1**[1]

2310 **3** 1 **Zomerlust**[28] 5903 8-8-9 86 .... (v) RobertWinston 1 92
(J J Quinn) *in tch: hdwy over 2f out: chsng ldrs over 2f out: styd on same pce* **16/1**

1040 **4** 2¾ **Joseph Henry**[20] 6175 8-8-6 88 .... BillyCray(5) 3 87
(D Nicholls) *led: hdd over 1f out: one pce* **25/1**

6216 **5** nse **Docofthebay (IRE)**[13] 6357 6-8-13 90 .... PJMcDonald 12 89
(J A Glover) *sn prom: hung lft over 2f out: kpt on fnl f* **20/1**

0100 **6** 2¼ **Prime Exhibit**[20] 6177 5-9-5 96 .... PaulHanagan 18 89+
(R A Fahey) *t.k.h in rr: effrt and nt clr run 2f out: swtchd lft over 1f out: r.o* **15/2**[2]

4300 **7** ½ **Internationaldebut (IRE)**[21] 6142 5-8-7 84 oh2 .... FrankieMcDonald 10 75
(P T Midgley) *hld up towards rr: hdwy over 2f out: n.m.r and edgd lft over 1f out: kpt on same pce* **25/1**

2433 **8** 1¼ **Misplaced Fortune**[20] 6175 5-8-9 89 .... Louis-PhilippeBeuzelin(3) 20 77
(N Tinkler) *swtchd lft sn after s: in rr: hdwy over 2f out: kpt on: nvr nr ldrs* **18/1**

1200 **9** 2¼ **Gap Princess (IRE)**[20] 6175 6-8-12 89 .... SilvestreDeSousa 16 71
(G A Harker) *hld up in rr: hdwy over 2f out: nt clr run over 1f out: nvr nr ldrs* **33/1**

6210 **10** 1¼ **Esprit De Midas**[13] 6357 4-8-13 90 .... JamieSpencer 19 68
(K A Ryan) *hld up: swtchd lft after s: hdwy ins over 3f out: wknd over 1f out* **25/1**

4000 **11** 2¼ **Kaptain Kirkup (IRE)**[28] 5911 3-9-7 100 .... TomEaves 14 72
(M Dods) *hld up in rr: effrt over 2f out: kpt on: nvr nr ldrs* **20/1**

-003 **12** ¾ **Mastership (IRE)**[21] 6142 6-8-7 84 .... (p) DavidProbert 6 54
(J J Quinn) *mid-div: effrt over 2f out: nvr a factor* **9/1**

5011 **13** 1¾ **My Kingdom (IRE)**[13] 6357 4-8-10 92 .... (t) JohnFahy(5) 15 58
(H Morrison) *hld up in rr: hdwy far side over 2f out: chsng ldrs over 1f out: sn wknd* **8/1**[3]

1035 **14** 1 **Golden Shaheen (IRE)**[13] 6357 3-8-9 88 .... (b) RichardHills 5 51
(M Johnston) *in rr: hdwy to chse ldrs on inner over 2f out: wknd over 1f out* **18/1**

0240 **15** 3¾ **Advanced**[13] 6349 7-9-3 97 .... AmyRyan(3) 13 50
(K A Ryan) *in rr: drvn 3f out: nvr on terms* **14/1**

06-5 **16** 1 **Without Prejudice (USA)**[147] 2091 5-8-10 87 .... (v) DarryllHolland 2 37
(J Noseda) *chsd ldrs on inner: wkng whn hmpd over 1f out: eased* **20/1**

6410 **17** 1¾ **Little Scotland**[19] 6221 3-8-9 88 .... JimmyQuinn 17 33
(R A Fahey) *a towards rr* **50/1**

5504 **18** 3¼ **Academy Blues (USA)**[13] 6357 5-8-10 87 .... AndrewMullen 11 24
(D Nicholls) *dwlt: sn chsng ldrs: lost pl 2f out: eased* **25/1**

5525 **19** 27 **Desert Creek (IRE)**[27] 5950 4-9-0 91 .... JimmyFortune 9 —
(Sir Michael Stoute) *wnt rt s: mid-div: rdn and lost pl over 2f out: sn heavily eased: t.o* **5/1**[1]

1m 29.44s (4.14) **Going Correction** +0.825s/f (Soft)

WFA 3 from 4yo+ 2lb 19 Ran SP% **127.7**

Speed ratings (Par 109): **109,108,107,103,103 101,100,99,96,95 92,91,89,88,84 83,81,77,46**

toteswingers:1&2:£30.80, 1&3:£38.90, 2&3:£22.20 CSF £133.63 CT £2135.61 TOTE £36.50: £5.80, £1.70, £2.80, £7.00; EX 194.60 Trifecta £1261.70 Part won. Pool: £1,705.04 - 0.50 winning units..

Owner The Pontoon Partnership **Bred** Wellsummers Farm & Hammarsfield B'Stock **Trained** Musley Bank, N Yorks

FOCUS

This ultra-competitive handicap again saw the main action develop down the centre of the home straight, but despite there being a solid pace few managed to land a serious blow, but for which the form could be rated higher. The winner progressed again but the second was unable to confirm his apparent Redcar improvement.

NOTEBOOK

Justonefortheroad, 1lb out of the weights, forged to the front near the line under strong handling from Saleem Golam. The winner had done all of his previous winning on quick ground, but showed he acts on this sort of surface when running well in defeat at Ayr last time, and his proven stamina was a big asset on this drop back a furlong. It rates a career-best effort and he could be the sort to land a big handicap next term. (op 20-1)

Eton Rifles(IRE) posted his best effort to date when second in Listed company at Redcar last weekend, and is due to race off a 10lb higher mark in future, so it wasn't surprising to see him out again quickly. He proved popular and, after travelling well just off the pace, was produced to lead nearing the final furlong. His jockey became a little unbalanced near the end as things got tight, but he was probably just done with at that stage and ultimately the winner outstayed him. Things will be much tougher for him from now on. (op 6-1 tchd 9-2)

Zomerlust is a course specialist and he rates the most sensible guide for this form. He had plenty in his favour and ran very close to his best.

Joseph Henry made a bold bid form the front on this return to the extra furlong, but remains weighted to his best.

Docofthebay(IRE) enjoyed this return to a more conventional track and ran a solid race in defeat. He had beaten the winner off a 6lb lower mark when ending his losing run at Ayr two runs back, so is another that helps to set the standard here. (op 25-1)

Prime Exhibit met support back over his optimum distance with the ground in his favour. He proved free after being heavily restrained, but was travelling powerfully right out the back around 3f out. He momentarily had to wait for his challenge passing the 2f pole, but looking at the way he stayed on with purpose he was surely given too much to do. He is one to side with next time. (op 8-1 tchd 9-1)

Internationaldebut(IRE), 2lb out of the handicap, ran one of his better races but remains a very hard horse to actually win with. (op 33-1)

Misplaced Fortune, another that attracted support, moved nicely through the race before her stamina for the longer trip clearly gave way. (op 20-1 tchd 16-1)

My Kingdom(IRE) was another 6lb higher in this quest for the hat-trick, but his talented rider's claim helped negate that rise. He was going well on the far side, but being held up here proved a disadvantage and he is happiest on less conventional tracks than this. He was later reported to have been unsuited by the going. Official explanation: jockey said the gelding was unsuited by the Soft, Good to Soft in places going (op 10-1)

Desert Creek(IRE) looked to have a fair bit in his favour, but he was one of the first in trouble after turning into the home straight, and presumably something went amiss. Connections were unable to offer explanation and he was later routine tested. (op 9-2)

6722 E B F READ PAUL NICHOLLS EXCLUSIVELY ON BETFAIR MAIDEN STKS 6f

3:55 (3:56) (Class 3) 2-Y-O £6,605 (£1,965; £982; £490) Stalls Centre

Form RPR

0024 **1** **Rudegirl (IRE)**[19] 6230 2-8-12 78 .... SilvestreDeSousa 3 75
(N Tinkler) *wnt rt s: mde all: kpt on gamely fnl f: all out* **4/1**[3]

0 **2** ½ **Commended**[21] 6145 2-9-3 0 .... MichaelHills 5 79
(B W Hills) *bmpd s: sn w ldrs: no ex fnl 50yds* **11/4**[1]

3 1 **Iceblast** 2-9-3 0 .... DavidNolan 7 76
(M W Easterby) *swvd rt and hmpd s: hld up towards rr: effrt over 2f out: chsng ldrs 1f out: kpt on same pce last 100yds* **40/1**

4 6 **Questionnaire (IRE)** 2-8-12 0 .... DarryllHolland 8 53
(N J Vaughan) *wnt lft s: sn chsng ldrs: wknd over 1f out* **33/1**

65 **5** 3¼ **Cat Island**[24] 6058 2-8-12 0 .... RichardHills 2 43
(M H Tompkins) *chsd ldrs: wknd over 1f out* **25/1**

6 4 **What About You (IRE)** 2-9-3 0 .... PaulHanagan 4 36
(R A Fahey) *wnt lft s: sn trcking ldrs: upsides whn hung bdly lft over 1f out: sn wknd* **3/1**[2]

050 **7** *12* **Queen O'The Desert (IRE)**[21] 6157 2-8-12 72.........(t) JimmyFortune 1 —
(A M Balding) *w ldrs: wknd over 1f out: eased ins fnl f* **5/1**
8 *11* **Shirataki (IRE)** 2-9-3 0...................................... FrankieDettori 6 —
(M Johnston) *n.m.r sn after s: sn outpcd and in rr: hdwy wd outside over 2f out: sn lost pl and eased* **11/2**

1m 18.18s (6.28) **Going Correction** +0.825s/f (Soft) **8** Ran SP% **112.9**
Speed ratings (Par 99): **91,90,89,81,76 71,55,40**
toteswingers:1&2:£3.90, 1&3:£10.90, 2&3:£17.30 CSF £14.96 TOTE £4.20: £1.70, £1.30, £5.10; EX 19.10 Trifecta £504.60 Pool: £934.20 - 1.37 winning units..
Owner Jonathon And James White **Bred** Spratstown Bloodstock Ltd **Trained** Langton, N Yorks

FOCUS
This modest juvenile maiden was the fourth consecutive race on the card that saw the leaders dominate late throughout. It was run at a solid pace and once more the runners shunned either rail.

NOTEBOOK
Rudegirl(IRE) made most and ran out a tenacious winner, shedding her maiden tag at the fifth time of asking. She was handed an official mark of 78 after posing a career-best in a sales race in Ireland last month, and proved that to be spot-on here. The positive tactics on this drop back a furlong proved ideal so this now looks her optimum distance, and she clearly enjoyed the underfoot conditions. She could well make her mark in a nursery. (tchd 7-2 and 9-2)
Commended was backed to step up on the form of his debut eighth at Newbury last month and had every chance, but found the winner too strong near the finish. He got a bit warm beforehand and this added experience should bring him on again, so it wouldn't be surprising to see him go one better if reverting to less testing ground on his next outing. (tchd 10-3 in places)
Iceblast ◆, bred for speed, was unconsidered in the betting for this racecourse debut but ran a big race in defeat. He showed his inexperience from the gates, but travelled up strongly nearing the final furlong and only tired out of things nearing the end. This experience will not be lost on him and he is well up to winning a maiden.
Questionnaire(IRE) is by the leading first-season sire and attracted support on her debut. She travelled nicely in midfield, but lacked the tactical pace to stay with the principals from the furlong marker. Her pedigree suggests a stiffer test is what she wants, and good ground may also suit ideally. (op 40-1 tchd 25-1)
Cat Island still looked in need of this experience and is now eligible for nurseries. She should fare better next year. (op 18-1)
What About You(IRE) is bred to make his mark this year and was solid in the betting. He looked a threat passing 2f out, but struggled when asked for maximum effort on this ground as he began to hang markedly to his left. He should come on nicely for this introduction and ought to get a lot closer when faced with a sounder surface, as the dam's side of his pedigree strongly implies. (tchd 10-3 in a place)
Queen O'The Desert(IRE) was done with around 2f out on this return to maiden company, but surely needs quicker ground. (op 13-2)
Shirataki(IRE) is bred to need further and he looked all at sea on this soft ground. (op 5-1 tchd 9-2)

6723 PARSONAGE COUNTRY HOUSE HOTEL H'CAP — 5f
4:30 (4:30) (Class 4) (0-85,85) 3-Y-O+ **£6,540** (£1,946; £972; £485) **Stalls** Centre

Form RPR
4505 **1** **Haajes**[13] 6364 6-9-2 **83**...................................... PaulPickard(3) 20 94
(P T Midgley) *in rr: gd hdwy stands' side 2f out: edgd lft and r.o wl to ld nr fin* **7/1**[3]
0303 **2** *hd* **Russian Spirit**[10] 6446 4-9-5 **83**.......................... PhilipRobinson 1 93
(M A Jarvis) *w ldr: led over 1f out: hdd and no ex clsng stages* **8/1**
0213 **3** *1 ¼* **Mango Music**[21] 6140 7-8-13 **77**.......................... PaulHanagan 18 83
(R A Fahey) *mid-div: hdwy over 2f out: chsng ldrs over 1f out: styd on same pce fnl 150yds* **6/1**[2]
1000 **4** *1* **Walvis Bay (IRE)**[13] 6364 3-9-6 **84**...................... MickyFenton 6 86
(T P Tate) *prom: hdwy to chse ldrs over 1f out: styd on same pce* **25/1**
0060 **5** *¾* **Ishetoo**[48] 5302 6-9-0 **78**...................................... JimmyFortune 19 77
(Ollie Pears) *bhd: hdwy stands' side over 1f out: styd on wl ins fnl f* **12/1**
0306 **6** *1 ¼* **Strike Up The Band**[13] 6364 7-9-2 **85**................ BillyCray(5) 13 80
(D Nicholls) *led: hdd over 1f out: fdd* **9/1**
4260 **7** *shd* **Discanti (IRE)**[33] 5787 5-9-7 **85**......................(t) DuranFentiman 4 79
(T D Easterby) *chsd ldrs: kpt on same pce appr fnl f* **20/1**
0200 **8** *1 ¼* **Magical Macey (USA)**[21] 6140 3-8-13 **82**.............. DeanHeslop(5) 10 72
(T D Barron) *chsd ldrs: wknd appr fnl f* **25/1**
13-0 **9** *1* **Nadeen (IRE)**[13] 6358 3-9-0 **78**.......................... SilvestreDeSousa 9 64
(Michael Smith) *mid-div: hdwy over 2f out: kpt on: nvr ldrs* **33/1**
1104 **10** *½* **Mey Blossom**[27] 5941 5-8-13 **80**......................... MichaelStainton(3) 2 64
(R M Whitaker) *in rr: hdwy over 2f out: wknd appr fnl f* **16/1**
0400 **11** *½* **Floor Show**[42] 5480 4-8-11 **75**.............................. JackMitchell 8 58
(N Wilson) *s.i.s: sme hdwy 2f out: nvr a factor* **20/1**
0600 **12** *2 ¼* **Oldjoesaid**[21] 6142 6-9-2 **80**..............................(t) JamieSpencer 11 55
(K A Ryan) *s.i.s: in rr: hdwy over 1f out: nvr a factor* **5/1**[1]
2000 **13** *½* **Lucky Dan (IRE)**[13] 6358 4-8-6 **75**...................... AdamBeschizza(5) 3 48
(Paul Green) *bhd: hdwy 2f out: nvr on terms* **11/1**
0100 **14** *1 ½* **Niran (IRE)**[132] 2542 3-9-5 **83**.......................... AndrewElliott 14 50
(Mrs R A Carr) *chsd ldrs: wknd over 1f out* **50/1**
0104 **15** *1* **Mon Brav**[48] 5309 3-9-1 **79**...................................(v) DavidNolan 12 43
(D Carroll) *dwlt: a in rr* **16/1**
5110 **16** *1* **Kylladdie**[141] 2260 3-8-13 **77**.............................. FrankieDettori 7 37
(S Gollings) *in rr-div: bhd and eased over 1f out* **12/1**
0000 **17** *nk* **Luscivious**[3] 6663 6-8-11 **75**..............................(b) PJMcDonald 15 34
(J A Glover) *mid-div: lost pl 2f out* **25/1**

63.02 secs (3.72) **Going Correction** +0.825s/f (Soft) **17** Ran SP% **126.0**
Speed ratings (Par 105): **103,102,100,99,97 95,95,93,92,91 90,86,86,83,82 80,80**
toteswingers:1&2:£9.60, 1&3:£11.60, 2&3:£4.70 CSF £57.92 CT £379.80 TOTE £9.00: £2.20, £2.30, £1.80, £6.10; EX 38.90 Trifecta £145.70 Pool: £1,044.19 - 5.30 winning units..
Owner N Lomas, A Taylor Snr, A Taylor Jnr **Bred** Irish National Stud **Trained** Westow, N Yorks

FOCUS
A typically wide-open sprint handicap for the class, run at a strong early pace. The form looks solid enough with the winner back to his early-summer level.

6724 FUTURE CLEANING SERVICES "HANDS AND HEELS" APPRENTICE H'CAP — 1m 2f 88y
5:00 (5:01) (Class 4) (0-85,85) 4-Y-O+ **£6,540** (£1,946; £972; £485) **Stalls** Low

Form RPR
4523 **1** **Veiled Applause**[22] 6105 7-8-9 **76**........................ ShaneBKelly(3) 3 85
(J J Quinn) *in rr: hdwy over 2f out: styd on to ld last 100yds* **7/2**[2]
1261 **2** *½* **King Zeal (IRE)**[14] 6328 6-8-12 **76**...................... JamesRogers 9 84+
(B D Leavy) *led: hdd and no ex ins fnl f* **5/1**[3]
4002 **3** *nk* **Red Jade**[12] 6396 5-9-7 **85**.................................. AdamBeschizza 7 93
(R A Fahey) *hld up: hdwy over 3f out: chal over 2f out: no ex fnl 100yds* **3/1**[1]
0/00 **4** *8* **Boucheron**[87] 3974 5-8-7 **74**.............................. MarzenaJeziorek(3) 2 67
(R A Fahey) *mid-div: hdwy to chse ldrs over 3f out: outpcd appr fnl f* **7/1**
0360 **5** *nk* **Prince Of Johanne (IRE)**[69] 4594 4-8-9 **76**.......(p) MatthewCosham(3) 1 68
(T P Tate) *sn pushed along towards rr: hdwy on inner over 3f out: hung lft and rdr dropped whip over 2f out: wknd over 1f out* **14/1**
0206 **6** *7* **Rosbay (IRE)**[6] 6573 6-8-8 **72**..............................(p) AdamCarter 4 51
(T D Easterby) *chsd ldrs: drvn and outpcd over 3f out: wknd over 2f out* **13/2**
0000 **7** *1* **Follow The Flag (IRE)**[7] 6534 6-9-0 **81**..............(p) NoraLooby(3) 10 58
(A J McCabe) *mid-div: pushed along 6f out: hdwy to chse ldrs over 3f out: wknd over 1f out* **22/1**
0-00 **8** *22* **Motafarred (IRE)**[55] 5070 8-8-7 **71** oh2....................(t) HarryBentley 6 6
(Miss T Jackson) *chsd ldrs: lost pl over 2f out: eased whn bhd: t.o* **33/1**
6060 **9** *7* **Trans Sonic**[13] 6367 7-8-7 **71** oh2.............................. RyanPowell 8 —
(D O'Meara) *chsd ldrs: lost pl over 3f out: sn bhd: t.o* **20/1**

2m 15.65s (3.15) **Going Correction** +0.45s/f (Yiel) **9** Ran SP% **108.4**
Speed ratings (Par 105): **105,104,104,97,97 92,91,73,68**
toteswingers:1&2:£2.30, 1&3:£2.50, 2&3:£3.20 CSF £18.45 CT £48.90 TOTE £4.70: £1.80, £1.60, £1.30; EX 17.20 Trifecta £17.50 Pool: £486.60 - 20.46 winning units. Place 6 £378.69; Place 5 £88.59.
Owner Far 2 Many Sues **Bred** P J McCalmont **Trained** Settrington, N Yorks
■ Desert Vision was withdrawn (14/1, tried to burst out of stalls). Deduct 5p in the £ under R4.

FOCUS
Not a bad race of its type. There was a decent early pace on and once again three came clear late on. Sound form, rated around the winner.
T/Jkpt: Not won. T/Plt: £189.10 to a £1 stake. Pool of £122,579.72 - 473.17 winning tickets
T/Qpdt: £13.10 to a £1 stake. Pool of £10,113.72 - 571.00 winning tickets WG

6594 DUNDALK (A.W) (L-H)
Friday, October 8

OFFICIAL GOING: Standard

6726a IRISH STALLION FARMS EUROPEAN BREEDERS FUND MEDIAN AUCTION MAIDEN — 7f (P)
7:00 (7:00) 2-Y-O **£8,243** (£1,911; £836; £477)

RPR
1 **Tradition (IRE)**[24] 6066 2-9-3 .... JMurtagh 3 79
(David Wachman, Ire) *a.p: led or disp ld: drvn along to ld under 2f out: asserted 1f out: kpt on wl ins fnl f* **9/4**[1]
2 *1* **Equus Ferus (IRE)**[19] 6229 2-9-3 61.......................... RPCleary 8 76
(Ms Joanna Morgan, Ire) *in rr of mid-div on inner: 7th 1/2-way: swtchd rt early st: impr into 2nd over 1f out: kpt on wl wout rching wnr* **20/1**
3 *1* **Walfa (IRE)** 2-8-12 .... WJSupple 5 69
(P D Deegan, Ire) *in rr of mid-div: rdn and hdwy ent st: wnt 5th over 1f out: kpt on ins fnl f* **33/1**
4 *¾* **Music Pearl (IRE)**[14] 6338 2-8-12 .... KLatham 10 67
(G M Lyons, Ire) *hld up in rr: 14th appr st: hdwy on outer fr over 2f out: wnt 4th 1f out: kpt on ins fnl f* **10/3**[2]
5 *3 ½* **File And Paint (IRE)**[9] 6481 2-8-12 72...................... KJManning 14 58
(J S Bolger, Ire) *trckd ldrs in 4th: hdwy to join issue early st: hdd under 2f out and sn no ex: wknd fnl f* **9/1**
6 *4* **Norma Talmadge (IRE)**[5] 6594 2-8-12 .... PJSmullen 9 47
(Andrew Oliver, Ire) *chsd ldrs: 6th 1/2-way: impr ent st to dispute briefly 2f out: sn hdd and no ex: wknd* **16/1**
7 *hd* **Thunder Gulf** 2-9-3 .... CDHayes 1 52
(P D Deegan, Ire) *nvr bttr than mid-div: kpt on one pce in st* **25/1**
8 *shd* **Marvada (IRE)** 2-8-12 .... DPMcDonogh 13 47
(K J Condon, Ire) *in rr of mid-div: kpt on one pce in st wout threatening* **14/1**
9 *shd* **Distinguish (IRE)**[13] 6353 2-8-12 .... GregFairley 11 46
(M Johnston) *prom: disp ld: drvn along early st: sn hdd: no ex under 2f out: sn wknd* **7/2**[3]
10 *2* **Painted Fingers (IRE)**[44] 5427 2-8-12 .... WJLee 4 41
(Timothy Doyle, Ire) *chsd ldrs: 5th 1/2-way: pushed along ent st: no ex fr under 2f out* **50/1**
11 *½* **Pre Tax Profit (IRE)** 2-9-3 .... NGMcCullagh 6 45
(Reginald Roberts, Ire) *slowly away and a towards rr* **25/1**
12 *3* **Click And Go (IRE)**[47] 5339 2-8-12 .... PBBeggy 2 32
(P F McEnery, Ire) *trckd ldrs on inner racing keenly: 3rd 1/2-way: no ex fr 2f out: sn wknd* **50/1**
13 *nk* **Opinionated (IRE)** 2-8-9 .... GFCarroll(3) 12 31
(M Halford, Ire) *a bhd* **16/1**
14 *2 ½* **Molly Me (IRE)** 2-8-13 ow1.. FMBerry 7 26
(P D Deegan, Ire) *a bhd* **20/1**

1m 24.25s (84.25) **14** Ran SP% **128.6**
CSF £58.70 TOTE £2.80: £1.02, £5.50, £13.20; DF 52.30.
Owner Mrs John Magnier **Bred** Mrs Brid Cosgrove **Trained** Goolds Cross, Co Tipperary

NOTEBOOK
Tradition(IRE) is clearly progressive on this display. Ridden to the front early and spurning the opportunity to get some cover, he gradually upped the tempo and, even when a couple of late challenges developed, was always in control. He won snugly and should be one to look forward to next year, as a mile shouldn't inconvenience him. (op 5/2 tchd 2/1)
Equus Ferus(IRE) looks one with enough ability to win an ordinary maiden, and good ground would seem important. He got cover on the inside and wasn't in the most promising position turning into the straight but did run on well inside the last when getting a clear passage. The winner was far too good, but he should win a race and is reasonably handicapped for a nursery.
Walfa(IRE) ran a solid race and will improve. Held up just off the pace, she was being ridden along to improve before the turn in, but when the penny dropped she picked up nicely and ran on quite well. An extra furlong shouldn't trouble her and she could have a future.
Music Pearl(IRE) had a huge amount to do. Racing in last place and seemingly going nowhere at halfway, she had to come quite wide in the straight and, despite picking up well, hung right all the way up the straight. The way she ran may be due to greenness and she probably deserves another chance.
File And Paint(IRE) raced keenly in the leading group and weakened inside the last. (op 8/1)
Distinguish(IRE) disputed with the winner for much of the journey but faded tamely inside the final quarter-mile.

6727a IRISH STALLION FARMS EUROPEAN BREEDERS FUND STAR APPEAL STKS (LISTED RACE) — 7f (P)
7:30 (7:30) 2-Y-O **£34,513** (£10,088; £4,778; £1,592)

RPR
1 **Warning Flag (USA)**[33] 5793 2-9-1 86.......................... JMurtagh 5 98
(David Wachman, Ire) *mde virtually all: strly pressed and jnd 2f out: led again u.p jst under 1f out: swished tail and kpt on wl* **2/1**[1]

2 1 1/4 **Park Avenue (IRE)**[5] 6596 2-9-1 91 JPO'Brien 3 95
(A P O'Brien, Ire) *trckd ldrs on inner in 3rd: swtchd rt ent st: rdn to chal 1 1/2f out: jnd issue briefly 1f out: hdd and no imp u.p ins fnl f* **6/1**[3]

3 hd **Tell The Wind (IRE)**[14] 6339 2-8-12 88 DPMcDonogh 9 91
(Kevin Prendergast, Ire) *a.p: 2nd 1/2-way: impr to dispute ld 2f out: hdd u.p jst ins fnl f: no imp and kpt on same pce* **8/1**

4 2 1/2 **Juliet Capulet (IRE)**[12] 6401 2-8-12 86 (b) JAHeffernan 7 85
(A P O'Brien, Ire) *in rr of mid-div: sme hdwy ent st: wnt mod 4th over 1f out: kpt on same pce wout threatening* **14/1**

5 1 1/4 **Foolproof (IRE)**[61] 4880 2-9-1 87 WJLee 8 84
(John Joseph Murphy, Ire) *settled in rr: sme hdwy on outer ent st: mod 5th over 1f out: kpt on one pce* **25/1**

6 1 **Satin Love (USA)**[20] 6191 2-9-1 GregFairley 1 82
(M Johnston) *chsd ldrs on inner: pushed along in 6th ent st: no ex fr 1 1/2f out* **7/2**[2]

7 2 1/2 **Act Of Love (IRE)**[19] 6230 2-8-12 80 (b) CO'Donoghue 4 72
(David Marnane, Ire) *chsd ldrs racing keenly: 4th 1/2-way: no ex u.p fr under 2f out* **12/1**

8 hd **Posh Cracker (USA)**[7] 6545 2-8-12 (t) KLatham 6 72
(G M Lyons, Ire) *rrd leaving stalls: in tch towards rr: no ex fr 2f out* **8/1**

9 nk **Stage Master (USA)**[12] 6399 2-9-1 WMLordan 2 74
(David Wachman, Ire) *a towards rr* **9/1**

10 1 **Brown Pete (IRE)**[7] 6544 2-9-1 PBBeggy 10 71
(Paul W Flynn, Ire) *chsd ldrs on outer: 5th 1/2-way: no ex fr 2f out: wknd* **12/1**

1m 23.8s (83.80) **10** Ran SP% **128.0**
CSF £16.24 TOTE £2.70: £1.20, £2.00, £1.90; DF 14.60.
Owner Michael Tabor **Bred** Good Vibes Syndicate **Trained** Goolds Cross, Co Tipperary

NOTEBOOK
Warning Flag(USA) pulled out all the stops. Making all on the inside rail, he was joined and briefly headed as the second and third came at him inside the 1 1/2f, but what he produced under pressure was impressive as he continued to respond despite his tail swishing and eventually wore down his two main opponents. His tail-swishing doesn't stop him, and he is one to look forward to over middle distances next season. (op 11/4 tchd 3/1)
Park Avenue(IRE) is improving, and this surface seems responsible. Racing just off the pace, he made good headway to join issue with the winner inside the 2f point and kept going to the line, but the winner had too many guns. This is probably his optimum trip for now. (op 11/2 tchd 13/2)
Tell The Wind(IRE) improved on a career-best effort here the previous month. Racing up with the pace, she had every chance when heading the winner over 1f out but couldn't sustain it inside the last half-furlong. (op 8/1 tchd 7/1)
Juliet Capulet(IRE) was taking a small drop in class and ran well but doesn't look as progressive as one or two of the others. Racing in mid-division, she didn't get going until inside the last furlong and ran on without threatening. She probably wants a mile.
Foolproof(IRE) was stepping up in trip and did his best work late without threatening.
Satin Love(USA) never travelled and was beaten at the top of the straight. (op 7/2 tchd 4/1)

6730a CROWNE PLAZA RACE & STAY PACKAGE H'CAP 1m 4f (P)
9:00 (9:01) (60-85,85) 3-Y-O+ **£6,411** (£1,486; £650; £371)

RPR

1 **Realisation (USA)**[4] 6630 3-9-1 79 GregFairley 6 86
(M Johnston) *a.p: trckd ldr in 2nd: 3rd 5f out: hdwy to chal early st: led under 2f out: kpt on u.p: strly pressed wl ins fnl f: hld on* **9/4**[1]

2 hd **The Pier (IRE)**[152] 1950 4-10-0 85 WJLee 5 92+
(Joseph G Murphy, Ire) *trckd ldrs: 6th 1/2-way: 5th on outer under 2f out: kpt on u.p to go 2nd ins fnl f: styd on wl clsng stages: jst failed* **25/1**

3 3 **Kalacan (IRE)**[19] 6233 4-9-8 79 JMurtagh 3 81
(G M Lyons, Ire) *in rr of mid-div: 9th on inner 2f out: wnt 5th 1f out: kpt on fnl f wout rching ldrs* **8/1**[3]

4 hd **Home Secretary**[14] 6341 6-9-5 76 (t) PBBeggy 12 78
(Garvan Donnelly, Ire) *mid-div: hdwy into 4th appr st: rdn to go 2nd over 1f out: no ex ins fnl f* **20/1**

5 1/2 **Final Flashback (IRE)**[13] 6381 5-9-10 84 GFCarroll(3) 13 85
(Patrick J Flynn, Ire) *prom: wnt 2nd after 1/2-way: disp fr 4f out: led u.p ent st: hdd under 2f out: sn no ex* **12/1**

6 1 1/2 **Maal (IRE)**[14] 6341 7-9-8 79 (t) CO'Donoghue 11 78
(David Marnane, Ire) *hld up: sme hdwy early st: 6th over 1f out: no imp and kpt on one pce* **11/1**

7 2 1/2 **All About Timing (IRE)**[36] 5706 5-9-7 78 (b) KJManning 4 73
(J T Gorman, Ire) *chsd ldrs: 5th 1/2-way: 7th u.p early st: no imp and kpt on one pce* **33/1**

8 4 **Lesoto Diamond (IRE)**[14] 6341 8-9-3 74 JAHeffernan 8 62
(P A Fahy, Ire) *chsd ldrs: 7th 1/2-way: no imp u.p fr 1 1/2f out* **33/1**

9 3 1/2 **Solo Performer (IRE)**[12] 6404 5-9-4 82 DCByrne(7) 9 65
(H Rogers, Ire) *nvr a factor* **10/1**

10 3 1/2 **Chapter Nine (IRE)**[42] 5194 4-9-4 75 (b[1]) CDHayes 1 52
(J G Coogan, Ire) *a towards rr* **25/1**

11 3 **Righteous Man (IRE)**[103] 3492 3-9-7 85 (b) FMBerry 7 57
(Mrs John Harrington, Ire) *led: jnd 4f out: hdd ent st: no ex 2f out: wknd* **9/1**

12 1 1/2 **Al Dafa (USA)**[16] 3606 3-8-11 75 DPMcDonogh 2 45
(Gordon Elliott, Ire) *nvr a factor* **12/1**

13 dist **Scots Gaelic (IRE)**[13] 6378 3-9-3 81 PJSmullen 10 —
(Patrick J Flynn, Ire) *mid-div: 9th 1/2-way: no ex ent st: wknd: t.o* **4/1**[2]

P **Emmpat (IRE)**[21] 5464 12-9-9 85 (t) JPO'Brien(5) 14 —
(C F Swan, Ire) *trckd ldrs: 4th 1/2-way: no ex ent st: wknd: p.u injured 1f out* **12/1**

2m 29.14s (149.14)
WFA 3 from 4yo+ 7lb **14** Ran SP% **130.7**
CSF £77.49 CT £420.23 TOTE £2.30: £1.50, £13.60, £2.10; DF 127.50.
Owner Sheikh Hamdan Bin Mohammed Al Maktoum **Bred** Darley **Trained** Middleham Moor, N Yorks

FOCUS
The fourth and fifth are the best guides to the level.
NOTEBOOK
Realisation(USA) kept finding a bit in front and, while he got tired close home, he had enough in reserve to hold on. Content to take a lead while the wind blew in their faces in the back straight, Greg Fairley went for his race early in the straight and got a length or two, which proved crucial as he had just enough in hand to hold the runner-up. Realisation could return and, with a positive ride, win over a shorter trip. (op 5/2 tchd 2/1)
The Pier(IRE), held up just off the pace, stayed on strongly all the way to the line and would have got there in another stride. Versatile as to ground, he doesn't have to return here to get his going and this showed that there may be a handicap in him before the end of the season.
Kalacan(IRE) was held up off the pace and, despite never getting into the contest, stayed on well and did good late work on the inside. He benefited from horses coming back to him and is good enough to win a similar handicap, being versatile as to trip. (op 9/1)
Home Secretary gradually improved his position and looked to be travelling well just behind the leaders turning into the straight. However, he was unable to find a huge amount off the bridle and came home at the same pace.
Final Flashback(IRE) raced close to the pace for most of the way and was driven up to dispute it entering the straight. He ran out of steam once the winner made his move and kept on at the same pace. (op 10/1)
Emmpat(IRE) broke down very badly close home and had to be put down.

6731 - 6732a (Foreign Racing) - See Raceform Interactive

6386 ASCOT (R-H)
Saturday, October 9

OFFICIAL GOING: Straight course - good to soft (6.7); round course - soft (6.2)
Rail on round course moved 3yds ins the outside line from 10f to home straight increasing distances of 12f race by 12yds, 10f by 9yds and 1m by 3yds.
Wind: Moderate, across Weather: Low cloud

6733 CARRAIG INSURANCE HYPERION CONDITIONS STKS 7f
1:55 (1:56) (Class 2) 2-Y-O **£6,916** (£2,071; £1,035; £518; £258) **Stalls** Low

Form RPR

2004 1 **Dubawi Gold**[31] 5850 2-9-0 93 TomEaves 1 104
(M Dods) *mde all: drvn and c readily clr appr fnl f: unchal* **25/1**

1 2 3 1/2 **Tazahum (USA)**[30] 5893 2-9-0 85 RichardHills 2 95
(Sir Michael Stoute) *t.k.h fr stalls and stdd to dispute cl 3rd: pushed along and one pce 2f out: styd on u.p fnl f to take 2nd cl home but nvr any ch w unchal wnr* **11/4**[2]

1321 3 1/2 **Big Issue (IRE)**[10] 6475 2-9-0 107 RichardHughes 5 94
(R Hannon) *disp 3rd tl rdn over 2f out and sn chsng wnr but no imp: edgd lft over 1f out: no ex and lost 2nd cl home* **5/6**[1]

413 4 3 1/2 **Catalyze**[31] 5849 2-9-0 87 (t) JimmyFortune 4 85
(A M Balding) *chsd wnr: rdn over 2f out: sn lost 2nd: wknd over 1f out* **8/1**[3]

4104 5 5 **Memen (IRE)**[50] 5257 2-9-0 92 RyanMoore 3 73
(P F I Cole) *rdn 3f out: a in last and lost tch ins fnl 2f* **8/1**[3]

1m 29.31s (1.31) **Going Correction** +0.40s/f (Good) **5** Ran SP% **107.3**
Speed ratings (Par 101): **108,104,103,99,93**
CSF £86.10 TOTE £19.80: £5.10, £2.10; EX 69.90.
Owner Andrew Tinkler **Bred** A H Bennett **Trained** Denton, Co Durham

FOCUS
The ground was officially good to soft but the race time was not that bad and the jockeys reported it was riding on the dead side. This conditions event often throws up a useful performer, the best recent winners being subsequent Group 3 scorers Confront and Charlie Farnsbarns. Despite the small field this was an interesting contest but it produced a shock result.
NOTEBOOK
Dubawi Gold, a winner over 6f on fast ground and placed in Listed company, had been held in Group company since. However, up in trip and racing on soft ground for the first time, he set off in front and had his rivals in trouble 2f out. He found more for pressure and eventually ran out an emphatic winner. (tchd 33-1)
Tazahum(USA), a debut winner over 7f on Polytrack, was keen early on this turf debut. He kept on under pressure without ever looking likely to overhaul the winner. (op 9-4)
Big Issue(IRE), a dual winner at 6f and placed in Listed and Group company, was proven on soft ground and had plenty in hand judged on official ratings. He moved up threateningly at halfway but it was clear before the furlong marker he was making no impression on the leader, and he eventually lost second near the line. (op Evens)
Catalyze, a 7f winner on fast but placed in hot nursery last time at Doncaster on easy ground, tracked the leader early but was beaten 2f out, and may not have gone through the ground as well this time. (op 17-2)
Memen(IRE), winner at six and 7f on fast ground, appeared to handle soft ground last time but was being rowed along and in trouble soon after halfway. (tchd 17-2)

6734 SODEXO PRESTIGE CORNWALLIS STKS (GROUP 3) 5f
2:30 (2:30) (Class 1) 2-Y-O
£22,708 (£8,608; £4,308; £2,148; £1,076; £540) **Stalls** Low

Form RPR

1110 1 **Electric Waves (IRE)**[29] 5907 2-8-11 101 RichardMullen 9 105
(E S McMahon) *chsd ldrs: led 3f out: sn rdn: styd on strly thrght fnl f* **7/1**

0045 2 2 1/4 **Move In Time**[7] 6568 2-9-0 94 TomEaves 3 100
(B Smart) *chsd ldrs: rdn 1/2-way: chsd wnr ins fnl 2f: kpt on u.p but no imp fnl f: hld on wl for 2nd last strides* **25/1**

212 3 shd **Darajaat (USA)**[15] 6317 2-8-11 83 RichardHills 1 97
(M P Tregoning) *chsd ldrs: rdn along fr 2f out: kpt on wl fnl f to press for 2nd cl home but nvr any imp on wnr* **10/1**

1602 4 1 1/4 **Dinkum Diamond (IRE)**[29] 5907 2-9-0 108 DaneO'Neill 12 95
(H Candy) *sn chsng ldrs: rdn 1/2-way: styd on same pce fnl f* **7/2**[1]

1320 5 1/2 **Cape To Rio (IRE)**[51] 5245 2-9-0 105 RyanMoore 13 93
(R Hannon) *in rr: sn pushed along: hdwy over 1f out: kpt on wl fnl f and gng on cl home but nt rch ldrs* **11/1**

1601 6 nk **Arctic Feeling (IRE)**[22] 6141 2-9-0 101 JimmyFortune 11 92
(R A Fahey) *in rr: rdn 2f out: hdwy over 1f out: kpt on fnl f but nvr gng pce to get into contention* **14/1**

512 7 1 **Pabusar**[52] 5221 2-9-0 105 JimCrowley 8 89
(R M Beckett) *s.i.s towards rr: hdwy 1/2-way: drvn to chse ldrs 2f out but nvr on terms: wknd fnl 120yds* **13/2**[3]

211 8 1 1/4 **Invincible Ridge (IRE)**[21] 6191 2-9-0 93 RichardHughes 5 84
(R Hannon) *broke wl: trckd ldrs tl outpcd 1/2-way: sn pushed along: kpt on again ins fnl f but nvr a threat* **5/1**[2]

51 9 3/4 **Anadolu (IRE)**[90] 3939 2-8-11 0 PJSmullen 10 78
(Tracey Collins, Ire) *chsd ldrs: rdn 1/2-way: wknd fnl f* **25/1**

1133 10 3/4 **Loki's Revenge**[5] 6627 2-9-0 78 SteveDrowne 4 79
(W Jarvis) *broke wl but bdly outpcd and adrift in rr after 2f: stl plenty to do and last over 1f out: styd on strly ins fnl f: fin strly* **50/1**

2215 11 1 1/4 **Lexi's Hero (IRE)**[28] 5939 2-9-0 89 StevieDonohoe 14 74
(K A Ryan) *chsd ldrs: rdn 3f out: wknd wl over 1f out* **50/1**

116 12 nk **Marine Commando**[71] 4538 2-9-0 104 JMurtagh 6 73
(R A Fahey) *rdn 1/2-way: a outpcd* **17/2**

5031 13 1 1/4 **Jolah**[11] 6435 2-8-11 71 SebSanders 7 66
(C E Brittain) *bhd fr 1/2-way* **50/1**

2353 14 3 1/4 **The Thrill Is Gone**[22] 6141 2-8-11 101 WilliamBuick 2 54
(M R Channon) *led 2f: wknd 2f out: eased whn no ch* **14/1**

61.21 secs (0.71) **Going Correction** +0.40s/f (Good) **14** Ran SP% **119.6**
Speed ratings (Par 105): **110,106,106,104,103 102,101,99,98,96 94,94,92,87**
toteswingers: 1&2 £37.50, 1&3 £14.70, 2&3 £40.40 CSF £179.66 TOTE £10.00: £3.60, £7.90, £4.40; EX 246.60 Trifecta £1660.40 Pool: £2,468.26 - 1.10 winning units..
Owner J C Fretwell **Bred** Ms Michelle Lyons **Trained** Lichfield, Staffs
■ The Cornwallis Stakes is to switch to Newmarket next season.

The Form Book, Raceform Ltd, Compton, RG20 6NL

FOCUS
A good Group 3 for sprinting juveniles. Although a number of failed to fulfil the promise shown when winning this, Dominica did go on to take the King's Stand over C&D the following season, while Amour Propre won the Palace House Stakes. The pace seemed good from the start but nothing got into it from off the pace, and the first three were in the leading quartet throughout.

NOTEBOOK
Electric Waves(IRE), a three-time 5f winner; including a Listed race, on good and easy ground, had a bit to find with Dinkum Diamond on Flying Childers form but she jumped well from the gates, disputed the lead throughout and asserted entering the final furlong to score readily. It is notoriously difficult for 3yo sprinters to make their mark but she has a bit of scope and will have options against her own sex. (op 6-1)
Move In Time, a 6f winner on good but placed in a sales race over 5f, had put up fair efforts in Listed company since. Another to race close up from the start, he stuck to his task although no match for the winner. (op 33-1)
Darajaat(USA), a winner over 6f on Polytrack and placed over 61/2f since, was down in trip and up in grade but travelled well up with the pace only to have nothing left at the business end. (op 12-1)
Dinkum Diamond(IRE), runner-up to Zebedee in the Flying Childers last time with a couple of these, including today's winner, behind, raced wide of the leading group and, although staying on, could never land a serious blow. (op 4-1 tchd 9-2 in places)
Cape To Rio(IRE), a dual 5f winner in the spring on good and easy ground was another with a bit to find with Dinkum Diamond (on Sandown form). He stayed on well from the back in the closing stages and can be given extra credit as he raced widest of all. (op 12-1)
Arctic Feeling(IRE), a three-time 5f winner including at Listed level, was another who had finished behind the favourite at Doncaster. He came from off the pace and that was not the place to be as it turned out. (op 16-1)
Pabusar, a winner over 6f on good and runner-up in good Listed race last time, chased the leaders throughout but could make no headway in the latter stages. (op 5-1)
Invincible Ridge(IRE), a dual winner over 6f who acts on fast and easy ground, was up in grade and down in trip. He travelled well enough on the heels of the leaders until halfway but got left behind when the race began in earnest. (op 13-2)
Lexi's Hero(IRE) Official explanation: jockey said colt hung right throughout
Marine Commando won the Windsor Castle over C&D in June but had finished well held in the Richmond Stakes after a break. This drop back in trip on softer ground brought no improvement on that and he has something to prove now. (op 9-1 tchd 8-1)

6735 MODELS 1 BENGOUGH STKS (GROUP 3) — 6f
3:05 (3:07) (Class 1) 3-Y-O+

£34,062 (£12,912; £6,462; £3,222; £1,614; £810) **Stalls** Low

Form	Pos	Dist	Horse / details	RPR
6131	**1**		**Bewitched (IRE)**[27] 6009 3-9-1 105 ...(t) JMurtagh 5 (Charles O'Brien, Ire) *hld up in rr: rdn and hdwy over 1f out: str run ins fnl f: hung rt fnl 100yds and led nr fin* **6/1**[2]	112+
1034	**2**	¾	**Genki (IRE)**[21] 6177 6-9-1 111 ...(v) SteveDrowne 17 (R Charlton) *in rr: rdn and gd hdwy over 2f out: styd on u.p to ld fnl 120yds: hdd and carried rt nr fin* **6/1**[2]	109
2222	**3**	*1*	**Secret Witness**[14] 6363 4-9-1 92 ...(b) JoeFanning 18 (R A Harris) *pressed ldrs tl slt ld 3f out: styd on u.p tl hdd fnl 120yds: styd on same pce clsng stages* **50/1**	105
0432	**4**	½	**Iver Bridge Lad**[7] 6564 3-9-0 105 ...(b) AdamKirby 6 (J Ryan) *in tch: hrd drvn and styd on u.p fnl f but nvr quite gng pce to chal* **12/1**	104
3-01	**5**	*hd*	**Brave Prospector**[25] 6063 5-9-1 104 ... RichardMullen 12 (P W Chapple-Hyam) *chsd ldrs: rdn to chal 1f out: styng on same pce whn sltly hmpd fnl 20yds* **25/1**	103
20-4	**6**	*1 ¼*	**Huntdown (USA)**[22] 6147 4-9-1 110 ... PJSmullen 11 (Saeed Bin Suroor) *pressed ldrs: rdn and stl rt there 2f out: outpcd u.p ins fnl f* **16/1**	99
4610	**7**	*1 ½*	**Doncaster Rover (USA)**[35] 5744 4-9-1 108 ... RobertWinston 3 (D H Brown) *chsd ldrs: rdn fr 1/2-way: styd on same pce fr over 1f out* **11/1**	94
4-60	**8**	*shd*	**Mr David (USA)**[29] 5911 3-9-0 100 ... SebSanders 7 (B J Meehan) *chsd ldrs: rdn over 2f out: one pce fnl f* **40/1**	94
0100	**9**	*1*	**Mister Hughie (IRE)**[6] 6608 3-9-0 106 ... JimmyFortune 15 (M R Channon) *towards rr: rdn and hdwy over 1f out: styd on same pce fnl f* **25/1**	91
1U50	**10**	*3 ¼*	**Triple Aspect (IRE)**[21] 6194 4-9-5 108 ... LiamJones 19 (W J Haggas) *in rr: rdn over 3f out: styd on u.p fnl f but nvr in contention* **14/1**	84
0311	**11**	*1 ½*	**Redford (IRE)**[14] 6349 5-9-1 111 ... RichardHughes 16 (D Nicholls) *hld up in rr: rdn ins fnl 2f: sme prog fnl f but nvr any ch* **5/2**[1]	76
3102	**12**	*1 ½*	**Rash Judgement**[19] 6241 5-9-1 94 ... IanMongan 4 (E J Alston) *chsd ldrs tl wknd 2f out* **66/1**	71
0000	**13**	*1 ¼*	**Jimmy Styles**[14] 6349 6-9-1 102 ... LukeMorris 14 (C G Cox) *in tch and rdn 1/2-way: wknd 2f out* **20/1**	67
50/0	**14**	*2 ¼*	**Alhaban (IRE)**[22] 6147 4-9-1 97 ... DaneO'Neill 9 (R A Harris) *chsd ldrs over 3f* **100/1**	60
222-	**15**	*nk*	**Taajub (IRE)**[364] 6660 3-9-0 108 ... RichardHills 2 (W J Haggas) *spd 3f* **10/1**[3]	59
5500	**16**	*1 ¾*	**Edge Closer**[70] 4576 6-9-1 99 ...(b1) PatDobbs 8 (R Hannon) *led tl hdd 3f out: sn wknd* **66/1**	53
10-6	**17**	*1 ¾*	**Royal Rock**[25] 6063 6-9-1 109 ... GeorgeBaker 13 (C F Wall) *hmpd ins fnl 3f: a in rr* **14/1**	47

1m 14.85s (0.45) **Going Correction** +0.40s/f (Good)
WFA 3 from 4yo+ 1lb **17** Ran SP% **122.3**
Speed ratings (Par 113): **113,112,110,110,109 108,106,105,104,100 98,96,94,91,91 88,86**
toteswingers: 1&2 £6.70, 1&3 £24.80, 2&3 £33.10 CSF £38.76 TOTE £5.40: £1.70, £2.60, £12.40; EX 34.70 Trifecta £2045.20 Pool: £3,344.29 - 1.21 winning units..
Owner Mrs J Magnier & Mrs J O'Brien **Bred** Monsieur J C Coude **Trained** Straffan, Co Kildare
■ Stewards' Enquiry : J Murtagh caution: careless riding

FOCUS
This recently instituted Group 3 has been won by a battle-hardened sprinter on both previous renewals. It attracted a big ield including the 2009 winner but was an ordinary race for the grade.

NOTEBOOK
Bewitched(IRE) ◆, a winner at 5f and 6f, including Listed and Group 3s, was held up off the pace early and did not appear to be making much headway under pressure inside the final 2f. However, she hit top gear inside the last and, despite edging right, proved too strong for the runner-up. She could make up into a top-class sprinter next season. (op 8-1)
Genki(IRE), a multiple 6f winner including twice over C&D, had finished third in the Group 1 Haydock Sprint Cup and fourth in the Ayr Gold Cup on his previous two starts. More consistent since having headgear fitted, he came to win his race entering the final furlong, only to be run down by the filly late on. He deserves to pick up another race before the end of the season. (op 11-2 tchd 5-1)
Secret Witness is a consistent handicapper but was up in grade. He ran arguably a personal best, having been in the firing line from the start. (tchd 66-1 in a place)
Iver Bridge Lad, a winner at 5f and 6f including Listed level, has been running well in handicaps with blinkers on of late, including being touched off the previous weekend. He was keen early as usual but stayed on well, just missing out on the places. (op 14-1)
Brave Prospector, third in this last year but lightly raced since, travelled well in the slipstream of the leaders and looked a possible winner when coming to challenge inside the final 2f. However, his effort petered out under pressure. (op 16-1)
Huntdown(USA) had been placed in Group company but had been lightly raced of late, showed pace early before fading when the challenges arrived.
Doncaster Rover(USA), a three-time winner over 6f (twice in Listed company), was being stoked along at halfway before staying on late without threatening. (op 12-1)
Mr David(USA), lightly raced since finishing fourth in the Gimcrack last year and held this season, offered more encouragement, showing plenty of pace before tiring in the last furlong or so. (op 33-1 tchd 100-1 in a place)
Mister Hughie(IRE), who finished well beaten in the Prix de l'Abbaye on very soft the previous weekend, came from well back to reach his final position. (op 18-1 tchd 33-1 in a place)
Triple Aspect(IRE) also came from well back to reach his final position. (tchd 12-1)
Redford(IRE) came into this in blinding form, having won the Ayr Gold Cup and then the totesport Challenge Cup over 7f here. Held up under a confident ride, he never got close to making a challenge and this has to go down as disappointing, especially considering both the ninth and tenth raced behind him in the early stages. Official explanation: jockey said gelding ran flat (op 11-4 tchd 3-1)
Royal Rock never got into contention after racing in mid-division, eventually finishing last. (op 10-1)

6736 LADBROKES.COM STKS (HERITAGE H'CAP) — 1m 4f
3:40 (3:40) (Class 2) (0-105,104) 3-Y-O+

£46,732 (£13,995; £6,997; £3,502; £1,747; £877) **Stalls** High

Form	Pos	Dist	Horse / details	RPR
0111	**1**		**Vulcanite (IRE)**[84] 4153 3-8-10 **97** ... JimCrowley 19 (R M Beckett) *stdd in tch: hdwy fr 3f out: led ins fnl 2f: styd on gamely u.p fnl f* **8/1**[3]	105+
602	**2**	¾	**Sirvino**[16] 6304 5-9-1 **95** ... TomEaves 14 (T D Barron) *chsd ldrs: rdn and one pce over 2f out: styd on u.p fnl f to take 2nd ins fnl f and kpt on but a hld by wnr* **12/1**	101
40	**3**	*hd*	**Siberian Tiger (IRE)**[28] 5949 5-8-11 **91** ...(p) RobertWinston 17 (M Wigham) *chsd ldrs: rdn: hung rt and lost position ins fnl 2f: rallied u.p fnl f and kpt on cl home but a hld by wnr* **12/1**	97
0003	**4**	*nk*	**The Betchworth Kid**[14] 6362 5-8-10 **95** ... JohnFahy(5) 6 (A King) *hld up in rr: hdwy on ins over 2f out: styd on wl u.p fnl f and gng on cl home but no imp on wnr* **14/1**	101+
0001	**5**	*hd*	**Red Merlin (IRE)**[5] 6630 5-9-2 **96** 6ex ...(v) AdamKirby 16 (C G Cox) *stdd towards rr: hdwy on ins over 2f out and kpt on u.p fnl f* **12/1**	101
4500	**6**	*shd*	**Montaff**[74] 4461 4-9-5 **99** ... JMurtagh 13 (M R Channon) *stdd towards rr: hdwy over 2f out: styd on fnl f: gng on cl home* **20/1**	104
0532	**7**	*1*	**Prompter**[13] 6387 3-9-0 **104** ... MartinLane(3) 3 (M L W Bell) *in rr: hdwy u.p on outside fr 2f out: kpt on fnl f: nt rch ldrs* **7/1**[2]	107
0532	**8**	*4*	**Chilly Filly (IRE)**[9] 6493 4-8-12 **92** ... JoeFanning 2 (M Johnston) *in rr and sn outpcd: rdn 3f out: styd on fr over 1f out and gng on cl home but nvr a threat* **12/1**	89
4065	**9**	*1 ¼*	**Icon Dream (IRE)**[24] 6101 3-9-0 **101** ...(vt) JimmyFortune 15 (David Wachman, Ire) *in tch: rdn and hdwy whn hmpd over 2f out: kpt on fnl f but nvr a threat* **20/1**	96
1013	**10**	¾	**The Fonz**[13] 6387 4-8-13 **93** ... RyanMoore 7 (Sir Michael Stoute) *mid-div 1/2-way: rdn and sme hdwy u.p fr 2f out: nvr rchd ldrs: sn hung lft: wknd ins fnl f* **6/1**[1]	87
521-	**11**	*hd*	**Hunterview**[154] 7018 4-8-13 **93** ...(b) WilliamBuick 10 (D E Pipe) *chsd ldrs: wnt 2nd 5f out: slt ld u.p appr fnl 2f: hdd sn after: wknd qckly fnl f* **14/1**	87
1510	**12**	*3 ¾*	**Mount Athos (IRE)**[29] 5908 3-8-8 **95** ... SebSanders 18 (J W Hills) *chsd ldr: rdn 4f out: styd disputing 2nd 2f out: wknd over 1f out* **7/1**[2]	83
0513	**13**	¾	**Spirit Is Needed (IRE)**[11] 6437 4-8-11 **91** ...(b) RoystonFfrench 5 (M Johnston) *sn towards rr: stl plenty to do 2f out: mod prog ins fnl f* **40/1**	77
0226	**14**	*nk*	**Magaling (IRE)**[21] 6193 4-8-5 **88** ... JamesSullivan(3) 8 (M W Easterby) *sn led: hdd appr fnl 2f: wknd wl over 1f out* **10/1**	74
-305	**15**	*13*	**Man Of Iron (USA)**[35] 5749 4-9-10 **104** ... J-PGuillambert 1 (L M Cumani) *chsd ldrs: rdn 4f out: wknd qckly 2f out* **33/1**	69
1255	**16**	*44*	**Magicalmysterytour (IRE)**[13] 6387 7-8-9 **89** ... StevieDonohoe 4 (W J Musson) *a towards rr: t.o* **14/1**	—

2m 38.2s (5.70) **Going Correction** +0.70s/f (Yiel)
WFA 3 from 4yo+ 7lb **16** Ran SP% **125.2**
Speed ratings (Par 109): **109,108,108,108,108 107,107,104,103,103 103,100,100,99,91 61**
toteswingers: 1&2 £16.70, 1&3 £23.70, 2&3 £27.30 CSF £98.70 CT £1170.95 TOTE £9.00: £2.60, £2.80, £2.80, £3.70; EX 83.70 Trifecta £2178.50 Part won. Pool: £2,944.00 - 0.50 winning units..
Owner Pearl Bloodstock Ltd **Bred** Barouche Stud Ireland Ltd **Trained** Whitsbury, Hants
■ Stewards' Enquiry : Jim Crowley caution: use of whip

FOCUS
A strong, valuable handicap in which three of the previous four winners were 3yo, all of whom went on to score at Group level. This year's line-up again looked strong and, with the big field, it produced a good finish.

NOTEBOOK
Vulcanite(IRE) ◆ had won three of his four previous starts on turf at up to 1m4f, all on a sound surface, but had been raised 10lb for his last success and was also returning from a 12-week break. Never far away, he came through to lead early in the straight and stuck on gamely under pressure to hold off a number of challenges. He looks sure to be aimed at the November Handicap now he has proved himself on the ground, and will go to Doncaster with a major chance. (tchd 7-1)
Sirvino, a multiple winner last season culminating in the John Smith's Cup, put up better effort last time after a quiet spell and was just 3lb above his last winning mark. Having won his last three starts on right-handed tracks, he ran a fine race on this first try at the trip and could be ready to score again before long. (op 10-1 tchd 9-1)
Siberian Tiger(IRE) has won on all sorts of ground, including over hurdles. He ran his best race since returning to the Flat, and could take on the winner again at Doncaster before returning to hurdles.
The Betchworth Kid ◆ was progressive last season for another yard and then made up into fair hurdler. He ran his best race on the Flat this season over 1m6f on soft last time, and built on that off 9lb below his last winning mark. He could win again on the Flat before long, but should be ready for a return to hurdles if that is the preferred option. (tchd 16-1)
Red Merlin(IRE), who completed a hat-trick when winning Old Newton Cup in 2009, gained his first success since when taking a Warwick handicap over 1m2f last time. Raised 6lb for that, he stayed on up the inside in the straight, missing out narrowly on a place in the frame. (op 14-1)

Montaff had previously shown his best form on soft, including finishing second to Opinion Poll in April. Held in Group company on faster ground, he was dropped in grade on this return from over ten weeks off and stayed on well in the straight. There is a staying race in him on this evidence. (op 25-1)

Prompter had not won since his juvenile days but had posted decent efforts in handicaps, including on his first try at the trip over C&D last time. Suited by good or easy ground, he travelled well off the pace but was forced to race wide throughout from his draw, and could not pick up sufficiently to mount a challenge. (tchd 6-1)

The Fonz, a dual winner on a sound surface at around this trip earlier in the season but behind Prompter here last time on easy ground, was 6lb above his last winning mark. Like his old rival, he ended up trying to make his ground on the outside and had nothing left in the closing stages, the ground was probably not ideal either. (op 8-1)

Hunterview Official explanation: jockey said gelding stopped quickly

Mount Athos(IRE), whose wins this summer were on fast ground, had been well beaten on his only try on soft and, 11lb above last winning mark, the result was the same here after he showed up prominently early. (op 8-1)

Spirit Is Needed(IRE) Official explanation: jockey said gelding never travelled

Magicalmysterytour(IRE) Official explanation: jockey said gelding lost its action

6737 JAGUAR XJ AUTUMN STKS (GROUP 3) 1m (R)

4:15 (4:16) (Class 1) 2-Y-O

£22,708 (£8,608; £4,308; £2,148; £1,076; £540) Stalls High

Form				RPR
541	1		**Abjer (FR)**[26] 6036 2-9-0 80 ... RichardHills 2 (C E Brittain) *trckd ldrs: pushed along to go 2nd over 2f out: styd on wl to ld fnl 150yds: kpt on strly* **33/1**	104
11	2	1 ¾	**Pausanias**[24] 6083 2-9-0 99 ... RichardHughes 7 (R Hannon) *hld up in rr: hdwy fr 2f out: rdn and styd on wl thrght fnl f to take 2nd cl home but no imp on wnr* **9/1**[3]	100
421	3	½	**Dux Scholar**[30] 5871 2-9-0 87 ... RyanMoore 6 (Sir Michael Stoute) *trckd ldrs: str run on ins to ld over 2f out: hdd and no ex fnl 150yds: wknd and lost 2nd cl home* **7/2**[2]	99
U11	4	2	**Toolain (IRE)**[77] 4355 2-9-0 105 ... PhilipRobinson 5 (M A Jarvis) *in tch: pushed along and nt clr run over 2f out: edgd rt and hdwy over 1f out: kpt on fnl f but nvr rchd ldrs* **2/1**[1]	95
1	5	2 ¾	**Baptist (USA)**[21] 6190 2-9-0 85 ... JimmyFortune 8 (A M Balding) *in rr tl hdwy on ins to get wl in tch over 2f out: nvr quite rchd ldrs and wknd over 1f out* **10/1**	89
1	6	4	**Masked Marvel**[24] 6087 2-9-0 0 ... WilliamBuick 1 (J H M Gosden) *trckd ldrs: rdn and hdwy on outside 3f out: nvr quite on terms and wknd ins fnl 2f* **7/2**[2]	80
0402	7	2	**Al Madina (IRE)**[29] 5910 2-8-11 100 ... TomEaves 4 (B Smart) *trckd ldrs: rdn and wl there 2f out: fading whn hmpd over 1f out* **11/1**	72
6	8	11	**Dream Catcher (FR)**[41] 2-9-0 0 ... RichardMullen 3 (D Nicholls) *led tl hdd over 2f out: sn btn* **25/1**	51

1m 44.84s (4.14) **Going Correction** +0.70s/f (Yiel) 8 Ran SP% **112.0**

Speed ratings (Par 105): **107,105,104,102,100 96,94,83**

toteswingers: 1&2 £12.50, 1&3 £10.50, 2&3 £3.40 CSF £285.97 TOTE £24.60: £4.00, £2.30, £1.60; EX 228.30 Trifecta £1225.30 Pool: £12,253.99 - 7.40 winning units..

Owner Mohammed Al Shafar **Bred** Malcolm Parrish **Trained** Newmarket, Suffolk

■ Another race set to switch to Newmarket in 2011.

FOCUS

A decent juvenile Group 3 that is often won by a progressive performer. The best recent scorers have been the multiple Group winners Nayef and Kite Wood. There was plenty of interest in this year's line-up, especially as six of the field had been successful last time out, but there was another surprise result.

NOTEBOOK

Abjer(FR), whose win came at 1m1f on good ground at Redcar, was up in grade but has clearly improved since that success and showed plenty of courage to battle back to the front after looking held. His trainer will no doubt be looking at bigger targets.

Pausanias, a winner on his debut over 7f on fast ground at Goodwood, had dead-heated at Kempton next time. Up in trip and grade and on different ground, he stayed on all the way to the line, having been held up, without ever looking likely to win. He will appreciate the return to better ground. (op 5-1)

Dux Scholar, the winner of a 1m maiden on good and with form on fast and soft, got a good split up the rail and came to lead inside the final 2f before finding the winner too determined inside the last furlong. (op 5-1)

Toolain(IRE) who beat two subsequent winners over 7f on Polytrack then won a Listed race over 7f here, was up in trip and grade. He never saw much daylight at any stage and, although by a sire whose progeny go well on soft ground, seemed to be less effective on it. (op 9-4)

Baptist(USA), a winner on debut from a more experienced subsequent winner over 7f on fast, was up in trip and grade on different ground and gave the impression this came too soon in his career. (op 9-1 tchd 8-1)

Masked Marvel, a 260,000euros son of Montjeu, was a winner on his debut in a 1m Sandown maiden. He got involved in some early scrimmaging but was close enough turning in. He was eased in the straight once his chance had gone. (tchd 4-1 and 9-2 in a place)

Al Madina(IRE), a surprise runner-up to the subsequent Fillies' Mile winner White Moonstone in the May Hill, was far too keen in the early stages and paid for it in the straight. (tchd 12-1)

6738 DAVID & TONI EYLES H'CAP 1m 2f

4:50 (4:51) (Class 2) (0-105,102) 3-Y-O+

£9,969 (£2,985; £1,492; £747; £372; £187) Stalls High

Form				RPR
0026	1		**Kings Destiny**[21] 6179 4-9-8 100 ... PhilipRobinson 2 (M A Jarvis) *trckd ldr: chal 3f out: led wl over 2f out: styd on wl u.p ins fnl f* **5/1**	108
1001	2	½	**Rock N Roll Ransom**[15] 6318 3-8-13 96 ... J-PGuillambert 9 (L M Cumani) *trckd ldrs: rdn and styd on fnl 2f: chsd wnr over 1f out and styd on wl fnl f but a hld* **5/2**[2]	103
20-0	3	1 ¼	**Moyenne Corniche**[28] 5951 5-9-4 96 ... JimmyFortune 4 (M L W Bell) *t.k.h: hld up in rr: hdwy on outside over 2f out: styd on u.p to take 3rd jst ins fnl f but nt rch ldng duo* **25/1**	101
1013	4	1 ¾	**Spanish Duke (IRE)**[30] 5879 3-9-0 97 ... RichardHughes 8 (J L Dunlop) *t.k.h: hld up in rr tl rapid hdwy to trck ldrs 4f out: rdn to chse wnr 2f out: no imp and lost 2nd over 1f out: wknd fnl f and lost 3rd nr fin* **2/1**[1]	98
	5	1	**Seven Summits (IRE)**[89] 4001 3-8-12 95 ... RyanMoore 10 (J Noseda) *in rr: pushed along over 2f out: styd on same pce u.p over 1f out* **9/2**[3]	94
0630	6	1	**Thin Red Line (IRE)**[21] 6193 4-9-1 93 ... TomEaves 6 (M Dods) *chsd ldrs: rdn 3f out: wknd ins fnl 2f* **10/1**	90
2540	7	14	**Suits Me**[21] 6179 7-9-10 102 ... MickyFenton 7 (T P Tate) *led: jnd 3f out: hdd wl over 2f out: sn btn* **25/1**	71

2m 14.6s (7.60) **Going Correction** +0.70s/f (Yiel)

WFA 3 from 4yo+ 5lb 7 Ran SP% **113.5**

Speed ratings (Par 109): **97,96,95,94,93 92,81**

toteswingers: 1&2 £8.70, 1&3 £10.80, 2&3 £4.60 CSF £17.66 CT £276.79 TOTE £5.60: £2.60, £2.30; EX 23.30 Trifecta £270.60 Pool: £1,199.71 - 3.28 winning units..

Owner Dennis Yardy **Bred** D A Yardy **Trained** Newmarket, Suffolk

FOCUS

A high-class and tightly knit handicap that fell to subsequent Royal Ascot winner Cill Rialaig in 2009.

NOTEBOOK

Kings Destiny, a winner at up to 1m4f on soft, but effective at 1m2f on fast, had finished runner-up in the 1m4f heritage handicap earlier on the card last season. Racing off 2lb higher but faced with a slightly easier task, he disputed the lead throughout and, after kicking for home off the turn, put his stamina to good use to hold off the persistent runner-up. He should be winning again and, as he handles Polytrack, the Churchill Stakes at Lingfield next month might prove a suitable target. (op 6-1 tchd 7-1)

Rock N Roll Ransom ◆ is lightly raced but had won three of five starts, including one over C&D. Despite being 8lb above his last winning mark, he ran his race if perhaps a little too keen early on. He looks the sort to make up into a cracking 4-y-o for the yard. (op 2-1 tchd 11-4 in a place)

Moyenne Corniche, a 1m winner on easy ground but effective at up to 1m2f on soft ground, had been well beaten on his only previous start this year. He finished well from off the pace to show that much of his ability remains. (tchd 20-1)

Spanish Duke(IRE), a four-time winner at up to 1m2f, acts on fast but is suited by easy ground. He came around his field on the run towards the straight but had nothing left under pressure from over a furlong out. He is 9lb above his last winning mark and the handicapper appears in charge now. (tchd 15-8)

Seven Summits(IRE), a 1m2f winner on Polytrack for Aidan O'Brien but effective over 1m1f on fast, was having his first run for a new stable and failed to make an impression on this easier surface. (op 15-2)

Thin Red Line(IRE), a Polytrack winner at 1m4f but effective at 1m2f on good and easy ground, was 6lb above last winning mark and faded after having his chance early in the straight. (tchd 12-1)

Suits Me handles most ground on turf but is better known as a Polytrack performer. He made the running but was given no peace by the winner and faded in the straight. He will be seen to much better effect back on Polytrack, and he could well meet the winner again in the Churchill Stakes next month. (op 20-1)

6739 BRITISH CHAMPIONS DAY APPRENTICE H'CAP 5f

5:25 (5:27) (Class 4) (0-85,85) 3-Y-O+

£4,984 (£1,492; £746; £373; £186; £93) Stalls Low

Form				RPR
2211	1		**Humidor (IRE)**[17] 6280 3-9-5 83 ... MatthewDavies 5 (George Baker) *chsd ldrs: drvn to ld appr fnl f: hld on all out* **6/1**[3]	94
4535	2	nse	**Ancient Cross**[22] 6142 6-9-7 85 ... (t) JamesSullivan 4 (M W Easterby) *chsd ldrs: rdn and chsd wnr ins fnl f: str run cl home: jst failed* **4/1**[1]	96
4360	3	1 ½	**Even Bolder**[11] 6440 7-8-2 71 oh3 ... HarryBentley(5) 1 (E A Wheeler) *chsd ldrs: racd wd towards stands' side fr 1/2-way but styd on wl to take 3rd wl ins fnl f but nt rch ldng duo* **10/1**	77
3316	4	¾	**Boogie Waltzer**[42] 5528 3-8-5 74 ... (t) RyanClark(5) 13 (S C Williams) *chsd ldrs: rdn and styd on fnl 2f: kpt on ins fnl f but nvr gng pce of ldng duo* **25/1**	77
0034	5	hd	**Lost In Paris (IRE)**[19] 6245 4-8-12 79 ... (v) LanceBetts(3) 6 (T D Easterby) *led tl hdd appr fnl f: wknd u.p fnl 150yds* **5/1**[2]	81
3004	6	1 ½	**Rapid Water**[10] 6478 4-8-11 75 ... (b) SimonPearce 14 (A M Balding) *in tch: rdn and styd on fnl 2f: nt rch ldrs* **12/1**	72
-050	7	1 ½	**Just For Mary**[13] 6400 6-9-4 82 ... AndreaAtzeni 11 (Daniel Mark Loughnane, Ire) *in rr: racd towards far side and hdwy over 1f out: styd on fnl f but nvr a threat* **9/1**	73
3560	8	¾	**Red Avalanche (IRE)**[19] 6253 3-8-9 78 ... (b[1]) DuilioDaSilva(5) 16 (P F I Cole) *chsd ldrs: rdn 3f out: wknd appr fnl f* **25/1**	67
5560	9	½	**Invincible Lad (IRE)**[14] 6358 6-8-13 80 ... (p) BillyCray(3) 3 (E J Alston) *wnt lft s: racd alone stands' side and a struggling to go pce* **12/1**	67
0460	10	1	**The Strig**[19] 6253 3-8-5 72 ... TobyAtkinson(3) 8 (S C Williams) *chsd ldrs: rdn 3f out: wknd appr fnl f* **33/1**	55
1033	11	1	**Fair Passion**[8] 6539 3-8-8 72 ... MarcHalford 9 (D Shaw) *s.i.s: sn chsng ldrs: wknd over 1f out* **25/1**	52
41	12	hd	**Arctic Lynx (IRE)**[25] 6060 3-8-7 71 oh1 ... KierenFox 7 (J R Best) *sn drvn to chse ldrs: wknd ins fnl 2f* **5/1**[2]	50
1412	13	hd	**Magical Speedfit (IRE)**[11] 6440 5-8-6 75 ... RyanPowell(5) 15 (G G Margarson) *racd towards far side: outpcd most of way* **14/1**	53
0000	14	2 ¼	**Quarrel (USA)**[15] 6321 3-9-4 85 ... JohnFahy(3) 17 (W J Haggas) *stdd s: a towards rr* **20/1**	55
001	15	hd	**Commander Wish**[3] 6679 7-8-0 71 6ex oh13 ... VictoriaFletcher(7) 2 (Lucinda Featherstone) *hmpd s: a in rr* **25/1**	40
0520	16	¾	**Solemn**[14] 6364 5-9-7 85 ... (b) MartinLane 12 (J M Bradley) *chsd ldrs to 1/2-way* **20/1**	52

61.76 secs (1.26) **Going Correction** +0.40s/f (Good) 16 Ran SP% **136.6**

Speed ratings (Par 105): **105,104,102,101,101 98,96,95,94,92 91,90,90,86,86 85**

toteswingers: 1&2 £6.40, 1&3 £32.30, 2&3 £28.80 CSF £30.98 CT £214.18 TOTE £7.30: £2.30, £1.80, £3.50, £5.60; EX 46.80 Trifecta £522.30 Pool: £1,362.40 - 1.93 winning units. Place 6 £1,593.19, Place 5 £461.65.

Owner M Khan X2 **Bred** Yeomanstown Stud **Trained** Moreton Morrell, Warwicks

■ Stewards' Enquiry : Matthew Davies two-day ban: used whip with excessive and in the incorrect place (Oct 25-26)

FOCUS

A good-sized field for this competitive apprentices' sprint handicap and a desperate finish between two of the leading young riders. The time was over half a second slower than the earlier juvenile Group 3.

T/Plt: £1,759.80 to a £1 stake. Pool of £135,920.81. 56.38 winning tickets. T/Qpdt: £96.80 to a £1 stake. Pool of £10,377.49. 79.30 winning tickets. ST

[6711] WOLVERHAMPTON (A.W) (L-H)

Saturday, October 9

OFFICIAL GOING: Standard changing to standard to fast after race 2 (6.10)

Wind: Fresh, against Weather: Overcast

6740 BETDAQ.COM NURSERY 5f 216y(P)

5:40 (5:41) (Class 6) (0-65,65) 2-Y-O £1,706 (£503; £252) Stalls Low

Form RPR

3031 1 **One Cool Bex**[24] 6072 2-9-4 62 (e) PatCosgrave 10 68
(P J McBride) *hld up in tch: led over 1f out: rdn and hung rt ins fnl f: hung lft nr fin: jst hld on* 13/2[3]

50 2 shd **Saucy Buck (IRE)**[26] 6035 2-9-5 63 SamHitchcott 8 69
(M R Channon) *hld up: hdwy over 1f out: r.o: bmpd nr fin: jst failed* 10/1

0450 3 1 1/4 **Brave Battle**[16] 6308 2-9-6 64 PatDobbs 4 66
(R Hannon) *a.p: rdn over 1f out: edgd lft ins fnl f: styd on* 11/4[1]

0050 4 1/2 **Wandering Lad**[26] 6035 2-9-3 61 DavidNolan 13 61
(D Carroll) *chsd ldrs: rdn and ev ch over 1f out: hung lft ins fnl f: styd on same pce* 16/1

2604 5 1 1/4 **Piccoluck**[24] 6075 2-9-7 65 (tp) DuranFentiman 2 62
(Mrs D J Sanderson) *mid-div: rdn 1/2-way: hdwy over 1f out: r.o: nt rch ldrs* 10/1

4310 6 1 1/4 **Country Waltz**[3] 6674 2-9-1 59 CathyGannon 9 52
(M R Channon) *chsd ldr: led 1/2-way: rdn and hdd over 1f out: hmpd ins fnl f: no ex* 7/2[2]

0624 7 3/4 **Rylee Mooch**[4] 6645 2-9-0 58 PaulEddery 5 49
(R C Guest) *led to 1/2-way: rdn over 1f out: wknd ins fnl f* 13/2[3]

4040 8 nk **Mr Optimistic**[24] 6075 2-9-6 64 LiamKeniry 6 54
(R A Fahey) *hld up: plld hrd: hdwy over 1f out: wknd ins fnl f* 16/1

6455 9 5 **Swendab (IRE)**[12] 6419 2-9-7 65 LukeMorris 3 40
(J G M O'Shea) *hld up: stmbld after 100yds: nvr on terms* 14/1

4405 10 1/2 **Mystica (IRE)**[67] 4677 2-9-4 62 JamesDoyle 1 35
(D J S Ffrench Davis) *prom: rdn over 2f out: wknd over 1f out* 20/1

0540 11 1 1/2 **Deva Le Deva (IRE)**[18] 6264 2-9-0 63 RossAtkinson(5) 7 32
(Tom Dascombe) *hld up: rdn over 2f out: a in rr* 25/1

1m 14.98s (-0.02) **Going Correction** -0.075s/f (Stan) 11 Ran SP% 120.8

Speed ratings (Par 93): **97,96,95,94,92 91,90,89,83,82 80**

toteswingers:1&2:£10.80, 1&3:£5.80, 2&3:£11.20 CSF £71.92 CT £227.18 TOTE £4.60: £1.20, £4.40, £2.90; EX 84.30.

Owner J Burns **Bred** Belgrave Bloodstock Ltd **Trained** Newmarket, Suffolk

■ Stewards' Enquiry : Pat Cosgrave caution: careless riding

FOCUS

A moderate nursery.

NOTEBOOK

One Cool Bex was perhaps value for a greater margin of victory as he drifted away from the whip twice inside the final furlong, first right and then left (on the latter occasion bumping the runner-up, but the result stood after an inquiry). At the same time, however, he had also strayed off a true line close home before landing a Beverley seller on his previous outing, and it remains to be seen how long it is before this trait start costing him races. (op 11-2)

Saucy Buck(IRE) came as close as he ever has to winning a nursery, having been dropped 14lb since his first appearance in one and 6lb since the last on this surface. There should be a comparable contest in him around here on this evidence from this sort of mark. (op 12-1)

Brave Battle, who was gambled on, may have run the first two closer had the gaps appeared inside the final furlong, but was still well enough held to suggest a win might still have been beyond him. It was a fair first effort in handicap company, though, and he too could find a small opening this winter. Official explanation: jockey said that the colt lost a shoe (op 13-2)

Wandering Lad handled this artificial surface far better than the Fibresand of his racecourse debut, though is yet to see out a race entirely convincingly. (op 12-1)

Country Waltz, on whom Cathy Gannon was a late jockey change, had made all for victory at Leicester two starts previously. On her toes in the preliminaries, she found neither the muddling early gallop nor the rivalry of Rylee Mooch for the early lead at all to her liking and declined to settle. She may need another soft lead if she is to double her tally. Official explanation: jockey said that the filly's saddle slipped slightly (tchd 3-1)

Rylee Mooch, available at as low as 9-2 in mid-afternoon, hadn't front-run in a race before this, and the effort left him a spent force turning in. (op 11-2 tchd 5-1)

6741 THE BLACK COUNTRY'S ONLY RACECOURSE H'CAP 5f 216y(P)

6:10 (6:15) (Class 6) (0-60,62) 3-Y-O+ £1,706 (£503; £252) Stalls Low

Form RPR

2112 1 **Kinigi (IRE)**[10] 6455 4-9-2 60 (b) AndrewHeffernan(3) 2 75
(R A Harris) *chsd ldrs: led over 1f out: rdn out* 3/1[1]

2001 2 2 **White Shift (IRE)**[10] 6455 4-9-7 62 KirstyMilczarek 11 71+
(P Howling) *mid-div: hdwy over 2f out: rdn to chse wnr and edgd lft fnl f: r.o* 8/1

5400 3 3 **Espy**[10] 6456 5-9-2 57 PatrickMathers 1 56
(I W McInnes) *s.i.s: hdwy 5f out: rdn over 1f out: no ex ins fnl f* 16/1

060 4 1/2 **Time Medicean**[24] 6073 4-9-4 59 TonyCulhane 4 57
(P T Midgley) *hld up: pushed along over 2f out: hung lft over 1f out: r.o: nt trble ldrs* 7/2[2]

0500 5 nse **Dispol Grand (IRE)**[24] 6073 4-9-5 60 FrankieMcDonald 10 58
(P T Midgley) *led early: chsd ldr: rdn and ev ch over 1f out: no ex ins fnl f* 33/1

0020 6 shd **Avow (USA)**[10] 6456 3-9-4 60 (b) NeilChalmers 6 57
(J J Bridger) *chsd ldrs: rdn over 2f out: no ex fnl f* 20/1

0135 7 nk **Charlie Delta**[10] 6455 7-8-12 60 (b) JakePayne(7) 8 56
(R A Harris) *s.i.s: hld up: hdwy over 2f out: rdn over 1f out: sn hung lft: no ex ins fnl f* 10/1

0600 8 1/2 **Ride A White Swan**[35] 5764 5-9-5 60 (p) LukeMorris 12 55
(D Shaw) *hld up: nt clr run and swtchd rt ins fnl f: nvr nrr* 10/1

1060 9 1 1/2 **Only A Game (IRE)**[26] 6025 5-9-0 58 (vt) GaryBartley(3) 9 48
(I W McInnes) *hld up: rdn over 2f out: hdwy over 1f out: n.m.r ins fnl f: n.d* 18/1

4253 10 1 1/4 **Bateleur**[12] 6421 6-8-11 59 MatthewLawson(7) 5 45
(M R Channon) *s.i.s: hld up: rdn over 2f out: n.d* 13/2[3]

-060 11 5 **Alsufooh (USA)**[141] 2274 3-8-11 60 ThomasWhite(7) 7 30
(D Shaw) *sn led: rdn and hdd over 1f out: wkng whn hmpd ins fnl f* 33/1

0005 12 1 3/4 **Ocean Rosie (IRE)**[38] 5669 3-9-4 60 (v) CathyGannon 3 24
(Miss J Feilden) *mid-div: rdn over 3f out: wknd over 2f out* 12/1

1m 14.48s (-0.52) **Going Correction** -0.075s/f (Stan)

WFA 3 from 4yo+ 1lb 12 Ran SP% 119.3

Speed ratings (Par 101): **100,97,93,92,92 92,92,91,89,87 81,78**

toteswingers: 1&2 £5.30, 1&3 £12.00, 2&3 £20.20 CSF £26.98 CT £334.98 TOTE £4.10: £1.30, £3.70, £9.10; EX 30.10.

Owner Brian Hicks **Bred** Corduff Stud **Trained** Earlswood, Monmouths

FOCUS

More early pace on in this 0-60 than the slightly higher banded nursery which preceded it, and the winning time was half a second faster. The going was changed to standard to fast from standard afterwards.

Charlie Delta Official explanation: jockey said that the gelding was struck into

6742 BET EURO 2012 QUALIFIERS - BETDAQ MAIDEN STKS (DIV I) 1m 141y(P)

6:40 (6:41) (Class 5) 2-Y-O £1,774 (£523; £262) Stalls Low

Form RPR

4 1 **Irons On Fire (USA)**[15] 6334 2-9-3 0 SebSanders 12 73
(B J Meehan) *chsd ldr: rdn to ld 1f out: hung lft: r.o* 5/1[2]

3 2 1/2 **Ajeeb (USA)**[27] 5985 2-9-3 0 LiamKeniry 7 72
(D M Simcock) *hld up: hdwy over 2f out: rdn over 1f out: r.o to go 2nd nr fin: nt rch wnr* 7/1

2 3 3/4 **Jaridh (USA)**[21] 6211 2-9-3 0 RichardHughes 9 70
(Saeed Bin Suroor) *led: rdn and hdd over 1f out: hung lft ins fnl f: styd on: lost 2nd nr fin* 4/5[1]

63 4 1 1/4 **Oversteer (USA)**[16] 6305 2-9-3 0 RobertHavlin 10 68
(J H M Gosden) *swtchd lft sn after s: hld up in tch 7f out: rdn and hung lft fr over 1f out: styd on* 6/1[3]

0 5 nk **Swift Blade (IRE)**[19] 6249 2-9-3 0 PatCosgrave 3 67
(W J Knight) *chsd ldrs: rdn and hung lft over 1f out: styd on* 33/1

03 6 2 3/4 **Plattsburgh (USA)**[19] 6249 2-9-3 0 RoystonFfrench 1 61
(Mahmood Al Zarooni) *chsd ldrs: rdn over 1f out: looked hld whn hmpd ins fnl f* 12/1

00 7 14 **Xenophon**[12] 6414 2-9-3 0 (t) LukeMorris 5 32
(G D Blake) *mid-div: drvna long 1/2-way: lost tch over 2f out* 100/1

0 8 1 **Coastal Bequest (IRE)**[24] 6092 2-9-3 0 PatDobbs 11 30
(Sir Michael Stoute) *s.i.s: hld up and a in rr: drvn along 1/2-way: wknd over 2f out* 25/1

0 9 1 1/4 **Diamond City (IRE)**[23] 6128 2-9-3 0 DuranFentiman 8 27
(Mrs D J Sanderson) *hld up: rdn 1/2-way: a in rr: lost tch fnl 3f* 100/1

0 10 26 **Steel Rain**[29] 5900 2-9-0 0 AndrewHeffernan(3) 4 —
(Mrs N S Evans) *prom tl rdn and wknd over 2f out: t.o* 100/1

1m 51.04s (0.54) **Going Correction** -0.075s/f (Stan) 10 Ran SP% 116.5

Speed ratings (Par 95): **94,93,92,91,91 89,76,75,74,51**

toteswingers:1&2:£3.60, 1&3:£1.30, 2&3:£2.70 CSF £38.26 TOTE £3.60: £1.10, £3.80, £1.40; EX 34.20.

Owner Gold Group International Ltd **Bred** Woodford Thoroughbreds LLC **Trained** Manton, Wilts

FOCUS

Ultimately the faster of the two 1m maidens on the card, although the early fractions had seemed no better than steady.

NOTEBOOK

Irons On Fire(USA), as with so many from his yard, stepped up markedly from first outing to second, taking the extra furlong in his stride as readily as both his recent 7f debut here and the exploits of his immediate family suggested he might. A protracted battle with longtime leader Jaridh was entitled to take something out of him, but there was still enough in reserve with which to hold off the flying runner-up. He looks a fair prospect, though he holds no fancy entries at present. (tchd 4-1)

Ajeeb(USA) ◆, under pressure from some way out before good late gains on debut at Ffos Las, seemed more comfortable with the job in hand this time around and may have run the winner closer still with another 25 yards to travel. A win in an identical Polytrack contest to this in the coming weeks appears a formality. (op 8-1 tchd 6-1)

Jaridh(USA) had created a very favourable impression on debut over course and distance a month earlier, grasping what was required when set alight from the rear and nearly upsetting a John Gosden 4-11 favourite. The response when asked to quicken leaving the back straight this time suggests finding enough late tactical speed at the end of a more prominent ride is an issue rather than necessarily seeing out this trip, and it would not surprise to see more patient tactics reverted to next time. (op 10-11 tchd 11-10)

Oversteer(USA) didn't pick up quite as well as it looked he might early in the straight, and this first try of an artificial surface didn't constitute a big step up on previous efforts. He can at least go the handicap route now. (op 13-2)

Swift Blade(IRE) shaped with a little promise and might want further before too long.

6743 BET EURO 2012 QUALIFIERS - BETDAQ MAIDEN STKS (DIV II) 1m 141y(P)

7:10 (7:12) (Class 5) 2-Y-O £1,774 (£523; £262) Stalls Low

Form RPR

60 1 **Oasis Storm**[30] 5878 2-9-3 0 PhillipMakin 5 77
(M Dods) *trckd ldrs: rdn 2f out: r.o to ld post* 12/1

2 nse **Maywood** 2-9-3 0 RoystonFfrench 11 77
(Mahmood Al Zarooni) *s.i.s: hdwy over 6f out: rdn to ld wl ins fnl f: hdd post* 9/1

543 3 1 1/4 **Claret'N'Blue (USA)**[24] 6088 2-9-3 80 RichardHughes 8 74
(B J Meehan) *chsd ldrs: rdn to ld and hung lft ins fnl f: sn hdd: styd on same pce* 11/4[2]

4 1/2 **Taqaat (USA)** 2-9-3 0 TadhgO'Shea 10 73
(M Johnston) *w ldr: rdn and hung lft fr over 1f out: unable qck wl ins fnl f* 10/1

532 5 nse **Riot Police (USA)**[17] 6278 2-9-3 75 RobertHavlin 3 73
(J H M Gosden) *led: rdn over 1f out: hdd and unable qck ins fnl f* 85/40[1]

56 6 nk **Scented**[22] 6155 2-8-12 0 LiamJones 6 67
(W J Haggas) *chsd ldrs: rdn over 2f out: swtchd rt ins fnl f: r.o* 7/2[3]

00 7 3 1/4 **Salaamie**[10] 6473 2-9-3 0 JoeFanning 9 65
(E A L Dunlop) *hdwy over 6f out: rdn over 2f out: no ex fnl f* 50/1

8 7 **Smirfys Emerald (IRE)** 2-9-3 0 DuranFentiman 2 51
(Mrs D J Sanderson) *s.i.s: sn pushed along in rr: rdn over 2f out: sn wknd* 100/1

0 9 4 **Easydoesit (IRE)**[9] 6514 2-9-3 0 CathyGannon 4 42
(D Donovan) *hld up: a in rr: rdn and wknd over 3f out* 100/1

00 10 7 **Blade**[18] 6268 2-9-3 0 LukeMorris 1 28
(W M Brisbourne) *mid-div: drvn along 1/2-way: wknd over 3f out* 100/1

11 21 **Final Liberation (FR)** 2-9-3 0 SebSanders 7 —
(Sir Mark Prescott) *s.i.s: outpcd: t.o fnl 3f* 20/1

1m 51.31s (0.81) **Going Correction** -0.075s/f (Stan) 11 Ran SP% 117.4

Speed ratings (Par 95): **93,92,91,91,91 91,88,81,78,72 53**

toteswingers: 1&2 £22.00, 1&3 £9.60, 2&3 £3.10 CSF £111.10 TOTE £14.50: £5.00, £1.20, £1.20; EX 155.10.

Owner Andrew Tinkler **Bred** J G Davis **Trained** Denton, Co Durham

FOCUS

The slower of the two maidens.

NOTEBOOK

Oasis Storm finished with enough of a flourish to land the spoils in the dying strides despite not having the guidance of the inner rail that the runner-up enjoyed. Just midfield in two good-ground turf contests over 7f-1m previously, connections (who had been no better than 'hopeful' here) believe 1m2f-1m4f and another winter will be required for him to come into his own, and he will not been seen out again this year. (op 14-1)

Maywood ◆, a 350,000gns first foal of a half-sister to Group 3 1m1f winner Charlie Farnsbarns, got everything right on debut bar the start, losing more ground on the winner in being among the slowest away than he lost the race by. A Derby entry, he should be able to land one of these easily enough if kept on the go this autumn, with the 1m1f trip around here probably as likely to suit him. Official explanation: jockey said colt hung left and lost a shoe (op 16-1)
Claret'N'Blue(USA), edgy in the preliminaries and kept tightly hold of on the way down, had been keeping better company than this on all three previous starts, including a Listed contest second time out, but didn't quite appear to know what to do once hitting the front for the first time ever in a race. It's hoped he can learn enough from the experience to land a routine maiden, as his current mark of 80 doesn't look especially competitive for an immediate switch to handicaps. (op 3-1)
Taqaat(USA), out of a half-sister to unbeatable juvenile Alhaarth, was still green to post despite making his fourth racecourse appearance. Given no peace up front for over 6f, unsurprisingly he could not muster another turn of foot once challenged, but looks to have the raw material to take a small maiden granted an uncontested lead. (op 9-1)
Riot Police(USA) paid for becoming engaged in a duel up front with the fourth horse. He may do better with an uncontested lead but a mark of 75 doesn't look an obvious gift. (op 2-1 tchd 9-4)
Scented Official explanation: jockey said that the filly was denied a clear run

6744 BET MULTIPLES - BETDAQ H'CAP — 2m 119y(P)
7:40 (7:40) (Class 5) (0-70,68) 4-Y-0+ — £2,115 (£624; £312) Stalls Low

Form / RPR
5021 1 **Resplendent Ace (IRE)**[8] 6538 6-9-0 61 ... J-PGuillambert 1 — 69
(P Howling) *hld up: pushed along 6f out: drvn over 3f out: hdwy over 1f out: styd on u.p to ld post* 4/1[3]
5342 2 nse **Red Kestrel (USA)**[26] 6028 5-9-0 68 ... JulieBurke(7) 7 — 76
(K A Ryan) *led: hdd over 6f out: chsd ldr tl led again over 2f out: rdn ins fnl f: hdd post* 7/2[2]
2300 3 1 1/4 **Pearl (IRE)**[14] 6373 6-8-2 49 oh4 ...(tp) CathyGannon 8 — 56
(Mrs A M Thorpe) *prom: chsd ldr 14f out to over 6f out: remained handy: rdn over 1f out: styd on* 9/1
5350 4 2 1/4 **Bushy Dell (IRE)**[206] 910 5-8-6 58 ... AdamBeschizza(5) 6 — 62
(Miss J Feilden) *chsd ldr 2f: remained handy: rdn to chse ldr over 1f out: styd on same pce ins fnl f* 14/1
5026 5 2 3/4 **Chocolate Caramel (USA)**[23] 6109 8-9-1 62 ... PaulMulrennan 2 — 63
(R A Fahey) *prom: rdn over 2f out: wknd fnl f* 11/2
0005 6 2 **Paint The Town Red**[23] 6121 5-8-4 51 ... JoeFanning 5 — 49
(H J Collingridge) *hld up: hdwy over 2f out: rdn over 1f out: wknd ins fnl f* 14/1
6004 7 2 1/2 **Taste The Wine (IRE)**[9] 6502 4-9-1 62 ... RichardHughes 4 — 57
(J S Moore) *hld up: rdn over 3f out: hdwy u.p over 1f out: wknd ins fnl f* 3/1[1]
-260 8 9 **Babilu**[36] 5722 5-8-10 57 ...(p) LiamKeniry 3 — 41
(D Burchell) *chsd ldrs tl led over 6f out: rdn and hdd over 2f out: wknd over 1f out* 12/1

3m 42.19s (0.39) **Going Correction** -0.075s/f (Stan) 8 Ran SP% 113.6
Speed ratings (Par 103): **96,95,95,94,93 92,90,86**
toteswingers: 1&2 £3.70, 1&3 £9.90, 2&3 £8.20 CSF £18.17 CT £116.47 TOTE £5.00: £1.70, £1.10, £3.60; EX 20.90.
Owner Paul Howling **Bred** Newlands House Stud **Trained** Newmarket, Suffolk
FOCUS
Not especially strong for the grade, with only four runners rated within 11lb of the ratings ceiling.
Paint The Town Red Official explanation: jockey said that the gelding lost a right fore shoe

6745 BREEDERS' CUP LIVE ONLY ON ATR NURSERY — 7f 32y(P)
8:10 (8:11) (Class 4) (0-85,85) 2-Y-0 — £3,594 (£1,069; £534; £266) Stalls High

Form / RPR
2103 1 **Tinkertown (IRE)**[19] 6254 2-9-5 83 ... JamieSpencer 6 — 87
(P F I Cole) *hld up in last turning for home: swtchd lft and hdwy over 1f out: rdn to ld wl ins fnl f: r.o* 15/2[2]
31 2 3/4 **Male Model**[17] 6293 2-9-7 85 ... RoystonFfrench 2 — 87
(Mahmood Al Zarooni) *s.i.s: sn mid-div: nt clr run over 2f out: hdwy over 1f out: rdn and ev ch wl ins fnl f: styd on* 6/4[1]
6100 3 1/2 **Kalkan Bay**[28] 5947 2-8-7 71 ... PaulHanagan 7 — 72
(Jedd O'Keeffe) *led: rdn over 1f out: edgd lft and hdd wl ins fnl f: one pce* 16/1
5000 4 1 1/2 **Believe It Or Not (IRE)**[31] 5856 2-8-9 73 ... RichardHughes 4 — 70
(J S Moore) *hld up: hdwy over 1f out: no imp wl ins fnl f* 12/1
4020 5 3/4 **Pick A Little**[11] 6435 2-8-7 71 ... TadhgO'Shea 8 — 66
(B W Duke) *a.p: pushed along 1/2-way: rdn over 2f out: styd on same pce ins fnl f* 40/1
3100 6 1/2 **Lenjawi Pride**[15] 6317 2-9-4 82 ... RichardKingscote 5 — 76
(Tom Dascombe) *prom: rdn over 1f out: no ex wl ins fnl f* 12/1
0210 7 1/2 **Restless Bay (IRE)**[9] 6513 2-8-9 73 ...(p) PaulMulrennan 9 — 66
(R Hollinshead) *hld up: hdwy over 1f out: sn rdn: no ex wl ins fnl f* 8/1[3]
5150 8 shd **Persian Herald**[13] 6386 2-9-5 83 ... DaneO'Neill 12 — 76
(Pat Eddery) *dwlt: hld up: nt clr run over 1f out: sn rdn and hung lft: nt trble ldrs* 12/1
5331 9 shd **Dazzling Valentine**[8] 6521 2-8-8 72 ... SamHitchcott 11 — 64
(A Bailey) *chsd ldrs: rdn and ev ch over 1f out: no ex ins fnl f* 16/1
2225 10 7 **Ajaafa**[23] 6130 2-8-5 69 ...(p) JoeFanning 10 — 44
(J G Given) *chsd ldr: rdn over 2f out: wknd fnl f* 20/1
3204 11 2 1/4 **Orchid Street (USA)**[14] 6354 2-8-13 77 ...(v[1]) SebSanders 1 — 47
(Mrs A Duffield) *chsd ldrs: wkng whn hmpd over 1f out* 9/1

1m 28.8s (-0.80) **Going Correction** -0.075s/f (Stan) 11 Ran SP% 114.9
Speed ratings (Par 97): **101,100,99,97,97 96,95,95,95,87 85**
toteswingers: 1&2 £2.70, 1&3 £59.20, 2&3 £12.90 CSF £18.54 CT £178.11 TOTE £3.50: £1.10, £1.10, £10.00; EX 13.20.
Owner Mrs Fitri Hay **Bred** Corrin Stud **Trained** Whatcombe, Oxon
FOCUS
A reasonable nursery.
NOTEBOOK
Tinkertown(IRE) enjoyed a smart ride from Jamie Spencer. Last but still full of running turning in, a rapid dive for the inner rail offered the colt an alternative to trying to thread through a heavily bunching field without incident, which he accepted with aplomb. Other than a failure on soft at Newmarket two runs previously, he has maintained a gently progressive profile all season, and this probably rates another career best. (op 7-1)
Male Model ◆ looked unlucky not to have run the winner closer. A poor start negated the advantage of his stall two draw, and having worked his way to sixth or seventh turning in he endured a troubled passage through the crowds. He's certainly not for deserting in similar contests yet. Official explanation: jockey said that the colt missed the break (tchd 11-8)
Kalkan Bay gave it a good go on what was both his all-weather debut and the first time he's been asked to make all, though there was nothing left to hit back with once the first two collared him. Additionally unraced over a 7f this sharp previously, he may be good enough to hold on under similar tactics in a lower-graded contest over this course and distance. (op 25-1)
Believe It Or Not(IRE) improved markedly on his last-place finish in both previous nursery outings, but a few pounds off his mark may speed up his return to winning ways quicker than the extra furlong he got here.
Restless Bay(IRE)'s best effort in three previous nursery starts came in the only one of those over 6f, which he won, at this venue. A return to that trip might be worth a try judged on this second failure to build on that win since then. (op 17-2 tchd 10-1)
Orchid Street(USA)'s first-time visor had already set her alight on the way to post, and she had nothing left to offer even before a bump in the straight finished her off. (op 17-2 tchd 10-1)

6746 ATTHERACES.COM/BREEDERSCUP MAIDEN STKS — 5f 20y(P)
8:40 (8:40) (Class 5) 3-Y-0+ — £2,115 (£624; £312) Stalls Low

Form / RPR
6 1 **Doc Hay (USA)**[5] 6638 3-9-3 0 ... JamieSpencer 10 — 71+
(P F I Cole) *trckd ldr: rdn to ld 1f out: r.o: edgd rt nr fin* 11/4[2]
225 2 nk **Bushwhacker (AUS)**[16] 6310 5-9-3 70 ...(b) PaulHanagan 5 — 70
(W R Muir) *hld up: hdwy over 1f out: rdn and ev ch ins fnl f: r.o: hmpd last strides* 9/4[1]
-236 3 nk **Sparking**[44] 5438 3-8-12 59 ... GrahamGibbons 3 — 64
(T D Barron) *chsd ldrs: led wl over 1f out: sn rdn and hdd: r.o* 5/1
3044 4 1 1/4 **Praesepe**[57] 5044 3-8-12 67 ... LiamJones 4 — 60
(W J Haggas) *prom: outpcd over 3f out: rallied over 1f out: rdn and edgd rt ins fnl f: no imp towards fin* 9/2[3]
6353 5 2 1/4 **Luisa Tetrazzini (IRE)**[21] 6206 4-8-7 54 ... MarkCoumbe(5) 11 — 51+
(D Bourton) *s.s: outpcd: r.o ins fnl f: nrst fin* 9/1
0303 6 1 1/4 **Captain Bluebird (IRE)**[15] 6330 3-9-3 52 ... CathyGannon 12 — 52
(D Donovan) *chsd ldrs: rdn over 1f out: no ex fnl f* 14/1
2660 7 1 **True Red (IRE)**[28] 5957 3-8-9 48 ...(b) AndrewHefferman(3) 8 — 43
(Mrs N S Evans) *led and wl lft s: rdn and hdd wl over 1f out: wknd ins fnl f* 40/1
5000 8 3 3/4 **One Cat Diesel (IRE)**[15] 6332 3-9-3 42 ...(bt) PatrickMathers 9 — 35
(H A McWilliams) *prom: rdn 1/2-way: wknd over 1f out* 66/1
6605 9 1 3/4 **Riggs (IRE)**[54] 5153 4-9-3 30 ... DavidNolan 7 — 29
(Peter Grayson) *hmpd s: hdwy 1/2-way: sn rdn and wknd* 100/1
00 10 11 **Shesasnip**[37] 5700 3-8-12 0 ... LiamKeniry 1 — —
(R Hollinshead) *a in rr: bhd fr 1/2-way* 66/1

62.14 secs (-0.16) **Going Correction** -0.075s/f (Stan) 10 Ran SP% 115.4
Speed ratings (Par 103): **98,97,97,95,91 89,87,81,79,61**
toteswingers: 1&2 £1.70, 1&3 £3.40, 2&3 £4.70 CSF £9.18 TOTE £5.40: £1.10, £2.70, £2.50; EX 7.50.
Owner Mrs Fitri Hay **Bred** Colts Neck Stables Llc **Trained** Whatcombe, Oxon
■ Stewards' Enquiry : Jamie Spencer caution: careless riding
FOCUS
Relatively few to consider in a weak-looking all-ages sprint maiden, but at least the early pace was decent.

6747 BREEDERS' CUP LIVE ONLY ON ATR H'CAP — 1m 4f 50y(P)
9:10 (9:11) (Class 6) (0-60,61) 3-Y-0 — £1,706 (£503; £252) Stalls Low

Form / RPR
4316 1 **New Code**[16] 6314 3-9-6 59 ... RichardHughes 6 — 67+
(W R Muir) *hld up: hmpd sn after s: hdwy over 1f out: r.o to ld nr fin* 9/2[2]
5656 2 nk **Stoical (IRE)**[15] 6336 3-9-6 59 ... DaneO'Neill 5 — 65
(W Jarvis) *hld up: hdwy over 1f out: rdn to ld ins fnl f: edgd lft: hdd nr fin* 8/1
0302 3 2 1/4 **Firehawk**[29] 5923 3-9-1 54 ... CathyGannon 2 — 56
(P D Evans) *prom: rdn over 3f out: hung rt 1f out: styd on same pce ins fnl f* 9/2[2]
6524 4 hd **Ella Grace (USA)**[18] 6266 3-9-6 59 ... PaulHanagan 1 — 61
(R A Fahey) *hld up: hdwy over 1f out: sn rdn into ins fnl f: styd on same pce* 6/1[3]
5 2 **The Dukes Arch (USA)**[57] 5062 3-9-6 59 ...(b[1]) PatCosgrave 8 — 57
(Peter Fahey, Ire) *chsd ldrs: led over 2f out: rdn and hung rt 1f out: hdd and no ex ins fnl f* 25/1
6430 6 shd **Catbells (IRE)**[9] 6495 3-9-3 56 ...(p) SamHitchcott 3 — 58+
(A Bailey) *led 2f: chsd ldrs: nt clr run over 2f out: rdn over 1f out: styd on same pce* 22/1
4321 7 2 1/4 **Miss Whippy**[7] 6579 3-8-13 52 ... KirstyMilczarek 9 — 47
(P Howling) *hmpd sn after s: hld up: hdwy over 2f out: rdn whn hmpd ins fnl f: sn btn* 11/1
4441 8 1 1/4 **Frameit (IRE)**[8] 6525 3-9-8 61 ...(vt) LiamKeniry 4 — 54
(Tim Vaughan) *prom: rdn over 2f out: wknd fnl f* 16/1
5000 9 3 **Mary Helen**[17] 6287 3-9-1 54 ... LiamJones 12 — 42
(W M Brisbourne) *s.i.s: hld up: hdwy over 3f out: rdn to chse ldr 2f out: wknd over 1f out* 40/1
-223 10 13 **Honoured (IRE)**[8] 6526 3-9-4 57 ...(b[1]) SebSanders 7 — 24
(Sir Mark Prescott) *s.i.s: hmpd sn after s: hdwy to ld 10f out: rdn and hdd over 2f out: sn wknd* 3/1[1]
4052 11 1 3/4 **Shoot The Pot (IRE)**[17] 6287 3-9-5 58 ... StephenCraine 11 — 22
(J Mackie) *s.i.s: hmpd sn after s: hdwy 1/2-way: rdn and wknd over 2f out* 16/1

2m 40.4s (-0.70) **Going Correction** -0.075s/f (Stan) 11 Ran SP% 117.5
Speed ratings (Par 99): **99,98,97,97,95 95,94,93,91,82 81**
toteswingers: 1&2 £6.40, 1&3 £7.50, 2&3 £15.00 CSF £39.45 CT £172.64 TOTE £5.90: £2.80, £3.40, £2.60; EX 32.00 Place 6 £41.44, Place 5 £20.79.
Owner Mrs D Edginton **Bred** Foursome Thoroughbreds **Trained** Lambourn, Berks
■ Stewards' Enquiry : Pat Cosgrave two-day ban: careless riding (Oct 25 - 26)
FOCUS
Trouble in running on more than one occasion here, and several performances are best ignored.
Miss Whippy Official explanation: jockey said that the filly suffered interference both at the start and in the home straight
T/Plt: £19.80 to a £1 stake. Pool of £62,834.40. 2,314.37 winning tickets. T/Qpdt: £6.80 to a £1 stake. Pool of £9,860.43. 1,065.77 winning tickets. CR

6719 YORK (L-H)
Saturday, October 9
OFFICIAL GOING: Soft (good to soft in places; 5.8)
Races on inside line on home bend reducing races of one mile and over by 27yds.
Wind: Light, half against Weather: Overcast

6748 CORAL BACKING SUE RYDER CARE E B F MAIDEN STKS — 7f
1:45 (1:46) (Class 2) 2-Y-0 — £7,447 (£2,216; £1,107; £553) Stalls Low

Form / RPR
6 1 **Namibian (IRE)**[17] 6278 2-9-3 0 ... GregFairley 2 — 82
(M Johnston) *dwlt and pushed along on inner: sn in tch: hdwy 3f out: rdn to chal 2f out and sn led: edgd rt and clr ent fnl f: styd on wl* 8/1

4420 **2** 3 1/2 **Nicola's Dream**[28] 5947 2-8-12 68 BarryMcHugh 5 68
(R A Fahey) *a chsng ldrs: rdn along over 2f out: drvn over 1f out and kpt on u.p fnl f: tk 2nd nr fin* **14/1**

06 **3** 1/2 **Escala**[7] 6575 2-8-12 0 WilliamCarson 14 67
(M D Squance) *midfield: hdwy on stands' rail 1/2-way: rdn along over 2f out: styd on ent fnl f: tk 3rd nr fin* **100/1**

0 **4** *hd* **King Ferdinand**[22] 6153 2-9-3 0 DavidProbert 4 71
(A M Balding) *led: rdn along over 2f out: hdd wl over 1f out: sn drvn and wknd ins fnl f* **9/2**[2]

5 **5** 1/2 **Maraheb**[21] 6196 2-9-3 0 TadhgO'Shea 6 70
(J L Dunlop) *trckd ldr: hdwy and cl up 1/2-way: rdn wl over 2f out and grad wknd* **9/2**[2]

00 **6** *7* **Inca Blue**[7] 6566 2-9-3 0 GrahamGibbons 1 53
(T D Easterby) *dwlt: a towards rr* **50/1**

02 **7** 3/4 **Spey Song (IRE)**[20] 6222 2-8-12 0 TomQueally 7 46
(J D Bethell) *in tch: hdwy to chse ldrs 3f out: rdn over 2f out and sn wknd* **4/1**[1]

8 1 1/4 **L'Ami Louis (IRE)** 2-9-3 0 FergusSweeney 9 48
(H Candy) *in rr: sme hdwy over 2f out: n.d* **14/1**

9 3 3/4 **Vantaa (IRE)** 2-9-3 0 PaulHanagan 11 38
(R A Fahey) *s.i.s: a in rr* **5/1**[3]

0 **10** *10* **Boston Court (IRE)**[11] 6443 2-9-3 0 ShaneKelly 13 13
(B J Meehan) *in tch: rdn along over 3f out: sn lost pl and bhd fnl 2f* **33/1**

0 **11** *6* **Kwik Time**[23] 6111 2-9-3 0 PhillipMakin 8 —
(R Bastiman) *a in rr* **150/1**

0 **P** **Indian Jack (IRE)**[30] 5878 2-9-3 0 SamHitchcott 12 —
(A Bailey) *t.k.h: trckd ldrs tl unbalanced and lost pl after 2f: sn bhd and p.u over 3f out: dismntd* **7/1**

1m 32.63s (7.33) **Going Correction** +0.925s/f (Soft) **12** Ran SP% **116.5**
Speed ratings (Par 101): **95,91,90,90,89 81,80,79,75,63 56,—**
toteswingers: 1&2 £15.30, 1&3 £98.20, 2&3 £73.30 CSF £110.64 TOTE £11.00: £3.10, £3.00, £9.50; EX 161.30 TRIFECTA Not won..
Owner Sheikh Hamdan Bin Mohammed Al Maktoum **Bred** Hascombe And Valiant Studs **Trained** Middleham Moor, N Yorks
■ Stewards' Enquiry : Tom Queally trainer said that the filly was unsuited by the Soft, Good to Soft in places going

FOCUS
Not that strong a maiden for the course, the 68-rated runner-up clearly the guide to the level of the form, but the winner was impressive and a few of the others are also likely to improve in due course.

NOTEBOOK
Namibian(IRE) was very green on last month's Goodwood debut and improved plenty with that behind him, clearly being suited to the testing conditions and emerging well on top at the finish. He has the scope to go on again next year, when he'll stay at least 1m, and is potentially useful. (op 9-1)
Nicola's Dream ran right up to the pick of her previous form. There's no indication she's going to prove much better than this, but she should pick up a race at some stage, while this also shows she is versatile regards ground. (op 12-1)
Escala left her two previous efforts well behind. There's some speed in her pedigree but this increased test of stamina clearly suited her as she stuck on well. Handicaps are also an option after this.
King Ferdinand was better than the bare result and remains open to improvement. Last off the bridle, having cut out the running, he left the impression that this trip under these conditions stretched his stamina.
Maraheb showed clear signs of inexperience off the bridle, so it's reasonable to expect there'll be more to come from this well-bred sort, and he'll be suited by 1m on this evidence. (op 5-1)
Inca Blue has had three quick runs in maidens and is almost certainly the type who'll do better in handicaps next year. (op 66-1)
Spey Song(IRE)'s Hamilton form set the standard but she didn't come anywhere near reproducing it, with the softer conditions presumably against her. Official explanation: trainer said filly was unsuited by the soft (good to soft patches) ground (tchd 9-2 in a place)
L'Ami Louis(IRE), an Elusive City colt, travelled comfortably for a fair way under restraint before getting tired in the conditions and is sure to leave this form behind before long. (op 10-1)
Vantaa(IRE), a son of Shamardal, didn't achieve much on his debut but was presumably the choice of Paul Hanagan over the runner-up and can be expected to do a good bit better in future.
Indian Jack(IRE) Official explanation: jockey said gelding lost its action; vet said gelding had been struck into behind

6749 CORAL.CO.UK STKS (H'CAP) 1m
2:15 (2:17) (Class 2) (0-100,100) 3-Y-O+ **£12,952** (£3,854; £1,926; £962) **Stalls** Low

Form RPR
6452 **1** **Gunner Lindley (IRE)**[9] 6510 3-8-9 88 MichaelHills 6 99
(B W Hills) *chsd ldr: led 6f out: hld on gamely* **8/1**[3]

1331 **2** 1/2 **Pintura**[7] 6556 3-8-4 86 SophieDoyle(3) 16 95
(D M Simcock) *in rr: hdwy over 3f out: styd on to chse wnr ins fnl f: no ex towards fin* **12/1**

4016 **3** 1 3/4 **Osteopathic Remedy (IRE)**[21] 6180 6-9-2 92 PhillipMakin 19 97+
(M Dods) *t.k.h in rr: effrt and nt clr run 3f out: styd on to take 3rd nr fin* **20/1**

5414 **4** *1* **Medici Pearl**[15] 6327 6-8-11 87 DavidAllan 8 90
(T D Easterby) *trckd ldrs: chal 2f out: styd on same pce fnl f* **12/1**

0432 **5** 2 1/2 **Charlie Cool**[7] 6567 7-9-5 95 (b) PJMcDonald 13 92+
(Mrs R A Carr) *hld up in rr: hdwy and swtchd lft over 1f out: kpt on: nt rch ldrs* **22/1**

1152 **6** *nk* **Smarty Socks (IRE)**[36] 5736 6-9-3 93 SilvestreDeSousa 18 90
(D O'Meara) *in rr: gd hdwy to r upsides towards centre 2f out: wknd fnl f* **10/1**

0000 **7** *nk* **Extraterrestrial**[21] 6180 6-8-13 89 PaulHanagan 11 85
(R A Fahey) *prom: stmbld and lost pl after 2f: styd on fnl 2f: nt rch ldrs* **15/2**[2]

0131 **8** *hd* **Brick Red**[13] 6391 3-8-9 88 DavidProbert 5 83
(A M Balding) *trckd ldrs: drvn over 3f out: one pce fnl 2f* **4/1**[1]

0606 **9** 1 1/2 **Mont Agel**[28] 5951 3-9-4 97 TomQueally 10 89
(M L W Bell) *mid-div: effrt over 2f out: nvr rchd ldrs* **25/1**

5001 **10** 3/4 **Kiwi Bay**[7] 6567 5-9-7 97 DarryllHolland 3 87
(M Dods) *mid-div: effrt over 2f out: nvr trbld ldrs* **16/1**

3000 **11** 3/4 **Bonnie Charlie**[14] 6349 4-9-0 90 ShaneKelly 9 79
(W J Haggas) *s.i.s: sn in mid-div: effrt 3f out: nvr a factor* **33/1**

1220 **12** 1/2 **City Of The Kings (IRE)**[40] 5605 5-8-11 90 MichaelO'Connell(3) 12 77
(G A Harker) *in rr: effrt towards centre and hung lft over 2f out: nvr a factor* **33/1**

1164 **13** 1 1/2 **Sunnyside Tom (IRE)**[17] 6296 6-8-6 87 LeeTopliss(5) 20 71
(R A Fahey) *t.k.h: trckd ldrs: lost pl over 4f out: swtchd lft over 1f out: n.d* **33/1**

-454 **14** 3 1/4 **Layali Al Andalus**[21] 6195 3-9-7 100 (vt) TadhgO'Shea 14 76
(Saeed Bin Suroor) *s.i.s: hld up towards rr: sme hdwy and swtchd lft over 2f out: hung lft over 1f out: sn wknd* **28/1**

0000 **15** *10* **Balcarce Nov (ARG)**[21] 6180 5-9-7 97 JamieSpencer 7 50
(T P Tate) *led 2f: hung lft over 3f out: wknd over 2f out: eased whn bhd* **16/1**

0150 **16** *2* **Autumn Riches**[11] 6447 3-8-8 87 AdrianNicholls 1 36
(M Johnston) *chsd ldrs: drvn centre over 3f out: hung lft and lost pl 2f out: sn eased and bhd* **12/1**

0656 **17** 1 1/4 **Dubai Dynamo**[7] 6577 5-8-9 85 (b) AndrewElliott 17 31
(Mrs R A Carr) *chsd ldrs: lost pl over 4f out: eased whn bhd* **50/1**

-200 **18** 3 3/4 **Pallantes Cross**[21] 6203 3-9-0 93 GregFairley 2 30
(M Johnston) *prom: drvn over 4f out: lost pl over 2f out: eased whn bhd* **33/1**

0040 **19** 2 1/2 **Caldercruix (USA)**[7] 6567 3-8-10 89 AndrewMullen 15 21
(T P Tate) *chsd ldrs: lost pl over 2f out: eased whn bhd* **50/1**

5125 **P** **Silver Rime (FR)**[51] 5242 5-8-12 88 LNewman 4 —
(Miss L A Perratt) *s.i.s: sme hdwy towards centre over 3f out: eased over 1f out: p.u and dismntd ins fnl f* **16/1**

1m 43.31s (4.51) **Going Correction** +0.70s/f (Yiel)
WFA 3 from 4yo+ 3lb **20** Ran SP% **124.8**
Speed ratings (Par 109): **105,104,102,101,99 98,98,98,96,96 95,94,93,90,80 78,76,73,70,—**
toteswingers: 1&2 £16.40, 1&3 £43.60, 2&3 £51.20 CSF £88.85 CT £1909.51 TOTE £9.10: £2.10, £3.50, £4.90, £3.70; EX 95.00 TRIFECTA Not won..
Owner P McNamara, N Browne, S Richards **Bred** Marston Stud **Trained** Lambourn, Berks

FOCUS
A pretty useful contest. The gallop looked sound enough under the conditions, with the field coming towards the near side in the straight.

NOTEBOOK
Gunner Lindley(IRE) clearly handles soft ground well and went one better than at Newmarket last week, showing a likeable attitude too, having been in the firing line throughout. The fact he goes so well in the mud is sure to continue to hold him in good stead for the rest of the season and he's fresher than most for the time of year. (tchd 15-2)
Pintura is another who goes particularly well on bad ground and ran well from a 6lb higher mark than Epsom. He should continue to give a good account. (op 14-1)
Osteopathic Remedy(IRE) has yet to win off a mark this high but that could change before long judged on this, as he would have been closer with more luck in running, having to wait for it to open up for him after being dropped into the rear from his wide draw. (op 25-1)
Medici Pearl is another proven mudlark and ran well, while giving the impression her 5lb rise for winning a small-field event at Hamilton leaves her with little in hand of her mark. (op 9-1)
Charlie Cool was beaten twice in claiming company last month but backed up last weekend's Redcar second, finishing well from off the pace. (op 25-1 tchd 20-1)
Smarty Socks(IRE) has had a good year and remains at the top of his game, seeming to pay in the end for making a rapid move from the rear to the head of affairs.
Extraterrestrial is on a good mark and is likely to pop up at some stage, things not going his way as he stumbled early and was also tight for room a couple of times in the final 2f. (tchd 7-1)
Brick Red had been going the right way and perhaps deserves another chance to show himself still on the up back under less testing conditions. (op 9-2)
Kiwi Bay was found out by an 8lb rise for Redcar, while none of the remainder offered hope that they'll be winning handicaps soon. (op 14-1)
Silver Rime(FR) Official explanation: jockey said that the gelding lost action

6750 CORAL STKS (H'CAP) 2m 2f
2:45 (2:45) (Class 4) (0-85,82) 3-Y-O+ **£7,123** (£2,119; £1,059; £529) **Stalls** Low

Form RPR
2103 **1** **Act Of Kalanisi (IRE)**[13] 6397 4-9-7 75 GregFairley 1 83
(M Johnston) *trckd ldrs on inner: hdwy over 4f out: cl up 3f out: rdn to ld over 2f out: drvn over 1f out: kpt on gamely u.p fnl f* **9/1**

01-0 **2** 3/4 **Sphinx (FR)**[188] 1101 12-9-4 72 (b) PaulMulrennan 8 79
(E W Tuer) *hld up and bhd: stdy hdwy over 4f out: rdn to chse ldrs 2f out: styd on to chal ins fnl f: ev ch tl drvn and no ex last 50yds* **25/1**

4136 **3** *1* **Bollin Judith**[9] 6516 4-9-0 68 (t) DavidAllan 3 74
(T D Easterby) *trckd ldng pair: hdwy 5f out: led over 3f out: rdn and hdd over 2f out: sn drvn and kpt on same pce fnl f* **14/1**

0-30 **4** 3/4 **Dulcie**[27] 5996 4-9-4 77 AshleyMorgan(5) 7 82
(M H Tompkins) *hld up in rr: hdwy 5f out: rdn to chse ldrs over 2f out: drvn over 1f out: kpt on same pce ins fnl f* **7/1**[3]

2611 **5** *nk* **Descaro (USA)**[22] 6143 4-9-2 70 SilvestreDeSousa 6 75
(D O'Meara) *hld up towards rr: hdwy 5f out: chsd ldrs 3f out: rdn over 2f out: drvn wl over 1f out and kpt on same pce* **9/4**[1]

5442 **6** *17* **Tillietudlem (FR)**[22] 6143 4-8-13 67 PaulHanagan 5 53
(J S Goldie) *led: rdn along and styd far side over 4f out: sn hdd and grad wknd* **10/1**

-004 **7** *12* **Nemo Spirit (IRE)**[9] 6493 5-10-0 82 RichardKingscote 9 55
(Tom Dascombe) *cl up: rdn along 5f out: wknd 4f out* **15/2**

6611 **8** 1 1/2 **Dubara Reef (IRE)**[14] 6359 3-8-3 69 (p) HayleyTurner 10 40
(Paul Green) *hld up in tch: rdn along 5f out: wknd 4f out: bhd whn eased fnl 2f* **9/1**

5214 **9** 3 1/4 **Head Hunted**[27] 5996 3-8-2 68 DavidProbert 2 36
(D M Simcock) *hld up towards rr: hdwy to trck ldrs 1/2-way: rdn along over 4f out: sn wknd: bhd and eased fnl 2f* **9/2**[2]

-540 **10** *19* **Folk Tune (IRE)**[21] 6185 7-9-4 75 IanBrennan(3) 4 22
(J J Quinn) *in tch: rdn along over 5f out: sn wknd: bhd and eased fnl 2f* **40/1**

4m 8.85s (10.45) **Going Correction** +0.70s/f (Yiel)
WFA 3 from 4yo+ 12lb **10** Ran SP% **115.3**
Speed ratings (Par 105): **104,103,103,102,102 95,89,89,87,79**
toteswingers: 1&2 £49.70, 1&3 £21.70, 2&3 £39.50 CSF £204.14 CT £3087.93 TOTE £10.30: £2.50, £4.80, £3.80; EX 264.20 Trifecta £745.20 Part won. Pool of £1,007.10 - 0.44 winning units..
Owner Mrs Joan Keaney **Bred** Mrs Joan Keaney **Trained** Middleham Moor, N Yorks

FOCUS
A fair staying event. They went a sensible gallop but conditions meant the emphasis was still firmly on stamina.
Bollin Judith Official explanation: jockey said that the filly hung left
Head Hunted Official explanation: trainer was unable to offer any explanation for the poor performance shown

6751 CORAL ROCKINGHAM STKS (LISTED RACE) 6f
3:20 (3:21) (Class 1) 2-Y-O **£23,704** (£8,964; £4,480; £2,240) **Stalls** Centre

Form RPR
5 **1** **Katla (IRE)**[13] 6401 2-8-10 0 ow1 WJLee 6 106
(J F Grogan, Ire) *hld up in tch: smooth hdwy over 2f out: sn cl up: qcknd to ld over 1f out: sn clr: rdn out* **5/1**[3]

113 **2** *6* **Barefoot Lady (IRE)**[21] 6176 2-8-9 97 PaulHanagan 7 87
(R A Fahey) *trckd ldrs: pushed along and n.m.r 1/2-way: rdn and outpcd 2f out: drvn and styd on appr fnl f: tk 2nd nr fin: no ch w wnr* **11/4**[1]

31 **3** *nk* **Carrignavar (USA)**[29] 5914 2-8-9 79 EJMcNamara 5 86
(R M Beckett) *chsd ldrs: rdn along over 2f out: drvn wl over 1f out: kpt on same pce* **11/1**

13 **4** *1 1/4* **None Shall Sleep (IRE)**[60] 4934 2-9-0 88 GregFairley 2 87
(P F I Cole) *awkward s and s.i.s: effrt and sme hdwy on outer 1/2-way: rdn along over 2f out: sn btn* **14/1**

1213 **5** *1 1/4* **Easy Ticket (IRE)**[21] 6191 2-9-0 94 GrahamGibbons 1 84
(D H Brown) *cl up: led after 2f: jnd and rdn 2f out: drvn and hdd over 1f out: wknd ins fnl f* **9/2**[2]

110 **6** *1/2* **Murbeh (IRE)**[30] 5880 2-9-0 95 TadhgO'Shea 4 82
(B J Meehan) *awkward s: hld up in tch: hdwy to trck ldr 1/2-way: rdn along over 2f out and sn wknd* **5/1**[3]

1303 **7** *30* **Ballista (IRE)**[7] 6568 2-9-0 94 RichardKingscote 8 —
(Tom Dascombe) *led 2f: sn rdn along and wknd 1/2-way: sn bhd and eased* **5/1**[3]

1m 17.94s (6.04) **Going Correction** +0.925s/f (Soft) 7 Ran SP% **109.8**
Speed ratings (Par 103): **96,88,87,85,84 83,43**
toteswingers: 1&2 £1.30, 1&3 £8.20, 2&3 £4.50 CSF £17.59 TOTE £6.60: £3.20, £1.70; EX 12.00 Trifecta £146.00 Pool of £1,180.52 - 5.98 winning units..
Owner J F Grogan **Bred** John Grogan **Trained** Cashel, Co Tipperary
■ A first British winner for John Grogan, with his only horse in training.

FOCUS
A one-sided Listed event, but the likelihood is that the majority simply failed to run up to their best under the conditions, rather than that the winner found massive improvement.

NOTEBOOK
Katla(IRE)'s previous form entitled her to go close, but she absolutely routed her field, clearly revelling in the conditions. What the form's worth isn't easy to know but she'd clearly be entitled to respect even in Group company when the mud's flying. (op 9-2 tchd 4-1)
Barefoot Lady(IRE) never looked comfortable under these more testing conditions and it's hard to believe she got anywhere near the form she showed at Ayr last time, though the way she stuck to her task does at least reaffirm the view that she's going to be well suited by 7f-plus. (tchd 3-1)
Carrignavar(USA) now has a Listed place to her name, which doesn't harm her value, but it's doubtful this represents much of an improvement on her Sandown maiden form, those she beat all being below their best. (op 8-1)
None Shall Sleep(IRE), gelded since finishing third to Forjatt in a Nottingham minor event two months ago, wasn't discredited upped in class, particularly after a slow start. He's stoutly bred on the dam's side, so it's not out of the question longer trips may bring a bit more out of him.
Easy Ticket(IRE) patently failed to get home under the conditions, looking a clear second-best until his stamina gave out inside the last. His nursery form is strong and he's up to making a mark at this level. (op 4-1)
Murbeh(IRE) had faced much quicker conditions previously and presumably didn't handle the ground as he was certainly a fair way off his previous form. Official explanation: jockey said that the gelding lost action (op 6-1)
Ballista(IRE) had performed well on soft ground at Redcar a week ago but was in trouble before halfway. Official explanation: jockey said that the colt ran flat (op 6-1)

6752 CORAL SPRINT TROPHY (HERITAGE H'CAP) 6f
3:55 (3:57) (Class 2) (0-105,105) 3-Y-O £48,570 (£14,452; £7,222; £3,607) Stalls Centre

Form RPR

1222 **1** **Fathsta (IRE)**[14] 6357 5-8-13 94 SilvestreDeSousa 15 107
(D M Simcock) *trckd ldrs towards stands' side: hdwy to ld over 1f out: forged clr* **14/1**

6040 **2** *3 1/4* **Damien (IRE)**[21] 6177 4-9-3 98 WilliamCarson 8 101
(B W Hills) *mid-div: effrt over 2f out: r.o to take 2nd last 50yds* **18/1**

0615 **3** *1* **Irish Heartbeat (IRE)**[21] 6175 5-9-1 96 PaulHanagan 2 95
(R A Fahey) *trckd ldrs towards far side: edgd rt over 1f out: drifted rt and kpt on same pce ins fnl f* **7/1**[2]

3020 **4** *2* **Parisian Pyramid (IRE)**[21] 6177 4-9-4 99 StephenCraine 4 92
(K A Ryan) *trckd ldrs towards far side: swtchd lft and kpt on same pce ins fnl f* **40/1**

4021 **5** *nse* **Tajneed (IRE)**[49] 5302 7-9-9 104 AdrianNicholls 14 97
(D Nicholls) *chsd ldrs: kpt on same pce fnl f* **12/1**

0013 **6** *3/4* **Quest For Success (IRE)**[9] 6508 5-9-2 100 IanBrennan(3) 19 90
(R A Fahey) *mid-div: effrt over 2f out: styd on fnl f* **16/1**

6003 **7** *1/2* **Brae Hill (IRE)**[7] 6564 4-9-0 95 PJMcDonald 1 84
(R A Fahey) *overall ldr far side: edgd rt over 2f out: hdd over 1f out: kpt on same pce* **40/1**

6300 **8** *shd* **Secret Asset (IRE)**[9] 6508 5-8-9 97 LewisWalsh(7) 3 86
(Jane Chapple-Hyam) *chsd ldrs towards far side: kpt on same pce appr fnl f* **50/1**

2306 **9** *nk* **Manassas (IRE)**[21] 6175 5-9-0 95 ShaneKelly 11 83
(B J Meehan) *chsd ldrs: swtchd rt towards stands' side over 2f out: kpt on same pce appr fnl f* **16/1**

0200 **10** *3 1/2* **Kaldoun Kingdom (IRE)**[21] 6177 5-9-5 105 LeeTopliss(5) 20 81
(R A Fahey) *hld up towards rr: effrt over 2f out: kpt on ins fnl f: nvr a factor* **14/1**

0110 **11** *4* **Poet's Place (USA)**[21] 6177 5-9-7 102 PhillipMakin 7 66
(T D Barron) *chsd ldrs towards far side: wknd over 1f out* **9/2**[1]

1100 **12** *3/4* **Masamah (IRE)**[21] 6194 4-9-7 102 PaulMulrennan 12 63
(K A Ryan) *racd towards far side: w ldrs: wknd over 1f out: eased ins fnl f* **25/1**

3010 **13** *6* **Hawkeyethenoo (IRE)**[21] 6177 4-9-2 97 TomQueally 18 39
(J S Goldie) *in rr stands' side: hdwy over 2f out: chsng ldrs over 1f out: wknd and heavily eased last 150yds* **10/1**[3]

0064 **14** *10* **Knot In Wood (IRE)**[19] 6241 8-9-2 100 BarryMcHugh(3) 10 10
(R A Fahey) *in rr: drvn over 2f out: sn bhd: eased* **12/1**

4400 **15** *4 1/2* **Rileyskeepingfaith**[13] 6390 4-9-6 101 (v) DarryllHolland 17 —
(M R Channon) *in rr and sn drvn along: bhd fnl 2f: eased* **16/1**

0500 **16** *3 3/4* **Able Master (IRE)**[21] 6175 4-9-0 95 (p) NickyMackay 5 —
(J R Gask) *racd towards far side: prom tl lost pl over 2f out: sn bhd and eased* **16/1**

0211 **17** *1/2* **Colonel Mak**[21] 6175 3-9-4 100 GrahamGibbons 16 —
(T D Barron) *hld up in mid-div: effrt over 2f out: sn wknd and eased* **12/1**

110P **18** *4* **Gramercy (IRE)**[14] 6349 3-9-3 99 JamieSpencer 13 —
(M L W Bell) *dwlt: in rr and sn given reminders: bhd and eased over 1f out* **16/1**

1005 **19** *2 1/2* **Swilly Ferry (USA)**[29] 5911 3-9-6 102 MichaelHills 6 —
(B W Hills) *in rr-div towards far side: bhd fnl 2f: eased* **28/1**

0300 **20** *2* **Signor Peltro**[21] 6177 7-9-5 100 FergusSweeney 9 —
(H Candy) *in rr: bhd fnl 2f: eased* **16/1**

1m 16.07s (4.17) **Going Correction** +0.925s/f (Soft)
WFA 3 from 4yo+ 1lb 20 Ran SP% **130.9**
Speed ratings (Par 109): **109,104,103,100,100 99,98,98,98,93 88,87,79,66,60 55,54,49,45,43**
toteswingers: 1&2 £48.30, 1&3 £35.10, 2&3 £27.30 CSF £246.81 CT £1984.65 TOTE £15.90: £2.90, £5.00, £1.90, £16.00; EX 264.60 Trifecta £3993.30 Pool of £49,107.78 - 9.10 winning units..
Owner Dr Marwan Koukash **Bred** Brian Miller **Trained** Newmarket, Suffolk

FOCUS
As always, a smart and competitive sprint handicap. They were fanned out across the track, the winner coming more towards the near side.

NOTEBOOK
Fathsta(IRE) has been in really good form of late but stepped it up another notch here to defy a career-high mark, bursting clear towards the near side approaching the final 1f. He'll be up in the low 100s when reassessed and will need to improve again to defy that mark.
Damien(IRE) has only a maiden win to his name but the ability has always been there and he ran his best race of the season, impressing with the way he travelled. He hasn't had many runs on soft ground but has always gone well on it. (op 25-1)
Irish Heartbeat(IRE) is right back in form and will remain one to bear in mind, though he doesn't always deliver that much off the bridle and will need things to drop right. His rider was possibly unaware of the winner making his move wide of him but the fact he was even run out of second late on suggests he can't be considered unlucky. (op 8-1)
Parisian Pyramid(IRE) put an abysmal run in the Ayr Gold Cup behind him but there's nothing in his record to suggest he's up to winning one of these off his current mark.
Tajneed(IRE) wasn't discredited but tends to save his best efforts for Ripon. (op 14-1 tchd 9-1)
Quest For Success(IRE) continues in form but has had plenty of chances from this sort of mark now. (tchd 18-1)
Brae Hill(IRE) has done most of his recent racing at 7f but has always looked to have the speed for sprint trips and ran respectably. (op 50-1)
Poet's Place(USA) was strong as favourite but clearly wasn't himself, the writing being on the wall from some way out. He's still got very few miles on the clock and it would be no surprise to see him get back on the up next year. Official explanation: jockey said that the gelding was never travelling (op 6-1 tchd 13-2 in places)
Hawkeyethenoo(IRE) is another whose progress appears to have stalled for now but, like Poet's Place, it would be no shock to see him pull out a bit more next year. (tchd 9-1)
Knot In Wood(IRE) has had a good record over the years and might have been expected to do better, given he wasn't beaten far in the Ayr Gold Cup last month and had come down another 2lb in the weights.
Rileyskeepingfaith Official explanation: trainer said that the gelding was unsuited by the Soft, Good to Soft in places going.
Colonel Mak came into this at the top of his game but clearly wasn't himself, being beaten too far to blame a 7lb rise for Ayr.
Signor Peltro Official explanation: jockey said that the gelding had no more to give.

6753 CORAL TV STKS (H'CAP) 1m 2f 88y
4:30 (4:31) (Class 4) (0-80,79) 3-Y-O £6,540 (£1,946; £972; £485) Stalls Low

Form RPR

6304 **1** **Tres Coronas (IRE)**[27] 6002 3-9-7 79 GrahamGibbons 17 88
(T D Barron) *dwlt and swtchd lft s: hld up in rr: hdwy 4f out: n.m.r and swtchd lft wl over 2f out: rdn to chse ldrs over 1f out: led ent fnl f: kpt on* **33/1**

4440 **2** *1 1/4* **Ejteyaaz**[14] 6355 3-9-1 78 LeeTopliss(5) 15 85
(R A Fahey) *towards rr: effrt over 3f out: rdn over 2f out: drvn to chse ldrs and edgd rt ins fnl f: styd on wl u.p towards fin* **18/1**

032 **3** *1* **Shallow Bay**[28] 5971 3-9-1 73 PaulHanagan 5 78+
(W R Swinburn) *midfield: hdwy over 4f out: rdn to chse ldrs over 2f out: drvn and ev ch over 1f out: kpt on same pce fnl f* **3/1**[1]

331 **4** *1* **Titivation**[10] 6470 3-9-5 77 HayleyTurner 19 80
(M L W Bell) *in rr: hdwy over 4f out: rdn along wl over 2f out: drvn over 1f out: styd on ins fnl f: nrst fin* **15/2**[3]

1000 **5** *nse* **Monkton Vale (IRE)**[24] 6074 3-9-1 73 (b[1]) JackMitchell 2 76
(R A Fahey) *trckd ldrs: hdwy over 4f out: led over 3f out: rdn and hdd over 2f out: drvn and one pce over 1f out* **25/1**

3404 **6** *3 1/4* **Law To Himself (IRE)**[28] 5942 3-8-12 70 DavidAllan 8 67
(G A Swinbank) *in tch: hdwy to chse ldrs 4f out: rdn along 3f out: drvn 2f out and sn one pce* **20/1**

2411 **7** *2 1/2* **The Caped Crusader (IRE)**[28] 5942 3-9-0 75 BarryMcHugh(3) 12 67
(Ollie Pears) *hld up in midfield: hdwy over 3f out: in tch whn nt clr run over 2f out: sn swtchd lft and rdn: no imp* **9/2**[2]

311 **8** *3/4* **Hail Bold Chief (USA)**[18] 6266 3-9-2 74 PJMcDonald 4 65
(G A Swinbank) *trckd ldrs: hdwy 4f out: rdn along wl over 2f out: drvn wl over 1f out and grad wknd* **11/1**

9 *1 3/4* **Royal And Ancient (IRE)**[14] 3342 3-8-13 74 Louis-PhilippeBeuzelin(3) 11 61
(M F Harris) *in rr and sn pushed along: hdwy 3f out: rdn and hung rt over 2f out: sn no imp* **50/1**

0100 **10** *4 1/2* **Think Its All Over (USA)**[52] 5217 3-9-5 77 JamieSpencer 14 56
(T P Tate) *in tch rdn along 1/2-way: sn lost pl and bhd fnl 3f* **14/1**

6106 **11** *3 3/4* **Cherry Bee**[13] 6395 3-8-12 70 GregFairley 18 42
(M Johnston) *hld up: hdwy on outer over 2f out: sn rdn and n.d* **25/1**

3000 **12** *1 3/4* **Layla's Dancer**[14] 6355 3-9-3 75 StephenCraine 1 43
(R A Fahey) *led 2f: cl up tl rdn along over 4f out and sn wknd* **20/1**

000 **13** *16* **Take It To The Max**[16] 6304 3-9-5 77 (t) PaulMulrennan 13 15
(G M Moore) *trckd ldrs: hdwy 1/2-way and sn cl up: led over 3f out: rdn and hdd over 2f out: grad wknd* **14/1**

0000 **14** *2 1/2* **Beneath**[23] 6122 3-8-9 67 FrannyNorton 3 —
(K A Ryan) *cl up: led after 2f: hdd 1/2-way: rdn along 4f out and sn wknd* **33/1**

6505 **15** *4* **Christmas Light**[35] 5759 3-9-2 74 SilvestreDeSousa 16 —
(D O'Meara) *a towards rr* **12/1**

1040 **16** *5* **Syrian**[10] 6467 3-9-5 77 ShaneKelly 7 —
(Ian Williams) *v.s.a and bhd: sme hdwy 4f out: sn rdn and nvr a factor* **20/1**

0240 **17** *30* **Blues Music (IRE)**[11] 6447 3-9-7 79 (p) MichaelHills 10 —
(B W Hills) *cl up: led 1/2-way: rdn along and hdd over 3f out: sn drvn and wknd* **25/1**

5220 **P** **Southern Cape (IRE)**[23] 6122 3-8-4 67 DeclanCannon(5) 9 —
(D J Coakley) *midfield: lost action and lost pl qckly bef 1/2-way: sn p.u* **20/1**

2m 18.18s (5.68) **Going Correction** +0.70s/f (Yiel) 18 Ran SP% **128.0**
Speed ratings (Par 103): **105,104,103,102,102 99,97,97,95,92 89,87,74,72,69 65,41,—**
toteswingers: 1&2 £51.90, 1&3 £25.40, 2&3 £16.90 CSF £502.53 CT £2336.63 TOTE £53.10: £8.30, £4.70, £1.90, £1.70; EX 938.20 TRIFECTA Not won..
Owner J Cringan & D Pryde **Bred** Denis McDonnell **Trained** Maunby, N Yorks
■ Stewards' Enquiry : Lee Topliss two-day ban: used whip with excessive frequency (Oct 25, TBA)

The Form Book, Raceform Ltd, Compton, RG20 6NL

FOCUS
A fairly useful 3-y-o event. They went hard up front in the conditions and it was no surprise that the principals came from off the gallop.
Christmas Light Official explanation: jockey said that the filly had no more to give

6754 COLDSTREAM GUARDS ASSOCIATION STKS (H'CAP) 1m 4f
5:05 (5:05) (Class 4) (0-85,85) 3-Y-0+ **£6,540** (£1,946; £972; £485) **Stalls** Centre

Form				RPR
1033	1		**Tepmokea (IRE)**[21] 6193 4-9-12 **85** ... PaulHanagan 5	95
			(R A Fahey) *hld up in midfield: hdwy to trck ldrs 3f out: led and edgd rt over 1f out: hdd last 75yds: hrd rdn and rallied to ld post* **10/3**[1]	
0211	2	*nse*	**Pertemps Networks**[23] 6109 6-8-12 **71** oh1 ... GrahamGibbons 3	81
			(M W Easterby) *hld up towards rr: hdwy over 3f out: styd on to ld narrowly last 75yds: hdd post* **9/2**[2]	
0111	3	*1 3/4*	**Kathleen Frances**[28] 5953 3-8-6 **77** ... AshleyMorgan(5) 10	84
			(M H Tompkins) *trckd ldrs: led over 2f out tl over 1f out: sn hmpd and swtchd lft: kpt on same pce last 100yds* **5/1**[3]	
4-11	4	*hd*	**Leslingtaylor (IRE)**[7] 6573 8-8-13 **79** ... ShaneBKelly(7) 6	86
			(J J Quinn) *s.i.s: in rr: effrt 4f out: chsng ldrs over 2f out: hmpd 1f out: edgd rt and styd on ins fnl f* **12/1**	
4344	5	*2 3/4*	**Rockfella**[58] 5002 4-8-13 **72** ... DarryllHolland 2	74
			(D J Coakley) *chsd ldrs: chal over 3f out: one pce fnl 2f* **16/1**	
6001	6	*1 3/4*	**Alsahil (USA)**[16] 6306 4-8-9 **75** ... JamesRogers(7) 12	75
			(Micky Hammond) *racd wd early: led after 1f: hdd over 2f out: edgd rt 1f out: one pce* **33/1**	
211	7	*1 1/4*	**Maybe I Wont**[40] 5591 5-8-9 **71** oh2 ... RussKennemore(3) 11	69
			(Lucinda Featherstone) *in rr: hdwy over 3f out: sn chsng ldrs: wknd appr fnl f* **25/1**	
133	8	*3 1/4*	**George Adamson (IRE)**[35] 5757 4-9-1 **74** ... PJMcDonald 13	66+
			(G A Swinbank) *hld up in rr: hdwy over 3f out: swtchd rt over 2f out: one pce whn checked jst ins fnl f* **25/1**	
0353	9	*15*	**Becausewecan (USA)**[7] 6565 4-9-8 **81** ... GregFairley 8	49
			(M Johnston) *chsd ldr: rdn to chal 4f out: wknd 3f out: sn bhd: eased* **9/2**[2]	
6220	10	*3 1/4*	**Arashi**[15] 6322 4-8-12 **71** oh4 ... (v) SilvestreDeSousa 9	34
			(Lucinda Featherstone) *chsd ldrs: wknd over 2f out: eased whn bhd* **25/1**	
4000	11	*hd*	**Porgy**[16] 6304 5-9-4 **82** ... LeeTopliss(5) 14	45
			(R A Fahey) *s.i.s: swtchd lft s: hdwy over 5f out: hung lft and lost pl over 2f out* **20/1**	
1412	12	*8*	**Beat The Rush**[84] 4153 3-9-2 **85** ... BarryMcHugh(3) 1	35
			(Julie Camacho) *t.k.h: led 1f: trckd ldrs: rdn over 3f out: lost pl over 2f out: eased whn bhd* **13/2**	

2m 39.9s (6.70) **Going Correction** +0.70s/f (Yiel)
WFA 3 from 4yo+ 7lb **12 Ran SP% 122.3**
Speed ratings (Par 105): **105,104,103,103,101 100,99,97,87,85 85,80**
toteswingers: 1&2 £5.30, 1&3 £5.90, 2&3 £7.60 CSF £17.27 CT £76.84 TOTE £4.10: £1.70, £2.20, £2.30; EX 22.60 Trifecta £234.40 Pool of £912.31 - 2.88 winning units. Place 6 £7,131.61, Place 5 £719.40.
Owner Keep Racing **Bred** J H A Baggen **Trained** Musley Bank, N Yorks

FOCUS
No reason to doubt the merit of this form.
Beat The Rush Official explanation: trainer said that the gelding was unsuited by the Soft, Good to Soft in places going
T/Jkpt: Not won. T/Plt: £2,649.80 to a £1 stake. Pool of £140,295.38. 38.65 winning tickets. T/Qpdt: £162.20 to a £1 stake. Pool of £10,448.21. 38.65 winning tickets. JR

6602 BELMONT PARK (L-H)
Saturday, October 9
OFFICIAL GOING: Dirt: fast; turf: good

6756a CHAMPAGNE STKS (GRADE 1) (2YO) (DIRT) 1m
10:09 (10:13) 2-Y-0
£111,111 (£37,037; £18,518; £9,259; £5,555; £3,703)

			RPR
1		**Uncle Mo (USA)**[42] 2-8-10 0 ... JRVelazquez 3	116
		(Todd Pletcher, U.S.A) *disp ld or shaded lded fr the off: wnt on 2f out: qcknd clr 1 1/2f out: rn a little green in front: steadily plld away* **1/5**[1]	
2	*4 3/4*	**Mountain Town (USA)** 2-8-10 0 ... CVelasquez 5	106
		(Richard Dutrow Jr, U.S.A) *settled in 5th: hdwy on outside 3f out: 3rd on outside 2f out: tk 2nd w 1 1/2f to run: kpt on wl: plld clr of others but no ch w wnr* **9/1**[3]	
3	*9 3/4*	**I'm Steppin' It Up (USA)**[90] 2-8-10 0 ... (b) DCohen 4	87
		(Anthony Pecoraro, U.S.A) *disp ld and pressed ldr fr the s: gave best to wnr 2f out: rdn appr fnl f: wknd* **225/10**	
4	*nk*	**Settle For Medal (USA)**[33] 5827 2-8-10 0 ... JLezcano 2	86
		(Mark Hennig, U.S.A) *racd in last: sme mod late prog: nvr in contention* **118/10**	
5	*1 1/2*	**Meridian Magic (USA)** 2-8-10 0 ... ASolis 1	83
		(Nicholas Zito, U.S.A) *racd in 4th: no imp on ldrs fnl 2f* **29/1**	
6	*3 1/2*	**Brother In Arms (USA)**[76] 2-8-10 0 ... (b) EPrado 6	76
		(Kelly Breen, U.S.A) *disp ld v early: sn racd in 3rd: rdn over 2f out: drifted rt and wknd appr fnl 1 1/2f* **68/10**[2]	

1m 34.51s (94.51) **6 Ran SP% 121.6**
PARI-MUTUEL (all including $2 stakes): WIN 2.40; PLACE (1-2) 2.10, 4.70; SHOW (1-2-3) 2.10, 3.70, 5.20; SF 11.40.
Owner Repole Stable **Bred** D Michael Cavey Dvm **Trained** USA

NOTEBOOK
Uncle Mo(USA) ◆ is North America's answer to Frankel. Sent off at 1-5 after scoring by more than 14l on debut at Saratoga, he was hassled by long shot I'm Steppin' It Up and set quick opening fractions, but he still powered away in the straight to record a time which tied Seattle Slew for the second-fastest Champagne at the distance, just a fifth of a second slower than Devil's Bag in 1983. Held in the highest regard by Todd Pletcher, he should be extremely hard to beat in the Breeders' Cup Juvenile.

6732 KEENELAND (L-H)
Saturday, October 9
OFFICIAL GOING: Polytrack: fast; turf: firm

6757a ABU DHABI FIRST LADY STKS (GRADE 1) (3YO+ FILLIES & MARES) (TURF) 1m
9:42 (9:44) 3-Y-0+
£148,148 (£49,382; £24,691; £12,345; £7,407; £1,234)

			RPR
1		**Proviso**[70] 5-8-12 0 ... MESmith 7	114
		(William Mott, U.S.A) *hld up in rr: 8th 1 1/2f out: hdwy on outside: r.o strly fnl f to ld cl home* **13/10**[1]	
2	*1/2*	**C. S. Silk (USA)**[20] 4-8-12 0 ... KDesormeaux 1	113
		(Dale Romans, U.S.A) *a.p: chsd ldr fr 1 1/2f out: led fnl 50yds: ct cl home: no ex* **20/1**	
3	*nse*	**Gotta Have Her (USA)**[33] 6-8-12 0 ... GKGomez 3	113
		(Jenine Sahadi, U.S.A) *hld up in last pl: hdwy on outside appr fnl f: fin wl: nvr nrr* **8/1**	
4	*nk*	**Fantasia**[126] 4-8-12 0 ... JRLeparoux 2	112
		(Jonathan Sheppard, U.S.A) *racd in 6th: short of room appr fnl f and swtchd outside: r.o but swtchd ins fnl 80yds and fnd gap on rail: r.o wl* **41/5**	
5	*1/2*	**Wasted Tears (USA)**[54] 5-8-12 0 ... RMaragh 8	111
		(Bart B Evans, U.S.A) *disp ld early but sn chsng ldr: led 3 1/2f out: hdd fnl 50yds: no ex* **31/10**[2]	
6	*1 1/2*	**Dynaslew (USA)**[42] 4-8-12 0 ... JJCastellano 4	107
		(Seth Benzel, U.S.A) *racd in 5th: rdn 1 1/2f out: wnt 3rd 1f out: unable qck u.p* **48/10**[3]	
7	*1*	**Kiss Mine (USA)**[63] 4-8-12 0 ... JKCourt 6	105
		(David Vance, U.S.A) *racd in midfield: cl up over 1f out: nt qckn* **158/10**	
8	*4 1/4*	**Cure For Sale (ARG)**[13] 6-8-12 0 ... (b) MMena 9	95
		(Raja Malek, U.S.A) *racd in 4th and 5th for much of the r: rdn and wknd fnl 300yds* **88/1**	
9	*9 1/4*	**West Hope (BRZ)**[56] 5-8-12 0 ... GretaKuntzweiler 5	74
		(Eduardo Caramori, U.S.A) *2nd earlY but sn led: hdd 3 1/2f out: wknd fnl 300yds* **77/1**	

1m 34.81s (94.81) **9 Ran SP% 120.2**
PARI-MUTUEL (all including $2 stakes): WIN 4.60; PLACE (1-2) 3.20, 13.00; SHOW (1-2-3) 2.10, 8.40, 4.40; SF 79.00.
Owner Juddmonte Farms **Bred** Juddmonte Farms Ltd **Trained** USA

NOTEBOOK
Proviso came from an unpromising position to win and now goes for the Breeders' Cup Mile.

6759a SHADWELL TURF MILE STKS (GRADE 1) (3YO+) (TURF) 1m
10:45 (10:47) 3-Y-0+
£222,222 (£74,074; £37,037; £18,518; £11,111; £7,407)

			RPR
1		**Gio Ponti (USA)**[49] 5321 5-9-0 0 ... RADominguez 4	116
		(Christophe Clement, U.S.A) *patiently rdn wl off the pce: clsd up fr 2f out: smooth hdwy fr 1 1/2f out (despite being bmpd) to ld fnl 100yds: comf* **4/5**[1]	
2	*1*	**Society's Chairman (CAN)**[33] 7-9-0 0 ... JRLeparoux 5	114
		(Roger L Attfield, Canada) *settled in last: hdwy on outside over 1f out to ld appr fnl 110yds: sn hdd: no ex as wnr qcknd by* **181/10**	
3	*1 1/4*	**Courageous Cat (USA)**[196] 1025 4-9-0 0 ... PValenzuela 3	111
		(William Mott, U.S.A) *racd in 4th: clsd up 2f out: led ins fnl f: sn rdn: hdd appr fnl 110yds: no ex* **33/10**[3]	
4	*2*	**Get Stormy (USA)**[43] 4-9-0 0 ... JJCastellano 1	107
		(Thomas Bush, U.S.A) *a.p: unable qck appr fnl f* **29/10**[2]	
5	*6 1/4*	**Enriched (USA)**[42] 5-9-0 0 ... (b) GKGomez 6	92
		(Doug O'Neill, U.S.A) *trckd ldr: led 2 1/2f out: hdd ins fnl f: fdd* **79/10**	
6	*1 3/4*	**Acting Zippy (USA)**[174] 5-9-0 0 ... (b) EMMartinJr 2	88
		(William Bennett, U.S.A) *led: hdd 2 1/2f out: rallied to stay prom: wknd qckly fnl f* **60/1**	

1m 35.06s (95.06) **6 Ran SP% 122.6**
PARI-MUTUEL (all including $2 stakes): WIN 3.60; PLACE (1-2) 2.60, 8.00; SHOW (1-2-3) 2.10, 3.40, 2.80; SF 32.80.
Owner Castleton Lyons Farm **Bred** Kilboy Estate Inc **Trained** USA

NOTEBOOK
Gio Ponti(USA) ◆ could be the one to deny Goldikova a third Breeders' Cup Mile. While the bare form of his 21/4l beating of Courageous Cat (beaten 1/2l into second by Goldikova at last year's BC) cannot be taken literally seeing as that one was returning from a break, he won with a lot in hand. He's done most of his racing at around 1m2f, and was second to Zenyatta in last year's Classic, but a stronger traveller with a fine turn of foot, it's quite possible he's even better over 1m. On his last start at this distance, he won a Grade 1 in March 2009 and he's now 4-5 at the trip.

6640 MAISONS-LAFFITTE (R-H)
Saturday, October 9
OFFICIAL GOING: Turf: very soft

6760a PRIX ECLIPSE (GROUP 3) (2YO) (TURF) 6f (S)
1:30 (12:00) 2-Y-0 **£35,398** (£14,159; £10,619; £7,079; £3,539)

			RPR
1		**Split Trois (FR)**[18] 6277 2-8-8 0 ... Christophe-PatriceLemaire 7	101
		(Y De Nicolay, France) *bkmarker fr s and stl in rr 1f out whn swtchd away fr stands' side: fnd split: qcknd wl: fin strly to get up on line* **182/10**	
2	*shd*	**Captain Chop (FR)**[48] 5347 2-8-11 0 ... FlavienPrat 1	104
		(D Guillemin, France) *led fr s on rail: rdn 1 1/2f out: r.o wl ins fnl f and only ct fnl strides* **9/1**	
3	*hd*	**Spirit Of Battle (USA)**[18] 6277 2-8-11 0 ... MickaelBarzalona 2	103
		(A Fabre, France) *racd in midfield: swtchd away fr rails to make chal 1 1/2f out: r.o wl to chal for ld 100yds out: no ex fnl 25yds* **4/1**[3]	
4	*2*	**Khawatim**[69] 4637 2-8-11 0 ... ChristopheSoumillon 3	97
		(J-C Rouget, France) *racd in 3rd: rdn 1 1/2f out: no ex ins fnl f: styd on* **23/10**[2]	

5 snk **Chinese Wall (IRE)**[26] 6044 2-8-8 0 .... ThierryJarnet 5 93
(D Guillemin, France) *racd towards rr on outside: rdn 1 1/2f out: r.o: no ex fnl 100yds* 9/5[1]
6 1/2 **Boccalino (GER)**[26] 6044 2-8-11 0 .... StephanePasquier 4 95
(H-A Pantall, France) *racd in 2nd: u.p 1f out: r.o: no ex fnl 100yds* 53/10
1m 16.9s (3.50) 6 Ran SP% 117.1
PARI-MUTUEL (all including 1 euro stakes): WIN 19.20. PLACES: 6.20, 3.50. SF: 106.60.
Owner Christian Henry De Villeneuve **Bred** Nicholas J Hughes **Trained** France

6761a PRIX LE FABULEUX (LISTED RACE) (3YO) (TURF) 1m 1f
2:40 (12:00) 3-Y-0 £24,336 (£9,734; £7,300; £4,867; £2,433)

RPR
1 **Royal Revival**[15] 6344 3-9-2 0 .... Pierre-CharlesBoudot 7 99
(A Fabre, France) 9/2[2]
2 1 **Rysckly (FR)**[55] 3-9-2 0 .... Christophe-PatriceLemaire 9 97
(Y De Nicolay, France) 9/1
3 2 1/2 **Atlantis Star**[23] 6123 3-9-2 0 .... MickaelBarzalona 1 92
(Saeed Bin Suroor) *broke wl: racd in 4th on stands' side as field split: u.str.p 1 1/2f out: wnt 2nd 1f out: led briefly 100yds out: sn hdd and no ex fnl 50yds* 15/1
4 3/4 **Don Bosco (FR)**[25] 3-9-2 0 .... GregoryBenoist 2 90
(D Smaga, France) 17/1
5 hd **Roche Ambeau (FR)**[28] 5981 3-8-13 0 .... AnthonyCrastus 3 87
(E Lellouche, France) 12/1
6 3/4 **Wolverine (FR)**[16] 6315 3-9-2 0 .... SebastienMaillot 5 88
(M Boutin, France) 32/1
7 1 **Persiste Et Signe (FR)**[140] 2357 3-9-2 0 .... ThierryThulliez 10 86
(N Clement, France) 3/1[1]
8 8 **Tagar Bere (FR)**[29] 5935 3-9-2 0 .... FranckBlondel 6 69
(M Pimbonnet, France) 73/10[3]
9 15 **Muhtaker**[29] 5935 3-9-2 0 .... IoritzMendizabal 8 38
(J E Hammond, France) 73/10[3]
10 1/2 **Street Lair (USA)**[53] 3-9-2 0 .... ChristopheSoumillon 4 37
(J-C Rouget, France) 9/2[2]
2m 0.20s (5.50) 10 Ran SP% 118.0
PARI-MUTUEL (all including 1 euro stakes): WIN 4.10 (Royal Revival coupled with Atlantis Star). PLACES: 2.00, 3.10, 4.40. DF: 33.40. SF: 46.10.
Owner Godolphin SNC **Bred** Newsells Park Stud Limited **Trained** Chantilly, France

NOTEBOOK
Atlantis Star, winner of a conditions race at Wolverhampton on his reappearance, had very different conditions to deal with here but ran a solid race in defeat.

6238 SAN SIRO (R-H)
Saturday, October 9
OFFICIAL GOING: Turf: soft

6762a PREMIO GRAN CRITERIUM (GROUP 1) (2YO COLTS & FILLIES) (TURF) 1m
2:40 (3:03) 2-Y-0 £119,469 (£52,566; £28,672; £14,336)

RPR
1 **Biondetti (USA)**[35] 5751 2-8-11 0 .... AhmedAjtebi 5 105
(Mahmood Al Zarooni) *slowly away: settled midfield: produced fnl 2f: rdn to ld 1f out: styd on wl fnl f* 23/20[1]
2 1/2 **Singapore Lilly (IRE)**[35] 5746 2-8-8 0 .... NeilCallan 7 101
(M R Channon) *slowly away: towards rr for 5f: rdn ent st: gd hdwy ent fnl 1 1/2f: clst fnl 100yds* 23/10[2]
3 2 3/4 **Billy Budd (IRE)**[20] 2-8-11 0 .... FabioBranca 4 98
(S Botti, Italy) *broke wl to ld: set gd pce: lened ent st to take clr ld: chal 1f out: hrd rdn and no rspnse fnl 100yds* 13/2
4 2 1/2 **Meracus (IRE)**[35] 2-8-11 0 .... MircoDemuro 3 92
(S Botti, Italy) *settled in 2nd for 5f: rdn and ev ch fnl 2f: styd on* 31/10[3]
5 snk **Fairyhall** 2-8-11 0 .... DarioVargiu 2 92
(B Grizzetti, Italy) *settled in 3rd after 1f: moved 2nd ent fnl 2f: hrd rdn and no imp ent fnl f* 98/10
6 3 1/2 **Reventon** 2-8-11 0 .... CColombi 8 84
(B Grizzetti, Italy) *slowly away and hld up in rr: rdn to stay in tch ent st: no imp under hrd ride fnl 3f* 36/1
7 1 1/4 **Ksenia (ITY)**[27] 2-8-8 0 .... LManiezzi 6 78
(Maria Rita Salvioni, Italy) *mid-div on outer tl ent st: rdn 3f out to stay in tch: sn btn* 67/1
8 shd **Arma Mani (IRE)**[13] 2-8-11 0 .... UmbertoRispoli 1 80
(B Grizzetti, Italy) *broke wl: settled midfield on inner: niggled to stay in tch fnl 4f: hrd rdn and no imp fnl 2f* 161/10
1m 41.5s (-0.60) 8 Ran SP% 133.8
WIN (incl. 1 euro stake): 2.17. PLACES: 1.20, 1.29, 1.67. DF: 3.72.
Owner Godolphin **Bred** Palides Investments N V Inc **Trained** Newmarket, Suffolk

NOTEBOOK
Biondetti(USA), winner of his first two starts, including when making all in a conditions event at Kempton last time, was up in class and he was ridden more patiently here before coming through to lead a furlong out. The extra furlong suited him.
Singapore Lilly(IRE), a winner in Listed company at Haydock last time out, coped well with the softer ground and closed down the winner inside the last, but he always had her measure.

6763a PREMIO VERZIERE (GROUP 3) (3YO+ FILLIES & MARES) (TURF) 1m 2f
3:15 (3:32) 3-Y-0+ £35,398 (£15,575; £8,495; £4,247)

RPR
1 **Irini (GER)**[20] 6234 4-9-0 0 .... LManiezzi 4 101
(H J Groschel, Germany) *settled in rr for 6f: hdwy fnl 2f on outer: rdn ent fnl f and sn in command: comf* 77/20[3]
2 2 1/2 **Tech Exceed (GER)**[27] 3-8-13 0 .... EPedroza 9 100
(A Wohler, Germany) *broke wl: settled 3rd for 5f: rdn to ld ent fnl 1 1/2f: chal fnl f: no answer to wnr* 4/5[1]
3 1 **Sakheart**[20] 4-9-0 0 .... UmbertoRispoli 8 95
(V Luka Jr, Czech Republic) *slowly away: settled in mid-div for 5f: rdn fnl 2f and ev ch: styd on one pce fnl f* 92/10
4 1 **Ephigenie (IRE)**[48] 5345 4-9-0 0 .... DominiqueBoeuf 2 94
(T Mundry, Germany) *nr rr tl ent st: outpcd and last ent fnl 3f: gd hdwy under hrd ride fnl 1 1/2f* 101/10
5 snk **Amare**[27] 6011 3-8-9 0 .... EFrank 1 94
(T Mundry, Germany) *rdn to go 2nd after 1f: high hd carriage whn asked 3f out: hrd rdn fnl 2f: styd on* 198/10
6 2 1/4 **Lolamar (ITY)**[104] 3495 3-8-9 0 .... FabioBranca 7 90
(S Botti, Italy) *broke wl to ld: 2 l clr ent st: chal ent fnl 1 1/2f: hrd rdn and btn ent fnl f: eased fnl 100yds* 31/10[2]
7 3 **Tremoto**[104] 5-9-0 0 .... (b) SDiana 6 84
(F & L Camici, Italy) *broke wl: settled mid-div: 4th ent st: outpcd fnl 2f: hrd rdn and no imp* 163/10
8 2 1/2 **Saldennahe (GER)**[27] 6011 3-8-9 0 .... AStarke 1 79
(P Schiergen, Germany) *broke wl: settled to r midfield: hdwy and ev ch fnl 2f: hrd rdn and sn btn: eased fnl f* 4/5[1]
9 2 1/4 **Ragiam (ITY)**[55] 5-9-0 0 .... NPinna 5 74
(S Botti, Italy) *in rr: effrt and no imp fnl 2f* 31/10[2]
2m 5.60s (-1.10)
WFA 3 from 4yo+ 5lb 9 Ran SP% 209.9
WIN (incl. 1 euro stake): 4.87. PLACES: 1.65, 1.20, 1.95. DF: 5.27.
Owner J Frey **Bred** Gestut Evershorst **Trained** Germany

6764a PREMIO VITTORIO DI CAPUA (GROUP 1) (3YO+) (TURF) 1m
3:50 (4:07) 3-Y-0+ £119,469 (£52,566; £28,672; £14,336)

RPR
1 **Rio De La Plata (USA)**[34] 5801 5-9-0 0 .... FrankieDettori 2 115
(Saeed Bin Suroor) *slowly away: settled mid-div on inner for 4f: hdwy ent st to go 3rd: produced to ld fnl 1 1/2f: hrd rdn fnl f to keep in command* 27/20[1]
2 snk **Vanjura (GER)**[35] 5782 3-8-7 0 .... APietsch 6 111
(R Dzubasz, Germany) *mid-div: trckd eventual wnr for 5f: hrd rdn fnl 1 1/2f: a being hld by wnr* 197/10
3 1 1/4 **Worthadd (IRE)**[154] 1945 3-8-10 0 .... MircoDemuro 8 111
(Vittorio Caruso, Italy) *broke wl to trck ldr for 4f: 2nd ent st: lost position under patient ride 2f out: chal ldrs and ev ch 1 1/2f out tl hrd rdn: styd on* 37/20[2]
4 1 1/4 **Sehrezad (IRE)**[62] 4888 5-9-0 0 .... JiriPalik 12 109
(Andreas Lowe, Germany) *settled in 4th for 5f: outpcd ent fnl 2f: styd on u.str ride fnl f* 32/1
5 shd **Rockhorse (IRE)**[20] 5-9-0 0 .... DarioVargiu 7 109
(B Grizzetti, Italy) *hld up in rr on outer: effrt and little imp ent fnl 2f: styd on fnl f* 70/1
6 shd **Pressing (IRE)**[34] 5803 7-9-0 0 .... NeilCallan 5 109
(M A Jarvis) *settled in 5th tl ent st: hdwy to dispute ld briefly ent fnl f: chal and no imp under hrd ride fnl f* 69/20[3]
7 1 1/4 **Miles Gloriosus (USA)**[20] 7-9-0 0 .... LManiezzi 11 106
(Maria Rita Salvioni, Italy) *slowly away and hld up nr rr for 6f: rdn and little imp 2f out: styd on* 61/1
8 1 1/4 **Liliside (FR)**[38] 5673 3-8-7 0 .... Francois-XavierBertras 10 99
(F Rohaut, France) *mid-div tl ent st: rdn and no imp fnl 2f* 67/10
9 3 **Earl Of Fire (GER)**[39] 5649 5-9-0 0 .... DominiqueBoeuf 9 96
(W Baltromei, Germany) *broke wl to ld: chal ent fnl 3f: hdd 2 1/2f out: hrd rdn fnl 2f and sn btn: eased fnl f* 185/10
10 snk **Estejo (GER)**[20] 6-9-0 0 .... MEsposito 3 96
(R Rohne, Germany) *broke wl to trck ldr tl ent st: led 2 1/2f out: chal 2f out: hrd rdn and sn btn: eased fnl f* 174/10
11 10 **Selmis**[161] 1712 6-9-0 0 .... SUrru 1 73
(Vittorio Caruso, Italy) *slowly away: a in rr* 37/20[2]
1m 38.2s (-3.90)
WFA 3 from 5yo+ 3lb 11 Ran SP% 169.6
WIN (incl. 1 euro stake): 2.36. PLACES: 1.30, 2.20, 1.29. DF: 43.13.
Owner Godolphin **Bred** Jose De Camargo, Robert N Clay Et Al **Trained** Newmarket, Suffolk

NOTEBOOK
Rio De La Plata(USA), narrowly beaten in the Moulin last time out, is not usually at his best on soft ground, but apparently the surface was riding more like good to soft, and he coped with it well enough to take this sub-standard Group 1. His trainer suggested they would now look for another race at this level before the season is out.
Pressing(IRE), winner of a Group 2 race in Turkey last time out, may have still been feeling the effects of that run as he didn't quite perform to his very best here.

6765a PREMIO SERGIO CUMANI (GROUP 3) (3YO+ FILLIES & MARES) (TURF) 1m
5:00 (12:00) 3-Y-0+ £35,398 (£15,575; £8,495; £4,247)

RPR
1 **Sajjhaa**[14] 6346 3-8-9 0 .... NeilCallan 7 113
(M A Jarvis) *trckd ldrs in 5th on outer: rdn and hdwy to chal for ld fnl 1 1/2f: hrd rdn fnl f and drvn clr fnl 100yds* 85/40[1]
2 1 1/2 **Aspectoflove (IRE)**[14] 6346 4-8-13 0 .... FrankieDettori 9 111
(Saeed Bin Suroor) *slowly away: rdn to go mid-div: hdwy on inner sntering st to go 4th: rdn to ld briefly 1f out: chal and btn fnl 100yds* 3/1[2]
3 1 **Rockatella (IRE)**[39] 5649 3-8-9 0 .... KKerekes 8 107
(W Hefter, Germany) *broke wl to ld for 2f: then trckd ldr ent st: rdn to ld and ev ch 2f out: hdd 1f out: chal and styd on one pce fnl f* 102/10
4 2 **Magic Eye (IRE)**[36] 5739 5-8-13 0 .... APietsch 4 104
(Andreas Lowe, Germany) *rdn to move 4th after 3f: effrt 2f out: hrd rdn fnl f: styd on one pce* 36/1
5 1 1/2 **Alta Fedelta**[118] 4-9-2 0 .... MircoDemuro 12 103
(Vittorio Caruso, Italy) *hld up patiently in rr tl 2f out: rdn and immediate hdwy to go 4th on inner 1f out: one pce fnl f* 122/10
6 1 1/4 **Mahamaya (GER)**[20] 3-8-13 0 .... ADeVries 6 100
(A Trybuhl, Germany) *trckd ldrs for 5f: drvn to chal 2f out: sn one pce* 158/10
7 1 1/4 **Corcovada (IRE)**[58] 5139 3-8-9 0 .... UmbertoRispoli 14 93
(V Luka Jr, Czech Republic) *settled mid-div tl ent st: rdn fnl 2 1/2f and no imp: styd on one pce* 38/1
8 nse **Artica (GER)**[87] 4035 3-8-9 0 .... EFrank 3 93
(T Mundry, Germany) *hld up nr rr: hdwy ent st: nvr able to chal* 67/1
9 1 1/4 **Aslana (IRE)**[36] 5739 3-8-13 0 .... AStarke 5 94
(P Schiergen, Germany) *hld up nr rr: hdwy and sltly hmpd 2 1/2f out: styd on one pce fnl 1 1/2f* 103/20[3]
10 1 1/2 **Three French Hens (IRE)**[27] 4-8-13 0 .... THellier 2 88
(Mario Hofer, Germany) *in rr: effrt 3f out on inner: wknd fnl f* 58/1
11 1 3/4 **Prakasa (FR)**[39] 5649 3-8-13 0 .... EPedroza 11 87
(W Hickst, Germany) *in tch on outer for 5f: effrt and one pce fnl 2f* 27/4
12 1/2 **Vattene (IRE)**[6] 5-8-13 0 .... MKolmarkaj 10 83
(M Gasparini, Italy) *nr rr: little imp whn asked for effrt 3f out* 21/1

13 hd **Ravenel (GER)**[20] 4-8-13 0 .... MEsposito 1 82
(R Rohne, Germany) *led after 2f tl 2f out: wknd fr 1 1/2f out* **27/4**

14 4 1/2 **Monblue**[6] 3-8-9 0 .... DarioVargiu 13 71
(B Grizzetti, Italy) *mid-div: outpcd 2f out* **137/10**

15 8 **Destination Place (IRE)**[111] 4-8-13 0 .... LManiezzi 15 54
(Maria Rita Salvioni, Italy) *trckd ldrs for 6f: outpcd and eased fnl f* **147/1**

1m 38.2s (-3.90)
WFA 3 from 4yo+ 3lb 15 Ran SP% **142.0**
WIN (incl. 1 euro stake); 3.12. PLACES: 1.53, 1.56, 2.73. DF: 5.88.
Owner Sheikh Ahmed Al Maktoum **Bred** Darley **Trained** Newmarket, Suffolk

NOTEBOOK
Sajjhaa reversed Ascot form with Aspectoflove despite being 2lb worse off at the weights with the Godolphin filly. This ground seemed to suit her well. She won't race again this year but the expectation is that she'll stay in training as a 4-y-o.
Aspectoflove(IRE) couldn't confirm Ascot form with Sajjhaa despite being 2lb better off at the weights. It's possible she hit the front too soon.

6411 BATH (L-H)
Sunday, October 10

OFFICIAL GOING: Good to soft (6.5)
Wind: brisk wind behind Weather: sunny

6769 TOTEPLACEPOT NURSERY 5f 11y
2:25 (2:26) (Class 5) (0-75,75) 2-Y-O **£2,272** (£671; £335) **Stalls** Centre

Form RPR
1320 1 **Diamond Vine (IRE)**[13] 6426 2-9-5 **71** .... DavidProbert 8 76
(R A Harris) *squeezed up s: sn pushed along towards rr: hdwy on outer fr over 2f out: r.o wl to ld fnl strides* **7/1**

1322 2 hd **Millyluvstobouggie**[12] 6445 2-9-7 **73** .... LukeMorris 1 77
(C G Cox) *wnt sltly rt s: chsd ldrs: rdn 2f out: led ent fnl f: ct fnl strides* **3/1**[1]

0230 3 3/4 **Indian Shuffle (IRE)**[19] 6271 2-9-2 **68** .... RichardKingscote 14 70
(J G Portman) *chsd ldrs on outer: rdn over 2f out: kpt on ins fnl f: no ex towards fin* **16/1**

3314 4 2 1/2 **Best Be Careful (IRE)**[67] 4688 2-9-0 **66** .... LiamKeniry 10 59
(M D I Usher) *prom: rdn to ld over 1f out: hdd ent fnl f: no ex* **16/1**

6400 5 1 1/2 **Silk Bounty**[8] 6568 2-9-2 **68** .... PaulMulrennan 12 55
(J G Given) *mid-div: rdn over 2f out: hdwy to chse ldrs whn hmpd jst over 1f out: kpt on same pce* **13/2**[3]

000 6 hd **Dreams Of Glory**[39] 5651 2-7-7 **52** ow2 .... HarryBentley(7) 13 38
(R J Hodges) *chsd ldrs: rdn 2f out: one pce fnl f* **40/1**

020 7 1 3/4 **Coconut Ice**[12] 6445 2-9-2 **73** .... RossAtkinson(5) 4 53
(Tom Dascombe) *chsd ldrs: rdn over 2f out: bmpd jst over 1f out: fdd ins fnl f* **10/1**

2061 8 hd **West Leake Bridge (IRE)**[4] 6675 2-9-9 **75** 6ex .... MichaelHills 9 54
(B W Hills) *sn led: rdn and hdd over 1f out: wknd ins fnl f* **5/1**[2]

0466 9 hd **Scommettitrice (IRE)**[17] 6307 2-9-0 **66** .... RobertWinston 7 45
(R A Harris) *squeezed out s: a struggling towards rr* **16/1**

0046 10 1 1/2 **Master Macho (IRE)**[19] 6271 2-8-8 **63** .... AndrewHeffernan(3) 2 36
(M R Channon) *chsd ldrs: rdn over 2f out: wknd over 1f out* **10/1**

066 11 3 **Kingfisher Blue (IRE)**[15] 6369 2-8-2 **57** .... SophieDoyle(3) 6 20
(J A Osborne) *s.i.s: a towards rr* **14/1**

6246 12 2 1/4 **Silca Conegliano (IRE)**[18] 6286 2-8-11 **63** .... CathyGannon 5 17
(M R Channon) *s.i.s: a towards rr* **20/1**

000 13 hd **Avon Causeway**[58] 5029 2-7-7 **52** oh5 ow2 .... (b[1]) RyanPowell(7) 3 6
(J M Bradley) *sn pushed along in mid-div: bhd fnl 3f* **80/1**

62.66 secs (0.16) **Going Correction** +0.025s/f (Good) 13 Ran SP% **118.4**
Speed ratings (Par 95): **99,98,97,93,91 90,87,87,87,84 80,76,76**
toteswingers:1&2:£4.60, 1&3:£15.70, 2&3:£10.60 CSF £27.47 CT £342.50 TOTE £7.50: £3.10, £1.10, £8.60; EX 33.70 Trifecta £319.10 Part won. Pool: £431.29 - 0.63 winning units..
Owner A Powell, A Holdsworth & G Wheeler **Bred** Michael O'Mahony **Trained** Earlswood, Monmouths

FOCUS
After a dry night and morning, the ground was officially good to soft. There was a brisk wind chasing the runners up the home straight. This was a run-of-the-mill nursery in which a few looked overrated.

NOTEBOOK
Diamond Vine(IRE), who had finished second off a 2lb lower mark here early in September, underlined his liking for this course. He was not the quickest away and, having been backed at each-way prices beforehand, had to make his challenge out wide after the home bend. He looked set for only a place 1f out, but responded well to driving and forced his head in front in the dying strides. (op 10-1)
Millyluvstobouggie had finished in the frame from this sort of mark on her last three outings and looks an ideal yardstick for the form. Never too far off the pace, with a position close to the inside rail, she battled on bravely under pressure but could not quite hold off the winner. (tchd 11-4)
Indian Shuffle(IRE), in the first three on two previous visits here, was another to demonstrate again that this track suits him. Always in the front rank, he stayed on bravely without quite showing the finishing zip of the two ahead of him at the post. (op 14-1)
Best Be Careful(IRE), a winner on fast ground at Lingfield in July, proved she can handle these easier conditions. Prominent throughout and in front at the 2f marker, she could not quite maintain the gallop but ran commendably all the same.
Silk Bounty, outclassed in a Listed event at Redcar on his previous start, fared better in this more suitable grade. He might even have finished a little closer had he not been slightly hampered just over 1f from home. (op 8-1)
Dreams Of Glory, whose apprentice rider put up 2lb overweight, ran as well as could be expected. He chased the pace early on, before fading out of contention in the closing stages. (op 100-1)
West Leake Bridge(IRE), carrying a 6lb penalty for a maiden win at Nottingham four days earlier, was ultimately disappointing. In front early on, he dropped away towards the business end. (op 4-1)
Scommettitrice(IRE)'s rider reported the filly suffered interference shortly after the start. Official explanation: jockey said the filly suffered interference shortly after the start (op 20-1)

6770 E B F & TOTEEXACTA FLEXI BETTING MAIDEN FILLIES' STKS 1m 5y
3:00 (3:00) (Class 5) 2-Y-O **£2,978** (£886; £442; £221) **Stalls** Low

Form RPR
4 1 **Inimitable Romanee (USA)**[38] 5691 2-9-0 0 .... JimmyFortune 10 76
(Mrs A J Perrett) *trckd ldrs: squeezed up over 5f out: chalng whn sltly hmpd jst over 1f out: sn led: r.o strly: comf* **11/4**[1]

63 2 3 1/4 **Pandorica**[15] 6360 2-9-0 0 .... LukeMorris 15 69
(C G Cox) *rn freely to post: sn trcking ldr: led over 2f out: sn rdn: edgd rt and hdd jst over 1f out: styd on but sn no ch w wnr* **8/1**

0 3 3/4 **Lady Bridget**[23] 6155 2-9-0 0 .... MichaelHills 3 67
(B W Hills) *led at gd pce: rdn whn hdd over 2f out: styd on but no ch w wnr ent fnl f* **13/2**[3]

00 4 3/4 **Chesnut Coffee**[23] 6154 2-9-0 0 .... LiamJones 2 66
(D M Simcock) *chsd ldrs: rdn 3f out: styd on same pce fnl 2f* **22/1**

00 5 3/4 **Lady Barastar (IRE)**[37] 5724 2-9-0 0 .... FergusSweeney 7 64
(W R Swinburn) *hmpd s: towards rr: hdwy over 4f out: rdn over 2f out: styd on same pce* **40/1**

6 1/2 **Hairstyle** 2-9-0 0 .... RyanMoore 6 63
(Sir Michael Stoute) *towards rr of mid-div: rdn and stdy prog fr 3f out: styd on but nvr gng pce to rch ldrs* **7/2**[2]

4 7 1 1/4 **Geblah (IRE)**[66] 4747 2-9-0 0 .... JackMitchell 16 60
(D M Simcock) *in tch: awkward on bnd over 4f out: effrt whn edgd lft over 2f out: wknd ent fnl f* **8/1**

05 8 1/2 **Heart Felt**[11] 6469 2-9-0 0 .... PatDobbs 14 59
(R Hannon) *in tch: rdn 3f out: wknd over 1f out* **14/1**

9 1 1/4 **Torpedo Run** 2-8-11 0 .... PatrickHills(3) 12 56
(R Hannon) *hld up towards rr: rdn 3f out: sme hdwy 2f out: wknd ins fnl f* **40/1**

024 10 1/2 **Areopagitica**[17] 6307 2-8-11 59 .... (p) RussKennemore(3) 11 55
(J L Flint) *s.i.s: rdn 3f out: a towards rr* **25/1**

11 1/2 **Director's Dream (IRE)** 2-9-0 0 .... DavidProbert 4 54
(P Winkworth) *in tch: rdn wl over 2f out: wknd over 1f out* **25/1**

12 nk **Flo Motion (IRE)** 2-9-0 0 .... RobertWinston 5 53
(J W Hills) *mid-div: rdn over 3f out: wknd over 1f out* **50/1**

0 13 2 1/4 **Mujarah (IRE)**[23] 6154 2-9-0 0 .... TadhgO'Shea 13 48
(J L Dunlop) *rdn 3f out: a towards rr* **25/1**

14 9 **Dixie Land Band** 2-9-0 0 .... RobertHavlin 8 29
(A B Haynes) *mid-div tl wknd on outer over 3f out* **100/1**

15 3 1/4 **Delagoa Bay (IRE)** 2-9-0 0 .... LiamKeniry 9 21
(S Kirk) *s.i.s: sn pushed along: a towards rr* **66/1**

1m 43.48s (2.68) **Going Correction** +0.20s/f (Good) 15 Ran SP% **116.3**
Speed ratings (Par 92): **94,90,90,89,88 88,86,86,85,84 84,83,81,72,69**
toteswingers:1&2:£5.30, 1&3:£5.40, 2&3:£7.50 CSF £21.24 TOTE £3.10: £1.20, £3.10, £3.40; EX 25.20 Trifecta £92.70 Pool: £547.66 - 4.37 winning units..
Owner Mrs Marlene Brody **Bred** Gallagher's Shiraz Llc **Trained** Pulborough, W Sussex

FOCUS
An ordinary juvenile fillies' maiden, those with form looking limited on paper.

NOTEBOOK
Inimitable Romanee(USA), slowly away and hampered when fourth on her Salisbury debut, got a much better start this time and broke her duck in decisive fashion. Always close to the pace, she was travelling ominously strongly 2f out and quickened into the lead approaching the last. Once in front, she drew clear comfortably, suggesting she can win again. That is likely to be next season, as the plan is to put her away after this, and her future probably lies in handicaps. (op 3-1)
Pandorica, a solid third at Haydock last time, again ran creditably, despite bucking and kicking on the way to post. Never far away, she led briefly before the winner swept by and then stayed on gamely. It should not be impossible to find her a winning opportunity in similar company. (op 15-2 tchd 17-2)
Lady Bridget, who had finished in midfield in a Newmarket maiden first time out, seemed to appreciate this less demanding task. She led into the home straight and, while she lacked the winner's change of gear, plugged on gamely in the closing stages. (op 5-1 tchd 9-2)
Chesnut Coffee, who had previously finished in midfield in maidens at Doncaster and Newmarket, looks a feasible marker for the form. Never too far off the pace, she too stayed on towards the line without nearly matching the winner's finishing kick. (op 25-1 tchd 20-1)
Lady Barastar(IRE), having her first run on turf after two moderate all-weather efforts, is another to peg the level achieved by the principals. She will need to make a marked step forward to land a maiden.
Hairstyle, a newcomer whose dam won the Yorkshire Oaks and ran second in the St Leger, was made favourite. She never appeared likely to collect, however, racing in mid-field from the start and failing to make any significant late progress. (op 10-3)

6771 TOTESUPER7 H'CAP 1m 5y
3:35 (3:35) (Class 4) (0-85,81) 3-Y-O **£4,209** (£1,252; £625; £312) **Stalls** Low

Form RPR
0302 1 **Aerodynamic (IRE)**[11] 6467 3-9-7 **81** .... RobertWinston 3 87
(Pat Eddery) *in tch: rdn over 2f out: hrd drvn to chal over 1f out: led narrowly ins fnl f: all out* **2/1**[1]

0600 2 hd **Duplicity**[15] 6358 3-9-6 **80** .... PatDobbs 5 86
(R Hannon) *led: rdn whn hrd pressed fr over 2f out: battled on: narrowly hdd ins fnl f: kpt on gamely* **20/1**

1205 3 hd **Purple Gallery (IRE)**[11] 6467 3-8-12 **79** .... (p) RyanPowell(7) 7 84
(J S Moore) *in tch: hdwy 3f out: upsides ldr over 2f out: rdn ent fnl f: nt qckn but kpt on* **11/2**[3]

6-60 4 5 **Poor Prince**[60] 4956 3-9-0 **74** .... LukeMorris 1 68
(C G Cox) *chsd ldrs: rdn over 2f out: nt pce to chal: fdd fnl f* **11/1**

4356 5 4 1/2 **Rockabilly Rebel**[12] 6438 3-8-9 **69** .... MichaelHills 6 52
(B W Hills) *chsd ldr: rdn over 2f out: wknd over 1f out* **9/2**[2]

2120 6 2 1/4 **Gifted Apakay (USA)**[22] 6204 3-9-4 **78** .... JimmyFortune 8 56
(E A L Dunlop) *hld up in last pair: rdn over 2f out: little imp: wknd over 1f out* **9/2**[2]

5-00 7 10 **Rosie's Magic**[121] 2925 3-8-7 **67** oh22 .... AdrianLayt 4 22
(F J Brennan) *in tch: rdn over 3f out: sn wknd* **100/1**

2055 8 15 **Warm Memories**[59] 5007 3-8-10 **70** .... RyanMoore 2 —
(Sir Michael Stoute) *stdd s: tk str hold in last: rdn 3f out: sn wknd* **7/1**

1m 41.75s (0.95) **Going Correction** +0.20s/f (Good) 8 Ran SP% **111.7**
Speed ratings (Par 103): **103,102,102,97,93 90,80,65**
toteswingers:1&2:£7.50, 1&3:£3.90, 2&3:£17.30 CSF £44.36 CT £188.04 TOTE £2.60: £1.90, £9.50, £1.40; EX 23.20 Trifecta £65.70 Pool: £571.79 - 6.44 winning units..
Owner Mrs Gay Smith **Bred** Swettenham, Carradale, S Cosgrove & T Stack **Trained** Nether Winchendon, Bucks

FOCUS
Just a fair handicap, with the top weight rated 81.
Rockabilly Rebel Official explanation: jockey said that the gelding hung left handed
Gifted Apakay(USA) Official explanation: jockey said that the filly ran flat
Warm Memories Official explanation: jockey said that colt ran too free

6772 TOTETRIFECTA FLEXI BETTING FILLIES' H'CAP 5f 161y
4:10 (4:12) (Class 4) (0-80,78) 3-Y-O+ **£4,209** (£1,252; £625; £312) **Stalls** Centre

Form RPR
1505 1 **Ray Of Joy**[40] 5628 4-9-7 **77** .... PatDobbs 2 85
(J R Jenkins) *in tch: nt clr run over 1f out: qcknd up wl whn gap appeared jst ins fnl f: r.o strly to ld fnl 75yds: readily* **25/1**

2031 2 3/4 **Superior Edge**[12] 6466 3-8-12 **74** .... DeclanCannon(5) 4 80
(B Palling) *chsd ldrs: rdn over 2f out: kpt on ins fnl f: wnt 2nd towards fin* **11/2**[3]

-050 **3** *nk* **Sharpened Edge**[142] 2280 4-9-2 72 DavidProbert 8 77
(B Palling) *sn led: rdn whn hdd over 2f out: kpt pressing ldr: regained ld briefly fnl 100yds: no ex* **16/1**
2166 **4** *½* **Dream Number (IRE)**[13] 6421 3-8-10 67 FergusSweeney 3 70
(W R Muir) *prom: led over 2f out: sn rdn: hdd fnl 100yds: no ex* **14/1**
1303 **5** *½* **Russian Rave**[11] 6478 4-9-1 71 RichardKingscote 1 72
(J G Portman) *in tch: rdn over 2f out: nt pce to mount chal* **13/2**
64 **6** *1* **Requisite**[22] 6207 5-9-3 73 (v) CathyGannon 5 71
(I A Wood) *sn pushed along towards rr: styd on fr over 1f out: nvr trbld ldrs* **17/2**
1241 **7** *¾* **Grand Zafeen**[9] 6524 3-9-0 78 MatthewLawson(7) 7 73
(M R Channon) *s.i.s: towards rr: rdn 3f out: sme hdwy over 1f out: one pce fnl f* **8/1**
4200 **8** *hd* **Our Piccadilly (IRE)**[9] 6539 5-9-0 70 (v[1]) LiamKeniry 6 65
(W S Kittow) *travelled wl trcking ldrs: rdn jst over 1f out: fnd little* **10/1**
2360 **9** *¾* **Key Light (IRE)**[26] 6057 3-8-8 70 (t) AmyScott(5) 9 62
(J W Hills) *towards rr: sn pushed along: nvr gng pce to get on terms* **16/1**
3130 **10** *1 ½* **Basle**[11] 6487 3-9-6 77 JimmyFortune 10 64
(Miss Gay Kelleway) *reluctant at s: s.i.s: swtchd rt over 1f out: a towards rr* **5/1**[2]
0201 **11** *2 ½* **Yurituni**[17] 6303 3-9-6 77 (b) RyanMoore 11 56
(Eve Johnson Houghton) *racd wd: prom: rdn over 2f out: wknd ent fnl f: eased* **9/2**[1]

1m 11.04s (-0.16) **Going Correction** +0.025s/f (Good)
WFA 3 from 4yo+ 1lb **11 Ran SP% 116.6**
Speed ratings (Par 102): **102,101,100,99,99 97,96,96,95,93 90**
toteswingers:1&2:£19.70, 1&3:£28.80, 2&3:£14.60 CSF £156.10 CT £2335.02 TOTE £35.70: £8.80, £2.70, £5.90; EX 133.80 Trifecta £260.40 Part won. Pool: £351.91 - 0.10 winning units..
Owner Robin Stevens **Bred** D R Tucker **Trained** Royston, Herts

FOCUS
A competitive fillies' handicap.

6773 TOTEPOOL A BETTER WAY TO BET MAIDEN STKS 5f 161y
4:45 (4:47) (Class 5) 3-Y-0+ **£2,590** (£770; £385; £192) **Stalls** Centre

Form RPR
4322 **1** **Nadinska**[6] 6638 3-8-12 56 CathyGannon 9 64
(M R Channon) *s.i.s: hdwy on outer over 3f out: rdn over 2f out: r.o ins fnl f: led fnl 75yds: rdn out* **2/1**[1]
302 **2** *¾* **Bilash**[11] 6466 3-9-3 66 TonyCulhane 2 67
(R Hollinshead) *trckd ldrs: rdn over 2f out: led fnl 100yds: sn hdd: no ex* **4/1**[3]
0330 **3** *1* **Aalsmeer**[11] 6466 3-8-12 66 (p) RyanMoore 8 58
(Karen George) *prom: rdn 2f out: led over 1f out: hdd fnl 100yds: kpt on same pce* **3/1**[2]
54 **4** *¾* **Brewers Boy**[59] 5007 3-9-0 0 JamesMillman(3) 4 61
(B R Millman) *led: rdn and hdd over 1f out: kpt on same pce* **10/1**
0 **5** *1* **Old Peg**[6] 6638 5-8-8 0 MarkCoumbe(5) 10 53
(D Bourton) *s.i.s: towards rr: rdn and hdwy 2f out: swtchd rt over 1f out: no further imp* **7/1**
4665 **6** *6* **Rose Bed (IRE)**[13] 6420 3-8-9 43 KellyHarrison(3) 6 33
(M G Quinlan) *prom: rdn over 2f out: wknd over 1f out* **33/1**
5006 **7** *1* **Dancing Again**[27] 6025 4-8-13 42 DavidProbert 5 30
(E A Wheeler) *dwlt: towards rr: rdn and hdwy over 2f out: wknd over 1f out* **33/1**
004 **8** *4 ½* **Gessabelle**[18] 6285 3-8-12 49 (t) RobertWinston 1 15
(P S McEntee) *chsd ldrs: rdn whn swtchd rt over 2f out: wknd over 1f out* **33/1**
9 *1* **Book Smart (IRE)**[122] 2915 3-8-12 0 SladeO'Hara(5) 11 16
(Miss Gay Kelleway) *towards rr: nvr gng pce to get on terms* **66/1**
5-00 **10** *hd* **Fiftyfourth Street**[82] 4225 4-9-4 63 (t) FergusSweeney 3 16
(P J Makin) *stmbld leaving stalls: mainly towards rr* **25/1**
000- **11** *13* **Deo Valente (IRE)**[304] 7703 5-9-4 47 (t) LiamKeniry 7 —
(J M Bradley) *unruly loading: trckd ldrs: rdn over 2f out: sn btn* **66/1**

1m 11.7s (0.50) **Going Correction** +0.025s/f (Good)
WFA 3 from 4yo+ 1lb **11 Ran SP% 115.6**
Speed ratings (Par 103): **97,96,94,93,92 84,83,77,75,75 58**
toteswingers:1&2:£2.90, 1&3:£2.20, 2&3:£3.00 CSF £9.32 TOTE £3.90: £2.20, £1.10, £1.20; EX 8.70 Trifecta £19.30 Pool: £569.89 - 21.74 winning units.
Owner Norman Court Stud **Bred** Mr & Mrs P Trant **Trained** West Ilsley, Berks

FOCUS
A modest maiden and several looked out of their depth.

6774 TOTESWINGER FLEXI BETTING APPRENTICE H'CAP 1m 3f 144y
5:20 (5:20) (Class 5) (0-75,75) 3-Y-0+ **£2,286** (£675; £337) **Stalls** Low

Form RPR
4436 **1** **Pelham Crescent (IRE)**[56] 5115 7-9-4 72 ThomasBrown(5) 6 82
(B Palling) *rrd leaving stalls: hld up: hdwy fr 3f out: led wl over 1f out: styd on: rdn out* **8/1**
0120 **2** *1 ½* **Raktiman (IRE)**[23] 6152 3-8-9 68 (p) SoniaEaton(3) 3 75
(Tom Dascombe) *slowly away: towards rr: hdwy 3f out: sn rdn: ev ch over 1f out: styd on but no ex* **6/1**[3]
4424 **3** *1* **Mykingdomforahorse**[16] 6322 4-9-4 70 (v) MatthewLawson(3) 9 76
(M R Channon) *in tch: rdn over 3f out: hdwy over 2f out: squeezed through gap on rails over 1f out: styd on same pce* **7/2**[2]
3615 **4** *5* **Potentiale (IRE)**[32] 5859 6-9-9 75 (p) HollyHall(3) 7 72+
(J W Hills) *trckd clr ldr tl rn wd on bnd over 4f out: rdn over 2f out: fdd fnl f* **6/1**[3]
6502 **5** *nk* **Lucky Breeze (IRE)**[13] 6424 3-9-4 74 HarryBentley 4 71
(W J Knight) *awkward leaving stalls: hld up: rdn 3f out: sme late prog past btn horses: nvr a factor* **8/1**
0135 **6** *3 ½* **Blue Tango (IRE)**[38] 5680 4-9-4 70 (p) NatashaEaton(3) 5 61
(Mrs A J Perrett) *in tch: rdn wl over 2f out: wknd over 1f out* **9/1**
4105 **7** *¾* **Mr Money Maker**[13] 6422 3-8-11 72 MatthewCosham(5) 8 62
(J L Flint) *led: sn clr: rdn over 2f out: hdd wl over 1f out: wknd fnl f* **9/1**
2011 **8** *nk* **Jasmeno**[40] 5625 3-9-2 72 (t) RosieJessop 2 61
(H Morrison) *t.k.h: trckd ldrs: wnt 2nd over 4f out: rdn wl over 2f out: wknd over 1f out* **10/3**[1]

2m 33.41s (2.81) **Going Correction** +0.20s/f (Good)
WFA 3 from 4yo+ 7lb **8 Ran SP% 116.1**
Speed ratings (Par 103): **98,97,96,93,92 90,89,89**
toteswingers:1&2:£10.50, 1&3:£8.20, 2&3:£5.30 CSF £55.78 CT £200.15 TOTE £11.30: £2.30, £2.60, £1.90; EX 85.00 Trifecta £375.60 Part won. Pool of £507.65 - 0.84 winning units. Place 6 £71.16; Place 5 £33.03..
Owner Wayne Devine **Bred** Cathal M Ryan **Trained** Tredodridge, Vale Of Glamorgan

FOCUS
An uninspiring finale, with the top weight rated 75.
Mr Money Maker Official explanation: jockey said gelding hung left-handed throughout

T/Jkpt: Not won. T/Plt: £23.50 to a £1 stake. Pool of £65,719.39 - 2,036.35 winning tickets T/Qpdt: £12.70 to a £1 stake. Pool of £5,775.54 - 333.90 winning tickets TM

6278 GOODWOOD (R-H)
Sunday, October 10

OFFICIAL GOING: Good to soft
Lower bend dolled out 7yds, straight dolled out 7yds to the 2f pole, top bend dolled out 3yds all races on round course increased in distance by 12yds.
Wind: Fresh, half behind Weather: Glorious

6775 THREE MUSKETEERS TROPHY (HANDICAP FOR NATIONAL HUNT JOCKEYS) 2m
2:00 (2:00) (Class 5) (0-70,68) 4-Y-0+ **£2,914** (£867; £433; £216) **Stalls** Low

Form RPR
2-04 **1** **Bugsy's Boy**[144] 874 6-11-12 68 DavidEngland 7 77
(George Baker) *prom: wnt 2nd over 7f out: drvn to ld wl over 2f out: clr over 1f out: styd on wl* **15/2**[3]
3222 **2** *4* **Mohanad (IRE)**[11] 6480 4-11-9 65 JamieGoldstein 6 69
(Miss Sheena West) *hld up in tch: trckd ldrs gng wl 3f out: plld out and rdn wl over 1f out: fnd little: kpt on to take 2nd ins fnl f* **5/2**[1]
-010 **3** *1 ½* **Karky Schultz (GER)**[26] 6065 5-11-4 60 FelixDeGiles 2 62
(J M P Eustace) *hld up in midfield: clsd on ldrs gng easily over 3f out: chsd wnr over 2f out: sn rdn and fnd nil: lost 2nd ins fnl f* **16/1**
55-0 **4** *1* **Double Whammy**[95] 3780 4-11-7 63 MattieBatchelor 12 64
(Jamie Poulton) *prom: cl up and rdn 3f out: sn nt qckn and outpcd: kpt on fnl f* **40/1**
6/05 **5** *2 ¾* **Osolomio (IRE)**[12] 6114 7-11-12 68 (b[1]) AlanO'Keeffe 10 66
(Jennie Candlish) *led: hrd rdn and hdd wl over 2f out: grad fdd* **16/1**
536 **6** *18* **William's Way**[47] 5382 8-11-2 58 (t) WillKennedy 11 34
(I A Wood) *hld up in last: prog on outer to trck ldrs over 4f out: wknd 3f out: sn bhd* **15/2**[3]
1104 **7** *2 ¼* **Where's Susie**[6] 6639 5-11-12 68 (p) ChristianWilliams 4 42
(M Madgwick) *in tch: rdn over 3f out: wknd wl over 2f out: sn wl bhd* **8/1**
4605 **8** *25* **Honorable Endeavor**[29] 5963 4-10-7 49 oh3 (v) LiamTreadwell 1 —
(E F Vaughan) *chsd ldr to over 7f out: rdn and wknd rapidly over 3f out: t.o* **10/1**
3006 **9** *5* **Binnion Bay (IRE)**[29] 5962 9-10-7 49 (b) ColinBolger 9 —
(J J Bridger) *s.s: a in rr: wknd 5f out: t.o* **50/1**
4222 **10** *7* **Zelos Diktator**[27] 6021 4-11-2 58 (p) RichardHughes 8 —
(G L Moore) *prom: lost pl 1/2-way: rdn at rr of main gp over 4f out: wknd 3f out: eased 2f out: t.o* **4/1**[2]
00-0 **11** *12* **Sahara Sunshine**[227] 263 5-11-0 56 LeightonAspell 5 —
(Mrs L J Mongan) *stdd s: a in rr: lost tch over 4f out: t.o* **20/1**

3m 36.86s (7.86) **Going Correction** +0.225s/f (Good) **11 Ran SP% 113.2**
Speed ratings (Par 103): **89,87,86,85,84 75,74,61,59,55 49**
toteswingers:1&2:£4.30, 1&3:£20.10, 2&3:£9.80 CSF £25.02 CT £291.47 TOTE £8.00: £2.70, £1.80, £6.90; EX 28.60.
Owner Seaton Partnership **Bred** Mrs R S Evans **Trained** Moreton Morrell, Warwicks
■ David England's first Flat win.

FOCUS
A low-grade staying handicap restricted to jockeys with a National Hunt licence.
Zelos Diktator Official explanation: jockey said gelding stopped quickly

6776 TOYO TIRES SPEED STKS (H'CAP) 6f
2:35 (2:36) (Class 3) (0-95,93) 3-Y-0+ **£6,476** (£1,927; £963; £481) **Stalls** Low

Form RPR
2315 **1** **R Woody**[31] 5884 3-9-3 89 GeorgeBaker 11 98
(D K Ivory) *pressed ldrs: pushed into ld 2f out: rdn over 1f out: kpt on wl* **11/2**[3]
3320 **2** *¾* **Lochan Mor**[11] 6478 4-8-8 79 JamieSpencer 8 86
(M L W Bell) *led: hrd rdn and hdd 2f out: edgd lft 1f out: kpt on u.p* **10/1**
0035 **3** *1* **We Have A Dream**[15] 6363 5-9-2 87 NeilCallan 9 91
(W R Muir) *pressed ldr to 1/2-way: styd cl up: drvn over 1f out: bmpd ins fnl f: kpt on* **14/1**
0030 **4** *hd* **Baldemar**[23] 6142 5-9-2 87 PaulHanagan 10 90
(R A Fahey) *chsd ldrs: rdn 2f out: kpt on same pce: nvr able to chal* **9/1**
0006 **5** *½* **One Way Or Another (AUS)**[90] 3969 7-8-10 86 JohnFahy(5) 7 88
(J R Gask) *dwlt: chsd ldrs: drvn and effrt on outer of gp over 2f out: nt qckn 1f out: one pce* **9/1**
5043 **6** *¾* **Pretty Bonnie**[10] 6509 5-8-10 84 NataliaGemelova(3) 2 83
(A E Price) *pressed ldrs: nt qckn 2f out: one pce whn sltly checked ins fnl f* **25/1**
0316 **7** *¾* **Fleeting Echo**[15] 6351 3-9-7 93 RichardHughes 3 90
(R Hannon) *in tch in midfield: shkn up and no prog over 2f out: one pce after* **9/1**
2501 **8** *shd* **Summerinthecity (IRE)**[15] 6363 3-9-6 92 DarryllHolland 13 88
(J Noseda) *hld up in rr: effrt over 2f out: one pce and no imp on ldrs* **9/2**[1]
0004 **9** *hd* **Kellys Eye (IRE)**[16] 6319 3-9-7 93 GrahamGibbons 1 89
(D H Brown) *towards rr: rdn and no prog over 2f out: kpt on fnl f* **11/1**
25 **10** *2 ¼* **Avertor**[29] 5966 4-8-11 82 (b[1]) SteveDrowne 4 71
(R Charlton) *t.k.h: hld up in rr: shkn up and no prog over 2f out* **5/1**[2]
0404 **11** *5* **Olynard (IRE)**[20] 6256 4-9-4 89 JimCrowley 6 62
(R M Beckett) *hld up wl in rr: shkn up and no prog over 2f out: wknd over 1f out* **20/1**
0000 **12** *4* **Rum King (USA)**[16] 6321 3-8-13 85 DaneO'Neill 5 45
(R Hannon) *dwlt: a in last pair: struggling over 2f out* **66/1**
06-0 **13** *8* **Roodle**[38] 5694 3-9-2 88 TomQueally 12 22
(Eve Johnson Houghton) *chsd ldrs: rdn 1/2-way: wknd rapidly over 2f out: t.o* **28/1**

1m 12.18s (-0.02) **Going Correction** +0.175s/f (Good)
WFA 3 from 4yo+ 1lb **13 Ran SP% 117.9**
Speed ratings (Par 107): **107,106,104,104,103 102,101,101,101,98 91,86,75**
toteswingers:1&2:£12.40, 1&3:£16.70, 2&3:£18.70 CSF £56.17 CT £736.53 TOTE £6.40: £1.90, £4.50, £4.70; EX 68.00.
Owner Quintessential Thoroughbreds Solar Syn **Bred** R, D And M Close **Trained** Radlett, Herts

FOCUS
This had looked a competitive sprint handicap, but little got into it.

NOTEBOOK
R Woody, who got going too late at Doncaster off this new career-high mark latest, prospered under a more positive ride this time and, having gone on 2f out, he always looked to be pulling out enough to hold on. It will take another significant step forward for her defy another rise, but he's only three and may well be up to it. (op 7-1)
Lochan Mor, below form at Salisbury latest, had earlier finished second off this mark at Haydock and he returned to that form here. (op 11-1 tchd 14-1)

The Form Book, Raceform Ltd, Compton, RG20 6NL

We Have A Dream was up there throughout and rallied inside the final furlong, but never quite looked like getting back up. (op 11-1)
Baldemar, well down the field in the Ayr Bronze Cup, found this easier and ran considerably better. (tchd 10-1 in a place)
One Way Or Another(AUS) ran okay but again gave the impression this trip is on the short side. (op 15-2 tchd 7-1)
Summerinthecity(IRE), 5lb higher than when winning at Haydock, never got into it (op 5-1)
Avertor showed little in the first-time blinkers. (tchd 4-1)

6777 E B F GOODWOOD RACEHORSE OWNERS GROUP NURSERY 7f
3:10 (3:10) (Class 4) (0-80,78) 2-Y-O £4,533 (£1,348; £674; £336) Stalls High

Form RPR
330 1 **Double Dealer**[17] 6301 2-9-7 **78** RoystonFfrench 9 80
(Mahmood Al Zarooni) *t.k.h: hld up bhd ldng pair: c between them to ld jst over 1f out: drvn out and r.o wl* **4/1**[2]
3065 2 1 1/2 **Uncle Dermot (IRE)**[24] 6126 2-8-10 **67** DaneO'Neill 6 65
(B G Powell) *t.k.h: hld up in 6th: swtchd out wd and effrt over 1f out: r.o to take 2nd ins fnl f: no imp on wnr* **14/1**
036 3 2 1/2 **Colebrooke**[28] 5985 2-9-1 **72** GregFairley 2 64
(M Johnston) *led 3f: w ldr to jst over 1f out: fdd fnl f* **6/1**[3]
14 4 nk **Mutual Force (USA)**[47] 5392 2-9-0 **78** AntiocoMurgia[(7)] 4 69
(Mahmood Al Zarooni) *hld up in detached last: reminders and no prog over 2f out: styd on wl last 150yds: nrly snatched 3rd* **7/2**[1]
333 5 hd **Inside**[20] 6240 2-8-3 **60** PaulHanagan 7 51
(R A Fahey) *w ldr: led after 3f: hdd jst over 1f out: wknd ins fnl f* **7/2**[1]
060 6 1/2 **Sleeping Wolf**[4] 6673 2-8-2 **59** FrankieMcDonald 5 49
(R Hannon) *pressed ldrs: hanging lft and reminders fr 3f out: sn lost pl: n.d over 1f out* **20/1**
0030 7 1 **Oliver's Gold**[8] 6560 2-8-5 **65** (p) MartinLane[(3)] 8 52
(Mrs A J Perrett) *sn trckd ldng pair: nt qckn 2f out: grad fdd* **4/1**[2]

1m 29.8s (2.90) **Going Correction** +0.225s/f (Good) 7 Ran SP% **110.2**
Speed ratings (Par 97): **92,90,87,87,86 86,85**
toteswingers:1&2:£8.80, 1&3:£4.00, 2&3:£10.20 CSF £50.82 CT £309.54 TOTE £6.00: £3.70, £7.90; EX 61.30.
Owner Godolphin **Bred** Brinkley Stud Sas **Trained** Newmarket, Suffolk

FOCUS
A modest nursery.

NOTEBOOK
Double Dealer, a beaten favourite on each of his last two starts, was particularly disappointing over 6f at Pontefract latest, but the step back up in trip and switch to handicaps enabled him to find enough improvement to get off the mark. On this evidence he will stay 1m. (op 11-2)
Uncle Dermot(IRE) ran his best race to date. He appreciated the return to 7f and if anything gave the impression 1m would suit better. (tchd 12-1)
Colebrooke looked a likely improver switched to handicaps, but having made the running, he was unable to march the front pair inside the final furlong. (tchd 5-1)
Mutual Force(USA), well held in a 1m novice stakes at Yarmouth latest, was ridden out of his ground and, despite keeping on well late, he couldn't quite reach the leaders. He can safely be rated better than the bare form. (op 4-1)
Inside didn't improve as expected for the step up to 7f/switch to handicaps. (op 10-3 tchd 3-1)
Sleeping Wolf didn't get home. Official explanation: jockey said that the colt hung left under pressure (op 14-1)
Oliver's Gold proved bitterly disappointing in the first-time cheekpieces. (op 3-1)

6778 BET AT BLUESQ.COM MEDIAN AUCTION MAIDEN STKS 6f
3:45 (3:46) (Class 5) 2-Y-O £2,590 (£770; £385; £192) Stalls Low

Form RPR
222 1 **Celtic Sixpence (IRE)**[23] 6161 2-8-12 70 PaulHanagan 1 74
(M G Quinlan) *led or disp: modest pce to 1/2-way: rousted along to assert over 1f out: drvn out last 150yds* **2/1**[2]
35 2 2 1/2 **Its You Again**[138] 2413 2-9-3 0 WilliamCarson 6 72
(M G Quinlan) *trckd ldng pair: tried to chal 2f out: nt qckn over 1f out: one pce after* **14/1**
32 3 nk **New Latin (IRE)**[16] 6324 2-9-3 0 GregFairley 9 71
(M Johnston) *disp ld at stdy pce to over 2f out: sn rdn and outpcd: kpt on fnl f* **13/8**[1]
4 3 **Obiter Dicta** 2-8-12 0 DaneO'Neill 7 57
(H Candy) *hld up last: outpcd and shkn up over 2f out: kpt on ins fnl f* **7/1**
00 5 1/2 **Mister Ben Vereen**[23] 6145 2-9-3 0 SebSanders 4 60
(Eve Johnson Houghton) *hld up in tch: outpcd fr 2f out: fdd* **14/1**
4 6 3 **Rambo Will**[24] 6126 2-9-3 0 (b[1]) JimCrowley 8 51
(J R Jenkins) *hanging rt thrght: in tch: stl on terms over 1f out: hanging more markedly and eased* **11/2**[3]

1m 15.01s (2.81) **Going Correction** +0.175s/f (Good) 6 Ran SP% **112.6**
Speed ratings (Par 95): **88,84,84,80,79 75**
toteswingers:1&2:£2.90, 1&3:£1.20, 2&3:£5.10 CSF £27.78 TOTE £2.80: £1.50, £5.10; EX 24.40.
Owner Burns Farm Racing **Bred** Burns Farm Stud **Trained** Newmarket, Suffolk
■ Certral (14/1) was withdrawn after unseating her rider in the paddock. Deduct 5p in the £ under R4.

FOCUS
Not much of a maiden.

NOTEBOOK
Celtic Sixpence(IRE), runner-up on each of her three previous starts, made most of the running for a ready success. She's the type with more to offer in nurseries. Official explanation: one - day ban: use of whip (Oct 25) (old market op 5-2 tchd 15-8, new market op 15-8)
Its You Again, a stablemate to the winner, appreciated the step up to 6f and could do better still in nurseries. (old market op 11-1 tchd 12-1, new market op 10-1)
New Latin(IRE), who has a rather scratchy action, has now been a beaten favourite on all three starts and looks in need of a seventh furlong. (old market op 13-8 tchd 2-1, new market op 7-4)
Obiter Dicta, whose dam is from a good family, is bred to need further than this and shaped quite encouragingly. (old market op 12-1 tchd 10-1, new market op 8-1)
Mister Ben Vereen is now qualified for a nursery mark. (old market op 16-1 tchd 20-1, new market op 16-1)
Rambo Will failed to build on his debut effort, never looking happy in the first-time blinkers. Official explanation: jockey said that the colt hung right throughout (old market op 11-2 tchd 13-2, new market op 6-1)

6779 BLUE SQUARE BET E B F MAIDEN STKS 1m 1f
4:20 (4:21) (Class 4) 2-Y-O £5,180 (£1,541; £770; £384) Stalls High

Form RPR
2 1 **Weapon Of Choice (IRE)**[29] 5954 2-9-0 0 MartinLane[(3)] 6 80
(D M Simcock) *trckd ldng pair: led 3f out: readily drew clr fr 2f out: comf* **10/11**[1]
6 2 3 1/2 **Kadoodd (IRE)**[11] 6473 2-9-3 0 RichardHughes 2 73
(M R Channon) *trckd ldr: pushed along 4f out: upsides 3f out: chsd wnr after: readily hld* **11/2**[3]
3 10 **Hidden Valley** 2-8-12 0 NeilChalmers 5 48
(A M Balding) *hld up in 4th: shkn up and cl enough 3f out: wnt 3rd 2f out but rn green: lft bhd by ldng pair after* **12/1**
4 4 **Iron Step** 2-9-3 0 JimCrowley 1 45
(E A L Dunlop) *dwlt: hld up last: effrt 4f out: sn rdn: outpcd by ldrs over 2f out: no ch after* **14/1**
0246 5 9 **Flodden (USA)**[20] 6249 2-9-3 75 JamieSpencer 3 27
(P F I Cole) *led: rdn and hdd 3f out: immediately btn: wknd over 1f out: heavily eased last 100yds* **5/2**[2]
60 6 16 **Senor Tibor (USA)**[12] 6443 2-9-3 0 EddieCreighton 4 —
(E J Creighton) *rdn to stay in tch: wknd 4f out: wl t.o* **66/1**

1m 58.61s (2.31) **Going Correction** +0.225s/f (Good) 6 Ran SP% **112.2**
Speed ratings (Par 97): **98,94,86,82,74 60**
toteswingers:1&2:£1.50, 2&3:£4.60, 1&3:£3.30 CSF £6.58 TOTE £2.10: £1.50, £3.50; EX 4.80.
Owner Trillium Place Racing **Bred** Stone Ridge Farm **Trained** Newmarket, Suffolk

FOCUS
Not the most competitive maiden.

NOTEBOOK
Weapon Of Choice(IRE) stayed on strongly to win quite comfortably. Runner-up to a useful sort over 1m at the course on debut, this was easier, and he probably showed improved form. There should be more to come in nurseries. (op 5-6 tchd Evens and 8-11 in a place)
Kadoodd(IRE) improved markedly on his debut effort, finishing clear of the remainder, and he looks a middle-distance handicap prospect. (op 6-1 tchd 5-1)
Hidden Valley, from a family the yard has done well with, was beaten a long way, but she looked in need of the experience and should do better at three. (op 11-1 tchd 9-1)
Iron Step has a rather unspectacular pedigree and he offered little promise for the immediate future. (op 16-1 tchd 12-1)
Flodden(USA) was particularly disappointing for a second straight time and looks one to avoid. (op 11-4 tchd 3-1)

6780 EXCLUSIVE LIVE SHOWS AT BLUESQ.COM STKS (H'CAP) 1m
4:55 (4:57) (Class 4) (0-85,85) 3-Y-O+ £3,885 (£1,156; £577; £288) Stalls High

Form RPR
0000 1 **Sarah Park (IRE)**[14] 6391 5-9-2 **80** NeilCallan 5 90
(B J Meehan) *trckd ldr: rdn to ld over 1f out: styd on wl* **16/1**
5050 2 1 3/4 **General Eliott (IRE)**[25] 6097 5-9-1 **79** ShaneKelly 6 85
(P F I Cole) *led: drvn and hdd over 1f out: wl hld fnl f: jst kpt 2nd* **16/1**
6056 3 hd **Edgewater (IRE)**[11] 6478 3-8-8 **75** GregFairley 13 81
(J Akehurst) *chsd ldrs in 7th: rdn wl over 2f out: styd on fr over 1f out: nrly snatched 2nd* **20/1**
5122 4 2 1/4 **Beaumont's Party (IRE)**[30] 5919 3-8-9 **76** SteveDrowne 1 76
(R Hannon) *racd wd thrght: sn in midfield: rdn over 2f out: styd on to take 4th fnl f* **11/1**
0642 5 1 1/4 **Bullet Man (USA)**[21] 6223 5-9-0 **78** PaulHanagan 15 75
(R A Fahey) *settled in midfield: urged along 3f out: looking for room over 2f out: styd on fnl f: n.d* **6/1**[1]
0000 6 1 **Seek The Fair Land**[8] 6558 4-9-2 **80** (b) PatCosgrave 3 75
(J R Boyle) *chsd ldng trio: rdn to go 3rd briefly over 1f out: fdd fnl f* **25/1**
461 7 1/2 **Beaver Patrol (IRE)**[39] 5652 8-8-11 **80** (v) JohnFahy[(5)] 10 74
(Eve Johnson Houghton) *chsd ldng quartet: rdn and nt qckn 2f out: grad outpcd* **20/1**
2005 8 nk **Mishrif (USA)**[8] 6558 4-8-13 **77** (v) DaneO'Neill 7 70
(J R Jenkins) *pressed ldng pair: nt qckn 2f out: wknd over 1f out* **22/1**
1646 9 1 1/2 **Salient**[28] 5993 6-8-10 **77** KierenFox[(3)] 11 67
(M J Attwater) *chsd ldrs on inner in 6th: nt qckn over 2f out: fdd* **20/1**
1021 10 nse **Master Mylo (IRE)**[29] 5968 3-8-12 **79** JimCrowley 14 69
(D K Ivory) *taken down early: hld up in rr: shuffled along over 2f out: nvr nr ldrs* **8/1**[3]
0501 11 hd **Compton Blue**[33] 5833 4-9-0 **78** (b) RichardHughes 4 67
(R Hannon) *settled wl in rr: shkn up over 2f out: no prog and btn after* **13/2**[2]
5254 12 nse **Satwa Laird**[17] 6312 4-9-4 **85** MartinLane[(3)] 16 74
(E A L Dunlop) *settled in midfield on inner: looking for room and rdn over 2f out: no prog* **6/1**[1]
13 1 3/4 **Noguchi (IRE)**[169] 5-9-1 **79** DarryllHolland 9 64
(J Noseda) *dwlt: hld up in last: rdn and no prog over 2f out* **16/1**
6164 14 3/4 **Kavachi (IRE)**[28] 5994 7-9-4 **82** GeorgeBaker 2 65
(G L Moore) *dropped in fr wd draw: hld up wl in rr: shkn up and no prog over 2f out* **14/1**
5364 15 shd **Jordaura**[38] 5702 4-9-6 **84** JamieSpencer 8 67
(J R Holt) *a wl in rr: brought wd and rdn over 2f out: no prog* **6/1**[1]
0000 16 1 3/4 **Kalypso King (USA)**[58] 5030 3-9-4 **85** StephenCraine 12 64
(S Kirk) *awkward s: hld up wl in rr on inner: rdn and no prog over 2f out: sn btn* **50/1**

1m 40.52s (0.62) **Going Correction** +0.225s/f (Good)
WFA 3 from 4yo+ 3lb 16 Ran SP% **124.4**
Speed ratings (Par 105): **105,103,103,100,99 98,98,97,96,96 96,95,94,93,93 91**
toteswingers:1&2:£83.10, 1&3:£107.20, 2&3:£112.10 CSF £230.51 CT £5284.32 TOTE £19.70: £4.60, £5.50, £5.90, £2.10; EX 358.20.
Owner Mrs J & D E Cash **Bred** George S O'Malley **Trained** Manton, Wilts

FOCUS
Another race where little got into it from off the pace.
Sarah Park(IRE) Official explanation: trainer said, regarding the apparent improvement of form, that the mare needed the run at Ascot, which was her first for over two months having had a break from racing to recover from splints
Noguchi(IRE) Official explanation: jockey said gelding was slowly away
Kalypso King(USA) Official explanation: jockey said the colt hung left

6781 PLAY ROULETTE AT BLUESQ.COM STKS (H'CAP) 1m 4f
5:30 (5:31) (Class 5) (0-75,75) 3-Y-O £2,590 (£770; £385; £192) Stalls Low

Form RPR
4002 1 **Dynamic Drive (IRE)**[13] 6427 3-9-6 **74** AdamKirby 9 84
(W R Swinburn) *chsd ldrs: shkn up over 3f out: clsd to ld over 2f out: drvn clr over 1f out: styd on* **6/1**[3]
-506 2 2 1/2 **Seaside Sizzler**[33] 5832 3-8-13 **67** (bt) JimCrowley 2 73
(R M Beckett) *sn in last pair: rdn in last bef 1/2-way and nt keen: prog u.p 3f out: styd on to take 2nd 1f out: nt rch wnr* **20/1**
3523 3 4 1/2 **Kerchak (USA)**[32] 5868 3-9-2 **75** JohnFahy[(5)] 6 74
(W Jarvis) *rousted along early: in tch: rdn and prog on outer to chal over 2f out: chsd wnr to 1f out: fdd* **7/2**[1]
3641 4 4 1/2 **Beat Route**[9] 6526 3-8-7 **66** JemmaMarshall[(5)] 4 58
(M J Attwater) *chsd ldng pair: clsd to dispute ld over 2f out: wknd over 1f out* **25/1**
2305 5 5 **Donna Elvira**[45] 5444 3-9-4 **72** RichardHughes 7 56
(R Hannon) *led and sn clr: c bk over 3f out: hdd and btn over 2f out* **8/1**

0231 **6** *hd* **Iron Condor**[18] 6290 3-9-0 **68** .... PaulHanagan 5 51
(J M P Eustace) *chsd ldrs: clsd to chal u.p over 2f out: wknd wl over 1f out* **7/2**[1]

2223 **7** *5* **Fascination (IRE)**[13] 6415 3-9-2 **73** .... MartinLane(3) 10 48
(M L W Bell) *chsd ldr: clsd over 3f out: sn rdn: wknd over 2f out* **8/1**

5056 **8** *23* **Street Entertainer (IRE)**[11] 6480 3-9-0 **68** .... (p) NeilCallan 3 —
(Mrs A J Perrett) *trckd ldrs: gng wl enough 4f out: rdn and wknd rapidly 3f out: virtually p.u fnl f* **6/1**[3]

4213 **9** *8* **Shianda**[9] 6525 3-8-7 **61** .... (b) JamieSpencer 8 —
(G L Moore) *hld up in last pair: rdn in 8th over 4f out: hung bdly rt over 2f out: t.o* **5/1**[2]

400 **10** *½* **Rio Prince**[27] 6020 3-8-7 **61** oh15 .... NeilChalmers 1 —
(J J Bridger) *a in rr: rdn over 5f out: sn wknd: t.o* **80/1**

2m 42.13s (3.73) **Going Correction** +0.225s/f (Good) **10** Ran SP% **121.7**
Speed ratings (Par 101): **96,94,91,88,85 84,81,66,60,60**
toteswingers:1&2:£8.80, 1&3:£6.30, 2&3:£21.10 CSF £121.52 CT £491.56 TOTE £8.30: £2.60, £4.20, £1.40; EX 117.30 Place 6 £505.54; Place 5 £244.31.
Owner P W Harris **Bred** Pendley Farm **Trained** Aldbury, Herts

FOCUS
A modest handicap.
Kerchak(USA) Official explanation: jockey said colt ran in snatches
T/Plt: £990.40 to a £1 stake. Pool of £82,767.04 - 61.00 winning tickets T/Qpdt: £174.90 to a £1 stake. Pool of £5,650.08 - 23.90 winning tickets JN

6782 - (Foreign Racing) - See Raceform Interactive

6399 CURRAGH (R-H)
Sunday, October 10

OFFICIAL GOING: Yielding to soft

6783a JERSEY RACING CLUB TESTIMONIAL STKS (LISTED RACE) 6f
2:45 (2:46) 3-Y-O+ **£24,446** (£7,146; £3,384; £1,128)

RPR

1 **Luisant**[14] 6402 7-9-3 108 .... CO'Donoghue 11 114
(J A Nash, Ire) *settled in mid-div on outer: 6th 1/2-way: smooth hdwy to chal over 1f out: led and edgd lft ins fnl f: styd on wl* **3/1**[2]

2 *2½* **Definightly**[22] 6175 4-9-6 .... (b) KJManning 8 109
(R Charlton) *trckd ldrs in 4th: travelled wl to chal after 1/2-way: led under 2f and sn strly pressed: rdn and hdd ins fnl f: kpt on but no ch w wnr* **11/4**[1]

3 *4* **Song Of My Heart (IRE)**[60] 4977 3-8-13 98 .... (b) JMurtagh 6 90
(David Wachman, Ire) *settled towards rr: stdy hdwy into 5th 1/2-way: rdn fr 2f out: kpt on one pce to go 3rd ins fnl f* **8/1**

4 *¾* **Snaefell (IRE)**[28] 6009 6-9-8 108 .... (b) PJSmullen 5 96
(M Halford, Ire) *prom on stands' rail: led briefly after 1/2-way: rdn and hdd under 2f out: no ex fr 1f out* **4/1**[3]

5 *shd* **Jumbajukiba**[7] 6617 7-9-3 100 .... (b) FMBerry 3 90
(Mrs John Harrington, Ire) *led: strly pressed and hdd after 1/2-way: no ex u.p in 4th fr over 1f out* **9/1**

6 *1* **Walk On Bye (IRE)**[28] 6009 3-8-13 100 .... (b[1]) WMLordan 2 84
(T Stack, Ire) *slowly away: in tch on outer bef 1/2-way: 6th 2f out: sn rdn and no imp* **12/1**

7 *1* **Velvet Flicker (IRE)**[92] 3928 3-9-2 102 .... DPMcDonogh 7 84
(Kevin Prendergast, Ire) *in rr of mid-div: 7th 1/2-way: no imp u.p fr over 1f out* **20/1**

8 *1¼* **Money Trader (IRE)**[28] 6008 3-9-2 86 .... CDHayes 9 80
(J T Gorman, Ire) *nvr a factor* **40/1**

9 *¾* **Barack (IRE)**[14] 6402 4-9-3 97 .... (b) BACurtis 4 78
(Francis Ennis, Ire) *prom early: drvn along and lost pl fr 1/2-way* **8/1**

10 *3½* **Bay Knight (IRE)**[14] 6400 4-9-3 97 .... NGMcCullagh 1 66
(K J Condon, Ire) *a towards rr* **16/1**

1m 13.58s (-1.42) **Going Correction** +0.075s/f (Good)
WFA 3 from 4yo+ 1lb **10** Ran SP% **124.7**
Speed ratings: **112,108,103,102,102 100,99,97,96,92**
CSF £12.69 TOTE £4.30: £1.50, £1.50, £2.20; DF 20.40.
Owner J A McCarthy **Bred** Petra Bloodstock Agency Ltd **Trained** The Curragh, Co. Kildare

FOCUS
The decisive winner travelled well and has been rated to his best.

NOTEBOOK
Luisant travelled very well off the pace, although when he loomed up to take on the runner-up there might have been doubts in the mind of many as to what he would find. There were no worries though as he eased past inside the final furlong and kept on well despite just edging left towards the rail. He'll finish his season in a Listed race at Leopardstown at the end of the month and looks certain to run his race. (op 10/3 tchd 7/2)
Definightly was pulled out of a more competitive contest a bit closer to home the previous day and it was a good decision. He was close to the pace and travelled very well in his own right, but was just outpaced by a better horse inside the last. He put plenty of distance between himself and the remainder, though, and seems to be very much a soft-ground horse. A return to Ireland at some stage would appear likely. (op 3/1)
Song Of My Heart(IRE) appeared to appreciate the drop in class but not the drop in trip. She was being ridden to go the pace from halfway but did keep on to reasonable effect inside the last. One imagines that she won't be running over this type of trip in the near future. (op 8/1 tchd 15/2)
Snaefell(IRE) was ridden closer to the pace this time, moving into a challenging position a little bit sooner than would be the norm with him, but he faded a little bit tamely when the race really took shape inside the last 1½f. (op 4/1 tchd 10/3)
Jumbajukiba hasn't shown too many signs of being anything like the force of old this season. He didn't run badly here, trying to make all and weakening when better horses came to challenge, but he was still well short of his best. (op 9/1 tchd 10/1)
Walk On Bye(IRE) didn't run too badly and kept on past beaten horses after being quite slowly into her stride. (op 10/1)

6784a LANWADES & STAFFORDSTOWN STUDS STKS (LISTED RACE) (FILLIES) 1m
3:15 (3:15) 2-Y-O **£25,309** (£7,398; £3,504; £1,168)

RPR

1 **Gemstone (IRE)**[28] 6005 2-8-12 86 .... JMurtagh 4 85
(A P O'Brien, Ire) *mde virtually all: drvn along fr 2f out: styd on wl u.p ins fnl f* **7/1**

2 *1¼* **Rising Wind (IRE)**[26] 6067 2-8-12 .... CDHayes 7 82
(Kevin Prendergast, Ire) *towards rr: 8th 3f out: sme hdwy into 5th over 1f out: sn swtchd lft: styd on wl u.p fnl f to go 2nd cl home* **4/1**[2]

3 *nk* **Hurricane Havoc (IRE)**[13] 6431 2-8-12 .... KJManning 3 82
(J S Bolger, Ire) *settled towards rr: hdwy fr 3f out: rdn to chal and wnt 2nd over 1f out: no imp u.p ins fnl f* **2/1**[1]

4 *2½* **Luxurious (IRE)**[28] 6005 2-8-12 88 .... JPO'Brien 9 76
(A P O'Brien, Ire) *prom: 2nd 1/2-way: rdn fr over 2f out: no imp in 3rd 1f out: no ex ins fnl f* **6/1**

5 *1¼* **Hadrian's Waltz (IRE)**[9] 6545 2-8-12 .... JAHeffernan 8 73
(David Wachman, Ire) *chsd ldrs: 4th 1/2-way: drvn along 2f out: no imp whn carried lft 1f out: kpt on one pce* **20/1**

6 *1* **Betrothed (IRE)** 2-8-12 .... WMLordan 5 71
(T Stack, Ire) *towards rr: pushed along bef 1/2-way: kpt on fr over 1f out wout threatening* **20/1**

7 *4½* **Hope Of An Angel (IRE)**[14] 6401 2-8-12 84 .... (p) MHarley 1 61
(Niall Moran, Ire) *chsd ldrs: 3rd 1/2-way: no ex u.p fr 2f out* **16/1**

8 *2½* **Negotiate**[42] 5570 2-8-12 .... PJSmullen 2 56
(Andrew Oliver, Ire) *trckd ldrs: 5th 1/2-way: 3rd over 2f out: sn no ex u.p: wknd* **14/1**

9 *½* **Bonita Star**[8] 6563 2-8-12 .... SamHitchcott 10 55
(M R Channon) *mid-div best: no ex fr 2f out* **14/1**

10 *9* **Aris (IRE)**[28] 6005 2-8-12 .... FMBerry 6 35
(P J Prendergast, Ire) *mid-div: 6th 1/2-way: no ex and wknd fr 2f out: eased fnl f* **9/2**[3]

1m 46.48s (0.48) **Going Correction** +0.075s/f (Good) **10** Ran SP% **127.0**
Speed ratings: **100,98,98,95,94 93,89,86,86,77**
CSF £38.54 TOTE £7.20: £1.80, £1.90, £1.40; DF 62.10.
Owner Derrick Smith **Bred** Airlie Stud **Trained** Ballydoyle, Co Tipperary

FOCUS
This was run at a slow pace.

NOTEBOOK
Gemstone(IRE) benefited from an excellent tactical ride, going to the front and kicking on 3f out. She stayed well to boot and the chasing group were unable to make any impression on her. She has rediscovered her best form late in the year, is a filly likely to stay middle distances next year and is very adaptable as to ground. (op 6/1)
Rising Wind(IRE) ◆ got up in the last stride to win her maiden at Listowel and again here wasn't suited by the lack of pace and was tapped for speed when the tempo quickened in the straight. In the end she picked up in taking fashion and stayed on very well inside the last, but she looks certain to come into her own when stepped up to middle distances next year.
Hurricane Havoc(IRE) was unlikely to have been suited by how the race was run, but she did improve to chase the leaders over a furlong out and had every chance but just couldn't make an impression. She did keep going well enough, although not quite as well as the runner-up, and there wouldn't appear to be too many excuses. One wouldn't be quite as confident with her that she'll be effective over middle distances next year. (op 5/2)
Luxurious(IRE) helped to set the mostly unsatisfactory gallop and she kept on at one pace when challenged by the winner over 2f from the finish. (op 6/1 tchd 13/2)
Hadrian's Waltz(IRE) ◆ looks a progressive filly who will probably get a bit further in time once winning her maiden. She raced just off the pace and kept going at the same pace inside the final furlong. A maiden success should be a formality for her.
Betrothed(IRE) justified the decision to run her in this company on her debut as she ran on past beaten fillies inside the final furlong or so. She probably stays quite well and is certain to improve.
Aris(IRE) Official explanation: jockey said filly raced freely for the first half of this race and weakened quickly thereafter; vet said filly was found to be blowing hard post-race; trainer later said filly was found to have mucus following a post-race endoscopic examination

6786a GO RACING IN KILDARE FESTIVAL FINALE STKS (LISTED RACE) 1m 4f
4:15 (4:17) 3-Y-O+ **£24,446** (£7,146; £3,384; £1,128)

RPR

1 **Hazarafa (IRE)**[114] 3185 3-8-11 96 .... BACurtis 1 99+
(John M Oxx, Ire) *chsd clr ldr in 3rd: clsr in 2nd ent st: rdn to chal fr 2f out: led 1f out: kpt on wl u.p fnl f* **12/1**

2 *1¾* **Roses For The Lady (IRE)**[31] 5881 4-9-7 .... FMBerry 7 99
(John M Oxx, Ire) *led: clr bef 1/2-way: reduced advantage appr st: rdn and strly pressed fr over 2f out: hdd 1f out: no ex u.p: kpt on one pce* **3/1**[2]

3 *2* **Celtic Soprano (IRE)**[21] 6231 5-9-4 91 .... WJSupple 5 93
(P D Deegan, Ire) *hld up in rr of mid-div: mod 7th 1/2-way: hdwy into 4th appr st: 3rd over 2f out: sn rdn and no imp fr over 1f out* **14/1**

4 *8* **Lady Lupus (IRE)**[15] 6379 3-8-11 103 .... (b) JPO'Brien 3 80
(A P O'Brien, Ire) *chsd clr ldr in 5th: clsr in 3rd appr st: sn drvn along: no ex in 4th fr 2f out* **6/1**[3]

5 *nk* **Montbretia**[25] 6095 5-9-4 93 .... WMLordan 2 80
(Edward P Harty, Ire) *mid-div: 6th 1/2-way: in tch appr st: rdn and no ex in 5th fr 2f out* **16/1**

6 *2* **Zaralabad (IRE)**[30] 5932 6-9-7 95 .... (t) WJLee 13 80
(C F Swan, Ire) *in rr of mid-div: 8th 1/2-way: rdn in mod 7th 2f out: kpt on one pce* **16/1**

7 *shd* **Karasiyra (IRE)**[70] 4631 3-9-0 96 .... NGMcCullagh 11 79
(John M Oxx, Ire) *chsd clr ldr in 2nd: rdn and dropped to 5th appr st: no ex fr over 2f out* **12/1**

8 *4½* **Rain Forest**[150] 2067 3-9-0 .... JMurtagh 10 72
(A P O'Brien, Ire) *chsd clr ldr in 4th: clsr and niggled along appr st: sn no ex* **11/4**[1]

9 *2* **Harriers Call (IRE)**[29] 5978 5-9-4 103 .... KLatham 9 66
(J C Hayden, Ire) *a towards rr* **15/2**

10 *3½* **Zerashan (IRE)**[49] 5341 3-9-0 96 .... DPMcDonogh 8 63
(M Halford, Ire) *a bhd* **10/1**

11 *1* **Syann (IRE)**[41] 5619 3-8-11 .... CO'Donoghue 4 59
(David Marnane, Ire) *mid-div: dropped to 9th after 1/2-way: no ex appr st* **12/1**

2m 41.88s (2.78) **Going Correction** +0.375s/f (Good)
WFA 3 from 4yo+ 7lb **11** Ran SP% **128.3**
Speed ratings: **105,103,102,97,96 95,95,92,91,88 88**
CSF £52.46 TOTE £19.30: £4.90, £1.40, £5.30; DF 115.80.
Owner H H Aga Khan **Bred** His Highness The Aga Khan's St **Trained** Currabeg, Co Kildare

FOCUS
The gradually progressive first three have all been rated to slight personal bests.

NOTEBOOK
Hazarafa(IRE) came good here on what may have been her final racecourse appearance. Well ridden by Curtis, who had her in the ideal position from which to mount her challenge, she came under pressure early in the straight but responded admirably and stayed on strongly all the way to the line. She just had too many guns for her stable companion on this ground and did it well in the end. (op 14/1)
Roses For The Lady(IRE), positively ridden by Fran Berry, opened up a nice early lead and kept battling on under pressure in the straight but was unable to give 10lb to her stable companion. It might just have been her best run of the season and, had the ground been a bit deeper, she could have been very hard to beat. (op 3/1 tchd 7/2)
Celtic Soprano(IRE) put up her best effort to date in stakes company. Racing in the rear of mid-division, she made reasonably smooth headway to get into a challenging position early in the straight and, despite not picking up as one might have expected when let down, did keep on well inside the last while not making any real impression. She takes her racing well and is probably versatile as to trip, so it's likely that she'll run again this season.

Lady Lupus(IRE) raced just behind the early pace and moved up to chase the leader early in the straight, but she ran out of steam inside the last 1½f. (op 8/1)
Montbretia was never a factor before staying on inside the last furlong.
Rain Forest raced handily early on but weakened in the straight, running well below the form she had shown in winning her two starts early in the season. It would be hard to put such a disappointing effort solely down to the easier surface. (op 9/4)
Zerashan(IRE) Official explanation: trainer said colt suffered abrasions to his hock while in the stalls and was found to be lame post-race

6785 - 6789a (Foreign Racing) - See Raceform Interactive

4640 DUSSELDORF (R-H)

Sunday, October 10

OFFICIAL GOING: Turf: soft

6790a OBERBURGERMEISTER DIRK ELBERS PREIS (EX FRANKFURTER STUTENPREIS) (GROUP 3) (3YO+ FILLIES & MARES) 1m 3f

2:45 (3:08) 3-Y-0+

£28,318 (£9,734; £4,867; £2,654; £1,769; £1,327)

RPR

1 Pearl Banks[57] 5108 4-9-4 0 Francois-XavierBertras 7 112
(F Rohaut, France) *broke fast: disp ld tl led on bk st hill: r.o wl in st: saw off all chals: comf* **17/10[1]**

2 1 ½ Ovambo Queen (GER)[49] 5345 3-8-11 0 HenkGrewe 5 108
(Dr A Bolte, Germany) *broke fast to briefly share ld w eventual wnr: first to chal ldr in st: r.o gamely* **23/5**

3 1 ¾ Nicea (GER)[21] 6239 3-8-11 0 AStarke 3 105
(P Schiergen, Germany) *settled in 5th: shkn up ent st: qcknd wl: r.o wl fnl f* **29/10[2]**

4 hd Indian Breeze (GER)[35] 5805 3-8-11 0 ADeVries 4 105
(J Hirschberger, Germany) *settled in 4th: mde early move in st: r.o wl but no threat to ldrs* **37/10[3]**

5 2 ½ Margarita (GER)[32] 5870 4-9-4 0 THellier 2 101
(M Munch, Germany) *broke wl to be prom: r.o wl in st but no threat to ldrs* **188/10**

6 ¾ Semina (GER)[70] 4640 3-8-11 0 EFrank 8 99
(S Smrczek, Germany) *broke wl and tried to ld but had to be settled bhd ldrs: threatened briefly at end of bk st: quick to chal in st: sn one pce* **213/10**

7 ¾ Power Eva (GER)[14] 3-8-11 0 WPanov 6 97
(H J Groschel, Germany) *bkmarker fr s: effrt but no ex in st: wknd* **147/10**

8 3 Lagalp (GER)[39] 5672 3-8-11 0 FilipMinarik 1 92
(P Schiergen, Germany) *a towards rr: nvr figured* **53/10**

2m 20.54s (140.54)
WFA 3 from 4yo 6lb 8 Ran SP% **133.6**
WIN (incl. 10 euro stake): 27. PLACES: 11, 13, 11. SF: 119.
Owner Scea Haras De Saint Pair **Bred** 6c Racing **Trained** Sauvagnon, France

6791a GROSSER PREIS DER LANDESHAUPSTADT DUSSELDORF (GROUP 3) (3YO+) (TURF) 1m 110y

4:00 (12:00) 3-Y-0+

£28,318 (£9,734; £4,867; £2,654; £1,769; £1,327)

RPR

1 Alianthus (GER)[14] 6408 5-9-6 0 ADeVries 3 110
(J Hirschberger, Germany) *reluctant to load: broke fast to ld: set solid pce: r.o wl in st to see off all chals: comf* **6/5[1]**

2 1 ¾ Noble Alpha (IRE)[14] 6408 3-8-13 0 THellier 5 103
(Mario Hofer, Germany) *settled in 4th: trckd ldr: rn freely: effrt in st: r.o wl to chse ldr home* **19/10[2]**

3 2 Sanjii Danon (GER)[63] 4888 4-9-2 0 APietsch 6 98
(W Hickst, Germany) *settled midfield: shkn up early in st: r.o wl: fin strly fnl f* **91/10**

4 7 Setareh (GER)[21] 5-9-2 0 EFrank 9 82
(P Olsanik, Germany) *racd promly: mde early move in st: no imp on ldrs* **27/1**

5 3 Tertullus (FR)[49] 5350 7-9-4 0 EspenSki 7 78
(Rune Haugen, Norway) *bkmarker fr s: produced early in st but hit traffic problems: r.o wl fnl f* **139/10**

6 shd Torres (GER)[112] 3251 4-9-2 0 JiriPalik 4 75
(Frau E Mader, Germany) *racd bhd ldrs: rn freely: threatened briefly in st: no imp* **184/10**

7 4 ½ Big Hunter (FR)[106] 3-8-13 0 HenkGrewe 8 66
(E Kurdu, Germany) *a in rr: nvr a threat* **11/2[3]**

8 2 ½ Schutzenjunker (GER)[43] 5542 5-9-2 0 DPorcu 2 60
(Uwe Ostmann, Germany) *broke wl to trck pce in 2nd: threatened briefly on fnl turn: sn wknd* **13/2**

1m 44.34s (-3.24)
WFA 3 from 4yo+ 3lb 8 Ran SP% **134.0**
WIN (incl 10 euro stake): 22. PLACES: 10, 11, 17. SF: 44.
Owner Baron G Von Ullmann **Bred** Gestut Karlshof **Trained** Germany

6665 KEMPTON (A.W) (R-H)

Monday, October 11

OFFICIAL GOING: Standard
Wind: medium, across Weather: bright and sunny

6794 BET SHANGHAI MASTERS TENNIS - BETDAQ H'CAP 1m (P)

2:20 (2:20) (Class 6) (0-65,68) 3-Y-0+ £1,637 (£483; £241) Stalls High

Form RPR

00-0 1 April Fool[9] 6581 6-9-4 64 (v) TomMcLaughlin 6 75
(R A Harris) *mde all: sn clr: jnd and rdn over 2f out: drvn clr again over 1f out: kpt on wl fnl f* **50/1**

0053 2 1 ½ Lord Of The Dance (IRE)[23] 6210 4-9-2 62 LukeMorris 3 70
(W M Brisbourne) *hld up in rr: rdn and hdwy over 2f out: n.m.r over 1f out: drvn and hdwy between horses ent fnl f: chsd wnr fnl 150yds: r.o but nvr able to rch wnr* **8/1**

6061 3 1 ½ Swiftly Done (IRE)[7] 6629 3-9-0 68 6ex (v) NeilFarley(5) 8 73
(D Carroll) *dwlt: hld up in last trio: rdn and hdwy over 2f out: chsd clr wnr jst over 1f out tl jst ins fnl f: kpt on same pce and no imp fnl 100yds* **5/1[3]**

0530 4 nk Opera Prince[12] 6472 5-9-4 64 (p) RyanMoore 10 68
(Lady Herries) *racd in midfield: rdn and unable qck over 2f out: hdwy u.p to chse ldrs 1f out: kpt on: nvr gng pce to rch wnr* **9/2[2]**

0636 5 6 Final Drive (IRE)[9] 6581 4-9-4 64 StevieDonohoe 12 54
(J Ryan) *s.i.s: bhd: switching rt looking for run over 2f out: kpt on past btn horses fnl f: n.d* **9/1**

-654 6 1 ¾ Plenty O'Toole[21] 6243 3-9-2 65 KierenFallon 5 51
(Mrs D J Sanderson) *chsd wnr: rdn to chal and clr of field over 2f out: btn over 1f out: lost 2nd jst over 1f out: fdd fnl f* **10/3[1]**

40 7 1 ½ French Art[37] 5756 5-9-4 64 (p) TomEaves 4 47
(N Tinkler) *chsd ldrs: wnt 3rd over 4f out: drvn and unable qck jst over 2f out: wknd u.p over 1f out* **17/2**

0005 8 ¾ Zubova[15] 6395 3-9-2 65 (t) TedDurcan 11 46
(D Shaw) *dwlt: sn bustled along and in midfield: rdn and struggling 3f out: wl btn fnl 2f* **12/1**

403- 9 1 ¼ Valkov[320] 7513 3-8-13 65 KierenFox(3) 9 43
(E A Wheeler) *racd in midfield: rdn and struggling over 3f out: wl btn fnl 2f* **33/1**

1002 10 20 Hip Hip Hooray[12] 6452 4-9-5 65 FergusSweeney 7 —
(L A Dace) *racd in midfield: rdn and no prog over 3f out: wl btn fnl 2f: heavily eased fnl f: t.o* **9/1**

5000 11 21 Heliocentric[132] 2620 3-9-2 65 NeilCallan 14 —
(B Palling) *chsd ldrs tl rdn and losing pl 1/2-way: t.o fnl 2f* **25/1**

1m 38.86s (-0.94) **Going Correction** -0.10s/f (Stan)
WFA 3 from 4yo+ 3lb 11 Ran SP% **116.0**
Speed ratings (Par 101): **100,98,97,96,90 88,87,86,85,65 44**
Tote Swingers: 1&2 £41.70, 1&3 £23.50, 2&3 £8.20 CSF £403.29 CT £2418.31 TOTE £46.60: £12.90, £3.90, £1.10; EX 499.70.
Owner Ridge House Stables Ltd **Bred** Miss B Swire **Trained** Earlswood, Monmouths

FOCUS
A modest, uncompetitive handicap, but the form seems sound enough rated around the runner-up and third.
April Fool Official explanation: trainer said, regarding apparent improvement in form, that the gelding was better suited by being able to dominate
Zubova Official explanation: jockey said filly had no more to give
Hip Hip Hooray Official explanation: jockey said filly never travelled and moved poorly

6795 BET EURO 2012 FOOTBALL - BETDAQ CLAIMING STKS 1m (P)

2:50 (2:52) (Class 5) 2-Y-0 £2,286 (£675; £337) Stalls High

Form RPR

3500 1 King Of Aquitaine (IRE)[23] 6184 2-9-4 77 (b[1]) NeilCallan 7 80
(K A Ryan) *chsd ldrs: rdn to chse ldr over 2f out: drvn and hung lft fr wl over 1f out: led ent fnl f: kpt on fnl f* **7/1[3]**

0446 2 1 ¾ Right Said Fred (IRE)[24] 6156 2-8-13 71 (p) PatCosgrave 11 71
(R M Beckett) *in tch in midfield: rdn and unable qck over 2f out: no prog tl hdwy ins fnl f: kpt on wl to go 2nd last strides: nvr gng to rch wnr* **4/1[2]**

1563 3 hd Water Ice[18] 6307 2-8-8 74 RichardKingscote 4 66
(Tom Dascombe) *chsd ldr for 2f: styd chsng ldrs: hung lft bnd 3f out: rdn and hung lft fr 2f out: kpt on u.p fnl f: wnt 3rd last strides: nvr gng pce to rch wnr* **9/4[1]**

2335 4 hd Kissing Clara (IRE)[14] 6412 2-7-13 65 (p) RyanPowell(7) 2 63
(J S Moore) *chsd ldrs: wnt 2nd after 2f tl led over 3f out: rdn and hung lft ent fnl f: hdd ent fnl f: stl hanging and one pce after: lost 2 pls nr fin* **7/1[3]**

0000 5 1 ¾ Imaginary World (IRE)[42] 5602 2-8-7 46 AdrianNicholls 12 60
(E S McMahon) *s.i.s: sn pushed along and nt trng in last pair: rdn and c wd over 2f out: styd on wl ins fnl f: nvr trbld ldrs* **20/1**

0400 6 6 Elusive Vine (IRE)[39] 5701 2-8-1 48 ow1 AndrewHeffernan(3) 5 43
(R A Harris) *chsd ldrs tl wknd u.p jst over 2f out: wl btn fnl f* **66/1**

00 7 1 ¾ Glenavon[14] 6414 2-8-13 0 (b[1]) RyanMoore 14 48
(Mrs A J Perrett) *s.i.s: sn rdn along in rr: sme prog u.p on inner jst over 2f out: no prog and wl btn 1f out* **7/1[3]**

2110 8 3 ¾ Lord Of The Storm[12] 6471 2-8-10 71 SophieDoyle(3) 3 40
(W G M Turner) *racd in midfield: rdn and no prog over 2f out: wl btn fnl 2f* **20/1**

0340 9 6 Red Jacaranda[25] 6129 2-8-2 50 FrannyNorton 6 15
(C A Dwyer) *a towards rr: swtchd rt and effrt over 2f out: no prog and wl btn fnl 2f* **25/1**

000 10 3 Blade Pirate[25] 6129 2-8-6 50 MarcHalford 9 12
(J Ryan) *sn pushed up to ld: hdd over 3f out: wknd u.p over 2f out: wl bhd and eased ins fnl f* **100/1**

650 11 1 ¾ Paris Is Burning[24] 6146 2-8-6 66 LukeMorris 13 8
(J S Moore) *hld up towards rr: rdn and no prog over 2f out: sn wl btn: eased ins fnl f* **14/1**

0000 12 2 ¾ Adzing (IRE)[41] 5630 2-8-9 45 JoeFanning 10 5
(R A Harris) *chsd ldrs tl rdn and wknd wl over 2f out: wl bhd and eased ins fnl f* **100/1**

66 13 27 Already Basking (CAN)[30] 5954 2-9-7 0 JamieSpencer 8 —
(P F I Cole) *wd and racd awkwardly: bhd fr 1/2-way: t.o and eased fnl 2f* **20/1**

1m 39.92s (0.12) **Going Correction** -0.10s/f (Stan) 13 Ran SP% **116.5**
Speed ratings (Par 95): **95,93,93,92,91 85,83,79,73,70 68,66,39**
Tote Swingers: 1&2 £6.80, 1&3 £6.20, 2&3 £2.00 CSF £31.71 TOTE £7.70: £3.00, £1.30, £1.10; EX 42.00.
Owner Mrs Ger O'Driscoll **Bred** Cathal & Paul McCarthy **Trained** Hambleton, N Yorks

FOCUS
A fair juvenile claimer in which, somewhat strangely, the action unfolded middle to stands' side. The runner-up is the best guide to the form.

NOTEBOOK
King Of Aquitaine(IRE) had lost his way on his last three starts, but the combination of the step up in trip, switch to Polytrack and fitting of blinkers clearly suited. He was a bit keen early, but still found plenty for pressure, despite ending up stands' side. Whether he can repeat this sort of form remains to be seen. (op 15-2 tchd 13-2)
Right Said Fred(IRE), upped in trip, switched to Polytrack and fitted with cheekpieces, plugged on without matching the winner's speed. (op 7-2)
Water Ice didn't handle going right-handed for the first time, losing ground when hanging on the bend and coming off the bridle before the straight. She would have been 7lb worse off with the winner in handicap. (op 5-2)
Kissing Clara(IRE), reported to have lost her action in the closing stages last time, didn't help herself by hanging left and was one-paced. (op 5-1)

Imaginary World(IRE), upped in trip, raced out the back after missing the break and got going too late to threaten. (op 22-1 tchd 25-1)

6796 BETDAQ.COM E B F MAIDEN FILLIES' STKS 6f (P)
3:25 (3:26) (Class 4) 2-Y-O £4,630 (£1,377; £688; £343) Stalls High

Form RPR

2 **1** **Googlette (IRE)**[136] 2505 2-9-0 0 JamieSpencer 1 85
(E F Vaughan) *led and crossed to rail: rdn ent fnl 2f: clr over 1f out: styd on wl* **13/8**[1]

606 **2** 2 ¼ **Strictly Pink (IRE)**[11] 6512 2-9-0 77 LukeMorris 8 78
(A Bailey) *chsd ldrs: rdn over 2f out: chsd clr wnr jst over 1f out: hrd drvn and kpt on same pce fnl f* **16/1**

3 1 **Sand Owl** 2-9-0 0 RyanMoore 4 75
(P W Chapple-Hyam) *in tch in midfield: rn green and hung lft bnd 4f out tl 3f out: rdn over 2f out: hdwy over 1f out: kpt on ins fnl f: nvr able to chal* **8/1**

4 ½ **Nabah** 2-9-0 0 NeilCallan 11 74
(C E Brittain) *wnt rt s: rdn and no prog over 2f out: hdwy u.p over 1f out: swtchd rt jst ins fnl f: gng on fin: nvr trbld ldrs* **33/1**

0244 **5** 3 ¼ **Grandmas Dream**[37] 5748 2-9-0 77 RichardHughes 3 64
(G C Bravery) *chsd wnr: rdn wl over 2f out: outpcd by wnr 2f out: lost 2nd jst over 1f out: wknd ins fnl f* **12/1**

6 nk **Dubai Queen (USA)** 2-9-0 0 KierenFallon 12 63
(L M Cumani) *hmpd leaving stalls and v.s.i.s: bhd: pushed along over 2f out: sme hdwy 2f out: no imp after: nvr trbld ldrs* **7/2**[2]

06 **7** 1 **Abeer (USA)**[21] 6248 2-9-0 0 RichardHills 6 60
(E A L Dunlop) *chsd ldrs: rdn and nt pce of wnr 2f out: edgd lft and wknd ent fnl f* **16/1**

62 **8** 3 ¾ **Les Verguettes (IRE)**[40] 5657 2-9-0 0 PatCosgrave 7 49
(Stef Higgins) *in tch: rdn ent fnl 3f: wknd u.p over 2f out* **9/2**[3]

0 **9** 6 **Piccolete**[24] 6146 2-9-0 0 FrannyNorton 10 31
(R Hannon) *a towards rr: n.d* **33/1**

10 ½ **Red Remanso (IRE)** 2-9-0 0 AdamKirby 5 29
(B W Hills) *s.i.s: a in rr* **50/1**

0 **11** ½ **Lucky Royale**[10] 6520 2-9-0 0 JamesDoyle 9 28
(S Kirk) *in tch in midfield: rdn and struggling 3f out: sn wknd* **100/1**

1m 12.25s (-0.85) **Going Correction** -0.10s/f (Stan) 11 Ran SP% **117.9**
Speed ratings (Par 94): **101,98,96,96,91 91,89,84,76,76 75**
Tote Swingers: 1&2 £10.00, 1&3 £3.80, 2&3 £26.90 CSF £31.58 TOTE £3.50: £2.20, £10.50, £2.60; EX 39.50.
Owner Pearl Bloodstock Ltd **Bred** Ged O'Leary **Trained** Newmarket, Suffolk

FOCUS
A fair fillies' maiden in which the runner-up set a pretty solid standard and the winner confirmed her good debut impresssion.

NOTEBOOK
Googlette(IRE) overcame both stall one and an absence of 136 days. She had had finished a good second on debut in a decent Newmarket maiden and showed she's gone the right way since then. There should be more to come. (op 2-1, tchd 9-4 in places)
Strictly Pink(IRE), trying Polytrack for the first time, seemed to have her chance and ran well. Officially rated 77, she helps give the form a solid look. (op 20-1, tchd 25-1 in a place)
Sand Owl, a 30,000gns purchase, ran green and didn't handle the bend all that well, losing ground. She ran on in the straight, though, showing plenty of ability, and should come on for this. (op 10-1)
Nabah, a 32,000gns purchase, out of a French 7f and 1m (Listed) juvenile winner, has been entered in Saturday's Rockfel. She raced off the pace following a sluggish start but finished well and should come on for the run. (op 28-1)
Grandmas Dream was well placed but finished tamely, now looking flattered by her official rating of 77. Official explanation: jockey said filly lost its action closing stages (tchd 11-1 and 14-1)
Dubai Queen(USA) ◆, a half-sister to top-class miler Dubawi, out of a high-class multiple 1m2f-1m3f winner, was very slowly away and ran green early before then swinging extremely wide into the straight. She should come on a great deal for the run. Official explanation: jockey said filly suffered interference at the start (op 9-4)
Les Verguettes(IRE) was nowhere near the form she showed when runner-up over C&D on her previous start. (op 7-1)

6797 BETDAQ THE BETTING EXCHANGE H'CAP 1m 4f (P)
4:00 (4:01) (Class 4) (0-85,85) 3-Y-O+ £3,885 (£1,156; £577; £288) Stalls Centre

Form RPR

50-0 **1** **Hendersyde (USA)**[31] 5922 5-9-11 82 AdamKirby 3 91
(W R Swinburn) *hld up in midfield: hdwy over 2f out: rdn to chse ldrs 2f out: led over 1f out: edgd rt u.p jst ins fnl f: styd on wl: rdn out* **16/1**

3513 **2** 1 **Sea Change (IRE)**[19] 6282 3-9-3 81 RichardHughes 1 88
(J Noseda) *chsd ldr after 1f: rdn to ld over 2f out: hdd and drvn over 1f out: styd on same pce u.p fnl f: edgd rt nr fin* **7/1**[3]

0400 **3** shd **Stand Guard**[14] 6428 6-9-7 81 AndrewHeffernan(3) 10 88
(P Howling) *in tch in midfield: effrt and rdn ent fnl 2f: swtchd rt and drvn to chse ldrs over 1f out: kpt on same pce fnl 100yds* **40/1**

-331 **4** 1 **Giants Play (USA)**[21] 6250 3-9-3 81 RyanMoore 13 87
(Sir Michael Stoute) *chsd ldrs: rdn to press ldrs ent fnl 2f: unable qck u.p over 1f out: one pce fnl f* **9/4**[1]

-323 **5** ½ **Ateeb**[17] 6331 4-9-2 73 (b[1]) RichardHills 7 78
(E A L Dunlop) *t.k.h: stdd after s: hld up towards rr: hdwy and swtchd lft jst over 2f out: chsd ldrs u.p ent fnl f: keeping on same pce and n.m.r fnl 100yds* **6/1**[2]

2063 **6** nk **Brouhaha**[18] 6312 6-9-10 81 RichardKingscote 2 85
(Tom Dascombe) *hld up towards rr: c wd and rdn over 2f out: kpt on wl u.p fnl f: nt rch ldrs* **20/1**

0006 **7** 1 **Franco Is My Name**[14] 6428 4-9-9 80 TomMcLaughlin 6 83
(P R Hedger) *short of room s: hld up in last trio: rdn and hdwy ent fnl 2f: swtchd rt and rdn over 1f out: kpt on same pce and no imp fnl f* **16/1**

303 **8** 9 **Aphrodisia**[14] 6427 6-9-3 74 JamieSpencer 8 62
(Ian Williams) *hld up in last trio: rdn and effrt over 2f out: no prog and wl btn over 1f out* **8/1**

2315 **9** 1 ¾ **Exemplary**[19] 6282 3-9-7 85 JoeFanning 12 71
(M Johnston) *in tch: rdn and unable qck over 2f out: wknd ent fnl 2f: wl btn over 1f out* **7/1**[3]

0400 **10** 1 ¼ **Kidlat**[110] 3318 5-9-6 77 MickyFenton 9 61
(A Bailey) *led tl rdn and hdd over 2f out: wknd wl over 1f out* **40/1**

0110 **11** 2 ¾ **Phoenix Flight (IRE)**[76] 3974 5-9-12 83 LeeVickers 4 62
(H J Evans) *stdd s: hld up in rr: rdn and no hdwy over 2f out: n.d* **25/1**

5313 **12** 9 **Silent Act (USA)**[60] 5008 4-9-5 76 NeilCallan 5 41
(Mrs A J Perrett) *wnt rt s: hld up in tch: rdn and unable qck ent fnl 3f: wknd over 2f out* **9/1**

1504 **13** 1 ¾ **Chalice Welcome**[12] 6449 7-9-10 81 GeorgeBaker 11 43
(N B King) *in tch: shuffled bk and dropped towards rr over 3f out: pushed along and no prog over 2f out: wl btn after* **14/1**

1340 **14** 19 **Jawaab (IRE)**[78] 4400 6-9-8 79 TedDurcan 14 —
(Mark Buckley) *chsd ldrs tl lost pl qckly 4f out: t.o and eased fnl 2f* **20/1**

2m 32.6s (-1.90) **Going Correction** -0.10s/f (Stan)
WFA 3 from 4yo+ 7lb 14 Ran SP% **127.8**
Speed ratings (Par 105): **102,101,101,100,100 100,99,93,92,91 89,83,82,69**
Tote Swingers: 1&2 £22.10, 1&3 £79.50, 2&3 £58.70 CSF £124.06 CT £4430.37 TOTE £28.20: £5.00, £2.00, £9.90; EX 211.30.
Owner P W Harris **Bred** Iron County Farms Inc **Trained** Aldbury, Herts

FOCUS
A fair handicap and they seemed to go an even gallop. The winner is rated back to last autumn's form.
Aphrodisia Official explanation: trainer said mare failed to stay mile and a half in higher grade
Chalice Welcome Official explanation: jockey said gelding had no more to give
Jawaab(IRE) Official explanation: jockey said gelding stopped quickly

6798 BET ASIAN H'CAPS - BETDAQ HANDICAP (DIV I) 6f (P)
4:30 (4:31) (Class 4) (0-85,88) 3-Y-O+ £3,561 (£1,059; £529; £264) Stalls High

Form RPR

5311 **1** **Green Park (IRE)**[7] 6625 7-9-6 88 6ex (b) NeilFarley(5) 6 101
(D Carroll) *chsd ldrs: rdn to ld wl over 1f out: r.o wl and a holding runner-up ins fnl f* **8/1**

1241 **2** nk **Barq (IRE)**[21] 6253 3-9-7 85 (tp) TedDurcan 4 97
(Saeed Bin Suroor) *chsd ldr: rdn and ev ch wl fr wl over 1f out: clr w wnr fnl f: a jst hld* **3/1**[1]

2616 **3** 4 ½ **Qudwah (IRE)**[83] 4231 3-9-5 83 RichardHills 11 81
(M A Jarvis) *hld up in midfield: rdn and hdwy jst over 2f out: chsd clr ldng pair jst over 1f out: no imp fnl f* **12/1**

4046 **4** ¾ **Rule Of Nature**[21] 6253 3-9-3 81 RyanMoore 2 76+
(Sir Michael Stoute) *sltly hmpd at s and s.i.s: bhd: rdn and hdwy jst over 2f out: kpt on: nvr trbld ldrs* **8/1**

3360 **5** 1 **Viking Spirit**[45] 5495 8-8-12 75 JamieSpencer 12 67
(W R Swinburn) *t.k.h: hld up in midfeld: effrt and swtchd rt 2f out: sn drvn: outpcd by ldng pair jst over 1f out: no ch fnl f* **13/2**[3]

4406 **6** 1 ¾ **Fivefold (USA)**[19] 6280 3-9-0 78 JoeFanning 5 64
(J Akehurst) *chsd ldrs on outer: rdn over 2f out: wknd ent fnl 2f* **25/1**

2-06 **7** 2 ½ **Al Gillani (IRE)**[29] 5995 5-9-5 82 PatCosgrave 7 60
(J R Boyle) *in tch: rdn and unable qck ent fnl 2f: wknd over 1f out* **16/1**

4263 **8** 2 ¼ **Quasi Congaree (GER)**[73] 4551 4-9-1 78 (t) GeorgeBaker 9 49
(I A Wood) *chsd ldrs: effrt and rdn to press ldrs wl over 1f out: sn outpcd: wknd jst over 1f out: wl btn and eased ins fnl f* **16/1**

5031 **9** 2 ¾ **Illustrious Prince (IRE)**[11] 6501 3-9-3 81 (v) RichardHughes 3 43
(J Noseda) *wnt lft s: sn swtchd rt: a bhd* **5/1**[2]

6260 **10** shd **Peter Island (FR)**[11] 6501 7-8-13 76 (v) AdamKirby 10 38
(J Gallagher) *led tl rdn and hdd wl over 1f out: sn fdd* **11/1**

1033 **11** nse **Duster**[20] 6274 3-9-2 80 SteveDrowne 1 42
(H Morrison) *a outpcd in rr* **14/1**

1m 11.19s (-1.91) **Going Correction** -0.10s/f (Stan)
WFA 3 from 4yo+ 1lb 11 Ran SP% **115.5**
Speed ratings (Par 105): **108,107,101,100,99 96,93,90,86,86 86**
Tote Swingers: 1&2 £5.00, 1&3 £19.60, 2&3 £10.90 CSF £31.56 CT £294.87 TOTE £5.30: £1.30, £1.10, £5.40; EX 29.40.
Owner G A Fixings Ltd **Bred** James Burns And A Moynan **Trained** Sledmere, E Yorks

FOCUS
A fair, competitive sprint handicap run at a strong pace and the time was 0.60 seconds quicker than the second division. A personal best from the in-form winner.
Illustrious Prince(IRE) Official explanation: jockey said gelding ran flat

6799 BET ASIAN H'CAPS - BETDAQ HANDICAP (DIV II) 6f (P)
5:00 (5:03) (Class 4) (0-85,84) 3-Y-O+ £3,561 (£1,059; £529; £264) Stalls High

Form RPR

5032 **1** **Swiss Cross**[23] 6198 3-9-1 79 (vt) NeilCallan 5 91
(G A Butler) *chsd ldrs: rdn to chal over 1f out: drvn ahd ins fnl f: styd on wl: rdn out* **4/1**[1]

4006 **2** 1 ¾ **Living It Large (FR)**[13] 6446 3-9-4 82 (b) TedDurcan 11 88
(R F Fisher) *led: rdn wl over 1f out: hdd ins fnl f: nt pce of wnr fnl 75yds* **11/1**

3662 **3** ¾ **Vhujon (IRE)**[10] 6537 5-8-10 78 AdamBeschizza(5) 2 82
(P D Evans) *in tch in midfield: rdn ent fnl 3f: kpt on u.p ins fnl f: nt pce to rch ldrs* **8/1**[3]

5105 **4** ½ **Baby Strange**[10] 6539 6-9-7 84 FrannyNorton 3 86
(D Shaw) *hld up towards rr: hdwy ent fnl 2f: sn rdn: kpt on steadily ins fnl f: nt rch ldrs* **10/1**

646 **5** nk **Requisite**[1] 6772 5-8-7 73 (v) SophieDoyle(3) 7 74
(I A Wood) *sn outpcd in rr: rdn 4f out: c wd over 2f out: r.o wl ins fnl f: nt rch ldrs* **16/1**

-014 **6** nk **Silaah**[24] 6140 6-9-6 83 (p) AdrianNicholls 4 83
(D Nicholls) *awkward s and s.i.s: bhd: swtchd ins and effrt ent fnl 2f: switching lft over 1f out: r.o fnl f: nt rch ldrs* **4/1**[1]

6005 **7** ¾ **Soap Wars**[23] 6198 5-9-5 82 RichardHughes 8 80
(J A Osborne) *chsd ldrs: rdn to press ldr wl over 1f out: btn jst over 1f out: wknd fnl f* **7/1**[2]

5000 **8** 3 ½ **Admiral Cochrane (IRE)**[68] 4699 3-9-2 80 JoeFanning 1 67
(W Jarvis) *a in rr: rdn 3f out: nvr trbld ldrs* **40/1**

4600 **9** nk **Sarah's Art (IRE)**[11] 6501 7-9-1 78 (t) PatCosgrave 6 64
(Stef Higgins) *towards rr: rdn and effrt over 2f out: nvr trbld ldrs* **20/1**

0500 **10** 2 **Clifton Bridge**[21] 6253 3-8-13 77 (b) RichardKingscote 10 57
(R M Beckett) *chsd ldr tl wl over 1f out: sn drvn and wknd* **16/1**

5130 **11** nse **Bahamian Lad**[41] 5647 5-9-3 80 (p) AdamKirby 9 59
(R Hollinshead) *in tch: rdn ent fnl 2f: wknd u.p over 1f out* **12/1**

2204 **12** 3 **Tasmeem (IRE)**[16] 6358 3-8-13 77 (b) TomEaves 12 47
(R A Fahey) *t.k.h early: hld up towards rr: hmpd over 4f out: rdn and no rspnse over 2f out: wl bhd over 1f out* **8/1**[3]

1m 11.79s (-1.31) **Going Correction** -0.10s/f (Stan)
WFA 3 from 5yo+ 1lb 12 Ran SP% **118.8**
Speed ratings (Par 105): **104,101,100,100,99 99,98,93,93,90 90,86**
Tote Swingers: 1&2 £9.20, 1&3 £6.20, 2&3 £18.60 CSF £49.78 CT £346.36 TOTE £4.70: £2.20, £2.10, £1.40; EX 46.70.
Owner A D Spence **Bred** Lordship Stud **Trained** Newmarket, Suffolk

FOCUS
The time was 0.60 seconds slower than the first division but the form looks sound enough despite a biggish step up from the winner.

6800 BET MULTIPLES - BETDAQ H'CAP (DIV I) 7f (P)
5:30 (5:33) (Class 5) (0-75,75) 3-Y-O+ **£1,944** (£574; £287) **Stalls** High

Form RPR

3136 **1** **Merchant Of Medici**[23] 6197 3-9-5 **75**........................ GeorgeBaker 12 86+
(W R Muir) *hld up in last trio: rdn 3f out: hdwy and nt clr run over 1f out tl gd hdwy ent fnl f: led ins fnl f: sn in command: eased nr fin* **4/1**[1]

1500 **2** *1 ¼* **Noble Greek (USA)**[10] 6524 3-8-10 **69**.................... KierenFox(3) 8 76
(J R Best) *hld up in tch: effrt and rdn ent fnl 2f: chsd ldr jst over 1f out: ev ch ins fnl f tl nt pce of wnr fnl 100yds* **50/1**

112 **3** *½* **Tislaam (IRE)**[19] 6292 3-8-12 **68**.....................(p) JamesDoyle 6 74
(A J McCabe) *chsd ldr over 5f out: led over 2f out: rdn wl over 1f out: hdd and nt pce of wnr ins fnl f* **15/2**

0020 **4** *1 ¾* **Fardyieh**[43] 5561 3-8-11 **67**.....................(t) NeilCallan 13 68
(C E Brittain) *towards rr: hdwy towards inner ent fnl 2f: chsd ldrs and drvn ent fnl f: styd on same pce after* **14/1**

42-0 **5** *shd* **Tuxedo**[30] 5964 5-9-2 **70**.................... WilliamCarson 5 72
(P W Hiatt) *in tch on outer: rdn and effrt over 2f out: styd on same pce u.p fr over 1f out* **16/1**

5022 **6** *1* **Hand Painted**[10] 6524 4-9-4 **72**.................... RichardHughes 14 71
(P J Makin) *in tch in midfield: rdn and effrt wl over 1f out: no real prog and kpt on same pce fnl f* **9/2**[2]

5300 **7** *¾* **Flip Flop (IRE)**[26] 6090 3-9-5 **75**.................... SteveDrowne 10 71
(B W Hills) *chsd ldrs: rdn and unable qck jst over 2f out: one pce and no threat to ldrs fr over 1f out* **12/1**

4233 **8** *nk* **Desert Icon (IRE)**[19] 6280 4-8-8 **69**.....................(v) HarryBentley(7) 2 65
(W J Knight) *stdd and swtchd rt after s: hld up towards rr: hdwy into midfield 1/2-way: rdn and effrt over 2f out: no prog and no threat to ldrs fnl 2f* **14/1**

0600 **9** *1 ¾* **Gallantry**[14] 6430 8-9-4 **75**.................... MichaelStainton(3) 3 67
(P Howling) *s.i.s: sn bustled along in rr: sme prog wl over 1f out: nvr trbld ldrs* **14/1**

3223 **10** *½* **George Benjamin**[7] 6622 3-9-5 **75**.................... AdrianNicholls 9 64
(D Nicholls) *led tl over 5f out: chsd ldrs after: rdn and effrt towards inner ent fnl 2f: wknd jst over 1f out* **11/2**[3]

3000 **11** *3 ¾* **Best Trip (IRE)**[30] 5964 3-9-0 **70**.................... FrannyNorton 4 49
(R C Guest) *chsd ldr tl led and crossed to rail over 5f out: rdn and hdd over 2f out: wknd qckly over 1f out: wl bhd and eased ins fnl f* **33/1**

4244 **12** *6* **Billberry**[26] 6098 5-9-2 **70**.....................(vt) RyanMoore 7 34
(S C Williams) *hld up in rr: rdn and no rspnse over 2f out: n.d* **12/1**

1455 **13** *3* **Cuthbert (IRE)**[30] 5968 3-9-3 **73**.....................(p) JoeFanning 11 28
(W Jarvis) *in tch in midfield: rdn and lost pl jst over 2f out: bhd over 1f out: eased ins fnl f* **10/1**

1m 25.07s (-0.93) **Going Correction** -0.10s/f (Stan)
WFA 3 from 4yo+ 2lb **13** Ran SP% **120.6**
Speed ratings (Par 103): **101,99,99,97,96 95,94,94,92,91 87,80,77**
Tote Swingers: 1&2 £39.20, 1&3 £9.60, 2&3 £57.50 CSF £207.32 CT £1514.43 TOTE £9.20: £2.50, £16.50, £1.90; EX 352.40.
Owner S Jones & R Haim **Bred** Cheveley Park Stud Ltd **Trained** Lambourn, Berks

FOCUS
A modest handicap run at a good pace. The time was 0.07 seconds quicker than the second division. A 5lb best from the winner, woth the third looking the best guide.

6801 BET MULTIPLES - BETDAQ H'CAP (DIV II) 7f (P)
6:00 (6:02) (Class 5) (0-75,75) 3-Y-O+ **£1,944** (£574; £287) **Stalls** High

Form RPR

4345 **1** **Sheer Force (IRE)**[23] 6208 3-9-2 **72**.....................(v) NeilCallan 12 81
(W J Knight) *in tch in midfield: n.m.r over 2f out: rdn and gd hdwy over 1f out: led ins fnl f: r.o wl* **14/1**

5603 **2** *1 ¼* **Tiger Star**[10] 6540 3-8-11 **67**.................... TomMcLaughlin 5 73
(J M P Eustace) *s.i.s: sn bustled along in rr: hdwy on outer over 2f out: drvn and ev ch jst over 1f out tl nt pce of wnr fnl 100yds: kpt on* **6/1**[2]

-350 **3** *shd* **Slugger O'Toole**[7] 6629 5-9-5 **73**.....................(v) WilliamCarson 2 80
(S C Williams) *short of room s and s.i.s: bhd: rdn and effrt on outer over 2f out: hdwy to chse ldrs jst over 1f out: kpt on u.p fnl f: wnt 3rd last stride* **14/1**

5531 **4** *½* **Smart Endeavour (USA)**[16] 6371 4-9-3 **71**.....................(v) AdamKirby 13 76
(W R Swinburn) *hld up in tch: effrt and swtchd ins ent fnl 2f: drvn to ld over 1f out: hdd and nt pce of wnr fnl 100yds: lost 2 pls after* **10/3**[1]

0025 **5** *½* **Army Of Stars (IRE)**[11] 6503 4-9-4 **75**.....................(p) SophieDoyle(3) 1 79
(J A Osborne) *wnt rt s: in tch: rdn over 2f out: drvn to chse ldrs over 1f out: no ex and one pce ins fnl f* **8/1**

2030 **6** *1* **Gazboolou**[26] 6085 6-9-0 **71**.................... KierenFox(3) 4 72
(David Pinder) *towards rr: nt clr run over 2f out: hdwy over 1f out: kpt on u.p fnl f: nt rch ldrs* **25/1**

3210 **7** *hd* **Harting Hill**[9] 6580 5-8-12 **66**.................... RyanMoore 9 67
(M P Tregoning) *in rr: nt clr run and detached over 2f out: plenty to do and switching lft ent fnl 2f: r.o wl fnl f: nt rch ldrs* **13/2**[3]

4324 **8** *1* **Pan American**[10] 6523 3-9-4 **74**.................... RichardHughes 7 71
(P J Makin) *in tch: rdn and effrt ent fnl 2f: kpt on same pce fr over 1f out* **10/1**

550 **9** *¾* **Chilli Green**[121] 2968 3-9-1 **71**.................... JamieMackay 6 66
(J Akehurst) *led: rdn and hdd over 1f out: btn whn n.m.r jst ins fnl f: wknd after* **40/1**

0112 **10** *½* **Tukitinyasok (IRE)**[47] 5421 3-9-2 **72**.....................(p) TomEaves 3 66
(R F Fisher) *chsd ldr over 5f out: rdn over 2f out: btn jst over 1f out: wknd fnl f* **6/1**[2]

0400 **11** *2 ¼* **Step In Time (IRE)**[15] 6394 3-9-0 **70**.................... JoeFanning 8 58
(M Johnston) *sn bustled along to chse ldrs: wknd u.p wl over 1f out* **25/1**

6505 **12** *5* **Victorian Bounty**[10] 6524 5-9-5 **73**.....................(p) MickyFenton 10 48
(Stef Higgins) *plld hrd: chsd ldrs: losing pl and swtchd rt jst over 2f out: wknd wl over 1f out* **16/1**

1m 25.14s (-0.86) **Going Correction** -0.10s/f (Stan)
WFA 3 from 4yo+ 2lb **12** Ran SP% **114.5**
Speed ratings (Par 103): **100,98,98,97,97 96,95,94,93,93 90,85**
Tote Swingers: 1&2 £20.30, 1&3 £24.60, 2&3 £24.60. totesuper7: Win: Not won. Place: Not won. CSF £90.75 CT £1220.82 TOTE £11.40: £8.30, £3.60, £5.80; EX 113.20 Place 6: £265.92 Place 5: £55.31..
Owner Bluehills Racing Limited **Bred** Victor Stud Bloodstock Ltd **Trained** Patching, W Sussex

FOCUS
The time was only fractionally slower than the first division. The form looks best rated around the runner-up.
T/Plt: £101.90 to a £1 stake. Pool of £58,547. 419.24 winning tickets. T/Qpdt: £44.80 to a £1 stake. Pool of £4,590. 75.80 winning tickets. SP

6473 SALISBURY (R-H)
Monday, October 11

OFFICIAL GOING: Good to soft (soft for first 100yds in 7f races and in the dip at 2.5f; 7.5)
Wind: mild breeze behind Weather: sunny

6802 BATHWICK TYRES MAIDEN AUCTION STKS 6f 212y
2:10 (2:11) (Class 5) 2-Y-O **£2,914** (£867; £433; £216) **Stalls** High

Form RPR

1 **Chef** 2-8-13 0.................... JimmyFortune 1 79
(A M Balding) *trckd ldrs: chal 2f out: sn rdn: led narrowly ins fnl f: kpt on wl: drvn out* **6/1**[3]

32 **2** *hd* **Songsmith**[24] 6158 2-8-13 0.................... JimCrowley 11 78
(Mrs L Wadham) *disp ld: rdn over 1f out: kpt on gamely whn narrowly hdd ins fnl f: jst hld* **2/1**[1]

4255 **3** *2 ¾* **Standout**[12] 6471 2-8-10 66.................... DaneO'Neill 2 68
(R Hannon) *hld up towards rr: hdwy 3f out: rdn to chse ldrs 2f out: kpt on ins fnl f* **7/1**

336 **4** *nk* **Sylas Ings**[42] 5587 2-8-11 78.................... JackMitchell 12 68
(P M Phelan) *disp ld: rdn 3f out: kpt holding ev ch tl fnl 100yds: no ex: lost 3rd nr fin* **4/1**[2]

0235 **5** *½* **Looksmart**[18] 6309 2-8-8 72.................... FrankieMcDonald 5 64
(R Hannon) *chsd ldrs: rdn over 2f out: kpt on same pce* **14/1**

30 **6** *1* **Heart In Motion (IRE)**[16] 6369 2-8-6 0.................... ChrisCatlin 3 59
(M R Channon) *mid-div: rdn and no imp 2f out: kpt on ins fnl f* **10/1**

7 *1 ¼* **Ice Nelly (IRE)** 2-8-7 0 ow1.................... SteveDrowne 10 57
(H Morrison) *s.i.s: towards rr: pushed along 3f out: hdwy 2f out: no further imp fnl f* **10/1**

8 *6* **Noble Defender** 2-8-7 0.................... JohnFahy(5) 9 46
(W S Kittow) *mid-div: rdn 3f out: wknd over 1f out* **25/1**

6 **9** *dht* **Matavia Bay (IRE)**[94] 3842 2-8-9 0.................... RichardMullen 4 43
(A P Jarvis) *mid-div: rdn over 2f out: wknd over 1f out* **33/1**

65 **10** *¾* **Iron Green (FR)**[19] 6278 2-8-10 0.................... HayleyTurner 7 43
(Mrs H S Main) *a towards rr* **20/1**

00 **11** *1 ¼* **Our Folly**[91] 3964 2-8-11 0.................... LiamKeniry 8 40
(W S Kittow) *trckd ldrs: rdn over 2f out: sn wknd* **150/1**

12 *¾* **Blue Maisey** 2-8-4 0.................... JimmyQuinn 6 31
(Miss S L Davison) *s.i.s: a towards rr* **100/1**

1m 30.56s (1.56) **Going Correction** +0.075s/f (Good) **12** Ran SP% **118.2**
Speed ratings (Par 95): **94,93,90,90,89 88,87,80,80,79 78,77**
Tote Swingers: 1&2 £4.10, 1&3 £6.50, 2&3 £3.70 CSF £17.57 TOTE £6.60: £2.20, £1.10, £2.00; EX 14.80.
Owner Brook Farm Bloodstock **Bred** Bloomsbury Stud **Trained** Kingsclere, Hants

FOCUS
Although the ground had dried out since the previous meeting, the going was still good to soft with soft patches. The stands' rail was dolled out considerably, leaving the track relatively narrow all the way up the straight and they raced towards the far side. The jockeys reported that the ground was sticky. A fair maiden auction stakes and the form appears sound.

NOTEBOOK
Chef ◆, from a good Bloomsbury Stud family and by a soft-ground sire, overcame having to race on the outside of his field throughout to gain a narrow victory. He travelled well into contention and, after striking the front entering the last furlong, stuck on under pressure to hold off a more experienced opponent. He has a Racing Post Trophy and Derby entry, so is clearly well thought-of, and looks the type to make up into a decent 3-y-o. (op 5-1 tchd 7-1)
Songsmith had been placed in maidens on good and soft ground and helped set the standard. Always close up, he had every chance but could not find a change of gear despite doing nothing wrong. He looks as though further will suit and he now qualifies for handicaps. (op 5-2)
Standout had posted modest efforts in five previous starts but looked a big threat when coming to challenge inside the final 2f. He could not sustain his effort though, and faded in the last furlong. A return to handicaps looks in order. (op 15-2 tchd 8-1)
Sylas Ings had put up fair efforts in maidens at six to 7f on a sound surface. Despite being trotted up at the start he ran a decent race from the front, only giving way inside the last 2f. He was beaten when he jinked near the line. (op 5-1 tchd 7-2)
Looksmart, placed three times in five starts, all over 6f on fast ground, helped set the standard off 72 but, up in trip and trying soft ground for the first time, she ran well enough having been close up throughout. She could not quicken in the ground but still finished on the heels of the placed horses, getting a bump from the fourth near the line. (tchd 12-1)
Heart In Motion(IRE) made a promising debut over 6f on Polytrack, but failed to build on it over 5f at same track next time. Up in trip for this turf debut, she was noted staying on in the closing stages and now qualifies for a handicap mark. (op 12-1)
Ice Nelly(IRE), from the family of Flying Nelly but retained cheaply at the sales, was slowly away but stayed on steadily from halfway and should come on a fair amount for the experience. (op 9-1)

6803 BATHWICK TYRES MAIDEN FILLIES' STKS (DIV I) 6f 212y
2:40 (2:43) (Class 5) 2-Y-O **£2,590** (£770; £385; £192) **Stalls** High

Form RPR

1 **Pandorea** 2-9-0 0.................... DaneO'Neill 8 79+
(H Candy) *mde all: r.o wl fnl f: readily* **6/1**[3]

2 **2** *1* **Desert Shine (IRE)**[11] 6511 2-9-0 0.................... HayleyTurner 7 76
(M L W Bell) *trckd wnr: rdn over 2f out: kpt on but a being readily hld by wnr fnl f* **2/1**[1]

3 *3 ½* **Follow My Dream** 2-9-0 0.................... WilliamBuick 11 67
(J H M Gosden) *trckd ldrs: rdn over 2f out: kpt on same pce* **4/1**[2]

4 *¾* **Tanassuq (USA)** 2-9-0 0.................... TadhgO'Shea 6 65
(J L Dunlop) *trckd ldrs: rdn over 3f out: kpt on same pce fnl 2f* **14/1**

5 *nse* **Mafeteng** 2-9-0 0.................... JimmyFortune 9 65
(J L Dunlop) *little slowly away: mid-div: rdn over 2f out: styd on ins fnl f* **25/1**

6 *1 ¼* **Mrs Dee Bee (IRE)** 2-9-0 0.................... MichaelHills 12 62
(B W Hills) *mid-div: rdn over 2f out: kpt on same pce* **10/1**

7 *nse* **Destiny Of Dreams** 2-9-0 0.................... LiamKeniry 4 61
(Miss Jo Crowley) *mid-div: rdn over 2f out: no imp* **33/1**

0 **8** *3 ½* **Teazel**[13] 6443 2-9-0 0.................... SteveDrowne 3 52
(D J S Ffrench Davis) *trckd ldrs: rdn over 2f out: wknd ent fnl f* **33/1**

9 *hd* **Secoya** 2-9-0 0.................... JimCrowley 5 52
(R M Beckett) *s.i.s: towards rr: swtchd lft over 2f out: sn rdn: no imp* **14/1**

10 *nse* **Striking Veil (USA)** 2-9-0 0.................... RichardMullen 1 52
(Sir Michael Stoute) *mid-div: rdn over 2f out: wknd fnl f* **11/1**

11 *4 ½* **Border Abby** 2-9-0 0.................... DavidProbert 10 40
(Rae Guest) *s.i.s: a towards rr* **20/1**

12 *1* **Melody Belle (IRE)** 2-9-0 0 ChrisCatlin 2 37
(T B P Coles) *s.i.s: towards rr: effrt 3f out: wknd over 1f out* **50/1**

1m 31.87s (2.87) **Going Correction** +0.075s/f (Good) **12** Ran SP% **114.8**
Speed ratings (Par 92): **86,84,80,80,79 78,78,74,74,74 69,67**
Tote Swingers: 1&2 £3.70, 1&3 £5.90, 2&3 £3.00 CSF £16.62 TOTE £7.10: £2.70, £1.10, £1.30.

Owner Girsonfield Ltd **Bred** Girsonfield Ltd **Trained** Kingston Warren, Oxon

FOCUS

Last year's winner of this fillies' maiden had previous experience but only two in today's line-up had run, and each of those just the once. The time was 1.31secs slower than the opening race.

NOTEBOOK

Pandorea ♦, the first foal of a 7f winner from the family of Gorse, who won on his debut at this track, clearly knew her job on this debut and made all the running. She came away in quite impressive style and looks sure to go on from this, although she might need the ground on the soft side to produce her best. (op 9-1)

Desert Shine(IRE) made a promising debut over 7f on soft ground and was never far away. However, she had nothing in reserve when the winner picked up from the front, although she was clear of the rest. She should win one of these before long. (tchd 7-4 and 9-4)

Follow My Dream, a half-sister to Pipedreamer from a good Cheveley Park Stud family, was always in the leading group but could only stay on at one pace in the last 2f. She should be better for the experience. (op 7-2)

Tanassuq(USA), a half-sister to seven winners including Bahri and Bahhare, stayed on from off the pace despite not looking totally suited by the soft ground. (op 12-1 tchd 16-1)

Mafeteng, the third foal of a 1m4f-1m6f Listed winner from the family of Petoski, finished strongly from the rear on this debut and should make up into a fair sort over middle-distances next season. (op 16-1)

Mrs Dee Bee(IRE), a 32,000euros half-sister to winners at 6f/7f and a stayer, chased the leaders throughout and is another who will appreciate further next year. (tchd 9-1 and 12-1)

Destiny Of Dreams, a 28,000gns half-sister to a 5f AW winner, ran a decent race on this debut and could be interesting on Polytrack next time. (tchd 28-1)

6804 BATHWICK TYRES MAIDEN FILLIES' STKS (DIV II) 6f 212y

3:15 (3:16) (Class 5) 2-Y-O **£2,590** (£770; £385; £192) **Stalls** High

Form RPR

1 **Flood Plain** 2-9-0 0 WilliamBuick 5 80+
(J H M Gosden) *trckd ldrs: rdn to ld narrowly over 1f out: r.o wl to assert fnl 100yds: readily* **5/1**[3]

3 2 *1¾* **Super (IRE)**[13] 6441 2-9-0 0 HayleyTurner 6 75
(R Hannon) *trckd ldrs: rdn and ev ch over 1f out: nt pce of wnr fnl 100yds but drew clr of remainder* **10/3**[1]

2 3 *6* **Celani**[12] 6451 2-9-0 0 ChrisCatlin 2 59
(Andrew Turnell) *hld up towards rr: hdwy over 2f out: sn rdn: styd on same pce fnl f* **11/2**

4 *½* **Misty Isles** 2-9-0 0 LiamKeniry 4 58
(Mrs H S Main) *s.i.s: sn mid-div: swtchd lft over 2f out: sn rdn: r.o wl ins fnl f* **50/1**

5 *1* **Amerthyst** 2-9-0 0 DaneO'Neill 12 56
(Miss Jo Crowley) *led: rdn and hdd over 1f out: sn hld: fdd fnl 75yds and lost 2 pls* **20/1**

6 *1½* **Zafaraan** 2-9-0 0 JimmyFortune 3 52
(P W Chapple-Hyam) *trckd ldrs: rdn over 2f out: kpt on same pce* **16/1**

7 *4* **Carousel** 2-9-0 0 JimCrowley 11 41
(R M Beckett) *little s.i.s: sn trcking ldrs: lost pl whn pushed along over 3f out: nvr bk on terms: wknd 1f out* **4/1**[2]

8 *3* **Miss Topsy Turvy (IRE)** 2-9-0 0 JimmyQuinn 8 33
(J L Dunlop) *s.i.s: mainly towards rr* **8/1**

9 *½* **Plug In Baby** 2-8-11 0 RobertLButler(3) 7 32
(Nick Mitchell) *nvr bttr than mid-div* **100/1**

4 10 *nk* **Dancerella**[45] 5488 2-9-0 0 PhilipRobinson 1 31
(D R C Elsworth) *trckd ldrs: rdn over 3f out: wknd 2f out* **8/1**

11 *9* **Queen Carmel (IRE)** 2-9-0 0 TadhgO'Shea 10 8
(B J Meehan) *s.i.s: sn pushed along: bhd fnl 3f* **20/1**

6 12 *1* **Sue's Dream**[34] 5836 2-9-0 0 RichardMullen 9 —
(A P Jarvis) *towards rr of midfield tl wknd wl over 2f out* **50/1**

1m 30.5s (1.50) **Going Correction** +0.075s/f (Good) **12** Ran SP% **117.7**
Speed ratings (Par 92): **94,92,85,84,83 81,77,73,73,72 62,61**
Tote Swingers: 1&2 £3.50, 1&3 £5.10, 2&3 £3.00 CSF £20.77 TOTE £4.00: £1.20, £1.30, £3.20; EX 19.30.

Owner K Abdulla **Bred** Juddmonte Farms Ltd **Trained** Newmarket, Suffolk

FOCUS

The second leg of this fillies' maiden and again the majority were making their debuts. The time was the best of the three juvenile races.

NOTEBOOK

Flood Plain ♦, a half-sister to winners at 7f and 1m out of a miler from a good Juddmonte family, was prominent throughout on this debut. She drew away when put under pressure, and looks the sort who can go on to better things.

Super(IRE), a 60,000euros purchase, raced off the pace after starting slowly but finished well on debut over 6f on good. She tracked the leader from the start and, although she had to wait for a gap, got out on plenty of time and was upsides the winner entering the final furlong. She found that rival too strong in the end but was clear of the rest, and there are races to be won with her. (tchd 7-2)

Celani, a daughter of the lightly raced 2002 Derby fourth Jelani out of a mare that won at two, made a promising debut over 7f on Polytrack. She moved up to join the leaders over 2f out but was unable to go with the principals soon afterwards. She looks to have the scope to make a decent 3-y-o. (op 4-1)

Misty Isles, a half-sister to winners at varying trips out of a smart 7f winner, missed the break but was soon tracking the leaders and stayed on nicely in the closing stages. (op 80-1)

Amerthyst, a cheaply bought half-sister to winners at six and 7f, made much of the running and, although unable to hold on in the closing stages, looks capable of more that paying her way. (op 25-1)

Zafaraan, a half-sister to a 7f 3-y-o winner out of a mare who was a half-sister to four juvenile winners, ran a nice race and can be expected to build on this. (op 14-1)

Carousel, a homebred half-sister to a 1m winner at three out of 1m-1m2f winner in Italy, was very well backed but was in trouble at halfway before keeping on in the closing stages. She had clearly been showing something at home and better can be expected next time. (op 10-1)

6805 BATHWICK TYRES BOURNEMOUTH H'CAP 6f 212y

3:45 (3:48) (Class 4) (0-85,85) 3-Y-O **£4,209** (£1,252; £625; £312) **Stalls** High

Form RPR

1034 1 **Sard**[39] 5677 3-8-11 **75** PhilipRobinson 10 88
(M A Jarvis) *mde all: rdn clr over 1f out: styd on strly: comf* **12/1**

1140 2 *3¼* **Imperial Delight**[12] 6478 3-9-4 **82** DaneO'Neill 1 86
(H Candy) *hld up towards rr: hdwy over 3f out: rdn over 2f out: chsd wnr over 1f out: drifted rt: kpt on but no ch* **11/1**

2534 3 *1½* **First Cat**[15] 6391 3-9-7 **85** FrankieMcDonald 11 85
(R Hannon) *s.i.s: bhd: hdwy whn swtchd lft 2f out: sn rdn: wnt 3rd ent fnl f: kpt on but no ch w front pair* **9/2**[3]

3503 4 *2½* **Kurtanella**[34] 5834 3-9-0 **78** JimmyFortune 6 71
(R Hannon) *hld up towards rr: no imp u.str.p whn hmpd over 2f out: swtchd lft: styd on ins fnl f: wnt 4th nr fin* **14/1**

4014 5 *½* **Spa's Dancer (IRE)**[23] 6197 3-9-1 **79** FrankieDettori 7 71
(J W Hills) *awkward leaving stalls: sn mid-div: rdn over 2f out: styd on same pce* **7/2**[1]

4002 6 *1¼* **Kings Bayonet**[20] 6274 3-9-3 **81** WilliamBuick 8 70
(H R A Cecil) *trckd ldrs: rdn over 2f out: wknd jst over 1f out* **4/1**[2]

P010 7 *1¾* **En Fuego**[23] 6197 3-9-0 **78** JackMitchell 4 62
(P W Chapple-Hyam) *mid-div: rdn over 2f out: wknd fnl f* **33/1**

2144 8 *6* **Touch Tone**[19] 6291 3-9-0 **78** MichaelHills 12 46
(B W Hills) *trckd ldrs: rdn over 2f out: sn wknd* **8/1**

1060 9 *½* **Perfect Ch'I (IRE)**[23] 6212 3-8-3 **72** JohnFahy(5) 3 38
(I A Wood) *s.i.s: mid-div on outer: rdn 3f out: wknd over 1f out* **20/1**

0040 10 *8* **Water Gipsy**[27] 6057 3-8-7 **71** oh1 (p) LiamKeniry 2 16
(G L Moore) *hld up and a bhd* **33/1**

4565 11 *¾* **Burghley**[33] 5861 3-9-0 **78** RichardMullen 5 21
(M L W Bell) *mid-div: rdn over 3f out: wknd over 2f out* **17/2**

5300 12 *¾* **Lenkiewicz**[16] 6351 3-8-10 **74** TadhgO'Shea 9 15
(B R Millman) *trckd wnr: rdn over 2f out: wknd over 1f out* **22/1**

1m 28.98s (-0.02) **Going Correction** +0.075s/f (Good) **12** Ran SP% **119.7**
Speed ratings (Par 103): **103,99,97,94,94 92,90,83,83,74 73,72**
Tote Swingers: 1&2 £11.10, 1&3 £12.90, 2&3 £17.30 CSF £131.86 CT £701.07 TOTE £18.60: £3.60, £4.40, £1.50; EX 178.00.

Owner Tony Bloom **Bred** Jeremy Green And Sons **Trained** Newmarket, Suffolk

FOCUS

A fair 3-y-o handicap and the time was over 1.5secs faster than the quickest of the juvenile races. The winner improved for a change of tactics, with the runner-up the best guide.

Burghley Official explanation: jockey said gelding was unsuited by the good to soft ground

6806 BATHWICK TYRES FREE ADMISSION RACEDAY CONDITIONS STKS 6f 212y

4:20 (4:20) (Class 2) 3-Y-O+

£8,723 (£2,612; £1,306; £653; £326; £163) **Stalls** High

Form RPR

3312 1 **Secrecy**[37] 5741 4-9-5 110 FrankieDettori 7 108+
(Saeed Bin Suroor) *hld up in last pair but in tch: nt clr run briefly 2f out: swtchd lft over 1f out: led ins fnl f: nudged out: cleverly* **1/2**[1]

2100 2 *¾* **Balducci**[30] 5948 3-9-0 96 JimmyFortune 2 102
(A M Balding) *chsd ldr: rdn to chal over 1f out: ev ch ins fnl f: hld nring fin* **9/1**[3]

3500 3 *2¼* **Nasri**[31] 5911 4-9-2 92 WilliamBuick 1 97
(D M Simcock) *hld up last but in tch: rdn 2f out: no imp tl r.o ins fnl f: wnt 3rd nr fin* **16/1**

0041 4 *1* **Carnaby Street (IRE)**[9] 6564 3-9-5 102 DaneO'Neill 6 98
(R Hannon) *trckd ldrs: rdn 2f out: kpt on but nt pce to chal* **11/2**[2]

0060 5 *hd* **Prince Of Dance**[24] 6147 4-9-7 98 LiamKeniry 5 99
(J R Gask) *led: rdn over 1f out: hdd jst ins fnl f: no ex whn lost 2 pls nr fin* **14/1**

2020 6 *nk* **Layline (IRE)**[18] 6312 3-9-0 88 (b) JimCrowley 4 92
(R M Beckett) *racd keenly: trckd ldrs: rdn 2f out: hung rt: kpt on same pce* **28/1**

1m 29.24s (0.24) **Going Correction** +0.075s/f (Good)
WFA 3 from 4yo 2lb **6** Ran SP% **108.0**
Speed ratings (Par 109): **101,100,97,96,96 95**
Tote Swingers: 1&2 £1.40, 1&3 £3.50, 2&3 £4.80 CSF £5.18 TOTE £1.30: £1.50, £1.20; EX 5.70.

Owner Godolphin **Bred** Whatton Manor Stud **Trained** Newmarket, Suffolk

FOCUS

A good conditions stakes not far short of Listed class and a comfortable success for the favourite. The time was 0.26secs slower than the preceding handicap. The form is not the most solid and the winner did not need to be at his best.

NOTEBOOK

Secrecy, a consistent sort who is effective on any ground, was held up in the rear before picking up nicely when a gap appeared, and ultimately won cosily, as the ratings suggested he should. He finished behind a subsequent Group 3 winner last time and looks up to winning at Listed level. (op 4-7 tchd 4-6 in places)

Balducci, having his first try on ground softer than good, ran well and did his best to give the winner a race. He seems to be back in form and, already proven on Polytrack, might find an opening on that surface. (tchd 10-1)

Nasri has been hit and miss this season after good efforts in Pattern company last year. This was better and small fields seem to suit him best.

Carnaby Street(IRE), a narrow winner at Newmarket last time, likes soft ground but was under pressure some way out and might have found this going too sticky. (op 9-2)

Prince Of Dance has struggled to capture last year's form but likes soft ground and ran a fair race from the front. (op 12-1)

Layline(IRE) had a lot to do on the ratings and did not help his chance by being too keen early on. (op 22-1 tchd 33-1)

6807 BATHWICK TYRES ANDOVER H'CAP 1m 1f 198y

4:50 (4:51) (Class 4) (0-85,80) 3-Y-O+ **£4,209** (£1,252; £625; £312) **Stalls** High

Form RPR

1100 1 **Rosco Flyer (IRE)**[32] 5888 4-9-2 **72** DaneO'Neill 5 81
(R A Teal) *hld up in last pair but in tch: hdwy 3f out: rdn 2f out: styd on ins fnl f: drifted rt: led fnl strides* **12/1**

0312 2 *hd* **Captain Dancer (IRE)**[5] 6677 4-9-9 **79** MichaelHills 6 88
(B W Hills) *trckd ldrs: rdn to ld ins fnl f: kpt on but edgd lft: hdd fnl strides* **11/8**[1]

1123 3 *1¼* **Rock The Stars (IRE)**[14] 6422 3-8-0 **66** AmyScott(5) 4 72
(J W Hills) *trckd ldrs: rdn over 2f out: kpt on ins fnl f: cl 3rd but hld whn short of room nring fin* **15/2**

-033 4 *1¼* **Pittodrie Star (IRE)**[9] 6556 3-8-9 **70** (p) DavidProbert 7 75
(A M Balding) *sn led: rdn 2f out: sn narrowly hdd: kpt on w ev ch: hung lft ins fnl f: hld nring fin* **4/1**[2]

100 5 *3¼* **Kensei (IRE)**[52] 5266 3-8-13 **74** JimCrowley 1 74
(R M Beckett) *trckd ldr: rdn to ld narrowly over 1f out: hdd ins fnl f: disputing cl 4th but hld whn squeezed out towards fin* **9/2**[3]

3110 **6** 7 **Ashkalara**[16] 6361 3-8-6 **67** JimmyQuinn 3 50
(H S Howe) *hld up in last pair but in tch: effrt over 2f out: wknd over 1f out* **15/2**

2m 12.36s (2.46) **Going Correction** +0.30s/f (Good)
WFA 3 from 4yo+ 5lb 6 Ran SP% **111.5**
Speed ratings (Par 105): **102,101,100,99,97 91**
Tote Swingers: 1&2 £3.90, 1&3 £5.90, 2&3 £2.40 CSF £28.86 CT £133.40 TOTE £11.50: £5.50, £1.70; EX 27.60.
Owner Chris Simpson, Miss Elizabeth Ross **Bred** Ms Amy Mulligan **Trained** Ashtead, Surrey

FOCUS
A fair handicap in which the pace was not strong and five of the six were abreast over 1f out. The runners came quite close in the closing stages. The first two are rated to form.
Pittodrie Star(IRE) Official explanation: jockey said gelding hung left-handed

6808 BATHWICK TYRES "SEASON FINALE" H'CAP 1m 6f 21y
5:20 (5:21) (Class 3) (0-95,93) 3-Y-0+ **£6,476** (£1,927; £963; £481)

Form RPR
4200 **1** **Woolfall Treasure**[16] 6352 5-10-0 **93** (v) WilliamBuick 12 102
(G L Moore) *trckd ldr: c wdst of all in centre over 3f out: rdn to ld over 2f out: edgd lft: styd on wl to draw clr fnl f* **11/1**

0461 **2** 4 1/2 **Lethal Glaze (IRE)**[9] 6565 4-9-13 **92** DaneO'Neill 11 95
(R Hannon) *trckd ldrs: c down centre fr over 3f out: rdn wl over 2f out: sn chsng wnr: styd on but wl hld ent fnl f* **8/1**[3]

5432 **3** 1 1/4 **Dakiyah (IRE)**[60] 5002 6-9-2 **81** (p) JimCrowley 9 82
(Mrs L J Mongan) *trckd ldrs: rdn and ch over 2f out: styd on same pce fr over 1f out* **8/1**[3]

6010 **4** nk **Crocus Rose**[31] 5908 4-9-0 **79** JimmyQuinn 6 80
(H J L Dunlop) *mid-div: rdn 3f out: hdwy over 2f out: styd on wout threatening* **20/1**

0-01 **5** 2 **It's A Date**[162] 1736 5-9-6 **85** FergusSweeney 7 83
(A King) *led: rdn 3f out: hdd over 2f out: sn one pce* **13/2**[2]

1060 **6** 1 **Final Victory**[15] 6387 4-9-9 **88** (v[1]) LiamKeniry 1 84
(A M Balding) *hld up towards rr: rdn wl over 2f out: no imp tl styd on fnl f: nvr trbld ldrs* **14/1**

0600 **7** 5 **Perfect Shot (IRE)**[16] 6352 4-9-7 **86** RichardMullen 10 75
(J L Dunlop) *rdn 3f out: a towards rr* **20/1**

1535 **8** 3/4 **Montparnasse (IRE)**[23] 6201 3-8-13 **87** TadhgO'Shea 8 75
(B J Meehan) *hld up bhd: nudged along and hdwy on inner 5f out: effrt over 3f out: sn btn* **9/4**[1]

3043 **9** 1 **Hevelius**[25] 6131 5-9-1 **85** (v[1]) JohnFahy(5) 5 72
(W R Swinburn) *mid-div: hdwy over 3f out: sn rdn: wknd over 1f out* **10/1**

4-06 **10** 17 **Numide (FR)**[29] 5989 7-9-8 **90** JamesMillman(3) 3 53
(B R Millman) *trckd ldrs after 2f tl wknd over 3f out* **50/1**

0/00 **11** 1 3/4 **Pippa Greene**[9] 6565 6-9-1 **80** JimmyFortune 2 41
(P F I Cole) *a towards rr* **28/1**

3212 **12** dist **Isobar (GER)**[14] 6428 4-9-2 **81** J-PGuillambert 4 —
(L M Cumani) *mid-div: wkng whn virtually p.u over 1f out* **13/2**[2]

3m 8.86s (1.46) **Going Correction** +0.30s/f (Good)
WFA 3 from 4yo+ 9lb 12 Ran SP% **118.7**
Speed ratings (Par 107): **107,104,103,103,102 101,98,98,97,88 87,—**
Tote Swingers: 1&2 £8.00, 1&3 £28.50, 2&3 £32.20 CSF £91.83 CT £753.18 TOTE £12.30: £3.70, £3.30, £3.40 Place 6: £14.68 Place 5: £9.49..
Owner Andrew Bradmore **Bred** Serpentine Bloodstock Et Al **Trained** Lower Beeding, W Sussex

FOCUS
A decent staying handicap in which the subsequent high-class hurdler and Northumberland Plate winner Overturn gained his first-ever success last season. Not many showed their form and the race is rated around the winner.

NOTEBOOK
Woolfall Treasure, a C&D winner who also ran well on his other start here, was never far away and his rider brought him wide in the straight. He went clear inside the last 2f and never looked like getting caught. (tchd 12-1)
Lethal Glaze(IRE) who stays this trip, came into this off the back of a win over 1m4f on soft ground earlier in the month. He ran a good race off 6lb higher but, after following the winner through, could make no further impression. (op 9-1 tchd 10-1)
Dakiyah(IRE) is a consistent performer and she handled the ground well enough. She had her chance but could not find an extra gear, and may be ideally suited by shorter. (op 9-1)
Crocus Rose was racing over her optimum trip but was held up and appeared to clip heels and stumble slightly around 4f from home. She stayed on under pressure in the latter stages without ever looking likely to trouble the principals.
It's A Date came into this with a record of two wins in three starts here. He made the running on this return from five and a half months off, but that fact and the stick ground probably found him out and he had no more to offer when headed around the 2f pole. (op 8-1)
Final Victory, wearing a visor for the first time on this step back up in trip, was keen early but was being ridden and making no progress over 3f out. He ran past beaten horses in the latter stages though. (op 12-1)
Montparnasse(IRE) had never raced on soft ground and he did not appear to enjoy the experience. His rider was not hard on him once his chance had gone. (op 10-3 tchd 7-2)
Hevelius acts on this ground and had a visor on for the first time. He joined the leaders going well 4f out but did not appear to get home. (op 11-1)
Isobar(GER), another who had never raced on the ground, clearly failed to handle it and was eased right down in the closing stages. Official explanation: jockey said colt lost its action (op 7-2)
T/Plt: £14.20 to a £1 stake. Pool of £49,682. 2,537.76 winning tickets. T/Qpdt: £9.20 to a £1 stake. Pool of £3,816.00. 306 winning tickets. TM

6632 WINDSOR (R-H)
Monday, October 11

OFFICIAL GOING: Good to soft (good in places; 7.9)
Wind: Light, half-against Weather: Sunny

6809 TRAINER MAGAZINE NOW ON ITUNES NURSERY (DIV I) 1m 67y
2:00 (2:00) (Class 5) (0-75,75) 2-Y-O **£1,944** (£574; £287) **Stalls** High

Form RPR
550 **1** **Mountain Range (IRE)**[19] 6279 2-8-11 **68** Louis-PhilippeBeuzelin(3) 11 73
(J L Dunlop) *stdd s: hld up in 9th: rdn 3f out and sn swtchd to outer: prog 2f out: sustained effrt to ld last 100yds* **8/1**[2]

6222 **2** 1 **Jacobs Son**[52] 5256 2-9-7 **75** (v[1]) RobertHavlin 7 78
(R A Mills) *prom: led 5f out: rdn and looked in command against rail over 1f out: hdd and one pce last 100yds* **15/8**[1]

2350 **3** 2 3/4 **Bowermaster (USA)**[33] 5849 2-9-7 **75** AhmedAjtebi 9 72
(Mahmood Al Zarooni) *prom: chsd ldr 3f out: nt qckn u.p 2f out: lost 2nd and one pce over 1f out* **8/1**[2]

445 **4** 1 1/2 **My Little Star (IRE)**[18] 6305 2-8-11 **65** RobertWinston 10 58
(B W Hills) *chsd ldrs: rdn 3f out: cl enough 2f out: sn outpcd* **8/1**[2]

660 **5** 1/2 **Blue Dazzler (IRE)**[12] 6473 2-8-13 **70** MartinLane(3) 1 62
(Mrs A J Perrett) *in tch: effrt on outer 3f out: rdn and wknd over 1f out* **10/1**

636 **6** 3/4 **September Draw (USA)**[34] 5829 2-9-0 **68** PatDobbs 6 59
(R Hannon) *trckd ldrs: shkn up and outpcd 2f out: kpt on but nvr on terms after* **8/1**[2]

500 **7** 3 1/4 **Swaninstockwell (IRE)**[31] 5914 2-8-6 **60** CathyGannon 5 44
(P M Phelan) *led 3f: rdn over 3f out: steadily wknd fnl 2f: eased fnl 100yds* **9/1**[3]

0100 **8** 6 **Rafella (IRE)**[32] 5882 2-9-0 **71** (b) EJMcNamara(3) 3 41
(R M Beckett) *chsd ldr 2f: hanging bnd after: rdn 3f out: wknd tamely 2f out* **20/1**

4030 **9** 3 3/4 **Silver Shine (IRE)**[24] 6163 2-8-2 **56** (b[1]) PaulHanagan 2 18
(W J Haggas) *s.s: last to 1/2-way: rdn 2f out: no prog* **20/1**

5325 **10** 13 **Ihavenotime (IRE)**[18] 6302 2-8-12 **66** SamHitchcott 4 —
(M R Channon) *struggling in last trio by 1/2-way: t.o* **25/1**

1m 44.7s **Going Correction** +0.05s/f (Good) 10 Ran SP% **111.7**
Speed ratings (Par 95): **102,101,98,96,96 95,92,86,82,69**
Tote Swingers: 1&2 £7.20, 1&3 £12.40, 2&3 £4.80 CSF £21.63 CT £119.16 TOTE £7.60: £2.90, £1.10, £3.20; EX 29.80 Trifecta £97.90 Pool: £251.51 - 1.90 winning units..
Owner Sir Philip Wroughton **Bred** Holborn Trust Co **Trained** Arundel, W Sussex

FOCUS
This was a moderate nursery, but there were some potential improvers lurking. Despite the ground expected to be on the easy side the runners stuck to the stands' side in the home straight, but the winner was the one that came down the centre with his challenge.

NOTEBOOK
Mountain Range(IRE) ran out a ready winner on his nursery debut. Despite the ground expected to be on the easy side the runners stuck to the stands' side in the home straight, but he was the one that came down the centre with his challenge. John Dunlop has his team in top order at present, but there was no obvious confidence about him in the market for this first run out of maiden company. He rates value for further as he had to come around the houses from 3f out, and still looked green when asked to win the race. This ground evidently suited and it will be interesting to see how much he is put up for this as there should be more to come from him before the season's end. Official explanation: trainer's rep said, regarding apparent improvement in form, that the gelding suffered interference last time out and was also better suited by the easier ground. (tchd 9-1)
Jacobs Son came into this having finished second on his last three outings and proved popular in a first-time visor. He was given a positive ride and showed guts to get to the front in the home straight, but he was a sitting duck for the winner late on and again found one too good. He is a solid benchmark and deserves to find a race. (op 5-2 tchd 11-4)
Bowermaster(USA) looked a big threat nearing the 3f marker, but he proved laboured under maximum pressure and was made to look one paced. This was a step back in the right direction and reverting to quicker ground may be what he wants, but he is one of his powerful owner's lesser lights. (op 10-1 tchd 7-1)
My Little Star(IRE), making her nursery debut, made good headway 4f out, but again left the impression a drop to 7f may suit ideally in the short term. (tchd 15-2)
Blue Dazzler(IRE), another having his first outing out of maidens, showed up more encouragingly for this return to quicker ground but looks more of a 3-y-o in the making. (op 8-1 tchd 13-2)
September Draw(USA) proved somewhat disappointing on this switch to a nursery and is just struggling to find her ideal trip. (tchd 9-1)
Silver Shine(IRE) Official explanation: jockey said gelding reared as stalls opened

6810 TRAINER MAGAZINE NOW ON ITUNES NURSERY (DIV II) 1m 67y
2:30 (2:30) (Class 5) (0-75,75) 2-Y-O **£1,944** (£574; £287) **Stalls** High

Form RPR
0040 **1** **Aldwick Bay (IRE)**[15] 6386 2-9-1 **69** PatDobbs 5 77
(R Hannon) *mde all: racd against rail in st: pushed clr fr 2f out: styd on wl* **20/1**

040 **2** 2 3/4 **Dr Darcey**[74] 4499 2-8-2 **56** CathyGannon 3 58
(R Hannon) *chsd wnr: drvn 3f out: no imp fr 2f out but kpt on for 2nd* **16/1**

1354 **3** nk **Majestic Dream (IRE)**[15] 6386 2-9-5 **73** (v) ShaneKelly 6 74
(W R Swinburn) *t.k.h: hld up in midfield: shkn up 2f out: prog over 1f out: styd on to press for 2nd ins fnl f* **11/2**[3]

033 **4** 1 1/2 **Rocky Rebel**[38] 5724 2-9-4 **75** EJMcNamara(3) 9 73
(R M Beckett) *dwlt: hld up in last trio: effrt towards outer over 2f out: one pce over 1f out* **5/2**[1]

065 **5** 1 1/4 **Elusivity (IRE)**[44] 5523 2-9-0 **68** PaulMulrennan 2 63
(B J Meehan) *hld up in last pair: gng wl enough whn nt clr run 2f out to over 1f out: rdn and nt qckn fnl f* **12/1**

104 **6** nk **Mary Boyle**[25] 6129 2-8-1 **55** PaulHanagan 1 49
(A J McCabe) *hld up last early: wd bnd 5f out: prog into midfield on outer sn after: rdn over 2f out: wknd over 1f out* **8/1**

463 **7** 3/4 **Coachlight**[39] 5676 2-9-3 **71** IanMongan 7 64
(J L Dunlop) *trckd ldrs: rdn and nt qckn over 2f out: wknd jst over 1f out* **9/2**[2]

4044 **8** 1 1/2 **Ice Magic**[27] 6059 2-8-2 **61** ow1 (b) AshleyMorgan(5) 10 50
(M H Tompkins) *hld up: awkward bnd over 5f out: shkn up and nt qckn 2f out: no ch after* **15/2**

055 **9** 2 3/4 **Denices Moonlight**[69] 4682 2-8-13 **67** GregFairley 8 50
(M Johnston) *chsd ldng pair: steadily lost pl fr over 2f out* **12/1**

0000 **10** 7 **Kyncraighe (IRE)**[20] 6271 2-8-11 **65** (t) SebSanders 4 33
(Eve Johnson Houghton) *sltly awkward bnd over 5f out whn in midfield: effrt on outer over 2f out: wknd rapidly over 1f out* **50/1**

1m 45.28s (0.58) **Going Correction** +0.05s/f (Good) 10 Ran SP% **113.0**
Speed ratings (Par 95): **99,96,95,94,93 92,92,90,87,80**
Tote Swingers: 1&2 £38.70, 1&3 £20.10, 2&3 £18.50 CSF £293.53 CT £1995.87 TOTE £16.50: £6.20, £4.40, £2.50; EX 111.60 TRIFECTA Not won..
Owner Mrs Ann Williams **Bred** Ailesbury Bloodstock **Trained** East Everleigh, Wilts

FOCUS
The general opinion of riders after the opener confirmed that the ground was riding on the soft side of good, as was officially advertised. This second division of the nursery looked wide open. It was run at a sound enough pace and again the field stuck to the stands' side.

NOTEBOOK
Aldwick Bay(IRE) raced hard against the near rail in the home straight and made all to get off the mark at the fifth time of asking. He didn't fire at Ascot on his nursery debut last time, but was backed that day and left the impression this sort of test was what he needed. He clearly relished the distance and, while he did get the run of things out in front, he could've been called the winner passing the furlong marker. (tchd 18-1)
Dr Darcey, who attracted support, kept on to make it a 1-2 for his yard and showed his best form to date on this nursery debut. He got the trip without too much fuss and has now found his sort of level. (op 12-1)
Majestic Dream(IRE) finished comfortably in front of the winner at Ascot last time out, but he was racing in a second-time visor here and didn't help his cause by refusing to settle early on. He too got the trip okay, but probably needs quicker ground to shine over it. (op 4-1 tchd 7-2)
Rocky Rebel, placed on his last two outings, was well backed for this switch to a nursery. He was patiently ridden over slightly stiffer test and left the impression more positive handling was required. (op 7-2 tchd 4-1)

Elusivity(IRE) ◆ was stepping up from 6f on this nursery debut and was ridden to get the trip. He moved nicely into contention 3f out, but had to wait for his challenge and that cost him some valuable ground. He still didn't pick up all that well when in the clear, though, and is another that probably wants better ground over this far. There is definitely one of these to be won with him. (tchd 14-1)

Mary Boyle was drawn in stall one and had to come widest of all with her effort off the home turn. This better company ultimately proved too much for her. Official explanation: jockey said filly hung right (tchd 9-1)

Coachlight, another making his nursery debut, travelled sweetly and had his chance but failed to get home on this easier surface. He looks well worth a drop back to 7f in this sphere. (op 4-1 tchd 7-2)

Ice Magic Official explanation: jockey said colt suffered interference on bend

6811 EUROPEAN BREEDERS' FUND MAIDEN STKS 6f

3:05 (3:06) (Class 5) 2-Y-O £3,043 (£905; £452; £226) Stalls High

Form				RPR
04	1		**Sensational Love (IRE)**[81] 4299 2-8-12 0 RobertHavlin 2 (R A Mills) *t.k.h: hld up in 4th: prog to ld over 1f out: drvn fnl f: jst hld on* 9/1	68
002	2	nse	**Ceffyl Gwell**[7] 6626 2-9-3 0 PatDobbs 7 (R Hannon) *hld up in 6th: prog 2f out: rdn to chse wnr fnl f: str chal last 100yds: jst failed* 15/8[1]	73
06	3	2 ¾	**Tony Hollis**[24] 6145 2-9-3 0 IanMongan 5 (B R Millman) *chsd ldr: led briefly over 1f out: outpcd fnl f* 12/1	65
50	4	hd	**Cheylesmore (IRE)**[12] 6458 2-9-3 0 WilliamCarson 12 (S C Williams) *taken down early: hld up in 7th: swtchd to outer 1/2-way: prog 2f out: kpt on one pce fnl f* 33/1	64
	5	½	**State Senator (USA)** 2-9-3 0 SebSanders 9 (Sir Mark Prescott) *dwlt: wl off the pce in last trio: inclined to hang and jst shuffled along fr over 2f out: styd on steadily: nrst fin: do bttr* 9/1	69+
020	6	nk	**Putin (IRE)**[63] 4902 2-9-3 69 CathyGannon 6 (D Haydn Jones) *chsd ldrs in 5th: drvn over 2f out: grad outpcd fr over 1f out* 9/1	62
	7	3 ¼	**Seadream** 2-9-3 0 TravisBlock 13 (M D I Usher) *uns rdr and bolted to post: rn green in rr: rdn 2f out: n.d but kpt on: nt disgracd* 50/1	52
00	8	2 ¾	**Deveze (IRE)**[14] 6419 2-8-12 0 PaulHanagan 14 (J W Hills) *led to over 1f out: wknd* 20/1	39
	9	1	**Fair Value (IRE)** 2-8-12 0 KirstyMilczarek 10 (S Dow) *t.k.h: hld up in 8th: racd wd fr 1/2-way: wknd over 1f out* 25/1	36
000	10	hd	**One Cool Chick**[34] 5829 2-8-12 50 NeilChalmers 4 (J J Bridger) *chsd ldng pair to 2f out: wknd* 100/1	35
	11	8	**Web Of Dreams (IRE)** 2-9-3 0 PaulMulrennan 11 (B J Meehan) *s.s: sn struggling in last: a wl bhd* 5/1[2]	16
	12	8	**Birdwatcher (IRE)** 2-9-3 0 GregFairley 1 (M Johnston) *sn drvn in rr: bhd fr 1/2-way: t.o* 15/2[3]	—
00	13	17	**Tea And Sympathy**[28] 6034 2-8-12 0 (p) NickyMackay 3 (J R Holt) *dwlt: a bhd: wl t.o* 100/1	—

1m 16.11s (3.11) **Going Correction** +0.30s/f (Good) 13 Ran SP% **116.4**

Speed ratings (Par 95): **91,90,87,87,86 85,81,77,76,76 65,55,32**

Tote Swingers: 1&2 £5.40, 1&3 £31.30, 2&3 £7.80 CSF £24.22 TOTE £5.80: £2.20, £1.10, £6.20; EX 35.30 Trifecta £282.40 Pool: £427.50 - 1.12 winning units..

Owner J E Harley **Bred** Michael Morrissey **Trained** Headley, Surrey

FOCUS

The first pair came clear from the furlong marker in this modest juvenile maiden. The fifth looks the one to take from the race.

NOTEBOOK

Sensational Love(IRE), having her third outing, was returning from an 81-day break and dropping back a furlong on this slower ground did the trick. This was her yard's third winner at the track in the past week, and she has evidently done well for her time off the track as it was a clear personal-best. A mark in the mid 70s can now be expected for nurseries and she is open to improvement in that sphere, but connections believe she will really come into her own next year. (tchd 17-2 and 11-1 in a place)

Ceffyl Gwell just lost out on heavy ground over this trip at Warwick a week earlier and was the one to beat here. He held every chance and only lost out by a whisker, but ultimately just looked to find this that little bit too sharp. There really ought to be a race for him over a stiffer test before that long. (op 9-4 tchd 7-4)

Tony Hollis posted his best effort yet under a positive ride and is now eligible for nurseries. Another furlong should suit him before long. (op 14-1 tchd 16-1)

Cheylesmore(IRE) was keeping on encouragingly down the centre of the track from 2f out and posted his most encouraging display to date. He too now qualifies for nurseries. (op 20-1)

State Senator(USA) ◆, who has some lofty entries for next year, proved too green to do himself full justice and shaped as though this was an insufficient test of stamina. He's one to be interested in next time. Official explanation: jockey said, regarding running and riding, that his orders were to finish as close as he could without frightening the colt which is big and green, losing its action twice during the race, tried to keep it balanced and push out to the line. (op 13-2 tchd 10-1)

Putin(IRE) attracted support on his return from a 63-day break. His previous three outings had all been over C&D on contrasting ground and he left the clear impression here he would come on for the run. Another furlong could also now help his cause. Cathy Gannon later reported he had hung right. Official explanation: jockey said colt hung right (op 11-1)

Seadream got loose beforehand and proved distinctly green through the race. He was noted keeping on steadily late in the day, however, and should learn a deal for this initial experience. (op 40-1)

Web Of Dreams(IRE) was backed for this racecourse debut and was starting over a suitable trip looking at his pedigree. His fate was apparent from a very early stage, though, and the run was badly needed. (op 7-1 tchd 9-2)

Birdwatcher(IRE) is out of a 1m winner that has already produced six previous winners. He proved easy to back and never figured, looking very green in rear. (op 13-2 tchd 17-2)

6812 GOT THE FEELING, GET TO LADBROKES H'CAP 6f

3:35 (3:37) (Class 5) (0-70,70) 3-Y-O+ £2,286 (£675; £337) Stalls High

Form				RPR
4154	1		**Cardinal**[11] 6515 5-9-2 65 ShaneKelly 15 (R M H Cowell) *hld up nr side: jst abt last 2f out and looking for room gng strly: repeatedly swtchd lft over 1f out: storming run fnl f to ld last 100yds* 11/2[2]	79+
6040	2	1 ¼	**Ivory Silk**[16] 6374 5-9-0 68 (b) TobyAtkinson(5) 5 (J R Gask) *dwlt: hld up wl in rr: prog on wd outside over 2f out: narrow ld over 1f out: hdd and outpcd last 100yds* 14/1	75
4201	3	shd	**Bathwick Xaara**[6] 6656 3-8-11 66 6ex AdamBeschizza(5) 6 (J G Portman) *towards rr: rdn and prog on outer fr 1/2-way: drvn to chal fnl f: outpcd last 100yds* 5/1[1]	73
0520	4	1 ¾	**Kensington (IRE)**[5] 6679 9-9-3 66 RobertWinston 3 (A J McCabe) *pressed ldrs: hrd rdn 2f out: nrly upsides jst over 1f out: one pce* 16/1	67
0500	5	¾	**King's Caprice**[13] 6444 9-9-6 69 PatDobbs 11 (J C Fox) *taken down early: hld up wl in rr: rdn 2f out: styd on wl last 150yds: nrst fin* 12/1	68
0241	6	1	**Hatta Stream (IRE)**[11] 6515 4-9-4 70 SimonPearce(3) 1 (J Pearce) *dwlt: racd wd: towards rr: prog fr 1/2-way: drvn to chal over 1f out: wknd fnl f* 8/1	66
64	7	1 ¾	**Doctor Hilary**[42] 5614 8-8-12 64 EJMcNamara(3) 10 (M R Hoad) *w ldrs on inner: led over 2f out to over 1f out: sn btn* 16/1	54
410	8	1 ¼	**Arctic Lynx (IRE)**[2] 6739 3-9-3 70 KierenFox(3) 9 (J R Best) *mde most to jst over 2f out: grad wknd* 8/1	56
4150	9	1 ¼	**Bobs Dreamflight**[10] 6523 4-8-13 67 JamesO'Reilly(5) 16 (D K Ivory) *cl up on inner: rdn and trying to stay on whn hmpd 1f out: no ch after* 10/1	53
0052	10	1	**Picansort**[67] 4760 3-9-1 65 PaulHanagan 14 (B R Johnson) *trckd ldrs on inner: shkn up 2f out: edgd lft and nt qckn over 1f out: sn lost pl* 15/2[3]	44
2414	11	1 ½	**Elsie's Orphan**[10] 6524 3-9-2 66 SebSanders 7 (P R Chamings) *chsd ldrs: pushed along 1/2-way: no prog 2f out: eased whn btn fnl f* 16/1	40
0300	12	2	**Excellent Aim**[88] 4063 3-9-1 65 StevieDonohoe 12 (Jane Chapple-Hyam) *cl up on inner: rdn and lost pl 2f out: sn no ch* 33/1	33
3100	13	nk	**St Ignatius**[37] 5769 3-9-3 67 (b) SamHitchcott 13 (K O Cunningham-Brown) *w ldrs to 2f out: wknd* 66/1	34
0000	14	2 ¼	**Princess Valerina**[23] 6207 6-8-13 65 MartinLane(3) 8 (D Haydn Jones) *taken down early: hld up in rr: hmpd over 3f out: swtchd wd and rdn over 2f out: no prog whn rdr dropped whip over 1f out: b.b.v* 25/1	25
0100	15	¾	**C'Mon You Irons (IRE)**[26] 6078 5-9-5 68 WilliamCarson 4 (M R Hoad) *sn pushed along in midfield: wd and wknd u.p 2f out* 20/1	25
0-00	16	12	**Running Mate (IRE)**[61] 4956 3-9-4 68 IanMongan 2 (Miss Jo Crowley) *nvr bttr than midfield: wknd 2f out: virtually p.u ins fnl f* 40/1	—

1m 14.25s (1.25) **Going Correction** +0.30s/f (Good)

WFA 3 from 4yo+ 1lb 16 Ran SP% **122.6**

Speed ratings (Par 103): **103,101,101,98,97 96,94,92,90,89 87,84,84,81,80 64**

Tote Swingers: 1&2 £18.00, 1&3 £11.60, 2&3 £11.70 CSF £76.42 CT £434.64 TOTE £3.20: £1.02, £4.70, £1.60, £5.40; EX 82.20 Trifecta £80.40 Pool: £197.91 - 1.82 winning units..

Owner Mrs J May **Bred** The Queen **Trained** Six Mile Bottom, Cambs

■ Stewards' Enquiry : E J McNamara one-day ban: careless riding (Oct 25)

FOCUS

Things don't come much more open than this moderate sprint handicap. It was run at a decent tempo and the runners were spread out from the near rail to centre from 2f out. The winner is better than the bare form.

Princess Valerina Official explanation: trainer said mare bled from the nose

6813 BET AFTER THE OFF AT LADBROKES.COM H'CAP 1m 2f 7y

4:10 (4:10) (Class 4) (0-85,85) 3-Y-O £3,885 (£1,156; £577; £288) Stalls Low

Form				RPR
0022	1		**Ingleby Spirit**[17] 6327 3-9-5 83 PaulHanagan 9 (R A Fahey) *dwlt: hld up towards rr: drvn and prog over 1f out: styd on wl fnl f between rivals: led post* 7/2[1]	91
1260	2	nse	**Miss Antonia (IRE)**[16] 6361 3-9-0 78 IanMongan 6 (H R A Cecil) *sn led: styd against rail in st: drvn 2f out: hung lft fnl f: hdd post* 15/2	86
1213	3	nk	**First Post (IRE)**[31] 5918 3-9-1 79 CathyGannon 4 (D Haydn Jones) *hld up in tch: prog on outer over 2f out: chsd ldr over 1f out but hanging lft: upsides ins fnl f: hung lft and nt qckn nr fin* 5/1[2]	86
0362	4	nse	**Paintball (IRE)**[30] 5953 3-8-12 76 ShaneKelly 2 (W R Muir) *stdd s: hld up last: effrt against rail 2f out: drvn and styd on fnl f: nt quite get there* 15/2	83
2143	5	1	**Higgy's Ragazzo (FR)**[30] 5953 3-9-0 78 PatDobbs 5 (R Hannon) *prom: drvn and lost pl 2f out: nt clr run over 1f out: styd on again fnl f* 11/2[3]	85+
6222	6	shd	**Dream On Buddy (IRE)**[20] 6266 3-8-10 74 RobertWinston 1 (B W Hills) *hld up in last pair: wd bnd 6f out to 5f out: prog on wd outside over 2f out: drvn and hanging over 1f out: nt qckn fnl f* 6/1	79
0220	7	1 ¼	**Valiant Knight (FR)**[13] 6447 3-8-13 80 PatrickHills(3) 3 (R Hannon) *trckd ldrs: wnt 3rd 2f out: cl enough over 1f out: wknd ins fnl f* 14/1	83
0240	8	3	**Gallant Eagle (IRE)**[128] 2742 3-9-0 78 TravisBlock 10 (S Kirk) *t.k.h: prom: drvn and lost pl wl over 1f out: wknd fnl f* 18/1	75
1113	9	2 ½	**Explorator (IRE)**[79] 4381 3-9-4 85 MatthewDavies(3) 8 (George Baker) *chsd ldr to 3f out: sn lost pl u.p* 12/1	77

2m 7.44s (-1.26) **Going Correction** +0.05s/f (Good) 9 Ran SP% **111.7**

Speed ratings (Par 103): **107,106,106,106,105 105,104,102,100**

Tote Swingers: 1&2 £27.30, 1&3 £4.30, 2&3 £10.40 CSF £28.54 CT £126.88 TOTE £3.90: £2.70, £1.60, £1.10; EX 26.20 Trifecta £50.60 Pool: £597.16 - 8.72 winning units..

Owner Percy/Green Racing **Bred** Barton Stud And Peter Botham **Trained** Musley Bank, N Yorks

■ Stewards' Enquiry : Matthew Davies one-day ban: careless riding (Oct 27)

FOCUS

Despite this modest 3-y-o handicap being run at a solid early pace there was still a blanket finish. Solid form, the first six within a pound of their marks.

First Post(IRE) Official explanation: jockey said gelding hung left

6814 BET IN-PLAY AT LADBROKES.COM MAIDEN STKS (DIV I) 1m 67y

4:40 (4:40) (Class 5) 3-Y-O+ £1,944 (£574; £287) Stalls High

Form				RPR
032	1		**Launchpad**[12] 6470 3-9-3 80 KierenFallon 2 (L M Cumani) *chsd ldr: lft in ld 5f out: mde rest: drvn and kpt on fnl f* 11/8[1]	76+
0-24	2	1	**Gift Of Love (IRE)**[30] 5971 3-8-12 65 RobertWinston 10 (D R C Elsworth) *prom: lft 2nd 5f out: drvn to press wnr over 1f out: kpt on but a hld* 7/2[3]	69
36-	3	4	**Loyaliste (FR)**[371] 6533 3-9-3 0 PatDobbs 5 (R Hannon) *trckd ldrs: shkn up to chse ldng pair wl over 1f out: no imp* 12/1	65
66	4	2 ¾	**Mackenzie Spiers**[45] 5474 3-8-12 0 IanMongan 1 (B R Millman) *t.k.h: cl up: lft 3rd bnd 5f out: no imp 2f out: wknd over 1f out* 50/1	53
66	5	2 ½	**Supatov (USA)**[11] 6496 3-8-12 0 RobertHavlin 11 (H Morrison) *hld up in rr: rchd 5th over 2f out: nudged along and nvr nr ldrs: eased fnl f: do bttr* 33/1	47+
	6	4 ½	**The Brown Bomber (IRE)**[190] 4-9-3 0 AlanCreighton(3) 9 (Luke Comer, Ire) *t.k.h early: trckd ldrs: rdn 3f out: sn btn* 100/1	42
0623	7	nk	**Waabel**[44] 5524 3-9-3 77 PaulHanagan 7 (Jim Best) *t.k.h: led: virtually rn off the crse bnd 5f out: lost all ch* 15/8[2]	41+

04 **8** *2 ¼* **Fair Breeze**[34] 5839 3-8-11 0 ow2 .... EJMcNamara(3) 8 33
(R T Phillips) *stdd s: hld up in rr: gng wl enough 3f out: nudged along 2f out: wknd* **50/1**

9 *2 ¼* **Spacecraft (IRE)** 3-9-3 0 .... SebSanders 4 31
(C N Kellett) *s.s: a last: nvr on terms* **100/1**

1m 46.15s (1.45) **Going Correction** +0.05s/f (Good)
WFA 3 from 4yo+ 3lb 9 Ran SP% **115.6**
Speed ratings (Par 103): **94,93,89,86,83 79,78,76,74**
Tote Swingers: 1&2 £1.80, 1&3 £4.90, 2&3 £6.00 CSF £6.58 TOTE £2.30: £1.10, £1.10, £3.90; EX 6.50 TRIFECTA Pool: £951.92 - 21.58 winning units..
Owner Mrs Angie Silver **Bred** Cheveley Park Stud Ltd **Trained** Newmarket, Suffolk
■ Stewards' Enquiry : E J McNamara three-day ban: weighed in 2lb heavy (Oct 26-28)

FOCUS
An ordinary maiden, run at a modest pace and the first pair dominated in the home straight. The form is rated around the runner-up and the winner did not need to match his Nottingham latest.
Mackenzie Spiers Official explanation: jockey said filly ran too freely
Waabel Official explanation: jockey said gelding ran too freely and was unable to steer round bend
Spacecraft(IRE) Official explanation: jockey said gelding was slowly away

6815 BET IN-PLAY AT LADBROKES.COM MAIDEN STKS (DIV II) 1m 67y
5:10 (5:13) (Class 5) 3-Y-0+ **£1,944** (£574; £287) **Stalls** High

Form RPR

1 **Constant Craving** 3-8-12 0 .... LukeMorris 7 70+
(C G Cox) *trckd ldng pair to over 3f out: sn rdn: rallied and swtchd lft wl over 1f out: r.o to ld last 100yds* **25/1**

023 **2** *1* **Land And Sea**[32] 5872 3-8-12 68 .... RobertWinston 8 68
(B W Hills) *led: drvn over 1f out: hdd and outpcd last 100yds* **7/2**[2]

6 **3** *nk* **Jaldarshaan (IRE)**[45] 5493 3-8-12 0 .... TravisBlock 10 67
(W J H Ratcliffe) *t.k.h: hld up towards rr: nt clr run briefly over 2f out: shkn up over 1f out: styd on to take 3rd last strides* **33/1**

2 **4** *hd* **Colour Scheme (IRE)**[177] 1387 3-9-3 0 .... (t) ShaneKelly 9 72
(B J Meehan) *trckd ldr: rdn to chal 2f out: nt qckn and hld over 1f out: lost pl fnl f* **5/4**[1]

5 **5** *1 ¼* **Myboyalfie (USA)**[12] 6470 3-9-3 0 .... PaulHanagan 4 69
(J R Jenkins) *hld up in rr: gng strly but only 8th 2f out: nudged along and styd on takingly fnl f* **25/1**

04 **6** *½* **Point North (IRE)**[7] 6624 3-9-3 0 .... (t) DarryllHolland 1 68+
(J Noseda) *stdd s: hld up in detached last pair: sme prog towards outer over 2f out: swtchd ins and rn into trble over 1f out: nudged along and kpt on wl: do bttr* **5/1**[3]

0 **7** *4* **Polly Floyer**[151] 2051 3-8-12 0 .... IanMongan 2 54
(W R Swinburn) *t.k.h: hld up: prog to go 3rd over 3f out: wknd wl over 1f out* **5/1**[3]

0000 **8** *1 ½* **Lily Eva**[33] 5864 4-9-1 42 .... CathyGannon 6 50?
(D Donovan) *in tch: rdn on outer over 2f out: sn wknd* **50/1**

9 *2 ¼* **Maydream** 3-8-12 0 .... SamHitchcott 5 45
(J C Fox) *s.s: a last and wl off the pce* **80/1**

0 **R** **Boldly Go**[11] 6496 3-9-3 0 .... PatDobbs 3 —
(R Hannon) *t.k.h: in tch tl rn out off of the crse bnd 5f out* **50/1**

1m 44.55s (-0.15) **Going Correction** +0.05s/f (Good)
WFA 3 from 4yo 3lb 10 Ran SP% **115.8**
Speed ratings (Par 103): **102,101,100,100,99 98,94,93,91,—**
Tote Swingers: 1&2 £12.10, 1&3 £26.30, 2&3 £14.10 CSF £106.28 TOTE £40.70: £7.90, £1.50, £9.00; EX 195.80 TRIFECTA Not won..
Owner Mascalls Stud **Bred** Mascalls Stud **Trained** Lambourn, Berks

FOCUS
This second division of the extended 1m maiden was the quicker and more interesting of the pair. There was a decent enough pace on and there were a host of chances. There are doubts over the form with the favourite disappointing and the race has been rated around the runner-up.
Point North(IRE) Official explanation: jockey said colt hung badly right
Maydream Official explanation: jockey said filly was slowly away
Boldly Go Official explanation: jockey said gelding hung left which caused saddle to slip, then ducked left and unseated

6816 BET ON THE GO WITH LADBROKES MOBILE H'CAP 1m 3f 135y
5:40 (5:41) (Class 5) (0-70,69) 3-Y-0 **£2,286** (£675; £337) **Stalls** Low

Form RPR

4430 **1** **Chicane**[17] 6336 3-8-13 **64** .... (v[1]) MartinLane(3) 8 72
(W J Haggas) *hld up towards rr: gd prog on outer over 3f out: led over 2f out: clr fnl f: rdn out* **9/1**

0012 **2** *1* **Sancho Panza**[27] 6065 3-8-7 **55** oh3 .... CathyGannon 12 61
(Miss J Feilden) *hld up: last over 3f out: gd prog on outer fr 2f out: wnt 2nd ins fnl f: too much to do* **8/1**[3]

5533 **3** *1 ½* **Dr Finley (IRE)**[16] 4545 3-9-0 **65** .... SimonPearce(3) 10 69
(J Pearce) *settled midfield: drvn 4f out and struggling: prog u.p over 2f out: kpt on fnl f* **9/1**

6005 **4** *1 ¾* **Captain Cool (IRE)**[40] 5653 3-8-9 **57** .... SamHitchcott 2 58
(R Hannon) *prom: drvn against rail to dispute 2nd wl over 1f out: fdd ins fnl f* **14/1**

2261 **5** *nk* **Broadway Dancer**[21] 6244 3-9-7 **69** .... PaulHanagan 3 69
(R A Fahey) *hld up in tch: prog over 3f out: drvn to dispute 2nd over 1f out: fdd fnl f* **8/1**[3]

3250 **6** *2 ¼* **Ice Viking (IRE)**[22] 6225 3-9-0 **62** .... (b) PaulMulrennan 9 58
(J G Given) *hld up in tch: gng bttr than most 3f out: rdn and no rspnse 2f out* **9/1**

000- **7** *2 ½* **Belle Zorro**[367] 6627 3-8-7 **55** oh1 .... HayleyTurner 5 47
(M L W Bell) *chsd ldrs: rdn 3f out: grad wknd fnl 2f* **4/1**[1]

4420 **8** *2 ½* **Thundering Home**[37] 5753 3-8-10 **58** .... ShaneKelly 6 46
(M J Attwater) *hld up in last pair: effrt on outer over 3f out: no prog over 1f out: wknd* **22/1**

2130 **9** *2 ½* **Now What**[19] 6290 3-9-4 **66** .... StephenCraine 1 50
(J G Portman) *mostly trckd ldr: led 4f out to over 2f out: wknd* **12/1**

6444 **10** *3 ½* **Wavertree Bounty**[9] 6574 3-8-7 **55** oh7 .... MarcHalford 14 33
(J Ryan) *prom: lost pl on inner over 3f out: swtchd out over 2f out: no prog* **40/1**

4-10 **11** *19* **Jinto**[27] 6065 3-9-4 **66** .... JamieSpencer 13 11
(R M H Cowell) *t.k.h: led to 4f out: sn wknd: virtually p.u over 1f out* **9/2**[2]

005 **P** **Spring Stock**[45] 5474 3-8-13 **61** .... DarryllHolland 7 —
(B G Powell) *sn bhd: t.o whn p.u 5f out* **16/1**

2m 29.8s (0.30) **Going Correction** +0.05s/f (Good) 12 Ran SP% **117.4**
Speed ratings (Par 101): **101,100,99,98,97 96,94,93,91,89 76,—**
Tote Swingers: 1&2 £10.30, 1&3 £16.70, 2&3 £19.30 CSF £78.44 CT £673.38 TOTE £12.50: £3.90, £3.70, £4.80; EX 90.00 TRIFECTA Not won. Place 6: £54.04 Place 5: £35.22..
Owner St Albans Bloodstock LLP **Bred** Eurostrait Ltd **Trained** Newmarket, Suffolk

FOCUS
A moderate middle-distance handicap for 3-y-os. It was run at a fair tempo but this does not look form to be too positive about. The winner rated a small personal best.
Sancho Panza ◆ Official explanation: jockey said gelding hung right
Jinto Official explanation: jockey said gelding lost its action
Spring Stock Official explanation: jockey said filly moved poorly
T/Jkpt: Not won. T/Plt: £34.10 to a £1 stake. Pool of £69,979. 1,495.81 winning tickets. T/Qpdt: £5.60 to a £1 stake. Pool of £6,085. 793.95 winning tickets. JN

6823 - 6824a (Foreign Racing) - See Raceform Interactive

6651 LEICESTER (R-H)
Tuesday, October 12

OFFICIAL GOING: Good to soft (6.6)
Wind: Light, across. Weather: Overcast

6825 WYMESWOLD CONDITIONS STKS 7f 9y
2:10 (2:10) (Class 3) 2-Y-0 **£5,046** (£1,510; £755; £377) **Stalls** Low

Form RPR

531 **1** **Marked Card (IRE)**[14] 6436 2-8-13 77 .... RichardMullen 1 84+
(P W Chapple-Hyam) *mde virtually all: rdn over 1f out: r.o wl* **7/4**[2]

623 **2** *2 ¾* **Yair Hill (IRE)**[31] 5954 2-8-13 82 .... TedDurcan 3 77
(J L Dunlop) *plld hrd and prom: trckd wnr over 4f out: rdn over 1f out: hung lft and styd on same pce ins fnl f* **5/4**[1]

6 **3** *3* **Red Mercury (IRE)**[12] 6514 2-8-13 0 .... ChrisCatlin 2 70
(M R Channon) *chsd wnr to over 4f out: rdn over 2f out: styd on same pce appr fnl f* **14/1**

4 *1 ¼* **Al Mayasah (IRE)** 2-8-8 0 .... WilliamBuick 4 61+
(D M Simcock) *hld up: hdwy over 2f out: rdn over 1f out: no ex fnl f* **3/1**[3]

1m 30.79s (4.59) **Going Correction** +0.35s/f (Good) 4 Ran SP% **112.5**
Speed ratings (Par 99): **87,83,80,79**
CSF £4.55 TOTE £3.00; EX 5.10.
Owner J C Fretwell **Bred** Yeomanstown Stud **Trained** Newmarket, Suffolk

FOCUS
An uncompetitive conditions event in which the quartet raced tight against the nearside rail and the order hardly changed. The pace was ordinary. The form is rated around the second and third.

NOTEBOOK
Marked Card(IRE), successful on quicker ground at Brighton last month, was sent straight to the front and kept up the gallop to see off his only conceivable danger. He looks the finished article now, but this form may not add up to much as, even though he is officially rated 5lb lower than the runner-up, it looked more of a case of that rival not running to his mark. (tchd 15-8)
Yair Hill(IRE) had every chance to overhaul the winner, but didn't look as brave and appeared a bit wayward once held inside the final furlong. He has now twice been disappointing since chasing home the smart Saamidd at a respectful distance at Newbury and has plenty of questions to answer. (op 13-8 tchd 7-4)
Red Mercury(IRE) showed promise on similar ground on his Warwick debut, but raced keenly enough early and found little off the bridle. He needs more time. (tchd 16-1)
Al Mayasah(IRE), a 48,000gns half-sister to three winners at up to 1m2f, never threatened but she looked in need of the run and ought to do better. (op 10-3 tchd 5-2)

6826 WHISSENDINE (S) STKS 7f 9y
2:40 (2:40) (Class 6) 3-4-Y-0 **£1,942** (£578; £288; £144) **Stalls** Low

Form RPR

4300 **1** **Toby Tyler**[7] 6664 4-8-12 61 .... (v[1]) TonyCulhane 8 67+
(P T Midgley) *hld up: hdwy 1/2-way: rdn to ld over 1f out: styd on wl* **6/1**[3]

0600 **2** *2* **Dark Moment**[20] 6295 4-8-9 62 .... BarryMcHugh(3) 13 60
(Ollie Pears) *hld up: rdn over 2f out: hdwy over 1f out: edgd lft: styd on* **9/2**[2]

0 **3** *nse* **Chez Vrony**[190] 1127 4-8-12 0 .... ChrisCatlin 14 60
(D Morris) *s.i.s: swtchd rt and hdwy over 1f out: styd on* **100/1**

1101 **4** *½* **Fault**[14] 6439 4-9-3 77 .... (t) SebSanders 1 63+
(Stef Higgins) *hld up: rdn over 2f out: swtchd rt and hdwy over 1f out: nt rch ldrs* **2/1**[1]

4000 **5** *½* **Magenta Strait**[15] 6413 3-8-3 52 .... JackDuern(7) 4 56
(R Hollinshead) *s.s: swtchd rt and hdwy over 1f out: styd on* **50/1**

0120 **6** *3 ½* **Rising Kheleyf (IRE)**[34] 5852 4-9-0 67 .... (p) GaryBartley(3) 6 53+
(John A Harris) *hld up in tch: plld hrd: hmpd and lost pl 1/2-way: styd on fr over 1f out* **8/1**

6000 **7** *¾* **Jibrrya**[11] 6540 3-8-10 57 .... JoeFanning 3 45
(D Nicholls) *hld up: hdwy 1/2-way: rdn over 2f out: wknd ins fnl f* **12/1**

0000 **8** *2 ¾* **Glan Y Mor (IRE)**[11] 6527 3-8-5 42 .... (p) LiamJones 11 32
(A W Carroll) *chsd ldrs: rdn over 2f out: wknd over 1f out* **50/1**

4644 **9** *hd* **Thaliwarru**[7] 6657 3-9-1 64 .... (p) SteveDrowne 7 42
(J R Gask) *prom: n.m.r 1/2-way: sn rdn: wknd over 1f out* **8/1**

0015 **10** *2 ¾* **Scooby Dee**[10] 6579 3-8-7 49 .... (p) AmyRyan(3) 2 29
(R M Whitaker) *hld up: rdn over 2f out: n.d* **14/1**

0000 **11** *nk* **Trading Nation (USA)**[24] 6186 4-8-9 46 .... RobertLButler(3) 5 29
(P W Hiatt) *chsd ldrs: led 3f out: rdn: hdd & wknd over 1f out* **66/1**

004 **12** *1 ¾* **Boundless Applause**[44] 5559 4-8-4 43 .... MartinLane(3) 12 20
(I A Wood) *chsd ldrs: rdn and ev ch over 2f out: wknd over 1f out* **40/1**

0062 **13** *5* **Saigon Kitty (IRE)**[11] 6522 3-8-2 58 .... KierenFox(3) 10 —
(J R Best) *chsd ldrs: led over 4f out: rdn and hdd 3f out: wknd over 1f out* **12/1**

4600 **14** *6* **Truly Magic**[22] 6255 3-8-5 45 .... JimmyQuinn 9 —
(H J L Dunlop) *led: hdd over 4f out: wknd over 2f out* **33/1**

1m 28.64s (2.44) **Going Correction** +0.35s/f (Good)
WFA 3 from 4yo 2lb 14 Ran SP% **121.9**
Speed ratings (Par 101): **100,97,97,97,96 92,91,88,88,85 84,82,77,70**
Tote Swingers:1&2:£6.20, 2&3:£92.20, 1&3:£87.70 CSF £32.68 TOTE £7.20: £3.10, £2.10, £14.50; EX 28.80 TRIFECTA Not won..There was no bid for the winner. Fault was the subject of a friendly claim.
Owner Anthony D Copley **Bred** Whitsbury Manor Stud **Trained** Westow, N Yorks

FOCUS
A weakish seller. Although the runners again came up the stands' rail, it was noticeable that the first three home all came from off the pace down the wide outside of the field. With the favourite disappointing the winner probably only had to run to his recent form.
Saigon Kitty(IRE) Official explanation: jockey said filly ran too free

6827 E B F REFERENCE POINT MAIDEN STKS (DIV I) 7f 9y
3:10 (3:10) (Class 4) 2-Y-0 **£4,209** (£1,252; £625; £312) **Stalls** Low

Form RPR

4 **1** **Marden (IRE)**[46] 5491 2-9-0 0 .... ShaneKelly 7 82+
(B J Meehan) *dwlt: hdwy over 4f out: pushed along to ld 1f out: rdn and r.o wl* **5/6**[1]

3 **2** *3 ½* **Muffraaj**[18] 6324 2-9-0 0 .... WilliamBuick 10 73
(D M Simcock) *a.p: rdn and ev ch over 1f out: styd on same pce* **20/1**

5 **3** *½* **Danadana (IRE)**[18] 6334 2-9-0 0 .... KierenFallon 6 72
(L M Cumani) *chsd ldr tl led over 2f out: rdn and hdd 1f out: edgd rt: styd on same pce* **11/2**[2]

4 **4** 1 1/4 **Indian Emperor (IRE)**[17] 6365 2-9-0 0 PhilipRobinson 4 69
(M A Jarvis) *led over 4f: ev ch over 1f out: no ex ins fnl f* **11/2**[2]

5 *shd* **Raahin (IRE)** 2-9-0 0 RichardHills 3 69+
(Sir Michael Stoute) *s.i.s: hld up: hdwy over 1f out: nrst fin* **15/2**[3]

50 **6** 2 1/2 **Hot Spice**[20] 6278 2-9-0 0 TedDurcan 1 65+
(J L Dunlop) *s.i.s: hld up: pushed along 1/2-way: hung rt over 1f out: r.o ins fnl f: nvr nrr* **80/1**

00 **7** 5 **Control Chief**[24] 6200 2-9-0 0 JimCrowley 8 50
(R M Beckett) *chsd ldrs tl rdn and wknd over 1f out* **18/1**

00 **8** 3/4 **Love Nest**[65] 4856 2-9-0 0 JimmyQuinn 2 48
(J L Dunlop) *mid-div: rdn 1/2-way: wknd 2f out* **100/1**

9 1/2 **Waterford Star (IRE)** 2-9-0 0 JoeFanning 9 47
(M Johnston) *s.i.s: sn pushed along and a in rr* **33/1**

00 **10** 1/2 **Fire Fighter (IRE)**[10] 6569 2-9-0 0 SebSanders 11 46
(Sir Mark Prescott) *s.i.s: outpcd* **100/1**

11 7 **Daddyow** 2-9-0 0 DavidProbert 5 28
(B Palling) *prom: rdn 1/2-way: wknd over 2f out* **100/1**

1m 28.3s (2.10) **Going Correction** +0.35s/f (Good) **11** Ran SP% **114.3**
Speed ratings (Par 97): **102,98,97,96,95 93,87,86,85,85 77**
Tote Swingers:1&2:£5.90, 2&3:£6.80, 1&3:£2.30 CSF £25.31 TOTE £1.60: £1.10, £3.90, £3.40; EX 21.00 Trifecta £152.30 Pool £841.89 - 4.09 winning units..

Owner Sangster Families **Bred** Rockhart Trading Ltd **Trained** Manton, Wilts

FOCUS
An interesting maiden and a few of these look nice prospects for next season. The bare form is fair and the winner progressed from his promising debut. Unlike in the previous two races, the field came down the centre of the track. The winning time was 0.34 seconds faster than the older horses in the seller and 2.49 seconds faster than the opening 2-y-o conditions event.

NOTEBOOK
Marden(IRE) ◆ was surrounded by subsequent winners when a very promising fourth of 15 on his Newmarket debut back in August and was a warm order to improve plenty from that. Despite a slow start, he was still able to produce a telling turn of foot to lead well inside the last furlong and win going away, but he still looked a bit green at the end of the race and he is very likely to improve again. (op Evens)

Muffraaj ◆, a well-beaten third of five on his Haydock debut, also improved from his initial outing. Despite racing away from the others closer to the far rail, he had every chance and wasn't beaten until well inside the last furlong. There are races to be won with him. (op 22-1)

Danadana(IRE), a fair fifth of nine on his Wolverhampton debut last month, was always close to the pace and kept on despite hanging about under pressure inside the last furlong. He is bred to stay much further than this and looks one for next season. (tchd 6-1)

Indian Emperor(IRE) didn't get home over 1m on soft ground on his Haydock debut and again didn't get home here, despite the shorter trip. He may need better ground to show his best. (op 9-2)

Raahin(IRE), a 200,000gns half-brother to a winning miler, made steady late progress without ever being touched with the whip. There is plenty of improvement to come from him. (op 17-2 tchd 10-1)

Hot Spice, who looked clueless in his first two starts, never threatened here either but is bred to stay and now gets a mark. (op 125-1)

6828 E B F REFERENCE POINT MAIDEN STKS (DIV II) 7f 9y
3:40 (3:40) (Class 4) 2-Y-O **£4,209** (£1,252; £625; £312) **Stalls** Low

Form RPR

1 **Naqshabban (USA)** 2-9-0 0 KierenFallon 4 75+
(L M Cumani) *hld up in tch: shkn up to ld wl ins fnl f: readily* **9/1**

2 3/4 **Moonscape** 2-9-0 0 RyanMoore 5 73
(Sir Michael Stoute) *chsd ldr tl led 2f out: rdn and hdd over 1f out: edgd rt and ev ch ins fnl f: r.o* **2/1**[1]

3 *nk* **Long Awaited (IRE)** 2-9-0 0 PhilipRobinson 3 72
(M A Jarvis) *chsd ldrs: rdn to ld over 1f out: edgd rt and hdd wl ins fnl f* **11/4**[2]

4 2 1/2 **Mungo Park** 2-9-0 0 JoeFanning 8 66
(M Johnston) *chsd ldrs: rdn and ev ch over 1f out: styd on same pce ins fnl f* **6/1**[3]

035 **5** 3 1/4 **Number Theory**[27] 6070 2-9-0 72 NickyMackay 2 59
(J R Holt) *led: rdn and hdd 2f out: wknd ins fnl f* **8/1**

5 **6** 1 **Experimentalist**[13] 6474 2-9-0 0 SteveDrowne 7 55
(H Morrison) *hld up: hdwy 1/2-way: edgd lft and wknd over 1f out* **11/1**

7 4 **Twinkled** 2-9-0 0 HayleyTurner 6 45
(M L W Bell) *hld up in tch: rdn over 2f out: wknd wl over 1f out* **16/1**

8 9 **Silver Tiger** 2-9-0 0 JackMitchell 10 23
(C F Wall) *dwlt: hld up: rdn and wknd over 2f out* **20/1**

1m 29.32s (3.12) **Going Correction** +0.35s/f (Good) **8** Ran SP% **112.6**
Speed ratings (Par 97): **96,95,94,91,88 87,82,72**
Tote Swingers:1&2:£4.50, 2&3:£1.60, 1&3:£5.70 CSF £26.56 TOTE £12.30: £4.30, £1.10, £1.10; EX 21.50 Trifecta £40.10 Pool £623.51 - 11.48 winning units..

Owner Sheikh Mohammed Obaid Al Maktoum **Bred** Darley **Trained** Newmarket, Suffolk

FOCUS
Again the runners came down the centre and there were four in a line across the track inside the last furlong. This didn't look quite as strong as the first division and the winning time was over a second slower. The winner looks the type to do a good deal better.

NOTEBOOK
Naqshabban(USA) ◆, out of a winning half-sister to his useful stablemate Afsare, was full of himself in the paddock beforehand but did nothing wrong once under way. He had to be switched towards the far rail in order to get a run and looked like finishing third well inside the last furlong, but he quickened up for a second time and in the end won a bit cosily. Being a gelding, he should be around for a few years yet and looks well up to winning some nice prizes with improvement to come. (op 8-1 tchd 10-1)

Moonscape ◆, out of a winning half-sister to Medicean, had every chance and kept on well despite coming under pressure fully 2f from home. He should have little trouble going one better. (op 5-2)

Long Awaited(IRE), a 55,000gns half-sister to two winners, took a while to warm to his task but eventually responded to pressure to just about hit the front inside the last furlong, only to then be worried out of it close home. He should have learnt plenty from this. (op 3-1 tchd 10-3)

Mungo Park, a 150,000gns half-brother to three winners including the useful stayer Keenes Day, was bang there until fading well inside the last furlong and should do better with this run under his belt. (op 5-1 tchd 13-2)

Number Theory, officially rated 72 after showing ability in three maidens, set the pace until over a furlong from home. He remains vulnerable to unexposed rivals, but at least provides the benchmark to the form. (op 9-1 tchd 7-1)

Experimentalist, green when a well-beaten fifth of 12 in a 1m soft-ground Salisbury maiden on debut, fared a little better here but looks a long-term handicap prospect. (tchd 10-1 and 12-1)

Twinkled, a 36,000gns gelding out of a 1m winner on Polytrack, pulled too hard on this debut. (op 14-1)

Silver Tiger, a 37,000gns colt out of a winner over 1m4f, fluffed the start and finished tailed off but could still be one for handicaps over further in due course. (op 22-1)

6829 FOSSE WAY CLASSIFIED CLAIMING STKS 1m 3f 183y
4:10 (4:11) (Class 5) 3-5-Y-O **£2,266** (£674; £337; £168) **Stalls** High

Form RPR

4316 **1** **Bondage (IRE)**[25] 6166 3-9-1 69 (t[1]) PatCosgrave 6 68
(J R Fanshawe) *trckd ldr tl led over 2f out: rdn over 1f out: edgd lft ins fnl f: styd on* **3/1**[2]

0412 **2** *hd* **Country Road (IRE)**[18] 6331 4-9-4 70 (be) KierenFox(3) 5 67
(A W Carroll) *plld hrd and prom: rdn and ev ch fr over 1f out: sn hung lft: styd on* **11/4**[1]

-242 **3** 2 1/4 **Not In The Clock (USA)**[10] 6554 3-9-3 62 SteveDrowne 7 66
(J R Best) *a.p: rdn over 2f out: styd on same pce* **4/1**[3]

3444 **4** 2 **Easy Terms**[13] 6476 3-8-10 63 ow1 (v[1]) JamesMillman(3) 1 59
(B R Millman) *hld up: hdwy over 2f out: rdn over 1f out: no ex ins fnl f* **8/1**

0534 **5** *shd* **Marafong**[22] 6257 3-8-5 45 JimmyQuinn 4 51
(Miss J Feilden) *broke wl sn stdd and lost pl: rdn over 2f out: styd on same pce fnl f* **33/1**

0522 **6** 2 **Into The Light**[38] 5765 5-9-1 64 GrahamGibbons 3 51?
(E S McMahon) *led: rdn and hdd over 2f out: wknd fnl f* **9/2**

6353 **7** 4 1/2 **Dane Cottage**[8] 6637 3-8-5 55 (v) CathyGannon 2 41
(P D Evans) *hld up: hdwy over 2f out: rdn and wknd over 1f out* **14/1**

2m 39.42s (5.52) **Going Correction** +0.35s/f (Good)
WFA 3 from 4yo+ 7lb **7** Ran SP% **110.6**
Speed ratings (Par 103): **95,94,93,92,91 90,87**
Tote Swingers:1&2:£1.90, 2&3:£2.90, 1&3:£3.70 CSF £10.87 TOTE £4.10: £2.30, £1.10; EX 10.60.

Owner Mrs Andrew Crawshaw & Mrs J Fanshawe **Bred** Mesnil Investments Ltd & Carrigbeg Stud **Trained** Newmarket, Suffolk

FOCUS
A modest early pace for this claimer and not a race to live long in the memory, even though it was quite a dramatic race. Muddling and dubious form.

Country Road(IRE) Official explanation: jockey said gelding hung left

6830 WREAKE FILLIES' CONDITIONS STKS 1m 60y
4:40 (4:40) (Class 3) 3-Y-O+ **£5,677** (£1,699; £849; £424; £211) **Stalls** High

Form RPR

-420 **1** **Long Lashes (USA)**[17] 6346 3-8-9 102 (p) FrankieDettori 3 95+
(Saeed Bin Suroor) *chsd ldr tl led over 1f out: styd on wl* **5/2**[1]

224 **2** 1 1/4 **Seradim**[62] 4950 4-8-12 86 JimmyFortune 8 92
(P F I Cole) *dwlt: hld up: hdwy over 1f out: rdn and r.o wl to go 2nd nr fin: nt rch wnr* **16/1**

0-30 **3** 3/4 **Super Sleuth (IRE)**[118] 3067 4-8-12 100 KierenFallon 6 90
(B J Meehan) *chsd ldrs: rdn over 1f out: chsd wnr wl ins fnl f to nr fin: styd on same pce* **3/1**[2]

0115 **4** 1 **Titbit**[39] 5728 3-8-12 84 RyanMoore 7 91
(H R A Cecil) *hld up: hdwy over 2f out: rdn over 1f out: styd on* **8/1**[3]

16 **5** 1/2 **Decorative (IRE)**[52] 5305 3-8-9 96 PhilipRobinson 9 86
(M A Jarvis) *led: racd keenly: rdn and hdd over 1f out: no ex ins fnl f* **5/2**[1]

0160 **6** *hd* **Whirly Dancer**[18] 6321 3-8-12 83 IanMongan 2 89
(H R A Cecil) *hld up: hdwy over 2f out: rdn over 1f out: no ex ins fnl f* **33/1**

401 **7** 5 **Personified (GER)**[18] 6332 3-8-9 73 LiamKeniry 4 75
(E F Vaughan) *hld up: rdn over 2f out: wknd over 1f out* **50/1**

0420 **8** 1 3/4 **Za Za Zoom (IRE)**[33] 5883 3-8-9 98 MichaelHills 1 79
(B W Hills) *prom: rdn over 2f out: hung rt and wknd over 1f out: eased ins fnl f* **14/1**

1m 45.95s (0.85) **Going Correction** +0.35s/f (Good)
WFA 3 from 4yo+ 3lb **8** Ran SP% **110.7**
Speed ratings (Par 104): **109,107,107,106,105 105,100,98**
Tote Swingers:1&2:£5.70, 2&3:£7.40, 1&3:£2.20 CSF £40.61 TOTE £2.70: £1.10, £4.80, £1.10; EX 35.20 Trifecta £109.50 Pool £1,129.09 - 7.63 winning units..

Owner Godolphin **Bred** Robert V Lapenta & Nicholas P Zito **Trained** Newmarket, Suffolk

FOCUS
An interesting fillies' conditions event run at an uneven tempo.With the third and fifth below form this didn't take much winning, with the runner-up the best guide.

NOTEBOOK
Long Lashes(USA) belatedly resumed winning ways on this drop in class. She bombed out when first tried in cheekpieces at Ascot 17 days earlier, but she had also run below par at that venue in last year's Fillies' Mile and clearly doesn't enjoy the track. Frankie Dettori kept closest tabs on the front-runner through the race and was perfectly placed to strike when things got serious from the two-furlong marker. She came right away and ought to be high on confidence after this first success since winning the Group 3 Sweet Solera on her debut for Godolphin last term. With that in mind connections would do well to get her out again before the season's end as she is obviously versatile as regards underfoot conditions. Her trainer later confirmed it was now very much the plan to find her another race back up in grade. (op 9-4)

Seradim, returning from a 62-day absence, is more talented than her official mark of 86 implies. However, she has become an extremely difficult horse to get right and, while she was motoring home off the uneven pace here, it's certainly not the first time she has got going too late in the day. (op 20-1 tchd 14-1)

Super Sleuth(IRE) was having her first outing for 118 days and attracted support, despite having been very edgy beforehand and unseating her rider at one stage. She had her chance and may not have been suited by the way the race unfolded, but still could've been expected to fare better in this easier company. Surely reverting to maiden company is worth a try now to gain that elusive first success. (op 5-1)

Titbit would've probably enjoyed more of a test over this sharper test returning to turf and wasn't at all disgraced. She has few miles on the clock and remains open to improvement. (tchd 7-1)

Decorative(IRE), well behind the winner when flopping at Sandown on her previous outing, has been very patiently handled by connections and was expected to fare a lot better on this return to easy ground. She was ridden a lot more aggressively this time and had very much the run of the race, but lacked any sort of acceleration when asked for maximum effort nearing the final furlong. It's now a case of back to the drawing boards for her operation. (op 2-1 tchd 3-1)

Whirly Dancer bounced back to form on ground that suits, but consistency has not been her strong suit and she is not the most simple filly to place. (op 25-1 tchd 22-1)

Za Za Zoom(IRE) Official explanation: jockey said filly hyung right

6831 E B F SOAR MAIDEN STKS 1m 60y
5:10 (5:11) (Class 4) 2-Y-O **£4,533** (£1,348; £674; £336) **Stalls** High

Form RPR

30 **1** **Sadler's Risk (IRE)**[10] 6560 2-9-3 0 JoeFanning 2 77
(M Johnston) *mde all: rdn and hung lft ins fnl f: sn edgd rt: r.o: hmpd nr fin* **5/1**[3]

2 *shd* **Sea Moon** 2-9-3 0 RyanMoore 4 79+
(Sir Michael Stoute) *hld up: hdwy 2f out: rdn: edgd rt and r.o wl ins fnl f: jst failed* **5/4**[1]

3 1 3/4 **Estourah (IRE)** 2-9-3 0 FrankieDettori 3 73+
(Saeed Bin Suroor) *chsd ldrs: rdn and nt clr run ins fnl f: styd on same pce* **7/2**[2]

0 4 2 3/4 **First Battalion (IRE)**[27] 6092 2-9-3 0 JimmyFortune 7 67+
(Sir Michael Stoute) *hld up: hdwy 2f out: shkn up over 1f out: r.o: nt rch ldrs* **10/1**

0 5 nk **Rosairlie (IRE)**[30] 5985 2-8-12 0 JimmyQuinn 14 61
(H J L Dunlop) *hld up: hdwy over 4f out: rdn over 2f out: styd on* **50/1**

6 2 1/2 **Madrasa (IRE)** 2-9-3 0 RichardMullen 8 61
(E S McMahon) *pushed along in rr early: hdwy over 2f out: rdn over 1f out: swtchd lft ins fnl f: styd on* **66/1**

04 7 shd **Tileyf (IRE)**[13] 6474 2-8-12 0 JohnFahy[(5)] 5 61
(C G Cox) *chsd ldrs: rdn over 2f out: no ex fnl f* **50/1**

8 3 **Pretty Diamond (IRE)** 2-8-12 0 GregFairley 12 49
(M Johnston) *mid-div: rdn over 3f out: n.d* **50/1**

0 9 shd **Tiger's Pride**[33] 5878 2-9-0 0 MartinLane[(3)] 13 54
(J Gallagher) *prom: rdn over 2f out: sn wknd* **100/1**

10 1/2 **Golestan Palace (IRE)** 2-9-3 0 KierenFallon 6 55+
(L M Cumani) *s.s: hld up: hdwy over 2f out: sn wknd* **10/1**

00 11 2 1/4 **Toucan Tango (IRE)**[24] 6190 2-9-3 0 JackMitchell 10 48
(P W Chapple-Hyam) *s.i.s: hld up: rdn over 2f out: n.d* **40/1**

05 12 5 **Breton Star**[26] 6127 2-9-3 0 NickyMackay 1 37
(D M Simcock) *chsd wnr tl rdn over 2f out: wknd over 1f out* **50/1**

00 13 9 **Invent**[8] 6634 2-9-3 0 SebSanders 11 17
(Sir Mark Prescott) *hld up: hdwy over 4f out: wknd over 2f out* **100/1**

14 7 **Veloce (IRE)** 2-9-3 0 TedDurcan 9 —
(J L Dunlop) *s.s: a in rr: lost tch fnl 3f* **50/1**

1m 49.06s (3.96) **Going Correction** +0.35s/f (Good) **14** Ran SP% **117.2**
Speed ratings (Par 97): **94,93,92,89,89 86,86,83,83,82 80,75,66,59**
Tote Swingers:1&2:£2.80, 2&3:£2.40, 1&3:£2.90 CSF £10.92 TOTE £3.10: £1.10, £1.10, £1.60; EX 16.50 Trifecta £22.40 Pool £843.41 - 27.79 winning units..
Owner R S Brookhouse **Bred** Smythson **Trained** Middleham Moor, N Yorks

FOCUS

An interesting maiden even though they bet 40-1 bar five. There should be plenty of winners coming out of it although the bare form is only limited.

NOTEBOOK

Sadler's Risk(IRE) had little chance in the Tattersalls Millions 2YO Trophy last time, but had previously shown ability in similar conditions over this trip on his Haydock debut and he put his experience to good use with an all-the-way success. He did edge left inside the last furlong, intimidating the third horse and eventually bumping the runner-up near the line, but the stewards allowed him to keep the race. He can win more races, but wouldn't beat the second if they met again. (tchd 9-2 and 11-2)

Sea Moon ◆, a half-brother to Brian Boru, Listed winner Kitty O'Shea and Soviet Moon (the dam of Workforce), was all the rage to make a winning debut, but not much went right for him as he was always trapped out wide from his outside draw. He finished well, only just failing to get up, and will prove the best of these in time. (tchd 6-5 and 11-8 in places)

Estourah(IRE) ◆, a 75,000gns half-brother to a winning plater and a winning hurdler, travelled particularly well behind the leaders and still had every chance entering the last furlong. He was slightly inconvenienced when the winner hung across him, but not enough to affect his finishing position. He should get off the mark before too long. (op 5-2)

First Battalion(IRE), well beaten on similar ground on his Yarmouth debut, looked very much the stable's second string but he was nonetheless a springer in the market. Given plenty to do, he made up a lot of ground down the wide outside and is the type to come into his own over middle distances next year. (op 25-1 tchd 28-1)

Rosairlie(IRE), well beaten on her Ffos Las debut, still looked green here but she showed a lot more and obviously has some ability.

Madrasa(IRE) ◆, a £20,000 gelding and half-brother to several winners both here and abroad, was another to make up ground from off the pace up the inside rail and this was a promising enough debut.

Tileyf(IRE) improved from his first start to his second and again ran well here until fading over a furlong from home. He becomes of greater interest now that he gets a nursery mark. (op 66-1 tchd 40-1)

6832 STEWARDS H'CAP 1m 1f 218y
5:40 (5:40) (Class 5) (0-75,75) 3-Y-O+ **£2,266** (£674; £337; £168) **Stalls** High

Form RPR

1500 1 **Goodlukin Lucy**[112] 3298 3-9-2 **72** JimCrowley 13 83
(Pat Eddery) *hld up in tch: rdn to ld over 1f out: styd on wl* **16/1**

2612 2 3/4 **Nisaal (IRE)**[22] 6261 5-8-13 **71** JulieBurke[(7)] 1 80
(A W Carroll) *s.i.s and hmpd s: hdwy over 2f out: rdn and hung rt ins fnl f: styd on* **9/2**[2]

0030 3 1 3/4 **Best Prospect (IRE)**[24] 6181 8-9-7 **72** (tp) PhillipMakin 10 78
(M Dods) *hld up: swtchd lft and hdwy over 1f out: rdn and ev ch ins fnl f: fnd nil* **9/1**[3]

0400 4 nk **Hail Tiberius**[27] 6074 3-8-13 **69** GrahamGibbons 6 74
(T D Walford) *a.p: rdn over 1f out: styd on u.p* **20/1**

/2-4 5 shd **Beetuna (IRE)**[11] 6543 5-9-4 **74** MarkCoumbe[(5)] 15 79
(D Bourton) *hld up: hdwy over 1f out: r.o: nt rch ldrs* **33/1**

156 6 1 **Oriental Cavalier**[18] 6322 4-9-7 **75** RussKennemore[(3)] 8 78
(Mark Buckley) *prom: led over 2f out: rdn and hdd over 1f out: no ex ins fnl f* **9/2**[2]

342- 7 2 **Astrodiva**[364] 6766 4-8-6 **62** AshleyMorgan[(5)] 2 61
(M H Tompkins) *hld up in tch: rdn and ev ch over 1f out: no ex ins fnl f* **10/1**

4406 8 1/2 **Yossi (IRE)**[11] 6065 6-8-10 **61** oh1 (b) GregFairley 11 59
(R C Guest) *chsd ldr tl led over 3f out: rdn and hdd over 2f out: edgd rt and no ex fnl f* **14/1**

0002 9 nk **Bajan Flash**[48] 5411 3-8-11 **67** (p) KierenFallon 14 64
(D Nicholls) *s.i.s and edgd rt s: sn chsng ldrs: rdn over 1f out: no ex fnl f* **4/1**[1]

0064 10 hd **Nevada Desert (IRE)**[5] 6699 10-8-7 **61** oh1 AmyRyan[(3)] 3 58
(R M Whitaker) *s.s: hld up: hdwy u.p over 1f out: nt trble ldrs* **25/1**

0505 11 1 3/4 **Agapanthus (GER)**[27] 6091 5-9-6 **71** MickyFenton 7 64
(B J Curley) *hld up: pushed along 1/2-way: nvr on terms* **16/1**

1126 12 3/4 **Gross Prophet**[20] 6288 5-9-7 **72** SteveDrowne 12 64
(A J Lidderdale) *prom: rdn over 3f out: wknd over 1f out* **16/1**

0605 13 2 3/4 **Edgeworth (IRE)**[75] 4498 4-9-3 **68** GeorgeBaker 5 54
(B G Powell) *chsd ldrs: rdn and ev ch over 2f out: wknd over 1f out* **12/1**

0526 14 9 **Magnitude**[28] 6051 5-8-10 **61** oh6 PaulQuinn 16 29
(B P J Baugh) *hld up: pushed along 1/2-way: a in rr: bhd fnl 2f* **33/1**

5150 15 10 **All Guns Firing (IRE)**[181] 1296 4-8-11 **62** JoeFanning 9 10
(D Carroll) *led: rdn and hdd over 3f out: wknd over 2f out: t.o* **33/1**

2m 10.53s (2.63) **Going Correction** +0.35s/f (Good)
WFA 3 from 4yo+ 5lb **15** Ran SP% **124.9**
Speed ratings (Par 103): **103,102,101,100,100 99,98,97,97,97 96,95,93,86,78**
Tote Swingers:1&2:£27.20, 2&3:£13.10, 1&3:£46.00. totesuper7: Win: Not won. Place: £42.90. CSF £84.26 CT £706.94 TOTE £25.30: £6.90, £1.10, £4.60; EX 189.80 TRIFECTA Not won. Place 6 £36.63, Place 5 £8.13..
Owner Evergreen Racing **Bred** Moretail Ventures **Trained** Nether Winchendon, Bucks
■ Stewards' Enquiry : Mark Coumbe ten-day ban: breach of Rule (B) 59.4 (Oct 26-Nov 4)

FOCUS

An ordinary handicap, though quite a competitive one with only a couple of lengths covering about eight horses passing the furlong pole. The winner was much improved, the form rated around the second and third.

Beetuna(IRE) ◆ Official explanation: jockey said, regarding running and riding, that his orders were to settle the gelding in behind and make his run from about 2f out; trainer said his instructions were to drop the gelding in and make its run turning for home.

Bajan Flash Official explanation: jockey said colt was a poor mover

T/Plt: £63.80 to a £1 stake. Pool of £76,913.31. 879.07 winning tickets. T/Qpdt: £5.40 to a £1 stake. Pool of £7,233.04. 975.96 winning tickets. CR

6457 NEWCASTLE (L-H)
Tuesday, October 12

6833 Meeting Abandoned - False Ground

6794 KEMPTON (A.W) (R-H)
Wednesday, October 13

OFFICIAL GOING: Standard

Wind: Light, half against Weather: Cloudy

6841 KIA VENGA CLAIMING STKS 1m 2f (P)
5:40 (5:41) (Class 6) 3-4-Y-O **£1,637** (£483; £241) **Stalls** High

Form RPR

502 1 **Whistleinthewind (IRE)**[28] 6091 3-9-6 85 (v[1]) RyanMoore 8 76+
(G L Moore) *pushed up to ld: mde all: drvn clr bnd 2f out: in n.d after: rdn out* **5/4**[1]

60 2 2 1/4 **Officer In Command (USA)**[40] 5727 4-9-8 78 (b[1]) LiamKeniry 2 68
(J S Moore) *chsd wnr: outpcd 2f out: kpt on but nvr a threat after* **12/1**

0606 3 1 1/2 **Exceedthewildman**[40] 5728 3-8-13 83 (p) RyanPowell[(7)] 6 68+
(J S Moore) *hld up last: stl there whn c extremely wd bnd 2f out: gd prog over 1f out to take 3rd last 75yds: hopeless task* **15/2**[3]

0202 4 1/2 **Gearbox (IRE)**[12] 6535 4-9-2 56 MartinLane[(3)] 3 61
(H J L Dunlop) *trckd ldrs: outpcd 2f out: kpt on same pce after* **16/1**

0005 5 shd **Lucky Punt**[14] 6450 4-9-8 85 FergusSweeney 1 64
(B G Powell) *racd wd: in tch: outpcd 2f out: wnt 3rd briefly fnl f: one pce* **12/1**

6432 6 1 3/4 **Flighty Frances (IRE)**[8] 6652 3-8-2 72 PaulHanagan 7 45
(D R C Elsworth) *hld up in 6th: rdn and no prog over 2f out: no imp after* **3/1**[2]

5460 7 nse **Zelos Spirit**[23] 6255 3-8-1 42 DavidProbert 4 44?
(Rae Guest) *a towards rr: outpcd fr 2f out* **50/1**

2050 8 3 1/4 **Pebblesonthebeach**[19] 6336 3-9-0 68 (p) SteveDrowne 5 51
(J W Hills) *n.m.r sn after s: hld up: wd bnd 2f out: n.d after: wknd fnl f* **12/1**

-006 9 1 1/2 **Royal Defence (IRE)**[35] 5859 4-9-8 77 J-PGuillambert 9 51
(N P Littmoden) *t.k.h early: trckd ldng pair: rdn over 2f out: wknd qckly over 1f out* **25/1**

2m 8.25s (0.25) **Going Correction** -0.125s/f (Stan)
WFA 3 from 4yo 5lb **9** Ran SP% **116.0**
Speed ratings (Par 101): **94,92,91,90,90 89,89,86,85**
toteswingers:1&2:£6.10, 1&3:£3.20, 2&3:£6.20 CSF £18.68 TOTE £2.10: £1.02, £2.80, £2.10; EX 17.00.Flighty Frances was claimed by J. L. Flint for £5,000.
Owner R A Green **Bred** Mervyn Stewkesbury **Trained** Lower Beeding, W Sussex

FOCUS

A muddling claimer with the form held down by the fourth and seventh.

Flighty Frances(IRE) Official explanation: jockey said filly never travelled

Pebblesonthebeach Official explanation: jockey said gelding hung left-handed

6842 COME JUMP RACING THIS SUNDAY CLAIMING STKS 6f (P)
6:10 (6:12) (Class 6) 2-Y-O **£1,637** (£483; £241) **Stalls** High

Form RPR

5510 1 **Rosina Grey**[12] 6528 2-8-11 85 JamesMillman[(3)] 4 78+
(B R Millman) *hld up and racd wd in rr: wanting to hang rt fr over 2f out: prog over 1f out: cajoled along and styd on to ld post* **5/1**[2]

2231 2 nse **Chevise (IRE)**[35] 5865 2-8-4 75 (t) MartinLane[(3)] 5 71+
(R M Beckett) *wl plcd: effrt 2f out: drvn to ld 1f out: styd on: hdd post* **5/1**[2]

4230 3 1 **My Lord**[15] 6435 2-8-7 74 MatthewDavies[(3)] 9 71
(W G M Turner) *dwlt: hld up wl in rr: prog on inner over 2f out: drvn and styd on fnl f to take 3rd nr fin* **16/1**

2205 4 1/2 **Captain Dimitrios**[19] 6325 2-8-13 73 CathyGannon 3 72
(P D Evans) *pressed ldr: led narrowly over 2f out: drvn and hdd 1f out: one pce* **8/1**[3]

1001 5 shd **Bilko Pak (IRE)**[33] 5921 2-9-5 85 RichardHughes 2 79
(R Hannon) *forced to r wd in midfield: drvn over 2f out: tried to cl on ldrs over 1f out: one pce and hld whn short of room ins fnl f* **7/2**[1]

0050 6 hd **Silence Is Bliss (IRE)**[25] 6191 2-8-13 74 (p) LiamKeniry 11 71
(J S Moore) *hld up in midfield: effrt over 2f out: nt clr run over 1f out tl ins fnl f: drvn and styd on wl last 100yds* **11/1**

1546 7 nk **Magic Cross**[7] 6674 2-8-1 57 (t) DavidProbert 1 59
(P J McBride) *dwlt: hld up wl in rr: plld out wd over 2f out: prog over 1f out: clsd on ldng gp fnl f: one pce last 100yds* **25/1**

1042 8 1 1/2 **Fifth Ave**[9] 6636 2-8-11 83 SophieDoyle[(3)] 10 67
(J A Osborne) *chsd ldng pair to over 2f out: sn rdn: one pce and lost pls ins fnl f: wknd nr fin* **7/2**[1]

4520 9 1 3/4 **Silly Billy (IRE)**[20] 6311 2-8-9 67 SteveDrowne 7 57
(S Kirk) *led: rdn and narrowly hdd over 2f out: pressed ldr to over 1f out: wknd ins fnl f* **16/1**

0 10 3 1/4 **Lisselton Cross**[34] 5895 2-8-9 0 FergusSweeney 12 47
(M R Bosley) *hld up wl in rr: prog on inner over 2f out: no hdwy over 1f out: wknd fnl f* **100/1**

0 11 12 **He'Sahit (FR)**[13] 6500 2-8-12 0 IanMongan 6 14
(P R Hedger) *t.k.h in midfield: wknd rapidly over 2f out: sn bhd* **66/1**

00 12 21 **Street Cred (IRE)**[14] 6451 2-8-4 0 WilliamCarson 8 —
(P Burgoyne) *prom tl wknd rapidly wl over 2f out: t.o* **100/1**

1m 12.87s (-0.23) **Going Correction** -0.125s/f (Stan) **12 Ran SP% 116.3**
Speed ratings (Par 93): **96,95,94,93,93 93,93,91,88,84 68,40**
toteswingers:1&2:£5.70, 1&3:£16.30, 2&3:£9.20 CSF £29.23 TOTE £10.60: £4.00, £1.50, £11.20; EX 35.30.
Owner P Gibbins M Daly **Bred** The Three Point Partnership **Trained** Kentisbeare, Devon

FOCUS
A modest claimer and the field finished rather compressed. The winner is better than this on her day.

NOTEBOOK
Rosina Grey was best in at the weights in this claimer but she's not an easy ride, and it required the kid-glove treatment from her rider to get her home by the narrowest of margins. She had the race run to suit with the leaders going off quite quick, but when challenging down the outside in the straight she made things difficult for her rider by continually hanging right. With minimal recourse to the whip, though, Millman got her home right on the line. This is her trip. (op 11-2 tchd 6-1)
Chevise(IRE), winner of a maiden over course and distance last time out, was never too far off the pace and was trapped quite wide around the bend, so in the circumstances she ran well. She can win something similar. (op 9-2 tchd 4-1)
My Lord, held up towards the back, nipped through on the inside rail in the closing stages to take third. He seems a pretty consistent sort at this level. (op 14-1)
Captain Dimitrios was rushed up from his low draw to dispute the lead and paid for that early effort in the closing stages. (op 11-1 tchd 12-1)
Bilko Pak(IRE), winner of his previous two starts on Polytrack, had a poor draw, his rider was unable to tuck him in and he ended up racing just about widest of all. He can do better granted better luck with the draw. (op 3-1)
Fifth Ave was a little disappointing as she seemed to enjoy a good run through tracking the leader on the rail, but found little under pressure in the straight. (tchd 10-3)

6843 DIGIBET CASINO MAIDEN STKS (DIV I) 1m (P)
6:40 (6:43) (Class 4) 2-Y-O **£2,914** (£867; £433; £216) **Stalls** High

Form RPR
2 1 **Badeel (USA)**[30] 6036 2-9-3 0 FrankieDettori 5 77
(Saeed Bin Suroor) *led after 1f: mde most after: shkn up and drew at least 3 l clr over 1f out: drvn fnl f: jst hld on* **4/7**[1]

2 shd **Crimson China (USA)** 2-9-3 0 ShaneKelly 8 77+
(B J Meehan) *dwlt: pushed along in midfield 1/2-way and off the pce: prog into 4th 3f out: rdn and hdwy to go 2nd jst over 1f out: clsd on wnr: jst failed* **33/1**

0 3 3 ¾ **Fennica (USA)**[15] 6443 2-8-12 0 RobertHavlin 1 63
(J H M Gosden) *chsd ldng pair after 2f to over 1f out: kpt on same pce to regain 3rd ins fnl f* **14/1**

6 4 ½ **Alfouzy**[26] 6154 2-8-12 0 PhilipRobinson 7 62
(M A Jarvis) *dwlt: wl in rr: pushed along and wnt 5th 3f out: nvr on terms but kpt on steadily fr over 1f out* **15/2**[3]

3 5 3 **Mariners Lodge (USA)**[21] 6278 2-9-3 0 AhmedAjtebi 4 60
(Mahmood Al Zarooni) *t.k.h: led 1f: pressed wnr: upsides over 3f out to over 2f out: wknd over 1f out* **7/2**[2]

0 6 6 **Dark And Dangerous (IRE)**[28] 6087 2-9-3 0 AdamKirby 9 46
(P Winkworth) *dwlt: sn pushed along in rr: nvr a factor* **50/1**

7 2 ¼ **Deceptive** 2-8-12 0 SteveDrowne 3 36
(R Charlton) *chsd ldng trio after 2f to 3f out: rn green and sn wknd* **25/1**

8 8 **Neighbourhood (USA)** 2-9-3 0 GregFairley 10 23
(M Johnston) *hmpd after 2f and dropped to last: virtually t.o over 3f out: no real prog after* **14/1**

0 9 1 ¼ **Black Iceman**[26] 6159 2-9-3 0 MickyFenton 2 20
(J Pearce) *prom early: struggling in rr by 1/2-way: wl bhd fnl 3f* **100/1**

1m 38.77s (-1.03) **Going Correction** -0.125s/f (Stan) **9 Ran SP% 120.7**
Speed ratings (Par 97): **100,99,96,95,92 86,84,76,75**
toteswingers:1&2:£6.20, 1&3:£3.40, 2&3:£40.50 CSF £35.41 TOTE £1.20: £1.02, £15.90, £2.90; EX 25.50.
Owner Godolphin **Bred** Shadwell Farm LLC **Trained** Newmarket, Suffolk

FOCUS
This looked a decent maiden on paper, and the pace and final time were good, but the favourite was made to work hard and only just hung on. Probably just average form.

NOTEBOOK
Badeel(USA) was sent off odds-on to win over 1m1f at Redcar on his debut and was unlucky to bump into a subsequent Group 3 winner, but with that experience under his belt he looked sure to take plenty of beating. Sent into the lead early on, he saw off the Godolphin second string with two furlongs to run and, with proven stamina, looked set for a cosy success, but the runner-up came home strongly and in the end the line came just in time. It'll be interesting to see how he gets on in better company, but his pedigree is all about middle distances next season, and that is when he'll be seen at his best. (op 8-11)
Crimson China(USA) ◆ quickened up really well from a furlong and a half down and almost got up on the line to upset the odds-on favourite. A son of Giant's Causeway out of a half-sister to Elusive City, he hails from a stable whose 2-y-os rarely win first time out, so this has to go down as a most promising effort. He looks sure to take plenty of beating next time, before being upped in grade.
Fennica(USA), who chased the leading pair for a long time until tiring in the straight, was only keeping on one-paced when hampered by the winner approaching the furlong pole. Very well bred, she's the type to do better at three. (op 12-1)
Alfouzy was given plenty to do but stayed on quite pleasingly while still looking green. She can probably win a maiden, but will also be eligible for handicaps after one more run. Official explanation: jockey said filly got upset in stalls and was slowly away (op 9-1)
Mariners Lodge(USA), who was stepping up in distance from 7f, raced alongside the winner for much of the way but couldn't stay with him over the final two furlongs. A drop back to 7f should see him pick up an ordinary AW maiden. (op 10-3 tchd 3-1)
Deceptive looked very much in need of the experience on her debut. Official explanation: jockey said filly ran green

6844 DIGIBET CASINO MAIDEN STKS (DIV II) 1m (P)
7:10 (7:11) (Class 4) 2-Y-O **£2,914** (£867; £433; £216) **Stalls** High

Form RPR
1 **Primevere (IRE)** 2-8-12 0 SteveDrowne 7 81+
(R Charlton) *settled in rr: shkn up 2f out: prog over 1f out: rdn and r.o to ld last 100yds: readily: promising* **16/1**

2 1 **Laatafreet (IRE)** 2-9-3 0 FrankieDettori 9 83+
(Saeed Bin Suroor) *slowest away: rcvrd to chse ldrs: swtchd lft and prog over 2f out: led over 1f out and sn more than a l clr: hdd and outpcd last 100yds* **6/4**[1]

6 3 2 **Shooting Line (IRE)**[28] 6087 2-9-3 0 AdamKirby 4 79
(W R Swinburn) *trckd ldrs: effrt 2f out: rdn to go 2nd briefly 1f out: one pce after* **25/1**

04 4 3 ¾ **Silverware (USA)**[21] 6278 2-9-3 0 RichardHughes 5 70
(R Hannon) *led: rdn over 2f out: hdd & wknd over 1f out* **9/1**[2]

25 5 1 ¾ **Charles Fosterkane**[26] 6159 2-9-0 0 KierenFox(3) 10 66
(J R Best) *prom: rdn to chse ldr over 2f out: hd quite high and nt qckn: wknd over 1f out* **14/1**[3]

4 6 hd **Circus Star (USA)**[26] 6159 2-9-3 0 KierenFallon 2 66
(B J Meehan) *pressed ldr but pushed along bef 1/2-way to do so: lost pl over 2f out: wknd over 1f out* **6/4**[1]

6 7 5 **Achalas (IRE)**[13] 6497 2-9-3 0 IanMongan 1 54
(Mrs H S Main) *racd wd: hld up: outpcd fr over 2f out: no ch after* **50/1**

8 nk **Halifax (IRE)** 2-9-3 0 GregFairley 3 53
(M Johnston) *s.i.s: rn green in detached last and pushed along: nvr a factor* **16/1**

00 9 4 **Carrauntoohil (IRE)**[36] 5829 2-8-12 0 J-PGuillambert 6 39
(Miss Amy Weaver) *a in rr: brief effrt on inner over 2f out: sn wknd* **100/1**

0 10 26 **Come On Eileen (IRE)**[55] 5239 2-8-9 0 AndrewHeffernan(3) 8 —
(R C Guest) *dwlt: a in rr: wknd rapidly over 2f out: t.o* **66/1**

1m 38.13s (-1.67) **Going Correction** -0.125s/f (Stan) **10 Ran SP% 116.7**
Speed ratings (Par 97): **103,102,100,96,94 94,89,89,85,59**
toteswingers:1&2:£7.50, 1&3:£66.10, 2&3:£9.80 CSF £40.25 TOTE £13.30: £2.50, £1.10, £8.00; EX 81.00.
Owner A E Oppenheimer **Bred** Hascombe And Valiant Studs **Trained** Beckhampton, Wilts
■ Stewards' Enquiry : Frankie Dettori one-day ban; carless riding (Oct 27)

FOCUS
The quicker of the two divisions by 0.64sec, and a new 2-y-o course record in a race fought out by a couple of newcomers, both by Singspiel. They both look to have bright futures and this looks a race to be positive about.

NOTEBOOK
Primevere(IRE) ◆ travelled well for much of the race, but she got a bump from the runner-up early in the straight and was then crossed by the third soon afterwards. However, once she was switched to the outside and got rolling she stayed on strongly to win a shade cosily. She has plenty of size, should improve from two to three and on pedigree she'll be suited by middle distances next year. Apparently she'd been showing quite a bit at home, so this was not totally unexpected.
Laatafreet(IRE), a half-brother to Honolulu, who stayed particularly well, missed the break and had to be rushed up to make up the lost ground. Angled off the rail early in the straight, he went to the front going well a furlong out, only to be run down by the strong staying winner. He should have little trouble going one better soon. (op 13-8 tchd 11-8)
Shooting Line(IRE) couldn't make his previous experience tell against the first two but stepped up on his debut effort, and there's better to come from him, perhaps once handicapped. (op 28-1)
Silverware(USA) was given every chance from the front and simply wasn't good enough. He'll have better opportunities if his attentions are switched to handicaps. (tchd 10-1)
Charles Fosterkane, who has a dirt pedigree, did better back on the AW, and looks the type who could do well on the AW over the winter. (op 12-1)
Circus Star(USA) was the disappointment of the race, failing to build on his promising debut effort at Newmarket. Given his pedigree this surface should have been more to his liking. (op 13-8)

6845 DIGIBET CONDITIONS STKS 1m (P)
7:40 (7:40) (Class 3) 2-Y-O **£5,504** (£1,637; £818; £408) **Stalls** High

Form RPR
1110 1 **Byrony (IRE)**[19] 6317 2-8-9 90 RichardHughes 6 77+
(R Hannon) *mde all: set dawdling pce for 3f: qcknd dramatically over 3f out: nvr less than 2 l clr after: rdn out* **9/4**[2]

12 2 3 ¼ **Seattle Drive (IRE)**[26] 6149 2-9-0 93 DaneO'Neill 3 75+
(D R C Elsworth) *plld hrd bhd wnr's slow pce for 3f: settled in 3rd fr 1/2-way: up against it once pce qcknd over 3f out: wnt 2nd again over 2f out: no imp* **4/6**[1]

0601 3 1 ½ **Joyously**[13] 6500 2-8-9 70 ow3 RobertLButler(3) 4 69+
(P Butler) *hld up: chsd wnr 5f out to over 2f out: outpcd and one pce* **33/1**

4 5 **Navigation Track** 2-8-12 0 WilliamBuick 5 58+
(D M Simcock) *dwlt: hld up in last: outpcd fr 3f out: no imp after* **13/2**[3]

1m 46.02s (6.22) **Going Correction** -0.125s/f (Stan) **4 Ran SP% 107.0**
Speed ratings (Par 99): **63,59,58,53**
CSF £4.12 TOTE £5.50; EX 3.50.
Owner Axom XXIII **Bred** Mr & Mrs C Booth **Trained** East Everleigh, Wilts

FOCUS
Just the four runners, and a tactical affair with no gallop at all early and the winning rider dictating. The third governs the form.

NOTEBOOK
Byrony(IRE) was allowed the most uncontested of uncontested leads and dominated at a crawl. Asked to quicken from 3f out, the filly immediately took a couple of lengths lead and was never going to be caught. This success taught us nothing, apart from confirming her preference for Polytrack, having run poorly on good to soft ground on turf last time out. (op 5-2 tchd 11-4)
Seattle Drive(IRE) raced keenly at Newbury last time so it was no surprise to see him fail to settle off this pedestrian gallop. While he still looked to have something in the tank with two and a half furlongs to run, once Dane O'Neill went for him it was soon obvious there was nothing there, and the winner pulled even further clear. Perhaps the jockey was under instructions not to go on even if there was no pace, but the way he was ridden here gave him little chance. (tchd 8-13)
Joyously, having her first start for her new trainer having left David Evans, had little chance on the ratings, and her performance underlines the dubious value of the form.
Navigation Track, the only newcomer in the line-up, was held up in last and Buick's only hope was probably to kick for home first and perhaps catch those in front off guard. Instead, he waited for the leader to begin the sprint and predictably made little headway once in line for home. (op 6-1)

6846 DIGIBET.COM H'CAP 1m 3f (P)
8:10 (8:11) (Class 5) (0-70,70) 3-Y-O+ **£2,286** (£675; £337) **Stalls** High

Form RPR
0-03 1 **Loden**[21] 6290 3-9-3 68 KierenFallon 6 79+
(L M Cumani) *t.k.h: hld up in 5th: wnt 2nd 2f out gng wl: drvn to cl over 1f out: led jst ins fnl f: styd on wl* **13/8**[1]

3552 2 1 **Lady Lam**[13] 6518 4-9-0 59 (t) RichardHughes 3 68
(S Kirk) *hld up in 8th: prog on outer 2f out: clsd over 1f out: wnt 2nd ins fnl f: styd on but no imp on wnr last 100yds* **16/1**

5003 3 ½ **Wasara**[21] 6287 3-8-6 57 HayleyTurner 4 65
(Miss Amy Weaver) *hld up in last quartet: prog fr 3f out: chsd ldrs over 1f out: styd on: nvr quite able to chal* **25/1**

5221 4 1 ¾ **Celestial Girl**[12] 6527 3-9-5 70 ChrisCatlin 12 75
(H Morrison) *hld up in 10th: prog on outer fr 3f out: drvn 2f out: styd on but nvr cl enough to chal* **11/2**[2]

1321 5 1 ¼ **Josr's Magic (IRE)**[21] 6289 6-9-8 67 JimmyQuinn 8 70
(P R Hedger) *trckd ldng pair: led on inner over 2f out gng strly: hdd & wknd jst ins fnl f* **10/1**

2460 6 1 ¼ **Ghufa (IRE)**[29] 6055 6-9-7 69 SimonPearce(3) 9 69
(J Pearce) *hld up in last quartet: wdst of all bnd 3f out and u.p: styd on fr 2f out: nrst fin* **25/1**

4360 **7** *3 1/4* **Lord Theo**[19] 6331 6-9-10 **69**........ J-PGuillambert 14 64
(N P Littmoden) *hld up in 7th: effrt on inner over 2f out: no imp on ldrs over 1f out: wknd fnl f* **28/1**

0233 **8** *1 3/4* **Strategic Mission (IRE)**[7] 6677 5-9-8 **67**........ PaulHanagan 5 58
(P F I Cole) *chsd ldng trio: drvn wl over 2f out: steadily wknd* **7/1**[3]

0402 **9** *1 3/4* **Mister Bit (IRE)**[12] 6527 3-8-11 **65**........ KierenFox(3) 1 53
(J R Best) *hld up in last: sme prog over 2f out to midfield over 1f out: no hdwy after* **14/1**

3116 **10** *8* **Aurora Sky (IRE)**[16] 6427 4-9-8 **67**........ LiamKeniry 2 41
(J Akehurst) *pressed ldr to over 2f out: sn wknd* **14/1**

1310 **11** *2 1/2* **Moscow Oznick**[16] 6427 5-9-7 **66**........(v) CathyGannon 7 35
(D Donovan) *led to over 2f out: wknd qckly* **25/1**

5-5 **12** *1 3/4* **Holden Eagle**[146] 2240 5-9-8 **67**........ SteveDrowne 11 33
(A G Newcombe) *hld up in 9th: nudged along over 3f out: no prog whn reminder over 1f out: hanging sn after and wknd* **50/1**

4000 **13** *2 1/4* **Shifting Gold (IRE)**[12] 6543 4-9-1 **60**........(p) FergusSweeney 13 22
(K A Ryan) *a in last quartet: struggling over 3f out: sn wl bhd* **40/1**

5113 **14** *shd* **Seattle Speight (USA)**[66] 4873 3-8-9 **67**........(v) HarryBentley(7) 10 29
(W J Knight) *hld up in 6th: lost pl 3f out: sn wknd and bhd* **14/1**

2m 18.59s (-3.31) **Going Correction** -0.125s/f (Stan)
WFA 3 from 4yo+ 6lb **14** Ran SP% **120.3**
Speed ratings (Par 103): **107,106,105,104,103 102,100,99,97,92 90,89,87,87**
toteswingers:1&2:£12.60, 1&3:£8.10, 2&3:£26.20 CSF £28.31 CT £502.26 TOTE £3.70: £2.70, £5.00, £6.50; EX 48.40.
Owner Fittocks Stud **Bred** Fittocks Stud **Trained** Newmarket, Suffolk

FOCUS
A bit of a gamble was landed in this ordinary handicap, which was strong run. The winner was unexposed and did best of the prominent runners, and the form makes sense.

6847 RACING UK H'CAP (DIV I) 6f (P)
8:40 (8:43) (Class 6) (0-52,52) 3-Y-0+ **£1,364** (£403; £201) **Stalls** High

Form RPR

0430 **1** **Swansea Jack**[58] 5162 3-8-10 **49**........(t) WilliamCarson 10 57
(S C Williams) *chsd ldrs: effrt and eased towards outer 2f out: shkn up and prog over 1f out: drvn to ld ins fnl f: styd on strly nr fin* **11/4**[1]

4024 **2** *3/4* **Ayam Zainah**[33] 5926 3-8-13 **52**........(v) CathyGannon 8 58
(M R Channon) *chsd ldrs: struggling to hold pl bef 1/2-way: swtchd lft over 2f out: sn lost pl: drvn and r.o over 1f out: tk 2nd nr fin* **6/1**[3]

4364 **3** *3/4* **Mansii**[25] 6206 5-9-0 **52**........(t) DaneO'Neill 6 56
(P J McBride) *hld up towards rr: prog 2f out: drvn and upsides ins fnl f: outpcd after* **8/1**

2532 **4** *1 1/4* **Shakespeare's Son**[27] 6119 5-9-0 **52**........(p) RichardHughes 4 52
(H J Evans) *stdd s: hld up wl in rr: prog towards inner 2f out: drvn to ld 1f out: hdd and fdd ins fnl f* **7/2**[2]

3036 **5** *1/2* **Captain Bluebird (IRE)**[4] 6746 3-8-13 **52**........(b) JamesDoyle 3 50
(D Donovan) *restless in stalls: chsd ldr: nt qckn 2f out: lost 2nd jst over 1f out: one pce after* **12/1**

5600 **6** *1/2* **Izzi Mill (USA)**[45] 5562 4-8-9 **52**........(e[1]) JohnFahy(5) 5 48
(P W D'Arcy) *chsd ldrs: hanging bdly and lost pl over 2f out: styd on again u.p fnl f* **25/1**

0460 **7** *hd* **Nativity**[32] 5960 4-9-0 **52**........(p) SamHitchcott 2 48
(J L Spearing) *hld up and swtchd fr wd draw: pushed along fr 2f out: keeping on whn rdn fnl f: nvr nr ldrs* **20/1**

3026 **8** *1 1/4* **Barraland**[8] 6644 5-8-12 **50**........(p) TonyCulhane 7 42
(George Baker) *led: hdd & wknd 1f out* **14/1**

4200 **9** *1 1/4* **Guildenstern (IRE)**[33] 5926 8-9-0 **52**........ JimmyQuinn 11 40
(P Howling) *hld up towards rr: prog on inner 2f out: cl enough over 1f out: rdn and fnd nil* **8/1**

164 **10** *1* **Pavement Games**[13] 6490 3-8-8 **50**........ KierenFox(3) 12 35
(R C Guest) *v awkward s: mostly last: rdn 2f out: one pce and no imp* **10/1**

0565 **11** *3 3/4* **Barberhoney**[40] 5729 3-8-8 **50**........ AndrewHeffernan(3) 9 23
(J R Jenkins) *chsd ldng pair to over 1f out: wknd rapidly* **20/1**

6-00 **12** *1* **One Cool Slash (IRE)**[113] 3292 3-8-10 **49**........ LiamKeniry 1 18
(M J McGrath) *racd wd: nvr bttr than midfield: dropped to rr and btn over 2f out* **33/1**

1m 12.21s (-0.89) **Going Correction** -0.125s/f (Stan)
WFA 3 from 4yo+ 1lb **12** Ran SP% **125.2**
Speed ratings (Par 101): **100,99,98,96,95 95,94,93,91,90 85,83**
toteswingers:1&2:£4.10, 1&3:£4.50, 2&3:£15.40 CSF £19.57 CT £125.02 TOTE £7.20: £2.30, £2.10, £2.60; EX 29.50.
Owner K J Mercer **Bred** Usk Valley Stud **Trained** Newmarket, Suffolk

FOCUS
A poor handicap and a heavily-gambled winner. The time was a bit quicker than the second division and the third is the best guide.
Swansea Jack Official explanation: trainer's rep said, regarding apparent improvement in form, that this was the gelding's first run on the all-weather

6848 RACING UK H'CAP (DIV II) 6f (P)
9:10 (9:10) (Class 6) (0-52,52) 3-Y-0+ **£1,364** (£403; £201) **Stalls** High

Form RPR

0265 **1** **Embra (IRE)**[14] 6464 5-8-11 **52**........(p) RobertLButler(3) 3 63
(T J Etherington) *hld up in 7th: shkn up and prog on outer 2f out: drvn to cl and take narrow ld ins fnl f: hld on* **11/1**

6314 **2** *nk* **Mushy Peas (IRE)**[31] 5990 3-8-10 **49**........ CathyGannon 10 59
(P D Evans) *sn pushed along in 4th: prog u.p to ld over 1f out: hdd ins fnl f: kpt on wl: a hld* **11/4**[1]

0200 **3** *1 1/2* **Metropolitan Chief**[19] 6329 6-9-0 **52**........ LiamKeniry 7 57
(P Burgoyne) *awkward s: hld up in last trio: swtchd out wd 2f out: prog over 1f out: styd on to take 3rd ins fnl f* **16/1**

2300 **4** *1 1/2* **Bold Ring**[83] 4298 4-9-0 **52**........ EddieCreighton 4 52
(E J Creighton) *chsd ldng quartet: rdn and nt qckn 2f out: tried to cl 1f out: kpt on same pce* **20/1**

-000 **5** *2* **Mister Fantastic**[27] 6125 4-9-0 **52**........(b[1]) PaulHanagan 9 46
(N J Vaughan) *chsd ldr: hrd rdn 2f out: lost 2nd over 1f out: fdd fnl f* **7/2**[3]

2053 **6** *1 1/4* **Rigid**[11] 6579 3-8-13 **52**........ RichardHughes 5 42
(A W Carroll) *hld up in 6th: drvn and fnd nil over 1f out: no imp after* **3/1**[2]

3005 **7** *1 1/4* **Inquisitress**[32] 5962 6-8-13 **51**........ NeilChalmers 1 37
(J J Bridger) *mostly in last trio: shkn up 2f out: one pce and no threat* **10/1**

0000 **8** *4 1/2* **Angle Of Attack (IRE)**[14] 6464 5-8-10 **48**........ JimmyQuinn 6 19
(A D Brown) *led to over 1f out: wknd qckly* **16/1**

0400 **9** *1 3/4* **Drubinca**[28] 6076 3-8-11 **50**........(v) WilliamCarson 2 16
(S C Williams) *outpcd in last and a detached* **14/1**

2300 **10** *nk* **Cheshire Lady (IRE)**[40] 5730 3-8-11 **50**........ LiamJones 8 15
(W M Brisbourne) *racd wd: pressed ldng pair to over 2f out: wknd rapidly* **20/1**

1m 12.65s (-0.45) **Going Correction** -0.125s/f (Stan)
WFA 3 from 4yo+ 1lb **10** Ran SP% **119.3**
Speed ratings (Par 101): **98,97,95,93,90 89,87,81,79,78**
toteswingers:1&2:£10.70, 1&3:£13.10, 2&3:£12.80 CSF £42.39 CT £503.50 TOTE £12.20: £5.10, £3.00, £8.60; EX 73.20 Place 6 £89.56; Place 5 £56.20.
Owner The Carpe Diem Partnership **Bred** Michael Kavanagh **Trained** Norton, N Yorks

FOCUS
The leaders went off too fast and it paid to be held up. The winning time was 0.44sec slower than the first division. The runer-up is rated 5lb better than his turf form.
Drubinca Official explanation: jockey said gelding never travelled
T/Plt: £260.10 to a £1 stake. Pool:£65,104.56 - 182.72 winning tickets T/Qpdt: £89.10 to a £1 stake. Pool:£8,865.00 - 73.60 winning tickets JN

6520 LINGFIELD (L-H)
Wednesday, October 13

OFFICIAL GOING: Standard
Wind: modest, half against Weather: overcast, dry

6849 EUROPEAN BREEDERS' FUND SOMAC SERVICES MAIDEN STKS 7f (P)
2:00 (2:00) (Class 5) 2-Y-O **£2,978** (£886; £442; £221) **Stalls** Low

Form RPR

25 **1** **Muntasib (USA)**[54] 5263 2-9-3 0........ RichardHills 6 75
(M P Tregoning) *chsd ldr: rdn to ld ent fnl f: kpt on wl fnl f: rdn out* **9/2**[3]

24 **2** *1/2* **Yojimbo (IRE)**[15] 6443 2-9-3 0........ RichardHughes 2 74
(M R Channon) *trckd ldrs: swtchd lft and effrt over 1f out: pressed wnr thrght fnl f: kpt on but a hld* **11/4**[1]

26 **3** *2 3/4* **Jalors (IRE)**[14] 6457 2-9-3 0........ JoeFanning 4 67
(M Johnston) *led: rdn ent fnl 2f: hdd ent fnl f: nt pce of ldng pair and btn ins fnl f* **10/1**

00 **4** *nk* **Palm Pilot (IRE)**[14] 6469 2-8-12 0........ JimCrowley 7 61
(E A L Dunlop) *hld up in rr of main gp: rdn and hdwy over 1f out: r.o wl fnl f: gng on strly fin: nt rch ldrs* **33/1**

00 **5** *1 1/4* **Honkers Bonkers**[39] 5761 2-9-3 0........ JamesDoyle 3 63
(A J McCabe) *in tch: effrt and rdn to chse ldrs over 1f out: outpcd and btn fnl f* **100/1**

342 **6** *2 3/4* **Apollo D'Negro (IRE)**[11] 6575 2-9-3 74........(b[1]) LukeMorris 8 56
(C G Cox) *in tch: rdn and unable qck over 1f out: one pce and wl hld fnl f* **17/2**

7 *2 3/4* **Medaille D'Or** 2-8-12 0........ PhilipRobinson 14 44
(M A Jarvis) *s.i.s: rn green in rr: hdwy and in tch on outer 3f out: rn green and outpcd bnd over 2f out: n.d after* **12/1**

8 *3* **Obsession (IRE)** 2-9-3 0........(v[1]) RyanMoore 1 41
(J Noseda) *v s.i.s: detached in last and rdn along thrght: modest hdwy fnl f: n.d* **9/1**

0 **9** *1* **L'Hermitage (IRE)**[25] 6190 2-9-3 0........ KierenFallon 13 38
(B J Meehan) *sn outpcd and rdn along in rr: wl btn whn rn wd bnd 2f out: n.d* **10/3**[2]

00 **10** *shd* **Bella Nemica**[15] 6441 2-8-12 0........ EddieCreighton 9 33
(E J Creighton) *in tch: rdn and struggling jst over 2f out: wl btn whn edgd lft jst ins fnl f* **250/1**

0 **11** *1* **Golden Compass**[139] 2474 2-8-12 0........ SaleemGolam 5 30
(G C Bravery) *hld up wl in tch: rdn and wknd over 2f out: wl bhd fnl f* **22/1**

12 *18* **Jessica Ashton** 2-8-12 0........ TadhgO'Shea 11 —
(J Gallagher) *v.s.a: a detached in last pair: t.o fnl 2f* **100/1**

1m 24.92s (0.12) **Going Correction** 0.0s/f (Stan) **12** Ran SP% **114.9**
Speed ratings (Par 95): **99,98,95,94,93 90,87,83,82,82 81,60**
toteswingers:1&2:£2.80, 1&3:£8.50, 2&3:£5.10 CSF £16.29 TOTE £4.80: £1.80, £1.90, £2.80; EX 18.60 Trifecta £90.90 Pool: £416.71 - 3.39 winning units..
Owner Hamdan Al Maktoum **Bred** Branch Equine Llc **Trained** Lambourn, Berks

FOCUS
Just a fair maiden. The time and the principals set the level.

NOTEBOOK
Muntasib(USA), always well placed, ran on strongly and built on the form he showed on his first two starts. He's quite a big type, but handled this tight track well and has the scope to go improving. (tchd 5-1)
Yojimbo(IRE) ran another solid race but he's yet to really progress from his promising debut second to Fury and, as such, he's vulnerable in this sort of company. A step up to 1m should help, though, and nurseries are now an option. (op 3-1tchd 10-3 in places)
Jalors(IRE) didn't act on soft ground over 1m last time, and these conditions suited better. He's now qualified for a handicap mark. (op 9-1 tchd 11-1)
Palm Pilot(IRE) was set a bit to do and wasn't given a hard time, but she finished well. She wants further and should find her level in handicaps. (op 25-1)
Honkers Bonkers is now qualified for an official rating and should find easier opportunities.
Apollo D'Negro(IRE) didn't get much cover early on and was a bit keen in first-time blinkers, not running to his mark of 74. (op 8-1 tchd 10-1)
Medaille D'Or, a half-sister to numerous minor winners, out of a US 1m4f Grade 2 winner, was badly in need of the experience. Official explanation: jockey said filly ran green, particularly on the bends (tchd 14-1)
Obsession(IRE) had a visor fitted for his debut but it didn't wake him up much - he started slowly and needed to be driven along early to take an interest. (op 8-1)
L'Hermitage(IRE) shaped nicely on debut over 7f at Newbury and is from a stable whose youngsters often improve for a run, but he was never really going. Perhaps the track and/or surface didn't suit, and a wide draw was no help, so he'll be worth another chance to confirm that initial promise. (op 4-1 tchd 11-4)

6850 EUROPEAN BREEDERS' FUND PREMIER SHOWFREIGHT NOVICE STKS 1m (P)
2:30 (2:31) (Class 4) 2-Y-O **£4,144** (£1,233; £616; £307) **Stalls** High

Form RPR

0 **1** **Garde Cotiere (USA)**[12] 6532 2-9-0 0........ RyanMoore 5 94+
(J Noseda) *travelled wl: chsd ldr 5f out: rdn to ld ent fnl f: styd on strly fnl f: comf* **15/8**[1]

3213 **2** *4* **Enabling (IRE)**[26] 6149 2-9-5 **91**........ RichardHughes 2 90
(R Hannon) *led for 1f: chsd ldr tl 5f out: drvn and effrt jst over 2f out: chsd wnr jst ins fnl f: no imp and btn fnl 100yds: eased towards fin* **10/3**[3]

3123 **3** *3 3/4* **Owain (USA)**[7] 6667 2-9-2 **78**........ CathyGannon 1 78
(C A Dwyer) *hld up in tch: rdn to chse ldng pair jst over 2f out: drvn wl over 1f out: plugged on to go modest 3rd ins fnl f: no ch w wnr* **5/1**

14 **4** *1 1/2* **Cloud Rock**[26] 6149 2-9-2 **85**........ JimmyFortune 4 75
(P W Chapple-Hyam) *chsd ldr tl led after 1f: rdn 2f out: hdd ent fnl f: wknd fnl 150yds* **9/4**[2]

5 *10* **Sawahill** 2-8-9 0 .... NeilCallan 3 45
(C E Brittain) *dwlt: in tch tl struggling and rdn over 2f out: wl btn over 1f out* **25/1**

06 **6** *16* **Trojan Touch (USA)**[7] 6667 2-9-0 0 .... EddieCreighton 6 13
(C A Dwyer) *wl in tch: rdn and lost tch over 2f out: wl bhd and eased ins fnl f* **250/1**

1m 37.6s (-0.60) **Going Correction** 0.0s/f (Stan) **6** Ran SP% **109.5**
Speed ratings (Par 97): **103,99,95,93,83 67**
toteswingers:1&2:£2.20, 1&3:£2.50, 2&3:£2.10 CSF £8.07 TOTE £2.70: £1.40, £1.60; EX 7.40.
Owner Sir Robert Ogden **Bred** Haras Du Mezeray & Ships Commodities Int **Trained** Newmarket, Suffolk

FOCUS
A good novice event. The time was quicker than both divisions of the Class 5 handicap for older horses. The form stacks up at face value and the winner impressed.

NOTEBOOK
Garde Cotiere(USA) justified strong market support. He ran green and found 7f an insufficient test on debut in a big-field Newmarket maiden, but has clearly made good progress. Although a touch keen early, he was basically just travelling with enthusiasm and powered away when getting first run on the runner-up entering the straight. He has plenty of scope and could be a pattern horse in the making (was entered in Racing Post Trophy, and is in the Irish Guineas). (op 9-4 tchd 5-2)
Enabling(IRE) was weak in the market but went some way to confirming the improvement he showed when a staying-on third in the Haynes, Hanson & Clark at Newbury, though he again lacked the pace to get into a winning position. He had to wait for a clear run entering the straight, but was basically just no match at all for the smart winner. An official rating of around 91 could make him tricky to place, but he may benefit from a step up in trip. (op 9-4 tchd 7-2)
Owain(USA), trying his furthest trip to date, got away on terms this time (missed break last three starts), but raced off the pace and lacked the speed of the front two. He ran a very similar race in a 6f novice event on the Kempton on his previous start and basically isn't up to this level, indeed his new official mark of 85 looks a shade too high. (tchd 9-2)
Cloud Rock didn't settle and was then outpaced when behind Enabling at Newbury on his previous start, so a forward ride looked a good move this time, but he found disappointingly little for pressure. The surface should have been okay (sire has good record on Polytrack), but he was a cheap purchase and it's now looking doubtful he'll progress. Official explanation: jockey said colt moved poorly under pressure (op 10-3)
Sawahill started slowly and ran in snatches, needing the experience. (op 20-1 tchd 16-1)

6851 CAROL SHEPPARD'S BIRTHDAY CREW SUPPORTING H.A.M. H'CAP (DIV I) 1m (P)
3:00 (3:00) (Class 5) (0-75,75) 3-Y-0+ **£2,047** (£604; £151; £151) **Stalls** High

Form RPR

3544 **1** **Cativo Cavallino**[21] 6292 7-8-4 61 .... NataliaGemelova(3) 4 68
(J E Long) *sn pushed up to ld after 1f: mde rest: qcknd ent fnl 2f: hld on wl fnl f* **14/1**

6000 **2** *½* **Green Earth (IRE)**[35] 5866 3-9-2 73 ....(p) NeilCallan 11 79
(Mrs A J Perrett) *t.k.h: hld up wl in tch: effrt and rdn to press ldrs ent fnl f: ev ch fnl 150yds: a jst hld* **16/1**

5222 **3** *1* **Plutocraft**[34] 5887 3-8-13 70 .... PatCosgrave 2 74
(J R Fanshawe) *hld up wl in tch in midfield: rdn and effrt wl over 1f out: kpt on wl u.p ins fnl f: nt rch ldrs* **11/2**[2]

223 **3** *dht* **Abhar (USA)**[16] 6430 3-9-1 75 .... KierenFox(3) 6 79
(J R Best) *t.k.h: led for 1f: chsd wnr after: ev ch and rdn over 1f out: no ex and btn fnl 75yds* **5/1**[1]

1406 **5** *1 ¼* **Seasonal Cross**[15] 6444 5-9-6 74 .... HayleyTurner 10 75
(S Dow) *stdd after s: hld up in tch in midfield: effrt and rdn wl over 1f out: styd on same pce and no imp ins fnl f* **15/2**

5003 **6** *shd* **Copper Penny**[11] 6580 3-9-4 75 .... TedDurcan 12 75
(D R Lanigan) *wl in tch on outer: rdn to chse ldrs jst over 1f out: styd on same pce fnl f* **6/1**[3]

0503 **7** *½* **Silent Oasis**[22] 6275 4-8-13 67 .... FergusSweeney 5 66
(B G Powell) *hld up wl in tch in midfield: rdn and effrt wl over 1f out: hanging lft and one pce fr over 1f out* **20/1**

0025 **8** *1* **Prince Of Thebes (IRE)**[16] 6430 9-9-7 75 .... LukeMorris 3 72
(M J Attwater) *chsd ldrs: rdn jst over 2f out: drvn and btn jst over 1f out: styd on same pce fnl f* **15/2**

0360 **9** *nk* **Basra (IRE)**[96] 3863 7-9-7 75 .... IanMongan 1 71
(Miss Jo Crowley) *hld up wl in tch in rr: rdn and effrt wl over 1f out: kpt on fnl f: nvr able to chal* **14/1**

6020 **10** *hd* **Expensive Problem**[21] 6289 7-9-0 71 .... AndrewHeffernan(3) 8 67
(R J Smith) *stdd after s: t.k.h: hld up in tch in rr: rdn and effrt wl over 1f out: no imp* **7/1**

000 **11** *4 ½* **Conry (IRE)**[26] 6167 4-9-5 73 .... StephenCraine 9 58
(Patrick Morris) *taken down early: stdd after s: t.k.h: hld up in tch in rr: rdn and no prog wl over 1f out: n.d* **12/1**

6500 **12** *1 ¾* **Bennelong**[207] 943 4-8-12 69 ....(t) SimonPearce(3) 7 50
(G C Bravery) *stdd s: hld up in tch in rr: rdn and no hdwy ent fnl 2f: wl bhd fnl f* **33/1**

1m 38.5s (0.30) **Going Correction** 0.0s/f (Stan)
WFA 3 from 4yo+ 3lb **12** Ran SP% **117.0**
Speed ratings (Par 103): **98,97,96,96,95 95,94,93,93,93 88,86**
PL: Plutocraft £1.10, Abhar £0.60 .T/C: CC&GE&PC £702.67, CC&GE&AH £648.98.
toteswingers:CC&GE:£54.70, GE&CC:£14.20, CC&GE:£12.40, GE&PC:£10.00, 1&2:£8.30 CSF £216.76 TOTE £15.40: £5.30, £6.10; EX 241.60 TRIFECTA Not won..
Owner P Saxon **Bred** Miss A M Rees **Trained** Caterham, Surrey

FOCUS
A modest handicap and form to treat with caution as Cativo Cavallino was allowed to set a steady pace under a well-judged ride, resulting in a time 0.73 seconds slower than the second division, won by Three Ducks. The front four are rated close to their marks but the form is not that solid.

6852 CAROL SHEPPARD'S BIRTHDAY CREW SUPPORTING H.A.M. H'CAP (DIV II) 1m (P)
3:35 (3:35) (Class 5) (0-75,75) 3-Y-0+ **£2,047** (£604; £302) **Stalls** High

Form RPR

2234 **1** **Three Ducks**[15] 6444 4-9-7 75 .... RichardHughes 6 82+
(R Hannon) *hld up wl in tch: trckd ldrs and looking for gap ent fnl f: rdn and hdwy ins fnl f: led fnl 75yds: rdn out* **8/1**

202 **2** *nk* **The Happy Hammer (IRE)**[14] 6456 4-8-7 61 .... ChrisCatlin 8 68
(Eugene Stanford) *led tl hdd 2f out: stl ev ch and rdn over 1f out: edgd rt jst ins fnl f: kpt on wl* **14/1**

1054 **3** *nk* **Kiss A Prince**[14] 6479 4-9-4 72 ....(b) JimmyFortune 12 78
(D K Ivory) *stdd s: t.k.h: hld up in tch in rr: rdn and hdwy on outer over 1f out: r.o wl ins fnl f: nt quite rch ldrs* **7/1**[3]

00-0 **4** *hd* **Final Verse**[273] 151 7-9-7 75 .... TadhgO'Shea 3 81
(Miss Tor Sturgis) *stdd after s: hld in tch in rr: hdwy and rdn over 1f out: flashed tail u.p 1f out: r.o wl ins fnl f: nt quite rch ldrs* **12/1**

3021 **5** *¾* **Recalcitrant**[30] 6023 7-8-10 67 .... SimonPearce(3) 4 71
(S Dow) *chsd ldr: rdn to ld 2f out: drvn over 1f out: hdd fnl 75ys: no ex towards fin* **16/1**

0000 **6** *¾* **Kilburn**[33] 5919 6-9-2 70 ....(p) TedDurcan 1 72
(A J Lidderdale) *chsd ldrs on inner: rdn and effrt ent fnl 2f: kpt on same pce u.p fnl f* **28/1**

5021 **7** *½* **Tap Dance Way (IRE)**[59] 5113 3-9-1 72 .... LiamKeniry 9 73
(P R Chamings) *t.k.h: hld up wl in tch: rdn and chsd ldrs ent fnl 2f: drvn and one pce over 1f out: swtchd lft ins fnl f* **14/1**

2-52 **8** *nk* **Dancing Queen (IRE)**[35] 5866 3-9-2 73 .... GeorgeBaker 7 73
(M A Magnusson) *hld up in tch towards rr: switching rt and looking for run jst over 2f out: rdn and kpt on same pce fr over 1f out* **2/1**[1]

0515 **9** *hd* **Walcot Square (IRE)**[25] 6197 3-9-4 75 .... WilliamBuick 2 75
(R Charlton) *hld up in tch towards rr: rdn over 2f out: kpt on but nvr gng pce to rch ldrs* **6/1**[2]

0-00 **10** *½* **Maswerte (IRE)**[112] 3330 4-9-5 73 .... JimCrowley 11 72
(M Wigham) *chsd ldng pair: outpcd and lost pl ent fnl 2f: btn and kpt on same pce fnl f* **22/1**

2660 **11** *6* **Trafalgar Square**[9] 6632 8-8-12 66 ....(v) NeilCallan 10 51
(M J Attwater) *reminder sn after s: in tch towards rr: hdwy on outer over 3f out: rdn and wknd over 2f out* **12/1**

603R **R** **Sir Frank Wappat**[27] 6105 3-9-3 74 .... KierenFallon 5 —
(M Johnston) *ref to r* **14/1**

1m 37.77s (-0.43) **Going Correction** 0.0s/f (Stan)
WFA 3 from 4yo+ 3lb **12** Ran SP% **120.3**
Speed ratings (Par 103): **102,101,101,101,100 99,99,98,98,98 92,—**
toteswingers:1&2:£10.30, 1&3:£7.20, 2&3:£19.20 CSF £116.47 CT £845.87 TOTE £5.10: £1.70, £4.10, £2.40; EX 72.00 TRIFECTA Not won..
Owner Mrs James Wigan **Bred** Mrs James Wigan **Trained** East Everleigh, Wilts

FOCUS
A typically tight Lingfield handicap, though the pace was fair with The Happy Hammer and Recalcitrant disputing the lead for a long way. The winning time was 0.73 seconds faster than the steadily run first division. Ordinary form which seems sound overall.

6853 L & M BODY REPAIRS LEGENDARY CLASSIFIED CLAIMING STKS (DIV I) 7f (P)
4:05 (4:05) (Class 6) 3-Y-0+ **£1,706** (£503; £252) **Stalls** Low

Form RPR

060 **1** **Fol Liam**[18] 6371 4-8-0 62 ow2 ....(p) AndrewHeffernan(3) 12 67
(A J McCabe) *in tch in midfield: rdn over 2f out: str run u.p fnl f to ld fnl 50yds* **12/1**

3454 **2** *1 ¼* **Faited To Pretend (IRE)**[28] 6078 3-8-7 67 .... ChrisCatlin 7 69
(M Botti) *racd keenly: sn led: rdn over 1f out: clr ins fnl f tl wknd and hdd fnl 50yds* **9/2**[2]

2312 **3** *nk* **Perfect Friend**[18] 6370 4-9-1 70 .... RichardHughes 3 75
(S Kirk) *chsd ldrs: rdn over 2f out: drvn 2f out: chsd ldr jst over 1f out: kpt on same pce u.p ins fnl f* **15/8**[1]

0560 **4** *½* **Super Frank (IRE)**[30] 6025 7-8-1 70 ....(b) LukeMorris 5 60
(J Akehurst) *in tch in midfield: hmpd 6f out: hdwy to trck ldrs gng wl ent fnl 2f: sn swtchd rt and drvn wl 1f out: fnd little and no prog over 1f out: plugged on again fnl 100yds* **15/2**

0620 **5** *1 ½* **Know No Fear**[30] 6025 5-7-12 57 ....(p) AmyScott(5) 11 58
(A J Lidderdale) *t.k.h: in tch: hmpd 6f out: hdwy to chse ldr 4f out: rdn wl over 1f out: lost 2nd jst over 1f out: kpt on same pce fnl f* **25/1**

3020 **6** *3 ½* **I Confess**[15] 6439 5-7-12 65 ....(b) SimonPearce(3) 6 46
(G C Bravery) *chsd ldrs: rdn over 2f out: wknd u.p over 1f out* **5/1**[3]

4100 **7** *¾* **Lopinot (IRE)**[153] 2053 7-8-7 63 ....(v) LiamKeniry 9 50
(M R Bosley) *stdd s: racd in last trio: hdwy into midfield ent fnl 2f: rdn and no prog fr over 1f out* **16/1**

00-0 **8** *nk* **Sir Ike (IRE)**[34] 5877 5-8-9 58 ....(tp) FergusSweeney 10 52
(W S Kittow) *stdd s: hld up in rr: rdn wl over 1f out: nvr trbld ldrs* **16/1**

0-06 **9** *nse* **Public Image**[201] 986 4-8-4 46 .... MartinLane(3) 8 49
(Jamie Poulton) *dwlt: a in rr: nvr trbld ldrs* **33/1**

5020 **10** *shd* **King's Sabre**[14] 6452 4-8-3 65 .... JimmyQuinn 1 45
(D Bourton) *taken down early: stdd s: hld up in last trio: hmpd 6f out: nvr trbld ldrs* **10/1**

1-04 **11** *3 ¾* **Shark Man (IRE)**[7] 4132 3-7-13 67 ow1 ....(p) SophieDoyle(3) 2 36
(Andrew Reid) *hld up in midfield: hmpd 6f out: rdn and wknd 2f out: wl bhd fnl f* **14/1**

1m 24.9s (0.10) **Going Correction** 0.0s/f (Stan)
WFA 3 from 4yo+ 2lb **11** Ran SP% **123.4**
Speed ratings (Par 101): **99,97,97,96,94 90,90,89,89,89 85**
toteswingers:1&2:£17.50, 1&3:£8.30, 2&3:£2.40 CSF £68.61 TOTE £18.10: £3.90, £1.30, £2.00; EX 91.30 Trifecta £167.50 Pool: £355.57 - 1.57 winning units..
Owner A C Timms **Bred** Adrian Smith **Trained** Averham Park, Notts
■ Stewards' Enquiry : Andrew Heffernan four-day ban: careless riding (Oct 27-30)

FOCUS
A modest claimer run in a time 0.68 seconds quicker than the second division. The form makes some sense buit should not be taken too literally.

6854 L & M BODY REPAIRS LEGENDARY CLASSIFIED CLAIMING STKS (DIV II) 7f (P)
4:40 (4:41) (Class 6) 3-Y-0+ **£1,706** (£503; £252) **Stalls** Low

Form RPR

0442 **1** **Hierarch (IRE)**[16] 6413 3-8-9 69 .... RichardHughes 9 66
(R Hannon) *chsd ldrs: wnt 2nd 5f out: rdn and ev ch ent fnl 2f: led 1f out: kpt on up: rdn out* **5/2**[1]

0000 **2** *1* **Rubenstar (IRE)**[18] 6370 7-8-3 66 .... CathyGannon 10 57
(Patrick Morris) *stdd s: hld up in tch in rr: hdwy into midfield jst over 2f out: rdn over 1f out: kpt on fnl f: wnt 2nd on post* **15/2**

0306 **3** *nse* **Dvinsky (USA)**[12] 6524 9-8-3 67 ....(b) JimmyQuinn 4 57
(P Howling) *t.k.h: hld up wl in tch: rdn and effrt to join ldrs ent fnl f: drvn and styd on same pce fnl 150yds: lost 2nd on post* **9/1**

000 **4** *hd* **Fernando Torres**[13] 6515 4-8-4 56 .... KellyHarrison(3) 12 60
(N P Littmoden) *led: rdn wl over 1f out: hdd 1f out: styd on same pce fnl 100yds* **28/1**

03 **5** *¾* **The Winged Assasin (USA)**[18] 6371 4-8-1 66 .... JamieMackay 6 52
(M Wigham) *stdd s: hld up in tch in rr: hdwy over 1f out swtchd rt jst ins fnl f: keeping on but hld whn nt clr run and eased towards fin* **11/2**[3]

0452 **6** *1* **Lady Kent (IRE)**[26] 6164 4-8-6 68 .... SamHitchcott 5 54
(J R Boyle) *hld up in tch in rr: hdwy on inner jst over 2f out: rdn to chse ldrs ent fnl f: keeping on same pce whn nt clr run and swtchd rt fnl 100yds* **7/2**[2]

4005 **7** *shd* **Another Magic Man (USA)**[9] 6632 3-8-6 69 .... KierenFox(3) 7 58
(J R Best) *in tch: hdwy to chse ldrs and rdn jst over 2f out: outpcd over 1f out: keeping on same pce and btn whn pushed rt jst ins fnl f* **6/1**

5000 **8** *1* **Shaded Edge**[28] 6085 6-8-11 63 JamesDoyle 11 56
(D W P Arbuthnot) *chsd ldrs: drvn ent fnl 2f: ev ch ent fnl f: wknd qckly fnl 100yds* **14/1**

4200 **9** *hd* **Wise Up**[12] 6541 3-8-7 67 EddieCreighton 3 53
(C A Dwyer) *in tch in midfield: racing awkwardly and dropped to rr 3f out: kpt on same pce and n.d fnl 2f* **33/1**

1m 25.58s (0.78) **Going Correction** 0.0s/f (Stan)
WFA 3 from 4yo+ 2lb **9** Ran SP% **115.3**
Speed ratings (Par 101): **95,93,93,93,92 91,91,90,90**
toteswingers:1&2:£4.40, 1&3:£4.60, 2&3:£7.40 CSF £21.95 TOTE £2.30: £1.02, £3.70, £3.40; EX 28.70 Trifecta £115.20 Pool: £512.52 - 3.29 winning units..Hierarch was claimed by D. J. Flood for £10,000.
Owner Highclere Thoroughbred Racing(Emil Adam) **Bred** Castlemartin Stud And Skymarc Farm **Trained** East Everleigh, Wilts
■ Stewards' Enquiry : Jamie Mackay three-day ban: careless riding (Oct 27-29)

FOCUS
The pace was steady, resulting in a time 0.68 seconds slower than the first division. Muddling form rated through the fourth, and the winner did not need to improve.
The Winged Assasin(USA) Official explanation: jockey said gelding suffered interference in running

6855 SWEETWOODS GOLF CLUB H'CAP 2m (P)
5:15 (5:15) (Class 6) (0-65,63) 3-Y-O+ **£2,047** (£604; £302) **Stalls** Low

Form RPR

60-0 **1** **King's Realm (IRE)**[12] 6527 3-9-3 **62** SebSanders 4 71+
(Sir Mark Prescott) *stdd s: hld up in rr: swtchd rt and gd hdwy on outer over 3f out: rdn to ld jst over 2f out: hung lft u.p over 1f out: styd on wl to forge ahd ins fnl f* **7/1**

1-02 **2** *1 ¾* **Dansilver**[13] 6502 6-9-10 **58** RichardHughes 9 65
(A W Carroll) *hld up in tch towards rr: stdy hdwy fr 9f out: ev ch and rdn ent fnl 2f: no ex and btn fnl 100yds* **9/2**[2]

0544 **3** *½* **Carnac (IRE)**[18] 6373 4-9-3 **51** (b) JamesDoyle 1 58+
(A J McCabe) *hld up in tch: shuffled bk towards rr and nt clr run briefly jst over 2f out: sn switching rt and rdn: kpt on u.p fnl f to go 3rd fnl 50yds* **6/1**[3]

54-2 **4** *½* **Wester Ross (IRE)**[18] 5722 6-9-10 **58** LukeMorris 10 64
(J M P Eustace) *dwlt: sn bustled along and hdwy to chse ldrs after 2f: wnt 2nd 7f out tl led over 3f out: rdn and hdd jst over 2f out: kpt on same pce u.p after* **6/1**[3]

0202 **5** *4* **Mymateeric**[22] 6272 4-8-11 **48** SimonPearce[(3)] 3 49
(J Pearce) *in tch towards rr: pushed along 8f out: rdn and effrt over 2f out: outpcd by ldrs ent fnl 2f: kpt on same pce after* **8/1**

4-04 **6** *1 ¼* **Slew Charm (FR)**[231] 426 8-9-7 **55** (t) TravisBlock 12 55
(Noel T Chance) *stdd s: hld up in rr: hdwy 4f out: rdn and chsd ldrs ent fnl 2f: no prog and wknd u.p over 1f out* **10/1**

221 **7** *2 ¾* **Marcus Antonius**[22] 6273 3-9-0 **59** PatCosgrave 11 55
(J R Boyle) *t.k.h: chsd ldrs tl wnt 2nd 10f out tl 7f out: styd chsng ldrs: n.m.r on inner bnd jst over 2f out: wknd u.p over 1f out* **7/2**[1]

6020 **8** *½* **Mixing**[13] 6502 8-8-6 **45** JemmaMarshall[(5)] 8 41
(M J Attwater) *t.k.h: hld up wl in tch: rdn and outpcd over 2f out: no ch w ldrs fr wl over 1f out* **40/1**

500 **9** *8* **Shannon Falls (FR)**[84] 4257 6-9-2 **50** DaneO'Neill 5 36
(Miss Jo Crowley) *stdd s: hld up in rr: rdn and struggling over 2f out: wl btn fnl 2f* **25/1**

0640 **10** *1* **Whitley Bay (USA)**[22] 6272 3-8-0 **45** JimmyQuinn 6 30
(J R Best) *chsd ldrs tl wknd u.p over 2f out: wl bhd over 1f out* **25/1**

0006 **11** *28* **Belvidera**[9] 6637 4-8-11 **45** (v) LiamJones 14 —
(A W Carroll) *sn led: hdd and rdn over 3f out: sn dropped out and bhd: t.o fnl 2f* **66/1**

/-00 **12** *3* **Noddies Way**[27] 6114 7-9-0 **48** JimCrowley 2 —
(J F Panvert) *sn bustled along to chse ldr: lost 2nd 10f out: lost pl qckly u.p 4f out: t.o fnl 2f* **20/1**

3m 25.32s (-0.38) **Going Correction** 0.0s/f (Stan)
WFA 3 from 4yo+ 11lb **12** Ran SP% **118.1**
Speed ratings (Par 101): **100,99,98,98,96 96,94,94,90,89 75,74**
toteswingers:1&2:£7.20, 1&3:£14.40, 2&3:£9.30 CSF £36.14 CT £203.67 TOTE £9.90: £3.30, £2.30, £2.60; EX 46.60 Trifecta £167.50 Pool: £366.74 - 1.62 winning units..
Owner P J McSwiney - Osborne House **Bred** Swordlestown Stud **Trained** Newmarket, Suffolk

FOCUS
A modest staying handicap run at a reasonable gallop. The form is rated around the second to fourth.
King's Realm(IRE) Official explanation: trainer's rep said, regarding apparent improvement in form, that the gelding was suited by the longer distance and had improved in fitness.

6856 TAGWORLDWIDE.COM H'CAP 1m 2f (P)
5:45 (5:45) (Class 5) (0-70,70) 3-Y-O **£2,388** (£705; £352) **Stalls** Low

Form RPR

443 **1** **Piano**[32] 5971 3-9-4 **67** WilliamBuick 7 80+
(J H M Gosden) *hld up in tch towards rr: nt clr run on inner jst over 2f out: hdwy and switching rt wl over 1f out: stl only 6th 1f out: str run fnl 100yds to ld last strides* **2/1**[1]

0003 **2** *nk* **Trailblazing**[8] 6664 3-9-7 **70** (b) JoeFanning 13 82
(M Johnston) *hld up in tch in midfield: hdwy 3f out: rdn to ld ent fnl 2f: clr ins fnl f: kpt on tl hdd last strides* **14/1**

3056 **3** *2 ¾* **Eltheeb**[35] 5858 3-9-6 **69** (b[1]) RichardHills 9 75
(J L Dunlop) *dwlt: sn pushed along and hdwy into midfield: swtchd rt and gd hdwy over 2f out: ev ch and rdn 2f out: btn 1f out: kpt on same pce after* **8/1**

0321 **4** *2 ½* **D'Urberville**[21] 6287 3-9-1 **64** JimmyQuinn 8 65
(J R Jenkins) *chsd ldrs: rdn ent fnl 2f: wknd u.p jst over 1f out* **11/1**

355 **5** *nk* **Pedantic**[36] 5839 3-9-2 **65** KierenFallon 5 65
(L M Cumani) *hld up in tch in midfield: hdwy over 2f out: rdn and no prog fr wl over 1f out* **5/1**[3]

0600 **6** *1 ¾* **Sunset Place**[30] 6020 3-8-11 **60** LukeMorris 3 57
(C G Cox) *chsd ldrs: rdn over 2f out: wknd u.p over 1f out* **50/1**

2224 **7** *1 ½* **Azaday (IRE)**[21] 6290 3-9-6 **69** GeorgeBaker 6 63
(C F Wall) *led tl 6f out: rdn to ld again over 2f out tl ent fnl 2f: wknd ent fnl f: fdd fnl 100yds* **4/1**[2]

006 **8** *¾* **Lingfield Bound (IRE)**[27] 6122 3-9-3 **69** KierenFox[(3)] 10 61
(J R Best) *hld up in last trio: rdn and effrt on outer wl over 2f out: wd and no prog bnd ent fnl 2f: n.d after* **12/1**

4-30 **9** *nk* **Spirit Of Love (IRE)**[19] 6332 3-9-3 **66** StephenCraine 12 58
(M Wigham) *stdd s: hld up in last trio: pushed along and sme hdwy over 2f out: stl plenty to do whn nt clr run bnd 2f out: n.d after* **28/1**

630- **10** *1 ½* **Masterful Act (USA)**[385] 6211 3-9-7 **70** TonyCulhane 2 59
(E F Vaughan) *hld up in last trio: rdn and hanging lft over 1f out: nvr trbld ldrs* **40/1**

250 **11** *hd* **My Sister**[34] 5887 3-8-12 **61** HayleyTurner 4 49
(M D I Usher) *in tch in midfield: rdn and struggling whn sltly hmpd ent fnl 2f: sn wl btn* **18/1**

0632 **12** *8* **Layla's Lexi**[23] 6257 3-9-3 **66** StevieDonohoe 14 38
(Ian Williams) *chsd ldrs tl rdn and wknd over 2f out: bhd whn n.m.r bnd ent fnl 2f* **16/1**

4 **13** *11* **Vezere (USA)**[22] 6275 3-9-4 **67** SebSanders 11 17
(S Dow) *t.k.h: chsd ldr tl led 6f out: rdn and hdd over 2f out: sn wknd* **25/1**

2m 4.93s (-1.67) **Going Correction** 0.0s/f (Stan) **13** Ran SP% **126.6**
Speed ratings (Par 101): **106,105,103,101,101 99,98,98,97,96 96,90,81**
toteswingers:1&2:£7.60, 1&3:£6.30, 2&3:£20.40 CSF £35.24 CT £203.99 TOTE £3.00: £1.40, £6.20, £4.50; EX 47.10 Trifecta £155.50 Pool: £449.85 - 2.14 winning units. Place 6 £53.28; Place 5 £30.11.
Owner Cheveley Park Stud **Bred** Cheveley Park Stud Ltd **Trained** Newmarket, Suffolk

FOCUS
A fair 3-y-o contest run at a good pace and won in extraordinary fashion by handicap debutante Piano, who came from an impossible-looking position. She looks better than the bare form, which has been rated slightly positively.
T/Plt: £35.60 to a £1 stake. Pool:£58,904.46 - 1,205.96 winning tickets T/Qpdt: £18.50 to a £1 stake. Pool:£4,592.28 - 183.30 winning tickets SP

6435 BRIGHTON (L-H)
Thursday, October 14

OFFICIAL GOING: Good (good to soft in places; 7.8)
Wind: modest, half behind Weather: bright and sunny

6858 DIGIBET.COM H'CAP 5f 59y
2:30 (2:30) (Class 5) (0-75,75) 3-Y-O+ **£2,331** (£693; £346; £173) **Stalls** Centre

Form RPR

1121 **1** **Kinigi (IRE)**[5] 6741 4-8-9 **66** 6ex (b) AndrewHeffernan[(3)] 2 81
(R A Harris) *chsd ldrs: rdn and effrt 2f out: led over 1f out: r.o strly and clr ins fnl f: readily* **9/4**[1]

0454 **2** *3* **Make My Dream**[16] 6440 7-9-1 **69** CathyGannon 3 73
(J Gallagher) *hld up in tch in rr: effrt on far side and rdn 2f out: kpt on to chse clr wnr ins fnl f: no imp fnl 100yds* **13/2**

2050 **3** *¾* **Whiskey Junction**[13] 6523 6-9-4 **72** ShaneKelly 6 73
(M Quinn) *led: rdn and hdd ent fnl 2f: outpcd by wnr ent fnl f: styd on same pce ins fnl f* **14/1**

0051 **4** *½* **Colorus (IRE)**[22] 6284 7-8-6 **67** (v) MatthewCosham[(7)] 7 67
(W J H Ratcliffe) *w ldrs: rdn to ld ent fnl 2f: hdd over 1f out: outpcd by wnr ent fnl f: kpt on same pce after* **14/1**

0664 **5** *shd* **Highland Harvest**[16] 6439 6-9-0 **68** StevieDonohoe 9 67
(Jamie Poulton) *hld up wl in tch: rdn and hanging lft over 1f out: continued hanging and styd on same pce ins fnl f* **10/1**

1004 **6** *½* **Cut The Cackle (IRE)**[10] 6637 4-9-4 **75** (b) RobertLButler[(3)] 1 73
(P Butler) *v.s.a: bhd: effrt on far side 2f out: drvn and hdwy over 1f out: kpt on same pce and swtchd rt ins fnl f* **33/1**

4613 **7** *1 ¼* **Love You Louis**[44] 5628 4-9-7 **75** RichardHughes 8 68
(J R Jenkins) *stdd s: hld up wl in tch: rdn and effrt over 1f out: drvn and btn 1f out: wknd fnl 100yds* **11/2**[2]

6006 **8** *nk* **Athwaab**[13] 6523 3-8-9 **63** WilliamCarson 10 55
(M G Quinlan) *in tch on outer: rdn and no prog over 1f out: no ch w wnr ins fnl f* **14/1**

0320 **9** *1* **Triple Dream**[16] 6440 5-9-6 **74** (p) LiamKeniry 4 63
(J M Bradley) *pressed ldr: rdn 1/2-way: wknd u.p over 1f out* **12/1**

0256 **10** *¾* **Rocker**[16] 6440 6-9-6 **74** GeorgeBaker 5 60
(G L Moore) *bmpd s: in tch in rr: rdn and effrt wl over 1f out: drvn and btn jst over 1f out: wknd ins fnl f* **6/1**[3]

61.30 secs (-1.00) **Going Correction** -0.175s/f (Firm) **10** Ran SP% **113.5**
Speed ratings (Par 103): **101,96,95,94,94 93,91,90,89,87**
CSF £16.11 CT £162.86 TOTE £2.50: £1.10, £1.80, £5.80; EX 19.20 Trifecta £300.60 Pool: £654.15 - 1.61 winning units..
Owner Brian Hicks **Bred** Corduff Stud **Trained** Earlswood, Monmouths

FOCUS
The inside rail was dolled out six yards from the 6f to 3f marker, but not as far as it was at the previous meeting. A drying day aided by a breeze behind the runners in the straight allowed the ground to dry out to good, good to soft in places. A fair and quite tightly knit sprint handicap in which the runners were spread across the track once the false rail ended, but the majority ended up towards the far side. Another step up from the winner, with the form rated around the runner-up.

6859 EUROPEAN BREEDERS' FUND MEDIAN AUCTION MAIDEN STKS 7f 214y
3:00 (3:01) (Class 5) 2-Y-O **£3,154** (£944; £472; £236; £117) **Stalls** Centre

Form RPR

2320 **1** **Fly By White (IRE)**[15] 6471 2-8-12 72 RichardHughes 10 72
(R Hannon) *t.k.h: chsd ldr tl led 6f out: mde rest: rdn and forged clr jst over 1f out: in command ins fnl f: eased nr fin* **7/2**[1]

53 **2** *3 ½* **Suddenly Susan (IRE)**[14] 6497 2-8-12 0 DarryllHolland 5 64
(J Noseda) *led tl 6f out: chsd wnr after: rdn 4f out: chal u.p over 2f out: edgd rt and no ex over 1f out: edgd lft and plugged on same pce ins fnl f* **7/2**[1]

0400 **3** *½* **Captain Sharpe**[28] 6129 2-9-3 55 LukeMorris 7 68
(H J L Dunlop) *chsd ldrs: effrt and unable qck wl over 2f out: drvn and kpt on same pce fr over 1f out* **100/1**

4354 **4** *1 ½* **Cornish Quest**[28] 6130 2-9-3 68 LiamJones 2 65
(M H Tompkins) *chsd ldrs: effrt u.p to chse ldng pair over 2f out: btn over 1f out: plugged on same pce ins fnl f* **10/1**

3332 **5** *2 ¼* **Zakon (IRE)**[17] 6411 2-9-3 72 (v[1]) ShaneKelly 3 60
(D J Coakley) *t.k.h: hld up in midfield: rdn and nt qckn over 2f out: drvn and no prog 2f out* **4/1**[2]

03 **6** *¾* **Afaara (IRE)**[10] 6635 2-8-12 0 DaneO'Neill 8 53
(Mrs A J Perrett) *t.k.h: in tch in midfield: rdn and outpcd ent fnl f: n.d fnl 2f: plugged on again ins fnl f* **6/1**[3]

0 **7** *1 ½* **Desert Location**[15] 6468 2-8-12 0 HayleyTurner 6 50
(M L W Bell) *dwlt: racd in midfield: rdn and struggling 1/2-way: sn outpcd and n.d fr wl over 2f out* **12/1**

0 **8** *3* **Mystic Edge**[15] 6469 2-8-12 0 J-PGuillambert 4 43
(M L W Bell) *stdd s: racd in last trio: rdn and struggling over 3f out: wl btn fnl 3f* **40/1**

00 **9** *5* **Bumbling Bertie**[27] 6159 2-9-3 0 DavidProbert 11 37
(A M Balding) *dwlt: sn pushed along and rn green: struggling over 4f out: u.p and wl btn 3f out* **40/1**

4 **10** *10* **Dancing All Night**[10] 6628 2-8-12 0 ChrisCatlin 9 10
(M R Channon) *stdd s: a in rr: lost tch over 3f out* **15/2**

000 **11** *9* **Blade Pirate**[3] 6795 2-9-3 50 (be) StevieDonohoe 1 —
(J Ryan) *stdd and dropped in bhd after s: a last: lost tch over 3f out: t.o* **100/1**

1m 35.17s (-0.83) **Going Correction** -0.175s/f (Firm) **11** Ran SP% **114.1**
Speed ratings (Par 95): **97,93,93,91,89 88,87,84,79,69 60**
CSF £14.99 TOTE £3.50: £1.10, £1.30, £18.00; EX 13.20 Trifecta £534.40 Part won. Pool: £722.25 - 0.74 winning units..
Owner Turf Club 2008 **Bred** Lynch Bages,Samac Ltd & Brittas Hse Stud **Trained** East Everleigh, Wilts

FOCUS
An ordinary auction maiden in which they ended up racing centre to stands' side and it proved best to race close to the pace.

NOTEBOOK
Fly By White(IRE) had some decent form earlier in the season but did not get home over 1m2f on soft on her previous start. However, much happier back on this better ground, Hughes went on before halfway and the filly was always holding off her rivals in the last couple of furlongs. She should be up to winning a handicap at around this trip. (op 10-3 tchd 3-1)
Suddenly Susan(IRE) had shown plenty of promise in two starts at shorter. She made the early running and kept battling on in pursuit of the winner in the straight, despite wandering about on the camber. She should be capable of breaking her maiden on a more conventional track. (op 10-3 tchd 4-1)
Captain Sharpe, rated just 55 after five starts in maidens and nurseries (one a seller), had the headgear left off and appeared to run well above himself, at the same time limiting the form.
Cornish Quest, another stepping up in trip, ran his race without ever looking likely to beat the winner, and might be best off in handicaps off his current mark. (op 8-1)
Zakon(IRE) had been pretty consistent previously and was proven at the trip. However, he was too keen in the first-time visor and could make no impression in the closing stages. (tchd 9-2)
Afaara(IRE) ran well over this trip on soft last time, but proved less effective held up on this better ground. She at least qualifies for handicaps now. (op 13-2 tchd 7-1 and 11-2)
Blade Pirate Official explanation: jockey said gelding hung left

6860 BRIGHTON SQUARE "HEART OF LANES" H'CAP 1m 1f 209y
3:30 (3:32) (Class 6) (0-60,60) 3-Y-O+ **£1,942** (£578; £288; £144) **Stalls** High

Form RPR

/003 **1** **Broughtons Dream**[46] 5559 4-8-12 48 StevieDonohoe 5 61
(W J Musson) *t.k.h: hld up in tch in midfield: rdn to chse ldr over 1f out: led 1f out: r.o wl: rdn out* **20/1**

4306 **2** *nk* **Catbells (IRE)**[5] 6747 3-9-1 56 (p) RobertWinston 2 68
(A Bailey) *dwlt: sn chsng ldrs: trckd ldrs gng wl ent fnl 2f: rdn to ld over 1f out: hdd 1f out: r.o and drew clr w wnr ins fnl f: a jst hld* **9/2**[1]

0040 **3** *5* **Rocky Mood (IRE)**[40] 5766 3-9-2 57 (p) LukeMorris 4 62+
(W R Swinburn) *in tch in midfield: rdn and effrt to chse ldrs whn hmpd 2f out: no ch w ldng pair: kpt on u.p ins fnl f* **12/1**

4424 **4** *nk* **Prince Valentine**[43] 5655 9-8-11 47 (p) RichardHughes 6 48
(G L Moore) *hld up in midfield: rdn and effrt ent fnl 2f: drvn and pressing for 3rd 1f out: kpt on: no imp on ldng pair* **10/1**

3342 **5** *nk* **Corrib (IRE)**[35] 5873 7-9-0 50 (p) DavidProbert 7 51
(B Palling) *hld up in tch in rr: rdn over 2f out: hdwy u.p over 1f out: kpt on same pce and no ch w ldng pair fnl f* **9/2**[1]

4020 **6** *1 ¾* **Optimistic Duke (IRE)**[12] 4448 3-8-11 52 HayleyTurner 11 49
(W R Muir) *chsd ldrs: rdn over 2f out: unable qck u.p whn hmpd 2f out: one pce after* **16/1**

0060 **7** *½* **It's A Mans World**[28] 6125 4-8-6 49 RyanPowell(7) 15 45
(Ian Williams) *t.k.h: chsd ldr tl led 8f out: edging rt fr 3f out and on stands' rail whn rdn and hdd over 1f out: wknd ent fnl f* **25/1**

6000 **8** *1 ½* **On The Cusp (IRE)**[29] 6098 3-8-8 52 ow1 (b) RobertLButler(3) 8 45
(P Butler) *t.k.h: hld up in tch in midfield: hdwy to chse ldrs and rdn whn edgd rt 2f out: wknd over 1f out* **33/1**

0454 **9** *3 ¾* **Golden Prospect**[99] 3787 6-9-10 60 PaulFitzsimons 3 46
(Miss J R Tooth) *stdd s: t.k.h: hld up in tch in rr: hdwy on inner over 4f out: rdn and btn 2f out* **25/1**

2600 **10** *½* **Outland (IRE)**[30] 6065 4-9-6 56 GeorgeBaker 10 41
(J R Jenkins) *led for 2f: chsd ldrs after: squeezed for room and lost pl ent fnl 2f: wl btn over 1f out* **15/2**[2]

43-0 **11** *½* **Forty Thirty (IRE)**[77] 3723 4-9-5 55 JamieGoldstein 12 39
(Miss Sheena West) *in tch towards rr: rdn and effrt but stl plenty to do whn hmpd 2f out: n.d after* **17/2**[3]

6030 **12** *3* **Joinedupwriting**[8] 6669 5-9-7 57 J-PGuillambert 16 35
(R M Whitaker) *stdd s: hld up in rr: rdn and struggling over 3f out: n.d* **14/1**

0003 **13** *2 ½* **House Point**[15] 6460 3-9-2 57 WilliamCarson 14 30
(S C Williams) *a towards rr: rdn and effrt 4f out: wknd over 2f out: sn bhd: eased ins fnl f* **9/1**

4440 **F** **Wavertree Bounty**[3] 6816 3-8-7 48 MarcHalford 9 —
(J Ryan) *chsd ldrs: rdn 4f out: drvn and struggling whn short of room: clipped heels and fell heavily 2f out* **14/1**

2m 2.90s (-0.70) **Going Correction** -0.175s/f (Firm)
WFA 3 from 4yo+ 5lb **14** Ran SP% **120.0**
Speed ratings (Par 101): **95,94,90,90,90 88,88,87,84,83 83,81,79,—**
toteswingers:1&2: £20.70, 2&3: £15.40, 1&3: £33.70 CSF £103.69 CT £1160.31 TOTE £28.20: £6.00, £1.90, £4.70; EX 156.90 TRIFECTA Not won..
Owner Broughton Thermal Insulation **Bred** M E Broughton **Trained** Newmarket, Suffolk
■ Stewards' Enquiry : Ryan Powell eight-day ban: careless riding (Oct 28-Nov 4)

FOCUS
A big field for this low-grade handicap and it became something of a rough race with general bunching inside the last 2f. Very modest form, with the winner up a stone.

6861 EUROPEAN BREEDERS' FUND MAIDEN STKS 1m 3f 196y
4:00 (4:04) (Class 5) 3-Y-O+ **£3,217** (£962; £481; £240; £119) **Stalls** High

Form RPR

042 **1** **Gakalina (IRE)**[9] 6661 3-8-12 0 DarryllHolland 5 77
(J Noseda) *chsd ldr: rdn and ev ch over 3f out: drvn to ld wl over 1f out: outbattled runner-up and hld on ins fnl f* **11/4**[1]

4223 **2** *nk* **Bombadero (IRE)**[9] 6661 3-9-3 78 (b) TedDurcan 1 82
(J L Dunlop) *sn chsng ldrs: swtchd rt and rdn 3f out: chsd wnr and hung rt u.p over 1f out: edgd lft and ev ch ins fnl f: nt qckn u.p and hld fnl 75yds* **10/3**[2]

-323 **3** *2 ¼* **Strictly Lambada**[24] 6250 3-8-12 75 RobertHavlin 8 73
(J H M Gosden) *chsd ldrs: clr in ldng quartet over 4f out: drvn to chse ldng pair over 1f out: one pce and btn fnl 150yds: eased towards fin* **7/2**[3]

302 **4** *14* **Momkinzain (USA)**[12] 6557 3-9-3 80 RichardHughes 10 56
(M R Channon) *led: early reminder: pressed and more reminders 5f out: rdn ent fnl 3f: hdd wl over 1f out: sn eased and wl btn 1f out* **4/1**

40 **5** *1* **Blackmore**[21] 6313 3-9-3 0 AmirQuinn 7 54
(Miss J Feilden) *short of room s: hld up in last pair: lost tch w ldrs 5f out: pushed along and sme hdwy whn hmpd 2f out: wnt poor 5th wl over 1f out: nvr trbld ldrs* **66/1**

00 **6** *7* **Precious Spring (IRE)**[24] 6250 3-8-12 0 TomMcLaughlin 3 38
(E A L Dunlop) *in tch: rdn and lost tch w ldrs wl over 4f out: no ch fnl 3f* **25/1**

7 *½* **Paloma Blanca (IRE)**[17] 6434 3-8-12 66 RobertWinston 6 37
(A Bailey) *a towards rr: chsd ldng quartet but toiling bdly wl over 4f out: no ch fnl 4f* **10/1**

0-0 **8** *1 ½* **Velvet Nayef**[24] 6250 4-9-2 0 SimonPearce(3) 9 35
(J Pearce) *a towards rr: lost tch qckly wl over 4f out: wl bhd fnl 3f* **100/1**

0 **9** *13* **Beseech (USA)**[52] 5366 3-8-12 0 CathyGannon 2 14
(Miss J Feilden) *hld up in rr: rdn and toiling 5f out: t.o over 3f out* **100/1**

0- **10** *42* **Sing Of Run**[409] 5499 3-9-3 0 (t) LiamKeniry 11 —
(L Corcoran) *in tch in midfield: lost pl qckly and hung lft 5f out: t.o and eased fr over 3f out* **100/1**

2m 32.3s (-0.40) **Going Correction** -0.175s/f (Firm)
WFA 3 from 4yo 7lb **10** Ran SP% **109.4**
Speed ratings (Par 103): **94,93,92,82,82 77,77,76,67,39**
toteswingers:1&2: £2.30, 2&3: £2.70, 1&3: £3.60 CSF £10.86 TOTE £3.20: £1.10, £1.90, £2.00; EX 12.50 Trifecta £27.70 Pool: £1079.69 - 28.75 winning units..
Owner Nurlan Bizakov **Bred** John Connaughton **Trained** Newmarket, Suffolk
■ Stewards' Enquiry : Ted Durcan four-day ban: struck colt in annoyance (Oct 28-31)

FOCUS
A decent older-horse maiden for the time of year but the market concerned only five, and only four of those were in contention inside the last 2f. The runner-up is the best guide and the winner did not need to match his Southwell latest.
Momkinzain(USA) Official explanation: jockey said colt hung badly left
Blackmore Official explanation: jockey said gelding did not come down the hill
Paloma Blanca(IRE) Official explanation: jockey said filly did not handle the track

6862 BRIGHTONANDHOVEJOBS.COM H'CAP (DIV I) 7f 214y
4:30 (4:33) (Class 6) (0-60,60) 3-Y-O **£1,619** (£481; £240; £120) **Stalls** Centre

Form RPR

305 **1** **One Hit Wonder**[10] 6633 3-9-7 60 LiamKeniry 2 71+
(Mouse Hamilton-Fairley) *in tch in midfield: pushed along 4f out: rdn and hdwy to chal over 1f out: led ent fnl f: r.o wl and clr fnl 100yds: comf* **3/1**[1]

14 **2** *2 ¼* **Ermyntrude**[50] 5414 3-8-9 53 JemmaMarshall(5) 10 57
(P M Phelan) *chsd ldrs: wnt 2nd over 2f out: rdn to ld over 1f out: hdd ent fnl f: nt gng pce of wnr fnl 150yds: kpt on to hold 2nd* **9/2**[3]

0005 **3** *1* **Tarita (IRE)**[15] 6452 3-9-7 60 (t) RichardHughes 11 62
(R Hannon) *in tch: effrt and rdn to chse ldrs over 1f out: drvn and kpt on same pce ins fnl f* **13/2**

3020 **4** *1 ¾* **Farmers Dream (IRE)**[41] 5710 3-9-4 57 CathyGannon 5 55
(J L Spearing) *stdd s: t.k.h: hld up in rr: rdn and racd awkwardly downhill 3f out: drvn and hdwy to chse ldrs over 1f out: no imp and btn ins fnl f* **8/1**

00 **5** *½* **Zagarock**[19] 6375 3-9-2 55 RobertWinston 1 52
(B Palling) *chsd ldr tl over 2f out: wknd u.p over 1f out* **9/1**

0335 **6** *1* **Eye Of Eternity**[35] 5877 3-9-3 56 DavidProbert 7 50
(Rae Guest) *short of room and hmpd s: hld up in last trio: effrt and n.m.r ent fnl 2f: hung lft u.p and no hdwy over 1f out* **7/2**[2]

0050 **7** *2 ½* **Fashion Tycoon (IRE)**[48] 5469 3-8-4 46 oh1 SimonPearce(3) 9 34
(M F Harris) *hld up in tch towards rr: rdn and effrt ent fnl 2f: no prog and wl hld over 1f out* **28/1**

0305 **8** *½* **Giulietta Da Vinci**[13] 6522 3-9-2 58 (p) AndrewHeffernan(3) 3 45
(S Woodman) *led: rdn over 2f out: drvn and hdd over 1f out: wknd qckly jst over 1f out* **16/1**

0006 **9** *3* **Lilli Palmer (IRE)**[58] 5175 3-8-10 49 PaulFitzsimons 4 29
(Miss J R Tooth) *a towards rr: pushed along over 4f out: wknd 2f out* **33/1**

0000 **10** *4* **Brody's Boy**[43] 5650 3-8-10 49 ow1 (bt) AmirQuinn 8 20
(G L Moore) *wnt lft s: t.k.h: chsd ldrs: rdn ent fnl 2f: drvn and wknd over 1f out* **20/1**

1m 36.07s (0.07) **Going Correction** -0.175s/f (Firm) **10** Ran SP% **116.9**
Speed ratings (Par 99): **92,89,88,87,86 85,83,82,79,75**
toteswingers:1&2: £5.00, 2&3: £7.40, 1&3: £3.30 CSF £16.24 CT £83.88 TOTE £3.70: £2.10, £1.50, £1.60; EX 17.80 Trifecta £42.90 Pool: £919.53 - 15.83 winning units..
Owner More Money Than Sense Partnership **Bred** Elsdon Farms **Trained** Bramshill, Hants

FOCUS
A moderate but competitive race for the first division of this 3-y-o handicap. It was slightly quicker than division II. The winner posted a small personal best with the third and fifth close to their marks.

6863 BRIGHTONANDHOVEJOBS.COM H'CAP (DIV II) 7f 214y
5:00 (5:01) (Class 6) (0-60,60) 3-Y-O **£1,619** (£481; £240; £120) **Stalls** Centre

Form RPR

6660 **1** **Fire Raiser**[13] 6527 3-9-5 58 DavidProbert 7 65
(A M Balding) *t.k.h: hld up in last trio: swtchd rt and effrt wl over 2f out: drvn to chse ldrs over 1f out: kpt on u.p to ld fnl 75yds: drvn out* **4/1**[2]

0540 **2** *¾* **Whisper Wind**[14] 6518 3-9-4 57 (b) GeorgeBaker 4 62
(G L Moore) *t.k.h: hld up wl in tch: effrt to press ldr over 1f out: rdn to ld ins fnl f: drvn and hdd fnl 75yds: no ex* **7/1**

5520 **3** *1* **Via Aurelia (IRE)**[30] 6060 3-9-4 57 (v) HayleyTurner 3 60
(J R Fanshawe) *stdd s: t.k.h: hld up in tch in rr: hdwy over 1f out: swtchd lft and pressed ldrs gng wl ent fnl 2f: shkn up and fnd nil jst ins fnl f: btn fnl 75yds* **7/1**

3524 **4** *¾* **Little Meadow (IRE)**[13] 6527 3-8-7 51 AmyBaker(5) 8 52
(Miss J Feilden) *t.k.h: hld up wl in tch: rdn ent fnl 2f: edging lft u.p and swtchd rt over 1f out: kpt on same pce ins fnl f* **7/1**

00-4 **5** *1* **Madame Boot (FR)**[20] 6332 3-9-7 60 RichardHughes 6 59
(P J Makin) *chsd ldr: rdn and pressing wnr ent fnl 2f: stl ev ch ch and drvn over 1f out: wknd u.p ins fnl f* **5/1**[3]

4004 **6** *2* **Chateau Zara**[35] 5877 3-9-2 55 TedDurcan 5 49
(C G Cox) *racd keenly: led: rdn ent fnl 2f: hrd pressed over 1f out: hung lft ent fnl f: hdd ins fnl f: wknd fnl 100yds* **7/2**[1]

2400 **7** *2* **Green Community (USA)**[35] 5873 3-9-4 57 LiamKeniry 9 47
(E F Vaughan) *t.k.h: chsd ldrs: rdn and unable qck ent fnl 2f: drvn over 1f out: wknd jst ins fnl f* **14/1**

00-0 **8** *7* **Seeker Rainbow**[62] 5028 3-8-4 46 oh1 SimonPearce(3) 10 19
(Mrs L C Jewell) *t.k.h: in tch on outer: effrt and rdn ent fnl 3f: wknd qckly jst over 2f out* **40/1**

0030 **9** *hd* **Rock D'Argent (IRE)**[190] 1162 3-9-3 56 RobertHavlin 1 29
(A B Haynes) *a bhd: struggling over 3f out: wl bhd over 2f out* **33/1**

034 **10** *1 ¼* **Force To Spend**[34] 5927 3-8-10 **49**................................ J-PGuillambert 2 19
(N P Littmoden) *plld hrd: hld up in tch towards rr: rdn and hdwy ent fnl 2f: btn ent fnl f: heavily eased whn no ch fnl 100yds* **16/1**

1m 36.63s (0.63) **Going Correction** -0.175s/f (Firm) **10** Ran SP% **114.3**
Speed ratings (Par 99): **89,88,87,86,85 83,81,74,74,73**
toteswingers:1&2: £6.50, 2&3: £8.60, 1&3: £4.80 CSF £31.51 CT £188.83 TOTE £3.60: £1.10, £3.30, £4.90; EX 39.00 Trifecta £287.10 Pool: £845.99 - 2.18 winning units..
Owner Kingsclere Racing CLub **Bred** Kingsclere Stud **Trained** Kingsclere, Hants

FOCUS
The second leg of the handicap was run 0.56secs slower than the first division. The winner rates a small personal best.
Green Community(USA) Official explanation: jockey said filly was unsuited by the track
Seeker Rainbow Official explanation: vet said filly returned lame

6864 BOOK YOUR CHRISTMAS ROYALE PARTY NOW H'CAP 6f 209y
5:30 (5:30) (Class 5) (0-70,70) 3-Y-O+ £2,331 (£693; £346; £173) Stalls Centre

Form RPR

2365 **1** **Daddy's Gift (IRE)**[15] 6479 4-8-12 **60**................................ LiamKeniry 13 69
(R Hannon) *chsd ldrs: rdn and ev ch over 1f out: drvn ins fnl f: led fnl 50yds: all out* **16/1**

5450 **2** *½* **Desert Falls**[8] 6672 4-8-7 **55** oh2.................................... HayleyTurner 16 63
(R M Whitaker) *led: rdn ent fnl 2f: kpt on gamely u.p tl hdd and no ex fnl 50yds* **16/1**

5345 **3** *2 ¼* **Al Jaadi**[35] 5891 3-9-2 **66**.. J-PGuillambert 4 67
(W Jarvis) *chsd ldrs: rdn over 2f out: chsd ldng pair and drvn over 1f out: no ex and btn fnl 100yds* **14/1**

0531 **4** *nk* **Grand Vizier (IRE)**[31] 6024 6-9-7 **69**.............................. JackMitchell 14 70+
(C F Wall) *v.s.a and reminders sn after s: bhd and pushed along: rdn and c nrest stands' rail 3f out: stl plenty to do over 1f out: styd on strly ins fnl f: nvr gng pce to rch ldrs* **9/2**[2]

1224 **5** *nk* **Eager To Bow (IRE)**[31] 6023 4-9-4 **66**.......................... GeorgeBaker 10 66
(P R Chamings) *hld up in tch in midfield: rdn and hdwy ent fnl 2f: chsd ldrs and drvn ent fnl f: edging lft and btn fnl 150yds* **3/1**[1]

0023 **6** *½* **Ivory Lace**[31] 6023 9-9-3 **68**.................................. AndrewHeffernan(3) 8 67
(S Woodman) *hld up towards rr: rdn and effrt jst over 2f out: swtchd rt and drvn ins over 1f out: styd on wl ins fnl f: nvr trbld ldrs* **14/1**

4300 **7** *¾* **Child Of Our Time (IRE)**[20] 6336 3-9-3 **67**.................. RobertWinston 7 63
(P W Chapple-Hyam) *in tch: pushed along 4f out: drvn and effrt to chse ldrs over 1f out: one pce and btn ins fnl f* **33/1**

5062 **8** *1 ¼* **Abhainn (IRE)**[31] 6024 4-8-7 **55** oh3................................ DavidProbert 12 49
(B Palling) *in tch in midfield: hdwy to chse ldrs 3f out: rdn over 2f out: wknd ent fnl f* **9/1**[3]

6-00 **9** *½* **Braddock (IRE)**[40] 5764 7-8-4 **55** oh1..........................(t) SimonPearce(3) 5 47
(K O Cunningham-Brown) *chsd ldr tl 2f out: rdn and n.m.r over 1f out: wknd ent fnl f* **80/1**

0000 **10** *¾* **Nubar Boy**[12] 6572 3-8-12 **62**......................................(v) TomMcLaughlin 1 51
(P D Evans) *stdd s: t.k.h: hld up towards rr: rdn and hdwy ent fnl 2f: no prog and btn 1f out* **10/1**

3160 **11** *½* **Phluke**[24] 6261 9-8-5 **60**...(v) DanielBlackett(7) 9 49
(Eve Johnson Houghton) *hld up towards rr: rdn and no hdwy 2f out: nvr trbld ldrs* **28/1**

4040 **12** *hd* **Ocean Countess (IRE)**[31] 6023 4-9-1 **66**.................. KellyHarrison(3) 6 54
(Miss J Feilden) *a towards rr: pushed along over 4f out: rdn and effrt over 2f out: kpt on same pce: n.d* **16/1**

3214 **13** *nk* **The Human League**[13] 6541 3-8-11 **68**.................. MatthewLawson(7) 15 55
(M R Channon) *in tch in midfield: effrt and rdn over 2f out: hrd drvn and wknd over 1f out* **12/1**

3440 **14** *shd* **Decency (IRE)**[22] 6292 3-8-13 **63**................................ DarryllHolland 11 49
(H J L Dunlop) *hld up in rr: rdn and effrt wl over 1f out: nvr trbld ldrs* **33/1**

2660 **15** *2 ¾* **Starry Mount**[7] 6692 3-9-6 **70**....................................(p) RobertHavlin 3 49
(A B Haynes) *racd in midfield: lost pl and rdn over 3f out: wl btn over 1f out* **14/1**

5340 **16** *11* **Gundaroo**[31] 6024 3-8-12 **62**.. TedDurcan 2 —
(J L Dunlop) *midfield tl lost pl and hung rt bnd 4f out: continued to hang rt and wl btn over 2f out: eased ins fnl f* **14/1**

1m 22.8s (-0.30) **Going Correction** -0.175s/f (Firm)
WFA 3 from 4yo+ 2lb **16** Ran SP% **124.8**
Speed ratings (Par 103): **94,93,90,90,90 89,88,87,86,85 85,85,84,84,81 68**
toteswingers:1&2: £44.00, 2&3: £48.10, 1&3: £40.60 CSF £250.76 CT £3815.45 TOTE £20.90: £2.60, £5.90, £4.90, £1.20; EX 525.10 TRIFECTA Not won. Place 6: £35.54 Place 5: £18.95.
Owner Charlee & Hollie Allan **Bred** Vincent Dunne **Trained** East Everleigh, Wilts

FOCUS
Another big field for this modest handicap but again it paid to race close to the pace. There are doubts over the form with the winner having been beaten in sellers this year.
Grand Vizier(IRE) Official explanation: jockey said gelding was slowly away
T/Jkpt: Not won. T/Plt: £69.80 to a £1 stake. Pool of £72,029.02 - 752.51 winning tickets. T/Qpdt: £29.50 to a £1 stake. Pool of £5,057.62 - 126.65 winning tickets. SP

6841 KEMPTON (A.W) (R-H)
Thursday, October 14

OFFICIAL GOING: Standard
Wind: Light, half against Weather: Overcast

6865 BETDAQ THE BETTING EXCHANGE CLASSIFIED STKS 1m (P)
5:20 (5:20) (Class 6) 3-Y-O+ £1,637 (£483; £241) Stalls High

Form RPR

2600 **1** **Lady Of Garmoran (USA)**[8] 6672 3-8-7 55............(b) DuilioDaSilva(7) 8 61
(P F I Cole) *mde virtually all: drew clr over 2f out: rdn over 1f out: kpt on* **14/1**

0400 **2** *2* **Queenie's Star (IRE)**[8] 6672 3-9-0 55............................... JimCrowley 3 56
(M J Attwater) *racd wd: hld up in 8th: rdn over 2f out: prog over 1f out: styd on to take 2nd last 100yds* **33/1**

5026 **3** *2* **Aqua Vitae (IRE)**[41] 5730 3-9-0 55.............................. DaneO'Neill 14 52
(Miss Tor Sturgis) *trckd ldrs in 6th: gng bttr than most 3f out: effrt on inner over 2f out: chsd wnr 1f out: no imp: lost 2nd last 100yds* **8/1**

2400 **4** *2* **King's Approach (IRE)**[13] 6522 3-9-0 55......................(p) LukeMorris 7 47
(R A Harris) *racd freely early: pressed wnr: nt qckn fr 3f out: no imp after: lost 2nd and fdd 1f out* **10/1**

06-0 **5** *½* **Cunning Plan (IRE)**[166] 1694 3-9-0 54............................ LiamJones 13 46
(P W Chapple-Hyam) *nvr gng wl in midfield: reminders over 5f out: u.p fr 1/2-way: kpt on fnl 2f: nrst fin* **12/1**

-600 **6** *nse* **I'Lldoit**[13] 6536 3-8-9 55.. JohnFahy(5) 11 46
(H J Evans) *settled in midfield: scrubbed along bef 1/2-way: nvr gng pce to rch ldrs: kpt on* **8/1**

6060 **7** *2 ¼* **Bill's Story**[13] 6540 3-9-0 55.. ChrisCatlin 12 41
(M R Channon) *dwlt: last tl 1 1/2-way: rdn and plugged on fr over 2f out: n.d* **15/2**[3]

00-0 **8** *nk* **Richardlionheart (USA)**[15] 6476 4-9-3 40.............. FrankieMcDonald 6 40
(M Madgwick) *sn t.k.h: hld up in rr: pushed along over 2f out: v modest late prog* **100/1**

00-0 **9** *¾* **Original Dancer (IRE)**[38] 5815 3-9-0 51......................... GregFairley 10 38
(M Johnston) *dropped to last and pushed along 1/2-way: wl bhd 3f out: kpt on fnl 2f on inner* **7/1**[2]

6624 **10** *2* **Trecase**[22] 6287 3-9-0 55... JimmyFortune 9 34
(A W Carroll) *chsd ldng pair: rdn over 3f out: lost pl over 2f out: steadily wknd: eased fnl f* **5/2**[1]

600/ **11** *1 ¾* **Dancing Belle**[792] 4987 5-9-3 46...................................... ShaneKelly 2 30
(J R Jenkins) *a wl in rr: lft bhd fr 3f out* **28/1**

0060 **12** *6* **Chocolate Cookie (IRE)**[135] 2634 3-9-0 55...............(t) SaleemGolam 5 16
(Miss M E Rowland) *sn pushed up to chse ldrs in 5th: wknd rapidly 2f out* **20/1**

0066 **13** *4* **Retrato (USA)**[15] 6454 3-9-0 47.....................................(bt[1]) RichardMullen 1 7
(Rae Guest) *trckd ldrs tl wknd rapidly wl over 2f out* **12/1**

1m 39.11s (-0.69) **Going Correction** -0.125s/f (Stan)
WFA 3 from 4yo+ 3lb **13** Ran SP% **118.3**
Speed ratings (Par 101): **98,96,94,92,91 91,89,88,88,86 84,78,74**
toteswingers:1&2: £108.00, 2&3 £16.10, 1&3 £13.50 CSF £418.04 TOTE £15.30: £3.30, £17.70, £2.00; EX 945.80.
Owner Mrs Fitri Hay **Bred** B Wayne Hughes **Trained** Whatcombe, Oxon

FOCUS
Seven horses were rated within 1lb on official ratings in this low-grade classified stakes and four were comfortably clear of the remainder at the junction of the two tracks.
Lady Of Garmoran(USA) Official explanation: trainer's rep said, regarding apparent improvement in form, that the filly had benefited from the re-fitting of blinkers

6866 BETDAQEXTRA.COM MAIDEN AUCTION FILLIES' STKS 7f (P)
5:50 (5:56) (Class 5) 2-Y-O £2,286 (£675; £337) Stalls High

Form RPR

5 **1** **Poyle Judy**[17] 6425 2-8-2 0...................................... JohnFahy(5) 4 73
(R M Beckett) *hld up towards rr: prog over 2f out: chsd ldr over 1f out: clsd ins fnl f: rdn to ld last 75yds* **14/1**

334 **2** *1 ½* **Whitecrest**[27] 6161 2-8-7 67... SamHitchcott 6 69
(J L Spearing) *prom on outer: prog to ld over 2f out: clr w wnr over 1f out: hdd last 75yds* **8/1**[3]

32 **3** *2 ¼* **Our Gal**[9] 6651 2-8-10 0... WilliamCarson 7 66
(M G Quinlan) *hld up in midfield: pushed along and effrt over 2f out: styd on fr over 1f out to take 3rd ins fnl f* **5/4**[1]

00 **4** *¾* **Saint Helena (IRE)**[27] 6158 2-8-10 0................................ DaneO'Neill 10 64
(H J L Dunlop) *reluctant to enter stalls: prom: rdn and nt qckn over 2f out: styd on again fr over 1f out: tk 4th nr fin* **14/1**

0 **5** *½* **Arctic Maiden**[27] 6153 2-8-8 0.. SaleemGolam 5 61
(W J Musson) *hld up wl in rr: pushed along over 2f out: prog on inner over 1f out: styd on to take 5th nr fin* **40/1**

025 **6** *¾* **Grecian Goddess (IRE)**[27] 6154 2-8-9 69 ow2................ ShaneKelly 2 60
(J Ryan) *gd spd fr wd draw to ld: sn crossed to rail: hdd over 2f out: sn outpcd* **6/1**[2]

0 **7** *½* **Theavonfilly**[36] 5865 2-8-7 0.. LiamJones 8 57
(R A Teal) *chsd ldrs: nt qckn and lost pl over 2f out: kpt on same pce after* **100/1**

64 **8** *nk* **Petrichor**[13] 6521 2-8-12 0.. JimmyFortune 12 61
(E F Vaughan) *hld up in midfield: n.m.r briefly over 2f out: jst pushed along and kpt on same pce fr over 1f out* **8/1**[3]

9 *shd* **Phase Shift** 2-8-12 0.. JimCrowley 3 61
(W R Muir) *rn green in rr and racd wd: lost grnd bnd 3f out: pushed along over 2f out: sme late prog* **20/1**

3003 **10** *1* **Alexs Rainbow (USA)**[14] 6513 2-8-2 62.................. JulieBurke(7) 14 55
(J Gallagher) *chsd ldr to over 2f out: one pce u.p after: wknd ins fnl f* **9/1**

60 **11** *½* **Stilettoesinthemud (IRE)**[30] 6047 2-8-9 0.................. RichardMullen 9 54
(J G Given) *prom: rdn wl over 2f out: lost pl wl over 1f out: wknd ins fnl f* **20/1**

0 **12** *½* **Burst Of Applause (IRE)**[36] 5865 2-8-11 0..................... ChrisCatlin 11 54
(M G Quinlan) *stdd s: a wl in rr: pushed along and one pce fnl 2f* **33/1**

00 **13** *3* **Generous Genella**[27] 6155 2-8-12 0................................. GregFairley 13 48
(Miss J Feilden) *prom in last after 2f: a bhd* **33/1**

0 **14** *2 ¼* **Misefi**[24] 6247 2-8-9 0.. LukeMorris 1 39
(M R Bosley) *dwlt and wnt lft s: racd wd in rr: wdst of all bnd 3f out: struggling after* **100/1**

1m 26.18s (0.18) **Going Correction** -0.125s/f (Stan) **14** Ran SP% **124.1**
Speed ratings (Par 92): **93,91,88,87,87 86,85,85,85,84 83,83,79,77**
toteswingers:1&2: £14.00, 2&3: £3.00, 1&3 £6.10 CSF £118.53 TOTE £19.60: £4.20, £1.80, £1.10; EX 148.20.
Owner Cecil And Miss Alison Wiggins **Bred** Cecil And Miss Alison Wiggins **Trained** Whitsbury, Hants

FOCUS
A weak fillies' maiden auction race. Some proved very awkward to load and the race was off six minutes after the advertised time.

NOTEBOOK
Poyle Judy, from a stable back on the scoreboard, had shown a glimmer of ability on her debut here two weeks ago and did not go unbacked. Making ground from midfield, she emerged as the sole challenger to the leader. She readily mastered her and was firmly in command at the line. A leggy type, she should improve again and be competitive in handicap company from a mark in the low 70s. (op 16-1 tchd 12-1)
Whitecrest, having her fourth start and rated 67, was quite keen. After taking charge she saw off all but the winner, but was very much second best in the end.
Our Gal, who achieved an RPR of 75 when runner-up on her second start at Leicester a week earlier, was one of the first to load and was in the stalls for some time on her first try on the all-weather. Racing in midfield, she was flat out turning in and, although keeping on all the way to the line, she never threatened the first two. (op 11-10 tchd 11-8)
Saint Helena(IRE), having her third start and her first taste of the all-weather, gave serious problems at the gate. She is now qualified for a handicap mark but looks tricky. (op 20-1 tchd 12-1)
Arctic Maiden stayed on from the rear hard against the far-side rail and may improve again.
Grecian Goddess(IRE), a cheap purchase rated 69 and having her fourth start, took them along on her all-weather debut but in the end came up well short. (op 9-1)

Petrichor showed ability without being any way knocked about and may do better in handicap company at three. (tchd 9-1)

6867 TRY BETDAQ FOR AN EXCHANGE NURSERY (DIV I) 6f (P)
6:20 (6:29) (Class 6) (0-65,66) 2-Y-O **£1,364** (£403; £201) **Stalls** High

Form				RPR
502	1		**Saucy Buck (IRE)**[5] 6740 2-9-5 **63** ... SamHitchcott 9 *(M R Channon) chsd ldng trio: rdn over 2f out: prog wl over 1f out: clsd to ld jst ins fnl f: sn clr* **11/10**[1]	69
2650	2	2	**Avalon Bay**[23] 6271 2-9-3 **61** ... DaneO'Neill 7 *(Pat Eddery) t.k.h: hld up in 5th: prog 2f out: styd on fnl f to take 2nd last strides* **4/1**[2]	61
5230	3	½	**Kokojo (IRE)**[29] 6086 2-9-2 **65** ... JohnFahy(5) 4 *(B G Powell) bmpd s: sn prom: rdn to chse ldr 2f out: clsd 1f out: wnr wnt by: lost 2nd last strides* **15/2**[3]	64
060	4	1 ¼	**Pleasant Humor (USA)**[20] 6333 2-8-7 **51** ...(v[1]) RichardMullen 5 *(R M H Cowell) wnt lft s and bmpd rival: led: gng strly 2f out: hdd & wknd jst ins fnl f* **20/1**	46
0050	5	1 ½	**Freedom Trail**[47] 5527 2-9-6 **64** ... JimCrowley 2 *(D R C Elsworth) bmpd s: hld up in last trio: pushed along and prog fr 2f out: wnt 5th ins fnl f: one pce after* **20/1**	54
5066	6	4	**Cool Land (IRE)**[6] 6711 2-9-0 **58** ... LukeMorris 12 *(R A Harris) awkward s: plld hrd: hld up in 6th: rdn 1/2-way: sn struggling* **12/1**	36
000	7	hd	**Make My Mark (IRE)**[73] 4658 2-8-8 **52** ... ChrisCatlin 3 *(F Jordan) bmpd s: hld up in rr and racd wd: pushed along and no prog 2f out* **33/1**	30
0616	8	½	**Brave Tiger (IRE)**[31] 6035 2-8-13 **57** ...(t) LiamJones 6 *(S C Williams) plld hrd: chsd ldr to 2f out: wknd rapidly over 1f out* **10/1**	33
000	9	½	**Torteval (IRE)**[123] 3000 2-8-7 **51** ow1 ... WilliamCarson 1 *(P D Evans) dwlt and intimidated s: a last: plld out wd over 2f out: no prog* **16/1**	26

1m 13.88s (0.78) **Going Correction** -0.125s/f (Stan) **9** Ran SP% **114.5**
Speed ratings (Par 93): **89,86,85,84,82 76,76,75,75**
toteswingers:1&2: £2.30, 2&3: £4.50, 1&3: £2.90 CSF £5.14 CT £21.48 TOTE £2.70: £1.30, £1.10, £1.90; EX 7.50.
Owner M Channon **Bred** T Sherman **Trained** West Ilsley, Berks

FOCUS
A 50-65 nursery but a seller in all but name for a meagre first prize. The start was delayed five minutes after a withdrawn horse burst out of the stalls and did a lap of the track.

NOTEBOOK
Saucy Buck(IRE), having his 12th start, had started life in nursery company from a stone higher mark. Just denied at Wolverhampton on his previous start, he made quite hard work of it but was right on top at the finish. (tchd 5-4)
Avalon Bay, runner-up here from a 1lb higher mark on his nursery debut four outings ago, is an edgy, keen-going type. Very keen early and inclined to hang left under pressure, he kept on to secure second spot without ever threatening to trouble the winner. (op 5-1)
Kokojo(IRE), stepping up in trip, took a hefty bump at the start. This was her seventh start and she looks fully exposed. (op 8-1)
Pleasant Humor(USA), who had three runs in less than three weeks last month to qualify for a handicap mark, went left exiting the stalls in a first-time visor, hampering those drawn on his outside. Very keen, he took them along but was swallowed up in the end. (op 12-1)
Freedom Trail, one of those inconvenienced by Pleasant Humour at the start, never threatened to enter the argument on her handicap debut. (op 16-1 tchd 25-1)
Brave Tiger(IRE), who made all from a 10lb higher mark over 5f here two outings ago, was much too keen and stopped to nothing in the final furlong. (op 9-1 tchd 11-1)

6868 TRY BETDAQ FOR AN EXCHANGE NURSERY (DIV II) 6f (P)
6:50 (6:54) (Class 6) (0-65,65) 2-Y-O **£1,364** (£403; £201) **Stalls** High

Form				RPR
6061	1		**Cinderkamp**[9] 6645 2-9-7 **65** 6ex ... JimmyFortune 4 *(E F Vaughan) stdd s: hld up towards rr: gd prog fr 2f out: led last 150yds: stormed clr* **5/2**[1]	77
6601	2	3 ½	**Duquesa (IRE)**[8] 6674 2-9-5 **63** 6ex ... CathyGannon 10 *(P D Evans) sn pushed along in rr: u.p and struggling over 2f out: prog over 1f out: styd on wl ins fnl f to take 2nd last stride* **15/2**	65
3263	3	shd	**Misscomplacent**[21] 6311 2-9-3 **61** ...(b[1]) SebSanders 5 *(Mrs A Duffield) trckd ldr after 2f: led 2f out: hdd and outpcd last 150yds: lost 2nd post* **7/1**[3]	62
0300	4	1 ½	**Venus Empress**[12] 6576 2-8-10 **54** ... RichardMullen 8 *(E S McMahon) chsd ldr 2f: drvn over 2f out: tried to cl 1f out: sn outpcd* **16/1**	51
000	5	nse	**Silbury (IRE)**[15] 6465 2-8-8 **52** ... SteveDrowne 9 *(R Charlton) hld up in midfield: prog to go 4th over 2f out: tried to cl jst over 1f out: outpcd after* **15/2**	49
2020	6	2 ¾	**Maggie's Treasure (IRE)**[17] 6426 2-9-7 **65** ... TadhgO'Shea 6 *(J Gallagher) led to 2f out: wknd ins fnl f* **14/1**	53
0004	7	nse	**Urban Kode (IRE)**[8] 6673 2-8-9 **53** ... ShaneKelly 2 *(P D Evans) rn v wd bnd over 4f out and again 3f out: wl in rr: shkn up 2f out: kpt on ins fnl f* **20/1**	41
000	8	¾	**Juarla (IRE)**[21] 6308 2-8-6 **50** ...(t) LukeMorris 11 *(R A Harris) chsd ldng trio: rdn over 3f out: struggling over 2f out: grad wknd* **33/1**	36
643	9	3 ¼	**Madame Solitaire**[16] 6436 2-9-1 **59** ... RichardHughes 12 *(R Hannon) wnt lft s: nvr bttr than midfield: pushed along over 3f out: no prog 2f out: eased ins fnl f* **7/2**[2]	35
506	10	3	**Hi Note**[17] 6425 2-8-13 **57** ... ChrisCatlin 3 *(M R Channon) a wl in rr: struggling over 2f out* **25/1**	24
5300	11	1 ¾	**Bouzy**[29] 6081 2-9-1 **59** ... JimCrowley 7 *(P Winkworth) chsd ldrs: wknd over 2f out: heavily eased ins fnl f* **14/1**	21
060	12	5	**Lord Cornwall (IRE)**[40] 5763 2-8-7 **51** ... LiamJones 1 *(J R Gask) mostly last: nvr a factor* **25/1**	—

1m 12.28s (-0.82) **Going Correction** -0.125s/f (Stan) **12** Ran SP% **121.4**
Speed ratings (Par 93): **100,95,95,93,93 89,89,88,84,80 77,71**
toteswingers:1&2: £3.30, 2&3: £5.20, 1&3: £4.90 CSF £21.16 CT £122.93 TOTE £7.40: £2.70, £5.90, £1.10; EX 19.30.
Owner Ali Saeed **Bred** Baron F Von Oppenheim **Trained** Newmarket, Suffolk

FOCUS
Part two but much more strength in depth, with a fast-improving winner and a time 1.6 seconds quicker.

NOTEBOOK
Cinderkamp, off the mark at the fifth attempt over 5f at Catterick, defied a 6lb penalty on her all-weather debut. Confidently ridden, she showed a decent turn of foot to cut down the leader and score in good style in the end. She may well be capable of defying another penalty. (op 7-2, tchd 4-1 in a place)
Duquesa(IRE), penalised for her Nottingham success, took a bump at the start and was left with a fair bit to do. She stayed on in good style down the outer to snatch second spot and deserves credit for this. (op 13-2 tchd 8-1)
Misscomplacent, tried in blinkers on her ninth start, continues to knock on the door, but after taking charge was readily run down by the winner then edged out by the runner-up. She has had plenty of chances now. (op 15-2)
Venus Empress was keen and, after taking them along in the early stages, faded late on. Beaten in selling company on her three most recent starts, 5f holds out more hope for her. (op 20-1)
Silbury(IRE), from a high-profile stable and making her handicap debut, ran her best race so far on her fourth start, but she lacks size and scope. (op 8-1)
Maggie's Treasure(IRE) soon pulled his way to the front and, even though dropping back in trip, he again failed to get home. (tchd 16-1)
Madame Solitaire, who went left exiting the stalls, was driven along to chase the leaders on her handicap debut but was on the retreat once in line for home. She does not seem to be progressing at all.
Bouzy Official explanation: jockey said filly had no more to give

6869 BETDAQ ON 0870 178 1221 MAIDEN STKS 6f (P)
7:20 (7:24) (Class 5) 2-Y-O **£2,286** (£675; £337) **Stalls** High

Form				RPR
2	1		**Pearl Ice**[13] 6520 2-9-3 0 ... SebSanders 4 *(Sir Mark Prescott) chsd ldr: rdn and no imp over 2f out: clsd qckly over 1f out: led jst ins fnl f: sn clr* **1/2**[1]	85+
4004	2	4 ½	**Saskia's Dream**[14] 6513 2-8-12 68 ... TedDurcan 3 *(Jane Chapple-Hyam) hld up last: rdn to go modest 3rd over 1f out: kpt on fnl f to take 2nd nr fin* **12/1**	67
052	3	1 ¼	**Three Sparrows (IRE)**[7] 6688 2-9-3 0 ... RichardHughes 1 *(R Hannon) led: 3 l clr and gng best 2f out: rdn over 1f out: wknd and hdd jst ins fnl f: lost 2nd nr fin* **10/3**[2]	68
03	4	3 ¼	**Blowing Bubbles (USA)**[7] 6697 2-8-12 0 ... SteveDrowne 2 *(B J Meehan) racd wd: hld up: outpcd fr 1/2-way: no imp after* **13/2**[3]	53
00	5	3 ¼	**Fajer Al Kuwait**[59] 5160 2-9-3 0 ...(t) KirstyMilczarek 6 *(G Prodromou) chsd ldng pair: outpcd fr 1/2-way: wknd over 1f out* **80/1**	48
6006	6	4 ½	**Shutupandrive**[24] 6258 2-8-12 45 ... TravisBlock 5 *(M D I Usher) in tch to 1/2-way: sn btn* **66/1**	30

1m 12.3s (-0.80) **Going Correction** -0.125s/f (Stan) **6** Ran SP% **113.5**
Speed ratings (Par 95): **100,94,92,88,83 77**
toteswingers:1&2: £2.40, 2&3: £3.10, 1&3: £1.10 CSF £8.53 TOTE £1.50: £1.10, £6.70; EX 7.40.
Owner Pearl Bloodstock Ltd **Bred** Canary Thoroughbreds **Trained** Newmarket, Suffolk

FOCUS
An uncompetitive maiden.

NOTEBOOK
Pearl Ice, a grand stamp of a colt, had to be rousted along to keep the pacesetter in his sights and, like when runner-up on his debut at Lingfield, he still looked very inexperienced. He was right on top at the finish and looks a fine prospect for sprint handicaps at three from a mark in the low 80s. (op 8-11)
Saskia's Dream, blanketed for stalls entry, was having her seventh start and has a rating of just 68. She stayed on from off the pace to snatch second spot near the line and this may well have flattered her. Official explanation: trainer's rep said filly was in season (op 14-1)
Three Sparrows(IRE), runner-up on his third start at Newbury, was in the stalls for over four minutes after an unruly horse was eventually withdrawn after being given far too many chances by the starting team. He had the outside draw but kicked four lengths clear with over two furlongs to run. Readily run down by the winner, he was very leg weary when edged out of runner-up spot near the line. (op 11-4 tchd 7-2)
Blowing Bubbles(USA), ponied to post, was far too keen on his third start and will need to learn to settle better if she is to progress and stay as far as her pedigree suggests she might. (op 6-1 tchd 15-2)

6870 BETDAQ.COM NURSERY 7f (P)
7:50 (7:51) (Class 2) 2-Y-O
£6,916 (£2,071; £1,035; £518; £258; £129) **Stalls** High

Form				RPR
1	1		**Pearl Arch (IRE)**[38] 5814 2-8-10 **77** ...(t) WilliamBuick 1 *(B J Meehan) sn prom fr wd draw: led over 2f out: drvn and edgd lft 1f out: styd on wl* **15/2**[3]	83
521	2	nk	**Sagramor**[14] 6498 2-9-0 **81** ... SteveDrowne 6 *(H Morrison) hld up in midfield: lost pl sltly over 2f out: prog on outer wl over 1f out: chal ins fnl f: drifted lft: hld nr fin* **7/2**[2]	86
21	3	2 ¾	**Blue Tiger's Eye (IRE)**[30] 6053 2-9-7 **88** ... TedDurcan 11 *(Saeed Bin Suroor) trckd ldng pair: cl up 2f out: sn nt qckn u.p: wnt 3rd again ins fnl f: outpcd* **15/8**[1]	86
001	4	½	**Ebony Song (USA)**[31] 6019 2-8-1 **68** ...(t) JimmyQuinn 8 *(J Noseda) dwlt: hld up wl in rr: effrt over 2f out: hanging and nt qckn wl over 1f out: styd on ins fnl f: nrst fin* **14/1**	65
2300	5	hd	**My Son Max**[56] 5245 2-9-2 **83** ... RichardHughes 3 *(R Hannon) hld up in rr: pushed along over 2f out: styd on fr over 1f out: n.d* **12/1**	79
1204	6	1 ¾	**Colorado Gold**[29] 6088 2-9-4 **85** ...(b) JimmyFortune 10 *(P F I Cole) led 1f: trckd ldr: led briefly wl over 2f out: outpcd fr over 1f out* **20/1**	77
1103	7	nk	**Jollywood (IRE)**[32] 5987 2-8-9 **76** ... HayleyTurner 12 *(R Hannon) hld up bhd ldrs: prog on inner to chal 2f out: wknd ins fnl f* **33/1**	67
401	8	nk	**Mutajare (IRE)**[40] 5762 2-9-4 **85** ... TadhgO'Shea 4 *(M Johnston) racd wd: hld up: prog arnd rivals to go prom over 2f out: nt qckn over 1f out: steadily lost pl* **8/1**	75
052	9	¾	**L'Astre De Choisir (IRE)**[21] 6309 2-8-6 **73** ... LukeMorris 7 *(W R Swinburn) hld up in midfield: pushed along 1/2-way: prog u.p 2f out: wknd ins fnl f* **20/1**	61
3122	10	7	**Introvert (IRE)**[29] 6088 2-9-6 **87** ... RoystonFfrench 2 *(Mahmood Al Zarooni) hld up in rr: stmbld bdly after 2f: nt rcvr: wl in rr after* **12/1**	57
0000	11	¾	**Jamaica Grande**[8] 6667 2-7-5 **65** oh8 ... JessicaSteven(7) 9 *(T T Clement) led after 1f to wl over 2f out: qckly dropped out* **100/1**	33

1m 24.76s (-1.24) **Going Correction** -0.125s/f (Stan) **11** Ran SP% **115.4**
Speed ratings (Par 101): **102,101,98,97,97 95,95,95,94,86 85**
toteswingers:1&2: £6.40, 2&3: £2.00, 1&3: £2.70 CSF £31.93 CT £70.92 TOTE £8.00: £3.00, £1.40, £1.10; EX 42.50.
Owner Pearl Bloodstock Ltd **Bred** E Mulhern, J Flynn & Mrs M Haughey **Trained** Manton, Wilts
■ Stewards' Enquiry : Steve Drowne five-day ban: careless riding (Oct 28-Nov 1)

FOCUS
Quite a valuable and highly competitive 65-88 nursery handicap and, with four last-time-out winners filling the frame, the form looks rock solid.

The Form Book, Raceform Ltd, Compton, RG20 6NL

NOTEBOOK

Pearl Arch(IRE) has a good reputation and had the outside draw to overcome. He showed a willing attitude and seemed to relish the surface on his handicap debut. He looks likely to progress further and is a decent prospect. (op 9-1)

Sagramor, off the mark at his third attempt here, was left short of room leaving the stalls. He made his effort on the outer and ran on in honest fashion to make the winner pull out all the stops. He deserves plenty of credit for this. (op 3-1)

Blue Tiger's Eye(IRE), after a tardy start, was quite keen and ran out of racing room on the heels of the leaders once in line for home. When in the clear he did not do a lot and this may be as good as he is. (op 2-1, tchd 9-4 in a place)

Ebony Song(USA), who struggled to open his account at the third attempt at Brighton, did not have the rub of the green and can be rated third best on merit. (tchd 16-1)

My Son Max, settled off the pace, put in some solid late work. This marked a return to form on his nursery debut and on his all-weather debut, back after a two-month break. (op 14-1)

Colorado Gold, who had blinkers reapplied, helped force the pace but he came up well short in the end and, with nine races under his belt already, he looks regressive. Official explanation: jockey said colt hung left (op 16-1)

Mutajare(IRE) was forced to take avoidance measures at the end of the back straight and in the circumstances did well to finish as close as he did.

Introvert(IRE), the Godolphin second string, lost all chance when seeming to strike heels exiting the back straight. (op 11-1)

6871 BET CHAMPIONS DAY - BETDAQ H'CAP — 2m (P)

8:20 (8:21) (Class 6) (0-60,59) 3-Y-O — **£1,637** (£483; £241) **Stalls** High

Form — RPR

0435 **1** **Tower**[13] 6525 3-9-3 **55** ..... KirstyMilczarek 6 — 59
(G Prodromou) *t.k.h: hld up in last pair: stl there over 2f out: gd prog on outer fr 2f out: r.o wl ins fnl f to ld nr fin* **8/1**

0430 **2** *hd* **Storm Hawk (IRE)**[13] 6525 3-8-12 **57** ..... (p) JamesRogers(7) 13 — 61
(Pat Eddery) *hld up in midfield: prog on inner fr over 2f out: drvn to ld narrowly ent fnl f: hdd nr fin* **8/1**

0000 **3** *½* **Admiral Rodney**[13] 6525 3-8-12 **50** ..... MickyFenton 5 — 54
(Mrs P Sly) *hld up wl in rr: gd prog on outer over 2f out: jnd ldr jst over 1f out: wouldn't overtake: styd on bhd ldng pair after* **20/1**

0000 **4** *1 ¼* **Defence Of Realm (GER)**[98] 3829 3-9-7 **59** ..... (p) TonyCulhane 3 — 61
(George Baker) *pressed ldrs: drvn to ld over 1f out: hdd and no ex ent fnl f* **5/1**[2]

3343 **5** *½* **Jennerous Blue**[23] 6273 3-8-10 **48** ..... (p) PaulQuinn 4 — 49
(D K Ivory) *t.k.h: prom on inner: lost pl sltly over 3f out: cl 4th again 2f out but nt qckn: styd on same pce after* **3/1**[1]

6020 **6** *3* **Jewellery (IRE)**[19] 6373 3-9-7 **59** ..... (v[1]) HayleyTurner 11 — 57
(J R Fanshawe) *trckd ldrs: pushed along over 2f out: sn lost pl bdly: no ch over 1f out: nudged along and passed 4 rivals ins fnl f* **6/1**[3]

0600 **7** *hd* **Kargarann (IRE)**[15] 6454 3-8-3 **46** ..... JohnFahy(5) 7 — 44
(Stef Higgins) *s.v.s: in tch in last: drvn and prog on inner 2f out: no hdwy 1f out* **25/1**

0405 **8** *1* **Voysey (IRE)**[13] 6526 3-9-3 **55** ..... (bt) JimCrowley 8 — 51
(Mrs A J Perrett) *w ldr: drvn over 2f out: fdd over 1f out* **5/1**[2]

0003 **9** *1 ¾* **Kitty Koo (IRE)**[14] 6517 3-8-0 **45** ..... JulieBurke(7) 10 — 39
(A W Carroll) *t.k.h: trckd ldrs: rdn over 2f out: wkng whn hmpd over 1f out* **20/1**

000 **10** *2 ½* **Sea Tobougie**[37] 5832 3-8-5 **48** ..... AmyBaker(5) 2 — 39
(M D I Usher) *dwlt: hld up in rr: prog on outer to go prom over 3f out: wknd 2f out* **66/1**

0060 **11** *½* **Amylyn**[70] 4765 3-8-2 **45** ..... TobyAtkinson(5) 14 — 36
(J R Holt) *hld up wl in rr: pushed along and no prog over 2f out* **66/1**

6646 **12** *2* **Oak Leaves**[13] 6526 3-8-10 **48** ..... RichardHughes 1 — 36
(J G Portman) *mde most to over 1f out: wknd and eased* **11/1**

00-0 **13** *34* **Ring Of Fire**[34] 5925 3-8-12 **50** ..... LiamJones 9 — —
(J L Spearing) *t.k.h: hld up: rapid prog and prom after 6f: wknd rapidly 3f out: virtually p.u* **50/1**

3m 34.5s (4.40) **Going Correction** -0.125s/f (Stan) — **13** Ran SP% **121.5**

Speed ratings (Par 99): **84,83,83,83,82 81,81,80,79,78 78,77,60**

toteswingers:1&2 £4.30, 2&3 £74.50, 1&3 £44.40 CSF £66.70 CT £1250.35 TOTE £12.10: £2.90, £4.00, £6.50; EX 69.30.

Owner Fahed Al Dabbous **Bred** Cheveley Park Stud Ltd **Trained** East Harling, Norfolk

FOCUS

A low-grade 45-59 stayers' handicap run at a very steady pace and the dash for home did not begin until once in line for home. It is hard to rate the form too positively.

Jewellery(IRE) Official explanation: jockey said filly was denied a clear run

Voysey(IRE) Official explanation: jockey said colt pulled up lame

Ring Of Fire Official explanation: jockey said colt ran too free

6872 BETDAQ.COM H'CAP — 1m 4f (P)

8:50 (8:50) (Class 4) (0-85,82) 3-Y-O — **£3,885** (£1,156; £577; £288) **Stalls** Centre

Form — RPR

6204 **1** **Fantastic Strike (IRE)**[12] 6554 3-8-7 **68** ..... GregFairley 3 — 79
(M Johnston) *hld up: prog to trck ldr 1/2-way: rdn to ld narrowly over 2f out: grad asserted ins fnl f* **8/1**

2100 **2** *4* **Deauville Post (FR)**[55] 5273 3-9-1 **76** ..... RichardHughes 1 — 81
(R Hannon) *prom and racd wd: led and qcknd after 4f: drvn 3f out: hdd over 2f out: pressed wnr after tl no ex ins fnl f* **5/1**[3]

2510 **3** *3 ¼* **On Khee**[19] 6361 3-9-2 **77** ..... SteveDrowne 2 — 77
(H Morrison) *hld up: rdn to go 3rd over 2f out: no imp on ldng pair after* **9/2**[2]

3-15 **4** *12* **Ipswich Lad**[162] 1823 3-9-3 **78** ..... (b[1]) DavidProbert 5 — 59
(A M Balding) *hld up: drvn 1/2-way: sn lost tch: wl bhd fnl 3f* **14/1**

31 **5** *10* **Beggar's Opera (IRE)**[209] 928 3-9-5 **80** ..... (t) WilliamBuick 4 — 71
(J H M Gosden) *pressed ldr 4f: styd prom: cl 3rd 3f out: sn shkn up and wknd: eased over 1f out* **2/1**[1]

3224 **6** *20* **Sierra Alpha**[65] 4933 3-9-7 **82** ..... PatDobbs 6 — 15
(Mrs A J Perrett) *mde most 4f: drvn 5f out: sn lost tch: t.o* **2/1**[1]

2m 31.44s (-3.06) **Going Correction** -0.125s/f (Stan) — **6** Ran SP% **119.3**

Speed ratings (Par 103): **105,102,100,92,85 72**

toteswingers:1&2 £7.00, 2&3 £5.80, 1&3 £5.80 CSF £49.26 TOTE £13.80: £6.30, £6.10; EX 46.80 Place 6: £28.94 Place 5: £2.71.

Owner Brian Yeardley Continental Ltd **Bred** Victor Stud Bloodstock Ltd **Trained** Middleham Moor, N Yorks

FOCUS

A competitive 68-82 three-year-old stayers' handicap on paper, but it saw abysmal efforts from the two market leaders and only the first three home ran to their form. The pace was stop-start for the first half-mile. There are grounds for rating the form a bit higher, but the winner looks the best guide.

Beggar's Opera(IRE) Official explanation: jockey said colt lost its action

Sierra Alpha Official explanation: vet said colt bled from the nose

T/Plt: £26.90 to a £1 stake. Pool of £53,377.96 - 1,447.96 winning tickets. T/Qpdt: £3.10 to a £1 stake. Pool of £10,550.27 - 2,477.19 winning tickets JN

6673 NOTTINGHAM (L-H)

Thursday, October 14

OFFICIAL GOING: Good (good to soft in places)

6873 EUROPEAN BREEDERS' FUND MAIDEN STKS (DIV I) — 1m 75y

2:10 (2:11) (Class 5) 2-Y-O — **£3,238** (£963; £481; £240) **Stalls** Centre

Form — RPR

43 **1** **Defence Of Duress (IRE)**[31] 6036 2-9-3 0 ..... JamieSpencer 3 — 79+
(T P Tate) *mde all: rdn along wl over 2f out: drvn and edgd rt wl over 1f out: kpt on wl u.p ins fnl f* **3/1**[2]

2 *2 ¼* **Little Rocky** 2-9-3 0 ..... WilliamBuick 6 — 74
(D M Simcock) *hld up in rr: hdwy on wd outside over 2f out: rdn to chse ldrs over 1f out: drvn to chse wnr ins fnl f: sn no imp* **8/1**

5 **3** *1* **Discovery Bay**[26] 6190 2-9-3 0 ..... SteveDrowne 10 — 72
(R Charlton) *hld up in midfield: hdwy over 4f out: niggled along 3f out: rdn over 2f out: kpt on same pce: tk 3rd nr fin* **2/1**[1]

0006 **4** *shd* **Thank You Joy**[29] 6082 2-8-5 45 ..... DannyBrock(7) 5 — 67
(J R Jenkins) *trckd ldrs: hdwy on inner 4f out: rdn along wl over 2f out: drvn over 1f out: kpt on same pce* **200/1**

00 **5** *hd* **Dragonera**[15] 6468 2-8-12 0 ..... KierenFallon 9 — 66
(E A L Dunlop) *trckd ldrs: hdwy to chse wnr over 3f out: rdn over 2f out: drvn over 1f out: wknd ins fnl f* **14/1**

6 *4* **Raajih** 2-9-3 0 ..... TadhgO'Shea 1 — 62
(J H M Gosden) *s.i.s and sn rdn along: hdwy on inner to trck ldrs after 1 1/2f: pushed along wl over 3f out: rdn wl over 2f out and sn btn* **11/2**

0 **7** *nk* **Maharana (USA)**[14] 6504 2-9-3 0 ..... PaulHanagan 11 — 62
(M L W Bell) *hld up in rr: sme hdwy over 2f out: sn rdn and n.d* **9/2**[3]

8 *4 ½* **Look For Love** 2-9-3 0 ..... GrahamGibbons 2 — 52
(R Hollinshead) *dwlt: a in rr* **66/1**

0 **9** *6* **Nella Sofia**[27] 6158 2-8-12 0 ..... PaulMulrennan 4 — 34
(J G Given) *chsd wnr: rdn along 4f out: sn wknd* **100/1**

0 **10** *2 ½* **Intombi**[15] 6469 2-8-12 0 ..... JamesDoyle 7 — 28
(A J McCabe) *chsd ldrs: rdn along 4f out: sn wknd* **100/1**

1m 49.4s (3.80) **Going Correction** +0.30s/f (Good) — **10** Ran SP% **113.6**

Speed ratings (Par 95): **93,90,89,89,89 85,85,80,74,72**

toteswingers:1&2: £4.60, 2&3: £4.50, 1&3: £2.10 CSF £26.45 TOTE £4.10: £2.30, £2.70, £1.02; EX 31.00.

Owner Mrs Fitri Hay **Bred** Alan Byrne & Tinnakill Bloodstock **Trained** Tadcaster, N Yorks

FOCUS

The form of this maiden is let down by the proximity of 45-rated Thank You Joy, but the time wasn't too bad, being only 0.35 seconds slower than Elas Diamond, impressive winner of the second division.

NOTEBOOK

Defence Of Duress(IRE) found this easier than the Redcar maiden he finished third in last time (winner followed up in Autumn Stakes, runner-up won Kempton maiden) and ran out a convincing winner under a well-judged front-running ride. He should get at least 1m4f next year and is a useful handicapper in the making.

Little Rocky, out of a useful 7f-1m winner, made good headway out wide in the straight from well off the gallop. There's better to come, though his knee action suggests he might not enjoy fast ground. (op 10-1)

Discovery Bay didn't really build on the promise of his debut effort. He was hanging left when first produced with his challenge in the straight and basically didn't knuckle down for pressure, possibly still green. Official explanation: jockey said colt hung left (op 9-4 tchd 5-2)

Thank You Joy looked well exposed as just moderate and, though clearly running well, she holds the form down. (op 250-1)

Dragonera was well placed and had her chance, but she didn't see her race out. She might find her level in modest middle-distance handicaps next year.

Raajih needed the experience, missing the break and then offering little for pressure in the straight. He's another who will want middle distances next season. (tchd 5-1)

Maharana(USA) showed ability on debut at Newmarket, but was disappointing this time, never looking likely to get competitive. (op 4-1)

6874 EUROPEAN BREEDERS' FUND MAIDEN STKS (DIV II) — 1m 75y

2:40 (2:42) (Class 5) 2-Y-O — **£3,238** (£963; £481; £240) **Stalls** Centre

Form — RPR

2 **1** **Elas Diamond**[27] 6154 2-8-12 0 ..... RyanMoore 1 — 88+
(J Noseda) *mde all: clr fr over 2f out: shkn up and styd on strly fr over 1f out* **8/15**[1]

2 *12* **Mulaqen** 2-9-3 0 ..... TadhgO'Shea 9 — 67
(M P Tregoning) *prom: hdwy to chse wnr and hung lft over 2f out: sn outpcd* **18/1**

3 *1 ¾* **Madison Square (USA)** 2-9-3 0 ..... AhmedAjtebi 2 — 63
(Mahmood Al Zarooni) *chsd ldrs: rdn over 3f out: outpcd fr over 2f out* **10/1**

4 *1* **Susan Stroman** 2-8-12 0 ..... PaulHanagan 5 — 56
(E A L Dunlop) *s.i.s: pushed along 1/2-way: r.o ins fnl f: nvr nrr* **16/1**

5 *¾* **Watercourse (IRE)** 2-9-3 0 ..... PhilipRobinson 8 — 59
(M A Jarvis) *broke wl: sn lost pl: hdwy over 1f out: nvr on terms* **7/1**[2]

0 **6** *2 ¼* **Lordofthehouse (IRE)**[14] 6504 2-9-3 0 ..... KierenFallon 10 — 54
(W J Haggas) *s.i.s: hdwy 6f out: rdn over 3f out: sn outpcd* **8/1**[3]

00 **7** *2 ½* **Hawridge Knight**[14] 6514 2-9-0 0 ..... JamesMillman(3) 3 — 48
(B R Millman) *prom: rdn over 3f out: sn lost pl* **100/1**

0 **8** *6* **Rattleyurjewellery**[21] 6301 2-8-12 0 ..... MickyFenton 4 — 30
(D H Brown) *sn chsng wnr: rdn over 3f out: hung lft and wknd fr over 2f out* **100/1**

00 **9** *½* **Kepler's Law**[8] 6676 2-9-3 0 ..... SebSanders 6 — 34
(Sir Mark Prescott) *mid-div: wknd over 3f out* **100/1**

10 *2* **Bobby Dazzler (IRE)** 2-9-3 0 ..... SteveDrowne 7 — 30
(S Kirk) *s.i.s: a in rr: bhd fr 1/2-way* **40/1**

11 *14* **X Rated** 2-9-3 0 ..... JamesDoyle 11 — —
(A J McCabe) *s.i.s: in rr and rdn 1/2-way: sn wknd: t.o* **66/1**

1m 49.05s (3.45) **Going Correction** +0.30s/f (Good) — **11** Ran SP% **116.0**

Speed ratings (Par 95): **94,82,80,79,78 76,73,67,67,65 51**

toteswingers:1&2: £5.20, 2&3: £22.60, 1&3: £2.90 CSF £12.72 TOTE £1.50: £1.10, £4.30, £2.70; EX 10.30.

Owner Newsells Park Stud **Bred** Newsells Park Stud Limited **Trained** Newmarket, Suffolk

FOCUS

A visually impressive winner, and though the time was somewhat surprisingly only 0.35 seconds quicker than the ordinary looking first division, hand times suggest Elas Diamond covered the final 3f around 1.70 seconds faster than Defence Of Duress, who made all in the opening leg.

NOTEBOOK

Elas Diamond extended in good style in the straight to draw clear of rivals who patently weren't up to much on the day, confirming the promise shown when second Khawlah (third in Group 3 next time) on debut. Out of Lancashire Oaks winner Ela Athena, she should stay further and could be smart. (op 4-7 tchd 1-2)

Mulaqen, a 30,000gns half-brother to 6f winner Boule Masquee, ran green under pressure and was no match at all for the winner. (op 22-1)

Madison Square(USA) is a half-brother to US dirt winners Seattle Hoofer and Star Meteor, out of a 7f Grade 2 winner, so soft turf probably didn't suit and he was beaten a long way. (tchd 12-1)

Susan Stroman, the first foal of a 1m1f winner and second in the Ribblesdale, wasn't best away and raced off the pace, but she made some modest late headway. She ought to come on a bundle for this and can do a lot better over middle distances next season. (op 12-1)

Watercourse(IRE), a 50,000gns purchase, was never seen with a chance and probably needs more time and distance. (op 6-1)

Lordofthehouse(IRE), a close relation to George Washington and Grandera, is a big horse and is some way off fulfilling his potential. (tchd 9-1)

6875 WILLOUGHBY SUBARU NURSERY — 1m 75y

3:10 (3:12) (Class 5) (0-70,70) 2-Y-O — £2,914 (£867; £433; £216) Stalls Centre

Form				RPR
0365	1		**Plea**[12] 6555 2-9-4 67 ... WilliamBuick 5 (J H M Gosden) *hld up towards rr: swtchd rt to wd outside and hdwy 3f out: rdn and hung lft over 1f out: drvn to chal ins fnl f: kpt on to ld nr fin* **6/1**[2]	71
1160	2	hd	**Ninfea (IRE)**[7] 6690 2-9-5 68 ...(p) JamesDoyle 6 (S Kirk) *in tch: hdwy over 3f out and sn pushed along: rdn to chse ldrs 2f out: drvn: edgd lft and led wl ins fnl f: hdd and no ex towards fin* **22/1**	72
0300	3	2 ¾	**Beer Flush (IRE)**[15] 6471 2-9-0 63 ... AndrewElliott 9 (Jedd O'Keeffe) *led after 1f: rdn clr wl over 2f out: drvn over 1f out: hdd wl ins fnl f: one pce* **25/1**	61
6644	4	hd	**Fimias (IRE)**[17] 6426 2-9-5 68 ... KierenFallon 2 (L M Cumani) *midfield: effrt over 3f out and sn pushed along: swtchd lft and rdn wl over 1f out: kpt on u.p ins fnl f: nrst fin* **15/8**[1]	65
5340	5	½	**Little Miss Take**[63] 4984 2-9-3 66 ... RichardKingscote 17 (Tom Dascombe) *prom: trckd ldr after 2f: rdn along over 2f out: drvn over 1f out: wknd ins fnl f* **66/1**	62
4560	6	¾	**Classic Voice (IRE)**[14] 6513 2-9-0 63 ... RyanMoore 16 (R Hannon) *in tch: hdwy on outer 3f out: rdn to chse ldrs whn n.m.r over 1f out: one pce after* **10/1**	57
500	7	½	**Oetzi**[45] 5587 2-9-0 63 ow1 ... AdamKirby 10 (A P Jarvis) *dwlt and in rr: hdwy over 2f out: sn rdn and kpt on ins fnl f: nrst fin* **66/1**	56
0403	8	nk	**Fastada (IRE)**[51] 5389 2-9-2 65 ... StephenCraine 3 (J G Portman) *in tch on inner: hdwy to chse ldrs 3f out: rdn 2f out and grad wknd* **25/1**	58
4525	9	hd	**Barista (IRE)**[7] 6695 2-9-4 67 ... TadhgO'Shea 7 (M R Channon) *dwlt and hld up in rr: hdwy and nt clr run on inner 5f out: swtchd rt and rdn 3f out: kpt on appr fnl f: nt rch ldrs* **12/1**	59
0060	10	1 ¼	**C P Joe (IRE)**[7] 6695 2-9-0 63 ... FrannyNorton 11 (Paul Green) *hld up in rr: hdwy 3f out: n.m.r and swtchd lft 2f out: styng on whn nt clr run ins fnl f: nt rch ldrs* **33/1**	52
4214	11	3 ½	**Regimental (IRE)**[9] 6647 2-9-7 70 ... PaulHanagan 15 (Mrs A Duffield) *chsd ldrs: rdn along over 3f out: grad wknd* **15/2**[3]	52
0564	12	5	**Marc De Savoie (IRE)**[15] 6471 2-9-2 65 ... JamieSpencer 8 (K A Ryan) *led 1f: prom tl rdn along over 3f out and sn wknd* **11/1**	36
0140	13	1 ¼	**Sky Diamond (IRE)**[12] 6568 2-9-2 65 ... PaulMulrennan 13 (J G Given) *nvr bttr than midfield* **28/1**	33
5230	14	9	**Mark Harbour (IRE)**[17] 6412 2-9-4 67 ... PatDobbs 14 (R Hannon) *a towards rr* **20/1**	15
004	15	½	**Mirabile Visu**[16] 6441 2-9-4 67 ... SebSanders 1 (Mrs H S Main) *midfield: rdn along 4f out: sn wknd* **33/1**	14
6000	16	12	**Hero From Zero (IRE)**[43] 5659 2-9-2 65 ... PatCosgrave 12 (B J Meehan) *a in rr* **33/1**	—

1m 49.46s (3.86) **Going Correction** +0.30s/f (Good) — **16** Ran SP% **118.0**

Speed ratings (Par 95): **92,91,89,88,88 87,87,86,86,85 81,76,75,66,66 54**

toteswingers:1&2: £26.10, 2&3: £112.90, 1&3: £33.40 CSF £132.32 CT £3041.29 TOTE £5.70: £2.30, £6.60, £7.80, £1.02; EX 127.60.

Owner Highclere & The Duke Of Devonshire **Bred** The Duke Of Devonshire **Trained** Newmarket, Suffolk

FOCUS

A modest nursery run at a reasonable pace. The time was respectable, being only slightly slower than both divisions of the juvenile maiden.

NOTEBOOK

Plea is not straightforward, that was evident in his previous races (wore blinkers second and third start), and he once again showed wayward tendencies, so credit to William Buick for managing to win on him. He was produced extremely wide in the straight, probably a shrewd move seeing as he avoided getting in a battle until late on, and despite continually edging left, was persuaded to put his head in front. This half-brother to high-class stayer Ask is evidently talented, and it's hoped he can go on from this - that's not out of the question seeing as he'll be suited by a lot further next year, by which time he might have grown up a bit. (op 5-1 tchd 9-2)

Ninfea(IRE), tyried in cheekpieces, ran much better than at Newbury last time, clearly benefiting from the step back up in trip. She is due to be eased 3lb and will have an obvious chance if turned out off her new mark before the handicapper has second thoughts. (op 20-1 tchd 16-1)

Beer Flush(IRE) responded well to a positive ride on this drop in trip and simply just found a couple too good. (tchd 33-1)

Fimias(IRE) ran okay without improving as one might have hoped for the step up in trip and switch to turf. (tchd 2-1)

Little Miss Take had every chance, but she was up in trip after a break of two months and didn't see her race out. (op 50-1)

Oetzi took an age to pick up, but was running on quite well in the closing stages until eased near the line and we've yet to see the best of him.

6876 WILDGOOSECONSTRUCTION.CO.UK MAIDEN STKS — 1m 2f 50y

3:40 (3:44) (Class 5) 3-Y-O — £2,590 (£770; £385; £192) Stalls Low

Form				RPR
4-	1		**Pekan Star**[412] 5401 3-9-3 0 ... PhilipRobinson 1 (M A Jarvis) *sn chsng ldrs: led over 2f out: rdn out* **9/1**	91+
0	2	1 ¾	**Cape Dutch (IRE)**[154] 2043 3-9-3 0 ... AhmedAjtebi 14 (Mahmood Al Zarooni) *hld up: hdwy over 1f out: hung lft and r.o wl ins fnl f: nt rch wnr* **40/1**	86+
5-	3	1 ¾	**Local Hero (GER)**[485] 2997 3-9-3 0 ... PaulHanagan 16 (S Gollings) *hld up: hdwy over 3f out: rdn over 1f out: r.o: wnt 3rd towards fin* **66/1**	82
	4	1	**Tax Break** 3-9-3 0 ... JoeFanning 15 (M Johnston) *hld up in tch: chal over 2f out: sn hung lft: no ex and lost 2nd wl ins fnl f* **33/1**	80+
	5	1 ¾	**Arabian History (USA)** 3-9-3 0 ...(t) FrankieDettori 7 (Saeed Bin Suroor) *pushed along in rr early: hdwy u.p over 2f out: styd on: nt gng pce to chal* **7/2**[2]	77+
02-2	6	¾	**Protaras (USA)**[185] 1268 3-9-3 80 ... IanMongan 4 (H R A Cecil) *chsd ldrs: rdn over 2f out: hung lft over 1f out: styd on same pce* **5/1**[3]	75
-3	7	nk	**Highland Park (IRE)**[28] 6115 3-9-3 0 ... RyanMoore 9 (Sir Michael Stoute) *chsd ldrs: rdn over 3f out: styd on same pce appr fnl f* **7/4**[1]	75
0362	8	½	**Weathervane**[28] 6115 3-9-3 77 ... WilliamBuick 12 (J H M Gosden) *prom: rdn over 3f out: styd on same pce appr fnl f* **7/1**	74
00	9	1 ¾	**Justazippy**[14] 6499 3-8-12 0 ... JamesDoyle 8 (A J McCabe) *chsd ldr tl led 4f out: rdn and hdd over 2f out: edgd lft and wknd over 1f out* **100/1**	65
4	10	4 ½	**Room For A View**[15] 6470 3-8-12 0 ... PatDobbs 5 (M P Tregoning) *mid-div: rdn over 3f out: wknd 2f out* **50/1**	56
	11	4 ½	**Sulliman** 3-8-10 0 ... LewisWalsh(7) 3 (Jane Chapple-Hyam) *s.i.s: sn outpcd: nvr nrr* **80/1**	52
53	12	shd	**Miss Kingwood**[14] 6499 3-8-12 0 ... KierenFallon 13 (M P Tregoning) *s.i.s: hld up: nvr on terms* **16/1**	47
60	13	3 ¼	**Eurasian**[43] 5665 3-9-3 0 ... PatCosgrave 11 (D M Simcock) *prom: rdn over 3f out: wknd over 2f out* **100/1**	45
66	14	3 ¼	**Raghdaan**[15] 6476 3-9-3 0 ... PhillipMakin 10 (P W Hiatt) *hld up: pushed along 1/2-way: wknd over 3f out* **150/1**	39
0	15	14	**Stardust Dancer**[15] 6470 3-9-3 0 ... SilvestreDeSousa 2 (Paul Green) *s.i.s: a in rr* **100/1**	—
0-	16	¾	**Fourlanends**[404] 5668 3-9-0 0 ... BarryMcHugh(3) 6 (N Wilson) *plld hrd: led: hdd 4f out: wknd over 2f out* **150/1**	—

2m 14.24s (2.54) **Going Correction** +0.30s/f (Good) — **16** Ran SP% **118.0**

Speed ratings (Par 101): **101,99,98,97,96 95,95,94,93,89 86,86,83,80,69 69**

CSF £325.36 TOTE £10.80: £2.70, £10.60, £5.30; EX 365.30.

Owner H R H Sultan Ahmad Shah **Bred** Ecurie Les Monceaux **Trained** Newmarket, Suffolk

FOCUS

An interesting older-horse maiden for the time of year, with plenty of late-maturing types representing powerful connections. The form horses were not at their best but was the winner was a big improver. The time was 1.37 seconds slower than the following handicap won by the 94-rated Psychic Ability.

Miss Kingwood Official explanation: jockey said filly hung

6877 DENMAN - BUILDING FOR YOU - H'CAP — 1m 2f 50y

4:10 (4:11) (Class 3) (0-95,95) 3-Y-O+ — £7,771 (£2,312; £1,155; £577) Stalls Low

Form				RPR
1201	1		**Psychic Ability (USA)**[33] 5970 3-9-4 94 ...(v) FrankieDettori 7 (Saeed Bin Suroor) *led 1f: chsd ldr: effrt and cl up 3f out: rdn to chal over 2f out: led 1 1/2f out and sn drvn: hld on wl towards fin* **2/1**[1]	104+
0610	2	nk	**Jo'Burg (USA)**[12] 6562 6-8-12 88 ... JamesO'Reilly(5) 11 (J O'Reilly) *hld up towards rr: stdy hdwy on outer 3f out: rdn wl over 1f out: drvn and edgd lft ins fnl f: styd on strly towards fin: jst hld* **7/1**[2]	97+
1061	3	½	**Bencoolen (IRE)**[18] 6396 5-9-1 89 ... MichaelO'Connell(3) 2 (D Nicholls) *trckd ldr: hdwy on inner to ld 3f out: rdn over 2f out: drvn and hdd 1 1/2f out: kpt on same pce ins fnl f* **20/1**	97
3020	4	½	**Shavansky**[18] 6391 6-9-5 93 ... JamesMillman(3) 8 (B R Millman) *s.i.s and in rr: hdwy 1/2-way: effrt to chse ldrs over 2f out and sn rdn: swtchd rt and drvn ins fnl f: kpt on: nrst fin* **25/1**	100
3000	5	1 ¼	**Roman Republic (FR)**[58] 5188 4-9-10 95 ... AhmedAjtebi 1 (Saeed Bin Suroor) *in tch: hdwy to chse ldrs 1/2-way: rdn along over 2f out: drvn over 1f out: kpt on same pce* **9/1**	100
4345	6	3	**Oratory (IRE)**[18] 6391 4-9-7 92 ... RyanMoore 16 (R Hannon) *dwlt and hld up in rr: hdwy 3f out: swtchd rt and rdn 2f out: kpt on ins fnl f: nrst fin* **8/1**[3]	91
0134	7	2 ¼	**Plaisterer**[12] 6552 5-9-3 88 ... IanMongan 15 (C F Wall) *chsd ldrs: rdn along over 3f out: drvn wl over 2f out and grad wknd* **20/1**	82
0404	8	2	**Cloudy Start**[28] 6123 4-9-8 93 ...(t) FergusSweeney 3 (J A Osborne) *chsd ldng pair: rdn along 3f out: drvn over 2f out and grad wknd* **33/1**	83
4225	9	¾	**Play It Sam**[20] 6327 4-9-3 88 ... AdamKirby 6 (W R Swinburn) *midfield: hdwy to chse ldrs 3f out: rdn over 2f out: drvn wl over 1f out and sn wknd* **11/1**	77
0434	10	nk	**Reve De Nuit (USA)**[13] 6534 4-9-3 88 ... PatCosgrave 13 (A J McCabe) *nvr bttr than midfield* **8/1**[3]	76
1036	11	3 ¼	**Granston (IRE)**[26] 6185 9-9-2 87 ... GrahamGibbons 5 (J D Bethell) *chsd ldrs: rdn along over 3f out: sn wknd* **33/1**	68
0000	12	1 ¾	**Aspectus (IRE)**[21] 6312 7-9-2 90 ... SophieDoyle(3) 4 (J A Osborne) *in tch: hdwy to chse ldrs 1/2-way: rdn along over 3f out and sn wknd* **50/1**	68
4205	13	hd	**Lucky Dance (BRZ)**[10] 6630 8-9-2 87 ...(b) MickyFenton 12 (T T Clement) *hld up: a in rr* **66/1**	65
3000	14	½	**Shadows Lengthen**[96] 3921 4-9-0 88 ...(b) JamesSullivan(3) 14 (M W Easterby) *led after 1f: rdn along and hdd 3f out: sn wknd* **20/1**	65
350-	15	1 ¼	**Laterly (IRE)**[301] 7789 5-9-4 89 ... PaulHanagan 10 (S Gollings) *a towards rr* **33/1**	63
0005	16	3 ¼	**Classic Colori (IRE)**[26] 6203 3-9-5 95 ... RichardKingscote 9 (Tom Dascombe) *a in rr* **11/1**	63

2m 12.87s (1.17) **Going Correction** +0.30s/f (Good)

WFA 3 from 4yo+ 5lb — **16** Ran SP% **125.1**

Speed ratings (Par 107): **107,106,106,105,104 102,100,99,98,98 95,94,94,93,92 90**

toteswingers:1&2: £5.60, 2&3: £29.50, 1&3: £6.50 CSF £13.52 CT £234.11 TOTE £2.40: £1.10, £2.30, £3.30, £4.40; EX 17.30.

Owner Godolphin **Bred** Flaxman Holdings Ltd **Trained** Newmarket, Suffolk

FOCUS

A fair handicap run at a reasonable enough pace, and the time was 1.37 seconds quicker than the earlier maiden won by Pekan Star. Sound form and the winner looks capable of better still.

NOTEBOOK

Psychic Ability(USA) was raised only 2lb for his success at Sandown last time, when he defeated subsequent winner Kings Destiny, and showed himself to still be well handicapped. The type who only seems to do enough, the hat-trick is a possibility. (op 9-4)

Jo'Burg(USA), seventh in the Cambridgeshire (and best of those stands' side) on debut for this yard, ran another good race off a 2lb lower mark, but just got going too late. He should remain competitive. (op 11-2 tchd 8-1)

Bencoolen(IRE) had every chance but found this slightly tougher than the claimer he won last time. (op 18-1)

Shavansky travelled well to a point but took a while to pick up when first under pressure, before running on. Official explanation: jockey said gelding missed the break (op 28-1 tchd 33-1)

Roman Republic(FR) ran respectably after an absence of 58 days. (op 16-1)

Laterly(IRE) Official explanation: jockey said gelding hung left-handed in straight

6878 RACING UK ON CHANNEL 432 MAIDEN AUCTION STKS 6f 15y
4:40 (4:43) (Class 5) 2-Y-O £2,729 (£806; £403) Stalls High

Form RPR
4 1 **Soweto Star (IRE)**[27] 6153 2-8-12 0 JimmyQuinn 4 73
(J R Best) *chsd ldr: rdn over 1f out: r.o to ld nr fin* 4/1[2]
2 hd **Steps (IRE)** 2-8-13 0 PhilipRobinson 12 73
(M A Jarvis) *sn prom: rdn and ev ch ins fnl f: r.o* 9/2[3]
3533 3 nk **Eland Ally**[44] 5637 2-8-11 68 MickyFenton 1 71
(T P Tate) *led: rdn and hung rt over 1f out: hdd nr fin* 9/1
04 4 4 **Bertiewhittle**[21] 6301 2-8-10 0 GrahamGibbons 14 58
(T D Barron) *hld up: hdwy over 1f out: r.o: nt trble ldrs* 10/1
5 1 **Dickie's Lad (IRE)** 2-8-13 0 JamieSpencer 7 58
(K A Ryan) *hld up: hdwy over 1f out: nvr trbld ldrs* 25/1
055 6 nk **Homeboy (IRE)**[22] 6293 2-8-11 66 PatDobbs 2 55
(M P Tregoning) *chsd ldrs: rdn over 1f out: no ex ins fnl f* 16/1
0 7 nk **Pearl Blue (IRE)**[16] 6441 2-8-7 0 FergusSweeney 11 50
(C F Wall) *hld up: hdwy over 1f out: no imp ins fnl f* 33/1
0 8 5 **Midnight Trader (IRE)**[27] 6153 2-8-12 0 TonyCulhane 10 40
(P W D'Arcy) *s.i.s: hdwy over 4f out: rdn and wknd over 1f out* 7/2[1]
0223 9 1 **Three Scoops**[10] 6628 2-8-1 51 (t) SophieDoyle(3) 6 29
(D J S Ffrench Davis) *chsd ldrs tl rdn and wknd over 2f out* 20/1
10 hd **Amelia's Surprise** 2-8-5 0 AndrewElliott 8 29
(M L W Bell) *dwlt: outpcd* 50/1
00 11 2 3/4 **Dreamweaving (IRE)**[21] 6301 2-8-4 50 SilvestreDeSousa 13 20
(N Tinkler) *mid-div: rdn over 3f out: wknd over 2f out* 100/1
0046 12 13 **Millies Dancer (IRE)**[29] 6072 2-8-3 42 JamesSullivan(3) 9 —
(M G Quinlan) *hld up: rdn and wknd over 2f out* 150/1
043 U **Barnet Fair**[8] 6666 2-8-9 0 KierenFallon 3 —
(R C Guest) *rrd and uns rdr s* 4/1[2]

1m 15.28s (0.38) **Going Correction** +0.025s/f (Good) 13 Ran SP% **120.5**
Speed ratings (Par 95): **98,97,97,92,90 90,89,83,81,81 77,60,—**
toteswingers:1&2: £7.10, 2&3: £10.70, 1&3: £4.70 CSF £21.42 TOTE £4.80: £1.60, £1.70, £4.50; EX 35.80.
Owner Hucking Horses IV **Bred** Lady Of Talent Syndicate **Trained** Hucking, Kent

FOCUS
The proximity of 68-rated Eland Ally suggests this form is no more than fair. Add to that the race lost one of the more fancied runners when Barnet Fair reared and unseated his rider as the stalls opened. They raced up the middle of the track.

NOTEBOOK
Soweto Star(IRE) confirmed the promise he showed when an eyecatching fourth on debut in an ordinary Newmarket maiden, but he was forced to work hard. He reportedly didn't like the ground according to his jockey, so there should be better to come. (op 3-1)
Steps(IRE), a 20,000gns purchase, is not all that big but evidently has ability and just failed. He should win a similar race, but doesn't appeal as one to follow in the long term. (op 11-4 tchd 5-1)
Eland Ally responded well to a really positive ride and had his chance. This is as good as he is. (op 15-2 tchd 12-1)
Bertiewhittle shaped respectably, looking the type who will do better now he can switch to handicaps. (op 16-1)
Dickie's Lad(IRE), a 20,000gns purchase, hung left under pressure and needed the experience. (op 16-1)
Midnight Trader(IRE), nine places behind Soweto Star on debut at Newmarket, was backed in from 20-1 on course, but failed to justify the support. (op 20-1)
Millies Dancer(IRE) Official explanation: jockey said filly jumped right leaving stalls

6879 PADDOCKS CONFERENCE CENTRE H'CAP 6f 15y
5:10 (5:11) (Class 5) (0-75,75) 3-Y-O £2,590 (£770; £385; £192) Stalls High

Form RPR
2305 1 **Piddie's Power**[27] 6164 3-9-0 68 GrahamGibbons 4 77
(E S McMahon) *mde all: rdn clr over 1f out: drvn ins fnl f: kpt on wl towards fin* 9/1
4403 2 1 1/4 **Hulcote Rose (IRE)**[15] 6479 3-8-9 63 JamieSpencer 9 68+
(S Kirk) *dwlt and in rr: pushed along 1/2-way: hdwy on wd outside 2f out: rdn over 1f out: chsd wnr and hung lft ins fnl f: drvn and no imp towards fin* 11/2[2]
0312 3 1 3/4 **Superior Edge**[4] 6772 3-9-1 74 DeclanCannon(5) 12 73
(B Palling) *t.k.h: chsd ldrs: hdwy to chse wnr 2f out: sn rdn and one pce ins fnl f* 4/1[1]
3211 4 nk **Jack Luey**[62] 5046 3-9-2 73 IanBrennan(3) 5 71
(L A Mullaney) *in tch: hdwy over 2f out: rdn to chse ldrs and wandered over 1f out: hld whn n.m.r and swtchd rt ins fnl f* 17/2
5600 5 3 1/2 **Bossy Kitty**[15] 6466 3-8-8 62 SilvestreDeSousa 11 49
(N Tinkler) *trckd ldrs: swtchd rt and hdwy 2f out: rdn and n.m.r over 1f out: sn one pce* 8/1
052 6 3/4 **Coin From Heaven (IRE)**[15] 6461 3-9-7 75 PaulHanagan 7 60
(R A Fahey) *towards rr: hdwy 2f out: sn rdn and n.d* 12/1
565 7 nk **Super Yellow**[8] 6679 3-9-1 69 FergusSweeney 3 53
(J A Osborne) *prom: rdn along over 2f out: grad wknd* 16/1
1550 8 1 1/4 **Kings 'n Dreams**[26] 6198 3-9-4 72 (b) PhilipRobinson 2 52
(D K Ivory) *chsd ldrs: rdn wl over 1f out: grad wknd* 15/2[3]
0560 9 3 1/4 **Gertmegalush (IRE)**[13] 6540 3-8-10 67 (p) BarryMcHugh(3) 13 36
(John A Harris) *chsd ldrs: cl up 1/2-way: sn rdn and wknd* 33/1
4040 10 1/2 **Transmit (IRE)**[25] 6226 3-9-0 68 (b) DavidAllan 8 36
(T D Easterby) *dwlt: a in rr* 18/1
-100 11 2 1/2 **Johannesgray (IRE)**[134] 2656 3-9-4 75 MichaelO'Connell(3) 10 35
(D Nicholls) *dwlt: hdwy and cl up after 1f: rdn along over 2f out: sn hung lft and wknd* 22/1
0001 12 nk **Durham Express (IRE)**[15] 6461 3-9-4 72 (p) PhillipMakin 6 31
(M Dods) *a in rr* 14/1
6130 13 3 **Chushka**[31] 6040 3-9-1 69 (v) TomEaves 1 18
(B Smart) *wnt lft s: bhd fr 1/2-way* 16/1

1m 15.12s (0.22) **Going Correction** +0.025s/f (Good) 13 Ran SP% **117.5**
Speed ratings (Par 101): **99,97,95,94,89 88,88,86,82,81 78,78,74**
toteswingers:1&2: £12.40, 2&3: £6.30, 1&3: £11.90 CSF £56.81 CT £239.87 TOTE £6.30: £3.00, £2.30, £2.10.
Owner The Brookfield Stud & Partners **Bred** The Dunnet Lads **Trained** Lichfield, Staffs

FOCUS
A modest sprint handicap in which the main action unfolded up the middle of the track. Not many got involved and the time was relatively slow. The winner is rated up 5lb.

6880 DG CARS FIRST CORPORATE CHOICE-01159 500 500 H'CAP 5f 13y
5:40 (5:42) (Class 6) (0-65,71) 3-Y-O+ £1,706 (£503; £252) Stalls High

Form RPR
0003 1 **Tamarind Hill (IRE)**[16] 6440 3-8-11 60 (b) DeclanCannon(5) 17 71
(A J McCabe) *chsd ldrs: rdn to ld over 1f out: r.o wl* 14/1
5030 2 2 **Danum Dancer**[8] 6679 6-8-11 55 (b) SilvestreDeSousa 13 59
(N Bycroft) *s.i.s: hdwy over 2f out: rdn over 1f out: r.o* 8/1[3]
0010 3 1/2 **Bouncy Bouncy (IRE)**[20] 6329 3-8-11 55 (t) JamieSpencer 14 57
(M L W Bell) *hld up: hdwy over 1f out: rdn and hung lft ins fnl f: r.o* 9/1
1541 4 1 **Cardinal**[3] 6812 5-9-13 71 6ex FrankieDettori 3 69+
(R M H Cowell) *awkward leaving stalls: hld up: hdwy 2f out: rdn over 1f out: styd on same pce ins fnl f* 13/8[1]
0011 5 nk **Avertuoso**[9] 6643 6-9-6 71 6ex (v) AdamCarter(7) 11 68+
(B Smart) *s.s: bhd: r.o wl ins fnl f: nvr nrr* 11/2[2]
5326 6 2 3/4 **First Swallow**[82] 4373 5-9-3 61 (t) PaulHanagan 9 48
(D H Brown) *led: rdn and hdd over 1f out: wknd ins fnl f* 11/1
00-0 7 1/2 **Senate Majority**[14] 6515 3-8-13 57 DavidAllan 12 43
(T D Easterby) *prom: rdn over 2f out: wknd ins fnl f* 20/1
0300 8 shd **Speak The Truth (IRE)**[14] 6515 4-9-4 62 (p) PatCosgrave 2 47
(J R Boyle) *chsd ldrs: rdn over 1f out: wknd ins fnl f* 22/1
2600 9 2 1/4 **Stolt (IRE)**[12] 6572 6-9-4 65 BarryMcHugh(3) 10 42
(N Wilson) *w ldr: rdn and ev ch 2f out: wknd ins fnl f* 40/1
4251 10 nk **Wreningham**[46] 5562 5-8-11 62 RyanClark(7) 8 38
(S C Williams) *chsd ldrs: rdn and ev ch over 1f out: wknd ins fnl f* 14/1
0420 11 nse **Mr Funshine**[159] 1915 5-8-11 55 GrahamGibbons 4 31
(D Shaw) *hld up: rdn over 1f out: nvr on terms* 50/1
1103 12 1 1/2 **Towy Boy (IRE)**[13] 6536 5-8-11 60 (bt) BillyCray(5) 5 31
(I A Wood) *prom: rdn 1/2-way: wknd over 1f out* 25/1
0503 13 hd **Fromsong (IRE)**[22] 6292 12-8-13 57 PhilipRobinson 7 27
(D K Ivory) *chsd ldrs: rdn 1/2-way: wknd over 1f out* 20/1
4053 14 1/2 **Drumpellier (IRE)**[18] 6392 3-8-11 58 PaulPickard(3) 1 26
(S G West) *mid-div: drvn along 1/2-way: wknd over 1f out* 33/1
6100 15 9 **Alacity (IRE)**[50] 5422 4-8-11 55 FrannyNorton 6 —
(N Bycroft) *s.i.s: sn pushed along in rr: bhd fnl 2f* 40/1

60.91 secs (-0.09) **Going Correction** +0.025s/f (Good) 15 Ran SP% **123.8**
Speed ratings (Par 101): **101,97,97,95,94 90,89,89,85,85 85,83,82,81,67**
toteswingers:1&2: £22.00, 2&3: £14.80, 1&3: £32.20. totesuper7: Win: Not won. Place: Not won. CSF £112.27 CT £737.48 TOTE £20.00: £5.30, £2.20, £5.60; EX 169.20 Place 6: £197.72 Place 5: £135.03.
Owner A C Timms **Bred** Ballylinch Stud **Trained** Averham Park, Notts

FOCUS
A moderate contest in which the action unfolded middle to stands' side, and six of the first nine were drawn in double figures. Not many showed their form but the exposed winner posted a pesonal best.
Avertuoso Official explanation: jockey said gelding reared in stalls
T/Plt: £184.00 to a £1 stake. Pool of £51,534.83 - 204.42 winning tickets. T/Qpdt: £319.00 to a £1 stake. Pool of £3,311.34 - 7.68 winning tickets. JR

BORDEAUX LE BOUSCAT (R-H)
Thursday, October 14

OFFICIAL GOING: Turf: good

6881a PRIX ANDRE BABOIN (GRAND PRIX DES PROVINCES) (GROUP 3) (3YO+) (TURF) 1m 1f 110y
2:45 (12:00) 3-Y-O+ £35,398 (£14,159; £10,619; £7,079; £3,539)

RPR
1 **Zibimix (IRE)**[25] 6234 6-8-11 0 GregoryBenoist 7 103
(X Nakkachdji, France) *racd in 4th: rdn to chal 1 1/2f out: qcknd wl to grab ld 1f out: sn clr: comf* 17/5[2]
2 1 **Thai Haku (IRE)**[21] 6316 3-8-5 0 Christophe-PatriceLemaire 4 100
(M Delzangles, France) *racd in 5th on rail: swtchd wdr arnd fnl turn: qcknd wl 1 1/2f out: r.o wl fnl f wout threatening wnr* 31/1
3 nk **Skins Game**[19] 6384 4-9-1 0 IoritzMendizabal 3 104
(J-C Rouget, France) *racd towards rr: swtchd wd and qcknd 1 1/2f out: r.o wl fnl f wout threatening* 6/1[3]
4 2 1/2 **Pont Des Arts (FR)**[18] 6-9-1 0 FredericSpanu 1 99
(A Scharer, Germany) *led: hdd 1f out: r.o fnl f* 16/1
5 nk **Wealthy (IRE)**[25] 6219 3-8-11 0 Pierre-CharlesBoudot 6 100
(A Fabre, France) *racd in 3rd along rail: threatened briefly early in st: failed to qckn: r.o one pce* 6/4[1]
6 nk **Pallodio (IRE)**[165] 1747 5-9-1 0 DavyBonilla 2 98
(J E Hammond, France) *racd in rr: rdn early in st: failed to qckn: styd on* 6/1[3]
7 2 **Starlish (IRE)**[20] 6344 5-9-1 0 AnthonyCrastus 8 94
(E Lellouche, France) *trckd ldr racing on outside: rdn but no rspnse fr 2f out: fdd* 17/2
8 1 1/2 **Macondo (FR)**[32] 5-8-11 0 Roberto-CarlosMontenegro 5 87
(X Thomas-Demeaulte, France) *racd towards rr: rdn early in st : no ex* 17/1

2m 3.25s (123.25)
WFA 3 from 4yo+ 4lb 8 Ran SP% **116.4**
WIN (incl. 1 euro stake): 4.40. PLACES: 1.90, 6.30, 2.40. DF: 52.20. SF: 84.50.
Owner Antoine Boucher **Bred** Wertheimer Et Frere **Trained** France

6559 NEWMARKET (R-H)
Friday, October 15

OFFICIAL GOING: Good (stands' side 7.7, centre 7.8, far side 8.0)
Wind: virtually nil Weather: overcast

6882 EBF PRESTIGE VEHICLES MAIDEN STKS 6f
1:45 (1:46) (Class 4) 2-Y-O £5,180 (£1,541; £770; £384) Stalls Centre

Form RPR
20 1 **Desert Law (IRE)**[27] 6192 2-9-3 0 JimmyFortune 13 88
(A M Balding) *dwlt: sn rcvrd and chsd ldng pair: wnt 2nd over 2f out: rdn to ld ent fnl f: r.o strly: comf* 7/4[1]
3220 2 2 3/4 **Jinky**[13] 6568 2-9-3 85 RichardHughes 9 80
(M R Channon) *led: rdn ent fnl 2f: hdd ent fnl f: sn outpcd and no ch w wnr fnl 150yds: eased towards fin* 3/1[2]
63 3 3/4 **Cape Rambler**[91] 4110 2-9-3 0 DaneO'Neill 7 78
(H Candy) *chsd ldr tl over 2f out: rdn and outpcd by ldng pair over 1f out: kpt on same pce ins fnl f* 16/1
62 4 1/2 **Lamasaas (USA)**[72] 4709 2-9-3 0 RichardHills 6 76
(B W Hills) *stdd after s: hld up towards rr: pushed along and hdwy on far side ent fnl 2f: chsd ldng trio and edgd lft u.p ent fnl f: kpt on and pressing for 3rd ins fnl f: nvr trbld ldrs* 7/1

5 *6* **Trojan Nights (USA)** 2-9-3 0 KierenFallon 10 58
(W J Haggas) *dwlt: pushed along and hdwy to chse ldrs after 2f: rdn and outpcd ent fnl 2f: wl btn over 1f out* **12/1**

0 6 *1 ¼* **Stirling Bridge**[28] 6153 2-9-3 0 SteveDrowne 2 54
(W Jarvis) *hld up in tch in midfield: rdn and outpcd ent fnl 2f: no ch fr over 1f out* **50/1**

0 7 *2 ¾* **Wom**[28] 6153 2-9-3 0 MichaelHills 1 46
(W J Haggas) *s.i.s: t.k.h: hld up in rr: hdwy past btn horses fr over 1f out: kpt on: nvr trbld ldrs* **25/1**

3 8 *1* **Loving Thought**[16] 6451 2-8-12 0 TomQueally 12 38
(H R A Cecil) *dwlt: hld up towards rr: swtchd rt and hdwy over 2f out: sn struggling u.p: wl btn over 1f out* **6/1**[3]

9 *2* **Salesiano** 2-9-3 0 NeilCallan 5 37
(P J Makin) *chsd ldrs tl rdn and wknd u.p over 2f out: wl btn over 1f out* **50/1**

10 *4* **Giotto (IRE)** 2-9-3 0 J-PGuillambert 3 25
(N P Littmoden) *t.k.h: rn green and hld up in tch towards rr: rdn and struggling wl over 2f out: wl bhd fnl 2f* **80/1**

0 11 *3* **Cairanne**[30] 6092 2-8-12 0 JimmyQuinn 8 11
(T Keddy) *chsd ldrs tl rdn and wknd over 2f out: wl bhd fr wl over 1f out* **125/1**

12 *2 ½* **Bluberry** 2-8-12 0 RyanMoore 4 4
(G L Moore) *rn green: in tch tl 1/2-way: steadily dropped out: wl bhd fnl f* **20/1**

1m 12.43s (0.23) **Going Correction** +0.05s/f (Good) **12** Ran SP% **116.3**
Speed ratings (Par 97): **100,96,95,94,86 85,81,80,77,72 68,64**
toteswingers:1&2:£2.40, 1&3:£7.60, 2&3:£7.40 CSF £6.22 TOTE £2.60: £1.50, £1.60, £3.50; EX 8.60 Trifecta £48.90 Pool: £298.86 - 4.52 winning units..
Owner J C Smith **Bred** Littleton Stud **Trained** Kingsclere, Hants
■ Question Times (7/1) was withdrawn on vet's advice. Deduct 10p in the £ under R4. New market formed.

FOCUS
The favourite had taken this maiden seven times in the previous nine years, including the last five, and that trend continued. The first three horses home held those positions throughout and little else ever got into it.

NOTEBOOK
Desert Law(IRE) ◆ pulled too hard when last of seven in the Mill Reef, but the application of a cross noseband saw him settle much better in a handy position. Having travelled well, he had little difficulty in cutting down the leader and won going away. He will be put away now and looks a nice prospect for next season. (old market op 9-4, new market op 15-8)
Jinky, the most experienced in the field, has an official rating of 85 after making the frame in his first four starts and then finishing seventh in the totepool Two-Year-Old Trophy. He did his best to make all, but was up against a classy rival and had no answer to him from the furlong pole. He has a race in him, but lacks the scope of most of these rivals. (old market op 10-3 tchd 11-4)
Cape Rambler, a remote third behind Dream Ahead at Nottingham when last seen in July, was always in about the same place and kept on all the way to the line. He now gets a mark and looks the type to come into his own at three. (old market op 20-1 tchd 22-1)
Lamasaas(USA), who missed the break in his first two starts but showed some ability, was the only one to make up any appreciable ground from off the pace and also now gets a mark. (new market op 8-1)
Trojan Nights(USA) ◆, a half-brother to 13 winners of which at least five turned out to be useful, ran green on this debut but showed that there is something there to work on and the experience will not be lost. (old market op 14-1 tchd 16-1)
Stirling Bridge ◆, 11th of 17 on his debut over C&D last month, was by no means knocked about and gave the impression he is capable of lot more than he has shown so far. Although by a top-class sprinter, there is plenty of stamina on the dam's side and the way he ran here suggests he will get further. (old market op 66-1)
Loving Thought, a promising third of 12 over 7f on her Kempton debut last month, didn't improve from that and she appeared to be racing awkwardly in the Dip. (old market op 15-2 tchd 9-1, new market op 13-2)

6883 E B F ANGLO HIBERNIAN BLOODSTOCK INSURANCE MAIDEN STKS 1m

2:20 (2:24) (Class 4) 2-Y-O £5,180 (£1,541; £770; £384) **Stalls** Centre

Form RPR

04 1 **Argocat (IRE)**[16] 6473 2-9-3 0 FrankieDettori 8 87
(P F I Cole) *chsd ldr tl led over 6f out: rdn and hdd wl over 2f out: sltly outpcd by ldng pair and drvn over 1f out: rallied ins fnl f: carried lft fnl 100yds: kpt on gamely to ld last strides* **11/1**

42 2 *hd* **El Muqbil (IRE)**[56] 5277 2-9-3 0 RichardHills 3 87
(B J Meehan) *rrd s: sn in tch: chsd ldrs over 3f out: rdn and ev ch over 2f out: clr w rival and led over 1f out: hung rt u.p 1f out: forged ahd ins fnl f: hung lft fnl 100yds: hdd last strides* **5/4**[1]

3 *1 ½* **Suhaili** 2-9-3 0 PhilipRobinson 2 84
(M A Jarvis) *in tch in midfield: rdn and outpcd by ldng trio 3f out: styd on again over 1f out: kpt on wl fnl f: wnt 3rd towards fin* **10/1**

4 *1* **Splendid Light** 2-9-3 0 WilliamBuick 17 81
(J H M Gosden) *w ldrs: rdn to ld wl over 2f out: hdd but clr w runner-up over 1f out: hld hd high u.p and pushed rt 1f out: btn ins fnl f: wknd fnl 75yds* **6/1**[3]

5 *1 ¼* **Laughing Jack** 2-9-3 0 JamieSpencer 18 78
(M L W Bell) *broke wl: t.k.h: led tl over 6f out: stdd and chsd ldrs after: rdn and outpcd by ldng trio 3f out: no threat to ldrs over 1f out: kpt on again ins fnl f* **11/2**[2]

0 6 *½* **Malanos (IRE)**[28] 6159 2-9-3 0 DaneO'Neill 4 77+
(D R C Elsworth) *in tch in midfield: rdn and outpcd over 3f out: styd on again fr over 1f out: keeping on wl ins fnl f: nt pce to threaten ldrs* **66/1**

7 *nk* **Quiz Mistress** 2-8-12 0 StevieDonohoe 12 72+
(G A Butler) *s.i.s: sn in tch in midfield: rdn and outpcd ent fnl 3f: no ch w ldrs whn nt clr run and swtchd rt over 1f out: kpt on again ins fnl f: keeping on fin* **66/1**

8 *1 ¼* **Thubiaan (USA)** 2-9-3 0 TadhgO'Shea 10 74
(W J Haggas) *chsd ldrs: rdn and outpcd 3f out: kpt on same pce and no threat to ldrs fr wl over 1f out* **28/1**

9 *¾* **Divinite Green (IRE)** 2-9-3 0 JackMitchell 15 72
(P W Chapple-Hyam) *v.s.a: rcvrd and in tch in midfield after 1f: rdn and hdwy to chse ldrs over 4f out: rdn and outpcd 3f out: styd on same pce u.p fr over 1f out* **100/1**

10 *2 ¼* **Sea Soldier (IRE)** 2-9-3 0 JimmyFortune 1 67
(A M Balding) *s.i.s: bhd: pushed along and sme hdwy over 3f out: kpt on steadily after: nvr trbld ldrs* **16/1**

11 *½* **Cry Fury** 2-9-3 0 SteveDrowne 7 66+
(R Charlton) *s.i.s: in tch in midfield: lost pl and rdn along over 4f out: n.d and kpt on same pce fr over 1f out* **33/1**

12 *hd* **Wayward Glance** 2-9-3 0 RyanMoore 16 65
(M L W Bell) *in tch towards rr: rdn along and outpcd 4f out: kpt on same pce and n.d after* **25/1**

13 *hd* **Diverting** 2-8-12 0 LiamKeniry 6 60
(W Jarvis) *awkward s and v.s.a: bhd: rdn and struggling over 4f out: sme hdwy over 1f out: n.d* **100/1**

14 *2* **Gladstone (IRE)** 2-9-3 0 ShaneKelly 9 60
(W J Haggas) *stdd s: in tch towards rr: rdn and outpcd 4f out: plugging on same pce: rn geen and hanging rt fr over 2f out* **66/1**

15 *½* **Romeo Montague** 2-9-3 0 NeilCallan 19 59
(E A L Dunlop) *stdd s: hld up in tch: rdn and struggling over 3f out: no ch fnl 2f* **100/1**

0 16 *4 ½* **Old Boy Ted**[15] 6504 2-9-3 0 JimmyQuinn 11 49
(M H Tompkins) *a in rr: rdn and struggling fr 1/2-way: n.d* **100/1**

17 *1* **Proud Chieftain** 2-9-0 0 GilmarPereira(3) 14 46
(H J Collingridge) *wnt rt s and slowly away: bhd: hdwy into midfield 5f out: rdn and wknd over 3f out:* **100/1**

5 18 *24* **Yas Marina (USA)**[13] 6566 2-9-3 0 AhmedAjtebi 13 —
(Mahmood Al Zarooni) *in tch in midfield: lost pl and rn green over 4f out: wl bhd and virtually p.u ins fnl f* **16/1**

1m 40.05s (1.45) **Going Correction** +0.05s/f (Good) **18** Ran SP% **123.0**
Speed ratings (Par 97): **94,93,92,91,90 89,89,88,87,85 84,84,84,82,81 77,76,52**
toteswingers:1&2:£3.90, 1&3:£14.30, 2&3:£5.10 CSF £23.92 TOTE £13.90: £3.20, £1.10, £3.30; EX 34.50 Trifecta £186.90 Pool: £719.97 - 2.85 winning units..
Owner Mrs Fitri Hay **Bred** B Bellaud & Caragh Bloodstock **Trained** Whatcombe, Oxon

FOCUS
Plenty of interesting types on show, but the time was disappointing, being 2.59 seconds (around 15l) slower than the following conditions event won by Mantoba, albeit that looked a hot race. That said, the runner-up, who recorded RPRs in the 80s on his first two starts, helps give the form a solid look. The action mainly unfolded up the middle of the track.

NOTEBOOK
Argocat(IRE) improved a good deal on his first two efforts with a strong staying performance, rallying when headed having been outpaced. Paul Cole considers him very much a 3-y-o prospect who will want middle-distances, and said he won't run him again this year. (op 14-1 tchd 16-1)
El Muqbil(IRE), just as in the Convivial maiden at York over 7f last time, looked the winner when taking over before finding one too strong in the closing stages. Not quite seeing his races out just yet, the impression is we haven't seen the best of him and he could do better in time. (op Evens tchd 11-8 and 6-4 in places)
Suhaili, a 165,000gns half-brother to five winners, out of an Oaks third, is in the English and Irish Derby. He kept on nicely after getting outpaced and looks a decent prospect middle-distance prospect. (op 8-1)
Splendid Light ◆, described by his trainer as a "nice horse for next year", has a giant stride and ran a big race until getting unbalanced and changing his legs leaving the Dip. There should be much better to come and he appeals as one to follow. (op 8-1)
Laughing Jack's rider stopped pushing with about half a furlong to go, but the colt still ran on. There should be better to come. (op 8-1)
Malanos(IRE) improved on his debut effort and looks the type to continue to go the right way.
Quiz Mistress, one of only two fillies, missed the break and was outpaced, before keeping on. She's another who should do well over further.

6884 BET AT BLUESQ.COM HOUGHTON CONDITIONS STKS 1m

2:55 (2:56) (Class 2) 2-Y-O

£8,723 (£2,612; £1,306; £653; £326; £163) **Stalls** Centre

Form RPR

41 1 **Mantoba**[17] 6443 2-9-3 76 (t) FrankieDettori 2 102
(B J Meehan) *a.p: led wl over 2f out: hrd pressed and sn rdn: r.o strly to assert fnl 75yds: rdn out* **8/1**[3]

1 2 *2 ¼* **Loving Spirit**[14] 6532 2-9-3 0 RobertHavlin 10 97
(J A R Toller) *trckd ldrs: rdn over 2f out: ev ch jst ins fnl f: no ex fnl 75yds* **15/8**[1]

1 3 *1 ½* **Dordogne (IRE)**[23] 6279 2-9-3 90 KierenFallon 8 93
(M Johnston) *prom: led 4f out: rdn whn narrowly hdd wl over 2f out: kpt pressing wnr tl no ex fnl 100yds* **15/8**[1]

4 *4 ½* **Whey Sauce (JPN)** 2-8-7 0 JackMitchell 1 73
(P W Chapple-Hyam) *hld up in tch: smooth hdwy 3f out: sn rdn to chal: kpt on same pce fnl 2f* **20/1**

1 5 *9* **Pivotman**[16] 6474 2-9-3 85 NeilCallan 5 62
(Mrs A J Perrett) *s.i.s: sn trcking ldrs: rdn over 3f out: wknd over 2f out* **7/2**[2]

0 6 *¾* **Emmeline Pankhurst (IRE)**[144] 2389 2-8-7 0 JimmyQuinn 6 51
(Miss J Feilden) *trckd ldrs: rdn over 3f out: wknd over 2f out* **40/1**

0000 7 *17* **Jamaica Grande**[1] 6870 2-8-12 57 DavidProbert 4 17
(T T Clement) *trckd ldrs: rdn 3f out: sn wknd* **150/1**

3000 8 *10* **Callipygos**[10] 6646 2-8-7 56 LauraPike 7 —
(P S McEntee) *led tl 4f out: wknd 3f out* **150/1**

9 *½* **Generous Pursuit** 2-8-7 0 AdamBeschizza 9 —
(P S McEntee) *dwlt: pushed along towards rr fr over 4f out: wknd over 3f out* **150/1**

000 10 *62* **Huckle Duckle (IRE)**[31] 6058 2-8-7 30 (vt[1]) TobyAtkinson 3 —
(P S McEntee) *awkward leaving stalls: sn struggling in rr: wknd over 3f out* **150/1**

1m 37.46s (-1.14) **Going Correction** +0.05s/f (Good) **10** Ran SP% **112.7**
Speed ratings (Par 101): **107,104,103,98,89 89,72,62,61,—**
toteswingers:1&2:£4.00, 1&3:£2.70, 2&3:£1.90 CSF £22.55 TOTE £8.90: £1.90, £1.10, £1.40; EX 26.70 Trifecta £36.40 Pool: £1,532.85 - 31.10 winning units..
Owner Manton Racing Partnership **Bred** Kirtlington Stud **Trained** Manton, Wilts
■ Stewards' Enquiry : Robert Havlin caution: careless riding.

FOCUS
Not as competitive as the numbers would suggest with only half the field holding realistic chances (the four outsiders were available at 1000-1 to good money on a leading exchange throughout the day), but still a decent contest featuring three that had won their only previous starts very impressively. Again they raced down the centre and the winning time was 2.59 seconds quicker than the preceding maiden.

NOTEBOOK
Mantoba ◆ responded well to the tongue tie when improving from his debut to win a 7f Newbury maiden last month, though the form of that race had yet to be truly boosted. However, the colt took another major step forward with this success and he certainly had to do it the hard way, as he was involved in a three-way battle for the advantage for most of the way. However, despite coming under strong pressure over a furlong from home, he still managed to produce an impressive turn of foot up the rising ground to put daylight between himself and his two nearest pursuers. He may run in either the Criterium du Saint-Cloud or the Breeders' Cup Juvenile Turf and, as his dam was successful at up to 1m6f, he should have little trouble staying middle distances next year. (tchd 15-2)
Loving Spirit ◆, up a furlong after slamming 16 rivals on debut in a soft-ground maiden here last month (eighth horse won a Lingfield novice event impressively two days earlier), moved into contention over 2f from home and had every chance, but he couldn't match the winner's turn of foot running out of the Dip. His breeding suggests that he will be well suited by middle distances next season. (tchd 7-4 and 2-1)

Dordogne(IRE), down a furlong after bolting up on his debut at Goodwood last month (race has already produced a couple of winners from amongst the also-rans), tried to make the most of his proven stamina, but the winner stuck to him limpet-like and, when bettered by his rival, he tended to run green and hung about in the Dip. A return to further will suit him and the Zetland Stakes over an extra 2f back here at the end of the month may be the ideal race for him. (op 7-4 tchd 2-1 and 9-4 in places)

Whey Sauce(JPN) ◆, related to some smart performers in both Japan and the US, faced a monumental task on this debut but she emerges with a lot of credit. Having travelled well throughout, she made smooth progress towards the nearside to challenge for the lead passing the 2f pole, but then seemed to blow up as lack of a previous run began to tell. She still finished a very long way clear of the others and is a filly with a bright future.

Pivotman, easy winner of a soft-ground Salisbury maiden over this trip on debut, was the disappointment of the race. He was off the bridle and going nowhere from some way out here and perhaps the form of the Salisbury race is modest, or maybe he needs genuinely testing ground to show his best. (op 4-1 tchd 9-2 in places)

Emmeline Pankhurst(IRE), not seen since finishing a well-beaten seventh of nine on her Leicester debut in May, did much the best of the outsiders and she will find easier opportunities than this. (op 33-1)

6885 RICHARD HAMBRO DARLEY STKS (GROUP 3) 1m 1f

3:30 (3:31) (Class 1) 3-Y-O+

£32,358 (£12,266; £6,138; £3,060; £1,533; £769) **Stalls** Centre

Form				RPR
3331	**1**		**Tazeez (USA)**[27] 6195 6-9-3 118 RichardHills 6 (J H M Gosden) *chsd ldr: rdn to ld over 1f out: edgd lft u.p fnl f: kpt on wl* **3/1**[1]	115+
4422	**2**	*3/4*	**Steele Tango (USA)**[13] 6562 5-9-3 107 LiamKeniry 7 (R A Teal) *in tch in midfield: rdn and effrt ent 3f out: chsd ldrs and drvn over 1f out: chsd wnr fnl 100yds: kpt on wl* **7/1**[3]	113
13-5	**3**	*1 1/4*	**Mastery**[202] 1027 4-9-3 117 DaraghO'Donohoe 10 (Saeed Bin Suroor) *hld up towards rr: hdwy 3f out: rdn to chse ldrs over 1f out: kpt on same pce ins fnl f: wnt 3rd nr fin* **10/1**	110
-063	**4**	*nse*	**Al Zir (USA)**[37] 5853 3-8-13 109 (t) TedDurcan 1 (Saeed Bin Suroor) *rring in stalls: in tch in midfield: rdn and effrt 3f out: drvn and chsd wnr over 1f out: keeping on same pce and hld whn nt clr run and swtchd rt fnl 100yds: lost 3rd nr fin* **15/2**	111+
2141	**5**	*2 1/2*	**Vesuve (IRE)**[27] 6179 4-9-3 110 FrankieDettori 5 (Saeed Bin Suroor) *rring in stalls: chsd ldrs: rdn 3f out: chsd ldng pair and drvn over 1f out: wknd ins fnl f* **4/1**[2]	105
1003	**6**	*3 1/2*	**Cockney Class (USA)**[7] 6709 3-8-13 88 SteveDrowne 4 (B J Meehan) *stdd s: hld up in rr: rdn and effrt ent fnl 3f: drvn and hdwy 2f out: no imp u.p fr over 1f out: nvr trbld ldrs* **50/1**	98
4400	**7**	*1 3/4*	**Fanunalter**[41] 5741 4-9-3 106 DarryllHolland 9 (M Botti) *hld up in rr: hdwy over 3f out: rdn and no prog ent fnl 2f: wknd wl over 1f out* **9/1**	94
3546	**8**	*1 1/2*	**The Cheka (IRE)**[104] 3704 4-9-3 110 WilliamBuick 15 (Eve Johnson Houghton) *hld up in tch in midfield: rdn and unable qck over 2f out: wknd wl over 1f out* **10/1**	91
	9	*nk*	**Letty**[19] 3-8-10 0 NeilCallan 13 (A Friebert, Hungary) *racd keenly: led and racd alone tl over 3f out: rdn and hdd over 1f out: wknd ent fnl f* **100/1**	87
1-65	**10**	*1*	**Mac Love**[34] 5951 9-9-3 113 MickyFenton 14 (Stef Higgins) *stdd and swtchd lft after s: t.k.h: hld up in rr: rdn and effrt on far side over 2f out: no hdwy: n.d* **25/1**	88
1530	**11**	*2 3/4*	**Field Of Dream**[56] 5274 3-8-13 108 KierenFallon 8 (L M Cumani) *hld up in tch towards rr: rdn and effrt over 3f: wknd over 2f out* **25/1**	82
0-56	**12**	*4 1/2*	**Runaway**[61] 5134 8-9-3 107 JimmyFortune 11 (R Pritchard-Gordon, France) *stdd s: hld up in tch: rdn and strugggling ent fnl 3f: wl btn whn hung lft ent fnl f: eased ins fnl f* **50/1**	73
0210	**13**	*14*	**Royal Destination (IRE)**[27] 6193 5-9-3 105 RyanMoore 12 (J Noseda) *chsd ldrs tl 4f out: sn u.p and losing pl: wl bhd over 1f out: eased ins fnl f: t.o* **12/1**	43

1m 49.74s (-1.96) **Going Correction** +0.05s/f (Good)
WFA 3 from 4yo+ 4lb **13** Ran SP% **117.7**
Speed ratings (Par 113): **110,109,108,108,105 102,101,99,99,98 96,92,79**
toteswingers:1&2:£4.70, 1&3:£7.70, 2&3:£13.20 CSF £22.69 TOTE £3.50: £1.50, £2.40, £3.50; EX 12.40 Trifecta £169.00 Pool: £1,327.27 - 5.81 winning units..
Owner Hamdan Al Maktoum **Bred** Clovelly Farms **Trained** Newmarket, Suffolk

■ Stewards' Enquiry : Richard Hills two-day ban: careless riding (Oct 29-30)
Liam Keniry one-day ban: used whip with excessive frequency (Oct 29)

FOCUS
The field started off up the middle of the track, but gradually edged over towards the stands' side. The runner-up is a pretty sound guide to the form.

NOTEBOOK
Tazeez(USA) beat Steele Tango into second for the fourth time, and in total the John Gosden-trained runner now leads the head-to-head 5-0. He is also now 3-3 over C&D, and proved he doesn't need the cheekpieces he had fitted last time. As good as ever at the age of six, there's a nice prize to be won with Tazeez somewhere abroad, though probably not at one of the major foreign meetings. John Gosden said he will consider races in the US (third in Arlington Million only previous start in States) and Hong Kong. (op 11-4 tchd 10-3)

Steele Tango(USA), winner of this last year and runner-up in the Cambridgeshire over C&D off a mark of 103 on his previous start, ran another honest race. (op 13-2)

Mastery, having only his third start since winning last year's St Leger, and his first outing since a surprisingly close-up effort in the Dubai World Cup, was racing over a trip well short of his best and needed the race according to Saeed Bin Suroor, so this was a noteworthy effort. (op 14-1)

Al Zir(USA) is a fine physical specimen who surely hasn't fulfilled his potential. Fitted with a tongue-tie for the first time, he came with a threatening looking run towards the stands' side in the closing stages, but was inclined to hang right and didn't look comfortable on the undulations, his effort flattening out late on. He would, though, have been third had he not been short of room against the near rail close home. Considering his US pedigree, he'll be interesting if ever switched to dirt, or more likely synthetics at next year's Dubai Carnival. (op 7-1 tchd 8-1)

Vesuve(IRE) was the choice of Frankie Dettori over the third and fourth, but he found this tougher than the Ayr Listed race he won on his previous start, simply not looking good enough. (op 7-2)

Cockney Class(USA) won a 1m Musselburgh handicap on good to soft off a mark of just 88 on his previous start, so clearly had plenty to find in this company, but he acquitted himself with credit, especially as he was set quite a bit to do. (op 66-1)

Fanunalter was not at his best. (op 12-1)

The Cheka(IRE) offered little after an absence of 104 days. (op 16-1 tchd 20-1 in places)

Field Of Dream Official explanation: jockey said colt had no more to give

6886 LANWADES STUD SEVERALS STKS (LISTED RACE) (F&M) 1m 2f

4:05 (4:09) (Class 1) 3-Y-O+

£19,869 (£7,532; £3,769; £1,879; £941; £472) **Stalls** Centre

Form				RPR
1-	**1**		**Modeyra**[357] 6992 3-8-11 88 FrankieDettori 1 (Saeed Bin Suroor) *settled towards rr of mid-div: qcknd up wl on stands' side rail 2f out to ld jst ins fnl f: r.o wl: readily* **13/2**[2]	110+
4201	**2**	*1 1/2*	**Timepiece**[121] 3071 3-9-0 111 TomQueally 5 (H R A Cecil) *mid-div: hdwy 3f out: rdn whn short of room and swtchd lft over 1f out: styd on to chse wnr ins fnl f: a being hld* **15/8**[1]	111+
5304	**3**	*1 1/2*	**Middle Club**[14] 6551 3-8-11 108 RichardHughes 13 (R Hannon) *prom: rdn over 2f out: ev ch ent fnl f: kpt on but no ex* **9/1**[3]	102
1102	**4**	*shd*	**Sea Of Heartbreak (IRE)**[33] 5989 3-8-11 92 SteveDrowne 12 (R Charlton) *mid-div: hdwy 3f out: rdn 2f out: led briefly ent fnl f: kpt on but no ex* **10/1**	102
2546	**5**	*1 3/4*	**Bikini Babe (IRE)**[34] 5938 3-8-11 105 NeilCallan 4 (M Johnston) *trckd ldrs: rdn over 2f out: styd on same pce* **20/1**	98
5045	**6**	*1 1/2*	**Three Moons (IRE)**[14] 6533 4-9-2 99 DaneO'Neill 3 (H J L Dunlop) *sn led: rdn and narrowly hdd 2f out: ev ch ent fnl f: one pce* **25/1**	95
4355	**7**	*3/4*	**Totally Ours**[40] 5805 3-8-11 94 RichardMullen 2 (W R Muir) *hld up towards rr: rdn 3f out: styd on but nvr gng pce to rch ldrs* **40/1**	94
3414	**8**	*shd*	**Principal Role (USA)**[120] 3101 3-9-0 103 IanMongan 8 (H R A Cecil) *t.k.h: trckd ldrs: rdn and ev ch over 2f out: edgd lft and fdd fnl f* **13/2**[2]	97
1600	**9**	*1/2*	**Some Sunny Day**[21] 6320 4-9-2 82 HayleyTurner 11 (H Morrison) *hld up bhd: rdn over 2f out: sn hung rt: little imp* **100/1**	93?
1440	**10**	*nk*	**Island Sunset (IRE)**[113] 3368 4-9-2 85 DavidProbert 15 (W R Muir) *mid-div on outer: hdwy 4f out: sn rdn: fdd ins fnl f* **100/1**	92?
3020	**11**	*1/2*	**Clarietta**[14] 6551 3-8-11 95 TedDurcan 6 (J L Dunlop) *w ldr: rdn to ld 2f out: hdd jst ins fnl f: fdd* **50/1**	91
4023	**12**	*nk*	**Mudaaraah**[65] 4957 3-8-11 105 RichardHills 14 (J L Dunlop) *sn swtchd lft: towards rr: rdn over 2f out: nvr any imp* **10/1**	90
1206	**13**	*3 3/4*	**Eldalil**[57] 5249 3-8-11 106 TadhgO'Shea 10 (Sir Michael Stoute) *mid-div: rdn over 2f out: wknd fnl f* **16/1**	83
3022	**14**	*17*	**Fanditha (IRE)**[17] 6447 4-9-2 85 (p) KierenFallon 9 (L M Cumani) *little slowly away: mid-div: rdn 4f out: hung rt and wknd ent fnl f* **14/1**	49

2m 4.19s (-1.61) **Going Correction** +0.05s/f (Good)
WFA 3 from 4yo 5lb **14** Ran SP% **117.2**
Speed ratings (Par 111): **108,106,105,105,104 102,102,102,101,101 101,100,97,84**
toteswingers:1&2:£3.00, 1&3:£8.10, 2&3:£4.70 CSF £17.49 TOTE £6.90: £2.30, £1.50, £3.20; EX 18.40 Trifecta £74.70 Pool: £1,010.98 - 10.01 winning units..
Owner Godolphin **Bred** Darley **Trained** Newmarket, Suffolk

FOCUS
A competitive fillies' Listed race and although the runners started off racing up the middle of the track, they gradually edged over towards the stands' rail as the contest progressed. The front pair are a bit above this grade and better than the bare form.

NOTEBOOK
Modeyra ◆ has had her problems and hadn't been seen since beating Gertrude Bell on her Doncaster debut a year ago, but she represented a yard that had taken this three times in the previous six runnings. Ridden with plenty of confidence, she was switched over to the stands' rail over 2f from home and quickened up smartly to hit the front at the furlong pole and win going away. She remains totally unexposed and may have another run before the end of the year, but she could be even better as a 4-y-o and certainly looks capable of winning something better than this. (op 6-1 tchd 7-1)

Timepiece, not seen since winning the Sandringham at Royal Ascot, was joint best-in at these weights. Off the bridle behind the leaders over 2f from home, she had a problem trying to get through a gap between Three Moons and Clarietta over a furlong from home and, by the time she did, the winner was away and clear. It's doubtful she would have won with a clear run, but she certainly would have been closer. (op 9-4)

Middle Club, the other joint best-in at the weights, was always up there and, despite coming under pressure a fair way out, stuck to her task gamely. She has shown her very best form abroad, so it wouldn't be a surprise to see her on her travels again in the coming weeks. (op 10-1)

Sea Of Heartbreak(IRE), back down to probably her best trip, ran a splendid race as not only was she up against an unexposed winner, she had 16lb to find with the second and third at these weights and also raced out towards the centre of the track, whilst the first three came more towards the nearside rail. (op 12-1)

Bikini Babe(IRE), who has run several decent races at this level and higher and had a decent chance on official ratings, ran on up the stands' rail after coming under pressure over 2f from home, but she on a losing run of 16 since winning her maiden on her second start at two. (op 22-1 tchd 25-1)

Three Moons(IRE), held in similar company since winning a Folkestone maiden in April of last year, set the pace but had little left after being headed 2f from home.

Totally Ours has performed well in defeat since switching to turf and tried at this level, but although she made up some late ground she never looked like winning. (op 33-1 tchd 50-1 and 100-1 in places)

Principal Role(USA), representing the same owner/trainer combination as the runner-up, had been off since appearing not to stay the extra 2f in the Ribblesdale and ran here as though the race was needed. (op 8-1 tchd 6-1)

Clarietta ended up well beaten, but she ran better than her finishing position would suggest considering she was pretty keen early. (op 33-1)

6887 E B F NATIONAL STUD BOADICEA FILLIES' STKS (LISTED RACE) 6f

4:40 (4:42) (Class 1) 3-Y-O+

£19,869 (£7,532; £3,769; £1,879; £941; £472) **Stalls** Centre

Form				RPR
3121	**1**		**Dever Dream**[36] 5883 3-9-1 105 RyanMoore 10 (W J Haggas) *dwlt: bhd: stl plenty to do and rdn 2f out: hdwy and switching lft over 1f out: chsd ldrs on stands' rail ins fnl f: r.o strly to ld towards fin* **7/4**[1]	102+
1110	**2**	*3/4*	**Wake Up Call**[20] 6351 4-9-0 89 ow1 GeorgeBaker 8 (C F Wall) *hld up in midfield: hdwy ent fnl 2f: swtchd rt and rdn over 1f out: drvn to ld fnl 100yds: hdd and no ex towards fin* **14/1**	98
5401	**3**	*hd*	**Amitola (IRE)**[15] 6509 3-8-12 89 JamieSpencer 1 (T D Barron) *racd towards stands' rail: chsd ldr: rdn and wnt rt over 1f out: hrd drvn and ev ch 1f out: kpt on same pce fnl 100yds* **14/1**	96
1001	**4**	*1 3/4*	**Curtains**[17] 6438 3-8-12 85 TomQueally 5 (S Dow) *led: rdn ent fnl 2f: edgd rt u.p over 1f out: hdd fnl 100yds: wknd towards fin* **40/1**	91

1200 **5** *3 1/4* **Beyond Desire**[27] 6194 3-9-1 97 NeilCallan 9 83
(M A Jarvis) *chsd ldrs: rdn over 2f out: hrd drvn to press ldr and carried rt jst over 1f out: wknd ins fnl f* **8/1**

0431 **6** *hd* **Doric Lady**[17] 6446 5-8-13 81 KirstyMilczarek 3 80
(J A R Toller) *in tch: effrt to chse ldrs over 2f out: drvn and unable qck whn short of room and swtchd lft jst over 1f out: wknd qckly ins fnl f* **40/1**

0553 **7** *2* **Electric Feel**[20] 6351 3-8-12 100 WilliamBuick 4 73
(M Botti) *swtchd lft after s and racd towards stands' rail: rdn and unable qck over 2f out: wknd u.p over 1f out* **13/2**[3]

4240 **8** *nk* **Arabian Pearl (IRE)**[34] 5937 4-8-13 75 (b) JackMitchell 11 72
(P W Chapple-Hyam) *t.k.h: chsd ldrs: rdn and struggling over 2f out: wknd wl over 1f out* **100/1**

1513 **9** *shd* **Arabian Mirage**[34] 5952 4-8-13 95 KierenFallon 2 72
(B J Meehan) *chsd ldrs: rdn over 2f out: stl pressing ldrs but one pce whn sltly hmpd over 1f out: wknd u.p ent fnl f* **9/1**

423 **10** *nk* **Poppet's Lovein**[29] 6113 4-8-13 82 (p) StevieDonohoe 12 71
(A B Haynes) *stdd s: hld up in tch in rr: swtchd rt and effrt over 2f out: no hdwy and btn over 1f out* **66/1**

0222 **11** *3/4* **Golden Destiny (IRE)**[27] 6194 4-8-13 105 (b) RichardHughes 14 69
(P J Makin) *in tch towards rr: rdn over 3f out: nvr gng pce to rch ldrs* **9/2**[2]

4030 **12** *2 1/2* **Sea Of Leaves (USA)**[27] 6175 4-8-13 89 JimmyFortune 6 61
(J S Goldie) *bhd: rdn and no prog 3f out: n.d* **14/1**

6502 **13** *2 3/4* **Fly Silca Fly (IRE)**[17] 6438 3-8-12 80 TedDurcan 7 52
(M R Channon) *towards rr: rdn and struggling 3f out: wl btn and edgd rt over 1f out* **100/1**

3041 **14** *6* **Sakhee's Pearl**[23] 6291 4-8-13 79 (b) MichaelHills 13 33
(Miss Gay Kelleway) *chsd ldrs tl rdn and wknd over 2f out: wl bhd fnl f* **66/1**

1m 11.34s (-0.86) **Going Correction** +0.05s/f (Good)
WFA 3 from 4yo+ 1lb **14** Ran SP% **118.8**
Speed ratings (Par 108): **107,106,105,103,99 98,96,95,95,95 94,90,87,79**
toteswingers:1&2:£8.60, 1&3:£7.80, 2&3:£23.30 CSF £29.07 TOTE £2.90: £1.30, £4.10, £4.30; EX 30.90 TRIFECTA Pool: £1,418.78 - 3.75 winning units..
Owner Pearl Bloodstock Ltd **Bred** F C T Wilson **Trained** Newmarket, Suffolk

FOCUS

An ordinary fillies' Listed contest. They raced middle-to-stands' side.

NOTEBOOK

Dever Dream raced out the back after missing the break and briefly looked in trouble when first off the bridle over 2f out, but it turned out she had a big finishing kick in reserve and picked up best of all when switched left. This was a sixth win from nine starts, and a second consecutive Listed contest, adding to the 7f event she picked up at Doncaster. The drop in trip didn't seem to suit ideally, and though her class got her through, a return to further should suit. (op 2-1)

Wake Up Call was below form in a Listed race at Ascot (got loose beforehand) last time, but she proved herself up to this class with a fine effort. She's open to further improvement, possibly back at 7f. (op 10-1)

Amitola(IRE), drawn lowest of all, was kept towards the stands' side from the off while most of the others raced up the middle and stuck on well for pressure. She had the same chance as the runner-up judged on official figures. (op 12-1)

Curtains, a handicap winner off just 80 over 7f at Brighton on her previous start, received a really positive ride and stuck on well, finishing nicely clear of the remainder. (tchd 33-1)

Beyond Desire, for the third race in succession, was below form. (op 9-1 tchd 10-1 in places)

Golden Destiny(IRE) hails from a yard not in much form and was never going, running well below the form she showed when second from the front in a 5f Group 3 at Newbury on her previous start. (op 5-1)

6888 BLUE SQUARE EXCLUSIVE LIVE SHOWS H'CAP 7f

5:15 (5:15) (Class 2) (0-105,102) 3-Y-0+

£9,969 (£2,985; £1,492; £747; £372; £187) **Stalls** Centre

Form RPR

2165 **1** **Docofthebay (IRE)**[7] 6721 6-8-12 90 (b) IanMongan 29 99
(J A Glover) *racd far side: in tch in midfield: effrt ent fnl 2f: switching lft and chsd ldrs over 1f out: r.o wl u.p to ld fnl 50yds: drvn out* **33/1**

0534 **2** *1/2* **Golden Desert (IRE)**[20] 6349 6-9-7 99 RyanMoore 6 107+
(R A Mills) *racd stands' side: hld up in tch in gp: rdn and effrt wl over 1f out: led gp but stl plenty to do overall ins fnl f: r.o strly to go 2nd nr fin: nt rch wnr: 1st of 9 in gp* **12/1**[3]

1005 **3** *nk* **Camerooney**[13] 6562 7-8-9 90 IanBrennan(3) 15 97
(B Ellison) *racd in centre: led that gp and prom overall: rdn wl over 1f out: chsd overall ldrs 1f out: kpt on gamely ins fnl f: 1st of 8 in gp* **18/1**

523 **4** *1/2* **Imperial Guest**[20] 6349 4-9-2 94 TomQueally 27 100
(G G Margarson) *racd far side: in tch: rdn and effrt ent fnl 2f: ev ch and drvn jst over 1f out: led and edgd rt ins fnl f: hdd and lost 2 pls fnl 50yds: 2nd of 13 in gp* **10/1**[2]

1000 **5** *hd* **No Hubris (USA)**[98] 3867 3-8-10 90 JamieSpencer 17 94
(P F I Cole) *racd far side: overall ldr: rdn wl over 1f out: hrd pressed ent fnl f: hdd ins fnl f: n.m.r and no ex fnl 100yds: 3rd of 13 in gp* **50/1**

0213 **6** *1* **Greensward**[35] 5903 4-8-7 85 DaraghO'Donohoe 19 88
(B J Meehan) *racd in centre: hld up towards rr of gp: hdwy 3f out: rdn 2f out: stl plenty to do over 1f out: kpt on wl ins fnl f: nt rch ldrs: 2nd of 8 in gp* **33/1**

3113 **7** *nse* **Horseradish**[20] 6363 3-8-13 93 HayleyTurner 25 94
(M L W Bell) *racd far side: stdd s: hld up in rr: hdwy 3f out: chsd ldrs and rdn over 1f out: kpt on same pce and no imp ins fnl f: 4th of 13 in gp* **16/1**

4160 **8** *nk* **Citrus Star (USA)**[20] 6349 3-9-7 101 GeorgeBaker 28 102
(C F Wall) *racd far side: chsd ldrs: rdn to press ldr wl over 1f out: ev ch and drvn ent fnl f: n.m.r and btn fnl 75yds: 5th of 13 in gp* **33/1**

6002 **9** *1/2* **Decent Fella (IRE)**[27] 6205 4-8-7 85 (v) LiamKeniry 8 85
(A M Balding) *racd stands' side: chsd gp ldr: rdn ent fnl 2f: kpt on same pce and no threat to overall ldrs fnl f: 2nd of 9 in gp* **14/1**

1152 **10** *nk* **Zero Money (IRE)**[27] 6178 4-8-12 90 SteveDrowne 7 89
(R Charlton) *racd stands' side: in tch: rdn ent fnl 2f: one pce and hld whn n.m.r jst ins fnl f: kpt on: 3rd of 9 in gp* **16/1**

0030 **11** *1/2* **Spirit Of Sharjah (IRE)**[34] 5950 5-9-1 98 AdamBeschizza(5) 14 96
(Miss J Feilden) *racd in centre: t.k.h: hld up in midfield: rdn and effrt ent fnl 2f: kpt on u.p ins fnl f: unable to rch ldrs: 3rd of 8 in gp* **33/1**

0210 **12** *1/2* **Rulesn'regulations**[20] 6349 4-9-9 101 RobertHavlin 18 98
(Matthew Salaman) *racd far side: hld up in tch: rdn and effrt jst over 2f out: styd on same pce and hld fr over 1f out: 6th of 13 in gp* **40/1**

0620 **13** *nk* **Leviathan**[21] 6327 3-8-9 89 MickyFenton 24 84+
(T P Tate) *racd far side: bhd: rdn 3f out: stl plenty to do over 1f out: styd on wl ins fnl f: gng on fin: nvr trbld ldrs: 7th of 13 in gp* **14/1**

0550 **14** *shd* **Viva Vettori**[13] 6562 6-8-6 84 DavidProbert 1 80
(D R C Elsworth) *racd stands' side: in tch: rdn and effrt ent fnl 2f: styng on same pce whn nt clr run and swtchd rt ent fnl f: no threat to ldrs after: 4th of 9 in gp* **16/1**

1061 **15** *nse* **Hajoum (IRE)**[12] 6597 4-9-9 101 6ex FrankieDettori 23 97
(M Johnston) *racd far side: chsd ldrs tl wl over 1f out: wknd u.p over 1f out: 8th of 13 in gp* **8/1**[1]

0660 **16** *1 1/4* **Gallagher**[20] 6349 4-9-2 97 RussKennemore(3) 30 89
(B J Meehan) *racd far side: chsd ldrs: rdn 2f out: wknd over 1f out: 9th of 13 in gp* **16/1**

030 **17** *1/2* **Wannabe King**[20] 6349 4-9-10 102 (p) TedDurcan 21 93
(D R Lanigan) *racd far side: hld up in tch: rdn ent fnl 2f: wknd u.p over 1f out: 10th of 13 in gp* **33/1**

4452 **18** *shd* **Mass Rally (IRE)**[21] 6321 3-9-4 98 (vt) WilliamBuick 9 88
(J H M Gosden) *racd stands' side: hld up towards rr: shkn up and effrt 2f out: rdn and no hdwy wl over 1f out: wl hld fnl f: eased towards fin: 5th of 9 in gp* **14/1**

3103 **19** *hd* **Zomerlust**[7] 6721 8-8-8 86 (v) SaleemGolam 13 76
(J J Quinn) *racd in centre: chsd gp ldr: rdn over 2f out: no prog u.p over 1f out: wknd fnl f: 4th of 8 in gp* **50/1**

0160 **20** *nk* **Sailorman (IRE)**[21] 6321 3-8-9 89 RichardHills 2 77
(M Johnston) *racd stands' side: led gp but chsng ldrs at best overall: rdn ent fnl 2f: btn jst over 1f out: wknd fnl f: 6th of 9 in gp* **40/1**

4220 **21** *nk* **Santefisio**[13] 6564 4-8-9 87 NeilCallan 10 75
(P J Makin) *racd in centre: t.k.h: hld up towards rr: rdn and no real prog ent fnl 2f: nvr trbld ldrs: 5th of 8 in gp* **14/1**

3030 **22** *nse* **Webbow (IRE)**[19] 6391 8-8-12 90 (p) JimmyFortune 3 78
(N Tinkler) *racd stands' side: in tch in gp: rdn and no prog ent fnl 2f: kpt on same pce after and nvr trbld ldrs: 7th of 9 in gp* **20/1**

0000 **23** *1/2* **Flipando (IRE)**[27] 6177 9-9-3 95 DaneO'Neill 22 82
(T D Barron) *racd far side: stdd s: hld up in rr: rdn and effrt 2f out: nvr trbld ldrs: 11th of 13 in gp* **66/1**

6-50 **24** *3/4* **Without Prejudice (USA)**[7] 6721 5-8-9 87 (v) DarrylHolland 20 72
(J Noseda) *racd far side: a in rr and sn rdn along: n.d: 12th of 13 in gp* **50/1**

1000 **25** *1/2* **Damika (IRE)**[20] 6363 7-9-2 97 MichaelStainton(3) 12 81
(R M Whitaker) *racd in centre: chsd ldrs: rdn over 2f out: wknd u.p wl over 1f out: wl btn fnl f: 6th of 8 in gp* **33/1**

5540 **26** *3/4* **Big Noise**[83] 4358 6-8-8 89 Louis-PhilippeBeuzelin(3) 11 71
(Dr J D Scargill) *racd in centre: a in rr: pushed along 1/2-way: rdn and wknd ent fnl 2f: wl btn and hung lft over 1f out: 7th of 8 in gp* **33/1**

0000 **27** *1/2* **Marajaa (IRE)**[20] 6349 8-8-12 90 JamieMackay 4 70
(W J Musson) *racd stands' side: stdd s: hld up in rr: n.d: 8th of 9 in gp* **33/1**

320 **28** *3/4* **Bramshaw (USA)**[21] 6321 3-8-5 85 JimmyQuinn 16 62
(Mrs A J Perrett) *racd in centre: t.k.h: hld up in midfield: rdn and no prog ent fnl 2f: wl btn over 1f out: 8th of 8 in gp* **16/1**

321 **29** *18* **Kajima**[63] 5030 3-9-0 94 RichardHughes 5 23
(R Hannon) *racd stands' side: a in rr: btn ent fnl 2f: virtually p.u fnl f: t.o: 9th of 9 in gp* **66/1**

2520 **30** *25* **Swop (IRE)**[34] 5948 7-9-8 100 KierenFallon 26 —
(L M Cumani) *racd far side: in tch in midfield: wknd qckly ent fnl 2f: heavily eased and virtually p.u fr wl over 1f out: t.o: 13th of 13 in gp* **14/1**

1m 24.14s (-1.26) **Going Correction** +0.05s/f (Good)
WFA 3 from 4yo+ 2lb **30** Ran SP% **140.9**
Speed ratings (Par 109): **109,108,108,107,107 106,106,105,105,104 104,103,103,103,103 101,101,101,100,100 100,100,99,98,**
toteswingers:1&2:£157.20, 1&3:Not won, 2&3:£104.80 CSF £379.99 CT £7290.54 TOTE £54.80: £8.00, £4.10, £8.10, £4.40; EX 1562.00 TRIFECTA Not won..
Owner Paul J Dixon **Bred** G And Mrs Middlebrook **Trained** Babworth, Notts
■ Stewards' Enquiry : Tom Queally two-day ban: careless riding (Oct 29-30)

FOCUS

As competitive and difficult to solve a handicap as you could wish for, hence they went 8-1 the field. They split into three groups early with the largest group of 13 racing far side, nine racing against the nearside rail whilst eight came up the centre. The fact that the first three horses home raced in each of the three groups suggests there was no great bias. Probably not form to be too positive about.

NOTEBOOK

Docofthebay(IRE) was still 6lb higher than when winning at Ayr three starts ago, but his second place off 8lb higher in the 2007 Cambridgeshire showed that he has what it takes to run well in a huge field when in the mood. With the blinkers back on, he was ridden with plenty of confidence in the far-side group before being produced to hit the front around 50 yards from home. However, judging by his profile in recent years, whether he will reproduce this next time is anyone's guess.

Golden Desert(IRE) had run really well off this mark (1lb lower than for his last win) in his previous two starts, including when fourth behind Redford in a red-hot handicap at Ascot last time, and he ran another cracker here. Held up in the nearside group, he took off entering the final furlong and finished strongly despite hanging right up the final climb. He deserves to get his head back in front. (tchd 11-1)

Camerooney, six times a winner this year and a fine fifth off this mark in the Cambridgeshire last time, led the centre group the whole way and kept on right to the line. He remains at the top of his game. (op 16-1)

Imperial Guest, whose four career wins have come over 6f, was put up 2lb after finishing a fine third behind Redford in the Totesport.com Challenge Cup at Ascot last month. Always close up in the far-side group, he looked to have timed it right when leading inside the final furlong, but he didn't quite get up the hill and was run out of the first three. It appears that this trip is right on the limit of his stamina, especially on a stiff track like this. (op 14-1)

No Hubris(USA), having just his seventh start, hadn't been seen since running poorly on the July Course three months earlier, but he made most of the running towards the far side until blowing up entering the last furlong. (op 40-1)

Greensward, still 6lb higher than when winning on Polytrack two starts ago, was held up in the centre group but ran on late and was never closer than at the line.

Horseradish, yet to finish worse than third in eight previous starts, was successful in his only previous try over this far and ran on over the last 2f here. He remains unexposed over the trip.

Citrus Star(USA), beaten a long way at Ascot last time, ran well until the furlong pole and probably needs an easier 7f than this.

Decent Fella(IRE) ran an improved race in the first-time visor over 1m here last month and stayed on up the stands' rail. He is still lightly raced, but may need a return to further. (tchd 16-1)

Zero Money(IRE), raised 4lb for his narrow defeat by Docofthebay at Ayr last month, was another running on against the stands' rail towards the end.

Viva Vettori Official explanation: jockey said horse was denied a clear run

Hajoum(IRE), carrying a 6lb penalty for his Dundalk success earlier this month, appeared to have every chance in the far-side group but found little after coming under pressure entering the Dip. (op 11-1)

Big Noise Official explanation: jockey said horse never travelled

Kajima Official explanation: jockey said gelding lost its action

Swop(IRE) Official explanation: jockey said gelding lost its action

6889 BLUE SQUARE BET H'CAP — 1m 4f

5:50 (5:53) (Class 2) (0-105,105) 3-Y-O+

£9,969 (£2,985; £1,492; £747; £372; £187) **Stalls** Centre

Form				RPR
6-11	**1**		**Willing Foe (USA)**[35] 5913 3-8-8 **92** ... FrankieDettori 7 (Saeed Bin Suroor) *hld up towards rr: stdy prog fr 5f out: shkn up over 1f out: led ins fnl f: styd on wl* **11/10**[1]	105+
1442	**2**	1 ½	**Times Up**[34] 5949 4-9-5 **96** ... RyanMoore 10 (J L Dunlop) *hld up towards rr: hdwy 3f out: sn rdn: styd on fnl f: wnt 2nd nr fin* **11/1**	104
20-1	**3**	½	**Ottoman Empire (FR)**[42] 5723 4-9-7 **98** ... TedDurcan 9 (D R Lanigan) *trckd ldrs: rdn over 2f out: led ent fnl f: sn hdd: no ex: lost 2nd nr fin* **6/1**[2]	105
2605	**4**	½	**Right Step**[21] 6318 3-7-12 **89** ... HarryBentley(7) 8 (A P Jarvis) *mid-div: hdwy over 2f out: sn rdn: swtchd rt 1f out: styd on* **33/1**	95
2361	**5**	1	**Life And Soul (IRE)**[19] 6387 3-8-9 **93** ... NeilCallan 6 (Mrs A J Perrett) *mid-div: rdn 3f out: styd on but nvr gng pce to get on terms w ldrs* **6/1**[2]	98
2143	**6**	2	**Classic Punch (IRE)**[41] 5749 7-10-0 **105** ... JamieSpencer 5 (D R C Elsworth) *led: clr w one other after 2f: rdn over 2f out: kpt on gamely tl hdd ent fnl f: no ex* **20/1**	107
6200	**7**	hd	**Classic Vintage (USA)**[80] 4461 4-9-3 **94** ... KierenFallon 3 (Mrs A J Perrett) *trckd ldrs: rdn wl over 2f out: fdd ins fnl f* **14/1**	95
3004	**8**	22	**Rashaad (USA)**[36] 5879 3-8-12 **96** ... RichardHills 4 (B W Hills) *a towards rr: lost tch fr 2f out* **8/1**[3]	62
0000	**9**	3 ¼	**Chiberta King**[19] 6387 4-9-4 **95** ... JimmyFortune 1 (A M Balding) *mid-div: rdn 3f out: wknd 2f out* **16/1**	56
5206	**10**	1 ¾	**Private Story (USA)**[10] 6654 3-8-13 **97** ... RichardHughes 2 (R Hannon) *a towards rr: lost tch fr 2f out* **50/1**	55
0620	**11**	1 ¾	**Seeking The Buck (USA)**[69] 4818 6-8-10 **87** ...(p) DaneO'Neill 11 (W J Greatrex) *chsd ldr clr of remainder after 2f: racd towards centre alone: rdn over 3f out: sn btn* **66/1**	42

2m 30.63s (-1.37) **Going Correction** +0.05s/f (Good)

WFA 3 from 4yo+ 7lb — **11** Ran SP% **119.3**

Speed ratings (Par 109): **106,105,104,104,103 102,102,87,85,84 83**

toteswingers:1&2:£2.80, 2&3:£7.10, 1&3:£4.00. totesuper7: Win: Not won. Place: £47.40. CSF £7.71 CT £51.02 TOTE £1.90: £1.10, £1.80, £3.70; EX 5.70 Trifecta £27.30 Pool: £852.17 - 23.04 winning units. Place 6 £8.41; Place 5 £5.98.

Owner Godolphin **Bred** Stonerside Stable **Trained** Newmarket, Suffolk

FOCUS

A decent handicap run at a reasonable pace. The winner did not need to improve on the bare form and is possibly better than a handicapper. The runner-up is a sound guide.

NOTEBOOK

Willing Foe(USA), twice a tidy winner against decent 3-y-o opposition over 1m2f at Doncaster this year, looked to have been let in lightly off a mark of 92 for his handicap debut, but was tackling older opposition for the first time and they were a good, solid bunch. He needed this long trip, as his breeding suggested (brother to a Ribblesdale winner), and after taking a few strides to get going when first under pressure and still looking green on this first taste of an undulating track, he was nicely on top at the finish. The November Handicap is the obvious target should he race in Britain again this year, though he's so far been given at least 35 days between his races, and his main objective will no doubt be the Dubai Carnival. (op 6-5 tchd 5-4)

Times Up had recorded an improved RPR on his last four starts and this will probably be another. He shapes as though he'll be worth another try over further at some stage. (op 11-2 tchd 5-1)

Ottoman Empire(FR), a big horse, didn't handle the Dip on his last run at this track in 2009 and, though he was better this time around, he still didn't look comfortable on the undulations. His three wins to date have been gained on the AW, not a total surprise seeing as he doesn't want extremes of going on turf, but he might be able to win a race on this surface on a flat, galloping track. (op 9-1 tchd 8-1)

Right Step lacks consistency, but this was a solid effort and he'll be worth another try at this trip.

Life And Soul(IRE) was found out by the combination of a 3lb higher mark and better company than when winning at Ascot last time. (op 9-1)

Classic Punch(IRE) had a tough task conceding upwards of 7lb all around, and faded after setting a good pace. (op 18-1)

T/Jkpt: Not won. T/Plt: £5.50 to a £1 stake. Pool of £88,334.17 - 11,554.36 winning tickets T/Qpdt: £3.50 to a £1 stake. Pool of £5,286.33 - 1,105.28 winning tickets SP

6566 REDCAR (L-H)

Friday, October 15

OFFICIAL GOING: Good (7.6)

Wind: fresh 1/2 against Weather: overcast, very cool and breezy, drizzle

6890 FOLLOW REDCAR RACING ON FACEBOOK LADIES' H'CAP (FOR LADY AMATEUR RIDERS) — 1m 2f

1:30 (1:31) (Class 6) (0-60,60) 3-Y-O+ **£1,648** (£507; £253) **Stalls** Low

Form				RPR
1651	**1**		**Dean Iarracht (IRE)**[24] 6269 4-10-2 **60** ...(p) MissAngelaBarnes(5) 5 (Miss Tracy Waggott) *t.k.h: midfield: hdwy 4f out: swtchd outside and effrt 2f out: str run ent fnl f: styd on wl to ld nr line* **13/2**[3]	69
4024	**2**	hd	**Chantilly Pearl (USA)**[23] 6298 4-10-4 **57** ... MrsCBartley 11 (J G Given) *trckd ldrs: smooth hdwy 4f out: swtchd rt and cl up 3f out: led over 2f out: pushed clr over 1f out: rdn ins fnl f: hdd and no ex nr line* **6/1**[2]	66
4404	**3**	2 ½	**Lakeman (IRE)**[16] 6462 4-10-3 **56** ...(b) MissSBrotherton 4 (B Ellison) *trckd ldrs on inner: effrt and n.m.r 2f out: nt clr run and swtchd rt to outer over 1f out: rdn and styd on ins fnl f* **7/1**	60+
00-2	**4**	¾	**Prince Rhyddarch**[25] 6242 5-10-2 **55** ... MissADeniel 3 (M Dods) *plld hrd: hld up towards rr: hdwy 3f out: rdn to chse ldrs whn n.m.r wl over 1f out: kpt on ins fnl f* **7/1**	58
0336	**5**	1 ¾	**Ingleby King (USA)**[29] 6125 4-9-7 **53** ...(b) MissSRussell(7) 1 (T D Barron) *wnt bdly lft and almost uns rdr s: bhd untl hdwy wl over 2f out: rdn and kpt on fnl f: nrst fin* **12/1**	52
30-0	**6**	hd	**Active Asset (IRE)**[184] 1296 8-9-11 **55** ... MissJoannaMason(5) 7 (D C Griffiths) *in tch: hdwy to chse ldrs over 3f out: rdn 2f out: sn edgd lft and one pce* **20/1**	54
5030	**7**	½	**Maybeme**[10] 6649 4-9-9 **53** ... MissHCuthbert(5) 6 (N Bycroft) *s.i.s and bhd: hdwy wl over 2f out: sn rdn and kpt on fnl f: nrst fin* **16/1**	51
-060	**8**	nk	**Monfils Monfils (USA)**[15] 6518 8-9-8 **54** ... MissSMStaveley(7) 10 (P A Kirby) *prom: cl up 1/2-way: rdn along wl over 3f out: drvn 2f out and kpt on same pce* **33/1**	51
32-0	**9**	4	**Flora's Pride**[193] 1113 6-9-9 **53** ... MissPhillipaTutty(5) 13 (K G Reveley) *hld up: a towards rr* **16/1**	42
0020	**10**	nk	**Orpen Wide (IRE)**[16] 6472 8-9-13 **59** ...(bt) MissJessicaLodge(7) 15 (M C Chapman) *led: rdn along 4f out: hdd wl over 2f out and grad wknd* **50/1**	47
6535	**11**	¾	**Silly Gilly (IRE)**[24] 6269 6-9-12 **54** ... MissMMullineaux(3) 2 (R E Barr) *chsd ldng pair: hdwy and cl up over 3f out: rdn to ld briefly wl over 2f out: sn hdd & wknd* **12/1**	41
5305	**12**	1 ¼	**Petrocelli**[12] 6463 3-9-9 **58** ... MissLAlexander(5) 9 (W Storey) *in tch on inner: pushed along 1/2-way: rdn 4f out and sn wknd* **50/1**	42
6120	**13**	1 ¼	**Tropical Duke (IRE)**[10] 6650 4-10-2 **60** ... MissVBarr(5) 12 (R E Barr) *dwlt: hld up: a in rr* **11/2**[1]	42
0400	**14**	1 ½	**Hurricane Thomas (IRE)**[15] 6518 6-9-11 **57** ... MissGTutty(7) 14 (R A Fahey) *chsd ldrs: rdn along over 3f out: sn wknd* **20/1**	36
3500	**15**	2 ¾	**Refuse To Wait (IRE)**[46] 5598 3-9-8 **57** ... MissRKneller(5) 8 (T D Easterby) *a towards rr: bhd fr over 2f out* **16/1**	30

2m 10.68s (3.58) **Going Correction** +0.15s/f (Good)

WFA 3 from 4yo+ 5lb — **15** Ran SP% **117.4**

Speed ratings (Par 101): **91,90,88,88,86 86,86,86,82,82 82,81,80,78,76**

toteswingers:1&2:£4.40, 1&3:£12.40, 2&3:£10.60 CSF £41.00 CT £282.33 TOTE £9.50: £2.30, £2.10, £2.40; EX 48.60.

Owner Michael Howarth **Bred** Ken Carroll **Trained** Spennymoor, Co Durham

■ Stewards' Enquiry : Miss Joanna Mason one-day ban: careless riding (tbn)

Miss S Brotherton caution: careless riding.

FOCUS

A damp day and the ground had eased to good all over prior to this weak opening handicap for lady amateur riders. It was run at a sound pace and the form makes sense, with a small personal best from the winner.

Ingleby King(USA) Official explanation: jockey said gelding suffered interference in running

6891 MARKET CROSS JEWELLERS CLAIMING STKS — 7f

2:00 (2:02) (Class 6) 2-Y-O **£1,706** (£503; £252) **Stalls** Centre

Form				RPR
1440	**1**		**Lady Del Sol**[59] 5187 2-8-0 76 ... PaulHanagan 13 (G R Oldroyd) *trckd ldrs: led over 3f out: clr over 1f out: edgd lft: pushed out* **5/4**[1]	56+
000	**2**	2 ¾	**Hartforth**[30] 6070 2-8-13 49 ...(b[1]) GrahamGibbons 6 (J D Bethell) *mid-div: effrt 3f out: styd on to take 2nd 1f out: no imp* **80/1**	62
	3	¾	**Delaney's Dream** 2-8-13 0 ... AdrianNicholls 1 (D Nicholls) *dwlt: hdwy over 2f out: edgd rt over 1f out: styd on wl to take 3rd nr fin* **12/1**[3]	60
3006	**4**	1 ½	**None Sweeter**[9] 6673 2-7-13 56 ow1 ... DuranFentiman 8 (T D Easterby) *led tl over 3f out: kpt on same pce fnl 2f* **33/1**	42
2	**5**	½	**Yorketa**[16] 6459 2-8-5 0 ... PatrickDonaghy(3) 2 (M Dods) *mid-div: hdwy over 2f out: edgd rt and one pce over 1f out* **16/1**	50
4306	**6**	6	**Bachelor Knight (IRE)**[35] 5921 2-8-0 67 ... AmyRyan(3) 12 (R A Fahey) *mid-div: effrt over 2f out: nvr nr ldrs* **12/1**[3]	29
3555	**7**	½	**Crown Ridge (IRE)**[9] 6674 2-8-9 54 ... TomEaves 14 (M R Channon) *mid-div: effrt 3f out: wkng whn hmpd over 1f out* **20/1**	34
0004	**8**	nk	**Miss Cosette (IRE)**[50] 5434 2-7-13 47 ... KellyHarrison(3) 7 (T D Barron) *in rr: sme hdwy and hmpd over 2f out: nvr nr ldrs* **22/1**	26
000	**9**	6	**Maunby Rumba (IRE)**[13] 6566 2-8-0 35 ow2 ...(v[1]) AndrewMullen 3 (B M R Haslam) *s.i.s: sme hdwy over 2f out: nvr on terms* **100/1**	—
0400	**10**	2 ¼	**Face The Future**[7] 6717 2-8-13 63 ...(bt[1]) PhillipMakin 20 (M Dods) *chsd ldrs: rdn and hung rt over 2f out: edgd rt and wknd over 1f out* **25/1**	16
06	**11**	¾	**Dark Times (IRE)**[50] 5434 2-7-7 48 ...(v[1]) NeilFarley(5) 9 (Mrs K Burke) *chsd ldrs: wknd over 1f out* **33/1**	—
00	**12**	nk	**Always De Man (IRE)**[7] 6712 2-8-5 0 ... JoeFanning 10 (M Johnston) *in rr: drvn and hmpd over 2f out: nvr a factor* **22/1**	—
0406	**13**	1	**Bright Dictator (IRE)**[23] 6300 2-7-12 46 ... PaulQuinn 5 (J G Given) *chsd ldrs: wknd 2f out* **33/1**	—
6000	**14**	3 ½	**Auburn Lady**[23] 6294 2-8-0 52 ...(b[1]) SilvestreDeSousa 18 (A D Brown) *mid-div: lost pl 3f out* **66/1**	—
4502	**15**	4 ½	**Bernisdale**[13] 6569 2-8-12 67 ... PJMcDonald 17 (G M Moore) *in rr: drvn 3f out: nvr on terms* **10/1**[2]	—
1230	**16**	1 ¼	**Chilworth Lass (IRE)**[30] 6082 2-8-0 54 ow3...(v) AndrewHeffernan(3) 19 (M R Channon) *hld up in mid-div: effrt over 2f out: sn wknd* **10/1**[2]	—
060	**17**	1 ¼	**Classic Gem (IRE)**[29] 6118 2-8-5 52 ow1 ...(v[1]) RichardKingscote 4 (Tom Dascombe) *chsd ldrs: wknd over 2f out* **66/1**	—
00	**17**	dht	**Zoom In**[13] 6566 2-8-4 0 ... JamesSullivan(3) 15 (Mrs L Stubbs) *a towards rr* **50/1**	—
1450	**19**	10	**Two Feet Of Snow (IRE)**[7] 6719 2-8-1 68 ow1 ... PatrickMathers 11 (I W McInnes) *s.i.s: in rr: bhd fnl 3f: eased* **16/1**	—
4000	**20**	8	**Logans Rose**[32] 6036 2-8-4 40 ow1 ...(b[1]) AndrewElliott 16 (A D Brown) *in rr: bhd fnl 3f: eased* **100/1**	—

1m 26.98s (2.48) **Going Correction** +0.15s/f (Good) — **20** Ran SP% **124.1**

Speed ratings (Par 93): **91,87,87,85,84 77,77,76,70,67 66,66,65,61,56 54,53,53,41,32**

toteswingers:1&2:£29.30, 1&3:£4.70, 2&3:£102.50 CSF £171.31 TOTE £2.00: £1.10, £12.80, £5.30; EX 150.30.Lady Del Sol was claimed by Mrs Marjorie Fife for £6,000.

Owner R C Bond **Bred** Bond Thoroughbred Corporation **Trained** Brawby, N Yorks

FOCUS

Despite the large numbers this juvenile claimer was all about the 76-rated Lady Del Sol.

NOTEBOOK

Lady Del Sol duly obliged as she was entitled to at the weights. She won her maiden here in June and has generally run close to her current mark in defeat since, though she wasn't sighted after a slow start in a good nursery at York on her previous outing. Returning from a 59-day break, she was drawn in the right place and got a no-nonsense ride from Paul Hanagan. The extra furlong posed her no problems and she is better than this class, but her head carriage wasn't overly convincing under pressure, and one wonders if she has already reached her peak. She was later claimed to join Marjorie Fife. (op 2-1)

Hartforth holds the form down with an official mark of 49, but this was a drop in class and first-time blinkers clearly improved him.

Delaney's Dream ◆ was making his debut in lowly company, and if there is a horse to take out of the race it is this already gelded son of Distant Music. He was the only one to really get involved from off the pace and stayed on with purpose, so should really be capable of winning one of these granted the normal improvement for the experience. (op 8-1 tchd 14-1)

None Sweeter, whose previous best effort was when third in a 6f maiden here, ran well under a positive ride and returned to something like her best. Similar tactics back over 6f in this class could see her finish closer.

Yorketa didn't achieve too much when second on debut at Newcastle 16 days earlier and this confirms her sort of level. She remains open to a little improvement. (op 20-1)

Bernisdale Official explanation: jockey said filly never travelled

6892 EUROPEAN BREEDERS' FUND MAIDEN FILLIES' STKS (DIV I) 6f
2:35 (2:37) (Class 5) 2-Y-O £3,238 (£963; £481; £240) **Stalls** Centre

Form RPR

2 **1** **Blanche Dubawi (IRE)**[42] 5719 2-9-0 0 PaulHanagan 4 80
(M G Quinlan) *prom: cl up 1/2-way: led 2f out: rdn clr and hung lft ent fnl f: kpt on* **6/4**[1]

5 **2** *3 ½* **Map Of Heaven**[17] 6441 2-9-0 0 LiamJones 5 70
(W J Haggas) *trckd ldrs: swtchd rt and hdwy 2f out: sn chsng wnr: rdn ent fnl f and sn no imp* **7/4**[2]

53 **3** *3 ½* **Sovereign Street**[22] 6301 2-9-0 0 SebSanders 9 59
(Mrs A Duffield) *stdd s and hld up in rr: hdwy over 2f out: rdn to chse ldrs wl over 1f out: sn one pce* **8/1**[3]

053 **4** *1* **I Got You Babe (IRE)**[15] 6488 2-8-11 60 AndrewHeffernan(3) 6 56
(R C Guest) *cl up on outer: effrt and ch over 2f out: sn rdn and kpt on same pce* **25/1**

3230 **5** *6* **Hortensis**[7] 6719 2-9-0 65 DavidAllan 2 38
(T D Easterby) *led to 1/2-way: rdn along over 2f out and sn wknd* **12/1**

6 *1 ¾* **Majestic Millie (IRE)** 2-9-0 0 SilvestreDeSousa 3 33
(D O'Meara) *in tch: rdn along 1/2-way: sn outpcd* **20/1**

00 **7** *nk* **Bigalo's Vera B**[62] 5099 2-8-9 0 (e[1]) DeclanCannon(5) 8 32
(L A Mullaney) *in rr: outpcd and bhd fr 1/2-way* **100/1**

8 *5* **Pyrenean** 2-9-0 0 PaulMulrennan 11 17
(J G Given) *a towards rr: outpcd and bhd fr 1/2-way* **50/1**

9 *1* **Spontaneity (IRE)** 2-9-0 0 TomEaves 1 14
(B Smart) *dwlt: sn chsng ldrs: led 1/2-way: rdn along over 2f out: sn hdd & wknd qckly appr fnl f* **12/1**

10 *4 ½* **Willbeme** 2-8-11 0 MarkLawson(3) 7 —
(N Bycroft) *s.i.s: a bhd* **100/1**

11 *1 ¾* **Loughtownlady (IRE)** 2-8-11 0 MichaelO'Connell(3) 10 —
(G A Harker) *chsd ldrs on outer: rdn along 1/2-way: sn wknd* **66/1**

1m 12.47s (0.67) **Going Correction** +0.15s/f (Good) **11** Ran SP% **116.9**
Speed ratings (Par 92): **101,96,91,90,82 80,79,72,71,65 63**
toteswingers:1&2:£1.50, 1&3:£4.10, 2&3:£3.80 CSF £4.00 TOTE £2.60: £1.30, £1.10, £3.20; EX 4.20.
Owner Burns Farm Racing **Bred** Burns Farm Stud **Trained** Newmarket, Suffolk

FOCUS
The betting suggested this fillies' juvenile maiden was a match between the two clear market leaders and they duly filled the first two places. It was run at solid pace and the form is straightforward.

NOTEBOOK
Blanche Dubawi(IRE) created a decent impression when second on debut at Kempton in a better maiden than this race six weeks earlier, and she got off the mark with a decisive display. She was never far away and it was clear nearing the final furlong she was the one to be on. She hung left when put under maximum pressure, but that was likely down to greenness and she looks a useful performer in the making. It will be interesting to see how the handicapper rates this and connections now plan to put her away for next season. (op 7-4 tchd 2-1)
Map Of Heaven, green on debut at Newbury, attracted strong support to open her account yet still showed her inexperience and was never a serious threat to the winner. She was doing her best work towards the finish and ought to come on again, but already looks more of a nursery type. (op 9-4 tchd 13-8)
Sovereign Street was ridden with a bit more patience again and probably ran close to her previous level, so rates the benchmark. She now qualifies for nurseries. (op 15-2 tchd 9-1)
I Got You Babe(IRE) travelled nicely on the front end and, while she lacked a change of gear, kept on under pressure towards the finish. She will appreciate switching into a moderate nursery. (op 16-1)
Hortensis returned to something like her previous level, but remains winless after eight outings and looks fully exposed.
Spontaneity(IRE) comes from a decent sprinting family known for winning first time out, has . She proved easy to back for this belated debut, however, and is clearly more a late-maturing sort. There could be a deal of improvement in her down the line. (op 10-1)

6893 EUROPEAN BREEDERS' FUND MAIDEN FILLIES' STKS (DIV II) 6f
3:10 (3:10) (Class 5) 2-Y-O £3,238 (£963; £481; £120; £120) **Stalls** Centre

Form RPR

1 **Watneya** 2-9-0 0 LiamJones 6 67
(W J Haggas) *s.i.s: hdwy over 2f out: swtchd rt over 1f out: r.o wl to ld wl ins fnl f* **7/2**[2]

06 **2** *1 ½* **Cootehill Lass (IRE)**[16] 6459 2-8-11 0 MichaelO'Connell(3) 8 62
(G A Harker) *swtchd lft s: mid-div: hdwy 2f out: led jst ins fnl f: hdd and no ex last 50yds* **66/1**

05 **3** *3* **Pizzarra**[16] 6459 2-9-0 0 PaulMulrennan 1 53
(J G Given) *led after 1f: edgd lft and hdd jst ins fnl f: kpt on same pce* **5/1**[3]

04 **4** *2* **Rhal (IRE)**[16] 6459 2-9-0 0 TomEaves 3 47
(B Smart) *chsd ldrs: hung lft and wknd fnl f* **7/1**

52 **4** *nse* **Shesastar**[24] 6263 2-9-0 0 GrahamGibbons 10 47
(T D Barron) *chsd ldrs: hung lft and wknd appr fnl f* **5/2**[1]

6 **6** *nk* **Tahitian Princess (IRE)**[13] 6566 2-9-0 0 RoystonFfrench 9 46
(Mrs A Duffield) *s.i.s: kpt on appr fnl f: nvr nr ldrs* **10/1**

6000 **7** *1 ¾* **Playful Girl (IRE)**[23] 6300 2-9-0 49 DavidAllan 7 41
(T D Easterby) *in rr-div: hdwy over 2f out: sn wknd* **40/1**

050 **8** *3 ¾* **Bon Appetit**[13] 6566 2-8-11 57 BarryMcHugh(3) 5 29
(N Tinkler) *t.k.h: led 1f: trckd ldrs: lost pl wl over 1f out* **10/1**

0 **9** *7* **Skiddaw View**[10] 6646 2-9-0 0 SilvestreDeSousa 4 8
(A D Brown) *mid-div: hung lft and lost pl 2f out* **40/1**

0320 **10** *14* **Infectious (IRE)**[46] 5602 2-9-0 62 PaulHanagan 2 —
(D H Brown) *s.i.s: sn chsng ldrs: lost pl over 2f out: sn bhd: eased* **8/1**

1m 13.96s (2.16) **Going Correction** +0.15s/f (Good) **10** Ran SP% **115.6**
Speed ratings (Par 92): **91,89,85,82,82 81,79,74,65,46**
toteswingers:1&2:£36.70, 1&3:£8.80, 2&3:£41.70 CSF £212.35 TOTE £5.00: £2.40, £24.30, £1.20; EX 326.30.
Owner Sheikh Ahmed Al Maktoum **Bred** J Breslin **Trained** Newmarket, Suffolk

FOCUS
The second division of the fillies' maiden and it was by some way weaker than the first.

NOTEBOOK
Watneya, the sole debutante, made a tardy start and got a touch outpaced off the brisk early pace, but the further she went the better she was. She was always going to get there at the business end, ought to have little trouble with another furlong and rates a fair prospect as she has scope. (op 9-2 tchd 10-3)
Cootehill Lass(IRE) came through to have every chance and posted a clear personal-best effort, finishing nicely clear in second. This return to a sounder surface helped and she now has the option of nurseries.
Pizzarra made her way to the front after a furlong or so and enjoyed this return to better ground. This half-sister to her stable's former star juvenile Wunders Dream looks well worth a try over the minimum trip, and is another that can now enter nurseries. (tchd 9-2)
Rhal(IRE) was always to the fore, but hung markedly left under maximum pressure and failed to reverse last-time-out form with the third on this better ground. She is yet another that is now qualified for a mark. (op 8-1)
Shesastar was the one to beat on the level her two previous runs. She failed to see it out like the principals after coming there with her chance, but getting so warm beforehand cannot have helped and she ought to find her feet in nurseries. (op 8-1)
Tahitian Princess(IRE) still looked distinctly green and got outpaced early out the back. She kept on late in the day and should go forward again for the run. (tchd 14-1)

6894 HOLD YOUR CHRISTMAS PARTY HERE MEDIAN AUCTION MAIDEN STKS 1m
3:45 (3:46) (Class 6) 2-Y-O £1,706 (£503; £252) **Stalls** Centre

Form RPR

2 **1** **Glencadam Gold (IRE)**[9] 6676 2-9-3 0 PaulHanagan 14 77
(H R A Cecil) *cl up: led wl over 2f out and sn rdn: drvn ent fnl f: sn hung lft: kpt on wl towards fin* **10/11**[1]

4 **2** *2 ¾* **Captain Brown**[17] 6436 2-9-3 0 SebSanders 5 71
(Sir Mark Prescott) *sltly hmpd s and towards rr: hdwy to trck ldrs 1/2-way: effrt over 2f out: rdn to chse wnr over 1f out: edgd lft and one pce ins fnl f* **7/2**[3]

00 **3** *10* **Inca Chief**[20] 6365 2-9-3 0 SilvestreDeSousa 8 48
(Mrs A Duffield) *prom: hdwy and cl up 1/2-way: rdn to chal wl over 2f out and ev ch tl drvn and outpcd over 1f out* **33/1**

4 *½* **Getabuzz** 2-9-3 0 GrahamGibbons 15 47
(T D Easterby) *dwlt and towards rr: stdy hdwy over 3f out: swtchd rt and rdn wl over 1f out: styd on strly ins fnl f: nrst fin* **50/1**

0 **5** *nk* **Kieron's Dream (IRE)**[24] 6268 2-9-3 0 AndrewElliott 7 46
(Jedd O'Keeffe) *prom: rdn along and outpcd 2f out: kpt on u.p fnl f* **80/1**

0 **6** *1* **Coin Box**[38] 5841 2-8-12 0 RoystonFfrench 10 39
(Mahmood Al Zarooni) *led: pushed along over 3f out: sn hdd & wknd over 2f out* **5/2**[2]

0060 **7** *9* **Phair Winter**[10] 6658 2-8-12 45 DuranFentiman 12 18
(A D Brown) *outpcd and in rr tl styd on fnl 2f: nvr a factor* **100/1**

04 **8** *2* **Wolds Agent**[31] 6046 2-9-3 0 DavidAllan 2 18
(T D Easterby) *nvr bttr than midfield* **16/1**

0000 **9** *¾* **Good Faith**[16] 6457 2-9-3 37 PJMcDonald 3 17
(G M Moore) *in tch: rdn along over 3f out: sn wknd* **100/1**

0 **10** *1 ¾* **Hot Toddie**[13] 6566 2-8-12 0 PaulMulrennan 17 7
(J G Given) *chsd ldrs on wd outside: rdn along over 3f out: sn wknd* **33/1**

06 **11** *1 ¼* **Miss T**[15] 6511 2-8-12 0 LeeVickers 9 5
(J G Given) *a in midfield* **66/1**

00 **12** *9* **Our Mate Joe (IRE)**[24] 6268 2-9-0 0 MichaelO'Connell(3) 13 —
(G A Harker) *a in rr: bhd fnl 3f* **80/1**

00 **13** *1 ¼* **Primo Muscovado**[8] 6697 2-9-3 0 LiamJones 11 —
(M Mullineaux) *bhd fr 1/2-way* **100/1**

0 **14** *¾* **Geminus (IRE)**[26] 6222 2-9-3 0 TomEaves 6 —
(Jedd O'Keeffe) *chsd ldrs: rdn along 1/2-way: sn wknd* **80/1**

15 *2 ¼* **Staerough View** 2-9-0 0 PaulPickard(3) 16 —
(K G Reveley) *sn outpcd and a bhd* **100/1**

4 **16** *17* **Blue Ronnie (IRE)**[16] 6457 2-9-0 0 PatrickDonaghy(3) 1 —
(B M R Haslam) *wnt lft s: sn chsng ldrs on wd outside: rdn along 1/2-way: sn wknd* **50/1**

1m 41.83s (3.83) **Going Correction** +0.15s/f (Good) **16** Ran SP% **128.0**
Speed ratings (Par 93): **86,83,73,72,72 71,62,60,59,57 56,47,46,45,43 26**
toteswingers:1&2:£1.60, 1&3:£15.80, 2&3:£22.30 CSF £4.60 TOTE £2.00: £1.10, £1.30, £7.20; EX 6.20.
Owner Angus Dundee Distillers plc **Bred** Roalso Ltd **Trained** Newmarket, Suffolk

FOCUS
An uncompetitive maiden despite the big field with only three considered in the market.

NOTEBOOK
Glencadam Gold(IRE) made a promising debut behind a stable companion on soft ground and built on that here. Always in the front rank, he went on over 2f out and kept galloping all the way to the line. He looks the sort to improve next season and, with stayers in his pedigree, will appreciate middle-distances at least in time. (tchd Evens)
Captain Brown, who ran green on his debut behind a subsequent winner at Brighton, was settled early before moving into contention as the winner went on. He had every chance but showed a marked tendency to hang left, and swished his tail under pressure. He looks less than straightforward at present, although it might be greenness, but is in the right hands for any quirks to be sorted out. (op 9-2)
Inca Chief, having his third start, improved considerably on previous efforts, racing prominently until tiring from over a furlong out. He now qualifies for a handicap mark and should not be too badly treated in that sphere. (op 40-1)
Getabuzz, a gelded debutant, is a brother to a juvenile 7f scorer out of a multiple winner. He ran with promise under a considerate ride and can be expected to do a fair bit better in time.
Coin Box, who was unsuited by the track and ground on her debut, made the running this time but was quickly done with when headed by the winner and has a fair bit to prove now. (tchd 11-4)

6895 SAM HALL MEMORIAL H'CAP 1m 6f 19y
4:20 (4:20) (Class 5) (0-75,81) 3-Y-O+ £2,072 (£616; £308; £153) **Stalls** Low

Form RPR

4446 **1** **Bollin Greta**[26] 6224 5-9-5 66 (t) DavidAllan 13 76
(T D Easterby) *s.i.s: hld up in rr: hdwy over 3f out: swtchd ins over 1f out: styd on to ld last 150yds* **8/1**

1251 **2** *1* **Saute**[8] 6693 4-9-9 70 (p) AdamKirby 3 79
(W R Swinburn) *w ldrs: led over 3f out: hdd and no ex ins fnl f* **13/2**[3]

3330 **3** *1* **Capable Guest (IRE)**[29] 6114 8-9-0 61 PJMcDonald 7 68
(G M Moore) *in rr-div: hdwy over 3f out: chsng ldrs over 1f out: kpt on same pce fnl f* **22/1**

4511 **4** *1 ¼* **Chookie Hamilton**[7] 6707 6-10-1 81 6ex LeeTopliss(5) 8 86
(V P Donoghue) *prom: effrt over 3f out: kpt on same pce appr fnl f* **9/1**

3410 **5** *nk* **Mohawk Ridge**[29] 6109 4-9-4 65 (p) TomEaves 1 70
(M Dods) *trckd ldrs: wnt 2nd over 2f out: kpt on one pce appr fnl f* **33/1**

5360 **6** *6* **French Hollow**[29] 6114 5-8-12 62 BarryMcHugh(3) 9 59
(T J Fitzgerald) *in tch on outer: t.k.h: effrt 3f out: wknd over 1f out* **25/1**

3210 **7** *2* **Petella**[8] 6693 4-8-13 60 PaulHanagan 11 54
(C W Thornton) *in rr: hdwy on wd outside 3f out: kpt on appr fnl f: nvr nr ldrs* **17/2**

0/0- **8** *shd* **Categorical**[195] 1242 7-8-11 61 PaulPickard(3) 4 55
(K G Reveley) *hld up in rr: hdwy on ins over 3f out: nvr nr ldrs* **25/1**

4345 **9** *2 ½* **Simple Jim (FR)**[14] 6538 6-9-0 61 SilvestreDeSousa 16 51
(D O'Meara) *in rr-div: hdwy u.p over 3f out: swtchd lft over 1f out: nvr a factor* **6/1**[2]

4330 **10** *5* **Red Fama**[15] 6516 6-9-4 65 DuranFentiman 12 48
(N Bycroft) *s.i.s: in rr: nvr on terms* **28/1**

5051 **11** 1 3/4 **Drop The Hammer**[10] 6649 4-8-8 **60** 6ex....................(b) JohnFahy(5) 10 41
(D O'Meara) *hood removed v late: hdwy to ld after 1f: hdd over 2f out: sn lost pl* **10/1**

3-20 **12** 1 3/4 **Tricky Situation**[15] 6516 4-9-6 **67**.............................. GrahamGibbons 2 45
(D H Brown) *led 1f: chsd ldrs: drvn over 3f out: lost pl 3f out* **28/1**

1112 **13** 3 1/2 **Tobernea (IRE)**[7] 6707 3-9-2 **72** 6ex................................ JoeFanning 14 45
(M Johnston) *chsd ldrs: wknd 3f out* **3/1**[1]

0245 **14** 3 1/2 **Finellas Fortune**[10] 6649 5-8-9 **56**.......................... PaulMulrennan 5 24
(G M Moore) *mid-div: drvn over 5f out: sn lost pl* **33/1**

5400 **15** 3 **Layla's Boy**[11] 6623 3-8-9 **65**.. RoystonFfrench 15 29
(J Mackie) *mid-div: effrt over 3f out: sn wknd* **100/1**

2040 **16** 72 **Twist Again (IRE)**[90] 4141 4-9-12 **73**............................... SebSanders 6 —
(P Howling) *in rr-div: bhd and eased 3f out: virtually p.u: wl t.o* **28/1**

3m 5.60s (0.90) **Going Correction** +0.15s/f (Good)
WFA 3 from 4yo+ 9lb **16** Ran SP% **122.6**
Speed ratings (Par 103): **103,102,101,101,100 97,96,96,94,92 91,90,88,86,84 43**
toteswingers:1&2:£9.60, 1&3:£43.80, 2&3:£35.60 CSF £52.65 CT £1124.36 TOTE £8.70: £2.00, £1.80, £6.80, £2.50; EX 48.30.
Owner Sir Neil Westbrook **Bred** Sir Neil & Exors Of Late Lady Westbrook **Trained** Great Habton, N Yorks

FOCUS
A wide-open staying handicap. There was a decent pace on and the form should work out, with the first five finishing clear. The winner is rated back to her best.
Simple Jim(FR) Official explanation: jockey said gelding had no more to give

6896 RACING UK ON SKY 432 MAIDEN STKS 6f
4:55 (4:59) (Class 5) 3-Y-0+ **£2,072** (£616; £308; £153) **Stalls** Centre

Form RPR

1 **Benato The Great (IRE)** 4-9-1 0.......................... MichaelO'Connell(3) 8 67+
(R C Guest) *trckd ldrs: smooth hdwy to chse ldr 2f out: rdn to ld ent fnl f: edgd lft and kpt on wl* **16/1**

00/ **2** 2 **Always Gunner**[726] 6837 4-8-13 0............................ JamesO'Reilly(5) 10 61
(J O'Reilly) *led: rdn along 2f out: drvn and hdd ent fnl f: kpt on* **66/1**

5-44 **3** 1 1/4 **Tsar Bomba (USA)**[43] 5686 3-9-3 62....................... GrahamGibbons 13 57
(T D Barron) *midfield: hdwy and in tch 2f out: rdn to chse ldrs over 1f out: drvn and edgd lft ent fnl f: sn no imp* **3/1**[1]

4402 **4** 1/2 **Accamelia**[16] 6464 4-8-13 48................................... PaulMulrennan 15 50
(C W Fairhurst) *swtchd lft s and hld up towards rr: hdwy 2f out: sn swtchd rt and rdn over 1f out: kpt on ins fnl f: nrest fnish* **9/1**

000 **5** 1 **Boy The Bell**[35] 5906 3-8-10 53.................................. JosephYoung(7) 1 52
(M Mullineaux) *in tch on wd outside: hdwy 3f out: rdn and edgd rt 2f out: drvn and kpt on u.p ins fnl f: nrst fin* **16/1**

6 1/2 **Amy Thorpe** 3-8-9 0.. PaulPickard(3) 4 45
(O Brennan) *dwlt and towards rr: hdwy on outer over 2f out: sn rdn to chse ldrs and kpt on same pce fnl f* **80/1**

5050 **7** 3/4 **Hairy Maclary**[41] 5758 3-9-3 49.. DavidAllan 11 48
(T D Easterby) *prom: rdn along over 2f out: grad wknd* **12/1**

8 3/4 **Watch The Flame**[59] 5189 4-9-0 43 ow1.........................(t) AdamKirby 7 41
(M G Quinlan) *towards rr: effrt over 2f out and sn rdn: kpt on u.p fnl f: nrst fin* **28/1**

-323 **9** 5 **Hambleton**[53] 5359 3-9-3 60.......................................(b[1]) TomEaves 12 29
(B Smart) *prom: rdn along over 2f out: sn wknd* **7/1**[2]

0000 **10** 1/2 **Media Jury**[47] 5548 3-8-12 45...................................(p) NeilFarley(5) 6 28
(J S Wainwright) *midfield: rdn along and chsd ldrs 1/2-way: sn drvn: edgd lft and wknd over 2f out* **100/1**

40 **11** 2 1/4 **Reset To Fit**[16] 6470 3-9-3 0...................................... PaulHanagan 3 21
(E J Alston) *in tch: rdn along wl over 2f out: sn n.m.r and wknd* **8/1**[3]

0000 **12** 1 1/4 **Northumberland**[71] 4760 4-9-1 47....................... AndrewHeffernan(3) 5 17
(M C Chapman) *a in midfield: hmpd over 2f out* **100/1**

0 **13** nk **Kings Craic**[181] 1401 3-9-3 0... DavidNolan 9 16
(D Carroll) *chsd ldrs: rdn along over 2f out: sn wknd* **25/1**

-605 **14** 1/2 **Paradise Spectre**[33] 6000 3-9-3 75.............................. AndrewElliott 16 14
(Mrs K Burke) *midfield: effrt wl over 2f out: sn rdn and n.d* **3/1**[1]

-545 **15** 12 **Erfaan (USA)**[39] 5816 3-9-0 60.............................(p) BarryMcHugh(3) 2 —
(Julie Camacho) *hld up: hdwy towards outer whn hmpd over 2f out: no ch and eased after* **12/1**

16 5 **Regythelion** 4-9-4 0.. AndrewMullen 17 —
(F Watson) *wnt rt s: sn outpcd and bhd* **100/1**

17 2 1/4 **Matilda May** 3-8-12 0... PatrickMathers 14 —
(C J Teague) *dwlt: sn rdn along and a in rr* **100/1**

1m 15.03s (3.23) **Going Correction** +0.15s/f (Good)
WFA 3 from 4yo 1lb **17** Ran SP% **124.7**
Speed ratings (Par 103): **84,81,79,79,77 77,76,75,68,67 64,63,62,61,45 39,36**
toteswingers:1&2:£97.70, 1&3:£17.80, 2&3:£65.40 CSF £848.96 TOTE £21.80: £6.10, £13.50, £1.70; EX 1727.00.
Owner Miss Alison Ibbotson **Bred** Glending Bloodstock **Trained** Stainforth, S Yorks
■ Stewards' Enquiry : Neil Farley two-day ban: careless riding (Oct 29-30)

FOCUS
This was a desperately weak maiden and again no surprise therefore to see a newcomer winning. The bare form is questionable, limited by the fourth.
Paradise Spectre Official explanation: jockey said colt had no more to give

6897 THANKS & SEE YOU NEXT SEASON H'CAP 7f
5:30 (5:30) (Class 5) (0-70,70) 3-Y-O **£2,072** (£616; £308; £153) **Stalls** Centre

Form RPR

6204 **1** **White Dart**[71] 4742 3-9-5 **68**... PaulMulrennan 2 76
(M R Channon) *hld up: hdwy over 2f out: led 1f out: styd on strly: v readily* **12/1**

2230 **2** 3 3/4 **Jupiter Fidius**[24] 6266 3-8-8 **64**............................(p) ShaneBKelly(7) 8 62
(Mrs K Walton) *led: hdd 1f out: kpt on same pce* **8/1**[3]

0000 **3** nse **Celestial Tryst**[25] 6243 3-8-9 **58**................................. PJMcDonald 1 56
(G M Moore) *hld up in rr: hdwy over 2f out: kpt on fnl f* **28/1**

5306 **4** 1 **Reddy To Star (IRE)**[14] 6522 3-8-6 **58** ow1.............. BarryMcHugh(3) 13 53
(Julie Camacho) *hld up in mid-div: hdwy over 2f out: kpt on same pce fnl f* **33/1**

3004 **5** 1 3/4 **William Morgan (IRE)**[49] 5484 3-9-7 **70**........................ PaulHanagan 3 60
(R A Fahey) *hld up: effrt and nt clr run over 3f out: kpt on same pce fnl 2f* **4/1**[1]

4331 **6** 3 **Chookie Avon**[7] 6710 3-8-12 **61** 6ex.........................(p) AdrianNicholls 4 43
(V P Donoghue) *trckd ldrs: effrt 2f out: one pce* **7/1**[2]

5565 **7** hd **Kirkby's Gem**[27] 6186 3-8-4 **56** oh11........................... PaulPickard(3) 11 38
(A Berry) *in rr: hdwy 2f out: kpt on ins fnl f* **100/1**

6062 **8** 4 1/2 **Choc'A'Moca (IRE)**[10] 6643 3-8-4 **58**........................(v) NeilFarley(5) 14 28
(D Carroll) *chsd ldrs: wknd over 1f out* **12/1**

9 3/4 **Muqalad (IRE)**[112] 3418 3-9-5 **68**....................................... TomEaves 15 36
(B Smart) *dwlt: hld up: hdwy over 2f out: sn rdn and hung lft: nvr a threat* **9/1**

0226 **10** nse **Uddy Mac**[16] 6460 3-8-4 **56** oh2................................ KellyHarrison(3) 9 23
(N Bycroft) *chsd ldrs: drvn over 2f out: wl outpcd whn hmpd over 1f out* **28/1**

4023 **11** nk **Hades (IRE)**[16] 6462 3-9-1 **64**.. DavidAllan 7 31
(T D Easterby) *t.k.h: trckd ldr: lost pl over 2f out* **4/1**[1]

2154 **12** 2 1/4 **Viking Warrior (IRE)**[28] 6144 3-9-2 **68**.................. PatrickDonaghy(3) 16 28
(M Dods) *chsd ldrs: rdn and wknd over 2f out* **12/1**

0025 **13** 1/2 **Tombellini (IRE)**[10] 6655 3-8-8 **57**................................... PaulQuinn 12 16
(D Nicholls) *mid-div: lost pl and hmpd over 1f out: eased ins fnl f* **28/1**

4040 **14** 8 **Bahamian Jazz (IRE)**[32] 6040 3-8-11 **60**........................... SebSanders 6 —
(R Bastiman) *t.k.h: w ldrs: hung bdly rt and bit slipped 2f out: sn wknd and heavily eased* **20/1**

6005 **15** 5 **Taborcillo**[27] 6188 3-8-7 **56** oh1.................................. GrahamGibbons 5 —
(T D Barron) *dwlt: in mid-div: lost pl over 2f out: eased ins fnl f* **16/1**

1m 28.55s (4.05) **Going Correction** +0.15s/f (Good) **15** Ran SP% **121.6**
Speed ratings (Par 101): **82,77,77,76,74 71,70,65,64,64 64,61,61,52,46**
toteswingers:1&2:£22.40, 1&3:£102.20, 2&3:£60.40 CSF £97.83 CT £2706.27 TOTE £18.60: £5.50, £3.10, £9.60; EX 200.30 Place 6 £42.57; Place 5 £18.93.
Owner Leon Crouch **Bred** Jeremy Gompertz **Trained** West Ilsley, Berks

FOCUS
This moderate handicap was another wide-open race. The form is sound enough but most of these are exposed and/or regressive. An exception is the winner who posted a clear personal best.
Bahamian Jazz(IRE) Official explanation: jockey said gelding hung right throughout
T/Plt: £47.90 to a £1 stake. Pool:£43,842.42 - 666.89 winning tickets T/Qpdt: £9.50 to a £1 stake. Pool:£3,953.15 - 305.20 winning tickets JR

6740 WOLVERHAMPTON (A.W) (L-H)
Friday, October 15

OFFICIAL GOING: Standard
Wind: Fresh across Weather: Overcast

6898 BETDAQ ON 0870 178 1221 APPRENTICE H'CAP 5f 216y(P)
5:35 (5:36) (Class 6) (0-65,65) 3-Y-0+ **£1,706** (£503; £252) **Stalls** Low

Form RPR

1320 **1** **Forever's Girl**[8] 6700 4-9-3 **65**................................... AdamCarter(3) 7 75
(G R Oldroyd) *a.p: led over 1f out: edgd lft ins fnl f: rdn out* **7/2**[2]

4412 **2** 1 1/4 **Cavitie**[35] 5920 4-9-3 **62**.. AshleyMorgan 9 68
(Andrew Reid) *prom: rdn to chse wnr fnl f: styd on same pce* **3/1**[1]

0000 **3** 3/4 **Bahamian Kid**[7] 6713 5-8-10 **62**..................................(v) JackDuern(7) 2 66
(R Hollinshead) *in rr: hdwy over 2f out: swtchd lft over 1f out: styd on* **16/1**

0513 **4** 3/4 **Mary's Pet**[171] 1593 3-9-4 **64**.. AmyBaker 12 65+
(J Akehurst) *hdwy over 4f out: rdn over 1f out: styd on* **10/1**

2023 **5** 1 **Simple Rhythm**[63] 5048 4-8-11 **61**............................ NatashaEaton(5) 13 59
(J Ryan) *prom: chsd ldr 4f out: led 2f out: rdn and hdd over 1f out: no ex ins fnl f* **14/1**

2006 **6** 3/4 **Valmina**[43] 5698 3-9-2 **65**.. JulieBurke(3) 8 61
(A W Carroll) *prom: pushed along and n.m.r 1/2-way: sn outpcd: styd on u.p ins fnl f* **10/1**

4400 **7** hd **Nacho Libre**[20] 6371 5-8-12 **62**.........................(b) DavidSimmonson(5) 11 57
(M W Easterby) *mid-div: hdwy over 1f out: nt rch ldrs* **25/1**

-450 **8** hd **Mighty Aphrodite**[105] 3620 3-8-11 **62**................. StephanieBancroft(5) 6 56
(Miss Olivia Maylam) *hld up: r.o ins fnl f: nvr nrr* **66/1**

-550 **9** hd **Bouggie Daize**[47] 5557 4-8-10 **62**.............................(b[1]) ThomasDyer(7) 3 56
(C G Cox) *s.i.s: sn pushed along in rr: r.o ins fnl f: nvr nrr* **12/1**

4013 **10** 1 1/4 **Romantic Queen**[14] 6537 4-9-6 **65**.............................(t) RossAtkinson 4 55
(George Baker) *dwlt: hld up: shkn up over 1f out: nvr on terms* **13/2**[3]

0 **11** 2 1/4 **Flyjack (USA)**[7] 6713 3-9-4 **64**.. BillyCray 1 46
(Mrs L Williamson) *mid-div: sme hdwy whn hung rt 3f out: sn wknd* **33/1**

1200 **12** nk **Philosophers Stone (FR)**[19] 6392 3-9-3 **63**.............(b[1]) DeanHeslop 10 45
(T D Barron) *sn led: rdn and hdd 2f out: wknd fnl f* **33/1**

0660 **13** shd **Replicator**[23] 6292 5-8-11 **61**.......................................(e) LeonnaMayor(5) 5 42
(P L Gilligan) *led early: chsd ldr to 4f out: remained handy: rdn over 2f out: wknd fnl f* **14/1**

1m 15.12s (0.12) **Going Correction** -0.10s/f (Stan)
WFA 3 from 4yo+ 1lb **13** Ran SP% **116.9**
Speed ratings (Par 101): **95,93,92,91,90 89,88,88,88,86 83,83,83**
toteswingers: 1&2 £2.20, 1&3 £19.20, 2&3 £16.30. CSF £13.53 CT £152.64 TOTE £5.20: £2.00, £1.10, £10.00; EX 16.80.
Owner R C Bond **Bred** R C Bond **Trained** Brawby, N Yorks

FOCUS
A tight apprentice handicap comprising horses rated 61-65. The gallop was reasonable and the winner raced down the centre in the straight. The winner recorded a personal best to reverse last month's C/D form with the runner-up.

6899 EUROPEAN BREEDERS' FUND MEDIAN AUCTION MAIDEN STKS 5f 216y(P)
6:10 (6:10) (Class 5) 2-Y-O **£3,139** (£926; £463) **Stalls** Low

Form RPR

4055 **1** **Reposer (IRE)**[114] 3315 2-9-3 82....................................... LukeMorris 6 76
(J R Best) *mde all: rdn over 1f out: hung rt fnl f: styd on* **7/2**[3]

33 **2** 1/2 **Elusive Prince**[24] 6264 2-9-3 0.. PhillipMakin 3 75
(T D Barron) *a.p: pushed along over 2f out: rdn to chse wnr fnl f: sn ev ch: unable qck nr fin* **5/2**[2]

0 **3** 3 1/4 **Redvers (IRE)**[28] 6146 2-9-3 0.. JimCrowley 1 65
(R M Beckett) *chsd ldrs: pushed along 1/2-way: rdn to chse wnr over 1f out tl styd on same pce fnl f* **15/8**[1]

50 **4** 1/2 **Whipphound**[21] 6334 2-9-3 0.................................... TomMcLaughlin 8 63
(W M Brisbourne) *chsd wnr tl rdn over 1f out: sn hung lft: no ex fnl f* **12/1**

033 **5** 11 **Arabella Fenella**[10] 6658 2-8-12 0....................................... ShaneKelly 2 25
(R M H Cowell) *pushed along in rr early: rdn over 2f out: sn wknd* **11/1**

6 nk **See The Storm** 2-9-3 0.. StephenCraine 4 29
(Patrick Morris) *hld up: hdwy over 2f out: rdn and wknd over 1f out* **50/1**

7 6 **Chillianwallah** 2-9-3 0... RichardKingscote 7 11
(J W Unett) *s.s: outpcd* **25/1**

00 **8** 4 1/2 **Sarojini**[16] 6465 2-8-12 0... ChrisCatlin 5 —
(J A Glover) *broke wl enough: sn outpcd* **50/1**

1m 14.26s (-0.74) **Going Correction** -0.10s/f (Stan) **8** Ran SP% **109.4**
Speed ratings (Par 95): **100,99,95,94,79 79,71,65**
toteswingers: 1&2 £2.20, 1&3 £2.60, 2&3 £2.20. CSF £11.46 TOTE £3.40: £1.10, £1.10, £1.30; EX 10.50.
Owner John Foulger & Simon Malcolm **Bred** Keene Bloodstock Ltd **Trained** Hucking, Kent

FOCUS
Very little depth to a maiden in which the gallop was ordinary. The first two pulled clear and the winner came down the centre in the straight.

NOTEBOOK
Reposer(IRE), gelded since his last run in June, had good prospects on the pick of his turf form and probably didn't have to improve too much to win on this all-weather debut in workmanlike fashion after edging right under pressure in the straight. He should stay 7f but he'll have to improve if he is to follow up in handicap company from his current mark of 82. (op 4-1 tchd 3-1)
Elusive Prince, who was well supported, duly improved for the step back up to 6f and registered his best effort on this all-weather debut. He's now qualified for a mark and it'll be a surprise if he isn't placed to best advantage by his shrewd trainer this winter. (op 2-1)
Redvers(IRE) raced with the choke out on this all-weather debut but bettered the form shown on his debut at Newbury. This half-brother to Chester Cup winner Mamlook (as well as several other winners over a variety of distances) should have no problems with 7f and is the type to improve as he learns to settle better. (op 5-2 tchd 11-4)
Whipphound had shown only a modest level of form in two previous starts and his proximity confirmed this form is nothing special. He should do better returned to further in handicaps, although he didn't really impress with the way he wanted to hang left when pressure was applied. (op 14-1 tchd 16-1)

6900 ASD METAL SERVICES NURSERY — 5f 20y(P)
6:40 (6:41) (Class 4) (0-85,90) 2-Y-O — **£3,594** (£1,069; £534; £266) **Stalls** Low

Form / RPR
2314 **1** **Ahtoug**[86] 4262 2-9-5 **82** ... AhmedAjtebi 4 — 91
(Mahmood Al Zarooni) *a.p: nt clr run over 1f out: led 1f out: sn clr: comf* **5/1**[2]
0451 **2** *2 ¾* **Phoebs**[11] 6636 2-9-13 **90** 6ex ... JimCrowley 1 — 89
(R A Mills) *hld up: hdwy over 1f out: sn rdn: styd on* **5/1**[2]
6341 **3** *nk* **Key Lago (IRE)**[20] 6369 2-8-10 **73** ... (p) PhillipMakin 2 — 71
(M Dods) *s.i.s: hld up: hdwy and nt clr run over 1f out: swtchd rt: r.o u.p ins fnl f: wnt 3rd nr fin: nt rch ldrs* **7/2**[1]
2140 **4** *hd* **Major Muscari (IRE)**[32] 6030 2-9-5 **82** ... (b[1]) JamesDoyle 7 — 79
(A J McCabe) *trckd ldrs: led over 1f out: sn rdn and hdd: styd on same pce* **8/1**[3]
2120 **5** *½* **Johnny Hancocks (IRE)**[17] 6435 2-8-7 **77** ... RyanPowell[(7)] 5 — 72
(P D Evans) *a.p: rdn and ev ch over 1f out: styd on same pce ins fnl f* **16/1**
0034 **6** *3* **Turn The Tide**[55] 5293 2-9-3 **80** ... RobertWinston 13 — 65
(A Bailey) *mid-div: rdn over 2f out: hung lft fr over 1f out: nt trble ldrs* **40/1**
1000 **7** *¾* **The Sydney Arms (IRE)**[63] 5036 2-9-4 **81** ... PatDobbs 3 — 63
(R Hannon) *hld up: plld hrd: rdn over 1f out: n.d* **16/1**
0651 **8** *1* **Sacrosanctus**[37] 5863 2-8-12 **75** ... ChrisCatlin 9 — 53
(J A Glover) *s.i.s: nvr on terms* **8/1**[3]
0332 **9** *2 ½* **My Love Fajer (IRE)**[23] 6286 2-8-9 **72** ... WilliamCarson 6 — 41
(G Prodromou) *chsd ldr: rdn and ev ch 2f out: wknd ins fnl f* **14/1**
152 **10** *1* **Fred Willetts (IRE)**[35] 5901 2-8-12 **75** ... PatCosgrave 11 — 41
(P D Evans) *sn outpcd* **14/1**
0310 **11** *hd* **Abzolutely (IRE)**[32] 6030 2-8-7 **70** ... CathyGannon 12 — 35
(D O'Meara) *led: rdn over 2f out: hdd over 1f out: sn hung rt: wknd fnl f* **16/1**
1434 **12** *5* **Lord Avon**[111] 3426 2-9-4 **84** ... JackDean[(3)] 8 — 31
(W G M Turner) *mid-div: rdn and wknd 1/2-way* **50/1**

61.56 secs (-0.74) **Going Correction** -0.10s/f (Stan) **12 Ran SP% 113.2**
Speed ratings (Par 97): **101,96,96,95,95 90,89,87,83,81 81,73**
toteswingers: 1&2 £4.90, 1&3 £5.10, 2&3 £1.70. CSF £28.67 CT £93.35 TOTE £7.40: £2.50, £1.80, £1.60; EX 28.30.
Owner Godolphin **Bred** Darley **Trained** Newmarket, Suffolk

FOCUS
Several previous winners in a useful nursery. The pace was a strong one and those held up had the edge. The winner came down the centre.

NOTEBOOK
Ahtoug ◆, who ran creditably in a race that threw up winners on his nursery debut, had the race run to suit and turned in a much-improved effort to win with plenty in hand on this all-weather debut. He'll be up in the weights for this and he did get things teed up for him to an extent but he should prove equally effective over 6f and may well be capable of better on this surface. (tchd 9-2)
Phoebs, who had won her only previous start on Polytrack and came here on the back of a soft-ground win, ran up to her best under her penalty in a race that suited those ridden with a degree of patience. She will be 2lb lower in future handicaps and should continue to give it her best shot either on this surface or when returned to turf. (op 9-2)
Key Lago(IRE) had the race run to suit and ran well on this nursery debut with the cheekpieces again fitted. He's the type who needs things to pan out ideally but is capable of winning again when things do and there'll be easier opportunities this winter. Official explanation: jockey said colt was slowly away (op 11-4)
Major Muscari(IRE) ran creditably returned to Polytrack in first-time blinkers and may be a bit better than the bare form suggest as he fared the best of those who raced up with the strong pace throughout. He's capable of winning in a lesser grade. (op 11-1 tchd 12-1)
Johnny Hancocks(IRE) appreciated the return to this trip and put a below-par run over 6f firmly behind him back on Polytrack. He has little in hand from his current mark but he should continue to give a good account, especially when it looks as though he will be able to dominate.
Turn The Tide wasn't disgraced from the widest draw on this first run on Polytrack returned to the minimum trip. However, she will have to fare better if she is to win a similarly competitive handicap from her current mark.
Sacrosanctus had raced up with the pace when winning both his previous starts on Polytrack but wasn't at his best after losing ground at the start. He'll be worth another chance, especially in a less competitive event. Official explanation: jockey said gelding missed the break
Abzolutely(IRE) Official explanation: jockey said filly hung right

6901 BET PREMIER LEAGUE FOOTBALL - BETDAQ NURSERY (DIV I) — 7f 32y(P)
7:10 (7:12) (Class 5) (0-70,70) 2-Y-O — **£1,774** (£523; £262) **Stalls** High

Form / RPR
1436 **1** **Fifth Dimension (IRE)**[16] 6453 2-9-7 **70** ... FergusSweeney 2 — 72
(J A Osborne) *hld up in tch: led over 1f out: rdn and hung lft ins fnl f: r.o* **8/1**
545 **2** *nk* **Lord Of Persia (USA)**[62] 5074 2-9-6 **69** ... JimCrowley 5 — 70
(R M Beckett) *a.p: chsd wnr over 1f out: sn rdn and ev ch: r.o* **6/1**
2236 **3** *2 ½* **So Is She (IRE)**[29] 6102 2-9-4 **67** ... (v) RobertWinston 8 — 62
(A Bailey) *hld up: hdwy over 1f out: sn rdn: and looked reluctant: no imp ins fnl f* **14/1**
5340 **4** *2 ¼* **Tokum (IRE)**[13] 6560 2-9-5 **68** ... ShaneKelly 1 — 58
(J Noseda) *hld up: hdwy over 2f out: rdn over 1f out: styd on same pce fnl f* **9/2**[3]
000 **5** *5* **Talkhees (IRE)**[42] 5719 2-8-7 **56** ... TadhgO'Shea 12 — 33
(B J Meehan) *chsd ldr 6f out: rdn and ev ch over 1f out: wknd fnl f* **20/1**
3505 **6** *½* **Apazine (USA)**[28] 6162 2-9-3 **66** ... NickyMackay 11 — 42
(J H M Gosden) *hdwy over 5f out: rdn over 1f out: wknd fnl f* **9/1**
0061 **7** *nk* **Diplomasi**[7] 6717 2-9-4 **67** 6ex ... ChrisCatlin 10 — 42
(C E Brittain) *prom: pushed along and hung rt fr 1/2-way: sn lost pl: n.d after* **7/2**[1]
1 **8** *5* **Striking Priorite**[128] 2867 2-9-7 **70** ... PatDobbs 6 — 33
(R Charlton) *hld up: effrt on outside over 2f out: sn wknd: eased fnl f* **4/1**[2]
0024 **9** *½* **Marina Belle**[15] 6488 2-8-11 **60** ... PhillipMakin 9 — 22
(M Johnston) *sn led: rdn and hdd over 1f out: wknd fnl f* **20/1**
5500 **10** *12* **Minus Tolerance**[18] 6411 2-7-9 **47** oh2 ... SophieDoyle[(3)] 4 — —
(Miss S L Davison) *chsd ldrs: rdn 1/2-way: wknd over 2f out* **100/1**

1m 29.91s (0.31) **Going Correction** -0.10s/f (Stan) **10 Ran SP% 113.0**
Speed ratings (Par 95): **94,93,90,88,82 81,81,75,75,61**
toteswingers: 1&2 £9.20, 1&3 £11.70, 2&3 £12.20. CSF £52.34 CT £658.77 TOTE £15.80: £4.90, £3.10, £2.30; EX 53.90.
Owner Hearn, Durkan & Pennick **Bred** Rathbarry Stud **Trained** Upper Lambourn, Berks

FOCUS
Division one of a modest nursery but a race that took less winning than seemed likely with the two market-leaders disappointing. The gallop was only fair and the winner raced centre to far side late on.

NOTEBOOK
Fifth Dimension(IRE) hadn't been at his best over 1m on his previous start but showed that to be all wrong and did enough, despite edging left, to maintain his unbeaten record over this course and distance. He's worth another chance over 1m and is lightly raced enough to be open to a little improvement. (tchd 10-1)
Lord Of Persia(USA) ◆ showed improved form on this all-weather and nursery debut and first run beyond 6f and is the one to take from the race. This scopey sort pulled a couple of lengths clear of the third, is the type to progress further and it'll be a surprise if he isn't up to winning a similar event. (op 7-1 tchd 15-2)
So Is She(IRE) had disappointed at Ayr on her previous start but fared better back up in trip on this all-weather debut with the visor again fitted. She's a fairly reliable yardstick but she looks exposed and is likely to remain vulnerable against the more progressive or better handicapped sorts in this grade. (op 12-1 tchd 16-1)
Tokum(IRE)'s form has a patchy look to it and he has yet to win a race but he wasn't disgraced back on Polytrack, leaving the impression that a stiffer overall test of stamina would have suited. However, he wouldn't be one to take too short a price about next time. (op 8-1)
Talkhees(IRE), who had hinted at ability in maidens, had the run of the race on this nursery debut but, while not totally disgraced, she will have to show a fair bit more before she is a solid betting proposition. (op 16-1)
Diplomasi, who showed improved form to win over the extended 1m at this course on his nursery debut, attracted support but failed to reproduce that after racing keenly over this shorter trip. Given he is only lightly raced, he is probably worth another chance. (op 5-1 tchd 11-2)
Striking Priorite, the least experienced member of this field, was very easy to back and was well beaten after racing keenly on the wide outside on this nursery debut after a break of over four months. His rider reported the bit slipped through his mouth, causing him to hang right, and he too will be worth another chance. Official explanation: jockey said bit pulled through gelding's mouth and it hung right (op 9-4 tchd 2-1)

6902 BET PREMIER LEAGUE FOOTBALL - BETDAQ NURSERY (DIV II) — 7f 32y(P)
7:40 (7:42) (Class 5) (0-70,70) 2-Y-O — **£1,774** (£523; £262) **Stalls** High

Form / RPR
3043 **1** **Jibaal (IRE)**[29] 6130 2-9-6 **68** ... TadhgO'Shea 2 — 73
(M Johnston) *led: rdn and hdd wl over 1f out: rallied to ld 1f out: edgd lft nr fin: all out* **7/2**[2]
0205 **2** *nse* **Falkland Flyer (IRE)**[8] 6690 2-9-7 **69** ... SamHitchcott 1 — 74
(M R Channon) *a.p: rdn and ev ch fnl f: r.o* **14/1**
6032 **3** *2 ½* **Polar Auroras**[28] 6162 2-9-4 **66** ... RobertWinston 7 — 65
(Pat Eddery) *hld up in tch: rdn over 2f out: hung lft over 1f out: hung rt ins fnl f: styd on: wnt 3rd nr fin* **8/1**
0300 **4** *nse* **Bonjour Bongee**[13] 6576 2-8-11 **59** ... (b) JamesDoyle 4 — 58
(A J McCabe) *chsd wnr: led wl over 1f out: rdn and hdd 1f out: styd on same pce ins fnl f: lost 3rd nr fin* **66/1**
053 **5** *4* **Franciscan**[16] 6465 2-9-5 **67** ... J-PGuillambert 3 — 56
(L M Cumani) *chsd ldrs: rdn 1/2-way: outpcd fr over 2f out* **11/8**[1]
0401 **6** *½* **Azlaa**[8] 6695 2-9-8 **70** 6ex ... PatDobbs 5 — 58
(R Hannon) *hld up: rdn over 1f out: styd on ins fnl f: nvr nrr* **4/1**[3]
5336 **7** *1 ¼* **Lady Platinum Club**[33] 5998 2-9-0 **69** ... (p) AdamCarter[(7)] 12 — 54
(G R Oldroyd) *dwlt: hld up: sme hdwy over 2f out: sn rdn and hung lft: n.d* **50/1**
356 **8** *2* **Whitstable Native**[14] 6520 2-9-4 **66** ... LukeMorris 11 — 46
(J R Best) *trckd ldrs: racd keenly: rdn and wknd over 1f out* **40/1**
6355 **9** *1 ¼* **Not So Bright (USA)**[22] 6311 2-8-11 **59** ... JimCrowley 8 — 36
(J G Given) *hld up: nt clr run 3f out: n.d* **12/1**
6500 **10** *2 ¾* **Granny Anne (IRE)**[17] 6435 2-8-7 **55** ... ChrisCatlin 10 — 25
(A Bailey) *s.i.s: a in rr* **80/1**
5466 **11** *1* **Dancing With Fire**[70] 4788 2-7-9 **46** oh1 ... SophieDoyle[(3)] 9 — 13
(D Donovan) *hld up: rdn over 4f out: a in rr* **125/1**
055 **12** *7* **Melbury**[13] 6575 2-9-1 **63** ... KirstyMilczarek 6 — 13
(P Howling) *chsd ldrs: rdn 1/2-way: wknd over 2f out* **28/1**

1m 29.15s (-0.45) **Going Correction** -0.10s/f (Stan) **12 Ran SP% 121.2**
Speed ratings (Par 95): **98,97,95,95,90 89,88,86,84,81 80,72**
toteswingers: 1&2 £11.10, 1&3 £3.60, 2&3 £20.00. CSF £50.13 CT £382.72 TOTE £3.20: £1.10, £5.70, £3.20; EX 47.90.
Owner Hamdan Al Maktoum **Bred** Liam Cashman And M Fahy **Trained** Middleham Moor, N Yorks

FOCUS
The second division of an ordinary nursery and another race in which the market leader proved disappointing. The ordinary gallop favoured those up with the pace and the first two raced centre-to-far side in the straight.

NOTEBOOK
Jibaal(IRE) had shown ability at a modest level up to this trip on turf but was allowed to do his own thing in front on this all-weather debut and, as with many from this yard, showed a tremendous attitude under pressure. He won't be going up much for this, should prove equally effective over 1m and appeals as the sort to win again. (op 11-2)
Falkland Flyer(IRE) had mainly been disappointing since winning his maiden on turf but he had the run of the race and ran as well as he ever has done returned to Polytrack. He'll be 2lb lower until he is reassessed but his record suggests he wouldn't be certain to build on this next time.
Polar Auroras isn't fully exposed and left the impression that either a stronger overall test of stamina over this trip or the step up to 1m would have been more to her liking. She looks capable of picking up a run-of-the-mill event on Polytrack. (op 7-1)
Bonjour Bongee also had the run of the race and returned to form returned to this longer trip. This seemed the limit of his stamina and, although the drop to 6f may be more to his liking, his record suggests he'd be anything but guaranteed to put it all in next time.
Franciscan had been expected to show improved form back over this trip in ordinary nursery company but proved disappointing. However he didn't travel with any fluency in this moderately run race and left the impression an even stiffer test would suit. He's in good hands and is worth another chance. Official explanation: trainer had no explanation for the poor form shown (op 15-8 tchd 2-1)

The Form Book, Raceform Ltd, Compton, RG20 6NL

Azlaa, under a penalty for her course-and-distance win, wasn't seen to best effect attempting to come from a long way off the pace in a race run at just an ordinary gallop. She will be 1lb lower in future and should do better granted a stiffer test over this trip or over 1m. (op 3-1 tchd 9-2)

6903 ATTHERACES.COM/BREEDERSCUP H'CAP 7f 32y(P)
8:10 (8:12) (Class 6) (0-60,60) 3-Y-O+ £1,706 (£503; £252) Stalls High

Form				RPR
0052	1		**Annes Rocket (IRE)**[7] 6713 5-9-4 60 PatDobbs 10	68+
			(J C Fox) *dwlt: hld up: hdwy and hmpd over 1f out: nt clr run and swtchd rt ins fnl f: sn rdn to ld r.o* **7/1**[2]	
1323	2	½	**Pipers Piping (IRE)**[9] 6671 4-9-1 60 (p) MichaelStainton(3) 11	67
			(P Howling) *hld up: hdwy u.p and hung lft fr over 1f out: ev ch ins fnl f: r.o* **7/2**[1]	
0130	3	¾	**Woolston Ferry (IRE)**[9] 6671 4-9-3 59 FergusSweeney 7	66+
			(David Pinder) *hld up: nt clr run fr over 1f out tl swtchd rt ins fnl f: fin wl* **16/1**[3]	
0042	4	nk	**Unlimited**[9] 6671 8-8-11 60 JulieBurke(7) 1	64
			(A W Carroll) *sn pushed along and prom: lost pl 6f out: hdwy over 1f out: rdn and ev ch ins fnl f: unable qck towards fin* **7/2**[1]	
0003	5	1	**Quaestor (IRE)**[28] 6168 3-9-2 60 RichardKingscote 8	60
			(Tom Dascombe) *chsd ldrs: rdn and hung lft fr over 1f out: no ex wl ins fnl f* **22/1**	
0460	6	1	**Far View (IRE)**[18] 6421 3-9-2 60 ChrisCatlin 2	57
			(J W Hills) *led: plld hrd: rdn over 1f out: hdd and unable qck wl ins fnl f* **7/1**[2]	
0500	7	1 ¾	**Suzhou**[34] 5972 3-9-2 60 CathyGannon 12	53
			(D J Coakley) *mid-div: drvn along over 4f out: hdwy over 2f out: styng on same pce whn hmpd ins fnl f* **25/1**	
000	8	½	**Pearly Wey**[49] 5496 7-9-4 60 (e1) RoystonFfrench 6	52
			(I W McInnes) *mid-div: hdwy 1/2-way: rdn over 1f out: styng on same pce whn hmpd ins fnl f* **33/1**	
-400	9	6	**Irish Jugger (USA)**[102] 3739 3-8-13 60 JamesMillman(3) 9	35
			(B R Millman) *mid-div: hdwy over 4f out: rdn and wknd over 2f out* **20/1**	
040P	10	7	**First Term**[49] 5469 3-9-2 60 TomMcLaughlin 5	16
			(M S Saunders) *chsd ldrs: rdn and ev ch over 2f out: hmpd and wknd fnl f* **66/1**	
	11	14	**Delek (IRE)**[52] 5399 4-9-3 59 JimCrowley 4	—
			(J G Portman) *chsd ldrs: rdn over 2f out: wknd over 1f out* **50/1**	

1m 29.14s (-0.46) **Going Correction** -0.10s/f (Stan)
WFA 3 from 4yo+ 2lb 11 Ran SP% 94.7
Speed ratings (Par 101): **98,97,96,96,95 93,91,91,84,76 60**
toteswingers: 1&2 £3.30, 1&3 £12.70, 2&3 £5.70. CSF £18.65 CT £191.00 TOTE £6.50: £1.50, £1.10, £6.30; EX 11.00.
Owner The Cross Keys Racing Club **Bred** S Coughlan **Trained** Collingbourne Ducis, Wilts
■ Rain On The Wind (4/1) was withdrawn after breaking out of the stalls. Deduct 20p in the £ under R4.
■ Stewards' Enquiry : Pat Dobbs 1st incident one-day ban: careless riding (Oct 29) 2nd, one-day ban: careless riding (Oct 30)
Michael Stainton one-day ban: careless riding (Oct 29)

FOCUS
Another very tight handicap featuring horses rated either 59 or 60. The pace wasn't noticeably strong but the hold-up horses came to the fore in the closing stages. The winner raced centre-to-far-side in the straight and is rated to his best.

6904 BET NEWMARKET CHAMPIONS DAY - BETDAQ H'CAP 1m 141y(P)
8:40 (8:40) (Class 4) (0-85,84) 3-Y-O+ £3,594 (£1,069; £534; £266) Stalls Low

Form				RPR
1000	1		**Ahlawy (IRE)**[8] 6701 7-9-5 78 (t) LeeVickers 7	86
			(F Sheridan) *s.i.s: hld up: hdwy 3f out: led over 1f out: hrd rdn and edgd lft ins fnl f: all out* **66/1**	
0000	2	nk	**Jarrow (IRE)**[17] 6438 3-8-11 74 (b1) JoeFanning 9	81
			(M Johnston) *hld up: hdwy over 1f out: rdn to chse wnr ins fnl f: styd on* **8/1**[3]	
-053	3	1 ¼	**Fine Sight**[106] 3594 3-9-3 80 StevieDonohoe 2	84+
			(G A Butler) *mid-div: rdn over 3f out: hdwy over 2f out: styd on* **7/1**[2]	
161	4	1 ½	**Mazamorra (USA)**[20] 6372 3-9-4 81 ChrisCatlin 10	82
			(M Botti) *prom: led 2f out: rdn and hdd over 1f out: styd on same pce ins fnl f* **5/2**[1]	
1100	5	hd	**Agent Archie (USA)**[99] 3824 3-9-7 84 LukeMorris 11	84
			(J R Best) *in rr: last and drvn along 5f out: r.o u.p ins fnl f: nvr nrr* **16/1**	
6064	6	1 ¼	**Templetuohy Max (IRE)**[26] 6223 5-9-1 74 (v) PatCosgrave 12	71
			(J D Bethell) *hld up: hdwy over 2f out: sn rdn: edgd lft and no ex fnl f* **25/1**	
2053	7	¾	**Purple Gallery (IRE)**[5] 6771 3-8-9 79 (p) RyanPowell(7) 6	74
			(J S Moore) *hld up: hdwy over 2f out: rdn over 1f out: no ex fnl f* **9/1**	
6146	8	13	**Tewin Wood**[24] 6274 3-8-13 76 RobertWinston 1	42
			(A Bailey) *prom: pushed along 4f out: sn wknd* **33/1**	
6510	9	hd	**William Van Gogh**[20] 6366 3-8-11 77 PatrickHills(3) 13	42
			(J H M Gosden) *s.s: a in rr* **9/1**	
3200	10	nk	**Celtic Change (IRE)**[13] 6567 6-9-10 83 (bt) PhillipMakin 5	47
			(M Dods) *prom: chsd ldr over 5f out tl led over 2f out: sn hdd: wknd fnl f* **9/1**	
0060	11	2	**Wigram's Turn (USA)**[20] 6374 5-9-2 78 JamesSullivan(3) 8	38
			(M W Easterby) *prom: drvn along 1/2-way: wknd over 2f out* **33/1**	
0004	12	25	**Inheritor (IRE)**[15] 6503 4-9-7 80 (p) RoystonFfrench 4	—
			(B Smart) *chsd ldr 3f: rdn and wknd over 2f out: t.o* **12/1**	
2026	13	8	**Aultcharn (FR)**[8] 6701 3-9-1 78 (b) ShaneKelly 3	—
			(B J Meehan) *led: rdn and hdd over 2f out: sn wknd and eased: t.o* **9/1**	

1m 49.07s (-1.43) **Going Correction** -0.10s/f (Stan)
WFA 3 from 4yo+ 4lb 13 Ran SP% 117.0
Speed ratings (Par 105): **102,101,100,99,99 98,97,85,85,85 83,61,54**
toteswingers: 1&2 £139.00, 1&3 £73.10, 2&3 £8.60. CSF £518.54 CT £4287.34 TOTE £68.00: £3.50, £2.50, £1.90; EX 402.30.
Owner Frank Sheridan **Bred** Castlemartin Stud And Skymarc Farm **Trained** Averham Park, Notts
■ Stewards' Enquiry : Lee Vickers four-day ban: used whip with excessive frequency without giving gelding time to respond (Oct 29-Nov 1)

FOCUS
Mainly exposed performers in a fair handicap. The pace was sound and those held up again had the edge late on. The winner edged towards the far rail in the closing stages. There are doubts over the form with the favourite a bit disappointing and the race is rated around the third.

William Van Gogh Official explanation: jockey said colt hung left

6905 CELEBRATE CHRISTMAS AT WOLVERHAMPTON RACECOURSE CLASSIFIED STKS 1m 1f 103y(P)
9:10 (9:11) (Class 6) 3-Y-O+ £1,706 (£503; £252) Stalls Low

Form				RPR
2350	1		**Star Addition**[68] 4867 4-9-2 55 RobertWinston 5	61
			(E J Alston) *s.i.s: hld up: hdwy and swtchd rt over 1f out: rdn to ld wl ins fnl f* **11/2**[3]	
6045	2	¾	**Join Up**[21] 6335 4-8-11 50 RossAtkinson(5) 9	59
			(W M Brisbourne) *hld up: hdwy over 2f out: led over 1f out: rdn and hdd wl ins fnl f* **12/1**	
5502	3	1	**Tallawalla (IRE)**[13] 6579 3-8-12 55 CathyGannon 3	58
			(M R Channon) *hld up: hdwy over 2f out: rdn and swtchd lft over 1f out: styd on* **7/2**[1]	
642	4	shd	**James Pollard (IRE)**[16] 6472 5-9-2 53 (t) StevieDonohoe 7	57
			(B J Llewellyn) *mid-div: hdwy over 3f out: rdn over 1f out: styd on* **16/1**	
044	5	2	**Carter**[41] 5770 4-9-2 52 (v1) ShaneKelly 4	53
			(W M Brisbourne) *chsd ldrs: rdn over 1f out: styd on same pce fnl f* **9/2**[2]	
0243	6	6	**Saving Grace**[103] 3707 4-9-2 54 PatCosgrave 10	40
			(E J Alston) *chsd ldr tl led 3f out: rdn and hdd over 1f out: wknd ins fnl f* **9/2**[2]	
0001	7	2 ¾	**Princess Aliuska**[32] 6037 5-9-2 50 SilvestreDeSousa 13	34
			(C Smith) *hld up: rdn over 3f out: nvr on terms* **10/1**	
0000	8	hd	**Lily Eva**[4] 6815 4-8-13 42 SophieDoyle(3) 6	34
			(D Donovan) *chsd ldrs tl rdn and wknd over 2f out* **28/1**	
00-0	9	2 ¼	**Bishop Rock (USA)**[24] 6269 4-9-2 50 PhillipMakin 2	29
			(N Tinkler) *hld up: rdn over 2f out: nvr on terms* **33/1**	
3	10	5	**Storms Over (USA)**[16] 6454 3-8-9 51 RobertLButler(3) 8	19
			(B W Duke) *chsd ldrs tl rdn and wknd over 1f out* **14/1**	
/004	11	3 ¾	**Dora Explora**[26] 4361 6-8-13 47 (p) RussKennemore(3) 1	11
			(Mrs L C Jewell) *chsd ldrs: rdn over 3f out: wknd over 2f out* **40/1**	
	12	4	**Dream Dream Dream (IRE)**[35] 5931 3-8-12 53 ChrisCatlin 12	3
			(K M Prendergast) *led: racd keenly: hdd 3f out: wknd over 2f out* **25/1**	

2m 1.23s (-0.47) **Going Correction** -0.10s/f (Stan)
WFA 3 from 4yo+ 4lb 12 Ran SP% 116.0
Speed ratings (Par 101): **98,97,96,96,94 89,86,86,84,80 76,73**
toteswingers: 1&2 £12.00, 1&3 £6.00, 2&3 £8.60. CSF £65.20 TOTE £7.00: £2.90, £2.10, £3.60; EX 73.30 Place 6: £63.15, Place 5: £41.10..
Owner John & Maria Thompson & Paul Buist **Bred** J E Jackson **Trained** Longton, Lancs

FOCUS
A low-grade classified event and a race that is unlikely to be throwing up many winners. The pace was reasonable and this was another race on the card that suited the hold-up horses. The winner came down the centre.
Star Addition Official explanation: trainer had no explanation for the apparent improvement in form
Princess Aliuska Official explanation: jockey said mare hung right
T/Plt: £103.20 to a £1 stake. Pool:£73,703.89 - 521.22 winning tickets T/Qpdt: £35.00 to a £1 stake. Pool:£10,104.10 - 213.40 winning tickets CR

6906 - (Foreign Racing) - See Raceform Interactive

6725 DUNDALK (A.W) (L-H)
Friday, October 15

OFFICIAL GOING: Standard

6907a DUNDALK STADIUM ON FACEBOOK H'CAP 7f (P)
7:00 (7:01) (70-100,100) 3-Y-O+ £12,367 (£3,615; £1,712; £570)

			RPR
1		**Banna Boirche (IRE)**[12] 6597 4-9-1 87 JMurtagh 2	93+
		(M Halford, Ire) *hld up towards rr: rdn in 8th over 1f out: rn fnl f to ld ins fnl 100yds* **9/4**[1]	
2	1 ½	**Alsalwa (IRE)**[7] 6728 3-8-13 87 DPMcDonogh 7	89
		(Kevin Prendergast, Ire) *chsd ldr in 2nd: rdn to ld under 2f out: strly pressed ins fnl f: hdd ins fnl 100yds and no ex* **6/1**[3]	
3	shd	**Mountain Coral (IRE)**[12] 6597 6-9-0 86 NGMcCullagh 12	88
		(F Oakes, Ire) *chsd ldrs: 4th 1/2-way: rdn into 2nd 1 1/2f out: kpt on to chal ins fnl f: no ex fnl 100yds* **20/1**	
4	½	**Maundy Money**[19] 6400 7-9-5 98 (t) SHJames(7) 8	98
		(David Marnane, Ire) *chsd ldrs: 5th 1/2-way: rdn into 4th 1 1/2f out: no ex ins fnl f: kpt on same pce* **25/1**	
5	hd	**Captain Ramius (IRE)**[20] 6357 4-9-5 91 FMBerry 11	91+
		(K A Ryan) *hld up towards rr: swtchd wd under 2f out: rdn in 13th over 1f out: r.o fnl f* **4/1**[2]	
6	hd	**He's Got Rhythm (IRE)**[12] 6597 5-9-2 88 KJManning 6	87
		(David Marnane, Ire) *mid-div: hdwy into 6th 2f out: rdn in 5th and no ex 1f out: kpt on same pce fnl f* **9/1**	
7	hd	**Collingwood (IRE)**[34] 5973 8-9-2 88 ow1 (bt) MsKWalsh 1	87
		(T M Walsh, Ire) *mid-div: rdn in 9th 2f out: no imp in 7th 1f out: kpt on one pce* **12/1**	
8	1 ¼	**Award Ceremony (IRE)**[12] 6597 5-9-1 87 (bt) PJSmullen 4	82
		(D K Weld, Ire) *chsd ldrs: 3rd 1/2-way: rdn to chal under 2f out: no ex in 3rd 1f out: wknd fnl f* **7/1**	
9	shd	**Toufan Express**[12] 6597 8-8-9 88 RPWhelan(7) 5	83
		(Adrian McGuinness, Ire) *chsd ldrs: 6th 1/2-way: rdn in 8th 2f out: no imp in 6th 1f out: wknd fnl f* **16/1**	
10	1	**Copper Dock (IRE)**[7] 6728 6-8-12 87 BACurtis(3) 10	79
		(T G McCourt, Ire) *mid-div: rdn in 11th 2f out: sn no ex* **20/1**	
11	1	**Hard Rock City (USA)**[12] 6597 10-9-0 93 DCByrne(7) 14	83
		(M J Grassick, Ire) *in rr of mid-div for most: nvr a factor* **14/1**	
12	1 ¼	**Full Title (IRE)**[38] 5845 7-8-6 85 CPHoban(7) 13	71
		(Reginald Roberts, Ire) *sn chsd ldrs: 7th 1/2-way: rdn 2f out: sn no ex* **14/1**	
13	hd	**Silenceofthewind (USA)**[462] 3817 3-9-3 91 CDHayes 9	77
		(James J Hartnett, Ire) *a towards rr* **16/1**	
14	6	**Quinmaster (USA)**[425] 5080 8-9-11 100 AFernandes(3) 3	70
		(M Halford, Ire) *led: rdn and hdd under 2f out: no ex and wknd* **20/1**	

1m 24.13s (84.13)
WFA 3 from 4yo+ 2lb 14 Ran SP% 138.5
CSF £17.43 CT £255.74 TOTE £3.00: £1.30, £2.30, £7.10; DF 13.20.
Owner Paul Rooney **Bred** Joseph Tierney **Trained** Doneany, Co Kildare
■ Stewards' Enquiry : J Murtagh advice: careless riding

FOCUS
The handicapper got this one right as they finished mostly in a heap. The form is rated around the fourth and seventh.

NOTEBOOK

Banna Boirche(IRE) won snugly and is likely to get a small hike. Held up off the pace, Johnny Murtagh had to make a move to daylight which involved him taking two or three other horses out with him, but when his mount saw daylight he picked up and won going away in the style of a classy individual. He looks to be improving, and with his penchant for this surface not in question, he'll pay to follow between now and the end of the season. (op 7/2)

Alsalwa(IRE), consistent but without a win since early in the season, gave a glimpse as to why she doesn't win very often. She travelled strongly at the head of the leading group and still looked to be travelling by far the best when getting to the front well over a furlong out, but when asked to pick up she didn't find as much as it appeared she would and couldn't get away from her opponents. She still should win a handicap before the season is out, but she certainly flattered to deceive somewhat here. (op 13/2)

Mountain Coral(IRE) had a tremendous campaign in the summer of last year which saw him shoot up the handicap, but off his lowest mark for a while he ran a very solid race and gave signs that he could soon be ready to win again. He was ridden more prominently than usual and stuck at it in the straight without ever getting to the front. It was an encouraging display. (op 16/1)

Maundy Money has mixed the good with the bad this season and this was one of his better efforts. Racing just off the pace, he came off the bridle before the straight and got caught in a pocket towards the inside and had to be switched. But he was only marginally unlucky in what was a decent run. (op 20/1)

Captain Ramius(IRE), held up in rear, was last and switched to the outside early in the straight. He came under pressure and it took him a while to pick up but he kept on strongly inside the last. He should be more effective at a mile on this evidence.

He's Got Rhythm(IRE) was done no favours by the winner's move to the outside early in the straight. However it didn't affect his momentum much and he kept going. (op 10/1)

Collingwood(IRE) never saw much daylight. (op 11/1)

Award Ceremony(IRE) faded inside the last having been ridden positively. (op 17/2)

6910a BUY A RACING POST BONUS YEARLING CANDIDATE H'CAP 1m 2f 150y(P)

8:30 (8:34) (60-90,90) 3-Y-O+ £8,243 (£1,911; £836; £477)

Pos	Dist	Horse / details	RPR
1		**Licence To Till (USA)**[22] 6304 3-9-6 87 GregFairley 4 (M Johnston) *chsd ldr: led after 2f: rdn to assert over 1f out: kpt on fnl f: pressed cl home* **3/1**[1]	93
2	nk	**Prospectorous (IRE)**[14] 6549 6-9-10 86 (tp) JMurtagh 8 (J P Dempsey, Ire) *led: hdd after 2f: 2nd 1/2-way: rdn 1 1/2f out: kpt on fnl f to press wnr cl home* **9/2**[2]	91
3	3 ½	**Kevkat (IRE)**[81] 2368 9-8-13 80 JPO'Brien(5) 7 (Eoin Griffin, Ire) *chsd ldrs: 4th 1/2-way: rdn 2f out: 3rd and no imp 1f out: kpt on same pce fnl f* **16/1**	78
4	2 ½	**Celendine**[26] 6231 3-9-5 86 FMBerry 10 (John M Oxx, Ire) *chsd ldrs: 3rd 1/2-way: rdn 2f out: no ex over 1f out: kpt on same pce* **8/1**[3]	80
5	¾	**Strandfield Lady (IRE)**[9] 6685 5-8-11 80 (p) DCByrne(7) 3 (H Rogers, Ire) *chsd ldrs: 6th 1/2-way: rdn in 5th 2f out: no imp in 4th 1f out: kpt on same pce fnl f* **8/1**[3]	72
6	hd	**Grand Opera (IRE)**[32] 5845 7-8-12 84 (b) JMMoore(10) 5 (Gordon Elliott, Ire) *mid-div: 7th 1/2-way: rdn in 8th 2f out: kpt on same pce fr over 1f out* **14/1**	75
7	1	**High Importance (USA)**[33] 5797 3-9-2 83 KJManning 9 (A J Martin, Ire) *chsd ldrs: 5th 1/2-way: rdn in 6th 2f out: no ex 1 1/2f out: kpt on one pce* **12/1**	73
8	½	**Carefree Smile (IRE)**[47] 5572 4-9-6 82 (b) PJSmullen 13 (D K Weld, Ire) *mid-div: 8th 1/2-way: rdn in 7th 2f out: kpt on one pce fr over 1f out* **9/1**	70
9	1 ¼	**Matraash (USA)**[14] 6549 4-9-8 84 JAHeffernan 14 (Mrs Sarah Dawson, Ire) *in rr of mid-div thrght: nvr a factor* **18/1**	70
10	shd	**Cul A Dun (IRE)**[4] 6823 4-9-1 84 SHJames(7) 12 (John Joseph Murphy, Ire) *in rr of mid-div: 9th 1/2-way: rdn and no imp 2f out: kpt on one pce* **10/1**	76
11	nk	**Lonesome Maverick (IRE)**[20] 5130 6-9-8 84 (b) CDHayes 11 (Donal Kinsella, Ire) *in rr of mid-div thrght: nvr a factor* **16/1**	69
12	1	**Sugar Baby Love (IRE)**[12] 6599 4-9-0 81 (t) APThornton(5) 2 (Patrick Martin, Ire) *a towards rr* **11/1**	64
13	1 ¼	**Lord Kenmare (USA)**[12] 6597 4-9-7 90 (p) CPHoban(7) 1 (M Halford, Ire) *a towards rr* **20/1**	71
14	5	**Spirit Of Xaar (IRE)**[30] 6100 4-9-10 86 DPMcDonogh 6 (David Marnane, Ire) *s.i.s: a towards rr* **20/1**	57

2m 12.59s (132.59)
WFA 3 from 4yo+ 6lb 14 Ran SP% **133.7**
CSF £17.40 CT £200.40 TOTE £2.60: £2.30, £1.40, £5.60; DF 16.80.
Owner The Vine Accord **Bred** John Hettinger **Trained** Middleham Moor, N Yorks

FOCUS

Another successful raid from one of Mark Johnston's middle-grade handicappers. The first two are on the upgrade.

NOTEBOOK

Licence To Till(USA) won in trademark fashion. Getting to the front early on, he dictated the pace and kicked on in the straight. It proved crucial as the runner-up was coming at him inside the final furlong, although the winning rider felt he had a bit more up his sleeve should he have needed it. He's tough with a bit of class. (op 11/4)

Prospectorous(IRE), tough and consistent, ended up the last challenger as the first two pulled clear inside the last. He tracked the leader to the straight and was caught out by that rival quickening on. He stayed on and came home strongly inside the last, but needed to be closer to the winner early in the straight and the result may well be different should they meet again. (op 5/1)

Kevkat(IRE) doesn't quite possess the ability of old. Having raced just off the pace he didn't have the speed to go with the winner over a furlong out and came home at one pace.

Celendine was prominent early but was under pressure and one-paced from early in the straight in a race that not many horses got into. (op 7/1)

Strandfield Lady(IRE) chased the leaders on the inside and travelled well for most of the journey but didn't pick up when asked to do so early in the straight and just kept on at the same pace. She's had a terrific season and, if getting a break now, certainly deserves it. The handicapper may well have her measure. (op 10/1)

6911 - 6914a (Foreign Racing) - See Raceform Interactive

6643 CATTERICK (L-H)

Saturday, October 16

OFFICIAL GOING: Good (good to soft in places; 8.3)

6915 TOTEPLACEPOT APPRENTICE CLAIMING STKS 1m 3f 214y

1:45 (1:45) (Class 6) 3-Y-O+ £2,047 (£604; £302) Stalls High

Form	Pos	Dist	Horse / details	RPR
1636	1		**Eijaaz (IRE)**[11] 6650 9-9-4 61 (p) MichaelO'Connell 14 (G A Harker) *hld up towards rr: hdwy on outer over 4f out: cruised up on bit 2f out: shkn up to ld ent fnl f: jst hld on* **5/1**[2]	64+
6040	2	shd	**Lady Norlela**[66] 4945 4-8-5 42 TimothyAyres(7) 1 (B S Rothwell) *in tch on inner: lost pl over 4f out: hdwy on inner over 2f out: chsd ldrs and nt clr run over 1f out: swtchd rt ins fnl f: fin strly: jst failed* **80/1**	55+
0000	3	¾	**Robby Bobby**[24] 6297 5-9-8 67 AmyRyan 13 (M Johnston) *hld up towards rr: gd hdwy 1/2-way: trckd ldrs 4f out: effrt over 2f out: sn rdn to chal and led briefly jst over 1f out: hung lft drvn and hdd ent fnl f: no ex towards fin* **9/2**[1]	64
0020	4	nk	**Bold Marc (IRE)**[21] 6375 8-9-1 63 NeilFarley(5) 6 (Mrs K Burke) *trckd ldrs: hdwy 3f out: rdn to chse ldrs and n.m.r over 1f out: drvn and one pce fnl f* **9/2**[1]	61
1434	5	1	**Oddsmaker (IRE)**[8] 6707 9-9-5 59 (t) IanBrennan 5 (M A Barnes) *led: rdn along wl over 2f out: drvn and hdd over 1f out: sn n.m.r and wknd ins fnl f* **5/1**[2]	59
4006	6	1 ¼	**Jenny Soba**[19] 6416 7-8-8 50 VictoriaFletcher(7) 10 (Lucinda Featherstone) *chsd ldrs: rdn along over 3f out: drvn wl over 1f out: kpt on same pce* **22/1**	53
500	7	1 ¾	**Inside Knowledge (USA)**[14] 6571 4-9-0 44 BillyCray(3) 11 (G Woodward) *midfield: rdn along and outpcd 4f out: styng on whn hung lft over 1f out: sn no imp* **125/1**	52
0602	8	½	**Without Equal**[25] 6262 4-8-9 48 DeanHeslop(3) 12 (N Wilson) *chsd ldrs: hdwy on inner over 2f out: drvn over 1f out: hld whn nt clr run and hmpd ins fnl f* **20/1**	46
3300	9	½	**Dimashq**[33] 6033 8-8-13 43 PaulPickard 3 (P T Midgley) *prom: chsd ldr over 2f out: sn rdn and n.m.r wl over 1f out: sn rdn and grad wknd* **20/1**	46
5304	10	2 ¾	**Lucayan Dancer**[49] 5515 10-8-13 60 TerenceFury(7) 9 (N Bycroft) *hld up towards rr: effrt over 3f out: sn rdn and n.d* **12/1**	49
0265	11	5	**Chocolate Caramel (USA)**[7] 6744 8-9-0 61 LeeTopliss(3) 15 (R A Fahey) *a in rr* **11/2**[3]	38
6464	12	¾	**Mojeerr**[17] 6472 4-9-0 50 (b) DeclanCannon(3) 7 (A J McCabe) *a towards rr* **14/1**	37
50-	13	13	**Bluegrass Lion (USA)**[326] 7504 4-9-5 0 PatrickDonaghy(3) 8 (Mrs L Williamson) *a in rr: bhd fnl 3f* **80/1**	21
000/	14	11	**Bottomless Wallet**[1232] 2253 9-8-10 50 LanceBetts(3) 2 (F Watson) *chsd ldr: rdn along over 3f out: wknd over 2f out* **200/1**	—

2m 40.81s (1.91) **Going Correction** +0.175s/f (Good) 14 Ran SP% **117.1**
Speed ratings (Par 101): **100,99,99,99,98 97,96,96,95,94 90,90,81,74**
Tote Swingers: 1&2 £72.20, 1&3 £7.20, 2&3 £79.40 CSF £371.49 TOTE £5.40: £1.80, £31.60, £2.50; EX 639.10.
Owner A S Ward **Bred** Shadwell Estate Company Limited **Trained** Thirkleby, N Yorks
■ Stewards' Enquiry : Amy Ryan seven-day ban: careless riding (Oct 30-Nov 5)

FOCUS

A poor race, but quite a dramatic one. The form is limited by the runner-up and seventh and is not worth taking too literally.

6916 TOTESWINGER FLEXI BETTING NOVICE STKS 5f

2:15 (2:15) (Class 4) 2-Y-O £3,238 (£963; £481; £240) Stalls Low

Form	Pos	Dist	Horse / details	RPR
0100	1		**El Viento (FR)**[14] 6568 2-9-2 88 (b) BarryMcHugh(3) 6 (R A Fahey) *outpcd and reminders sn after s: in rr: gd hdwy over 1f out: styd on strly to ld post* **3/1**[1]	82
3201	2	shd	**Diamond Vine (IRE)**[6] 6769 2-9-2 71 TomMcLaughlin 12 (R A Harris) *outpcd and reminders after s: in rr: gd hdwy on wd outside over 1f out: led last 50yds: hdd post* **12/1**	79
31	3	1 ½	**Captain Kolo (IRE)**[11] 6646 2-9-5 77 DavidAllan 8 (T D Easterby) *s.i.s: sn mid-div: hdwy and swtchd rt appr fnl f: r.o* **7/2**[2]	76
013	4	shd	**Style And Panache (IRE)**[12] 6636 2-9-0 78 LeeTopliss(5) 7 (P D Evans) *chsd ldrs: kpt on same pce fnl f* **11/1**	76
1	5	shd	**Yellow Dandy (IRE)**[19] 6419 2-9-0 74 CathyGannon 11 (Liam McAteer, Ire) *chsd ldrs: led 1f out: hdd and no ex last 50yds* **14/1**	71
2201	6	1 ¾	**Nine Before Ten (IRE)**[28] 6182 2-9-0 75 GregFairley 2 (Mrs D J Sanderson) *led tl 1f out: wknd ins fnl f* **11/2**[3]	64
4454	7	¾	**Defence Council (IRE)**[48] 5547 2-9-2 76 PaulMulrennan 1 (J Howard Johnson) *dwlt: sn chsng ldrs: one pce appr fnl f* **25/1**	64
0050	8	¾	**On The High Tops (IRE)**[14] 6568 2-9-2 80 MickyFenton 9 (T P Tate) *chsd ldrs: one pce appr fnl f* **28/1**	61
2104	9	3	**Where's Romeo (IRE)**[12] 6636 2-9-5 84 GrahamGibbons 5 (D H Brown) *chsd ldrs: wknd 1f out: eased ins fnl f* **7/2**[2]	53+
4004	10	1 ¾	**Cerejeira (IRE)**[22] 6323 2-8-9 49 DuranFentiman 10 (E J Alston) *sn outpcd and in rr: bhd fnl 2f* **100/1**	37
0	11	1	**Georgian Silver**[110] 3498 2-8-9 0 LNewman 4 (A G Foster) *s.i.s: sn mid-div: lost pl over 1f out* **200/1**	33

61.04 secs (1.24) **Going Correction** +0.225s/f (Good) 11 Ran SP% **116.3**
Speed ratings (Par 97): **99,98,96,96,96 93,92,90,86,83 81**
Tote Swingers: 1&2 £8.30, 1&3 £4.70, 2&3 £7.70 CSF £39.11 TOTE £3.60: £2.20, £6.30, £1.10; EX 35.50.
Owner John Nicholls Ltd/David Kilburn **Bred** Ballykilbride Stud **Trained** Musley Bank, N Yorks
■ Stewards' Enquiry : Tom McLaughlin two-day ban: used whip with excessive frequency (Oct 30-31)

FOCUS

A decent novice event with nine of the 11 runners previous winners, but the leaders may have done too much early with the first three coming from well off the pace. Straightforward but limited form.

NOTEBOOK

El Viento(FR) had upwards of 4lb in hand of his rivals at these weights after his eighth place in the Totepool Two-Year-Old Trophy, but he didn't look likely to win this for a long way as he had to be given reminders after breaking slowly and was still last and being ridden passing the 2f pole. However, he then found his stride and weaved through the field to hit the front almost on the line. He will be suited by a return to a stiffer test. (op 11-4 tchd 5-2)

Diamond Vine(IRE) came into this in winning form, but had plenty on at these weights (he had a stone to find with the winner) and not much really went right for him here. He also missed the break and was forced to race almost on his own out in the centre of the track, yet was produced to win his race and was only caught on the line. (op 11-1)

Captain Kolo(IRE), winner of a C&D maiden earlier this month, ran on from over a furlong out but looked held when becoming short of room in the final 50 yards. (tchd 4-1)

Style And Panache(IRE) was always up there and fared best of the prominent racers, but she lacks the scope of a few of these with this being her 13th start. (op 10-1 tchd 12-1)

Yellow Dandy(IRE) made a successful raid to win a Ffos Las maiden last month and she had every chance here after having raced up with the pace, but she tended to hang about under pressure inside the last furlong. (op 16-1)

Nine Before Ten(IRE), all-the-way winner of a 6f maiden here last month, attempted the same tactics over this shorter trip but may have gone off too quick as she didn't get home. (op 7-1 tchd 15-2)

Where's Romeo(IRE) was entitled to need his return from four months off at Windsor 12 days earlier, but was disappointing here and faded tamely inside the last furlong. (op 9-2)

6917 BET TOTEPOOL ON ALL UK RACING H'CAP (DIV I) 7f
2:50 (2:50) (Class 5) (0-75,75) 3-Y-0+ **£2,266** (£674; £337; £168) **Stalls Low**

Form RPR
1431 **1** **Cara's Request (AUS)**20 6394 5-9-7 **75** AdrianNicholls 3 89
(D Nicholls) *mde all: rdn clr 2f out: kpt on strly fnl f* **3/1**1
2230 **2** *2* **Solar Spirit (IRE)**32 6048 5-8-11 **72** ShaneBKelly(7) 10 81
(J J Quinn) *in tch: hdwy over 2f out: rdn to chse wnr ins fnl f: no imp towards fin* **8/1**
4611 **3** *1* **Northern Flyer (GER)**28 6189 4-8-7 **64** (p) IanBrennan(3) 11 70+
(J J Quinn) *towards rr: hdwy on outer over 2f out: rdn wl over 1f out: kpt on ins fnl f* **5/1**3
1430 **4** *3* **Offspring**30 6113 3-8-13 **69** DuranFentiman 5 66
(T D Easterby) *trckd ldrs: hdwy 3f out and sn chsng wnr: drvn over 1f out and kpt on same pce* **14/1**
0200 **5** *1 1/2* **Hits Only Jude (IRE)**8 6710 7-8-2 **61** NeilFarley(5) 6 55
(D Carroll) *chsd ldrs: rdn along over 2f out: drvn wl over 1f out and sn one pce* **8/1**
0000 **6** *3/4* **Ubenkor (IRE)**16 6491 5-8-7 **61** oh3 PJMcDonald 1 53
(M Herrington) *in tch: effrt and hdwy over 2f out: sn rdn and n.d* **22/1**
4000 **7** *3 1/2* **White Deer (USA)**25 6267 6-8-13 **70** (v) MichaelO'Connell(3) 4 53
(G A Harker) *a towards rr* **16/1**
5050 **8** *1 1/2* **Christmas Light**7 6753 3-8-10 **71** JohnFahy(5) 2 49
(D O'Meara) *chsd ldrs on inner: rdn along 3f out: drvn over 2f out and sn wknd* **10/3**2
0025 **9** *1 1/2* **Chambers (IRE)**43 5732 4-8-4 **61** oh4 PaulPickard(3) 9 36
(E J Alston) *dwlt: a in rr* **16/1**
0000 **10** *2 3/4* **Ishe Mac**30 6113 4-9-0 **68** GrahamGibbons 7 35
(N Bycroft) *chsd wnr: rdn along 3f out: sn wknd* **14/1**

1m 26.56s (-0.44) **Going Correction** +0.175s/f (Good)
WFA 3 from 4yo+ 2lb **10** Ran SP% **116.4**
Speed ratings (Par 103): **109,106,105,102,100 99,95,93,92,89**
Tote Swingers: 1&2 £4.60, 1&3 £1.10, 2&3 £7.10 CSF £27.51 CT £119.38 TOTE £4.40: £2.90, £1.20, £1.60; EX 26.30.
Owner Stewart Aitken **Bred** S Aitken **Trained** Sessay, N Yorks

FOCUS
An ordinary handicap and there was only ever one horse in it. The form is rated slightly positively with the runner-up to this year's best.
Ishe Mac Official explanation: jockey said filly had no more to give

6918 TOTEPOOL CATTERICK DASH (H'CAP) 5f
3:25 (3:25) (Class 2) (0-100,100) 3-Y-0+ **£9,714** (£2,890; £1,444; £721) **Stalls Low**

Form RPR
1 **Thats A Fret (IRE)**20 6400 4-8-7 **86** GregFairley 4 94
(Liam McAteer, Ire) *chsd ldrs: swtchd rt over 1f out: led 1f out: jst hld on* **8/1**2
1060 **2** *hd* **Favourite Girl (IRE)**28 6175 4-8-11 **90** (v) DuranFentiman 13 98
(T D Easterby) *chsd ldrs: wnt 2nd jst ins fnl f: r.o: no ex nr fin* **20/1**
0000 **3** *shd* **Johannes (IRE)**28 6177 7-8-10 **94** LeeTopliss(5) 12 101+
(R A Fahey) *sn outpcd and in rr: gd hdwy over 1f out: str run fnl 100yds: jst failed* **8/1**2
0053 **4** *1 1/2* **Fathom Five (IRE)**26 6256 6-8-12 **91** SebSanders 14 93
(C F Wall) *s.i.s: mid-div on outer: chsng ldrs over 1f out: kpt on same pce ins fnl f* **11/1**
4300 **5** *1/2* **Duchess Dora (IRE)**21 6364 3-8-8 **90** IanBrennan(3) 11 90
(J J Quinn) *chsd ldrs: kpt on same pce fnl f* **18/1**
2000 **6** *1/2* **Pavershooz**28 6175 5-8-8 **87** AndrewElliott 1 85
(N Wilson) *chsd ldrs: kpt on same pce appr fnl f* **12/1**
4002 **7** *3/4* **Archers Road (IRE)**8 6706 3-9-0 **93** PaulMulrennan 9 89+
(T D Barron) *in tch: nt clr run 2f out: styd on wl ins fnl f* **14/1**
0100 **8** *shd* **Tabaret**37 5884 7-8-5 **87** (b1) AmyRyan(3) 3 82
(R M Whitaker) *led: hdd 1f out: wknd ins fnl f* **22/1**
1506 **9** *hd* **Star Rover (IRE)**11 6663 3-9-0 **93** CathyGannon 8 88
(P D Evans) *sn in rr: hdwy over 1f out: nvr on terms* **25/1**
6005 **10** *3/4* **Our Jonathan**25 6265 3-9-4 **97** PJMcDonald 15 89
(K A Ryan) *in rr on outer: hdwy over 1f out: nvr a factor* **20/1**
0060 **11** *nse* **Moorhouse Lad**13 6608 7-9-0 **100** AdamCarter(7) 7 92
(B Smart) *chsd ldrs: wknd over 1f out* **17/2**3
3111 **12** *3/4* **Green Park (IRE)**5 6798 7-8-10 **94** 6ex (b) NeilFarley(5) 5 83
(D Carroll) *chsd ldrs: outpcd over 2f out* **17/2**3
1000 **13** *3/4* **Hotham**28 6175 7-8-11 **93** BarryMcHugh(3) 2 79
(N Wilson) *s.i.s: sn mid-div: outpcd and lost pl over 2f out* **25/1**
3113 **14** *nk* **Hazelrigg (IRE)**21 6364 5-8-9 **88** (be) DavidAllan 6 73
(T D Easterby) *s.i.s: in rr: nvr on terms* **9/2**1
2000 **15** *2* **Judge 'n Jury**13 6608 6-9-5 **98** (t) TomMcLaughlin 10 76
(R A Harris) *chsd ldrs: wknd over 1f out* **9/1**

59.78 secs (-0.02) **Going Correction** +0.225s/f (Good) **15** Ran SP% **121.0**
Speed ratings (Par 109): **109,108,108,106,105 104,103,103,102,101 101,100,99,98,95**
Tote Swingers: 1&2 £53.30, 1&3 £15.70, 2&3 £56.00 CSF £165.42 CT £1352.57 TOTE £9.10: £3.90, £8.00, £3.60; EX 240.30 TRIFECTA Not won..
Owner Mrs Marie Cusack **Bred** Mrs M Cusack **Trained** Navan, Co Meath

FOCUS
A fiercely competitive sprint handicap featuring a couple who had contested the Prix de l'Abbaye 13 days earlier, though neither figured in the finish. The draw didn't appear to play a major part because although the winner was drawn low, the next four home were all drawn in double figures. The pace was unsurprisingly rapid. The progressive winner is rated as having improved again.

NOTEBOOK
Thats A Fret(IRE) was 5lb higher than when winning a valuable 6f handicap on softer ground at the Curragh last month, but although connections were concerned by the shorter trip he does have winning form over the minimum on quick ground and the key to him here was probably the decent pace. He travelled well just behind the leaders and, having hit the front passing the furlong pole, kept on to just about last home with nothing to spare. He is described as a tough sort by his trainer, who thinks he will carry on improving. (op 11-1)
Favourite Girl(IRE) has found life tougher in races such as the Great St Wilfid and Ayr Silver Cup since winning four times earlier in the season, but she ran a blinder, especially as she was trapped out wide down the centre of the track. She never stopped galloping and was only just denied. (tchd 25-1)
Johannes(IRE) ◆, unplaced in red-hot sprint handicaps since winning at York on his reappearance, is now 1lb lower than for that success and was well supported in the market. He can be considered unlucky too, as he was outpaced and under pressure early and enjoyed anything but a trouble-free passage, but he finished with a real flourish and only just failed to get up. (op 12-1)
Fathom Five(IRE) was another to run a fine race from a wide draw and he had every chance a furlong from home. He remains on a winning mark, but his last two successes have come in the same race on his seasonal reappearance at Epsom. (op 12-1)
Duchess Dora(IRE) was by no means disgraced and is now 4lb lower than when winning on her Sandown reappearance. (op 20-1 tchd 25-1)
Pavershooz had every chance against the inside rail and has slipped to a mark 1lb lower than for his last win at Ayr in July of last year.
Archers Road(IRE) ◆, raised 1lb after running much better to go down narrowly at Musselburgh eight days earlier, was staying on at the line and still looks capable of winning off this mark. Official explanation: jockey said gelding was denied a clear run
Tabaret was successful in a first-time visor three starts back and this time was making his debut in blinkers. He showed dazzling early speed to take them along, but had shot his bolt a furlong from home. (tchd 20-1)
Green Park(IRE), carrying a 6lb penalty in his bid for a four-timer following three wins over 6f, lost his place at halfway and there was no way back. (tchd 8-1 and 9-1)
Hazelrigg(IRE), who has been called some names in the past, was on his best behaviour last month with two wins and a fine third off this inflated mark, but he missed the break here and didn't seem to fancy it at all, though he was reported to have been struck into. Official explanation: jockey said gelding was struck into (op 4-1)

6919 TOTEPOOL A BETTER WAY TO BET MEDIAN AUCTION MAIDEN STKS 7f
4:00 (4:01) (Class 5) 2-Y-0 **£2,797** (£826; £413) **Stalls Low**

Form RPR
33 **1** **Tasfeya**22 6334 2-9-3 0 TadhgO'Shea 7 78+
(M Johnston) *mde all: rdn clr over 1f out: kpt on strly* **5/4**1
6534 **2** *3 1/4* **Icy Blue**8 6704 2-9-0 64 AmyRyan(3) 4 70
(R M Whitaker) *in tch: hdwy on wd outside 2f out: rdn to chse ldrs over 1f out: hung bdly lft ins fnl f: kpt on* **12/1**
6045 **3** *2 1/4* **Piccoluck**7 6740 2-9-3 65 (t) PaulMulrennan 10 64
(Mrs D J Sanderson) *t.k.h: trckd ldrs: hdwy over 2f out: rdn over 1f out: chsng wnr ins fnl f whn n.m.r last 75yds and one pce* **14/1**
40 **4** *1* **Benidorm**16 6498 2-9-3 0 JamesDoyle 8 61
(A J McCabe) *chsd wnr: rdn along 2f out: drvn over 1f out: keeping on same pce whn hmpd ins fnl f* **25/1**
523 **5** *2* **Candys Girl**37 5885 2-8-12 77 HayleyTurner 1 51
(M L W Bell) *chsd ldrs on inner: rdn along over 2f out: sn drvn and grad wknd* **3/1**2
03 **6** *shd* **Snow Ridge**8 6712 2-9-3 0 SebSanders 9 56
(Sir Mark Prescott) *trckd ldrs: hdwy over 2f out: rdn wl over 1f out: drvn and one pce whn n.m.r ent fnl f: sn wknd* **5/1**3
05 **7** *8* **Sandy Lonnen**80 4480 2-9-3 0 PJMcDonald 2 35
(J Howard Johnson) *a towards rr* **66/1**
8 *1/2* **Crowned Supreme (IRE)**55 5339 2-9-3 0 (b1) CathyGannon 13 34
(Liam McAteer, Ire) *s.i.s: a in rr* **80/1**
9 *10* **Dikanta** 2-8-12 0 MarkCoumbe(5) 12 8
(A Berry) *s.i.s: a in rr* **100/1**
000 **10** *17* **Red Snapper (IRE)**25 6263 2-9-3 45 DuranFentiman 5 —
(J R Weymes) *lost many l s and a bhd* **100/1**
60 **11** *3 1/2* **Sangar**14 6569 2-8-9 0 BarryMcHugh(3) 11 —
(Ollie Pears) *dwlt: sn in tch: rdn along and hdwy to chse ldrs whn stmbld bdly and lost action home turn: sn bhd and eased* **10/1**

1m 28.14s (1.14) **Going Correction** +0.175s/f (Good) **11** Ran SP% **118.1**
Speed ratings (Par 95): **100,96,93,92,90 90,81,80,69,49 45**
Tote Swingers: 1&2 £4.70, 1&3 £5.30, 2&3 £10.90 CSF £18.84 TOTE £2.40: £1.30, £4.50, £4.40; EX 20.00.
Owner Hamdan Al Maktoum **Bred** Shadwell Estate Co Ltd **Trained** Middleham Moor, N Yorks

FOCUS
Not much strength in depth to this maiden and another race dominated by the pacesetter. The winner basically ran to form.

NOTEBOOK
Tasfeya had been beaten less than a length each time when third in maidens at Newcastle and Wolverhampton and probably only needed repeat those efforts in order to take this. Well backed and soon in front, he never looked likely to be caught over the last 2f and his future depends on how the handicapper interprets this comfortable defeat of rivals rated 64 and 65, but connections expect him to make a nice 3-y-o. (op 7-4 tchd 15-8)
Icy Blue had already shown some ability in maiden/nursery company and ran creditably here as he didn't appear to handle the track at all. He was awkward passing the 2f pole and although he then ran on, he was inclined to hang to his left all the way to the line. He does lack scope. (op 9-1 tchd 17-2)
Piccoluck was rated 1lb higher than the runner-up after showing some ability in maiden/nursery company, but his stamina for this trip was an issue and although he travelled very kindly behind the leaders, he found nothing like as much as had seemed likely when coming under pressure. He is also starting to look exposed.
Benidorm failed to build on his promising Beverley debut on Polytrack next time, but ran a little better here. He lacked a turn of foot over this sharp 7f and ideally needs a stiffer test, but he now gets a mark which widens his options. (op 20-1)
Candys Girl was disappointing stepped up to 6f at Epsom last time having previously been beaten narrowly in a Catterick maiden that has worked out well, but she dropped out tamely over this extra furlong and ran nowhere near her mark of 77. (op 11-4 tchd 5-2)
Snow Ridge, making his turf debut after showing ability in two Polytrack maidens, did not improve for the different surface but now qualifies for handicaps. (tchd 9-2 and 11-2)
Red Snapper(IRE) Official explanation: jockey said gelding was reluctant to race
Sangar was reported to have stumbled on the bend and lost her action. Official explanation: jockey said filly slipped on bend and lost its action (op 12-1)

6920 TOTEEXACTA FLEXI BETTING FILLIES' NURSERY 7f
4:35 (4:35) (Class 4) (0-85,79) 2-Y-0 **£3,885** (£1,156; £577; £288) **Stalls Low**

Form RPR
5412 **1** **First Class Favour (IRE)**11 6647 2-9-2 **79** LanceBetts(5) 10 80
(T D Easterby) *mde all: rdn over 2f out: drvn appr fnl f and kpt on strly* **11/2**3
0030 **2** *2 3/4* **Child Bride**14 6563 2-8-10 **71** IanBrennan(3) 4 65
(P F I Cole) *s.i.s and in rr: hdwy over 2f out: sn rdn and styd on strly fnl f: nt rch wnr* **5/1**2
21 **3** *1* **Nawaashi**33 6034 2-9-5 **77** TadhgO'Shea 2 68
(M Johnston) *chsd ldng pair on inner: rdn along and sltly outpcd wl over 2f out: swtchd rt and drvn over 1f out: kpt on same pce fnl f* **5/2**1
3260 **4** *3/4* **Millies Folly**14 6568 2-8-5 **68** NeilFarley(5) 3 57
(D Carroll) *chsd ldrs: hdwy and cl up over 2f out: sn rdn and ev ch tl drvn and wknd appr fnl f* **14/1**
1003 **5** *2 1/4* **Bay Of Fires (IRE)**11 6647 2-8-12 **75** JohnFahy(5) 12 58
(D O'Meara) *sn chsng wnr: rdn along and ch 2f out: drvn over 1f out: wknd fnl f* **15/2**
315 **6** *3/4* **Biaraafa (IRE)**34 5998 2-8-13 **71** HayleyTurner 6 53
(M L W Bell) *midfield: edgd rt 3f out: sn rdn and no imp* **8/1**
10 **7** *1 1/4* **Cosmic Moon**28 6174 2-8-12 **75** LeeTopliss(5) 11 53
(R A Fahey) *dwlt and bhd: sme late hdwy whn slipped and lost action home turn: no imp after* **9/1**

2400 **8** *nk* **Damascus Symphony**[11] 6647 2-8-4 **62**......................(p) AndrewElliott 9 39
(J D Bethell) *in tch: hdwy to chse ldrs whn bmpd and rn wd home turn: sn rdn and wknd* **50/1**

043 **9** *3/4* **Kaua'i Girl**[17] 6459 2-8-9 **67**.. RoystonFfrench 8 43
(Mrs A Duffield) *a in rr* **40/1**

603 **10** *7* **Gainsboroughs Best (IRE)**[16] 6511 2-8-10 **71**......... GilmarPereira(3) 1 28
(W J Haggas) *towards rr: hdwy on inner and in tch 1/2-way: sn rdn and wknd* **20/1**

042 **11** *14* **Baileys Moneypenny**[24] 6293 2-9-4 **76**....................... PaulMulrennan 7 —
(J G Given) *towards rr: effrt on outer wl over 2f out: sn rdn and wknd: bhd and eased fnl f* **10/1**

1m 28.56s (1.56) **Going Correction** +0.175s/f (Good) **11** Ran SP% **118.4**
Speed ratings (Par 94): **98,94,93,92,90 89,88,87,86,78 62**
Tote Swingers: 1&2 £8.20, 1&3 £3.90, 2&3 £4.40 CSF £32.85 CT £87.89 TOTE £6.50: £1.90, £1.80, £1.40; EX 50.20.
Owner S A Heley **Bred** Oghill House Stud **Trained** Great Habton, N Yorks
■ Stewards' Enquiry : Lance Betts one-day ban: used whip with excessive frequency (Oct 30)

FOCUS
A fair fillies' nursery and another well-judged front-running ride. Apart from the runner-up, the other principals all raced handily. The winning time was 0.42 seconds slower than the preceding maiden. The winner did it in some style but the form is limited.

NOTEBOOK
First Class Favour(IRE) came into this with a course record of 3-4, but was put up another 2lb for her narrow defeat here 11 days earlier. However, despite having to work in order to gain the early advantage from her wide draw, she travelled powerfully in front and found plenty when asked to keep her rivals at bay inside the last 2f. She obviously loves it here and is proving a tough filly. (op 6-1)
Child Bride ran better than her finishing position would suggest upped to this trip at Newmarket last time and also ran well here, as she was the only one to make up any appreciable ground from off the pace. In fact, she gave herself an awful lot to do and did well to finish a clear second. On this evidence she may be worth a try over 1m. (op 11-2 tchd 9-2)
Nawaashi was returning from three months off when scraping home from three subsequent winners in a Redcar maiden last month. Making her nursery debut, she was handy from the off but became outpaced on the home bend before running on again when switched to the wide outside. She still showed signs of greenness in the latter stages, so may yet be capable of better. (op 11-4 tchd 3-1)
Millies Folly had no chance in the Totepool Two-Year-Old Trophy last time, but was always close to the pace and had every chance here. She is still looking for her first win, however, and is starting to look exposed.
Bay Of Fires(IRE), a winner over C&D, finished less than a length behind First Class Favour back here earlier this month and enjoyed a 2lb pull, but she was beaten further this time having had every chance and may not have been at her best. (op 9-1 tchd 7-1)
Biaraafa(IRE), a disappointing favourite on soft ground at Newcastle last time, found very little off the bridle and her stamina for this longer trip remains questionable.
Cosmic Moon was reported to have stumbled on the bend and lost her action. Official explanation: jockey said filly stumbled on bend and lost its action (op 15-2 tchd 10-1)
Baileys Moneypenny Official explanation: jockey said filly had no more to give

6921 TOTETRIFECTA FLEXI BETTING H'CAP 1m 5f 175y
5:10 (5:12) (Class 6) (0-60,60) 3-Y-0+ **£1,942** (£578; £288; £144) **Stalls** Low

Form RPR

5002 **1** **Aaman (IRE)**[15] 6538 4-8-13 **54**....................................... RyanClark(7) 10 77
(E F Vaughan) *prom: led after 3f: clr over 6f out: shkn up 2f out and styd on strly: unchal* **6/1**[2]

5366 **2** *8* **Madamlily (IRE)**[28] 6187 4-9-7 **58**.............................. IanBrennan(3) 1 66
(J J Quinn) *in tch on inner: hdwy to chse ldrs over 3f out: rdn 2f out: n.m.r and swtchd rt over 1f out: drvn to chse wnr ins fnl f: no imp* **8/1**

-040 **3** *5* **Moonlight Blaze**[11] 6660 3-8-5 **48**.............................. RoystonFfrench 4 49
(C W Fairhurst) *prom: chsd wnr over 2f out: sn rdn and kpt on same pce* **25/1**

056 **4** *1 1/2* **Spahi (FR)**[161] 1925 4-9-7 **60**... JohnFahy(5) 3 59
(D O'Meara) *hld up towards rr: hdwy over 4f out: rdn to chse ldrs over 2f out: drvn over 1f out and kpt on same pce* **13/2**[3]

2304 **5** *1 1/4* **Tivers Song (USA)**[15] 6538 6-8-9 **46**....................(b) BarryMcHugh(3) 15 43
(John A Harris) *hld up towards rr: sme hdwy on outer 3f out: sn rdn and nvr nr ldrs* **16/1**

0336 **6** *2 1/2* **Aalya (IRE)**[12] 6623 3-9-2 **59**..................................... GregFairley 5 53
(P W Chapple-Hyam) *hld up: sme hdwy over 3f out: nvr a factor* **7/1**

2226 **7** *7* **Zefooha (FR)**[33] 6028 6-9-12 **60**............................(p) GrahamGibbons 7 43
(T D Walford) *led 3f: chsd wnr: rdn along 3f out: drvn over 2f out and sn wknd* **9/2**[1]

40-0 **8** *2 1/4* **Veronicas Boy**[18] 41 4-9-0 **48**..................................... PJMcDonald 12 28
(G M Moore) *towards rr and rdn along 1/2-way: nvr a factor* **20/1**

3035 **9** *3 1/2* **La Bacouetteuse (FR)**[20] 6397 5-9-4 **57**...................... LeeTopliss(5) 13 32
(A G Foster) *trckied ldrs: hdwy over 5f out: rdn wl over 2f out and sn wknd* **9/1**

0501 **10** *1/2* **Dream Risk (FR)**[13] 5203 4-9-4 **55**...........................(t) KellyHarrison(3) 8 29
(Mrs K Walton) *chsd ldrs: rdn along over 4f out: sn wknd* **17/2**

/126 **11** *1 3/4* **Dan's Heir**[68] 4900 8-9-3 **56**.......................................(p) DeanHeslop(5) 2 28
(W Storey) *midfield: rdn along over 5f out and sn outpcd* **10/1**

P0 **12** *18* **Treason Trial**[24] 4246 9-8-13 **50**........................... MichaelO'Connell(3) 14 —
(A Crook) *a in rr: bhd fnl 3f* **40/1**

600 **13** *7* **Penshurst Lad (IRE)**[35] 5971 3-8-7 **50**......................... HayleyTurner 6 —
(R T Phillips) *dwlt: a in rr: bhd fnl 3f* **33/1**

-300 **14** *30* **Frankie Falco**[175] 1520 4-8-13 **50**.......................... RussKennemore(3) 11 —
(G Fierro) *in tch: racd wd bk st: sn lost pl and bhd fnl 3f* **80/1**

3m 5.15s (1.55) **Going Correction** +0.175s/f (Good)
WFA 3 from 4yo+ 9lb **14** Ran SP% **120.1**
Speed ratings (Par 101): **102,97,94,93,93 91,87,86,84,84 83,72,68,51**
Tote Swingers: 1&2 £11.50, 1&3 £33.50, 2&3 £47.60 CSF £50.49 CT £1132.26 TOTE £5.70: £2.40, £1.90, £13.40; EX 54.20 Trifecta £289.50 Part won. Pool: £391.34 - 0.63 winning units..
Owner Mohammed Rashid **Bred** Darley **Trained** Newmarket, Suffolk

FOCUS
A moderate staying handicap and very few ever got into it. The winner was in the best place up front and is rated in line with his Polytrack form.
Dream Risk(FR) Official explanation: jockey said filly never travelled
Frankie Falco Official explanation: jockey said colt hung right throughout

6922 BET TOTEPOOL ON ALL UK RACING H'CAP (DIV II OF 2.50) 7f
5:45 (5:45) (Class 5) (0-75,73) 3-Y-0+ **£2,266** (£674; £337; £168) **Stalls** Low

Form RPR

0600 **1** **Trans Sonic**[8] 6724 7-8-9 **66**...(b) JohnFahy(5) 4 79
(D O'Meara) *sn chsng ldrs: led wl over 1f out: kpt on wl towards fin* **10/1**

0040 **2** *1* **Captain Macarry (IRE)**[56] 5287 5-9-0 **69**....................(v) IanBrennan(3) 6 79
(J J Quinn) *trckd ldrs: chal over 1f out: no ex clsng stages* **11/4**[2]

0124 **3** *5* **Ryedane (IRE)**[8] 6714 8-9-7 **73**...(b) DavidAllan 9 70
(T D Easterby) *chsd ldrs: styd far side in home st: kpt on same pce fnl 2f* **17/2**

0303 **4** *1* **Nuit Sombre (IRE)**[40] 5820 10-8-7 **62** ow2.......(p) MichaelO'Connell(3) 3 56
(G A Harker) *led tl wl over 1f out: kpt on one pce* **12/1**

6133 **5** *nk* **Eastern Hills**[12] 6633 5-8-2 **59** oh2.................................(p) NeilFarley(5) 1 52+
(A J McCabe) *stmbld s: detached in last 2: hdwy on outside 2f out: nvr nr ldrs* **2/1**[1]

0235 **6** *1/2* **Real Diamond**[16] 6494 4-8-5 **60** oh2 ow1.................... BarryMcHugh(3) 7 52
(Ollie Pears) *chsd ldrs: one pce fnl 2f* **8/1**[3]

1004 **7** *1 3/4* **Island Chief**[14] 6571 4-8-13 **72**.............................. DavidSimmonson(7) 8 59
(M W Easterby) *s.s: in rr: detached in last 2: styd far side initially in home st: edgd rt 2f out: kpt on: nvr nr ldrs* **25/1**

4000 **8** *3/4* **Tatiana Romanova (USA)**[20] 6395 3-8-6 **65**................ LeeTopliss(5) 11 50
(R A Fahey) *s.i.s: sn chsng ldrs on outside: reminders over 3f out: wknd over 1f out* **28/1**

3520 **9** *1 1/4* **Norville (IRE)**[12] 6633 3-9-1 **69**.................................. CathyGannon 10 51
(P D Evans) *prom: drvn and sltly outpcd over 3f out: wknd 2f out* **12/1**

0500 **10** *2 3/4* **The Hermitage (IRE)**[30] 6108 3-9-4 **72**.............................. GregFairley 2 46
(M Johnston) *in rr: styd far side in home st: bhd fnl 2f* **16/1**

1m 27.63s (0.63) **Going Correction** +0.175s/f (Good)
WFA 3 from 4yo+ 2lb **10** Ran SP% **119.3**
Speed ratings (Par 103): **103,101,96,95,94 94,92,91,89,86**
Tote Swingers: 1&2 £10.40, 1&3 £11.00, 2&3 £4.60 CSF £38.60 CT £253.26 TOTE £18.20: £5.10, £2.70, £1.10; EX 52.40 Place 6: £35.37 Place 5: £15.51..
Owner Mrs Lynne Lumley **Bred** I A Balding **Trained** Nawton, N Yorks

FOCUS
A messy race with several of the runners deciding to come up the centre of the track after turning in and the front pair pulled well clear. The winning time was 1.07 seconds slower than the first division. The race is rated around the runner-up to this year's form.
Eastern Hills Official explanation: trainer said gelding stumbled at start
T/Plt: £50.70 to a £1 stake. Pool:£41,784 - 600.58 winning tickets T/Qpdt: £19.40 to a £1 stake. Pool:£2,944 - 111.98 winning tickets JR

6882 NEWMARKET (Rowley Mile) (R-H)
Saturday, October 16

OFFICIAL GOING: Good to soft
Wind: medium, half behind Weather: bright spells, showers earlier

6923 VICTOR CHANDLER CHALLENGE STKS (GROUP 2) 7f
1:50 (1:51) (Class 1) 3-Y-O+
£51,093 (£19,368; £9,693; £4,833; £2,421; £1,215) **Stalls** Low

Form RPR

2053 **1** **Red Jazz (USA)**[21] 6350 3-9-1 120................................ RobertWinston 7 121
(B W Hills) *racd on stands' side: chsd ldrs: rdn to ld overall over 2f out: kpt on wl fnl firlong: forged clr fnl 150yds: rdn out* **5/1**[2]

0226 **2** *2 1/4* **Cat Junior (USA)**[35] 5946 5-9-3 113...............................(vt) RichardHills 10 116
(B J Meehan) *racd on stands' side: chsd ldrs: chsd ldng pair 2f out: drvn over 1f out: kpt on same pce ins fnl f: snatched 2nd on post* **14/1**

1042 **3** *nse* **Main Aim**[49] 5518 5-9-3 111..(v[1]) RyanMoore 3 116
(Sir Michael Stoute) *racd on stands' side: chsd overall ldr tl led 3f out: sn rdn and hdd: drvn over 1f out: no ex and btn ins fnl f: lost 2nd on post* **12/1**

35-1 **4** *1/2* **Delegator**[29] 6147 4-9-3 121.. FrankieDettori 11 115+
(Saeed Bin Suroor) *lw: racd in centre tl gps merged over 2f out: hld up towards rr: hdwy 1/2-way: chsng ldrs and rdn whn n.m.r over 1f out: styd on same pce u.p ins fnl f* **6/4**[1]

3013 **5** *3/4* **Mabait**[41] 5803 4-9-3 114... KierenFallon 1 112
(L M Cumani) *racd stands' side: in tch: effrt and rdn over 2f out: sn switching rt: drvn to chse ldrs over 1f out: one pce and no imp fnl f: n.m.r towards fin* **25/1**

0235 **6** *1/2* **High Standing (USA)**[35] 5946 5-9-3 109......................... JamieSpencer 2 111
(W J Haggas) *racd stands' side: stdd s: hld up in last trio: rdn and effrt ent fnl 2f: drvn and kpt on steadily fnl f: nvr gng pce to rch ldrs* **20/1**

6020 **7** *3/4* **Sir Gerry (USA)**[14] 6570 5-9-3 114.................................... GeorgeBaker 6 109
(C A Dwyer) *racd stands' side: stdd s: hld up in last trio: rdn and effrt ent fnl 2f: kpt on ins fnl f: nvr able to chal* **50/1**

0264 **8** *3 1/2* **Duff (IRE)**[35] 5946 7-9-3 110..(v[1]) PJSmullen 9 100
(Edward Lynam, Ire) *racd in centre tl gps merged over 2f out: overall ldr tl rdn and hdd 3f out: wknd u.p over 1f out* **20/1**

4334 **9** *3/4* **Himalya (IRE)**[20] 6390 4-9-3 111...................................... TomQueally 4 98
(J Noseda) *ponied to s: racd stands' side: awkward leaving stalls: in tch in midfield: rdn and effrt ent fnl 3f: no imp u.p over 1f out: wknd fnl f* **16/1**

3601 **10** *nse* **Harrison George (IRE)**[14] 6570 5-9-3 111........................ PaulHanagan 13 98
(R A Fahey) *racd in centre tl gps merged 2f out: in tch: rdn and effrt 2f out: hung rt u.p wl over 1f out: sn wknd* **33/1**

3562 **11** *nk* **Dream Eater (IRE)**[41] 5803 5-9-3 116...........................(t) JimmyFortune 5 97
(A M Balding) *racd stands' side: t.k.h: hld up in last trio: hdwy 1/2-way: rdn ent 2f out: no prog and btn over 1f out: wknd ins fnl f* **8/1**[3]

4432 **12** *5* **Blue Angel (IRE)**[21] 6351 3-8-12 102.................................(b) JMurtagh 8 79
(R Hannon) *racd in centre tl gps merged over 2f out: a bhd: rdn and struggling 1/2-way* **50/1**

6510 **13** *14* **Shakespearean (IRE)**[35] 5946 3-9-5 116........................(t) TedDurcan 14 48
(Saeed Bin Suroor) *racd in centre tl gps merged over 2f out: chsd ldrs tl rdn fnl 3f: wknd qckly ent fnl 2f: wl bhd and heavily eased ins fnl f* **18/1**

2525 **14** *3* **Golden Stream (IRE)**[63] 5081 4-9-0 103........................ WilliamBuick 12 34
(Sir Michael Stoute) *racd in centre tl gps merged over 2f out: in tch in midfield: rdn and struggling 1/2-way: wl bhd fnl 2f: heavily eased ins fnl f* **50/1**

1m 26.04s (0.64) **Going Correction** +0.30s/f (Good)
WFA 3 from 4yo+ 2lb **14** Ran SP% **115.5**
Speed ratings (Par 115): **108,105,105,104,103 103,102,98,97,97 97,91,75,72**
toteswingers:1&2:£9.20, 1&3:£6.90, 2&3:£12.40 CSF £63.60 TOTE £6.50: £2.40, £3.80, £2.20; EX 67.90 Trifecta £197.30 Pool: £2,939.59 - 11.02 winning units..
Owner R J Arculli **Bred** William F Murphy & Annabel Murphy **Trained** Lambourn, Berks
■ Stewards' Enquiry : Frankie Dettori caution: careless riding.

FOCUS
Following 2mm of rain overnight and another 2mm in the morning, the going was changed to good to soft. They were racing on fresh ground on the near-side track. They split into two groups and the advantage was very much with those who raced closest to the stands' side. The front three basically ran to from, the winner confirming his Queen Elizabeth Stakes improvement.

NOTEBOOK

Red Jazz(USA) boasted the best recent form, having finished a half-length third in the Queen Elizabeth II Stakes last time out. The drop in class, coupled with a return to the C&D over which he won the Free Handicap, did the trick and, having been up there from the start, he responded well to a strong drive to win by a clear margin, enhancing his trainer's record in the race (four winners in the last 11 years). It mattered not one bit that he got a little stirred up in the prelims, as he has done that in the past. He could go to Dubai in the spring and will be trained with the likes of the Lockinge and Queen Anne in mind for next season. (op 11-2, tchd 6-1 in places)

Cat Junior(USA), who raced towards the outer of the stands' side group, carried his head a little high under pressure but kept on reasonably well. Runner-up in this race two years ago, he repeated that feat, but he has only won one of his last 21 starts and remains quite a tricky ride.

Main Aim, visored for the first time, took full advantage of his low draw to make the running on the stands' side. He kept on quite well after being headed, improving a place on his fourth in this race last year, but having once looked likely to make up into a high-class performer, his level has very much plateaued now. (op 11-1 tchd 10-1)

Delegator made a pleasing reappearance at Newbury last month and was expected to have come on for that. Last year's Guineas runner-up found himself in the wrong group here, though, having been drawn in stall 11, and while he came through to do best of that bunch, he could never quite get competitive. Having had such a short campaign he could still go for the Breeders' Cup Mile, a race in which he was fifth last year. (tchd 7-4 in a place and 13-8 in places)

Mabait tracked Main Aim on the stands' side before being switched out wider to challenge. He put up a solid effort and had few excuses the way the race unfolded. (op 16-1)

High Standing(USA) kept on from the back of the field along the apparently favoured stands' rail, but never threatened the principals in a race in which the pace held up pretty well. He is still a fair guide to the level of the form, though. (op 16-1)

Sir Gerry(USA) could have done without the overnight and morning rain easing the ground. (op 33-1)

Duff(IRE) was another who probably found the ground softer than ideal, and in addition he raced in the centre group, away from the seemingly favoured stands' side. (tchd 25-1)

Himalya(IRE) is very difficult to win with, has had a long season and was not quite at his best. (op 18-1)

Harrison George(IRE) had conditions to suit but he is no more than a Listed-class horse, and this was a bit too competitive for him.

Dream Eater(IRE) had a decent enough pace to run off but proved disappointing, even allowing for his poor win record. Official explanation: jockey said horse was unsuited by the good to soft ground (op 12-1)

Blue Angel(IRE) Official explanation: jockey said filly was unsuited by the good to soft ground

6924 DUBAI DEWHURST STKS (GROUP 1) (ENTIRE COLTS & FILLIES) 7f

2:25 (2:26) (Class 1) 2-Y-O

£180,074 (£68,261; £34,162; £17,033; £8,532; £4,282) **Stalls** Low

Form					RPR
111	**1**		**Frankel**[21] 6347 2-9-1 123 (H R A Cecil) *lw: hmpd sn after s: t.k.h: hld up in last pair: smooth hdwy ent fnl 3f: shkn up to ld over 1f out: in command whn rn green and edging rt fnl f: pushed out: comf* **4/6**[1]	TomQueally 4	127+
	2	*2 1/4*	**Roderic O'Connor (IRE)**[112] 3469 2-9-1 0 (A P O'Brien, Ire) *str: led: rdn ent fnl 2f: hdd over 1f out: drvn and btn 1f out: no threat to wnr but kpt on for clr 2nd fnl f* **25/1**	JMurtagh 6	120
2225	**3**	*2 3/4*	**Glor Na Mara (IRE)**[35] 5975 2-9-1 0 (J S Bolger, Ire) *w'like: scope: str: n.m.r and hmpd sn after s: chsd ldng pair: rdn and effrt ent fnl 2f: outpcd u.p over 1f out: kpt on same pce after* **33/1**	KJManning 5	113
2113	**4**	*hd*	**Waiter's Dream**[35] 5943 2-9-1 109 (B J Meehan) *chsd ldr: pushed along and pressed ldr ent fnl 3f: drvn and unable qck over 2f out: outpcd and wl hld fr over 1f out* **50/1**	KierenFallon 1	112
111	**5**	*1 3/4*	**Dream Ahead (USA)**[15] 6531 2-9-1 128 (D M Simcock) *wnt rt and stdd s: t.k.h: hld up in last pair: swtchd rt and effrt over 2f out: rdn and hanging lft ent fnl 2f: no hdwy and wandered u.p over 1f out: sn wl btn* **5/2**[2]	WilliamBuick 2	108
11	**6**	*10*	**Saamidd**[35] 5943 2-9-1 115 (Saeed Bin Suroor) *hmpd s: t.k.h: hld up in midfield: rdn over 2f out: sn struggling: wl btn over 1f out: eased ins fnl f* **7/1**[3]	FrankieDettori 3	82

1m 25.73s (0.33) **Going Correction** +0.30s/f (Good) **6** Ran SP% **109.8**

Speed ratings (Par 109): **110,107,104,104,102 90**

toteswingers:1&2:£3.00, 1&3:£5.80, 2&3:£14.20 CSF £20.07 TOTE £1.50: £1.10, £7.40; EX 17.50.

Owner K Abdulla **Bred** Juddmonte Farms Ltd **Trained** Newmarket, Suffolk

FOCUS

The most eagerly awaited 2yo race for many years, featuring three unbeaten colts with sky-high reputations and the form in the book to back it up. As it turned out, two of the trio failed to turn up, but that should not detract too much from the winner, who confirmed he is as brilliant a juvenile as we have seen for many years. The runner-up set a reasonable pace and the time was 0.31sec quicker than the older horses in the Challenge Stakes. Frankel, up 4lb, now rates the joint-third best 2yo since RPRs began, behind only Arazi (134) and Celtic Swing (133). Dream Ahead was 17lb off his Middle Park figure.

NOTEBOOK

Frankel looked freakishly good in his wide-margin victories at Doncaster and in Ascot's Royal Lodge Stakes, and his work on the gallops since had been spectacular, but this was his first tilt at Group 1 company and much his stiffest task to date. He was calm in the preliminaries and went to post better than at Ascot, but was keen early on at the rear of the field after a bump leaving the stalls set him alight. Improving quickly down the outside at halfway, reminiscent of his mid-race move in the Royal Lodge, he swept past the runner-up and only had to be pushed out for a very comfortable success, Tom Queally not needing to use his stick on him. Henry Cecil's first Dewhurst winner since Diesis in 1982, he is now a short price for the 2,000 Guineas and Cecil mentioned the St James's Palace Stakes too, appearing to rule out the Derby at this stage, although the colt promises to stay at least 1m2f further down the line. While the below-par efforts of his chief opponents hold down the form of this victory, he is a special prospect and, at this stage, it is hard to see anything derailing him in the Guineas, providing he comes through the winter in good nick. He is likely to have a prep race, perhaps in the Greenham. Faster ground is unlikely to prove a problem for him. (op 4-5, tchd 5-6 in a place)

Roderic O'Connor(IRE) was the only representative of a stable that had three of the first four home 12 months ago, inlcuding winner Beethoven, but Ballydoyle have not sent out a 2yo winner in Britain this year. He had not been seen since taking a Curragh maiden on Irish Derby day in late June, when he enjoyed a very easy lead, and he showed bare form a long way removed from the level attained by the big three here. Smartly away to get over and claim the stands' rail, which had looked very much the place to be in the opener, he dictated the pace. He could do nothing to repel the favourite but maintained the gallop to hold a clear second. Perhaps he is a shade flattered by this, in that he enjoyed the run of the race, but he is undoubtedly a high-class colt and a nice middle-distance prospect for next year. In the meantime, connections are not ruling out another run this season. (op 22-1 tchd 28-1 and 33-1 in a place)

Glor Na Mara(IRE), whose stable won this three years running from 2006 to 2008, most notably with Derby/Champion Stakes victor New Approach, remains a high-class maiden but has now been placed four times in Group company, with his second to Zoffany in the Phoenix Stakes at this level the pick of his previous efforts. He was below par in soft ground in the National Stakes last time but bounced back with this solid run and is a decent guide to the strength of the form. His trainer believes he won't get beyond a mile next year. (op 40-1)

Waiter's Dream was found wanting behind Saamidd at Doncaster and faced a stiff task in this company. He tracked the pace and had no obvious excuse, but this honest effort underlines that he is a smart colt who should pay his way when avoiding the biggest guns next season. (op 66-1, tchd 100-1 in a place)

Dream Ahead(USA), whose superb nine-length demolition of his Middle Park rivals came on an easy surface, appeared to have his ground, but William Buick reported afterwards that his mount had found conditions too loose this time. Attempting his third Group 1 victory, having landed Deauville's Prix Morny, the colt was top-rated to the tune of 5lb by the BHA and by 2lb on RPRs, and officially put up the best performance in the Middle Park for two decades. After diving right leaving the stalls he was held up in rear, a little keen early, and attempted to follow Frankel down the outside when the winner made his forward move. The response was not there and he showed signs of wanting to hang when brought under pressure, although there was no repeat of the left-hand drift he showed in the Middle Park and on his debut at Nottingham. More than one respected paddock watcher thought that the colt had run up a little light, and while his connections deserve every credit for not ducking a showdown with Frankel, this perhaps came too soon for him. It might also be noted that his Middle Park victory came on a day when winning margins were exaggerated because of the ground. The 7f trip was not a problem but he is yet to tackle fast ground, which is likely to prevail on 2,000 Guineas day. He'll head straight to Newmarket. Official explanation: trainer had no explanation for the poor form shown (tchd 11-4)

Saamidd, a very easy winner of Doncaster's Champagne Stakes, was supplemented for this at a fee of £20,000 but did not give connections a run for their money. After showing reluctance to enter the stalls, he failed to pick up at all when shaken up and was eased right down from the furlong pole, finishing a long way behind Waiter's Dream, whom he had beaten at Doncaster. Connections blamed the ground and the aim remains the 2,000 Guineas for a colt they regard as likely to make a better 3-y-o. Official explanation: jockey said colt was unsuited by the good to soft ground (op 13-2)

6925 EMIRATES AIRLINE CHAMPION STKS (GROUP 1) 1m 2f

3:00 (3:07) (Class 1) 3-Y-O+

£213,739 (£81,022; £40,549; £20,218; £10,127; £5,082) **Stalls** Low

Form					RPR
2123	**1**		**Twice Over**[42] 5775 5-9-3 125 (H R A Cecil) *lw: t.k.h: chsd ldrs after 2f: rdn to ld 2f out: clr and edgd rt 1f out: styd on wl: rdn out* **7/2**[2]	TomQueally 7	126
1-01	**2**	*1 3/4*	**Vision D'Etat (FR)**[63] 5107 5-9-3 117 (E Libaud, France) *stdd after s: t.k.h: hld up in midfield: hmpd after 1f: rdn and effrt 3f out: drvn to chse clr wnr ent fnl f: kpt on wl but nvr gng to rch wnr* **3/1**[1]	OlivierPeslier 6	123
1041	**3**	*3/4*	**Debussy (IRE)**[56] 5321 4-9-3 120 (J H M Gosden) *lw: led and set stdy gallop: rdn and qcknd ent fnl 3f: hdd 2f out: sn drvn: kpt on same pce fr over 1f out* **10/1**	WilliamBuick 4	121
-161	**4**	*3/4*	**Gitano Hernando**[15] 6548 4-9-3 117 (M Botti) *lw: broke wl: t.k.h: grad stdd bk and hld up in midfield: rdn and effrt 3f out: switching rt and drvn over 1f out: kpt on ins fnl f: nt pce to rch ldrs* **15/2**	KierenFallon 2	120+
1122	**5**	*3/4*	**Wigmore Hall (IRE)**[38] 5853 3-8-12 112 (M L W Bell) *stdd s: hld up in tch in last tio: hdwy and swtchd rt over 2f out: kpt on same pce u.p fr over 1f out* **16/1**	JamieSpencer 3	118
-136	**6**	*1*	**Glass Harmonium (IRE)**[122] 3068 4-9-3 115 (Sir Michael Stoute) *stdd s: t.k.h and sn trcking ldrs: rdn 3f out: nt pce of ldrs and drvn 2f out: wknd u.p over 1f out* **14/1**	RyanMoore 8	116
1141	**7**	*3/4*	**Fuisse (FR)**[41] 5801 4-9-3 120 (Mme C Head-Maarek, France) *w'like: stdd s: hld up in rr: rdn over 3f out: no prog tl kpt on fnl f: nvr trbld ldrs* **6/1**[3]	(t) StephanePasquier 11	115
0222	**8**	*2 1/4*	**Sri Putra**[41] 5804 4-9-3 117 (M A Jarvis) *lw: stdd s: plld hrd: hld up wl in tch in midfield: rdn and outpcd 3f out: plugged on same pce and n.d fnl 2f* **25/1**	(b[1]) PhilipRobinson 9	110
0211	**9**	*3*	**Poet's Voice**[21] 6350 3-8-12 122 (Saeed Bin Suroor) *lw: plld hrd: chsd ldr for 2f: styd trcking ldrs: swtchd rt and rdn wl over 2f out: wknd over 1f out* **6/1**[3]	(t) FrankieDettori 5	104
46-4	**10**	*19*	**Alwaary (USA)**[15] 6533 4-9-3 109 (J H M Gosden) *in tch in rr: rdn and btn over 2f out: wl bhd and eased ins fnl f* **33/1**	RichardHills 1	66

2m 8.54s (2.74) **Going Correction** +0.30s/f (Good)

WFA 3 from 4yo+ 5lb **10** Ran SP% **116.0**

Speed ratings (Par 117): **101,99,99,98,97 97,96,94,92,77**

toteswingers:1&2:£2.70, 1&3:£9.50, 2&3:£8.40 CSF £14.34 CT £94.87 TOTE £4.50: £1.50, £1.20, £4.30; EX 14.20 Trifecta £102.70 Pool: £17,816.11 - 128.34 winning units..

Owner K Abdulla **Bred** Juddmonte Farms Ltd **Trained** Newmarket, Suffolk

■ Twice Over joins a select group headed by Brigadier Gerard following back-to-back wins here.

FOCUS

The final running of the Champion Stakes on the Rowley Mile before its move to Ascot as part of a revamped Champions Day in 2011, and a competitive heat, featuring six individual Group or Grade 1 winners. It proved a tactical race and very few got into it from off the pace. It was a bit of a muddling race though the form makes sense at face value. The winner is rated 3lb better than last year's mark in this race.

NOTEBOOK

Twice Over has tended to be found out in the very top company over the years, but he is a solid, consistent Group 1 performer and, back at his favourite track, he repeated last year's success in this race, in no small part due to a fine ride from Tom Queally, who made sure his mount was prominently placed in what soon became clear would be a steadily run race. Tracking the leader one off the rail, he settled better than many of his rivals and, when the pace finally lifted approaching the 3f pole, he was in prime position to take over and force the others to play catch-up. The climb from the Dip here has always seemed to suit and he took his course record to five wins from seven starts. Another tilt at the Dubai World Cup beckons in the spring. (op 9-2)

Vision D'Etat(FR), who one might have expected to be familiar enough with steadily run races, given that he's trained in France, still raced keenly and threw his head around off the pedestrian gallop he encountered here, having also been free to post. Tracking Twice Over, who got first run on him, he had his chance, but the Cecil horse had more in reserve and pulled away in the closing stages. A top performer over this distance, he is fresher than most at this time of year having got jarred up in Dubai in the spring and missed most of the campaign. He could well appreciate a return to a turning track, and it is easy to see him going back to Hong Kong and repeating last year's success in the Cup. (tchd 5-2 and 10-3)

Debussy(IRE) is another who has shown his best form on a turning track, but he could not help but run well here given what an easy lead he was handed. Left alone in front and with the stands' rail to help, he took full advantage, setting a steady gallop before beginning a sprint for home approaching the 3f marker. He could not hold off a couple of high-class rivals, but third place was well deserved for the ride alone, and he is another who now has the Breeders' Cup Turf on his agenda. (op 12-1 tchd 8-1)

Gitano Hernando, who returned from a setback in the spring to win at Dundalk last time out, is much better known as an all-weather performer, but he does act on turf and this was a solid effort considering the race was not run to suit and he did not get the clearest of runs either. He remains a possible for the Breeders' Cup, where he could run in the Classic or the Turf, and one would imagine that once again he will be prepared for the Dubai World Cup in the spring, a race in which he was sent off favourite this year. (op 8-1 tchd 7-1)

Wigmore Hall(IRE), a consistent sort who tends to travel well in his races and is suited by a strong pace to run off, did not exactly have things pan out to his liking, but he kept on quite well to post a solid effort on this rise in class. (tchd 18-1)
Glass Harmonium(IRE) had been off the track since finding the ground too quick at Royal Ascot, but he has won when fresh before, so that was not such a concern. He still had to prove he was up to this level, though, and this race did not really answer the question, as he got little cover towards the outside of the pack and consequently raced far too keenly in what was a steadily run affair. (tchd 16-1)
Fuisse(FR), who was ponied to the start, was trying a trip this far for the first time since finishing runner-up in last year's Prix du Jockey Club. Held up at the back of the field, he could not make up any ground when the principals quickened and, while the race was not run to suit, he did not prove his stamina. He now retires to stud. (op 7-1 tchd 15-2)
Sri Putra, whose best form is on a sounder surface, saw too much daylight and did not settle on the outside. His rider later confirmed that the colt was unsuited by the ground. Official explanation: jockey said colt was unsuited by the good to soft ground (op 22-1)
Poet's Voice was something of a tearaway earlier in his career and his connections even toyed with going sprinting (he ran in the Middle Park on his final start last year), but they finally got him to settle this summer, which resulted in wins in the Celebration Mile and Queen Elizabeth II Stakes. This step up in distance was an experiment, but it went horribly wrong as, predictably off the steady early gallop, he pulled really hard and gave himself no chance of seeing out the race. Official explanation: jockey said colt ran too freely (op 5-1 tchd 13-2)
Alwaary(USA) ran well in the King George last year and is clearly still quite highly regarded at home. Too free on his reappearance in a Listed race here at the last meeting, he was expected to have come on for that, but in the event failed to pick up. He probably needs better ground to show his best anyway. (tchd 50-1 in a place)

6926 TOTESPORT.COM CESAREWITCH (HERITAGE H'CAP) 2m 2f
3:40 (3:46) (Class 2) 3-Y-0+

£99,696 (£29,856; £14,928; £7,472; £3,728; £1,872) **Stalls** Centre

Form				RPR
0203	1		**Aaim To Prosper (IRE)**[21] 6352 6-7-13 **87**. Louis-PhilippeBeuzelin(3) 30 (B J Meehan) *hld up in midfield: hdwy to chse ldrs 6f out: rdn to ld wl over 3f out: clr wl over 1f out: pressed ins fnl f: hld on wl* **16/1**	95+
1603	2	nk	**La Vecchia Scuola (IRE)**[16] 6493 6-8-9 **94**. WilliamBuick 16 (J S Goldie) *hld up in rr: hdwy on outer 3f out: rdn to chse clr wnr jst over 1f out: str run u.p to chal ins fnl f: jst hld nr fin* **33/1**	102
2320	3	1 ¾	**Plymouth Rock (IRE)**[36] 5908 4-8-8 **93**. (v) DarryllHolland 13 (J Noseda) *t.k.h: hld up in rr: hdwy on far rail 4f out: nt clr run and switching lft fr over 2f out: stl plenty to do and hdwy on outer over 1f out: edging lft but r.o strly fnl f: nt rch ldrs* **50/1**	99+
4633	4	1	**Ocean's Minstrel**[28] 6201 4-7-13 **87**. MartinLane(3) 17 (J Ryan) *lw: hld up towards rr: hdwy on far rail whn nt clr run 4f out tl 3f out: switching lft after: stl plenty to do over 1f out: str run fnl f: wnt 4th nr fin: unable to rch ldrs* **14/1**	92+
3500	5	½	**Palomar (USA)**[21] 5790 8-7-13 **84** oh6 ow1. JimmyQuinn 28 (B Ellison) *t.k.h: hld up in rr: hdwy over 4f out: nt clr run and swtchd lft over 3f out: nt clr run again 2f out tl swtchd rt and hdwy over 1f out: kpt on fnl f: unable to rch ldrs* **28/1**	88+
0/63	6	¾	**Sentry Duty (FR)**[81] 4461 8-9-3 **102**. OlivierPeslier 26 (N J Henderson) *hld up in rr: swtchd lft to outer and n.m.r over 4f out: nt clr run 3f out tl rdn and hdwy 2f out: edging rt and kpt on fr over 1f out: nvr able to rch ldrs* **9/1**[3]	106
0236	7	2	**Dazzling Light (UAE)**[28] 6181 5-7-5 **83** oh3. HarryBentley(7) 31 (J S Goldie) *hld up towards rr: hdwy over 5f out: prom in gp chsng clr wnr and edgd rt u.p 2f out: plugged on same pce fr over 1f out* **80/1**	84
2251	8	shd	**My Arch**[70] 4846 8-8-4 **89**. FrannyNorton 25 (Ollie Pears) *lw: in tch in midfield: n.m.r over 5f out: rdn and effrt 4f out: edging rt u.p ent fnl 2f: styd on same pce fr over 1f out* **12/1**	90
4222	9	½	**Red Cadeaux**[28] 6201 4-8-10 **95**. (b¹) JMurtagh 5 (E A L Dunlop) *hld up in rr: hdwy over 4f out: rdn to chse clr ldr 2f out tl over 1f out: 3rd and btn 1f out: wknd ins fnl f* **8/1**[2]	96+
5303	10	4	**Swingkeel (IRE)**[44] 5696 5-8-13 **98**. (p) JimmyFortune 20 (J L Dunlop) *lw: hld up towards rr: hdwy 5f out: nt clr run over 2f out tl swtchd rt over 1f out: rdn and plugged on fnl f: nvr trbld ldrs* **33/1**	94
5001	11	1 ¼	**Hawk Mountain (UAE)**[57] 5278 5-8-0 **85**. SilvestreDeSousa 19 (J J Quinn) *t.k.h: in tch: n.m.r and shuffled bk over 5f out: rallied and hdwy to chse ldrs and hung rt u.p 2f out: wknd qckly wl over 1f out* **25/1**	80
3114	12	3	**Simonside**[28] 6201 7-7-5 **79** 4ex oh4. NoelGarbutt(7) 15 (B Ellison) *t.k.h: hld up towards rr: hdwy over 5f out: rdn and hanging rt ent fnl 2f: no prog fr wl over 1f out* **50/1**	75
2003	13	2	**Dazinski**[19] 6423 4-8-2 **87**. NickyMackay 8 (M H Tompkins) *hld up towards reer: hdwy 8f out: rdn over 3f out: drvn and wknd ent fnl 2f* **100/1**	76
1530	14	½	**Deauville Flyer**[57] 5278 4-8-8 **93**. KierenFallon 22 (T D Easterby) *chsd ldrs: rdn 3f out: wknd ent fnl 2f: eased whn wl btn ins fnl f* **12/1**	82
1620	15	¾	**Rangefinder**[21] 6362 6-8-7 **92**. StevieDonohoe 21 (Jane Chapple-Hyam) *in tch in midfield: rdn and struggling 4f out: wl btn whn hung lft ent fnl 2f* **50/1**	80
0651	16	2 ¾	**Precision Break (USA)**[36] 5908 5-8-12 **97** 4ex. (t) JamieSpencer 29 (P F I Cole) *lw: chsd ldrs: rdn and short of room 6f out: lost pl 4f out: wl btn over 2f out* **16/1**	82
56-0	17	shd	**Kayf Aramis**[28] 6201 8-7-12 **83**. DavidProbert 11 (N A Twiston-Davies) *in tch: hdwy to chse ldrs 10f out: rdn and struggling 6f out: wknd over 3f out: no ch fnl 2f: eased ent fnl f* **14/1**	68
1031	18	nk	**Act Of Kalanisi (IRE)**[7] 6750 4-7-12 **80** 7ex. AndreaAtzeni 18 (M Johnston) *sn chsng ldr: led 6f out tl rdn and hdd wl over 3f out: wknd over 2f out: eased fnl f* **33/1**	68
1402	19	2 ½	**Cotillion**[30] 6131 4-8-2 **87**. JoeFanning 2 (Ian Williams) *hld up towards rr: hdwy 8f out: rdn to chse wnr 3f out tl wl over 1f out: sn wknd* **50/1**	69
01/4	20	2 ½	**Majestic Concorde (IRE)**[80] 1821 7-9-2 **101**. PJSmullen 9 (D K Weld, Ire) *hld up towards rr: rdn and struggling 5f out: wl bhd over 2f out: nvr trbld ldrs* **16/1**	80
3611	21	hd	**Royal Trooper (IRE)**[16] 6516 4-7-10 **81** 7ex ow1. JamesSullivan(3) 14 (J G Given) *in tch: n.m.r and travelling wl 6f out: hdwy to chse ldrs ent fnl 3f: wknd and hung rt u.p 2f out: eased fnl f* **66/1**	63
	22	6	**Universal Truth (IRE)**[81] 5533 5-7-9 **87** ow1. (v¹) LFRoche(7) 32 (D K Weld, Ire) *t.k.h: hld up in tch on rail: rdn and effrt 3f out: wknd 2f out: eased fr over 1f out* **15/2**[1]	59
3111	23	nk	**Lang Shining (IRE)**[17] 6450 6-8-0 **88** 7ex. SophieDoyle(3) 24 (J A Osborne) *lw: in tch: rdn and struggling 6f out: lost pl over 3f out: no ch fr over 2f out* **100/1**	60
4330	24	shd	**Dayia (IRE)**[36] 5909 6-8-3 **91**. SimonPearce(3) 27 (J Pearce) *chsd ldrs: rdn and hung rt ent 4f out: wknd wl over 2f out: eased ins fnl f* **16/1**	63
5061	25	17	**Ajaan**[12] 6621 6-9-5 **104** 4ex. TomQueally 4 (H R A Cecil) *hld up towards rr: rdn and no prog ent fnl 4f: t.o and eased ins fnl f* **33/1**	57
-122	26	nse	**Gala Evening**[154] 2126 8-8-13 **98**. AdamKirby 10 (J A B Old) *lw: ld up towards rr: rdn and struggling over 3f out: wl btn 2f out: eased ins fnl f: t.o* **40/1**	51
	27	17	**Admiral Barry (IRE)**[35] 5977 5-8-9 **94** 4ex. CDHayes 7 (Eoin Griffin, Ire) *lw: in tch: hdwy 7f out: swtchd lft and rdn over 3f out: sn struggling: wl btn fnl 2f: eased ins fnl f: t.o* **14/1**	28
/512	28	7	**Bergo (GER)**[49] 5517 7-9-10 **109**. RyanMoore 6 (G L Moore) *racd wd tl 10f out: a towards rr: struggling 5f out: lost tch 4f out: t.o and eased ins fnl f* **33/1**	36
1002	29	4 ½	**Arab League (IRE)**[16] 6516 5-7-12 **86** oh3 ow3. AndrewHeffernan(3) 1 (R J Price) *t.k.h: in tch: hdwy to chse ldrs 8f out: lost pl u.p 6f out: wl bhd fnl 3f: t.o and eased ins fnl f* **100/1**	—
0010	30	3 ½	**Cosmic Sun**[16] 6493 4-8-2 **87** 4ex. (p) PaulHanagan 23 (R A Fahey) *sn led: hdd 10f out: wknd qckly 4f out: wl bhd fnl 2f: eased fnl f: t.o* **40/1**	—
20	31	17	**Swinging Hawk (GER)**[106] 3634 4-8-3 **88**. LiamJones 12 (Ian Williams) *chsd ldrs tl led 10f out tl 6f out: wknd quickly 4f out: t.o and eased fnl f* **40/1**	—
-000	32	4 ½	**Noddies Way**[3] 6855 7-7-10 **84** oh29 ow1. (p) NataliaGemelova(3) 3 (J F Panvert) *racd wd tl 10f out: a bhd: lost tch 7f out: t.o fnl 5f* **200/1**	—

3m 59.1s (2.30) **Going Correction** +0.30s/f (Good) **32** Ran SP% **135.1**
Speed ratings (Par 109): **106,105,105,104,104 104,103,103,102,101 100,99,98,98,97 96,96,96,95,94 94,91,91,91,83 83,76,7**
toteswingers:1&2:£496.30, 1&3:£386.00, 2&3:£589.60 CSF £498.61 CT £22643.50 TOTE £19.10: £4.40, £9.90, £14.10, £4.90; EX 882.40 Trifecta £18984.20 Part won. Pool: £25,654.44 - 0.10 winning units..
Owner CGA Racing Partnership 2 **Bred** Stephanie Hanly **Trained** Manton, Wilts

FOCUS
A typically competitive renewal of this historic handicap, which provided a thorough test of stamina. The 3-y-o Darley Sun won 12 months ago, but there were no members of the younger generation in the line-up this year. The winner was never far from the pace but most of those who chased him home came from the rear, and there were some hard-luck stories. Once more a high draw proved beneficial in the Cesarewitch. The third and fourth are rated at face value despite having to weave through.

NOTEBOOK
Aaim To Prosper(IRE), who came out of stall 30, became the seventh winner in the last ten years to be drawn 25 or higher. He could not hold his initial very prominent pitch but was still well enough placed and, after kicking clear plenty soon enough, he held on well when the mare came at him. He had been seventh in this last year, when racing a little keenly in first-time blinkers, and was racing off a mark 2lb higher after some solid efforts in marathon handicaps this season.
La Vecchia Scuola(IRE) travelled well in rear before closing to go after the winner but, having reached his quarters, she could not get by. This was a brave effort from a versatile mare and it cannot be said that she did not stay. She could drop back to 1m4f for the November Handicap at Doncaster. (tchd 40-1 in a place)
Plymouth Rock(IRE) was arguably an unlucky loser. He was tucked away at the back and his rider's attempts at a forward move on the inside were thwarted repeatedly. Eventually switched for a run, at a point when the winner had already kicked for home, he finished fast down the outside. He is a frustrating animal, a beaten favourite four times this year, but is capable when things go his way and he got the longer trip well. (tchd 100-1 in a place)
Ocean's Minstrel had finished well in third in the Cesarewitch Trial here last month and again came home strongly, having been looking for room in a similar position to Plymouth Rock at a crucial stage. He will have a break now before going hurdling and is likely to do well at that game. (op 16-1)
Palomar(USA), who won a valuable handicap hurdle last time, was well drawn and was another finishing well from the back after meeting trouble. This was a fine effort from effectively 9lb out of the weights. (op 25-1)
Sentry Duty(FR), whose trainer won this in 2003 and 2008, became his only runner after Ghimaar met with a setback. Given a break since finishing third at Glorious Goodwood, he ran a sound race with no real excuses. (op 8-1 tchd 10-1)
Dazzling Light(UAE), a stablemate of the runner-up, was favourably drawn and she ran a solid race from 3lb out of the weights over this longer trip. (op 66-1)
My Arch, kept for this after winning over 2m on the July course in August, ran respectably without landing a serious blow.
Red Cadeaux, runner-up to Theola (an absentee due to injury here) in the trial for this last month, was able to race off 3lb lower here. Blinkered for the first time, he ran well out of stall 5 but faded inside the last after looking set to make the frame. (op 12-1)
Swingkeel(IRE) Official explanation: jockey said gelding suffered interference in running
Hawk Mountain(UAE), 3lb badly in under the penalty he picked up at the Ebor meeting, ran an honest race but did not quite see out this trip in the ground.
Deauville Flyer ◆ showed up well for a long way but was another whose stamina was failing him late on. There should be a decent handicap in him next season.
Cotillion, who was 3lb ahead of the handicapper, was another to run well before fading. (tchd 100-1 in a place)
Majestic Concorde(IRE), who ran well over fences in the Galway Plate last time, was never really in the hunt from an unfavourable draw. (op 20-1)
Universal Truth(IRE), winner of a maiden hurdle at Galway last time, was well drawn and had the assistance of a first-time visor, but was rather keen early on and did not get home. It emerged that he picked up an injury, probably a sress fracture to his pelvis, and he will be sidelined for six months. Official explanation: jockey said gelding ran too free (op 8-1)
Admiral Barry(IRE), a long-time ante-post fancy, was officially 5lb well in, but he was unlucky with the draw and his chance had gone with 3f to run.
Swinging Hawk(GER) Official explanation: jockey said colt ran too keen

6927 ROCKFEL STKS (GROUP 2) (FILLIES) 7f
4:15 (4:18) (Class 1) 2-Y-0

£56,770 (£21,520; £10,770; £5,370; £2,690; £1,350) **Stalls** Low

Form				RPR
313	1		**Cape Dollar (IRE)**[49] 5519 2-8-12 98. RyanMoore 8 (Sir Michael Stoute) *hld up in tch: rdn and hdwy wl over 2f out: drvn to chse ldr wl over 1f out: edging rt u.p and ld ins fnl f: hld on wl: all out* **7/2**[2]	104
1226	2	½	**Cochabamba (IRE)**[15] 6528 2-8-12 99. JackMitchell 12 (R A Teal) *stdd s: hld up in tch in last trio: swtchd rt and effrt jst over 2f out: chsd ldng trio over 1f out: drvn and ev ch ins fnl f: kpt on wl: a jst hld* **12/1**	103
15	3	hd	**I Love Me**[14] 6559 2-8-12 95. JimmyFortune 5 (A M Balding) *lengthy: lw: t.k.h: chsd ldr: rdn to ld ent fnl 2f: sn edgd lft: drvn and edgd rt fr over 1f out: hdd ins fnl f: kpt on but a hld after* **9/4**[1]	102
4	4	3	**Nabah**[5] 6796 2-8-12 0. TomQueally 7 (C E Brittain) *leggy: stdd s: hld up in tch in last trio: nt clr run 3f out tl over 2f out: hdwy and rn green over 1f out: kpt on to go 4th ins fnl f: nvr able to chal ldrs* **22/1**	95+

The Form Book, Raceform Ltd, Compton, RG20 6NL

16 **5** ½ **Date With Destiny (IRE)**[49] 5519 2-8-12 93........................ JMurtagh 6 93
(R Hannon) *lengthy: t.k.h: hld up in tch: rdn and effrt 3f out: sn edgd rt u.p and outpcd over 2f out: no ch w ldng trio and kpt on same pce fr over 1f out* **11/1**

3 **6** 1 ¼ **Hurricane Havoc (IRE)**[6] 6784 2-8-12 0........................... KJManning 2 90
(J S Bolger, Ire) *str: hld up wl in tch: rdn and effrt whn n.m.r 2f out: drvn and outpcd by ldng trio wl over 1f out: wl hld fnl f* **11/1**

040 **7** ¾ **Sonning Rose (IRE)**[20] 6401 2-8-12 97............................... NeilCallan 3 88
(M R Channon) *bmpd s: sn in tch: rdn and lost pl jst over 2f out: no threat to ldrs and styd on same pce u.p fr over 1f out* **25/1**

21 **8** 9 **Submission**[26] 6248 2-8-12 79... KierenFallon 1 64
(L M Cumani) *w'like: t.k.h: chsd ldrs: nt clr run and shuffled bk to last over 1f out: wl bhd and no ch whn swtchd rt jst over 1f out: nvr able to rcvr* **14/1**

01 **9** ¾ **Shim Sham (IRE)**[44] 5692 2-8-12 0................................. WilliamBuick 4 63
(B J Meehan) *wnt lft s: racd keenly: led tl hdd ent fnl 2f: sn rdn and lost pl: wl btn over 1f out: eased ins fnl f* **11/1**

21 **10** 1 ¼ **Abtasaamah (USA)**[11] 6658 2-8-12 85......................... FrankieDettori 9 59
(Saeed Bin Suroor) *athletic: chsd ldrs: rdn and unable qck over 2f out: wknd qckly u.p over 1f out: eased ins fnl f* **5/1**[3]

1m 26.91s (1.51) **Going Correction** +0.30s/f (Good) **10** Ran SP% **117.2**
Speed ratings (Par 104): **103,102,102,98,98 96,95,85,84,83**
toteswingers:1&2:£9.80, 1&3:£2.80, 2&3:£9.40 CSF £45.42 TOTE £3.90: £1.50, £3.90, £1.60; EX 42.80 Trifecta £75.30 Pool: £2,074.88 - 20.37 winning units..
Owner Saeed Suhail **Bred** Rabbah Bloodstock Limited **Trained** Newmarket, Suffolk

FOCUS
A Group 2 that has, in recent years, built up a really good record of throwing up serious 1,000 Guineas candidates, and, while this did not look a special race on paper, the first fillies' Classic has an open look to it and one of the three who came clear here might yet develop into a player over the winter. The winning time was a respectable - 1.18sec slower than the Dewhurst.

NOTEBOOK
Cape Dollar(IRE) ◆ finished one place behind Cochabamba when the pair were placed behind Theyskens' Theory in the Prestige Stakes, but both raced keenly that day in a race dominated by the winner from the front, and the more solid gallop they got to run off here suited them better. The winner, who was stuck on the outside of the pack most of the way, came under pressure with 2f to run but kept responding, especially after hitting the rising ground, and was always just doing enough in the closing stages. A daughter of Cape Cross out of a Kingmambo mare, it will be a big surprise if she does not improve plenty for a return to quick ground, while she will get a mile easily, and probably stay further than that in time. She was dismissed as a 50-1 shot for the Guineas by Stan James afterwards, which might be a mistake. (op 5-1 tchd 11-2 in places)
Cochabamba(IRE) was disappointing in the Oh So Sharp Stakes over this C&D last time, but the ground was softer that day (almost 2sec slower winning time) and she returned to form here. Despite bagging the worst draw and being held up in last, she picked up well to fight out the finish, and she looks to have every chance of progressing into a smart 3-y-o.
I Love Me ◆, who took a valuable sales race on her debut and ran a blinder from a poor draw here at the last meeting, was never far off the pace and was last off the bridle. She was run down by two rivals who were more patiently ridden in the closing stages, but it was still a great effort and, given her pedigree, she is another likely to be seen in an even better light on quicker ground. A mile will suit her next year and it won't be a surprise at all to see her turn out for the Guineas in the spring. (op 3-1 tchd 7-2 in a place)
Nabah ◆ ran with promise on her debut in a 6f Polytrack maiden just six days earlier and, while this was a huge step up in class, her trainer has never been one to worry about that sort of thing. Still a bit green, she was continually denied a clear run until inside the last, at which point she stayed on really well. This was an eyecatching effort, the extra furlong suited her - as one would expect given her pedigree - and she can surely only improve further. (op 40-1)
Date With Destiny(IRE) could not handle the soft ground in the Prestige Stakes and no doubt found these conditions less than ideal too. Having raced keenly, she dropped back to the rear of the field before running on again late, and is another capable of better next year given quick ground. (op 9-1)
Hurricane Havoc(IRE), third in a Listed race over 1m at the Curragh six days earlier, could not go with the principals when the pace quickened. (tchd 12-1)
Sonning Rose(IRE), the most experienced filly in the line-up, has shown all her best form on good ground or faster. (op 20-1)
Submission, whose pedigree suggests she will be wanting middle distances next season, tracked the leader on the stands' side but was far too keen and, after the gaps did not open for her and she was squeezed out, she wasn't beaten up in a lost cause. Official explanation: jockey said filly lost its action going into the dip (op 10-1)
Shim Sham(IRE) is a sister to Decado, who enjoyed some cut in the ground, but she did too much in front here and was beaten with 2f to run. (op 8-1)
Abtasaamah(USA), easy winner of a Fibresand maiden last time out, got unbalanced and was eased in the closing stages. She can leave this form behind in time. (tchd 9-2)

6928 PRIDE STKS (GROUP 2) (F&M) 1m 4f
4:50 (4:52) (Class 1) 3-Y-O+

£51,093 (£19,368; £9,693; £4,833; £2,421; £1,215) **Stalls** Centre

Form RPR

152- **1** **Crystal Capella**[364] 6853 5-9-3 114.................................. RyanMoore 12 120
(Sir Michael Stoute) *lw: hld up in tch in midfield: rdn and hdwy 3f out: drvn to chse ldr ent fnl 2f: led over 1f out: clr 1f out: edgd rt u.p but r.o strly* **4/1**[1]

1011 **2** 4 ½ **Myplacelater**[15] 6533 3-8-10 110...................................... PaulHanagan 6 112
(D R C Elsworth) *stdd s: hld up in rr: hdwy on outer over 3f out: rdn and chsd ldrs ent fnl 2f: chsd clr wnr ent fnl f: no imp* **9/1**

4122 **3** 1 ½ **She's Our Mark**[21] 6379 6-9-3 107... DMGrant 13 110
(Patrick J Flynn, Ire) *t.k.h: hld up in tch in midfield: drvn and effrt 2f out: edging lft u.p fr wl over 1f out: kpt on fnl f to go 3rd towards fin: no threat to wnr* **12/1**

3166 **4** 1 **Barshiba (IRE)**[58] 5248 6-9-5 110................................. JamieSpencer 2 110
(D R C Elsworth) *led: rdn over 2f out: hrd drvn and hdd over 1f out: edgd rt u.p and btn 1f out: lost 3rd towards fin* **16/1**

0306 **5** 1 ½ **Saphira's Fire (IRE)**[29] 6148 5-9-3 100.......................... NeilCallan 5 106
(W R Muir) *hld up in tch in rr: pushed along and effrt wl over 2f out: drvn and no imp over 1f out* **66/1**

-000 **6** ½ **You'll Be Mine (USA)**[21] 6379 3-8-10 97............................ JMurtagh 1 105
(A P O'Brien, Ire) *chsd ldr: rdn 3f out: lost 2nd ent fnl 2f: wknd u.p over 1f out* **33/1**

2443 **7** 1 ¾ **Meeznah (USA)**[37] 5881 3-8-10 113................................. TedDurcan 11 102
(D R Lanigan) *lw: hld up in tch: rdn and effrt whn n.m.r 3f out: rdn and edging rt whn hmpd over 2f out: n.d after* **13/2**[2]

0202 **8** 4 ½ **High Heeled (IRE)**[14] 6591 4-9-3 114............................... WilliamBuick 9 95
(J H M Gosden) *hld up in tch towards rr: rdn and effrt 3f out: drvn and no prog ent fnl 2f: wl btn over 1f out* **4/1**[1]

0432 **9** 40 **Rumoush (USA)**[37] 5881 3-8-10 107................................. RichardHills 4 31
(M P Tregoning) *lw: chsd ldr: rdn 3f out: drvn and btn over 2f out: eased fnl 2f: t.o* **4/1**[1]

3131 **10** 1 ¼ **Eleanora Duse (IRE)**[34] 6007 3-8-12 115..................... FrankieDettori 10 31
(Sir Michael Stoute) *chsd ldrs: rdn 3f out: wknd qckly 2f out: heavily eased fr wl over 1f out: t.o* **7/1**[3]

300 **11** 16 **Tinaar (USA)**[79] 4507 4-9-3 95... TomQueally 8 —
(G A Butler) *hld up in rr: lost tch over 4f out: wl t.o fnl 3f* **50/1**

6105 **12** 3 ½ **Brushing**[22] 6320 4-9-3 102.. KierenFallon 3 —
(M H Tompkins) *bhd and rdn 4f out: sn lost tch: wl t.o fnl 3f:* **33/1**

2m 34.73s (2.73) **Going Correction** +0.30s/f (Good)
WFA 3 from 4yo+ 7lb **12** Ran SP% **118.7**
Speed ratings (Par 115): **102,99,98,97,96 96,94,91,65,64 53,51**
toteswingers:1&2:£6.60, 1&3:£8.90, 2&3:£12.10 CSF £40.71 TOTE £5.30: £2.20, £3.10, £2.90; EX 39.60 TRIFECTA Pool: £7,528.53 - 8.54 winning units..
Owner Sir Evelyn De Rothschild **Bred** Southcourt Stud **Trained** Newmarket, Suffolk

FOCUS
The third - and highest quality - renewal to date of this distaff Group 2, which is to be switched to Ascot with boosted prize money next year. The pace was sound and the fourth home took the field over to the stands' rail on entering the long straight. The winner goes well fresh and looks better than ever, but few of these gave their running. The fifth limits the form a little.

NOTEBOOK
Crystal Capella ◆, who won the inaugural running of this event, was touched off by Ashalanda in it a year ago and had not been seen since. Travelling well before striking for home, she stayed on really strongly for an emphatic victory. She has a tendency to throw splints which makes her hard to train, but is a high-class and supremely tough mare who is capable of better still. Connections are hoping she receives an invitation to the Hong Kong Vase in December, where she would take on the males, and were she to stay in training at six then there would be several tempting targets. (tchd 7-2)
Myplacelater has been in fine form in recent weeks and she followed her win in a course-and-distance Listed race with another fine effort, albeit never threatening the clear-cut winner. She will stay in training and there may be further improvement in her. (op 7-1 tchd 13-2)
She's Our Mark found herself on the outside of the bunch when the field tacked over but stayed on well once finding her way to the rail. She is tough and consistent, and a good guide to the strength of the form. (op 10-1 tchd 9-1)
Barshiba(IRE) heads to the paddocks now after another honest performance. She retires the winner of seven races, including back-to-back Lancahire Oaks. (tchd 20-1)
Saphira's Fire(IRE) had been third in both the previous editions of this race and she ran well again on a course that she seems to like. (tchd 100-1 in a place)
You'll Be Mine(USA) has not lived up to the promise of her juvenile campaign but this was a bertter run after three very moderate efforts this season. Her stamina was just waning late on. Official explanation: jockey said filly had no more to give
Meeznah(USA) has been unable to build on that cracking effort at Epsom and she ran a rather lacklustre race here, perhaps finding the ground against her. Official explanation: jockey said filly was unsuited by the good to soft ground (op 8-1)
High Heeled(IRE), another for whom Epsom proved a seasonal high spot, when third in the Coronation Cup, had run her previous four races in France. She could never get involved on this return to racing in Britain. (op 11-2)
Rumoush(USA) was back to form in the Park Hill last time but failed to give her running here and was eased right down when beaten. Official explanation: jockey said filly lost its action (op 11-2)
Eleanora Duse(IRE) short-headed She's Our Mark to take the Group 2 Blandford Stakes last time but was 2lb worse off. The winner's stablemate weakened disappointingly and was below the form she showed both at the Curragh and in the Yorkshire Oaks. Official explanation: jockey said filly ran flat
Tinaar(USA) Official explanation: jockey said filly never travelled

6929 JOCKEY CLUB CUP (GROUP 3) 2m
5:25 (5:28) (Class 1) 3-Y-O+

£32,358 (£12,266; £6,138; £3,060; £1,533; £769) **Stalls** Centre

Form RPR

0624 **1** **Tastahil (IRE)**[20] 6388 6-9-0 111.................................. WilliamBuick 7 115
(B W Hills) *chsd ldr tl led 9f out: mde rest: rdn over 2f out: styd on wl: in command 1f out: eased towards fin* **10/3**[2]

1133 **2** 5 **Motrice**[36] 5909 3-8-1 108.. SilvestreDeSousa 1 106
(Sir Mark Prescott) *stdd and dropped in bhd after s: hld up in last: shkn up 12f out: hdwy to chse ldrs 6f out: drvn over 2f out: chsd clr wnr jst over 1f out: no imp* **7/4**[1]

1560 **3** 2 ½ **Buxted (IRE)**[42] 5749 4-9-0 100... JimCrowley 3 106
(R A Mills) *hld up in last trio: hdwy to chse ldrs 6f out: rdn and btn over 2f out: no ch w wnr and edgd rt u.p over 1f out: plugged on to go 3rd ins fnl f* **14/1**

0100 **4** 1 ¼ **Akmal**[59] 5218 4-9-5 109.. RichardHills 8 110
(J L Dunlop) *lw: in tch in midfield: hdwy to chse ldr 7f out: rdn over 2f out: wknd u.p over 1f out: wl btn and lost 2 pls fnl f* **6/1**[3]

0503 **5** 1 ¼ **Snoqualmie Girl (IRE)**[22] 6320 4-8-11 103...............(p) JamieSpencer 5 100
(D R C Elsworth) *t.k.h: hld up in last trio: hdwy to trck ldrs 6f out: rdn and hung rt 2f out: sn swtchd lft and drvn: wknd over 1f out* **9/1**

2531 **6** 53 **Bramalea**[22] 6322 5-8-11 85... KierenFallon 4 36
(B W Duke) *led: styd towards far side 10f out: hdd 9f out: rdn and dropped out qckly 6f out: wl t.o fnl 4f* **20/1**

4104 **7** 3 **Lady Eclair (IRE)**[36] 5908 4-8-11 97................................. JoeFanning 2 33
(M Johnston) *chsd ldrs: rdn and struggling over 4f out: lost tch 4f out: wl t.o fnl 3f* **13/2**

141 **8** 48 **Lady Hestia (USA)**[50] 5497 5-8-11 76................................. TedDurcan 6 —
(M P Tregoning) *chsd ldrs tl struggling u.p over 6f out: lost tch 5f out: wl t.o fnl 4f* **33/1**

3m 29.9s (-0.60) **Going Correction** +0.30s/f (Good)
WFA 3 from 4yo+ 10lb **8** Ran SP% **111.4**
Speed ratings (Par 113): **113,110,109,108,108 81,80,56**
toteswingers:1&2:£1.80, 1&3:£7.90, 2&3:£6.20 CSF £9.03 TOTE £4.00: £1.80, £1.10, £4.40; EX 9.40 Trifecta £62.80 Pool: £1,575.16 - 18.56 winning units. Place 6 £227.17; Place 5 £50.57.
Owner Hamdan Al Maktoum **Bred** Darley **Trained** Lambourn, Berks

FOCUS
With Patkai a non-runner, this had the look of a weak race, as only one of these (Akmal) had previously been successful in Group company. The winner looks the best guide to a race that probably doesn't want viewing too positively. The runner-up could not match her Doncaster form.

NOTEBOOK
Tastahil(IRE), although not previously successful at this level, had shown the form required when runner-up in the Doncaster Cup two starts back. A poor effort at Ascot last time left question marks, but he bounced back to form here, taking up the running before halfway and pulling nicely clear in the closing stages. His strike-rate remains an ordinary one, but a bit of give suits him and he was found a good opening here. (tchd 3-1)
Motrice, only narrowly behind Tastahil in the Doncaster Cup, was unable to reverse that form, probably as a result of the ground turning more in the favour of Barry Hills's gelding, but it was still a sound effort from this very progressive filly. (op 2-1 tchd 5-2)
Buxted(IRE) did not show a great deal on his return from a break on his favoured Polytrack surface in early September, but his trainer has been in good form this month and this was a much more encouraging display, especially as it is questionable whether he was totally at home on the ground. (op 12-1)

Akmal, who won this last year, had to give weight all round. He has run all his best races from the front, but his last two efforts when leading had been disappointing. In a change of tactics he was held up this time, but he failed to bounce back to form on ground that was undoubtedly softer than ideal. (op 5-1 tchd 9-2)
Snoqualmie Girl(IRE) ran a better race in first-time cheekpieces on her previous start, and the headgear was on again, but she had never before run over a distance this far and, having raced keenly early, it simply proved too much for her. (op 10-1 tchd 11-1)
Bramalea won an ordinary handicap at Ascot by a long way last time out, but getting into the frame here required a big step up even on that effort. Having made the early running, she dropped right out and was eased in the closing stages.
Lady Eclair(IRE), who has been on the go since March, racking up seven wins from 16 starts, also failed to make the jump from handicaps. (op 8-1)
Lady Hestia(USA) had most to find on official ratings and was predictably outclassed. (op 25-1)
T/Jkpt: £9,325.70 to a £1 stake. Pool:£26,269.81 - 2.00 winning tickets T/Plt: £353.40 to a £1 stake. Pool:£191,039.16 - 394.55 winning tickets T/Qpdt: £55.20 to a £1 stake. Pool:£13,319.64 - 178.45 winning tickets SP

[6898] WOLVERHAMPTON (A.W) (L-H)

Saturday, October 16

OFFICIAL GOING: Standard

Wind: Fresh against Weather: Cloudy with sunny spells

6930 PLAY SLOTS AT TOTESPORT.COM H'CAP (DIV I) 1m 1f 103y(P)

5:30 (5:30) (Class 6) (0-65,64) 3-Y-0+ £1,364 (£403; £201) Stalls Low

Form RPR
0066 1 **Twisted**[30] 6116 4-9-4 **56** (b[1]) PhillipMakin 6 70
(M W Easterby) *a.p: chsd ldr over 2f out: rdn to ld over 1f out: r.o wl* **7/2**[1]
0500 2 3 ¾ **Watchmaker**[10] 6669 7-9-8 **60** SamHitchcott 7 66
(Miss Tor Sturgis) *mid-div: hdwy over 2f out: rdn to go 2nd ins fnl f: no ch w wnr* **18/1**
-003 3 1 ½ **New Beginning (IRE)**[29] 6165 6-9-9 **61** (p) GeorgeBaker 10 64
(J Mackie) *chsd ldr over 8f out: led 5f out: rdn and hdd over 1f out: styd on same pce* **7/2**[1]
121 4 ¾ **Nolecce**[17] 6462 3-9-3 **62** KierenFox(3) 9 63
(R C Guest) *hld up: racd keenly: hdwy over 2f out: rdn and edgd lft over 1f out: styd on same pce ins fnl f* **7/2**[1]
56-4 5 1 ½ **Forbidden (IRE)**[29] 6165 7-9-10 **62** (t) RobertWinston 11 60
(Daniel Mark Loughnane, Ire) *hld up: plld hrd: hdwy over 2f out: rdn over 1f out: no ex ins fnl f* **8/1**[2]
0041 6 nk **Empress Leizu (IRE)**[14] 6574 3-8-10 **59** JulieBurke(7) 5 56
(A W Carroll) *prom: pushed along and nt clr run over 2f out: sn lost pl: r.o u.p ins fnl f* **10/1**[3]
460 7 hd **Sumner (IRE)**[10] 4648 6-9-10 **62** (v) PatCosgrave 13 59
(P D Evans) *s.i.s: in rr: pushed along 4f out: r.o ins fnl f: nvr nrr* **33/1**
0064 8 3 ¼ **St Savarin (FR)**[11] 6660 9-8-10 **51** RobertLButler(3) 1 41
(M S Tuck) *s.i.s: hld up: nvr nr to chal* **28/1**
0000 9 4 ½ **Tell Halaf**[24] 6292 3-9-1 **57** LiamKeniry 4 38
(M G Quinlan) *hld up: nvr on terms* **33/1**
3204 10 nse **Bideeya (USA)**[80] 4482 3-9-7 **63** (p) SteveDrowne 3 44
(C E Brittain) *led 1f: chsd ldrs: rdn over 2f out: wknd over 1f out* **16/1**
443 11 5 **Crimson Empire (USA)**[26] 6244 3-9-8 **64** TomEaves 8 34
(B Smart) *chsd ldr: led over 8f out: hdd 5f out: chsd ldr again tl rdn over 2f out: sn wknd* **16/1**
0045 12 6 **Sounds Of Thunder**[17] 6476 3-9-7 **63** (b) DaneO'Neill 12 21
(H J L Dunlop) *trckd ldrs: rdn over 3f out: wknd 2f out* **25/1**

2m 0.90s (-0.80) **Going Correction** -0.05s/f (Stan)
WFA 3 from 4yo+ 4lb 12 Ran SP% **117.1**
Speed ratings (Par 101): **101,97,96,95,94 94,93,91,87,86 82,77**
Tote Swingers: 1&2 £2.60, 1&3 £4.10, 2&3 £2.70 CSF £73.56 CT £235.04 TOTE £4.20: £1.30, £4.00, £1.80; EX 91.00.
Owner Steve Hull **Bred** Highclere Stud **Trained** Sheriff Hutton, N Yorks

FOCUS
Just an ordinary handicap for the grade and the pace was only a fair one. The time was similar to division II and the winner built on his recent better effort.

6931 SHANE ELTON MEMORIAL MAIDEN STKS 5f 20y(P)

6:00 (6:00) (Class 5) 3-Y-0+ £2,388 (£705; £352) Stalls Low

Form RPR
04 1 **Cloth Ears**[12] 6638 4-8-7 0 AdamBeschizza(5) 12 63
(P S McEntee) *chsd ldr: rdn to ld ins fnl f: styd on* **14/1**
3303 2 nk **Aalsmeer**[6] 6773 3-8-12 66 (p) SteveDrowne 10 62
(Karen George) *chsd ldrs: rdn over 1f out: r.o* **4/1**[2]
2252 3 nk **Bushwhacker (AUS)**[7] 6746 5-9-3 68 (b) GeorgeBaker 9 66
(W R Muir) *s.i.s: hld up: hdwy over 1f out: rdn ins fnl f: nt run on* **10/11**[1]
0- 4 3 ¼ **Estonia**[427] 5026 3-8-12 0 WilliamCarson 2 49
(M D Squance) *s.i.s: hld up: hdwy over 1f out: nt trble ldrs* **12/1**[3]
00 5 ¾ **Francis Albert**[28] 6206 4-8-10 49 (b) JosephYoung(7) 11 52
(M Mullineaux) *led and plld hrd: rdn: hung rt and hdd ins fnl f: no ex* **14/1**
6440 6 1 ¼ **Billionaire Boy (IRE)**[26] 6246 3-8-12 48 RossAtkinson(5) 5 47
(Patrick Morris) *chsd ldrs: rdn over 1f out: no ex fnl f* **20/1**
0262 7 ¾ **Sharp Shoes**[16] 6490 3-8-12 51 (p) RosieJessop(5) 8 44
(Mrs A Duffield) *s.i.s and stmbld sn after s: in rr: rdn over 1f out: nvr nrr* **12/1**[3]
8 nk **Suttonia (IRE)**[161] 1936 4-8-12 42 SamHitchcott 6 38
(Noel T Chance) *sn pushed along in rr: nvr on terms* **33/1**
/ 9 2 ¾ **Woodwind** 5-8-5 0 ThomasWhite(7) 4 28
(D Shaw) *s.i.s: sn outpcd* **33/1**
-000 10 nk **Ariel Bender**[20] 6392 3-9-3 28 LiamKeniry 3 32
(Peter Grayson) *mid-div: drvn along 1/2-way: sn wknd* **100/1**
2634 11 3 ¼ **A Pocketful Of Rye (IRE)**[43] 5730 3-8-5 53 LeonnaMayor(7) 7 16
(P Howling) *s.i.s: a bhd* **16/1**
0000 12 2 ½ **Whispering Ridge**[68] 4908 3-9-0 28 (v) KierenFox(3) 1 12
(M Wellings) *prom and sn pushed along: rdn 1/2-way: wknd over 1f out* **100/1**

61.95 secs (-0.35) **Going Correction** -0.05s/f (Stan) 12 Ran SP% **119.6**
Speed ratings (Par 103): **100,99,99,93,92 90,89,88,84,84 78,74**
Tote Swingers: 1&2 £7.30, 1&3 £4.30, 2&3 £2.20 CSF £67.81 TOTE £18.40: £6.20, £1.10, £2.20; EX 96.30.
Owner Steve Shore **Bred** Caroline Shore **Trained** Newmarket, Suffolk

FOCUS
A very weak maiden but one run at a decent pace and there didn't look to be any hard-luck stories. The fifth and sixth help set the lowly standard.

Bushwhacker(AUS) Official explanation: vet said gelding struck into itself

6932 PLAY BINGO AT TOTESPORT.COM CLAIMING STKS 5f 20y(P)

6:30 (6:30) (Class 6) 3-Y-0+ £1,706 (£503; £252) Stalls Low

Form RPR
0000 1 **Matsunosuke**[18] 6446 8-9-1 99 TomMcLaughlin 12 81
(R A Harris) *hld up: hdwy 1/2-way: rdn to ld and hung lft ins fnl f: r.o* **7/2**[2]
325 2 hd **Elhamri**[9] 6700 6-8-11 69 LiamKeniry 13 76
(S Kirk) *chsd ldrs: rdn and ev ch ins fnl f: carried lft: r.o* **5/1**
0100 3 1 ½ **Prince James**[26] 6246 3-8-8 65 JamesSullivan(3) 9 71+
(M W Easterby) *hld up: rdn over 1f out: r.o ins fnl f: wnt 3rd towards fin: nt rch ldrs* **33/1**
6000 4 ¾ **Royal Intruder**[41] 5791 5-8-11 82 RobertWinston 5 68
(S Donohoe, Ire) *chsd ldrs: nt clr run over 1f out: r.o* **5/1**
4401 5 1 ¼ **Six Diamonds**[21] 6368 3-8-6 74 NickyMackay 3 58
(H Morrison) *disp ld tl led wl over 1f out: rdn: hdd and no ex ins fnl f* **11/4**[1]
5050 6 nk **Victorian Bounty**[5] 6801 5-9-1 73 (p) PatCosgrave 4 66
(Stef Higgins) *disp ld tl rdn and hung rt wl over 1f out: styd on same pce ins fnl f* **9/2**[3]
400 7 1 ¼ **Six Wives**[30] 6103 3-8-2 68 WilliamCarson 7 49
(J A Glover) *s.i.s: hdwy over 1f out: no ex ins fnl f* **16/1**
0000 8 2 ½ **Ginobili (IRE)**[17] 6455 4-8-0 57 (e) RosieJessop(5) 11 43
(Andrew Reid) *dwlt: in rr and rdn 1/2-way: n.d* **33/1**

61.39 secs (-0.91) **Going Correction** -0.05s/f (Stan) 8 Ran SP% **112.2**
Speed ratings (Par 101): **105,104,102,101,99 98,96,92**
Tote Swingers: 1&2 £3.20, 1&3 £13.80, 2&3 £11.20 CSF £20.48 TOTE £3.00: £1.10, £2.90, £9.50; EX 15.10.Six Diamonds was claimed by Mr S. Arnold for £8,000.
Owner S Mares **Bred** R Coogan **Trained** Earlswood, Monmouths

FOCUS
A wide variety of abilities on display in the claimer and though it went to the one with the highest rating, the pace wasn't strong and the overall result looks muddling. It is hard to know what ability the winner retains and the runner-up looks the best guide.
Prince James ◆ Official explanation: jockey said colt was denied a clear run

6933 BREEDERS' CUP LIVE ONLY ON ATR H'CAP 2m 119y(P)

7:00 (7:01) (Class 6) (0-65,65) 3-Y-0+ £1,706 (£503; £252) Stalls Low

Form RPR
3161 1 **New Code**[7] 6747 3-9-3 **64** GeorgeBaker 10 75+
(W R Muir) *hld up: hdwy over 3f out: led over 1f out: shkn up and styd on wl* **7/2**[2]
3003 2 2 ¾ **Pearl (IRE)**[7] 6744 6-8-13 **50** (tp) ShaneKelly 11 56
(Mrs A M Thorpe) *led 1f: a.p: chsd ldr over 3f out: rdn and ev ch over 1f out: styd on same pce ins fnl f* **8/1**[3]
-124 3 1 **Dart**[221] 835 6-10-0 **65** PhillipMakin 7 70
(J Mackie) *hld up: hdwy over 6f out: rdn and ev ch over 1f out: no ex ins fnl f* **8/1**[3]
211 4 5 **If I Had Him (IRE)**[142] 2476 6-9-13 **64** TonyCulhane 6 63
(George Baker) *prom: chsd ldr over 10f out: led 5f out: rdn and hdd over 1f out: wknd ins fnl f* **7/4**[1]
050 5 6 **Delorain (IRE)**[163] 1849 7-8-2 **46** (vt) LauraPike(7) 3 37
(W B Stone) *led after 1f: sn hdd: led again over 13f out: hdd 5f out: sn rdn along: wknd over 2f out* **12/1**
0-0 6 1 **Share Option**[162] 584 8-8-9 **49** KierenFox(3) 5 39
(A W Carroll) *hld up: sme hdwy over 2f out: sn rdn: n.d* **10/1**
0000 7 3 ¼ **Transfered (IRE)**[46] 5631 4-8-4 **46** oh1 AdamBeschizza(5) 12 32
(Lucinda Featherstone) *hld up: hdwy over 6f out: rdn over 3f out: wknd over 1f out* **50/1**
1-00 8 1 **Follow The Dream**[230] 748 7-9-10 **61** SteveDrowne 9 46
(Karen George) *hld up: rdn over 3f out: n.d* **16/1**
2005 9 ¾ **Davana**[11] 6660 4-8-7 **47** (v[1]) MartinLane(3) 4 31
(W J H Ratcliffe) *prom: rdn along over 6f out: wknd over 4f out* **16/1**
4005 10 10 **Wee Ziggy**[10] 6120 7-8-3 **47** JosephYoung(7) 1 19
(M Mullineaux) *hld up in tch: wknd over 5f out* **50/1**
00 11 6 **Najca De Thaix (FR)**[17] 6450 9-8-9 **46** oh1 SamHitchcott 2 11
(J L Spearing) *led 15f out: hdd over 13f out: chsd ldrs: drvn along over 5f out: sn wknd* **66/1**
000- 12 1 ¾ **Beyonda Dream**[306] 7751 4-8-9 **46** oh1 NeilChalmers 8 9
(Lucinda Featherstone) *hld up: a in rr* **66/1**

3m 39.35s (-2.45) **Going Correction** -0.05s/f (Stan)
WFA 3 from 4yo+ 10lb 12 Ran SP% **116.3**
Speed ratings (Par 101): **103,101,101,98,96 95,94,93,93,88 85,84**
Tote Swingers: 1&2 £8.90, 1&3 £4.90, 2&3 £9.60 CSF £30.70 CT £208.41 TOTE £3.70: £1.20, £3.80, £1.60; EX 38.70.
Owner Mrs D Edginton **Bred** Foursome Thoroughbreds **Trained** Lambourn, Berks

FOCUS
A modest handicap in which the pace for the first circuit was only fair. The winner improved again for the step up in trip but this was not a strong race for the grade.

6934 PLAY BLACKJACK AT TOTESPORT.COM H'CAP 1m 141y(P)

7:30 (7:30) (Class 6) (0-65,67) 3-Y-0+ £1,706 (£503; £252) Stalls Low

Form RPR
0532 1 **Lord Of The Dance (IRE)**[5] 6794 4-9-7 **62** TomMcLaughlin 9 73
(W M Brisbourne) *chsd ldrs: led 3f out: pushed clr over 1f out: rdn out* **5/1**[1]
0032 2 3 ½ **Dream Of Fortune (IRE)**[8] 6718 6-9-9 **67** (bt) RichardEvans(3) 4 70
(P D Evans) *a.p: rdn over 1f out: chsd wnr ins fnl f: no imp* **6/1**[2]
0060 3 ½ **Abriachan**[21] 6370 3-9-5 **64** WilliamCarson 8 66
(M G Quinlan) *led 1f: chsd ldr to over 3f out: rdn over 1f out: styd on* **6/1**[2]
60-6 4 hd **Royal Willy (IRE)**[10] 6671 4-9-4 **59** SteveDrowne 12 60+
(W Jarvis) *hld up: hdwy over 2f out: rdn over 1f out: styd on* **8/1**[3]
3350 5 nk **Just Jimmy (IRE)**[12] 6632 5-9-1 **61** AdamBeschizza(5) 6 62
(P D Evans) *mid-div: hdwy over 3f out: rdn over 1f out: styd on* **12/1**
2265 6 nse **Just Timmy Marcus**[8] 6713 4-9-10 **65** (b) TonyCulhane 3 66+
(B P J Baugh) *hld up: r.o ins fnl f: nt trble ldrs* **9/1**
6620 7 nk **Powerful Pierre**[15] 6541 3-9-6 **65** TomEaves 10 65
(I W McInnes) *hld up: hdwy over 3f out: rdn over 2f out: styd on* **33/1**
0266 8 1 **Rascal In The Mix (USA)**[21] 6372 4-9-7 **65** (p) MichaelStainton(3) 11 63
(R M Whitaker) *led 7f out: hdd 3f out: rdn over 1f out: no ex ins fnl f* **16/1**
5004 9 1 ¼ **Confrontation**[37] 5891 3-9-0 **62** MartinLane(3) 5 57
(D M Simcock) *chsd ldrs: rdn over 2f out: no ex fnl f* **16/1**
3166 10 2 ¾ **Beat Up**[8] 6718 4-9-8 **63** (p) DaneO'Neill 2 51
(G D Blake) *hld up: rdn over 3f out: n.d* **10/1**
554 11 1 **La Columbina**[40] 5813 5-9-2 **57** LeeVickers 1 43
(H J Evans) *hld up: rdn over 2f out: a in rr* **33/1**

0463 **12** 3 ½ **Yourgolftravel Com**[42] 5767 5-9-3 **58**.......... GeorgeBaker 7 36
(M Wigham) *s.i.s and hmpd s: hld up: a in rr* **5/1**[1]

1m 52.55s (2.05) **Going Correction** -0.05s/f (Stan)
WFA 3 from 4yo+ 4lb 12 Ran SP% **117.4**
Speed ratings (Par 101): **88,84,84,84,84 83,83,82,81,79 78,75**
Tote Swingers: 1&2 £2.60, 1&3 £12.60, 2&3 £14.40 CSF £33.79 CT £185.86 TOTE £7.60: £2.70, £1.70, £2.80; EX 35.30.
Owner D C Rutter & H Clewlow **Bred** Bridgewater Equine Ltd **Trained** Great Ness, Shropshire

FOCUS
Another modest handicap run at a steady pace and the prominently-ridden winner had it in the bag as soon he moved to the front turning for home. The form is not rated too positively.
Yourgolftravel Com Official explanation: jockey said gelding was hampered at start; vet said gelding finished distressed

6935 PLAY ROULETTE AT TOTESPORT.COM H'CAP 1m 141y(P)
8:00 (8:01) (Class 5) (0-70,70) 3-Y-0+ **£2,729** (£806; £403) **Stalls** Low

Form RPR
3230 **1** **Elijah Pepper (USA)**[30] 6116 5-9-6 **66**.......... GrahamGibbons 11 76
(T D Barron) *chsd ldr tl led 6f out: rdn over 1f out: r.o* **4/1**[2]
-002 **2** ½ **Star Links (USA)**[15] 6546 4-9-9 **69**..........(p) RobertWinston 8 78
(S Donohoe, Ire) *a.p: rdn and hung lft over 1f out: chsd wnr fnl f: r.o* **7/1**
0460 **3** ½ **Cookie Crumbles (IRE)**[39] 5833 3-9-4 **68**.......... GeorgeBaker 2 76+
(C F Wall) *hld up: hdwy over 2f out: rdn over 1f out: rdr lost reins briefly ins fnl f: r.o* **9/1**
3536 **4** 1 ½ **Vertigo On Course (IRE)**[29] 6165 5-9-0 **60**.......... PaulHanagan 3 64
(R A Fahey) *a.p: rdn over 2f out: hung rt ins fnl f: styd on same pce* **9/2**[3]
0301 **5** 1 **Cross The Boss (IRE)**[22] 6335 3-8-11 **61**..........(t) PhillipMakin 12 63+
(B M R Haslam) *hld up: hmpd over 2f out: styd on fr over 1f out: nt rch ldrs* **9/4**[1]
1612 **6** ¾ **Aussie Blue (IRE)**[14] 6580 6-9-7 **70**.......... MichaelStainton[(3)] 7 70
(R M Whitaker) *led: hdd 6f out: chsd ldrs: rdn over 1f out: no ex fnl f* **8/1**
0400 **7** 4 ½ **Toga Tiger (IRE)**[14] 6580 3-9-0 **64**.......... TonyCulhane 6 54
(P T Midgley) *hld up: rdn over 2f out: n.d* **50/1**
0600 **8** 2 **Justcallmehandsome**[8] 6718 8-8-12 **65**..........(v) KatiaScallan[(7)] 9 50
(D J S Ffrench Davis) *prom: rdn over 2f out: wknd over 1f out* **20/1**
3300 **9** ½ **Blue Spinnaker (IRE)**[24] 6297 11-9-4 **67**.......... JamesSullivan[(3)] 5 51
(M W Easterby) *hld up: pushed along 5f out: nvr on terms* **33/1**
3505 **10** 1 **Tanforan**[16] 6495 8-8-12 **58**.......... SteveDrowne 1 40
(B P J Baugh) *hld up: bhd fnl 3f* **28/1**
0000 **11** 1 **Takajan (IRE)**[29] 6168 3-8-4 **57**.......... Louis-PhilippeBeuzelin[(3)] 10 37
(W M Brisbourne) *trckd ldrs: racd keenly: ev ch 2f out: sn rdn and wknd* **50/1**

1m 49.73s (-0.77) **Going Correction** -0.05s/f (Stan)
WFA 3 from 4yo+ 4lb 11 Ran SP% **117.6**
Speed ratings (Par 103): **101,100,100,98,97 97,93,91,91,90 89**
Tote Swingers: 1&2 £10.30, 1&3 £10.10, 2&3 £13.30 CSF £30.23 CT £241.43 TOTE £7.20: £3.50, £4.30, £5.80; EX 35.80.
Owner Wensleydale Bacon Limited **Bred** Liberation Farm & Oratis Thoroughbreds **Trained** Maunby, N Yorks

FOCUS
A reasonably competitive handicap for the grade but it was another run at a steady pace and once again those ridden prominently were favoured. It was a bit of a messy race but the first two are rated to this year's turf form.

6936 ATTHERACES.COM/BREEDERSCUP MEDIAN AUCTION MAIDEN STKS 1m 1f 103y(P)
8:30 (8:31) (Class 6) 2-Y-0 **£1,706** (£503; £252) **Stalls** Low

Form RPR
33 **1** **Tenby Lady (USA)**[8] 6711 2-8-12 0.......... SebSanders 5 67
(Sir Mark Prescott) *dwlt: hld up: hdwy 5f out: chsd ldr over 2f out: rdn over 1f out: hung lft ins fnl f: styd on to ld nr fin* **4/5**[1]
4362 **2** ¾ **Zamina (IRE)**[15] 6542 2-8-12 67.......... LiamKeniry 8 66
(S Kirk) *led after 1f: pushed clr 2f out: rdn and hung lft ins fnl f: hdd nr fin* **4/1**[2]
450 **3** ½ **Swift Alhaarth (IRE)**[65] 4993 2-9-3 67.......... JoeFanning 4 70
(M Johnston) *trckd ldrs: plld hrd: rdn and hung lft fr over 1f out: r.o* **7/1**
003 **4** 2 **Windsor Knights**[15] 6542 2-9-3 67..........(b) JamesDoyle 1 66
(A J Lidderdale) *hld up: drvn along 5f out: styd on ins fnl f: nvr nrr* **33/1**
64 **5** shd **Operateur (IRE)**[15] 6542 2-9-3 0.......... PaulHanagan 3 66
(B M R Haslam) *led 1f: chsd ldrs: rdn over 1f out: no ex ins fnl f* **6/1**[3]
60 **6** 1 ¼ **Varlak**[12] 6628 2-9-3 0.......... DavidProbert 6 63
(D Donovan) *hld up: rdn over 3f out: hdwy and hung lft fr over 1f out: styd on same pce fnl f* **80/1**
0060 **7** 5 **Dolcezza (IRE)**[19] 6411 2-8-12 55.......... PatCosgrave 2 49
(B J Meehan) *prom: rdn 4f out: wknd over 1f out* **40/1**
3333 **8** 9 **Papas Fritas**[8] 6717 2-9-3 65..........(b) ShaneKelly 7 37
(B J Meehan) *prom: chsd ldr over 6f out tl rdn over 2f out: wknd and eased over 1f out* **8/1**

2m 2.33s (0.63) **Going Correction** -0.05s/f (Stan) 8 Ran SP% **120.1**
Speed ratings (Par 93): **95,94,93,92,92 90,86,78**
Tote Swingers: 1&2 £1.80, 1&3 £2.40, 2&3 £4.50 CSF £4.63 TOTE £2.90: £1.10, £1.20, £2.20; EX 5.60.
Owner David F O'Rourke **Bred** O'Rourke's Silver Springs Stud Farm Llc **Trained** Newmarket, Suffolk
■ Stewards' Enquiry : Liam Keniry two-day ban: careless riding (Oct 30-31)

FOCUS
No more than a fair maiden in which half of the field had already shown their hand. Again, the pace wasn't strong.

NOTEBOOK
Tenby Lady(USA) looked to hold marginally the best claims and though she won only narrowly and made hard of work of it, she probably deserves her effort upgrading a little given that she did most of her running out wide after missing the break and still looked babyish when put under pressure. This trip suits her better than shorter, and she looks the type that might improve more with experience as well as when getting into a more strongly-run race. (op Evens)
Zamina(IRE) was entitled to finish runner-up on form and was given every chance to win the race after stealing a couple of lengths off the home turn, but she's only modest and not really up to the standard usually expected of a maiden winner. Nurseries will provide her with easier options. (op 7-2)
Swift Alhaarth(IRE)'s form has been hard to get a handle on so far but this was a return to form and he travelled well through the race, still running on at the finish. He looks to have some scope about him and might yet be open to more progress. (op 10-1 tchd 11-1)
Windsor Knights had finished three lengths behind Zamina here last time and virtually replicated that effort with the headgear retained, though he was hard at work from some way out before staying on and would have got much closer to turning the form around had the race been more strongly run.
Operateur(IRE) had also run in the same race as Zamina last time and this effort was another step forward. He'll be seen to better effect put over 1m2f or more now he is qualified for a mark. (op 7-1 tchd 8-1)
Varlak needed this for a mark and seemed to step up on previous efforts but was probably helped to some degree by the steady tempo at which the race was run. Modest nurseries look the way forward for him. Official explanation: jockey said colt hung left-handed
Papas Fritas dropped away quickly coming off the home turn. Stamina surely wasn't an issue given the steady pace and given that he is proven on the surface, this was disappointing. (tchd 15-2)

6937 PLAY SLOTS AT TOTESPORT.COM H'CAP (DIV II OF 5.30) 1m 1f 103y(P)
9:00 (9:00) (Class 6) (0-65,65) 3-Y-0+ **£1,364** (£403; £201) **Stalls** Low

Form RPR
4443 **1** **Astound**[10] 6668 3-9-8 **64**..........(v) TomMcLaughlin 11 74
(P D Evans) *hld up: rdn over 3f out: hdwy over 2f out: r.o to ld wl ins fnl f* **9/2**[2]
4353 **2** 1 ¼ **Guga (IRE)**[24] 6298 4-9-10 **62**..........(p) PaulHanagan 10 69
(J Mackie) *chsd ldr: led over 1f out: rdn and hdd wl ins fnl f* **4/1**[1]
-554 **3** 1 ¾ **George Baker (IRE)**[17] 6452 3-9-0 **59**.......... MatthewDavies[(3)] 6 63
(George Baker) *hld up: hdwy over 1f out: r.o: nt rch ldrs* **9/1**
0526 **4** ½ **Bentley**[14] 6578 6-9-2 **57**.......... JamesSullivan[(3)] 2 60
(B P J Baugh) *led: rdn and hdd over 1f out: no ex ins fnl f* **8/1**
6050 **5** ½ **Iptkaar (USA)**[49] 5541 3-9-6 **62**..........(b) SebSanders 8 64
(C E Brittain) *hld up: r.o ins fnl f: nrst fin* **12/1**
-400 **6** 1 ¼ **Richo**[32] 6051 4-9-1 **56**..........(p) EJMcNamara[(3)] 3 55
(S A Harris) *hld up: rdn over 2f out: styd on ins fnl f: nvr nrr* **33/1**
4400 **7** hd **Gwenllian (IRE)**[47] 5585 3-9-2 **58**.......... TomEaves 5 57
(Ian Williams) *prom: rdn over 2f out: no ex* **25/1**
3501 **8** nk **Highland Love**[21] 6375 5-9-7 **59**.......... TonyCulhane 13 57
(Jedd O'Keeffe) *prom: rdn over 2f out: no ex fnl f* **8/1**
9 1 ¾ **Jade Express (IRE)**[34] 6004 3-9-0 **56**.......... ShaneKelly 1 50
(Daniel Mark Loughnane, Ire) *hld up: hdwy u.p over 1f out: wknd ins fnl f* **25/1**
5564 **10** 4 **Munaawer (USA)**[22] 6326 3-9-9 **65**..........(b) GrahamGibbons 12 51
(J D Bethell) *chsd ldrs: rdn over 2f out: wknd over 1f out* **13/2**[3]
6520 **11** 7 **Belle Park**[22] 6335 3-8-13 **55**.......... JamieMackay 9 26
(Karen George) *hld up: rdn over 2f out: a in rr* **14/1**
3466 **12** 8 **Lago Indiano (IRE)**[33] 6042 3-9-9 **65**.......... LiamKeniry 4 19
(Peter Fahey, Ire) *chsd ldrs tl rdn and wknd over 2f out* **33/1**
2640 **P** **Widow Bird (IRE)**[27] 6225 3-9-7 **63**.......... SteveDrowne 7 —
(H Morrison) *hld up: bhd whn p.u 6f out* **10/1**

2m 1.05s (-0.65) **Going Correction** -0.05s/f (Stan)
WFA 3 from 4yo+ 4lb 13 Ran SP% **120.8**
Speed ratings (Par 101): **100,98,97,96,96 95,95,94,93,89 83,76,—**
Tote Swingers: 1&2 £5.50, 1&3 £7.90, 2&3 £8.10 CSF £22.13 CT £157.11 TOTE £4.80: £1.40, £2.50, £1.10; EX 19.80 Place 6: £63.26 Place 5: £37.35..
Owner Mrs I M Folkes **Bred** Darley **Trained** Pandy, Monmouths

FOCUS
Another modest event, run at a fair pace. The winner has not had many chances needs her effort upgrading, despite the limitations of the opposition. The second is rated to his best.
Jade Express(IRE) Official explanation: jockey said filly hung right throughout
T/Plt: £74.40 to a £1 stake. Pool:£56,419.80 - 568.29 winning tickets. T/Qpdt: £35.60 to a £1 stake. Pool:£9,310.98 - 35.60 winning tickets CR

6938 - 6945a (Foreign Racing) - See Raceform Interactive

6766 CAULFIELD (R-H)
Saturday, October 16

6946a DAVID JONES CUP (GROUP 3 H'CAP) (3YO+) (TURF) 1m 2f
5:20 (12:00) 3-Y-0+
£42,083 (£12,500; £6,250; £3,125; £1,736; £1,388)

RPR
1 **Ginga Dude (NZ)**[14] 7-8-8 **0**.......... MichaelWalker 10 113
(Graeme Boyd, New Zealand) **13/2**[3]
2 2 **Purple (AUS)**[14] 5-8-8 **0**..........(b) MarkZahra 8 109
(Peter Snowden, Australia) **5/2**[1]
3 1 ½ **Zoomin (NZ)** 6-8-5 **0**..........(b) GlenBoss 1 103
(Michael Kent, Australia) **7/1**
4 1 **Dream Pedlar (AUS)**[234] 6-8-6 **0** ow1..........(b) DannyNikolic 9 102
(Troy Blacker, Australia) **60/1**
5 1 **Rainbow Styling (NZ)**[22] 6345 6-8-10 **0**.......... ChrisMunce 7 104
(Michael, Wayne & John Hawkes, Australia) **13/2**[3]
6 ½ **C'Est La Guerre (NZ)**[14] 6-9-0 **0**.......... NicholasHall 5 107
(Robert Hickmott, Australia) **5/1**[2]
7 1 **Becqu Adoree (FR)**[76] 4624 4-8-6 **0** ow1.......... GeraldMosse 11 97
(L M Cumani) *pushed along to go early pce but sn rushed up on outside fr rr and settled in 6th: rdn 2f out and c five-wd into st (stl 6th) w 1 1/2f to run: unable qck u.p ins fnl f* **25/1**
8 hd **Token Of Honour (AUS)**[28] 4-8-5 **0**..........(p) DeanYendall 12 96
(David Hayes, Australia) **16/1**
9 ½ **Stanstill (IRE)**[83] 4400 4-8-5 **0**.......... CraigAWilliams 2 95
(Michael Kent, Australia) **66/1**
10 3 ½ **Crocodile Canyon (NZ)** 6-8-5 **0**.......... MarkDuPlessis 4 88
(Howie Mathews, New Zealand) **30/1**
11 1 ½ **The Fuzz (NZ)**[42] 8-8-9 **0**..........(bt) BradRawiller 3 89
(David Hayes, Australia) **66/1**
12 5 **Playwright (NZ)**[250] 6-8-7 **0**.......... StevenKing 6 77
(Steve Richards, Australia) **20/1**
13 4 **Empires Choice (NZ)**[7] 6767 7-8-10 **0**..........(b) LukeNolen 13 72
(Bart Cummings, Australia) **16/1**

2m 6.68s (126.68)
WFA 3 from 4yo+ 5lb 13 Ran SP% **112.6**
PARI-MUTUEL (NSW TAB - all including au$1 stakes): WIN 7.60 PLACE 2.40, 1.60, 2.50; DF 13.60 SF 34.60.
Owner G Boyd & Mrs R M Yovich **Bred** Willow Park Ltd **Trained** New Zealand

NOTEBOOK
Ginga Dude(NZ), a Group 1 performer in New Zealand, made virtually all of the running for a comfortable success. He nicked a good advantage from the front as the tempo increased and was never going to be caught.
Purple(AUS) didn't always have the room her rider would have hoped for, and made good ground on Ginga Dude in the final half a furlong.
Becqu Adoree(FR) travelled strongly in midfield but lacked a turn of pace at a crucial stage and was readily held.

Stanstill(IRE), having his first start since leaving Alan Swinbank, soon got prominent but was hard ridden as the field turned into the home straight and steadily weakened.

6947a BMW CAULFIELD CUP (GROUP 1 H'CAP) (3YO+) (TURF) 1m 4f

6:05 (6:05) 3-Y-O+

£888,888 (£208,333; £111,111; £61,111; £50,000; £41,666)

RPR

1 **Descarado (NZ)**13 4-8-4 0 ChrisMunce 15 119
(Gai Waterhouse, Australia) *a.p: hdwy to ld over 1 1/2f out: sn rdn and styd on gamely u.p* **16/1**

2 *1* **Harris Tweed (NZ)**13 5-8-7 0 (t) BradRawiller 8 118
(Murray & Bjorn Baker, New Zealand) *prom early: settled midfield after 3f: hdwy fnl 3f to go 6th 2f out travelling wl: c wd into st (1 1/2f out): r.o wl u.p to go 2nd fnl 200yds: no ex cl home* **16/1**

3 *1 1/4* **Monaco Consul (NZ)**13 4-8-7 0 (t) CraigAWilliams 12 118
(Michael Moroney, Australia) *hld up towards rr: hdwy on outside 3 1/2f out to go 5th w 2f to run: r.o wl st to go 3rd fnl f: no ex fnl 75yds* **20/1**

4 *hd* **Shocking (AUS)**13 5-9-0 0 (bt) MichaelRodd 10 123+
(Mark Kavanagh, Australia) *hld up towards rr: hdwy on ins over 3f out: sn rdn and nowhere to go 2f out: swtchd outside and c 5-wd fnl bnd: 11th on ins fnl f and styd on wl on outside: nvr nrr* **7/2**1

5 *1/2* **Manighar (FR)**55 5349 4-8-7 0 DamienOliver 3 115
(L M Cumani) *settled in midfield: 12th 3f out: pushed along and hdwy on ins 2f out: 7th st (1 1/2f out): twice swtchd to outside (appr and ins fnl f): styd on u.p: nrest at fin* **14/1**

6 *1 1/4* **Mr Medici (IRE)**139 5-8-9 0 GeraldMosse 13 115
(L Ho, Hong Kong) *trckd ldrs: 5th 3f out: rdn 2f out: wnt 2nd st (1 1/2f out): rdn and one pce fnl f: no ex fnl 100yds* **16/1**

7 *3 1/4* **Zavite (NZ)**13 8-8-7 0 BenMelham 16 108
(Anthony Cummings, Australia) *in rr: hdwy on wd outside over 2f out but stl bhd st (1 1/2f out): styd on wl fnl f: nvr plcd to chal* **100/1**

8 *3/4* **Metal Bender (NZ)**13 5-8-11 0 (b) HughBowman 2 110
(Chris Waller, Australia) *racd in middle of pack: 8th st: one pce fnl f* **10/1**

9 *2* **Herculian Prince (NZ)**14 5-8-6 0 4ex GlynSchofield 5 102
(Gai Waterhouse, Australia) *led after 1f: hdd 6f out and trckd ldr: disp ld 3f out: hdd over 1 1/2f out: unable qck* **8/1**3

10 *3/4* **Triple Honour (NZ)**14 6-8-7 0 (bt) LarryCassidy 9 102
(Chris Waller, Australia) *racd in midfield: hdwy on outside to ld 6f out: jnd w 3f to run: hdd over 1 1/2f out: one pce* **25/1**

11 *1/2* **Alcopop (AUS)**7 6767 6-8-6 0 MarkZahra 18 100
(Jake Stephens, Australia) *bhd: rapid hdwy on outside ins fnl 3f: 6th fnl bhd but on wd outside: rdn and wknd st* **5/1**2

12 *1* **Tokai Trick (JPN)**167 8-8-8 0 ShinjiFujita 17 101
(Kenji Nonaka, Japan) *racd in fnl 3rd: hdwy on outside 4f out: 6th 2 1/2f out: sn u.p: wkng whn squeezed out fnl 300yds* **80/1**

13 *1 1/2* **Mourayan (IRE)**14 4-8-6 0 (b) NicholasHall 4 96
(Robert Hickmott, Australia) *chsd ldrs (in abt 8th pl): rdn and no imp st: wknd ins fnl f* **20/1**

14 *1 1/4* **Red Ruler (NZ)**7 6767 6-8-6 0 MarkDuPlessis 1 94
(John Sargent, New Zealand) *led early: hdd after 1f: settled in ldng gp: 4th 3f out: rdn 1 1/2f out: wknd fnl f* **80/1**

15 *2 1/4* **Valdemoro (AUS)**28 4-7-12 0 (b) JasonMaskiell 11 85
(Tony Vasil, Australia) *a bhd: nvr threatened* **60/1**

16 *3/4* **Buccellati**13 6-8-7 0 (v) StevenKing 14 90
(Tony Noonan, Australia) *hld up: prog 3f out: rdn and btn st: nvr beyond mid-div* **80/1**

17 *1 1/2* **Faint Perfume (AUS)**13 4-8-3 0 (b1) GlenBoss 6 86
(Bart Cummings, Australia) *racd in fnl 3rd: hdwy 3f out: 10th 2f out (abt 6 l off ldr): sn rdn and wknd qckly* **9/1**

18 *6* **Dariana (AUS)**13 4-8-2 0 (b) LukeNolen 7 75
(Bart Cummings, Australia) *nvr plcd to chal: eased fnl f* **25/1**

2m 35.69s (155.69) **18** Ran SP% **117.0**

PARI-MUTUEL (NSW TAB - all including au$1 stakes): WIN 19.20 PLACE 5.10, 4.10, 6.60; DF 144.20 SF 276.20.

Owner D A & Mrs R J Henderson Et Al **Bred** W S McQuoid **Trained** Australia

FOCUS

This is probably not form to get too carried away with considering the going (a few of these didn't seem to handle it), and it saw the first three return to their best after being mainly well held or behind some they faced here.

NOTEBOOK

Descarado(NZ), beaten a long way in the Turnbull Stakes last time when behind six he reopposed here, was well positioned throughout despite breaking from a wide draw and responded to pressure to sustain his effort once in front. He appears versatile with regards to trip, as his three previous wins ranged from 6f to 1m2f, so this victory was breaking new ground for him, although he was a good second over 1m4f in the AJC Derby last season.

Harris Tweed(NZ), another to be up there throughout, had come into this off the back of a success in Listed company, and had no doubts about this stamina. He is often difficult to predict accurately, and had been well beaten on his two previous starts at Caulfield, including in this race last season.

Monaco Consul(NZ), a place behind Descarado in the AJC Derby last April, but two places in front of that horse when 12th in the Turnbull, hadn't been showing that this sort of performance was coming, but he stayed on well after being bustled to the head of affairs turning back in. Monaco Consul's trainer was happy with his final effort before Flemington.

Shocking(AUS) ◆, carrying top weight here, would have won with more luck. Dropped in behind from the start, he travelled comfortably towards the rear but found no room when it was needed, and then came about nine horses wide to get in the clear. Nothing was finishing better in the heavy conditions than him, and he surely would have won with a clear passage. This was a big prize missed but those on him for Flemington will have been delighted with the effort.

Manighar(FR) wasn't disgraced on two tries over 1m4f in the summer (fast ground both times), but it wasn't a big surprise to see him return to his very best in France last time when there was ease underfoot. With conditions looking to be in his favour here, he ran a satisfactory race without being knocked about, and connections will no doubt be delighted with the performance.

Mr Medici(IRE) ◆ hadn't gone anti-clockwise since leaving Ireland for Hong Kong so this probably came as a bit of a shock for him. Close up throughout, and said to have over-raced by Mosse, he arguably ran one of the most eyecatching races in ground that would not have been ideal for him.

Zavite(NZ) ◆ was knocked wider than Shocking turning in and stayed on really well down the home straight. He stays extreme distances and should improve on his rear-field effort at Flemington last November if turning up this season.

Metal Bender(NZ) has been in good form since his winter, but there was a doubt about him staying this distance. He wasn't beaten far in the 2009 AJC Australian Derby, but only finished eighth. The rain that fell almost certainly wasn't in his favour and he went nowhere quickly after being hard ridden as the race took shape.

Herculian Prince(NZ), the better-fancied stablemate of the winner, didn't have a lot of negatives against his chance, as he came into this contest off the back of a Group 1 success at Randwick over 1m4f, which secured his trainer's 100th Group 1 winner. Drawn well here, he was always prominent but offered little once the pack closed in, and he came home at the one pace.

Alcopop(AUS) sprung to the head of the betting for this after chasing home potential superstar So You Think in the Yalumba Stakes last weekend. It was an eyecatching performance but he was easily held that day by the winner, and had been handed a modest draw here to say the least. Forced to settled towards the rear, his rider made a quick move heading towards the final bend but it soon came to little.

Tokai Trick(JPN) has looked to want further than this trip in his homeland and never threatened.

Mourayan(IRE) had run over some bizarre trips since going south, and showed his first piece of form, unsurprisingly, when behind Herculian Prince in the Metropolitan last time over 1m4f - he was in front far too early in that and didn't appear to be relish being there. He got in here because of non-runners and failed to make much impression.

Faint Perfume(AUS), wearing blinkers for the first time, got bumped going into the first bend and has struggled to make much impression since her reappearance at the end of August. Glen Boss said the mare panicked and went out of control after the incident. Mosse, rider of Mr Medici, was suspended for 10 meetings for his part in the coming together, but becomes clear to ride again on October 28th.

Dariana(AUS), this season's Queensland Derby winner, was thought not to want the ground heavy, and so it proved.

6235 WOODBINE (R-H)

Saturday, October 16

OFFICIAL GOING: Turf: good

6949a NEARCTIC STKS (GRADE 1) (3YO+) (TURF) 6f

9:23 (12:00) 3-Y-O+

£176,470 (£58,823; £32,352; £21,176; £8,823; £235)

RPR

1 **Serious Attitude (IRE)**20 6390 4-8-2 0 GKGomez 10 113
(Rae Guest) *help up: 10th fnl turn (over 2f out): hdwy 2f out and swtchd outside ins fnl f: qcknd to ld 160yds out: r.o wl and drew clr fnl 100yds* **231/10**

2 *2 1/2* **Grand Adventure (USA)**27 6237 4-8-9 0 PHusbands 2 112
(Mark Frostad, Canada) *racd in midfield (nvr far off pce): 5th on rail 2f out: qcknd and led fnl f: hdd 160yds out: r.o but nt pce of wnr* **9/2**2

3 *3 1/4* **Fatal Bullet (USA)**48 5-8-5 0 (b) ERosaDaSilva 9 98
(Reade Baker, Canada) *a.p (3rd for much of the way): outside of line of 3 turning for hom (over 2f out): rdn and nt qckn fnl f* **21/4**3

4 *nk* **Field Commission (CAN)**48 5-8-7 0 (b) JJCastellano 1 99
(Daniel J Vella, Canada) *settled towards rr: last over 3f out: hdwy appr fnl f: r.o wl last 160yds: nvr nrr* **129/10**

5 *nk* **Bridgetown (USA)**40 3-8-3 0 ElvisTrujillo 3 95
(Kenneth McPeek, U.S.A) *broke wl and led: jnd after abt 300yds: ins of line of 3 turning for home: hdd appr fnl f and sn wknd* **23/10**1

6 *1/2* **Sneaking Uponyou (USA)**76 4-8-5 0 AGarcia 8 94
(Jamie Ness, U.S.A) *broke will: jnd ldr after 300yds: middle of line of 3 turning for home: led appr fnl f: hdd sn after: rdn and fdd fnl 160yds* **185/10**

7 *1 1/4* **Signature Red (USA)**27 6237 4-8-9 0 LContreras 7 94
(Sid Attard, Canada) *hld up in fnl 3rd: hdwy 3f out: cl 8th on outside st (over 2f out): rdn and nt qckn fnl 300 yds* **219/10**

8 *3/4* **Bogue Chitto (USA)**40 6-8-6 0 ow1 (b) GOlguin 4 89
(Ian Howard, Canada) *chsd ldrs: cl 5th and ev ch st (over 2f out): wknd u.p fnl f* **34/1**

9 *1/2* **Towzee (NZ)**40 8-8-5 0 ERamsammy 5 86
(Brian A Lynch, Canada) *hld up: hdwy to go midfield on rail 2f out: unable qck: n.d* **35/1**

10 *nk* **Amico Fritz (GER)**13 6608 4-8-9 0 Christophe-PatriceLemaire 6 89
(H-A Pantall, France) *racd in the main pack: hdwy over 2 1/2f out to go 5th ins fnl 2f: sn rdn and unable qck: fdd last 110yds* **41/5**

11 *1 1/4* **Woodbourne (CAN)**27 6237 6-8-5 0 ChantalSutherland 12 81
(Robert Tiller, Canada) *chsd ldrs: 6th st (over 2f out): sn btn* **185/10**

12 *nse* **Balthazaar's Gift (IRE)**35 5946 7-8-9 0 LukeMorris 11 85
(C G Cox) *dwlt and last: 3rd last over 2f out: no imp u.p: nvr a threat* **25/4**

69.37 secs (69.37)

WFA 3 from 4yo+ 1lb **12** Ran SP% **120.7**

PARI-MUTUEL (all including $2 stake): WIN 48.20; PLACE (1-2) 20.30, 6.20; SHOW (1-2-3) 10.50, 4.30, 4.60; SF 368.30.

Owner Derek J Willis & Rae Guest **Bred** Paddy Twomey **Trained** Newmarket, Suffolk

NOTEBOOK

Serious Attitude(IRE), the 2008 Cheveley Park winner, had recorded a three-figure RPR just once in six starts since a Group 3 success at York in July 2009, but was using Lasix for the first time and Garrett Gomez was a positive jockey booking. Sensibly dropped in from stall ten, she had only one behind once in line for the finish, but the leaders soon wilted up the long straight. This was a "Win and You're In" for the Breeders' Cup Turf Sprint, but that race is to be to run over 5f this year, and is not a Grade 1, so instead she will head straight to Fasig-Tipton November sale, where she should fetch big money.

Amico Fritz(GER), who didn't use Lasix, was well enough placed but failed to pick up for pressure, running well below his European form.

Balthazaar's Gift(IRE), another runner kept off Lasix, was always struggling after a slow start. He's better over 7f.

6950a E P TAYLOR STKS (GRADE 1) (3YO+ FILLIES & MARES) (TURF) 1m 2f (T)

10:03 (10:04) 3-Y-O+

£352,941 (£117,647; £64,705; £35,294; £17,647; £235)

RPR

1 **Reggane**22 6344 4-8-12 0 ChristopheSoumillon 5 112
(A De Royer-Dupre, France) **104/10**

2 *1* **Miss Keller (IRE)**27 6235 4-8-12 0 JJCastellano 6 110
(Roger L Attfield, Canada) **69/20**3

3 *1 3/4* **Shalanaya (IRE)**55 5348 4-8-12 0 Christophe-PatriceLemaire 1 107
(M Delzangles, France) **67/20**2

4 *3/4* **Contredanse (IRE)**55 5346 3-8-8 0 GKGomez 7 106
(L M Cumani) **51/20**1

5 *nk* **Pachattack (USA)**56 5320 4-8-12 0 ChantalSutherland 9 104
(G A Butler) **159/10**

6 *1/2* **Akarlina (FR)**22 6344 4-8-12 0 ThierryThulliez 10 103
(N Clement, France) **54/10**

7 *1* **Gallic Star (IRE)**55 5346 3-8-8 0 ChrisCatlin 8 102
(M R Channon) **61/1**

8 *hd* **Lahaleeb (IRE)**14 6561 4-8-12 0 (b1) JohnEgan 2 101
(P W D'Arcy) **214/10**

9 2 3/4 **Silver Grey (IRE)**[31] 6095 3-8-8 0 RobertHavlin 4 97
(R Ingram) 49/1
10 2 1/4 **Mekong Melody (IRE)**[20] 5-8-12 0 PHusbands 3 91
(Roger L Attfield, Canada) 103/10
2m 3.38s (-0.64)
WFA 3 from 4yo+ 5lb **10** Ran SP% **120.9**
PARI-MUTUEL (all including $2 stake): WIN 22.80; PLACE (1-2) 8.60, 4.60; SHOW (1-2-3) 5.40, 3.10, 3.50; SF 115.90.
Owner Haras De La Perelle **Bred** Haras De La Perelle **Trained** Chantilly, France

NOTEBOOK
Reggane had mainly struggled since finishing second to Ghanaati in last year's Coronation Stakes at Royal Ascot, her only win since then coming in a minor Listed race three starts back, though a slow pace hadn't helped in her last two races. Partnered by the world-class Christophe Soumillon for the first time, she had the race run to suit and picked up smartly under a well-timed ride. This was a "Win and You're In" for the Breeders' Cup Filly & Mare Turf and she could take her chance.
Shalanaya(IRE) was always well placed, and though briefly short of room early in the straight, had her chance. She could only find the one pace, however, and looks a shadow of the filly who won last year's Prix de l'Opera.
Contredanse(IRE) did little to disprove the theory that she was flattered by her proximity to subsequent Prix de l'Opera winner Lily Of The Valley in a Deauville Group 3 last time.
Pachattack(USA) got away from the stalls much better than in the Beverly D, but was still waited with. She went very wide into the straight and got going too late.
Gallic Star(IRE) didn't get the clearest of runs in the straight, but was not unlucky.
Lahaleeb(IRE) had blinkers fitted and was using Lasix for the first time, but she did not return to the form she showed when winning this race last year.
Silver Grey(IRE) was out of her depth.

6951a PATTISON CANADIAN INTERNATIONAL (GRADE 1) (3YO+) (TURF) 1m 4f (T)
10:40 (10:46) 3-Y-O+
£705,882 (£235,294; £129,411; £70,588; £42,352; £235)

RPR
1 **Joshua Tree (IRE)**[35] 5945 3-8-10 0 CO'Donoghue 7 115
(A P O'Brien, Ire) 23/5[3]
2 hd **Mores Wells**[34] 6017 6-9-0 0 (b) SebastienMaillot 3 112
(R Gibson, France) 205/10
3 nse **Redwood**[27] 6236 4-9-0 0 MichaelHills 8 112
(B W Hills) 11/5[1]
4 1/2 **Al Khali (USA)**[35] 4-9-0 0 AGarcia 5 111
(William Mott, U.S.A) 109/20
5 3/4 **Fifty Proof (CAN)**[27] 6236 4-9-0 0 JStein 9 110
(Ian Black, Canada) 69/10
6 nk **Chinchon (IRE)**[34] 6015 5-9-0 0 GKGomez 2 109
(C Laffon-Parias, France) 13/4[2]
7 1 1/2 **Simmard (USA)**[35] 5-9-0 0 (b) JJCastellano 4 107
(Roger L Attfield, Canada) 166/10
8 nk **Marsh Side (USA)**[27] 6236 7-9-0 0 EPrado 6 107
(Neil Drysdale, U.S.A) 117/10
9 1/2 **Memorial Maniac (USA)**[27] 6236 5-9-0 0 (b) JamesGraham 1 106
(Larry Demeritte, U.S.A) 50/1
2m 32.72s (3.12)
WFA 3 from 4yo+ 7lb **9** Ran SP% **121.0**
PARI-MUTUEL (all including $2 stake): WIN 11.20; PLACE (1-2) 6.90, 15.10; SHOW (1-2-3) 4.30, 7.60, 2.50; SF 171.50.
Owner D Smith, Mrs J Magnier, M Tabor **Bred** Castlemartin Stud And Skymarc Farm **Trained** Ballydoyle, Co Tipperary

NOTEBOOK
Joshua Tree(IRE) delayed the start after losing a shoe in the paddock, though he seemed calm on the way to post. Having travelled well in about mid-division, he made good headway to take third early in the straight, but Colm O'Donoghue sensibly waited a few strides before going for everything, clearly knowing not to commit what would have been too soon up this relatively long Woodbine straight. The winner, who was on Lasix for the first time, appreciated the drop back in trip after struggling to be competitive in the St Leger and may even have the speed for 1m2f. This victory has earned him a place in the Breeders' Cup Turf, however, and he'll probably be worth his place in the line-up.
Mores Wells, like 2006 winner Collier Hill, came into this after victory in the Stockholm Cup, but didn't use Lasix. He was short of room when trying to follow Joshua Tree through over a furlong out and, having finished well when in the open, the margin of defeat suggests he may have been unlucky.
Redwood had everything go his way when he landed the Northern Dancer on his previous start, but not on this occasion. Unlike when slowly away last time, he wasn't sent for a rails run, Michael Hills, no doubt aware he was unlikely to enjoy such a ground-saving trip in this more competitive race, and when trying to close between horses in the straight, he became involved in a barging match. While his run was never checked, that can't have helped. He again went without Lasix.
Al Khali(USA), a Grade 2 winner at Belmont last time, is another who can be described as unlucky. He got caught up in the interference around a furlong out, being baulked when looking for a run, and then finished strongly when switched out widest of all.

6769 BATH (L-H)
Sunday, October 17

OFFICIAL GOING: Good (7.8)
Wind: Virtually nil Weather: Sunny

6952 BRIGHTVIEW WINDOWS H'CAP (DIV I) 5f 161y
1:40 (1:40) (Class 6) (0-58,65) 3-Y-O+ **£1,295** (£385; £192; £96) **Stalls** Centre

Form RPR
5165 1 **Wooden King (IRE)**[16] 6536 5-9-3 56 TomMcLaughlin 1 65
(M S Saunders) *mde all: rdn over 2f out: hld on: all out* 4/1[2]
0533 2 nk **Cwmni**[38] 5875 4-9-0 58 DeclanCannon(5) 10 66
(B Palling) *towards rr of mid-div: rdn and hdwy over 2f out: kpt on but edgd lft ins fnl f: wnt 2nd fnl stride* 4/1[2]
0000 3 shd **Captain Kallis (IRE)**[26] 6270 4-8-9 48 JamesDoyle 6 56
(D J S Ffrench Davis) *chsd wnr: rdn to chal over 1f out: kpt on towards fin* 10/1
0064 4 2 1/4 **Cocktail Party (IRE)**[48] 5580 4-8-7 46 (v) JimmyQuinn 8 46
(J W Unett) *plld hrd towards rr: hdwy over 2f out: sn rdn: kpt on fnl f* 22/1
1400 5 1 1/2 **Stamford Blue**[17] 6515 9-8-11 57 (b) JakePayne(7) 11 52
(R A Harris) *chsd ldrs on outer: rdn over 2f out: kpt on same pce fnl f* 7/2[1]
4050 6 3/4 **Liel**[118] 3255 4-9-5 58 ShaneKelly 5 51
(B J Meehan) *mid-div: rdn 3f out: nvr any imp* 11/1

3221 7 2 1/2 **Nadinska**[7] 6773 3-9-11 65 6ex CathyGannon 7 50
(M R Channon) *s.i.s: towards rr: rdn over 2f out: nt pce to get on terms* 5/1[3]
050 8 4 **Swingle**[51] 5474 3-9-0 54 DaneO'Neill 2 25
(D Haydn Jones) *mid-div: rdn over 2f out: wknd ent fnl f* 12/1
2010 9 2 1/2 **Boga (IRE)**[38] 5876 3-8-13 53 WilliamCarson 4 16
(R J Hodges) *trckd wnr: rdn over 2f out: wknd over 1f out* 33/1
0060 10 2 3/4 **Little Buddy**[12] 6655 3-8-3 46 oh1 SophieDoyle(3) 9 —
(R J Price) *s.i.s: a towards rr* 80/1
1m 11.45s (0.25) **Going Correction** -0.05s/f (Good)
WFA 3 from 4yo+ 1lb **10** Ran SP% **112.5**
Speed ratings (Par 101): **96,95,95,92,90 89,86,80,77,73**
toteswingers: 1&2 £4.90, 1&3 £6.90, 2&3 £8.50 CSF £19.26 CT £149.28 TOTE £5.10: £2.10, £2.50, £3.10; EX 18.00 Trifecta £63.60 Pool: £107.44 - 1.25 winning units..
Owner Pat Hancock **Bred** Terence E Connelly **Trained** Green Ore, Somerset
■ Stewards' Enquiry : Tom McLaughlin two-day ban: used whip with excessive frequency (Nov 1-2)
Declan Cannon two-day ban: used whip with excessive frequency (Oct 31-Nov 1)

FOCUS
The ground had dried out to good all round. An ordinary handicap.

6953 PROFAB WINDOWS SW MAIDEN STKS 1m 5y
2:10 (2:13) (Class 5) 2-Y-O **£2,007** (£597; £298; £149) **Stalls** Low

Form RPR
02 1 **Census (IRE)**[18] 6473 2-9-3 0 RyanMoore 15 78+
(R Hannon) *little slowly away: trckd ldrs: clipped heels on bnd over 4f out: rdn to ld over 1f out: in command fnl f: readily* 4/5[1]
6 2 3 **Elfine (IRE)**[12] 6651 2-8-12 0 DaneO'Neill 13 63
(H J L Dunlop) *led: did nt handle bnd and hdd over 4f out: chsd ldrs: rdn over 2f out: styd on to chse wnr fnl f but readily hld* 25/1
6 3 1 **Conjuror's Bluff**[13] 6635 2-9-3 0 JimCrowley 4 66
(R Hannon) *mid-div: hdwy over 2f out: sn rdn: styd on same pce* 20/1
6 4 1/2 **Whiplash Willie**[18] 6474 2-9-3 0 JimmyFortune 1 65+
(A M Balding) *prom: lft in ld on bnd over 5f out: rdn and hdd wl over 2f out: styd on same pce* 20/1
2 5 nk **Ru'Oud**[51] 5498 2-9-3 0 TedDurcan 5 64
(Saeed Bin Suroor) *trckd ldrs: led wl over 2f out: rdn and hdd wl over 1f out: kpt on same pce* 9/4[2]
5 6 8 **Secret Edge**[13] 6634 2-9-3 0 FergusSweeney 3 46
(A King) *s.i.s: sn in mid-div: rdn over 2f out: little imp* 28/1
00 7 3/4 **Captain Bellamy (USA)**[10] 6689 2-9-3 0 SteveDrowne 9 44
(H Morrison) *a in mid-div* 100/1
0 8 1/2 **Sum Satisfaction**[18] 6473 2-9-3 0 IanMongan 2 43
(Miss Tor Sturgis) *s.i.s: t.k.h in mid-div: rdn over 2f out: no imp* 125/1
0000 9 shd **Adzing (IRE)**[6] 6795 2-9-3 45 LukeMorris 10 42
(R A Harris) *trckd ldrs: rdn 3f out: wknd 2f out* 200/1
00 10 1 1/4 **Fleeting Tiger**[18] 6474 2-9-3 0 JimmyQuinn 12 40
(J L Dunlop) *sn bhd* 100/1
0 11 1 3/4 **Ishikawa (IRE)**[97] 3961 2-9-3 0 AdamKirby 6 36
(A King) *mid-div: rdn wl over 2f out: wknd ent fnl f* 100/1
00 12 12 **Emperorsnewclothes (IRE)**[13] 6628 2-9-0 0 (p) MatthewDavies(3) 7 8
(George Baker) *a towards rr* 150/1
13 20 **Midnight Moon** 2-9-3 0 DaraghO'Donohoe 8 —
(Saeed Bin Suroor) *v.s.a: a detached in last: t.o* 12/1[3]
00 14 4 **Titian Queen**[135] 2687 2-8-9 0 SophieDoyle(3) 11 —
(Mrs P N Dutfield) *sn bhd: t.o* 200/1
1m 41.88s (1.08) **Going Correction** -0.05s/f (Good) **14** Ran SP% **116.3**
Speed ratings (Par 95): **92,89,88,87,87 79,78,77,77,76 74,62,42,38**
toteswingers: 1&2 £7.40, 1&3 £5.70, 2&3 £25.90 CSF £32.23 TOTE £1.90: £1.10, £5.50, £7.50; EX 32.90 Trifecta £85.70 Pool: £265.36 - 2.29 winning units..
Owner Highclere Thoroughbred Racing (Beeswing) **Bred** Brian Williamson **Trained** East Everleigh, Wilts

FOCUS
Despite the big field the market only wanted to know two of these, and in fact it spoke pretty loudly for the chance of Census. He was well in command, but the likes of the seventh and nionth suggest this is very limited form.

NOTEBOOK
Census(IRE), despite having to be backed out of the stalls beforehand after Come On The Irons reared up in the adjoining stall and got his front legs stuck over his gate, overcame his wide draw, having to be rushed up early and running green to come home strongly and get off the mark at the third attempt. He'll be better for a winter on his back and should make up into a nice middle-distance horse next year. (op 6-4)
Elfine(IRE) got a good break from her wide draw and crossed over to make the early running. This was a step up on her debut effort, the extra furlong suited, and although she's by Invincible Spirit, she doesn't look short of stamina. (op 22-1)
Conjuror's Bluff, stablemate of the winner, was another to improve for his debut. One more run will make him eligible for handicaps, which is when he'll be of more interest. (op 14-1)
Whiplash Willie made the most of his low draw to get a prominent early position, and didn't run too badly. There's loads of stamina in his pedigree and it won't be until he tackles 1m4f plus next year that the best will be seen of him. (tchd 18-1)
Ru'Oud looked to have plenty going for him, but he failed to build on his promising debut at Thirsk. He got first run on the winner early in the straight, but was soon headed and weakened disappointingly. (op 7-4 tchd 5-2)
Secret Edge was outpaced by the principals but stayed on to be best of the rest. He'll do better next year. (op 25-1 tchd 33-1)

6954 EXPRESS GLAZING & E B F MAIDEN STKS 5f 11y
2:40 (2:43) (Class 5) 2-Y-O **£3,076** (£915; £457; £228) **Stalls** Centre

Form RPR
0343 1 **Forty Proof (IRE)**[20] 6419 2-8-12 71 AdamBeschizza(5) 12 74
(W J Knight) *hld up: hdwy over 2f out: led wl over 1f out: edgd lft: r.o strly: rdn out* 4/1[2]
06 2 3 1/4 **Sluggsy Morant**[67] 4954 2-9-3 0 DaneO'Neill 8 66+
(H Candy) *little slowly away: sn chsng ldrs: rdn over 2f out: kpt on ins fnl f: wnt 2nd towards fin: no ch w wnr* 11/2[3]
3440 3 1 **Till Dawn (IRE)**[11] 6674 2-8-12 53 JimmyQuinn 1 54
(A W Carroll) *chsd ldrs: rdn over 2f out: wnt 2nd jst ins fnl f tl no ex towards fin* 50/1
35 4 1/2 **Loved To Bits**[16] 6520 2-8-12 0 FergusSweeney 14 52
(P J Makin) *wnt rt s: towards rr: rdn and hdwy over 1f out: styd on fnl f* 20/1
4323 5 1/2 **Imogen Louise (IRE)**[27] 6259 2-8-12 69 PhilipRobinson 15 50
(D Haydn Jones) *hmpd leaving stalls: towards rr: hdwy over 1f out: kpt on ins fnl f: nrst fin* 4/1[2]

0 **6** ½ **Just For Leo (IRE)**[15] 6568 2-9-3 65 CathyGannon 9 53
(P D Evans) *prom: rdn and ev ch 2f out: kpt on same pce fr over 1f out* **18/1**

2340 **7** ¾ **Barking (IRE)**[19] 6445 2-9-3 70 RyanMoore 10 59+
(R Hannon) *hld up towards rr: rdn and hdwy whn hmpd over 1f out: nt best of runs ins fnl f: no further imp* **7/2**[1]

4 **8** *hd* **Lady Mango (IRE)**[10] 6697 2-8-12 0 LukeMorris 6 45
(R A Harris) *hmpd sn after s: disp ld tl wnr swept by over 1f out: fdd* **8/1**

9 *hd* **Certral** 2-8-9 0 MatthewDavies(3) 16 50+
(George Baker) *s.i.s: racd green: bhd: plenty to do 2f out: r.o wl whn swtchd lft ins fnl f: nrst fin: improve* **50/1**

0600 **10** *hd* **Palindromic (IRE)**[11] 6674 2-9-3 49 (b) LiamKeniry 7 48
(J R Gask) *hmpd sn after s: mid-div: travelling wl whn nt clr run over 1f out: swtchd rt: sn rdn: nt qckn* **100/1**

60 **11** *hd* **Bobbyow**[18] 6465 2-8-12 0 DeclanCannon(5) 2 48
(B Palling) *hmpd sn after s: disp ld tl wnr swept by over 1f out: sn wknd* **40/1**

12 4 ½ **Albany Rose (IRE)** 2-8-12 0 SteveDrowne 4 27
(Rae Guest) *chsd ldrs: rdn over 2f out: wknd over 1f out* **28/1**

4446 **13** *3* **Partout Le Magasin**[11] 6666 2-9-3 71 (p) JimCrowley 3 21
(J S Moore) *short of room sn after s: disp ld tl wekaned over 1f out* **25/1**

14 ¾ **Lady Titticaca** 2-8-12 0 RichardKingscote 13 13
(R J Hodges) *a towards rr* **100/1**

4000 **15** *10* **Terrys Flutter**[133] 2785 2-8-9 0 SophieDoyle(3) 17 —
(M A Allen) *chsd ldrs on outer for 3f: sn wknd* **150/1**

16 *48* **Kitty Fisher** 2-8-12 0 WilliamCarson 11 —
(R J Hodges) *sn wl bhd: t.o* **66/1**

62.45 secs (-0.05) **Going Correction** -0.05s/f (Good) **16** Ran SP% **116.5**
Speed ratings (Par 95): **98,92,91,90,89 88,87,87,86,86 86,79,74,73,57** —
toteswingers: 1&2 £6.00, 1&3 £27.60, 2&3 £32.40 CSF £23.09 TOTE £5.80: £1.30, £2.70, £9.60; EX 36.90 TRIFECTA Not won..
Owner G Roddick **Bred** David Jamison Bloodstock And G Roddick **Trained** Patching, W Sussex

FOCUS
A weak, rather rough maiden. The winner produced a minor personal best and the runner-up is better than the bare form.

NOTEBOOK
Forty Proof(IRE) has been very consistent, running to an RPR of between 63 and 68 in each of his previous five starts, and it's doubtful he had to improve a great deal on that to get off the mark here. Held up off the pace, while the runner-up got into all sorts of trouble towards the inside, he was delivered with his challenge out wide by Beschizza, who as a result had the luxury of easing up close home. This trip seems to suit the colt well. (op 9-2)
Sluggsy Morant found the gap he was going for 2f out closing in front of him, and after being switched twice he finally stayed on towards the inside to take second. He'd have gone much closer with a clear run. Handicaps now become an option. (op 6-1 tchd 13-2)
Till Dawn(IRE) found 6f in soft ground far too much of a test last time and proved much happier back over the minimum trip on this better surface. (op 40-1)
Loved To Bits, wide throughout, ran a sound race on her turf debut, and is another now eligible for a mark. It wouldn't be a surprise if her trainer found her a nursery back on the Polytrack at Lingfield. (op 16-1)
Imogen Louise(IRE) struggled to go the pace but stayed on late. She doesn't appear to be progressing, though. Official explanation: jockey said filly was hampered leaving stalls (tchd 9-2)
Barking(IRE) is another who isn't progressing, although he shouldn't be too harshly judged on this effort as his path was continually blocked and he got no sort of run. Official explanation: jockey said colt was denied a clear run (tchd 4-1)
Lady Mango(IRE) Official explanation: jockey said filly was hampered leaving stalls
Bobbyow Official explanation: jockey said colt hung right on leaving stalls

6955 MODERN GLASS H'CAP 2m 1f 34y
3:15 (3:15) (Class 5) (0-75,71) 3-Y-O **£2,007** (£597; £298; £149) **Stalls** Centre

Form RPR

4153 **1** **Sula Two**[19] 6448 3-9-7 71 RichardKingscote 5 80
(R J Hodges) *in tch: tk narrow advantage over 2f out: hrd pressed and sn rdn: styd on gamely: edgd lft fnl f: all out* **6/1**

2120 **2** ¾ **Albeed**[31] 6132 3-9-5 69 JimmyQuinn 1 77
(J L Dunlop) *trckd ldrs: rdn to chal fr over 2f out: remained w ev ch but leaned on by wnr fnl f: no ex fnl 50yds* **10/1**

4232 **3** 2 ¾ **Viviani (IRE)**[20] 6416 3-8-13 63 (t) JimCrowley 6 68
(Mrs A J Perrett) *trckd ldrs: rdn wl over 2f out: styd on same pce* **11/2**

1154 **4** ½ **Bravo Bravo**[26] 6272 3-8-6 56 CathyGannon 7 60
(M R Channon) *hld up in last pair: rdn wl over 2f out: styd on same pce: nvr able to chal* **4/1**[2]

5103 **5** *7* **Budva**[47] 5646 3-9-0 64 JimmyFortune 2 60
(H Morrison) *led for 8f: trckd ldr: led 3f out: sn rdn and hdd: styd chsng ldrs tl wknd fnl 120yds* **12/1**

0524 **6** *6* **High Ransom**[89] 4230 3-9-5 69 (b[1]) PhilipRobinson 4 58
(M A Jarvis) *racd keenly: trckd ldr: led after 8f: sn clr: rdn and hdd 3f out: sn hld: wknd over 1f out* **9/2**[3]

0512 **7** 2 ¾ **Al Shababiya (IRE)**[22] 6373 3-8-8 63 AdamBeschizza(5) 8 49
(D M Simcock) *hld up last: rdn 3f out: nvr able to get on terms: wknd over 1f out* **11/4**[1]

-050 **8** 2 ¾ **Daryainur (IRE)**[16] 6527 3-8-2 52 oh7 FrankieMcDonald 3 34
(F J Brennan) *stmbld leaving stalls: in last trio but in tch: rdn 3f out: wknd 2f out* **66/1**

3m 50.19s (-1.71) **Going Correction** -0.05s/f (Good) **8** Ran SP% **112.8**
Speed ratings (Par 101): **102,101,100,100,96 94,92,91**
toteswingers: 1&2 £8.70, 1&3 £5.80, 2&3 £4.40 CSF £61.36 CT £346.08 TOTE £10.50: £1.60, £4.60, £2.10; EX 43.20 Trifecta £220.00 Pool: £297.30 - 0.63 winning units..
Owner Richard Prince **Bred** D R Tucker **Trained** Charlton Mackrell, Somerset

FOCUS
Quite a competitive little staying handicap.
High Ransom Official explanation: jockey said filly was unsuited by the good ground

6956 BRIGHTVIEW WINDOWS H'CAP (DIV II) 5f 161y
3:50 (3:51) (Class 6) (0-58,58) 3-Y-O+ **£1,295** (£385; £192; £96) **Stalls** Centre

Form RPR

00-0 **1** **Final Rhapsody**[31] 6133 4-8-9 48 ow1 StevieDonohoe 10 59
(W J Musson) *hld up towards rr: racd wd: rdn and hdwy over 1f out: str run but edgd lft ins fnl f: led fnl stride* **20/1**

0031 **2** *hd* **Rio Royale (IRE)**[61] 5169 4-9-5 58 (p) JimCrowley 6 68
(Mrs A J Perrett) *pushed along in mid-div fr over 3f out: rdn and hdwy 2f out: r.o to ld nring fin: hdd fnl stride* **12/1**[1]

4006 **3** ½ **Durgan**[18] 6455 4-9-2 55 (p) SteveDrowne 5 63
(Mrs L C Jewell) *trckd ldrs: rdn to chal whn bmpd wl over 1f out: led jst ins fnl f: no ex whn hdd nring fin* **9/1**

006 **4** 3 ½ **Ellen Vannin (IRE)**[27] 6255 3-9-0 54 (b) CathyGannon 8 51
(Eve Johnson Houghton) *dropped to rr after being squeezed out after 1f: sn rdn: no imp tl styd on ins fnl f: snatched 4th fnl stride* **16/1**

4222 **5** *hd* **Best One**[16] 6536 6-9-2 55 (b) LukeMorris 13 51
(R A Harris) *trckd ldrs: rdn to chal whn bmpd wl over 1f out: no ex ins fnl f* **6/1**[2]

6 *nse* **Leahness (IRE)**[76] 4665 3-8-6 46 oh1 HayleyTurner 7 42
(Patrick Morris) *stdd s: rdn 2f out: styd on but nvr gng pce to get involved* **14/1**

0600 **7** ½ **Figaro Flyer (IRE)**[18] 6455 7-8-11 50 J-PGuillambert 9 44
(P Howling) *mid-div: rdn and hdwy to chse ldrs 2f out: wknd fnl 100yds* **7/1**[3]

6044 **8** *hd* **Green Lagonda (AUS)**[16] 6536 8-9-1 57 ow1 (p) RichardEvans(3) 3 51
(P D Evans) *prom: led over 2f out: sn rdn: hdd jst ins fnl f: no ex* **8/1**

2042 **9** *shd* **Commandingpresence (USA)**[11] 6672 4-9-2 55 NeilChalmers 4 48
(J J Bridger) *hld up: hdwy whn nt clr run 3f out: sn rdn: styd on same pce fnl 2f* **15/2**

2310 **10** 3 ¼ **The Jailer**[32] 6078 7-9-2 58 (p) RussKennemore(3) 1 41
(J G M O'Shea) *sn led: rdn and hdd over 2f out: wknd ent fnl f* **8/1**

4030 **11** *5* **Novastasia (IRE)**[48] 5579 4-8-8 47 oh1 ow1 (p) FergusSweeney 12 13
(D K Ivory) *chsd ldrs: rdn over 2f out: wknd ent fnl f: eased* **40/1**

0005 **12** *nse* **Miss Tenacious**[48] 5586 3-8-6 46 oh1 WilliamCarson 11 12
(R J Hodges) *sn outpcd: a in rr* **33/1**

2004 **13** ½ **Crystallize**[44] 5711 4-9-4 57 TomMcLaughlin 2 21
(A B Haynes) *s.i.s: nvr bttr than mid-div: wknd ent fnl f* **12/1**

1m 11.68s (0.48) **Going Correction** -0.05s/f (Good)
WFA 3 from 4yo+ 1lb **13** Ran SP% **116.5**
Speed ratings (Par 101): **94,93,93,88,88 88,87,87,87,82 76,75,75**
toteswingers: 1&2 £26.10, 1&3 £51.70, 2&3 £12.10 CSF £121.70 CT £1077.86 TOTE £31.60: £7.20, £1.20, £3.10; EX 183.60 TRIFECTA Not won..
Owner The Survivors **Bred** Compton Down Stud **Trained** Newmarket, Suffolk

FOCUS
There was plenty of pace on here and the race was set up for a closer. The winning time was marginally slower than the first division.
Final Rhapsody Official explanation: trainer had no explanation for the apparent improvement in form

6957 ASHTON GLASS H'CAP 1m 5f 22y
4:25 (4:25) (Class 4) (0-80,80) 3-Y-O+ **£3,594** (£1,069; £534; £266) **Stalls** Low

Form RPR

0021 **1** **Dynamic Drive (IRE)**[7] 6781 3-9-8 80 6ex AdamKirby 3 92+
(W R Swinburn) *trckd ldrs: shkn up over 2f out: chal ent fnl f: tk narrow advantage fnl 100yds: pushed out* **11/8**[1]

4006 **2** *nk* **Soundbyte**[17] 6502 5-8-13 63 FergusSweeney 4 71
(J Gallagher) *trckd ldrs: led 2f out: sn rdn and hrd pressed: kpt on gamely whn narrowly hdd fnl 100yds: hld nr fin* **25/1**

4361 **3** *2* **Pelham Crescent (IRE)**[7] 6774 7-9-1 72 ThomasBrown(7) 6 77+
(B Palling) *hld up in last: rdn wl over 2f out: hdwy and hung rt over 1f out: styd on: snatched 3rd fnl strides* **11/2**[3]

43/1 **4** *nk* **Oldrik (GER)**[30] 6152 7-9-9 76 (p) EJMcNamara(3) 10 81
(P J Hobbs) *racd keenly: hld up: hdwy 3f out: rdn to chal 2f out: no ex ent fnl f: lost 3rd fnl strides* **3/1**[2]

1040 **5** 1 ¾ **Turjuman (USA)**[102] 3781 5-9-7 71 StevieDonohoe 2 73
(W J Musson) *in tch: rdn wl over 2f out: styd on same pce* **28/1**

2501 **6** 1 ¾ **Lombok**[11] 6668 4-9-8 72 HayleyTurner 11 72
(M L W Bell) *trckd ldr: led after 3f: rdn and hdd 2f out: wknd ins fnl f* **11/1**

1330 **7** *5* **Mecox Bay (IRE)**[39] 5868 3-9-0 72 JimmyFortune 1 64
(A M Balding) *led for 3f: trckd ldr: rdn wl over 2f out: wknd over 1f out* **8/1**

0-6 **8** 4 ½ **Zafranagar (IRE)**[197] 355 5-8-12 69 GeorgeDowning(7) 9 55
(A W Carroll) *rdn 3f out: a towards rr* **50/1**

0000 **9** *8* **If I Were A Boy (IRE)**[15] 6556 3-9-3 75 JamesDoyle 8 49
(D J S Ffrench Davis) *in tch: c wdst fr 3f out: effrt sn after: wknd over 1f out* **28/1**

2m 52.72s (0.72) **Going Correction** -0.05s/f (Good)
WFA 3 from 4yo+ 8lb **9** Ran SP% **114.6**
Speed ratings (Par 105): **95,94,93,93,92 91,88,85,80**
toteswingers: 1&2 £11.00, 1&3 £2.80, 2&3 £22.50 CSF £45.05 CT £152.10 TOTE £2.60: £1.60, £5.50, £1.80; EX 41.50 Trifecta £333.80 Pool: £451.16 - 0.73 winning units..
Owner P W Harris **Bred** Pendley Farm **Trained** Aldbury, Herts

FOCUS
Another race notable for a gamble landed on a well-backed favourite.
Oldrik(GER) Official explanation: jockey said he dropped reins inside final furlong

6958 BETFAIR RACING EXCELLENCE APPRENTICE TRAINING SERIES H'CAP 1m 5y
5:00 (5:00) (Class 5) (0-75,75) 3-Y-O+ **£2,007** (£597; £298; £149) **Stalls** Low

Form RPR

0434 **1** **Music Maestro (IRE)**[20] 6413 3-7-12 61 oh1 DanielHarris(7) 5 73
(B W Hills) *chsd ldng pair: led over 2f out: styd on wl: pushed out* **12/1**

0105 **2** 3 ¾ **Boom And Bust (IRE)**[26] 6276 3-8-9 70 KatiaScallan(5) 11 73
(M P Tregoning) *hld up: hdwy fr 3f out: chsd wnr wl over 1f out: styd on but a being hld* **14/1**

6433 **3** 2 ¾ **Effigy**[19] 6444 6-9-8 75 AmyScott 10 72
(H Candy) *towards rr: pushed along over 5f out: rdn 3f out: styd on fnl 2f: wnt 3rd ins fnl f* **3/1**[2]

0642 **4** 1 ½ **Zebrano**[22] 6366 4-9-8 75 (b) AdamBeschizza 7 69
(A B Haynes) *dwlt: pushed along and rcvrd to midfield after 1f: rdn to chse wnr briefly 2f out: styd on same pce fnl f* **5/1**[3]

2020 **5** ¾ **Bidable**[13] 6629 6-8-12 70 ThomasBrown(5) 9 62
(B Palling) *hld up: hdwy 3f out: sn rdn: styd on same pce fr over 1f out: edgd lft whn rdr dropped reins ins fnl f* **20/1**

2112 **6** *6* **Lutine Charlie (IRE)**[13] 6632 3-8-8 69 (p) MatthewCosham(5) 6 47
(J L Flint) *disp ld at decent pce tl over 2f out: wknd fnl f* **7/4**[1]

0100 **7** *6* **Cavendish Road (IRE)**[16] 6543 4-9-5 72 (t) RyanClark 8 36
(N J Vaughan) *mid-div: rdn 3f out: wknd over 1f out* **25/1**

1600 **8** 1 ¾ **Phluke**[3] 6864 9-8-1 61 oh1 (v) DanielBlackett(7) 1 21
(Eve Johnson Houghton) *disp ld at decent pce tl over 2f out: sn wknd* **25/1**

141- **9** *13* **Don Pietro**[418] 5243 7-8-10 68 JakePayne(5) 2 —
(F J Brennan) *chsd ldrs: rdn over 3f out: wknd 2f out* **9/1**

1m 39.68s (-1.12) **Going Correction** -0.05s/f (Good)
WFA 3 from 4yo+ 3lb **9** Ran SP% **114.8**
Speed ratings (Par 103): **103,99,96,95,94 88,82,80,67**
toteswingers: 1&2 £6.90, 1&3 £5.50, 2&3 £7.60 CSF £156.62 CT £637.15 TOTE £14.50: £2.80, £3.10, £1.70; EX 69.10 Trifecta £300.60 Pool: £406.32 - 1.00 winning units..
Owner Triermore Stud **Bred** Adjalisa Syndicate **Trained** Lambourn, Berks
■ Daniel Harris's first winner.

FOCUS
An ordinary race won by the bottom weight.

6959 BILL LUKER MEMORIAL FILLIES' H'CAP — 1m 2f 46y
5:30 (5:30) (Class 5) (0-70,70) 3-Y-0+ — £2,007 (£597; £298; £149) Stalls Low

Form — RPR

34 **1** **Ocean Transit (IRE)**[118] 3257 5-9-4 69 .... AdamBeschizza(5) 11 — 76
(R J Price) *trckd ldrs: led wl over 2f out: sn hrd pressed and rdn: kpt on gamely: hld on on nod* **16/1**

4211 **2** *nse* **Oriental Girl**[38] 5873 5-9-10 70 ....(p) LiamKeniry 2 — 77
(J S Moore) *mid-div: hdwy u.p over 1f out: kpt on to hold ev ch ins fnl f: lost on nod* **7/2**[1]

4260 **3** *3/4* **Shades Of Grey**[65] 5038 3-9-3 68 .... AdamKirby 9 — 75+
(C G Cox) *trckd ldrs: rdn 2f out: short of room jst over 1f out: styd on* **16/1**

006 **4** *nk* **Regency Girl (IRE)**[20] 6415 3-8-4 62 ....(p) KatiaScallan(7) 3 — 67+
(M P Tregoning) *hld up towards rr: c wdst of all over 3f out: hdwy over 2f out: hung lft: kpt on ins fnl f: nt quite rch ldrs* **33/1**

4236 **5** *shd* **Madame Excelerate**[13] 6629 3-9-3 68 .... TomMcLaughlin 8 — 73
(W M Brisbourne) *w ldr: led after 4f: rdn and hdd wl over 2f out: remained w ev ch: no ex fnl 100yds* **7/1**[3]

2335 **6** *nk* **Sensationally**[39] 5860 3-9-2 67 .... JimCrowley 10 — 71
(R M Beckett) *hld up towards rr: smooth hdwy on outer 2f out: sn rdn: styd on but no ex fnl 100yds* **14/1**

3046 **7** *3 3/4* **It's Dubai Dolly**[36] 5972 4-9-7 67 .... JamesDoyle 15 — 64
(A J Lidderdale) *led for 4f: styd prom: rdn and ev ch over 2f out: fdd ins fnl f* **12/1**

0650 **8** *1/2* **Make Amends (IRE)**[10] 6691 5-9-8 68 .... HayleyTurner 14 — 64
(R J Hodges) *mid-div: rdn wl over 2f out: nt pce to get on terms* **25/1**

2235 **9** *1/2* **Dancing Storm**[13] 6639 7-9-2 62 .... IanMongan 4 — 57
(W S Kittow) *rrd up leaving stalls and lost 12 l: midfield after 2f: effrt over 2f out: one pce fnl f* **6/1**[2]

0452 **10** *nk* **On The Feather**[11] 6678 4-9-9 69 .... JamesMillman 7 — 63
(B R Millman) *nvr bttr than mid-div* **16/1**

1051 **11** *1* **Broughtons Swinger**[48] 5611 3-9-0 65 .... StevieDonohoe 5 — 57
(W J Musson) *trckd ldrs: rdn over 2f out: wknd ent fnl f* **10/1**

5303 **12** *nk* **Choral Festival**[13] 6639 4-9-0 60 .... NeilChalmers 16 — 51
(J J Bridger) *hld up: hdwy over 2f out: effrt over 1f out: wknd fnl f* **12/1**

3436 **13** *1 1/2* **Chasse Coeur**[17] 6517 3-8-10 61 ....(v[1]) JimmyFortune 12 — 49
(A M Balding) *mid-div: rdn over 2f out: wknd 1f out* **20/1**

-644 **14** *7* **Craighall**[65] 5056 3-8-13 64 .... SteveDrowne 1 — 38
(D M Simcock) *a towards rr: eased whn btn over 1f out* **7/1**[3]

2m 10.36s (-0.64) **Going Correction** -0.05s/f (Good)
WFA 3 from 4yo+ 5lb — **14** Ran SP% **121.8**
Speed ratings (Par 100): **100,99,99,99,99 98,95,95,95,94 93,93,92,86**
toteswingers: 1&2 £15.50, 1&3 £33.90, 2&3 £11.30 CSF £70.53 CT £948.26 TOTE £24.00: £4.30, £1.50, £5.00; EX 63.90 Trifecta £150.00 Pool: £202.76 - 0.44 winning units. Place 6 £163.86, Place 5 £80.33..
Owner Ocean's Five **Bred** Mike Channon Bloodstock Ltd **Trained** Ullingswick, H'fords

FOCUS
An open race on paper and a tight finish.
Dancing Storm Official explanation: jockey said mare slipped in stalls
Broughtons Swinger Official explanation: jockey said filly banged its head in stalls
T/Jkpt: Not won. T/Plt: £230.90 to a £1 stake. Pool: £66,811.50. 211.15 winning tickets. T/Qpdt: £68.60 to a £1 stake. Pool: £4,998.11. 53.90 winning tickets. TM

6457 NEWCASTLE (L-H)
Sunday, October 17

OFFICIAL GOING: Heavy (4.6)
Wind: Moderate, half against Weather: Cloudy

6960 ROBSON & PRESCOTT VETERINARY GROUP H'CAP — 1m 3y(S)
2:00 (2:00) (Class 2) (0-100,95) 3-Y-O£8,831 (£2,643; £1,321; £660; £329) Stalls Centre

Form — RPR

0163 **1** **Osteopathic Remedy (IRE)**[8] 6749 6-9-7 92 .... TomEaves 1 — 103
(M Dods) *hld up: racd keenly: smooth hdwy to trck ldrs over 2f out: rdn to ld over 1f out: drvn out* **11/2**[2]

20-0 **2** *2* **The Fifth Member (IRE)**[21] 6391 6-9-1 86 .... PatCosgrave 2 — 92
(J R Boyle) *w ldr: led over 2f out: drvn whn hdd over 1f out: kpt on ins fnl f* **11/2**[2]

3304 **3** *2 1/4* **Faithful Ruler (USA)**[13] 6630 6-8-6 82 .... LeeTopliss(5) 8 — 83
(R A Fahey) *chsd ldrs: rdn over 2f out: kpt on same pce* **12/1**

2200 **4** *1 1/4* **City Of The Kings (IRE)**[8] 6749 5-9-1 89 .... MichaelO'Connell(3) 5 — 87
(G A Harker) *hld up: rdn 3f out: no imp tl kpt on ins fnl f: n.d* **20/1**

6100 **5** *hd* **Bullwhip (IRE)**[15] 6564 3-9-7 95 ....(v[1]) NickyMackay 3 — 93
(J H M Gosden) *trckd ldrs: rdn over 2f out: sn one pce: wknd ins fnl f* **13/2**[3]

3123 **6** *1 1/2* **Arabian Spirit**[17] 6510 5-9-1 86 .... PaulHanagan 6 — 80
(R A Fahey) *trckd ldrs: rdn over 2f out: wknd ins fnl f* **3/1**[1]

1001 **7** *4 1/2* **Scrapper Smith (IRE)**[22] 6367 4-8-7 78 .... PJMcDonald 4 — 62
(A C Whillans) *v.s.a: hld up: rdn over 2f out: sn no imp* **13/2**[3]

3001 **8** *12* **Al Farahidi (USA)**[13] 6620 3-9-6 94 .... GregFairley 7 — 50
(M Johnston) *led narrowly: rdn whn hdd over 2f out: rdn over 2f out: sn wknd* **14/1**

0103 **P** **Secretive**[12] 6659 3-9-2 90 ....(b) RoystonFfrench 9 — —
(M Johnston) *trckd ldrs: rdn 4f out: sn wknd: t.o whn p.u ins fnl f* **9/1**

1m 50.22s (6.82) **Going Correction** +1.10s/f (Soft)
WFA 3 from 4yo+ 3lb — **9** Ran SP% **111.6**
Speed ratings (Par 109): **109,107,104,103,103 101,97,85,—**
toteswingers: 1&2 £7.40, 1&3 £5.70, 2&3 £25.90 CSF £34.00 CT £340.79 TOTE £4.80: £1.30, £1.10, £6.20; EX 26.20.
Owner Kevin Kirkup **Bred** Airlie Stud **Trained** Denton, Co Durham

FOCUS
The course had dried out since losing its fixture last Tuesday but the ground was still officially described as heavy. The top two were some way below the ceiling of the weights for this decent handicap. They went a fair pace in the conditions and finished quite well strung out racing down the centre of track.

NOTEBOOK
Osteopathic Remedy(IRE) picked up decent prizes in big-field handicaps at Thirsk and Ripon earlier in the season and was a creditable third of 20 at York last time. There was a slight doubt whether this potentially tactical affair would play to his strengths but he settled quite well and was always in control after cruising to the front 1f out. Things will get tougher again after this first success off a mark in the 90s but he is as good as ever at the age of six and may be able to record a ninth career win this autumn. (op 4-1)

The Fifth Member(IRE) was well backed and ran a decent race under a prominent ride on his second run after ten months off. He should continue to work his way back and it is encouraging that he was successful during this month in 2007 and 2008 and went close to repeating the trend off 1lb lower at Windsor last autumn. (op 8-1)

Faithful Ruler(USA) had a bit to prove after uncharacteristic capitulations at Ayr and Warwick, but plugged on well for some minor prize-money. He has received some charity from the handicapper and is just 1lb higher than when shooting clear on good ground at Ayr last September. (op 14-1 tchd 16-1)

City Of The Kings(IRE) did some decent late work and can probably be marked up a bit because he has done most of his winning on fast ground. He can run hot and cold, but could pose a threat next time if building on this revived effort. (op 25-1 tchd 33-1)

Bullwhip(IRE) couldn't respond when the pace quickened and has not improved for the application of a visor. (tchd 7-1)

Arabian Spirit had gone close in both runs since winning at Ayr in August, but he was lacklustre this time, which was disappointing because he has plenty of form and a win on very testing ground. (op 11-4)

Scrapper Smith(IRE) made life very difficult for himself by standing still for a few moments when the stalls opened. (op 8-1)

Secretive Official explanation: jockey said colt had no more to give

6961 COUNTRYSIDE ALLIANCE H'CAP — 1m 3y(S)
2:30 (2:30) (Class 4) (0-80,79) 3-Y-O — £4,219 (£1,255; £627; £313) Stalls Centre

Form — RPR

-200 **1** **Medicinal Compound**[18] 6467 3-9-0 79 .... JulieBurke(7) 9 — 95
(K A Ryan) *led narrowly: rdn over 2f out: drvn clr fnl f: easily* **9/1**

424 **2** *11* **Mark Twain (IRE)**[10] 6692 3-8-13 74 .... MartinLane(3) 6 — 65
(D M Simcock) *hld up: rdn over 3f out: kpt on fr over 1f out: tk 2nd fnl 100yds: no match for wnr* **5/2**[1]

4601 **3** *1 3/4* **Master Of Dance (IRE)**[18] 6463 3-9-2 74 .... PaulMulrennan 4 — 61
(J G Given) *w ldr: rdn 3f out: stl ev ch over 1f out: wknd fnl f: lost 2nd fnl 100yds* **4/1**[3]

6530 **4** *3/4* **Muwalla**[18] 6467 3-8-7 65 .... GrahamGibbons 5 — 50
(J D Bethell) *chsd ldrs: rdn over 3f out: sn one pce: wknd ins fnl f* **3/1**[2]

0410 **5** *6* **Opening Nite (IRE)**[15] 6573 3-9-0 72 ....(b) PaulHanagan 8 — 43
(R A Fahey) *hld up: hdwy to trck ldrs 3f out: rdn 2f out: wknd over 1f out: eased fnl 75yds* **13/2**

2110 **6** *71* **Fibs And Flannel**[159] 2002 3-9-5 77 .... DavidAllan 2 — —
(T D Easterby) *dwlt: sn chsd ldrs: rdn over 3f out: sn wknd: t.o whn eased over 1f out* **7/1**

1m 50.36s (6.96) **Going Correction** +1.10s/f (Soft) — **6** Ran SP% **109.4**
Speed ratings (Par 103): **109,98,96,95,89 18**
toteswingers: 1&2 £4.50, 1&3 £8.30, 2&3 £2.70 CSF £30.10 CT £95.93 TOTE £15.10: £6.60, £3.20; EX 44.50.
Owner Hambleton Racing Ltd XIII **Bred** Mr & Mrs G Middlebrook **Trained** Hambleton, N Yorks

FOCUS
This handicap was weakened by three withdrawals. They were very tightly grouped in a steadily run race for a long way, and the outsider eventually powered clear for a runaway win.
Medicinal Compound Official explanation: trainer's rep said, regarding apparent improvement in form, that the gelding was slowly away last time and was better suited by the testing conditions.
Fibs And Flannel Official explanation: jockey said gelding had no more to give

6962 NORTHERN HUNTS H'CAP — 6f
3:00 (3:02) (Class 4) (0-85,85) 3-Y-O+ — £4,403 (£1,310; £654; £327) Stalls Centre

Form — RPR

0-00 **1** **Magic Cat**[30] 6140 4-9-0 77 .... AndrewElliott 14 — 87
(Mrs K Burke) *hld up: rdn over 2f out: hdwy and edgd lft over 1f out: r.o strly ins fnl f: led post* **22/1**

3202 **2** *shd* **Lochan Mor**[7] 6776 4-8-13 79 .... MartinLane(3) 8 — 89
(M L W Bell) *prom: rdn to ld over 2f out: drvn clr over 1f out: chal fnl 50yds: hdd post* **9/2**[1]

004 **3** *5* **Icelandic**[13] 6625 8-9-7 84 ....(t) SilvestreDeSousa 10 — 78
(F Sheridan) *hld up: rdn over 3f out: hdwy to chse ldrs over 1f out: kpt on ins fnl f: nvr threatened ldng pair* **7/1**[3]

0163 **4** *2 1/2* **Northern Bolt**[9] 6708 5-8-10 73 ....(b) PatrickMathers 13 — 59
(I W McInnes) *s.i.s: sn chsd along towards rr: kpt on fr over 1f out: n.d* **25/1**

2133 **5** *1/2* **Mango Music**[9] 6723 7-9-0 77 .... PaulHanagan 6 — 61
(R A Fahey) *led after 2f: rdn whn hdd over 2f out: stl 2nd over 1f out: wknd ins fnl f* **5/1**[2]

1506 **6** *1 1/2* **Great Charm (IRE)**[22] 6358 5-9-2 79 .... PaulMulrennan 1 — 59
(E J Alston) *prom: effrt over 2f out: stl ev ch wl over 1f out: wknd ins fnl f* **15/2**

6051 **7** *1/2* **Ingleby Arch (USA)**[178] 1491 7-8-7 70 .... GrahamGibbons 16 — 48
(T D Barron) *sn chsd ldrs: outpcd 1/2-way: kpt on again ins fnl f* **20/1**

0251 **8** *1 1/2* **Flaneur**[35] 6000 3-9-2 80 ....(b) DavidAllan 3 — 53
(T D Easterby) *chsd ldrs: drvn over 2f out: wknd over 1f out* **7/1**[3]

1021 **9** *3* **Captain Royale (IRE)**[17] 6492 5-8-6 72 ....(p) JamesSullivan(3) 12 — 36
(Miss Tracy Waggott) *prom on outer: rdn over 2f out: wknd over 1f out* **7/1**[3]

6310 **10** *nse* **Ginger Ted (IRE)**[30] 6142 3-9-4 85 ....(p) AndrewHeffernan(3) 4 — 48
(R C Guest) *hld up: rdn over 2f out: sn no imp* **14/1**

5600 **11** *1/2* **Horatio Carter**[22] 6357 5-9-1 83 ....(p) DaleSwift(5) 9 — 45
(Michael Smith) *chsd ldrs: rdn over 3f out: wknd over 1f out* **15/2**

0-06 **12** *4* **Sloop Johnb**[27] 6245 4-8-5 73 .... LeeTopliss(5) 5 — 22
(R A Fahey) *rrd s: sn chsd ldrs: wknd 2f out* **50/1**

5020 **13** *5* **Where's Reiley (USA)**[16] 6539 4-8-2 70 .... DeanHeslop(5) 7 — —
(T D Barron) *trckd ldrs: lost pl over 3f out: sn bhd* **33/1**

0002 **14** *8* **Wyatt Earp (IRE)**[45] 5684 9-8-10 73 ....(p) GregFairley 2 — —
(P Salmon) *led for 2f: rdn over 3f out: sn wknd: eased fnl f* **33/1**

1m 20.38s (5.78) **Going Correction** +1.10s/f (Soft)
WFA 3 from 4yo+ 1lb — **14** Ran SP% **123.3**
Speed ratings (Par 105): **105,104,98,94,94 92,91,89,85,85 84,79,72,62**
toteswingers: 1&2 £29.00, 1&3 £30.00, 2&3 £6.80 CSF £114.39 CT £795.19 TOTE £39.00: £7.50, £1.70, £3.30; EX 175.20.
Owner Ray Bailey **Bred** R Bailey **Trained** Middleham Moor, North Yorks

FOCUS
A competitive handicap, involving three last-time-out winners and five others who finished placed on their previous start. They raced centre to far side and the first two pulled clear. Bonnie Prince Blue was withdrawn after bursting through the stalls before they were ready to go.

Sloop Johnb Official explanation: jockey said gelding missed the break

6963 COUNTRYSIDE ALLIANCE RACE FOR REPEAL H'CAP 7f

3:35 (3:35) (Class 4) (0-85,83) 3-Y-0+ **£4,403** (£1,310; £654; £327) **Stalls** Centre

Form RPR

0521 1 **Amethyst Dawn (IRE)**[9] 6709 4-9-7 **82** DavidAllan 16 93+
(T D Easterby) *racd alone against stands' rail: mde most: rdn over 2f out: drvn and kpt on wl ins fnl f* **9/2**[2]

-400 2 ½ **Spinning**[9] 6709 7-9-5 **80** (b) GrahamGibbons 10 90
(T D Barron) *hld up in midfield: rdn and outpcd over 3f out: drvn and hdwy to chse ldrs over 1f out: kpt on wl ins fnl f* **20/1**

2135 3 2 **Ming Meng (IRE)**[19] 6438 3-8-13 **76** PaulMulrennan 9 80
(M L W Bell) *chsd ldrs: hdwy over 2f out: rdn and ev ch over 1f out: kpt on tl no ex and lost 2nd nr fin* **14/1**

0400 4 ½ **Game Lad**[22] 6366 8-9-3 **78** (t) PJMcDonald 12 81
(T D Easterby) *hld up: hdwy over 2f out: chsd ldrs over 1f out: kpt on ins fnl f* **16/1**

6000 5 4 ½ **Turn Me On (IRE)**[21] 6394 7-8-11 **79** LukeStrong(7) 11 70
(T D Walford) *chsd ldrs: rdn over 2f out: kpt on tl no ex ins fnl f* **40/1**

313 6 2 ¼ **Tariq Too**[22] 6367 3-8-9 **75** MartinLane(3) 8 59
(D M Simcock) *in tch: hdwy to chse ldrs over 2f out: rdn over 1f out: no ex ins fnl f* **7/2**[1]

2624 7 1 **Miss Bootylishes**[22] 6367 5-8-9 **75** AmyBaker(5) 6 57
(A B Haynes) *hld up: rdn 3f out: hdwy to chse ldrs over 1f out: wknd ins fnl f* **12/1**

1603 8 hd **Barren Brook**[13] 6620 3-9-3 **83** JamesSullivan(3) 15 64
(M W Easterby) *in tch: rdn over 2f out: sn no imp* **12/1**

4265 9 11 **Whispered Times (USA)**[15] 6567 3-8-9 **75** (p) AndrewHeffernan(3) 5 26
(Miss Tracy Waggott) *prom: rdn over 2f out: wknd over 1f out* **20/1**

-046 10 4 **Rock 'N' Royal**[36] 5937 3-9-1 **78** PaulHanagan 14 18
(R A Fahey) *midfield: rdn over 2f out: nvr on terms* **7/1**[3]

0164 11 2 ¼ **Ursula (IRE)**[28] 6221 4-9-4 **79** AndrewElliott 4 14
(Mrs K Burke) *prom tl wknd over 2f out* **12/1**

0060 12 7 **Pravda Street**[15] 6564 5-9-2 **77** (v[1]) TomEaves 1 —
(P F I Cole) *in tch towards far side: rdn over 3f out and sn lost pl: wknd over 2f out* **33/1**

0105 13 2 **Shotley Mac**[25] 6296 6-9-5 **80** (b) FrannyNorton 2 —
(N Bycroft) *in tch: drvn over 2f out and sn lost pl: eased over 1f out* **14/1**

2-10 14 30 **Masked Dance (IRE)**[137] 2656 3-9-3 **83** (p) AmyRyan(3) 3 —
(K A Ryan) *prom tl wknd 3f out* **18/1**

0500 15 23 **Aldermoor (USA)**[51] 5495 4-9-7 **82** PatCosgrave 13 —
(S C Williams) *hld up: bhd fr 1/2-way* **20/1**

1m 36.51s (7.81) **Going Correction** +1.10s/f (Soft)
WFA 3 from 4yo+ 2lb **15** Ran SP% **120.1**
Speed ratings (Par 105): **99,98,96,95,90 87,86,86,73,69 66,58,56,22,—**
toteswingers: 1&2 £24.20, 1&3 £13.20, 2&3 £40.00 CSF £99.01 CT £1208.53 TOTE £4.60: £2.70, £7.30, £6.30; EX 122.30.

Owner D A West **Bred** W Kane **Trained** Great Habton, N Yorks

FOCUS
They were spread all across the track in this decent handicap and it looked really hard work on the taxing ground.

6964 BEAGLERS' MAIDEN STKS 7f

4:10 (4:11) (Class 5) 2-Y-0 **£3,497** (£1,040; £520; £259) **Stalls** Centre

Form RPR

1 **Mystic Winds** 2-8-12 0 DavidAllan 2 69
(B Ellison) *dwlt: sn in tch centre: rdn and hdwy over 2f out: led narrowly over 1f out: kpt on wl u.p ins fnl f* **7/1**[2]

50 2 nk **Private Cowboy (IRE)**[15] 6560 2-9-3 0 PaulHanagan 5 73
(M G Quinlan) *racd keenly: w ldr centre: led 3f out: rdn whn hdd narrowly over 1f out: kpt on and chal again ins fnl f: hld nr fin* **8/11**[1]

3 6 **Pursuing** 2-8-12 0 TomEaves 1 53
(B Smart) *s.i.s: hld up centre: hdwy to trck ldng pair over 2f out: rdn 2f out: sn one pce* **7/1**[2]

4 3 **Wrekin Sunset** 2-8-12 0 AndrewElliott 8 46
(Mrs K Burke) *dwlt: in tch stands' side: rdn and edgd lft over 3f out: sn no imp* **10/1**[3]

0000 5 19 **Carver County (IRE)**[25] 6294 2-9-3 41 (p) GrahamGibbons 4 —
(K A Ryan) *led overall: rdn whn hdd 3f out: sn wknd* **33/1**

00 6 ¾ **Hobbesian War**[25] 6293 2-9-3 0 MickyFenton 9 —
(T P Tate) *led stands' side trio: rdn over 2f out: sn wknd* **16/1**

7 4 ½ **Valentine's Gift** 2-9-3 0 FrannyNorton 7 —
(N Bycroft) *hld up centre: rdn over 3f out: a bhd* **25/1**

06 8 3 ¼ **Vodka Red (IRE)**[18] 6458 2-8-12 0 LeeTopliss(5) 3 —
(R Johnson) *prom centre tl wknd qckly over 3f out* **33/1**

0 9 25 **Voovoo (IRE)**[16] 6542 2-8-12 0 SilvestreDeSousa 6 —
(D O'Meara) *in tch stands' side: rdn and lost pl over 3f out: sn bhd* **12/1**

1m 36.75s (8.05) **Going Correction** +1.10s/f (Soft) **9** Ran SP% **115.3**
Speed ratings (Par 95): **98,97,90,87,65 64,59,55,27**
toteswingers: 1&2 £2.50, 1&3 £4.20, 2&3 £2.50 CSF £12.25 TOTE £9.40: £3.10, £1.10, £1.90; EX 20.20.

Owner Koo's Racing Club **Bred** Mystic Meg Limited **Trained** Norton, N Yorks

FOCUS
A weak maiden but pleasing efforts from the first two. A newcomer just foiled a massive gamble on the favourite and the pair finished a long way clear, with few of these giving their running on the ground.

NOTEBOOK
Mystic Winds travelled smoothly on debut and showed a good attitude to fight off the rallying favourite. It is hard to rate the form, but this was a promising start by an £18,000 breeze-up buy who is a half-sister to Marvo, a multiple 7f-1m1f winner on good/soft ground. (tchd 8-1)

Private Cowboy(IRE) was never a factor in a hot Newmarket sales race last time, but set a clear standard on his 4l fifth of ten in a 1m Ffos Las maiden on debut last month. Very heavily backed, he was never far away but couldn't overhaul a rival who travelled a bit better for most of the way. This was an expensive setback but was a solid enough effort and he could have run into a decent type. (op 11-8 tchd 6-4 and 4-6)

Pursuing showed a bit of promise, staying on steadily on debut. She should improve for the experience and has a pedigree that is a blend of middle-distance and sprinting influences. (op 13-2 tchd 11-2 and 15-2)

Wrekin Sunset showed a glimmer of ability on her first run. She is out of a 1m2f winning half-sister to a fair dual middle-distance winner and should do better with time and a stiffer test. (op 7-1)

6965 MASTER OF FOXHOUNDS H'CAP 5f

4:45 (4:45) (Class 5) (0-70,70) 3-Y-0+ **£3,108** (£924; £462; £230) **Stalls** Centre

Form RPR

6560 1 **Foreign Rhythm (IRE)**[18] 6464 5-8-5 **57** NataliaGemelova(3) 12 68
(R E Barr) *bhd centre: outpcd 3f out: stl plenty to do over 1f out: r.o strly ins fnl f: led fnl 75yds* **25/1**

2-30 2 1 ¾ **Bedloe's Island (IRE)**[15] 6572 5-9-6 **69** FrannyNorton 8 74+
(N Bycroft) *trckd ldrs centre: rdn and hdwy to ld 1f out: kpt on tl hdd and no ex fnl 75yds* **9/1**

0302 3 3 ¼ **Wicked Wilma (IRE)**[9] 6708 6-9-0 **63** (t) RoystonFfrench 7 56
(A Berry) *trckd ldrs centre: rdn and ev ch over 1f out: kpt on ins fnl f* **14/1**

4314 4 hd **Ballarina**[27] 6246 4-8-8 **57** PaulMulrennan 6 49
(E J Alston) *led centre: rdn over 1f out: hdd 1f out: no ex ins fnl f: lost 3rd nr fin* **16/1**

0302 5 nk **Danum Dancer**[3] 6880 6-8-7 **56** oh2 (b) SilvestreDeSousa 5 47
(N Bycroft) *chsd ldrs centre: rdn over 2f out: kpt on same pce ins fnl f* **3/1**[1]

0510 6 ¾ **Tenancy (IRE)**[12] 6643 6-8-6 **60** (b) BillyCray(5) 9 49
(S A Harris) *w ldr centre: rdn and outpcd over 2f out: kpt on again ins fnl f* **7/1**[3]

0000 7 2 ¼ **Top Bid**[11] 6679 6-9-1 **64** GrahamGibbons 4 44
(T D Easterby) *hld up centre: rdn over 2f out: kpt on same pce: n.d* **12/1**

0602 8 2 **Sands Of Dee (USA)**[12] 6644 3-8-8 **57** PJMcDonald 1 30
(J A Glover) *prom far side: rdn over 2f out: wknd over 1f out* **6/1**[2]

0055 9 3 ¼ **Cross Of Lorraine (IRE)**[21] 6398 7-8-11 **60** (b) PaulHanagan 14 22
(C Grant) *in tch towards stands' side: rdn over 2f out: sn no imp* **8/1**

0020 10 7 **La Capriosa**[10] 6700 4-9-7 **70** TomEaves 13 6
(J A Glover) *prom stands' side: rdn over 2f out: wknd over 1f out* **16/1**

6620 11 2 ¾ **Your Gifted (IRE)**[158] 2026 3-8-5 **57** AmyRyan(3) 16 —
(Patrick Morris) *s.i.s: hld up stands' side: nvr on terms* **33/1**

0000 12 5 **Pawan (IRE)**[26] 6265 10-9-2 **70** (p) AnnStokell(5) 10 —
(Miss A Stokell) *s.i.s: sn chsd along in rr stands' side: a bhd* **33/1**

3006 13 ½ **Sir Louis**[28] 6226 3-8-6 **58** BarryMcHugh(3) 11 —
(R A Fahey) *in tch stands' side: rdn over 2f out: sn wknd* **14/1**

0136 14 14 **Bravely (IRE)**[21] 6398 6-8-11 **60** DavidAllan 3 —
(T D Easterby) *in tch towards far side: wknd qckly over 2f out: eased over 1f out* **10/1**

65.85 secs (4.75) **Going Correction** +1.10s/f (Soft) **14** Ran SP% **124.5**
Speed ratings (Par 103): **106,103,98,97,97 96,92,89,84,72 68,60,59,37**
toteswingers: 1&2 £53.80, 1&3 £93.90, 2&3 £18.60 CSF £240.42 CT £3290.82 TOTE £44.80: £13.60, £2.20, £5.00; EX 372.50.

Owner P Cartmell **Bred** Yeomanstown Stud **Trained** Seamer, N Yorks

FOCUS
An ordinary handicap in which there was a surprise winner. The small group who raced near the stands' side finished well beaten.

Foreign Rhythm(IRE) Official explanation: trainer had no explanation for the apparent improvement in form

Pawan(IRE) Official explanation: jockey said gelding was unsuited by the heavy ground

Bravely(IRE) Official explanation: jockey said gelding had no more to give

6966 RURAL RETAILER MEDIAN AUCTION MAIDEN STKS 7f

5:20 (5:22) (Class 6) 3-5-Y-0 **£2,331** (£693; £346; £173) **Stalls** Centre

Form RPR

1 **Hakuna Matata** 3-9-3 0 PaulHanagan 4 73+
(B Ellison) *in tch: hdwy to trck ldrs over 3f out: rdn to ld 2f out: drvn and kpt on wl ins fnl f* **3/1**[2]

0 2 2 ½ **Fama Mac**[31] 6115 3-9-3 0 FrannyNorton 11 65
(N Bycroft) *midfield: rdn to chse ldrs over 2f out: kpt on to take 2nd ins fnl f: no imp on wnr* **50/1**

5450 3 3 ¼ **Spread Boy (IRE)**[9] 6710 3-9-3 60 TomEaves 7 56
(A Berry) *trckd ldrs: hdwy and ev ch over 2f out: kpt on same pce* **7/1**

-036 4 ¾ **Brink**[106] 3662 3-8-9 57 BarryMcHugh(3) 10 49
(T J Pitt) *prom: rdn to ld over 2f out: sn hdd: kpt on tl no ex ins fnl f* **7/1**

4 5 10 **Machir Bay**[27] 6244 3-9-3 0 PaulMulrennan 13 27
(V P Donoghue) *hld up in midfield: rdn over 3f out: sn no imp* **14/1**

50 6 ¾ **Maxi Moo (IRE)**[13] 6624 3-9-0 0 MichaelO'Connell(3) 14 25
(G A Harker) *dwlt: outpcd in rr tl kpt on fnl 2f: n.d* **17/2**

2425 7 2 **Ezra Church (IRE)**[10] 6696 3-9-3 72 (b[1]) GrahamGibbons 9 20
(T D Barron) *led: rdn whn hdd over 2f out: sn wknd* **11/4**[1]

4350 8 hd **Lathaat**[44] 5713 3-8-12 60 TadhgO'Shea 2 14
(J L Dunlop) *s.i.s: sn outpcd in rr: a bhd* **11/2**[3]

640 9 ¾ **Anna's Boy**[32] 6077 3-9-3 40 RoystonFfrench 6 17
(A Berry) *dwlt: midfield: rdn and outpcd over 3f out: nvr on terms* **50/1**

0660 10 8 **Mujada**[32] 6077 5-9-0 37 SilvestreDeSousa 12 —
(D O'Meara) *trckd ldrs: rdn over 3f out: sn wknd* **28/1**

560- 11 2 **Blue Rum (IRE)**[334] 7421 3-9-0 53 PaulPickard(3) 1 —
(A Kirtley) *trckd ldrs: wknd over 3f out* **33/1**

50 12 5 **Seven Sons**[13] 6624 3-9-3 0 LNewman 3 —
(I W McInnes) *prom: wknd qckly over 3f out* **100/1**

0 13 ¾ **Pengula (IRE)**[13] 6624 3-8-12 0 PJMcDonald 8 —
(R Johnson) *s.i.s: a bhd* **100/1**

04- 14 dist **Charles Bear**[303] 7799 3-8-12 0 PatrickMathers 5 —
(Bruce Hellier) *prom tl wknd qckly 3f out: t.o whn eased over 1f out* **33/1**

1m 37.56s (8.86) **Going Correction** +1.10s/f (Soft)
WFA 3 from 5yo 2lb **14** Ran SP% **124.5**
Speed ratings (Par 101): **93,90,86,85,74 73,71,70,69,60 58,52,51,—**
toteswingers: 1&2 £42.50, 1&3 £8.30, 2&3 £75.20 CSF £164.54 TOTE £4.60: £2.10, £18.70, £3.70; EX 188.90 Place 6 £512.87, Place 5 £188.60.

Owner Sekura Group **Bred** Mrs J A Chapman **Trained** Norton, N Yorks

FOCUS
A modest maiden auction.

Maxi Moo(IRE) Official explanation: jockey said gelding finished lame behind but returned sound

Seven Sons Official explanation: trainer said gelding was unsuited by the heavy ground

T/Plt: £282.40 to a £1 stake. Pool: £82,426.19. 213.07 winning tickets. T/Qpdt: £40.90 to a £1 stake. Pool: £6,015.42. 108.80 winning tickets. AS

6967 - 6970a (Foreign Racing) - See Raceform Interactive

4663 NAAS (L-H)

Sunday, October 17

OFFICIAL GOING: Flat course - good; hurdle course - good to firm

6971a WOODLAND PARK 100 CLUB OCTOBER H'CAP (PREMIER HANDICAP) 1m 4f

5:15 (5:15) 3-Y-O+ £23,008 (£6,725; £3,185; £1,061)

RPR

1 **Gimli's Rock (IRE)**[7] 4561 4-9-0 84 (b) FMBerry 14 90+
(Mrs John Harrington, Ire) *hld up early: impr into 6th on outer 4f out: 4th 2f out: rdn to ld under 1f out: sn clr: eased cl home* **8/1**

2 2 ½ **Final Flashback (IRE)**[9] 6730 5-8-11 84 GFCarroll(3) 3 86
(Patrick J Flynn, Ire) *trckd ldrs in 4th: rdn to chal fr 2f out: cl 2nd over 1f out: kpt on u.p* **25/1**

3 shd **Table Mountain (IRE)**[11] 6687 3-8-10 87 ow1 JMurtagh 5 88
(A P O'Brien, Ire) *hld up: 11th 4f out: prog early st: 5th on inner 1 1/2f out: kpt on u.p ins fnl f* **9/4**[1]

4 shd **Zaralabad (IRE)**[7] 6786 6-9-3 94 (t) TCCarroll(7) 10 95
(C F Swan, Ire) *trckd ldrs: 7th 1/2-way: prog on outer early st: 5th under 2f out: rdn to ld narrowly under 1 1/2f out: hdd under 1f out: kpt on u.p* **25/1**

5 2 **The Pier (IRE)**[9] 6730 4-9-4 88 WJLee 4 86
(Joseph G Murphy, Ire) *trckd ldrs: 5th 4f out: 2nd and chal over 2f out: kpt on same pce u.p fr over 1f out* **8/1**

6 1 ¼ **Celtic Dane (IRE)**[7] 6787 6-9-3 87 CDHayes 15 83
(Kevin Prendergast, Ire) *towards rr: styd on wout threatening fr over 2f out* **25/1**

7 hd **Knight Eagle (IRE)**[21] 6404 3-9-0 98 SHJames(7) 12 94
(Kevin Prendergast, Ire) *mid-div: 9th into st: kpt on same pce fr 2f out* **14/1**

8 nk **Greenbelt Star**[11] 6682 4-8-10 80 KLatham 9 75
(Mrs John Harrington, Ire) *towards rr: brought wd early st: kpt on wl fr over 1f out* **20/1**

9 1 ¾ **Prince Chaparral (IRE)**[16] 6549 4-9-6 90 (t) DMGrant 16 82
(Patrick J Flynn, Ire) *prom: 3rd 4f out: rdn to chal early st: no ex fr 1 1/2f out* **16/1**

10 1 ¼ **La Chassotte (FR)**[43] 5776 3-9-2 96 BACurtis(3) 7 86
(Gerard O'Leary, Ire) *hld up in tch: rdn and one pce st* **12/1**

11 1 ½ **Tovaria**[8] 5977 6-9-5 89 KJManning 13 77
(Edward P Harty, Ire) *towards rr: rdn and kpt on same pce st* **25/1**

12 ½ **Capellanus (IRE)**[246] 4-9-7 91 WMLordan 2 78
(E J O'Grady, Ire) *mid-div: 8th 1/2-way: wknd st* **25/1**

13 shd **Elusive Ridge (IRE)**[16] 6549 4-8-8 85 DCByrne(7) 11 72
(H Rogers, Ire) *cl 2nd: led early st: sn strly pressed: hdd & wknd under 1 1/2f out* **25/1**

14 8 **Mister Angry (IRE)**[71] 4815 3-9-2 93 DPMcDonogh 1 67
(M Johnston) *led: j. path after 1f: rdn and hdd early st: sn wknd: eased fnl f* **4/1**[2]

15 1 ½ **Natural High (IRE)**[36] 5977 5-9-7 91 PJSmullen 8 63
(D K Weld, Ire) *chsd ldrs: 6th 1/2-way: rdn 4f out: wknd early st: eased fnl f* **5/1**[3]

16 16 **Alajan (IRE)**[7] 6787 4-9-0 84 (b) JAHeffernan 6 30
(William J Fitzpatrick, Ire) *a bhd* **12/1**

2m 32.67s (152.67)
WFA 3 from 4yo+ 7lb **16 Ran SP% 145.4**
CSF £218.28 CT £609.84 TOTE £10.30: £2.20, £5.70, £1.50, £5.40; DF 205.60.
Owner Geoffrey Ruddock **Bred** Mrs Ann Marie O'Brien **Trained** Moone, Co Kildare

FOCUS
This looked fairly open on paper, but it produced an emphatic winner. The runner-up and fourth have been rated to their best.

NOTEBOOK
Gimli's Rock(IRE) has been out of the frame only once in ten starts this year and won this with plenty to spare. Having been on the go since March, he is probably due for a break. (op 10/1 tchd 15/2)
Final Flashback(IRE) proved with this effort that he is still competitive off the mark that he attained after his final win last year. He emerged best in a battle for second with the gambled-on favourite Table Mountain and Zaralabad, who ran a fine race over a trip that is probably a little short of his best.
Table Mountain(IRE) stuck to his task having had a fair bit to do before the straight. (op 3/1)
Zaralabad(IRE) had a brief spell in the lead until headed early in the last furlong.
The Pier(IRE) is fairly high in the official ratings after winning three races last season. He ran a sound race on only his second run having had a break during the summer. (op 9/1)
Alajan(IRE) Official explanation: trainer said gelding swallowerd its tongue during the race

6913 LONGCHAMP (R-H)

Sunday, October 17

OFFICIAL GOING: Turf: good to soft

6973a PRIX DE CONDE (GROUP 3) (2YO) (TURF) 1m 1f

1:35 (12:00) 2-Y-O £35,398 (£14,159; £10,619; £7,079; £3,539)

RPR

1 **Prairie Star (FR)**[30] 2-8-11 0 AnthonyCrastus 5 102
(E Lellouche, France) *settled in 2nd: qcknd to ld 1 1/2f out: r.o wl fnl f to hold off chalrs on both sides: a in command* **11/8**[2]

2 nk **Bubble Chic (FR)**[16] 2-8-11 0 StephanePasquier 1 101
(G Botti, Italy) *racd in 3rd on rail: swtchd away fr rail 1f out: hrd rdn and r.o strly fnl 100yds: clst at fin* **6/1**[3]

3 nse **Kreem**[16] 2-8-11 0 OlivierPeslier 3 101
(A Fabre, France) *sn led: hdd 1 1/2f out: battled bk fnl f: r.o wl* **5/4**[1]

4 4 **Zack Yield (FR)**[30] 6173 2-8-11 0 (b[1]) Christophe-PatriceLemaire 2 93
(A Lamotte D'Argy, France) *racd in 4th: rdn but no ex fnl f: styd on* **10/1**

5 ½ **Such A Maj (FR)**[21] 2-8-11 0 DavyBonilla 4 92
(Mme M Bollack-Badel, France) *bkmarker fr s: rdn but no ex 1 1/2f out: styd on* **20/1**

1m 59.5s (7.90) **Going Correction** +1.025s/f (Soft) **5 Ran SP% 114.7**
Speed ratings: **105,104,104,101,100**
WIN (incl. 1 euro stake): 2.20. PLACES: 1.30, 2.00. SF: 6.70.
Owner Ecurie Wildenstein **Bred** Dayton Investments Ltd **Trained** Lamorlaye, France

FOCUS
One of the weaker renewals of this event.

NOTEBOOK
Prairie Star(FR) won comfortably under a well-judged ride. He could go for the Group 1 Criterium de Saint-Cloud now.

6974a PRIX DU CONSEIL DE PARIS (GROUP 2) (3YO+) (TURF) 1m 4f

2:40 (12:00) 3-Y-O+ £65,575 (£25,309; £12,079; £8,053; £4,026)

RPR

1 **Prince Bishop (IRE)**[29] 6219 3-8-11 0 OlivierPeslier 3 118
(A Fabre, France) *racd in 5th: qcknd wl 1 1/2f out: tk ld 1f out: r.o wl fnl 100yds to hold off str chal of runner-up* **7/1**

2 snk **Cirrus Des Aigles (FR)**[15] 6592 4-9-6 0 FranckBlondel 1 120
(Mme C Barande-Barbe, France) *initially racd in 2nd: then dropped bk to 3rd on rail: short of room over 1f out: swtchd away fr rail: qckd wl: fnd split between horses: chsd ldr: chal for ld fnl 50yds: no ex cl home* **7/4**[1]

3 3 **Shimraan (FR)**[15] 6592 3-9-0 0 Christophe-PatriceLemaire 4 116
(A De Royer-Dupre, France) *racd towards rr: rdn 1 1/2f out: wnt 3rd ins fnl f: styd on* **3/1**[2]

4 1 ½ **Timos (GER)**[14] 6612 5-9-2 0 IoritzMendizabal 7 109
(T Doumen, France) *initially 3rd: wnt 2nd after 4f: rdn early in st: tk ld 2f out: hdd 1 1/2f out: hrd rdn and styd on fnl f* **7/1**

5 nse **Aizavoski (IRE)**[46] 5674 4-9-2 0 AnthonyCrastus 2 109
(E Lellouche, France) *racd in 4th: hrd rdn 2f out: styd on* **10/1**

6 1 ½ **Zack Hall (FR)**[24] 6315 3-8-9 0 ThierryThulliez 6 106
(M Delzangles, France) *bkmarker fr s: swtchd wd outside in st: styd on* **11/2**[3]

7 4 **Almail (USA)**[36] 5982 4-9-2 0 DavyBonilla 5 100
(F Head, France) *sn led: stl in front ent st: rdn 2f out and hdd: r.o: fdd fnl f: eased* **20/1**

2m 40.8s (10.40) **Going Correction** +1.025s/f (Soft)
WFA 3 from 4yo+ 7lb **7 Ran SP% 115.6**
Speed ratings: **106,105,103,102,102 101,99**
WIN (incl. 1 euro stake): 9.10. PLACES: 3.20, 1.70. SF: 27.80.
Owner Godolphin SNC **Bred** Thurso Limited **Trained** Chantilly, France

NOTEBOOK
Prince Bishop(IRE) completed a four-timer on this rise in class to Group 2 company, albeit he was fortunate to hold off the unlucky in running runner-up. He's now likely to head off for a winter in Dubai.
Cirrus Des Aigles(FR), the Prix Dollar winner, endured a luckless run, only finding room when it was too late, and ran well in the circumstances. He has been invited to the Japan Cup, but his trainer would rather drop him back to 1m2f for the Hong Kong Cup. She added that she still believes him to be "a phenomenal racehorse."
Shimraan(FR), who was giving 3lb to the winner, stayed on to take third and will apparently be kept in training as a 4-y-o.

6762 SAN SIRO (R-H)

Sunday, October 17

OFFICIAL GOING: Turf: very soft

6975a PREMIO DORMELLO (GROUP 3) (2YO FILLIES) (TURF) 1m

2:40 (2:57) 2-Y-O £48,672 (£21,415; £11,681; £5,840)

RPR

1 **Adamantina**[21] 2-8-11 0 MircoDemuro 9 103
(Vittorio Caruso, Italy) *broke wl to trck ldr tl ent st: eased to centre of trck fnl 2 1/2f: led 2f out: drvn out fnl f* **21/10**[2]

2 1 ¼ **Stay Alive (IRE)**[21] 2-8-11 0 DarioVargiu 7 100
(B Grizzetti, Italy) *trckd ldrs tl ent st: effrt 2f out to stay in tch: hrd rdn and wnt 2nd ent fnl f: nt pce to chal* **153/10**

3 2 ¼ **Singapore Lilly (IRE)**[8] 6762 2-8-11 0 NeilCallan 4 95
(M R Channon) *settled midfield: hrd rdn fnl 2f: styd on for 3rd fnl 100yds* **4/5**[1]

4 1 ¼ **Kagera**[21] 2-8-11 0 CColombi 3 92
(B Grizzetti, Italy) *broke wl to ld: set gd pce: hrd rdn whn chal and hdd ent fnl 2f: sn btn: lost 3rd fnl 100yds* **128/10**

5 2 ½ **Ksenia (ITY)**[8] 6762 2-8-11 0 GMarcelli 12 87
(R Menichetti, Italy) *in rr: prog fnl 2f under hrd ride: styd on* **172/10**

6 ½ **Simply Noble (GER)** 2-8-11 0 GBietolini 2 86
(Andreas Lowe, Germany) *mid-div: rdn and outpcd 2f out: nvr nr ldrs* **128/10**

7 6 **Seia (ITY)**[21] 2-8-11 0 AStarke 13 72
(Mario Hofer, Germany) *hld up nr rr on outer: effrt 3f out: no imp* **38/1**

8 ½ **Bint Modelliste** 2-8-11 0 (b) UmbertoRispoli 5 71
(D Gambarota, Italy) *in rr: effrt on outer 2f out: kpt on under hrd ride fnl f* **41/1**

9 3 **March Madness**[35] 2-8-11 0 FabioBranca 11 65
(S Botti, Italy) *in tch on outer for 4f: hrd rdn and no imp fnl 2f: wknd: eased fnl f* **71/10**[3]

10 ¾ **Black Raja (USA)**[21] 2-8-11 0 LManiezzi 1 63
(R Menichetti, Italy) *broke wl to trck ldrs for 4f: rdn ent st to stay in tch: one pce fnl 2f: eased fnl f* **172/10**

11 dist **Zakumi (IRE)** 2-8-11 0 CDemuro 6 —
(L Riccardi, Italy) *mid-div tl ent st: effrt to stay in tch 3f out: sn wknd and eased fnl 2f* **128/10**

1m 45.7s (3.60) **11 Ran SP% 144.0**
WIN (incl. 1 euro stake): 3.10. PLACES: 1.20, 1.69, 1.11. DF: 26.45.
Owner Incolinx **Bred** Azienda Agricola Rosati Colarieti **Trained** Italy

NOTEBOOK
Singapore Lilly(IRE) ran well to finish second in a Group 1 here the previous weekend, but was a little disappointing here, failing to build on that effort back against her own sex. Perhaps the race came a bit too soon.

6976a PREMIO OMENONI (GROUP 3) (3YO+) (TURF) 5f

3:15 (3:36) 3-Y-O+ £35,398 (£15,575; £8,495; £4,247)

RPR

1 **Jakor (ITY)**[28] 6238 4-9-0 0 PierantonioConvertino 9 104
(M Marcialis, Italy) *broke wl: trckd ldrs for 2 1/2f: led ent fnl 2f: clr ent fnl f: rdn and kpt on* **95/40**[1]

2 nk **Charming Woman (IRE)**[42] 5802 3-9-0 0 MircoDemuro 2 103
(Vittorio Caruso, Italy) *v.s.a: moved rt and hdwy on outer 2f out: rdn fnl f to chal ldr: a hld* **63/20**[3]

3 2 1/4 **Farrel (IRE)**28 6238 5-9-0 0 DarioVargiu 7 95
(B Grizzetti, Italy) *broke wl: lost position and struggling fnl 2f: hrd rdn and proged to stay on fnl 300yds* **3/1**2
4 3/4 **Golden Ramon (IRE)**91 4185 3-8-10 0 CColombi 11 88
(B Grizzetti, Italy) *led: rdn and hdd 2f out: styd on same pce* **37/4**
5 snk **Ekin**28 6238 5-9-0 0 UmbertoRispoli 10 92
(P Riccioni, Italy) *settled midfield on outer: rdn to stay in tch 2f out: outpcd and styd on fnl f* **8/1**
6 1/2 **Above Limits (IRE)**28 6238 3-8-10 0 NeilCallan 3 86
(D M Simcock) *broke wl to share ld tl 1/2-way: hrd rdn ent fnl 2f: no imp* **104/10**
7 6 **Dagda Mor (ITY)**28 6238 3-9-0 0 FabioBranca 6 68
(S Botti, Italy) *in tch tl last 2 1/2f: rdn and sn u.p: eased fnl f* **27/1**
8 3 **Black Mambazo (IRE)**133 2804 5-9-0 0 GMarcelli 4 57
(L Riccardi, Italy) *midfield tl 1/2-way: hrd rdn and no imp: eased fnl f* **18/5**
9 9 **Cry Of Liberty (IRE)**182 1419 3-8-10 0 CDemuro 1 21
(L Riccardi, Italy) *in tch tl 1/2-way: outpcd and eased fnl 2f* **37/4**

61.10 secs (1.90) 9 Ran SP% **143.4**
WIN (incl. 1 euro stake): 3.37. PLACES: 1.41, 1.57, 1.51. DF: 7.57.
Owner Scuderia Marwins **Bred** Sofim Scuderia Alessia **Trained** Italy

NOTEBOOK
Above Limits(IRE) faced a stiffer task up in grade and, having shown early speed, dropped out in the latter stages in this testing ground.

6977a GRAN PREMIO DEL JOCKEY CLUB (GROUP 1) (3YO+) (TURF) 1m 4f
3:55 (12:00) 3-Y-O+ £119,469 (£52,566; £28,672; £14,336)

RPR
1 **Rainbow Peak (IRE)**30 6148 4-9-4 0 NeilCallan 3 119
(M A Jarvis) *racd in midfield tl ent st: edgd rt and hdwy ent fnl 2 1/2f: chal to ld ent fnl f: led 1f out: hrd rdn to hold on u.p nr fin* **97/20**
2 shd **Lord Chaparral (IRE)**14 3-8-13 0 MircoDemuro 1 121
(R Brogi, Italy) *broke wl to ld after 1f: set stdy pce: rdn to go 2 l clr ent fnl 2f: chal fnl 1 1/2f and hdd 1f out: styd on fnl f u.str ride to go cl* **218/10**
3 6 1/2 **Cavalryman**14 6612 4-9-4 0 FrankieDettori 5 108
(Saeed Bin Suroor) *trckd ldr: rdn to chal 3f out: ev ch: btn ent fnl 300yds: styd on one pce to hold 3rd fnl strides* **31/20**1
4 hd **Night Magic (GER)**21 6410 4-9-1 0 KKerekes 7 105
(W Figge, Germany) *settled to trck ldrs: produced to chal fnl 3f: sn hrd rdn and little imp: styd on fnl f* **53/20**2
5 3 1/2 **Jakkalberry (IRE)**61 5186 4-9-4 0 FabioBranca 6 103
(E Botti, Italy) *hld up in rr tl ent st: effrt and hdwy 3f out: one pce fnl 2f* **17/4**3
6 nk **Indian Days**42 5804 5-9-4 0 AlanMunro 4 102
(J G Given) *hld up nr rr tl ent st: hrd rdn to stay in tch fnl 3f: wknd* **87/10**
7 12 **Quijano (GER)**21 6410 8-9-4 0 AStarke 2 83
(P Schiergen, Germany) *trckd ldrs on inner tl ent st: effrt 3f out: hrd rdn and sn wknd: eased fnl f* **78/10**
8 3/4 **Halicarnassus (IRE)**21 6389 6-9-4 0 SamHitchcott 9 82
(M R Channon) *in rr: rdn to stay in tch ent st: no imp* **51/1**
9 10 **Cima De Triomphe (IRE)**15 6592 5-9-4 0 DarioVargiu 8 66
(B Grizzetti, Italy) *midfield on outer: rdn 3f out: sn btn and eased fnl 2f* **34/1**

2m 36.1s (4.60)
WFA 3 from 4yo+ 7lb 9 Ran SP% **133.6**
WIN (incl. 1 euro stake): 5.83. PLACES: 1.99, 4.13, 1.51. DF: 117.49.
Owner P D Savill **Bred** P D Savill **Trained** Newmarket, Suffolk

NOTEBOOK
Rainbow Peak(IRE) narrowly held off Lord Chaparral to record his first win at the highest level, and in the process gave a boost to his Newbury conqueror Dangerous Midge, who is heading for the Breeders' Cup Turf. The winner, who has progressed from handicaps this term, is an improving sort, enjoyed the soft ground and should be capable of further success at the top level. He could well return to Italy for the Group 1 Premio Roma at the Capannelle on November 7.
Lord Chaparral(IRE), a Listed winner last time out, excelled himself, although he did enjoy the run of things out in front.
Cavalryman, unlucky in running in the Arc, looked to have less to do in this company but couldn't stay in touch with the first two when things got serious. This was clearly a below-par performance and perhaps came a bit quick after the Arc.
Indian Days didn't have the race run to suit in the same way as when coming home strongly to take a Group 2 in Turkey last month.
Halicarnassus(IRE), who has done all his winning on quicker ground than this, was up against it class-wise, too.

6618 PONTEFRACT (L-H)
Monday, October 18

OFFICIAL GOING: Good (7.5)
Wind: light 1/2 behind Weather: overcast

6978 TOTEPLACEPOT NURSERY (DIV I) 1m 4y
2:10 (2:10) (Class 5) (0-75,75) 2-Y-O £2,590 (£770; £385; £192) Stalls Low

Form RPR
6644 1 **Unknown Rebel (IRE)**10 6717 2-8-7 61 SilvestreDeSousa 12 64
(K A Ryan) *chsd ldrs: led over 1f out: hld on towards fin* **20/1**
15 2 1/2 **Lucy Limelites**18 6513 2-9-3 71 PaulHanagan 5 73
(R Charlton) *mid-div: hdwy over 1f out: str run fnl f: edgd lft clsng stages: jst hld* **9/2**1
5052 3 3/4 **My Mate Jake (IRE)**32 6130 2-9-3 71 MickyFenton 3 71
(J G Given) *w ldr: led 3f out: hdd over 1f out: kpt on same pce ins fnl f* **17/2**
5641 4 nk **Itzakindamagic (IRE)**25 6302 2-9-4 72 KierenFallon 10 72
(M Johnston) *chsd ldrs: outpcd over 1f out: styd on wl fnl 75yds* **6/1**2
4336 5 3/4 **Night Singer**89 4242 2-8-3 60 IanBrennan(3) 6 58
(J Howard Johnson) *mid-div: hdwy over 2f out: keeping on whn hmpd towards fin* **28/1**
5042 6 3/4 **Paco Belle (IRE)**18 6500 2-8-13 67 RyanMoore 8 63
(R Hannon) *in rr: hdwy over 2f out: nt clr run and swtchd rt over 1f out: r.o: nt rch ldrs* **11/1**
4066 7 1 **Dunmore Boy (IRE)**11 6694 2-8-5 62 ow3 BarryMcHugh(3) 14 56
(R A Fahey) *chsd ldrs: one pce fnl 2f* **33/1**
6530 8 hd **Downtown Boy (IRE)**42 5818 2-8-1 55 AndrewMullen 13 48
(T P Tate) *chsd ldrs: one pce fnl 2f* **50/1**
2020 9 2 **Bradbury (IRE)**18 6505 2-8-12 66 (b) GrahamGibbons 11 55
(J D Bethell) *chsd ldrs: fdd fnl f* **14/1**
540 10 shd **Deep Applause**31 6138 2-9-2 70 TomEaves 2 59
(M Dods) *dwlt: hld up towards rr: hdwy and hung rt over 1f out: nvr nr ldrs* **8/1**
000 11 6 **Lejaam**19 6474 2-9-6 74 TadhgO'Shea 7 49
(J L Dunlop) *hld up in rr: bhd fnl 2f* **14/1**
5641 12 3 1/4 **Tapis Libre**26 6300 2-8-9 66 JamesSullivan(3) 17 33
(M W Easterby) *s.i.s: a in rr* **22/1**
040 13 4 **Kodicil (IRE)**33 6070 2-7-13 53 DuranFentiman 16 11
(T D Walford) *prom: lost pl after 2f: sn in rr* **50/1**
0306 14 3 3/4 **High Kickin**10 6717 2-7-13 58 (p) DeclanCannon(5) 15 7
(A J McCabe) *swtchd rt s: t.k.h in rr: hung rt bnd 2f out* **28/1**
300 15 2 1/2 **Last Destination (IRE)**14 6619 2-9-1 72 KellyHarrison(3) 9 16
(N Tinkler) *led tl 3f out: sn wknd* **66/1**
0550 16 19 **Acute (IRE)**19 6471 2-9-0 68 JamieSpencer 1 —
(B J Meehan) *in rr: bhd 2f out: eased ins fnl f: t.o* **10/1**
3503 P **Bowermaster (USA)**7 6809 2-9-7 75 AhmedAjtebi 4 —
(Mahmood Al Zarooni) *hld up towards rr: p.u after 2f: fatally injured* **13/2**3

1m 46.68s (0.78) **Going Correction** +0.075s/f (Good) 17 Ran SP% **122.6**
Speed ratings (Par 95): **99,98,97,97,96 95,94,94,92,92 86,83,79,75,73 54,—**
toteswingers:1&2:£26.60, 1&3:£25.00, 2&3:£10.40 CSF £101.39 CT £881.71 TOTE £27.00: £4.30, £1.50, £3.20, £1.40; EX 205.10.
Owner D Reilly & Mrs C Reilly **Bred** Kilfrush Stud **Trained** Hambleton, N Yorks

FOCUS
A dry run up to the meeting, which was run on significantly quicker ground than the fixture here the previous Monday. The riders reported the ground to be as described. A handful of unexposed sorts in the first division of an ordinary but open-looking nursery. The gallop was only fair and those attempting to come from the back of the field were at a disadvantage.

NOTEBOOK
Unknown Rebel(IRE) was starting to look exposed but he is a reliable yardstick who got first run and showed a good attitude in the closing stages. He shouldn't be going up too much for this and should continue to give a good account on either turf or Polytrack. (op 16-1)
Lucy Limelites ◆, as her pedigree suggested, appreciated the step up to this trip and, although she took a bit of time to find full stride, she made up plenty of ground in the straight to register a career-best effort on the quickest ground she has encountered to fare the best of those who came from just behind the pace. A stronger overall gallop would have suited and she's more than capable of making amends. (tchd 4-1 and 5-1)
My Mate Jake(IRE), who attracted support, had the run of the race against the inside rail and again ran creditably returned to this longer trip. His pedigree suggests he should be equally effective on artificial surfaces and he is lightly raced enough to be open to a little improvement. (op 12-1)
Itzakindamagic(IRE), who beat a subsequent winner in convincing fashion over C&D on her previous start, had the run of the race and ran creditably from this 8lb higher mark. She is bred to stay at least 1m2f, she is in very good hands and will be worth another chance granted a stiffer test of stamina. (op 11-2 tchd 7-1)
Night Singer isn't fully exposed and ran creditably after a three-month break on his first start over this longer trip in a race that didn't really suit the hold-up horses. A stronger end-to-end gallop would have suited and he's capable of picking up an ordinary event. (op 33-1)
Paco Belle(IRE) was far from disgraced returned to turf from this 7lb higher mark for the first time since her debut in a race that suited those up with the pace. She should be able to win a run-of-the-mill event. (op 12-1)
Deep Applause, loaded with a stalls blanket, was nibbled at in the market and wasn't disgraced on this nursery debut. He wasn't knocked about and will be one to keep an eye on in a similar event in the near future. (op 10-1)
Bowermaster(USA) looked to have claims in this company but broke down early on and sadly had to be put down. (op 7-1 tchd 8-1)

6979 TOTEPLACEPOT NURSERY (DIV II) 1m 4y
2:40 (2:40) (Class 5) (0-75,75) 2-Y-O £2,590 (£770; £385; £192) Stalls Low

Form RPR
0242 1 **One Lucky Lady**16 6555 2-9-0 68 MichaelHills 2 75
(B W Hills) *led after 1f: styd on strly to forge clr fnl f* **4/1**2
1 2 2 1/2 **Tahaamah**24 6333 2-9-4 72 JamieSpencer 9 73
(Saeed Bin Suroor) *trckd ldrs: chal over 2f out: kpt on same pce fnl f* **6/5**1
2553 3 nk **Standout**7 6802 2-8-12 66 RyanMoore 17 67
(R Hannon) *dwlt: sn in mid-div: hdwy on outer over 2f out: styd on wl fnl f* **10/1**3
6021 4 nse **Amistress**21 6412 2-8-1 55 SilvestreDeSousa 12 55
(Eve Johnson Houghton) *chsd ldrs: kpt on same pce appr fnl f* **14/1**
0150 5 2 **Fairlie Dinkum**18 6513 2-9-3 71 TomEaves 3 67
(B Smart) *trckd ldrs: t.k.h: kpt on same pce fnl 2f* **28/1**
6013 6 1 3/4 **Joyously**5 6845 2-8-13 70 RobertLButler(3) 11 62
(P Butler) *dwlt: swtchd lft after s: in rr: hdwy over 2f out: hung lft over 1f out: kpt on: nvr trbld ldrs* **33/1**
0540 7 8 **Cotton Spirit**19 6471 2-8-11 65 PaulHanagan 5 38
(R A Fahey) *led 1f: chsd ldrs: drvn over 3f out: lost pl over 1f out* **14/1**
001 8 3/4 **Newport Arch**66 5040 2-8-13 70 IanBrennan(3) 1 42
(J J Quinn) *dwlt: drvn along detached in last: sme hdwy 3f out: wknd over 1f out* **14/1**
0300 9 1 1/2 **Market Maker (IRE)**30 6184 2-8-7 61 ow1 DavidAllan 14 29
(T D Easterby) *dwlt: in rr: sme hdwy 2f out: nvr on terms* **66/1**
600 10 1 3/4 **Katiesister**31 6138 2-8-4 58 ChrisCatlin 13 22
(J S Goldie) *in rr: sme hdwy 2f out: nvr a factor* **40/1**
0360 11 1 **King Kurt (IRE)**40 5849 2-8-13 67 PJMcDonald 6 29
(K A Ryan) *mid-div: drvn and lost pl 3f out* **40/1**
560 12 nk **Domino Effect (IRE)**86 4368 2-7-11 54 ow1 JamesSullivan(3) 10 15
(J Howard Johnson) *chsd ldrs on outside: lost pl over 1f out* **100/1**
202 13 3 1/4 **Mia Madonna**19 6469 2-9-4 72 PatCosgrave 7 26
(B J Meehan) *sn chsng ldrs: wknd 2f out* **14/1**
1350 14 1 **Fabiello**13 6647 2-9-7 75 RichardKingscote 8 26
(Tom Dascombe) *in tch: drvn 3f out: sn lost pl* **66/1**

1m 46.94s (1.04) **Going Correction** +0.075s/f (Good) 14 Ran SP% **116.5**
Speed ratings (Par 95): **97,94,94,94,92 90,82,81,80,78 77,77,73,72**
toteswingers:1&2:£2.10, 1&3:£7.10, 2&3:£4.80 CSF £8.35 CT £45.24 TOTE £3.90: £1.20, £1.30, £3.00; EX 10.30.
Owner S W Group Logistics Limited **Bred** Ken Knox **Trained** Lambourn, Berks

FOCUS
A handful of unexposed sorts in an ordinary nursery. The gallop was an ordinary one, suiting those up with the pace and the first six finished clear.

NOTEBOOK
One Lucky Lady, back on a sound surface, had the run of the race and showed a good attitude to beat the heavily backed market leader and in the process to get off the mark at the sixth attempt. She is a consistent sort who goes on most ground and, although things were in her favour, she should continue to give a good account. (op 5-1)

Tahaamah, looked potentially well treated on this turf and nursery debut judging on the favourable impression he created on Polytrack on his debut and it was not surprising he attracted a good deal of support. However, while he bettered that debut effort in terms of form, he didn't do his prospects any good by taking a strong hold in the first half of the race. He's more than capable of winning on turf over either this trip or back over 7f but he'll have to settle a good deal better if he is to fulfil his potential. (op 5-4 tchd 11-8)
Standout ◆ was nibbled at in the market and shaped as though better than the bare form after racing wide throughout from the outside draw and after making ground from off the pace against two rivals that were at the head of affairs throughout. He has had a few chances but he's capable of winning in similar company. (op 12-1 tchd 14-1)
Amistress, who scored at Bath at the end of last month, was far from disgraced in this stronger event from this 10lb higher mark. She should have no problems with 1m2f and she may be capable of a little better. (op 12-1)
Fairlie Dinkum had been soundly beaten in soft ground on her previous start but she had the run of the racefared better back on a sound surface. She hasn't had many chances , is bred to stay a bit further in due course and she too may be able to win another small race. (op 25-1 tchd 33-1)
Joyously wasn't disgraced in a race that didn't suit the hold-up horses on only this second run for the yard. She has won on a sound surface and on Polytrack but she is likely to remain vulnerable to the less-exposed and better handicapped sorts in this type of event. (op 28-1)

6980 TOTESWINGER FLEXI BETTING MAIDEN AUCTION STKS 6f
3:10 (3:10) (Class 5) 2-Y-O **£2,914** (£867; £433; £216) **Stalls** Low

Form				RPR
33	1		**Fieldgunner Kirkup (GER)**[65] 5092 2-8-12 0 .... GrahamGibbons 9 (T D Barron) *s.i.s: hld up: hdwy over 2f out: styd on ins to ld last 75yds: kpt on wl* **7/2**[2]	74
2223	2	1 1/4	**Insolenceofoffice (IRE)**[10] 6705 2-8-11 72 .... SilvestreDeSousa 3 (Mrs A Duffield) *w ldr: t.k.h: drvn 3f out: led over 2f out: edgd rt 1f out: hdd and no ex ins fnl f* **6/4**[1]	69
	3	1 1/4	**Boogie Shoes** 2-8-13 0 .... PhilipRobinson 4 (M A Jarvis) *chsd ldrs: pushed along 3f out: kpt on wl ins fnl f* **7/2**[2]	68
2236	4	1/2	**Moral Issue**[16] 6569 2-8-8 70 ....(t) PatrickDonaghy(3) 5 (Jedd O'Keeffe) *led tl over 2f out: cl up tl fdd fnl 50yds* **8/1**	64
45	5	1/2	**Flash City (ITY)**[65] 5092 2-9-0 0 .... TomEaves 10 (B Smart) *chsd ldrs on outer: kpt on same pce appr fnl f* **7/1**[3]	66
00	6	7	**Cannon Bolt (IRE)**[10] 6704 2-8-10 0 .... DavidAllan 6 (R Bastiman) *a in rr: nvr on terms* **100/1**	41
6	7	4	**Spin A Wish**[44] 5755 2-8-2 0 .... AmyRyan(3) 7 (R M Whitaker) *chsd ldrs: lost pl over 1f out* **40/1**	24
	8	1	**Crystallus (IRE)** 2-8-8 0 .... TadhgO'Shea 1 (Mrs A Duffield) *hood stl on whn stalls opened: s.s: nvr on terms* **33/1**	24
6000	9	4	**Sleights Boy (IRE)**[12] 6674 2-8-7 59 ....(b) BarryMcHugh(3) 8 (I W McInnes) *trckd ldrs: drvn 3f out: sn wknd* **100/1**	14
00	10	2 3/4	**Kwik Time**[9] 6748 2-8-12 0 .... JimmyQuinn 11 (R Bastiman) *s.i.s: sn chsng ldrs on outer: lost pl over 3f out* **100/1**	7

1m 17.51s (0.61) **Going Correction** +0.075s/f (Good) **10 Ran SP% 116.4**
Speed ratings (Par 95): **98,96,94,94,93 84,78,77,72,68**
toteswingers:1&2:£1.70, 1&3:£3.90, 2&3:£2.90 CSF £9.06 TOTE £4.00: £1.50, £1.10, £2.30; EX 10.70.
Owner Kevin Kirkup **Bred** I And D Meinke **Trained** Maunby, N Yorks

FOCUS
A maiden lacking anything in the race of strength in depth and one in which those with previous experience were no more than fair at best. The gallop was an ordinary one and the first five pulled clear.

NOTEBOOK
Fieldgunner Kirkup(GER), gelded since his previous start in August, had shown ability at a modest level on his two previous starts and turned in his best effort returned to a sound surface to beat a reliable yardstick with a bit in hand. He shapes as though he'll improve further for the step up to 7f and he appeals as the sort to make his mark in handicap company. (tchd 11-4)
Insolenceofoffice(IRE), the well-backed market leader, is a reliable yardstick who had the run of the race and seemed to give it his best shot - despite edging off a true line late on - back over 6f and back on a sound surface. He's capable of winning an ordinary race and he should continue to give it his best shot but he's vulnerable to the better types in this grade and a mark of 72 leaves him with little margin for error in nurseries. (op 9-4 tchd 5-2)
Boogie Shoes ◆, a 20,000 yearling half-brother to a 1m2f Listed winner Splashdown, ran well against more experienced rivals, despite proving easy to back and despite his apparent greenness on this racecourse debut, and is the one to take from the race. This good-bodied sort should be better for this outing, should have no problems with 7f and can pick up a similar event at the very least. (op 5-2 tchd 4-1)
Moral Issue, back in trip and back on a sound surface in a first-time tongue-tie, helped to force the issue but once again underlined his vulnerability in this type of event and he'll have to step up on what he's achieved to date to defy his current mark of 70 in nursery company. (op 7-1)
Flash City(ITY), having his first run for two months, finished a bit further behind the winner than he did at Ripon but he has now run to a similar level on all his three starts and he'll be seen to better effect in run-of-the-mill nursery company. (op 8-1 tchd 9-1)
Crystallus(IRE) Official explanation: jockey said he was late in removing blindfold because the filly was very nervous and his orders were to leave the blindfold on as late as possible but, as he tried to remove it, it had become caught on a buckle.

6981 TOTESUPER7 H'CAP (DIV I) 5f
3:40 (3:40) (Class 4) (0-85,85) 3-Y-O+ **£4,209** (£1,252; £625; £312) **Stalls** Low

Form				RPR
0210	1		**Captain Royale (IRE)**[1] 6962 5-8-5 72 ....(p) MartinLane(3) 5 (Miss Tracy Waggott) *chsd ldrs: led appr fnl f: kpt on wl* **10/1**	83
3032	2	1	**Russian Spirit**[10] 6723 4-9-7 85 .... PhilipRobinson 7 (M A Jarvis) *led over 1f: w ldr: chal 1f out: kpt on same pce ins fnl f* **10/3**[1]	92
3066	3	1/2	**Strike Up The Band**[10] 6723 7-9-6 84 .... AdrianNicholls 3 (D Nicholls) *sltly hmpd s: mid-div: effrt on ins whn nt clr run over 2f out: styd on to chse ldrs 1f out: kpt on same pce* **8/1**	89+
4010	4	hd	**Evelyn May (IRE)**[28] 6256 4-8-11 75 .... MichaelHills 4 (B W Hills) *wnt lft s: chsd ldrs: nt clr run and swtchd rt over 1f out: r.o wl fnl 100yds* **14/1**	79
4120	5	1	**Legal Eagle (IRE)**[23] 6358 5-9-2 80 ....(p) JamieSpencer 8 (Paul Green) *w ldr: led over 3f out tl appr fnl f: kpt on one pce* **12/1**	81
0006	6	1/2	**Titus Andronicus (IRE)**[10] 6708 4-8-11 75 ....(p) PaulHanagan 12 (R A Fahey) *trckd ldrs: effrt over 1f out: kpt on same pce* **28/1**	74
0605	7	1 1/4	**Ishetoo**[10] 6723 6-9-0 78 .... RyanMoore 11 (Ollie Pears) *towards rr: rdn and kpt on fnl 2f: nvr a threat* **13/2**[3]	73+
2010	8	hd	**Yurituni**[8] 6772 3-8-13 77 ....(b) KierenFallon 10 (Eve Johnson Houghton) *dwlt: in tch on outside: one pce fnl 2f* **14/1**	71
3214	9	1/2	**Captain Scooby**[16] 6572 4-8-7 74 .... MichaelStainton(3) 9 (R M Whitaker) *in rr: hdwy and swtchd outside over 1f out: nvr on terms* **12/1**	66+
6400	10	1 3/4	**Medici Time**[31] 6142 5-9-4 82 ....(v) GrahamGibbons 1 (T D Easterby) *dwlt: in rr: effrt on ins whn hmpd over 2f out: no threat after* **4/1**[2]	68
2615	11	3 1/4	**Mr Wolf**[37] 5941 9-8-12 79 ....(p) IanBrennan(3) 13 (J J Quinn) *chsd ldrs on wd outside: wknd over 1f out* **12/1**	53
0006	12	2	**Electioneer (USA)**[13] 6664 3-8-4 71 oh1 ....(e) JamesSullivan(3) 2 (M W Easterby) *s.i.s: in rr and drvn along: bhd fnl 2f* **16/1**	38

62.94 secs (-0.36) **Going Correction** +0.075s/f (Good) **12 Ran SP% 122.4**
Speed ratings (Par 105): **105,103,102,102,100 99,97,97,96,93 88,85**
toteswingers:1&2:£4.40, 1&3:£21.50, 2&3:£5.10 CSF £44.69 CT £292.38 TOTE £12.20: £3.90, £1.80, £3.50; EX 60.20.
Owner H Conlon **Bred** Skymarc Farm Inc **Trained** Spennymoor, Co Durham
■ Martin Lane, leading the apprentice title, lost the right to claim after this win.

FOCUS
Exposed sorts in a reasonable handicap. The gallop was sound but those held up could never land a blow. It was quicker than division II. The winner confirmed his Ayr running, with the next three close to form.

6982 TOTEPOOL SILVER TANKARD STKS (LISTED RACE) 1m 4y
4:10 (4:10) (Class 1) 2-Y-O
£15,895 (£6,025; £3,015; £1,503; £753; £378) **Stalls** Low

Form				RPR
132	1		**Zenella**[14] 6627 2-8-11 92 .... PaulHanagan 4 (Mrs A Duffield) *led: drvn 2 l clr 2f out: hld on gamely* **10/1**	87
1113	2	1 3/4	**Royal Exchange**[18] 6507 2-9-5 103 .... RyanMoore 6 (R Hannon) *chsd ldrs: lost pl and dropped bk last bnd after 2f: hdwy 3f out: n.m.r over 1f out: styd on same pce to take n.d 2nd clsng stages* **8/13**[1]	91
210	3	hd	**Rigolleto (IRE)**[62] 5184 2-9-2 83 .... ChrisCatlin 1 (M R Channon) *trckd ldrs: drvn over 2f out: styd on same pce* **40/1**	88
5101	4	1	**Star Surprise**[37] 5969 2-9-2 85 .... JamieSpencer 5 (M L W Bell) *w ldr: hung lft and reminders over 2f out: chsng ldr whn hung bdly lft over 1f out: one pce* **14/1**	85
21	5	1 1/2	**Weapon Of Choice (IRE)**[8] 6779 2-9-2 0 .... MartinLane 2 (D M Simcock) *trckd ldrs: drvn over 2f out: one pce* **9/2**[2]	82
2151	6	18	**Time To Work (IRE)**[16] 6555 2-9-2 84 .... DavidProbert 3 (A M Balding) *s.i.s: sn chsng ldrs: drvn over 4f out: lost pl over 2f out: bhd and eased over 1f out* **8/1**[3]	40

1m 45.28s (-0.62) **Going Correction** +0.075s/f (Good) **6 Ran SP% 109.4**
Speed ratings (Par 103): **106,104,104,103,101 83**
toteswingers:1&2:£2.60, 1&3:£6.60, 2&3:£5.50 CSF £16.02 TOTE £10.30: £5.00, £1.10; EX 14.00.
Owner S E Sangster **Bred** Dukes Stud & Vanquish Bloodstock Ltd **Trained** Constable Burton, N Yorks

FOCUS
Several smart sorts on the roll-of-honour for this race, the pick being Comic Strip (renamed Viva Pataca and top class in Hong Kong) in 2004 and multiple Group 2/3 winner Bandari in 2001, but this didn't look a strong Listed event given the proximity of the 80-odd rated horses filling the minor placings. Plus a moderate gallop that only picked up turning for home means the bare form has a shaky look to it.

NOTEBOOK
Zenella, the only filly in the field, was the second-highest of these on official ratings and, although easy to back, she returned to winning ways under a perfectly judged front-running ride on this first outing over 1m. She may have been flattered by getting an uncontested lead against her main market rival that looked to lack anything in the way of tactical pace but, although there was plenty to like about her attitude under pressure, she'll have to raise her game again or be afforded the same rope in front if she is to hold her own in Group company next season. (op 8-1)
Royal Exchange, the clear form-choice, looked sure to be suited by the return to 1m, but he lacks much in the way of pace and wasn't seen to best effect after being dropped out last in a moderately run race back on a sound surface and was always going to struggle to peg back the deficit when the pace quickened round the home turn. Nevertheless he'll be well worth another chance in similar company when it looks as though his stamina will be more fully tested. (op 4-6 tchd 8-15)
Rigolleto(IRE), from a yard that has won this race three times in the last four seasons and four times since 2000, had his limitations exposed in Group 3 company in August, but he ran creditably in the face of a stiff task (only rated 83) on this first run over 1m. While he may be flattered in this moderately run race, it will be interesting to see how the handicapper reacts and he should be able to win again in ordinary company granted a stiffer test of stamina. (op 28-1)
Star Surprise faced a tough task at the weights and wasn't disgraced in a muddling event, despite being unable to get his own way in front stepping up from nursery company. He is another who may be flattered by his proximity given the way this race panned out and he'll be of more interest back in nurseries when it looks as though he will be able to dominate. Official explanation: jockey said colt hung left (op 10-1)
Weapon Of Choice(IRE), up a fair way in grade after winning a Goodwood maiden in gritty style, wasn't seen to best effect over this shorter trip. The tempo of this race didn't look to suit but he has plenty of physical scope and he will be worth another chance in a lesser event in a race placing more of an emphasis on stamina. (op 11-2 tchd 6-1)
Time To Work(IRE) was a long way below the form he had shown when beating One Lucky Lady (earlier nursery winner on this card) in heavy ground at Epsom on his previous start. He has also won on a sound surface and is worth another chance. (tchd 10-1)

6983 TOTEEXACTA FLEXI BETTING BLUFF COVE H'CAP 2m 1f 216y
4:40 (4:40) (Class 5) (0-75,75) 3-Y-O+ **£2,914** (£867; £433; £216) **Stalls** Low

Form				RPR
2602	1		**Dan Buoy (FR)**[32] 6114 7-8-12 64 ....(b) BillyCray(5) 7 (R C Guest) *led: stdd pce 9f out: qcknd 6f out: styd on gamely: all out* **4/1**[1]	72
6411	2	hd	**Lava Lamp (GER)**[64] 5119 3-8-12 70 ....(v) SilvestreDeSousa 2 (G A Harker) *trckd ldrs: pushed along 5f out: wnt 2nd over 1f out: almost upsides last 75yds: jst hld* **4/1**[1]	78
5051	3	3 3/4	**Dubai Phantom (USA)**[37] 5963 3-8-5 66 .... MartinLane(3) 6 (D M Simcock) *in rr: drvn over 5f out: styd on one pce to take n.d 3rd jst ins fnl f* **7/1**	70
1363	4	2 1/4	**Bollin Judith**[9] 6750 4-9-7 68 ....(t) DavidAllan 3 (T D Easterby) *chsd ldrs: wknd jst ins fnl f* **5/1**[3]	70
4426	5	3	**Tillietudlem (FR)**[9] 6750 4-9-4 65 .... KierenFallon 1 (J S Goldie) *chsd ldrs: pushed along 6f out: wknd 1f out* **9/2**[2]	63
1533	6	shd	**Fair Spin**[13] 6648 10-8-4 58 oh7 ow2 ....(v) JamesRogers(7) 4 (Micky Hammond) *in rr: hdwy over 3f out: wknd over 1f out* **20/1**	56
3006	7	9	**Strikemaster (IRE)**[13] 6648 4-8-9 56 oh1 ....(b) PaulHanagan 8 (B Ellison) *hld up: hdwy to trck ldrs 6f out: wknd 2f out: eased ins fnl f* **8/1**	44
50-1	8	17	**Woody Waller**[188] 1277 5-9-11 75 .... IanBrennan(3) 5 (J Howard Johnson) *hld up in rr: drvn 3f out: wknd 2f out: eased ins fnl f* **17/2**	45

4m 3.47s (7.27) **Going Correction** +0.075s/f (Good)
WFA 3 from 4yo+ 11lb **8 Ran SP% 113.7**
Speed ratings (Par 103): **86,85,84,83,81 81,77,70**
toteswingers:1&2:£2.90, 1&3:£4.70, 2&3:£4.20 CSF £19.82 CT £106.83 TOTE £5.20: £2.30, £1.60, £2.10; EX 14.50.
Owner Bamboozelem **Bred** London Thoroughbred Services **Trained** Stainforth, S Yorks

■ Stewards' Enquiry : Billy Cray caution: used whip with excessive frequency.
Silvestre De Sousa one-day ban: used whip in incorrect place (Nov 1)

FOCUS
An ordinary handicap in which all bar one of the runners had won a race this season. The gallop was a reasonable one and the winner is rated to last month's C/D form.

6984 TOTETRIFECTA FLEXI BETTING H'CAP 1m 2f 6y
5:10 (5:12) (Class 5) (0-75,75) 3-Y-0+ **£2,914** (£867; £433; £216) **Stalls** Low

Form RPR
3311 **1** **Sharp Sovereign (USA)**[28] 6242 4-9-1 **65** .... SilvestreDeSousa 6 74
(T D Barron) *mde all: hrd drvn over 1f out: hld on gamely* **5/1**[1]
2104 **2** *1* **Saint Thomas (IRE)**[21] 6422 3-9-2 **71** .... JimmyQuinn 3 78
(J Mackie) *trckd ldrs: hung lft 1f out: styd on to chse wnr last 150yds: no ex* **14/1**
2-45 **3** *½* **Beetuna (IRE)**[6] 6832 5-9-5 **74** .... MarkCoumbe(5) 2 82+
(D Bourton) *hld up in midfield: hdwy 2f out: nt clr run and swtchd rt over 1f out: fin wl* **13/2**[2]
4123 **4** *nk* **Sharakti (IRE)**[14] 6623 3-8-9 **69** ....(p) DeclanCannon(5) 9 75
(A J McCabe) *sn chjasing ldrs: chal 2f out: kpt on same pce fnl f* **8/1**[3]
0000 **5** *1* **Jack Dawkins (USA)**[23] 6367 5-9-3 **67** .... AdrianNicholls 7 71
(D Nicholls) *hld up towards rr: hdwy over 2f out: chsng ldrs over 1f out: kpt on same pce* **28/1**
0530 **6** *nk* **Sanctuary**[16] 6573 4-9-9 **73** .... TomEaves 1 76
(B Smart) *chsd ldrs: effrt over 3f out: outpcd whn n.m.r 2f out: kpt on same pce fnl f* **16/1**
0000 **7** *nse* **Karaka Jack**[21] 6430 3-9-6 **75** .... KierenFallon 17 78
(M Johnston) *in tch on outer: drvn to chse ldrs over 3f out: edgd lft 2f out one pce* **14/1**
653 **8** *5* **Mashatu**[14] 6624 3-9-0 **69** .... PatCosgrave 11 62
(J R Fanshawe) *hld up in tch: effrt over 2f out: one pce whn n.m.r jst ins fnl f: wknd and eased last 75yds* **10/1**
2003 **9** *nk* **Knight's Victory (IRE)**[16] 6571 4-8-10 **63** .... MichaelStainton(3) 10 55
(Michael Smith) *s.s: detached in last: styd on fnl 2f: nvr on terms* **28/1**
4546 **10** *1¾* **Carlitos Spirit (IRE)**[19] 6462 6-8-13 **68** .... DaleSwift(5) 16 57
(I W McInnes) *s.s: hld up in rr: nvr on terms* **66/1**
0034 **11** *1* **Dream Of Olwyn (IRE)**[24] 6328 5-9-1 **65** .... MickyFenton 5 52
(J G Given) *trckd ldrs: t.k.h: hmpd and lost pl 2f out* **20/1**
1405 **12** *2* **Umverti**[13] 6650 5-9-9 **73** .... FrannyNorton 13 56
(N Bycroft) *in rr: sn drvn along: sme hdwy over 2f out: wknd over 1f out* **16/1**
3422 **13** *nk* **Raleigh Quay (IRE)**[32] 6112 3-9-6 **75** .... PaulHanagan 15 57
(Micky Hammond) *a in rr* **8/1**[3]
2500 **14** *1¼* **Huntingfortreasure**[19] 6467 3-9-4 **73** ....(p) DavidAllan 14 53
(M Dods) *s.i.s: drvn 4f out: sme hdwy whn hmpd over 2f out: sn wknd* **20/1**
0040 **15** *24* **Amanda Carter**[22] 6397 6-9-2 **69** .... BarryMcHugh(3) 12 —
(R A Fahey) *chsd ldrs: lost pl over 2f out: bhd whn eased ins fnl f: t.o* **20/1**
2413 **16** *15* **Scarab (IRE)**[16] 6573 5-9-5 **69** ....(p) GrahamGibbons 4 —
(T D Walford) *trckd ldrs: wkng whn hmpd 2f out: sn eased and bhd: virtually p.u: t.o* **8/1**[3]

2m 14.22s (0.52) **Going Correction** +0.075s/f (Good)
WFA 3 from 4yo+ 5lb **16** Ran SP% **120.2**
Speed ratings (Par 103): **100,99,98,98,97 97,97,93,93,91 91,89,89,88,69 57**
toteswingers:1&2:£16.70, 1&3:£8.90, 2&3:£29.20 CSF £66.73 CT £467.62 TOTE £4.30: £1.30, £3.60, £2.30, £2.10; EX 91.70 TRIFECTA Not won..
Owner Raymond Miquel **Bred** James Sumter Carter **Trained** Maunby, N Yorks
■ Stewards' Enquiry : Mark Coumbe two-day ban: used whip without giving gelding time to respond (Nov 5-6); caution: careless riding.
Kieren Fallon two-day ban: careless riding (Nov 1-2)

FOCUS
Largely exposed performers in an ordinary handicap in which a few met trouble rounding the home turn. The gallop was reasonable but this was another race on the day that went to one that was right up with the pace throughout. The fourth helps with the level of the form.
Umverti Official explanation: jockey said blindfold has to be left on as late as possible but as he went to remove it, it had become caught on a buckle, causing the mare to miss the break.

6985 TOTESUPER7 H'CAP (DIV II) 5f
5:40 (5:42) (Class 4) (0-85,85) 3-Y-0+ **£4,209** (£1,252; £625; £312) **Stalls** Low

Form RPR
5113 **1** **Divertimenti (IRE)**[30] 6198 6-8-12 **76** ....(b) JimmyQuinn 11 85
(S R Bowring) *mde all: edgd lft fr outside draw: edgd rt and hld on gamely fnl f* **12/1**[3]
4235 **2** *1* **Grissom (IRE)**[14] 6625 4-8-11 **75** ....(t) PaulHanagan 3 80
(T D Easterby) *mid-div: hdwy to chse ldrs and plld wd 1f out: styd on to take 2nd last 50yds* **3/1**[1]
3000 **3** *½* **Internationaldebut (IRE)**[10] 6721 5-9-4 **82** .... MickyFenton 4 86+
(P T Midgley) *stdd s: hld up in rr: nt clr run on ins over 2f out and over 1f out: styd on ins fnl f: snatched 3rd on line* **6/1**[2]
3110 **4** *shd* **Select Committee**[16] 6572 5-8-3 **74** ....(v) ShaneBKelly(7) 8 77
(J J Quinn) *chsd ldrs: wnt 2nd last 150yds: kpt on same pce* **16/1**
3303 **5** *1¾* **The Nifty Fox**[10] 6706 6-9-7 **85** .... DavidAllan 5 82
(T D Easterby) *in rr: hdwy over 2f out: kpt on fnl f: nvr threatened ldrs* **6/1**[2]
5142 **6** *1* **Night Trade (IRE)**[28] 6245 3-9-2 **80** ....(p) SilvestreDeSousa 9 73
(Mrs D J Sanderson) *w ldrs: fdd last 50yds* **14/1**
2000 **7** *½* **Magical Macey (USA)**[10] 6723 3-9-2 **80** .... GrahamGibbons 12 72
(T D Barron) *swtchd lft s: in rr: hdwy 2f out: sn n.m.r: nvr rchd ldrs* **16/1**
2114 **8** *¾* **Jack Luey**[4] 6879 3-8-6 **73** .... IanBrennan(3) 1 64
(L A Mullaney) *fly-leaped s: sn chsng ldrs: wkng whn hmpd and eased last 50yds* **6/1**[2]
1040 **9** *¾* **Mon Brav**[10] 6723 3-8-8 **77** ....(v) NeilFarley(5) 10 63
(D Carroll) *chsd ldrs: wknd over 1f out* **25/1**
0100 **10** *2* **Falasteen (IRE)**[23] 6364 3-9-6 **84** .... TomEaves 6 63
(R A Fahey) *in rr: effrt outer 2f out: nvr a factor* **33/1**
0046 **11** *1¼* **Cut The Cackle (IRE)**[4] 6858 4-8-3 **72** ....(b) DeclanCannon(5) 13 46
(P Butler) *s.i.s: in rr: sme hdwy 3f out: hung lft and wknd 2f out* **40/1**

63.48 secs (0.18) **Going Correction** +0.075s/f (Good) **11** Ran SP% **103.2**
Speed ratings (Par 105): **101,99,98,98,95 94,93,92,90,87 85**
toteswingers:1&2:£6.00, 1&3:£14.70, 2&3:£4.70 CSF £37.68 CT £179.75 TOTE £11.10: £2.70, £1.10, £2.90; EX 41.50 Place 6 £7.90; Place 5 £3.44..
Owner K Nicholls **Bred** Airlie Stud **Trained** Edwinstowe, Notts

FOCUS
A fair handicap in which the gallop was a decent one but yet another race that went to one making all the running. The form is taken at face value but the winner may not merit full credit for this.
Jack Luey Official explanation: jockey said gelding was denied a clear run
T/Jkpt: Not won. T/Plt: £6.20 to a £1 stake. Pool:£74,670.20 - 8,671.56 winning tickets T/Qpdt: £3.20 to a £1 stake. Pool:£4,190.20 - 966.54 winning tickets WG

6809 WINDSOR (R-H)
Monday, October 18

OFFICIAL GOING: Good to firm (good in places; 9.6)
Stands' rail dolled out 6yds at 6f and 2½yards at the winning post.
Wind: Moderate, behind Weather: Cloudy

6986 TOTEPLACEPOT MEDIAN AUCTION MAIDEN STKS 5f 10y
2:00 (2:00) (Class 5) 2-Y-O **£2,286** (£675; £337) **Stalls** High

Form RPR
6 **1** **Glas Burn**[20] 6441 2-8-12 0 .... JimCrowley 1 74
(J G Portman) *hld up: smooth hdwy over 2f out: led in centre over 1f out: sn in command: eased nr fin* **9/1**
3300 **2** *¾* **Magic Stella**[40] 5856 2-8-12 75 .... SebSanders 3 71
(A P Jarvis) *prom: led 2f out tl over 1f out: nt pce of wnr: kpt on nr fin: a comf hld* **5/2**[2]
2 **3** *3½* **Pantella (IRE)**[33] 6075 2-8-12 0 .... NeilCallan 4 58
(K A Ryan) *in tch in 5th: rdn to chse ldng pair 2f out: one pce appr fnl f* **15/8**[1]
02 **4** *1¾* **Oh So Kool**[19] 6458 2-9-3 0 .... WilliamCarson 6 57
(S C Williams) *towards rr tl shkn up and r.o fnl 2f: nvr nrr* **7/1**[3]
4050 **5** *2* **Mystica (IRE)**[9] 6740 2-8-12 56 ....(b[1]) JamesDoyle 5 45
(D J S Ffrench Davis) *prom tl wknd 2f out* **50/1**
630 **6** *hd* **Gottcher**[70] 4896 2-9-3 69 .... DaneO'Neill 9 49
(T D Barron) *sn led: hdd & wknd 2f out* **7/1**[3]
00 **7** *1* **Cliffords Reprieve**[11] 6688 2-9-0 0 .... KierenFox(3) 10 46
(E A Wheeler) *a abt same pl: n.d* **100/1**
6620 **8** *6* **Vetvey (IRE)**[16] 6575 2-9-3 60 .... GregFairley 8 24
(M Johnston) *broke wl: chsd ldrs over 2f: qckly lost pl* **11/1**
9 *½* **Heavenly Pursuit** 2-8-12 0 .... StephenCraine 7 17
(J R Boyle) *s.s: outpcd: a bhd* **50/1**
10 *2* **Queens Troop** 2-8-12 0 .... SamHitchcott 2 10
(D K Ivory) *s.i.s: outpcd: a bhd* **100/1**

59.51 secs (-0.79) **Going Correction** -0.225s/f (Firm) **10** Ran SP% **112.6**
Speed ratings (Par 95): **97,95,90,87,84 83,82,72,71,68**
toteswingers:1&2:£5.90, 1&3:£4.50, 2&3:£1.80 CSF £30.65 TOTE £13.30: £2.70, £1.40, £1.30; EX 48.00 Trifecta £53.80 Pool: £759.58 - 10.43 winning units..
Owner Jaliza Partnership **Bred** Mill House Stud **Trained** Compton, Berks

FOCUS
An ordinary maiden, run at a solid pace. The first two came down the middle.

NOTEBOOK
Glas Burn ran with promise at Newbury last month, but was dropping back to the minimum trip and had the outside stall to contend with. There is pace in her pedigree, though, and she got off the mark with a ready effort, easing down near the finish. The decent early pace was a help over this sharper test, there should be some more to come and she looks a fair prospect for sprint handicaps. (op 12-1 tchd 8-1)
Magic Stella was not that surprisingly doing her best work towards the finish on this return to 5f and returned to form, but is somewhat flattered by her proximity to the winner. This was her eighth outing and she rates the benchmark even if her current mark looks beyond her (op 7-2)
Pantella(IRE) looked the one to be on if building on the level of her debut second at Beverley last month, but she lacked the pace to get seriously involved on this sharper track. Returning to a stiffer test should only help and she isn't one to abandon yet. (op 2-1)
Oh So Kool ◆ had tried to make all on desperate ground when second at Newcastle last time out. Very easy to back here, he found things happening too quickly but now qualifies for a mark and is one to keep an eye on in that sphere. (op 7-2)
Gottcher was having his fourth outing and first run for 70 days. He showed decent early speed, but ultimately dropped out tamely and a mark of 69 probably flatters him at this stage. He was later reported to have hung left. Official explanation: jockey said gelding hung left (op 9-1 tchd 13-2)

6987 ATTHERACES.COM CLAIMING STKS 6f
2:30 (2:30) (Class 6) 3-Y-O+ **£1,706** (£503; £252) **Stalls** High

Form RPR
0400 **1** **Sunrise Safari (IRE)**[17] 6537 7-8-8 81 ....(v) LeeTopliss(5) 8 86
(R A Fahey) *mid-div: drvn along over 2f out: hdwy over 1f out: swtchd lft and fnd gap: edgd lft: r.o to ld nr fin* **8/1**[3]
0506 **2** *½* **Victorian Bounty**[2] 6932 5-8-4 73 .... JohnFahy(5) 3 80
(Stef Higgins) *led: hrd rdn and kpt on fnl f: hdd nr fin* **10/1**
2520 **3** *½* **Maze (IRE)**[18] 6503 5-9-1 78 .... SebSanders 4 84
(A W Carroll) *pressed ldr: drvn to chal over 1f out: nt qckn fnl 100yds* **10/1**
0463 **4** *¾* **Green Manalishi**[23] 6368 9-9-7 80 ....(tp) NeilCallan 5 88
(K A Ryan) *chsd ldrs: hrd rdn over 1f out: one pce fnl f* **14/1**
0050 **5** *nk* **Soap Wars**[7] 6799 5-9-2 82 .... FergusSweeney 16 82
(J A Osborne) *settled in midfield on stands' rail: hdwy and nt clr run over 1f out: kpt on fnl f* **17/2**
6505 **6** *nse* **Macdillon**[19] 6478 4-8-13 77 ....(p) IanMongan 14 79
(W S Kittow) *chsd ldrs: hrd rdn over 1f out: no ex fnl f* **17/2**
1500 **7** *1¾* **Bobs Dreamflight**[7] 6812 4-8-12 67 .... SamHitchcott 10 72
(D K Ivory) *mid-div: rdn along over 2f out: no imp* **66/1**
6623 **8** *nk* **Vhujon (IRE)**[7] 6799 5-8-7 78 .... AdamBeschizza(5) 9 71
(P D Evans) *hld up towards rr: hdwy towards far side over 2f out: wknd over 1f out* **4/1**[1]
6005 **9** *3¼* **Cerito**[17] 6523 4-8-1 68 ....(p) JemmaMarshall(5) 12 55
(J R Boyle) *hld up towards rr: rdn and n.d fnl 2f* **40/1**
5200 **10** *nk* **Universal Circus**[20] 6439 3-8-3 70 .... LukeMorris 11 52
(M R Channon) *n.m.r sn after s: sn in rr* **40/1**
1500 **11** *¾* **Lujeanie**[19] 6478 4-9-5 80 ....(p) JimCrowley 13 65
(D K Ivory) *a bhd* **6/1**[2]
0250 **12** *7* **Steelcut**[17] 6523 6-8-8 72 .... HayleyTurner 1 31
(Andrew Reid) *prom: rdn over 2f out: sn wknd* **25/1**
4432 **U** **Cape Melody**[10] 6714 4-8-6 74 .... NickyMackay 2 —
(H Morrison) *dwlt: hdwy and in tch 4f out: 6th whn no room: stmbld and uns rdr ins fnl 3f* **6/1**[2]

1m 11.5s (-1.50) **Going Correction** -0.225s/f (Firm)
WFA 3 from 4yo+ 1lb **13** Ran SP% **115.8**
Speed ratings (Par 101): **101,100,99,98,98 98,95,95,91,90 89,80,—**
toteswingers:1&2:£22.10, 1&3:£20.50, 2&3:£20.50 CSF £80.59 TOTE £10.60: £3.50, £4.40, £3.10; EX 131.30 TRIFECTA Not won..
Owner Timeform Betfair Racing Club Ltd **Bred** Mervyn Stewkesbury **Trained** Musley Bank, N Yorks
■ Stewards' Enquiry : Lee Topliss two-day ban: careless riding (Nov 1-2)

FOCUS
A fair claimer and a wide-open contest. It was run at a sound pace and again the winner came down the middle late on. The form makes sense at face value but the time was modest compared with the 2yos in the next.

6988 TOTEQUADPOT NURSERY (DIV I) 6f
3:00 (3:00) (Class 5) (0-75,75) 2-Y-O **£1,944** (£574; £287) **Stalls** High

Form RPR
016 **1** **Picabo (IRE)**[24] 6317 2-8-12 **66**........ HayleyTurner 12 72
(Mrs L Wadham) *s.s: hld up in midfield: hdwy 2f out: led over 1f out: hung bdly lft: rdn out* **5/2**[1]
520 **2** *1 ¼* **Fred Willetts (IRE)**[3] 6900 2-9-4 **75**........(b) RichardEvans(3) 5 77
(P D Evans) *prom: drvn along over 2f out: nt qckn ins fnl f* **8/1**
3431 **3** *hd* **Prophet In A Dream**[12] 6673 2-8-11 **68**........ AndrewHeffernan(3) 7 69
(M R Channon) *chsd ldrs: hrd rdn wl over 1f out: one pce ins fnl f* **7/2**[2]
050 **4** *¾* **Danceyourselfdizzy (IRE)**[19] 6474 2-8-11 **65**........ JimmyFortune 9 64
(R Hannon) *mid-div tl rdn and hdwy fr 2f out: 4th and styng on whn hung lft ins fnl f* **13/2**[3]
4600 **5** *2 ½* **Reginald Claude**[30] 6191 2-8-11 **70**........ LeeNewnes(5) 2 61
(M D I Usher) *missed break and hmpd s: bhd tl rdn and styd on fnl 2f* **40/1**
6401 **6** *2 ¼* **Reachtothestars (USA)**[16] 6575 2-9-5 **73**........(t) JimCrowley 10 57
(M Dods) *t.k.h: led after 1f tl hrd rdn and wknd over 1f out* **14/1**
0335 **7** *3 ½* **Shostakovich (IRE)**[12] 6673 2-8-1 **52** ow3........ LukeMorris 3 28
(S Kirk) *missed break and hmpd s: bhd: drvn along over 2f out: nvr rchd ldrs* **16/1**
0206 **8** *shd* **Putin (IRE)**[7] 6811 2-9-1 **69**........ DaneO'Neill 11 41
(D Haydn Jones) *led 1f: prom tl hrd rdn and wknd 2f out* **20/1**
0344 **9** *3 ¾* **Livia Quarta (IRE)**[59] 5268 2-7-12 **52** oh3........ AndreaAtzeni 6 12
(E J Creighton) *dwlt: sn in midfield: rdn and no hdwy 2f out: eased whn btn fnl f* **100/1**
1530 **10** *1 ¾* **Arctic Mirage**[11] 6690 2-9-4 **72**........ WilliamCarson 4 27
(M Blanshard) *sn outpcd towards rr* **14/1**
205 **11** *2 ½* **Bahri Sheen (IRE)**[40] 5865 2-9-4 **72**........ SteveDrowne 8 19
(J R Best) *s.s: a bhd* **13/2**[3]
6506 **12** *3* **Go**[18] 6498 2-8-6 **60**........(b¹) FrankieMcDonald 1 —
(R Hannon) *wnt rt s: sn in midfield: hung rt and reminders thrght: hrd rdn and wknd qckly over 2f out* **50/1**

1m 11.88s (-1.12) **Going Correction** -0.225s/f (Firm) **12** Ran SP% **117.9**
Speed ratings (Par 95): **98,96,96,95,91 88,84,83,78,76 73,69**
toteswingers:1&2:£5.00, 1&3:£2.40, 2&3:£6.70 CSF £31.80 CT £72.33 TOTE £4.40: £2.80, £2.50, £1.10; EX 22.42 TRIFECTA Pool: £314.37 - 4.45 winning units..
Owner Tom Ford **Bred** A B Mulholland **Trained** Newmarket, Suffolk

FOCUS
A moderate nursery, run at a sound pace. This time the first three ended up towards the far side.

NOTEBOOK
Picabo(IRE) was well backed throughout the day and resumed winning ways with a fair bit left in the tank. She got to the leaders going easily enough nearing the furlong marker, but once in front hung badly left and finished towards the far rail. She was found out in much better company on tacky ground at Ascot last time, but proved too classy off for this opposition off a 1lb lower mark and the slight drop back in trip on this sharper track was right up her street. Her hanging was likely still down to inexperience and she could well defy a likely rise. (op 9-4 tchd 2-1 and 11-4 and 3-1 in a place)
Fred Willetts(IRE) flopped on the AW three days earlier, but had been running well on turf prior to that and this was a definite return to form back up a furlong in lesser company. He was carried over when the winner hung, but it made no real difference to the overall result. (tchd 7-1)
Prophet In A Dream was 8lb higher than when winning well at Nottingham 12 days previously, but still proved popular. He posted a solid effort in defeat, on ground probably a bit quicker than he cares for over this trip, and may be able to win again this year. (op 9-2)
Danceyourselfdizzy(IRE) was making his nursery debut and dropping back from 1m. He got going late in the day and enjoyed this return to a sounder surface. He ought to make his mark in one of these before too long, perhaps when racing over another furlong. He was later reported to have hung left. Official explanation: jockey said colt hyung left (op 12-1)
Reginald Claude, down in class with the cheekpieces abandoned, was taken off his feet through the early parts after a messy start. He stayed on late in the day and probably does want easier ground over a stiffer test to be seen at his best. Official explanation: jockey said colt suffered interference at start (tchd 50-1)
Reachtothestars(USA), off the mark on his AW debut 16 days earlier, wasn't able to dictate on this return to a nursery but still travelled sweetly in a handy position. He paid late on for taking a keen early hold, though, and looks worth another try back on Polytrack. (op 8-1)
Bahri Sheen(IRE) Official explanation: jockey said colt never travelled
Go Official explanation: jockey said colt hung badly right

6989 TOTEQUADPOT NURSERY (DIV II) 6f
3:30 (3:30) (Class 5) (0-75,75) 2-Y-O **£1,944** (£574; £287) **Stalls** High

Form RPR
3106 **1** **Country Waltz**[9] 6740 2-8-3 **60** ow3........ AndrewHeffernan(3) 9 63
(M R Channon) *mde all: drvn over 2 l clr 2f out: hld on wl fnl f* **14/1**
240 **2** *1* **Karate (IRE)**[12] 6666 2-9-2 **70**........ GregFairley 7 70
(M Johnston) *prom: hrd rdn and outpcd by wnr 2f out: kpt on fnl f* **8/1**
241 **3** *½* **Latin Lashes (USA)**[26] 6286 2-9-4 **72**........ JimmyFortune 1 71
(R Hannon) *wnt lft s: hld up in rr: gd hdwy to dispute 2nd 1f out: kpt on* **13/2**[2]
221 **4** *shd* **Enthusing (IRE)**[31] 6146 2-9-7 **75**........ DaneO'Neill 3 73
(D R C Elsworth) *t.k.h towards rr: hdwy to chse ldrs 2f out: kpt on fnl f* **2/1**[1]
0144 **5** *2 ½* **Ruby Alexander (IRE)**[28] 6259 2-8-2 **61**........(b) JohnFahy(5) 4 52
(R M Beckett) *towards rr: rdn and sme hdwy fnl 2f: nt pce to chal* **18/1**
0000 **6** *shd* **Make My Mark (IRE)**[4] 6867 2-7-12 **52**........ AndreaAtzeni 6 42
(F Jordan) *prom tl hrd rdn and no ex over 1f out* **66/1**
010 **7** *nk* **Malice Or Mischief (IRE)**[12] 6670 2-9-5 **73**........ NeilCallan 10 63
(A W Carroll) *mid-div: hdwy over 2f out: sn rdn and one pce* **7/1**[3]
5200 **8** *2 ½* **Silly Billy (IRE)**[5] 6842 2-8-13 **67**........ LiamKeniry 11 49
(S Kirk) *mid-div: hrd rdn and hung lft fr over 1f out: n.d* **8/1**
4660 **9** *10* **Scommettitrice (IRE)**[8] 6769 2-8-12 **66**........ LukeMorris 2 18
(R A Harris) *stdd s: a towards rr: no ch and edging rt whn hmpd ins fnl 2f* **33/1**
2303 **10** *3* **Indian Shuffle (IRE)**[8] 6769 2-8-9 **68**........ AdamBeschizza(5) 5 11
(J G Portman) *in tch tl wknd qckly 3f out* **7/1**[3]
5406 **P** **Milldown Magic**[21] 6419 2-9-2 **70**........ JamesMillman 8 —
(B R Millman) *chsd ldrs over 3f: wkng whn p.u ins fnl 2f: fatally injured* **25/1**

1m 12.28s (-0.72) **Going Correction** -0.225s/f (Firm) **11** Ran SP% **114.1**
Speed ratings (Par 95): **95,93,93,92,89 89,89,85,72,68** —
toteswingers:1&2:£22.90, 1&3:£12.90, 2&3:£7.30 CSF £116.09 CT £815.33 TOTE £17.70: £4.20, £1.70, £2.40; EX 229.00 Trifecta £410.40 Part won. Pool: £554.61 - 0.33 winning units..
Owner Ridgeway Downs Racing **Bred** Mike Channon Bloodstock Ltd **Trained** West Ilsley, Berks

FOCUS
The second division of the nursery and it looked slightly stronger than the first. The field raced more towards the centre from the home turn and again the main action was nearer the far rail late on.

NOTEBOOK
Country Waltz was friendless in the betting ring, but she made all in ready fashion on this return to turf. She responded strongly when asked everything nearing the furlong pole and wasn't in any serious danger thereafter. She is now 2-2 when leading from the start and it rates a career-best effort. (op 9-1)
Karate(IRE) ◆ shaped a lot more encouragingly again on this step back up from 5f and has evidently begun life in this sphere on a workable mark. He has now finished second on his two outings on turf, he proved suited by the quick ground and can go one better in one of these on a stiffer track. (tchd 9-1)
Latin Lashes(USA) made it third time lucky on her AW debut last time out and was back up a furlong for this nursery debut. She took time to settle, but had her chance and turned in a sound display. She has few miles on the clock and can defy this mark before long. (op 5-1 tchd 9-2 and 7-1 in a place)
Enthusing(IRE), off the mark at the fourth attempt at Newbury a month earlier, found things happening to bit too quickly for him on this sharper circuit. He probably wants a slightly easier surface to be at his most effective and is another that can win off his current mark. (op 5-2 tchd 11-4)

6990 TOTEEXACTA H'CAP 1m 2f 7y
4:00 (4:00) (Class 4) (0-85,87) 3-Y-O+ **£3,885** (£1,156; £577; £288) **Stalls** Centre

Form RPR
3605 **1** **Prince Of Johanne (IRE)**[10] 6724 4-8-8 **73**........(p) JohnFahy(5) 10 85
(T P Tate) *dwlt: hld up in rr: swtchd rt and hdwy 2f out: styd on in centre to ld 100yds out: drvn out* **12/1**
4355 **2** *1* **The Which Doctor**[19] 6449 5-9-8 **82**........(p) TomQueally 3 92
(J Noseda) *hld up in rr of midfield: effrt and hmpd 3f out: hdwy in centre 2f out: pressed wnr fnl 100yds: kpt on* **6/1**[3]
0460 **3** *½* **Safari Sunup (IRE)**[20] 6437 5-9-9 **83**........ LukeMorris 11 92
(P Winkworth) *chsd ldrs: hrd rdn in centre 2f out: styd on same pce* **10/1**
3021 **4** *1 ¼* **Aerodynamic (IRE)**[8] 6771 3-9-8 **87** 6ex........ RobertWinston 7 93
(Pat Eddery) *sn prom: led towards far side 3f out: hrd rdn and hdd 1f out: no ex* **9/2**[2]
3036 **5** *¾* **Tinshu (IRE)**[88] 4306 4-9-10 **84**........ DaneO'Neill 6 89
(D Haydn Jones) *hld up in midfield: smooth hdwy 3f out: led towards far side 1f out: hdd & wknd 100yds out* **12/1**
0315 **6** *1 ¼* **Ramona Chase**[16] 6552 5-9-8 **82**........(t) NeilCallan 9 84
(M J Attwater) *chsd ldrs tl outpcd in centre fnl 2f* **20/1**
512- **7** *1 ½* **Brilliana**[404] 5771 4-9-8 **82**........ TedDurcan 8 81
(D R Lanigan) *mid-div: styd alone on stands' rail fr 3f out: no imp* **9/4**[1]
610 **8** *1* **Inspirina (IRE)**[20] 6437 6-9-8 **82**........ J-PGuillambert 2 79
(R Ford) *hld up in midfield: hdwy and prom 3f out: wknd over 1f out* **40/1**
0-03 **9** *1 ¾* **Silverglas (IRE)**[26] 6288 4-9-1 **75**........ JimCrowley 1 69
(W J Knight) *bhd: rdn and sme hdwy over 2f out: sn wknd* **8/1**
0362 **10** *¾* **Sohcahtoa (IRE)**[19] 6476 4-9-6 **80**........(b) JimmyFortune 4 72
(R Hannon) *prom: outpcd and rdn 4f out: wknd over 2f out* **11/1**
4000 **11** *6* **Kidlat**[7] 6797 5-9-3 **77**........ SebSanders 13 57
(A Bailey) *rdn up fr rr to ld after 3f: hdd & wknd 3f out* **50/1**
6 **12** *6* **Shalambar (IRE)**[14] 6630 4-9-1 **75**........ TonyCulhane 12 43
(A W Carroll) *sn wl bhd* **50/1**
50 **13** *3 ¾* **Time Square (FR)**[37] 5953 3-8-10 **75**........ ShaneKelly 5 36
(A W Carroll) *led 3f: prom tl wknd over 2f out* **100/1**

2m 4.96s (-3.74) **Going Correction** -0.225s/f (Firm)
WFA 3 from 4yo+ 5lb **13** Ran SP% **119.3**
Speed ratings (Par 105): **105,104,103,102,102 101,100,99,97,97 92,87,84**
toteswingers:1&2:£11.10, 1&3:£21.70, 2&3:£13.60 CSF £79.65 CT £761.32 TOTE £12.90: £3.60, £2.20, £4.60; EX 61.20 Trifecta £316.20 Part won. Pool: £427.36 - 0.50 winning units..
Owner David Storey **Bred** T J Rooney And Corduff Stud **Trained** Tadcaster, N Yorks
■ Stewards' Enquiry : Luke Morris two-day ban: careless riding (Nov 1-2)

FOCUS
A modest handicap in which there were a host of chances as the runner spread out across the home straight. Once more the centre proved the place to be, however. The form looks sound with the runner-up a good guide, and the winner and third were well handicapped on the their early-season form.
Time Square(FR) Official explanation: jockey said gelding ran too freely

6991 CSP H'CAP (DIV I) 1m 67y
4:30 (4:30) (Class 5) (0-70,74) 3-Y-O+ **£1,944** (£574; £287) **Stalls** High

Form RPR
5234 **1** **Song To The Moon (IRE)**[14] 6629 3-9-5 **70**........(b¹) JimmyFortune 12 82
(A M Balding) *chsd ldrs: effrt over 2f out: led ins fnl f: rdn clr* **15/8**[1]
050 **2** *2 ¼* **Ermyn Express**[14] 6633 3-8-0 **56**........ JemmaMarshall(5) 9 63
(P M Phelan) *chsd ldr: drvn to chal 1f out: nt pce of wnr* **20/1**
0-01 **3** *1 ¼* **April Fool**[7] 6794 6-9-12 **74** 6ex........(v) TomMcLaughlin 1 78
(R A Harris) *racd freely: led and sn 4 l clr at gd pce: hdd and no ex ins fnl f* **16/1**
4332 **4** *½* **Osgood**[14] 6633 3-9-5 **70**........ SamHitchcott 8 73
(M R Channon) *dwlt: sn chsng ldrs: gng wl tl rdn over 2f out: styd on same pce* **11/2**[2]
4125 **5** *½* **Catchanova (IRE)**[21] 6413 3-8-13 **64**........ TomQueally 5 66
(Eve Johnson Houghton) *hld up in 6th: chsd ldrs and hrd rdn 2f out: no ex fnl f* **11/2**[2]
2325 **6** *1 ¾* **Hellbender (IRE)**[13] 6664 4-9-1 **63**........(t) LiamKeniry 3 61
(S Kirk) *towards rr: sme hdwy and hrd rdn 2f out: nt rch ldrs* **11/1**[3]
61 **7** *2 ¾* **Croeso Cusan**[14] 6633 5-9-7 **69**........ SebSanders 2 60
(J L Spearing) *stdd s: hld up in rr: rdn and sme hdwy 2f out: nvr able to chal* **11/1**[3]
-040 **8** *¾* **Montelissima (IRE)**[37] 5958 3-8-11 **62**........ JimCrowley 13 52
(E A L Dunlop) *a in mid-div: rdn and no hdwy fnl 3f* **12/1**
-200 **9** *19* **Meer Und Wind (GER)**[24] 6336 3-8-12 **63**........(b) TedDurcan 11 9
(P R Webber) *hrd rdn 5f out: a bhd* **16/1**
0100 **10** *5* **George Thisby**[21] 6421 4-9-4 **66**........ JamesMillman 6 —
(B R Millman) *awkward s: a in rr gp* **25/1**
0-00 **11** *39* **Sir Ike (IRE)**[5] 6853 5-9-1 **63**........(tp) IanMongan 4 —
(W S Kittow) *s.i.s: sn chsng ldrs: rdn 3f out: sn wknd* **16/1**

1m 41.46s (-3.24) **Going Correction** -0.225s/f (Firm)
WFA 3 from 4yo+ 3lb **11** Ran SP% **116.2**
Speed ratings (Par 103): **107,104,103,103,102 100,98,97,78,73 34**
toteswingers:1&2:£16.60, 1&3:£9.20, 2&3:£31.10 CSF £45.22 CT £482.10 TOTE £2.60: £1.20, £9.80, £3.30; EX 56.30 TRIFECTA Not won..
Owner John K Gale **Bred** Michael Woodlock & Seamus Kennedy **Trained** Kingsclere, Hants

FOCUS
A moderate handicap, run at a decent pace.

Sir Ike(IRE) Official explanation: jockey said gelding stopped quickly

6992 CSP H'CAP (DIV II) 1m 67y
5:00 (5:02) (Class 5) (0-70,70) 3-Y-O+ £1,944 (£574; £287) Stalls High

Form RPR
4410 1 **Rosedale**30 6197 3-9-1 67 TedDurcan 12 76
(J A R Toller) *mid-div: pushed along over 3f out: swtchd towards far side and hdwy to ld over 1f out: drvn out* 15/2[3]
2524 2 3/4 **Diggeratt (USA)**10 6718 4-9-2 70 LeeTopliss(5) 10 77
(R A Fahey) *chsd ldrs: hrd rdn in centre 2f out: styd on wl nr fin* 7/2[1]
0236 3 1/2 **Ivory Lace**4 6864 9-9-2 68 AndrewHeffernan(3) 11 74
(S Woodman) *dwlt: t.k.h in midfield: rdn and hdwy in centre over 1f out: chsd ldrs fnl f: kpt on* 12/1
0066 4 3 **Saturn Way (GR)**14 6633 4-9-4 67 JimCrowley 5 66
(P R Chamings) *prom: led towards far side over 2f out tl over 1f out: no ex* 6/1[2]
3545 5 1 1/2 **Night Sky**36 5988 3-8-11 63 (p) FergusSweeney 4 59
(P J Makin) *chsd ldr: led briefly 3f out: wknd over 1f out* 20/1
0320 6 2 **Mellifera**47 5664 3-8-12 69 (v1) JohnFahy(5) 3 60
(W R Swinburn) *towards rr: hrd rdn 2f out: sme late hdwy* 6/1[2]
1363 7 nk **Frank Street**19 6452 4-8-7 56 (t) LiamKeniry 2 46
(Eve Johnson Houghton) *in tch tl outpcd and btn 3f out* 15/2[3]
4000 8 3/4 **Ajool (USA)**14 6632 3-8-11 63 TonyCulhane 8 52
(P W D'Arcy) *towards rr: rdn and n.d fnl 3f* 28/1
1301 9 nse **Batgirl**33 6098 3-8-13 65 TomMcLaughlin 9 54
(John Berry) *bhd: hrd rdn over 2f out: modest hdwy over 1f out: eased whn no imp* 6/1[2]
-500 10 2 **Florio Vincitore (IRE)**48 5647 3-9-4 70 EddieCreighton 6 54
(E J Creighton) *dwlt: a bhd* 40/1
03-0 11 2 **Valkov**7 6794 3-8-10 65 KierenFox(3) 1 44
(E A Wheeler) *in tch: nt handle bnd and lost pl over 6f out: hrd rdn and wknd over 2f out* 40/1
4500 12 1 1/4 **Meydan Dubai (IRE)**14 6633 5-9-0 63 (b1) SteveDrowne 7 40
(J R Best) *led tl 3f out: hrd rdn and wknd 2f out* 12/1

1m 42.38s (-2.32) **Going Correction** -0.225s/f (Firm)
WFA 3 from 4yo+ 3lb 12 Ran SP% 117.1
Speed ratings (Par 103): **102,101,100,97,96 94,93,93,93,91 89,87**
toteswingers:1&2:£6.00, 1&3:£16.20, 2&3:£9.80 CSF £32.18 CT £259.57 TOTE £14.00: £4.70, £1.10, £5.80; EX 43.90 Trifecta £218.40 Pool: £342.49 - 1.16 winning units..
Owner Alan Gibson **Bred** Alan Gibson **Trained** Newmarket, Suffolk

FOCUS
This second division of the extended 1m handicap was another ordinary affair. It was run at a fair pace. The winner stepped up on her Yarmouth win and the next two ran to form.
Frank Street Official explanation: trainer said gelding was unsuited by the good to firm ground
Batgirl Official explanation: trainer said filly did not handle the bend

6993 DOMINO'S PIZZA BEST TURNED OUT HORSE H'CAP 1m 2f 7y
5:30 (5:30) (Class 6) (0-65,70) 3-Y-O £1,706 (£503; £252) Stalls Centre

Form RPR
2040 1 **Rodrigo De Freitas (IRE)**17 6527 3-9-0 58 (v1) TomQueally 16 68
(J R Boyle) *hld up in rr: hdwy over 2f out: led in centre wl over 1f out: edgd lft: drvn clr* 20/1
2 2 1 1/2 **Marrimeclaire (IRE)**31 6165 3-9-4 62 ShaneKelly 3 69
(B J McMath) *hld up in rr: hdwy to press wnr towards far side wl over 1f out: nt qckn ins fnl f* 9/1
5311 3 1 **Kenyan Cat**18 6518 3-9-4 62 TedDurcan 14 67+
(George Baker) *towards rr: rdn 3f out: r.o in centre fnl 2f: nrst fin* 6/1[3]
0120 4 3/4 **Pennfield Pirate**19 6472 3-9-4 62 SteveDrowne 13 66
(H Morrison) *chsd ldrs: drvn to chal in centre 2f out: one pce* 9/1
-242 5 1 1/2 **Gift Of Love (IRE)**7 6814 3-9-7 65 RobertWinston 9 68+
(D R C Elsworth) *sn in midfield: hdwy to press ldrs towards far side 2f out: one pce* 4/1[1]
2130 6 2 1/4 **Shianda**8 6781 3-9-3 61 (b) GeorgeBaker 5 57
(G L Moore) *chsd ldrs: led over 5f out tl hdd in centre wl over 1f out: sn wknd* 16/1
4431 7 nk **Astound**2 6937 3-9-12 70 6ex (v) TomMcLaughlin 1 65
(P D Evans) *chsd ldrs: towards far side and rdn whn bmpd ins fnl 2f: sn btn* 7/1
5244 8 1 **Ella Grace (USA)**9 6747 3-8-10 59 LeeTopliss(5) 11 52
(R A Fahey) *in tch: hrd rdn in centre 2f out: one pce* 9/2[2]
6003 9 6 **Tammela**66 5034 3-9-2 60 SebSanders 8 41
(A P Jarvis) *led tl over 5f out: prom in centre tl wknd over 1f out* 33/1
0500 10 1 1/2 **Zawadi**19 6454 3-8-7 51 oh1 HayleyTurner 15 29
(R M Beckett) *a in mid-div* 33/1
304 11 8 **Bizarrely (IRE)**30 6212 3-9-4 62 StevieDonohoe 7 24
(J Pearce) *in tch: wnt prom 4f out: no room towards far side and bmpd ins fnl 2f: eased* 16/1
0506 12 1/2 **Hedonist (IRE)**17 6525 3-8-11 55 LiamKeniry 12 16
(J R Gask) *in tch tl wknd 3f out* 25/1
500 13 4 1/2 **Sonnellino**18 6496 3-8-13 62 (b1) AdamBeschizza(5) 6 14
(J R Holt) *lost 15 l s: a bhd* 40/1
0413 14 4 **Ting Ting (USA)**109 3582 3-9-2 60 StephenCraine 2 4
(J R Boyle) *a towards rr: n.d fnl 3f* 20/1
2032 15 25 **Amends (USA)**65 5072 3-9-4 62 LukeMorris 10 —
(J R Best) *t.k.h: prom tl wknd over 3f out* 20/1

2m 6.98s (-1.72) **Going Correction** -0.225s/f (Firm) 15 Ran SP% 123.2
Speed ratings (Par 99): **97,95,95,94,93 91,91,90,85,84 77,77,73,70,50**
toteswingers:1&2:£6.00, 1&3:£14.70, 2&3:£4.70 CSF £180.24 CT £1236.59 TOTE £27.10: £6.70, £3.30, £1.70; EX 630.10 TRIFECTA Not won. Place 6 £288.38; Place 5 £205.33..
Owner The Rodrigo De Freitas Partnership **Bred** Castlemartin Stud And Skymarc Farm **Trained** Epsom, Surrey
■ Stewards' Enquiry : Stevie Donohoe caution: careless riding.

FOCUS
A weak 3-y-o handicap. It was run at an uneven pace but the form seems sound enough, with the winner recording a clear personal best.
Shianda Official explanation: jockey said filly hung right under pressure
Amends(USA) Official explanation: jockey said gelding stopped quickly
T/Plt: £391.50 to a £1 stake. Pool:£71,532.48 - 133.35 winning tickets T/Qpdt: £38.50 to a £1 stake. Pool:£7,255.93 - 139.30 winning tickets LM

6849 LINGFIELD (L-H)
Tuesday, October 19

OFFICIAL GOING: Standard
Wind: Moderate, across Weather: Sunny intervals

6994 NEWS INTERNATIONAL MAIDEN AUCTION STKS 7f (P)
2:30 (2:31) (Class 6) 2-Y-O £2,047 (£604; £302) Stalls Low

Form RPR
1 **The Holyman (IRE)** 2-8-13 FergusSweeney 8 78+
(Miss Jo Crowley) *mid-div: hdwy 2f out: led ins fnl f: hld on wl: all out* 25/1
0254 2 hd **Masonic Lady (IRE)**19 6497 2-8-3 71 (b) AdamBeschizza(5) 9 72+
(W J Haggas) *chsd ldrs: c to centre in st: drvn to chal fnl f: r.o* 4/1[2]
0 3 3 3/4 **Hurricane Lady (IRE)**20 6451 2-8-5 JohnFahy(5) 4 65
(W R Swinburn) *in tch: rdn to chse ldrs on ins ent st: kpt on to take 3rd fnl 50yds* 10/3[1]
2355 4 1 **Looksmart**8 6802 2-8-8 68 LiamKeniry 7 60
(R Hannon) *mainly chsd ldr tl no ex 1f out* 6/1[3]
05 5 hd **Seeking Glory**19 6497 2-9-1 PaulHanagan 11 66
(E A L Dunlop) *sn led: rdn over 1f out: hdd & wknd ins fnl f* 6/1[3]
0 6 hd **Foxtrot Golf (IRE)**133 2839 2-8-13 FrankieMcDonald 12 64
(P Winkworth) *dwlt: rdn in rr early: hdwy ent st: styd on fnl f* 50/1
3364 7 1 3/4 **Sylas Ings**8 6802 2-8-11 78 (t) IanMongan 5 57
(P M Phelan) *prom tl wknd over 1f out* 10/3[1]
0 8 2 **Warden Bond**32 6158 2-8-9 WilliamCarson 10 50
(S C Williams) *sn pushed along towards rr: n.d* 33/1
50 9 nk **Quite A Catch (IRE)**105 3769 2-8-13 RichardKingscote 2 53
(J G Portman) *mid-div on rail: lost pl and struggling 3f out: n.d after* 14/1
10 13 **Trust Me Boy** 2-8-8 NataliaGemelova(3) 6 18
(J E Long) *s.s: a wl bhd* 20/1
000 11 14 **Nice Chimes (IRE)**21 6436 2-8-4 25 DavidProbert 3 —
(B W Duke) *mid-div tl wknd over 3f out* 100/1

1m 25.2s (0.40) **Going Correction** -0.025s/f (Stan) 11 Ran SP% 115.9
Speed ratings (Par 93): **96,95,91,90,90 89,87,85,85,70 54**
Tote Swingers: 1&2 £15.80, 1&3 £20.00, 2&3 £5.30 CSF £117.18 TOTE £31.50: £9.70, £2.80, £1.10; EX 149.40.
Owner Kilstone Limited **Bred** Old Carhue Stud **Trained** Whitcombe, Dorset
■ Stewards' Enquiry : Adam Beschizza three-day ban: weighed-in 2lb heavy (Nov 2-4)

FOCUS
An ordinary maiden with questionable depth, but a nice start from the winner. The second has an uneven profile.

NOTEBOOK
The Holyman(IRE), out of a once-raced half-sister to Coventry winner Red Sea, clearly has a fair amount of ability and is open to improvement. The trainer's assistant, ex-jockey Tony Clark, reports the winner to be more of a 3-y-o prospect. (tchd 20-1)
Masonic Lady(IRE) came wide into the straight and, though running on, she was always being held. Her jockey weighed in 2lb heavier than he weighed out and was consequently banned for three days. A race might fall her way at some stage, but she's not one to be following. (op 3-1 tchd 11-4 and 9-2)
Hurricane Lady(IRE), just as on debut at Kempton, finished well from off the pace, a creditable effort considering she raced against the far rail in the straight. She should stay further. (op 5-1)
Looksmart ran no more than respectably and is not progressing. (op 13-2 tchd 11-2)
Seeking Glory was asked to try and make all, which is rarely easy at Lingfield, and edged left in the straight as he faded, proving unable to reverse recent Kempton placings with Masonic Lady. (tchd 7-1)
Foxtrot Golf(IRE) stepped up on the form he showed on debut 133 days earlier, giving the impression he'll come on again for the run. (op 66-1)
Sylas Ings, with tongue-tie re-fitted and trying Polytrack for the first time, ran nowhere near his official mark of 78. (op 3-1 tchd 7-2)

6995 E B F MENZIES DISTRIBUTION MEDIAN AUCTION MAIDEN STKS 6f (P)
3:00 (3:00) (Class 5) 2-Y-O £3,070 (£906; £453) Stalls Low

Form RPR
4503 1 **Brave Battle**10 6740 2-9-3 64 JimmyFortune 1 69
(R Hannon) *led 1f: chsd ldr after: drvn to ld again 100yds out* 3/1[2]
4 2 3/4 **Missile Command (IRE)**17 6575 2-9-3 0 NeilCallan 6 67
(W J Haggas) *led after 1f: rdn and hdd 100yds out: nt qckn* 1/2[1]
3 2 3/4 **Arowana (IRE)** 2-8-12 0 LiamJones 3 54+
(W J Haggas) *pushed along in rr early: in tch after 2f: outpcd 2f out: styng on at fin* 10/1[3]
4 1 1/2 **Isingy Red (FR)** 2-9-3 0 StephenCraine 5 54
(J R Boyle) *chsd ldrs: rdn and sltly wd bnd into st: no ex over 1f out* 16/1
5 9 **Frozen Over** 2-9-3 0 FergusSweeney 2 27
(W S Kittow) *s.i.s: in tch towards rr: wknd 2f out* 28/1
000 6 5 **Huckle Duckle (IRE)**4 6884 2-8-7 30 (v) TobyAtkinson(5) 4 7
(P S McEntee) *in tch tl wknd over 2f out* 100/1

1m 12.38s (0.48) **Going Correction** -0.025s/f (Stan) 6 Ran SP% 111.1
Speed ratings (Par 95): **95,94,90,88,76 69**
Tote Swingers: 1&2 £1.10, 1&3 £1.40, 2&3 £1.20 CSF £4.72 TOTE £3.80: £2.50, £1.10; EX 5.20.
Owner D W Barker **Bred** Lady Whent **Trained** East Everleigh, Wilts

FOCUS
A modest maiden with the exposed winner rated back to his best.

NOTEBOOK
Brave Battle came into this officially rated only 64 and sets the standard. This was a straightforward success and he should be competitive back in handicaps. (tchd 11-4 and 10-3)
Missile Command(IRE) showed ability when beaten at 11-8 on debut at Wolverhampton, but seemed to run below that level this time. He raced freely in front and offered little when challenged, maybe not being helped by sticking to the far rail. A drop to 5f should suit. (op 4-9 tchd 4-7)
Arowana(IRE) ◆, a 17,000gns purchase out of a useful prolific sprinter, was badly in need of the experience but showed ability. She's open to a deal of improvement. (op 14-1)
Isingy Red(FR), a 39,000euros first foal of a 1m winner in France (also winner over fences), ran to only a moderate level. (op 25-1)

6996 TELEGRAPH MEDIA GROUP (S) STKS 6f (P)
3:30 (3:30) (Class 6) 3-Y-O £2,047 (£604; £302) Stalls High

Form RPR
1354 1 **Avonvalley**14 6656 3-8-11 67 MatthewDavies(3) 8 64
(George Baker) *stdd s and swtchd ins: hld up in rr: effrt and rn v wd bnd ent st: rapid hdwy to ld fnl 50yds* 3/1[2]
014 2 1 **Kate Skate**40 5890 3-8-11 60 KierenFox(3) 6 61
(Miss Gay Kelleway) *prom: drvn into narrow ld 1f out: hdd and nt qckn fnl 50yds* 10/1

5600 **3** ½ **Red Avalanche (IRE)**[10] 6739 3-9-0 75......................(bt) PaulHanagan 7 59
(P F I Cole) *hld up in 6th: rdn 2f out: styd on fnl f: nvr nrr* **11/8**[1]
0520 **4** nk **Coolree Star (IRE)**[19] 6515 3-9-0 58.................................. IanMongan 2 58
(J A Glover) *led: rdn and hdd 1f out: no ex fnl 50yds* **15/2**[3]
1345 **5** 1 **Watch Chain (IRE)**[62] 5206 3-9-0 55......................... AshleyMorgan(5) 5 60
(M H Tompkins) *towards rr: effrt and hrd rdn over 1f out: unable to chal* **20/1**
40-6 **6** hd **Excelling (IRE)**[24] 6368 3-8-9 73................................ FergusSweeney 3 49
(P J Makin) *chsd ldr: chal 2f out tl no ex ins fnl f* **8/1**
0206 **7** 1 ¼ **Avow (USA)**[10] 6741 3-9-5 59.......................................(b) NeilChalmers 4 55
(J J Bridger) *in tch in 5th: pushed along over 3f out: effrt and hrd rdn over 1f out: fdd fnl f* **16/1**
2053 **8** 5 **Gilderoy**[13] 5926 3-9-0 50...(p) JamesDoyle 1 34
(D J S Ffrench Davis) *chsd ldrs: rdn over 2f out: wknd over 1f out* **40/1**
1m 12.0s (0.10) **Going Correction** -0.025s/f (Stan) **8** Ran SP% **112.2**
Speed ratings (Par 99): **98,96,96,95,94 94,92,85**
Tote Swingers: 1&2 £5.60, 1&3 £2.10, 2&3 £3.90 CSF £31.32 TOTE £3.30: £1.10, £3.70, £2.40; EX 30.90.The winner was bought in for 5,400gns. Red Avalanche was claimed by Ms. Stef Higgins for £6,000.
Owner George Baker & Partners **Bred** Ercan Dogan **Trained** Moreton Morrell, Warwicks
FOCUS
A weak seller, but the form seems sound if limited.

6997 DAILY MAIL H'CAP 6f (P)
4:00 (4:01) (Class 5) (0-70,70) 3-Y-O+ **£2,388** (£705; £352) **Stalls** Low

Form RPR
3252 **1** **Elhamri**[3] 6932 6-9-6 69... JamesDoyle 1 78
(S Kirk) *mid-div on rail: sltly hmpd 1st bend: hdwy over 1f out: drvn to ld ins fnl f: hld on wl* **6/1**[3]
5100 **2** 1 **Frequency**[11] 6714 3-9-3 67.. J-PGuillambert 7 73
(Miss Amy Weaver) *stdd s: patiently rdn in rr: gd hdwy on ins over 1f out: r.o to take 2nd wl ins fnl f: hld fnl 50yds* **20/1**
1645 **3** hd **Scottish Glen**[27] 6292 4-9-0 63.. JimCrowley 9 68+
(P R Chamings) *towards rr: wd st: gd hdwy fr over 1f out: fin wl* **9/2**[1]
6060 **4** ½ **Private Olley**[40] 5890 3-9-0 64... DaneO'Neill 6 68
(J Akehurst) *led: hrd rdn over 1f out: hdd and no ex ins fnl f* **16/1**
0066 **5** 1 ¼ **Valmina**[4] 6898 3-9-1 65... NeilCallan 2 65
(A W Carroll) *chsd ldrs: sltly hmpd 1st bend: drvn to chal 1f out: sn btn* **13/2**
1601 **6** hd **Mack's Sister**[20] 6456 3-9-0 64... RobertHavlin 12 63
(D K Ivory) *trckd ldrs: effrt 2f out: hrd rdn and btn over 1f out* **5/1**[2]
3063 **7** hd **Dvinsky (USA)**[6] 6854 9-9-4 67...(b) IanMongan 3 65
(P Howling) *prom tl outpcd and btn 2f out* **10/1**
5503 **8** 1 ¾ **Sherjawy (IRE)**[18] 6523 6-9-2 70............ GemmaGracey-Davison(5) 10 63
(Miss Z C Davison) *chsd ldr tl wknd wl over 1f out* **16/1**
0060 **9** ½ **Goodwood Maestro**[40] 5890 3-8-12 62......................(b) JimmyFortune 5 53
(J L Dunlop) *towards rr: mod effrt and wd st: n.d* **20/1**
022 **10** 2 ¼ **Littlemisssunshine (IRE)**[26] 6303 5-9-5 68...................(t) LiamKeniry 4 52
(T B P Coles) *mid-div tl wknd over 2f out* **5/1**[2]
14- **11** 9 **Bellini Rose (IRE)**[348] 7251 3-9-6 70............................... SteveDrowne 8 25
(J R Gask) *stdd s: hld up in 6th: rdn 3f out: wknd 2f out* **16/1**
1m 11.17s (-0.73) **Going Correction** -0.025s/f (Stan)
WFA 3 from 4yo+ 1lb **11** Ran SP% **115.4**
Speed ratings (Par 103): **103,101,101,100,99 98,98,96,95,92 80**
Tote Swingers: 1&2 £23.50, 1&3 £5.30, 2&3 £9.10 CSF £116.15 CT £592.27 TOTE £9.30: £1.50, £9.90, £1.50; EX 113.70.
Owner Liam Breslin **Bred** Highfield Stud Ltd **Trained** Upper Lambourn, Berks
■ Stewards' Enquiry : James Doyle one-day ban: careless riding (Nov 3)
Dane O'Neill two-day ban: careless riding (Nov 3-4)
FOCUS
A modest but competitive sprint handicap. The winner only needed to run to his recent claimer form.

6998 CITIPOST DIRECT DISTRIBUTION H'CAP 5f (P)
4:30 (4:31) (Class 5) (0-75,75) 3-Y-O+ **£2,388** (£705; £352) **Stalls** High

Form RPR
2246 **1** **Freddie's Girl (USA)**[19] 6501 3-9-0 74............................. JohnFahy(5) 1 82
(Stef Higgins) *sn led: hrd rdn and hdd over 1f out: rallied to ld again fnl stride* **6/1**[3]
3603 **2** shd **Even Bolder**[10] 6739 7-8-13 71.. KierenFox(3) 6 79
(E A Wheeler) *dwlt: hdwy to chse ldrs on inner over 3f out: slt ld over 1f out: hrd rdn and kpt on fnl f: hdd on line* **5/1**[2]
0401 **3** nk **Ajjaadd (USA)**[21] 6440 4-9-2 71.. SteveDrowne 5 78+
(T E Powell) *leapt in air leaving stalls and missed break: bhd tl hdwy over 2f out: chsd ldng pair fnl f: clsd grad to line* **3/1**[1]
3200 **4** 1 ¾ **Triple Dream**[5] 6858 5-9-5 74...(p) LiamKeniry 3 75
(J M Bradley) *t.k.h in 5th: effrt 2f out: one pce appr fnl f* **14/1**
4034 **5** ¾ **Di Stefano**[26] 6303 3-9-5 74.. AdrianNicholls 9 72
(D Nicholls) *bhd: wd st: hung lft and hrd rdn over 1f out: gd hdwy fnl f* **7/1**
3026 **6** nk **Jigajig**[11] 6714 3-9-2 71...(p) PaulHanagan 4 68
(K A Ryan) *prom on outer tl rdn and btn ent st* **8/1**
0464 **7** ¾ **Kummel Excess (IRE)**[20] 6466 3-9-1 73.............. MatthewDavies(3) 10 67
(George Baker) *dwlt: outpcd in rr: nvr trbld ldrs* **12/1**
4045 **8** ¾ **Brandywell Boy (IRE)**[21] 6446 7-9-6 75.............................. JamesDoyle 7 66
(D J S Ffrench Davis) *sn towards rr: rdn over 2f out: n.d* **12/1**
000 **9** ½ **Incomparable**[26] 6303 5-9-2 71... IanMongan 8 61
(J A Glover) *in tch on outer tl wknd over 1f out* **14/1**
3005 **10** nk **Danny's Choice**[21] 6440 3-9-4 73.................................(p) JimCrowley 2 62
(R M Beckett) *pressed ldr tl hrd rdn and wknd over 1f out* **9/1**
58.45 secs (-0.35) **Going Correction** -0.025s/f (Stan) **10** Ran SP% **118.3**
Speed ratings (Par 103): **101,100,100,97,96 95,94,93,92,92**
Tote Swingers: 1&2 £6.00, 1&3 £3.40, 2&3 £3.60 CSF £36.67 CT £112.09 TOTE £5.50: £2.10, £1.20, £2.30; EX 36.00.
Owner Mrs Anne & Fred Cowley **Bred** Respite Farm Inc **Trained** Lambourn, Berks
FOCUS
An ordinary sprint handicap. The game winner produced a small personal best.
Ajjaadd(USA) Official explanation: jockey said gelding reared on leaving stalls causing him to lose an iron
Kummel Excess(IRE) Official explanation: jockey said filly was denied a clear run
Brandywell Boy(IRE) Official explanation: jockey said gelding was denied a clear run

6999 SMITHS NEWS APPRENTICE H'CAP 1m 4f (P)
5:00 (5:01) (Class 6) (0-60,60) 3-Y-O+ **£2,047** (£604; £302) **Stalls** Low

Form RPR
0432 **1** **Jovial (IRE)**[17] 6574 3-8-12 52... JohnFahy 9 65+
(D J Coakley) *hld up in midfield: smooth hdwy 3f out: led 2f out: drvn clr 1f out: readily* **5/2**[1]
3644 **2** 5 **Lunar River (FR)**[24] 6375 7-9-3 53..........................(t) JamesRogers(3) 14 58
(David Pinder) *chsd ldrs: drvn to take 2nd ins fnl f: one pce* **9/1**[3]
006 **3** nk **Byrd In Hand (IRE)**[18] 6527 3-9-0 57............................ RyanClark(3) 16 61
(J J Bridger) *mid-div on outer: hdwy 3f out: chsd wnr 2f out tl ins fnl f: styd on same pce* **12/1**
3102 **4** shd **Larkrise Star**[18] 6526 3-9-5 59.................................... AdamBeschizza 2 63
(D K Ivory) *chsd ldrs: sltly outpcd 3f out: rallied and styd on fnl f* **7/2**[2]
2304 **5** 1 ½ **Rose Aurora**[18] 6525 3-8-2 47..................................(v[1]) KatiaScallan(5) 13 49+
(M P Tregoning) *hld up towards rr: shkn up and r.o appr fnl f: going on wl at fin* **12/1**
6046 **6** nse **Petsas Pleasure**[14] 6662 4-9-1 48.......................................(p) DaleSwift 8 50
(Ollie Pears) *mid-div: rdn and styd on fnl 2f: nt rch ldrs* **14/1**
6500 **7** 3 ¼ **Forgotten Army (IRE)**[27] 6290 3-9-4 58.................... AshleyMorgan 12 54
(M H Tompkins) *bhd: rdn whn bmpd wl over 2f out: sme late hdwy* **16/1**
0660 **8** 5 **Given A Choice (IRE)**[25] 6328 8-9-3 55.............(p) SophieSilvester(5) 10 43
(J Pearce) *s.s: rdn along early: bhd tl modest late hdwy* **25/1**
0004 **9** 3 **Pictures (IRE)**[20] 6454 3-8-8 51.................................... RyanPowell(3) 7 35
(J J Bridger) *prom: led 3f out tl 2f out: sn wknd* **22/1**
00-6 **10** hd **Mater Mater**[75] 4746 3-9-6 60.. LeeTopliss 5 43
(Andrew Reid) *towards rr: rdn into midfield 4f out: outpcd fnl 3f* **33/1**
3003 **11** 4 ½ **Pedasus (USA)**[42] 5840 4-9-12 59............................(p) RossAtkinson 15 35
(T Keddy) *s.s: outpcd in rr: drvn along 5f out: n.d whn bmpd wl over 2f out* **25/1**
0606 **12** 16 **Shooting Party (IRE)**[13] 6668 4-9-6 56..................... CharlesEddery(3) 3 6
(R Hannon) *led 4f: prom tl wknd 3f out: no ch whn eased over 1f out* **10/1**
5400 **13** 2 ¾ **Turner's Touch**[48] 5663 8-8-6 46.............................(b) ChelseyBanks(7) 4 —
(G L Moore) *s.s: settled in midfield on rail: kidded along whn wnt rt and bmpd wl over 2f out: stopped qckly* **33/1**
-610 **14** 7 **Ptolomeos**[24] 6375 7-9-8 58.................. GemmaGracey-Davison(3) 6 —
(S Regan) *prom: led after 4f tl 3f out: sn wknd* **33/1**
6330 **15** 54 **Sunset Boulevard (IRE)**[13] 6669 7-9-10 57................. TobyAtkinson 1 —
(Jim Best) *mid-div tl wknd over 3f out* **12/1**
2m 32.87s (-0.13) **Going Correction** -0.025s/f (Stan)
WFA 3 from 4yo+ 7lb **15** Ran SP% **126.4**
Speed ratings (Par 101): **99,95,95,95,94 94,92,88,86,86 83,73,71,66,30**
Tote Swingers: 1&2 £7.40, 1&3 £11.70, 2&3 £13.30 CSF £24.41 CT £235.79 TOTE £3.30: £1.60, £1.80, £6.50; EX 34.50 Place 6: £9.42 Place 5: £4.82..
Owner Chris Van Hoorn **Bred** Genesis Green Stud Ltd **Trained** West Ilsley, Berks
FOCUS
Plenty of runners, but few of them were up to much. The winner was the least exposed and he produced a clear personal best. The second is rated in line with her recent form.
T/Jkpt: Not won. T/Plt: £17.50 to a £1 stake. Pool:£66,527 - 2,764.04 winning tickets T/Qpdt: £6.60 to a £1 stake. Pool:£4,963 - 551.02 winning tickets LM

6126 YARMOUTH (L-H)
Tuesday, October 19

OFFICIAL GOING: Soft (4.9)
Wind: Fresh half-behind Weather: Cloudy with sunny spells

7000 EUROPEAN BREEDERS' FUND MAIDEN FILLIES' STKS (DIV I) 1m 3y
1:50 (1:52) (Class 5) 2-Y-O **£2,838** (£849; £424; £212; £105) **Stalls** High

Form RPR
24 **1** **Aneedah (IRE)**[17] 6559 2-9-0 0.. WilliamBuick 8 86+
(J H M Gosden) *mde all: shkn up over 1f out: sn clr: eased nr fin* **1/5**[1]
2 3 ½ **Dancing Rain (IRE)** 2-9-0 0... MichaelHills 5 74
(W J Haggas) *stdd s: hld up: hdwy over 1f out: r.o to go 2nd nr fin: no ch w wnr* **22/1**
3 shd **Arizona Jewel** 2-9-0 0.. TomQueally 2 76+
(H R A Cecil) *a.p: chsd wnr over 3f out: rdn over 1f out: no ex fnl f: lost 2nd nr fin* **7/1**[2]
6 **4** hd **Insieme (IRE)**[20] 6469 2-9-0 0.. AdamKirby 9 74
(M Botti) *chsd ldrs: rdn over 2f out: styd on same pce appr fnl f* **20/1**[3]
5 1 ¾ **Polly Holder (IRE)** 2-9-0 0.. LukeMorris 1 70
(A Bailey) *hld up: rdn over 3f out: styd on fr over 1f out: nvr trbld ldrs* **100/1**
6 2 ¼ **Run On Ruby (FR)** 2-9-0 0... TedDurcan 7 65
(D R Lanigan) *s.i.s: hdwy 1/2-way: rdn and edgd lft over 2f out: sn outpcd* **50/1**
06 **7** 13 **Handicraft (IRE)**[21] 6436 2-9-0 0....................................... GregFairley 3 36
(M Johnston) *chsd wnr over 4f: wknd over 2f out* **50/1**
0 **8** 3 ½ **Mrs Lovely**[32] 6159 2-9-0 0.. TonyCulhane 4 29
(P W D'Arcy) *hld up in tch: plld hrd: wknd 3f out* **150/1**
0 **9** 9 **The Absent Mare**[20] 6451 2-9-0 0..................................(t) LeeVickers 10 —
(F Sheridan) *hld up: wknd over 3f out: t.o* **250/1**
1m 45.76s (5.16) **Going Correction** +0.45s/f (Yiel) **9** Ran SP% **110.9**
Speed ratings (Par 92): **92,88,88,88,86 84,71,67,58**
Tote Swingers: 1&2 £2.90, 1&3 £1.50, 2&3 £2.30 CSF £8.96 TOTE £1.20: £1.02, £3.60, £1.30; EX 7.00 Trifecta £14.70 Pool: £1061.11 - 53.10 winning units..
Owner Ali Saeed **Bred** Sunderland Holdings Ltd **Trained** Newmarket, Suffolk
FOCUS
Probably the stronger of the two divisions (despite time being 0.21secs slower) and a good opportunity for 1-5 shot Aneedah to get off the mark. The overall form may be rated a shade high but the winner did it very easily and it is worth giving a chance to the race.
NOTEBOOK
Aneedah(IRE) had an ideal opportunity to get off the mark, having finished fourth in a valuable sales race at Newmarket latest, and she had no trouble at odds of 1-5. Although John Gosden had expressed a doubt about the ground, she always looked comfortable in front and drew clear inside the final 2f, clearly appreciating the step up to 1m. She'll presumably step back up in grade when returning next season. (op 3-10)
Dancing Rain(IRE), a £200,000 sister to 7f-1m winner Captain Dancer, just getting up for second. She looked green when first coming under pressure, but really grasped what was required inside the final furlong and she's sure to prove popular for a maiden next time, with improvement anticipated. (op 20-1)
Arizona Jewel ◆, a half-sister to high-class middle-distance performer Powerscourt, as well as Kind, the dam of Frankel, was never far away and challenged from over 2f out, but she tired late on and nearly missed out on the places. Better ground will suit and this experience will do her no harm, so she'll be expected to win an ordinary maiden. (op 5-1)

Insieme(IRE), a never-nearer sixth at Nottingham on debut, improved on that, keeping on right the way to the line, and she too looks capable of winning an ordinary maiden. (op 18-1)
Polly Holder(IRE), half-sister to a couple of sprint winners, kept on late and fared better than her 100-1 odds implied. She'll find easier opportunities. (op 125-1)
Run On Ruby(FR), a £65,000 half-sister to a 1m-1m1f winner, never got into it having been slowly away but runners from the yard often improve for a run.
Handicraft(IRE) should do better once handicapping. (op 40-1)

7001 EUROPEAN BREEDERS' FUND MAIDEN FILLIES' STKS (DIV II) 1m 3y
2:20 (2:22) (Class 5) 2-Y-O **£2,838** (£849; £424; £212; £105) **Stalls** High

Form	Pos	Dist	Horse	Jockey / SP	RPR
20	1		**Mohedian Lady (IRE)**[17] 6559 2-9-0 0 — (M L W Bell) *chsd ldrs: led over 2f out: shkn up over 1f out: r.o wl*	JamieSpencer 1 — 1/1[1]	83+
2	2	2½	**Moonsail**[24] 6360 2-9-0 0 — (Mahmood Al Zarooni) *trckd ldrs: racd keenly: rdn over 1f out: styd on same pce fnl f*	AhmedAjtebi 9 — 7/2[2]	77
	3	½	**Hunza Dancer (IRE)** 2-9-0 0 — (J H M Gosden) *s.i.s: hld up: hdwy over 3f out: rdn over 1f out: no ex ins fnl f*	WilliamBuick 2 — 8/1	75+
	4	2¼	**Piece D'Or (IRE)** 2-9-0 0 — (Sir Michael Stoute) *s.s: hld up: hdwy over 3f out: rdn over 1f out: styd on same pce*	RyanMoore 3 — 6/1[3]	70+
	5	2½	**Cyber Star** 2-9-0 0 — (J R Fanshawe) *s.i.s: hld up: hdwy over 2f out: nt trble ldrs*	PatCosgrave 8 — 33/1	65+
	6	3¼	**Peira** 2-9-0 0 — (Jane Chapple-Hyam) *hld up: plld hrd: rdn over 2f out: n.d*	JimmyQuinn 4 — 80/1	58
	7	2¾	**Cotton Grass** 2-9-0 0 — (M H Tompkins) *s.s: bhd: pushed along over 3f out: nvr on terms*	MichaelHills 7 — 100/1	52
	8	7	**Allez Leulah (IRE)** 2-9-0 0 — (M Johnston) *led over 5f: rdn and wknd over 1f out*	GregFairley 5 — 33/1	36
0	9	3¾	**Fully Armed (IRE)**[15] 6628 2-8-11 0 — (Rae Guest) *hld up in tch: wknd over 2f out*	MartinLane(3) 6 — 125/1	28
4	10	nk	**Makheelah**[136] 2740 2-9-0 0 — (C E Brittain) *chsd ldrs tl rdn and wknd over 2f out*	ChrisCatlin 10 — 14/1	27

1m 45.55s (4.95) **Going Correction** +0.45s/f (Yiel) **10 Ran SP% 113.2**
Speed ratings (Par 92): **93,90,90,87,85 82,79,72,68,68**
Tote Swingers: 1&2 £1.80, 1&3 £2.70, 2&3 £3.70 CSF £4.22 TOTE £2.20: £1.10, £1.20, £3.60; EX 5.10 Trifecta £17.40 Pool: £750.10 - 31.81 winning units..
Owner Mrs Olivia Hoare **Bred** Kildaragh Stud **Trained** Newmarket, Suffolk

FOCUS
More competitive than the first division (time 0.21secs quicker), this also went to the favourite. The level of the form is fluid but has been rated around the balance of the front pair.

NOTEBOOK
Mohedian Lady(IRE), ninth in the same Newmarket sales race as Aneedah, winner of the first division, stayed on best under a positive ride. The return to 1m was clearly in her favour and she's expected to stay 1m4f next season. (op 5-4 after 11-8 in places)
Moonsail, runner-up over this trip on debut, was a bit keen in a prominent position, but she still saw it out well despite carrying her head a touch high. A daughter of Oaks winner Kazzia, she'll improve for a longer trip next season. (op 3-1)
Hunza Dancer(IRE), an £80,000 sister to Air Chief Marshall, closed in good style and had her chance, but couldn't see it out as strongly as the front pair. She'll learn from this and looks another ready-made maiden winner. (op 13-2)
Piece D'Or(IRE) ◆, from an excellent family, made a pleasing debut back in fourth and is probably the one to take from the race. Not the best away, she gradually made ground on the outside of the field and kept on inside the final furlong without threatening to win. It's likely 1m2f will suit next season and she rates a promising 3-y-o prospect. (op 8-1 tchd 11-2)
Cyber Star, first foal of a 1m4f winner, showed her inexperience but did keep on late and should improve. (tchd 40-1)
Allez Leulah(IRE), a 7,000gns purchase, weakened late on but should improve for some better ground. (op 20-1)
Makheelah failed to build on a promising first effort, although it was her first run since June and it's possible the ground was too taxing.

7002 EUROPEAN BREEDERS' FUND MAIDEN STKS 6f 3y
2:50 (2:51) (Class 5) 2-Y-O **£3,154** (£944; £472; £236; £117) **Stalls** High

Form	Pos	Dist	Horse	Jockey / SP	RPR
	1		**Hallelujah** 2-8-12 0 — (J R Fanshawe) *chsd ldrs: rdn to ld over 1f out: r.o*	PatCosgrave 2 — 20/1	76+
6	2	½	**Fettuccine (IRE)**[114] 3482 2-8-12 0 — (J Noseda) *chsd ldrs: ld jst ins fnl 2f: hdd and rdn over 1f out: styd on*	RyanMoore 1 — 4/1[1]	75
	3	2	**Unex Goya (IRE)** 2-9-3 0 — (W J Haggas) *s.i.s: sn pushed along in rr: rdn and hung lft over 1f out: r.o wl to go 3rd towards fin: nt trble ldrs*	MichaelHills 4 — 17/2	77+
6	4	¾	**Flying Arch (USA)**[58] 5324 2-8-12 0 — (L M Cumani) *chsd ldrs: led over 2f out: hdd jst ins fnl 2f: rdn over 1f out: styd on same pce*	KierenFallon 10 — 11/2[3]	66
	5	1¼	**Paperetto** 2-9-3 0 — (R A Mills) *s.s: hdwy 1/2-way: rdn and ev ch over 1f out: no ex ins fnl f*	StevieDonohoe 7 — 4/1[1]	68
65	6	1¾	**Beacon Hill (IRE)**[140] 2621 2-9-3 0 — (J H M Gosden) *trckd ldrs: rdn and edgd rt over 1f out: hung lft and wknd fnl f*	WilliamBuick 5 — 9/2[2]	62
	7	¾	**Munaaseb** 2-9-3 0 — (E A L Dunlop) *hld up: hdwy 2f out: wknd ins fnl f*	RichardHills 8 — 12/1	60
0000	8	6	**Jamaica Grande**[4] 6884 2-9-3 52 — (T T Clement) *led to over 2f out: wknd over 1f out*	(p) SamHitchcott 6 — 100/1	42
	9	1½	**Dangerous Illusion (IRE)** 2-8-12 0 — (M Quinn) *hld up: a in rr: wknd 2f out*	ShaneKelly 3 — 66/1	33
2	10	2¼	**Luckbealadytonight (IRE)**[14] 6658 2-8-12 0 — (M Johnston) *w ldr: rdn and ev ch over 2f out: wknd over 1f out*	GregFairley 9 — 6/1	26

1m 17.22s (2.82) **Going Correction** +0.45s/f (Yiel) **10 Ran SP% 113.3**
Speed ratings (Par 95): **99,98,95,94,93 90,89,81,79,76**
Tote Swingers: 1&2 £7.50, 1&3 £24.80, 2&3 £9.10 CSF £95.10 TOTE £32.90: £7.50, £1.10, £2.50; EX 282.80 Trifecta £402.50 Part won. Pool: £543.99 - 0.63 winning units..
Owner Chippenham Lodge Stud **Bred** Chippenham Lodge Stud Ltd **Trained** Newmarket, Suffolk

FOCUS
An open-looking sprint maiden. The form is pitched around the lower level for the race avaerages of recent years, but might have been underrated with some nice types on show.

NOTEBOOK
Hallelujah, half-sister to dual 5f winner Tom Folan, picked up well to lead and stayed on strongly to provide her trainer with a first 2-y-o winner of the season. She had been working encouragingly and her trainer views her as a sprinter.
Fettuccine(IRE), last of six in a conditions race at Windsor back in June, was expected to post an improved display, despite there being a doubt over the suitability of the ground, and she duly did, but couldn't stay on as well as the winner. (op 7-2 tchd 9-2)
Unex Goya(IRE), a son of Medicean, was nibbled at beforehand and, despite being slowly away and hanging when first coming under pressure, he did stay on nicely for third. A step up to 7f will suit and he looks capable of winning maiden. (op 14-1)
Flying Arch(USA) improved on his initial effort and looks one for handicaps in time. (op 5-1 tchd 6-1)
Paperetto, bred to go in the ground, being a son of Selkirk, was very backed beforehand and briefly made a forward move, but the lack of a run seemed to tell late on. (op 5-1)
Beacon Hill(IRE), returning from a 140-day absence, appeared to dislike the ground, but on the plus side he's now qualified for a mark. (tchd 4-1 and 5-1)
Munaaseb, who has a high-class sprinting pedigree, deserves another chance on better ground. (op 8-1)
Jamaica Grande Official explanation: jockey said colt hung right
Luckbealadytonight(IRE) may appreciate a return to AW, having finished second on Fibresand earlier in the month. (tchd 5-1)

7003 EASTERN POWER SYSTEMS (S) STKS 1m 3f 101y
3:20 (3:20) (Class 6) 3-Y-O **£1,554** (£462; £231; £115) **Stalls** Low

Form	Pos	Dist	Horse	Jockey / SP	RPR
22-0	1		**Edward Whymper**[110] 3606 3-8-12 65 — (M H Tompkins) *mid-div: hdwy over 3f out: rdn to ld 1f out: styd on*	JimmyQuinn 8 — 11/2[2]	59
0000	2	1½	**Mary Helen**[10] 6747 3-8-7 48 — (W M Brisbourne) *hld up: hdwy u.p over 2f out: styd on to go 2nd post: nt rch wnr*	LukeMorris 9 — 16/1	51
0451	3	nse	**Miss Wendy**[28] 6262 3-9-0 53 — (M H Tompkins) *chsd ldrs: led over 4f out: rdn and hdd 1f out: styd on same pce: lost 2nd post*	TomQueally 7 — 11/2[2]	58
6646	4	6	**Baggsy (IRE)**[16] 3113 3-8-7 47 — (Miss J Feilden) *led 1f: chsd ldrs: rdn over 3f out: wknd fnl f*	GregFairley 5 — 50/1	41
-000	5	½	**Ildiko (USA)**[27] 6290 3-8-8 60 ow1 — (Sir Mark Prescott) *prom: chsd ldr over 4f out: rdn and hung lft over 1f out: wknd ins fnl f*	(b[1]) SebSanders 6 — 9/1	41
5-51	6	19	**State Visit**[20] 6476 3-9-5 75 — (Miss Amy Weaver) *led after 1f: rdn and hdd over 4f out: wknd over 2f out*	(v[1]) KierenFallon 2 — 13/8[1]	20
4430	7	½	**Shercon (IRE)**[124] 3113 3-8-9 49 — (N Tinkler) *hld up: wknd over 3f out*	Louis-PhilippeBeuzelin(3) 3 — 40/1	12
0403	8	½	**Half Sister (IRE)**[14] 6652 3-8-7 53 — (M E Rimmer) *sn pushed along and prom: rdn over 3f out: sn wknd*	(p) JamieMackay 1 — 15/2[3]	6
3530	9	1¼	**Dane Cottage**[7] 6829 3-9-0 55 — (P D Evans) *hld up: rdn and wknd over 3f out*	(v) PatCosgrave 10 — 14/1	11
40	10	58	**Kathindi (IRE)**[44] 3960 3-9-5 57 — (N B King) *s.s: sn drvn along and a in rr: t.o fr 1/2-way*	(b) HayleyTurner 11 — 33/1	—
	11	43	**Bombardino (IRE)** 3-8-9 0 — (G Prodromou) *s.i.s and sn pushed along in rr: stmbld 10f out: t.o fr 1/2-way*	AshleyHamblett(3) 4 — 22/1	—

2m 38.77s (10.07) **Going Correction** +0.45s/f (Yiel) **11 Ran SP% 114.9**
Speed ratings (Par 99): **81,79,79,75,75 61,60,60,59,17** —
Tote Swingers: 1&2 £21.50, 1&3 £5.90, 2&3 £14.00 CSF £82.90 TOTE £8.70: £2.20, £3.20, £1.30; EX 101.80 Trifecta £349.80 Part won. Pool: £472.83 - 0.50 winning units..The winner was bought in for 4,600gns.
Owner P A Sakal **Bred** P A And Mrs D G Sakal **Trained** Newmarket, Suffolk

FOCUS
A poor seller and a slow-motion finish in the ground. The favourite ran poorly and the winner didn't need to match his 2yo form.
State Visit Official explanation: trainer had no explanation for the poor form shown
Kathindi(IRE) Official explanation: trainer said gelding was unsuited by the soft ground
Bombardino(IRE) Official explanation: jockey said gelding stumbled shortly after start

7004 AVENUE PUB NURSERY 1m 3y
3:50 (3:51) (Class 6) (0-60,60) 2-Y-O **£1,942** (£578; £288; £144) **Stalls** High

Form	Pos	Dist	Horse	Jockey / SP	RPR
0000	1		**Slumbering Sioux**[13] 6674 2-9-5 **59** — (H J L Dunlop) *hld up: hdwy u.p over 1f out: styd on to ld nr fin*	AdamKirby 13 — 20/1	63
0061	2	shd	**Salvationist**[33] 6129 2-8-13 **56** — (J L Dunlop) *chsd ldrs: rdn and ev ch fr over 1f out: styd on*	MartinLane(3) 10 — 9/2[1]	60
0650	3	nk	**Indian Wish (USA)**[34] 6081 2-9-2 **56** — (M L W Bell) *led: rdn and hdd over 2f out: rallied to ld over 1f out: hdd nr fin*	JamieSpencer 9 — 9/1[3]	59
065	4	1¾	**Anton Dolin (IRE)**[41] 5857 2-9-6 **60** — (J L Dunlop) *hld up: hdwy over 2f out: sn rdn and hung lft: nt rch ldrs*	TedDurcan 15 — 8/1[2]	59+
4305	5	4½	**Eduardo**[27] 6300 2-9-1 **58** — (Jedd O'Keeffe) *chsd ldrs: led over 2f out: rdn and hdd over 1f out: wknd ins fnl f*	MichaelO'Connell(3) 4 — 14/1	48
600	6	1¼	**Sukhothai (USA)**[29] 6248 2-9-4 **58** — (H R A Cecil) *hld up: racd keenly: hdwy and hung lft over 2f out: nt trble ldrs*	TomQueally 5 — 11/1	45
000	7	1½	**Chillie Peppar**[22] 6425 2-9-3 **57** — (G Prodromou) *hld up: plld hrd: hdwy over 3f out: rdn and wknd over 1f out*	KirstyMilczarek 12 — 20/1	41
056	8	¾	**Castlemorris King**[26] 6305 2-9-1 **60** — (M C Chapman) *hld up: hdwy over 3f out: sn rdn: wknd over 1f out*	MarkCoumbe(5) 16 — 80/1	42
005	9	¾	**Milly Filly**[24] 6360 2-9-3 **57** — (Miss Amy Weaver) *chsd ldrs: rdn over 2f out: wknd over 1f out*	KierenFallon 1 — 12/1	37
600	10	¾	**Izzet**[28] 6268 2-9-6 **60** — (M H Tompkins) *s.s: hdwy over 4f out: rdn and wknd over 1f out*	JimmyQuinn 3 — 20/1	39
5454	11	¾	**Scoglio**[13] 6674 2-9-6 **60** — (F Sheridan) *mid-div: rdn over 3f out: wknd over 1f out*	LeeVickers 8 — 8/1[2]	37
2065	12	23	**Pahente**[48] 5660 2-9-6 **60** — (J S Moore) *chsd ldrs: rdn and hung lft over 4f out: wknd over 2f out*	LukeMorris 11 — 33/1	—
0026	13	41	**May's Boy**[22] 6411 2-9-1 **60** — (M D I Usher) *hld up: hdwy over 4f out: rdn and wknd over 3f out: t.o*	LeeNewnes(5) 2 — 12/1	—
5565	14	9	**Al Rannan**[11] 6717 2-9-6 **60** — (E A L Dunlop) *chsd ldrs tl rdn and wknd over 2f out: t.o*	WilliamBuick 6 — 10/1	—
0032	P		**Chadford**[27] 6300 2-9-3 **57** — (T D Walford) *hld up: rdn over 2f out: bhd whn p.u ins fnl f*	GrahamGibbons 14 — 12/1	—

1m 46.79s (6.19) **Going Correction** +0.45s/f (Yiel) **15 Ran SP% 116.0**
Speed ratings (Par 93): **87,86,86,84,80 79,77,76,76,75 74,51,10,1,—**
Tote Swingers: 1&2 £27.90, 1&3 £47.80, 2&3 £8.70 CSF £98.17 CT £885.32 TOTE £34.50: £13.90, £1.60, £2.30; EX 196.90 TRIFECTA Not won..
Owner The Wigwam Partnership **Bred** R F And S D Knipe **Trained** Lambourn, Berks
■ Stewards' Enquiry : Martin Lane four-day ban: used whip with excessive frequency down shoulder in the forehand (Nov 2-5)

FOCUS
A competitive nursery and there was little to separate the front three at the line. The first four came clear and the form is solid if limited. The time was over a second slower than either division of the fillies' maiden.

NOTEBOOK

Slumbering Sioux, unplaced in four previous attempts, including on her recent nursery debut over 6f, proved well suited by the extra 2f and stayed on strongly to get up close home. She should have more to offer at a modest level. Official explanation: trainer's rep said, regarding apparent improvement in form, that the filly had been denied a clear run on its last start and the stable are coming into form. (op 16-1)

Salvationist, 5lb higher in a better race, took another step forward, only losing out narrowly. (tchd 11-2)

Indian Wish(USA) appreciated the return to turf and ran considerably better than she had done on her handicap debut at Kempton. (op 14-1)

Anton Dolin(IRE) ◆ left behind the form shown in maidens, keeping on to finish clear of the remainder, although he didn't help his chance by hanging. He can improve again. (tchd 9-1)

Eduardo again ran well and can find a small race at some stage. (op 16-1)

Sukhothai(USA) improved on what she'd shown in maidens, despite hanging and possibly not liking the ground. We've still to see the best of her. (op 10-1 tchd 9-1)

Scoglio was a non-stayer on this step up in trip. (op 17-2 tchd 7-1)

May's Boy Official explanation: trainer's rep said colt had a breathing problem

Al Rannan Official explanation: trainer rep said colt was unsuited by the soft ground

Chadford was pulled up and presumably went wrong. Official explanation: jockey said gelding lost its action (op 11-1 tchd 10-1)

7005 AVENUE PUB H'CAP — 1m 3y

4:20 (4:21) (Class 6) (0-60,60) 3-Y-O+ — **£1,942** (£578; £288; £144) — **Stalls** High

Form — RPR

5606 **1** **Inpursuitoffreedom**[116] 3413 3-9-6 **60**........................ JamieSpencer 16 70+
(P J McBride) *swtchd to r centre sn after s: hld up: hdwy over 2f out: rdn to ld overall over 1f out: r.o* **8/1**[3]

0010 **2** *2* **Nicholas Pocock (IRE)**[18] 6534 4-9-7 **58**........................ TomEaves 9 63+
(B Ellison) *racd centre: hld up: hdwy over 2f out: rdn to ld overall over 1f out: sn hdd: styd on same pce ins fnl f: 2nd of 10 in gp* **7/4**[1]

F240 **3** *nk* **Louisiana Gift (IRE)**[46] 5710 3-9-4 **58**........................(v[1]) SebSanders 8 62
(J W Hills) *racd centre: hld up: hdwy over 1f out: styd on: nt rch ldrs: 3rd of 10 in gp* **25/1**

5013 **4** *4 ½* **Exopuntia**[35] 6062 4-8-13 **50**........................ TonyCulhane 10 44
(Miss J Feilden) *racd centre: chsd ldr tl led that gp over 3f out: rdn and hdd over 1f out: wknd ins fnl f: 4th of 10 in gp* **8/1**[3]

0030 **5** *¾* **House Point**[5] 6860 3-9-3 **57**........................ AdamKirby 15 49
(S C Williams) *racd stands' side: chsd ldrs: led that gp and overall ldr over 2f out: rdn and hung rt over 1f out: sn hdd: wknd ins fnl f: 1st of 3 in gp* **9/1**

0650 **6** *9* **Transfixed (IRE)**[66] 5073 3-8-11 **54**........................ MartinLane(3) 11 26
(P D Evans) *racd centre: hld up in tch: racd keenly: rdn and wknd over 1f out: 5th of 10 in gp* **33/1**

0024 **7** *1 ¼* **Big Boom**[13] 6679 5-9-4 **55**........................ PatCosgrave 12 24
(M Quinn) *racd stands' side: overall ldr over 5f: wknd over 1f out: 2nd of 3 in gp* **11/1**

0231 **8** *6* **Big Sur**[41] 5864 4-9-7 **58**........................ StevieDonohoe 2 13
(T Keddy) *racd centre: s.i.s: hdwy over 6f out: wknd 2f out: eased fnl f: 6th of 10 in gp* **4/1**[2]

0000 **9** *shd* **Jonnie Skull (IRE)**[38] 5964 4-9-2 **53**........................(b) LukeMorris 14 —
(M D Squance) *chsd ldr stands' side tl over 2f out: sn wknd: last of 3 in gp* **33/1**

4600 **10** *1* **Diamondgeezer Luke (IRE)**[13] 6243 3-8-12 **55**(p) Louis-PhilippeBeuzelin(3) 3 —
(Patrick Morris) *racd centre: hld up in tch: plld hrd: wknd over 2f out: 7th of 10 in gp* **50/1**

3050 **11** *1 ¾* **Gra Adhmhar (IRE)**[41] 5867 3-9-4 **58**........................(p) KirstyMilczarek 1 —
(G Prodromou) *racd centre: chsd ldrs: rdn over 3f out: sn wknd: 8th of 10 in gp* **40/1**

0640 **12** *8* **Young Simon**[14] 6657 3-9-5 **59**........................(v) TomQueally 5 —
(G G Margarson) *racd centre: prom: rdn over 3f out: sn wknd: 9th of 10 in gp* **28/1**

0600 **13** *nk* **Jemimaville (IRE)**[75] 4762 3-8-13 **53**........................ TravisBlock 4 —
(G C Bravery) *led centre over 4f: wknd over 2f: last of 10 in gp* **40/1**

1m 45.2s (4.60) **Going Correction** +0.45s/f (Yiel)
WFA 3 from 4yo+ 3lb — **13** Ran SP% **116.9**
Speed ratings (Par 101): **95,93,92,88,87 78,77,71,71,70 68,60,60**
Tote Swingers: 1&2 £5.00, 1&3 £19.60, 2&3 £10.90 CSF £20.49 CT £359.18 TOTE £8.10: £2.70, £1.10, £6.70; EX 34.90 Trifecta £372.40 Part won. Pool: £503.32 - 0.72 winning units..
Owner P J McBride **Bred** Lord Fairhaven **Trained** Newmarket, Suffolk

FOCUS

A low-grade handicap. Three of them raced in a group stands' side. Only the first three home showed their form and it's not form to be too positive about.

Young Simon Official explanation: trainer said gelding lost a shoe

7006 DIGIBET.COM H'CAP — 7f 3y

4:50 (4:51) (Class 6) (0-65,65) 3-Y-O+ — **£1,942** (£578; £288; £144) — **Stalls** High

Form — RPR

0135 **1** **Franki J**[17] 6574 3-8-5 **54**........................ SophieDoyle(3) 9 75
(D Donovan) *mde all: rdn clr fr over 1f out: easily* **16/1**

0651 **2** *9* **Cheddar George**[13] 6671 4-9-4 **62**........................ JamieSpencer 1 59
(P W Chapple-Hyam) *stdd s: hld up: swtchd rt over 1f out: r.o u.p ins fnl f: nvr any ch* **11/4**[1]

1400 **3** *1* **Red Dagger (IRE)**[20] 6472 4-8-7 **54**........................ Louis-PhilippeBeuzelin(3) 2 48
(R J Price) *hld up: rdn over 2f out: styd on: nvr trbld ldrs* **18/1**

0065 **4** *hd* **Bel Cantor**[19] 6515 7-8-13 **64**........................(p) MatthewCosham(7) 12 57
(W J H Ratcliffe) *chsd ldrs: rdn over 2f out: outpcd fr over 1f out* **16/1**

1362 **5** *hd* **Yankee Storm**[34] 6098 5-9-0 **58**........................(v) JimmyQuinn 13 51
(H J Collingridge) *hld up: hdwy over 2f out: rdn over 1f out: no ex fnl f* **6/1**[2]

4230 **6** *½* **Chinese Democracy (USA)**[18] 6541 3-9-1 **61**........(v) PatCosgrave 15 53
(P D Evans) *trckd ldrs: racd keenly: rdn over 1f out: no ex fnl f: hmpd nr fin* **25/1**

0235 **7** *1 ¼* **Simple Rhythm**[4] 6898 4-9-4 **65**........................ MartinLane(3) 4 53
(J Ryan) *chsd ldrs: rdn over 2f out: wknd fnl f* **12/1**

0006 **8** *3 ¼* **Carnivore**[59] 5287 8-9-7 **65**........................ GrahamGibbons 11 44
(T D Barron) *hld up: hdwy u.p over 1f out: nt trble ldrs* **10/1**

0010 **9** *2 ¼* **Royal Holiday (IRE)**[39] 5923 3-8-8 **54**........................ TomEaves 10 27
(B Ellison) *prom: rdn over 2f out: wknd over 1f out* **28/1**

2004 **10** *1* **Hayek**[34] 6093 3-9-0 **60**........................ SilvestreDeSousa 3 31
(W Jarvis) *in rr and pushed along: sme hdwy u.p over 2f out: sn wknd* **20/1**

2021 **11** *1 ½* **Katmai River (IRE)**[14] 6657 3-8-7 **58**........................ AmyBaker(5) 8 25
(M D I Usher) *s.i.s: sn pushed along and a in rr* **10/1**

423 **12** *½* **Meia Noite**[22] 6420 3-9-2 **62**........................ TedDurcan 5 27
(C F Wall) *chsd ldrs: rdn over 2f out: wknd over 1f out: eased* **7/1**[3]

50 **13** *22* **Jemima Nicholas**[64] 5163 3-9-0 **60**........................(b[1]) DarryllHolland 7 —
(W J Haggas) *trckd ldrs tl rdn and wknd over 2f out: t.o* **25/1**

2040 **14** *¾* **Bideeya (USA)**[3] 6930 3-9-3 **63**........................(b[1]) ChrisCatlin 14 —
(C E Brittain) *sn pushed along in rr: bhd fr 1/2-way: t.o* **25/1**

0050 **15** *8* **Ocean Rosie (IRE)**[10] 6741 3-8-11 **57**........................ SebSanders 6 —
(Miss J Feilden) *chsd wnr tl rdn 1/2-way: wknd over 2f out: eased: t.o* **50/1**

1m 29.5s (2.90) **Going Correction** +0.45s/f (Yiel)
WFA 3 from 4yo+ 2lb — **15** Ran SP% **118.1**
Speed ratings (Par 101): **101,90,89,89,89 88,87,83,80,79 77,77,52,51,42**
Tote Swingers: 1&2 £17.60, 1&3 £39.40, 2&3 £12.50 CSF £53.16 CT £846.17 TOTE £19.80: £6.00, £1.30, £5.90; EX 154.10 TRIFECTA Not won..
Owner River Racing **Bred** Mrs A M Upsdell **Trained** Newmarket, Suffolk

FOCUS

Few got into this with the winner making all up the stands' rail. Big improvement from the winner, and her effort could have been rated higher.

Meia Noite Official explanation: jockey said filly had no more to give

7007 SPACE MARKETING ADVERTISING DESIGN H'CAP — 6f 3y

5:20 (5:20) (Class 6) (0-60,60) 3-Y-O+ — **£1,942** (£578; £288; £144) — **Stalls** High

Form — RPR

4235 **1** **Downhill Skier (IRE)**[20] 6456 6-9-3 **56**........................ TomMcLaughlin 8 65
(W M Brisbourne) *a.p: led 2f out: sn rdn: styd on gamely* **5/1**[3]

1032 **2** *nk* **Bermondsey Bob (IRE)**[13] 6679 4-9-7 **60**........................ DarryllHolland 1 68
(J L Spearing) *w ldrs: rdn over 1f out: styd on* **7/2**[1]

6020 **3** *1* **Sands Of Dee (USA)**[2] 6965 3-9-3 **57**........................ TomQueally 3 62
(J A Glover) *chsd ldrs: rdn over 1f out: styd on* **13/2**

010 **4** *½* **Commander Wish**[10] 6739 7-9-2 **58**........................ AmyRyan(3) 11 61
(Lucinda Featherstone) *hld up: hdwy over 2f out: rdn over 1f out: styd on* **14/1**

5000 **5** *3 ½* **Footstepsofspring (FR)**[27] 6292 3-9-5 **59**........................ TonyCulhane 9 51
(W J Musson) *prom: rdn over 2f out: no ex fnl f* **14/1**

0400 **6** *2 ¾* **Scruffy Skip (IRE)**[14] 6664 5-9-0 **53**........................(b) SebSanders 14 36
(Mrs C A Dunnett) *led 4f: wknd fnl f* **14/1**

6140 **7** *hd* **Eye For The Girls**[13] 6679 4-9-2 **55**........................ SamHitchcott 6 37
(M R Channon) *prom: rdn 1/2-way: wknd ins fnl f* **12/1**

6200 **8** *½* **Pragmatist**[68] 5010 6-9-6 **59**........................ JamesMillman 10 40
(B R Millman) *s.i.s: hdwy over 2f out: wknd fnl f* **11/1**

0100 **9** *4* **Zeffirelli**[35] 6061 5-9-0 **56**........................ MartinLane(3) 15 24
(M Quinn) *chsd ldrs: rdn 1/2-way: wknd over 1f out* **25/1**

5500 **10** *¾* **Memphis Man**[20] 6455 7-9-4 **60**........................ RichardEvans(3) 7 26
(P D Evans) *s.i.s: hld up: rdn 1/2-way: a in rr* **9/2**[2]

2230 **11** *2 ¼* **Guto**[20] 6464 7-9-6 **59**........................ TravisBlock 4 17
(W J H Ratcliffe) *chsd ldrs tl rdn and wknd over 1f out* **16/1**

0040 **12** *9* **Fuzzy Cat**[23] 6398 4-9-2 **55**........................ GrahamGibbons 16 —
(T D Barron) *sn pushed along and prom: wknd fr 1/2-way* **12/1**

1m 17.8s (3.40) **Going Correction** +0.45s/f (Yiel)
WFA 3 from 4yo+ 1lb — **12** Ran SP% **123.9**
Speed ratings (Par 101): **95,94,93,92,87 84,84,83,78,77 74,62**
Tote Swingers: 1&2 £3.70, 1&3 £6.40, 2&3 £4.20. totesuper7: Win: Not won. Place: £52.80. CSF £23.94 CT £121.90 TOTE £5.90: £1.40, £2.30, £3.60; EX 28.10 Trifecta £108.20 Pool: £394.80 - 2.70 winning units. Place 6: £33.23 Place 5: £31.84..
Owner Miss P D Insull **Bred** Swettenham Stud **Trained** Great Ness, Shropshire

FOCUS

A modest but competitive sprint handicap, and straightforward form.

T/Plt: £140.60 to a £1 stake. Pool: £57,937 - 300.63 winning tickets T/Qpdt: £105.10 to a £1 stake. Pool:£3,723 - 26.20 winning tickets CR

5622 DEAUVILLE (R-H)

Tuesday, October 19

OFFICIAL GOING: Turf: soft; fibresand: standard

7008a PRIX DES RESERVOIRS - HARAS D'ETREHAM (GROUP 3) (2YO FILLIES) (TURF) — 1m (R)

1:40 (12:00) 2-Y-O — **£35,398** (£14,159; £10,619; £7,079; £3,539)

RPR

1 **Espirita (FR)**[72] 4884 2-8-9 0........................ AnthonyCrastus 4 106
(E Lellouche, France) *broke wl to trck ldr in 3rd: tk clsr order ent st: rdn to ld 1 1/2f out: qcknd clr fnl f: comf* **39/10**[2]

2 *3* **Footsteppy (IRE)**[36] 2-8-9 0........................ Christophe-PatriceLemaire 7 99
(S Wattel, France) *racd towards rr: mde gd prog on outside 1 1/2f out: r.o wl fnl f to take 2nd cl home* **17/2**

3 *1 ½* **Nova Step**[43] 5826 2-8-9 0........................ Francois-XavierBertras 8 96
(F Rohaut, France) *racd in midfield: qckned wl on outer 1 1/2f out: chsd ldr but no ex fnl f: lost 2nd cl home* **1/1**[1]

4 *1* **Like Afleet (USA)**[28] 6277 2-8-9 0........................ StephanePasquier 5 94
(P Demercastel, France) *racd in 6th following eventual wnr: mde gd prog early in st in centre of trck: r.o fnl f* **14/1**

5 *½* **Nosail (FR)**[32] 2-8-10 0 ow1........................ OlivierPeslier 2 94
(F Head, France) *trckd ldr fr s: hrd rdn early in st: no ex fnl f* **7/1**[3]

6 *5* **Angel Of Harlem (FR)**[10] 2-8-9 0........................ IoritzMendizabal 1 82
(E J O'Neill, France) *racd towards rr on rail: rdn early in st: no ex: wknd* **25/1**

7 *6* **Tawaaleef (USA)**[34] 2-8-10 0 ow1........................ ChristopheSoumillon 3 70
(J E Hammond, France) *led fr s: rdn early in st: hdd 1 1/2f out: sn btn: wknd* **11/1**

8 *5* **Ana Style (FR)**[18] 2-8-9 0........................ GregoryBenoist 6 58
(P Demercastel, France) *broke wl: pulling hrd on outside: nvr settled: rdn early in st: sn wknd* **18/1**

1m 45.2s (4.40) — **8** Ran SP% **117.5**
WIN (incl. 1 euro stake): 4.90. PLACES: 1.40, 1.60, 1.10. DF: 14.00. SF: 32.70.
Owner Bruno Mettoudi **Bred** S C A La Perrigne & Elevage De Courteilles **Trained** Lamorlaye, France

NOTEBOOK

Espirita(FR) had had a minor setback, which explains her absence since August, but she came back to win with a fair bit in hand, and will now be put away for the winter, with the Prix de la Grotte and the Poule d'Essai des Pouliches her early-season targets next year.

7009a PRIX DU BOIS BOURDON (CLAIMER) (2YO) (TURF) 6f

2:10 (12:00) 2-Y-0 **£9,292** (£3,716; £2,787; £1,858; £929)

RPR

1 **Gwenhwyfar (IRE)**[20] 2-8-4 0 RufusVergette(7) 12 80
(A Fabre, France) **11/1**

2 *snk* **Gavriel (USA)**[20] 2-9-1 0 StephanePasquier 14 84
(G Botti, Italy) **9/2**[2]

3 *½* **Valerius Maximus**[11] 6719 2-9-4 0 ChristopheSoumillon 7 85
(P F I Cole) *bkmarker fr s: swtchd to stands' rail after 1f: rdn 3f out: qckn wl to chal 1f out: r.o u.p: no ex fnl 50yds* **5/2**[1]

4 *snk* **Platine Rose (FR)**[17] 6589 2-8-11 0 OlivierPeslier 9 78
(D Prod'Homme, France) **9/2**[2]

5 *2* **Germanico (IRE)**[20] 2-9-1 0 JeromeClaudic 13 76
(C Laffon-Parias, France) **45/1**

6 *1* **Kialoskar (IRE)** 2-8-5 0 WilliamsSaraiva(3) 4 66
(T Lemer, France) **14/1**

7 *½* **Chiqueta (FR)** 2-8-11 0 JohanVictoire 10 67
(C Gourdain, France) **29/1**

8 *2* **Gone Fighting (FR)**[6] 2-8-8 0 TristanNormand(3) 2 61
(Y De Nicolay, France) **35/1**

9 *1* **Glamorous Emma (IRE)**[32] 2-8-8 0 ASanna 1 55
(G Botti, Italy) **58/1**

10 *½* **Gasolina (FR)** 2-8-8 0 IoritzMendizabal 5 54
(C Gourdain, France) **9/1**[3]

0 **Magic Cat (FR)**[123] 2-8-5 0 WenceslasWalter(3) 6 —
(H Fortineau, France) **95/1**

0 **Give It To Me (FR)**[75] 2-8-8 0 HenkGrewe 11 —
(Mario Hofer, Germany) **27/1**

0 **Skipping Stones (IRE)**[15] 2-8-10 0 EddyHardouin(8) 3 —
(Robert Collet, France) **36/1**

0 **Indian Arrow (FR)** 2-9-1 0 ThomasMessina(3) 16 —
(F Doumen, France) **12/1**

0 **Crick Court (FR)** 2-8-6 0 (p) AlexandreChampenois(5) 15 —
(D De Waele, France) **39/1**

1m 13.7s (2.70) **15** Ran SP% **117.4**

WIN (incl. 1 euro stake): 12.50. PLACES: 2.80, 1.90, 1.80. DF: 21.20. SF: 68.50.

Owner Mme Andre Fabre **Bred** Mme A Fabre **Trained** Chantilly, France

NOTEBOOK

Valerius Maximus, winner of a Wolverhampton maiden two starts back, lost his race at the start, but picked up well from off the pace, and it was a good effort in the end to take third.

6419 FFOS LAS (L-H)

Wednesday, October 20

OFFICIAL GOING: Good (7.8)

Wind: Light, against Weather: Fine

7010 O'BRIEN CHARTERED ACCOUNTANTS MEDIAN AUCTION MAIDEN STKS 1m (R)

2:30 (2:31) (Class 5) 2-Y-0 **£2,914** (£867; £433; £216) **Stalls** Low

Form RPR

0 1 **Rastaban**[32] 6190 2-9-3 0 JoeFanning 4 75
(W J Haggas) *dwlt: hld up: hdwy 2f out: chsd ldr over 1f out: upsides and str chal ins fnl f: r.o to ld post* **5/1**[3]

03 2 *shd* **Lady Bridget**[10] 6770 2-8-12 0 RobertWinston 5 70
(B W Hills) *t.k.h: led: rdn over 1f out: hrd pressed and jnd ins fnl f: hdd post* **11/4**[2]

2 3 *4* **Never Never Land**[12] 6712 2-9-3 0 WilliamBuick 3 66
(J H M Gosden) *midfield: effrt to chse ldrs 2f out: no imp on front pair fnl f* **5/6**[1]

04 4 *1* **Sisindu (IRE)**[40] 5900 2-9-0 0 JamesSullivan(3) 2 64
(B J Meehan) *t.k.h: trckd ldrs: rdn wl over 1f out: one pce ins fnl f* **9/1**

0 5 *nk* **Promenadia**[21] 6468 2-8-12 0 SteveDrowne 7 58
(R Charlton) *racd keenly: hld up in rr: swtchd rt and hdwy 3f out: rdn to chse ldr briefly over 1f out: no ex fnl 100yds* **20/1**

0 6 *2¼* **Nutshell**[48] 5692 2-8-12 0 JamesDoyle 8 53
(H J L Dunlop) *sn moved up to r w ldr: pushed along over 2f out: wknd wl over 1f out* **100/1**

00 7 *2¾* **Mrs Neat (IRE)**[20] 6511 2-8-12 0 LiamKeniry 6 46
(S Kirk) *towards rr: niggled along after 2f: impr to trck ldrs 5f out: rdn over 2f out: wknd over 1f out* **100/1**

1m 44.41s (3.91) **Going Correction** +0.225s/f (Good) **7** Ran SP% **114.6**

Speed ratings (Par 95): **89,88,84,83,83 81,78**

Tote Swingers: 1&2 £2.10 CSF £19.17 TOTE £4.80: £1.40, £1.40; EX 26.30 Trifecta £25.90 Pool: £623.80 - 17.81 winning units..

Owner Abdulla Al Khalifa **Bred** Sheikh Abdullah Bin Isa Al-Khalifa **Trained** Newmarket, Suffolk

FOCUS

The ground had eased to good after some overnight rain. A tight little maiden and most of the field held some sort of chance over a furlong out. The first two finished clear and the form is modest but straightforward.

NOTEBOOK

Rastaban had shown promise on debut in a Newbury maiden and duly built on that to get off the mark at the second time of asking. Nudged along after missing the break slightly, he showed a determined attitude to eventually wear down the runner-up as the finish neared. He had come in for some late support for this step up in trip which he saw out well, and looks a horse for next season. (op 7-1)

Lady Bridget had progressed with each outing and remains progressive after a solid effort in defeat. She was only just run out of it in the closing stages and can gain compensation before long. (tchd 5-2 and 3-1)

Never Never Land, on turf debut, was all the rage in the market after not getting the best of runs on his racecourse debut. He was close enough if good enough over a furlong out but could only stay on at the same pace. (op 10-11 tchd Evens)

Sisindu(IRE) was another to have progressed with each run and set a fair standard overall. He raced a little keenly but had his chance before his effort flattened out inside the final furlong. (tchd 12-1)

Promenadia beat only one home on debut, but the yard's debut runners do tend to improve for the run and this was a step in the right direction, and she can only build upon this. (op 18-1 tchd 33-1)

7011 BLUEFIN INSURANCE H'CAP 1m 6f (R)

3:05 (3:05) (Class 5) (0-70,69) 3-Y-0+ **£3,238** (£963; £481; £240) **Stalls** Low

Form RPR

0204 1 **Quinsman**[12] 6715 4-9-13 **68** LiamKeniry 9 76
(J S Moore) *hld up: hdwy 3f out: rdn to ld 1f out: styd on ins fnl f: in command towards fin* **9/2**[2]

00-5 2 *1½* **Stormy Morning**[14] 6668 4-9-2 **60** MartinLane(3) 2 66
(Mrs Lawney Hill) *trckd ldrs: rdn to chal over 2f out: nt qckn sn after: kpt on to take 2nd wl ins fnl f: no imp on wnr* **8/1**

1305 3 *1¾* **Peintre D'Argent (IRE)**[26] 6331 4-9-5 **67** HarryBentley(7) 5 70
(W J Knight) *in tch: led over 2f out: rdn and hdd 1f out: no ex towards fin* **7/2**[1]

306/ 4 *1½* **Rio Gael (IRE)**[10] 7443 4-9-2 **57** RobertWinston 6 58
(P Bowen) *led at stdy pce: rdn over 3f out: hdd over 2f out: kpt on same pce u.p fr over 1f out: fdd fnl 100yds* **9/2**[2]

0054 5 *½* **Starshine**[14] 6668 3-8-8 **63** JohnFahy(5) 3 64
(R Charlton) *midfield: pushed along over 3f out: outpcd 2f out: kpt on u.p ins fnl f: unable to trble ldrs* **7/1**[3]

2620 6 *3¼* **Chincoteague (IRE)**[64] 5179 4-9-10 **68** JamesSullivan(3) 4 64
(B J Meehan) *prom tl rdn and wknd over 2f out* **12/1**

4630 7 *7* **Special Cuvee**[49] 5663 4-8-11 **52** (tp) SebSanders 8 38
(Mrs A M Thorpe) *s.i.s: hld up: rdn over 2f out: no imp: no ch fr over 1f out* **40/1**

6000 8 *36* **Outland (IRE)**[6] 6860 4-9-1 **56** WilliamBuick 7 —
(J R Jenkins) *s.i.s: hld up: hdwy over 7f out: sn prom: brought wd into st over 4f out: wknd 3f out: eased whn wl btn over 1f out: t.o* **12/1**

2232 9 *nk* **Oxford City (IRE)**[159] 2081 6-10-0 **69** (t) FergusSweeney 1 —
(P M Phelan) *midfield: rdn 3f out: sn wknd: eased whn wl btn fnl f: t.o* **8/1**

3m 18.58s (14.78) **Going Correction** +0.225s/f (Good)

WFA 3 from 4yo+ 9lb **9** Ran SP% **111.1**

Speed ratings (Par 103): **66,65,64,63,63 61,57,36,36**

Tote Swingers: 1&2 £7.10, 1&3 £3.70, 2&3 £10.50 CSF £37.88 CT £133.98 TOTE £5.60: £2.20, £3.30, £1.10; EX 21.70 Trifecta £128.40 Pool: £416.57 - 2.40 winning units..

Owner Donald M Kerr **Bred** Mr & Mrs G Middlebrook **Trained** Upper Lambourn, Berks

FOCUS

A steady pace for this staying handicap.

7012 INSIDER DEALMAKER H'CAP 1m (R)

3:40 (3:41) (Class 4) (0-85,85) 3-Y-0+ **£5,154** (£1,533; £766; £382) **Stalls** Low

Form RPR

1040 1 **Space War**[21] 6467 3-9-4 **85** WilliamBuick 8 100+
(J H M Gosden) *midfield: hdwy over 2f out: led ent fnl f: r.o wl towards fin* **5/1**[1]

1130 2 *1¾* **Lutine Bell**[56] 5421 3-8-10 **77** (v[1]) SebSanders 6 88
(Sir Mark Prescott) *towards rr: hdwy under 3f out: hung lft and led jst over 2f out: hdd ent fnl f: kpt on but hld towards fin* **16/1**

1361 3 *2¼* **Merchant Of Medici**[9] 6800 3-9-0 **81** 6ex JimmyFortune 2 87+
(W R Muir) *hld up: hdwy 3f out: rdn to chse ldrs over 1f out: styd on u.p ins fnl f: nt quite pce to chal front 2* **7/1**[3]

100 4 *hd* **Baylini**[22] 6447 6-8-9 **76** SophieDoyle(3) 7 81
(J A Osborne) *towards rr: rdn and hdwy over 2f out: chsd ldrs over 1f out: styd on u.p ins fnl f whn chalng for 3rd: nt quite pce of front 2* **18/1**

2400 5 *4½* **Gallant Eagle (IRE)**[9] 6813 3-8-11 **78** LiamKeniry 14 73
(S Kirk) *midfield: rdn over 2f out: hdwy over 1f out: hung lft sltly: kpt on ins fnl f: no imp on front quartet* **16/1**

1510 6 *2* **Night Lily (IRE)**[25] 6346 4-8-13 **82** JohnFahy(5) 10 72
(P W D'Arcy) *midfield: hdwy 3f out: rdn to chse ldrs 2f out: wknd 1f out* **10/1**

0131 7 *7* **First In The Queue (IRE)**[13] 6692 3-8-10 **77** TravisBlock 4 51
(S Kirk) *led for 1f: remained prom: rdn and wknd 2f out* **12/1**

606 8 *1* **Huzzah (IRE)**[32] 6204 5-9-5 **83** RobertWinston 3 55
(B W Hills) *midfield: pushed along 3f out: no imp: rdn and btn 2f out* **13/2**[2]

14 9 *¾* **Daboos (USA)**[23] 6430 3-8-12 **79** TadhgO'Shea 5 49
(M P Tregoning) *hld up: u.p over 2f out: nt clr run briefly whn no real imp over 1f out: nvr on terms w ldrs* **7/1**[3]

0010 10 *1¾* **Hidden Glory**[13] 6701 3-8-5 **79** JamesRogers(7) 13 45
(Pat Eddery) *worked hrd to ld after 1f: hdd jst over 2f out: sn wknd* **14/1**

2303 11 *2¾* **Aflaam (IRE)**[18] 6558 5-8-5 **72** (t) AndrewHeffernan(3) 11 32
(R A Harris) *midfield: rdn over 2f out: no imp: wknd wl over 1f out* **10/1**

1545 12 *1¾* **Munsarim (IRE)**[33] 6151 3-8-10 **80** MartinLane(3) 9 36
(J L Dunlop) *trckd ldrs: pushed along over 3f out: wknd over 2f out* **9/1**

2310 13 *1* **Sennockian Storm (USA)**[35] 6097 3-8-6 **73** JoeFanning 12 27
(M Johnston) *chsd ldrs tl rdn and wknd over 2f out* **14/1**

0600 14 *25* **The Cayterers**[18] 6562 8-9-4 **85** MichaelGeran(3) 1 —
(A W Carroll) *towards rr: struggling and bhd fnl 3f* **16/1**

1m 41.28s (0.78) **Going Correction** +0.225s/f (Good)

WFA 3 from 4yo+ 3lb **14** Ran SP% **127.1**

Speed ratings (Par 105): **105,103,101,100,96 94,87,86,85,83 81,79,78,53**

Tote Swingers: 1&2 £24.40, 1&3 £13.90, 2&3 £42.00 CSF £92.53 CT £596.02 TOTE £7.30: £2.50, £9.10, £3.80; EX 160.00 TRIFECTA Not won..

Owner H R H Princess Haya Of Jordan **Bred** Shutford Stud And O F Waller **Trained** Newmarket, Suffolk

FOCUS

A competitive handicap.

Night Lily(IRE) Official explanation: jockey said filly was unsuited by the good ground

7013 INSIDER DEALMAKER MAIDEN STKS 6f

4:10 (4:14) (Class 5) 3-Y-0+ **£2,914** (£867; £433; £216) **Stalls** High

Form RPR

R 1 **Delaware Dancer (IRE)**[65] 5153 3-8-12 0 LiamKeniry 4 64
(J R Gask) *hld up in rr: nt clr run over 2f out: swtchd lft and hdwy over 1f out: r.o ins fnl f: led towards fin* **20/1**

544 2 *½* **Brewers Boy**[10] 6773 3-9-3 0 JamesMillman 1 67
(B R Millman) *led: rdn over 1f out: worn down towards fin* **13/2**

0036 3 *1* **Romancea (USA)**[39] 5960 3-8-9 58 MartinLane(3) 7 59
(E F Vaughan) *hld up: rdn over 2f out: tried to chal over 1f out: edgd lft whn ch ins fnl f: nt qckn towards fin* **8/1**

4 *2¾* **Red Rhythm** 3-9-3 0 J-PGuillambert 8 55
(L M Cumani) *racd freely w ldr tl pushed along 2f out: nt qckn over 1f out: one pce fnl 110yds* **7/1**

0444 **5** 1 3/4 **Praesepe**[11] 6746 3-8-12 57 ....(b1) WilliamBuick 6 45
(W J Haggas) *wnt lft s: in tch: effrt and edgd lft over 1f out: sn trying to chal: no ex fnl 120yds* **9/2**[2]

3200 **6** 1/2 **Acquaviva**[16] 6638 3-8-7 60 ....(p) JohnFahy(5) 5 43
(Eve Johnson Houghton) *prom: rdn over 1f out: sn outpcd: no imp after* **22/1**

432 **7** 3/4 **French Fantasy**[53] 5535 3-8-12 55 ....(t) SteveDrowne 9 41
(H Morrison) *prom: rdn 2f out: u.p whn n.m.r over 1f out: no imp after* **3/1**[1]

0 **8** 5 **Hidden Destiny**[16] 6638 3-9-3 0 .... FergusSweeney 3 30
(P J Makin) *dwlt: wnt lft s: hld up in tch: hung lft u.p wl over 1f out: sn wknd* **17/2**

63 **9** 1/2 **Jaldarshaan (IRE)**[9] 6815 3-8-12 0 .... TravisBlock 2 23
(W J H Ratcliffe) *dwlt: wnt lft s: prom: rdn 2f out: wknd over 1f out* **5/1**[3]

1m 11.77s (2.07) **Going Correction** +0.225s/f (Good) 9 Ran SP% **116.4**
Speed ratings (Par 103): **95,94,93,89,87 86,85,78,78**
Tote Swingers: 1&2 £26.40, 1&3 £23.70, 2&3 £10.30 CSF £144.95 TOTE £24.60: £6.90, £1.30, £3.80; EX 187.60 TRIFECTA Not won..
Owner The Delaware Dancer Partnership **Bred** Barronstown Stud And Cobra **Trained** Sutton Veny, Wilts

FOCUS
An ordinary maiden run at a decent pace, and there was a rather surprising outcome.

7014 H M PLANT HITACHI H'CAP 6f
4:45 (4:47) (Class 3) (0-95,95) 3-Y-0+ **£7,771** (£2,312; £1,155; £577) **Stalls** High

Form RPR

4000 **1** **Pastoral Player**[40] 5911 3-9-3 92 .... SteveDrowne 5 102
(H Morrison) *dwlt: hld up: hdwy wl over 1f out: r.o ins fnl f: led towards fin* **4/1**[2]

4030 **2** 1/2 **Below Zero (IRE)**[18] 6564 3-9-1 90 .... JoeFanning 4 98
(M Johnston) *led: rdn over 1f out: hdd towards fin* **12/1**

3011 **3** 1 1/2 **Drawnfromthepast (IRE)**[19] 6539 5-9-4 95 .... SophieDoyle(3) 3 98
(J A Osborne) *a.p: rdn and ch over 1f out: nt qckn fnl 75yds* **7/1**

1035 **4** 3/4 **Street Power (USA)**[100] 3969 5-8-10 84 .... LiamKeniry 7 85
(J R Gask) *dwlt: hld up: hdwy whn lugged lft fr 2f out: styd on towards fin: nt quite pce to rch ldrs* **17/2**

000 **5** hd **Shifting Star (IRE)**[23] 6429 5-8-6 85 ....(p) JohnFahy(5) 1 85
(W R Swinburn) *in tch: rdn over 2f out: chsng ldrs whn nt qckn over 1f out: styd on same pce ins fnl f* **5/1**[3]

3126 **6** 3 1/2 **Barons Spy (IRE)**[30] 6256 9-8-5 82 .... AndrewHeffernan(3) 8 71
(R J Price) *hld up: rdn 2f out: no imp: kpt on modly ins fnl f: nvr a threat* **16/1**

3-03 **7** 3/4 **Tellelle (IRE)**[12] 6728 4-8-7 84 .... MartinLane(3) 2 71
(Liam McAteer, Ire) *in tch: rdn over 2f out: wknd over 1f out* **15/2**

0353 **8** 7 **We Have A Dream**[10] 6776 5-8-13 87 .... JimmyFortune 6 51
(W R Muir) *prom: rdn 2f out: wknd over 1f out* **3/1**[1]

5060 **9** 1 1/4 **Star Rover (IRE)**[4] 6918 3-9-1 93 .... RichardEvans(3) 9 53
(P D Evans) *prom: rdn over 2f out: struggling to hold pl whn n.m.r 2f out: sn wknd* **16/1**

1m 10.0s (0.30) **Going Correction** +0.225s/f (Good)
WFA 3 from 4yo+ 1lb 9 Ran SP% **115.9**
Speed ratings (Par 107): **107,106,104,103,103 98,97,88,86**
Tote Swingers: 1&2 £12.80, 1&3 £4.70, 2&3 £12.10 CSF £50.94 CT £327.08 TOTE £5.70: £2.10, £4.10, £2.50; EX 57.80 Trifecta £309.70 Pool: £493.87 - 1.18 winning units..
Owner The Pursuits Partnership **Bred** Whitsbury Manor Stud & Pigeon House Stud **Trained** East Ilsley, Berks

FOCUS
A decent standard of sprinters on offer, but with the fast-improving Kuanyao becoming a late withdrawal, it took a little shine of the race.

NOTEBOOK
Pastoral Player has more often than not set himself some difficult tasks with some tardy starts and again was slowly away, but he can be a strong traveller, which held him in good stead, and after squeezing through a gap over a furlong out, he quickened up well to reel in the long-time leader. The stable are in form and he remains a very capable sprinter on his day. (tchd 9-2)
Below Zero(IRE) took up his customary role at the head of affairs and made this a decent test. This was one of his better efforts away from Chester, where he seems to go best. (op 11-1 tchd 9-1)
Drawnfromthepast(IRE) was coming here off the back of somewhat a revival with two wins around Wolverhampton and posted another solid effort to confirm present his well-being. (op 11-2)
Street Power(USA) ran with promise after slightly missing the break and will be of much interest when back at Kempton where he is 6-7. (op 9-1 tchd 8-1)
Shifting Star(IRE) is slipping to a dangerous mark if he can rekindle his form, but he could not find the pace to lay down a serious challenge. (op 8-1)
Tellelle(IRE) was the subject of a strong whisper beforehand, but after chasing the pace was a spent force entering the final furlong. (op 7-1 tchd 8-1)

7015 INSIDER DEALMAKER APPRENTICE H'CAP 1m 2f (R)
5:20 (5:20) (Class 5) (0-70,70) 3-Y-0+ **£2,914** (£867; £433; £216) **Stalls** Low

Form RPR

424 **1** **James Pollard (IRE)**[5] 6905 5-8-10 56 oh3 ....(t) AndrewHeffernan 10 62
(B J Llewellyn) *hld up: hdwy over 3f out: led over 1f out: r.o wl to draw clr and in command ins fnl f* **11/2**[3]

253- **2** 6 **Josephine Malines**[42] 5364 6-8-4 57 oh6 ow1 ..(p) MatthewCosham(7) 3 51
(J L Flint) *hld up: hdwy 3f out: rdn and nt qckn 2f out: styd on ins fnl f to take 2nd fnl stride: no ch w wnr* **5/1**[2]

0546 **3** shd **Edition**[16] 6632 3-8-8 62 .... TobyAtkinson(3) 5 56
(J R Gask) *midfield: rdn and hdwy over 1f out: styd on ins fnl f: but only chalng for pls* **6/1**

02 **4** shd **Officer In Command (USA)**[7] 6841 4-9-5 70 ....(b) RyanPowell(5) 9 64
(J S Moore) *prom: led over 3f out: rdn 2f out: hdd over 1f out: outpcd by wnr ins fnl f: lost 2nd fnl stride* **7/1**

4444 **5** 1/2 **Easy Terms**[8] 6829 3-8-12 63 ....(v) JamesMillman 1 56
(B R Millman) *prom: rdn 3f out: nt qckn over 1f out: kpt on u.p whn chalng for pls ins fnl f: hld for pls cl home* **8/1**

0025 **6** 6 **Spring Secret**[19] 6543 4-9-4 67 .... DeclanCannon(3) 4 48
(B Palling) *midfield: niggled along 5f out: rdn over 4f out: wknd 2f out* **4/1**[1]

3/ **7** 1 3/4 **Apt Son (USA)**[34] 6136 5-9-10 70 .... MichaelO'Connell 6 47
(Francis Ennis, Ire) *chsd ldrs: rdn over 2f out: wknd over 1f out* **10/1**

2100 **8** 4 1/2 **Sandy Shaw**[39] 5959 3-8-12 68 .... HollyHall(5) 2 36
(J W Hills) *led: hdd over 3f out: rdn and wknd over 2f out* **8/1**

0440 **9** 21 **Mountain Pass (USA)**[40] 5905 8-8-3 56 oh6 ....(p) KevinLundie(7) 7 —
(B J Llewellyn) *completely missed break: bhd: rdn over 3f out: t.o fnl 2f* **50/1**

2m 14.15s (5.75) **Going Correction** +0.225s/f (Good)
WFA 3 from 4yo+ 5lb 9 Ran SP% **112.1**
Speed ratings (Par 103): **86,81,81,81,80 75,74,70,54**
Tote Swingers: 1&2 £5.30, 1&3 £5.30, 2&3 £6.60 CSF £31.81 CT £168.11 TOTE £8.40: £3.80, £1.10, £2.00; EX 37.50 Trifecta £261.90 Part won. Pool: £354.03 - 0.50 winning units..
Owner Granville Reynolds **Bred** Gainsborough Stud Management Ltd **Trained** Fochriw, Caerphilly

FOCUS
A very tricky low-grade apprentice handicap.
Spring Secret Official explanation: jockey said gelding never travelled
T/Jkpt: Not won. T/Plt: £2,053.50 to a £1 stake. Pool:£66,472 - 23.63 winning tickets T/Qpdt: £301.80 to a £1 stake. Pool:£6,404 - 15.70 winning tickets DO

6865 KEMPTON (A.W) (R-H)
Wednesday, October 20

OFFICIAL GOING: Standard
Wind: virtually nil Weather: dry, chilly

7016 KIA SPORTAGE NURSERY (DIV I) 5f (P)
5:50 (5:51) (Class 6) (0-60,60) 2-Y-O **£1,364** (£403; £201) **Stalls** High

Form RPR

0063 **1** **Miss Toldyaso (IRE)**[37] 6035 2-8-4 48 .... AdamBeschizza(5) 8 54
(M G Quinlan) *chsd ldr: rdn ent fnl 2f: chsd ldr jst over 1f out: led fnl 100yds: r.o wl: rdn out* **5/1**[2]

4403 **2** 1 **Till Dawn (IRE)**[3] 6954 2-9-0 53 .... JimmyQuinn 5 55
(A W Carroll) *dwlt: hld up towards rr: rdn and hanging rt wl over 1f out: hdwy ent fnl f: r.o wl to go 2nd last strides* **9/2**[1]

0253 **3** hd **Regal Bullet (IRE)**[14] 6674 2-9-2 55 .... SamHitchcott 6 57
(D K Ivory) *dwlt: t.k.h: hld up in rr: stl plenty to do over 1f out: gd hdwy ent fnl f: r.o strly to snatch 3rd on post* **5/1**[2]

0430 **4** shd **Je Suis Unrockstar**[14] 6674 2-9-1 54 ....(p) PJMcDonald 3 55
(J A Glover) *taken down early: led: rdn wl over 1f out: hdd fnl 100yds: no ex and lost 2 pls last strides* **10/1**

0005 **5** 2 **Bendigedig**[25] 6369 2-8-13 52 .... DavidProbert 2 46
(S Kirk) *chsd ldrs: rdn ent fnl 2f: drvn and styd on same pce fr over 1f out* **25/1**

306 **6** 1 1/4 **Mini Bon Bon**[18] 6576 2-9-6 59 ....(b1) PaulHanagan 7 49
(A Bailey) *in tch in midfield: rdn and effrt 2f out: styd on same pce u.p fr over 1f out* **9/1**

5040 **7** 1 1/4 **Majestic Ridge (IRE)**[18] 6576 2-9-2 55 .... LukeMorris 4 40
(R A Harris) *dwlt: sn bustled along and hdwy to chse ldr tl over 1f out: wknd fnl f* **33/1**

0000 **8** 1 1/2 **Mayfair Princess**[15] 6645 2-9-4 57 ....(t) ChrisCatlin 10 37
(P S McEntee) *hld up towards rr: rdn and hdwy on inner wl over 1f out: no prog ent fnl f: wknd ins fnl f* **25/1**

055 **9** 3 1/2 **Glitter Bug (IRE)**[113] 3528 2-8-6 45 .... SilvestreDeSousa 9 12
(M Johnston) *in tch in midfield: rdn and unable qck ent fnl 2f: wknd over 1f out: wl btn fnl f* **9/2**[1]

000 **10** 1 **Danehill Deb**[125] 3126 2-8-6 45 .... WilliamCarson 11 9
(B De Haan) *dwlt: a in rr: v wd and rdn bnd 2f out: no prog: n.d* **33/1**

6000 **11** 7 **Newzflash**[14] 6673 2-8-10 49 ....(b1) GrahamGibbons 12 —
(T D Barron) *broke wl: sn rdn and nvr travelling wl: steadily lost pl tl bhd ent fnl 2f: sn lost tch* **11/2**[3]

60.29 secs (-0.21) **Going Correction** -0.175s/f (Stan) 11 Ran SP% **117.7**
Speed ratings (Par 93): **94,92,92,91,88 86,84,82,76,75 63**
Tote Swingers: 1&2 £5.50, 1&3 £3.80, 2&3 £4.00 CSF £26.65 CT £117.84 TOTE £5.50: £3.40, £1.20, £2.10; EX 30.30.
Owner Toldyaso Partnership **Bred** Rathdown Stud Ltd **Trained** Newmarket, Suffolk

FOCUS
This was a weak, low-grade nursery. The front pair are the best guide to the form, which is pretty limited.

NOTEBOOK
Miss Toldyaso(IRE) grabbed a good position tracking the pace on the rail and picked up nicely in the straight once switched. She was fully entitled to win this on the form of her narrow defeat at Redcar last time. Despite her trainer's reservations, this sharp 5f proved very much in her favour. (tchd 11-2)
Till Dawn(IRE) backed up a good run at Bath three days earlier with another solid effort. She's proving pretty consistent and is taking her racing well. Official explanation: jockey said filly suffered interference (op 4-1)
Regal Bullet(IRE) struggled to go the early pace, but finished his race off well. A return to 6f will probably be in his favour. (op 9-2 tchd 11-2)
Je Suis Unrockstar, who went to post very early, had a low draw, but showed good early pace to dispute the lead. That effort cost him in the end, but he showed enough to suggest he's capable of winning a minor race, either on Polytrack or at Southwell, where he ran so well on his second start. (op 12-1 tchd 9-1)
Mini Bon Bon raced wider than most. (op 10-1 tchd 8-1 and 11-1 in places)
Glitter Bug(IRE) had been beaten a long way in each of his three starts in maidens, but had been gelded and given a break since his last outing. Officially 14lb out of the handicap, despite carrying bottom weight, his chance looked remote on paper, but there were plenty prepared to give him another chance and he was solid in the market. On this evidence, though, heâ€˜s has little to offer. (op 8-1)

7017 KIA SPORTAGE NURSERY (DIV II) 5f (P)
6:20 (6:22) (Class 6) (0-60,60) 2-Y-O **£1,364** (£403; £201) **Stalls** High

Form RPR

406 **1** **Even Stevens**[14] 6675 2-8-11 50 .... PJMcDonald 8 51
(J A Glover) *towards rr: hmpd and wnt wd bnd over 3f out: hdwy and rdn 3f out: chsd ldrs and swtchd lft over 1f out: r.o wl to ld post* **9/1**

0066 **2** nse **Shutupandrive**[6] 6869 2-8-6 45 ....(v1) HayleyTurner 11 46
(M D I Usher) *dwlt: sn rdn and rcvrd to chse ldrs: lft 2nd bnd over 3f out: rdn to chal over 1f out: led last strides tl hdd on post* **25/1**

6160 **3** nk **Brave Tiger (IRE)**[6] 6867 2-9-3 56 ....(t) DavidProbert 12 56
(S C Williams) *dwlt: sn rdn along and rcvrd to ld over 3f out: rdn wl over 1f out: kpt on gamely u.p tl hdd and lost 2 pls last strides* **5/2**[1]

2300 **4** 1/2 **Chester Deelyte (IRE)**[15] 6645 2-8-6 48 .... PatrickDonaghy(3) 9 46
(Mrs L Williamson) *in midfield wh hung lft and lost pl on bnd over 3f out: rallied u.p over 1f out: r.o wl ins fnl f: nt rch ldrs* **28/1**

2633 **4** dht **Misscomplacent**[6] 6868 2-9-7 60 ....(b) PaulMulrennan 5 59
(Mrs A Duffield) *chsd ldrs: hmpd and carried lft bnd over 3f out: sn rdn and rcvrd to chse ldrs 3f out: ev ch and drvn over 1f out: unable qck wl ins fnl f* **4/1**[2]

U060 **6** *nk* **Misty Morn**[15] 6645 2-9-2 **55**........ SilvestreDeSousa 6 52
(A D Brown) *led tl over 3f out: sn hung bdly lft on bnd and lost pl: rdn and rallied to chse ldrs and rdn wl over 1f out: styd on same pce ins fnl f* **8/1**

0000 **7** *nse* **King Bling (IRE)**[34] 6129 2-8-7 **46**........(b[1]) ChrisCatlin 1 43
(S Kirk) *dwlt: sn rdn along and outpcd in rr: hdwy on outer ent fnl f: styd on wl fnl f: nt rch ldrs* **14/1**

0000 **8** *1/2* **High Avon**[14] 6673 2-9-1 **54**........ SamHitchcott 7 49
(D K Ivory) *dwlt: sn rdn along and outpcd in last trio: hdwy ent fnl f: styd on wl u.p fnl f: nt rch ldrs* **13/2**[3]

4504 **9** *1/2* **Fairy Tales**[42] 5863 2-8-6 **45**........ NeilChalmers 2 41+
(J J Bridger) *t.k.h: hld up towards rr: hdwy jst over 1f out: chsng ldrs and running on whn nt clr run fnl 75yds: no ch* **50/1**

0605 **10** *1/2* **Amber Mist**[32] 6209 2-8-10 **52**........ KierenFox(3) 10 43
(David Pinder) *taken down early: chsd ldrs: hung lft bnd over 3f out: midfield after: rdn and hanging rt over 1f out: swtchd lft ins fnl f: kpt on but nt pce to chal* **8/1**

6000 **11** *2 1/4* **Melodize**[29] 6271 2-9-1 **54**........(t) GeorgeBaker 3 37
(W R Muir) *midfield but sn pushed along: towards rr and rdn over 1f out: hung rt and no prog after* **12/1**

0600 **12** *1/2* **Molly Mylenis**[18] 6576 2-9-6 **59**........ PaulHanagan 4 40
(P D Evans) *chsd ldrs but sn rdn along: hmpd and carried wd bnd over 3f out: lost pl and n.d after* **25/1**

60.91 secs (0.41) **Going Correction** -0.175s/f (Stan) **12** Ran SP% **121.6**
Speed ratings (Par 93): **89,88,88,87,87 87,87,86,85,84 81,80**
Tote Swingers: 1&2 £39.60, 1&3 £6.60, 2&3 £24.20 CSF £222.40 CT £737.89 TOTE £14.90: £4.60, £9.80, £1.80; EX 187.90.
Owner Paul J Dixon **Bred** Mrs Yvette Dixon **Trained** Babworth, Notts

FOCUS
There was plenty of early pace on here and several ran wide on the bend. That gave the advantage to the leader Brave Tiger and his pursuer Shutupandrive, but in the end the pair were run down in the shadow of the post. The winning time was 0.62sec slower than the first division. They finished very much in a heap and this is form to be against.

NOTEBOOK
Even Stevens, who was running in a handicap for the first time, was one of those forced wide around the bend, so it's to his credit he was able to make up the lost ground and just get up on the line. His dam won on Fibresand, so there's every chance he'll handle the other AW surface, too. (op 8-1)
Shutupandrive ran a better race for the fitting of a visor for the first time, although it has to be said she very much enjoyed the run of the race. (op 33-1)
Brave Tiger(IRE) made all round here last month and, although not best away this time, he was soon up there. When most of the others went wide around the bend, he was handed a big advantage, but he couldn't hold the field off, and in hindsight he'd probably been forced to go off just a bit too quick early. (op 7-2)
Chester Deelyte(IRE), running on the AW for the first time, ran a more encouraging race than of late. (op 25-1)
Misscomplacent, wearing cheekpieces this time, had a handy early position, but was carried wide around the bend, and in the circumstances she did well to finish as close as she did. (op 25-1)
Misty Morn was fast away and led going into the bend, but she didn't handle it at all and went very wide, carrying others with her. Official explanation: jockey said filly hung left (op 15-2 tchd 9-1)
Fairy Tales Official explanation: jockey said filly was denied a clear run
Amber Mist Official explanation: jockey said filly was denied a clear run

7018 REMEMBER BE MY ROYAL H'CAP — 5f (P)
6:50 (6:50) (Class 6) (0-55,58) 3-Y-O+ **£1,637** (£483; £241) **Stalls** High

Form RPR

2225 **1** **Best One**[3] 6956 6-9-2 **55**........(b) LukeMorris 6 63
(R A Harris) *dwlt: racd in midfield: rdn and effrt over 1f out: chsd ldr jst ins fnl f: r.o wl to ld fnl 75yds* **11/2**[2]

000- **2** *nk* **Sir Don (IRE)**[412] 5610 11-8-13 **52**........(tp) SilvestreDeSousa 7 59
(Mrs D J Sanderson) *led: sn clr: rdn over 1f out: hdd and no ex fnl 75yds* **25/1**

2651 **3** *1* **Embra (IRE)**[7] 6848 5-9-2 58 6ex........(p) RobertLButler(3) 10 63+
(T J Etherington) *hld up in midfield: rdn and effrt over 1f out: nt clr run and swtchd lft 1f out: kpt on u.p fnl f* **6/1**[3]

0460 **4** *shd* **Stargazing (IRE)**[20] 6515 4-9-2 **55**........(v[1]) ShaneKelly 9 58
(B J Meehan) *s.i.s: sn rdn along and detached in last: hdwy jst over 1f out: swtchd lft ins fnl f: r.o wl: nt rch ldrs* **11/2**[2]

3345 **5** *1* **Black Baccara**[73] 4861 3-9-1 **54**........(p) TomMcLaughlin 12 53
(P S McEntee) *hld up in rr: hdwy and rdn on outer wl over 1f out: kpt on ins fnl f: nt rch ldrs* **16/1**

2441 **6** *1* **Duke Of Rainford**[14] 6665 3-8-13 **52**........ PaulHanagan 5 48
(M Herrington) *chsd clr ldr: rdn over 1f out: edgd sltly lft u.p 1f out: wknd ins fnl f* **7/1**

5431 **7** *1/2* **Almaty Express**[32] 6206 8-9-0 **53**........(b) DarryllHolland 11 47
(J R Weymes) *towards rr: pushed along and effrt on inner over 1f out: kpt on steadily fnl f: nvr gng pce to rch ldrs* **4/1**[1]

0-60 **8** *1/2* **Villaruz (IRE)**[121] 3280 4-9-1 **54**........(be) StephenCraine 8 46
(D Flood) *chsd ldrs: rdn and unsble to qckn over 1f out: hung rt and wknd 1f out* **15/2**

0300 **9** *1 1/2* **Spoof Master (IRE)**[21] 6456 6-8-13 **55**........ SimonPearce(3) 3 42
(J Pearce) *in midfield on outer: rdn and struggling over 2f out: no threat to ldrs after* **10/1**

0600 **10** *1/2* **Alsufooh (USA)**[11] 6741 3-9-2 **55**........ AdamKirby 4 40
(D Shaw) *stdd s: t.k.h: hld up in rr: nvr trbld ldrs* **33/1**

2400 **11** *1 3/4* **Kheley (IRE)**[130] 2957 4-8-13 **55**........ KierenFox(3) 1 34
(W M Brisbourne) *in tch: rdn and struggling ent fnl 2f: wl btn 1f out* **14/1**

59.28 secs (-1.22) **Going Correction** -0.175s/f (Stan) **11** Ran SP% **117.7**
Speed ratings (Par 101): **102,101,99,99,98 96,95,94,92,91 88**
Tote Swingers: 1&2 £24.70, 1&3 £6.70, 2&3 £39.30 CSF £132.59 CT £857.36 TOTE £7.10: £1.20, £13.20, £4.50; EX 226.00.
Owner The Govin Partnership **Bred** Darley **Trained** Earlswood, Monmouths

FOCUS
Ordinary sprint handicap form.

7019 DIGIBET.COM CLAIMING STKS — 1m (P)
7:20 (7:20) (Class 6) 3-Y-O **£1,637** (£483; £241) **Stalls** High

Form RPR

0002 **1** **Green Earth (IRE)**[7] 6851 3-9-3 73........(p) NeilCallan 10 76
(Mrs A J Perrett) *hld up in tch: hdwy to chse ldrs gng wl over 1f out: rdn to ld 1f out: drvn and r.o wl fnl f* **9/2**[2]

4300 **2** *1* **Pastello**[16] 6633 3-8-6 68........ FrankieMcDonald 2 63
(R Hannon) *stdd after s and dropped to last pair: sn pushed along: hdwy ent fnl 2f: swtchd lft jst over 1f out: pressed wnr fnl 150yds: kpt on but a hld* **14/1**

0230 **3** *1 3/4* **Lean Machine**[12] 6718 3-9-1 65........ LukeMorris 1 68
(R A Harris) *stdd s: bhd: rdn over 3f out: stl bhd and drvn over 2f out: hdwy over 1f out: r.o strly fnl f: nt rch ldrs* **16/1**

2131 **4** *1/2* **Indian Valley (USA)**[16] 6622 3-9-2 75........ DavidProbert 13 68
(Rae Guest) *hld up towards rr: nt clr run towards inner over 2f out: rdn and gd hdwy 2f out: led jst over 1f out: sn hdd: outpcd and no threat to ldng pair fnl f* **7/2**[1]

4115 **5** *1/2* **Sabatini (IRE)**[18] 6577 3-8-11 72........ ChrisCatlin 12 62
(J Pearce) *in tch in midfield: rdn and effrt ent fnl 2f: styd on same pce and no imp fnl f* **9/2**[2]

-063 **6** *1 1/4* **Rich Boy**[19] 6522 3-8-13 64........ DaneO'Neill 14 61
(Mrs L J Mongan) *hld up in tch: hdwy on inner jst over 2f out: chsd ldrs and drvn over 1f out: wknd fnl f* **12/1**

4421 **7** *2 1/4* **Hierarch (IRE)**[7] 6854 3-8-12 69........(v[1]) AdamBeschizza(5) 3 60
(D Flood) *sn in tch and pushed along: rdn and nt qckn jst over 2f out: hrd drvn and outpcd over 1f out* **15/2**[3]

0050 **8** *1 1/2* **Another Magic Man (USA)**[7] 6854 3-9-1 68........ GeorgeBaker 4 54
(J R Best) *chsd ldr after 2f: rdn over 2f out: wknd u.p over 1f out* **20/1**

6546 **9** *2 3/4* **Plenty O'Toole**[9] 6794 3-9-7 65........ SilvestreDeSousa 7 54
(Mrs D J Sanderson) *sn led: rdn over 2f out: drvn and hdd jst over 1f out: fdd fnl f* **8/1**

-040 **10** *4* **Shark Man (IRE)**[7] 6853 3-8-9 67 ow2........(v[1]) RussKennemore(3) 11 36
(Andrew Reid) *led early: chsd ldrs after tl wknd u.p jst over 2f out* **33/1**

3000 **11** *2 3/4* **Excellent Aim**[9] 6812 3-8-13 65........ StevieDonohoe 9 30
(Jane Chapple-Hyam) *chsd ldrs: rdn over 3f out: wknd over 2f out: wl btn over 1f out* **33/1**

12 *19* **Mororatorio (IRE)** 3-9-6 0........ EddieCreighton 5 —
(Mrs D J Sanderson) *s.i.s: a bhd: lost tch and eased ent fnl 2f: t.o* **66/1**

6 **13** *1/2* **Broughtons Bandit**[15] 6652 3-8-12 0........ TonyCulhane 6 —
(W J Musson) *a towards rr: in last pair and lost tch over 2f out: t.o* **33/1**

1m 38.07s (-1.73) **Going Correction** -0.175s/f (Stan) **13** Ran SP% **116.8**
Speed ratings (Par 99): **101,100,98,97,97 96,93,92,89,85 82,63,63**
Tote Swingers: 1&2 £26.80, 1&3 £12.00, 2&3 £47.80 CSF £60.38 TOTE £6.40: £2.60, £5.80, £5.10; EX 88.20.Green Earth was claimed by Mr P. Wheatley for £12, 000.
Owner The Green Dot Partnership **Bred** Woodcote Stud Ltd **Trained** Pulborough, W Sussex

FOCUS
There was competition up front here and the principals came from off the pace.
Mororatorio(IRE) Official explanation: jockey said gelding lost its action

7020 DIGIBET CASINO MAIDEN STKS — 7f (P)
7:50 (7:52) (Class 4) 2-Y-O **£3,238** (£963; £481; £240) **Stalls** High

Form RPR

02 **1** **Terdaad (IRE)**[30] 6249 2-9-3 0........(p) FrankieDettori 9 78+
(Saeed Bin Suroor) *t.k.h: hld up in midfield: nt clr run ent fnl 2f: sn swtchd lft: rdn and gd hdwy to ld jst ins fnl f: r.o wl: eased towards fin* **13/8**[2]

00 **2** *1 1/2* **Kuala Limper (IRE)**[19] 6532 2-9-3 0........ DaneO'Neill 5 74
(D R C Elsworth) *wnt lft s: in tch towards rr: pushed along over 2f out: rdn and hdwy over 1f out: chsd wnr ins fnl f: kpt on* **100/1**

6 **3** *1* **Midnight Maasai**[68] 5032 2-9-3 0........ PhilipRobinson 14 72
(C G Cox) *led tl 5f out: chsd ldr after tl rdn to ld again over 1f out: hdd ins fnl f: styd on same pce after* **20/1**

62 **4** *3/4* **Puttingonthestyle (IRE)**[22] 6442 2-9-3 0........ RyanMoore 8 70
(R Hannon) *chsd ldr tl 5f out: styd handy: rdn and ev ch wl over 1f out: no ex and btn ins fnl f* **6/1**[3]

00 **5** *2 1/2* **Odin (IRE)**[33] 6159 2-9-3 0........ RobertWinston 6 63+
(D R C Elsworth) *sltly hmpd s: in tch in midfield: rdn and sltly outpcd over 2f out: styd on steadily ins fnl f: nt pce to threaten ldrs* **66/1**

6 **6** *nk* **Daa'Iman**[98] 4021 2-8-12 0........ NeilCallan 1 57
(C E Brittain) *in tch in midfield: rdn and effrt jst over 2f out: drvn and outpcd jst over 1f out: one pce and n.d fnl f* **33/1**

00 **7** *1 3/4* **Pivot Bridge**[22] 6443 2-9-3 0........ MichaelHills 12 58+
(B W Hills) *stdd after s: t.k.h: hld up in rr of main gp: pushed along and effrt on inner 2f out: kpt on steadily fnl f: nvr trbld ldrs* **40/1**

00 **8** *1 1/2* **Ministry**[20] 6497 2-9-3 0........ JimmyQuinn 13 54
(J R Best) *stdd after s: hld up in rr of main gp: rdn and sme hdwy over 1f out: nvr trbld ldrs* **100/1**

40 **9** *1 1/4* **Aloneinthestreet (USA)**[35] 6087 2-9-3 0........ KierenFallon 7 51
(M Johnston) *towards rr of main gp: pushed along and effrt ent fnl 2f: nvr gng pce to threaten ldrs* **20/1**

52 **10** *nk* **Mutayaser**[35] 6087 2-9-3 0........ RichardHills 11 50
(Sir Michael Stoute) *in tch: swtchd ins and effrt to press ldrs 2f out: rdn over 1f out: btn ent fnl f: wknd* **6/4**[1]

36 **11** *5* **Old Possum (USA)**[36] 6053 2-9-3 0........(b[1]) AhmedAjtebi 2 37
(Mahmood Al Zarooni) *t.k.h: chsd ldrs tl led 5f out: rdn and hdd over 1f out: wknd qckly* **40/1**

12 *35* **Talkin Italian** 2-8-12 0........ JimCrowley 3 —
(H Morrison) *stdd s: rn green and sn lost tch in last: t.o after 2f* **50/1**

1m 25.46s (-0.54) **Going Correction** -0.175s/f (Stan) **12** Ran SP% **115.2**
Speed ratings (Par 97): **96,94,93,92,89 89,87,85,83,83 77,37**
Tote Swingers: 1&2 £24.10, 1&3 £6.80, 2&3 £41.20 CSF £173.52 TOTE £1.90: £1.10, £32.40, £5.40; EX 122.90.
Owner Godolphin **Bred** Darley **Trained** Newmarket, Suffolk

FOCUS
Just fair form. The winner was the clear form pick and quite a decisive winner.

NOTEBOOK
Terdaad(IRE) finished second here last time but that form hasn't worked out at all well, and he was hardly impressive here, but he did enough to win and coped perfectly well with the drop back to 7f. He's a brother to a 1m2f winner but his dam, who won over 7f, is a sister to top-class sprinter Iffraaj, and he was keen enough here in the first-time cheekpieces, so it remains to be seen what his trip will be next year. (op 6-4 tchd 7-4)
Kuala Limper(IRE) responded to pressure to stay on down the outside for second. This was a big step up on his previous two efforts, and connections will no doubt be hoping the handicapper doesn't react too harshly.
Midnight Maasai didn't run badly in Saamidd's maiden on his debut, and this was a nice step up on his return from a two-month break. He needs one more run for a mark and will be interesting once handicapped.
Puttingonthestyle(IRE) probably ran to a similar level as in his previous two starts. He now has the handicap option, and probably won't be inconvenienced by a drop back to 6f in that sphere. (tchd 5-1 and 13-2)
Odin(IRE), who raced wide for much of the way, is eligible for a mark now and will probably be suited by longer distances in handicaps.
Daa'Iman, drawn worst of all, didn't really build on her debut effort, which came three months earlier. (tchd 28-1)
Ministry Official explanation: jockey said colt was slowly away

Mutayaser was bitterly disappointing, weakening right out inside the final furlong and a half. This wasn't his true form, but he'll get a mark now and he'll surely be seen to better effect in handicaps next year. (op 13-8 tchd 7-4)

7021 DIGIBET MAIDEN FILLIES' STKS 6f (P)

8:20 (8:21) (Class 5) 2-Y-O £2,286 (£675; £337) Stalls High

Form RPR

1 **Instance** 2-9-0 0 FrankieDettori 8 74+
(J Noseda) *pushed lft s: hld up in tch: hdwy over 2f out: rdn and ev ch 1f out: r.o wl fnl f to ld on post* **2/1**[1]

6062 2 *nse* **Strictly Pink (IRE)**[9] 6796 2-9-0 77 PaulHanagan 9 74
(A Bailey) *wnt lft s: chsd ldrs: wnt 2nd over 1f out: rdn and edgd lft over 1f out: led 1f out: hrd drvn and r.o wl fnl f: hdd on post* **5/2**[2]

3 *1* **Little Curtsey** 2-9-0 0 RobertHavlin 2 71+
(H Morrison) *hld up in tch: hdwy to chse ldrs and nt clr run 2f out: sn swtchd lft: chsd ldng pair ins fnl f: r.o wl* **11/1**

4 *3 1/4* **Beso (IRE)** 2-9-0 0 KierenFallon 11 65+
(L M Cumani) *sn pushed along in rr: hdwy on outer ent fnl f: kpt on wl to go 4th nr fin: nvr trbld ldrs* **8/1**

0 5 *nk* **Acclamatory**[33] 6153 2-9-0 0 WilliamCarson 7 60
(S C Williams) *hld up towards rr: pushed along ent fnl 2f: no real prog tl styd on ins fnl f: nvr trbld ldrs* **40/1**

60 6 *hd* **Bird In The Wind (USA)**[22] 6441 2-9-0 0 JimCrowley 3 60
(R M Beckett) *led: rdn over 2f out: drvn and hdd 1f out: wknd ins fnl f* **25/1**

3 7 *1* **Elegant Muse**[151] 2338 2-9-0 0 ShaneKelly 5 57
(W R Swinburn) *t.k.h: hld up in tch: hdwy to chse ldrs over 3f out: effrt and hung lft 2f out: sn outpcd and no threat to ldrs fr over 1f out* **10/3**[3]

00 8 *3 3/4* **Melancholy Hill (IRE)**[30] 6248 2-9-0 0 NeilCallan 4 46
(P F I Cole) *in tch towards rr: rdn and hanging rt over 2f out: swtchd lft ent fnl 2f: no prog* **66/1**

0000 9 *2 1/2* **Callipygos**[5] 6884 2-9-0 50 (be[1]) TomMcLaughlin 10 38
(P S McEntee) *a in last pair: rdn and effrt on inner ent fnl 2f: no hdwy: n.d* **100/1**

10 *1 1/4* **Oh What's Occuring** 2-9-0 0 ChrisCatlin 1 34
(T T Clement) *chsd ldr tl over 2f out: sn wknd: wl bhd over 1f out* **100/1**

1m 13.08s (-0.02) **Going Correction** -0.175s/f (Stan) **10** Ran SP% **114.2**
Speed ratings (Par 92): **93,92,91,87,86 86,85,80,76,75**
Tote Swingers: 1&2 £3.10, 1&3 £4.30, 2&3 £5.50 CSF £6.81 TOTE £3.40: £1.10, £1.10, £2.40; EX 10.50.
Owner The Hon William Vestey **Bred** T R G Vestey **Trained** Newmarket, Suffolk

FOCUS
A tight finish to what was probably a fair maiden. The fiorm is limited by the time and some of those down the field.

NOTEBOOK
Instance holds an Irish 1,000 Guineas entry and was sent off favourite ahead of a couple of rivals in the market who had some solid form to their names. Evidently fairly well regarded, she came there travelling strongly approaching the final furlong but was forced to dig deep when Strictly Pink would not go away. It's to her credit that she responded so well for pressure on her debut, and it'll be interesting to see how she progresses. She's a half-sister to a 1m4f winner and her dam won over 1m2f, but she's by Invincible Spirit and she showed plenty of pace here. (op 15-8 tchd 9-4)
Strictly Pink(IRE) did everything right but just came up short. She certainly didn't shirk it in the battle to the line, and she should have other opportunities to win a similar race. (op 7-2)
Little Curtsey ◆, a newcomer by Royal Applause, ran a promising race behind the front two for a stable whose juveniles invariably come on a good deal for their debuts. She's out of Tychy, who won plenty of races for Stuart Williams, and it'll be a surprise if she doesn't win her fair share too. (op 12-1 tchd 10-1)
Beso(IRE) ◆, whose dam was a smart sprinter, was green for most of the race but stayed on well under hands-and-heels riding in the straight. She looks sure to come on a bundle for this and could well win something similar next time. (op 13-2)
Acclamatory will be one for handicaps after one more run, while \bBird In The Wind\p, who crossed over from trap three to lead and was given a positive ride, has that option now open to her, and should do better in that sphere.
Elegant Muse, third to Margot Did on her debut back in May, hadn't run since, suggesting all had not been well, and, having raced keenly widest of all, she weakened out of contention inside the final furlong and a half. (op 3-1 tchd 7-2)

7022 TENDONOLOGY: TENDON TREATMENT FOR RACEHORSES MEDIAN AUCTION MAIDEN STKS 1m 4f (P)

8:50 (8:51) (Class 5) 3-5-Y-O £2,286 (£675; £337) Stalls Centre

Form RPR

-304 1 **Penangdouble O One**[39] 5958 3-9-3 69 (t) JimCrowley 1 65+
(R M Beckett) *in tch in midfield: hdwy to chse ldrs over 3f out: rdn to ld 2f out: hld on wl u.p fnl f* **7/2**[2]

3 2 *3/4* **Treacle Tart**[154] 2231 5-9-5 0 RobertWinston 6 59+
(P Charalambous) *t.k.h: hld up towards rr: hdwy over 3f out: rdn and edgd rt ent fnl 2f: pressed wnr fnl f: kpt on u.p but a hld* **7/1**[3]

45 3 *1/2* **Hibba (USA)**[30] 6250 3-8-12 0 RichardHills 2 58+
(M P Tregoning) *stdd s: hld up in rr: hdwy over 3f out: swtchd ins and effrt to press ldrs 2f: drvn and kpt on same pce fr over 1f out* **8/1**

36-3 4 *2* **Loyaliste (FR)**[9] 6814 3-9-3 0 RyanMoore 4 60+
(R Hannon) *dwlt: in tch in midfield: rdn and chsd ldrs over 3f out: drvn and keeping on same pce whn nt clr run and swtchd lft 2f out: kpt on one pce after* **7/2**[2]

000 5 *shd* **Suhailah**[49] 5666 4-9-2 40 KierenFox[(3)] 8 55
(M J Attwater) *chsd ldrs: rdn ent fnl 3f: nt clr run over 2f out: drvn and hung lft fr over 1f out: styd on same pce after* **100/1**

-522 6 *13* **Gay Mirage (GER)**[156] 2175 3-8-12 68 (b) PhilipRobinson 3 34
(M A Jarvis) *hdwy to join ldr after 2f: rdn and nt qckn over 2f out: wknd qckly 2f out* **2/1**[1]

3040 7 *7* **Elvira Madigan**[21] 6480 3-8-12 67 DavidProbert 10 23
(A M Balding) *led: rdn over 2f out: hdd 2f out: sn wknd: eased ins fnl f* **15/2**

0 8 *37* **Rannoch Moor**[223] 864 3-9-3 0 GeorgeBaker 9 —
(M P Tregoning) *a towards rr: pushed along over 8f out: lost tch over 4f out: t.o and eased fnl 2f* **20/1**

9 *7* **Waypost**[75] 4-9-7 0 RobertLButler[(3)] 7 —
(D G Bridgwater) *s.i.s: nvr gng wl in rr: lost tch 5f out: t.o fnl 3f* **100/1**

0 10 *43* **Alhudhud (USA)**[20] 6499 4-9-10 0 (t) AndreaAtzeni 5 —
(K A Morgan) *chsd ldr for 2f: pushed along over 8f out: chsd ldrs after tl lost pl qckly wl over 3f out: t.o and virtually p.u fnl 2f* **100/1**

2m 32.05s (-2.45) **Going Correction** -0.175s/f (Stan)
WFA 3 from 4yo+ 7lb **10** Ran SP% **120.9**
Speed ratings (Par 103): **101,100,100,98,98 90,85,60,56,27**
Tote Swingers: 1&2 £14.40, 1&3 £8.90, 2&3 £12.00 CSF £28.95 TOTE £3.00: £1.10, £1.90, £2.80; EX 27.20.
Owner Mrs A K H Ooi **Bred** Mrs A K H Ooi **Trained** Whitsbury, Hants

FOCUS
Poor maiden form rated around the fully exposed fifth.
Alhudhud(USA) Official explanation: jockey said gelding had no more to give

7023 BOOK YOUR CHRISTMAS PARTY AT KEMPTON H'CAP 1m (P)

9:20 (9:21) (Class 6) (0-52,55) 3-Y-O+ £1,637 (£483; £241) Stalls High

Form RPR

0005 1 **Esteem Lord**[105] 3786 4-8-13 50 JimCrowley 10 61+
(D K Ivory) *staedied s: hld up in rr: stl last pair and switching lft 2f out: str run fr over 1f out to ld fnl 75yds: in command towards fin* **8/1**

0452 2 *1* **Join Up**[5] 6905 4-8-8 50 RossAtkinson[(5)] 14 59
(W M Brisbourne) *hld up in midfield: swtchd ins and gd hdwy ent fnl 2f: drvn to ld over 1f out: hdd and no ex fnl 75yds* **5/1**[2]

4301 3 *shd* **Swansea Jack**[7] 6847 3-9-1 55 6ex (t) WilliamCarson 9 64+
(S C Williams) *t.k.h: hld up in last trio: nt clr run and switching lft fr over 2f out: eventually in the clr on wd outside ent fnl f: edgd rt u.p but r.o strly fnl f :nvr able to chal* **13/8**[1]

0405 4 *1 1/2* **Straight And Level (CAN)**[42] 5864 5-9-0 51 (v) DaneO'Neill 12 56
(Miss Jo Crowley) *t.k.h: hld up wl in tch: rdn and effrt over 1f out: hrd drvn and ev ch over 1f out: styd on same pce fnl f* **13/2**[3]

2000 5 *1/2* **Guildenstern (IRE)**[7] 6847 8-9-1 52 JimmyQuinn 13 56
(P Howling) *stdd s: hld up in last trio: hdwy on inner over 2f out: swtchd ins and gd hdwy to chse ldrs wl over 1f out: no imp u.p fnl f* **25/1**

650 6 *hd* **Pab Special (IRE)**[81] 4591 7-9-1 52 AdamKirby 2 56
(B R Johnson) *stdd s: hld up towards rr: hdwy 3f out: rdn and in tch whn nt clr run 2f out: kpt on same pce u.p fnl f* **33/1**

0050 7 *shd* **Feet Of Fury**[82] 4547 4-9-0 51 PJMcDonald 8 54
(Ian Williams) *dwlt: in tch in midfield: nt clr run over 2f out tl 2f out: kpt on u.p fnl f* **16/1**

0040 8 *1/2* **Crystallize**[3] 6956 4-8-9 51 (p) AmyBaker[(5)] 6 53
(A B Haynes) *chsd ldrs: rdn and ev ch over 1f out: no ex and one pced fnl f* **20/1**

340 9 *3* **Acropolis (IRE)**[21] 6450 9-8-13 50 NeilCallan 3 45
(A W Carroll) *t.k.h: hld up in tch in midfield: rdn and nt qckn wl over 1f out: outpcd ent fnl f* **20/1**

0050 10 *3 3/4* **Inquisitress**[7] 6848 6-9-0 51 NeilChalmers 4 38
(J J Bridger) *hld up in tch: hdwy over 2f out: rdn to chse ldrs 2f out: wknd ent fnl f* **16/1**

/1-0 11 *1 3/4* **Ain't Talkin'**[148] 2419 4-8-10 50 KierenFox[(3)] 11 33
(M J Attwater) *chsd ldrs: rdn and nt qckning whn bdly hmpd and lost pl jst over 2f out: no ch w ldrs fr over 1f out* **40/1**

0060 12 *6* **Prince Rossi (IRE)**[131] 2920 6-9-1 52 (v) PaulHanagan 1 21
(A E Price) *led tl rdn and hdd over 2f out: wknd wl over 1f out* **12/1**

0040 13 *1* **Fiancee (IRE)**[69] 4987 4-9-1 52 (v) GeorgeBaker 5 19
(R Brotherton) *chsd ldr tl rdn to ld jst over 2f out: hdd over 1f out: sn wknd* **25/1**

6000 14 *8* **Deely Plaza**[30] 6255 3-8-12 52 (v[1]) AndreaAtzeni 7 —
(J A Glover) *dwlt: sn chsng ldrs: rdn and struggling wl over 2f out: wl bhd and eased ins fnl f* **50/1**

1m 38.55s (-1.25) **Going Correction** -0.175s/f (Stan)
WFA 3 from 4yo+ 3lb **14** Ran SP% **123.2**
Speed ratings (Par 101): **99,98,97,96,95 95,95,95,92,88 86,80,79,71**
Tote Swingers: 1&2 £9.60, 1&3 £6.70, 2&3 £4.00 CSF £44.93 CT £99.87 TOTE £8.00: £1.90, £2.60, £1.10; EX 55.10.
Owner Bill Brown & Ian Brown **Bred** G Davey & Exors Of The Late J Davey **Trained** Radlett, Herts

FOCUS
A competitive handicap run at a good gallop – four of the first six were at the back of the field turning in.
Fiancee(IRE) Official explanation: jockey said filly hung badly right
T/Plt: £125.50 to a £1 stake. Pool:£82,042 - 477.05 winning tickets T/Qpdt: £27 to a £1 stake. Pool:£7,905 - 216.60 winning tickets SP

7030 - 7031a (Foreign Racing) - See Raceform Interactive

GEELONG (L-H)

Wednesday, October 20

OFFICIAL GOING: Turf: good to soft

7032a CENTREBET.COM GEELONG CUP (GROUP 3 H'CAP) (3YO+) (TURF) 1m 4f 7y

6:00 (12:00) 3-Y-O+

£83,333 (£22,500; £11,250; £5,625; £3,125; £2,500)

RPR

1 **Americain (USA)**[59] 5349 5-9-2 0 GeraldMosse 1 116
(A De Royer-Dupre, France) *settled 5th on rail: shuffled bk and nowhere to go fr 3f out: 10th and travelling strly fnl turn but bhd wall of horses: blocked st: swtchd off rail and checked appr 1f out: wnt through gap and qcknd to ld fnl 110yds* **10/1**

2 *hd* **Moudre (AUS)**[11] 6766 5-8-8 0 (b) CraigAWilliams 10 108
(Ciaron Maher, Australia) *settled towards rr: hdwy on outside over 3f out: c wd into st in abt 8th pl: r.o u.p to ld 1f out: hdd fnl 110yds: no ex* **9/2**[1]

3 *1/2* **Exceptionally (NZ)**[17] 4-8-6 0 ow1 DannyNikolic 3 107
(Terry & Karina O'Sullivan, Australia) *racd in midfield: 7th 3 1/2f out: swtchd outside and bmpd Count Encosta: styd on u.str.p to take 3rd ins fnl 110yds* **11/2**[3]

4 *1/2* **Mr Charlie (NZ)**[18] 5-8-5 0 (b) LukeNolen 2 103
(Peter G Moody, Australia) *racd in midfield travelling strly on rail: lost pl 4f out: 11th 3f out but stl gng wl: trckd wnr rnd fnl bnd: short of room 1f out: gap c ins fnl f: styd on but nt qckn fnl 100yds* **7/1**

5 *shd* **Macedonian (NZ)**[18] 5-8-5 0 (b) DwayneDunn 4 103
(Peter G Moody, Australia) *settled in middle 3rd: rapid hdwy on outside 4f out and pressed two ldrs fr 3 1/2f out: in line of three outside Miles Above and The Hombre 3f out: led 1 1/2f out tl hdd 1f out: kpt on at one pce u.str driving* **50/1**

6 *nk* **Count Encosta (AUS)**[18] 4-8-5 0 (p) CraigNewitt 13 105
(John P Thompson, Australia) *w.w in fnl 4: mde grnd on outside 3f out: c 8 wd into st: bmpd by Exceptionally but styd on to be nrest at fin* **12/1**

7 *3/4* **Saint Encosta (AUS)**[18] 4-8-6 0 ow1 (b) JamesWinks 8 105
(John P Thompson, Australia) *hld up towards rr: 14th st (1 1/2f out): plld wd and styd on wout ever threatening* **80/1**

8 *1* **Once Were Wild (AUS)**[18] 4-8-9 0 NashRawiller 5 106
(Gai Waterhouse, Australia) *a.p: on heels of ldng trio turning for home: twice denied a run appr fnl f: kpt on* **13/2**

9 2 **Apprehend (AUS)**[11] 6766 5-8-5 **0**..............................(t) JasonMaskiell 6 97
(Tony Vasil, Australia) *chsd ldrs (4th or 5th much of the way): rdn and nt qckn 1 1/2f out: wknd fnl f* **30/1**

10 ¾ **The Hombre (AUS)**[18] 4-8-5 **0**.................................... MarkDuPlessis 7 98
(John Bary, New Zealand) *led early: hdd after1 1/2f: jnd ldr 3 1/2f out: in middle of line of 3 outside Miles Above and ins Macedonian 3f out: led briefly st (1 1/2f out) but sn rdn and wknd* **9/1**

11 ½ **Drunken Sailor (IRE)**[53] 5517 5-9-0 **0**..........................(b) BrettPrebble 9 104
(L M Cumani) *hld up: hdwy on outside 4f out: 4th on outside fnl turn: rdn and nt qckn immediately whn squeezed out by Moudre and Macedonian appr fnl f: sn btn* **5/1**[2]

12 1 **Gallant Lady (AUS)**[193] 4-8-5 **0**......................................(t) BlakeShinn 11 95
(Lee Freedman, Australia) *towards rr: hdwy into midfield 3f out: wknd st* **20/1**

13 ¾ **No Wine No Song (AUS)**[18] 9-9-0 **0**..........................(b) JimCassidy 14 101
(Kevin Moses, Australia) *a bhd: pushed along fr 3f out: nvr figured* **20/1**

14 1 ¾ **Miles Above (AUS)**[732] 5-8-5 **0**......................................(bt) GlenBoss 12 89
(Denis Daffy, Australia) *2nd early: pushed up to ld after 1 1/2f: jnd 3 1/2f out: on ins of The Hombre and Macedonian 3f out: hdd st: sn wknd* **30/1**

15 shd **Kerdem (IRE)**[226] 7-8-5 **0**..(t) MichellePayne 15 89
(Patrick Payne, Australia) *a bhd: nvr a factor* **100/1**

2m 30.35s (150.35) **15** Ran SP% **123.0**
PARI-MUTUEL (NSW TAB - all including au$1 stakes): WIN 12.20 PLACE 4.00, 2.10, 2.50; DF 36.50 SF 79.20.
Owner G T Ryan, K L Bamford, & Mrs C O Bamford **Bred** Wertheimer Et Frere **Trained** Chantilly, France

NOTEBOOK
Americain(USA), having his first run since late August, got trapped in as the field rounded the home bend but managed to find a clear passage and get to the front in time. This was a fine performance under top weight, a feat not matched in this race for quite some time. A horse specifically purchased by his owner for the Melbourne Cup after proving unsuccessful in America, the handicapper has handed him a 0.5kg penalty for the Melbourne Cup, a race he was already assured of getting in, but he looks sure to have a leading chance at Flemington.
Drunken Sailor(IRE), who really needed to win this so he could make the line-up at Flemington in early November, came with a good effort as the tempo increased, one that looked as though it could take him to the front, but it soon petered out. The horse returned with a bloodstained near-fore hoof.

6858 BRIGHTON (L-H)

Thursday, October 21

OFFICIAL GOING: Good
All races on inner line and distances as advertised.
Wind: Light, half against Weather: Sunny

7033 RYAN MOORE THREE CLASSIC WINS 2010 H'CAP — 5f 213y
2:00 (2:00) (Class 4) (0-80,80) 3-Y-O+ **£4,533** (£1,348; £674; £336) **Stalls** Low

Form RPR

3605 1 **Viking Spirit**[10] 6798 8-9-2 **75**.. LukeMorris 14 84+
(W R Swinburn) *dwlt: bhd: hdwy and hmpd over 1f out: drvn to ld nr fin* **14/1**

0031 2 nk **Earlsmedic**[24] 6421 5-8-13 **72**...................................(v) WilliamCarson 15 80
(S C Williams) *mid-div: rdn and hdwy over 1f out: led ins fnl f: kpt on u.p: hdd nr fin* **6/1**[2]

0622 3 ¾ **Imprimis Tagula (IRE)**[17] 6625 6-8-9 **75**.......................(v) HobieGill(7) 2 81
(A Bailey) *mid-div on rail: outpcd 4f out: hdwy over 2f out: disp ld over 1f out tl ins fnl f: nt qckn fnl 50yds* **15/2**

5204 4 hd **Kensington (IRE)**[10] 6812 9-8-4 **66** oh1........................ MartinLane(3) 1 71
(A J McCabe) *led tl over 2f out: hrd rdn and ev ch ins fnl f: one pce* **16/1**

5020 5 ¾ **Fly Silca Fly (IRE)**[6] 6887 3-9-6 **80**............................... ChrisCatlin 7 83
(M R Channon) *hmpd s: bhd: rdn 4f out: r.o fr over 1f out: nvr nrr* **14/1**

0-10 6 1 ¼ **Elusive Hawk (IRE)**[33] 6198 6-9-0 **73**........................ TomQueally 10 72
(B J Curley) *w ldrs: disp ld over 1f out tl wknd ins fnl f* **12/1**

3215 7 1 ½ **Timeteam (IRE)**[23] 6439 4-9-4 **77**...................................... RyanMoore 4 71
(G L Moore) *s.s: bhd: rdn over 2f out: sme hdwy on far rail over 1f out: nt rch ldrs* **16/1**

-100 8 nse **Highland Quaich**[33] 6204 3-9-4 **78**.................................. DaneO'Neill 5 72
(D R C Elsworth) *t.k.h: chsd ldrs tl hrd rdn and no ex over 1f out* **16/1**

1211 9 4 **Kinigi (IRE)**[7] 6858 4-8-12 **74** 6ex.....................(b) AndrewHeffernan(3) 12 55
(R A Harris) *chsd ldrs on outer: hrd rdn and wknd over 1f out* **4/1**[1]

0-21 10 1 **Zip Lock (IRE)**[21] 6496 4-9-7 **80**................................... DarryllHolland 6 58
(J Noseda) *chsd ldrs 4f: hrd rdn and btn whn n.m.r over 1f out* **7/1**[3]

0031 11 1 ½ **Tamarind Hill (IRE)**[7] 6880 3-8-1 **66** 6ex.............(b) DeclanCannon(5) 11 39
(A J McCabe) *chsd ldrs 3f: sn lost pl* **12/1**

5143 12 2 ½ **Billy Red**[49] 5678 6-9-4 **77**..(b) FergusSweeney 9 42
(J R Jenkins) *w ldr: led over 2f out tl wknd qckly over 1f out* **14/1**

1214 13 10 **Desperate Dan**[64] 5212 9-9-4 **77**.......................................(v) NeilCallan 8 10
(A B Haynes) *mid-div tl drvn along and wknd 2f out* **14/1**

1m 10.92s (0.72) **Going Correction** +0.075s/f (Good)
WFA 3 from 4yo+ 1lb **13** Ran SP% **118.2**
Speed ratings (Par 105): **98,97,96,96,95 93,91,91,86,84 82,79,66**
toteswingers: 1&2 £11.10, 1&3 £18.80, 2&3 £11.60. CSF £94.79 CT £711.57 TOTE £11.70: £3.80, £2.90, £3.10; EX 92.70 TRIFECTA Not won..
Owner The Masterminds **Bred** Bearstone Stud **Trained** Aldbury, Herts

FOCUS
A fair sprint handicap in which most of the runners raced slightly away from the inside rail, though one did stick close to it. The first three came from well off the pace. The winner finally took advantage of a sliding mark.
Billy Red Official explanation: jockey said gelding had no more to give

7034 TARPAN VODKA MEDIAN AUCTION MAIDEN STKS — 6f 209y
2:30 (2:30) (Class 5) 2-Y-O **£2,266** (£674; £337; £168) **Stalls** Low

Form RPR

56 1 **My Vindication (USA)**[14] 6689 2-9-3 .... RyanMoore 10 70
(R Hannon) *chsd ldrs: hrd rdn and hung lft 2f out: led ins fnl f: drvn out* **5/2**[1]

03 2 ½ **Labore**[19] 6569 2-9-3 .... NeilCallan 9 69
(M Botti) *pressed ldr: led over 2f out tl over 1f out: hrd rdn and ev ch ins fnl f: r.o* **6/1**[3]

4003 3 ½ **Captain Sharpe**[7] 6859 2-9-3 55.................................... LukeMorris 2 67
(H J L Dunlop) *prom: hrd rdn 2f out: kpt on fnl f* **10/1**

06 4 1 ¼ **Street Band (IRE)**[22] 6465 2-9-3 .... DaneO'Neill 4 64
(H Candy) *led tl over 2f out: slt ld over 1f out tl no ex ins fnl f* **6/1**[3]

00 5 4 ½ **Sandtail (IRE)**[31] 6247 2-8-12 .... SebSanders 3 47
(J W Hills) *mid-div: mod effrt 2f out: no imp* **22/1**

0 6 2 ½ **Plug In Baby**[10] 6804 2-8-9 .... RobertLButler(3) 7 41
(Nick Mitchell) *stdd s: bhd: rdn 3f out: nvr nr ldrs* **150/1**

4 7 12 **Norse Wing**[52] 5583 2-8-12 .... JimCrowley 8 10
(R M Beckett) *mid-div tl wknd over 2f out* **10/3**[2]

0 8 9 **Awesome Asset (USA)**[118] 3411 2-8-12 .... DarryllHolland 6 —
(J Noseda) *a towards rr: rdn and bhd fnl 3f* **10/1**

405 9 8 **Rowan Ridge**[52] 5587 2-9-3 75.. PatCosgrave 5 —
(J R Boyle) *nvr gng wl: in tch tl wknd over 2f out: eased whn no ch wl over 1f out* **9/1**

1m 24.37s (1.27) **Going Correction** +0.075s/f (Good) **9** Ran SP% **113.4**
Speed ratings (Par 95): **95,94,93,92,87 84,70,60,51**
toteswingers: 1&2 £2.80, 1&3 £5.50, 2&3 £4.70. CSF £17.53 TOTE £3.20: £1.40, £2.50, £2.20; EX 21.50 Trifecta £171.10 Pool: £374.70 - 1.62 winning units..
Owner Sir David Seale **Bred** Peter E Blum & Gerry Dilger **Trained** East Everleigh, Wilts

FOCUS
An ordinary maiden with several hanging on the track, a couple disappointing, and there were four in a line 50yds from the post.

NOTEBOOK
My Vindication(USA) was taking on much easier company than on his first two starts, but a win here looked very unlikely as he didn't respond immediately when ridden on the wide outside passing the 2f pole. However, he eventually found his stride and flew home to lead around 50yds out. His pedigree could make him of even more interest on sand. (op 7-2)
Labore, third in a weak-looking Redcar maiden earlier this month, had every chance but hung about over a furlong out and, although he ran on, the winner was finishing much quicker. Ordinary handicaps look to be his future. (op 11-2 tchd 9-2)
Captain Sharpe, officially rated 70 and third of 11 at 100-1 in a similar event over a furlong further here the previous week, was close enough if good enough but he too hung all over the place throughout the last 2f and lacks anything in the way of scope. (op 12-1)
Street Band(IRE) showed ability on his second start and was bred to appreciate this extra furlong. Soon in front, he looked to have shaken off his nearest pursuers a furlong out, but he started to struggle and was run right out of it in the last 50yds. He now qualifies for nurseries. (op 11-2 tchd 5-1)
Sandtail(IRE), unplaced at 100-1 on her first two starts, plugged on from off the pace and may do better now that she gets a mark. (op 25-1)
Norse Wing, a staying-on fourth of ten over 1m on her Bath debut in August, was beaten over 2f from home though the drop in trip may not have been ideal. (op 11-4 tchd 7-2)
Awesome Asset(USA) was disappointing and her absence since finishing a well-beaten third favourite on debut at Newmarket in June now looks more than a coincidence. She was reported to have been unsuited by the track. Official explanation: trainer said filly was unsuited by the track (op 8-1)

7035 BRITVIC SOFT DRINKS NURSERY — 6f 209y
3:05 (3:05) (Class 5) (0-75,76) 2-Y-O **£2,266** (£674; £337; £168) **Stalls** Low

Form RPR

5550 1 **Crown Ridge (IRE)**[6] 6891 2-8-1 **53**................................ CathyGannon 7 60
(M R Channon) *dwlt: bhd: rdn 5f out: gd hdwy over 1f out: disp ld fnl 100yds: jst prevailed* **10/1**

2052 2 nse **Falkland Flyer (IRE)**[6] 6902 2-9-1 **67**............................. SamHitchcott 6 74
(M R Channon) *mid-div: rdn and hdwy 2f out: slt ld ins fnl f: disp ld fnl 100yds: jst pipped* **4/1**[2]

4435 3 2 ¼ **Cathcart Castle**[24] 6426 2-8-5 **60**........................ AndrewHeffernan(3) 9 61
(M R Channon) *hld up in tch: rdn to join ldrs 2f out: nvr got on top: fdd fnl 100yds* **10/1**

0000 4 1 ¼ **Hero From Zero (IRE)**[7] 6875 2-8-13 **65**..................(b[1]) HayleyTurner 11 63
(B J Meehan) *mid-div: rdn and hdwy over 2f out: swtchd rt over 1f out: styd on fnl f* **50/1**

0014 5 1 ¼ **Ebony Song (USA)**[7] 6870 2-9-2 **68**.............................(t) DarryllHolland 3 63
(J Noseda) *chsd ldrs: pushed along after 2f: one pce fnl 2f* **5/1**[3]

6444 6 ¾ **Fimias (IRE)**[7] 6875 2-9-2 **68**... KierenFallon 5 61
(L M Cumani) *sn led: wnt rt 2f out: hdd & wknd ins fnl f* **7/2**[1]

0205 7 2 **Pick A Little**[12] 6745 2-9-0 **69**.................................... RobertLButler(3) 15 57
(B W Duke) *bhd: hrd rdn over 2f out: sme late hdwy wd of others on stands' rail: nvr rchd ldrs* **33/1**

2400 8 nse **Summer Jasmine**[20] 6521 2-8-4 **56**.............................. LukeMorris 10 43
(H J L Dunlop) *bhd: rdn and sme hdwy 2f out: n.d* **66/1**

3424 9 4 **High On The Hog (IRE)**[48] 5709 2-8-12 **67**.. Louis-PhilippeBeuzelin(3) 4 44
(J L Dunlop) *a towards rr: drvn along and n.d fnl 2f* **12/1**

0652 10 1 ¼ **Uncle Dermot (IRE)**[11] 6777 2-9-1 **67**............................ DaneO'Neill 1 41
(B G Powell) *s.s: bhd: rdn and sme hdwy on ins 2f out: no further prog* **14/1**

135 11 3 ¾ **Fluvial (IRE)**[31] 6259 2-9-6 **72**.. AhmedAjtebi 2 36
(Mahmood Al Zarooni) *chsd ldrs: hrd rdn 2f out: wknd over 1f out: eased whn no ch fnl f* **12/1**

0400 12 3 ¾ **Velvet Underground (IRE)**[25] 6386 2-9-7 **73**...............(b) ShaneKelly 8 27
(B J Meehan) *prom: rdn whn hmpd and lost pl 2f out: nt rcvr* **20/1**

530 13 ½ **Mishtaag**[22] 6465 2-9-5 **71**.. ChrisCatlin 16 24
(C E Brittain) *prom: rdn whn hmpd and lost pl 2f out: nt rcvr* **12/1**

1m 24.49s (1.39) **Going Correction** +0.075s/f (Good) **13** Ran SP% **118.0**
Speed ratings (Par 95): **95,94,92,90,89 88,86,86,81,80 76,71,71**
toteswingers: 1&2 £13.70, 1&3 £19.80, 2&3 £11.80. CSF £47.73 CT £419.98 TOTE £11.00: £2.90, £2.10, £2.80; EX 54.20 Trifecta £207.10 Part won. Pool: £279.96 - 0.73 winning units..
Owner Box 41 **Bred** Pat Grogan **Trained** West Ilsley, Berks

FOCUS
A competitive nursery, but a messy race. The field came more towards the centre of the track than in the previous contests, but again several hung and they ended up all over the track. It resulted in a 1-2-3 for trainer Mick Channon.

NOTEBOOK
Crown Ridge(IRE) didn't appear to get home when tried over this trip for the first time at Redcar six stays earlier, but he certainly had to stay this time. He was out the back and seemingly going nowhere for a long way, but picked up on meeting the rising ground and stole the race from the runner-up right on the line to break his duck at the 12th attempt. (op 16-1)
Falkland Flyer(IRE), in the same ownership as the winner and 2lb lower than when beaten a whisker at Wolverhampton six days earlier, looked to have timed his effort just right until mugged right on the line. He is already due to go up 5lb, which won't help. (op 5-1)
Cathcart Castle was always close to the pace on the wide outside and had every chance, but hung away to his left inside the last 2f and was run out of it. He is running consistently well in defeat. (op 17-2)
Hero From Zero(IRE) had run poorly since a promising debut and was tried in blinkers, but performed a bit better here especially as he was under the cosh a long way out. (op 40-1)
Ebony Song(USA) had excuses last time and had previously proved his effectiveness here when winning a maiden over C&D. He was another to keep on despite coming under a ride a fair way out. (tchd 9-2 and 11-2)

Fimias(IRE) has lacked finishing pace in his previous outings so was given a positive ride from the start, but he hung badly away to his right over 2f out and was then carried back down the camber by the hanging Cathcart Castle once beaten. He looks one to have serious reservations about. (op 9-2 tchd 3-1)
High On The Hog(IRE) was reported to have never been travelling. Official explanation: jockey said colt never travelled

7036 EUROPEAN BREEDERS' FUND MAIDEN STKS 7f 214y
3:35 (3:35) (Class 5) 2-Y-O **£3,561** (£1,059; £529; £264) **Stalls** Low

Form RPR
2 **1** **Maywood**[12] 6743 2-9-3 0 AhmedAjtebi 2 81
(Mahmood Al Zarooni) *hld up in tch: smooth hdwy to join ldr 3f out: led over 1f out: rdn out* **13/2**
5242 **2** 1 ¾ **Choral**[17] 6634 2-8-12 73 RyanMoore 9 72
(R Hannon) *in tch: lost pl 5f out: rallied 2f out: chsd wnr 1f out: kpt on: a hld* **9/2**[3]
222 **3** 2 ¼ **Tiger Webb**[28] 6305 2-9-3 79 TomQueally 8 72
(H R A Cecil) *chsd ldrs: rdn over 3f out: one pce fnl f* **2/1**[1]
3236 **4** 1 ½ **Buckland (IRE)**[15] 6670 2-9-3 83 KierenFallon 5 68
(B J Meehan) *led: drvn along and hdd over 1f out: no ex fnl f* **9/4**[2]
65 **5** 5 **Undulant Way**[21] 6511 2-8-12 0 NeilCallan 1 52
(Mrs A J Perrett) *t.k.h: prom tl wknd over 1f out* **10/1**
000 **6** 6 **Kepler's Law**[7] 6874 2-9-3 0 SebSanders 10 43+
(Sir Mark Prescott) *bhd: rdn 3f out: nvr nr ldrs* **80/1**
50 **7** 4 **Trend (IRE)**[17] 6634 2-9-3 0 HayleyTurner 6 34
(M L W Bell) *a bhd: no ch fnl 3f* **25/1**
4 **8** ½ **Iron Step**[11] 6779 2-9-3 0 JimCrowley 3 33
(E A L Dunlop) *a towards rr: rdn and bhd fnl 3f* **33/1**
056 **9** 21 **Jeeran**[21] 6504 2-9-3 77 ChrisCatlin 7 —
(C E Brittain) *prom: rdn 4f out: wknd 3f out* **33/1**

1m 36.49s (0.49) **Going Correction** +0.075s/f (Good) 9 Ran SP% 115.7
Speed ratings (Par 95): **100,98,96,94,89 83,79,79,58**
toteswingers: 1&2 £4.30, 1&3 £3.90, 2&3 £1.80. CSF £34.70 TOTE £9.60: £2.70, £1.30, £1.10; EX 36.10 Trifecta £102.20 Pool: £744.79 - 5.39 winning units..
Owner Godolphin **Bred** Wood Hall Stud Limited **Trained** Newmarket, Suffolk

FOCUS
Just a fair maiden in which it paid to race handily and the pace was decent. This time the runners made a beeline for the nearside rail after straightening up.

NOTEBOOK
Maywood had been beaten a nose on his Wolverhampton debut 12 days earlier, so his starting price looked generous based on that. Content to track the pace, he was produced to hit the front over a furlong out and ran straight and true to the line. Although not the best Godolphin colt in training, he is expected to make up into an even better 3-y-o and should win more races. (op 5-1 tchd 7-1)
Choral, rated 77 after showing plenty of ability in turf/Polytrack maidens, did best of those held up and made her effort much wider than the other principals, who came up the stands' rail. This was another creditable effort, but she doesn't seem to be progressing. (op 5-1 tchd 11-2)
Tiger Webb, rated 79 after finishing runner-up in his first three starts (the last two as a short-priced favourite), had to be shoved along to take closer order 3f from home and could only stay on at one pace. He is starting to run out of excuses. (op 9-4)
Buckland(IRE), rated 83, set a solid pace from the start but was starting to hang away from the nearside rail over a furlong out and was soon headed. He hasn't built on early promise, including in headgear, so it's hard to know where he goes from here. (op 11-4tchd 3-1 in a place)
Undulant Way again ran with some promise and looks the type to improve in nurseries. (op 12-1)

7037 BRAKES FOR FRESH IDEAS H'CAP 7f 214y
4:05 (4:05) (Class 6) (0-65,66) 3-Y-O+ **£1,942** (£578; £288; £144) **Stalls** Low

Form RPR
5230 **1** **Leitzu (IRE)**[34] 6144 3-9-2 60 ChrisCatlin 2 68
(M R Channon) *in tch: effrt on outer 2f out: led 1f out: drvn out* **11/1**
0020 **2** ½ **Ice Cool Lady (IRE)**[20] 6540 3-9-7 65 (v) LukeMorris 13 72
(W R Swinburn) *prom: rdn over 2f out: hung lft and outpcd over 1f out: rallied to take 2nd nr fin* **25/1**
0046 **3** 1 ½ **Chateau Zara**[7] 6863 3-8-11 55 SebSanders 3 58
(C G Cox) *prom: led over 2f out: hrd rdn and hdd 1f out: one pce* **17/2**
0543 **4** ½ **Collect Art (IRE)**[24] 6413 3-9-5 63 StevieDonohoe 10 65+
(A B Haynes) *stdd s: t.k.h in rr: drvn along and r.o fnl 2f: nrst fin* **17/2**
6506 **5** ½ **Transfixed (IRE)**[2] 7005 3-8-10 54 CathyGannon 4 55
(P D Evans) *w ldrs tl no ex fnl f* **25/1**
3651 **6** ½ **Daddy's Gift (IRE)**[7] 6864 4-9-11 66 6ex RyanMoore 8 66
(R Hannon) *towards rr: hdwy and n.m.r over 1f out: no imp fnl f* **6/1**[2]
0230 **7** hd **Isabella Romee (IRE)**[30] 6269 4-8-4 52 LewisWalsh(7) 14 51
(Jane Chapple-Hyam) *dwlt: sn in tch on outer: hrd rdn 2f out: styd on same pce* **9/1**
1152 **8** 1 **Fire King**[48] 5710 4-9-4 59 (p) NeilCallan 11 56
(A B Haynes) *hld up in midfield: rdn and hung lft 2f out: no imp* **3/1**[1]
4000 **9** 1 ½ **Chantilly Dancer (IRE)**[69] 5039 4-8-4 48 oh3 Louis-PhilippeBeuzelin(3) 6 42
(M Quinn) *towards rr: rdn 3f out: hdwy 2f out: no ex fnl f* **50/1**
0001 **10** 1 ¼ **Goodbye Cash (IRE)**[15] 6672 6-9-0 58 AndrewHeffernan(3) 9 49
(R J Smith) *led tl over 2f out: hrd rdn and wknd over 1f out* **16/1**
5402 **11** ½ **Whisper Wind**[7] 6863 3-8-10 57 (b) MartinLane(3) 5 47
(G L Moore) *dwlt: a in rr gp: drvn along and n.d fnl 2f* **15/2**[3]
0012 **12** 2 ¾ **Signora Frasi (IRE)**[40] 5962 5-9-5 60 FergusSweeney 1 43
(A G Newcombe) *towards rr: sme hdwy 5f out: wknd 2f out* **12/1**
0460 **13** ¾ **Miss Kitty Grey (IRE)**[37] 6061 3-8-7 58 NathanAlison(7) 7 40
(J R Boyle) *bhd: mod effrt on ins 2f out: sn wknd* **50/1**

1m 37.04s (1.04) **Going Correction** +0.075s/f (Good)
WFA 3 from 4yo+ 3lb 13 Ran SP% 115.6
Speed ratings (Par 101): **97,96,95,94,94 93,93,92,90,89 89,86,85**
toteswinger: 1&2 £49.60, 1&3 £28.70, 2&3 £41.00. CSF £260.99 CT £2498.44 TOTE £12.70: £3.60, £9.90, £2.40; EX 263.90 Trifecta £221.70 Part won. Pool: £299.69 - 0.20 winning units..
Owner Upsan Downs Racing **Bred** Newhall Ltd **Trained** West Ilsley, Berks

FOCUS
A modest handicap. The field came up the centre of the track turning for home, though they all eventually edged back towards the inside rail. The winner is rated to this year's form.
Daddy's Gift(IRE) Official explanation: jockey said filly was denied a clear run

7038 TARPAN VODKA H'CAP 1m 1f 209y
4:40 (4:40) (Class 6) (0-65,65) 3-Y-O+ **£1,942** (£578; £288; £144) **Stalls** High

Form RPR
3062 **1** **Catbells (IRE)**[7] 6860 3-8-10 56 (p) CathyGannon 3 72
(A Bailey) *t.k.h: trckd ldrs: led over 4f out: drvn clr 2f out: readily* **9/4**[1]
3206 **2** 7 **Mayfair's Future**[38] 6021 5-8-10 51 oh1 (p) NeilCallan 1 53
(J R Jenkins) *prom: wnt 2nd 2f out: nt pce of wnr* **17/2**
6050 **3** 3 ½ **Merrymadcap (IRE)**[71] 4958 8-9-0 60 AdamBeschizza(5) 5 55
(Matthew Salaman) *chsd ldrs: outpcd and struggling to hold pl 3f out: styd on same pce to take mod 3rd over 1f out* **10/1**
5244 **4** 1 **Little Meadow (IRE)**[7] 6863 3-8-0 51 AmyBaker(5) 7 44
(Miss J Feilden) *bhd: hdwy and nt clr run over 2f out: swtchd outside: hung lft and styd on same pce: nvr nr to chal* **10/1**
400 **5** 2 ½ **Rezwaan**[17] 6632 3-9-0 65 (v[1]) DeclanCannon(5) 8 53
(M J McGrath) *t.k.h towards rr: rdn and hdwy over 2f out: hung lft and wknd wl over 1f out* **40/1**
4020 **6** shd **Quality Mover (USA)**[20] 6527 3-9-0 63 MartinLane(3) 9 51
(D M Simcock) *dwlt: bhd: rdn over 3f out: mod hdwy 2f out: n.d* **12/1**
2 **7** 17 **Timocracy**[50] 5148 5-9-10 65 StevieDonohoe 2 19
(A B Haynes) *slt ld tl over 4f out: sn rdn: wknd 2f out: eased whn wl btn* **15/2**[3]
6256 **8** 2 ¼ **Santa Margherita**[14] 6691 3-9-3 63 SebSanders 4 12
(H J L Dunlop) *w ldrs tl edgd lft and wknd over 2f out: eased whn no ch over 1f out* **14/1**
4244 **9** 11 **Prince Valentine**[7] 6860 9-8-10 51 oh4 (p) AmirQuinn 10 —
(G L Moore) *hld up in midfield: rdn over 3f out: wknd over 2f out* **33/1**
1215 **10** 19 **Baoli**[45] 5812 3-9-5 65 KierenFallon 6 —
(L M Cumani) *dwlt: sn chsng ldrs: rdn over 4f out: wknd over 2f out* **7/2**[2]

2m 4.09s (0.49) **Going Correction** +0.075s/f (Good)
WFA 3 from 5yo+ 5lb 10 Ran SP% 113.2
Speed ratings (Par 101): **101,95,92,91,89 89,76,74,65,50**
toteswingers: 1&2 £6.00, 1&3 £6.20, 2&3 £14.30. CSF £21.38 CT £157.02 TOTE £3.60: £1.30, £2.60, £2.90; EX 31.00 Trifecta £114.30 Pool: £488.16 - 3.16 winning units..
Owner C M & Mrs S A Martin **Bred** Mrs Mary Rose Hayes **Trained** Newmarket, Suffolk

FOCUS
nother modest handicap and a one-horse race, with Catbells probably bettering last week's C/D run.
Santa Margherita Official explanation: jockey said filly lost its action

7039 BOOK YOUR CHRISTMAS ROYALE PARTY NOW APPRENTICE H'CAP 1m 3f 196y
5:10 (5:10) (Class 6) (0-55,55) 3-Y-O+ **£1,942** (£578; £288; £144) **Stalls** High

Form RPR
30 **1** **Derby Desire (IRE)**[15] 6671 6-9-3 52 JamesRogers(3) 12 61
(D Donovan) *trckd ldrs: led 2f out: hld on wl: rdn out* **33/1**
1436 **2** nk **Dovedon Angel**[50] 5663 4-9-2 48 DeclanCannon 7 56
(Miss Gay Kelleway) *hld up towards rr: hdwy to ld on outer 3f out: hdd 2f out: kpt on: chalng to line: jst hld* **8/1**
5055 **3** 5 **Always De One**[134] 2878 3-8-10 49 AdamBeschizza 10 49
(Miss J Feilden) *in tch: hrd rdn over 2f out: wnt 3rd over 1f out: nt pce of ldng pair* **20/1**
3045 **4** 2 ½ **Rose Aurora**[2] 6999 3-8-3 47 (v) KatiaScallan(5) 1 43
(M P Tregoning) *prom: nt clr run 3f out: swtchd rt over 2f out: one pce* **6/1**[3]
4300 **5** ¾ **Iguacu**[16] 6662 6-9-1 47 (p) AshleyMorgan 14 42
(George Baker) *in tch: hrd rdn over 2f out: sn outpcd* **10/1**
652 **6** 1 ¼ **Court Wing (IRE)**[16] 6660 4-9-1 47 TobyAtkinson 5 40
(R J Price) *mid-div: drvn along 3f out: styd on same pce: hung lft: nvr able to chal* **14/1**
0530 **7** 2 ½ **Lovely Eyes (IRE)**[20] 6526 3-8-9 55 AliceHaynes(7) 2 50+
(D M Simcock) *hld up towards rr: sme hdwy whn hmpd 3f out: fair 6th and styng on whn bdly hmpd on rail wl over 1f out: no ch after* **8/1**
0254 **8** 1 ¾ **Quince (IRE)**[15] 6669 7-9-2 53 (v) SophieSilvester(5) 5 39
(J Pearce) *bhd: sme hdwy 2f out: n.d* **9/1**
5443 **9** 1 ¾ **Carnac (IRE)**[8] 6855 4-9-2 51 (b) NeilFarley(3) 13 34
(A J McCabe) *chsd ldrs: rdn 4f out: wknd over 2f out* **9/2**[1]
3023 **10** 4 **Firehawk**[12] 6747 3-8-10 54 MatthewCosham(5) 4 31
(P D Evans) *led tl 3f out: 5th and wkng whn edgd lft wl over 1f out* **5/1**[2]
0505 **11** ½ **Foxtrot Bravo (IRE)**[17] 6637 4-8-13 45 (b) AmyBaker 11 21
(Miss S L Davison) *a towards rr: n.d fnl 3f* **22/1**
0360 **12** 6 **Blue Zealot (IRE)**[41] 5923 3-8-4 48 (v[1]) IanBurns(5) 9 15
(M L W Bell) *prom tl wknd 5f out* **14/1**
4-00 **13** 33 **Spanish Cross (IRE)**[16] 6661 5-8-8 47 RichardOld(7) 8 —
(G Prodromou) *lost 10 l at the s and rdr lost iron: a wl bhd: t.o fnl 4f* **66/1**

2m 35.73s (3.03) **Going Correction** +0.075s/f (Good)
WFA 3 from 4yo+ 7lb 13 Ran SP% 117.3
Speed ratings (Par 101): **92,91,88,86,86 85,83,82,81,78 78,74,52**
toteswingers: 1&2 £70.60, 1&3 £43.80, 2&3 £22.30. CSF £266.81 CT £5368.72 TOTE £49.10: £12.70, £2.40, £8.10; EX 242.50 TRIFECTA Not won. Place 6: £289.55, Place 5: £87.66..
Owner River Racing **Bred** Miss Ann Hennessy **Trained** Newmarket, Suffolk

FOCUS
A moderate race with eight of the 13 runners maidens coming into it and the form is difficult form to gauge.
Spanish Cross(IRE) Official explanation: jockey said mare stumbled on leaving stalls causing him to lose irons
T/Jkpt: Not won. T/Plt: £654.00 to a £1 stake. Pool:£76,091.07 - 84.93 winning tickets T/Qpdt: £112.00 to a £1 stake. Pool:£7,705.15 - 50.90 winning tickets LM

7016 KEMPTON (A.W) (R-H)
Thursday, October 21

OFFICIAL GOING: Standard
Wind: Moderate across Weather: Dry

7040 BET EUROPA LEAGUE FOOTBALL - BETDAQ CLAIMING STKS 5f (P)
5:40 (5:43) (Class 6) 2-Y-O **£1,637** (£483; £241) **Stalls** High

Form RPR
2312 **1** **Chevise (IRE)**[8] 6842 2-9-2 75 (t) JimCrowley 11 73
(R M Beckett) *s.i.s: in rr tl drvn and gd hdwy appr fnl f: str run to ld fnl 50yds: won gng away* **1/1**[1]
4200 **2** ¾ **Volcanic Dust (IRE)**[23] 6435 2-9-2 66 WilliamBuick 12 70
(E A L Dunlop) *hld up towards rr but in tch: drvn and gd hdwy over 1f out: wnt 2nd ins fnl f: qcknd to chal fnl 120yds: styd on but outpcd by wnr fnl 50yds: tk 2nd on line* **13/2**[2]
4401 **3** nse **Second Encore**[19] 6576 2-9-0 68 LiamKeniry 5 68
(J S Moore) *led: rdn over 1f out: jnd fnl 120yds: hdd and nt qcknd fnl 50yds* **12/1**
200 **4** 2 ¼ **Coconut Ice**[11] 6769 2-8-11 73 RossAtkinson(5) 10 62
(Tom Dascombe) *chsd ldrs: drvn ins fnl 2f: styd on one pce ins fnl f* **8/1**[3]
5444 **5** shd **Darwin Star**[15] 6666 2-9-2 63 JimmyQuinn 2 62
(D K Ivory) *chsd ldr: rdn over 2f out: lost 2nd ins fnl f and one pce* **16/1**

0334 **6** *shd* **Saltergate**[19] 6576 2-9-1 64 (p) PaulHanagan 9 60
(N Tinkler) *chsd ldrs: rdn 2f out: one pce appr fnl f* **20/1**

2250 **7** *shd* **Ajaafa**[12] 6745 2-8-9 67 (p) PaulMulrennan 6 54
(J G Given) *chsd ldrs: outpcd appr fnl f: kpt on again cl home* **16/1**

0440 **8** *5* **Royalorien**[24] 6426 2-9-2 67 ShaneKelly 3 43
(W J Knight) *racd on outside and in tch: chsd ldrs bnd ins fnl 2f: sn wknd* **14/1**

1100 **9** *3* **Tedious**[19] 6576 2-9-1 75 DaneO'Neill 7 31
(S Kirk) *sn bhd: eased whn no ch fnl f* **10/1**

60.13 secs (-0.37) **Going Correction** -0.20s/f (Stan) **9 Ran SP% 114.4**
Speed ratings (Par 93): **94,92,92,89,88 88,88,80,75**
toteswingers: 1&2 £2.30, 1&3 £4.30, 2&3 £5.50. CSF £7.61 TOTE £1.80: £1.10, £2.90, £5.00; EX 7.30.Ajaafa was claimed by Michael Attwater for £2,000. Chevise was claimed by Mustafa Khan for £8,000.
Owner R Roberts **Bred** Paul And Mrs Jenny Green **Trained** Whitsbury, Hants

FOCUS
Not much between the pick of the runners on adjusted official figures but several had been below-par in recent runs and it perhaps wasn't as competitive as the ratings made out. The pace was only fair with the field well bunched on the home turn.

NOTEBOOK
Chevise(IRE) was having her first run at 5f and did well to overcome a slow start and a poor position on the home turn given the early gallop, showing a good turn of foot to catch rivals that had got first run. She'll win more races if kept on the go this winter. (op 5-4)
Volcanic Dust(IRE) had a bit to do at the weights and would have preferred a stronger pace given that she was keen early (as she is inclined to be) but considering she too made her effort from a poor position, this has to go down as a respectable run. (op 6-1 tchd 5-1)
Second Encore had a bit to find with the winner on adjusted official ratings but had been good enough to land a maiden earlier in the year and gave it her best shot trying to follow up her recent selling win on Polytrack. That said, she had the run of the race and can have no excuses. (op 7-1)
Coconut Ice just won the battle for fourth despite once again running below the form she showed when second in a nursery at Musselburgh last month. (op 10-1 tchd 15-2)
Darwin Star looked to have a lot on at the weights and from a poor draw to boot, but was helped greatly by a smart break and a prominent position on the home turn. This form might turn out to flatter her. (tchd 11-1)
Saltergate had plenty to find on these terms and never threatened to play a serious role. (op 16-1)
Ajaafa showed a bit more than in his last two runs despite not impressing with his head carriage. (op 20-1)
Royalorien wasn't well drawn or helped by racing widest of all. (tchd 16-1)
Tedious ran poorly for the second time in a row and looks one to have reservations about for now. (tchd 9-1 and 11-1)

7041 BETDAQ POKER H'CAP 5f (P)
6:10 (6:12) (Class 4) (0-85,85) 3-Y-0+ **£3,885** (£1,156; £577; £288) **Stalls** High

Form RPR

0030 **1** **Piscean (USA)**[31] 6256 5-9-4 82 AdamKirby 6 99+
(T Keddy) *hld up in rr: stdy hdwy over 1f out: qcknd to ld fnl 120yds: comf* **7/1**

4506 **2** *1 ¼* **Sutton Veny (IRE)**[24] 6429 4-9-3 81 SteveDrowne 12 94
(J R Gask) *led: hrd drvn over 1f out: hdd and outpcd fnl 120yds* **5/1**[2]

0330 **3** *1 ¼* **Fair Passion**[12] 6739 3-8-11 75 DaneO'Neill 9 83
(D Shaw) *hld up towards rr: stdy hdwy fr 2f out: drvn to dispute 2nd appr fnl f: kpt on same pce* **10/1**

2000 **4** *hd* **Sir Geoffrey (IRE)**[26] 6374 4-8-11 75 (b) PJMcDonald 5 82
(J A Glover) *chsd ldr: rdn wl over 1f out: styd on same pce ins fnl f* **25/1**

0416 **5** *1* **Anne Of Kiev (IRE)**[142] 2635 5-9-3 81 (t) LukeMorris 3 85+
(J R Gask) *s.i.s: in rr tl hdwy appr fnl f: styd on wl fnl 120yds: gng on cl home* **11/1**

0-46 **6** *1 ¼* **Toms Laughter**[20] 6539 6-9-6 84 (vt[1]) PaulHanagan 7 83
(D H Brown) *s.i.s: in rr: pushed along over 1f out: kpt on wl fnl 120yds: gng on cl home* **10/1**

3164 **7** *½* **Boogie Waltzer**[12] 6739 3-8-3 74 (t) RyanClark[(7)] 11 71
(S C Williams) *chsd ldrs: rdn ins fnl 2f: wknd ins fnl f* **8/1**

6005 **8** *nk* **Lewyn**[32] 6221 3-9-7 85 (t) FergusSweeney 1 81
(K A Ryan) *chsd ldrs tl wknd fnl f* **40/1**

0455 **9** *½* **Tomintoul Singer (IRE)**[37] 6063 3-9-5 83 TomQueally 10 78
(H R A Cecil) *in tch: n.m.r on ins 1/2-way: swtchd lft to outside wl over 1f out but nvr any imp on ldrs* **6/1**[3]

5030 **10** *hd* **Sherjawy (IRE)**[2] 6997 6-8-7 71 oh1 SamHitchcott 4 65
(Miss Z C Davison) *mid-div and rdn 1/2-way: sn bhd* **20/1**

0062 **11** *½* **Living It Large (FR)**[10] 6799 3-9-4 82 (b) TedDurcan 8 77+
(R F Fisher) *spd to 1/2-way* **4/1**[1]

5200 **12** *5* **Solemn**[12] 6739 5-9-5 83 (b) LiamKeniry 2 57
(J M Bradley) *racd towards outside: a in rr* **33/1**

58.50 secs (-2.00) **Going Correction** -0.20s/f (Stan) **12 Ran SP% 115.1**
Speed ratings (Par 105): **108,106,104,103,102 100,99,98,98,97 96,88**
toteswingers: 1&2 £5.50, 1&3 £14.70, 2&3 £12.70. CSF £38.80 CT £356.19 TOTE £6.80: £2.50, £2.00, £1.90; EX 56.30.
Owner Andrew Duffield **Bred** Connie And John Iacuone **Trained** Newmarket, Suffolk

FOCUS
A competitive sprint that was run at a good pace with the result appearing the right one and no obvious hard-luck stories. Good form for the grade.
Living It Large(FR) Official explanation: jockey said, regarding running, that the colt was unable to dictate.

7042 BET MULTIPLES - BETDAQ H'CAP 1m 2f (P)
6:40 (6:42) (Class 5) (0-75,75) 3-Y-0 **£2,286** (£675; £337) **Stalls** High

Form RPR

6314 **1** **Snow Magic (IRE)**[19] 6580 3-9-3 71 PatCosgrave 6 86+
(J R Fanshawe) *hld up towards rr: hdwy and n.m.r whn swtchd lft to outside over 1f out: str run ins fnl f to ld cl home: readily* **7/1**[3]

5403 **2** *½* **Elmfield Giant (USA)**[20] 6543 3-9-2 70 PaulHanagan 2 82
(R A Fahey) *in tch: hdwy over 2f out: drvn to ld ins fnl f: hdd and outpcd cl home* **14/1**

2233 **3** *3* **Abhar (USA)**[8] 6851 3-9-4 75 KierenFox[(3)] 7 81
(J R Best) *chsd ldrs: drvn to ld wl over 1f out: hdd ins fnl f: readily outpcd by ldng duo fnl 100yds* **14/1**

1464 **4** *1* **Onyx Of Arabia (IRE)**[78] 4698 3-9-4 72 (b) ShaneKelly 1 76
(B J Meehan) *in rr: rdn and hdwy on ins fr 2f out: styd on thrght fnl f but nvr a threat* **25/1**

1000 **5** *nk* **Think Its All Over (USA)**[12] 6753 3-9-7 75 JamieSpencer 11 78
(T P Tate) *led tl hdd wl over 1f out: wknd fnl f* **12/1**

0536 **6** *1* **Streets Of War (USA)**[19] 6580 3-9-5 73 JackMitchell 3 74
(P W Chapple-Hyam) *towards rr: hdwy 3f out: drvn to chse ldrs 2f out: wl there over 1f out: wknd ins fnl f* **33/1**

1614 **7** *½* **Dhan Dhana (IRE)**[34] 6166 3-8-13 72 JohnFahy[(5)] 12 72
(W J Haggas) *chsd ldr tl ins fnl 2f: wknd over 1f out* **9/1**

6-33 **8** *nk* **Alubari**[26] 6356 3-9-4 72 AdamKirby 9 72+
(W R Swinburn) *in tch tl rdn and lost position over 3f out: styd on again u.p fnl f but nvr any ch* **9/2**[2]

5001 **9** *1 ¼* **Goodlukin Lucy**[9] 6832 3-9-6 74 6ex JimCrowley 5 71
(Pat Eddery) *towards rr: pushed along 2f out: kpt on fnl f but nvr any ch* **10/1**

4542 **10** *1 ¼* **Tamtara**[35] 6122 3-9-5 73 KierenFallon 8 71
(Mrs A J Perrett) *chsd ldrs: rdn over 2f out: wknd qckly ins fnl f* **9/1**

0031 **11** *¾* **Bakongo (IRE)**[13] 6718 3-9-6 74 HayleyTurner 10 67
(M L W Bell) *chsd ldrs tl wknd 2f out* **14/1**

4112 **12** *¾* **Destiny Blue (IRE)**[14] 6692 3-9-6 74 PaulMulrennan 14 66
(J A Osborne) *rdn and awkward bnd after 2f: styd chsng ldrs tl wknd u.p 2f out* **4/1**[1]

2054 **13** *2 ½* **Scorn (USA)**[24] 6415 3-9-4 72 (v[1]) WilliamBuick 13 59
(J H M Gosden) *bhd most of way* **16/1**

4200 **14** *13* **Thundering Home**[10] 6816 3-8-13 72 JemmaMarshall[(5)] 4 33
(M J Attwater) *rdn after s: a towards rr* **66/1**

2m 4.71s (-3.29) **Going Correction** -0.20s/f (Stan) **14 Ran SP% 121.6**
Speed ratings (Par 101): **105,104,102,101,101 100,99,99,98,97 97,96,94,84**
toteswingers: 1&2 £20.30, 1&3 £18.90, 2&3 £41.20. CSF £100.97 CT £1351.70 TOTE £7.10: £2.70, £2.10, £4.20; EX 103.90.
Owner Nigel & Carolyn Elwes **Bred** Aylesfield Farms Stud Ltd **Trained** Newmarket, Suffolk

FOCUS
A well-contested race for the grade, with plenty of recent winning form represented, and run at a good gallop so the form should stand up well. Personal bests from the first two with the fourth helping set the standard.

7043 BETDAQ ON FACEBOOK MAIDEN STKS 1m 3f (P)
7:10 (7:12) (Class 5) 3-Y-0+ **£2,286** (£675; £337) **Stalls** High

Form RPR

3620 **1** **Weathervane**[7] 6876 3-9-3 77 WilliamBuick 14 84
(J H M Gosden) *hld up in mid-div: hdwy 4f out: led ins fnl 2f: drvn and styd on strly fnl f* **5/1**[3]

0625 **2** *1 ½* **Herostatus**[16] 6661 3-9-3 79 GregFairley 10 81
(M Johnston) *in rr and rdn over 4f out: hdwy on ins over 2f out: hld hd high and sn hanging lft: styd on to chse wnr fnl f but a hld: wnt lft again cl home* **7/2**[1]

3422 **3** *1 ¾* **Mascarene (USA)**[24] 6415 3-8-12 76 RyanMoore 12 73
(Sir Michael Stoute) *mid-div: hdwy over 2f out: disp 2nd over 1f out: no imp on wnr and one pce whn carried lft cl home* **7/2**[1]

6562 **4** *6* **Stoical (IRE)**[12] 6747 3-9-3 62 DaneO'Neill 5 67
(W Jarvis) *in rr: hdwy fr 3f out: nvr nr ldrs and one pce fnl 2f* **11/1**

43- **5** *3 ¼* **Muzo (USA)**[364] 6974 4-9-9 0 FrannyNorton 6 61
(C A Dwyer) *wl behnd tl r.o fr ins fnl 2f: kpt on wl past wkng horse fnl f* **16/1**

0264 **6** *1* **Cast Of Stars (IRE)**[24] 6427 3-9-3 72 (v) JimCrowley 11 59
(R M Beckett) *trckd ldrs: led ins fnl 3f: hdd ins fnl 2f and sn wknd* **9/2**[2]

502 **7** *4 ½* **Dhaafer**[133] 2899 3-9-3 74 JamieSpencer 2 51
(A King) *in rr tl rapid hdwy to chse ldrs 7f out: wknd insde fnl 2f* **6/1**

/000 **8** *1 ¾* **Wrecking Crew (IRE)**[52] 5584 6-9-9 50 JamesMillman 8 48
(B R Millman) *in rr tl sme prog on outside 3f out: nvr anywhere nr ldrs* **66/1**

0 **9** *½* **Epsom Girl**[21] 6499 3-8-7 0 JemmaMarshall[(5)] 9 42
(P M Phelan) *chsd ldrs to 3f out: sn wknd* **66/1**

6 **10** *3 ¾* **King Of The Titans (IRE)**[63] 4348 7-9-6 0 (v[1]) AshleyHamblett[(3)] 7 40
(P L Gilligan) *led tl hdd ins fnl 3f: sn wknd* **66/1**

0-0 **11** *8* **Morning Drive**[24] 6415 3-8-12 0 TedDurcan 3 21
(W R Swinburn) *chsd ldrs: rdn 4f out: wknd 3f out* **50/1**

0 **12** *3 ¾* **Surprise Us**[16] 6661 3-9-3 0 (p) PaulMulrennan 1 19
(Mrs A Duffield) *pressed ldrs tl wknd 3f out* **100/1**

0/ **13** *30* **Greenbank Destiny**[713] 7221 4-9-4 0 LiamKeniry 4 —
(P R Hedger) *slowly away: a bhd: t.o* **66/1**

2m 18.44s (-3.46) **Going Correction** -0.20s/f (Stan)
WFA 3 from 4yo+ 6lb **13 Ran SP% 116.7**
Speed ratings (Par 103): **104,102,101,97,94 94,90,89,89,86 80,78,56**
toteswingers: 1&2 £8.90, 1&3 £6.20, 2&3 £1.80. CSF £22.02 TOTE £5.70: £2.30, £1.10, £2.40; EX 28.00.
Owner Cheveley Park Stud **Bred** Cheveley Park Stud Ltd **Trained** Newmarket, Suffolk

FOCUS
Just a fair maiden that was run at an ordinary gallop. The winner confirmed Pontefract form with the second.

7044 BET PREMIER LEAGUE FOOTBALL - BETDAQ H'CAP (DIV I) 1m 4f (P)
7:40 (7:42) (Class 4) (0-80,80) 3-Y-0+ **£3,561** (£1,059; £529; £264) **Stalls** Centre

Form RPR

0400 **1** **Ellemujie**[23] 6447 5-9-9 77 (p) AdamKirby 3 86
(D K Ivory) *hld up in rr tl rapid hdwy on ins over 2f out: qcknd to trck ldr ins fnl f: led fnl 120yds: comf* **8/1**

5016 **2** *¾* **Lombok**[4] 6957 4-9-4 72 HayleyTurner 11 80
(M L W Bell) *chsd ldrs: drvn to ld over 1f out: hdd and outpcd fnl 120yds* **7/1**[3]

313 **3** *2 ¾* **Status Symbol (IRE)**[36] 6091 5-9-10 78 WilliamCarson 9 85+
(G C Bravery) *hld up towards rr: hdwy over 2f out: styng on wl whn nt clr run and hmpd over 1f out: one pce after* **4/1**[1]

4422 **4** *nk* **Barliffey (IRE)**[49] 5679 5-9-2 70 (p) TomQueally 6 73
(D J Coakley) *t.k.h: trckd ldrs: rdn ins fnl 3f: outpcd by ldng trio fnl f* **12/1**

2000 **5** *½* **High On A Hill (IRE)**[26] 6359 3-8-12 73 LiamKeniry 12 75
(S Kirk) *chsd ldrs: rdn and losing pl whn swtchd lft over 1f out: styd on again fnl f but nvr a threat* **33/1**

1231 **6** *1 ¾* **Carlton Scroop (FR)**[15] 6669 7-8-11 68 (b) KierenFox[(3)] 2 68
(A W Carroll) *in rr tl hdwy to chse ldrs 4f out: rdn 3f out: wknd over 1f out* **15/2**

2332 **7** *nse* **Beauchamp Xiara**[66] 5146 4-9-4 72 DaneO'Neill 4 71
(H Candy) *towards rr: hdwy and swtchd lft to outside over 2f out: kpt on fnl f but nvr any ch* **8/1**

0005 **8** *¾* **Monkton Vale (IRE)**[12] 6753 3-8-11 72 (b) PaulHanagan 10 70
(R A Fahey) *in tch: rdn and effrt fr 3f out: nvr rchd ldrs and wknd fnl f* **9/1**

3235 **9** *½* **Ateeb**[10] 6797 4-9-5 73 (v[1]) TadhgO'Shea 1 70
(E A L Dunlop) *sn led: rdn and qcknd over 3f out: hdd appr fnl 2f: wknd fnl f* **13/2**[2]

255 **10** *¾* **Chain Of Events**[26] 6288 3-8-12 73 CathyGannon 8 69
(N B King) *trckd ldr tl led over 2f out: hdd over 1f out: wknd qckly* **25/1**

200 **11** *¾* **Encircled**[24] 6428 6-9-12 80 ShaneKelly 5 75
(J R Jenkins) *t.k.h towards rr: c wd into st 3f out and nvr rchd ldrs* **28/1**

00 **12** *shd* **Epsom Salts**[33] 6201 5-9-1 **74**................................ JemmaMarshall(5) 7 69
(P M Phelan) *hld up in rr: pushed along and styd on same pce fnl 2f* **9/1**

2m 34.79s (0.29) **Going Correction** -0.20s/f (Stan)
WFA 3 from 4yo+ 7lb **12** Ran SP% **117.7**
Speed ratings (Par 105): **91,90,88,88,88 86,86,86,86,85 85,85**
toteswingers: 1&2 £11.10, 1&3 £12.30, 2&3 £7.50. CSF £61.34 CT £260.40 TOTE £10.80: £3.40, £2.90, £3.00; EX 80.40.
Owner Mrs J A Cornwell **Bred** Mrs J A Cornwell **Trained** Radlett, Herts

FOCUS
A fair handicap, but with few obvious front-runners in the lineup, it was run at a sedate pace and turned into a sprint finish. The form promises to be unreliable but the winner did well to come from the rear. The race is rated around the second.
Status Symbol(IRE) ◆ Official explanation: jockey said gelding was denied a clear run

7045 BET PREMIER LEAGUE FOOTBALL - BETDAQ H'CAP (DIV II) 1m 4f (P)
8:10 (8:12) (Class 4) (0-80,80) 3-Y-0+ **£3,561** (£1,059; £529; £264) **Stalls** Centre

Form RPR
3501 **1** **Spensley (IRE)**[24] 6427 4-9-6 **74**.. KierenFallon 8 86+
(J R Fanshawe) *s.i.s: in rr whn hmpd 7f out: hdwy and nt clr run 2f out: sn swtchd lft to outside and str run fnl f to ld last stride* **5/2**[2]

1 **2** *shd* **Modun (IRE)**[30] 6275 3-9-4 **79**.. RyanMoore 1 91+
(Sir Michael Stoute) *in tch: drvn: hdwy and green 2f out: r.o wl to ld appr fnl f: hung lft u.p fnl 50yds: ct last strides* **1/1**[1]

3330 **3** *2 ¼* **Argaum (IRE)**[27] 6331 3-8-11 **72**.. TedDurcan 10 80
(W R Swinburn) *led 1f: styd trcking ldr tl led again over 3f out: rdn over 2f out: hdd appr fnl f: outpcd by ldng duo fnl 150yds* **15/2**

5244 **4** *2* **Alfonso The Wise (IRE)**[15] 6678 3-9-0 **75**................(p) WilliamBuick 11 80
(J Noseda) *hld up in rr off pce: shkn up: hung rt and nt keen over 2f out: pushed along and styd on to take wl hld 4th fnl 80yds* **6/1**[3]

0030 **5** *2 ¾* **Archie Rice (USA)**[17] 6639 4-9-2 **70**........................... StevieDonohoe 2 70
(T Keddy) *in rr and hmpd 7f out: hdwy to chse ldrs ins fnl 2f: no imp and wknd fnl f* **50/1**

6502 **6** *1 ½* **Rowan Tiger**[17] 6639 4-9-9 **77**.. PatCosgrave 5 75
(J R Boyle) *chsd ldrs: wnt 2nd briefly over 2f out: wknd over 1f out* **14/1**

4310 **7** *13* **Ethics Girl (IRE)**[33] 6199 4-9-4 **72**.. FrannyNorton 4 49
(John Berry) *in tch whn hmpd 7f out: hdwy 3f out and in tch 2f out: wknd and eased appr fnl f* **25/1**

-200 **8** *16* **Tricky Situation**[6] 6895 4-8-12 **66**.. PaulHanagan 3 18
(D H Brown) *led after 1f: hdd over 3f out: sn btn* **40/1**

365- **P** **Straits Of Hormuz (USA)**[376] 6671 4-9-8 **76**.................. JimCrowley 9 —
(Ian Williams) *chsng ldrs whn p.u bdly lame 7f out* **66/1**

2m 30.16s (-4.34) **Going Correction** -0.20s/f (Stan)
WFA 3 from 4yo+ 7lb **9** Ran SP% **121.0**
Speed ratings (Par 105): **106,105,104,103,101 100,91,80,—**
toteswingers: 1&2 £1.80, 1&3 £4.70, 2&3 £3.40. CSF £5.55 CT £15.94 TOTE £2.30: £1.60, £1.30, £2.70; EX 5.60.
Owner Axom (XV) **Bred** Mount Coote Stud And M H Dixon **Trained** Newmarket, Suffolk

FOCUS
An interesting handicap in which the two least-exposed horses came to the fore in a race run at a good gallop. It was a record time, although the track was slick, and the form is rated on the positive side.

7046 BET ASIAN H'CAPS - BETDAQ HANDICAP (DIV I) 7f (P)
8:40 (8:45) (Class 5) (0-75,78) 3-Y-0+ **£1,944** (£574; £287) **Stalls** High

Form RPR
465 **1** **Requisite**[10] 6799 5-9-4 **73**..(v) MartinLane(3) 4 82
(I A Wood) *hld up in rr: str run on outside fr 2f out to ld ins fnl f: styd on wl clsng stages* **11/1**

302 **2** *¾* **Slikback Jack (IRE)**[19] 6581 3-9-5 **73**........................... PaulHanagan 7 79
(J A Glover) *chsd ldrs: drvn to chal 1f out: tk def 2nd clsng stages but a hld by wnr* **7/1**[3]

3451 **3** *¾* **Sheer Force (IRE)**[10] 6801 3-9-5 **78** 6ex.....................(v) JohnFahy(5) 14 82
(W J Knight) *s.i.s: in rr: gd hdwy fr 2f out to chal 1f out: kpt on same pce ins fnl f* **7/2**[2]

0330 **4** *nse* **Cut And Thrust (IRE)**[131] 2959 4-9-0 **69**........................... KierenFox(3) 10 74
(M Wellings) *chsd ldrs: led over 2f out: jnd 1f out: hdd ins fnl f: styd on same pce* **20/1**

3123 **5** *nse* **Perfect Friend**[8] 6853 4-9-4 **70**.. LiamKeniry 1 75
(S Kirk) *in rr: hdwy towards outside 2f out: chsd ldrs 1f out: one pce ins fnl f* **12/1**

2141 **6** *1 ¼* **Darcey**[13] 6714 4-9-7 **73**.. CathyGannon 6 78+
(Miss Amy Weaver) *t.k.h: hld up in rr: gd hdwy whn bdly hmpd and snatched up over 1f out: swtchd lft fnl f and fin strly: nt rcvr* **11/1**

3321 **7** *½* **Bianca De Medici**[20] 6540 3-9-6 **74**........................... SteveDrowne 13 73
(H Morrison) *chsd ldrs: pushed along 3f out: drvn to chal 1f out: wknd ins fnl f and eased cl home* **5/2**[1]

6500 **8** *1 ¾* **Fazza**[26] 6370 3-8-13 **67**.. DavidProbert 5 61
(D W P Arbuthnot) *chsd ldrs: rdn over 2f out: wknd 1f out* **20/1**

0306 **9** *shd* **Gazboolou**[10] 6801 6-9-5 **71**.. FergusSweeney 9 66
(David Pinder) *awkward leaving stalls: in rr: hdwy and n.m.r wl over 1f out: styd on fnl f but nvr a threat* **16/1**

3151 **10** *1 ¼* **Rough Rock (IRE)**[30] 6274 5-8-6 **63**........................... AdamBeschizza(5) 2 55
(C A Dwyer) *chsd ldrs tl wknd u.p wl over 1f out* **10/1**

2440 **11** *½* **Billberry**[10] 6800 5-9-4 **70**..(tp) AdamKirby 12 60
(S C Williams) *in tch: rdn and one pce over 2f out: rallied u.str.p over 1f out but nvr on terms: sn wknd* **25/1**

0500 **12** *3 ¾* **Another Magic Man (USA)**[1] 7019 3-9-0 **68**............ StevieDonohoe 11 47
(J R Best) *led tl hdd over 2f out: sn btn* **33/1**

1m 25.19s (-0.81) **Going Correction** -0.20s/f (Stan)
WFA 3 from 4yo+ 2lb **12** Ran SP% **118.9**
Speed ratings (Par 103): **96,95,94,94,94 92,92,90,90,88 88,83**
toteswingers: 1&2 £12.80, 1&3 £18.00, 2&3 £5.80. CSF £81.81 CT £334.98 TOTE £23.60: £6.10, £1.50, £1.50; EX 106.90.
Owner Paddy Barrett **Bred** Darley **Trained** Upper Lambourn, Berks
■ Stewards' Enquiry : Martin Lane one-day: careless riding (Nov 6)
David Probert caution: careless riding.

FOCUS
A competitive handicap and a tight finish after the field were almost in a line at the furlong pole. The winner came from last but it wasn't necessarily an advantage to be held up. It was slower than division one but the form seems sound enough.
Gazboolou Official explanation: jockey said gelding anticipated the start and hit the stalls

7047 BET ASIAN H'CAPS - BETDAQ HANDICAP (DIV II) 7f (P)
9:10 (9:17) (Class 5) (0-75,75) 3-Y-0+ **£1,944** (£574; £287) **Stalls** High

Form RPR
3256 **1** **Hellbender (IRE)**[3] 6991 4-9-3 **71**..(t) LiamKeniry 4 83
(S Kirk) *hld up in rr: hdwy over 2f out: drvn and qcknd to ld appr fnl f: drvn out* **7/1**

1320 **2** *2 ¼* **Headache**[99] 4024 5-8-13 **70**..(t) RobertLButler(3) 9 76
(B W Duke) *chsd ldrs: rdn over 2f out: styd on u.p to chse wnr ins fnl f but no imp* **33/1**

2143 **3** *¾* **Valencha**[42] 5896 3-9-2 **72**.. SteveDrowne 6 75
(H Morrison) *in tch: rdn and one pce 2f out: swtchd lft to outside over 1f out and kpt on wl fnl f to take 3rd cl home but nvr any ch w wnr* **6/1**[3]

335 **4** *nk* **Copperwood**[36] 6085 5-9-1 **69**.. DaneO'Neill 8 72
(M Blanshard) *in rr: hdwy fr 2f out to chse ldrs over 1f out: kpt on ins fnl f* **16/1**

223 **5** *½* **Rondeau (GR)**[42] 5889 5-9-5 **73**.. JimCrowley 7 75
(P R Chamings) *mid-div: rdn and hdwy over 2f out: chsd ldrs over 1f out but nvr on terms and kpt on one pce ins fnl f* **12/1**

3503 **6** *¾* **Slugger O'Toole**[10] 6801 5-9-2 **70**...........................(v) WilliamCarson 11 70
(S C Williams) *taken down early: reluctant to load: bmpd s and bhd: c wd into st and stl plenty to do 2f out: kpt on fnl f: nvr a threat* **4/1**[1]

0255 **7** *¾* **Army Of Stars (IRE)**[10] 6801 4-9-4 **75**.....................(p) SophieDoyle(3) 14 73
(J A Osborne) *led: jnd over 3f out but kpt slt advantage tl hdd over 1f out: wknd ins fnl f* **11/1**

5314 **8** *¾* **Smart Endeavour (USA)**[10] 6801 4-8-12 **71**.............(v) JohnFahy(5) 13 67
(W R Swinburn) *bmpd s: sn rcvrd to trck ldr and chal fr over 3f out tl led briefly over 1f out: sn hdd: wknd ins fnl f* **6/1**[3]

6032 **9** *¾* **Tiger Star**[10] 6801 3-8-11 **67**..(b) LukeMorris 10 60
(J M P Eustace) *wnt rt s: sn chsng ldrs: wknd u.p over 1f out* **11/2**[2]

1000 **10** *nse* **He's Invincible**[14] 6692 3-9-4 **74**...........................(b) ShaneKelly 1 67
(B J Meehan) *in rr: stl bhd whn swtchd rt to ins over 2f out: sme prog u.p over 1f out but nvr nr ldrs and wknd ins fnl f* **25/1**

0446 **11** *nk* **Spinning Bailiwick**[16] 6656 4-9-0 **68**........................... RyanMoore 3 61
(G L Moore) *a in rr* **12/1**

0-00 **12** *½* **Koraleva Tectona (IRE)**[17] 6629 5-8-9 **70**............ JamesRogers(7) 5 61
(Pat Eddery) *chsd ldrs tl wknd over 2f out* **33/1**

0000 **13** *25* **Shaded Edge**[8] 6854 6-8-9 **63**.. HayleyTurner 2 —
(D W P Arbuthnot) *a in rr: t.o* **33/1**

1m 24.73s (-1.27) **Going Correction** -0.20s/f (Stan)
WFA 3 from 4yo+ 2lb **13** Ran SP% **118.7**
Speed ratings (Par 103): **99,96,95,95,94 93,92,92,91,91 90,90,61**
toteswingers: 1&2 £54.10, 1&3 £15.40, 2&3 £56.00. CSF £227.31 CT £1452.59 TOTE £8.20: £2.60, £8.60, £1.20; EX 109.30 Place 6: £55.05, Place 5: £41.44..
Owner Mike Newbould **Bred** James Lombard **Trained** Upper Lambourn, Berks

FOCUS
Perhaps not quite as competitive as the first division but still an open betting heat and form likely to stand up given that the field were soon well strung out. It was the faster division and the winner is rated back towards his best.
T/Plt: £166.20 to a £1 stake. Pool:£64,770.60 - 284.33 winning tickets T/Qpdt: £29.20 to a £1 stake. Pool:£7,653.77 - 193.40 winning tickets ST

6488 AYR (L-H)
Friday, October 22

OFFICIAL GOING: Good to soft changing to soft after race 5 (4:05)
Back straight out 4m home bend out 6m, home straight out 8m from innermost line, increasing distances on round course by about 18yds.
Wind: Fairly strong, against Weather: Cloudy

7049 EUROPEAN BREEDERS' FUND/SCOTTISH POPPY APPEAL MAIDEN STKS 1m
1:55 (2:00) (Class 4) 2-Y-O **£4,533** (£1,348; £674; £336) **Stalls** High

Form RPR
1 **Eternal Ruler (IRE)** 2-9-3 0.. PJMcDonald 2 74+
(G A Swinbank) *s.i.s: hld up: hdwy on outside over 2f out: chsng ldrs and effrt whn rn green over 1f out: styd on wl to ld towards fin* **7/1**

04 **2** *nk* **Sam Nombulist**[29] 6305 2-9-0 0........................... MichaelStainton(3) 4 71
(R M Whitaker) *t.k.h: cl up: rdn to ld appr fnl f: kpt on: hdd towards fin* **16/1**

6323 **3** *3 ¼* **Sabratha (IRE)**[14] 6704 2-8-9 59........................... JamesSullivan(3) 9 59
(Miss L A Perratt) *t.k.h: cl up: led 1/2-way to appr fnl f: sn no ex* **12/1**

3362 **4** *2 ½* **Fenella Fudge**[22] 6512 2-8-12 85.. PaulMulrennan 1 53
(J G Given) *trckd ldrs: effrt and drvn over 2f out: no ex over 1f out* **11/8**[1]

0 **5** *1 ½* **Another For Joe**[20] 6569 2-9-0 0........................... GaryBartley(3) 8 55
(J S Goldie) *hld up in tch: rdn along over 2f out: no imp over 1f out* **66/1**

6 *1* **Patriotic (IRE)** 2-9-3 0.. JoeFanning 6 53+
(M Johnston) *hld up: rdn whn n.m.r and swtchd rt over 2f out: n.d after* **4/1**[2]

4 **7** *2* **Newby Lodge (IRE)**[30] 6293 2-8-12 0.. TomEaves 7 43
(B Smart) *prom: rdn and wandered over 2f out: sn outpcd* **5/1**[3]

00 **8** *12* **Nay Secret**[18] 6618 2-8-10 0.. PaulNorton(7) 5 22
(J S Goldie) *dwlt: bhd: drvn 1/2-way: wknd over 2f out: t.o* **100/1**

0 **9** *19* **Sheedal (IRE)**[98] 4103 2-8-12 0.. PhillipMakin 3 —
(Miss L A Perratt) *led to over 3f out: wknd over 2f out: eased whn no ch fnl f: t.o* **100/1**

1m 48.89s (5.09) **Going Correction** +0.65s/f (Yiel) **9** Ran SP% **108.3**
Speed ratings (Par 97): **100,99,96,93,92 91,89,77,58**
toteswingers:1&2:£18.40, 1&3:£9.50, 2&3:£11.80 CSF £96.79 TOTE £9.80: £2.80, £4.00, £1.50; EX 79.00.
Owner Mrs E Walters **Bred** B Kennedy **Trained** Melsonby, N Yorks
■ Stewards' Enquiry : P J McDonald one-day ban: used whip with excessive frequency (Nov 5)

FOCUS
Round course: Back straight out 4m home bend out 6m, home straight out 8m from innermost line, increasing distances on Round course by about 18yds. The rail was out 4m in the back straight, 6m on the home bend, and 8m from the innermost line in the home straight, adding around 18yds to races over 7f plus. The ground was changed to good to soft all round before the meeting started, though some of the riders in this opener felt it was softer than that. An ordinary maiden and although the early pace was modest, it looked hard work for these juveniles with the winning time 9.98 seconds outside standard, though the rail movements should be taken into account and they were racing into a headwind. The third helps anchor the form.

NOTEBOOK

Eternal Ruler(IRE), retained for 18,000gns as a yearling, is a half-brother to three winners at up to 2m including the smart Villa Sciarra. He did very well to win this as he gave away a lot of ground at the start and then raced very green once under way, but he was still able to pick up and grab the race almost on the line. He was well backed beforehand, which suggested someone knew that he had ability, and this big type should develop into a nice performer at around 1m2f next season. (op 12-1)

Sam Nombulist hinted at ability in his first two starts and looked the likely winner when sent to the front over a furlong out, but he held his head high and was run down late. He now gets a mark, but the head carriage is a slight worry. (op 20-1 tchd 14-1)

Sabratha(IRE) ran well considering she pulled hard early and was in front from 4f out to 2f out, but she has already been beaten in a selling nursery and is only rated 58, so her proximity doesn't exactly boost the form. (op 10-1)

Fenella Fudge was the form horse of the race having been placed in three of her first four starts and finished sixth in the May Hill. She travelled well behind the leaders, but found little under maximum pressure and this was a major step backwards. Official explanation: jockey said filly never travelled (op Evens tchd 10-11)

Another For Joe, well beaten on his Redcar debut, ran a little better here but looks more of a long-term handicap prospect. (op 50-1)

Patriotic(IRE)'s stable won this with the high-class Corsica last year, though he had already raced three times, and this half-brother to Dhaular Dhar and Proclaim proved too green to do himself justice on debut. (op 9-2 tchd 5-1)

7050 GMC CORSEHILL NURSERY 6f

2:25 (2:27) (Class 5) (0-75,72) 2-Y-O £2,590 (£770; £385; £192) Stalls Centre

Form RPR

0233 **1** **Tro Nesa (IRE)**[27] 6354 2-9-7 **72** PhillipMakin 7 78
(Mrs A Duffield) *in tch: effrt over 1f out: led ins fnl f: styd on strly* **7/1**[3]

6440 **2** 1 ¾ **Rothesay Chancer**[14] 6705 2-8-7 **58** JoeFanning 3 59
(J S Goldie) *prom: hdwy to ld over 1f out: hdd ins fnl f: kpt on: nt pce of wnr* **13/2**[2]

2301 **3** ½ **Indian Giver**[23] 6459 2-9-2 **67** PatrickMathers 9 66
(H A McWilliams) *dwlt: hld up: swtchd lft and hdwy over 2f out: chal and hung lft over 1f out: no ex wl ins fnl f* **20/1**

3025 **4** nk **Eilean Mor**[18] 6619 2-8-12 **66** GaryBartley(3) 8 64
(J S Goldie) *bhd: pushed along over 2f out: hdwy and edgd lft over 1f out: styd on fnl f: nrst fin* **12/1**

4313 **5** 2 **Prophet In A Dream**[4] 6988 2-9-3 **68** ChrisCatlin 1 60
(M R Channon) *cl up: led over 2f to 1f out: sn drvn and one pce* **9/4**[1]

1040 **6** ½ **Peppercorn Rent (IRE)**[16] 6674 2-8-2 **53** (e) DuranFentiman 5 44
(T D Easterby) *prom: drvn and outpcd over 2f out: kpt on fnl f: n.d* **33/1**

0346 **7** nk **Ted's Brother (IRE)**[18] 6619 2-9-0 **65** FrannyNorton 11 55
(R C Guest) *hld up: rdn over 2f out: no imp fr over 1f out* **9/1**

4050 **8** hd **Philharmonic Hall**[22] 6513 2-8-10 **66** LeeTopliss(5) 4 55
(R A Fahey) *cl up: rdn and ev ch over 2f out: no ex fr over 1f out* **11/1**

3302 **9** 2 ¾ **Madam Markievicz (IRE)**[20] 6576 2-9-4 **69** (p) TomEaves 6 50
(M Dods) *hld up bhd ldng gp: drvn over 2f out: btn fnl f* **16/1**

3550 **10** 1 **Not So Bright (USA)**[7] 6902 2-8-8 **59** PaulMulrennan 2 37
(J G Given) *led to over 2f out: edgd rt and sn wknd* **11/1**

3624 **11** 21 **Saxonette**[14] 6705 2-8-8 **62** JamesSullivan(3) 10 —
(Miss L A Perratt) *prom tl drvn and wknd over 2f out: t.o* **8/1**

1m 17.59s (3.99) **Going Correction** +0.60s/f (Yiel) 11 Ran SP% **115.7**

Speed ratings (Par 95): **97,94,94,93,90 90,89,89,85,84 56**

toteswingers:1&2:£4.20, 1&3:£5.10, 2&3:£31.50 CSF £51.12 CT £882.82 TOTE £7.40: £2.30, £3.60, £7.60; EX 64.80.

Owner Rasio Cymru Racing **Bred** Lynnlodge Stud & Arthur Finnan **Trained** Constable Burton, N Yorks

FOCUS

A competitive little nursery.

NOTEBOOK

Tro Nesa(IRE) had made the frame five times from seven starts since making a winning racecourse debut, so she deserved this success. The ground had come right for her and the way she flew home after being held up suggests she could go in again soon, provided underfoot conditions are suitable. (op 13-2 tchd 8-1)

Rothesay Chancer, minus the cheekpieces this time, was expected to appreciate this return to 6f having been dropped 5lb since his last run, so a big run was no surprise. He looked like winning until the filly was unleashed and it's surely only a matter of time before he breaks his duck. (op 9-1)

Indian Giver, making her nursery debut, had been raised 7lb for her easy win in a heavy-ground maiden at Newcastle last month and may have been unlucky not to have gone even closer here. Firstly, she missed the break and lost ground, and then hung away to the far rail under pressure 2f from home when in with every chance. Unfortunately she already is due to go up another 4lb which will make life more difficult. (op 14-1)

Eilean Mor, often placed but yet to win, didn't get going until it was too late but he finished well and may prefer a stiffer test. (op 10-1)

Prophet In A Dream, still 8lb higher than when winning at Nottingham two starts back, should have appreciated this ground more than at Windsor four days earlier, but having travelled well up with the leaders towards the far side, he faded rather disappointingly. (op 11-4)

Peppercorn Rent(IRE), who hadn't been disgraced in nurseries the last twice having won a Ripon seller in July, showed up early and ran on again after getting outpaced mid-race. (tchd 28-1)

Saxonette Official explanation: jockey said filly lost its action

7051 POPPYSCOTLAND SUPPORTING OUR HEROES H'CAP 6f

2:55 (2:56) (Class 6) (0-65,65) 3-Y-0+ £1,942 (£578; £288; £144) Stalls Centre

Form RPR

0552 **1** **Charles Parnell (IRE)**[22] 6515 7-8-13 **60** MichaelStainton(3) 12 71
(S P Griffiths) *missed break: bhd: hdwy over 2f out: led appr fnl f: drvn out* **5/1**[2]

0202 **2** 2 **Dubai Hills**[22] 6492 4-9-0 **65** AdamCarter(7) 14 69
(B Smart) *chsd ldrs: rdn and ev ch over 1f out: kpt on fnl f: nt pce of wnr* **11/4**[1]

6560 **3** 1 ¼ **Dower Glen**[22] 6490 3-7-13 **51** oh2 (v[1]) ShirleyTeasdale(7) 2 51
(V P Donoghue) *wnt rt s: led and sn clr: rdn over 2f out: hdd appr fnl f: kpt on same pce* **80/1**

4-30 **4** 2 ¼ **Benny The Bear**[50] 5686 3-8-13 **58** PaulMulrennan 8 51
(Miss L A Perratt) *carried rt s: prom: drvn over 2f out: kpt on u.p ins fnl f* **25/1**

6315 **5** ½ **Music Festival (USA)**[22] 6492 3-9-3 **62** JoeFanning 10 53
(J S Goldie) *carried bdly rt s: towards rr: gd hdwy over 1f out: styd on wl fnl f: nrst fin* **9/1**

2030 **6** 2 ¾ **Carnival Dream**[28] 6329 5-8-8 **52** PatrickMathers 3 35
(H A McWilliams) *dwlt: bhd: hdwy 2f out: no imp fnl f* **14/1**

3003 **7** hd **Monte Mayor One**[22] 6491 3-8-13 **61** IanBrennan(3) 13 43
(P Monteith) *towards rr: rdn over 2f out: hdwy over 1f out: nvr able to chal* **12/1**

6000 **8** 2 ¼ **Stolt (IRE)**[8] 6880 6-9-7 **65** PJMcDonald 11 40
(N Wilson) *in tch: rdn over 2f out: wknd over 1f out* **50/1**

2520 **9** 2 **Peter's Gift (IRE)**[23] 6460 4-9-0 **58** (b) ChrisCatlin 5 26
(K A Ryan) *carried rt s: sn bhd: drvn 1/2-way: nvr able to chal* **11/1**

4205 **10** 2 ¼ **Newbury Street**[78] 4749 3-9-6 **65** AndrewElliott 16 26
(P F Holmes) *chsd clr ldr: rdn over 2f out: hung lft and wknd over 1f out* **33/1**

0303 **11** 1 **Cheyenne Red (IRE)**[22] 6492 4-9-7 **65** (b[1]) PhillipMakin 7 23
(M Dods) *hmpd s: in tch tl rdn and wknd over 1f out* **6/1**[3]

0000 **12** 2 **Reach For The Sky (IRE)**[33] 6226 3-8-3 **51** oh1 JamesSullivan(3) 1 3
(A Berry) *bhd: rdn along 1/2-way: nvr on terms* **100/1**

2300 **13** 6 **Lindoro**[36] 6110 5-9-4 **65** (be) AndrewHeffernan(3) 15 —
(K M Prendergast) *midfield: reminders 1/2-way: wknd over 2f out* **8/1**

004 **14** 3 ¾ **Distant Sun (USA)**[14] 6708 6-9-5 **63** TomEaves 6 —
(Miss L A Perratt) *hmpd s: sn bhd and drvn along: no ch fr 1/2-way* **25/1**

1m 18.04s (4.44) **Going Correction** +0.60s/f (Yiel)

WFA 3 from 4yo+ 1lb 14 Ran SP% **116.2**

Speed ratings (Par 101): **94,91,89,86,86 82,82,79,76,73 72,69,61,56**

toteswingers:1&2:£3.00, 1&3:£61.60, 2&3:£37.80 CSF £17.36 CT £1000.52 TOTE £4.50: £2.20, £1.90, £17.60; EX 13.50.

Owner J N Griffiths **Bred** R And Mrs R Hodgins **Trained** Easingwold, N Yorks

■ Stewards' Enquiry : Michael Stainton three-day ban: used whip with excessive frequency (Nov 5,6,8)

FOCUS

A modest sprint handicap and dubious form with Dower Glen lunging away to her right exiting the stalls and all but wiping out the six drawn closest to her on that side, namely Carnival Dream, Peter's Gift, Distant Sun, Cheyenne Red, Benny The Bear and Music Festival. Few got into the race as a result and the winning time was 0.45 seconds slower than the nursery.

Cheyenne Red(IRE) Official explanation: jockey said gelding never travelled

7052 POPPYSCOTLAND SMALL THINGS BIG DIFFERENCE H'CAP 5f

3:30 (3:30) (Class 5) (0-70,70) 3-Y-O £2,590 (£770; £385; £192) Stalls Centre

Form RPR

4305 **1** **Dancing Freddy (IRE)**[23] 6466 3-9-7 **70** (p) PaulMulrennan 1 75
(J G Given) *mde all: rdn over 1f out: strly pressed wl ins fnl f: jst hld on* **7/2**[3]

0211 **2** nse **Red Roar (IRE)**[26] 6392 3-9-1 **64** FrannyNorton 2 69+
(A Berry) *chsd wnr: effrt and drvn over 1f out: chal wl ins fnl f: jst failed* **10/3**[2]

0620 **3** 1 ½ **Choc'A'Moca (IRE)**[7] 6897 3-8-4 **58** (v) NeilFarley(5) 7 57
(D Carroll) *prom: effrt over 2f out: outpcd wl over 1f out: kpt on fnl f* **11/4**[1]

61 **4** ¾ **Doc Hay (USA)**[13] 6746 3-9-6 **69** TomEaves 3 66
(P F I Cole) *prom: effrt and drvn wl over 1f out: kpt on same pce fnl f* **9/2**

0560 **5** 4 ½ **Ya Boy Sir (IRE)**[36] 6103 3-8-7 **59** (v[1]) JamesSullivan(3) 5 40
(N Wilson) *rrd s: hld up: effrt 2f out: wknd ent fnl f* **14/1**

-005 **6** 9 **Sumay Buoy (IRE)**[26] 6392 3-8-2 **51** oh3 AndrewMullen 4 —
(Mrs J C McGregor) *trckd ldrs tl wknd over 2f out* **33/1**

4300 **7** 1 ¼ **Kalahari Desert (IRE)**[15] 6696 3-8-4 **53** PaulQuinn 6 —
(R M Whitaker) *prom tl rdn and wknd over 1f out* **6/1**

62.61 secs (2.51) **Going Correction** +0.60s/f (Yiel) 7 Ran SP% **114.0**

Speed ratings (Par 101): **103,102,100,99,92 77,75**

toteswingers:1&2:£4.30, 1&3:£3.00, 2&3:£2.50 CSF £15.50 TOTE £5.20: £2.80, £2.30; EX 16.50.

Owner Danethorpe Racing Partnership **Bred** Vincent Duignan **Trained** Willoughton, Lincs

FOCUS

The rain started to come down before this race. Last year this handicap was won by Hawkeyethenoo off a mark of 63 (now rated 96) but it would be a surprise if any of these improved as much as he hasrated around the exposed winner. The race was dominated by prominent racers.

Ya Boy Sir(IRE) Official explanation: jockey said colt missed the break

Sumay Buoy(IRE) Official explanation: jockey said colt was unsuited by the good to soft ground

Kalahari Desert(IRE) Official explanation: jockey said gelding had no more to give

7053 DAILY RECORD H'CAP 1m 2f

4:05 (4:05) (Class 4) (0-85,85) 3-Y-0+ £5,180 (£1,541; £770; £384) Stalls High

Form RPR

14-0 **1** **Bagber**[17] 6650 4-8-12 **73** AndrewMullen 9 82
(P Monteith) *prom: rdn and hdwy to ld appr fnl f: styd on strly* **33/1**

5231 **2** 1 ¼ **Veiled Applause**[14] 6724 7-9-3 **81** IanBrennan(3) 6 87+
(J J Quinn) *hld up: nt clr run and swtchd over 2f out: hdwy to chse wnr ins fnl f: r.o* **9/2**[2]

3202 **3** 1 ½ **Royal Straight**[26] 6393 5-8-5 **71** oh4 NeilFarley(5) 10 74
(Miss L A Perratt) *dwlt: towards rr: hdwy to ld over 2f out to appr fnl f: kpt on same pce* **12/1**

3311 **4** hd **Diamond Duchess (IRE)**[15] 6691 3-9-4 **84** (b) ChrisCatlin 8 87+
(D R Lanigan) *towards rr: drvn and outpcd over 4f out: styd on wl fr 2f out: nrst fin* **4/1**[1]

3262 **5** ¾ **Veroon (IRE)**[21] 6543 4-9-1 **76** (p) PaulMulrennan 14 77
(J G Given) *trckd ldrs: effrt over 2f out: one pce over 1f out* **12/1**

1103 **6** ½ **High Resolution**[58] 5408 3-8-12 **81** JamesSullivan(3) 7 81
(Miss L A Perratt) *hld up: hdwy and in tch 2f out: sn rdn and kpt on same pce* **18/1**

0303 **7** 2 ½ **Best Prospect (IRE)**[10] 6832 8-8-11 **72** (tp) PhillipMakin 12 67
(M Dods) *s.i.s: hld up: hdwy over 2f out: sn rdn and no imp* **11/1**

0306 **8** 1 ¾ **Oneofapear (IRE)**[37] 6096 4-9-10 **85** PJMcDonald 3 77
(G A Swinbank) *midfield on outside: rdn and edgd lft over 2f out: sn outpcd* **20/1**

6425 **9** 1 **Bullet Man (USA)**[12] 6780 5-8-12 **78** LeeTopliss(5) 1 68
(R A Fahey) *midfield: drvn along over 2f out: sn outpcd: n.d after* **10/1**

1513 **10** 7 **Casino Night**[14] 6710 5-8-7 **71** oh4 AndrewHeffernan(3) 2 47
(Miss L A Perratt) *hld up ins: drvn 3f out: btn fnl 2f* **20/1**

4510 **11** nk **Tamarillo Grove (IRE)**[31] 6266 3-8-7 **73** TomEaves 11 48
(B Smart) *led to over 2f out: sn wknd* **14/1**

2055 **12** 17 **Snow Dancer (IRE)**[48] 5757 6-9-0 **75** PatrickMathers 13 16
(H A McWilliams) *bhd: drvn over 3f out: sn btn* **33/1**

0000 **13** 2 **Layla's Dancer**[13] 6753 3-8-6 **72** FrannyNorton 4 9
(R A Fahey) *in tch tl rdn and wknd over 2f out* **8/1**[3]

3150 **14** 11 **Exemplary**[11] 6797 3-9-5 **85** JoeFanning 5 —
(M Johnston) *chsd ldr: rdn over 3f out: sn struggling* **14/1**

2m 17.01s (5.01) **Going Correction** +0.65s/f (Yiel)

WFA 3 from 4yo+ 5lb 14 Ran SP% **116.1**

Speed ratings (Par 105): **105,104,102,102,102 101,99,98,97,91 91,78,76,67**

toteswingers:1&2:£49.30, 1&3:£86.10, 2&3:£25.40 CSF £164.68 CT £1910.33 TOTE £58.90: £16.50, £2.10, £5.70; EX 349.20.

Owner Allan McLuckie **Bred** Stowell Hill Ltd & Major & Mrs R B Kennard **Trained** Rosewell, Midlothian

■ Stewards' Enquiry : Neil Farley one-day ban: used whip with excessive frequency (Nov 5)
Andrew Mullen three-day ban: used whip with excessive frequency (Nov 5,6,8)

FOCUS
This competitive handicap was run in miserable conditions. The surprise winner matched last year's AW best.

7054 JIMMY & CAROL-ANNE DEANS 10TH ANNIVERSARY H'CAP (DIV I) 1m 1f 20y
4:40 (4:40) (Class 5) (0-70,70) 3-Y-O+ £2,266 (£674; £337; £168) Stalls High

Form RPR
1-2 **1** **Kiama Bay (IRE)**30 6297 4-9-2 62 IanBrennan(3) 2 74+
(J J Quinn) *hld up: gd hdwy on outside 2f out: led ins fnl f: kpt on wl* **13/2**
5003 **2** 1 1/4 **Edas**39 6032 8-9-4 64 KellyHarrison(3) 13 73
(T A K Cuthbert) *hld up in midfield on outside: hdwy to ld wl over 1f out: hdd ins fnl f: kpt on* **12/1**
0-04 **3** 2 **Pokfulham (IRE)**22 6495 4-8-12 55 (v) ChrisCatlin 12 59
(J S Goldie) *trckd ldr: rdn over 2f out: kpt on same pce fnl f* **12/1**
126- **4** 1/2 **Grandad Bill (IRE)**188 6768 7-9-1 61 GaryBartley(3) 11 64
(J S Goldie) *bhd tl hdwy over 1f out: nrst fin* **6/1**3
0242 **5** 3/4 **Chantilly Pearl (USA)**7 6890 4-9-0 57 PaulMulrennan 5 58
(J G Given) *hld up on ins: effrt over 2f out: no imp over 1f out* **9/2**1
0040 **6** 4 1/2 **Mississippian (IRE)**67 5155 6-8-10 53 oh4 PJMcDonald 10 44
(Mrs R Dobbin) *prom: effrt and drvn over 2f out: wknd appr fnl f* **33/1**
1346 **7** 1 **Frontline Phantom (IRE)**33 6225 3-8-13 60 AndrewElliott 7 49
(Mrs K Burke) *prom: drvn over 2f out: wknd over 1f out* **10/1**
0050 **8** 1 3/4 **Deadly Secret (USA)**14 6710 4-9-3 65 LeeTopliss(5) 8 50
(R A Fahey) *led tl hdd wl over 1f out: sn wknd* **14/1**
0350 **9** 7 **Wigwam Willie (IRE)**27 6367 8-9-10 67 (tp) PhillipMakin 3 37
(K A Ryan) *hld up: drvn 3f out: nvr able to chal* **16/1**
0505 **10** 7 **Finsbury**26 6396 7-9-1 58 TomEaves 6 13
(Miss L A Perratt) *stdd s: hld up: rdn 3f out: nvr on terms* **33/1**
0356 **11** 20 **Real Desire**57 5439 4-8-10 53 oh5 AndrewMullen 1 —
(P Monteith) *in tch: rdn over 3f out: sn wknd* **25/1**
0032 **12** 30 **Trailblazing**9 6856 3-9-9 70 (b) JoeFanning 9 —
(M Johnston) *bhd: hmpd after 3f: sn struggling: t.o* **11/2**2
6633 **U** **Botham (USA)**22 6495 6-8-8 58 PaulNorton(7) 4 —
(J S Goldie) *hld up: stmbld and uns rdr after 3f* **10/1**

2m 4.31s (5.91) **Going Correction** +0.75s/f (Yiel)
WFA 3 from 4yo+ 4lb 13 Ran SP% 117.0
Speed ratings (Par 103): **103,101,100,99,99 95,94,92,86,80 62,35,—**
toteswingers:1&2:£20.10, 1&3:£13.70, 2&3:£42.80 CSF £78.83 CT £909.53 TOTE £6.40: £1.70, £7.10, £5.30; EX 62.40.
Owner Mrs S Quinn **Bred** Tipper House Stud **Trained** Settrington, N Yorks

FOCUS
The ground was changed to soft before this race. An ordinary handicap and the first two horses home ended up closer to the stands' rail. It was quicker than division II and the winner is rated up 6lb.
Trailblazing Official explanation: jockey said gelding was hampered by a fallen rider

7055 WILLIAM AITKEN 18TH BIRTHDAY H'CAP (DIV II OF 4.40) 1m 1f 20y
5:15 (5:15) (Class 5) (0-70,70) 3-Y-O+ £2,266 (£674; £337; £168) Stalls High

Form RPR
3324 **1** **Osgood**4 6991 3-9-9 70 ChrisCatlin 7 79
(M R Channon) *mde all: rdn 2f out: kpt on wl fnl f: jst hld on* **4/1**1
4043 **2** hd **Lakeman (IRE)**7 6890 4-8-13 56 (b) TomEaves 11 65
(B Ellison) *prom: rdn over 2f out: styd on u.p fnl f: jst hld* **7/1**
3113 **3** 2 1/4 **Social Rhythm**26 6395 6-9-3 67 GarryWhillans(7) 12 71
(A C Whillans) *hld up: hdwy over 2f out: kpt on fnl f: nt rch first two* **6/1**3
200- **4** 2 **Ulysees (IRE)**356 7174 11-8-10 53 oh5 JoeFanning 2 53
(J S Goldie) *prom: drvn over 2f out: one pce over 1f out* **25/1**
356 **5** nk **Shethoughtshewas (IRE)**61 5337 3-9-4 65 PJMcDonald 6 64
(G A Swinbank) *trckd ldrs: drvn over 2f out: no ex over 1f out* **20/1**
3164 **6** hd **Wood Fair**38 6065 3-8-4 56 NeilFarley(5) 8 55
(Mrs K Burke) *dwlt: bhd: rdn 3f out: hdwy over 1f out: styd on wl fnl f* **5/1**2
2000 **7** 1 1/4 **Shy Glance (USA)**22 6495 8-9-1 58 (p) PaulMulrennan 13 54
(P Monteith) *midfield: drvn over 2f out: sn outpcd: n.d after* **25/1**
3003 **8** 3/4 **Cool Baranca (GER)**33 6223 4-9-7 67 JamesSullivan(3) 4 62
(P Monteith) *t.k.h early: in tch: drvn over 2f out: sn outpcd* **11/1**
0300 **9** 8 **Joinedupwriting**8 6860 5-8-11 57 MichaelStainton(3) 5 35
(R M Whitaker) *in tch: drvn and outpcd over 2f out: sn btn* **20/1**
4200 **10** 1 3/4 **Houston Dynimo (IRE)**20 6573 5-9-5 65 IanBrennan(3) 3 39
(N G Richards) *s.i.s: rdn in rr 3f out: nvr on terms* **13/2**
4460 **11** 2 **Stellite**36 6107 10-9-3 63 GaryBartley(3) 10 33
(J S Goldie) *hld up: rdn over 2f out: sn btn* **18/1**
0536 **12** 9 **Aldaado (IRE)**139 2766 4-9-4 61 (b1) PhillipMakin 1 12
(M Dods) *chsd wnr tl rdn and wknd 2f out* **8/1**

2m 6.53s (8.13) **Going Correction** +0.75s/f (Yiel)
WFA 3 from 4yo+ 4lb 12 Ran SP% 118.7
Speed ratings (Par 103): **93,92,90,89,88 88,87,86,79,78 76,68**
toteswingers:1&2:£6.20, 1&3:£3.40, 2&3:£4.60 CSF £29.92 CT £165.72 TOTE £4.70: £1.30, £2.20, £2.20; EX 23.80.
Owner Billy Parish **Bred** Eurostrait Ltd **Trained** West Ilsley, Berks
■ Stewards' Enquiry : Chris Catlin two-day ban: used whip with excessive frequency in incorrect place (Nov 5-6)

FOCUS
The early pace was only modest in this handicap and the winning time was 2.22 seconds slower than the first division. This time the whole field made for the centre of the track on turning in. The fourth lends doubts to the form, but the race has been rated at face value with the winner and second to their best.

7056 EVENT-A-LOO H'CAP 7f 50y
5:45 (5:46) (Class 5) (0-70,74) 3-Y-O+ £2,590 (£770; £385; £192) Stalls High

Form RPR
241 **1** **Out Of Nothing**48 5766 7-8-9 61 AndrewHeffernan(3) 14 75
(K M Prendergast) *pressed ldr: led over 2f out: rdn clr fnl f* **7/1**3
0060 **2** 4 1/2 **Violent Velocity (IRE)**56 5500 7-8-13 65 IanBrennan(3) 10 67
(J J Quinn) *hld up: hdwy 2f out: chsd wnr ins fnl f: no imp* **5/1**1
5354 **3** 1 1/2 **North Central (USA)**14 6710 3-8-11 62 (p) LNewman 4 60
(J S Goldie) *led: rdn and hdd over 2f out: kpt on same pce fnl f* **20/1**
3316 **4** 1 **Chookie Avon**7 6897 3-8-9 60 (p) JoeFanning 11 55
(V P Donoghue) *hld up: hdwy over 2f out: edgd lft over 1f out: no imp fnl f* **14/1**
5364 **5** 2 1/2 **Vertigo On Course (IRE)**6 6935 5-8-11 60 PJMcDonald 9 48
(R A Fahey) *prom: rdn and outpcd over 2f out: sme late hdwy: nvr on terms* **5/1**1
2012 **6** nse **Emeralds Spirit (IRE)**14 6710 3-8-9 63 KellyHarrison(3) 8 51
(J R Weymes) *t.k.h: hld up: pushed along over 2f out: styd on ins fnl f: n.d* **12/1**
3536 **7** nk **Berbice (IRE)**14 6710 5-9-1 67 JamesSullivan(3) 12 54
(Miss L A Perratt) *trckd ldrs: effrt wl over 1f out: wknd ent fnl f* **12/1**
5362 **8** 2 3/4 **Geojimali**22 6494 8-8-11 60 (p) ChrisCatlin 13 40
(J S Goldie) *s.i.s: bhd: detached and struggling 1/2-way: sme hdwy over 1f out: n.d* **12/1**
5064 **9** nk **Celtic Lynn (IRE)**23 6460 5-9-4 67 PhillipMakin 2 46
(M Dods) *hld up: effrt over 2f out: no further imp over 1f out* **10/1**
0 **10** 2 **Muqalad (IRE)**7 6897 3-9-3 68 TomEaves 3 42
(B Smart) *t.k.h: cl up: rdn over 2f out: wknd wl over 1f out* **20/1**
0000 **11** 9 **Deadly Encounter (IRE)**26 6394 4-9-2 70 (v1) LeeTopliss(5) 5 19
(R A Fahey) *midfield: drvn and outpcd over 2f out: n.d after* **10/1**
0656 **12** 20 **Mister Jingles**31 6267 7-8-7 56 (b) FrannyNorton 7 —
(R M Whitaker) *in tch: rdn over 2f out: sn wknd: t.o* **20/1**
2041 **13** 4 **White Dart**7 6897 3-9-9 74 6ex PaulMulrennan 1 —
(M R Channon) *midfield on ins: struggling over 2f out: sn btn: t.o* **13/2**2

1m 38.28s (4.88) **Going Correction** +0.75s/f (Yiel)
WFA 3 from 4yo+ 2lb 13 Ran SP% 121.4
Speed ratings (Par 103): **102,96,95,94,91 91,90,87,87,84 74,51,47**
toteswingers:1&2:£16.80, 1&3:£26.40, 2&3:£30.90. totesuper7: WIN: Not won. PLACE: 1,306.50. CSF £41.23 CT £681.51 TOTE £9.40: £3.10, £2.30, £6.30; EX 71.20 Place 6: £973.91, Place 5: £162.96.
Owner Phoenix Brothers **Bred** E Young And Sons **Trained** Matlon, N Yorks
■ Stewards' Enquiry : Andrew Heffernan caution: used whip with excessive frequency.

FOCUS
Another routine handicap, run at just a fair pace, and they again came centre-to-stands' side up the home straight.
White Dart Official explanation: jockey said gelding never travelled and hung right
T/Plt: £1,715.30 to a £1 stake. Pool:£58,981.21 - 25.10 winning tickets T/Qpdt: £48.20 to a £1 stake. Pool:£5,903.34 - 90.50 winning tickets RY

5943 DONCASTER (L-H)
Friday, October 22

OFFICIAL GOING: Good (good to soft in places; 7.4)
Wind: moderate 1/2 against Weather: fine but breezy

7057 HRH PRINCESS ROYAL E B F MAIDEN FILLIES' STKS 1m (S)
2:15 (2:16) (Class 4) 2-Y-O £4,047 (£1,204; £601; £300) Stalls High

Form RPR
2 **1** **Devastation**23 6468 2-9-0 0 WilliamBuick 1 82
(J H M Gosden) *trckd ldrs: led 3f out: 3 l clr 1f out: hld on towards fin* **2/1**2
2 1/2 **Izzi Top** 2-9-0 0 RobertHavlin 12 81+
(J H M Gosden) *dwlt: hld up towards rr: hdwy and swtchd lft 2f out: chsd wnr 1f out: styd on strly: promising r* **33/1**
4 **3** 1 3/4 **Encore Une Annee**24 6442 2-9-0 0 JimCrowley 14 77
(R M Beckett) *hld up in mid-div: hdwy over 2f out: styd on strly fnl f: will do bttr* **8/1**3
4 2 1/2 **Mantatisi** 2-9-0 0 PatCosgrave 10 71
(J R Fanshawe) *in tch: effrt over 2f out: chsng wnr over 1f out: kpt on same pce* **40/1**
020 **5** 1 1/2 **Spey Song (IRE)**13 6748 2-9-0 79 PaulHanagan 16 68
(J D Bethell) *chsd ldrs: one pce fnl 2f* **14/1**
2 **6** 1/2 **Complexion**32 6248 2-9-0 0 RyanMoore 4 67
(Sir Michael Stoute) *w ldrs: racd keenly: pushed along 3f out: fdd fnl f* **15/8**1
7 1 1/4 **Armoise** 2-9-0 0 SebSanders 7 64
(M Botti) *s.i.s: mid-div: hdwy 3f out: kpt on: nvr rchd ldrs* **28/1**
8 3/4 **Reem Star** 2-9-0 0 TomMcLaughlin 8 62
(E A L Dunlop) *in rr: sn drvn along: kpt on fnl 2f: nvr nr ldrs* **100/1**
9 3/4 **Jeu De Vivre (IRE)** 2-9-0 0 KierenFallon 5 60
(M Johnston) *dwlt: sn chsng ldrs: wknd over 1f out* **20/1**
00 **10** 1 **Mujarah (IRE)**12 6770 2-9-0 0 RichardHills 15 58
(J L Dunlop) *hld up in rr: sme hdwy 2f out: nvr a factor* **66/1**
11 3 1/2 **May Burnett (IRE)** 2-9-0 0 (t) MickyFenton 17 50
(B S Rothwell) *in rr: nvr a factor* **200/1**
3 **12** nk **Sugar Hiccup (IRE)**17 6651 2-9-0 0 LukeMorris 9 49
(C G Cox) *chsd ldrs: lost pl 2f out* **12/1**
13 1/2 **Supreme Seductress (IRE)** 2-9-0 0 MichaelHills 13 48
(B W Hills) *in rr: nvr on terms* **25/1**
0 **14** nk **Alluring Star**27 6360 2-9-0 0 GrahamGibbons 3 47
(M W Easterby) *led tl 3f out: wknd over 1f out* **200/1**
0563 **15** 1 1/4 **Willow's Wish**23 6457 2-8-11 50 PatrickDonaghy(3) 11 45
(G M Moore) *mid-div: drvn 3f out: sn wknd* **200/1**
16 5 **Bailadeira** 2-8-9 0 DaleSwift(5) 6 33
(T J Etherington) *mid-div: drvn over 3f out: sn lost pl* **100/1**
17 15 **Felt** 2-9-0 0 DavidAllan 2 —
(J G Given) *sn chsng ldrs on outside: hung lft and lost pl over 2f out: sn bhd: t.o* **100/1**

1m 42.77s (3.47) **Going Correction** +0.15s/f (Good) 17 Ran SP% 117.0
Speed ratings (Par 94): **88,87,85,83,81 81,80,79,78,77 74,73,73,72,71 66,51**
toteswingers:1&2:£15.70, 1&3:£5.00, 2&3:£41.20 CSF £77.56 TOTE £2.80: £1.10, £6.80, £2.60; EX 55.10 Trifecta £659.40 Part won. Pool: £891.13 - 0.64 winning units..
Owner Duke Of Roxburghe **Bred** Floors Farming **Trained** Newmarket, Suffolk

FOCUS
This is often a good juvenile fillies' maiden. They raced down the centre of the track and there was just an ordinary pace on, with the ground looking on the easy side of good. The Gosden pair came clear and the form is decent.

NOTEBOOK
Devastation is the second foal of the top-class Attraction and had run a big race when going down narrowly on debut at Nottingham last month. She looked to have come on for that experience and seemed sure to win nicely when stretching clear of the field at the two-furlong pole. However, she was typing up inside the final furlong and only just held off her stablemate at the business end. It was probably a case of her idling somewhat due to inexperience, an opinion later confirmed by her rider, and this scopey filly should make up into a decent horse over further at three. (op 5-2)
Izzi Top ◆ is a stablemate of the winner and very much the second string. She was ridden out the back early on, but really caught the eye making ground effortlessly around 2f out, where her rider met some trouble. She was hardly fully extended to get closer thereafter, but continually made up ground towards the finish and would've surely made a winning debut under more vigorous handling (rider never went for the whip). She has a choice pedigree, should be suited by stepping up to 1m2f next year and looks a surefire winner of a maiden before going onto better things.
Encore Une Annee ◆ was doing her best work towards the finish on this step up in trip and bettered the level of her Newbury debut last month. She has a definite future and will relish stepping up in trip next term. (op 15-2 tchd 13-2)
Mantatisi ◆, whose pedigree suggests a mix of speed and stamina, showed a nice level of ability and clearly stays well enough. She ought to come on for the initial experience and win a maiden. (op 33-1)

Spey Song(IRE), a beaten favourite last time, showed more again for this return to better ground and looks good enough to win an ordinary maiden. With an official mark of 79 she helps to set the level here. (op 12-1 tchd 16-1)

Complexion, who got going late when second on debut over 7f at Kempton, was on her toes beforehand yet met strong support on this switch to turf. She raced a lot more positively this time, indeed she did too much through the first 2f, and produced a limited response when eventually asked for her effort. She is better than this, but the run goes some way to confirming her limitations. (op 2-1 tchd 7-4)

Armoise has a nice middle-distance pedigree and posted an encouraging debut effort considering the outing looked needed. She ought to step up nicely on this next time out. (op 33-1)

Sugar Hiccup(IRE), easy to back, failed to improve as might have been expected for the extra furlong and switch to a sounder surface. She now has a bit to prove. (op 9-1)

7058 "TOOL@RREST" DROP STOPS HERE E B F MAIDEN STKS 7f

2:45 (2:53) (Class 4) 2-Y-O **£4,047** (£1,204; £601; £300) **Stalls** High

Form RPR

3 **1** **Bridgefield (USA)**[21] 6532 2-9-3 0 ..... AhmedAjtebi 20 81
(Mahmood Al Zarooni) *trckd ldrs: hdwy 1/2-way: chal jst over 2f out: sn led: rdn over 1f out: styd on strly u.p fnl f* **9/2**[1]

2 *1 1/4* **Kirthill (IRE)** 2-9-3 0 ..... KierenFallon 13 77
(L M Cumani) *hld up towards rr: hdwy 3f out: trckd ldrs 2f out: sn rdn and styd on u.p fnl f* **16/1**

2 **3** *1/2* **Sirius Prospect (USA)**[24] 6443 2-9-3 0 ..... PhilipRobinson 19 76
(D K Ivory) *led: rdn along and jnd over 2f out: hdd wl over 1f out and sn drvn: one pce fnl f* **9/2**[1]

03 **4** *hd* **Red Lover**[24] 6443 2-9-3 0 ..... JimCrowley 12 75
(E A L Dunlop) *hld up towards rr: hdwy 1/2-way: trckd ldrs over 2f out: rdn to chse wnr wl over 1f out: drvn and one pce fnl f* **7/1**[3]

6 **5** *2 1/2* **Figaro**[21] 6532 2-9-3 0 ..... MichaelHills 18 69
(W J Haggas) *hld up towards rr: hdwy wl over 2f out: rdn over 1f out: kpt on ins fnl f: nrst fin* **13/2**[2]

6 *3/4* **Fadhaa (IRE)** 2-9-3 0 ..... RichardHills 5 67
(B W Hills) *s.i.s: smooth hdwy after 2f: cl up 1/2-way: rdn over 2f out and grad wknd* **12/1**

05 **7** *1 1/4* **Lightning Cloud (IRE)**[22] 6488 2-9-3 0 ..... RobertWinston 15 64
(K A Ryan) *hld up and bhd: hdwy wl over 2f out: swtchd lft over 1f out: kpt on fnl f: nrst fin* **100/1**

8 *1 1/2* **Steenbok (IRE)** 2-9-3 0 ..... WilliamBuick 17 60
(J H M Gosden) *chsd ldrs: rdn along over 2f out: sn wknd* **11/1**

2 **9** *1* **Calaf**[36] 6126 2-9-3 0 ..... StevieDonohoe 4 57
(Jane Chapple-Hyam) *dwlt: hdwy to trck ldrs bef 1/2-way: rdn along over 2f out: grad wknd* **16/1**

00 **10** *1* **Korngold**[24] 6442 2-9-3 0 ..... TedDurcan 14 55
(J L Dunlop) *hld up and bhd tl sme late hdwy* **33/1**

04 **11** *shd* **Levitate**[15] 6689 2-9-3 0 ..... RyanMoore 11 54
(Sir Michael Stoute) *in tch: rdn along bef 1/2-way: sn outpcd* **9/2**[1]

0 **12** *7* **Ride The Wind**[24] 6441 2-8-12 0 ..... SebSanders 3 31
(C F Wall) *dwlt: a towards rr* **50/1**

13 *4* **Dashing Eddie (IRE)** 2-9-3 0 ..... JamieSpencer 1 26
(K A Ryan) *hmpd s: a outpcd in rr* **40/1**

0 **14** *1/2* **Greenhead High**[21] 6532 2-9-3 0 ..... J-PGuillambert 6 25
(P Howling) *cl up: rdn along 1/2-way: sn wknd* **200/1**

15 *1 1/2* **Mint Imperial (IRE)** 2-9-3 0 ..... PatCosgrave 9 21
(Miss Amy Weaver) *a in rr* **100/1**

0 **16** *3/4* **Scottish Lake**[29] 6301 2-9-3 0 ..... JimmyQuinn 16 19
(Jedd O'Keeffe) *a in rr* **100/1**

00 **17** *1 3/4* **Cottam Donny**[23] 6458 2-8-10 0 ..... JohnCavanagh(7) 8 14
(M Brittain) *a in rr: bhd fr 1/2-way* **200/1**

00 **18** *10* **Oakwell (IRE)**[20] 6566 2-9-3 0 ..... MickyFenton 2 —
(Miss S E Hall) *trckd ldrs: hdwy and cl up after 3f: rdn along 3f out: sn wknd: bhd fnl 2f* **200/1**

1m 27.92s (1.62) **Going Correction** +0.15s/f (Good) **18** Ran SP% **120.0**
Speed ratings (Par 97): **96,94,94,93,90 90,88,86,85,84 84,76,71,71,69 68,66,55**
toteswingers:1&2:£14.80, 1&3:£5.20, 2&3:£17.80 CSF £78.42 TOTE £4.80: £1.90, £5.00, £1.60; EX 71.40 Trifecta £721.90 Part won. Pool: £975.59 - 0.83 winning units..

Owner Godolphin **Bred** B M Kelley **Trained** Newmarket, Suffolk

FOCUS

A fair juvenile maiden with a wide-open look about it. There was a fair pace on down the centre of the track and the form looks straightforward enough, rated around the third and fourth.

NOTEBOOK

Bridgefield(USA) readily got off the mark at the second time of asking. He showed the clear benefit of his debut experience at Newmarket 21 days previously, which came in a good race on softer ground, and rates value for a little further as he didn't look to be doing a great deal out in front nearing the finish. Another furlong will not bother him as he matures and he rates a very useful prospect. (tchd 7-2 and 5-1)

Kirthill(IRE) ◆ is bred to get a bit further next year and was doing all of his best work late in the day here. He ought to improve a good deal for this experience and should prove very hard to beat on his next assignment.

Sirius Prospect(USA) finished a pleasing second to the promising Mantoba at Newbury on debut last month and held every chance, running very close to his previous level. This added experience will not be lost on him and he remains a horse of potential. (tchd 6-1)

Red Lover again travelled nicely and was produced with every chance, but rather flattened out towards the finish. He still ran right up to his last-time-out form with the third and now qualifies for nurseries. (op 11-2 tchd 15-2)

Figaro ◆ was expected to step up on the level of his Newmarket debut and he posted a more encouraging effort, shaping as though another furlong would suit ideally. He will be winning races in due course. (op 7-1 tchd 15-2 and 6-1)

Fadhaa(IRE), whose dam won over 1m2f and is a half-sister to Sakhee, was not the best out of the gates but still showed up nicely for a long way. He should last a good bit longer next time out.

Lightning Cloud(IRE) ◆ proved well suited by stepping back up a furlong and turned in a career-best. He should do better as he matures and is one to keep an eye on now he qualifies for nurseries.

Steenbok(IRE) caught the eye on breeding, but doesn't have much scope and proved very easy to back for this racecourse debut. He tired late on, but ought to step up for the experience and one could see him enjoying a switch to Polytrack. (op 9-1 tchd 12-1)

Calaf, a close second on debut at Yarmouth last time, was expected to enjoy this stiffer test but failed to see it out and dropping back a furlong looks on the cards. (op 14-1 tchd 12-1)

Levitate was an eyecatcher at Newbury last time so it wasn't surprising to see him attract support here. However, he once again proved too green to do himself justice and dropping back a furlong didn't help. He is looking more of a handicap prospect for next year, for which he is now eligible. (op 8-1)

7059 BETFAIR SUPPORTS SIA AND HEARTBEAT APPEAL NURSERY 1m (S)

3:20 (3:23) (Class 2) 2-Y-O **£6,670** (£1,984; £991; £495) **Stalls** High

Form RPR

2212 **1** **Humdrum**[20] 6563 2-8-10 **76** ..... RyanMoore 7 82
(R Hannon) *trckd ldrs: chal over 1f out: r.o to ld fnl stride* **10/3**[1]

0101 **2** *shd* **Mariachi Man**[22] 6505 2-9-7 **87** ..... DavidAllan 9 93
(T D Easterby) *w ldr: edgd lft over 2f out: led wl over 1f out: hdd post* **9/2**[3]

61 **3** *2 1/4* **Namibian (IRE)**[13] 6748 2-9-2 **82** ..... KierenFallon 2 83
(M Johnston) *sn outpcd in rr and drvn along: hdwy 5f out: wnt 3rd over 1f out: kpt on same pce* **7/2**[2]

153 **4** *1/2* **Dads Amigo**[120] 3364 2-9-3 **83** ..... JamieSpencer 8 83
(D H Brown) *hld up: effrt over 2f out: kpt on fnl f* **28/1**

0622 **5** *1 1/4* **Golden Blaze**[26] 6386 2-8-2 **68** ..... JimmyQuinn 4 65
(James Moffatt) *led tl wl over 1f out: one pce* **10/1**

631 **6** *1* **Lady Gar Gar**[20] 6569 2-8-2 **68** ..... SilvestreDeSousa 1 63
(G R Oldroyd) *trckd ldrs on outside: swtchd rt over 3f out: effrt stands' side rail over 2f out: one pce: hung lft last 100yds* **8/1**

312 **7** *3* **Goldenveil (IRE)**[36] 6104 2-9-2 **82** ..... PaulHanagan 5 70
(R A Fahey) *trckd ldrs: t.k.h: effrt over 2f out: hung lft and wknd over 1f out* **13/2**

4630 **8** *4 1/2* **Coachlight**[11] 6810 2-8-5 **71** ..... (b[1]) MartinLane 6 48
(J L Dunlop) *chsd ldrs: lost pl over 2f out* **33/1**

003 **9** *1* **Hollow Tree**[15] 6689 2-8-6 **75** ..... SimonPearce(3) 3 50
(A M Balding) *trckd ldrs: drvn 3f out: sn lost pl* **12/1**

1m 41.29s (1.99) **Going Correction** +0.15s/f (Good) **9** Ran SP% **111.1**
Speed ratings (Par 101): **96,95,93,93,91 90,87,83,82**
toteswingers:1&2:£3.30, 1&3:£3.10, 2&3:£4.30 CSF £17.44 CT £52.37 TOTE £3.70: £1.40, £1.60, £1.50; EX 16.40 Trifecta £24.40 Pool: £942.35 - 28.43 winning units..

Owner The Queen **Bred** The Queen **Trained** East Everleigh, Wilts

FOCUS

A competitive nursery. The main action was down the centre of the track late on and the form looks good, despite there being no more than an average pace on.

NOTEBOOK

Humdrum deservedly got back to winning ways and registered a second career success. She shaped better than the bare form when a strong-finishing second on soft ground at Newmarket last time, for which she was raised 2lb, and she got a more straightforward ride over this extra furlong. It was her best effort yet, she enjoys a bit of cut in the ground and there should be more to come from her over an even stiffer test as a 3-y-o. (op 7-2 tchd 4-1)

Mariachi Man was a very game winner at Newmarket 22 days earlier and went down fighting off this 5lb higher mark. This imposing colt was a clear second best, needs some cut underfoot and the best of him has very likely still to be seen. (op 10-3)

Namibian(IRE) comfortably landed his maiden on soft ground at York 13 days earlier and looked fairly treated for this nursery debut over the extra furlong. However, he raced very lazily through the first half of the race and was coming back at the first pair far too late in the day. He should be given the benefit of the doubt as this was just his third outing, and more positive handling is probably required. (tchd 10-3)

Dads Amigo ◆, stepping up two furlongs, was making his nursery debut after a 120-day absence and was awash with sweat. Given a very patient ride, he would've no doubt preferred a stronger pace and looks well worth another chance over this trip. (op 33-1)

Golden Blaze had narrowly found one too good on his last two outings and was up 4lb for his latest effort at Ascot. He got a positive ride, but was done with from the furlong marker and may prefer a quicker surface. (op 12-1 tchd 14-1)

Lady Gar Gar, off the mark at Redcar 20 days previously, originally made her challenge towards the stands' rail before drifting towards the middle when held late on. The extra furlong proved beyond her at this stage, but she does appear weighted to win a nursery back over 7f. (tchd 7-1)

Goldenveil(IRE), who endured a hard race in defeat at Ayr on her previous outing, looked to pay for running somewhat with the choke out. She is another that could prove happier back over 7f in the short term. (op 7-1 tchd 8-1)

7060 SOVEREIGN HEALTH CARE H'CAP 6f

3:55 (3:58) (Class 2) (0-105,105) 3-Y-O+ **£9,714** (£2,890; £1,444; £721) **Stalls** High

Form RPR

0201 **1** **Mac's Power (IRE)**[25] 6429 4-8-10 **90** ..... (t) PatCosgrave 17 103+
(J R Fanshawe) *stdd s and hld up in rr: hdwy 2f out: effrt and n.m.r over 1f out: rdn and qcknd ent fnl f: led last 100yds* **8/1**[2]

2100 **2** *1 1/2* **Esprit De Midas**[14] 6721 4-8-9 **89** ..... StevieDonohoe 20 97
(K A Ryan) *hld up in rr: hdwy on wd outside wl over 1f out: rdn and kpt on strly ins fnl f* **50/1**

2400 **3** *3/4* **Enderby Spirit (GR)**[42] 5911 4-8-10 **90** ..... (p) JimCrowley 6 96
(B Smart) *trckd ldrs: gd hdwy on inner over 1f out: rdn to ld ent fnl f: drvn and hdd last 100yds: one pce* **33/1**

5342 **4** *nk* **Golden Desert (IRE)**[7] 6888 6-9-5 **99** ..... RyanMoore 16 104
(R A Mills) *t.k.h: trckd ldrs: effrt 2f out: sn rdn and ch tl drvn and kpt on same pce ins fnl f* **5/1**[1]

5352 **5** *nk* **Ancient Cross**[13] 6739 6-8-9 **89** ..... (t) GrahamGibbons 21 93
(M W Easterby) *in tch on outer: hdwy 2f out: rdn to chse ldrs over 1f out: drvn and one pce ins fnl f* **10/1**[3]

0640 **6** *3/4* **Knot In Wood (IRE)**[13] 6752 8-9-4 **98** ..... FrankieDettori 9 99
(R A Fahey) *chsd ldrs: hdwy over 2f out: rdn to chal wl over 1f out: and sn led: drvn and hdd ent fnl f: one pce* **16/1**

0215 **7** *nse* **Tajneed (IRE)**[13] 6752 7-9-6 **103** ..... MichaelO'Connell(3) 3 104
(D Nicholls) *led: rdn along over 2f out: hdd wl over 1f out: sn drvn and grad wknd* **18/1**

0040 **8** *shd* **Kellys Eye (IRE)**[12] 6776 3-8-12 **93** ..... JamieSpencer 2 94+
(D H Brown) *hld up towards rr: hdwy whn nt clr run over 1f out: sn swtchd rt: rdn and styd on wl fnl f: nrst fin* **20/1**

4324 **9** *1 1/4* **Iver Bridge Lad**[13] 6735 3-9-10 **105** ..... (b) KierenFallon 12 102
(J Ryan) *midfield: pushed along 1/2-way: rdn and hdwy over 1f out: sn drvn and one pce* **14/1**

0605 **10** *1/2* **Prince Of Dance**[11] 6806 4-9-4 **98** ..... SteveDrowne 1 93
(J R Gask) *in tch: hdwy 2f out: sn rdn and no imp fnl f* **20/1**

2223 **11** *shd* **Secret Witness**[13] 6735 4-9-6 **100** ..... (b) TomMcLaughlin 14 95
(R A Harris) *prom: rdn along over 2f out: drvn 1f out and sn wknd* **14/1**

0204 **12** *hd* **Parisian Pyramid (IRE)**[13] 6752 4-9-4 **98** ..... StephenCraine 7 92
(K A Ryan) *prom: rdn along 2f out: grad wknd* **33/1**

1506 **13** *nk* **Rasaman (IRE)**[14] 6706 6-8-1 **88** ..... HarryBentley(7) 22 81
(J S Goldie) *chsd ldrs: rdn along over 2f out and sn wknd* **40/1**

0136 **14** *1/2* **Quest For Success (IRE)**[13] 6752 5-9-0 **99** ..... AdamBeschizza(5) 15 91
(R A Fahey) *prom: effrt over 2f out: sn rdn and ch tl drvn: edgd lft and wknd ent fnl f* **16/1**

2400 **15** *shd* **Advanced**[14] 6721 7-8-12 **95** AmyRyan(3) 8 86
(K A Ryan) *chsd ldrs: pushed along whn n.m.r over 2f out: sn rdn and wknd* **20/1**

0430 **16** *nk* **Singeur (IRE)**[41] 5944 3-9-0 **95** SilvestreDeSousa 19 85
(R Bastiman) *hld up in tch: effrt and n.m.r 2f out: sn swtchd rt: rdn and btn over 1f out* **16/1**

1054 **17** *½* **Baby Strange**[11] 6799 6-8-8 **93** DaleSwift(5) 4 82+
(D Shaw) *v.s.a and bhd tl sme late hdwy* **14/1**

5010 **18** *nk* **Summerinthecity (IRE)**[12] 6776 3-8-11 **92** DarryllHolland 13 80
(J Noseda) *hld up: hdwy 2f out: sn rdn and btn* **14/1**

1020 **19** *4 ½* **Rash Judgement**[13] 6735 5-9-0 **94** RobertWinston 10 67
(E J Alston) *chsd ldrs: rdn along 2f out: sn drvn and wknd* **66/1**

0404 **20** *1 ¾* **Joseph Henry**[14] 6721 8-8-7 **87** AdrianNicholls 11 55
(D Nicholls) *cl up: rdn along over 2f out: sn wknd* **14/1**

0-04 **21** *23* **Flying Statesman (USA)**[27] 6363 3-8-8 **89** PaulHanagan 18 —
(R A Fahey) *in tch: pushed along 1/2-way: rdn and wknd qckly 2f out: sn bhd and eased* **10/1**[3]

1m 13.05s (-0.55) **Going Correction** +0.15s/f (Good)
WFA 3 from 4yo+ 1lb **21** Ran SP% **128.3**
Speed ratings (Par 109): **109,107,106,105,105 104,104,104,102,101 101,101,100,100,100 99,99,98,92,90 59**
toteswingers:1&2:£62.30, 1&3:£51.90, 2&3:Not won CSF £386.03 CT £12145.26 TOTE £11.50: £3.20, £14.40, £10.60, £1.50; EX 516.80 TRIFECTA Not won..
Owner Michael McDonnell **Bred** Ballyhane Stud **Trained** Newmarket, Suffolk

FOCUS
A decent sprint handicap and it was highly competitive. The field pretty much shunned the stands' side of the track and it was run at a solid pace. Strong form, with a 6lb personal best from the winner.

NOTEBOOK
Mac's Power(IRE) ◆ was 5lb higher for a ready success at Kempton last month and he followed up on this return to turf in great style. Very patiently ridden, he travelled strongly and his rider timed his challenge perfectly. He obviously likes this venue as his form figures here now read - 2171 - and a fast-run 6f now looks very much his optimum trip. Another rise is now forthcoming but he could well have more to offer in this division next season, when a campaign could well be based around a crack at the Wokingham Handicap at Royal Ascot.
Esprit De Midas ◆ had failed to fire over 7f the last twice, but was a good winner over this trip three runs back and this was much more like it again from him. He came from a long way back, making his effort more towards the near side, and clearly enjoys some cut on turf. He needs things to fall right, but is capable of defying this mark.
Enderby Spirit(GR), with cheekpieces replacing a visor, raced near the far rail and, asked for everything nearing the furlong marker, held every chance. He hasn't won since last July, but has dropped to a decent mark now and this was a definite return to form. (op 28-1)
Golden Desert(IRE) had his chance, but looked to find this that bit too sharp dropping back from 7f and has become hard to win with. He still rates the benchmark. (op 6-1)
Ancient Cross made smooth headway from 2f out, but he is a fiendishly hard horse to actually win with and flattened out late on. (op 14-1 tchd 9-1)
Tajneed(IRE) ran a solid enough race from the front and is another that sets the standard. (op 20-1)
Kellys Eye(IRE) ◆ fared best of the 3-y-os. He was ridden out the back and hadn't been asked any sort of question nearing the furlong marker. There was a gap for him, but his rider waited and it soon closed as Ancient Cross elected to take it. That saw him having to switch right over to the stands' side and he ultimately finished with something left in the tank. He should've finished closer and he could well be the type to improve as a 4-y-o. (tchd 18-1 and 22-1)
Joseph Henry Official explanation: jockey said gelding hung left throughout
Flying Statesman(USA) Official explanation: jockey said gelding lost its action

7061 RACING POST / SIS BETTING SHOP MANAGER H'CAP 1m 6f 132y
4:30 (4:32) (Class 4) (0-85,88) 3-Y-O+ **£5,180** (£1,541; £770; £384) **Stalls** Low

Form RPR

-213 **1** **Ashbrittle**[40] 5989 3-9-10 **88** (v[1]) JimCrowley 6 97+
(R M Beckett) *trckd ldrs: wnt 2nd over 1f out: styd on to ld last 50yds* **7/1**[2]

2120 **2** *¾* **Comedy Act**[63] 5273 3-9-7 **85** SebSanders 13 93
(Sir Mark Prescott) *racd wd early: chsd ldr: led 4f out: hdd and no ex wl ins fnl f* **8/1**

0-00 **3** *1 ¼* **Spring Jim**[20] 6565 9-9-12 **81** KierenFallon 7 87+
(J R Fanshawe) *hld up towards rr: hdwy 7f out: nt clr run and swtchd outside over 2f out: edgd lft and styd on wl fnl f: tk 3rd last 75yds* **14/1**

0104 **4** *½* **Crocus Rose**[11] 6808 4-9-10 **79** JimmyQuinn 12 85
(H J L Dunlop) *in tch: effrt and chsng ldrs over 2f out: styd on same pce ins fnl f* **16/1**

000 **5** *½* **Pevensey (IRE)**[105] 3873 8-9-11 **80** (p) GrahamGibbons 11 85
(J J Quinn) *mid-div: hdwy on ins to chal over 3f out: kpt on same pce appr fnl f* **11/1**

6115 **6** *nk* **Descaro (USA)**[13] 6750 4-9-0 **69** SilvestreDeSousa 17 74
(D O'Meara) *chsd ldrs: one pce fnl 2f: n.m.r towards fin* **15/2**[3]

4211 **7** *½* **Regal Park (IRE)**[24] 6448 3-9-8 **86** (p) RyanMoore 16 90+
(J Noseda) *dwlt: in rr: hdwy 3f out: nt clr run over 1f out: one pce whn nt clr run 100yds out* **3/1**[1]

2066 **8** *1 ½* **Bow To No One (IRE)**[27] 6352 4-9-7 **83** HarryBentley(7) 19 85+
(A P Jarvis) *hld up in rr: hdwy over 2f out: edgd lft and kpt on: n.m.r wl ins fnl f: nvr rchd ldrs* **25/1**

113 **9** *7* **Broughtons Point**[53] 5612 4-9-0 **69** JamieMackay 15 61
(W J Musson) *gave problems s: swtchd lft after s: in rr: nvr a factor* **25/1**

0504 **10** *¾* **Camps Bay (USA)**[34] 6181 6-9-6 **80** DaleSwift(5) 20 71
(B Ellison) *swtchd lft s: in rr: effrt over 3f out: nvr a factor* **25/1**

5336 **11** *6* **Rare Ruby (IRE)**[36] 6114 6-9-1 **70** StephenCraine 10 53
(Jennie Candlish) *swtchd lft s: sn chsng ldrs: wknd 2f out* **33/1**

0055 **12** *nk* **Highland Legacy**[80] 4686 6-9-6 **75** JamieSpencer 4 58
(M L W Bell) *in rr: sme hdwy and swtchd lft over 2f out: nvr on terms* **16/1**

4 **13** *shd* **Mashdood (USA)**[17] 6661 4-9-1 **73** RobertLButler(3) 9 56
(P W Hiatt) *chsd ldrs: lost pl over 1f out* **100/1**

4501 **14** *nk* **Missionaire (USA)**[20] 6554 3-9-0 **83** (p) AdamBeschizza(5) 2 65
(W J Knight) *chsd ldrs: lost pl over 2f out* **9/1**

2234 **15** *1 ½* **Omokoroa (IRE)**[27] 6352 4-9-8 **77** MichaelHills 3 57
(M H Tompkins) *prom: chsng ldrs 3f out: wknd over 1f out* **12/1**

0020 **16** *½* **Arab League (IRE)**[6] 6926 5-9-8 **77** WilliamCarson 8 57
(R J Price) *mid-div: hdwy on inner 4f out: lost pl over 2f out* **28/1**

0016 **17** *4* **Alsahil (USA)**[13] 6754 4-8-10 **72** JamesRogers(7) 1 46
(Micky Hammond) *led: hdd 4f out: edgd rt and lost pl over 2f out* **33/1**

2003 **18** *30* **Red Wine**[52] 5631 11-8-9 **64** oh3 DavidAllan 14 —
(J A Glover) *t.k.h in rr: effrt and swtchd outside 3f out: wknd over 1f out: heavily eased: t.o* **33/1**

3m 8.23s (0.83) **Going Correction** +0.15s/f (Good)
WFA 3 from 4yo+ 9lb **18** Ran SP% **129.6**
Speed ratings (Par 105): **103,102,101,101,101 101,100,100,96,96 92,92,92,92,91 91,89,73**
toteswingers:1&2:£13.10, 1&3:£17.50, 2&3:£28.10 CSF £59.76 CT £794.97 TOTE £8.00: £1.90, £2.80, £3.40, £3.90; EX 81.40 TRIFECTA Not won..
Owner J L Rowsell **Bred** Ashbrittle Stud **Trained** Whitsbury, Hants
■ Stewards' Enquiry : Jim Crowley caution: used whip with excessive frequency
Seb Sanders one-day ban: used whip with excessive frequency (Nov 5)

FOCUS
This fair staying handicap was run at an average sort of pace and the first pair were never far away from front end. Little got involved from the rear but this is still form to treat fairly positively. The third helps with the standard.

7062 PERTEMPS H'CAP 1m 2f 60y
5:05 (5:05) (Class 4) (0-80,79) 3-Y-O+ **£3,885** (£1,156; £577; £288) **Stalls** Low

Form RPR

44-1 **1** **Bourne**[168] 1883 4-9-8 **77** KierenFallon 2 87+
(L M Cumani) *trckd ldrs on inner: hdwy over 3f out: swtchd rt and rdn to chse ldng pair over 1f out: drvn and styd on ins fnl f to ld last 100yds* **5/1**[2]

1233 **2** *½* **Rock The Stars (IRE)**[11] 6807 3-8-1 **66** AmyScott(5) 8 75
(J W Hills) *trckd ldrs: hdwy 3f out: rdn to chal and wandered 2f out: drvn: edgd lft and ev ch ent fnl f: kpt on* **33/1**

5532 **3** *shd* **Zahoo (IRE)**[15] 6691 3-9-5 **79** RichardHills 12 88+
(J L Dunlop) *hld up towards rr: hdwy 3f out: n.m.r and swtchd rt over 2f out: rdn to chse ldrs over 1f out: edgd lft and kpt on fnl f* **13/2**[3]

0343 **4** *shd* **Aneel**[20] 6557 3-9-2 **76** RyanMoore 1 85
(J Noseda) *trckd ldrs on inner: hdwy 3f out: swtchd rt and rdn to ld 2f out: drvn ent fnl f: hdd and no ex last 100yds* **25/1**

5000 **5** *1 ¾* **Wing Play (IRE)**[28] 6322 5-8-12 **72** (v[1]) AdamBeschizza(5) 6 77
(H Morrison) *t.k.h: trckd ldrs: effrt and nt much 3f out: sn swtchd rt and rdn over 2f out: swtchd rt again and drvn over 1f out: kpt on ins fnl f* **25/1**

21 **6** *1* **Dark Promise**[36] 6115 3-9-4 **78** PhilipRobinson 15 81+
(M A Jarvis) *midfield on wd outside: hdwy 1/2-way: rdn to chse ldrs whn hung lft over 2f out: drvn wl over 1f out: sn one pce* **5/2**[1]

2612 **7** *3 ¼* **King Zeal (IRE)**[14] 6724 6-9-3 **79** JamesRogers(7) 5 76
(B D Leavy) *trckd ldr: hdwy and cl up over 4f out: led 3f out: rdn 2f out: sn hdd and drvn: hld whn n.m.r over 1f out* **12/1**

0000 **8** *¾* **Follow The Flag (IRE)**[14] 6724 6-9-10 **79** (p) JamesDoyle 14 75
(A J McCabe) *midfield: effrt on outer over 3f out: rdn 2f out and sn no imp* **40/1**

542 **9** *shd* **Path Of Peace**[26] 6395 3-9-4 **78** GrahamGibbons 4 74
(J D Bethell) *hld up in midfield on inner: hdwy over 3f out: rdn to chse ldrs over 2f out: sn drvn and btn* **16/1**

-453 **10** *¾* **Beetuna (IRE)**[4] 6984 5-9-0 **74** MarkCoumbe(5) 17 68+
(D Bourton) *stdd s and hld up in rr: hdwy over 3f out: rdn over 2f out: n.d* **7/1**

2653 **11** *2 ½* **Prince Of Dreams**[16] 6678 3-9-0 **74** (t) ShaneKelly 18 63
(W J Knight) *t.k.h: a towards rr* **40/1**

221 **12** *1 ½* **Tarooq (USA)**[46] 5815 4-9-4 **73** FrankieDettori 3 60
(R A Fahey) *set stdy pce: qcknd over 4f out: rdn and hdd 3f out: drvn and wknd 2f out* **12/1**

3410 **13** *1 ¼* **Ailsa Craig (IRE)**[27] 6361 4-9-9 **78** DavidAllan 9 62
(E W Tuer) *hld up: hdwy over 4f out: chsng ldrs whn hmpd over 2f out: nt rcvr* **25/1**

0640 **14** *2 ¼* **Nevada Desert (IRE)**[10] 6832 10-8-7 **65** oh8 AmyRyan(3) 7 45
(R M Whitaker) *s.i.s: a in rr* **50/1**

0334 **15** *2 ¼* **Pittodrie Star (IRE)**[11] 6807 3-8-10 **70** (p) DavidProbert 16 46
(A M Balding) *a towards* **28/1**

/33- **16** *3 ½* **Orbitor**[545] 1512 4-9-3 **75** MatthewDavies(3) 13 44
(George Baker) *a towards rr* **50/1**

2060 **17** *5* **Wise Dennis**[36] 6105 8-9-1 **77** HarryBentley(7) 11 37
(A P Jarvis) *hld up: a in rr* **50/1**

-200 **18** *5* **Toledo Gold (IRE)**[26] 6394 4-9-1 **70** RobertWinston 10 20
(E J Alston) *chsd ldrs: rdn along over 3f out: sn wknd* **100/1**

2m 9.57s (0.17) **Going Correction** +0.15s/f (Good)
WFA 3 from 4yo+ 5lb **18** Ran SP% **122.0**
Speed ratings (Par 105): **105,104,104,104,103 102,99,99,98,98 96,95,94,92,90 87,83,79**
toteswingers:1&2:£27.90, 1&3:£6.40, 2&3:£34.50 CSF £170.18 CT £1103.28 TOTE £5.00: £1.90, £4.10, £1.60, £4.80; EX 189.00 TRIFECTA Not won..
Owner Aston House Stud **Bred** Aston House Stud **Trained** Newmarket, Suffolk

FOCUS
This fair handicap was another very competitive affair. It was run at an uneven pace, though, and racing prominently looked a definite advantage. Interesting form, with mostly unexposed types dominating.
Beetuna(IRE) Official explanation: jockey said gelding slipped coming out of stalls
Pittodrie Star(IRE) Official explanation: jockey said gelding hung left

7063 SIR RODNEY AND LADY WALKER E.A.R.S. APPRENTICE H'CAP 1m (S)
5:35 (5:35) (Class 5) (0-75,74) 3-Y-O+ **£3,238** (£963; £481; £240) **Stalls** High

Form RPR

0500 **1** **Bond City (IRE)**[15] 6701 8-9-7 **74** YoannBonnefoy 1 81
(G R Oldroyd) *t.k.h: w ldr: led 3f out: pushed 3 l clr appr fnl f: hld on towards fin* **16/1**

0332 **2** *¾* **Glenmuir (IRE)**[23] 6462 7-9-0 **67** (p) ShaneBKelly 6 72+
(J J Quinn) *hld up towards rr: hdwy over 2f out: carried hd high: kpt on to take 2nd last 50yds* **4/1**[2]

6122 **3** *½* **Nisaal (IRE)**[10] 6832 5-9-4 **71** MartinSeidl 7 75
(A W Carroll) *stdd s: hld up in rr: hdwy over 2f out: hung bdly lft: styd on to take 3rd nr fin* **9/2**[3]

4302 **4** *1 ¼* **Daring Dream (GER)**[36] 6108 5-9-5 **72** JulieBurke 5 73+
(J S Goldie) *hld up in mid-div: effrt over 2f out: chsd wnr jst ins fnl f: kpt on same pce* **7/2**[1]

0011 **5** *2* **Astrodonna**[23] 6479 5-9-1 **68** StefanoMura 8 65
(M H Tompkins) *hld up in rr: styd on fnl 2f: nvr rchd ldrs* **10/1**

215 **6** *3 ¼* **Frontline Girl (IRE)**[27] 6367 4-9-6 **73** PasqualeSalis 4 62
(Mrs K Burke) *w ldr: drvn 3f out: sn outpcd: wknd over 1f out* **4/1**[2]

1000 **7** *1* **Cavendish Road (IRE)**[5] 6958 4-9-5 **72** AntoineHamelin 3 59
(N J Vaughan) *trckd ldrs: effrt over 2f out: wknd over 1f out* **22/1**

0100 **8** *3 ¼* **Border Owl (IRE)**[69] 5071 5-9-0 **67** RyanClark 9 46
(P Salmon) *hld up in mid-div: hdwy to chal over 2f out: wknd jst ins fnl f* **14/1**

5460 **9** *4 ½* **Carlitos Spirit (IRE)**[4] 6984 6-9-1 **68** (v) PatrickGibson 2 37
(I W McInnes) *trckd ldrs: t.k.h: led 3f out: hung rt and lost pl 2f out* **12/1**

1m 40.62s (1.32) **Going Correction** +0.15s/f (Good) **9** Ran SP% **114.1**
Speed ratings (Par 103): **99,98,97,96,94 91,90,87,82**
toteswingers:1&2:£11.40, 1&3:£11.30, 2&3:£2.70 CSF £78.09 CT £345.55 TOTE £17.90: £3.00, £1.20, £1.50; EX 111.40 Trifecta £435.30 Part won. Pool: £588.34 - 0.20 winning units. Place 6: £141.29, Place 5: £63.83.
Owner R C Bond **Bred** David Ryan **Trained** Brawby, N Yorks
■ Stewards' Enquiry : Julie Burke caution: used whip with excessive frequency.

FOCUS
A moderate handicap that was run at an ordinary pace. Once again the middle of the track was the place to be. The form is rated around the winner to his summer form.
T/Jkpt: £24,939.50 to a £1 stake. Pool:£52,689.12 - 1.50 winning tickets T/Plt: £67.30 to a £1 stake. Pool:£99,098.07 - 1,073.36 winning tickets T/Qpdt: £20.70 to a £1 stake. Pool:£8,564.43 - 306.14 winning tickets WG

6930 WOLVERHAMPTON (A.W) (L-H)
Friday, October 22

OFFICIAL GOING: Standard
Wind: Fresh behind Weather: Overcast

7064 BETDAQ THE BETTING EXCHANGE CLASSIFIED STKS 5f 216y(P)
5:40 (5:40) (Class 6) 3-Y-0+ £1,706 (£503; £252) Stalls Low

Form RPR
0005 **1** **Ajara (IRE)**[21] 6537 4-9-1 55 RichardKingscote 10 65
(Tom Dascombe) *chsd ldr tl led over 1f out: rdn clr fnl f* 5/1[1]
3560 **2** 2 ¾ **Gemma's Delight (IRE)**[32] 6261 3-9-0 55 (p) KirstyMilczarek 6 56+
(J W Unett) *hld up: rdn and r.o ins fnl f: no ch w wnr* 8/1
3455 **3** 1 ¼ **Black Baccara**[2] 7018 3-9-0 54 (p) AdamKirby 8 52
(P S McEntee) *hld up: hdwy over 1f out: rdn and edgd lft ins fnl f: styd on* 6/1[3]
5350 **4** hd **Lordsbury Pride (USA)**[21] 6523 3-8-11 55 (b[1]) KierenFox(3) 1 52
(J R Best) *chsd ldrs: rdn and ev ch over 1f out: styd on same pce* 14/1
6330 **5** hd **Itsthursdayalready**[28] 6329 3-9-0 54 LiamJones 3 51
(W M Brisbourne) *hld up in tch: plld hrd: rdn over 1f out: styd on same pce ins fnl f* 5/1[1]
5436 **6** shd **Ruler's Honour (IRE)**[30] 6285 3-9-0 54 (p) LeeVickers 2 51
(T J Etherington) *chsd ldrs: rdn over 1f out: no ex ins fnl f* 22/1
6040 **7** nk **Bidruma**[43] 5898 3-9-0 55 TonyCulhane 4 50
(Mike Murphy) *led: hdd over 1f out: sn rdn and hung lft: no ex ins fnl f* 15/2
0000 **8** nk **Talent Scout (IRE)**[30] 6296 4-9-1 55 LiamKeniry 9 49+
(T D Walford) *s.i.s: hld up: r.o ins fnl f: nrst fin* 11/1
6060 **9** ¾ **Music Lover**[23] 6456 3-9-0 52 LukeMorris 12 46
(J F Panvert) *broke wl: sn stdd and lost pl: rdn and r.o ins fnl f: nvr trbld ldrs* 40/1
5340 **10** ¾ **Fathey (IRE)**[37] 6098 4-9-1 53 GregFairley 5 44
(C Smith) *s.i.s: hld up: hdwy over 2f out: wknd ins fnl f* 11/2[2]
0005 **11** 1 ½ **Boy The Bell**[7] 6896 3-9-0 53 SamHitchcott 11 39
(M Mullineaux) *hld up in tch: rdn over 2f out: wknd over 1f out* 18/1
5450 **12** 6 **Erfaan (USA)**[7] 6896 3-9-0 55 (p) BarryMcHugh 7 20
(Julie Camacho) *plld hrd and prom: rdn over 2f out: wknd over 1f out* 20/1

1m 14.64s (-0.36) **Going Correction** -0.025s/f (Stan)
WFA 3 from 4yo 1lb 12 Ran SP% **117.7**
Speed ratings (Par 101): **101,97,95,95,95 95,94,94,93,92 90,82**
toteswingers:1&2:£10.70, 1&3:£8.40, 2&3:£16.30 CSF £43.27 TOTE £4.90: £2.80, £6.30, £2.00; EX 63.80.
Owner Butt Scholes **Bred** Rozelle Bloodstock **Trained** Malpas, Cheshire
■ Stewards' Enquiry : Richard Kingscote one-day ban: careless riding (Nov 5); one-day ban: failed to ride to draw (Nov 6)

FOCUS
A low-grade affair but a fair pace gave everyone a chance. Limited but sound form.

7065 TRY BETDAQ FOR AN EXCHANGE MAIDEN STKS 5f 216y(P)
6:15 (6:18) (Class 5) 2-Y-0 £2,914 (£867; £433; £216) Stalls Low

Form RPR
423 **1** **Silver Ocean (USA)**[21] 6520 2-9-0 78 EJMcNamara(3) 1 77
(R M Beckett) *chsd ldrs: led over 1f out: rdn and hung lft ins fnl f: r.o* 9/4[1]
52 **2** 1 ¼ **Khaleeji**[15] 6697 2-9-3 0 DaneO'Neill 2 73
(J W Hills) *a.p: rdn and swtchd lft over 1f out: nt clr run and swtchd rt ins fnl f: r.o* 11/4[2]
0 **3** 1 ¼ **Spin Cast**[36] 6126 2-9-3 0 (v[1]) AdamKirby 11 70
(W R Swinburn) *mid-div: drvn along over 2f out: hdwy over 1f out: r.o u.p* 25/1
54 **4** ¾ **Royal Talisman**[14] 6711 2-9-3 0 LiamKeniry 3 67
(Matthew Salaman) *led early: chsd ldrs: rdn and ev ch over 1f out: styd on same pce ins fnl f* 12/1
034 **5** 1 ½ **Blowing Bubbles (USA)**[8] 6869 2-8-12 0 WilliamBuick 7 58
(B J Meehan) *ponied to the s: sn led: rdn and hdd over 1f out: no ex ins fnl f* 7/1
02 **6** nk **Crimson Cloud**[17] 6646 2-8-12 0 PaulHanagan 4 57
(R A Fahey) *prom: rdn over 1f out: no ex fnl f* 3/1[3]
06 **7** 9 **Cadmium Loch**[14] 6712 2-9-0 0 RussKennemore(3) 6 35
(R Hollinshead) *hld up: hdwy 2f out: sn rdn: wknd fnl f* 100/1
8 2 ¾ **Irish Boy (IRE)** 2-9-3 0 TravisBlock 8 27
(W J H Ratcliffe) *sn outpcd: nvr nrr* 80/1
9 2 ¼ **Saubestre** 2-9-3 0 LiamJones 5 20
(J R Best) *s.s: outpcd* 50/1
05 **10** hd **Taverners Jubilee**[38] 6045 2-8-12 0 RossAtkinson(5) 10 19
(Patrick Morris) *hld up: drvn over 3f out: a in rr* 100/1
11 3 ½ **Walshestown Lad (IRE)** 2-9-3 0 LukeMorris 9 9
(R A Harris) *prom: chsd ldr over 3f out tl rdn and hung rt over 2f out: sn wknd* 66/1

1m 15.38s (0.38) **Going Correction** -0.025s/f (Stan) 11 Ran SP% **113.1**
Speed ratings (Par 95): **96,94,92,91,89 89,77,73,70,70 65**
toteswingers:1&2:£1.70, 1&3:£11.10, 2&3:£10.50 CSF £7.99 TOTE £2.30: £1.10, £1.20, £5.40; EX 8.40.
Owner M Nelmes-Crocker **Bred** Sun Valley Farm **Trained** Whitsbury, Hants

FOCUS
A fair AW maiden on the figures.

NOTEBOOK
Silver Ocean(USA) went into this rated a highly respectable 78, and his maiden form is solid over this trip and 5f. He won with a bit in hand and should go on from here. (op 5-2)
Khaleeji has done well in three races, one on turf, and all at 6f. He is now qualified for handicaps but has every chance of landing a maiden first. (tchd 5-2 and 3-1)
Spin Cast ran a more satisfactory race in a first-time visor, so it is worth using again. This was a sound AW debut and he can do better if continuing to respond to the headgear, with 7f likely to suit. (op 28-1)
Royal Talisman has shown ability in 6f and 7f maidens but needs to improve a little to win one, so a switch to handicaps is worth considering. (op 16-1)
Blowing Bubbles(USA), ponied to the start 20 minutes before race-time, was worth trying with these more positive tactics but she has been well beaten in her last two races. (op 6-1)
Crimson Cloud wants to hang right, so Kempton might suit better. (tchd 4-1)

7066 BETDAQ.COM NURSERY 1m 141y(P)
6:45 (6:47) (Class 4) (0-80,80) 2-Y-0 £3,011 (£896; £447; £223) Stalls Low

Form RPR
061 **1** **Buxfizz (USA)**[18] 6634 2-9-7 80 PaulHanagan 5 85
(R A Mills) *hld up in tch: pushed along 3f out: rdn to ld over 1f out: hung lft ins fnl f: r.o* 10/3[2]
0410 **2** ½ **Wafeira**[20] 6563 2-9-5 78 TomQueally 1 82
(H R A Cecil) *a.p: rdn and ev ch fr over 1f out: hung lft ins fnl f: r.o* 5/2[1]
5433 **3** 3 **Claret'N'Blue (USA)**[13] 6743 2-9-4 77 SebSanders 8 75
(B J Meehan) *hld up: hdwy 4f out: rdn to ld wl over 1f out: sn hdd: styd on same pce ins fnl f* 6/1[3]
2050 **4** 4 **Ollon (USA)**[41] 5947 2-8-13 72 BarryMcHugh 2 61
(R A Fahey) *s.i.s: hld up: rdn over 2f out: nvr on terms* 7/1
0142 **5** ½ **Captain Loui (IRE)**[15] 6694 2-8-3 65 (p) SimonPearce(3) 9 53
(D Burchell) *led: rdn over 2f out: hdd over 1f out: wknd fnl f* 12/1
0240 **6** 2 ¼ **Areopagitica**[12] 6770 2-8-0 59 (p) CathyGannon 7 43
(J L Flint) *prom: chsd ldr 4f out: rdn over 2f out: wknd fnl f* 22/1
144 **7** 1 **Mutual Force (USA)**[12] 6777 2-9-5 78 AhmedAjtebi 6 59
(Mahmood Al Zarooni) *hld up: rdn over 2f out: a in rr* 13/2
3310 **8** nk **Dazzling Valentine**[13] 6745 2-8-13 72 LukeMorris 4 53
(A Bailey) *chsd ldr over 4f: rdn over 2f out: wknd over 1f out* 12/1

1m 50.09s (-0.41) **Going Correction** -0.025s/f (Stan) 8 Ran SP% **111.5**
Speed ratings (Par 97): **100,99,96,93,92 90,90,89**
toteswingers:1&2:£3.10, 1&3:£3.80, 2&3:£2.00 CSF £11.45 CT £45.02 TOTE £7.00: £2.60, £1.30, £2.00; EX 14.00.
Owner Buxted Partnership **Bred** Darley **Trained** Headley, Surrey

FOCUS
A decent AW nursery, with the top-ranked winner rated 80.

NOTEBOOK
Buxfizz(USA), a maiden winner on soft last time, transferred that improved form to sand on his second run on Polytrack. He looks the sort to stand his racing and should continue to improve. (op 4-1)
Wafeira, stepping back up in trip, ran a solid race in defeat. She goes well on Polytrack and should find a winning opportunity. (tchd 9-4 and 11-4)
Claret'N'Blue(USA), admirably consistent, was beaten by two reasonable nursery types here, so this sort of mark may well be low enough to get him off the mark. (op 8-1)
Ollon(USA) made a creditable AW debut but probably needs a stronger gallop. He should be suited by this trip or a little further. (op 9-1)
Captain Loui(IRE) ran as if 7f suits him better. (op 8-1)
Areopagitica has some ability and should do better in this company when she comes down a few pounds. (op 20-1)

7067 GREAT OFFERS AT WOLVERHAMPTON-RACECOURSE.CO.UK H'CAP 2m 119y(P)
7:15 (7:16) (Class 4) (0-80,81) 3-Y-0+ £3,594 (£1,069; £534; £266) Stalls Low

Form RPR
2320 **1** **Saggiatore**[23] 6480 3-9-4 72 PaulHanagan 6 82+
(E A L Dunlop) *chsd ldrs: pushed along over 5f out: hdwy to ld over 2f out: sn rdn clr: styd on* 13/2
2134 **2** 3 **Joseph Lister**[27] 6359 3-9-13 81 WilliamBuick 1 87
(J H M Gosden) *hld up: rdn over 3f out: hdwy over 2f out: chsd wnr over 1f out: no imp ins fnl f* 3/1[2]
3314 **3** 1 ¾ **Sir Freddie**[25] 6416 4-9-9 70 JohnFahy(3) 8 74
(Lady Herries) *led: hdd 15f out: chsd ldr tl 7f out: remained handy: outpcd over 2f out: rallied over 1f out: styd on* 9/2[3]
2345 **4** 2 ¼ **Rawnaq (IRE)**[24] 6448 3-9-6 74 TadhgO'Shea 5 75
(M Johnston) *led 15f out: rdn and hdd over 3f out: styd on same pce appr fnl f* 5/1
13P5 **5** 3 ¾ **Corr Point (IRE)**[25] 6424 3-9-5 73 (t) FergusSweeney 2 70
(J A Osborne) *hld up: hdwy 2f out: wknd fnl f* 20/1
4450 **6** 1 ¾ **Calculating (IRE)**[15] 6693 6-9-9 72 LeeNewnes(5) 4 67
(M D I Usher) *s.i.s: hld up: hdwy 1/2-way: rdn over 2f out: wknd over 1f out* 25/1
0-01 **7** 2 **King's Realm (IRE)**[9] 6855 3-9-0 68 6ex SebSanders 3 60
(Sir Mark Prescott) *hld up: hdwy 1/2-way: chsd ldr 7f out tl rdn to ld over 3f out: hdd over 2f out: wknd over 1f out* 5/2[1]

3m 40.02s (-1.78) **Going Correction** -0.025s/f (Stan)
WFA 3 from 4yo+ 10lb 7 Ran SP% **110.4**
Speed ratings (Par 105): **103,101,100,99,97 97,96**
toteswingers:1&2:£4.20, 1&3:£4.70, 2&3:£2.80 CSF £24.41 CT £90.56 TOTE £5.70: £2.50, £2.00; EX 24.90.
Owner Cliveden Stud **Bred** Cliveden Stud Ltd **Trained** Newmarket, Suffolk

FOCUS
The generous early pace soon had them stretched out by 15 lengths and the first two both came from the ruck. The time was reasonable and the form looks sound.

7068 HAPPY 50TH BIRTHDAY STEVE ARIES H'CAP 1m 1f 103y(P)
7:45 (7:45) (Class 6) (0-60,60) 3-Y-0+ £1,706 (£503; £252) Stalls Low

Form RPR
1300 **1** **Strike Force**[31] 6269 6-9-7 57 (t) CathyGannon 7 71
(Miss Olivia Maylam) *hld up: hdwy over 2f out: led over 1f out: rdn clr fnl f* 12/1
5002 **2** 5 **Watchmaker**[6] 6930 7-9-10 60 (p) FergusSweeney 12 63+
(Miss Tor Sturgis) *chsd ldr tl led 5f out: rdn and hdd over 1f out: no ex fnl f* 9/2[3]
0005 **3** ½ **Bubbly Braveheart (IRE)**[19] 6020 3-9-6 60 LukeMorris 3 62
(A Bailey) *hld up: rdn over 2f out: styd on u.p fr over 1f out: nt trble ldrs* 7/1
0-64 **4** ½ **Royal Willy (IRE)**[6] 6934 4-9-9 59 PaulHanagan 8 60
(W Jarvis) *hld up: hdwy over 3f out: rdn and hung lft over 1f out: no ex fnl f* 7/2[1]
5264 **5** 3 ¼ **Bentley**[6] 6937 6-9-4 57 JohnFahy(3) 11 51
(B P J Baugh) *led over 4f: chsd ldr tl rdn over 1f out: wknd fnl f* 11/1
2510 **6** nk **Jezza**[74] 4913 4-9-3 53 StevieDonohoe 9 46
(V R A Dartnall) *dwlt: bhd: pushed along 1/2-way: styd on ins fnl f: nvr nrr* 16/1
6500 **7** nk **Diamond Daisy (IRE)**[90] 4394 4-9-10 60 SamHitchcott 6 53
(Mrs A Duffield) *chsd ldrs: drvn along over 5f out: wknd over 1f out* 40/1
0206 **8** 2 ¾ **Indian Violet (IRE)**[22] 6495 4-9-2 52 AdamKirby 5 39
(D W Thompson) *hld up: rdn over 3f out: nvr on terms* 20/1
4050 **9** ½ **Bernix**[14] 6718 8-9-10 60 (p) J-PGuillambert 10 46
(N Tinkler) *prom: rdn over 3f out: wknd wl over 1f out* 25/1
-050 **10** ½ **The Grey One (IRE)**[20] 6581 7-9-9 59 (p) LiamKeniry 4 44
(J M Bradley) *prom: rdn over 3f out: wknd wl over 1f out* 12/1

4315 **11** *7* **Pattern Mark**[27] 6375 4-9-6 **56**......(p) BarryMcHugh 2 26
(Ollie Pears) *mid-div: rdn over 3f out: wknd over 2f out* **4/1**[2]
2m 0.20s (-1.50) **Going Correction** -0.025s/f (Stan)
WFA 3 from 4yo+ 4lb **11** Ran SP% **113.6**
Speed ratings (Par 101): **105,100,100,99,96 96,96,93,93,92 86**
toteswingers:1&2:£9.20, 1&3:£18.80, 2&3:£9.30 CSF £61.63 CT £411.11 TOTE £20.10: £4.60, £1.80, £4.30; EX 85.60.
Owner Miss A L Hutchinson **Bred** Cheveley Park Stud Ltd **Trained** Newmarket, Suffolk
FOCUS
A decent gallop helped the winner come from the rear. He is rated back to his best, with the runner-up close to his latest form.
Pattern Mark Official explanation: jockey said gelding ran flat

7069 BREEDERS' CUP LIVE ONLY ON ATR MEDIAN AUCTION MAIDEN STKS 1m 1f 103y(P)
8:15 (8:16) (Class 6) 3-5-Y-O £1,706 (£503; £252) Stalls Low

Form RPR
2223 **1** **Plutocraft**[9] 6851 3-9-3 70...... PatCosgrave 4 75
(J R Fanshawe) *a.p: led 1f out: rdn out* **15/8**[1]
-366 **2** *2* **Hill Tribe**[77] 4786 3-8-12 71...... SteveDrowne 10 66
(J R Gask) *chsd ldr tl led 2f out: rdn and hdd 1f out: styd on same pce* **9/2**[2]
2553 **3** *nk* **Swift Return**[28] 6332 3-9-3 67......(v) WilliamCarson 6 70
(S C Williams) *hld up in tch: rdn over 1f out: edgd lft and styd on same pce ins fnl f* **12/1**
52 **4** *1* **Sennybridge**[14] 6716 3-8-12 0...... DaneO'Neill 9 63
(J W Hills) *chsd ldrs: rdn over 1f out: no ex ins fnl f* **5/1**[3]
432P **5** *6* **Resuscitator (USA)**[66] 5171 3-9-3 75......(v) SebSanders 7 55
(Mrs H S Main) *chsd ldrs: rdn over 1f out: wknd fnl f* **9/1**
0 **6** *½* **Just Zak**[62] 5303 5-9-7 0...... GregFairley 12 54
(O Brennan) *hld up: hdwy over 2f out: wknd over 1f out* **200/1**
00 **7** *7* **Rhythm Stick**[41] 5971 3-9-3 0...... CathyGannon 11 40
(John Berry) *hld up: a in rr* **33/1**
00 **8** *1* **Arakette (IRE)**[14] 6716 3-8-12 0...... RobertHavlin 8 32
(A B Haynes) *sn led: rdn and hdd 2f out: wknd over 1f out* **100/1**
66 **9** *½* **Mr Howe**[14] 6716 3-9-3 0...... BarryMcHugh 13 36
(T J Fitzgerald) *hld up: hdwy over 2f out: rdn: hung lft and wknd over 1f out* **80/1**
10 *10* **Beyond Rubies** 3-8-12 0...... TomQueally 2 10
(H R A Cecil) *dwlt: hld up: rdn and wknd over 2f out* **9/2**[2]
11 *2 ¼* **Big Bad Boo** 4-9-0 0...... AlexEdwards(7) 1 11
(J W Unett) *mid-div: lost pl 1/2-way: sn wknd* **66/1**
12 *4* **Avon Ferry** 3-8-7 0...... AmyBaker(5) 3 —
(A B Haynes) *s.s: outpcd* **100/1**
2m 0.73s (-0.97) **Going Correction** -0.025s/f (Stan)
WFA 3 from 4yo+ 4lb **12** Ran SP% **113.7**
Speed ratings (Par 101): **103,101,100,100,94 94,88,87,86,77 75,72**
toteswingers:1&2:£3.20, 1&3:£4.80, 2&3:£9.80 CSF £9.63 TOTE £2.40: £1.10, £2.80, £1.10; EX 11.50.
Owner The Owl Society **Bred** Howard Barton Stud **Trained** Newmarket, Suffolk
FOCUS
A middling maiden run at a good gallop. The form is best judged around the third.

7070 ATTHERACES.COM/BREEDERSCUP H'CAP (DIV I) 1m 141y(P)
8:45 (8:46) (Class 6) (0-55,55) 3-Y-O+ £1,364 (£403; £201) Stalls Low

Form RPR
065 **1** **Zafeen's Pearl**[224] 872 3-8-8 **50**...... SamHitchcott 3 56
(D K Ivory) *prom: chsd ldr over 6f out: rdn and hmpd over 1f out: r.o to ld post* **8/1**
5023 **2** *nse* **Tallawalla (IRE)**[7] 6905 3-8-13 **55**...... CathyGannon 4 61+
(M R Channon) *hld up: hmpd over 7f out: hdwy over 2f out: rdn to ld wl ins fnl f: hdd post* **4/1**[2]
0403 **3** *hd* **Rocky Mood (IRE)**[8] 6860 3-8-9 **51**......(p) LukeMorris 8 57
(W R Swinburn) *led: rdn and swvd rt over 1f out: hung lft and hdd wl ins fnl f* **7/2**[1]
5006 **4** *1 ½* **Piccolo Express**[34] 6188 4-8-10 **48**...... J-PGuillambert 7 50
(B P J Baugh) *hld up: hmpd over 7f out: hdwy over 6f out: rdn over 1f out: no ex towards fin* **25/1**
0000 **5** *1* **Royal Patriot (IRE)**[42] 5926 3-8-2 **47**...... JohnFahy(3) 10 47
(Paul Green) *hld up: hdwy u.p over 1f out: nt rch ldrs* **25/1**
2534 **6** *1 ½* **Tres Froide (FR)**[28] 6335 5-8-12 **50**......(p) PaulHanagan 6 46
(N Tinkler) *chsd ldrs: rdn over 2f out: no ex ins fnl f* **4/1**[2]
002- **7** *3* **Royal Island (IRE)**[392] 6256 8-9-3 **55**...... VinceSlattery 11 44
(M G Quinlan) *trckd ldrs: plld hrd: rdn over 1f out: no ex fnl f* **5/1**[3]
0030 **8** *4 ½* **Bold Hawk**[83] 4591 4-8-13 **54**......(tp) KierenFox(3) 13 33
(Mrs C A Dunnett) *hld up: rdn 1/2-way: nvr on terms* **50/1**
2302 **9** *5* **Libre**[38] 6062 10-8-5 **48**...... AshleyMorgan(5) 2 16
(F Jordan) *mid-div: wknd over 2f out* **9/1**
6000 **10** *11* **Boxer Shorts**[43] 5875 4-8-4 **49**......(t) JosephYoung(7) 5 —
(M Mullineaux) *hld up: hmpd over 7f out: wknd 4f out* **66/1**
000 **11** *27* **Ettrick Mill**[120] 3374 4-8-10 **48**......(p) LiamKeniry 9 —
(J M Bradley) *hld up: wknd wl over 2f out: t.o* **25/1**
1m 52.54s (2.04) **Going Correction** -0.025s/f (Stan)
WFA 3 from 4yo+ 4lb **11** Ran SP% **115.0**
Speed ratings (Par 101): **89,88,88,87,86 85,82,78,74,64 40**
toteswingers:1&2:£5.60, 1&3:£7.40, 2&3:£3.80 CSF £37.15 CT £136.20 TOTE £16.10: £5.50, £1.10, £2.20; EX 60.10.
Owner Radlett Racing **Bred** Mr And Mrs L Baker **Trained** Radlett, Herts
■ Stewards' Enquiry : Vince Slattery six-day ban: careless riding (Nov 5,6,8,10-12)
J-P Guillambert three-day ban: weighed in 2lb heavy (Nov 5,6,8)
FOCUS
The pace was unsatisfactory, and consequently a number of runners were too keen, until the tempo increased 3f out. Weak form, rated through the runner-up.

7071 ATTHERACES.COM/BREEDERSCUP H'CAP (DIV II) 1m 141y(P)
9:15 (9:16) (Class 6) (0-55,54) 3-Y-O+ £1,364 (£403; £201) Stalls Low

Form RPR
4522 **1** **Join Up**[2] 7023 4-8-8 **50**...... RossAtkinson(5) 7 57
(W M Brisbourne) *hld up: hdwy over 2f out: chsd ldr over 1f out: rdn to ld wl ins fnl f* **5/2**[1]
0520 **2** *1* **Herecomethegirls**[50] 5704 4-8-11 **51** ow2......(b[1]) JackDean(3) 8 56
(W G M Turner) *hld up in tch: led over 2f out: rdn and hung lft over 1f out: hdd wl ins fnl f* **7/2**[2]
32 **3** *1 ¼* **Chichen Daawe**[37] 6076 4-9-1 **52**...... PaulHanagan 12 54
(B Ellison) *chsd ldrs tl led over 3f out: rdn and hdd over 2f out: nt clr run over 1f out: styd on* **7/2**[2]
6000 **4** *1 ¼* **Escardo (GER)**[107] 3787 7-8-11 **48**...... TonyCulhane 4 47
(D G Bridgwater) *hld up: hdwy over 2f out: rdn over 1f out: styd on same pce ins fnl f* **33/1**
0000 **5** *4* **Hilbre Court (USA)**[35] 6165 5-8-12 **54**......(bt) DeclanCannon(5) 1 44
(B P J Baugh) *chsd ldrs: rdn over 2f out: wknd fnl f* **10/1**
0605 **6** *2 ¾* **Woodsley House (IRE)**[16] 6672 8-9-2 **53**...... RobertHavlin 3 37
(T T Clement) *prom: rdn over 2f out: sn wknd* **11/1**
4005 **7** *¾* **Mullitovermaurice**[48] 5767 4-8-11 **48**......(p) StephenCraine 10 30
(Patrick Morris) *chsd ldrs tl rdn over 2f out: sn wknd* **8/1**[3]
060 **8** *12* **Wingate Street**[14] 6716 3-8-6 **47**...... CathyGannon 2 1
(P D Evans) *sn led: hdd over 3f out: wknd wl over 1f out* **20/1**
60-0 **9** *9* **Bold Bomber**[143] 2629 4-8-5 **45**...... JohnFahy(3) 13 —
(Paul Green) *hld up: a in rr: bhd fnl 4f: t.o* **28/1**
00/0 **10** *8* **Always Baileys (IRE)**[19] 5635 7-8-6 **46**...... NataliaGemelova(3) 5 —
(Mrs P Ford) *hld up: a in rr: bhd fnl 6f: t.o* **50/1**
1m 51.09s (0.59) **Going Correction** -0.025s/f (Stan)
WFA 3 from 4yo+ 4lb **10** Ran SP% **114.7**
Speed ratings (Par 101): **96,95,94,92,89 86,86,75,67,60**
toteswingers:1&2:£3.80, 1&3:£1.20, 2&3:£4.10 CSF £10.48 CT £29.64 TOTE £4.80: £2.80, £2.00, £1.10; EX 13.40 Place 6: £60.23, Place 5: £23.21.
Owner P R Kirk **Bred** A Reid **Trained** Great Ness, Shropshire
FOCUS
A better pace than division one, though a promising early gallop eased a bit turning into the back straight. The form is very limited but probably sound. The winner didn't need to match his recent best.
T/Plt: £47.90 to a £1 stake. Pool:£93,290.82 - 1,420.87 winning tickets T/Qpdt: £15.50 to a £1 stake. Pool:£9,725.52 - 463.20 winning tickets CR

7072 - (Foreign Racing) - See Raceform Interactive

6906 DUNDALK (A.W) (L-H)
Friday, October 22

OFFICIAL GOING: Standard

7073a MERCURY STKS (LISTED RACE) 5f (P)
7:00 (7:01) 2-Y-O+ £24,446 (£7,146; £3,384; £1,128)

RPR
1 **Invincible Ash (IRE)**[54] 5569 5-9-11 104......(p) GFCarroll 2 102
(M Halford, Ire) *chsd ldrs: 4th 1/2-way: rdn to chal in 2nd 1f out: led fnl 150yds: kpt on wl* **13/2**[3]
2 *¾* **Hitchens (IRE)**[34] 6177 5-9-11...... FMBerry 5 99
(T D Barron) *mid-div: 9th 1/2-way: rdn in 8th 2f out: styd on in 6th 1f out: kpt on wl fnl f* **10/3**[1]
3 *nk* **Luisant**[12] 6783 7-10-0 109...... CO'Donoghue 8 101+
(J A Nash, Ire) *hld up towards rr: late hdwy in 8th 1f out: r.o wl fnl f* **10/3**[1]
4 *hd* **Knock Stars (IRE)**[5] 6969 2-8-4 95...... CDHayes 3 88
(Patrick Martin, Ire) *mid-div: 8th 1/2-way: hdwy in 6th 2f out: nt clr run over 1f out: rdn into 4th 1f out: kpt on fnl f* **12/1**
5 *¾* **Bajan Tryst (USA)**[41] 5944 4-9-11...... PJSmullen 7 95
(K A Ryan) *chsd ldrs: 5th 1/2-way: rdn into 3rd 1f out: drifted sltly lft: no ex ins fnl f: kpt on same pce* **13/2**[3]
6 *nk* **Calm Bay (IRE)**[2] 7024 4-9-11 92......(bt) KJManning 9 93
(H Rogers, Ire) *led: rdn and chal 1f out: hdd fnl 150yds: no ex and kpt on same pce* **25/1**
7 *¾* **Velvet Flicker (IRE)**[12] 6783 3-9-11 102...... DPMcDonogh 4 92
(Kevin Prendergast, Ire) *hld up towards rr: rdn and no imp 2f out: kpt on same pce fr over 1f out* **16/1**
8 *1 ½* **Della'Alba (IRE)**[41] 5973 3-9-8 84...... WMLordan 13 83
(M Halford, Ire) *towards rr for most: rdn and no imp 2f out: kpt on one pce fr over 1f out* **33/1**
9 *hd* **Sampers (IRE)**[14] 6728 4-9-8 85......(p) KLatham 12 85
(M Halford, Ire) *chsd ldrs: 3rd 1/2-way: rdn 2f out: no ex in 5th whn hmpd 1f out: kpt on one pce* **25/1**
10 *nk* **Jaconet (USA)**[105] 3875 5-9-11......(b) JAHeffernan 1 81
(T D Barron) *chsd ldrs: 6th 1/2-way: rdn in 7th 2f out: sn no ex* **13/2**[3]
11 *3* **Taajub (IRE)**[13] 6735 3-9-11...... JMurtagh 6 74
(W J Haggas) *chsd ldrs: 7th 1/2-way: rdn and no ex 2f out* **6/1**[2]
12 *hd* **Ladie's Choice (IRE)**[42] 5907 2-8-4 98...... BACurtis 10 63
(M J Tynan, Ire) *chsd ldr: 2nd 1/2-way: rdn 2f out: no ex and wknd fr over 1f out* **16/1**
13 *4 ½* **Tough Regime (IRE)**[2] 7024 3-9-8 50......(t) PBBeggy 11 54
(Paul W Flynn, Ire) *mid-div: rdn and wknd 2f out* **50/1**
58.10 secs (58.10)
WFA 2 from 3yo+ 18lb **13** Ran SP% **132.5**
CSF £30.79 TOTE £8.40: £2.20, £2.10, £1.70; DF 39.90.
Owner P J Condron **Bred** Mrs Sandra Maye **Trained** Doneany, Co Kildare
FOCUS
A decent Listed race which has been rated through the front-running sixth.
NOTEBOOK
Invincible Ash(IRE) returned from a break and gained her third victory on this surface. She broke well and had a good position towards the inside the whole way around. She was guaranteed to find under pressure and that kicked in when she looked beaten for a few strides over a furlong out, but she was tough and got her head back in front inside the last. A proper good-ground and much improved filly this season, she has a great attitude and her trainer said she's likely to go to Dubai over the winter.
Hitchens(IRE) made a rare foray out of handicap company and justified the decision to bring him over for this contest. He almost certainly found the trip inadequate as he only really got going inside the last furlong and, despite his reasonable draw, ended up coming home on the outside. He finished well but the winner had his measure. (op 3/1)
Luisant just couldn't go the pace and had a wall of horses in front of him entering the straight. Pulled to the outside inside the final furlong and a half, he came home well but just had too much ground to make up. (op 4/1)
Knock Stars(IRE), a 2yo, ran tremendously well even given the fact she had a considerable weight allowance. She showed some reasonable speed in mid-division and was starting to make some headway in the straight when not getting the racing room she needed and, in the end, she kept on inside the last. It was a very good effort and gives hope that she could be a stakes-class sprinter next year. (op 10/1)
Bajan Tryst(USA) showed some decent speed himself and had every chance when mounting a challenge over a furlong out, but his effort flattened out inside the last and he drifted off a true line as well. (op 11/2 tchd 7/1)
Calm Bay(IRE) showed tremendous pace, but just couldn't last out against this class of opponent.

Velvet Flicker(IRE) made some late ground without threatening, having struggled to go the pace.

7078a CHRISTMAS PARTIES AT DUNDALK H'CAP 1m 2f 150y(P)
9:25 (9:29) (50-70,75) 3-Y-0+ £5,190 (£1,203; £526; £300)

RPR

1 **Force Of Habit**[85] 4525 4-9-9 65 (b) PJSmullen 3 74+
(D K Weld, Ire) *chsd ldrs: 3rd 1/2-way: hdwy in 2nd 2f out: sn led: rdn and kpt on strly fr over 1f out* 3/1[1]

2 4 **Accompanist**[14] 6729 7-9-12 68 (p) KLatham 1 69
(T G McCourt, Ire) *chsd ldrs: 6th 1/2-way: hdwy into 4th 2f out: rdn in 5th 1 1/2f out: 4th 1f out: kpt on fnl f: 2nd cl home* 16/1

3 ½ **Flattery**[78] 4771 4-9-9 65 JMurtagh 8 65+
(Charles O'Brien, Ire) *in rr of mid-div: hdwy in 9th 3f out: rdn in 8th 2f out: styd on in 6th 1f out: kpt on same pce fnl f: 3rd cl home* 3/1[1]

4 shd **Jeangeorges (IRE)**[56] 5506 4-9-9 65 (p) DMGrant 6 65
(Patrick J Flynn, Ire) *chsd ldrs: 4th 1/2-way: rdn into 2nd 1 1/2f out: no imp on ldr over 1f out: no ex ins fnl f: dropped to 4th cl home* 8/1

5 shd **Bay Swallow (IRE)**[14] 6729 4-9-9 68 (p) GFCarroll(3) 2 68
(Patrick J Flynn, Ire) *led: hdd after 1f: regained ld 3f out: rdn and hdd under 2f out: no ex in 3rd 1 1/2f out: kpt on same pce* 12/1

6 1 ½ **Lynott (IRE)**[9] 6787 7-9-4 70 (t) CTKeane(10) 14 67
(Gerard Keane, Ire) *dwlt: towards rr: 10th 1/2-way: rdn 2f out: 8th 1f out: kpt on same pce fnl f* 16/1

7 nk **Broadway Dancer**[11] 6816 3-9-8 69 FMBerry 10 66
(R A Fahey) *chsd ldrs: 7th 1/2-way: hdwy into 5th 2f out: rdn in 4th 1 1/2f out: no ex in 5th 1f out: kpt on one pce* 7/1[3]

8 ½ **Fleeting Moment (IRE)**[15] 5844 5-9-7 70 (p) DCByrne(7) 4 65
(Patrick Martin, Ire) *mid-div: rdn in 9th 2f out: no ex in 7th 1f out: kpt on one pce* 12/1

9 ½ **Global Recovery (IRE)**[34] 6215 3-9-5 66 KJManning 7 61
(J S Bolger, Ire) *s.i.s: towards rr: sme late hdwy into 10th 1f out: no imp and kpt on one pce* 16/1

10 4 **Moriches (IRE)**[62] 5318 3-9-6 67 WMLordan 13 54
(T Stack, Ire) *mid-div: rdn and no imp over 3f out* 20/1

11 nk **Hampstead Heath (IRE)**[21] 6546 5-9-10 66 (b) CO'Donoghue 12 52
(David Marnane, Ire) *chsd ldrs: 5th 1/2-way: rdn and wknd 3f out* 12/1

12 1 **Spring Hawk (IRE)**[14] 6729 4-9-9 68 BACurtis(3) 9 52
(T G McCourt, Ire) *chsd ldrs: 5th 1/2-way: rdn in 6th 2f out: no ex over 1f out: wknd* 6/1[2]

13 ½ **Another Jayjay (IRE)**[14] 6729 9-9-10 66 (tp) WJSupple 11 49
(M Halford, Ire) *led after 1f: rdn and hdd 3f out: wknd over 2f out* 14/1

14 28 **Meyyal (USA)**[78] 4771 4-10-0 70 JAHeffernan 5 —
(Mrs Sarah Dawson, Ire) *a towards rr: wknd bef st: t.o* 25/1

2m 14.6s (134.60)
WFA 3 from 4yo+ 6lb 14 Ran SP% **143.9**
CSF £71.82 CT £176.37 TOTE £3.30: £2.30, £3.70, £2.30; DF 70.50.
Owner Dr R Lambe **Bred** Grundy Bloodstock S R L **Trained** The Curragh, Co Kildare
■ Stewards' Enquiry : C T Keane severe caution: used whip with excessive frequency

FOCUS
The form is rated through the third, fourth and fifth.

NOTEBOOK
Force Of Habit is a class above this sort of opposition at his best and a healthy hike may await him, but he's good enough to be more than competitive in a better handicap Sitting off the pace in a race where the two front-runners went off too quickly, he got to the front well over 1f out and really extended inside the last to win going away. He is likely to see some action over jumps later in the season. (op 7/2)
Accompanist ran his best race for a while. Racing in mid-division, he travelled reasonably well to the straight and began to close 2f out. The winner then showed himself to be in a different league, but this horse kept on well enough. He's capable of winning a handicap, but catching him on the right day is the key. (op 16/1 tchd 14/1)
Flattery found herself behind a wall of horses when travelling well early in the straight. She kept on towards the outside in the final furlong without threatening. (op 7/2)
Jeangeorges(IRE) was certainly close enough in the straight, but couldn't cope with the winner's change of gear and just kept on at the same pace.
Bay Swallow(IRE) was the first to come under pressure before the straight. She seemed likely to drop away, but kept going on the inside rail.
T/Jkpt: Not Won. T/Plt: @5,934.00 to a @1 stake. Pool:@20,279.53 - 3 winning tickets II

7057 DONCASTER (L-H)
Saturday, October 23

OFFICIAL GOING: Good (good to soft in places; 7.5)
Wind: Moderate 1/2 against Weather: Overcast, breezy

7079 40% BETTER OFF ON BETFAIR SP H'CAP 5f
1:55 (1:58) (Class 2) (0-100,99) 3-Y-0+
£31,155 (£9,330; £4,665; £2,335; £1,165; £585) Stalls High

Form RPR

5002 1 **Hoof It**[28] 6364 3-9-2 94 KierenFallon 1 106
(M W Easterby) *prom towards far side: effrt 2f out: styd on wl to ld towards fin* 10/1[2]

0002 2 nk **Noble Storm (USA)**[18] 6663 4-9-6 98 GrahamGibbons 15 109
(E S McMahon) *w ldrs: led over 1f out: hdd and no ex last 50yds* 14/1

0020 3 1 ¼ **Whozthecat (IRE)**[15] 6706 3-8-5 88 (v) NeilFarley(5) 18 94
(D Carroll) *chsd ldrs towards stands' side: hung lft over 1f out: styd on same pce last 150yds* 50/1

5211 4 shd **Cheveton**[28] 6364 6-9-0 97 DaleSwift(5) 20 103
(R J Price) *dwlt: sn chsng ldrs stands' side: styd on same pce ins fnl f* 10/1[2]

03-5 5 hd **Waffle (IRE)**[18] 6663 4-9-7 99 FrankieDettori 16 104
(J Noseda) *hld up in midfield stands' side: effrt over 2f out: hung lft over 1f out: styd on wl ins fnl f* 14/1

4045 6 nk **Anglezarke (IRE)**[23] 6508 4-9-2 94 (b) PaulHanagan 13 98
(R A Fahey) *in rr-div: hdwy 2f out: styd on ins fnl f* 14/1

0050 7 ½ **Our Jonathan**[7] 6918 3-9-2 94 StevieDonohoe 14 96
(K A Ryan) *towards rr stands' side: hdwy over 1f out: fin wl* 33/1

0003 8 nk **Johannes (IRE)**[7] 6918 7-9-0 97 LeeTopliss(5) 11 98
(R A Fahey) *mid-div: hdwy 2f out: kpt on fnl f* 12/1[3]

0000 9 nk **Judge 'n Jury**[7] 6918 6-9-3 95 JoeFanning 7 95
(R A Harris) *w ldr: led over 3f out: hdd over 1f out: fdd* 25/1

4330 10 nse **Misplaced Fortune**[15] 6721 5-8-6 89 (v) AdamBeschizza(5) 8 89
(N Tinkler) *in rr: hdwy over 1f out: kpt on ins fnl f* 22/1

3-21 11 ½ **Harry Patch**[60] 5393 4-9-0 92 NeilCallan 3 90
(M A Jarvis) *s.i.s: sn chsng ldrs far side: kpt on same pce fnl f* 3/1[1]

2010 12 ½ **Confessional**[42] 5944 3-9-1 93 (e) DavidAllan 21 90
(T D Easterby) *mid-div: hdwy to chse ldrs stands' side 2f out: one pce appr fnl f* 16/1

0042 13 ½ **Edinburgh Knight (IRE)**[33] 6253 3-8-9 87 TonyCulhane 10 85+
(P W D'Arcy) *s.i.s: in rr: hdwy 2f out: keeping on same pce whn nt clr run towards fin* 20/1

3000 14 nk **Secret Asset (IRE)**[14] 6752 5-8-10 95 LewisWalsh(7) 9 89
(Jane Chapple-Hyam) *mid-div: effrt and edgd lft over 2f out: one pce appr fnl f* 33/1

0602 15 nk **Favourite Girl (IRE)**[7] 6918 4-9-1 93 (v) DuranFentiman 2 86
(T D Easterby) *led tl over 3f out: wknd over 1f out: hmpd ins fnl f* 18/1

1 16 nse **Thats A Fret (IRE)**[7] 6918 4-8-12 90 RobertWinston 6 95+
(Liam McAteer, Ire) *chsd ldrs: drvn 2f out: sn outpcd: hmpd and edgd lft ins fnl f* 14/1

3005 17 nk **Duchess Dora (IRE)**[7] 6918 3-8-8 89 IanBrennan(3) 22 80
(J J Quinn) *mid-div stands' side: nvr a threat* 25/1

0000 18 2 **Hotham**[7] 6918 7-9-0 92 BarryMcHugh 5 76
(N Wilson) *chsd ldrs: wknd 2f out* 50/1

4520 19 ½ **Coolminx (IRE)**[36] 6142 3-8-9 87 (p) TomEaves 12 69
(R A Fahey) *mid-div: effrt over 2f out: sn lost pl* 28/1

5060 20 nk **Rasaman (IRE)**[1] 7060 6-8-10 88 (v) PaulMulrennan 4 69
(J S Goldie) *a in rr* 50/1

0560 21 9 **Arganil (USA)**[35] 6177 5-9-2 94 SilvestreDeSousa 19 43
(K A Ryan) *s.s: a bhd stands' side: eased ins fnl f* 25/1

58.23 secs (-2.27) **Going Correction** -0.225s/f (Firm) 21 Ran SP% **124.5**
Speed ratings (Par 109): **109,108,106,106,106 105,104,104,103,103 102,102,101,100,100 100,99,96,95,95 80**
toteswingers: 1&2 £174.70, 1&3 £174.70, 2&3 £42.60. CSF £122.34 CT £6638.26 TOTE £9.10: £2.10, £4.90, £11.20, £3.60; EX 261.90 TRIFECTA Not won..
Owner A Chandler & L Westwood **Bred** Bond Thoroughbred Corporation **Trained** Sheriff Hutton, N Yorks
■ Stewards' Enquiry : Robert Winston caution: careless riding.
Neil Farley two-day ban: careless riding (Nov 6,8)

FOCUS
This decent sprint handicap was seriously competitive. The previous day's action saw most of the races develop down the centre of the home straight, and despite runners being drawn across the track in this opener they once again shunned either of the rails. It was run at a quick pace, but only the winner managed to land a serious blow from off the pace. He progressed again with the runner-up back to his best.

NOTEBOOK
Hoof It, drawn in stall one, turned in a career-best effort when returned to this trip at Haydock when only just denied by Cheveton last month and went one better with a decent effort. He was ridden a bit more patiently and it was obvious nearing the business end he would reel back the runner-up. He did his winning on quick ground in the summer, but evidently relishes some cut over the minimum trip and strongly appeals as the type to improve further next year. Indeed he may well make up into a pattern performer as a 4-y-o. (op 11-1)
Noble Storm(USA) was comfortably held by the winner at Haydock on his penultimate outing, but ran close to his best again at Southwell last time out and he made a bold bid on this return to turf. A 5lb rise put him back up to this last winning mark but it just found him out. He was a clear second-best, though, and does deserve to find an opening this term. (op 16-1)
Whozthecat(IRE) has developed into a tricky customer and, not for the first time, was awash with sweat. He is clearly still improving, however, as this rates a clear personal-best in defeat. His connections can certainly find less competitive assignments for him in the coming weeks and this proves his versatility regards ground.
Cheveton was up another 5lb for his short-head success over the winner at Haydock last month and he ran a perfectly respectable race in defeat in his quest for a hat-trick. He helps to give the form a decent look. (tchd 11-1)
Waffle(IRE) finished third in this race last year on his handicap debut off a 1lb higher mark. He proved easy to back on this return from Fibresand, but improved on his last-time-out form with the runner-up racing on 7lb better terms with that rival. This was only his second outing of the year and he could progress again next time.
Anglezarke(IRE) caught the eye somewhat in staying on towards the finish. She looks to be nearing a return to her best and this was just her second outing in a handicap for her current yard. (op 16-1)
Our Jonathan was keeping on strongly late in the day and really wants a stiffer test, but he has become hard to predict this term. (op 40-1)
Johannes(IRE) is another that ideally wants more of a test and this wasn't a bad effort on ground easy enough for his liking. (op 14-1)
Harry Patch was 5lb higher than when winning on soft ground at Yarmouth on his previous outing 60 days earlier. He missed the Ayr Gold Cup due to a setback and, not the best away this time, never looked that happy more towards the far side in a mid-field position. He is too lightly raced to be writing off. (op 7-2)

7080 THEBETTINGSITE.COM STKS (REGISTERED AS THE DONCASTER STAKES) (LISTED RACE) 6f
2:25 (2:29) (Class 1) 2-Y-O £14,815 (£5,602; £2,800; £1,400) Stalls High

Form RPR

51 1 **Earl Of Leitrim (IRE)**[24] 6465 2-9-1 86 ShaneKelly 3 102
(B J Meehan) *sn drvn along in rr: hdwy over 2f out: hung lft and styd on to ld last 50yds* 11/1

431 2 ½ **Night Carnation**[44] 5885 2-8-10 79 FrannyNorton 7 96
(A M Balding) *trckd ldrs: effrt over 2f out: tk 2nd last 50yds: no ex* 25/1

2221 3 1 ½ **Galtymore Lad**[24] 6477 2-9-1 109 KierenFallon 2 96
(M R Channon) *trckd ldr towards far side: led overall jst ins fnl f: hung lft: hdd clsng stages* 11/10[1]

3205 4 1 ¾ **Cape To Rio (IRE)**[14] 6734 2-9-1 102 JMurtagh 4 91
(R Hannon) *led centre gp and overall ldr 3f out: kpt on same pce appr fnl f* 5/1[3]

2110 5 ½ **Invincible Ridge (IRE)**[14] 6734 2-9-1 92 PatDobbs 6 89
(R Hannon) *trckd ldrs: effrt over 1f out: kpt on same pce* 9/1

0131 6 2 ½ **Signs In The Sand**[17] 6667 2-9-1 98 FrankieDettori 1 82
(Saeed Bin Suroor) *racd upsides towards far side: racd freely: overall ldr 3f out: hung lft and hdd jst ins fnl f: wknd and eased* 7/2[2]

1025 7 4 ½ **Little Lion Man**[49] 5748 2-9-1 85 NeilCallan 8 68
(P W Chapple-Hyam) *hld up towards rr: effrt over 2f out: lost pl over 1f out* 50/1

6346 8 ½ **Belle Bayardo (IRE)**[19] 6627 2-9-1 93 TomMcLaughlin 5 67
(R A Harris) *sn chsng ldrs: lost pl over 2f out* 50/1

1m 11.79s (-1.81) **Going Correction** -0.225s/f (Firm) 8 Ran SP% **112.6**
Speed ratings (Par 103): **103,102,100,98,97 94,88,87**
toteswingers: 1&2 £11.70, 1&3 £3.60, 2&3 £6.30. CSF £216.04 TOTE £13.00: £2.90, £4.40, £1.10; EX 98.90 Trifecta £461.00 Pool: £1,451.65 - 2.33 winning units..
Owner Gallagher Equine Ltd **Bred** Gordon Phillips **Trained** Manton, Wilts

FOCUS
A tricky Listed race that looked more open than the betting implied.

The Form Book, Raceform Ltd, Compton, RG20 6NL

NOTEBOOK

Earl Of Leitrim(IRE), having only his third start, had reportedly improved at home and he coped well with the cut in the ground, staying on strongly inside the final furlong, having initially been outpaced, to just get the better of outsider Night Carnation. Clearly progressing fast, he will improve for a longer trip next season and looks a decent prospect. (op 10-1 tchd 12-1)

Night Carnation, the lowest-rated runner in the field, having won a modest Epsom maiden on her third start, was never far away and briefly looked the winner inside the final furlong, but she couldn't quite see it out as well as Earl Of Leitrim. She has proved well suited by the drop to 6f and connections will no doubt be eager to get a win into her at pattern-level from a breeding perspective. (tchd 22-1)

Galtymore Lad set a high standard for the others to aim at, having twice finished second to Wootton Bassett in valuable sales races before winning a minor contest at Salisbury latest. He went on over 1f out, but started to edge across to the far rail and was run out of it in the final 100 yards. This was a bit disappointing, and for all that better ground probably suits best, he clearly has his limitations and will be tough to place next season. (tchd 6-5 in places)

Cape To Rio(IRE), fifth in the Cornwallis latest, enjoyed the bit of cut in the ground and kept on better than expected, again finishing just ahead of stablemate Invincible Ridge. (op 6-1)

Invincible Ridge(IRE) didn't improve as much as expected for the return to 6f. (tchd 8-1)

Signs In The Sand didn't see it out, having raced freely, and consistency is already becoming a problem for the daughter of Cape Cross. (tchd 4-1)

Little Lion Man continues to struggle in pattern-company. (tchd 40-1)

Belle Bayardo(IRE), having his 14th run of the campaign, found himself outclassed. (op 40-1)

7081 RACING POST TROPHY (GROUP 1) (ENTIRE COLTS & FILLIES) 1m (S)

2:55 (2:58) (Class 1) 2-Y-O

£140,789 (£53,369; £26,709; £13,317; £6,671; £3,348) **Stalls** High

Form RPR

21 **1** **Casamento (IRE)**[27] 6403 2-9-0 0 FrankieDettori 3 121
(M Halford, Ire) *trckd ldrs: pushed lft after 1f: led over 2f out: edgd rt and styd on wl fnl f* **2/1**[1]

2 ¾ **Seville (GER)**[20] 6616 2-9-0 0 CO'Donoghue 8 119
(A P O'Brien, Ire) *racd wd towards stands' side: trckd ldrs: effrt over 2f out: sn chsng wnr: styd on ins fnl f: a jst hld* **8/1**

3 2 **Master Of Hounds (USA)**[104] 3936 2-9-0 0 JMurtagh 6 115
(A P O'Brien, Ire) *hld up in rr: effrt over 2f out: chsng ldrs over 1f out: styd on same pce* **15/2**

11 **4** ¾ **Native Khan (FR)**[63] 5306 2-9-0 106 PaulHanagan 7 113
(E A L Dunlop) *hld up in rr: effrt over 2f out: sn outpcd: styd on fnl f* **17/2**

1 **5** 1 ¾ **Dunboyne Express (IRE)**[97] 4176 2-9-0 0 DPMcDonogh 4 109
(Kevin Prendergast, Ire) *trckd ldrs: racd keenly: hmpd after 1f: edgd rt over 1f out: one pce* **4/1**[2]

14 **6** 2 ¼ **Karam Albaari (IRE)**[42] 5943 2-9-0 109 JimmyQuinn 2 104
(J R Jenkins) *trckd ldrs: t.k.h: hmpd after 1f: effrt over 2f out: wknd over 1f out* **40/1**

U114 **7** *hd* **Toolain (IRE)**[14] 6737 2-9-0 105 (b[1]) NeilCallan 5 103
(M A Jarvis) *trckd ldr: racd keenly: edgd lft after 1f: lost pl over 1f out* **20/1**

114 **8** 1 **Zaidan (USA)**[70] 5079 2-9-0 109 SebSanders 10 101
(C E Brittain) *s.i.s: hdwy 4f out: chsng ldrs over 2f out: wknd over 1f out* **16/1**

0041 **9** 6 **Dubawi Gold**[14] 6733 2-9-0 99 TomEaves 1 87
(M Dods) *led: qcknd 3f out: edgd rt and hdd over 2f out: lost pl over 1f out* **20/1**

11 **10** 4 ½ **Titus Mills (IRE)**[46] 5831 2-9-0 108 KierenFallon 9 77
(B J Meehan) *trckd ldrs: effrt over 2f out: wknd over 1f out* **13/2**[3]

1m 37.03s (-2.27) **Going Correction** -0.225s/f (Firm) 2y crse rec **10** Ran SP% **117.9**

Speed ratings (Par 109): **102,101,99,98,96 94,94,93,87,82**

toteswingers: 1&2 £5.60, 1&3 £4.60, 2&3 £11.20. CSF £18.54 TOTE £2.00: £1.10, £2.80, £2.50; EX 21.40 Trifecta £109.20 Pool: £11,904.38 - 80.61 winning units..

Owner Sheikh Mohammed **Bred** D And J Cantillon & C & K Canning **Trained** Doneany, Co Kildare

■ Michael Halford's first Group 1 winner.

FOCUS

It was a mixed bunch in attendance this year and there was a very strong Irish challenge. They raced down the centre of the track and there was just an average early pace on. Things began to get serious nearing the three-furlong marker and the first pair dominated throughout the final 2f, making their efforts more towards the stands' side late on. Strong form. Casamento rates the third best 2yo on RPRs, 6lb behind Frankel, and second only to St Nicholas Abbey in the last ten winners of this race.

NOTEBOOK

Casamento(IRE), who was supplemented for the race, made it three wins from four career outings with a game display on his return to the top level, completing the task with a fair amount left in the tank, and gave his trainer a first winner in this class. He didn't need to his best when coming home a clear-cut winner in the Group 2 Beresford Stakes over this trip at the Curragh in September - the same race that last year's stunning winner St Nicholas Abbey landed before coming here - and his short-head defeat to the unbeaten Pathfork in the National Stakes over 7f at the same venue earlier that month made him the clear form pick in this field. Frankie Dettori was aboard for this British debut and he delivered him to lead nearing 2f out. Seville threw down a strong challenge at the furlong marker and looked a big danger, but the winner was probably idling somewhat as he picked up again to assert his authority nearing the finish. It was great to see Sheikh Mohammed's colours back on a British racecourse and Casamento will now transfer to Godolphin for his Classic season. As for next term he was later cut as short as 7/1 second favourite in the ante-post betting for the 2,000 Guineas behind the outstanding Frankel. This event is much better known as a pointer for the following year's Derby, though, and he was also promoted to a clear second favourite, again behind Frankel, for the big one next June. Looking at his pedigree there is a fair bit of speed there, which would bode well for the Guineas and his trainer later said this horse is certainly not short of gears. He clearly also stays well, however, and should have no trouble stepping up in distance at three. His sire Shamardal's progeny have tended to be more milers or 1m2f performers to date, but he has had winners up to 2m. His dam was best at 1m, but her sire Always Fair is a decent stamina influence. All considered he must have a good chance of getting the Derby trip and his return will be eagerly awaited, but there is the niggling concern about how Godolphin's 3-y-os most often emerge from a winter in Dubai needing their first run back. (op 3-1)

Seville(GER) came out on top of the O'Brien pair and he was the only one to give the winner a serious race. He arrived here having taken the same conditions race at Tipperary last month that High Chaparral won before landing this in 2001, and was open to any amount of improvement. He was never far away through the early parts and raced more towards the near side. He responded strongly to pressure from 2f out and momentarily looked like getting on top, but the winner always just had his measure inside the final half furlong. He still looked a little green and his pedigree strongly suggests stepping up to around 1m4f will suit him next term and so it wasn't at all surprising to see him cut as short as 10/1 (Ladbrokes) for the Derby. (tchd 9-1)

Master Of Hounds(USA), the pick of Johnny Murtagh, was having his first run since landing his maiden at the fourth time of asking back in July. This was obviously a big step up, but he was very closely matched with the unbeaten Dunboyne Express and there was a good chance the extra distance would help him. He stayed on without ever really threatening the first pair and left the impression more of a test would've seen him in a better light. The ground was also probably easy enough for his liking and he should make up into very nice horse at around 1m2f next term, but he wouldn't be certain to get further than that. (op 13-2 tchd 8-1)

Native Khan(FR) made it 2-2 when readily winning the Group 3 Solario Stakes and bypassed last week's Dewhurst for this. He had something to prove on the slower surface, but his sire's progeny do have a decent record on soft ground and he went through it without that much fuss - though connections later said he didn't enjoy it. Indeed he was another that shaped as though a stronger early pace would've been more to his liking over this extra furlong and he remains a decent prospect. (op 9-1 tchd 8-1)

Dunboyne Express(IRE) came into this unbeaten in two previous outings and, another that bypassed the Dewhurst, was having his first run since decisively winning the Group 3 Anglesey Stakes over an extended 6f in July. He showed a real liking for easy ground that day and proved popular here. Despite getting a bump through the early stages, he had his chance and ultimately failed to see out the longer trip that well after taking a keen hold. Perhaps the run was needed somewhat, as he is bred to get further as he matures, and it connections later reported him to have come back a little distressed from the race. It's unlikely the best of him has yet been seen. (op 9-2)

Karam Albaari(IRE) finished fourth in the Group 2 Champagne Stakes behind Saamid at this venue on his second outing last month and met some support at big odds in the ante-post betting for this race, for which he was supplemented. He came under pressure a long way out and was well beaten, but kept on fairly well inside the final furlong. He should be up to winning a Listed race at least and ought to enjoy racing over even further next term. (op 33-1tchd 50-1 in a place)

Toolain(IRE) did plenty through the early parts in first-time blinkers and that spoilt his cause. A drop back down in class is what he wants, though, and he could well land a decent race when reverting to quicker ground as a 3-y-o. (op 18-1)

Zaidan(USA) was very disappointing on easy ground at Newbury on his previous outing 70 days previously, where connections firmly believed he wasn't right. He was drawn nearest to the stands' rail on this return, but was taken over towards the far side for his effort and once again looked uneasy with some cut in the ground.

Dubawi Gold found this too hot and he failed to last home from the front on this further step up in distance. (op 16-1 tchd 14-1)

Titus Mills(IRE) produced a tame effort and something presumably went amiss with him. (op 6-1 tchd 7-1)

7082 RICHARD JAMES HONE MEMORIAL "HANDS AND HEELS" APPRENTICE SERIES FINAL H'CAP 7f

3:30 (3:30) (Class 5) (0-75,75) 3-Y-O **£3,885** (£1,156; £577; £288) **Stalls** High

Form RPR

0235 **1** **Ginger Grey (IRE)**[57] 5494 3-8-12 **66** (b) DaleSwift 14 77
(D O'Meara) *hld up in rr: gd hdwy 2f out: styd on wl to ld 1f out: drvn out* **12/1**

31 **2** 1 ¼ **Junket**[19] 6638 3-9-2 **70** RyanPowell 9 78+
(Dr J D Scargill) *hld up in mid-div: effrt and hung lft over 2f out: n.m.r over 1f out: upsides jst ins fnl f: no ex* **10/3**[1]

0006 **3** 3 **Adam De Beaulieu (USA)**[15] 6713 3-8-4 **61** oh2 (t) IanBurns[(3)] 5 61
(B M R Haslam) *trckd ldrs: edgd lft and led over 1f out: hdd 1f out: one pce* **33/1**

0526 **4** 1 ½ **Coin From Heaven (IRE)**[9] 6879 3-9-3 **74** MarzenaJeziorek[(3)] 12 70
(R A Fahey) *hld up in mid-div: effrt over 2f out: kpt on same pce fnl f* **20/1**

123 **5** *shd* **Tislaam (IRE)**[12] 6800 3-9-0 **68** (p) NeilFarley 3 64
(A J McCabe) *trckd ldrs: led over 3f out: hdd and hmpd over 1f out: wknd ins fnl f* **8/1**[3]

4341 **6** *nk* **Music Maestro (IRE)**[6] 6958 3-8-9 **66** 6ex DanielHarris[(3)] 11 61
(B W Hills) *trckd ldrs: effrt 2f out: kpt on one pce* **9/2**[2]

4060 **7** 1 **Luv U Noo**[24] 6460 3-8-4 **61** oh1 (p) MatthewCosham[(3)] 6 53
(B Ellison) *dwlt: hdwy to chse ldrs over 3f out: one pce appr fnl f* **25/1**

0600 **8** 3 ½ **Perfect Ch'I (IRE)**[12] 6805 3-9-2 **70** JamesRogers 1 53
(I A Wood) *sn chsng ldrs: wknd over 1f out* **33/1**

055 **9** ½ **Safwaan**[19] 6624 3-8-13 **67** AdamBeschizza 2 48
(W J Haggas) *dwlt: in rr: swtchd rt after 1f: sme hdwy 2f out: nvr a factor* **9/2**[2]

0003 **10** 9 **Celestial Tryst**[8] 6897 3-8-7 **61** oh3 AdamCarter 10 18
(G M Moore) *sn chsng ldrs: wknd 2f out* **16/1**

1540 **11** 2 ¼ **Mark Anthony (IRE)**[24] 6466 3-9-5 **73** JulieBurke 7 24
(K A Ryan) *w ldrs: wknd over 2f out* **16/1**

0-20 **12** 7 **Mad Millie (IRE)**[22] 6540 3-8-4 **61** oh3 NoelGarbutt[(3)] 4 —
(D O'Meara) *led: hdd over 3f out: sn lost pl* **18/1**

2302 **13** 14 **Jupiter Fidius**[8] 6897 3-8-7 **64** (p) ShaneBKelly[(3)] 8 —
(Mrs K Walton) *in rr and sn drvn along: bhd fnl 2f* **12/1**

1m 25.53s (-0.77) **Going Correction** -0.225s/f (Firm) **13** Ran SP% **117.5**

Speed ratings (Par 101): **95,93,90,88,88 87,86,82,82,71 69,61,45**

toteswingers: 1&2 £9.80, 1&3 £77.40, 2&3 £29.00. CSF £48.71 CT £1337.92 TOTE £14.50: £3.80, £1.80, £10.00; EX 56.40 TRIFECTA Not won..

Owner Liam, Johnny & Mecca Too **Bred** B Kennedy **Trained** Nawton, N Yorks

■ Stewards' Enquiry : Ian Burns two-day ban: careless riding (Nov 6,8)

FOCUS

The final of the 'hands and heels' series, and it was always going to be competitive. The exposed winner posted a small personal best.

7083 BARRY HILLS BIOGRAPHY CONDITIONS STKS 7f

4:05 (4:05) (Class 2) 3-Y-O+

£9,346 (£2,799; £1,399; £700; £349; £175) **Stalls** High

Form RPR

-056 **1** **Inler (IRE)**[21] 6570 3-8-9 95 KierenFallon 4 110
(B J Meehan) *hmpd s: trckd ldrs: led over 2f out: edgd rt and styd on fnl f* **7/1**

6416 **2** 1 ½ **Ashram (IRE)**[36] 6147 4-9-4 109 (v) FrankieDettori 10 113
(Saeed Bin Suroor) *hmpd s: hld up: hdwy over 2f out: sn chsng ldrs: kpt on to take 2nd towards fin* **3/1**[1]

1323 **3** 1 ¼ **Flambeau**[69] 5120 3-8-4 98 PaulHanagan 1 98
(H Candy) *wnt rt s: trckd ldrs: kpt on same pce fnl f* **7/2**[2]

2000 **4** 1 **Mia's Boy**[28] 6349 6-9-0 101 BarryMcHugh 2 103
(C A Dwyer) *n.m.r s: in rr: hdwy over 2f out: sn chsng ldrs: kpt on same pce appr fnl f* **9/2**[3]

0630 **5** 7 **Summer Fete (IRE)**[44] 5883 4-8-6 97 RichardMullen 5 76
(B Smart) *hmpd s: t.k.h towards rr: effrt over 2f out: wknd over 1f out* **10/1**

4200 **6** 1 **Za Za Zoom (IRE)**[11] 6830 3-8-4 96 FrannyNorton 9 73
(B W Hills) *wnt rt s: sn chsng ldrs: wknd over 1f out* **20/1**

0/00 **7** 5 **Alhaban (IRE)**[14] 6735 4-8-11 93 TomMcLaughlin 3 65
(R A Harris) *in rr: effrt over 2f out: wknd over 1f out* **50/1**

0206 **8** 4 ½ **Layline (IRE)**[12] 6806 3-8-9 88 (b) JackMitchell 6 53
(R M Beckett) *wnt lft s: t.k.h in rr: edgd rt 3f out: sn wknd* **25/1**

-434 **9** *hd* **City Style (USA)**[56] 5516 4-8-11 103 AhmedAjtebi 11 52
(Mahmood Al Zarooni) *hld up in rr: drvn and nt keen over 3f out: lost pl over 2f out* **11/2**

565 **10** *2 ¼* **Welsh Emperor (IRE)**[54] 5609 11-8-11 **100**................(b) TonyCulhane 8 46
(T P Tate) *led: hdd over 2f out: sn lost pl: eased over 1f out* **33/1**

1m 23.86s (-2.44) **Going Correction** -0.225s/f (Firm)
WFA 3 from 4yo+ 2lb **10** Ran SP% **115.9**
Speed ratings (Par 109): **104,102,100,99,91 90,84,79,79,76**
toteswingers: 1&2 £5.10, 1&3 £6.20, 2&3 £2.80. CSF £27.05 TOTE £8.20: £2.60, £1.60, £2.00; EX 35.80 Trifecta £85.20 Pool: £795.72 - 6.91 winning units..
Owner Sangster Family **Bred** D And J Cantillon & C & K Canning **Trained** Manton, Wilts

FOCUS
What had looked an open conditions event was won in good style by one-time Guineas fancy Inler. This was a clear best from him and the form seems sound enough rated around the runner-up.

NOTEBOOK
Inler(IRE), who had clearly improved a lot for his recent debut for Brian Meehan, won this in good style. Although interfered with at the start, he travelled sweetly under Kieren Fallon and stayed on well to win with plenty in hand, despite drifting across to the stands' rail. This is as far as he wants to go, and he rates a smart prospect for next season, when connections will presumably turn their focus to sprints. (op 8-1)
Ashram(IRE), another done no favours leaving the gate, ran well, but did look vulnerable conceding weight all round and it was no surprise to see him find something too good. (op 7-2)
Flambeau looked a big player at the weights and she had her chance, but lacked the class of the winner. (tchd 10-3)
Mia's Boy has struggled of late in handicaps, and he ran better in this less competitive race. (op 6-1)
Summer Fete(IRE) was entitled to finish closer on the pick of her efforts. (tchd 11-1)
City Style(USA) has proved a touch disappointing this season, and looks one to avoid now following this rather disconcerting effort. Official explanation: jockey said gelding ran flat (op 5-1 tchd 6-1)
Welsh Emperor(IRE) Official explanation: jockey said gelding lost its action

7084 CROWNHOTEL-BAWTRY.COM H'CAP 1m 4f
4:40 (4:41) (Class 3) (0-95,95) 3-Y-O+ **£6,476** (£1,927; £963; £481) **Stalls** Low

Form RPR
035- **1** **Salden Licht**[191] 7293 6-9-12 **95**.................................. PaulMulrennan 15 106
(A King) *swtchd lft s: hld up in rr: hdwy: nt clr run and swtchd ins over 2f out: led over 1f out: jst hld on* **28/1**
1 **2** *hd* **Alazan (IRE)**[38] 6091 4-8-12 **81**.................................. FrankieDettori 7 92+
(P J Hobbs) *hld up in mid-div: nt clr run over 2f out: gd hdwy over 1f out: styd on wl: jst failed* **4/1**[1]
2000 **3** *1 ¾* **Classic Vintage (USA)**[8] 6889 4-9-7 **90**........................ NeilCallan 16 98
(Mrs A J Perrett) *prom: nt clr run over 2f out: styd on wl fnl f: tk 3rd last 75yds* **16/1**
0402 **4** *1* **Tominator**[16] 6698 3-8-10 **86**.................................. TonyCulhane 14 92
(R Hollinshead) *swtchd lft s: in rr: hdwy on outside over 2f out: hung lft over 1f out: kpt on same pce* **40/1**
0136 **5** *1* **Sunny Game**[28] 6362 3-8-6 **82**.................................. RichardMullen 8 87+
(M L W Bell) *trckd ldrs: t.k.h: one pce fnl 2f* **10/1**
0023 **6** *1 ½* **Red Jade**[15] 6724 5-9-4 **87**.................................. PaulHanagan 12 89
(R A Fahey) *mid-div: effrt over 2f out: kpt on fnl f: nvr trbld ldrs* **9/1**[3]
1100 **7** *1* **Epic (IRE)**[21] 6565 3-8-10 **86**..............................(b) KierenFallon 4 87
(M Johnston) *in rr: hdwy on inner over 3f out: upsides over 2f out: wknd appr fnl f* **16/1**
3355 **8** *1 ¼* **Arlequin**[28] 6355 3-8-13 **89**.................................. DarryllHolland 6 88
(J D Bethell) *in rr: hdwy on ins over 3f out: led over 2f out: hung lft and hdd over 1f out: wknd* **11/1**
006 **9** *½* **Bothy**[21] 6565 4-8-11 **85**.................................. DaleSwift(5) 5 83
(B Ellison) *led: hdd over 2f out: wknd over 1f out* **25/1**
1264 **10** *1* **Tajaarub**[122] 3335 3-8-5 **81** oh3.................................. FrannyNorton 3 77
(B W Hills) *trckd ldrs: wknd fnl 2f* **12/1**
0040 **11** *1 ¼* **Crackentorp**[28] 6362 5-9-7 **90**.................................. GrahamGibbons 18 84
(T D Easterby) *prom: effrt over 2f out: one pce* **25/1**
1312 **12** *hd* **Kings Troop**[31] 6283 4-9-1 **84**.................................. FergusSweeney 1 78
(A King) *chsd ldrs: one pce fnl 2f* **14/1**
3051 **13** *½* **Arizona John (IRE)**[35] 6185 5-8-10 **84**.................. DeclanCannon(5) 17 77
(J Mackie) *in rr: hdwy over 2f out: kpt on fnl f* **33/1**
6003 **14** *4 ½* **Centennial (IRE)**[19] 6630 5-9-5 **88**..............................(b) SebSanders 2 74
(Jonjo O'Neill) *in rr: hmpd 6f out: nvr on terms* **33/1**
5520 **15** *¾* **Trip The Light**[48] 5786 5-8-13 **87**..............................(v) LeeTopliss(5) 13 72
(R A Fahey) *chsd ldrs: lost pl over 2f out* **66/1**
1144 **16** *nk* **Nave (USA)**[33] 6251 3-8-10 **86**.................................. JoeFanning 9 70
(M Johnston) *chsd ldrs: ev ch tl wknd over 2f out* **16/1**
55 **17** *2* **Ella**[44] 5879 6-9-2 **85**.................................. PJMcDonald 19 66
(G A Swinbank) *trckd ldrs: effrt over 2f out: sn wknd* **10/1**
5 **18** *10* **Seven Summits (IRE)**[14] 6738 3-9-2 **92**.......................... JMurtagh 20 57
(J Noseda) *chsd ldrs: lost pl over 2f out: eased whn bhd* **8/1**[2]
0360 **19** *3* **Granston (IRE)**[9] 6877 9-9-2 **85**.................................. RobertWinston 11 45
(J D Bethell) *chsd ldrs: lost pl over 2f out: bhd whn eased* **50/1**
2153 **P** **Sagamore**[33] 6251 3-8-11 **87**.................................. RobertHavlin 10 —
(J H M Gosden) *in rr: p.u 6f out* **12/1**

2m 31.78s (-3.12) **Going Correction** -0.225s/f (Firm)
WFA 3 from 4yo+ 7lb **20** Ran SP% **130.2**
Speed ratings (Par 107): **101,100,99,99,98 97,96,95,95,94 94,93,93,90,90 89,88,81,79,—**
toteswingers: 1&2 £28.70, 1&3 £71.80, 2&3 £20.50. CSF £135.23 CT £1948.35 TOTE £42.90: £7.00, £1.80, £5.60, £7.60; EX 219.30 TRIFECTA Not won..
Owner Dai Griffiths **Bred** Gestut Wittekindshof **Trained** Barbury Castle, Wilts

FOCUS
A good handicap that proved a decent test at the distance, with two 'jumpers' Salden Licht and Alazan fighting out the finish. Salden Licht got back to near his old French Flat form, with the second up 5lb and the next two close to their marks.

NOTEBOOK
Salden Licht, who was conceding at least 5lb to all his rivals, was placed behind subsequent Group 1 hero Rainbow Peak off 1lb lower last season, and he showed himself to be a smart novice hurdler earlier in the year. He wasn't for passing having struck for home, willingly sticking his neck out under pressure when strongly pressed close home. He'll be entitled to return for the November Handicap over C&D next month before going back hurdling, where he has the potential to develop into a top handicapper. (op 22-1)
Alazan(IRE), up 7lb for winning over 1m2f at Sandown on his return to the Flat, was faced with more of a test this time, but he saw it out well and some will argue he'd have won had he not been briefly denied a clear run. He too remains capable of better as a hurdler. (op 7-2 tchd 10-3)
Classic Vintage(USA), another briefly stopped in his run, is back on a decent mark and this was easily his best effort since the spring. (tchd 18-1)
Tominator, back to form when second at Wolverhampton latest, shaped surprisingly well in this much stronger contest, making good ground from the rear and shaping as though he'd stay further in time.
Sunny Game was a bit keen, but saw it out well enough and could be worth another try over further. (op 9-1)
Red Jade kept grinding away but never looked likely to win. (op 10-1 tchd 8-1)
Epic(IRE) remains too high in the weights and he failed to get home. (op 28-1)
Arlequin hung late on having made swift headway to lead. Official explanation: jockey said colt hung left (op 20-1)
Centennial(IRE) Official explanation: jockey said horse suffered interference in running
Seven Summits(IRE) failed to improve for the step up in trip, quickly losing his pitch and ending up well held. (op 12-1)
Sagamore quickly went wrong and was pulled up. (op 11-1)

7085 UNIVERSAL RECYCLING NURSERY 7f
5:15 (5:16) (Class 2) 2-Y-O **£6,670** (£1,984; £991; £495) **Stalls** High

Form RPR
3543 **1** **Majestic Dream (IRE)**[12] 6810 2-8-5 **73**........................(v) JoeFanning 7 82
(W R Swinburn) *trckd ldrs: led 2f out: edgd rt ins fnl f: hld on wl* **33/1**
12 **2** *1 ¼* **Unex El Greco**[16] 6690 2-9-4 **86**.................................. DarryllHolland 13 92+
(J H M Gosden) *dwlt and wnt rt s: bhd: gd hdwy over 1f out: edgd lft ins fnl f: no ex last 50yds* **85/40**[1]
0660 **3** *2* **Planet Waves (IRE)**[23] 6505 2-8-9 **77** ow1..................... SebSanders 10 78
(C E Brittain) *mid-div: hdwy to chal over 1f out: kpt on same pce ins fnl f* **16/1**
13 **4** *1 ¼* **Jaaryah (IRE)**[17] 6670 2-9-7 **89**.................................. FrankieDettori 11 88
(M A Jarvis) *hld up in rr: gd hdwy whn nt clr run 2f out: kpt on same pce ins fnl f* **9/2**[2]
0001 **5** *3* **Honeymead (IRE)**[21] 6563 2-9-0 **82**.............................. PaulHanagan 16 72
(R A Fahey) *hld up in rr: hdwy whn nt clr run over 1f out: kpt on: nvr rchd ldrs* **6/1**[3]
010 **6** *nk* **The Mellor Fella**[43] 5901 2-8-8 **81**.............................. LeeTopliss(5) 8 70
(R A Fahey) *chsd ldrs: edgd rt over 1f out: one pce* **66/1**
4410 **7** *¾* **Loukoumi**[23] 6505 2-8-8 **76**.................................. TomEaves 9 63
(B Smart) *mid-div: effrt and n.m.r 2f out: kpt on same pce* **33/1**
1123 **8** *¾* **Maggie Mey (IRE)**[15] 6719 2-8-4 **72**......................... SilvestreDeSousa 15 58
(D O'Meara) *chsd ldrs: nt clr run over 1f out: kpt on towards fin* **10/1**
1303 **9** *2 ½* **Royal Opera**[16] 6690 2-8-7 **75**.................................. JimmyQuinn 12 54
(B R Millman) *hld up in mid-div: effrt over 2f out: wknd over 1f out* **16/1**
6126 **10** *2 ½* **Highlife Dancer**[16] 6690 2-8-1 **76** ow1..................... MatthewLawson(7) 6 48
(M R Channon) *mid-div: effrt over 2f out: hung lft and wknd over 1f out* **50/1**
1 **11** *nk* **Stamp Duty (IRE)**[24] 6458 2-8-11 **79**........................... BarryMcHugh 14 50
(Ollie Pears) *hld up in rr: nvr on terms* **16/1**
2604 **12** *2 ½* **Millies Folly**[7] 6920 2-7-7 **66** oh1.................................. NeilFarley(5) 1 31
(D Carroll) *led towards far side: edgd rt 3f out: hdd & wknd 2f out* **33/1**
0363 **13** *3 ½* **Colebrooke**[13] 6777 2-8-2 **70**.................................. AdrianNicholls 5 26
(M Johnston) *chsd ldrs: rdn over 2f out: lost pl over 1f out* **33/1**
312 **14** *9* **Male Model**[14] 6745 2-9-5 **87**.................................. AhmedAjtebi 4 19
(Mahmood Al Zarooni) *gave problems in stalls: trckd ldrs: t.k.h: hung bdly lft over 2f out: sn lost pl: eased whn bhd* **9/1**
0241 **15** *3* **Rudegirl (IRE)**[15] 6722 2-8-10 **78**.............................. KierenFallon 2 —
(N Tinkler) *chsd ldrs on outside: edgd rt and lost pl 2f out: eased whn bhd* **16/1**

1m 26.04s (-0.26) **Going Correction** -0.225s/f (Firm) **15** Ran SP% **122.3**
Speed ratings (Par 101): **92,90,88,86,83 83,82,81,78,75 75,72,68,58,54**
toteswingers: 1&2 £22.40, 1&3 £83.20, 2&3 £13.00. CSF £100.62 CT £1276.55 TOTE £49.10: £7.00, £1.40, £5.50; EX 102.90 Trifecta £860.40 Place 6: £137.03, Place 5: £26.33Part won. Pool: £1,162.77 - 0.10 winning units..
Owner Mark Goodall **Bred** Thomas Hassett **Trained** Aldbury, Herts
■ Stewards' Enquiry : Lee Topliss three-day ban: careless riding (Nov 6,8,10)

FOCUS
A decent nursery with only five of the 15-strong field having failed to reach the frame on their previous outing. There was a sound pace on and once more the main action came down the centre of the track.

NOTEBOOK
Majestic Dream(IRE) took it up going strongly nearing the furlong marker and kept on resolutely to regain the winning thread. He had run consistently in defeat the last twice, but the drop back a furlong on this ground did the trick. A strong pace on quick ground back over 1m next year should be much to his liking, but for now this is definitely his optimum trip and rates a clear personal-best effort. (op 16-1)
Unex El Greco, a beaten favourite on his nursery debut last time, again came in for strong support despite being 5lb higher. He did plenty wrong in the race, however, and clearly has some temperament issues. He made a very tardy start, but got going as the race developed and looked as though he would pick up the winner passing the furlong marker as he quickened. He hung markedly left when it really mattered, though, as was the case on his previous outing, and really threw it away. It wouldn't be surprising to see some headgear applied next time. (op 11-4 tchd 3-1 and 2-1)
Planet Waves(IRE), whose rider put up 1lb overweight, travelled as well as anything through the race and was asked for his effort in between the final 2f. He lacked a real turn of foot, though, and it may be that returning to 1m on a sounder surface will work the oracle. He has now run two solid races over C&D so rates a good benchmark. (op 22-1)
Jaaryah(IRE) posted an improved effort off this mark when third on her second outing at Kempton on her return 17 days earlier. She too moved nicely off the pace and emerged with her chance, but failed to see it out like the principals. This was her first run on turf, though, and it's possible the ground was easier than she cares for. She does give the form a solid look. (tchd 3-1)
Honeymead(IRE) was up 4lb for winning at Newmarket on softer ground 21 days earlier, and that form was boosted when the runner-up went in at this venue the previous day. She wasn't helped when hampered, but this return to a flatter track didn't suit either, as she lacked the tactical pace to go with the principals. A return to a stiffer test can see her back in the winner's enclosure. (op 13-2)
The Mellor Fella posted an improved effort under a positive ride, but probably wants a return to quicker ground over this far.
Loukoumi returned to form back over this shorter trip.
Maggie Mey(IRE) was badly hampered around the furlong marker and is better than the bare form. (op 12-1)
Male Model Official explanation: jockey said colt ran flat
T/Jkpt: Not won. T/Plt: £70.20 to a £1 stake. Pool:£123,129.99 - 1,279.46 winning tickets. T/Qpdt: £10.40 to a £1 stake. Pool:£6,968.58 - 495.75 winning tickets. WG

7040 KEMPTON (A.W) (R-H)
Saturday, October 23

OFFICIAL GOING: Standard
Wind: medium, half against Weather: showers earlier, brightening up

7086 BET NFL - BETDAQ MAIDEN STKS 1m (P)
5:45 (5:54) (Class 5) 3-Y-O+ **£2,286** (£675; £337) **Stalls** High

Form RPR
3 **1** **Morning Chief (IRE)**[24] 6470 3-9-3 0.............................. PhilipRobinson 8 76
(C G Cox) *dwlt: sn pushed along and hdwy to chse ldrs after 2f: rdn ent fnl 2f: kpt on wl u.p to ld ins fnl f: rdn out* **7/4**[1]

0 **2** *1* **Majestic Bright**[147] 2548 3-8-12 0................................. KirstyMilczarek 3 69+
(L M Cumani) *in tch on outer: rdn and chsd ldrs 2f out: edgd lft over 1f out: chsd wnr ins fnl f: kpt on* **5/1**[3]

5 **3** *hd* **Marching Home**[124] 3275 3-9-3 0.....................................(t) LukeMorris 5 73
(W R Swinburn) *hld up in tch: hdwy over 2f out: rdn and outpcd 2f out: rallied over 1f out: kpt on wl fnl f: pressing for 2nd nr fin* **15/2**

02 **4** *3 1/4* **Chris's Ridge**[23] 6496 3-9-3 0.. RichardHughes 6 66
(B J Meehan) *led: rdn and qcknd ent fnl 2f: clr over 1f out: hdd ins fnl f: sn btn: fdd and eased towards fin* **9/4**[2]

0 **5** *1/2* **Khateer**[211] 997 3-9-3 0... ChrisCatlin 11 65
(C E Brittain) *in tch in midfield: rdn and unable qck jst over 2f out: styd on same pce fr over 1f out* **16/1**

0 **6** *4 1/2* **Annie Bonita**[141] 2718 3-8-12 0.. PatCosgrave 13 50
(P R Hedger) *t.k.h: chsd ldrs: nt clr run over 2f out: sn swtchd lft: rdn and wknd qckly wl over 1f out* **50/1**

7 *1 1/4* **Etoile Filante (IRE)** 3-8-9 0.. SimonPearce(3) 7 47
(J R Gask) *s.i.s: a towards rr: nvr trbld ldrs* **33/1**

64 **8** *nse* **My Name Is Bert**[16] 6696 4-9-3 0............................ RussKennemore(3) 1 52
(Lucinda Featherstone) *in tch on outer: pushed along 6f out: rdn and struggling over 2f out: no ch after* **25/1**

9 *2 1/4* **Dashwood** 3-9-3 0... WilliamCarson 4 46
(G C Bravery) *s.i.s: racd in last trio: rdn and wknd over 2f out* **33/1**

10 *6* **Jane's Gift** 3-8-5 0.. NathanAlison(7) 14 28
(J Akehurst) *s.i.s: a last trio: rdn and lost tch qckly over 2f out* **66/1**

6 **11** *1 1/2* **The Brown Bomber (IRE)**[12] 6814 4-9-3 0............ AlanCreighton(3) 12 29
(Luke Comer, Ire) *chsd ldr for 2f: styd chsng ldrs tl wknd qckly over 2f out: bhd fnl 2f* **100/1**

1m 40.64s (0.84) **Going Correction** -0.025s/f (Stan)
WFA 3 from 4yo 3lb **11** Ran SP% **115.6**
Speed ratings (Par 103): **94,93,92,89,89 84,83,83,81,75 73**
toteswingers:1&2 £2.70, 2&3 £5.90, 1&3 £4.70 CSF £10.19 TOTE £3.20: £1.20, £1.50, £1.80; EX 14.30.
Owner Stephen W Barrow **Bred** G Callanan **Trained** Lambourn, Berks

FOCUS
An ordinary maiden at best, run in a slow time compared with the following nursery. The first three were all biggish improvers.
Chris's Ridge Official explanation: jockey said gelding stumbled 100 yards out and lost its action
Jane's Gift Official explanation: jockey said filly stumbled 3f out

7087 BET PREMIER LEAGUE FOOTBALL - BETDAQ NURSERY 1m (P)
6:15 (6:20) (Class 5) (0-75,75) 2-Y-O £2,286 (£675; £337) **Stalls** High

Form RPR

5606 **1** **Classic Voice (IRE)**[9] 6875 2-8-6 **60**.............................. DavidProbert 7 71
(R Hannon) *sn pushed along in towards rr: hung lft bnd over 4f out: last and rdn over 2f out: str run on outer over 1f out: led ins fnl f: sn clr: readily* **8/1**

4462 **2** *3 1/4* **Right Said Fred (IRE)**[12] 6795 2-9-0 **71**.................(v[1]) EJMcNamara(3) 2 74
(R M Beckett) *led: rdn ent fnl 2f: hdd over 1f out: hung lft u.p ins fnl f: no ch w wnr fnl 100yds: kpt on* **14/1**

0005 **3** *3/4* **Night Witch (IRE)**[17] 6676 2-8-11 **65**......................... EddieCreighton 14 66
(E J Creighton) *dwlt: sn rdn along and rcvrd to chse ldrs: rdn and n.m.r ent fnl 2f: swtchd rt wl over 1f out: drvn to ld jst over 1f out: hdd ins fnl f: no ch w wnr after: lost 2nd fnl 100yds* **33/1**

5041 **4** *shd* **Whodathought (IRE)**[26] 6411 2-9-3 **71**....................(b) RichardHughes 5 72
(R Hannon) *towards rr: hdwy into midfield and pushed along 4f out: rdn and hdwy to chse ldrs over 1f out: one pce and no ch w wnr ins fnl f* **6/1**[2]

445 **5** *2 1/4* **Entrance**[15] 6711 2-9-2 **70**.. JamieSpencer 11 66
(E A L Dunlop) *stdd s: hld up in rr: swtchd ins and hdwy 2f out: chsd ldrs over 1f out: wknd ins fnl f* **8/1**

204 **6** *hd* **Pencarrow**[46] 5841 2-9-5 **73**... JimmyFortune 6 69
(Mahmood Al Zarooni) *s.i.s: bhd: rdn and hdwy ent fnl 2f: swtchd rt wl over 1f out: no imp ins fnl f* **8/1**

5633 **7** *3/4* **Water Ice**[12] 6795 2-9-4 **72**....................................... RichardKingscote 13 66
(Tom Dascombe) *t.k.h: chsd ldrs: rdn to chse ldr over 2f out: carried lft and wknd ins fnl f* **20/1**

3034 **8** *1 1/2* **Ivan Vasilevich (IRE)**[26] 6412 2-8-10 **64**.......................... PatCosgrave 8 54
(Jane Chapple-Hyam) *chsd ldrs tl wknd u.p over 2f out* **8/1**

6012 **9** *1/2* **Duquesa (IRE)**[9] 6868 2-8-10 **64**...................................... CathyGannon 9 53
(P D Evans) *t.k.h: hld up in rr: rdn and effrt on outer wl over 2f out: nvr trbld ldrs* **9/2**[1]

5325 **10** *1* **Riot Police (USA)**[14] 6743 2-9-7 **75**...........................(v[1]) SaleemGolam 4 62
(J H M Gosden) *t.k.h: chsd ldrs: rdn and effrt over 2f out: wknd over 1f out* **13/2**[3]

040 **11** *2 3/4* **Violet Ray (USA)**[24] 6473 2-9-5 **73**..................................(t) JimCrowley 1 54
(R M Beckett) *racd in midfield: rdn and struggling wl over 2f out: sn btn* **10/1**

0400 **12** *12* **Meandmyshadow**[15] 6719 2-9-0 **68**.................................... DaneO'Neill 3 21
(A D Brown) *chsd ldr tl over 2f out: sn wknd: eased ins fnl f* **33/1**

1m 39.85s (0.05) **Going Correction** -0.025s/f (Stan) **12** Ran SP% **116.6**
Speed ratings (Par 95): **98,94,94,93,91 91,90,89,88,87 84,72**
toteswingers:1&2 £42.10, 2&3 £115.40, 1&3 £44.20 CSF £110.00 CT £3490.61 TOTE £13.10: £4.00, £4.30, £11.60; EX 158.20.
Owner Byerley Thoroughbred Racing **Bred** G Flannery Developments **Trained** East Everleigh, Wilts
■ Stewards' Enquiry : E J McNamara one-day ban: careless riding (Nov 6)

FOCUS
An open race but a surprise winner.

NOTEBOOK
Classic Voice(IRE) has looked very modest to date, under a variety of different conditions, but proved a revelation here, and was backed at decent odds to do so. Still last turning into the straight, he made a sweeping move down the wide outside to pass all of his rivals and scoot clear in the final furlong, in the style of a horse well ahead of his mark. He had run on Polytrack, over this trip, and in handicaps before, so it's hard to know where this improvement came from, but this was a huge step forward and it will be interesting to see if connections try to get him out under a penalty, as he'd surely take some stopping if able to repeat this level of performance. (op 9-1)
Right Said Fred(IRE) kept on well despite edging to his left in the straight and he is gradually improving, while his stable are enjoying a really good spell. (op 12-1)
Night Witch(IRE) had to work hard early to get a good pitch having dwelt from the stalls and that took its toll at the business end, where she failed to sustain her effort having hit the front. This was her best effort so far though and she's going to be interesting next time. (op 25-1)
Whodathought(IRE), a winner off 3lb lower at Bath last time, couldn't quite repeat that level of form on his first try on Polytrack. Official explanation: jockey said colt ducked left and right throughout (op 5-1 tchd 9-2)

Duquesa(IRE) Official explanation: jockey said filly had no more to give

7088 BET IN-RUNNING - BETDAQ MAIDEN AUCTION STKS 6f (P)
6:45 (6:46) (Class 5) 2-Y-O £2,286 (£675; £337) **Stalls** High

Form RPR

1 **War Painter** 2-8-13 0... RichardHughes 8 82+
(S Kirk) *chsd ldrs: swtchd ins and effrt 2f out: qcknd to ld jst over 1f out: sn rdn clr: r.o strly: readily* **7/4**[1]

5350 **2** *3* **Buddy Miracle**[29] 6317 2-8-4 70.. DavidProbert 5 64
(A M Balding) *t.k.h: hld up in tch: rdn and effrt ent fnl 2f: chsd wnr 1f out: nt gng pce of wnr and wl hld after* **13/2**

3354 **3** *1 3/4* **Kissing Clara (IRE)**[12] 6795 2-8-5 64..............................(p) LukeMorris 6 60
(J S Moore) *led: rdn ent fnl 2f: hdd jst over 1f out: outpcd ins fnl f* **4/1**[3]

3030 **4** *3/4* **Indian Shuffle (IRE)**[5] 6989 2-8-13 69.............................. JimCrowley 3 66
(J G Portman) *chsd ldr: rdn to press ldr wl over 1f out: outpcd by wnr 1f out: one pce and wl hld after* **8/1**

5 *1/2* **Woop Woop (IRE)** 2-8-3 0... JohnFahy(3) 7 57
(Stef Higgins) *in tch in rr: hdwy and swtchd lft ent fnl 2f: kpt on but no ch w wnr ins fnl f* **12/1**

3 **6** *nk* **Arowana (IRE)**[4] 6995 2-8-9 0.. LiamJones 9 59
(W J Haggas) *in tch in midfield: rdn over 2f out: swtchd lft wl over 1f out: kpt on: nvr gng pce to threaten wnr* **7/2**[2]

0000 **7** *7* **King Bling (IRE)**[3] 7017 2-9-0 46.....................................(b) ChrisCatlin 1 43
(S Kirk) *s.i.s: sn in tch: chsd ldrs 4f out: rdn and wknd 2f out: wl btn whn edgd rt over 1f out* **66/1**

500 **8** *3* **Amore Et Labore**[22] 6542 2-9-0 50..................................... LiamKeniry 4 34
(S Kirk) *hld up in last pair: rdn and struggling 3f out: lost tch jst over 2f out* **50/1**

1m 13.69s (0.59) **Going Correction** -0.025s/f (Stan) **8** Ran SP% **114.2**
Speed ratings (Par 95): **95,91,88,87,87 86,77,73**
toteswingers:1&2 £2.60, 2&3 £4.60, 1&3 £2.30 CSF £13.91 TOTE £3.20: £1.10, £1.60, £1.10; EX 14.90.
Owner Abbott Racing, D Boocock & R J Brennan **Bred** R J Brennan And D Boocock **Trained** Upper Lambourn, Berks

FOCUS
A weak maiden in which most were exposed as modest and Buddy Miracle set the standard with an official mark of 70.

NOTEBOOK
War Painter was solid in the market on his debut and, with Richard Hughes a significant booking, he proved more than equal to the task, coming clear in the final furlong. Although a little keen early, he clearly knew his job well and proved different league to his rivals. It was a good performance but the form is nothing to get excited about, although his trainer said afterwards that he was a big backward horse who was expected to do much better next year. (op 13-8 tchd 15-8)
Buddy Miracle was the solid one in this field and he ran his race again but is clearly vulnerable to anything with a bit of class in maiden company. He'll find a race at some point though and is at least consistent. (op 6-1)
Kissing Clara(IRE) extended her record to 0-13 but, like Buddy Miracle, appeared to run her race once again. Her handicap mark is on the slide and low grade handicaps/claimers/sellers look her best chance of success. (op 11-2)
Indian Shuffle(IRE) isn't progressing but at least he bounced back having blotted his copybook in handicap company at Windsor last time. Official explanation: vet said gelding lost its right hind shoe (op 12-1)
Woop Woop(IRE) shaped encouragingly, keeping on steadily from off the pace and, given she has more of a miler's pedigree, looks likely to do much better when upped in trip. (op 16-1 tchd 10-1)
Arowana(IRE) was a bit disappointing and didn't build on her Lingfield debut. (op 11-4 tchd 4-1 in places)

7089 BETDAQ ON 0870 178 1221 CLAIMING STKS 1m 4f (P)
7:15 (7:17) (Class 6) 3-Y-O+ £1,637 (£483; £241) **Stalls** Centre

Form RPR

5131 **1** **Talenti (IRE)**[16] 6699 7-9-6 70..(t) DaneO'Neill 10 75
(Mrs Lawney Hill) *racd in midfield: dropped in rr main gp but stl in tch 6f out: rdn wl over 2f out: hdwy u.p over 1f out: chal ins fnl f: led nr fin* **7/2**[2]

5504 **2** *shd* **Kames Park (IRE)**[27] 6393 8-9-8 69............................... JamieSpencer 1 77
(R C Guest) *stdd s: hld up in last pair: rdn and hdwy over 1f out: led ins fnl f: hdd nr fin* **6/1**

6154 **3** *3* **Potentiale (IRE)**[13] 6774 6-9-12 74................................... GeorgeBaker 3 76
(J W Hills) *stdd s: hld up in last trio: rdn and hdwy 2f out: drvn to press ldrs 1f out: wknd fnl 100yds* **15/2**

4122 **4** *1 3/4* **Country Road (IRE)**[11] 6829 4-9-10 74........................ RichardHughes 6 71
(A W Carroll) *chsd ldrs: rdn to press ldrs jst over 2f out: sn hung bdly lft and racing on stands' rail over 1f out: kpt on same pce u.p after* **11/4**[1]

1356 **5** *1/2* **Blue Tango (IRE)**[13] 6774 4-9-12 72..............................(v) JimCrowley 7 72
(Mrs A J Perrett) *chsd ldrs: rdn and effrt jst over 2f out: drvn to ld wl over 1f out: hdd ins fnl f: wknd* **8/1**

2024 **6** *3* **Gearbox (IRE)**[10] 6841 4-9-2 59... AdamKirby 11 58
(H J L Dunlop) *led for 1f: chsd ldr after: rdn and ev ch over 2f out tl wl over 1f out: wknd ent fnl f* **20/1**

0050 **7** *9* **Sri Kuantan (IRE)**[18] 6662 6-8-11 38........................(t) MarkCoumbe(5) 2 43
(D Bourton) *awkward s: sn pushed along and ld after 1f: rdn over 2f out: hdd wl over 1f out: wknd u.p over 1f out* **20/1**

/00- **8** *4 1/2* **Animator**[520] 2200 5-9-12 68.. ChrisCatlin 5 46
(M Hill) *t.k.h: hld up in last pair: rdn and effrt over 2f out: wknd wl over 1f out* **33/1**

0003 **9** *2 1/2* **Robby Bobby**[7] 6915 5-9-10 74... GregFairley 4 40
(M Johnston) *in tch in midfield: clipped heels and stmbld 6f out: rdn ent fnl 3f: wknd over 2f out* **5/1**[3]

2m 35.26s (0.76) **Going Correction** -0.025s/f (Stan) **9** Ran SP% **115.2**
Speed ratings (Par 101): **96,95,93,92,92 90,84,81,79**
.Gearbox was claimed by J. Darby for £2000.\n\x\x
Owner Alan Hill **Bred** Watership Down Stud **Trained** Aston Rowant, Oxon

FOCUS
Not much depth to this ordinary claimer, and there were doubts over much. The form is rated around the front pair.
Country Road(IRE) Official explanation: jockey said gelding hung left

7090 BET ASIAN H'CAPS - BETDAQ HANDICAP 1m 3f (P)
7:45 (7:47) (Class 4) (0-85,85) 3-Y-O £3,885 (£1,156; £577; £288) **Stalls** High

Form RPR

4431 **1** **Piano**[10] 6856 3-8-10 **74**... WilliamBuick 4 86+
(J H M Gosden) *hld up in last pair: swtchd ins and gd hdwy ent fnl 2f: rdn to ld and flashed tail 1f out: hung lft u.p: r.o strly fnl 100yds* **11/8**[1]

2032 **2** 1 ¾ **Akhmatova**[16] 6701 3-9-5 **83** DaneO'Neill 9 92
(G A Butler) *hld up in tch towards rr: hdwy to chse ldrs over 2f out: swtchd lft and rdn ent fnl 2f: led over 1f out tl 1f out: nt gng pce of wnr fnl 100yds: kpt on* **8/1**

5114 **3** nk **Lyric Poet (USA)**[45] 5868 3-8-13 **77** (t) WilliamCarson 3 85
(G C Bravery) *hld up in tch towards rr: hdwy over 2f out: swtchd rt and rdn to chse ldrs over 1f out: keeping on same pce whn carried lft and sltly hmpd ins fnl f* **7/1**[3]

1100 **4** ¾ **Cosimo de Medici**[25] 6447 3-9-2 **80** (t) SteveDrowne 5 87
(H Morrison) *hld up in last pair: stl bhd and rdn over 2f out: hdwy to chse ldrs and nt clr run 1f out: swtchd rt and chsd ldng trio ins fnl f: no imp fnl 75yds* **33/1**

1110 **5** 1 **Captain John Nixon**[92] 4334 3-9-5 **83** JimCrowley 8 88
(Pat Eddery) *chsd ldrs: rdn and ev ch ent fnl 2f: no ex 1f out: btn whn pushed lft ins fnl f* **10/1**

2041 **6** 4 **Fantastic Strike (IRE)**[9] 6872 3-8-10 **74** GregFairley 6 72
(M Johnston) *chsd ldrs: rdn wl over 2f out: wknd u.p over 1f out* **6/1**[2]

5021 **7** hd **Whistleinthewind (IRE)**[10] 6841 3-9-7 **85** (v) GeorgeBaker 10 82
(G L Moore) *led for 1f: chsd ldr after tl rdn to ld ent fnl 2f: hdd over 1f out: wknd jst over 1f out* **20/1**

5326 **8** 14 **Formulation (IRE)**[22] 6543 3-8-8 **72** ow1 RichardHughes 2 44
(H Morrison) *led after 1f: rdn over 2f out: hdd ent fnl 2f: sn wknd: wl bhd ins fnl f* **6/1**[2]

13- **9** nse **Magician's Cape (IRE)**[374] 6779 3-9-4 **85** Louis-PhilippeBeuzelin(3) 1 57
(Sir Michael Stoute) *t.k.h: hld up in tch towards rr: rdn and no hdwy over 2f out: wl bhd over 1f out* **20/1**

0000 **10** 2 ¾ **Kalypso King (USA)**[13] 6780 3-8-13 **77** StephenCraine 7 44
(S Kirk) *stdd s: hld up in tch: lost pl qckly over 2f out: wl bhd fnl 2f* **50/1**

2m 19.72s (-2.18) **Going Correction** -0.025s/f (Stan) 10 Ran SP% **117.8**
Speed ratings (Par 103): **106,104,104,103,103 100,100,90,89,87**
toteswingers:1&2 £5.90, 2&3 £8.70, 1&3 £2.60 CSF £12.57 CT £60.23 TOTE £2.50: £1.20, £2.50, £1.10; EX 17.80.
Owner Cheveley Park Stud **Bred** Cheveley Park Stud Ltd **Trained** Newmarket, Suffolk
■ Stewards' Enquiry : William Buick one-day ban: careless riding (Nov 6)

FOCUS
The best race of the night, so no surprise it produced the best time. Decent form and the winner can probably do better.
Formulation(IRE) Official explanation: jockey said colt ran too free

7091 BETDAQ THE BETTING EXCHANGE H'CAP (DIV I) 7f (P)
8:15 (8:15) (Class 4) (0-85,85) 3-Y-0+ **£3,561** (£794; £794; £264) **Stalls** High

Form RPR

1460 **1** **Nazreef**[22] 6534 3-9-2 **82** (t) TravisBlock 13 91+
(H Morrison) *chsd ldr tl 4f out: rdn to chse ldr again over 2f out: drvn and ev ch over 1f out: led ins fnl f: idled towards fin* **11/2**

0232 **2** ½ **L'Hirondelle (IRE)**[41] 5997 6-9-6 **84** JimCrowley 9 92
(M J Attwater) *racd off the pce in midfield: swtchd lft and hdwy wl over 2f out: rdn to chal wl over 1f out: led jst over 1f out tl hdd and no ex ins fnl f* **5/1**[3]

1314 **2** dht **Space Station**[21] 6558 4-9-5 **83** (b) HayleyTurner 5 91+
(S Dow) *stdd and dropped in bhd after s: hld up wl bhd: rdn and hdwy on outer over 1f out: r.o strly u.p ins fnl f: nt quite rch wnr* **4/1**[1]

0000 **4** hd **Lowther**[21] 6564 5-9-0 **85** (be) NatashaEaton(7) 2 92
(A Bailey) *sn nudged along towards rr: reminder 5f out: hdwy on outer ent fnl 2f: chsd ldrs jst ins fnl f: kpt on wl* **20/1**

0410 **5** 1 ½ **Hazzard County (USA)**[23] 6503 6-8-10 **81** LauraPike(7) 10 84
(D M Simcock) *hld up off the pce towards rr: hdwy over 2f out: swtchd rt and pressed ldrs over 1f out: ev ch jst ins fnl f: edgd lft and no ex fnl 100yds* **10/1**

-000 **6** 1 ½ **Elspeth's Boy (USA)**[129] 3081 3-8-13 **79** SteveDrowne 11 78
(J R Best) *chsd ldrs: rdn and effrt ent fnl 2f: hmpd and swtchd lft jst over 1f out: styd on same pce after* **20/1**

0310 **7** 1 ½ **Chief Exec**[23] 6503 8-8-10 **74** (b) LukeMorris 12 69
(J R Gask) *sn wl bhd in last: swtchd ins and gd hdwy jst over 2f out: no imp over 1f out* **20/1**

111 **8** ½ **Global Village (IRE)**[183] 1509 5-9-3 **81** WilliamCarson 6 75
(G C Bravery) *racd in midfield: hdwy and in tch over 2f out: sn swtchd lft and rdn: styd on same pce and no imp fr over 1f out* **9/2**[2]

000 **9** 1 ¼ **Palisades Park**[42] 5967 3-9-4 **84** RichardHughes 1 75
(R Hannon) *stdd and dropped in bhd after s: hld up in rr: hdwy over 2f out: rdn and no prog over 1f out: no threat to ldrs ins fnl f* **25/1**

0405 **10** 2 **Arachnophobia (IRE)**[46] 5834 4-9-2 **80** DaneO'Neill 3 65
(Pat Eddery) *wl off the pce towards rr: rdn and effrt wl over 2f out: plugged on same pce u.p fnl 2f: nvr trbld ldrs* **14/1**

4250 **11** ¾ **Mambo Spirit (IRE)**[23] 6503 6-9-1 **79** PatCosgrave 8 62
(Stef Higgins) *led: rdn over 2f out: hdd over 1f out: wknd ins fnl f* **10/1**

-000 **12** 8 **Secret Queen**[127] 3158 3-8-13 **79** DavidProbert 14 41
(M Hill) *chsd ldrs: rdn 3f out: wknd u.p wl over 1f out* **50/1**

4066 **13** ¾ **Fivefold (USA)**[12] 6798 3-8-9 **75** MartinLane 4 35
(J Akehurst) *chsd ldrs: wnt 2nd 4f out tl over 2f out: sn wknd* **25/1**

1m 24.89s (-1.11) **Going Correction** -0.025s/f (Stan)
WFA 3 from 4yo+ 2lb 13 Ran SP% **119.0**
Speed ratings (Par 105): **105,104,104,104,102 100,99,98,97,94 93,84,83**
CSF £12.32 CT £61.82 TOTE £10.70: £4.40; EX 28.70.
Owner Deborah Collett & M J Watson **Bred** M J Watson **Trained** East Ilsley, Berks
■ Stewards' Enquiry : Jim Crowley caution: careless riding.

FOCUS
A really good finish to this competitive handicap, which was run at a decent gallop but was slightly slower than division II. The form basically looks sound.
Global Village(IRE) Official explanation: trainer said gelding lost a shoe

7092 BETDAQ THE BETTING EXCHANGE H'CAP (DIV II) 7f (P)
8:45 (8:47) (Class 4) (0-85,85) 3-Y-0+ **£3,561** (£1,059; £529; £264) **Stalls** High

Form RPR

0052 **1** **Primaeval**[23] 6503 4-9-7 **85** (v) HayleyTurner 8 97+
(J R Fanshawe) *stdd s: t.k.h: hld up in last pair: stl plenty to do over 2f out: switching lft and gd hdwy wl over 1f out: led jst ins fnl f: sn clr and r.o strly: readily* **2/1**[1]

0132 **2** 2 ¼ **Dingaan (IRE)**[25] 6439 7-9-2 **80** DavidProbert 12 86
(A M Balding) *t.k.h: hld up towards rr: rdn and hdwy wl over 1f out: chsd clr wnr ins fnl f: no ch w wnr: kpt on* **10/1**

3223 **3** ½ **Fantasy Gladiator**[23] 6501 4-8-9 **73** (p) LiamKeniry 7 78
(R M H Cowell) *t.k.h: hld up towards rr: pushed along and hdwy ent fnl 2f: rdn and kpt on ins fnl f: wnt 3rd nr fin* **5/1**[2]

4461 **4** ½ **Red Gulch**[35] 6197 3-9-3 **83** DaneO'Neill 5 86
(E A L Dunlop) *hld up in tch: rdn to chse ldr 2f out: ev ch jst over 1f out: led ins fnl f: sn hdd and no ch w wnr: kpt on same pce and lost 2 pls after* **8/1**[3]

0041 **5** 1 **Samarinda (USA)**[21] 6577 7-9-4 **82** (p) MickyFenton 6 83
(Mrs P Sly) *led: rdn 2f out: hdd jst ins fnl f: no ex ins fnl f* **22/1**

0000 **6** ½ **Admiral Cochrane (IRE)**[12] 6799 3-8-10 **76** JimCrowley 9 75
(W Jarvis) *hld up towards rr: rdn and effrt over 2f out: no hdwy tl kpt on ins fnl f: nvr trbld ldrs* **33/1**

4236 **7** ½ **Thunderball**[23] 6510 4-9-3 **81** IanMongan 11 79
(J A Glover) *chsd ldrs: rdn to chse wnr and edgd rt jst over 2f out tl 2f out: kpt on same pce fr over 1f out* **8/1**[3]

2005 **8** ½ **Unshakable Will (IRE)**[41] 6002 3-8-13 **79** (v[1]) TomEaves 13 76
(B Smart) *chsd ldrs: effrt on inner and chsng ldrs whn pushed rt jst over 1f out: kpt on same pce fr over 1f out* **25/1**

0030 **9** 1 ¼ **Mastership (IRE)**[15] 6721 6-9-6 **84** (p) GeorgeBaker 10 77
(J J Quinn) *hld up towards rr: hdwy on inner over 2f out: rdn and no prog ent fnl f: nvr trbld ldrs* **8/1**[3]

0200 **10** 1 **Planet Red (IRE)**[73] 4963 3-9-2 **82** RichardHughes 1 72
(R Hannon) *stdd s: hld up in rr: rdn 3f out: nvr trbld ldrs* **25/1**

0450 **11** 5 **Protector (SAF)**[19] 6625 9-9-0 **78** (t) PatCosgrave 14 55
(T T Clement) *in tch: rdn and wknd jst over 2f out: wl btn ins fnl f* **40/1**

2135 **12** 3 **Defector (IRE)**[23] 6501 4-8-13 **77** JamieSpencer 3 46
(D Bourton) *wnt lft s: chsd ldr tl jst over 2f out: sn bmpd and pushed rt: wknd 2f out* **14/1**

430 **13** 2 ½ **Nezami (IRE)**[23] 6503 5-9-0 **78** GregFairley 2 40
(J Akehurst) *hmpd s and s.i.s: sn in tch in midfield on outer: rdn over 3f out: wknd over 2f out* **16/1**

1m 24.67s (-1.33) **Going Correction** -0.025s/f (Stan)
WFA 3 from 4yo+ 2lb 13 Ran SP% **122.4**
Speed ratings (Par 105): **106,103,102,102,101 100,100,99,98,96 91,87,84**
toteswingers:1&2 £3.50, 2&3 £5.80, 1&3 £4.50 CSF £22.19 CT £94.11 TOTE £3.60: £2.20, £3.90, £1.10; EX 18.10.
Owner Lord Vestey **Bred** Stowell Park Stud **Trained** Newmarket, Suffolk

FOCUS
Not as competitive as the first division but it was slightly quicker. An improved effort from the winner, with the form rated around the third.
Defector(IRE) Official explanation: jockey said gelding suffered interference in running

7093 BETDAQ.COM H'CAP 6f (P)
9:15 (9:16) (Class 5) (0-75,80) 3-Y-0+ **£2,286** (£675; £337) **Stalls** High

Form RPR

2416 **1** **Hatta Stream (IRE)**[12] 6812 4-9-2 **73** SimonPearce(3) 9 85
(J Pearce) *in tch: effrt to chse ldr ent fnl 2f: rdn to ld jst over 1f out: kpt on wl under hands and heels ins fnl f* **6/1**[2]

4100 **2** 1 **Arctic Lynx (IRE)**[12] 6812 3-8-13 **68** HayleyTurner 4 77
(J R Best) *stdd s: hld up in last trio: rdn and gd hdwy over 1f out: chsd wnr fnl f: r.o: a hld* **12/1**

30-2 **3** 2 **Dear Maurice**[22] 6523 6-9-7 **75** (t) IanMongan 11 77
(T B P Coles) *chsd ldrs: rdn to press ldrs wl over 1f out: drvn over 1f out: no ex and btn fnl 150yds* **4/1**[1]

0-16 **4** 2 **Alis Aquilae (IRE)**[98] 4148 4-9-4 **75** RobertLButler(3) 12 71+
(T J Etherington) *stdd s: hld up in midfield: shuffled bk and towards rr wl over 2f out: hdwy 2f out: nt clr run over 1f out tl 1f out: kpt on: nvr able to chal* **13/2**[3]

3210 **5** 1 **Erebus (IRE)**[24] 6461 3-9-2 **71** RichardHughes 3 64
(S Kirk) *hld up towards rr: rdn and hdwy over 2f out: no prog u.p fr over 1f out* **15/2**

0654 **6** nse **Lord Of The Reins (IRE)**[23] 6501 6-9-1 **69** PaulMulrennan 1 62
(J G Given) *stdd and dropped in bhd after s: hld up in rr: rdn over 2f out: nvr trbld ldrs* **8/1**

10 **7** ¾ **Yes We Can**[23] 6501 3-8-12 **67** SteveDrowne 5 57
(J R Gask) *bhd: rdn wl over 2f out: kpt on fr over 1f out: nvr trbld ldrs* **14/1**

2461 **8** nse **Freddie's Girl (USA)**[4] 6998 3-9-8 **80** 6ex JohnFahy(3) 2 70
(Stef Higgins) *w ldr tl led over 2f out: drvn wl over 1f out: hdd jst over 1f out: wknd ins fnl f* **9/1**

1000 **9** 1 **C'Mon You Irons (IRE)**[12] 6812 5-8-13 **70** KierenFox(3) 6 57
(M R Hoad) *chsd ldrs: drvn and unable qck over 2f out: wknd wl over 1f out* **25/1**

2310 **10** hd **Starwatch**[25] 6438 3-9-1 **70** NeilChalmers 10 56
(J J Bridger) *led tl hdd and rdn over 2f out: wknd over 1f out* **25/1**

1002 **11** nk **Kersivay**[187] 1428 4-9-3 **71** PatCosgrave 8 56
(P D Evans) *hld up towards rr: hdwy into midfield and rdn jst over 2f out: no hdwy over 1f out: wknd ins fnl f* **16/1**

4051 **12** 4 **Gracie's Gift (IRE)**[23] 6491 8-8-11 **65** (v) JamieSpencer 7 37
(R C Guest) *in tch on outer: rdn and hung rt over 2f out: sn wknd* **6/1**[2]

1m 12.64s (-0.46) **Going Correction** -0.025s/f (Stan)
WFA 3 from 4yo+ 1lb 12 Ran SP% **122.7**
Speed ratings (Par 103): **102,100,98,95,94 93,92,92,91,91 90,85**
toteswingers:1&2 £54.70, 2&3 £10.10, 1&3 £25.30 CSF £78.95 CT £329.61 TOTE £13.90: £3.40, £2.70, £2.50; EX 130.10 Place 6: £88.90 Place 5: £56.96.
Owner Macniler Racing Partnership **Bred** T W Bloodstock Ltd **Trained** Newmarket, Suffolk

FOCUS
An ordinary handicap run at a sound pace. A length personal best from the winner.
C'Mon You Irons(IRE) Official explanation: jockey said gelding hung left
Gracie's Gift(IRE) Official explanation: trainer's rep said gelding was unsuited by the surface
T/Plt: £337.00 to a £1 stake. Pool of £57,170.76 - 123.81 winning tickets. T/Qpdt: £7.30 to a £1 stake. Pool of £8,995.76 - 908.15 winning tickets. SP

6688 NEWBURY (L-H)
Saturday, October 23

OFFICIAL GOING: Good to soft (good in places) changing to good to soft after race 1 (1.30)
Rail realignment increased distances on round course by about 30m.
Wind: Moderate ahead Weather: Sunny intervals

7094 WADE WILLIS 50TH BIRTHDAY E B F MAIDEN STKS (DIV I) 1m (S)
1:30 (1:33) (Class 4) 2-Y-0 **£4,209** (£1,252; £625; £312) **Stalls** Centre

Form RPR

5 **1** **Al Kazeem**[16] 6689 2-9-3 0 SteveDrowne 1 87+
(R Charlton) *trckd ldrs: slt advantage wl over 2f out: pushed along and qcknd over 1f out: pushed out ins fnl f: readily* **5/1**[1]

2 1 **Thimaar (USA)** 2-9-3 0 RichardHills 5 85+
(J H M Gosden) *trckd ldrs: chal wl over 2f out tl over 1f out: drvn and styd on wl to chse wnr ins fnl f: a hld but c wl clr of 3rd* **5/1**[1]

3 9 **Tonnerre (IRE)** 2-9-3 0 RyanMoore 14 65
(Sir Michael Stoute) *in rr tl pushed along and hdwy over 2f out: sn green but kpt on to take wl hld 3rd fnl f* **5/1**[1]

4 hd **Goodness** 2-9-0 0 Louis-PhilippeBeuzelin(3) 15 65
(Sir Michael Stoute) *in rr tl hdwy fr 3f out: styng on but no ch w ldng duo whn swtchd rt ins fnl f: styd on to press for wl hld 3rd cl home* **25/1**

5 2 1/4 **Sandusky** 2-9-3 0 WilliamBuick 9 60
(Mahmood Al Zarooni) *chsd ldrs: hanging lft over 3f out: chal sn after and stl ev ch over 2f out: wknd over 1f out and no ch whn hung lft again ins fnl f* **12/1**

06 6 3/4 **Mrs Greeley**[25] 6442 2-8-12 0 JimCrowley 4 53
(Eve Johnson Houghton) *s.i.s: sn mid-div: chsd ldrs fr 1/2-way: rdn over 2f out: wknd wl over 1f out* **12/1**

0 7 nk **Xclaim**[24] 6474 2-9-3 0 AdamKirby 12 57
(C G Cox) *in tch: pushed along and one pce 1/2-way: mod prog again fnl f* **50/1**

5 8 4 **Great Shot**[24] 6473 2-9-3 0 LiamKeniry 2 49
(S Kirk) *mde most tl narrowly hdd wl over 2f out: wknd wl over 1f out* **7/1**[2]

50 9 5 **Tijori (IRE)**[56] 5523 2-9-3 0 RichardHughes 13 38
(R Hannon) *in tch: rdn over 3f out: no imp on ldrs and no ch fnl 2f* **9/1**[3]

0 10 1/2 **Web Of Dreams (IRE)**[12] 6811 2-9-3 0 (t) JamieSpencer 6 36
(B J Meehan) *trckd ldrs: rdn to chal 3f out: hung lft and wknd ins fnl 2f* **25/1**

0 11 1 1/4 **Miss Topsy Turvy (IRE)**[12] 6804 2-8-12 0 TedDurcan 3 29
(J L Dunlop) *s.i.s: in rr: pushed along and sme prog 1/2-way: nvr nr ldrs* **33/1**

12 3/4 **Beat Of The Blues** 2-9-3 0 JimmyFortune 17 32
(A M Balding) *s.i.s: in rr: rdn and green 1/2-way: nvr beyond mid-div* **20/1**

0 13 1/2 **Deceptive**[10] 6843 2-8-12 0 HayleyTurner 7 26
(R Charlton) *in tch: rdn 1/2-way and sn wknd* **40/1**

0 14 3/4 **Viking Storm**[16] 6689 2-9-3 0 DaneO'Neill 19 29
(H J L Dunlop) *in tch: rdn 3f out and sn bhd* **33/1**

15 3/4 **Orange Ace** 2-9-3 0 TomQueally 11 28
(P F I Cole) *chsd ldrs over 4f* **20/1**

16 6 **Elfaaten (USA)** 2-9-3 0 TadhgO'Shea 8 14
(M P Tregoning) *early spd: sn in rr* **22/1**

0 17 24 **Guards Chapel**[38] 6092 2-9-3 0 J-PGuillambert 18 —
(L M Cumani) *s.i.s: in rr: sn rdn and lost tch* **28/1**

1m 44.17s (4.47) **Going Correction** +0.60s/f (Yiel) **17** Ran SP% **123.2**
Speed ratings (Par 97): **101,100,91,90,88 87,87,83,78,78 76,76,75,74,74 68,44**
toteswingers: 1&2 £5.90, 1&3 £5.70, 2&3 £3.20. CSF £24.33 TOTE £5.70: £2.10, £2.60, £2.40; EX 25.00.

Owner D J Deer **Bred** D J And Mrs Deer **Trained** Beckhampton, Wilts

FOCUS
An open-looking maiden, but the first two came well clear.

NOTEBOOK
Al Kazeem showed ability when in need of the experience on his debut and the benefit of that outing proved decisive in seeing off a useful-looking newcomer in Thimaar. The winner travelled well through the race, quickened up smartly, and gives the impression that he will be suited by faster ground, and another 2f should be within his compass next year. There could be a nice prize in him down the road. (op 11-2)
Thimaar(USA) travelled strongly, but in the end the lack of a previous outing found him out. He finished well clear of the rest, though, and this well-bred son of Dynaformer looks sure to make up into a decent middle-distance performer next season. (op 11-2 tchd 6-1)
Tonnerre(IRE) ran green but was keeping on in taking fashion at the finish. There is no shortage of stamina in his pedigree and it won't be until he tackles 1m4f-plus that he will be seen at his best. (op 11-2 tchd 6-1)
Goodness was chopped for room a furlong out and had to switched, but for which he would have edged third. He should not have any trouble getting another 2f.
Sandusky carried his head to one side, hanging left, for much of the race, which did not help his chance. Hopefully it was just greenness.
Mrs Greeley battled on fairly well and is now eligible for a mark. She should be able to find a race in modest company. (op 11-1)
Xclaim, who ran as though needing the race on his debut, lasted longer this time, but he is another for whom handicaps will see him in a better light.
Great Shot had the benefit of a previous run but he raced too freely in front here and the result was that he had little left for the finish. (op 8-1 tchd 13-2)
Tijori(IRE) was stepping up from 6f but neither his pedigree nor previous races had suggested it would suit him. He did not get home and will make more appeal in handicaps back over shorter. (op 11-1 tchd 12-1)
Web Of Dreams(IRE), wearing a tongue-tie for the first time, was another stepping up 2f in distance, and he was another who found the trip in this ground too much of a test. Jamie Spencer later confirmed that the colt was unsuited by the good to soft ground. Official explanation: jockey said colt was unsuited by the good to soft ground

7095 JOHN SMITH'S EXTRA SMOOTH STKS (REGISTERED AS THE HORRIS HILL STAKES) (GROUP 3) (C&G) 7f (S)

2:05 (2:05) (Class 1) 2-Y-O

£21,288 (£8,070; £4,038; £2,013; £1,008; £506) **Stalls** Centre

Form RPR

5322 1 **Klammer**[28] 6347 2-8-12 103 JamieSpencer 3 105
(Jane Chapple-Hyam) *stdd in last pl: stdy hdwy over 2f out: effrt and swtchd lft over 1f out: styd on wl u.p fnl f: led post* **6/1**

4213 2 nse **Dux Scholar**[14] 6737 2-8-12 98 RyanMoore 11 105
(Sir Michael Stoute) *hld up bhd ldng gp: hdwy over 2f out: hung lft u.p and led ins fnl f: ct post* **7/2**[1]

123 3 nk **Elzaam (AUS)**[107] 3823 2-8-12 112 (b[1]) RichardHills 5 104
(M A Jarvis) *t.k.h: led: rdn over 1f out: hdd ins fnl f: rallied: hld cl home* **9/2**[2]

340 4 4 1/2 **Madawi**[21] 6560 2-8-12 94 TomQueally 2 93
(C E Brittain) *hld up: drvn and outpcd over 2f out: styd on wl to take 4th pl cl home: no ch w first three* **7/1**

3213 5 hd **Big Issue (IRE)**[14] 6733 2-8-12 107 RichardHughes 6 92
(R Hannon) *w ldr: rdn over 2f out: outpcd fr over 1f out* **5/1**[3]

4311 6 1/2 **Azrael**[36] 6156 2-8-12 86 JamesDoyle 4 91
(A J McCabe) *trckd ldrs: drvn and outpcd over 2f out: kpt on last 100yds: no imp* **25/1**

0332 7 1 1/4 **Surrey Star (IRE)**[23] 6507 2-8-12 104 JohnFahy 10 88
(R A Teal) *t.k.h: cl up: rdn over 2f out: no ex over 1f out: wknd ins fnl f* **8/1**

13 8 3 3/4 **Sensei (IRE)**[70] 5079 2-8-12 90 AdamKirby 8 79
(M G Quinlan) *hld up: drvn along over 2f out: sn btn* **66/1**

1 9 16 **Well Sharp**[36] 6138 2-8-12 82 JimCrowley 7 39
(M Dods) *in tch: rdn along 1/2-way: wknd over 2f out: t.o* **10/1**

01 10 1 1/4 **Norse Blues**[25] 6442 2-8-12 80 LiamKeniry 9 36
(S Kirk) *t.k.h: trckd ldrs tl lost pl qckly over 2f out: sn struggling: t.o* **20/1**

1m 28.21s (2.51) **Going Correction** +0.60s/f (Yiel) **10** Ran SP% **114.2**
Speed ratings (Par 105): **109,108,108,103,103 102,101,96,78,77**
toteswingers: 1&2 £4.00, 1&3 £2.90, 2&3 £1.30. CSF £26.13 TOTE £7.80: £2.30, £1.90, £1.70; EX 31.20 Trifecta £111.30 Pool: £889.58 - 5.91 winning units..

Owner Yan Wah Wu **Bred** Ermyn Lodge Stud Limited **Trained** Dalham, Suffolk

FOCUS
Rarely one of the more important juvenile Group races, and the form again looks nothing out of the ordinary, though there was a notable boost to Frankel's Royal Lodge effort courtesy of the winner. The time was good, however, being much quicker than the two later 7f races, albeit the ground surely deteriorated somewhat. The action unfolded up the centre of the track.

NOTEBOOK
Klammer was having his first outing since being thrashed 10l by Frankel at Ascot. The drop back from 1m didn't inconvenience him, for all that he only got up in the last stride, and he picked up really well on the soft ground. His mind very much needed making up when brought with his challenge from well off the pace, with his head carriage slightly awkward at one point, but Jamie Spencer said the horse got hit on the head by Richard Hills's whip, and that was probably the reason. He will reportedly continue his career in Hong Kong. (op 8-1)
Dux Scholar, dropped in trip after fading into third in the Autumn Stakes over 1m, didn't help himself by being inclined to hang left under pressure, but he still showed smart form in defeat. He probably won't mind going back over further next year. (tchd 4-1)
Elzaam(AUS), fitted with blinkers for his first start in 107 days, came here rather than the Dewhurst. Last seen finishing third in the July Stakes, he was a bit keen in front through the early stages but still saw out the extra furlong, finishing well clear of the remainder. He'll probably prefer better ground and there's more to come. (op 7-2)
Madawi ◆ was under pressure a long way out and took an age to respond, but he finally ran on in the closing stages and looked to cross the line with something left, albeit he was passing beaten horses. He seems sure to improve when stepped up in trip, indeed he could be quite smart over middle-distances next year, and is one to keep in mind. (op 10-1)
Big Issue(IRE) raced freely through the early stages and didn't see his race out on ground softer than ideal. He's capable of better.
Azrael was taking a big jump in class after winning a Newmarket nursery off 83, and the soft ground was an unknown, but he performed with credit. Official explanation: jockey said colt was unsuited by the good to soft ground (op 28-1)
Surrey Star(IRE) made no impression and the form of the Newmarket Group 3 in which he finished a close second last time is not working out. The colt has been sold to race in the USA. (tchd 15-2)

7096 JOHN SMITH'S STKS (REGISTERED AS THE ST SIMON STAKES) (GROUP 3) 1m 4f 5y

2:40 (2:40) (Class 1) 3-Y-O+

£32,358 (£12,266; £6,138; £3,060; £1,533; £769) **Stalls** Low

Form RPR

0 1 **Clowance**[189] 1382 5-9-0 110 RichardHughes 2 111+
(R Charlton) *hld up in tch: hdwy whn nt clr run 2f out and sn swtchd rt: drvn and qcknd fnl f to ld fnl 120yds: pushed clr: readily* **7/2**[1]

3134 2 2 **Poet**[21] 6592 5-9-6 114 AdamKirby 6 114
(C G Cox) *trckd ldr tl led 3f out: narrowly hdd 2f out: styd chalng u.p and upsides fnl 120yds: sn outpcd by wnr but kpt on wl for 2nd* **9/2**[3]

-152 3 1 1/2 **Dreamspeed (IRE)**[22] 6533 3-8-10 103 JimmyFortune 1 108
(A M Balding) *trckd ldrs: slt ld 2f out: styd hrd pressed tl hdd & wknd fnl 120yds* **12/1**

4232 4 2 **Jedi**[43] 5908 4-9-3 97 RyanMoore 3 105
(Sir Michael Stoute) *in rr but in tch: hdwy u.p whn hmpd: swtchd rt over 2f out and lost momentum: kpt on u.p fnl f but no imp on ldng trio* **15/2**

1-12 5 1 3/4 **La De Two (IRE)**[51] 5696 4-9-3 109 (t) DaraghO'Donohoe 7 102
(Saeed Bin Suroor) *s.i.s: sn in tch: chsng ldrs whn hung lft fr over 3f out: rdn: hung bdly lft and nt run on appr fnl 2f* **8/1**

5124 6 1/2 **Hot Prospect**[31] 6281 3-8-10 110 PhilipRobinson 4 102
(M A Jarvis) *hld up in rr: hdwy fr 3f out: trckd ldrs over 1f out: reminders sn after and wknd fnl f* **4/1**[2]

2012 7 6 **Whispering Gallery**[27] 6389 4-9-3 111 TedDurcan 5 92
(Saeed Bin Suroor) *led: hdd 3f out: styd chalng u.p over 2f out: wknd sn after* **9/2**[3]

0400 8 16 **Ted Spread**[23] 6506 3-8-13 100 TomQueally 8 69
(M H Tompkins) *in rr: racd on outside and hdwy 4 out: nvr quite rchd ldrs: hung lft and wknd ins fnl 3f* **20/1**

2m 40.45s (4.95) **Going Correction** +0.75s/f (Yiel)
WFA 3 from 4yo+ 7lb **8** Ran SP% **113.9**
Speed ratings (Par 113): **113,111,110,109,108 107,103,93**
toteswingers: 1&2 £4.80, 1&3 £12.70, 2&3 £10.70. CSF £19.24 TOTE £4.70: £1.20, £1.80, £4.00; EX 21.40 Trifecta £273.40 Pool: £1,167.83 - 3.16 winning units..

Owner Seasons Holidays **Bred** B Hurley **Trained** Beckhampton, Wilts

FOCUS
This had the look of a competitive Group 3, but in the end the well-backed favourite Clowance came through to win quite readily. The winner loved the ground but did not need to match her top efforts with her main form rivals below their best.

NOTEBOOK
Clowance, the only mare in the field, hasn't stood much racing over the years and was disappointing on her only previous start this term in the John Porter Stakes (ground too quick), but she was best in at these weights and conditions had come in her favour. In addition, her liking for this track and proven ability to win when fresh suggested a big run was on the cards, and she duly delivered in style. Her owner is keen to keep her in training as a 6-y-o. (op 5-1)
Poet likes to lead but had to accept being taken along by the Godolphin first string this time. He responded well to pressure and kept battling away, but the winner always had his measure. It was a good effort under his penalty, especially as deeper ground suits him ideally. (op 6-1)
Dreamspeed(IRE) appreciates a little cut and posted another career-best in defeat. He's quietly progressing and appeals as the type to make an even better 4-y-o. (op 11-1 tchd 14-1)
Jedi was one of the two worst in at the weights but he appreciates plenty of cut in the ground. Staying on when others had cried enough, he posted a respectable effort on this step up in class. (op 10-1 tchd 7-1)
La De Two(IRE) showed he stays further than this at Salisbury last time, but the ground was good that day and these more testing conditions found him out. He hung badly under pressure and his rider reported that the colt didn't handle the good to soft ground. Official explanation: jockey said colt was unsuited by the good to soft ground (op 15-2 tchd 7-1)
Hot Prospect handles this sort of ground but his stamina for the trip, which was unproven, let him down. (op 9-2)
Whispering Gallery, whose trainer had warned would not want the ground too soft, weakened quickly once headed, his rider reporting that the gelding ran flat. Official explanation: jockey said gelding ran flat (op 10-3)

Ted Spread, who was expected to relish conditions, ran a stinker, and clearly all is not well with him at the moment. (tchd 22-1 in a place)

7097 E B F BATHWICK TYRES FILLIES' H'CAP 7f (S)
3:10 (3:13) (Class 3) (0-95,92) 3-Y-0+ **£9,066** (£2,697; £1,348; £673) **Stalls** Centre

Form RPR
4250 **1** **Gouray Girl (IRE)**[29] 6319 3-9-4 **89** JamieSpencer 10 102+
(W R Swinburn) *hld up: hdwy on outside of gp 2f out: led ins fnl f: drvn out* **6/1**[1]
0054 **2** *1* **Bahati (IRE)**[28] 6346 3-9-4 **89** RichardKingscote 9 99
(J G Portman) *hld up in midfield: hdwy and edgd lft fr over 2f out: chsd wnr ins fnl f: kpt on* **14/1**
0341 **3** *½* **Sard**[12] 6805 3-8-11 **82** PhilipRobinson 12 91+
(M A Jarvis) *led: rdn over 1f out: hdd ins fnl f: kpt on u.p* **6/1**[1]
3160 **4** *1* **Fleeting Echo**[13] 6776 3-9-7 **92** RichardHughes 8 98
(R Hannon) *t.k.h: hld up in tch: stdy hdwy to chse ldrs over 1f out: drvn and one pce fnl f* **10/1**
3166 **5** *nk* **Perfect Silence**[28] 6346 5-8-10 **82** (b) JohnFahy(3) 13 87+
(C G Cox) *hld up: hdwy 2f out: rdn and kpt on fnl f: nrst fin* **14/1**
4144 **6** *1 ¾* **Medici Pearl**[14] 6749 6-9-4 **87** TedDurcan 2 87
(T D Easterby) *in tch: effrt on outside of gp over 2f out: no ex fnl f* **15/2**[2]
0000 **7** *nk* **Victoria Sponge (IRE)**[28] 6346 4-8-11 **80** DaneO'Neill 17 80+
(S C Williams) *missed break: bhd: rdn and hdwy nr side of gp 2f out: kpt on fnl f: nrst fin* **12/1**
2044 **8** *hd* **Sioux Rising (IRE)**[23] 6509 4-8-12 **81** RyanMoore 15 80
(R A Fahey) *hld up: effrt on nr side of gp 2f out: kpt on fnl f: nvr rchd ldrs* **8/1**[3]
0400 **9** *1* **Perfect Flight**[19] 6625 5-8-8 **77** KirstyMilczarek 14 73
(M Blanshard) *trckd ldrs: drvn over 2f out: no ex fr over 1f out* **40/1**
0160 **10** *1* **Hairspray**[29] 6319 3-8-11 **82** CathyGannon 5 76
(M R Channon) *midfield: nt clr run and swtchd lft over 2f out: sn rdn and no imp* **28/1**
2050 **11** *½* **Bintalwaadi**[28] 6346 3-9-2 **87** RichardHills 1 79
(E A L Dunlop) *prom: smooth hdwy on outside of gp over 2f out: rdn and wknd over 1f out* **16/1**
4100 **12** *hd* **Little Scotland**[15] 6721 3-9-0 **85** (p) JimmyFortune 18 77
(R A Fahey) *in tch on nr side of gp: rdn over 2f out: wknd over 1f out* **22/1**
41 **13** *nse* **Island Rhapsody**[178] 1622 3-8-5 **76** oh1 DavidProbert 7 68
(A M Balding) *hld up: drvn over 2f out: nvr able to chal* **16/1**
1 **14** *2* **Bella Noir**[37] 5487 3-8-11 **82** AndrewElliott 4 68
(Mrs K Burke) *cl up: drvn along over 3f out: wknd over 2f out* **10/1**
0436 **15** *2 ½* **Pretty Bonnie**[13] 6776 5-8-11 **83** NataliaGemelova(3) 6 63
(A E Price) *midfield: rdn over 3f out: wknd over 2f out* **20/1**
2020 **16** *16* **Mistic Magic (IRE)**[28] 6346 3-9-4 **89** (b) TomQueally 3 25
(P F I Cole) *cl up tl rdn and wknd qckly over 2f out: t.o* **33/1**

1m 29.19s (3.49) **Going Correction** +0.60s/f (Yiel)
WFA 3 from 4yo+ 2lb **16** Ran SP% **120.4**
Speed ratings (Par 104): **104,102,102,101,100 98,98,98,97,95 95,95,95,92,89 71**
toteswingers: 1&2 £30.30, 1&3 £7.20, 2&3 £29.40. CSF £82.48 CT £533.78 TOTE £6.80: £1.80, £3.50, £2.20, £2.80; EX 84.00 Trifecta £1150.10 Pool: £103,754.40 - 66.75 winning units..
Owner Alan Le Herissier **Bred** George S O'Malley **Trained** Aldbury, Herts

FOCUS
A good fillies' handicap but perhaps not as competitive as the betting suggests. They raced up the middle of the track. The winner produced a clear personal best and the form could be rated a little higher.

NOTEBOOK
Gouray Girl(IRE) produced a career best on this first attempt at 7f, adding to her debut maiden win. This was only her ninth start and she looks set to progress into a smart type. (op 13-2)
Bahati(IRE), dropped in trip after finishing fourth over 1m in a Listed handicap at Ascot, ran about as well as she ever has. (op 12-1)
Sard was a bit free in front through the early stages but stuck on well. She was 7lb higher than when making all at Salisbury last time, but still has more to offer. (op 13-2)
Fleeting Echo briefly looked a player about a furlong out, but her effort came to nothing. Her last two wins have been gained at 7f, but she looks worth another go over 6f. (op 11-1 tchd 9-1)
Perfect Silence took a while to pick up but was going on at the finish. She will be worth another try over 1m, although the effect of the blinkers seems to have worn off. (tchd 12-1)
Medici Pearl had the ground to suit and has won off this mark, so a little better could have been expected. (tchd 8-1)
Victoria Sponge(IRE), not for the first time, lost several lengths with a slow start, and she looked reluctant to race, having her head in the air when asked to leave the stalls. In the circumstances, she did well to get so close. (op 14-1)

7098 JOHN MOORE AND BIDDESTONE STUD MEMORIAL STKS (REGISTERED AS THE RADLEY STAKES) (LISTED) (FILLIES) 7f (S)
3:40 (3:44) (Class 1) 2-Y-0
£13,340 (£5,057; £2,530; £1,261; £632; £317) **Stalls** Centre

Form RPR
1 **1** **Zoowraa**[21] 6566 2-8-12 0 PhilipRobinson 5 101+
(M A Jarvis) *racd towards far side and trckd ldr: led ins fnl 2f: drvn and qcknd clr fnl f* **3/1**[1]
1 **2** *3 ¼* **Flood Plain**[12] 6804 2-8-12 0 WilliamBuick 11 92+
(J H M Gosden) *racd towards centre crse fr 1/2-way: rdn and styd on to chse wnr fnl f but a wl hld* **8/1**
012 **3** *1 ¾* **Sweetie Time**[79] 4748 2-8-12 90 JamieSpencer 12 88
(M L W Bell) *stdd s: racd stands' side tl swtchd lft towards centre crse over 2f out: r.o u.p to take 3rd cl home: no imprssion on ldng duo* **20/1**
1 **4** *½* **Face Reality (USA)**[25] 6441 2-8-12 78 RichardHughes 1 87
(R Hannon) *racd far side: t.k.h and led: hdd ins fnl 2f: styd chsng wnr tl 1f out: wknd fnl 120yds and lost 3rd cl home* **12/1**
1 **5** *½* **Tuscania**[24] 6451 2-8-12 0 RyanMoore 13 86
(Sir Michael Stoute) *racd towards stands' side and in tch: rdn and styd on fnl 2f: no ex fnl 120yds* **7/1**[3]
511 **6** *1 ¼* **Winter's Night (IRE)**[29] 6317 2-8-12 83 LukeMorris 10 82
(C G Cox) *t.k.h: racd towards centre crse fr 1/2-way: rdn 2f out: wknd 1f out* **8/1**
06 **7** *1 ½* **Cloud Illusions (USA)**[68] 5147 2-8-12 0 DaneO'Neill 4 79
(Mrs H S Main) *racd far side: chsd ldrs: rdn over 2f out: wknd over 1f out* **125/1**
0254 **8** *1* **Ladyanne (IRE)**[22] 6528 2-8-12 93 TomQueally 15 76
(S Kirk) *racd stands' side: in tch: rdn 3f out: wknd over 1f out* **20/1**
46 **9** *¾* **Blessed Biata (USA)**[21] 6559 2-8-12 0 JimCrowley 9 74
(W J Haggas) *s.i.s: sn rcvrd and racd towards centre 1/2-way: rdn over 2f out: sn btn* **5/1**[2]
1455 **10** *1 ¼* **Lily Again**[22] 6528 2-9-1 98 (b1) JimmyFortune 3 74
(P F I Cole) *racd towards far side: chsd ldrs and rdn over 2f out: wknd over 1f out* **20/1**
063 **11** *5* **Escala**[14] 6748 2-8-12 67 WilliamCarson 6 59
(M D Squance) *racd towards centre crse fr 1/2-way: sn rdn and btn* **100/1**
1 **12** *hd* **Golden Delicious**[16] 6688 2-8-12 83 SteveDrowne 2 58
(H Morrison) *racd towards far side: in tch: rdn and hdwy to chse ldrs 3f out: wknd 2f out* **8/1**
6346 **13** *½* **Mortitia**[22] 6530 2-8-12 95 TedDurcan 7 57
(B J Meehan) *racd far side: sme hdwy fr 3f out: sn wknd* **10/1**
50 **14** *8* **Mawjoodah**[133] 2958 2-8-12 0 ChrisCatlin 14 37
(C E Brittain) *racd towards centre crse fr 1/2-way and bried effrt: nvr on terms and sn wknd* **100/1**

1m 30.52s (4.82) **Going Correction** +0.60s/f (Yiel) **14** Ran SP% **121.3**
Speed ratings (Par 100): **96,92,90,89,89 87,86,84,84,82 76,76,76,66**
toteswingers: 1&2 £5.20, 1&3 £11.00, 2&3 £29.10. CSF £25.67 TOTE £4.20: £1.60, £3.40, £4.90; EX 23.40 Trifecta £311.80 Pool: £1,230.50 - 2.92 winning units..
Owner Sheikh Ahmed Al Maktoum **Bred** Darley **Trained** Newmarket, Suffolk

FOCUS
This looked a competitive Listed race as it featured several interesting fillies from top yards, including five who came here on the back of debut maiden wins. The field initially split into two groups, but then both spread out so that runners were right across the track.

NOTEBOOK
Zoowraa came from the far-side group. Having tracked the leader for much of the way, she quickened up really well to take over and drew clear to win by a comfortable margin. She is clearly a smart performer in the making and should have little difficulty with another furlong next year, so a general quote afterwards of 16-1 for the 1,000 Guineas did not come as a surprise, especially considering how open the race looks at the moment. A note of caution was sounded by her connections, though, as she is not that big and will need to winter well to progress. (op 7-2)
Flood Plain, who did best of those who raced in the stands' side group, is another very useful prospect for next season, when she probably won't be wanting to go beyond a mile. (op 6-1)
Sweetie Time came from off the pace in the stands' side group, challenging up the centre of the track, and saw out this longer trip well. She has prospects of getting a mile next year on this evidence. (op 16-1)
Face Reality(USA) made the running on the far side and had a lot of her rivals on the stretch 2f out, but she didn't really see it out. She might be more effective over this distance next year, but surely won't be inconvenienced by a return to 6f. (tchd 14-1)
Tuscania, who won her maiden on Polytrack, couldn't go with her owner's other filly in the race (Flood Plain) when that one quickened up, but she stayed on well enough and is another who should do better at three. Official explanation: jockey said filly became upset in stalls (op 8-1)
Winter's Night(IRE) won a nursery at Ascot off 72 last time out and, while this required more, conditions promised to suit. She showed pace in the stands' side group but raced a bit keenly, meaning she had less in the locker for the closing stages. (op 15-2)
Cloud Illusions(USA) stepped up significantly on the form of her first two starts, appreciating the extra furlong and softer ground to record a fine effort in defeat. This is not going to do her upcoming handicap mark any good, though. (op 150-1)
Ladyanne(IRE), who raced closest to the stands' rail throughout, did nothing to boost the form of Havant's Oh So Sharp Stakes, in which she finished fourth. (op 16-1)
Blessed Biata(USA) was below the form she showed when a close fourth in a valuable sales race at Newmarket last time. This ground was probably just too testing for her. (op 13-2)
Golden Delicious, who won her maiden in good style here first time out, was disappointing. She's better than this and can be given another chance next year. (op 9-1)

7099 WADE WILLIS 50TH BIRTHDAY E B F MAIDEN STKS (DIV II) 1m (S)
4:15 (4:17) (Class 4) 2-Y-0 **£4,209** (£1,252; £625; £312) **Stalls** Centre

Form RPR
2 **1** **Carlton House (USA)**[24] 6474 2-9-3 0 RyanMoore 14 95+
(Sir Michael Stoute) *cl up: led over 2f out: shkn up to go clr fr over 1f out: impressive* **3/1**[2]
2 *9* **Yaseer (IRE)** 2-9-3 0 TadhgO'Shea 8 75
(M P Tregoning) *hld up: hdwy 2f out: chsd (clr) wnr appr fnl f: no imp: bttr for r* **40/1**
3 **3** *2* **Estourah (IRE)**[11] 6831 2-9-3 0 TedDurcan 17 71
(Saeed Bin Suroor) *prom: hdwy to chse wnr over 2f out to appr fnl f: kpt on same pce* **2/1**[1]
5 **4** *7* **Muqtarrib (IRE)**[23] 6504 2-9-3 0 RichardHills 15 56
(B J Meehan) *hld up in tch: effrt and edgd lft over 2f out: sn outpcd* **7/2**[3]
05 **5** *hd* **Spirit Of Gondree (IRE)**[23] 6514 2-9-3 0 JimCrowley 16 55
(J L Dunlop) *hld up in midfield: stdy hdwy over 2f out: rdn and outpcd wl over 1f out* **33/1**
04 **6** *¾* **Sergeant Troy (IRE)**[19] 6635 2-9-3 0 HayleyTurner 13 54
(R Charlton) *dwlt: t.k.h and sn midfield: shkn up and outpcd over 2f out: sn no imp* **12/1**
7 *2 ¼* **Swindy** 2-9-3 0 TomQueally 1 49
(P F I Cole) *towards rr: outpcd 3f out: sme late hdwy: nvr rchd ldrs* **33/1**
8 *1 ½* **Atlas Shrugged (IRE)** 2-9-3 0 AdamKirby 5 45
(C G Cox) *dwlt: bhd and early reminders: sme hdwy appr fnl f: nvr on terms* **33/1**
9 *2 ¾* **Silenzio** 2-9-3 0 RichardHughes 4 46+
(R Hannon) *trckd ldrs: rdn over 2f out: 4th and hld whn eased over 1f out: sddle slipped* **16/1**
60 **10** *nk* **Achalas (IRE)**[10] 6844 2-9-3 0 LiamKeniry 7 39
(Mrs H S Main) *towards rr: rdn along 1/2-way: sme late hdwy: nvr on terms* **100/1**
11 *hd* **Sirius Superstar** 2-9-3 0 JimmyFortune 18 38
(A M Balding) *dwlt: bhd and pushed along: styd on fnl f: nvr on terms* **14/1**
12 *½* **Praxios** 2-9-3 0 J-PGuillambert 11 37
(L M Cumani) *midfield: drvn and outpcd over 2f out: sn btn* **28/1**
13 *2 ½* **Barnmore** 2-9-3 0 DaneO'Neill 12 32
(P R Hedger) *t.k.h in midfield: struggling over 2f out: sn btn* **100/1**
0 **14** *1* **Veloce (IRE)**[11] 6831 2-9-3 0 MartinLane 2 29
(J L Dunlop) *in tch: rdn over 3f out: sn lost pl* **100/1**
0 **15** *nk* **Camberley Two**[43] 5916 2-9-3 0 SteveDrowne 3 29
(R Charlton) *trckd ldrs tl rdn and wknd wl over 2f out* **66/1**
16 *nk* **Phantom House** 2-8-9 0 RobertLButler(3) 19 23
(B W Duke) *dwlt: bhd: pushed along 1/2-way: nvr on terms* **100/1**
17 *12* **Pani Ash** 2-8-12 0 IanMongan 10 —
(P M Phelan) *cl up tl rdn and wknd qckly fr over 2f out: t.o* **100/1**
18 *10* **Ecological (IRE)**[51] 2-9-3 0 JamieSpencer 9 —
(Rune Haugen, Norway) *led to over 2f out: sn rdn and wknd: t.o* **20/1**

1m 44.06s (4.36) **Going Correction** +0.60s/f (Yiel) **18** Ran SP% **126.7**
Speed ratings (Par 97): **102,93,91,84,83 83,80,79,76,76 76,75,73,72,71 71,59,49**
toteswingers: 1&2 £29.60, 1&3 £1.40, 2&3 £19.70. CSF £136.21 TOTE £2.90: £1.40, £11.60, £1.50; EX 128.00.
Owner The Queen **Bred** Darley **Trained** Newmarket, Suffolk

FOCUS
Despite the ground surely deteriorating a little as the meeting progressed, Carlton House, who had some well-connected rivals strung out, recorded a time 0.11 seconds quicker than the first division, and it will be a surprise if he's not a Group horse.

NOTEBOOK

Carlton House(USA) ◆ fairly tanked along for much of the way before running on really strongly when let go, looking a strong-galloping type with a sustained finishing effort, rather than a quickener. Clearly this was a big improvement on the form he showed when runner-up under similar conditions at Salisbury on debut. By a Dubai World Cup winner, out of a Bustino mare who won at Group 2 level over 1m2f, and a half-brother to smart stayer Friston Forest, he will have no trouble staying middle distances next year. At this early stage he enters Derby calculations, albeit with much still to prove, and Paddy Power are a standout 25-1. (op 5-2)

Yaseer(IRE) carried the owner's second colours and was ignored in the betting, but he made an encouraging debut. Out of a smart triple 1m winner, he was clear of the remainder and should improve. (tchd 33-1)

Estourah(IRE) was 11l adrift of the winner, but was in turn a long way clear of the rest. It's hard to know which way he has gone from his debut. Time will tell. (op 5-2)

Muqtarrib(IRE) shaped well on his debut when the ground was soft, but he did not confirm that promise and perhaps didn't take to an easy surface second time around. (op 4-1)

Spirit Of Gondree(IRE) has inherited stamina from the dam's side of his pedigree and should do better in handicaps over further next year.

Sergeant Troy(IRE) should find his level now he's eligible for an official mark. (op 16-1)

Silenzio ◆ is certainly one to note. He wasn't far behind the winner when his saddle slipped inside the final 2f, at which point Richard Hughes stopped riding. Official explanation: jockey said saddle slipped (tchd 14-1)

7100 JOHN SMITH'S TILEHURST ROYAL BRITISH LEGION CLUB H'CAP 1m 2f 6y

4:50 (4:50) (Class 2) (0-100,97) 3-Y-0+

£9,346 (£2,799; £1,399; £700; £349; £175) Stalls Low

Form				RPR
1142	1		**Lost In The Moment (IRE)**[22] 6534 3-8-13 **91**.............(p) RyanMoore 6	104
			(J Noseda) *trckd ldrs: drvn to ld and edgd lft fr ins fnl 2f: drvn out* **11/2**[2]	
6054	2	1 ¾	**Right Step**[8] 6889 3-8-3 **88**............ HarryBentley(7) 13	98
			(A P Jarvis) *in rr and racd towards outside: hdwy fr 3f out: hrd drvn fr 2f out and styd on to chse wnr fnl f but a hld* **20/1**	
0060	3	1 ¾	**Brunston**[21] 6562 4-9-0 **87**............ JamieSpencer 4	93
			(R Charlton) *trckd ldrs: led briefly appr fnl 2f: sn hdd: styd chsng wnr tl 1f out: kpt on same pce* **16/1**	
1561	4	½	**Oriental Cat**[17] 6677 3-8-13 **91**............ WilliamBuick 15	96
			(J H M Gosden) *hld up in rr: hdwy on ins fr 3f out: hrd drvn fr 2f out and kpt on fnl f but nvr gng pce to trble ldrs* **5/1**[1]	
1201	5	½	**Resurge (IRE)**[21] 6552 5-9-7 **94**............ IanMongan 8	98+
			(W S Kittow) *hld up in rr: hdwy and nt clr run over 2f out: swtchd lft sn after and kpt on fnl f: nt rch ldrs* **20/1**	
4400	6	4 ½	**Cumulus Nimbus**[35] 6193 3-9-1 **93**............ RichardHughes 5	88
			(R Hannon) *s.i.s: sn in mid-div: rdn to chse ldrs over 2f out: wknd fnl f* **11/2**[2]	
5430	7	¾	**Proponent (IRE)**[21] 6562 6-9-10 **97**............ TedDurcan 11	91
			(R Charlton) *racd on outer and chsd ldrs: rdn over 2f out: wknd over 1f out* **10/1**	
2000	8	nk	**Admission**[35] 6203 3-9-5 **97**............ HayleyTurner 3	90
			(M L W Bell) *in rr: rdn and sme hdwy over 2f out: nvr rchd ldrs and wknd over 1f out* **40/1**	
4340	9	1	**Reve De Nuit (USA)**[9] 6877 4-9-1 **88**............ JamesDoyle 1	79
			(A J McCabe) *t.k.h: chsd ldrs: rdn 3f out: wknd 2f out* **40/1**	
1521	10	1	**Julienas (IRE)**[24] 6449 3-9-3 **95**............ AdamKirby 16	84
			(W R Swinburn) *trckd ldr: chal fr 6f out: led ins fnl 4f: hdd over 2f out: sn hung bdly lft and wknd* **12/1**	
3334	11	3	**Sandor**[21] 6562 4-9-8 **95**............(v) SteveDrowne 7	78
			(P J Makin) *in rr: effrt and n.m.r over 2f out: nvr any ch and sn bhd* **17/2**	
0134	12	1 ½	**Spanish Duke (IRE)**[14] 6738 3-9-4 **96**............ TomQueally 14	76
			(J L Dunlop) *t.k.h: racd towards outside: rdn: hung lft and wknd 2f out* **6/1**[3]	
5400	13	2 ½	**Suits Me**[14] 6738 7-9-9 **96**............ MickyFenton 9	71
			(T P Tate) *led tl hdd ins fnl 4f: wknd over 2f out* **66/1**	
-003	14	2	**Unbreak My Heart (IRE)**[29] 6327 5-9-0 **87**............ RichardHills 2	58
			(R A Fahey) *nvr bttr than mid-div: bhd fnl 3f* **16/1**	
6461	15	5	**Dubai Crest**[26] 6428 4-8-13 **86**............ JimCrowley 12	47
			(Mrs A J Perrett) *racd towards outside: nvr bttr than mid-div and bhd fnl 3f* **33/1**	
0-03	16	9	**Moyenne Corniche**[14] 6738 5-9-9 **96**............ JimmyFortune 10	39
			(M L W Bell) *t.k.h: racd towards outside: towards rr most of way* **20/1**	

2m 13.93s (5.13) **Going Correction** +0.75s/f (Yiel)
WFA 3 from 4yo+ 5lb **16** Ran SP% **124.4**
Speed ratings (Par 109): **109,107,106,105,105 101,101,100,100,99 96,95,93,92,88 80**
toteswingers: 1&2 £42.80, 1&3 £24.50, 2&3 £148.20. CSF £118.44 CT £1690.00 TOTE £5.80: £1.80, £4.90, £4.80, £1.90; EX 177.80.
Owner M Tabor & Mrs Susan Roy **Bred** Rockhart Trading Ltd **Trained** Newmarket, Suffolk

FOCUS

The 3-y-os looked the ones to concentrate on here, and that age group provided the first two home. A fair handicap run in testing conditions, and reasonably sound form.

NOTEBOOK

Lost In The Moment(IRE) has a progressive profile and had gone close off 2lb lower at Newmarket last time. Clearly at home on this sort of surface, and stepping back up to 1m2f, he won well, but it's clear he still has his quirks as he was continually hanging left in the closing stages and also flashed his tail under pressure. That said, the cheekpieces clearly had a positive effect and there is probably more to come from him. (op 7-1 tchd 15-2)

Right Step has been slightly in and out this season but his best efforts, including when beaten narrowly at Glorious Goodwood off 2lb lower, gave him every chance if the combination of a drop back to 1m2f and soft ground did the trick. This was a good effort, but he'll go up in the handicap again now, which won't help his chances of adding to his maiden race win. (op 16-1)

Brunston sprang a surprise in the Spring Cup, which was a rough race, earlier in the season, but he's struggled off higher marks since. Back down to a rating 1lb higher, he ran a lot better here for a stable finishing the season strongly.

Oriental Cat, a winner in similar conditions at Nottingham last time, had a 9lb higher mark to overcome here and that proved just beyond him. It was still a good effort, though, and he remains on the upgrade. (op 9-2 tchd 11-2)

Resurge(IRE), another coming here on the back of a career-best effort, didn't enjoy a clear run through and shaped like he could have finished third with more luck. Testing ground seems to bring out the best in him. (tchd 18-1)

Cumulus Nimbus was another for whom a case could easily be made on his best form, but ground this soft was an unknown and he didn't really pick up on it. He'll be of interest again when back on a decent surface. (tchd 9-2)

Proponent(IRE) remains handicapped up to the hilt but is a consistent performer and once again ran his race.

Admission looks a difficult horse to place off his current mark.

Julienas(IRE) has a pedigree that suggests he'll be much happier back on a sound surface, or on the Polytrack, on which he's already been successful. Official explanation: jockey said colt hung left (op 14-1)

Sandor, fourth in the Cambridgeshire last time out, was up 3lb and ran as though he'd had enough for the year. (op 9-1 tchd 8-1)

Spanish Duke(IRE) had conditions to suit but raced much too keenly and simply gave himself little chance of getting home. (op 7-1 tchd 11-2)

7101 FRANK OSGOOD MEMORIAL LADY JOCKEYS' H'CAP (FOR LADY AMATEUR RIDERS) 1m 4f 5y

5:25 (5:25) (Class 5) (0-75,75) 4-Y-0+ **£3,123** (£968; £484; £242) Stalls Low

Form				RPR
/061	1		**Pocketwood**[24] 6480 8-10-4 **75**............ MissZoeLilly(3) 4	82
			(A J Lidderdale) *hld up in midfield: effrt over 3f out: rdn and drifted to stands' rail fr over 1f out: styd on wl fnl f: led towards fin* **6/1**[3]	
3150	2	¾	**Maslak (IRE)**[44] 5888 6-9-9 **70**............ MissCBoxall(7) 2	76
			(P W Hiatt) *led: rdn over 2f out: kpt on fnl f: hdd towards fin* **25/1**	
01/0	3	1 ½	**Tuanku (IRE)**[26] 6428 5-9-9 **68**............ MissRachelKing(5) 1	71
			(A King) *trckd ldrs: pushed along and outpcd over 2f out: kpt on ins fnl f* **17/2**	
250	4	1 ¼	**Sir Boss (IRE)**[56] 5530 5-9-11 **68**............ MissMMullineaux(3) 3	69
			(M Mullineaux) *trckd ldrs: shkn up over 2f out: no ex ins fnl f* **20/1**	
/004	5	½	**Boucheron**[15] 6724 5-9-12 **71**............ MrsVFahey(5) 12	72
			(R A Fahey) *trckd ldr: outpcd over 2f out: rallied over 1f out: one pce fnl f* **5/1**[2]	
3-06	6	2 ½	**Beau Fighter**[21] 6554 5-9-11 **65**............ MissGAndrews 9	62
			(G L Moore) *hld up: hdwy over 2f out: edgd lft and kpt on fnl f: nrst fin* **7/1**	
42-0	7	1 ½	**Astrodiva**[11] 6832 4-9-0 **61** oh1............ MissNMcCaffrey(7) 11	55
			(M H Tompkins) *t.k.h: hld up in midfield: shkn up over 2f out: sn no imp* **14/1**	
3360	8	3 ¼	**Abayaan**[48] 5788 4-9-9 **70**............ MissAZetterholm(7) 6	59
			(Jane Chapple-Hyam) *hld up in midfield on ins: outpcd 3f out: n.d after* **12/1**	
4243	9	5	**Mykingdomforahorse**[13] 6774 4-10-2 **70**............(v) MissEJJones 7	51
			(M R Channon) *plld hrd in tch: outpcd over 2f out: edgd rt and sn btn* **4/1**[1]	
5530	10	6	**Yonder**[46] 5828 6-9-0 **61** oh7............(t) MissNDumelow(7) 10	32
			(H Morrison) *in tch on outside tl wknd fr over 3f out* **25/1**	
/0-0	11	¾	**Mister Benedictine**[59] 4621 7-9-0 **61**............(t) MissCEReid(7) 5	31
			(B W Duke) *t.k.h: in tch tl wknd over 3f out* **33/1**	
0405	12	2 ½	**Turjuman (USA)**[6] 6957 5-9-10 **71**............ MissLaurenShea(7) 8	37
			(W J Musson) *hld up: struggling over 3f out: nvr on terms* **10/1**	
40	13	1	**Hollow Green (IRE)**[23] 6516 4-10-7 **75**............ MrsEEvans 13	40
			(P D Evans) *bhd: struggling over 3f out: sn btn* **12/1**	

2m 45.6s (10.10) **Going Correction** +0.75s/f (Yiel) **13** Ran SP% **120.5**
Speed ratings (Par 103): **96,95,94,93,93 91,90,88,85,81 80,79,78**
toteswingers: 1&2 £24.30, 1&3 £12.50, 2&3 £25.90. CSF £155.21 CT £1287.10 TOTE £8.60: £3.30, £11.20, £1.10; EX 187.20 Place 6: £29.36, Place 5: £14.86..
Owner The Sw1ft Buck Partnership **Bred** M J Lewin **Trained** Eastbury, Berks
■ Stewards' Enquiry : Miss Zoe Lilly nine-day ban: used whip with excessive frequency (tbn)

FOCUS

A typical amateur riders' event run in testing ground. Not form to be too positive about.

T/Plt: £21.70 to a £1 stake. Pool:£89,343.03 - 3,003.88 winning tickets. T/Qpdt: £10.90 to a £1 stake. Pool:£4,432.05 - 299.08 winning tickets. RY

5805 BADEN-BADEN (L-H)

Saturday, October 23

OFFICIAL GOING: Turf: soft

7102a ENGELBERT STRAUSS TROPHY (GROUP 3) (3YO+) (TURF) 1m 3f

3:45 (12:00) 3-Y-0+

£28,318 (£9,734; £4,867; £2,654; £1,769; £1,327)

			RPR
1		**Durban Thunder (GER)**[34] 6234 4-9-2 0............ NRichter 9	102
		(T Mundry, Germany) *broke wl: settled in 3rd: tk ld into 1st turn: set gd pce: led into st: r.o wl: wandered off st line but battled hrd ins fnl f to hold off chalr on line* **67/10**	
2	nse	**Representing (USA)**[34] 6234 6-9-2 0............ MlleAnne-SophiePacault 6	102
		(Mlle A-S Pacault, France) *settled in midfield: r.o wl in st: had to work to find clr run: jnd ldr ins fnl f: battled hrd to line: jst failed* **227/10**	
3	nk	**Liang Kay (GER)**[20] 6612 5-9-2 0............ StephanePasquier 3	101
		(Uwe Ostmann, Germany) *settled in midfield: r.o wl u.p in st: battled to line: narrowly btn* **7/5**[1]	
4	nk	**Lyssio (GER)**[34] 6234 3-8-8 0............ AStarke 7	99
		(P Schiergen, Germany) *a bkmarker: shkn up in st: r.o wl to threaten ins fnl f: no ex cl home* **61/10**[3]	
5	2	**Agent Secret (IRE)**[70] 5107 4-9-4 0............ Francois-XavierBertras 5	100
		(F Rohaut, France) *settled in midfield: r.o wl in st wout threatening ldrs* **7/2**[2]	
6	4	**Next Vision (IRE)**[41] 6011 4-9-0 0............ ADeVries 4	89
		(J Hirschberger, Germany) *initially led: then settled 2nd: trcking pce: sn btn ent st* **161/10**	
7	2 ½	**Falun (GER)**[20] 6606 4-9-2 0............ EFrank 10	87
		(A Trybuhl, Germany) *towards rr fr s: briefly threatened in st: no ex: wknd* **42/1**	
8	nk	**Touch Of Hawk (FR)**[41] 6017 4-9-4 0............ LennartHammer-Hansen 2	88
		(Wido Neuroth, Norway) *hld up in 4th: threatened briefly early in st: r.o: wknd fnl f* **94/10**	
9	4	**Altair Star (IRE)**[52] 5671 3-8-8 0............ FilipMinarik 8	77
		(P Schiergen, Germany) *settled bhd ldrs: ev ch ent st: no ex* **29/1**	
10	hd	**Zaungast (IRE)**[55] 6-9-2 0............ APietsch 1	79
		(W Hickst, Germany) *settled in 4th: flattered briefly early in st: sn btn* **68/10**	
11	4	**Derwisch (IRE)**[34] 6234 4-9-0 0............ EPedroza 11	70
		(A Wohler, Germany) *a towards rr: sn btn in st* **43/1**	

2m 23.31s (4.04)
WFA 3 from 4yo+ 6lb **11** Ran SP% **131.4**
WIN (incl.10 euro stake): 77. PLACES: 21, 36, 12. SF: 2,439..
Owner Stall Tinsdal **Bred** Frau M Sohl **Trained** Germany

[6975] SAN SIRO (R-H)
Saturday, October 23

OFFICIAL GOING: Turf: good

7103a ST LEGER ITALIANO (GROUP 3) (3YO+) (TURF) 1m 6f
3:10 (12:00) 3-Y-O+ £35,398 (£15,575; £8,495; £4,247)

RPR

1 **Burma Gold (IRE)**[41] 6011 3-8-5 0 JiriPalik 2 96
(P Schiergen, Germany) *settled mid-div: patiently rdn tl 2 1/2f out: swtchd rt and hdwy to ld fnl 150yds: hrd rdn fnl 100yds to keep command* **27/10**[3]

2 ¾ **Ryan (IRE)**[21] 7-8-13 0 (b) UmbertoRispoli 1 94
(J Hanacek, Slovakia) *broke wl to share ld briefly: trckd ldr: produced to chal 3f out: led 2 1/2f out tl ent fnl f: hrd pressed u.str ride to hold 2nd* **12/5**[2]

3 shd **Cima De Pluie**[21] 3-8-5 0 DarioVargiu 5 95
(B Grizzetti, Italy) *hld up in rr: hdwy ent st to move 3rd 2f out: chal for ld fnl 300yds: led briefly ent fnl f: hrd rdn: styd on* **216/10**

4 ¾ **Caudillo (GER)**[21] 7-8-13 0 PierantonioConvertino 3 93
(Dr A Bolte, Germany) *hld up in rr: rdn to stay in tch 3f out: styd on fnl 300yds under v hrd ride* **11/5**[1]

5 6 **Baschar**[34] 6239 3-8-5 0 MircoDemuro 6 86
(M G Mintchev, Germany) *settled mid-div on outer: in tch ent fnl 3f: hrd rdn and no imp: btn and eased fnl f* **13/4**

6 4 **Orluna (GER)**[21] 3-8-2 0 MEsposito 4 77
(R Rohne, Germany) *broke to ld: chal 3f out: no answer fnl 2f: sn btn* **58/10**

3m 4.20s (184.20)
WFA 3 from 7yo 9lb **6** Ran SP% **130.3**
WIN (incl. 1 euro stake): 3.70. PLACES: 2.06, 1.72. DF: 17.60.
Owner Gestut Ammerland **Bred** Gestut Ammerland **Trained** Germany

[7102] BADEN-BADEN (L-H)
Sunday, October 24

OFFICIAL GOING: Turf: heavy

7108a COOLMORE STUD PREIS DER WINTERKONIGIN 2010 (GROUP 3) (2YO FILLIES) (TURF) 1m
3:40 (12:00) 2-Y-O

£53,097 (£20,353; £9,734; £5,309; £2,654; £1,769)

RPR

1 **Djumama (IRE)** 2-9-2 0 ADeVries 8 102
(Andreas Lowe, Germany) *broke wl: settled in 2nd: r.o wl in st: qcknd wl fnl f: led 150yds out: comf* **139/10**

2 ¾ **Aigrette Garzette (IRE)** 2-9-2 0 AStarke 3 100
(P Schiergen, Germany) *broke fast then settled in prom position: r.o wl in st: grabbed ld 250yds out: ct 150yds out* **7/5**[1]

3 1 **Danedream (GER)**[21] 6609 2-9-2 0 FilipMinarik 10 98
(P Schiergen, Germany) *failed to settle early on then racd promly: shkn up early in st: picked up wl 1f out: fin fast* **5/1**[3]

4 nk **Lips Poison (GER)** 2-9-2 0 (b[1]) AHelfenbein 6 97
(Andreas Lowe, Germany) *broke wl: racd freely: sent to ld ent bk st: led into home st: r.o wl: hdd 1f out: styd on* **87/10**

5 1 ¼ **Dalarna (GER)** 2-9-2 0 APietsch 2 95
(W Hickst, Germany) *broke wl: racd in ldng gp: mde early move in st: no ex fnl 2f* **104/10**

6 2 ½ **Wolkenburg (GER)** 2-9-2 0 THellier 7 89
(P Schiergen, Germany) *bkmarker fr s: picked up in st but only passed btn runners* **4/1**[2]

7 1 **Global Magic (GER)** 2-9-2 0 EPedroza 11 87
(A Wohler, Germany) *s.i.s: proged towards end of bk st: rdn early in home st but no ex: fdd* **17/2**

8 3 ½ **Turia (GER)** 2-9-2 0 DPorcu 4 79
(Uwe Ostmann, Germany) *a in rr: nvr figured* **15/1**

9 ¾ **Temida (IRE)** 2-9-2 0 EFrank 1 78
(M G Mintchev, Germany) *broke wl: led briefly: then settled: sn tired arnd fnl turn: qckly btn* **28/1**

10 **Achinora** 2-9-2 0 PJWerning 9 78
(M G Mintchev, Germany) *racd in midfield: nvr figured* **58/1**

11 5 **Sword Style (GER)** 2-9-2 0 HenkGrewe 5 67
(Mario Hofer, Germany) *racd in 6th: r.o arnd fnl turn: sn btn in home st* **231/10**

1m 48.34s (9.23) **11** Ran SP% **130.2**
WIN (incl. 10 euro stake): 149. PLACES: 29, 13, 23. SF: 473.
Owner Stall Phillip I **Bred** Colin Kennedy **Trained** Germany

[2152] CAPANNELLE (R-H)
Sunday, October 24

OFFICIAL GOING: Turf: soft

7109a PREMIO LYDIA TESIO (GROUP 1) (3YO+ FILLIES & MARES) (TURF) 1m 2f
4:00 (12:00) 3-Y-O+ £119,469 (£52,566; £28,672; £14,336)

RPR

1 **Aoife Alainn (IRE)**[21] 3-8-10 0 UmbertoRispoli 7 117
(M Guarnieri, Italy) *hld up in rr: hdwy 4f out to move 6th: rdn ent fnl 2f to move 3rd: led 1f out: rdn and pushed clr fnl 100yds* **18/1**

2 2 ½ **Antara (GER)**[21] 6613 4-9-0 0 FrankieDettori 5 111
(Saeed Bin Suroor) *broke wl to trck ldr: produced to chal ldr 3f out: led ent fnl 2f: hrd rdn and sn btn by eventual wnr 1f out: one pce fnl f* **4/9**[1]

3 2 **Soberania (GER)**[28] 6410 4-9-0 0 MircoDemuro 1 107
(A Wohler, Germany) *broke wl to ld tl 3f out: chal by eventual 2nd bwteen 3f and 2f markers: hrd rdn and no ex whn btn ent fnl f* **341/100**[2]

4 3 ½ **Tremoto**[15] 6763 5-9-0 0 (b) SDiana 3 100
(F & L Camici, Italy) *broke wl to trck ldrs tl ent st: ct for pce 3 1/2f out and lost several l: styd on under hrd ride fnl 2f whn no ch of catching 1st 3* **241/10**

5 2 ¼ **Quiza Quiza Quiza**[315] 4-9-0 0 JMurtagh 6 96
(L Riccardi, Italy) *settled in 4th on outer: hrd rdn fr 3f out: sn one pce and styd on under hrd ride fnl f* **25/4**[3]

6 2 **Suchita Devious (ITY)**[21] 4-9-0 0 PAragoni 2 92
(S Bietolini, Italy) *hld up in rr: struggled to stay in tch ent st: hrd rdn and styd on past btn horses fnl 300yds* **34/1**

7 1 ¼ **She Is Great (IRE)**[21] 3-8-10 0 (b) SUrru 9 90
(Vittorio Caruso, Italy) *mid-div tl ent st: rdn handily to move 3rd 3f out: sn hrd rdn and one pce fnl 2f* **183/20**

8 2 ½ **Cronsa (GER)**[21] 3-8-10 0 FabioBranca 8 85
(S Botti, Italy) *mid-div: hrd rdn to stay in tch 4f out: no imp and btn 2f out* **169/10**

2m 4.30s (1.00)
WFA 3 from 4yo+ 5lb **8** Ran SP% **133.3**
WIN (incl. 1 euro stake): 19.01. PLACES: 1.87, 1.10, 1.31. DF: 57.13.
Owner Soc All M Guarnieri **Bred** Deer Forest Stud **Trained** Italy

NOTEBOOK

Aoife Alainn(IRE) had just one rival behind her turning for home but she quickened up in great style to go by the field and cross the line nicely clear. The exagerrated waiting tactics worked a treat.

Antara(GER), disappointing at Longchamp last time out, was nevertheless sent off a warm favourite against these lesser rivals. She was given every chance but firmly put in her place by the winner.

[6973] LONGCHAMP (R-H)
Sunday, October 24

OFFICIAL GOING: Turf: soft

7110a PRIX ROYAL-OAK (GROUP 1) (3YO+) (TURF) 1m 7f 110y
3:10 (12:00) 3-Y-O+ £126,415 (£50,575; £25,287; £12,632; £6,327)

RPR

1 **Gentoo (FR)**[21] 6607 6-9-4 0 (p) Christophe-PatriceLemaire 5 113
(A Lyon, France) *w.w towards rr: hit traffic problems in st: whn clr qcknd wl ins fnl f to take command: comf* **11/4**[1]

2 ½ **Celtic Celeb (IRE)**[22] 6590 3-8-9 0 ThierryThulliez 7 113
(F Doumen, France) *tk ld on settling down after 2f: rdn to go clr early in st: saw off all chals tl ct ins fnl f: r.o* **10/1**

3 1 ½ **Opinion Poll (IRE)**[44] 5909 4-9-4 0 PhilipRobinson 6 110
(M A Jarvis) *a.p on outside: first to chal ldr 1 1/2f out: r.o wl: no ex fnl 100yds* **5/1**[2]

4 ½ **Maria Royal (IRE)**[22] 6591 3-8-6 0 ThierryJarnet 8 108
(A De Royer-Dupre, France) *towards rr: mde prog bef st: r.o wl fnl 2f wout threatening ldrs* **10/1**

5 hd **Blek (FR)**[21] 6607 5-9-4 0 YohannBourgois 3 110
(E Lellouche, France) *racd bhd ldrs along rail: r.o in st wout threatening* **13/2**[3]

6 ½ **Watar (IRE)**[42] 6016 5-9-4 0 DavyBonilla 10 109
(F Head, France) *w.w: mde prog bef st: rdn and r.o wout threatening* **10/1**

7 2 **Peinture Rare (IRE)**[22] 6591 4-9-1 0 AnthonyCrastus 4 104
(E Lellouche, France) *prom bhd ldrs: threatened briefly 1 1/2f out: no ex fnl f* **12/1**

8 5 **Vulcanite (IRE)**[15] 6736 3-8-9 0 JimCrowley 9 102
(R M Beckett) *bkmarker fr s: nvr figured in st* **12/1**

9 1 **Flying Cross (IRE)**[43] 5976 3-8-9 0 WilliamBuick 2 101
(J H M Gosden) *prom fr s: rdn bef st: tk ld briefly 2f out: rdn but no ex: wknd* **5/1**[2]

10 6 **Winter Dream (IRE)**[21] 6607 6-9-4 0 IoritzMendizabal 1 94
(Robert Collet, France) *racd in 3rd on rail: rdn early in st: no ex: wknd* **14/1**

3m 36.0s (14.50) **Going Correction** +0.525s/f (Yiel)
WFA 3 from 4yo+ 9lb **10** Ran SP% **122.7**
Speed ratings: **84,83,83,82,82 82,81,78,78,75**
WIN (incl. 1 euro stake): 2.50. PLACES: 1.40, 2.40, 2.50. DF: 11.00. SF: 17.90.
Owner Serge Tripier-Mondancin **Bred** Jean-Claude Seroul **Trained** France

FOCUS

Despite its close proximity to the Prix du Cadran (French Gold Cup), the Prix Royal-Oak (French St Leger) over 1m7f1/2f has proven more suited to stayers than middle distance performers in recent seasons. The like of Yeats and Westerner have won this in recent years, but this running did not look the toughest Group 1.

NOTEBOOK

Gentoo(FR) showed he was a cut above these to win this in comfortable enough fashion and make it four from four since upped to 1m7f-plus. These conditions clearly play to his strengths and he was also happier with the stop-start pace than some of his rivals. Having been held up towards the rear as they crawled through the first mile or so, he had just three behind as they straightened up, and although he was slightly short of room as his rider attempted to angle him out late in the straight, he always had the measure of these and could have won by further. He has been a model of consistency in the second half of this season, and has now won four of his last eight starts, finishing second in the other four. This will be his lot for his sixth year, with Ascot's Gold Cup a possible target next season. Although there are seemingly few stars among the staying division at present, the fact he seems better suited when there is cut in the ground must count against him in the mid-summer feature, and he may be better suited to the races he has won at home in the backend of this season.

Celtic Celeb(IRE)'s win in Group 2 company here on Arc weekend did not look much at the time, but he proved that was no fluke with a respectable run on this second try over a longer trip. His rider was able to boss it from the front from the off and he had enough left to see off the challenge of Flying Cross at the top of the straight, only to be headed by the winner late on. There could be more to come from this 3-y-o over staying trips in the future.

Opinion Poll(IRE) was one of four who finished in a heap behind the front two. He was more at home on this ground than when disappointing in the Doncaster Cup last time but the staccato gallop did not play to his strengths. (op 9-2)

Maria Royal(IRE) was again able to come off a slow pace. She had no problems with the extra 3f and looks worth persevering with over these longer trips.

Blek(FR) ran a better race than in the Cadran, which was evidently too far for him. (op 6-1)

Watar(IRE) again drifted when coming under pressure. It was a respectable enough run, though.

Peinture Rare(IRE) never got in the mix over this trip, even though she is bred to stay.

Vulcanite(IRE) has been going well in handicap company this season but was never a factor in this better company.

The Form Book, Raceform Ltd, Compton, RG20 6NL

Flying Cross(IRE), having his first start for new connections, came to challenge at the top of the straight but it proved to be short-lived. It is not often that horses improve for leaving Aidan O'Brien, and it remains to be seen if John Gosden can get any more out of him.

Winter Dream(IRE) raced close to the rails in company with Blek in the early stages. He left his previous form behind when finishing second in the Cadran last time but on the evidence of this, it was more his ability to cope with testing conditions that day than a sudden improvement in form that resulted in him getting so close. He dropped away tamely here.

7086 KEMPTON (A.W) (R-H)

Monday, October 25

OFFICIAL GOING: Standard

Wind: Almost nil Weather: Fine, sunny

7111 TRY BETDAQ FOR AN EXCHANGE H'CAP 1m 2f (P)

2:10 (2:10) (Class 5) (0-75,75) 3-Y-O+ **£2,286** (£675; £337) **Stalls** High

Form RPR

0323 **1** **Shallow Bay**[16] 6753 3-9-4 **74** AdamKirby 9 91+
(W R Swinburn) *prom: trckd ldr 1/2-way: led over 2f out: rdn wl clr over 1f out: eased last 100yds* **11/8**[1]

0005 **2** 2 1/2 **Striding Edge (IRE)**[17] 6718 4-9-2 **67** JimCrowley 7 74
(W R Muir) *hld up in last trio: pushed along and effrt on outer over 2f out: prog over 1f out: wnt 2nd last 150yds: no ch w wnr* **12/1**

-520 **3** 2 **Dancing Queen (IRE)**[12] 6852 3-9-3 **73** RyanMoore 6 76
(M A Magnusson) *led 4f: styd prom: drvn to chse wnr over 1f out to last 150yds: one pce* **11/2**[3]

3215 **4** 3/4 **Josr's Magic (IRE)**[12] 6846 6-9-2 **67** TomMcLaughlin 2 69
(P R Hedger) *hld up in tch: effrt 2f out: swtchd lft jst over 1f out: plugged on one pce after* **8/1**

4235 **5** 1 3/4 **Diamond Twister (USA)**[26] 6472 4-8-13 **67** KierenFox(3) 1 65
(J R Best) *prog to ld after 4f: hdd over 2f out: wknd over 1f out* **33/1**

0040 **6** 4 1/2 **Burma Rock (IRE)**[26] 6449 4-9-9 **74** KierenFallon 3 63
(L M Cumani) *chsd ldrs: u.p disputing 3rd over 2f out: wknd over 1f out* **5/1**[2]

0-15 **7** 1 1/4 **Savaronola (USA)**[97] 4227 5-9-1 **66** TomQueally 4 53
(B J Curley) *hld up in last trio: pushed along and no prog over 2f out: rdn and wknd over 1f out* **7/1**

4002 **8** 3 3/4 **Free Tussy (ARG)**[18] 6699 6-9-10 **75** (bt) PatDobbs 8 54
(G L Moore) *chsd ldrs: rdn on inner 3f out: wknd wl over 1f out* **25/1**

400 **9** 13 **Craicajack (IRE)**[156] 2334 3-8-8 **64** ow1 EddieCreighton 5 17
(E J Creighton) *hld up last: rdn over 4f out: sn bhd: t.o* **66/1**

2m 5.65s (-2.35) **Going Correction** -0.05s/f (Stan)
WFA 3 from 4yo+ 5lb **9** Ran SP% **113.7**
Speed ratings (Par 103): **107,105,103,102,101 97,96,93,83**
toteswingers:1&2:£6.60, 1&3:£2.10, 2&3:£10.70 CSF £19.28 CT £71.04 TOTE £2.80: £1.50, £4.90, £1.90; EX 24.10.
Owner M H Dixon **Bred** M H Dixon **Trained** Aldbury, Herts

FOCUS

A fair handicap in which the relatively unexposed favourite shot clear for an emphatic win. He was value for more like 5l.

7112 BETDAQ.COM MAIDEN STKS 7f (P)

2:40 (2:40) (Class 4) 2-Y-O **£3,238** (£963; £481; £240) **Stalls** High

Form RPR

22 **1** **Splash Point (USA)**[52] 5717 2-9-3 0 AhmedAjtebi 8 85
(Mahmood Al Zarooni) *mde all: drew 2 l clr 2f out: rdn over 1f out: hld on* **7/1**[3]

33 **2** 1/2 **Zain Shamardal (IRE)**[26] 6474 2-9-3 0 WilliamBuick 5 84
(B J Meehan) *trckd ldrs: rdn to chse wnr on inner wl over 1f out: swtchd lft fnl f: no imp tl styd on last 100yds: clsng fin* **13/8**[1]

3 2 **Failasoof (USA)** 2-9-3 0 MichaelHills 12 79
(B W Hills) *hld up in rr: prog on inner fr 1/2-way: wnt 4th over 2f out: shkn up to cl on ldrs over 1f out: one pce after* **40/1**

0 **4** 1 1/4 **Sultah (USA)**[53] 5691 2-8-12 0 RichardHills 1 70
(B W Hills) *chsd wnr: pushed along over 3f out: nt qckn and lost 2nd wl over 1f out: one pce after* **11/1**

5 hd **Laajooj (IRE)** 2-9-3 0 PhilipRobinson 7 75
(M A Jarvis) *dwlt: sn in midfield: shkn up and effrt over 2f out: kpt on one pce fr over 1f out* **7/4**[2]

04 **6** 6 **Deny**[37] 6190 2-9-3 0 RyanMoore 6 59
(Sir Michael Stoute) *s.i.s: racd on outer in rr: outpcd fr 3f out: nvr on terms after* **10/1**

7 2 1/2 **Ebtihaj** 2-8-12 0 TomQueally 3 48
(R Hannon) *dwlt: rn green and sn wl bhd in last: nvr a factor but passed wkng rivals last 2f* **100/1**

40 **8** 7 **Distinguish (IRE)**[17] 6726 2-8-12 0 SilvestreDeSousa 9 29
(M Johnston) *a in rr: brief effrt over 2f out: sn wknd* **33/1**

9 3 **Dysios (IRE)** 2-9-3 0 KierenFallon 4 27
(L M Cumani) *prom to 1/2-way: sn wknd and wl bhd* **25/1**

23 **10** 1 1/4 **Jaridh (USA)**[16] 6742 2-9-3 0 (p) TedDurcan 2 23
(Saeed Bin Suroor) *t.k.h: prom tl wknd rapidly jst over 3f out* **12/1**

1m 25.55s (-0.45) **Going Correction** -0.05s/f (Stan) **10** Ran SP% **122.3**
Speed ratings (Par 97): **100,99,97,95,95 88,85,77,74,72**
toteswingers:1&2:£2.90, 1&3:£13.60, 2&3:£18.20 CSF £19.42 TOTE £5.20: £1.40, £1.30, £7.70; EX 20.10.
Owner Godolphin **Bred** WinStar Farm LLC **Trained** Newmarket, Suffolk

FOCUS

There was plenty of activity in the market for this decent maiden. It was run at a fair pace and the first five pulled clear. The form is rated around the time and the runner-up.

NOTEBOOK

Splash Point(USA) was prominent in the betting when runner-up in both previous maiden runs, the latest when 2l behind a rival who ran well off 83 on nursery debut. The return to 7f looked a good move and he travelled very smoothly under a positive ride from a good draw and was never in serious danger. The form looks solid rated around the second and this probably represents a decent burst of improvement by a nice type, who should have a very profitable future. (tchd 8-1)

Zain Shamardal(IRE) seemed to get bogged down in soft ground on his second run but had leading claims on his third of four behind two previous winners in a Salisbury novice stakes event on debut. He gave it a decent try to justify a big on-course market move but couldn't quite get to the leader who was always travelling a bit better. (op 9-4 tchd 5-4)

Failasoof(USA) was sent off at a big price but ran an eye-catching race on debut and finished just ahead of his shorter-priced stable companion who was running for the same connections. This Derby-entered colt is an imposing $650,000 brother to Temple City a 1m4f US Grade 3 winner. He should have a similar race at his mercy next time and is an interesting prospect for the future.

Sultah(USA) couldn't land a blow after finding some trouble in a 7f Salisbury maiden on debut but she showed up well here. She is not very big but this was a step forward by the second foal of a useful dual 6f winner. (op 12-1)

Laajooj(IRE) attracted plenty of support throughout the day but he was probably undone by his inexperience and couldn't quite get into the firing line. However, this was a promising start by the son of Azamour who cost 150,000gns and is a half-brother to a classy 7f/1m performer in France/US. (op 2-1 tchd 5-2 and 11-4 in places)

Deny was forced wide for a long way and couldn't build on his 5l fourth at Newbury last time. (op 12-1 tchd 14-1)

Jaridh(USA) was also stuck on the outside from his tough draw but he went out very quickly with cheekpieces tried, which was disappointing from a colt who had fair form claims. (op 8-1)

7113 BETDAQ THE BETTING EXCHANGE MAIDEN FILLIES' STKS 1m (P)

3:10 (3:12) (Class 5) 2-Y-O **£2,286** (£675; £337) **Stalls** High

Form RPR

4 **1** **Charleston Lady**[26] 6451 2-9-0 0 JimCrowley 10 75+
(R M Beckett) *t.k.h early: prom: trckd ldr over 4f out: shkn up over 2f out: clsd suddenly to ld last 150yds: decisively* **15/8**[1]

5 **2** 1 **Oceanway (USA)**[55] 5643 2-9-0 0 SilvestreDeSousa 1 73
(M Johnston) *prom: led over 5f out: rdn 2 l clr 2f out: hdd and outpcd last 150yds* **33/1**

3 1 1/4 **Bow River Arch (USA)** 2-9-0 0 AdamKirby 6 70+
(J Noseda) *reluctant to enter stalls: settled in rr: prog to go 4th over 2f out: clsd to take 3rd over 1f out: styd on fnl f* **12/1**

4 **4** 5 **Alareen (USA)**[72] 5066 2-9-0 0 TedDurcan 13 58
(Saeed Bin Suroor) *slowest away: rousted along and sn prom: rdn to chse ldng pair over 2f out to over 1f out: wknd* **4/1**[3]

5 1 1/4 **Monicalew** 2-9-0 0 ShaneKelly 9 55
(W R Swinburn) *settled in rr: pushed along 3f out: sn outpcd: rn green but kpt on steadily fr over 1f out* **66/1**

6 nse **Whispered** 2-9-0 0 RyanMoore 3 55
(Sir Michael Stoute) *hld up in last pair: pushed along over 2f out: styd on in decent style fnl f: nrst fin* **12/1**

4 **7** 3 3/4 **Susan Stroman**[11] 6874 2-9-0 0 TomQueally 8 47
(E A L Dunlop) *chsd ldrs: outpcd fr 3f out: steadily fdd* **25/1**

5 **8** 3 1/2 **Viking Rose (IRE)**[26] 6451 2-9-0 0 TomMcLaughlin 7 39
(J M P Eustace) *broke wl but sn restrained to last pair: shkn up on inner over 2f out: no great prog* **25/1**

4 **9** 3 **Fortunateencounter (FR)**[38] 6155 2-9-0 0 WilliamBuick 4 32
(J H M Gosden) *prog fr rr to go prom 5f out: rdn and wknd wl over 2f out: eased whn no ch fnl f* **9/4**[2]

0 **10** 3/4 **Elusive Diva (IRE)**[24] 6520 2-9-0 0 EddieCreighton 2 30
(E J Creighton) *a towards rr: lft bhd fr 3f out* **40/1**

0 **11** 1/2 **Torpedo Run**[15] 6770 2-9-0 0 KierenFallon 11 29
(R Hannon) *led to over 5f out: sn lost pl: wl in rr over 2f out: eased fnl f* **66/1**

1m 39.5s (-0.30) **Going Correction** -0.05s/f (Stan) **11** Ran SP% **117.0**
Speed ratings (Par 92): **99,98,96,91,90 90,86,83,80,79 78**
toteswingers:1&2:£8.40, 1&3:£7.30, 2&3:£21.70 CSF £77.17 TOTE £2.90: £1.10, £4.90, £3.90; EX 43.80.
Owner R A Pegum **Bred** Mrs J Chandris **Trained** Whitsbury, Hants

FOCUS

Not many got involved in this fillies' maiden and the first three finished clear. The winner was heavily backed and looks a nice type, but the form is only fair.

NOTEBOOK

Charleston Lady got the hang of things late when staying on well to nearly snatch third in a 7f maiden here last month. After moving smoothly for a long way it looked like she might have trouble reeling in the trailblazer halfway up the straight in this race but the overdrive kicked in and she eventually landed a gamble with something in hand. A Hurricane Run half-sister to a smart Japanese miler, she has a good physique and looks a decent prospect for middle-distance handicaps. (op 5-2 tchd 7-4)

Oceanway(USA), the second foal of a 1m2f winner, put in a brave bid under an attacking ride from a tough draw and has stepped up significantly on her fifth of six in a 6f Southwell maiden on debut. (op 25-1)

Bow River Arch(USA) was supported at big prices and put in a promising staying on effort on debut. She should learn a lot from the experience and is a scopey $190,000 half-sister to Mibar, a 1m Listed winner as a 2-y-o in Italy. (op 20-1)

Alareen(USA) did some eye-catching late work after a slow start when 12l fourth in a decent Doncaster maiden on debut but she still looked inexperienced in this contest and faded under a more prominent ride. (op 5-1)

Monicalew stayed on steadily from a long way back on debut. She is a half-sister to 7f winner/Ribblesdale second Eldalil and is likely to come into her own over middle-distances next year. Official explanation: jockey said filly suffered interference early stages (op 100-1)

Whispered also showed some promise from some way back. She is out of an unraced half-sister to a stack of winners and should improve with time and distance. (op 10-1)

Fortunateencounter(FR) Official explanation: trainer's rep said, regarding running, that the filly ran flat and lost a left-fore shoe.

7114 BETDAQ ON FACEBOOK H'CAP (DIV I) 1m (P)

3:40 (3:40) (Class 4) (0-80,80) 3-Y-O+ **£3,561** (£1,059; £529; £264) **Stalls** High

Form RPR

1330 **1** **Warning Song (USA)**[70] 5142 3-9-1 **77** TomQueally 8 85+
(Mrs A J Perrett) *hld up in midfield: pushed along over 2f out: bk on bridle over 1f out: set alight and led last 150yds: in command after* **11/1**

355P **2** 1 1/4 **Squall**[37] 6205 3-9-0 **76** WilliamBuick 9 81
(J Noseda) *trckd ldng pair: drvn to chal and narrow ld wl over 1f out: hdd ent fnl f: styd on* **8/1**[3]

1000 **3** hd **Highland Quaich**[4] 7033 3-9-2 **78** HayleyTurner 6 83
(D R C Elsworth) *hld up in rr: prog on inner 2f out: drvn to chal and upsides 1f out: styd on* **14/1**

2040 **4** nk **Qalahari (IRE)**[29] 6409 4-9-6 **79** RobertWinston 4 83
(D J Coakley) *hld up in rr: urged along over 2f out: prog over 1f out: styd on fnl f to take 4th nr fin* **8/1**[3]

6605 **5** 1/2 **Getcarter**[35] 6252 4-9-4 **77** RyanMoore 10 80
(R Hannon) *trckd ldrs on inner: looking for room 2f out: nt qckn over 1f out: styd on fnl f: nvr able to chal* **11/4**[1]

0210 **6** 1 **Master Mylo (IRE)**[15] 6780 3-9-3 **79** WilliamCarson 3 79+
(D K Ivory) *stdd s: hld up last: plenty to do and coaxed along 2f out: styd on fnl f: no ch* **10/1**

3065 **7** shd **Blue Lyric**[46] 5887 3-8-13 **75** KierenFallon 2 75
(L M Cumani) *trckd ldng trio: effrt to chal 2f out: led briefly ent fnl f: sn wknd* **15/2**[2]

4210 **8** 1 3/4 **Chat De La Burg (USA)**[37] 6197 3-8-12 **77** KierenFox(3) 5 73
(J R Best) *led: hdd narrowly wl over 1f out: wknd fnl f* **17/2**

1-00 **9** nk **Eolith**[25] 6510 3-9-4 **80** JimCrowley 1 75
(W J Knight) *pressed ldr: upsides 2f out tl wknd qckly fnl f* **15/2**[2]

4000 **10** 3¾ **Highly Regal (IRE)**[35] 6252 5-9-4 **80** .... JohnFahy(3) 7 67
(R A Teal) *racd wd in midfield: drvn and fnd nil over 2f out: sn btn* **10/1**

1m 38.71s (-1.09) **Going Correction** -0.05s/f (Stan)
WFA 3 from 4yo+ 3lb 10 Ran SP% **116.1**
Speed ratings (Par 105): **103,101,101,101,100 99,99,97,97,93**
toteswingers:1&2:£8.30, 1&3:£30.80, 2&3:£24.50 CSF £95.48 CT £1244.94 TOTE £10.10: £2.90, £2.40, £5.40; EX 79.50.
Owner G Harwood & G Bailey **Bred** Bloodstock Holdings Llc **Trained** Pulborough, W Sussex

FOCUS
Not a very strong race for the grade. All of the runners had been beaten more than 4l on their previous start and they finished in a bit of a bunch. It was the quicker division.

7115 BETDAQ ON FACEBOOK H'CAP (DIV II) 1m (P)
4:10 (4:10) (Class 4) (0-80,80) 3-Y-O+ **£3,561** (£1,059; £529; £264) **Stalls** High

Form RPR

-630 **1** **Mustakmil (IRE)**[26] 6449 4-9-7 **80** .... HayleyTurner 9 88
(S Dow) *settled midfield: prog to 4th 2f out: hrd rdn to chse ldr ins fnl f: styd on wl nr fin to ld post* **7/2**[2]

0223 **2** *shd* **Willow Dancer (IRE)**[18] 6701 6-9-1 **74** ....(p) AdamKirby 10 82
(W R Swinburn) *led 2f: styd prom: chsd ldr over 2f out: clsd to ld 1f out: drvn and styd on: hdd post* **3/1**[1]

0250 **3** *1* **Prince Of Thebes (IRE)**[12] 6851 9-8-12 **74** .... KierenFox(3) 6 80
(M J Attwater) *pushed along in 6th pl 1/2-way: prog on outer to press ldrs 3f out: nt qckn over 2f out: styd on again fr over 1f out: tk 3rd nr fin* **12/1**

6002 **4** *nk* **Duplicity**[15] 6771 3-9-4 **80** .... TedDurcan 8 85
(R Hannon) *chsd ldrs: drvn and nt qckn wl over 2f out: no prog tl styd on wl fnl f* **9/2**[3]

0050 **5** *1½* **Mishrif (USA)**[15] 6780 4-9-2 **75** ....(v) KierenFallon 5 77
(J R Jenkins) *t.k.h: led after 2f: 2 l clr 2f out: hdd & wknd 1f out* **8/1**

0563 **6** *½* **Edgewater (IRE)**[15] 6780 3-9-3 **79** .... TomQueally 4 79
(J Akehurst) *prom: chsd ldr over 4f out to over 2f out: fdd over 1f out* **9/1**

6000 **7** *1* **Gallantry**[14] 6800 8-8-7 **73** .... IanBurns(7) 3 71
(P Howling) *a towards rr: shkn up and no progres over 2f out* **25/1**

2000 **8** *1¼* **Lisahane Bog**[25] 6503 3-9-0 **76** .... TomMcLaughlin 7 71
(P R Hedger) *s.s: a in rr: drvn on inner over 2f out: no prog* **25/1**

0400 **9** *1½* **Dinner Date**[26] 6449 8-8-4 **70** .... SophieSilvester(7) 2 62
(T Keddy) *s.s: hld up in last pair: pushed along and no prog over 2f out* **16/1**

5005 **10** *nk* **Charlie Smirke (USA)**[18] 6701 4-9-4 **77** .... RyanMoore 1 68
(G L Moore) *hld up in last pair: pushed along and no prog over 2f out* **11/1**

1m 38.95s (-0.85) **Going Correction** -0.05s/f (Stan)
WFA 3 from 4yo+ 3lb 10 Ran SP% **116.1**
Speed ratings (Par 105): **102,101,100,100,99 98,97,96,94,94**
toteswingers:1&2:£3.10, 1&3:£11.50, 2&3:£6.70 CSF £14.36 CT £108.71 TOTE £5.40: £2.30, £1.60, £3.50; EX 15.50.
Owner Simon Caunce **Bred** Shadwell Estate Company Limited **Trained** Epsom, Surrey
■ Stewards' Enquiry : Adam Kirby two-day ban: used whip in incorrect place (Nov 8,10)

FOCUS
There was an exciting finish to the second divison of this handicap. The pace was not very strong and the time was a bit slower than the first division. Slightly muddling form.

7116 BET IN-RUNNING - BETDAQ NURSERY 6f (P)
4:40 (4:41) (Class 3) (0-90,90) 2-Y-O **£5,504** (£1,637; £818; £408) **Stalls** High

Form RPR

3111 **1** **Jack Smudge**[21] 6619 2-9-0 **83** .... PaulMulrennan 5 86
(J G Given) *pressed ldr: led over 3f out: rdn and hdd wl over 1f out: led again ent fnl f: edgd lft nr fin: hld on* **7/2**[1]

3135 **2** *shd* **Prophet In A Dream**[3] 7050 2-7-13 **68** .... SilvestreDeSousa 6 71
(M R Channon) *trckd ldrs: effrt over 2f out: styd on to chal fnl f: nudged by wnr nr fin: jst hld* **7/1**

0161 **3** *1½* **Picabo (IRE)**[7] 6988 2-8-3 **72** 6ex .... HayleyTurner 4 71
(Mrs L Wadham) *hld up in tch: effrt over 2f out: stuck bhd ldng pair over 1f out: styd on but nvr cl enough to chal* **4/1**[2]

2104 **4** *2½* **Gold Pearl (USA)**[37] 6191 2-9-0 **83** .... JimCrowley 1 74
(S C Williams) *hld up in cl tch: rdn and nt qckn 2f out: steadily outpcd* **4/1**[2]

0523 **5** *nse* **Three Sparrows (IRE)**[11] 6869 2-8-8 **77** .... RyanMoore 7 68
(R Hannon) *led to over 3f out: drvn on inner to ld again wl over 1f out: hdd & wknd ent fnl f* **13/2**

134 **6** *3¼* **None Shall Sleep (IRE)**[16] 6751 2-9-7 **90** .... KierenFallon 2 71
(P F I Cole) *tk fierce hold: hld up tl prog rnd outside to press ldr over 3f out: wknd 2f out* **9/2**[3]

1061 **7** *½* **Country Waltz**[7] 6989 2-7-5 **63** 6ex .... IanBurns(7) 3 47
(M R Channon) *mostly last: struggling wl over 2f out: sn btn* **12/1**

1m 13.36s (0.26) **Going Correction** -0.05s/f (Stan) 7 Ran SP% **113.9**
Speed ratings (Par 99): **96,95,93,90,90 86,85**
totesngers:1&2:£4.20, 1&3:£2.60, 2&3:£5.80 CSF £27.80 TOTE £5.90: £3.20, £2.20; EX 30.00.
Owner Danethorpe Racing Partnership **Bred** P And Mrs A G Venner **Trained** Willoughton, Lincs
■ Stewards' Enquiry : Paul Mulrennan one-day ban: careless riding (Nov 8)

FOCUS
A hot nursery, involving three last-time-out winners. The pace was very steady but the progressive winner put in a gutsy performance to complete a four-timer. The second is rated right back to his best.

NOTEBOOK
Jack Smudge has been highly versatile regarding ground conditions and completed a hat-trick in a Pontefract nursery early this month. He had a 6lb rise and another hike in grade to deal with on AW debut but put in a tremendously gritty effort to continue his golden spell. He was always in the right place in a steadily run sprint but there is no sign of his progress levelling out and he could take some stopping in a bid to make it five wins in a row next time. (op 4-1 tchd 10-3)
Prophet In A Dream has seen plenty of action this year but is a reliable type and emerges with credit for posing the biggest threat to a highly progressive rival. This dual winner should continue run well and is effective at 5f-7f on most types of surface. (op 8-1)
Picabo(IRE) scored with quite a bit in hand despite hanging left in a Windsor nursery last week. She came up short in her attempt to defy a penalty but didn't get the strong pace that suits her hold-up style and was short of room in the final furlong. She could resume her progress if things unfold better next time. (op 3-1)
Gold Pearl(USA) couldn't get into a threatening position out wide. His profile is not particularly progressive but his high-class half-sister Arch Swing found several jolts of improvement at 7f-1m and there could be more to come in a strongly run race over a stiffer test. (op 9-2 tchd 11-2)
Three Sparrows(IRE) looked a possible winner when hitting the front approaching the final furlong but he couldn't hang in there on nursery debut. He is out of a multiple winning miler and is bred to stay quite a bit further than this but he showed enough speed here to suggest a drop to 5f might suit. (tchd 6-1 and 15-2)
None Shall Sleep(IRE) attracted support but he dropped away after taking a strong hold out wide on nursery debut. (op 6-1)

7117 BET BREEDERS' CUP - BETDAQ H'CAP 1m 4f (P)
5:10 (5:13) (Class 6) (0-60,59) 3-Y-O **£1,637** (£483; £241) **Stalls** Centre

Form RPR

4321 **1** **Jovial (IRE)**[6] 6999 3-8-10 **51** .... JohnFahy(3) 7 60+
(D J Coakley) *trckd ldrs: smooth prog to ld 2f out: shkn up and sn clr: comf* **10/11**[1]

00-0 **2** *3* **Belle Zorro**[14] 6816 3-9-0 **52** .... TomQueally 1 56
(M L W Bell) *led to 1/2-way: led again briefly over 2f out: sn outpcd by wnr: plugged on* **16/1**

0232 **3** *¾* **Motirani**[22] 6080 3-9-2 **57** .... SimonPearce(3) 4 60
(J Pearce) *prom: rdn to chal over 2f out: sn outpcd: kpt on* **33/1**

0033 **4** *½* **Wasara**[12] 6846 3-9-7 **59** .... PaulMulrennan 9 61+
(Miss Amy Weaver) *hld up last: gd prog on inner over 2f out: rdn to cl on ldrs over 1f out: one pce fnl f* **9/1**[3]

416 **5** *¾* **Empress Leizu (IRE)**[9] 6930 3-9-6 **58** .... ShaneKelly 8 59
(A W Carroll) *hld up: prog to trck ldrs on outer 1/2-way: rdn and nt qckn over 2f out: one pce after* **25/1**

5402 **6** *1½* **Belle Boleyn**[24] 6525 3-9-4 **56** .... TedDurcan 13 55+
(C F Wall) *hld up towards rr: effrt over 3f out: nt qckn in midfield over 2f out: one pce after* **14/1**

0040 **7** *nse* **Pictures (IRE)**[6] 6999 3-8-10 **51** .... KierenFox(3) 11 50
(J J Bridger) *hld up wl in rr: drvn on outer over 2f out: kpt on: nvr gng pce to threaten* **50/1**

0054 **8** *hd* **Captain Cool (IRE)**[14] 6816 3-8-12 **50** .... RyanMoore 3 48
(R Hannon) *chsd ldr 5f: styd prom: drvn over 2f out: fdd* **11/2**[2]

0066 **9** *1½* **Charpoy Cobra**[25] 6499 3-9-0 **52** .... JimCrowley 6 48
(J A R Toller) *stdd s: hld up wl in rr: effrt on outer over 2f out: no significant prog* **40/1**

0206 **10** *1¾* **Jewellery (IRE)**[11] 6871 3-9-5 **57** ....(v) HayleyTurner 5 50
(J R Fanshawe) *hld up in midfield: prog to ld 1/2-way: hdd & wknd over 2f out* **9/1**[3]

3210 **11** *3* **Miss Whippy**[16] 6747 3-8-13 **51** .... KierenFallon 12 39
(P Howling) *trckd ldrs on inner: steadily lost pl fr 4f out: struggling over 2f out* **20/1**

600 **12** *4* **Eurasian**[11] 6876 3-9-3 **55** .... SilvestreDeSousa 10 37
(D M Simcock) *settled in midfield: lost pl fr 1/2-way: last over 2f out: no ch after* **100/1**

-600 **13** *16* **Bonamassa**[26] 6454 3-8-9 **47** .... WilliamCarson 14 3
(M J Attwater) *a in rr: wknd 3f out: t.o* **100/1**

2m 35.98s (1.48) **Going Correction** -0.05s/f (Stan) 13 Ran SP% **118.2**
Speed ratings (Par 99): **93,91,90,90,89 88,88,88,87,86 84,81,71**
toteswingers:1&2:£5.10, 1&3:£9.50, 2&3:£6.30 CSF £16.74 CT £306.88 TOTE £2.40: £1.40, £5.10, £4.70; EX 23.80 Place 6: £134.86 Place 5: £88.48..
Owner Chris Van Hoorn **Bred** Genesis Green Stud Ltd **Trained** West Ilsley, Berks

FOCUS
A modest handicap run at a reasonable pace and the well treated, hot favourite did the job in good style. He did not need to match his latest.
Wasara Official explanation: jockey said filly missed the break
T/Jkpt: £8,846.30 to a £1 stake. Pool:£18,689.43 - 1.50 winning tickets T/Plt: £148.20 to a £1 stake. Pool:£57,946.11 - 285.35 winning tickets T/Qpdt: £141.10 to a £1 stake. Pool:£4,388.00 - 23.00 winning tickets JN

6825 LEICESTER (R-H)
Monday, October 25

OFFICIAL GOING: Heavy (soft in places; 5.5)
False rail from round course bend to 1f marker increased distances on round course by 9yds.
Wind: Light behind Weather: Fine and sunny

7118 HAYMARKET NURSERY (DIV I) 7f 9y
2:00 (2:00) (Class 6) (0-65,65) 2-Y-O **£1,619** (£481; £240; £120) **Stalls** Low

Form RPR

034 **1** **Mega Mount (IRE)**[18] 6695 2-9-6 **64** ....(v) JackMitchell 15 70
(R M Beckett) *chsd ldrs: led over 4f out: rdn over 1f out: r.o* **11/2**[2]

3600 **2** *½* **Las Verglas Star (IRE)**[21] 6619 2-9-7 **65** .... BarryMcHugh 10 70
(R A Fahey) *chsd ldrs: rdn over 1f out: edgd rt ins fnl f: r.o* **12/1**

0120 **3** *5* **Duquesa (IRE)**[2] 7087 2-9-1 **64** .... DeclanCannon(5) 2 56+
(P D Evans) *hld up: hdwy u.p and hung rt over 1f out: styd on to go 3rd post: nvr nrr* **7/1**[3]

4040 **4** *shd* **Phoenix Flame**[18] 6695 2-9-2 **60** .... SebSanders 12 52
(A J McCabe) *chsd ldrs: rdn over 2f out: no ex appr fnl f: lost 3rd post* **14/1**

2305 **5** *1½* **Hortensis**[10] 6892 2-9-5 **63** .... DavidAllan 14 51
(T D Easterby) *hld up: rdn over 2f out: r.o ins fnl f: nvr nrr* **12/1**

000 **6** *½* **Iwantobreakfree**[33] 6278 2-8-1 **48** ow3 .... Louis-PhilippeBeuzelin(3) 13 35
(P D Evans) *mid-div: hdwy u.p over 2f out: wknd fnl f* **66/1**

030 **7** *½* **Icelady**[41] 6058 2-8-2 **46** .... AndreaAtzeni 11 32
(R M H Cowell) *s.i.s: hdwy over 5f out: rdn over 2f out: styd on same pce* **28/1**

0000 **8** *5* **Playful Girl (IRE)**[10] 6893 2-8-9 **53** .... GrahamGibbons 3 26
(T D Easterby) *led: hdd over 4f out: chsd ldrs: rdn 1/2-way: wknd over 1f out* **50/1**

640 **9** *½* **Bathwick Scanno (IRE)**[37] 6209 2-8-13 **57** .... CathyGannon 5 29
(P D Evans) *hld up: nvr on terms* **25/1**

0005 **10** *¾* **Silbury (IRE)**[11] 6868 2-8-6 **50** .... RichardMullen 9 20
(R Charlton) *plld hrd and prom: rdn over 2f out: sn wknd* **11/2**[2]

4353 **11** *7* **Cathcart Castle**[4] 7035 2-9-2 **60** .... RichardHughes 16 13
(M R Channon) *hld up in tch: rdn over 1f out: sn wknd* **3/1**[1]

060 **12** *12* **Silver Tigress**[41] 6047 2-8-7 **51** .... TomEaves 1 —
(C W Thornton) *mid-div: rdn 1/2-way: wknd over 2f out: t.o* **16/1**

000 **13** *29* **Shutterbug**[38] 6158 2-8-10 **54** .... NeilCallan 4 —
(S C Williams) *mid-div: rdn 1/2-way: sn wknd: t.o* **10/1**

1m 30.55s (4.35) **Going Correction** +0.45s/f (Yiel) 13 Ran SP% **116.0**
Speed ratings (Par 93): **93,92,86,86,84 84,83,78,77,76 68,54,21**
toteswingers:1&2:£11.20, 1&3:£4.60, 2&3:£13.80 CSF £65.62 CT £484.10 TOTE £4.60: £1.30, £5.20, £2.00; EX 71.60 Trifecta £105.40 Pool: £270.80 - 1.90 winning units..
Owner R Roberts **Bred** Rathbarry Stud **Trained** Whitsbury, Hants
■ Stewards' Enquiry : Barry McHugh three-day ban: used whip with excessive frequency (Nov 8,10,11)

The Form Book, Raceform Ltd, Compton, RG20 6NL

FOCUS
The time of this opening nursery was 6.2secs outside RP standard, very much suggesting it was testing. The first two finished clear and the runner-up helps with the level.

NOTEBOOK
Mega Mount(IRE) had finished fourth off this mark at Wolverhampton latest, and with the visor retained, he turned in a career-best effort return to turf, not being at all inconvenienced by the testing ground. (op 9-2 tchd 6-1)
Las Verglas Star(IRE), going without the blinkers this time, had run well in soft ground before, off 10lb higher, so it was no surprise to see him put in a good effort. (op 11-1)
Duquesa(IRE), a soft-ground winner off 7lb lower earlier in the month, didn't help her rider by hanging, but was never near the front two. (op 5-1)
Phoenix Flame, well behind Mega Mount latest, got a lot closer here, just losing out on third. (op 16-1 tchd 12-1)
Hortensis had run well off 1lb higher back in the summer and the way she kept on suggests 1m may suit. (tchd 11-1)
Iwantobreakfree, whose rider was putting up 3lb overweight, improved on the very moderate form shown in maidens. (op 100-1)
Icelady, beaten 12l or more all three maiden starts, was up to 7f for the first time and kept on late, suggesting she'd have been closer with a better start. (op 33-1)
Silbury(IRE) failed to run her race and clearly struggled with the ground (op 13-2 tchd 7-1)
Cathcart Castle has been proving consistent and was expected to go close once more, but didn't handle the conditions. Official explanation: jockey said colt stopped quickly (op 9-2)

7119 E B F FOSSE WAY MAIDEN STKS — 5f 218y
2:30 (2:31) (Class 4) 2-Y-O — **£4,533** (£1,348; £674; £336) — **Stalls** Low

Form — RPR
2202 1 **Jinky**[10] 6882 2-9-3 83 ... RichardHughes 5 — 81
(M R Channon) *led: hdd over 2f out: rdn and ev ch fr over 1f out: styd on u.p to ld nr fin* **10/11**[1]
633 2 hd **Cape Rambler**[10] 6882 2-9-3 81 ... DaneO'Neill 1 — 80
(H Candy) *chsd wnr tl led over 2f out: sn rdn and hung rt: hdd nr fin* **5/2**[2]
3 3½ **Flynn's Boy** 2-9-3 0 ... JimmyFortune 4 — 70
(Rae Guest) *prom: outpcd 4f out: rallied over 1f out: styd on same pce ins fnl f* **22/1**
42 4 1¾ **Lion Court (IRE)**[19] 6675 2-9-3 0 ... SebSanders 2 — 65
(Sir Mark Prescott) *chsd ldrs: pushed along 1/2-way: no ex fnl f* **6/1**[3]
5 4 **Secret Lake** 2-8-9 0 ... Louis-PhilippeBeuzelin(3) 3 — 48
(Jane Chapple-Hyam) *dwlt: outpcd* **10/1**

1m 16.94s (3.94) **Going Correction** +0.45s/f (Yiel) — **5 Ran SP% 108.7**
Speed ratings (Par 97): **91,90,86,83,78**
CSF £3.27 TOTE £1.70: £1.10, £2.20; EX 3.60.
Owner John Breslin **Bred** J Breslin **Trained** West Ilsley, Berks
■ Stewards' Enquiry : Dane O'Neill one-day ban: used whip with excessive frequency (Nov 8)

FOCUS
The front two came clear in what was a fair maiden. The winner was the marginal pre-race form choice.

NOTEBOOK
Jinky just got back up under a determined drive from Richard Hughes. Although unproven in this sort of ground, so was the runner-up, whom he had finished ahead of at Newmarket latest, and he showed a willing attitude. He won't find winning easy in handicaps, but should benefit from an extra furlong. (op Evens tchd 11-10)
Cape Rambler, 3/4l behind the winner at Newmarket, edged ahead two out and briefly looked to be holding his old rival, but started to hang and was just run out of it. (tchd 9-4)
Flynn's Boy, an already gelded son of Tobougg, clearly coped okay with the ground and was keeping on as though 7f would suit. (op 18-1 tchd 25-1)
Lion Court(IRE) was a little disappointing considering he had run well on soft ground previously, but he may bounce back on better ground once handicapping. (op 11-2 tchd 13-2)
Secret Lake, whose sire gets plenty of soft-ground winners, wasn't the best away and was always struggling. Official explanation: jockey said filly missed the break (op 11-1 tchd 12-1 and 8-1)

7120 SIR GORDON RICHARDS CONDITIONS STKS — 1m 3f 183y
3:00 (3:00) (Class 3) 3-Y-O+ — **£5,677** (£1,699; £849; £424) — **Stalls** High

Form — RPR
2004 1 **Peligroso (FR)**[53] 5696 4-9-2 105 ... FrankieDettori 3 — 107+
(Saeed Bin Suroor) *mde all: clr fr 8f out: eased fnl 2f: canter* **1/4**[1]
4323 2 10 **Dakiyah (IRE)**[14] 6808 6-8-11 81 ... (p) IanMongan 2 — 82
(Mrs L J Mongan) *prom: chsd wnr fr over 8f out: rdn 4f out: no imp* **6/1**[2]
3 33 **Nodforms Violet (IRE)**[106] 6-9-2 0 ... PhillipMakin 4 — —
(Karen McLintock) *s.i.s: sn rcvrd to chse wnr tl over 8f out: hmpd over 6f out: sn wknd: t.o* **33/1**
-300 4 38 **Via Galilei (IRE)**[128] 3194 5-9-2 95 ... RichardHughes 1 — —
(G L Moore) *hld up: rdn and wknd over 4f out: t.o* **17/2**[3]

2m 39.06s (5.16) **Going Correction** +0.70s/f (Yiel) — **4 Ran SP% 107.8**
Speed ratings (Par 107): **110,103,81,56**
CSF £2.18 TOTE £1.40; EX 2.20.
Owner Godolphin **Bred** S R L Undosa **Trained** Newmarket, Suffolk

FOCUS
About as uncompetitive a race as you'll find, disappointing considering the prize-money on offer. A non event form-wise.

NOTEBOOK
Peligroso(FR), a Group 3 winner in similar conditions when trained in Germany, barely broke sweat to win, cantering clear of his floundering rivals. He'll have harder workouts at home and could win another one of these before the season's out. (op 1-3 tchd 4-11 and 2-9)
Dakiyah(IRE) faced a near impossible task against the winner, in receipt of only 5lb, and she ran about as well as could have been expected. (tchd 8-1)
Nodforms Violet(IRE), a former bumper winner, pottered round for some third-place money. (op 28-1 tchd 50-1)
Via Galilei(IRE), 7l behind the winner at Lingfield earlier in the year, has run well in testing ground before, so this disconcerting performance is hard to explain. (op 7-1 tchd 13-2 and 9-1)

7121 LEICESTER RACECOURSE CONFERENCE CENTRE H'CAP — 1m 60y
3:30 (3:30) (Class 3) (0-90,89) 3-Y-O+ **£5,677** (£1,699; £849; £424; £211) — **Stalls** High

Form — RPR
01 1 **Green Destiny (IRE)**[116] 3586 3-8-8 **82** ... AdamBeschizza(5) 14 — 93+
(W J Haggas) *hld up: hdwy over 1f out: r.o to ld wl ins fnl f* **9/2**[1]
165 2 1½ **Agony And Ecstasy**[23] 6556 3-9-1 **84** ... (t) JackMitchell 13 — 91
(R M Beckett) *led: rdn over 1f out: hdd wl ins fnl f* **14/1**
12 3 hd **Heddwyn (IRE)**[176] 1730 3-9-4 **87** ... SebSanders 2 — 94+
(M P Tregoning) *hld up: hdwy and hung rt over 1f out: r.o* **9/2**[1]
4033 4 nse **One Scoop Or Two**[21] 6629 4-8-8 **77** ow2 ... RussKennemore(3) 3 — 83
(R Hollinshead) *chsd ldrs: rdn over 1f out: r.o* **17/2**
0423 5 ¾ **Fastnet Storm (IRE)**[32] 6304 4-9-7 **87** ... NeilCallan 11 — 92
(T P Tate) *a.p: chsd ldr over 2f out: rdn over 1f out: no ex towards fin* **8/1**[3]
6424 6 2½ **Zebrano**[8] 6958 4-8-9 **75** ... (b) RobertHavlin 12 — 74
(A B Haynes) *s.i.s: hld up: rdn over 2f out: styd on fnl f: nvr trbld ldrs* **8/1**[3]
3640 7 2¾ **Jordaura**[15] 6780 4-9-2 **82** ... GrahamGibbons 7 — 74
(J R Holt) *prom: rdn over 2f out: styd on same pce appr fnl f* **9/1**
1640 8 8 **Kavachi (IRE)**[15] 6780 7-9-1 **81** ... RichardHughes 1 — 55
(G L Moore) *s.i.s: hld up: rdn over 3f out: nvr on terms* **16/1**
0000 9 1½ **Extraterrestrial**[16] 6749 6-9-7 **87** ... TomEaves 5 — 57
(R A Fahey) *hld up in tch: rdn over 2f out: nt run on* **5/1**[2]
5400 10 2¾ **Guilded Warrior**[31] 6327 7-9-4 **87** ... Louis-PhilippeBeuzelin(3) 4 — 51
(W S Kittow) *chsd ldr tl rdn over 2f out: wknd over 1f out* **20/1**

1m 50.39s (5.29) **Going Correction** +0.70s/f (Yiel)
WFA 3 from 4yo+ 3lb — **10 Ran SP% 113.1**
Speed ratings (Par 107): **101,99,99,99,98 96,93,85,83,81**
toteswingers:1&2:£15.60, 1&3:£3.10, 2&3:£15.20 CSF £65.32 CT £304.19 TOTE £4.30: £1.90, £2.80, £2.00; EX 70.70 Trifecta £158.30 Pool: £213.92 - 1.00 winning units..
Owner Saleh Al Homaizi & Imad Al Sagar **Bred** Mubkera Syndicate **Trained** Newmarket, Suffolk

FOCUS
A fair handicap. The winner and third are unexposed and the form is rated around the runner-up.

NOTEBOOK
Green Destiny(IRE) ◆, off since narrowly winning a Haydock maiden in the summer, the form of which had worked out extremely well, looked potentially well treated off a mark of 82 and he just about got away with the heavy ground, coming through late under a well-timed ride. A promising type with next season in mind, he could develop into a smart handicapper and maybe even a pattern-performer given time. (op 13-2 tchd 7-1)
Agony And Ecstasy appeared not to handle heavy ground at Epsom latest, but she got the lead here and, although unable to hold on, it was a definite step back in the right direction. (op 16-1 tchd 12-1)
Heddwyn(IRE) ◆, having only his third start, had finished second in a good Newmarket handicap when last seen in May, and the testing ground helped somewhat to offset the 2f drop in trip. He was going on well at the finish and rates a very useful handicap prospect for next season. (op 11-2)
One Scoop Or Two, for whom ground conditions weren't a problem, kept on late and just missed third. This was a good effort considering his rider was putting up 2lb overweight. (op 11-1)
Fastnet Storm(IRE) failed to lead as he likes to, but did keep boxing on. (op 5-1)
Zebrano bounced back from a below-par effort at Bath and would have been closer but for a slow start. Official explanation: jockey said gelding was denied a clear run (op 9-1)
Extraterrestrial remains unable to capitalise on an attractive mark and his attitude looked questionable late on. (op 9-2 tchd 4-1)

7122 GUMLEY CLAIMING STKS — 7f 9y
4:00 (4:00) (Class 5) 3-4-Y-O — **£2,266** (£674; £337; £168) — **Stalls** Low

Form — RPR
0042 1 **Just Five (IRE)**[56] 5596 4-8-13 74 ... PhillipMakin 1 — 79+
(M Dods) *chsd ldrs: led over 2f out: clr fnl f: eased towards fin* **3/1**[2]
2060 2 3¼ **Dr Wintringham (IRE)**[28] 6430 4-8-9 76 ow1 ... RichardHughes 5 — 66
(Karen George) *hld up: hdwy and nt clr run over 2f out: rdn over 1f out: no imp: wnt 2nd last strides* **9/4**[1]
0005 3 nk **Magenta Strait**[13] 6826 3-7-5 52 ... KevinLundie(7) 11 — 56
(R Hollinshead) *s.s: hld up: hdwy over 2f out: sn rdn: styd on same pce fnl f: eased last strides* **20/1**
0045 4 1¾ **William Morgan (IRE)**[10] 6897 3-8-7 69 ... TomEaves 7 — 60
(R A Fahey) *prom: rdn 1/2-way: no ex fnl f* **5/1**[3]
03 5 ½ **Chez Vrony**[13] 6826 4-8-7 0 ... ChrisCatlin 8 — 57
(D Morris) *hld up: rdn over 2f out: r.o ins fnl f: nvr nrr* **12/1**
3154 6 2 **Castle Myth (USA)**[26] 6463 4-8-2 59 ... IanBrennan(3) 6 — 50
(B Ellison) *mid-div: drvn along 1/2-way: wknd over 1f out* **10/1**
0050 7 ½ **Cerito**[7] 6987 4-7-13 68 ow1 ... (v1) JulieBurke(7) 4 — 49
(J R Boyle) *led over 4f: wknd fnl f* **14/1**
6002 8 9 **Dark Moment**[13] 6826 4-8-5 60 ... BarryMcHugh 3 — 24
(Ollie Pears) *prom: rdn over 2f out: sn wknd* **7/1**
4050 9 5 **Musical Delight**[44] 5962 3-7-10 53 ... HarryBentley(7) 9 — 10
(A P Jarvis) *chsd ldrs tl rdn and wknd over 2f out* **40/1**
-000 10 7 **Rosie's Magic**[15] 6771 3-8-6 37 ... AdrianLayt 10 — —
(F J Brennan) *sn pushed along in rr: wknd 3f out* **125/1**

1m 30.65s (4.45) **Going Correction** +0.55s/f (Yiel)
WFA 3 from 4yo 2lb — **10 Ran SP% 116.4**
Speed ratings (Par 103): **96,92,91,89,89 87,86,76,70,62**
toteswingers:1&2:£2.60, 1&3:£9.60, 2&3:£12.50 CSF £9.99 TOTE £6.20: £1.10, £2.00, £7.80; EX 13.70 Trifecta £123.20 Pool: £774.33 - 4.65 winning units..
Owner Mrs C E Dods **Bred** Rathbarry Stud **Trained** Denton, Co Durham

FOCUS
An uncompetitive claimer. The winner was the only one of the form horses to give their running on the ground.

7123 HOBY MEDIAN AUCTION MAIDEN FILLIES' STKS — 5f 218y
4:30 (4:30) (Class 6) 2-Y-O — **£1,942** (£578; £288; £144) — **Stalls** Low

Form — RPR
422 1 **Show Rainbow**[17] 6711 2-9-0 74 ... RichardHughes 4 — 76
(M R Channon) *mde all: rdn clr fr over 1f out: comf* **2/1**[1]
2 4 **Swimsuit** 2-9-0 0 ... NeilCallan 5 — 64+
(M A Jarvis) *chsd ldrs: outpcd over 2f out: rallied fnl f: wnt 2nd towards fin: no ch w wnr* **16/1**
3 ½ **Bless You** 2-9-0 0 ... DaneO'Neill 2 — 63+
(H Candy) *chsd ldrs: rdn over 1f out: no ex ins fnl f: lost 2nd nr fin* **5/1**[3]
3 4 1¼ **Follow My Dream**[14] 6803 2-9-0 0 ... RobertHavlin 8 — 62+
(J H M Gosden) *chsd ldrs: rdn over 1f out: wknd wl ins fnl f* **6/1**
0 5 7 **Lady Deanie (IRE)**[43] 5985 2-9-0 0 ... CathyGannon 6 — 38
(B Palling) *chsd ldrs: rdn over 2f out: wknd over 1f out* **50/1**
662 6 3 **Miss Exhibitionist**[41] 6058 2-9-0 74 ... JimmyFortune 10 — 29
(P W Chapple-Hyam) *chsd ldrs tl rdn and wknd over 1f out* **3/1**[2]
7 1 **Zeavola (IRE)** 2-9-0 0 ... NeilChalmers 11 — 26
(A M Balding) *prom: rdn and hung rt over 1f out: sn wknd* **33/1**
05 8 ½ **Caramella Brownie**[23] 6569 2-9-0 0 ... DavidAllan 12 — 24
(T D Easterby) *s.i.s: sn prom: rdn and wknd over 1f out* **8/1**
6 9 ¾ **Romantic Girl (IRE)**[55] 5643 2-8-11 0 ... RussKennemore(3) 7 — 22
(A G Juckes) *hld up: wknd over 2f out* **200/1**
10 4½ **Suga Shot** 2-9-0 0 ... AdrianLayt 3 — 9
(F J Brennan) *s.i.s: a in rr* **150/1**
0 11 1¼ **The Datai**[40] 6075 2-8-11 0 ... GaryBartley(3) 1 — 5
(I W McInnes) *sn outpcd* **200/1**
0 12 5 **Cool Water Oasis**[33] 6278 2-9-0 0 ... RichardMullen 9 — —
(G L Moore) *s.i.s: hdwy over 3f out: wknd 2f out* **100/1**

1m 16.61s (3.61) **Going Correction** +0.55s/f (Yiel) — **12 Ran SP% 113.8**
Speed ratings (Par 90): **97,91,91,89,80 76,74,74,73,67 65,58**
toteswingers:1&2:£6.40, 1&3:£5.10, 2&3:£3.70 CSF £35.51 TOTE £2.80: £1.50, £1.90, £1.30; EX 37.50 Trifecta £143.60 Pool: £887.30 - 4.57 winning units..
Owner Jaber Abdullah **Bred** Follow The Flag Partnership **Trained** West Ilsley, Berks

FOCUS
An ordinary maiden run in bad ground. The winner is the best guide to the form.

NOTEBOOK
Show Rainbow was well ridden by Ricahrd Hughes, who had clearly taken note of the stands'-rail bias in the previous race and was quick to grab a lead. The filly gradually came clear, winning with plenty in hand. She could develop into a fair handicapper at three. (op 5-2 tchd 11-4 in places)
Swimsuit, a half-sister to five-time winner La Zamorra, stayed on again to take second and will benefit from an extra furlong. She should win an ordinary maiden. (op 12-1)
Bless You, from a yard that traditionally does well with its juveniles, was strong in the market and showed enough to suggest she'll be winning races, with better ground expected to suit. (op 15-2)
Follow My Dream proved one-paced under pressure, racing a good bit off the rail, but this half-sister to Pipedreamer should fare an awful lot better over further next year. (op 4-1)
Miss Exhibitionist failed to reproduce the form of her Newmarket second and clearly didn't like the ground. (op 5-2)

7124 HAYMARKET NURSERY (DIV II) 7f 9y
5:00 (5:01) (Class 6) (0-65,64) 2-Y-O £1,619 (£481; £240; £120) Stalls Low

Form RPR
5250 1 **Barista (IRE)**[11] 6875 2-9-7 64 RichardHughes 1 72
(M R Channon) chsd ldrs: led 5f out: rdn clr fr over 1f out: eased wl ins fnl f 3/1[1]
4540 2 2 1/4 **Scoglio**[6] 7004 2-9-3 60 (b[1]) LeeVickers 16 59+
(F Sheridan) hld up: hdwy over 1f out: r.o to go 2nd ins fnl f: no ch w wnr 12/1
2230 3 1 3/4 **Three Scoops**[11] 6878 2-8-10 53 (t) NeilCallan 3 48
(D J S Ffrench Davis) chsd ldrs: rdn over 1f out: styd on same pce fnl f 17/2
1046 4 1 3/4 **Mary Boyle**[14] 6810 2-8-6 54 DeclanCannon(5) 4 44
(A J McCabe) hld up: hdwy over 1f out: nvr nrr 6/1[2]
0530 5 2 3/4 **Mediplomat**[40] 6081 2-9-4 61 (v[1]) ChrisCatlin 8 44
(M Botti) hld up: hdwy over 2f out: rdn over 1f out: wknd ins fnl f 13/2[3]
0000 6 2 1/2 **Torteval (IRE)**[11] 6867 2-8-0 46 Louis-PhilippeBeuzelin(3) 14 23
(P D Evans) chsd ldrs: rdn 1/2-way: wknd fnl f 25/1
1400 7 hd **Sky Diamond (IRE)**[11] 6875 2-9-5 62 TomEaves 12 39
(J G Given) prom: rdn over 2f out: wknd over 1f out 9/1
0050 8 1/2 **Arctic Reach**[17] 6717 2-9-0 57 SebSanders 7 32
(G D Blake) chsd ldrs: rdn over 2f out: sn wknd 18/1
006 9 1/2 **Inca Blue**[16] 6748 2-8-13 56 GrahamGibbons 15 30
(T D Easterby) chsd ldrs: rdn 1/2-way: wknd over 1f out 7/1
0000 10 4 **Bernie's Tune**[56] 5613 2-8-7 50 FrankieMcDonald 13 14
(J L Spearing) s.i.s: hdwy over 5f out: rdn over 2f out: wknd over 1f out 20/1
4660 11 1 1/2 **Dancing With Fire**[10] 6902 2-7-13 45 (v[1]) SophieDoyle(3) 6 5
(D Donovan) chsd ldrs: pushed along and lost pl 5f out: bhd fr 1/2-way 40/1
4250 12 2 1/2 **Alensgrove (IRE)**[40] 6071 2-9-7 64 TonyCulhane 5 18
(P T Midgley) hld up: hdwy u.p on outside over 1f out: wknd fnl f 20/1
340 13 nk **Mollyow (IRE)**[111] 3769 2-9-6 63 JimmyFortune 2 16
(B Palling) led 2f: wknd 3f out 25/1

1m 31.13s (4.93) **Going Correction** +0.55s/f (Yiel) 13 Ran SP% 118.3
Speed ratings (Par 93): **93,90,88,86,83 80,80,79,79,74 72,69,69**
toteswingers:1&2:£12.30, 1&3:£6.20, 2&3:£22.20 CSF £37.14 CT £290.08 TOTE £3.00: £1.60, £4.60, £2.50; EX 54.30 Trifecta £542.80 Pool: £762.97 - 1.04 winning units..
Owner Mrs T Burns **Bred** Rathasker Stud **Trained** West Ilsley, Berks

FOCUS
This didn't prove as competitive as the first division, with Richard Hughes, followed by Neil Callan, still being the only rider alert to the massive stands' rail bias. The winner produced a clear best but the runner-up limits the form.

NOTEBOOK
Barista(IRE), with just a selling win to his name in 11 previous tries, raced keenly, but saw it out well having established a lead, being called the winner with over 2f to run. He raced against the favoured stands' rail. (op 7-2 tchd 4-1 and 11-4)
Scoglio, drawn out in 16, stayed on late to record an improved effort in the first-time blinkers. (op 17-2)
Three Scoops is largely consistent and he kept on well against the rail for another placed effort. (op 11-1)
Mary Boyle stayed on late and may have benefited from a more forceful ride on this drop in trip (op 8-1)
Mediplomat made good headway through the field in the first-time visor, but he wasn't on the best ground ultimately faded. (op 11-2 tchd 7-1)
Alensgrove(IRE) Official explanation: jockey said filly hung right-handed

7125 AMATEUR JOCKEYS' ASSOCIATION INSURE THEIR MEMBERS H'CAP (FOR GENTLEMEN AMATEUR RIDERS) 7f 9y
5:30 (5:30) (Class 5) (0-70,68) 3-Y-O+ £2,307 (£709; £354) Stalls Low

Form RPR
1335 1 **Eastern Hills**[9] 6922 5-10-0 57 (p) MrPCollington(3) 5 69
(A J McCabe) chsd ldrs: rdn to ld ins fnl f: r.o 5/1[1]
2140 2 3/4 **The Human League**[11] 6864 3-10-4 67 MrCBishop(7) 7 77
(M R Channon) a.p: led wl over 1f out: rdn: edgd rt and hdd ins fnl f: styd on same pce 17/2
2005 3 6 **Hits Only Jude (IRE)**[9] 6917 7-9-12 59 MrJHarney(7) 17 53
(D Carroll) trckd ldr far side tl led that pair 1/2-way: rdn and hung lft over 1f out: no ex fnl f 12/1
3001 4 2 **Toby Tyler**[13] 6826 4-10-10 64 (v) MrSWalker 14 52
(P T Midgley) hld up: hdwy over 2f out: rdn over 1f out: nt rch ldrs 7/1
0435 5 1/2 **Bid For Gold**[25] 6491 6-9-13 57 oh1 (p) MrJHamer(3) 3 43
(Jedd O'Keeffe) s.i.s: hld up: swtchd rt and hdwy over 1f out: styd on: nt trble ldrs 16/1
5350 6 nk **Silly Gilly (IRE)**[10] 6890 6-9-9 57 oh4 MrJNewman(5) 4 40
(R E Barr) in rr: rdn over 2f out: r.o ins fnl f: nrst fin 13/2[3]
4564 7 1/2 **The Name Is Frank**[28] 6421 5-10-5 62 (t) MrPJTolman(3) 9 47
(Mark Gillard) chsd ldr: rdn 1/2-way: wknd over 1f out 16/1
4605 8 1 1/2 **Cruise Control**[17] 6716 4-9-9 57 oh9 MrBJPoste(5) 12 35
(R J Price) hld up: hdwy over 2f out: wknd over 1f out 40/1
5061 9 5 **Sea Salt**[33] 6295 7-10-11 68 MrJMQuinlan(3) 10 35
(R E Barr) led: rdn and hdd wl over 1f out: sn wknd 20/1
6213 10 nse **Mr Udagawa**[20] 6657 4-10-4 63 (p) MrRJWilliams(5) 16 30
(B J Llewellyn) prom: rdn 1/2-way: wknd over 1f out 6/1[2]
0322 11 3 1/4 **Bermondsey Bob (IRE)**[6] 7007 4-10-6 60 MrSDobson 18 18
(J L Spearing) led far side duo to 1/2-way: wknd 2f out 8/1
500 12 2 1/2 **Lethal**[110] 3777 7-10-3 60 MrMPrice(3) 13 12
(R J Price) chsd ldrs tl rdn and wknd wl over 1f out 22/1
0406 13 1/2 **Mississippian (IRE)**[3] 7054 6-9-9 57 oh8 MrAdamNicol(5) 11 4
(Mrs R Dobbin) s.i.s: sn pushed along and a in rr 11/1
14 13 **Jenny's Pride (IRE)**[203] 1114 4-9-9 57 oh11 MrTGarner(5) 6 —
(John A Harris) hld up: rdn over 4f out: a in rr: t.o 28/1
600- 15 5 **Edge End**[339] 7460 6-9-7 57 oh10 MrCEllingham(7) 1 —
(Mrs L Williamson) mid-div: wknd 1/2-way: t.o 100/1
5200 16 1/2 **Set To Go**[89] 4475 3-9-11 60 (b) MrCVitler(7) 2 —
(Miss N A Lloyd-Beavis) prom over 4f: t.o 80/1
00-0 17 28 **White Ledger (IRE)**[56] 5586 11-9-9 57 oh12 (p) MrOGarner(5) 15 —
(R E Peacock) prom: rdn 1/2-way: sn bhd: t.o 125/1

1m 31.38s (5.18) **Going Correction** +0.55s/f (Yiel)
WFA 3 from 4yo+ 2lb 17 Ran SP% 124.2
Speed ratings (Par 103): **92,91,84,82,81 81,80,78,73,73 69,66,65,51,45 44,12**
toteswingers:1&2:£11.20, 1&3:£4.60, 2&3:£13.80. totesuper7: WIN: Not won. PLACE: £502.90. CSF £44.81 CT £515.55 TOTE £5.40: £2.20, £2.70, £5.20, £3.10; EX 70.20 Trifecta £200.10 Pool: £343.55 - 1.27 winning units. Place 6: £14.62 Place 5: £3.63.
Owner Charles Wentworth **Bred** Azienda Agricola Patrizia **Trained** Averham Park, Notts

FOCUS
The stands' rail was again the place to be and the front pair drew clear. The winner is rated up 3lb on recent best.
Sea Salt Official explanation: jockey said saddle slipped
T/Plt: £20.70 to a £1 stake. Pool:£51,188.93 - 1,803.65 winning tickets T/Qpdt: £5.60 to a £1 stake. Pool:£3,549.75 - 464.90 winning tickets CR

6658 SOUTHWELL (L-H)
Monday, October 25

OFFICIAL GOING: Standard
Wind: Virtually nil Weather: Fine and dry

7126 BRAMLEY APPLE CELEBRATION MEDIAN AUCTION MAIDEN STKS 1m (F)
2:20 (2:20) (Class 6) 2-Y-O £1,569 (£463; £231) Stalls Low

Form RPR
0224 1 **Top Care (USA)**[27] 6435 2-9-3 78 JoeFanning 7 82+
(M Johnston) trckd ldrs: hdwy on outer 3f out: rdn to chse ldr 2f out: styd on to ld ent fnl f: drvn out 5/4[1]
532 2 3 **Suddenly Susan (IRE)**[11] 6859 2-8-12 68 DarryllHolland 2 69
(J Noseda) led: rdn clr over 2f out: drvn and jnd over 1f out: hdd ent fnl f and one pce 9/4[2]
3405 3 10 **Little Miss Take**[11] 6875 2-8-7 65 RossAtkinson(5) 8 46
(Tom Dascombe) a.p: effrt to chse ldr 3f out: rdn over 2f out: drvn wl over 1f out and sn one pce 6/1[3]
0603 4 2 3/4 **Munro's Dragon**[39] 6129 2-8-12 51 AshleyMorgan(5) 5 45
(M H Tompkins) chsd ldrs: hdwy 3f out: rdn over 2f out: sn drvn and one pce 17/2
0000 5 3/4 **Pinotage**[21] 6618 2-9-0 45 MichaelStainton(3) 1 43
(R M Whitaker) cl up on inner: pushed along after 2f and sn lost pl: towards rr fr 1/2-way 66/1
00 6 1 3/4 **Warrant**[25] 6504 2-9-3 0 LiamKeniry 9 39
(P Howling) a in rr 25/1
0 7 1 **X Rated**[11] 6874 2-9-3 0 JamesDoyle 3 37
(A J McCabe) dwlt: rapid hdwy to join ldrs after 1f: cl up on inner tl rdn along 3f out and sn wknd 20/1
0 8 4 **Devon Delight**[26] 6469 2-8-12 0 PJMcDonald 6 23
(R M H Cowell) in tch: rdn along over 3f out: sn wknd 66/1
00 9 30 **Voovoo (IRE)**[8] 6964 2-8-12 0 DuranFentiman 4 —
(D O'Meara) a in rr: bhd fr 1/2-way 100/1

1m 43.38s (-0.32) **Going Correction** +0.125s/f (Slow) 9 Ran SP% 112.6
Speed ratings (Par 93): **106,103,93,90,89 87,86,82,52**
toteswingers:1&2:£1.10, 1&3:£2.30, 2&3:£4.00 CSF £3.82 TOTE £3.20: £1.50, £1.02, £2.00; EX 4.20.
Owner Ahmed Jaber **Bred** Charles H Wacker **Trained** Middleham Moor, N Yorks

FOCUS
A modest race but a decent time being 0.58 seconds faster than the later Class 5 handicap for older horses. The first two came clear, with a small personal best from the winner.

NOTEBOOK
Top Care(USA) had raced exclusively at around 6f in his seven previous starts, but this significant step up in trip clearly suited, and he handled the surface okay. He was hanging left from some way out, but that didn't stop him and he basically outstayed the runner-up. He should get even further, although may not run again this season according to connections. (op 10-11)
Suddenly Susan(IRE) has started to go in her coat, but she had her chance under a positive ride and did little wrong. (op 5-2 tchd 11-4)
Little Miss Take wasn't running on inside the final furlong, looking a bit awkward (maybe she didn't appreciate the Fibresand), and she's yet to prove her stamina. (op 13-2)
Munro's Dragon, rated only 51, puts this form into perspective. (op 12-1)

7127 PM ENGINEERING CONTRACTORS LTD NOVICE STKS 6f (F)
2:50 (2:50) (Class 4) 2-Y-O £3,043 (£905; £452; £226) Stalls Low

Form RPR
1206 1 **Lord Of The Stars (USA)**[56] 5604 2-9-5 93 MartinLane 4 91+
(R M Beckett) mde all: shkn up and qcknd clr 2f out: readily 4/9[1]
1006 2 4 1/2 **Lenjawi Pride**[16] 6745 2-8-9 78 RossAtkinson(5) 3 72
(Tom Dascombe) trckd ldng pair: hdwy to chse wnr over 2f out and sn rdn: drvn over 1f out and sn one pce 5/1[3]
60 3 4 1/2 **Spin A Wish**[7] 6980 2-8-6 0 AmyRyan(3) 2 53
(R M Whitaker) chsd wnr on inner: rdn along wl over 2f out: drvn wl over 1f out and kpt on same pce 50/1
1404 4 1/2 **Major Muscari (IRE)**[10] 6900 2-9-5 81 (b) JamesDoyle 1 62
(A J McCabe) trckd ldrs: effrt 2f out and sn rdn: drvn over 1f out: sn edgd lft and one pce 3/1[2]

1m 17.49s (0.99) **Going Correction** +0.125s/f (Slow) 4 Ran SP% 112.9
Speed ratings (Par 97): **98,92,86,85**
CSF £3.48 TOTE £1.30; EX 3.40.
Owner Mogeely Stud & Mrs Maura Gittins **Bred** JMJ Racing Stables LLC **Trained** Whitsbury, Hants
■ Stewards' Enquiry : Amy Ryan caution: used whip down shoulder in the forehand.

FOCUS
An uncompetitive novice event and the winner was the clear pre-race form choice.

NOTEBOOK
Lord Of The Stars(USA), who had 10lb in hand over the runner-up on official figures, was a class apart. He had contested a Listed race when last seen in August, so this represented a notable ease in grade, and he handled the Fibresand at the first attempt without any problems. (op 1-2, tchd 8-15 after early 4-6, 8-13 and 4-7 in places)
Lenjawi Pride showed a notable knee action, so this surface should have been okay, but she was predictably outclassed by the winner. (op 4-1 tchd 11-2)
Spin A Wish was out of her depth, but this was only her third run and handicaps are now an option.

The Form Book, Raceform Ltd, Compton, RG20 6NL

Major Muscari(IRE) ran nowhere near his official mark of 81 and seemingly didn't take to the Fibresand. (op 9-2)

7128 BETDAQ ON 0870 178 1221 H'CAP 1m (F)
3:20 (3:21) (Class 5) (0-70,70) 3-Y-O+ £2,115 (£624; £312) Stalls Low

Form RPR

6205 1 **Know No Fear**[12] 6853 5-8-8 57..............(p) FergusSweeney 8 67
(A J Lidderdale) *hld up in tch: smooth hdwy over 2f out: rdn to ld over 1f out: kpt on fnl f* 25/1

0005 2 1 3/4 **Hilbre Court (USA)**[3] 7071 5-8-7 56 oh2..............(bt) PatrickMathers 6 62
(B P J Baugh) *trckd ldrs: smooth hdwy to ld 2f out: rdn hdd over 1f out: kpt on u.p fnl f* 17/2

0050 3 hd **Betteras Bertie**[39] 6116 7-8-8 57.............. FrannyNorton 12 63
(M Brittain) *dwlt: hdwy on outer 1/2-way: rdn to chse ldrs wl over 1f out: drvn and kpt on ins fnl f: nrst fin* 25/1

0100 4 2 **Royal Holiday (IRE)**[6] 7006 3-8-10 62.............. PJMcDonald 3 63
(B Ellison) *hld up: hdwy on wd outside over 2f out: rdn and hung lft over 1f out: kpt on u.p fnl f* 7/1[2]

5560 5 1/2 **My One Weakness (IRE)**[37] 6189 3-8-5 57.............. MartinLane 9 57
(B Ellison) *dwlt and in rr: hdwy over 2f out: sn rdn and kpt on fnl f: nrst fin* 8/1[3]

2660 6 1 1/2 **Rascal In The Mix (USA)**[9] 6934 4-8-12 64..............(p) AmyRyan(3) 7 61
(R M Whitaker) *dwlt and towards rr: hdwy on inner over 3f out: rdn wl over 1f out: drvn and no imp fnl f* 20/1

5621 7 1 3/4 **Elusive Warrior (USA)**[20] 6664 7-9-0 70..............(p) NoraLooby(7) 11 63
(A J McCabe) *led: rdn along 3f out: hdd over 2f out: sn drvn and grad wknd* 8/1[3]

3304 8 3/4 **Full Victory (IRE)**[21] 6633 8-8-10 59.............. LiamKeniry 14 50
(R A Farrant) *in tch: hdwy 3f out: rdn along over 2f out and sn no imp* 16/1

0503 9 8 **Postman**[26] 6472 4-8-9 65..............(p) AdamCarter(7) 5 38
(B Smart) *in rr and sn rdn along: a bhd* 7/2[1]

3532 10 2 3/4 **Guga (IRE)**[9] 6937 4-9-2 65..............(p) JoeFanning 2 31
(J Mackie) *cl up on inner: rdn along wl over 2f out: sn wknd* 7/1[2]

0260 11 1 **Stef And Stelio**[24] 6522 3-8-11 63..............(p) StevieDonohoe 10 27
(G A Butler) *a towards rr* 25/1

6126 12 2 3/4 **Aussie Blue (IRE)**[9] 6935 6-9-3 69.............. MichaelStainton(3) 4 27
(R M Whitaker) *prom: rdn along 3f out: wknd over 2f out* 8/1[3]

500- 13 4 1/2 **Byron Bay**[318] 7349 8-8-4 56 oh1.............. JamesSullivan(3) 13 3
(R Johnson) *cl up: rdn along 3f out: sn drvn and wknd* 66/1

5000 14 6 **Bennelong**[12] 6851 4-9-2 65..............(tp) DarrylHolland 1 —
(G C Bravery) *in tch: rdn along 3f out: wknd over 2f out* 33/1

1m 43.96s (0.26) **Going Correction** +0.125s/f (Slow)
WFA 3 from 4yo+ 3lb 14 Ran SP% **117.7**
Speed ratings (Par 103): **103,101,101,99,98 97,95,94,86,83 82,80,75,69**
toteswingers:1&2:£37.60, 1&3:£61.00, 2&3:£61.00 CSF £207.20 CT £5442.63 TOTE £26.90: £7.90, £3.80, £10.40; EX 384.60.
Owner C S J Beek **Bred** B Bargh **Trained** Eastbury, Berks

FOCUS
A modest but competitive handicap run in a poor time, being 0.58 seconds slower than earlier 2-y-o maiden. Very ordinary form.
Postman Official explanation: jockey said, regarding running, that the gelding never travelled
Guga(IRE) Official explanation: trainer had no explanation for the poor form shown

7129 BETDAQ.COM MAIDEN STKS 7f (F)
3:50 (3:52) (Class 5) 3-Y-O+ £2,115 (£624; £312) Stalls Low

Form RPR

032 1 **Divine Call**[20] 6655 3-9-3 75.............. LiamJones 6 85+
(W J Haggas) *trckd ldng pair: smooth hdwy to ld wl over 2f out: pushed clr wl over 1f out: comf* 4/7[1]

3463 2 2 1/2 **Lay Claim (USA)**[21] 6638 3-9-3 72..............(p) JamesDoyle 4 75
(A J McCabe) *trckd ldrs: hdwy to chse wnr wl over 2f out and sn rdn: drvn wl over 1f out and no imp* 3/1[2]

53 3 6 **Catching Zeds**[54] 5658 3-8-12 0.............. PJMcDonald 1 54
(Ian Williams) *chsd ldr on inner: hdwy to ld briefly 3f out: sn hdd and rdn: drvn and one pce fnl 2f* 6/1[3]

4 11 **King Bertolini (IRE)** 3-9-3 0.............. DuranFentiman 3 29
(D O'Meara) *rdn along and outpcd in rr: bhd 1/2-way: swtchd outside and hdwy over 2f out: kpt on fnl f: nvr a factor* 33/1

0060 5 1 3/4 **Proud Tuscan**[69] 5171 3-9-3 47.............. SteveDrowne 7 25
(A J McCabe) *chsd ldrs: rdn along 1/2-way: sn wknd* 50/1

05 6 4 1/2 **Old Peg**[15] 6773 5-8-9 0.............. MarkCoumbe(5) 9 —
(D Bourton) *a in rr: outpcd fr 1/2-way* 16/1

0 7 4 **Matilda May**[10] 6896 3-8-12 0.............. PatrickMathers 2 —
(C J Teague) *a in rr: outpcd fr 1/2-way* 66/1

0-0 8 1 **Fourlanends**[11] 6876 3-9-0 0.............. JamesSullivan(3) 8 —
(N Wilson) *led: rdn along 1/2-way: sn hdd & wknd wl over 2f out* 33/1

1m 30.32s (0.02) **Going Correction** +0.125s/f (Slow)
WFA 3 from 5yo 2lb 8 Ran SP% **118.2**
Speed ratings (Par 103): **104,101,94,81,79 74,70,68**
toteswingers:1&2:£1.50, 1&3:£1.90, 2&3:£1.70 CSF £2.61 TOTE £1.60: £1.02, £1.20, £1.50; EX 3.40.
Owner Cheveley Park Stud **Bred** Cheveley Park Stud Ltd **Trained** Newmarket, Suffolk

FOCUS
A weak and uncompetitive maiden, and straightforward form. The winner can do better.

7130 BETDAQ THE BETTING EXCHANGE H'CAP 1m 4f (F)
4:20 (4:20) (Class 4) (0-85,85) 3-Y-O+ £3,626 (£1,079; £539; £269) Stalls Low

Form RPR

0055 1 **Lucky Punt**[12] 6841 4-9-12 84.............. FergusSweeney 7 96+
(B G Powell) *a cl up: effrt to ld wl over 2f out: rdn and hung rt to stands' rail over 1f out: drvn and kpt on wl fnl f* 10/1

3530 2 2 1/2 **Becausewecan (USA)**[16] 6754 4-9-8 80.............. JoeFanning 6 86
(M Johnston) *led: rdn along 3f out and sn hdd: drvn 2f out: kpt on u.p fnl f to regain 2nd nr fin* 3/1[2]

1-15 3 1 1/2 **Powerful Melody (USA)**[30] 6359 3-9-6 85..............(v[1]) DaraghO'Donohoe 4 89
(Saeed Bin Suroor) *s.i.s: reluctant and reminders first f and in rr tl hdwy over 4f out: rdn wl over 2f out: styd on u.p fnl f: tk 3rd nr line* 9/2[3]

0412 4 shd **Bivouac (UAE)**[17] 6715 6-9-5 77.............. PJMcDonald 2 80
(G A Swinbank) *trckd ldrs: smooth hdwy 4f out: cl up 3f out: rdn to chse wnr over 2f out: drvn over 1f out and kpt on same pce: lost 3rd nr line* 9/2[3]

0533 5 21 **Fine Sight**[10] 6904 3-9-3 82..............(p) StevieDonohoe 1 52
(G A Butler) *prom: pushed along over 4f out: sn rdn and wknd 3f out* 8/1

0-44 6 30 **Taikoo**[25] 6516 5-9-6 78.............. SteveDrowne 5 —
(H Morrison) *trckd ldrs: pushed along 1/2-way: rdn and lost pl 5f out: sn bhd: t.o and virtually p.u fnl 2f* 9/4[1]

2m 40.38s (-0.62) **Going Correction** +0.125s/f (Slow)
WFA 3 from 4yo+ 7lb 6 Ran SP% **112.3**
Speed ratings (Par 105): **107,105,104,104,90 70**
toteswingers:1&2:£6.40, 1&3:£5.10, 2&3:£3.70 CSF £39.82 TOTE £18.80: £7.80, £3.10; EX 44.70.
Owner I S Smith **Bred** S A Douch **Trained** Upper Lambourn, Berks

FOCUS
A fair handicap, weakened by the favourite's poor run. The winner was back to his best.
Taikoo Official explanation: trainer had no explanation for the poor form shown

7131 BREEDERS' CUP LIVE ONLY ON ATR APPRENTICE H'CAP (DIV I) 6f (F)
4:50 (4:52) (Class 6) (0-55,55) 3-Y-O+ £1,364 (£403; £201) Stalls Low

Form RPR

0000 1 **Takajan (IRE)**[9] 6935 3-9-0 54.............. JamesRogers 8 64
(W M Brisbourne) *chsd ldrs: hdwy on outer over 2f out: rdn to ld over 1f out: drvn out* 6/1[3]

6304 2 2 1/2 **Best Known Secret (IRE)**[20] 6643 4-8-6 48.............. RichardRowe(3) 4 50
(C C Bealby) *trckd ldrs on inner: hdwy over 2f out: rdn wl over 1f out: chsd wnr ent fnl f: no imp towards fin* 6/1[3]

656/ 3 2 1/2 **Compton Micky**[1379] 137 9-8-0 46 oh1..............(p) ChristopherGraham(7) 7 40
(O Brennan) *chsd ldrs: hdwy over 2f out: rdn wl over 1f out: kpt on ins fnl f* 25/1

0000 4 1 3/4 **Russian Brigadier**[51] 5758 3-8-6 46 oh1.............. JohnCavanagh 5 34
(M Brittain) *cl up: rdn and ev ch over 2f out: drvn and outpcd wl over 1f out: kpt on u.p fnl f* 25/1

0040 5 hd **Boundless Applause**[13] 6826 4-8-7 46 oh1.............. NeilFarley 11 34
(I A Wood) *slt ld: rdn along 2f out: drvn and hdd over 1f out: wknd fnl f* 14/1

040 6 1 **Gessabelle**[15] 6773 3-8-6 46 oh1..............(t) RyanClark 6 31
(P S McEntee) *midfield: hdwy over 2f out: rdn wl over 1f out: no imp fnl f* 18/1

0060 7 1/2 **Fyodorovich (USA)**[104] 3976 5-8-2 46 oh1..............(v) NoraLooby(5) 3 29
(A J McCabe) *dwlt: rdn along in midfield 1/2-way: wd st: sme late hdwy* 4/1[2]

0004 8 1 1/2 **Sophie's Beau (USA)**[40] 6076 3-8-7 52..............(t) LeonnaMayor(5) 12 30
(M C Chapman) *wnt rt s: rapid hdwy to join ldrs after 1f and sn cl up: rdn and ev ch over 2f out: sn drvn and wknd wl over 1f out* 10/1

6600 9 5 **Mujada**[8] 6966 5-8-2 46 oh1.............. ShaneBKelly(5) 9 8
(D O'Meara) *nvr bttr than midfield* 14/1

3404 10 hd **Final Salute**[53] 5688 4-9-2 55..............(v) AdamCarter 1 17
(B Smart) *dwlt: a in rr* 10/3[1]

640 11 13 **Pavement Games**[12] 6847 3-8-4 49..............(v[1]) SeanPalmer(5) 2 —
(R C Guest) *free to s: a in rr* 12/1

00/ 12 2 3/4 **Miss Red Eye (IRE)**[466] 4027 5-8-4 46 oh1.....(b[1]) MatthewLawson(3) 10 —
(Luke Comer, Ire) *s.i.s: a bhd* 25/1

1m 17.99s (1.49) **Going Correction** +0.125s/f (Slow)
WFA 3 from 4yo+ 1lb 12 Ran SP% **118.6**
Speed ratings (Par 101): **95,91,88,86,85 84,83,81,75,74 57,53**
toteswingers:1&2:£10.10, 1&3:£42.90, 2&3:£29.60 CSF £40.88 CT £825.24 TOTE £8.90: £2.50, £2.50, £7.90; EX 47.90.
Owner Stephen Jones **Bred** His Highness The Aga Khan's Studs S C **Trained** Great Ness, Shropshire
■ Stewards' Enquiry : Ryan Clark two-day ban: careless riding (Nov 8 & remedial training)

FOCUS
The time was 0.20 seconds slower than the second division. A weak handicap with the majority out of the weights.
Russian Brigadier Official explanation: jockey said gelding hung left
Final Salute Official explanation: jockey said gelding suffered interference in running

7132 BREEDERS' CUP LIVE ONLY ON ATR APPRENTICE H'CAP (DIV II) 6f (F)
5:20 (5:22) (Class 6) (0-55,54) 3-Y-O+ £1,364 (£403; £201) Stalls Low

Form RPR

4055 1 **Darcy's Pride (IRE)**[39] 6110 6-8-9 52.............. ShaneBKelly(5) 4 63
(P T Midgley) *trckd ldrs: hdwy on inner 2f out: rdn over 1f out: styd on to ld ins fnl f: kpt on wl towards fin* 6/1[3]

0003 2 1 1/2 **Captain Kallis (IRE)**[8] 6952 4-8-10 48.............. JamesRogers 6 54
(D J S Ffrench Davis) *chsd ldrs: hdwy over 2f out: rdn wl over 1f out: styd on u.p fnl f* 11/4[1]

6655 3 3/4 **Norcroft**[40] 6098 8-8-7 45..............(b) RyanClark 12 49
(Mrs C A Dunnett) *midfield: wd st: hdwy 2f out: sn rdn and kpt on u.p fnl f: tk 3rd nr fin* 11/1

3662 4 shd **Desert Strike**[37] 6206 4-8-11 54..............(p) NoraLooby(5) 9 58
(A J McCabe) *chsd ldrs: hdwy on outer to chal 2f out: rdn to ld over 1f out: hdd ins fnl f: wknd last 100yds* 5/1[2]

-043 5 1 3/4 **Whaston (IRE)**[20] 6660 5-8-11 49.............. GarryWhillans 7 47+
(Miss P Robson) *sn outpcd and bhd: wd st: hdwy wl over 1f out: sn rdn and styd on fnl f: nrst fin* 5/1[2]

0050 6 4 **Marsh's Gift**[40] 6076 3-8-6 45..............(p) AdamCarter 5 30
(C J Teague) *s.i.s and bhd tl styd on fnl 2f: nvr a factor* 20/1

6003 7 1/2 **Prigsnov Dancer (IRE)**[59] 5485 5-8-4 45..........(p) MatthewLawson(3) 8 29
(O Brennan) *t.k.h: cl up: rdn to ld 2f out: sn drvn and edgd lft: hdd & wknd over 1f out* 16/1

0200 8 1 1/2 **Sea Crest**[26] 6464 4-8-9 47.............. JohnCavanagh 3 26
(M Brittain) *rdn along 1/2-way: a towards rr* 20/1

0000 9 1 1/4 **Angle Of Attack (IRE)**[12] 6848 5-8-7 45..............(v) NeilFarley 1 20
(A D Brown) *prom on inner: rdn along over 2f out: sn drvn and wknd* 7/1

05-0 10 3 3/4 **Italian Dame**[26] 6464 4-8-2 45.............. DavidSimmonson(5) 11 8
(J R Turner) *a in rr* 50/1

042 11 1 1/2 **Baby Judge (IRE)**[30] 4761 3-8-3 47.............. LeonnaMayor(5) 10 5
(M C Chapman) *a in rr* 20/1

3605 12 2 **Lieu Day Louie (IRE)**[20] 6644 3-8-6 45.............. RyanPowell 2 —
(N Wilson) *led: rdn along 3f out: sn drvn and hdd 2f out: sn wknd* 40/1

1m 17.79s (1.29) **Going Correction** +0.125s/f (Slow)
WFA 3 from 4yo+ 1lb 12 Ran SP% **119.7**
Speed ratings (Par 101): **96,94,93,92,90 85,84,82,80,75 73,71**
toteswingers:1&2:£5.10, 1&3:£9.50, 2&3:£6.30 CSF £21.45 CT £185.25 TOTE £5.70: £1.50, £1.10, £6.30; EX 23.70 Place 6: £205.06 Place 5: £168.61..
Owner T Shepherd & A Turton **Bred** Leo Cox **Trained** Westow, N Yorks
■ Stewards' Enquiry : Ryan Powell one-day ban: used whip above shoulder height (Nov 8)

FOCUS
A moderate contest, but the time was 0.20 seconds quicker than the first division. Not quite as weak as division 1.
T/Plt: £576.10 to a £1 stake. Pool:£49,465.16 - 62.67 winning tickets T/Qpdt: £204.10 to a £1 stake. Pool:£4,304.31 - 15.60 winning tickets JR

7133 - 7134a (Foreign Racing) - See Raceform Interactive

5771 LEOPARDSTOWN (L-H)

Monday, October 25

OFFICIAL GOING: Good to firm (good in straight)

7135a JRA KILLAVULLAN STKS (GROUP 3) 7f

2:25 (2:29) 2-Y-O **£28,761** (£8,407; £3,982; £1,327)

RPR

1 **Dubai Prince (IRE)**[30] 6383 2-9-1 .... PJSmullen 8 111+
(D K Weld, Ire) *trckd ldrs in 3rd: hdwy ent st: led 1 1/2f out: sn qcknd clr: kpt on wl fnl f: impressive* **4/9**[1]

2 3 ½ **Warning Flag (USA)**[17] 6727 2-9-1 100 .... JMurtagh 2 100
(David Wachman, Ire) *trckd ldrs in 4th: 5th and outpcd ent st: mod 3rd 1f out: r.o last 100yds* **4/1**[2]

3 1 ¾ **Park Avenue (IRE)**[17] 6727 2-9-1 96 .... CO'Donoghue 6 95
(A P O'Brien, Ire) *trckd ldrs in 5th: rdn in 4th ent st: mod 2nd 1f out: sn no ex* **12/1**

4 4 **Ruling (IRE)**[8] 6967 2-9-1 .... JAHeffernan 7 85
(A P O'Brien, Ire) *hld up: prog into mod 6th ent st: kpt on same pce* **11/1**[3]

5 2 **Petronius Maximus (IRE)**[8] 6969 2-9-1 96 .... SMLevey 4 79
(A P O'Brien, Ire) *cl 2nd: led ent st: hdd 1 1/2f out: sn no ex* **16/1**

6 nk **Obligada (IRE)**[8] 6969 2-8-12 86 .... CDHayes 1 76
(Kevin Prendergast, Ire) *lost grnd s: hld up in rr: kpt on same pce st* **25/1**

7 1 ¾ **Oor Jock (IRE)**[8] 6969 2-9-1 96 .... DPMcDonogh 5 74
(D K Weld, Ire) *chsd ldrs in 6th: no imp st* **16/1**

8 1 **Catalpa Sail (IRE)**[3] 7072 2-9-1 78 .... SMGorey 3 71
(D K Weld, Ire) *led: set str pce: hdd ent st: wknd 1 1/2f out* **50/1**

1m 28.13s (-0.57) **Going Correction** +0.125s/f (Good) 8 Ran SP% **122.8**
Speed ratings: **108,104,102,97,95 94,92,91**
CSF £2.99 TOTE £1.40: £1.02, £1.30, £1.90; DF 3.20.
Owner Sheikh Mohammed **Bred** Mrs Eithne Hamilton **Trained** The Curragh, Co Kildare

FOCUS

Strong Group 3 form, underpinned by the second and third. Dubai Prince impressed and is clearly a colt of high potential.

NOTEBOOK

Dubai Prince(IRE) ◆ produced a performance full of class to have connections dreaming of big things next season. Clearly 7f was always going to be a bit short for him, but the way the race was run helped to offset that. Catalpa Sail made it a good test from the outset and his stablemate was perfectly placed ahead of the fourth horse but going a nice even pace. It would not be true to say that he travelled entirely smoothly throughout - that is purely because 7f is as short as he really wants - but it was very impressive how quickly he went from third to the lead and the race was over in a matter of seconds.Typical of a son of Shamardal, this colt is ground-versatile, tough and uncomplicated. His dam won five races over middle distances - one of them over 1m5f - so everything points to him being a Derby horse, like Grey Swallow, who won this race for Dermot Weld back in 2003. There is no doubt he is a top-class prospect over middle distances, whether that be with his present trainer or Godolphin. He may yet run in the Grand Criterium at Saint Cloud over 1m2f next month and he would take some stopping. (op 8/15)

Warning Flag(USA) gives the form a very solid look. Rated 100, he seemed to run his race, running on well in the final furlong. He has had a good season but probably wants at least 1m ideally. (op 4/1 tchd 9/2)

Park Avenue(IRE), 96-rated, was simply a little outclassed. He had finished a similar distance behind the runner-up at Dundalk last time and this is as good as he is. (op 12/1 tchd 14/1)

Ruling(IRE), winner of a maiden on his debut, struggled stepped up in class here. (op 10/1 tchd 12/1)

7136 - 7141a (Foreign Racing) - See Raceform Interactive

6915 CATTERICK (L-H)

Tuesday, October 26

OFFICIAL GOING: Good to soft (soft in places; 7.1)

Wind: moderate, half behind Weather: Overcast, but dry

7142 COWTHORPE MEDIAN AUCTION MAIDEN STKS 5f 212y

1:50 (1:51) (Class 6) 2-Y-O **£2,047** (£604; £302) **Stalls** Low

Form RPR

04 1 **Magnini (IRE)**[36] 6240 2-9-3 0 .... PhillipMakin 5 74
(K A Ryan) *mde all: drvn and hung lft over 1f out: kpt on ins fnl f* **11/1**

352 2 1 ¼ **Its You Again**[16] 6778 2-9-3 74 .... PaulHanagan 4 70
(M G Quinlan) *chsd ldr: rdn over 2f out: drvn and kpt on ins fnl f: nvr rch wnr* **5/2**[1]

3 2 ¼ **Deliberation (IRE)** 2-9-3 0 .... BarryMcHugh 3 63
(Ollie Pears) *s.i.s: hld up: hdwy to chse ldrs over 1f out: rdn and kpt on ins fnl f* **16/1**

3 4 nk **Delaney's Dream**[11] 6891 2-9-3 0 .... AdrianNicholls 7 62+
(D Nicholls) *chsd ldrs: rdn and outpcd over 2f out: drvn and kpt on again ins fnl f* **7/2**[3]

2 5 nk **Norton Girl**[35] 6264 2-8-9 0 .... IanBrennan(3) 9 56
(J J Quinn) *in tch: hdwy to chse ldrs 2f out: kpt on same pce* **11/4**[2]

600 6 9 **Bobbyow**[9] 6954 2-9-3 0 .... DavidProbert 10 34
(B Palling) *midfield: rdn over 2f out: wknd over 1f out* **25/1**

7 3 ½ **Bigalo's Princessa** 2-8-7 0 .... DeclanCannon(5) 8 19
(L A Mullaney) *chsd ldrs on outer tl wknd qckly over 2f out* **150/1**

66 8 2 **Tahitian Princess (IRE)**[11] 6893 2-8-12 0 .... RoystonFfrench 2 13
(Mrs A Duffield) *dwlt: hld up: rdn over 2f out: sn no imp* **33/1**

9 5 **Indigo Sands (IRE)** 2-8-12 0 .... BillyCray(5) 6 3
(A Berry) *slowly away: a bhd* **150/1**

6 10 5 **Majestic Millie (IRE)**[11] 6892 2-8-12 0 .... SilvestreDeSousa 1 —
(D O'Meara) *prom tl wknd qckly over 2f out: eased ins fnl f* **11/2**

1m 17.43s (3.83) **Going Correction** +0.625s/f (Yiel) 10 Ran SP% **115.2**
Speed ratings (Par 93): **99,97,94,93,93 81,76,74,67,60**
toteswingers:1&2 £5.10, 2&3 £9.40, 1&3 £12.50 CSF £37.90 TOTE £18.90: £4.90, £1.10, £6.50; EX 51.90.
Owner Mrs T Marnane **Bred** Buttinelli Mariangela **Trained** Hambleton, N Yorks

FOCUS

Winning jockey Phillip Makin described the ground as "mainly soft", a view supported by the time. An ordinary maiden in which the stands' rail was the place to be in the straight. Straightforward but limited form with the runner-up helping set the level.

NOTEBOOK

Magnini(IRE) benefited from a positive ride and soon grabbing the fence once in line for the finish. He handled the undulations particularly well and never looked in much danger of being caught. This was a significant improvement on his first two efforts and he looks set to make a fair handicapper, though he may not run again this year according to connections. (tchd 12-1)

Its You Again didn't travel anywhere near as well as the winner, being under pressure a fair way out and hanging on entering the straight, basically finding things happening too quickly on this sharp track. A step up to 7f should suit. (op 11-4 tchd 10-3)

Deliberation(IRE) ◆ is one to take from the race. An already gelded half-brother to seven winners, he lost ground at the start but kept on gradually, a particularly creditable effort considering he raced off the stands' rail in the straight.

Delaney's Dream predictably found this tougher than the Redcar claimer in which he was third on debut. (op 11-4)

Norton Girl shaped nicely enough when runner-up over 5f on debut, but somewhat surprisingly failed to go the required speed on this step up in trip. Perhaps a more galloping track will suit better. (tchd 3-1 in a place)

Tahitian Princess(IRE) Official explanation: jockey said filly stumbled turning in and had no more to give thereafter

Indigo Sands(IRE) Official explanation: jockey said gelding hung left

Majestic Millie(IRE), for whom there was money, was eventually well beaten but showed more ability. She displayed good early speed to get a handy position, before then finding nothing in the straight, quite possibly not handling the ground and/or track, and was heavily eased from over 1f out. Official explanation: jockey said filly had no more to give (op 14-1)

7143 TURFTV.CO.UK H'CAP (DIV I) 7f

2:20 (2:20) (Class 4) (0-85,85) 3-Y-O+ **£3,367** (£1,002; £500; £250) **Stalls** Low

Form RPR

0043 1 **Icelandic**[9] 6962 8-9-6 84 .... (t) SilvestreDeSousa 11 93
(F Sheridan) *s.i.s: hld up: rdn and hdwy to chse ldrs over 1f out: drvn and r.o wl to ld ins fnl f* **11/2**[2]

0151 2 ¾ **Glenridding**[24] 6558 6-9-2 85 .... (p) DaleSwift(5) 5 92
(J G Given) *w ldr: led after 3f: rdn over 2f out: drvn whn hdd ins fnl f: kpt on* **15/2**

6001 3 1 **Trans Sonic**[10] 6922 7-8-6 73 .... (b) JohnFahy(3) 2 77
(D O'Meara) *chsd ldrs: rdn over 2f out: ev ch over 1f out: kpt on ins fnl f* **7/1**

5340 4 shd **Keys Of Cyprus**[26] 6510 8-9-3 81 .... AdrianNicholls 1 85
(D Nicholls) *in tch: chsd ldrs towards inner after 3f: rdn and hdwy to chal over 1f out: kpt on ins fnl f* **4/1**[1]

1120 5 hd **Tukitinyasok (IRE)**[15] 6801 3-9-3 83 .... (p) TomEaves 8 86
(R F Fisher) *prom on outer: rdn over 2f out: stl ev ch 1f out: kpt on* **16/1**

0040 6 1 **Everymanforhimself (IRE)**[31] 6363 6-9-5 83 .... (b) PhillipMakin 4 84
(K A Ryan) *in tch: rdn and hdwy to chse ldrs over 1f out: kpt on same pce* **13/2**[3]

1443 7 ¾ **Mujaadel (USA)**[24] 6567 5-8-12 76 .... (p) PaulHanagan 3 75
(D Nicholls) *midfield: rdn over 2f out: sn one pce* **7/1**

0005 8 hd **Turn Me On (IRE)**[9] 6963 7-8-8 79 .... LukeStrong(7) 10 77
(T D Walford) *dwlt: hld up: rdn over 1f out: kpt on ins fnl f: n.d* **22/1**

1050 9 ¾ **Shotley Mac**[9] 6963 6-9-2 80 .... (b) FrannyNorton 12 76
(N Bycroft) *hld up: rdn over 2f out: n.d* **16/1**

0250 10 1 ½ **Vito Volterra (IRE)**[59] 5533 3-8-6 75 .... MichaelStainton(3) 6 67
(Michael Smith) *w ldrs: racd keenly: rdn over 2f out: wknd over 1f out* **20/1**

4004 11 12 **Game Lad**[9] 6963 8-9-0 78 .... (t) DavidAllan 9 38
(T D Easterby) *hld up: a towards rr* **12/1**

6150 12 5 **Mr Wolf**[8] 6981 9-8-12 79 .... (p) IanBrennan(3) 7 25
(J J Quinn) *led: hdd after 3f and sn lost pl: wknd over 2f out* **33/1**

1m 30.43s (3.43) **Going Correction** +0.625s/f (Yiel)
WFA 3 from 5yo+ 2lb 12 Ran SP% **117.0**
Speed ratings (Par 105): **105,104,103,102,102 101,100,100,99,97 84,78**
toteswingers:1&2 £8.60, 2&3 £8.40, 1&3 £9.20 CSF £44.56 CT £297.83 TOTE £6.70: £3.40, £2.90, £2.70; EX 50.90.
Owner Scuderia A4/5 **Bred** Cheveley Park Stud Ltd **Trained** Averham Park, Notts

FOCUS

Unlike in the opener, the winner did not race against the stands' rail in the straight. The time was 0.43 seconds slower than the second division. The form looks sound.

7144 GO RACING AT WETHERBY THIS FRIDAY H'CAP 5f 212y

2:50 (2:50) (Class 5) (0-75,75) 3-Y-O **£2,072** (£616; £308; £153) **Stalls** Low

Form RPR

1654 1 **Spinning Spirit (IRE)**[27] 6461 3-8-7 61 .... SilvestreDeSousa 6 66
(J G Given) *trckd ldrs: led jst ins fnl f: edgd lft and styd on* **7/2**[1]

0345 2 ¾ **Di Stefano**[7] 6998 3-9-6 74 .... AdrianNicholls 4 77
(D Nicholls) *trckd ldrs: almost upsides jst ins fnl f: no ex* **11/2**[3]

1000 3 1 ½ **Johannesgray (IRE)**[12] 6879 3-9-1 72 .... MichaelO'Connell(3) 7 70
(D Nicholls) *led: hdd jst ins fnl f: kpt on same pce* **9/1**

1100 4 nk **Kylladdie**[18] 6723 3-9-2 75 .... DaleSwift(5) 8 72
(S Gollings) *chsd ldrs: effrt over 2f out: styd on ins fnl f* **9/1**

3-00 5 ½ **Nadeen (IRE)**[18] 6723 3-9-4 75 .... MichaelStainton(3) 5 70
(Michael Smith) *rrd s: hdwy over 3f out: chsng ldrs towards centre over 1f out: one pce* **13/2**

4503 6 2 ¾ **Spread Boy (IRE)**[9] 6966 3-8-7 61 oh1 .... TomEaves 1 47
(A Berry) *in rr: drvn: hmpd and lost pl over 3f out: kpt on ins fnl f* **8/1**

0060 7 ½ **Electioneer (USA)**[8] 6981 3-9-2 70 .... GrahamGibbons 2 55
(M W Easterby) *in rr: drvn over 4f out: nvr a factor* **15/2**

4640 8 8 **Arch Walker (IRE)**[34] 6295 3-8-8 62 .... PaulHanagan 3 29
(Jedd O'Keeffe) *prom: n.m.r and lost pl over 3f out: bhd whn eased last 100yds* **4/1**[2]

1m 16.95s (3.35) **Going Correction** +0.625s/f (Yiel) 8 Ran SP% **113.8**
Speed ratings (Par 101): **102,101,99,98,97 94,93,82**
toteswingers:1&2 £2.90, 2&3 £13.30, 1&3 £10.20 CSF £22.66 CT £157.53 TOTE £6.00: £3.00, £3.20, £6.80; EX 16.20.
Owner R Jones & Patrick B Doyle Construction **Bred** T Pabst **Trained** Willoughton, Lincs

FOCUS

They raced middle to stands' side. It was hard to seriously fancy any of these and this is weak form for the class, rated around the winner. The race was notable, however, for yet another quality ride from Silvestre de Sousa, who continues to impress.

Arch Walker(IRE) Official explanation: jockey said gelding failed to handle the bend

7145 CATTERICKBRIDGE.CO.UK H'CAP 1m 7f 177y

3:20 (3:20) (Class 5) (0-70,66) 3-Y-O+ **£2,072** (£616; £308; £153) **Stalls** Low

Form RPR

0403 1 **Moonlight Blaze**[10] 6921 3-8-0 48 oh1 ow1 .... DuranFentiman 5 59
(C W Fairhurst) *w ldr: rdn to ld narrowly wl over 2f out: drvn and kpt on wl ins fnl f* **10/1**

4414 2 1 ½ **Danceintothelight**[13] 6650 3-8-11 62 .... KellyHarrison(3) 4 71
(Micky Hammond) *trckd ldrs: rdn over 2f out: chal 2f out tl 1f out: edgd lft and no ex ins fnl f* **4/1**[2]

4200 3 7 **Elite Land**[37] 6224 7-9-8 65 .... DaleSwift(5) 8 66
(B Ellison) *hld up: hdwy 7f out: rdn over 3f out: kpt on: nvr rchd ldrs* **4/1**[2]

1260 **4** 1/2 **Dan's Heir**[10] 6921 8-8-12 **55** DeanHeslop(5) 3 55
(W Storey) *hld up: brief hdwy 7f out: rdn over 4f out: no imp tl kpt on strly fr over 1f out: nrst fin* **12/1**
0510 **5** 4 **Drop The Hammer**[11] 6895 4-9-10 **62** (b) SilvestreDeSousa 1 57
(D O'Meara) *dwlt: sn led: rdn whn hdd wl over 2f out: wknd over 1f out* **11/4**[1]
/0-0 **6** 13 **Categorical**[11] 6895 7-9-5 **57** TonyCulhane 7 37
(K G Reveley) *hld up: hdwy 7f out: rdn over 4f out: sn no imp* **15/2**[3]
0-60 **7** 17 **Young Firth**[22] 6631 3-8-2 **50** FrannyNorton 11 9
(J R Norton) *midfield: rdn over 5f out: sn bhd* **80/1**
1435 **8** 15 **Bright Sparky (GER)**[31] 6373 7-8-7 **48** (vt) JamesSullivan(3) 2 —
(M W Easterby) *trckd ldrs: reminders bef 1/2-way: rdn and lost pl over 6f out: sn bhd* **14/1**
0/3- **9** 28 **Spear Thistle**[205] 7248 8-10-0 **66** (p) StephenCraine 10 —
(C J Mann) *trckd ldrs: reminders bef 1/2-way: rdn and lost pl 7f out: sn bhd* **16/1**
0 **10** 60 **Don't Hurry Love (IRE)**[79] 4863 3-8-1 **52** ow3 (p) JohnFahy(3) 12 —
(T J Pitt) *s.i.s: hld up: t.o fnl 6f* **22/1**

3m 43.24s (11.24) **Going Correction** +0.625s/f (Yiel)
WFA 3 from 4yo+ 10lb **10** Ran SP% **113.3**
Speed ratings (Par 103): **96,95,91,91,89 83,74,67,53,23**
toteswingers:1&2 £10.80, 2&3 £5.30, 1&3 £8.20 CSF £48.39 CT £187.91 TOTE £13.70: £3.40, £2.40, £1.10; EX 53.80.
Owner The PQD Partnership **Bred** Mrs R D Peacock **Trained** Middleham Moor, N Yorks

FOCUS
The field were strung out and, with it hard to make up significant amounts of ground on the soft conditions, those held up had next to no chance. They raced middle to stands' side in the closing stages. The form is taken at face value, with the front pair, who finished clear, rated to their best.
Drop The Hammer Official explanation: jockey said blindfold became caught on blinkers and filly was slowly away

7146 TURFTV.CO.UK H'CAP (DIV II) 7f
3:50 (3:50) (Class 4) (0-85,84) 3-Y-O+ **£3,367** (£1,002; £500; £250) **Stalls Low**

Form RPR
2302 **1** **Solar Spirit (IRE)**[10] 6917 5-8-7 **73** IanBrennan(3) 9 87
(J J Quinn) *s.i.s: hdwy on outside to trck ldrs over 4f out: swtchd lft appr fnl f: r.o wl to ld last 150yds: readily* **6/1**[3]
4311 **2** 2 1/2 **Cara's Request (AUS)**[10] 6917 5-9-3 **80** AdrianNicholls 12 87
(D Nicholls) *set str pce: wnt clr 4f out: hdd ins fnl f: no ex* **3/1**[1]
-001 **3** nk **Magic Cat**[9] 6962 4-9-6 **83** 6ex AndrewElliott 8 89
(Mrs K Burke) *sn chsng ldrs: kpt on same pce ins fnl f* **6/1**[3]
000 **4** 1 1/4 **Conry (IRE)**[13] 6851 4-9-3 **80** SilvestreDeSousa 7 83+
(Patrick Morris) *in rr div: hdwy towards centre over 2f out: hung lft and kpt on same pce appr fnl f* **5/1**[2]
5400 **5** 1/2 **Snow Bay**[40] 6105 4-9-4 **81** GregFairley 10 82
(D Nicholls) *trckd ldr: t.k.h: one pce ins fnl f* **10/1**
0040 **6** 2 1/2 **Island Chief**[10] 6922 4-8-7 **70** GrahamGibbons 6 65
(M W Easterby) *chsd ldrs: drvn and lost pl over 4f out: kpt on ins fnl f* **40/1**
0006 **7** 1 3/4 **Last Sovereign**[26] 6503 6-8-11 **79** (p) JamesO'Reilly(5) 4 69
(J O'Reilly) *s.i.s: drvn 4f out: sme hdwy towards centre over 2f out: nvr a factor* **14/1**
3161 **8** 7 **Malcheek (IRE)**[54] 5703 8-9-7 **84** DavidAllan 3 55
(T D Easterby) *t.k.h in midfield: effrt towards centre over 2f out: sn wknd* **16/1**
3030 **9** 2 **Elusive Sue (USA)**[51] 5789 3-8-12 **77** PaulHanagan 2 43
(R A Fahey) *sn chsng ldrs: lost pl over 2f out* **20/1**
0003 **10** 1 3/4 **Internationaldebut (IRE)**[8] 6985 5-9-5 **82** TonyCulhane 1 43
(P T Midgley) *dwlt: t.k.h in rr: drvn 4f out: bhd fnl 2f* **5/1**[2]

1m 30.0s (3.00) **Going Correction** +0.625s/f (Yiel)
WFA 3 from 4yo+ 2lb **10** Ran SP% **115.7**
Speed ratings (Par 105): **107,104,103,102,101 98,96,88,86,84**
toteswingers:1&2 £2.90, 2&3 £6.40, 1&3 not won. CSF £24.13 CT £106.89 TOTE £8.50: £2.80, £1.60, £2.30; EX 26.10.
Owner Christopher James Allan **Bred** Paul Hensey **Trained** Settrington, N Yorks

FOCUS
The second leg of this handicap was 0.43 seconds faster than the first. Fair form.
Conry(IRE) Official explanation: jockey said gelding hung left
Malcheek(IRE) Official explanation: jockey said gelding ran too free
Internationaldebut(IRE) Official explanation: jockey said gelding was unsuited by the good to soft (soft in places) ground

7147 RACING UK ON SKY 432 H'CAP (DIV I) 1m 3f 214y
4:20 (4:21) (Class 6) (0-60,60) 3-Y-O+ **£1,706** (£503; £252) **Stalls High**

Form RPR
0060 **1** **Emirate Isle**[21] 6648 6-9-0 **48** (p) PJMcDonald 4 57
(B Storey) *hld up in midfield: rdn and hdwy to chse ldrs over 4f out: drvn over 1f out: kpt on to ld fnl 100yds* **33/1**
2-00 **2** nk **Flora's Pride**[11] 6890 6-9-3 **51** TonyCulhane 12 60
(K G Reveley) *hld up: hdwy on outer to trck ldrs 5f out: rdn to chal fr over 2f out: led narrowly 1f out: hdd fnl 100yds: kpt on* **12/1**
1144 **3** 2 **Straversjoy**[22] 6631 3-9-5 **60** GrahamGibbons 6 66
(R Hollinshead) *midfield: hdwy to trck ldrs 6f out: rdn to ld narrowly over 2f out: hdd 1f out: no ex fnl 100yds* **7/2**[1]
5300 **4** 4 **Miereveld**[24] 6571 3-8-6 **47** SilvestreDeSousa 9 46
(B Ellison) *midfield: drvn 4f out: chsd ldrs 2f out: kpt on* **10/1**
4060 **5** 3 **Yossi (IRE)**[14] 6832 6-9-10 **58** (b) PaulHanagan 8 53
(R C Guest) *sn led: rdn whn hdd over 2f out: wknd ins fnl f* **5/1**[2]
410 **6** 1 **Deejan (IRE)**[31] 6373 5-9-12 **60** DavidProbert 15 53
(B Palling) *prom: rdn 4f out: lost pl over 2f out: wknd 1f out* **5/1**[2]
0300 **7** 7 **Maybeme**[11] 6890 4-9-2 **50** FrannyNorton 14 32
(N Bycroft) *hld up: rdn over 3f out: n.d* **8/1**
0000 **8** 3 1/2 **Shanavaz**[21] 6648 4-8-12 **46** oh1 (p) LeeVickers 5 22
(C J Teague) *sn prom: rdn and lost pl over 4f out: wknd 3f out* **80/1**
5300 **9** 8 **Fantastic Storm**[27] 6472 3-8-2 **46** oh1 (v) PaulPickard(3) 11 9
(R Bastiman) *trckd ldrs: rdn over 4f out: wknd over 2f out* **16/1**
0650 **10** 3 1/2 **Classic Contours (USA)**[86] 4246 4-9-9 **60** IanBrennan(3) 3 18
(J J Quinn) *midfield: rdn over 4f out: sn no imp* **13/2**[3]
000/ **11** 9 **Strathaird (IRE)**[800] 6505 6-8-9 **46** oh1 (v[1]) KellyHarrison(3) 10 —
(A Crook) *s.i.s: hld up: a bhd* **100/1**
0000 **12** 1 1/2 **Transfered (IRE)**[10] 6933 4-8-9 **46** oh1 RussKennemore(3) 7 —
(Lucinda Featherstone) *hld up: rdn over 5f out: a towards rr* **25/1**
6345 **13** 15 **Red Valerian Two (IRE)**[190] 1422 3-8-9 **50** BarryMcHugh 2 —
(P T Midgley) *hld up: rdn over 5f out: a towards rr* **20/1**
14 39 **Waldsee (GER)**[350] 5-9-8 **56** JamesDoyle 1 —
(S Curran) *midfield: lost pl over 4f out: sn wknd: eased fnl 2f* **18/1**
20/0 **15** 23 **Gramm**[131] 3119 7-8-11 **52** DavidSimmonson(7) 13 —
(G P Kelly) *trckd ldrs: lost pl qckly after 4f: t.o fnl 5f* **66/1**

2m 47.79s (8.89) **Going Correction** +0.625s/f (Yiel)
WFA 3 from 4yo+ 7lb **15** Ran SP% **123.2**
Speed ratings (Par 101): **95,94,93,90,88 88,83,81,75,73 67,66,56,30,15**
toteswingers:1&2 £80.60, 2&3 £12.50, 1&3 £31.00 CSF £382.37 CT £1759.83 TOTE £45.20: £13.80, £1.70, £2.00; EX 326.90.
Owner John Wade **Bred** J Wade **Trained** Boltonfellend, Cumbria
■ Trainer Brian Storey's first Flat winner.
■ Stewards' Enquiry : P J McDonald four-day ban: used whip with excessive frequency (Nov 10-13)

FOCUS
A moderate contest in which they raced middle to stands' side. It was the quicker division. The winner showed his first Flat form for two years, but the form seems sound.
Waldsee(GER) Official explanation: jockey said gelding lost its action but returned sound
Gramm Official explanation: trainer said gelding was unsuited by the good to soft (soft in places) ground

7148 COME RACING AGAIN NEXT TUESDAY H'CAP 5f
4:50 (4:50) (Class 6) (0-65,68) 3-Y-O+ **£2,047** (£604; £302) **Stalls Low**

Form RPR
4061 **1** **Fashion Icon (USA)**[21] 6644 4-8-8 **52** (b) SilvestreDeSousa 7 64
(D O'Meara) *w ldr: led after 1f and crossed to stands' side rail: kpt on wl ins fnl f* **7/2**[1]
3541 **2** 1 1/4 **Avonvalley**[7] 6996 3-9-5 **68** 6ex AdamBeschizza(5) 1 75
(George Baker) *mid-div towards centre: hdwy 2f out: chsd wnr 1f out: edgd rt: kpt on same pce* **11/2**[3]
3266 **3** 4 1/2 **First Swallow**[12] 6880 5-9-2 **60** (t) PhillipMakin 8 51
(D H Brown) *led 1f: chsd ldrs: one pce ins fnl f* **6/1**
0504 **4** 1/2 **Miss Daawe**[41] 6073 6-8-9 **58** DaleSwift(5) 12 47
(B Ellison) *chsd ldrs: outpcd over 2f out: kpt on ins fnl f* **5/1**[2]
1003 **5** nse **Prince James**[10] 6932 3-9-1 **62** JamesSullivan(3) 3 51+
(M W Easterby) *dwlt: sn outpcd and in rr: hdwy in centre 1f out: fin wl* **12/1**
5200 **6** 1 1/4 **Liberty Ship**[41] 6073 5-9-6 **64** (b) PaulHanagan 9 49
(J D Bethell) *chsd ldrs: wknd fnl f* **8/1**
0400 **7** 1/2 **Ursus**[38] 6189 5-8-11 **55** RoystonFfrench 10 38
(C R Wilson) *mid-div: effrt 2f out: one pce whn n.m.r ins fnl f* **9/1**
2050 **8** nk **Newbury Street**[4] 7051 3-9-7 **65** AndrewElliott 6 47
(P F Holmes) *chsd ldrs towards centre: wknd over 1f out* **22/1**
6200 **9** 1 3/4 **Your Gifted (IRE)**[9] 6965 3-8-13 **57** StephenCraine 11 32
(Patrick Morris) *mid-div: hdwy over 2f out: wknd ins fnl f* **25/1**
5230 **10** 2 3/4 **Gower Sophia**[27] 6464 3-8-7 **51** oh1 FrannyNorton 13 16
(M Brittain) *chsd ldrs: lost pl over 2f out* **12/1**
0000 **11** 1 **Azygous**[41] 6073 7-8-7 **51** oh2 BarryMcHugh 5 13
(G P Kelly) *sn outpcd and in rr* **28/1**
0500 **12** 10 **Miacarla**[36] 6246 7-8-7 **51** oh6 (p) PatrickMathers 4 —
(H A McWilliams) *hood removed v late: sn outpcd and in rr: bhd whn eased* **50/1**

61.72 secs (1.92) **Going Correction** +0.425s/f (Yiel) **12** Ran SP% **118.7**
Speed ratings (Par 101): **101,99,91,91,90 88,88,87,84,80 78,62**
toteswingers:1&2 £3.20, 2&3 £10.50, 1&3 £4.40 CSF £21.30 CT £115.40 TOTE £3.70: £1.60, £3.60, £1.10; EX 28.10.
Owner Trendy Ladies **Bred** Mr & Mrs Theodore Kuster **Trained** Nawton, N Yorks

FOCUS
A moderate contest in which Silvestre De Sousa was once again seen to good effect, improving his tremendous record at Catterick to 37-177 - he's ridden more winners here than anywhere else in Britain. First-season trainer David O'Meara also deserves a mention, this being his 24th victory of the campaign, and together the partnership moved on to 18-71. The winner is rated to the best view of her previous form.

7149 RACING UK ON SKY 432 H'CAP (DIV II) 1m 3f 214y
5:20 (5:20) (Class 6) (0-60,60) 3-Y-O+ **£1,706** (£503; £252) **Stalls High**

Form RPR
6020 **1** **Without Equal**[10] 6915 4-9-0 **48** PJMcDonald 3 56
(N Wilson) *midfield: reminders over 8f out: hdwy to chse ldrs over 6f out: led wl over 3f out: drvn over 1f out: jst hld on* **20/1**
0402 **2** nk **Lady Norlela**[10] 6915 4-8-12 **53** TimothyAyres(7) 14 60
(B S Rothwell) *hld up: sltly hmpd on inner wl over 2f out: racd alone far side st: hdwy 2f out: chal 1f out: ev ch ins fnl f: edgd rt ins fnl 100yds: jst failed* **14/1**
0232 **3** nse **Rosewin (IRE)**[21] 6649 4-9-8 **59** JamesSullivan(3) 4 66
(Ollie Pears) *midfield: rdn to chse ldrs 4f out: drvn 3f out: styd on wl u.p ins fnl f: jst failed* **6/4**[1]
2003 **4** 6 **Leaving Alone (USA)**[33] 6306 3-8-10 **58** (p) AdamCarter(7) 5 55
(E W Tuer) *chsd ldrs: rdn over 3f out: sn one pce* **10/1**
0564 **5** hd **Spahi (FR)**[10] 6921 4-9-9 **57** SilvestreDeSousa 6 54+
(D O'Meara) *hld up: racd keenly: smooth hdwy to trck ldrs over 2f out: rdn over 1f out: sn one pce: wknd ins fnl f* **7/2**[2]
0304 **6** 2 3/4 **Barbirolli**[21] 6662 8-8-5 **46** oh1 LauraPike(7) 7 39
(W B Stone) *midfield: hdwy 7f out: prom 4f out: rdn 3f out: wknd over 1f out* **12/1**
0500 **7** 1/2 **The Midshipmaid**[22] 6623 3-8-2 **46** oh1 AmyRyan(3) 13 38
(Lucinda Featherstone) *sn led: hdd wl over 3f out: wknd over 1f out* **66/1**
600/ **8** 2 **Little Lily Morgan**[148] 600 7-8-9 **46** oh1 PaulPickard(3) 11 35
(R Bastiman) *slowly away: hld up: n.d* **100/1**
00-0 **9** 1 1/4 **Diktalina**[31] 5940 4-8-13 **50** (tp) RussKennemore(3) 10 37
(Mrs A M Thorpe) *trckd ldrs tl wknd over 3f out* **7/1**[3]
5000 **10** 8 **Refuse To Wait (IRE)**[11] 6890 3-8-12 **53** (b) DavidAllan 12 27
(T D Easterby) *prom tl wknd over 4f out* **20/1**
6003 **11** 35 **Bold Indian (IRE)**[35] 6269 6-9-4 **52** PhillipMakin 2 —
(M E Sowersby) *hld up in midfield: rdn over 3f out: sn wknd* **14/1**
-50P **12** dist **Ilkley**[62] 5423 3-8-7 **48** GrahamGibbons 9 —
(M W Easterby) *trckd ldrs: lost pl over 7f out: sn wknd: t.o whn virtually p.u over 1f out* **28/1**

2m 49.33s (10.43) **Going Correction** +0.625s/f (Yiel)
WFA 3 from 4yo+ 7lb **12** Ran SP% **120.3**
Speed ratings (Par 101): **90,89,89,85,85 83,83,82,81,75 52,—**
toteswingers:1&2 £16.40, 2&3 £4.90, 1&3 £8.70 totesuper7: Win: Not won. Place: Not won. CSF £265.17 CT £682.86 TOTE £28.70: £6.00, £5.30, £1.40; EX 149.20 Place 6 £138.59 Place 5: £51.13.
Owner K Fitzsimons **Bred** The Brookfield Stud **Trained** Sandhutton, N Yorks

FOCUS
The time was 1.54 seconds slower than the first division and the form is not the most convincing.
Refuse To Wait(IRE) Official explanation: jockey said filly suffered interference in running
T/Jkpt: Not won. T/Plt: £38.10 to a £1 stake. Pool of £60,976.80 - 1,165.98 winning tickets.
T/Qpdt: £19.40 to a £1 stake. Pool of £4,968.92 - 188.60 winning tickets. AS

7000 YARMOUTH (L-H)

Tuesday, October 26

OFFICIAL GOING: Heavy (soft in places) changing to heavy after race 4 (3.00)

Wind: fresh, across Weather: cold, light rain

7150 EUROPEAN BREEDERS' FUND BET365.COM MAIDEN STKS 7f 3y

1:30 (1:31) (Class 5) 2-Y-O £2,978 (£886; £442; £221) Stalls High

Form RPR

1 **First Mohican** 2-9-3 0 IanMongan 8 77
(H R A Cecil) *hld up in tch: hdwy to join ldrs: ev ch 2f out: rn green and hanging lft after: led ins fnl f: stl hanging: forged ahd fnl 75yds* **12/1**[3]

3 2 2 **Long Awaited (IRE)**[14] 6828 2-9-3 0 PhilipRobinson 2 73
(M A Jarvis) *trckd ldrs: hdwy to ld wl over 1f out: rdn along and clr w wnr over 1f out: hdd ins fnl f: wknd towards fin* **4/9**[1]

0 3 ¾ **Orthodox Lad**[39] 6153 2-9-0 0 KierenFox(3) 6 70
(J R Best) *in tch: rdn and effrt to chse ldrs over 1f out: edging lft but kpt on ins fnl f* **100/1**

0 4 shd **Tidal Star**[39] 6158 2-9-3 0 AdamKirby 5 70
(M G Quinlan) *stdd s: hld up in last pair: effrt to chse clr ldng pair and rn green over 1f out: kpt on ins fnl f* **33/1**

0 5 8 **Twinkled**[14] 6828 2-9-3 0 HayleyTurner 7 50
(M L W Bell) *stdd s: in tch in rr but sn niggled along: rdn and struggling 1/2-way: no ch fr wl over 2f out* **40/1**

32 6 1 ¾ **Above All**[28] 6442 2-9-3 0 RichardHills 1 45
(W J Haggas) *led tl ent fnl 2f: immediately dropped out: wl btn over 1f out* **11/4**[2]

04 7 11 **Ace Master**[20] 6675 2-8-10 0 RyanClark(7) 3 —
(S R Bowring) *chsd ldr tl led ent fnl 2f: sn rdn and hdd wl over 1f out: immediately dropped out: wl bhd ent fnl f* **100/1**

1m 36.18s (9.58) **Going Correction** +1.20s/f (Soft) **7** Ran SP% **111.0**
Speed ratings (Par 95): **93,90,89,89,80 78,66**
toteswingers:1&2 £2.20, 2&3 £10.60, 1&3 £7.20 CSF £17.40 TOTE £9.40: £4.70, £1.10; EX 10.50 Trifecta £247.20 Pool: £444.41 - 1.33 winning units..
Owner W H Ponsonby **Bred** Bottisham Heath Stud **Trained** Newmarket, Suffolk
■ Stewards' Enquiry : Ian Mongan caution: used whip down shoulder in the forehand,

FOCUS
After a dry night, racing began on ground that was officially heavy, soft in places. However, rain started to fall before the opener, which was a moderate juvenile maiden. They raced up the centre of the course. The first four finished clear and the form is rated tentatively around the winner.

NOTEBOOK
First Mohican, a colt with a Derby entry, made an encouraging start to his career. Held up in touch in the early stages, he eased into fourth 3f out and made his challenge towards the stands' side of the field. Responding well to pressure, he quickened up to lead inside the last furlong and scored with a little in hand. Judged strictly on this effort, he will probably be contesting handicaps next season. (op 10-1 tchd 14-1)
Long Awaited(IRE), third over this trip in an ordinary maiden at Leicester on his only previous start, failed to justify surprisingly short odds. Never far off the pace, he led 2f out, but was unable to establish a decisive advantage and failed to quicken when the winner came alongside. (op 4-7 tchd 4-6 in places)
Orthodox Lad, not beaten all that far at Newmarket on his only previous outing, improved on that display. He raced in fourth for much of the journey and gained a place in the closing stages. Despite slight doubts on pedigree, he stayed this trip well.
Tidal Star, a well-beaten favourite for his debut while in a different yard, was another to show more on his second start. He will need to progress significantly again, though, in order to land an average maiden. (op 28-1)
Twinkled had shown a glimmer of ability behind Long Awaited on his debut, but failed to build on it here. He was never in the hunt. (op 50-1)
Above All, who had dead-heated for second in a below-average Newbury maiden last time, did nothing to advertise that form. He led until 3f out, but was soon left behind when the principals kicked for home. (op 5-2)
Ace Master Official explanation: trainer said gelding was unsuited by the heavy (soft in places) ground

7151 BET365 NURSERY 7f 3y

2:00 (2:00) (Class 5) (0-75,75) 2-Y-O £2,266 (£674; £337; £168) Stalls High

Form RPR

0005 1 **Focail Maith**[29] 6411 2-8-9 **63** ow1 (b[1]) StevieDonohoe 3 71
(J Ryan) *chsd ldrs: rdn to ld and edgd lft over 1f out: drvn clr ins fnl f: in command whn hung lft towards fin* **7/1**

624 2 3 ¾ **Avid Kale**[53] 5724 2-9-5 **73** ChrisCatlin 1 72
(M Botti) *in tch: rdn and effrt over 2f out: pressed wnr u.p over 1f out: wknd ins fnl f* **7/2**[3]

0535 3 3 ½ **Franciscan**[11] 6902 2-8-13 **67** KierenFallon 5 58
(L M Cumani) *stmbld s: in tch in last pair: rdn over 3f out: struggling u.p over 2f out: no ch w ldrs fr over 1f out: kpt on u.p to go modest 3rd fnl 75yds* **11/4**[2]

2110 4 2 ¼ **Cometh**[32] 6317 2-9-2 **70** MartinLane 6 54
(N P Littmoden) *racd keenly: chsd ldr tl led jst over 2f out: sn rdn: hdd over 1f out: wknd ent fnl f* **5/2**[1]

5413 5 2 ¼ **Hawk Moth (IRE)**[27] 6453 2-8-13 **67** CathyGannon 4 46
(J L Spearing) *stdd s: hld up in last pair: rdn and effrt wl over 2f out: no prog and wl btn over 1f out* **6/1**

004 6 10 **Gothic Chick**[26] 6512 2-9-0 **68** (p) JamieMackay 7 22
(Miss Amy Weaver) *racd keenly: led tl jst over 2f out: sn dropped out: wl bhd over 1f out* **18/1**

1m 35.87s (9.27) **Going Correction** +1.20s/f (Soft) **6** Ran SP% **109.5**
Speed ratings (Par 95): **95,90,86,84,81 70**
toteswingers:1&2 £4.60, 2&3 £1.30, 1&3 £4.90 CSF £29.74 TOTE £10.30: £3.90, £3.40; EX 39.90.
Owner Cathal Fegan **Bred** D Robb **Trained** Newmarket, Suffolk

FOCUS
Just a run-of-the-mill nursery. This time they raced a few horse widths off the stands' rail. The form has been rated conservatively given the conditions and the time of year.

NOTEBOOK
Focail Maith, whose best form gave him a major chance, was fitted with first-time blinkers and they had the desired effect. Despite carrying 1lb overweight, he was always chasing the pace and quickened best in the closing stages. He wandered a little on the softening ground, but still scored decisively. Whether he can follow-up once reassessed, though, remains to be seen. Official explanation: trainer said, regarding apparent improvement in form, that the colt benefited from the first time blinkers and was suited by the heavy (soft in places) ground (op 6-1 tchd 15-2)
Avid Kale was making his first appearance in a handicap after three mildly encouraging runs in maidens, and has clearly been given a rating from which he can be competitive. Close up from the start, he plugged on gamely without exhibiting the winner's finishing kick. (op 5-1)
Franciscan, third to two subsequent winners at Nottingham in late-September, lost ground when seeming to stumble at the start. That meant he was always playing catch-up and, although he finished quite powerfully, he could never get to grips with the first two. Kieren Fallon reported that the colt lost his two front shoes. Official explanation: jockey said colt lost both front shoes (op 5-2 tchd 3-1)
Cometh, who made all when scoring over C&D in mid-September, was rather disappointing. She raced in second early on and led briefly 2f out, but then faded tamely. It may just be that her rating is now too high. (op 11-4 tchd 3-1)
Hawk Moth(IRE), a solid third off this mark at Kempton last time out, did not seem nearly as effective on this switch to turf. (op 5-1 tchd 9-2)
Gothic Chick had apparently shown improvement when filling fourth at Warwick last time out, but that performance had come in a slowly-run affair and there remains a suspicion that she was flattered. (op 14-1 tchd 12-1 and 20-1)

7152 EUROPEAN BREEDERS' FUND BET365 MAIDEN STKS 1m 3y

2:30 (2:32) (Class 5) 2-Y-O £2,901 (£868; £434; £217; £108) Stalls High

Form RPR

2 1 **Sea Moon**[14] 6831 2-9-3 0 RyanMoore 12 82+
(Sir Michael Stoute) *chsd ldrs: hdwy to ld on bit over 2f out: rdn along hands and heels and hanging lft fr over 1f out: clr w rival 1f out: stl hanging asserted ins fnl f* **1/5**[1]

2 2 1 **Little Rocky**[12] 6873 2-9-3 0 WilliamBuick 3 80+
(D M Simcock) *hld up towards rr: hdwy to chse ldrs 3f out: rdn to chal over 1f out: clr w wnr 1f out: no ex and btn fnl 75yds* **10/1**[3]

3 9 **Hawawi** 2-9-3 0 TedDurcan 1 62+
(D R Lanigan) *wnt lft s and s.i.s: hld up in rr: hdwy and rn green wl over 2f out: kpt on to go modest 3rd ins fnl f: nvr trbld ldrs* **33/1**

4 1 **Raw Spirit (GER)** 2-9-3 0 FrankieDettori 7 60+
(Saeed Bin Suroor) *stdd s: hld up in rr: hdwy 1/2-way: chsd ldng pair and rdn wl over 1f out: wknd over 1f out: lost 3rd ins fnl f* **13/2**[2]

5 4 **Aussie Dollar (IRE)** 2-9-3 0 JimmyFortune 15 49
(A M Balding) *in tch in midfield: rdn and effrt to chse ldrs over 2f out: wknd over 1f out: 5th and wl btn ins fnl f* **50/1**

0 6 5 **Border Abby**[15] 6803 2-8-12 0 MartinLane 14 33
(Rae Guest) *in tch in midfield: rdn and effrt to chse ldrs over 2f out: wknd wl over 1f out: wl btn ins fnl f* **80/1**

00 7 1 ¼ **Maharana (USA)**[12] 6873 2-9-3 0 JamieSpencer 5 35
(M L W Bell) *in tch in midfield: hdwy to chse ldrs and rdn 3f out: wknd qckly wl over 1f out* **20/1**

00 8 6 **If What And Maybe**[26] 6504 2-9-3 0 AdamKirby 6 22
(J Ryan) *led: rdn ent fnl 3f: hdd over 2f out: wknd 2f out: sn wl btn* **100/1**

00 9 5 **Easydoesit (IRE)**[17] 6743 2-9-3 0 CathyGannon 8 11
(D Donovan) *chsd ldr tl wl over 2f out: sn struggling u.p: wl btn fnl 2f: t.o* **200/1**

10 1 **Flying Power** 2-9-3 0 ChrisCatlin 9 9
(D R Lanigan) *stdd s: hld up in rr: rdn ent fnl 3f: sme hdwy over 2f out: struggling and btn 2f out: no ch over 1f out: t.o* **100/1**

11 6 **Strangelittlegirl** 2-8-12 0 StevieDonohoe 2 —
(P Leech) *a bhd: rdn and struggling 1/2-way: t.o fnl 2f* **100/1**

12 2 ¼ **Durante Alighieri** 2-9-3 0 IanMongan 13 —
(H R A Cecil) *awkward leaving stalls and s.i.s: hld up towards rr: rdn and effrt ent fnl 3f: sn btn and wl bhd: t.o* **12/1**

0 13 15 **Final Liberation (FR)**[17] 6743 2-9-3 0 SebSanders 10 —
(Sir Mark Prescott) *a towards rr: rdn and lost tch over 3f out: t.o fnl 2f* **150/1**

0 14 30 **Generous Pursuit**[11] 6884 2-8-12 0 TomMcLaughlin 4 —
(P S McEntee) *chsd ldrs tl over 3f out: sn lost pl: wl t.o fnl 2f* **250/1**

1m 50.93s (10.33) **Going Correction** +1.325s/f (Soft) **14** Ran SP% **128.9**
Speed ratings (Par 95): **101,100,91,90,86 81,79,73,68,67 61,59,44,14**
toteswingers:1&2 £2.50, 2&3 £14.50, 1&3 £8.20 CSF £4.07 TOTE £1.40: £1.02, £1.90, £7.70; EX 5.40 Trifecta £50.40 Pool of : £576.67 - 8.46 winning units..
Owner K Abdulla **Bred** Juddmonte Farms Ltd **Trained** Newmarket, Suffolk
■ Stewards' Enquiry : William Buick caution: used whip down shoulder in the forehand

FOCUS
An interesting two-year-old maiden, featuring a hot-favourite and a clutch of well-bred newcomers. They raced up the centre. Good efforts from the first two to pull well clear, and promise from the third and fourth.

NOTEBOOK
Sea Moon, touched off at Leicester when market-leader on his only previous start, was backed this time to the exclusion of all the rest and duly went one better. A relative of Derby/Arc hero Workforce, he was no better than workmanlike, however, and will need to do a lot better in order to live up to his promising pedigree. The ground will not have helped, of course, and his jockey was not hard on him, but nobody should get over-excited about the standard he needed to achieve to register this victory. (op 2-5 tchd 1-2 in a place)
Little Rocky, second in an ordinary Nottingham maiden first time out, improved on that effort and kept the winner honest throughout the final furlong. Having been held up in the early stages, he went into second 2f out and kept galloping all the way to the line. (op 9-1)
Hawawi, a first-time-out son of Motivator, made an encouraging start to his career. Well in arrears early on, he picked off at least a half-dozen rivals in the the last couple of furlongs. He ought to be able to win a maiden at some stage and will probably stay middle-distances next term. (tchd 40-1)
Raw Spirit(GER), a 160,000gns newcomer with a Derby entry, was another to suggest that there is better to come. Ridden patiently, he was plugging on gamely in the closing stages. (op 11-2)
Aussie Dollar(IRE), yet another newcomer from a smart family, ran creditably enough, even though he was a long way behind the principals. He was unable to quicken in the final furlong, after racing in midfield from the outset, but will surely show more as he matures.
Border Abby improved on a modest debut effort at Salisbury. She had been slowly away there, but broke better here and was always in the leading five or six.

7153 BET365 H'CAP 7f 3y

3:00 (3:02) (Class 6) (0-60,60) 3-Y-O £1,942 (£578; £288; £144) Stalls High

Form RPR

1351 1 **Franki J**[7] 7006 3-9-5 **60** 6ex SophieDoyle(3) 4 77+
(D Donovan) *mde all: clr fr over 2f out: pushed out: easily* **6/4**[1]

5203 2 6 **Via Aurelia (IRE)**[12] 6863 3-9-5 **57** (b[1]) HayleyTurner 12 58
(J R Fanshawe) *stdd s: hld up in rr: hdwy and swtchd lft over 2f out: chsd clr wnr 2f out: rdn over 1f out: no imp and wl hld after* **7/1**[3]

555 3 1 ½ **Miss Blink**[42] 6060 3-8-11 **49** RobertWinston 10 46
(R Bastiman) *towards rr: rdn and nt clr run wl over 3f out: hdwy over 2f out: swtchd lft over 1f out: no ch w wnr but kpt on u.p to go 3rd fnl 100yds* **33/1**

3064 4 1 ¼ **Reddy To Star (IRE)**[11] 6897 3-9-5 **57** PaulMulrennan 13 50
(Julie Camacho) *racd in midfield: rdn over 3f out: switching lft ent fnl 2f: no ch w wnr fnl 2f: plugged on u.p* **33/1**

006 5 1 **Zarius**[21] 6655 3-9-5 **57** TedDurcan 6 48
(C F Wall) *t.k.h: hld up in tch: rdn and effrt over 2f out: hung rt and outpcd by wnr 2f out: plugged on same pce and wl btn over 1f out* **33/1**

-030 **6** 1 ½ **Dudley**[25] 6522 3-8-11 **49**......(p) CathyGannon 3 36
(J G Portman) *in tch in midfield: rdn and effrt over 2f out: chsd ldng pair wl over 1f out: no prog and wl btn over 1f out* **50/1**

0305 **7** 10 **House Point**[7] 7005 3-9-2 **54**......(p) AdamKirby 1 14+
(S C Williams) *racd in centre trio: s.i.s: sn pushed along and reminder after 1f: nvr bttr than midfield overall: wl btn fnl 2f* **9/2**[2]

0306 **8** 10 **Thewinnatakesitall**[27] 6464 3-8-5 **46**......(p) Louis-PhilippeBeuzelin(3) 11 —
(N Tinkler) *racd keenly: chsd wnr tl 1/2-way: sn struggling: wl btn ent fnl 2f* **66/1**

2302 **9** 2 ¾ **Broctune Papa Gio**[50] 5821 3-8-12 **50**...... NeilCallan 9 —
(K G Reveley) *chsd ldrs: wnt 2nd 1/2-way tl 2f out: sn wknd: wl btn and eased ins fnl f: t.o* **7/1**[3]

0 **10** 1 ¼ **Book Smart (IRE)**[16] 6773 3-8-4 **45**...... KierenFox(3) 7 —
(Miss Gay Kelleway) *towards rr and rdn over 4f out: wl bhd fnl 2f: eased ins fnl f: t.o* **100/1**

4606 **11** 2 ¾ **Far View (IRE)**[11] 6903 3-9-6 **58**......(t) SebSanders 8 —
(J W Hills) *stdd s: t.k.h: hld up in rr: hdwy over 3f out: rdn and hung lft over 2f out: sn wknd: wl bhd and eased ins fnl f: t.o* **16/1**

02 **12** 3 ¾ **No Complaining (IRE)**[53] 5729 3-8-11 **49**...... MickyFenton 14 —
(B J Curley) *restless in stalls: chsd ldrs tl over 3f out: sn lost pl and wl bhd fnl 2f: eased ins fnl f* **14/1**

-443 **13** 3 ¼ **Tsar Bomba (USA)**[11] 6896 3-9-7 **59**...... JamieSpencer 5 —
(T D Barron) *racd in centre trio: nvr trbld ldrs: wl bhd fnl 2f: eased ins fnl f: t.o* **7/1**[3]

4600 **14** ½ **Miss Kitty Grey (IRE)**[5] 7037 3-9-6 **58**...... JimmyFortune 2 —
(J R Boyle) *racd in centre trio: nvr trbld ldrs: wl bhd fnl 2f: eased ins fnl f: t.o* **33/1**

1m 35.97s (9.37) **Going Correction** +1.325s/f (Soft) **14 Ran SP% 124.4**
Speed ratings (Par 99): **99,92,90,89,87 86,74,63,60,58 55,51,47,47**
toteswingers:1&2 £4.90, 2&3 £4.00, 1&3 £6.50 CSF £12.32 CT £272.43 TOTE £2.70: £1.40, £2.40, £6.10; EX 12.30 Trifecta £355.50 Pool: £643.81 - 1.34 winning units..
Owner River Racing **Bred** Mrs A M Upsdell **Trained** Newmarket, Suffolk

FOCUS
A moderate handicap, with the penalised top weight rated 60. The field spilt into two groups, with the larger contingent closer to the stands' rail. The winner last week's romp in this weak race.

7154 BET365.COM H'CAP (DIV I) 5f 43y
3:30 (3:33) (Class 6) (0-60,60) 3-Y-0+ **£1,619** (£481; £240; £120) **Stalls** High

Form RPR

142 **1** **Kate Skate**[7] 6996 3-9-4 **60**...... KierenFox(3) 9 67
(Miss Gay Kelleway) *hld up in tch in rr: rdn and hdwy on outer over 2f out: chsd ldr wl over 1f out: kpt on wl to ld ins fnl f: rdn out* **10/1**

6203 **2** 1 **Choc'A'Moca (IRE)**[4] 7052 3-8-11 **55**......(v) NeilFarley(5) 5 58
(D Carroll) *pressed ldrs tl led ent fnl 2f: sn rdn: clr over 1f out: hdd and no ex ins fnl f* **3/1**[1]

0103 **3** 2 ¼ **Bouncy Bouncy (IRE)**[12] 6880 3-9-2 **55**......(t) HayleyTurner 11 50
(M L W Bell) *hld up in tch towards rr: nt clr run over 2f out: rdn wl over 1f out: no ch w ldng pair: kpt on ins fnl f to go 3rd fnl 50yds* **11/2**

3000 **4** ¾ **Speak The Truth (IRE)**[12] 6880 4-9-7 **60**......(p) JimmyFortune 8 52
(J R Boyle) *in tch: rdn and effrt ent fnl 2f: chsd ldng pair u.p over 1f out: no prog and btn fnl 150yds: lost 3rd fnl 50yds* **7/1**

3625 **5** 1 ¼ **Yankee Storm**[7] 7006 5-9-5 **58**......(v) DarryllHolland 7 46
(H J Collingridge) *hld up in tch towards rr: rdn and effrt ent fnl 2f: no imp u.p ent fnl f* **7/2**[2]

0000 **6** nk **Ariel Bender**[10] 6931 3-8-0 **46** oh1......(b) LeonnaMayor(7) 10 33
(Peter Grayson) *hld up in rr: rdn and no prog 2f out: styd on wl past btn horses ins fnl f: nvr trbld ldrs* **100/1**

6360 **7** 2 **Tartufo Dolce (IRE)**[27] 6464 3-9-4 **57**...... PaulMulrennan 3 36
(J G Given) *w ldrs: rdn and sltly outpcd whn short of room and swtchd rt 2f out: sn drvn: wknd jst over 1f out* **33/1**

4200 **8** 11 **Mr Funshine**[12] 6880 5-8-13 **52**...... NeilCallan 2 —
(D Shaw) *led: rdn and hdd ent fnl 2f: sn edgd rt u.p: wknd over 1f out: wl btn and eased ins fnl f* **9/1**

3053 **9** ¾ **Gracie's Games**[21] 6656 4-8-10 **54**......(v) TobyAtkinson(5) 1 —
(R J Price) *wnt lft s: sn in tch in midfield: rdn and unable qck over 2f out: wknd 2f out: wl btn and eased ins fnl f* **5/1**[3]

5000 **10** 7 **Albaher**[40] 6119 4-8-7 **46** oh1......(b) PaulEddery 4 —
(Peter Grayson) *racd keenly: chsd ldrs: rdn and struggling 1/2-way: bhd fnl 2f: eased ins fnl f* **66/1**

1m 10.28s (7.58) **Going Correction** +1.45s/f (Soft) **10 Ran SP% 116.3**
Speed ratings (Par 101): **97,95,91,90,88 88,84,67,66,54**
toteswingers:1&2 £4.90, 2&3 £4.00, 1&3 £6.50 CSF £39.92 CT £191.95 TOTE £9.70: £2.20, £2.00, £2.10; EX 59.30 Trifecta £168.30 Pool of £518.84 - 2.28 winning units..
Owner Nightmare Partnership **Bred** R A Instone **Trained** Exning, Suffolk
■ Stewards' Enquiry : Kieren Fox one-day ban: used whip with excessive frequency (Nov 10)

FOCUS
A modest contest, but apparently competitive on paper. Most of these headed for the stands' rail after leaving the stalls. A length personal best from the winner.

7155 BET365.COM H'CAP (DIV II) 5f 43y
4:00 (4:01) (Class 6) (0-60,60) 3-Y-0+ **£1,619** (£481; £240; £120) **Stalls** High

Form RPR

0200 **1** **First Blade**[40] 6110 4-9-7 **60**......(b) RobertWinston 7 69+
(S R Bowring) *towards rr: sn pushed along and hdwy over 2f out: squeezed between horses and rdn to chse ldr over 1f out: led ins fnl f: styd on strly and clr towards fin* **11/2**[3]

445/ **2** 1 ¼ **Dontforgeturshovel**[693] 7530 4-8-4 **46**...... SimonPearce(3) 1 50
(J Pearce) *dropped in bhd after s: sn pushed along in rr: hdwy and n.m.r 2f out: swtchd lft and wnt between horses over 1f out: rdn and chsd ldng pair ent fnl f: wnt 2nd and kpt on same pce fnl 100yds* **10/1**

2300 **3** 2 ¾ **Guto**[7] 7007 7-8-13 **59**...... MatthewCosham(7) 10 53
(W J H Ratcliffe) *chsd ldrs tl led 1/2-way: rdn wl over 1f out: hdd ins fnl f: wknd fnl 100yds* **4/1**[2]

0500 **4** 1 ¾ **Mr Skipiton (IRE)**[20] 6679 5-9-2 **55**...... TomMcLaughlin 8 42
(B J McMath) *dwlt and short of room s: sn bustled along in rr: hdwy u.p over 1f out: chsd ldng trio 1f out: wknd u.p ins fnl f* **7/2**[1]

0240 **5** 3 **Big Boom**[7] 7005 5-9-2 **55**......(b) MartinLane 6 32
(M Quinn) *nvr gng wl: sn pushed along in midfield: edgd lft u.p and dropped to rr ent fnl 2f: no ch w ldrs: plugged on u.p fr over 1f out* **7/2**[1]

6000 **6** 3 **Alsufooh (USA)**[6] 7018 3-9-2 **55**...... AdamKirby 3 21
(D Shaw) *a towards rr: rdn along over 3f out: nvr gng pce to trble ldrs* **16/1**

0400 **7** nk **Spring Horizon (IRE)**[34] 6285 4-8-7 **46** oh1......(p) KirstyMilczarek 5 11
(Miss Z C Davison) *led tl 1/2-way: wknd u.p wl over 1f out* **22/1**

6600 **8** ½ **Replicator**[11] 6898 5-9-2 **58**......(e) AshleyHamblett(3) 9 21
(P L Gilligan) *in tch: effrt to chse ldrs and pushed lft wl over 1f out: sn wknd u.p: wl btn and eased ins fnl f* **10/1**

6000 **9** 6 **Jemimaville (IRE)**[7] 7005 3-9-0 **53**......(v) WilliamCarson 4 —
(G C Bravery) *taken down early: w ldr tl 1/2-way: struggling u.p whn pushed lft wl over 1f out: sn bhd: eased ins fnl f* **16/1**

1m 10.52s (7.82) **Going Correction** +1.45s/f (Soft) **9 Ran SP% 114.1**
Speed ratings (Par 101): **95,93,88,85,81 76,75,74,65**
toteswingers:1&2 £7.50, 2&3 £6.10, 1&3 £6.80 CSF £58.09 CT £244.34 TOTE £5.00: £1.30, £3.20, £2.70; EX 85.50 Trifecta £267.90 Part won. Pool of £362.13 - 0.64 winning units..
Owner S R Bowring **Bred** S R Bowring **Trained** Edwinstowe, Notts

FOCUS
There seemed less depth to this second division of a very modest sprint handicap. A small best on turf from the winner.

7156 FINANCIALS AT BET365.COM H'CAP 1m 1f
4:30 (4:30) (Class 6) (0-60,64) 3-Y-0 **£1,942** (£578; £288; £144) **Stalls** Low

Form RPR

6303 **1** **Cuckoo Rock (IRE)**[53] 5729 3-9-1 **52**......(p) CathyGannon 1 62
(J G Portman) *stdd s: hld up towards rr: hdwy over 3f out: chsd clr ldr over 1f out: clsd ent fnl f: led fnl 150yds: sn clr: pushed out* **12/1**

440F **2** 6 **Wavertree Bounty**[12] 6860 3-8-10 **47**...... KirstyMilczarek 7 44
(J Ryan) *chsd ldr: led gng wl over 2f out: sn clr: rdn over 1f out: hdd fnl 150yds: sn btn* **8/1**

25 **3** 7 **Dandarrell**[34] 6297 3-9-5 **56**...... PaulMulrennan 12 38
(Julie Camacho) *led: rdn and hdd over 2f out: sn wl outpcd by ldr: 3rd and wl btn over 1f out* **10/1**

2403 **4** ½ **Louisiana Gift (IRE)**[7] 7005 3-9-7 **58**......(v) SebSanders 11 39
(J W Hills) *hld up in last trio: drvn and effrt 3 out: no ch w ldrs after: plugged on to go modest 4th ins fnl f: n.d* **4/1**[1]

4300 **5** 4 **Shercon (IRE)**[7] 7003 3-8-12 **49**...... J-PGuillambert 2 22
(N Tinkler) *in tch in midfield: rdn and effrt 3f out: no prog over 2f out: 4th and wl btn 2f out* **66/1**

6-05 **6** 6 **Cunning Plan (IRE)**[12] 6865 3-9-2 **53**...... LiamJones 5 13
(P W Chapple-Hyam) *in tch in midfield: rdn over 4f out: edgd rt u.p 3f out: wl btn after* **22/1**

0320 **7** 5 **Miss Chaumiere**[55] 5654 3-9-0 **51**......(v) JamieSpencer 4 1
(M L W Bell) *chsd ldrs: drvn over 3f out: wknd u.p 3f out: wl btn after: eased ins fnl f* **9/2**[2]

0000 **8** 2 **On The Cusp (IRE)**[12] 6860 3-8-9 **49**...... RobertLButler(3) 9 —
(P Butler) *stdd s: hld up in rr: swtchd rt and rdn ent fnl 3f: no hdwy and wl btn fnl 3f: eased ins fnl f* **33/1**

-222 **9** 11 **Master Of Song**[73] 5064 3-9-1 **52**......(p) RobertWinston 3 —
(S R Bowring) *chsd ldrs: rdn and struggling whn sltly hmpd ent fnl 4f: t.o and virtually p.u ins fnl f* **11/2**

0401 **10** 6 **Rodrigo De Freitas (IRE)**[8] 6993 3-9-13 **64** 6ex..(v) TomMcLaughlin 10 —
(J R Boyle) *s.i.s: nvr gng wl and sn rdn along: lost tch over 3f out: t.o and virtually p.u ins fnl f* **5/1**[3]

0244 **11** 12 **Lady Brickhouse**[24] 6579 3-8-11 **48**...... SaleemGolam 13 —
(M D Squance) *chsd ldrs: rdn to go 3rd and edgd lft ent fnl 3f: wknd qckly 3f out: t.o and virtually p.u fr over 1f out* **20/1**

0066 **12** 1 ½ **Asterales**[24] 6574 3-8-12 **49**...... StevieDonohoe 14 —
(W J Musson) *hld up towards rr: rdn and effrt on outer over 3f out: no hdwy and wl btn 3f out: t.o and virtually p.u fr over 1f out* **14/1**

2m 9.02s (13.22) **Going Correction** +1.45s/f (Soft) **12 Ran SP% 118.3**
Speed ratings (Par 99): **99,93,87,87,83 78,73,71,62,56 46,44**
toteswingers:1&2 £26.90, 2&3 £18.10, 1&3 £19.10 CSF £100.31 CT £1020.50 TOTE £11.70: £3.40, £3.10, £1.90; EX 136.40 TRIFECTA Not won..
Owner Prof C D Green **Bred** Prof C Green **Trained** Compton, Berks
■ Stewards' Enquiry : Robert L Butler one-day ban: used whip when out of contention (Nov 10)

FOCUS
A moderate contest, in which several looked out of their depth. They went a decent gallop, given the ground, and finished well strung out. Not form to take too positively.
Master Of Song Official explanation: trainer said gelding was unsuited by the heavy ground

7157 CASINO AT BET365.COM H'CAP 1m 6f 17y
5:00 (5:00) (Class 6) (0-55,55) 4-Y-0+ **£1,942** (£578; £288; £144) **Stalls** High

Form RPR

6526 **1** **Court Wing (IRE)**[5] 7039 4-8-5 **47**...... AndrewHeffernan(3) 1 58
(R J Price) *t.k.h early: chsd ldrs: squeezed through on inner to chal ent fnl 2f: rdn to ld over 1f out: idled and edgd rt u.p over 1f out: styd on wl fnl f* **12/1**

14/5 **2** 3 ½ **Zed Candy (FR)**[112] 3760 7-8-13 **52**...... J-PGuillambert 2 58
(R Ford) *t.k.h early: led: rdn 3f out: hdd ent fnl 2f: kpt on same pce u.p fr over 1f out* **8/1**

000 **3** ¾ **Inside Knowledge (USA)**[10] 6915 4-8-11 **50**...... KirstyMilczarek 13 55
(G Woodward) *t.k.h: chsd ldrs 12f out: wnt 2nd 9f out tl over 2f out: kpt on same pce u.p fr over 1f out* **40/1**

650/ **4** 1 **Spice Bar**[81] 3547 6-8-4 **48**...... NeilFarley(5) 6 52
(D Carroll) *stdd s: hld up in rr: hdwy and n.m.r over 3f out: chsd ldrs u.p 2f out: plugged on same pce fr over 1f out* **9/1**

301 **5** 2 **Derby Desire (IRE)**[5] 7039 6-8-6 **52**...... JamesRogers(7) 8 53
(D Donovan) *chsd ldr tl 9f out: styd chsng ldrs: led ent fnl 2f: hdd and rdn over 1f out: wknd ins fnl f* **9/2**[2]

0-00 **6** 7 **Velvet Nayef**[12] 6861 4-8-4 **46** oh1...... SimonPearce(3) 7 37
(J Pearce) *in tch: rdn and struggling 3f out: one pce and wl btn fnl 2f* **25/1**

0060 **7** 1 ¼ **Strikemaster (IRE)**[8] 6983 4-9-2 **55**...... MartinLane 4 44
(B Ellison) *s.i.s: hld up towards rr: rdn and effrt over 3f out: sn struggling: wl btn fnl 2f* **5/1**[3]

0335 **8** 2 **Sparkaway**[19] 6693 4-8-12 **51**......(b) StevieDonohoe 12 37
(W J Musson) *s.i.s: sn bustled along and racd in midfield: rdn and effrt ent fnl 3f: drvn and btn over 2f out* **9/4**[1]

54 **9** 5 **Sanctum**[43] 6022 4-8-10 **52**...... Louis-PhilippeBeuzelin(3) 9 31
(Dr J D Scargill) *s.i.s: sn in tch in midfield: n.m.r and shuffled bk over 3f out: swtchd to outer and rdn wl over 2f out: no hdwy and wl btn fnl 2f* **8/1**

2540 **10** 8 **Quince (IRE)**[5] 7039 7-9-0 **53**......(v) MickyFenton 11 21
(J Pearce) *hld up in tch in rr: rdn and short-lived effrt 3f out: sn btn: eased ins fnl f* **20/1**

50-0 **11** 31 **Bluegrass Lion (USA)**[10] 6915 4-8-11 **50**...... SaleemGolam 3 —
(Mrs L Williamson) *s.i.s: sn in tch in midfield: rdn and wknd over 3f out: t.o and virtually p.u fr over 1f out* **66/1**

0000 **12** 36 **Jenny Dawson (IRE)**[63] 5380 4-8-7 **46** oh1...... ChrisCatlin 5 —
(John Berry) *a in rr: lost tch 6f out: wl t.o fnl 4f* **50/1**

3m 32.2s (24.60) **Going Correction** +1.45s/f (Soft) **12 Ran SP% 120.0**
Speed ratings (Par 101): **87,85,84,84,82 78,78,77,74,69 51,31**
toteswingers:1&2 £10.20, 2&3 £30.80, 1&3 £26.90 CSF £100.77 CT £3716.77 TOTE £10.70: £3.60, £2.20, £11.10; EX 118.40 TRIFECTA Not won. Place 6: £57.43 Place 5: £47.65.

Owner Court Reclamation & Salvage Ltd **Bred** Crandon Park Stud **Trained** Ullingswick, H'fords

FOCUS

A low-grade finale, the top weight being rated just 55. They went a steady pace until quickening in the home straight. The form is rated through the third.

Sparkaway Official explanation: trainer's rep said gelding was unsuited by the heavy ground

Quince(IRE) Official explanation: jockey said gelding had no more to give

T/Plt: £45.80 to a £1 stake. Pool of £57,720.88 - 918.21 winning tickets. T/Qpdt: £6.80 to a £1 stake. Pool of £5,271.23 - 570.10 winning tickets. SP

6702 SAINT-CLOUD (L-H)

Tuesday, October 26

OFFICIAL GOING: Turf: very soft

7160a PRIX DE FLORE (GROUP 3) (3YO+ FILLIES & MARES) (TURF) 1m 2f 110y

2:15 (12:00) 3-Y-O+ **£35,398** (£14,159; £10,619; £7,079; £3,539)

RPR

1 **Valasyra (FR)**[25] 6551 3-8-7 0 .... GregoryBenoist 12 111
(A De Royer-Dupre, France) *towards rr tl st: mde gd prog on outside: qcknd wl fnl f to chse ldr: got up in fnl strides* **32/1**

2 ¾ **Board Meeting (IRE)**[23] 6613 4-8-11 0 ....(b[1]) AnthonyCrastus 7 108
(E Lellouche, France) *sn sent to ld: tk clr advantage 2f out: qcknd wl: clr ent fnl 100yds: r.o wl: ct fnl strides* **10/1**

3 ¾ **La Boum (GER)**[24] 6591 7-8-11 0 .... IoritzMendizabal 8 107
(Robert Collet, France) *racd towards rr: mde gradual prog in st: qcknd wl 1f out: fin strly fnl 100yds* **73/10**

4 snk **Rosanara (FR)**[23] 6613 3-8-7 0 .... Christophe-PatriceLemaire 13 108
(A De Royer-Dupre, France) *towards rr tl st: mde gd prog trcking eventual wnr 2f out: r.o wl fnl f: fin strly* **33/10[1]**

5 ¾ **Aviate**[24] 6561 3-8-10 0 .... TomQueally 9 110
(H R A Cecil) *sn prom: qcknd early in st: wnt 2nd 1f out: no ex fnl 100yds* **16/1**

6 ¾ **Fleur Enchantee (FR)**[23] 6613 6-8-11 0 ....(p) StephanePasquier 6 103
(P Van De Poele, France) *racd midfield: rdn early in st: hrd rdn to chse ldr: wknd ins fnl f* **44/5**

6 dht **Baahama (IRE)**[25] 6551 3-8-8 0 ow1 .... OlivierPeslier 2 106
(A Fabre, France) *racd in 5th: rdn 1 1/2f out: no ex fnl f* **43/10[2]**

8 ¾ **Indian Breeze (GER)**[16] 6790 3-8-7 0 .... FranckBlondel 3 104
(J Hirschberger, Germany) *trckd ldr fr s: outpcd 2f out: styd on fnl f* **29/1**

9 1 ½ **Deluxe (USA)**[55] 5672 3-8-7 0 .... MaximeGuyon 11 101
(A Fabre, France) *racd in midfield: rdn but no ex 2f out* **58/10[3]**

10 2 **Tech Exceed (GER)**[17] 6763 3-8-10 0 .... DominiqueBoeuf 4 100
(A Wohler, Germany) *racd in midfield on rail: rdn ent s: sn wknd* **18/1**

0 **Tangaspeed (FR)**[220] 953 5-8-11 0 .... DavyBonilla 10 —
(R Laplanche, France) *bkmarker fr s: nvr figured in st* **43/1**

0 **Waajida**[44] 3-8-7 0 .... ThierryThulliez 5 —
(J Cagan, Czech Republic) *prom fr s: rdn 1 1/2f out: sn wknd* **47/1**

0 **Lady's Purse**[44] 6013 3-8-10 0 .... JohanVictoire 1 —
(H-A Pantall, France) *a towards rr: nvr figured in st* **14/1**

2m 19.6s

WFA 3 from 4yo+ 5lb **13** Ran SP% **116.7**

WIN (incl. 1 euro stake): 3.80 (Valasyra coupled with Rosanara). PLACES: 6.60, 4.00, 3.00. DF: 159.30. SF: 246.90.

Owner H H Aga Khan **Bred** Haras De S.A. Aga Khan Scea **Trained** Chantilly, France

NOTEBOOK

Valasyra(FR) picked up nicely from off the pace to lead close home. It was a taking performance and a big step up on her previous efforts, but it's unclear whether she will be kept in training as a 4-y-o.

Aviate travelled well enough but failed to pick up in the ground. Perhaps it was softer than ideal.

7111 KEMPTON (A.W) (R-H)

Wednesday, October 27

OFFICIAL GOING: Standard

Wind: Almost nil Weather: Fine, mild

7161 KIA VENGA CLASSIFIED STKS 7f (P)

5:40 (5:41) (Class 6) 3-Y-O+ **£1,637** (£483; £241) **Stalls High**

Form RPR

3013 1 **Swansea Jack**[7] 7023 3-9-0 54 ....(t) WilliamCarson 3 62+
(S C Williams) *trckd ldng trio: pushed into ld over 1f out: wandered both ways but clr fnl f: a holding on* **11/10[1]**

0242 2 1 **Ayam Zainah**[14] 6847 3-9-0 55 .... RichardHughes 10 59+
(M R Channon) *sn settled in midfield: rdn wl over 2f out: prog over 1f out: wnt 2nd ins fnl f: clsd on wnr but nvr able to chal* **10/3[2]**

5604 3 1 ¾ **Olympic Dream**[27] 6494 4-9-2 55 ....(p) PatDobbs 8 54
(M Herrington) *taken down early: hld up towards rr: pushed along 2f out: prog over 1f out: shkn up and r.o fnl f to take 3rd nr fin* **20/1**

0065 4 ½ **Alnaseem (USA)**[28] 6454 3-9-0 50 .... PhillipMakin 2 53
(M W Easterby) *led: rdn and pressed 2f out: hdd over 1f out: one pce fnl f* **20/1**

3603 5 ¾ **Anaya**[20] 6696 3-9-0 54 ....(b) NeilCallan 5 51
(D Bourton) *s.i.s: rousted along and prog to chse ldr after 2f: drvn over 2f out to chal: one pce over 1f out* **16/1**

-500 6 1 **Eclipsed (USA)**[26] 6522 3-8-11 48 .... KierenFox[(3)] 14 48
(J R Best) *pushed along in midfield after 3f: effrt u.p 2f out: nvr gng pce to chal* **66/1**

664 7 ½ **Mackenzie Spiers**[16] 6814 3-9-0 55 .... JamesMillman 11 47
(B R Millman) *hld up and sn last: shovelled along over 2f out: styd on past several rivals fnl 2f: nvr nr ldrs* **20/1**

5003 8 hd **Blue Zephyr**[21] 6672 3-9-0 55 ....(tp) LeeVickers 12 46
(D C Griffiths) *chsd ldng quartet: drvn to cl on them 2f out: wknd fnl f* **11/1[3]**

4000 9 1 **Gwenllian (IRE)**[11] 6937 3-9-0 55 .... SaleemGolam 7 44
(Ian Williams) *nvr bttr than midfield: no imp on ldrs u.p over 1f out* **25/1**

0430 10 2 ¼ **Freedom Pass (USA)**[48] 5898 3-9-0 55 .... JimCrowley 6 38
(J A R Toller) *chsd ldr 2f: styd prom: rdn to chal jst over 2f out: wknd jst over 1f out* **12/1**

0000 11 1 ½ **Battleship Grey**[37] 6255 3-9-0 42 .... SamHitchcott 1 33
(D K Ivory) *racd wd: hld up in rr: shkn up and no prog over 2f out* **100/1**

600 12 ¾ **Vertumnus**[121] 3521 3-9-0 55 .... J-PGuillambert 13 31
(N P Littmoden) *dwlt: hld up in rr: rdn on inner 2f out: sn struggling* **66/1**

0-00 13 ½ **Wet Feet**[27] 6496 3-9-0 55 ....(t) LiamKeniry 9 30
(P R Chamings) *hld up wl in rr: no prog 2f out: reminders and wknd over 1f out* **50/1**

0263 14 shd **Aqua Vitae (IRE)**[13] 6865 3-9-0 54 .... FergusSweeney 4 30
(Miss Tor Sturgis) *nvr bttr than midfield on outer: wknd 2f out* **25/1**

1m 26.14s (0.14) **Going Correction** -0.05s/f (Stan)

WFA 3 from 4yo 2lb **14** Ran SP% **120.5**

Speed ratings (Par 101): **97,95,93,93,92 91,90,90,89,86 85,84,83,83**

toteswingers:1&2:£1.70, 2&3:£13.90, 1&3:£6.40 CSF £3.67 TOTE £2.60: £1.80, £1.10, £6.40; EX 3.70.

Owner K J Mercer **Bred** Usk Valley Stud **Trained** Newmarket, Suffolk

FOCUS

A modest 0-55 classified where no less than eight of the field were rated on the maximum with three just 1lb below and in which two were backed to exclusion of the others. It is doubtful the winner had to match his recent best.

Eclipsed(USA) Official explanation: jockey said gelding hung left

Mackenzie Spiers Official explanation: jockey said filly hung left

7162 BOOK NOW FOR BOXING DAY H'CAP 7f (P)

6:10 (6:12) (Class 6) (0-65,65) 3-Y-O+ **£1,637** (£483; £241) **Stalls High**

Form RPR

0600 1 **Devil You Know (IRE)**[22] 6664 4-9-5 65 ....(t) PhillipMakin 7 73+
(M W Easterby) *racd keenly: mde all: drew 3 l clr 2f out: same ld fnl f: a holding on* **20/1**

2100 2 ¾ **Harting Hill**[16] 6801 5-9-5 65 .... RichardHughes 4 71+
(M P Tregoning) *stdd s: hld up in rr: rdn and prog 2f out: styd on fnl f: tk 2nd last strides: too much to do* **9/2[1]**

0204 3 shd **Profligate (IRE)**[23] 6632 3-9-3 65 .... JimCrowley 10 71
(W Jarvis) *hld up in midfield: prog over 2f out w hd to one side: chsd clr wnr over 1f out: clsd fnl f but lost 2nd last strides* **7/1[3]**

U04 4 ¾ **Landucci**[66] 5325 9-9-3 63 ....(p) SebSanders 8 67
(S Curran) *prom: rdn to dispute 2nd fr over 1f out: kpt on fnl f but nvr able to chal* **14/1**

1563 5 ½ **Emiratesdotcom**[19] 6713 4-9-3 63 .... LiamKeniry 11 66
(J M Bradley) *trckd ldrs: rdn and effrt 2f out: pressed for pl over 1f out: nt qckn* **9/2[1]**

035 6 1 **The Winged Assasin (USA)**[14] 6854 4-9-5 65 .... DarryllHolland 6 65
(M Wigham) *chsd ldrs: rdn and outpcd over 2f out: kpt on same pce after* **8/1**

0521 7 ½ **Annes Rocket (IRE)**[12] 6903 5-9-3 63 .... PatDobbs 13 62+
(J C Fox) *hld up in last pair: pushed along 2f out: kpt on but nvr rchd ldrs: too much to do* **13/2[2]**

5000 8 2 ¾ **Bobs Dreamflight**[9] 6987 4-9-3 63 .... SamHitchcott 2 54
(D K Ivory) *chsd wnr: outpcd over 2f out: lost 2nd over 1f out: wknd qckly fnl f* **16/1**

0012 9 ½ **White Shift (IRE)**[18] 6741 4-9-2 65 .... KierenFox[(3)] 14 55
(P Howling) *mostly in midfield: rdn over 2f out: no prog over 1f out: wknd fnl f* **11/1**

4000 10 ½ **Fayre Bella**[22] 6656 3-9-3 65 .... FergusSweeney 3 53
(J Gallagher) *hld up in rr: rdn and no prog 2f out: wknd fnl f* **50/1**

3050 11 2 ½ **Mountrath**[20] 6692 3-9-3 65 .... WilliamCarson 5 47
(B R Johnson) *a wl in rr: struggling u.p 3f out* **12/1**

5134 12 3 **Mary's Pet**[12] 6898 3-9-2 64 .... J-PGuillambert 12 38
(J Akehurst) *a wl in rr: struggling over 2f out* **10/1**

4006 13 6 **Scruffy Skip (IRE)**[8] 7007 5-9-4 64 ....(p) SaleemGolam 9 21
(Mrs C A Dunnett) *chsd ldng pair: rdn 1/2-way: wknd rapidly over 2f out* **25/1**

1m 25.94s (-0.06) **Going Correction** -0.05s/f (Stan)

WFA 3 from 4yo+ 2lb **13** Ran SP% **121.5**

Speed ratings (Par 101): **98,97,97,96,95 94,93,90,90,89 86,83,76**

toteswingers:1&2:£26.10, 1&3:£43.40, 2&3:£5.10 CSF £107.95 CT £737.76 TOTE £32.20: £9.70, £1.40, £3.40; EX 180.00.

Owner Mrs Jean Turpin **Bred** Joseph Stewart Investments **Trained** Sheriff Hutton, N Yorks

FOCUS

Modest form. The winner had a pretty easy time of it up front but the form is taken at face value.

Devil You Know(IRE) Official explanation: trainer's rep said, regarding apparent improvement in form, that the gelding is well suited by the track having won previously

7163 DIGIBET.COM MAIDEN AUCTION STKS (DIV I) 1m (P)

6:40 (6:42) (Class 4) 2-Y-O **£2,914** (£867; £433; £216) **Stalls High**

Form RPR

032 1 **Twice Bitten**[27] 6497 2-8-11 78 .... RichardHughes 7 77
(J A R Toller) *trckd ldng pair: wnt 2nd wl over 1f out: hrd rdn to ld narrowly ins fnl f: pushed out nr fin* **4/5[1]**

2542 2 hd **Masonic Lady (IRE)**[8] 6994 2-8-3 71 ....(b) AdamBeschizza[(5)] 4 74
(W J Haggas) *chsd ldr: led over 2f out: sn hrd rdn: narrowly hdd ins fnl f: styd on wl: jst hld* **6/1[2]**

60 3 6 **Matavia Bay (IRE)**[16] 6802 2-8-2 0 .... HarryBentley[(7)] 8 61
(A P Jarvis) *t.k.h: hld up in tch: outpcd in 4th over 2f out: tk modest 3rd ins fnl f* **100/1**

0 4 shd **Ice Nelly (IRE)**[16] 6802 2-8-6 0 .... ChrisCatlin 9 58+
(H Morrison) *dwlt: t.k.h towards rr: outpcd over 2f out: kpt on fnl f to press for modest 3rd nr fin* **9/1[3]**

04 5 2 ¾ **Face Value**[27] 6498 2-9-2 0 .... JimmyFortune 11 61
(B J Meehan) *dwlt: hld up in rr: outpcd fr over 2f out: kpt on fr over 1f out* **6/1[2]**

0256 6 nse **Grecian Goddess (IRE)**[13] 6866 2-8-4 68 .... KirstyMilczarek 6 49
(J Ryan) *led to over 2f out: wknd over 1f out* **12/1**

00 7 nk **Theavonfilly**[13] 6866 2-8-4 0 .... LiamJones 5 48
(R A Teal) *chsd ldrs: rdn 1/2-way: outpcd fr over 2f out: no ch after* **100/1**

8 3 ½ **Oratouch (IRE)** 2-8-6 0 .... TobyAtkinson[(5)] 2 47
(M Botti) *dwlt: mostly in last trio: nvr a factor* **40/1**

00 9 hd **Fire N'Brimstone**[20] 6688 2-8-11 0 .... FrankieMcDonald 10 47
(Mouse Hamilton-Fairley) *walked to post: dwlt: nvr bttr than midfield: struggling towards rr 3f out: sn btn* **100/1**

0 10 2 ¼ **High Samana**[20] 6689 2-9-2 0 .... JimCrowley 1 47
(R M Beckett) *dwlt: racd wd: rchd midfield 1/2-way: dropped to last pair over 2f out: nt involved after* **25/1**

11 ½ **Kambis** 2-8-11 0 .... KierenFallon 3 41
(L M Cumani) *dwlt: rn green and mostly in last trio: lft bhd fr over 2f out* **25/1**

1m 39.42s (-0.38) **Going Correction** -0.05s/f (Stan) **11** Ran SP% **114.9**

Speed ratings (Par 97): **99,98,92,92,89 89,89,86,85,83 83**

toteswingers:1&2:£2.00, 1&3:£21.20, 2&3:£49.20 CSF £5.32 TOTE £1.70: £1.10, £1.30, £44.00; EX 6.20.

Owner The Cobra Partnership **Bred** M E Wates **Trained** Newmarket, Suffolk

FOCUS

A weak maiden. The first two finished clear and this is straightforward form with the winner rated to his recent mark.

NOTEBOOK

Twice Bitten, the highest of those rated with a mark of 78, appeared to appreciate this move up from 7f, and although the winning margin was narrow it's possible there was a bit more to come. Patiently ridden, he looked likely to score readily, but his rider was tight for room with his whip hand in the final 50 yards and resorted to just hands and heels. Connections are now likely to put him away for the year. (op 10-11 tchd evens in places)

Masonic Lady(IRE) had finished about three and a half lengths behind Twice Bitten when they were second and fourth to Dubarshi 28 days earlier, and she is rated 7lb inferior on official ratings. This extra furlong suited her well and she has a pedigree that suggests she will stay further. (op 7-1)

Matavia Bay(IRE) is now due a mark and showed improvement on his previous run when 6l behind Ice Nelly.

Ice Nelly(IRE) once again showed promise and will be interesting through the winter in handicaps after another run to attain a rating. (tchd 10-1)

Face Value ◆ ran an eyecatching race and is certainly one to look out for now he is due a rating. He was staying on well over this first attempt at 1m and will be suited by further when handicapping. (op 4-1)

Grecian Goddess(IRE) is rated 68 and will probably drop for this. She handles the surface well, and handicaps are calling now. (op 20-1)

7164 DIGIBET.COM MAIDEN AUCTION STKS (DIV II) 1m (P)

7:10 (7:13) (Class 4) 2-Y-O £2,914 (£867; £433; £216) **Stalls** High

Form RPR

1 **Burj Alzain (IRE)** 2-8-11 0 NeilCallan 6 76
(G A Butler) *trckd ldrs gng wl: wnt 3rd over 2f out: effrt on inner over 1f out: rdn to ld ins fnl f: readily* **10/1**

004 2 1 ½ **Saint Helena (IRE)**[13] 6866 2-8-8 70 ow2 RichardHughes 1 70
(H J L Dunlop) *trckd ldr: chal over 2f out: rdn to ld jst over 1f out: hdd and outpcd ins fnl f* **7/1**[3]

63 3 3 **Romantic Wish**[105] 4021 2-8-6 0 RichardKingscote 8 61
(R A Mills) *racd v freely early: led: drvn and hdd jst over 1f out: fdd* **11/8**[1]

56 4 1 ¾ **Experimentalist**[15] 6828 2-9-2 0 SteveDrowne 11 67
(H Morrison) *mostly chsd ldng pair to over 2f out: clr of rest but fading in 4th over 1f out* **17/2**

5 6 **Tinaheely (IRE)** 2-8-8 0 CathyGannon 5 45
(J G Portman) *in tch: outpcd fr 3f out: wnt poor 5th over 2f out: no imp after* **33/1**

6 4 ½ **Alemaratiya** 2-8-6 0 EddieCreighton 10 33
(D M Simcock) *dwlt: hld up in rr: wl outpcd fr 3f out: v modest late prog* **16/1**

06 7 6 **Emmeline Pankhurst (IRE)**[12] 6884 2-8-6 0 AdamBeschizza(5) 3 24
(Miss J Feilden) *prom on outer: rdn 1/2-way: lost tch and struggling wl over 2f out* **12/1**

8 2 **Crossword** 2-8-9 0 ChrisCatlin 4 18
(M Botti) *a towards rr: rdn over 3f out: sn lft bhd* **7/2**[2]

0 9 ¾ **Near The Mark (IRE)**[107] 3964 2-8-11 0 DarryllHolland 9 18
(M Wigham) *nvr bttr than midfield: pushed along sn after 1/2-way: wknd over 2f out* **40/1**

5040 10 4 **Laffraaj (IRE)**[57] 5626 2-8-2 48 JamesRogers(7) 7 7
(Pat Eddery) *dwlt: sn detached in last: nvr a factor* **33/1**

00 11 7 **Oceans Destination**[27] 6504 2-8-12 0 ow1 JimmyFortune 2 —
(J Ryan) *hld up in rr: wl bhd fnl 3f: t.o* **66/1**

1m 39.76s (-0.04) **Going Correction** -0.05s/f (Stan) **11** Ran SP% **119.8**

Speed ratings (Par 97): **98,96,93,91,85 81,75,73,72,68 61**

toteswingers:1&2:£10.80, 1&3:£3.70, 2&3:£2.10 CSF £77.84 TOTE £23.90: £7.00, £1.20, £1.10; EX 108.00.

Owner Asaad Al Banwan **Bred** Shadwell Estate Company Limited **Trained** Newmarket, Suffolk

FOCUS

This second division of the maiden did not appear to have quite the quality of the first with the highest of those rated, Saint Helena on 70, finishing second, but the time was only fractionally slower. The form is rated around the runner-up.

NOTEBOOK

Burj Alzain(IRE), a half-brother to a 7f winner on this surface, won nicely on debut. There is no reason to believe he will not stay a bit further. (tchd 9-1 and 12-1)

Saint Helena(IRE)'s previous three outings had been over 7f and the step up suited her despite a moderate draw. If connections persevere this year then she can win a race of this calibre or a handicap off a mark that should not change. (op 9-2 tchd 15-2)

Romantic Wish was coming back from a 105-day absense and that, combined with being too keen and over a furlong longer trip, was too much for him. On the plus side he should be reasonably handicapped after this third run and is one to be with next time. Official explanation: jockey said filly ran too freely (op 7-4 tchd 2-1 in a place)

Experimentalist showed more resolution than on his two previous outings and, despite being by a sire whose influence is for speed, he stayed on well enough on this move up to a mile without ever looking a threat. He had to give upwards of 5lb all round which made things harder. (op 8-1)

Tinaheely(IRE) showed some ability on debut.

Alemaratiya was nibbled in the market but was too immature to do herself justice. (op 33-1)

7165 DIGIBET CASINO NURSERY 1m (P)

7:40 (7:41) (Class 2) 2-Y-O

£6,916 (£2,071; £1,035; £518; £258; £129) **Stalls** High

Form RPR

21 1 **Flag Officer**[19] 6711 2-8-13 80 TedDurcan 5 85+
(Saeed Bin Suroor) *trckd ldr: led over 2f out: drvn over 1f out: styd on fnl f: hld on nr fin* **5/4**[1]

3144 2 ½ **Golden Tempest (IRE)**[21] 6670 2-8-11 78 ShaneKelly 1 82
(W R Swinburn) *hld up in 7th: prog 1/2-way: trckd ldrs gng strly over 2f out: rdn over 1f out: wnt 2nd last 150yds: clsd on wnr fin* **6/1**[2]

1031 3 ¾ **Tinkertown (IRE)**[18] 6745 2-9-7 88 JimmyFortune 6 90+
(P F I Cole) *s.i.s: hld up last: drvn and stl only 7th over 1f out: r.o fnl f to take 3rd last 75yds: nrst fin* **15/2**

0401 4 ¾ **Aldwick Bay (IRE)**[16] 6810 2-8-9 76 RichardHughes 2 76
(R Hannon) *trckd ldng pair: drvn to take 2nd wl over 1f out and tried to chal: hld fnl f and sn lost pl* **13/2**[3]

1602 5 1 ¼ **Ninfea (IRE)**[13] 6875 2-8-5 72 ChrisCatlin 3 69
(S Kirk) *t.k.h: hld up towards rr: effrt on inner 2f out: nt qckn over 1f out: one pce* **10/1**

5410 6 2 ½ **Hawdyerwheesht**[25] 6568 2-9-1 82 KierenFallon 7 74
(M Johnston) *chsd ldng pair to over 2f out: nt qckn and sn lost pl: no hdwy over 1f out* **8/1**

0136 7 2 **Joyously**[9] 6979 2-8-2 72 JohnFahy(3) 8 59
(P Butler) *led to over 2f out: wknd over 1f out* **20/1**

0034 8 16 **Windsor Knights**[11] 6936 2-8-1 68 (b) CathyGannon 4 18
(A J Lidderdale) *sn pushed along: in tch to 3f out: wknd: t.o* **25/1**

1m 39.02s (-0.78) **Going Correction** -0.05s/f (Stan) **8** Ran SP% **112.6**

Speed ratings (Par 101): **101,100,99,99,97 95,93,77**

toteswingers:1&2:£2.50, 1&3:£2.30, 2&3:£6.40 CSF £8.70 CT £39.25 TOTE £2.30: £1.10, £1.60, £3.80; EX 10.70.

Owner Godolphin **Bred** Floors Farming And Dominic Burke **Trained** Newmarket, Suffolk

FOCUS

Quite a competitive handicap on paper. The winner is progressing and the form is quite solid rated around the principals.

NOTEBOOK

Flag Officer's second-time-out win at Wolverhampton eight days earlier had gained credibility following the wins of the second and third on their next appearance. The move up a furlong to 1m off a debut mark of 80 was also in his favour and he certainly needed it as he had to be firmely driven to assert. Quite where he goes from here is debatable as this was workmanlike at best despite him being much sharper than last time when tardy from the stalls. (op 6-4)

Golden Tempest(IRE) was still keen enough and is now exposed at this level, but she still came with a strong flourish to keep Flag Officer honest in the run to the line. She is 12lb higher than when winning over 6f here in early September and will rise again. However, if she ever truely dropped her bit she could win one of these as she seems to try. (op 13-2 tchd 11-2)

Tinkertown(IRE) made things very hard for himself and in the circumstances did extremely well to finish so close. After a tardy start he was still last turning for home and came wide. The move back to 1m suited him as nothing finished better despite rising 5lb for winning over 7f at Wolverhampton 18 days earlier. (op 6-1)

Aldwick Bay(IRE) was making his debut on this surface off a 7lb higher mark after winning an extended 1m handicap by just under 3l at Windsor 16 days earlier. He didn't last home anywhere near so well this time. (op 11-2)

Ninfea(IRE) didn't have the cheekpieces on which almost got her home over 1m at Nottingham 13 days previously off a 4lb lower mark. (op 9-1)

Hawdyerwheesht was another making his debut on this surface but didn't seem to last home at this first try at 1m. (op 9-1)

Windsor Knights Official explanation: jockey said gelding had no more to give

7166 DIGIBET MEDIAN AUCTION MAIDEN STKS 6f (P)

8:10 (8:12) (Class 5) 3-4-Y-O £2,286 (£675; £337) **Stalls** High

Form RPR

5025 1 **Wallis**[35] 6291 3-8-12 75 KierenFallon 3 60+
(L M Cumani) *hld up in 8th: plld to outer and gd prog 2f out: led jst ins fnl f: hung rt but sn in command* **4/6**[1]

4366 2 2 **Ruler's Honour (IRE)**[5] 7064 3-9-3 54 (p) LeeVickers 10 59
(T J Etherington) *trckd ldng pair: chsd ldr briefly over 1f out: sltly hmpd and outpcd ins fnl f: kpt on to take 2nd again last 100yds* **20/1**

00 3 1 **Hidden Destiny**[7] 7013 3-9-3 0 FergusSweeney 9 56
(P J Makin) *chsd ldr: led over 2f out: drvn 2 l clr over 1f out: hdd and outpcd jst ins fnl f* **28/1**

4423 4 2 ¼ **Millden**[56] 5668 3-8-12 64 AmyScott(5) 7 49
(H Candy) *chsd ldng trio: urged along and nt qckn whn nudged by rival 2f out: one pce after* **7/1**[2]

-605 5 1 ¾ **Cane Cat (IRE)**[21] 6665 3-8-12 48 (t) NeilCallan 4 38
(A W Carroll) *chsd ldrs: nt qckn 2f out: grad outpcd over 1f out* **40/1**

005 6 1 **Ice Road Trucker (IRE)**[23] 6638 3-9-3 45 RichardHughes 1 40
(J R Boyle) *hld up last: shkn up over 2f out: modest late prog: nvr a factor* **16/1**

5 7 1 **Hippique**[27] 6496 3-8-12 0 JimmyFortune 8 32
(A M Balding) *mostly in last pair: rdn 1/2-way: struggling after: kpt on nr fin* **15/2**[3]

0000 8 2 ½ **Outshine**[33] 6330 3-8-12 49 (tp) ChrisCatlin 12 24
(Karen George) *led to over 2f out: sn wknd* **33/1**

0-4 9 1 ¼ **Estonia**[11] 6931 3-8-12 0 WilliamCarson 11 20
(M D Squance) *chsd ldrs: drvn and effrt on inner 2f out: wknd over 1f out* **12/1**

5600 10 15 **Jubilant Lady (USA)**[19] 6716 3-8-12 47 (b[1]) JimCrowley 5 —
(B Smart) *racd wd: a in rr: wknd over 2f out: t.o* **20/1**

1m 13.02s (-0.08) **Going Correction** -0.05s/f (Stan) **10** Ran SP% **116.2**

Speed ratings (Par 103): **98,95,94,91,88 87,86,82,81,61**

toteswingers:1&2:£5.60, 1&3:£10.80, 2&3:£25.40 CSF £21.93 TOTE £1.70: £1.10, £7.60, £8.60; EX 15.20.

Owner Fittocks Stud **Bred** Fittocks Stud **Trained** Newmarket, Suffolk

FOCUS

Maidens over 5f-6f at this time of the season are often weak and this was no exception.

7167 EPSOM OWNERS & TRAINERS AWARDS DINNER H'CAP 1m 4f (P)

8:40 (8:42) (Class 6) (0-65,65) 3-Y-O+ £1,637 (£483; £241) **Stalls** Centre

Form RPR

-164 1 **Sovento (GER)**[12] 6911 6-9-3 59 JohnFahy(3) 11 68
(Shaun Harley, Ire) *stdd s: hld up in last pair: gd prog on inner over 2f out to press ldrs over 1f out: shkn up to ld ins fnl f: readily* **9/1**

2423 2 ¾ **Not In The Clock (USA)**[15] 6829 3-9-5 65 SteveDrowne 13 73
(J R Best) *trckd ldng pair: chal 2f out: drvn to ld briefly 1f out: styd on same pce* **9/1**

0062 3 1 ½ **Soundbyte**[10] 6957 5-9-10 63 FergusSweeney 12 69
(J Gallagher) *hld up towards rr: clsd on ldrs over 2f out: drvn over 1f out: styd on to take 3rd nr fin* **11/2**[3]

5-30 4 ¾ **Eagle Nebula**[71] 5180 6-9-5 58 (p) RichardHughes 9 62
(B R Johnson) *chsd ldng trio: clsd to ld 2f out: hdd and one pce 1f out* **8/1**

3504 5 ½ **Bushy Dell (IRE)**[18] 6744 5-9-0 58 AdamBeschizza(5) 4 62
(Miss J Feilden) *racd wd: hld up in midfield: effrt over 2f out: tried to cl on ldrs over 1f out: kpt on same pce* **20/1**

020 6 ½ **Setter's Princess**[137] 2952 4-9-2 55 GeorgeBaker 6 58
(R J Hodges) *hld up towards rr: prog over 2f out: tried to cl over 1f out: one pce fnl f* **50/1**

4003 7 ½ **Faith Jicaro (IRE)**[25] 6578 3-9-4 64 (v[1]) DarryllHolland 8 66
(N J Vaughan) *hld up towards rr: effrt over 2f out: tried to cl on ldrs over 1f out: sn one pce* **16/1**

0310 8 nk **Kayaan**[23] 6623 3-9-4 64 MickyFenton 1 66+
(Mrs P Sly) *s.s: hld up in last pair: brought wd bnd 3f out: prog 2f out: effrt flattened out fnl f* **7/1**

2200 9 2 ½ **Megalala (IRE)**[21] 6668 9-9-10 63 NeilChalmers 5 61
(J J Bridger) *chsd ldrs: rdn in 6th 3f out: cl enough u.p 2f out: grad fdd* **40/1**

0-60 10 1 ¾ **Squad**[25] 6554 4-9-12 65 SebSanders 3 60
(S Dow) *hld up in last trio: nt clr run briefly over 2f out: no prog over 1f out* **20/1**

6000 11 *11* **Hatch A Plan (IRE)**[139] 2894 9-8-12 **51** oh3........... FrankieMcDonald 14 28
(Mouse Hamilton-Fairley) *chsd ldrs: rdn 4f out: 5th 3f out: wknd rapidly jst over 2f out* **100/1**

-005 12 *10* **Allanit (GER)**[46] 5959 6-9-4 **57**..........................[1] TomQueally 10 18
(B J Curley) *led at decent but nt breakneck pce: rdn 3f out: hdd & wknd 2f out: eased: t.o* **5/1**[2]

6000 13 *1 ¼* **Look Officer (USA)**[28] 6454 4-8-12 **51**..................... TomMcLaughlin 7 10
(Miss M E Rowland) *chsd ldr to over 2f out: wknd rapidly: t.o* **66/1**

0661 14 *10* **Twisted**[11] 6930 4-9-11 **64**.....................................(b) PhillipMakin 2 7
(M W Easterby) *chsd ldrs: rdn 4f out: sn wknd: t.o* **5/2**[1]

2m 32.97s (-1.53) **Going Correction** -0.05s/f (Stan)
WFA 3 from 4yo+ 7lb **14** Ran SP% **126.5**
Speed ratings (Par 101): **103,102,101,101,100 100,100,99,98,96 89,82,82,75**
toteswingers:1&2:£19.90, 1&3:£18.40, 2&3:£8.00 CSF £87.18 CT £502.84 TOTE £15.00: £4.40, £5.10, £1.80; EX 105.40.
Owner Lough Derg Syndicate **Bred** Achim Stahn **Trained** Letterkenny, Co Donegal

FOCUS
A trappy contest. They finished in a bit of a heap but the time was not bad and the form is taken at face value.
Setter's Princess Official explanation: jockey said filly was denied a clear run
Faith Jicaro(IRE) Official explanation: jockey said filly hung
Hatch A Plan(IRE) Official explanation: jockey said gelding was denied a clear run
Twisted Official explanation: jockey said gelding never travelled

7168 PANORAMIC H'CAP 1m (P)
9:10 (9:12) (Class 6) (0-60,63) 3-Y-0+ **£1,637** (£483; £241) **Stalls** High

Form RPR
5044 1 **Al Aqabah (IRE)**[21] 6671 5-8-13 **58**..................(b[1]) AdamBeschizza(5) 12 68
(B Gubby) *nt that wl away but pushed up to trck ldrs: prog on outer 2f out: drvn to ld last 150yds: styd on wl: asserted nr fin* **7/2**[1]

1303 2 *1* **Woolston Ferry (IRE)**[12] 6903 4-9-5 **59**................... RichardHughes 10 67
(David Pinder) *hld up in midfield: prog on outer over 2f out: drvn to chal 1f out: styd on but hld last 100yds* **6/1**[3]

1000 3 *1 ¾* **Sovereignty (JPN)**[21] 6671 8-9-1 **58**.................... SophieDoyle(3) 6 62
(D K Ivory) *taken down early and free to post: t.k.h: hld up in tch: prog 1/2-way and sn prom: led over 2f out: worn down last 150yds* **10/1**

1225 4 *2 ¼* **Mr Chocolate Drop (IRE)**[39] 6189 6-9-6 **60**.................(t) AdamKirby 4 59
(Miss M E Rowland) *hld up in last pair: pushed along and sme prog 2f out: drvn and styd on to take 4th ins fnl f: no imp on ldrs* **6/1**[3]

0300 5 *4* **Teen Ager (FR)**[112] 3777 6-9-5 **59**.......................... TomMcLaughlin 11 49
(P Burgoyne) *chsd ldng pair: rdn over 2f out: wknd over 1f out* **33/1**

0300 6 *hd* **Distant Waters**[46] 5958 3-8-10 **60**............................. HarryBentley(7) 5 49
(A P Jarvis) *hld up wl in rr on outer: urged along and no real prog 2f out: modest late hdwy* **40/1**

4000 7 *nse* **Fine Ruler (IRE)**[247] 663 6-9-4 **58**.............................. GeorgeBaker 9 47
(M R Bosley) *hld up in rr: tried to cl on ldrs 2f out: no hdwy over 1f out: wknd fnl f* **20/1**

2051 8 *1 ¾* **Know No Fear**[2] 7128 5-9-9 **63** 6ex..............................(p) KierenFallon 8 48
(A J Lidderdale) *wl in rr: last and struggling over 2f out: no ch after* **4/1**[2]

0010 9 *½* **Goodbye Cash (IRE)**[6] 7037 6-9-1 **58**....................... RobertLButler(3) 7 42
(R J Smith) *pressed ldr to over 2f out: wknd wl over 1f out* **16/1**

0500 10 *1 ½* **The Grey One (IRE)**[5] 7068 7-9-5 **59**..............................(p) LiamKeniry 2 39
(J M Bradley) *chsd ldrs: rdn and lost pl 2f out: wknd* **20/1**

0035 11 *2 ¼* **Quaestor (IRE)**[12] 6903 3-9-2 **59**.......................... RichardKingscote 13 34
(Tom Dascombe) *led at str pce to over 2f out: sn wknd* **12/1**

-430 12 *2 ¼* **Lend A Grand (IRE)**[21] 6671 6-9-5 **59**........................ IanMongan 14 29
(Miss Jo Crowley) *chsd ldrs on inner: lost pl sn after 1/2-way: struggling over 2f out* **15/2**

1m 39.01s (-0.79) **Going Correction** -0.05s/f (Stan)
WFA 3 from 4yo+ 3lb **12** Ran SP% **120.1**
Speed ratings (Par 101): **101,100,98,96,92 91,91,90,89,88 85,83**
toteswingers:1&2:£5.60, 1&3:£5.70, 2&3:£8.00 CSF £23.65 CT £199.23 TOTE £3.00: £1.20, £1.70, £4.50; EX 16.20 Place 6 £6.92, Place 5 £5.52..
Owner Brian Gubby **Bred** Ocal Bloodstock **Trained** Bagshot, Surrey
■ Stewards' Enquiry : Adam Beschizza one-day ban: careless riding (Nov 10)

FOCUS
A moderate handicap in which the winner improved to something like her old form.
Know No Fear Official explanation: jockey said gelding ran flat
T/Plt: £10.30 to a £1 stake. Pool:£61,765.38 - 4,367.08 winning tickets T/Qpdt: £2.20 to a £1 stake. Pool:£7,780.08 - 2,588.92 winning tickets JN

6704 MUSSELBURGH (R-H)
Wednesday, October 27

OFFICIAL GOING: Round course - good to soft (soft in places); straight course - soft (good to soft in places; 5.3)
Wind: Fresh, half against Weather: Fine and dry

7169 TURFTV H'CAP (DIV I) 5f
1:40 (1:40) (Class 5) (0-75,75) 3-Y-0+ **£2,914** (£867; £433; £216) **Stalls** Low

Form RPR
2352 1 **Grissom (IRE)**[9] 6985 4-9-7 **75**.......................... PaulHanagan 4 84
(T D Easterby) *cl up: led 1/2-way: rdn over 1f out: drvn ins fnl f: kpt on wl* **13/8**[1]

4152 2 *nk* **Sandwith**[31] 6398 7-8-8 **62**..............................(v) LNewman 5 70
(A G Foster) *dwlt: hld up towards rr: hdwy 1/2-way: chsd ldrs over 1f out: swtchd lft and rdn to chal ent fnl f: sn drvn and ev ch tl no ex last 50yds* **7/1**

-060 3 *1 ½* **Sloop Johnb**[10] 6962 4-9-0 **73**........................ LeeTopliss(5) 10 76
(R A Fahey) *dwlt: in tch: hdwy on outer over 2f out: rdn to chal and hung lft over 1f out: kpt on same pce* **28/1**

5360 4 *1 ¼* **Berbice (IRE)**[5] 7056 5-8-10 **67**..................... JamesSullivan(3) 8 65
(Miss L A Perratt) *dwlt: hld up towards rr: hdwy 2f out: rdn to chse ldrs over 1f out: sn no imp* **9/1**

040 5 *½* **Distant Sun (USA)**[5] 7051 6-8-6 **63**.................. IanBrennan(3) 7 59
(Miss L A Perratt) *dwlt: hdwy over 2f out: rdn over 1f out: no imp fnl f* **33/1**

0262 6 *4 ½* **Atlantic Beach**[40] 6140 5-9-7 **75**......................(b) SilvestreDeSousa 11 55
(D O'Meara) *qckly away and cl up: rdn along over 2f out: sn wknd* **13/2**[3]

1460 7 *¾* **Musical Bridge**[34] 6303 4-8-13 **67**.....................(b) TomEaves 6 44
(Mrs L Williamson) *hld up towards rr whn sltly hmpd after 1 1/2f: in rr after* **22/1**

0115 8 *1 ¼* **Avertuoso**[13] 6880 6-8-9 **70**..........................(v) AdamCarter(7) 2 43
(B Smart) *led: rdn along and hdd 1/2-way: drvn over 1f out and sn wknd* **6/1**[2]

1405 9 *4* **Cayman Fox**[19] 6706 5-9-3 **71**........................... PJMcDonald 3 29
(Miss L A Perratt) *dwlt: trckd ldrs whn stmbld bdly after 1 1/2f: towards rr after* **15/2**

64.13 secs (3.73) **Going Correction** +0.75s/f (Yiel) **9** Ran SP% **110.7**
Speed ratings (Par 103): **100,99,97,95,94 87,85,83,77**
toteswingers:1&2:£7.80, 1&3:£8.30, 2&3:£8.80 CSF £12.19 CT £210.35 TOTE £3.20: £1.90, £1.50, £6.90; EX 9.00 TRIFECTA Not won..
Owner Jim & Helen Bowers **Bred** Michael McGlynn **Trained** Great Habton, N Yorks
■ Stewards' Enquiry : Silvestre De Sousa five-day ban: carless riding (Nov 10-13,15)
Paul Hanagan one-day ban: used whip with excessive frequency (Nov 10)

FOCUS
Minimal rain overnight had only slightly affected the going, but the time was modest due in part to the brisk headwind. The first division of this ordinary sprint handicap, and slightly slower than the second. The form is rated around the winner.

7170 ICOPAL ROOFING CONTRACTOR AMATEUR RIDERS' H'CAP 5f
2:10 (2:11) (Class 6) (0-60,63) 3-Y-0+ **£1,873** (£581; £290; £145) **Stalls** Low

Form RPR
0203 1 **Sands Of Dee (USA)**[8] 7007 3-10-13 **59** ow2.............. MrMSeston 10 68
(J A Glover) *cl up: led 2f out and sn rdn: drvn over 1f out: edgd rt ins fnl f: kpt on wl towards fin* **4/1**[1]

3044 2 *1 ¼* **Monsieur Harvey**[28] 6464 4-9-10 **47**..................... MrJNewman(5) 9 52
(B Smart) *trckd ldrs: hdwy and cl up 1/2-way: rdn to chal over 1f out and ev ch tl drvn and no ex wl ins fnl f* **9/2**[2]

3643 3 *½* **Mansii**[14] 6847 5-10-4 **53**.....................................(t) MrJMQuinlan(3) 2 56
(P J McBride) *in tch: rdn along and outpcd 1/2-way: hdwy wl over 1f out: sn swtchd rt and rdn: drvn and kpt on ins fnl f* **5/1**[3]

0611 4 *shd* **Fashion Icon (USA)**[1] 7148 4-10-5 **58** 6ex..................(p) MrSMurray(7) 3 60
(D O'Meara) *led: hdd 2f out and grad wknd appr fnl f* **11/2**

0550 5 *1 ¾* **Cross Of Lorraine (IRE)**[10] 6965 7-10-7 **60**............(b) MissCJones(7) 6 56
(C Grant) *hmpd s and bhd: swtchd rt to outer and hdwy wl over 1f out: sn edgd rt and kpt on fnl f* **10/1**

0000 6 *4 ½* **Angelofthenorth**[19] 6708 8-10-0 **46** oh1........................ MrSDobson 5 26
(C J Teague) *hmpd s and bhd tl sme late hdwy* **33/1**

000/ 7 *2 ¾* **Eilean Eeve**[749] 6573 4-9-9 **46** oh1..................... MrGJCockburn(5) 4 16
(A G Foster) *wnt rt s: chsd ldrs: rdn along bef 1/2-way and sn wknd* **40/1**

0553 8 *shd* **Attrition**[22] 6643 3-10-0 **53**................................... MrAJones(7) 7 23
(Andrew Reid) *chsd ldrs: rdn along 2f out: grad wknd* **10/1**

0530 9 *½* **Drumpellier (IRE)**[13] 6880 3-10-9 **55**........................ MrSWalker 11 23
(S G West) *in tch: hdwy to chse ldrs 2f out: sn rdn and wknd over 1f out* **13/2**

2000 10 *1* **Philosophers Stone (FR)**[12] 6898 3-10-6 **59**.......... MissSRussell(7) 12 23
(T D Barron) *racd wd: chsd ldrs to 1/2-way: sn wknd* **16/1**

65.57 secs (5.17) **Going Correction** +0.75s/f (Yiel) **10** Ran SP% **113.0**
Speed ratings (Par 101): **88,86,85,85,82 75,70,70,69,68**
toteswingers:1&2:£5.00, 1&3:£3.30, 2&3:£3.50 CSF £21.08 CT £91.87 TOTE £6.00: £2.90, £1.40, £1.50; EX 25.00.
Owner Paul J Dixon & Brian Morton **Bred** Mike Abraham **Trained** Babworth, Notts
■ Stewards' Enquiry : Mr G J Cockburn caution: used whip when out of contention
Mr M Seston four-day ban: used whip with excessive frequency (Nov 17,23,29,30)
Miss S Russell caution: used whip when out of contention
Mr A Jones caution: used whip when out of contention

FOCUS
A moderate amateur riders' sprint run 0.74secs slower than the opener. The winner reversed recent Catterick form with the fourth.

7171 R&M ENGINEERING LTD, UGIE ON TOUR (S) STKS 1m 1f
2:40 (2:41) (Class 6) 3-Y-0+ **£1,942** (£578; £288; £144) **Stalls** High

Form RPR
3000 1 **Opus Maximus (IRE)**[19] 6709 5-9-6 85...................... JoeFanning 13 74
(M Johnston) *chsd ldng pair: hdwy over 2f out: rdn wl over 1f out: chsd ldr whn n.m.r ins fnl f: sn swtchd lft and drvn: styd on to ld nr fin* **15/8**[2]

0323 2 *nk* **King Of The Moors (USA)**[31] 6396 7-9-6 63...........(b) FrannyNorton 12 73
(D Bourton) *led: rdn clr wl over 2f out: drvn over 1f out: hung rt ins fnl f: hdd and no ex nr fin* **8/1**[3]

5050 3 *4 ½* **Finsbury**[5] 7054 7-9-6 58.. TomEaves 3 63
(Miss L A Perratt) *hld up towards rr: hdwy 3f out: rdn to chse ldrs 2f out: drvn and n.m.r over 1f out: kpt on towards fin* **80/1**

5010 4 *hd* **Kimberley Downs (USA)**[14] 5436 4-9-3 65.................. GaryBartley(3) 1 63
(N Wilson) *chsd ldr: rdn along 3f out: drvn 2f out: grad wknd appr fnl f* **25/1**

034 5 *nk* **Ra Junior (USA)**[31] 6396 4-8-11 64........................... PaulPickard(3) 10 56
(P T Midgley) *in tch: hdwy on outer to chse ldrs wl over 2f out: sn rdn: drvn and one pce appr fnl f* **14/1**

3211 6 *1 ½* **Fremen (USA)**[35] 6296 10-9-6 85............................ AdrianNicholls 4 59
(D Nicholls) *trckd ldrs: effrt over 2f out and sn pushed along: rdn wl over 1f out: wknd appr fnl f* **5/4**[1]

1130 7 *1 ¼* **Abbondanza (IRE)**[95] 4354 7-9-3 80...................... MichaelGeran(3) 5 56
(D Nicholls) *hld up towards rr: sme hdwy 3f out: sn rdn along and n.d* **10/1**

00 8 *4* **Balance On Time (IRE)**[37] 6242 4-8-6 41................. JamesSullivan(3) 8 36
(Miss L A Perratt) *in tch: hdwy to chse ldrs 3f out: effrt on inner to chal over 2f out and ev ch: sn rdn and wknd* **125/1**

9 *9* **Walleyd (IRE)** 3-8-10 0..................................... LNewman 11 21
(Miss L A Perratt) *s.i.s: a bhd* **200/1**

030/ 10 *1 ¼* **Beverly Hill Billy**[535] 4894 6-8-9 0........................ LeeTopliss(5) 9 19
(Miss S E Forster) *s.i.s: a bhd* **33/1**

400 11 *5* **Anna's Boy**[10] 6966 3-8-10 40................................ RoystonFfrench 6 —
(A Berry) *a bhd* **150/1**

1m 59.72s (5.82) **Going Correction** +0.575s/f (Yiel)
WFA 3 from 4yo+ 4lb **11** Ran SP% **116.1**
Speed ratings (Par 101): **97,96,92,92,92 90,89,86,78,77 72**
toteswingers:1&2:£3.10, 1&3:£22.40, 2&3:£21.10 CSF £16.61 TOTE £2.60: £1.10, £1.80, £9.90; EX 15.80.There was no bid for the winner.
Owner Jim McGrath **Bred** Mrs Anne Marie Burns **Trained** Middleham Moor, N Yorks

FOCUS
A wide range of abilities amongst the runners in this seller in which three stood out on official marks, and although one of those won the other two failed to make the frame. The form does not look solid.

7172 EUROPEAN BREEDERS' FUND MAIDEN STKS 1m
3:15 (3:15) (Class 3) 2-Y-O **£6,476** (£1,927; £963; £481) **Stalls** High

Form RPR
1 **Our Dynasty (IRE)** 2-9-0 0.................................... IanBrennan(3) 2 80+
(J J Quinn) *trckd ldrs: pushed along and green 3f out: swtchd rt and hdwy over 2f out: rdn to ld 1 1/2f out: kpt on wl fnl f* **9/4**[2]

6 **2** *1* **Blue Destination**82 4803 2-9-3 0 (t) PaulHanagan 4 78+
(P J McBride) *trckd ldrs: hdwy 3f out: rdn to ld briefly wl over 1f out: sn hdd and drvn: kpt on u.p fnl f* **5/4**1

2340 **3** *4* **Hoppy's Flyer (FR)**58 5622 2-8-9 85 RussKennemore(3) 9 64
(P A Kirby) *sn led: rdn along over 2f out: drvn and hdd wl over 1f out: sn edgd rt and kpt on same pce* **10/1**

4 *10* **Stansonnit** 2-9-3 0 PJMcDonald 8 47+
(G A Swinbank) *dwlt and green in rr: hdwy over 3f out: kpt on fnl 2f: nvr nr ldrs: bttr for r* **10/1**

5342 **5** *½* **Icy Blue**11 6919 2-9-0 70 AmyRyan(3) 1 46+
(R M Whitaker) *wnt lft s: towards rr: hdwy on outer 1/2-way: rdn to chse ldrs wl over 2f out: sn drvn and n.d* **8/1**3

0 **6** *3½* **Pretty Diamond (IRE)**15 6831 2-8-12 0 JoeFanning 7 33
(M Johnston) *chsd ldrs: rdn along 3f out: drvn over 2f out and sn wknd* **16/1**

0 **7** *3¼* **Waterford Star (IRE)**15 6827 2-9-3 0 SilvestreDeSousa 3 31
(M Johnston) *dwlt: a towards rr* **25/1**

0 **8** *hd* **Shirocco Vice (IRE)**32 6360 2-8-7 0 LeeTopliss(5) 10 26
(R A Fahey) *a towards rr* **100/1**

00 **9** *14* **Fearless Poet (IRE)**35 6293 2-9-3 0 TomEaves 6 —
(B Smart) *cl up: rdn along 3f out: wknd over 2f out* **80/1**

00 **10** *9* **Sheedal (IRE)**5 7049 2-8-9 0 JamesSullivan(3) 5 —
(Miss L A Perratt) *a towards rr* **250/1**

00 **11** *14* **Immacolata (IRE)**57 5640 2-8-5 10 VictorSantos(7) 11 —
(A Berry) *chsd ldrs 3f: sn lost pl and bhd* **300/1**

1m 46.59s (5.39) **Going Correction** +0.575s/f (Yiel) **11** Ran SP% **117.2**
Speed ratings (Par 99): **96,95,91,81,80 77,73,73,59,50 36**
toteswingers:1&2:£2.00, 1&3:£5.40, 2&3:£3.20 CSF £5.35 TOTE £4.10: £2.10, £1.10, £2.50; EX 7.50.
Owner Mrs S Quinn **Bred** E Puerari, Janus B/S & Oceanic B/S **Trained** Settrington, N Yorks

FOCUS
Quite a valuable maiden, but not many could be seriously fancied and these juveniles found this a proper test of stamina in the conditions. The field came more towards the centre of the track once in line for home, but ended up against the far rail. The race produced a one-two for sire Dubai Destination. The time was decent and it was a nice start from the winner.

NOTEBOOK
Our Dynasty(IRE) ◆, a 52,000euros 2-y-o and half-brother to a dual winner at up to 1m1f in France, was well backed earlier in the day. He did show signs of greenness in the middle of the field rounding the home turn, but responded to the pressure and found himself in front after being switched to the inside rail over a furlong from home. He saw his race out really well and, apparently held in some regard by connections, looks a colt with a future. (op 5-2 tchd 11-4)
Blue Destination, given a break since a promising debut in a Newmarket maiden in August which has since worked out extremely well, had a tongue tie on this time. He held every chance a furlong from home, but couldn't cope with the winner and tended to hang about inside the last furlong. Of the pair, he looked the one with no previous experience and this big, scopey colt should make up into a nice 3-y-o. (op 11-8 tchd 6-4)
Hoppy's Flyer(FR), making her debut for the yard after finishing in the frame in maiden/conditions events both here and in France for Tom Dascombe, didn't seem to stay this trip in soft ground at Deauville last time and, having held a clear advantage starting up the home straight, she didn't see this out either. A return to 7f will help, but she doesn't justify an official mark of 85. (op 12-1 tchd 9-1)
Stansonnit was never in the race, but he did make up some late ground from well off the pace over the last 2f. A 20,000gns yearling, he has a real blend of speed and stamina in his pedigree, but judging by this debut effort he looks a stayer. (op 9-1 tchd 8-1)
Icy Blue, officially rated 70, had been gradually getting closer to winning but this trip again appeared beyond him in the conditions and he has had more chances than most. (op 7-1 tchd 13-2)

7173 WEATHERBYS BLOODSTOCK INSURANCE WILLIE PARK TROPHY H'CAP 2m
3:50 (3:50) (Class 2) (0-100,88) 3-Y-O+
£10,592 (£3,172; £1,586; £793; £396; £198) **Stalls** Low

Form RPR
5005 **1** **Palomar (USA)**11 6926 8-9-11 85 PaulHanagan 4 99+
(B Ellison) *hld up in rr: smooth hdwy over 4f out: trckd ldrs 3f out: led 2f out and sn rdn: put hd in air and drvn fnl f: kpt on* **3/1**1

5006 **2** *3¼* **Bowdler's Magic**31 6387 3-9-3 87 SilvestreDeSousa 6 95
(M Johnston) *trckd ldrs: hdwy 3f out: rdn to chse wnr wl over 1f out: drvn to chal and ev ch ent fnl f: sn edgd rt and one pce* **7/2**2

1552 **3** *9* **Bollin Felix**32 6362 6-10-0 88 (v) DavidAllan 1 85
(T D Easterby) *trckd ldrs: hdwy 1/2-way: led 4f out: rdn and hdd 2f out: sn drvn and one pce* **11/2**3

3205 **4** *6* **Atlantic Tiger (IRE)**32 6352 3-9-2 86 JoeFanning 7 76
(M Johnston) *prom: rdn along over 4f out: wknd 3f out* **11/2**3

5114 **5** *1* **Chookie Hamilton**12 6895 6-9-8 82 TomEaves 3 71
(V P Donoghue) *hld up in tch: effrt and sme hdwy 4f out: sn rdn and n.d* **8/1**

2131 **6** *2½* **Graceful Descent (FR)**27 6493 5-9-6 80 FrannyNorton 2 66
(J S Goldie) *trckd ldrs: hdwy to chse ldr over 3f out: rdn wl over 2f out: sn wknd* **11/2**3

034- **7** *30* **Battle Planner (USA)**382 6671 4-9-4 78 PJMcDonald 8 28
(V P Donoghue) *a towards rr: rdn along 6f out: sn outpcd and bhd* **28/1**

1205 **8** *30* **Wicked Daze (IRE)**40 6143 7-9-3 80 JamesSullivan(3) 5 —
(Miss L A Perratt) *led: rdn along and hdd over 4f out: sn wknd* **22/1**

3m 38.95s (5.45) **Going Correction** +0.575s/f (Yiel)
WFA 3 from 4yo+ 10lb **8** Ran SP% **112.3**
Speed ratings (Par 109): **109,107,102,99,99 98,83,68**
toteswingers:1&2:£3.80, 1&3:£3.80, 2&3:£4.60 CSF £13.08 CT £52.69 TOTE £4.40: £1.10, £1.90, £2.10; EX 18.50.
Owner Koo's Racing Club **Bred** Juddmonte Farms Inc **Trained** Norton, N Yorks

FOCUS
A decent and tightly knit staying handicap but in the end only two mattered and they were well strung out behind. The winner is rated back towards his old best.

NOTEBOOK
Palomar(USA) has always been a talented individual but his current trainer has got him firing on all cylinders at present, having won a valuable hurdle at Market Rasen before running a good fifth in the Cesarewitch. He travelled well in rear before cutting through his field early in the straight and, despite showing he still has a kink or two once going on 2f out, he came away to win decisively. He is likely to be aimed at the Ladbroke Hurdle at Ascot before Christmas. (op 10-3 tchd 7-2)
Bowdler's Magic, trying his longest trip to-date, handles this ground well enough and was the only one to give the winner a race. He has dropped back to a more competitive mark now. (op 11-2)
Bollin Felix likes soft ground and was soon racing prominently. However, he was easily brushed aside by the first two after going on at the end of the back straight. (op 5-1)
Atlantic Tiger(IRE) whose wins have both been at 1m4f on Polytrack, appears to stay and handles this ground. He was tracking the pace when carried back by the weakening early leader turning for home, and could never get competitive afterwards. He can be forgiven this. (op 13-2 tchd 5-1)
Chookie Hamilton has had a good season but was struggling soon after halfway here. (op 6-1)
Graceful Descent(FR) has been running well but this was a step up in both class and trip and she did not appear to get home. (op 4-1 tchd 7-2)

7174 WEATHERBYS BANK NURSERY 5f
4:25 (4:26) (Class 4) (0-85,78) 2-Y-O
£3,885 (£1,156; £577; £288) **Stalls** Low

Form RPR
3200 **1** **Berberana (IRE)**25 6568 2-9-5 76 DavidAllan 4 82
(T D Easterby) *trckd ldrs: hdwy on inner wl over 1f out: rdn to chal ent fnl f: kpt on to ld last 100yds* **7/2**2

5516 **2** *1* **Black Annis Bower**33 6325 2-8-7 67 JamesSullivan(3) 8 69
(M W Easterby) *in tch: hdwy on outer 2f out: rdn to chal over 1f out: led jst ins fnl f: drvn: hdd and nt qckn last 100yds* **20/1**

5522 **3** *1* **Crimson Knot (IRE)**19 6705 2-9-7 78 PaulHanagan 7 77
(A Berry) *trckd ldrs: smooth hdwy to ld 2f out: rdn over 1f out: drvn and hdd jst ins fnl f: kpt on same pce* **9/2**3

15 **4** *¾* **Yellow Dandy (IRE)**11 6916 2-9-0 74 MichaelO'Connell(3) 5 70
(Liam McAteer, Ire) *cl up: rdn 2f out and ev ch tl drvn and one pce ent fnl f* **9/1**

4402 **5** *hd* **Rothesay Chancer**5 7050 2-8-1 58 JoeFanning 6 53+
(J S Goldie) *dwlt: rdn along and outpcd in rr: hdwy wl over 1f out: kpt on ins fnl f: eased nr fin: fin lame* **9/2**3

314 **6** *1¼* **Lady Paris (IRE)**19 6719 2-9-6 77 TomEaves 1 68
(B Smart) *dwlt and in rr: hdwy wl over 1f out: effrt and nt clr run ins fnl f: no ch after* **3/1**1

3100 **7** *17* **Abzolutely (IRE)**12 6900 2-8-13 70 SilvestreDeSousa 3 —
(D O'Meara) *led: rdn along and hdd 2f out: sn drvn and wknd: eased fnl f* **6/1**

64.02 secs (3.62) **Going Correction** +0.75s/f (Yiel) **7** Ran SP% **112.6**
Speed ratings (Par 97): **101,99,97,96,96 94,67**
toteswingers:1&2:£18.00, 1&3:£3.80, 2&3:£8.40 CSF £62.18 CT £316.91 TOTE £4.50: £2.00, £16.60; EX 112.40.
Owner D A West **Bred** Patrick F Kelly And M J Foley **Trained** Great Habton, N Yorks

FOCUS
A fair nursery run 0.81secs faster than the quickest of the earlier races over the trip. Things got tight in the last 2f. The winner was back to her Haydock form from last month.

NOTEBOOK
Berberana(IRE) has been taking on some decent company of late and the drop in grade clearly helped her. She tracked the pace early and then got a gap nearest the rail 2f out. She took a while to come through but finished strongest of all in the last furlong and scored decisively. (op 5-1)
Black Annis Bower has been running over further of late but the drop in trip did not inconvenience her and she ran well from the outside draw, looking the winner until inside the last furlong. (op 18-1)
Crimson Knot(IRE) is a regular here, having her eighth race over C&D this season. She travelled well before taking the lead inside the last 2f but could not sustain her effort in the closing stages. She is pretty consistent and helps set the standard. (op 7-2 tchd 10-3)
Yellow Dandy(IRE), the Irish raider, handles some cut but might be better on a sounder surface. She had her chance but was a little short of room in the closing stages, and had no more to offer under pressure. (op 8-1)
Rothesay Chancer tends to miss the break but has run well here before and came to have a chance entering the final furlong but was eased near the line, his rider reporting that the colt felt lame. He is probably worth another go over 6f. Official explanation: vet said colt returned lame behind (tchd 5-1)
Lady Paris(IRE) looked a bit unlucky as she did not get the best of breaks then had nowhere to go over a furlong out when looking for a run. Although she did not pick up after than, she can be forgiven this effort. Official explanation: jockey said filly was denied a clear run (op 10-3)
Abzolutely(IRE) got upset in the stalls but broke well enough to make the early running, before being seen off in the last 2f. (op 15-2 tchd 8-1)

7175 TURFTV H'CAP (DIV II OF 1.40) 5f
5:00 (5:00) (Class 5) (0-75,75) 3-Y-O+
£2,914 (£867; £433; £216) **Stalls** Low

Form RPR
0200 **1** **La Capriosa**10 6965 4-9-2 70 DavidAllan 4 78
(J A Glover) *a cl up: chal 2f out: rdn over 1f out: styd on to ld last 100yds: drvn and kpt on gamely nr fin* **7/1**

3021 **2** *nk* **Highland Warrior**31 6398 11-8-12 69 PaulPickard(3) 10 76
(P T Midgley) *dwlt and pushed along in rr: hdwy on outer wl over 1f out: rdn to chse ldrs ent fnl f: chal and ev ch whn edgd rt last 100yds: nt qckn nr line* **5/1**2

3520 **3** *hd* **Secret Venue**20 6700 4-8-10 67 (v) MichaelO'Connell(3) 1 73
(Jedd O'Keeffe) *led: rdn along wl over 1f out: drvn ent fnl f: hdd and no ex last 100yds* **15/2**

3023 **4** *2¾* **Wicked Wilma (IRE)**10 6965 6-8-9 63 (t) RoystonFfrench 6 59
(A Berry) *bmpd s and towards rr: hdwy to trck ldrs 1/2-way: rdn over 1f out: kpt on ins fnl f* **11/2**3

5001 **5** *1¼* **Lesley's Choice**19 6708 4-9-7 75 (v) PaulHanagan 8 67
(Miss L A Perratt) *cl up on outer: rdn 2f out and ev ch tl drvn and wknd appr fnl f* **4/1**1

1055 **6** *nk* **Mandarin Spirit (IRE)**19 6708 10-8-12 66 (b) PJMcDonald 5 57
(Miss L A Perratt) *chsd ldrs: hdwy over 2f out: rdn wl over 1f out and sn btn* **18/1**

0100 **7** *½* **Bosun Breese**25 6572 5-9-0 73 (b1) DeanHeslop(5) 7 62
(T D Barron) *cl up: rdn along over 2f out: grad wknd* **14/1**

0510 **8** *5* **Arriva La Diva**44 6031 4-8-6 63 JamesSullivan(3) 3 34
(Miss L A Perratt) *chsd ldrs: rdn along 1/2-way: sn wknd* **12/1**

1104 **9** *1½* **Select Committee**9 6985 5-9-3 74 (v) IanBrennan(3) 2 39
(J J Quinn) *sn rdn along: outpcd and bhd fr 1/2-way* **4/1**1

63.70 secs (3.30) **Going Correction** +0.75s/f (Yiel) **9** Ran SP% **115.9**
Speed ratings (Par 103): **103,102,102,97,95 95,94,86,84**
toteswingers:1&2:£10.90, 1&3:£7.30, 2&3:£6.30 CSF £42.05 CT £273.53 TOTE £7.90: £2.10, £2.40, £2.50; EX 41.70.
Owner Paul J Dixon **Bred** Slatch Farm Stud **Trained** Babworth, Notts
■ Stewards' Enquiry : David Allan caution: used whip with excessive frequency.

FOCUS
The second leg of this modest handicap was run 1.13secs faster than the first and was the quickest time of the day over the trip, although the headwind might have eased a little and the ground dried out. The form looks sound.

7176 SCOTTISH RACING YOUR BETTER BET H'CAP 1m 6f
5:30 (5:30) (Class 6) (0-65,65) 3-Y-O+
£1,942 (£578; £288; £144) **Stalls** High

Form RPR
4105 **1** **Mohawk Ridge**12 6895 4-9-9 65 (p) LeeTopliss(5) 8 74
(M Dods) *trckd ldrs: effrt over 3f out and sn cl up: rdn to chal wl over 2f out: drvn to ld over 1f out: styd on gamely* **6/1**3

0213 **2** *1½* **Hong Kong Island (IRE)**19 6707 3-9-5 65 PaulHanagan 3 71
(A G Foster) *trckd ldrs: hdwy over 4f out: rdn to ld 3f out: sn jnd and drvn: hdd over 1f out: sn hung rt and no ex* **15/8**1

4345 **3** *5* **Oddsmaker (IRE)**[11] 6915 9-9-8 **59**..................................(t) JoeFanning 9 58
(M A Barnes) *led: pushed along over 5f out: rdn and hdd over 3f out: drvn and kpt on same pce fnl 2f* **9/2**[2]

3500 **4** *3/4* **Maid Of Meft**[41] 6109 3-9-0 **60**... PJMcDonald 4 58
(Miss L A Perratt) *hld up towards rr: hdwy over 3f out: rdn wl over 3f out: drvn and kpt on same pce fnl 2f* **50/1**

1146 **5** *7* **Ballade De La Mer**[32] 6373 4-8-10 **47**..............................(p) LNewman 2 35
(A G Foster) *hld up in rr: hdwy and in tch over 3f out: sn rdn and btn over 2f out* **16/1**

00 **6** *3 1/2* **Hunters Belt (IRE)**[41] 6109 6-9-8 **62**..........................(p) GaryBartley(3) 5 45
(N Wilson) *prom: hdwy to chse ldr after 5f: led over 3f out: sn rdn and hdd 3f out: sn drvn and wknd* **16/1**

6140 **7** *30* **Silent Lucidity (IRE)**[41] 6109 6-9-4 **55**..................................(p) DavidAllan 6 —
(P D Niven) *chsd ldrs: rdn along over 3f out: sn wknd* **9/2**[2]

3-05 **8** *8* **Toshi (USA)**[19] 6707 8-8-13 **50**.. FrannyNorton 1 —
(J S Goldie) *a in rr: rdn along 1/2-way: sn bhd* **7/1**

3m 16.43s (11.13) **Going Correction** +0.575s/f (Yiel)
WFA 3 from 4yo+ 9lb **8** Ran SP% **111.7**
Speed ratings (Par 101): **91,90,87,86,82 80,63,59**
toteswingers:1&2:£3.20, 1&3:£5.50, 2&3:£2.40. totesuper7: Win: Not won. Place: Not won. CSF £16.82 CT £53.61 TOTE £6.10: £2.30, £1.90, £1.20; EX 25.30 Place 6: £35.06, Place 5 £18.78..
Owner Doug Graham **Bred** Old Mill Stud Ltd And Oomswell Ltd **Trained** Denton, Co Durham

FOCUS

A moderate staying handicap in which they went a good gallop and it developed into a war of attrition, with the first two finishing clear. The winner posted a personal best.
Toshi(USA) Official explanation: jockey said gelding moved poorly throughout
T/Plt: £112.30 to a £1 stake. Pool:£44,600.94 - 289.84 winning tickets T/Qpdt: £26.80 to a £1 stake. Pool:£3,770.88 - 104.10 winning tickets JR

6873 NOTTINGHAM (L-H)

Wednesday, October 27

OFFICIAL GOING: Good to soft (soft in places) changing to soft (good to soft in places) after race 2 (2:00)
All race son inner course.
Wind: Light against Weather: Fine

7177 EXCLUSIVE NETWORKS PROUDLY PARTNERS EXINDA (S) STKS 1m 75y

1:30 (1:30) (Class 6) 2-Y-O £1,706 (£503; £252) **Stalls** Centre

Form RPR

1 **Brand Bob (IRE)**[72] 5165 2-8-11 0.. DaneO'Neill 16 63
(Miss Amy Weaver) *a.p: chsd ldr 6f out: led over 2f out: rdn out* **11/2**[2]

6400 **2** *nk* **Bathwick Scanno (IRE)**[2] 7118 2-8-11 57.................... CathyGannon 2 62
(P D Evans) *hld up: hdwy over 3f out: rdn to chse wnr over 1f out: r.o* **14/1**

050 **3** *4* **Fire Crystal**[39] 6209 2-8-6 54.. EddieCreighton 9 48
(M R Channon) *s.i.s: hld up: hdwy over 3f out: rdn and hung lft over 1f out: styd on same pce fnl f* **12/1**

2200 **4** *1* **Calormen**[58] 5581 2-8-11 56.. DarryllHolland 15 51
(A G Juckes) *hld up: hdwy u.p and hung lft fr over 1f out: nt trble ldrs* **40/1**

000 **5** *2* **Gypsy Legend (IRE)**[34] 6307 2-8-6 55........................... DavidProbert 5 42+
(S Kirk) *hld up: hdwy over 2f out: nt rch ldrs* **6/1**[3]

0 **6** *nk* **Lynchpin**[26] 6542 2-8-11 0....................................... TomMcLaughlin 4 46
(R A Harris) *chsd ldrs: rdn over 2f out: wknd fnl f* **66/1**

0 **7** *1* **Seadream**[16] 6811 2-8-11 0... TravisBlock 17 44
(M D I Usher) *plld hrd: led 7f out: hdd over 2f out: wknd fnl f* **16/1**

50 **8** *shd* **Simmons**[39] 6209 2-8-6 0.. AndreaAtzeni 6 39
(Matthew Salaman) *s.i.s: hld up: hdwy u.p over 1f out: nvr on terms* **14/1**

003 **9** *1/2* **Neytiri**[30] 6425 2-8-6 60... HayleyTurner 8 37
(R M Beckett) *led 1f: chsd ldrs: rdn over 1f out: wknd ins fnl f* **11/4**[1]

0000 **10** *3/4* **Erythrina (IRE)**[56] 5660 2-8-6 52........................... FrankieMcDonald 13 36
(B G Powell) *prom: rdn over 2f out: sn wknd* **66/1**

000 **11** *1 1/4* **Boogie Star**[30] 6414 2-8-11 59.......................................(p) LiamKeniry 11 38
(J S Moore) *chsd ldrs tl rdn and wknd over 2f out* **14/1**

0 **12** *3* **Jessica Ashton**[14] 6849 2-8-6 0... MartinLane 12 26
(J Gallagher) *s.i.s: a in rr* **100/1**

600 **13** *23* **Chagal (IRE)**[51] 5814 2-8-11 53...................................... PhillipMakin 7 —
(K A Ryan) *sn pushed along and a in rr: t.o* **12/1**

64 **14** *21* **Libertia**[83] 4729 2-8-6 0... ChrisCatlin 1 —
(A G Newcombe) *hld up in tch: racd keenly: rdn and wknd over 3f out: t.o* **14/1**

0000 **15** *43* **Appyjack**[40] 6162 2-8-11 55..(t) RichardHughes 10 —
(J S Moore) *hld up: a in rr: bhd fnl 4f: t.o* **12/1**

1m 51.78s (2.18) **Going Correction** 0.0s/f (Good) **15** Ran SP% **118.4**
Speed ratings (Par 93): **89,88,84,83,81 81,80,80,79,79 77,74,51,30,—**
toteswingers:1&2:£17.80, 1&3:£18.70, 2&3:£54.00 CSF £77.70 TOTE £3.80: £1.30, £5.50, £5.80; EX 87.90 TRIFECTA Not won..There was no bid for the winner.
Owner Miss A Weaver **Bred** Anamoine Ltd **Trained** Newmarket, Suffolk

FOCUS

Following 4.5mm of rain the previous day and overnight, the ground had eased to good to soft, soft in places (GoingStick 6.2). There was a stiff breeze in the runners' faces up the straight and it proved a stiff test of stamina. An ordinary seller where the first two finished clear. The winner is rated to his Irish form.

NOTEBOOK

Brand Bob(IRE) was having his first race for a new stable following three maiden starts in Ireland. A good start helped as he overcame a tricky outside draw and the drop in class, coupled with the step up in trip and softer ground, all helped see him get off the mark. He hadn't run for ten weeks so there might be some improvement to come. (op 4-1)
Bathwick Scanno(IRE), making a quick reappearance after finishing down the field on his nursery debut two days earlier, stayed on well to throw down a late challenge to the winner. The longer trip really suited him. (op 20-1)
Fire Crystal, in midfield in a similar race over 7f on Polytrack last time, couldn't go with the first two in the closing stages but seemed to get the trip all right. (op 16-1)
Calormen has plenty of speed in his pedigree so it's no surprise that he's spent his career so far running over sprint distances, but he actually ran well on this big step up in trip. Official explanation: jockey said colt hung left (op 33-1)
Gypsy Legend(IRE) was given every chance but didn't seem to see out the trip. (op 8-1)

Neytiri, another stepping up in trip, was up there throughout but found the final 2f tough going. (op 9-4 tchd 3-1 in a place)

7178 E B F EXCLUSIVE NETWORKS PROUDLY PARTNERS KASPERSKY OATH COLTS' AND GELDINGS' MAIDEN STKS (DIV I) 1m 75y

2:00 (2:01) (Class 4) 2-Y-O £4,209 (£1,252; £625; £312) **Stalls** Centre

Form RPR

25 **1** **Parlour Games**[28] 6457 2-9-0 0...................................... AhmedAjtebi 12 77
(Mahmood Al Zarooni) *chsd ldrs: led over 3f out: rdn out* **7/1**

2 *1 1/2* **Ittirad (USA)** 2-9-0 0.. PhilipRobinson 10 74+
(M A Jarvis) *hld up: hdwy over 3f out: rdn to chse wnr over 1f out: no imp wl ins fnl f* **11/2**

0 **3** *3* **Albert Bridge**[28] 6474 2-9-0 0................................ RichardKingscote 8 69+
(R M Beckett) *broke wl: sn pushed along and lost pl: hdwy over 1f out: r.o: nt rch ldrs* **4/1**[3]

0 **4** *2 3/4* **Romeo Montague**[12] 6883 2-9-0 0.............................. TomMcLaughlin 1 61+
(E A L Dunlop) *s.s: in rr: hdwy over 1f out: nt trble ldrs* **66/1**

0 **5** *2* **Sea Soldier (IRE)**[12] 6883 2-9-0 0................................ JimmyFortune 3 57
(A M Balding) *chsd ldrs: rdn over 2f out: wknd fnl f* **5/2**[1]

404 **6** *6* **Benidorm**[11] 6919 2-9-0 65... JamesDoyle 7 43
(A J McCabe) *chsd ldrs: rdn over 2f out: wknd fnl f* **33/1**

7 *2 1/4* **Spifer (IRE)** 2-9-0 0.. KierenFallon 2 39
(L M Cumani) *prom: nt clr run over 2f out: wknd over 1f out* **14/1**

00 **8** *1* **Ishikawa (IRE)**[10] 6953 2-9-0 0..................................... FergusSweeney 5 36
(A King) *plld hrd and prom: wknd over 1f out* **150/1**

06 **9** *1* **Lordofthehouse (IRE)**[13] 6874 2-9-0 0............................. RyanMoore 9 34
(W J Haggas) *s.s: sn pushed along and a in rr* **16/1**

10 *14* **Szabo's Destiny** 2-9-0 0... PaulMulrennan 11 —
(J G Given) *dwlt: pushed along in rr: rdn 5f out: lost tch fr over 3f out: t.o* **100/1**

11 *1 1/4* **Emerald Royal** 2-9-0 0... EddieCreighton 6 —
(E J Creighton) *s.s: a in rr: bhd fnl 3f: t.o* **150/1**

63 **12** *6* **Conjuror's Bluff**[10] 6953 2-9-0 0................................... RichardHughes 4 —
(R Hannon) *led: hdd over 3f out: wknd over 2f out: t.o* **7/2**[2]

1m 50.06s (0.46) **Going Correction** 0.0s/f (Good) **12** Ran SP% **118.0**
Speed ratings (Par 97): **97,95,92,89,87 81,79,78,77,63 62,56**
toteswingers:1&2:£5.00, 1&3:£3.30, 2&3:£3.50 CSF £44.90 TOTE £7.10: £2.60, £2.50, £1.80; EX 24.40 Trifecta £142.40 Pool of : £506.32 - 2.63 winning units..
Owner Godolphin **Bred** Darley **Trained** Newmarket, Suffolk

FOCUS

Probably just a fair maiden. The winner bounced back and the form is rated around his debut effort and the weaker members of this field.

NOTEBOOK

Parlour Games was very disappointing at Newcastle on his previous start but the ground was bottomless that day and, while it was on the soft side here, conditions weren't quite as testing. His debut effort still made him the one to beat in this company and he got the job done well enough, staying on strongly to score. Despite his breeding, he doesn't look anything special, but better ground should help and he should make up into a middle-distance horse next year. (op 11-2)
Ittirad(USA), a newcomer by Dubai Destination out of Oaks runner-up Noushkey, ran a promising race behind the more experienced winner. He's another who'll be suited by further next year and quicker ground ought to suit him. (op 9-2 tchd 6-1)
Albert Bridge, like on his debut, was well backed beforehand. He clearly shows quite a bit at home, but he was still green here and only got going very late to take third. He'll stay a good deal further next season and should win handicaps. (op 8-1)
Romeo Montague fell out of the stalls and could never get competitive, but he did stay on through beaten horses and he'll be another for handicaps after one more run.
Sea Soldier(IRE) didn't really see his race out having been prominent from the off. He's bred to make a better 3-y-o, though. (op 7-2)
Benidorm, about whom there was a stamina query, probably wasn't good enough anyway, but he appeared to fail to get home. (op 25-1)
Spifer(IRE) showed signs of greenness and is another who will only be seen at his best with a winter on his back. Official explanation: jockey said colt had no more to give (op 10-1)
Conjuror's Bluff was disappointing, but he's now had the three required starts for a mark. Official explanation: jockey said colt stopped quickly (op 10-3 tchd 11-4)

7179 E B F EXCLUSIVE NETWORKS PROUDLY PARTNERS KASPERSKY OATH COLTS' AND GELDINGS' MAIDEN STKS (DIV II) 1m 75y

2:30 (2:31) (Class 4) 2-Y-O £4,209 (£1,252; £625; £312) **Stalls** Centre

Form RPR

54 **1** **Charles Camoin (IRE)**[45] 5985 2-9-0 0......................... RichardHughes 2 77
(S Kirk) *trckd ldr: drvn over 3f out: hung lft and led over 1f out: hld on towards fin* **13/2**[2]

0 **2** *3/4* **Wayward Glance**[12] 6883 2-9-0 0................................. JamieSpencer 12 75
(M L W Bell) *v awkward to load: led: hdd over 1f out: no ex last 75yds* **20/1**

56 **3** *3 1/4* **Secret Edge**[10] 6953 2-9-0 0....................................... FergusSweeney 8 68+
(A King) *trckd ldrs: drvn over 3f out: outpcd over 2f out: styd on to take 3rd last 100yds* **33/1**

4 *1 3/4* **High Jinx (IRE)** 2-9-0 0... WilliamBuick 4 64+
(J R Fanshawe) *s.i.s: sn mid-div: outpcd over 3f out: styd on fnl f* **14/1**[3]

2 **5** *nk* **Academy (IRE)**[27] 6504 2-9-0 0.. RyanMoore 1 64
(Sir Michael Stoute) *dwlt: sn trcking ldrs: upsides and hrd drvn over 2f out: wknd fnl f* **2/11**[1]

6 *nk* **Midlothian (IRE)** 2-9-0 0.......................................(t) AhmedAjtebi 11 63
(Mahmood Al Zarooni) *in tch: drvn 4f out: sn wl outpcd: kpt on fnl f* **14/1**[3]

000 **7** *10* **Invent**[15] 6831 2-9-0 0... SebSanders 3 41
(Sir Mark Prescott) *chsd ldrs: drvn over 3f out: wknd over 2f out* **66/1**

000 **8** *3 1/4* **Our Folly**[16] 6802 2-9-0 45...(v[1]) IanMongan 10 34
(W S Kittow) *in rr: drvn 4f out: sn bhd* **100/1**

0 **9** *nse* **Look For Love**[13] 6873 2-9-0 0................................... GrahamGibbons 7 34
(R Hollinshead) *trckd ldrs: hung lft and lost pl over 2f out* **80/1**

0 **10** *19* **Bollin Harry**[130] 3222 2-9-0 0..................................... RobertWinston 9 —
(T D Easterby) *s.i.s: in rr: bhd fnl 3f: t.o* **66/1**

11 *7* **Newgate Dani** 2-9-0 0... BarryMcHugh 6 —
(N Bycroft) *s.s: a detached in last: t.o* **100/1**

1m 50.81s (1.21) **Going Correction** +0.175s/f (Good) **11** Ran SP% **125.2**
Speed ratings (Par 97): **100,99,96,94,93 93,83,80,80,61 54**
toteswingers:1&2:£6.30, 1&3:£10.70, 2&3:£31.80 CSF £120.25 TOTE £8.50: £1.30, £3.70, £6.90; EX 131.40 Trifecta £552.00 Part won. Pool: £746.05 - 0.94 winning units..
Owner C Wright & The Hon Mrs J M Corbett **Bred** Pat Grogan **Trained** Upper Lambourn, Berks

FOCUS

The ground was officially changed to soft, good to soft in places before this race. The slower of the two divisions by 0.75sec. The winner improved but the favourite was disappointing. The time and the likes of the eighth limit the form.

NOTEBOOK

Charles Camoin(IRE) had put up solid efforts in his first two starts but still looked to have plenty on his plate taking on the Stoute hotpot, but with that one disappointing it took less winning than had looked likely, and his greater experience saw him through in his battle with the once-raced Wayward Glance in the closing stages. His pedigree suggests he'll be a middle-distance colt next season. (op 7-1 tchd 15-2)

Wayward Glance, who hinted at ability on his debut at Newmarket, showed the benefit of that outing, made much of the running, and was last off the bridle. He has the makings of a decent middle-distance handicapper next season.

Secret Edge, whose pedigree suggests this sort of ground ought to suit, stayed on well to take third without troubling the first two. He's now eligible for a mark and should do better in handicap company.

High Jinx(IRE), whose stable is in great form, did best of the newcomers and wasn't beaten up to finish where he did. There's more to come from him.

Academy(IRE) was sent off a very short price to go one better than on his debut when making a good impression behind a more experienced Godolphin colt. He just didn't pick up for pressure, though, and presumably the ground just wasn't to his liking. (op 2-9 tchd 1-4 in places)

Midlothian(IRE) ran very green and will surely know a lot more next time. He could do with better ground too. (tchd 12-1)

7180 EXCLUSIVE NETWORKS PROUDLY PARTNERS NETWORK INSTRUMENTS H'CAP 5f 13y

3:05 (3:06) (Class 5) (0-75,78) 3-Y-0+ **£2,590** (£770; £385; £192) **Stalls** High

Form RPR

0503 **1** **Sharpened Edge**[17] 6772 4-9-5 **73** DavidProbert 15 81
(B Palling) *chsd ldrs: rdn to ld and hung lft ins fnl f: r.o* **14/1**

0503 **2** *nk* **Whiskey Junction**[13] 6858 6-9-3 **71** SebSanders 14 78
(M Quinn) *prom: outpcd 3f out: r.o wl ins fnl f: nt quite get up* **20/1**

2602 **3** *hd* **Milton Of Campsie**[117] 3622 5-9-5 **73** RobertWinston 16 79
(J Balding) *hld up: hdwy over 1f out: r.o wl* **20/1**

04 **4** *½* **Equuleus Pictor**[43] 6064 6-9-7 **75** DarryllHolland 8 79+
(J L Spearing) *hld up: hdwy u.p over 1f out: r.o* **10/1**

3213 **5** *nk* **Westwood**[23] 6625 5-9-4 **72** DaneO'Neill 7 75
(D Haydn Jones) *led overall: rdn over 1f out: hdd and unable qck ins fnl f* **11/2**[3]

4542 **6** *nse* **Make My Dream**[13] 6858 7-9-2 **70** WilliamBuick 17 73
(J Gallagher) *mid-div: hdwy over 1f out: r.o* **5/1**[2]

2644 **7** *1* **Spring Green**[26] 6539 4-9-5 **73** (b[1]) SteveDrowne 10 73
(H Morrison) *s.s: bhd: r.o wl ins fnl f: nrst fin* **9/1**

2101 **8** *nk* **Captain Royale (IRE)**[9] 6981 5-9-10 **78** 6ex (p) MartinLane 13 77
(Miss Tracy Waggott) *chsd ldrs: rdn over 1f out: styng on same pce whn hmpd ins fnl f* **9/1**

1350 **9** *½* **Ace Of Spies (IRE)**[43] 6057 5-9-4 **72** HayleyTurner 12 69
(C R Dore) *mid-div: rdn 1/2-way: styd on ins fnl f: nt pce to chal* **25/1**

6130 **10** *nk* **Love You Louis**[13] 6858 4-9-6 **74** RichardHughes 11 70
(J R Jenkins) *chsd ldrs: rdn over 1f out: no ex ins fnl f* **14/1**

302 **11** *shd* **Bedloe's Island (IRE)**[10] 6965 5-9-1 **69** (p) GrahamGibbons 5 64
(N Bycroft) *s.s: sn mid-div: rdn 1/2-way: nvr nrr* **9/2**[1]

4015 **12** *3 ¾* **Six Diamonds**[11] 6932 3-9-1 **72** RobertLButler(3) 2 54
(P Butler) *chsd ldr on far side tl outpcd fr 1/2-way* **40/1**

0004 **13** *1 ¾* **Sir Geoffrey (IRE)**[6] 7041 4-9-7 **75** (b) IanMongan 3 51
(J A Glover) *led far side duo: rdn over 1f out: wknd ins fnl f* **9/1**

2004 **14** *nk* **Triple Dream**[8] 6998 5-9-4 **72** (p) RichardKingscote 9 46
(J M Bradley) *mid-div: sn drvn along: outpcd fr 1/2-way* **25/1**

0460 **15** *½* **Cut The Cackle (IRE)**[9] 6985 4-8-11 **72** NathanAlison(7) 1 45
(P Butler) *s.s: a bhd* **50/1**

3460 **16** *3 ¼* **Grudge**[47] 5915 5-9-3 **71** (be) BarryMcHugh 6 32
(C R Dore) *prom: rdn 1/2-way: wknd over 1f out* **66/1**

63.25 secs (2.25) **Going Correction** +0.525s/f (Yiel) **16** Ran SP% **125.8**

Speed ratings (Par 103): **103,102,102,101,100 100,99,98,97,97 97,91,88,88,87 82**

toteswingers:1&2:£40.30, 1&3:£43.40, 2&3:£19.00 CSF £277.49 CT £3054.88 TOTE £17.00: £2.70, £4.60, £5.80, £2.80; EX 279.70 TRIFECTA Not won..

Owner Christopher & Annabelle Mason **Bred** Christopher J Mason **Trained** Tredodridge, Vale Of Glamorgan

FOCUS

They raced right across the track here but a stands'-side draw proved a nice advantage, with the first three home drawn in the top four boxes. Fairly sound, if ordinary form.

Bedloe's Island(IRE) Official explanation: jockey said gelding hit its head on leaving stalls

7181 EXCLUSIVE NETWORKS PROUDLY PARTNERS IMPERVA H'CAP 2m 9y

3:40 (3:40) (Class 6) (0-65,65) 3-Y-0+ **£1,706** (£503; £252) **Stalls** Low

Form RPR

4040 **1** **Gaselee (USA)**[20] 6693 4-9-12 **63** MartinLane 2 73
(Rae Guest) *led after 1f: pushed over 3 l clr 3f out: hld on gamely* **16/1**

-002 **2** *¾* **Warne's Way (IRE)**[20] 6693 7-9-13 **64** (b) GeorgeBaker 10 73
(B G Powell) *trckd ldrs: wnt 2nd over 3f out: kpt on fnl f: a jst hld* **12/1**

0545 **3** *3 ½* **Starshine**[7] 7011 3-9-2 **63** RyanMoore 6 68
(R Charlton) *mid-div: effrt over 3f out: kpt on to take n.d 3rd nr fin* **11/2**[1]

3303 **4** *½* **Capable Guest (IRE)**[12] 6895 8-9-12 **63** ShaneKelly 3 67
(G M Moore) *trckd ldrs: effrt over 3f out: 3rd 2f out: one pce* **8/1**[3]

4506 **5** *1 ¼* **Calculating (IRE)**[5] 7067 6-9-2 **58** LeeNewnes(5) 7 61
(M D I Usher) *trckd ldrs: effrt over 3f out: one pce* **20/1**

600- **6** *¾* **Arctic Wings (IRE)**[186] 7635 6-9-4 **62** GeorgeDowning(7) 1 64
(A W Carroll) *t.k.h in mid-div: n.m.r over 5f out: effrt over 3f out: one pce* **50/1**

2100 **7** *¾* **Petella**[12] 6895 4-9-7 **58** WilliamBuick 11 59
(C W Thornton) *in rr: shkn up over 5f out: brought v wd 4f out: kpt on: nvr nr ldrs* **6/1**[2]

3465 **8** *hd* **Unawatuna**[22] 6648 5-8-13 **53** KellyHarrison(3) 13 54
(Mrs K Walton) *mid-div: pushed along 7f out: one pce fnl 3f* **20/1**

5101 **9** *10* **Short Supply (USA)**[22] 6660 4-9-2 **53** GrahamGibbons 4 42
(T D Walford) *led 1f: chsd ldrs: pushed along 6f out: wknd and eased 2f out* **20/1**

-405 **10** *6* **M'Lady Rousseur (IRE)**[27] 6502 4-9-6 **57** DaneO'Neill 12 39
(C C Bealby) *in rr-div: hung lft and wknd over 3f out* **14/1**

0350 **11** *11* **Two Oclock John**[25] 6578 4-9-8 **59** JackMitchell 8 27
(T T Clement) *in rr: sme hdwy 3f out: nvr on terms* **40/1**

1440 **12** *1 ½* **Sendali (FR)**[22] 6649 6-9-1 **52** PhilipRobinson 14 19
(J D Bethell) *in rr: nvr on terms* **16/1**

6061 **13** *6* **Cotton King**[34] 6314 3-9-2 **63** (vt) TomMcLaughlin 16 22
(T B P Coles) *hld up in mid-div: drvn 4f out: sn wknd* **8/1**[3]

4430 **14** *hd* **Carnac (IRE)**[6] 7039 4-9-0 **51** (v[1]) JamesDoyle 17 10
(A J McCabe) *w ldrs: reminder 6f out: wknd over 2f out: sn eased* **14/1**

1243 **15** *6* **Dart**[11] 6933 6-10-0 **65** RobertWinston 5 17
(J Mackie) *mid-div: hdwy 10f out: drvn 6f out: lost pl 4f out* **16/1**

2506 **16** *8* **Ice Viking (IRE)**[16] 6816 3-8-13 **60** (b) PaulMulrennan 9 2
(J G Given) *mid-div: lost pl over 3f out: bhd and eased 2f out* **11/1**

211P **17** *12* **Vertueux (FR)**[83] 4737 5-9-10 **61** RichardHughes 15 —
(A W Carroll) *in rr: hdwy 7f out: lost pl over 3f out: sn bhd and eased* **10/1**

3m 40.46s (4.46) **Going Correction** +0.175s/f (Good)

WFA 3 from 4yo+ 10lb **17** Ran SP% **126.7**

Speed ratings (Par 101): **95,94,92,92,92 91,91,91,86,83 77,76,73,73,70 66,60**

toteswingers:1&2:£75.00, 1&3:£22.90, 2&3:£14.50 CSF £189.68 CT £1215.74 TOTE £29.60: £5.70, £3.30, £1.90, £3.20; EX 305.00 TRIFECTA Not won..

Owner Mrs Paula Smith **Bred** Flaxman Holdings Ltd **Trained** Newmarket, Suffolk

FOCUS

A moderate staying handicap. The form looks sound enough.

Carnac(IRE) Official explanation: jockey said gelding stopped quickly

Ice Viking(IRE) Official explanation: jockey said gelding had no more to give

Vertueux(FR) Official explanation: jockey said gelding had no more to give

7182 EXCLUSIVE NETWORKS PROUDLY PARTNERS FORTINET H'CAP 1m 75y

4:15 (4:16) (Class 4) (0-85,85) 3-Y-0+ **£6,152** (£1,830; £914; £456) **Stalls** Centre

Form RPR

6362 **1** **South Cape**[31] 6391 7-9-7 **85** RyanMoore 9 94
(G L Moore) *hld up: hdwy over 2f out: rdn to ld ins fnl f: r.o* **9/2**[1]

1000 **2** *1* **West End Lad**[39] 6205 7-8-13 **77** (b) DaneO'Neill 4 83
(S R Bowring) *a.p: rdn and ev ch ins fnl f: styd on* **12/1**

2312 **3** *¾* **Ken's Girl**[23] 6629 6-8-12 **76** ow1 IanMongan 15 81
(W S Kittow) *led: rdn over 1f out: hdd and unable qck ins fnl f* **10/1**

0000 **4** *1* **Club Tahiti**[29] 6444 4-8-7 **71** DavidProbert 6 73
(A W Carroll) *chsd ldrs: rdn over 1f out: styd on* **12/1**

2215 **5** *nse* **Ours (IRE)**[23] 6629 7-8-9 **73** (p) BarryMcHugh 3 75
(John A Harris) *s.i.s: hld up: hdwy over 1f out: styd on* **16/1**

3640 **6** *¾* **Norwegian Dancer (UAE)**[21] 6677 4-8-12 **76** GrahamGibbons 16 77
(E S McMahon) *trckd ldrs: racd keenly: rdn over 2f out: no ex wl ins fnl f* **10/1**

300 **7** *shd* **Spying**[32] 6355 3-9-3 **84** JackMitchell 5 84
(Mrs A Duffield) *dwlt: hld up: hdwy over 3f out: rdn over 1f out: no ex ins fnl f* **9/1**

3150 **8** *1 ½* **Lastkingofscotland (IRE)**[37] 6260 4-8-10 **74** (v) HayleyTurner 8 71
(C R Dore) *hld up: hdwy 2f out: sn rdn: no ex ins fnl f* **20/1**

0314 **9** *3 ¼* **Harriet's Girl**[31] 6395 4-9-1 **79** AndrewElliott 7 68
(Mrs K Burke) *chsd ldr: rdn and ev ch over 2f out: wknd ins fnl f* **16/1**

000 **10** *hd* **Hurricane Hymnbook (USA)**[20] 6701 5-8-9 **73** TonyCulhane 14 62
(W J Musson) *hld up: rdn over 3f out: nvr on terms* **28/1**

5010 **11** *2* **Compton Blue**[17] 6780 4-9-0 **78** (b) RichardHughes 10 62
(R Hannon) *hld up: plld hrd: rdn over 2f out: wknd over 1f out* **16/1**

4002 **12** *4 ½* **Spinning**[10] 6963 7-9-2 **80** (b) JamieSpencer 17 54
(T D Barron) *hld up: drvn along over 5f out: nvr on terms* **13/2**[2]

005- **13** *1 ¾* **Humungous (IRE)**[496] 3067 7-9-6 **84** MickyFenton 12 54
(C R Egerton) *dwlt: hld up: rdn over 4f out: a in rr* **40/1**

0610 **14** *3 ¾* **Cobo Bay**[53] 5753 5-9-7 **85** (b) RobertWinston 11 46
(C R Dore) *chsd ldrs: rdn: hung lft and wknd over 2f out: eased over 1f out* **16/1**

1335 **15** *15* **Dabbers Ridge (IRE)**[32] 6366 8-8-12 **76** DuranFentiman 1 3
(I W McInnes) *prom tl rdn and wknd over 2f out: t.o* **33/1**

-115 **16** *17* **Naddwah**[84] 4699 3-8-12 **79** PhilipRobinson 13 —
(M A Jarvis) *mid-div: wknd 3f out: t.o* **7/1**[3]

1m 49.84s (0.24) **Going Correction** +0.175s/f (Good)

WFA 3 from 4yo+ 3lb **16** Ran SP% **124.7**

Speed ratings (Par 105): **105,104,103,102,102 101,101,99,96,96 94,89,88,84,69 52**

toteswingers:1&2:£13.20, 1&3:£7.60, 2&3:£25.70 CSF £57.55 CT £552.00 TOTE £4.00: £1.10, £4.10, £1.90, £3.40; EX 74.00 Trifecta £183.20 Pool of : £279.86 - 1.13 winning units..

Owner Heart Of The South Racing **Bred** John And Mrs Caroline Penny **Trained** Lower Beeding, W Sussex

FOCUS

One for the course specialists, and ordinary late-season form.

Naddwah Official explanation: jockey said filly had no more to give

7183 EXCLUSIVE NETWORKS PROUDLY PARTNERS SAFENET MAIDEN STKS 1m 75y

4:50 (4:51) (Class 5) 3-Y-0 **£2,914** (£867; £433; £216) **Stalls** Centre

Form RPR

046 **1** **Point North (IRE)**[16] 6815 3-9-3 0 (t) WilliamBuick 12 84+
(J Noseda) *trckd ldrs: t.k.h: edgd rt and chsd ldr over 1f out: styd on to ld last 75yds* **9/4**[2]

5 **2** *1 ¾* **Chiefdom Prince (IRE)**[195] 1325 3-9-3 0 RyanMoore 7 80+
(Sir Michael Stoute) *led 1f: led over 3f out: over 3 l clr appr fnl f: rdn and hdd fnl 75yds: no ex* **5/6**[1]

3 *8* **Yensi** 3-8-12 0 TonyCulhane 13 57
(George Baker) *in rr-div: hdwy to chse ldr 3f out: kpt on one pce fnl 2f* **25/1**

4 **4** *¾* **Handsome King**[22] 6655 3-9-3 0 RobertWinston 10 60
(J R Jenkins) *t.k.h in rr: hdwy over 3f out: sn chsng ldrs: hung lft and one pce fnl 2f* **20/1**

0 **5** *7* **Spacecraft (IRE)**[16] 6814 3-9-3 0 IanMongan 5 44
(C N Kellett) *dwlt: hdwy to chse ldrs 4f out: wknd over 2f out* **66/1**

02 **6** *hd* **Fama Mac**[10] 6966 3-9-3 0 GrahamGibbons 6 43
(N Bycroft) *led after 1f: set stdy pce: hdd over 5f out: cl up tl wknd over 2f out* **15/2**[3]

7 *4* **Rustic Deacon** 3-9-3 0 StevieDonohoe 9 34
(W J Musson) *t.k.h: sn trcking ldrs: lost pl over 2f out* **33/1**

8 *3 ¼* **Penbryn (USA)** 3-9-3 0 MartinLane 1 27
(N P Littmoden) *s.s: hdwy on ins to chse ldrs over 3f out: wknd 2f out* **16/1**

9 *nk* **Drivemode** 3-9-3 0 MickyFenton 11 26
(Dr J D Scargill) *in rr: sn pushed along: bhd fnl 4f* **66/1**

10 *23* **Great Show** 3-8-12 0 DavidProbert 4 —
(R A Harris) *in rr-div: hdwy to chse ldrs 4f out: sn wknd: bhd fnl 2f: t.o* **66/1**

11 *1* **Saremma** 3-8-12 0 TomMcLaughlin 3 —
(R A Harris) *s.i.s: hdwy to trck ldrs after 2f: led over 5f out tl over 3f out: sn wknd: bhd fnl 2f: t.o* **100/1**

1m 50.47s (0.87) **Going Correction** +0.175s/f (Good) **11** Ran SP% **120.0**

Speed ratings (Par 101): **102,100,92,91,84 84,80,77,76,53 52**

toteswingers:1&2:£1.20, 1&3:£9.60, 2&3:£7.60 CSF £4.31 TOTE £2.60: £1.10, £1.10, £4.80; EX 5.00 Trifecta £38.10 Pool of : £594.18 - 11.54 winning units..

Owner Sir Robert Ogden **Bred** Barronstown Stud **Trained** Newmarket, Suffolk

FOCUS
A two-horse race on paper, and that's how it turned out. They pulled clear of some dubious opposition.

7184 AJA INSURE THEIR MEMBERS H'CAP (FOR LADY AMATEUR RIDERS) 1m 2f 50y
5:20 (5:20) (Class 6) (0-65,65) 3-Y-0+ **£1,648** (£507; £253) **Stalls** Low

Form RPR
4000 1 **Hurricane Thomas (IRE)**[12] 6890 6-9-6 **55**.......... MissPhillipaTutty(5) 4 64
(R A Fahey) *chsd ldrs: led 1f out: styd on* **16/1**
3113 2 ¾ **Kenyan Cat**[9] 6993 3-9-11 **63**.................................. MissRJefferson(3) 14 71
(George Baker) *a.p: rdn and ev ch 1f out: styd on* **2/1**[1]
460 3 1 **Eastern Magic**[90] 4521 3-9-11 **65**................................ MissRKneller(5) 11 71+
(R Hollinshead) *hld up: hdwy u.p over 1f out: r.o to go 3rd nr fin: nt rch ldrs* **14/1**
6650 4 ½ **Wiseman's Diamond (USA)**[41] 6116 5-9-13 **62**........ MissWGibson(5) 8 67
(P T Midgley) *chsd ldrs: led over 3f out: rdn and hdd 1f out: styd on same pce: lost 3rd nr fin* **12/1**
0160 5 3 ¼ **Rebellious Spirit**[21] 6669 7-10-5 **63**.............................. MissEJJones 13 62
(S Curran) *hld up: hdwy over 3f out: rdn over 2f out: no ex fnl f* **12/1**
03 6 nk **Heredias (GER)**[27] 6518 4-9-11 **62**................ MissBeckyBrisbourne(7) 5 60
(W M Brisbourne) *hld up: r.o ins fnl f: nvr nrr* **9/2**[2]
7 4 **Mezarat (ITY)**[49] 5-10-0 **65**..............................(t) MissAZetterholm(7) 1 55
(S C Williams) *s.i.s: hld up: nt clr run over 3f out: hdwy over 2f out: wknd over 1f out* **18/1**
0011 8 hd **Bollin Freddie**[125] 3370 6-10-4 **62**.................................... MissADeniel 2 52
(A J Lockwood) *hld up: hdwy over 3f out: wknd over 1f out* **7/1**[3]
0406 9 2 ½ **Dragon Slayer (IRE)**[28] 6472 8-10-7 **65**...................... MissGAndrews 6 50
(John A Harris) *s.i.s: hld up: rdn over 1f out: n.d* **14/1**
4200 10 hd **King Columbo (IRE)**[37] 6261 5-9-12 **63**.................... MissSBirkett(7) 12 48
(Miss J Feilden) *chsd ldrs tl wknd over 2f out* **16/1**
4000 11 1 ¾ **Craicajack (IRE)**[2] 7111 3-9-9 **63**............................ MissJFerguson(5) 3 45
(E J Creighton) *chsd ldrs: rdn and ev ch over 2f out: wknd over 1f out* **33/1**
2500 12 6 **Daniel Thomas (IRE)**[21] 6669 8-9-13 **62**................(tp) MissMBryant(5) 9 32
(P Butler) *s.i.s: hdwy 6f out: wknd 3f out* **25/1**
505- 13 19 **Miss Porky**[484] 2950 4-9-11 **60**.................. MissSusannahWileman(5) 15 —
(C N Kellett) *led: racd keenly: hdd & wknd over 3f out* **50/1**

2m 19.61s (5.31) **Going Correction** +0.175s/f (Good)
WFA 3 from 4yo+ 5lb **13** Ran SP% **118.5**
Speed ratings (Par 101): **85,84,83,83,80 80,77,77,75,74 73,68,53**
toteswingers:1&2:£16.90, 1&3:£46.80, 2&3:£9.70 CSF £46.95 CT £485.59 TOTE £22.30: £7.50, £2.50, £5.30; EX 96.40 TRIFECTA Not won. Place 6: £1880.14, Place 5 £514.95..
Owner N D Tutty **Bred** P D Savill **Trained** Musley Bank, N Yorks
■ Stewards' Enquiry : Miss J Ferguson caution: used whip when gelding showed no response

FOCUS
A modest handicap. Ordinary form, with the winner back to his best.
T/Jkpt: Not won. T/Plt: £2,295.00 to a £1 stake. Pool:£52,032.22 - 16.55 winning tickets T/Qpdt: £201.40 to a £1 stake. Pool:£4,982.74 - 18.30 winning tickets CR

6994 LINGFIELD (L-H)
Thursday, October 28

OFFICIAL GOING: Standard
Wind: Fresh, half behind Weather: Overcast

7185 E B F WEATHERBYS "MY STABLE" MAIDEN FILLIES' STKS 7f (P)
1:40 (1:41) (Class 5) 2-Y-0 **£3,302** (£982; £491; £245) **Stalls** Low

Form RPR
40 1 **Adorable Choice (IRE)**[39] 6230 2-9-0 0............... RichardKingscote 11 72
(Tom Dascombe) *w ldr: led over 4f out: drvn over 1f out: hld on nr fin* **33/1**
6 2 ½ **Dubai Queen (USA)**[17] 6796 2-9-0 0.............................. KierenFallon 13 73+
(L M Cumani) *dwlt: t.k.h: hld up in 9th and racd wd: effrt over 1f out: r.o wl to take 2nd nr fin: too much to do* **5/4**[1]
00 3 1 **Cinta**[23] 6651 2-9-0 0... RyanMoore 2 68
(M Botti) *trckd ldrs on inner: effrt 2f out: disp 2nd ent fnl f: styd on same pce* **10/1**[3]
5225 4 hd **Bakoura**[49] 5882 2-9-0 73.. RichardHills 12 68
(J L Dunlop) *pressed ldng pair: rdn to chse wnr wl over 1f out: no imp: one pce ins fnl f* **10/3**[2]
5 nse **Birdolini** 2-9-0 0... FergusSweeney 14 67
(A King) *racd wd: wl in tch: rdn and cl enough over 1f out: one pce ins fnl f* **100/1**
3 6 3 ½ **Waltzing Cat (USA)**[34] 6323 2-9-0 0.............................. SebSanders 7 61+
(Sir Mark Prescott) *dwlt: mostly last tl effrt on outer over 2f out: styd on ins fnl f: n.d* **40/1**
00 7 nk **Desert Location**[14] 6859 2-9-0 0.................................... HayleyTurner 8 58+
(M L W Bell) *settled in last trio: pushed along 2f out: kpt on steadily: nrst fin* **33/1**
8 nse **Judgement** 2-9-0 0.. WilliamBuick 1 59+
(J H M Gosden) *dwlt: wl in rr: last and pushed along over 2f out: sme prog on inner over 1f out: shkn up and kpt on* **10/1**[3]
06 9 1 ¼ **Royal Reason**[22] 6676 2-9-0 0.................................. SamHitchcott 6 54
(M R Channon) *led to over 4f out: chsd wnr to wl over 1f out: wknd* **66/1**
0 10 2 ¼ **Deslaya (IRE)**[23] 6651 2-9-0 0.. TomQueally 10 48
(H R A Cecil) *trckd ldrs: gng wl enough 3f out: lost pl 2f out: pushed along and fdd* **14/1**
30 11 1 **Poppy**[30] 6441 2-9-0 0.. RichardHughes 3 46+
(R Hannon) *settled in rr: pushed along and no prog wl over 1f out* **12/1**
12 ¾ **All Honesty** 2-9-0 0.. JimCrowley 5 44+
(W J Knight) *sn towards rr: shkn up over 2f out: btn after* **33/1**

1m 25.06s (0.26) **Going Correction** 0.0s/f (Stan) **12** Ran SP% **113.8**
Speed ratings (Par 92): **98,97,96,96,96 92,91,91,90,87 86,85**
Tote Swingers: 1&2 £12.20, 1&3 £31.10, 2&3 £5.70 CSF £70.71 TOTE £31.40: £5.40, £1.40, £3.50; EX 109.00 TRIFECTA Not won..
Owner John Brown **Bred** John O'Connor **Trained** Malpas, Cheshire

FOCUS
A modest fillies' maiden, although the time was respectable after an early dawdle. No better than fair form. The runner-up ought to have won.

NOTEBOOK
Adorable Choice(IRE) had been relatively highly tried on her first two starts, and although well beaten in an Irish sales race latest, had shown ability on debut when fourth in a Polytrack conditions race, so it was a surprise to see her dismissed at 33-1. Like the favourite, she was drawn wide, but she enjoyed a much better trip than that rival, Richard Kingscote doing well to soon get her across to make much of the running. Despite sticking towards the usually unfavoured far rail in the straight, she found plenty to hold on. She can probably do better again, albeit she still has to prove herself on turf. Official explanation: trainer's rep said, regarding apparent improvement in form, that the filly was better suited by the all-weather surface and was badly drawn on its last run.
Dubai Queen(USA), a real eyecatcher on debut over 6f at Kempton (met trouble leaving the stalls after slow start, ran green and taken wide into straight), was well backed to confirm that promise. However, she again received a bit of a bump on leaving the gates following another sluggish beginning, and then was keen for the first furlong or so while stuck wide without much cover. She then had to be nudged along, never really looking happy, and it was only in the straight that she got going, but too late. There's no doubt that she's better than we've seen so far, but she is still immature and needs to learn to break better. (tchd 6-5, 11-8 in a place)
Cinta, fitted with a sheepskin noseband, was never far away towards the inside and kept on in the straight, improving on her first two efforts. She'll be suited by further in due course and can do better, with handicaps now an option. (op 20-1)
Bakoura was well placed turning into the straight, but she hung fire when first coming under serious pressure and was one-paced. It's questionable whether she ran to her official mark of 73. (op 3-1 tchd 7-2 in a place)
Birdolini ◆, drawn 14, raced widest for just about most of the contest but was still there at the finish and clearly has plenty of ability. The first foal of a prolific 6f-7f winner, she's one to keep in mind.
Waltzing Cat(USA) was set an impossible task and wasn't given a particularly hard race, but it's a fair bet we'll see better when she goes handicapping. (op 33-1)
All Honesty Official explanation: jockey said bit slipped through filly's mouth

7186 E B F SHOWCASING STANDING AT WHITSBURY MANOR STUD MAIDEN STKS 7f (P)
2:10 (2:11) (Class 5) 2-Y-0 **£3,302** (£982; £491; £245) **Stalls** Low

Form RPR
0 1 **Tullius (IRE)**[103] 4131 2-9-3 0.. JimCrowley 6 76
(P Winkworth) *pressed ldng pair: rdn to ld narrowly over 1f out: styd on wl: jst hld on* **25/1**
2 nse **Sunday Bess (JPN)** 2-8-12 0................................ RichardKingscote 5 71+
(Tom Dascombe) *trckd ldr: chal 2f out: upsides over 1f out: pressed wnr after: jst failed* **4/1**[2]
4 3 1 ¼ **Motivado**[29] 6458 2-9-3 0.. SebSanders 4 73+
(Sir Mark Prescott) *in tch in last pair and racd wd: shkn up and rn green wl over 1f out: prog to press ldng pair ins fnl f: kpt on* **15/2**[3]
5 4 2 ¼ **Trojan Nights (USA)**[13] 6882 2-9-3 0............................. KierenFallon 1 67
(W J Haggas) *dwlt: trckd ldrs: rdn to chal over 1f out: nt qckn and sn outpcd* **5/4**[1]
5 ¾ **Hugely Exciting** 2-9-3 0.. LukeMorris 2 65
(J S Moore) *trckd ldrs: cl enough over 1f out: nt qckn and outpcd after* **16/1**
00 6 hd **Sammy Alexander**[119] 3602 2-9-3 0................................ AndreaAtzeni 7 65
(D M Simcock) *in tch in last pair: effrt on inner and cl enough over 1f out: sn fdd* **20/1**
63 7 3 ¾ **Red Mercury (IRE)**[16] 6825 2-9-3 0............................ RichardHughes 3 58
(M R Channon) *led: rdn over 2f out: hdd & wknd over 1f out: eased* **4/1**[2]

1m 25.85s (1.05) **Going Correction** 0.0s/f (Stan) **7** Ran SP% **110.7**
Speed ratings (Par 95): **94,93,92,89,89 88,84**
Tote Swingers: 1&2 £4.60, 1&3 £17.10, 2&3 £15.40 CSF £113.65 TOTE £45.70: £12.80, £3.50; EX 169.10.
Owner Kennet Valley Thoroughbreds VI **Bred** Sc Archi Romani **Trained** Chiddingfold, Surrey

FOCUS
A couple of the more likely types disappointed, and as such the bare form seems no better than fair, a view supported by a time 0.79 seconds slower than Adorable Choice recorded in the earlier modest-looking fillies' maiden. Indeed, this was the slowest of five races over 7f on the card. However, that said, in time one or two these could be very useful. The form has been rated around the race averages.

NOTEBOOK
Tullius(IRE) showed nothing on his only previous start on quick turf in July, but had been gelded and was bred to take to this surface, being a half-brother to a Polytrack winner (another sibling was successful in the US, likewise his dam). Always close up, he battled on well in the straight to get the better of a protracted duel with the runner-up, showing a fair amount of ability. He should come on again. Official explanation: trainer said, regarding apparent improvement in form, that the gelding had benefitted from being gelded since its last run.
Sunday Bess(JPN) ◆, the only filly in the line-up, cost JPY33,000,000 (around £255,000) as a foal, and was the first runner in Britain for Japanese superstar Deep Impact, while her dam was a champion filly on turf in Chile. Reported by her owner beforehand to go "extremely well on the gallops", she was solid in the market and just failed to make a successful debut. She should stay further and looks a useful enough prospect. (op 5-1 tchd 11-2 and 7-2)
Motivado ◆ raced further back than the front two, came widest into the straight and wasn't hit with the whip, but this was still an improvement on his debut effort. A fine, big type, who is bred to want middle-distances, he could be very useful next year and will be of particular interest when sent handicapping. (tchd 7-1 and 8-1)
Trojan Nights(USA) was one of the disappointments. He showed ability in a decent 6f turf maiden on debut, and was expected to do better under these conditions with the benefit of that experience, but he found little for pressure, even allowing for sticking towards the inside rail. (op 11-8 tchd 6-4)
Hugely Exciting was described beforehand by Stan Moore as "a nice horse to follow on the AW this winter." He got outpaced in the straight and should stay further. (op 25-1)
Sammy Alexander hinted at ability on his debut for this yard after a break of 119 days and could do okay in handicaps. (op 28-1)
Red Mercury(IRE) had appeared to be going the right way, but he was weak in the market and proved disappointing on this switch to Polytrack (previously raced exclusively on easy turf). (op 11-4)

7187 LINGFIELD PARK BREEDERS' DAY H'CAP 7f (P)
2:40 (2:42) (Class 3) (0-95,95) 3-Y-0+ **£6,476** (£1,927; £963; £481) **Stalls** Low

Form RPR
21-1 1 **Quick Wit**[29] 6467 3-9-4 **94**.. FrankieDettori 14 111+
(Saeed Bin Suroor) *t.k.h: racd v wd early: trckd ldng trio: shkn up to ld jst ins fnl f: pushed out and nvr in serious danger* **8/11**[1]
6003 2 1 ¼ **Mr Willis**[106] 4030 4-8-10 **87**.. KierenFox(3) 2 95+
(J R Best) *hld up in 7th and off the pce: effrt 2f out: rdn and r.o fnl f to take 2nd last 75yds* **20/1**
0006 3 nk **Seek The Fair Land**[18] 6780 4-8-12 **86**........................(b) TomQueally 11 93
(J R Boyle) *trckd ldrs: taken wd and drvn 2f out: styd on to dispute 2nd ins fnl f: no imp on wnr* **16/1**

2210 **4** ½ **Woodcote Place**[47] 5950 7-8-12 **86**........ WilliamBuick 5 92
(P R Chamings) *trckd ldrs: shkn up 2f out: styd on fnl f: nt pce to chal* **20/1**

1050 **5** *nk* **Den's Gift (IRE)**[54] 5750 6-8-8 **85**........(b) JohnFahy(3) 12 90
(C G Cox) *pressed ldr: rdn and upsides jst over 1f out: outpcd fnl f* **8/1**[2]

0000 **6** ½ **Bravo Echo**[40] 6204 4-9-5 **93**........ LukeMorris 1 97
(M J Attwater) *pressed ldng pair: rdn to chal over 1f out: sn outpcd* **20/1**

2200 **7** *hd* **Santefisio**[13] 6888 4-8-11 **85**........ JimmyFortune 13 88
(P J Makin) *hld up in 8th: rdn over 1f out: styd on wl fnl f: nrst fin* **8/1**[2]

0000 **8** 1½ **Flipando (IRE)**[13] 6888 9-9-5 **93**........ RyanMoore 4 92
(T D Barron) *taken down early: hld up in last trio and wl off the pce: same pl 2f out: nudged along and styd on fnl f: nvr nr ldrs* **16/1**

2006 **9** *hd* **Venutius**[34] 6321 3-8-13 **89**........ GrahamGibbons 6 88
(E S McMahon) *led: hrd pressed 2f out: hdd & wknd jst ins fnl f* **12/1**[3]

6636 **10** 1¾ **Excellerator (IRE)**[48] 5903 4-8-13 **90**........(t) MatthewDavies(3) 9 84
(George Baker) *a in last trio: rdn over 2f out: no prog* **40/1**

5040 **11** *nse* **Titan Triumph**[35] 6312 6-8-9 **83**........(t) JimCrowley 8 77
(W J Knight) *hld up in last trio: rdn and no prog 2f out* **20/1**

1m 23.47s (-1.33) **Going Correction** 0.0s/f (Stan)
WFA 3 from 4yo+ 2lb **11** Ran SP% **121.1**
Speed ratings (Par 107): **107,105,105,104,104 103,103,101,101,99 99**
Tote Swingers: 1&2 £4.30, 1&3 £5.40, 2&3 £10.40 CSF £24.61 CT £157.69 TOTE £2.00: £1.10, £4.50, £3.40; EX 12.80 Trifecta £137.60 Pool: £504.03 - 2.71 winning units..
Owner Godolphin **Bred** Ptarmigan Bloodstock Limited **Trained** Newmarket, Suffolk

FOCUS
Last year this handicap was won by the then lightly raced Sirocco Breeze, who went on to win twice at the Dubai Carnival, and Quick Wit is another obvious improver for the same connections, unsurprisingly recording much the quickest time of the five 7f races. The winner was value for further and the form looks solid behind him.

NOTEBOOK
Quick Wit ◆ looked a notch or two better than this level, overcoming the widest stall to defy an 11lb rise for his taking Nottingham win (1m, good to soft). The drop back in trip and switch to Polytrack didn't inconvenience, and he recorded a victory that is likely to ensure he'll make the cut for Carnival races next year, while also starting the new campaign on a workable mark. He should have plenty of options, too, with Tapeta and Turf both set to suit. (op Evens tchd 11-10 in a place)
Mr Willis hadn't been seen since July, but has won when fresh. He ran well behind a rival probably some way ahead of the handicapper.
Seek The Fair Land appreciated the return to Polytrack and ran well after coming wide into the straight. (op 14-1)
Woodcote Place looked to have something to offer when appearing slightly short of room for much of the straight, and he was probably second best. Official explanation: jockey said gelding was denied a clear run (op 16-1)
Den's Gift(IRE) had his chance under a positive ride but isn't particularly well handicapped. (op 14-1 tchd 16-1)

7188 E B F NORMANDIE STUD FLEUR DE LYS FILLIES' STKS (LISTED RACE) 1m (P)

3:10 (3:13) (Class 1) 3-Y-O+

£19,869 (£7,532; £3,769; £1,879; £941; £472) **Stalls** High

Form RPR

5012 **1** **Aspectoflove (IRE)**[19] 6765 4-9-3 106........ FrankieDettori 10 103
(Saeed Bin Suroor) *trckd ldr: shkn up 2f out: one of many chalng 1f out: pressed ldr after: drvn to ld last strides* **11/10**[1]

2220 **2** *shd* **Mosqueras Romance**[33] 6351 4-9-0 102........ RyanMoore 6 100
(M Botti) *trckd ldrs: rdn to chal over 1f out: narrow ld ent fnl f: hdd last strides* **9/2**[2]

1635 **3** ½ **Forest Crown**[33] 6346 3-8-11 92........ JimCrowley 11 98
(R M Beckett) *hld up towards rr: effrt on outer wl over 1f out: r.o ins fnl f to take 3rd last strides* **10/1**

3650 **4** *nk* **Siyaadah**[134] 3071 3-8-11 102........ AhmedAjtebi 7 98
(Mahmood Al Zarooni) *hld up towards rr: shkn up over 1f out: gd prog ent fnl f: wnt 3rd briefly nr fin: nvr cl enough to chal* **25/1**

5 **5** ¾ **Kameruka**[32] 6409 4-9-0 87........ AdamKirby 8 96?
(R Pritchard-Gordon, France) *hld up in midfield: quick move on outer to ld narrowly jst over 2f out: hdd and nt qckn ent fnl f* **50/1**

-303 **6** ½ **Super Sleuth (IRE)**[16] 6830 4-9-0 96........ KierenFallon 9 95
(B J Meehan) *led after 1f: narrowly hdd jst over 2f out: stl disputing ld 1f out: fdd* **11/2**[3]

0001 **7** ½ **Sarah Park (IRE)**[18] 6780 5-9-0 86........ NeilCallan 2 94
(B J Meehan) *wl in tch in midfield: 6th and rdn over 1f out: no prog: wl hld whn hmpd nr fin* **20/1**

340 **8** 1 **What's Up Pussycat (IRE)**[60] 5553 4-9-0 94........ WilliamBuick 4 91
(D M Simcock) *settled in last pair: shkn up over 2f out: one pce and no imp on ldrs* **25/1**

0643 **9** 1 **Lady Darshaan (IRE)**[117] 3694 3-8-11 104........ RichardHughes 3 89
(J S Moore) *led 1f: styd cl up: effrt on inner wl over 1f out: sn fdd* **8/1**

3421 **10** 1½ **Faithful One (IRE)**[57] 5662 3-8-11 86........ ChrisCatlin 1 86
(D R Lanigan) *dwlt: sn in tch in midfield: nt qckn 2f out: no prog after* **25/1**

5220 **11** 1 **Gobama**[33] 6346 3-8-11 85........ SebSanders 12 83
(J W Hills) *dropped in fr wd draw and hld up last: rdn and no prog 2f out* **66/1**

1m 36.71s (-1.49) **Going Correction** 0.0s/f (Stan)
WFA 3 from 4yo+ 3lb **11** Ran SP% **121.1**
Speed ratings (Par 108): **107,106,106,106,105 104,104,103,102,100 99**
Tote Swingers: 1&2 £2.50, 1&3 £4.60, 2&3 £11.00 CSF £5.71 TOTE £2.50: £1.40, £1.40, £2.40; EX 7.70 Trifecta £64.70 Pool: £619.48 - 7.08 winning units..
Owner Godolphin **Bred** Patrick Cassidy **Trained** Newmarket, Suffolk
■ Stewards' Enquiry : Ahmed Ajtebi one-day ban: careless riding (Nov 11)

FOCUS
An ordinary Listed contest but quite muddling form with some lesser fillies not far.

NOTEBOOK
Aspectoflove(IRE) produced a smart effort considering she was conceding upwards of 3lb all round. Representing last year's winning jockey/owner/trainer, she maintained her good run of form and is now 3-3 on Polytrack, adding to a couple of victories she gained at Dundalk when with John Oxx. If she goes back to Dubai for the Carnival, presumably she'll try to improve on last year's second placings in the Cape Verdi and Balanchine. However, both of those races have been upgraded to Group 2 status, which may be beyond her, and considering her fine record on synthetics, her best chance may come on the Tapeta. (op 11-8)
Mosqueras Romance was just denied, but she still enhanced her fine record on Polytrack, her form figures on the surface now reading 321222. (op 13-2)
Forest Crown came very wide into the straight but still ran on to pick up some more black type. This half-sister to Crowded House is a valuable broodmare prospect. (tchd 12-1)
Siyaadah ran much better than on her two turf outings earlier this year, appreciating the return to a synthetic surface after a break of 134 days, although her head was a bit high under pressure. Presumably she'll head back out to Dubai. (tchd 33-1)
Kameruka, a 50-1 shot whose French form looked no better than useful, wasn't that far away at the finish, so it may be that she actually benefited from an enterprising ride. (op 40-1)
Super Sleuth(IRE), trying Polytrack for the first time, didn't improve on the form she showed on her return from a break at Leicester. (op 9-2 tchd 4-1 and 6-1)
Sarah Park(IRE) found this tougher than the Goodwood handicap she won off 80 last time, though still fared better than when tenth in this last year. (op 16-1)
Lady Darshaan(IRE) soon emptied under pressure and was well below form on this first taste of Polytrack. (op 9-1 tchd 7-1)

7189 E B F COCKNEY REBEL FIRST CROP SUCCESS RIVER EDEN FILLIES' STKS (LISTED RACE) 1m 5f (P)

3:40 (3:42) (Class 1) 3-Y-O+

£19,869 (£7,532; £3,769; £1,879; £941; £472) **Stalls** Low

Form RPR

610- **1** **Baila Me (GER)**[355] 7293 5-9-2 105........ FrankieDettori 2 99+
(Saeed Bin Suroor) *led at mod pce: kicked on 3f out: narrowly hdd over 1f out: styd on u.p to ld again last strides* **5/4**[1]

3042 **2** *nse* **Rosika**[71] 5220 4-9-2 102........ RyanMoore 11 99+
(Sir Michael Stoute) *trckd ldrs: prog on outer over 2f out: rdn to ld narrowly over 1f out: styd on: hdd last strides* **15/8**[2]

3314 **3** ½ **Giants Play (USA)**[17] 6797 3-8-8 81........ RichardMullen 13 98
(Sir Michael Stoute) *wl in tch in midfield: prog on outer over 2f out: drvn and r.o to take 3rd last 75yds: gaining at fin* **33/1**

3-53 **4** ¾ **Copperbeech (IRE)**[70] 5249 4-9-2 96........ NeilCallan 6 97
(Saeed Bin Suroor) *trckd wnr 2f: styd prom: rdn to chse ldng pair over 1f out: styd on but lost 3rd last 75yds* **20/1**

3360 **5** 1¼ **Lady Artemisia (IRE)**[34] 6320 4-9-2 100........ WilliamBuick 1 95
(M Botti) *hld up wl in rr: plenty to do 2f out: swtchd out and prog over 1f out: hanging lft but styd on: nrst fin* **25/1**

3152 **6** 1¼ **Roxy Flyer (IRE)**[40] 6199 3-8-8 90........ JimmyQuinn 4 93
(Mrs A J Perrett) *trckd ldrs on inner: effrt 2f out: one pce and no imp fnl f* **16/1**

1420 **7** ½ **Nezhenka**[20] 6715 3-8-9 87 ow1........ SebSanders 8 94
(Sir Mark Prescott) *hld up in last pair: pushed along and styd on steadily 2f out: nvr nr ldrs* **50/1**

5110 **8** ¾ **Wild Rose**[55] 5723 3-8-8 92........(t) HayleyTurner 5 91
(M L W Bell) *hld up wl in rr: effrt on inner wl over 1f out: kpt on: nt pce to threaten* **25/1**

2133 **9** *shd* **Western Pearl**[28] 6506 3-8-8 95........ ShaneKelly 12 91
(W J Knight) *t.k.h: trckd wnr after 2f to wl over 1f out: sn wknd* **10/1**[3]

6000 **10** 2¼ **Some Sunny Day**[13] 6886 4-9-2 90........ JimmyFortune 9 88?
(H Morrison) *hld up in last pair: plenty to do over 2f out: brt wdst of all and effrt wl over 1f out: no prog fnl f* **66/1**

3-0 **11** 1 **Funday**[47] 5970 4-9-2 82........ GeorgeBaker 3 86?
(G L Moore) *prom: rdn over 2f out: wknd wl over 1f out* **100/1**

0421 **12** 3 **Gakalina (IRE)**[14] 6861 3-8-8 75........ DarryllHolland 10 82
(J Noseda) *wl in tch in midfield: rdn and wknd fr 2f out* **50/1**

053 **13** ½ **Just Lille (IRE)**[20] 6715 7-9-2 92........(p) KierenFallon 14 81
(Mrs A Duffield) *prom: rdn 3f out: wknd 2f out* **14/1**

1310 **14** 17 **Mujdeya**[43] 6095 3-8-8 95........ RichardHills 7 56
(J H M Gosden) *racd wd: hld up: brief effrt over 3f out: wknd 2f out: eased: t.o* **25/1**

2m 42.42s (-3.58) **Going Correction** 0.0s/f (Stan) course record
WFA 3 from 4yo+ 8lb **14** Ran SP% **126.5**
Speed ratings (Par 108): **111,110,110,110,109 108,108,107,107,106 105,103,103,93**
Tote Swingers: 1&2 £1.60, 1&3 £21.70, 2&3 £18.30 CSF £3.38 TOTE £3.00: £1.30, £1.40, £7.70; EX 5.60 Trifecta £56.70 Pool: £843.82 - 11.01 winning units..
Owner Godolphin **Bred** Gestut Karlshof **Trained** Newmarket, Suffolk

FOCUS
A weak Listed race, won by Baila Me for the second year running. The pace was not bad but the form is still a bit messy, and though the first pair were not at their best.

NOTEBOOK
Baila Me(GER) went from the front, which isn't easy over this trip on the Lingfield Polytrack, but the rider got it spot on, setting a steady pace before kicking on in just enough time. The mare, through no fault of her own or Dettori's, ended up against the unfavoured far rail late on, and was narrowly headed, but she battled back to regain to lead in the final strides. She had only been seen once since her success in this 12 months ago, finishing well beaten in the November Handicap, but she clearly retains plenty of ability. It's not certain that she'll go to Dubai for the Carnival. (op 6-5 tchd 13-8)
Rosika, the Ebor runner-up, was beaten 4l into second by Baila Me in this last season, but she's an improved filly and only just failed to reverse form. (op 11-4 tchd 3-1 in places)
Giants Play(USA) did not look up to this class, but she disproved that view with a fine effort. This was valuable black type for a filly with a top-class pedigree.
Copperbeech(IRE) had no obvious excuse and ran respectably after a 70-day absence. (op 22-1)
Lady Artemisia(IRE) raced further back than those who finished ahead of her, although she didn't help herself by hanging left. Her only win to date came in a maiden. (tchd 20-1)
Nezhenka was set a bit to do and didn't get the clearest of runs through, but she wasn't unlucky. (op 40-1)
Wild Rose was in an unpromising position throughout. (op 33-1)

7190 BLUE SQUARE WINTER CARNIVAL COMING SOON H'CAP 1m 2f (P)

4:10 (4:13) (Class 5) (0-75,75) 3-Y-O+ **£2,388** (£705; £352) **Stalls** Low

Form RPR

0543 **1** **Kiss A Prince**[15] 6852 4-9-7 **72**........(b) JimmyFortune 4 80
(D K Ivory) *t.k.h: hld up in last trio: prog 2f out: str run on outer fnl f to ld last 75yds* **4/1**[2]

5030 **2** ¾ **Silent Oasis**[15] 6851 4-9-0 **65**........ FergusSweeney 5 72
(B G Powell) *trckd ldng trio: prog to jnd ldrs 2f out: led over 1f out w hd to one side: hdd and outpcd last 75yds* **11/1**

6006 **3** 1¼ **Halsion Chancer**[38] 6252 6-9-10 **75**........ GeorgeBaker 1 79
(J R Best) *hld up in 5th: clsd on ldrs 2f out: rdn to chal fnl f: no ex last 150yds* **6/1**[3]

1200 **4** ¾ **Negotiation (IRE)**[20] 6718 4-9-3 **68**........ WilliamBuick 10 71
(M Quinn) *trckd ldr: rdn to chal and upsides over 1f out: fdd fnl f* **14/1**

4210 **5** 1¼ **Hierarch (IRE)**[8] 7019 3-9-0 **70**........(b[1]) StephenCraine 11 70
(D Flood) *hld up in last trio: smooth prog fr 3f out to trck ldrs over 1f out: sn rdn and fnd nil* **16/1**

6300 **6** ½ **King Supreme (IRE)**[29] 6480 5-9-2 **67**........(b) RyanMoore 8 66
(R Hannon) *chsd ldrs in 6th: rdn over 3f out: sn lost pl: last 2f out: kpt on again fnl f* **7/2**[1]

3600 **7** 2½ **Basra (IRE)**[15] 6851 7-9-8 **73**........ IanMongan 9 67
(Miss Jo Crowley) *hld up in 7th: effrt over 2f out: no prog and btn over 1f out* **7/1**

3600 **8** 1¼ **Lord Theo**[15] 6846 6-9-1 **66**........ J-PGuillambert 2 58
(N P Littmoden) *pushed up to ld at gd pce: hdd & wknd over 1f out* **12/1**

060 **9** *1 ¼* **Lingfield Bound (IRE)**[15] 6856 3-8-11 **67**........................ JimmyQuinn 3 56
(J R Best) *chsd ldng pair to over 2f out: sn wknd* **6/1**[3]

2350 **10** *6* **Atacama Sunrise**[29] 6452 4-8-5 **63**........................ CharlotteKerton(7) 6 40
(G Prodromou) *t.k.h: hld up in last pair: pushed along and no prog 2f out: wknd* **33/1**

2m 4.54s (-2.06) **Going Correction** 0.0s/f (Stan)
WFA 3 from 4yo+ 5lb **10** Ran SP% **114.8**
Speed ratings (Par 103): **108,107,106,105,104 104,102,101,100,95**
Tote Swingers: 1&2 £5.80, 1&3 £4.20, 2&3 £13.30 CSF £46.67 CT £261.00 TOTE £5.00: £1.80, £3.20, £1.70; EX 53.50 TRIFECTA Not won..

Owner A Pryer **Bred** Baroness, Magnusson, Myriade, Redmyre **Trained** Radlett, Herts

FOCUS
A modest handicap run at a good pace. The runner-up helps set the standard.

Atacama Sunrise Official explanation: jockey said filly stopped quickly

7191 ATTHERACES.COM/BREEDERSCUP APPRENTICE H'CAP (DIV I) 7f (P)
4:40 (4:41) (Class 6) (0-60,60) 3-Y-0+ **£1,706** (£503; £252) **Stalls** Low

Form RPR

3004 **1** **Bold Ring**[15] 6848 4-8-9 **51**........................ JulieBurke(3) 4 59
(E J Creighton) *mostly chsd ldng pair: effrt between them over 1f out: led ins fnl f: rdn out* **10/1**

2066 **2** *¾* **Posy Fossil (USA)**[27] 6540 3-9-2 **60**........................(tp) RyanClark(3) 8 66
(S C Williams) *trckd ldr: rdn to ld over 1f out: hdd ins fnl f: kpt on: a hld* **4/1**[2]

3455 **3** *nk* **Watch Chain (IRE)**[9] 6996 3-9-0 **55**........................ AshleyMorgan 11 60
(M H Tompkins) *hld up in midfield: prog to go 4th wl over 1f out: shkn up and styd on: nvr chal* **6/1**

6001 **4** *1 ¼* **Lady Of Garmoran (USA)**[14] 6865 3-8-13 **57**.........(b) DuilioDaSilva(3) 6 59
(P F I Cole) *led at decent pce to over 1f out: fdd fnl f* **5/1**[3]

6000 **5** *1 ¼* **Phluke**[11] 6958 9-8-8 **54**........................(v) DanielBlackett(7) 7 52
(Eve Johnson Houghton) *trckd ldrs: nt qckn and outpcd 2f out: kpt on fnl f* **12/1**

3232 **6** *½* **Pipers Piping (IRE)**[13] 6903 4-9-2 **60**...................(p) LeonnaMayor(5) 10 57
(P Howling) *stdd s: hld up last: effrt on wd outside bnd 2f out: styd on: nvr on terms* **3/1**[1]

0620 **7** *2 ¼* **Saigon Kitty (IRE)**[16] 6826 3-8-12 **58**........................ IanBurns(5) 5 49
(J R Best) *sn in last pair: rdn on wd outside 1/2-way: no real prog* **14/1**

1-00 **8** *nk* **Ain't Talkin**[8] 7023 4-8-11 **50**........................ DeclanCannon 3 40
(M J Attwater) *chsd ldrs: rdn over 2f out: steadily wknd* **12/1**

0 **9** *1 ¼* **Watch The Flame**[13] 6896 4-8-2 **46** oh1...................(t) RichardRowe(5) 9 33
(M G Quinlan) *a towards rr: rdn and struggling over 2f out* **25/1**

0000 **10** *¾* **Chat De Soie (IRE)**[44] 6054 3-8-5 **46** oh1...................(b) RossAtkinson 2 31
(J S Moore) *rn in snatches: struggling fr 3f out: no prog after* **33/1**

0500 **11** *11* **Gra Adhmhar (IRE)**[9] 7005 3-9-3 **58**........................(v[1]) BillyCray 1 13
(G Prodromou) *nvr on terms w ldrs: u.p and struggling wl over 2f out: t.o* **16/1**

1m 25.26s (0.46) **Going Correction** 0.0s/f (Stan)
WFA 3 from 4yo+ 2lb **11** Ran SP% **119.8**
Speed ratings (Par 101): **97,96,95,94,92 92,89,89,88,87 74**
Tote Swingers: 1&2 £11.30, 1&3 £10.10, 2&3 £4.60 CSF £50.75 CT £273.53 TOTE £14.30: £3.90, £2.10, £2.20; EX 70.70 Trifecta £223.90 Part won. Pool: £302.65 - 0.10 winning units..

Owner Daniel Creighton **Bred** J A Pickering & T Pears **Trained** Wormshill, Kent

FOCUS
A moderate apprentices' handicap run in a time 0.37 seconds slower than the second division. Straightforward form.

7192 ATTHERACES.COM/BREEDERSCUP APPRENTICE H'CAP (DIV II) 7f (P)
5:10 (5:10) (Class 6) (0-60,60) 3-Y-0+ **£1,706** (£503; £252) **Stalls** Low

Form RPR

0115 **1** **Paphos**[27] 6541 3-9-2 **58**........................(v) RyanClark(3) 7 72+
(S C Williams) *trckd ldng pair: led over 2f out: wd bnd sn after: clr over 1f out: rdn out* **7/4**[1]

3000 **2** *3* **Batchworth Blaise**[86] 4681 7-9-6 **57**........................ BillyCray 2 63
(E A Wheeler) *dwlt: hld up last: prog 2f out: hanging over 1f out: styd on wl to take 2nd nr fin* **7/1**

0000 **3** *½* **Song Of Praise**[34] 6329 4-8-11 **51**........................ DuilioDaSilva(3) 6 56
(M Blanshard) *hld up in last pair: prog fr 1/2-way: chsd wnr over 1f out: no imp: lost 2nd nr fin* **12/1**

546 **4** *2 ¾* **Ever Cheerful**[22] 6672 9-9-2 **53**........................(p) AmyBaker 5 51
(A B Haynes) *t.k.h: w ldr: led 1/2-way to over 2f out: wknd over 1f out* **12/1**

0060 **5** *5* **Cavalry Guard (USA)**[218] 976 6-8-8 **48**...................(b) JulieBurke(3) 8 32
(T D McCarthy) *racd wd: in tch: effrt 3f out: lft bhd over 2f out* **25/1**

0620 **6** *1 ½* **Abhainn (IRE)**[14] 6864 4-9-1 **52**........................ DeclanCannon 10 32
(B Palling) *prom: lost pl 1/2-way u.p: last 2f: no ch after* **13/2**[3]

020 **7** *½* **Royal Envoy (IRE)**[170] 1998 7-8-11 **55**........................ LauraSimpson(7) 1 34
(P Howling) *in tch to 3f out: pushed along and steadily wknd* **25/1**

4500 **8** *2* **Mighty Aphrodite**[13] 6898 3-9-7 **60**........................ RossAtkinson 4 33
(Miss Olivia Maylam) *chsd ldrs: lft bhd fr 3f out: no ch fnl 2f* **7/1**

6510 **9** *shd* **Cool Kitten (IRE)**[60] 5559 3-9-1 **57**........................(v) HarryBentley(3) 3 30
(W J Knight) *led to 1/2-way: wknd over 2f out* **11/2**[2]

1m 24.89s (0.09) **Going Correction** 0.0s/f (Stan)
WFA 3 from 4yo+ 2lb **9** Ran SP% **113.2**
Speed ratings (Par 101): **99,95,95,91,86 84,83,81,81**
Tote Swingers: 1&2 £4.90, 1&3 £6.10, 2&3 £15.70 CSF £13.96 CT £109.36 TOTE £2.90: £1.60, £2.00, £4.70; EX 15.30 TRIFECTA Pool: £440.87 - 1.71 winning units. Place 6: £39.27 Place 5: £22.85..

Owner Stuart C Williams **Bred** L Ellinas And Old Mill Stud Ltd **Trained** Newmarket, Suffolk

FOCUS
The time was 0.37 seconds quicker than the first division and it's fair to say Paphos was much the best of both legs. The form is rated around the third's recent best.

T/Jkpt: Not won. T/Plt: £81.60 to a £1 stake. Pool:£59,484.71 - 531.88 winning tickets T/Qpdt: £2.80 to a £1 stake. Pool:£6,183.80 - 1,619.70 winning tickets JN

7064 WOLVERHAMPTON (A.W) (L-H)
Thursday, October 28

OFFICIAL GOING: Standard
Wind: Light, half-behind Weather: Cloudy

7193 BET MULTIPLES - BETDAQ H'CAP (DIV I) 5f 20y(P)
5:20 (5:26) (Class 5) (0-70,70) 3-Y-0+ **£1,774** (£523; £262) **Stalls** Low

Form RPR

0001 **1** **Grand Stitch (USA)**[27] 6536 4-8-11 **65**........................(v) NeilFarley(5) 3 79+
(D Carroll) *mde all: abt 3 l clr 2f out: rdn ins fnl f: r.o wl and a in command* **11/4**[1]

6242 **2** *1 ¾* **Riflessione**[21] 6700 4-9-7 **70**........................(b) DavidProbert 2 78
(R A Harris) *in tch: effrt to chse wnr over 1f out: no imp ins fnl f* **7/2**[2]

000 **3** *3* **Hypnosis**[20] 6708 7-9-5 **68**........................ RichardHughes 9 65
(N Wilson) *midfield: pushed along 3f out: hdwy over 1f out: kpt on ins fnl f: nt pce to rch front 2* **16/1**

2110 **4** *1 ½* **Bubbly Bellini (IRE)**[17] 6822 3-8-13 **62**........................(p) CathyGannon 8 54
(Lee Smyth, Ire) *in rr: hdwy over 1f out: styd on ins fnl f: nt pce to chal ldrs* **25/1**

1553 **5** *1* **Star Twilight**[36] 6299 3-8-12 **61**........................(v) RobertWinston 6 49
(D Shaw) *hld up: effrt and hdwy 2f out: chsd ldrs over 1f out: one pce ins fnl f* **10/1**

1664 **6** *¼* **Cape Royal**[30] 6446 10-9-1 **64**........................(bt) LiamKeniry 4 51
(J M Bradley) *n.m.r sn after s: chsd wnr after 1f: lost 2nd u.p over 1f out: wknd ins fnl f* **11/2**[3]

0000 **7** *½* **Canadian Danehill (IRE)**[21] 6700 8-9-2 **65**...................(p) DavidAllan 7 51
(R M H Cowell) *in tch: rdn and outpcd over 2f out: wl btn over 1f out* **10/1**

2050 **8** *¾* **Poppy Golightly**[76] 5031 3-8-9 **63**........................ AdamBeschizza(5) 10 46
(R J Hodges) *dwlt: bhd: pushed along over 2f out: nvr on terms* **33/1**

3006 **9** *2* **Maryolini**[29] 6456 5-8-4 **56**........................ Louis-PhilippeBeuzelin(3) 1 32
(T Keddy) *chsd ldrs tl rdn and wknd over 2f out* **7/1**

-500 **10** *2 ½* **Harry Up**[108] 3958 9-9-0 **63**........................(p) JamesDoyle 5 30
(Andrew Reid) *chsd ldrs: rdn 2f out: wknd over 1f out* **25/1**

0400 **11** *23* **Micky Mac (IRE)**[22] 6679 6-8-8 **60**........................ KellyHarrison(3) 11 —
(C J Teague) *a outpcd and bhd* **20/1**

61.57 secs (-0.73) **Going Correction** -0.025s/f (Stan) **11** Ran SP% **116.2**
Speed ratings (Par 103): **104,101,96,94,92 92,91,90,86,82 46**
Tote Swingers: 1&2 £2.10, 1&3 £6.70, 2&3 £7.90 CSF £11.27 CT £130.04 TOTE £4.20: £1.80, £1.10, £2.70; EX 9.50.

Owner Danny Fantom **Bred** Fortress Pacific Equine Llc **Trained** Sledmere, E Yorks

FOCUS
The course had been rotavated to a depth of between 5.5 inches and 6 inches on Tuesday, but had settled down again and the ground was officially standard with the time being 1.37 seconds slower than the RP standard. It was faster than the second division. Some veterans, who are some way past their best, and mainly exposed younger horses contested this sprint handicap. The winner looked better than the bare form, with the runner-up the best guide.

Micky Mac(IRE) Official explanation: jockey said gelding hung left throughout and stopped quickly

7194 BET MULTIPLES - BETDAQ H'CAP (DIV II) 5f 20y(P)
5:50 (5:51) (Class 5) (0-70,69) 3-Y-0+ **£1,774** (£523; £262) **Stalls** Low

Form RPR

5066 **1** **Perlachy**[21] 6700 6-8-13 **64**........................(v) KellyHarrison(3) 4 72
(D Shaw) *midfield: hdwy over 2f out: chsd ldr over 1f out: r.o u.p to ld towards fin: jst hld on fnl strides* **8/1**

3061 **2** *nse* **Speedyfix**[36] 6285 3-9-1 **63**........................(v) DavidProbert 3 71
(Mrs C A Dunnett) *bhd: rdn and hdwy over 1f out: r.o ins fnl f: clsd qckly fnl strides: jst failed* **13/2**[3]

3124 **3** *¾* **Island Legend (IRE)**[21] 6700 4-9-7 **69**........................(p) LiamKeniry 2 74+
(J M Bradley) *led: rdn over 1f out: hdd towards fin: no ex fnl strides* **9/2**[1]

1664 **4** *1* **Dream Number (IRE)**[18] 6772 3-8-13 **61**........................ PhillipMakin 1 62
(W R Muir) *midfield: rdn and hdwy over 1f out: styd on ins fnl f: nt quite pce to chal ldrs* **5/1**[2]

3032 **5** *¾* **Aalsmeer**[12] 6931 3-9-0 **62**........................(p) TomMcLaughlin 5 61
(Karen George) *midfield: pushed along over 2f out: rdn over 1f out: styd on ins fnl f: nt quite pce to rch ldrs* **5/1**[2]

1125 **6** *1* **Rio's Girl**[36] 6299 3-8-8 **59**........................ AmyRyan(3) 6 54
(R M Whitaker) *chsd ldrs: shkn up when n.m.r briefly over 1f out: one pce ins fnl f* **7/1**

00 **7** *4 ½* **Ridley Didley (IRE)**[42] 6103 5-9-5 **67**........................ RichardHughes 10 46
(N Wilson) *chsd ldrs: wnt 2nd 3f out: rdn and lost 2nd over 1f out: wknd fnl f* **7/1**

0600 **8** *½* **Silver Prelude**[36] 6292 9-9-2 **64**........................(t) WilliamCarson 9 41
(S C Williams) *chsd ldr to 3f out: rdn over 1f out: wknd fnl f* **16/1**

0000 **9** *7* **Ponting (IRE)**[23] 6664 4-9-1 **63**........................ TonyCulhane 8 15
(P T Midgley) *bhd: wl outpcd fr over 2f out* **50/1**

3400 **10** *1 ¼* **Thoughtsofstardom**[20] 6714 7-8-12 **65**........................ TobyAtkinson(5) 7 12
(P S McEntee) *bhd: wl outpcd fr over 2f out: nvr on terms* **40/1**

62.35 secs (0.05) **Going Correction** -0.025s/f (Stan) **10** Ran SP% **111.2**
Speed ratings (Par 103): **98,97,96,95,93 92,85,84,73,71**
Tote Swingers: 1&2 £4.20, 1&3 £4.30, 2&3 £3.90 CSF £56.16 CT £215.34 TOTE £6.90: £3.10, £1.90, £2.00; EX 67.50.

Owner Mrs N Macauley **Bred** J James **Trained** Sproxton, Leics

FOCUS
Mainly exposed sorts in the second division of the 5f handicap, for which the time was significantly slower than the previous heat. The winner was close to his best with the third the best guide.

7195 BET IN RUNNING - BETDAQ H'CAP 5f 216y(P)
6:20 (6:20) (Class 6) (0-60,60) 3-Y-0+ **£1,706** (£503; £252) **Stalls** Low

Form RPR

220 **1** **Mottley Crewe**[39] 6226 3-9-3 **60**........................ TomEaves 7 71
(M Dods) *sn w ldr: led over 2f out: rdn over 1f out: kpt on wl towards fin* **11/1**

4502 **2** *1 ¼* **Desert Falls**[14] 6864 4-9-0 **59**........................ MichaelStainton(3) 2 66
(R M Whitaker) *chsd ldrs: wnt 2nd 2f out: styd on u.p fnl f: no real imp on wnr* **13/2**[3]

5332 **3** *nk* **Cwmni**[11] 6952 4-9-2 **58**........................ DavidProbert 5 64
(B Palling) *hld up in midfield: rdn and hdwy 2f out: sn chsd ldrs: styd on ins fnl f: nt quite gng pce of front 2* **6/1**[2]

5340 **4** *¾* **Tawzeea (IRE)**[20] 6713 5-9-4 **60**........................(bt[1]) PhillipMakin 1 64
(M Dods) *hld up: hdwy over 1f out: sn chsd ldrs: styd on same pce fnl 100yds* **11/2**[1]

0003 **5** *nk* **Bahamian Kid**[13] 6898 5-8-11 **60**.....(v) JackDuern(7) 10 63+
(R Hollinshead) *bhd: nt clr run over 1f out: sn plld wd: hdwy ins fnl f: styd on and hung lft towards fin: nt pce to chal* **8/1**

1350 **6** *2* **Charlie Delta**[19] 6741 7-9-4 **60**.....(b) PaulHanagan 8 56
(R A Harris) *midfield: u.p over 1f out: one pce ins fnl f: nvr able to chal* **10/1**

3-00 **7** *½* **Richelieu**[17] 6820 8-9-2 **58**.....(p) RobertWinston 6 53
(Lee Smyth, Ire) *hld up: pushed along over 3f out: sme hdwy over 1f out: one pce ins fnl f* **8/1**

0540 **8** *4 ½* **Pherousa**[31] 6421 3-9-2 **59**..... FrannyNorton 11 39
(M Blanshard) *racd keenly in midfield: rdn over 1f out: no imp whn n.m.r and hmpd ins fnl f: nvr a danger* **20/1**

0000 **9** *8* **Maxwell Hawke (IRE)**[64] 5405 4-9-4 **60**.....(t) RichardKingscote 3 15
(Tom Dascombe) *chsd ldrs: rdn wl over 1f out: sn wknd* **14/1**

605 **10** *¾* **Silver Linnet (IRE)**[129] 3277 3-9-3 **60**..... WilliamCarson 13 12
(M G Quinlan) *s.i.s: a bhd* **33/1**

0030 **11** *hd* **Connor's Choice**[20] 6713 5-8-13 **58**..... SimonPearce(3) 4 10
(Andrew Turnell) *led: rdn and hdd over 2f out: wknd over 1f out* **14/1**

5005 **12** *½* **Dispol Grand (IRE)**[19] 6741 4-9-3 **59**..... TonyCulhane 9 9
(P T Midgley) *chsd ldrs tl rdn and wknd over 2f out* **22/1**

0650 **13** *nk* **Tyrannosaurus Rex (IRE)**[26] 6572 6-9-4 **60**..... LukeMorris 12 9
(D Shaw) *midfield tl rdn and wknd over 2f out* **14/1**

1m 15.52s (0.52) **Going Correction** -0.025s/f (Stan)
WFA 3 from 4yo+ 1lb 13 Ran SP% **114.7**
Speed ratings (Par 101): **95,93,92,91,91 88,88,82,71,70 70,69,69**
Tote Swingers: 1&2 £20.10, 1&3 £4.90, 2&3 £6.70 CSF £75.52 CT £472.99 TOTE £21.00: £6.70, £5.70, £1.10; EX 87.90.
Owner Crewe And Nantwich Racing Club **Bred** Longdon Stud Ltd **Trained** Denton, Co Durham

FOCUS
A low-grade 6f handicap in which the early pace was no more than ordinary. A clear personal best from the winner, with the form rated around the next three.
Silver Linnet(IRE) Official explanation: jockey said filly stumbled out of the gates

7196 BET ASIAN H'CAPS - BETDAQ HANDICAP 1m 5f 194y(P)
6:50 (6:50) (Class 3) (0-95,95) 3-Y-O+ **£5,677** (£1,699; £849; £424; £211) **Stalls** Low

Form RPR
0300 **1** **Mystery Star (IRE)**[20] 6720 5-10-0 **95**..... RichardHughes 4 105
(M H Tompkins) *hld up bhd ldrs: effrt 2f out: wnt 2nd over 1f out: sn chalng: led ins fnl f: styd on and in command ins fnl 75yds: pushed out cl home* **8/1**

6402 **2** *1 ¼* **Desert Recluse (IRE)**[33] 6352 3-8-11 **92**..... AdamBeschizza(5) 2 100
(Pat Eddery) *chsd ldr: led over 2f out: rdn over 1f out: sn pressed: hdd ins fnl f: hld ins fnl 75yds* **6/4**[1]

0044 **3** *4 ½* **Record Breaker (IRE)**[30] 6437 6-9-9 **90**.....(b) JoeFanning 3 92
(M Johnston) *in rr early: trckd ldrs after 3f: rdn and outpcd 2f out: kpt on to take 3rd ins fnl f: n.d to front 2* **5/1**

0636 **4** *2* **Brouhaha**[17] 6797 6-8-12 **79**..... RichardKingscote 5 78
(Tom Dascombe) *in rr after 2f: rdn and outpcd over 2f out: plugged on at one pce ins fnl f: nvr able to chal* **4/1**[3]

3164 **5** *½* **Proud Times (USA)**[33] 6362 4-9-6 **87**..... PJMcDonald 1 85
(G A Swinbank) *led: hdd over 2f out: rdn and outpcd over 1f out: wknd ins fnl f* **3/1**[2]

3m 4.18s (-1.82) **Going Correction** -0.025s/f (Stan)
WFA 3 from 4yo+ 9lb 5 Ran SP% **112.8**
Speed ratings (Par 107): **104,103,100,99,99**
CSF £21.13 TOTE £9.30: £10.40, £1.20; EX 14.50.
Owner John Brenchley **Bred** R Coffey **Trained** Newmarket, Suffolk

FOCUS
A 76-95 handicap but not reliable form as the pace was moderate and it developed into a sprint over the last 3f. The race is rated around the front pair.

NOTEBOOK
Mystery Star(IRE) had run two desperate races on his last two starts but reportedly pulled a muscle on the first occasion and failed to handle the soft ground at York last time. He's proven on the surface and was back to form here showing the best turn of foot in the straight. He ran off 95, and is likely to have only limited opportunities on the domestic scene in the next few months. (tchd 13-2)
Desert Recluse(IRE) was running off a mark of 92 which indicates the improvement he's shown this year as his last all-weather success was off 66. In a muddling race, he just lost out in a sprint finish. Considering he gets 2m, he would almost certainly have been better suited by a stronger pace. However, despite his rise up the weights, he showed he's still capable of being competitive. (op 9-4)
Record Breaker(IRE) is 6lb higher on the all-weather than on turf, but has struggled to make his mark in handicaps this season. (tchd 6-1)
Brouhaha goes well on the track but, even though he may not have been suited by the way the race panned out, he didn't shape with any great encouragement.
Proud Times(USA) had the run of the race, as his rider dictated matters, but he was readily outpaced when the sprint began. This wasn't his true form. (op 5-2 tchd 9-4)

7197 ENJOY THE PARTY PACK GROUP OFFER CLAIMING STKS 1m 1f 103y(P)
7:20 (7:21) (Class 5) 2-Y-O **£2,115** (£624; £312) **Stalls** Low

Form RPR
0005 **1** **Imaginary World (IRE)**[17] 6795 2-8-10 60..... RichardMullen 4 69
(E S McMahon) *trckd ldrs: led 3f out: rdn 2f out: r.o and kpt finding more: wl on top fnl 75yds* **10/1**

566 **2** *2 ¼* **Scented**[19] 6743 2-9-2 69..... RichardHughes 8 71
(W J Haggas) *led for 1f: trckd ldrs after: pushed along for a few strides over 3f out: wnt cl 2nd over 2f out: sn rdn: hung lft over 1f out: no ex fnl 75yds* **8/13**[1]

4330 **3** *5* **Sheila's Star (IRE)**[43] 6081 2-8-9 66..... LukeMorris 5 55
(J S Moore) *hld up: rdn over 3f out: sn outpcd: styd on to take 3rd 1f out: nt trble front 2* **8/1**[3]

0440 **4** *4 ½* **Roi Du Boeuf (IRE)**[29] 6471 2-9-4 62..... MartinLane 10 55
(D M Simcock) *prom: rdn 3f out: outpcd by ldrs wl over 1f out: wknd fnl f* **9/2**[2]

000 **5** *2 ¾* **Senor Sassi (USA)**[40] 6209 2-8-12 50.....(p) LiamKeniry 7 44
(J S Moore) *t.k.h: in tch: pushed along 3f out: sn wknd* **66/1**

210 **6** *6* **Rather Cool**[36] 6300 2-8-11 56.....(p) PaulHanagan 9 31
(A B Haynes) *rushed up to ld after 1f: rdn and hdd 3f out: wknd 2f out* **14/1**

000 **7** *1 ½* **Always De Man (IRE)**[13] 6891 2-8-12 52..... JoeFanning 6 29
(M Johnston) *s.i.s: bhd: sn pushed along: nvr on terms* **25/1**

0000 **8** *1 ½* **Adzing (IRE)**[11] 6953 2-8-11 41..... DavidProbert 1 26
(R A Harris) *awkward s: bhd: rdn 4f out: nvr on terms* **100/1**

600 **9** *34* **Georgina Bailey (IRE)**[130] 3237 2-8-6 55.....(p) AdamBeschizza(5) 2 —
(A J McCabe) *broke wl: prom: lost pl over 5f out: lost tch over 3f out: t.o* **66/1**

040 **10** *13* **Will Barrow**[50] 5857 2-8-7 49.....(b1) MatthewDavies(3) 3 —
(J R Boyle) *in tch: lost pl after 1f: sn bhd: lost tch 4f out: t.o* **80/1**

2m 1.31s (-0.39) **Going Correction** -0.025s/f (Stan) 10 Ran SP% **116.0**
Speed ratings (Par 95): **100,98,93,89,87 81,80,79,48,37**
Tote Swingers: 1&2 £2.80, 1&3 £1.30, 2&3 £6.60 CSF £16.50 TOTE £10.40: £2.50, £1.50, £1.40; EX 22.20.
Owner J C Fretwell **Bred** Denis McDonnell **Trained** Lichfield, Staffs

FOCUS
This was a fair juvenile claimer for the course, the pace was fair and they finished well strung out. Sound form, with the winner on the upgrade.

NOTEBOOK
Imaginary World(IRE) has improved for the step up in trip. Rated just 48 after her first four starts, she improved significantly when stepped up to 1m last time at Kempton and confirmed that with a game win over this extended 1m1f. She was one of a handful with a chance on official ratings and she showed the right attitude. Another win in this grade would be on the cards. (op 9-1)
Scented, rated 69 after showing promise in maidens, was giving the winner 6lb and though she had every chance on this drop in grade, she edged left under pressure and lacked the battling qualities of the winner. She may find a similar race but doesn't look one to take a short price about. (tchd 8-11 in places)
Sheila's Star(IRE), who has a mark of 66, didn't run to that, though she kept on under some strong driving to finish a well-beaten third. She may need to be relegated to selling company to find a winning opportunity. (op 15-2)
Roi Du Boeuf(IRE) had no easy task giving weight away all round, but ran a disappointing race on his first run on the surface. (op 5-1)
Senor Sassi(USA) shaped creditably with first-time cheekpieces but is no better than plating class. (op 80-1)
Will Barrow Official explanation: vet said colt finished lame

7198 BREEDERS' CUP LIVE ONLY ON ATR MAIDEN FILLIES' STKS 1m 141y(P)
7:50 (7:52) (Class 5) 2-Y-O **£2,978** (£886; £442; £221) **Stalls** Low

Form RPR
00 **1** **Rumh (GER)**[26] 6559 2-9-0 0..... RichardMullen 1 87+
(Saeed Bin Suroor) *mde all: r.o wl to draw clr ins fnl f: pushed out* **2/1**[2]

30 **2** *6* **Electra Star**[91] 4508 2-9-0 0..... RichardHughes 7 75
(W J Haggas) *trckd ldrs: effrt over 3f out: chsd wnr over 2f out: sn rdn: hung lft over 1f out: no ex and no ch ins fnl f* **7/2**[3]

5 **3** *7* **Polly Holder (IRE)**[9] 7000 2-9-0 0..... LukeMorris 10 59
(A Bailey) *bhd: pushed along 5f out: styd on fr over 1f out: wnt 3rd wl ins fnl f: nt trble front 2* **33/1**

4 *1* **Apparel (IRE)** 2-9-0 0..... PaulHanagan 6 57+
(E A L Dunlop) *towards rr: pushed along briefly after 1f: effrt into midfield 3f out: kpt on fr over 1f out but nt pce to trble ldrs* **14/1**

0 **5** *½* **Lady Gabrielle (IRE)**[27] 6532 2-9-0 0..... MickyFenton 5 56
(M L W Bell) *midfield: pushed along 4f out: nvr able to get on terms w ldrs* **50/1**

3 **6** *2* **Matilda's Waltz**[41] 6154 2-9-0 0..... JimCrowley 2 51
(R M Beckett) *trckd ldrs: pushed along 5f out: chsd wnr 3f out tl over 2f out: sn outpcd by ldrs: wknd ins fnl f:* **6/4**[1]

64 **7** *1 ½* **Magic Of The Sea (IRE)**[42] 6118 2-9-0 0..... ChrisCatlin 4 48
(M Botti) *in rr: pushed along 3f out: nvr on terms* **16/1**

40 **8** *4 ½* **Geblah (IRE)**[18] 6770 2-9-0 0..... TomQueally 3 39
(D M Simcock) *chsd wnr: pushed along 4f out: lost pl 3f out: wknd over 2f out* **33/1**

0 **9** *1 ¼* **Delagoa Bay (IRE)**[18] 6770 2-9-0 0..... LiamKeniry 8 36
(S Kirk) *in tch: rdn 3f out: sn wknd* **100/1**

0 **10** *2 ½* **Dixie Land Band**[18] 6770 2-9-0 0..... RobertHavlin 9 31
(A B Haynes) *hld up: u.p 3f out: sn lft wl bhd* **100/1**

1m 49.75s (-0.75) **Going Correction** -0.025s/f (Stan) 10 Ran SP% **117.9**
Speed ratings (Par 92): **102,96,90,89,89 87,86,82,80,78**
Tote Swingers: 1&2 £13.20, 1&3 £3.10, 2&3 £16.10 CSF £9.43 TOTE £3.20: £1.10, £1.40, £7.70; EX 10.70.
Owner Godolphin **Bred** Stiftung Gestut Fahrhof **Trained** Newmarket, Suffolk

FOCUS
This was a competitive juvenile fillies' maiden for the course but the pace was no more than ordinary and there were only two in it from 3f out. The winner confirmed her debut promise and looks a nice prospect.

NOTEBOOK
Rumh(GER), who had stepped up markedly on her debut run when in midfield in a valuable fillies' sales race at Newmarket last time, had the run of the race but left the impression she would have won anyway. Making all, with her rider dictating the gallop, she stretched clear in the straight and ran out a ready winner. She's bred to stay further than this, is an improving sort and should make up into a decent filly over middle distances next year. (op 7-4 tchd 13-8 and 9-4 in a place)
Electra Star is probably a decent yardstick to the form as she'd shown promise on both previous starts, notably on her debut at Newbury. She drew away with the winner from the home turn but was clearly outpointed and wasn't knocked about when held. She'll find a race. (op 9-2)
Polly Holder(IRE), who showed a little promise on her debut at Yarmouth last week, did so again here. Although she was never travelling at any stage, she ran on to take third without troubling the front pair. She'll do better in handicaps over middle distances next season.
Apparel(IRE) was rather uneasy in the market but showed a degree of promise and should improve for the run. (op 11-1)
Lady Gabrielle(IRE) shaped better than on her debut.
Matilda's Waltz was the disappointment of the race, having run such a promising race on her debut at Newmarket and been sent off favourite. Although she raced close to the pace, her rider never seemed happy and she looked ill-suited by either the surface or the track, or perhaps both, and is likely to prove much better than she showed here. Official explanation: jockey had no explanation for the poor form shown (op 2-1)
Magic Of The Sea(IRE) was keen early and made a little ground after being dropped right out early on. She is now qualified for a handicap mark. (op 14-1)
Geblah(IRE) Official explanation: jockey said filly hung left-handed in home straight

7199 ATTHERACES.COM/BREEDERSCUP H'CAP 1m 141y(P)
8:20 (8:21) (Class 7) (0-50,50) 3-Y-O+ **£1,364** (£403; £201) **Stalls** Low

Form RPR
055/ **1** **Master Of Light**[64] 5430 5-9-0 **49**..... RichardHughes 9 62+
(Ms Joanna Morgan, Ire) *a.p: led 2f out: rdn over 1f out: drew clr ins fnl f: r.o wl* **5/2**[1]

0004 **2** *4* **Escardo (GER)**[6] 7071 7-8-13 **48**..... TonyCulhane 3 52
(D G Bridgwater) *midfield: pushed along over 2f out: hdwy whn swtchd lft over 1f out: styd on to take 2nd wl ins fnl f: nt trble wnr* **16/1**

6234 **3** *½* **Al Rayanah**[44] 6061 7-9-0 **49**.....(p) KirstyMilczarek 10 55+
(G Prodromou) *hld up: nt clr run wl over 1f out: hdwy sn after: nt clr run again briefly ins fnl f: gng on at fin* **8/1**

400 **4** *½* **Acropolis (IRE)**[8] 7023 9-9-1 **50**..... CathyGannon 5 52
(A W Carroll) *in tch: effrt 2f out: nt qckn over 1f out: styd on same pce ins fnl f* **18/1**

0505 **5** 1/2 **Napoletano (ITY)**[36] 6298 4-9-1 **50**.................. PaulHanagan 7 49
(R Johnson) *led: rdn and hdd 2f out: outpcd by wnr over 1f out: wknd fnl 75yds* **16/1**

020 **6** 1/2 **Navajo Joe (IRE)**[62] 5486 5-8-11 **49**.................. JamesSullivan(3) 11 47
(R Johnson) *hld up: hdwy on outer over 3f out: rdn 2f out whn chsng ldrs: one pce ins fnl f* **33/1**

00 **7** 1 1/4 **Mackintosh (IRE)**[114] 3758 4-9-0 **49**.................. StephenCraine 6 44
(Patrick Morris) *hld up: hdwy gng wl over 2f out: rdn over 1f out: nt pick up: wknd ins fnl f* **66/1**

3425 **8** 3 1/2 **Corrib (IRE)**[14] 6860 7-9-0 **49**..................(p) NeilChalmers 8 36
(B Palling) *missed break: bhd: rdn over 2f out: nvr able to get competitive* **6/1**

2040 **9** hd **Dream Express (IRE)**[52] 5817 5-9-0 **49**.................. ChrisCatlin 4 36
(D W Thompson) *prom tl wknd 2f out* **33/1**

5202 **10** 1 1/2 **Herecomethegirls**[6] 7071 4-9-0 **49**..................(b) LukeMorris 1 32
(W G M Turner) *midfield: pushed along 5f out: wknd 3f out* **9/2**[2]

445 **11** 3 3/4 **Carter**[13] 6905 4-9-1 **50**..................(v) TomMcLaughlin 13 25
(W M Brisbourne) *chsd ldr 7f out tl rdn wl over 2f out: wknd wl over 1f out* **11/2**[3]

3020 **12** 7 **Libre**[6] 7070 10-8-8 **48**.................. AshleyMorgan(5) 2 7
(F Jordan) *hld up in midfield: rdn and wknd over 3f out* **25/1**

0000 **13** 45 **Boxer Shorts**[6] 7070 4-8-7 **49**.................. JosephYoung(7) 12 —
(M Mullineaux) *hld up: bhd and struggling 5f out: nvr on terms: t.o* **100/1**

1m 50.33s (-0.17) **Going Correction** -0.025s/f (Stan) **13** Ran SP% **116.8**
Speed ratings (Par 97): **99,95,95,94,93 93,92,89,88,87 84,77,37**
Tote Swingers: 1&2 £5.10, 1&3 £11.60, 2&3 £13.40 CSF £44.20 CT £293.63 TOTE £2.70: £1.50, £6.20, £3.00; EX 61.50.
Owner West Meets East Syndicate **Bred** Miss Jackie Penny **Trained** Ballivor, Co Meath

FOCUS
Not only a low-grade handicap, the rating band being 45-50, but few came into the race in much form and the race had a moderate look about it. It still looks an improved effort from the winner.
Al Rayanah Official explanation: jockey said mare was denied a clear run
Acropolis(IRE) Official explanation: jockey said gelding hung left
Corrib(IRE) Official explanation: jockey said mare was slowly into stride
Boxer Shorts Official explanation: trainer said gelding had breathing problems

7200 BREEDERS' CUP LIVE ONLY ON ATR H'CAP 1m 1f 103y(P)
8:50 (8:54) (Class 6) (0-55,55) 3-Y-O+ **£1,706** (£503; £252) **Stalls** Low

Form RPR

510 **1** **Querido (GER)**[226] 898 6-9-2 **52**..................(t) LiamKeniry 10 61+
(G Brown) *in tch: dropped to midfield 7f out: hdwy gng wl 2f out: led jst over 1f out: r.o ins fnl f: rdn out* **16/1**

5346 **2** 1 **Tres Froide (FR)**[6] 7070 5-9-0 **50**..................(p) TomEaves 9 56
(N Tinkler) *hld up: hdwy 2f out: rdn over 1f out: r.o ins fnl f: wnt 2nd fnl 75yds: nt quite rch wnr* **22/1**

0400 **3** 1 1/2 **Ocean Countess (IRE)**[14] 6864 4-9-4 **54**.................. CathyGannon 6 57
(Miss J Feilden) *hld up: pushed along over 2f out: rdn and hung lft whn hdwy over 1f out: r.o and clsd towards fin* **25/1**

4 3/4 **An Mhi (IRE)**[53] 5794 5-9-4 **54**.................. RichardHughes 3 55
(Ms Joanna Morgan, Ire) *trckd ldrs: led on inner wl over 2f out: hdd jst over 1f out: no ex fnl 75yds* **5/2**[2]

000/ **5** hd **Abydos**[705] 7427 6-9-0 **50**.................. TomQueally 8 51
(B J Curley) *chsd ldr: chalng 3f out: rdn and nt qckn over 1f out: styd on same pce ins fnl f* **11/8**[1]

0240 **6** 1 **Masterofceremonies**[28] 6518 7-9-2 **52**..................(v) TomMcLaughlin 5 51
(W M Brisbourne) *missed break: rdn along and bhd: hdwy to chse ldrs 5f out: rdn whn chalng 3f out: nt qckn over 1f out: wknd fnl 100yds* **15/2**[3]

0-06 **7** 6 **Active Asset (IRE)**[13] 6890 8-9-2 **52**.................. PaulHanagan 12 38
(D C Griffiths) *in tch on outer: pushed along over 3f out: sn wknd* **8/1**

2003 **8** 3 **Noche De Reyes**[20] 6716 5-9-5 **55**.................. RobertWinston 1 35
(E J Alston) *led: rdn 3f out: hdd wl over 2f out: wknd wl over 1f out* **18/1**

4060 **9** 1 **Barodine**[130] 2955 7-8-9 **50**.................. AdamBeschizza(5) 4 28
(R J Hodges) *in tch: rdn over 2f out: sn wknd* **28/1**

0000 **10** 1/2 **All About You (IRE)**[122] 3521 4-9-3 **53**.................. KirstyMilczarek 7 30
(P Howling) *hld up: struggling fnl 3f: nvr on terms* **40/1**

2m 2.11s (0.41) **Going Correction** -0.025s/f (Stan) **10** Ran SP% **118.8**
Speed ratings (Par 101): **97,96,94,94,93 93,87,85,84,83**
Tote Swingers: 1&2 £15.30, 1&3 £13.10, 2&3 £16.10 CSF £318.94 CT £8440.16 TOTE £25.20: £5.30, £5.10, £6.90; EX 159.30 Place 6: £24.50 Place 5: £16.80..
Owner Miss Emma Wettern **Bred** Gestut Brummerhof **Trained** East Garston, Berks
■ Stewards' Enquiry : Adam Beschizza caution: used whip when out of contention.

FOCUS
An ordinary 46-55 handicap which featured two well-backed runners but the pair both ran below expectations. Weak form, to which the runner-up looks the best guide.
T/Plt: £16.00 to a £1 stake. Pool:£78,566.38 - 3,572.12 winning tickets T/Qpdt: £8.30 to a £1 stake. Pool:£10,428.55 - 925.17 winning tickets DO

6923 NEWMARKET (Rowley Mile) (R-H)
Friday, October 29

OFFICIAL GOING: Good to soft (good in places; 7.5)
Stands' side section of Rowley Mile used.
Wind: strong, half against Weather: overcast, chilly wind

7201 UKUNPUBLISHED.CO.UK E B F MAIDEN STKS 6f
1:15 (1:16) (Class 4) 2-Y-O **£4,533** (£1,348; £674; £336) **Stalls** High

Form RPR

00 **1** **My Delirium**[22] 6697 2-8-9 0.................. JohnFahy(3) 9 79
(R M Beckett) *leggy: unf: chsd ldrs: rdn to chse ldr over 2f out: chal over 1f out: led ins fnl f: styd on wl: rdn out* **80/1**

02 **2** 1 1/2 **Commended**[21] 6722 2-9-3 0.................. MichaelHills 11 80
(B W Hills) *led: rdn wl over 1f out: hrd pressed and drvn jst over 1f out: hdd ins fnl f: kpt on same pce fnl 100yds* **6/4**[1]

63 **3** 1 3/4 **Cultural Desert**[42] 6153 2-9-3 0.................. JimCrowley 3 74
(R M Beckett) *racd in centre tl gps merged 1/2-way: chsd ldrs: rdn ent fnl 2f: chsd ldng pair over 1f out: styd on same pce and no imp u.p fnl f* **9/2**[2]

4 2 1/4 **Guided Missile (IRE)** 2-8-12 0.................. JimmyFortune 4 64+
(A M Balding) *w'like: str: bit bkwd: racd in centre tl gps merged 1/2-way: racd in midfield overall: hdwy 1/2-way: chsd ldng quartet wl over 1f out: kpt on fnl f: nt rch ldrs* **8/1**

53 **5** 1 3/4 **Mr Dream Maker (IRE)**[45] 6046 2-9-3 0.................. SaleemGolam 12 62
(Ian Williams) *unf: chsd ldrs tl over 2f out: sn rdn: wknd over 1f out* **40/1**

0 **6** 1 1/2 **Sim Sala Bim**[42] 6153 2-9-3 0.................. WilliamCarson 8 60+
(S C Williams) *stdd after s: bhd: stl plenty to do ent fnl 2f: rdn and hdwy wl over 1f out: styd on steadily fnl f: nvr trbld ldrs* **25/1**

7 2 3/4 **Jawhar (IRE)** 2-9-3 0.................. TadhgO'Shea 15 50
(W J Haggas) *leggy: stdd s: hld up in rr: lost tch w ldrs over 2f out: plugged on steadily fr over 1f out: n.d* **20/1**

8 2 1/2 **Centre Stage** 2-9-3 0.................. JackMitchell 10 42+
(G G Margarson) *w'like: racd in midfield: rdn and struggling 1/2-way: wl btn whn hmpd over 2f out: plugged on same pce and n.d after* **100/1**

9 1 3/4 **Art Thief** 2-9-3 0.................. RichardHughes 13 37+
(S Kirk) *unf: chsd ldrs: rdn and struggling over 3f out: wkng whn edgd lft wl over 2f out: wl btn fnl 2f* **16/1**

10 1/2 **Paradise Place** 2-8-12 0.................. RyanMoore 7 30
(J Noseda) *leggy: scope: sn pushed along towards rr: n.d* **10/1**

11 1 1/4 **Cape Classic (IRE)** 2-9-3 0.................. KierenFallon 1 32
(W J Haggas) *w'like: str: scope: gd bodied: bit bkwd: racd in centre tl gps merged 1/2-way: s.i.s: a in rr: nvr trbld ldrs* **7/1**[3]

0 **12** 1 **Storm Runner (IRE)**[56] 5717 2-9-3 0.................. SebSanders 2 29
(G G Margarson) *leggy: on toes: racd in centre tl gps merged 1/2-way: a towards rr: n.d* **100/1**

0000 **13** nk **Chillie Peppar**[10] 7004 2-9-3 57.................. KirstyMilczarek 6 28
(G Prodromou) *racd in centre tl gps merged 1/2-way: chsd ldrs tl rdn and btn over 2f out: wknd wl over 1f out* **100/1**

0 **14** 2 1/4 **Sabys Gem (IRE)**[81] 4902 2-9-3 0.................. JamieSpencer 5 21
(M Wigham) *w'like: racd in centre tl gps merged 1/2-way: a towards rr: bhd and edging rt wl over 2f out: n.d* **66/1**

0 **15** 18 **Alspritza**[30] 6465 2-8-12 0.................. NeilCallan 14 —
(C F Wall) *leggy: unf: warm: a in rr: lost tch over 2f out: t.o and edging lft fnl f* **100/1**

1m 15.28s (3.08) **Going Correction** +0.625s/f (Yiel) **15** Ran SP% **114.5**
Speed ratings (Par 97): **104,102,99,96,94 92,88,85,83,82 80,79,78,75,51**
Tote Swingers: 1&2 £43.70, 1&3 £2.70, 2&3 £54.90 CSF £186.18 TOTE £159.40: £29.50, £1.30, £1.60; EX 962.70 TRIFECTA Not won..
Owner P K Gardner **Bred** Springcombe Park Stud **Trained** Whitsbury, Hants

FOCUS
An interesting maiden, if not the classiest, and the field split into two early with nine starting up the far rail and six up the centre, but the nearside bunch gradually moved across so that the groups had merged on reaching the 3f pole. There seemed no fluke about the winner's performance, with the time, second and third fitting in.

NOTEBOOK
My Delirium had been well beaten in a couple of modest median auction maidens on turf and Polytrack recently and looked an impossible winner to find, hence her monster starting price. There seemed no fluke about this, however, as she was always up with the pace in the far-side group and saw her race out well after leading a furlong from home. She should have a future as a handicapper over this trip or a little further next year. (op 100-1)
Commended, from a stable with a decent record in this race and narrowly beaten by a 78-rated rival at York earlier this month, tried to make all and managed to hold off all bar the winner. He now gets a mark and should win a race, but he obviously has his limitations. (op 15-8 tchd 2-1 in a place)
Cultural Desert, a stable companion of My Delirium and just in front of a subsequent winner when third of 17 in a C&D maiden last month, started off leading the centre-field group and had every chance, but he was done for finishing speed. He also now qualifies for nurseries. (op 7-2)
Guided Missile(IRE) ◆, a sister to the smart sprinter Dark Missile, proved green in the early stages but she stayed on very nicely under hands-and-heels riding over the last 2f to emerge much the best of the newcomers. She looks a nice prospect and seems likely to emerge the best of these. (op 9-1)
Mr Dream Maker(IRE), who was warm beforehand, showed up for a long way and also now qualifies for a mark, but he has shaped as though in need of further than this.
Sim Sala Bim, over 4l behind Cultural Desert on debut over C&D last month, ran on from the rear over the last 2f but still looked green as he held his head high in the air. He is bred to appreciate middle distances, so should really come into his own over further next year.
Jawhar(IRE) ◆, already gelded and out of a half-sister to Trans Island and Welsh Diva, became short of room when staying on over 2f from home, but still showed enough to suggest there is some ability there. (op 22-1)
Centre Stage, retained for 3,000gns as a yearling and a half-brother to a modest winning sprinter, proved as green as grass and wasn't helped by being hampered by the weakening Art Thief over 2f from home, but he did offer a glimmer of promise.
Cape Classic(IRE) ◆, retained for 320,000gns as a yearling and a half-brother to two winning stable companions, including the Group 1 sprinter King's Apostle, was another to show signs of greenness from an early stage and is likely to fare quite a bit better next time. (op 13-2 tchd 11-2)

7202 CHRISTINE KILKER MEMORIAL E B F MAIDEN STKS (C&G) (DIV I) 7f
1:50 (1:51) (Class 4) 2-Y-O **£4,209** (£1,252; £625; £312) **Stalls** High

Form RPR

1 **Dogs May Bark** 2-9-0 0.................. JimmyFortune 3 86+
(P W Chapple-Hyam) *w'like: scope: str: in tch in midfield: pushed along and hdwy 1/2-way: chsd ldr 2f out: drvn and edgd lft wl over 1f out: led ins fnl f: kpt on: drvn out* **16/1**

4 **2** 1 **Dean Swift**[39] 6254 2-9-0 0.................. ShaneKelly 2 84+
(B J Meehan) *w'like: scope: lengthy: hld up in tch: rdn and effrt to chsd ldng pair 2f out: ev ch and edgd lft u.p over 1f out: styd on same pce fnl 100yds* **11/4**[1]

005 **3** 1 1/2 **Odin (IRE)**[9] 7020 2-9-0 0.................. RobertWinston 8 80
(D R C Elsworth) *led: rdn 2f out: wandered u.p over 1f out: hdd ins fnl f: edgd lft and no ex fnl 150yds* **11/1**

4 2 1/2 **Communicator** 2-9-0 0.................. JamieSpencer 9 74+
(M L W Bell) *w'like: stdd and short of room after s: bhd: swtchd lft and hdwy over 2f out: rdn to chse ldng trio over 1f out: rn green and edgd rt after: kpt on same pce fnl f* **17/2**

5 2 3/4 **Sinfonico (IRE)** 2-9-0 0.................. RichardHughes 10 67+
(R Hannon) *w'like: attr: scope: in tch: n.m.r over 2f out: rdn and hdwy ent fnl 2f: outpcd by ldng trio and carried rt over 1f out: one pce and wl hld fnl f* **8/1**

6 2 1/4 **Looking On** 2-9-0 0.................. DaneO'Neill 7 61
(H Candy) *unf: scope: lengthy: bit bkwd: in tch: rdn and effrt jst over 2f out: outpcd and carried rt over 1f out: wknd jst over 1f out* **6/1**[3]

7 2 3/4 **Grandad Mac** 2-8-7 0.................. LewisWalsh(7) 1 54
(Jane Chapple-Hyam) *str: scope: bit bkwd: s.i.s: a towards rr: pushed along over 4f out: sme hdwy 1/2-way: rdn and wknd ent fnl 2f* **28/1**

00 **8** 4 1/2 **Wom**[14] 6882 2-9-0 0.................. MichaelHills 6 43
(W J Haggas) *lw: chsd ldr tl 2f out: sn rdn and wknd: wl btn over 1f out* **16/1**

00 **9** 2 3/4 **Old Boy Ted**[14] 6883 2-9-0 0.................. JimmyQuinn 5 36
(M H Tompkins) *bhd: pushed along and edging rt over 2f out: nvr trbld ldrs* **66/1**

04 **10** 4 **First Battalion (IRE)**[17] 6831 2-9-0 0.................. RyanMoore 11 26
(Sir Michael Stoute) *w'like: w ldrs tl 4f out: sn rdn along: lost pl 1/2-way: wl btn fnl 2f* **7/2**[2]

The Form Book, Raceform Ltd, Compton, RG20 6NL

0 11 5 **Ninth Parallel (USA)**[31] 6442 2-9-0 0 KierenFallon 4 14
(B J Meehan) *s.i.s: a towards rr: lost tch over 2f out* **22/1**

1m 29.0s (3.60) **Going Correction** +0.625s/f (Yiel) 11 Ran SP% **114.2**
Speed ratings (Par 97): **104,102,101,98,95 92,89,84,81,76 70**
Tote Swingers: 1&2 £13.90, 1&3 £29.50, 2&3 £6.90 CSF £57.25 TOTE £21.70: £4.90, £1.10, £3.10; EX 90.30 TRIFECTA Not won..
Owner Paul Hancock **Bred** Grove Farm Stud **Trained** Newmarket, Suffolk

FOCUS
This maiden has tended to produce handicappers rather than pattern performers but often falls to a major yard, although not necessarily a local one. A decent debut effort from the winner, and both the placed horses are improvers.

NOTEBOOK
Dogs May Bark, who cost less at the breeze-ups than as a yearling, is half-brother to three winners at 5-10f including the prolific Sherjawy. He was not the quickest away on this debut but settled in the pack before making good headway to take the lead over a furlong out. He ran on too well for his more experienced opponents and looks capable of winning more races next season. (op 20-1)
Dean Swift, who finished last of four behind two subsequent winners on his debut over 7f, had Group 1 juvenile race entries before that and was backed into favouritism. He tracked the pace before coming through to deliver his challenge, only to have no answer to the winner up the hill. He should not be too long in winning a maiden. (op 4-1 tchd 9-2)
Odin(IRE) had put up three modest efforts in maidens at 7f-1m, his best effort being on his previous start on Polytrack. Warm beforehand, he helped make the running but could only keep on at the one pace in the latter stages. He is probably the best guide to what is just a fair level of form. (tchd 9-1)
Communicator ◆, a half-brother to a 1m1f juvenile winner out of a mare who won at 6f but is also related to middle-distance winners, put up an eyecatching performance considering he looked pretty green for much of the race. He has a Derby entry and, while he might not quite live up to that, he looks one to bear in mind for next year. (op 12-1)
Sinfonico(IRE), a 55,000gns half-brother to five winners at 5f-1m2f including Bustan, was making his debut for top yard. He ran with some promise and will no doubt come on for the outing. (op 7-1 tchd 17-2)
Looking On, a third foal of a three-time winner, including first time out at two and three, was supported earlier in the day but ran as if he needs more time, having tracked the pace before being unable to go on once the race began in earnest. (op 13-2)
Grandad Mac had already been through the sales ring three times before this debut, and his price had decreased each time. This half-brother to the useful Jelani and four other winners ran as if in need of the experience, staying on in the manner of a colt who will need longer trips in time. (op 22-1)
First Battalion(IRE), who improved on his debut when fourth in a Leicester maiden over a mile, drifted out from favouritism and ran disappointingly, losing his pitch before halfway and finishing out the back. He is now eligible for a mark but needs to put this effort behind him. (op 9-4)

7203 CHRISTINE KILKER MEMORIAL E B F MAIDEN STKS (C&G) (DIV II) 7f
2:25 (2:25) (Class 4) 2-Y-O **£4,209** (£1,252; £625; £312) **Stalls** High

Form RPR
1 **Western Aristocrat (USA)** 2-9-0 0 RyanMoore 2 86+
(J Noseda) *gd sort: scope: hld up in tch: pushed along to chal wl over 1f out: rdn to ld over 1f out: styd on strly fnl f: easily* **3/1**[1]
06 2 3 ¾ **Malanos (IRE)**[14] 6883 2-9-0 0 DaneO'Neill 5 77
(D R C Elsworth) *w ldr tl led 2f out: sn rdn and hdd over 1f out: no ch w wnr ins fnl f: kpt on to hold 2nd* **4/1**[2]
3 ¾ **Lyric Street (IRE)** 2-9-0 0 KierenFallon 11 75+
(L M Cumani) *w'like: attr: scope: s.i.s: sn in tch in midfield: swtchd lft to outer and hdwy 4f out: chsd ldrs and rdn 2f out: unable qck over 1f out: kpt on again but no ch w wnr ins fnl f* **6/1**
4 nse **Guisho (IRE)** 2-9-0 0 ShaneKelly 3 75
(B J Meehan) *w'like; lengthy: plld hrd: hld up trcking ldrs: rdn and effrt wl over 1f out: hung rt and no prog over 1f out: one pce fnl f* **11/1**
5 nk **Maqaraat (IRE)** 2-9-0 0 TadhgO'Shea 9 76+
(B W Hills) *lengthy: s.i.s: bhd: hdwy and hanging rt over 1f out: nudged along and kpt on fnl f: gng on at fin: nvr trbld ldrs* **9/2**[3]
6 ¾ **Piave (IRE)** 2-9-0 0 JimmyFortune 8 72
(P W Chapple-Hyam) *athletic: led tl 2f out: sn rdn: outpcd by wnr ent fnl f: wknd and lost 3 pls fnl 150yds* **15/2**
7 1 ¼ **Dictate** 2-9-0 0 MichaelHills 1 69+
(M H Tompkins) *lengthy: athletic: s.i.s: sn swtchd rt and in tch towards rr: rdn and hdwy into midfield 3f out: rdn and unable qck 2f out: wl hld and plugged on same pce after* **33/1**
8 1 ¾ **Islesman** 2-9-0 0 SebSanders 6 65
(Mrs H S Main) *w'like: cl cpld: s.i.s: t.k.h: rn green and hld up in rr: hdwy 1/2-way: chsd ldrs and rdn ent fnl 2f: wknd over 1f out* **40/1**
9 2 ¼ **Star Rebel** 2-9-0 0 JamieSpencer 10 59
(Jane Chapple-Hyam) *str: bit bkwd: chsd ldrs: rdn and struggling over 2f out: wknd 2f out* **11/1**
0 10 3 ¾ **Tommy Tiger**[28] 6532 2-9-0 0 WilliamCarson 7 50
(S C Williams) *str: t.k.h: hld up in tch towards rr: rdn and lost tch jst over 2f out* **50/1**
11 7 **Amor Patrice** 2-9-0 0 JamesMillman 4 32
(L Montague Hall) *w'like: bit bkwd: wnt lft s: in tch in midfield: rdn and struggling 1/2-way: wl bhd fnl 2f* **50/1**

1m 31.52s (6.12) **Going Correction** +0.625s/f (Yiel) 11 Ran SP% **115.2**
Speed ratings (Par 97): **90,85,84,84,84 83,82,80,77,73 65**
Tote Swingers: 1&2 £4.30, 1&3 £4.10, 2&3 £5.50 CSF £14.10 TOTE £4.50: £2.00, £1.60, £2.00; EX 20.80 Trifecta £50.90 Pool: £459.72 - 6.67 winning units..
Owner Tom Ludt **Bred** Grapestock Llc **Trained** Newmarket, Suffolk

FOCUS
A steady pace and the winning time was 2.52 seconds slower than the first division, but several of these offered promise for the future. The winner looks potentially smart.

NOTEBOOK
Western Aristocrat(USA) ◆, out of a 1m2f winner in France, travelled powerfully behind the leaders and quickened up impressively when asked over a furlong from home. He should get 1m without any problem and looks a nice prospect for next season. (op 7-2 tchd 4-1)
Malanos(IRE) finished a staying-on sixth of 18 on his second start over 1m here a fortnight earlier so wouldn't necessarily have been suited by the shorter trip, but he was given a positive ride and helped force the pace until the winner was produced over a furlong from home. He now gets a mark and will win races. (tchd 9-2)
Lyric Street(IRE) proved friendless in the market and showed signs of inexperience once under way, but this 100,000gns yearling and half-brother to a couple of smart performers on the continent kept on going after being switched outside. He should make up into a better 3-y-o. (op 7-2)
Guisho(IRE) ◆, retained for 30,000euros as a yearling and a half-brother to two winners including the smart Sir Parky, was keen early but then travelled well and ran on again after getting outpaced passing the 2f pole. He should win races in due course. (op 14-1 tchd 10-1)
Maqaraat(IRE) ◆, unsold for 120,000euros as a yearling and a half-brother to two winners including the Group 3 winner Marionnaud, was another to show signs of greenness but he was noted staying on late without being by any means knocked about. He was reportedly denied a clear run, but whatever the case he is certainly one for the notebook. Official explanation: jockey said colt was denied a clear run (op 11-2)
Piave(IRE), a half-brother to six winners including the smart Morena Park, helped force the pace for a long way alongside Malanos and should have learnt plenty from the experience. (op 9-1)
Dictate, a half-brother to five winners including the smart pair Jammaal and Mus-If, was held up after missing the break but made some late progress without being given a hard time. He is bred to stay much further than this and looks one for staying handicaps in due course. (op 25-1)
Amor Patrice Official explanation: jockey said colt ran green

7204 EUROPEAN BREEDERS' FUND BOSRA SHAM FILLIES' STKS (LISTED RACE) 6f
3:00 (3:00) (Class 1) 2-Y-O
£13,340 (£5,057; £2,530; £1,261; £632; £317) **Stalls** High

Form RPR
5240 1 **Sweet Cecily (IRE)**[28] 6530 2-8-12 99 RichardHughes 1 97
(R Hannon) *chsd ldrs: rdn over 2f out: drvn and ev ch ent fnl f: led fnl 100yds: kpt on wl* **5/1**[3]
34 2 ½ **Question Times**[42] 6150 2-8-12 0 JackMitchell 6 96
(P W Chapple-Hyam) *taken down early: stdd after s: hld up in tch in last trio: shkn up wl over 1f out: rdn and hdwy 1f out: chsd wnr fnl 50yds: hld towards fin* **14/1**
310 3 ½ **Sharnberry**[28] 6530 2-8-12 94 RyanMoore 7 94
(E A L Dunlop) *t.k.h: hld up in tch: rdn and effrt 2f out: ev ch jst over 1f out: no ex and one pce fnl 100yds* **7/2**[2]
61 4 ¾ **Glas Burn**[11] 6986 2-8-12 0 JimCrowley 3 92
(J G Portman) *stdd s: hld up in tch in last trio: rdn ent fnl 2f: chsd ldrs and drvn over 1f out: kpt on same pce ins fnl f* **16/1**
031 5 ½ **Barbieri (IRE)**[23] 6666 2-8-12 71 JamieSpencer 2 90
(J R Gask) *lw: stdd s: hld up in tch in rr: swtchd rt and effrt 2f out: hdwy over 1f out: kpt on ins fnl f* **33/1**
115 6 ¾ **Fifth Commandment (IRE)**[69] 5293 2-8-12 88 FergusSweeney 5 88
(J A Osborne) *led: rdn ent fnl 2f: edgd rt u.p ent fnl f: hdd fnl 100yds: wknd towards fin* **25/1**
1224 7 shd **Ragsah (IRE)**[28] 6530 2-8-12 100 FrankieDettori 4 88
(Saeed Bin Suroor) *hld up wl in tch: rdn and effrt 2f out: unable qck and n.m.r jst over 1f out: styd on same pce fnl f* **1/1**[1]
1050 8 3 ¾ **Dress Up (IRE)**[31] 6445 2-8-12 80 KierenFallon 8 76
(S Kirk) *chsd ldr: rdn ent fnl 2f: wknd jst ins fnl f: eased towards fin* **16/1**

1m 15.81s (3.61) **Going Correction** +0.625s/f (Yiel) 8 Ran SP% **114.1**
Speed ratings (Par 100): **100,99,98,97,97 96,95,90**
Tote Swingers: 1&2 £7.60, 1&3 £2.80, 2&3 £6.60 CSF £69.75 TOTE £6.80: £2.10, £3.50, £1.30; EX 83.10 Trifecta £383.10 Pool: £1,330.72 - 2.57 winning units..
Owner Mrs J Wood **Bred** Knocklong House Stud **Trained** East Everleigh, Wilts

FOCUS
This Listed race usually falls to an in-form filly, and there were several fitting that criteria. It did not look the strongest race for the grade, and that was backed up by the time, which was 0.53secs slower than the opening maiden, although they did race up the centre of the track this time. The field finished compressed and the winner looks the best guide to the form.

NOTEBOOK
Sweet Cecily(IRE) had beaten Ragsah 6l when the latter was making her debut in June. She had made the frame in Listed company since but was 10l behind her old rival in the Cheveley Park on her previous outing. She was settled after breaking well and found the most under pressure up the hill. She will be aimed at one of the 1000 Guineas trials in the spring. (op 6-1 tchd 9-2)
Question Times had finished in the frame in maidens at around 7f but was dropping in trip and up in grade. Held up at the back, the shorter distance seemed to help her get home and she finished well to earn black type. She should be well up to winning races at this trip. (tchd 16-1)
Sharnberry finished 2 3/4l behind Ragsah in the Cheveley Park with today's winner behind her. She was never far away if a little keen early but had her chance before not having a change of gear up the hill. (tchd 10-3)
Glas Burn, a 5f fast-ground maiden winner on her second start, was up in trip and grade. She looked a threat when produced to challenge in the Dip but her effort flattened out in the last furlong.
Barbieri(IRE), a 5f Polytrack winner who was well beaten on her only try on turf, was held up at the back before staying on up the hill to finish on the heels of the placed horses.
Fifth Commandment(IRE), a three-time winner at 5-6f on a sound surface, as sual made the running on this step up in grade and return from a break but could not sustain it in the closing stages. (op 28-1 tchd 22-1)
Ragsah(IRE) was the big disappointment. A 7f Polytrack winner but runner-up in a Group 3 and fourth in the Cheveley Park since, when she had today's winner and third behind, should have run much better and appeared to have no excuses, so she has probably had enough for the time being. (tchd 10-11 and 11-10 in a place)
Dress Up(IRE), a 5f winner on easy ground, has been beaten in a nursery since and this was asking a lot. She showed up early but was beaten in the Dip. (tchd 14-1)

7205 BETFAIR APPRENTICE TRAINING SERIES FINAL STKS (H'CAP) 1m
3:35 (3:35) (Class 5) (0-75,75) 3-Y-O **£6,476** (£1,927; £963; £481) **Stalls** High

Form RPR
6061 1 **Inpursuitoffreedom**[10] 7005 3-8-9 66 6ex JulieBurke(3) 5 76+
(P J McBride) *stdd s: hld up in last: hdwy gng wl over 3f out: rdn over 1f out: chsd clr ldr ent fnl f: kpt on wl to ld towards fin* **3/1**[1]
5016 2 ¾ **Tilsworth Glenboy**[22] 6692 3-8-9 68 DannyBrock(5) 8 76
(J R Jenkins) *hld up in tch: trckd ldrs and nt clr run ent fnl 2f: swtchd rt ent fnl 2f: sn rdn and qcknd to ld wl over 1f out: clr over 1f out: kpt on tl hdd and no ex towards fin* **16/1**
2110 3 3 **Mr Harmoosh (IRE)**[43] 6122 3-9-7 75 AdamBeschizza 3 76
(E F Vaughan) *hld up in tch: rdn to chse ldr wl over 1f out tl ent fnl f: styd on same pce* **8/1**
3440 4 2 ¾ **Ostentation**[58] 5662 3-8-12 66 RyanClark 4 61
(R A Teal) *t.k.h: chsd ldrs: rdn ent fnl 2f: outpcd and hmpd over 1f out: sn swtchd lft: styd on but no ch w ldrs after* **9/1**
-604 5 4 ½ **Olney Lass**[135] 3091 3-8-12 66 JamesRogers 9 50
(Mike Murphy) *hld up in last trio: struggling and dropped to last over 3f out: swtchd to outer and styd on past btn horses fr over 1f out: nvr trbld ldrs* **25/1**
0000 6 ½ **Take It To The Max**[20] 6753 3-9-6 74 (t) DaleSwift 7 57
(G M Moore) *swtg: t.k.h: chsd ldr tl over 2f out: wknd wl over 1f out: wl btn fnl f* **5/1**[3]
6000 7 2 **Perfect Ch'I (IRE)**[6] 7082 3-9-2 70 (p) LeeTopliss 10 49
(I A Wood) *s.i.s: bustled along early: hmpd after 1f out: rdn and wknd over 2f out: wl btn over 1f out* **33/1**
1126 8 ½ **Lutine Charlie (IRE)**[12] 6958 3-8-12 69 (p) DavidKenny(3) 2 46
(J L Flint) *t.k.h: chsd ldrs tl led over 2f out tl wl over 1f out: wknd qckly over 1f out* **6/1**

1234 **9** *2* **Sharakti (IRE)**[11] 6984 3-9-1 **69**........ JohnFahy 6 42
(A J McCabe) *taken down early: led tl rdn and hdd over 2f out: wknd wl over 1f out: wl bhd fnl f* **4/1**[2]

1050 **10** *14* **Mr Money Maker**[19] 6774 3-8-11 **70**........ MatthewCosham(5) 11 11
(J L Flint) *t.k.h: chsd ldrs tl over 3f out: wknd over 2f out: t.o fnl f* **11/1**

1m 44.11s (5.51) **Going Correction** +0.625s/f (Yiel) **10** Ran SP% **118.1**
Speed ratings (Par 101): **97,96,93,90,86 85,83,83,81,67**
Tote Swingers: 1&2 £11.90, 1&3 £3.40, 2&3 £17.00 CSF £54.57 CT £365.18 TOTE £4.60: £2.00, £4.30, £1.80; EX 70.70 TRIFECTA Not won..
Owner P J McBride **Bred** Lord Fairhaven **Trained** Newmarket, Suffolk

FOCUS
A fair handicap and they went a reasonable pace with a disputed lead, setting things up for the closers. The winner is on the upgrade, unlike most of these.

7206 E B F NEWMARKET RACECOURSES THANKS JOHN TAYLOR FILLIES' H'CAP 1m 4f

4:10 (4:10) (Class 3) (0-90,90) 3-Y-O+

£7,477 (£2,239; £1,119; £560; £279; £140) **Stalls** Centre

Form RPR

5323 **1** **Zahoo (IRE)**[7] 7062 3-8-10 **79**........ TadhgO'Shea 6 98+
(J L Dunlop) *stdd s: hld up in rr: hdwy to trck ldrs gng wl over 2f out: pushed rt and bmpd rival over 1f out: clr w ldr 1f out: pushed ahd ins fnl f: idled but sn in command* **15/2**

2261 **2** *1 ½* **Calatrava Cape (IRE)**[41] 6199 3-9-7 **90**........ RyanMoore 1 106
(J L Dunlop) *lw: stdd s: hld up in rr: hdwy gng wl 3f out: rdn to ld wl over 1f out: clr w wnr 1f out: hdd and no ex ins fnl f* **7/2**[2]

3224 **3** *9* **Nafura**[41] 6199 3-9-5 **88**........(p) FrankieDettori 4 90
(Saeed Bin Suroor) *led: rdn over 2f out: hdd: edgd rt u.p over 1f out: sn btn* **11/2**[3]

216 **4** *2* **Dark Promise**[7] 7062 3-8-9 **78**........ PhilipRobinson 3 77
(M A Jarvis) *chsd ldrs: rdn and ev ch over 2f out: wknd over 1f out: wl btn fnl f* **3/1**[1]

0442 **5** *nk* **Issabella Gem (IRE)**[34] 6361 3-8-9 **78**........ RichardHughes 11 76
(C G Cox) *in tch: hdwy to chse ldrs 5f out: rdn 3f out: wkng whn bmpd over 1f out: wl btn fnl f* **11/1**

1165 **6** *11* **Critical Path (IRE)**[41] 6199 4-9-5 **81**........ JimmyFortune 5 62+
(A M Balding) *lw: in tch in midfield: hdwy to chse ldrs and rdn 3f out: btn 2f out: sn wknd* **14/1**

432 **7** *2 ½* **Dazzle The Crowd (IRE)**[39] 6250 3-8-8 **77**........ RobertHavlin 7 54+
(J H M Gosden) *in tch: rdn ent fnl 3f: btn whn hung lft ent fnl 2f: wl btn and eased ins fnl f* **18/1**

12-0 **8** *7* **Brilliana**[11] 6990 4-9-6 **82**........ RichardMullen 9 48
(D R Lanigan) *taken down early: in tch: struggling u.p over 3f out: wl btn fnl 2f: eased ins fnl f: t.o* **20/1**

2454 **9** *10* **Ragdollianna**[22] 6693 6-8-12 **74** oh5........ WilliamCarson 10 24
(M J McGrath) *stdd s: hld up in midfield: rdn and struggling 4f out: wl bhd over 2f out: eased ins fnl f: t.o* **40/1**

613 **10** *¾* **Sea Of Galilee**[77] 5056 3-9-1 **84**........ DaneO'Neill 8 32
(H Candy) *chsd ldrs tl wknd u.p over 4f out: wl bhd over 2f out: eased ins fnl f: t.o* **7/1**

1340 **11** *50* **Plaisterer**[15] 6877 5-9-11 **87**........ SebSanders 12 —
(C F Wall) *in tch tl 5f out: sn dropped out: wl t.o and virtually p.u fnl 2f* **33/1**

3220 **12** *1 ¾* **Mildoura (FR)**[89] 4624 5-9-12 **88**........ IanMongan 2 —
(Mrs L J Mongan) *taken down early: in tch: rdn and struggling ent 4f out: wl t.o and virtually p.u fnl 2f* **33/1**

2m 38.04s (6.04) **Going Correction** +0.625s/f (Yiel)
WFA 3 from 4yo+ 7lb **12** Ran SP% **120.2**
Speed ratings (Par 104): **104,103,97,95,95 88,86,81,75,74 41,40**
Tote Swingers: 1&2 £6.10, 1&3 £4.80, 2&3 £4.70 CSF £33.16 CT £160.79 TOTE £9.10: £3.00, £1.90, £1.50; EX 29.00 Trifecta £104.10 Pool: £1,229.12 - 8.73 winning units..
Owner Hamdan Al Maktoum **Bred** Shadwell Estate Company Limited **Trained** Arundel, W Sussex

FOCUS
A decent and tightly knit fillies' handicap in which recent successes have been equally divided between 3-y-os and the older fillies. This time the younger generation dominated with the first five all from that age group, and the John Dunlop pair came clear. The field raced up the stands' side in the straight. The first pair are progressive.

NOTEBOOK
Zahoo(IRE), a 1m winner on fast but with form at up to this trip on good and softer ground, needs to be held onto as long as possible and Tadhg O'Shea performed the task to perfection. Held up at the back, she came through just behind her stable companion and proved quicker up the hill. This should help her confidence for if she stays in training next season. (op 11-2 tchd 5-1)
Calatrava Cape(IRE), a 1m4f winner on good and fast ground and well suited by Newmarket, was raised 6lb for her last success when today's third and sixth were behind. She came through looking likely to supplement that success but her stable companion was travelling equally as well, and found more up the hill. (tchd 3-1)
Nafura finished not far behind Calatrava Cape here last time and was 5lb better off. She made the running but could not respond when her old rival and the winner swept past. (op 13-2)
Dark Promise, a lightly raced 1m2f winner from the family of Oaks winner Love Divine, was up in trip but was ridden positively. She kept galloping but had nothing in reserve when the principals arrived on the scene. (op 9-2 tchd 5-1 in places)
Issabella Gem(IRE) appears to stay 1m4f and acts on this ground, and she moved up travelling well. However, she was passed on either side by the principals and done no favours on the run into the Dip, from which point she was one-paced. (op 10-1)
Critical Path(IRE) was behind Calatrava Cape and Nafura over C&D last time but despite being better off with both of those, finished further behind. (tchd 16-1)
Sea Of Galilee, a winner over 1m2f on easy going, was trying a new trip but was beaten before stamina became an issue. (op 8-1)
Plaisterer's rider reported the mare was never travelling. Official explanation: jockey said mare never travelled (tchd 28-1)

7207 NGK SPARK PLUGS CONDITIONS STKS 6f

4:45 (4:46) (Class 3) 2-3-Y-O

£6,231 (£1,866; £933; £467; £233; £117) **Stalls** High

Form RPR

1100 **1** **Morache Music**[27] 6568 2-8-3 88........ SilvestreDeSousa 4 94+
(P J Makin) *lw: in tch: hdwy to ld gng wl ent fnl 2f: rdn clr and edgd rt over 1f out: pushed out fnl f: easily* **4/9**[1]

3100 **2** *4* **Ginger Ted (IRE)**[12] 6962 3-9-8 85........(p) J-PGuillambert 5 87
(R C Guest) *stdd after s: t.k.h: hld up in rr: hdwy ent fnl 2f: rdn and chsd clr wnr over 1f out: kpt on but no imp fnl f* **5/1**[2]

410 **3** *4 ½* **Island Rhapsody**[6] 7097 3-9-6 75........ JimmyFortune 8 71
(A M Balding) *chsd ldr: rdn ent fnl 2f: nt pce of wnr over 1f out: 3rd and wl btn ent fnl f* **13/2**[3]

0000 **4** *6* **Jamaica Grande**[10] 7002 2-7-10 52........(p) JessicaSteven(7) 9 50
(T T Clement) *chsd ldrs tl outpcd over 2f out: no ch w ldrs fnl 2f: plugged on ins fnl f: wnt poor 4th last stride* **66/1**

0 **5** *shd* **Dangerous Illusion (IRE)**[10] 7002 2-7-12 0........ AndreaAtzeni 7 45
(M Quinn) *t.k.h: chsd ldrs: rdn and struggling ent fnl 2f: wl btn over 1f out* **50/1**

3320 **6** *½* **My Love Fajer (IRE)**[14] 6900 2-8-3 72........ KirstyMilczarek 2 48
(G Prodromou) *taken down early: led tl ent fnl 2f: wknd qckly over 1f out* **14/1**

01-0 **7** *3* **Gypsy Jazz (IRE)**[143] 1514 3-8-12 67........ AnnStokell(5) 3 39
(Miss A Stokell) *taken down early: a towards rr: rdn and wl btn over 2f out* **40/1**

2112 **8** *shd* **Red Roar (IRE)**[7] 7052 3-9-6 64........ FrannyNorton 6 42
(A Berry) *t.k.h: in tch tl rdn and btn over 2f out: wl bhd over 1f out* **11/1**

0-40 **9** *21* **Estonia**[2] 7166 3-9-3 0........ WilliamCarson 1 —
(M D Squance) *t.k.h: chsd ldrs tl 1/2-way: sn struggling: wl bhd and eased fnl f* **66/1**

1m 16.12s (3.92) **Going Correction** +0.625s/f (Yiel) **9** Ran SP% **121.6**
Speed ratings: **98,92,86,78,78 77,73,73,45**
Tote Swingers: 1&2 £1.70, 1&3 £1.80, 2&3 £3.30 CSF £3.44 TOTE £1.50: £1.10, £1.60, £1.40; EX 3.40 Trifecta £9.70 Pool: £1,331.51 - 101.34 winning units..
Owner R P Marchant, D M Ahier, Mrs E Lee **Bred** Michael E Broughton **Trained** Ogbourne Maisey, Wilts

FOCUS
An uncompetitive conditions race and a modest early pace resulted in the slowest of the three 6f races on the card. This had been won by a 2-y-o seven times in the previous eight runnings, including by Paco Boy three years ago, and that trend continued. A tricky race to rate but the winner probably stepped up on his Windsor win.

NOTEBOOK
Morache Music, who is suited by these conditions and had been taking on better company lately, had upwards of 16lb in hand of these rivals at the weights and won like it, despite hanging over to the inside rail after leading 2f from home. He only achieved what he was entitled to on these terms, but given his liking for soft ground connections may look for a Listed race in France for him. (op 8-15 tchd 4-7 and 8-13 in places)
Ginger Ted(IRE), twice disappointing since winning at Newcastle in August, ran on from the back of the field but was in vain pursuit of the favourite over the last furlong. He does seem to have two ways of running, but probably ran close to his mark here.
Island Rhapsody was reappearing six days after running moderately on her return from six months off/turf debut at Newbury six days earlier. She had every chance and although outpaced by the front pair over the last furlong or so, this was better. Still lightly raced, she has already proved herself on the Kempton Polytrack so should have plenty of opportunities if kept on the go through the winter. (op 7-1)
Jamaica Grande, 0-14 coming into this, had little chance on these terms (being 41lb badly in with the winner) and achieved nothing in running on up the inside rail for a remote fourth. (op 100-1)
My Love Fajer(IRE), rated 72, had the second-best chance at the weights after placing in three modest maidens and a nursery and should technically have done better, but he raced too keenly in front early and eventually paid for it. Official explanation: jockey said colt pulled hard (op 20-1)
Red Roar(IRE) Official explanation: jockey said filly ran keen early and had no more to give

7208 NORFOLK RACING CLUB M D THOMPSON ELECTRICAL H'CAP 2m

5:20 (5:21) (Class 3) (0-90,90) 3-Y-O+ **£6,476** (£1,927; £963; £481) **Stalls** Centre

Form RPR

125 **1** **Hawridge Star (IRE)**[30] 6480 8-8-10 **72**........ RichardHughes 2 81
(W S Kittow) *taken down early: hld up in rr: clsd 5f out: rdn over 2f out: drvn and hdwy to join ldrs over 1f out: led ins fnl f: styd on wl* **10/3**[2]

1501 **2** *1 ¾* **Saborido (USA)**[32] 6416 4-8-13 **75**........ JimCrowley 7 82
(Mrs A J Perrett) *lw: chsd ldng pair: clsd over 4f out: rdn to ld over 1f out: edgd rt u.p and hdd ins fnl f: no ex fnl 100yds* **11/2**[3]

3 *shd* **Afsoun (FR)**[181] 8-10-0 **90**........ SebSanders 1 96
(N B King) *taken down early: stdd and dropped in bhd after s: hld up in rr: clsd over 4f out: rdn and unable qck ent fnl 2f: styd on again ins fnl f* **7/1**

2550 **4** *1 ¾* **Magicalmysterytour (IRE)**[20] 6736 7-9-12 **88**........(t) StevieDonohoe 5 92
(W J Musson) *hld up off the pce towards rr: hdwy 5f out: pressed ldrs and rdn wl over 1f out: no ex and btn fnl 100yds* **11/2**[3]

4310 **5** *nk* **Hawridge King**[54] 5788 8-8-11 **73**........ JamesMillman 8 77
(W S Kittow) *taken down early: racd in midfield: clsd 5f out: rdn and unable qck over 2f out: swtchd rt over 1f out: styd on same pce* **12/1**

-015 **6** *2* **It's A Date**[18] 6808 5-9-8 **84**........ FergusSweeney 4 86
(A King) *led: rdn ent fnl 2f: hdd over 1f out: wknd ins fnl f* **6/1**

0653 **P** **Rock Soleil**[22] 6693 6-8-10 **72** oh1 ow1........ JamieSpencer 6 —
(Jane Chapple-Hyam) *chsd ldr tl rdn and lost pl over 2f out: in rr whn lost action: p.u and dismntd over 1f out* **3/1**[1]

3m 39.46s (8.96) **Going Correction** +0.625s/f (Yiel)
WFA 3 from 4yo+ 10lb **7** Ran SP% **113.3**
Speed ratings (Par 107): **102,101,101,100,100 99,—**
Tote Swingers: 1&2 £3.00, 1&3 £3.60, 2&3 £4.00 CSF £21.40 CT £118.50 TOTE £4.10: £2.30, £2.70; EX 17.90 Trifecta £63.70 Pool: £752.85 - 8.74 winning units. Place 6: £60.87 Place 5: £41.39..
Owner Eric Gadsden **Bred** Seamus Murphy **Trained** Blackborough, Devon

FOCUS
A fair staying handicap that in 2009 fell to the subsequent Cesarewitch winner Aaim To Prosper. The runners came up the centre in the straight. The form is rated at face value.

NOTEBOOK
Hawridge Star(IRE) had not won beyond 1m6f on the Flat, although he had been beaten a short head over 2m on soft. He came under pressure over 2f out but put his stamina to good use and proved strongest up the hill. (op 7-2 tchd 3-1)
Saborido(USA), a multiple winner at 1m6f-2m1f, was 6lb higher than for his last success. He is best on a sound surface and, although he ran well, had nothing more to offer in the last furlong. (op 4-1)
Afsoun(FR) is best known as a high-class hurdler and had never run on Flat in this country, but was a useful staying handicapper in France years ago. Having his first run for new connections and first start since the beginning of May, he moved into contention before his effort flattened out in the closing stages. (op 6-1)
Magicalmysterytour(IRE) had gained recent wins over 1m4f and 1m5f on good and soft ground but was trying his longest trip to-date. Wearing a tongue tie for the first time, he moved up travelling well but in the end did not appear to get home. (tchd 5-1)
Hawridge King, a stable companion of the winner and short-headed in this race last year, was the first under pressure but kept going and was finishing as well as anything. (op 8-1 tchd 7-1)
It's A Date's only run over this distance was over two years ago on Polytrack. He made the running but despite dictating what looked a fairly steady gallop, he did not appear to stay the trip. (tchd 13-2)
Rock Soleil was backed into favourite but came under pressure around half a mile from home, dropped away and was pulled up as if something had gone amiss. (op 7-1)
T/Plt: £58.10 to a £1 stake. Pool:£73,711.62 - 779.65 winning tickets T/Qpdt: £16.20 to a £1 stake. Pool:£5,368.23 - 244.60 winning tickets SP

[7193]WOLVERHAMPTON (A.W) (L-H)

Friday, October 29

OFFICIAL GOING: Standard

Wind: Fresh behind Weather: Overcast

7209 CE PROPERTY SERVICES GROUP FILLIES' H'CAP — 7f 32y(P)

5:40 (5:40) (Class 5) (0-75,75) 3-Y-O+ — **£2,115** (£624; £312) Stalls High

Form — RPR

1102 **1** **Whispering Spirit (IRE)**[34] 6372 4-9-7 **75**....(v) PaulHanagan 3 — 85
(Mrs A Duffield) *chsd ldrs: led over 2f out: rdn and hung lft fnl f: r.o* **7/2**[1]

1416 **2** 1 1/4 **Darcey**[8] 7046 4-9-5 **73**.... CathyGannon 6 — 80
(Miss Amy Weaver) *a.p: rdn to chse wnr over 1f out: r.o* **5/1**[2]

034 **3** 1/2 **Maid To Dream**[29] 6496 3-8-8 **64**....(p) WilliamBuick 1 — 70
(J H M Gosden) *hld up in tch: chsd wnr wl over 1f out: sn rdn: styd on* **10/1**

0410 **4** 1 3/4 **Piquante**[38] 6267 4-8-10 **67**.... Louis-PhilippeBeuzelin(3) 9 — 68
(N Tinkler) *hld up: racd keenly: hdwy over 1f out: r.o* **25/1**

0553 **5** nse **Mount Juliet (IRE)**[28] 6541 3-8-10 **66**.... ChrisCatlin 2 — 67+
(M Botti) *hld up: r.o u.p ins fnl f: nvr nrr* **11/2**[3]

5500 **6** 1/2 **Chilli Green**[18] 6801 3-8-12 **68**.... DarryllHolland 11 — 67
(J Akehurst) *plld hrd and prom: rdn and edgd lft over 1f out: styd on* **25/1**

4110 **7** 4 1/2 **Sweet Gale (IRE)**[21] 6714 6-9-2 **70**.... AndrewMullen 5 — 57
(Mike Murphy) *dwlt: hld up: hdwy u.p over 1f out: wknd ins fnl f* **10/1**

4526 **8** 2 1/2 **Lady Kent (IRE)**[16] 6854 4-8-13 **67**.... StephenCraine 10 — 48
(J R Boyle) *chsd ldr tl led over 2f out: sn hdd: rdn and wknd over 1f out* **22/1**

0102 **9** nk **Amber Sunset**[27] 6558 4-9-5 **73**.... NeilCallan 12 — 53
(D Morris) *hld up: hdwy over 2f out: rdn whn nt clr run 1f out: wknd fnl f* **14/1**

0006 **10** 3 1/4 **Kingston Acacia**[37] 6291 3-9-2 **72**.... DavidProbert 4 — 43
(A M Balding) *led: rdn: hung rt and hdd over 2f out: wknd fnl f* **11/1**

0- **11** 1 3/4 **Moonlight Cass (IRE)**[397] 6317 3-8-12 **68**.... LukeMorris 8 — 34
(J R Gask) *hld up: drvn along 3f out: wknd 2f out* **40/1**

0051 **12** 4 1/2 **Ajara (IRE)**[7] 7064 4-8-4 **61** 6ex.... RossAtkinson(3) 7 — 15
(Tom Dascombe) *hld up: rdn over 2f out: a in rr* **7/1**

1m 29.13s (-0.47) **Going Correction** +0.025s/f (Slow) — **12** Ran SP% **114.4**
WFA 3 from 4yo+ 2lb
Speed ratings (Par 100): **103,101,101,99,98 98,93,90,90,86 84,79**
toteswingers:1&2:£2.10, 1&3:£4.60, 2&3:£14.60 CSF £18.37 CT £160.20 TOTE £4.00: £2.60, £1.70, £2.30; EX 16.90.
Owner Middleham Park Racing XLII **Bred** David Barry **Trained** Constable Burton, N Yorks

FOCUS
Mainly exposed performers in this ordinary fillies' handicap. The gallop soon steadied and those attempting to come from off the pace were at a disadvantage. The first six finished clear and the winner raced towards the inside rail in the straight. The first three all showed improvement.
Piquante Official explanation: jockey said filly ran too free
Kingston Acacia Official explanation: jockey said filly hung right-handed

7210 BREEDERS' CUP LIVE ONLY ON ATR MEDIAN AUCTION MAIDEN STKS — 7f 32y(P)

6:10 (6:12) (Class 5) 2-Y-O — **£2,115** (£624; £312) Stalls High

Form — RPR

23 **1** **Never Never Land**[9] 7010 2-9-3 0.... WilliamBuick 8 — 72+
(J H M Gosden) *chsd ldrs: led over 1f out: rdn out* **4/7**[1]

0303 **2** 3 **Educated Son**[22] 6695 2-9-3 61.... ShaneKelly 11 — 65+
(W R Muir) *hld up: hdwy over 1f out: sn rdn and hung lft: styd on* **7/1**[3]

3360 **3** 1 3/4 **Lady Platinum Club**[14] 6902 2-8-12 67....(p) TomEaves 9 — 57
(G R Oldroyd) *chsd ldr 6f out tl led 3f out: rdn and hdd over 1f out: styng on same pce whn hmpd ins fnl f* **11/1**

204 **4** 1 **Podgies Boy (IRE)**[41] 6182 2-9-3 0.... PaulHanagan 7 — 58
(R A Fahey) *hld up: hdwy over 2f out: rdn over 1f out: styd on same pce* **6/1**[2]

0 **5** 3/4 **Areef (IRE)**[21] 6712 2-8-12 0.... HayleyTurner 6 — 51
(M L W Bell) *chsd ldrs: rdn over 1f out: no ex ins fnl f* **12/1**

06 **6** 3 1/2 **Nutshell**[9] 7010 2-8-12 0.... JamesDoyle 10 — 43
(H J L Dunlop) *led 4f: sn rdn: wknd fnl f* **40/1**

0666 **7** 10 **Cool Land (IRE)**[15] 6867 2-9-3 56.... LukeMorris 2 — 23
(R A Harris) *prom: lost pl 6f out: sn pushed along: wknd 3f out* **80/1**

60 **8** 8 **Tourmaline (IRE)**[32] 6425 2-8-12 0.... JoeFanning 5 — —
(P W Chapple-Hyam) *hld up in tch: rdn over 2f out: sn wknd* **33/1**

1m 30.78s (1.18) **Going Correction** +0.025s/f (Slow) — **8** Ran SP% **113.1**
Speed ratings (Par 95): **94,90,88,87,86 82,71,62**
toteswingers:1&2:£2.00, 1&3:£1.90, 2&3:£3.80 CSF £4.97 TOTE £1.50: £1.10, £1.40, £2.30; EX 4.50.
Owner H R H Princess Haya Of Jordan **Bred** Peter E Clinton **Trained** Newmarket, Suffolk

FOCUS
Very little depth in this modest maiden. The gallop was an ordinary one and the winner came down the centre in the straight. The second and third govern the form.

NOTEBOOK
Never Never Land, turned over at a short price on his turf debut last time, was well supported and didn't have to improve to make the most of this straightforward opportunity returned to Polytrack. He is in good hands and may do better in ordinary handicaps. (op 4-6 tchd 8-15)
Educated Son, who had previously turned in an improved effort when in front of a couple of subsequent winners on his all-weather/nursery debut last time, at least matched that form. The return to handicaps will be the way forward but the way he hung under pressure was disconcerting, so he may not be one for maximum faith. Official explanation: jockey said gelding hung left-handed (op 8-1)
Lady Platinum Club, ridden more prominently than at this course last time, seemed to give it her best shot but she is likely to remain vulnerable in this grade and her current handicap mark of 67 leaves her with little margin for error. (op 12-1)
Podgies Boy(IRE), who had shown ability on a sound surface, failed to build on those efforts upped in distance and switched to Polytrack for the first time. Ordinary handicaps will be the way forward with him. (op 5-1)
Areef(IRE) fared better than she had done on her racecourse debut over this course and distance earlier in the month. She is bred to be effective over this trip in due course and may do better in handicaps. (op 9-1)

7211 CLEANEVENT NURSERY — 5f 20y(P)

6:40 (6:41) (Class 5) (0-75,75) 2-Y-O — **£2,115** (£624; £312) Stalls Low

Form — RPR

0311 **1** **One Cool Bex**[20] 6740 2-8-12 **66**....(e) PaulHanagan 9 — 74
(P J McBride) *hld up: hdwy over 1f out: led ins fnl f: rdn out* **11/4**[1]

205 **2** 2 1/4 **Johnny Hancocks (IRE)**[14] 6900 2-9-6 **74**.... CathyGannon 1 — 74
(P D Evans) *led: rdn over 1f out: hdd and unable qck ins fnl f* **11/4**[1]

4005 **3** 1 1/4 **Silk Bounty**[19] 6769 2-8-12 **66**....(b[1]) PaulMulrennan 8 — 62
(J G Given) *chsd ldrs: rdn and hung lft fr over 1f out: styd on same pce ins fnl f* **15/2**[3]

3144 **4** 1 **Best Be Careful (IRE)**[19] 6769 2-8-11 **65**.... HayleyTurner 3 — 57
(M D I Usher) *a.p: rdn over 1f out: no ex ins fnl f* **17/2**

6510 **5** 1 1/4 **Sacrosanctus**[14] 6900 2-9-7 **75**.... DarryllHolland 6 — 62
(J A Glover) *hld up: hdwy over 1f out: no imp ins fnl f* **8/1**

2552 **6** 2 3/4 **Wild Hysteria (IRE)**[46] 6035 2-8-5 **59**.... AndrewMullen 7 — 37
(T P Tate) *chsd ldrs: rdn 1/2-way: wknd fnl f* **13/2**[2]

3000 **7** 1/2 **Henrys Air**[51] 5862 2-8-6 **60**.... LukeMorris 4 — 36
(D G Bridgwater) *sn pushed along in rr: nvr on terms* **20/1**

4040 **8** 2 1/2 **Instructress**[38] 6271 2-9-0 **68**....(p) WilliamBuick 5 — 35
(R M H Cowell) *chsd ldr: rdn whn hmpd over 1f out: wknd ins fnl f* **16/1**

6100 **9** 3 1/4 **Upark Flyer**[36] 6311 2-8-5 **62**....(v) RossAtkinson(3) 2 — 17
(Patrick Morris) *s.s: plld hrd and hdwy 4f out: rdn 1/2-way: wknd wl over 1f out* **33/1**

62.82 secs (0.52) **Going Correction** +0.025s/f (Slow) — **9** Ran SP% **113.7**
Speed ratings (Par 95): **96,92,90,88,86 82,81,77,72**
toteswingers:1&2:£2.20, 1&3:£3.50, 2&3:£4.90 CSF £9.32 CT £48.73 TOTE £2.80: £1.10, £1.10, £3.10; EX 9.20.
Owner J Burns **Bred** Belgrave Bloodstock Ltd **Trained** Newmarket, Suffolk

FOCUS
A couple of recent winners in another ordinary handicap. The gallop was a decent one and the winner came down the centre in the straight. The winner continues on the up and the form has a sound feel.

NOTEBOOK
One Cool Bex, whose last win from a 4lb lower mark came in a race that has thrown up numerous winners, had the race run to suit and showed a good turn of foot to settle the issue in the straight. He's progressing quickly and, although he may not be entirely straightforward, he may be able to extend the winning run on sand granted a good gallop. (op 2-1)
Johnny Hancocks(IRE) is a reliable yardstick and helped to force a decent gallop, but he looked to give it his best shot from this 3lb lower mark. He's vulnerable to an improver from his current mark but should continue to go well over this trip on sand, especially when it looks as though he will be able to dominate. (op 10-3)
Silk Bounty ran creditably returned to Polytrack after racing on the outside with blinkers fitted for the first time. However, he didn't look the most straightforward once pressure was applied and he may have to drop further in the weights before opening his account. (op 10-1 tchd 7-1)
Best Be Careful(IRE) probably ran to a similar level on this all-weather debut as she had done on her two previous nursery starts. She isn't fully exposed, but she'll have to improve to win a similar event on either turf or Polytrack from her current mark. (op 9-1 tchd 8-1)
Sacrosanctus, who missed the break when losing his unbeaten record on Polytrack last time, again forfeited ground at the start but, in truth, could have been expected to pick up a little better in the straight given the way things unfolded. He may be worth another try over 6f. Official explanation: jockey said gelding was slowly away (op 15-2)
Wild Hysteria(IRE) had run to his best at Redcar last time but failed by a long chalk to confirm that promise on this all-weather debut. He looks one to tread carefully with at present. (op 15-2 tchd 9-1)
Instructress Official explanation: jockey said saddle slipped

7212 CE RISK, SAFETY & SECURITY H'CAP — 5f 216y(P)

7:10 (7:10) (Class 4) (0-85,85) 3-Y-O+ — **£3,594** (£1,069; £534; £266) Stalls Low

Form — RPR

0-00 **1** **Mister Laurel**[50] 5884 4-8-8 **77**....(b) LeeTopliss(5) 1 — 89
(R A Fahey) *a.p: led 2f out: rdn over 1f out: r.o: comf* **16/1**

0006 **2** 1 3/4 **Pavershooz**[13] 6918 5-9-7 **85**.... DuranFentiman 11 — 91
(N Wilson) *chsd ldrs: rdn over 1f out: edgd lft and styd on to go 2nd nr fin* **12/1**

250 **3** hd **Avertor**[19] 6776 4-9-3 **81**.... WilliamBuick 3 — 87+
(R Charlton) *hld up: racd keenly: rdn over 2f out: r.o wl u.p ins fnl f: wnt 3rd nr fin: nt rch ldrs* **3/1**[1]

0600 **4** 1/2 **Marvellous Value (IRE)**[42] 6142 5-9-2 **80**.... PhillipMakin 10 — 84+
(M Dods) *hld up: hdwy over 2f out: rdn over 1f out: r.o* **13/2**[3]

0004 **5** hd **Walvis Bay (IRE)**[21] 6723 3-9-4 **83**.... MickyFenton 13 — 87
(T P Tate) *chsd ldrs: rdn over 1f out: no ex ins fnl f* **20/1**

-222 **6** 1 **Excellent Show**[261] 492 4-8-11 **82**.... AdamCarter(7) 5 — 82
(B Smart) *mid-div: pushed along and hdwy over 2f out: styd on: nt trble ldrs* **7/1**

500- **7** 1 1/2 **Diriculous**[373] 6949 6-9-7 **85**.... NeilCallan 4 — 81
(R A Mills) *dwlt: plld hrd: hdwy and hmpd over 3f out: rdn over 1f out: styd on same pce ins fnl f* **10/1**

0620 **8** 3/4 **Living It Large (FR)**[8] 7041 3-9-4 **83**....(b) PaulHanagan 2 — 76
(R F Fisher) *led: rdn and hdd 2f out: no ex fnl f* **15/2**

1350 **9** nk **Defector (IRE)**[6] 7092 4-8-10 **77**.... RossAtkinson(3) 8 — 69
(D Bourton) *hld up: hdwy over 1f out: no ex ins fnl f* **16/1**

4000 **10** hd **Onceaponatime (IRE)**[132] 3216 5-9-5 **83**.... LukeMorris 12 — 75
(M D Squance) *hld up: styd on ins fnl f: nvr on terms* **40/1**

6000 **11** 1/2 **Sarah's Art (IRE)**[18] 6799 7-8-8 **75**....(t) JohnFahy(3) 7 — 65
(Stef Higgins) *s.s: a bhd* **20/1**

1205 **12** 1 1/2 **Legal Eagle (IRE)**[11] 6981 5-9-2 **80**....(p) MartinLane 6 — 65
(Paul Green) *chsd ldrs: rdn over 2f out: wknd over 1f out* **12/1**

0004 **13** 4 **Royal Intruder**[13] 6932 5-9-0 **78**....(p) RichardHughes 9 — 61
(S Donohoe, Ire) *trckd ldrs: shkn up over 1f out: eased whn btn ins fnl f* **6/1**[2]

1m 14.3s (-0.70) **Going Correction** +0.025s/f (Slow) — **13** Ran SP% **125.1**
WFA 3 from 4yo+ 1lb
Speed ratings (Par 105): **105,102,102,101,101 100,98,97,96,96 95,93,88**
toteswingers:1&2:£26.30, 1&3:£24.70, 2&3:£9.60 CSF £199.67 CT £769.09 TOTE £29.80: £9.40, £5.00, £1.90; EX 397.00.
Owner The Cosmic Cases **Bred** Mrs M Bryce **Trained** Musley Bank, N Yorks

FOCUS
Not too many in-form types in this reasonable handicap but, although the gallop seemed sound, those attempting to make ground from the rear could never land a blow. The winner, who raced in the centre in the straight, is rated to his 3yo best.
Royal Intruder Official explanation: jockey said gelding moved poorly in the home straight

7213 ATTHERACES.COM/BREEDERSCUP H'CAP — 2m 119y(P)

7:40 (7:40) (Class 6) (0-60,58) 3-Y-O+ — **£1,706** (£503; £252) Stalls Low

Form — RPR

3435 **1** **Jennerous Blue**[15] 6871 3-8-7 **47**....(p) PaulQuinn 3 — 55
(D K Ivory) *s.i.s: hld up: pushed along 6f out: hdwy over 2f out: rdn to chse ldr over 1f out: styd on u.p to ld nr fin* **13/2**[3]

430- **2** 3/4 **Mystified (IRE)**[377] 6558 7-9-8 **52**....(tp) PaulHanagan 10 — 59
(R F Fisher) *led: rdn clr 2f out: hdd nr fin* **9/1**

0505 **3** 1 1/4 **Delorain (IRE)**[13] 6933 7-8-8 **45**....(vt) LauraPike(7) 12 — 51
(W B Stone) *a.p: chsd ldr 12f out: rdn over 2f out: styd on* **14/1**

000/ **4** *9* **Cashel Bay (USA)**[208] 4614 12-8-13 **46**..................(t) AlanCreighton(3) 8 41
(Luke Comer, Ire) *hld up: hdwy 4f out: rdn over 2f out: hung lft and wknd over 1f out* **33/1**

0-06 **5** *5* **Share Option**[13] 6933 8-9-2 **46**.. NeilCallan 6 35
(A W Carroll) *hld up: hdwy 7f out: rdn over 2f out: wknd over 1f out* **12/1**

6000 **6** *7* **Kargarann (IRE)**[15] 6871 3-8-2 **45**.................................... JohnFahy(3) 7 25
(Stef Higgins) *dwlt: bhd: drvn along over 3f out: nvr nrr* **20/1**

/00- **7** *hd* **Cat Six (USA)**[197] 4373 6-8-8 **45**.................................... AlexEdwards(7) 4 25
(T R Gretton) *prom tl wknd over 2f out: hmpd wl over 1f out* **10/3**[1]

-000 **8** *17* **Follow The Dream**[13] 6933 7-10-0 **58**.......................... DarryllHolland 5 18
(Karen George) *s.i.s: a in rr: t.o* **16/1**

0056 **9** *2 1/2* **Paint The Town Red**[20] 6744 5-9-5 **49**............................. JoeFanning 2 6
(H J Collingridge) *hld up: rdn over 3f out: wknd over 2f out: t.o* **16/1**

2025 **10** *6* **Mymateeric**[16] 6855 4-9-0 **47**.. SimonPearce(3) 1 —
(J Pearce) *chsd ldrs tl wknd over 3f out: bhd whn hmpd wl over 1f out: t.o* **9/1**

0-00 **11** *71* **Bold Bomber**[7] 7071 4-9-1 **45**.. MartinLane 9 —
(Paul Green) *chsd ldrs tl rdn and wknd 4f out: t.o* **100/1**

0032 **U** **Pearl (IRE)**[13] 6933 6-9-6 **50**....................................(tp) RichardHughes 13 —
(Mrs A M Thorpe) *chsd ldrs: rdn over 3f out: wknd over 2f out: hmpd and uns rdr wl over 1f out* **7/2**[2]

0003 **U** **Admiral Rodney**[15] 6871 3-8-10 **50**.............................. MickyFenton 11 —
(Mrs P Sly) *hld up: hdwy over 2f out: 6th and styng on whn broke down and uns rdr wl over 1f out* **17/2**

3m 41.21s (-0.59) **Going Correction** +0.025s/f (Slow)
WFA 3 from 4yo+ 10lb 13 Ran SP% **124.0**
Speed ratings (Par 101): **102,101,101,96,94 91,91,83,81,79 45,—,—**
toteswingers:1&2:£14.40, 1&3:£16.90, 2&3:£12.40 CSF £65.55 CT £811.94 TOTE £9.50: £3.80, £3.50, £5.30; EX 83.40.
Owner Mrs J A Cornwell & Cynthia Smith **Bred** Mrs J A Cornwell **Trained** Radlett, Herts

FOCUS
A low-grade handicap, run at an ordinary gallop, in which the two market leaders failed to run to their best. The race was eventful in the straight and the first three, who finished clear, came down the centre. The second is the best guide and the form is not rated too positively.

7214 CLEANWASTESOLUTIONS H'CAP 1m 141y(P)
8:10 (8:12) (Class 5) (0-70,70) 3-Y-O+ £2,115 (£624; £312) Stalls Low

Form RPR

0022 **1** **Star Links (USA)**[13] 6935 4-9-10 **70**.......................(p) RichardHughes 11 79
(S Donohoe, Ire) *hld up: hmpd over 3f out: hdwy over 2f out: jst hld on* **11/2**[3]

0102 **2** *nk* **Nicholas Pocock (IRE)**[10] 7005 4-8-12 **58**................. PaulHanagan 12 66
(B Ellison) *swtchd lft sn after s: hld up: hdwy over 2f out: rdn to chse wnr ins fnl f: styd on* **9/4**[1]

2303 **3** *1 1/4* **Lean Machine**[9] 7019 3-9-1 **65**.. LukeMorris 10 70
(R A Harris) *trckd ldrs: plld hrd: stdd and lost pl over 6f out: hmpd over 3f out: hdwy over 2f out: sn rdn: styd on* **10/1**

3001 **4** *3/4* **Strike Force**[7] 7068 6-8-12 **63** 6ex.........................(t) AdamBeschizza(5) 3 66+
(Miss Olivia Maylam) *hld up: hdwy over 1f out: r.o: nt rch ldrs* **7/2**[2]

2656 **5** *1/2* **Just Timmy Marcus**[13] 6934 4-9-5 **65**....................(b) GrahamGibbons 5 67
(B P J Baugh) *a.p: chsd ldr over 2f out: led over 1f out: sn rdn: hdd and hung rt: no ex ins fnl f* **7/1**

5321 **6** *3/4* **Lord Of The Dance (IRE)**[13] 6934 4-9-8 **68**............ TomMcLaughlin 1 68
(W M Brisbourne) *prom: chsd ldr 5f out: led over 3f out: rdn and hdd over 1f out: no ex ins fnl f* **11/2**[3]

0205 **7** *12* **Bidable**[12] 6958 6-9-5 **70**.. DeclanCannon(5) 8 43
(B Palling) *sn pushed along and prom: rdn over 2f out: sn wknd* **18/1**

0050 **8** *1* **Kumbeshwar**[31] 6438 3-9-0 **67**................................ RichardEvans(3) 2 38
(P D Evans) *chsd ldr over 3f: hmpd and lost pl over 3f out: sn bhd* **28/1**

5000 **9** *61* **French Applause (IRE)**[37] 6296 4-8-10 **56** oh2.........(b[1]) MickyFenton 6 —
(T P Tate) *led: clr 6f out: hdd & wknd over 3f out: t.o* **25/1**

1m 50.47s (-0.03) **Going Correction** +0.025s/f (Slow)
WFA 3 from 4yo+ 4lb 9 Ran SP% **117.9**
Speed ratings (Par 103): **101,100,99,98,98 97,87,86,32**
toteswingers:1&2:£3.00, 1&3:£7.20, 2&3:£6.70 CSF £18.70 CT £117.77 TOTE £5.90: £2.10, £1.90, £3.50; EX 17.50 Place 6 £40.44; Place 5 £21.96.
Owner G Dolan/M McVitie/G Venamore/Mrs M Dolan **Bred** Shell Bloodstock **Trained** Cootehill Road, Co Cavan

FOCUS
A modest handicap in which a fair pace steadied around halfway. The winner came down the centre in the straight. The front three ran basically to form at face value.
T/Plt: £60.40 to a £1 stake. Pool:£87,043.42 - 1,051.29 winning tickets T/Qpdt: £26.00 to a £1 stake. Pool:£8,825.28 - 250.70 winning tickets CR

7215 - 7216a (Foreign Racing) - See Raceform Interactive

7072 DUNDALK (A.W) (L-H)
Friday, October 29

OFFICIAL GOING: Standard

7217a CROWNE PLAZA RACE & STAY PACKAGE H'CAP 6f (P)
7:30 (7:31) 3-Y-O+ £12,367 (£3,615; £1,712; £570)

RPR

1 **Take Ten**[32] 6429 3-8-8 83.. GregFairley 1 99
(M Johnston) *sn led: rdn and kpt on strly fr over 1f out: comf* **9/2**[2]

2 *3* **Noverre To Go (IRE)**[41] 6177 4-9-9 97.................(t) RichardKingscote 3 103
(Tom Dascombe) *chsd ldr in 2nd: rdn 2f out: no imp on ldr over 1f out: kpt on same pce* **11/2**[3]

3 *nk* **Banna Boirche (IRE)**[14] 6907 4-9-7 95.............................. JMurtagh 7 100+
(M Halford, Ire) *mid-div: 9th 1/2-way: rdn into 6th 1 1/2f out: 4th 1f out: kpt on fnl f* **11/2**[3]

4 *1 1/2* **Mountain Coral (IRE)**[14] 6907 6-8-12 86..................... NGMcCullagh 2 86
(F Oakes, Ire) *chsd ldrs: 3rd 1/2-way: rdn 2f out: no ex over 1f out: kpt on same pce* **8/1**

5 *1/2* **Solent Ridge (IRE)**[33] 6400 5-8-10 84.................................. KLatham 4 83
(G M Lyons, Ire) *mid-div early: 7th 1/2-way: rdn in 5th 2f out: no ex over 1f out: kpt on same pce* **20/1**

6 *1 1/4* **Copper Dock (IRE)**[14] 6907 6-8-10 84................................ CDHayes 5 79
(T G McCourt, Ire) *hld up towards rr: sme late hdwy in 8th 1f out: kpt on same pce fnl f* **16/1**

7 *1 1/4* **Tweedy (IRE)**[21] 6728 3-9-4 93.. WMLordan 10 84
(Edward Lynam, Ire) *chsd ldrs early: 8th 1/2-way: rdn 2f out: no imp and kpt on one pce* **7/2**[1]

8 *1/2* **Collingwood (IRE)**[14] 6907 8-8-13 87..............................(bt) WJLee 14 76
(T M Walsh, Ire) *towards rr: no imp 2f out: kpt on one pce* **16/1**

9 *nk* **Velvet Flicker (IRE)**[7] 7073 3-9-4 100............................ SHJames(7) 12 88
(Kevin Prendergast, Ire) *towards rr: no imp 2f out: kpt on one pce* **20/1**

10 *1/2* **Della'Alba (IRE)**[7] 7073 3-8-6 84.................................... GFCarroll(3) 8 70
(M Halford, Ire) *chsd ldrs: 6th 1/2-way: rdn in 4th 2f out: no ex in 5th 1f out: wknd* **20/1**

11 *shd* **Tornadodancer (IRE)**[103] 4180 7-8-5 82......................(b) BACurtis(3) 9 68
(T G McCourt, Ire) *mid-div best: rdn and wknd over 2f out* **20/1**

12 *4 1/2* **Cheviot (USA)**[9] 7024 4-9-2 90.................................(p) DPMcDonogh 11 62
(Reginald Roberts, Ire) *chsd ldrs: 4th 1/2-way: rdn in 6th 2f out: sn no ex and wknd* **8/1**

13 *hd* **Johnstown Lad (IRE)**[13] 6938 6-8-11 85.............................(t) WJSupple 6 56
(Daniel Mark Loughnane, Ire) *a towards rr* **12/1**

14 *5* **Calm Bay (IRE)**[7] 7073 4-9-4 92...(t) KJManning 13 47
(H Rogers, Ire) *chsd ldrs: 5th 1/2-way: rdn and wknd 2f out: hmpd 1 1/2f out* **14/1**

1m 10.4s (70.40)
WFA 3 from 4yo+ 1lb 14 Ran SP% **138.6**
CSF £32.60 CT £147.75 TOTE £5.00: £1.80, £2.00, £2.80; DF 19.70.
Owner Sheikh Hamdan Bin Mohammed Al Maktoum **Bred** Whitsbury Manor Stud And Mrs M E Slade **Trained** Middleham Moor, N Yorks

FOCUS
The front-running winner has been rated back to his 2009 best, with the fifth just off his recent best.

NOTEBOOK
Take Ten could be called the winner a long way from home. Jockey Greg Fairley took full advantage of his draw in stall one and was soon at the head of affairs. None of his rivals wanted to force the pace, so he was allowed the luxury of a soft lead, which runners from this stable thrive on. He kicked clear at the 2f pole and never looked in danger of being reeled in. He was value for more than the winning margin.
Noverre To Go(IRE) was always prominent but, despite staying on gamely in the home straight, could never get close to the winner. (op 6/1 tchd 5/1)
Banna Boirche(IRE) was bidding to follow up his smooth course success earlier in the month, but the drop down to 6f proved an inconvenience and he got going too late. He can regain the winning thread when returning to 7f. (op 4/1)
Mountain Coral(IRE) finished third behind Banna Boirche on his previous start and again finished behind Michael Halford's charge despite being better off at the weights. This was his second good run on the bounce after some inconsistent efforts and he could pick up a less competitive contest here before the turn of the year. (op 10/1)
Tweedy(IRE) was well supported to supplement her impressive C&D success earlier in the month but didn't race with the same zest as that outing and weakened in the home straight to finish a disappointing seventh. She may have disliked the kickback and may be better suited to forcing the pace. (op 5/1)
Tornadodancer(IRE) Official explanation: jockey said gelding lost its place in the early stages but ran on well at the finish

7218 - 7222a (Foreign Racing) - See Raceform Interactive

7049 AYR (L-H)
Saturday, October 30

OFFICIAL GOING: Heavy (7.1)
Wind: Fresh, half against Weather: Cloudy

7223 EUROPEAN BREEDERS' FUND MAIDEN STKS 7f 50y
1:35 (1:35) (Class 5) 2-Y-O £3,238 (£963; £481; £240) Stalls High

Form RPR

3 **1** **Fine Threads**[30] 6512 2-8-12 0.. RobertWinston 5 71+
(B W Hills) *prom: pushed along and outpcd over 2f out: rallied over 1f out: styd on wl fnl f: led post* **11/10**[1]

3233 **2** *nse* **Sabratha (IRE)**[8] 7049 2-8-9 60................................ JamesSullivan(3) 7 71
(Miss L A Perratt) *hld up in tch: hdwy to ld over 1f out: kpt on fnl f: hdd last stride* **11/2**[3]

4 **3** *2* **Coax**[26] 6626 2-9-3 0.. GregFairley 8 71
(M Johnston) *led: qcknd over 2f out: hdd over 1f out: kpt on same pce fnl f* **11/2**[3]

0 **4** *3 3/4* **Jeu De Vivre (IRE)**[8] 7057 2-8-12 0.................................... JoeFanning 1 57
(M Johnston) *t.k.h: trckd ldrs: pushed along over 2f out: wknd over 1f out* **3/1**[2]

0 **5** *18* **Crowned Supreme (IRE)**[14] 6919 2-9-3 0......................(b) DavidAllan 6 18
(Liam McAteer, Ire) *chsd ldr: rdn over 2f out: sn wknd* **25/1**

0 **6** *36* **Tinzo (IRE)**[42] 6182 2-9-3 0.................................... SilvestreDeSousa 2 —
(A Berry) *hld up in tch: struggling 1/2-way: sn lost tch* **80/1**

1m 38.34s (4.94) **Going Correction** +0.575s/f (Yiel) 6 Ran SP% **108.5**
Speed ratings (Par 95): **94,93,91,87,66 25**
toteswingers:1&2:£1.10, 1&3:£2.30, 2&3:£4.00 CSF £7.12 TOTE £1.80: £1.10, £2.70; EX 5.50.
Owner Lady Bamford **Bred** Lady Bamford **Trained** Lambourn, Berks

FOCUS
A modest maiden that produced a desperate finish in bad ground. The runner-up rates a significant improver but the conditions lend doubts.

NOTEBOOK
Fine Threads was the form choice based on her debut over this trip on soft ground at Warwick, but she had to work hard in the conditions to just prevail. She looked in trouble 2f out but kept trying and got to the front in the last few strides. She will appreciate further in time. (op 5-6 tchd 5-4 in a place)
Sabratha(IRE), having her eighth start and placed in the last three on softish ground, was backed beforehand and travelled well into contention. She looked the winner when going on over a furlong out but could not pick up again under pressure, and was caught virtually on the line. She deserves to pick up a small race, but the fact she is rated only 60 indicates the level of this form. (op 13-2 tchd 5-1)
Coax was stepping up in trip but made the running and kept on after being headed, doing better than his more fancied stablemate. (op 13-2)
Jeu De Vivre(IRE) did not appear to handle the ground and was in trouble before the quarter-mile pole. (op 7-2 tchd 11-4)

7224 JOHN SMITH'S NURSERY 6f
2:10 (2:10) (Class 5) (0-75,71) 2-Y-O £2,590 (£770; £385; £192) Stalls Low

Form RPR

3066 **1** **Bachelor Knight (IRE)**[15] 6891 2-8-5 **60**........................ LeeTopliss(5) 1 64
(R A Fahey) *dived rt s: sn cl up: led over 2f out: rdn and styd on wl fnl f* **11/1**

044 **2** *3/4* **Bertiewhittle**[16] 6878 2-8-12 **62**...................................... PhillipMakin 3 64
(T D Barron) *hmpd s: t.k.h and sn trckd ldrs: rdn and sltly outpcd 2f out: rallied over 1f out: kpt on fnl f* **7/2**[2]

3465 **3** *1 3/4* **Red Marling (IRE)**[26] 6627 2-9-7 **71**............................ RobertWinston 7 68
(B W Hills) *cl up: rdn and ev ch over 2f out: one pce fnl f* **9/2**[3]

6025 **4** *1 1/4* **Dotty Darroch**[25] 6645 2-8-9 **59**................................ SilvestreDeSousa 4 52
(R Bastiman) *prom: rdn along over 2f out: kpt on same pce fnl f* **20/1**

0254 **5** *nse* **Eilean Mor**[8] 7050 2-8-12 **65** GaryBartley(3) 6 58
(J S Goldie) *hld up: effrt over 2f out: no imp fnl f* **6/1**

4002 **6** *2 1/2* **Hernando Torres**[24] 6674 2-8-5 **58** JamesSullivan(3) 5 43
(M W Easterby) *hld up in tch: effrt over 2f out: wknd over 1f out* **3/1**[1]

062 **7** *3* **Cootehill Lass (IRE)**[15] 6893 2-9-4 **71** MichaelO'Connell(3) 8 47
(G A Harker) *dwlt and wnt rt s: hld up: hdwy over 2f out: wknd over 1f out* **20/1**

2402 **8** *19* **Karate (IRE)**[12] 6989 2-9-7 **71** JoeFanning 2 —
(M Johnston) *checked s: sn led: hdd over 2f out: wknd qckly and eased over 1f out* **13/2**

1m 17.66s (4.06) **Going Correction** +0.575s/f (Yiel) **8** Ran SP% **110.9**
Speed ratings (Par 95): **95,94,91,90,89 86,82,57**
toteswingers:1&2:£29.80, 1&3:£18.10, 2&3:£4.70 CSF £46.39 CT £194.57 TOTE £12.10: £2.70, £1.80, £1.90; EX 50.60.
Owner Lets Go Racing 1 **Bred** Angelo Robiati **Trained** Musley Bank, N Yorks

FOCUS
The stalls were on the far side for this ordinary nursery and it ended with something of a slow-motion finish, although full credit goes to Lee Topliss for his ride on the winner. Not form to be positive about.

NOTEBOOK
Bachelor Knight(IRE) won twice on fast ground earlier in the season but has struggled of late in claimers and sellers, and his rating had slipped 10lb in his last three runs. He swerved sharply right out of the stalls and his rider did well to keep the partnership intact. He recovered well, though, and the gelding made all the running. The fact that he was good enough to win limits the form, but he handled the heavy ground well on his first try on it. Official explanation: trainer had no explanation for the apparent improvement in form (op 16-1)
Bertiewhittle, another tackling testing ground for the first time was backed on this handicap debut and ran well, despite being hampered by the winner's antics at the start, but without being unable to get past that rival. (tchd 5-1 in a place)
Red Marling(IRE) seemed to handle this ground last time and ran his race but his best effort was on fast going. (tchd 4-1)
Dotty Darroch, like the third, did not run too badly but looks better suited by a sound surface. (op 40-1)
Eilean Mor has had a number of chances and stayed on having been held up off the pace. (op 8-1)
Hernando Torres was another held up and, after making some headway from the halfway mark, failed to make an impression in the last 2f. (op 7-2)
Cootehill Lass(IRE) was a market drifter and was never competitive having been held up. (op 10-1)
Karate(IRE) was a major drifter and, after being hampered by the winner at the start, raced prominently until dropping away quickly from halfway. Official explanation: trainer had no explanation for the poor form shown (op 4-1 tchd 7-2)

7225 ADVANCE CONSTRUCTION H'CAP 6f
2:45 (2:48) (Class 5) (0-75,71) 3-Y-O+ **£2,590** (£770; £385; £192) **Stalls** Low

Form RPR

0510 **1** **Ingleby Arch (USA)**[13] 6962 7-9-5 **68** PhillipMakin 4 76
(T D Barron) *cl up: drvn 1/2-way: rallied: led ins fnl f: hld on wl* **7/1**

4213 **2** *1/2* **Lake Chini (IRE)**[24] 6679 8-8-13 **65** (b) JamesSullivan(3) 11 71
(M W Easterby) *hld up in tch: rdn and hdwy on outside over 1f out: ev ch ins fnl f: hld towards fin* **7/1**

3604 **3** *hd* **Berbice (IRE)**[3] 7169 5-9-2 **65** DavidAllan 10 70
(Miss L A Perratt) *t.k.h: hld up in tch: smooth hdwy 2f out: rdn to chal ins fnl f: put hd in air: nt go past* **5/1**[1]

0010 **4** *3/4* **Durham Express (IRE)**[16] 6879 3-9-7 **71** (p) PaulMulrennan 12 74
(M Dods) *led tl rdn and hdd ins fnl f: kpt on same pce* **8/1**

-304 **5** *1 3/4* **Benny The Bear**[8] 7051 3-8-7 **57** SilvestreDeSousa 8 54
(Miss L A Perratt) *in tch: rdn over 2f out: kpt on same pce fnl f* **11/2**[2]

3155 **6** *4* **Music Festival (USA)**[8] 7051 3-8-11 **61** JoeFanning 2 46
(J S Goldie) *in tch: rdn over 2f out: edgd lft and wknd over 1f out* **6/1**[3]

0030 **7** *3* **Monte Mayor One**[8] 7051 3-8-10 **60** AndrewMullen 5 35
(P Monteith) *cl up: rdn 1/2-way: wknd over 1f out* **12/1**

0456 **8** *2* **Hold On Tiger (IRE)**[30] 6490 3-7-13 **56** oh3 ShirleyTeasdale(7) 9 25
(V P Donoghue) *cl up tl rdn and wknd wl over 1f out* **20/1**

/05- **9** *nk* **Zhukhov (IRE)**[19] 6822 7-9-6 **69** PJMcDonald 13 37
(T G McCourt, Ire) *in tch tl rdn and wknd over 2f out* **8/1**

1m 17.7s (4.10) **Going Correction** +0.575s/f (Yiel)
WFA 3 from 4yo+ 1lb **9** Ran SP% **106.0**
Speed ratings (Par 103): **95,94,94,93,90 85,81,78,78**
toteswingers:1&2:£9.80, 1&3:£8.70, 2&3:£11.10 CSF £47.16 CT £221.12 TOTE £8.20: £2.40, £1.80, £2.00; EX 34.70.
Owner Dave Scott **Bred** Alexander-Groves Thoroughbreds **Trained** Maunby, N Yorks
■ The Bear (14/1) and Orchid Wing (33/1) were withdrawn at the stalls. Rule 4 applies: deduction 5p in £ from all bets.
■ Stewards' Enquiry : David Allan caution: used whip with excessive frequency.

FOCUS
Two non-runners and two more withdrawn at the start reduced this field by almost a third and it produced another desperate, slow-motion finish. Again they raced towards the far rail. The form makes sense at face value but perhaps should not be taken literally.

7226 JOHN SMITH'S EXTRA SMOOTH H'CAP 1m 7f
3:20 (3:20) (Class 4) (0-85,79) 3-Y-O+
£5,607 (£1,679; £839; £420; £209; £105)

Form RPR

4141 **1** **Lady Bluesky**[25] 6648 7-8-13 **64** AndrewMullen 1 72
(A C Whillans) *hld up in tch: hdwy 3f out: led over 1f out: edgd lft u.p ins fnl f: styd on wl* **7/2**[2]

3634 **2** *1/2* **Bollin Judith**[12] 6983 4-9-2 **67** (t) DavidAllan 8 74
(T D Easterby) *trckd ldrs: drvn and outpcd over 2f out: rallied over 1f out: chsd wnr ins fnl f: r.o* **11/2**

1-02 **3** *3/4* **Sphinx (FR)**[21] 6750 12-9-8 **73** (b) PhillipMakin 7 79
(E W Tuer) *hld up last but in tch: stdy hdwy and cl up 1/2-way: effrt on outside over 2f out: kpt on u.p fnl f* **3/1**[1]

6110 **4** *1 1/2* **Royal Trooper (IRE)**[14] 6926 4-10-0 **79** PaulMulrennan 9 83
(J G Given) *led to over 2f out: rdn and rallied: kpt on same pce fnl f* **6/1**

1021 **5** *nk* **Royal Swain (IRE)**[25] 6650 4-9-13 **78** PJMcDonald 3 82
(G A Swinbank) *t.k.h: cl up: led over 2f tl over 1f out: edgd lft: no ex fnl f* **4/1**[3]

2112 **6** *16* **Pertemps Networks**[21] 6754 6-9-10 **75** GrahamGibbons 2 58
(M W Easterby) *prom: drvn and outpcd over 3f out: lost tch fnl 2f* **11/2**

3m 40.2s (19.80) **Going Correction** +0.575s/f (Yiel)
WFA 3 from 4yo+ 9lb **6** Ran SP% **112.3**
Speed ratings (Par 105): **70,69,69,68,68 59**
toteswingers:1&2:£3.40, 1&3:£4.10, 2&3:£7.20 CSF £22.42 CT £62.40 TOTE £4.50: £1.30, £3.50; EX 24.50.
Owner Mrs S Harrow Mrs L M Whillans **Bred** C E Whiteley **Trained** Newmill-On-Slitrig, Borders

FOCUS
A flip start for this stayers' event and not surprisingly the pace was steady in the conditions. There was a bunch finish and this is not form to take too literally.

7227 JOHN SMITH'S NO NONSENSE H'CAP 1m
3:55 (3:55) (Class 3) (0-90,88) 3-Y-O+ **£7,771** (£2,312; £1,155; £577) **Stalls** Low

Form RPR

0-02 **1** **The Fifth Member (IRE)**[13] 6960 6-9-5 **86** StephenCraine 11 95
(J R Boyle) *cl up: led gng wl over 2f out: drvn out fnl f* **11/2**[3]

5211 **2** *3/4* **Amethyst Dawn (IRE)**[13] 6963 4-9-6 **87** DavidAllan 4 94
(T D Easterby) *cl up: drvn and outpcd over 2f out: rallied to chse wnr over 1f out: kpt on fin* **5/1**[2]

1236 **3** *1/2* **Arabian Spirit**[13] 6960 5-9-5 **86** PaulMulrennan 9 92
(R A Fahey) *midfield: effrt over 2f out: kpt on u.p ins fnl f* **8/1**

3043 **4** *1 3/4* **Faithful Ruler (USA)**[13] 6960 6-8-9 **81** LeeTopliss(5) 8 83
(R A Fahey) *hld up: hdwy on outside over 2f out: rdn and kpt on same pce appr fnl f* **12/1**

2230 **5** *nk* **Dolphin Rock**[29] 6534 3-8-12 **82** PhillipMakin 6 83
(T D Barron) *led tl hdd over 2f out: sn rdn and kpt on same pce* **9/2**[1]

1036 **6** *1* **High Resolution**[8] 7053 3-8-10 **80** SilvestreDeSousa 5 79
(Miss L A Perratt) *hld up: rdn and swtchd rt over 2f out: hdwy over 1f out: nvr able to chal* **10/1**

0100 **7** *nk* **Northern Fling**[28] 6562 6-9-2 **86** GaryBartley(3) 3 84
(J S Goldie) *bhd: drvn over 2f out: styd on wl fnl f: nrst fin* **16/1**

3024 **8** *2 1/2* **Daring Dream (GER)**[8] 7063 5-8-7 **74** oh2 JoeFanning 2 66
(J S Goldie) *prom: drvn over 2f out: wknd over 1f out* **14/1**

2260 **9** *2 1/2* **Magaling (IRE)**[21] 6736 4-9-7 **88** GrahamGibbons 12 75
(M W Easterby) *in tch: rdn and outpcd 2f out: sn btn* **5/1**[2]

125P **10** *2* **Silver Rime (FR)**[21] 6749 5-9-7 **88** LNewman 10 70
(Miss L A Perratt) *hld up in tch: drvn over 2f out: sn btn* **25/1**

2004 **11** *1 1/2* **City Of The Kings (IRE)**[13] 6960 5-9-4 **88** MichaelO'Connell(3) 7 67
(G A Harker) *bhd: rdn over 3f out: nvr on terms* **22/1**

1m 46.7s (2.90) **Going Correction** +0.575s/f (Yiel)
WFA 3 from 4yo+ 3lb **11** Ran SP% **115.5**
Speed ratings (Par 107): **108,107,106,105,104 103,103,100,98,96 94**
toteswingers:1&2:£5.30, 1&3:£9.20, 2&3:£3.10 CSF £32.52 CT £223.49 TOTE £5.00: £1.60, £1.80, £3.10; EX 13.40.
Owner Epsom Equine Spa Partnership **Bred** Ms Amy Mulligan **Trained** Epsom, Surrey
■ Stewards' Enquiry : Stephen Craine three-day ban: used whip with excessive frequency (Nov 13,15,16)
David Allan one-day ban: used whip with excessive frequency (Nov 13)

FOCUS
A decent race for this feature event. The winner ran to his best with the next two to their marks.

NOTEBOOK
The Fifth Member(IRE) had come up all the way from Epsom and the journey proved worthwhile. Always in the leading trio, he went on 2f out travelling well and found more for pressure to hold on. He handles most surfaces but has a particularly good record on heavy ground and, having just his third start of the year, looks set to win more races on the all-weather this winter. (op 13-2)
Amethyst Dawn(IRE) has been in fine form, winning her last two, including one on heavy ground. She had to be ridden to challenge but kept on well all the way to the line, and might be able to defy this career-high mark. (tchd 4-1)
Arabian Spirit ran two good races over C&D earlier in the autumn, winning one, and came through to challenge entering the last furlong. This was creditable but he looks more effective on better ground. (op 15-2)
Faithful Ruler(USA) handles heavy but was a market drifter. He ran pretty well on a track he likes, having scored over C&D last season, his last success. (op 8-1)
Dolphin Rock was backed into favouritism and made the running, but he could respond when the winner went past. (op 9-1)
Magaling(IRE) handles fast and easy ground but had been well held on two previous tries on soft and this even more testing ground found him out. He was beaten 3f out. (op 4-1)

7228 JOHN SMITH'S H'CAP 1m 2f
4:30 (4:30) (Class 4) (0-80,80) 3-Y-O+
£4,984 (£1,492; £746; £373; £186; £93) **Stalls** Low

Form RPR

3030 **1** **Best Prospect (IRE)**[8] 7053 8-9-1 **70** (vt) PhillipMakin 9 83+
(M Dods) *hld up: smooth hdwy over 2f out: led on bit ins fnl f: canter* **9/2**[1]

5014 **2** *2 3/4* **Starla Dancer (GER)**[23] 6691 4-9-5 **79** LeeTopliss(5) 4 83
(R A Fahey) *prom: led and rdn over 2f out: hdd ins fnl f: no ch w easy wnr* **13/2**

3111 **3** *4* **Sharp Sovereign (USA)**[12] 6984 4-9-1 **70** SilvestreDeSousa 1 66
(T D Barron) *led 1f: cl up: drvn and outpcd over 3f out: rallied 2f out: no ex ins fnl f* **9/2**[1]

4200 **4** *4 1/2* **Hurlingham**[25] 6650 6-8-11 **66** (b) PaulMulrennan 7 53
(M W Easterby) *hld up in tch: effrt and hdwy over 2f out: rdn and wknd appr fnl f* **11/1**

5130 **5** *1 1/4* **Casino Night**[8] 7053 5-8-11 **66** JoeFanning 8 51
(Miss L A Perratt) *dwlt: hdwy to ld after 1f: rdn and hdd over 2f out: sn outpcd: n.d after* **9/1**

4-01 **6** *1* **Bagber**[8] 7053 4-9-8 **77** AndrewMullen 2 60
(P Monteith) *trckd ldrs: rdn and ev ch over 2f out: wknd over 1f out* **5/1**[2]

2023 **7** *17* **Royal Straight**[8] 7053 5-8-12 **70** JamesSullivan(3) 3 19
(Miss L A Perratt) *hld up: effrt over 2f out: sn btn* **6/1**[3]

6511 **8** *15* **Dean Iarracht (IRE)**[15] 6890 4-8-10 **65** oh1 RobertWinston 6 —
(Miss Tracy Waggott) *midfield: rdn over 2f out: wknd wl over 1f out* **9/1**

2000 **9** *79* **Gumnd (IRE)**[140] 2970 3-9-6 **80** GrahamGibbons 5 —
(J D Bethell) *bhd: lost tch 1/2-way: t.o* **22/1**

2m 19.47s (7.47) **Going Correction** +0.875s/f (Soft)
WFA 3 from 4yo+ 5lb **9** Ran SP% **113.3**
Speed ratings (Par 105): **105,102,99,96,95 94,80,68,5**
toteswingers:1&2:£4.20, 1&3:£5.40, 2&3:£5.50 CSF £33.02 CT £137.45 TOTE £6.30: £2.10, £1.60, £1.90; EX 41.40.
Owner D Neale **Bred** Farmers Hill Stud **Trained** Denton, Co Durham

FOCUS
A competitive-looking handicap on paper but it proved to be an easy success for Best Prospect. This could underrate him, but this is not form to go overboard about.
Dean Iarracht(IRE) Official explanation: jockey said gelding was unsuited by the heavy ground
Gumnd(IRE) Official explanation: jockey said gelding never travelled

7229 BUY JOHN SMITH'S AT AYR RACECOURSE H'CAP (DIV I) 1m 1f 20y
5:00 (5:00) (Class 6) (0-60,60) 3-Y-O+ **£1,619** (£481; £240; £120) **Stalls** Low

Form RPR

0432 **1** **Lakeman (IRE)**[8] 7055 4-9-9 **59** (b) DavidAllan 12 68+
(B Ellison) *pressed ldr: led over 3f out: qcknd over 2f out: hld on wl fnl f* **7/2**[2]

4060 **2** ¾ **Mississippian (IRE)**[5] 7125 6-8-12 **48**........................ PaulMulrennan 11 55
(Mrs R Dobbin) *dwlt: hld up: hdwy on outside over 2f out: chsd wnr and edgd lft over 1f out: kpt on fnl f* **8/1**

5520 **3** 2 ¾ **Broughtons Silk**[54] 5821 5-8-10 **46**........................ PJMcDonald 9 47
(A C Whillans) *hld up: hdwy on outside over 2f out: egded lft over 1f out: kpt on fnl f: nt rch first two* **12/1**

-043 **4** hd **Pokfulham (IRE)**[8] 7054 4-8-11 **54**........................(v) PaulNorton(7) 2 55
(J S Goldie) *in tch: rdn over 2f out: no imp tl styd on wl fnl f: nvr able to chal* **9/4**[1]

0350 **5** 1 ¾ **La Bacouetteuse (FR)**[14] 6921 5-9-3 **53**........................ LNewman 8 50
(A G Foster) *cl up tl rdn and no ex over 1f out* **15/2**

0602 **6** 1 **Lordship (IRE)**[25] 6657 6-8-12 **55**........................ JakePayne(7) 10 49
(A W Carroll) *plld hrd: set stdy pce tl hdd over 3f out: one pce fr 2f out* **5/1**[3]

7 1 ¼ **Young Lochinvar (IRE)**[90] 4634 6-9-10 **60**........................ AndrewMullen 4 52
(John G Carr, Ire) *prom: rdn over 2f out: kpt on same pce over 1f out* **22/1**

000 **8** 1 **Balance On Time (IRE)**[3] 7171 4-8-6 **47** oh1 ow1........ LeeTopliss(5) 5 37
(Miss L A Perratt) *dwlt: hld up: effrt on ins over 2f out: nvr able to chal* **25/1**

-500 **9** 31 **Meml**[176] 1887 4-8-10 **46** oh1........................ GrahamGibbons 6 —
(J D Bethell) *trckd ldrs tl rdn and wknd over 2f out: t.o* **16/1**

0450 **10** 17 **Charity Fair**[47] 6026 3-8-6 **46** oh1........................ SilvestreDeSousa 7 —
(A Berry) *towards rr: struggling over 3f out: t.o* **33/1**

2m 6.29s (7.89) **Going Correction** +0.875s/f (Soft)
WFA 3 from 4yo+ 4lb **10** Ran SP% **117.2**
Speed ratings (Par 101): **99,98,95,95,94 93,92,91,63,48**
toteswingers:1&2:£4.70, 1&3:£9.30, 2&3:£7.00 CSF £31.05 CT £305.04 TOTE £4.10: £1.60, £2.00, £4.60; EX 37.90.
Owner The Country Stayers **Bred** Tally-Ho Stud **Trained** Norton, N Yorks

FOCUS
The first division of this weak handicap and a good tactical ride from David Allan. The winner probably only had to run to his recent form.

7230 PLUMBSTORE LTD H'CAP (DIV II OF 5.00) 1m 1f 20y
5:30 (5:31) (Class 6) (0-60,60) 3-Y-0+ **£1,619** (£481; £240; £120) **Stalls** Low

Form RPR

00-4 **1** **Ulysees (IRE)**[8] 7055 11-8-13 **49**........................ JoeFanning 1 58+
(J S Goldie) *hld up: smooth hdwy and prom over 2f out: sn rdn: led over 1f out: styd on strly* **5/1**[2]

0000 **2** 3 ½ **Funky Munky**[28] 6571 5-8-10 **46** oh1........................(t) DavidAllan 11 47
(A C Whillans) *prom: effrt and ev ch over 2f out: kpt on u.p fnl f: nt rch wnr* **7/1**[3]

633U **3** 1 ¾ **Botham (USA)**[8] 7054 6-9-1 **58**........................ PaulNorton(7) 6 55
(J S Goldie) *hld up: rdn over 2f out: hdwy over 1f out: kpt on same pce fnl f* **4/1**[1]

6406 **4** 2 **Papa's Princess**[65] 5216 6-8-10 **46** oh1........................ RobertWinston 3 39
(James Moffatt) *cl up: led over 2f out tl over 1f out: sn outpcd* **12/1**

3365 **5** ¾ **Ingleby King (USA)**[15] 6890 4-9-2 **52**........................(b) PhillipMakin 10 43
(T D Barron) *hld up towards rr: effrt over 2f out: sn rdn and hung bdly rt: no imp fr over 1f out* **4/1**[1]

543- **6** 1 ½ **Laura's Lady (IRE)**[483] 3614 4-9-3 **53**........................ PJMcDonald 4 41
(G A Swinbank) *hld up: rdn and outpcd 1/2-way: hdwy and edgd lft 2f out: nvr rchd ldrs* **5/1**[2]

7 7 **Tommy's Star (IRE)**[33] 6433 7-9-7 **57**........................ AndrewMullen 2 30
(John G Carr, Ire) *midfield: drvn along 1/2-way: wknd fr over 2f out* **20/1**

1500 **8** 6 **All Guns Firing (IRE)**[18] 6832 4-9-7 **60**........... MichaelO'Connell(3) 12 20
(D Carroll) *sn led and clr: hdd 1/2-way: wknd over 2f out* **14/1**

6000 **9** 10 **Singing Scott (IRE)**[45] 6076 3-8-6 **46** oh1........................ SilvestreDeSousa 8 —
(R Bastiman) *in tch tl rdn and wknd fr 3f out* **33/1**

000 **10** 7 **Catcher Of Dreams (IRE)**[47] 6029 4-8-11 **47**........................ LNewman 9 —
(A G Foster) *cl up: led 1/2-way to over 2f out: sn wknd* **16/1**

2m 6.78s (8.38) **Going Correction** +0.875s/f (Soft)
WFA 3 from 4yo+ 4lb **10** Ran SP% **113.8**
Speed ratings (Par 101): **97,93,92,90,89 88,82,77,68,61**
toteswingers:1&2:£11.10, 1&3:£5.30, 2&3:£6.80 CSF £38.86 CT £152.26 TOTE £5.30: £1.80, £2.40, £1.80; EX 43.70 Place 6 £92.10, Place 5 £13.60.
Owner Johnny Higgins **Bred** Sweetmans Bloodstock **Trained** Uplawmoor, E Renfrews

FOCUS
The second division of this low-grade handicap was run just under half a second slower than the first. Few got into this and the winner is rated to his best form of the past couple of years.
Ingleby King(USA) Official explanation: jockey said gelding hung right
T/Plt: £92.10 to a £1 stake. Pool: £52,126.59. 412.86 winning tickets. T/Qpdt: £13.60 to a £1 stake. Pool: £4,042.89. 219.80 winning tickets. RY

7201
NEWMARKET (Rowley Mile) (R-H)
Saturday, October 30

OFFICIAL GOING: Good to soft (7.1)
Stands' side section of Rowley Mile used.
Wind: fresh, half against Weather: light cloud, dry

7231 BET365.COM E B F MAIDEN FILLIES' STKS (DIV I) 7f
12:50 (12:51) (Class 4) 2-Y-0 **£4,209** (£1,252; £625; £312) **Stalls** Low

Form RPR

0 **1** **Make A Dance (USA)**[40] 6247 2-9-0 0........................ MichaelHills 13 85+
(B W Hills) *chsd ldrs: rdn to chal over 1f out: led ent fnl f: r.o wl: comf* **6/1**[1]

00 **2** 4 **Vita Lika**[28] 6559 2-9-0 0........................ ShaneKelly 11 75
(B J Meehan) *wnt lft s: chsd ldr: rdn 2f out: led over 1f out: sn hdd: nvr gng pce of wnr fnl f but kpt on for 2nd* **6/1**[1]

3 ¾ **Elmaam** 2-9-0 0........................ TadhgO'Shea 9 73+
(W J Haggas) *in tch: outpcd jst over 2f out: pushed along and styd on again over 1f out: gng on wl fin: no threat to wnr* **25/1**

0042 **4** ½ **Saskia's Dream**[16] 6869 2-9-0 72........................ JamieSpencer 6 72
(Jane Chapple-Hyam) *led: rdn 2f out: hdd over 1f out: no ex and kpt on same pce fnl f* **11/1**

5 2 **Five Hearts** 2-9-0 0........................ JimmyQuinn 19 68+
(M H Tompkins) *stdd s: t.k.h: hld up towards rr: hdwy and swtchd lft 2f out: styd on wl fnl f: nvr trbld ldrs* **100/1**

0 **6** 1 ¾ **Making Eyes (IRE)**[32] 6443 2-9-0 0........................ SebSanders 16 63
(C F Wall) *chsd ldrs: rdn ent fnl 2f: 4th and btn over 1f out: wknd fnl f* **16/1**

7 3 ¼ **Lunar Phase (IRE)** 2-9-0 0........................ LukeMorris 1 54+
(C G Cox) *s.i.s: bhd and sn pushed along: hdwy 2f out: styd on steadily fnl f: n.d* **25/1**

00 **8** hd **Mystic Edge**[16] 6859 2-9-0 0........................ HayleyTurner 5 54
(M L W Bell) *racd in midfield: rdn and outpcd over 2f out: kpt on again fnl f: no ch w ldrs* **100/1**

9 ¾ **Regal Salute** 2-9-0 0........................ RichardHughes 10 52+
(J Noseda) *pushed lft s: in tch: pushed along and struggling 3f out: wl btn fnl 2f* **10/1**

0 **10** nk **Diverting**[15] 6883 2-9-0 0........................ KierenFallon 14 51
(W Jarvis) *in tch: rdn and outpcd wl over 2f out: plugged on one pce and wl hld fnl 2f* **33/1**

11 1 **Starlight Walk** 2-9-0 0........................ FergusSweeney 12 49
(R Charlton) *a towards rr: rdn and no hdwy over 3f out: wl btn fnl 2f* **22/1**

12 nk **Moon Over Water (IRE)** 2-9-0 0........................ PhilipRobinson 18 48
(M A Jarvis) *in tch in midfield: rdn and wknd ent fnl 3f: wl btn fnl 2f* **8/1**[3]

13 1 ¼ **Midas Moment** 2-9-0 0........................ RichardMullen 2 45
(W R Muir) *chsd ldrs: rdn over 2f out: btn wl over 1f out: wknd qckly fnl f* **16/1**

14 2 ½ **Young Jackie** 2-9-0 0........................ NeilCallan 17 39
(G G Margarson) *in tch in midfield: rdn and struggling 3f out: wl btn fnl 2f* **66/1**

15 nk **Rosaria** 2-9-0 0........................ JimmyFortune 3 38+
(R Hannon) *s.i.s: a bhd* **25/1**

0 **16** 2 ½ **Carousel**[19] 6804 2-9-0 0........................ JimCrowley 7 32
(R M Beckett) *racd in midfield: rdn over 2f out: sn wknd: wl btn and edgd rt over 1f out* **14/1**

17 ½ **Spectacle** 2-9-0 0........................ RyanMoore 20 30
(Sir Michael Stoute) *s.i.s: a bhd: lost tch 3f out* **6/1**[1]

18 2 **Moment Juste** 2-9-0 0........................ WilliamBuick 8 25
(J H M Gosden) *s.i.s: a bhd: lost tch 3f out* **7/1**[2]

19 26 **Blueberry Fizz (IRE)** 2-9-0 0........................ KirstyMilczarek 15 —
(J Ryan) *s.i.s: sn rdn along and nvr gng wl in last: t.o fr 1/2-way* **100/1**

1m 28.1s (2.70) **Going Correction** +0.50s/f (Yiel) **19** Ran SP% **125.6**
Speed ratings (Par 94): **104,99,98,98,95 93,90,89,88,88 87,87,85,82,82 79,79,76,47**
toteswingers:1&2:£17.00, 1&3:£36.80, 2&3:£152.90 CSF £37.35 TOTE £7.80: £2.60, £2.90, £6.80; EX 80.80 TRIFECTA Not won..
Owner K Abdulla **Bred** Juddmonte Farms Inc **Trained** Lambourn, Berks

FOCUS
Following 1.2mm of rain overnight, the going was changed slightly to good to soft all round (GoingStick 7.1). The first division of a maiden that has thrown up several Pattern-class fillies in recent years, most notably Sariska. While it should again produce winners, it is difficult to rate the race highly for the time being, and very few got into it from off the pace. The time was 0.61sec faster than the second division and the fourth and eighth are the guides to the level.

NOTEBOOK
Make A Dance(USA) had things go against her on her debut at Kempton, but that experience had clearly done her some good as she looked far more professional here, breaking well and racing prominently throughout. She drew clear on the rise from the Dip and shapes very much like a filly who will appreciate a longer trip next season - her dam stayed 1m2f. (op 8-1)
Vita Lika arrived here with a couple of duck eggs next to her name, but the latest of those came in competitive sales race. That was enough to entitle her to co-favouritism, and she ran a fine race in defeat. Closely related to Vital Equine, 1m should suit her next year. (op 15-2 tchd 8-1)
Elmaam did best of those who did not race in the front rank, and despite showing signs of inexperience and carrying her head a touch high when asked to make up ground, she finished her race off well to take third. She can only improve for this.
Saskia's Dream, the most experienced filly in the line-up, has an official mark of 72, and it would be difficult to rate her as having running any better than that here. (op 10-1 tchd 9-1)
Five Hearts ◆ was friendless in the market, so this performance, in which she didn't get a clear passage through and ran green, must go down as a promising effort. She surely has the ability to win a maiden on this evidence, and perhaps her trainer can find a race on the Polytrack for her before the year is out. Her dam was a multiple 1m2f winner, but her sire is an influence for speed, so it remains to be seen what her best trip will be. (op 80-1)
Making Eyes(IRE) showed up well for a long way before dropping out quickly on the climb out of the Dip. This was a big step up on her debut effort and she certainly looks to be going the right way. (op 18-1)
Lunar Phase(IRE) struggled to go the pace and ran green before staying on past beaten horses. There's a fair amount of stamina in her pedigree and she'll be wanting at least 1m2f next year. (op 33-1)
Mystic Edge has now had the three runs required for a mark and will surely find things easier in handicap company.
Regal Salute was fairly prominent in the betting on this debut. She kept pace with the principals for a long way, wasn't beaten up when her chance had gone. (op 8-1)
Moon Over Water(IRE) was another fairly prominent in the betting on this debut. A 100,000gns half-sister to Dubai World Cup winner Moon Ballad, she was too green to show her true ability on her debut. (op 15-2)
Spectacle is a half-sister to Workforce, but with Dalakhani being her sire, she has more stamina in her pedigree than him. Reported beforehand as being weak and backward, and likely to need the race, she ran very green and was never seriously involved. She should do a lot better next year over 1m4f plus. (tchd 13-2)
Moment Juste was another far too green to do herself justice, but she's a half-sister to several smart performers and could well leave this form well behind next year. (op 15-2)
Blueberry Fizz(IRE) Official explanation: jockey said filly was slowly away

7232 BET365.COM E B F MAIDEN FILLIES' STKS (DIV II) 7f
1:25 (1:27) (Class 4) 2-Y-0 **£4,209** (£1,252; £625; £312) **Stalls** Low

Form RPR

3 **1** **Qushchi**[23] 6688 2-9-0 0........................ JimCrowley 6 75
(W Jarvis) *in tch: rdn 2f out: ev ch and drvn ent fnl f: kpt on wl u.p to ld fnl 50yds* **11/1**

2422 **2** 1 **Choral**[9] 7036 2-9-0 77........................ RichardHughes 3 72
(R Hannon) *broke wl: sn stdd and hld up tch: hdwy to chse ldr 2f out: led over 1f out: drvn ent fnl f: hdd and no ex fnl 50yds* **11/2**[2]

3 nse **Joviality** 2-9-0 0........................ WilliamBuick 15 72+
(J H M Gosden) *awkward s and s.i.s: t.k.h: hld up in rr: swtchd rt and gd hdwy on far side wl over 1f out: chsd ldng trio: rn green and hung lft over 1f out: pressed ldrs ins fnl f: one pce fnl 100yds* **5/1**[1]

4 ½ **Field Of Miracles (IRE)** 2-9-0 0........................ RobertHavlin 12 71+
(J H M Gosden) *s.i.s: t.k.h: hld up in rr: gd hdwy 3f out: chsd ldrs over 1f out: edging rt and kpt on wl fnl f: nt rch ldrs* **16/1**

4 **5** nk **Port Hollow**[30] 6511 2-9-0 0........................ MichaelHills 11 70
(B W Hills) *led: rdn ent fnl 2f: hdd over 1f out: drvn ent fnl f: no ex fnl 100yds* **8/1**[3]

6 4 **Rien Ne Vas Plus (IRE)** 2-9-0 0........................ RyanMoore 5 63+
(Sir Michael Stoute) *towards rr: outpcd and pushed along 1/2-way: rallied over 1f out: styd on wl fnl f: gng on wl fin: nvr trbld ldrs* **10/1**

0 **7** 1 ¾ **Moonlight Mystery**[25] 6651 2-9-0 0........................ JackMitchell 1 56
(C F Wall) *in tch in midfield: rdn and unable qck over 2f out: no threat to ldrs and styd on same pce fr over 1f out* **66/1**

4 **8** ½ **Obiter Dicta**[20] 6778 2-9-0 0 DaneO'Neill 7 54
(H Candy) *hld up towards rr: hdwy on far side over 2f out: kpt on same pce and no imp fr over 1f out* **16/1**

9 *nk* **Kublahara (IRE)** 2-9-0 0 JimmyFortune 8 54
(A M Balding) *chsd ldrs: rdn over 2f out: wknd u.p wl over 1f out* **33/1**

10 ½ **Romany Stone (IRE)** 2-9-0 0 NeilCallan 14 52
(M A Jarvis) *chsd ldr tl 2f out: wknd u.p over 1f out* **8/1**[3]

11 ¾ **Imperial Fong** 2-9-0 0 HayleyTurner 19 50
(D R C Elsworth) *stdd and swtchd rt after s: hld up towards rr: rdn and outpcd jst over 3f out: plugged on same pce and wl hld fnl 2f* **50/1**

323 **12** *hd* **Our Gal**[16] 6866 2-9-0 74 WilliamCarson 18 50
(M G Quinlan) *chsd ldrs: rdn over 2f out: drvn and btn wl over 1f out* **12/1**

0 **13** ¾ **Cotton Grass**[11] 7001 2-9-0 0 JimmyQuinn 16 48
(M H Tompkins) *sltly hmpd s and s.i.s: a towards rr: rdn and kpt on same pce fr over 2f out: nvr trbld ldrs* **100/1**

14 *nk* **Tafaneen (USA)** 2-9-0 0 TadhgO'Shea 9 47+
(M A Jarvis) *in tch: pushed along and struggling ent fnl 3f: no threat to ldrs fnl 2f* **14/1**

0 **15** ¾ **Melody Belle (IRE)**[19] 6803 2-8-11 0 (t) SophieDoyle(3) 17 45
(T B P Coles) *in tch tl rdn and struggling ent fnl 3f: no threat to ldrs fnl 2f* **150/1**

16 *7* **Hopscotch** 2-9-0 0 JamieSpencer 13 28
(M L W Bell) *s.i.s: a in rr: rdn and struggling fr 1/2-way: n.d* **14/1**

17 *30* **She Ain't A Saint** 2-9-0 0 FrankieDettori 4 —
(Jane Chapple-Hyam) *hld up towards rr: sme hdwy 1/2-way: wknd over 2f out: wl bhd and virtually p.u ins fnl f* **10/1**

18 *12* **Ssafa** 2-9-0 0 SebSanders 2 —
(J W Hills) *s.i.s: hld up in tch towards rr: hdwy 1/2-way: btn ent fnl 2f: eased and virtually p.u fr over 1f out: t.o* **66/1**

1m 28.71s (3.31) **Going Correction** +0.50s/f (Yiel) **18** Ran SP% **123.1**
Speed ratings (Par 94): **101,99,99,99,98 94,92,91,91,90 89,89,88,88,87 79,45,31**
toteswingers:1&2:£14.80, 1&3:£25.60, 2&3:£5.10 CSF £69.02 TOTE £15.40: £4.10, £1.90, £2.80; EX 81.20 TRIFECTA Not won..
Owner Gillian, Lady Howard De Walden **Bred** Avington Manor Stud **Trained** Newmarket, Suffolk

FOCUS
The winning time was 0.61sec slower than the first division and the front five came clear, but plenty of winners should come out of it. The runner-up sets the level.

NOTEBOOK
Qushchi had proved green both before and during her Newbury debut this month, though she still finished a respectable third of ten. Much more the finished article this time, she still showed signs of greenness entering the Dip and took a while to hit her stride, but she bounded up the hill to hit the front 25yds from home and really stuck her neck out. Her breeding suggests that she ought to get 1m, though not much further, and she should go on to better things at three. (op 14-1)
Choral held an official rating of 77 after finishing runner-up in three of her six previous outings (all over 1m) and seemed likely to break her duck at the seventh attempt when leading over a furlong from home, but she hung left up the final climb and was run out of it. She has the ability to win races and is the benchmark to the form, but a few of those behind her here are likely to improve past her. (op 5-1 tchd 6-1)
Joviality ◆, a 200,000gns half-sister to two winners at up to 1m, was probably unfortunate not to make a winning debut. Slowly into stride, she pulled hard and ran extremely green in the early stages and, even after making her move towards the far side entering the last 2f, she started to hang again running out of the Dip. She would be very short odds to beat the front pair were they to meet again and she looks a nice prospect for next season. (op 7-1)
Field Of Miracles(IRE) ◆ also proved green, fluffing the start and giving herself plenty to do, but she stayed on in eye-catching style over the last 2f, despite hanging about, and was still going forward at the line. A 155,000gns half-sister to the 1m2f winner Sour Mash, there will be races to be won with her next term. (tchd 14-1)
Port Hollow, fourth of ten on her debut in an ordinary Warwick maiden last month, proved weak in the market but set a fair pace until collared over a furlong from home. (op 6-1 tchd 14-1 in a place)
Rien Ne Vas Plus(IRE), a half-sister to four winners including the stable's Derby winner North Light, the very useful Researched and the smart stayer Cover Up, was another to run green at the back of the field early but she stayed on in the latter stages to snatch a remote sixth. This effort suggests that she has inherited more of the stamina of her dam rather than the speed of her sire, and she seems sure to improve over the winter. (tchd 9-1)
Moonlight Mystery, last of ten on her Leicester debut this month, improved from that and stayed on without being by any means knocked about. She looks one for handicaps in due course.
Kublahara(IRE), out of a winning miler who was herself a half-sister to a winner over 1m6f, showed up among the leading group for a long way and seems sure to come on plenty for the run. (op 28-1)
Imperial Fong, a sister to the useful miler Gobama and a half-sister to two other winners, was noted staying on late without being given a hard time and better can be expected. (op 66-1)
Tafaneen(USA), a $700,000 half-sister to a Flat/hurdles winner and a bumper winner, wasn't knocked about on this debut and gave the impression that she is capable of a lot better.
Ssafa Official explanation: jockey said filly lost its action

7233 CASINO AT BET365.COM H'CAP 1m
2:00 (2:00) (Class 2) (0-105,100) 3-Y-0+

£9,346 (£2,799; £1,399; £700; £349; £175) **Stalls** Low

Form RPR
1310 **1** **Brick Red**[21] 6749 3-8-11 **88** JimmyFortune 11 97+
(A M Balding) *stdd s: hld up in tch: hdwy over 3f out: drvn to chse ldrs over 1f out: r.o wl to ld fnl 75yds: rdn out* **9/2**[1]

5050 **2** 1¼ **Beauchamp Xerxes**[92] 4537 4-9-12 **100** DaneO'Neill 7 106
(G A Butler) *led: rdn and fnd ex 2f out: clr over 1f out: drvn ent fnl f: hdd and no ex fnl 75yds* **18/1**

5500 **3** ½ **Viva Vettori**[15] 6888 6-8-10 **84** (b[1]) WilliamBuick 5 89
(D R C Elsworth) *stdd s: hld up in rr: hdwy over 2f out: swtchd rt and effrt u.p wl over 1f out: kpt on to go 3rd wl ins fnl f* **13/2**

0230 **4** *1* **Directorship**[28] 6562 4-8-12 **86** JimCrowley 2 91+
(P R Chamings) *t.k.h: hld up in midfield: nt clr run and shuffled bk over 2f out: swtchd lft 2f out: hdwy and edging rt u.p over 1f out: kpt on fnl 100yds: nt rch ldrs* **10/1**

0021 **5** *hd* **Signor Verdi**[91] 4603 3-8-9 **86** RichardHughes 1 89+
(B J Meehan) *chsd ldrs: rdn and chsd ldng pair wl over 1f out: kpt on same pce fnl f: hld whn n.m.r fnl 50yds* **5/1**[2]

3010 **6** *nk* **Emirates Dream (USA)**[28] 6562 3-9-7 **98** (p) FrankieDettori 3 99
(Saeed Bin Suroor) *wnt rt s: sn chsng ldr: rdn and nt pce of wnr 2f out: rallied u.p ent fnl f: styd on same pce fnl 150yds* **15/2**

5520 **7** 2¼ **Vainglory (USA)**[72] 5247 6-9-6 **94** MartinLane 10 90
(D M Simcock) *chsd ldrs: rdn and outpcd 2f out: keeping on same pce and hld whn pushed sltly rt ent fnl f* **22/1**

4022 **8** ¾ **Sand Skier**[26] 6620 3-9-1 **92** KierenFallon 6 86
(M Johnston) *chsd ldrs: rdn and unable qck 3f out: keeping on same pce u.p whn pushed sltly rt and n.m.r ent fnl f* **6/1**[3]

-000 **9** *7* **Big Bay (USA)**[140] 2971 4-8-9 **83** NeilCallan 4 61
(Jane Chapple-Hyam) *restless in stalls: rdn over 4f out: styd in tch tl wknd u.p 2f out* **50/1**

5343 **10** ½ **First Cat**[19] 6805 3-8-7 **84** DavidProbert 13 61
(R Hannon) *t.k.h: hld up in tch in midfield: rdn and effrt over 2f out: no prog and wkng whn pushed sltly rt wl over 1f out* **8/1**

300 **11** 1½ **Wannabe King**[15] 6888 4-9-12 **100** (p) ChrisCatlin 8 74
(D R Lanigan) *hld up towards rr: rdn and effrt over 2f out: hanging rt and no hdwy 2f out: wl btn over 1f out* **16/1**

2050 **12** 4½ **Lucky Dance (BRZ)**[16] 6877 8-8-9 **83** RobertHavlin 12 46
(T T Clement) *hld up towards rr: lost tch ent fnl 2f: eased wl ins fnl f* **25/1**

1m 40.66s (2.06) **Going Correction** +0.50s/f (Yiel)
WFA 3 from 4yo+ 3lb **12** Ran SP% **115.7**
Speed ratings (Par 109): **109,107,107,106,106 105,103,102,95,95 93,89**
toteswingers:1&2:£24.20, 1&3:£5.90, 2&3:£31.50 CSF £82.16 CT £533.03 TOTE £5.10: £1.70, £5.60, £2.50; EX 119.90 TRIFECTA Not won..
Owner Brick Racing **Bred** Raimon Bloodstock **Trained** Kingsclere, Hants

FOCUS
A decent, open-looking handicap. They came stands' side this time. The form is sound, rated around the second, with another step up from the winner.

NOTEBOOK
Brick Red had to be switched around horses to challenge but saw the trip out strongly to score. He'd found the ground just too soft at York last time but he appreciates a little dig, and conditions here proved perfect. His trainer has the Lincoln in mind for him next year. (op 11-2)
Beauchamp Xerxes, running for the first time since July, held the pack off for most of the race, but was eventually reeled in. Presumably he'll be kept going on the Polytrack as he might be capable of nicking a Listed race some time this winter on that surface. (op 16-1 tchd 14-1)
Viva Vettori, who remains winless on turf, didn't settle particularly well in the first-time blinkers so in the circumstances he ran quite well. He's rated 15lb higher on the AW and is another who will surely be chasing further success in Listed company on Polytrack this winter. (op 7-1 tchd 6-1)
Directorship raced quite near the stands' rail for most of the way and didn't enjoy the clearest of runs, although he's not one to be making too many excuses for as he only has a maiden win to his name in 15 starts. Official explanation: jockey said gelding was denied a clear run (op 11-1)
Signor Verdi looked an improving colt when last seen in July, but this ground was an unknown (hampered previous try on easy ground). He didn't really pick up on it and, while he might have needed the run, its just as possible that he needs a faster surface to be seen at his best. (op 11-2 tchd 6-1)
Emirates Dream(USA) looked well placed chasing the leader for much of the race, but he didn't quite see it out. This was a little disappointing considering he was proven in the conditions. (op 7-1)
Vainglory(USA), who was returning from a 72-day break and is weighted up to the hilt at the moment. (op 20-1)
Sand Skier ran as though he's had enough for the time being.

7234 BET365 BEN MARSHALL STKS (LISTED RACE) 1m
2:35 (2:35) (Class 1) 3-Y-0+

£19,869 (£7,532; £3,769; £1,879; £941; £472) **Stalls** Low

Form RPR
1-5 **1** **Kingsfort (USA)**[28] 6570 3-8-11 110 DaraghO'Donohoe 4 113
(Saeed Bin Suroor) *chsd ldng pair: rdn to chse ldr 2f out: drvn to chal over 1f out: led ins fnl f: styd on wl* **10/1**

5460 **2** 1¼ **The Cheka (IRE)**[15] 6885 4-9-0 107 (p) KierenFallon 1 110
(Eve Johnson Houghton) *chsd ldr: pushed along to ld 3f out: rdn over 2f out: clr w wnr wl over 1f out: hdd ins fnl f: no ex fnl 100yds* **15/2**

1002 **3** 2¼ **Balducci**[19] 6806 3-8-11 96 JimmyFortune 7 105+
(A M Balding) *stdd s: hld up off the pce in last trio: hdwy 3f out: rdn and chsd clr ldng pair wl over 1f out: kpt on fnl f but nvr gng pce to rch ldrs* **14/1**

3121 **4** 1¾ **Secrecy**[19] 6806 4-9-0 110 JamieSpencer 3 101
(Saeed Bin Suroor) *stdd s: hld up in last pair: hdwy wl over 2f out: chsd clr ldng pair and drvn over 1f out: kpt on same pce and no imp after* **15/8**[1]

0004 **5** *2* **Mia's Boy**[7] 7083 6-9-0 100 BarryMcHugh 5 96
(C A Dwyer) *racd off the pce in midfield: rdn and unable qck over 2f out: edgd rt u.p 2f out: nvr trbld ldrs* **14/1**

0 **6** *8* **Letty**[15] 6885 3-8-6 90 DavidProbert 2 73
(A Friebert, Hungary) *led: hdd 3f out: sn rdn: wknd u.p wl over 1f out* **40/1**

2110 **7** 3¾ **Nationalism**[28] 6562 3-8-11 102 (b[1]) WilliamBuick 6 69
(J H M Gosden) *stdd s: hld up in last trio: rdn and no rspnse ent fnl 3f: n.d* **9/2**[3]

0235 **8** *6* **Alexandros**[29] 6529 5-9-0 112 (v[1]) FrankieDettori 8 73
(Saeed Bin Suroor) *hld up off the pce in midfield: rdn and no hdwy over 2f out: wkng whn n.m.r 2f out: wl btn after: eased fnl f* **10/3**[2]

1m 40.27s (1.67) **Going Correction** +0.50s/f (Yiel)
WFA 3 from 4yo+ 3lb **8** Ran SP% **112.7**
Speed ratings (Par 111): **111,109,107,105,103 95,92,86**
toteswingers:1&2:£7.30, 1&3:£9.30, 2&3:£10.30 CSF £79.22 TOTE £12.60: £3.00, £2.30, £2.60; EX 85.30 Trifecta £745.30 Pool: £1,309.32 - 1.30 winning units..
Owner Godolphin **Bred** Airlie Stud **Trained** Newmarket, Suffolk

FOCUS
A messy Listed contest in which it paid to race close to the pace set by the free-running Letty, with the first two home the ones to slipstream the Hungarian filly in the early stages. The winning time was 0.39sec faster than the preceding handicap. Muddling Listed form, rated around the runner-up. Kingsfort returned to something like his 2yo form.

NOTEBOOK
Kingsfort(USA), Godolphin's apparent third-string, was a top-class 2-y-o in Ireland last year but a modest fifth of ten on his belated reappearance/debut for the yard at Redcar this month. He had every chance on adjusted ratings and was given a good ride by O'Donohoe, who always had him in a good position with those held up struggling to pick up. He quickened up well to hit the front inside the last furlong and although the form may be dubious, this did at least show that he retains ability. He remains totally unexposed and is now likely to head for the Dubai Carnival. (op 8-1)
The Cheka(IRE), disappointing since decent efforts in defeat behind Paco Boy in the both the Bet365 Mile and Lockinge in the spring, had cheekpieces on for the first time and they appeared to bring about something of a return to form. Having tracked the pacemaker early, he took over passing the 3f pole and did his best, but was outstayed by the Godolphin colt. (op 8-1 tchd 7-1)
Balducci, beaten by Secrecy at Salisbury this month, turned that form around and stayed on up the nearside rail from over a furlong out to fare best of those held up. This was a fair effort at the weights. (tchd 12-1)
Secrecy, never out of the first three in all ten previous outings, lost that record here but things didn't really go his way. He seemed to be ridden to beat Alexandros, as he slipstreamed him from the off, but when it became obvious that his stable companion was going nowhere fast, he found himself too far out of his ground and was never going to get close to the leading pair. (op 9-4 tchd 5-2 in places)
Mia's Boy, mainly disappointing since finishing runner-up three times at this level in the spring, had plenty on at these weights and probably ran close to his mark. (tchd 12-1)

Nationalism was blinkered for the first time following his modest effort from an unfavourable draw when favourite for the Cambridgeshire, but it soon became obvious that the headgear wasn't having a positive effect. Official explanation: jockey said colt lost its action (op 11-2)
Alexandros, tried in a visor following a modest effort in a Group 3 over C&D earlier this month, was the choice of Dettori but he disappointed again and found nothing off the bridle inside the last 3f. Official explanation: jockey said horse never travelled (op 3-1 tchd 7-2)

7235 BET365.COM E B F MONTROSE FILLIES' STKS (LISTED RACE) 1m

3:10 (3:12) (Class 1) 2-Y-O

£14,192 (£5,380; £2,692; £1,342; £672; £337) **Stalls** Low

Form RPR
21 **1** **Blue Bunting (USA)**[77] 5066 2-8-12 89 AhmedAjtebi 7 99+
(Mahmood Al Zarooni) *trckd ldr: ev ch and rdn 2f out: led over 1f out: hdd 1f out: kpt on gamely to ld again fnl 100yds: styd on wl* **10/1**
21 **2** *1* **Elas Diamond**[16] 6874 2-8-12 93 RyanMoore 12 97+
(J Noseda) *trckd ldr: ev ch and rdn 2f out: drvn to ld 1f out: hung rt and hdd fnl 100yds: stl hanging and no ex after* **7/4**[1]
1213 **3** *nse* **Whisper Louise (IRE)**[28] 6563 2-8-12 89 MickyFenton 1 97
(Mrs P Sly) *hld up in stands' side trio: hdwy ent fnl 2f: rdn to chse ldrs over 1f out: edging rt u.p but kpt on wl fnl f* **14/1**
241 **4** *2* **Aneedah (IRE)**[11] 7000 2-8-12 95 WilliamBuick 2 92
(J H M Gosden) *racd keenly: led stands' side trio: chsd ldrs overall: rdn and ev ch over 1f out: no ex and btn fnl 150yds* **9/2**[2]
44 **5** *nk* **Nabah**[14] 6927 2-8-12 0 NeilCallan 5 92
(C E Brittain) *t.k.h: hld up in tch: rdn ent fnl 2f: edgd lft and sltly outpcd over 1f out: rallied u.p and edgd rt fnl f: kpt on* **7/1**[3]
1 **6** *2 ½* **Matula (IRE)**[48] 5985 2-8-12 79 JimCrowley 9 86
(R M Beckett) *stdd s: hld up in tch in last pair: hdwy to chse ldrs over 2f out: rdn 2f out: wknd u.p 1f out* **16/1**
14 **7** *1* **Face Reality (USA)**[7] 7098 2-8-12 91 RichardHughes 6 84
(R Hannon) *stdd s: hld up wl in tch in last pair: hdwy over 2f out: styd on same pce and no imp ent fnl f* **16/1**
051 **8** *2* **Isolate**[25] 6651 2-8-12 78 JimmyFortune 8 80
(H Morrison) *led: rdn ent fnl 2f: hdd over 1f out: wknd ent fnl f* **33/1**
4 **9** *1 ¼* **Whey Sauce (JPN)**[15] 6884 2-8-12 0 JackMitchell 4 77
(P W Chapple-Hyam) *t.k.h: hld up chsng ldrs: rdn ent fnl 2f: btn over 1f out: wknd fnl f* **12/1**
3 **10** *3 ¼* **Parvana (IRE)**[43] 6150 2-8-12 0 JamieSpencer 11 70
(W J Haggas) *hld up wl in tch: rdn jst over 2f out: sn struggling: wl btn over 1f out* **15/2**
3 **11** *9* **Pursuing**[13] 6964 2-8-12 0 TomEaves 3 50
(B Smart) *chsd ldr in stands' side trio: rdn and struggling over 2f out: sn bhd* **100/1**

1m 41.65s (3.05) **Going Correction** +0.50s/f (Yiel) **11 Ran SP% 118.0**
Speed ratings (Par 100): **104,103,102,100,100 98,97,95,93,90 81**
toteswingers:1&2:£6.60, 1&3:£12.70, 2&3:£8.20 CSF £27.83 TOTE £9.00: £2.50, £1.60, £3.10; EX 33.10 Trifecta £253.00 Pool: £1,203.78 - 3.52 winning units..
Owner Godolphin **Bred** B M Kelley **Trained** Newmarket, Suffolk

FOCUS
With so little separating the best 2-y-o fillies around, this looked a potentially informative Listed contest, providing something with a chance to make its mark on the betting for next year's Classics. Indeed, in the previous seven years the race has thrown up two Oaks winners in Ouija Board (third in 2003) and Midday (fourth in 2008), an Oaks runner-up in Something Exciting (second in 2004), and a 1,000 Guineas third in Super Sleuth (second in 2008), so it's a race not to be dismissed. The field split into two groups, with three runners coming stands' side and the rest heading up the middle, and it's difficult to know whether there was a draw advantage. The form looks routine for the grade.

NOTEBOOK
Blue Bunting(USA) appreciated every yard of the mile at Doncaster last time and once again she was strongest at the finish on this step up in class. A half-sister to a dual winner over 2m plus, she is clearly going to have no trouble with 1m4f next year, and has the potential to develop into an Oaks candidate, but her connections pointed the way towards a campaign in Dubai, with the UAE 1000 Guineas and Oaks in mind. (op 9-1)
Elas Diamond, runaway winner of a Nottingham maiden last time out, travelled comfortably just behind the leader and picked up well exiting the Dip, but the winner just saw it out that bit better. She remains an interesting prospect for next season, when she should have no trouble with 1m2f, and will perhaps stay 1m4f. (op 9-4 tchd 5-2 in a place)
Whisper Louise(IRE), by far the most exposed filly in the line-up, came from off the pace to do best of the trio who raced in the stands' side group. She got the longer trip without any problem and, clearly thriving on racing, has done nothing but progress this season. (op 10-1)
Aneedah(IRE), who made all to win her maiden last time, led two others on the stands' side and kept on well. She's not sure to want to go any further than this next year. (tchd 5-1)
Nabah failed to strongly advertise the Rockfel form as she only finished slightly nearer the winner here than she did in that Group 2. She took a while to get into full stride but was closing at the finish, and the likelihood is that she'll do better over further on quicker ground next year. (tchd 15-2 tchd 8-1 in places)
Matula(IRE), easy winner of a Ffos Las maiden on her debut, was taking a big step up in class, but she acquitted herself well despite racing keenly, quickening with the principals initially, before weakening inside the last. There's more to come from her next year and she should be well up to winning at this level. (op 12-1 tchd 11-1)
Face Reality(USA), about whom there were stamina doubts, failed to get home, and a return to shorter will be in her favour. By a dirt sire out of a mare who won on an AW surface, it would be interesting to see her given an outing on the Polytrack.
Isolate, who made the running up the centre, didn't find the ground playing to her strengths as much as at Leicester last time. (op 25-1)
Whey Sauce(JPN) couldn't get cover early and as a result she failed to settle. (op 14-1)
Parvana(IRE) was one of the first under pressure and dropped out very tamely. This was clearly not her true form and perhaps she was simply over the top. (op 17-2 tchd 9-1)

7236 BET365 ZETLAND CONDITIONS STKS 1m 2f

3:45 (3:45) (Class 2) 2-Y-O

£7,477 (£2,239; £1,119; £560; £279; £140) **Stalls** Low

Form RPR
0112 **1** **Indigo Way**[30] 6505 2-9-0 88 RyanMoore 9 100
(B J Meehan) *hld up in rr of main gp: pushed along and hdwy 4f out: drvn to chse ldr and swtchd rt over 1f out: styd on wl to ld ins fnl f: battled on gamely* **11/2**[3]
1224 **2** *shd* **Measuring Time**[28] 6560 2-9-3 105 RichardHughes 8 103
(R Hannon) *chsd ldrs: wnt 2nd 4f out: pushed into ld 3f out: rdn and edgd lft over 2f out: clr over 1f out: drvn and hdd ins fnl f: rallied gamely: jst hld* **4/1**[2]
11 **3** *3 ¼* **Picture Editor**[25] 6653 2-9-3 91 IanMongan 5 97
(H R A Cecil) *in tch: hdwy to chse ldrs over 3f out: rdn and n.m.r wl over 2f out: swtchd rt and chsd ldng pair u.p 2f out: no imp over 1f out: wknd ins fnl f* **4/6**[1]
14 **4** *9* **Shooting Gallery**[23] 6702 2-9-0 90 AhmedAjtebi 4 78
(Mahmood Al Zarooni) *stdd s: t.k.h: hld up in rr of main gp: hdwy to chse ldrs 4f out: rdn and wknd 2f out* **8/1**
0423 **5** *1 ¾* **Barathea Dancer (IRE)**[28] 6555 2-8-9 74 KierenFallon 10 70
(R A Teal) *racd keenly: led tl hdd and rdn 3f out: btn 2f out: wknd* **33/1**
62 **6** *6* **Kadoodd (IRE)**[20] 6779 2-9-0 0 ChrisCatlin 7 64
(M R Channon) *in tch in midfield: rdn and struggling over 3f out: no ch fr over 2f out* **33/1**
0000 **7** *28* **Blade Pirate**[16] 6859 2-9-0 45 MichaelHills 2 14
(J Ryan) *stdd s: t.k.h early: hld up in rr: lost tch 4f out: t.o* **150/1**
0611 **8** *nk* **Buxfizz (USA)**[8] 7066 2-9-0 85 JimCrowley 6 13
(R A Mills) *t.k.h early: hld up in tch in midfield: rdn and wknd over 3f out: eased fr over 1f out: t.o* **14/1**
000 **9** *10* **Oceans Destination**[3] 7164 2-9-0 0 (b[1]) SophieDoyle 3 —
(J Ryan) *sn struggling in rr: t.o 5f out* **150/1**
0306 **10** *1* **Point Du Jour (FR)**[33] 6426 2-9-0 76 NeilCallan 1 —
(I A Wood) *t.k.h: chsd ldr tl 4f out: sn dropped out: t.o and virtually p.u fr over 1f out* **80/1**

2m 9.65s (3.85) **Going Correction** +0.50s/f (Yiel) **10 Ran SP% 121.6**
Speed ratings (Par 101): **104,103,101,94,92 87,65,65,57,56**
toteswingers:1&2:£3.30, 1&3:£2.50, 2&3:£1.90 CSF £28.71 TOTE £7.20: £1.80, £1.90, £1.10; EX 35.60 Trifecta £24.30 Pool: £839.49 - 25.54 winning units..
Owner N Attenborough,Mrs L Mann,Mrs L Way **Bred** Mrs Johnny Eddis **Trained** Manton, Wilts

FOCUS
Not as competitive as the numbers would suggest as half the field started 33-1 or longer, but this was a severe test of stamina for these youngsters and they finished well spread out. Twice Over in 2007 would be by far the highest-profile winner of this race in recent years. The form looks straightforward rated around the placed horses.

NOTEBOOK
Indigo Way, thwarted by a whisker in his hat-trick bid in a 1m soft-ground nursery here last time, looked a likely stayer judged on recent efforts and so it proved as stamina was at a premium here. He was well off the pace and being ridden along 3f from home, but he warmed to the task and managed to get to the front well inside the last furlong before grinding out victory. He looks a nice staying prospect for next year, especially when there is some cut in the ground. (op 6-1 tchd 13-2)
Measuring Time was by far the highest rated in this field, mainly on account of his narrow defeat in the Solario, and his breeding suggested this trip should be within range. Sent for home passing the 2f pole, he edged over to the stands' rail but it still looked as though he would take some catching and it was only well inside the last furlong that he was worn down. He tries very hard and stays well, but he may not be the easiest to place next season with an official mark of 105. Official explanation: jockey said colt hung left (tchd 9-2 in a place)
Picture Editor came into this a general 12-1 co-second favourite for the Derby following his defeat of an odds-on shot (who had previously run Frankel close) on his debut at Doncaster, before winning a three-runner non-event on heavy ground at Leicester at odds of 1-14. He was already under pressure when forced to switch right over 2f from home and it was only his class that gave his supporters hope for as long as it did, but he ended up well held by the front pair. This was disappointing, but the Leicester win may have given the wrong impression over his ground requirements and perhaps he really needs it quicker. Either way, he is worth another chance. (op 8-13 tchd 8-11 in places)
Shooting Gallery, fourth of five in a Saint-Cloud Group 3 this month, has looked a stayer and moved strongly into contention 3f out, but he appeared to have run his race when hampered against the nearside rail a furlong later. (op 10-1 tchd 11-1 in a place)
Barathea Dancer(IRE), placed in a couple of 1m nurseries, made much of the running but she was keen enough early and that was always likely to tell.
Kadoodd(IRE) found little once off the bridle 3f out, but at least now qualifies for a mark. (tchd 28-1)

7237 BET365 JAMES SEYMOUR STKS (LISTED RACE) 1m 2f

4:20 (4:20) (Class 1) 3-Y-O+

£19,869 (£7,532; £3,769; £1,879; £941; £472) **Stalls** Low

Form RPR
2012 **1** **Timepiece**[15] 6886 3-8-11 111 IanMongan 8 112+
(H R A Cecil) *chsd ldrs: rdn to chse ldr ent fnl 3f: drvn to ld over 1f out: sn hung bdly lft and racing on stands' rail 1f out: styd on wl to draw clr fnl f* **2/1**[2]
2614 **2** *3 ½* **Prince Siegfried (FR)**[49] 5951 4-9-3 110 (v[1]) WilliamBuick 7 106
(Saeed Bin Suroor) *led: qcknd gallop and clr 3f out: rdn and pressed over 2f out: hdd over 1f out: wknd ins fnl f* **7/1**
-356 **3** *nk* **Nideeb**[29] 6529 3-8-12 99 NeilCallan 2 105
(C E Brittain) *t.k.h: hld up wl in tch: rdn and outpcd 3f out: rallied u.p over 1f out: wnt 3rd ins fnl f: pressing for 2nd nr fin: no ch w wnr* **33/1**
4006 **4** *2 ¼* **Cumulus Nimbus**[7] 7100 3-8-12 92 RyanMoore 1 101+
(R Hannon) *stdd s: t.k.h: hld up in rr: pushed along and outpcd ent fnl 3f: hdwy u.p over 1f out: kpt on to go 4th ins fnl f: nvr trbld ldrs* **16/1**
1012 **5** *2 ¼* **Penitent**[29] 6529 4-9-7 113 RichardHughes 6 100
(W J Haggas) *in tch in midfield: pushed along over 3f out: rdn and chsd ldng pair over 1f out: no imp: wknd and lost 2 pls ins fnl f* **11/2**[3]
0-43 **6** *1 ¾* **Kirklees (IRE)**[22] 6720 6-9-3 109 FrankieDettori 3 93
(Saeed Bin Suroor) *chsd ldr tl ent fnl 3f: sn rdn and unable qck: wl btn over 1f out* **7/4**[1]
40-4 **7** *11* **Spring Of Fame (USA)**[261] 517 4-9-3 110 DaraghO'Donohoe 5 71
(Saeed Bin Suroor) *hld up in last pair: lost tch 3f out: wl bhd fnl 2f: eased ins fnl f* **22/1**

2m 11.02s (5.22) **Going Correction** +0.50s/f (Yiel)
WFA 3 from 4yo+ 5lb **7 Ran SP% 110.8**
Speed ratings (Par 111): **99,96,95,94,92 90,82**
toteswingers:1&2:£2.70, 1&3:£9.70, 2&3:£15.60 CSF £15.25 TOTE £3.30: £1.80, £4.10; EX 19.30 Trifecta £312.80 Pool: £815.88 - 1.93 winning units..
Owner K Abdulla **Bred** Juddmonte Farms Ltd **Trained** Newmarket, Suffolk

FOCUS
A solid enough race on paper for its Listed status. The form is muddling though and the winner did not need to be at her best.

NOTEBOOK
Timepiece was a leading Oaks candidate earlier in the campaign and, while things didn't work out in that regard, she's since found success over shorter, winning the Sandringham Handicap and now this Listed race, her first success beyond 1m. Just about best in at the weights, she was better for her return to action here at the last meeting and quickened up nicely to take over, before hanging left all the way over to the stands' side rail. She had plenty left in the tank, though, and kept on well to run out a clear winner. She has her quirks - she hung left when denied in the Lingfield Oaks Trial earlier in the year - but clearly has plenty of ability, too, and it wouldn't be a surprise if she made up into an even better 4-y-o. There must be a big temptation to keep her in training too, as she's yet to score at Group level. (op 9-4)
Prince Siegfried(FR), runner-up in this race last year, wore a visor for the first time and tried to make every yard. His last three victories were all-the-way wins, and so credit goes to the winner for seeing him off as he was very much allowed the run of the things here. (op 6-1 tchd 11-2)
Nideeb ran a sound race against rivals rated more than 10lb better than him, but is likely to remain a difficult horse to place. (op 25-1)

The Form Book, Raceform Ltd, Compton, RG20 6NL

Cumulus Nimbus, the lowest rated horse in the field, became detached from the rest half a mile out and his rider appeared to be accepting the situation, but he kept nudging along and, as some of the principals weakened, he was able to stay on for a position that flatters him. (tchd 20-1)
Penitent, for whom this longer trip was the concern beforehand, simply failed to get home. A return to 1m is surely in order now. (op 4-1 tchd 6-1)
Kirklees(IRE) was the Godolphin first string on jockey bookings, but he failed to pick up in the ground and almost certainly found conditions too testing. He's far more at home on a sounder surface or Polytrack. (op 2-1 tchd 9-4 in places)
Spring Of Fame(USA) never really threatened to land a blow, but then again his best form is over shorter than this and he hadn't run since February, so he's fully entitled to come on for it. (op 20-1)

7238 FINANCIALS AT BET365.COM H'CAP — 7f
4:55 (4:55) (Class 4) (0-85,85) 3-Y-O+ — £4,533 (£1,348; £674; £336) Stalls Low

Form — RPR

0111 **1** **Clumber Place**[31] 6460 4-8-7 **71** .... FrannyNorton 9 — 80
(R C Guest) chsd ldr tl led 3f out: rdn ent fnl 2f: hdd over 1f out: kpt on gamely to ld again fnl 100yds: all out **11/1**

0330 **2** *hd* **Duster**[19] 6798 3-8-13 **79** .... RichardHughes 17 — 88
(H Morrison) led tl 3f out: styd prom: rdn and sltly outpcd over 1f out: rallied gamely u.p ins fnl f: pressed wnr nr fin: nt quite rch wnr **16/1**

2-14 **3** *nk* **Call To Reason (IRE)**[48] 5993 3-9-3 **83** .... RyanMoore 16 — 91+
(J Noseda) hld up towards rr: pushed along and hdwy over 2f out: swtchd rt and hdwy u.p to chse ldrs 1f out: kpt on wl fnl f: nt quite rch ldrs **4/1**[1]

2136 **4** *nk* **Greensward**[15] 6888 4-9-7 **85** .... KierenFallon 4 — 92+
(B J Meehan) hld up in midfield: hdwy jst over 2f out: rdn to ld over 1f out: drvn and hdd fnl 100yds: no ex and lost 2 pls towards fin **4/1**[1]

610 **5** *2 3/4* **Beaver Patrol (IRE)**[20] 6780 8-8-11 **78**....(v) Louis-PhilippeBeuzelin(3) 15 — 78
(Eve Johnson Houghton) chsd ldrs: rdn and unable qck ent fnl 2f: kpt on same pce u.p fr over 1f out **33/1**

-512 **6** *hd* **Lord Aeryn (IRE)**[22] 6709 3-8-13 **79** .... BarryMcHugh 8 — 78
(R A Fahey) in tch in midfield: hdwy over 2f out: rdn and ev ch over 1f out: keeping on same whn n.m.r and lost pl jst over 1f out: styd on same pce after **15/2**[2]

0065 **7** *1/2* **One Way Or Another (AUS)**[20] 6776 7-9-7 **85** .... LukeMorris 20 — 83
(J R Gask) stdd s: hld up towards rr: hdwy gng wl over 2f out: rdn and effrt wl over 1f out: drvn and no hdwy 1f out: wknd ins fnl f **8/1**[3]

4101 **8** *1 1/2* **Rosedale**[12] 6992 3-8-5 **71** oh1 .... TadhgO'Shea 10 — 65
(J A R Toller) hld up in tch in midfield: rdn and effrt ent fnl 2f: edgd rt u.p over 1f out: kpt on fnl f: nvr gng pce to rch ldrs **14/1**

1510 **9** *nk* **Rough Rock (IRE)**[9] 7046 5-8-4 **73** .... AdamBeschizza(5) 19 — 66
(C A Dwyer) in tch: rdn and unable qck ent fnl 2f: styd on same pce u.p fr jst over 1f out **25/1**

0000 **10** *1/2* **Victoria Sponge (IRE)**[7] 7097 4-9-1 **79** ....(p) NeilCallan 13 — 70
(S C Williams) s.i.s: in rr: hdwy into midfield 1/2-way: rdn and unable qck 2f out: one pce and no imp fr over 1f out **11/1**

3506 **11** *1* **Spitfire**[26] 6625 5-9-4 **82** .... JimmyQuinn 14 — 71
(J R Jenkins) hld up in midfield: rdn and effrt ent fnl 2f: wknd u.p ent fnl f **20/1**

4651 **12** *2 1/4* **Requisite**[9] 7046 5-8-12 **76** ....(v) MartinLane 2 — 59
(I A Wood) hld up towards rr: hdwy 3f out: rdn ent fnl 2f: wknd u.p over 1f out **22/1**

3356 **13** *1/2* **Suffolk Punch (IRE)**[28] 6564 3-9-2 **82** ....(v[1]) JimmyFortune 11 — 63
(A M Balding) chsd ldrs: rdn over 2f out: wknd u.p wl over 1f out: wl btn fnl f **10/1**

2500 **14** *3/4* **Mambo Spirit (IRE)**[7] 7091 6-8-10 **77** .... JohnFahy(3) 5 — 56
(Stef Higgins) chsd ldrs tl rdn and struggling over 2f out: wl hld fr over 1f out **33/1**

0000 **15** *2 1/4* **Quarrel (USA)**[21] 6739 3-9-0 **80** .... MichaelHills 18 — 53
(W J Haggas) stdd s: t.k.h: hld up towards rr: rdn and effrt wl over 1f out: no hdwy: nvr trbld ldrs **40/1**

2000 **16** *1* **Nightjar (USA)**[58] 5703 5-9-0 **78** .... DarryllHolland 7 — 49
(K A Ryan) hld up towards rr: rdn and no prog over 2f out: n.d **25/1**

4500 **17** *3 1/4* **Protector (SAF)**[7] 7092 9-8-11 **75** ....(t) RobertHavlin 12 — 37
(T T Clement) a in rr: rdn and struggling 3f out: wl bhd fnl 2f **40/1**

0000 **18** *1 3/4* **Rum King (USA)**[20] 6776 3-9-0 **80** .... JimCrowley 3 — 37
(R Hannon) stdd s: t.k.h: hld up in rr: n.d **66/1**

2400 **19** *11* **Arabian Pearl (IRE)**[15] 6887 4-8-11 **75** ....(b) JackMitchell 1 — —
(P W Chapple-Hyam) racd alone on stands' side: nvr trbld ldrs: wl bhd fnl 2f: eased ins fnl f **25/1**

1m 27.91s (2.51) **Going Correction** +0.50s/f (Yiel)
WFA 3 from 4yo+ 2lb — 19 Ran SP% 134.1
Speed ratings (Par 105): **105,104,104,104,100 100,100,98,98,97 96,93,93,92,89 88,84,82,70**
toteswingers:1&2:£22.20, 1&3:£8.70, 2&3:£14.30 CSF £170.24 CT £870.38 TOTE £11.70: £2.80, £4.00, £2.00, £1.50; EX 269.90 Trifecta £598.50 Part won. Pool: £808.84 - 0.10 winning units. Place 6 £203.12, Place 5 £54.99.
Owner The Clumber Park Syndicate **Bred** Worksop Manor Stud **Trained** Stainforth, S Yorks

FOCUS
A devilishly trappy handicap in which the bulk of the field raced centre to far-side, though Arabian Pearl ran a solo up the stands' rail without much success. This race had been won by a 3-y-o in six of the seven previous years, but it went to the older brigade this time. The first two were always up with the pace and the winner produced a clear personal best.
Nightjar(USA) Official explanation: jockey said gelding hung right
T/Plt: £211.50 to a £1 stake. Pool:£78,316.27 - 270.20 winning tickets T/Qpdt: £59.40 to a £1 stake. Pool:£7,563.94 - 94.17 winning tickets SP

7209 WOLVERHAMPTON (A.W) (L-H)
Saturday, October 30

OFFICIAL GOING: Standard
Wind: Light behind Weather: Overcast

7239 GOT THE FEELING? GET TO LADBROKES H'CAP — 5f 216y(P)
6:50 (6:51) (Class 5) (0-70,71) 3-Y-O+ — £2,388 (£705; £352) Stalls Low

Form — RPR

5062 **1** **Victorian Bounty**[12] 6987 5-9-8 **71** .... MickyFenton 6 — 80
(Stef Higgins) sn led: rdn and hdd over 1f out: rallied to ld post **15/2**

300 **2** *hd* **Rainy Night**[22] 6714 4-9-4 **67** ....(p) PaulHanagan 1 — 76
(R Hollinshead) chsd ldrs: led over 1f out: sn rdn: hdd post **6/1**[3]

3201 **3** *1/2* **Forever's Girl**[15] 6898 4-8-13 **69** .... AdamCarter(7) 5 — 76
(G R Oldroyd) hld up: hdwy and nt clr run over 1f out: r.o to go 3rd post: nt rch ldrs **9/2**[2]

614 **4** *nk* **Doc Hay (USA)**[8] 7052 3-9-4 **68** .... ShaneKelly 2 — 74
(P F I Cole) hld up: hdwy 2f out: rdn and ev ch over 1f out: styd on same pce: lost 3rd post **4/1**[1]

0665 **5** *2* **Methaaly (IRE)**[22] 6714 7-8-11 **67** ....(be) JosephYoung(7) 11 — 67
(M Mullineaux) hood removed sltly late: hld up: r.o ins fnl f: nrst fin **25/1**

1000 **6** *3/4* **Bosun Breese**[3] 7175 5-9-7 **70** .... RichardHughes 12 — 67
(T D Barron) led early: chsd wnr tl rdn 2f out: edgd lft and no ex ins fnl f **7/1**

2000 **7** *2 1/4* **Gwilym (GER)**[38] 6280 7-9-7 **70** .... DaneO'Neill 4 — 60
(D Haydn Jones) prom: rdn over 1f out: no ex fnl f **14/1**

3545 **8** *1 3/4* **Shaluca**[78] 5044 3-9-1 **65** .... SebSanders 10 — 49
(E S McMahon) prom: rdn over 2f out: edgd lft and wknd over 1f out **10/1**

0000 **9** *1* **Blown It (USA)**[30] 6492 4-8-13 **62** .... FergusSweeney 3 — 43
(J S Goldie) chsd ldrs: rdn over 2f out: wknd over 1f out **9/1**

5010 **10** *1* **Rothesay Dancer**[30] 6491 7-9-3 **66** .... ChrisCatlin 7 — 44
(J S Goldie) hld up: rdn over 2f out: a in rr **28/1**

3200 **11** *4 1/2* **Toms Return**[29] 6524 3-9-3 **67** .... GeorgeBaker 13 — 31
(J R Best) hld up: rdn over 1f out: a in rr **16/1**

1m 14.7s (-0.30) **Going Correction** 0.0s/f (Stan)
WFA 3 from 4yo+ 1lb — 11 Ran SP% 115.7
Speed ratings (Par 103): **102,101,101,100,98 97,94,91,90,89 83**
toteswingers:1&2:£8.50, 1&3:£5.40, 2&3:£5.70 CSF £51.16 CT £231.68 TOTE £8.60: £3.50, £1.30, £1.20; EX 56.50.
Owner David Gilbert **Bred** Mrs P D Gray And H Farr **Trained** Lambourn, Berks

FOCUS
A run-of-the-mill sprint. It didn't pay to sit too far back, nothing ever seriously threatening from well off the pace. Straightforward form.

7240 EUROPEAN BREEDERS' FUND MEDIAN AUCTION MAIDEN STKS — 5f 216y(P)
7:20 (7:20) (Class 5) 2-Y-O — £2,978 (£886; £442; £221) Stalls Low

Form — RPR

3002 **1** **Magic Stella**[12] 6986 2-8-12 **75** .... RichardHughes 4 — 70
(A P Jarvis) sn led: rdn and hdd over 1f out: rallied to ld ins fnl f: r.o **9/4**[2]

0622 **2** *1 1/4* **Strictly Pink (IRE)**[10] 7021 2-8-12 **78** .... PaulHanagan 8 — 66
(A Bailey) chsd wnr tl led over 1f out: sn rdn and hung lft: hdd and unable qck ins fnl f **10/11**[1]

6345 **3** *1/2* **Crucis Abbey (IRE)**[26] 6628 2-9-3 **67** .... WilliamCarson 9 — 70
(J W Unett) chsd ldrs: rdn and hung lft over 1f out: r.o **12/1**

4 *3/4* **Green Apple** 2-8-12 0 .... FergusSweeney 5 — 63+
(P J Makin) dwlt: hld up: hdwy over 1f out: r.o **18/1**

5 *3 3/4* **Russian Winter** 2-9-0 0 .... RobertLButler(3) 6 — 56
(T J Etherington) hld up in tch: rdn over 1f out: edgd lft and wknd fnl f **33/1**

6 *1 1/4* **Three Opera Divas** 2-8-12 0 .... GregFairley 2 — 48
(M Johnston) chsd ldrs: rdn over 2f out: hung lft and wknd over 1f out **18/1**

0523 **7** *1 1/2* **Rowan Spirit (IRE)**[25] 6646 2-9-3 **69** .... SebSanders 1 — 51
(W M Brisbourne) hld up: sme hdwy whn hmpd over 1f out: nvr on terms **9/1**[3]

0 **8** *1 1/4* **Ladydolly**[23] 6697 2-8-12 0 .... CathyGannon 3 — 39
(R Brotherton) s.i.s: sn pushed along and a in rr **80/1**

1m 15.36s (0.36) **Going Correction** 0.0s/f (Stan) — 8 Ran SP% 115.5
Speed ratings (Par 95): **97,95,94,93,88 87,85,83**
toteswingers:1&2:£1.10, 1&3:£4.40, 2&3:£2.40 CSF £4.65 TOTE £3.80: £1.80, £1.10, £1.40; EX 5.90.
Owner Philip Milburn **Bred** Philip Milburn **Trained** Twyford, Bucks

FOCUS
A maiden which was always likely to develop into a match. The form looks pretty weak with the third the best guide.

NOTEBOOK
Magic Stella rallied when headed to get off the mark at the ninth time of asking. She may not prove the easiest to place from now on, having already had her limitations exposed in handicaps, but she did at least show a likeable attitude under pressure. (tchd 5-2)
Strictly Pink(IRE) has now finished runner-up on her last three starts and should go one better before long if kept on the go, maidens only likely to get weaker as we head into winter, though it could be argued she didn't find as much as looked likely having appeared to be going a bit better than the winner turning in. (tchd Evens)
Crucis Abbey(IRE) had made the frame on his two previous tries on Polytrack and wasted no time putting a below-par effort on testing ground last time behind him, though he's starting to look a bit exposed now. (op 16-1)
Green Apple, a daughter of Needwood Blade out of a useful 6f/7f winner, made a promising start and is sure to improve, probably enough to go close in a similar event next time, running green for much of the way (started slowly) but keeping on well once she finally got the hang of things. (op 16-1 tchd 20-1)
Russian Winter, a gelded son of Tobougg out of a winning sprinter, hinted at ability and is entitled to improve for this initial experience. Official explanation: jockey said gelding hung left in straight
Three Opera Divas hails from a leading yard but there was no strength behind her in the market and she didn't show any immediate promise. (tchd 16-1)
Rowan Spirit(IRE)'s effort is best ignored as, having travelled comfortably enough under restraint, he was threatening to make some headway when cut off against the rail approaching the final furlong. (op 8-1)

7241 BEST ODDS GUARANTEED AT LADBROKES.COM H'CAP — 7f 32y(P)
7:50 (7:51) (Class 5) (0-70,70) 3-Y-O+ — £2,388 (£705; £352) Stalls High

Form — RPR

2022 **1** **The Happy Hammer (IRE)**[17] 6852 4-8-12 **61** .... WilliamCarson 3 — 65
(Eugene Stanford) chsd ldrs: rdn to ld ins fnl f: jst hld on **7/2**[1]

3060 **2** *nk* **Gazboolou**[9] 7046 6-8-12 **68** .... JamesRogers(7) 7 — 72+
(David Pinder) hld up: rdn over 1f out: r.o wl ins fnl f: nt quite rch wnr **8/1**

00 **3** *hd* **Mr Lu**[22] 6710 5-8-9 **58** .... ChrisCatlin 9 — 61
(J S Goldie) a.p: rdn over 1f out: hung lft ins fnl f: r.o **33/1**

240 **4** *hd* **Buxton**[45] 6085 6-9-7 **70** ....(t) RobertHavlin 10 — 72+
(R Ingram) s.i.s: hld up: r.o wl ins fnl f: nrst fin **16/1**

405 **5** *nk* **Royal Blade (IRE)**[61] 5588 3-8-2 **60** .... HarryBentley(7) 4 — 62
(A P Jarvis) led: rdn and hung rt over 1f out: hdd ins fnl f: styd on **25/1**

5005 **6** *3/4* **King's Caprice**[19] 6812 9-9-2 **65** .... LukeMorris 11 — 65+
(J C Fox) s.i.s: hld up: rdn over 1f out: r.o wl ins fnl f: nrst fin **14/1**

0324 **7** *1* **Cape Kimberley**[52] 5852 3-9-1 **66** .... PaulHanagan 1 — 63
(A G Newcombe) chsd ldrs: rdn over 1f out: no ex wl ins fnl f **7/2**[1]

5521 **8** *hd* **Charles Parnell (IRE)**[8] 7051 7-9-1 **67** .... MichaelStainton(3) 8 — 63
(S P Griffiths) s.i.s: hdwy to chse ldr over 5f out: rdn over 1f out: no ex wl ins fnl f **9/1**

2602 **9** *1 1/2* **Cawdor (IRE)**[30] 6491 4-9-4 **67** .... KierenFallon 6 — 59
(Mrs L Stubbs) sn pushed along in rr: hdwy u.p over 1f out: no ex wl ins fnl f **7/1**[2]

3036 **10** ½ **Liberty Trail (IRE)**[35] 6371 4-8-8 57 CathyGannon 5 48
(P D Evans) *hld up in tch: outpcd 1/2-way: n.d after* **10/1**

0002 **11** 2 **Rubenstar (IRE)**[17] 6854 7-9-3 66 RichardHughes 2 52
(Patrick Morris) *hld up: hdwy over 2f out: rdn over 1f out: wknd ins fnl f* **15/2**[3]

1m 29.24s (-0.36) **Going Correction** 0.0s/f (Stan)
WFA 3 from 4yo+ 2lb 11 Ran SP% **118.2**
Speed ratings (Par 103): **102,101,101,101,100 100,98,98,96,96 94**
toteswingers:1&2:£14.60, 1&3:£32.70, 2&3:£50.10 CSF £32.18 CT £814.19 TOTE £3.10: £1.40, £3.80, £8.30; EX 27.60.
Owner Newmarket Connections Ltd **Bred** Rathbarry Stud **Trained** Newmarket, Suffolk

FOCUS
Just an ordinary handicap, the bunched finish suggesting it didn't contain many ahead of their marks either. Prominent runners seemed favoured and the form is rated around the winner.

7242 BET IN-PLAY AT LADBROKES.COM MAIDEN AUCTION STKS 1m 141y(P)
8:20 (8:20) (Class 5) 2-Y-O £2,266 (£674; £337; £168) Stalls Low

Form RPR

52 **1** **Mattoral**[30] 6498 2-9-1 0 SebSanders 5 74
(P J Makin) *a.p: chsd ldr over 6f out: rdn over 1f out: led ins fnl f: all out* **9/4**[1]

2 **2** hd **Copper Canyon**[60] 5626 2-8-9 0 FergusSweeney 8 68
(A B Haynes) *s.i.s: hdwy over 6f out: shkn up over 2f out: rdn and edgd lft ins fnl f: r.o* **6/1**[2]

0 **3** ½ **Phase Shift**[16] 6866 2-8-10 0 RichardHughes 1 68
(W R Muir) *chsd ldr 2f: remained handy: rdn and swtchd rt over 1f out: r.o* **9/1**

3622 **4** 1¼ **Zamina (IRE)**[14] 6936 2-8-1 67 JohnFahy(3) 4 59
(S Kirk) *led: rdn over 1f out: hdd and unable qck insde fnl f* **9/4**[1]

53 **5** 2½ **Polly Holder (IRE)**[2] 7198 2-8-7 0 CathyGannon 7 57
(A Bailey) *hld up: rdn over 1f out: styd on ins fnl f: nvr trbld ldrs* **8/1**

6 **6** 6 **Dancing Cavalier (IRE)**[26] 6628 2-8-12 0 LukeMorris 6 49
(R Hollinshead) *hld up in tch: rdn over 2f out: wknd over 1f out* **33/1**

7 2¼ **Lovers Peace (IRE)** 2-8-4 0 PaulHanagan 2 36
(J J Quinn) *s.i.s: hld up: effrt over 2f out: wknd over 1f out* **15/2**[3]

00 **8** 13 **Mariyah**[115] 3785 2-8-7 0 WilliamCarson 3 12
(M Blanshard) *chsd ldrs: lost pl over 6f out: sn drvn along: wknd over 2f out* **100/1**

1m 51.85s (1.35) **Going Correction** 0.0s/f (Stan) 8 Ran SP% **112.6**
Speed ratings (Par 95): **94,93,93,92,90 84,82,71**
toteswingers:1&2:£2.70, 1&3:£6.10, 2&3:£6.00 CSF £16.06 TOTE £3.00: £1.60, £5.30, £6.30; EX 12.40.
Owner Mattoral Partners **Bred** Howard Barton Stud **Trained** Ogbourne Maisey, Wilts
■ Stewards' Enquiry : John Fahy two-day ban: used whip with excessive force (Nov 13,15)

FOCUS
Fair form in this maiden rated around the first two. It was run at a steady tempo.

NOTEBOOK
Mattoral had nothing of Sagramor's quality to contend with this time and got off the mark at the third time of asking, digging deep under strong pressure to just hold on. He's bred to be suited by further still and could be the type to go on again next year for a yard which tends to bring its charges on steadily. (op 7-4 tchd 5-2)
Copper Canyon has now finished runner-up on both starts and shouldn't remain a maiden much longer, a greater emphasis on stamina likely to see him do better still, finding the line coming just too soon here. (op 5-1)
Phase Shift had clearly learnt plenty from her recent debut as this was a definite step up, seeing out the longer trip well. She's entitled to go on again.
Zamina(IRE) looked to hold good claims at these weights but faded out of contention late on, almost certainly a little below her best. She'd been runner-up over further here last time so lack of stamina can't have been an issue. (op 3-1 tchd 2-1)
Polly Holder(IRE) was a well-beaten third here the other day and again never seriously threatened, though handicaps are at least an option for her after this. (op 12-1)
Lovers Peace(IRE) didn't achieve anything at the first time of asking but is in good hands and entitled to improve for the experience. (op 8-1)

7243 LADBROKES.COM H'CAP 1m 1f 103y(P)
8:50 (8:50) (Class 3) (0-90,90) 3-Y-O+ **£6,308** (£1,888; £944; £472; £235) Stalls Low

Form RPR

0365 **1** **Tinshu (IRE)**[12] 6990 4-9-6 86 DaneO'Neill 1 95
(D Haydn Jones) *chsd ldrs: rdn to ld over 1f out: r.o* **9/1**

0334 **2** ½ **One Scoop Or Two**[5] 7121 4-8-8 77 oh1 ow1 RussKennemore(3) 4 85
(R Hollinshead) *chsd ldr tl led over 2f out: rdn and hdd over 1f out: r.o* **16/1**

004 **3** ½ **Baylini**[10] 7012 6-9-4 87 SophieDoyle(3) 10 94
(J A Osborne) *hld up: hdwy over 3f out: rdn over 1f out: r.o* **20/1**

5202 **4** shd **Audemar (IRE)**[37] 6312 4-9-10 90 RichardHughes 2 97
(E F Vaughan) *hld up: hdwy over 1f out: sn rdn: styd on* **5/2**[1]

-000 **5** ½ **Wedding March (IRE)**[62] 5553 3-9-6 90 TadhgO'Shea 5 96
(Saeed Bin Suroor) *a.p: chsd ldr over 2f out: sn rdn: styd on* **9/1**

2426 **6** 1 **Dylanesque**[33] 6430 3-8-12 82 PhilipRobinson 8 86
(M A Jarvis) *a.p: rdn over 1f out: styd on* **12/1**

0322 **7** nse **Akhmatova**[7] 7090 3-8-13 83 PaulHanagan 11 87
(G A Butler) *dwlt: hld up: hdwy over 2f out: rdn over 1f out: styd on ins fnl f* **7/2**[2]

0400 **8** 11 **Invincible Force (IRE)**[35] 6363 6-9-9 89 (p) FrannyNorton 3 70
(Paul Green) *led 7f: wknd over 1f out* **50/1**

2312 **9** ½ **Veiled Applause**[8] 7053 7-8-9 78 IanBrennan(3) 9 58
(J J Quinn) *hld up in tch: pushed along over 3f out: wknd over 2f out* **6/1**[3]

034- **10** 4 **Royal Amnesty**[412] 5915 7-8-10 76 (b) MartinLane 7 47
(V P Donoghue) *s.i.s: hld up: a in rr* **40/1**

0320 **11** 10 **Trailblazing**[8] 7054 3-8-6 76 oh1 (b) GregFairley 6 26
(M Johnston) *sn pushed along in rr: bhd fnl 6f* **14/1**

1m 59.38s (-2.32) **Going Correction** 0.0s/f (Stan)
WFA 3 from 4yo+ 4lb 11 Ran SP% **114.5**
Speed ratings (Par 107): **110,109,109,109,108 107,107,97,97,93 84**
toteswingers:1&2:£14.40, 1&3:£18.40, 2&3:£39.10 CSF £136.18 CT £2769.68 TOTE £5.40: £1.10, £5.70, £6.90; EX 119.20.
Owner Llewelyn, Runeckles **Bred** Mrs M L Parry & P M Steele-Mortimer **Trained** Efail Isaf, Rhondda C Taff

FOCUS
A fairly useful handicap. The gallop was by no means steady but the front two were both handy throughout, the fourth a little better than the bare result after faring best of those patiently ridden. The form looks solid.

NOTEBOOK
Tinshu(IRE) recorded a brace of wins on Polytrack around this time last year and was right back to her best on her second outing after a break. Her record on this surface is one of steady progression so she's no forlorn hope to defy a small rise in the weights. (op 12-1)
One Scoop Or Two is proving most consistent and ran another blinder. He doesn't have much in hand of his mark now but his reliability will continue to hold him in good stead. (op 14-1 tchd 12-1)
Baylini has been busier than usual on turf this year but she's always been capable of a higher level of form on AW and ran her usual sound race. (tchd 25-1)
Audemar(IRE) goes really well on this surface and has now run two sound races since returning from a mid-season break, travelling with his usual fluency but ending up with a bit to do in relation to the leading pair. He's off a career-high mark now but it won't necessarily prove beyond him when he gets a race run to suit. (op 11-4 tchd 3-1)
Wedding March(IRE) has been given a chance by the handicapper and fared better than previously for this yard switched to AW for the first time, but there's no real sign of her recapturing her juvenile form in France. (op 8-1)
Dylanesque wasn't discredited but this is just further evidence that her mark is high enough at present. (op 10-1)
Akhmatova came into this at the very top of her game and probably remains in form, as she ended up a bit further back than ideal after being dropped in from her wide stall. (op 9-2 tchd 10-3)
Veiled Applause came here on the back of two really good efforts on turf and might have been expected to do better as he's got winning form over C&D earlier in his career. (op 5-1)
Trailblazing was runner-up on this surface at Lingfield earlier in the month but has now run abysmally on both starts since, and was the first beaten here. (tchd 16-1)

7244 BREEDERS' CUP LIVE ONLY ON ATR MAIDEN STKS 1m 1f 103y(P)
9:20 (9:20) (Class 5) 3-Y-O+ £2,388 (£705; £352) Stalls Low

Form RPR

23 **1** **Mongoose Alert (IRE)**[23] 6699 8-9-7 0 StevieDonohoe 9 76+
(W J Musson) *hld up: hdwy over 3f out: nt clr run and swtchd rt ins fnl f: r.o to ld towards fin* **11/4**[2]

2 1 **Imagination (IRE)**[27] 6598 3-8-12 0 RichardHughes 1 69
(Richard Brabazon, Ire) *trckd ldrs: led over 1f out: rdn and hung lft ins fnl f: hdd towards fin* **5/6**[1]

05 **3** 3½ **Khateer**[7] 7086 3-9-3 0 ChrisCatlin 5 67
(C E Brittain) *chsd ldrs: rdn over 2f out: styd on same pce ins fnl f* **5/1**[3]

4 2 **Secret Era** 3-8-12 0 PaulHanagan 12 58
(W R Muir) *sn led: rdn over 2f out: hdd over 1f out: no ex ins fnl f* **12/1**

00 **5** 1½ **Western Eyes (IRE)**[183] 1654 3-8-12 0 ShaneKelly 10 55
(B J Meehan) *hld up: hdwy fr over 1f out: nt trble ldrs* **33/1**

6 16 **Mystic Halo** 7-9-2 0 MartinLane 4 21
(L Corcoran) *sn pushed along and a in rr: lost tch fr over 3f out* **66/1**

7 7 **Let's Face Facts** 3-8-12 0 GregFairley 6 —
(J S Goldie) *a in rr: lost tch fr over 3f out* **20/1**

8 3½ **Cawthorne**[22] 4-9-4 0 IanBrennan(3) 3 —
(M W Easterby) *hld up: wknd over 3f out* **40/1**

9 ¾ **La Chemme**[10] 4-8-9 0 JackDuern(7) 11 —
(R Hollinshead) *chsd ldrs tl wknd over 3f out* **66/1**

2m 0.93s (-0.77) **Going Correction** 0.0s/f (Stan)
WFA 3 from 4yo+ 4lb 9 Ran SP% **118.7**
Speed ratings (Par 103): **103,102,99,97,95 81,75,72,71**
toteswingers:1&2:£1.20, 1&3:£1.80, 2&3:£2.50 CSF £5.38 TOTE £3.60: £1.30, £1.10, £1.30; EX 8.10 Place 6 £92.77; Place 5 £35.36.
Owner Python Partners **Bred** D And Mrs Noonan **Trained** Newmarket, Suffolk

FOCUS
A maiden which lacked depth and the pair with the best form coming into it ended up dominating. Modest form.
T/Plt: £143.20 to a £1 stake. Pool: £93,221.90 - 475.13 winning tickets. T/Qpdt: £49.70 to a £1 stake. Pool: £7,504.23 - 111.70 winning tickets. CR

7245 - 7247a (Foreign Racing) - See Raceform Interactive

7185 LINGFIELD (L-H)
Sunday, October 31

OFFICIAL GOING: Standard
Wind: nil Weather: light rain

7248 ATTHERACES.COM/BREEDERSCUP MEDIAN AUCTION MAIDEN STKS 1m (P)
12:40 (12:40) (Class 6) 2-Y-O £2,047 (£604; £302) Stalls High

Form RPR

64 **1** **Whiplash Willie**[14] 6953 2-9-3 0 RichardHughes 1 75
(A M Balding) *chsd ldrs: rdn over 2f out: drvn to chal ent fnl f: kpt on wl to ld towards fin* **9/2**[3]

0 **2** hd **O Ma Lad (IRE)**[58] 5724 2-9-3 0 JamesDoyle 12 74
(S Kirk) *sn chsng ldr: rdn and ev ch over 2f out: drvn to ld 1f out: kpt on wl tl hdd and no ex towards fin* **100/1**

0 **3** 1½ **Destiny Of Dreams**[20] 6803 2-8-12 0 IanMongan 11 66
(Miss Jo Crowley) *chsd ldrs: sltly outpcd and rdn bnd 2f out: kpt on u.p ins fnl f* **12/1**

2 **4** ¾ **Mulaqen**[17] 6874 2-9-3 0 TadhgO'Shea 4 69
(M P Tregoning) *led: rdn jst over 2f out: hdd 1f out: styd on same pce fnl f* **9/4**[1]

5 ½ **Tropical Beat** 2-9-3 0 JimCrowley 5 68
(H Morrison) *t.k.h: hld up in midfield: hdwy to chse ldrs ent fnl 2f: rdn and swtchd lft over 1f out: styd on same pce ins fnl f* **28/1**

6 6 **Arizona High** 2-9-3 0 DavidProbert 8 54
(A M Balding) *towards rr: rdn 4f out: no ch w ldrs 2f out: kpt on steadily fr over 1f out* **25/1**

46 **7** nk **Circus Star (USA)**[18] 6844 2-9-3 0 ShaneKelly 6 53
(B J Meehan) *restless in stalls: s.i.s: hld up towards rr: rdn and hdwy into midfield over 2f out: no imp fnl 2f: nvr trbld ldrs* **4/1**[2]

0 **8** 1¼ **Proud Chieftain**[16] 6883 2-9-3 0 JoeFanning 7 50
(H J Collingridge) *racd in midfield: rdn and outpcd over 2f out: styd on same pce and no ch w ldrs fnl 2f* **66/1**

9 16 **Chenonceau (IRE)** 2-8-12 0 PaulHanagan 10 9
(E A L Dunlop) *s.i.s: a in rr: lost tch over 2f out* **14/1**

10 nk **Simpulse** 2-8-12 0 AdrianLayt 2 8
(F J Brennan) *chsd ldrs: rdn and lost pl over 3f out: bhd fnl 2f* **100/1**

11 2 **Cantor** 2-9-3 0 WilliamBuick 3 22+
(J H M Gosden) *midfield tl rdn along and dropped to rr 5f out: wl bhd over 2f out* **7/1**

U **Ballistic (USA)** 2-9-3 0 NickyMackay 9 —
(J H M Gosden) *s.i.s: in rr: rdn and sme hdwy ent fnl 2f: stl plenty to do whn lost action: stmbld bdly and uns rdr over 2f out: fataly injured* **11/1**

1m 37.5s (-0.70) **Going Correction** +0.025s/f (Slow) 12 Ran SP% **114.9**
Speed ratings (Par 93): **104,103,102,101,101 95,94,93,77,77 75,—**
toteswingers: 1&2 £28.40, 1&3 £8.00, 2&3 £49.70 CSF £411.01 TOTE £3.60: £1.50, £20.00, £4.20; EX 129.10 TRIFECTA Not won..
Owner J C & S R Hitchins **Bred** J C & S R Hitchins **Trained** Kingsclere, Hants

The Form Book, Raceform Ltd, Compton, RG20 6NL

FOCUS
Not a strong maiden auction. The pace was decent and they finished well strung out behind the first five. The winner stepped up and the form has been given a chance through the race averages.

NOTEBOOK
Whiplash Willie attracted steady support throughout the morning and showed a resilient attitude to grind his way into the lead in the closing stages on his third run. A progressive type who is out of a 1m2f winner and closely related to a 2m Polytrack winner, he should continue to improve and will be suited by a stiffer test. (tchd 10-3)
O Ma Lad(IRE) ran green when never out of rear division in a similar course-and-distance maiden on debut. This half-brother to 7f/1m4f (Listed) winner Raydiya was sent off at another big price but put in a bold bid from a wide draw and has improved significantly on his debut form.
Destiny Of Dreams showed ability when seventh in a steadily run Salisbury fillies' maiden on debut and this Dubai Destination half-sister to a 5f Polytrack winner has built on that with a solid effort switched to the all-weather. (tchd 16-1)
Mulaqen, a 30,000gns half-brother to 6f winner Boule Masquee, was well backed to improve on his second behind a runaway winner at Nottingham on debut, but he couldn't repel the finishers under a front-running ride. (op 3-1)
Tropical Beat, a half-brother to 1m2f winner Dr Brass (off a mark of 72), shaped with promise on debut and should have learned plenty from the experience. (op 25-1)
Arizona High did some late work from some way back on debut. He has already been gelded but is out of a well-related dam who has produced a pair of 1m4f winners on Polytrack, and middle-distances should suit next season.
Circus Star(USA) made things tough for himself by starting slowly after dipping down in the stalls, but he was laboured when he got going and put in his second disappointing run since a promising 66-1 fourth at Newmarket on debut. He was reported to have got upset in the stalls. Official explanation: jockey said colt was upset in stalls (op 7-2 tchd 10-3)
Cantor, a close relative to top-class multiple 1m-1m2f winner Chorist, ran very green and was never sighted on debut. (op 11-2 tchd 15-2)

7249 TRY BETDAQ FOR AN EXCHANGE H'CAP (DIV I) 6f (P)
1:10 (1:10) (Class 6) (0-55,62) 3-Y-O+ **£1,706** (£503; £252) **Stalls** Low

Form				RPR
0312	**1**		**Rio Royale (IRE)**[14] 6956 4-9-2 **55**...(p) JimCrowley 12 (Mrs A J Perrett) *chsd ldrs: rdn and ev ch ent fnl 2f: drvn ahd ins fnl f: r.o wl* **7/2**[1]	65
3504	**2**	1 ½	**Lordsbury Pride (USA)**[9] 7064 3-8-10 **53**...(v[1]) KierenFox[(3)] 5 (J R Best) *t.k.h: trckd ldng trio: rdn and effrt to press ldrs ent fnl f: nt pce of wnr fnl 75yds: kpt on* **7/1**	58
0603	**3**	hd	**Cheery Cat (USA)**[65] 5482 6-8-11 **50**...(p) LukeMorris 6 (J Balding) *w ldr tl led 4f out: jnd and rdn ent fnl 2f: drvn over 1f out: hdd ins fnl f: nt pce of wnr fnl 100yds: lost 2nd last strides* **6/1**[3]	54
0600	**4**	½	**Only A Game (IRE)**[22] 6741 5-9-2 **55**...(tp) PaulHanagan 3 (I W McInnes) *in tch: rdn and effrt over 1f out: edging lft 1f out: kpt on u.p ins fnl f* **7/1**	58
2003	**5**	¾	**Metropolitan Chief**[18] 6848 6-8-13 **52**... TomQueally 11 (P Burgoyne) *t.k.h: hld up wl in tch on outer: rdn and effrt wl over 1f out: hanging lft fr over 1f out: kpt on same pce fnl f* **12/1**	52
4000	**6**	shd	**Kheley (IRE)**[11] 7018 4-8-13 **52**... ShaneKelly 4 (W M Brisbourne) *stdd after s: t.k.h early: hld up wl in tch in last pair: rdn and effrt over 1f out: kpt on ins fnl f: no threat to wnr* **8/1**	52
6000	**7**	nk	**Figaro Flyer (IRE)**[14] 6956 7-9-1 **54**... J-PGuillambert 2 (P Howling) *wl in tch in midfield: rdn and effrt over 1f out: keeping on same pce and hld whn n.m.r towards fin* **14/1**	53
0104	**8**	shd	**Commander Wish**[12] 7007 7-8-12 **51**... RichardHughes 8 (Lucinda Featherstone) *stdd and dropped in bhd after s: hld up wl in tch in last pair: looking for run over 1f out: nt clr run fr over 1f out tl ins fnl f: kpt on: nvr able to chal* **4/1**[2]	50+
0-01	**9**	½	**Final Rhapsody**[14] 6956 4-9-4 **57**... StevieDonohoe 1 (W J Musson) *led tl 4f out: chsd ldr after tl 2f out: wknd u.p ins fnl f: btn whn nt clr run and eased towards fin* **10/1**	54

1m 12.86s (0.96) **Going Correction** +0.025s/f (Slow)
WFA 3 from 4yo+ 1lb **9** Ran SP% **116.1**
Speed ratings (Par 101): **94,92,91,91,90 89,89,89,88**
toteswingers: 1&2 £5.10, 1&3 £4.60, 2&3 £7.90 CSF £28.43 CT £143.54 TOTE £3.00: £1.20, £3.00, £2.70; EX 28.20 Trifecta £156.30 Pool: £211.27 - 1.00 winning units..
Owner Mrs Amanda Perrett **Bred** Glending Bloodstock **Trained** Pulborough, W Sussex

FOCUS
There was a lively market for this ordinary handicap. It was run at a fairly steady pace and the hold-up runners struggled to land a blow. The race is rated around the winner's recent turf form.
Metropolitan Chief Official explanation: jockey said gelding hung left
Commander Wish Official explanation: jockey said gelding was denied a clear run

7250 TRY BETDAQ FOR AN EXCHANGE H'CAP (DIV II) 6f (P)
1:40 (1:40) (Class 6) (0-55,58) 3-Y-O+ **£1,706** (£503; £252) **Stalls** Low

Form				RPR
0041	**1**		**Bold Ring**[3] 7191 4-8-5 **51**... JulieBurke[(7)] 8 (E J Creighton) *in tch in midfield: swtchd rt and effrt over 1f out: r.o wl u.p to ld ins fnl f: hld on wl towards fin* **9/2**[1]	59
5000	**2**	nk	**Meydan Dubai (IRE)**[13] 6992 5-8-10 **49**...(b) HayleyTurner 3 (J R Best) *hld up wl in tch in rr: nt clr run 2f out tl over 1f out: hdwy ent fnl f: pressed wnr fnl 75yds: r.o but hld towards fin* **7/1**	56+
0063	**3**	½	**Durgan**[14] 6956 4-9-3 **56**...(p) RichardHughes 11 (Mrs L C Jewell) *in tch on outer: rdn and effrt over 1f out: styd on wl u.p fnl 150yds: nt quite rch ldng pair* **6/1**[3]	61+
1650	**4**	¾	**Dualagi**[32] 6455 6-9-2 **55**... GeorgeBaker 2 (M R Bosley) *hld up wl in tch in rr: hmpd bnd 5f out: effrt and looking for run on inner wl over 1f out: swtchd rt and hdwy to chse ldrs 1f out: styd on same pce u.p fnl 100yds* **10/1**	58
2251	**5**	hd	**Best One**[11] 7018 6-9-5 **58**...(b) LukeMorris 10 (R A Harris) *stdd s: hld up wl in tch in rr: nt clr run 2f out: rdn and gd hdwy ent fnl f: chsd ldrs and hanging lft u.p ins fnl f: no imp fnl 75yds* **8/1**	60
3142	**6**	nk	**Mushy Peas (IRE)**[18] 6848 3-8-11 **51**... MartinLane 4 (P D Evans) *led: rdn ent fnl 2f: hdd ins fnl f: no ex fnl 100yds* **5/1**[2]	52
-040	**7**	¾	**Polemica (IRE)**[26] 6656 4-8-13 **52**...(t) SilvestreDeSousa 7 (F Sheridan) *in tch: effrt and hanging lft over 1f out: styd on same pce and no imp fnl 150yds* **14/1**	51
3305	**8**	½	**Itsthursdayalready**[9] 7064 3-8-13 **53**... ShaneKelly 12 (W M Brisbourne) *taken down early: hld up wl in tch in rr on outer: rdn and effrt over 1f out: kpt on wl fnl 150yds: nvr able to chal* **11/1**	50
3000	**9**	1	**Spoof Master (IRE)**[11] 7018 6-8-10 **52**... SimonPearce[(3)] 9 (J Pearce) *chsd ldrs on outer: rdn over 1f out: wknd ent fnl f* **25/1**	46
0500	**10**	4 ½	**Suhayl Star (IRE)**[141] 2964 6-9-0 **53**... WilliamCarson 1 (P Burgoyne) *taken down early: t.k.h: hld up wl in tch in midfield on inner: rdn ent fnl 2f: wknd ent fnl f* **16/1**	33
45-	**11**	3 ½	**Jonny Ebeneezer**[520] 2436 11-9-1 **54**...(b) StephenCraine 5 (D Flood) *taken down early: w ldr: rdn ent fnl 2f: wknd over 1f out* **33/1**	23
4000	**12**	9	**Hatman Jack (IRE)**[48] 6018 4-8-9 **48**...(tp) FergusSweeney 6 (B G Powell) *racd keenly: w ldrs tl wknd qckly wl over 1f out: wl btn and eased ins fnl f* **14/1**	—

1m 12.9s (1.00) **Going Correction** +0.025s/f (Slow)
WFA 3 from 4yo+ 1lb **12** Ran SP% **116.2**
Speed ratings (Par 101): **94,93,92,91,91 91,90,89,88,82 77,65**
toteswingers: 1&2 £8.10, 1&3 £7.60, 2&3 £10.50 CSF £34.80 CT £193.56 TOTE £5.60: £1.80, £3.60, £2.70; EX 51.50 TRIFECTA Not won..
Owner Daniel Creighton **Bred** J A Pickering & T Pears **Trained** Wormshill, Kent

FOCUS
The second division of a modest handicap. The early tempo was not strong, but the leaders were swamped in the final furlong. The winner ran to the same mark as her recent win.
Dualagi Official explanation: jockey said mare was denied a clear run
Hatman Jack(IRE) Official explanation: jockey said gelding had no more to give

7251 BETDAQ ON 0870 178 1221 CLAIMING STKS 1m 2f (P)
2:15 (2:15) (Class 6) 3-Y-O+ **£2,047** (£604; £302) **Stalls** Low

Form				RPR
0322	**1**		**Dream Of Fortune (IRE)**[15] 6934 6-9-1 67...(bt) TomQueally 6 (P D Evans) *chsd ldng pair and clr of field: clsd 3f out: rdn to ld ent fnl 2f: kpt on wl u.p fnl f* **11/1**	73+
0021	**2**	1	**Green Earth (IRE)**[11] 7019 3-9-5 75...(p) IanMongan 11 (P M Phelan) *chsd ldng trio and clr of field: clsd 3f out: rdn to chse wnr and swtchd lft over 1f out: kpt on same pce u.p ins fnl f* **13/2**[3]	79
2601	**3**	2 ¾	**Fujin Dancer (FR)**[42] 6223 5-9-6 72...(p) PaulHanagan 12 (K A Ryan) *hld up wl off the pce towards rr: hdwy but stl plenty to do 3f out: rdn along ent fnl 2f: styd on wl fr over 1f out to go 3rd ins fnl f: clsng on ldrs fin: nvr able to chal* **13/2**[3]	70+
2105	**4**	6	**Hierarch (IRE)**[3] 7190 3-9-2 70...(b) StephenCraine 5 (D Flood) *hld up wl off the pce towards rr: stl wl bhd and nt clr run 3f out tl 2f out: rdn and kpt on fr over 1f out: wnt 4th nr fin: nvr trbld ldrs* **16/1**	59
1110	**5**	nk	**Lang Shining (IRE)**[15] 6926 6-9-7 85... SophieDoyle[(3)] 13 (J A Osborne) *racd wl off the pce in midfield: rdn along and effrt over 2f out: plugged on u.p ins fnl f: nvr trbld ldrs* **3/1**[1]	61
3232	**6**	shd	**King Of The Moors (USA)**[4] 7171 7-8-7 58...(b) BillyCray[(5)] 2 (D Bourton) *led and set gd gallop: rdn and hdd ent fnl 2f: 3rd and btn over 1f out: fdd fnl f* **12/1**	49
6106	**7**	½	**Ocean Of Peace (FR)**[65] 5468 7-9-0 45... LukeMorris 9 (M R Bosley) *taken down early: racd wl off the pce in midfield: rdn and effrt over 2f out: no imp fnl 2f: n.d* **66/1**	50
0001	**8**	2 ½	**Ahlawy (IRE)**[16] 6904 7-9-5 83...(t) SilvestreDeSousa 1 (F Sheridan) *v.s.a: wl bhd: rdn 4f out: sme prog u.p 2f out: n.d* **9/2**[2]	50
0030	**9**	¾	**Robby Bobby**[8] 7089 5-8-13 72...(b[1]) JoeFanning 3 (M Johnston) *chsd ldr and clr of field: rdn over 2f out: wknd u.p wl over 1f out: fdd bdly ent fnl f* **7/1**	42
	10	nk	**Poesmulligan (IRE)**[13] 4-8-12 0...(p) FrankieMcDonald 7 (Mrs L C Jewell) *s.i.s: hld up wl off the pce in rr: rdn over 2f out: n.d* **100/1**	41
4020	**11**	1 ¾	**Mount Hadley (USA)**[25] 3318 6-9-0 70...(bt) RichardHughes 4 (D E Pipe) *racd wl off the pce in midfield: rdn and no real prog over 2f out: wl btn and eased ins fnl f* **9/1**	39
0/	**12**	7	**Between Dreams**[7] 2717 7-8-5 0... SimonPearce[(3)] 10 (Andrew Turnell) *racd wl off the pce in midfield: rdn 4f out: dropped to rr and wl btn fr over 2f out* **100/1**	19
0-00	**13**	28	**Richardlionheart (USA)**[17] 6865 4-9-2 40... GeorgeBaker 8 (M Madgwick) *stdd after s: racd wl off the pce in midfield: rdn and struggling 4f out: wl bhd over 2f out: virtually p.u fr over 1f out: t.o* **100/1**	—

2m 4.74s (-1.86) **Going Correction** +0.025s/f (Slow)
WFA 3 from 4yo+ 5lb **13** Ran SP% **118.7**
Speed ratings (Par 101): **108,107,105,100,99 99,99,97,96,96 95,89,67**
toteswingers: 1&2 £12.30, 1&3 £12.20, 2&3 £10.50 CSF £80.55 TOTE £12.50: £4.30, £3.50, £1.80; EX 85.70 Trifecta £316.50 Part won. Pool: £427.71 - 0.63 winning units..The winner was subject to a friendly claim. Robby Bobby was claimed by Mrs L. J. Mongan for £5,000.
Owner Mrs I M Folkes **Bred** Newborough Stud **Trained** Pandy, Monmouths

FOCUS
A fair claimer run at a strong pace and in a good time for the grade. The pacesetters probably went off too fast, while the hold-up performers struggled to get involved and it was the two runners who raced just off the leaders who fought the finish. The form is rated around the front pair.
Ahlawy(IRE) Official explanation: jockey said gelding was slowly away
Poesmulligan(IRE) Official explanation: jockey said gelding ran green

7252 BETDAQ THE BETTING EXCHANGE H'CAP 1m 5f (P)
2:50 (2:50) (Class 4) (0-85,82) 3-Y-O+ **£4,533** (£1,348; £674; £336) **Stalls** Low

Form				RPR
6252	**1**		**Herostatus**[10] 7043 3-9-0 **78**... PaulHanagan 7 (M Johnston) *chsd ldrs tl led 10f out: wandered and hdd over 3f out: sn rdn and stl ev ch after: led again jst over 2f out: veered rt ent fnl f: drvn and edgd lft fnl f: styd on* **15/8**[1]	87+
315	**2**	1 ¼	**Beggar's Opera (IRE)**[17] 6872 3-9-2 **80**...(t) WilliamBuick 4 (J H M Gosden) *led tl 10f out: styd chsng ldr tl led over 3f out: hdd and rdn jst over 2f out: keeping on u.p whn hmpd and pushed rt ent fnl f: rallied to chse wnr again ins fnl f: kpt on* **3/1**[2]	87+
3232	**3**	½	**Dakiyah (IRE)**[6] 7120 6-9-11 **81**...(p) IanMongan 1 (Mrs L J Mongan) *in tch: n.m.r 3f out tl over 2f out: rdn and effrt to chse ldrs ent fnl f: chsd wnr briefly fnl 100yds: one pce after* **7/2**[3]	86
000	**4**	1 ½	**Encircled**[10] 7044 6-9-7 **77**... RichardHughes 5 (J R Jenkins) *stdd after s: hld up in tch in last pair: hdwy to chse ldrs over 2f out: drvn and chsd wnr fnl f tl fnl 100yds: no ex* **9/1**	80
150	**5**	3 ¼	**Silent Applause**[56] 5790 7-8-12 **68** oh1...(v) LukeMorris 6 (Dr J D Scargill) *in tch: rdn to chse ldng pair over 2f out: hung rt and lost pl bnd 2f out: edgd lft u.p and btn over 1f out* **10/1**	65
-060	**6**	3 ¾	**Numide (FR)**[20] 6808 7-9-12 **82**... JamesMillman 3 (B R Millman) *stdd s: hld up in tch in last pair: rdn and effrt whn rn wd and lost pl bnd ent fnl 2f: n.d after* **16/1**	73
0/05	**7**	1 ½	**Dalhaan (USA)**[156] 2495 5-9-3 **73**... JimCrowley 2 (Ian Williams) *chsd ldr tl over 2f out: wknd qckly 2f out* **12/1**	62

2m 47.1s (1.10) **Going Correction** +0.025s/f (Slow)
WFA 3 from 5yo+ 8lb **7** Ran SP% **114.7**
Speed ratings (Par 105): **97,96,95,95,93 90,89**
toteswingers: 1&2 £1.80, 1&3 £2.20, 2&3 £2.30 CSF £7.71 TOTE £2.90: £1.80, £2.30; EX 7.70.
Owner Sheikh Hamdan Bin Mohammed Al Maktoum **Bred** Darley **Trained** Middleham Moor, N Yorks

FOCUS
A fair handicap run at a steady pace. The winner scored with something to spare, despite showing some wayward tendencies, and the unexposed front pair are potentially better than the bare form.

7253 BET PREMIER LEAGUE FOOTBALL - BETDAQ FILLIES' H'CAP 1m 2f (P)
3:20 (3:20) (Class 4) (0-80,79) 3-Y-O+ £4,533 (£1,348; £674; £336) Stalls Low

Form RPR
1160 1 **Aurora Sky (IRE)**[18] 6846 4-8-11 66 RichardHughes 7 73
(J Akehurst) *t.k.h: chsd ldr tl over 2f out: sn rdn: drvn to ld ent fnl f: hld on gamely wl ins fnl f: all out* 15/2

21U4 2 shd **Bahamian Music (IRE)**[36] 6361 3-9-5 79 PaulHanagan 2 86
(R A Fahey) *in tch in last pair: rdn and effrt over 2f out: ev ch ent fnl f: kpt on wl u.p: jst hld fnl 50yds* 5/2[1]

0502 3 1 **Countess Comet (IRE)**[34] 6422 3-9-5 79 JimCrowley 4 84
(R M Beckett) *chsd ldrs: effrt to press ldr over 2f out: rdn and ev ch 2f out tl no ex and btn fnl 50yds* 11/2

21 4 1 1/4 **Commerce**[23] 6716 3-8-8 68 HayleyTurner 3 70
(S Dow) *t.k.h: chsd ldrs: rdn and effrt wl over 1f out: styd on same pce u.p ins fnl f* 11/4[2]

625 5 2 1/4 **Sentosa**[40] 6275 3-8-11 71 TomQueally 1 69
(H R A Cecil) *dwlt: t.k.h: hld up in tch in last pair: hdwy on outer to chse ldrs wl over 3f out: hung lft and wknd ent fnl f* 8/1

51-6 6 11 **Addahab (USA)**[171] 2047 3-9-1 75 (p) DaraghO'Donohoe 5 57
(Saeed Bin Suroor) *dwlt: sn pushed up to ld: rdn ent fnl 2f: hdd ent fnl f: wknd qckly 1f out* 9/2[3]

2m 5.71s (-0.89) **Going Correction** +0.025s/f (Slow)
WFA 3 from 4yo 5lb 6 Ran SP% **111.7**
Speed ratings (Par 102): **104,103,103,102,100 91**
toteswingers: 1&2 £4.50, 1&3 £3.30, 2&3 £2.50 CSF £26.25 TOTE £4.70: £1.80, £2.30; EX 18.80.
Owner M Chandler **Bred** Roland Alder & Morton Bloodstock **Trained** Epsom, Surrey
■ Stewards' Enquiry : Richard Hughes one-day ban: used whip with excessive frequency (Nov 15)
Paul Hanagan one-day ban: used whip with excessive frequency (Nov 15)

FOCUS
An interesting fillies' handicap and there was an exciting finish involving runners ridden by championship contenders Richard Hughes and Paul Hanagan. The pace was only steady and this is muddling form.

7254 TRY BETDAQ FOR AN EXCHANGE H'CAP 5f (P)
3:55 (3:56) (Class 3) (0-95,93) 3-Y-O+ £7,123 (£2,119; £1,059; £529) Stalls High

Form RPR
0301 1 **Piscean (USA)**[10] 7041 5-9-3 89 GeorgeBaker 5 102+
(T Keddy) *hld up in rr: effrt and nt clr run over 1f out: swtchd lft and gd hdwy ent fnl f: led fnl 100yds: sn in command: comf* 5/1[2]

1430 2 1 **Billy Red**[10] 7033 6-8-13 85 (b) FergusSweeney 7 92
(J R Jenkins) *stdd after s: t.k.h: hld up trcking ldrs: rdn and unable qck over 1f out: rallied u.p fnl 100yds: r.o wl to go 2nd last strides* 25/1

1060 3 hd **Lenny Bee**[115] 3828 4-9-4 90 JimCrowley 6 96
(D H Brown) *dwlt: hld up in tch towards rr: rdn and gd hdwy ent fnl f: ev ch ins fnl f: nt pce of wnr fnl 100yds: lost 2nd last strides* 5/1[2]

2120 4 1 **Secret Millionaire (IRE)**[34] 6429 3-9-4 90 RichardHughes 1 93
(Patrick Morris) *taken down early: t.k.h: hld up wl in tch: nt clr run briefly over 1f out: sn rdn to chal: ev ch and drvn 1f out: no ex fnl 100yds* 9/2[1]

62 5 hd **Ziggy Lee**[30] 6539 4-9-0 86 WilliamCarson 9 88+
(S C Williams) *towards rr on outer: rdn and wd bnd 2f out: styd on wl ins fnl f: nt rch ldrs* 7/1

6450 6 1 3/4 **Le Toreador**[26] 6663 5-9-1 87 (tp) PaulHanagan 2 83
(K A Ryan) *broke wl and wnt rt s: led: rdn and edgd rt wl over 1f out: hdd fnl 100yds: wknd towards fin* 11/1

0014 7 hd **Curtains**[16] 6887 3-8-13 85 SebSanders 3 80
(S Dow) *towards rr: rdn and effrt on inner ent fnl 2f: wknd fnl f* 11/2[3]

0000 8 3/4 **Judge 'n Jury**[8] 7079 6-9-7 93 LukeMorris 10 85
(R A Harris) *t.k.h: hld up in tch: hdwy to press ldrs ent fnl 2f: drvn over 1f out: wknd ins fnl f* 9/1

0023 9 3 1/2 **Nickel Silver**[26] 6663 5-9-7 93 (v) TomEaves 8 73
(B Smart) *pressed ldr: rdn 2f out: wknd qckly jst over 1f out* 13/2

5005 10 shd **Love Delta (USA)**[164] 2260 3-9-6 92 JoeFanning 4 71
(M Johnston) *s.i.s: a outpcd in rr* 22/1

58.26 secs (-0.54) **Going Correction** +0.025s/f (Slow) 10 Ran SP% **119.3**
Speed ratings (Par 107): **105,103,103,101,101 98,98,96,91,91**
toteswingers: 1&2 £19.00, 1&3 £9.60, 2&3 £37.90 CSF £122.04 CT £664.88 TOTE £4.50: £2.20, £8.50, £2.20; EX 157.70 TRIFECTA Not won..
Owner Andrew Duffield **Bred** Connie And John Iacuone **Trained** Newmarket, Suffolk

FOCUS
A decent handicap run at a good pace, although perhaps not as strong a gallop as seemed likely. Sound form.

NOTEBOOK
Piscean(USA) appreciated the switch back to Polytrack when a stylish come-from-behind winner with cheekpieces removed at Kempton last time, and he repeated the trick to defy a 7lb rise here, and improve his AW record to 2271211. He can miss the break and take a while to get going, but this represents a personal best, and he could continue the golden spell. (op 11-2)
Billy Red is better known as a trailblazer, but he ran a big race under more patient tactics switched back to 5f here. He is 1lb higher than his best winning mark, but this six-time Polytrack winner had a good spell last winter and may be closing in on a tenth career success.
Lenny Bee lost his form quickly after readily winning a Beverley handicap off 5lb lower in April, but he had been given some time off and returned with a good effort. Equally effective on fast-turf/Polytrack, he could be poised to strike again soon. (op 13-2)
Secret Millionaire(IRE) didn't find much at Kempton last time, but the step back up to 6f probably backfired and he gave a decent response back at his optimum trip. He has a generally progressive profile and should continue to be dangerous in useful 5f handicaps. (op 11-2)
Ziggy Lee, second over this trip at Wolverhampton last time, did well to get as close as he did from a long way back after being forced widest of all. (op 5-1)
Le Toreador couldn't hang in there after setting a decent pace. (op 12-1 tchd 10-1)
Curtains excelled herself when 40-1 fourth behind the hugely progressive Dever Dream in a 6f Listed race at Newmarket last time. Her mark was unaltered, but she couldn't land a blow back in a handicap. (op 15-2)

7255 BETDAQEXTRA.COM H'CAP 1m (P)
4:25 (4:25) (Class 5) (0-70,70) 3-Y-O+ £2,729 (£806; £403) Stalls High

Form RPR
0006 1 **Kilburn**[18] 6852 6-9-5 68 (b[1]) JamesDoyle 7 78+
(A J Lidderdale) *s.i.s: bhd: rdn over 2f out: swtchd lft and str run over 1f out: led jst ins fnl f: sn clr: r.o wl* 9/1

056U 2 1 1/2 **Emeebee**[76] 5157 4-9-3 66 StevieDonohoe 3 73
(W J Musson) *hld up in tch in midfield: pushed along and effrt ent fnl 2f: rdn over 1f out: chsd wnr ins fnl f: kpt on* 12/1

3115 3 1 1/2 **Super Duplex**[29] 6554 3-9-1 67 IanMongan 2 70+
(P M Phelan) *s.i.s: t.k.h early: pushed along over 3f out: stl last over 1f out: gd hdwy 1f out: r.o wl to go 3rd fnl 75yds: nt rch ldrs* 12/1

4412 4 3/4 **Sweet Secret**[32] 6479 3-9-2 68 (b) RichardHughes 9 69
(R Hannon) *in tch in midfield: rdn and unable qck over 2f out: kpt on same pce u.p fnl f* 9/4[1]

3400 5 1 3/4 **Dichoh**[32] 6479 7-9-6 69 (v) PaulHanagan 12 66
(M Madgwick) *towards rr: hdwy on outer 3f out: wd bnd and rdn ent fnl 2f: kpt on ins fnl f: nvr gng pce to trble ldrs* 20/1

5604 6 nse **Super Frank (IRE)**[18] 6853 7-9-2 65 (b) JoeFanning 10 62+
(J Akehurst) *t.k.h: hld up in tch: hdwy to chse ldrs 3f out: ev ch over 1f out: rdn to ld 1f out: sn hdd and btn: fdd fnl 100yds* 20/1

0215 7 2 **Recalcitrant**[18] 6852 7-9-1 67 SimonPearce[(3)] 5 60
(S Dow) *led: rdn ent fnl 2f: hdd jst ins fnl f: wknd qckly fnl 150yds* 14/1

-013 8 1 **April Fool**[13] 6991 6-9-7 70 (v) LukeMorris 6 60
(R A Harris) *awkward leaving stalls: sn pushed up to join ldr: rdn ent fnl 2f: stl ev ch tl wknd qckly jst ins fnl f* 8/1[3]

3030 9 1/2 **Aflaam (IRE)**[11] 7012 5-9-0 66 (t) AndrewHeffernan[(3)] 11 55
(R A Harris) *chsd ldrs: rdn and unable qck over 2f out: wknd over 1f out* 11/2[2]

5200 10 3/4 **Norville (IRE)**[15] 6922 3-9-1 67 MartinLane 4 54
(P D Evans) *t.k.h: hld up wl in tch: rdn and effrt jst over 2f out: wknd ent fnl f* 16/1

0040 11 1 1/2 **Knightfire (IRE)**[23] 6714 3-9-0 69 JohnFahy[(3)] 1 53
(W R Swinburn) *t.k.h: hld up in tch on inner: rdn and wknd over 1f out* 20/1

3011 12 1 1/2 **So Surreal (IRE)**[23] 6713 3-9-0 66 (b) GeorgeBaker 8 47
(G L Moore) *hld up towards rr: rdn and no prog wl over 1f out: no ch and eased wl ins fnl f* 10/1

1m 36.74s (-1.46) **Going Correction** +0.025s/f (Slow)
WFA 3 from 4yo+ 3lb 12 Ran SP% **118.6**
Speed ratings (Par 103): **108,106,105,104,102 102,100,99,98,98 96,95**
toteswingers: 1&2 £23.40, 1&3 £27.30, 2&3 £17.30. Totesuper7: Win: £1,902.90. Place: £250.30. CSF £108.48 CT £1305.68 TOTE £14.20: £3.60, £6.00, £4.70; EX 236.10 TRIFECTA Not won. Place 6 £109.86, Place 5 £19.81..
Owner Royal Windsor Racing Club **Bred** B Walters **Trained** Eastbury, Berks

FOCUS
A competitive handicap. The first three all came from some way off the decent pace. Sound form.
T/Plt: £266.60 to a £1 stake. Pool: £68,912.95. 188.64 winning tickets. T/Qpdt: £26.00 to a £1 stake. Pool: £6,392.91. 181.69 winning tickets. SP

7134 LEOPARDSTOWN (L-H)
Sunday, October 31

OFFICIAL GOING: Yielding to soft changing to soft after race 1 (12.35)

7256a IRISH STALLION FARMS EUROPEAN BREEDERS FUND FILLIES MAIDEN 7f
12:35 (12:38) 2-Y-O £10,685 (£2,477; £1,084; £619)

RPR
1 **Manieree (IRE)**[15] 6945 2-9-0 FMBerry 15 82
(John M Oxx, Ire) *chsd ldr in 2nd: impr to ld 2f out: rdn and kpt on wl fr over 1f out: pressed cl home* 10/3[2]

2 1/2 **Wonder Of Wonders (USA)** 2-9-0 JAHeffernan 5 81+
(A P O'Brien, Ire) *mid-div: 8th 1/2-way: hdwy into 6th 2f out: rdn into 4th 1f out: kpt on fnl f: pressed wnr cl home* 9/1

3 1 1/4 **Asheerah**[42] 6228 2-9-0 DPMcDonogh 6 78
(Kevin Prendergast, Ire) *chsd ldrs: 4th 1/2-way: rdn in 3rd 2f out: styd on to 2nd over 1f out: kpt on same pce fnl f* 9/4[1]

4 5 **Puzzled (IRE)** 2-9-0 CDHayes 18 65
(Andrew Oliver, Ire) *s.i.s: towards rr: pushed along in 13th 2f out: 7th over 1f out: kpt on wl fnl f* 25/1

5 1 1/4 **Future Generation (IRE)**[16] 6908 2-9-0 KLatham 11 62
(G M Lyons, Ire) *led: rdn and hdd 2f out: no ex in 3rd 1f out: kpt on same pce* 12/1

6 1 1/4 **Living On Promises (IRE)**[21] 6782 2-9-0 WMLordan 10 59
(David Wachman, Ire) *chsd ldrs: 6th 1/2-way: rdn in 7th 2f out: no imp in 5th 1f out: kpt on same pce* 11/2[3]

7 3 1/2 **Cloud Hawk (IRE)**[20] 6817 2-8-9 MHarley[(5)] 1 50
(T J O'Mara, Ire) *chsd ldrs: 5th 1/2-way: rdn in 4th 2f out: no ex in 6th 1f out: kpt on one pce* 66/1

8 1 1/2 **Empowering (IRE)** 2-8-9 SMLevey[(5)] 4 46
(A P O'Brien, Ire) *mid-div: rdn into 8th 2f out: no ex over 1f out: kpt on one pce* 20/1

9 shd **Spice Power (IRE)** 2-9-0 PBBeggy 9 46
(Edward Lynam, Ire) *hld up towards rr: no imp 2f out: sme late hdwy fr over 1f out* 25/1

10 1/2 **Cailin Coillteach**[11] 7027 2-8-11 BACurtis[(3)] 7 45
(Andrew Oliver, Ire) *in rr of mid-div: rdn and no imp 2f out: kpt on one pce* 12/1

11 2 1/2 **Lady's Locket (IRE)**[6] 7134 2-9-0 RPCleary 2 39
(Andrew Oliver, Ire) *towards rr for most: sme late hdwy: nvr a factor* 14/1

12 3 **Croce Rossa (IRE)**[44] 6161 2-8-11 GFCarroll[(3)] 12 31
(J R Boyle) *mid-div: rdn and no ex ent st* 33/1

13 2 1/2 **Vasoni (IRE)**[14] 6968 2-9-0 72 WJSupple 16 25
(Timothy Doyle, Ire) *chsd ldrs: 3rd 1/2-way: rdn in 5th 2f out: no ex and wknd* 25/1

14 3/4 **Good Shot Noreen (IRE)** 2-9-0 WJLee 3 23
(T Stack, Ire) *slowly away: towards rr for most: nvr a factor* 25/1

15 2 **Thistle Thunder (IRE)** 2-9-0 MCHussey 13 18
(Tracey Collins, Ire) *chsd ldrs: 7th 1/2-way: rdn in 9th 2f out: no ex and wknd* 12/1

16 2 1/2 **Newlands Princess (IRE)**[55] 5822 2-9-0 NGMcCullagh 17 12
(Denis W Cullen, Ire) *a towards rr* 20/1

17 1 3/4 **Dananna (IRE)**[20] 6817 2-9-0 DMGrant 14 7
(Timothy Doyle, Ire) *mid-div: rdn and wknd ent st* 66/1

18 20 **Whipped (IRE)**[14] 6968 2-9-0 DJMoran 8 —
(Matthieu Palussiere, Ire) *a towards rr: t.o* 66/1

1m 34.45s (5.75) **Going Correction** +1.025s/f (Soft) 18 Ran SP% **141.3**
Speed ratings: **108,107,106,100,98 97,93,91,91,91 88,84,81,81,78 75,73,51**
CSF £35.24 TOTE £4.10: £1.60, £3.00, £1.40; DF 40.00.
Owner Maxwell Morris **Bred** Max Morris **Trained** Currabeg, Co Kildare

FOCUS
The race has been rated around the balance of the principals.

NOTEBOOK
Manieree(IRE) followed up a promising debut at Cork two weeks previously. She overcame her bad draw by getting close to the front very early on, took it up before the straight, lengthened nicely and kept on well. The runner-up did close but the winner had been out on front for long enough and might just have been idling a bit close to the line. She'll improve and has every chance of staying middle distances next year. (op 3/1 tchd 7/2)
Wonder Of Wonders(USA) ◆ was an alarming market drifter but ran a very promising race and appears to be a filly with a real future. Racing in mid-division, she began to close up in the straight but ran green and she only got the hang of things very slowly. One would expect considerable improvement from her. (op 11/2)
Asheerah appeared to have no excuses. She had an ideal position tucked in behind the leaders most of the way and picked up for a few strides when asked to chase the winner early in the straight. She just didn't get home inside the last. (op 11/4 tchd 3/1)
Puzzled(IRE) ◆ completely blew the start and had only about three or four horses behind her turning in, but she picked up well inside the last furlong and a half and came home well. She may well be seen in a Dundalk maiden but looks a filly of considerable promise for next year.
Future Generation(IRE) should be a filly that will improve next year over a trip. She raced quite keenly in front and just faded inside the final furlong and a half. (op 14/1)
Spice Power(IRE) Official explanation: jockey said filly hung left and ran very green early on but stayed on well in this race

7257 - 7263a (Foreign Racing) - See Raceform Interactive

7109 CAPANNELLE (R-H)
Sunday, October 31

OFFICIAL GOING: Turf: very soft

7264a PREMIO GUIDO BERADELLI (GROUP 3) (2YO) (TURF) 1m 1f
3:10 (12:00) 2-Y-O **£35,398** (£15,575; £8,495; £4,247)

RPR

1 **Duel (IRE)**[28] 2-8-11 0 .... MircoDemuro 4 —
(Vittorio Caruso, Italy) *settled mid-div on outer for 4f: proged ent st to share ld: tk ld 4f out: rdn 3f out to go a l clr: pushed out 2 l clr ent fnl f: rdn to keep command fnl 100yds* **11/20**[1]

2 ½ **Lui Den** 2-8-11 0 .... CDemuro 7 —
(A Renzoni, Italy) *slowly away: hld up nr rr for 5f: rdn ent st to stay in tch: hrd rdn ent fnl 2f: styd on gamely fnl f to go cl last 100yds* **14/1**

3 1½ **Fairyhall**[22] 6762 2-8-11 0 .... DarioVargiu 2 —
(B Grizzetti, Italy) *trckd ldrs tl ent st: shkn up to chal 2f out: hrd rdn and one pce fnl 300yds* **42/10**[2]

4 nk **Hallo Heart (IRE)** 2-8-11 0 .... MPasquale 6 —
(R Betti, Italy) *shared ld after 1f: plld hrd and lost position: wnt 4th ent st: rdn to chal ldr 3 1/2f out: hrd rdn fnl 2f: styd on one pce* **79/10**

5 4 **Palazzo Reale**[35] 2-8-11 0 .... UmbertoRispoli 3 —
(R Biondi, Italy) *broke wl to ld tl ent st: shkn up and rdn 3f out to stay in tch w ldr: hrd rdn and btn 2f out* **89/20**[3]

6 2 **Street Honor (IRE)** 2-8-11 0 .... GBietolini 1 —
(A Peraino, Italy) *slowly away: hld up nr rr tl ent st: styd on fnl 3f under hrd ride* **159/10**

7 3 **Passaggio (ITY)** 2-8-11 0 .... GMarcelli 9 —
(A Cascio, Italy) *slowly away and in rr: rdn and no imp 4f out* **73/1**

8 3½ **Gabby's Brother (IRE)** 2-8-11 0 .... SDiana 5 —
(M Oppo, Italy) *mid-div tl ent st: rdn and no imp 3 1/2f out: eased fnl f* **27/1**

9 7 **Olmo On Line (USA)**[35] 2-8-11 0 .... CFiocchi 8 —
(R Menichetti, Italy) *settled mid-div: rdn ent st to stay in tch: sn one pce: eased fnl 1 1/2f* **37/1**

1m 54.1s (-0.60) 9 Ran SP% **133.5**
WIN (incl. 1 euro stake): 1.55. PLACES: 1.13, 2.12, 1.66. DF: 9.35.
Owner Incolinx **Bred** Scuderia Incolinx **Trained** Italy

NOTEBOOK
Duel(IRE) confirmed the favourable impression he created in a runaway maiden success. The win meant that his trainer has won a third of the Group races run in Italy this season, including the 2,000 Guineas and Derby.

7160 SAINT-CLOUD (L-H)
Sunday, October 31

OFFICIAL GOING: Turf: heavy

7265a CRITERIUM INTERNATIONAL (GROUP 1) (2YO COLTS & FILLIES) (TURF) 1m
1:35 (12:00) 2-Y-O **£126,415** (£50,575; £25,287; £12,632; £6,327)

RPR

1 **Roderic O'Connor (IRE)**[15] 6924 2-9-0 0 .... JMurtagh 10 120+
(A P O'Brien, Ire) *amongst early ldrs: racd on outer: qcknd wl early in st: wnt clr: began to drift lft: stened: drifted sharply rt towards stands' side: hrd rdn 100yds: r.o again: comf* **5/2**[2]

2 1½ **Salto (IRE)**[22] 2-9-0 0 .... OlivierPeslier 7 117
(F Head, France) *bkmarker tl st: rdn 1 1/2f out: wnt 2nd 1f out: r.o wl: briefly threatened wnr 100yds out: a hld* **14/1**

3 5 **Maiguri (IRE)**[28] 6610 2-9-0 0 .... JohanVictoire 5 106
(C Baillet, France) *racd bhd ldrs: hrd rdn to follow eventual wnr in st: hdd for 2nd 1f out: styd on wl* **9/1**

4 snk **Rerouted (USA)**[31] 6507 2-9-0 0 .... MichaelHills 1 105
(B W Hills) *amongst early ldrs fr s racing on ins rail: rdn early in st: r.o fnl f* **20/1**

5 4 **French Navy**[43] 6218 2-9-0 0 .... MaximeGuyon 6 97
(A Fabre, France) *racd bhd ldrs: unable qck early in st: styd on one pce* **2/1**[1]

6 8 **Private Jet (FR)**[24] 6702 2-9-0 0 .... StephanePasquier 3 79
(H-A Pantall, France) *amongst early ldrs: hrd rdn early in st: no ex: fdd 1 1/2f out* **25/1**

7 3 **Havane Smoker**[43] 6218 2-9-0 0 .... IoritzMendizabal 9 72+
(J-C Rouget, France) *w.w towards rr: hrd rdn early in st: no ex: fdd* **7/1**[3]

8 hd **Pisco Sour (USA)**[29] 6560 2-9-0 0 .... JimmyFortune 4 72
(H Morrison) *prom fr s: hrd rdn to chse eventual wnr early in st: sn wknd* **20/1**

9 8 **Ziyarid (IRE)**[24] 2-9-0 0 .... Christophe-PatriceLemaire 8 54+
(A De Royer-Dupre, France) *racd on outside bhd ldrs: rdn but no ex in st: wknd* **10/1**

10 1½ **Abjer (FR)**[22] 6737 2-9-0 0 .... RichardHills 2 51
(C E Brittain) *racd bhd ldrs on rail: wknd qckly in st* **14/1**

1m 45.7s (-1.80) 10 Ran SP% **120.2**
WIN (incl. 1 euro stake): 3.80. PLACES: 2.20, 4.60, 3.00. DF: 41.40. SF: 102.80.
Owner Mrs Magnier/M Tabor/D Smith/Sangster Family **Bred** Swettenham Stud **Trained** Ballydoyle, Co Tipperary

FOCUS
Straightforward form, the winner confirming his Dewhurst improvement.

NOTEBOOK
Roderic O'Connor(IRE) gave his trainer back-to-back wins in the race and paid a big compliment to Frankel despite hanging badly over to the stands' rail when in front. He is now a top-priced 12-1 for the Derby, but will be trained for the 2,000 Guineas first for which he was cut to a top-priced 14-1.
Salto(IRE) briefly looked dangerous but was well held in the final furlong. He finished clear of the rest.
Rerouted(USA) was always up there and never stopped trying. He is probably not quite up to this class, but can still win more Group races espcially when there is cut in the ground.
French Navy, twice in front of Salto at Deauville, found the ground too sticky and lost his unbeaten record.
Pisco Sour(USA) didn't get home in the conditions and was probably just not good enough.
Abjer(FR) is proven over the trip and on soft ground, so this was disappointing.

7266a PRIX PERTH (GROUP 3) (3YO+) (TURF) 1m
2:40 (12:00) 3-Y-O+ **£35,398** (£14,159; £10,619; £7,079; £3,539)

RPR

1 **Rajsaman (FR)**[43] 6219 3-9-1 0 .... DavyBonilla 9 110
(F Head, France) *broke bdly: lost several l: in rr ent st: swtchd towards stands' side: qcknd wl 1 1/2f out: r.o strly ins fnl f: ct ldr 25yds out: comf* **4/1**[1]

2 1 **Alianthus (GER)**[21] 6791 5-9-6 0 .... ADeVries 3 110
(J Hirschberger, Germany) *led fr s: set gd pce: stl in front ent fnl f: hrd rdn: r.o wl: ct 25yds out: r.o* **10/1**

3 hd **Skins Game**[17] 6881 4-9-1 0 .... IoritzMendizabal 2 105
(J-C Rouget, France) *racd towards rr: qcknd wl towards stands' side 1f out: fin strly: jst missed 2nd* **11/1**

4 nk **Usbeke (GER)**[28] 6606 4-9-1 0 .... ThierryThulliez 7 104
(J-P Carvalho, Germany) *sn prom: qcknd wl whn swtchd towards stands' side: r.o wl fnl 50yds* **33/1**

5 2 **Keredari (IRE)**[28] 6617 3-8-11 0 .... Christophe-PatriceLemaire 8 98
(John M Oxx, Ire) *chsd ldr fr s: hrd rdn to chal 1 1/2f out: no ex fnl f* **4/1**[1]

6 ½ **Royal Revival**[22] 6761 3-8-11 0 .... MaximeGuyon 4 97
(A Fabre, France) *towards rr: rdn but no ex: styd on fnl f* **6/1**[2]

7 1½ **Devoted To You (IRE)**[6] 7140 3-8-8 0 .... CO'Donoghue 1 91
(A P O'Brien, Ire) *prom: proged in centre of trck in st: no ex fnl f: styd on* **14/1**

8 ¾ **Polytechnicien (USA)**[23] 4-9-1 0 .... OlivierPeslier 5 93
(A Fabre, France) *prom fr s: rdn early in st: r.o 1 1/2f out but no ex fnl f: fdd* **8/1**

9 hd **Colonial (IRE)**[36] 6384 3-8-11 0 .... MickaelBarzalona 11 91
(A Fabre, France) *w.w: qcknd on wd outside in st: rdn but fdd 1f out* **6/1**[2]

10 15 **Kali (GER)**[147] 2801 3-9-0 0 .... StephanePasquier 6 60
(Mme M Bollack-Badel, France) *sn prom: rdn but no rspnse early in st: sn wknd* **7/1**[3]

1m 45.4s (-2.10)
WFA 3 from 4yo+ 3lb 10 Ran SP% **119.2**
WIN (incl. 1 euro stake): 7.20. PLACES: 2.60, 3.10, 2.80. DF: 27.40. SF: 54.10.
Owner Saeed Nasser Alromaithi **Bred** Haras De Son Altesse L'Aga Khan Scea **Trained** France

NOTEBOOK
Rajsaman(FR), making his debut for the yard, did well to win this as he gave away a lot of ground with a slow start, but he eventually showed a decent turn of foot when the gap appeared to win comfortably. He may run in the Hong Kong Mile, if invited, before being campaigned in Dubai.

7267 - (Foreign Racing) - See Raceform Interactive

7239 WOLVERHAMPTON (A.W) (L-H)
Monday, November 1

OFFICIAL GOING: Standard
Wind: Light, half-behind Weather: Overcast and cold, turning fine

7268 BET PREMIER LEAGUE FOOTBALL - BETDAQ MAIDEN STKS (DIV I) 5f 20y(P)
1:10 (1:10) (Class 5) 2-Y-O **£2,047** (£604; £302) **Stalls** Low

Form RPR

62 1 **Manoori (IRE)**[26] 6666 2-8-12 0 .... TedDurcan 3 70+
(C F Wall) *in tch: led over 1f out: r.o wl to draw clr ins fnl f: comf* **4/6**[1]

4040 2 5 **Gunalt Joy**[27] 6645 2-8-9 47 .... JamesSullivan(3) 6 52
(M W Easterby) *towards rr: sn outpcd: hdwy 2f out: rdn whn proging 1f out: r.o ins fnl f: rdn 2nd fnl 75yds: nt pce to threaten wnr* **100/1**

0400 3 ¾ **Mr Optimistic**[23] 6740 2-9-3 62 .... BarryMcHugh 11 54
(R A Fahey) *led: qcknd 2f out: rdn and hdd over 1f out: sn outpcd by wnr: lost 2nd and no ex fnl 75yds* **20/1**

0 4 2¼ **Crystallus (IRE)**[14] 6980 2-8-12 0 .... PaulHanagan 10 41
(Mrs A Duffield) *dwlt: in midfield: hung rt 3f out: hdwy whn hung lft over 1f out: styd on ins fnl f: nt gng pce to rch ldrs* **12/1**

06 5 2¼ **Quadra Hop (IRE)**[98] 4432 2-9-3 0 .... DavidProbert 4 38
(B Palling) *chsd ldrs: rdn wl over 1f out: sn wknd* **16/1**

24 6 ½ **Hygrove Gal**[27] 6646 2-8-12 0 .... TomEaves 8 31
(B Smart) *racd on outer: chsd ldrs tl rdn and wknd over 1f out* **11/2**[2]

4 7 nk **Questionnaire (IRE)**[24] 6722 2-8-12 0 .... DarryllHolland 1 30
(N J Vaughan) *chsd ldr tl rdn over 1f out: sn wknd* **6/1**[3]

3004 8 1½ **Chester Deelyte (IRE)**[12] 7017 2-8-9 48 .... PatrickDonaghy(3) 9 25
(Mrs L Williamson) *midfield: pushed along 1/2-way: sn outpcd: nvr a danger* **33/1**

000 9 1½ **Deveze (IRE)**[21] 6811 2-8-12 50 .... RichardHughes 7 19
(J W Hills) *racd keenly: midfield: pushed along 3f out: wknd wl over 1f out* **50/1**

6 10 3¾ **Go Maggie Go (IRE)**[170] 2111 2-8-12 0 .... PhillipMakin 5 6
(K A Ryan) *sn bhd and outpcd: eased whn n.d fnl f* **25/1**

00 11 ½ **False Promises**[72] 5298 2-8-10 0 .... ThomasWhite(7) 13 9
(D Shaw) *a outpcd and bhd* **100/1**

560 12 1½ **Renesmee (IRE)**[84] 4890 2-8-5 0 .... LeonnaMayor(7) 12 —
(Peter Grayson) *a bhd* **150/1**

5 **13** *1 1/2* **Cruise Racer (IRE)**[117] 3770 2-9-3 0............................ StephenCraine 2 —
(Patrick Morris) *awkward leaving stalls: a outpcd and bhd* **125/1**

61.95 secs (-0.35) **Going Correction** -0.025s/f (Stan) 13 Ran SP% **120.2**
Speed ratings (Par 96): **101,93,91,88,84 83,83,80,78,72 71,69,66**
toteswingers:1&2:£27.10, 1&3:£7.60, 2&3:£128.90 CSF £154.92 TOTE £1.40: £1.02, £26.30, £6.40; EX 115.80 TRIFECTA Not won..
Owner Hassan Al Abdulmalik **Bred** T J Monaghan **Trained** Newmarket, Suffolk

FOCUS
Very little strength in depth, but a time 0.79 seconds quicker than the second division. The winner was in total command but the form is rated negatively through the second and third.

NOTEBOOK
Manoori(IRE) was readily confirming the promise of her improved second at Kempton, outclassing this lot to win with plenty in hand. She's obviously inherited loads of speed from the dam's side of her pedigree and looks useful. (op 10-11)
Gunalt Joy ran on after being outpaced, performing some way above her official mark of 47.
Mr Optimistic was suited by the drop in trip but still didn't see his race out. Low-grade handicaps may offer his best hope. (op 18-1)
Crystallus(IRE) Official explanation: jockey said the filly was difficult to steer around the bend
Hygrove Gal seems to be going the wrong way. (op 3-1)
Questionnaire(IRE) failed to progress from her debut. (op 15-2 tchd 11-2)
Go Maggie Go(IRE) reportedly did not face the kickback. Official explanation: jockey said the filly ran green and wouldn't face the kickback (op 33-1)

7269 BET PREMIER LEAGUE FOOTBALL - BETDAQ MAIDEN STKS (DIV II) 5f 20y(P)

1:40 (1:40) (Class 5) 2-Y-O **£2,047** (£604; £302) **Stalls** Low

Form RPR
232 **1** **Insolenceofoffice (IRE)**[14] 6980 2-9-3 72...................(p) PaulHanagan 9 69
(Mrs A Duffield) *a.p: led wl over 1f out: rdn and edgd lft ins fnl f: a doing enough towards fin* **4/6**[1]
3263 **2** *1/2* **Lady Kildare (IRE)**[49] 6030 2-8-9 70...................... PatrickDonaghy(3) 12 62
(Jedd O'Keeffe) *midfield: effrt and hdwy 2f out: rdn over 1f out: r.o towards fin: nt quite gng pce of wnr* **11/2**[3]
40 **3** *1* **Lady Mango (IRE)**[15] 6954 2-8-12 0........................... RichardHughes 8 59
(R A Harris) *led: hdd over 2f out: rdn and nt qckn over 1f out: kpt on ins fnl f but a hld* **9/2**[2]
3300 **4** *nk* **Paper Dreams (IRE)**[25] 6694 2-8-12 59........................... PhillipMakin 3 58
(K A Ryan) *chsd ldrs: rdn and tried to chal 1f out: styd on same pce wl ins fnl f* **14/1**
0 **5** *hd* **Spontaneity (IRE)**[17] 6892 2-8-12 0.................................. TomEaves 13 57
(B Smart) *hld up: rdn and hdwy 1f out: styd on ins fnl f: one pce fnl 50yds* **25/1**
0500 **6** *nse* **Bon Appetit**[17] 6893 2-8-12 55... BarryMcHugh 6 57
(N Tinkler) *racd keenly: w ldr: led over 2f out: rdn and hdd wl over 1f out: no ex fnl 50yds* **25/1**
06 **7** *3/4* **Just For Leo (IRE)**[15] 6954 2-9-3 62.......................... CathyGannon 4 59
(P D Evans) *chsd ldrs: rdn and nt qckn over 1f out: one pce fnl f* **10/1**
00 **8** *4* **Skiddaw View**[17] 6893 2-8-12 0................................... DaneO'Neill 1 40
(A D Brown) *towards rr: effrt over 1f out: no imp on ldrs: one pce fnl f* **100/1**
000 **9** *5* **Sarojini**[17] 6899 2-8-12 40..(b[1]) DavidProbert 5 22
(J A Glover) *a outpcd and bhd: nvr on terms* **66/1**
10 *1/2* **Ngina** 2-8-12 0.. MartinLane 11 20
(D Shaw) *missed break: wl bhd and outpcd: nvr on terms* **66/1**
0 **11** *1 1/2* **Tough Customer**[37] 6369 2-9-3 0.................................. VinceSlattery 7 19
(G Brown) *bmpd s: bhd: outpcd fr 3f out: nvr on terms* **100/1**
0 **12** *22* **Lady Titticaca**[15] 6954 2-8-12 0.............................. RichardKingscote 10 —
(R J Hodges) *racd on outer: chsd ldrs tl rdn and wknd over 2f out* **100/1**

62.74 secs (0.44) **Going Correction** -0.025s/f (Stan) 12 Ran SP% **123.0**
Speed ratings (Par 96): **95,94,92,92,91 91,90,84,76,75 72,37**
toteswingers:1&2:£2.10, 1&3:£2.00, 2&3:£3.50 CSF £4.89 TOTE £1.50: £1.02, £1.80, £2.10; EX 6.20 Trifecta £14.60 Pool: £1419.36 - 21.25 winning units..
Owner S E Sangster **Bred** Gerard Kennedy **Trained** Constable Burton, N Yorks

FOCUS
A weak maiden run in a time 0.79 seconds slower than the first division. The first two are rated below their best, but the form could be pitched up to 5lb higher.

NOTEBOOK
Insolenceofoffice(IRE), fitted with cheekpieces for the first time, was forced wide into the straight but still ran to something like his official mark of 72 to gain his first success at the seventh attempt. (op 10-11)
Lady Kildare(IRE) took too long to get going in the straight and may have been slightly below her official rating, seeing as she had 3lb in hand over the winner at the weights. (tchd 5-1)
Lady Mango(IRE) had her chance on the pace, but wasn't quite good enough. She's one for low-grade handicaps. (tchd 5-1)
Paper Dreams(IRE) was unsuited by the drop in distance, shaping as though 6f may be her trip.
Spontaneity(IRE) travelled okay, but then had to wait for a clear run and didn't see her race out when in the open.
Lady Titticaca Official explanation: jockey said the filly hung right-handed throughout

7270 BET CHAMPIONS LEAGUE FOOTBALL H'CAP 1m 5f 194y(P)

2:15 (2:16) (Class 6) (0-60,60) 3-Y-O+ **£1,706** (£503; £252) **Stalls** Low

Form RPR
5355 **1** **Prickles**[56] 5811 5-8-12 46 oh1.. DarryllHolland 8 54
(Karen George) *mde all: rdn over 1f out: all out towards fin* **22/1**
003 **2** *nk* **Inside Knowledge (USA)**[6] 7157 4-8-13 47...................... MartinLane 6 55
(G Woodward) *chsd ldrs: rdn over 2f out: chsd wnr over 1f out: r.o ins fnl f: clsd nr fin* **20/1**
4351 **3** *2 1/4* **Tower**[18] 6871 3-9-2 58.. KirstyMilczarek 12 62+
(G Prodromou) *hld up: rdn and hdwy over 1f out: edgd lft ins fnl f: styd on: nt rch front pair* **10/1**
5 **4** *hd* **The Dukes Arch (USA)**[23] 6747 3-9-1 57.....................(b) LiamKeniry 11 61
(Peter Fahey, Ire) *midfield: hdwy over 2f out: edgd lft ins fnl f: styd on: nt pce to get to front pair* **8/1**[3]
5013 **5** *2* **Leyte Gulf (USA)**[31] 6538 7-9-12 60.................................. DaneO'Neill 7 61+
(C C Bealby) *hld up: rdn and hdwy over 1f out: hung lft ins fnl f: sn nt clr run briefly: nvr rchd ldrs* **7/2**[1]
4662 **6** *1* **Locum**[44] 6187 5-9-11 59... RichardHughes 9 59
(M H Tompkins) *chsd ldrs: wnt 2nd over 2f out: rdn and lost 2nd wl over 1f out: no imp ins fnl f: wl btn fnl 100yds* **7/2**[1]
0030 **7** *1 3/4* **Red Wine**[10] 7061 11-9-1 49... PhillipMakin 3 47
(J A Glover) *hld up: hdwy into midfield wl over 1f out: n.m.r and hmpd ent fnl f: no imp after* **20/1**
6400 **8** *3/4* **Whitley Bay (USA)**[19] 6855 3-8-1 46 oh1......................... KierenFox(3) 5 46+
(J R Best) *midfield: pushed along 4f out: rdn 2f out: keeping on same pce u.p whn carried lft wl ins fnl f: sn eased* **25/1**
6600 **9** *1* **Given A Choice (IRE)**[13] 6999 8-9-4 52.......................(p) DavidProbert 2 47
(J Pearce) *midfield: rdn and hdwy over 2f out: wknd over 1f out* **33/1**
/6-6 **10** *1 3/4* **Watch Out**[120] 748 6-8-12 46 oh1.................................... CathyGannon 1 39
(D Burchell) *midfield tl rdn and wknd 3f out* **14/1**
-000 **11** *1/2* **Ramora (USA)**[26] 6669 4-9-7 60...................................... KylieManser(5) 4 52
(Miss Olivia Maylam) *hld up: struggling over 2f out: nvr on terms* **40/1**
-436 **12** *13* **Weybridge Light**[243] 777 5-9-12 60............................... GeorgeBaker 10 34
(M R Bosley) *chsd ldr tl over 2f out: rdn and wknd over 1f out* **10/1**
5524 **13** *31* **Stanley Rigby**[157] 2489 4-8-13 47.................................... PaulHanagan 13 —
(R A Fahey) *in rr: rdn over 4f out: nvr on terms: t.o* **9/2**[2]

3m 5.48s (-0.52) **Going Correction** -0.025s/f (Stan)
WFA 3 from 4yo+ 8lb 13 Ran SP% **121.7**
Speed ratings (Par 101): **100,99,98,98,97 96,95,95,94,93 93,86,68**
toteswingers:1&2:£31.90, 1&3:£57.70, 2&3:£40.90 CSF £382.83 CT £4626.17 TOTE £44.40: £8.00, £7.60, £3.70; EX 754.00 TRIFECTA Not won..
Owner P J H George **Bred** R E Baskerville **Trained** Higher Eastington, Devon
■ Stewards' Enquiry : Paul Hanagan two-day ban: careless riding (16-17 Nov)

FOCUS
Darryll Holland is up there with the best when riding from the front, as he demonstrated once again aboard the winner, setting a stop-start gallop that meant the chasers were unable to get into any sort of a rhythm. The time was reasonable and the form is rated around the winner.
Locum Official explanation: vet said gelding lost a front shoe

7271 TRY BETDAQ FOR AN EXCHANGE (S) STKS 7f 32y(P)

2:50 (2:50) (Class 6) 2-Y-O **£1,706** (£503; £252) **Stalls** High

Form RPR
3543 **1** **Kissing Clara (IRE)**[9] 7088 2-8-6 64............................(p) CathyGannon 2 59
(J S Moore) *mde all: rdn 2f out: abt 3 l clr over 1f out: kpt on wl towards fin* **11/4**[2]
2000 **2** *1* **Silly Billy (IRE)**[14] 6989 2-8-9 64...................................... LukeRowe(7) 5 67
(S Kirk) *midfield: hdwy 3f out: wnt 2nd ent fnl f: hung lft and r.o: nt quite get to wnr* **25/1**
25 **3** *3 1/2* **Yorketa**[17] 6891 2-8-3 0... PatrickDonaghy(3) 3 48
(M Dods) *racd keenly in tch: rdn and outpcd over 2f out: hdwy to chse ldrs over 1f out: no imp and styd on same pce fnl 75yds* **9/1**
0506 **4** *shd* **Silence Is Bliss (IRE)**[19] 6842 2-9-2 75...................... RichardHughes 8 58
(J S Moore) *prom: rdn 2f out: nt qckn over 1f out: no ex fnl 100yds* **3/1**[3]
00 **5** *3 1/4* **Farmer's Wife**[32] 6512 2-8-6 0.. LiamJones 11 40
(W J Haggas) *hld up: pushed along over 2f out: hdwy over 1f out: nvr able to chal ldrs* **33/1**
500 **6** *2 1/4* **Simmons**[5] 7177 2-8-3 0.. KierenFox(3) 6 34
(Matthew Salaman) *bhd: pushed along 5f out: kpt on over 1f out: nvr rchd chalng position* **40/1**
042 **7** *1/2* **Soviet Spring (IRE)**[35] 6425 2-8-11 68........................ JimmyFortune 4 38
(A M Balding) *racd keenly: prom: rdn 2f out: wknd fnl f* **2/1**[1]
2050 **8** *1* **Pick A Little**[11] 7035 2-9-2 67.................................... PaulHanagan 9 41
(B W Duke) *in tch: lost pl 5f out: hdwy over 3f out: no imp on ldrs: wknd over 1f out* **8/1**
04 **9** *2 3/4* **Speed Gene (IRE)**[154] 2591 2-8-6 0.......................... FrankieMcDonald 10 24
(M R Bosley) *hld up: u.p over 2f out: nvr on terms* **80/1**
0 **10** *2* **Ameliana**[60] 5701 2-8-3 0... KellyHarrison(3) 1 19
(M G Quinlan) *dwlt: sn chsd ldrs: rdn and wknd over 2f out* **66/1**
0 **11** *36* **Kitty Fisher**[15] 6954 2-8-6 0..................................(b[1]) RichardKingscote 7 —
(R J Hodges) *dwlt: hld up: brief effrt into midfield 3f out: wknd over 2f out: t.o* **100/1**

1m 30.34s (0.74) **Going Correction** -0.025s/f (Stan) 11 Ran SP% **119.1**
Speed ratings (Par 94): **94,92,88,88,85 82,81,80,77,75 34**
toteswingers:1&2:£14.30, 1&3:£5.20, 2&3:£17.00 CSF £75.29 TOTE £3.80: £1.40, £3.00, £5.30; EX 62.90 Trifecta £439.50 Pool: £593.95 - 1.00 winning units..There was no bid for the winner.
Owner D Hanafin **Bred** Keogh Family **Trained** Upper Lambourn, Berks

FOCUS
A modest seller. The winner had a pretty easy time of it up front and the second anchors the level.

NOTEBOOK
Kissing Clara(IRE), back up in trip, gained her first success at the 14th attempt. The race rather fell in her lap, though, with the second and third not knuckling down for pressure, and she might struggle to follow up. (op 10-3)
Silly Billy(IRE) ruined his chance by continually hanging badly left in the straight - he probably would have won had he stayed straight. His apprentice proved unable to correct him, but it would be unfair to be too critical considering he was having his first ride in public. Whatever the case, this was a respectable effort from the runner-up given that he would have been 10lb better off with the winner in a handicap. (op 20-1)
Yorketa carried her head a bit awkwardly, but more than anything she continually pricked her ears. She basically wasn't concentrating and has plenty of growing up to do, though she clearly has ability. (op 8-1)
Silence Is Bliss(IRE) was handily placed but found little for pressure and was a tired horse when losing third late on. Official explanation: jockey said the gelding moved poorly in the closing stages (op 7-2)
Soviet Spring(IRE) was nowhere near the form he showed when runner-up in a 6f maiden at Kempton on his previous start. Official explanation: jockey said that the colt ran too free (op 5-2 tchd 11-4)
Speed Gene(IRE) Official explanation: vet said the filly was struck into on its rear hind

7272 WOLVERHAMPTON-RACECOURSE.CO.UK MAIDEN STKS 7f 32y(P)

3:20 (3:20) (Class 5) 2-Y-O **£2,388** (£705; £352) **Stalls** High

Form RPR
00 **1** **Angelic Upstart (IRE)**[25] 6689 2-9-3 0......................... JimmyFortune 10 71
(A M Balding) *midfield: hdwy on outer over 2f out: r.o ins fnl f: str run towards fin to ld fnl stride* **6/1**
5452 **2** *nk* **Lord Of Persia (USA)**[17] 6901 2-9-3 73........................... JimCrowley 4 70
(R M Beckett) *chsd ldrs: wnt 2nd over 1f out: r.o to ld 150yds out: worn down fnl stride* **5/4**[1]
0655 **3** *1 3/4* **Elusivity (IRE)**[21] 6810 2-9-3 68............................... RichardHughes 5 66
(B J Meehan) *led: rdn over 1f out: hdd fnl 150yds: no ex towards fin* **4/1**[3]
4 *3* **Moonlight Dash** 2-9-3 0... TedDurcan 6 58
(Saeed Bin Suroor) *s.i.s: hld up: rdn and hdwy wl over 1f out: styd on ins fnl f: nt rch ldrs* **7/2**[2]
5 *1* **Samarkand (IRE)** 2-9-3 0.. SebSanders 2 56+
(Sir Mark Prescott) *dwlt: bhd: styd on fr over 1f out: nt rch ldrs: can do bttr* **16/1**
0002 **6** *2 3/4* **Hartforth**[17] 6891 2-9-3 70..(b) GrahamGibbons 7 49
(J D Bethell) *in tch: pushed along and outpcd over 2f out: kpt on u.p over 1f out but no imp on ldrs* **12/1**
4000 **7** *hd* **Algurayn (IRE)**[60] 5701 2-9-3 62.................................. KirstyMilczarek 9 49
(G Prodromou) *prom: w ldr 5f out tl rdn 2f out: nt qckn over 1f out: wknd ins fnl f* **100/1**

500 **8** 2 ¼ **Safe Haven (IRE)**[34] 6436 2-8-12 55 RobertWinston 1 38
(A Bailey) *racd keenly in midfield: hdwy 2f out: wknd ins fnl f* **66/1**

0 **9** 4 ½ **Irish Boy (IRE)**[10] 7065 2-9-3 0 TravisBlock 8 32
(W J H Ratcliffe) *sn chsd ldr: lost 2nd 5f out: remained prom: rdn and wknd wl over 1f out* **100/1**

00 **10** ½ **Steel Rain**[23] 6742 2-9-0 0 AndrewHeffernan(3) 3 31
(Mrs N S Evans) *hld up: rdn over 1f out: nvr on terms* **100/1**

1m 30.09s (0.49) **Going Correction** -0.025s/f (Stan) **10** Ran SP% **119.0**
Speed ratings (Par 96): **96,95,93,90,89 85,85,83,78,77**
toteswingers:1&2:£3.80, 1&3:£4.40, 2&3:£2.50 CSF £14.32 TOTE £11.40: £1.20, £1.10, £1.40; EX 19.60 Trifecta £74.00 Pool: £551.18 - 5.51 winning units..
Owner Barry Burdett **Bred** Swordlestown Stud **Trained** Kingsclere, Hants

FOCUS
The time was only 0.25 seconds faster than Kissing Clara recorded in the earlier juvenile seller, and this was just a modest maiden. The second and third set the level.

NOTEBOOK
Angelic Upstart(IRE) was down the field on his first two starts, but they were much better races than this one. The combination of the class drop and switch to Polytrack evidently suited, although he needed all of the 7f trip. He may stay 1m2f in time and should make a fair handicapper. (op 8-1)
Lord Of Persia(USA), runner-up in a C&D nursery off 69 on his previous start, was well placed throughout and had every chance, but he was worn down in the final strides. A similarly ordinary race should come his way at some stage, and he might have the speed for 6f. (op 11-8 tchd 6-4 in a place)
Elusivity(IRE), trying Polytrack for the first time, was hassled up front by a couple of outsiders and that softened him up, meaning he had little left when strongly challenged in the straight. (op 6-1)
Moonlight Dash, a half-brother to 7f 2-y-o winner Daheeya, out of a useful middle-distance performer, was never seen with a chance after missing the break and needed the experience. He's going to want a fair bit further. (op 5-2 tchd 4-1)
Samarkand(IRE), who has plenty of size, wasn't given a hard time and looks all over a 3-y-o handicapper in the making. (tchd 20-1)

7273 ENJOY THE PARTY PACK GROUP OFFER H'CAP 1m 141y(P)
3:55 (3:55) (Class 6) (0-65,64) 3-Y-O **£1,706** (£503; £252) Stalls Low

Form RPR

2362 **1** **Blue Moon**[31] 6541 3-9-7 64 PaulHanagan 8 73+
(K A Ryan) *midfield: pushed along 3 out: rdn and gd hdwy on outer 2f out: led 1f out: edgd lft ins fnl f whn pressed: kpt finding more towards fin* **5/2**[2]

0611 **2** ½ **Inpursuitoffreedom**[3] 7205 3-9-7 64 RichardHughes 2 72+
(P J McBride) *midfield: hdwy gng wl 2f out: wnt 2nd 1f out: str chal ins fnl f: hld towards fin* **10/11**[1]

6200 **3** 2 ¼ **Powerful Pierre**[16] 6934 3-9-7 64 TomEaves 11 67
(I W McInnes) *trckd ldrs: led wl over 1f out: rdn and hdd 1f out: styd on same pce u.p fnl 100yds* **33/1**

040 **4** nk **Bizarrely (IRE)**[14] 6993 3-9-0 60 SimonPearce(3) 5 62
(J Pearce) *hld up: rdn and hdwy over 1f out: chsd ldrs ins fnl f: styd on same pce and no imp fnl 50yds* **9/1**[3]

522- **5** 1 ¾ **Capacity (IRE)**[10] 7077 3-9-2 59 (v[1]) CathyGannon 10 57+
(T G McCourt, Ire) *in rr: rdn and hdwy over 1f out: styd on ins fnl f: no imp on ldrs fnl 50yds* **16/1**

4350 **6** nk **Director General (USA)**[58] 5758 3-9-1 58 (b[1]) BarryMcHugh 9 57
(Julie Camacho) *prom: led over 2f out: rdn and hdd wl over 1f out: u.p whn n.m.r 1f out: kpt on same pce and no imp on ldrs after* **33/1**

-300 **7** 1 **Spirit Of Love (IRE)**[19] 6856 3-9-6 63 StephenCraine 4 58
(M Wigham) *hld up: rdn and hdwy over 1f out: kpt on ins fnl f: no further imp and kpt on same pce fnl 100yds* **20/1**

4460 **8** ½ **Penrod Ballantyne (IRE)**[134] 3243 3-9-5 62 TedDurcan 6 56
(Karen George) *hld up: rdn 2f out: no imp on ldrs: one pce fnl f* **50/1**

5055 **9** 1 ¾ **Ruby Dazzler**[46] 6124 3-9-0 57 (t) VinceSlattery 13 47
(S Lycett) *trckd ldrs: rdn over 1f out: sn wknd* **80/1**

6-10 **10** ¾ **Orpen Arms (IRE)**[193] 1488 3-9-6 63 PaulMulrennan 12 51
(R A Fahey) *hld up: rdn over 1f out: no imp* **33/1**

320 **11** ¾ **Angelena Ballerina (IRE)**[44] 6212 3-9-0 57 (v) DarryllHolland 7 44
(Karen George) *in tch: u.p and wkng whn checked over 1f out* **14/1**

0000 **12** 3 ½ **Ajool (USA)**[14] 6992 3-9-1 58 SebSanders 1 37
(P W D'Arcy) *led: rdn and hdd over 2f out: wknd over 1f out* **16/1**

000 **13** 2 **Princess Of Troy (IRE)**[178] 1861 3-8-9 52 MartinLane 3 26
(P D Evans) *trckd ldrs: rdn over 2f out: wknd over 1f out* **20/1**

1m 50.44s (-0.06) **Going Correction** -0.025s/f (Stan) **13** Ran SP% **130.9**
Speed ratings (Par 98): **99,98,96,96,94 94,93,93,91,90 90,87,85**
toteswingers:1&2:£1.70, 1&3:£15.80, 2&3:£15.60 CSF £5.27 CT £70.00 TOTE £3.60: £1.10, £1.10, £15.50; EX 8.00 Trifecta £92.90 Pool: £778.79 - 6.20 winning units..
Owner Guy Reed **Bred** Theakston Stud **Trained** Hambleton, N Yorks

FOCUS
Not a bad handicap for the grade, dominated by the front two in the market, who were both really well backed. There are one or etow doubts over the form but the first two are capable of better.

7274 BREEDERS' CUP LIVE ONLY ON ATR H'CAP 1m 141y(P)
4:30 (4:30) (Class 4) (0-80,78) 3-Y-O+ **£3,885** (£1,156; £577; £144; £144) Stalls Low

Form RPR

2301 **1** **Elijah Pepper (USA)**[16] 6935 5-8-12 69 GrahamGibbons 2 79
(T D Barron) *chsd ldrs: effrt whn swtchd rt jst over 1f out: r.o ins fnl f: led towards fin* **8/1**

0646 **2** ½ **Templetuohy Max (IRE)**[17] 6904 5-9-1 72 (v) RichardHughes 1 80
(J D Bethell) *hld up: hdwy 2f out: rdn over 1f out: chalng and ev ch wl ins fnl f: hld towards fin* **11/1**

2232 **3** ¾ **Willow Dancer (IRE)**[7] 7115 6-9-3 74 (p) AdamKirby 7 81
(W R Swinburn) *prom: chsd ldr over 3f out: rdn to ld over 1f out: hdd and no ex towards fin* **7/2**[1]

2325 **4** nk **Ilie Nastase (FR)**[62] 5624 6-9-5 76 LiamKeniry 9 82
(C R Dore) *hld up: hdwy over 1f out: r.o and clsd towards fin: nt quite pce to chal* **33/1**

2226 **4** dht **Dream On Buddy (IRE)**[21] 6813 3-9-0 74 RobertWinston 5 80
(B W Hills) *midfield: rdn 3f out: hdwy over 2f out: hrd rdn to chse ldrs over 1f out: r.o towards fin: nt pce to rch ldrs* **11/2**[3]

0231 **6** 1 ¾ **Sir Bruno (FR)**[31] 6541 3-9-0 74 (p) DavidProbert 6 76
(B Palling) *prom: rdn 3f out: chalng ent fnl f: no ex fnl 75yds* **16/1**

1512 **7** 4 ½ **Glenridding**[6] 7143 6-9-4 75 (p) PaulMulrennan 10 67
(J G Given) *led: tried to slip the field 2f out: rdn and hdd over 1f out: fdd ins fnl f* **10/1**

3022 **8** 9 **Slikback Jack (IRE)**[11] 7046 3-9-0 74 PaulHanagan 3 45
(J A Glover) *dwlt: in rr: rdn 3f out: wl outpcd after* **11/2**[3]

0000 **9** ¾ **Stevie Gee (IRE)**[25] 6701 6-8-12 72 IanBrennan(3) 4 41
(Ian Williams) *s.s: a bhd: wl adrift wl over 2f out* **20/1**

3342 **10** 2 ¾ **One Scoop Or Two**[7] 7243 4-9-1 75 RussKennemore(3) 8 38
(R Hollinshead) *in tch: rdn 3f out: wknd over 2f out* **9/2**[2]

040 **11** 2 ¾ **Inheritor (IRE)**[17] 6904 4-9-7 78 (p) TomEaves 11 35
(B Smart) *hld up: rdn over 2f out: sn lft wl bhd* **33/1**

1m 48.89s (-1.61) **Going Correction** -0.025s/f (Stan)
WFA 3 from 4yo+ 3lb **11** Ran SP% **116.2**
Speed ratings (Par 105): **106,105,104,104,104 103,99,91,90,87 85**
toteswingers:1&2:£10.40, 1&3:£6.00, 2&3:£7.80 CSF £89.25 CT £369.97 TOTE £7.70: £2.60, £4.00, £1.10; EX 110.30 TRIFECTA Not won..
Owner Wensleydale Bacon Limited **Bred** Liberation Farm & Oratis Thoroughbreds **Trained** Maunby, N Yorks

FOCUS
A fair handicap. Sound form, with a 3lb best from the winner and the next four close to their marks.
Stevie Gee(IRE) Official explanation: jockey said that the gelding was never travelling

7275 ATTHERACES.COM/BREEDERSCUP H'CAP 1m 4f 50y(P)
5:00 (5:00) (Class 5) (0-70,70) 3-Y-O+ **£2,388** (£705; £352) Stalls Low

Form RPR

4660 **1** **Naheell**[125] 3522 4-8-10 56 oh5 KirstyMilczarek 4 68
(G Prodromou) *in tch: effrt over 2f out: led wl over 1f out: sn clr and edgd lft: r.o wl and in command after* **40/1**

3000 **2** 3 **Trachonitis (IRE)**[29] 6427 6-9-8 68 PaulHanagan 3 75
(J R Jenkins) *in rr: hdwy over 2f out: rdn to take 2nd 1f out: styd on ins fnl f but nvr able to trble wnr* **33/1**

4606 **3** 1 ¼ **Ghufa (IRE)**[19] 6846 6-9-4 67 SimonPearce(3) 7 72
(J Pearce) *hld up: hdwy over 2f out: sn rdn: chsd ldrs over 1f out: kpt on ins fnl f wout threatening* **10/1**

1443 **4** 2 ¾ **Straversjoy**[6] 7147 3-8-8 60 GrahamGibbons 6 61+
(R Hollinshead) *hld up in midfield: nt clr run 3f out: hdwy whn nt clr run again over 1f out: styd on ins fnl f wout troubling ldrs* **3/1**[2]

0030 **5** ¾ **Faith Jicaro (IRE)**[5] 7167 3-8-12 64 (b[1]) DarryllHolland 9 64
(N J Vaughan) *chsd ldrs: led over 4f out: hdd wl over 1f out: wknd fnl f* **20/1**

4224 **6** 1 ½ **Barliffey (IRE)**[11] 7044 5-9-10 70 RobertWinston 8 67
(D J Coakley) *s.i.s: hld up: nt clr run 3f out: sn rdn: nvr able to trble ldrs* **6/1**[3]

062 **7** shd **Knockdolian (IRE)**[26] 6669 3-9-1 67 RichardHughes 10 64
(R Charlton) *midfield: hdwy over 3f out: sn cl up: rdn 2f out: wknd over 1f out: eased whn wl btn wl ins fnl f* **11/10**[1]

/40- **8** 12 **Barndeh (IRE)**[40] 4632 7-8-10 56 CathyGannon 5 34
(T G McCourt, Ire) *stmbld s: hld up: pushed along 4f out: hdwy 3f out: rdn to chse ldrs 2f out: wknd over 1f out* **66/1**

4520 **9** nk **On The Feather**[15] 6959 4-9-4 64 JamesMillman 1 41
(B R Millman) *chsd ldrs: pushed along over 3f out: sn wknd* **28/1**

2-30 **10** 3 ½ **Little Richard (IRE)**[280] 293 11-8-7 56 oh1 (p) KierenFox(3) 11 28
(M Wellings) *chsd ldr tl over 5f out: pushed along over 3f out: wknd wl over 2f out* **50/1**

2213 **11** ½ **Colonel Sherman (USA)**[177] 1919 5-8-11 60 RussKennemore(3) 2 31
(P A Kirby) *racd keenly: led: hdd over 4f out: rdn and wknd over 2f out* **11/1**

2m 39.8s (-1.30) **Going Correction** -0.025s/f (Stan)
WFA 3 from 4yo+ 6lb **11** Ran SP% **121.4**
Speed ratings (Par 103): **103,101,100,98,97 96,96,88,88,86 85**
toteswingers:1&2:£60.20, 1&3:£81.40, 2&3:£33.80. Totesuper7: Win: Not won. Place: £286.30. CSF £956.62 CT £13336.18 TOTE £63.20: £11.00, £8.90, £1.70; EX 323.40 Trifecta £601.80 Part won. Pool: £813.36 - 0.73 winning units..
Owner Fahed Al Dabbous **Bred** Darley **Trained** East Harling, Norfolk

FOCUS
The front two in the market both disappointed and this is weak form for the class. Through the opening stages the pace was just steady, before increasing down the back straight. The surprise winner was back to last winter's form.
Straversjoy Official explanation: jockey said that the filly was denied a clear run
T/Plt: £64.60 to a £1 stake. Pool:£57,762.72 - 652.07 winning tickets T/Qpdt: £37.80 to a £1stake. Pool:£5,165.08 - 100.87 winning tickets DO

6857 MAISONS-LAFFITTE (R-H)
Monday, November 1

OFFICIAL GOING: Turf: very soft

7276a PRIX MIESQUE (GROUP 3) (2YO FILLIES) (TURF) 7f (S)
1:15 (12:00) 2-Y-O **£35,398** (£14,159; £10,619; £7,079; £3,539)

RPR

1 **Izalia (FR)**[27] 2-8-11 0 FranckBlondel 7 92
(F Rossi, France) *racd in 4th pulling freely: gd prog 2f out: led 1f out: r.o wl* **76/10**

2 ¾ **Gypsy Highway (IRE)**[20] 2-8-11 0 GregoryBenoist 2 90
(D Smaga, France) *towards rr fr s: swtchd towards outside 1f out: qcknd wl: fin strly wout troubling wnr* **33/10**[3]

3 1 **Angel Of Harlem (FR)**[13] 7008 2-8-11 0 IoritzMendizabal 5 88
(E J O'Neill, France) *sent st to ld: hdd by wnr 1f out: r.o gamely fnl f* **12/1**

4 ½ **Whip And Win (FR)**[24] 2-8-11 0 OlivierPeslier 1 87
(Robert Collet, France) *w.w towards rr: hit traffic problems 2f out whn making move: dropped bk towards rr: rdn and fin wl fnl f* **2/1**[1]

5 1 **Moranda (FR)**[6] 7158 2-8-11 0 MaximeGuyon 3 84
(C Boutin, France) *sn prom: rdn 1 1/2f out: r.o: hmpd ins fnl f* **21/1**

6 nk **Butterfly Hill (FR)**[12] 2-8-11 0 Christophe-PatriceLemaire 6 83
(P Bary, France) *racd towards rr on outer: proged 2f out: hrd rdn but no ex fnl f* **3/1**[2]

7 2 ½ **Heidikly (FR)**[36] 2-8-11 0 EddyDelbarba 8 77
(B De Montzey, France) *sn prom: outpcd 1 1/2f out: sn wknd* **12/1**

8 8 **Ana Style (FR)**[13] 7008 2-8-11 0 StephanePasquier 9 57
(P Demercastel, France) *w.w towards rr: rdn 1 1/2f out: no ex: wknd* **26/1**

1m 29.9s (1.60) **8** Ran SP% **116.9**
WIN (incl. 1 euro stake): 8.60. PLACES: 2.70, 1.80, 3.20. DF: 15.40. SF: 39.20.
Owner Jean-Claude Seroul **Bred** J-C Seroul **Trained** France

FOCUS
Pre-race figures suggest that the low level of this form is about right, but time may tell otherwise.

NOTEBOOK
Izalia(FR), who had to be supplemented for this, ran out a brace winner of a rough race and had to survive a stewards' inquiry and a couple of objections. Her trainer would like to return here with her next spring for the Prix Imprudence.

7277a CRITERIUM DE MAISONS-LAFFITTE (GROUP 2) (2YO) (TURF) 6f (S)
1:45 (12:00) 2-Y-O £95,840 (£36,991; £17,654; £11,769; £5,884)

RPR
1 **Blu Constellation (ITY)**[30] 2-9-0 0 MircoDemuro 6 119+
(Vittorio Caruso, Italy) *racd bhd the ldng gp: qckng wl to ld 1 1/2f out: sn clr: easily* **19/2**
2 6 **Wizz Kid (IRE)**[99] 4419 2-8-10 0 IoritzMendizabal 3 97
(Robert Collet, France) *racd bhd early ldr: rdn and r.o wl to take 2nd ins fnl f: no threat to wnr* **9/1**
3 1 ½ **Katla (IRE)**[23] 6751 2-8-10 0 WJLee 7 93
(J F Grogan, Ire) *w.w towards rr: proged 1 1/2f out: r.o wl fnl f: lost 2nd cl home* **32/1**
4 1 **Exciting Life (IRE)**[36] 2-9-0 0 MSrnec 2 94
(T Kluczynski, Poland) *sn prom: no answer to wnr 1 1/2f out: r.o wl fnl f* **50/1**
5 ½ **Captain Chop (FR)**[23] 6760 2-9-0 0 FlavienPrat 11 92
(D Guillemin, France) *settled towards rr: proged on outside 1 1/2f out: r.o fnl f* **22/1**
6 ½ **Spirit Of Battle (USA)**[23] 6760 2-9-0 0 MaximeGuyon 12 91
(A Fabre, France) *in rr on outside fr s: failed to qckn 1f out: styd on* **10/1**
7 1 ½ **Temps Au Temps (IRE)**[20] 6913 2-9-0 0 GregoryBenoist 4 86
(M Delzangles, France) *racd in midfield towards stands' rail: no ex fnl f* **8/1**[3]
8 nk **Approve (IRE)**[31] 6531 2-9-0 0 StephanePasquier 10 85
(W J Haggas) *racd promly fr s: rdn 1 1/2f out: no ex: sn wknd* **9/2**[2]
9 ¾ **Broox (IRE)**[49] 6044 2-9-0 0 OlivierPeslier 1 83
(E J O'Neill, France) *sent st to ld: hdd by wnr over 1 1/2f out: qckly wknd* **2/1**[1]
10 ½ **Split Trois (FR)**[23] 6760 2-8-10 0 Pierre-CharlesBoudot 9 77
(Y De Nicolay, France) *prom fr s: rdn 1 1/2f out: no ex* **22/1**
0 **Keratiya (FR)**[52] 5907 2-8-10 0 Christophe-PatriceLemaire 13 —
(J-C Rouget, France) *broke slowly: racd towards rr: rdn 2f out: no ex: wknd* **12/1**
0 **Boccalino (GER)**[23] 6760 2-9-0 0 MickaelBarzalona 8 —
(H-A Pantall, France) *nvr figured* **46/1**
0 **Dancing Dynamite (GER)**[50] 2-9-0 0 ThierryThulliez 5 —
(H-W Hiller, Germany) *nvr figured* **36/1**

1m 14.4s (1.00) **13** Ran SP% **117.5**
WIN (incl. 1 euro stake): 10.50. PLACES: 3.80, 3.80, 9.10. DF: 63.60. SF: 111.60.
Owner Incolinx **Bred** Azienda Agricola Loreto Luciani **Trained** Italy

FOCUS
The winner's wide-margin vicitory can't be taken too literally in this end-of-season race in bad ground, and it could be that he is either flattered or underplayed by this rating.

NOTEBOOK
Blu Constellation(ITY) absolutely bolted up to win his fourth race in a row. He is expected to be kept to sprint distances and may appear at Royal Ascot next year.
Approve(IRE) faded into eighth and connections blamed the ground. He is now to be retired to stud in Ireland.

7278a PRIX DE SEINE-ET-OISE (GROUP 3) (3YO+) (TURF) 6f (S)
2:15 (12:00) 3-Y-O+ £35,398 (£14,159; £10,619; £7,079; £3,539)

RPR
1 **Definightly**[22] 6783 4-8-11 0 (b) ThierryThulliez 1 113
(R Charlton) *sn led gp on stands' rail: qcknd wl 1 1/2f out: r.o wl fnl f: comf* **18/1**
2 1 ½ **Alcohuaz (CHI)**[28] 6640 5-8-11 0 MaximeGuyon 2 108
(Lennart Reuterskiold Jr, Sweden) *racd bhd ldr on stands' rail: rdn 1f out: threatened eventual wnr briefly 100yds out: r.o wl: a hld* **15/2**[3]
3 8 **Dalghar (FR)**[36] 6390 4-9-0 0 Christophe-PatriceLemaire 11 85
(A De Royer-Dupre, France) *led gp in centre of trck: rdn 1 1/2f out: styd on wout threatening ldrs ins fnl f: jst hld 3rd on line* **6/4**[1]
4 shd **Mar Adentro (FR)**[29] 6608 4-8-11 0 (p) ThierryJarnet 9 82
(R Chotard, France) *w.w towards rr in centre of trck: proged wl 1 1/f out: styd on wl fnl 100yds: jst missed 3rd* **43/10**[2]
5 2 ½ **Salut L'Africain (FR)**[28] 6640 5-8-11 0 (p) FranckBlondel 14 74
(Robert Collet, France) *w.w on outside: proged 1f out: r.o* **37/1**
6 nk **Tiza (SAF)**[28] 6640 8-8-11 0 (p) GregoryBenoist 6 73
(A De Royer-Dupre, France) *w.w towards rr: clsd 1f out: r.o but no threat to ldrs* **17/1**
7 nk **Rock Of Nassau (FR)**[17] 4-8-11 0 DavyBonilla 8 72
(F Head, France) *bkmarker of outside gp: rdn 1 1/2f out: no ex: fdd* **36/1**
8 1 ½ **Arctic (IRE)**[29] 6608 3-8-11 0 JAHeffernan 4 67
(Tracey Collins, Ire) *w.w in outer gp: rdn 1 1/2f out: no ex: sn wknd* **16/1**
9 hd **Fred Lalloupet**[28] 6640 3-8-11 0 OlivierPeslier 5 67
(D Smaga, France) *racd bhd ldrs in outer gp: rdn 1 1/2f out: sn wknd* **29/1**
10 3 **Nuit De Glace (FR)**[4] 6-8-8 0 SebastienMaillot 3 54
(Mlle Valerie Boussin, France) *racd bhd ldrs on stands' rail: unable qck 1 1/2f out: wknd* **20/1**
0 **Skyteam (FR)**[4] 6-8-11 0 (p) MatthieuAutier 10 —
(M Boutin, France) *sn prom on outside: rdn but failed to qckn 1 1/2f out: wknd* **76/1**
0 **Main Aim**[16] 6923 5-9-0 0 (b) StephanePasquier 7 —
(Sir Michael Stoute) *sn prom in centre of trck: rdn but nt qckn 1 1/2f out: sn fdd* **78/10**
0 **Bluster (FR)**[29] 6608 4-8-11 0 IoritzMendizabal 12 —
(Robert Collet, France) *prom on outside fr s: rdn 1 1/2f out: no ex: sn fdd* **25/1**

1m 13.1s (-0.30) **13** Ran SP% **117.3**
WIN (incl. 1 euro stake): 18.70. PLACES: 3.70, 2.30, 1.50. DF: 39.40. SF: 157.40.
Owner S Emmet And Miss R Emmet **Bred** S Emmet And Miss R Emmet **Trained** Beckhampton, Wilts

NOTEBOOK
Definightly was given a well-judged ride as his jockey utilised the strip of ground tight against the stands' rail. He will be kept to soft ground in the future and his trainer believes he has enough speed to become a Prix de l'Abbaye contender.
Main Aim, tried in blinkers, didn't get home despite the shorter trip and disappointed again.

7142 CATTERICK (L-H)
Tuesday, November 2

OFFICIAL GOING: Soft (7.2) changing to soft (heavy in places) after race 4 (3.15)
Wind: Fresh, half-behind Weather: Changeable, heavy showers and very breezy, persistent rain after race 4

7279 YORKSHIRE4X4.COM ADVENTURE ACTIVITIES MAIDEN AUCTION STKS 5f 212y
1:45 (1:46) (Class 6) 2-Y-O £2,047 (£604; £302) Stalls Low

Form RPR
34 1 **Delaney's Dream**[7] 7142 2-8-9 0 AdrianNicholls 12 70
(D Nicholls) *chsd ldrs: chal over 2f out: crowded ins fnl f: styd on to ld post* **7/4**[1]
02 2 shd **Monsieur Jamie**[56] 5836 2-8-9 0 DarryllHolland 3 70
(J R Jenkins) *led over 1f: w ldr: led over 2f out: edgd rt over 1f out: hdd post* **9/4**[2]
00 3 7 **Joe Le Taxi (IRE)**[33] 6498 2-9-2 0 GregFairley 8 56
(M Johnston) *chsd ldrs: sn drvn along: hung lft and kpt on one pce fnl 2f* **9/1**
500 4 6 **Whipperoo (IRE)**[57] 5818 2-8-0 43 ow1 JulieBurke(7) 6 29
(Patrick Morris) *s.i.s: hdwy over 2f out: nvr nr ldrs* **33/1**
5 ½ **These Dreams** 2-8-4 0 FrannyNorton 4 24
(R C Guest) *s.v.s: hdwy over 3f out: kpt on fnl 2f: nvr nr ldrs* **10/1**
0 6 ¾ **Littlepromisedland (IRE)**[102] 4336 2-8-1 0 JamesSullivan(3) 7 22
(R C Guest) *mid-div: nvr nr ldrs* **100/1**
60 7 ½ **Majestic Millie (IRE)**[7] 7142 2-8-4 0 SilvestreDeSousa 1 20
(D O'Meara) *w ldr: led over 4f out tl over 2f out: wknd over 1f out* **16/1**
8 14 **Diamond Sunrise (IRE)** 2-8-8 0 PJMcDonald 11 —
(N Wilson) *prom: lost pl over 2f out: sn bhd* **25/1**
050 9 4 ½ **Caramella Brownie**[8] 7123 2-8-4 0 DuranFentiman 2 —
(T D Easterby) *awkward to load: s.s: a bhd* **9/2**[3]
0 10 6 **Indigo Sands (IRE)**[7] 7142 2-8-6 0 (b[1]) PaulPickard(3) 9 —
(A Berry) *sn mid-div: lost pl over 2f out* **100/1**
000 11 1 **Mujapiste (IRE)**[28] 6646 2-7-13 40 (t) DeclanCannon(5) 10 —
(L A Mullaney) *chsd ldrs: lost pl 3f out: sn bhd* **100/1**

1m 17.32s (3.72) **Going Correction** +0.425s/f (Yiel) **11** Ran SP% **120.0**
Speed ratings (Par 94): **92,91,82,74,73 72,72,53,47,39 38**
Tote Swingers:1&2:£1.90, 2&3:£6.10, 1&3:£4.20 CSF £5.79 TOTE £2.90: £1.10, £1.70, £1.80; EX 6.40 Trifecta £30.40 Pool £594.23 - 14.45 winning units..
Owner Middleham Park Racing XXXIX **Bred** Bambi Bloodstock **Trained** Sessay, N Yorks

FOCUS
A weak juvenile maiden and not a race to take too literally. As is nearly always the case at this venue when the ground is deep, the runners came stands' side off the home bend, and the first two came well clear in a bobbing finish.

NOTEBOOK
Delaney's Dream stuck his head down where it mattered most and opened his account at the third attempt. He was housed on the wide outside, but that enabled him to bag the favoured stands' rail in the home straight and it no doubt helped his cause. This softer ground brought his stamina into play over this distance and he is the sort that can go on and take a nursery if kept on the go during the winter. (op 2-1 tchd 9-4)
Monsieur Jamie met support when second on the AW 56 days earlier and again proved popular. He was drawn towards the inside and was never far away, but that meant he had to forfeit the near rail to the winner. Despite racing off it, though, he posted a brave effort and only just lost out at the line. He should be well up to getting off the mark back on the AW, and is now qualified for nurseries. (op 2-1 tchd 15-8)
Joe Le Taxi(IRE) was outpaced after a furlong or so, but kept gamely to his task and this was a clear personal-best effort. He too is now eligible for a mark and, despite being a half-brother to sprinters, looks set to enjoy another furlong. (tchd 10-1)
Whipperoo(IRE), whose claiming rider put up 1lb overweight, plugged on to grab fourth near the finish and helps to put the form into perspective. (op 25-1)
These Dreams, bred to enjoy a bit further, fell out of the gates and was always playing catch up. She did make up some ground, though, and should come on a bundle for the initial experience. (op 18-1)
Littlepromisedland(IRE), the second of the Richard Guest runners, finished out the back over 5f on debut in July. She again got outpaced over this stiffer test, but left the impression she could have a future when switching to handicaps. (tchd 80-1)
Majestic Millie(IRE), who was well backed over C&D a week earlier, once again showed bright early speed before dropping out. She is one to keep an eye on now she is qualified for a mark. (op 12-1)
Caramella Brownie, well backed, proved reluctant to load and was always trailing after a tardy start. (op 8-1)

7280 JOE HOPWOOD MEMORIAL NURSERY 7f
2:15 (2:15) (Class 4) (0-85,80) 2-Y-O £3,043 (£905; £452; £226) Stalls Low

Form RPR
2501 1 **Barista (IRE)**[8] 7124 2-8-11 **70** 6ex PaulMulrennan 3 78
(M R Channon) *mde all: styd on strly: readily* **7/2**[3]
331 2 3 ¼ **Tasfeya**[17] 6919 2-9-4 **77** TadhgO'Shea 6 77
(M Johnston) *chsd ldrs: hung lft and styd on to take 2nd last 75yds: no imp* **5/2**[1]
2362 3 2 ½ **Grand Duchy**[33] 6513 2-9-7 **80** SilvestreDeSousa 1 74
(Mahmood Al Zarooni) *chsd wnr: drvn over 2f out: hung rt: fdd last 100yds* **11/4**[2]
3460 4 9 **Ted's Brother (IRE)**[11] 7050 2-8-4 **63** FrannyNorton 5 34
(R C Guest) *chsd ldrs: outpcd over 4f out: sme hdwy 2f out: nvr a factor* **9/1**
2331 5 7 **Tro Nesa (IRE)**[11] 7050 2-9-6 **79** PhillipMakin 4 33
(Mrs A Duffield) *s.i.s: hrd drvn and outpcd over 4f out: sn lost pl* **8/1**
1003 6 35 **Kalkan Bay**[24] 6745 2-8-13 **72** PJMcDonald 2 —
(Jedd O'Keeffe) *drvn along in rr: lost pl after 2f: t.o over 3f out: virtually p.u* **8/1**

1m 30.24s (3.24) **Going Correction** +0.425s/f (Yiel) **6** Ran SP% **109.7**
Speed ratings (Par 98): **98,94,91,81,73 33**
Tote Swingers:1&2:£2.40, 2&3:£1.70, 1&3:£1.60 CSF £12.04 TOTE £4.10: £2.00, £1.10; EX 9.60.
Owner Mrs T Burns **Bred** Rathasker Stud **Trained** West Ilsley, Berks

FOCUS
A modest nursery, run at a sound pace. Once again the stands' side was the place to be in the home straight and the runners hardly changed their positions from the start. The winner relished the ground but this was a typical Catterick race for the time of year.

NOTEBOOK

Barista(IRE) came up the stands' rail when winning at Leicester eight days earlier and grabbing it again here saw him follow up in ready fashion. He made most of the running and his tactical speed on this surface enabled him to grab the rail once tracking across without much fuss. He is versatile regards ground, but is clearly very effective when the mud is flying and this rates his best effort yet. He was already due to race off a 4lb higher mark, however, so things will be plenty tougher from now on. (op 3-1 tchd 11-4)

Tasfeya made all when off the mark at the third attempt over C&D 17 days earlier, but wasn't able to boss the race on this nursery debut. He also looked a little uneasy at times on this softer ground and does have scope, so it's probably best not to be fully judging him on this effort.

Grand Duchy got a nice sit just off the pace early on, but got a little tapped for toe when the winner kicked into the home turn and was unable to raise his game in the straight. His 6lb rise for finishing second at Warwick last month looks a bit harsh. (tchd 3-1)

Ted's Brother(IRE) adopted a mid-field position over this extra furlong and failed to make a sufficient impact, but did reverse last-time-out form with Tro Nesa. (op 12-1 tchd 14-1)

Tro Nesa(IRE) was upped 7lb for her success at Ayr 11 days earlier and, held up to get this longer trip, her fate was sealed before the home turn. She is better than this. (op 7-1)

Kalkan Bay, who didn't go unbacked, was outpaced pretty much from the off and didn't handle the ground. Official explanation: jockey said gelding was unsuited by the soft ground (op 11-1)

7281 GO RACING IN YORKSHIRE CLAIMING STKS 5f
2:45 (2:45) (Class 6) 3-Y-O+ **£1,706** (£503; £252) **Stalls** Low

Form RPR

5412 **1** **Avonvalley**[7] 7148 3-8-1 62 FrannyNorton 5 69
(George Baker) *w ldr: styd on to ld last 100yds: kpt on wl towards fin* **13/8**[1]

4035 **2** ½ **Galpin Junior (USA)**[31] 6572 4-8-6 71 SilvestreDeSousa 7 72
(Mrs R A Carr) *chsd ldrs: outpcd over 2f out: kpt on to chal ins fnl f: no ex* **11/4**[2]

2626 **3** ¾ **Atlantic Beach**[6] 7169 5-9-0 75 (b) PaulMulrennan 8 78
(D O'Meara) *led: hdd and no ex ins fnl f* **11/2**

0234 **4** 1 **Wicked Wilma (IRE)**[6] 7175 6-8-4 62 (t) PaulPickard(3) 1 67
(A Berry) *w ldrs on outside: edgd lft and kpt on same pce last 150yds* **5/1**[3]

2356 **5** 1 **Real Diamond**[17] 6922 4-7-11 57 ow1 (p) JamesSullivan(3) 3 56
(Ollie Pears) *chsd ldrs: outpcd over 2f out: hung rt and kpt on fnl f* **9/1**

0000 **6** 24 **Jibrrya**[21] 6826 3-8-4 55 AdrianNicholls 6 —
(D Nicholls) *chsd ldrs: outpcd and lost pl over 2f out: eased whn bhd ins fnl f: t.o* **20/1**

62.70 secs (2.90) **Going Correction** +0.625s/f (Yiel) **6** Ran SP% **111.6**

Speed ratings (Par 101): **101,100,99,97,95 57**

Tote Swingers:1&2:£1.50, 2&3:£2.30, 1&3:£2.20 CSF £6.20 TOTE £2.80: £2.80, £1.10; EX 7.20 Trifecta £27.00 Pool £478.71 - 13.09 winning units..Avonvalley was claimed by Peter Grayson for £6,000.

Owner George Baker & Partners **Bred** Ercan Dogan **Trained** Moreton Morrell, Warwicks

FOCUS

Once again the far side was shunned in this 5f claimer, but the first two made their efforts more towards the middle of the track. The winner did not need to match her C/D latest form.

7282 HAMBLETON MAIDEN STKS 1m 3f 214y
3:15 (3:16) (Class 5) 3-Y-O+ **£2,072** (£616; £308; £153) **Stalls** High

Form RPR

5-3 **1** **Local Hero (GER)**[19] 6876 3-9-3 0 DarryllHolland 12 88+
(S Gollings) *in rr: hmpd and pushed along bnd over 7f out: gd hdwy over 5f out: led over 2f out: styd on wl: readily* **7/2**[3]

2-26 **2** 2¼ **Protaras (USA)**[19] 6876 3-9-3 78 IanMongan 14 82
(H R A Cecil) *sn trcking ldrs: drvn over 2f out: chsd wnr over 1f out: no imp* **3/1**[1]

2225 **3** 7 **Astral Flower**[33] 6499 3-8-12 73 SilvestreDeSousa 2 66
(Sir Michael Stoute) *chsd ldrs: rdn to chal over 2f out: wknd appr fnl f* **7/2**[3]

3233 **4** ½ **Strictly Lambada**[19] 6861 3-8-12 72 RobertHavlin 9 65
(J H M Gosden) *w ldrs: led after 2f: reminders over 3f out: hdd over 2f out: wknd over 1f out* **10/3**[2]

/64- **5** 10 **Broughton Beck (IRE)**[617] 659 4-9-6 56 IanBrennan(3) 11 54
(R F Fisher) *mid-div: outpcd and lost pl over 3f out* **100/1**

3-53 **6** 1 **Dr Valentine (FR)**[178] 834 4-9-9 64 PhillipMakin 7 52
(Mrs A Duffield) *hld up towards rr: hmpd bnd over 7f out: hdwy 6f out: drvn and outpcd over 3f out* **33/1**

5226 **7** 28 **Gay Mirage (GER)**[13] 7022 3-8-12 68 (v[1]) PhilipRobinson 1 —
(M A Jarvis) *w ldrs: drvn 6f out: lost pl over 3f out: bhd whn eased over 1f out: t.o* **15/2**

3 **8** 2¼ **Nodforms Violet (IRE)**[8] 7120 6-9-9 0 GregFairley 5 —
(Karen McLintock) *s.i.s: in rr: bhd 6f out: sn t.o* **16/1**

45 **9** 6 **Machir Bay**[16] 6966 3-9-3 0 PaulMulrennan 13 —
(V P Donoghue) *mid-div: lost pl 5f out: sn bhd: t.o 3f out* **100/1**

00/0 **10** 4 **Bottomless Wallet**[17] 6915 9-9-4 47 TomEaves 10 —
(F Watson) *chsd ldrs: lost pl over 5f out: sn bhd: t.o 3f out* **250/1**

11 2 **Ballyday (IRE)**[1458] 8-9-9 0 PaddyAspell 3 —
(F Watson) *sn in rr: bhd 5f out: sn t.o* **250/1**

0- **12** 76 **Mon Mon (IRE)**[332] 7638 3-8-12 0 PJMcDonald 6 —
(B Storey) *rn wout declared tongue-tie: t.k.h: led 2f: lost pl over 6f out: sn bhd: t.o over 4f out: virtually p.u* **100/1**

2m 46.45s (7.55) **Going Correction** +0.775s/f (Yiel)

WFA 3 from 4yo+ 6lb **12** Ran SP% **116.9**

Speed ratings (Par 103): **105,103,98,98,91 91,72,71,67,64 63,12**

Tote Swingers:1&2:£3.70, 2&3:£3.00, 1&3:£4.40 CSF £14.29 TOTE £5.80: £2.40, £1.40, £1.10; EX 23.50 Trifecta £71.50 Pool £847.80 - 8.76 winning units..

Owner P J Martin **Bred** Gestut Evershorst **Trained** Scamblesby, Lincs

FOCUS

A weak maiden, run at a fair enough pace and the first four dominated. Straightforward form with the first two improving to pull clear. The next pair are becoming disappointing.

Gay Mirage(GER) Official explanation: jockey said filly was unsuited by the soft (heavy in places) ground

7283 RACINGUK.COM H'CAP 7f
3:45 (3:45) (Class 4) (0-80,80) 3-Y-O+ **£3,691** (£1,098; £548; £274) **Stalls** Low

Form RPR

3112 **1** **Cara's Request (AUS)**[7] 7146 5-9-7 80 AdrianNicholls 1 89
(D Nicholls) *mde all: drvn over 2f out: edgd lft ins fnl f: hld on gamely* **10/3**[1]

0004 **2** ½ **Conry (IRE)**[7] 7146 4-9-0 80 JulieBurke(7) 12 88+
(Patrick Morris) *in rr: hdwy over 3f out: effrt against stands' rail and hmpd wl over 1f out: swtchd lft: styd on to take 2nd nr fin* **11/2**

0013 **3** nk **Trans Sonic**[7] 7143 7-9-0 73 (b) SilvestreDeSousa 13 80
(D O'Meara) *chsd ldrs: wnt 2nd over 3f out: styd on same pce last 75yds* **5/1**[3]

3021 **4** ¾ **Solar Spirit (IRE)**[7] 7146 5-9-3 79 6ex IanBrennan(3) 11 84
(J J Quinn) *trckd ldrs: effrt over 2f out: edgd rt: styd on fnl f: no ex* **4/1**[2]

0050 **5** 4 **Turn Me On (IRE)**[7] 7143 7-8-11 77 LukeStrong(7) 10 71
(T D Walford) *s.i.s: in rr: hdwy towards centre 2f out: nvr nr ldrs* **11/1**

6013 **6** 1 **Master Of Dance (IRE)**[16] 6961 3-9-0 74 PaulMulrennan 5 66
(J G Given) *sn chsng ldrs: fdd appr fnl f* **20/1**

0030 **7** 1½ **Feeling Fresh (IRE)**[38] 6366 5-8-13 72 PhillipMakin 6 60
(Paul Green) *mid-div: hdwy 3f out: wkng whn hmpd over 1f out* **25/1**

0406 **8** ½ **Island Chief**[7] 7146 4-8-8 70 (p) JamesSullivan(3) 14 56
(M W Easterby) *towards rr on outer: sme hdwy on stands' side whn nt clr run over 1f out: swtchd lft: kpt on* **33/1**

0460 **9** ¾ **Rock 'N' Royal**[16] 6963 3-9-2 76 BarryMcHugh 15 60
(R A Fahey) *s.i.s: sn prom on outside: edgd rt and wknd over 1f out* **20/1**

1634 **10** 3¾ **Northern Bolt**[16] 6962 5-8-13 72 (b) PatrickMathers 7 46
(I W McInnes) *s.i.s: a towards rr* **20/1**

0500 **11** 4 **Shotley Mac**[7] 7143 6-9-5 78 (b) FrannyNorton 9 41
(N Bycroft) *hld up in tch: lost pl over 4f out* **14/1**

1106 **12** 3½ **Fibs And Flannel**[16] 6961 3-9-1 75 DavidAllan 4 30
(T D Easterby) *hld up in midfield: hdwy over 3f out: drvn over 2f out: lost pl wl over 1f out* **28/1**

1500 **13** 4 **Mr Wolf**[7] 7143 9-8-11 77 (p) ShaneBKelly(7) 2 21
(J J Quinn) *hmpd s: chsd ldrs: styd far side over 2f out: lost pl over 1f out: sn bhd* **40/1**

5264 **14** 1 **Coin From Heaven (IRE)**[10] 7082 3-8-13 73 TomEaves 3 14
(R A Fahey) *s.i.s: mid-div: lost pl over 3f out* **22/1**

1m 31.51s (4.51) **Going Correction** +0.775s/f (Yiel)

WFA 3 from 4yo+ 1lb **14** Ran SP% **121.4**

Speed ratings (Par 105): **105,104,104,103,98 97,95,95,94,90 85,81,77,76**

Tote Swingers:1&2:£3.90, 2&3:£6.80, 1&3:£3.10 CSF £18.69 CT £95.63 TOTE £3.00: £1.10, £4.00, £2.20; EX 26.70 Trifecta £53.10 Pool £537.52 - 7.48 winning units..

Owner Stewart Aitken **Bred** S Aitken **Trained** Sessay, N Yorks

■ Stewards' Enquiry : Ian Brennan four-day ban: careless riding (Nov 16-19)

Barry McHugh two-day ban: careless riding (Nov 16-17)

FOCUS

The ground was officially eased to soft, heavy in places after the maiden. A modest handicap in which over half of the field had run over C&D a week previously. Few got into serious contention off the solid early pace. The form looks sound despite the ground and time of year.

7284 NATIONAL HUNT SEASON STARTS ON 1ST DECEMBER H'CAP 1m 5f 175y
4:15 (4:15) (Class 5) (0-75,71) 3-Y-O+ **£2,072** (£616; £308; £153) **Stalls** Low

Form RPR

6110 **1** **Dubara Reef (IRE)**[24] 6750 3-9-1 66 (p) GregFairley 14 73
(Paul Green) *w ldr: led after 5f: jnd over 2f out: kpt on gamely fnl f* **12/1**

4461 **2** 1¼ **Bollin Greta**[18] 6895 5-10-0 71 (t) DavidAllan 13 76
(T D Easterby) *hld up in rr: hdwy 7f out: sn trcking ldrs: effrt over 2f out: kpt on to chal jst ins fnl f: no ex* **11/2**[3]

3213 **3** 1¼ **Affinity**[29] 6631 3-9-4 69 IanMongan 2 72
(H R A Cecil) *trckd ldrs: chal over 2f out: kpt on same pce fnl f* **8/1**

3362 **4** ½ **Puy D'Arnac (FR)**[47] 6109 7-10-0 71 PJMcDonald 9 74
(G A Swinbank) *hld up: hdwy to trck ldrs over 7f out: effrt over 2f out: kpt on same pce over 1f out* **9/2**[2]

1162 **5** 1 **Beat The Shower**[37] 6397 4-9-13 70 FrannyNorton 1 71+
(P D Niven) *hld up in tch: drvn over 3f out: kpt on one pce fnl 2f* **10/3**[1]

3606 **6** ½ **French Hollow**[18] 6895 5-9-3 60 PaulMulrennan 12 60
(T J Fitzgerald) *t.k.h in rr: hdwy over 5f out: one pce fnl 2f* **12/1**

7 2¼ **Not Til Monday (IRE)**[32] 4636 4-9-11 68 DarryllHolland 3 65
(J R Jenkins) *led 5f: chsd ldrs: n.m.r over 1f out: one pce whn n.m.r ins fnl f: eased* **12/1**

054- **8** 4½ **Hernando's Boy**[381] 6845 9-8-9 55 KellyHarrison(3) 8 46
(K G Reveley) *in rr div: hdwy over 3f out: chsd ldrs over 1f out: wknd fnl 100yds: nvr on terms* **28/1**

0066 **9** 1¼ **Jenny Soba**[17] 6915 7-8-6 52 MichaelStainton(3) 11 41
(Lucinda Featherstone) *chsd ldrs: drvn 6f out: wknd over 1f out* **22/1**

5645 **10** 1½ **Spahi (FR)**[7] 7149 4-9-0 57 SilvestreDeSousa 6 44
(D O'Meara) *hld up in rr: sme hdwy over 2f out: wknd over 1f out* **9/1**

0/6- **11** 2¼ **Pegasus Prince (USA)**[174] 7505 6-8-10 56 PaulPickard(3) 4 40
(K G Reveley) *stdd s: hld up in rr: nvr on terms* **20/1**

6361 **12** 1 **Eijaaz (IRE)**[17] 6915 9-9-2 62 (p) MichaelO'Connell(3) 5 45
(G A Harker) *hld up in rr: hdwy 7f out: chsd ldrs over 3f out: edgd lft and one pce over 1f out* **20/1**

500- **13** shd **Melange (USA)**[225] 2772 4-8-12 55 (t) TomEaves 10 37
(G A Charlton) *trckd ldrs: lost pl over 3f out: sn bhd* **33/1**

3m 20.02s (16.42) **Going Correction** +1.125s/f (Soft)

WFA 3 from 4yo+ 8lb **13** Ran SP% **121.1**

Speed ratings (Par 103): **98,97,96,96,95 95,94,91,90,90 88,88,88**

Tote Swingers:1&2:£7.70, 2&3:£8.90, 1&3:£9.70 CSF £72.03 CT £575.03 TOTE £16.60: £5.70, £2.00, £2.00; EX 110.70 Trifecta £335.60 Part won. Pool £453.58 - 0.62 winning units..

Owner The Four Aces **Bred** M Duffy **Trained** Lydiate, Merseyside

FOCUS

A competitive staying handicap for the class that was always going to prove a real test on such ground. Fair form, and pretty sound.

T/Jkpt: £10,259.70 to a £1 stake. Pool:£79,476.96. 5.50 winning tickets. T/Plt: £11.40 to a £1 stake. Pool:£73,093.01. 4,649.52 winning tickets. T/Qpdt: £7.10 to a £1 stake. Pool:£3,339.50. 344.20 winning tickets. WG

7161 KEMPTON (A.W) (R-H)
Tuesday, November 2

OFFICIAL GOING: Standard

Wind: Brisk, behind. Weather: Overcast

7285 DALMORE SIXTY FOUR YEAR OLD H'CAP 5f (P)
2:25 (2:26) (Class 5) (0-75,75) 3-Y-O+ **£2,286** (£675; £337) **Stalls** High

Form RPR

1300 **1** **Love You Louis**[6] 7180 4-8-13 67 RichardHughes 4 79
(J R Jenkins) *mde all: drvn over 1f out: styd on wl fnl f: unchal* **8/1**

3303 **2** 1¾ **Fair Passion**[12] 7041 3-9-6 74 JimmyQuinn 11 80
(D Shaw) *chsd ldrs: rdn and styd on wl fnl f: edgd rt and tk 2nd fnl 120yds but no imp on wnr* **4/1**[2]

6546 **3** ¾ **Lord Of The Reins (IRE)**[10] 7093 6-9-0 68 PaulHanagan 6 71
(J G Given) *in rr but in tch: hdwy fr 2f out: drvn and styd on fnl f to take 3rd fnl 100yds: kpt on but no imp on ldng duo* **7/1**

1243 **4** 2 1/4 **Island Legend (IRE)**[5] 7194 4-9-1 **69**...............................(p) LiamKeniry 9 64
(J M Bradley) *chsd wnr: rdn and no imp ins fnl 2f: lost 2nd fnl 120yds and sn wknd* **9/2**[3]
4013 **5** 1 1/4 **Ajjaadd (USA)**[14] 6998 4-9-4 **72**.. SteveDrowne 7 62
(T E Powell) *towards rr early: hdwy 1/2-way: rdn and hung rt ins fnl 2f: kpt on again fnl f* **7/2**[1]
3100 **6** 3/4 **Starwatch**[10] 7093 3-9-1 **69**... NeilChalmers 3 57
(J J Bridger) *in rr: pushed along over 1f out: r.o ins fnl f: fin wl* **66/1**
4250 **7** 1/2 **Wanchai Whisper**[34] 6466 3-8-9 **66**.................(p) AndrewHeffernan(3) 5 52
(P R Hedger) *unruly stalls: in rr: pushed along over 1f out: r.o fnl 120yds: fin wl* **12/1**
0010 **8** *shd* **Zowington**[45] 6198 8-9-1 **69**..(v) WilliamCarson 10 55
(S C Williams) *s.i.s: hung rt and carried hd high home turn ins fnl 2f: nt look keen but kpt on cl home* **16/1**
13-0 **9** *hd* **Wellington Fair**[73] 5309 3-9-7 **75**.................................. SamHitchcott 12 60
(Miss Tor Sturgis) *t.k.h: chsd ldrs tl wknd fnl f* **50/1**
6440 **10** 4 1/2 **Spring Green**[6] 7180 4-9-5 **73**...(b) JimCrowley 2 42
(H Morrison) *chsd ldrs tl hung lft: v wd and wknd bnd ins fnl 2f* **7/1**

59.36 secs (-1.14) **Going Correction** 0.0s/f (Stan) **10** Ran SP% **113.5**
Speed ratings (Par 103): **109,106,105,101,99 98,97,97,96,89**
Tote Swingers:1&2:£6.30, 2&3:£6.80, 1&3:£7.50 CSF £38.93 CT £242.04 TOTE £13.70: £3.00, £1.20, £1.90; EX 50.90.
Owner J Pepper **Bred** Mrs Wendy Jenkins **Trained** Royston, Herts

FOCUS
A tightly knit sprint handicap. The winner made all in a good time and just he is just as good on Polytrack as on turf.

7286 WHYTE AND MACKAY H'CAP 1m 2f (P)
2:55 (2:56) (Class 6) (0-65,65) 3-Y-0+ **£1,637** (£483; £241) **Stalls** High

Form RPR
5522 **1** **Lady Lam**[20] 6846 4-9-7 **62**...(t) RichardHughes 8 70
(S Kirk) *mid-div: pushed along over 2f out: rdn and styd on fr over 1f out: kpt on thrght fnl f to ld cl home* **15/8**[1]
0053 **2** *nk* **Bubbly Braveheart (IRE)**[11] 7068 3-9-1 **60**................ RobertWinston 9 67
(A Bailey) *led 2f: styd chsng ldr: chal 3f out: led again ins fnl 2f: hrd drvn fnl f: hdd and no ex cl home* **6/1**[2]
2600 **3** *nk* **Blackstone Vegas**[11] 5864 4-8-10 **51**............................... JoeFanning 10 58
(D Shaw) *chsd ldrs tl rdn and one pce fr 2f out: rallied ins fnl f and styd on strly fnl 100yds: gng on cl home* **20/1**
2062 **4** *nk* **Mayfair's Future**[12] 7038 5-8-10 **51** oh1.....................(p) StephenCraine 7 57
(J R Jenkins) *trckd ldrs: rdn to chse wnr fr 2f out: ev ch fnl f untl no ex fnl 25yds* **12/1**
6166 **5** 1 3/4 **Adoyen Spice**[27] 6669 3-9-0 **59**.. PaulHanagan 14 62
(Mike Murphy) *chsd ldrs: rdn along 2f out: styd on same pce fnl f* **15/2**[3]
0400 **6** 3 1/2 **Pictures (IRE)**[8] 7117 3-8-3 **51** oh1.................................... KierenFox(3) 1 47
(J J Bridger) *in rr: pushed along 2f out: styd on u.p fnl f but no imp on ldrs* **20/1**
30 **7** *nk* **Storms Over (USA)**[18] 6905 3-8-6 **51** oh1........................ JimmyQuinn 6 46
(B W Duke) *s.i.s: in rr: rdn: hdwy and hung rt ins fnl 2f: styd on fnl f but nvr any threat* **50/1**
0310 **8** *nk* **Carr Hall (IRE)**[172] 2081 7-9-10 **65**...................................... NeilCallan 4 60
(A W Carroll) *in tch 1/2-way: pushed along and hdwy fr 3f out: nvr gng pce to rch ldrs and one pce appr fnl f* **12/1**
0364 **9** *nk* **Singbella**[99] 4422 4-9-0 **58**...(p) JohnFahy(3) 3 52
(C G Cox) *in rr: stl plenty to do 2f out: sme hdwy ins fnl f* **9/1**
0022 **10** 1 3/4 **Watchmaker**[11] 7068 7-9-5 **60**..(p) FergusSweeney 12 50
(Miss Tor Sturgis) *in tch: rdn 2f out: wknd over 1f out* **8/1**
02-0 **11** 2 1/4 **Looks Like Slim**[182] 1796 3-8-10 **55**.................................. ChrisCatlin 13 41
(B De Haan) *w ldr: led after 2f: hdd ins fnl 2f: wknd 2f out* **50/1**
0-60 **12** *10* **Mater Mater**[14] 6999 3-8-10 **55**.. J-PGuillambert 11 21
(Andrew Reid) *s.i.s: a in rr* **25/1**
2400 **13** *7* **Katchmore (IRE)**[144] 2935 3-9-6 **65**................................... JimCrowley 2 17
(M Blanshard) *chsd ldrs and racd wd: wknd 4f out: v wd bnd ins fnl 2f and eased whn no ch* **40/1**
6-00 **14** 1/2 **Weald Park (USA)**[270] 429 4-9-4 **62**.......................... SimonPearce(3) 5 13
(J Pearce) *chsd ldrs tl wknd ins fnl 3f* **10/1**

2m 7.21s (-0.79) **Going Correction** 0.0s/f (Stan)
WFA 3 from 4yo+ 4lb **14** Ran SP% **126.2**
Speed ratings (Par 101): **103,102,102,102,100 98,97,97,97,95 94,86,80,80**
Tote Swingers:1&2:£4.30, 2&3:£16.50, 1&3:£11.00 CSF £12.15 CT £183.92 TOTE £3.00: £1.10, £2.70, £7.10; EX 18.10.
Owner J B J Richards **Bred** J B J Richards **Trained** Upper Lambourn, Berks

FOCUS
A modest but pretty competitive handicap and a close finish. The form looks sound and the winner produced a length personal best.

7287 FETTERCAIRN H'CAP 1m 2f (P)
3:25 (3:25) (Class 2) (0-100,105) 3-Y-0+
£9,221 (£2,761; £1,380; £691; £344; £173) **Stalls** High

Form RPR
0-13 **1** **Ottoman Empire (FR)**[18] 6889 4-9-8 **98**........................ RichardMullen 7 108+
(D R Lanigan) *trckd ldrs: hdwy on ins whn n.m.r: edgd rt and hit rail ins fnl 2f: drvn to chal appr fnl f: one pce ins fnl f tl rallied fnl 50yds to ld last stride* **5/4**[1]
403 **2** *shd* **Greylami (IRE)**[60] 5723 5-9-3 **93**.. JimCrowley 1 101
(R A Mills) *hld up in rr but in tch: hdwy on outside fr 2f out to ld over 1f out: drvn: edgd rt and kpt on wl fnl f: hdd and no ex last stride* **3/1**[2]
242 **3** *3* **Seradim**[21] 6830 4-8-10 **86**.. RichardHughes 3 88
(P F I Cole) *chsd ldr: drvn to chal over 1f out: outpcd ins fnl f* **8/1**
200 **4** 3/4 **Changing The Guard**[45] 6193 4-8-10 **86** oh1................ PaulHanagan 5 87
(R A Fahey) *plld hrd early and settled in tch after 2f: rdn over 2f out and no imp on ldrs: one pce fr over 1f out* **6/1**[3]
1300 **5** 2 1/4 **Mafeking (UAE)**[186] 1665 6-9-1 **91**.................................... ChrisCatlin 8 87
(M R Hoad) *led: edgd rt ins fnl 2f: hdd over 1f out and sn wknd* **12/1**
1055 **6** *11* **Highland Glen**[90] 4711 4-10-1 **105**.....................................(t) TedDurcan 4 79
(Saeed Bin Suroor) *in rr: rdn 3f out: fnd nthing and sn wl bhd* **11/1**

2m 6.09s (-1.91) **Going Correction** 0.0s/f (Stan) **6** Ran SP% **110.9**
Speed ratings (Par 109): **107,106,104,103,102 93**
Tote Swingers:1&2:£1.70, 2&3:£2.20, 1&3:£2.10 CSF £4.98 CT £17.59 TOTE £2.50: £2.20, £1.80; EX 6.20.
Owner Miss Yvonne Jacques & Plantation Stud **Bred** S C E A Haras De La Perelle **Trained** Newmarket, Suffolk

FOCUS
Reasonable prizemoney produced a fair line-up for this decent handicap, although interest was tempered slightly by a couple of defections. The time was 1.21 secs faster than the preceding handicap and the first two came clear. The winner is a bit better than the bare form.

NOTEBOOK
Ottoman Empire(FR) was beaten by the top weight here last September but was better off at the weights and came into this in good heart. He tracked the leader from the start but was short of room when looking to get through early in the straight. It did not stop him though and, once in the clear, he was able to wear down the runner-up near the line. He is now 3-4 here and effective at 1m2f-1m4f, although his trainer believers the latter trip is just a little too far. he will have a short break now before being prepared for a trip to the Dubai Carnival. (tchd 6-4 in places)
Greylami(IRE) is a consistent performer and twice a winner on this track. Held up at the back, he made his ground around the outside on the turn and it looked as though he would score when hitting the front. However, the winner got his gap on the inside and caught him near the line. He is a good yardstick and is likely to win his share; he has done particularly well here in the early spring. (op 4-1)
Seradim has gone close this season without winning but was stepping up in trip. She was ridden close to the pace and, despite being a little keen, made a bold bid until fading in the last furlong. (op 6-1)
Changing The Guard, another who was keen early, settled off the pace but could not pick up once in line for home. (tchd 11-2)
Mafeking(UAE), returning from a summer break, made the running before fading in the straight. This outing should put him right, and he should pay his way again this winter. (op 10-1)
Highland Glen was beaten on the home turn and seems to have gone the wrong way since winning on his debut for connections at Meydan in February, after which he was off for a good while. (op 8-1)

7288 ISLE OF JURA MEDIAN AUCTION MAIDEN STKS 1m (P)
3:55 (3:55) (Class 6) 3-5-Y-O **£1,637** (£483; £241) **Stalls** High

Form RPR
40 **1** **Room For A View**[19] 6876 3-8-12 0...................................(p) TedDurcan 3 65+
(M P Tregoning) *chsd ldrs: rdn over 3f out: styd on to chal appr fnl 2f: led wl over 1f out: rdn ins fnl f: styd on strly* **10/1**
44 **2** 1 1/4 **Handsome King**[6] 7183 3-9-3 0.. RichardHughes 1 67
(J R Jenkins) *chsd ldrs tl pushed along and lost position 3f out: rallied and kpt on appr fnl f: kpt on wl fnl 120yds: tk 2nd cl home: no ch w wnr* **7/1**[3]
065 **3** *hd* **Marksbury**[61] 5700 3-8-12 **56**.. PaulHanagan 5 62
(J M P Eustace) *trckd ldrs: chal fr over 4f out tl slt ld wl over 2f out: sn rdn: hdd wl over 1f out: styd chsng wnr but no imp: lost 2nd cl home* **8/1**
40 **4** 2 1/2 **Vezere (USA)**[20] 6856 3-8-12 64.. SebSanders 4 56
(S Dow) *in rr tl stdy hdwy on outer fr over 3f out: styd on to chse ldrs ins fnl 2f: one pce fnl f* **8/1**
05 **5** 1 3/4 **Flying Cherry (IRE)**[62] 5658 3-8-12 0............................. FergusSweeney 7 52
(Miss Jo Crowley) *in tch: chsd ldrs over 3f out: drvn and hung lft 1f out: styd same pce ins fnl f* **25/1**
3 **6** 1 3/4 **Asterisk**[28] 6655 3-8-12 0... CathyGannon 6 48
(John Berry) *in tch: t.k.h and edgd rt after 2f: sn bhd: rdn and hdwy on outside bnd 3f out: hung lft over 2f out: edgd rt u.p over 1f out: kpt on fnl f* **11/4**[1]
000 **7** 1 1/4 **Mouchez**[29] 6637 3-9-3 39.. SamHitchcott 10 50
(D K Ivory) *hmpd after 2f: styd in tch: rdn over 2f out and styd on same pce* **66/1**
0060 **8** 1 3/4 **Gibraltar Lass (USA)**[28] 6656 3-8-12 45.......................... JimmyQuinn 13 41
(H J Collingridge) *chsd ldrs: rdn over 2f out: wknd over 1f out* **66/1**
06 **9** 1/2 **Annie Bonita**[10] 7086 3-8-9 0... JohnFahy(3) 12 40
(P R Hedger) *s.i.s: hmpd after 2f: hdwy on ins over 1f out: kpt on but nvr a threat* **12/1**
10 3/4 **Princess Runner** 3-8-12 0.. SteveDrowne 11 38+
(J R Gask) *slowly away: hmpd after 2f: veered lft and v green: stl in rr: rn green and hung bdly lft 2f out: sme prog fnl f* **20/1**
00 **11** 1 3/4 **Prince Blue**[28] 6655 3-9-0 0.. SimonPearce(3) 8 39
(G G Margarson) *sn led: jnd over 4f out: hdd over 2f out and sn wknd* **66/1**
56- **12** *2* **Suntrap**[405] 6199 3-9-3 0.. JimCrowley 9 34
(W J Knight) *in tch whn hmpd after 2f: sn bhd* **3/1**[2]
0050 **13** 1 1/2 **Aldorable**[29] 6638 3-8-12 43.. LiamKeniry 14 26
(R A Teal) *in tch whn hmpd after 2f: sme hdwy on ins fr 3f out: nvr rchd ldrs and wknd 2f out* **50/1**
00 **14** 1 1/4 **Boldly Go**[22] 6815 3-9-0 0... PatrickHills(3) 2 28
(R Hannon) *a in rr* **33/1**

1m 40.7s (0.90) **Going Correction** 0.0s/f (Stan) **14** Ran SP% **121.2**
Speed ratings (Par 101): **95,93,93,91,89 87,86,84,84,83 81,79,78,76**
Tote Swingers:1&2:£9.30, 2&3:£5.00, 1&3:£8.80 CSF £75.03 TOTE £12.10: £2.20, £1.60, £3.00; EX 125.20.
Owner Efemera Stud **Bred** N A Penston **Trained** Lambourn, Berks

FOCUS
A weak older-horse maiden, although a number had only limited experience. The winner did not need to improve much on her debut form.

7289 GLAYVA H'CAP 6f (P)
4:25 (4:27) (Class 3) (0-95,94) 3-Y-0+ **£6,281** (£1,869; £934; £466) **Stalls** High

Form RPR
5062 **1** **Sutton Veny (IRE)**[12] 7041 4-8-10 **83**............................... SteveDrowne 3 96+
(J R Gask) *trckd ldrs: drvn and qcknd to ld appr fnl f: styd on strly* **8/1**[3]
005 **2** 1 1/2 **Shifting Star (IRE)**[13] 7014 5-8-11 **84**............................. HayleyTurner 7 90
(W R Swinburn) *chsd ldrs: rdn and styd on to chse wnr fnl 75yds: no imp but hld on wl for 2nd cl home* **8/1**[3]
5051 **3** *hd* **Ray Of Joy**[23] 6772 4-8-11 **84**.. FergusSweeney 5 89+
(J R Jenkins) *in rr: stl plenty to do whn swtchd lft ins fnl 2f and str run fnl f to cl on 2nd last strides but no ch w wnr* **25/1**
3530 **4** 1/2 **We Have A Dream**[13] 7014 5-8-13 **86**................................ JimCrowley 10 90
(W R Muir) *disp ld tl slt advantage appr fnl 2f: hdd appr fnl f styd in 2nd tl wknd fnl 75yds* **14/1**
0540 **5** 1 1/4 **Baby Strange**[11] 7060 6-8-11 **84**.................................... PaulHanagan 11 84
(D Shaw) *in tch: rdn and no imp on ldrs fnl 2f* **9/2**[1]
0530 **6** *hd* **Yer Woman (IRE)**[39] 6319 3-9-6 **93**............................... RichardHughes 9 92
(R Hannon) *in rr: rdn over 2f out: rdn and sme hdwy fr 2f out: nvr gng pce to rch ldrs* **8/1**[3]
0321 **7** *1* **Swiss Cross**[22] 6799 3-8-12 **85**......................................(vt) NeilCallan 2 81
(G A Butler) *s.i.s: sn mid-div: hdwy on outside over 2f out: nvr rchd ldrs and styd on same pce* **5/1**[2]
4000 **8** *1* **Fullandby (IRE)**[38] 6363 8-9-7 **94**..................................... TedDurcan 1 87
(T J Etherington) *in rr: outpcd tl sme prog ins fnl f* **14/1**
0400 **9** *1* **Tourist**[43] 6256 5-9-2 **89**... JimmyQuinn 8 79
(D Shaw) *outpcd most of way* **33/1**
6223 **10** *1* **Imprimis Tagula (IRE)**[12] 7033 6-8-13 **86**..................(v) RobertWinston 4 72
(A Bailey) *chsd ldrs tl wknd ins fnl 2f* **8/1**[3]
0302 **11** *shd* **Below Zero (IRE)**[13] 7014 3-9-5 **92**................................. JoeFanning 12 78
(M Johnston) *disp ld tl appr fnl 2f: sn btn* **5/1**[2]

1006 **12** 2¾ **Harlech Castle**^{65} 5551 5-9-1 **88**..............................(b) StephenCraine 6 65
(J R Boyle) *a outpcd* **66/1**

1m 11.46s (-1.64) **Going Correction** 0.0s/f (Stan) **12** Ran SP% **117.6**
Speed ratings (Par 107): **110,108,107,107,105 105,103,102,101,99 99,96**
Tote Swingers:1&2:£12.60, 2&3:£22.30, 1&3:£31.70 CSF £68.99 CT £1535.67 TOTE £8.20: £2.20, £3.70, £8.50; EX 66.40.
Owner The Sutton Veny Syndicate **Bred** Rathbarry Stud **Trained** Sutton Veny, Wilts

FOCUS
Another good handicap, this time a sprint. The pace was decent and the form looks fairly sound. The winner improved again on this step up to 6f.

NOTEBOOK
Sutton Veny(IRE) was given a good ride by Steve Drowne. The filly broke well and was able to take up a pitch behind the leaders, getting a good tow before being pulled out 2f out. Once in the clear she swept past her rivals and scored decisively. Her record over C&D is now 4-5 and this was her highest winning mark. She should remain competitive, even after reassessment. (op 6-1)
Shifting Star(IRE) has shown he handles this track in the past, despite not winning for over two years. With the cheekpieces left off this time, he was never far away and stuck on well in the closing stages. He is well handicapped on his old form if this signals a revival. (op 15-2 tchd 7-1)
Ray Of Joy has gained three of her four successes over C&D but was 7lb higher than for her success at Bath last time. Held up at the back, she came with a late flourish down the outside and will find easier opportunities around here this winter. (tchd 33-1)
We Have A Dream, never out of the first two in three previous appearances here, made the running alongside Below Zero but could not sustain his effort once headed by the winner. (tchd 16-1)
Baby Strange appeared to have a good pitch on the rail early but could not pick up, although he kept staying on. He has an entry at Doncaster on Saturday, a track that suits him well. (op 6-1)
Yer Woman(IRE) was 2-3 over C&D coming into this but failed to land a blow having been held up early. (op 9-1 tchd 10-1)
Swiss Cross was being pushed along to hold his place some way from home and never got into a challenging position. (op 11-2 tchd 6-1)

7290 RICHARD PATERSON ALL WEATHER "HANDS & HEELS" APPRENTICE SERIES H'CAP (RACING EXCELLENCE INITIATIVE) 1m (P)

4:55 (4:55) (Class 5) (0-75,73) 3-Y-O+ **£2,286** (£675; £337) **Stalls** High

Form RPR
4000 **1** **Dinner Date**^{8} 7115 8-9-1 **70**..............................(b^{1}) LucyBarry$^{(3)}$ 8 80
(T Keddy) *trckd ldrs on ins: pushed along to ld over 1f out: kpt on wl* **6/1**
1002 **2** 2¾ **Harting Hill**^{6} 7162 5-8-10 **65**.............................. KatiaScallan$^{(3)}$ 4 69
(M P Tregoning) *t.k.h: chsd ldr: led on outer over 4f out: jnd 2f out: one pce into 3rd 1f out: styd on agan to go 2nd fnl 100yds: no ch w wnr* **5/2**^{1}
5000 **3** 1 **Florio Vincitore (IRE)**^{15} 6992 3-9-2 **70**.............................. MatthewLawson 5 72
(E J Creighton) *led tl narrowly hdd over 4f out: styd pressing ldr and chal 2f out tl over 1f out: no ch w wnr ins fnl f: wknd and lost 2nd fnl 100yds* **8/1**
-000 **4** 1¼ **San Antonio**^{81} 5039 10-8-8 **65**..............................(b) ChristyMews$^{(5)}$ 3 64
(Mrs P Sly) *trckd ldrs on outer: rdn and styd on same pce fr over 1f out* **11/1**
0000 **5** 1¾ **Gallantry**^{8} 7115 8-9-4 **73**.............................. IanBurns$^{(3)}$ 1 68
(P Howling) *s.i.s: sn rcvrd to chse ldrs: wknd 2f out* **3/1**^{2}
3100 **6** 5 **Chief Exec**^{10} 7091 8-9-7 **73**..............................(b) NatashaEaton 2 56
(J R Gask) *s.i.s: a towards rr* **11/2**^{3}
2060 **7** 4 **Avow (USA)**^{14} 6996 3-8-2 **59** oh2..............................(b) MatthewCosham$^{(3)}$ 7 33
(J J Bridger) *chsd ldrs tl wknd ins fnl 3f* **12/1**
0000 **8** 8 **Warrior Nation (FR)**^{64} 5586 4-8-4 **59** oh14..............................(t) HobieGill$^{(3)}$ 6 15
(A J Chamberlain) *stdd off pce s: a in rr* **66/1**

1m 40.27s (0.47) **Going Correction** 0.0s/f (Stan)
WFA 3 from 4yo+ 2lb **8** Ran SP% **111.9**
Speed ratings (Par 103): **97,94,93,92,90 85,81,73**
Tote Swingers:1&2:£4.80, 2&3:£5.30, 1&3:£9.20 CSF £20.44 CT £119.42 TOTE £6.20: £2.00, £1.10, £1.40; EX 23.30.
Owner Mrs H Keddy **Bred** J M Greetham **Trained** Newmarket, Suffolk

FOCUS
An ordinary 'hands and heels' apprentice handicap. Muddling form, with the runner-up about the only solid guide.
T/Plt: £75.20 to a £1 stake. Pool:£74,800.49. 726.07 winning tickets. T/Qpdt: £32.70 to a £1 stake. Pool:£4,547.06. 102.80 winning tickets. ST

7245 FLEMINGTON (L-H)

Tuesday, November 2

OFFICIAL GOING: Turf: soft

7291a EMIRATES MELBOURNE CUP (GROUP 1) (H'CAP) (3YO+) (TURF) 2m

4:00 (12:00) 3-Y-O+
£2,097,222 (£500,000; £250,000; £138,888; £97,222; £69,444)

RPR
1 **Americain (USA)**^{13} 7032 5-8-8 **0** 1ex.............................. GeraldMosse 11 125+
(A De Royer-Dupre, France) *travelled wl in midfield: shkned up 3f out and sed to cl: 8th 2f out: rdn and running on down centre of trck: 5th 1 1/2f out: led appr fnl 110yds: won gng away* **12/1**
2 2¾ **Maluckyday (NZ)**^{3} 7245 4-8-0 **0** 2ex..............................(p) LukeNolen 5 118
(Michael, Wayne & John Hawkes, Australia) *settled in 10th (half-l in front of eventual wnr): smooth prog ins fnl 4f: 7th 2 1/2f out: rdn over 1 1/2f out: 3rd and jst over 1 l down ent fnl f: styd on u.p (drifting lft) to take 2nd fnl 50yds* **8/1**^{2}
3 ½ **So You Think (NZ)**^{3} 7246 4-8-11 **0**.............................. StevenArnold 2 128
(Bart Cummings, Australia) *a gng wl in 6th or 7th: clsd up 4f out: 5th and clsng on outside 2 1/2f out: led over 1 1/2f out: sn rdn and r.o: hdd appr fnl 110yds: unable qck: lost 2nd fnl 50yds* **2/1**^{1}
4 1¾ **Zipping (AUS)**^{10} 7107 9-8-10 **0**.............................. NicholasHall 15 121
(Robert Hickmott, Australia) *settled towards rr: last 3f out: c wdst of all fnl bnd: rdn and r.o outside whole field: 19th 2f out: styd on strly u.p: 6th ent fnl f: kpt on to go 4th fnl 25yds* **25/1**
5 ½ **Harris Tweed (NZ)**^{17} 6947 5-8-7 **0**..............................(t) BradRawiller 12 118
(Murray & Bjorn Baker, New Zealand) *a.p (trckd wnr for much of the way): briefly disp ld appr 2 out: sn rdn and nt qckn: wknd fnl 50yds and lost 4th 25yds out* **25/1**
6 ¾ **Holberg (UAE)**^{41} 6281 4-8-6 **0**.............................. FrankieDettori 9 116
(Saeed Bin Suroor) *settled in 5th or 6th: stl wl plcd and gng wl 3f out: lost pl and rdn 2 1/2f out (in abt 10th): styd on fnl 300yds wout really qckning* **20/1**
7 3 **Manighar (FR)**^{17} 6947 4-8-7 **0**.............................. DamienOliver 19 113
(L M Cumani) *settled towards rr: rdn and hdwy 3f out: 16th 2f out: styd on u.p tl one pce ins fnl 150yds* **25/1**
8 shd **Precedence (NZ)**^{10} 7106 5-8-6 **0** 7ex.............................. JamesWinks 14 112
(Bart Cummings, Australia) *among bkmarkers tl styd on fr 2 1/2f out: nrest at fin* **20/1**
9 1½ **Illustrious Blue**^{76} 5218 7-8-9 **0**.............................. GlenBoss 8 114
(W J Knight) *dwlt s and qckly swtchd to rail and settled in midfield (abt 12th): clsd up and gng nicely 3f out: disputing 7th and rdn appr 2f out: kpt on but unable qck fnl 300yds* **50/1**
10 1¼ **Mr Medici (IRE)**^{17} 6947 5-8-9 **0**.............................. DarrenBeadman 4 112
(L Ho, Hong Kong) *chsd ldrs: 5th and gng ok 3f out: disputing 3rd 2f out: sn rdn and nt qckn: fdd fnl f* **60/1**
11 nk **Once Were Wild (AUS)**^{3} 7245 4-8-2 **0**.............................. JimCassidy 10 109
(Gai Waterhouse, Australia) *broke wl and led after 1f: pushed along and hdd appr 2f out: dropped away fnl 300yds* **30/1**
12 nk **Tokai Trick (JPN)**^{17} 6947 8-8-8 **0**.............................. ShinjiFujita 3 111
(Kenji Nonaka, Japan) *racd in abt 8th: hdwy to go 3rd 3f out: one of v few to stay on ins fnl turn: disp ld u.p appr 2f out: hdd appr fnl 1 1/2f: sn btn* **100/1**
13 ¾ **Shoot Out (AUS)**^{3} 7246 4-8-9 **0**.............................. CoreyBrown 16 115
(John Wallace, Australia) *racd in midfield: rdn and no imp fnl 3f* **25/1**
14 1¾ **Monaco Consul (NZ)**^{17} 6947 4-8-7 **0**..............................(t) CraigAWilliams 13 111
(Michael Moroney, Australia) *hld up towards rr: styd on ins rail fnl turn: nvr in contention* **30/1**
15 2¾ **Master O'Reilly (NZ)**^{10} 7106 8-8-7 **0**.............................. VladDuric 17 104
(Danny O'Brien, Australia) *a bhd: n.d* **200/1**
16 ½ **Campanologist (USA)**^{46} 6148 5-8-11 **0**.............................. KerrinMcEvoy 18 107
(Saeed Bin Suroor) *hld up in fnl 3rd: pushed along 3f out: 18th 1 1/2f out: rdn and no imp* **66/1**
17 ½ **Profound Beauty (IRE)**^{52} 5976 6-8-7 **0**.............................. PJSmullen 21 103
(D K Weld, Ire) *settled in 18th: rdn 2f out: no imp* **30/1**
18 shd **Shocking (AUS)**^{3} 7246 5-9-0 **0**..............................(bt) MichaelRodd 23 110
(Mark Kavanagh, Australia) *hld up: last and rdn appr 2f out: nvr seen w a ch* **11/1**^{3}
19 1 **Red Ruler (NZ)**^{3} 7245 6-8-6 **0**.............................. MarkDuPlessis 7 101
(John Sargent, New Zealand) *nvr threatened* **300/1**
20 3 **Buccellati**^{17} 6947 6-8-7 **0**..............................(v) StevenKing 20 98
(Tony Noonan, Australia) *nvr a factor* **300/1**
21 12 **Linton (AUS)**^{3} 7245 4-8-3 **0** 3ex.............................. BrettPrebble 22 85
(Robert Hickmott, Australia) *a bhd: nvr a factor* **25/1**
22 12 **Zavite (NZ)**^{17} 6947 8-8-7 **0**..............................(b) MichaelWalker 6 72
(Anthony Cummings, Australia) *settled in 4th: rdn and lost pl 3 1/2f out: wknd fnl 2f* **150/1**
P **Descarado (NZ)**^{3} 7246 4-8-7 **0** 3ex.............................. NashRawiller 1 —
(Gai Waterhouse, Australia) *set stdy gallop tl hdd after 1f: settled in share of 2nd/3rd: pressed ldr v cl 2 1/2f out to all but share ld: rdn appr 2f out but nt qckn: rdr looked down twice and eased 150yds out: sn p.u: dismntd* **12/1**

3m 26.87s (7.23) **23** Ran SP% **114.5**
PARI-MUTUEL (NSW TAB - all including au$1 stakes): WIN 12.30 PLACE 3.60, 3.00, 2.10; DF 59.50 SF 138.00.
Owner G T Ryan, K L Bamford, & Mrs C O Bamford **Bred** Wertheimer Et Frere **Trained** Chantilly, France
■ The first French-trained Melbourne Cup winner.

FOCUS
The 150th running of the Melbourne Cup. The early pace appeared modest, but the three market leaders filled the places and the form is sound.

NOTEBOOK
Americain(USA) won in style, pulling clear of his rivals takingly. Owned by an Australian partnership who started their search for a runner in this race five years previously, he already looked to have a strong chance on his French form after a moderate spell in America. But he managed to gain a victory in the Geelong Cup on the way to this success under top weight, a feat not achieved often. Connections suggested that he could go for the Hong Kong Vase, and then have a campaign geared towards another attempt at this race next year.
Maluckyday(NZ), who was bidding to emulate Shocking by winning the Lexus Stakes before taking this, fully justified his connections' decision to race him here and he will almost certainly now be one of the favourites for 2011.
So You Think(NZ) took a strong early grip under Steven Arnold. The jockey did a fine job trying to settle him as they started down the back straight, but the horse was still inclined to take a pull under restraint. The pair cruised into contention in ominous style at the top of the home straight, still arguably over-racing, and got to the front about 300 metres out. But the energy he had exerted took its toll and he didn't have much left when challenged on both sides. It was a tremendous effort by a horse all eyes were focused on and if he races on he is likely to be retired) he will be very hard to beat at trips up to 1m4f. Coolmore have purchased a majority share in him, and he may race for Aidan O'Brien in 2011.
Zipping(AUS) had been showing there was plenty of life left in him when taking a pair of Group 1s this year, including the Turnbull Stakes, which contained plenty who re-opposed here. Finishing fourth for the third time in this famous contest, he was widest of the field turning in, but kept on well in the final stages and was catching the first three who had gone beyond recall. A closer position about 400 metres out could have seen him trouble the winner.
Harris Tweed(NZ), who ran fifth behind Shocking last season, came from a stable whose owner/trainer combination landed the Victoria Derby the previous weekend. He needed to reverse form with Descarado on their Caulfield Cup meeting, which he was able to do so under a prominent ride, although the jockey reported afterwards that it wasn't the plan to be so handy. Good effort though it was, he regularly doesn't find as much under pressure as seems likely.
Holberg(UAE) had looked unlikely to make the line-up at one point because of his position down the list of runners, but was always the preferred choice of Frankie Dettori. Given an intelligent ride considering he definitely stays, he kept on in good style to claim an honourable sixth despite his jockey reporting that his mount wasn't enjoying the ground.
Manighar(FR)'s stablemate Bauer was a late absentee. He seemed to compromise his chance by pulling far too hard in the rear for much of the contest and then needed riding quite strongly to get into a challenging position on the home bend. It looked as though he may have met some traffic on turning in and was forced to delay his challenge just a little longer than his jockey would have liked, but how much ground he lost can only be guessed at. His effort behind Americain in the Prix Kergorlay, when giving that rival 2lb, suggests he was entitled to be thereabouts, so it's a shame he wasn't closer to the leaders at the crucial point of the race. Damien Oliver said the ground was too loose for his mount.
Precedence(NZ) looked to have every chance considering his form, but he didn't have any gears when needed. The ground may have been too slow for him and he will no doubt come back next year with a leading chance if he can build on this effort.
Illustrious Blue, purchased by the Australia Bloodstock Syndicate since his last start at York, looked to be travelling well under a quiet ride by Glen Boss over 600 metres out before getting outpaced. He quickly found his stride again and stayed on towards the far rail without ever quite getting involved. It was a decent performance on ground that would not have been ideal and he could be interesting next year if the going is on the quick side.

Mr Medici(IRE), a consistent performer in Hong Kong at the highest level, shaped really well in the Caulfield Cup but gave the firm impression he doesn't stay 2m.
Once Were Wild(AUS) was allowed to do her own thing without any pressure. As had been the case in the Lexus Stakes, she folded in the final stages, seemingly proving she isn't the strongest of finishers.
Tokai Trick(JPN), never dangerous in the Caulfield Cup, stays well in Japan but had done his winning on firm ground so the rain-affected track wouldn't have been to his liking. His jockey made a move towards the inside rail, a part of the track that didn't seem favoured considering where the principals finished.
Shoot Out(AUS) has plenty of good form in Group 1s, but the trip appeared to stretch him to a limit he couldn't achieve, and he was another to be one-paced.
Campanologist(USA), who claimed two German Group 1 victories over 1m4f this year, including one in soft ground, never got involved.
Profound Beauty(IRE) travelled nicely early on, but could make little progress from the rear rounding the final bend. She may have met a little traffic, but even when in the clear she was made to look slow. This was not the mare we saw dominating in Ireland, albeit against some modest horses for the level she was racing in, so something was possibly wrong.
Shocking(AUS) put in a lacklustre performance, even allowing for the fact he was drawn wide. The rider reported afterwards that his mount ripped a plate off round the back and had pulled up a bit lame.
Linton(AUS) had a nightmare which was readily explained by his rider who said his mount hung all the way and wasn't comfortable in the going at all. He then slipped quite badly on the home turn and lost both his action and his confidence.
Descarado(NZ) was sadly pulled up over 300 metres out after holding every chance.

7285 KEMPTON (A.W) (R-H)

Wednesday, November 3

OFFICIAL GOING: Standard

Wind: Fresh, half behind Weather: Overcast

7292 KIA SPORTAGE H'CAP — 1m 2f (P)

4:35 (4:38) (Class 4) (0-85,85) 4-Y-O+ £3,885 (£1,156; £577; £288) Stalls High

Form				RPR
0060	1		**Franco Is My Name**[23] 6797 4-8-11 78 ... KierenFox(3) 6 — (P R Hedger) stdd s: hld up last: smooth prog on outer fr 3f out: reminder 1f out and rdr immediately dropped whip: pushed into ld last 100yds: comf 11/4[1]	86+
3114	2	nk	**Denton (NZ)**[68] 5475 7-9-4 85 ... (t) SimonPearce(3) 4 — (J R Gask) led 2f: trckd ldr: rdn to ld again over 1f out: styd on: hdd and readily hld last 100yds 5/1	92
1001	3	½	**Rosco Flyer (IRE)**[23] 6807 4-8-12 76 ... DarryllHolland 3 — (R A Teal) chsd ldng pair: rdn to cl over 1f out: tried to chal fnl f: a hld 10/1	82
4001	4	¾	**Ellemujie**[13] 7044 5-9-5 83 ... (p) AdamKirby 2 — (D K Ivory) stdd s: hld up in 6th: effrt 2f out: nt clr run jst over 1f out: rdn and r.o fnl f: nvr able to chal 7/2[3]	89+
5614	5	3 ¾	**High Office**[41] 6304 4-9-7 85 ... PaulHanagan 9 — (R A Fahey) trckd ldng pair: rdn and nt qckn over 1f out: sn btn 10/3[2]	82
4441	6	1	**Sequillo**[74] 5311 4-9-4 82 ... (b) IanMongan 7 — (R Hannon) led after 2f and hung lft bnd sn after: pushed along and hdd over 1f out: fnd nil 10/1	77
5306	7	3	**Sanctuary**[16] 6984 4-8-9 73 ... TomEaves 8 — (B Smart) hld up in 5th: pushed along 3f out: wknd over 1f out 12/1	62

2m 6.61s (-1.39) **Going Correction** -0.075s/f (Stan) 7 Ran SP% **114.5**
Speed ratings (Par 105): **102,101,101,100,97 96,94**
toteswingers:1&2 £3.20, 2&3 £4.10, 1&3 £5.60 CSF £16.90 CT £117.97 TOTE £4.90: £1.80, £3.80; EX 23.60.
Owner P C F Racing Ltd **Bred** J J Whelan **Trained** Dogmersfield, Hampshire

FOCUS
Several fairly recent winners in a fair handicap. The gallop was just an ordinary one and the winner raced down the centre in the straight. He is rated back to his best.
Rosco Flyer(IRE) Official explanation: vet said gelding lost it's right fore shoe

7293 BOXINGDAYRACES.CO.UK H'CAP — 1m 2f (P)

5:05 (5:06) (Class 4) (0-85,84) 3-Y-O £3,885 (£1,156; £577; £288) Stalls High

Form				RPR
415	1		**Akinoshirabe (JPN)**[134] 3298 3-9-3 80 ... KierenFallon 6 — (L M Cumani) trckd ldng trio: clsd 2f out: shkn up to ld jst over 1f out: sn wl in command: plenty in hand 5/2[1]	98+
1613	2	3	**Sharedah (IRE)**[67] 5529 3-9-7 84 ... RichardHills 3 — (Sir Michael Stoute) trckd ldng pair: wnt 2nd and pressed ldr 1/2-way: led over 3f out: hdd jst over 1f out: easily outpcd 7/2[2]	93
6210	3	1 ¼	**Tenessee**[28] 6677 3-9-3 80 ... LukeMorris 4 — (C G Cox) chsd ldr to 1/2-way: sn u.p: kpt on thrght fnl 4f but easily outpcd over 1f out 8/1	86
1143	4	½	**Lyric Poet (USA)**[11] 7090 3-9-0 77 ... (t) WilliamCarson 1 — (G C Bravery) s.i.s: hld up in 7th: prog to go 4th 2f out: sn outpcd: pressed for 3rd 1f out: one pce 6/1	82
4032	5	6	**Elmfield Giant (USA)**[13] 7042 3-8-12 75 ... PaulHanagan 5 — (R A Fahey) hld up in midfield: shkn up and nt qckn wl over 1f out: wknd 5/1[3]	68
1005	6	2 ½	**Agent Archie (USA)**[19] 6904 3-9-6 83 ... SteveDrowne 2 — (J R Best) hld up in 6th: pushed along wl over 2f out: sn outpcd and no ch 7/1	71
0400	7	8	**Syrian**[25] 6753 3-8-12 75 ... StevieDonohoe 7 — (Ian Williams) s.v.s: plld hrd early: hld up last: already outpcd whn asked for effrt over 1f out: fnd nil: wknd 14/1	47
550	8	12	**Chain Of Events**[13] 7044 3-8-4 70 ... SimonPearce(3) 8 — (N B King) led to over 3f out: wknd rapidly over 2f out: t.o 33/1	18

2m 4.48s (-3.52) **Going Correction** -0.075s/f (Stan) 8 Ran SP% **115.0**
Speed ratings (Par 104): **111,108,107,107,102 100,94,84**
CSF £11.37 CT £59.45 TOTE £2.50: £1.10, £3.50, £5.30; EX 8.10.
Owner N L Tinkler **Bred** Darley Japan K K **Trained** Newmarket, Suffolk

FOCUS
Another useful handicap in which a fair gallop picked up around halfway and a race over two seconds quicker than the opener. The winner raced towards the centre to far side in the straight. Potentially good form, rated around the second and third.
Syrian Official explanation: jockey said gelding ran too free

7294 EUROPEAN BREEDERS' FUND MAIDEN STKS — 6f (P)

5:35 (5:35) (Class 5) 2-Y-O £3,076 (£915; £457; £228) Stalls High

Form				RPR
40	1		**St Augustine (IRE)**[35] 6465 2-9-0 0 ... KierenFox(3) 3 — (J R Best) chsd ldrs in 4th: rdn over 2f out: clsd to ld 1f out: styd on and sn clr 33/1	79+
2	2	2 ¼	**Steps (IRE)**[20] 6878 2-9-3 0 ... PhilipRobinson 7 — (M A Jarvis) led at str pce but pressed tl over 2f out: sn drvn: hdd 1f out: sn btn 9/4[1]	72
50	3	shd	**Daffydowndilly**[32] 6559 2-8-12 0 ... SteveDrowne 2 — (H Morrison) hld up off the pce in midfield: rdn and no prog in 5th over 2f out: r.o last 150yds: nrly snatched 2nd 5/1[3]	67
0225	4	1 ½	**Enlightening (IRE)**[28] 6675 2-9-3 75 ... StevieDonohoe 6 — (R Hannon) w ldr at str pce to over 2f out: lost 2nd over 1f out: wknd 13/2	67
	5	nk	**Elvira Delight (IRE)** 2-8-12 0 ... DarryllHolland 4 — (J Noseda) nt on terms in midfield: shkn up over 2f out and no prog: kpt on ins fnl f 14/1	61+
5	6	2	**Paperetto**[15] 7002 2-9-3 0 ... KierenFallon 8 — (R A Mills) s.i.s: rcvrd to chse ldng pair: rdn over 2f out: lost 3rd over 1f out: wknd 10/3[2]	60
323	7	hd	**New Latin (IRE)**[24] 6778 2-9-3 74 ... PaulHanagan 5 — (M Johnston) a in last pair: chsd along bef 1/2-way: no prog over 2f out and wanting to hang lft: kpt on ins fnl f 5/1[3]	60
0	8	10	**Suga Shot**[9] 7123 2-8-12 0 ... AdrianLayt 1 — (F J Brennan) s.i.s: a in last pair: wl bhd fnl 2f 100/1	25

1m 13.04s (-0.06) **Going Correction** -0.075s/f (Stan) 8 Ran SP% **111.1**
Speed ratings (Par 96): **97,94,93,91,91 88,88,75**
toteswingers:1&2 £11.40, 2&3 £4.70, 1&3 £11.60 CSF £101.24 TOTE £48.70: £15.90, £1.20, £1.90; EX 120.50.
Owner B Malt, S Malcolm & S Gabriel **Bred** Paget Bloodstock **Trained** Hucking, Kent

FOCUS
No more than a fair maiden. The gallop was a reasonable one and the winner raced centre to far side in the straight.

NOTEBOOK
St Augustine(IRE), who failed to build on a bit of debut promise at Nottingham last time, turned in his best effort on this all-weather debut to spring a surprise. This wasn't a strong maiden but it will be interesting to see if this form can be built on in ordinary handicap company this winter.
Steps(IRE) had shown promise on his turf debut and he probably ran to a similar level on this first run on Polytrack after racing with the choke out in the first half of the race. He's nothing out of the ordinary but remains capable of picking up an uncompetitive race in this grade. (op 2-1 tchd 5-2 in a place)
Daffydowndilly, well beaten in soft ground last time after showing promise over 7f on her debut, left the impression on this all-weather debut that the return to that longer trip would be very much to her liking. She is now qualified for a mark and she should be able to pick up an ordinary event. (op 11-2 tchd 6-1)
Enlightening(IRE) hadn't been seen to best effect in testing ground on her previous start but, while he fared better on this Polytrack debut, he has had a few chances and is likely to remain vulnerable to the better types in this grade or from his mark of 75 when sent into handicaps. (op 7-1 tchd 6-1)
Elvira Delight(IRE), who was easy to back on this racecourse debut, took the eye on pedigree as a half-sister to dual King's Stand winner Equiano but she looks to have more in the way of stamina than that relative. She wasn't knocked about after showing signs of greenness and should come on for the experience. (op 16-1)
Paperetto had shown promise in soft ground on his debut but failed to build on that, despite getting the perfect tow into this race. He may need time to strengthen up and may do better in ordinary handicaps in due course. (op 7-2 tchd 3-1)
New Latin(IRE) had shown bits of fair form on turf but found this trip on Polytrack an insufficient test of stamina (rider reported he was slowly away and never travelling) on this all-weather debut. He should fare better upped to 7f or beyond and remains capable of picking up a small event.
Official explanation: jockey said colt was slowly away and was never travelling (op 9-2 tchd 11-2)

7295 DIGIBET.COM NURSERY (DIV I) — 1m (P)

6:05 (6:06) (Class 6) (0-65,68) 2-Y-O £1,364 (£403; £201) Stalls High

Form				RPR
650	1		**Skeleton (IRE)**[47] 6158 2-8-9 53 ... (b[1]) SilvestreDeSousa 9 — (W J Haggas) hld up in 10th: looking for room in last trio over 2f out: rapid prog on outer over 1f out: hung lft: r.o wl to ld last strides 7/1	58
0051	2	hd	**Focail Maith**[8] 7151 2-9-10 68 6ex ... (b) StevieDonohoe 13 — (J Ryan) chsd ldrs: shkn up over 2f out: prog to chse ldr over 1f out: hung lft but led last 100yds: hdd fnl strides 9/2[2]	73
0260	3	2	**May's Boy**[15] 7004 2-9-2 60 ... (p) AdamKirby 12 — (M D I Usher) led: drvn 2 l clr wl over 1f out: hdd and outpcd last 100yds 66/1	60
3032	4	hd	**Educated Son**[5] 7210 2-9-3 61 ... ShaneKelly 1 — (W R Muir) hld up in last pair: prog over 2f out: rdn over 1f out: styd on: nt pce to chal 6/1[3]	60
00	5	2 ½	**Knox Overstreet**[89] 4802 2-9-5 63 ... SamHitchcott 7 — (M R Channon) racd wd in midfield: struggling u.p over 2f out: kpt on again ins fnl f 15/8[1]	57
6004	6	1 ¼	**Orange Ketchup (IRE)**[27] 6694 2-8-11 62 ... DuilioDaSilva(7) 10 — (P F I Cole) settled midfield: hrd rdn and nt qckn over 2f out: tried to rally over 1f out: no hdwy ins fnl f 16/1	53
00	7	½	**On Wings Of Love (IRE)**[26] 6717 2-9-0 58 ... (p) LukeMorris 6 — (A Bailey) hld up in last quartet: prog over 2f out: nt rch ldrs over 1f out: fdd ins fnl f 50/1	48
4054	8	1 ¼	**Blaze On By**[49] 6081 2-8-6 50 ... NeilChalmers 4 — (J J Bridger) hld up in last quartet: prog over 2f out: effrt flattened out over 1f out: wknd 33/1	37
5650	9	1 ¾	**Al Rannan**[15] 7004 2-9-2 60 ... TomMcLaughlin 11 — (E A L Dunlop) prom on inner: rdn to chse ldr 2f out to over 1f out: wknd 33/1	43
5640	10	½	**Marc De Savoie (IRE)**[20] 6875 2-9-5 63 ... PaulHanagan 8 — (K A Ryan) pressed ldr to wl over 2f out: nt qckn u.p: lost pl and wknd sn after 12/1	45
4454	11	4 ½	**My Little Star (IRE)**[23] 6809 2-9-5 63 ... MichaelHills 3 — (B W Hills) racd on outer: chsd ldng pair: rdn wl over 2f out: sn wknd 10/1	34
036	12	2 ¼	**Afaara (IRE)**[20] 6859 2-9-7 65 ... JimCrowley 2 — (Mrs A J Perrett) racd wd in midfield: wdst of all bnd into st: sn struggling 12/1	31
3000	13	4	**Lady Excellentia (IRE)**[28] 6673 2-8-11 55 ... SteveDrowne 5 — (A B Haynes) slowest away: hld up in last pair: briefest of effrts on inner over 2f out: sn wknd 100/1	12

000 **14** *11* **Touch Of Red (USA)**[55] 5893 2-9-1 **59**.............................. IanMongan 14 —
(R Hannon) *prom: hanging and wknd v rapidly 2f out: t.o* **33/1**

1m 39.95s (0.15) **Going Correction** -0.075s/f (Stan) **14** Ran SP% **123.4**
Speed ratings (Par 94): **96,95,93,93,91 89,89,88,86,85 81,79,75,64**
toteswingers:1&2 £9.70, 2&3 £25.50, 1&3 £26.80 CSF £38.18 CT £1972.56 TOTE £8.10: £3.60, £1.20, £9.30; EX 44.40.
Owner Raymond Tooth **Bred** Darley **Trained** Newmarket, Suffolk

FOCUS
Several unexposed sorts in a modest handicap. The gallop was an ordinary one and the first two ended up towards the stands side.

NOTEBOOK
Skeleton(IRE) attracted support and duly turned in an improved effort. She was set a fair bit to do on this all-weather/nursery debut in the first-time blinkers and beat a previous scorer who will be 3lb higher in future. She should have no problems with a bit further and is capable of further success on Polytrack if the headgear has the desired effect again. Official explanation: trainer's rep said, regarding the apparent improvement in form shown, it was the first time the filly wore blinkers (op 8-1)
Focail Maith had turned in an improved effort to score in first-time blinkers in heavy ground on his previous start and he ran creditably back up in trip from this 5lb higher mark, despite edging towards the stands side late on. He'll be 3lb higher in future but should be able to win a race on artificial surfaces. (op 5-1 tchd 6-1)
May's Boy ran creditably returned to Polytrack with the cheekpieces refitted and, on this evidence, should prove equally effective over 7f. However his overall form has a patchy look to it and it remains to be seen whether this will be reproduced or built on next time.
Educated Son ran creditably returned to handicap company after meeting trouble when starting to make ground. He'll be 5lb higher in future and may not be entirely straightforward but has the ability to win an ordinary event when things drop right. (op 5-1)
Knox Overstreet took a good hold to post and in the race itself on this first start for new connections and failed to justify the market support. He stuck on surprisingly well in the closing stages on this all-weather debut and first run over 1m but is going to have to settle if he is to progress. (op 9-4 tchd 5-2)
Orange Ketchup(IRE), who has had a few chances, doesn't look to have much in the way of pace and but it wouldn't surprise to see him step up on this form when allowed to tackle 1m2f.

7296 DIGIBET.COM NURSERY (DIV II) — 1m (P)
6:35 (6:35) (Class 6) (0-65,65) 2-Y-O **£1,364** (£403; £100; £100) **Stalls** High

Form RPR

0321 **1** **Ree's Rascal (IRE)**[49] 6082 2-9-5 **63**.............................. StephenCraine 9 69+
(J R Boyle) *mounted on crse: trckd ldrs: smooth prog on outer to ld over 2f out: drew 3 l clr over 1f out: pushed out and a gng to hold on* **11/4**[1]

6002 **2** *1* **Las Verglas Star (IRE)**[9] 7118 2-9-7 **65**........................ PaulHanagan 14 69
(R A Fahey) *hld up bhd ldrs gng wl: effrt over 2f out: drvn over 1f out: jst won battle for 2nd and clsd on wnr: nvr able to chal* **15/2**

060 **3** *nk* **Handicraft (IRE)**[15] 7000 2-8-1 **45**.......................... SilvestreDeSousa 12 48
(M Johnston) *led 1f: styd prom: drvn over 2f out: disp 2nd in clsng pack ins fnl f: styd on* **15/2**

0402 **3** *dht* **Dr Darcey**[23] 6810 2-8-13 **57**... DarryllHolland 1 60
(R Hannon) *sn pushed up to go prom: hrd rdn to chse wnr 2f out: grad clsd ins fnl f: lost 2nd nr fin* **9/2**[2]

0100 **5** *hd* **History Repeating**[37] 6412 2-8-4 **55**.................................. IanBurns(7) 6 58
(M D I Usher) *chsd ldrs: bmpd along furiously fr over 2f out: clsd to chal for 2nd ins fnl f: kpt on* **66/1**

5056 **6** *2 1/4* **Dubai Glory**[35] 6471 2-9-3 **61**....................................(b[1]) TomMcLaughlin 5 59
(E A L Dunlop) *s.i.s and pushed along early in last: effrt and v wd bnd 3f out: drvn and kpt on fnl 2f: n.d* **10/1**

050 **7** *4 1/2* **A Little Bit Dusty**[48] 6129 2-9-2 **63**................................... KierenFox(3) 13 50
(W G M Turner) *drvn to stay in tch after 2f: effrt u.p over 2f out: sn btn* **50/1**

050 **8** *3 1/4* **Heart Felt**[24] 6770 2-9-7 **65**... JimCrowley 8 45+
(R Hannon) *t.k.h: hld up in last trio: reminder 3f out: hanging over 2f out: passed a few toiling rivals fr over 1f out* **20/1**

5060 **9** *4 1/2* **Hi Note**[20] 6868 2-8-9 **53**.. ChrisCatlin 2 23
(M R Channon) *s.i.s: wl in rr: rchd 8th 1/2-way: no prog over 2f out: wknd* **50/1**

6210 **10** *hd* **Countrywide Flame**[49] 6082 2-8-8 **59**............................ JulieBurke(7) 10 28
(K A Ryan) *led after 1f to over 4f out: led over 3f out to over 2f out: wknd* **11/2**[3]

6040 **11** *18* **Millies Folly**[11] 7085 2-9-0 **63**...(b[1]) NeilFarley(5) 7 —
(D Carroll) *t.k.h: w ldrs: led over 4f out to over 2f out: wknd rapidly: t.o* **11/1**

5020 **12** *6* **Russian Ice**[27] 6694 2-9-1 **59**.. SamHitchcott 11 —
(D K Ivory) *s.i.s: sn drvn: last and wkng over 3f out: t.o* **20/1**

1m 40.24s (0.44) **Going Correction** -0.075s/f (Stan) **12** Ran SP% **116.1**
Speed ratings (Par 94): **94,93,92,92,92 90,85,82,78,77 59,53**PL: Handicraft 0.70, Dr Darcey 0.60. TRICAST: Ree's Rascal/Las Verglas Star/Dr Darcey £45.92, RR/LVS/Handicraft £70.95 toteswingers:1&2:£4.80, 2& Dr Darcey £1.50, 2& Handicraft £4.00, 1& Dr Darcey £1.80, 1& Handicraft £3.90 CSF £21.84 TOTE £4.70: £2.20, £3.00, £27Owner Walter Hayford Trifecta £Bred Pier House Stud Trained.

FOCUS
Division two of a modest nursery and one in which the gallop was fair. The winner came down the centre in the straight.

NOTEBOOK
Ree's Rascal(IRE) notched his second course-and-distance success and did so in the manner of one that had a fair bit more in hand than the winning margin suggested. This strong-travelling sort should prove equally effective when held on to for longer or even back over 7f and, although he'll be up in the weights for this, he should be able to add to his tally in the near future. (op 5-2 tchd 3-1 in places)
Las Verglas Star(IRE) had fared better with the blinkers left off in heavy ground last time and ran creditably from a decent draw against a progressive winner on his first run over this trip and on this first run on Polytrack. However he'll have to raise his game to win on this surface as he's due to go up 5lb in future. (op 5-1)
Dr Darcey's turf record is one of steady improvement and he was far from disgraced on this debut on artificial surfaces. It'll be a bit of a surprise if he can't be placed to best advantage on Polytrack in the coming months. (op 10-1)
Handicraft(IRE) ◆, a half-sister to Winter Derby winner and Group 1-placed Hattan, hadn't shown much in turf maidens but duly turned in an improved effort on this surface from her bargain-basement mark on this nursery debut. She left the strong impression that the step up to 1m2f would suit and she's more than capable of winning a race in this grade. (op 10-1)
History Repeating had been soundly beaten in handicaps for her current yard but fared a good deal better on this all-weather debut. She should be equally effective over 1m2f and is lightly raced enough to be open to further progress.
Dubai Glory, backed at double-figure odds in the first-time blinkers, wasn't disgraced after being dropped out back on Polytrack over this shorter trip. A stronger overall gallop would have suited but she may not be one to place maximum faith in. (op 16-1 tchd 9-1)
Countrywide Flame, who showed improved form to beat the winner over course-and-distance in September, was a long way below that level behind the same rival for the second outing in succession. He is one to tread carefully with at present. (op 6-1)

7297 DIGIBET FLOODLIT STKS (LISTED RACE) — 1m 4f (P)
7:05 (7:07) (Class 1) 3-Y-O+
£14,483 (£14,483; £3,984; £1,986; £995; £499) **Stalls** Centre

Form RPR

3-53 **1** **Mastery**[19] 6885 4-9-3 **117**.. TedDurcan 5 113
(Saeed Bin Suroor) *trckd ldr to 1/2-way: styd cl up: drvn to ld wl over 1f out: narrowly hdd nr fin: forced dead-heat post* **1/2**[1]

0050 **1** *dht* **Dansili Dancer**[74] 5307 8-9-3 **108**.. AdamKirby 8 113
(C G Cox) *hld up in 7th: shkn up and prog over 2f out: wnt 2nd fnl f: sn chalng: hrd drvn and narrow ld nr fin: jnd on the nod* **11/1**

-120 **3** *3* **Age Of Reason (UAE)**[165] 2345 5-9-3 **108**......................... RichardHills 1 108
(Saeed Bin Suroor) *hld up in midfield: wnt 4th 5f out: rdn and effrt over 2f out: nt qckn wl over 1f out: kpt on same pce after* **20/1**

3050 **4** *1 1/4* **Man Of Iron (USA)**[25] 6736 4-9-3 **109**.........................(b[1]) KierenFallon 10 106
(L M Cumani) *prom: chsd ldr 1/2-way: drvn to chal 2f out: upsides wl over 1f out: sn fdd* **8/1**[3]

3133 **5** *1 3/4* **Status Symbol (IRE)**[13] 7044 5-9-3 **78**......................... WilliamCarson 6 103
(G C Bravery) *trckd ldng trio: lost pl sltly 5f out: renewed effrt and rdn 3f out: no imp fnl 2f* **50/1**

1450 **6** *1/2* **Once More Dubai (USA)**[60] 5749 5-9-3 **107**.............(bt) DarryllHolland 2 103
(Saeed Bin Suroor) *dwlt: hld up last: coaxed along and effrt on outer 2f out: tried to cl on ldrs 1f out: wknd rapidly last 100yds* **25/1**

-140 **7** *1 1/4* **Dansant**[33] 6548 6-9-3 **102**..(v[1]) JimCrowley 9 101
(G A Butler) *awkward s: hld up in 8th: shkn up and no rspnse over 2f out: no ch after: r.o fnl 100yds* **15/2**[2]

1436 **8** *1 1/4* **Classic Punch (IRE)**[19] 6889 7-9-3 **105**........................... PaulHanagan 3 99
(D R C Elsworth) *led: hrd pressed and rdn 3f out: hdd & wknd wl over 1f out: eased* **12/1**

3200 **9** *7* **Munsef**[123] 3672 8-9-3 **105**... StevieDonohoe 4 87
(Ian Williams) *chsd ldrs tl wknd over 2f out:* **40/1**

2m 32.9s (-1.60) **Going Correction** -0.075s/f (Stan) **9** Ran SP% **118.6**
Speed ratings (Par 111): **102,102,100,99,98 97,96,96,91**
WIN: Dansili Dancer £11.10 Mastery £0.60 PL: DD £4.70, M £1.02. EX: Dansili Dancer/ Mastery £4.40, M/DD £11.50 CSF: DD/M £8.53, M/DD £3.57 toteswingers DD & M:£3.60, Dansili Dancer &3: £21.30, Mastery &3:£5.80 CSF £3.57 TOTE £11.10: £4.70, £4.60; EX 11.50.
Owner Godolphin **Bred** Darley **Trained** Newmarket, Suffolk
Owner The Loyal Troupers **Bred** The Magic Slipper Partnership **Trained** Lambourn, Berks

FOCUS
A good-quality Listed event featuring two of the three previous winners and one in which all bar one of the runners were rated 102 or above. However the gallop was only a steady one to the straight and this bare form may not be entirely reliable, something backed up by the proximity of the 78-rated fifth. The dead-heaters came down the centre in the straight. Dansili Dancer is rated to his Rosebery form with Mastery not at his best.

NOTEBOOK
Mastery, the clear pick on official ratings, was wisely ridden close to the ordinary gallop and, while he lacks anything in the way of a turn of foot, he again displayed admirable battling qualities in the closing stages to dead-heat on the line. He's ideally suited by a much stronger stamina test over this trip and he'll now reportedly be aimed at the Hong Kong Vase, in which he'll need a good gallop. (tchd 10-1)
Dansili Dancer, the winner of the Rosebery Handicap over 1m3f here in March, confirmed himself a smart performer on the surface when dead-heating with a higher rated rival and deserves extra credit as he was dropped out in a race run at just a moderate gallop. A more truly run race would have seen him in a more favourable light and, although he could follow a Winter Derby campaign, he'll also be of interest if sent to Dubai this winter. (tchd 10-1)
Age Of Reason(UAE), turned over at odds-on in this race last year, put a poor run at York firmly behind him. He too has little in the way of a change of gear and this 1m6f turf winner at Meydan in February, who also won on turf at the 2009 Dubai Carnival, will be worth a second look back in the UAE early in the new year. (op 16-1)
Man Of Iron(USA) had beaten Mastery in the Breeders' Cup Marathon on Pro-Ride last year but he's been below that level since and he failed to confirm those placings in this muddling event, despite the presence of the first-time blinkers. He too will be seen to better effect granted a much stiffer stamina test. (op 11-1 tchd 12-1)
Status Symbol(IRE) is almost certainly flattered by his proximity in a moderately run race in this markedly stronger grade. He's a lightly raced sort who is open to further progress but his short-term future rests at the door of the handicapper.
Once More Dubai(USA), who showed a good turn of foot to beat Age Of Reason in this race last year, didn't come into this race in much form and remains below his best, again not looking the most straightforward under pressure. He remains one to have reservations about at present. (tchd 20-1)
Dansant, who won this in 2007, had a bit to find strictly on official ratings but was again a fair way below his best with the first-time visor replacing the blinkers he sported on his previous start. He may do better without the headgear in a more truly run race but he'll have to show a fair bit more before he's a solid betting proposition, though it later transpired he banged his head on the stalls. Official explanation: jockey said horse banged his head on the stalls (op 7-1 tchd 8-1)

7298 DIGIBET CASINO H'CAP — 1m (P)
7:35 (7:35) (Class 6) (0-65,65) 3-Y-O+ **£1,637** (£483; £241) **Stalls** High

Form RPR

0202 **1** **Ice Cool Lady (IRE)**[13] 7037 3-9-0 **60**...............................(v) LukeMorris 9 72
(W R Swinburn) *trckd ldr: rdn to ld over 1f out: romped away ins fnl f* **12/1**

0003 **2** *3 3/4* **Sovereignty (JPN)**[7] 7168 8-8-11 **58**.......................... SophieDoyle(3) 12 61+
(D K Ivory) *plld v hrd: hld up in midfield: hanging 2f out: plld out over 1f out: r.o wl ins fnl f to take 2nd last strides* **11/1**

6365 **3** *1/2* **Final Drive (IRE)**[23] 6794 4-9-4 **62**................................ StevieDonohoe 5 64+
(J Ryan) *rn wout declared tongue-strap: stdd s: hld up in last pair: stl there 2f out: nudged along and gd prog jst over 1f out: r.o to take 3rd nr fin* **15/2**[2]

0-45 **4** *hd* **Madame Boot (FR)**[20] 6863 3-8-12 **58**.............................(p) JimCrowley 7 60
(P J Makin) *chsd ldng trio: wnt 3rd 2f out and drvn: outpcd 1f out: chsd wnr briefly ins fnl f: kpt on* **25/1**

3-00 **5** *1/2* **Serious Drinking (USA)**[107] 4206 4-9-6 **64**...................... AdamKirby 8 65+
(W R Swinburn) *hld up wl in rr: rdn and gd prog fr 2f out: styd on to dispute 2nd last 75yds: no ex* **20/1**

3140 **6** *hd* **Leelu**[35] 6479 4-9-3 **61**.. LiamKeniry 10 61
(D W P Arbuthnot) *racd freely: led: mod pce to 1/2-way: hdd over 1f out: lost several pls nr fin* **12/1**

0603 **7** *hd* **Abriachan**[18] 6934 3-9-3 **63**... PaulHanagan 4 63
(M G Quinlan) *t.k.h: chsd ldrs on outer: drvn over 2f out: kpt on same pce u.p fr over 1f out* **10/1**[3]

2254 **8** *1 1/2* **Mr Chocolate Drop (IRE)**[7] 7168 6-9-2 **60**...........(t) SilvestreDeSousa 6 56
(Miss M E Rowland) *tk fierce hold: hld up in midfield: nt qckn over 2f out: no real imp on ldrs after* **14/1**

0664 **9** *1* **Saturn Way (GR)**[16] 6992 4-9-7 **65**................ GeorgeBaker 13 59
(P R Chamings) *hld up in midfield: chsd ldrs 2f out: hanging and nt qckn over 1f out: wknd ins fnl f* **15/2**[2]

6512 **10** *1/2* **Cheddar George**[15] 7006 4-9-4 **62**................ DarrylHolland 3 55+
(P W Chapple-Hyam) *t.k.h: hld up in last pair: swtchd to inner and effrt 2f out: sme prog over 1f out: effrt fizzled out ins fnl f: b.b.v* **7/4**[1]

0636 **11** *2 3/4* **Rich Boy**[14] 7019 3-8-12 **63**................(p) JemmaMarshall(5) 11 49
(Mrs L J Mongan) *t.k.h: trckd ldng pair to 2f out: wknd qckly over 1f out* **33/1**

0650 **12** *2* **Prince Namid**[88] 4839 8-9-4 **62**................ WilliamCarson 2 44
(J A T De Giles) *t.k.h: hld up in rr and racd wd: rdn and no prog over 2f out: struggling after* **50/1**

42-3 **13** *hd* **Almahaza (IRE)**[237] 857 6-9-3 **61**................ NeilChalmers 14 42
(A J Chamberlain) *t.k.h: restrained towards rr on inner after 2f: wknd 2f out* **20/1**

1m 39.22s (-0.58) **Going Correction** -0.075s/f (Stan) **13** Ran SP% **117.6**
WFA 3 from 4yo+ 2lb
Speed ratings (Par 101): **99,95,94,94,94 93,93,92,91,90 87,85,85**
toteswingers:1&2 £9.00, 2&3 £33.60, 1&3 £24.10 CSF £125.75 CT £1096.24 TOTE £18.70: £4.90, £2.00, £3.30; EX 123.80.
Owner London Market Racing Club **Bred** Lodge Park Stud **Trained** Aldbury, Herts
■ Stewards' Enquiry : Jemma Marshall one-day ban: careless riding (Nov 17)

FOCUS
Mainly exposed sorts in a modest handicap and one in which the gallop was an ordinary one until lifting early in the straight. The winner came down the centre. He is rated to his turf latest with the fourth and fifth limiting the form slightly.
Cheddar George Official explanation: vet said gelding bled from the nose

7299 PANORAMIC H'CAP 7f (P)
8:05 (8:06) (Class 6) (0-55,57) 3-Y-O+ **£1,637** (£483; £241) **Stalls** High

Form RPR

00- **1** **Taurakina**[164] 4-9-2 **55**................ AndreaAtzeni 12 73+
(M Botti) *mde all: spreadeagled field after 3f: nt less than 4 l ahd fr 3f out: rdn over 1f out: kpt on steadily* **3/1**[1]

0411 **2** *4* **Bold Ring**[3] 7250 4-8-11 **57** 6ex................ JulieBurke(7) 6 64
(E J Creighton) *trckd ldng quartet but wl off the pce: prog to go 2nd 2f out: sn clr of rest: no imp on wnr after* **5/1**[2]

4006 **3** *2 1/4* **Richo**[18] 6937 4-9-1 **54**................(p) ChrisCatlin 10 55
(S A Harris) *hld up wl in rr and off the pce: rdn over 2f out and no prog: gd hdwy jst over 1f out: r.o to take 3rd last 100yds* **15/2**

-000 **4** *1 3/4* **Braddock (IRE)**[20] 6864 7-8-13 **52**................(t) LiamKeniry 13 48
(K O Cunningham-Brown) *hld up in 6th and wl off the pce: rdn over 2f out: kpt on one pce: n.d* **25/1**

600 **5** *nk* **Villaruz (IRE)**[14] 7018 4-8-13 **52**................(b) StephenCraine 14 47
(D Flood) *hld up wl off the pce in 7th: gng bttr than rest of chsng pack over 2f out: rdn and v limited rspnse over 1f out: wnt 3rd briefly ins fnl f* **25/1**

464 **6** *3/4* **Ever Cheerful**[6] 7192 9-9-0 **53**................(p) SteveDrowne 7 46
(A B Haynes) *chsd wnr after 2f to 2f out: steadily fdd over 1f out* **25/1**

02-0 **7** *3/4* **Royal Island (IRE)**[12] 7070 8-9-0 **53**................ AdamKirby 1 44
(M G Quinlan) *dropped in fr wd draw and hld up wl in rr: str reminders 3f out: modest prog over 1f out* **20/1**

6004 **8** *3/4* **Only A Game (IRE)**[3] 7249 5-9-2 **55**................(tp) PaulHanagan 9 44
(I W McInnes) *nvr bttr than midfield and wl off the pce: no real imp u.p fnl 2f* **7/1**[3]

4600 **9** *1 1/4* **Nativity**[21] 6847 4-8-12 **51**................(p) SamHitchcott 11 37
(J L Spearing) *chsd ldng trio tl fdd fr 2f out* **25/1**

5543 **10** *2 3/4* **Namu**[150] 2779 7-9-2 **55**................(p) JimCrowley 3 34
(Miss T Spearing) *swtchd to inner fr wd draw: hld up last: shkn up over 2f out: nvr a factor* **10/1**

4400 **11** *2 3/4* **Mind The Monarch**[89] 4790 3-8-11 **54**................ KierenFox(3) 4 25
(R A Teal) *a towards rr and wl off the pce: rdn and struggling over 2f out* **40/1**

600/ **12** *1* **River Bounty**[737] 7013 5-9-2 **55**................ TedDurcan 8 23
(A P Jarvis) *chsd wnr 2f: rdn in 3rd 1/2-way: wknd over 2f out* **20/1**

1m 25.3s (-0.70) **Going Correction** -0.075s/f (Stan) **12** Ran SP% **102.4**
WFA 3 from 4yo+ 1lb
Speed ratings (Par 101): **101,96,93,91,91 90,89,88,87,84 81,80**
toteswingers:1&2 £3.90, 2&3 £13.00, 1&3 £7.00 CSF £10.84 CT £63.41 TOTE £3.70: £1.60, £2.80, £2.20.
Owner A Rosati-Colarieti **Bred** Azienda Agricola Rosati Colarieti **Trained** Newmarket, Suffolk

FOCUS
What had looked a fairly open handicap was turned into a procession by the well-backed market leader, who was another on the night to race down the centre. The pace was soon reasonable. The ex-Italian winner looks much better than this grade but overall it was a weak race.
T/Plt: £33.50 to a £1 stake. Pool of £67,342.58 - 1,466.22 winning tickets. T/Qpdt: £7.70 to a £1 stake. Pool of £8,419.60 - 808.00 winning tickets. JN

7177 NOTTINGHAM (L-H)
Wednesday, November 3

OFFICIAL GOING: Heavy (soft in places) changing to heavy after race 6 (2.55)
Wind: nil Weather: rainy

7300 JOHN A STEPHENS BULWELL STONE H'CAP 5f 13y
12:15 (12:17) (Class 6) (0-55,55) 3-Y-O+ **£1,706** (£503; £252) **Stalls** High

Form RPR

2620 **1** **Sharp Shoes**[18] 6931 3-8-12 **51**................(p) SilvestreDeSousa 11 62
(Mrs A Duffield) *cl up: led over 3f out: rdn clr over 1f out: kpt on* **10/1**

4024 **2** *nk* **Accamelia**[19] 6896 4-8-11 **50**................ PaulMulrennan 14 60
(C W Fairhurst) *hld up in tch: hdwy 2f out: swtchd lft and rdn over 1f out: chsd wnr ins fnl f: styd on wl towards fin* **11/2**[2]

0000 **3** *2 1/2* **Jemimaville (IRE)**[8] 7155 3-8-8 **47**................(v) WilliamCarson 6 48
(G C Bravery) *towards rr: hdwy 2f out: sn rdn and styd on ins fnl f: nrst fin* **66/1**

0442 **4** *nk* **Monsieur Harvey**[7] 7170 4-8-7 **46** oh1................ TomEaves 8 46
(B Smart) *trckd ldrs: hdwy and cl up 2f out: sn rdn and ev ch tl one pce appr fnl f* **8/1**[3]

4604 **5** *1 1/4* **Stargazing (IRE)**[14] 7018 4-9-2 **55**................(v) ShaneKelly 12 50
(B J Meehan) *chsd ldrs: rdn along wl over 1f out: drvn and one pce appr fnl f* **10/1**

0000 **6** *shd* **Elegant Dancer (IRE)**[32] 6574 3-8-4 **46** oh1.......... JamesSullivan(3) 13 41
(Paul Green) *sn outpcd and rdn along in rr: hdwy 2f out: swtchd lft over 1f out: kpt on u.p ins fnl f: nrst fin* **33/1**

0020 **7** *3/4* **Bertbrand**[163] 2381 5-8-10 **49**................(v) DavidAllan 9 41
(I W McInnes) *chsd ldrs: rdn along 2f out: drvn over 1f out and sn wknd* **50/1**

3344 **8** *nk* **Miss Polly Plum**[43] 6270 3-8-8 **50**................ KellyHarrison(3) 10 41
(C A Dwyer) *led: hdd over 3f out: cl up tl rdn and wknd over 2f out and grad wknd* **20/1**

2032 **9** *1* **Choc'A'Moca (IRE)**[8] 7154 3-8-11 **55**................(v) NeilFarley(5) 15 43
(D Carroll) *trckd ldrs: n.m.r after 1 1/2f: pushed along 2f out: sn rdn: edgd lft and wknd* **7/2**[1]

0644 **10** *3/4* **Cocktail Party (IRE)**[17] 6952 4-8-7 **46** oh1................(v) GrahamGibbons 1 31
(J W Unett) *nvr bttr than midfield* **12/1**

0005 **11** *1 1/2* **Pinball (IRE)**[46] 6206 4-8-9 **48**................(b) PJMcDonald 4 28
(Mrs L Williamson) *blind removed late and v.s.a: bhd tl kpt on fnl 2f* **16/1**

2240 **12** *shd* **Hart Of Gold**[55] 5875 6-8-13 **52**................(p) LukeMorris 16 31
(R A Harris) *chsd ldrs: rdn along over 2f out: sn drvn and wknd* **14/1**

3540 **13** *4 1/2* **Exceedingly Good (IRE)**[28] 6679 4-8-13 **52**................ JimmyQuinn 2 15
(S R Bowring) *sltly hmpd s: in tch on outer: rdn along over 2f out and sn wknd* **25/1**

0551 **14** *3/4* **Darcy's Pride (IRE)**[9] 7132 6-8-6 **52**................ ShaneBKelly(7) 3 12
(P T Midgley) *wnt lft s: a in rr* **8/1**[3]

066- **15** *hd* **Chifah**[527] 2319 3-8-10 **52**................ IanBrennan(3) 5 12
(R J Price) *towards rr: rdn along and outpcd bef 1/2-way: sn bhd* **40/1**

0100 **16** *1* **Boga (IRE)**[17] 6952 3-8-12 **51**................ RichardKingscote 17 7
(R J Hodges) *a towards rr: rdn along bef 1/2-way: sn outpcd and bhd* **33/1**

63.85 secs (2.85) **Going Correction** +0.60s/f (Yiel) **16** Ran SP% **118.6**
Speed ratings (Par 101): **101,100,96,96,94 93,92,92,90,89 87,86,79,78,78 76**
toteswingers:1&2 £15.40, 2&3 £107.10, 1&3 £109.30 CSF £58.24 CT £3588.60 TOTE £13.50: £2.60, £1.80, £14.70, £2.20; EX 93.50 TRIFECTA Not won..
Owner T P McMahon and D McMahon **Bred** Mrs Mary Rowlands **Trained** Constable Burton, N Yorks

FOCUS
Following 8mm of rain overnight the ground was changed to heavy, soft in places (GoingStick 5.5). A low-grade sprint handicap in which few got seriously involved. They raced towards the stands' side rail in this weak late-season handicap. The form is rated around the winner.
Pinball(IRE) Official explanation: jockey said filly was slowly away

7301 HALLGARTEN DRUITT NURSERY 5f 13y
12:45 (12:46) (Class 5) (0-70,68) 2-Y-O **£2,590** (£770; £385; £192) **Stalls** High

Form RPR

5162 **1** **Black Annis Bower**[7] 7174 2-9-3 **67**................ JamesSullivan(3) 12 74
(M W Easterby) *trckd ldrs: led over 1f out: styd on wl* **11/2**[2]

062 **2** *1 1/4* **Sluggsy Morant**[17] 6954 2-9-1 **67**................ AmyScott(5) 10 72+
(H Candy) *stdd s: hld up in rr: effrt and hdwy whn nt clr run 2f out: nt clr run and swtchd lft 1f out: styd on strly: fin wl: snatched 2nd nr fin* **5/1**[1]

0631 **3** *hd* **Miss Toldyaso (IRE)**[14] 7016 2-8-6 **53**................ NickyMackay 16 54
(M G Quinlan) *trckd ldrs: wnt 2nd over 1f out: styd on same pce ins fnl f* **6/1**[3]

6006 **4** *nk* **Bobbyow**[8] 7142 2-8-12 **59**................ DavidProbert 1 59
(B Palling) *in tch: hdwy on wd outside 2f out: kpt on ins fnl f* **25/1**

041 **5** *nk* **Sensational Love (IRE)**[23] 6811 2-9-7 **68**................ RobertHavlin 11 67
(R A Mills) *stdd s: hld up: hdwy over 2f out: sn chsng ldrs: styd on same pce ins fnl f* **10/1**

066 **6** *1* **Mini Bon Bon**[14] 7016 2-8-10 **57**................(v) SilvestreDeSousa 9 53
(A Bailey) *chsd ldr: led 3f out: hdd over 1f out: fdd jst ins fnl f* **8/1**

3004 **7** *1/2* **Bonjour Bongee**[19] 6902 2-8-12 **59**................(v) JamesDoyle 6 53
(A J McCabe) *chsd ldrs: drvn and outpcd over 2f out: kpt on ins fnl f* **10/1**

0533 **8** *1 1/2* **Jambo Bibi (IRE)**[55] 5894 2-9-3 **64**................ RichardHughes 5 52
(R Hannon) *chsd ldrs: outpcd and lost pl over 2f out: hdwy over 1f out: kpt on fnl 75yds* **15/2**

6506 **9** *nk* **Be A Good Lady**[29] 6658 2-8-7 **54**................(p) FrankieMcDonald 7 41
(P T Midgley) *dwlt: t.k.h in rr: outpcd over 2f out: keeping on whn n.m.r 1f out* **80/1**

6050 **10** *3/4* **Amber Mist**[14] 7017 2-8-3 **50**................ LukeMorris 13 35
(David Pinder) *chsd ldrs: outpcd 2f out: sn wknd* **25/1**

006 **11** *1 1/2* **Hobbesian War**[17] 6964 2-7-12 **45**................ AndrewMullen 14 24
(T P Tate) *dwlt: sn drvn along and outpcd in rr* **12/1**

2550 **12** *3/4* **Kheya (IRE)**[29] 6646 2-9-1 **62**................ PJMcDonald 2 38
(G M Moore) *mid-div: effrt over 2f out: wknd over 1f out* **50/1**

6000 **13** *2 1/4* **Molly Mylenis**[14] 7017 2-8-9 **56**................(v) CathyGannon 15 24
(P D Evans) *led 2f: sn lost pl* **18/1**

063 **14** *1 1/2* **Tony Hollis**[23] 6811 2-9-5 **66**................ IanMongan 3 29
(B R Millman) *chsd ldrs: wknd over 2f out* **14/1**

64.90 secs (3.90) **Going Correction** +0.60s/f (Yiel) **14** Ran SP% **117.9**
Speed ratings (Par 96): **92,90,89,89,88 87,86,83,82,82 79,78,75,72**
toteswingers:1&2 £4.40, 2&3 £7.10, 1&3 £7.20 CSF £31.38 CT £177.37 TOTE £6.70: £2.20, £2.20, £3.20; EX 30.50 Trifecta £38.30 Pool: £208.43 - 4.02 winning units..
Owner Mrs A Jarvis **Bred** Mrs A Jarvis **Trained** Sheriff Hutton, N Yorks

FOCUS
A high draw proved an advantage in the first race and, while the first three came from double-figure stalls in this nursery, they didn't race bang up against the rail. Run-of-the-mill form.

NOTEBOOK
Black Annis Bower was 2lb well in following her second at Musselburgh and won quite cosily, albeit from an unlucky runner-up. Clearly very much at home in testing conditions, she shouldn't go up too much for this and looks the type who could strike early next spring granted favourable ground. (op 9-2 tchd 6-1)
Sluggsy Morant ◆ was the unlucky horse in the race as he got into all sorts of trouble as he tried to make up ground from behind. His finishing effort once in the clear was eyecatching and with a clear run he would probably have won, so it goes without saying that he should be kept in mind.
Official explanation: jockey said gelding was denied a clear run (op 9-2 tchd 4-1)
Miss Toldyaso(IRE), a winner on the Polytrack last time out, coped well with this very different ground, and ran a sound race off a 5lb higher mark, albeit with the benefit of the stands' rail. (tchd 11-2)
Bobbyow, running in a handicap for the first time, had the worst of the draw and raced widest of all, so in the circumstances this was a good effort. He's due to be dropped 3lb and might be able to find a race on the AW. (op 20-1)
Sensational Love(IRE) had the rail to help and ran all right, but perhaps conditions were a little too testing for her. (op 6-1)

7302 1STSECURITYSOLUTIONS.CO.UK MAIDEN STKS (DIV I) 1m 75y
1:15 (1:16) (Class 5) 2-Y-O **£2,914** (£867; £433; £216) **Stalls** Centre

Form RPR

0 **1** **Swindy**[11] 7099 2-9-3 0................ SilvestreDeSousa 8 74
(P F I Cole) *chsd ldrs: pushed along 1/2-way: hdwy wl over 2f out: rdn to chal wl over 1f out: drvn ent fnl f: styd on gamely to ld last 100yds* **7/1**

0P **2** ½ **Indian Jack (IRE)**[25] 6748 2-9-3 0 .... LukeMorris 3 73
(A Bailey) *sn led: hdd over 4f out and cl up tl led again 3f out: jnd and rdn wl over 1f out: drvn ent fnl f: hdd wl ins fnl f: no ex towards fin* **12/1**

0 **3** nse **Groomed (IRE)**[33] 6532 2-9-3 0 .... NeilCallan 14 73
(W J Haggas) *trckd ldrs on outer: hdwy 3f out: rdn to chse ldrs 2f out: drvn to chal over 1f out and ev ch tl edgd lft and no ex last 50yds* **5/1**[1]

4 3 ¼ **Duke Of Florence (IRE)** 2-9-3 0 .... JimCrowley 6 65+
(R Hannon) *s.i.s and reminders sn after s: in rr tl hdwy 3f out: rdn over 2f out: styd on wl ins fnl f: nrst fin* **25/1**

4 **5** hd **Wrekin Sunset**[17] 6964 2-8-9 0 .... MichaelO'Connell(3) 2 60
(Mrs K Burke) *chsd ldrs: effrt 3f out: rdn over 2f out: drvn wl over 1f out and kpt on same pce* **25/1**

6 1 ¼ **Layla's King** 2-9-3 0 .... StevieDonohoe 4 62
(Jane Chapple-Hyam) *green and towards rr: gd hdwy on inner over 3f out: chsd ldrs 2f out: sn rdn and one pce* **6/1**[2]

00 **7** 9 **Tanjung Agas (IRE)**[48] 6127 2-9-3 0 .... PhilipRobinson 13 42
(M A Jarvis) *racd wd: chsd ldrs: rdn along 3f out: wknd over 2f out* **9/1**

0 **8** nse **Golestan Palace (IRE)**[22] 6831 2-9-3 0 .... J-PGuillambert 1 42
(L M Cumani) *prom on inner: rdn along over 3f out: wknd over 2f out* **10/1**

9 ¾ **Ardlui (IRE)** 2-9-3 0 .... FergusSweeney 5 41
(H Candy) *in tch on inner: effrt over 3f out: sn rdn and n.d* **13/2**[3]

0 **10** nk **Dashing Eddie (IRE)**[12] 7058 2-9-3 0 .... StephenCraine 9 40
(K A Ryan) *a towards rr* **80/1**

0 **11** hd **Pyrenean**[19] 6892 2-8-12 0 .... PaulMulrennan 12 35
(J G Given) *midfield: hdwy to chse ldrs wl over 2f out: sn rdn and wknd wl over 1f out* **100/1**

0 **12** 1 **Phantom House**[11] 7099 2-8-9 0 .... (t) RobertLButler(3) 10 32
(B W Duke) *green and a in rr* **100/1**

13 17 **Baileys Agincourt** 2-9-3 0 .... GregFairley 7 —
(M Johnston) *s.i.s: green and sn pushed along in rr: bhd fr 1/2-way* **16/1**

3 **14** 4 ½ **Madison Square (USA)**[20] 6874 2-9-3 0 .... RichardHughes 11 —
(Mahmood Al Zarooni) *racd wd: prom: slt ld over 4f out: rdn and hdd 3f out: wknd qckly: bhd and eased fnl 2f* **5/1**[1]

1m 53.42s (3.82) **Going Correction** +0.375s/f (Good) **14** Ran SP% **117.0**
Speed ratings (Par 96): **95,94,94,91,91 89,80,80,79,79 79,78,61,56**
toteswingers:1&2 £31.30, 2&3 £18.30, 1&3 £7.50 CSF £82.97 TOTE £10.40: £2.30, £4.10, £1.60; EX 123.20 Trifecta £165.40 Pool: £223.57 - 1.00 winning units..
Owner Sir Martyn Arbib **Bred** The Aston House Stud **Trained** Whatcombe, Oxon

FOCUS
An ordinary looking maiden in which three with previous experience came clear. It proved a tough test in the ground.

NOTEBOOK
Swindy was well backed to improve dramatically on his debut effort behind Carlton House at Newbury, and he landed a bit of a gamble with a hard-fought success. He showed a really willing attitude under pressure and has the potential to develop into a nice middle-distance handicapper next season. (op 10-1)
Indian Jack(IRE), struck into at York last time, was interesting based on his debut effort behind Picture Editor at Doncaster, and ran well on ground he is bred to enjoy. (op 14-1 tchd 11-1)
Groomed(IRE) ran a promising race on debut at Newmarket and stepped up on that here. His sire is a speed influence, but there's plenty of stamina on his dam's side and it wouldn't be a surprise to see him get further next year. (tchd 4-1)
Duke Of Florence(IRE) ◆ was slowly away and raced very green, but came home really well without being asked for the maximum, shaping with a deal of promise on his debut. He'll come on plenty for the outing, and this half-brother to three-time Group 3 winner Caribbean Sunset is one to note for the future.
Wrekin Sunset kept plugging away and will no doubt be suited by stepping up to middle-distances next season.
Layla's King ◆, another who was slowly away and green early, responded to pressure and came with a challenge inside the final 2f, before weakening in the closing stages. He showed more than enough on his debut to suggest that he'll be winning races. (op 15-2 tchd 5-1)
Madison Square(USA), weak in the market, dropped out quickly once coming under pressure, and clearly failed to handle these testing conditions. Given his pedigree, he'll be of more interest on the AW. (op 7-2 tchd 11-2)

7303 1STSECURITYSOLUTIONS.CO.UK MAIDEN STKS (DIV II) 1m 75y
1:45 (1:45) (Class 5) 2-Y-O £2,914 (£867; £433; £216) **Stalls** Centre

Form RPR

0 **1** **Spyder**[64] 5629 2-9-3 0 .... LukeMorris 3 78
(Jane Chapple-Hyam) *w ldrs: rdn and outpcd over 2f out: hung rt and styd on to ld last 50yds* **9/1**

4 **2** ½ **Miss Diagnosis (IRE)**[49] 6087 2-8-12 0 .... JimCrowley 9 71+
(R M Beckett) *trckd ldrs: t.k.h: led 3f out: over 1 l ld and looking in command over 1f out: hdd and no ex last 50yds* **9/2**[3]

3 hd **Dauphine (IRE)** 2-8-12 0 .... DavidProbert 6 71
(A M Balding) *hld up towards rr: hdwy over 3f out: chsng ldrs jst ins fnl f: kpt on same pce last 50yds* **25/1**

4 2 ¾ **Unex Picasso** 2-9-3 0 .... NeilCallan 4 70
(W J Haggas) *s.i.s: t.k.h: hdwy 7f out: chsng ldrs over 3f out: fdd over 1f out* **4/1**[2]

4 **5** 5 **Mungo Park**[22] 6828 2-9-3 0 .... GregFairley 7 59
(M Johnston) *led 1f: chsd ldrs: drvn over 2f out: hung rt and wknd ins fnl f* **5/2**[1]

6 3 ½ **Peals And Plaudits** 2-9-3 0 .... TomMcLaughlin 8 51
(E A L Dunlop) *s.i.s: bhd and drvn along: hdwy 3f out: nvr nr ldrs* **100/1**

7 3 ½ **Joe Strummer (IRE)** 2-9-3 0 .... GeorgeBaker 12 44
(M L W Bell) *in rr: sme hdwy over 2f out: nvr nr ldrs* **16/1**

8 2 ½ **Circus Act** 2-9-3 0 .... RichardHughes 11 38
(Mahmood Al Zarooni) *trckd ldrs: wknd over 2f out* **4/1**[2]

00 **9** ½ **Final Liberation (FR)**[8] 7152 2-9-3 0 .... SebSanders 10 37
(Sir Mark Prescott) *a towards rr: nvr on terms* **125/1**

10 nk **Akrias (USA)** 2-9-3 0 .... J-PGuillambert 1 36
(L M Cumani) *s.s: hdwy into midfield 7f out: wknd over 2f out* **14/1**

11 ¾ **Cherrego (USA)** 2-8-12 0 .... ChrisCatlin 2 30
(B Palling) *drvn to ld after 1f: styd far side in home st and lft to r alone: hdd 3f out: sn wknd* **100/1**

0 **12** 2 ¾ **May Burnett (IRE)**[12] 7057 2-8-12 0 .... (t) DuranFentiman 13 24
(B S Rothwell) *mid-div: lost pl 3f out* **100/1**

13 5 **Bertie Blu Boy** 2-9-3 0 .... JamesDoyle 14 18
(Paul Green) *dwlt: in rr: hdwy 5f out: lost pl over 2f out: sn bhd* **100/1**

1m 53.45s (3.85) **Going Correction** +0.375s/f (Good) **13** Ran SP% **117.9**
Speed ratings (Par 96): **95,94,94,91,86 83,79,77,76,76 75,72,67**
toteswingers:1&2 £7.90, 2&3 £16.00, 1&3 £22.00 CSF £48.29 TOTE £10.90: £3.10, £1.50, £4.00; EX 46.30 TRIFECTA Not won..
Owner Miss Christina Blockley **Bred** Graham Aldrich & Miss Tracy Robinson **Trained** Dalham, Suffolk

FOCUS
This second division of the maiden was run in an almost identical time to the first leg. The level of the form is fluid.

NOTEBOOK
Spyder was prominent throughout and, although left behind when the runner-up moved easily to the front, he kept battling away and eventually got a second bite. A 200-1 shot when running creditably on debut, this was his first start for a new stable and he relished the step up to 1m. Stamina is clearly his strong suit. (op 14-1)
Miss Diagnosis(IRE) looked for a long way as though she would land the prize, as she travelled best of all and went clear off the front easily with 2 1/2f to run, but she began to paddle approaching the final furlong and couldn't hold on inside the final 100 yards. Although beaten, she shaped like the best horse in the race, and she looks sure to make up into a decent 3-y-o. (op 10-3)
Dauphine(IRE) was unfancied in the market and showed signs of inexperience, but she ran on really well from off the pace to take third. She should come on plenty. (op 20-1)
Unex Picasso fell out of the stalls but came through to have some sort of a chance approaching the final furlong, before weakening. Bred to stay well, he'll appreciate stepping up in trip next season. (op 7-1)
Mungo Park did not find the longer trip and softer ground helping him in any way. (op 9-4 tchd 11-4)
Circus Act has a pedigree that screams fast ground, so it was no great surprise to see him floundering in these conditions.

7304 1STSECURITYSOLUTIONS.CO.UK CONDITIONS STKS 1m 75y
2:20 (2:20) (Class 2) 3-Y-O+
£9,346 (£2,799; £1,399; £700; £349; £175) **Stalls** Centre

Form RPR

66 **1** **Sweet Child O'Mine**[96] 4548 3-8-3 77 .... FrannyNorton 4 82
(R C Guest) *in tch: hdwy 4f out: chsd ldrs wl over 2f out: rdn to chal wl over 1f out: led appr fnl f: kpt on wl towards fin* **10/1**

0002 **2** 1 ½ **West End Lad**[7] 7182 7-8-10 77 .... (b) FergusSweeney 6 84
(S R Bowring) *trckd ldng pair: effrt on stands' rail whn nt clr run and hmpd 3f out: swtchd lft and rdn over 2f out: drvn to chse wnr ent fnl f: kpt on same pce* **6/1**[3]

0054 **3** 2 ¾ **Blakey's Boy**[116] 3916 3-8-8 78 .... ChrisCatlin 9 78
(H J L Dunlop) *cl up: led after 1f: wd st to stands' rail: rdn along 3f out: drvn 2f out: hdd appr fnl f: sn one pce* **20/1**

2155 **4** ¾ **Ours (IRE)**[7] 7182 7-8-10 73 .... (b) BarryMcHugh 2 76
(John A Harris) *s.i.s and bhd: hdwy over 3f out: rdn 2f out: kpt on appr fnl f: nvr nr ldrs* **16/1**

0054 **5** 6 **Penderyn**[29] 6652 3-8-3 41 .... AndreaAtzeni 7 57?
(C Smith) *chsd ldrs: rdn along 3f out: drvn over 2f out and sn btn* **200/1**

6 3 ¼ **Caymans (AUS)**[585] 5-8-10 113 .... TedDurcan 1 55
(Saeed Bin Suroor) *t.k.h: trckd ldrs: hdwy on inner 4f out: rdn and cl up 3f out: sn drvn and btn whn hung rt 2f out: eased after* **7/4**[2]

11-2 **7** 1 **Sahara Kingdom (IRE)**[29] 6659 3-8-8 104 .... RichardHughes 8 52
(Saeed Bin Suroor) *led 1f: cl up: effrt to dispute ld over 3f out: rdn and ev ch over 2f out: sn drvn and edgd lft: hld whn bmpd and slipped 2f out: eased after* **5/4**[1]

1-00 **8** 30 **Gypsy Jazz (IRE)**[5] 7207 3-8-3 67 .... CathyGannon 3 —
(Miss A Stokell) *a in rr: outpcd and bhd fnl 3f* **100/1**

000 **9** 1 **Obe One**[122] 3711 10-8-10 40 .... VictorSantos 5 —
(A Berry) *dwlt: a in rr: bhd fnl 3f* **200/1**

1m 51.55s (1.95) **Going Correction** +0.375s/f (Good)
WFA 3 from 5yo+ 2lb **9** Ran SP% **116.8**
Speed ratings (Par 109): **105,103,100,100,94 90,89,59,58**
toteswingers:1&2 £5.20, 2&3 £9.40, 1&3 £12.80 CSF £67.92 TOTE £14.70: £2.40, £1.60, £3.30; EX 76.80 Trifecta £599.80 Part won..
Owner EERC **Bred** A Reid **Trained** Stainforth, S Yorks
■ Stewards' Enquiry : Chris Catlin one-day ban: careless riding (Nov 17)

FOCUS
If the ratings were to be believed this was a two-horse race between the Godolphin pair, but both came into the race with something to prove and in the event neither was even placed. Muddling form, modest for the grade.

NOTEBOOK
Sweet Child O'Mine was third best in at the weights and took full advantage of the Godolphin horses running well below their best. A dual winner on the Fibresand in the past, she should come on for this first outing in three months and will be of interest when returning to Southwell this winter. (op 14-1)
West End Lad was squeezed up near the rail early in the straight and had to be switched again when crossed by the winner approaching the final furlong, but he couldn't really be called unlucky. He has a good record here but is another capable of going on Fibresand, and he's better rated in that sphere. (op 8-1)
Blakey's Boy, previously trained by John Dunlop, last ran on soft ground when winning his maiden on debut. Despite having been off the track since July, he again showed his liking for a testing surface with a solid effort, although he did carry his head high under pressure.
Ours(IRE) was slowly away and trailed the field for most of the race, but he does tend to finish his races off well and once again he stayed on to be nearest at the finish. (op 20-1)
Caymans(AUS), placed in Grade 1 company in Australia for his previous stable, was best in at the weights but hadn't been seen out since March 2009. Weak in the market, he ran very much as though in need of the race. Official explanation: jockey said gelding was unsuited by the heavy, soft in places ground and lost its action (op 6-4)
Sahara Kingdom(IRE) had had a recent outing on Fibresand so fitness wasn't an issue for him, but he's an American-bred colt who'd never before run on turf, and it turned out that these very testing conditions were totally unsuitable. Official explanation: jockey said colt was unsuited by the heavy, soft in places ground (op 11-8)

7305 HALLGARTEN DRUITT H'CAP 1m 75y
2:55 (2:57) (Class 5) (0-70,70) 3-Y-O £2,266 (£674; £337; £168) **Stalls** Centre

Form RPR

0051 **1** **Flipping**[30] 6632 3-9-7 **68** .... FergusSweeney 10 84
(W S Kittow) *mde most: wd st to stands' rail: rdn clr 2f out: eased towards fin* **8/1**

3340 **2** 2 ¾ **Pittodrie Star (IRE)**[12] 7062 3-9-7 **68** .... DavidProbert 1 76
(A M Balding) *hld up towards rr: hdwy on inner over 3f out: rdn to chse ldrs 2f out: drvn and hung bdly rt ins fnl f: kpt on to take 2nd nr line* **11/2**[3]

3621 **3** shd **Blue Moon**[2] 7273 3-9-2 **70** 6ex .... JulieBurke(7) 2 77
(K A Ryan) *hld up in rr: gd hdwy towards inner 4f out: effrt to trck ldrs 3f out: rdn to chse wnr wl over 1f out: sn drvn and kpt on same pce: lost 2nd nr line* **5/1**[2]

0162 **4** 4 **Tilsworth Glenboy**[5] 7205 3-9-7 **68** .... StephenCraine 5 66
(J R Jenkins) *trckd ldrs: hdwy 3f out: rdn to chse ldrs 2f out: sn drvn and no imp* **6/1**

2365 **5** 1 ¼ **Madame Excelerate**[17] 6959 3-9-7 **68** .... TomMcLaughlin 7 63
(W M Brisbourne) *prom: effrt over 3f out: sn rdn along and chsd wnr tl drvn and wknd wl over 1f out* **16/1**

0463 **6** ½ **Chateau Zara**[13] 7037 3-8-4 54 .... JohnFahy(3) 11 48
(C G Cox) *in tch: effrt to chse ldrs 3f out: sn swtchd lft and rdn over 2f out: sn one pce* **6/1**

5625 **7** ½ **Tasza (USA)**[46] 6212 3-8-13 60 .... JamesDoyle 12 53
(A J McCabe) *in tch: hdwy and wd st: chsd ldrs over 3f out: sn rdn and wknd over 2f out* **33/1**

4124 **8** 6 **Sweet Secret**[3] 7255 3-9-7 68 ....(v[1]) RichardHughes 9 47
(R Hannon) *chsd wnr: wd st: rdn along 3f out: drvn and wknd qckly over 2f out: sn bhd and eased* **7/2**[1]

4005 **9** 2 ¼ **Rezwaan**[13] 7038 3-9-1 62 ....(v) ShaneKelly 4 36
(M J McGrath) *a towards rr* **20/1**

2000 **10** ½ **Norville (IRE)**[3] 7255 3-9-6 67 .... CathyGannon 3 40
(P D Evans) *a towards rr: rdn along over 3f out: nvr a factor* **33/1**

630 **11** 3 ¼ **Jaldarshaan (IRE)**[14] 7013 3-9-6 67 .... TravisBlock 6 32
(W J H Ratcliffe) *dwlt and in rr: hdwy on inner and in tch over 3f out: sn rdn and wknd wl over 2f out* **25/1**

1m 53.39s (3.79) **Going Correction** +0.525s/f (Yiel) **11 Ran SP% 114.3**
Speed ratings (Par 102): **102,99,99,95,93 93,92,86,84,84 80**
toteswingers:1&2 £8.90, 2&3 £7.90, 1&3 £10.20 CSF £47.74 CT £245.08 TOTE £9.40: £2.80, £2.20, £2.10; EX 55.90 TRIFECTA Not won..
Owner Reg Gifford **Bred** D R Tucker **Trained** Blackborough, Devon

FOCUS
This looked quite a competitive handicap. The winner had a pretty easy time in front and is rated back to his best.
Chateau Zara Official explanation: jockey said filly was unsuited by the heavy, soft in places ground

7306 B & M INSTALLATIONS H'CAP (DIV I) 1m 2f 50y
3:30 (3:32) (Class 5) (0-75,75) 3-Y-O+ **£2,266** (£674; £337; £168) **Stalls** Low

Form RPR

0256 **1** **Spring Secret**[14] 7015 4-9-0 65 .... RichardHughes 12 79
(B Palling) *trckd ldng pair on outer: wd to stands' rails over 4f out: rdn to ld 2f out: drvn clr ent fnl f: styd on wl* **17/2**

00- **2** 6 **Harry Hunt**[14] 7028 3-8-10 65 ....(b) CathyGannon 14 68
(Cecil Ross, Ire) *in tch on outer: hdwy 4f out: rdn to chse ldrs wl over 2f out: drvn and kpt on appr fnl f: no ch w wnr* **20/1**

0004 **3** 1 ¼ **Club Tahiti**[7] 7182 4-9-6 71 .... NeilCallan 9 71
(A W Carroll) *trckd ldrs on outer: hdwy over 4f out: led wl over 3f out: rdn and hdd 2f out: drvn and one pce appr fnl f* **9/2**[1]

0204 **4** 4 ½ **Bold Marc (IRE)**[18] 6915 8-8-8 62 .... MichaelO'Connell(3) 1 54
(Mrs K Burke) *hld up in tch on inner: hdwy 4f out: chsd ldrs 3f out: rdn and ch 2f out: sn drvn and wknd appr fnl f* **8/1**

3322 **5** ½ **Glenmuir (IRE)**[12] 7063 7-9-1 69 ....(p) IanBrennan(3) 11 60
(J J Quinn) *hld up in tch: hdwy over 4f out: rdn to chse ldrs 3f out: drvn over 2f out and sn wknd* **13/2**[2]

0005 **6** 4 ½ **Jack Dawkins (USA)**[16] 6984 5-9-2 67 .... AdrianNicholls 3 49
(D Nicholls) *in tch on inner: hdwy to chse ldrs 4f out: rdn 3f out: drvn over 2f out and sn wknd* **14/1**

0605 **7** nse **Yossi (IRE)**[8] 7147 6-8-3 61 oh3........(be) SeanPalmer(7) 8 43
(R C Guest) *dwlt and towards rr: hdwy over 3f out: sn rdn and nvr nr ldrs* **16/1**

2112 **8** 11 **Oriental Girl**[17] 6959 5-9-7 72 ....(p) LiamKeniry 13 33
(J S Moore) *hld up: sme hdwy over 4f out: rdn along over 3f out and n.d* **15/2**[3]

4130 **9** 2 ¼ **Scarab (IRE)**[16] 6984 5-9-4 69 ....(p) GrahamGibbons 7 26
(T D Walford) *led: rdn along over 4f out: hdd wl over 3f out and sn wknd* **13/2**[2]

3000 **10** 3 ¼ **Blue Spinnaker (IRE)**[18] 6935 11-8-11 65 .... JamesSullivan(3) 10 16
(M W Easterby) *a towards rr* **14/1**

0005 **11** 11 **Iron Out (USA)**[134] 3283 4-9-9 74 .... PaulMulrennan 5 4
(R Hollinshead) *chsd ldrs: rdn along 3f out: drvn and wknd over 2f out: sn bhd and eased* **14/1**

0-04 **12** 30 **Final Verse**[21] 6852 7-9-10 75 .... RobertWinston 4 —
(Miss Tor Sturgis) *cl up: rdn along 4f out: sn wknd* **17/2**

26-6 **13** 3 ¾ **Ensnare**[294] 151 5-9-4 72 .... RussKennemore(3) 6 —
(Mrs A Duffield) *towards rr on inner whn n.m.r and hmpd bnd after 4f: bhd after* **25/1**

4360 **14** 1 ¾ **General Tufto**[59] 5786 5-9-8 73 ....(b) AndreaAtzeni 2 —
(C Smith) *chsd ldrs: rdn along 1/2-way: sn wknd* **40/1**

2m 20.28s (5.98) **Going Correction** +0.525s/f (Yiel)
WFA 3 from 4yo+ 4lb **14 Ran SP% 121.8**
Speed ratings (Par 103): **97,92,91,87,87 83,83,74,72,70 61,37,34,33**
toteswingers:1&2 £21.20, 2&3 £38.30, 1&3 £7.20 CSF £172.78 CT £873.30 TOTE £7.50: £2.70, £6.70, £1.60; EX 176.40 Trifecta £213.70 Part won..
Owner Flying Eight Partnership **Bred** Canary Thoroughbreds **Trained** Tredodridge, Vale Of Glamorgan
■ Stewards' Enquiry : Sean Palmer caution: used whip when horse was showing no response

FOCUS
The official going was changed slightly to heavy all round. Few showed their form and the winner had the advantage of the stands' rail in the straight.
Final Verse Official explanation: jockey said gelding was unsuited by the heavy ground

7307 B & M INSTALLATIONS H'CAP (DIV II) 1m 2f 50y
4:05 (4:05) (Class 5) (0-75,75) 3-Y-O+ **£2,266** (£674; £337; £168) **Stalls** Low

Form RPR

341 **1** **Ocean Transit (IRE)**[17] 6959 5-9-4 72 .... IanBrennan(3) 10 86
(R J Price) *trckd ldrs: pushed along 5f out: led over 2f out: drew clr ins fnl f* **8/1**[3]

2332 **2** 3 ½ **Rock The Stars (IRE)**[12] 7062 3-9-0 69 .... SebSanders 9 76
(J W Hills) *prom: effrt over 3f out: kpt on to take 2nd jst ins fnl f: no imp* **7/2**[1]

0050 **3** 2 ¾ **Monkton Vale (IRE)**[13] 7044 3-9-3 72 ....(b) BarryMcHugh 8 74
(R A Fahey) *led tl over 2f out: outpcd over 1f out: kpt on to take modest 3rd nr fin* **9/1**

4252 **4** ¾ **Aegean Destiny**[29] 6650 3-8-3 63 .... DeclanCannon(5) 14 64
(J Mackie) *chsd ldrs: chal 3f out: wknd ins fnl f* **9/1**

4004 **5** 9 **Hail Tiberius**[22] 6832 3-9-0 69 .... GrahamGibbons 3 53
(T D Walford) *trckd ldrs: t.k.h: drvn 4f out: wknd over 2f out* **17/2**

003- **6** 1 ½ **Gordy Bee (USA)**[431] 5429 4-9-4 69 ....(e[1]) FrannyNorton 4 50
(R C Guest) *t.k.h towards rr: nvr a factor* **14/1**

-003 **7** nk **Dream In Waiting**[27] 6691 4-9-7 72 .... RichardHughes 13 52
(B J Meehan) *hld up in tch: hdwy to chse ldrs over 4f out: drvn 3f out: wknd wl over 1f out* **4/1**[2]

3320 **8** 6 **Beauchamp Xiara**[13] 7044 4-9-2 72 .... AmyScott(5) 2 41
(H Candy) *sn trcking ldrs: drvn over 3f out: wknd over 2f out* **9/1**

6500 **9** 9 **Make Amends (IRE)**[17] 6959 5-9-1 66 .... RichardKingscote 1 18
(R J Hodges) *s.i.s: drvn and sme hdwy 4f out: sn wknd* **33/1**

0020 **10** ½ **By Command**[120] 3768 5-8-8 62 .... RobertLButler(3) 6 13
(G A Ham) *hld up in rr: hrd drvn over 3f out: sn btn* **50/1**

0-20 **11** 18 **Curlew (IRE)**[50] 6056 4-9-10 75 .... JamesMillman 5 —
(C J Down) *s.i.s: drvn 6f out: sme hdwy 4f out: sn wknd: wl bhd fnl 2f* **33/1**

2411 **12** 8 **High Five Society**[64] 5635 6-9-3 73 ....(b) RyanClark(5) 12 —
(S R Bowring) *in rr: wl bhd and drvn 6f out: sme hdwy in centre over 3f out: wknd over 2f out: sn eased and bhd* **9/1**

2m 22.17s (7.87) **Going Correction** +0.525s/f (Yiel)
WFA 3 from 4yo+ 4lb **12 Ran SP% 118.4**
Speed ratings (Par 103): **89,86,84,83,76 75,74,69,62,62 47,41**
toteswingers:1&2 £8.80, 2&3 £8.70, 1&3 £17.70 CSF £35.58 CT £263.38 TOTE £14.10: £4.00, £1.90, £3.50; EX 37.90 Trifecta £320.40 Pool: £432.98 - 1.00 winning units..
Owner Ocean's Five **Bred** Mike Channon Bloodstock Ltd **Trained** Ullingswick, H'fords

FOCUS
The slower of the two divisions by 1.89sec. The winner is trated back to his best but again had the benefit of taking the wide route.
Aegean Destiny Official explanation: jockey said filly hung left in the straight
Curlew(IRE) Official explanation: jockey said gelding had no more to give
High Five Society Official explanation: jockey said gelding did not handle the heavy ground
T/Plt: £989.20 to a £1 stake. Pool of £59,897.49 - 44.20 winning tickets. T/Qpdt: £232.30 to a £1 stake. Pool of £3,391.66 - 10.80 winning tickets. JR

7292 KEMPTON (A.W) (R-H)
Thursday, November 4

OFFICIAL GOING: Standard
Wind: Fresh, half behind Weather: Fine but cloudy, mild

7309 BOOK KEMPTON TICKETS ON 0844 579 3008 MAIDEN AUCTION STKS 6f (P)
4:30 (4:31) (Class 5) 2-Y-O **£2,286** (£675; £337) **Stalls** High

Form RPR

1 **Richmond Fontaine** 2-8-10 0 .... KierenFox(3) 3 78+
(J R Best) *dwlt: rn green and wl off the pce in last: pushed along and sme prog over 2f out: gd hdwy to chse ldr jst ins fnl f: r.o to ld last strides* **14/1**

3502 **2** ½ **Buddy Miracle**[12] 7088 2-8-4 67 .... DavidProbert 4 67
(A M Balding) *trckd ldng pair and clr of rest: led over 2f out: 2 l up fnl f: hdd last strides* **9/2**[3]

3342 **3** 3 ½ **Whitecrest**[21] 6866 2-8-4 72 .... CathyGannon 2 57
(J L Spearing) *w ldr to 1/2-way: sn rdn: chsd new ldr over 1f out to ins fnl f: fdd* **33/10**[2]

5 **4** 1 ½ **Woop Woop (IRE)**[12] 7088 2-8-3 0 .... JohnFahy(3) 8 54
(Stef Higgins) *chsd ldng trio but nt on terms: drvn to try to cl fr over 2f out: one pce and no imp over 1f out* **3/1**[1]

504 **5** 3 **Whipphound**[20] 6899 2-8-10 68 ow1 .... KierenFallon 10 49
(W M Brisbourne) *didn't appear in paddock and mounted on crse: mde most to over 2f out: fdd over 1f out* **5/1**

00 **6** 1 **Lisselton Cross**[22] 6842 2-8-10 0 .... FergusSweeney 5 46
(M R Bosley) *settled in last trio and wl off the pce: pushed along and sme prog 2f out: no imp on ldrs 1f out: fdd* **66/1**

7 2 ¼ **Winniepeg** 2-8-7 0 .... LukeMorris 9 36
(C G Cox) *s.i.s: rdn in 7th after 2f: a struggling* **6/1**

8 1 ¾ **Pippa's Gift** 2-8-13 0 .... HayleyTurner 11 37
(W R Muir) *chsd ldng trio but nt on terms: pushed along and no prog over 2f out: wknd fnl f* **16/1**

00 **9** 3 **Burst Of Applause (IRE)**[21] 6866 2-8-8 0 .... WilliamCarson 12 23
(M G Quinlan) *rdn in 6th after 2f and wl off the pce: a struggling* **33/1**

00 **10** 3 ¾ **Hot Toddie**[20] 6894 2-8-5 0 .... ChrisCatlin 7 9
(J G Given) *a wl in rr: last and wl bhd over 2f out* **66/1**

1m 13.01s (-0.09) **Going Correction** -0.075s/f (Stan) **10 Ran SP% 115.9**
Speed ratings (Par 96): **97,96,91,89,85 84,81,79,75,70**
toteswingers:1&2:£11.40, 1&3:£6.90, 2&3:£2.00 CSF £74.96 TOTE £28.00: £7.80, £3.20, £1.10; EX 79.90.
Owner Hucking Horses IV **Bred** Kingwood Bloodstock **Trained** Hucking, Kent

FOCUS
Just a modest maiden, but a winner of at least fair ability. The time was 0.36 seconds quicker than the later Class 6 nursery. The second is the key to the form.

NOTEBOOK
Richmond Fontaine ◆ picked up in good style relative to the class, having been last at halfway. A 12,000gns half-brother to prolific 9.4f-1m4f AW winner Formidable Guest, out of a successful sprinter, he very much looked of the experience through the opening stages, but the combination of a sustained finishing effort, as well as the pace horses tiring, saw him claim an unlikely victory. There should be more to come. (op 16-1)
Buddy Miracle probably ran to the same sort of level as when filling this placing over C&D on her previous start. She might have the speed for 5f, but is not progressing. (op 4-1 tchd 3-1)
Whitecrest, dropped in trip after running second in a similarly weak event over 7f here last time, had a far from ideal draw and was hassled up front for most of the way by Whipphound. As a consequence, she had little left in the closing stages, and is slightly better than she showed. (op 3-1 tchd 7-2)
Woop Woop(IRE), on her second racecourse appearance, couldn't reverse debut placings with Buddy Miracle. She hung right when first in the straight, still looking a bit green, and was then one-paced under a hard ride. (op 5-1)
Whipphound did see his race out after going off a bit too fast. (op 4-1 tchd 6-1)

7310 PANORAMIC BAR & RESTAURANT MAIDEN STKS 7f (P)
5:00 (5:01) (Class 5) 3-Y-O+ **£2,286** (£675; £337) **Stalls** High

Form RPR

222 **1** **Entitled**[88] 4874 3-8-12 75 .... KierenFallon 5 81+
(Sir Michael Stoute) *slowest away: hld up in last trio: swift move to ld wl over 1f out: sn wl clr: pushed out* **4/11**[1]

63 **2** 6 **Sunset Kitty (USA)**[35] 6496 3-8-12 0 .... TedDurcan 8 65+
(W R Swinburn) *trckd ldrs: trying to cl whn short of room over 2f out as wnr sailed past: drvn to take 2nd 1f out: kpt on* **7/2**[2]

00 **3** 3 **Polly Floyer**[24] 6815 3-8-12 0 .... AdamKirby 3 57
(W R Swinburn) *t.k.h: chsd ldng pair: upsides 2f out: sn easily outpcd: wl btn 3rd ins fnl f* **7/1**[3]

0030 **4** 2 **South African Gold (USA)**[47] 6212 3-9-3 62 ....(p) MickyFenton 1 56
(J M P Eustace) *sn pressed ldr: upsides 2f out: nt qckn: wknd and wl btn 4th fnl f* **16/1**

0000 **5** *7* **Dolly Will Do**[84] 4989 3-8-12 40......(p) LiamKeniry 10 32
(N P Mulholland) *hld up in last trio: lft bhd fr 3f out: v modest late prog* **50/1**

/0 **6** *shd* **Woodwind**[19] 6931 5-8-6 0...... ThomasWhite(7) 7 32
(D Shaw) *chsd ldrs: lft bhd fr 3f out* **66/1**

00 **7** *1 ¼* **Rabbie Burns**[181] 1868 3-9-3 0...... JoeFanning 4 34
(V P Donoghue) *led to wl over 1f out: wknd rapidly* **33/1**

8 *1 ½* **Dolly Ann** 3-8-12 0...... KirstyMilczarek 9 25
(G Prodromou) *t.k.h: hld up in last trio: lft bhd fr 3f out* **33/1**

0 **9** *30* **Great Show**[8] 7183 3-8-9 0...... AndrewHeffernan(3) 2 —
(R A Harris) *chsd ldrs to 1/2-way: wknd: t.o* **50/1**

1m 25.7s (-0.30) **Going Correction** -0.075s/f (Stan)
WFA 3 from 5yo 1lb **9** Ran SP% **125.2**
Speed ratings (Par 103): **98,91,87,85,77 77,75,74,39**
toteswingers:1&2:£1.10, 1&3:£1.50, 2&3:£2.30 CSF £2.28 TOTE £1.50: £1.02, £1.40, £1.20; EX 2.60.
Owner Cheveley Park Stud **Bred** Cheveley Park Stud Ltd **Trained** Newmarket, Suffolk

FOCUS
An uncompetitive maiden in which Entitled totally outclassed her rivals. The time was ordinary and the form is rated around the winner.

7311 EUROPEAN BREEDERS' FUND MAIDEN FILLIES' STKS (DIV I) 7f (P)
5:30 (5:30) (Class 5) 2-Y-O £2,752 (£818; £409; £204) **Stalls** High

Form RPR

3 **1** **Little Curtsey**[15] 7021 2-9-0 0...... SteveDrowne 10 73+
(H Morrison) *trckd ldr 2f: styd prom: smooth effrt to ld 2f out: rdn out and a holding on* **5/4**[1]

2 *½* **Lady Rosamunde** 2-9-0 0...... RichardHughes 3 72+
(M P Tregoning) *t.k.h: hld up in rr: prog and shkn up 2f out: styd on to take 2nd last 100yds: clsd on wnr but a hld* **8/1**

0 **3** *½* **Blue Maisey**[24] 6802 2-9-0 0...... FergusSweeney 6 70
(Miss S L Davison) *chsd ldr after 2f to over 2f out: rdn to chse wnr over 1f out: styd on but lost 2nd last 100yds* **66/1**

4 *3 ½* **Herminella** 2-9-0 0...... DavidProbert 11 61
(W R Muir) *dwlt: chsd ldrs: styd on inner in st: nvr gng pce to threaten: kpt on* **40/1**

5 *½* **Almaasah (USA)** 2-9-0 0...... TedDurcan 1 60
(Saeed Bin Suroor) *restless in stalls: rn green on outer in midfield: reminder 1/2-way: struggling over 2f out: kpt on* **11/2**[3]

065 **6** *1* **Spade**[48] 6155 2-9-0 69...... DaneO'Neill 8 57
(D R C Elsworth) *chsd ldrs on outer: shkn up 2f out: hanging and nt qckn over 1f out: btn after* **9/4**[2]

6 **7** *½* **Run On Ruby (FR)**[16] 7000 2-9-0 0...... ChrisCatlin 5 56
(D R Lanigan) *dwlt: wl in rr: disputing last 2f out: nudged along and kpt on steadily: n.d* **14/1**

8 *½* **Frosty Friday** 2-9-0 0...... ShaneKelly 2 55
(J R Jenkins) *rn green in rr: last over 2f out: shkn up and styd on on fnl f* **66/1**

6 **9** *1* **Peira**[16] 7001 2-9-0 0...... JimmyQuinn 7 52
(Jane Chapple-Hyam) *led to 2f out: wknd rapidly over 1f out* **33/1**

0 **10** *1 ¾* **Zartina (IRE)**[28] 6688 2-9-0 0...... LiamKeniry 9 48
(S Kirk) *mostly in rr: shkn up 2f out: no prog over 1f out: wknd* **66/1**

06 **11** *1* **Plug In Baby**[14] 7034 2-8-11 0...... RobertLButler(3) 4 45
(Nick Mitchell) *chsd ldng trio after 2f to 3f out: wknd qckly* **66/1**

1m 27.33s (1.33) **Going Correction** -0.075s/f (Stan) **11** Ran SP% **119.7**
Speed ratings (Par 93): **89,88,87,83,83 82,81,81,79,77 76**
toteswingers:1&2:£3.70, 1&3:£30.20, 2&3:£38.60 CSF £12.57 TOTE £3.60: £1.10, £1.30, £36.00; EX 18.80.
Owner Lady Faringdon **Bred** L Ellinas & Old Mill Stud **Trained** East Ilsley, Berks

FOCUS
The bare form is no better than fair (time 1.41 seconds slower than Oceanway in second division), but a few of these ought to improve. The winner didn't need to step up much.

NOTEBOOK
Little Curtsey confirmed the promise she showed when third over 6f here on debut, finding enough after travelling well. She should make a fair handicapper at this trip and shorter. (tchd 11-10)
Lady Rosamunde, a half-sister to, among others, Oaks runner-up Meeznah, out of a useful 1m2f-1m4f (Listed) winner, made a respectable introduction. She was a bit keen early, and then ran green when first under pressure, but she's finished well enough.
Blue Maisey showed little on debut on easy turf (RPR 31) but she knew her job this time and clearly produced a much-improved performance. (op 100-1)
Herminella, a half-sister to 1m winner Dr Mathias, was never that far away against the inside rail and plugged on at the one pace.
Almaasah(USA) ◆, a sister to Breeders' Cup Juvenile/Kentucky Derby winner Street Sense, ran green, coming under pressure around the bend into the straight, and then hung right once in line for the finish, but she did seem to make some modest late progress. Her trainer has around a 50% strike-rate with his second-time out 2-y-os this year, so much better can be expected. (op 6-1 tchd 5-1)
Spade caught the eye over 1m on turf last time, but disappointed on this drop in trip and switch to Polytrack. Maybe she's had enough for the time being. (op 3-1)
Run On Ruby(FR) ◆, as on debut, hinted ability and can surely do better. (op 12-1 tchd 16-1)
Plug In Baby Official explanation: jockey said filly hung left in straight

7312 EUROPEAN BREEDERS' FUND MAIDEN FILLIES' STKS (DIV II) 7f (P)
6:00 (6:02) (Class 5) 2-Y-O £2,752 (£818; £409; £204) **Stalls** High

Form RPR

52 **1** **Oceanway (USA)**[10] 7113 2-9-0 0...... JoeFanning 2 85+
(M Johnston) *trckd ldng pair: led over 2f out: sn clr: shkn up and drew further away over 1f out: eased last 75yds* **5/4**[1]

44 **2** *8* **Alareen (USA)**[10] 7113 2-9-0 0...... (t) TedDurcan 4 64
(Saeed Bin Suroor) *chsd ldrs: rdn over 2f out: tk modest 2nd over 1f out: no imp on wnr* **9/4**[2]

3 *½* **Starstuded (IRE)** 2-9-0 0...... KierenFallon 3 63
(W J Haggas) *dwlt: hld up in tch: pushed along and prog over 2f out: wnt modest 3rd 1f out: catching runner-up at fin* **7/1**[3]

36 **4** *3* **Waltzing Cat (USA)**[7] 7185 2-9-0 0...... SebSanders 1 55+
(Sir Mark Prescott) *s.i.s: racd on outer in midfield and stl looked green: jst pushed along and kpt on steadily fnl 2f* **14/1**

5 *2 ¼* **Danish Pastry** 2-9-0 0...... SteveDrowne 5 49
(H Morrison) *s.s: detached in last and pushed along: rdr persisted and kpt on fr over 2f out* **8/1**

60 **6** *hd* **Corvette**[45] 6247 2-9-0 0...... JimmyQuinn 8 49
(J R Jenkins) *chsd ldng trio: shkn up and outpcd 2f out: drvn to dispute modest 3rd 1f out: fdd* **25/1**

0325 **7** *2 ¾* **Loves Theme (IRE)**[121] 3749 2-9-0 72...... RobertWinston 9 41
(A Bailey) *awkward s: pressed ldr to wl over 2f out: sn wknd* **16/1**

0 **8** *2 ¾* **Red Remanso (IRE)**[24] 6796 2-9-0 0...... MichaelHills 10 34
(B W Hills) *led to over 2f out: wknd over 1f out* **20/1**

0 **9** *nk* **Queen Carmel (IRE)**[24] 6804 2-9-0 0...... (b1) ShaneKelly 11 33
(B J Meehan) *reminder after 2f: struggling in rr 3f out* **50/1**

1m 25.92s (-0.08) **Going Correction** -0.075s/f (Stan) **9** Ran SP% **121.9**
Speed ratings (Par 93): **97,87,87,83,81 81,77,74,74**
toteswingers:1&2:£1.10, 1&3:£3.30, 2&3:£3.60 CSF £4.34 TOTE £3.40: £1.70, £1.70, £1.60; EX 6.10.
Owner Sheikh Hamdan Bin Mohammed Al Maktoum **Bred** Darley **Trained** Middleham Moor, N Yorks

FOCUS
Hard to be sure of the strength of the form, but a time 1.41 seconds quicker than the first division, as well as a wide winning margin, suggests Oceanway ran to a pretty useful level. She probably didn't beat much.

NOTEBOOK
Oceanway(USA) ◆, runner-up over 1m here last time, produced a good mix of speed and stamina on this drop in trip to thrash her rivals. She has the size to train on and should have no trouble staying at least a couple of furlongs further in time. (tchd 6-4 and 13-8 in places)
Alareen(USA) was a similar distance behind today's winner here last time, and is clearly no match at all for that one. She looks modest. (op 3-1)
Starstuded(IRE), a half-sister to nine winners, including some useful sprinters, out of a Lowther winner, started slowly and needed to be encouraged along pretty much throughout. She made only moderate progress in the straight, but ought to have learnt plenty. (op 13-2)
Waltzing Cat(USA) had the worst draw and raced widest of all for much of the way, in the process still looking immature. She's now eligible for handicaps and really ought to find her level. (tchd 16-1)
Danish Pastry wasn't going at all well early on, but made late progress and is open to a deal of improvement. (op 11-1)

7313 40% BETTER OFF ON BETFAIR SP NURSERY 6f (P)
6:30 (6:31) (Class 6) (0-65,65) 2-Y-O £1,637 (£483; £241) **Stalls** High

Form RPR

602 **1** **Queen Of Cash (IRE)**[65] 5643 2-9-3 62...... RichardHughes 3 68+
(H Morrison) *trckd ldng pair: effrt to ld wl over 1f out: drvn and in command fnl f* **7/2**[2]

0556 **2** *1 ¾* **Homeboy (IRE)**[21] 6878 2-9-3 62...... (v1) TedDurcan 1 63
(M P Tregoning) *dwlt: hld up but sn prog into midfield: hdwy over 2f out: rdn to chse wnr jst ins fnl f: styd on but no imp* **12/1**

2500 **3** *3 ¼* **Ajaafa**[14] 7040 2-9-4 63...... (p) CathyGannon 4 54
(M J Attwater) *hmpd after 1f and dropped to rr: wl off the pce tl drvn and prog over 2f out: styd on wl to take 3rd nr fin* **25/1**

6334 **4** *shd* **Misscomplacent**[15] 7017 2-9-2 61...... (b) PaulHanagan 6 52
(Mrs A Duffield) *led at str pce but sn jnd: hdd wl over 1f out: wknd fnl f* **7/1**[3]

6502 **5** *¾* **Avalon Bay**[21] 6867 2-9-3 62...... DaneO'Neill 2 50
(Pat Eddery) *w ldr after 1f to over 2f out: wknd over 1f out* **10/1**

050 **6** *3 ¼* **Sleeping Brave**[65] 5626 2-9-3 62...... StephenCraine 12 41
(J R Boyle) *chsd ldrs in 5th: shkn up 1/2-way: nt qckn over 2f out: wknd over 1f out* **14/1**

3554 **7** *½* **Looksmart**[16] 6994 2-9-6 65...... JimmyFortune 9 42
(R Hannon) *dwlt: wl off the pce in last gp after 2f: nvr a factor after: modest late prog* **16/1**

2460 **8** *½* **Silca Conegliano (IRE)**[25] 6769 2-9-2 61...... ChrisCatlin 7 37
(M R Channon) *sn wl off the pce in rr gp and racd wd: nvr a factor* **40/1**

5002 **9** *¾* **High Class Lady**[29] 6673 2-9-5 64...... LukeMorris 8 37
(W R Swinburn) *t.k.h: hld up in tch: hmpd after 1f and dropped to rr: wl off the pce after* **3/1**[1]

354 **10** *2 ¼* **Loved To Bits**[18] 6954 2-9-2 61...... FergusSweeney 11 28
(P J Makin) *chsd ldng trio: wknd 2f out* **8/1**

3560 **11** *1 ½* **Whitstable Native**[20] 6902 2-9-3 65...... KierenFox(3) 10 27
(J R Best) *stmbld bdly after 1f and dropped to rr: nvr able to rcvr* **16/1**

005 **12** *1* **Special Endeavour (IRE)**[35] 6498 2-9-3 62...... GeorgeBaker 5 21
(W R Muir) *bmpd s: chsd ldrs in 5th early: wknd 3f out* **11/1**

1m 13.37s (0.27) **Going Correction** -0.075s/f (Stan) **12** Ran SP% **120.7**
Speed ratings (Par 94): **95,92,88,88,87 82,82,81,80,77 75,74**
toteswingers:1&2:£16.40, 1&3:£14.30, 2&3:£35.50 CSF £46.49 CT £700.23 TOTE £3.70: £1.10, £5.70, £9.00; EX 71.70.
Owner Hugh Scott-Barrett And Partners **Bred** Grangemore Stud **Trained** East Ilsley, Berks

FOCUS
The pace was strong, but the time was 0.36 seconds slower than the earlier modest-looking juvenile maiden. Routine nursery form with more to come from the winner.

NOTEBOOK
Queen Of Cash(IRE) hadn't been seen for two months, but she returned in good order, readily confirming the promise she showed when runner-up in a Fibresand maiden over this trip last time. Well placed, she was always doing enough once asked and is probably up to defying a higher mark. (tchd 4-1)
Homeboy(IRE) had the worst draw, but the strong pace allowed him to find a position in mid-division. He ran on in the straight, appearing to respond to the first-time visor, and showed himself on a reasonable mark on his nursery debut.
Ajaafa, claimed for only £2,000 after finishing down the field over 5f here last time, made a respectable debut for new connections, just running on to claim an unlikely third having met trouble early. Official explanation: jockey said colt jumped awkwardly
Misscomplacent raced keenly in the lead through the opening stages and had little hope of seeing her race out after soon being taken on by Avalon Bay. (op 6-1)
High Class Lady was badly hampered by Whitstable Native after than one stumbled on the first bend, and she couldn't recover. (op 9-2)
Whitstable Native was pulling so hard going into the first bend that he seemed to clip heels (possibly the winner's heels) and consequently stumbled badly. He was lucky not to hit the deck.

7314 MIX BUSINESS WITH PLEASURE CLAIMING STKS 6f (P)
7:00 (7:00) (Class 6) 3-Y-O+ £1,637 (£483; £241) **Stalls** High

Form RPR

1322 **1** **Dingaan (IRE)**[12] 7092 7-9-0 81...... RichardHughes 1 78
(A M Balding) *stdd s: hld up in last: prog over 2f out: plld out over 1f out: produced to ld ins fnl f: sn clr* **13/8**[1]

6230 **2** *2 ½* **Vhujon (IRE)**[17] 6987 5-9-2 77...... PaulHanagan 4 72
(P D Evans) *settled in rr: prog 1/2-way: drvn to go 3rd over 1f out: clsd on ldng pair but wnr swooped by ins fnl f: tk 2nd nr fin* **3/1**[2]

6010 **3** *¾* **Italian Tom (IRE)**[57] 5855 3-9-7 77...... LukeMorris 10 75
(R A Harris) *chsd ldng trio: wnt 2nd over 2f out: drvn to cl and led briefly 1f out: sn outpcd* **14/1**

5030 **4** *1 ¼* **Fromsong (IRE)**[21] 6880 12-9-0 61...... SamHitchcott 5 64
(D K Ivory) *forced to r wd to dispute ld for 2f: led after and clr 1/2-way: hdd 1f out: fdd* **25/1**

340 **5** *2 ¼* **Force To Spend**[21] 6863 3-8-2 46...... KellyHarrison(3) 3 48
(N P Littmoden) *hld up in rr: pushed along in last pair over 2f out: rdn and prog over 1f out: no imp on ldrs fnl f* **100/1**

0203 **6** 3 3/4 **Elusive Fame (USA)**[65] 5647 4-9-6 80....(b) JoeFanning 11 51
(M Johnston) *chsd ldrs: rdn and no prog over 2f out: fdd* **7/1**[3]
0621 **7** 6 **Victorian Bounty**[5] 7239 5-9-0 71.... MickyFenton 8 26
(Stef Higgins) *disp ld 2f: hanging and nt qckn over 2f out: wknd* **3/1**[2]
1000 **8** 7 **St Ignatius**[24] 6812 3-9-0 63....(b) ChrisCatlin 7 3
(K O Cunningham-Brown) *nvr on terms w ldrs: struggling in rr over 2f out* **66/1**
0000 **9** 2 1/2 **Louie's Lad**[62] 5715 4-8-11 40.... NeilChalmers 9 —
(J J Bridger) *disp ld 2f: wknd rapidly fr 1/2-way* **66/1**

1m 12.36s (-0.74) **Going Correction** -0.075s/f (Stan) **9** Ran SP% **115.1**
Speed ratings (Par 101): **101,97,96,95,92 87,79,69,66**
toteswingers:1&2:£1.50, 1&3:£4.30, 2&3:£10.70 CSF £6.54 TOTE £1.70: £1.02, £1.40, £4.70; EX 4.60.Dingaan was claimed by Mr E. Grayson for £8,000.
Owner Lady C S Cadbury **Bred** Mrs Gill Wilson **Trained** Kingsclere, Hants

FOCUS
A good claimer which was strongly run. The form is rated around the fourth.
Victorian Bounty Official explanation: jockey said gelding hit its head on stalls

7315 KEMPTON.CO.UK H'CAP 1m 4f (P)
7:30 (7:30) (Class 6) (0-60,60) 3-Y-0+ £1,637 (£483; £241) Stalls Centre

Form RPR
-000 **1** **Danvilla**[43] 6290 3-9-4 **60**.... WilliamCarson 1 70+
(P R Webber) *wl away fr wdst draw and sn trckd ldrs: smooth prog on outer to ld over 2f out: sn jnd: forged clr last 100yds* **11/1**
1024 **2** 2 3/4 **Larkrise Star**[16] 6999 3-9-3 **59**.... RichardHughes 7 65
(D K Ivory) *hld up in midfield: prog 3f out: jnd wnr 2f out: upsides and clr of rest tl no ex last 100yds* **5/1**[3]
0325 **3** 3 1/2 **Dubburg (USA)**[29] 6669 5-9-8 **58**.... StevieDonohoe 6 58
(W J Musson) *hld up in last quartet: prog over 3f out: rchd 4th 2f out: sn outpcd: kpt on to take 3rd ins fnl f* **4/1**[2]
/000 **4** 3/4 **Jackson (BRZ)**[57] 5852 8-9-0 **50**....(b) PaulHanagan 9 49
(R C Guest) *t.k.h: trckd ldrs: effrt to chse ldr 3f out to over 2f out: outpcd fr wl over 1f out: lost 3rd fnl f* **7/2**[1]
206 **5** 8 **Setter's Princess**[8] 7167 4-9-5 **55**.... RichardKingscote 10 41
(R J Hodges) *trckd ldrs on inner: briefly trapped bhd wkng rival over 3f out: rdn and outpcd over 2f out: no ch after* **10/1**
0022 **6** 3/4 **Mister Frosty (IRE)**[30] 6662 4-9-5 **55**.... KirstyMilczarek 8 40
(G Prodromou) *led to over 2f out: steadily wknd* **11/2**
-000 **7** 2 1/4 **Mystic Touch**[46] 3264 4-9-0 **50**....(p) RobertHavlin 4 32
(A B Haynes) *hld up in 10th: effrt 3f out: wl outpcd fr 2f out: fdd* **50/1**
2220 **8** 2 **Zelos Diktator**[25] 6775 4-9-7 **57**.... GeorgeBaker 3 35
(G L Moore) *hld up in 9th: effrt on outer 3f out: rdn over 2f out: sn wknd* **10/1**
600 **9** 6 **Sumner (IRE)**[15] 6930 6-9-10 **60**....(bt) JimmyFortune 14 29
(P D Evans) *early reminders in last: effrt on outer 4f out: wknd over 2f out* **14/1**
2632 **10** nk **Magic Spirit**[7] 760 3-9-0 **56**....(b) SamHitchcott 2 24
(Miss Suzy Smith) *chsd ldr tl wknd qckly 3f out* **50/1**
3006 **11** hd **Distant Waters**[8] 7168 3-9-4 **60**.... TedDurcan 11 28
(A P Jarvis) *hld up in 8th on inner: drvn and wknd over 2f out* **33/1**
4-00 **12** 9 **Good Buy Dubai (USA)**[197] 1478 4-9-1 **51**.... EddieCreighton 13 5
(E J Creighton) *hld up in last trio: sltly hmpd after 4f: drvn and struggling in last pair 4f out: t.o* **33/1**
216/ **13** 16 **Ful Of Grace (IRE)**[13] 2641 6-9-0 **50**....(b) DaneO'Neill 12 —
(J D Frost) *urged along in last trio after 3f: wknd 4f out: t.o* **66/1**
0000 **14** 1/2 **Mekong Miss**[148] 2870 4-9-2 **52**.... LukeMorris 5 —
(D Shaw) *chsd ldng pair: wknd rapidly wl over 3f out: t.o* **16/1**

2m 32.44s (-2.06) **Going Correction** -0.075s/f (Stan)
WFA 3 from 4yo+ 6lb **14** Ran SP% **124.6**
Speed ratings (Par 101): **103,101,98,98,93 92,91,89,85,85 85,79,68,68**
toteswingers:1&2:£10.80, 1&3:£17.70, 2&3:£7.00 CSF £65.91 CT £268.26 TOTE £9.50: £2.30, £2.20, £2.20; EX 79.60.
Owner Shully Liebermann **Bred** Minster Stud **Trained** Mollington, Oxon

FOCUS
A moderate handicap but the time was fair for the grade. The form is rated around the runner-up.
Danvilla Official explanation: trainer said, regarding apparent improvement in form, that on its previous run the filly was slowly away and had been backward and green but appeared to be maturing.
Mister Frosty(IRE) Official explanation: jockey said gelding was unsuited by the surface and appears better suited to Southwell
Sumner(IRE) Official explanation: jockey said gelding did not face the blinkers

7316 KIA SPORTAGE H'CAP 1m 4f (P)
8:00 (8:01) (Class 5) (0-75,72) 3-Y-0 £2,286 (£675; £337) Stalls Centre

Form RPR
2316 **1** **Iron Condor**[25] 6781 3-9-7 **72**.... PaulHanagan 6 80+
(J M P Eustace) *t.k.h: hld up in last trio: prog to trck ldrs 3f out: rdn to ld jst over 1f out: styd on wl* **3/1**[1]
0064 **2** 1 3/4 **Regency Girl (IRE)**[18] 6959 3-8-5 **63**....(p) JulieBurke(7) 3 68
(M P Tregoning) *hld up in last trio: shkn up over 2f out: prog over 1f out: styd on fnl f to take 2nd last stride* **11/2**
0005 **3** shd **High On A Hill (IRE)**[14] 7044 3-9-7 **72**.... RichardHughes 1 77
(S Kirk) *trckd ldr: drvn to ld narrowly 2f out: hdd jst over 1f out: one pce fnl f: lost 2nd post* **5/1**[3]
0621 **4** 2 1/4 **Catbells (IRE)**[14] 7038 3-9-0 **65**....(p) CathyGannon 7 66
(A Bailey) *led 1f: styd cl up: rdn to chal 2f out: nt qckn over 1f out: fdd ins fnl f* **4/1**[2]
-650 **5** 4 **Perfect Vision**[28] 6691 3-9-1 **66**.... LukeMorris 4 61
(C G Cox) *led after 1f at mod pce: kicked on 3f out: hdd 2f out: steadily wknd* **10/1**
4504 **6** 6 **Lauberhorn**[38] 6424 3-9-0 **68**.... AndrewHeffernan(3) 2 53
(Eve Johnson Houghton) *in tch tl wknd u.p fr 3f out* **20/1**
063 **7** nk **Byrd In Hand (IRE)**[16] 6999 3-8-2 **58** oh1.... RyanClark(5) 5 43
(J J Bridger) *t.k.h: trckd ldrs: rdn 3f out: wknd over 2f out* **12/1**
-610 **8** 6 **Mme De Stael**[101] 4433 3-9-2 **67**....(b) SebSanders 8 42
(Sir Mark Prescott) *hld up in last trio: rdn over 3f out: fnd nil u.p over 2f out: wknd* **5/1**[3]

2m 33.54s (-0.96) **Going Correction** -0.075s/f (Stan) **8** Ran SP% **115.3**
Speed ratings (Par 102): **100,98,98,97,94 90,90,86**
toteswingers:1&2:£5.10, 1&3:£2.80, 2&3:£7.30 CSF £19.98 CT £79.34 TOTE £4.00: £1.20, £3.80, £2.10; EX 24.50.
Owner Harold Nass **Bred** Rockville Pike Partnership **Trained** Newmarket, Suffolk

FOCUS
The pace slowed down the back straight, with the field bunching up, and a relative sprint ensued in the closing stages. As a consequence, the time was 1.10 seconds slower than the earlier Class 6 handicap. The winner is rated to form.

T/Plt: £13.90 to a £1 stake. Pool:£66,303.14 - 3,475.50 winning tickets T/Qpdt: £8.40 to a £1 stake. Pool:£7,466.47 - 652.05 winning tickets JN

7248 LINGFIELD (L-H)
Thursday, November 4

OFFICIAL GOING: Standard
Wind: strong, half behind Weather: dry, breezy

7317 BET EUROPE LEAGUE FOOTBALL - BETDAQ NOVICE STKS 7f (P)
12:45 (12:45) (Class 4) 2-Y-O £3,238 (£963; £481; £240) Stalls Low

Form RPR
0341 **1** **Dubarshi**[35] 6497 2-9-2 82.... DaneO'Neill 1 83+
(Miss Jo Crowley) *stdd after s: hld up in tch in last: stl last but gng wl over 1f out: rdn and effrt 1f out: wnt between horses and qcknd to chal ins fnl f: r.o wl to ld towards fin* **10/3**[2]
1 **2** nk **War Painter**[12] 7088 2-9-2 83.... RichardHughes 3 82
(S Kirk) *trckd ldrs: rdn and effrt bnd 2f out: drvn and chse ldr jst ins fnl f: ev ch fnl 100yds: kpt on* **6/4**[1]
0512 **3** shd **Focail Maith**[1] 7295 2-9-2 62....(b) StevieDonohoe 2 82
(J Ryan) *chsd ldrs: effrt u.p on inner wl over 1f out: led 1f out: drvn ins fnl f: kpt on u.p tl hdd and lost 2 pls nr fin* **20/1**
5656 **4** 2 **Satin Love (USA)**[27] 6727 2-9-5 89.... JoeFanning 5 80
(M Johnston) *w ldr: rdn 2f out: stl ev ch tl wknd u.p ins fnl f* **7/2**[3]
01 **5** 1 3/4 **Conducting**[27] 6704 2-9-5 77.... ShaneKelly 4 75
(B J Meehan) *led: rdn wl over 1f out: hdd 1f out: sn wknd* **9/2**

1m 24.01s (-0.79) **Going Correction** 0.0s/f (Stan) **5** Ran SP% **108.2**
Speed ratings (Par 98): **104,103,103,101,99**
CSF £8.48 TOTE £4.10: £2.00, £1.40; EX 10.10.
Owner Kilstone Limited **Bred** R G Levin **Trained** Whitcombe, Dorset

FOCUS
The two previous winners of this race were both sent off short-priced favourites and had won their only previous starts, but that trend ended this time, albeit narrowly. The pace was decent thanks to a contested lead, but that merely set the race up for the winner. The form makes sense, rated around the front pair.

NOTEBOOK
Dubarshi had looked awkward when edging out a subsequent winner in a Kempton maiden auction last time, but he looked straightforward here and travelled very smoothly at the back of the field throughout. He didn't have much of a gap to go through well inside the last furlong, but was brave enough to take it and got up close to the line. (op 4-1)
War Painter justified market confidence when winning a 6f Kempton maiden on debut, but his lack of experience may have cost him here. He was always in a good position behind the leaders, but hung off the final bend and took a while to hit top stride. Despite that, he still looked like winning a furlong out before the winner was produced and he can probably improve again from this. (op 11-8 tchd 13-8)
Focail Maith, only beaten a head in a Kempton nursery the previous evening, was the most exposed in the field and was also worst in at the weights, so this was a fine effort. Having crept up the inside to lead entering the last furlong, he wasn't cut down until close to the line. (tchd 16-1 and 22-1)
Satin Love(USA), best in at the weights having mainly been tried in Pattern company since a successful racecourse debut, disputed the early lead but didn't get home and is likely to continue to be hard to place. (op 3-1 tchd 4-1)
Conducting, making his AW debut after making all to win a modest Musselburgh maiden, wasn't helped by the early attentions of Satin Love and was beaten a furlong from home. (op 5-1 tchd 4-1)

7318 BETDAQ THE BETTING EXCHANGE H'CAP 7f (P)
1:20 (1:21) (Class 3) (0-90,89) 3-Y-0+ £5,828 (£1,734; £866; £432) Stalls Low

Form RPR
1610 **1** **Malcheek (IRE)**[9] 7146 8-9-7 **89**.... DavidAllan 8 100
(T D Easterby) *led: sn hdd: chsd ldr after and a gng wl: led 3f out: mde rest: rdn clr over 1f out in command fnl f: comf* **20/1**
2104 **2** 2 1/4 **Woodcote Place**[7] 7187 7-9-4 **86**.... JimCrowley 7 91
(P R Chamings) *in tch in midfield: rdn and effrt ent fnl 2f: chsd clr wnr ins fnl f: kpt on but no threat to wnr* **13/2**
0063 **3** 1 1/2 **Seek The Fair Land**[7] 7187 4-9-4 **86**....(b) StephenCraine 2 87
(J R Boyle) *in tch in midfield: hdwy to chse ldrs 4f out: chsd ldr over 2f out: drvn and nt pce of wnr over 1f out: wl hld 1f out: lost 2nd ins fnl f* **4/1**[1]
0464 **4** nk **Rule Of Nature**[24] 6798 3-8-11 **80**.... RichardHughes 11 80
(Sir Michael Stoute) *stdd s: hld up in tch in rr: rdn and effrt jst over 2f out: drvn and kpt on same pce fr over 1f out* **6/1**
1000 **5** 1/2 **King's Colour**[35] 6510 5-9-2 **84**.... GeorgeBaker 4 85+
(B R Johnson) *hld up in rr: nt clr run ent fnl 2f tl swtchd lft and hdwy jst over 1f out: styd on same pce ins fnl f: nvr able to chal* **9/1**
3110 **6** 1/2 **Avon River**[134] 3334 3-9-4 **87**.... JimmyFortune 6 84
(R Hannon) *t.k.h early: hld up in last trio: dropped to last and pushed along over 4f out: hdwy over 1f out: styd on past btn horses fnl f: nvr trbld ldrs* **16/1**
2322 **7** shd **L'Hirondelle (IRE)**[12] 7091 6-9-2 **84**.... LukeMorris 3 81
(M J Attwater) *chsd ldrs: rdn and effrt over 2f out: outpcd u.p over 1f out: wknd ent fnl f* **11/2**[3]
1000 **8** 3/4 **Little Scotland**[12] 7097 3-9-0 **83**....(p) PaulHanagan 9 78
(R A Fahey) *in tch in midfield: rdn and effrt ent fnl 2f: wknd u.p over 1f out* **14/1**
6216 **9** 14 **For Life (IRE)**[86] 4930 8-8-5 **76**.... NataliaGemelova(3) 1 33
(J E Long) *taken down early: dwlt: sn pushed up to ld: hdd 3f out: rdn and wknd over 2f out: wl bhd and eased ins fnl f* **25/1**
0354 **10** 2 **Street Power (USA)**[15] 7014 5-9-7 **89**.... SteveDrowne 5 41
(J R Gask) *dwlt: in tch in midfield: rdn and effrt 2f out: btn jst over 1f out: eased ins fnl f: virtually p.u fnl 75yds* **9/2**[2]

1m 23.31s (-1.49) **Going Correction** 0.0s/f (Stan)
WFA 3 from 4yo+ 1lb **10** Ran SP% **112.3**
Speed ratings (Par 107): **108,105,103,103,102 102,102,101,85,82**
toteswingers:1&2:£21.30, 1&3:£20.30, 2&3:£9.60 CSF £139.42 CT £646.45 TOTE £18.70: £6.20, £3.20, £2.70; EX 142.20 TRIFECTA Not won..
Owner Habton Farms **Bred** Carrigbeg Stud **Trained** Great Habton, N Yorks

FOCUS
A decent handicap and a solid pace.

NOTEBOOK
Malcheek(IRE), a three-time winner at Wolverhampton, is a real 7f specialist having gained ten of his 11 previous successes over the trip. Despite being 4lb above his highest previous winning mark, he travelled powerfully behind the pacemaker before taking over 3f from home and an injection of pace from the front a furlong later had all his rivals floundering. (op 14-1)

Woodcote Place, 0-10 on Polytrack (runner-up five times) and just behind Seek The Fair Land over C&D the previous week, reversed that form despite being no better off. Always close up on the outside, rather than race widest around the final bend his rider manoeuvred him to the left and hoped for a clear run through. The tactic worked to an extent, even though he didn't collect the gold medal, and he will surely break his duck on this surface in the coming months. (op 7-1 tchd 11-2)
Seek The Fair Land, a five-time winner over this trip on Polytrack including two over C&D, held a great position throughout but couldn't go with the winner when he quickened 2f out and there seemed no excuses. (op 5-1)
Rule Of Nature came off the bridle at the back of the field turning in, but his finishing effort was too little too late. He is becoming expensive to follow and is still to win a handicap. (op 9-2)
King's Colour was successful on his last visit here a year ago, but his recent performances on turf hadn't been great. Even so, he would have finished closer had he not been held up behind the weakening Street Power and For Life over a furlong from home. Official explanation: jockey said gelding was denied a clear run (tchd 8-1 and 11-1)
For Life(IRE) set a solid pace, but he was contesting the highest-class handicap of his career and was beaten with 3f left to run.
Street Power(USA) was reported to have lost his action. Official explanation: jockey said gelding lost its action (op 11-2)

7319 COCKTAILS UN LIMITED H'CAP (DIV I) 6f (P)
1:55 (1:56) (Class 4) (0-80,80) 3-Y-0+ **£3,561** (£1,059; £529; £264) **Stalls** Low

Form RPR
4165 **1** **Anne Of Kiev (IRE)**[14] 7041 5-9-7 **80**....(t) LukeMorris 4 89+
(J R Gask) *hld up in tch in midfield: switching rt and effrt wl over 1f out: str run ins fnl f to ld fnl 50yds: r.o wl* **10/3**[1]
2630 **2** ½ **Quasi Congaree (GER)**[24] 6798 4-9-5 **78**....(t) DaneO'Neill 9 85
(I A Wood) *chsd ldrs: rdn to chse ldr ent fnl 2f: drvn and pressed wnr ins fnl f: kpt on* **12/1**
2521 **3** nse **Elhamri**[16] 6997 6-9-0 **73**.... HayleyTurner 11 80
(C R Dore) *chsd ldr tl led after 1f: rdn over 1f out: pressed and drvn ins fnl f: hdd and no ex fnl 50yds: lost 2nd on post* **5/1**[3]
1335 **4** 1 ½ **Mango Music**[18] 6962 7-8-7 **66** oh1.... PaulHanagan 3 68
(R A Fahey) *racd keenly: led for 1f: chsd ldr after tl ent fnl 2f: unable qck u.p over 1f out: one pce fnl f* **4/1**[2]
4610 **5** shd **Freddie's Girl (USA)**[12] 7093 3-9-4 **77**.... SebSanders 8 79
(Stef Higgins) *stdd s: hld up in tch in midfield: rdn and effrt over 1f out: styd on same pce ins fnl f* **9/1**
0450 **6** ½ **Brandywell Boy (IRE)**[16] 6998 7-8-10 **74**.... BillyCray(5) 5 74
(D J S Ffrench Davis) *t.k.h: hld up wl in tch: rdn and effrt 2f out: styd on same pce fr over 1f out* **20/1**
4032 **7** nse **Hulcote Rose (IRE)**[21] 6879 3-9-2 **75**.... RichardHughes 10 75
(S Kirk) *in tch towards rr: effrt ent fnl 2f: no prog u.p over 1f out: kpt on fnl 100yds: nt pce to chal ldrs* **15/2**
-060 **8** 3 ¾ **Al Gillani (IRE)**[24] 6798 5-9-6 **79**....(t) GeorgeBaker 2 67
(J R Boyle) *hld up in tch: rdn and effrt ent fnl 2f: no prog over 1f out: wknd ins fnl f* **10/1**
0160 **9** nk **Hinton Admiral**[70] 5454 6-8-10 **72**.... MichaelStainton(3) 12 59
(P Howling) *stdd and rrd as stalls opened: sn swtchd lft and hld up in rr: c towards centre wl over 1f out: no imp over 1f out: n.d* **25/1**
0500 **10** nse **Tony The Tap**[102] 4401 9-8-13 **79**.... JamesRogers(7) 7 66
(W R Muir) *short of room s: a in last pair: nvr trbld ldrs* **20/1**
0-00 **11** ½ **Mogok Ruby**[96] 4589 6-8-9 **68**.... WilliamCarson 6 53
(B R Johnson) *stdd and edgd rt s: hld up in tch towards rr: rdn and no hdwy over 1f out: nvr trbld ldrs* **40/1**

1m 11.67s (-0.23) **Going Correction** 0.0s/f (Stan) **11** Ran SP% **114.1**
Speed ratings (Par 105): **101,100,100,98,98 97,97,92,92,91 91**
toteswingers:1&2:£10.90, 1&3:£5.50, 2&3:£8.80 CSF £40.22 CT £199.68 TOTE £3.90: £1.20, £4.40, £1.50; EX 52.70 Trifecta £392.60 - 0.20 winning units..
Owner P Bamford **Bred** Deerfield Farm **Trained** Sutton Veny, Wilts

FOCUS
A fair sprint handicap and the pace was a good one. All the main action took place out in the centre of the track once into the straight.

7320 COCKTAILS UN LIMITED H'CAP (DIV II) 6f (P)
2:30 (2:30) (Class 4) (0-80,80) 3-Y-0+ **£3,561** (£1,059; £529; £264) **Stalls** Low

Form RPR
011 **1** **Ritual (IRE)**[46] 6226 3-9-5 **78**.... PaulHanagan 9 91+
(J Noseda) *awkward s: t.k.h: hld up in midfield on outer: effrt whn hmpd wl over 1f out: carried rt over 1f out: edgd lft u.p but qcknd ins fnl f: r.o wl to ld towards fin* **10/11**[1]
5000 **2** ½ **Lujeanie**[17] 6987 4-9-5 **78**....(p) AdamKirby 1 86
(D K Ivory) *in tch: rdn and swtchd lft over 1f out: led 1f out: hdd ins fnl f: kpt on u.p* **25/1**
6032 **3** hd **Even Bolder**[16] 6998 7-8-11 **73**.... KierenFox(3) 6 80
(E A Wheeler) *in tch in last trio: effrt and nt clr run 2f out: hdwy on inner and hung lft over 1f out: chsd ldr jst ins fnl f: led fnl 100yds: hdd and lost 2 pls towards fin* **12/1**
3116 **4** ½ **Micky P**[56] 5890 3-8-8 **67**.... WilliamCarson 2 72
(S C Williams) *hld up wl in tch: rdn and effrt ent fnl 2f: unable qck over 1f out: styd on again ins fnl f* **16/1**
1141 **5** 1 ¼ **Titus Gent**[34] 6523 5-9-1 **74**.... KirstyMilczarek 5 75
(R A Harris) *led: rdn and c towards centre st: hdd 1f out: wknd fnl 100yds* **9/2**[2]
0100 **6** hd **Yurituni**[17] 6981 3-9-3 **76**....(b) RichardHughes 11 77
(Eve Johnson Houghton) *chsd ldr: rdn ent fnl 2f: edging rt over 1f out: styd on same pce ins fnl f* **33/1**
3452 **7** shd **Di Stefano**[9] 7144 3-8-13 **72**.... AdrianNicholls 3 72
(D Nicholls) *t.k.h early: chsd ldrs: rdn and switching rt wl over 1f out: unable qck whn short of room and swtchd lft 1f out: kpt on same pce after* **7/1**[3]
0402 **8** 2 ½ **Ivory Silk**[24] 6812 5-9-1 **79**....(b) TobyAtkinson(5) 7 71
(J R Gask) *awkward leaving stalls and s.i.s: a in last pair: styd on same pce fr over 1f out: n.d* **16/1**
0660 **9** 1 **Fivefold (USA)**[12] 7091 3-9-0 **73**.... J-PGuillambert 4 62
(J Akehurst) *stdd s: t.k.h: hld up in tch in rr: rdn and no real prog over 1f out: nvr trbld ldrs* **25/1**

1m 11.5s (-0.40) **Going Correction** 0.0s/f (Stan) **9** Ran SP% **113.2**
Speed ratings (Par 105): **102,101,101,100,98 98,98,95,93**
toteswingers:1&2:£4.50, 1&3:£5.60, 2&3:£8.10 CSF £31.62 CT £175.17 TOTE £1.60: £1.10, £5.40, £3.50; EX 22.00 Trifecta £151.90 Pool: £531.69 - 2.59 winning units.
Owner Highclere Thoroughbred Racing Churchill **Bred** Agricola Del Parco **Trained** Newmarket, Suffolk
■ Stewards' Enquiry : Richard Hughes nineteen-day ban (18 under totting up procedure, 4 days deferred): careless riding (Nov 30 - Dec 14)

FOCUS
Not as competitive as the first division with a short-priced favourite, but quite a dramatic race and the winning time was 0.17 seconds faster than division one.
Even Bolder Official explanation: jockey said gelding hung

7321 BREEDERS' CUP LIVE ONLY ON ATR H'CAP 2m (P)
3:05 (3:05) (Class 5) (0-75,68) 3-Y-0+ **£2,590** (£770; £385; £192) **Stalls** Low

Form RPR
405 **1** **Blackmore**[21] 6861 3-8-11 **60**.... CathyGannon 2 68
(Miss J Feilden) *in tch: rdn over 2f out: n.m.r ent fnl 2f: sn drvn: swtchd rt ent fnl f: led ins fnl f: rn green and hung lft fnl 100yds: rdn out* **12/1**
-304 **2** nk **Eagle Nebula**[8] 7167 6-9-4 **58**.... GeorgeBaker 7 65
(B R Johnson) *hld up in tch: hdwy to chse ldrs over 2f out: rdn and hung lft over 1f out: ev ch ins fnl f: n.m.r fnl 100yds: hld towards fin* **5/1**
3006 **3** 1 ½ **King Supreme (IRE)**[7] 7190 5-9-13 **67**....(b) RichardHughes 5 72
(R Hannon) *chsd ldr tl 12f out: rdn to chse ldr again 4f out: led wl over 2f out: hrd drvn over 1f out: edgd rt and hdd ins fnl f: no ex and btn fnl 75yds* **4/1**[3]
366 **4** 2 ¼ **William's Way**[25] 6775 8-9-11 **65**....(t) NeilCallan 6 68
(I A Wood) *stdd s: hld up in rr: hdwy 4f out: jnd ldr and rdn ent fnl 2f: stl pressing ldr but one pce whn short of room ins fnl f: btn fnl 100yds* **6/1**
/6-0 **5** ½ **Sarando**[215] 164 5-9-8 **62**.... DaneO'Neill 4 65
(P R Webber) *in tch: chsd ldrs whn nt clr run on inner ent fnl 2f: rdn and unable qck over 1f out: no ex and btn ins fnl f* **10/3**[2]
0 **6** 24 **Paloma Blanca (IRE)**[21] 6861 3-9-2 **65**....(p) RobertWinston 3 38
(A Bailey) *towards rr tl hdwy to chse ldr 11f out: rdn and lost 2nd ent fnl 4f: sn dropped to rr and struggling: lost tch over 2f out* **16/1**
0045 **7** 23 **Boucheron**[12] 7101 5-10-0 **68**.... PaulHanagan 1 14
(R A Fahey) *led tl wl over 2f out: sn btn: t.o and eased fr over 1f out* **3/1**[1]

3m 24.51s (-1.19) **Going Correction** 0.0s/f (Stan)
WFA 3 from 5yo+ 9lb **7** Ran SP% **112.6**
Speed ratings (Par 103): **102,101,101,99,99 87,76**
toteswingers:1&2:£3.30, 1&3:£7.20, 2&3:£5.00 CSF £67.68 CT £284.48 TOTE £15.80: £7.60, £2.90; EX 71.10 Trifecta £344.30 Part won. Pool: £465.39 - 0.44 winning units..
Owner Good Company Partnership **Bred** Juddmonte Farms Ltd **Trained** Exning, Suffolk
■ Stewards' Enquiry : Richard Hughes First incident, two-day ban: careless riding (Nov 26-27); 2nd, two-day ban: careless riding (Nov 28-29)

FOCUS
A moderate stayers' handicap and, even though the pace was modest, the pair that helped force it both finished tailed off.

7322 BREEDERS' CUP LIVE ONLY ON ATR MAIDEN STKS 5f (P)
3:40 (3:40) (Class 5) 3-Y-0+ **£2,729** (£806; £403) **Stalls** High

Form RPR
0 **1** **Clear Praise (USA)**[35] 6496 3-9-3 0.... NeilCallan 2 71
(S Dow) *racd keenly: mde all: rdn and hung rt fr wl over 1f out: r.o strly to draw clr ins fnl f: readily* **2/1**[2]
0330 **2** 4 **Papageno**[43] 6285 3-9-3 59.... PaulHanagan 4 56
(J R Jenkins) *chsd wnr: rdn and pressed wnr 2f out: drvn over 1f out: nt pce of wnr ins fnl f* **5/4**[1]
6 **3** 1 ½ **Leahness (IRE)**[18] 6956 3-8-12 40.... RichardHughes 3 46
(Patrick Morris) *chsd ldrs: rdn and effrt ent fnl 2f: styd on same pce fr over 1f out* **9/2**[3]
406 **4** 2 ¾ **Billionaire Boy (IRE)**[19] 6931 3-9-3 48.... StephenCraine 1 41
(Patrick Morris) *t.k.h: chsd ldrs: rdn and unable qck ent fnl 2f: wl btn ent fnl f* **6/1**
6050 **5** 4 ½ **Riggs (IRE)**[26] 6746 4-9-3 38.... DaneO'Neill 5 25
(Peter Grayson) *in tch: rdn 1/2-way: wknd over 1f out: wl bhd fnl f* **33/1**

58.16 secs (-0.64) **Going Correction** 0.0s/f (Stan) **5** Ran SP% **113.2**
Speed ratings (Par 103): **105,98,96,91,84**
CSF £5.08 TOTE £3.60: £1.60, £1.10; EX 5.70.
Owner Chua, Moore, Goalen & Warner **Bred** Juddmonte Farms Inc **Trained** Epsom, Surrey

FOCUS
This is as bad as it gets.

7323 ATTHERACES.COM/BREEDERSCUP H'CAP 1m 2f (P)
4:10 (4:10) (Class 6) (0-65,65) 3-Y-0+ **£2,047** (£604; £302) **Stalls** Low

Form RPR
0502 **1** **Ermyn Express**[17] 6991 3-8-12 **56**.... IanMongan 1 64+
(P M Phelan) *chsd ldrs: wnt 2nd over 2f out: rdn to ld wl over 1f out: rn green and edgd rt u.p: hdd ins fnl f: rallied and hung lft u.p to ld again last stride* **10/1**
3653 **2** shd **Final Drive (IRE)**[1] 7298 4-9-8 **62**....(t) StevieDonohoe 4 70
(J Ryan) *stdd s: hld up towards rr: hdwy and n.m.r ent fnl 2f: rdn and gd hdwy over 1f out: led ins fnl f: kpt on: hdd last stride* **6/1**[3]
5304 **3** 1 ¼ **Opera Prince**[24] 6794 5-9-9 **63**....(p) SebSanders 8 68
(Lady Herries) *hld up towards rr: rdn and effrt over 1f out: styd on wl u.p ins fnl f: wnt 3rd towards fin* **11/2**[2]
42 **4** ½ **Ermyntrude**[21] 6862 3-8-4 **53**.... JemmaMarshall(5) 3 57
(P M Phelan) *chsd ldrs: rdn and effrt 2f out: swtchd lft 1f out: kpt on same pce ins fnl f* **25/1**
6442 **5** nse **Lunar River (FR)**[16] 6999 7-8-6 **53**....(t) JamesRogers(7) 13 57
(David Pinder) *stdd s: hld up in rr: hdwy on outer over 1f out: r.o ins fnl f: nt rch ldrs* **8/1**
0-55 **6** hd **Professor John (IRE)**[117] 3916 3-9-0 **58**....(v[1]) NeilCallan 14 62
(I A Wood) *hld up in tch in midfield: hdwy to chse ldrs ent fnl 2f: drvn over 1f out: styd on same pce fnl f* **25/1**
2-00 **7** 1 ¼ **Astrodiva**[12] 7101 4-8-12 **57**.... AshleyMorgan(5) 6 58
(M H Tompkins) *in tch: chsd ldrs 4f out: rdn and unable qck wl over 1f out: one pce and btn fnl 150yds* **12/1**
4020 **8** hd **Mister Bit (IRE)**[22] 6846 3-9-6 **64**.... GeorgeBaker 12 65
(J R Best) *stdd s: hld up in rr: hdwy jst over 2f out: kpt on u.p ins fnl f: nvr able to chal* **8/1**
0001 **9** shd **Hurricane Thomas (IRE)**[8] 7184 6-9-7 **61** 6ex.... PaulHanagan 7 61
(R A Fahey) *in tch in midfield: n.m.r and shuffled bk towards rr over 2f out: kpt on u.p ins fnl f: nvr able to chal* **9/1**
0320 **10** 2 ¼ **Amends (USA)**[17] 6993 3-9-4 **62**.... LiamJones 9 58
(J R Best) *hld up in last pair: effrt on inner jst over 2f out: kpt on same pce fr over 1f out: nvr trbld ldrs* **33/1**
2330 **11** ¾ **Vinces**[29] 6668 6-9-5 **64**.... TobyAtkinson(5) 10 58
(T D McCarthy) *dwlt: sn bustled along to r in midfield: rdn and n.m.r over 2f out: no real prog over 1f out* **25/1**
3214 **12** 1 ¼ **D'Urberville**[22] 6856 3-9-5 **63**.... RichardHughes 11 55
(J R Jenkins) *t.k.h: hld up in tch in midfield: rdn and no prog 2f out: n.d fnl f* **7/2**[1]

0500 **13** *1 ¼* **Mountrath**[8] 7162 3-9-2 **65** ... BillyCray(5) 2 54
(B R Johnson) *sn led: rdn and hdd wl over 1f out: drvn and wknd over 1f out* **33/1**

-606 **14** *3 ¼* **Levitation (IRE)**[54] 5958 4-9-8 **62** ... (v[1]) SamHitchcott 5 45
(W S Kittow) *chsd ldr tl over 2f out: sn struggling: wl btn over 1f out* **28/1**

2m 6.58s (-0.02) **Going Correction** 0.0s/f (Stan)
WFA 3 from 4yo+ 4lb **14** Ran SP% **121.8**
Speed ratings (Par 101): **100,99,98,98,98 98,97,97,97,95 94,93,92,90**
toteswingers:1&2:£13.70, 1&3:£10.80, 2&3:£7.70 CSF £64.12 CT £370.73 TOTE £11.50: £3.60, £1.70, £2.00; EX 104.90 TRIFECTA Not won..
Owner Ermyn Lodge Stud **Bred** Ermyn Lodge Stud Limited **Trained** Epsom, Surrey

FOCUS
A moderate if competitive handicap and a typical Lingfield finish.
T/Plt: £41.80 to a £1 stake. Pool:£40,301.72 - 703.24 winning tickets T/Qpdt: £11.30 to a £1 stake. Pool:£4,623.91 - 300.20 winning tickets SP

7126 SOUTHWELL (L-H)

Friday, November 5

OFFICIAL GOING: Standard
Wind: Light across Weather: Cloudy

7324 I'M A GOTH NURSERY 1m (F)

1:00 (1:00) (Class 4) (0-85,81) 2-Y-0 **£3,784** (£1,132; £566; £283; £141) **Stalls** Low

Form RPR

216 **1** **Makeynn**[34] 6555 2-9-7 **81** ... TedDurcan 2 88
(Saeed Bin Suroor) *trckd ldng pair: chsd ldr after 3f: wd st and sn chal: rdn to ld 1 1/2f out: kpt on* **13/8**[1]

4416 **2** *2 ½* **Il Battista**[56] 5901 2-9-7 **81** ... (p) JamesDoyle 7 82
(A J McCabe) *led: rdn along and jnd wl over 2f out: hdd 1 1 /2f out: sn drvn and kpt on same pce* **6/1**

0523 **3** *7* **My Mate Jake (IRE)**[18] 6978 2-8-11 **71** ... PaulMulrennan 3 56
(J G Given) *trckd ldrs: hdwy on outer and cl up over 3f out: rdn along wl over 2f out: edgd lft wl over 1f out and sn wknd* **5/1**[3]

5322 **4** *nk* **Suddenly Susan (IRE)**[11] 7126 2-8-8 **68** ... PaulHanagan 1 52
(J A Glover) *chsd ldrs on inner: pushed along 3f out: sn rdn and btn over 2f out* **3/1**[2]

5202 **5** *4 ½* **Fred Willetts (IRE)**[18] 6988 2-9-3 **77** ... TomMcLaughlin 4 51
(P D Evans) *sn rdn along and outpcd in rr: hdwy 3f out: kpt on fnl 2f: nvr nr ldrs* **14/1**

0004 **6** *6* **Beating Harmony**[36] 6500 2-8-5 **65** ... HayleyTurner 6 25
(Tom Dascombe) *a in rr: rdn along bef 1/2-way: sn outpcd and bhd* **25/1**

6414 **7** *8* **Itzakindamagic (IRE)**[18] 6978 2-8-12 **72** ... JoeFanning 5 14
(M Johnston) *dwlt: hdwy and in tch after 1f: chsd ldrs 1/2-way: rdn along over 3f out and sn wknd* **10/1**

1m 41.82s (-1.88) **Going Correction** -0.10s/f (Stan) **7** Ran SP% **113.7**
Speed ratings (Par 98): **105,102,95,95,90 84,76**
toteswingers:1&2 £3.20, 2&3 £5.50, 1&3 £2.60 CSF £11.86 TOTE £2.30: £1.10, £5.70; EX 14.20.
Owner Godolphin **Bred** Darley **Trained** Newmarket, Suffolk

FOCUS
Only the front two, both well suited by the surface, gave their true running, but the time was good, being 1.59 seconds faster than the folowing juvenile maiden won by Encore Une Annee.

NOTEBOOK
Makeynn was 4lb lower than when behind a couple of subsequent winners on his nursery debut (heavy ground at Epsom), and proved suited by the switch to Fibresand, as his breeding suggested. Not only he is a brother to a winner around here, but his sire Dubai Destination has a fantastic record with his Fibresand runners (this made it 8-36). The winner was adding to his Polytrack maiden success, and is clearly a force on the AW, but it remains to be seen whether he's as good on turf. (op 9-4)
Il Battista, gelded since last seen in August, proved suited by the return to Fibresand and, given a positive ride, ran well off an 11lb higher mark than when winning over 7f here earlier in the year. (op 5-1 tchd 13-2)
My Mate Jake(IRE) ran respectably without proving himself on the surface. Perhaps Polytrack will suit better. (op 7-1)
Suddenly Susan(IRE), debuting for a new stable, failed to match the form she showed when runner-up over C&D for Jeremy Noseda last time. Perhaps she's had enough for the year. (op 11-4 tchd 5-2 and 7-2)
Fred Willetts(IRE) was an unlikely stayer and never featured. (op 12-1)

7325 E B F BET BREEDERS' CUP - BETDAQ MAIDEN STKS 1m (F)

1:30 (1:30) (Class 5) 2-Y-O **£3,140** (£934; £467; £233) **Stalls** Low

Form RPR

43 **1** **Encore Une Annee**[14] 7057 2-8-12 0 ... JimCrowley 4 78+
(R M Beckett) *trckd ldrs: hdwy 3f out: cl up 2f out: rdn to ld over 1f out: clr ins fnl f: readily* **8/15**[1]

30 **2** *3 ¾* **Lexington Bay (IRE)**[139] 3190 2-9-3 0 ... PaulHanagan 2 72
(R A Fahey) *trckd ldrs on inner: rdn along to chse ldng pair over 2f out: sn outpcd: styd on u.p ins fnl f to take 2nd nr fin: no ch w wnr* **9/2**[3]

00 **3** *½* **X Rated**[11] 7126 2-9-3 0 ... JamesDoyle 5 71
(A J McCabe) *led: pushed along 3f out: jnd and rdn 2f out: hdd wl over 1f out: sn drvn and one pce ent fnl f: lost 2nd nr fin* **66/1**

4 **4** *9* **Raw Spirit (GER)**[10] 7152 2-9-3 0 ... TedDurcan 7 51
(Saeed Bin Suroor) *dwlt: in tch: pushed along over 3f out: rdn to chse ldrs and edgd lft 2f out: sn no imp* **7/2**[2]

0 **5** *6* **Szabo's Destiny**[9] 7178 2-9-3 0 ... PaulMulrennan 6 37
(J G Given) *chsd ldrs: rdn along and lost pl after 3f: swtchd to outer and wd st: n.d* **66/1**

0 **6** *2 ½* **Newgate Dani**[9] 7179 2-9-3 0 ... BarryMcHugh 9 31
(N Bycroft) *chsd ldrs on outer: rdn along over 3f out: sn wknd* **100/1**

00 **7** *1 ¾* **Look For Love**[9] 7179 2-9-3 0 ... GrahamGibbons 1 27
(R Hollinshead) *in tch on inner: rdn along over 3f out and sn wknd* **66/1**

8 *3 ¾* **Evelyns Diamond** 2-8-12 0 ... MickyFenton 3 13
(P T Midgley) *dwlt: sn rdn along and outpcd in rr: bhd fr 1/2-way* **50/1**

0 **9** *9* **Allez Leulah (IRE)**[17] 7001 2-8-12 0 ... JoeFanning 8 —
(M Johnston) *cl up: rdn along 3f out: sn wknd* **20/1**

1m 43.41s (-0.29) **Going Correction** -0.10s/f (Stan) **9** Ran SP% **117.8**
Speed ratings (Par 96): **97,93,92,83,77 75,73,69,60**
toteswingers:1&2 £1.60, 2&3 £15.00, 1&3 £10.60 CSF £3.41 TOTE £1.60: £1.02, £1.10, £17.80; EX 4.30 Trifecta £54.80 Pool: £607.25 - 8.20 winning units..
Owner Miss K Rausing **Bred** Miss K Rausing **Trained** Whitsbury, Hants

FOCUS
A reasonable maiden, although the time was slow, being 1.59 seconds off the time recorded by Makeynn in the opening Class 4 nursery.

NOTEBOOK
Encore Une Annee, well backed, confirmed the promise she showed in turf maidens over 7f-1m. A sister to a winner on this surface, it was no surprise the Fibresand suited and she won with plenty in hand. She'll want middle-distances next year. (op 8-11tchd 4-5 in places)
Lexington Bay(IRE) ◆ showed ability on debut but had been off since finishing down the field in the Chesham. He never threatened the winner, but stuck on well for second and this was a pleasing return. Handicaps are now an option and he should do well over further in due course. (op 4-1)
X Rated stepped up on his first two efforts with an encouraging performance. He didn't see his race out, but should stay better as he gets stronger, and he has the scope to progress into a fair handicapper.
Raw Spirit(GER) came off the bridle early on and was never going, failing to build on his debut effort. The surface seemed far from ideal. (op 10-3 tchd 3-1)

7326 BET ASIAN H'CAPS - BETDAQ HANDICAP 5f (F)

2:00 (2:00) (Class 4) (0-85,84) 3-Y-O+ **£3,885** (£1,156; £577; £288) **Stalls** High

Form RPR

0603 **1** **Sloop Johnb**[9] 7169 4-8-7 **70** oh2 ... (p) PaulHanagan 3 79
(R A Fahey) *prom: cl up 1/2-way: rdn wl over 1f out: drvn and edgd rt ins fnl f: kpt on to ld last 75yds* **6/1**[3]

0345 **2** *hd* **Lost In Paris (IRE)**[27] 6739 4-9-2 **79** ... (v) PaulMulrennan 10 87
(T D Easterby) *cl up: led 1/2-way: rdn over 1f out: drvn and edgd lft ins fnl f: hdd and no ex last 75yds* **6/1**[3]

0514 **3** *nk* **Colorus (IRE)**[22] 6858 7-8-1 **71** oh3 ow1 ... (v) MatthewCosham(7) 4 78
(W J H Ratcliffe) *chsd ldrs: hdwy on outer wl over 1f out: sn rdn and kpt on ins fnl f: nrst fin* **12/1**

3035 **4** *½* **The Nifty Fox**[18] 6985 6-9-6 **83** ... DavidAllan 5 88
(T D Easterby) *trckd ldrs: hdwy over 1f out: rdn and ch whn n.m.r ins fnl f: no ex towards fin* **9/2**[1]

2001 **5** *hd* **La Capriosa**[9] 7175 4-8-12 **75** 6ex ... AdrianNicholls 1 79
(J A Glover) *led: hdd 1/2-way and sn pushed along: rdn wl over 1f out: sn drvn and kpt on same pce* **6/1**[3]

4600 **6** *1 ½* **Grudge**[9] 7180 5-8-8 **71** ... (be) RobertWinston 12 70
(C R Dore) *prom on outer: rdn along over 2f out: drvn wl over 1f out and kpt on same pce* **33/1**

3500 **7** *1* **Ace Of Spies (IRE)**[9] 7180 5-8-9 **73** ... HayleyTurner 9 67
(C R Dore) *in tch: rdn along and sltly outpcd 1/2-way: drvn and kpt on ins fnl f* **16/1**

044 **8** *¾* **Equuleus Pictor**[9] 7180 6-8-12 **75** ... DarryllHolland 6 68
(J L Spearing) *swtchd lft sn after s: sn rdn along and a towards rr* **13/2**

0000 **9** *¾* **Pawan (IRE)**[19] 6965 10-8-5 **73** oh3 ow3 ... (b) AnnStokell(5) 8 63
(Miss A Stokell) *sn rdn along and outpcd in rr tl sme late hdwy* **33/1**

4311 **10** *hd* **Efistorm**[66] 5628 9-8-11 **74** ... (e[1]) LiamKeniry 11 63
(C R Dore) *prom: rdn along bef 1/2-way: sn wknd* **11/2**[2]

0200 **11** *2 ¼* **Where's Reiley (USA)**[19] 6962 4-8-11 **79** ... DeanHeslop(5) 7 60
(T D Barron) *in tch: sn rdn along and outpcd: bhd fr 1/2-way* **12/1**

000/ **12** *2* **Benwilt Breeze (IRE)**[113] 4078 8-9-7 **84** ... (t) TomEaves 2 58
(C J Teague) *s.i.s: a bhd* **33/1**

58.42 secs (-1.28) **Going Correction** -0.20s/f (Stan) **12** Ran SP% **119.8**
Speed ratings (Par 105): **102,101,101,100,100 97,96,94,93,93 89,86**
toteswingers:1&2 £7.90, 2&3 £17.70, 1&3 £14.10 CSF £41.74 CT £422.55 TOTE £6.60: £2.60, £2.50, £5.60; EX 58.40 Trifecta £294.40 Pool: £457.56 - 1.15 winning units..
Owner Jonathan Gill **Bred** Manor Farm Stud (rutland) **Trained** Musley Bank, N Yorks
■ Stewards' Enquiry : Paul Hanagan three-day ban: used whip with excessive frequency without giving gelding time to respond (Nov 19,20,23)

FOCUS
A fair, competitive sprint handicap. Somewhat surprisingly the front two had never previously raced on Fibresand.
Equuleus Pictor Official explanation: jockey said gelding missed the break
Efistorm Official explanation: jockey said gelding never travelled

7327 BET MULTIPLES - BETDAQ CLAIMING STKS 1m 3f (F)

2:30 (2:30) (Class 6) 3-Y-O+ **£1,706** (£503; £252) **Stalls** Low

Form RPR

5242 **1** **Diggeratt (USA)**[18] 6992 4-8-13 70 ... PaulHanagan 3 86
(R A Fahey) *trckd ldrs: hdwy to chse ldr 3f out: rdn to ld and hung lft 1 1/2f out: drvn and wandered ins fnl f: kpt on* **3/1**[2]

0551 **2** *2* **Lucky Punt**[11] 7130 4-9-12 84 ... FergusSweeney 10 95
(B G Powell) *trckd ldr: cl up 4f out: led over 3f out: rdn and jnd 2f out: hdd 1 1/2f out and sn drvn: rallied ins fnl f: no ex last 100yds* **8/15**[1]

4-45 **3** *10* **Grande Caiman (IRE)**[84] 5034 6-9-0 90 ... FrannyNorton 6 65
(G A Harker) *trckd ldrs: hdwy 4f out: rdn 3f out: drvn over 2f out: and kpt on same pce* **13/2**[3]

0104 **4** *hd* **Kimberley Downs (USA)**[9] 7171 4-9-5 75 ... GaryBartley(3) 5 73
(N Wilson) *led: rdn along 4f out: hdd over 3f out: sn drvn and kpt on same pce* **12/1**

0345 **5** *3* **Ra Junior (USA)**[9] 7171 4-9-0 64 ... MickyFenton 1 60
(P T Midgley) *chsd ldrs on inner: rdn along 4f out: drvn wl over 2f out and sn wknd* **20/1**

6300 **6** *1 ¼* **Special Cuvee**[16] 7011 4-9-0 49 ... (bt) HayleyTurner 2 57
(Mrs A M Thorpe) *s.i.s and in rr: stdy hdwy over 4f out: rdn and in tch over 2f out: sn drvn and no imp* **40/1**

6405 **7** *3 ¼* **Kingaroo (IRE)**[69] 5515 4-8-9 43 ... BillyCray(5) 8 52
(G Woodward) *hld up: a in rr* **40/1**

0-00 **8** *24* **Bluegrass Lion (USA)**[10] 7157 4-8-10 50 ... SaleemGolam 4 —
(Mrs L Williamson) *chsd ldrs on inner: rdn along 4f out: sn wknd* **100/1**

2m 25.83s (-2.17) **Going Correction** -0.10s/f (Stan)
WFA 3 from 4yo+ 5lb **8** Ran SP% **121.9**
Speed ratings (Par 101): **103,101,94,94,91 91,88,71**
toteswingers:1&2 £1.90, 2&3 £3.00, 1&3 £2.50 CSF £5.23 TOTE £3.30: £1.10, £1.10, £1.70; EX 6.70 Trifecta £21.30 Pool: £549.89 - 19.04 winning units..Diggeratt was claimed by Mr G Baker for £8,000.
Owner J A Rattigan **Bred** Hobby Horse Farm Inc **Trained** Musley Bank, N Yorks
■ Stewards' Enquiry : Paul Hanagan one-day ban: careless riding (Nov 24)

FOCUS
A fair claimer, although it only concerned the front two.

7328 BREEDERS' CUP LIVE ONLY ON ATR MAIDEN STKS 6f (F)

3:00 (3:00) (Class 5) 3-4-Y-O **£2,217** (£654; £327) **Stalls** Low

Form RPR

0-00 **1** **Senate Majority**[22] 6880 3-9-3 55 ... DavidAllan 10 64
(T D Easterby) *prom: hdwy to ld wl over 2f out: rdn clr over 1f out: kpt on strly* **15/2**

3042 **2** *2 ¼* **Best Known Secret (IRE)**[11] 7131 4-8-5 48 ... RichardRowe(7) 12 52
(C C Bealby) *towards rr and sn pushed along: hdwy 1/2-way: chsd ldrs 2f out: sn rdn and styd on ins fnl f* **11/1**

The Form Book, Raceform Ltd, Compton, RG20 6NL

6003 **3** *2 ¼* **We'll Deal Again**[53] 6031 3-9-3 62 PaulHanagan 4 50
(M W Easterby) *led: rdn along and hdd wl over 2f out: drvn over 1f out and kpt on same pce* **9/4**[1]

0306 **4** *1 ¼* **Dudley**[10] 7153 3-9-3 49 (p) JamesDoyle 14 46
(J G Portman) *chsd ldrs on outer: wd st and sn rdn: drvn wl over 1f out and kpt on same pce* **16/1**

0364 **5** *1 ¼* **Brink**[19] 6966 3-8-12 55 BarryMcHugh 3 37
(T J Pitt) *towards rr: hdwy over 2f out: sn rdn and kpt on fnl f: nvr nr ldrs* **10/1**

0000 **6** *hd* **Northumberland**[21] 6896 4-9-0 42 KellyHarrison(3) 11 41
(M C Chapman) *chsd ldrs on outer: rdn along 1/2-way: wd st: sn drvn and wknd* **100/1**

3466 **7** *nk* **Residency (IRE)**[30] 6679 4-9-3 58 (p) TomEaves 2 40
(B Smart) *chsd ldrs: hdwy 1/2-way: rdn over 2f out: drvn appr fnl f and sn wknd* **4/1**[2]

2363 **8** *hd* **Sparking**[27] 6746 3-8-12 61 GrahamGibbons 8 34
(T D Barron) *prom: rdn along wl over 2f out: sn drvn and wknd wl over 1f out* **9/2**[3]

0030 **9** *1* **Blue Zephyr**[9] 7161 3-9-0 55 (bt) AndrewHeffernan(3) 5 36
(D C Griffiths) *chsd ldrs: rdn along wl over 2f out: sn wknd* **12/1**

0506 **10** *8* **Marsh's Gift**[11] 7132 3-9-3 40 (p) PatrickMathers 7 11
(C J Teague) *s.i.s: a bhd* **80/1**

00 **11** *1 ¾* **Kings Craic**[21] 6896 3-9-3 0 DuranFentiman 1 5
(D Carroll) *prom on inner: rdn along wl over 2f out and sn wknd* **50/1**

0-06 **12** *8* **Champagne All Day**[90] 4853 4-9-3 38 FrannyNorton 13 —
(S P Griffiths) *a towards rr* **100/1**

6 **13** *4* **Bluegrass Gal (USA)**[69] 5514 4-8-12 0 SaleemGolam 6 —
(Mrs L Williamson) *a in rr* **100/1**

1m 15.78s (-0.72) **Going Correction** -0.10s/f (Stan) **13 Ran SP% 117.9**
Speed ratings (Par 103): **100,97,94,92,90 90,90,89,88,77 75,64,59**
toteswingers:1&2 £13.80, 2&3 £5.70, 1&3 £5.70 CSF £85.53 TOTE £14.30: £4.80, £6.10, £1.10; EX 89.80 TRIFECTA Not won..
Owner The Senators **Bred** Wheelers Land Stud **Trained** Great Habton, N Yorks

FOCUS
A moderate maiden - not form to dwell on.

7329 ATTHERACES.COM/BREEDERSCUP CONDITIONS STKS 5f (F)
3:30 (3:30) (Class 2) 3-Y-0+ **£9,146** (£2,737; £1,368; £684; £340) **Stalls High**

Form RPR

0022 **1** **Noble Storm (USA)**[13] 7079 4-8-11 102 GrahamGibbons 1 109+
(E S McMahon) *cl up: led 1/2-way: qcknd over 1f out: comf* **8/15**[1]

0050 **2** *2 ½* **Love Delta (USA)**[5] 7254 3-8-11 92 JoeFanning 2 100
(M Johnston) *chsd ldrs: hdwy to chse wnr wl over 1f out: sn rdn and no imp ins fnl f* **14/1**

0100 **3** *½* **Rowe Park**[99] 4505 7-8-11 101 SteveDrowne 5 98
(Mrs L C Jewell) *chsd ldrs: rdn along 2f out: drvn and kpt on same pce ins fnl f* **6/1**[3]

0446 **4** *5* **Fitz Flyer (IRE)**[125] 3674 4-8-11 98 PaulHanagan 4 80
(B Smart) *dwlt and in rr: swtchd lft to outer after 1f and sn pushed along: rdn 2f out: n.d* **9/2**[2]

200 **5** *4* **Angus Newz**[36] 6509 7-8-6 83 (v) FrannyNorton 3 61
(M Quinn) *j. off wl and prom but sn lost pl and wl adrift fr 1/2-way* **33/1**

041 **6** *2 ¼* **Cloth Ears**[20] 6931 4-8-9 63 RobertWinston 6 56
(P S McEntee) *led: hdd 1/2-way and sn rdn along: drvn wl over 1f out: sn wknd* **100/1**

57.16 secs (-2.54) **Going Correction** -0.20s/f (Stan) course record **6 Ran SP% 108.3**
Speed ratings (Par 109): **112,108,107,99,92 89**
toteswingers:1&2 £2.50, 2&3 £4.10, 1&3 not won. CSF £8.80 TOTE £1.80: £1.10, £2.90; EX 8.20.
Owner R L Bedding **Bred** Brereton C Jones **Trained** Lichfield, Staffs

FOCUS
A good conditions event.

NOTEBOOK
Noble Storm(USA) ◆ won with plenty in hand, not needing to be seriously asked. He had 10lb in hand over the runner-up, so was entitled to win well, but this was still impressive, and he's smart type. (op 8-13 tchd 4-6 in places)
Love Delta(USA) had won three of his previous four starts on Fibresand and ran well returned to his favoured surface. Although no match at all for the winner, he had some decent types in behind. (op 9-1)
Rowe Park, reported to have bled from the nose when last seen at Goodwood in July, made a pleasing return, despite being unable to extended his unbeaten record over C&D (was 2-2 coming into the race). This might have helped his confidence. (op 11-2 tchd 5-1)
Fitz Flyer(IRE) was never really going and failed to run up to his official mark of 98 on his debut for a new yard after a break of 125 days. Official explanation: jockey said gelding lost its action shortly after start (op 11-2 tchd 6-1)
Angus Newz, with a visor back on, was badly detached by halfway and only ran on past a beaten, vastly inferior rival. (op 20-1)

7330 BREEDERS' CUP LIVE ONLY ON ATR ALL WEATHER "HANDS AND HEELS" APPRENTICE SERIES H'CAP 1m 4f (F)
4:00 (4:00) (Class 5) (0-70,62) 3-Y-0+ **£2,266** (£674; £337; £168) **Stalls Low**

Form RPR

006 **1** **Hunters Belt (IRE)**[9] 7176 6-9-6 62 IanBurns(5) 6 70+
(N Wilson) *awkward s: hld up and bhd: stdy hdwy 4f out: str run on outer to chal 2f out: sn led and rdn clr over 1f out: kpt on* **13/2**[3]

0050 **2** *1* **Davana**[20] 6933 4-8-8 48 oh3 (p) MatthewCosham(5) 5 54
(W J H Ratcliffe) *in tch: hdwy 4f out: chsd ldrs 3f out: effrt and nt clr run 2f out: sn swtchd rt and rdn to chse wnr over 1f out: kpt on wl ins fnl f* **12/1**

-601 **3** *7* **Mexican Jay (USA)**[31] 6662 4-9-6 60 ShaneBKelly(3) 8 55
(B Smart) *led: jnd 1/2-way: rdn along and hdd 3f out: drvn over 2f out: kpt on same pce* **6/5**[1]

0600 **4** *1* **Monfils Monfils (USA)**[13] 6890 8-8-8 50 (p) LucyBarry(5) 4 44
(P A Kirby) *trckd ldrs: hdwy to chse ldng pair 4f out: rdn along 3f out: drvn and ev ch 2f out: sn one pce* **16/1**

0000 **5** *1 ½* **Antoella (IRE)**[12] 6336 3-8-5 48 oh1 RichardRowe 2 39
(P A Kirby) *hld up in rr: hdwy 1/2-way: rdn along to chse ldrs 3f out: sn drvn and no imp* **20/1**

0110 **6** *hd* **Bollin Freddie**[9] 7184 6-9-11 62 MatthewLawson 7 53
(A J Lockwood) *prom: cl up 1/2-way: rdn to ld 3f out: drvn over 2f out: sn hdd & wknd* **12/1**

3000 **7** *hd* **The Mighty Mod (USA)**[31] 6648 3-8-5 48 oh3 AlexEdwards 3 39
(M C Chapman) *a towards rr* **25/1**

6100 **8** *30* **Ptolomeos**[17] 6999 7-9-1 57 NoelGarbutt(5) 9 —
(S Regan) *midfield: hdwy to chse ldrs 1/2-way: rdn along over 4f out and sn wknd* **33/1**

305/ **9** *21* **Skye But N Ben**[15] 4966 6-8-11 48 oh3 (b) SoniaEaton 1 —
(M C Chapman) *cl up on inner: rdn along 1/2-way: sn lost pl and bhd fnl 3f* **7/2**[2]

2m 40.09s (-0.91) **Going Correction** -0.10s/f (Stan)
WFA 3 from 4yo+ 6lb **9 Ran SP% 113.8**
Speed ratings (Par 103): **99,98,93,93,92 91,91,71,57**
toteswingers:1&2 £5.00, 2&3 £20.30, 1&3 £47.70 CSF £76.28 CT £154.34 TOTE £9.10: £2.50, £2.60, £1.10; EX 53.30 TRIFECTA Not won..
Owner Mrs N C Wilson **Bred** Charlie Purcell **Trained** Sandhutton, N Yorks

FOCUS
A moderate apprentice handicap.
T/Plt: £45.70 to a £1 stake. Pool of £47,169.65 - 751.95 winning tickets. T/Qpdt: £10.30 to a £1 stake. Pool of £3,716.19 - 266.80 winning tickets. JR

7268 WOLVERHAMPTON (A.W) (L-H)
Friday, November 5

OFFICIAL GOING: Standard
Wind: Light, across Weather: Wet

7331 ATTHERACES.COM/BREEDERSCUP APPRENTICE H'CAP (DIV I) 5f 216y(P)
3:55 (3:57) (Class 5) (0-70,69) 3-Y-0+ **£1,774** (£523; £262) **Stalls Low**

Form RPR

2013 **1** **Forever's Girl**[6] 7239 4-9-2 69 AdamCarter(5) 9 82
(G R Oldroyd) *chsd ldrs: led over 2f out: r.o wl fnl f and drew clr fnl 100yds* **4/1**[2]

0500 **2** *3* **Loyal Royal (IRE)**[48] 6207 7-8-9 57 (bt) RussKennemore 12 61
(J M Bradley) *racd keenly: hld up: hdwy on outer over 2f out: styd on ins fnl f: tk 2nd towards fin: no imp on wnr* **33/1**

235 **3** *½* **Tislaam (IRE)**[13] 7082 3-9-6 68 (p) JohnFahy 1 70
(A J McCabe) *trckd ldrs: rdn over 1f out: styd on same pce ins fnl f* **3/1**[1]

002 **4** *hd* **Rainy Night**[6] 7239 4-8-12 67 (p) JackDuern(7) 2 69
(R Hollinshead) *trckd ldrs: pushed along and outpcd over 2f out: kpt on ins fnl f: nt pce of ldrs* **9/2**[3]

4553 **5** *½* **Black Baccara**[14] 7064 3-8-4 55 oh2 (p) AdamBeschizza(3) 10 55
(P S McEntee) *led for 1f: remained w ldr: chalng over 2f out: rdn and ev ch over 1f out: outpcd by wnr ent fnl f: no ex fnl 75yds* **16/1**

0063 **6** *1 ¼* **Adam De Beaulieu (USA)**[13] 7082 3-8-12 63 (t) PatrickDonaghy(3) 3 59
(B M R Haslam) *hld up: rdn over 1f out: kpt on ins fnl f: nt pce to trble ldrs* **15/2**

4000 **7** *1* **Nacho Libre**[21] 6898 5-8-12 60 (b) JamesSullivan 11 53
(M W Easterby) *bhd: pushed along over 2f out: sme late prog: nvr able to chal* **18/1**

0000 **8** *2* **Canadian Danehill (IRE)**[8] 7193 8-9-3 65 (p) IanBrennan 8 51
(R M H Cowell) *in tch: rdn and wknd over 2f out* **25/1**

2350 **9** *2 ¼* **Simple Rhythm**[17] 7006 4-8-8 59 TobyAtkinson(3) 4 38
(J Ryan) *led after 1f: hdd over 2f out: sn u.p: wknd jst over 1f out* **6/1**

2130 **10** *3 ¾* **Chjimes (IRE)**[102] 4428 6-9-0 62 (p) WilliamCarson 6 29
(C R Dore) *in rr: pushed along over 1f out: nvr able to get on terms* **12/1**

1m 14.93s (-0.07) **Going Correction** 0.0s/f (Stan) **10 Ran SP% 114.9**
Speed ratings (Par 103): **100,96,95,95,94 92,91,88,85,80**
toteswingers: 1&2 £23.30, 1&3 £2.40, 2&3 £23.10. CSF £120.77 CT £457.33 TOTE £8.90: £3.30, £10.90, £2.60; EX 123.90.
Owner R C Bond **Bred** R C Bond **Trained** Brawby, N Yorks

FOCUS
The pace was fairly steady in this apprentice handicap. It was an advantage to race prominently and nothing came out of the chasing pack.
Chjimes(IRE) Official explanation: vet said gelding lost left-hind shoe

7332 ATTHERACES.COM/BREEDERSCUP APPRENTICE H'CAP (DIV II) 5f 216y(P)
4:30 (4:31) (Class 5) (0-70,69) 3-Y-0+ **£1,774** (£523; £262) **Stalls Low**

Form RPR

6655 **1** **Methaaly (IRE)**[6] 7239 7-8-12 67 (be) JosephYoung(7) 5 82
(M Mullineaux) *trckd ldrs: chalng 3 wd over 2f out: sn chsd ldr: led 1f out: pushed clr fnl 100yds* **9/1**

0035 **2** *3 ¾* **Prince James**[10] 7148 3-8-10 65 DavidSimmonson(7) 3 68
(M W Easterby) *chsd ldr: led 3f out: rdn and hdd 1f out: outpcd by wnr fnl 100yds: no ex and jst hld on for 2nd cl home* **4/1**[1]

00 **3** *nse* **Clerical (USA)**[44] 6295 4-8-9 57 (p) WilliamCarson 9 60
(R M H Cowell) *hld up: pushed along over 3f out: rdn and hdwy 2f out: chsng ldrs and styng on whn rdr had whip knocked out of hand wl ins fnl f: jst failed to get 2nd but nt pce of wnr* **16/1**

0130 **4** *¾* **Romantic Queen**[21] 6898 4-9-2 64 (t) MatthewDavies 4 64
(George Baker) *hld up: hdwy over 1f out: styd on ins fnl f: clsd qckly towards fin* **6/1**[2]

5540 **5** *½* **Kipchak (IRE)**[41] 6372 5-8-11 64 (p) SophieSilvester(5) 7 63
(C R Dore) *led: hdd 3f out: chsd ldrs after: one pce ins fnl f* **7/1**[3]

2330 **6** *¾* **Desert Icon (IRE)**[25] 6800 4-8-12 67 AliceHaynes(7) 11 63
(D M Simcock) *hld up: u.p over 1f out: styd on ins fnl f: unable to rch ldrs* **8/1**

0000 **7** *3 ¾* **Top Bid**[19] 6965 6-8-11 62 LanceBetts(3) 8 46
(T D Easterby) *midfield: rdn and wknd over 1f out* **25/1**

4265 **8** *½* **Interchoice Star**[87] 4936 5-8-12 60 (p) RussKennemore 10 43
(R E Peacock) *towards rr: u.p over 2f out: nvr able to chal* **20/1**

3506 **9** *2* **Charlie Delta**[8] 7195 7-8-5 60 (b) JakePayne(7) 1 36
(R A Harris) *chsd ldrs tl wknd 3f out* **33/1**

446- **10** *nk* **Under Review (IRE)**[20] 6939 4-8-10 58 (t) IanBrennan 6 33
(Michael J Browne, Ire) *bhd: edgd rt u.p over 1f out: nvr on terms* **4/1**[1]

0020 **11** *3 ½* **Kersivay**[13] 7093 4-9-0 69 (b[1]) KevinLundie(7) 2 33
(P D Evans) *chsd ldrs: pushed along over 2f out: wknd u.p over 1f out* **14/1**

1m 14.45s (-0.55) **Going Correction** 0.0s/f (Stan) **11 Ran SP% 112.0**
Speed ratings (Par 103): **103,98,97,96,96 95,90,89,86,86 81**
toteswingers: 1&2 £6.30, 1&3 £19.00, 2&3 £13.80. CSF £41.60 CT £577.32 TOTE £14.00: £4.70, £1.50, £1.80; EX 44.90.
Owner Noel Racing **Bred** Scuderia Golden Horse S R L **Trained** Alpraham, Cheshire

FOCUS
It was raining heavily before the second division of this apprentice handicap. The prominent runners dominated and the race panned out almost exactly as the first division.

Under Review(IRE) Official explanation: jockey said gelding missed the break

7333 WOLVERHAMPTON-RACECOURSE.CO.UK NURSERY 5f 20y(P)

5:05 (5:06) (Class 4) (0-85,77) 2-Y-O **£3,011** (£896; £447; £223) **Stalls** Low

Form RPR

600 **1** **Pitkin**[77] 5277 2-7-11 **56** oh4 ow2 .... JamesSullivan(3) 1 65+
(M W Easterby) *chsd ldrs: effrt to ld over 1f out: edgd rt ins fnl f whn r.o wl and in command* **13/2**

3431 **2** *1 ¼* **Forty Proof (IRE)**[19] 6954 2-8-13 **74** .... AdamBeschizza(5) 5 78
(W J Knight) *bhd: hdwy over 1f out: rdn to take 2nd ins fnl f: styd on but nt trble wnr* **5/2**[1]

052 **3** *2 ¼* **Johnny Hancocks (IRE)**[7] 7211 2-9-4 **74** .... RichardHughes 3 70
(P D Evans) *led: jnd 2f out: rdn and hdd over 1f out: no ex fnl 100yds* **4/1**[2]

0134 **4** *2* **Style And Panache (IRE)**[20] 6916 2-9-7 **77** .... PaulHanagan 4 66
(P D Evans) *bhd: outpcd over 2f out: nvr able to get on terms w ldrs* **9/2**[3]

053 **5** *1 ¼* **Pizzarra**[21] 6893 2-8-8 **64** ow1 .... PaulMulrennan 2 48
(J G Given) *chsd ldr: upsides 2f out tl rdn over 1f out: wknd ins fnl f* **5/2**[1]

62.53 secs (0.23) **Going Correction** 0.0s/f (Stan) **5 Ran SP% 108.7**
Speed ratings (Par 98): **98,96,92,89,87**
toteswinger: 1&2 £11.90. CSF £22.20 TOTE £8.50: £4.20, £2.90; EX 29.20.
Owner Steve Hull **Bred** New Mill Farm Stud **Trained** Sheriff Hutton, N Yorks

FOCUS
A decent nursery run at a strong pace.

NOTEBOOK
Pitkin finished tailed off in his last two maiden runs but was a big market mover in the morning before this nursery/AW debut and produced a strong finishing surge to win with a bit in hand from out of the weights after 11 weeks off. He is a big scopey type who has a number of speedy winners in his pedigree and could have quite a bit more to offer. Official explanation: trainer's rep said, regarding apparent improvement in form, that the gelding appears to have benefitted from a ten-week break and seems to be steadily improving with time. (op 11-2 tchd 7-1)
Forty Proof(IRE) found a surge of improvement switched to hold-up tactics when powering clear in a 5f Bath maiden last month. Things did not look very promising when he was pushed along almost immediately after exiting the stalls on nursery/AW debut but he showed a good attitude to keep battling and shaped as if a return to 6f could inspire another step forward. (op 3-1)
Johnny Hancocks(IRE) did well to hang in there after setting a decent pace on his 19th run this year. He has come up a bit short since a big rise in the weights after his 4l victory at Ffos Las in September but he is a tough front-running sprinter who may be able to record a third win when away from progressive types. (op 10-3)
Style And Panache(IRE) put in her first lacklustre run since a 66-1 win in a competitive Newbury nursery off 2lb lower in September. It is possible a busy 14-race campaign is catching up with her, while there is also a question about how well she handled the surface on her first try on Polytrack. (op 4-1 tchd 5-1)
Pizzarra was up there for a long way but couldn't sustain her effort on nursery debut. (op 3-1 tchd 10-3)

7334 BREEDERS' CUP LIVE ONLY ON ATR H'CAP 5f 20y(P)

5:35 (5:36) (Class 6) (0-60,60) 3-Y-O+ **£1,569** (£463; £231) **Stalls** Low

Form RPR

1030 **1** **Towy Boy (IRE)**[22] 6880 5-9-6 **60** ....(bt) RichardHughes 2 74
(I A Wood) *chsd ldrs: r.o ins fnl f to ld fnl 100yds: pushed out cl home* **7/2**[1]

1651 **2** *1* **Wooden King (IRE)**[19] 6952 5-9-5 **59** .... TomMcLaughlin 9 69
(M S Saunders) *led: rdn over 1f out: hdd fnl 100yds: nt qckn cl home* **10/1**

0060 **3** *3* **Maryolini**[8] 7193 5-9-2 **56** .... JimmyQuinn 12 56
(T Keddy) *bhd: outpcd 2f out: hdwy over 1f out: styd on u.p ins fnl f: nt rch front pair* **25/1**

2-3 **4** *1* **Ability N Delivery**[54] 5990 5-9-6 **60** ....(b) PaulHanagan 8 56
(Michael J Browne, Ire) *chsd ldrs: wnt 2nd and upsides 3f out: rdn over 1f out: stl ev ch ent fnl f: no ex fnl 100yds* **5/1**[2]

2663 **5** *¾* **First Swallow**[10] 7148 5-9-3 **60** ....(t) JohnFahy(3) 7 53
(D H Brown) *in tch: rdn 2f out: kpt on same pce fr over 1f out: no imp fnl f* **8/1**

5655 **6** *shd* **Welcome Approach**[91] 4799 7-9-3 **57** .... PaulMulrennan 11 50+
(J R Weymes) *hld up: styd on ins fnl f: unable to rch ldrs* **14/1**

001 **7** *¾* **Triskaidekaphobia**[130] 3516 7-9-5 **59** ....(t) PaulFitzsimons 5 49
(Miss J R Tooth) *prom: rdn and outpcd 2f out: one pce and no imp ins fnl f: eased whn wl hld fnl 75yds* **25/1**

0004 **8** *nse* **Greek Secret**[37] 6455 7-8-12 **57** ....(b) JamesO'Reilly(5) 13 47
(J O'Reilly) *racd in midfield on outer: rdn over 3f out: outpcd wl over 1f out* **25/1**

6240 **9** *hd* **Sharp Bullet (IRE)**[35] 6536 4-9-5 **59** .... CathyGannon 1 48
(Bruce Hellier) *towards rr: n.m.r after 1f: u.p over 1f out: kpt on ins fnl f: nt pce to chal* **9/1**

2515 **10** *1* **Best One**[5] 7250 6-9-4 **58** ....(b) LukeMorris 3 44
(R A Harris) *midfield: pushed along 2f out: rdn over 1f out: no imp* **11/2**[3]

0236 **11** *½* **Flaxen Lake**[35] 6536 3-9-5 **59** ....(tp) LiamKeniry 4 43
(J M Bradley) *midfield: pushed along 2f out: rdn and wknd over 1f out* **16/1**

1000 **12** *1 ½* **Radiator Rooney (IRE)**[143] 3057 7-8-10 **57** .... JulieBurke(7) 6 36
(Patrick Morris) *hld up: u.p over 1f out: nvr on terms w ldrs* **20/1**

61.89 secs (-0.41) **Going Correction** 0.0s/f (Stan) **12 Ran SP% 113.3**
Speed ratings (Par 101): **103,101,96,95,93 93,92,92,92,90 89,87**
toteswingers: 1&2 £10.10, 1&3 £34.30, 2&3 £57.90. CSF £34.80 CT £751.43 TOTE £3.80: £1.40, £3.20, £12.30; EX 39.20.
Owner C R Lambourne **Bred** R W K Lewis **Trained** Upper Lambourn, Berks

FOCUS
An ordinary handicap run at a fair pace. The first two were clear of the third.

7335 HOTEL & CONFERENCING AT WOLVERHAMPTON MAIDEN STKS 7f 32y(P)

6:10 (6:12) (Class 5) 2-Y-O **£2,115** (£624; £312) **Stalls** High

Form RPR

02 **1** **Home Office**[28] 6704 2-9-3 0 .... PaulHanagan 11 81+
(M Johnston) *trckd ldrs: led over 2f out: rdn over 1f out: r.o ins fnl f: a doing enough cl home* **5/2**[2]

43 **2** *½* **Motivado**[8] 7186 2-9-3 0 .... StevieDonohoe 8 80+
(Sir Mark Prescott) *midfield: hdwy 3f out: chsd wnr over 1f out: styd on towards fin: nt quite pce of wnr and nvr gng to get there* **7/1**

0 **3** *7* **Cool Luke**[52] 6047 2-9-3 0 .... TomEaves 12 61
(G A Swinbank) *racd keenly: chsd ldrs: effrt on outer 2f out: outpcd over 1f out: kpt on ins fnl f but no ch w front pair* **50/1**

00 **4** *1 ½* **Valley Tiger**[48] 6196 2-9-3 0 .... RichardHughes 9 57
(W R Muir) *racd keenly: hld up: hdwy over 3f out: chsd ldrs over 1f out: one pce fnl f* **22/1**

03 **5** *shd* **Spin Cast**[14] 7065 2-9-3 0 ....(v) AdamKirby 7 57
(W R Swinburn) *hld up: pushed along 2f out: hdwy u.p over 1f out: no imp ins fnl f* **7/1**

6 *2 ½* **Royal Bonsai** 2-9-0 0 .... IanBrennan(3) 4 51
(J J Quinn) *bhd: pushed along 3f out: styd on ins fnl f: nvr able to get competitive* **66/1**

7 *hd* **Al Biruni (USA)** 2-9-3 0 .... TedDurcan 2 50
(Saeed Bin Suroor) *midfield: pushed along over 3f out: sn wknd* **4/1**[3]

32 **8** *1* **Muffraaj**[24] 6827 2-9-3 0 .... NeilCallan 1 48
(D M Simcock) *led for 1f: remained prom: ev ch 2f out: rdn and wknd over 1f out: eased whn wl btn fnl 100yds* **9/4**[1]

66 **9** *¾* **Dancing Cavalier (IRE)**[6] 7242 2-9-3 0 .... LukeMorris 6 46
(R Hollinshead) *hld up: pushed along 2f out: nvr able to get on terms* **100/1**

00 **10** *1 ¾* **Alluring Star**[14] 7057 2-8-5 0 .... DavidSimmonson(7) 3 37
(M W Easterby) *hld up: pushed along 2f out: nvr on terms* **100/1**

11 *½* **Samanda (IRE)** 2-9-3 0 .... KirstyMilczarek 5 40
(L M Cumani) *trckd ldrs tl pushed along and wknd 2f out* **22/1**

5 **12** *4 ½* **Decadence**[41] 6353 2-8-12 0 .... DavidAllan 10 24
(E J Alston) *led after 1f: hdd over 2f out: sn rdn: wknd over 1f out* **33/1**

1m 29.71s (0.11) **Going Correction** 0.0s/f (Stan) **12 Ran SP% 121.4**
Speed ratings (Par 96): **99,98,90,88,88 85,85,84,83,81 80,75**
toteswingers: 1&2 £5.50, 1&3 £57.90, 2&3 £20.60. CSF £19.97 TOTE £6.10: £2.40, £2.00, £17.20; EX 30.10.
Owner Sheikh Hamdan Bin Mohammed Al Maktoum **Bred** C A Cyzer **Trained** Middleham Moor, N Yorks

FOCUS
A competitive maiden. The first two pulled well clear and could be useful.

NOTEBOOK
Home Office stepped up considerably on his debut effort when a 14-1 second in a Musselburgh maiden last month. This first foal of a 7f/1m Polytrack winner had decent form claims on AW debut and was always in control after seizing the initiative around the final bend. He is a scopey type who is open to more improvement and should stay a bit further than this. (op 10-3 tchd 4-1)
Motivado was reported to have reared over backwards when led in early, but he was checked over and ran a big race on his third run to finish a long way clear of the third. An imposing son of Motivator who holds a Derby entry, he should continue to progress, particularly as he moves up in trip. (op 8-1)
Cool Luke stayed on nicely behind the clear front pair and has stepped up on his never-dangerous debut effort over 6f on soft at Haydock. He is a gelded brother to a 7f 2-y-o winner and should continue to get better with practice. (op 40-1)
Valley Tiger finished ahead of just one rival in both of his previous starts but he showed some sign of ability this time.
Spin Cast was a staying on third with a visor applied over 6f here last time. The step up in trip looked likely to suit but he was never dangerous and has not built on his previous promise. (op 13-2)
Al Biruni(USA), a $280,000 yearling who is a brother to 14.7f/2m winner Kasban, looked inexperienced and was never competitive over a trip on the sharp side on debut. He could improve significantly over a stiffer test next time. (tchd 9-2)
Muffraaj had a good chance on his runner-up effort behind a potentially useful odds-on shot at Leicester on his second start. He was solid in the market and prominent early on but was easily brushed aside early in the straight. (op 5-2 tchd 2-1)
Alluring Star Official explanation: vet said filly was struck into

7336 ATTHERACES.COM/BREEDERSCUP H'CAP 7f 32y(P)

6:40 (6:40) (Class 6) (0-62,63) 3-Y-O+ **£1,706** (£503; £252) **Stalls** High

Form RPR

2326 **1** **Pipers Piping (IRE)**[8] 7191 4-9-2 **60** ....(v1) RichardHughes 6 69
(P Howling) *midfield: hdwy over 2f out: proging whn swtchd lft over 1f out: r.o to ld wl ins fnl f: in control cl home* **3/1**[2]

5434 **2** *¾* **Collect Art (IRE)**[15] 7037 3-9-3 **62** .... StevieDonohoe 7 69
(A B Haynes) *in tch: rdn to ld wl over 1f out: hdd wl ins fnl f: kpt on but hld cl home* **11/8**[1]

0005 **3** *2 ¾* **Athaakeel (IRE)**[42] 6330 4-9-3 **61** .... LukeMorris 11 61
(R A Harris) *missed break: in rr: hdwy 2f out: styd on ins fnl f: nt rch front pair* **22/1**

4/5- **4** *1* **Kenton Street**[59] 5843 5-9-3 **61** .... PaulHanagan 10 58
(Michael J Browne, Ire) *racd keenly: chsd ldr: led over 2f out: rdn and hdd wl over 1f out: one pce ins fnl f* **16/1**

3505 **5** *1 ¼* **Just Jimmy (IRE)**[20] 6934 5-9-2 **60** .... CathyGannon 4 53
(P D Evans) *hld up: rdn and hdwy to chse ldrs over 1f out: no imp ins fnl f* **5/1**[3]

0510 **6** *¾* **Know No Fear**[9] 7168 5-9-5 **63** 6ex ....(p) FergusSweeney 8 54
(A J Lidderdale) *hld up: effrt on outer over 1f out: sn in midfield: no imp on ldrs* **9/1**

00 **7** *2 ½* **Muqalad (IRE)**[14] 7056 3-9-3 **62** ....(t) TomEaves 3 47
(B Smart) *racd keenly: trckd ldrs: pushed along 2f out: sn outpcd: wl btn 1f out* **20/1**

6050 **8** *½* **Sairaam (IRE)**[31] 6656 4-9-4 **62** .... NeilCallan 12 45
(C Smith) *chsd ldrs: chalng 2f out: wknd ent fnl f* **25/1**

1400 **9** *2 ½* **Ivestar (IRE)**[85] 4986 5-9-1 **62** ....(tp) PatrickDonaghy(3) 2 39
(B M R Haslam) *s.i.s: bhd: nvr able to get on terms* **28/1**

0000 **10** *3 ¼* **Jonnie Skull (IRE)**[17] 7005 4-9-4 **62** .... AdamKirby 1 30
(M D Squance) *led: rdn and hdd over 2f out: sn wknd* **40/1**

05-0 **11** *5* **Miss Porky**[9] 7184 4-9-2 **60** .... FrankieMcDonald 9 14
(C N Kellett) *midfield: effrt and hdwy over 2f out: wknd wl over 1f out* **100/1**

1m 29.84s (0.24) **Going Correction** 0.0s/f (Stan)
WFA 3 from 4yo+ 1lb **11 Ran SP% 119.5**
Speed ratings (Par 101): **98,97,94,92,91 90,87,87,84,80 74**
toteswingers: 1&2 £1.40, 1&3 £13.90, 2&3 £12.60. CSF £7.00 CT £77.80 TOTE £6.30: £2.10, £1.10, £8.80; EX 10.10.
Owner C N Wright **Bred** Drumhass Stud **Trained** Newmarket, Suffolk

FOCUS
A modest handicap but the two market leaders dominated and the form looks solid.
Jonnie Skull(IRE) Official explanation: jockey said gelding had no more to give

7337 GREAT OFFERS AT WOLVERHAMPTON-RACECOURSE.CO.UK H'CAP 1m 4f 50y(P)

7:10 (7:10) (Class 4) (0-80,80) 3-Y-O+ **£3,594** (£1,069; £534; £266) **Stalls** Low

Form RPR

3613 **1** **Pelham Crescent (IRE)**[19] 6957 7-9-5 **75** .... DavidProbert 10 84+
(B Palling) *hld up towards rr: stdy hdwy fr over 3f out: led over 1f out: rdn out and kpt on wl* **16/1**

1-21 **2** *½* **Kiama Bay (IRE)**[14] 7054 4-8-9 **68** .... IanBrennan(3) 6 76
(J J Quinn) *midfield: hdwy on outer 3f out: rdn and lugged lft to chse wnr but nt qckn over 1f out: styd on towards fin* **6/1**

The Form Book, Raceform Ltd, Compton, RG20 6NL

5040 **3** 1 **Camps Bay (USA)**14 7061 6-9-9 **79** DavidAllan 3 85
(B Ellison) *hld up: hdwy 2f out: chsd ldrs fnl f: styd on: hld cl home* **9/1**

00/4 **4** 1/2 **Samsons Son**34 6565 6-9-10 **80** RichardHughes 8 85
(A King) *midfield: pushed along 3f out: hdwy over 2f out: rdn to chse ldrs over 1f out: kpt on same pce fnl 75yds* **11/2**3

4530 **5** 2 3/4 **Beetuna (IRE)**14 7062 5-9-7 **77** PaulHanagan 11 78
(D Bourton) *hld up: hdwy 3f out: chsd ldr over 2f out: led wl over 1f out: sn hdd: wknd wl ins fnl f* **5/1**2

5040 **6** 8 **Penang Cinta**34 6554 7-8-12 **68** CathyGannon 5 56
(P D Evans) *midfield: rdn and hdwy over 3f out: wknd over 1f out* **50/1**

6152 **7** 1 1/4 **Mons Calpe (IRE)**34 6578 4-9-3 **73** (b) NeilCallan 1 59
(P F I Cole) *led: clr of remainder after 4f tl 4f out: rdn and hdd wl over 1f out: sn wknd* **12/1**

5042 **8** 5 **Kames Park (IRE)**13 7089 8-9-3 **73** JimmyQuinn 9 51
(R C Guest) *missed break: in rr: pushed along and sme hdwy over 1f out: nvr able to chal* **14/1**

0215 **9** 2 **Royal Swain (IRE)**6 7226 4-9-8 **78** TomEaves 4 53
(G A Swinbank) *midfield: rdn 4f out: wknd 3f out* **8/1**

5302 **10** 4 1/2 **Becausewecan (USA)**11 7130 4-9-10 **80** (b1) JoeFanning 7 48
(M Johnston) *racd keenly: w ldr and clr of remainder after 4f tl 4f out: rdn 3f out: sn lost 2nd and wknd* **7/2**1

0440 **11** 18 **Jeer (IRE)**58 5868 6-9-4 **74** (b) GrahamGibbons 2 13
(M W Easterby) *chsd clr ldrs: clsd over 3f out: wknd over 2f out* **16/1**

2m 38.34s (-2.76) **Going Correction** 0.0s/f (Stan) **11** Ran SP% **117.8**
Speed ratings (Par 105): **109,108,108,107,105 100,99,96,95,92 80**
toteswingers: 1&2 £15.50, 1&3 £33.20, 2&3 £18.70. CSF £109.28 CT £933.09 TOTE £25.40: £6.90, £3.00, £3.90; EX 87.30.
Owner Wayne Devine **Bred** Cathal M Ryan **Trained** Tredodridge, Vale Of Glamorgan

FOCUS
A fair handicap in which breakaway leaders dropped away quickly after going off too fast.
Kiama Bay(IRE) Official explanation: jockey said gelding hung right-handed throughout
Becausewecan(USA) Official explanation: trainer's rep had no explanation for the poor form shown

7338 BREEDERS' CUP LIVE ONLY ON ATR MAIDEN STKS 1m 1f 103y(P)
7:40 (7:41) (Class 5) 3-Y-O+ **£2,115** (£624; £312) **Stalls** Low

Form RPR

24 **1** **Colour Scheme (IRE)**25 6815 3-9-3 0 (t) RichardHughes 8 88+
(B J Meehan) *a.p: n.m.r wl over 3f out: led wl over 1f out: sn qcknd clr: r.o wl and in command after* **11/10**1

0-2 **2** 7 **Fashionable Gal (IRE)**126 3620 3-8-12 0 StevieDonohoe 6 68
(Sir Mark Prescott) *racd keenly: trckd ldrs: n.m.r and hmpd wl over 3f out: nt qckn wl over 1f out: hung lft and wnt 2nd 1f out: kpt on but no ch w wnr fnl f* **15/8**2

53 **3** 2 **Marching Home**13 7086 3-9-3 0 (t) AdamKirby 5 69
(W R Swinburn) *led: rdn and hdd wl over 1f out: sn outpcd: lost 2nd 1f out: one pce and btn fnl f* **5/1**3

0 **4** 3/4 **Penbryn (USA)**9 7183 3-9-3 0 NeilCallan 7 68
(N P Littmoden) *s.i.s: hld up: hdwy 3f out: lugged lft over 1f out: kpt on but unable to chal* **40/1**

44 **5** 8 **Star Hill**56 5902 3-8-12 0 FergusSweeney 10 46
(A King) *in tch: clsd over 3f out: chsd ldrs 2f out: wknd over 1f out* **11/1**

6 1/2 **Amazingreyce**14 5-8-12 0 IanBrennan(3) 4 45
(O Brennan) *dwlt: hld up: pushed along over 2f out: no imp* **50/1**

06 **7** 1 1/4 **Just Zak**14 7069 5-9-3 0 PaulPickard(3) 2 47
(O Brennan) *hmpd s: hld up: struggling 2f out: nvr on terms* **50/1**

0 **8** nk **Mororatorio (IRE)**16 7019 3-9-0 0 Louis-PhilippeBeuzelin(3) 1 46
(Mrs D J Sanderson) *handy: lost pl after 3f: pushed along and outpcd 3f out: n.d after* **100/1**

0 **9** 2 **Titanic Mill**228 963 3-9-3 0 (b1) LukeMorris 3 42
(N J Vaughan) *in tch: wknd over 3f out* **80/1**

3 **10** 1/2 **Kanace**185 1796 3-9-3 47 PaulMulrennan 9 41
(Mrs A Duffield) *racd keenly: hld up: hdwy to chse ldrs 6f out: pushed along and wknd under 2f out* **33/1**

2m 2.83s (1.13) **Going Correction** 0.0s/f (Stan)
WFA 3 from 5yo 3lb **10** Ran SP% **118.9**
Speed ratings (Par 103): **94,87,86,85,78 77,76,76,74,74**
toteswingers: 1&2 £1.20, 1&3 £1.60, 2&3 £2.30. CSF £3.33 TOTE £2.50: £1.10, £1.10, £1.10; EX 4.70.
Owner Paul & Jenny Green **Bred** Paul And Mrs Jenny Green **Trained** Manton, Wilts

FOCUS
A decent maiden. The favourite romped clear from the other two market leaders and Richard Hughes cut the gap to two in the jockeys' championship.
Kanace Official explanation: jockey said gelding hung left-handed
T/Plt: £58.50 to a £1 stake. Pool of £64,657.22 - 806.32 winning tickets. T/Qpdt: £16.40 to a £1 stake. Pool of £10,325.16 - 465.70 winning tickets. DO

1714 CHURCHILL DOWNS (L-H)
Friday, November 5

OFFICIAL GOING: Dirt: fast; turf: firm

7339a BREEDERS' CUP MARATHON (GRADE 3) (3YO+) (DIRT) 1m 6f
8:10 (8:11) 3-Y-O+ **£166,666** (£55,555; £30,555; £18,518; £9,259)

RPR

1 **Eldaafer (USA)**55 5-9-0 0 (b) JRVelazquez 4 107
(Diane Alvarado, U.S.A) *settled midfield disputing 5th: tk clsr order over 3 1/2f out: wnt 2nd gng wl appr fnl 2f: led nring 1f out: drvn clr* **12/1**

2 2 3/4 **Gabriel's Hill (USA)**37 6-9-0 0 JRLeparoux 6 103
(Seth Benzel, U.S.A) *sn led: qcknd 2 l clr 2f out: sn u.str.p: hdd nring 1f out: flashed tail and no ex: fin 3rd: plcd 2nd* **25/1**

3 1 **A. U. Miner (USA)**34 5-9-0 0 CHBorel 12 102
(Clark Hanna, U.S.A) *settled towards rr: hdwy 4f out: 7th and pushed along 3f out: running on whn hmpd and lost grnd 2 1/2f out: 10th 2f out: styd on u.p on outside: nvr nrr: fin 4th: plcd 3rd* **6/1**2

4 nse **Giant Oak (USA)**34 4-9-0 0 (b) GKGomez 8 102
(Chris Block, U.S.A) *hld up towards rr: next to last 3f out: hdwy on outside to go 5th 1 1/2f out: nt qckn u.p: fin 5th: plcd 4th* **5/1**1

5 1/2 **Alcomo (BRZ)**111 7-9-0 0 RBejarano 10 101
(Eduardo Caramori, U.S.A) *racd in midfield: hdwy on outside to go 6th 3f out: 4th 2f out: sn rdn and nt qckn: wknd fnl 110yds: fin 6th: plcd 5th* **9/1**

6 9 3/4 **Awesome Gem (USA)**33 6605 7-9-0 0 (b) DFlores 7 87
(Craig Dollase, U.S.A) *bhd (last much of way): hdwy 4f out: 10th and running on 3f out: sn pushed along: rdn 2f out: no imp: fin 7th: plcd 6th* **7/1**3

7 3 3/4 **Precision Break (USA)**20 6926 5-9-0 0 JamieSpencer 11 82
(P F I Cole) *trckd ldr: 2nd and pushed along 4f out: sn rdn: dropped away u.p over 2f out: fin 8th: plcd 7th* **8/1**

8 1/2 **Atoned (USA)**55 5-9-0 0 RAlbarado 1 81
(Neil J Howard, U.S.A) *settled in 3rd on rail: grad wknd fr over 2f out: fin 9th: plcd 8th* **20/1**

9 12 **Romp (ARG)**15 6-9-0 0 MGarcia 5 64
(Kristin Mulhall, U.S.A) *broke wl and led briefly: sn restrained in midfield: hmpd and nrly b.d 2 1/2f out: nt rcvr: fin 10th: plcd 9th* **40/1**

10 1 3/4 **Prince Will I Am (USA)**27 3-8-10 0 JJCastellano 2 107
(Michelle Nihei, U.S.A) *settled in middle of the field: 7th 1/2-way: qcknd and swtchd outside over 2 1/2f out (hampering Romp: Brt Horizon and A. U. Miner): cl 3rd and running on 2f out: styd on u.p: nt qckn fnl f: fin 2nd: disqualified* **6/1**2

11 nk **Bright Horizon**40 6404 3-8-10 0 JMurtagh 9 66
(A P O'Brien, Ire) *hld up: pushed along fr over 4f out: hdwy u.p 3f out: disputing 8th whn involved in scrimaging 2 1/2f out: fdd fnl 2f* **6/1**2

12 7 1/4 **Million Seller (USA)**25 4-8-11 0 JRose 3 48
(H Graham Motion, U.S.A) *a towards rr: last and btn ins fnl 4f* **50/1**

2m 59.62s (179.62)
WFA 3 from 4yo+ 8lb **12** Ran SP% **113.8**
PARI-MUTUEL (all including $2 stakes): WIN 23.20; PLACE (1-2) 12.00, 25.40; SHOW (1-2-3) 7.00, 13.20, 5.20; SF 453.60.
Owner leah Stables & Mansour Albaroudy **Bred** Shadwell Farm LLC **Trained** North America

FOCUS
Graded status now for a race that's still to prove its worth on the Breeders' Cup card. The first two runnings of the Marathon, staged on a synthetic surface, went to European challengers, hardly a surprise considering US runners aren't bred/trained for stamina. However, the race being held on dirt this year saw the home team well and truly dominate. The pace didn't seem particularly strong - the track record was lowered but this is a seldom-used distance.

NOTEBOOK
Eldaafer(USA) was claimed by these connections for just $20,000 in January 2009. He made no impression when seventh of ten in this race last year, but has done well since, winning three times prior to this, including at Grade 3 level latest, and added another in rather straightforward fashion. His chance was helped by avoiding some real carnage in behind, although he may well have won whatever the case.
Gabriel's Hill(USA) made the most of an easy lead, although he may deserve extra credit considering he stuck to the inside rail, which probably wasn't the place to be.
A. U. Miner(USA) lost his momentum in the incident on the bend, so to run as well as he did suggests he may have been an unlucky loser.
Giant Oak(USA) was up in trip, but still ran his usual sort of race, staying on all too late.
Precision Break(USA), racing on first-time Lasix, was ideally placed by Jamie Spencer, but it was noticeable he was on a loose rein going down the back straight, clearly not travelling on the bridle, and found little for pressure. He's bred to handle dirt, and is a four-time Polytrack winner back in Britain, but this was not his running. (op 9-1)
Romp(ARG) lost his chance when badly hampered on the bend into the straight.
Prince Will I Am(USA) was rightly disqualified. Trapped away against the inside rail in about mid-division for most of the journey, Castellano gave up waiting for a gap to appear as the field rounded the final bend, switching his mount off the fence to get into the clear. In doing so, he badly hampered Romp, whose jockey Martin Garcia did well to stay aboard. Also squeezed for room was A. U. Miner, and that one's rider Calvin Borel could easily have hit the deck, too. Extraordinary scenes followed, with Borel completely losing his cool around the winner's circle, having to be restrained after reportedly getting in a scuffle with Castellano. (op 11-2)
Bright Horizon won the Irish Cesarewitch by a wide margin off a mark of 91 on his previous start. However, he had been beaten on all three previous attempts off the turf (on Polytrack), and was never going this time. He could been have expected to run on past beaten horses once out of the kickback, but he found absolutely nothing. He used Lasix.

7340a BREEDERS' CUP JUVENILE FILLIES TURF (GRADE 2) (2YO FILLIES) 1m (T)
8:50 (8:51) 2-Y-O **£333,333** (£111,111; £61,111; £37,037; £18,518)

RPR

1 **More Than Real (USA)**48 2-8-10 0 GKGomez 11 112
(Todd Pletcher, U.S.A) *cut ins to run 5th (3 off the rail): qcknd 2f out and jinked lft: led 1 1/2f out: rdn clr ins fnl f* **14/1**

2 2 **Winter Memories (USA)**33 2-8-10 0 JLezcano 7 108
(James J Toner, U.S.A) *settled in 8th: tk clsr order 3f out: 6th and n.m.r 2 1/2f out: swtchd outside and r.o: boxed in bhd ldr and ins wnr 2f out: plld bk and swtchd outside 1 1/2f out: r.o and wnt 2nd ins fnl f: no imp* **6/4**1

3 hd **Kathmanblu (USA)**22 2-8-10 0 JRLeparoux 4 107
(Kenneth McPeek, U.S.A) *hld up towards rr: hdwy on outside fr 3f out: shared 10th 2f out (abt 8 l off ld): r.o wl to go 3rd 150yds out: jst failed to snatch 2nd* **10/1**3

4 2 1/4 **Forest Legend (USA)**28 6732 2-8-10 0 RADominguez 5 102
(Victoria Oliver, U.S.A) *last tl 2f out: sn rdn and swtchd outside: styd on wl to take 4th 110yds out: nrest at fin* **50/1**

5 1 1/2 **Together (IRE)**34 6559 2-8-10 0 JMurtagh 13 98
(A P O'Brien, Ire) *racd in fnl 3rd: next to last over 2 1/2f out: 11th and sing to run on u.p ins fnl 1 1/2f: styd on wout threatening ldrs* **11/2**2

6 3 1/4 **Wyomia (USA)**27 2-8-10 0 RBejarano 8 91
(Daniel J Vella, Canada) *racd in midfield: 6th and n.m.r on rail ins fnl 2f: stl 6th 1f out: unable qck* **12/1**

7 nk **Quiet Oasis (IRE)**40 6401 2-8-10 0 FrankieDettori 3 90
(B J Meehan) *a.p: chsd ldng pair for much of the r: 3rd on rail and short of room 2f out: sn rdn: wknd u.p fnl f* **14/1**

8 hd **New Normal (USA)**48 2-8-10 0 JJCastellano 10 90
(Mark Frostad, Canada) *travelled wl in middle of the pack: disputing 6th 2f out: sn rdn and unable qck* **12/1**

9 2 **Dos Lunas (USA)**28 6732 2-8-10 0 (b1) JKCourt 1 85
(John Glenney, U.S.A) *broke wl and led (disp ld for part of bkstretch w Fancy Point): u.p and hdd nring fnl 1 1/2f: wknd fnl f* **50/1**

10 nse **Fancy Point (USA)**33 2-8-10 0 KDesormeaux 9 85
(William Phipps, U.S.A) *trckd ldr (and disp ld for part of bkstretch): 2nd and rdn over 2f out: snatched up sn after: eased fnl f* **25/1**

11 1 **Tale Untold (USA)**34 6559 2-8-10 0 RyanMoore 2 83
(R Hannon) *settled in midfield: no imp fr over 2f out: nvr threatened* **14/1**

12 2 **Arch Support (USA)**33 2-8-10 0 EPrado 6 78
(Gary Contessa, U.S.A) *nvr beyond mid-div* **40/1**

13 2 1/2 **Allure D'Amour (USA)**19 2-8-10 0 JRVelazquez 14 72
(Todd Pletcher, U.S.A) *racd in fnl 3rd: rapid hdwy on outside 3 1/2f out: 7th 3f out: no imp fnl 2f* **22/1**

14 *33* **Flood Plain**[13] 7098 2-8-10 0............ WilliamBuick 12 —
(J H M Gosden) *slowly away: settled in rr: last 2f out: tailed-off and heavily eased fnl f* **16/1**

1m 36.61s (1.78) **14** Ran SP% **120.3**
PARI-MUTUEL (all including $2 stakes): WIN 29.20; PLACE (1-2) 9.20, 3.60; SHOW (1-2-3) 5.80, 2.60, 3.60; SF 76.40.
Owner Bobby Flay **Bred** Santucket Stables **Trained** USA

FOCUS
Like the Marathon earlier on the card, this race had Graded status for the first time. Somewhat surprisingly the Europeans have now come up short in all three runnings, but it's hard to get too excited by this form.

NOTEBOOK
More Than Real(USA) landed a Saratoga maiden on debut for a different stable, before finishing behind New Normal in a Woodbine Grade 3, but she's clearly made the greater progress of the two fillies. She was the winner on merit, for all that the runner-up didn't get the best of trips, and is clearly pretty smart.
Winter Memories(USA) came into the race 2-2, and had really impressed in a Belmont Grade 3 on yielding turf latest, but she wasn't quite good enough this time. She was short of room when held in by the winner at the top of the straight, but didn't run on well enough when in the clear to suggest she was unlucky. (op 15-8)
Kathmanblu(USA) raced further back than the first two finishers and had little room to manoeuvre when seemingly full of running on entering the straight. She finished well when in the open and might be better than she showed. (op 12-1)
Forest Legend(USA) ran an extraordinary race, staying on into fourth having been detached in last for much of the way. Surely she'll benefit from even just a slightly more forward ride. (op 40-1)
Together(IRE), using Lasix, was gradually dropped in from her wide draw, but didn't travel with much enthusiasm. She was short of room when still well behind rounding the final bend, but simply didn't have the legs to work her way into a challenging position. The Fillies' Mile runner-up has had a long season, this being her eighth start.
Quiet Oasis(IRE), racing on quick ground for the first time, and using Lasix, was beaten when short of room against the rail early in the straight, although she might have finished slightly closer with a clear run. It remains to be seen whether she's up to this sort of level. (op 12-1)
Tale Untold(USA) was a doubtful stayer and never got involved.
Flood Plain, who had finished runner-up in a Newbury Listed race last time, was very disappointing. According to William Buick, the filly slipped twice on the watered ground and she felt like she pulled up sore. (op 14-1)

7341a SENTIENT JET BREEDERS' CUP FILLY & MARE SPRINT (GRADE 1) (3YO+ FILLIES & MARES) (DIRT) 7f
9:30 (9:38) 3-Y-O+ **£333,333** (£111,111; £61,111; £37,037; £18,518)

RPR

1 **Dubai Majesty (USA)**[27] 5-8-12 0............ HJTheriotII 12 119
(W Bret Calhoun, U.S.A) *prom early: disputing 5th down far side: qcknd 3f out and disp ld 2f out (on outside of Gabby's Golden Gal and Champagne d'Oro): led ins fnl 2f: r.o wl: clr ins fnl f: comf* **9/1**

2 *2 ¼* **Switch (USA)**[33] 6603 3-8-10 0............ JRosario 9 112
(John W Sadler, U.S.A) *chsd ldrs in 4th: outpcd: over 2 1/2f out: 6th 2f out: styd on wl fnl f: tk 2nd fnl 110yds: no ch w wnr* **10/1**

3 *3* **Evening Jewel (USA)**[20] 6948 3-8-10 0............ VEspinoza 5 104
(James Cassidy, U.S.A) *hld up: tk clsr order 3 1/2f out: 6th and running on 2 1/2f out: u.p and disputing 4th 2f out: unable qck fnl f but kpt on gamely* **11/1**

4 *1 ½* **Champagne D'Oro (USA)**[27] 3-8-10 0............ MMena 13 100
(Eric J Guillot, U.S.A) *a.p: 3rd 4f out: disputing ld in between Gabby's Golden Gal and Dubai Majesty over 2f out: 2nd and rdn appr 1 1/2f out: fdd and lost 2nd fnl 150yds* **11/2[2]**

5 *1 ¾* **Sweet August Moon (USA)**[27] 5-8-12 0............ MESmith 8 96
(Brian Koriner, U.S.A) *sn last and detached: last and hdwy 3f out: 2nd last 2f out: r.o up outside: 8th 1 1/2f out: styd on u.p: n.d* **28/1**

6 *1* **Sara Louise (USA)**[41] 4-8-12 0............ FrankieDettori 2 94
(Saeed Bin Suroor) *missed break but sn settled next to last: pushed along 4f out: hdwy on rail to go 9th 3f out: swtchd outside and r.o u.p over 1 1/2f out: wnt 5th ins fnl f: one pce* **5/1[1]**

7 *1 ¾* **Informed Decision (USA)**[27] 5-8-12 0............(b) JRLeparoux 4 89
(Jonathan Sheppard, U.S.A) *hld up: rdn 3f out: last st: passed a few btn horses u.str.p* **6/1[3]**

8 *1 ½* **Rinterval (IRE)**[26] 5-8-12 0............ RBejarano 10 85
(Eric R Reed, U.S.A) *nvr beyond mid-div: no imp u.str.p fnl 2f* **33/1**

9 *½* **Jessica Is Back (USA)**[69] 6-8-12 0............ JJCastellano 11 83
(Martin D Wolfson, U.S.A) *settled in midfield: hdwy on outside 3 1/2f out: 4th and running on 2 1/2f out: fdd u.p ins fnl 2f* **14/1**

10 *nk* **Gabby's Golden Gal (USA)**[278] 4-8-12 0............ MGarcia 7 83
(Bob Baffert, U.S.A) *led: disp ld on ins of Champagne d'Oro and Dubai Majesty appr 2f out: sn hdd: wknd qckly u.p fnl 1 1/2f* **7/1**

11 *5 ¾* **Secret Gypsy (USA)**[55] 5-8-12 0............ RAlbarado 3 67
(Ronny Werner, U.S.A) *prom on rail: 2nd 3f out: sltly hmpd fnl turn: nowhere to go sn after (ins fnl 2f): unable qck u.p whn in clr fnl 300yds* **11/1**

12 *5 ¼* **Moontune Missy (USA)**[41] 4-8-12 0............ AGarcia 6 53
(Eoin Harty, U.S.A) *chsd ldrs tl rdn and grad wknd fnl 3 1/2f* **33/1**

13 *12 ½* **My Jen (USA)**[41] 3-8-10 0............ JRVelazquez 1 18
(Eddie Kenneally, U.S.A) *nvr really got beyond mid-div: rdn and wknd fnl 2 1/2f* **16/1**

1m 22.31s (82.31)
WFA 3 from 4yo+ 1lb **13** Ran SP% **116.5**
PARI-MUTUEL (all including $2 stakes): WIN 19.20; PLACE (1-2) 9.20, 8.80; SHOW (1-2-3) 6.00, 5.80, 5.60; SF 189.60.
Owner Martin Racing Stable LLC & Dan Morgan **Bred** Harold J Plumley **Trained** North America

FOCUS
This race was back on dirt for the first since the inaugural running in 2007. A competitive renewal, but the form is nothing special.

NOTEBOOK
Dubai Majesty(USA) gained her latest win in a Grade 2 on Polytrack, and has also won on turf, but she's every bit as good, if not better on dirt, as she proved in no uncertain terms. Supplemented at a cost of $90,000, she gained a straightforward victory, always going nicely in a stalking position before running on well once in the straight. (op 7-1)
Switch(USA) had looked something of a synthetic track specialist coming into this, and at a good one at that, having defeated Blind Luck earlier in the year, and more recently given Zenyatta a fright in the Lady's Secret, both races on Hollywood Park's Cushion Track. However, she clearly handled the dirt well, proving no match for the winner after that one got first run, but keeping on strongly.
Evening Jewel(USA) does most of her racing at around 1m-1m1f these days, and she lacked the early speed of the first two finishers on this drop in trip, but she finished well for a respectable third. (op 10-1)
Champagne D'Oro(USA), a Grade 1 winner over this trip at Saratoga on her previous start, was always handy and seemed to have her chance, although she probably wasn't on the best part of the track when drifting over to the inside rail in the straight.
Sara Louise(USA) had only been seen twice since finishing fourth in this last year, and just once this term. The surface was no problem (Graded winner on dirt), but her lack of race-sharpness told as she lost her chance with a slow start. In the circumstances she ran as well as could have been expected. (op 6-1)
Informed Decision(USA), last year's winner, was unsuited by the race being switched to dirt. It's true she has a C&D Grade 1 win to her name, but that wasn't a strong race and her very best form is on a synthetic surface. She was beaten before the straight and only ran on past beaten rivals. (op 11-2)

7342a GREY GOOSE BREEDERS' CUP JUVENILE FILLIES (GRADE 1) (2YO FILLIES) (DIRT) 1m 110y(D)
10:10 (12:00) 2-Y-O **£666,666** (£222,222; £122,222; £74,074; £37,037)

RPR

1 **Awesome Feather (USA)**[20] 2-8-10 0............ JASanchez 3 117
(Stanley I Gold, U.S.A) *sn settled in 3rd: wnt 2nd appr 3f out: pushed along and disp ld appr 2f out: hd-to-hd battle w runner-up tl wnt on narrowly ins fnl f: drvn clr fnl 100yds* **5/1[3]**

2 *2 ¼* **R Heat Lightning (USA)**[27] 6755 2-8-10 0............ JRVelazquez 2 112
(Todd Pletcher, U.S.A) *a up w cracking pce: led over 5f out: jnd by wnr appr fnl 2f: hd to hd battle w wnr tl hdd narrowly ins fnl f: no ex fnl 110yds* **9/2[2]**

3 *2 ¼* **Delightful Mary (USA)**[27] 2-8-10 0............ SXBridgmohan 8 107
(Mark Casse, Canada) *racd in 6th: rdn and hdwy over 3 1/2f out: wnt 3rd 2/12f out: nt qckn u.p fr 2f out: styd on again fnl 110yds* **12/1**

4 *1 ¼* **Believe In A. P. (USA)**[27] 2-8-10 0............ GKGomez 9 104+
(Richard Dutrow Jr, U.S.A) *bided time towards rr: 8th and sing to make hdwy on rail ins fnl 2 1/2f: 6th w under 2f to run: styd on u.p fnl f: n.d* **25/1**

5 *1 ¾* **Joyful Victory (CAN)**[27] 6755 2-8-10 0............ RADominguez 5 101
(Anthony Dutrow, U.S.A) *racd in 4th or 5th for much of the r: ct flat-footed over 3f out: hdwy to be a cl 5th and ev ch ins fnl 2f: unable qck* **20/1**

6 *3 ¼* **Theyskens' Theory (USA)**[41] 6348 2-8-10 0............ FrankieDettori 1 93
(B J Meehan) *a.p: led after 1 1/2f: hdd over 5f out and racd in 2nd on ins of ldr: rdn 3f out and lost 2nd: grad fdd u.p fnl 2f* **9/2[2]**

7 *2 ¼* **Tell A Kelly (USA)**[32] 6641 2-8-10 0............ CHBorel 11 88
(John W Sadler, U.S.A) *outpcd and bhd: sme hdwy on outside over 2f out: no imp fr 1 1/2f out: nvr in contention* **13/2**

8 *nk* **Harlan's Ruby (USA)**[28] 6732 2-8-10 0............ JRLeparoux 4 88
(Kenneth McPeek, U.S.A) *chsd ldrs (disp 4th for much of the way): rdn and dropped away fr over 2 1/2f out* **16/1**

9 *2* **Izshelegal (USA)**[32] 6641 2-8-10 0............(b[1]) MESmith 6 83
(Terry Knight, U.S.A) *chsd ldng half dozen tl rdn and btn over 2f out* **33/1**

10 *3* **Jordy Y (USA)**[28] 6732 2-8-10 0............ JRosario 12 77
(Wayne Catalano, U.S.A) *last: wl detached over 3f out: last and running on 2f out: wknd fnl f* **40/1**

11 *9 ¼* **Soundwave (USA)**[40] 2-8-10 0............ RAlbarado 10 56
(Ronny Werner, U.S.A) *midfield tl lost pl over 3f out: nvr a factor* **25/1**

12 *16 ½* **A Z Warrior (USA)**[27] 6755 2-8-10 0............ MGarcia 7 20
(Bob Baffert, U.S.A) *chsd ldrs in share of 6th tl rdn and wknd fnl 3f* **4/1[1]**

1m 45.17s (0.80) **12** Ran SP% **117.8**
PARI-MUTUEL (all including $2 stakes): WIN 10.40; PLACE (1-2) 5.40, 6.20; SHOW (1-2-3) 4.00, 4.20, 7.60; SF 57.80.
Owner Jacks Or Better Farm Inc **Bred** Jacks Or Better Farm Inc **Trained** USA

FOCUS
The pace was not overly strong and it paid to race prominently. The form is rated around the race averages.

NOTEBOOK
Awesome Feather(USA) was taking a marked step up in class having won her first five starts at Calder, including the three top races restricted to Florida bred fillies, but she proved well up to the task. She showed a mix of speed and stamina, sitting close to the ordinary pace before producing a sustained effort in that straight that saw her get the better of a brief dual with R Heat Lightning. This high-class juvenile is now a perfect 6-6, and apparently heads to the Fasig-Tipton Kentucky sales on November 7. (op 11-2)
R Heat Lightning(USA) had a bad trip when runner-up to A Z Warrior (something must have been amiss with that one) in the Frizette at Belmont last time, but she got a forward ride on this occasion and ran a fine race. She stuck more towards the inside rail in the straight than the winner, which probably didn't help, but she was basically second best.
Delightful Mary(USA), whose three previous runs were on synthetics at Woodbine, handled the dirt just fine, as her breeding suggested, but was no match for the front pair, who raced closer to the pace.
Believe In A. P.(USA) was up significantly in class after taking four goes to get off the mark, but she ran well, especially as she raced some way off the ordinary gallop.
Theyskens' Theory(USA), winner of the Prestige Stakes and third in the Fillies' Mile on turf in Britain, was well worth a shot on dirt being a half-sister to 2005 Juvenile winner Stevie Wonderboy, but she wasn't up to the task. Sticking to the apparently unfavoured inside rail probably didn't help.

7343a EMIRATES AIRLINE BREEDERS' CUP FILLY & MARE TURF (GRADE 1) (3YO+ FILLIES & MARES) 1m 3f (T)
10:50 (12:00) 3-Y-O+ **£666,666** (£222,222; £122,222; £74,074; £37,037)

RPR

1 **Shared Account (USA)**[34] 6583 4-8-12 0............ EPrado 5 110
(H Graham Motion, U.S.A) *trckd ldng trio on rail: wnt 3rd 6f out: disputing 3rd 2f out but short of room on rail: gap opened 1 1/2f out: scythed through it (gaining first run on runner-up) and disp ld 1f out bef qckly gained narrow advantage: r.o bravely* **33/1**

2 *nk* **Midday**[54] 6013 4-8-12 0............ TomQueally 7 110+
(H R A Cecil) *racd keenly early: settled on rail disputing 5th: pushed along 3f out: disputing 3rd and n.m.r 2f out: endured a bump or two: wnt through narrow gap to dispute ld 1f out: sn a hd down and r.o wl but unable qck past wnr* **1/1[1]**

3 *nk* **Keertana (USA)**[34] 6583 4-8-12 0............ JLezcano 4 109
(Thomas F Proctor, U.S.A) *settled towards rr: 9th but clsng 2 1/2f out: styd on u.p down outside fnl 2f: tk 3rd fnl 110yds* **40/1**

4 *1* **Red Desire (JPN)**[34] 6583 4-8-12 0............ KDesormeaux 10 107
(Mikio Matsunaga, Japan) *trckd ldng gp: 6th and running on 2 1/2f out: disputing 3rd ins fnl 2f: unable qck fnl f* **4/1[2]**

5 *nk* **Hot Cha Cha (USA)**[26] 4-8-12 0............ JamesGraham 8 107
(Phillip A Sims, U.S.A) *last: swtchd outside w less than 2f to go: r.o wl u.p fnl f: nvr nrr* **33/1**

6 *nk* **Forever Together (USA)**[34] 6583 6-8-12 0............ AnnaNapravnik 11 106
(Jonathan Sheppard, U.S.A) *towards rr (next to last for a long way): c wdst of all into st: last ins fnl 2f: styd on wout being able to change gear fnl f* **8/1**

6 *dht* **Eclair De Lune (GER)**[76] 5320 4-8-12 0............ JAlvarado 2 106
(Ronald McAnally, U.S.A) *trckd ldr: disp ld over 2f out: led 1 1/2f out: hdd appr fnl f: unable qck: fdd cl home* **7/1[3]**

8 nk **Hibaayeb**[33] 6604 3-8-9 0 FrankieDettori 9 108
(Saeed Bin Suroor) *racd in mdfield: cl 7th and ev ch over 2f out: forced wd fnl turn: rdn and n.m.r 1 1/2f out: kpt on wout qckning fnl f* **25/1**

9 1 3/4 **Miss Keller (IRE)**[20] 6950 4-8-12 0 JJCastellano 3 102
(Roger L Attfield, Canada) *hld up: hdwy on rail 2 1/2f out: squeezed through to dispute 3rd 1 1/2f out: n.m.r over 1f out: no ex fnl 150yds* **20/1**

10 4 1/2 **Harmonious (USA)**[20] 6948 3-8-9 0 JRosario 6 96
(John Shirreffs, U.S.A) *chsd ldrs: cl 3rd 2 1/2f out: pushed along whn squeezed out ins fnl 2f: nvr rcvrd* **16/1**

11 1 3/4 **Plumania**[33] 6612 4-8-12 0 OlivierPeslier 1 91
(A Fabre, France) *sn led: disp ld over 2f out: hdd 1 1/2f out: sn wknd* **20/1**

2m 17.74s (137.74)
WFA 3 from 4yo+ 5lb 11 Ran SP% **121.2**
PARI-MUTUEL (all including $2 stakes): WIN 94.00; PLACE (1-2) 21.80, 3.20; SHOW (1-2-3) 15.20, 2.20, 10.20; SF 295.20.
Owner Sagamore Farm **Bred** William A Carl **Trained** USA

FOCUS
This form is below the standard expected for a Grade 1, especially at such a big meeting. The two clear form picks, Midday and Red Desire, both failed to run to their best, and a steady pace resulted in plenty of these finding trouble, as well as the first eight being covered by less than 3l.

NOTEBOOK
Shared Account(USA) found the gap early in the straight that Midday was looking for, and the neck or so advantage she gained from that rival in doing so was maintained to the line in gusty fashion. She wasn't at her best on yielding turf behind Keertana and Red Desire in the Flower Bowl last time, but had previously finished a close second to Breeders' Cup Mile hope Provisio, and this was clearly a return to her best form.
Midday, the defending champion, ran as though a long, tough season had taken its toll. Given a similar ride to last year, being waited with towards the inside, she had little room once in the straight, and soon received a hefty enough bump. However, a gap quickly appeared had she been good enough, but despite trying, her usually potent change of pace was missing. It's to her credit that she stuck for second, in the end failing only narrowly. The runner-up was impressive when winning the Nassau and the Yorkshire Oaks earlier in the season, but when taking the latest of her three Group 1 wins this year, the Vermeille at Longchamp, she was much more workmanlike, indeed she was 10lb below her best RPR on that occasion. Despite having had the best part of two months to recover, she couldn't rediscover top form. (op 11-10 tchd 6-5)
Keertana(USA), only fourth in the Flower Bowl last time, ran a huge race considering she raced well off the gallop and then came about six-wide into the straight.
Red Desire(JPN)'s rider appeared over occupied by what Midday was up to, racing directly to that one's outside for the majority of the contest. As a consequence, the Japanese-trained filly had a wide trip, noticeably so into the straight, and was unable to pick up sufficiently. Even so, this was still a disappointing performance from a runner good enough to finish third in last year's Japan Cup. (op 7-2)
Hot Cha Cha(USA) was given too much to do and, having lost momentum when blocked as she looked for a run at the top of the straight, she took too long to get going.
Forever Together(USA), winner of this in 2008 and third last year, was yet again given an exaggerated hold-up ride and such one-dimensional tactics gave her no chance. She ended up about seven-wide around the turn into the straight and did well to get so close.
Hibaayeb, a Grade 1 winner at Hollywood Park on her previous start, didn't pick up well enough to take an opening towards the outside early in the straight and was forced back inside, where she again failed to respond to pressure.
Miss Keller(IRE) was short of room towards the inside when keeping on in the closing stages and is better than she showed.
Harmonious(USA) was possibly beginning to struggle when squeezed up early in the straight.
Plumania, runner-up to Midday in the Vermeille before a heavy defeat in the Arc, was allowed a soft enough lead but still weakened tamely. She didn't use Lasix and failed to prove herself on the quick ground, although she may just have had enough for the time being.

7344a BREEDERS' CUP LADIES' CLASSIC (GRADE 1) (3YO+ FILLIES & MARES) (DIRT) 1m 1f (D)
11:30 (11:30) 3-Y-0+ **£666,666** (£222,222; £122,222; £74,074; £37,037)

RPR

1 **Unrivaled Belle (USA)**[34] 6584 4-8-12 0 KDesormeaux 8 120
(William Mott, U.S.A) *settled in 5th: hdwy on outside over 3 1/2f out: led 3f out: r.o strly fnl 1 1/2f: responded wl to press* **8/1**

2 1 3/4 **Blind Luck (USA)**[34] 6614 3-8-10 0 (b) JRosario 10 118+
(Jerry Hollendorfer, U.S.A) *bhd (adrift of main pack): hdwy but stl 10th 2 1/2f out: 7th and running on 2f out: styd on u.p to go 2nd over 110yds out: no imp on wnr fnl 75yds* **15/8**[1]

3 1 **Havre De Grace (USA)**[34] 6614 3-8-10 0 JRose 11 116
(Anthony Dutrow, U.S.A) *racd in midfield: hdwy 3f out: 3rd and running on 2f out: wnt 2nd over 1f out: unable qck and lost 2nd appr fnl 110yds but kpt on* **7/1**[3]

4 7 1/2 **It's Tea Time (USA)**[26] 3-8-10 0 JRLeparoux 2 102
(George R Arnold II, U.S.A) *disp 6th for much of r: 6th and rdn 2 1/2f out: r.o to go 4th ins fnl 2f: kpt on at one pce fnl f* **25/1**

5 2 1/4 **Acoma (USA)**[26] 5-8-12 0 RAlbarado 9 97
(David M Carroll, U.S.A) *a.p: 2nd appr 2f out: sn rdn and wknd* **14/1**

6 nse **Acting Happy (USA)**[76] 3-8-10 0 (b[1]) JLezcano 5 97
(Richard Dutrow Jr, U.S.A) *chsd ldr racing keenly: rdn and lost pl fr 2 1/2f out* **16/1**

7 1 1/4 **Persistently (USA)**[34] 6584 4-8-12 0 (b) AGarcia 6 94
(Claude McGaughey III, U.S.A) *a bhd: rdn and btn over 2f out* **16/1**

8 3/4 **Milwaukee Appeal (CAN)**[26] 4-8-12 0 (b) RBejarano 4 93
(Scott H Fairlie, U.S.A) *chsd ldrs: midfield and rdn 2 1/2f out: no imp u.p st* **33/1**

9 3 1/4 **Seeking The Title (USA)**[34] 3-8-10 0 (b) CHBorel 7 88
(Dallas Stewart, U.S.A) *nvr a factor* **50/1**

10 8 1/4 **Malibu Prayer (USA)**[68] 4-8-12 0 GKGomez 3 71
(Todd Pletcher, U.S.A) *sn led on rail: hdd 3f out: grad wknd* **11/1**

P **Life At Ten (USA)**[34] 6584 5-8-12 0 JRVelazquez 1 —
(Todd Pletcher, U.S.A) *sn t.o: p.u 1/2-way* **7/2**[2]

1m 50.04s (110.04)
WFA 3 from 4yo+ 3lb 11 Ran SP% **116.1**
PARI-MUTUEL (all including $2 stakes): WIN 17.00; PLACE (1-2) 5.80, 3.20; SHOW (1-2-3) 4.20, 2.40, 4.00; SF 54.80.
Owner Peter Vegso & Gary Seidler **Bred** G Seidler & P Vegso **Trained** USA

FOCUS
Pace, or more specifically a lack of it, was the key to this race, with favourite Blind Luck simply not getting strong enough fractions to chase. That had much to do with Life At Ten, who was expected to go forward, running an absolute shocker.

NOTEBOOK
Unrivaled Belle(USA), much better placed than Blind Luck, was always holding that rival in the straight, crossing the line with plenty left. After beating Rachel Alexandra here in April, Unrivaled Belle had twice finished behind Life At Ten, so that rival's poor showing obviously made her task easier. (op 10-1)
Blind Luck(USA), North America's leading 3-y-o filly, did not have the race run to suit and in the circumstances she did really well to stay on for second. A deep closer very much in the mould of Zenyatta, she made fairly effortless looking headway before the straight, and for a split second it seemed as though her customary late drive would carry her to yet another narrow victory, but it soon became apparent that Unrivaled Belle wasn't stopping.
Havre De Grace(USA) had narrowly beaten Blind Luck last time, but she was getting 10lb on that occasion and unsurprisingly failed to confirm form. (op 13-2)
It's Tea Time(USA) has a Grade 3 win to her name on dirt, but that was a race switched from the turf. She's yet to truly convince on this surface and was beaten a long way.
Acoma(USA) has won on dirt but was nowhere near the form she showed when winning a Polytrack Grade 1 last time.
Life At Ten(USA) hardly raised a gallop before being pulled up. Her trainer Todd Pletcher said afterwards he had suspicions the filly was not right when being saddled, saying she was "abnormally quiet, almost sedated-like." She was apparently examined prior to entering the starting gates by a team of three vets, who "did not observe any physical problems." She was then examined after the race and again no problem was found. The next day, however, Pletcher revealed Life At Ten had simply 'tied-up', suffering cramps, but has responded well to treatment.

7079 DONCASTER (L-H)
Saturday, November 6

OFFICIAL GOING: Good to soft (soft in places; 6.6)
Wind: Light 1/2 against Weather: Fine and sunny

7345 TOTESPORT 0800 221 221 COCK O'THE NORTH E B F MAIDEN STKS (DIV I) 6f
12:15 (12:23) (Class 4) 2-Y-0 **£4,857** (£1,445; £722; £360) **Stalls** High

Form RPR

1 **Manaaber (USA)** 2-8-12 0 RichardHills 6 75+
(B W Hills) *hld up in tch: nt clr run and swtchd rt 2f out: hdwy wl over 1f out: rdn to chal ins fnl f: styd on to ld nr fin* **6/1**[3]

2 1/2 **Jamaican Bolt (IRE)** 2-9-3 0 TomEaves 4 78+
(B Smart) *sn led: pushed clr wl over 1f out: rdn ent fnl f: hdd and no ex towards fin* **5/1**[2]

3 nse **Skilful** 2-9-3 0 RobertHavlin 9 79+
(J H M Gosden) *hld up in midfield: swtchd rt and hdwy 2f out: rdn to chal ins fnl f: ev ch tl nt qckn nr fin* **12/1**

4 2 1/4 **Spinatrix** 2-8-12 0 PhillipMakin 3 66+
(M Dods) *midfield: hdwy 2f out: sn rdn and styd on ins fnl f: nrst fin* **28/1**

0022 5 shd **Ceffyl Gwell**[26] 6811 2-9-3 72 RichardHughes 12 71
(R Hannon) *trckd ldrs: hdwy over 2f out: rdn over 1f out and ev ch tl drvn and one pce ent fnl f* **4/1**[1]

6050 6 4 1/2 **Rational Act (IRE)**[29] 6711 2-9-3 53 DavidAllan 16 57
(T D Easterby) *cl up: rdn along over 2f out: grad wknd* **66/1**

7 3 1/2 **Miss Firefox** 2-8-12 0 LukeMorris 8 42
(N J Vaughan) *prom: pushed along 1/2-way: rdn over 2f out: grad wknd* **100/1**

0 8 1/2 **Vantaa (IRE)**[28] 6748 2-9-3 0 PaulHanagan 2 45
(R A Fahey) *cl up: rdn along over 2f out: sn wknd* **4/1**[1]

9 2 **Starbound (IRE)** 2-8-12 0 KierenFallon 10 34
(W J Haggas) *dwlt and towards rr: sme hdwy over 2f out: sn rdn and hung bdly lft: n.d* **5/1**[2]

0 10 1 **Bailadeira**[15] 7057 2-8-9 0 RobertLButler[(3)] 13 31
(T J Etherington) *a towards rr* **100/1**

00 11 hd **Tommy Tiger**[8] 7203 2-9-3 0 WilliamCarson 1 35
(S C Williams) *a towards rr* **50/1**

12 4 **Our Play (IRE)** 2-9-3 0 MichaelHills 7 23
(B W Hills) *a in rr* **14/1**

0 13 6 **Loughtownlady (IRE)**[22] 6892 2-8-12 0 SilvestreDeSousa 11 —
(G A Harker) *chsd ldrs: rdn along 1/2-way: sn wknd* **100/1**

0 14 3 **Dikanta**[21] 6919 2-9-3 0 PaulMulrennan 14 —
(A Berry) *chsd ldrs: rdn along 1/2-way: sn wknd* **100/1**

15 23 **Pope Potter** 2-9-0 0 AndrewHeffernan[(3)] 15 —
(R C Guest) *dwlt: a bhd* **50/1**

1m 14.05s (0.45) **Going Correction** +0.125s/f (Good) **15** Ran SP% **114.8**
Speed ratings (Par 98): **102,101,101,98,98 92,87,86,84,82 82,77,69,65,34**
toteswingers:1&2:£11.00, 1&3:£30.80, 2&3:£14.90 CSF £33.20 TOTE £6.70: £2.70, £2.50, £4.20; EX 44.40 Trifecta £259.20 Part won. Pool of £350.39 - 0.61 winning units.
Owner Hamdan Al Maktoum **Bred** Darley **Trained** Lambourn, Berks

FOCUS
The ground was described as good to soft, soft in places (GoingStick 6.6). Stall 16 didn't open first time round and a false start was declared, but none of the horses went beyond the four-furlong pole so it's unlikely too much harm was done to any of the runners' chances.

NOTEBOOK
Manaaber(USA) ran on well inside the final furlong to win a shade cosily on her debut. A daughter of Medicean out of a Group 3 winner in Italy, she looks sure to do better as a 3yo and should be suited by 1m. (op 13-2)
Jamaican Bolt(IRE), a son of Pivotal, was up there throughout and was only worn down inside the last. Presumably the bit of cut in the ground suited and he shouldn't have too much trouble winning his maiden if kept on the go on the all-weather. (op 8-1 tchd 17-2)
Skilful ◆ is bred to appreciate a good deal further in time - dam was a 1m4f winner - so this was a most encouraging debut. He looks sure to do a lot better next year. (op 10-1)
Spinatrix might not want to go too much further than this next year as she's by Diktat out of a speedy three-time 5f winner. (op 25-1)
Ceffyl Gwell set only a modest standard, and there's no reason to believe he didn't run close to his mark in defeat. (op 5-2)
Rational Act(IRE)'s stall failed to open and caused the false start, so he benefited from the others doing some running first time round. As a result he's probably flattered by his finishing position.
Vantaa(IRE), fancied when well beaten on debut, was again a market positive, but after being brought to have his chance on the outside he proved rather one-paced. He's clearly thought capable of better and might show it in handicaps next year. (op 5-1 tchd 11-2)
Starbound(IRE), a 400,000gns half-sister to Group 1 winning 2yo Alfred Nobel, was much too green to do herself justice on her debut, but she did show ability and is likely to do a lot better next time. (op 9-2)

7346 TOTESPORT 0800 221 221 COCK O'THE NORTH E B F MAIDEN STKS (DIV II) 6f
12:50 (12:52) (Class 4) 2-Y-0 **£4,857** (£1,445; £722; £360) **Stalls** High

Form RPR

1 **Seal Rock** 2-9-3 0 DaneO'Neill 8 84+
(H Candy) *hld up in midfield: effrt over 2f out: led jst ins fnl f: styd on wl* **11/1**

2 1 1/4 **Anoint** 2-9-3 0 KierenFallon 12 81+
(W J Haggas) *s.i.s: gd hdwy over 2f out: chal 1f out: styd on same pce* **9/2**[2]

62 **3** 1 ½ **Fettuccine (IRE)**[18] 7002 2-8-12 0................................ RichardHughes 6 71
(J Noseda) *t.k.h: w ldrs: led narrowly appr fnl f: hdd jst ins fnl f: no ex* **15/8**[1]

04 **4** ½ **Whistle On By**[75] 5372 2-9-3 0.. MichaelHills 9 75
(B W Hills) *led tl appr fnl f: kpt on same pce* **10/1**[3]

5 ½ **Countermarch** 2-8-12 0... JimmyFortune 7 68+
(R Hannon) *chsd ldrs: edgd rt and styd on same pce appr fnl f* **16/1**

3 **6** 3 ¼ **Iceblast**[29] 6722 2-9-3 0... PaulHanagan 13 64
(M W Easterby) *rr-div: hdwy over 2f out: hung lft: nvr rchd ldrs* **9/2**[2]

7 2 ¾ **Swing Door (IRE)** 2-8-12 0....................................... RobertWinston 11 50
(B W Hills) *s.i.s: in rr: hdwy and edgd rt 2f out: nvr nr ldrs* **20/1**

8 *hd* **Take Your Partner** 2-9-3 0... PhillipMakin 3 54
(K A Ryan) *chsd ldrs: wknd over 1f out* **66/1**

5 **9** ½ **Way Chief (FR)**[50] 6138 2-9-0 0................................ JamesSullivan(3) 15 53
(R A Fahey) *chsd ldrs: wknd over 1f out* **10/1**[3]

00 **10** 1 **Sabys Gem (IRE)**[8] 7201 2-9-3 0................................ StephenCraine 14 50
(M Wigham) *trckd ldrs: n.m.r and wknd 2f out* **125/1**

11 *nk* **Goal (IRE)** 2-9-3 0.. AdamKirby 1 49
(D C Griffiths) *s.s: sme hdwy and hung lft over 2f out: nvr a factor* **100/1**

05 **12** 1 **Kieron's Dream (IRE)**[22] 6894 2-9-0 0.................. PatrickDonaghy(3) 4 46
(Jedd O'Keeffe) *sn outpcd and drvn along: a in rr* **100/1**

40 **13** ½ **Soldiers Point**[74] 5385 2-9-3 0... TomEaves 10 45
(B Smart) *chsd ldrs: wknd 2f out* **33/1**

14 *nk* **The Auctioneer (IRE)** 2-9-3 0.................................... StevieDonohoe 2 44
(W J Musson) *sn outpcd and in rr* **66/1**

15 11 **Inde Country** 2-8-12 0.. LukeMorris 5 6
(N J Vaughan) *chsd ldrs: lost pl over 2f out: eased whn bhd* **66/1**

1m 14.16s (0.56) **Going Correction** +0.125s/f (Good) **15 Ran SP% 118.5**
Speed ratings (Par 98): **101,99,97,96,96 91,88,87,87,85 85,84,83,82,68**
toteswingers:1&2:£14.20, 1&3:£7.10, 2&3:£1.80 CSF £56.87 TOTE £10.60: £3.10, £2.30, £1.60; EX 73.90 Trifecta £258.70 Part won. Pool of £349.71 - 0.61 winning units..
Owner P A Deal **Bred** Mrs A D Bourne **Trained** Kingston Warren, Oxon

FOCUS
Very marginally the slower of the two divisions.

NOTEBOOK
Seal Rock got some good cover in behind the pace and picked up well when switched. He ran on really strongly to the line and put up a most pleasing debut. He could be the type to hit the ground running in sprint handicaps next spring. (tchd 10-1)
Anoint raced on the outside of the pack nearest the stands' rail and quickened up well to dispute the lead, but the winner just saw his race out the stronger. Closely related to Listed scorer Penitent, he should take a bit of beating next time. (op 6-1)
Fettuccine(IRE) looked to hold sound claims, but she raced keenly early and that probably cost her in the closing stages. Having had the three runs she could now switch to handicaps, but she could probably still find a maiden on the Polytrack if connections decide to keep her going in this sphere. (tchd 2-1 in places)
Whistle On By, returning from a 75-day break, was prominent throughout and ran his best race to date. Another now eligible for a mark, he'll be of more interest in handicaps. (op 12-1 tchd 9-1)
Countermarch, who briefly challenged on the wide outside, showed signs of inexperience and is fully expected to improve for this. A daughter of Selkirk out of a Daylami mare who won over 1m2f, she's obviously going to want a good deal further than this next year. (op 14-1)
Iceblast ran to a fair level at York on his debut but was a little disappointing in failing to build on that here, hanging left in the closing stages. (op 7-2)
The Auctioneer(IRE) Official explanation: vet said gelding lost a front shoe

7347 40 LIVE FOOTBALL MARKETS AT TOTESPORT.COM NURSERY 6f
1:25 (1:25) (Class 4) (0-85,83) 2-Y-O **£3,885** (£1,156; £577; £288) **Stalls** High

Form RPR

524 **1** **Shesastar**[22] 6893 2-8-1 63.. SilvestreDeSousa 5 69
(T D Barron) *hld up: hdwy to trck ldrs 1/2-way: effrt 2f out: rdn to ld ent fnl f: drvn and hld on wl towards fin* **14/1**

2425 **2** ½ **No Poppy (IRE)**[35] 6563 2-9-1 77................................... PaulHanagan 2 81
(T D Easterby) *cl up: rdn 2f out: sltly outpcd over 1f out: drvn and styd on to have ev ch ins fnl f: nt qckn towards fin* **7/2**[2]

011 **3** 1 **Dozy Joe**[94] 4696 2-9-5 81... NeilCallan 3 82
(I A Wood) *towards rr: hdwy over 2f out: swtchd lft and rdn over 1f out: styd on ins fnl f: nrst fin* **8/1**[3]

3522 **4** *nk* **Its You Again**[11] 7142 2-8-13 75.................................(b[1]) WilliamCarson 6 75
(M G Quinlan) *trckd ldrs: hdwy to ld 3f out: rdn wl over 1f out: drvn and hdd ent fnl f: one pce last 100yds* **25/1**

3425 **5** ½ **Icy Blue**[10] 7172 2-8-5 70.. AmyRyan(3) 4 69
(R M Whitaker) *midfield: hdwy over 2f out: rdn wl over 1f out: kpt on ins fnl f: nrst fin* **28/1**

31 **6** *nk* **Expose**[44] 6308 2-8-11 73... RichardHughes 14 71
(W J Haggas) *hld up in tch: smooth hdwy to trck ldrs over 2f out: effrt to chal over 1f out: sn rdn and ev ch tl drvn and one pce ins fnl f* **6/4**[1]

0534 **7** 1 ½ **I Got You Babe (IRE)**[22] 6892 2-7-13 61 ow1................ JimmyQuinn 10 54
(R C Guest) *t.k.h: hld up towards rr: hdwy 2f out: sn rdn and kpt on ins fnl f: nvr nr ldrs* **14/1**

2012 **8** *nk* **Diamond Vine (IRE)**[21] 6916 2-9-2 78............................... LukeMorris 8 70
(R A Harris) *chsd ldrs: rdn along wl over 2f out: drvn over 1f out and kpt on same pce* **16/1**

0400 **9** 1 ¼ **Serena's Pride**[29] 6719 2-9-6 82.. TedDurcan 12 71
(A P Jarvis) *cl up: rdn along 1/2-way: grad wknd* **33/1**

5031 **10** ½ **Brave Battle**[18] 6995 2-8-6 68.. CathyGannon 1 55
(R Hannon) *sn cl up on outer: rdn along wl over 2f out: drvn and wknd over 1f out* **20/1**

3055 **11** 1 ½ **Hortensis**[12] 7118 2-8-0 62 ow2.................................... DuranFentiman 9 45
(T D Easterby) *a in rr* **66/1**

4100 **12** ¾ **Dubai Celebration**[79] 5245 2-9-1 80......................... PatrickDonaghy(3) 7 60
(Jedd O'Keeffe) *led: hdd 1/2-way and sn pushed along: rdn 2f out and sn wknd* **28/1**

1026 **13** ¾ **Swiss Dream**[98] 4592 2-9-7 83... JimmyFortune 11 61
(D R C Elsworth) *hld up: a towards rr* **10/1**

1m 14.08s (0.48) **Going Correction** +0.125s/f (Good) **13 Ran SP% 121.6**
Speed ratings (Par 98): **101,100,99,98,97 97,95,95,93,92 90,89,88**
toteswingers:1&2:£13.50, 1&3:£25.80, 2&3:£2.20 CSF £59.33 CT £353.07 TOTE £17.60: £3.40, £1.80, £3.20; EX 69.30 TRIFECTA Not won..
Owner Star Alliance 4 - Lancs 2 Lincs **Bred** The Welcome Alliance **Trained** Maunby, N Yorks
■ Silvestre De Sousa's 100th winner of the turf season.
■ Stewards' Enquiry : Paul Hanagan four-day ban: used whip with excessive frequency without giving filly time to respond (Nov 25-28)

FOCUS
A competitive looking nursery.

NOTEBOOK
Shesastar got a bit stirred up before being turned over as favourite last time out. More relaxed this time, she responded well to a strong ride from Silvestre de Sousa and got up inside the last to win on her handicap debut. The easier ground presumably suited this daughter of Bahamian Bounty. (op 18-1)
No Poppy(IRE), who has been running to a consistent level, appreciated the return to 6f and rates the benchmark for the form. She'll go up again for this, so the handicapper could well remain in charge. (op 4-1 tchd 9-2 in a place)
Dozy Joe, put up 5lb for winning on the all-weather last time, got a bit outpaced before running on well at the finish. He might have needed this first run in three months and could win off this sort of mark back on the Polytrack, possibly over another furlong. (tchd 7-1)
Its You Again, wearing blinkers for the first time on his handicap debut, travelled strongly at the head of affairs, perhaps too strongly. He has the ability to win a similar race if settling a bit better. (op 22-1)
Icy Blue, who ran over 1m last time, acquitted himself well over this shorter trip, but he seems to be on a pretty stiff mark for what he's achieved.
Expose raced keenly and may have found conditions a little slower than ideal on this return to turf. (op 15-8 tchd 2-1 in places)

7348 BET ON LIVE FOOTBALL AT TOTESPORT.COM H'CAP 7f
2:00 (2:01) (Class 2) (0-105,104) 3-Y-O+**£23,961** (£7,129; £3,563; £1,779) **Stalls** High

Form RPR

1130 **1** **Horseradish**[22] 6888 3-8-13 93.. HayleyTurner 13 101+
(M L W Bell) *trckd ldrs: styd on fnl f: led nr fin* **12/1**

0622 **2** *shd* **Eton Rifles (IRE)**[29] 6721 5-8-13 92............................ PaulMulrennan 21 100
(J Howard Johnson) *swtchd lft after s: trckd ldrs: led 2f out: hdd appr fnl f: r.o: jst hld* **10/1**[3]

-210 **3** *hd* **Harry Patch**[14] 7079 4-8-13 92.. NeilCallan 1 99
(M A Jarvis) *in tch: hdwy over 2f out: r.o ins fnl f: jst hld* **17/2**[2]

3240 **4** *nk* **Iver Bridge Lad**[15] 7060 3-9-5 104.........................(b) AdamBeschizza(5) 3 111
(J Ryan) *hld up towards rr: hdwy and swtchd lft over 2f out: led appr fnl f: hdd fnl strides* **16/1**

1651 **5** ½ **Docofthebay (IRE)**[22] 6888 6-9-2 95..............................(b) IanMongan 16 100
(J A Glover) *hld up towards rr: hdwy over 2f out: styd on wl ins fnl f* **18/1**

2040 **6** 2 ¼ **Parisian Pyramid (IRE)**[15] 7060 4-9-3 96.................. StephenCraine 11 95
(K A Ryan) *mid-div: effrt over 2f out: kpt on fnl f: nvr nr ldrs* **50/1**

0010 **7** ½ **Kiwi Bay**[28] 6749 5-9-3 96... PJMcDonald 20 94
(M Dods) *hld up towards rr: kpt on fnl 2f: nvr nr ldrs* **33/1**

1505 **8** *nk* **Captain Ramius (IRE)**[22] 6907 4-8-11 90........................ PhillipMakin 8 87
(K A Ryan) *mid-div: hdwy over 2f out: nvr trbld ldrs* **22/1**

0402 **9** ½ **Damien (IRE)**[28] 6752 4-9-7 100...................................... MichaelHills 14 96
(B W Hills) *trckd ldrs: effrt 2f out: kpt on one pce* **7/1**[1]

1360 **10** 2 ½ **Quest For Success (IRE)**[15] 7060 5-9-4 97............... BarryMcHugh 12 86
(R A Fahey) *prom: effrt over 2f out: wknd over 1f out* **28/1**

10 **11** *hd* **Thats A Fret (IRE)**[14] 7079 4-8-12 91.......................... RichardHughes 5 79
(Liam McAteer, Ire) *towards rr: hdwy and n.m.r 2f out: nvr nr ldrs* **20/1**

4220 **12** 1 ½ **Kyllachy Star**[42] 6349 4-9-1 94.................................... StevieDonohoe 4 78
(R A Fahey) *in tch: effrt over 2f out: wknd over 1f out* **25/1**

4000 **13** *shd* **Advanced**[15] 7060 7-8-11 93.. AmyRyan(3) 10 77
(K A Ryan) *chsd ldrs: wknd appr fnl f* **28/1**

0110 **14** ½ **My Kingdom (IRE)**[29] 6721 4-8-13 92......................... AdrianNicholls 19 75
(D Nicholls) *dwlt: nvr a factor* **33/1**

2141 **15** 1 **Justonefortheroad**[29] 6721 4-8-11 90.......................... PaulHanagan 17 70
(R A Fahey) *hld up towards rr: effrt over 2f out: nvr a factor* **7/1**[1]

1526 **16** *nk* **Smarty Socks (IRE)**[28] 6749 6-9-0 93................... SilvestreDeSousa 2 72
(D O'Meara) *dwlt: sn mid-div: wknd over 1f out* **10/1**[3]

1631 **17** 4 ½ **Osteopathic Remedy (IRE)**[20] 6960 6-9-4 97................ TomEaves 18 64
(M Dods) *t.k.h in rr: nvr on terms* **16/1**

0510 **18** *nk* **Axiom**[42] 6349 6-9-10 103.. KierenFallon 6 69
(L M Cumani) *towards rr: sme hdwy over 2f out: n.m.r and lost pl over 1f out* **10/1**[3]

0053 **19** 5 **Camerooney**[22] 6888 7-8-10 92....................................... IanBrennan(3) 7 45
(B Ellison) *w ldrs: rdn over 2f out: sn lost pl* **12/1**

650 **20** 1 ¾ **Welsh Emperor (IRE)**[14] 7083 11-9-2 95...................(b) MickyFenton 15 43
(T P Tate) *w ldrs: led briefly over 2f out: wknd wl over 1f out: eased and bhd ins fnl f* **100/1**

0005 **21** 7 **No Hubris (USA)**[22] 6888 3-8-11 91............................. JimmyFortune 9 20
(P F I Cole) *led tl over 2f out: sn lost pl: eased whn bhd ins fnl f* **20/1**

1m 25.77s (-0.53) **Going Correction** +0.125s/f (Good)
WFA 3 from 4yo+ 1lb **21 Ran SP% 128.7**
Speed ratings (Par 109): **108,107,107,107,106 104,103,103,102,99 99,97,97,97,96 95,90,90,84,82 74**
toteswingers:1&2:£114.70, 1&3:£14.00, 2&3:£9.30 CSF £115.23 CT £1121.51 TOTE £13.30: £2.70, £3.20, £2.70, £4.60; EX 160.50 Trifecta £407.90 Pool: £1157.56- 2.10 winning units..
Owner Mrs G Rowland-Clark **Bred** Mrs F A Veasey **Trained** Newmarket, Suffolk
■ Stewards' Enquiry : Paul Mulrennan one-day ban: used whuip with excessive freauency in incorrect place(Nov 20)
Hayley Turner two-day ban: used whip with excessive frequency (Nov 20,23)

FOCUS
There was a tight finish to this 7f handicap.

NOTEBOOK
Horseradish just got his nose in front at the line. He travelled well behind the pace and battled on gamely to just edge ahead close home. Very consistent, he's only once finished out of the first three, and having had only the ten starts it wouldn't be a surprise if he improves again at four. He's just as good over 6f as he is over 7f.
Eton Rifles(IRE) has been running well this autumn and put up a great effort off a 5lb higher mark than when last seen. Another rise in the weights for being beaten won't be welcome, though. (op 11-1)
Harry Patch found 5f too short last time out, but he had his stamina to prove over this 7f trip. He got it well, finishing best of all to take third, and this lightly raced gelding should be capable of landing a decent pot next season when he gets a bit of cut in the ground. (op 8-1)
Iver Bridge Lad has had a busy, winless season, but he's run several good races in defeat and held his form particularly well.
Docofthebay(IRE) stayed on strongly down the outside but couldn't quite reach the places. He's done his winning on good ground or quicker so this was a decent effort.
Parisian Pyramid(IRE) does most of his racing over sprint distances and is another whose best form has come on quicker ground.
Damien(IRE) didn't see the trip out in the ground. (op 9-1)

Justonefortheroad, who appeared to have conditions to suit, was disappointing off a 6lb higher mark than when successful at York last time. (op 17-2)

7349 BET ON TOTESCOOP6 AT TOTESPORT.COM E B F GILLIES FILLIES' STKS (LISTED RACE) 1m 2f 60y

2:35 (2:35) (Class 1) 3-Y-O+ **£22,518** (£8,515; £4,256; £2,128) **Stalls** Low

Form RPR

3000 **1** **Ceilidh House**^{69} [5553] 3-8-10 93 (t) JimCrowley 17 103
(R M Beckett) *hld up and bhd: pushed along 3f out: rdn 2f out: swtchd outside and str run fr over 1f out: styd on wl to ld nr fin* **25/1**

3231 **2** ¾ **Zahoo (IRE)**^{8} [7206] 3-8-10 88 RichardHills 9 101+
(J L Dunlop) *hld up in midfield: stdy hdwy 3f out: swtchd rt and effrt wl over 1f out: rdn to ld ent fnl f: drvn and edgd lft fnl 100yds: hdd and no ex nr fin* **9/2^{2}**

3065 **3** *hd* **Saphira's Fire (IRE)**^{21} [6928] 5-9-0 103 HayleyTurner 16 101
(W R Muir) *stdd and swtchd lft s: hld up and bhd: stdy hdwy on inner 3f out: trckd ldrs 2f out: rdn over 1f out: styd on to chal jst ins fnl f and ev ch tl drvn and no ex towards fin* **20/1**

3-16 **4** 1 ¼ **Cheetah**^{52} [6095] 3-8-10 91 KierenFallon 7 98+
(L M Cumani) *hld up in midfield: hdwy 3f out: trckd ldrs and pushed along over 2f out: swtchd rt and rdn wl over 1f out: swtchd lft and styd on wl fnl f: nrst fin* **14/1**

4-30 **5** ½ **Hidden Brief**^{207} [1274] 4-9-0 90 PhilipRobinson 15 97
(M A Jarvis) *hld up and bhd: stdy hdwy on inner over 2f out: rdn wl over 1f out: drvn to chse ldrs ent fnl f: kpt on* **33/1**

1240 **6** ¾ **Starkat**^{42} [6361] 4-9-0 82 NeilCallan 4 96
(Jane Chapple-Hyam) *hld up towards rr: stdy hdwy 4f out: chsd ldrs 2f out: sn rdn and ch tl drvn and one pce ent fnl f* **66/1**

1-1 **7** *nk* **Modeyra**^{22} [6886] 3-8-13 108 TedDurcan 12 98
(Saeed Bin Suroor) *hld up in midfield: swtchd rt and hdwy 3f out: chsd ldrs 2f out: rdn to ld briefly jst over 1f out: drvn and hdd ent fnl f: wknd* **9/4^{1}**

562 **8** 3 ½ **Les Fazzani (IRE)**^{56} [5938] 6-9-3 108 PaulHanagan 6 92
(K A Ryan) *led: rdn along 3f out: drvn 2f out: hdd and hld whn n.m.r and wknd ins fnl f* **7/1^{3}**

4400 **9** 2 **Island Sunset (IRE)**^{22} [6886] 4-9-0 90 PhillipMakin 1 85
(W R Muir) *trckd ldng pair: rdn along over 3f out: drvn 2f out and grad wknd* **100/1**

3043 **10** *nse* **Middle Club**^{22} [6886] 3-8-10 108 RichardHughes 2 85
(R Hannon) *hld up in tch on inner: hdwy over 3f out: swtchd rt and effrt 2f out: sn rdn and wknd over 1f out* **8/1**

6214 **11** 6 **Fork Lightning (USA)**^{56} [5981] 3-8-10 92 SebSanders 8 73
(Sir Mark Prescott) *trckd ldrs: hdwy and cl up 1/2-way: rdn along over 3f out: hld whn n.m.r over 2f out: sn wknd* **33/1**

-534 **12** ½ **Copperbeech (IRE)**^{9} [7189] 4-9-0 96 DarryllHolland 14 73
(Saeed Bin Suroor) *cl up: rdn along 4f out: wknd 3f out* **12/1**

2210 **13** 9 **Marjury Daw (IRE)**^{42} [6361] 4-9-0 85 PaulMulrennan 3 55
(J G Given) *chsd ldrs: rdn along over 4f out: sn wknd* **66/1**

0200 **14** 11 **Clarietta**^{22} [6886] 3-8-10 95 ShaneKelly 10 35
(J L Dunlop) *hld up towards rr: stdy hdwy on outer over 3f out: in tch and rdn over 2f out: sn wknd* **40/1**

0010 **15** 8 **Goodlukin Lucy**^{16} [7042] 3-8-10 76 RobertWinston 18 19
(Pat Eddery) *midfield on outer: rdn along over 4f out: sn wknd* **50/1**

6-55 **16** 7 **Montbretia**^{27} [6786] 5-9-0 93 JimmyFortune 13 —
(Edward P Harty, Ire) *prom: rdn along over 4f out: sn wknd* **66/1**

431 **U** **All Annalena (IRE)**^{42} [6361] 4-9-0 89 DaneO'Neill 11 —
(Mrs L Wadham) *wnt down in stalls and uns rdr s* **11/1**

2m 9.66s (0.26) **Going Correction** +0.125s/f (Good)
WFA 3 from 4yo+ 4lb **17 Ran SP% 119.6**
Speed ratings (Par 108): **103,102,102,101,100 100,100,97,95,95 90,90,83,74,67 62,—**
toteswingers:1&2:£61.90, 1&3:£31.60, 2&3:£28.20 CSF £125.24 TOTE £30.40: £7.10, £2.30, £7.00; EX 204.30 TRIFECTA Not won..
Owner J H Richmond-Watson **Bred** Lawn Stud **Trained** Whitsbury, Hants

FOCUS

A big field of fillies chasing black type before the season ends.

NOTEBOOK

Ceilidh House looked a promising filly earlier in the campaign but ran poorly in the Oaks, and again at York, before showing a little at Goodwood on her last start. Given time off since then and fitted with a tongue-tie for the first time, she came from the clouds to get up inside the last. Cut in the ground appears to be important to her, and it looks as though she might stay in training as a 4-y-o. (op 22-1)

Zahoo(IRE) looked to have been brought with a well-timed challenge until Ceilidh House went by inside the last. She has really come good this autumn and there is probably more to come from her, so perhaps she'll be kept in training as a 4-y-o. (op 13-2)

Saphira's Fire(IRE) is on a long losing run, but she ran a solid race back at this correct level. (tchd 22-1)

Cheetah reversed Yarmouth form with Starkat on this less-testing ground. One of the least experienced fillies in the race, she still has room for improvement. (op 16-1)

Hidden Brief improved a little on her sixth in this race last year, and did run her best race of a shortened campaign, but quicker ground probably suits her best. (op 25-1)

Modeyra looked the one to beat on her Newmarket defeat of Timepiece, but that was only three weeks earlier and she wasn't quite able to back that up. She's capable of better and it wouldn't be a surprise to see her in action during the Dubai Carnival. (op 7-4 tchd 13-8 and 6-4 in places)

Les Fazzani(IRE), winner of this race in 2008 and fourth last year, had conditions to suit and, although asked to give 3lb all round, looked to hold solid claims. She was a little disappointing. (op 6-1)

Montbretia Official explanation: jockey said mare lost its action

7350 TOTESPORT.COM NOVEMBER H'CAP (HERITAGE HANDICAP) 1m 4f

3:10 (3:10) (Class 2) 3-Y-O+
£62,310 (£18,660; £9,330; £4,670; £2,330; £1,170) **Stalls** Low

Form RPR

4422 **1** **Times Up**^{22} [6889] 4-8-13 97 DaneO'Neill 9 109+
(J L Dunlop) *mid-div: hdwy far side over 3f out: led over 1f out: styd on strly* **14/1**

0034 **2** 1 ¾ **The Betchworth Kid**^{28} [6736] 5-8-6 95 AdamBeschizza$^{(5)}$ 17 104+
(A King) *swtchd lft after s: hld up in rr: swtchd outside and gd hdwy over 2f out: hung lft and styd on wl to chse wnr wl ins fnl f* **12/1**

4460 **3** *nk* **Simenon (IRE)**^{49} [6201] 3-8-5 95 DavidProbert 5 103
(A M Balding) *chsd ldrs: upsides over 2f out: styd on same pce fnl f* **12/1**

0003 **4** 1 ¼ **Classic Vintage (USA)**^{14} [7084] 4-8-9 93 JimCrowley 3 99
(Mrs A J Perrett) *mid-div: hdwy over 2f out: chsng ldrs over 1f out: styd on same pce* **25/1**

35-1 **5** *shd* **Salden Licht**^{14} [7084] 6-8-13 102 MHarley$^{(5)}$ 15 108
(A King) *hld up in rr: hdwy over 2f out: styd on wl fnl f* **16/1**

5320 **6** *hd* **Prompter**^{28} [6736] 3-8-13 103 HayleyTurner 11 109
(M L W Bell) *trckd ldrs: smooth hdwy over 2f out: kpt on same pce fnl f* **16/1**

0051 **7** 1 ¼ **Palomar (USA)**^{10} [7173] 8-8-6 90 SilvestreDeSousa 10 94
(B Ellison) *hld up in rr: hdwy far side over 3f out: edgd rt 2f out: kpt on fnl f* **10/1^{3}**

0331 **8** 1 ½ **Tepmokea (IRE)**^{28} [6754] 4-8-6 90 PaulHanagan 20 91
(R A Fahey) *swtchd lft after s: w ldr: t.k.h: led after 3f: hdd over 1f out: wknd fnl f* **10/1^{3}**

0204 **9** 2 **Shavansky**^{23} [6877] 6-8-9 93 JamesMillman 4 91
(B R Millman) *rr-div: effrt far side over 3f out: edgd rt and one pce fnl 2f* **50/1**

0603 **10** 1 ¾ **Brunston**^{14} [7100] 4-8-3 87 FrannyNorton 13 82
(R Charlton) *hld up in mid-div: effrt 3f out: nvr rchd ldrs* **22/1**

0-10 **11** 1 ½ **Prospect Wells (FR)**^{80} [5220] 5-9-10 108 PaulMulrennan 23 101
(J Howard Johnson) *swtchd lft sn after s: hld up towards rr: hdwy and n.m.r 2f out: kpt on fnl f* **66/1**

6022 **12** ½ **Sirvino**^{28} [6736] 5-8-13 97 PhillipMakin 18 89
(T D Barron) *trckd ldrs: upsides over 2f out: wknd over 1f out* **16/1**

4612 **13** ¾ **Lethal Glaze (IRE)**^{26} [6808] 4-8-6 93 JohnFahy$^{(3)}$ 25 84
(B Ellison) *mid-div: effrt over 3f out: nvr a factor* **33/1**

6200 **14** 1 ¾ **Rangefinder**^{21} [6926] 6-8-3 90 SophieDoyle$^{(3)}$ 6 78
(Jane Chapple-Hyam) *chsd ldrs: wknd over 2f out* **50/1**

6102 **15** *nse* **Jo'Burg (USA)**^{23} [6877] 6-8-6 90 DavidAllan 8 78
(J O'Reilly) *s.i.s: nvr on terms* **25/1**

0236 **16** 2 ¾ **Red Jade**^{14} [7084] 5-8-0 87 JamesSullivan$^{(3)}$ 19 71
(R A Fahey) *chsd ldrs: wknd 2f out* **40/1**

5006 **17** 1 ¾ **Montaff**^{28} [6736] 4-9-1 99 NeilCallan 7 80
(M R Channon) *mid-div: effrt 3f out: sn lost pl* **20/1**

3110 **18** 6 **Senate**^{49} [6193] 3-8-11 101 RichardHughes 14 72
(J H M Gosden) *hld up towards rr: effrt over 3f out: wknd over 2f out: eased whn bhd ins fnl f* **9/2^{1}**

-111 **19** *shd* **Willing Foe (USA)**^{22} [6889] 3-8-7 97 TedDurcan 2 68
(Saeed Bin Suroor) *sn trcking ldrs: lost pl over 2f out: eased whn bhd ins fnl f* **11/2^{2}**

0041 **20** 4 **Cracking Lass (IRE)**^{32} [6654] 3-8-4 94 JimmyQuinn 22 59
(R A Fahey) *mid-div: effrt 3f out: sn wknd: eased whn bhd ins fnl f* **25/1**

6306 **21** 2 ¼ **Thin Red Line (IRE)**^{28} [6738] 4-8-8 92 TomEaves 21 53
(M Dods) *chsd ldrs: lost pl 3f out* **40/1**

6032 **22** 9 **La Vecchia Scuola (IRE)**^{21} [6926] 6-9-0 98 KierenFallon 24 45
(J S Goldie) *sn chsng ldrs: lost pl 3f out: eased whn bhd ins fnl f* **22/1**

2m 32.62s (-2.28) **Going Correction** +0.125s/f (Good)
WFA 3 from 4yo+ 6lb **22 Ran SP% 129.7**
Speed ratings (Par 109): **112,110,110,109,109 109,108,107,106,105 104,103,103,102,102 100,99,95,95,92 91,85**
toteswingers:1&2:£60.30, 1&3:£75.00, 2&3:£43.80 CSF £152.64 CT £2114.08 TOTE £18.60: £3.70, £2.50, £4.00, £5.60; EX 279.90 Trifecta £5025.20 Pool: £44140.64 - 6.50 winning units..
Owner Mrs I H Stewart-Brown & M J Meacock **Bred** I Stewart-Brown And M Meacock **Trained** Arundel, W Sussex

FOCUS

A typically competitive renewal.

NOTEBOOK

Times Up won a shade cosily. Only 1lb higher than when runner-up to Willing Foe at Newmarket last time, he was meeting that rival on 4lb better terms and comprehensively turned the tables on this easier ground. He deserved this for a string of consistent efforts.

The Betchworth Kid, runner-up in this race in 2008, repeated the feat. A stronger pace from the off would have suited him better considering his style of running, but he still finished like a train, passing the whole field bar the winner in the straight. This sort of race brings out the best in him. (op 14-1)

Simenon(IRE) has been campaigned like a good horse this season, contesting Pattern races for the most part, and it was a clear case of his stamina giving out at Newmarket last time. He looked a big player down in distance off the same mark, and did run well, despite racing more to the fore than is normally wise in this race.

Classic Vintage(USA) bounced back to close to his best here on his last start and narrowly reversed form with Salden Licht this time, despite the ground being softer than ideal.

Salden Licht, put up 7lb for his C/D win last month, repeated last year's finishing position in this race. He has the potential to land a decent handicap over hurdles this winter.

Prompter ran a sound race considering he faced a pretty stiff task off a mark of 103. (op 18-1)

Palomar(USA) was keeping on nicely at the end, as one would expect of a gelding whose best trip is probably 2m. (op 14-1)

Tepmokea(IRE) got to the front and tried not to set too strong a pace, but this is a difficult race to win from the front and he was swamped approaching the final furlong. (op 12-1)

Senate had too much use made of him from a poor draw last time. Again drawn wider than ideal for a prominent racer, he was dropped in here and just didn't run to his best. (tchd 4-1 and 5-1 in places)

Willing Foe(USA) beat Times Up at Newmarket last time and, despite being 4lb worse off at the weights, looked to have every chance of confirming that form given his progressive profile. However, he finished well held and presumably failed to handle the easier ground. (op 13-2)

7351 BET ON BREEDERS CUP AT TOTESPORT.COM WENTWORTH STKS (LISTED RACE) 6f

3:40 (3:45) (Class 1) 3-Y-O+ **£29,630** (£11,205; £5,600; £2,800) **Stalls** High

Form RPR

0322 **1** **Russian Spirit**^{19} [6981] 4-8-12 85 PhilipRobinson 18 102
(M A Jarvis) *racd wd: cl up: led wl over 1f out: rdn ent fnl f: edgd lft and kpt on wl towards fin* **18/1**

6132 **2** *hd* **Hitchens (IRE)**^{15} [7073] 5-9-3 102 SilvestreDeSousa 15 106
(T D Barron) *chsd ldrs towards outer: hdwy over 2f out: rdn to chal and ev ch over 1f out: drvn ins fnl f: no ex towards fin* **11/2^{2}**

6100 **3** 1 **Doncaster Rover (USA)**^{28} [6735] 4-9-6 108 (b^{1}) RobertWinston 7 106
(D H Brown) *chsd ldrs: hdwy over 2f out: rdn and hung bdly rt over 1f out: drvn and kpt on fnl f* **13/2^{3}**

2011 **4** 2 **Mac's Power (IRE)**^{15} [7060] 4-9-3 97 (t) GeorgeBaker 8 96+
(J R Fanshawe) *hld up towards rr: smooth hdwy whn nt clr run over 1f out: sn swtchd lft and effrt whn nt clr run over 1f out: rdn and kpt on fnl f: nrst fin* **4/1^{1}**

2000 **5** 1 **Kaldoun Kingdom (IRE)**^{28} [6752] 5-9-3 103 PaulHanagan 1 93
(R A Fahey) *hld up in tch: hdwy on outer over 2f out: rdn to chal wl over 1f out and ev ch tl drvn and wknd ent fnl f* **7/1**

5024 **6** 1 **Croisultan (IRE)**^{6} [7259] 4-9-6 106 RichardHughes 10 93
(Liam McAteer, Ire) *cl up: rdn along 2f out: drvn over 1f out and grad wknd* **11/1**

3151 **7** ½ **R Woody**^{27} [6776] 3-9-3 93 AdamKirby 14 88
(D K Ivory) *prom: rdn along 2f out: sn drvn and grad wknd* **11/1**

0431 **8** 1 1/2 **Icelandic**[11] 7143 8-9-3 88 (t) DarryllHolland 5 84
(F Sheridan) *hld up: hdwy and n.m.r 2f out: sn swtchd lft and rdn over 1f out: kpt on ins fnl f: nt rch ldrs* **25/1**

5066 **9** nk **Great Charm (IRE)**[20] 6962 5-9-3 78 FrannyNorton 12 83
(E J Alston) *dwlt and rr tl styd on fnl 2f: nvr nr ldrs* **100/1**

0000 **10** nk **Fullandby (IRE)**[4] 7289 8-9-3 87 TedDurcan 19 82
(T J Etherington) *dwlt and swtchd lft s: bhd tl styd on fnl 2f: nvr nr ldrs* **25/1**

4003 **11** nk **Enderby Spirit (GR)**[15] 7060 4-9-3 90 (p) JimCrowley 3 81
(B Smart) *towards rr: sme late hdwy on inner: nvr nr ldrs* **25/1**

2310 **12** 1 1/4 **Esuvia (IRE)**[51] 6113 3-8-12 86 TomEaves 4 72
(B Smart) *cl up: rdn along over 2f out: drvn and edgd rt wl over 1f out: sn wknd* **80/1**

4316 **13** 3/4 **Doric Lady**[22] 6887 5-8-12 81 KirstyMilczarek 17 69
(J A R Toller) *in tch: rdn along over 2f out: sn wknd* **50/1**

2114 **14** 1/2 **Cheveton**[14] 7079 6-9-3 97 WilliamCarson 11 73
(R J Price) *dwlt and in rr: rdn along over 2f out: nvr a factor* **16/1**

5141 **15** 2 1/4 **Mirza**[38] 6478 3-9-3 87 NeilCallan 9 66
(Rae Guest) *midfield: rdn along over 2f out: n.d* **25/1**

232 **16** 1 3/4 **Tax Free (IRE)**[37] 6508 8-9-3 103 AdrianNicholls 2 60
(D Nicholls) *led: rdn along and hdd jst over 2f out: sn wknd* **10/1**

0456 **17** 2 1/2 **Anglezarke (IRE)**[14] 7079 4-8-12 93 (v1) BarryMcHugh 6 47
(R A Fahey) *cl up: rdn to ld jst over 2f out: sn drvn: hdd & wknd* **22/1**

1m 12.4s (-1.20) **Going Correction** +0.125s/f (Good) **17 Ran SP% 122.0**
Speed ratings (Par 111): **113,112,111,108,107 106,105,103,103,102 102,100,99,98,95 93,90**
toteswingers:1&2:£26.80, 1&3:£32.20, 2&3:£7.10 CSF £104.76 TOTE £19.00: £5.00, £2.40, £3.10; EX 108.50 TRIFECTA Not won..
Owner Cromhall Stud **Bred** Derek R Price **Trained** Newmarket, Suffolk
■ Paul Hanagan, fifth here, is the new champion jockey with 191 winners, two more than Richard Hughes.

FOCUS
The form of this Listed contest looks decidedly average.

NOTEBOOK
Russian Spirit has spent the majority of the campaign running over 5f, but she showed here that this is her best distance. Drawn high and racing apart from the rest for much of the race, she pulled clear with the runner-up approaching the last and just saw it out the better. Having raced off marks in the mid-80s all season, this was clearly a jump in class for the winner, and connections will no doubt be delighted to have bagged valuable black type with her. (op 20-1 tchd 16-1)
Hitchens(IRE) has recorded all five of his wins on fast ground so, despite being beaten by a filly rated much lower, this was a creditable performance in the circumstances. (op 8-1)
Doncaster Rover(USA), who was best in at the weights, wore blinkers for the first time. He probably didn't run quite up to his best on this drop in class. (op 9-1)
Mac's Power(IRE), buried in behind, didn't get the gaps when he needed them and his run was delayed. He finished well but it was all too late, and he shaped better than his finishing position indicates. Official explanation: jockey said gelding was denied a clear run (op 9-2)
Kaldoun Kingdom(IRE) goes well here - his last win came in a handicap over this course and distance on the opening weekend of the season - and this was another sound run from him. (op 15-2 tchd 8-1)
Croisultan(IRE), back over 6f, can't have the ground soft enough, and conditions here were probably not sufficiently testing. (op 9-1)
R Woody has been in good form of late but wasn't quite at his best on this step up in class. (op 12-1)
Icelandic, who won this race in 2008, is another who would have needed the ground to be far more testing for him to get involved. (tchd 16-1)

7352 BET INTO US POOLS AT TOTESPORT.COM APPRENTICE H'CAP 7f
4:10 (4:12) (Class 4) (0-85,84) 3-Y-O+ £3,885 (£1,156; £577; £288) Stalls High

Form RPR

1665 **1** **Perfect Silence**[14] 7097 5-8-11 **81** LucyBarry(7) 1 94
(C G Cox) *racd alone far side: w ldrs: led overall and edgd rt 3f out: kpt on wl fnl f* **12/1**

-001 **2** 2 1/4 **Mister Laurel**[8] 7212 4-9-5 **82** (b) JohnFahy 19 88+
(R A Fahey) *in rr: gd hdwy over 2f out: hrd rdn and chsd wnr fnl f: no imp* **8/1**[3]

4601 **3** 1/2 **Nazreef**[14] 7091 3-9-4 **82** (t) SophieDoyle 8 87
(H Morrison) *mid-div: hdwy over 2f out: styd on same pce fnl f* **15/2**[2]

3142 **4** nse **Space Station**[14] 7091 4-9-3 **83** (b) AdamBeschizza(3) 18 88
(S Dow) *hld up towards rr: hdwy over 2f out: styd on same pce fnl f* **11/2**[1]

2360 **5** 3 **Thunderball**[14] 7092 4-9-0 **80** (b) BillyCray(3) 13 77
(J A Glover) *trckd ldrs: hdwy to chse wnr over 2f out: wknd fnl f* **14/1**

0406 **6** 1 **Everymanforhimself (IRE)**[11] 7143 6-9-5 **82** (b) AmyRyan 10 76
(K A Ryan) *hld up in rr: hdwy over 2f out: kpt on fnl f* **16/1**

0650 **7** 3/4 **One Way Or Another (AUS)**[7] 7238 7-9-4 **84** TobyAtkinson(3) 15 76
(J R Gask) *hld up in midfield: effrt over 2f out: kpt on same pce appr fnl f* **15/2**[2]

0013 **8** 1 **Magic Cat**[11] 7146 4-9-2 **82** MHarley(3) 12 71
(Mrs K Burke) *in rr and sn drvn along: hdwy over 2f out: one pce appr fnl f* **10/1**

0210 **9** hd **Daaweitza**[35] 6567 7-9-3 **80** (b) IanBrennan 17 69
(B Ellison) *in rr: sme hdwy over 2f out: nvr nr ldrs* **33/1**

5306 **10** 1 **River Falcon**[41] 6394 10-8-9 **77** PaulNorton(5) 16 63
(J S Goldie) *towards rr: sme hdwy 2f out: nvr a factor* **22/1**

0040 **11** 3/4 **Game Lad**[11] 7143 8-8-10 **76** (tp) LanceBetts(3) 9 60
(T D Easterby) *mid-div: nvr a factor* **25/1**

2121 **12** 1/2 **Another Try (IRE)**[60] 5838 5-9-0 **77** MatthewDavies 3 60
(A P Jarvis) *chsd ldrs: wknd appr fnl f* **12/1**

-100 **13** 4 **Masked Dance (IRE)**[20] 6963 3-8-13 **82** (p) JulieBurke(5) 2 54
(K A Ryan) *led tl 3f out: wknd 2f out* **40/1**

1640 **14** 3/4 **Sunnyside Tom (IRE)**[28] 6749 6-9-0 **84** GeorgeChaloner(7) 14 54
(R A Fahey) *hld up towards rr: nvr a factor* **22/1**

2016 **15** 1 3/4 **Moody Tunes**[52] 6097 7-9-2 **79** MichaelGeran 4 44
(Mrs K Burke) *mid-div: effrt over 2f out: sn wknd* **25/1**

1426 **16** 5 **Night Trade (IRE)**[19] 6985 3-8-12 **79** (p) JamesO'Reilly(3) 5 31
(Mrs D J Sanderson) *chsd ldrs: hung rt and wknd 2f out: bhd whn eased ins fnl f* **40/1**

2320 **17** 2 1/4 **Fishforcompliments**[42] 6357 6-9-6 **83** (p) JamesSullivan 6 29
(R A Fahey) *hld up in mid-div: effrt over 2f out: sn wknd* **16/1**

5000 **18** 1 3/4 **Aldermoor (USA)**[20] 6963 4-9-2 **79** WilliamCarson 11 20
(S C Williams) *s.i.s: in rr: hdwy over 2f out: sn lost pl* **33/1**

00-5 **19** 2 **Mangham (IRE)**[242] 837 5-8-12 **78** AshleyMorgan(3) 20 14
(D H Brown) *t.k.h: sn trcking ldrs: wknd over 2f out* **33/1**

1131 **20** 5 **Divertimenti (IRE)**[19] 6985 6-8-12 **80** (b) RyanClark(5) 7 2
(S R Bowring) *s.s: a in rr: eased whn bhd ins fnl f* **16/1**

1m 26.26s (-0.04) **Going Correction** +0.125s/f (Good)
WFA 3 from 4yo+ 1lb **20 Ran SP% 128.9**
Speed ratings (Par 105): **105,102,101,101,98 97,96,95,95,93 93,92,87,87,85 79,76,74,72,66**
toteswingers:1&2:£16.40, 1&3:£22.90, 2&3:£10.50 CSF £95.99 CT £807.02 TOTE £13.10: £2.40, £3.00, £3.30, £2.30; EX 186.30 Trifecta £429.50 Part won. Pool of £406.34 - 0.30 winning units..
Owner Wild Beef Racing (Mr & Mrs R J Vines) **Bred** R J Vines **Trained** Lambourn, Berks
■ Thunderball was Jeremy Glover's last runner.
■ Stewards' Enquiry : John Fahy four-day ban: used whip with excessive frequency (Nov 20,23-25)

FOCUS
An open apprentice handicap brought the turf season to a close.
Night Trade(IRE) Official explanation: jockey said filly hung right
Divertimenti(IRE) Official explanation: trainer said gelding was unsuited by the good to soft (soft in places) ground
T/Jkpt: Not won. T/Plt: £1,347.80 to a £1 stake. Pool:£123,986.51 - 67.15 winning tickets T/Qpdt: £182.30 to a £1 stake. Pool:£11,830.19 - 48.00 winning tickets WG

7215 DUNDALK (A.W) (L-H)
Saturday, November 6

OFFICIAL GOING: Standard

7358a CARLINGFORD STKS (LISTED RACE) 1m 2f 150y(P)
9:00 (9:04) 3-Y-O+ £24,446 (£7,146; £3,384; £1,128)

RPR

1 **Shimmering Moment (USA)**[32] 6654 3-8-12 88 (b1) CDHayes 9 105
(James J Hartnett, Ire) *racd in 2nd: impr to chal over 3f out: rdn to ld early st: edgd clr over 1f out: styd on wl* **16/1**

2 3 **Bob Le Beau (IRE)**[36] 6549 3-9-1 103 ShaneFoley 2 102
(Mrs John Harrington, Ire) *reluctant to load: settled 8th: 9th ent st: rdr lost whip under 2f out: drvn out and styd on wl fr 1 1/2f out* **10/3**[1]

3 3/4 **Bikini Babe (IRE)**[22] 6886 3-8-12 GregFairley 6 98
(M Johnston) *led: strly pressed fr over 3f out: rdn and hdd early st: rallied u.p 1 1/2f out: kpt on same pce ins fnl f* **7/2**[2]

4 1 **You'll Be Mine (USA)**[12] 7140 3-8-12 103 JAHeffernan 13 96
(A P O'Brien, Ire) *mid-div: 7th 1/2-way: 8th st: prog under 2f out: 4th and styng on whn nt clr run and eased 100yds out* **8/1**

5 1 1/4 **Northgate (IRE)**[22] 6912 5-9-5 101 PJSmullen 4 95
(Joseph G Murphy, Ire) *trckd ldrs in 4th: rdn and one pce st* **6/1**[3]

6 3/4 **Indiana Gal (IRE)**[15] 7076 5-9-2 96 (p) CO'Donoghue 12 91
(Patrick Martin, Ire) *towards rr: sme prog after 1/2-way: 9th early st: kpt on same pce fr 1 1/2f out* **14/1**

7 nk **Barbadine (USA)**[43] 6343 3-8-12 95 (p) WMLordan 7 91
(David Wachman, Ire) *trckd ldrs in 3rd: rdn st: wknd fr over 1f out* **16/1**

8 1 1/4 **Miranda's Girl (IRE)**[8] 7218 5-9-2 76 (p) RPCleary 3 88
(Thomas Cleary, Ire) *chsd ldrs: 6th 3f out: no ex st* **33/1**

9 shd **Simla Sunset (IRE)**[17] 7030 4-9-2 87 (t) SMLevey 10 87
(P J Prendergast, Ire) *mid-div: 7th appr st: sn rdn and no imp* **25/1**

10 1 1/4 **Finicius (USA)**[63] 5774 6-9-5 105 (t) KJManning 8 88
(Eoin Griffin, Ire) *hld up towards rr: swtchd to outer for effrt ent st: rdn and no imp* **14/1**

11 1 3/4 **Riynaaz (IRE)**[12] 7140 3-8-12 FMBerry 11 83
(John M Oxx, Ire) *trckd ldrs in 5th: wknd early st* **17/2**

12 3 **Choose Me (IRE)**[12] 7140 4-9-2 106 DPMcDonogh 5 76
(Kevin Prendergast, Ire) *s.i.s and hld up towards rr: no imp st* **6/1**[3]

2m 12.29s (132.29)
WFA 3 from 4yo+ 5lb **12 Ran SP% 127.4**
CSF £73.95 TOTE £26.70: £4.60, £1.40, £2.20; DF 159.30.
Owner Mark Gittins **Bred** Dapple Bloodstock Et Al **Trained** Duleek, Co Meath

FOCUS
A surprise result to this Listed race, in which very few were in contention. A big pesonal bestd from the winner, with the third helping with the form.

NOTEBOOK
Shimmering Moment(USA), formerly with Henry Cecil, wore blinkers for the first time. Her rider was brave enough to take on a typical Mark Johnston pacesetter but it paid off. She had plenty to find at the weights, her rating based on UK form, but she is well accustomed to being ridden positively and was in control at the death, though there has to be the chance that the main horses underperformed at the end of a hard season. The owner will decide whether she stays in training or not. (op 14/1)
Bob Le Beau(IRE) did not fancy going into the stalls and he was the only one to get into it from off the pace. He is rated 15lb higher than the winner, but has been an excellent servant this season. (op 100/30 tchd 7/2)
Bikini Babe(IRE) did not get an entirely contested lead but showed good courage to rally when headed. She had every chance. (op 100/30)
You'll Be Mine(USA) was a little unlucky not to earn some black-type placing. She had momentum on her side when checked in the final furlong. She has been disappointing this season. (op 8/1 tchd 9/1)
Northgate(IRE) was never likely to win over this trip from where he had to come from. (op 10/1)
Indiana Gal(IRE) won the race last year but she has generally struggled since and never got remotely involved. (op 16/1)
Choose Me(IRE) might be feeling the effects of a tough campaign. (op 11/2)

7359 - (Foreign Racing) - See Raceform Interactive

7339 CHURCHILL DOWNS (L-H)
Saturday, November 6

OFFICIAL GOING: Dirt: fast;turf: firm

7360a BREEDERS' CUP JUVENILE TURF (GRADE 2) (2YO COLTS & GELDINGS) 1m (T)
5:50 (5:51) 2-Y-O £333,333 (£111,111; £61,111; £37,037; £18,518)

RPR

1 **Pluck (USA)**[49] 2-8-10 0 GKGomez 12 113+
(Todd Pletcher, U.S.A) *propped s and settled in last: sltly hmpd by faller on first bnd: racd 5 l adrift of field: shkn up 2 1/2f out: last but on terms w pack 2f out: pushed along and running on in 6th whn swtchd outside 1f out: led 75yds out* **9/1**

2 1 **Soldat (USA)**[34] 2-8-10 0 AGarcia 8 111
(Kiaran McLaughlin, U.S.A) *racd freely w ldrs early on: settled in 5th after 2f: 4th on rail 2f out: r.o u.p to ld 110yds out: hdd 75yds out: no ex* **7/1**[3]

The Form Book, Raceform Ltd, Compton, RG20 6NL

3	1 1/2	**Willcox Inn (USA)**[28] 6758 2-8-10 0 JRVelazquez 6 (Michael Stidham, U.S.A) *racd in midfield: 6th 3f out but sn outpcd and pushed along: looked to be making little imp in 7th 1f out: styd on wl u.p fnl 110yds to snatch 3rd on the line* **20/1**	108
4	hd	**Madman Diaries (USA)**[63] 2-8-10 0 (b) JASanchez 9 (Wesley A Ward, U.S.A) *led: pressed 4f out but sn asserted again: jst over 1 l up and u.p 2f out: r.o gamely: hdd appr fnl 110yds: unable qck* **20/1**	107
5	hd	**Banned (USA)**[20] 2-8-10 0 JRosario 7 (Thomas F Proctor, U.S.A) *settled in 4th: hdwy on outside 3f out: pressed ldr 2f out: sn strly rdn: all but led appr fnl 110yds: no ex* **8/1**	107
6	nk	**Master Of Hounds (USA)**[14] 7081 2-8-10 0 JMurtagh 4 (A P O'Brien, Ire) *dwlt s: settled towards rr: tk clsr order 3 1/2f out: disputing 7th over 2f out: sn u.p and nt qckn: styd on at one pce fnl 110yds* **10/3**[1]	106
7	nse	**Utley (USA)**[34] 6610 2-8-10 0 WilliamBuick 5 (J H M Gosden) *a in bk four: swtchd outside 2f out: styd on steadily u.p fnl f: nvr nr enough to be a threat* **6/1**[2]	106
8	1/2	**Humble And Hungry (USA)**[27] 2-8-10 0 OlivierPeslier 11 (Ignacio Correas IV, U.S.A) *stmbld s: sn rcvrd and chsd ldr tl rdn and wknd fnl f* **33/1**	105
9	2 1/4	**Air Support (USA)**[34] 2-8-10 0 RMaragh 3 (Claude McGaughey III, U.S.A) *trckd ldng pair: rdn and wknd ins fnl 2f* **8/1**	100
10	hd	**Mantoba**[22] 6884 2-8-10 0 FrankieDettori 2 (B J Meehan) *racd in midfield: 4 l off ld 2f out: sn rdn: wknd u.p 1 1/2f out* **6/1**[2]	99
11	3/4	**Deciphering Dreams (USA)**[34] 2-8-10 0 RADominguez 1 (Richard Dutrow Jr, U.S.A) *a bhd: nvr a factor* **28/1**	97
S		**Rough Sailing (USA)**[28] 6758 2-8-10 0 (b) AnnaNapravnik 10 (Michael Stidham, U.S.A) *towards rr and pulling hrd: lost hind legs first bnd and slipped up* **33/1**	—

1m 36.98s (2.15) **12** Ran SP% **115.2**

PARI-MUTUEL (all including $2 stakes): WIN 14.80; PLACE (1-2) 6.60, 5.20; SHOW (1-2-3) 5.00, 4.00, 8.80; SF 72.00.

Owner Team Valor International **Bred** Team Valor **Trained** USA

FOCUS

The fourth running of this race, and following wins for British-trained horses in the last two renewals, the prize stayed at home this time. Tricky form to gauge, but the seventh and tenth help.

NOTEBOOK

Pluck(USA), despite being slightly hampered by the faller on the first bend, he came from well off the pace to run down the entire field and win cosily. Events probably conspired in his favour as things turned out, but he looks pretty talented nonetheless.

Soldat(USA) mixed it with the leaders early before being dropped back to a stalking position. He saved ground on the inside and had his chance, but when the winner came by it looked as though he was standing still.

Willcox Inn(USA), a winner on Polytrack on his debut and third in a Grade 1 on dirt second time out, demonstrated his versatility again. He didn't have much room on the inside up the straight but stayed on well in the final stages to grab third.

Madman Diaries(USA), stepping up from 6f, took them along at a good clip and the only surprising thing was that he wasn't seen off before the half-furlong pole.

Banned(USA) was restrained back in fourth place early before attacking around the final bend, but try as he might he couldn't get past the leader Madman Diaries, and in the end the pair were run out of the places.

Master Of Hounds(USA), third in the Racing Post Trophy last time out, tracked Banned through as he challenged on the final bend but couldn't muster the pace to get in a real blow. It wasn't a bad run, but neither did he boost the form of the Doncaster race.

Utley(USA), fifth in the Prix Jean-Luc Lagardere on his final start, was expected to appreciate this quicker ground. He stayed on nicely in the closing stages and was never nearer than when they crossed the line, but the winner finished so much faster.

Mantoba looked to face a stiff task having only won a conditions race at Newmarket last time. Tightened up early and forced to drop back in the field, he stuck to the inside the whole way but was a beaten horse early in the straight.

7361a SENTIENT JET BREEDERS' CUP SPRINT (GRADE 1) (3YO+) (DIRT) 6f (D)

6:30 (6:31) 3-Y-0+ **£666,666** (£222,222; £122,222; £74,074; £37,037)

			RPR
1		**Big Drama (USA)**[63] 5779 4-9-0 0 (b) ECoa 1 (David Fawkes, U.S.A) *broke wl and led after 110yds: mde rest: 2 l clr ins fnl 2f: sn rdn and styd on gamely: nvr really chal* **5/1**[1]	122
2	1 1/2	**Hamazing Destiny (USA)**[54] 4-9-0 0 JRosario 4 (D Wayne Lukas, U.S.A) *racd in bk three: tk clsr order 2 1/2f out: 8th and running on up outside 1 1/2f out: styd on wl to take 2nd fnl 50yds: unable to rch wnr* **25/1**	118
3	nk	**Smiling Tiger (USA)**[27] 3-8-12 0 RBaze 5 (Jeff Bonde, U.S.A) *chsd ldng trio: qcknd to go 2nd 1 1/2f out: kpt on tl fdd sltly and lost 2nd fnl 50yds* **13/2**[2]	115
4	hd	**Supreme Summit (USA)**[27] 4-9-0 0 GKGomez 9 (Mike Puype, U.S.A) *wd: last fr 3f out: stl last 1 1/2f out but r.o u.p down wd outside to take 4th cl home: nvr nrr* **14/1**	116
5	1/2	**Warrior's Reward (USA)**[29] 4-9-0 0 JRLeparoux 12 (Ian Wilkes, U.S.A) *towards rr: smooth hdwy on outside over 2f out: 9th 1 1/2f out: styd on wout having pce to chal* **10/1**	115
6	nk	**Wise Dan (USA)**[29] 3-8-12 0 RBejarano 3 (Charles Lopresti, U.S.A) *midfield: 8th appr 2f out: styd on to go 3rd 1 1/2f out: no ex fnl 100yds* **8/1**	112
7	4	**Kinsale King (USA)**[120] 3870 5-9-0 0 (b) MGarcia 7 (Carl O'Callaghan, U.S.A) *chsd ldng gp: 6th 2 1/2f out: nt qckn u.p fr 1 1/2f out* **10/1**	102
8	3/4	**Cash Refund (USA)**[133] 4-9-0 0 (b) JRVelazquez 8 (Steve Margolis, U.S.A) *broke wl: led first 110yds: chsd ldr: 2nd and rdn whn bmpd by smiling tiger over 1 1/2f out: unable qck u.p* **20/1**	99
9	nk	**Riley Tucker (USA)**[35] 6582 5-9-0 0 (b) RADominguez 10 (Steven Asmussen, U.S.A) *racd in middle of pack: hdwy on outside to go 5th 2 1/2f out: no imp fnl 300yds* **12/1**	98
10	1 3/4	**Atta Boy Roy (USA)**[28] 5-9-0 0 CHBorel 11 (Valorie Lund, U.S.A) *a.p: cl 3rd on outside 2f out: sn rdn and nt qckn: wknd fnl 1 1/2f* **7/1**[3]	93
11	4 1/2	**Girolamo (USA)**[35] 6582 4-9-0 0 AGarcia 2 (Saeed Bin Suroor) *chsd ldrs on rail: 7th and pushed along 2 1/2f out: sn rdn and btn* **5/1**[1]	80
12	1/2	**Pashito The Che (USA)**[24] 4-9-0 0 JJCastellano 6 (Scott Lake, U.S.A) *nvr in contention: bhd fr 2f out* **25/1**	78

69.05 secs (-0.35) **12** Ran SP% **115.3**

PARI-MUTUEL (all including $2 stakes): WIN 12.40; PLACE (1-2) 7.00, 19.80; SHOW (1-2-3) 5.00, 12.20, 5.00; SF 254.80.

Owner Harold L Queen **Bred** Harold L Queen **Trained** USA

FOCUS

Two of the top sprinters in North America, Discreetly Mine and Majesticperfection, missed the race through injury, and as such, this was a far from vintage renewal. It paid to be prominent.

NOTEBOOK

Big Drama(USA) paid a big complement to the absent Majesticperfection, having been comprehensively defeated by that rival in a Saratoga Grade 1 in August. The winner looked to have the worst possible draw, but crucially he made a bright start and was soon in front. Sensibly taken away from the possibly unfavoured inside rail, his lead was never seriously threatened and he ran on well enough for a convincing success, his first at this level.

Hamazing Destiny(USA) stayed on from well off the pace without ever looking like the winner. This is as good as he is.

Smiling Tiger(USA), a dual Grade 1 winner on synthetics, including last time, was unproven on dirt but handled the surface well, keeping on having been handy throughout.

Supreme Summit(USA) raced in a detached last for much of the way but ran on for strong pressure down the outside in the straight.

Warrior's Reward(USA) travelled okay towards the rear but failed to pick up sufficiently when asked. He's probably better suited by 7f.

Girolamo(USA) looked a live contender judged on his Vosburgh win, but that was only a month ago and perhaps it took the edge off him. He was never going at any stage and finished up well beaten.

7362a BREEDERS' CUP TURF SPRINT (GRADE 2) (3YO+) 5f

7:15 (7:17) 3-Y-0+ **£333,333** (£111,111; £61,111; £37,037; £18,518)

			RPR
1		**Chamberlain Bridge (USA)**[28] 6-9-0 0 (b) HJTheriotII 1 (W Bret Calhoun, U.S.A) *settled in midfield on rail: shuffled bk appr 1/2-way: 8th 2f out: swtchd outside: r.o strly u.p appr fnl f: led fnl 50yds: won gng away* **6/1**[2]	121+
2	1 1/2	**Central City (USA)**[28] 4-9-0 0 (b) RAlbarado 2 (Ronny Werner, U.S.A) *broke wl and led: 2 l clr 1 1/2f out: r.o gamely u.p: hdd fnl 50yds: no ex* **12/1**	116
3	1 1/4	**Unzip Me (USA)**[36] 4-8-11 0 RBejarano 4 (Martin F Jones, U.S.A) *chsd along in middle of pack: 6th on rail 2f out: kpt on u.p fnl f* **9/1**	108
4	nse	**Bridgetown (USA)**[21] 6949 3-8-12 0 ElvisTrujillo 7 (Kenneth McPeek, U.S.A) *a.p: chsd ldr fr over 2f out: chal ldr ins fnl f: unable qck* **20/1**	109
5	nse	**Silver Timber (USA)**[28] 7-9-0 0 (b) JRLeparoux 5 (Chad C Brown, U.S.A) *chsd ldrs: 5th 1/2-way: 4th and keeping on u.p 1f out: checked 110yds out: styd on again cl home* **4/1**[1]	111
6	hd	**Due Date (USA)**[28] 5-9-0 0 (b) GKGomez 10 (Steve Margolis, U.S.A) *squeezed out early and racd in last: hdwy on rail 2f out: styd on wl fnl 150yds: nrest at fin* **20/1**	110
7	1 1/4	**Rose Catherine (USA)**[42] 3-8-9 0 JJCastellano 9 (Todd Pletcher, U.S.A) *racd in fnl 3rd: 12th 2f out: styd on fnl 300yds: n.d* **6/1**[2]	101
8	1/2	**California Flag (USA)**[28] 6-9-0 0 (b) VEspinoza 12 (Brian Koriner, U.S.A) *pushed along early fr outside draw: racd in rr: hdwy into midfield 2 1/2f out: no imp fr 1 1/2f out: styd on late* **14/1**	104
9	nk	**Grand Adventure (USA)**[21] 6949 4-9-0 0 PHusbands 11 (Mark Frostad, Canada) *in rr: forced v wd fnl turn: mde sme late hdwy: nvr in contention* **12/1**	103
10	1 1/4	**Quick Enough (USA)**[25] 6-9-0 0 PValenzuela 8 (Doug O'Neill, U.S.A) *a bhd* **8/1**[3]	98
11	hd	**Waveline (USA)**[36] 5-8-11 0 FrankieDettori 6 (B Cecil, U.S.A) *racd in 5th and 6th: rdn and unable qck 2f out: wknd fnl 110yds* **33/1**	94
12	3/4	**Tropic Storm (USA)**[28] 6-9-0 0 (b[1]) DFlores 13 (Craig Dollase, U.S.A) *chsd ldrs: 4th 1/2-way: rdn over 2f out: fdd appr fnl 110yds* **20/1**	95
13	hd	**Stradivinsky (USA)**[61] 7-9-0 0 JRVelazquez 3 (Richard Dutrow Jr, U.S.A) *gd early spd to chse ldr: cl 2nd and ev ch 2f out: began to drop away u.p fnl 1 1/2f* **10/1**	94
14	10	**Canadian Ballet (USA)**[22] 5-8-11 0 (b) KDesormeaux 14 (Linda Rice, U.S.A) *pressed ldng gp: lost pl 2 1/2f out: c v wd fnl bnd: last and unable to make any impact fnl 2f: eased fnl f* **40/1**	55

56.53 secs (56.53) **14** Ran SP% **120.5**

PARI-MUTUEL (all including $2 stakes): WIN 15.80; PLACE (1-2) 8.20, 9.80; SHOW (1-2-3) 5.60, 7.80, 7.00; SF 156.20.

Owner Carl R Moore Management LLC **Bred** Eugene Melnyk **Trained** North America

FOCUS

The third running of this event but, in contrast to the previous two years when it was run over 6.5f, this was the first time it had been staged over 5f. With plenty of horses in the race wanting to be up there making it, a strong pace looked assured, and it was no surprise to see the winner finishing late from behind. A high draw is very tough to overcome over this C&D, and that trend continued, with four of the first five drawn in the bottom five stalls. The winner is rated back to his C/D best.

NOTEBOOK

Chamberlain Bridge(USA) had good C&D form to his name and likes to challenge from off the pace, so he had quite a bit going for him. He saved ground on the inside for the first half of the race, before being switched out to challenge at just the right time in the straight. He came home really strongly once in the clear and, although things fell perfectly for him, credit must go to his rider, who very much played his part. It was a second success at the meeting for the trainer/jockey combination following Dubai Majesty's victory in the Filly & Mare Sprint the previous day.

Central City(USA) showed bright speed from his favourable gate, raced nearest the rail and held the call throughout until the winner ran him down inside the last. It was a fine effort in defeat.

Unzip Me(USA), eased back from disputing the early lead, was dropped in on the rail and that helped her stay on for the minor placing. She's probably at her best over 6f, though.

Bridgetown(USA), runner-up to Pounced in the Juvenile Turf last season, has since shown himself to be more effective over sprint distances. Drawn in stall seven, he showed good early speed but got trapped three wide the whole way round the bend. Although he challenged the runner-up strongly inside the last, that effort eventually told and he dropped out of the places close home. It was a mighty effort, though, and he was arguably the best horse in the race.

Silver Timber(USA) eventually got to the inside halfway round the bend and had his chance in the straight, but he wasn't quite good enough. He'd have probably edged third place had the winner not crossed slightly in front of him inside the last, though.

Due Date(USA) is a hold-up horse but had a tough draw to overcome. His rider eased him back early and dropped him in on the rail, and hoped the gaps would appear for him and allow him to challenge late. He was staying on at the finish up the inside and, while never really fast enough, it was a fair effort from a horse who wouldn't really be up to this level.

Rose Catherine(USA), the only 3-y-o filly in the line-up, had a tough draw and struggled to get involved having been caught wide much of the way.

California Flag(USA) won this race last year when it was run over an extra furlong and a half, and although she stayed on at the finish she wasn't quite quick enough over this shorter trip.

7363a GREY GOOSE BREEDERS' CUP JUVENILE (GRADE 1) (2YO COLTS & GELDINGS) (DIRT) 1m 110y(D)

7:55 (7:56) 2-Y-O £666,666 (£222,222; £122,222; £74,074; £37,037)

RPR

1 **Uncle Mo (USA)**28 6756 2-8-10 0 JRVelazquez 7 124+
(Todd Pletcher, U.S.A) *broke wl and qckly tk up position trcking ldr: smoothly jnd ldr over 2 1/2f out: led ins fnl 2f: sn clr: pushed out fnl f: impressive* 7/4[1]

2 4 1/4 **Boys At Tosconova (USA)**61 5827 2-8-10 0 RADominguez 2 115
(Richard Dutrow Jr, U.S.A) *disp 5th early: shared 3rd over 5f out: cl 3rd and pushed along 2f out: r.o u.p to take 2nd ins fnl 1 1/2f: no ch w wnr* 11/4[2]

3 6 **Rogue Romance (USA)**27 2-8-10 0 JRLeparoux 9 101
(Kenneth McPeek, U.S.A) *settled towards rr: hdwy over 2 1/2f out: 7th 2f out: styd on u.p to take 3rd fnl 110yds: nvr cl enough to chal* 16/1

4 1 3/4 **Biondetti (USA)**28 6762 2-8-10 0 AhmedAjtebi 1 98
(Mahmood Al Zarooni) *racd in midfield: 5th and clsng 3f out: rdn appr fnl 2f: disputing 4th 2f out (abt 1 l off ld): wnt 3rd but only plugging on 1f out: lost 3rd 110yds out* 16/1

5 2 1/2 **Stay Thirsty (USA)**61 5827 2-8-10 0 JJCastellano 6 92
(Todd Pletcher, U.S.A) *racd in 5th: hdwy on outside 2 1/2f out: on heels on ldng trio turning for home: sn rdn: wknd u.p* 10/1

6 1 **J P's Gusto (USA)**35 6587 2-8-10 0 PValenzuela 4 90
(David Hofmans, U.S.A) *settled in rr: mde sme prog fr 3f out: 8th 2f out: kpt on at one pce u.p: nvr in contention* 16/1

7 1/2 **Jaycito (USA)**35 6587 2-8-10 0 (b) MESmith 10 89
(Mike Mitchell, U.S.A) *last: rn v wd bnd into bkst: stl adrift in last 2f out: styd on fnl 300yds: n.d* 7/1[3]

8 nk **Riveting Reason (USA)**35 6587 2-8-10 0 (b1) VEspinoza 5 88
(Myung Kwon Cho, U.S.A) *broke wl and led: jnd by wnr 2 1/2f out: hdd ins fnl 2f: fdd u.p fr 1 1/2f out* 40/1

9 2 **J. B.'s Thunder (USA)**28 6758 2-8-10 0 SXBridgmohan 3 84
(Albert M Stall Jr, U.S.A) *prom in share of 3rd and 4th: rdn and lost pl 2 1/2f out: wknd 1 1/2f out: rdr twice looked down fnl f* 14/1

10 1/2 **Murjan (USA)**48 2-8-10 0 RBejarano 8 83
(Darrin Miller, U.S.A) *settled in middle of field early: lost pl 5f out: rdn and no imp fnl 3f* 33/1

1m 42.6s (-1.77) 10 Ran SP% 114.3
PARI-MUTUEL (all including $2 stakes): WIN 4.80; PLACE (1-2) 3.40, 4.20; SHOW (1-2-3) 2.60, 3.40, 4.20; SF 17.80.

Owner Repole Stable **Bred** D Michael Cavey Dvm **Trained** USA

FOCUS

A truly top-class performance from Uncle Mo, who looks a brilliant racehorse in the making. He is rated on a par with recenty winners of this event.

NOTEBOOK

Uncle Mo(USA) ◆ seemed the real deal coming into this, having won a Saratoga maiden on debut by more than 14l, before following up in an incredibly quick time in the Champagne Stakes, and he confirmed his status at the country's leading juvenile. The winning rider was oozing confidence down the back straight, looking around for dangers, and this colt, who has a huge stride, lengthened impressively when asked. What makes this performance particularly special is that the runner-up looks a high-class type in his own right and was in turn well clear of the rest, but could get nowhere near Uncle Mo. Incidentally, the time was 2.57 seconds quicker than Awesome Feather recorded in the fillies' equivalent the day before. Only Street Sense has won both this race and the Kentucky Derby but, interestingly enough, the year that horse won the Juvenile the race was staged at Churchill Downs. A lot can go wrong between now and next May, but Uncle Mo has the physical scope to make a 3-y-o and has now proven himself at the Derby track. The 8-1 available with Coral and Ladbrokes is fair.

Boys At Tosconova(USA), winner of the Grade 1 Hopeful Stakes over 7f at Saratoga on his previous start, ran a mighty race in second, pulling a long way clear of the others, but he just ran into an exceptional type.

Rogue Romance(USA) proved himself on dirt but was nowhere near the level of the front two.

Biondetti(USA), unbeaten in three starts in Europe, the latest an Italian Group 1, was far from ideally drawn but he travelled well, taking to the dirt through the opening stages. He didn't see his race out, though, fading in the straight.

Stay Thirsty(USA) ran below the form he showed when chasing home Boys At Tosconova on his previous start.

J P's Gusto(USA) has shown himself to be really smart on synthetics, but he wasn't the same horse switched to dirt.

Jaycito(USA), who had J P's Gusto behind when winning the Grade 1 Norfolk Stakes on synthetics last time, ran a bizarre race switched to the dirt. He got caught on heels on the first bend, and then heading down the back straight he went extremely wide, virtually going over to the far rail and ending up in a detached last. He did well to get so close.

7364a TVG BREEDERS' CUP MILE (GRADE 1) (3YO+) (TURF) 1m (T)

8:40 (8:40) 3-Y-O+ £666,666 (£222,222; £122,222; £74,074; £37,037)

RPR

1 **Goldikova (IRE)**34 6611 5-8-11 0 OlivierPeslier 10 125+
(F Head, France) *settled in 5th on outside first turn (bmpd w delegator): racd in 6th fr 5f out: hdwy on outside 1 1/2f out: qcknd to ld 160yds out: sn clr: r.o wl* 6/4[1]

2 1 3/4 **Gio Ponti (USA)**28 6759 5-9-0 0 RADominguez 3 123
(Christophe Clement, U.S.A) *hld up towards rr: began to cl over 2 1/2f out: 8th w 2f to run: r.o ins fnl 1 1/2f to take 2nd cl home: nvr threatened wnr* 5/1[2]

3 nk **The Usual Q. T. (USA)**48 6237 4-9-0 0 VEspinoza 7 122
(James Cassidy, U.S.A) *tk fierce hold first 2f: settled in 4th: outpcd briefly and lost a pl or two 2 1/2f out: sn running on again and disp 3rd 2f out: r.o fnl 300yds: no ex fnl 50yds and lost 2nd* 33/1

4 nse **Paco Boy (IRE)**34 6611 5-9-0 0 RyanMoore 6 122+
(R Hannon) *hld up in 8th: lost grnd fnl bnd and bk to next to last 2f out: r.o u.p fnl f: nvr nrr* 11/2[3]

5 3/4 **Court Vision (USA)**48 6237 5-9-0 0 (b) RAlbarado 4 120
(Richard Dutrow Jr, U.S.A) *settled in 7th (jst in front of paco boy): disputing 7th w goldikova 2f out: sn rdn: styd on wout having the pce to chal the first four* 16/1

6 nk **Sidney's Candy (USA)**83 3-8-11 0 JRosario 9 118
(John W Sadler, U.S.A) *smartly away and led: 2 l clr ins fnl 2f: r.o u.p: hdd by wnr 160yds out: wknd fnl 100yds* 7/1

7 3 **Proviso**28 6757 5-8-11 0 MESmith 11 110
(William Mott, U.S.A) *hld up towards rr: c wd and lost grnd fnl turn: last 2f out: no real imp* 10/1

8 hd **Delegator**21 6923 4-9-0 0 FrankieDettori 5 112
(Saeed Bin Suroor) *bmpd w goldikova first bnd: sn racing in ldng quartet: rdn and grad fdd appr 2f out* 16/1

9 2 1/2 **Society's Chairman (CAN)**28 6759 7-9-0 0 JRLeparoux 2 106
(Roger L Attfield, Canada) *bhd tl sme hdwy 1 1/2f out: no ex fnl f* 66/1

10 1/2 **Beethoven (IRE)**36 6548 3-8-11 0 (b) JMurtagh 1 104
(A P O'Brien, Ire) *w ldng trio: wnt 2nd 2f out: sn rdn: wknd fnl f* 25/1

11 5 1/2 **Get Stormy (USA)**28 6759 4-9-0 0 JJCastellano 8 93
(Thomas Bush, U.S.A) *chsd ldr in front trio: rdn and dropped away ins fnl 300yds* 50/1

1m 35.16s (0.33)
WFA 3 from 4yo+ 2lb 11 Ran SP% 115.6
PARI-MUTUEL (all including $2 stakes): WIN 4.60; PLACE (1-2) 3.20, 4.00; SHOW (1-2-3) 2.40, 3.20, 6.60; SF 18.20.

Owner Wertheimer & Frere **Bred** Wertheimer Et Frere **Trained** France

FOCUS

History was made in this 27th running of the Mile as Goldikova became the first three-time winner at the Breeders' Cup. She rates a cosy winner.

NOTEBOOK

Goldikova(IRE)'s outside draw and trouble in running looked the main obstacles to her recording a third consecutive win in this race, but she overcame the former and avoided the latter to sprint home for a most decisive victory. Although forced to race wider than ideal the whole way round, the decent pace up front helped her to settle well and, once into the straight and unleashed, she produced a most amazing burst of speed to swoop past those in front and win easily. Now the winner of 15 of her 21 starts, an incredible 12 of which have come in Group 1 company, she had been due to be retired at the end of this season, but there are now suggestions that her connections might be reconsidering. It would be some feat if she returned here next year and defended her title for a third time (Hills go 7-2), but right now there isn't a miler in the world that can touch her, so it's to be hoped that she does race on.

Gio Ponti(USA) looked the main home challenger on paper. Second in the Classic last season on the Pro-Ride surface at Santa Anita, he's not so good on dirt, so this race was considered a better option this time around. Having won the Grade 1 Turf Mile at Keeneland last time out, he came here at the top of his game, was given a fine, hold-up ride and delivered at the right time. He simply wasn't good enough to beat a superstar mare.

The Usual Q. T.(USA), who had his ideal conditions, made things hard for himself by failing to settle in the early stages, so it's to his credit that he didn't weaken out of things but got involved in the battle for the places. It no doubt helped that he was able to save ground on the inside.

Paco Boy(IRE), patiently ridden, was tracking Goldikova through but then dropped back on the turn out of the back straight before staying on strongly, but all too late, in the closing stages. This was the fifth time in five meetings that he's finished behind the mare. He now retires to stud. Ryan Moore said the ground was too quick for the horse and that he didn't handle the sharp bend.

Court Vision(USA), who defeated The Usual Q.T. in the Grade 1 Woodbine Mile last time out, couldn't confirm that form, but probably didn't run that far off the level of form he showed when fourth in this race last year.

Sidney's Candy(USA), one of two 3-y-os in the field, threatened to be let loose on the lead as he looked the only front-runner in the line-up, but in the event he set a true gallop and kicked for home quite some way out, which meant he was a sitting duck with a furlong to run. He has the potential for further improvement and could be much harder to catch if returning next year.

Proviso arrived here on the back of four straight wins in Grade 1 company. Ridden patiently as usual, she was forced widest of all rounding the turn into the straight and could never really get involved. She's better than this.

Delegator, not for the first time, failed to see out his race over a mile. His Celebration Mile win came in a tactical affair, but he has consistently shown that in a race run at a decent gallop he is vulnerable over this trip.

Beethoven(IRE), in second place turning in, dropped out tamely from there. Since running out a narrow winner of the Dewhurst, he's been consistently exposed as below the standard required to win at Group 1 level.

7365a BREEDERS' CUP DIRT MILE (GRADE 1) (3YO+) (DIRT) 1m

9:20 (9:22) 3-Y-O+ £333,333 (£111,111; £61,111; £37,037; £18,518)

RPR

1 **Dakota Phone (USA)**34 6605 5-9-0 0 JRosario 1 119
(Jerry Hollendorfer, U.S.A) *settled last (wl adrift of the main pack): hdwy on outside ins fnl 2f: 8th and styng on 1f out: r.o strly fnl 100yds to get up on line* 25/1

2 hd **Morning Line (USA)**42 3-8-11 0 JJCastellano 9 118
(Nicholas Zito, U.S.A) *a.p: on outside of three ldrs 3f out: led appr fnl 2f: r.o u.p: 2 l clr 110yds out: ct on line* 15/2

3 1 1/4 **Gayego (USA)**56 5-9-0 0 FrankieDettori 6 116
(Saeed Bin Suroor) *settled 9th on outside: r.o fr 2 1/2f out: 7th and styng on 1 1/2f out: wnt 3rd w 110yds to run: kpt on wl* 7/1[3]

4 3 **Cool Coal Man (USA)**34 6602 5-9-0 0 JRLeparoux 12 110
(Nicholas Zito, U.S.A) *racd in midfield: hdwy on outside over 2f out: wnt 2nd appr fnl f: wknd fnl 110yds* 28/1

5 nk **Tizway (USA)**34 6602 5-9-0 0 (b) RMaragh 2 109
(Harold James Bond, U.S.A) *a.p: in middle of line of three ldrs 3f out: 3rd ins fnl 2f: unable qck fr 1 1/2f out* 9/2[2]

6 1 1/2 **Vineyard Haven (USA)**63 5779 4-9-0 0 (b) AGarcia 11 106
(Saeed Bin Suroor) *broke smartly and led early: sn settled in share of 3rd: cl 4th 3f out: disputing 2nd and ev ch ins fnl 2f: n.m.r ins fnl f: unable qck* 8/1

7 nse **Thiskyhasnolimit (USA)**35 6588 3-8-11 0 HJTheriotll 7 105
(Steven Asmussen, U.S.A) *settled towards rr of main gp (mine that bird and dakota phone were wl adrift): hdwy over 2 1/2f out: disputing 5th 1 1/2f out: one pce fnl f: fdd fnl 75yds* 8/1

8 1/2 **Aikenite (USA)**22 3-8-11 0 JRVelazquez 3 104
(Todd Pletcher, U.S.A) *nvr beyond mid-div: nvr in contention* 40/1

9 4 **Hurricane Ike (USA)**42 3-8-11 0 (b) CHBorel 8 96
(John W Sadler, U.S.A) *sn led: ins line of three ldrs 3f out: 2nd and u.p 1 1/2f out: wknd fnl f* 20/1

10 nse **Mine That Bird (USA)**63 5780 4-9-0 0 (b) MESmith 10 97
(D Wayne Lukas, U.S.A) *wl adrift of main pack fr s: a bhd: nvr a factor* 20/1

11 1 1/2 **Here Comes Ben (USA)**63 5779 4-9-0 0 (b) ASolis 5 94
(Charles Lopresti, U.S.A) *disp 7th and 8th: tk clsr order on rail 3 1/2f out: 7th appr 1 1/2f out: no imp: fdd fnl f but nt given a hrd time* 3/1[1]

12 7 3/4 **Mad Flatter (USA)**21 5-9-0 0 JKCourt 4 79
(Jeffrey D Thornbury, U.S.A) *racd in 5th: grad fdd fr 2f out* 20/1

1m 35.29s (95.29)
WFA 3 from 4yo+ 2lb 12 Ran SP% 113.7
PARI-MUTUEL (all including $2 stakes): WIN 77.40; PLACE (1-2) 27.20, 7.40; SHOW (1-2-3) 14.60, 5.20, 6.80; SF 816.20.

Owner John Carver, Halo Farms et al **Bred** Cashmark Farms Inc & Dakota Stables **Trained** USA

FOCUS

After two successive runnings on synthetics at Santa Anita, the Dirt Mile was back on the surface it's named after. This looked a quality edition beforehand, but Dakota Phone, impossible to find beforehand, caused an upset.

NOTEBOOK

Dakota Phone(USA) had to prove himself on the surface, and in truth he simply didn't look good enough. However, he was well suited by being held up off the quick, disputed pace, and stayed on best of all down the outside in the straight.

Morning Line(USA) ◆, a Grade 2 winner on his previous start, ran a mighty race. Although beaten into second by an outsider, that doesn't tell the whole story - this was the performance of a top-class colt. Pretty much from the off he was caught up in a speed war with three others horses, all of whom dropped away (Tizway, Vineyard Haven and Hurricane Ike), so he did remarkably well to finish so close. A lightly raced improver, expect to see him back here next year for the Classic.

Gayego(USA), a close fourth in last year's Sprint, is better suited by this trip now and ran his race.

Cool Coal Man(USA), a stable companion of the runner-up, ran well without proving himself up to the class.

Tizway(USA) had solid form credentials, but paid for doing too much too soon.

Vineyard Haven(USA) was unable to dominate and ended up going too fast. He has won over this trip, but looks all speed these days.

Here Comes Ben(USA) outstayed the Sprint winner Big Drama when winning the Grade 1 Forego Stakes over 7f last time, but he proved hugely disappointing this time. The trip probably stretched him, but even so, a little better could have been expected.

7366a EMIRATES AIRLINE BREEDERS' CUP TURF (GRADE 1) (3YO+) 1m 4f (T)

10:00 (10:01) 3-Y-O£1,000,000 (£333,333; £183,333; £111,111; £55,555)

RPR

1 **Dangerous Midge (USA)**[50] 6148 4-9-0 0................(b[1]) FrankieDettori 7 121
(B J Meehan) *sn trcking ldr: rdn and pressed ldr fr 2 1/2f out: ct flat footed and 4th 1 1/2f out: styd on wl u.p fr 1f marker to ld ins fnl 100yds: eased cl home* **5/1[2]**

2 1 ¼ **Champ Pegasus (USA)**[33] 6642 4-9-0 0............................ JRosario 1 119
(Richard E Mandella, U.S.A) *led: pressed by wnr fr 2 1/2f out: hdd ins fnl 100yds: no ex* **16/1**

3 2 **Behkabad (FR)**[34] 6612 3-8-10 0............... Christophe-PatriceLemaire 6 118
(J-C Rouget, France) *settled in 3rd: outpcd for a few strides and pushed along 2 1/2f out: sn rcvrd and smooth hdwy on ins to go 2nd over 1 1/2f out: sn rdn and unable qck fnl f* **11/10[1]**

4 ½ **Winchester (USA)**[35] 6585 5-9-0 0...............................(b) CVelasquez 2 115
(Christophe Clement, U.S.A) *hld up in last pl: hdwy appr 1 1/2f out: 5th ins fnl f: styd on last 100yds: nt pce to chal* **8/1**

5 1 ½ **Debussy (IRE)**[21] 6925 4-9-0 0.. WilliamBuick 4 113
(J H M Gosden) *racd in 5th: hdwy 2f out to chal for 2nd fnl 1 1/2f: sn rdn: unable qck fnl f* **13/2[3]**

6 1 **Telling (USA)**[35] 6585 6-9-0 0.. JJCastellano 3 111
(Steve Hobby, U.S.A) *bided time in 4th: rdn and disp 3rd on outside of bekhabad 2 1/2f out: sn rdn: wknd fnl f* **25/1**

7 2 ½ **Al Khali (USA)**[21] 6951 4-9-0 0.. JRLeparoux 5 107
(William Mott, U.S.A) *a in bk two: bhd fr 1 1/2f out: nvr a factor* **13/2[3]**

2m 29.4s (149.40)
WFA 3 from 4yo+ 6lb **7 Ran SP% 111.8**
PARI-MUTUEL (all including $2 stakes): WIN 19.00; PLACE (1-2) 9.80, 9.00; SHOW (1-2-3) 5.20, 4.80, 2.40; SF 172.60.
Owner Iraj Parvizi **Bred** Tony Holmes & Dr Walter Zent **Trained** Manton, Wilts

FOCUS

The non-appearance of the Derby and Arc winner Workforce on account of the ground weakened the race significantly, as did the subsequent below-par run from the favourite Behkabad, so the bare form looks pretty ordinary for the grade. The early pace was only steady and it paid to race handily. The runner-up is the best guide to the form.

NOTEBOOK

Dangerous Midge(USA) is quite a lazy sort and so his trainer had decided to put blinkers on him for the first time, in the hope they would sharpen him up around this tight track. He was given a fine ride by Dettori, who had him well positioned throughout in what was a tactical affair. He kept him close when the leader began to wind things up leaving the back straight and, even though he got outpaced on the turn, managed to keep the colt within striking distance for the straight, where the colt's stamina really came into play. He came home strongly to win well in the end and give his trainer Brian Meehan a second win in the Turf, following Red Rocks in 2006. A real 1m4f horse, the Japan Cup and Sheema Classic are thought to be on his agenda next, and one would have to imagine that, being such a big sort, a more galloping track than this one would suit him ideally in future.

Champ Pegasus(USA) had won four of his previous five starts, his only defeat coming when stepped up to this distance. Stamina was clearly a concern for him, but he was given every chance of getting home the way the race panned out, as he got an uncontested lead, set a fairly steady pace and tried to nick it off the final bend. In the end he wasn't quite good enough, but it was still a good effort by the horse and jockey.

Behkabad(FR) was the disappointment of the race. Running without Lasix, he tracked Dangerous Midge most of the way and, although the front two put a bit of distance into him exiting the back straight, he was back in prime position entering the straight, where a gap opened up nicely for him on the inside. He didn't accelerate through it as had looked likely though, and could only keep on one-paced. It's possible the ground was too fast for him, but more likely is that this was just one hard race too many at the end of a long season which began back on April 1st. Having come up short here, it's now questionable whether he's done enough to earn a quick retirement to stud, so there must be every chance he'll stay in training as a 4-y-o.

Winchester(USA) is at his best held up way off the pace and brought with a strong, late challenge, but failed to get in a significant blow in this tactical affair.

Debussy(IRE) has looked better than ever this term, winning the Arlington Million and finishing third in the Champion Stakes in his last two starts, but stamina was a worry. Sure enough, having threatened to get involved in the battle for the places early in the straight, he weakened out of it in the closing stages, and the plan now is for him to drop back in trip, with the Dubai World Cup earmarked as his next big target.

Telling(USA), the outsider of the field, is a dual winner of the Grade 1 Sword Dancer at Saratoga, but his form at other tracks hasn't come close to matching that level.

7367a BREEDERS' CUP CLASSIC (GRADE 1) (3YO+) (DIRT) 1m 2f (D)

10:45 (10:46) 3-Y-O£1,666,666 (£555,555; £305,555; £185,185; £92,592)

RPR

1 **Blame (USA)**[35] 6586 4-9-0 0.. GKGomez 5 131
(Albert M Stall Jr, U.S.A) *settled towards rr: hdwy into midfield 2 1/2f out: qcknd appr 2f out: led 1 1/2f out: r.o u.p: 2 1/2 l up 110yds fr home: kpt on gamely: jst hld on* **11/2[3]**

2 hd **Zenyatta (USA)**[34] 6603 6-8-11 0.. MESmith 8 128+
(John Shirreffs, U.S.A) *dwlt at stalls and racd in last 5 l adrift of main gp: tk clsr order on bk st: at bk of tightly bunched field 2f out: swtchd outside appr fnl 1 1/2f and r.o: steadily cut down ldr: jst failed* **11/8[1]**

3 3 ½ **Fly Down (USA)**[35] 6586 3-8-10 0.................................... JRLeparoux 6 124
(Nicholas Zito, U.S.A) *hld up w only zenyatta bhd: tk clsr order fr 3f out: 10th ins fnl 2f (on heels of zenyatta): stl only 9th less than 1f fr home: styd on wl u.p to snatch 3rd cl home* **20/1**

4 nk **Lookin At Lucky (USA)**[35] 6588 3-8-10 0.......................... MGarcia 12 123
(Bob Baffert, U.S.A) *w.w in midfield: 6th 4f out: hdwy w 3f to run: 3rd and ev ch on outside 2f out: led briefly appr fnl 1 1/2f: sn hdd but cl 2nd ins fnl f: unable qck: lost 3rd cl home* **5/1[2]**

5 1 ¾ **Paddy O'Prado (USA)**[35] 6585 3-8-10 0....................... KDesormeaux 2 120
(Dale Romans, U.S.A) *hld up (jst fly down and zenyatta bhd): gd hdwy 2 1/2f out to dispute 5th passing 1 1/2f marker: unable qck u.p ins fnl f* **25/1**

6 3 ½ **Etched (USA)**[28] 5-9-0 0..(b) AGarcia 10 113
(Kiaran McLaughlin, U.S.A) *racd in 5th (more than 5 l adrift of ldng quartet): clsd qckly fr 3 1/2f out: led appr 2f out: hdd appr fnl 1 1/2f: wknd fnl 110yds* **40/1**

7 1 **Musket Man (USA)**[28] 4-9-0 0.. RMaragh 7 111
(Derek S Ryan, U.S.A) *w.w in middle of main pack: hdwy 2 1/2f out: disputing 5th 1 1/2f out: nt qckn fnl f* **25/1**

8 ½ **First Dude (USA)**[42] 3-8-10 0..(b) RAlbarado 4 110+
(Dale Romans, U.S.A) *led: hdd appr 2f out: unable qck (although squeezed for room on rail 1 1/2f out): wknd fnl 110yds* **33/1**

9 ½ **Pleasant Prince (USA)**[27] 3-8-10 0.................................... JRosario 9 109
(Wesley A Ward, U.S.A) *nvr in contention* **66/1**

10 3 ½ **Espoir City (JPN)**[26] 5-9-0 0.. TetsuzoSato 11 102+
(Akio Adachi, Japan) *trckd ldr in quartet that racd more than 5 l clr of rest: wnt 2nd over 2 1/2f out: pressed ldr into st: dropped away last 300yds* **25/1**

11 8 ¼ **Haynesfield (USA)**[35] 6586 4-9-0 0.............................. RADominguez 3 85+
(Steven Asmussen, U.S.A) *trckd ldr in quartet that racd wl clr of rest: 3rd and ev ch 2 1/2f out: wknd w less than 1 1/2f to go* **14/1**

12 6 ½ **Quality Road (USA)**[63] 5780 4-9-0 0.............................. JRVelazquez 1 72+
(Todd Pletcher, U.S.A) *settled in ldng quartet: racd more than 5 l clr of rest: rdn and fdd ins fnl 3f: bhd fr 2f out: eased* **7/1**

2m 2.28s (1.09)
WFA 3 from 4yo+ 4lb **12 Ran SP% 116.5**
PARI-MUTUEL (all including $2 stakes): WIN 12.40; PLACE (1-2) 4.40, 3.60; SHOW (1-2-3) 3.80, 2.80, 8.60; SF 33.20.
Owner Adele B Dilschneider & Claiborne Farm **Bred** Claiborne Farm & Adele B Dilschneider **Trained** USA

FOCUS

One of the most dramatic contests in the history of the Breeders' Cup, a race that will live forever in the memory. The pace was very strong and the third and fifth dictate the level.

NOTEBOOK

Blame(USA) isn't getting much attention right now, and history will remember him as 'the horse who beat Zenyatta', but he's a top-class colt in his own right. He was beaten into second by Haynesfield when that rival was allowed a soft lead in the Jockey Club Gold Cup on his previous start, but this scenario brought out the best in him, and he added to the two Grade 1s he picked up earlier in the year. The excellent Garrett Gomez got the tactics spot on, and the winner was brave when asked to take a narrow gap between rivals early in the straight. He now retires to stud.

Zenyatta(USA) was attempting to extend her unbeaten record to a scarcely believable 20 races, but she was beaten in the most agonising fashion. Away from the synthetic surfaces she's so used to, a slightly more pro-active ride than usual was called for, but the jockey got it horribly wrong. Mike Smith allowed Zenyatta to become detached from the field almost immediately. Passing the winning post for the first time, the mare was a good eight lengths behind the second-last horse, and heading away from the stands' she looked likely to be pulled up. The pace was strong, with four horses opening up a clear advantage going down the back straight, and though Zenyatta had made progress after finally being asked, latching on to the rear of the field, she was still a good 15 lengths off the lead. As the gallop slowed when the early leaders began to fall away on the final bend, the field bunched up, and although still at the back of the pack, it was now clear the favourite was full of running. However, just as she had begun to pass rivals, the momentum she'd started to build up was lost when her path was blocked at the top of the straight, and she was forced to switch around runners. When in the clear she soon came under severe whip pressure, often being given no time to respond, but she ran on gallantly. For much of the closing stages she looked likely to pull off the most unlikely of victories, but the line came a couple of strides too soon. This performance, even in defeat, has to be considered one of the most exceptional of all time.

Fly Down(USA), the Belmont Stakes runner-up, didn't have much room when trying to get going around the turn into the straight, but it's hard to argue he was anything other than third best.

Lookin At Lucky(USA) came wide into the straight and didn't see his race out after looking a big player. The Preakness winner has had a long season.

Paddy O'Prado(USA), who ran in this instead of the Turf, was back on dirt for the first time since his sixth in the Preakness, though he'd previously finished third in the Kentucky Derby. He stayed on from off the pace and was on the heels of the winner at the top of the straight, but he had no more to offer in the last furlong.

Etched(USA) led the main field chasing the four horses who were clear, but he made up his ground on those rivals too quickly, finding himself in front before the straight, and soon had little left. He still managed to confirm recent placings with Musket Man.

First Dude(USA) ◆ fared best of the quartet who raced clear, but had gone off too fast to offer any type of challenge. This fine, big horse is top-class 4-y-o prospect.

Quality Road(USA) had the worst draw, was stuck on the fence for much of the way and couldn't dominate.

7291 FLEMINGTON (L-H)

Saturday, November 6

OFFICIAL GOING: Turf: good to soft

7368a QUEEN'S CUP (GROUP 3 H'CAP) (3YO+) (TURF) 1m 5f

5:25 (12:00) 3-Y-0+

£88,888 (£25,000; £12,500; £6,250; £3,472; £2,777)

RPR

1 **Moudre (AUS)**[7] 7245 5-8-9 0......................................(b) CraigAWilliams 1 108
(Ciaron Maher, Australia) **11/4[1]**

2 ¾ **Capecover (NZ)**[14] 7106 8-8-11 0............................(b) MichellePayne 15 109
(Patrick Payne, Australia) **20/1**

3 shd **Persian Star (AUS)**[14] 7106 6-8-6 0.................................(tp) GlenBoss 8 104
(Robert Smerdon, Australia) **40/1**

4 ½ **Dream Pedlar (AUS)**[10] 6-8-6 0...............................(b) GlynSchofield 6 103
(Troy Blacker, Australia) **40/1**

5 ¾ **Above Average (IRE)**[14] 7106 4-8-9 0.........................(bt) CoreyBrown 5 105
(Lee Freedman, Australia) **6/1[2]**

6 shd **Exceptionally (NZ)**[17] 7032 4-8-6 0.............................. DannyNikolic 16 102
(Terry & Karina O'Sullivan, Australia) **8/1**

7 shd **Eastern Aria (UAE)**[58] 5881 4-8-11 0............................ KerrinMcEvoy 7 107
(M Johnston) *settled on outside of three horses in share of 5th: rdn over 3f out: styd on and disp 3rd 2f out: r.o at same pce but no imp* **7/1[3]**

8 ½ **My Bentley (NZ)**[10] 6-8-6 0... CraigNewitt 9 101
(Michael Kent, Australia) **25/1**

9 *shd* **Faint Perfume (AUS)**[7] 7246 4-8-10 0 .... MichaelRodd 14 105
(Bart Cummings, Australia) **16/1**
10 *nk* **Drunken Sailor (IRE)**[17] 7032 5-9-0 0 ....(b) MarkZahra 11 108
(L M Cumani) *slowly away: settled in rr: last st (2 1/2f out): styd on but nvr rchd chalng position: one pce fnl f* **11/1**
11 *1* **Mr Charlie (NZ)**[17] 7032 5-8-6 0 ....(b) DwayneDunn 10 99
(Peter G Moody, Australia) **8/1**
12 *3* **The Fuzz (NZ)**[10] 8-8-6 0 ....(bt) DeanYendall 13 94
(David Hayes, Australia) **100/1**
13 *1 ½* **Galizani (AUS)** 4-8-6 0 .... JamesWinks 12 92
(John P Thompson, Australia) **30/1**
14 *2 ¾* **Miss Darcey (AUS)**[357] 5-8-7 0 ow1 .... NicholasHall 2 89
(Anthony Cummings, Australia) **25/1**
15 *4* **No Wine No Song (AUS)**[17] 7032 9-9-0 0 ....(b) HughBowman 4 90
(Kevin Moses, Australia) **40/1**
16 *hd* **Sea Galleon (AUS)**[14] 7106 4-8-6 0 ....(bt) BenMelham 3 82
(Colin & Cindy Alderson, Australia) **30/1**

2m 45.22s (165.22) 16 Ran SP% **117.1**
PARI-MUTUEL (NSW TAB - all including au$1 stakes): WIN 3.80 PLACE 1.80, 4.80, 12.30; DF 44.80 SF 64.10.
Owner C B McKenna, Ms J M Thomson et al **Bred** Mrs L M Bensch **Trained** Australia

NOTEBOOK
Moudre(AUS) gained compensation for being ballotted out of both the Caulfield and Melbourne Cups.
Eastern Aria(UAE), the Park Hill winner, could never quite get close enough to challenge but was not beaten far.
Drunken Sailor(IRE), who missed the Caulfield Cup with a hoof problem, was unable to get into this.

7103 SAN SIRO (R-H)
Saturday, November 6

OFFICIAL GOING: Turf: good

7370a PREMIO CHIUSURA (GROUP 3) (2YO+) (TURF) 7f
2:45 (12:00) 2-Y-O+ **£35,398** (£15,575; £8,495; £4,247)

RPR
1 **Konig Concorde (GER)**[27] 6789 5-9-6 0 .... FilipMinarik 5 101
(C Sprengel, Germany) *broke wl to trck ldrs: chal and led ent fnl 2f: wnt 2 l clr ent fnl f: rdn out to keep command* **29/1**
2 *1 ¼* **Le Big (GER)**[27] 6789 6-9-6 0 .... AStarke 4 97
(U Stoltefuss, Germany) *slowly away: settled mid-div: bmpd and nt smooth ride 3f out: gd hdwy whn getting a run 2f out: clst fnl 100yds* **101/20[3]**
3 *1 ¼* **Glad Sky**[55] 4-9-6 0 .... APietsch 2 94
(W Gulcher, Germany) *settled mid-div on rail for 4f: rdn and nt clr run 2f out: rallied u.str ride to go 3rd fnl 50yds* **19/2**
4 *½* **Rosendhal (IRE)**[13] 3-9-6 0 ....(b) MMonteriso 9 94
(A Renzoni, Italy) *plld hrd 1f: settled mid-div for 4f: ct for pce 2f out: styd on under hrd ride fnl f* **28/1**
5 *nk* **Orife (IRE)**[54] 3-9-6 0 .... StephanePasquier 7 93
(G Botti, Italy) *slowly away: hld up nr rr: nt clr run 3f out: edgd lft and fnd rail 1f out: rallied u.str ride fnl 150yds* **106/10**
6 *½* **Rockhorse (IRE)**[13] 5-9-6 0 .... DarioVargiu 1 90
(B Grizzetti, Italy) *broke wl to ld: chal by eventual wnr over 2f out: sn hdd & wknd fnl f* **15/4[2]**
7 *½* **Alta Fedelta**[28] 6765 4-9-6 0 .... MircoDemuro 10 89
(Vittorio Caruso, Italy) *fell out of stalls: regained momentum and positioned on outer after 2f: rdn and effrt 2f out on wd outside: one pce fnl f* **13/2**
8 *2 ¼* **Farrel (IRE)**[20] 6976 5-9-6 0 .... CColombi 11 83
(B Grizzetti, Italy) *mid-div on outer for 5f: ct for pce and nr rr ent fnl 2f: hrd rdn to stay on fnl f* **132/10**
9 *nk* **Smooth Operator (GER)**[34] 6611 4-9-6 0 .... THellier 13 82
(Mario Hofer, Germany) *settled to trck ldrs on outer: outpcd ent fnl 2f: one pce fnl f* **27/10[1]**
10 *1* **Marshade (ITY)**[153] 3-9-6 0 .... FabioBranca 8 81
(S Botti, Italy) *trckd ldrs for 4f: produced and ev ch 2f out: sn one pced and btn: eased fnl f* **15/4[2]**
11 *2 ½* **Spinning Yarn**[153] 3-9-3 0 .... PierantonioConvertino 3 71
(B Grizzetti, Italy) *broke wl to trck ldrs in 3rd for 4f: rdn ent fnl 2f: sn wknd: eased fnl f* **44/1**
12 *3 ½* **Questi Amori (IRE)**[328] 7743 3-9-6 0 .... SSulas 6 64
(M Guarnieri, Italy) *in rr: nvr figured* **234/10**

1m 27.0s (-1.20)
WFA 3 from 4yo+ 1lb 12 Ran SP% **137.3**
WIN (incl. 1 euro stake): 29.58. PLACES: 7.17, 2.49, 3.36. DF: 59.77.
Owner Wolfgang Frohlich **Bred** Gestut Elsetal **Trained** Germany

6949 WOODBINE (R-H)
Saturday, November 6

OFFICIAL GOING: Polytrack: fast

7371a MAPLE LEAF STKS (F&M) (POLYTRACK) 1m 2f (D)
8:33 (8:33) 3-Y-O+ **£61,764** (£20,588; £11,323; £6,176; £3,088)

RPR
1 **Pachattack (USA)**[21] 6950 4-8-5 ....(b) ChantalSutherland 7 108
(G A Butler) **47/20[1]**
2 *5 ¾* **Impossible Time (CAN)**[30] 5-8-12 .... JCJones 3 103
(Roger L Attfield, Canada) **31/10[2]**
3 *1 ¼* **Satans Quick Chick (USA)**[34] 6603 4-8-5 ... RosemaryBHomeisterJr 1 94
(Eric R Reed, U.S.A) **67/20[3]**
4 *3* **Haka (USA)**[161] 4-8-9 .... TPizarro 8 92
(Christophe Clement, U.S.A) **9/1**
5 *2* **Deputy Darling (CAN)** 4-8-5 ....(b) ERamsammy 5 84
(Michael J Maker, U.S.A) **25/1**
6 *½* **Tasty Temptation (CAN)**[76] 4-8-9 .... LContreras 4 87
(Mark Casse, Canada) **5/1**
7 *5 ½* **Happy Clapper (CAN)**[41] 3-8-4 ow2 .... SCallaghan 6 75
(Michael J Doyle, Canada) **98/10**
8 *9 ½* **Greenapple Martini (CAN)** 4-8-5 ....(b) ERosaDaSilva 2 53
(Michael Mattine, Canada) **237/10**

2m 2.18s (122.18)
WFA 3 from 4yo+ 4lb 8 Ran SP% **121.1**

Owner M V Deegan **Bred** Dapple Broodmares 2004 **Trained** Newmarket, Suffolk

NOTEBOOK
Pachattack(USA), who was fitted with quarter-cup blinkers, made all the running and coasted home for a wide-margin win. She broke the track record.

7264 CAPANNELLE (R-H)
Sunday, November 7

OFFICIAL GOING: Turf: soft

7372a PREMIO RIBOT (GROUP 2) (3YO+) (TURF) 1m
1:50 (12:00) 3-Y-O+ **£61,946** (£27,256; £14,867; £7,433)

RPR
1 **Worthadd (IRE)**[29] 6764 3-9-1 0 .... MircoDemuro 6 111
(Vittorio Caruso, Italy) *broke wl: trckd ldr for 4f: led 3 1/2f out: shkn up 2f out: rdn 1 1/2f out whn chal on outer by eventual 2nd: kpt up to task and a in command fnl f* **4/6[1]**
2 *nk* **Sehrezad (IRE)**[29] 6764 5-9-2 0 .... JiriPalik 10 110
(Andreas Lowe, Germany) *trckd ldrs in 4th tl ent st: effrt ent fnl 3f: chal ldr 1 1/2f out: str run to go cl fnl 100yds* **49/10[2]**
3 *6* **Ransom Hope**[14] 5-9-2 0 .... CDemuro 4 96
(L Riccardi, Italy) *hld up in rr tl 1/2-way: rdn and little imp 3f out: hrd rdn and wl bk ent fnl 2f: kpt on fnl 200yds* **78/10**
4 *hd* **Indomito (GER)**[70] 5573 4-9-2 0 .... DavyBonilla 9 95
(P Vovcenko, Germany) *nr rr tl ent st: rdn 3f out: hrd rdn fnl 2f: kpt on fnl 200yds* **6/1[3]**
5 *2* **Noble Alpha (IRE)**[28] 6791 3-9-1 0 .... THellier 8 92
(Mario Hofer, Germany) *mid-div on outer tl ent st: prog 3f out to move 3rd: ev ch 2f out: sn one pce and lost 3rd fnl 100yds* **104/10**
6 *2 ½* **Red Kimi (IRE)**[14] 4-9-2 0 .... CColombi 5 85
(Riccardo Santini, Italy) *settled mid-div tl ent st: effrt 3f out: rdn and no ex 2f out* **68/1**
7 *1* **Le Vie Infinite (IRE)**[14] 3-9-1 0 .... GBietolini 1 84
(R Brogi, Italy) *hld up in rr on rail for 5f: edgd lft and fnd spce 3f out: hrd rdn to stay on: one pce* **166/10**
8 *1 ½* **Hiresh (IRE)** 3-9-1 0 .... MBelli 2 80
(Mario Vincis, Italy) *in rr for 5f: moved to outer and hrd rdn 2 1/2f out: sn no ex* **27/1**
9 *3* **Silver Arrow (ITY)**[14] 5-9-2 0 .... CFiocchi 3 72
(R Menichetti, Italy) *mid-div: effrt 4f out: sn one pce and eased 2 1/2f out* **118/10**
10 *4 ½* **Air Crew (USA)**[14] 3-9-1 0 .... LManiezzi 11 63
(R Menichetti, Italy) *broke wl to trck ldrs for 5f: rdn 2 1/2f out: sn btn* **118/10**
11 *2* **Back Hunting (USA)**[14] 3-9-1 0 .... DarioVargiu 7 58
(Gianluca Bietolini, Italy) *broke wl to ld tl 3 1/2f out whn chal by eventual wnr: hrd rdn: sn btn: eased* **28/1**

1m 35.8s (-4.00)
WFA 3 from 4yo+ 2lb 11 Ran SP% **141.1**
WIN (incl. 1 euro stake): 1.66. PLACES: 1.05, 1.22, 1.41. DF: 4.46.
Owner Incolinx **Bred** Compagnia Generale S R L **Trained** Italy

7373a PREMIO ROMA GBI RACING (GROUP 1) (3YO+) (TURF) 1m 2f
3:05 (12:00) 3-Y-O+ **£119,469** (£52,566; £28,672; £14,336)

RPR
1 **Rio De La Plata (USA)**[29] 6764 5-9-2 0 .... FrankieDettori 13 117
(Saeed Bin Suroor) *hld-up mid-div: hdfway 3f out to move 6th: wnt 3rd 2f out: rdn to chal ldr ent fnl f: sn led: rdn out to go clr fnl 150yds* **13/8[1]**
2 *2 ½* **Voila Ici (IRE)**[49] 6239 5-9-2 0 .... MircoDemuro 3 112
(Vittorio Caruso, Italy) *settled in 2nd to trck ldr tl ent st: effrt 3f out: rdn and wnt 1 l clr ent fnl 2f: pressed by eventual wnr 1f out: sn btn but hld on wl for 2nd* **71/20[2]**
3 *¾* **Estejo (GER)**[29] 6764 6-9-2 0 .... PierantonioConvertino 10 111
(R Rohne, Germany) *broke wl to ld tl 3f out: chal and sn chsng ldr: hld on u.str ride to hold 3rd fnl f* **59/1**
4 *nk* **Zazou (GER)**[36] 6592 3-9-0 0 .... THellier 4 112
(Mario Hofer, Germany) *mid-div on inner tl ent st: no room and hld up bhd horses tl 2f out: fnd spce but hmpd again 1 1/2f out: styd on wl fnl f* **102/10**
5 *nk* **Jakkalberry (IRE)**[21] 6977 4-9-2 0 .... FabioBranca 11 109
(E Botti, Italy) *hld up in rr tl ent st: effrt 3f out: hrd rdn and hdwy to go cl for 3rd fnl 100yds* **14/1**
6 *2 ½* **Saratoga Black (IRE)**[14] 3-9-0 0 .... GBietolini 1 106
(Gianluca Bietolini, Italy) *mid-div on inner: n.m.r and lost l 2f out: rallied under hrd ride fnl f* **65/1**
7 *nse* **Soberania (GER)**[14] 7109 4-8-13 0 .... CDemuro 2 101
(A Wohler, Germany) *trckd ldrs on inner tl ent st: efforet to stay in tch 3f out: hrd rdn in 3rd ent fnl 2f: one pce fnl 300yds* **29/1**
8 *2* **Titus Awarded (IRE)**[14] 3-9-0 0 .... SLandi 6 102
(A Renzoni, Italy) *nr rr tl ent st: effrt and hdwy 3f out: one pce whn hrd rdn fnl 2f* **81/1**
9 *snk* **Lord Chaparral (IRE)**[21] 6977 3-9-0 0 .... DarioVargiu 5 102
(R Brogi, Italy) *in tch in 5th tl 4f out: rdn and chal ldrs 2 1/2f out: hrd rdn and sn btn* **596/100**
10 *½* **Clowance**[15] 7096 5-8-13 0 .... JimmyFortune 8 96
(R Charlton) *settled to trck ldrs for 4f: briefly 2nd fnl turn: rdn to stay in tch 3 1/2f out: btn 2 1/2f out* **42/10[3]**
11 *2* **Flying Cloud (IRE)**[53] 6095 4-8-13 0 .... TedDurcan 16 92
(Saeed Bin Suroor) *in rr on outer tl home turn: effrt 4f out: sn one pce* **13/8[1]**
12 *4* **Miss Europa (IRE)**[71] 5542 4-8-13 0 .... AStarke 14 84
(P Schiergen, Germany) *hld up nr rr tl ent st: btn and eased ent fnl 2f* **193/10**
13 *1 ½* **Ansiei (ITY)**[14] 3-9-0 0 .... MMonteriso 7 86
(L Polito, Italy) *nr rr: effrt 4f out: no imp: sn btn* **215/10**

14 ½ **Permesso**[35] 5-9-2 0 .... GMarcelli 9 83
(G Pucciatti, Italy) *in rr: nvr figured* **31/1**

15 1 **Pedra Pompas**[35] 6-9-2 0 .... MKolmarkaj 12 81
(M Gasparini, Italy) *in tch w ldrs tl 4f out: sn btn and one pce* **36/1**

16 nk **Cima De Triomphe (IRE)**[21] 6977 5-9-2 0 .... CColombi 15 80
(B Grizzetti, Italy) *mid-div on outer tl 4f out: sn hrd rdn and no ex* **64/1**

2m 2.70s (-0.60)
WFA 3 from 4yo+ 4lb **16** Ran SP% **171.8**
WIN (incl. 1 euro stake): 2.66 (Rio de La Plata coupled with Flying Cloud). PLACES: 1.79, 1.81, 9.83. DF: 10.77.
Owner Godolphin **Bred** Jose De Camargo, Robert N Clay Et Al **Trained** Newmarket, Suffolk
■ This was Frankie Dettori's 100th Group One winner for Goldolphin.

NOTEBOOK
Rio De La Plata(USA) followed up his win in this grade at San Siro last month. He travelled well before leading at the furlong pole and pulling away, putting doubts over his stamina to rest.
Voila Ici(IRE) ran a gutsy race and held a clear advantage with two furlongs left.
Clowance wilted under pressure in the straight.
Flying Cloud(IRE) was retired after the race.

2019 JAGERSRO (R-H)
Sunday, November 7

OFFICIAL GOING: Dirt: standard

7374a JOCKEYKLUBBENS AVELSLOPNING (LISTED RACE) (3YO+ FILLIES & MARES) (DIRT) 1m 4f
3:33 (12:00) 3-Y-0+ **£21,645** (£10,822; £5,194; £3,463; £2,164)

RPR

1 **Demeanour (USA)**[56] 4-9-6 0 .... ValmirDeAzeredo 4 79
(Lars Bexell, Sweden) **40/1**

2 hd **La Zona (IRE)**[42] 4-9-6 0 .... Jan-ErikNeuroth 11 78
(Wido Neuroth, Norway) **105/10**[3]

3 1 ½ **Allannah Abu**[38] 6519 3-9-1 0 .... KimAndersen 5 77
(Sir Mark Prescott) *shkn up fr s to trck ldr: pushed along and dropped to 3rd 2 1/2f out: styd on fnl 1 1/2f: nt qckn fnl 110yds* **96/10**[2]

4 1 ½ **Double Up (SWE)**[364] 5-9-6 0 .... DinaDanekilde 1 74
(Bo Neuman, Sweden) **225/10**

5 1 ¾ **Una Hora (DEN)**[28] 6793 4-9-6 0 ....(b) RafaelSchistl 7 71
(Francisco Castro, Sweden) **134/10**

6 4 **What Budget**[77] 6-9-6 0 ....(b) ShaneKarlsson 2 64
(Arnfinn Lund, Norway) **35/1**

7 7 **Western Memory (USA)**[91] 3-9-1 0 .... Per-AndersGraberg 10 54
(Lennart Reuterskiold Jr, Sweden) **117/10**

8 2 ½ **Senorita Bloom (FR)** 3-9-1 0 .... LennartHammer-Hansen 3 50
(Fredrik Reuterskiold, Sweden) **169/10**

9 hd **Theatrical Award (NOR)**[28] 6793 5-9-6 0 .... CarlosLopez 8 49
(Michael Taylor, Norway) **1/2**[1]

10 6 **Freja (IRE)**[23] 3-9-1 0 .... JacobJohansen 6 40
(Bent Olsen, Denmark) **231/10**

11 dist **Sweet Baby Jane (IRE)**[23] 3-9-1 0 .... ManuelSantos 9 —
(Arnfinn Lund, Norway) **124/10**

2m 32.8s (152.80)
WFA 3 from 4yo+ 6lb **11** Ran SP% **126.3**
PARI-MUTUEL (all including 1sek stake): WIN 41.36; PLACE 6.53, 2.95, 3.14; DF 454.71.
Owner Lordagsklubben **Bred** Barronstown Stud **Trained** Sweden

NOTEBOOK
Allannah Abu was never far from the pace and stayed on for third.

7331 WOLVERHAMPTON (A.W) (L-H)
Monday, November 8

OFFICIAL GOING: Standard
Wind: Light half-against Weather: Light rain

7376 BETDAQ ON 0870 178 1221 H'CAP (DIV I) 7f 32y(P)
1:30 (1:30) (Class 5) (0-70,70) 3-Y-0+ **£1,683** (£501; £250; £62; £62) **Stalls High**

Form RPR

0042 1 **Conry (IRE)**[6] 7283 4-8-13 **69** .... JulieBurke(7) 8 77+
(Patrick Morris) *hld up: hdwy over 2f out: rdn over 1f out: hung lft fr over 1f out: r.o to ld nr fin* **11/4**[1]

3216 2 ½ **Lord Of The Dance (IRE)**[10] 7214 4-9-5 **68** .... TomMcLaughlin 4 74
(W M Brisbourne) *mid-div: sn pushed along: hdwy 1/2-way: rdn to ld wl ins fnl f: hdd nr fin* **5/1**[2]

6565 3 1 **Just Timmy Marcus**[10] 7214 4-9-1 **64** .... GrahamGibbons 1 68
(B P J Baugh) *a.p: rdn to ld insde fnl f: sn hdd and unable qck* **5/1**[2]

0056 4 1 ¼ **King's Caprice**[9] 7241 9-9-2 **65** .... LukeMorris 10 65
(J C Fox) *s.i.s: hld up: rdn over 1f out: r.o ins fnl f: nt rch ldrs* **8/1**

350 4 dht **Hobson**[62] 5838 5-9-7 **70** .... FergusSweeney 6 70
(Eve Johnson Houghton) *chsd ldrs: led 2f out: rdn and hdd ins fnl f: no ex* **16/1**

5000 6 shd **Suzhou**[24] 6903 3-8-8 **58** ....(v[1]) CathyGannon 11 58
(D J Coakley) *hld up: rdn over 1f out: swtchd lft and r.o ins fnl f: nvr nrr* **16/1**

0454 7 ¾ **William Morgan (IRE)**[14] 7122 3-8-10 **67** .... LauraBarry(7) 9 65
(R A Fahey) *hld up in tch: rdn over 2f out: styd on same pce appr fnl f* **25/1**

5106 8 1 ½ **Know No Fear**[3] 7336 5-8-5 **61** ....(v[1]) KatiaScallan(7) 3 55
(A J Lidderdale) *hld up in tch: rdn over 1f out: no ex ins fnl f* **18/1**

5022 9 nk **Desert Falls**[11] 7195 4-8-11 **60** .... HayleyTurner 2 53
(R M Whitaker) *chsd ldr: rdn and ev ch 2f out: no ex ins fnl f* **8/1**

10 7 **Mrs Batt (IRE)**[28] 6822 4-8-7 **56** oh3 ....(bt) ChrisCatlin 5 30
(John W Nicholson, Ire) *sn led: rdn and hdd 2f out: wknd over 1f out* **7/1**[3]

56/3 11 11 **Compton Micky**[14] 7131 9-8-0 **56** oh11 ....(p) ChristopherGraham(7) 7 1
(O Brennan) *s.i.s: hld up: rdn over 4f out: wknd over 2f out* **66/1**

1m 28.73s (-0.87) **Going Correction** -0.025s/f (Stan)
WFA 3 from 4yo+ 1lb **11** Ran SP% **117.1**
Speed ratings (Par 103): **103,102,101,99,99 99,98,97,96,88 76**
toteswingers:1&2 £4.60, 2&3 £5.20, 1&3 £5.10 CSF £15.84 CT £66.61 TOTE £4.30: £2.00, £1.10, £2.10; EX 20.50 Trifecta £101.00 Pool: £319.47 - 2.34 winning units..
Owner Liam Walsh, Timmy Birchall et al **Bred** Shay White **Trained** Tarporley, Cheshire

FOCUS
They went a reasonable pace, which helped the hold-up winner get there. The form looks sound if limited.

7377 BETDAQ ON 0870 178 1221 H'CAP (DIV II) 7f 32y(P)
2:05 (2:06) (Class 5) (0-70,70) 3-Y-0+ **£1,683** (£501; £250; £125) **Stalls High**

Form RPR

5200 1 **Peter's Gift (IRE)**[17] 7051 4-8-12 **61** ....(p) PhillipMakin 6 68
(K A Ryan) *hld up: hdwy over 2f out: rdn to ld ins fnl f: r.o* **20/1**

640 2 1 **My Name Is Bert**[16] 7086 4-8-8 **57** .... CathyGannon 3 61
(Lucinda Featherstone) *chsd ldr: rdn over 1f out: led ins fnl f: sn hdd and unable qck* **9/1**

5210 3 ¾ **Annes Rocket (IRE)**[12] 7162 5-9-0 **63** .... LukeMorris 4 65
(J C Fox) *s.i.s: hld up: hdwy over 1f out: nt clr run and swtchd rt ins fnl f: r.o: nt rch ldrs* **7/2**[1]

5535 4 hd **Mount Juliet (IRE)**[10] 7209 3-9-2 **66** .... ChrisCatlin 7 68
(M Botti) *hld up: hdwy 1/2-way: rdn and ev ch ins fnl f: styd on same pce* **4/1**[2]

0660 5 1 ¾ **Royal Box**[37] 6579 3-8-3 **56** oh4 ....(p) AndrewHeffernan(3) 1 53
(D Burchell) *led: rdn and hung lft over 1f out: hdd and no ex ins fnl f* **16/1**

3202 6 ¾ **Headache**[18] 7047 5-9-4 **70** ....(t) RobertLButler(3) 8 65
(B W Duke) *chsd ldrs: rdn over 1f out: no ex ins fnl f* **6/1**

3304 7 nse **Cut And Thrust (IRE)**[18] 7046 4-9-3 **69** .... KierenFox(3) 5 64
(M Wellings) *chsd ldrs: rdn over 2f out: nt clr run over 1f out: swtchd rt: styd on same pce* **9/2**[3]

4553 8 shd **Mighty Clarets (IRE)**[114] 4128 3-8-10 **67** .... LauraBarry(7) 10 62
(R A Fahey) *hld up: hdwy over 2f out: swtchd lft over 1f out: styd on same pce* **16/1**

0600 9 2 ¾ **Luv U Noo**[16] 7082 3-8-9 **59** ....(b[1]) TomEaves 9 46
(B Ellison) *s.i.s: hld up: rdn over 2f out: a in rr* **12/1**

3600 10 11 **Key Light (IRE)**[29] 6772 3-9-4 **68** ....(t) JimmyFortune 2 25
(J W Hills) *prom: lost pl 5f out: rdn over 2f out: wknd over 1f out* **9/1**

1m 28.87s (-0.73) **Going Correction** -0.025s/f (Stan)
WFA 3 from 4yo+ 1lb **10** Ran SP% **118.9**
Speed ratings (Par 103): **103,101,101,100,98 97,97,97,94,82**
toteswingers:1&2 £26.20, 2&3 £9.90, 1&3£13.00 CSF £191.98 CT £791.96 TOTE £21.40: £4.90, £2.10, £1.40; EX 188.40 TRIFECTA Not won..
Owner Mr & Mrs Julian And Rosie Richer **Bred** T C Chiang **Trained** Hambleton, N Yorks

FOCUS
Run in the same fashion as division one, with a fair pace, and in a similar time. The form is rated around the runner-up and fifth.

7378 ENJOY THE PARTY PACK GROUP OFFER CLAIMING STKS 7f 32y(P)
2:35 (2:37) (Class 6) 2-Y-0 **£1,619** (£481; £240; £120) **Stalls High**

Form RPR

2303 1 **My Lord**[26] 6842 2-8-8 74 .... KierenFox(3) 4 79
(W G M Turner) *a.p: rdn to ld wl ins fnl f: r.o* **5/1**[2]

0015 2 ½ **Bilko Pak (IRE)**[26] 6842 2-8-13 85 .... JimmyFortune 2 80
(R Hannon) *a.p: chsd ldr over 5f out: led wl over 1f out: rdn and hdd wl ins fnl f* **8/13**[1]

0010 3 2 **Sir Lunchalott**[39] 6500 2-8-9 70 ....(b) LukeMorris 5 71
(J S Moore) *led: rdn over 2f out: hdd wl over 1f out: styd on same pce ins fnl f* **13/2**[3]

2300 4 7 **Chilworth Lass (IRE)**[24] 6891 2-8-3 54 .... CathyGannon 1 48
(M R Channon) *chsd ldr to over 5f out: remained handy: rdn over 2f out: wknd ins fnl f* **12/1**

5305 5 1 ¼ **Mediplomat**[14] 7124 2-8-10 60 ....(t) ChrisCatlin 10 52
(M Botti) *hld up: hdwy over 2f out: sn rdn: wknd ins fnl f* **11/1**

0055 6 1 **Bendigedig**[19] 7016 2-8-1 52 .... JamieMackay 8 40
(S Kirk) *hld up in tch: rdn and wknd over 1f out: hung lft ins fnl f* **33/1**

4006 7 6 **Elusive Vine (IRE)**[28] 6795 2-8-1 48 ow3 .... AndrewHeffernan(3) 3 29
(R A Harris) *s.s: plld hrd and hdwy over 5f out: wknd over 2f out: hmpd over 1f out* **40/1**

0460 8 1 ¼ **Nalany**[128] 3678 2-8-1 42 ow1 ....(b[1]) FrankieMcDonald 7 22
(D Haydn Jones) *hld up: in rr and rdn 1/2-way: n.d* **66/1**

3400 9 hd **Red Jacaranda**[28] 6795 2-7-7 45 ....(v[1]) KatiaScallan(7) 9 21
(C A Dwyer) *hld up: effrt over 2f out: wkng whn hung lft over 1f out* **50/1**

0000 10 11 **Algurayn (IRE)**[7] 7272 2-8-9 62 .... WilliamCarson 6 3
(G Prodromou) *plld hrd early: hld up: bhd and rdn 1/2-way: t.o* **33/1**

1m 29.58s (-0.02) **Going Correction** -0.025s/f (Stan) **10** Ran SP% **119.7**
Speed ratings (Par 94): **99,98,96,88,86 85,78,77,77,64**
toteswingers:1&2 £2.10, 2&3 £2.30, 1&3 £4.80 CSF £8.48 TOTE £5.70: £1.20, £1.30, £1.40; EX 13.80 Trifecta £39.50 Pool: £524.56 - 9.81 winning units..
Owner Mrs M S Teversham **Bred** Mrs Monica Teversham **Trained** Sigwells, Somerset
■ Stewards' Enquiry : Katia Scallan two-day ban: careless riding (23-24 Oct)

FOCUS
The first three looked well ahead of the rest on previous form, and so it proved. They went a good dash to the first bend, but the tempo then steadied. The winner looked improved for the longer trip and the third sets the standard.

NOTEBOOK
My Lord has been generally running well since making a winning debut, and two previous runs on Polytrack showed he goes well on the surface. He is worth keeping to this longer distance and should be capable of winning a handicap. (op 11-2)
Bilko Pak(IRE), who had only previously run at 5f and 6f, stayed the extra furlong without suggesting it will improve him. Rated a lofty 85 for this grade, he was the best-in on official figures, but in his defence he was beaten only by another above-average sort at this level. (op 8-11)
Sir Lunchalott appreciated the drop back to 7f and, in finishing clear of the third, performed with credit. (op 6-1)
Chilworth Lass(IRE), who had lost her form in recent races, was beaten a long way. However, this was a little better than it looked because she had a tough task at the weights. (op 16-1)
Mediplomat has not achieved much in his two runs on Polytrack, but he had a hard job at the weights against the first three. (op 10-1)
Bendigedig has looked most effective in sellers.

7379 BET PREMIER LEAGUE FOOTBALL - BETDAQ NURSERY 7f 32y(P)
3:10 (3:11) (Class 4) (0-80,80) 2-Y-0 **£3,011** (£896; £447; £223) **Stalls High**

Form RPR

255 1 **Charles Fosterkane**[26] 6844 2-8-10 **72** .... KierenFox(3) 5 77+
(J R Best) *hld up: hdwy over 1f out: rdn to ld ins fnl f: carried hd high and hung rt: r.o wl* **4/1**[3]

6242 2 2 ¼ **Avid Kale**[13] 7151 2-9-0 **73** .... ChrisCatlin 2 72
(M Botti) *chsd ldrs: rdn to ld over 1f out: hdd and unable qck ins fnl f* **7/2**[2]

3060 3 1 ½ **Point Du Jour (FR)**[9] 7236 2-9-2 **75** .... TomMcLaughlin 7 71
(I A Wood) *s.s: hld up: plld hrd: hdwy over 1f out: r.o to go 3rd post: nt rch ldrs* **40/1**

41 4 *nse* **Gentleman Is Back (USA)**[45] 6334 2-9-7 **80**................ RobertHavlin 6 76
(J H M Gosden) *hld up in tch: plld hrd: swtchd rt over 1f out: rdn and r.o: nt trble ldrs* **10/11**[1]

5540 5 *2 ¾* **Looksmart**[4] 7313 2-8-6 **65**................ FrankieMcDonald 3 54
(R Hannon) *chsd ldrs: rdn over 2f out: nt clr run over 1f out: sn wknd* **11/1**

0000 6 *2* **Kyncraighe (IRE)**[28] 6810 2-7-8 **60**................ KatiaScallan(7) 1 44
(A J Lidderdale) *sn led: hung rt over 2f out: rdn and hdd over 1f out: wknd ins fnl f* **50/1**

0420 7 *¾* **Baileys Moneypenny**[23] 6920 2-9-2 **75**................ TomEaves 4 57
(J G Given) *chsd ldrs: rdn over 2f out: wknd ins fnl f* **16/1**

1m 29.94s (0.34) **Going Correction** -0.025s/f (Stan) 7 Ran SP% **113.2**
Speed ratings (Par 98): **97,94,92,92,89 87,86**
toteswingers:1&2 £2.10, 2&3 £16.30, 1&3 £10.30 CSF £17.98 TOTE £3.80: £1.90, £1.40; EX 17.10.
Owner John Mayne **Bred** J H Mayne **Trained** Hucking, Kent

FOCUS
Not a bad nursery, and the winner is likely to improve. The pace threatened to be good early on, but settled down as a middling one. The runner-up and sixth give a good line to the form.

NOTEBOOK
Charles Fosterkane ◆ found an easy run up the inner as the seven runners spread across the track in the home straight. His first three races were at 1m and a return to an extra furlong will not be a problem, but he did look highly effective at this trip. He looks progressive and is one to keep an eye on this winter. (op 6-1)
Avid Kale has done well in his last four races, including two nurseries, and it is only a matter of time before he wins. (op 9-2)
Point Du Jour(FR), trapped wide and pulling hard, is much more effective at 7f than further. He has yet to win but can go closer when gets a better run of the race. (op 33-1)
Gentleman Is Back(USA), making his handicap debut off top weight, ran respectably but he appeared to have been given several pounds too much. However, he was too headstrong and can probably do a bit better with experience. Official explanation: one-day ban: careless riding (23 Nov) (op 4-6 tchd Evens)
Looksmart has not progressed since switching to nurseries, so she looks too high in the weights. (op 16-1)
Kyncraighe(IRE) has lost his form, and this AW debut and return to front-running did not spark a revival. (op 66-1)
Baileys Moneypenny has finished last in both her nurseries, and her two runs on Polytrack have been modest. (op 14-1)

7380 WOLVERHAMPTON HOLIDAY INN H'CAP 5f 216y(P)
3:40 (3:42) (Class 7) (0-50,50) 4-Y-0+ £1,364 (£403; £201) Stalls Low

Form RPR

0050 1 **Pinball (IRE)**[5] 7300 4-8-13 **48**................(b) TomEaves 7 56
(Mrs L Williamson) *hld up in tch: shkn up over 1f out: rdn and hung rt ins fnl f: r.o to ld nr fin* **16/1**

6440 2 *shd* **Cocktail Party (IRE)**[5] 7300 4-8-10 **45**................ GrahamGibbons 8 53
(J W Unett) *hld up: nt clr run over 2f out: hdwy over 1f out: rdn to ld ins fnl f: sn hung rt: hdd nr fin* **12/1**

6033 3 *1 ¼* **Cheery Cat (USA)**[8] 7249 6-9-1 **50**................(p) LukeMorris 5 54
(J Balding) *chsd ldr: led over 1f out: sn rdn and hung lft: hdd and unable qck ins fnl f* **5/1**[2]

0400 4 *½* **Dream Express (IRE)**[11] 7199 5-9-0 **49**................ RobertWinston 9 51
(D W Thompson) *hld up: hdwy over 1f out: r.o wl* **10/1**

0306 4 *dht* **Carnival Dream**[17] 7051 5-9-1 **50**................ PatrickMathers 4 52
(H A McWilliams) *chsd ldrs: rdn over 2f out: r.o* **16/1**

2400 6 *½* **Hart Of Gold**[5] 7300 6-8-13 **48**................(b) TomMcLaughlin 2 49
(R A Harris) *led: rdn and hdd over 1f out: ev ch ins fnl f: styd on same pce* **8/1**

0002 7 *1 ½* **Meydan Dubai (IRE)**[8] 7250 5-9-0 **49**................(b) HayleyTurner 13 45
(J R Best) *s.s: hld up: styd on u.p ins fnl f: nt trble ldrs* **11/2**[3]

0400 8 *hd* **Fiancee (IRE)**[19] 7023 4-9-1 **50**................(b[1]) PhillipMakin 11 45
(R Brotherton) *hld up: rdn over 1f out: styd on ins fnl f: nvr trbld ldrs* **16/1**

0030 9 *½* **Prigsnov Dancer (IRE)**[14] 7132 5-8-7 **45**................(p) PaulPickard(3) 3 39
(O Brennan) *hld up: hdwy and nt clr run over 1f out: styd on same pce ins fnl f* **16/1**

45/2 10 *2 ¼* **Dontforgeturshovel**[13] 7155 4-8-12 **47**................ MickyFenton 1 34
(J Pearce) *sn pushed along and prom: rdn over 2f out: wknd ins fnl f* **7/2**[1]

000/ 11 *8* **Rich Harvest (USA)**[770] 6328 5-8-10 **45**................ JimmyQuinn 10 —
(R E Peacock) *prom: rdn over 2f out: wknd over 1f out* **33/1**

0200 12 *3 ¼* **Bertbrand**[5] 7300 5-9-0 **49**................(v) ChrisCatlin 6 —
(I W McInnes) *chsd ldrs: rdn over 2f out: wknd over 1f out* **16/1**

-000 13 *19* **Vanadium**[278] 388 8-8-5 **45**................ JemmaMarshall(5) 12 —
(A J Lidderdale) *sn outpcd: t.o* **25/1**

1m 15.24s (0.24) **Going Correction** -0.025s/f (Stan) 13 Ran SP% **118.4**
Speed ratings (Par 97): **97,96,95,94,94 93,91,91,90,87 77,72,47**
toteswingers:1&2 £23.90, 2&3 £10.00, 1&3 £15.10 CSF £193.97 CT £1110.13 TOTE £24.80: £5.40, £3.50, £1.60; EX 382.90 Trifecta £284.90 Part won. Pool of £385.06 - 0.62 winning units..

Owner D Manning, D Roycroft, P Kelly **Bred** John Morris **Trained** Saighton, Cheshire

FOCUS
A sprint that took little winning with the winner rated in line with this year's form.

7381 SPONSOR A RACE BY CALLING 01902 390000 MEDIAN AUCTION MAIDEN STKS 1m 4f 50y(P)
4:15 (4:16) (Class 6) 3-5-Y-0 £1,619 (£481; £240; £120) Stalls Low

Form RPR

32 1 **Treacle Tart**[19] 7022 5-9-3 0................ RobertWinston 4 66+
(P Charalambous) *a.p: chsd ldr over 2f out: led ins fnl f: styd on wl* **9/4**[2]

6206 2 *4 ½* **Chincoteague (IRE)**[19] 7011 4-9-3 65................ ShaneKelly 7 59
(B J Meehan) *chsd ldr tl led over 6f out: rdn over 1f out: hdd: hung rt and no ex ins fnl f* **7/1**[3]

530 3 *½* **Miss Kingwood**[25] 6876 3-8-11 0................ HayleyTurner 6 58+
(M P Tregoning) *led: hung rt almost thrght: hdd over 6f out: styd on same pce fnl 2f* **10/11**[1]

6464 4 *4* **Baggsy (IRE)**[7] 7003 3-8-11 46................ CathyGannon 1 52?
(Miss J Feilden) *hld up: drvn along over 7f out: hdwy over 2f out: wknd ins fnl f* **25/1**

06 5 *4* **Hecton Lad (USA)**[54] 6079 3-8-13 0................ KierenFox(3) 3 51?
(J R Best) *hld up: hdwy u.p over 3f out: wknd ins fnl f* **50/1**

5345 6 *3 ¾* **Marafong**[27] 6829 3-9-2 40................ GrahamGibbons 8 45?
(B P J Baugh) *stdd s: hld up: hdwy over 2f out: wknd over 1f out* **25/1**

2440 7 *45* **Lady Brickhouse**[13] 7156 3-8-11 48................ SaleemGolam 2 —
(M D Squance) *chsd ldrs: rdn over 5f out: wknd over 3f out: t.o* **33/1**

8 *nk* **Harrys** 3-9-2 0................ JimmyQuinn 5 —
(P Howling) *s.s: a in rr: bhd fnl 5f: t.o* **20/1**

2m 40.48s (-0.62) **Going Correction** -0.025s/f (Stan)
WFA 3 from 4yo+ 6lb 8 Ran SP% **113.0**
Speed ratings (Par 101): **101,98,97,95,92 89,59,59**
toteswingers:1&2 £2.90, 2&3 £3.10, 1&3 £1.40 CSF £15.72 TOTE £4.50: £2.10, £1.10, £1.10; EX 13.40 Trifecta £21.60 Pool: £780.87 - 26.69 winning units..
Owner P Charalambous **Bred** Middleton Stud **Trained** Newmarket, Suffolk

FOCUS
A routine maiden, but run at a solid pace and the form is limited by the fourth, fifth and sixth.
Miss Kingwood Official explanation: jockey said the filly hung badly right-handed throughout
Harrys Official explanation: trainer said that the gelding ran green

7382 BETDAQ.COM H'CAP 1m 141y(P)
4:45 (4:45) (Class 4) (0-85,85) 3-Y-0+ £3,594 (£1,069; £534; £266) Stalls Low

Form RPR

0 1 **Noguchi (IRE)**[29] 6780 5-8-13 **77**................ JimmyFortune 8 87+
(J Noseda) *hld up: hdwy over 1f out: qcknd to ld wl ins fnl f: r.o* **6/1**

0205 2 *1 ¼* **She's A Character**[35] 6620 3-8-11 **78**................(p) PhillipMakin 4 85
(R A Fahey) *chsd ldrs: rdn and ev ch wl ins fnl f: unable qck* **16/1**

6100 3 *1 ½* **Cobo Bay**[12] 7182 5-9-0 **78**................(b) RobertWinston 6 82
(C R Dore) *led: rdn and hung lft over 1f out: hdd wl ins fnl f* **15/2**

2625 4 *½* **Veroon (IRE)**[17] 7053 4-8-12 **76**................(p) TomEaves 3 78
(J G Given) *chsd ldrs: rdn over 1f out: styd on same pce ins fnl f* **5/1**[3]

6406 5 *2* **Norwegian Dancer (UAE)**[12] 7182 4-8-10 **74**................ GrahamGibbons 5 72
(E S McMahon) *prom: rdn over 2f out: styd on same pce fr over 1f out* **7/2**[2]

1500 6 *1 ¾* **Lastkingofscotland (IRE)**[12] 7182 4-8-9 **73**................(v) HayleyTurner 1 67
(C R Dore) *hld up in tch: lost pl wl over 2f out: n.d after* **15/2**

0000 7 *½* **Spectait**[67] 5702 8-9-7 **85**................ GeorgeBaker 2 78
(Jonjo O'Neill) *awkward leaving stalls: hld up: pushed along over 3f out: nvr on terms* **5/2**[1]

0010 8 *5* **Ahlawy (IRE)**[8] 7251 7-9-4 **82**................(t) LeeVickers 7 63
(F Sheridan) *s.i.s: hdwy over 6f out: chsd ldr 4f out tl rdn over 2f out: wknd over 1f out* **14/1**

1m 49.99s (-0.51) **Going Correction** -0.025s/f (Stan)
WFA 3 from 4yo+ 3lb 8 Ran SP% **117.8**
Speed ratings (Par 105): **101,99,98,98,96 94,94,89**
toteswingers:1&2 £4.80, 2&3 £9.70, 1&3 £9.70 totesuper7: Win: Not won. Place: £662.20 CSF £95.66 CT £739.17 TOTE £7.40: £2.20, £6.10, £3.70; EX 111.40 Trifecta £700.30 Pool: £993.67 - 1.05 winning units..
Owner The Honorable Earle I Mack **Bred** Cora Srl **Trained** Newmarket, Suffolk

FOCUS
An above-average Polytrack race, but the pace was disappointingly weak until the final bend, 3f out. The form is rated around the placed horses for now.
T/Jkpt: Not won. T/Plt: £69.00 to a £1 stake.Pool of £71,558.05 - 756.07 winning tickets. T/Qpdt: £6.50 to a £1 stake. Pool of £6,028.33 - 680.30 winning tickets. CR

7276 MAISONS-LAFFITTE (R-H)
Monday, November 8

OFFICIAL GOING: Turf: heavy

7383a PRIX D'ARCUEIL (CLAIMER) (2YO) (TURF) 6f (S)
11:50 (12:00) 2-Y-0 £11,061 (£4,424; £3,318; £2,212; £1,106)

RPR

1 **Gavriel (USA)**[20] 7009 2-9-1 0................ StephanePasquier 9 84
(G Botti, Italy) **5/1**[3]

2 *3* **Mister Segway (IRE)**[19] 2-8-11 0................ GregoryBenoist 1 71
(Robert Collet, France) **18/1**

3 *2* **Valerius Maximus**[20] 7009 2-9-5 0................ IoritzMendizabal 5 73
(P F I Cole) *broke wl: racd in midfield on stands' side: rdn 1 1/2f out: picked up wl and styd on u.p fnl f* **43/10**[2]

4 *1 ½* **Matreshka (IRE)**[82] 5226 2-8-8 0................ ThierryThulliez 7 58
(N Clement, France) **23/10**[1]

5 *3* **Gwenhwyfar (IRE)**[10] 7222 2-8-8 0................ MaximeGuyon 8 49
(C Boutin, France) **73/10**

6 *2* **Keisha (FR)**[26] 2-8-7 0................ RudyPimbonnet(8) 3 50
(C Laffon-Parias, France) **18/1**

7 *3* **Tupelo (IRE)**[28] 2-9-3 0................(p) SylvainRuis 12 43
(S Loeuillet, France) **15/1**

8 *nk* **El Cuerpo E L'Alma (USA)** 2-8-6 0................ EddyHardouin(5) 4 36
(G Botti, Italy) **42/1**

9 *hd* **Cerveza**[15] 2-9-1 0................ AnthonyCrastus 11 39
(C Laffon-Parias, France) **68/10**

10 *2* **Voix Des Aigles (FR)**[18] 2-8-6 0................ MatthieuAutier(5) 10 29
(Mme C Barande-Barbe, France) **38/1**

0 **Gone Fighting (FR)**[20] 7009 2-8-11 0................ Pierre-CharlesBoudot 2 —
(Y De Nicolay, France) **25/1**

1m 19.5s (6.10) 11 Ran SP% **116.2**
WIN (incl. 1 euro stake) 5.30 (Gavriel coupled with El Cuerpo E L'Alma). PLACES: 2.30, 4.60, 2.30. DF: 49.60. SF: 88.80.
Owner Selim Blanga Moghrabi **Bred** Ceka Ireland Ltd & Wiji Bloodstock **Trained** Italy

7309 KEMPTON (A.W) (R-H)
Wednesday, November 10

OFFICIAL GOING: Standard
Wind: Light, across Weather: Fine, crisp

7384 KIA SPORTAGE CONDITIONS STKS 1m 2f (P)
4:20 (4:20) (Class 3) 3-Y-0+ £6,281 (£1,869; £934; £466) Stalls High

Form RPR

3563 1 **Nideeb**[11] 7237 3-8-9 101................ NeilCallan 2 108
(C E Brittain) *trckd ldr: effrt 2f out: led over 1f out: shkn up and sn clr* **3/1**[2]

2465 2 *7* **Chock A Block (IRE)**[33] 6720 4-8-13 105................ RichardMullen 3 94
(Saeed Bin Suroor) *chsd ldng pair: pushed along 3f out: nt qckn 2f out: tk modest 2nd ins fnl f* **4/1**[3]

4000 3 *2 ¼* **Island Sunset (IRE)**[4] 7349 4-8-8 91................ ShaneKelly 1 85
(W R Muir) *stdd s: hld up last: pushed along and no prog 3f out: no ch after: tk modest 3rd nr fin* **11/2**

0041 4 1 3/4 **Peligroso (FR)**[16] 7120 4-9-7 105 TedDurcan 4 94
(Saeed Bin Suroor) *led at reasonable pce and unchal: gng best 2f out: hdd over 1f out: immediately btn* **11/10**[1]

2m 5.44s (-2.56) **Going Correction** +0.025s/f (Slow)
WFA 3 from 4yo 4lb 4 Ran SP% **108.0**
Speed ratings (Par 107): **111,105,103,102**
CSF £13.83 TOTE £4.60; EX 17.10.
Owner Saeed Manana **Bred** Rabbah Bloodstock Limited **Trained** Newmarket, Suffolk

FOCUS
A small but trappy field with three of the four making their all-weather debuts. The favourite folded tamely and this is not form to take too literally.

NOTEBOOK
Nideeb was an emphatic winner. The only 3-y-o in the field having made a belated reappearance in August, he had gradually run into form and was on an upward curve based on his latest run when dropped to Listed class and finishing 3 3/4l third to Timepiece over 1m2f at Newmarket 11 days earlier. The race conditions didn't favour him but the style and surface certainly did. It helped that he settled much better off a solid pace and won with any amount in hand in a time marginally below standard. He will rise from 101 having started this season off 106. (op 11-4 tchd 5-2)
Chock A Block(IRE) was the lesser fancied in the market of the two Godolphin runners and plugged on in his own time. He has been tried over further and on this evidence 1m2f is too short judged on this all-weather debut. (op 7-2 tchd 10-3)
Island Sunset(IRE) was poorly in at the race conditions and was always struggling despite three of her four wins coming on this surface. There will be easier options. (op 6-1 tchd 9-2)
Peligroso(FR) headed the market for Godolphin, being joint highest rated with his stablemate on 105. He likes to dominate as he showed when winning at Leicester 16 days earlier but in setting an even gallop he set the race up for the winner and went out limply when passed. Two of his three wins have been on heavy and this surface, on which he was making his debut, may not have suited. Regardless of that, he caved in too easily for comfort. (op 11-8 tchd 6-4 in a place)

7385 EUROPEAN BREEDERS' FUND MAIDEN STKS (DIV I) 7f (P)
4:50 (4:54) (Class 5) 2-Y-O £2,752 (£818; £409; £204) Stalls High

Form RPR

0 1 **Orange Ace**[18] 7094 2-9-3 0 NeilCallan 14 76+
(P F I Cole) *trckd ldrs: shkn up and swtchd lft over 1f out: r.o to ld ins fnl f: sn clr* **8/1**

0 2 1 1/2 **Silenzio**[18] 7099 2-9-3 0 JimmyFortune 8 72+
(R Hannon) *dwlt: hld up in rr: effrt and hanging in 10th over 2f out: rdn and gd prog on outer over 1f out: styd on wl to take 2nd nr fin* **3/1**[1]

002 3 hd **Kuala Limper (IRE)**[21] 7020 2-9-3 76 DaneO'Neill 9 72
(D R C Elsworth) *trckd ldrs: rdn over 2f out: prog over 1f out: styd on fnl f to press for 2nd nr fin* **7/2**[2]

06 4 1 1/2 **Foxtrot Golf (IRE)**[22] 6994 2-9-3 0 JimCrowley 10 68
(P Winkworth) *mde most: drvn and hdd over 1f out: upsides ins fnl f: fdd* **25/1**

3250 5 1/2 **Riot Police (USA)**[18] 7087 2-9-3 75 (b[1]) SaleemGolam 11 67
(J H M Gosden) *prom: chsd ldr over 2f out: narrow ld over 1f out: hdd & wknd ins fnl f* **9/1**

63 6 nk **Midnight Maasai**[21] 7020 2-9-3 0 LukeMorris 2 66
(C G Cox) *t.k.h: pressed ldr to over 2f out: sn u.p: nt qckn over 1f out: fdd* **6/1**[3]

7 3 **Top Diktat** 2-9-3 0 RichardMullen 13 58+
(Sir Michael Stoute) *a abt same pl: rdn fr 1/2-way: nt pce to threaten ldrs* **20/1**

4 8 3 1/4 **Isingy Red (FR)**[22] 6995 2-9-3 0 GeorgeBaker 3 50
(J R Boyle) *t.k.h: pressed ldrs on outer after 2f tl wknd over 1f out* **40/1**

9 1/2 **Club Oceanic** 2-9-3 0 JamieSpencer 4 48
(J Noseda) *dwlt: hld up last of main gp: plld out wd 2f out: jst pushed along and nvr on terms* **8/1**

10 2 1/4 **Like A Boy** 2-9-3 0 FergusSweeney 12 43
(P J Makin) *dwlt: wl in rr: effrt on inner over 2f out: wknd over 1f out* **80/1**

0 11 4 **Blueberry Fizz (IRE)**[11] 7231 2-8-12 0 TomMcLaughlin 6 27
(J Ryan) *in tch tl wknd over 2f out* **100/1**

12 nse **Mount Crystal (IRE)** 2-8-12 0 MichaelHills 1 27
(B W Hills) *dwlt: hld up in rr: hanging lft bnd 3f out: sn btn* **20/1**

13 2 1/4 **Mancunian (IRE)** 2-9-3 0 SteveDrowne 5 26
(J R Best) *s.s: t.o in last pair after 2f* **40/1**

0 14 24 **Birdwatcher (IRE)**[30] 6811 2-9-3 0 JoeFanning 7 —
(M Johnston) *dwlt: rn green: t.o in last pair after 2f* **25/1**

1m 26.79s (0.79) **Going Correction** +0.025s/f (Slow) 14 Ran SP% **118.0**
Speed ratings (Par 96): **96,94,94,92,91 91,88,84,83,81 76,76,73,46**
toteswingers:1&2 £8.50, 2&3 £3.10, 1&3 £8.90 CSF £28.81 TOTE £6.40: £2.10, £2.20, £1.40; EX 55.10.
Owner P de Camaret **Bred** Ecurie Des Monceaux **Trained** Whatcombe, Oxon

FOCUS
A difficult maiden to to get a handle on with the highest of those rated being 76.

NOTEBOOK
Orange Ace who had clearly benefitted from his debut over a furlong further at Newbury 18 days earlier. He showed a willing attitude and was staying on in a style suggesting he will get 1m if tried again this season. (op 10-1 tchd 11-1)
Silenzio has not been blessed with good fotune in his two runs so far, the saddle slipping on debut then a tardy start giving him a lot to do here. In the circumstances he did well to get so close as nothing finished better. (op 10-3 tchd 7-2)
Kuala Limper(IRE) was keen to post and finished best of those rated, 76. He was keen and in the circumstances saw the race out well enough. He might be worth a try in a nursery. (op 10-3 tchd 3-1)
Foxtrot Golf(IRE) was another that was very free early but stayed on encouragingly and is now due a rating which should be in the low-70s. (tchd 33-1)
Riot Police(USA), blinkered for the first time, was the other rated 76 and is now thoroughly exposed in both maidens and handicaps where he appears to lack a finishing kick over this trip or 1m. (op 8-1 tchd 10-1)
Midnight Maasai was also very keen but ran nearly the same race with Kuala Limper at Newbury 21 days previously. She is now due a mark and might be suited by the stronger pace of handicaps. (tchd 13-2)
Top Diktat was very stubborn to load but showed a willing enough attitude without ever looking a threat. (op 16-1)
Isingy Red(FR) needs another run for a mark and doesn't look a forlorn hope. (op 33-1)
Club Oceanic never got into the race but produced enough to think there are races to be won in the future. (op 7-1)

7386 EUROPEAN BREEDERS' FUND MAIDEN STKS (DIV II) 7f (P)
5:20 (5:26) (Class 5) 2-Y-O £2,752 (£818; £409; £204) Stalls High

Form RPR

23 1 **Sirius Prospect (USA)**[19] 7058 2-9-3 0 JimCrowley 11 78
(D K Ivory) *restless stalls: pressed ldrs: wnt 2nd 2f out: sn rdn: clsd to take narrow ld ins fnl f: a doing enough* **1/1**[1]

5 2 hd **Sinfonico (IRE)**[12] 7202 2-9-3 0 JimmyFortune 4 77
(R Hannon) *mde most: rdn 2l clr over 1f out: hdd ins fnl f: styd on wl: a jst hld* **8/1**

3 3 **Jameel (USA)** 2-9-3 0 TedDurcan 14 70
(Saeed Bin Suroor) *hld up in midfield: prog on inner 2f out: tk 3rd jst over 1f out: readily outpcd by ldng pair* **9/2**[2]

03 4 1/2 **Orthodox Lad**[15] 7150 2-9-3 0 JimmyQuinn 3 68
(J R Best) *pressed ldrs: shkn up and nt qckn 2f out: one pce and outpcd after* **20/1**

0 5 shd **Barnmore**[18] 7099 2-9-3 0 TomMcLaughlin 12 68+
(P R Hedger) *hld up in rr: shuffled along fr 2f out: gd prog fnl f: nrst fin: will improve* **40/1**

0 6 1 1/4 **Steenbok (IRE)**[19] 7058 2-9-3 0 SaleemGolam 5 65
(J H M Gosden) *t.k.h early: trckd ldrs on outer: pushed along over 2f out: one pce and outpcd* **5/1**[3]

7 2 1/2 **Old English (IRE)** 2-9-3 0 JoeFanning 2 58
(M Johnston) *restless stalls: gd spd fr wd draw and chsd ldr to 2f out: steadily wknd* **20/1**

00 8 hd **Warden Bond**[22] 6994 2-8-10 0 LauraPike[(7)] 7 58
(W B Stone) *nvr bttr than midfield: shuffled along and no imp on ldrs fr 2f out* **100/1**

06 9 1 **Dark And Dangerous (IRE)**[28] 6843 2-9-3 0 LukeMorris 8 55
(P Winkworth) *a towards rr: shkn up and no prog 2f out: nt on terms after* **66/1**

0 10 3 3/4 **Trust Me Boy**[22] 6994 2-9-3 0 SamHitchcott 9 46
(J E Long) *a in rr: u.p and struggling over 2f out* **100/1**

0 11 nk **Dysios (IRE)**[16] 7112 2-9-3 0 J-PGuillambert 13 45
(L M Cumani) *plld hrd early: chsd ldrs tl wknd over 2f out* **40/1**

12 15 **Jackstown Road (IRE)** 2-9-3 0 DaneO'Neill 10 6
(D R C Elsworth) *slowly away and rel to r early: jst in tch in last pair to 3f out: sn bhd: t.o* **33/1**

1m 28.17s (2.17) **Going Correction** +0.025s/f (Slow) 12 Ran SP% **116.8**
Speed ratings (Par 96): **88,87,84,83,83 82,79,79,78,73 73,56**
toteswingers:1&2 £2.70, 2&3 £5.50, 1&3 £1.90 CSF £8.77 TOTE £2.50: £1.20, £2.20, £1.30; EX 9.60.
Owner Miss N Yarrow **Bred** Brookdale And Dr Ted Folkerth **Trained** Radlett, Herts

FOCUS
From a form perspective this was harder to evaluate than the first division with no runner holding a rating and the time was 1.30sec slower.

NOTEBOOK
Sirius Prospect(USA) was the horse with the best public form, and prevailed - but only just. It was his experience gained in two previous attempts, when placed over over this distance, that saw him home but unlike those two races he didn't get to the front until the last stride. He has a willing attitude and judged on this will benefit from another furlong on this surface. Connections will now put him away until next year. (op 10-11 tchd 5-4)
Sinfonico(IRE) ◆ had showed potential on debut over this trip at Newmarket 12 days earlier and nearly stole it from the front. This looks the trip at present and he'll certainly win one of these if he runs again. (tchd 13-2)
Jameel(USA), out of the top-class filly Maid's Causeway, was just tapped for pace when the race started up the home straight but his pedigree suggests that middle distances next season will be the right passage. (op 7-2 tchd 5-1 and 11-2 in a place)
Orthodox Lad overcame a moderate draw to run a solid third race and is now due a mark which shouldn't be too high. (op 16-1 tchd 14-1)
Barnmore ◆ was the real eyecatcher in the race. Despite a moderate start and getting behind, nothing finished better. This was light years ahead of his debut and he's one to look for after one more race when he can be rated.
Steenbok(IRE) showed a bit more than on debut but was again readily beaten by Sirius Prospect and needs one more run to get a mark. (op 10-1 tchd 11-1)
Warden Bond is now due a mark and will win a modest handicap as this was much the best of his three runs. (tchd 66-1)
Dark And Dangerous(IRE) had been over 1m on his first two appearances and might need to go back to that trip now a mark can be allotted.

7387 DIGIBET H'CAP 1m 4f (P)
5:50 (5:57) (Class 6) (0-55,55) 3-Y-O £1,637 (£483; £241) Stalls Centre

Form RPR

5406 1 **Lucas Pitt**[62] 5873 3-8-13 52 JoeFanning 4 60
(M J Scudamore) *hld up in last trio: gd prog on outer 2f out to ld over 1f out: rdn clr ins fnl f* **8/1**

000 2 2 3/4 **Rhythm Stick**[19] 7069 3-8-13 52 DaneO'Neill 2 56
(John Berry) *hld up in midfield on outer: gd prog 2f out to chal over 1f out: chsd wnr after: readily lft bhd* **10/1**

305 3 1 1/2 **Lalika**[49] 6287 3-9-2 55 LukeMorris 8 56
(C G Cox) *led after 3f: gng strly over 2f out: hdd and outpcd over 1f out: drvn to hold on to 3rd* **5/1**[1]

0660 4 3/4 **Asterales**[15] 7156 3-8-7 46 ChrisCatlin 7 46
(W J Musson) *hld up in midfield: looking for room over 2f out: sme prog over 1f out: kpt on same pce* **12/1**

40F2 5 3/4 **Wavertree Bounty**[15] 7156 3-8-8 47 WilliamCarson 9 46
(J Ryan) *hld up towards rr: plld out 2f out: prog jst over 1f out: clsd on plcd horses ins fnl f: effrt petered out nr fin* **13/2**[3]

5-00 6 1/2 **Kingston Folly**[259] 677 3-9-2 55 NeilCallan 5 53
(A B Haynes) *stdd s: hld up in last trio: looking for room on inner over 2f out: rdn and kpt on one pce over 1f out* **50/1**

0002 7 2 **Mary Helen**[22] 7003 3-8-12 51 LiamJones 12 46
(W M Brisbourne) *hld up in midfield: nt clr run over 2f out: one pce and no imp over 1f out* **7/1**

-600 8 2 1/4 **Mater Mater**[8] 7286 3-9-2 55 (p) JimCrowley 3 46
(Andrew Reid) *hld up last: gng wl enough 3f out: plld out wd over 2f out: reminder and veered lft: modest late prog* **20/1**

0553 9 3/4 **Always De One**[20] 7039 3-8-9 48 CathyGannon 6 38
(Miss J Feilden) *trckd ldng pair to over 2f out: steadily wknd over 1f out* **8/1**

2400 10 1 1/2 **Port Hill**[90] 4991 3-9-2 55 ShaneKelly 14 43
(W M Brisbourne) *chsd ldrs: urged along most of way fr 5f out: effrt to dispute 2nd over 2f out: wknd over 1f out* **6/1**[2]

4030 11 hd **Half Sister (IRE)**[22] 7003 3-8-11 50 (t) SteveDrowne 1 37
(M E Rimmer) *racd wd: pressed ldrs: wknd 2f out* **20/1**

2100 12 3 1/2 **Miss Whippy**[16] 7117 3-8-9 51 KellyHarrison[(3)] 11 33
(P Howling) *led 3f: pressed ldr to over 2f out: wknd qckly over 1f out* **12/1**

2m 35.7s (1.20) **Going Correction** +0.025s/f (Slow) 12 Ran SP% **115.0**
Speed ratings (Par 98): **97,95,94,93,93 92,91,90,89,88 88,86**
CSF £80.71 CT £441.54 TOTE £6.00: £1.40, £2.30, £2.40; EX 97.10.
Owner Ted Bennett **Bred** M And Mrs V L Ritchie **Trained** Bromsash, Herefordshire
■ Stewards' Enquiry : Liam Jones two-day ban: careless riding (Nov 24-25)

FOCUS
An open handicap on paper made all the more suspect due to a modest early pace but, nevertheless, won with authority. Very moderate form, rated around the third.
Asterales Official explanation: vet said filly lost its left-fore shoe
Port Hill Official explanation: jockey said gelding hung right

7388 DIGIBET CASINO H'CAP 2m (P)
6:20 (6:27) (Class 6) (0-60,66) 3-Y-O+ **£1,637** (£483; £241) **Stalls** High

Form RPR

4051 **1** **Blackmore**[6] 7321 3-9-11 **66** 6ex CathyGannon 8 76
(Miss J Feilden) *nt gng wl in rr to 1/2-way: reminder after 3f: prog on inner 4f out: clsd over 2f out: drvn ahd over 1f out: styd on stoutly* **11/2**[2]

2340 **2** *1 ¼* **Miniyamba (IRE)**[60] 5963 3-9-4 **59** TedDurcan 1 68
(J L Dunlop) *hld up towards rr: prog fr 4f out to chse ldng pair 3f out: drvn to cl 2f out: chsd wnr jst over 1f out: one pce* **16/1**

3513 **3** *2 ¼* **Tower**[9] 7270 3-9-3 **58** JamieSpencer 14 64
(G Prodromou) *dropped out in last: stdy prog fr 6f out: chsd ldrs over 2f out: sn u.str.p and fnd nil: plugged into 3rd ins fnl f* **9/4**[1]

0-01 **4** *2 ¼* **Foreign King (USA)**[22] 6502 6-9-9 **55** IanMongan 13 58
(J W Mullins) *pressed ldrs: pushed up to ld 6f out: drvn over 2f out: hdd and one pce over 1f out* **11/1**

032U **5** *1* **Pearl (IRE)**[12] 7213 6-9-4 **50** (tp) ShaneKelly 12 52
(Mrs A M Thorpe) *trckd ldrs gng wl: wnt 2nd over 3f out: jnd ldr over 2f out gng strly: fdd rather tamely over 1f out* **11/1**

5053 **6** *5* **Delorain (IRE)**[12] 7213 7-8-8 **47** (vt) LauraPike(7) 6 43
(W B Stone) *mostly chsd ldr to over 3f out: steadily wknd fr over 2f out* **9/1**[3]

6362 **7** *8* **Happy Fleet**[48] 748 7-9-12 **58** DaneO'Neill 11 45
(R Curtis) *wl plcd bhd ldrs: gng bttr than most 4f out: drvn over 3f out: wknd qckly 2f out* **11/1**

5000 **8** *11* **Dongola (IRE)**[40] 6526 3-8-4 **45** LukeMorris 2 18
(P Winkworth) *chsd ldrs: rdn 6f out: no prog u.p over 3f out: wl btn in 8th over 2f out* **50/1**

060 **9** *3* **Pocket Too**[21] 1424 7-9-12 **58** (p) GeorgeBaker 3 28
(Matthew Salaman) *settled towards rr: dropped to bk of field 5f out: nvr on terms after* **16/1**

0500 **10** *8* **Stagecoach Emerald**[57] 6065 8-8-13 **50** (b) TobyAtkinson(5) 9 —
(T T Clement) *early reminders in last pair: nvr a factor: struggling fr 4f out* **40/1**

4043 **11** *1 ¼* **Astrovenus**[28] 6272 3-8-9 **50** JimmyQuinn 10 —
(M H Tompkins) *a towards rr: rdn 6f out: bhd fnl 4f* **25/1**

3366 **12** *6* **Aalya (IRE)**[25] 6921 3-9-1 **56** JimmyFortune 4 —
(P W Chapple-Hyam) *chsd ldrs: rdn 6f out: wknd fr 4f out* **14/1**

0603 **13** *42* **Annelko**[81] 5289 3-8-10 **51** SteveDrowne 7 —
(A B Haynes) *mde most to 6f out: wknd rapidly 4f out: eased and wl t.o* **12/1**

-006 **14** *4 ½* **Velvet Nayef**[15] 7157 4-8-13 **45** JackMitchell 5 —
(J Pearce) *hld up in rr: brief effrt 7f out: sn rdn and wknd rapidly: wl t.o* **25/1**

3m 30.25s (0.15) **Going Correction** +0.025s/f (Slow)
WFA 3 from 4yo+ 9lb **14** Ran SP% **119.4**
Speed ratings (Par 101): **100,99,98,97,96 94,90,84,83,79 78,75,54,52**
toteswingers:1&2 £28.50, 2&3 £9.00, 1&3 £3.50 CSF £86.36 CT £256.88 TOTE £5.20: £1.20, £5.60, £2.70; EX 69.10.
Owner Good Company Partnership **Bred** Juddmonte Farms Ltd **Trained** Exning, Suffolk
■ Stewards' Enquiry : Jamie Spencer two-day ban: used whip with excessive frequency without allowing gelding to respond (Nov 24-25)

FOCUS
Just an ordinary handicap, but the form looks sound and makes sense.
Annelko Official explanation: jockey said colt hung left

7389 DIGIBET.COM H'CAP 1m (P)
6:50 (6:56) (Class 5) (0-75,74) 3-Y-O **£2,286** (£675; £337) **Stalls** High

Form RPR

2322 **1** **Norman Orpen (IRE)**[47] 6332 3-9-6 **73** JamieSpencer 5 88+
(Jane Chapple-Hyam) *hld up in 7th and wl off the pce early: effrt whn rn into trble over 2f out: prog and swtiched lft over 1f out: pushed along and qcknd to ld last 150yds: won decisively* **9/2**[2]

6-34 **2** *1 ¼* **Loyaliste (FR)**[21] 7022 3-9-0 **67** JimmyFortune 1 77
(R Hannon) *trckd ldng trio: rdn and prog 2f out: led jst over 1f out: hdd last 150yds: styd on: readily hld* **10/1**

3-13 **3** *3* **Round Won (USA)**[182] 2025 3-9-7 **74** ShaneKelly 8 77
(W J Knight) *led at gd pce: hdd jst over 1f out: readily outpcd* **8/1**

1433 **4** *1* **Valencha**[20] 7047 3-9-5 **72** SteveDrowne 4 73
(H Morrison) *hld up in 6th: drvn and effrt on outer over 2f out: one pce fr over 1f out* **9/4**[1]

3033 **5** *nse* **Lean Machine**[12] 7214 3-8-12 **65** LukeMorris 2 66
(R A Harris) *chsd ldrs in 5th: drvn and effrt on inner 2f out: outpcd ins fnl f* **8/1**

-604 **6** *2 ½* **Poor Prince**[31] 6771 3-9-3 **70** FergusSweeney 7 65
(Mrs A M Batchelor) *trckd ldng pair: rdn to chse ldr wl over 2f out to wl over 1f out: wknd* **16/1**

0000 **7** *12* **Lisahane Bog**[16] 7115 3-9-6 **73** DaneO'Neill 6 40
(P R Hedger) *c out of the stalls wl after the rest: mostly detached in last: t.o* **7/1**[3]

2043 **8** *nk* **Profligate (IRE)**[14] 7162 3-8-12 **65** JimCrowley 3 32
(W Jarvis) *chsd ldr to wl over 2f out: wknd rapidly: t.o* **7/1**[3]

1m 39.31s (-0.49) **Going Correction** +0.025s/f (Slow) **8** Ran SP% **111.1**
Speed ratings (Par 102): **103,101,98,97,97 95,83,82**
toteswingers:1&2 £4.10, 2&3 £11.70, 1&3 £8.10 CSF £45.18 CT £339.64 TOTE £3.90: £1.10, £3.40, £3.60; EX 39.80.
Owner Gordon Li **Bred** Kevin Walsh **Trained** Dalham, Suffolk

FOCUS
A competitive mile handicap but won with considerable authority. It was just a modest race but the form is rated slightly positively.

7390 BOXINGDAYRACES.CO.UK H'CAP (DIV I) 6f (P)
7:20 (7:25) (Class 6) (0-65,65) 3-Y-O+ **£1,364** (£403; £201) **Stalls** High

Form RPR

0304 **1** **Nollaig Shona (IRE)**[69] 5695 3-9-1 **59** CathyGannon 10 67
(G Prodromou) *racd keenly: mde all: hrd pressed over 1f out: hld on gamely* **25/1**

0120 **2** *¾* **White Shift (IRE)**[14] 7162 4-9-7 **65** JimmyQuinn 5 71
(P Howling) *hld up in midfield: prog on inner over 2f out: chsd wnr wl over 1f out and styd against rail: nrly upsides ins fnl f: nt qckn* **10/1**

6644 **3** *hd* **Dream Number (IRE)**[13] 7194 3-9-2 **60** NeilCallan 8 65
(W R Muir) *wl in tch: pressed ldrs wl over 1f out: hrd rdn and kpt on: a hld* **11/2**[2]

2605 **4** *1 ½* **Bollywood Style**[140] 3322 5-9-0 **58** SteveDrowne 11 58
(J R Best) *chsd wnr to wl over 1f out: grad fdd last 150yds* **15/2**[3]

6513 **5** *¾* **Embra (IRE)**[21] 7018 5-9-0 **58** (p) TedDurcan 1 56+
(T J Etherington) *hld up in rr and racd wd: nt qckn over 2f out: styd on fnl f: nrst fin* **8/1**

4122 **6** *½* **Cavitie**[26] 6898 4-9-4 **62** JimCrowley 7 58
(Andrew Reid) *t.k.h early: chsd wnr to 1/2-way: rdn and nt qckn over 2f out: one pce after* **7/2**[1]

0200 **7** *½* **Sweet Avon**[44] 6421 3-9-2 **60** GeorgeBaker 2 55
(Matthew Salaman) *racd on outer: wl in tch: outpcd fr 2f out: no hdwy after* **14/1**

0612 **8** *1 ¼* **Speedyfix**[13] 7194 3-9-7 **65** (v) JimmyFortune 6 56
(Mrs C A Dunnett) *hld up in last trio: effrt and sme prog over 1f out: no hdwy and fdd ins fnl f* **10/1**

2351 **9** *½* **Downhill Skier (IRE)**[22] 7007 6-9-1 **59** TomMcLaughlin 3 48
(W M Brisbourne) *dwlt: detached in last: modest late prog: nvr a factor* **15/2**[3]

0000 **10** *1 ¾* **Bobs Dreamflight**[14] 7162 4-9-2 **60** SamHitchcott 4 43
(D K Ivory) *racd on outer: chsd wnr to wl over 2f out: wknd* **12/1**

4000 **11** *12* **Thoughtsofstardom**[13] 7194 7-8-13 **62** TobyAtkinson(5) 12 7
(P S McEntee) *hld up in last trio: wknd rapidly 2f out: t.o* **40/1**

1m 12.76s (-0.34) **Going Correction** +0.025s/f (Slow) **11** Ran SP% **111.1**
Speed ratings (Par 101): **103,102,101,99,98 98,97,95,95,92 76**
toteswingers:1&2 £49.70, 2&3 £5.70, 1&3 £33.40 CSF £218.96 CT £1184.89 TOTE £39.10: £7.90, £2.40, £2.10; EX 262.30.
Owner Fahed Al Dabbous **Bred** Pat Grogan **Trained** East Harling, Norfolk
■ Private Olley (6/1) was withdrawn after bolting to post: Rule 4 applies to all bets, deduct 10p in the £.

FOCUS
A tight handicap which lost a little of its edge with the late withdrawal of second favourite Private Olley. The time was faster than division 1 and little got involved, with the winner recording a clear personal best.
Downhill Skier(IRE) Official explanation: jockey said gelding hit starting gate, was slowly away and suffered interference

7391 BOXINGDAYRACES.CO.UK H'CAP (DIV II) 6f (P)
7:50 (7:53) (Class 6) (0-65,65) 3-Y-O+ **£1,364** (£403; £201) **Stalls** High

Form RPR

2000 **1** **Pragmatist**[22] 7007 6-8-13 **57** JamesMillman 12 64
(B R Millman) *hld up towards rr: prog on inner over 2f out: rdn to chal 1f out: styd on to ld nr fin* **10/1**

0000 **2** *nk* **Nubar Boy**[27] 6864 3-9-2 **60** GeorgeBaker 5 66+
(P D Evans) *hld up towards rr: looking for room fr 2f out: nt clr run and swtchd rt over 1f out: r.o wl fnl f: tk 2nd post* **8/1**

465 **3** *shd* **Laser Ruby**[49] 6285 3-9-2 **60** JimmyFortune 4 66
(A M Balding) *dwlt and n.m.r s: mostly last tl gd prog on inner fr over 2f out: drvn to ld 1f out: collared nr fin: lost 2nd post* **6/1**[2]

640 **4** *nk* **Doctor Hilary**[30] 6812 8-9-4 **62** (v) ChrisCatlin 10 67
(M R Hoad) *wl plcd bhd clr ldr: hanging and nt qckn fr over 2f out tl r.o ins fnl f: jst unable to chal* **8/1**

3350 **5** *¾* **Caramelita**[36] 6656 3-9-7 **65** JimCrowley 8 68
(J R Jenkins) *hld up in last trio: prog 2f out: chsd ldng pair wl ins fnl f: one pce and lost pl nr fin* **10/1**

6016 **6** *¾* **Mack's Sister**[22] 6997 3-9-6 **64** SteveDrowne 1 64+
(D K Ivory) *racd wd fr low draw and wl in rr: shkn up in last pair 2f out: styd on wl ins fnl f: nrst fin* **4/1**[1]

5000 **7** *½* **Lethal**[16] 7125 7-8-11 **58** AndrewHeffernan(3) 7 57
(R J Price) *chsd clr ldr to over 1f out: grad wknd* **10/1**

3500 **8** *2* **Simple Rhythm**[5] 7331 4-8-12 **59** RussKennemore(3) 9 51+
(J Ryan) *blasted off in front and sn 3 l clr: wknd and hdd 1f out* **15/2**[3]

1340 **9** *1* **Mary's Pet**[14] 7162 3-9-4 **62** J-PGuillambert 2 51
(J Akehurst) *dwlt: racd wd fr low draw and wl in rr: stl in last pair 2f out: kpt on same pce after* **16/1**

0630 **10** *¾* **Dvinsky (USA)**[22] 6997 9-9-7 **65** (b) JimmyQuinn 3 52
(P Howling) *racd on outer: chsd ldrs: no imp over 1f out: wknd* **9/1**

0000 **11** *1 ¼* **Fayre Bella**[14] 7162 3-9-2 **60** FergusSweeney 11 43
(J Gallagher) *nvr bttr than midfield: nt qckn 2f out: steadily fdd over 1f out* **16/1**

0300 **12** *1* **West Leake (IRE)**[42] 6456 4-9-1 **59** TomMcLaughlin 6 38
(P Burgoyne) *racd freely: prom bhd clr ldr tl lost pl wl over 1f out: n.m.r sn after and eased* **16/1**

1m 13.13s (0.03) **Going Correction** +0.025s/f (Slow) **12** Ran SP% **123.2**
Speed ratings (Par 101): **100,99,99,99,98 97,96,93,92,91 89,88**
toteswingers:1&2 £30.80, 2&3 £12.90, 1&3 £16.00 CSF £91.26 CT £541.80 TOTE £16.60: £5.70, £1.50, £3.50; EX 161.70.
Owner Mrs Jenny Willment **Bred** Mrs Jenny Willment **Trained** Kentisbeare, Devon

FOCUS
This was run at a strong gallop, but the pace collapsed and the time was slower than the first division. There was a bunch finish and the fiorm is rated around the winner, fourth and fifth.
Pragmatist Official explanation: trainer said, regarding apparent improvement in form, that the mare was better suited by the faster surface.
Nubar Boy Official explanation: jockey said gelding was denied a clear run
T/Plt: £76.60 to a £1 stake. Pool of £43,468.97 - 413.76 winning tickets. T/Qpdt: £14.50 to a £1 stake. Pool of £7,233.96 - 366.73 winning tickets. JN

7324 SOUTHWELL (L-H)
Wednesday, November 10

OFFICIAL GOING: Standard
Wind: moderate 1/2 behind Weather: fine and sunny but cold

7392 BET MULTIPLES - BETDAQ MAIDEN AUCTION STKS 5f (F)
12:30 (12:31) (Class 6) 2-Y-O **£1,619** (£481; £240; £120) **Stalls** High

Form RPR

022 **1** **Monsieur Jamie**[8] 7279 2-8-9 0 PaulMulrennan 4 62+
(J R Jenkins) *mde all: styd on wl to forge clr ins fnl f: readily* **10/11**[1]

2 *2 ½* **Arrivaderci** 2-8-3 0 AmyRyan(3) 12 50+
(R M Whitaker) *s.v.s: edgd lft towards centre: bhd: hdwy 2f out: r.o wl to take 2nd nr fin* **14/1**

00 **3** *½* **Georgian Silver**[25] 6916 2-7-13 0 NeilFarley(5) 1 46
(A G Foster) *chsd ldrs: kpt on same pce ins fnl f* **33/1**

4 1 **Verus Decorus (IRE)** 2-7-13 0 ow2 .... DannyBrock(7) 10 45
(Patrick Morris) *racd stands' side: mid-div: hdwy 2f out: styd on wl ins fnl f* **28/1**

0 5 nk **Diamond Sunrise (IRE)**[8] 7279 2-8-8 0 .... TomEaves 2 46
(N Wilson) *chsd wnr: kpt on same pce appr fnl f* **40/1**

0000 6 3/4 **Mujapiste (IRE)**[8] 7279 2-8-3 40 .... (tp) AndrewHeffernan(3) 5 41
(L A Mullaney) *chsd ldrs: one pce fnl 2f* **100/1**

000 7 2 1/4 **Emperorsnewclothes (IRE)**[24] 6953 2-8-3 35 ow1 .... (p) JulieBurke(7) 6 37
(George Baker) *sn outpcd and in rr towards stands' side: styd on appr fnl f: nvr a factor* **66/1**

000 8 1 **Hannah Cann**[82] 5269 2-7-13 20 ow2 .... LeonnaMayor(7) 3 29
(Peter Grayson) *dwlt: hld up towards rr: edgd rt over 2f out: nvr on terms* **200/1**

0064 9 nk **Lady On Top (IRE)**[131] 3636 2-8-6 51 .... LNewman 11 28
(Mrs P N Dutfield) *racd stands' side: a in rr* **33/1**

0304 10 5 **Indian Shuffle (IRE)**[18] 7088 2-8-13 69 .... RichardKingscote 7 17
(J G Portman) *sn in rr stands' side: reminders after 2f: sn bhd: eased ins fnl f* **5/2**[2]

403 11 2 3/4 **Silent Blessing**[68] 5733 2-8-11 62 .... (v) J-PGuillambert 9 5
(R M H Cowell) *racd stands' side: in rr: bhd fnl 2f: eased ins fnl f* **11/2**[3]

59.29 secs (-0.41) **Going Correction** -0.225s/f (Stan) 11 Ran SP% **117.8**
Speed ratings (Par 94): **94,90,89,87,87 85,82,80,80,72 67**
toteswingers:1&2 £5.60, 2&2 £40.30, 1&3 £9.30 CSF £16.27 TOTE £2.70: £1.30, £4.50, £10.70; EX 20.60 Trifecta £305.90 Part won. Pool of £413.38 - 0.50 winning units..

Owner Mark Goldstein & Stephen Pettman **Bred** Greg Parsons **Trained** Royston, Herts

FOCUS

A moderate maiden in which it paid to race middle to far side. The form is limited with some very lowly rated sorts not beaten far.

NOTEBOOK

Monsieur Jamie was the clear form pick and won as expected, keeping on best after displaying pace from the off. He had shown a reasonable level of ability over 6f on turf and was in no way inconvenienced by the drop in trip and switch to Fibresand. Things are set to get tougher, but he should be competitive in ordinary handicap company. (op Evens tchd 6-5)

Arrivaderci stood still as the stalls opened and lost several lengths. Having started from stall 12, she soon edged over towards the middle of the track, probably not a bad move considering low draws are often favoured over this C&D, and having been last 3f out, she finished well for second. While this is certainly not form to get carried away with, she has ability and should improve.

Georgian Silver stepped up markedly on her two turf efforts, although stall one may have put her at an advantage.

Verus Decorus(IRE), the first known foal of a 6f juvenile winner, ran to only a moderate level, but she did show speed towards the possibly unfavoured stands' rail and may do better. She carried 2lb overweight. (op 33-1)

Diamond Sunrise(IRE) showed speed up the centre of the track but didn't see her race out. (tchd 33-1)

Indian Shuffle(IRE) was struggling to keep up throughout and was ultimately well beaten. This was majorly disappointing, even allowing for him racing towards the possibly slower stands' side, and he was a long way below his official rating of 69 on this first Fibresand start. (op 7-2)

Silent Blessing showed nothing after a 68-day absence, but he had a rushed preparation according to Robert Cowell, who felt his runner was "probably a gallop short". (op 4-1)

7393 PLAY GOLF AT SOUTHWELL GOLF CLUB NURSERY (DIV I) 1m (F)

1:00 (1:01) (Class 5) (0-70,68) 2-Y-O **£1,910** (£564; £282) **Stalls** Low

Form RPR

000 1 **Geronimo Chief (IRE)**[65] 5814 2-8-6 **53** .... ChrisCatlin 4 58+
(B M R Haslam) *chsd ldrs: led over 4f out: hld on towards fin* **4/1**[3]

0404 2 3/4 **Phoenix Flame**[16] 7118 2-8-11 **58** .... RobertWinston 3 61
(A J McCabe) *w ldrs: chsd wnr over 2f out: kpt on same pce ins fnl f* **9/2**

0064 3 2 **Thank You Joy**[27] 6873 2-8-6 **60** .... DannyBrock(7) 2 58
(J R Jenkins) *t.k.h towards rr: effrt over 2f out: styd on fnl f: tk 3rd towards fin* **14/1**

0060 4 1 1/2 **Irie Ute**[82] 5256 2-9-1 **62** .... TravisBlock 6 60+
(S Kirk) *trckd ldrs: effrt and 3rd over 2f out: kpt on same pce ins fnl f* **18/1**

6224 5 1 **Zamina (IRE)**[11] 7242 2-9-5 **66** .... JamesDoyle 10 59
(S Kirk) *hld up in mid-div on outer: hdwy to trck ldrs over 3f out: one pce fnl 2f* **7/2**[2]

020 6 1/2 **Endaxi Mana Mou**[42] 6451 2-9-7 **68** .... WilliamCarson 8 60
(M G Quinlan) *s.i.s: hdwy on outer to chse ldrs 4f out: one pce fnl 2f* **10/1**

060 7 12 **Nippy Nikki**[46] 6360 2-7-7 **45** .... NeilFarley(5) 1 9
(J R Norton) *in rr: lost pl over 3f out: bhd fnl 2f* **33/1**

0000 8 1 1/4 **Terrys Flutter**[24] 6954 2-8-3 **50** .... (p) FrannyNorton 5 11
(M A Allen) *led tl over 4f out: lost pl over 1f out* **80/1**

0300 9 9 **Icelady**[16] 7118 2-7-12 **45** .... AndreaAtzeni 7 —
(R M H Cowell) *towards rr: sn drvn along: bhd fnl 3f* **22/1**

3003 10 4 **Beer Flush (IRE)**[27] 6875 2-8-12 **62** .... MichaelO'Connell(3) 9 —
(Jedd O'Keeffe) *towards rr: sn drvn along: lost pl over 2f out: sn bhd* **3/1**[1]

1m 44.17s (0.47) **Going Correction** -0.175s/f (Stan) 10 Ran SP% **114.9**
Speed ratings (Par 96): **90,89,87,85,84 84,72,71,62,58**
toteswingers:1&2 £4.80, 2&3 £10.20, 1&3 £8.60 CSF £21.67 CT £196.36 TOTE £5.80: £1.50, £1.60, £5.60; EX 27.30 Trifecta £183.20 Part won. Pool of £247.57 - 0.86 winning units..

Owner Mrs Sheila Mason & Robert Stipetic **Bred** Keene Bloodstock **Trained** Middleham Moor, N Yorks

■ Stewards' Enquiry : Robert Winston one-day ban: used whip with excessive frequency (Nov 24)

FOCUS

The time was 0.69 seconds slower than the second division, and almost a full second off the later juvenile seller win by 67-rated Podgies Boy. Clearly this moderate form with the runner-up setting the level.

NOTEBOOK

Geronimo Chief(IRE), returning from two months off, improved for the step up from 6f and the switch to Fibresand to become the third C&D winner for his dam Portorosa. He's clearly one to respect around here. Official explanation: trainer said, regarding apparent improvement in form, that the gelding may have benfited from a benevolent handicap mark and from running first time on the Fibresand. (op 7-2 tchd 9-2)

Phoenix Flame, back up in trip, was never far away and stuck on reasonably well, looking just the type her yard will find a race for this winter. (op 11-2)

Thank You Joy was soon behind, but she finished better than most. Her handicap mark was raised from 45 to 60 following a seemingly improved effort in a Nottingham maiden last time, and this performance goes some to proving that latest run was not a fluke.

Irie Ute, returning from 82 days off, didn't see his race out after being keen. This should have taken the freshness out of him and he may do better back over 7f. (op 22-1)

Zamina(IRE) offered little for pressure, running well below the form of her recent Polytrack efforts. She may do better away from Fibresand, but even so is probably one to have reservations about.

Beer Flush(IRE) responded well to a positive ride when third in a turf nursery on his previous start, but he was never going particularly well on this switch to Fibresand and was beaten a long way. (tchd 7-2)

7394 PLAY GOLF AT SOUTHWELL GOLF CLUB NURSERY (DIV II) 1m (F)

1:30 (1:30) (Class 5) (0-70,67) 2-Y-O **£1,910** (£564; £282) **Stalls** Low

Form RPR

003 1 **Battery Power**[40] 6521 2-8-12 **63** .... AshleyMorgan(5) 1 71+
(M H Tompkins) *hld up towards rr: hdwy whn hmpd and stmbld over 3f out: wnt 3rd over 1f out: styd on strly to ld last 50yds: won gng away* **11/2**[2]

0606 2 2 **Microlight**[69] 5682 2-8-9 **55** .... (e1) GrahamGibbons 8 58
(T D Easterby) *chsd ldrs: wnt 2nd over 3f out: edgd lft 2f out: led 1f out: hdd and no ex wl ins fnl f* **8/1**[3]

055 3 6 **Seeking Glory**[22] 6994 2-9-7 **67** .... TomMcLaughlin 3 57+
(E A L Dunlop) *led after 1f: qcknd 3f out: hdd 1f out: sn wknd* **5/1**[1]

3060 4 1 3/4 **High Kickin**[23] 6978 2-9-0 **60** .... (v1) JamesDoyle 2 46
(A J McCabe) *led 1f: chsd ldrs: outpcd and edgd rt over 2f out: one pce* **12/1**

0600 5 1 1/4 **Ad Vitam (IRE)**[91] 4967 2-7-13 **45** .... (t) JamieMackay 5 28
(S Kirk) *in rr and sn drvn along: kpt on fnl 2f: nvr nr ldrs* **50/1**

0040 6 hd **Miss Cosette (IRE)**[26] 6891 2-7-10 **47** .... NeilFarley(5) 4 29
(T D Barron) *in rr and sn drvn along: sme hdwy 2f out: nvr on terms* **5/1**[1]

4000 7 4 1/2 **Sky Diamond (IRE)**[16] 7124 2-9-2 **62** .... PaulMulrennan 9 34
(J G Given) *s.i.s: reminders after 2f: hdwy on outer to chse ldrs over 3f out: lost pl over 2f out* **9/1**

0461 8 9 **Callie's Angel**[37] 6628 2-9-1 **61** .... RobertWinston 10 12
(B Palling) *banged hd on gate: s.s: hdwy on outer 4f out: sn chsng ldrs: lost pl over 2f out* **11/2**[2]

000 9 3/4 **Mrs Neat (IRE)**[21] 7010 2-8-6 **52** .... (p) ChrisCatlin 6 —
(S Kirk) *chsd ldrs: drvn 4f out: sn lost pl* **14/1**

0550 10 8 **Glitter Bug (IRE)**[21] 7016 2-7-13 **45** .... AndreaAtzeni 7 —
(M Johnston) *chsd ldrs: hung lft and lost pl over 2f out: eased whn bhd towards fin* **9/1**

1m 43.48s (-0.22) **Going Correction** -0.175s/f (Stan) 10 Ran SP% **111.5**
Speed ratings (Par 96): **94,92,86,84,83 82,78,69,68,60**
toteswingers:1&2 £10.50, 2&3 £6.90, 1&3 £4.90 CSF £46.66 CT £232.04 TOTE £3.90: £1.50, £3.30, £4.20; EX 54.00 Trifecta £113.30 Part won. Pool of £153.15 - 0.10 winning units..

Owner H-Squared Electronics Ltd **Bred** Pollards Stables **Trained** Newmarket, Suffolk

FOCUS

A modest nursery run at a strong pace and the runner-up sets the level. The time was 0.69 seconds quicker than the first division, but 0.30 seconds off the 2-y-o seller.

NOTEBOOK

Battery Power is bred to stay well on the dam's side of her pedigree, so a fast-run race on this demanding surface suited well. She was off the pace through the early stages, and may even have clipped heels when stuck behind rivals on the bend into the straight, but she ran on strongly down the centre once in line for the finish, being helped by the leaders fading. She should be suited by further in due course. (tchd 6-1)

Microlight, upped in trip and fitted with eye-shields for the first time, ruined his chance by edging over to the usually unfavoured far rail in the straight. His performance can be upgraded slightly. (op 12-1)

Seeking Glory, upped in trip on his nursery debut, went off plenty fast enough under a really positive ride, and having been a good two or three lengths clear at the top of the straight, he had little left late on. He might want dropping back to 7f. (op 9-2 tchd 11-2)

High Kickin, with a visor replacing cheekpieces, seemed to have her chance. It remains to be proven that she wants a trip this far.

Miss Cosette(IRE), upped in distance, did not enjoy this first taste of Fibresand. She was soon behind and never featured at any stage. (op 6-1)

Callie's Angel lost ground when rearing slightly as the stalls opened, and though recovering to a point, he was under pressure and beaten before the straight. He won a Warwick maiden over 7f on heavy ground last time, but failed to prove himself under these conditions. Official explanation: jockey said colt banged it nose on leaving gates (op 7-2)

7395 BET ASIAN H'CAPS - BETDAQ NURSERY 6f (F)

2:00 (2:00) (Class 5) (0-70,69) 2-Y-O **£2,251** (£664; £332) **Stalls** Low

Form RPR

5230 1 **Rowan Spirit (IRE)**[11] 7240 2-9-7 **69** .... GrahamGibbons 7 76
(W M Brisbourne) *w ldrs on outer: led over 1f out: jst hld on* **8/1**[3]

6021 2 shd **Queen Of Cash (IRE)**[6] 7313 2-9-6 **68** 6ex .... RobertWinston 6 75
(H Morrison) *w ldrs: chal over 1f out: rallied ins fnl f: jst hld* **8/11**[1]

0000 3 1 3/4 **Henrys Air**[12] 7211 2-8-8 **56** .... WilliamCarson 4 57
(D G Bridgwater) *led tl over 1f out: kpt on same pce* **40/1**

1425 4 1 **Captain Loui (IRE)**[19] 7066 2-9-3 **65** .... (p) PaulMulrennan 5 63
(D Burchell) *chsd ldrs: edgd rt and kpt on one pce ins fnl f* **6/1**[2]

2635 5 2 1/4 **Cristaliyev**[35] 6666 2-9-6 **68** .... StephenCraine 3 60
(J R Boyle) *rrd s: hdwy to chse ldrs and hung rt over 3f out: one pce fnl 2f* **8/1**[3]

2303 6 hd **Three Scoops**[16] 7124 2-8-3 **51** .... (t) FrannyNorton 1 42
(D J S Ffrench Davis) *chsd ldrs: rdn and outpcd over 2f out: one pce* **8/1**[3]

603 7 5 **Spin A Wish**[16] 7127 2-8-9 **60** .... AmyRyan(3) 8 36
(R M Whitaker) *chsd ldrs on outer: lost pl 3f out* **25/1**

0046 8 7 **Gothic Chick**[15] 7151 2-9-3 **65** .... (p) JamieMackay 2 20
(Miss Amy Weaver) *chsd ldrs: outpcd over 2f out: sn lost pl* **33/1**

0004 9 2 3/4 **Jamaica Grande**[12] 7207 2-7-6 **47** .... (p) JessicaSteven(7) 9 —
(T T Clement) *towards rr on outer: hung rt and lost pl bnd over 3f out: sn bhd* **66/1**

1m 15.97s (-0.53) **Going Correction** -0.175s/f (Stan) 9 Ran SP% **116.2**
Speed ratings (Par 96): **96,95,93,92,89 88,82,72,69**
toteswingers:1&2 £2.70, 2&3 £12.80, 1&3 £13.50 CSF £14.11 CT £234.09 TOTE £14.90: £3.90, £1.10, £14.90; EX 19.60 Trifecta £188.20 Pool of £437.54 - 1.72 winning units..

Owner Deva Racing Captain Rio Partnership **Bred** Secret Justice Syndicate **Trained** Great Ness, Shropshire

FOCUS

A modest nursery with the first two improvers and the third back to previous course form.

NOTEBOOK

Rowan Spirit(IRE) handled the Fibresand well at the first attempt and built on a slightly unlucky effort at Wolverhampton. He was clearly reasonably treated for his handicap debut and can remain competitive. (tchd 15-2)

Queen Of Cash(IRE), 2lb well in under the penalty picked up for her success on her nursery debut at Kempton the previous week, was just held. She stuck on really gamely in the closing stages, briefly looking as though she may get back up, and her attitude should ensure she makes further progress. (op 10-11 tchd Evens)

Henrys Air came into this well out of form, but his second placing in a Polytrack maiden back in April showed he has ability, and this was a respectable performance.

Captain Loui(IRE) ran okay on this drop back from an extended 1m, but it may be that 7f is his optimum distance. (op 13-2 tchd 11-2)

7396 HOSPITALITY AT SOUTHWELL RACECOURSE (S) STKS 1m (F)
2:30 (2:30) (Class 6) 2-Y-O £1,619 (£481; £240; £120) Stalls Low

Form				RPR
2044	1		**Podgies Boy (IRE)**[12] 7210 2-8-11 67 PaulMulrennan 1 (R A Fahey) *in rr: effrt over 3f out: chsng ldrs over 2f out: led 1f out: kpt on wl* 5/1[3]	58
040	2	3/4	**Rath Maeve**[178] 2139 2-8-6 39 PaulQuinn 2 (A J McCabe) *chsd ldrs: kpt on and almost upsides over 1f out: no ex last 50yds* 100/1	51
0464	3	3/4	**Mary Boyle**[16] 7124 2-8-7 52 NeilFarley(5) 8 (A J McCabe) *sn in tch on outer: hdwy to chse ldr over 3f out: led over 1f out: sn hdd: kpt on same pce* 5/1[3]	56
253	4	1/2	**Yorketa**[9] 7271 2-8-7 0 ow1 TomEaves 10 (M Dods) *w ldr: led over 3f out: hdd over 1f out: one pce* 4/1[2]	49
2004	5	3 3/4	**Calormen**[14] 7177 2-8-9 56 ow1 RussKennemore(3) 9 (A G Juckes) *chsd ldrs: outpcd over 3f out: edgd lft and one pce over 1f out* 16/1	46
1	6	6	**Brand Bob (IRE)**[14] 7177 2-9-3 68 ChrisCatlin 11 (Miss Amy Weaver) *chsd ldrs: rdn and outpcd over 2f out: wknd over 1f out* 13/8[1]	37
0005	7	3/4	**Carver County (IRE)**[24] 6964 2-8-11 41 FrankieMcDonald 7 (Miss M E Rowland) *chsd ldrs: lost pl over 3f out* 66/1	29
0005	8	shd	**Gypsy Legend (IRE)**[14] 7177 2-8-6 54 JamieMackay 3 (S Kirk) *s.i.s: sn drvn along in rr: nvr on terms* 7/1	24
000	9	34	**Belles Boudier**[39] 6569 2-8-6 35 AndreaAtzeni 5 (G Woodward) *in rr and sn drvn along: lost pl over 3f out: sn bhd: t.o* 80/1	—
006	10	74	**Huckle Duckle (IRE)**[22] 6995 2-8-6 25 (p) WilliamCarson 4 (P S McEntee) *led tl over 3f out: sn lost pl and bhd: t.o 2f out: virtually p.u* 100/1	—

1m 43.18s (-0.52) **Going Correction** -0.175s/f (Stan) 10 Ran SP% **114.5**
Speed ratings (Par 94): **95,94,93,93,89 83,82,82,48,—**
toteswingers:1&2 £10.00, 2&3 £27.70, 1&3 £4.00 CSF £381.64 TOTE £7.40: £2.00, £15.70, £1.20; EX 159.80 TRIFECTA Not won..There was no bid for winner.
Owner G Devlin **Bred** Seamus Duffy **Trained** Musley Bank, N Yorks

FOCUS
The time was quicker than both divisions of the Class 5 nursery (0.99 faster than first leg, 0.30 quicker than the second), so probably a reasonable race for the grade. The winner is rated to his latest mark.

NOTEBOOK
Podgies Boy(IRE) handled Fibresand well at the first attempt and the step to 1m suited, too. He was off the pace towards the inside through the early stages, but picked up nicely when switched to the middle of the track in the straight to record a decisive success, his first at the fifth attempt. Although not that big, he should remain competitive at this sort of level. (op 3-1)
Rath Maeve, officially rated 39, clearly ran above her mark seeing as she had 23lb to find with the winner, and 7lb to find with the third. The step up from sprint trips evidently suited, and she deserves extra credit seeing as she stuck towards the unfavoured far rail for most of the way. (tchd 80-1)
Mary Boyle was off the pace early having started sluggishly, but she was then in front going around the final bend and surely must have used up a fair amount of energy to get there. She was still close up at the finish, though, and this was a respectable effort. (op 11-2 tchd 9-2)
Yorketa just as at Wolverhampton last time, didn't know how to knuckle down under pressure, again pricking her ears in the closing stages. She doesn't look ungenuine, it's seems to be immaturity more than anything, but she has the ability to win a race if learning to run on for pressure. Maybe headgear will help her concentrate. (op 10-3)
Brand Bob(IRE) was nowhere near the form he showed when winning a seller on his British debut on easy turf two weeks earlier, and seemingly this surface didn't suit. (op 11-4)

7397 BET IN RUNNING - BETDAQ (S) STKS 1m 4f (F)
3:00 (3:00) (Class 6) 3-Y-O+ £1,619 (£481; £240; £120) Stalls Low

Form				RPR
1044	1		**Kimberley Downs (USA)**[5] 7327 4-9-9 75 TomEaves 9 (N Wilson) *sn trcking ldr: led over 3f out: styd on ins fnl f* 14/1	75
1035	2	1 1/4	**Budva**[24] 6955 3-9-3 67 TravisBlock 5 (H Morrison) *drvn to ld after 1f: hdd over 3f out: styd on same pce ins fnl f: eased whn hld nr fin* 3/1[3]	74
-453	3	5	**Grande Caiman (IRE)**[5] 7327 6-9-4 90 FrannyNorton 7 (G A Harker) *in rr: hdwy 7f out: drvn over 5f out: wnt modest 3rd 3f out: kpt on one pce* 5/2[2]	61
0	4	8	**Mezarat (ITY)**[14] 7184 5-9-9 77 (t) AndreaAtzeni 3 (S C Williams) *mid-div: drvn over 5f out: kpt on one pce: tk modest 4th over 1f out* 15/8[1]	53
4513	5	9	**Miss Wendy**[22] 7003 3-8-7 58 AshleyMorgan(5) 1 (M H Tompkins) *led 1f: chsd ldrs: wknd over 2f out* 11/1	34
1050	6	12	**Black Falcon (IRE)**[36] 6660 10-9-9 50 (b) RobertWinston 6 (John A Harris) *sn trcking ldrs: hung bdly lft: hit rail: eased and lost pl over 3f out: sn bhd* 50/1	20
-004	7	4 1/2	**Feeling (IRE)**[18] 6051 6-8-13 40 (p) BillyCray(5) 8 (D Burchell) *in rr: drvn 7f out: lost pl over 5f out: sn bhd* 100/1	—
0	8	6	**Poesmulligan (IRE)**[10] 7251 4-9-4 0 FrankieMcDonald 4 (Mrs L C Jewell) *dwlt: in rr: bhd fnl 6f* 100/1	—
0000	9	hd	**Lava Steps (USA)**[123] 3901 4-9-4 60 MickyFenton 2 (P T Midgley) *s.i.s: mid-div: drvn 7f out: sn lost pl and bhd* 20/1	—
5660	10	7	**Suor Angelica (IRE)**[36] 6649 5-8-10 38 MatthewDavies(3) 10 (George Baker) *s.i.s: hdwy to chse ldrs after 2f: wknd and eased over 2f out: virtually p.u* 33/1	—

2m 37.53s (-3.47) **Going Correction** -0.175s/f (Stan)
WFA 3 from 4yo+ 6lb 10 Ran SP% **115.0**
Speed ratings (Par 101): **104,103,99,94,88 80,77,73,73,68**
toteswingers:1&2 £7.20, 2&3 £2.40, 1&3 £5.80 CSF £53.81 TOTE £5.70: £1.20, £2.40, £1.40; EX 58.70 Trifecta £120.60 Pool of £345.72 - 2.12 winning units..The winner was bought in for 8,500gns. Budva was claimed by J. L. Flint for £6000.
Owner Far 2 Many Sues **Bred** Gaines-Gentry Thoroughbreds **Trained** Sandhutton, N Yorks

FOCUS
A fair claimer in whichn the runner-up uis the best guide to the form.
Black Falcon(IRE) Official explanation: jockey said gelding hung left
Poesmulligan(IRE) Official explanation: jockey said gelding never travelled

7398 BOOK YOUR TICKETS ONLINE AT SOUTHWELL-RACECOURSE.CO.UK H'CAP 1m 6f (F)
3:30 (3:30) (Class 6) (0-60,60) 3-Y-O+ £1,619 (£481; £240; £120) Stalls Low

Form				RPR
106	1		**Jezza**[19] 7068 4-9-3 51 StevieDonohoe 10 (V R A Dartnall) *in rr: hrd drvn over 4f out: hdwy on ins over 3f out: led 2f out: styd on wl: eased nr fin* 8/1	62+
0242	2	2	**Mediterranean Sea (IRE)**[58] 6022 4-9-12 60 StephenCraine 8 (J R Jenkins) *hld up in rr: smooth hdwy to trck ldrs 7f out: edgd lft fr over 2f out: chsd wnr ins fnl f: no imp* 7/2[1]	67+
0502	3	nk	**Davana**[5] 7330 4-8-5 46 oh1 (p) MatthewCosham(7) 2 (W J H Ratcliffe) *in rr: hdwy over 4f out: outpcd 3f out: hdwy on outside 2f out: 6th appr fnl f: styd on wl* 13/2	53
1465	4	1 1/4	**Ballade De La Mer**[14] 7176 4-8-12 46 (p) LNewman 5 (A G Foster) *led tl 2f out: one pce: n.m.r wl ins fnl f* 20/1	51
1400	5	5	**Silent Lucidity (IRE)**[14] 7176 6-9-6 54 (p) TomEaves 1 (P D Niven) *chsd ldrs: hrd drvn over 4f out: fdd appr fnl f* 16/1	52
0046	6	3/4	**Pound Lane (IRE)**[36] 6660 4-8-12 46 oh1 RobertWinston 3 (Miss T Spearing) *trckd ldrs: drvn 3f out: wknd over 1f out* 7/1	43
0032	7	8	**Inside Knowledge (USA)**[9] 7270 4-8-13 47 AndreaAtzeni 9 (G Woodward) *s.i.s: hdwy on outside over 3f out: sn chsng ldrs: wknd over 2f out* 11/2[3]	33
0006	8	12	**Goodison Park**[33] 6707 3-7-13 46 oh1 (p) NeilFarley(5) 6 (A G Foster) *rn in snatches: in rr and reminders after 3f: hdwy on outside 6f out: sn given more reminders: lost pl 4f out: bhd and eased 2f out* 28/1	15
4205	9	3/4	**Astroleo**[28] 4765 4-8-7 46 AshleyMorgan(5) 4 (M H Tompkins) *prom: drvn over 5f out: lost pl 3f out* 12/1	14
/30-	10	3/4	**Fielder (IRE)**[588] 1073 5-9-12 60 RichardKingscote 11 (J G Portman) *chsd ldrs: n.m.r over 2f out: sn wknd: lame* 22/1	27
6013	11	12	**Mexican Jay (USA)**[5] 7330 4-9-5 60 AdamCarter(7) 7 (B Smart) *trckd ldr: lost pl over 3f out: heavily eased 2f out* 5/1[2]	10

3m 6.29s (-2.01) **Going Correction** -0.175s/f (Stan)
WFA 3 from 4yo+ 8lb 11 Ran SP% **117.4**
Speed ratings (Par 101): **98,96,96,95,93 92,88,81,80,80 73**
toteswingers:1&2 £10.60, 2&3 £5.70, 1&3 £12.50 CSF £35.08 CT £196.74 TOTE £7.20: £2.00, £1.20, £3.00; EX 38.60 Trifecta £205.40 Pool of £377.57- 1.36 winning units..
Owner Under The Radar **Bred** C P Ranson **Trained** Brayford, Devon

FOCUS
A moderate staying handicap rated around the third and fourth.
Fielder(IRE) Official explanation: vet said gelding finished lame
Mexican Jay(USA) Official explanation: jockey said filly ran flat

7399 ATHOS HERE FOR CHRISTMAS & NEW YEAR H'CAP 6f (F)
4:00 (4:02) (Class 5) (0-75,75) 3-Y-O+ £2,590 (£770; £385; £192) Stalls Low

Form				RPR
6210	1		**Victorian Bounty**[6] 7314 5-9-7 74 MickyFenton 8 (Stef Higgins) *led tl 3f out: rallied fnl f: styd on to ld nr fin* 14/1	85
-005	2	nk	**Nadeen (IRE)**[15] 7144 3-9-6 73 PaulMulrennan 6 (Michael Smith) *hld up: gd hdwy on inner to ld 3f out: edgd rt 2f out: hdd and no ex nr fin* 17/2	83
2022	3	1 1/2	**Dubai Hills**[19] 7051 4-8-5 65 AdamCarter(7) 5 (B Smart) *chsd ldrs: edgd rt and kpt on same pce over 1f out* 5/1[1]	70
5414	4	3 1/2	**Cardinal**[27] 6880 5-9-4 71 TomEaves 13 (R M H Cowell) *in rr: hdwy on outside to chse ldrs over 3f out: sn outpcd: kpt on fnl 2f* 6/1[3]	65
5405	5	hd	**Kipchak (IRE)**[5] 7332 5-8-4 64 (p) SophieSilvester(7) 9 (C R Dore) *trckd ldrs: outpcd 3f out: kpt on ins fnl f* 12/1	57
5000	6	3 1/2	**Ace Of Spies (IRE)**[5] 7326 5-9-3 70 RobertWinston 1 (C R Dore) *chsd ldrs: wknd over 1f out* 8/1	52
6023	7	1/2	**Milton Of Campsie**[14] 7180 5-9-7 74 FrannyNorton 2 (J Balding) *chsd ldrs: hung rt over 1f out: sn wknd* 10/1	54
2044	8	1/2	**Kensington (IRE)**[20] 7033 9-9-0 67 (p) JamesDoyle 10 (A J McCabe) *drvn to r w ldrs: lost pl 2f out* 16/1	46
5210	9	hd	**Charles Parnell (IRE)**[11] 7241 7-8-11 67 MichaelStainton(3) 11 (S P Griffiths) *rrd s: in rr: hdwy inner over 2f out: wknd over 1f out* 13/2	45
0654	10	3	**Bel Cantor**[22] 7006 7-8-3 63 (p) MatthewCosham(7) 3 (W J H Ratcliffe) *in rr: hdwy on ins over 2f out: wknd over 1f out* 11/2[2]	32
603	11	1 1/2	**Pilgrim Dancer (IRE)**[42] 6461 3-9-2 69 (v[1]) StephenCraine 12 (Patrick Morris) *sn chsng ldrs: lost pl over 2f out* 20/1	33

1m 14.87s (-1.63) **Going Correction** -0.175s/f (Stan) 11 Ran SP% **115.4**
Speed ratings (Par 103): **103,102,100,95,95 91,90,89,89,85 83**
toteswingers:1&2 £19.80, 2&3 £8.40, 1&3 £13.40 CSF £125.50 CT £683.67 TOTE £17.10: £6.90, £4.80, £2.10; EX 145.30 Trifecta £245.50 Part won. Pool of £331.78 - 0.43 winning units..
Owner David Gilbert **Bred** Mrs P D Gray And H Farr **Trained** Lambourn, Berks

FOCUS
A modest, but competitive enough handicap. The winner is rated to his turf best with the third to his recent best.
T/Plt: £67.90 to a £1 stake. Pool of £57,719.79 - 620.12 winning tickets. T/Qpdt: £11.10 to a £1 stake. Pool of £4,056.92 - 268.30 winning tickets. WG

7392 SOUTHWELL (L-H)
Thursday, November 11

OFFICIAL GOING: Standard
Wind: Fresh across Weather: Heavy frain showers

7400 MCGOW123 TV BRACKETS ON E BAY MAIDEN AUCTION STKS 7f (F)
12:20 (12:21) (Class 6) 2-Y-O £1,619 (£481; £240; £120) Stalls Low

Form				RPR
	1		**Brown Panther** 2-8-9 0 RichardKingscote 3 (Tom Dascombe) *prom: swtchd rt and hdwy 2f out: rdn to chal over 1f out: edgd lft and kpt on ins fnl f to ld last 50yds* 9/2[2]	69
0	2	1	**Flying Power**[16] 7152 2-8-9 0 TedDurcan 7 (D R Lanigan) *trckd ldrs: hdwy on outer 1/2-way to ld wl over 2f out: pushed clr wl over 1f out: rdn and hung bdly rt 1f out: drvn and sltly hmpd: hdd wl ins fnl f: kpt on towards fin* 10/1	67
5200	3	nk	**Laugh Or Cry**[44] 6445 2-8-9 68 NeilCallan 5 (P J Makin) *trckd ldrs: hdwy on inner over 2f out: rdn to chal 1f out: drvn and led wl ins fnl f: hdd and no ex last 50yds* 9/2[2]	66
0	4	2	**Dictate**[13] 7203 2-9-3 0 MichaelHills 8 (M H Tompkins) *s.i.s and in rr: hdwy 1/2-way: rdn to chse ldrs 2f out: sn drvn and kpt on same pce appr fnl f* 7/2[1]	69+

5006 **5** 7 **Bonniebridge**[69] 5709 2-8-6 50 ow2 FrannyNorton 11 40
(M E Rimmer) *towards rr: hdwy 3f out: rdn and in tch 2f out: sn no imp* **14/1**

00 **6** 6 **Colzium**[55] 6158 2-8-11 0 JimmyQuinn 4 29
(M H Tompkins) *s.i.s and bhd tl sme late hdwy* **40/1**

0 **7** 1 **Bigalo's Princessa**[16] 7142 2-8-4 0 DuranFentiman 2 19
(L A Mullaney) *led: rdn along 1/2-way: hdd wl over 2f out and sn wknd* **100/1**

00 **8** 1 ¾ **Come On Eileen (IRE)**[29] 6844 2-8-1 0 (e[1]) AndrewHeffernan(3) 10 15
(R C Guest) *a towards rr* **100/1**

3423 **9** nk **Whitecrest**[7] 7309 2-8-5 72 ow1 SamHitchcott 6 15
(J L Spearing) *prom: rdn along over 3f out: sn wknd* **7/2[1]**

10 1 **Gud Day (IRE)** 2-8-13 0 PaulMulrennan 1 20
(Mrs D J Sanderson) *sn rdn along and outpcd towards rr: bhd fr 1/2-way* **8/1[3]**

1m 29.3s (-1.00) **Going Correction** -0.20s/f (Stan) **10** Ran SP% **112.1**
Speed ratings (Par 94): **97,95,95,93,85 78,77,75,74,73**
toteswingers:1&2:£13.50, 1&3:£5.30, 2&3:£9.20 CSF £46.40 TOTE £5.00: £2.40, £4.00, £1.90; EX 63.90 TRIFECTA Not won..
Owner Owen Promotions Limited **Bred** Owen Promotions Ltd **Trained** Malpas, Cheshire

FOCUS
Conditions were riding on the fast side. An ordinary 2-y-o maiden with none of the runners having run here before.

NOTEBOOK
Brown Panther, green beforehand, is a homebred who has size and scope. Forced wide, he showed a good attitude to gain the upper hand in the closing stages. He should make a fair staying handicapper at three. (op 7-2 tchd 5-1)
Flying Power, 100-1 and tailed off on debut on heavy ground at Yarmouth two weeks earlier, swept to the front and looked in command, but he hung badly right and was worn down near the line. He still looks to have plenty to learn. (op 14-1)
Laugh Or Cry, rated 68, followed the first two drifting right-handed in the closing stages. He looks the marker for the overall value of the form. (op 5-1)
Dictate, drawn wide, lost ground at the start and was always going wide. He stuck on steadily in the home straight and looks to have further improvement in him. (op 4-1)
Bonniebridge, rated just 50, had the worst of the draw and was not disgraced. (op 33-1)
Whitecrest, an exposed filly rated 72, was flat out at halfway and dropped right away. Her mark flatters her. (op 11-4 tchd 5-2)

7401 BET MULTIPLES - BETDAQ H'CAP (DIV I) 7f (F)
12:50 (12:51) (Class 6) (0-60,60) 3-Y-O+ **£1,295** (£385; £192; £96) **Stalls** Low

Form RPR

0600 **1** **It's A Mans World**[28] 6860 4-8-0 **46** RyanPowell(7) 5 54
(Ian Williams) *hld up in tch: hdwy to chse ldrs 3f out: effrt to ld wl over 1f out: rdn ins fnl f: kpt on wl* **8/1**

1546 **2** 1 **Castle Myth (USA)**[17] 7122 4-9-5 **58** NeilCallan 9 63+
(B Ellison) *trckd ldrs: effrt over 2f out: rdn and n.m.r whn swtchd rt over 1f out: drvn and styd on wl fnl f* **11/2[1]**

0065 **3** 1 **Zarius**[16] 7153 3-9-1 **55** TedDurcan 6 57
(C F Wall) *in tch: hdwy to chse ldrs over 2f out: rdn and hung lft ent fnl f: kpt on towards fin* **14/1**

2134 **4** nk **Dancing Welcome**[36] 6671 4-9-0 **56** (b) RussKennemore(3) 2 58
(J M Bradley) *hld up: pushed along 1/2-way: hdwy over 2f out: swtchd lft and rdn wl over 1f out: drvn to chse ldrs ent fnl f: kpt on same pce* **13/2[2]**

0435 **5** shd **Whaston (IRE)**[17] 7132 5-8-10 **49** PaulMulrennan 14 51
(Miss P Robson) *trckd ldrs: hdwy on outer to ld wl over 2f out and sn rdn: hdd wl over 1f out: drvn and one pce fnl f* **9/1**

0134 **6** 1 **Exopuntia**[23] 7005 4-8-7 **49** MichaelStainton(3) 3 48+
(Miss J Feilden) *in rr: hdwy over 2f out: sn rdn and kpt on wl appr fnl f: nrst fin* **7/1[3]**

2300 **7** 3 ½ **Isabella Romee (IRE)**[21] 7037 4-8-4 **50** LewisWalsh(7) 10 39
(Jane Chapple-Hyam) *s.i.s and bhd tl styd on fnl 2f: nvr nr ldrs* **12/1**

0000 **8** shd **Ponting (IRE)**[14] 7194 4-9-4 **60** PaulPickard(3) 1 49
(P T Midgley) *trckd ldrs on inner: hdwy over 2f out: rdn and ev ch wl over 1f out: wknd appr fnl f* **28/1**

0210 **9** 7 **Katmai River (IRE)**[23] 7006 3-8-13 **58** LeeNewnes(5) 4 27
(M D I Usher) *sn rdn along: a towards rr* **7/1[3]**

600 **10** 5 **Kladester (USA)**[36] 6672 4-8-12 **51** (p) PhillipMakin 8 8
(M Herrington) *cl up: rdn along 3f out: sn drvn and wknd* **8/1**

11 1 **Arbiter (IRE)**[22] 7029 3-9-2 **56** ChrisCatlin 7 9
(Jarlath P Fahey, Ire) *led: rdn along 1/2-way: hdd wl over 2f and sn wknd* **16/1**

4000 **12** ¾ **Baraconti (IRE)**[43] 6463 3-9-4 **58** TomEaves 13 9
(Mrs R A Carr) *cl up: rdn along 3f out: sn wknd* **50/1**

00-0 **13** 4 **Byron Bay**[17] 7128 8-8-13 **52** (p) GrahamGibbons 11 —
(R Johnson) *chsd ldrs on outer: rdn along 1/2-way and sn wknd* **33/1**

1m 29.19s (-1.11) **Going Correction** -0.20s/f (Stan)
WFA 3 from 4yo+ 1lb **13** Ran SP% **114.5**
Speed ratings (Par 101): **98,96,95,95,95 94,90,90,82,76 75,74,69**
toteswingers:1&2:£10.00, 1&3:£22.90, 2&3:£9.40 CSF £48.56 CT £607.56 TOTE £11.50: £3.90, £1.80, £1.90; EX 47.10 TRIFECTA Not won..
Owner Ms S Howell **Bred** Cheveley Park Stud Ltd **Trained** Portway, Worcs

FOCUS
A low grade handicap. The winner is rated to this year's form.

7402 BET MULTIPLES - BETDAQ H'CAP (DIV II) 7f (F)
1:20 (1:20) (Class 6) (0-60,60) 3-Y-O+ **£1,295** (£385; £192; £96) **Stalls** Low

Form RPR

4553 **1** **Watch Chain (IRE)**[14] 7191 3-9-4 **57** MichaelHills 13 66
(M H Tompkins) *trckd ldrs: hdwy 2f out: swtchd lft and effrt to chal over 1f out: rdn to ld ins fnl f: kpt on wl* **7/1[3]**

0500 **2** ¾ **Feet Of Fury**[22] 7023 4-8-12 **50** PaulMulrennan 5 58
(Ian Williams) *t.k.h early: trckd ldrs: hdwy 3f out: led 2f out: rdn over 1f out: drvn and hdd ins fnl f: kpt on* **6/1[2]**

5605 **3** 1 ¾ **My One Weakness (IRE)**[17] 7128 3-9-2 **55** NeilCallan 12 57
(B Ellison) *dwlt and sn pushed along towards rr: rdn 1/2-way: hdwy on wd outside over 2f out: drvn to chal over 1f out: edgd lft ent fnl f and sn one pce* **9/2[1]**

0006 **4** 2 ¼ **Ubenkor (IRE)**[26] 6917 5-9-6 **58** TomEaves 3 55
(M Herrington) *midfield: hdwy on inner to chse ldrs over 2f out: rdn wl over 1f out: sn drvn and kpt on same pce* **12/1**

3400 **5** 2 ½ **Fathey (IRE)**[20] 7064 4-9-0 **52** PhillipMakin 9 42
(C Smith) *cl up: led 3f out: rdn and hdd 2f out: sn drvn and grad wknd* **12/1**

6553 **6** 4 **Norcroft**[17] 7132 8-8-7 **45** (b) CathyGannon 6 25
(Mrs C A Dunnett) *towards rr: sme hdwy fnl 2f: n.d* **10/1**

0530 **7** hd **Gilderoy**[23] 6996 3-8-11 **50** (p) JamesDoyle 1 28
(D J S Ffrench Davis) *chsd ldrs on inner: n.m.r 3f out: sn rdn and wknd fnl 2f* **20/1**

6560 **8** 2 ¾ **Mister Jingles**[20] 7056 7-8-13 **54** (v) MichaelStainton(3) 11 26
(R M Whitaker) *chsd ldrs: rdn along 3f out: wknd over 2f out* **25/1**

0000 **9** ½ **Refuse To Wait (IRE)**[16] 7149 3-8-10 **49** (b) GrahamGibbons 10 18
(T D Easterby) *nvr a factor* **16/1**

6026 **10** 3 **Lordship (IRE)**[12] 7229 6-8-10 **55** JakePayne(7) 8 17
(A W Carroll) *chsd ldrs: rdn along 3f out: sn wknd* **16/1**

0001 **11** 3 **Takajan (IRE)**[17] 7131 3-9-0 **60** JamesRogers(7) 14 13
(W M Brisbourne) *led: rdn along 1/2-way: sn hdd & wknd over 2f out* **8/1**

0002 **12** ½ **Funky Munky**[12] 7230 5-8-8 **46** (t) PatrickMathers 2 —
(A C Whillans) *sn rdn along and a in rr* **12/1**

5510 **13** 3 ½ **Darcy's Pride (IRE)**[8] 7300 6-8-12 **57** ShaneBKelly(7) 4 —
(P T Midgley) *blind removed late: v.s.a and a bhd* **14/1**

1m 29.4s (-0.90) **Going Correction** -0.20s/f (Stan)
WFA 3 from 4yo+ 1lb **13** Ran SP% **115.3**
Speed ratings (Par 101): **97,96,94,91,88 84,83,80,80,76 73,72,68**
toteswingers:1&2:£6.30, 1&3:£4.30, 2&3:£5.20 CSF £46.81 CT £217.29 TOTE £7.10: £2.30, £2.60, £1.90; EX 39.60 Trifecta £107.50 Part won. Pool of £145.40 - 0.43 winning units..
Owner Miss Clare Hollest **Bred** Miss S Von Schilcher **Trained** Newmarket, Suffolk

FOCUS
Part two and more of the same, but a bit slower than the first division. The form looks sound enough.
Darcy's Pride(IRE) Official explanation: jockey said, regarding late removal of blindfold, as the filly was difficult his orders were to leave it on as late as possible but when he tried to remove it, it had been tucked into the bridle too tightly.

7403 PLAY GOLF BEFORE RACING AT SOUTHWELL CLAIMING STKS 7f (F)
1:50 (1:50) (Class 6) 3-Y-O+ **£1,619** (£481; £240; £120) **Stalls** Low

Form RPR

5010 **1** **Salerosa (IRE)**[43] 6460 5-9-7 79 (p) PaulMulrennan 4 91+
(Mrs A Duffield) *trckd ldrs gng wl: smooth hdwy on inner over 2f out: led on bit wl over 1f out: rdn ins fnl f: kpt on wl towards fin* **16/1**

1014 **2** ½ **Fault**[30] 6826 4-8-12 75 (t) TomQueally 9 78
(Stef Higgins) *hld up in rr: hdwy 3f out: swtchd lft and effrt to chse ldrs wl over 1f out: rdn to chal on inner ins fnl f: ev ch tl nt qckn nr fin* **12/1**

4303 **3** 1 ¼ **Bonnie Prince Blue**[60] 5999 7-9-2 73 (v[1]) NeilCallan 10 79
(B Ellison) *hld up: hdwy wl over 2f out: rdn to chse ldrs over 1f out: drvn and kpt on wl towards fin* **7/1[3]**

0130 **4** 2 ½ **April Fool**[11] 7255 6-8-9 70 ow1 (v) TomMcLaughlin 12 65
(R A Harris) *chsd ldrs on outer: hdwy over 2f out: rdn wl over 1f out: edgd lft and kpt on same pce fnl f* **11/1**

1300 **5** ¾ **Abbondanza (IRE)**[15] 7171 7-9-3 88 MichaelO'Connell(3) 8 74
(D Nicholls) *prom: hdwy to chse ldr 3f out: rdn 2f out: drvn and ev ch over 1f out: wknd ins fnl f* **16/1**

420 **6** 1 ½ **Young Gladiator (IRE)**[56] 6110 5-8-7 66 (b) TomEaves 3 57
(Julie Camacho) *chsd ldrs: rdn along wl over 2f out: drvn and grad wknd fnl 2f* **14/1**

0053 **7** shd **Hits Only Jude (IRE)**[17] 7125 7-8-3 79 NeilFarley(5) 1 58
(D Carroll) *cl up on inner: led 1/2-way: jnd and rdn over 2f out: drvn and hdd wl over 1f out: grad wknd* **7/2[1]**

0421 **8** 1 **Just Five (IRE)**[17] 7122 4-9-6 78 PhillipMakin 6 67
(M Dods) *towards rr and sn rdn along: nvr a factor* **4/1[2]**

0004 **9** 1 **Quanah Parker (IRE)**[47] 6366 4-9-7 72 MichaelStainton(3) 11 68
(R M Whitaker) *towards rr: rdn along 1/2-way: nvr a factor* **16/1**

6210 **10** 1 ¾ **Elusive Warrior (USA)**[17] 7128 7-9-0 70 (p) JamesDoyle 2 53
(A J McCabe) *led: rdn along and hdd 1/2-way: wknd wl over 2f out* **10/1**

0602 **11** 4 ½ **Dr Wintringham (IRE)**[17] 7122 4-8-11 75 TedDurcan 5 38
(Karen George) *dwlt and a in rr* **11/1**

050 **12** 16 **Craicattack (IRE)**[78] 5424 3-8-9 65 (p) FrannyNorton 7 —
(Mrs S A Watt) *midfield: rdn along 1/2-way: sn wknd and bhd whn eased over 1f out* **66/1**

1m 28.8s (-1.50) **Going Correction** -0.20s/f (Stan)
WFA 3 from 4yo+ 1lb **12** Ran SP% **114.0**
Speed ratings (Par 101): **100,99,98,95,94 92,92,91,90,88 83,64**
toteswingers:1&2:£32.30, 1&3:£24.80, 2&3:£7.80 CSF £187.97 TOTE £29.00: £7.10, £3.00, £3.30; EX 197.00 TRIFECTA Not won..
Owner David K Barker & Phil White **Bred** Pedro Rosas **Trained** Constable Burton, N Yorks

FOCUS
A decent claimer run at a furious pace, although the time was ordinary compared with the earlier C/D races. The winner looked better than ever.

7404 CONTINENTAL-TREVOR BLAKE (S) STKS 6f (F)
2:20 (2:21) (Class 6) 2-Y-O **£1,619** (£481; £240; £120) **Stalls** Low

Form RPR

3350 **1** **Shostakovich (IRE)**[24] 6988 2-8-11 50 (p) JamesDoyle 4 65+
(S Kirk) *chsd ldr: hdwy to ld 2f out and sn clr: rdn and kpt on fnl f* **5/1[2]**

25 **2** 3 **Norton Girl**[16] 7142 2-8-6 0 WilliamCarson 6 51+
(J J Quinn) *chsd ldng pair: hdwy 2f out and sn rdn: drvn to chse wnr ins fnl f: no imp* **9/4[1]**

4000 **3** 4 **Local Diktator**[48] 6333 2-8-8 45 (t) AndrewHeffernan(3) 1 44
(R A Harris) *chsd ldrs on inner: hdwy over 2f out: sn rdn and kpt on same pce* **28/1**

5060 **4** 1 ½ **Be A Good Lady**[8] 7301 2-8-6 54 (p) FrankieMcDonald 12 35
(P T Midgley) *in tch: hdwy 1/2-way: rdn 2f out: chsd ldrs and edgd lft over 1f out: sn no imp* **25/1**

060 **5** 3 **Dark Times (IRE)**[27] 6891 2-8-6 48 (v) FrannyNorton 10 26
(Mrs K Burke) *led: rdn along over 2f out: sn hdd & wknd* **8/1**

000 **6** 2 ¾ **Bigalo's Vera B**[27] 6892 2-8-6 40 (be[1]) DuranFentiman 8 17
(L A Mullaney) *chsd ldrs: rdn along 1/2-way: sn outpcd* **33/1**

0000 **7** 5 **Callipygos**[22] 7021 2-8-6 45 CathyGannon 13 —
(P S McEntee) *a in rr* **25/1**

00 **8** 1 ¾ **Memimajic**[57] 6070 2-8-6 0 GrahamGibbons 11 —
(C W Fairhurst) *a bhd* **8/1**

0606 **9** nse **Misty Morn**[22] 7017 2-8-6 55 NeilFarley(5) 2 —
(A D Brown) *wnt rt s: a in rr* **7/1**

0 **10** 3 ¾ **Buon Compleanno (IRE)**[113] 4241 2-8-6 35 PaulQuinn 5 —
(A Berry) *a bhd* **100/1**

0335 **11** nk **Arabella Fenella**[27] 6899 2-8-6 58 ChrisCatlin 9 —
(R M H Cowell) *awkward s and dwlt: sn swtchd to wd outside: a bhd* **13/2[3]**

600 **12** *11* **Tourmaline (IRE)**[13] 7210 2-8-6 44..............................(b[1]) JimmyQuinn 3 —
(P W Chapple-Hyam) *in tch: rdn along bef 1/2-way: sn outpcd* **16/1**

1m 15.62s (-0.88) **Going Correction** -0.20s/f (Stan) 12 Ran SP% **116.4**
Speed ratings (Par 94): **97,93,87,85,81 78,71,69,68,63 63,48**
toteswingers:1&2:£3.90, 1&3:£18.10, 2&3:£18.20 CSF £15.41 TOTE £6.90: £2.90, £1.10, £9.80; EX 22.50 Trifecta £336.50 Part won. Pool of £454.83 - 0.61 winning units..The winner was bought in for £4,750.
Owner Dr J Wilson & S Kirk **Bred** Marchwood Aggregates **Trained** Upper Lambourn, Berks
■ Stewards' Enquiry : Andrew Heffernan one-day ban: used whip down shoulder in the forehand (Nov 25)

FOCUS
A low-grade juvenile race even by selling standards.

NOTEBOOK
Shostakovich(IRE), rated just 50, sported first-time cheekpieces on his AW bow after two below-par efforts. Free to post, he went head-to-head with the leader and quickly established an unassailable lead. He was retained at the auction. (op 6-1)
Norton Girl, runner-up on debut at Beverley in August, was dropping to plating company on her third start and first try on the AW. She couldn't stay with the winner once in line for home but stuck to her task to finish clear second best and can surely find a similar event. (op 2-1)
Local Diktator, rated just 45, was having his third start on the AW and his eighth in all. He stuck to the far side in the home straight unlike the first two. (op 25-1)
Be A Good Lady, rated just 49, was dropping to selling company for the first time on her sixth start. (op 28-1 tchd 22-1)
Dark Times(IRE), dropping back in trip on her AW debut, paid the price for taking on the winner up front. (op 12-1)

7405 BET ASIAN H'CAPS - BETDAQ HANDICAP 5f (F)
2:50 (2:50) (Class 5) (0-75,75) 3-Y-O+ **£2,590** (£770; £385; £192) **Stalls** High

Form RPR
0015 **1** **La Capriosa**[6] 7326 4-9-4 72.. TomQueally 9 81
(D Nicholls) *cl up: chal 2f out: rdn to ld over 1f out: drvn ins fnl f and hld on wl* **7/1**[2]
0352 **2** *nk* **Galpin Junior (USA)**[9] 7281 4-9-3 71.............................. TomEaves 10 79
(Mrs R A Carr) *trckd ldrs: rdn along and outpcd 1/2-way: hdwy over 1f out: swtchd lft and rdn ent fnl f: sn drvn to chal and ev ch tl nt qckn nr fin* **18/1**
440 **3** *3/4* **Equuleus Pictor**[6] 7326 6-9-7 75.. AdamKirby 6 80+
(J L Spearing) *in tch: rdn along and hdwy 2f out: chsd ldrs and n.m.r over 1f out: drvn and kpt on ins fnl f: nrst fin* **7/1**[2]
6646 **4** *1/2* **Cape Royal**[14] 7193 10-8-8 62............................(bt) RichardKingscote 11 66
(J M Bradley) *led: rdn 2f out: hdd over 1f out and sn drvn: one pce ins fnl f* **20/1**
2110 **5** *1/2* **Kinigi (IRE)**[21] 7033 4-9-4 75.............................(b) AndrewHeffernan(3) 4 77
(R A Harris) *in tch: hdwy 2f out: rdn wl over 1f out: sn edgd lft ent fnl f: kpt on: nrst fin* **7/1**[2]
5143 **6** *shd* **Colorus (IRE)**[6] 7326 7-8-6 67..............................(v) MatthewCosham(7) 3 68
(W J H Ratcliffe) *prom on wd outside: effrt 2f out: sn rdn and edgd rt over 1f out: drvn and one pce fnl f* **7/2**[1]
5032 **7** *3/4* **Whiskey Junction**[15] 7180 6-9-5 73.................................... ShaneKelly 2 72
(M Quinn) *rrd s and towards rr: hdwy on outer 2f out: rdn to chse ldrs and n.m.r over 1f out: swtchd lft and kpt on u.p towards fin* **10/1**
3032 **8** *1/2* **Fair Passion**[9] 7285 3-9-6 74.. JimmyQuinn 14 71
(D Shaw) *dwlt: sn trcking ldrs: effrt and cl up 1/2-way: rdn wl over 1f out and grad wknd* **8/1**[3]
6001 **9** *1 1/2* **Devil You Know (IRE)**[15] 7162 4-8-13 67................ GrahamGibbons 13 58
(M W Easterby) *hmpd s and sn swtchd lft: sn chsng ldrs: rdn along 2f out: grad wknd* **16/1**
3051 **10** *shd* **Dancing Freddy (IRE)**[20] 7052 3-9-4 72...................(p) PaulMulrennan 7 63
(J G Given) *cl up: rdn along over 2f out: grad wknd* **12/1**
0000 **11** *4* **Pawan (IRE)**[6] 7326 10-8-10 69 ow2...............................(b) AnnStokell(5) 5 46
(Miss A Stokell) *s.i.s and sn rdn along: a bhd* **40/1**
3000 **12** *hd* **Argentine (IRE)**[34] 6714 6-9-0 68.......................................(b) LNewman 12 44
(A G Foster) *hmpd s: a towards rr* **12/1**
2031 **13** *4 1/2* **Sands Of Dee (USA)**[15] 7170 3-8-9 63........................ DuranFentiman 8 23
(D Nicholls) *sn rdn along and outpcd in rr: bhd fr 1/2-way* **16/1**

57.76 secs (-1.94) **Going Correction** -0.30s/f (Stan) 13 Ran SP% **119.5**
Speed ratings (Par 103): **103,102,101,100,99 99,98,97,95,95 88,88,81**
toteswingers:1&2:£25.20, 1&3:£7.50, 2&3:£16.40 CSF £126.55 CT £923.22 TOTE £9.40: £3.40, £5.10, £2.60; EX 136.40 TRIFECTA Not won..
Owner Paul J Dixon **Bred** Slatch Farm Stud **Trained** Sessay, N Yorks

FOCUS
A competitive sprint handicap and the richest race on the eight-race card with the winner collecting a mere £2,590. Straightforward form.

7406 BETDAQ.COM MAIDEN STKS 7f (F)
3:20 (3:21) (Class 5) 3-Y-O **£2,388** (£705; £352) **Stalls** Low

Form RPR
0232 **1** **Land And Sea**[31] 6815 3-8-12 68.. MichaelHills 3 67+
(B W Hills) *cl up on inner: slt ld after 1f tl qcknd clr 2f out: shkn up and edgd lft ins fnl f: readily* **11/10**[1]
6045 **2** *5* **Olney Lass**[13] 7205 3-8-5 63.. JamesRogers(7) 11 53
(Mike Murphy) *chsd ldrs: rdn along over 2f out: drvn to chse wnr over 1f out: sn no imp* **7/1**
3230 **3** *4 1/2* **Hambleton**[27] 6896 3-9-3 58..(p) TomEaves 7 46
(B Smart) *chsd ldng pair on inner: rdn along and outpcd wl over 2f out: drvn and kpt on ins fnl f: tk mod 3rd nr line* **14/1**
5460 **4** *hd* **Plenty O'Toole**[22] 7019 3-9-3 62.....................................(b[1]) PaulMulrennan 4 46
(Mrs D J Sanderson) *led 1f: cl up tl rdn along wl over 2f out and grad wknd* **10/3**[2]
000 **5** *hd* **Lord Lansing (IRE)**[124] 3910 3-9-0 44................. MichaelO'Connell(3) 13 45
(Mrs K Burke) *chsd ldrs: rdn along and outpcd wl over 2f out: drvn and plugged on appr fnl f: n.d* **66/1**
50 **6** *4 1/2* **Majic Mojo**[104] 4556 3-8-9 0... MichaelStainton(3) 9 28
(R M Whitaker) *nvr nr ldrs* **50/1**
5060 **7** *1/2* **Marsh's Gift**[6] 7328 3-9-3 40...(p) CathyGannon 1 32
(C J Teague) *a towards rr* **80/1**
0600 **8** *5* **Little Buddy**[25] 6952 3-9-0 27.. AndrewHeffernan(3) 12 18
(R J Price) *a towards rr* **100/1**
9 *3* **Play The Blues (IRE)** 3-8-12 0.. SamHitchcott 2 5
(M A Allen) *in tch: rdn along wl over 2f out: sn wknd* **66/1**
00 **10** *17* **Matilda May**[17] 7129 3-8-12 0.. PatrickMathers 6 —
(C J Teague) *a in rr: bhd fnl 2f* **100/1**
11 *13* **Dorden** 3-8-7 0.. DeanHeslop(5) 5 —
(N Wilson) *dwlt: a bhd: t.o fnl 2f* **28/1**
12 *3 1/4* **Kassiodor (GER)** 3-9-3 0.. TomQueally 10 —
(B J Curley) *a towards rr: rdn along and outpcd bef 1/2-way: sn bhd and t.o fnl 2f* **11/2**[3]

1m 29.56s (-0.74) **Going Correction** -0.20s/f (Stan) 12 Ran SP% **116.9**
Speed ratings (Par 102): **96,90,85,84,84 79,78,73,69,50 35,31**
toteswingers:1&2:£2.70, 1&3:£3.50, 2&3:£10.90 CSF £9.35 TOTE £2.30: £2.10, £1.90, £2.00; EX 8.90 Trifecta £31.60 Pool of £550.29 - 12.85 winning units..
Owner K Abdulla **Bred** Juddmonte Farms Ltd **Trained** Lambourn, Berks

FOCUS
A weak maiden run in a slow time. The winner did not need to match her previous form.

7407 HOSPITALITY AT SOUTHWELL RACECOURSE H'CAP 1m 4f (F)
3:50 (3:50) (Class 6) (0-55,55) 3-Y-O+ **£1,619** (£481; £240; £120) **Stalls** Low

Form RPR
4050 **1** **Kingaroo (IRE)**[6] 7327 4-8-5 46 oh1.................................... BillyCray(5) 1 65
(G Woodward) *mde all: rdn clr over 2f out: styd on strly* **22/1**
0000 **2** *7* **Shifting Gold (IRE)**[29] 6846 4-9-2 55.................................(b) AmyRyan(3) 8 62
(K A Ryan) *dwlt and reminders s: sn rdn along in rr: hdwy on outer to join ldrs 1/2-way: cl up 4f out: rdn 3f out: drvn and kpt on fnl 2f: no ch w wnr* **5/1**[2]
253 **3** *1 1/2* **Dandarrell**[16] 7156 3-8-13 55... PaulMulrennan 10 60
(Julie Camacho) *in tch: hdwy to trckd ldrs over 3f out: rdn to chse ldng pair 2f out: sn drvn and no imp* **7/1**
6050 **4** *3* **Yossi (IRE)**[8] 7306 6-8-12 55...........................(be) SeanPalmer(7) 3 55
(R C Guest) *hld up towards rr: stdy hdwy on inner 4f out: rdn to chse ldrs and n.m.r 3f out: drvn wl over 1f out and sn one pce* **11/1**
0226 **5** *3* **Mister Frosty (IRE)**[7] 7315 4-9-5 55................................ CathyGannon 12 50
(G Prodromou) *hld up: hdwy on outer to chse ldrs 4f out: rdn over 3f out: drvn over 2f out and sn no imp* **11/2**[3]
5261 **6** *9* **Court Wing (IRE)**[16] 7157 4-9-0 53.................... AndrewHeffernan(3) 11 34
(R J Price) *hld up towards rr: sme hdwy on outer 4f out: rdn along 3f out and nvr a factor* **9/2**[1]
3551 **7** *1* **Prickles**[10] 7270 5-9-1 51 6ex... TedDurcan 14 30
(Karen George) *trckd ldrs on outer: hdwy 4f out: rdn over 3f out: sn wknd* **7/1**
3505 **8** *1 1/4* **La Bacouetteuse (FR)**[12] 7229 5-9-1 51................................. LNewman 2 28
(A G Foster) *trckd ldrs on inner: hdwy 4f out: rdn to chse wnr 3f out: sn drvn and wknd qckly over 2f out* **16/1**
-100 **9** *6* **Abulharith**[32] 6314 4-9-5 55...(p) JamesDoyle 9 23
(R A Harris) *cl up: rdn along over 4f out: sn wknd* **16/1**
00/5 **10** *6* **Abydos**[14] 7200 6-8-13 49... TomQueally 6 —
(B J Curley) *cl up: rdn along over 4f out: wknd qckly and bhd fnl 2f* **15/2**
0010 **11** *30* **Princess Aliuska**[27] 6905 5-9-0 50...................................... TomEaves 13 —
(C Smith) *sn outpcd and a bhd: t.o fnl 4f* **22/1**
050/ **12** *20* **Hugo Quick**[1142] 5728 6-8-12 48..................................... SamHitchcott 4 —
(J L Spearing) *a in rr: bhd fr 1/2-way: t.o fnl 4f* **66/1**

2m 38.58s (-2.42) **Going Correction** -0.20s/f (Stan)
WFA 3 from 4yo+ 6lb 12 Ran SP% **117.3**
Speed ratings (Par 101): **100,95,94,92,90 84,83,82,78,74 54,41**
toteswingers:1&2:£34.80, 1&3:£26.50, 2&3:£12.90. totesuper7: Win: Not won. Place: Not won. CSF £125.54 CT £869.42 TOTE £18.80: £4.30, £5.50, £3.10; EX 154.50 TRIFECTA Not won..
Owner J Pownall **Bred** Kevin Walsh **Trained** Maltby, S Yorks

FOCUS
A low-grade 46-55 finale run at a sound pace. The winner is rated back to something like his 3yo form.
T/Jkpt: Not won. T/Plt: £256.40 to a £1 stake. Pool:£54,616.88 - 155.50 winning tickets T/Qpdt: £35.20 to a £1 stake. Pool:£4,741.32 - 99.50 winning tickets JR

7376 WOLVERHAMPTON (A.W) (L-H)
Thursday, November 11

OFFICIAL GOING: Standard
Wind: Fresh behind Weather: Fine

7408 ENJOY THE PARTY PACK GROUP OFFER MEDIAN AUCTION MAIDEN STKS 5f 216y(P)
4:20 (4:21) (Class 6) 2-Y-O **£1,619** (£481; £240; £120) **Stalls** Low

Form RPR
44 **1** **Indian Emperor (IRE)**[30] 6827 2-9-3 0........................ PhilipRobinson 9 71+
(M A Jarvis) *chsd ldrs: led 2f out: rdn over 1f out: jst hld on* **11/8**[1]
3603 **2** *hd* **Lady Platinum Club**[13] 7210 2-8-5 62............................(p) AdamCarter(7) 12 65
(G R Oldroyd) *a.p: rdn to chse wnr over 1f out: r.o* **6/1**
30 **3** *nse* **Elegant Muse**[22] 7021 2-8-12 0.. LukeMorris 8 67+
(W R Swinburn) *hld up in tch: rdn over 1f out: r.o* **4/1**[3]
6 **4** *nk* **What About You (IRE)**[34] 6722 2-9-3 0..........................(t) PhillipMakin 3 71+
(R A Fahey) *prom: n.m.r and lost pl 5f out: hdwy over 1f out: r.o* **7/2**[2]
5 *3 3/4* **Consistant** 2-9-3 0.. JackMitchell 1 58
(B P J Baugh) *s.i.s: hld up: hdwy 2f out: rdn over 1f out: styd on same pce* **50/1**
40 **6** *1 1/4* **Shugar Rhi (IRE)**[45] 6419 2-8-12 0.................................... RobertWinston 2 49+
(B Palling) *pushed along and prom: lost pl over 5f out: hdwy u.p over 1f out: nt trble ldrs* **33/1**
05 **7** *1* **Twinkled**[16] 7150 2-8-10 0...................................... ThomasHemsley(7) 13 51
(M L W Bell) *sn pushed along in rr: styd on appr fnl f: nvr nrr* **50/1**
8 *nse* **Dunhoy (IRE)** 2-9-3 0.. MickyFenton 5 51
(Stef Higgins) *s.s: outpcd: styd on ins fnl f: nvr nrr* **33/1**
0 **9** *6* **Zeavola (IRE)**[17] 7123 2-8-12 0.. NeilChalmers 7 28+
(A M Balding) *sn led: rdn and hung rt over 2f out: sn hdd and eased: hung lft fr over 1f out* **20/1**
0 **10** *4 1/2* **Ngina**[10] 7269 2-8-12 0.. DaneO'Neill 4 15
(D Shaw) *s.i.s: hld up: effrt over 2f out: sn wknd* **100/1**
0 **11** *3 3/4* **Albany Rose (IRE)**[25] 6954 2-8-12 0................................ SteveDrowne 11 48+
(Rae Guest) *chsd ldrs: hmpd over 2f out: nt rcvr* **25/1**
0 **12** *2 3/4* **Honor Breeze (USA)**[69] 5724 2-8-9 0........................ MatthewDavies(3) 6 —
(Louise Best) *led early: chsd ldrs tl rdn and wknd over 1f out* **150/1**
00 **13** *2 1/4* **Greenhead High**[20] 7058 2-9-3 0.................................. J-PGuillambert 10 25+
(P Howling) *chsd ldrs: hmpd over 2f out: nt rcvr: eased* **100/1**

1m 16.1s (1.10) **Going Correction** +0.025s/f (Slow) 13 Ran SP% **119.7**
Speed ratings (Par 94): **93,92,92,92,87 85,84,84,76,70 65,61,58**
toteswingers:1&2:£3.00, 1&3:£1.90, 2&3:£4.20 CSF £9.58 TOTE £2.30: £1.10, £1.20, £1.80; EX 9.30.
Owner Mrs P Good **Bred** Wiji Bloodstock **Trained** Newmarket, Suffolk

FOCUS
A fair maiden in which those with experience held sway but it was run at a muddling gallop with plenty of trouble in running and there must be a big doubt whether the best horse won.

The Form Book, Raceform Ltd, Compton, RG20 6NL

NOTEBOOK

Indian Emperor(IRE)looked to hold just about the best form claims but the standard he set wasn't insuperable and he only scraped home, somewhat fortuitously, having been in the right position as the race was run. He's not bred to be anything special and ordinary handicaps look his level. (tchd 7-4)

Lady Platinum Club hadn't done much in two recent runs on Polytrack but she showed more like her earlier-season turf form here dropped back to 6f with a good effort, albeit that she was well-placed as the race developed. (op 10-1)

Elegant Muse is qualified for nurseries now and might do better in that sphere. She didn't have much room to manoeuvre in the straight after letting the winner get first run but kept on well and will likely be more effective at 7f. (tchd 7-2 and 9-2)

What About You(IRE) ◆ looked unlucky and would have won with an untroubled passage. Forced to rein back early on, putting him in a poor position, he met trouble turning in and from then on had next to no room to operate, nonetheless sticking on really well with his rider unable to ride him out properly. He can win a maiden before the year is out. (tchd 10-3)

Consistant hails from a yard that gets very few first-time-out winners but shaped well on his debut, possibly just needing the run after getting into the race smoothly on the home turn. He's related to plenty of winners and is probably up to winning a seller. (op 33-1)

Shugar Rhi(IRE) never threatened but will get more straightforward opportunities in low-grade nurseries.

Zeavola(IRE), who had looked green in the paddock, hung badly on the home turn, ending her chances in the process. Official explanation: jockey said filly hung badly right

Albany Rose(IRE) was badly hampered on the home turn.

Greenhead High was on course to post an improved effort when badly hampered on the home turn. He is now qualified for a mark. Official explanation: jockey said gelding suffered interference in runing

7409 GREAT OFFERS AT WOLVERHAMPTON-RACECOURSE.CO.UK CLAIMING STKS 5f 216y(P)

4:50 (4:51) (Class 6) 3-Y-0+ **£1,619** (£481; £240; £120) **Stalls** Low

Form				RPR
0001	**1**		**Matsunosuke**^{26} 6932 8-9-3 99 ... LukeMorris 1 (R A Harris) *trckd ldrs: led over 1f out: sn rdn: r.o: eased nr fin* **3/1**^{2}	86+
2230	**2**	1 ¼	**Imprimis Tagula (IRE)**^{9} 7289 6-9-7 86 ...(v) RobertWinston 4 (A Bailey) *chsd ldrs: sn pushed along: rdn over 2f out: styd on u.p to go 2nd post* **11/4**^{1}	84
4000	**3**	shd	**Tourist**^{9} 7289 5-9-7 89 ... DaneO'Neill 3 (D Shaw) *hld up: hdwy over 2f out: rdn to chse wnr fnl f: styd on: lost 2nd post* **11/4**^{1}	84
0010	**4**	1 ¼	**King's Wonder**^{41} 6537 5-8-11 79 ... PhillipMakin 8 (Mrs R A Carr) *hld up: racd keenly: hdwy over 1f out: styd on* **9/1**	70
/06	**5**	3 ½	**Woodwind**^{7} 7310 5-8-4 0 ... JoeFanning 7 (D Shaw) *s.i.s: hld up: hdwy over 1f out: wknd ins fnl f* **66/1**	51?
4055	**6**	nk	**Royal Blade (IRE)**^{12} 7241 3-8-6 60 ... AndreaAtzeni 5 (A P Jarvis) *chsd ldr tl led 1/2-way: rdn and hdd over 1f out: wknd ins fnl f* **12/1**	53
2226	**7**	12	**Weet A Surprise**^{217} 1192 5-8-6 78 ...(v) AlexEdwards$^{(7)}$ 6 (J W Unett) *prom: rdn over 2f out: sn wknd* **7/1**^{3}	21
0260	**8**	½	**Barraland**^{29} 6847 5-8-5 49 ow1 ...(p) MatthewDavies$^{(3)}$ 2 (George Baker) *led to 1/2-way: sn rdn: wknd fnl f* **50/1**	15

1m 14.99s (-0.01) **Going Correction** +0.025s/f (Slow) **8** Ran SP% **112.0**

Speed ratings (Par 101): **101,99,99,97,92 92,76,75**

toteswingers:1&2:£3.00, 1&3:£3.40, 2&3:£3.20 CSF £11.17 TOTE £4.30: £1.50, £1.30, £1.30; EX 10.90.Matsunosuke was subject to a friendy claim.

Owner S Mares **Bred** R Coogan **Trained** Earlswood, Monmouths

FOCUS

A decent claimer with five of the field having an official rating of 78 or more, but the winner stood out at the weights and won easily in a race run at no more than a fair tempo. The fifth and the time suggest caution over the form.

7410 BET TEST MATCH RUGBY - BETDAQ H'CAP 1m 5f 194y(P)

5:20 (5:21) (Class 4) (0-85,92) 3-Y-0+ **£3,594** (£1,069; £534; £266) **Stalls** Low

Form				RPR
3100	**1**		**Ethics Girl (IRE)**^{21} 7045 4-9-0 71 ... FrannyNorton 7 (John Berry) *hld up: hdwy over 2f out: led ins fnl f: hung lft: styd on wl* **20/1**	81
1004	**2**	1 ¼	**Cosimo de Medici**^{19} 7090 3-9-1 80 ...(t) SteveDrowne 8 (H Morrison) *hld up: hdwy to chse ldr over 2f out: led over 1f out: sn rdn and hung lft: hdd ins fnl f: styd on* **8/1**	88
0403	**3**	1 ¾	**Camps Bay (USA)**^{6} 7337 6-9-8 79 ... NeilCallan 4 (B Ellison) *s.i.s: hld up: hdwy over 1f out: sn rdn: styd on same pce ins fnl f* **7/2**^{2}	85
3152	**4**	½	**Beggar's Opera (IRE)**^{11} 7252 3-9-1 80 ...(t) RobertHavlin 8 (J H M Gosden) *hld up in tch: pushed along and hung lft fr over 4f out: led over 2f out: rdn and hdd over 1f out: styd on same pce* **9/2**^{3}	85
2622	**5**	10	**Valid Reason**^{55} 6152 3-9-1 80 ... JimCrowley 5 (D K Ivory) *chsd ldrs: rdn over 2f out: wknd over 1f out* **11/4**^{1}	71
4612	**6**	11	**Bollin Greta**^{9} 7284 5-9-0 71 ...(t) PhillipMakin 2 (T D Easterby) *led 1f: chsd ldr tl led again over 6f out: rdn and hdd over 2f out: wknd over 1f out* **15/2**	47
0010	**7**	3 ¼	**Satwa Gold (USA)**^{67} 5788 4-9-8 79 ... MickyFenton 3 (Stef Higgins) *chsd ldrs: rdn over 4f out: wknd 2f out* **15/2**	50
0000	**8**	17	**Shadows Lengthen**^{28} 6877 4-10-7 92 ...(b) GrahamGibbons 1 (M W Easterby) *led after 1f: hdd over 6f out: rdn and wknd over 2f out: t.o* **16/1**	39
00-0	**9**	1	**Animator**^{19} 7089 5-8-9 66 oh1 ... ChrisCatlin 6 (M Hill) *hld up: pushed along 6f out: bhd fnl 3f: t.o* **50/1**	12

3m 3.76s (-2.24) **Going Correction** +0.025s/f (Slow)

WFA 3 from 4yo+ 8lb **9** Ran SP% **114.3**

Speed ratings (Par 105): **107,106,105,105,99 93,91,81,80**

toteswingers:1&2:£27.30, 1&3:£13.80, 2&3:£6.70 CSF £168.34 CT £700.03 TOTE £19.80: £4.80, £3.80, £1.40; EX 202.00.

Owner The 1997 Partnership **Bred** Newsells Park Stud **Trained** Newmarket, Suffolk

FOCUS

A fairly useful handicap run at something of an uneven gallop. The form is rated at face value.

Ethics Girl(IRE) Official explanation: trainer said, regarding apparent improvement in form, that the filly was hampered in running last time.

Cosimo de Medici Official explanation: jockey said gelding hung left-handed

Beggar's Opera(IRE) Official explanation: jockey said colt hung left-handed

Satwa Gold(USA) Official explanation: jockey said colt hung left-handed

7411 BET CHELTENHAM OPEN MEETING - BETDAQ H'CAP 7f 32y(P)

5:50 (5:52) (Class 4) (0-85,85) 3-Y-0 **£3,594** (£1,069; £534; £266) **Stalls** High

Form				RPR
1302	**1**		**Lutine Bell**^{22} 7012 3-9-2 80 ...(b) NeilCallan 8 (Mike Murphy) *s.i.s: hld up: hdwy over 1f out: led 1f out: r.o strly* **9/2**^{1}	100
2306	**2**	6	**Tiradito (USA)**^{138} 3429 3-9-1 79 ...(p) ChrisCatlin 1 (M Botti) *a.p: rdn over 1f out: styd on same pce* **7/1**^{3}	83
1460	**3**	1	**Tewin Wood**^{27} 6904 3-8-11 75 ...(p) RobertWinston 2 (A Bailey) *led to 1/2-way: rdn to ld again over 1f out: sn hdd: styd on same pce* **12/1**	76
2316	**4**	¾	**Sir Bruno (FR)**^{10} 7274 3-8-10 74 ...(p) LukeMorris 3 (B Palling) *chsd ldrs: rdn over 1f out: no ex fnl f* **5/1**^{2}	73
5064	**5**	nk	**Master Leon**^{37} 6664 3-8-2 73 ...(v) AdamCarter$^{(7)}$ 9 (B Smart) *hld up: hdwy 5f out: led 1/2-way: rdn: hung rt and hdd over 1f out: no ex fnl f* **12/1**	71
410P	**6**	11	**Peadar Miguel**^{45} 6428 3-8-13 77 ... AdamKirby 4 (M G Quinlan) *hld up in tch: hung lft 1/2-way: rdn and wknd over 1f out* **20/1**	45
0650	**7**	2 ¼	**Blue Lyric**^{17} 7114 3-8-10 74 ... J-PGuillambert 7 (L M Cumani) *hld up: hdwy u.p over 2f out: wknd over 1f out* **8/1**	40
3000	**8**	½	**Spying**^{15} 7182 3-9-4 82 ... JackMitchell 6 (Mrs A Duffield) *hld up: nt clr run 1/2-way: nvr on terms* **5/1**^{2}	43
1004	**9**	nse	**Kylladdie**^{16} 7144 3-8-10 74 ... JamieSpencer 12 (S Gollings) *chsd ldrs: rdn over 2f out: hung lft and wknd over 1f out* **12/1**	35
6062	**10**	4 ½	**Breathless Kiss (USA)**^{63} 5896 3-9-0 78 ...(p) PhillipMakin 11 (K A Ryan) *hld up: a in rr: bhd whn rdr lost iron over 1f out* **8/1**	40
1000	**11**	58	**Niran (IRE)**^{34} 6723 3-9-7 85 ... JoeFanning 5 (Mrs R A Carr) *chsd ldrs tl wknd 1/2-way: t.o* **25/1**	—

1m 29.04s (-0.56) **Going Correction** +0.025s/f (Slow) **11** Ran SP% **117.9**

Speed ratings (Par 104): **104,97,96,95,94 82,79,79,79,73 7**

toteswingers:1&2:£8.20, 1&3:£9.70, 2&3:£18.70 CSF £35.97 CT £363.53 TOTE £4.50: £1.60, £4.00, £4.50; EX 38.00.

Owner M Murphy **Bred** Colin Valley Stud **Trained** Westoning, Beds

■ Stewards' Enquiry : Adam Carter two-day ban: careless riding (Nov 25-26)

FOCUS

What looked a competitive handicap was turned into a procession by the winner who managed to come from the back despite an ordinary gallop that favoured those ridden more prominently. The winner showed big improvement, the form rated at face value around the second and third.

Blue Lyric Official explanation: jockey said filly suffered interference in running

Niran(IRE) Official explanation: jockey said gelding stopped quickly

7412 SPONSOR A RACE BY CALLING 01902 390000 NURSERY 1m 141y(P)

6:20 (6:22) (Class 5) (0-75,73) 2-Y-0 **£2,007** (£597; £298; £149) **Stalls** Low

Form				RPR
032	**1**		**Labore**^{21} 7034 2-9-5 71 ... AdamKirby 3 (M Botti) *chsd ldrs: rdn to ld over 1f out: sn hung rt: hrd drvn and hung lft ins fnl f: r.o* **9/2**^{3}	77
0100	**2**	2 ¼	**Malice Or Mischief (IRE)**^{24} 6989 2-9-7 73 ... NeilCallan 5 (A W Carroll) *chsd ldr: rdn over 1f out: hung lft and styd on same pce ins fnl f* **8/1**	74
0300	**3**	1 ½	**Volcanic Ash (USA)**^{77} 5434 2-8-5 57 ... JoeFanning 4 (M Johnston) *led: rdn and hdd over 1f out: no ex ins fnl f* **13/2**	55
6501	**4**	1 ¼	**Skeleton (IRE)**^{8} 7295 2-8-4 59 6ex ...(b) GilmarPereira$^{(3)}$ 6 (W J Haggas) *s.i.s: hld up: rdn over 2f out: hung lft and styd on ins fnl f: nvr trbld ldrs* **7/2**^{2}	56
004	**5**	3 ¾	**Palm Pilot (IRE)**^{29} 6849 2-9-2 68 ... JimCrowley 1 (E A L Dunlop) *chsd ldrs: rdn over 2f out: wknd fnl f* **6/4**^{1}	56
0430	**6**	52	**Kaua'i Girl**^{26} 6920 2-8-10 62 ... JackMitchell 2 (Mrs A Duffield) *s.i.s: hld up: rdn 1/2-way: bhd fnl 3f: t.o* **8/1**	—

1m 51.24s (0.74) **Going Correction** +0.025s/f (Slow) **6** Ran SP% **116.0**

Speed ratings (Par 96): **97,95,93,92,89 43**

toteswingers:1&2:£3.40, 1&3:£5.20, 2&3:£4.90 CSF £39.34 TOTE £4.80: £4.70, £5.20; EX 17.10.

Owner Lok Ho Ting **Bred** Brook Stud Bloodstock Ltd **Trained** Newmarket, Suffolk

FOCUS

Not much strength in depth to this nursery but it was run at quite a solid gallop considering the small field.

NOTEBOOK

Labore had been improving gradually until now and, though he once again showed signs of running around in front, he was well on top at the line seeming well suited by the step up in trip despite what his pedigree might have suggested. Whether he beat much is open to question, but it would be surprising if there isn't a bit more still to come. (op 5-1)

Malice Or Mischief(IRE) was top weight despite his last win coming only in a claimer. He hadn't shown much in two runs for his current yard but this was more like his old form and he seemed to stay the trip fine. (op 15-2)

Volcanic Ash(USA) hadn't shown much on his nursery debut at Ayr last time but the longer trip and switch to Polytrack seemed to help him. He's only modest and the handicapper has him about right but given his running style here and pedigree, he's got to be worth a try on Fibresand. (op 6-1 tchd 7-1)

Skeleton(IRE) had presumably been helped by first-time blinkers last time but it was easy to see here why he wears headgear as he took an age to get going. A return to Kempton's longer straight together with a drop back in grade might be the key to him. (op 3-1)

Palm Pilot(IRE) was the disappointment of the race on her handicap debut. Progressive in three runs in maidens, she looked sure to be suited by the longer trip but she dropped out tamely after coming under pressure going into the far turn and didn't seem at ease with herself in the straight, carrying her head high. Official explanation: jockey said filly never travelled; vet said filly coughed on return (op 15-8 tchd 2-1)

Kaua'i Girl ran poorly in a nursery for the second time running on this her Polytrack debut. (op 12-1)

7413 HORIZONS RESTAURANT, THE PLACE TO DINE MEDIAN AUCTION MAIDEN STKS 1m 1f 103y(P)

6:50 (6:51) (Class 6) 3-4-Y-0 **£1,619** (£481; £240; £120) **Stalls** Low

Form				RPR
3	**1**		**Yensi**^{15} 7183 3-8-9 0 ... MatthewDavies$^{(3)}$ 2 (George Baker) *led 1f: chsd ldrs: led over 1f out: sn rdn and edgd lft: r.o* **11/4**^{2}	57+
22	**2**	1 ¼	**Marrimeclaire (IRE)**^{24} 6993 3-8-12 64 ... ShaneKelly 1 (B J McMath) *s.i.s: hld up: nt clr run 3f out: hdwy over 2f out: rdn to go 2nd ins fnl f: r.o: nt rch wnr* **1/1**^{1}	54+
0006	**3**	2	**Devon Diva**^{35} 6696 4-8-8 33 ... RichardRowe$^{(7)}$ 3 (M Hill) *chsd ldr tl led over 2f out: rdn and hdd over 1f out: edgd rt and no ex ins fnl f* **66/1**	49
/66-	**4**	3 ¼	**Money Money Money**^{539} 2204 4-9-1 60 ... JamesMillman 4 (B R Millman) *led over 8f out: set stdy pce: rdn and hdd over 2f out: wknd fnl f* **8/1**^{3}	42
	5	4	**No Time For Tears (IRE)** 3-8-12 0 ... DaneO'Neill 11 (Lucinda Featherstone) *hld up: hdwy over 5f out: rdn over 2f out: wknd over 1f out* **50/1**	35
0	**6**	1	**Etoile Filante (IRE)**^{19} 7086 3-8-12 0 ... SteveDrowne 9 (J R Gask) *hld up: rdn over 3f out: nvr trbld ldrs* **14/1**	33

00-0 7 *1* **Northern Champ (IRE)**[35] 6696 4-9-1 35................ MarkCoumbe(5) 10 35
(D Bourton) *hld up in tch: rdn over 2f out: sn wknd* **80/1**
0000 8 *11* **Whispering Ridge**[26] 6931 3-9-3 28................................ AdamKirby 7 12
(M Wellings) *stdd s: hld up: plld hrd: a in rr* **125/1**
00- 9 *15* **Sharp And Chic**[395] 6728 3-8-12 0................................ MickyFenton 6 —
(R Ford) *prom: rdn over 3f out: sn wknd: t.o* **100/1**

2m 3.63s (1.93) **Going Correction** +0.025s/f (Slow)
WFA 3 from 4yo 3lb **9** Ran SP% **100.9**
Speed ratings (Par 101): **92,90,89,86,82 81,80,71,57**
toteswingers:1&2:£1.20, 1&3:£10.60, 2&3:£10.00 CSF £4.44 TOTE £3.70: £1.40, £1.10, £13.90; EX 5.90.
Owner Wayne Hennessey **Bred** Michael Ng **Trained** Moreton Morrell, Warwicks

FOCUS
A weak maiden run at a steady pace, though the right two horses came to the fore, though perhaps not in the right order. Limited form and the winner did not need to improve much on her debut effort.

7414 BETDAQ ON 0870 178 1221 H'CAP 1m 1f 103y(P)
7:20 (7:20) (Class 4) (0-85,83) 3-Y-0+ £3,594 (£1,069; £534; £266) Stalls Low

Form RPR
6301 1 **Mustakmil (IRE)**[17] 7115 4-9-6 **82**................................ NeilCallan 5 93
(S Dow) *chsd ldrs: led over 1f out: sn rdn and hung lft: r.o* **3/1**[1]
6053 2 *1 ½* **Desert Vision**[43] 6449 6-9-7 **83**................................(vt) GrahamGibbons 3 91
(M W Easterby) *hld up: racd keenly: hdwy over 2f out: rdn to chse wnr and hmpd over 1f out: styd on same pce* **4/1**[2]
2210 3 *3 ½* **Tarooq (USA)**[20] 7062 4-8-10 **72**................................ JoeFanning 2 73
(R A Fahey) *chsd ldrs: rdn over 1f out: no ex ins fnl f* **6/1**
0050 4 *3 ¼* **Iron Out (USA)**[8] 7306 4-9-3 **79**................................ AdamKirby 4 73
(R Hollinshead) *sn led: rdn and hdd over 1f out: wknd fnl f* **20/1**
31 5 *1 ¼* **Morning Chief (IRE)**[19] 7086 3-8-8 **73**................................ PhilipRobinson 6 65
(C G Cox) *chsd ldr: rdn over 2f out: wknd over 1f out* **4/1**[2]
6 *1 ¾* **Roilos (IRE)**[57] 4-8-9 **71**................................(t) AndreaAtzeni 1 59
(M Botti) *hld up: rdn over 2f out: wknd over 1f out* **9/2**[3]
5636 7 *4 ½* **Edgewater (IRE)**[17] 7115 3-8-12 **77**................................ DaneO'Neill 7 56
(J Akehurst) *hld up: rdn over 2f out: sn wknd* **11/1**

2m 1.29s (-0.41) **Going Correction** +0.025s/f (Slow)
WFA 3 from 4yo+ 3lb **7** Ran SP% **110.6**
Speed ratings (Par 105): **102,100,97,94,93 92,88**
toteswingers:1&2:£3.80, 1&3:£3.80, 2&3:£4.50 CSF £14.06 TOTE £5.10: £1.30, £2.00; EX 15.60.
Owner Simon Caunce **Bred** Shadwell Estate Company Limited **Trained** Epsom, Surrey

FOCUS
A fair handicap run at a steady pace and the two market leaders came to the fore again. The winner produced a clear personal best.
T/Plt: £64.30 to a £1 stake. Pool:£80,308.19 - 910.33 winning tickets T/Qpdt: £40.00 to a £1 stake. Pool:£8,498.62 - 157.20 winning tickets CR

6519 TOULOUSE
Thursday, November 11
OFFICIAL GOING: Turf: heavy

7416a PRIX FILLE DE L'AIR (GROUP 3) (3YO+ FILLIES & MARES) (TURF) 1m 2f 110y
1:40 (12:00) 3-Y-0+ £35,398 (£14,159; £10,619; £7,079; £3,539)

RPR
1 **Ma Preference (FR)**[42] 6519 4-8-11 0................ StephanePasquier 2 98
(F Rohaut, France) *led sn after s: in front early in st: chal and briefly hdd 2f out: rdn and regained ld 1 1/2f out: r.o wl fnl f: comf* **122/10**
2 *1 ½* **La Boum (GER)**[16] 7160 7-8-11 0................ IoritzMendizabal 3 95
(Robert Collet, France) *towards rr: prog on ins early in st: swtchd towards stands' side: qcknd wl between rivals fnl f: clst at fin* **2/1**[1]
3 *nk* **Kartica**[18] 3-8-10 0 ow1................................ OlivierPeslier 5 98
(P Demercastel, France) *racd towards rr: dropped bk to last ent st: swtchd to stands' rail: qcknd 1 1/2f out: r.o wl fnl f* **11/1**
4 *nk* **Lake Palace**[42] 6519 4-8-11 0................ ThierryThulliez 4 93
(N Clement, France) *racd towards rr: slipped through on ins to go 4th 1 1/2f out: no ex fnl f: styd on* **19/1**
5 *1 ½* **Mary Boleyn (IRE)**[30] 6914 4-8-11 0................ Jean-BernardEyquem 7 90
(J E Hammond, France) *bkmarker tl end of bk st: slipped through on ins early in st to chal for ld: led briefly: sn hdd: r.o u.p fnl f* **14/1**
6 *¾* **Vertana (IRE)**[42] 6519 3-8-8 0................................ FabriceVeron 10 91
(H-A Pantall, France) *racd in 5th: swtchd towards stands' side early in st: r.o fnl 1 1/2f wout threatening ldrs* **14/1**
7 *nse* **Pearl Banks**[32] 6790 4-9-4 0................ Francois-XavierBertras 8 96
(F Rohaut, France) *led early: sn settled in 2nd: rdn early in st: no ex: fdd* **9/2**[3]
8 *¾* **Rock My Soul (IRE)**[25] 4-8-11 0................ GaetanMasure 6 87
(Uwe Ostmann, Germany) *towards rr fr s: rdn early in st: no ex: fdd fnl 1 1/2f* **30/1**
9 *¾* **Valasyra (FR)**[16] 7160 3-9-1 0................................ GregoryBenoist 9 95
(A De Royer-Dupre, France) *broke smartly: settled 4th: rdn early in st: no ex: fdd* **7/2**[2]
10 *1 ½* **Lady's Purse**[16] 7160 3-9-1 0................................(p) MaximeGuyon 1 92
(H-A Pantall, France) *racd in 3rd tl st: rdn but no ex: fdd* **13/1**

2m 22.43s (142.43)
WFA 3 from 4yo+ 4lb **10** Ran SP% **118.3**
WIN (incl. 1 euro stake): 13.20. PLACES: 2.60, 1.40, 3.20. DF: 10.00. SF: 39.10.
Owner Patrick Chedeville **Bred** P Chedeville & Mme A Tamagni-Bodmer **Trained** Sauvagnon, France

7317 LINGFIELD (L-H)
Friday, November 12
OFFICIAL GOING: Standard
Wind: fairly strong, half behind Weather: raining

7417 BET GRAND SLAM DARTS - BETDAQ NURSERY 7f (P)
12:55 (12:55) (Class 5) (0-75,74) 2-Y-0 £2,590 (£770; £385; £192) Stalls Low

Form RPR
633 1 **Romantic Wish**[16] 7164 2-9-3 **70**................................ RichardKingscote 10 73
(R A Mills) *stdd s and dropped in bhd: hld up in tch: hdwy on outer to chse ldrs over 2f out: styd on wl u.p ins fnl f to ld last strides* **5/1**[3]
01 2 *hd* **Tullius (IRE)**[15] 7186 2-9-7 **74**................................ JimCrowley 6 76
(P Winkworth) *led for 1f: chsd ldrs after: reminder over 4f out: rdn over 3f out: chsd ldng pair and drvn over 1f out: styd on wl to ld towards fin: hdd last strides* **7/2**[1]
6005 3 *hd* **Reginald Claude**[25] 6988 2-9-1 **68**................................ DaneO'Neill 4 70
(M D I Usher) *in tch in midfield: effrt and swtchd rt 2f out: nt clr run wl over 1f out: drvn and styd on wl fr over 1f out: ev ch fnl 50yds: kpt on* **12/1**
0414 4 *¾* **Whodathought (IRE)**[20] 7087 2-9-4 **71**................................(b) JimmyFortune 7 71
(R Hannon) *led after 1f: rdn ent fnl 2f: drvn over 1f out: kpt on tl hdd and lost 3 pls wl ins fnl f* **4/1**[2]
5021 5 *2 ¾* **Saucy Buck (IRE)**[29] 6867 2-9-2 **69**................................ SamHitchcott 2 62
(M R Channon) *wnt rt s: in tch: rdn and unable qck ent fnl 2f: styd on same pce and no imp fr over 1f out* **4/1**[2]
5000 6 *¾* **Swaninstockwell (IRE)**[32] 6809 2-8-7 **60**................................ ChrisCatlin 3 53+
(P M Phelan) *sightly hmpd s and s.i.s: in tch in last trio: rdn and no hdwy over 2f out: kpt on again ent fnl f: styd on steadily: nvr gng pce to threaten ldrs* **20/1**
000 7 *nk* **Salaamie**[34] 6743 2-8-12 **65**................................ JoeFanning 8 55
(E A L Dunlop) *chsd ldr over 4f out: drvn to press ldr ent fnl f: wknd fnl 100yds* **10/1**
005 8 *3 ¼* **Honkers Bonkers**[30] 6849 2-9-3 **70**................................ JamesDoyle 1 54
(A J McCabe) *chsd ldr tl over 4f out: swtchd rt and effrt wl over 1f out: wknd ent fnl f: wl btn and eased fnl 50yds* **16/1**
0000 9 *nk* **West Leake Melody**[37] 6673 2-8-3 **56**................................ WilliamCarson 9 37
(B W Hills) *rrd s and s.i.s: a last trio: rdn and no hdwy over 2f out* **16/1**
1006 10 *25* **Danube Dancer (IRE)**[78] 5452 2-8-12 **65**................................(p) LukeMorris 5 —
(J S Moore) *a in rr: rdn ent fnl 4f: lost tch jst over 2f out: eased fr over 1f out: t.o* **33/1**

1m 24.7s (-0.10) **Going Correction** -0.025s/f (Stan) **10** Ran SP% **115.1**
Speed ratings (Par 96): **99,98,98,97,94 93,93,89,89,60**
Tote Swingers: 1&2 £5.40, 1&3 £13.90, 2&3 £9.30 CSF £22.53 CT £203.36 TOTE £4.70: £1.90, £1.90, £4.60; EX 21.40 Trifecta £133.20 Part won. Pool: £180.00 - 0.42 winning units..
Owner Miss J A Leighs **Bred** Mervyn Stewkesbury **Trained** Headley, Surrey

FOCUS
A typical Lingfield finish, with the first three finishing wide and late to run down long-time leader Whodathought. Routine nursery form.

NOTEBOOK
Romantic Wish was a little disappointing at Kempton last time, but she had an excuse as she ran too free over 1m there. Back a furlong in distance on her handicap debut, she settled much better and, having raced widest of all throughout, saw her race out well. A half-sister to Golden Desert, who has six wins to his name, including three on the Polytrack, she looks the type who can also add to her tally on this surface, but the plan is apparently to put her away for the winter now. (tchd 9-2 and 11-2)
Tullius(IRE), narrow winner of a C&D maiden last time on his first start since being gelded, ran in snatches but was brought to have every chance. He's still quite green and is capable of better. (tchd 3-1)
Reginald Claude was one of the more exposed runners in the line-up but he didn't look badly handicapped on a mark of 68. He appreciated being stepped back up to 7f but any rise in the weights won't help his cause. (op 14-1 tchd 16-1)
Whodathought(IRE) ran an honest race from the front but, as is often the case around here, found himself a sitting duck on the inside rail as the closers finished out wider. (tchd 10-3)
Saucy Buck(IRE), under pressure coming down the hill, didn't run too badly off a 6lb higher mark, but he hardly looked to improve for the step up to 7f. (op 11-2)

7418 EUROPEAN BREEDERS' FUND MAIDEN STKS 5f (P)
1:30 (1:30) (Class 5) 2-Y-0 £2,914 (£867; £433; £216) Stalls High

Form RPR
026 1 **Crimson Cloud**[21] 7065 2-8-12 69................................ TomEaves 8 69
(R A Fahey) *pressed ldr thrght: rdn to ld ent fnl f: kpt on wl u.p* **10/1**
00 2 *nk* **Liberty Green (IRE)**[153] 2958 2-8-12 0................................ JamesDoyle 7 68
(A J McCabe) *led: hung rt bnd 4f out: rdn wl over 1f out: hdd ent fnl f: kpt on wl but a jst hld after* **40/1**
22 3 *hd* **Steps (IRE)**[9] 7294 2-9-3 0................................ PhilipRobinson 10 72
(M A Jarvis) *chsd ldng pair: rdn 2f out: hung lft and no prog jst over 1f out: rallied ins fnl f: styng on fin: nt quite rch ldng pair* **5/2**[2]
52 4 *3 ¼* **Map Of Heaven**[28] 6892 2-8-12 0................................ JoeFanning 3 56+
(W J Haggas) *s.i.s: bhd: rdn and hdwy to chse ldng quartet 2f out: no imp tl swtchd rt ins fnl f: kpt on fnl 75yds: nvr gng pce to trble ldrs* **6/4**[1]
5235 5 *½* **Three Sparrows (IRE)**[18] 7116 2-9-3 75................................ JimmyFortune 2 59
(R Hannon) *in tch: effrt on inner to chse ldrs wl over 1f out: drvn jst over 1f out: wknd ins fnl f* **3/1**[3]
0 6 *4 ½* **Walshestown Lad (IRE)**[21] 7065 2-9-3 0................................ ChrisCatlin 1 43
(R A Harris) *t.k.h early: hld up in last quartet: rdn and struggling over 2f out: wd bnd ent fnl 2f: wl hld after* **80/1**
0000 7 *¾* **Veuveveuvevoom**[70] 5719 2-8-12 20................................ FrankieMcDonald 6 35
(G P Enright) *in tch: rdn and struggling over 2f out: no ch w ldrs fr over 1f out* **100/1**
4600 8 *3 ¾* **Silca Conegliano (IRE)**[8] 7313 2-8-12 61................................ LukeMorris 9 21
(M R Channon) *s.i.s: a in rr: rdn and struggling over 3f out: wl btn fnl 2f* **22/1**
0 9 *1 ¼* **Cara Carmela**[63] 5914 2-8-12 0................................ WilliamCarson 5 17
(S C Williams) *s.i.s: a in rr: struggling and losing tch 3f out: wl btn after* **40/1**

58.36 secs (-0.44) **Going Correction** -0.025s/f (Stan) 2y crse rec **9** Ran SP% **114.1**
Speed ratings (Par 96): **102,101,101,96,95 88,86,80,78**
Tote Swingers: 1&2 £13.80, 1&3 £4.10, 2&3 £13.60 CSF £304.76 TOTE £13.20: £2.60, £7.80, £1.50; EX 311.90 TRIFECTA Not won..
Owner R A Fahey **Bred** Mrs Sheila Oakes **Trained** Musley Bank, N Yorks

FOCUS
No more than a modest maiden, limited by the likes of the seventh. A minor personal best from the winner.

NOTEBOOK

Crimson Cloud didn't get home over 6f at Wolverhampton last time and the drop back to the minimum proved in her favour, but she took a while to get the better of Liberty Green, despite being at an advantage in challenging on the outer. On the plus side, the handicapper can't do much to her rating on the back of this win. (op 12-1)

Liberty Green(IRE), off the track since June, made the running and took a bit of passing. This was her best effort to date, and handicaps are now an option for her. (op 50-1)

Steps(IRE), drawn widest of all, was staying on all too late down the outside and in her case the drop back from 6f wasn't a plus. She's another now eligible for a mark. (op 2-1 tchd 11-4)

Map Of Heaven struggled to get into it after being ponderous from the stalls. (op 7-4 tchd 11-8)

Three Sparrows(IRE), who couldn't lead over this shorter trip, stuck to the unfavoured inside in the straight and weakened in the closing stages. (tchd 7-2)

7419 BET TEST MATCH RUGBY - BETDAQ MAIDEN STKS 1m 4f (P)

2:05 (2:07) (Class 5) 3-Y-0+ **£2,388** (£705; £352) **Stalls** Low

Form RPR

0223 **1** **La Concorde (FR)**[78] 5445 3-8-12 75 JimmyFortune 9 71+
(Sir Michael Stoute) *led for 1f: chsd ldr after 1f led again ent fnl 3f: mde rest: c centre st: rdn and in command ins fnl f: comf* **7/4**[1]

2646 **2** *3* **Cast Of Stars (IRE)**[22] 7043 3-9-3 72 (b[1]) JimCrowley 8 72+
(R M Beckett) *t.k.h: hld up towards rr: hdwy over 5f out: chsd wnr over 2f out: drvn and effrt over 1f out: nt pce of wnr and btn fnl f* **11/4**[2]

50 **3** *nk* **Kitty Wells**[128] 3795 3-8-12 0 J-PGuillambert 11 66+
(L M Cumani) *hld up in last trio: pushed along and n.m.r wl over 2f out: hdwy and wd bnd 2f out: styd on wl ins fnl f: gng on fin: no threat to wnr* **5/1**[3]

4 *3 ¼* **Lisselan Courtesan (IRE)**[37] 6682 5-9-4 0 DaneO'Neill 2 61+
(Raymond Hurley, Ire) *in tch in midfield: rdn and effrt over 2f out: chsd ldng pair jst over 2f out: styd on same pce and wl hld fr over 1f out* **13/2**

5 *6* **Lisselan Grace (IRE)**[79] 5428 3-8-12 0 ChrisCatlin 4 51
(Raymond Hurley, Ire) *in tch: effrt and rdn 3f out: one pce and no ch w ldrs fnl 2f* **20/1**

0 **6** *4* **Maydream**[32] 6815 3-8-12 0 SamHitchcott 1 45
(J C Fox) *chsd ldrs: rdn and struggling ent fnl 3f: wknd over 2f out* **66/1**

00 **7** *1 ¼* **Rannoch Moor**[23] 7022 3-9-3 0 GeorgeBaker 7 48
(M P Tregoning) *rrd s: in tch in last trio: rdn and no hdwy wl over 2f out: nvr trbld ldrs* **25/1**

00 **8** *4 ½* **Poesmulligan (IRE)**[2] 7397 4-9-9 0 (p) FrankieMcDonald 5 41
(Mrs L C Jewell) *awkward s: rcvrd to ld after 1f: hdd ent fnl 3f: rdn and wknd jst over 2f out* **66/1**

60 **9** *1 ½* **The Brown Bomber (IRE)**[20] 7086 4-9-6 0 AlanCreighton(3) 6 38
(Luke Comer, Ire) *t.k.h early: chsd ldrs tl wknd u.p wl over 2f out* **66/1**

10 *1 ¾* **Maccool (IRE)** 4-9-9 0 TomQueally 3 36
(B J Curley) *hld up in tch in midfield: rdn and wknd over 2f out: wl bhd over 1f out* **10/1**

6 **11** *8* **Mystic Halo**[13] 7244 7-9-4 0 RobertWinston 10 18
(L Corcoran) *stdd s: hld up in tch in rr: rdn and lost tch 3f out: wl bhd fnl 2f* **50/1**

2m 32.63s (-0.37) **Going Correction** -0.025s/f (Stan)
WFA 3 from 4yo+ 6lb **11** Ran SP% **117.2**
Speed ratings (Par 103): **100,98,97,95,91 88,88,85,84,82 77**
Tote Swingers: 1&2 £1.80, 1&3 £3.80, 2&3 £3.50 CSF £6.14 TOTE £2.30: £1.30, £1.40, £1.20; EX 7.30 Trifecta £15.10 Pool: £723.80 - 35.38 winning units..
Owner Tsega Horses **Bred** Domaine De Montjeu **Trained** Newmarket, Suffolk

FOCUS

The market got this ordinary maiden right, with the first four returning in betting order. It was only steadily run and the outsiders finished rather too close for comfort.

Rannoch Moor Official explanation: jockey said colt reared leaving stalls

7420 EUROPEAN BREEDERS' FUND FILLIES' H'CAP 1m 2f (P)

2:40 (2:41) (Class 3) (0-90,87) 3-Y-O **£6,476** (£1,927; £963; £481) **Stalls** Low

Form RPR

3220 **1** **Akhmatova**[13] 7243 3-9-3 83 DaneO'Neill 1 94
(G A Butler) *hld up in tch: hdwy over 2f out: rdn ent fnl 2f: chal ent fnl f: led ins fnl f: r.o wl* **4/1**[3]

6453 **2** *1 ¼* **Sing Sweetly**[36] 6698 3-9-1 81 TomQueally 4 89
(G A Butler) *sn led: rdn and qcknd ent fnl 2f: hrd pressed ent fnl f: hdd ins fnl f: styd on same pce after* **7/2**[2]

2316 **3** *1 ½* **Babycakes (IRE)**[48] 6361 3-9-5 85 JamieSpencer 2 90+
(M L W Bell) *hld up in tch: rdn and unable qck ent fnl 2f: rallied ins fnl f: kpt on but nt pce to chal ldrs* **7/2**[2]

2243 **4** *1 ½* **Nafura**[14] 7206 3-9-7 87 (p) TedDurcan 6 89
(Saeed Bin Suroor) *chsd ldng pair: wnt 2nd 6f out: rdn and unable qck ent fnl 2f: one pce and wl hld fnl f* **3/1**[1]

614 **5** *1* **Mazamorra (USA)**[28] 6904 3-9-1 81 ChrisCatlin 5 81
(M Botti) *chsd ldr tl 6f out: styd chsng ldrs: rdn over 2f out: outpcd ent fnl 2f: one pce and wl hld ent fnl f* **6/1**

1300 **6** *4 ½* **Miss Mittagong (USA)**[51] 6291 3-9-0 80 JimCrowley 7 71
(R M Beckett) *in tch in rr: rdn and effrt whn wd bnd 2f out: sn outpcd and n.d after* **14/1**

2m 4.62s (-1.98) **Going Correction** -0.025s/f (Stan) **6** Ran SP% **110.4**
Speed ratings (Par 103): **106,105,103,102,101 98**
Tote Swingers: 1&2 £3.40, 1&3 £3.40, 2&3 £3.20 CSF £17.57 TOTE £4.50: £1.80, £5.30; EX 21.30.
Owner Trevor C Stewart **Bred** Sunny Days Ltd **Trained** Newmarket, Suffolk

FOCUS

A competitive little fillies' handicap run at a reasonable pace, and this is fair form.

NOTEBOOK

Akhmatova was supposed to run at Dundalk but had to be rerouted due to the bad weather. Held up off the pace, she attacked four wide off the home bend and wore down her stablemate inside the last. A better horse on the AW than on turf, her connections are keen to have a go for black type with her now, and have earmarked a Listed race at Deauville on 18th December. (op 9-2 tchd 5-1)

Sing Sweetly, back in distance, got an uncontested lead and kicked on the bend into the straight, but her stablemate was able to match her and just had a bit more pace at the finish. She only has a maiden win to her name but she ran well from the front here, and similar tactics could yet see her add to that tally. (op 9-2)

Babycakes(IRE), unsuited by soft ground last time out, appreciated the switch back to Polytrack and ran on well for third. A stronger all-round gallop would have suited her. (op 5-1)

Nafura, denied the lead this time, wasn't quite at her best, although she looks held off her current mark anyway. (op 2-1)

Mazamorra(USA) stuck to the unfavoured inside in the straight, which was no help to her chance. (op 5-1)

7421 BET CHELTENHAM OPEN MEETING - BETDAQ H'CAP 1m (P)

3:15 (3:16) (Class 5) (0-75,75) 3-Y-0+ **£2,388** (£705; £352) **Stalls** High

Form RPR

0063 **1** **Halsion Chancer**[15] 7190 6-9-6 75 GeorgeBaker 7 84
(J R Best) *broke wl: sn stdd and hld up in tch: hdwy to chse ldrs jst over 2f out: rdn over 1f out: led ins fnl f: r.o wl* **7/2**[1]

2233 **2** *½* **Fantasy Gladiator**[20] 7092 4-9-4 73 (p) JamieSpencer 3 81
(R M H Cowell) *anticipated s and broke early: sn stdd and hld up in last pair: hdwy on outer over 2f out: rdn and r.o over 1f out: pressed wnr fnl 75yds: hld towards fin* **9/2**[2]

5006 **3** *1 ¼* **Lastkingofscotland (IRE)**[4] 7382 4-9-4 73 (b) RobertWinston 6 78
(C R Dore) *chsd ldrs: rdn and ev ch ent fnl 2f: stl ev ch tl no ex fnl 100yds* **10/1**

2503 **4** *1 ¼* **Prince Of Thebes (IRE)**[18] 7115 9-9-5 74 RichardKingscote 2 76
(M J Attwater) *wl in tch in midfield: rdn and effrt 2f out: styd on same pce fnl f* **11/1**

0-23 **5** *½* **Dear Maurice**[20] 7093 6-9-6 75 (t) IanMongan 4 76
(T B P Coles) *stdd s: hld up in last pair: effrt towards inner wl over 1f out: drvn over 1f out: kpt on ins fnl f: nvr able to chal* **13/2**[3]

2404 **6** *½* **Buxton**[13] 7241 6-9-2 71 (t) RobertHavlin 11 71
(R Ingram) *stdd s: hld up in tch in last: rdn and hdwy on inner bnd ent fnl 2f: rdn over 1f out: no prog 1f out: wknd ins fnl f* **20/1**

3210 **7** *nse* **Bianca De Medici**[22] 7046 3-9-3 74 JimmyFortune 9 74
(H Morrison) *led after 1f: rdn and hrd pressed ent fnl 2f: kpt on wl tl hdd ins fnl f: fdd fnl 100yds* **15/2**

2235 **8** *nk* **Rondeau (GR)**[22] 7047 5-9-3 72 JimCrowley 8 71
(P R Chamings) *stdd after s: hld up in tch in last trio: rdn and effrt wl over 1f out: kpt on same pce after: nvr able to chal* **10/1**

6460 **9** *nk* **Salient**[33] 6780 6-9-1 71 JemmaMarshall(5) 5 73
(M J Attwater) *wl in tch in midfield: rdn and unable qck ent fnl 2f: kpt on one pce and no threat to ldrs fnl f* **16/1**

6551 **10** *¾* **Aviso (GER)**[41] 6581 6-9-2 71 TomQueally 12 68
(B J Curley) *t.k.h: chsd ldr over 6f out: ev ch and rdn ent fnl f: wknd jst over 1f out* **11/1**

1020 **11** *2* **Amber Sunset**[14] 7209 4-9-4 73 WilliamCarson 10 65
(D Morris) *broke wl: t.k.h: sn stdd and hld up in tch: rdn and lost pl bnd ent fnl 2f: n.d after* **25/1**

2102 **12** *2 ¼* **El Dececy (USA)**[38] 6664 6-9-5 74 (p) TedDurcan 1 61
(J Balding) *led for 1f: chsd ldrs after: rdn and struggling ent fnl 2f: wknd over 1f out* **20/1**

1m 37.21s (-0.99) **Going Correction** -0.025s/f (Stan)
WFA 3 from 4yo+ 2lb **12** Ran SP% **119.6**
Speed ratings (Par 103): **103,102,101,100,99 99,98,98,98,97 95,93**
Tote Swingers: 1&2 £5.10, 1&3 £9.70, 2&3 £8.90 CSF £18.11 CT £146.71 TOTE £6.90: £2.50, £1.70, £3.00; EX 28.20 Trifecta £206.00 Pool: £662.82 - 2.38 winning units..
Owner Halsion Ltd **Bred** Mrs S Hansford **Trained** Hucking, Kent

FOCUS

They went a fair pace up front and that suited the closers. Straightforward form.

7422 ASHURST WOOD APPRENTICE H'CAP 1m 5f (P)

3:45 (3:45) (Class 5) (0-70,66) 3-Y-0+ **£2,388** (£705; £352) **Stalls** Low

Form RPR

6601 **1** **Naheell**[11] 7275 4-9-3 57 6ex MatthewCosham(3) 3 66+
(G Prodromou) *in tch: effrt to ld 2f out: pushed along to assert ent fnl f: in command ins fnl f: pushed out* **11/4**[2]

0001 **2** *1 ¼* **Danvilla**[8] 7315 3-9-3 66 6ex IanBurns(5) 4 72+
(P R Webber) *hld up in last pair: rdn wl over 3f out: drvn and unable qck jst over 2f out: kpt on fnl 100yds to go 2nd last strides: no threat to wnr* **9/4**[1]

-332 **3** *nk* **Sheila's Castle**[128] 3780 6-9-6 60 LucyBarry(3) 6 66
(S Regan) *led: rdn and hdd 2f out: styd on same pce fnl f: lost 2nd last strides* **5/1**

0005 **4** *1* **Suhailah**[23] 7022 4-8-12 49 oh1 MatthewLawson 2 54
(M J Attwater) *chsd ldr tl 9f out: chsd ldrs after: rdn and unable qck ent fnl 2f: styd on same pce fr over 1f out* **20/1**

0135 **5** *1 ½* **Leyte Gulf (USA)**[11] 7270 7-9-9 60 RichardRowe 1 62
(C C Bealby) *stdd s: hld up in last pair: effrt on inner wl over 1f out: nt clr run over 1f out tl ins fnl f: nvr able to chal* **15/2**

0623 **6** *1* **Soundbyte**[16] 7167 5-9-7 63 DanielHarris(5) 5 64
(J Gallagher) *chsd ldrs: wnt 2nd 9f out: jnd ldr 5f out: ev ch and rdn over 2f out: unable qck wl over 1f out: wknd ent fnl f* **4/1**[3]

2m 46.06s (0.06) **Going Correction** -0.025s/f (Stan)
WFA 3 from 4yo+ 7lb **6** Ran SP% **110.6**
Speed ratings (Par 103): **98,97,97,96,95 94**
Tote Swingers: 1&2 £1.70, 1&3 £2.30, 2&3 £2.60 CSF £9.07 TOTE £2.50: £1.10, £3.60; EX 7.10.
Owner Fahed Al Dabbous **Bred** Darley **Trained** East Harling, Norfolk

FOCUS

A moderate event in which the winner pretty much matched his latest Wolverhampton win.

T/Plt: £60.50 to a £1 stake. Pool:£45,920.99 - 553.56 winning tickets T/Qpdt: £8.80 to a £1 stake. Pool:£4,163.94 - 346.60 winning tickets SP

7408 WOLVERHAMPTON (A.W) (L-H)

Friday, November 12

OFFICIAL GOING: Standard

Wind: Fresh behind Weather: Overcast

7423 BET MULTIPLES - BETDAQ NURSERY 5f 20y(P)

4:20 (4:21) (Class 5) (0-75,74) 2-Y-O **£2,007** (£597; £298; £149) **Stalls** Low

Form RPR

6001 **1** **Pitkin**[7] 7333 2-8-4 57 6ex ow1 GrahamGibbons 3 67+
(M W Easterby) *edgd rt s: sn prom: rdn to ld wl ins fnl f: r.o* **11/8**[1]

4312 **2** *1 ½* **Forty Proof (IRE)**[7] 7333 2-9-7 74 (v[1]) ShaneKelly 6 76
(W J Knight) *s.i.s: hld up: hdwy 1/2-way: rdn over 1f out: hung lft and r.o ins fnl f: wnt 2nd nr fin: nt rch wnr* **5/1**[2]

6313 **3** *nk* **Miss Toldyaso (IRE)**[9] 7301 2-7-13 55 ow2 KellyHarrison(3) 7 56
(M G Quinlan) *chsd ldr: led 1/2-way: rdn over 1f out: hdd wl ins fnl f: lost 2nd nr fin* **12/1**

4003 **4** *½* **Mr Optimistic**[11] 7268 2-8-9 62 DuranFentiman 4 61+
(R A Fahey) *hmpd s: hdwy and hmpd 1/2-way: rdn over 1f out: r.o: nt trble ldrs* **12/1**

0053 **5** *3* **Silk Bounty**[14] 7211 2-8-11 **64**.....................(b) PaulMulrennan 9 52
(J G Given) *chsd ldrs: rdn over 1f out: edgd lft and no ex ins fnl f* **6/1**[3]
0662 **6** *4* **Shutupandrive**[23] 7017 2-7-12 **51** oh6.....................(v) JamieMackay 2 25
(M D I Usher) *free to post: led to 1/2-way: wknd over 1f out* **66/1**
0415 **7** *hd* **Sensational Love (IRE)**[9] 7301 2-9-1 **68**..................... NeilCallan 11 41+
(R A Mills) *hld up: rdn over 1f out: nvr on terms* **10/1**
5006 **8** *1 1/4* **Bon Appetit**[11] 7269 2-8-2 **55**..................... CathyGannon 5 24
(N Tinkler) *hmpd s: plld hrd and prom: rdn 1/2-way: sn wknd* **20/1**
0402 **9** *3 1/2* **Gunalt Joy**[11] 7268 2-7-13 **52** oh4 ow1..................... JimmyQuinn 8 8
(M W Easterby) *mid-div: pushed along and lost pl 3f out: wknd 1/2-way* **11/1**
666 **10** *3* **Mini Bon Bon**[9] 7301 2-7-11 **57**.....................(v) JessicaSteven(7) 10 2
(A Bailey) *sn pushed along in rr: lost tch 1/2-way* **50/1**
62.00 secs (-0.30) **Going Correction** 0.0s/f (Stan) **10** Ran SP% **114.1**
Speed ratings (Par 96): **102,99,99,98,93 87,86,84,79,74**
toteswingers:1&2:£2.20, 1&3:£4.90, 2&3:£6.80 CSF £7.71 CT £56.66 TOTE £2.40: £1.50, £1.10, £2.60; EX 7.00.
Owner Steve Hull **Bred** New Mill Farm Stud **Trained** Sheriff Hutton, N Yorks

FOCUS
An ordinary nursery but the form looks sound, the winner confirming the good impression of his recent win here.

NOTEBOOK
Pitkin was always going to be hard to beat racing off effectively the same mark as when successful over C&D a week earlier. The handicapper will have his say now but he did it in pretty good style, and this son of Proclamation can be expected to stay on the upgrade for a good bit longer. He'll be well suited by 6f. (tchd 11-10)
Forty Proof(IRE), in a first-time visor, found Pitkin too good for the second start running but won't always run into one so far ahead of his mark, and is likely to add to his Bath maiden success before too long. He again finished in a manner which suggests he's well worth trying back over 6f. (op 6-1 tchd 7-1)
Miss Toldyaso(IRE) has done well since being switched to nurseries, and her likeable attitude should continue to hold her in good stead, but she does look vulnerable to less-exposed sorts after a 5lb rise for last month's Kempton win.
Mr Optimistic ran well here for the second start in a row but didn't have any excuses either and looks one of the yard's lesser lights at this stage. (tchd 16-1)
Silk Bounty didn't find much in the second-time blinkers and his attitude is already starting to look a bit questionable. (tchd 7-1)
Sensational Love(IRE) faced no easy task after being dropped in from her wide stall, and is perhaps worth another chance as she'd gone the right way before this. (tchd 11-1)

7424 CELEBRATE CHRISTMAS AT WOLVERHAMPTON RACECOURSE CLAIMING STKS 5f 20y(P)
4:50 (4:51) (Class 6) 2-Y-O **£1,619** (£481; £240; £120) **Stalls** Low

Form RPR
1 **Lady Prodee** 2-8-2 0..................... DuranFentiman 4 66+
(W G M Turner) *half-rrd s: bhd: swtchd lft and hdwy over 1f out: r.o u.p to ld nr fin* **22/1**
523 **2** *nk* **Johnny Hancocks (IRE)**[7] 7333 2-8-7 76..................... CathyGannon 5 70
(P D Evans) *led: rdn over 1f out: edgd rt ins fnl f: hdd nr fin* **7/4**[1]
5200 **3** *hd* **Golden Shine**[104] 4592 2-8-0 79..................... JulieBurke(7) 8 69
(A Bailey) *hld up in tch: rdn and ev ch ins fnl f: edgd rt: r.o* **3/1**[3]
0400 **4** *shd* **Instructress**[14] 7211 2-8-1 66..................... JimmyQuinn 2 63
(R M H Cowell) *chsd ldrs: hrd rdn and ev ch ins fnl f: r.o* **8/1**
0000 **5** *2 3/4* **Molly Mylenis**[9] 7301 2-8-0 56..................... AndreaAtzeni 3 52
(P D Evans) *prom: rdn 1/2-way: styd on same pce fnl f* **25/1**
4013 **6** *2 3/4* **Second Encore**[22] 7040 2-8-1 68..................... LukeMorris 6 43
(J S Moore) *prom: chsd ldr over 3f out: rdn and hung rt 1/2-way: no ex fnl f* **9/4**[2]
0 **7** *2* **Oh What's Occuring**[23] 7021 2-8-4 0 ow1..................... NeilChalmers 1 39
(T T Clement) *sn outpcd: nvr nrr* **66/1**
00 **8** *17* **He'Sahit (FR)**[30] 6842 2-8-2 0..................... AndrewHeffernan(3) 9 —
(P R Hedger) *chsd ldr tl hung lft over 3f out: wknd 1/2-way* **50/1**
62.74 secs (0.44) **Going Correction** 0.0s/f (Stan) **8** Ran SP% **114.9**
Speed ratings (Par 94): **96,95,95,95,90 86,83,55**
toteswingers:1&2:£7.90, 1&3:£10.40, 2&3:£1.60 CSF £60.25 TOTE £35.50: £7.80, £1.10, £1.10; EX 93.20.
Owner Mrs M S Teversham **Bred** Mrs Monica Teversham **Trained** Sigwells, Somerset

FOCUS
An above-average claimer that provided a thrilling finish. The form is modest rated through the runner-up.

NOTEBOOK
Lady Prodee ◆ overcame clear greenness to make a winning debut. This daughter of Proclamation reared as the stalls opened and looked clueless in rear until halfway but picked up really well as she got the hang of things in the straight. She can only improve and will be an interesting one for handicaps. (op 20-1)
Johnny Hancocks(IRE) is taking a busy campaign well, typically giving his all from the front, and he won't be long in getting back in the winner's enclosure if connections persevere at this level. (op 2-1)
Golden Shine had been picked up fairly cheaply from Mick Channon since last seen in July but showed all her ability remains intact, and there'll be races to be won with her this winter if she's kept to this company. (op 7-2)
Instructress put a below-par effort here last time behind her and will find weaker claimers than this during the winter. (op 7-1)
Molly Mylenis at least showed she's not a complete back number but she has essentially been disappointing since her Musselburgh maiden success in early summer. (op 22-1 tchd 20-1)
Second Encore came here in form and held sound claims at the weights so might have been expected to do better, fading out of it having been unable to dominate. (tchd 2-1)

7425 BETDAQEXTRA.COM H'CAP (DIV I) 5f 216y(P)
5:20 (5:21) (Class 6) (0-55,61) 3-Y-O+ **£1,295** (£385; £192; £96) **Stalls** Low

Form RPR
6624 **1** **Desert Strike**[18] 7132 4-8-8 **54**.....................(p) NoraLooby(7) 10 61
(A J McCabe) *trckd ldrs: plld hrd: hung rt over 2f out: rdn over 1f out: r.o to ld wl ins fnl f* **12/1**[3]
6062 **2** *1* **Equinity**[49] 6329 4-9-0 **53**.....................(t) MickyFenton 12 57
(J Pearce) *led 1f: remained handy: chsd ldr over 3f out: rdn and ev ch wl ins fnl f: styd on same pce* **9/1**[2]
5535 **3** *hd* **Black Baccara**[7] 7331 3-9-0 **53**.....................(p) AdamKirby 7 56
(P S McEntee) *trckd ldrs: plld hrd: rdn over 2f out: styd on* **12/1**[3]
00-1 **4** *nk* **Taurakina**[9] 7299 4-9-3 **61** 6ex..................... TobyAtkinson(5) 6 63+
(M Botti) *s.s: hdwy to ld 4f out: rdn over 1f out: hdd and no ex wl ins fnl f* **1/2**[1]
4416 **5** *1* **Duke Of Rainford**[23] 7018 3-8-13 **52**..................... PhillipMakin 3 51
(M Herrington) *hld up: hdwy over 1f out: running on whn hmpd wl insde fnl f* **16/1**
0300 **6** *1/2* **Connor's Choice**[15] 7195 5-9-2 **55**..................... LukeMorris 2 52
(Andrew Turnell) *prom: rdn over 1f out: styd on same pce ins fnl f* **28/1**
0160 **7** *hd* **Fair Bunny**[44] 6461 3-9-2 **55**.....................(b) JimmyQuinn 5 52
(A D Brown) *led 5f out: hdd 4f out: chsd ldrs: rdn over 2f out: no ex ins fnl f* **33/1**
0040 **8** *nk* **Only A Game (IRE)**[9] 7299 5-8-13 **55**.....................(vt) GaryBartley(3) 8 53+
(I W McInnes) *s.s: hdwy over 1f out: running on whn n.m.r wl ins fnl f* **20/1**
3050 **9** *1/2* **Itsthursdayalready**[12] 7250 3-9-0 **53**..................... ShaneKelly 13 47
(W M Brisbourne) *hld up: rdn over 1f out: styd on ins fnl f: n.d* **28/1**
200 **10** *3/4* **Royal Envoy (IRE)**[15] 7192 7-8-12 **54**..................... MichaelStainton(3) 11 46
(P Howling) *s.i.s: in rr and rdn 1/2-way: styd on ins fnl f: nvr nrr* **40/1**
356 **11** *1 3/4* **Sorrel Point**[114] 4256 7-8-13 **52**.....................(vt) CathyGannon 4 38
(H J Collingridge) *hld up: rdn over 1f out: n.d* **33/1**
1m 15.44s (0.44) **Going Correction** 0.0s/f (Stan) **11** Ran SP% **117.9**
Speed ratings (Par 101): **97,95,95,95,93 93,92,92,91,90 88**
toteswingers:1&2:£4.70, 1&3:£7.50, 2&3:£6.00 CSF £103.51 CT £1334.43 TOTE £10.70: £2.90, £2.00, £1.50; EX 46.40.
Owner Mrs M J McCabe **Bred** Mrs Mary Rowlands **Trained** Averham Park, Notts

FOCUS
The betting had this as a one-sided handicap but the favourite blew the start and this probably didn't take much winning. The time was a bit slower than division II.

7426 BETDAQEXTRA.COM H'CAP (DIV II) 5f 216y(P)
5:50 (5:51) (Class 6) (0-55,55) 3-Y-O+ **£1,295** (£385; £192; £96) **Stalls** Low

Form RPR
0360 **1** **Liberty Trail (IRE)**[13] 7241 4-9-2 **55**.....................(p) NeilCallan 11 63
(P D Evans) *chsd ldrs: rdn over 2f out: led ins fnl f: r.o* **5/1**[2]
5004 **2** *1/2* **Mr Skipiton (IRE)**[17] 7155 5-9-0 **53**..................... TomMcLaughlin 13 59
(B J McMath) *mid-div: hdwy over 2f out: rdn to ld 1f out: sn hdd: r.o* **12/1**
4310 **3** *nk* **Almaty Express**[23] 7018 8-8-7 **53**.....................(b) JulieBurke(7) 5 58
(J R Weymes) *chsd ldrs: rdn over 1f out: r.o* **6/1**[3]
3535 **4** *hd* **Luisa Tetrazzini (IRE)**[34] 6746 4-8-10 **54**..................... MarkCoumbe(5) 1 58+
(D Bourton) *s.s: hdwy over 1f out: hung lft and r.o: nt rch ldrs* **8/1**
5430 **5** *2* **Namu**[9] 7299 7-9-2 **55**..................... AdamKirby 3 53
(Miss T Spearing) *hld up: rdn over 1f out: r.o: nt trble ldrs* **7/1**
6000 **6** *nse* **Replicator**[17] 7155 5-8-13 **55**.....................(e) AshleyHamblett(3) 7 53
(P L Gilligan) *led 5f out: rdn and hdd 1f out: no ex* **20/1**
003 **7** *1/2* **Hidden Destiny**[16] 7166 3-9-2 **55**..................... FergusSweeney 10 51+
(P J Makin) *prom: nt clr run over 2f out: sn rdn: styd on* **9/2**[1]
0400 **8** *1/2* **Polemica (IRE)**[12] 7250 4-8-13 **52**.....................(bt[1]) LeeVickers 9 47
(F Sheridan) *s.i.s: hdwy over 2f out: rdn over 1f out: no imp* **20/1**
6340 **9** *nk* **A Pocketful Of Rye (IRE)**[27] 6931 3-8-10 **52**......... MichaelStainton(3) 2 46
(P Howling) *s.s: running on whn hmpd wl ins fnl f: nt rch ldrs* **25/1**
0000 **10** *2 1/4* **Spoof Master (IRE)**[12] 7250 6-8-13 **52**..................... MickyFenton 12 38
(J Pearce) *mid-div: rdn 1/2-way: nvr trbld ldrs* **22/1**
00-2 **11** *2 1/2* **Sir Don (IRE)**[23] 7018 11-9-1 **54**.....................(tp) StevieDonohoe 4 32
(Mrs D J Sanderson) *led 1f: chsd ldr: rdn over 2f out: wknd over 1f out* **9/1**
0053 **12** *2 1/4* **Magenta Strait**[18] 7122 3-8-9 **55**.....................(p) JackDuern(7) 6 26+
(R Hollinshead) *s.s: outpcd* **10/1**
1m 15.15s (0.15) **Going Correction** 0.0s/f (Stan) **12** Ran SP% **117.2**
Speed ratings (Par 101): **99,98,97,97,95 94,94,93,93,90 86,83**
toteswingers:1&2:£13.30, 1&3:£8.20, 2&3:£10.10 CSF £58.67 CT £375.24 TOTE £6.40: £2.30, £3.00, £2.70; EX 60.60.
Owner Mrs B Grainger **Bred** Clougher Partnership **Trained** Pandy, Monmouths

FOCUS
Very much run-of-the-mill fare. The time was slightly quicker than division I and the the form is straightforward, the winner matching his best for this yard.

7427 THE BLACK COUNTRY'S ONLY RACECOURSE MAIDEN STKS 7f 32y(P)
6:20 (6:22) (Class 5) 2-Y-O **£2,007** (£597; £298; £149) **Stalls** High

Form RPR
1 **Ho Ya Mal (IRE)** 2-9-3 0..................... EddieAhern 7 77+
(E A L Dunlop) *led 1f: chsd ldrs: shkn up to ld over 1f out: edged rt: r.o* **4/1**[3]
64 **2** *1 1/4* **Flying Arch (USA)**[24] 7002 2-8-12 0..................... J-PGuillambert 5 69
(L M Cumani) *hld up in tch: racd keenly: rdn and ev ch over 1f out: styd on same pce ins fnl f* **3/1**[2]
3 *1/2* **Rutland Boy** 2-9-3 0..................... TomMcLaughlin 1 73+
(E A L Dunlop) *hld up: hdwy over 2f out: rdn over 1f out: styd on* **16/1**
5 **4** *6* **Bill Page (USA)**[35] 6712 2-9-3 0..................... NeilCallan 9 58
(D M Simcock) *trckd ldrs: rdn and nt clr run over 1f out: wknd fnl f* **7/1**
23 **5** *1* **Celani**[32] 6804 2-8-12 0..................... CathyGannon 10 51
(Andrew Turnell) *led 6f out: hdd 5f out: led again over 3f out: rdn and hdd over 1f out: wknd fnl f* **11/4**[1]
0 **6** *4 1/2* **Cherrego (USA)**[9] 7303 2-8-12 0..................... LukeMorris 11 40
(B Palling) *mid-div: hdwy to ld 5f out: hdd over 3f out: rdn and wknd over 1f out* **22/1**
50 **7** *1/2* **Gekko (IRE)**[57] 6126 2-9-3 0..................... StephenCraine 4 43+
(Patrick Morris) *hld up: rdn over 1f out: n.d* **28/1**
00 **8** *2* **Shirocco Vice (IRE)**[16] 7172 2-8-5 0..................... LauraBarry(7) 8 33
(R A Fahey) *chsd ldrs tl rdn and wknd over 2f out* **66/1**
04 **9** *nse* **Tidal Star**[17] 7150 2-9-3 0..................... AdamKirby 2 38+
(M G Quinlan) *hld up: shkn up over 2f out: rdn over 1f out: n.d* **7/1**
10 *3 1/4* **Una Vita Pius (IRE)** 2-8-9 0..................... AshleyHamblett(3) 3 25
(P L Gilligan) *s.s: a in rr* **100/1**
11 *1* **Fire Commander** 2-9-3 0..................... GrahamGibbons 12 28
(B P J Baugh) *s.s: a in rr* **66/1**
00 **12** *15* **Barry Crockett (IRE)**[51] 6293 2-9-0 0..............(b[1]) AndrewHeffernan(3) 6 —
(Mrs L Williamson) *sn pushed along and a in rr: t.o* **100/1**
1m 30.57s (0.97) **Going Correction** 0.0s/f (Stan) **12** Ran SP% **115.3**
Speed ratings (Par 96): **94,92,92,85,84 78,78,76,75,72 71,53**
toteswingers:1&2:£13.30, 1&3:£8.20, 2&3:£10.10 CSF £15.30 TOTE £5.10: £2.00, £1.10, £4.30; EX 19.10.
Owner Ahmad Al Shaikh **Bred** Crone Stud Farms Ltd **Trained** Newmarket, Suffolk

FOCUS
Probably best to take a reasonably positive view of this form, certainly in regard to the first three, who pulled well clear. The form looks sound rated through the runner-up.

NOTEBOOK
Ho Ya Mal(IRE) ◆ attracted support and continued Ed Dunlop's fine strike-rate with juveniles at this track. This son of Shamardal certainly knew his job and only had to be nudged ahead by Eddie Ahern. He can be expected to go on from this. There's a bit of speed in his pedigree but he's likely to stay 1m on this evidence. (op 17-2 tchd 9-1)
Flying Arch(USA) is progressing with racing and should go one better before long. Her dam was a 1m winner as a juvenile and she's likely to do better as her stamina is drawn out a bit more. (op 11-4)

The Form Book, Raceform Ltd, Compton, RG20 6NL

Rutland Boy, a stablemate of the winner, made a promising start in his own right, travelling comfortably in midfield and quickening clear of the rest. He should be up to going close in a similar event next time.
Bill Page(USA) couldn't step up on last month's C&D debut but it's still early days and he remains the type to do better in due course, probably once eligible for handicaps. (op 5-1)
Celani has now been a little disappointing on both starts since her promising Kempton debut. She had no excuses here, fading after dictating the pace. (op 9-4 tchd 3-1)
Cherrego(USA) seemed to achieve a bit more than her debut but it's hardly a solid effort, weakening having been well placed up with the steady pace. (op 33-1)
Gekko(IRE) wasn't unduly knocked about on his third start and now has the option of handicaps. (op 33-1)
Shirocco Vice(IRE), who is bred to need a good bit further, is one to look out for next year off what will surely be a modest opening handicap mark.
Tidal Star never looked like repeating the form he showed when fourth at Yarmouth but is another who can now go down the handicap route. (op 13-2 tchd 6-1)

7428 ENJOY THE PARTY PACK GROUP OFFER H'CAP 1m 4f 50y(P)
6:50 (6:50) (Class 4) (0-85,84) 3-Y-O+ **£3,594** (£1,069; £534; £266) **Stalls** Low

Form RPR
1105 **1** **Captain John Nixon**[20] 7090 3-9-0 **80** .... AndreaAtzeni 6 90
(Pat Eddery) *chsd ldr tl led 3f out: rdn and hung lft over 1f out: styd on wl* **5/1**[2]
1042 **2** *2 1/4* **Saint Thomas (IRE)**[25] 6984 3-8-8 **74** .... GrahamGibbons 3 80
(J Mackie) *hld up: hdwy over 2f out: rdn to chse wnr and hung lft over 1f out: styd on same pce* **12/1**
5421 **3** *1* **Realisation (USA)**[35] 6730 3-9-4 **84** .... JoeFanning 7 89
(M Johnston) *a.p: rdn to chse wnr over 2f out to over 1f out: no ex ins fnl f: eased nr fin* **4/5**[1]
0510 **4** *nk* **Arizona John (IRE)**[20] 7084 5-9-10 **84** .... StephenCraine 5 88
(J Mackie) *hld up: hdwy over 2f out: rdn over 1f out: no ex ins fnl f* **14/1**
0550 **5** *5* **Snow Dancer (IRE)**[21] 7053 6-9-3 **77** .... PatrickMathers 4 73
(H A McWilliams) *hld up: sme hdwy 2f out: sn rdn and no imp* **25/1**
5335 **6** *13* **Fine Sight**[18] 7130 3-9-1 **81** .... StevieDonohoe 2 57
(G A Butler) *led: hdd 3f out: rdn and wknd over 1f out* **9/1**
4003 **7** *3* **Stand Guard**[32] 6797 6-9-7 **81** .... JimmyQuinn 1 52
(P Howling) *chsd ldrs: rdn over 4f out: wknd over 2f out* **8/1**[3]
42-3 **8** *24* **Can Can Star**[287] 341 7-9-9 **83** .... NeilCallan 8 15
(A W Carroll) *hld up: a in rr: wknd over 2f out: t.o* **16/1**
2m 37.94s (-3.16) **Going Correction** 0.0s/f (Stan)
WFA 3 from 5yo+ 6lb **8** Ran SP% **117.4**
Speed ratings (Par 105): **110,108,107,107,104 95,93,77**
toteswingers:1&2:£2.60, 1&3:£14.70, 2&3:£14.20 CSF £63.41 CT £95.46 TOTE £4.80: £1.30, £1.60, £2.00; EX 44.20.
Owner Paul Dean **Bred** Patrick Eddery Ltd **Trained** Nether Winchendon, Bucks

FOCUS
A fairly useful contest. It was run at just a modest gallop for the most part, the race not really beginning in earnest until the final 4f. The winner rates a 4lb personal best.

7429 STAY AT THE WOLVERHAMPTON HOLIDAY INN CLASSIFIED STKS 1m 1f 103y(P)
7:20 (7:21) (Class 6) 3-Y-O+ **£1,619** (£481; £240; £120) **Stalls** Low

Form RPR
4000 **1** **Irish Jugger (USA)**[28] 6903 3-8-12 55 .... JamesMillman 10 65
(B R Millman) *hld up: hdwy over 2f out: styd on to ld whn hmpd wl ins fnl f* **16/1**
2000 **2** *2* **All Moving Parts (USA)**[51] 6287 3-8-12 55 ....(v[1]) JamesDoyle 9 61+
(A J McCabe) *chsd ldr tl led 3f out: rdn clr over 1f out: hung rt and hdd wl ins fnl f* **8/1**
665 **3** *2 3/4* **Supatov (USA)**[32] 6814 3-8-12 52 .... SteveDrowne 12 55
(H Morrison) *chsd ldrs: pushed along 1/2-way: rdn to chse wnr over 2f out: hung lft over 1f out: no ex ins fnl f* **2/1**[1]
323 **4** *5* **Chichen Daawe**[21] 7071 4-9-1 52 .... DaneO'Neill 13 44
(B Ellison) *hld up in tch: rdn over 2f out: wknd over 1f out* **4/1**[2]
0654 **5** *1 3/4* **Alnaseem (USA)**[16] 7161 3-8-12 52 .... GrahamGibbons 8 41
(M W Easterby) *prom: rdn over 2f out: wknd over 1f out* **7/1**[3]
0000 **6** *3/4* **Mystic Touch**[8] 7315 4-9-1 50 ....(p) NeilCallan 11 38
(A B Haynes) *s.i.s: hld up: rdn over 1f out: styd on: n.d* **20/1**
0000 **7** *nse* **Mekong Miss**[8] 7315 4-9-1 52 .... LukeMorris 4 38
(D Shaw) *hld up: rdn over 2f out: styd on ins fnl f: nvr nrr* **33/1**
660 **8** *1/2* **Raghdaan**[29] 6876 3-8-12 50 .... CathyGannon 6 38
(P W Hiatt) *hld up: nvr on terms* **33/1**
9 *1 3/4* **Mary Spring Rice (IRE)**[90] 5102 4-9-1 47 .... ChrisCatlin 5 34
(Seamus Fahey, Ire) *s.i.s: a in rr* **20/1**
0050 **10** *nse* **Mullitovermaurice**[21] 7071 4-8-8 46 .... JulieBurke(7) 2 34
(Patrick Morris) *chsd ldrs: rdn over 3f out: wknd 2f out* **10/1**
000 **11** *7* **Vertumnus**[16] 7161 3-8-12 51 ....(p) J-PGuillambert 7 20
(N P Littmoden) *hld up: plld hrd: rdn over 2f out: sn wknd* **50/1**
-000 **12** *8* **Bluegrass Lion (USA)**[7] 7327 4-8-12 46 ....(b[1]) AndrewHeffernan(3) 1 —
(Mrs L Williamson) *led: rdn and hdd 3f out: wknd wl over 1f out* **100/1**
0000 **13** *1 3/4* **Marteau**[129] 3758 3-8-12 53 ....(t) PhillipMakin 3 —
(K A Ryan) *hld up in tch: wknd over 3f out* **20/1**
2m 1.03s (-0.67) **Going Correction** 0.0s/f (Stan)
WFA 3 from 4yo 3lb **13** Ran SP% **115.0**
Speed ratings (Par 101): **102,100,97,93,91 91,91,90,89,89 82,75,74**
toteswingers:1&2:£11.30, 1&3:£8.10, 2&3:£6.90 CSF £122.66 TOTE £21.40: £7.00, £2.70, £1.10; EX 110.80.
Owner The Irish Jugger Partnership **Bred** Richard S Kaster & Frederick C Wieting **Trained** Kentisbeare, Devon

FOCUS
A low-grade classified event, though the performances of the first two probably represent good form for the level. It was run at a sound pace.

7430 BET PREMIER LEAGUE FOOTBALL - BETDAQ H'CAP 1m 141y(P)
7:50 (7:53) (Class 2) (0-100,101) 3-Y-O£8,705 (£2,605; £1,302; £651; £324) **Stalls** Low

Form RPR
4235 **1** **Fastnet Storm (IRE)**[18] 7121 4-8-7 **86** .... GrahamGibbons 10 95
(T P Tate) *mde all: rdn and edgd rt over 1f out: styd on gamely* **16/1**
043 **2** *nk* **Baylini**[13] 7243 6-8-8 **87** .... JamesDoyle 2 95
(J A Osborne) *a.p: rdn over 1f out: edgd rt ins fnl f: r.o* **8/1**
2612 **3** *1 1/4* **Chapter And Verse (IRE)**[55] 6204 4-9-1 **94** .... AndreaAtzeni 13 99
(Mike Murphy) *hld up: hdwy over 3f out: rdn over 1f out: r.o* **7/1**[3]
0045 **4** *1/2* **Mia's Boy**[13] 7234 6-9-6 **99** .... EddieAhern 8 105+
(C A Dwyer) *hld up: hdwy and nt clr run fr over 1f out: r.o: nt rch ldrs* **7/2**[1]
0032 **5** *shd* **Mr Willis**[15] 7187 4-8-7 **89** .... KierenFox(3) 6 93+
(J R Best) *hld up: rdn over 1f out: r.o ins fnl f: nt rch ldrs* **5/1**[2]
0010 **6** *nk* **Sarah Park (IRE)**[15] 7188 5-8-11 **90** .... NeilCallan 11 93
(B J Meehan) *chsd wnr: rdn over 2f out: styd on same pce ins fnl f* **16/1**
0502 **7** *1/2* **Beauchamp Xerxes**[13] 7233 4-9-8 **101** .... DaneO'Neill 12 103
(G A Butler) *hld up: hdwy over 4f out: rdn over 1f out: styd on same pce ins fnl f* **9/1**
0006 **8** *hd* **Ceremonial Jade (UAE)**[81] 5370 7-9-4 **97** ....(t) AdamKirby 9 98
(M Botti) *hld up: hdwy over 1f out: rdn and edgd rt ins fnl f: no ex towards fin* **12/1**
0000 **9** *3 1/2* **Big Bay (USA)**[13] 7233 4-8-9 **88** ....(b[1]) LukeMorris 4 81
(Jane Chapple-Hyam) *hld up: n.m.r and lost pl over 3f out: hmpd 3f out: sn rdn: nvr trbld ldrs* **16/1**
2220 **10** *nse* **Ocean Legend (IRE)**[111] 4354 5-8-7 **86** oh1 .... LiamJones 5 79
(A W Carroll) *hld up in tch: rdn over 2f out: wknd fnl f* **33/1**
423 **11** *nk* **Seradim**[10] 7287 4-8-7 **86** .... ChrisCatlin 7 79
(P F I Cole) *chsd ldrs: rdn over 2f out: wknd fnl f* **14/1**
-114 **12** *nk* **Rjeef (IRE)**[210] 1352 3-8-9 **91** .... JoeFanning 1 84
(D M Simcock) *chsd ldrs: rdn over 2f out: wknd fnl f* **7/1**[3]
1m 50.28s (-0.22) **Going Correction** 0.0s/f (Stan)
WFA 3 from 4yo+ 3lb **12** Ran SP% **119.9**
Speed ratings (Par 109): **100,99,98,98,98 97,97,97,94,94 93,93**
toteswingers:1&2:£14.20, 1&3:£16.90, 2&3:£10.80 CSF £140.18 CT £1010.15 TOTE £23.30: £4.10, £3.30, £3.50; EX 168.50.
Owner The Kittywake Partnership **Bred** Norelands Bloodstock **Trained** Tadcaster, N Yorks

FOCUS
A useful contest, though the bare form has the potential to prove a bit muddling. The pace steadied in the back straight and a few were left with way too much to do turning in.

NOTEBOOK
Fastnet Storm(IRE) is a consistent sort who clearly took well to Polytrack at the first attempt, though his success undoubtedly owed plenty to a good ride from Gibbons, who steadied things down the back, and he'll do well to have things quite so much his own way next time.
Baylini doesn't know how to run a bad race and another fruitful winter campaign beckons, staying on strongly over a shorter trip than she usually tackles on Polytrack. (op 9-1 tchd 11-1)
Chapter And Verse(IRE) continues at the top of his game, deserving of a little extra credit after being caught wide/further back than ideal for much of the way. (tchd 13-2)
Mia's Boy, who endured a mid-season lull, is back in much better form on this evidence, ending up with a bit to do and also short of room in the straight before finishing strongly once in the clear. He's unlikely to be long in taking advantage of the mark he's dropped to. (op 4-1)
Mr Willis had shaped well when runner-up at Lingfield after a break last time and was much better than the result here, simply ending up with far too much to do before powering home late. (op 6-1 tchd 9-2)
Sarah Park(IRE) ran creditably but was well placed the way things went and looks handicapped to the hilt. (op 14-1)
Beauchamp Xerxes wasn't discredited but it will require a smart effort from him to defy his current mark.
Ceremonial Jade(UAE) travelled well but that's no surprise given his form over shorter and he wouldn't be certain to see out this trip in a more truly-run affair.
Big Bay(USA) fared no better for the fitting of blinkers. (op 25-1)
Rjeef(IRE) did well on Polytrack for Clive Brittain earlier in the year, winning twice at 7f, and was a good bit better than the bare result starting out for David Simcock, travelling well until lack of stamina/fitness began to tell. (op 11-2)
T/Plt: £107.30 to a £1 stake. Pool:£64,533.87 - 438.83 winning tickets T/Qpdt: £48.10 to a £1 stake. Pool:£7,554.35 - 116.10 winning tickets CR

7431 - 7437a (Foreign Racing) - See Raceform Interactive

7417 LINGFIELD (L-H)
Saturday, November 13

OFFICIAL GOING: Standard
Wind: very light, half behind Weather: overcast

7438 IN MEMORY OF CAROLINE ELIZABETH MCCARTHY CLAIMING STKS 1m (P)
12:30 (12:31) (Class 6) 3-Y-O **£1,706** (£503; £252) **Stalls** High

Form RPR
4000 **1** **Syrian**[10] 7293 3-9-2 72 .... JamieSpencer 6 72+
(Ian Williams) *s.i.s: hld up in last: hdwy gng wl and nt clr run ent fnl 2f: swtchd rt wl over 1f out: pushed along to ld jst ins fnl f: sn clr: comf* **4/1**[2]
2100 **2** *3 1/4* **Chat De La Burg (USA)**[19] 7114 3-9-2 76 .... KierenFox(3) 2 68
(J R Best) *taken down early: led tl over 4f out: styd w ldr: rdn ent fnl 2f: nt pce of wnr fnl 150yds: kpt on* **5/1**[3]
3 *nk* **Too Late Jones (USA)** 3-9-1 0 .... GeorgeBaker 10 63
(M A Magnusson) *hld up in tch: shkn up to chal over 1f out: rdn: rn green and hung lft u.p ent fnl f: nt pce of wnr fnl 150yds: kpt on* **15/2**
0066 **4** *nse* **Rainsborough**[79] 5455 3-8-12 49 .... JamesDoyle 7 60
(S Curran) *hld up in tch in last trio: hdwy on outer jst over 2f out: kpt on u.p fnl f: no threat to wnr* **100/1**
0212 **5** *2* **Green Earth (IRE)**[13] 7251 3-9-5 75 ....(p) IanMongan 4 62
(P M Phelan) *dwlt: sn pushed along and rcvrd to join ldr after 1f: led over 4f out: rdn ent fnl 2f: hdd jst ins fnl f: sn outpcd* **11/8**[1]
6000 **6** *1/2* **Miss Kitty Grey (IRE)**[18] 7153 3-7-9 50 ....(p) NathanAlison(7) 3 44
(J R Boyle) *in tch: effrt on inner to chse ldrs over 1f out: styd on same pce fnl f* **50/1**
2505 **7** *hd* **Wishformore (IRE)**[140] 3441 3-8-9 67 .... LukeMorris 8 51
(J S Moore) *in tch: n.m.r over 2f out: rdn and unable qck over 1f out: kpt on same pce and edgd rt ins fnl f* **8/1**
3050 **8** *1* **Giulietta Da Vinci**[30] 6862 3-8-3 53 ow1 .... AndrewHeffernan(3) 5 45
(S Woodman) *hld up in tch: nt clr run and squeezed out ent fnl 2f: styd on same pce u.p fr over 1f out* **33/1**
0003 **9** *1/2* **Florio Vincitore (IRE)**[11] 7290 3-8-11 68 .... AlanCreighton(3) 9 52
(E J Creighton) *chsd ldrs: rdn over 2f out: wknd u.p over 1f out* **16/1**
10 *29* **Fight Or Flight** 3-8-8 0 ow1 .... FergusSweeney 1 —
(B G Powell) *s.i.s: a bhd: rdn over 4f out: lost tch over 2f out* **66/1**
1m 37.28s (-0.92) **Going Correction** +0.05s/f (Slow) **10** Ran SP% **114.9**
Speed ratings (Par 98): **106,102,102,102,100 99,99,98,98,69**
toteswingers: 1&2 £5.50, 1&3 £5.30, 2&3 £7.30. CSF £23.62 TOTE £4.40: £1.10, £2.20, £2.70; EX 21.70 Trifecta £68.80 Pool: £373.20 - 4.01 winning units..
Owner Dr Marwan Koukash **Bred** Barry Walters **Trained** Portway, Worcs

FOCUS
A couple of fair sorts in an ordinary claimer but the proximity of the 49-rated fourth holds the form down. The gallop was only fair and the winner made his ground down the centre in the straight.

7439 RONNIE SMITH "THE GODFATHER" 80TH BIRTHDAY SURPRISE H'CAP 7f (P)
1:00 (1:00) (Class 5) (0-65,65) 3-Y-O+ **£2,388** (£705; £352) **Stalls** Low

Form RPR
6453 **1** **Scottish Glen**[25] 6997 4-9-4 **64**.. JimCrowley 3 75+
(P R Chamings) *hld up in tch: swtchd rt and effrt wl over 1f out: str run on outer to ld wl ins fnl f: kpt on wl* **4/1**[1]
5006 **2** *nk* **Chilli Green**[15] 7209 3-9-4 **65**.. DaneO'Neill 6 74
(J Akehurst) *t.k.h: chsd ldrs: rdn and effrt to ld 2f out: drvn and styd on ins fnl f: hdd wl ins fnl f: kpt on* **11/1**
0221 **3** *2 ¼* **The Happy Hammer (IRE)**[14] 7241 4-9-3 **63**.............. WilliamCarson 8 67
(Eugene Stanford) *in tch in midfield: rdn and effrt to press ldrs over 1f out: nt pce of ldng pair ins fnl f: kpt on* **6/1**[2]
0601 **4** *nk* **Fol Liam**[31] 6853 4-8-13 **62**..............................(p) AndrewHeffernan(3) 7 65
(A J McCabe) *in tch in midfield: hdwy over 2f out: chsd ldrs and drvn over 1f out: kpt on same pce ins fnl f* **11/1**
0020 **5** *¾* **Rubenstar (IRE)**[14] 7241 7-9-3 **63**.............................. JamieSpencer 1 64
(Patrick Morris) *stdd after s: hld up in rr: gd hdwy on inner ent fnl 2f: drvn and pressed ldrs over 1f out: outpcd ins fnl f* **16/1**
4055 **6** *½* **Kipchak (IRE)**[3] 7399 5-9-3 **63**..............................(p) RobertWinston 4 63
(C R Dore) *taken down early and led to s: chsd ldrs: rdn and effrt to press ldr on inner over 2f out: outpcd ins fnl f* **6/1**[2]
0000 **7** *nk* **Perfect Ch'l (IRE)**[15] 7205 3-9-4 **65**..............................(b[1]) TomQueally 10 63
(I A Wood) *sn pushed along to press ldr: rdn over 2f out: stl ev ch ent fnl f: wknd fnl 150yds* **25/1**
3261 **8** *1* **Pipers Piping (IRE)**[8] 7336 4-9-1 **64**..................(v) MichaelStainton(3) 2 60
(P Howling) *dwlt: bhd: rdn over 2f out: kpt on u.p on inner fnl f: nvr trbld ldrs* **12/1**
6046 **9** *hd* **Super Frank (IRE)**[13] 7255 7-9-3 **63**..............................(b) JoeFanning 5 61+
(J Akehurst) *hld up wl in tch: nt clr run over 1f out tl ent fnl f: styd on same pce after* **9/1**[3]
0520 **10** *shd* **Picansort**[33] 6812 3-9-4 **65**..............................(p) JackMitchell 13 59
(B R Johnson) *towards rr on outer: hdwy over 2f out: effrt towards inner over 1f out: styd on same pce and no prog fnl f* **14/1**
3032 **11** *¾* **Woolston Ferry (IRE)**[17] 7168 4-9-2 **62**.................. FergusSweeney 11 55
(David Pinder) *in tch: rdn and effrt ent fnl 2f: no real prog: nvr trbld ldrs* **9/1**[3]
2363 **12** *½* **Ivory Lace**[26] 6992 9-9-2 **62**.. GeorgeBaker 14 54
(S Woodman) *in tch: rdn and effrt towards outer ent fnl 2f: no prog: nvr trbld ldrs* **16/1**
0550 **13** *1* **Safwaan**[21] 7082 3-9-3 **64**.. StevieDonohoe 12 52
(W J Musson) *bhd: rdn over 4f out: n.d after* **16/1**
150 **14** *8* **Bookiesindex Girl (IRE)**[122] 4025 3-9-2 **63**.................. ShaneKelly 9 30
(J R Jenkins) *taken down early and led rdrless to s: led tl 2f out: sn wknd* **33/1**

1m 24.12s (-0.68) **Going Correction** +0.05s/f (Slow)
WFA 3 from 4yo+ 1lb **14** Ran SP% **124.0**
Speed ratings (Par 103): **105,104,102,101,100 100,99,98,98,98 97,97,95,86**
toteswingers: 1&2 £11.00, 1&3 £3.50, 2&3 £14.60. CSF £50.07 CT £271.50 TOTE £4.90: £1.80, £5.30, £1.80; EX 55.80 TRIFECTA Not won..
Owner The Foxford House Partnership **Bred** Mrs Ann Jenkins **Trained** Baughurst, Hants

FOCUS
A modest but very tight handicap comprising horses rated 62-65. The gallop was reasonable and the form looks reliable. The principals came down the centre in the straight.

7440 BET CHELTENHAM OPEN MEETING - BETDAQ MEDIAN AUCTION MAIDEN STKS 6f (P)
1:30 (1:32) (Class 6) 3-5-Y-O **£1,706** (£503; £252) **Stalls** Low

Form RPR
3-34 **1** **Baby Dottie**[157] 2871 3-8-12 69.. IanMongan 1 77
(P M Phelan) *wnt rt s: mde all: rdn wl clr over 1f out: easily* **10/11**[1]
2032 **2** *9* **Via Aurelia (IRE)**[18] 7153 3-8-12 57..............................(b) JamieSpencer 4 48
(J R Fanshawe) *hmpd s: in tch: rdn and effrt to chse wnr 2f out: sn swtchd rt: wl btn ent fnl f* **13/8**[2]
6400 **3** *2 ¼* **Young Simon**[25] 7005 3-9-3 55..............................(v) TomQueally 3 46
(G G Margarson) *hmpd s: chsd ldrs: rdn and outpcd 2f out: sn wknd and wl btn over 1f out* **16/1**[3]
0060 **4** *2 ¼* **Dancing Again**[34] 6773 4-8-9 42.. KierenFox(3) 2 34
(E A Wheeler) *chsd wnr: rdn wl over 2f out: lost 2nd 2f out: sn wknd* **25/1**
5000 **5** *½* **Dilys Maud**[73] 5669 3-8-12 54.. RichardThomas 7 32
(R Ingram) *sn bhd: rdn and lost tch 4f out: n.d after* **33/1**
0 **6** *½* **Some Yarn (IRE)**[240] 915 3-9-3 0......................(v[1]) FrankieMcDonald 5 36
(Mrs L C Jewell) *s.i.s: sn pushed along in last pair: rdn and lost tch over 3f out: n.d after* **100/1**

1m 11.03s (-0.87) **Going Correction** +0.05s/f (Slow) **6** Ran SP% **104.1**
Speed ratings (Par 101): **107,95,92,89,88 87**
toteswingers: 1&2 £1.10, 1&3 £1.90, 2&3 £1.90. CSF £2.11 TOTE £1.80: £1.40, £1.10; EX 1.70.
Owner Tony Smith **Bred** Tony J Smith **Trained** Epsom, Surrey
■ Intriguing Look (14/1) was withdrawn after proving unruly in the stalls. R4 applies, deduct 5p in the £.

FOCUS
A most uncompetitive maiden in which the pace was just an ordinary one. The winner came down the centre.

7441 BET TEST MATCH RUGBY - BETDAQ H'CAP (DIV I) 6f (P)
2:00 (2:00) (Class 5) (0-70,70) 3-Y-O+ **£2,047** (£604; £302) **Stalls** Low

Form RPR
1002 **1** **Arctic Lynx (IRE)**[21] 7093 3-9-7 **70**.. GeorgeBaker 7 83+
(J R Best) *t.k.h: hld up in tch: rdn and effrt over 1f out: rdn and qcknd ins fnl f: r.o wl to ld fnl 50yds* **3/1**[1]
2353 **2** *¾* **Tislaam (IRE)**[8] 7331 3-9-1 **67**..............................(p) AndrewHeffernan(3) 12 74
(A J McCabe) *taken down early: t.k.h: hld up in tch on outer: hdwy to chse ldrs over 2f out: rdn over 1f out: drvn to ld jst ins fnl f: hdd and no ex fnl 50yds* **11/2**[3]
5635 **3** *¾* **Emiratesdotcom**[17] 7162 4-9-0 **63**.......................... RichardKingscote 2 68
(J M Bradley) *hld up in tch on inner: rdn and effrt to press ldrs jst over 1f out: styd on same pce fnl 100yds* **7/1**
2422 **4** *hd* **Riflessione**[16] 7193 4-9-7 **70**..............................(b) JoeFanning 10 74
(R A Harris) *t.k.h: hld up in tch: hdwy on outer bnd 2f out: styd on wl u.p ins fnl f: nt rch ldrs* **5/1**[2]
0633 **5** *½* **Durgan**[13] 7250 4-8-8 **57**..............................(p) FrankieMcDonald 1 59
(Mrs L C Jewell) *led: rdn ent fnl 2f: hdd jst ins fnl f: no ex and outpcd fnl 150yds* **11/1**
6645 **6** *1 ¾* **Highland Harvest**[30] 6858 6-9-3 **66**.............................. StevieDonohoe 9 63
(Jamie Poulton) *in tch: rdn and effrt ent fnl 2f: styd on same pce u.p fr over 1f out* **16/1**
4600 **7** *½* **The Strig**[35] 6739 3-9-6 **69**.. WilliamCarson 3 64
(S C Williams) *hld up in tch in rr: effrt on inner over 1f out: no imp ins fnl f: nvr trbld ldrs* **16/1**
1202 **8** *1* **White Shift (IRE)**[3] 7390 4-9-2 **65**.. JimmyQuinn 8 57
(P Howling) *chsd ldrs: rdn and unable qck ent fnl 2f: drvn and wknd jst over 1f out* **11/2**[3]
-000 **9** *1 ¼* **Mogok Ruby**[9] 7319 6-9-2 **65**.. LukeMorris 4 53
(B R Johnson) *hld up in last pair: rdn and effrt wl over 1f out: no prog: nvr trbld ldrs* **14/1**
0000 **10** *1 ¼* **C'Mon You Irons (IRE)**[21] 7093 5-9-4 **67**.......................... JimCrowley 11 51
(M R Hoad) *pressed ldr tl wl over 1f out: wknd u.p ent fnl f* **16/1**

1m 12.2s (0.30) **Going Correction** +0.05s/f (Slow) **10** Ran SP% **117.6**
Speed ratings (Par 103): **100,99,98,97,97 94,94,92,91,89**
toteswingers: 1&2 £4.80, 1&3 £5.30, 2&3 £7.50. CSF £19.42 CT £110.49 TOTE £3.80: £1.60, £2.20, £2.30; EX 22.90 Trifecta £104.90 Pool: £472.12 - 3.33 winning units..
Owner Heading For The Rocks Partnership **Bred** Derek Veitch And Saleh Ali Hammadi **Trained** Hucking, Kent

FOCUS
A modest handicap in which the gallop was an ordinary one. The winner was another to race in the centre in the straight and left the impression he was a bit better than the bare form.

7442 BET TEST MATCH RUGBY - BETDAQ H'CAP (DIV II) 6f (P)
2:30 (2:30) (Class 5) (0-70,70) 3-Y-O+ **£2,047** (£604; £302) **Stalls** Low

Form RPR
14 **1** **Danzoe (IRE)**[76] 5562 3-9-3 **69**.. KierenFox(3) 5 78
(Mrs C A Dunnett) *hld up in tch: effrt on inner over 1f out: drvn and r.o wl to ld wl ins fnl f* **8/1**
0304 **2** *½* **Resplendent Alpha**[45] 6456 6-8-8 **57**..............................(b) JimmyQuinn 8 64
(P Howling) *stdd s: hld up in tch in rr: hdwy ent fnl f: burst between horses ins fnl f: r.o wl to go 2nd nr fin: nt quite rch wnr* **9/1**
0600 **3** *½* **Waterloo Dock**[110] 4435 5-8-13 **62**..............................(v) ChrisCatlin 9 68
(M Quinn) *w ldr: rdn 2f out: drvn to ld 1f out: hdd and no ex wl ins fnl f* **25/1**
3112 **4** *nk* **Dreamacha**[39] 6656 3-9-2 **65**.. WilliamCarson 10 70+
(S C Williams) *in tch on outer: effrt u.p 2f out: kpt on ins fnl f* **7/4**[1]
5002 **5** *nse* **Loyal Royal (IRE)**[8] 7331 7-8-8 **57**......................(bt) RichardKingscote 4 62
(J M Bradley) *t.k.h: hld up in tch in rr: hdwy jst over 2f out: swtchd lft over 1f out: hanging lft and nt clr run jst ins fnl f: r.o fnl 75yds: nt rch ldrs:* **10/1**
0300 **6** *nk* **Sherjawy (IRE)**[23] 7041 6-9-5 **68**.. SamHitchcott 2 72
(Miss Z C Davison) *chsd ldrs: effrt u.p 2f out: drvn and pressed ldrs ent fnl f: styd on same pce fnl 150yds* **16/1**
5426 **7** *1 ¼* **Make My Dream**[17] 7180 7-9-4 **67**.. CathyGannon 1 67
(J Gallagher) *stdd s: hld up in tch: rdn and effrt wl over 2f out: styd on same pce fr over 1f out* **6/1**[2]
0500 **8** *nk* **Cerito**[19] 7122 4-9-3 **66**..............................(v) TomQueally 12 65
(J R Boyle) *led: rdn 2f out: hdd 1f out: wknd ins fnl f* **8/1**
6660 **9** *1 ¼* **Charles Darwin (IRE)**[51] 6310 7-8-11 **60**.............................. DaneO'Neill 3 55
(M Blanshard) *chsd ldrs: rdn and unable qck over 1f out: one pce and wl hld fnl f* **12/1**
4121 **10** *nse* **Avonvalley**[11] 7281 3-9-7 **70**.. FergusSweeney 7 65
(Peter Grayson) *t.k.h: hld up in tch: rdn and effrt wl over 1f out: little rspnse and plugged on same pce after* **7/1**[3]
0-0 **11** *nk* **Moonlight Cass (IRE)**[15] 7209 3-9-2 **65**.......................... LukeMorris 6 59
(J R Gask) *in tch in midfield: rdn and unable qck over 1f out: one pce and wl hld fnl f* **16/1**
0-00 **12** *11* **Dubai Legend**[58] 6108 4-9-1 **64**.. DuranFentiman 11 22
(N Wilson) *in tch towards rr on outer: rdn and lost tch wl over 1f out* **25/1**

1m 11.7s (-0.20) **Going Correction** +0.05s/f (Slow) **12** Ran SP% **131.6**
Speed ratings (Par 103): **103,102,101,101,101 100,99,98,97,97 96,81**
toteswingers: 1&2 £9.70, 1&3 £40.30, 2&3 £41.10. CSF £87.10 CT £1767.28 TOTE £8.20: £2.20, £3.30, £9.10; EX 78.40 Trifecta £317.20 Pool: £694.61 - 1.62 winning units..
Owner The Smart Syndicate **Bred** Miss Anne Ormsby **Trained** Hingham, Norfolk

FOCUS
Division two of a modest handicap and one run at an ordinary gallop. Several finished in a heap and the winner was the only scorer on the card to race more towards the inside rail. The form is rated around the runner-up.

7443 LINGFIELD PARK MARRIOTT HOTEL & COUNTRY CLUB H'CAP 6f (P)
3:00 (3:01) (Class 2) (0-100,105) 3-Y-O+ **£9,714** (£2,890; £1,444; £721) **Stalls** Low

Form RPR
4051 **1** **Take Ten**[15] 7217 3-9-0 **93**.. JoeFanning 6 101
(M Johnston) *w ldr: rdn to ld 1f out: kpt on wl fnl f* **3/1**[2]
0420 **2** *½* **Edinburgh Knight (IRE)**[21] 7079 3-8-8 **87**.......................... LiamJones 4 93+
(P W D'Arcy) *hld up in tch in last pair: rdn and effrt over 1f out: kpt on wl u.p to chse wnr fnl 100yds: gng on fin: nt rch wnr* **5/2**[1]
0000 **3** *1 ¾* **Flipando (IRE)**[16] 7187 9-8-12 **91**.............................. GrahamGibbons 1 92
(T D Barron) *chsd ldrs: rdn and unable qck wl over 1f out: kpt on u.p ins fnl f* **8/1**
0011 **4** *¾* **Matsunosuke**[2] 7409 8-9-12 **105** 6ex.............................. LukeMorris 7 103
(R A Harris) *t.k.h: hld up in tch: hdwy to chse ldrs over 2f out: rdn over 1f out: outpcd ins fnl f* **12/1**
0003 **5** *1* **Tourist**[2] 7409 5-8-8 **87**.. JimmyQuinn 8 82
(D Shaw) *stdd s: hld up in tch in last: hdwy wl over 1f out: kpt on u.p ins fnl f: nvr gng pce to threaten ldrs* **14/1**
5600 **6** *¾* **Arganil (USA)**[21] 7079 5-9-7 **100**..............................(p) PhillipMakin 2 93
(K A Ryan) *hld up in tch in last trio: rdn and effrt over 1f out: kpt on same pce and no imp after* **7/1**[3]
0062 **7** *¾* **Pavershooz**[15] 7212 5-8-7 **86** oh1.. DuranFentiman 5 76
(N Wilson) *led: rdn ent fnl 2f: hdd 1f out: fdd ins fnl f* **8/1**
1410 **8** *3* **Mirza**[7] 7351 3-8-8 **87**.. ChrisCatlin 3 68
(Rae Guest) *in tch in midfield pushed along ent fnl 3f: rdn and dropped to rr whn n.m.r over 1f out: wl hld whn edgd lft ins fnl f* **12/1**

1m 11.25s (-0.65) **Going Correction** +0.05s/f (Slow) **8** Ran SP% **110.3**
Speed ratings (Par 109): **106,105,103,102,100 99,98,94**
toteswingers: 1&2 £1.80, 1&3 £4.20, 2&3 £4.50. CSF £10.10 CT £48.45 TOTE £2.90: £1.20, £1.80, £2.10; EX 7.80 Trifecta £121.30 Pool: £1,053.11 - 6.42 winning units..
Owner Sheikh Hamdan Bin Mohammed Al Maktoum **Bred** Whitsbury Manor Stud And Mrs M E Slade **Trained** Middleham Moor, N Yorks

FOCUS
A good-quality handicap but one in which the gallop was just an ordinary one. The winner came down the centre in the straight. There is a doubt over the solidity of the form.

The Form Book, Raceform Ltd, Compton, RG20 6NL

NOTEBOOK
Take Ten, who had run right up to his best at Dundalk from 10lb lower on his previous outing, was ideally placed and got first run to confirm he is smart on this surface. Things went his way but he will remain of interest in the better sprint handicaps on Polytrack if kept on the go this winter. (tchd 5-2 and 7-2)
Edinburgh Knight(IRE) ◆, having his first all-weather start since being gelded, shaped a bit better than the bare facts considering the in-form winner got first run. He would have been suited by a more strongly run race and is lightly raced enough to be open to further improvement. He should be able to pick up a decent handicap on this surface when things drop right. (op 9-4 tchd 2-1 and 11-4)
Flipando(IRE) had not been at his best since his last win in summer but shaped with a bit more encouragement, especially as an ordinary gallop over this trip would not have been in his favour. He is be worth another chance on Polytrack.
Matsunosuke has been seen to good effect in much less competitive company when winning all-weather claimers on his two previous starts and was anything but disgraced under his penalty from a 105 mark back in handicaps. He will be lower in the weights in future but is likely to remain vulnerable in similar handicaps.
Tourist ◆ was much better off at the weights with Matsunosuke on recent Wolverhampton form but failed to reverse placings back in handicap company. However, he is back on a fair mark, is fully effective on Fibresand and will be worth another chance given a more truly run race. (op 12-1)
Arganil(USA) showed himself smart on Polytrack earlier this year but was again below his best after taking a strong hold in the early stages with the headgear refitted. He needs to show a fair bit more. (op 12-1)
Pavershooz had run creditably on his recent all-weather debut at Wolverhampton but failed to confirm that promise. Although he has slipped to a fair mark, he may not be one for maximum faith. (op 7-1)

7444 JACKSBRIDGE CONDITIONS STKS 7f (P)
3:30 (3:30) (Class 3) 2-Y-O **£6,476** (£1,927; £963; £481) **Stalls** Low

Form RPR
1161 **1** **Talley Close**[39] 6647 2-9-3 89 PhillipMakin 5 89
(R A Fahey) chsd ldr: pushed along to ld wl over 1f out: rdn clr jst over 1f out: edgd lft fnl f: r.o wl **2/1**[1]
0113 **2** *1* **Dozy Joe**[7] 7347 2-9-3 82 DaneO'Neill 1 86
(I A Wood) chsd ldng pair: rdn and effrt wl over 1f out: chsd clr wnr 1f out: kpt on wl but a hld **5/1**
1233 **3** *3 ½* **Owain (USA)**[31] 6850 2-9-0 83 CathyGannon 3 74
(C A Dwyer) stdd s: t.k.h: hld up wl in tch: rdn and chsd ldrs wl over 1f out: outpcd jst over 1f out: wknd ins fnl f **9/2**[3]
4162 **4** *1 ½* **Il Battista**[8] 7324 2-9-0 84 (p) JamesDoyle 2 70
(A J McCabe) wnt rt s: led: rdn ent fnl 2f: hdd wl over 1f out: wknd ent fnl f **5/2**[2]
02 **5** *nk* **A Boy Named Suzi**[71] 5718 2-9-0 0 TomQueally 4 70
(M E Rimmer) hld up in tch in last: rdn and effrt wl over 1f out: stdy on same pce and no prog after **6/1**
1m 25.96s (1.16) **Going Correction** +0.05s/f (Slow) 5 Ran SP% **111.0**
Speed ratings (Par 100): **95,93,89,88,87**
CSF £12.20 TOTE £2.20: £1.50, £1.50; EX 9.70.
Owner Skeltools Ltd **Bred** A B Phipps **Trained** Musley Bank, N Yorks

FOCUS
Several useful sorts in a reasonable conditions event. The gallop was modest and the winner raced up the centre in the straight. Straightforward form, rated around the winner.

NOTEBOOK
Talley Close is a progressive sort who was always ideally placed and probably did not have to improve too much after getting first run to notch his fourth win on this all-weather debut. He is the type to make further progress and is capable of winning more races. (op 6-4)
Dozy Joe had a bit to find with the winner on official ratings but he turned in a creditable effort on this first run over 7f. A more truly run race would have been more to his liking and this steadily progressive sort should be able to win again on artificial surfaces. (op 4-1)
Owain(USA) did not improve for the step up to 1m on his previous start but shaped as though a much stiffer stamina test over this trip would have suited. However, his tendency to miss the break and to take a good hold is going to continue to make life difficult for him. (tchd 4-1)
Il Battista was allowed to set a modest gallop on this Polytrack debut but was readily swept aside in the straight. He may have been better served by making this a stronger test of stamina and will be of interest in similar company returned to Southwell. (op 11-2)
A Boy Named Suzi, the only maiden in the field, had something to find on these terms on this first run for his new trainer but, in any case, was not suited by a muddling gallop back in distance. He may do better back over 1m in ordinary handicap company. (tchd 7-1)

7445 BET GRAND SLAM DARTS - BETDAQ H'CAP 1m 2f (P)
4:00 (4:00) (Class 6) (0-60,60) 3-Y-O+ **£2,047** (£604; £302) **Stalls** Low

Form RPR
3500 **1** **Atacama Sunrise**[16] 7190 4-9-3 60 JulieBurke(7) 14 64+
(G Prodromou) hld up in rr: gd hdwy on outer 4f out: chsd clr ldr and edgd lft bnd jst over 2f out: drvn and ev ch whn carried rt ins fnl f: kpt on wl to ld nr fin **16/1**
4240 **2** *nk* **Sheila's Bond**[52] 6287 3-9-2 56 JamesDoyle 9 59
(J S Moore) hld up in tch towards rr: rdn and effrt whn hung lft bnd ent fnl 2f: styd on wl u.p ins fnl f: snatched 2nd last stride **9/1**
0000 **3** *shd* **Ajool (USA)**[12] 7273 3-9-1 55 LiamJones 11 58
(P W D'Arcy) t.k.h: trckd ldrs tl led 4f out: sn qcknd clr: rdn ent fnl 2f: hrd pressed and edgd rt u.p ins fnl f: hdd and lost 2 pls nr fin **16/1**
0051 **4** *1* **Esteem Lord**[24] 7023 4-9-6 56 JimCrowley 3 59+
(D K Ivory) t.k.h: hld up in tch: rdn and effrt on inner whn hmpd bnd ent fnl 2f: rallied fnl f: styd on wl: nt rch ldrs **5/1**[2]
0130 **5** *shd* **Litenup (IRE)**[72] 5704 4-9-4 54 TomQueally 1 55
(Miss Gay Kelleway) trckd ldrs: chsd ldng pair and rdn whn hmpd bnd ent fnl 2f: rallied u.p ins fnl f: kpt on **7/1**[3]
4425 **6** *4 ½* **Lunar River (FR)**[9] 7323 7-9-3 53 (t) FergusSweeney 10 45
(David Pinder) hld up in tch towards rr: hdwy ent fnl 4f: chsd ldrs and rdn jst over 2f out: wknd over 1f out **8/1**
4003 **7** *nk* **Ocean Countess (IRE)**[16] 7200 4-9-4 54 CathyGannon 4 45
(Miss J Feilden) dwlt: sn niggled along in last pair: reminders over 4f out: plugged on fr over 1f out: nvr trbld ldrs **8/1**
5021 **8** *½* **Ermyn Express**[9] 7323 3-9-6 60 IanMongan 2 50
(P M Phelan) hld up in tch: rdn and lost pl over 2f out: no threat to ldrs fnl 2f: kpt on ins fnl f **9/2**[1]
3015 **9** *shd* **Derby Desire (IRE)**[18] 7157 6-9-4 57 AndrewHeffernan(3) 5 47
(D Donovan) sn led and set stdy gallop: hdd 4f out: rdn and unable qck whn hmpd bnd ent fnl 2f: wknd over 1f out **10/1**
3031 **10** *1 ¾* **Cuckoo Rock (IRE)**[18] 7156 3-9-6 60 (p) RichardKingscote 13 47
(J G Portman) hld up in last trio: rdn and struggling jst over 4f out: n.d fnl 3f **8/1**
0500 **11** *17* **Brooklyn Spirit**[60] 6055 4-9-10 60 RichardThomas 6 13
(Mrs A M Batchelor) t.k.h: chsd ldr tl jst over 4f out: sn struggling: wl bhd fnl 2f **20/1**
2m 8.61s (2.01) **Going Correction** +0.05s/f (Slow)
WFA 3 from 4yo+ 4lb 11 Ran SP% **116.3**
Speed ratings (Par 101): **93,92,92,91,91 88,87,87,87,86 72**
toteswingers: 1&2 £19.50, 1&3 £34.00, 2&3 £17.30. CSF £151.01 CT £2342.88 TOTE £20.30: £4.60, £2.90, £6.90; EX 217.00 TRIFECTA Not won..
Owner George Prodromou **Bred** J R Furlong **Trained** East Harling, Norfolk
■ Stewards' Enquiry : Julie Burke three-day ban: careless riding (Nov 27-29)
Liam Jones caution: careless riding.

FOCUS
A few previous winners in a moderate finale. The gallop was an ordinary one and the first five, who pulled clear, raced down the centre in the straight. The second and fifth help with the standard.
T/Plt: £74.30 to a £1 stake. Pool:£48,860.38 - 479.98 winning tickets. T/Qpdt: £17.80 to a £1 stake. Pool:£3,925.72 - 162.80 winning tickets. SP

7423 WOLVERHAMPTON (A.W) (L-H)
Saturday, November 13

OFFICIAL GOING: Standard
Wind: Light behind Weather: Fine

7446 ENJOY THE RINGSIDE ENTERTAINMENT AFTER RACING H'CAP 5f 20y(P)
5:50 (5:52) (Class 5) (0-70,74) 3-Y-O+ **£2,007** (£597; £298; £149) **Stalls** Low

Form RPR
6006 **1** **Grudge**[8] 7326 5-9-5 68 (be) RobertWinston 6 77
(C R Dore) chsd ldr: rdn to ld over 1f out: sn hung lft: hdd wl ins fnl f: rallied to ld post **5/1**[2]
0546 **2** *shd* **The Tatling (IRE)**[68] 5809 13-8-10 62 RussKennemore(3) 11 71
(J M Bradley) hld up: hdwy 1/2-way: rdn to ld wl ins fnl f: hdd post **16/1**
2132 **3** *1 ¼* **Lake Chini (IRE)**[14] 7225 8-8-10 59 (b) GrahamGibbons 7 64+
(M W Easterby) sn pushed along in rr: hdwy u.p over 1f out: r.o to go 3rd nr fin **7/2**[1]
003 **4** *½* **Hypnosis**[16] 7193 7-9-4 67 TomEaves 2 70
(N Wilson) led: rdn and hdd over 1f out: styd on same pce ins fnl f **8/1**
6551 **5** *nk* **Methaaly (IRE)**[8] 7332 7-9-4 74 (be) JosephYoung(7) 9 76+
(M Mullineaux) bhd: r.o ins fnl f: nt rch ldrs **8/1**
2400 **6** *2 ¼* **Sharp Bullet (IRE)**[8] 7334 4-8-8 57 PatrickMathers 3 51
(Bruce Hellier) chsd ldrs: drvn along 1/2-way: edgd rt and no ex fnl f **11/1**
6050 **7** *2 ¼* **Silver Linnet (IRE)**[16] 7195 3-8-13 62 ow2 (b) AdamKirby 13 47
(M G Quinlan) in rr: styd on ins fnl f: nvr nrr **33/1**
0000 **8** *hd* **Canadian Danehill (IRE)**[8] 7331 8-8-11 60 (p) J-PGuillambert 4 45
(R M H Cowell) prom: drvn along 1/2-way: wknd fnl f **16/1**
6000 **9** *nk* **Silver Prelude**[16] 7194 9-8-13 62 (t) WilliamCarson 10 46
(S C Williams) mid-div: drvn along 1/2-way: one pce fnl 2f **25/1**
0040 **10** *2 ¾* **Triple Dream**[17] 7180 5-9-7 70 (p) NeilCallan 12 44
(J M Bradley) chsd ldrs: rdn 1/2-way: hung lft and wknd over 1f out **8/1**
0325 **11** *2 ¾* **Aalsmeer**[16] 7194 3-8-11 60 (p) TedDurcan 1 24
(Karen George) sn pushed along in rr: nvr on terms: eased fnl f **11/2**[3]
5000 **12** *2* **Harry Up**[16] 7193 9-8-7 59 (p) AmyRyan(3) 5 16
(Andrew Reid) chsd ldrs: rdn 1/2-way: wknd over 1f out **25/1**
61.64 secs (-0.66) **Going Correction** +0.075s/f (Slow) 12 Ran SP% **118.3**
Speed ratings (Par 103): **108,107,105,105,104 100,97,97,96,92 87,84**
Tote Swingers: 1&2 £18.60, 1&3 £4.30, 2&3 £14.60 CSF £80.04 CT £318.84 TOTE £7.10: £1.50, £5.90, £2.00; EX 95.50.
Owner Mrs Jennifer Marsh **Bred** D H Brailsford **Trained** Cowbit, Lincs

FOCUS
Not much recent placed form on show but an open contest, though one not run at the blistering pace that looked likely beforehand in view of the number of runners in it that usually race prominently. The winner was a length or so off his best form of the past year.
Aalsmeer Official explanation: jockey said filly became upset in stalls

7447 EUROPEAN BREEDERS' FUND MAIDEN FILLIES' STKS (DIV I) 7f 32y(P)
6:20 (6:23) (Class 5) 2-Y-O **£2,655** (£790; £394; £197) **Stalls** High

Form RPR
0 **1** **Midas Moment**[14] 7231 2-9-0 0 GeorgeBaker 11 71+
(W R Muir) trckd ldr: racd keenly: led over 4f out: rdn and hung lft ins fnl f: styd on **20/1**
0 **2** *nk* **Reem Star**[22] 7057 2-9-0 0 EddieAhern 2 70
(E A L Dunlop) hld up: hdwy over 2f out: rdn ins fnl f: r.o: nt quite get up **15/2**
4 **3** *1* **Beso (IRE)**[24] 7021 2-9-0 0 J-PGuillambert 10 68
(L M Cumani) hld up: hdwy u.p 1/2-way: hung lft over 1f out: r.o: wnt 3rd nr fin **9/4**[1]
34 **4** *shd* **Follow My Dream**[19] 7123 2-9-0 0 RobertHavlin 6 68
(J H M Gosden) chsd ldrs: rdn over 1f out: styd on **5/1**[3]
5 *2 ½* **Psychic's Dream** 2-9-0 0 ChrisCatlin 1 61
(M Botti) s.i.s: hld up: hdwy over 1f out: nt rch ldrs **15/2**
0 **6** *nk* **Medaille D'Or**[31] 6849 2-9-0 0 NeilCallan 7 61
(M A Jarvis) s.i.s: sn prom: rdn over 2f out: no ex ins fnl f **3/1**[2]
04 **7** *1 ¼* **Jeu De Vivre (IRE)**[14] 7223 2-9-0 0 GregFairley 9 58+
(M Johnston) led: hdd over 4f out: rdn over 2f out: no ex fnl f **12/1**
40 **8** *2 ¼* **Questionnaire (IRE)**[12] 7268 2-9-0 0 LukeMorris 5 52
(N J Vaughan) hld up: plld hrd: drvn along 1/2-way: n.d **33/1**
9 *1 ¼* **Jane's Legacy** 2-9-0 0 GrahamGibbons 8 49
(R Hollinshead) chsd ldrs tl wknd over 2f out **40/1**
10 *nk* **Dixie Gwalia** 2-8-7 0 LauraPike(7) 3 48
(D M Simcock) s.i.s: a in rr **66/1**
0 **11** *2 ¼* **Boushra**[42] 6575 2-9-0 0 TravisBlock 4 43
(S Kirk) s.i.s: a in rr **100/1**
0 **12** *10* **Felt**[22] 7057 2-9-0 0 PaulMulrennan 12 18
(J G Given) hld up: plld hrd: wknd over 2f out **125/1**
1m 30.0s (0.40) **Going Correction** +0.075s/f (Slow) 12 Ran SP% **117.1**
Speed ratings (Par 93): **100,99,98,98,95 95,93,91,89,89 86,75**
Tote Swingers: 1&2 £22.50, 1&3 £15.10, 2&3 £2.80 CSF £156.18 TOTE £29.80: £5.70, £2.90, £1.40; EX 273.70.
Owner Foursome Thoroughbreds **Bred** Foursome Thoroughbreds **Trained** Lambourn, Berks

FOCUS
This was run at something of a muddling pace with several pulling hard and the winner was able to make all. Just average form but there were a few interesting types on show.

NOTEBOOK
Midas Moment might have got first run on the others in the frame but there was still plenty to like about her performance, not least the fact that she was still on the bridle out in front while all behind were hard at work. For one whose dam comes from a good middle-distance family, she clearly possesses plenty of speed and, having improved a lot from her initial outing at Newmarket, seems certain to progress again. (op 16-1)
Reem Star was another to step up on what was a fairly quiet turf debut, keeping on in good style in the straight. The drop back in trip round here looked to count against her and she can win a similar event back at 1m if kept on the go this winter. (op 10-1 tchd 11-1)
Beso(IRE) just got third but was never travelling with the fluency of some of the others or ever threatened to finish any closer. She possibly still needed the experience having looked very green first time, and despite her pedigree might be in need of a longer trip too like most bred by her owners. (op 6-4)
Follow My Dream was back up 7f but once again lacked mid race speed and already looks in need of a further step up in trip. She appears no more than an ordinary handicapper at this stage. (op 9-2 tchd 11-2)
Psychic's Dream is a half-sister to a couple of winners, one of them useful in France at around 1m, and made an encouraging debut, keeping on without threatening from off the pace. Like most newcomers from this yard, she can be expected to improve. (op 12-1)
Medaille D'Or looked to have learned plenty from her initial run but perhaps still needed the run or suffered form her pre-race exertions (free to post), fading out of contention. Her pedigree is all about next year and she shouldn't be written off yet. (op 11-2)
Jeu De Vivre(IRE) is now qualified for nurseries. (op 10-1)
Questionnaire(IRE) is now qualified for nurseries.

7448 EUROPEAN BREEDERS' FUND MAIDEN FILLIES' STKS (DIV II) 7f 32y(P)
6:50 (6:52) (Class 5) 2-Y-O £2,655 (£790; £394; £197) **Stalls** High

Form RPR
4 **1** **Mantatisi**[22] 7057 2-9-0 0 GeorgeBaker 4 72+
(J R Fanshawe) *hld up: hdwy over 2f out: led 1f out: rdn out* **5/4**[1]
03 **2** *1* **Hurricane Lady (IRE)**[25] 6994 2-9-0 0 LukeMorris 1 70+
(W R Swinburn) *hld up: hdwy u.p over 1f out: swtchd rt ins fnl f: r.o wl: nt rch wnr* **6/1**[3]
0 **3** *nse* **Judgement**[16] 7185 2-9-0 0 RobertHavlin 2 69
(J H M Gosden) *hld up in tch: rdn and ev ch over 1f out: styd on* **5/1**[2]
4 *hd* **Al Khatma** 2-9-0 0 ChrisCatlin 11 69+
(M Botti) *hld up: hdwy over 1f out: r.o wl: nrst fin* **20/1**
40 **5** *2 1/4* **Susan Stroman**[19] 7113 2-9-0 0 EddieAhern 3 63+
(E A L Dunlop) *chsd ldr 1f: remained handy: rdn over 2f out: styd on same pce fnl f* **8/1**
6 *nse* **Verrazano** 2-9-0 0 PhillipMakin 8 63+
(K A Ryan) *s.i.s: in rr and drvn along 1/2-way: r.o ins fnl f: nvr nrr* **40/1**
60 **7** *3/4* **Peira**[9] 7311 2-9-0 0 JimmyQuinn 6 61
(Jane Chapple-Hyam) *chsd ldr 6f out: rdn and ev ch over 1f out: no ex ins fnl f* **40/1**
8 *1/2* **Fairy Familiar (USA)** 2-9-0 0 J-PGuillambert 12 60+
(L M Cumani) *hld up: hdwy 1/2-way: rdn to ld over 1f out: sn hdd: styd on same pce* **18/1**
0 **9** *2 1/4* **Certral**[27] 6954 2-9-0 0 StevieDonohoe 10 60+
(George Baker) *sn pushed along and a in rr* **10/1**
10 *1/2* **Shoodah** 2-9-0 0 NeilCallan 7 54
(D M Simcock) *prom: rdn over 2f out: wknd fnl f* **14/1**
6 **11** *1* **Three Opera Divas**[14] 7240 2-9-0 0 GregFairley 9 51
(M Johnston) *led: rdn and hdd over 1f out: wknd ins fnl f* **33/1**
12 *21* **Once Upon A Dream** 2-9-0 0 RobertWinston 5 —
(P Howling) *s.s: a in rr: bhd fr 1/2-way* **100/1**

1m 29.98s (0.38) **Going Correction** +0.075s/f (Slow) 12 Ran SP% **121.1**
Speed ratings (Par 93): **100,98,98,98,96 95,95,94,91,91 90,66**
Tote Swingers: 1&2 £4.10, 1&3 £1.10, 2&3 £3.10 CSF £8.64 TOTE £3.00: £1.90, £1.10, £1.70; EX 8.50.
Owner Lady Halifax **Bred** Lady Halifax **Trained** Newmarket, Suffolk

FOCUS
Never much between the runners at any stage here and probably just ordinary form, though a few look capable of better under different circumstances.

NOTEBOOK
Mantatisi looked to set a good standard and though dropping her in trip round here never really looked like backfiring, she didn't win with quite the authority her strength in the market suggested. That said, she impressed with the style with which she travelled for the most part and, by Motivator, might turn out to be fairly useful back up in trip next year. (op 11-8 tchd 6-4 in places)
Hurricane Lady(IRE) didn't look to be going anywhere on the home turn but really found her stride close home. Now qualified for a mark, she looks to be crying out for an increased test already. (tchd 11-2 and 13-2)
Judgement briefly disputed the lead inside the last and clearly improved a good deal on her debut when not given a hard time. She's well related and probably destined for better things, and would be an interesting runner if sent to Southwell for a maiden give her sire's record with his runners on Fibresand.
Al Khatma ◆ was retained very cheaply by her owner when sent to the Sales but shaped promisingly to fare best of the newcomers. She was a long way back leaving the back straight but stayed on really strongly and seems sure to improve as most from her yard do second time out. A longer trip will also suit.
Susan Stroman ◆ needed this for a mark and left the impression that she's a fair bit better than this, not knocked about and passing the post seemingly still with running left in her. She's bred to improve a good deal over middle distances next year and is one to keep an eye on. (op 16-1)
Verrazano shaped well considering her inexperience was evident, slowly away, on and off the bridle and then finally staying on from a poor position. She's from a good family and seems sure to improve. (op 33-1)
Fairy Familiar(USA) is a half-sister to a 1m4f winner out of a half-sister to Red Merlin and is more one for next year, but she showed up well for a long way and briefly looked dangerous when produced with her challenge before lack of race fitness seemed to find her out. (op 14-1)
Certral ◆ looks to have more to give and will be of interest once going handicapping. She was well behind turning for home but caught the eye going on well close home. Official explanation: jockey said filly ran green (op 8-1)

7449 BET MULTIPLES - BETDAQ H'CAP (DIV I) 1m 141y(P)
7:20 (7:20) (Class 6) (0-60,60) 3-Y-O+ £1,364 (£403; £201) **Stalls** Low

Form RPR
101 **1** **Querido (GER)**[16] 7200 6-9-3 56 (t) GeorgeBaker 3 66+
(G Brown) *chsd ldrs: rdn and hung lft fr over 1f out: styd on to ld nr fin* **5/2**[1]
2504 **2** *1/2* **Hector Spectre (IRE)**[70] 4914 4-9-1 54 (p) RobertWinston 10 63
(Mrs N S Evans) *sn led: rdn and hdd nr fin* **7/1**
3040 **3** *5* **Full Victory (IRE)**[19] 7128 8-9-5 58 (b) GrahamGibbons 6 56
(R A Farrant) *trckd ldrs: racd keenly: rdn and edgd lft over 1f out: styd on same pce* **10/1**
0204 **4** *nse* **Farmers Dream (IRE)**[30] 6862 3-9-0 56 AdamKirby 5 54
(J L Spearing) *hld up: hdwy u.p over 1f out: nt trble ldrs* **14/1**
0232 **5** *nk* **Tallawalla (IRE)**[22] 7070 3-9-1 57 CathyGannon 9 55
(M R Channon) *hld up: styd on u.p fr over 1f out: nvr nrr* **10/3**[2]
0/0- **6** *9* **Lend A Light**[627] 667 4-8-13 52 EddieAhern 8 28
(P J Hobbs) *hld up: plld hrd: hdwy to chse ldr over 5f out: rdn and wknd over 1f out* **9/2**[3]
-443 **7** *1 1/4* **King Of Connacht**[278] 469 7-9-7 60 LiamJones 1 33
(M Wellings) *broke wl: sn stdd and lost pl: effrt over 2f out: wknd over 1f out* **8/1**
3600 **8** *2* **Quadrifolio**[96] 4914 4-8-7 46 oh1 (t) GregFairley 11 15
(Paul Green) *chsd ldrs tl rdn and wknd over 2f out* **20/1**
0000 **9** *7* **Sue And Sue**[68] 5816 3-8-4 46 oh1 LukeMorris 4 —
(G Woodward) *hld up: a in rr: rdn and lost tch fnl 3f* **33/1**

1m 52.98s (2.48) **Going Correction** +0.075s/f (Slow)
WFA 3 from 4yo+ 3lb 9 Ran SP% **116.9**
Speed ratings (Par 101): **91,90,86,86,85 77,76,74,68**
Tote Swingers: 1&2 £5.60, 1&3 £5.40, 2&3 £7.00 CSF £20.98 CT £151.64 TOTE £5.30: £1.90, £3.80, £3.80; EX 25.50.
Owner Miss Emma Wettern **Bred** Gestut Brummerhof **Trained** East Garston, Berks

FOCUS
Only a modest handicap but quite competitive for its level. The pace was steady and it developed into a something of a sprint. The form is rated through the second but could be up to 5lb higher.
Lend A Light Official explanation: jockey said colt ran too free

7450 BET MULTIPLES - BETDAQ H'CAP (DIV II) 1m 141y(P)
7:50 (7:50) (Class 6) (0-60,59) 3-Y-O+ £1,364 (£403; £201) **Stalls** Low

Form RPR
1510 **1** **Cyril The Squirrel**[96] 4914 6-9-3 55 TedDurcan 6 64
(Karen George) *chsd ldr: rdn to ld 1f out: hung lft: r.o* **9/2**
5221 **2** *1 3/4* **Join Up**[22] 7071 4-8-13 54 RossAtkinson(3) 2 59+
(W M Brisbourne) *hld up: hdwy over 1f out: r.o wl: nt rch wnr* **3/1**[2]
5055 **3** *nk* **Just Jimmy (IRE)**[8] 7336 5-9-7 59 GeorgeBaker 8 63
(P D Evans) *hld up: hdwy over 5f out: rdn over 2f out: hung lft over 1f out: styd on* **4/1**[3]
3500 **4** *1* **Lujano**[68] 5820 5-9-6 58 PaulMulrennan 9 60
(Ollie Pears) *led: rdn and hdd 1f out: no ex* **11/4**[1]
0005 **5** *2 1/2* **Royal Patriot (IRE)**[22] 7070 3-8-5 46 GregFairley 4 43
(Paul Green) *hld up: plld hrd: hdwy over 1f out: styd on same pce fnl f* **14/1**
4064 **6** *1/2* **Papa's Princess**[14] 7230 6-8-7 45 JimmyQuinn 5 40
(James Moffatt) *chsd ldrs: rdn over 2f out: styd on same pce appr fnl f* **20/1**
0644 **7** *8* **Reddy To Star (IRE)**[18] 7153 3-9-1 56 TomEaves 7 34
(Julie Camacho) *chsd ldrs: rdn over 3f out: wknd wl over 1f out* **11/1**

1m 50.7s (0.20) **Going Correction** +0.075s/f (Slow)
WFA 3 from 4yo+ 3lb 7 Ran SP% **109.6**
Speed ratings (Par 101): **102,100,100,99,97 96,89**
Tote Swingers: 1&2 £2.00, 1&3 £3.40, 2&3 £3.60 CSF £16.80 CT £52.12 TOTE £3.40: £2.10, £1.20; EX 11.40.
Owner R E Baskerville **Bred** R E Baskerville **Trained** Higher Eastington, Devon

FOCUS
A weak affair run at a steady tempo and the form promises to be muddling. The form is rated around the second and third's recent form.

7451 BETDAQ.COM MAIDEN STKS 1m 141y(P)
8:20 (8:20) (Class 5) 3-Y-O+ £2,007 (£597; £298; £149) **Stalls** Low

Form RPR
2 **1** **Imagination (IRE)**[14] 7244 3-8-12 0 NeilCallan 3 66+
(Richard Brabazon, Ire) *led: hdd over 6f out: remained handy: led wl over 1f out: rdn and hung lft ins fnl f: r.o* **1/2**[1]
5 **2** *2 1/4* **Albertus Pictor**[305] 143 3-9-3 0 StevieDonohoe 1 71+
(Sir Mark Prescott) *s.i.s: sn prom: rdn to chse wnr over 1f out: styng on whn hmpd and snatched up towards fin* **9/4**[2]
3 *4* **Star In Flight** 3-9-3 0 ShaneKelly 7 57
(B J Meehan) *chsd ldr tl led over 6f out: rdn and hdd wl over 1f out: wknd ins fnl f* **14/1**[3]
30 **4** *shd* **Loyalty**[178] 2231 3-9-3 0 (v) PatrickMathers 5 56
(D Shaw) *s.i.s: in rr tl r.o ins fnl f: nvr nrr* **40/1**
05 **5** *6* **Spacecraft (IRE)**[17] 7183 3-9-3 0 JimmyQuinn 6 43
(C N Kellett) *s.i.s: a in rr* **66/1**
0P4 **6** *1/2* **Premier League**[43] 6522 3-9-3 0 RobertWinston 4 47
(Miss J Feilden) *prom: chsd ldr over 4f out: rdn and ev ch 2f out: wknd fnl f* **33/1**
0/0 **7** *10* **Between Dreams**[13] 7251 7-9-1 0 LukeMorris 2 12
(Andrew Turnell) *hld up: rdn and wknd over 2f out* **100/1**

1m 51.65s (1.15) **Going Correction** +0.075s/f (Slow)
WFA 3 from 7yo 3lb 7 Ran SP% **112.0**
Speed ratings (Par 103): **97,95,91,91,86 85,76**
Tote Swingers: 1&2 £1.20, 1&3 £1.60, 2&3 £1.10 CSF £1.72 TOTE £1.30: £1.10, £1.40; EX 2.00.
Owner Horse For Dubai Syndicate **Bred** Windflower Overseas **Trained** Curragh, Co Kildare
■ Stewards' Enquiry : Neil Callan two-day ban: careless riding (Nov 27-28)

FOCUS
A very uncompetitive maiden in which the two market leaders came to the fore at the end of a steadily-run race. The for mis rated around the winner and the second has been rated as dead-heating.
Premier League Official explanation: jockey said gelding had no more to give

7452 EUROPEAN BREEDERS' FUND MAIDEN STKS 1m 1f 103y(P)
8:50 (8:53) (Class 5) 2-Y-O £2,978 (£886; £442; £221) **Stalls** Low

Form RPR
0 **1** **Quiz Mistress**[29] 6883 2-8-12 0 NeilCallan 10 75+
(G A Butler) *hld up: hdwy over 5f out: rdn over 2f out: styd on to ld wl ins fnl f* **9/2**[2]
634 **2** *1* **Oversteer (USA)**[35] 6742 2-9-3 72 (b[1]) RobertHavlin 12 78
(J H M Gosden) *a.p: chsd ldr over 5f out: rdn and ev ch fr over 1f out: hung lft and nt run on* **8/1**
323 **3** *1/2* **Halfsin (IRE)**[38] 6676 2-9-3 83 AdamKirby 1 77
(M Botti) *led: rdn over 1f out: edgd lft and hdd wl ins fnl f* **4/6**[1]
4 *2* **For What (USA)** 2-9-3 0 ChrisCatlin 13 73+
(D R Lanigan) *sn pushed along in rr: hdwy over 4f out: r.o: nt trble ldrs* **28/1**
5 *1 3/4* **Jamr** 2-9-3 0 TedDurcan 3 70
(Saeed Bin Suroor) *s.i.s: sn drvn along to chse ldrs: rdn over 3f out: styd on same pce appr fnl f* **5/1**[3]

5 **6** 2 1/4 **Samarkand (IRE)**[12] 7272 2-9-3 0 StevieDonohoe 9 66+
(Sir Mark Prescott) *mid-div: rdn over 3f out: styd on fnl f: nvr trbld ldrs* **12/1**

00 **7** 8 **Dashing Eddie (IRE)**[10] 7302 2-9-3 0 PhillipMakin 8 51
(K A Ryan) *prom: pushed along 6f out: rdn over 2f out: wknd over 1f out* **50/1**

6 **8** 4 **Round Turn (IRE)**[47] 6414 2-9-3 0 GrahamGibbons 6 43+
(E S McMahon) *hld up: a in rr: rdn over 3f out: sn wknd* **50/1**

60 **9** 6 **Romantic Girl (IRE)**[19] 7123 2-8-9 0 RussKennemore(3) 11 27
(A G Juckes) *hld up: plld hrd: hmpd wl over 3f out: sn rdn and wknd* **100/1**

0 **10** 1 **Mint Imperial (IRE)**[22] 7058 2-9-3 0 FrankieMcDonald 4 30
(Miss Amy Weaver) *s.i.s: a in rr: wknd over 3f out* **80/1**

0 **11** 21 **Pope Potter**[7] 7345 2-9-0 0 AndrewHeffernan(3) 5 —
(R C Guest) *chsd ldrs: rdn 1/2-way: wknd over 3f out: t.o* **100/1**

0 **12** nk **Evelyns Diamond**[8] 7325 2-8-12 0 MickyFenton 2 —
(P T Midgley) *mid-div: wknd 1/2-way: t.o* **100/1**

2m 2.50s (0.80) **Going Correction** +0.075s/f (Slow) **12** Ran SP% **125.2**
Speed ratings (Par 96): **99,98,97,95,94 92,85,81,76,75 56,56**
Tote Swingers: 1&2 £3.10, 1&3 £1.80, 2&3 £2.60 CSF £41.82 TOTE £4.40: £1.30, £2.50, £1.30; EX 45.10.
Owner The Fairy Story Partnership **Bred** Deepwood Farm Stud **Trained** Newmarket, Suffolk

FOCUS
This turned into a good test of stamina for these youngsters. It was something of a mixed bag in terms of ability and is not an easy race to rate with confidence

NOTEBOOK
Quiz Mistress had looked a potential improver as well as in need of a longer trip when in midfield on her debut at Newmarket last month and benefited most from the race testing stamina, nowhere stronger than at the finish. There's plenty of class and stamina on the female side of her pedigree and she'll likely make up into a useful middle-distance filly next year. (op 4-1 tchd 7-2)
Oversteer(USA) ran a better race in first-time headgear, though he was probably helped by the longer trip as much as anything else, seeming to do little wrong but beaten only by a better animal at the weights. He's probably just a fair handicapper in the making but is good enough to win a maiden before the end of the year. (tchd 9-1)
Halfsin(IRE) looked to have the best form claims but probably wasn't quite at his best on the day, just beaten by a couple of stronger stayers at the trip. An official mark of 83 means he isn't going to be easy to place in handicaps. (op 11-10 tchd 6-5 in places)
For What(USA) ◆ did best of the newcomers and looks a potentially significant improver after looking extremely green early on but finishing his race to some purpose having been allowed plenty of time to find his stride. His half-brother Seeking The Buck is best around 1m2f, and a maiden should be his for the taking if seen again this year. (op 25-1)
Jamr was a bit tricky to load but he showed a fair level of ability once under way and looks a likely improver for a yard not averse keen on winning these races at this time of year. (tchd 9-2)
Samarkand(IRE) was never a serious threat but once again did enough to suggest he has a future, perhaps more in handicaps next year than in a maiden next time. (op 16-1)
Dashing Eddie(IRE) showed improved form switched to this surface but this run has rather blown his cover as far as handicaps are concerned.
Romantic Girl(IRE) Official explanation: jockey said filly was denied a clear run on final bend

7453 BETDAQ ON 0870 178 1221 FILLIES' H'CAP 1m 1f 103y(P)
9:20 (9:20) (Class 5) (0-70,70) 3-Y-O+ **£2,115** (£624; £312) **Stalls** Low

Form RPR

3356 **1** **Sensationally**[27] 6959 3-9-4 **67** RichardKingscote 5 73
(R M Beckett) *a.p: chsd ldr 7f out: rdn to ld 1f out: edgd lft: r.o* **7/1**[2]

6213 **2** 1/2 **Blue Moon**[10] 7305 3-9-0 **70** JulieBurke(7) 1 75+
(K A Ryan) *chsd ldrs: rdn and ev ch ins fnl f: r.o* **7/2**[1]

-005 **3** nk **Serious Drinking (USA)**[10] 7298 4-9-2 **62** AdamKirby 3 65+
(W R Swinburn) *hld up in tch: rdn over 1f out: edgd lft ins fnl f: r.o* **7/2**[1]

0540 **4** hd **Scorn (USA)**[23] 7042 3-9-5 **68** RobertHavlin 7 72
(J H M Gosden) *led: rdn and hdd 1f out: styd on* **14/1**[3]

6040 **5** 2 1/4 **Our Kes (IRE)**[247] 865 8-8-7 **53** oh7 JimmyQuinn 2 51
(P Howling) *hld up: hdwy u.p over 1f out: nvr trbld ldrs* **33/1**

222 **6** 2 1/2 **Marrimeclaire (IRE)**[2] 7413 3-9-1 **64** ShaneKelly 8 58
(B J McMath) *hld up: rdn over 2f out: nvr trbld ldrs* **7/2**[1]

6504 **7** 1 1/2 **Wiseman's Diamond (USA)**[17] 7184 5-9-1 **61** MickyFenton 6 51
(P T Midgley) *prom: rdn over 2f out: wknd over 1f out* **7/1**[2]

3662 **8** 1 **Hill Tribe**[22] 7069 3-9-1 **67** AndrewHeffernan(3) 4 56
(R C Guest) *hld up: rdn over 2f out: wknd over 1f out* **7/1**[2]

2m 3.91s (2.21) **Going Correction** +0.075s/f (Slow)
WFA 3 from 4yo+ 3lb **8** Ran SP% **113.8**
Speed ratings (Par 100): **93,92,92,92,90 87,86,85**
Tote Swingers: 1&2 £4.40, 1&3 £3.50, 2&3 £2.50 CSF £31.38 CT £100.17 TOTE £9.40: £1.80, £1.60, £1.80; EX 35.40.
Owner Helena Springfield Ltd **Bred** Meon Valley Stud **Trained** Whitsbury, Hants

FOCUS
An ordinary handicap to end the card but something of a tactical affair with the pace being steady. Muddling form.
Marrimeclaire(IRE) Official explanation: jockey said filly was in season
T/Plt: £12.70 to a £1 stake. Pool:£83,003.61 - 4,753.57 winning tickets. T/Qpdt: £3.90 to a £1 stake. Pool:£7,033.65 - 1,326.96 winning tickets. CR

7454 - 7455a (Foreign Racing) - See Raceform Interactive

7265 SAINT-CLOUD (L-H)
Saturday, November 13

OFFICIAL GOING: Turf: heavy

7456a CRITERIUM DE SAINT-CLOUD (GROUP 1) (2YO COLTS & FILLIES) (TURF) 1m 2f
1:05 (1:07) 2-Y-O **£126,415** (£50,575; £25,287; £12,632; £6,327)

RPR

1 **Recital (FR)**[24] 7025 2-9-0 0 JMurtagh 6 115+
(A P O'Brien, Ire) *amongst bkmarkers fr s: gd prog at end of bk st to cl bhd ldrs: fnd split towards outside early in st: qcknd to ld 1 1/2f out: rdn 1f out: sn wnt clr: easily* **3/1**[2]

2 5 **Bubble Chic (FR)**[27] 6973 2-9-0 0 StephanePasquier 8 106
(G Botti, Italy) *racd in mid-div: rdn early in st: followed eventual wnr: threatened briefly 1f out: nt qckn 100yds out: r.o wl for 2nd fnl 50yds* **7/1**

3 2 **Prairie Star (FR)**[27] 6973 2-9-0 0 AnthonyCrastus 9 102
(E Lellouche, France) *racd in 4th early on ins: dropped bk mid bk st: rdn early in st: wnt 2nd 1 1/2f out: wandered off st line 100yds out: losing 2nd fnl 50yds* **5/2**[1]

4 6 **Exodus**[38] 6684 2-9-0 0 JAHeffernan 3 92
(A P O'Brien, Ire) *amongst early ldrs: rdn early in st: no ex 1 1/2f out: styd on* **20/1**

5 nk **Quinindo (GER)**[34] 2-9-0 0 EPedroza 11 91
(A Wohler, Germany) *early ldr pulling freely on outer: settled in 3rd: rdn to ld early in st 2f out: no ex 1 1/2f out: styd on* **73/10**

6 snk **Creyente (IRE)**[20] 2-8-10 0 (b) RaphaelMarchelli 5 87
(S Wattel, France) *bkmarker fr s: rdn and styd on wl fnl 1 1/2f* **16/1**

7 3/4 **Kreem**[27] 6973 2-9-0 0 MaximeGuyon 4 89
(A Fabre, France) *racd bhd ldrs fr s: rdn early in st: no ex: styd on* **6/1**[3]

8 2 1/2 **Obligation (FR)**[13] 7260 2-9-0 0 CO'Donoghue 7 85
(A P O'Brien, Ire) *amongst bkmarkers fr s: rdn to be prom early in st towards wd outside: rdn 1 1/2f out: no ex: one pce* **17/1**

9 20 **Figli Fanesi (IRE)**[24] 2-9-0 0 DarioVargiu 10 49
(Vittorio Caruso, Italy) *prom early: rdn early in st but qckly wknd* **15/1**

10 dist **Rigolleto (IRE)**[26] 6982 2-9-0 0 OlivierPeslier 2 —
(M R Channon) *racd 2nd early: tk ld at end of bk st: rdn and qckly wknd early in st* **24/1**

2m 24.8s (8.80) **10** Ran SP% **118.9**
WIN (incl. 1 euro stake): 2.90 (Recital combined with Exodus & Obligation); PLACES: 1.50, 1.70, 1.40. DF: 24.20. SF: 26.70.
Owner Mrs Magnier/Tabor/Smith/Mordukhovitch **Bred** Mme Renee Geffroy & Caragh Bloodstock **Trained** Ballydoyle, Co Tipperary

FOCUS
Recital impressed in what is usually a weak Group 1 and is a very nice prospsct, but the second and third came from a weak Group 3.

NOTEBOOK
Recital(FR), a brother to Prix Ganay winner Corre Caminios and half-brother to Group-winning miler Racinger, won a Navan maiden on his debut last month. He came through from the rear to win this very easily under Johnny Murtagh, who announced this week that he won't be O'Brien's stable jockey next year. The colt has a nice blend of speed and stamina and is a smart prospect, who has been given a quote of 14/1 by Victor Chandler for next year's Investec Derby.
Bubble Chic(FR) was no match for the winner but reversed Prix de Conde form with Prairie Star over this longer trip.
Prairie Star(FR) ran his race over this extra furlong but was unable to confirm Longchamp form with today's runner-up.
Exodus created a good impression when winning his maiden by 9l but was well held behind his stablemate here.
Rigolleto(IRE) dropped out to finish last after making a lot of the early running.

7457a PRIX DENISY (LISTED RACE) (3YO+) (TURF) 1m 7f 110y
1:35 (1:35) 3-Y-O+ **£23,008** (£9,203; £6,902; £4,601; £2,300)

RPR

1 **Dayia (IRE)**[28] 6926 6-8-11 0 OlivierPeslier 5 99
(J Pearce) *racd in 3rd on inner: rdn 2f out: qcknd into ld 1 1/2f out: r.o wl: comf* **28/1**

2 1 1/2 **Cabimas**[20] 3-8-7 0 MickaelBarzalona 3 102
(P Schiergen, Germany) **15/1**

3 1/2 **Babyla**[18] 4-8-11 0 MaximeGuyon 9 96
(A Fabre, France) **6/4**[1]

4 3/4 **Gaselee (USA)**[17] 7181 4-8-11 0 ThierryThulliez 4 96
(Rae Guest) *broke wl to ld: stl in front early in st: rdn 2f out: nt qckn: styd on* **27/1**

5 1 1/2 **Winter Dream (IRE)**[20] 7110 6-9-7 0 ThierryJarnet 6 104
(Robert Collet, France) **58/10**[3]

6 hd **Plume Rose**[23] 7048 3-8-4 0 Pierre-CharlesBoudot 10 95
(Y De Nicolay, France) **15/1**

7 hd **Shawnee Saga (FR)**[18] 5-9-1 0 DominiqueBoeuf 2 97
(W Baltromei, Germany) **21/1**

8 6 **Shalangar (IRE)**[19] 3-8-7 0 GregoryBenoist 8 91
(A De Royer-Dupre, France) **6/1**

9 4 **Roatan**[18] 5-9-1 0 StephanePasquier 7 85
(P Bary, France) **19/5**[2]

10 20 **Dwilano (GER)**[20] 7-9-1 0 TheoBachelot 1 61
(N Sauer, Germany) **55/1**

3m 49.7s (11.00)
WFA 3 from 4yo+ 8lb **10** Ran SP% **115.7**
WIN (incl. 1 euro stake): 28.60. PLACES: 5.70, 3.30, 1.50. DF: 114.10. SF: 389.00.
Owner Lady Green **Bred** Shadwell Estate Company Limited **Trained** Newmarket, Suffolk

NOTEBOOK
Dayia(IRE), down the field in the Cesarewitch latest, handled the testing ground very well to gain a Listed win at the first attempt.
Gaselee(USA) ran creditably from the front but just missed out on some black type.

7372 CAPANNELLE (R-H)
Sunday, November 14

OFFICIAL GOING: Turf: heavy

7459a PREMIO CARLO & FRANCESCO ALOISI (EX PREMIO UMBRIA) (GROUP 3) (2YO+) (TURF) 6f
3:05 (3:17) 2-Y-O+ **£35,398** (£15,575; £8,495; £4,247)

RPR

1 **Rosendhal (IRE)**[8] 7370 3-9-8 0 (b) MMonteriso 10 103
(A Renzoni, Italy) *settled mid-div after 1f: prog between horses 3f out to trck ldrs: patiently rdn in 2nd 2f out: rdn 1 1/2f out to ld: hrd rdn fnl f to hold advantage* **183/20**

2 1 **Morgan Drive (IRE)**[138] 5-9-8 0 MKolmarkaj 5 100
(M Gasparini, Italy) *slowly away: hld up in rr: bkmarker and off the pce after 3f: hrd rdn 2 1/2f out and stl in rr: prog ent fnl 2f: hrd rdn and hdwy ent fnl f: fast-fining 2nd* **79/10**[3]

3 nse **Jiroft (ITY)**[56] 6238 3-9-8 0 PierantonioConvertino 7 100
(M Marcialis, Italy) *broke wl and prom for 3f: lef briefly 2f out: hrd rdn and one pce ent fnl f: ct fnl strides for 2nd* **102/10**

4 nse **Jakor (ITY)**[28] 6976 4-9-12 0 SLandi 2 104
(M Marcialis, Italy) *mid-div for 3f: 5th 2 1/2f out: rdn and high hd carriage 2f out: styd on under hrd ride fnl f* **87/10**

5 hd **Tony Douglas (IRE)**[190] 1944 6-9-8 0 PBorrelli 9 99
(A Di Dio, Italy) *rdn to stay in tch 3f out: one pce 2f out: hdwy whn chal on both sides fnl 150yds* **41/1**

6 1/2 **Charming Woman (IRE)**[28] 6976 3-9-8 0 FabioBranca 13 97
(Vittorio Caruso, Italy) *in tch on outer: produced 2 1/2f out to chal: ev ch 1 1/2f out: one pce ent fnl f whn 3rd: no ex fnl 100yds* **15/4**[2]

7 2 **Golden Joker (IRE)**[219] 6-9-8 0 PAragoni 14 91
(F Boccardelli, Italy) *broke wl to ld after 1f: a l clr ent fnl 2 1/2f: chal by eventual wnr 2f out: sn btn* **36/1**

8 *nk* **Farrel (IRE)**[8] 7370 5-9-8 0 ... CColombi 3 90
(B Grizzetti, Italy) *slowly away and in rr: rdn to stay in tch 5f out: hrd rdn 3f out: sme hdwy fnl 300yds* **162/10**
9 *2* **Definightly**[13] 7278 4-9-12 0 ... (b) SteveDrowne 1 88
(R Charlton) *broke wl to trck ldrs for 3f: wknd whn hrd rdn 2 1/2f out* **23/20**[1]
10 *1 3/4* **Madda's Force (ITY)**[119] 4185 4-9-5 0 ... MPasquale 4 75
(R Betti, Italy) *nr rr: rdn 3f out and sn no ex* **102/10**
11 *1* **Golden Dynamic (IRE)**[1169] 6-9-8 0 ... APolli 8 75
(E Galli, Italy) *nr rr: rdn 4f out to stay in tch: mid-div 3f out: btn 2f out* **131/10**
12 *4* **Thinking Robins (IRE)**[119] 4185 7-9-8 0 ... (b) SSulas 15 62
(Ottavio Di Paolo, Italy) *in rr on outer for 3f: rdn and sme hdwy 2f out: btn and eased ent fnl f* **32/1**
13 *6* **Black Mambazo (IRE)**[28] 6976 5-9-8 0 ... GMarcelli 12 43
(L Riccardi, Italy) *in tch w ldrs on outer for 2 1/2f: hrd rdn 3f out and sn one pce* **173/10**
14 *hd* **Golden Ramon (IRE)**[28] 6976 3-9-5 0 ... DarioVargiu 11 39
(B Grizzetti, Italy) *in tch in 3rd for 2f: caughgt for pce 3 1/2f out: rdn and sn btn* **14/1**
15 *1/2* **Remarque (IRE)**[190] 1944 5-9-8 0 ... (b) CDemuro 6 41
(L Riccardi, Italy) *swtchd lft to rail after 1f: rdn and mid-div 3f out: sn btn* **14/1**

1m 10.4s (0.10) **15** Ran SP% **156.6**
WIN (incl. 1 euro stake): 10.15. PLACES: 3.54, 3.99, 4.36. DF: 193.91.
Owner Allevamento Pian Di Neve SRL **Bred** Allevamento Pian Di Neve Srl **Trained** Italy

NOTEBOOK
Rosendhal(IRE) had failed to reach the first two in seven previous attempts in Group and Listed company.
Definightly, a winner in this grade at Maisons-Laffitte recently, was heavily backed but ran disappointingly.

KYOTO (R-H)
Sunday, November 14

OFFICIAL GOING: Turf: firm

7460a QUEEN ELIZABETH II COMMEMORATIVE CUP (GRADE 1) (3YO+ FILLIES & MARES) (TURF) 1m 3f
6:40 (12:00) 3-Y-0+ **£624,926** (£247,030; £156,804; £93,209; £59,920)

RPR
1 **Snow Fairy (IRE)**[64] 5945 3-8-7 0 ... RyanMoore 6 120
(E A L Dunlop) *settled midfield (abt 7th): bhd clr ldr (big gaps between 2nd: 3rd and 4th as wl): hdwy 2f out: r.o strly and swtchd to ins to ld appr fnl f: sn clr: impressive* **15/2**
2 *4* **Meisho Beluga (JPN)**[35] 5-8-11 0 ... KenichiIkezoe 9 112
(Kaneo Ikezoe, Japan) **21/10**[2]
3 *1 3/4* **Apapane (JPN)**[28] 3-8-7 0 ... MasayoshiEbina 5 110
(Sakae Kunieda, Japan) **17/10**[1]
4 *nse* **Little Amapola (JPN)**[28] 5-8-11 0 ... YuichiFukunaga 17 109
(Hiroyuki Nagahama, Japan) **213/10**
5 *3/4* **Hikaru Amaranthus (JPN)**[91] 4-8-11 0.. Christophe-PatriceLemaire 10 108
(Yasuo Ikee, Japan) **202/10**
6 *3/4* **Columbus Circle (JPN)**[28] 4-8-11 0 ... YutakaTake 1 106
(Futoshi Kojima, Japan) **62/1**
7 *nse* **Seraphic Romp (JPN)**[28] 6-8-11 0 ... HokutoMiyazaki 2 106
(Yoshinori Muto, Japan) **46/1**
8 *nk* **Brightia Pulse (JPN)**[28] 5-8-11 0 ... KotaFujioka 8 106
(Osamu Hirata, Japan) **109/1**
9 *1 1/4* **Saint Emilion (JPN)**[28] 3-8-7 0 ... MircoDemuro 7 104
(Masaaki Koga, Japan) **117/10**
10 *1 1/2* **Mood Indigo (JPN)**[28] 5-8-11 0 ... YugaKawada 15 101
(Yasuo Tomomichi, Japan) **158/1**
11 *hd* **Reginetta (JPN)**[91] 5-8-11 0 ... HideakiMiyuki 3 100
(Hidekazu Asami, Japan) **101/1**
12 *3/4* **Sing Like Bird (JPN)**[28] 5-8-11 0 ... RyotaSameshima 18 99
(Yasuo Tomomichi, Japan) **162/1**
13 *nk* **Sanrei Jasper (JPN)**[28] 8-8-11 0 ... YoshiyasuNanba 13 98
(Shigetada Takahashi, Japan) **350/1**
14 *nse* **Earth Symbol (JPN)**[36] 5-8-11 0 ... KatsuharuTanaka 14 98
(Yoshitada Munakata, Japan) **99/1**
15 *nk* **Animate Bio (JPN)**[28] 3-8-7 0 ... HirokiGoto 12 99
(Koji Maki, Japan) **31/5**[3]
16 *1 3/4* **Ave**[43] 6583 4-8-11 0 ... JJCastellano 16 95
(Roger L Attfield, Canada) **25/1**
17 *nk* **T M Precure (JPN)**[77] 7-8-11 0 ... KyosukeKokubun 4 94
(Tadao Igarashi, Japan) **77/1**

2m 12.5s (132.50) **17** Ran SP% **125.3**
WFA 3 from 4yo+ 5lb
PARI-MUTUEL (all including 100 ypj stake): WIN 850 SHOW 220, 120, 120 DF 1430 SF 3590.
Owner Anamoine Limited **Bred** Windflower Overseas Holdings Inc **Trained** Newmarket, Suffolk

NOTEBOOK
Snow Fairy(IRE) ◆, facing the best fillies and mares that Japan had to offer, was given a fantastic ride by Ryan Moore to win with plenty to spare. A move towards the inside of the course off the home bend saw her show tremendous acceleration on the firm track, and the race was soon over. The Japan Cup could be on the agenda next.
Meisho Beluga(JPN) came into this race off the back of a good win against Oken Bruce Lee, and did her usual by finishing strongly once in the clear. However, she was no match for the winner, who had gone before her jockey had time to react.
Apapane(JPN), who had taken the fillies' Triple Crown this season, was readily put in her place by the Oaks winner and was never seen with a winning chance.
Little Amapola(JPN), a previous winner of this, kept on and ran with credit without being a big danger.
Saint Emilion(JPN) seemingly disappointed for the second race in a row.

7446 WOLVERHAMPTON (A.W) (L-H)
Monday, November 15

OFFICIAL GOING: Standard
Wind: Light behind Weather: Fine and sunny

7461 BET GRAND SLAM DARTS - BETDAQ MAIDEN FILLIES' STKS 7f 32y(P)
1:40 (1:42) (Class 5) 3-Y-0+ **£2,007** (£597; £298; £149) **Stalls** High

Form RPR
003 1 **Polly Floyer**[11] 7310 3-8-12 61 ... AdamKirby 7 57+
(W R Swinburn) *mde all: rdn clr and swished tail over 1f out: eased towards fin* **4/6**[1]
0 2 *4 1/2* **La Chemme**[16] 7244 4-8-13 0 ... FergusSweeney 2 43
(R Hollinshead) *a.p: rdn to chse wnr 2f out: styd on same pce appr fnl f* **25/1**
3000 3 *3/4* **Cheshire Lady (IRE)**[33] 6848 3-8-12 47 ... (t) LiamJones 1 40
(W M Brisbourne) *hld up in tch: plld hrd: rdn over 1f out: styd on same pce* **12/1**
6 4 *1 3/4* **Amy Thorpe**[31] 6896 3-8-9 0 ... PaulPickard(3) 10 35
(O Brennan) *chsd ldrs: rdn over 2f out: styd on same pce appr fnl f* **8/1**[3]
0- 5 *2* **Aurora Lights**[324] 7843 3-8-5 0 ... LauraBarry(7) 12 30
(R A Fahey) *chsd ldrs: rdn over 2f out: edgd lft and wknd over 1f out* **14/1**
00 6 *4 1/2* **Cinderella**[151] 3125 3-8-12 0 ... CathyGannon 11 18
(Lucinda Featherstone) *in rr and rdn 1/2-way: nvr on terms* **66/1**
0600 7 *2 1/4* **Lilly Blue (IRE)**[72] 5767 4-8-13 41 ... (p) TomEaves 6 13
(R Brotherton) *s.i.s: hld up: n.d* **22/1**
60 8 *1 1/2* **Bluegrass Gal (USA)**[10] 7328 4-8-10 0 ... AndrewHeffernan(3) 3 —
(Mrs L Williamson) *hld up: rdn 1/2-way: a in rr* **100/1**
04-0 9 *3/4* **Charles Bear**[29] 6966 3-8-12 0 ... PatrickMathers 5 —
(Bruce Hellier) *s.s: a bhd* **20/1**
3-00 10 *1 1/2* **Marie Cuddy (IRE)**[47] 6470 3-8-12 57 ... ChrisCatlin 4 —
(Karen George) *hld up: rdn over 3f out: sn wknd* **9/2**[2]
400- 11 *3* **Superior Duchess**[344] 7652 5-8-6 45 ... LucyBarry(7) 8 —
(A J Chamberlain) *chsd wnr over 5f out tl rdn over 2f out: sn wknd* **50/1**
0/ 12 *43* **Red Rani**[857] 3916 5-8-13 0 ... GrahamGibbons 9 —
(R Hollinshead) *a in rr: t.o* **20/1**

1m 29.88s (0.28) **Going Correction** 0.0s/f (Stan)
WFA 3 from 4yo+ 1lb **12** Ran SP% **125.8**
Speed ratings (Par 100): **98,92,92,90,87 82,80,78,77,75 72,23**
toteswingers:1&2:£8.80, 1&3:£3.60, 2&3:£31.00 CSF £31.12 TOTE £1.70: £1.10, £7.00, £3.20; EX 26.80 Trifecta £130.50 Pool: £402.29 - 2.28 winning units..
Owner P W Harris **Bred** Pendley Farm **Trained** Aldbury, Herts

FOCUS
A very weak maiden and the easy winner didn't have to improve.

7462 GREAT OFFERS AT WOLVERHAMPTON-RACECOURSE.CO.UK (S) STKS 7f 32y(P)
2:10 (2:10) (Class 6) 3-Y-0+ **£1,535** (£453; £226) **Stalls** High

Form RPR
1 **The Big Haerth (IRE)**[17] 4-9-7 77 ... (t) AndreaAtzeni 6 73+
(S C Williams) *mde virtually all: rdn out* **8/13**[1]
1605 2 *1 1/2* **Rebellious Spirit**[19] 7184 7-9-7 62 ... LukeMorris 8 69
(S Curran) *chsd ldrs: rdn over 2f out: styd on to go 2nd nr fin* **20/1**
4164 3 *nk* **Apache Ridge (IRE)**[45] 6537 4-9-7 65 ... (p) PhillipMakin 5 68
(K A Ryan) *a.p: rdn to chse wnr over 1f out: styd on same pce ins fnl f: lost 2nd nr fin* **6/1**[2]
4540 4 *1* **William Morgan (IRE)**[7] 7376 3-8-7 67 ... GeorgeChaloner(7) 7 58
(R A Fahey) *broke wl: sn lost pl: pushed along 3f out: hung lft and r.o ins fnl f: nt trble ldrs* **8/1**[3]
550 5 *shd* **Ravi River (IRE)**[72] 5768 6-9-7 60 ... (v) GeorgeBaker 9 65
(P D Evans) *hld up: rdn over 2f out: r.o fnl f: nrst fin* **33/1**
4600 6 *2 3/4* **Penrod Ballantyne (IRE)**[14] 7273 3-9-0 59 ... ChrisCatlin 3 51
(Karen George) *prom: rdn over 2f out: styd on same pce appr fnl f* **16/1**
044 7 *1 3/4* **Landucci**[19] 7162 9-9-1 62 ... (p) JamesDoyle 1 47
(S Curran) *chsd wnr: rdn over 2f out: wknd fnl f* **6/1**[2]
4000 8 *4* **Bedouin Princess (IRE)**[39] 6696 3-8-9 42 ... CathyGannon 10 30
(Lucinda Featherstone) *rdn 1/2-way: a in rr* **100/1**
5- 9 *2 3/4* **Bravo Belle (IRE)**[377] 7217 3-8-9 0 ... FergusSweeney 4 23
(T H Caldwell) *hld up: rdn 1/2-way: sn wknd* **100/1**

1m 29.42s (-0.18) **Going Correction** 0.0s/f (Stan)
WFA 3 from 4yo+ 1lb **9** Ran SP% **117.2**
Speed ratings (Par 101): **101,99,98,97,97 94,92,87,84**
toteswingers:1&2:£7.50, 1&3:£2.20, 2&3:£8.80 CSF £20.18 TOTE £2.10: £1.50, £3.80, £1.10; EX 27.80 Trifecta £85.80 Pool: £326.12 - 2.81 winning units..The winner was bought in for 4,750gns.
Owner S Pecoraro **Bred** Hong Kong Breeders Club **Trained** Newmarket, Suffolk

FOCUS
It's hard to know if the ex-Italian winner is up to his BHA rating, and this form is rated around the runner-up.

7463 BET MULTIPLES - BETDAQ H'CAP 1m 4f 50y(P)
2:40 (2:41) (Class 5) (0-75,74) 3-Y-0+ **£2,007** (£597; £298; £149) **Stalls** Low

Form RPR
1224 1 **Country Road (IRE)**[23] 7089 4-9-8 **73** ... (be) AdamKirby 4 81
(A W Carroll) *chsd ldr tl wnt through on ins of stablemate to ld over 3f out: rdn over 1f out: styd on u.p* **5/2**[1]
2316 2 *2* **Carlton Scroop (FR)**[25] 7044 7-8-13 **67** ... KierenFox(3) 3 72
(A W Carroll) *led: hdd over 3f out: shkn up over 1f out: styd on* **11/2**
2000 3 *shd* **Houston Dynimo (IRE)**[24] 7055 5-9-2 **67** ... TomEaves 2 72
(N G Richards) *chsd ldrs: rdn over 2f out: styd on* **12/1**
0002 4 *1/2* **Trachonitis (IRE)**[14] 7275 6-9-3 **68** ... EddieAhern 6 72
(J R Jenkins) *hld up: hdwy over 6f out: shkn up over 1f out: styd on* **4/1**[3]
0305 5 *4* **Archie Rice (USA)**[25] 7045 4-9-2 **67** ... StevieDonohoe 1 65
(T Keddy) *hld up: rdn over 1f out: nvr on terms* **6/1**
566 6 *6* **Oriental Cavalier**[34] 6832 4-9-6 **74** ... RussKennemore(3) 5 62
(Mark Buckley) *prom: lost pl over 6f out: rdn and wknd over 2f out* **3/1**[2]

2m 39.57s (-1.53) **Going Correction** 0.0s/f (Stan) **6** Ran SP% **110.9**
Speed ratings (Par 103): **105,103,103,103,100 96**
toteswingers:1&2:£1.50, 1&3:£5.10, 2&3:£8.90 CSF £16.02 TOTE £3.00: £1.40, £6.80; EX 10.00.
Owner S Hussain & P O'Neill **Bred** Brittas House Stud & Lynch Bages & Samac **Trained** Cropthorne, Worcs

FOCUS
Something of an unsatisfactory race. Muddling form, rated around the runner-up.

The Form Book, Raceform Ltd, Compton, RG20 6NL

Country Road(IRE) Official explanation: jockey said, regarding running and riding that his orders were to jump out and get some cover but as the gelding tends to hang left, he felt it wise to stick to the rail.
Carlton Scroop(FR) Official explanation: jockey said, regarding running and riding, that his orders were to jump out, get off the rail as the going is always deeper and make the running on the gelding.
Oriental Cavalier Official explanation: jockey said gelding hung left-handed throughout

7464 SPONSOR A RACE BY CALLING 01902 390000 CLAIMING STKS 1m 141y(P)
3:10 (3:10) (Class 6) 2-Y-O **£1,457** (£433; £216; £108) **Stalls** Low

Form RPR
3303 **1** **Sheila's Star (IRE)**[18] 7197 2-8-3 62 LukeMorris 6 59
(J S Moore) *chsd ldr over 6f out: rdn whn hmpd wl over 1f out: carried rt sn after: styd on u.p to ld post* **15/8**[1]
005 **2** *shd* **Farmer's Wife**[14] 7271 2-8-1 49 FrannyNorton 2 57
(W J Haggas) *led 7f out: rdn and hung rt over 1f out: edgd lft ins fnl f: hdd post* **6/1**[3]
0 **3** *3 ¾* **Oratouch (IRE)**[19] 7163 2-8-9 0 ChrisCatlin 7 56
(M Botti) *s.i.s: hld up: hdwy over 1f out: r.o to go 3rd nr fin: nt trble ldrs* **4/1**[2]
500 **4** *nk* **A Little Bit Dusty**[12] 7296 2-8-7 60 KierenFox(3) 1 56
(W G M Turner) *led: hdd 7f out: chsd ldrs: rdn over 2f out: no ex ins fnl f: lost 3rd nr fin* **15/2**
4002 **5** *½* **Bathwick Scanno (IRE)**[19] 7177 2-8-7 66 CathyGannon 5 52
(P D Evans) *hld up: rdn over 2f out: hdwy over 1f out: no imp fnl f* **4/1**[2]
0000 **6** *1 ½* **Boogie Star**[19] 7177 2-7-13 55 (p) RyanPowell(7) 3 48
(J S Moore) *s.i.s: plld hrd and sn prom: rdn over 2f out: no ex fnl f* **25/1**
3060 **7** *1* **Stacey**[49] 6411 2-8-3 55 JimmyQuinn 4 43
(M Blanshard) *prom: rdn over 2f out: no ex fnl f* **10/1**
1m 52.44s (1.94) **Going Correction** 0.0s/f (Stan) **7** Ran SP% **113.8**
Speed ratings (Par 94): **91,90,87,87,86 85,84**
toteswingers:1&2:£3.70, 1&3:£2.90, 2&3:£2.70 CSF £13.55 TOTE £2.60: £1.30, £2.50; EX 13.00.Farmer's Wife was claimed by Mr B. J. Llewellyn for £5,000.
Owner Ray Styles & J S Moore **Bred** Albert Conneally **Trained** Upper Lambourn, Berks

FOCUS
They went quite steady early and the two up front dominated throughout.

NOTEBOOK
Sheila's Star(IRE), third in a similar race here last time out, was dropping back in distance, but she was given a prominent ride on a day when the pace was holding up and, despite being bumped and carried right by the runner-up in the straight, she just had her nose in front at the line. (tchd 9-4)
Farmer's Wife hadn't shown much in her first three starts and had a bit to find at the weights, but she was soon in front and made a bold bid. She showed she was still green when hanging right off the bend into the straight, though, and again when shown the whip approaching the final furlong. If she had held on at the line it's likely she'd have lost the race in the stewards' room. (op 11-2)
Oratouch(IRE), well held on her debut in maiden company, was taking on much lesser opposition here and ran respectably considering it was proving difficult to make up ground from off the pace, especially off a steady early gallop. (op 15-2)
A Little Bit Dusty, who had plenty to do giving weight all round, was off the bridle some way out. (op 8-1 tchd 7-1)
Bathwick Scanno(IRE) ran a decent race in a seller at Nottingham last time but didn't fare so well back on the AW. (op 10-3 tchd 11-4)

7465 BET IN RUNNING - BETDAQ H'CAP 2m 119y(P)
3:40 (3:40) (Class 5) (0-70,70) 3-Y-O+ **£2,007** (£597; £298; £149) **Stalls** Low

Form RPR
2430 **1** **Dart**[19] 7181 6-9-8 64 GeorgeBaker 5 71
(J Mackie) *hld up: hdwy over 3f out: led over 1f out: styd on wl* **15/2**[3]
/3-0 **2** *1 ½* **Master At Arms**[49] 6423 7-9-8 67 KierenFox(3) 9 71
(Daniel Mark Loughnane, Ire) *hld up: rdn over 1f out: edgd lft and r.o ins fnl f: wnt 2nd post: nt rch wnr* **3/1**[1]
4534 **3** *hd* **Stadium Of Light (IRE)**[47] 6450 3-8-10 61 TomEaves 7 65
(B Ellison) *chsd ldrs: pushed along over 3f out: led over 2f out: rdn and hdd over 1f out: styd on: lost 2nd post* **4/1**[2]
4410 **4** *1 ¾* **Frameit (IRE)**[14] 6747 3-8-9 60 (vt) PaulMulrennan 10 62
(J G Given) *hld up: hdwy over 4f out: rdn over 2f out: styd on* **12/1**
2650 **5** *¾* **Chocolate Caramel (USA)**[30] 6915 8-9-2 58 PhillipMakin 3 59
(R A Fahey) *hld up: rdn over 3f out: hdwy over 1f out: styd on* **16/1**
050 **6** *3 ½* **Dalhaan (USA)**[15] 7252 5-10-0 70 (p) EddieAhern 2 67
(Ian Williams) *chsd ldrs: rdn over 2f out: wknd fnl f* **14/1**
5535 **7** *½* **Divinatore**[151] 3127 4-8-12 54 (v[1]) FrannyNorton 1 50
(James Moffatt) *prom: outpcd over 3f out: styd on ins fnl f* **18/1**
6100 **8** *3 ¾* **Mme De Stael**[11] 7316 3-9-0 65 (b) StevieDonohoe 4 57
(Sir Mark Prescott) *sn led: hdd over 14f out: chsd ldr tl led again 4f out: rdn and hdd over 2f out: wknd fnl f* **10/1**
3422 **9** *3* **Red Kestrel (USA)**[37] 6744 5-9-7 70 JulieBurke(7) 8 58
(K A Ryan) *led over 14f out: hdd 4f out: sn rdn: wknd over 1f out* **3/1**[1]
3m 41.4s (-0.40) **Going Correction** 0.0s/f (Stan)
WFA 3 from 4yo+ 9lb **9** Ran SP% **116.4**
Speed ratings (Par 103): **100,99,99,98,98 96,96,94,92**
toteswingers:1&2:£7.10, 1&3:£5.00, 2&3:£4.00 CSF £30.54 CT £104.50 TOTE £6.30: £1.50, £1.30, £1.50; EX 39.90 Trifecta £139.60 Pool: £566.29 - 3.00 winning units..
Owner Caroline Lawson and Sarah Underwood **Bred** St Clare Hall Stud **Trained** Church Broughton , Derbys

FOCUS
An ordinary handicap and, although the early gallop was steady enough, the pace increased quite significantly when Mme De Stael took on Red Kestrel up front going out on the second circuit. This aided the cause of those held up off the pace, and the finish was eventually fought out by the two held up in rear early. The winner looks improved and the third and fourth set the standard.

7466 WOLVERHAMPTON-RACECOURSE.CO.UK H'CAP 5f 20y(P)
4:10 (4:11) (Class 3) (0-95,93) 3-Y-O+ **£5,828** (£1,734; £866; £432) **Stalls** Low

Form RPR
0203 **1** **Whozthecat (IRE)**[23] 7079 3-8-11 88 (v) NeilFarley(5) 2 98+
(D Carroll) *led: rdn and hdd wl ins fnl f: rallied to ld nr fin* **3/1**[1]
0603 **2** *nk* **Lenny Bee**[15] 7254 4-9-4 90 PaulMulrennan 9 99
(D H Brown) *chsd ldrs: rdn to ld wl ins fnl f: hdd nr fin* **9/2**[3]
030- **3** *1 ½* **Dark Lane**[423] 6050 4-8-7 79 JimmyQuinn 6 83+
(R A Fahey) *hld up: hdwy over 1f out: hung rt and r.o ins fnl f: nt rch ldrs* **13/2**
0050 **4** *hd* **Lewyn**[25] 7041 3-8-11 83 (t) PhillipMakin 5 86
(K A Ryan) *prom: rdn over 1f out: r.o* **16/1**
3011 **5** *¾* **Piscean (USA)**[15] 7254 5-9-7 93 AdamKirby 10 93+
(T Keddy) *bhd: hmpd 1/2-way: r.o wl ins fnl f: nrst fin* **3/1**[1]
4026 **6** *1 ¼* **Feelin Foxy**[81] 5435 6-8-7 79 oh1 TomEaves 11 75
(J G Given) *chsd ldrs: rdn over 1f out: styd on same pce* **28/1**
0000 **7** *hd* **Onceaponatime (IRE)**[17] 7212 5-8-10 82 LukeMorris 3 77
(M D Squance) *hld up: rdn over 1f out: r.o ins fnl f: nrst fin* **33/1**
3452 **8** *hd* **Lost In Paris (IRE)**[10] 7326 4-8-7 79 (v) GrahamGibbons 8 73
(T D Easterby) *w wnr tl pushed along 2f out: wknd ins fnl f* **7/2**[2]
005 **9** *2 ½* **Angus Newz**[10] 7329 7-8-7 79 FrannyNorton 7 64
(M Quinn) *mid-div: sn pushed along: no ch fr 1/2-way* **33/1**
0500 **10** *1 ½* **Just For Mary**[26] 7024 6-8-8 80 CathyGannon 4 60
(Daniel Mark Loughnane, Ire) *s.i.s: sn pushed along in rr: no ch fr 1/2-way* **20/1**
60.68 secs (-1.62) **Going Correction** 0.0s/f (Stan) **10** Ran SP% **123.7**
Speed ratings (Par 107): **112,111,109,108,107 105,105,104,100,98**
toteswingers:1&2:£4.90, 1&3:£6.00, 2&3:£8.60 CSF £17.33 CT £85.58 TOTE £3.80: £2.10, £1.50, £3.00; EX 23.30 Trifecta £239.00 Pool: £1,036.90 - 3.21 winning units..
Owner Ninerus **Bred** Liam Queally **Trained** Sledmere, E Yorks

FOCUS
A decent sprint handicap, and one in which the pace held up. The winner is potentially smart on the AW.

NOTEBOOK
Whozthecat(IRE) was quickly away from the inside-rail draw and held the call throughout, digging deep under pressure in the closing stages to hold off the runner-up. He showed he acts on Fibresand earlier in the year so should have a few options this winter, despite a climbing handicap mark. (op 4-1)
Lenny Bee tracked the winner through and had every chance in the straight, but he couldn't quite get by. He has the ability to win something similar. (op 5-1 tchd 11-2)
Dark Lane last ran in September 2009 and his winning form has come over 6f, so this has to go down as a promising effort. He'll be interesting if reverting to 6f next time. (op 11-2)
Lewyn, back down to her last winning mark, ran a better race back at her favourite track. (op 14-1)
Piscean(USA) was slowly away and struggled a little to go the early pace, but he finished like a train once in the clear up the straight. This was an eyecatching effort, especially as he ran into the back of horses on the turn in and the leaders weren't coming back. He remains on a mark he can win off when the cards fall right. Official explanation: jockey said gelding was outpaced early and denied a clear run final bend (op 7-2 tchd 9-2)
Lost In Paris(IRE), who ran well on the Fibresand last time out, mixed it up front with the winner early but couldn't stay with him in the straight. (op 9-2, tchd 5-1 in a place)

7467 WOLVERHAMPTON RACECOURSE - ALL CONFERENCING NEEDS MET H'CAP 1m 141y(P)
4:40 (4:40) (Class 6) (0-65,65) 3-Y-O+ **£1,706** (£503; £252) **Stalls** Low

Form RPR
6532 **1** **Final Drive (IRE)**[11] 7323 4-9-7 65 (t) StevieDonohoe 11 75
(J Ryan) *hld up: hdwy on outer over 2f out: rdn to ld 1f out: r.o wl* **11/4**[1]
0014 **2** *1 ¼* **Strike Force**[17] 7214 6-9-7 65 (t) CathyGannon 9 72
(Miss Olivia Maylam) *hld up: hdwy over 1f out: sn rdn: r.o* **9/2**[2]
0660 **3** *1* **Eastern Gift**[68] 5852 5-9-1 62 KierenFox(3) 6 67
(Miss Gay Kelleway) *hld up: hdwy over 1f out: styd on same pce ins fnl f* **20/1**
165 **4** *hd* **Empress Leizu (IRE)**[21] 7117 3-8-10 57 FergusSweeney 5 62+
(A W Carroll) *hld up in tch: rdn to ld over 1f out: sn edgd rt and hdd: styd on same pce* **8/1**
0500 **5** *2* **Kumbeshwar**[17] 7214 3-9-2 63 GeorgeBaker 8 64
(P D Evans) *led: rdn and over 1f out: no ex ins fnl f* **14/1**
2440 **6** *½* **Ella Grace (USA)**[28] 6993 3-8-12 59 PaulMulrennan 4 58
(R A Fahey) *prom: rdn over 2f out: edgd lft and no ex fnl f* **6/1**[3]
6-45 **7** *2 ¼* **Forbidden (IRE)**[30] 6930 7-8-10 61 (t) JulieBurke(7) 7 54
(Daniel Mark Loughnane, Ire) *hld up: rdn over 3f out: hung lft fr over 1f out: nvr trbld ldrs* **9/1**
5320 **8** *nk* **Guga (IRE)**[21] 7128 4-9-1 64 (p) RyanClark(5) 3 57
(J Mackie) *chsd ldrs: rdn over 1f out: wknd ins fnl f* **12/1**
2003 **9** *1 ½* **Powerful Pierre**[14] 7273 3-9-3 64 TomEaves 10 54
(I W McInnes) *chsd ldrs: rdn over 3f out: wknd ins fnl f* **16/1**
1200 **10** *nk* **Shared Moment (IRE)**[135] 3683 4-8-10 57 (p) AmyRyan(3) 1 45
(J Gallagher) *prom: rdn over 2f out: wknd fnl f* **33/1**
0003 **11** *2* **Steed**[57] 6226 3-8-13 60 PhillipMakin 2 45
(K A Ryan) *s.i.s: hld up: rdn over 3f out: n.d* **12/1**
6000 **12** *½* **Lord Theo**[18] 7190 6-9-4 62 (b) J-PGuillambert 12 49
(N P Littmoden) *chsd ldrs: rdn over 2f out: wkng whn hmpd ins fnl f* **12/1**
1m 49.41s (-1.09) **Going Correction** 0.0s/f (Stan)
WFA 3 from 4yo+ 3lb **12** Ran SP% **123.6**
Speed ratings (Par 101): **104,102,102,101,100 99,97,97,96,95 93,93**
toteswingers:1&2:£4.30, 1&3:£21.30, 2&3:£25.00. Totesuper7: Win: Not won. Place: £337.20. CSF £15.03 CT £218.72 TOTE £3.40: £1.20, £1.90, £7.00; EX 13.10 Trifecta £636.00 Part won. Pool: £859.49 - 0.70 winning units..
Owner Par 4 Racing **Bred** D Day & B Cantwell **Trained** Newmarket, Suffolk

FOCUS
They went a fair pace in this modest handicap, and the first three came from the rear. The form is rated around the runner-up.
T/Jkpt: £1,992.30 to a £1 stake. Pool:£113,648.68 - 40.50 winning tickets T/Plt: £35.60 to a £1 stake. Pool:£71,613.06 - 1,466.29 winning tickets T/Qpdt: £15.10 to a £1 stake. Pool:£5,376.74 - 263.30 winning tickets CR

7400 SOUTHWELL (L-H)
Tuesday, November 16

OFFICIAL GOING: Standard
Wind: Nil Weather: Dry and foggy, bright after second race.

7468 SOUTHWELL-RACECOURSE.CO.UK H'CAP (DIV I) 6f (F)
12:20 (12:20) (Class 6) (0-60,60) 3-Y-O+ **£1,364** (£403; £201) **Stalls** Low

Form RPR
0242 **1** **Accamelia**[13] 7300 4-9-1 54 PaulMulrennan 11 65
(C W Fairhurst) *trckd ldrs: hdwy 2f out: rdn over 1f out: styd on to ld last 100yds* **8/1**[3]
6241 **2** *nk* **Desert Strike**[4] 7425 4-9-0 60 6ex (p) NoraLooby(7) 13 70
(A J McCabe) *racd wd: in tch: hdwy nr stands' rails 2f out: rdn to chse ldrs over 1f out: ev ch ins fnl f: kpt on* **7/1**[2]
5030 **3** *½* **Cape Of Storms**[192] 1929 7-9-5 58 (b) TomEaves 5 66
(R Brotherton) *led: rdn along 2f out: drvn over 1f out: hdd and no ex last 100yds* **14/1**
1360 **4** *1 ¼* **Bravely (IRE)**[30] 6965 6-9-5 58 (e) RobertWinston 12 62
(T D Easterby) *chsd ldr: cl up wl over 2f out: rdn and ev ch over 1f out: drvn and one pce fnl f* **14/1**
1022 **5** *1 ½* **Nicholas Pocock (IRE)**[18] 7214 4-9-7 60 PhillipMakin 4 60
(B Ellison) *chsd ldrs: rdn along over 2f out: drvn and edgd lft wl over 1f out: no imp* **4/1**[1]

0000 **6** ¾ **Lujiana**[81] 5482 5-9-4 57 JoeFanning 8 54
(M Brittain) *chsd ldrs: rdn along wl over 2f out: drvn over 1f out and no imp* **10/1**

0422 **7** ¾ **Best Known Secret (IRE)**[11] 7328 4-8-2 48 RichardRowe(7) 14 43
(C C Bealby) *towards rr: hdwy over 2f out: swtchd rt and rdn wl over 1f out: kpt on: nrst fin* **8/1**[3]

0405 **8** ¾ **Boundless Applause**[22] 7131 4-8-7 46 oh1 CathyGannon 6 38
(I A Wood) *towards rr: rdn along 1/2-way: kpt on 2f out: nvr rchd ldrs* **50/1**

5-00 **9** 2¼ **Italian Dame**[22] 7132 4-8-7 46 oh1 (t) ChrisCatlin 10 31
(J R Turner) *wnt lft s: bhd tl sme late hdwy* **100/1**

4003 **10** ¾ **Espy**[38] 6741 5-9-4 57 PatrickMathers 2 40
(I W McInnes) *s.i.s: a towards rr* **20/1**

5460 **11** shd **Elkhorn**[71] 5817 8-8-7 46 (b) LiamJones 1 28
(Julie Camacho) *midfield: rdn along on inner 1/2-way: n.d* **25/1**

0000 **12** 1½ **Stonecrabstomorrow (IRE)**[45] 6577 7-8-11 55 MarkCoumbe(5) 7 33
(D Bourton) *a towards rr* **9/1**

1310 **13** 1¾ **Angaric (IRE)**[61] 6110 7-9-0 60 AdamCarter(7) 3 32
(B Smart) *prom on inner: rdn along 1/2-way: sn wknd* **11/1**

0053 **14** 7 **Athaakeel (IRE)**[11] 7336 4-9-7 60 LukeMorris 9 10
(R A Harris) *dwlt and sltly hmpd s: a bhd* **12/1**

1m 16.02s (-0.48) **Going Correction** -0.15s/f (Stan) 14 Ran SP% **114.7**
Speed ratings (Par 101): **97,96,95,94,92 91,90,89,86,85 85,83,80,71**
toteswingers:1&2:£11.30, 1&3:£14.80, 2&3:£18.40 CSF £57.96 CT £791.76 TOTE £15.60: £4.10, £2.30, £5.90; EX 82.90 TRIFECTA Not won..
Owner North Cheshire Trading & Storage Ltd **Bred** North Cheshire Trading And Storage Ltd **Trained** Middleham Moor, N Yorks

FOCUS
A moderate handicap. The time was 0.39 seconds quicker than the second leg, but slower than the Class 6 nursery won by the improving Shostakovich. The form is rated around the second and third.

7469 SOUTHWELL GOLF CLUB NURSERY 6f (F)
12:50 (12:50) (Class 6) (0-60,60) 2-Y-O £1,706 (£503; £252) Stalls Low

Form RPR

3501 **1** **Shostakovich (IRE)**[5] 7404 2-9-3 56 6ex (p) JamesDoyle 5 78
(S Kirk) *in tch: hdwy to ld wl over 2f out: rdn clr wl over 1f out: rdn out* **11/10**[1]

040 **2** 9 **Ace Master**[21] 7150 2-8-12 51 CathyGannon 11 46
(S R Bowring) *trckd ldrs: pushed along 1/2-way: hdwy to chse wnr wl over 1f out: sn drvn and kpt on: no ch w wnr* **14/1**

2533 **3** 2 **Regal Bullet (IRE)**[27] 7016 2-9-3 56 SamHitchcott 7 45
(D K Ivory) *in tch: hdwy over 2f out: rdn wl over 1f out: kpt on same pce* **11/2**[2]

4304 **4** 1¼ **Je Suis Unrockstar**[27] 7016 2-9-2 55 (p) PJMcDonald 12 40
(D Nicholls) *chsd ldrs: rdn over 2f out: drvn and edgd lft wl over 1f out and sn no imp* **13/2**[3]

0405 **5** 2 **Glenns Princess**[62] 6072 2-8-12 51 (b) PaulMulrennan 8 30
(R A Fahey) *in tch: rdn along wl over 2f out: n.d* **16/1**

0003 **6** 1¼ **Henrys Air**[6] 7395 2-9-3 56 WilliamCarson 14 32
(D G Bridgwater) *chsd ldrs on outer: rdn along 1/2-way: drvn and outpcd 2f out* **8/1**

0006 **7** nk **Kyncraighe (IRE)**[8] 7379 2-9-7 60 FergusSweeney 6 35
(A J Lidderdale) *led 2f: cl up tl rdn along wl over 2f out and sn wknd* **25/1**

0000 **8** ¾ **Vienna Woods (IRE)**[42] 6645 2-9-0 53 PhillipMakin 2 25
(B M R Haslam) *a towards rr* **50/1**

200 **9** 2¾ **Alantina**[95] 5047 2-8-0 46 DannyBrock(7) 1 —
(J R Jenkins) *s.i.s: a bhd* **22/1**

000 **10** 7 **Skiddaw View**[15] 7269 2-8-8 47 RobertWinston 4 —
(A D Brown) *a in rr: wd st and bhd fr over 2f out* **50/1**

0035 **11** ½ **Look'N'Listen (IRE)**[95] 5042 2-9-0 53 GrahamGibbons 3 —
(A D Brown) *cl up on inner: led after 2f: rdn along and hdd wl over 2f out: sn drvn and wknd* **22/1**

1m 15.73s (-0.77) **Going Correction** -0.15s/f (Stan) 11 Ran SP% **116.5**
Speed ratings (Par 94): **99,87,84,82,80 78,77,76,73,63 63**
toteswingers:1&2:£7.40, 1&3:£2.60, 2&3:£11.80 CSF £17.07 CT £62.89 TOTE £2.30: £1.10, £4.50, £1.40; EX 21.30 Trifecta £754.50 Pool: £1,152.20 - 1.13 winning units..
Owner Dr J Wilson & S Kirk **Bred** Marchwood Aggregates **Trained** Upper Lambourn, Berks
■ Stewards' Enquiry : James Doyle caution: used whip when clearly winning.
Robert Winston three-day ban: weighed in 2lb heavy (Nov 30,Dec 1-2)

FOCUS
A moderate contest, but Shostakovich showed himself better than this grade with a resounding victory. The time backs up the visual impression, being quicker than both divisions of the 46-60 older-horse handicap; the form looks solid and the winner could be rated a shade higher.

NOTEBOOK
Shostakovich(IRE) ◆'s first success was gained in a seller over C&D the previous week, but he's a good looker and is very much on the upgrade now. Officially 4lb well in, he raced up with a contested lead and carried his head at a bit of angle for most of the contest, but still readily outclassed this lot. He's 2-2 since being fitted with cheekpieces and switched to Fibresand, and there's more to come if he can go the right way mentally. (op 11-8)
Ace Master, switched to Fibresand for the first time on his nursery debut, was no match at all for an above-average type for the level. (op 16-1)
Regal Bullet(IRE) did not improve for the step up in trip and switch to Fibresand.. Official explanation: jockey said gelding hung right (op 7-1 tchd 8-1)
Je Suis Unrockstar, debuting for a new trainer, did not improve for the return to 6f and switch to Fibresand. (op 5-1 tchd 7-1)
Glenns Princess was well held on her first Fibresand start after a two-month break.

7470 BETDAQ THE BETTING EXCHANGE MEDIAN AUCTION MAIDEN STKS 1m (F)
1:20 (1:21) (Class 5) 2-Y-O £2,590 (£770; £385; £192) Stalls Low

Form RPR

1 **Ibn Bajjah (FR)** 2-9-3 0 TedDurcan 11 80+
(Saeed Bin Suroor) *trckd ldrs: hdwy over 3f out: chal over 2f out: rdn to ld wl over 1f out: edgd lft and clr ins fnl f* **13/8**[1]

0 **2** 6 **Frosty Friday**[12] 7311 2-8-12 0 FergusSweeney 8 62
(J R Jenkins) *a.p: led wl over 2f out: rdn and hdd wl over 1f out: kpt on same pce* **16/1**

04 **3** 2 **Ice Nelly (IRE)**[20] 7163 2-8-12 0 ChrisCatlin 9 58+
(H Morrison) *towards rr: swtchd outside and pushed along over 2f out: rdn to chse ldrs wl over 1f out: sn one pce* **7/2**[2]

05 **4** 1¼ **Szabo's Destiny**[11] 7325 2-9-3 0 PaulMulrennan 13 59
(J G Given) *in tch on wd outside: hdwy 3f out: rdn to chse ldrs 2f out: drvn over 1f out and kpt on same pce* **50/1**

003 **5** 1¼ **X Rated**[11] 7325 2-9-3 72 JamesDoyle 5 56
(A J McCabe) *led: rdn along 3f out: sn hdd: drvn and grad wknd fnl 2f* **4/1**[3]

000 **6** 2½ **Bodie**[81] 5498 2-9-3 0 MickyFenton 4 51
(Mrs P Sly) *trckd ldrs: hdwy 1/2-way: rdn to chse ldrs over 2f out: drvn wl over 1f out and grad wknd* **66/1**

00 **7** 1 **Waterford Star (IRE)**[20] 7172 2-9-3 0 JoeFanning 10 48+
(M Johnston) *rdn along: outpcd and bhd after 2f: sme hdwy on inner 2f out: nvr a factor* **12/1**

630 **8** ¾ **Escala**[24] 7098 2-8-12 67 WilliamCarson 2 41
(M D Squance) *cl up: rdn along 1/2-way: drvn 3f out and sn wknd* **15/2**

000 **9** 1¼ **Final Liberation (FR)**[13] 7303 2-9-3 0 StevieDonohoe 1 44
(Sir Mark Prescott) *sn rdn along and a in rr* **100/1**

0 **10** 5 **Bobby Dazzler (IRE)**[33] 6874 2-9-3 0 DavidProbert 3 32
(S Kirk) *dwlt: a in rr: bhd fr 1/2-way* **25/1**

00 **11** 4 **The Absent Mare**[28] 7000 2-8-12 0 (t) AndreaAtzeni 7 18
(F Sheridan) *chsd ldrs 2f: sn lost pl and bhd fnl 3f* **125/1**

00 **12** 1 **Melody Belle (IRE)**[17] 7232 2-8-9 0 (t) SophieDoyle(3) 12 16
(T B P Coles) *a in rr: bhd fnl 3f* **100/1**

1m 42.43s (-1.27) **Going Correction** -0.15s/f (Stan) 12 Ran SP% **115.7**
Speed ratings (Par 96): **100,94,92,90,89 87,86,85,84,79 75,74**
toteswingers:1&2:£8.90, 1&3:£2.60, 2&3:£8.00 CSF £30.70 TOTE £2.00: £1.10, £4.90, £2.20; EX 33.40 Trifecta £43.10 Pool: £366.10 - 2.62 winning units..
Owner Godolphin **Bred** Darley Stud Management Co Ltd **Trained** Newmarket, Suffolk

FOCUS
Put simply, Ibn Bajjah outclassed some modest rivals, enhancing his trainer's outstanding record on the Southwell Fibresand in the last five seasons to 8-17. The winner made a good start and can step up on this, while the sixth, seventh and ninth set the level.

NOTEBOOK
Ibn Bajjah(FR), a Derby entrant who's a half-brother to several winners, was never seriously challenged despite being inclined to edge left under pressure in the straight. It's impossible to know how good he may be, but he has the scope to make a useful type at least. (op 11-10, tchd 15-8 in a place)
Frosty Friday hinted at ability on her debut over 7f on Polytrack and seemed to step up a little, albeit she was no match at all for the winner. (op 20-1)
Ice Nelly(IRE) wasn't best away and got going much too late to threaten. Handicaps are now an option. (op 4-1)
Szabo's Destiny was well held, but still reversed recent C&D form with the disappointing X Rated. (op 100-1)
X Rated had offered encouragement last time, but this was a step backwards and, being quite a big 2-y-o, perhaps he's had enough for the time being. (op 5-1 tchd 7-2)

7471 INTRINSIC FINANCIAL SERVICE (S) STKS 7f (F)
1:50 (1:50) (Class 6) 2-Y-O £1,706 (£503; £252) Stalls Low

Form RPR

4000 **1** **Face The Future**[32] 6891 2-8-12 52 (p) PhillipMakin 1 58
(M Dods) *dwlt: sn trcking ldrs on inner: led 4f out: rdn 2f out: drvn over 1f out: hld on gamely* **9/1**

4442 **2** shd **Ivan's A Star (IRE)**[62] 6082 2-8-12 57 (p) LukeMorris 2 58
(J S Moore) *trckd ldrs: hdwy on inner 3f out: rdn to chal 2f out: hung rt over 1f out: sn drvn and edgd lft ins fnl f: ev ch tl no ex nr fin* **10/3**[2]

060 **3** 3¼ **Patricia's Hope**[46] 6521 2-8-7 52 (t[1]) LiamJones 6 45
(P W D'Arcy) *chsd ldrs: rdn along and outpcd 3f out: swtchd outside and drvn wl over 1f out: styd on ins fnl f* **18/1**

0030 **4** 1¼ **Neytiri**[20] 7177 2-8-7 58 RichardKingscote 3 41
(R M Beckett) *led 3f: rdn along 3f out: drvn over 2f out and sn one pce* **4/1**[3]

5020 **5** 1¾ **Bernisdale**[32] 6891 2-8-7 64 JoeFanning 4 38
(G M Moore) *chsd ldrs: rdn along over 2f out: n.d* **4/1**[3]

0660 **6** 1 **Dunmore Boy (IRE)**[29] 6978 2-8-12 59 TomEaves 7 39
(R A Fahey) *prom: chsd wnr 1/2-way: rdn along 3f out: sn drvn and wknd fnl 2f* **3/1**[1]

5000 **7** 5 **Amore Et Labore**[24] 7088 2-8-12 50 DavidProbert 9 28
(S Kirk) *prom: rdn along 1/2-way: sn wknd* **20/1**

8 13 **Bahri Beat (IRE)** 2-8-12 0 ChrisCatlin 5 —
(J R Norton) *s.i.s: a bhd* **40/1**

0000 **P** **Sarojini**[15] 7269 2-8-2 40 (p) BillyCray(5) 8 —
(D Nicholls) *s.i.s: a in rr: bhd whn p.u over 1f out: dismntd* **28/1**

1m 30.23s (-0.07) **Going Correction** -0.15s/f (Stan) 9 Ran SP% **114.0**
Speed ratings (Par 94): **94,93,90,88,86 85,79,65,—**
toteswingers:1&2:£4.60, 1&3:£16.30, 2&3:£6.10 CSF £37.82 TOTE £8.90: £3.70, £1.10, £7.10; EX 32.20 TRIFECTA Not won..There was no bid for the winner.
Owner Face The Future Partnership **Bred** Brook Stud Bloodstock Ltd **Trained** Denton, Co Durham

FOCUS
An ordinary seller that is straightforward to rate with the winner to his best.

NOTEBOOK
Face The Future offered nothing in blinkers and a tongue-tie at Redcar on his previous start, but proved well suited by the fitting of cheekpieces and switch to Fibresand, gaining his first success at the sixth attempt. He's got a long way to go to justify his 72,000gns price tag, but seemed to run above his official mark of 52 seeing as he had something to find at the weights with the next five finishers. (op 11-1 tchd 17-2)
Ivan's A Star(IRE), trying Fibresand for the first time after two months off, ruined his chance by continually hanging left in the straight, racing towards the often unfavoured far rail. He doesn't look one to rely on. (op 4-1)
Patricia's Hope, fitted with an eye-shield and a tongue-tie for the first time on her Fibresand debut, was given a positive ride but didn't see her race out. (op 16-1)
Neytiri ran some way below her official mark of 58 on her Fibresand debut and is going the wrong way. (op 7-2)
Bernisdale ran poorly for the second race in succession. (tchd 9-2)
Dunmore Boy(IRE) seemingly didn't take to the Fibresand. (tchd 11-4)
Sarojini Official explanation: jockey said filly lost its action but returned sound

7472 BETDAQ ON 08701781221 (S) STKS 1m (F)
2:20 (2:20) (Class 6) 3-Y-O+ £1,706 (£503; £252) Stalls Low

Form RPR

1304 **1** **April Fool**[5] 7403 6-9-6 70 (v) TomMcLaughlin 12 72
(R A Harris) *mde all: rdn clr over 1f out: kpt on* **4/7**[1]

3006 **2** 2¼ **Special Cuvee**[11] 7327 4-9-0 55 (bt) CathyGannon 11 61
(Mrs A M Thorpe) *s.i.s: towards rr: hdwy over 3f out: rdn over 2f out: styd on appr fnl f: nrst fin* **6/1**[2]

0000 **3** shd **White Deer (USA)**[31] 6917 6-8-11 58 (p) MichaelO'Connell(3) 6 61
(G A Harker) *prom: rdn along 1/2-way: drvn to chse wnr over 1f out: sn drvn: edgd rt and one pce* **13/2**[3]

0014 **4** 7 **Toby Tyler**[22] 7125 4-9-6 62 (v) MickyFenton 8 50
(P T Midgley) *trckd ldrs: hdwy 1/2-way: effrt to chal over 2f out: sn rdn and wknd over 1f out* **6/1**[2]

000/ **5** ¾ **Flaxton (UAE)**[707] 7619 5-8-7 44 JohnCavanagh(7) 1 43
(M Brittain) *cl up on inner: rdn along 3f out: drvn over 2f out and grad wknd* **28/1**

005- 6 20 **Fairys In A Storm (IRE)**537 2414 3-8-1 45 ow1......... ShaneBKelly(7) 5 —
(A J Lockwood) *a in rr: bhd fnl 3f* **20/1**

0/00 7 4 **Bottomless Wallet**14 7282 9-8-9 45.................................... TomEaves 4 —
(F Watson) *in tch: rdn along 1/2-way: sn wknd: bhd fnl 3f* **50/1**

050 8 3/4 **Mr Shammie**57 6255 3-8-9 8.. KellyHarrison(3) 2 —
(M G Quinlan) *towards rr: bhd fnl 3f* **80/1**

1m 42.44s (-1.26) **Going Correction** -0.15s/f (Stan)
WFA 3 from 4yo+ 2lb 8 Ran SP% **117.0**
Speed ratings (Par 101): **100,97,97,90,89 69,65,65**
toteswingers:1&2:£2.60, 1&3:£3.00, 2&3:£3.80 CSF £4.54 TOTE £1.30: £1.02, £1.70, £2.30; EX 4.70 Trifecta £14.70 Pool: £479.77 - 24.15 winning units..There was no bid for the winner.
Owner G B Balding **Bred** Miss B Swire **Trained** Earlswood, Monmouths
■ Stewards' Enquiry : Michael O'Connell caution: careless riding.

FOCUS
A weak and uncompetitive seller and the winner faced a straightforward task.
Special Cuvee Official explanation: jockey said gelding missed the break

7473 SOUTHWELL-RACECOURSE.CO.UK H'CAP (DIV II) 6f (F)
2:50 (2:52) (Class 6) (0-60,60) 3-Y-0+ £1,364 (£403; £201) Stalls Low

Form RPR

4040 1 **Final Salute**22 7131 4-8-8 54......................................(v) AdamCarter(7) 14 61
(B Smart) *chsd ldrs on wd outside: hdwy and cl up over 2f out: rdn to ld over 1f out: drvn ins fnl f: hld on gamely* **16/1**

0010 2 nse **Takajan (IRE)**5 7402 3-9-7 60.................................. TomMcLaughlin 13 67
(W M Brisbourne) *prom: hdwy on outer and cl up over 2f out: sn led: rdn and hdd over 1f out: drvn ins fnl f and ev ch tl edgd rt and no ex nr line* **10/1**

0636 3 shd **Adam De Beaulieu (USA)**11 7331 3-9-7 60.................(t) PhillipMakin 9 67
(B M R Haslam) *trckd ldrs: hdwy over 2f out: rdn and ev ch over 1f out: drvn ins fnl f: no ex nr fin* **7/2**2

0300 4 1 1/4 **Novastasia (IRE)**30 6956 4-8-7 46 oh1......................(b1) SamHitchcott 6 49
(D K Ivory) *hld up: towards rr: hdwy on inner wl over 2f out: rdn to chse ldrs wl over 1f out: drvn and kpt on same pce fnl f* **50/1**

-001 5 1 1/4 **Senate Majority**11 7328 3-9-7 60.............................. DuranFentiman 10 59
(T D Easterby) *prom: hdwy to chal over 2f out: sn rdn and ev ch tl drvn and wknd ent fnl f* **2/1**1

5400 6 hd **Exceedingly Good (IRE)**13 7300 4-8-11 50.............. CathyGannon 12 48
(S R Bowring) *towards rr: hdwy 2f out: sn rdn and styd on fnl f: nrst fin* **14/1**

0000 7 3 **Lethal**6 7391 7-9-2 58.. AndrewHeffernan(3) 4 47
(R J Price) *chsd ldrs: rdn along over 2f out: sn wknd* **8/1**3

5100 8 1 1/2 **Darcy's Pride (IRE)**5 7402 6-9-4 57............................ PaulMulrennan 1 41
(P T Midgley) *led: rdn along wl over 2f out: sn hdd & wknd* **16/1**

0600 9 1 **Fyodorovich (USA)**22 7131 5-8-0 46 oh1.................(v) NoraLooby(7) 11 27
(A J McCabe) *in tch: rdn along and n.m.r over 2f out: sn swtchd rt and wknd* **16/1**

6230 10 nk **Tobrata**81 5500 4-9-0 60.. JohnCavanagh(7) 8 40
(M Brittain) *bmpd sn after s: a in rr* **17/2**

3000 11 7 **Tag Team (IRE)**111 4478 9-8-9 48 ow1.....................(p) RobertWinston 5 5
(John A Harris) *cl up: rdn along wl over 2f out and sn wknd* **25/1**

0 12 1 1/4 **Suttonia (IRE)**31 6931 4-8-7 46 oh1.................................... ChrisCatlin 3 —
(Noel T Chance) *sn outpcd and a in rr* **33/1**

1m 16.41s (-0.09) **Going Correction** -0.15s/f (Stan) 12 Ran SP% **119.3**
Speed ratings (Par 101): **94,93,93,92,90 90,86,84,82,82 73,71**
toteswingers:1&2:£21.20, 1&3:£11.60, 2&3:£8.50 CSF £165.62 CT £710.38 TOTE £22.00: £5.50, £3.30, £2.00; EX 179.50 TRIFECTA Not won..
Owner Crossfields Racing & B Smart **Bred** Bricklow Ltd **Trained** Hambleton, N Yorks

FOCUS
The slower of the two divisions by 0.39 seconds. The winner is rated in line with this year's form.

7474 IT'S CHRISTMAS ALL YEAR ROUND H'CAP 1m (F)
3:20 (3:21) (Class 5) (0-70,69) 3-Y-0+ £2,266 (£674; £337; £168) Stalls Low

Form RPR

0600 1 **Mcconnell (USA)**57 6260 5-9-6 68.............................(b1) GeorgeBaker 5 80
(G L Moore) *trckd ldrs: smooth hdwy on inner over 2f out: rdn to chal over 1f out: led ins fnl f: rdn out* **13/8**1

3351 2 2 3/4 **Eastern Hills**22 7125 5-8-9 62..(p) NeilFarley(5) 1 68
(A J McCabe) *cl up: led over 4f out: rdn over 2f out: drvn over 1f out: hdd ins fnl f: kpt on same pce* **8/1**3

0030 3 1/2 **Florio Vincitore (IRE)**3 7438 3-9-1 68..................... AlanCreighton(3) 11 72
(E J Creighton) *prom: effrt over 2f out and sn cl up: rdn to chal wl over 1f out and ev ch tl drvn and one pce ins fnl f* **18/1**

03-6 4 1 **Gordy Bee (USA)**13 7307 4-9-5 67..............................(e) PaulEddery 14 70
(R C Guest) *trckd ldrs on outer: hdwy over 2f out: rdn wl over 1f out: kpt on same pce* **16/1**

0004 5 2 1/4 **San Antonio**14 7290 10-9-1 63.................................(b) MickyFenton 4 60
(Mrs P Sly) *chsd ldrs: rdn along over 2f out: drvn over 1f out and sn one pce* **22/1**

1000 6 1 1/2 **Border Owl (IRE)**25 7063 5-9-3 65.................................. GregFairley 6 59
(P Salmon) *chsd ldrs: rdn along 2f out: drvn wl over 1f out and sn no imp* **20/1**

6540 7 1 1/2 **Bel Cantor**6 7399 7-8-8 63..................................(p) MatthewCosham(7) 8 53
(W J H Ratcliffe) *sltly hmpd s and behnd: hdwy over 2f out: sn rdn and no imp* **16/1**

0115 8 4 **Astrodonna**25 7063 5-9-0 67...................................... AshleyMorgan(5) 3 48
(M H Tompkins) *towards rr: hdwy 1/2-way: rdn over 2f out: n.d* **11/1**

0000 9 6 **Jonnie Skull (IRE)**11 7336 4-8-9 57.............................(b) LukeMorris 13 24
(M D Squance) *led hdd over 4f out: rdn along over 3f out and sn wknd* **33/1**

10 1/2 **Pinsplitter (USA)**75 5705 3-9-4 68 ow1.........................(p) JamesDoyle 2 33
(A J McCabe) *chsd ldrs: rdn along 3f out: sn wknd* **40/1**

1004 11 7 **Royal Holiday (IRE)**22 7128 3-8-11 61............................ TomEaves 9 10
(B Ellison) *hmpd s: a in rr* **13/2**2

0040 12 2 1/4 **Ancient Times (USA)**55 5272 3-8-9 62............... RussKennemore(3) 10 6
(P A Kirby) *a in rr* **25/1**

0043 13 2 **Club Tahiti**13 7306 4-9-7 69.. DavidProbert 7 9
(A W Carroll) *a in rr* **13/2**2

0000 14 9 **Craicajack (IRE)**20 7184 3-8-6 56................................ CathyGannon 12 —
(E J Creighton) *a in rr* **50/1**

1m 41.84s (-1.86) **Going Correction** -0.15s/f (Stan)
WFA 3 from 4yo+ 2lb 14 Ran SP% **121.5**
Speed ratings (Par 103): **103,100,99,98,96 95,93,89,83,83 76,73,71,62**
toteswingers:1&2:£6.90, 1&3:£8.90, 2&3:£28.70 CSF £13.26 CT £188.01 TOTE £2.30: £1.10, £2.90, £5.70; EX 20.10 Trifecta £187.90 Pool: £424.26 - 1.67 winning units..
Owner B Siddle & B D Haynes **Bred** Hall Et Al Farm **Trained** Lower Beeding, W Sussex

FOCUS
A modest handicap but the time was relatively good. The second and fourth were close to their marks.
Bel Cantor Official explanation: jockey said horse suffered interference on leaving stalls
Club Tahiti Official explanation: jockey said filly did not face the kick back; vet said filly bled from the nose
Craicajack(IRE) Official explanation: jockey said gelding hung left

7475 BETDAQ.COM H'CAP 1m 4f (F)
3:50 (3:52) (Class 6) (0-60,60) 3-Y-0+ £1,706 (£503; £252) Stalls Low

Form RPR

0000 1 **Ramora (USA)**15 7270 4-9-1 56.................................... KylieManser(5) 2 65+
(Miss Olivia Maylam) *hld up in rr: gd hdwy on inner 5f out: trckd ldr 3f out: rdn to chal over 2f out: drvn to ld over 1f out: kpt on* **40/1**

0002 2 1/2 **Shifting Gold (IRE)**5 7407 4-9-2 55...........................(b) AmyRyan(3) 12 63
(K A Ryan) *sn chsng ldr: led 1/2-way: rdn along 3f out: jnd 2f out and sn drvn: hdd over 1f out: kpt on u.p fnl f* **5/1**3

5023 3 2 1/2 **Davana**6 7398 4-8-7 50...................................(p) MatthewCosham(7) 4 54
(W J H Ratcliffe) *chsd ldrs: hdwy 4f out: rdn along and sltly outpcd wl over 2f out: drvn and kpt on fnl f* **9/2**2

2500 4 1/2 **Jackie Kiely**96 4992 9-9-7 57..(tp) PhillipMakin 3 60
(R Brotherton) *hld up in rr: stdy hdwy over 3f out: rdn to chse ldng pair wl over 1f out: drvn and one pce ent fnl f* **16/1**

5000 5 6 **All Guns Firing (IRE)**17 7230 4-9-5 60.....................(b1) NeilFarley(5) 14 54
(D Carroll) *sn led and set str pce: hdd 1/2-way: rdn along over 4f out: drvn over 2f out and sn one pce* **16/1**

4362 6 1/2 **Dovedon Angel**26 7039 4-8-9 52.................................... JulieBurke(7) 9 45
(Miss Gay Kelleway) *hld up in rr: stdy hdwy over 4f out: chsd ldrs 3f out: rdn to chse ldng pair 2f out: sn drvn and wknd over 1f out* **10/3**1

0506 7 2 1/4 **Black Falcon (IRE)**6 7397 10-9-0 50..............................(p) RobertWinston 8 39
(John A Harris) *hld up in rr: hdwy 4f out: rdn and in tch over 2f out: sn drvn and btn* **20/1**

0-50 8 3/4 **Tallulah Mai**54 1059 3-9-1 57... LukeMorris 5 45
(Matthew Salaman) *in tch on inner: rdn along over 4f out: drvn 3f out and sn outpcd* **9/1**

3610 9 4 1/2 **Eijaaz (IRE)**14 7284 9-9-7 60..............................(p) MichaelO'Connell(3) 6 41
(G A Harker) *midfield: hdwy to chse ldrs over 5f out: rdn along over 3f out: sn wknd* **25/1**

6026 10 3 3/4 **Follow The Sun (IRE)**7 6518 6-9-2 52............................. PJMcDonald 13 27
(P D Niven) *chsd ldrs: rdn along over 4f out: sn wknd* **8/1**

-000 11 26 **Astrodiva**12 7323 4-9-0 55.. AshleyMorgan(5) 7 —
(M H Tompkins) *nvr bttr than midfield* **17/2**

0000 12 26 **Heliocentric**36 6794 3-9-4 60... DavidProbert 10 —
(B Palling) *prom: rdn along 1/2-way: sn wknd and bhd fnl 3f* **66/1**

2014 13 15 **Always Dixie (IRE)**56 6262 3-9-3 59................................ TomEaves 11 —
(A Crook) *in tch: rdn along after 4f: sn lost pl and bhd fr 1/2-way: t.o fnl 3f* **16/1**

2m 38.81s (-2.19) **Going Correction** -0.15s/f (Stan)
WFA 3 from 4yo+ 6lb 13 Ran SP% **119.8**
Speed ratings (Par 101): **101,100,99,98,94 94,92,92,89,86 69,52,42**
toteswingers:1&2:£39.90, 1&3:£46.50, 2&3:£5.40. Totesuper7: Win: Not won. Place: £151.60. CSF £226.27 CT £1108.88 TOTE £53.70: £30.60, £1.80, £2.30; EX 291.60 TRIFECTA Not won..
Owner Miss Olivia Maylam **Bred** Fred Seitz **Trained** Newmarket, Suffolk

FOCUS
A moderate handicap which was sound run. It has been rated around the third and fourth.
Ramora(USA) Official explanation: trainer said she had no explanation regarding the apparent improvement in form.
Black Falcon(IRE) Official explanation: jockey said gelding hung left and lost its action
T/Jkpt: Not won. T/Plt: £99.90 to a £1 stake. Pool:£57,911.34 - 423.16 winning tickets T/Qpdt: £13.80 to a £1 stake. Pool:£6,561.75 - 349.80 winning tickets JR

7384 KEMPTON (A.W) (R-H)
Wednesday, November 17

OFFICIAL GOING: Standard
Wind: Fresh, half behind Weather: Overcast, mostly raining from Race 3 onwards

7476 BOXINGDAYRACES.CO.UK APPRENTICE CLASSIFIED CLAIMING STKS 1m 2f (P)
4:10 (4:10) (Class 6) 3-Y-O £1,637 (£483; £241) Stalls High

Form RPR

3325 1 **Buona Sarah (IRE)**133 3789 3-8-13 64......................... NathanAlison(5) 6 73+
(J R Boyle) *hld up in 5th: prog to chse clr ldng pair over 2f out: readily clsd on inner over 1f out: led jst ins fnl f: pushed out* **6/1**

0303 2 1 1/4 **Florio Vincitore (IRE)**1 7474 3-8-13 68........... MatthewLawson(5) 1 70
(E J Creighton) *led: clr w one rival most of way: kicked on 3f out: hdd and one pce jst ins fnl f* **4/1**3

6600 3 6 **Starry Mount**34 6864 3-9-0 67..(p) BillyCray 3 54
(A B Haynes) *sn pushed along in 4th: rdn and struggling 3f out: kpt on fnl f to snatch modest 3rd post* **9/2**

5525 4 hd **Until The Man (IRE)**34 3714 3-9-4 67.......................(b1) MarcGoldstein 2 57
(Jim Best) *pressed ldr to over 1f out and mostly clr of rest: wknd fnl f: lost 3rd post* **10/3**1

0000 5 1 3/4 **Sea Tobougie**34 6871 3-8-8 45.. RyanPowell(3) 8 47
(M D I Usher) *hld up in last pair: pushed along 3f out: v modest late prog* **40/1**

6620 6 1 3/4 **Hill Tribe**4 7453 3-9-0 67... RossAtkinson 5 46
(R C Guest) *chsd clr ldng pair to over 2f out: hrd rdn and wknd over 1f out* **7/2**2

0500 7 1 1/2 **Aldorable**15 7288 3-8-9 41..(e1) JulieBurke(3) 4 41
(R A Teal) *stdd s: hld up in last pair: pushed along and no prog 3f out* **50/1**

0004 8 1 3/4 **Defence Of Realm (GER)**34 6871 3-9-3 59.............(p) DavidKenny(3) 7 46
(George Baker) *hld up in 6th: rdn 3f out: no prog 2f out: no ch after* **15/2**

2m 7.74s (-0.26) **Going Correction** 0.0s/f (Stan) 8 Ran SP% **113.9**
Speed ratings (Par 98): **101,100,95,95,93 92,91,89**
toteswingers:1&2 £6.00, 2&3 £4.90, 1&3 £6.70 CSF £29.95 TOTE £8.60: £2.10, £2.20, £1.90; EX 29.80.
Owner Mrs Pippa Boyle **Bred** Peter J Doyle Bloodstock Ltd **Trained** Epsom, Surrey

FOCUS
A moderate contest run at a decent enough gallop, courtesy of Florio Vincitore, who was chased by Until The Man, with the pair clear. The form is rated around the front two, but the fifth and sevent were close enough.

7477 KIA SPORTAGE H'CAP 5f (P)
4:40 (4:40) (Class 7) (0-50,50) 3-Y-0+ **£1,364** (£403; £201) **Stalls** High

Form RPR
0400 **1** **Bidruma**^{26} 7064 3-9-3 **50**........ NeilCallan 11 58
(Mike Murphy) *chsd ldng pair: rdn 1/2-way: wnt 2nd 1f out: hrd rdn and clsd to ld last strides* **4/1**^{2}
005 **2** *nk* **Francis Albert**^{32} 6931 4-8-10 **50**........(b) JosephYoung$^{(7)}$ 12 57
(M Mullineaux) *led: clr after 2f: stl 3 l up ent fnl f: sn c u.str.p: hdd last strides* **9/2**^{3}
3440 **3** *1 3/4* **Miss Polly Plum**^{14} 7300 3-8-12 **48**........(e^{1}) KellyHarrison$^{(3)}$ 9 49
(C A Dwyer) *chsd ldr: rdn 2f out: no imp and lost 2nd 1f out: clung on for 3rd* **5/2**^{1}
2600 **4** *hd* **Barraland**^{6} 7409 5-8-13 **49**........(v) MatthewDavies$^{(3)}$ 5 49+
(George Baker) *s.i.s: wl off the pce in last trio: c v wd bnd 2f out: styd on wl ins fnl f: nrly snatched 3rd* **12/1**
0053 **5** *shd* **Bluebok**^{42} 6665 9-8-13 **49**........(bt) RussKennemore$^{(3)}$ 4 49
(J M Bradley) *sn off the pce in 8th: rdn 2f out: kpt on fr over 1f out: nt gng pce to threaten* **12/1**
4000 **6** *3/4* **Mind The Monarch**^{14} 7299 3-8-10 **50**........(b^{1}) JulieBurke$^{(7)}$ 10 47
(R A Teal) *s.i.s: chsd ldrs in 5th but nt on terms: rdn 2f o ut: plugged on: n.d* **12/1**
5-0 **7** *2 1/4* **Jonny Ebeneezer**^{17} 7250 11-9-3 **50**........(be) StephenCraine 3 39
(D Flood) *settled last and wl off the pce: effrt 2f out: modest late prog: nvr a factor* **25/1**
5000 **8** *nk* **Suhayl Star (IRE)**^{17} 7250 6-9-3 **50**........ LukeMorris 7 38
(P Burgoyne) *chsd ldrs in 6th but nt on terms: rdn 1/2-way: brief effrt over 1f out: sn wknd* **14/1**
6600 **9** *1 1/4* **True Red (IRE)**^{39} 6746 3-8-12 **48**........(b) AndrewHeffernan$^{(3)}$ 6 31
(Mrs N S Evans) *racd wd in midfield: no prog over 1f out* **33/1**
004 **10** *nk* **Alana Banana (IRE)**^{42} 6665 3-9-3 **50**........ DaneO'Neill 1 32
(J Akehurst) *dwlt: mostly in last pair fr wd draw: forced v wd bnd 2f out: no ch after* **8/1**
1660 **11** *4 1/2* **Gleaming Spirit (IRE)**^{114} 4435 6-8-9 **49**........(v) LeonnaMayor$^{(7)}$ 8 15
(Peter Grayson) *chsd ldng trio to 2f out: wknd qckly* **33/1**

59.94 secs (-0.56) **Going Correction** 0.0s/f (Stan) **11** Ran SP% **117.3**
Speed ratings (Par 97): **104,103,100,100,100 99,95,94,92,92 85**
toteswingers:1&2 £3.80, 2&3 £3.00, 1&3 £3.30 CSF £21.89 CT £52.91 TOTE £3.40: £1.30, £3.60, £1.20; EX 26.00.
Owner The Chalfont Partnership **Bred** Ian H Stephenson **Trained** Westoning, Beds

FOCUS
A moderate sprint handicap in which a high draw was unsurprisingly a big advantage, with stall 11 beating 12 and 9. The form has been taken at face value.

7478 EUROPEAN BREEDERS' FUND MAIDEN STKS (DIV I) 7f (P)
5:10 (5:11) (Class 4) 2-Y-0 **£3,885** (£1,156; £577; £288) **Stalls** High

Form RPR
0P2 **1** **Indian Jack (IRE)**^{14} 7302 2-9-3 0........ LukeMorris 9 80+
(A Bailey) *t.k.h early: trckd ldr: shkn up to ld wl over 1f out: rdn and asserted ins fnl f* **9/2**
2 *1 1/2* **Hunter's Light (IRE)** 2-9-3 0........ TedDurcan 2 76
(Saeed Bin Suroor) *trckd ldng trio: shkn up 2f out: styd on to chse wnr last 100yds: no imp* **7/2**^{2}
0053 **3** *1 1/2* **Odin (IRE)**^{19} 7202 2-9-3 75........ RobertWinston 7 72
(D R C Elsworth) *trckd ldng quartet: urged along to cl 2f out: wnt 2nd jst over 1f out to last 100yds: nt qckn* **3/1**^{1}
4 *1 1/4* **Marie Rose** 2-8-12 0........ ShaneKelly 1 64+
(B J Meehan) *dwlt and swtchd to inner fr wd draw: hld up in 10th: prog over 2f out: shkn up and styd on to take 4th fnl f* **33/1**
5 *1 1/2* **Prince Of Burma (IRE)** 2-9-3 0........ RobertHavlin 3 66+
(J H M Gosden) *hld up in 9th and racd on outer: nudged along and kpt on steadily fnl 2f* **14/1**
05 **6** *nk* **Acclamatory**^{28} 7021 2-8-12 0........ WilliamCarson 10 59
(S C Williams) *chsd ldrs in 6th: swtchd lft over 2f out: no imp fr over 1f out* **40/1**
7 *nk* **Anna Fontenail** 2-8-12 0........ JamesMillman 8 58
(B R Millman) *hld up in 8th: pushed along and rn green over 2f out: kpt on steadily* **100/1**
43 **8** *1/2* **Coax**^{18} 7223 2-9-3 0........ JoeFanning 5 62
(M Johnston) *led to wl over 1f out: wknd* **4/1**^{3}
0 **9** *3/4* **Kublahara (IRE)**^{18} 7232 2-8-12 0........ JimmyFortune 12 54
(A M Balding) *trckd ldng pair: rdn to chal on inner 2f out: wknd over 1f out* **5/1**
0 **10** *11* **Emerald Royal**^{21} 7178 2-9-0 0........ AlanCreighton$^{(3)}$ 6 30
(E J Creighton) *dwlt: rousted along to rch 7th: rdn 3f out: sn wknd: t.o* **100/1**
11 *1/2* **Scarborough Lily** 2-8-12 0........ FergusSweeney 11 23
(E F Vaughan) *dwlt: a in last pair: t.o* **100/1**
0 **12** *2 1/2* **Strangelittlegirl**^{22} 7152 2-8-12 0........ StevieDonohoe 4 17
(P Leech) *a in last pair: t.o* **100/1**

1m 26.2s (0.20) **Going Correction** 0.0s/f (Stan) **12** Ran SP% **118.1**
Speed ratings (Par 98): **98,96,94,93,91 91,90,90,89,76 76,73**
toteswingers:1&2 £4.50, 2&3 £2.80, 1&3 £2.60 CSF £20.31 TOTE £7.90: £2.10, £1.40, £1.10; EX 27.60.
Owner Forza Azzurri **Bred** Waterford Hall Stud **Trained** Newmarket, Suffolk

FOCUS
Just a fair maiden, but one that's likely to produce a few winners. The pace was modest, and those prominent were at an advantage, yet the time was still 0.49 seconds quicker than the second division. The form is rated around the winner and third.

NOTEBOOK
Indian Jack(IRE) was pulled up after being struck into on his second start, but his efforts either side of that had been encouraging, the latest when second over 1m on heavy ground, and this was a straightforward success. The drop in trip and switch to Polytrack clearly didn't inconvenience him, and although he was a touch keen early on, he had been well placed and found plenty when asked. He should make a useful handicapper. (op 4-1)
Hunter's Light(IRE), who is out of a dual 1m2f winner, was a bit keen through the opening stages, racing close to the pace, but he stuck on in the straight. Many of his trainer's juveniles have been improving a good deal from their debuts this season and this one will warrant plenty of respect next time. (op 4-1)
Odin(IRE) produced an improved effort when third from the front over 7f at Newmarket last time but, returned to more patient tactics and back on Polytrack, he couldn't build on that performance. (op 11-4)
Marie Rose ◆ is a half-sister to 6f-7f winner Primaeval and 7f scorer Cigalas, out of a 6f Grade 2 juvenile winner in Australia. This debutant fared best of the fillies and also of those held up off the modest tempo. Dropped in from stall one, she never posed a threat, but kept on without being given a hard time. There should be plenty of improvement to come. (op 50-1)
Prince Of Burma(IRE) ◆, a 100,000euros first foal of a 6f-7f winner, caught the eye on debut, keeping on nicely without being given a hard time, having raced wide into the straight. A colt with a fluent action, quick surfaces are likely to suit best and he can do better. (op 16-1)
Acclamatory now has the option of handicaps, but although this was a respectable effort, it didn't look the sort of performance she'll improve significantly from in the short term. (op 33-1)
Anna Fontenail ◆, the first foal of a dual 1m4f winner, was not given a hard race, but kept on steadily and showed ability. She is likely to appreciate further in time and looks a nice enough long-term project.
Coax was allowed to set just an ordinary gallop, but his finishing effort was tame and this performance leaves him with much to prove, even with handicaps now an option.
Kublahara(IRE) was another not given a hard time in the straight and looks more of a handicap project. (op 7-1 tchd 8-1 in places)

7479 EUROPEAN BREEDERS' FUND MAIDEN STKS (DIV II) 7f (P)
5:40 (5:41) (Class 4) 2-Y-0 **£3,885** (£1,156; £577; £288) **Stalls** High

Form RPR
60 **1** **Run On Ruby (FR)**^{13} 7311 2-8-12 0........ TedDurcan 11 71
(D R Lanigan) *mde all: rdn and maintained gallop fnl 2f: unchal* **9/1**
640 **2** *2* **Sylas Ings**^{29} 6994 2-9-3 73........ IanMongan 8 71
(P M Phelan) *chsd wnr: rdn over 2f out: nt qckn and no imp: jst hld on for 2nd* **6/1**^{3}
0 **3** *shd* **Cape Classic (IRE)**^{19} 7201 2-9-3 0........ NeilCallan 4 71
(W J Haggas) *trckd ldng trio: wnt 3rd over 2f out: rdn and nt qckn wl over 1f out: kpt on ins fnl f: nrly snatched 2nd* **6/4**^{1}
4 *1* **Sleek Gold** 2-8-12 0........ ShaneKelly 9 63+
(B J Meehan) *hld up in 5th: pushed along over 2f out: kpt on steadily fr over 1f out: nrst fin* **12/1**
5 *2 1/4* **School For Scandal (IRE)** 2-9-3 0........ JoeFanning 10 62
(M Johnston) *chsd ldng pair to over 2f out: steadily fdd over 1f out* **5/1**^{2}
6 *1 3/4* **The Tichborne (IRE)** 2-9-3 0........ JackMitchell 5 57+
(R A Teal) *dwlt: hld up in last trio: pushed along over 2f out: kpt on: no threat* **66/1**
0 **7** *1 1/4* **Imperial Fong**^{18} 7232 2-8-12 0........ DaneO'Neill 3 49
(D R C Elsworth) *stdd s: hld up in abt 6th: pushed along and outpcd fr over 2f out* **7/1**
8 *6* **Icebuster** 2-9-3 0........ JamesMillman 1 38
(B R Millman) *v.s.a: a in last trio: nvr a factor* **50/1**
0 **9** *10* **Jackstown Road (IRE)**^{7} 7386 2-9-3 0........(b^{1}) RobertWinston 6 11
(D R C Elsworth) *dwlt and reluctant early: asked to play an active role and hung bdly lft bnds over 4f out and 3f out: sn bhd* **50/1**
0 **10** *nk* **Paradise Place**^{19} 7201 2-8-12 0........ JimmyFortune 2 —
(J Noseda) *in tch 4f: sn wknd and eased* **12/1**

1m 26.69s (0.69) **Going Correction** 0.0s/f (Stan) **10** Ran SP% **114.3**
Speed ratings (Par 98): **96,93,93,92,89 87,86,79,68,67**
toteswingers:1&2 £7.10, 2&3 £3.00, 1&3 £4.40 CSF £60.42 TOTE £20.30: £3.60, £2.30, £1.02; EX 43.50.
Owner Saif Ali & Saeed H Altayer **Bred** Victoria, Etienne & Julien Dubois **Trained** Newmarket, Suffolk

FOCUS
An ordinary maiden with Run On Ruby making all in a time 0.49 seconds slower than a modestly run first division. The bare form is pretty modest.

NOTEBOOK
Run On Ruby(FR) missed the break on her first two starts, but had still shown ability, indeed she was an eyecatcher over C&D last time when given a less than inspired ride by Chris Catlin, who wasn't at all hard on her. The filly had clearly benefited from those outings, soon being sent to the front after breaking much better on this occasion. Left alone in the lead, she ran on well and was never seriously threatened. (op 8-1 tchd 10-1)
Sylas Ings was unconvincing in second, for the fourth race in succession giving the impression this trip (even off an ordinary pace) stretched him. (op 13-2)
Cape Classic(IRE), a half-brother to the same owner and trainer's Diadem and Maurice de Gheest winner King's Apostle (didn't win until his fourth start), stepped up a good deal on for the form he showed when green on debut at Newmarket. He is, however, still a long way from the finished article. (op 2-1)
Sleek Gold, a half-sister to 1m2f winner Laish Ya Hajar and 6f scorer Muhajaar, out of a very smart 6f-7f juvenile winner, shaped nicely on debut. Much like her trainer's runner in the first division, she can do better. (op 11-1)
School For Scandal(IRE), a brother to 1m1f Polytrack winner Astound, didn't see his race out, but is entitled to come on for this. (op 4-1)
The Tichborne(IRE) ◆, an already gelded half-brother to 5f-6f winner Simpsons Mount, finished reasonably well from off the steady pace and clearly has ability. He can improve.
Icebuster Official explanation: jockey said gelding missed the break and hung left-handed

7480 DIGIBET CLAIMING STKS 1m 4f (P)
6:10 (6:11) (Class 6) 3-Y-0+ **£1,637** (£483; £241) **Stalls** Centre

Form RPR
1311 **1** **Talenti (IRE)**^{25} 7089 7-9-5 72........(t) DaneO'Neill 5 76
(Mrs Lawney Hill) *trckd ldrs: rdn over 2f out: struggling to cl tl styd on wl ins fnl f: led last strides* **13/8**^{1}
53/1 **2** *1/2* **Scary Movie (IRE)**^{251} 868 5-9-9 68........ RobertWinston 2 79
(D J Coakley) *trckd ldr: shkn up to ld over 2f out: jnd ins fnl f: hdd last strides* **11/2**^{3}
0420 **3** *1/2* **Kames Park (IRE)**^{12} 7337 8-9-7 70........ JimmyQuinn 3 76
(R C Guest) *stdd s: hld up in last pair: prog over 2f out: rdn to chal and upsides fnl f: nt qckn last 75yds* **7/2**^{2}
4050 **4** *2 1/2* **Turjuman (USA)**^{25} 7101 5-9-9 71........ StevieDonohoe 4 74
(W J Musson) *hld up in last pair: effrt on inner over 2f out: nt qckn over 1f out: one pce after* **11/2**^{3}
33-0 **5** *8* **Orbitor**^{26} 7062 4-9-7 71........(t) TedDurcan 6 59
(George Baker) *led: set slow pce for 2f and then stdy one: tried to kick on over 3f out: hdd over 2f out: wknd over 1f out* **9/1**
30-0 **6** *12* **Traphalgar (IRE)**^{149} 3278 5-9-4 77........ GeorgeBaker 1 37
(P D Evans) *trckd ldrs: rdn over 2f out: sn wknd: t.o* **9/1**

2m 40.19s (5.69) **Going Correction** 0.0s/f (Stan) **6** Ran SP% **111.1**
Speed ratings (Par 101): **81,80,80,78,73 65**
CSF £10.70 TOTE £3.70: £1.30, £1.80; EX 9.40.Talenti was claimed by D J Flood for £6,000.
Owner Alan Hill **Bred** Watership Down Stud **Trained** Aston Rowant, Oxon

FOCUS
A fair claimer, with 68 the lowest official rating on offer, but the pace, set by Orbitor, was steady and the time was over nine seconds above standard. Rather muddling form.

Traphalgar(IRE) Official explanation: jockey said gelding had no more to give

7481 DIGIBET.COM NURSERY 1m (P)
6:40 (6:41) (Class 2) 2-Y-O

£6,916 (£2,071; £1,035; £518; £258; £129) **Stalls** High

Form				RPR
1	**1**		**Burj Alzain (IRE)**[21] 7164 2-8-11 **77** NeilCallan 2 (G A Butler) *trckd ldng trio: drvn to cl on outer over 1f out: led last 150yds: r.o wl* **5/2**[2]	86+
11	**2**	1 1/4	**Pearl Arch (IRE)**[34] 6870 2-9-3 **83** (t) ShaneKelly 4 (B J Meehan) *sn trckd ldr: shkn up to ld narrowly 2f out: edgd lft over 1f out: hdd and one pce last 150yds* **11/10**[1]	89
641	**3**	1/2	**Whiplash Willie**[17] 7248 2-8-11 **77** JimmyFortune 7 (A M Balding) *sn settled in 3rd: rdn over 2f out: swtchd rt jst over 1f out: styd on: nt gng pce to chal* **9/1**	82
2241	**4**	1 1/2	**Top Care (USA)**[23] 7126 2-8-13 **79** GregFairley 8 (M Johnston) *chsd ldrs in 5th: rdn over 2f out: no imp tl kpt on ins fnl f to take 4th last stride* **7/1**[3]	80
2421	**5**	hd	**One Lucky Lady**[30] 6979 2-8-9 **75** MichaelHills 3 (B W Hills) *sn led at decent pce: narrowly hdd 2f out: fdd ins fnl f* **16/1**	76
5123	**6**	3	**Focail Maith**[13] 7317 2-9-3 **83** StevieDonohoe 6 (J Ryan) *hld up last: pushed along on inner over 2f out: one reminder over 1f out: nvr on terms* **16/1**	77
4235	**7**	5	**Barathea Dancer (IRE)**[18] 7236 2-8-8 **74** LukeMorris 5 (R A Teal) *t.k.h: hld up in last trio: pushed along over 2f out: sn lft bhd* **16/1**	57
6564	**8**	7	**Satin Love (USA)**[13] 7317 2-9-7 **87** (b[1]) JoeFanning 1 (M Johnston) *racd wd in last trio: pushed along over 2f out: sn lft wl bhd* **33/1**	53

1m 39.18s (-0.62) **Going Correction** 0.0s/f (Stan) **8** Ran SP% **119.3**
Speed ratings (Par 102): **103,101,101,99,99 96,91,84**
toteswingers:1&2 £1.10, 2&3 £5.70, 1&3 £3.50 CSF £5.89 CT £20.43 TOTE £3.90: £1.50, £1.10, £4.30; EX 7.10.
Owner Asaad Al Banwan **Bred** Shadwell Estate Company Limited **Trained** Newmarket, Suffolk

FOCUS
A good nursery run at a fair gallop. The first three are all improvers and the form makes sense.

NOTEBOOK
Burj Alzain(IRE) ◆ looked potentially well treated off a mark of 77, with the form of his C&D debut success boosted when the third-placed finisher won a nursery next time off 70, and so it proved. This was obviously tougher, but he again showed a likeable attitude, knuckling down well for pressure. He's still learning and is likely to improve again. (op 3-1)
Pearl Arch(IRE) ◆, a 6f turf maiden winner before landing a 7f nursery, ran an improved race on the figures, but the step up in trip didn't help. Raised 6lb, he was well placed throughout, but lacked the winner's stamina. This progressive colt can do better again back over shorter. (op 5-4 tchd 11-8 in places)
Whiplash Willie ◆ was trapped away behind the leader with little room early in the straight, and then after being switched left at the cutaway, he was again short of space around a furlong out. He still finished nicely when in the clear. This was an improvement on the form he showed when winning a Lingfield maiden last time and he very much gives the impression he'll progress again. His breeding suggest he could be quite useful over further in time. (tchd 10-1)
Top Care(USA) found this tougher than the Fibresand maiden he won on his previous start, but he showed he's going the right way. (op 6-1)
One Lucky Lady was up 7lb for her Pontefract success and found this company too hot. (op 20-1)

7482 DIGIBET CASINO CONDITIONS STKS 7f (P)
7:10 (7:10) (Class 3) 3-Y-O+ **£6,281** (£1,869; £934; £466) **Stalls** High

Form				RPR
5620	**1**		**Dream Eater (IRE)**[32] 6923 5-8-11 116 (t) JimmyFortune 7 (A M Balding) *hld up in 5th: stl there and plenty to do over 1f out: rdn and str run ins fnl f to ld last two strides* **5/4**[1]	104+
5013	**2**	nk	**Beauchamp Viceroy**[62] 6123 6-9-5 105 (b) DaneO'Neill 4 (G A Butler) *led: wound pce up fr 1/2-way: drvn over 1f out: styd on: collared last strides* **12/1**	111
3424	**3**	1	**Golden Desert (IRE)**[26] 7060 6-8-11 102 NeilCallan 2 (R A Mills) *t.k.h: trckd ldng trio: hanging and nt qckn 2f out: styd on ins fnl f after wnr flew past* **9/1**	100
2404	**4**	3/4	**Iver Bridge Lad**[11] 7348 3-8-10 105 (b) MichaelHills 6 (J Ryan) *rrd s: hld up last: pushed along and no prog over 2f out: rdn and r.o ins fnl f: nrst fin* **9/2**[3]	97+
4126	**5**	shd	**Invisible Man**[73] 5803 4-8-11 108 (b) TedDurcan 3 (Saeed Bin Suroor) *chsd ldr: rdn 2f out: no imp over 1f out: lost 2nd jst ins fnl f: one pce* **7/2**[2]	98
0000	**6**	1/2	**Atlantic Story (USA)**[115] 4413 8-9-5 108 (bt) GrahamGibbons 8 (M W Easterby) *trckd ldng pair: effrt on inner 2f out: pushed into 2nd jst ins fnl f: stl jst pushed and fdd last 100yds* **16/1**	105
6003	**7**	4	**Global City (IRE)**[58] 6241 4-8-11 102 (t) JoeFanning 1 (Saeed Bin Suroor) *stdd s: t.k.h: hld up in rr: shkn up over 2f out: nt qckn and sn btn* **16/1**	86

1m 25.17s (-0.83) **Going Correction** 0.0s/f (Stan)
WFA 3 from 4yo+ 1lb **7** Ran SP% **111.4**
Speed ratings (Par 107): **104,103,102,101,101 100,96**
toteswingers:1&2 £2.00, 2&3 £8.60, 1&3 £3.40 CSF £17.15 TOTE £2.60: £1.70, £9.70; EX 16.80.
Owner J C Smith **Bred** Stone Ridge Farm **Trained** Kingsclere, Hants

FOCUS
A good race but the pace was steady and the bare form is misleading. The form is rated around the runner-up and the winner is better than the bare figure.

NOTEBOOK
Dream Eater(IRE) had 19lb in hand over the runner-up at the weights but, unsurprisingly considering how the race unfolded, he ran nowhere near his official rating. The steady pace was no help at all to Jimmy Fortune, but the jockey remained determined to produce this tricky customer as late as possible. He was still sitting a good 3l off the runner-up with a furlong to run and the tactics were spot on. Despite carrying his head high when finally asked, Andrew Balding's runner had the necessary class to grab the long-time leader near the line. The winner is just 3-28, which is poor for a horse placed seven times in Group company, including at the highest level when third behind Goldikova in this season's Queen Anne. He might gain some confidence from this, and could go for the Hong Kong Mile if getting an invitation, while Dubai is said to be on the agenda next year, but he still doesn't appeal as one to follow. (op 11-8)
Beauchamp Viceroy, who was worst off at the weights on his return from a two-month break, was allowed to set a steady pace and, as such, is flattered.
Golden Desert(IRE) had recorded his top ten RPRs in double-figure fields. This type of race was no use to him and he compromised his chance by racing keenly, but he still performed with credit. (op 11-1)
Iver Bridge Lad reared as the stalls opened and was soon off the steady pace. He ran on, but would have preferred a stronger gallop. (op 7-2)
Invisible Man, returning from 73 days off, was well placed, but found disappointingly little for pressure. All four of his wins have been gained over 1m on turf. (tchd 4-1)
Atlantic Story(USA), back on his favoured surface, travelled well on his return from a 115-day break but found little when asked. (op 25-1)
Global City(IRE) raced without cover and pulled too hard.

7483 RACING AT SKYSPORTS.COM H'CAP 7f (P)
7:40 (7:41) (Class 5) (0-70,70) 3-Y-O+ **£2,286** (£675; £337) **Stalls** High

Form				RPR
2-05	**1**		**Tuxedo**[37] 6800 5-9-6 69 LukeMorris 13 (P W Hiatt) *hld up in tch: rousted along and prog fr 2f out to ld over 1f out: in command after: rdn out* **7/2**[1]	81+
4104	**2**	1 1/4	**Piquante**[19] 7209 4-9-0 66 KellyHarrison(3) 7 (N Tinkler) *t.k.h: hld up towards rr: prog 2f out: nt clr run briefly over 1f out: styd on to take 2nd ins fnl f: unable to chal* **11/1**	73
1600	**3**	1 1/4	**Hinton Admiral**[13] 7319 6-9-4 70 MichaelStainton(3) 14 (P Howling) *t.k.h: hld up towards rr: looking for room over 2f out: prog over 1f out: tk 3rd and styd on same pce fnl f* **25/1**	74
6300	**4**	nse	**Dvinsky (USA)**[7] 7391 9-9-2 65 (b) TomMcLaughlin 6 (P Howling) *pressed ldr: led 2f out to over 1f out: one pce fnl f* **25/1**	68
632	**5**	nk	**Sunset Kitty (USA)**[13] 7310 3-9-3 67 TedDurcan 4 (W R Swinburn) *t.k.h: hld up in rr on outer: rdn over 2f out: no prog tl r.o fnl f: nrst fin* **13/2**[3]	69+
0022	**6**	3/4	**Harting Hill**[15] 7290 5-9-2 65 GeorgeBaker 10 (M P Tregoning) *trckd ldrs: produced to chal over 1f out: fnd little and sn btn: lame* **4/1**[2]	66+
0005	**7**	1/2	**Gallantry**[15] 7290 8-9-7 70 JimmyQuinn 3 (P Howling) *dwlt: hld up wl in rr: prog on inner over 2f out: no imp on ldrs over 1f out: one pce* **20/1**	69
0602	**8**	1 3/4	**Gazboolou**[18] 7241 6-9-6 69 FergusSweeney 2 (David Pinder) *pressed ldng pair: rdn jst over 2f out: one pce and lost pl over 1f out* **14/1**	64
354	**9**	3/4	**Copperwood**[27] 7047 5-9-5 68 DaneO'Neill 5 (M Blanshard) *racd on outer in midfield: nt qckn over 2f out: no prog after* **9/1**	61
0000	**10**	2 1/2	**Hurricane Hymnbook (USA)**[21] 7182 5-9-7 70 StevieDonohoe 8 (W J Musson) *sltly awkward s: detached in last most of way: suddenly r.o ins fnl f: fin wl* **8/1**	56
6600	**11**	1/2	**Fivefold (USA)**[13] 7320 3-9-6 70 J-PGuillambert 12 (J Akehurst) *t.k.h early: hld up in last trio: shkn up and no prog over 2f out* **16/1**	53
0000	**12**	11	**Kalypso King (USA)**[25] 7090 3-9-6 70 JimmyFortune 9 (S Kirk) *t.k.h: hld up in midfield: wknd rapidly over 2f out: t.o* **20/1**	24
100	**13**	2 3/4	**Yes We Can**[25] 7093 3-9-1 65 SteveDrowne 1 (J R Gask) *gd spd fr outside draw to ld: hdd 2f out: wknd rapidly over 1f out: eased: t.o* **16/1**	11

1m 25.21s (-0.79) **Going Correction** 0.0s/f (Stan)
WFA 3 from 4yo+ 1lb **13** Ran SP% **120.6**
Speed ratings (Par 103): **104,102,101,101,100 99,99,97,96,93 93,80,77**
toteswingers:1&2 £14.90, 2&3 £95.00, 1&3 £31.60 CSF £40.48 CT £861.81 TOTE £7.30: £3.20, £6.30, £11.70; EX 43.60.
Owner Phil Kelly **Bred** Gainsborough Stud Management Ltd **Trained** Hook Norton, Oxon

FOCUS
A modest but competitive handicap, and the form looks pretty solid.
Harting Hill Official explanation: jockey said gelding was lame behind
Yes We Can Official explanation: jockey said filly had no more to give
T/Plt: £30.50 to a £1 stake.Pool of £55,293.35 - 1,319.56 winning tickets. T/Qpdt: £7.10 to a £1 stake. Pool of £8,557.04 - 891.18 winning tickets JN

7438 LINGFIELD (L-H)
Wednesday, November 17

OFFICIAL GOING: Standard
Wind: medium, half behind Weather: overcast

7484 BOB WARD THE SUN WINNER CLAIMING STKS 7f (P)
12:20 (12:21) (Class 6) 2-Y-O **£1,706** (£503; £252) **Stalls** Low

Form				RPR
0152	**1**		**Bilko Pak (IRE)**[9] 7378 2-8-8 85 DaneO'Neill 1 (R Hannon) *hld up wl in tch: effrt between horses ent fnl f: qcknd to ld ins fnl f: sn in command: r.o wl* **11/10**[1]	76+
6313	**2**	2	**Takeaway**[48] 6500 2-8-6 82 JoeFanning 4 (J R Boyle) *dwlt: sn rcvrd and pressing ldr: led ent fnl 4f: rdn and edgd rt wl over 1f out: hdd and nt pce of wnr ins fnl f: kpt on* **6/5**[2]	67
0103	**3**	nk	**Sir Lunchalott**[9] 7378 2-8-4 70 (b) LukeMorris 5 (J S Moore) *stdd s: t.k.h: sn trcking ldng pair: rdn and effrt ent fnl 2f: nt qckn u.p over 1f out: one pce ins fnl f* **10/1**[3]	64
000	**4**	1 3/4	**Melancholy Hill (IRE)**[28] 7021 2-7-12 54 DavidProbert 3 (P F I Cole) *stdd s: in tch in rr: rdn and effrt ent fnl 2f: hung lft and no imp over 1f out* **66/1**	53
05	**5**	3/4	**Arctic Maiden**[34] 6866 2-8-4 0 ow1 RichardKingscote 2 (W J Musson) *led tl ent fnl 4f: styd w ldr: rdn ent fnl 2f: stl ev ch tl ent fnl f: wknd fnl 150yds* **25/1**	57

1m 25.93s (1.13) **Going Correction** +0.075s/f (Slow) **5** Ran SP% **107.5**
Speed ratings (Par 94): **96,93,93,91,90**
CSF £2.53 TOTE £1.60: £1.10, £1.10; EX 2.40.Bilko Pak was claimed by J. G. Given for £12,000.
Owner Middleham Park Racing XLIII **Bred** Stuart Weld **Trained** East Everleigh, Wilts

FOCUS
An uncompetitive claimer, run at an ordinary pace. Muddling form, with the first pair not at their best.

NOTEBOOK
Bilko Pak(IRE), marginally best in at the weights, seemed to stay this trip at the first time of asking when runner-up at Wolverhampton nine days earlier and the way this race was run didn't place an emphasis on stamina. He was always travelling best and all that was required was for the gap to appear when he needed it. Fortunately one appeared a furlong out that a bus could be driven through and he made no mistake. He was claimed by James Given. (op 11-8)
Takeaway, a former stablemate of the winner, 2-4 on Polytrack coming into this, was given a more positive ride but had no answer to the winner's turn of foot from a furlong out. (op Evens tchd 5-4)
Sir Lunchalott had finished behind the two market leaders in his last two starts and did so again, but he didn't help himself by pulling early and then showed an awkward head-carriage turning for home. (op 9-1)
Melancholy Hill(IRE) is rated just 54 and made no impression from off the pace. (op 50-1)

Arctic Maiden showed up until inside the final furlong and will have more options now that she can be handicapped. (tchd 22-1)

7485 EUROPEAN BREEDERS' FUND MAIDEN STKS 6f (P)
12:50 (12:55) (Class 5) 2-Y-O £2,914 (£867; £433; £216) Stalls Low

Form RPR

1 **Fastest Magician (USA)** 2-9-3 0 GeorgeBaker 8 79+
(J Noseda) *hld up in tch in last trio: effrt and gd hdwy towards inner over 1f out: qckng to ld ins fnl f: sn in command: comf* 7/2[2]

503 2 1 ½ **Daffydowndilly**[14] 7294 2-8-12 72 SteveDrowne 3 66
(H Morrison) *led: rdn and qcknd 2f out: hdd and nt pce of wnr ins fnl f: kpt on* 6/4[1]

3 ½ **Palais Glide** 2-8-12 0 JimmyFortune 6 65+
(R Hannon) *in tch: effrt and rdn on outer over 1f out: kpt on wl to go 3rd ins fnl f* 14/1

00 4 1 ¼ **Cool Water Oasis**[23] 7123 2-8-12 0 AmirQuinn 1 60
(G L Moore) *s.i.s: t.k.h and sn wl in tch in midfield: n.m.r jst over 2f out: chsd ldrs and drvn over 1f out: styd on same pce ins fnl f* 100/1

5 1 **Robin Hoods Bay** 2-9-3 0 DaneO'Neill 4 64+
(E F Vaughan) *s.i.s: bhd: hdwy and swtchd lft jst over 1f out: styd on wl ins fnl f: nvr trbld ldrs* 16/1

36 6 shd **Arowana (IRE)**[25] 7088 2-8-12 0 LiamJones 11 57
(W J Haggas) *chsd ldrs: rdn and effrt ent fnl 2f: unable qck over 1f out: styd on same pce ins fnl f* 17/2

0 7 1 **Bluberry**[33] 6882 2-8-12 0 JoeFanning 5 54
(G L Moore) *t.k.h: hld up wl in tch: rdn and unable qck ent fnl 2f: styd on same pce fr over 1f out* 20/1

0 8 nk **Salesiano**[33] 6882 2-9-3 0 DavidProbert 7 58
(P J Makin) *chsd ldr: rdn ent fnl 2f: wknd jst over 1f out* 4/1[3]

0 9 2 ¾ **Bridget The Fidget**[171] 2561 2-8-5 0 JulieBurke(7) 2 44
(E J Creighton) *chsd ldrs: rdn and unable qck 2f out: wknd jst over 1f out* 100/1

10 ½ **Bedibyes** 2-8-9 0 RobertLButler(3) 12 42
(N R Mitchell) *swtchd lft s: in tch in rr and tail swishing: hdwy 3f out: pushed along and no hdwy wl over 1f out* 100/1

11 10 **Pink Sari** 2-8-12 0 FergusSweeney 9 10
(P J Makin) *in tch on outer: shkn up over 2f out: wknd wl over 1f out: wl btn and eased ins fnl f* 33/1

1m 14.73s (2.83) **Going Correction** +0.075s/f (Slow) 11 Ran SP% 116.0
Speed ratings (Par 96): **84,82,81,79,78 78,76,76,72,72 58**
toteswingers:1&2 £2.30, 2&3 £5.90, 1&3 £5.00 CSF £8.73 TOTE £3.90: £1.80, £1.10, £4.80; EX 11.60 Trifecta £30.40 Pool: £365.64 - 8.90 winning units..
Owner Charles E Fipke **Bred** Charles Fipke **Trained** Newmarket, Suffolk

FOCUS
Not a bad little maiden and a couple of these look interesting types for the future. The runner-up set a fair standard but there is a bit of doubt over what the bare form is worth.

NOTEBOOK
Fastest Magician(USA) raced at the back of the field early having been none too well away, but he enjoyed a charmed run though on the inside rounding the home bend and, despite making his effort close to the normally unfavoured inside rail, had little trouble in coasting to the front well inside the last furlong. An already-gelded half-brother to the stable's smart colt Awesome Act, he can go on to better things. (op 3-1 tchd 9-2)
Daffydowndilly, officially rated 72, got going too late when third dropped to this trip at Kempton last time but she was given a much more positive ride on this occasion. She did her best to make every yard, but came up against a nice prospect on the day. She has the option of handicaps, but should still be up to winning a routine AW maiden. (tchd 11-8 and 13-8 in places)
Palais Glide, a half-sister to five winning sprinters, stayed on nicely down the wide outside from the home turn and should be up to finding an ordinary maiden. (op 7-1)
Cool Water Oasis took a good grip in a prominent position early and was still racing keenly starting the home turn. She ran on well enough once off the bridle and this was a big improvement on her two turf efforts.
Robin Hoods Bay, the real eye-catcher, raced in last place after missing the break, but made a deal of late progress without being given by any means a hard time. The stewards looked into the performance and were told that the colt was a nervy type who needed to be dropped in. They stated that he had settled well, if showing his inexperience, and responded well when asked to run on past beaten horses despite carrying his head high and resenting the kickback. A half-brother to a 7f juvenile winner, he is bred to need middle distances and his next outing should be informative. Official explanation: jockey said, regarding running and riding, that his orders were, as the colt was a nervy type, to get it dropped in and settled, it settled well despite showing signs of inexperience, and when making its effort turning into the straight, responded well, running on through beaten horses despite carrying its head high due to the kickback. (op 25-1)
Arowana(IRE) had every chance starting up the straight, but didn't get home and she doesn't seem to be progressing. (op 8-1 tchd 10-1)

7486 BETDAQ FOR AN EXCHANGE NURSERY 1m (P)
1:20 (1:22) (Class 5) (0-75,73) 2-Y-O £2,729 (£806; £403) Stalls High

Form RPR

1002 1 **Malice Or Mischief (IRE)**[6] 7412 2-9-7 73 NeilCallan 1 78+
(A W Carroll) *dwlt: in tch towards rr: rdn over 2f out: hdwy and nt clr run over 1f out: swtchd sharply rt jst ins fnl f: r.o wl to ld fnl 50yds* 6/1[3]

4016 2 ½ **Azlaa**[33] 6902 2-9-3 69 JimmyFortune 3 72+
(R Hannon) *chsd ldrs: rdn and effrt wl over 1f out: ev ch ent fnl f: led ins fnl f tl hdd and no ex fnl 50yds* 7/2[1]

0053 3 ¾ **Night Witch (IRE)**[25] 7087 2-8-5 64 JulieBurke(7) 2 65
(E J Creighton) *dwlt: sn rcvrd and chsd ldrs: swtchd lft and rdn to chal jst over 1f out: ev ch ins fnl f: edgd rt and one pce fnl 100yds* 6/1[3]

0300 4 1 **Oliver's Gold**[38] 6777 2-8-10 62 JoeFanning 7 61
(Mrs A J Perrett) *dwlt: sn pushed along and rcvrd to r in midfield: rdn and effrt wl over 1f out: led 1f out tl hdd ins fnl f: wkng whn pushed rt and sltly hmpd wl ins fnl f* 11/2[2]

0046 5 2 **Beating Harmony**[12] 7324 2-8-11 63 RichardKingscote 8 59+
(Tom Dascombe) *in tch: rdn and effrt to press ldrs over 2f out: led wl over 1f out tl 1f out: wknd ins fnl f* 18/1

032 6 3 **Lady Bridget**[28] 7010 2-9-5 71 RobertWinston 4 58
(B W Hills) *s.i.s: in tch towards rr: rdn and effrt bnd 2f out: no real prog: nvr trbld ldrs* 7/2[1]

0400 7 1 **Violet Ray (USA)**[25] 7087 2-9-4 70 (b[1]) JimCrowley 6 55
(R M Beckett) *t.k.h: w ldr tl led 5f out tl over 2f out: wknd u.p over 1f out* 10/1

1360 8 1 ¾ **Joyously**[21] 7165 2-8-13 68 RobertLButler(3) 5 49
(P Butler) *s.i.s: a towards rr: rdn and no prog ent fnl 2f* 22/1

1005 9 ½ **History Repeating**[14] 7296 2-8-3 55 DavidProbert 10 35
(M D I Usher) *s.i.s: sn rdn along in rr: nvr trbld ldrs* 16/1

3250 10 12 **Loves Theme (IRE)**[13] 7312 2-9-2 68 LiamJones 9 20
(A Bailey) *led tl 5f out: chsd ldr tl led again over 2f out tl rdn and hdd wl over 1f out: wkng whn hmpd over 1f out: wl btn and eased ins fnl f* 66/1

1m 38.77s (0.57) **Going Correction** +0.075s/f (Slow) 10 Ran SP% 114.5
Speed ratings (Par 96): **100,99,98,97,95 92,91,90,89,77**
toteswingers:1&2 £4.20, 2&3 £4.30, 1&3 £5.20 CSF £26.74 CT £120.50 TOTE £5.50: £1.90, £1.10, £1.70; EX 25.60 Trifecta £120.90 Pool: £289.18 - 1.77 winning units..
Owner Bill Adams **Bred** Kilnamoragh Stud **Trained** Cropthorne, Worcs
■ Stewards' Enquiry : Julie Burke one-day ban: careless riding (Dec 1)

FOCUS
Just an ordinary nursery run at an even pace. The front pair are perhaps a biot better than the bare form.

NOTEBOOK
Malice Or Mischief(IRE) had run much better on his third start for the stable at Wolverhampton last time and the vibes from the yard before this race were very positive. Not that his supporters would have held out much hope halfway through the race, though, as he had lost a good early position and was receiving reminders before the home bend. However, once pulled out for his effort a furlong out, he quickened up smartly to lead close to the line, and there should be plenty more opportunities for him in the coming months. (op 9-2)
Azlaa didn't have the race run to suit at Wolverhampton last month, having won there a week earlier, and she may have been a bit unfortunate here too. She travelled like a dream behind the leaders on the inside, but her rider had no choice but to make his effort tight against the rail when the gap appeared and she nearly pulled it off, but the winner's late burst proved too much. She deserves to get her head back in front. (op 3-1 tchd 11-4)
Night Witch(IRE) travelled well just behind the leaders and had every chance. She has improved with every run and it is only a matter of time before she finds a similar contest. (op 9-2)
Oliver's Gold, making his AW debut, travelled as well as anything and came through to hold every chance a furlong out, but he then started to hang and was run out of it. (op 8-1)
Beating Harmony didn't handle the Fibresand on his debut for the yard last time and ran much better back on Polytrack. Sent to the front rounding the home bend, he had run his race when squeezed out inside the last furlong. (op 20-1)
Lady Bridget was making her nursery and AW debuts, but she hung off the final bend and soon had no chance. (op 9-2)

7487 BET ASIAN H'CAPS - BETDAQ HANDICAP 1m (P)
1:50 (1:50) (Class 6) (0-55,55) 3-Y-O+ £2,047 (£604; £302) Stalls High

Form RPR

000 1 **Sir Ike (IRE)**[30] 6991 5-9-0 53 (tp) ShaneKelly 4 61
(W S Kittow) *dwlt: towards rr: hdwy on outer over 2f out: chsd ldrs and rdn wl over 1f out: r.o wl to ld wl ins fnl f: rdn out* 33/1

6266 2 ½ **Fly By Nelly**[54] 6335 4-9-0 53 JimCrowley 11 60+
(M R Hoad) *stdd s: hld up towards rr: nt clr run jst over 2f out: hdwy and rdn wl over 1f out: swtchd rt jst over 1f out: r.o wl ins fnl f: wnt 2nd last strides: nt quite rch wnr* 8/1

24 3 hd **Ermyntrude**[13] 7323 3-8-12 53 IanMongan 7 58
(P M Phelan) *in tch in midfield: hdwy and n.m.r jst over 2f out: rdn and hdwy wl over 1f out: ev ch ins fnl f: no ex towards fin* 7/1[3]

0005 4 ¾ **Phluke**[20] 7191 9-8-12 51 (v) TomQueally 8 56
(Eve Johnson Houghton) *in tch in midfield: rdn and effrt to chse ldr ent fnl f: pressing ldrs but keeping on same pce whn nt clr run and swtchd lft ins fnl f: kpt on towards fin* 8/1

2212 5 nse **Join Up**[4] 7450 4-8-12 54 RossAtkinson(3) 12 59+
(W M Brisbourne) *stdd s: hld up in tch towards rr: hdwy over 2f out: led 2f out and sn rdn clr: edgd rt u.p and hdd wl ins fnl f: wknd towards fin* 7/2[1]

2645 6 3 **Bentley**[26] 7068 6-8-13 55 MatthewDavies(3) 1 53
(B P J Baugh) *in tch in midfield: rdn along 4f out: hdwy u.p to chse ldrs on inner over 1f out: wknd jst ins fnl f* 20/1

4054 7 2 ¾ **Straight And Level (CAN)**[28] 7023 5-8-12 51 (v) DaneO'Neill 9 42
(Miss Jo Crowley) *chsd ldr: rdn and ev ch ent fnl 2f: wknd over 1f out: wl hld and eased wl ins fnl f* 6/1[2]

4636 8 1 ¾ **Chateau Zara**[14] 7305 3-8-13 54 LukeMorris 6 40
(C G Cox) *in tch: rdn over 3f out: unable qck over 2f out: swtchd rt over 1f out: n.d after: wl btn and eased wl ins fnl f* 12/1

02-0 9 1 ½ **Daily Double**[67] 5962 4-9-0 53 DavidProbert 10 37
(M R Bosley) *stdd s: hld up towards rr: rdn and effrt on outer jst over 2f out: nvr trbld ldrs: wl btn and eased wl ins fnl f* 50/1

6650 10 2 **December**[140] 3566 4-8-8 50 (tp) KierenFox(3) 2 29
(Mrs C A Dunnett) *led: rdn jst over 2f out: hdd 2f out: wknd qckly over 1f out: wl btn and eased wl ins fnl f* 12/1

0003 11 ¾ **Ajool (USA)**[4] 7445 3-9-0 55 (b[1]) LiamJones 5 32
(P W D'Arcy) *racd awkwardly thrght: dwlt: sn rdn along and in tch: swtchd rt over 5f out: chsd ldrs and rdn 3f out: wknd ent fnl 2f* 6/1[2]

005 12 4 **Hilltop Artistry**[64] 6062 4-8-12 51 FergusSweeney 3 19
(J R Jenkins) *dwlt: a in rr and nvr gng wl: lost tch ent fnl 2f* 16/1

1m 37.41s (-0.79) **Going Correction** +0.075s/f (Slow)
WFA 3 from 4yo+ 2lb 12 Ran SP% 116.4
Speed ratings (Par 101): **106,105,105,104,104 101,98,97,95,93 92,88**
toteswingers:1&2 £28.70, 2&3 £10.50, 1&3 £24.20 CSF £270.73 CT £2109.72 TOTE £37.80: £11.90, £5.90, £2.70; EX 282.70 TRIFECTA Not won..
Owner Mrs J Scrivens **Bred** Martin Francis **Trained** Blackborough, Devon

FOCUS
A moderate handicap and little recent winning form amongst the 12 runners. The time was fair for the grade but the first five finished in a heap and the form is surely no better than average.

7488 CLAUDE DUVAL THE SUN PUNTER'S PAL H'CAP 7f (P)
2:20 (2:21) (Class 4) (0-85,85) 3-Y-O+ £4,209 (£1,252; £625; £312) Stalls Low

Form RPR

0004 1 **Lowther**[25] 7091 5-9-7 85 (be) RobertWinston 9 97
(A Bailey) *hld up in tch in midfield: hdwy gng wl over 2f out: shkn up to ld 1f out: rdn clr ins fnl f: r.o wl: readily* 13/2

0006 2 2 ¼ **Elspeth's Boy (USA)**[25] 7091 3-8-11 76 LukeMorris 3 84+
(J R Best) *in tch in midfield: rdn and effrt whn n.m.r over 1f out: kpt on wl u.p ins fnl f: wnt 2nd wl ins fnl f: no threat to wnr* 6/1[3]

6510 3 ½ **Requisite**[18] 7238 5-8-12 76 (v) CathyGannon 5 81
(I A Wood) *towards rr: rdn wl over 2f out: gd hdwy over 1f out: chsd ldrs ent fnl f: chsd clr wnr ins fnl f: no imp: lost 2nd wl ins fnl f* 16/1

4161 4 ½ **Hatta Stream (IRE)**[25] 7093 4-9-0 78 MickyFenton 6 81
(J Pearce) *in tch in midfield: effrt on inner and rdn over 1f out: chsd ldrs 1f out: styd on same pce fnl 150yds* 11/1

310 5 ½ **Regeneration (IRE)**[46] 6558 4-9-4 82 JimCrowley 4 84
(M L W Bell) *in tch: rdn to press ldr ent fnl 2f: led over 1f out tl 1f out: sn outpcd by wnr: styd on same pce fnl 150yds* 9/2[1]

2503 6 1 ¼ **Avertor**[19] 7212 4-9-3 81 SteveDrowne 13 80
(R Charlton) *stdd and dropped in bhd after s: t.k.h: hld up in rr: swtchd rt and hdwy ent fnl f: kpt on: nvr able to chal* 5/1[2]

0500 **7** *shd* **Cyflymder (IRE)**^{82} 5495 4-9-2 **80** JimmyFortune 11 78
(R Hannon) *stdd and dropped in bhd after s: hld up in rr: hdwy over 1f out: kpt on ins fnl f: nvr able to chal* **16/1**

3221 **8** *1 1/2* **Dingaan (IRE)**^{13} 7314 7-9-3 **81** GeorgeBaker 12 75
(Peter Grayson) *stdd s: hld up in rr: rdn and effrt wl over 1f out: swtchd lft 1f out: kpt on ins fnl f: nvr able to chal* **14/1**

0100 **9** *nk* **Beat Baby (IRE)**^{66} 6000 3-9-6 **85** JoeFanning 7 77
(M J Scudamore) *led tl 3f out: stl w ldr tl wknd u.p over 1f out* **40/1**

3254 **10** *nse* **Ilie Nastase (FR)**^{16} 7274 6-8-12 **76** TomQueally 14 69
(C R Dore) *a towards rr: rdn and sme hdwy on outer over 2f out: styd on same pce fr over 1f out* **11/1**

5120 **11** *1* **Glenridding**^{16} 7274 6-8-10 **74** (p) LiamJones 10 65
(J G Given) *pressed ldr: rdn to ld 3f out tl hdd over 1f out: wknd jst over 1f out* **11/1**

5203 **12** *2 1/2* **Maze (IRE)**^{30} 6987 5-8-11 **75** NeilCallan 1 59
(A W Carroll) *taken down early: chsd ldrs: rdn ent fnl 2f: wknd over 1f out* **20/1**

1241 **13** *12* **Urban Space**^{44} 6637 4-8-6 **77** SophieSilvester$^{(7)}$ 2 —
(C R Dore) *a in rr: rdn and toiling over 3f out: wl btn over 2f out* **25/1**

4550 **14** *9* **Cuthbert (IRE)**^{37} 6800 3-8-3 **71** KierenFox$^{(3)}$ 8 —
(W Jarvis) *in tch: rdn and effrt to join ldrs ent fnl 2f: btn jst over 1f out: heavily eased and virtually p.u ins fnl f* **18/1**

1m 23.44s (-1.36) **Going Correction** +0.075s/f (Slow)
WFA 3 from 4yo+ 1lb **14** Ran SP% **122.2**
Speed ratings (Par 105): **110,107,106,106,105 104,104,102,102,102 100,98,84,74**
toteswingers:1&2 £8.20, 2&3 £32.40, 1&3 £16.60 CSF £44.96 CT £628.40 TOTE £7.50: £3.50, £2.90, £6.10; EX 40.90 TRIFECTA Not won..
Owner L J Barratt **Bred** L J Barratt **Trained** Newmarket, Suffolk
■ A poignant winner, as the horse's owner Lowther Barratt, a former trainer, had died a few days before.

FOCUS
A fair handicap, run at a decent pace. The winner is rated in line with his best form.

7489 BACK AND LAY AT BETDAQ MAIDEN STKS 1m 2f (P)
2:50 (2:51) (Class 5) 3-Y-O+ £2,729 (£806; £403) Stalls Low

Form RPR

1 **Pertuis (IRE)**^{17} 4-9-7 70 LukeMorris 2 68
(H J L Dunlop) *chsd ldrs: effrt to ld ent fnl 2f: rdn clr over 1f out: kpt on wl ins fnl f* **6/1**^{2}

0-22 **2** *2 1/2* **Fashionable Gal (IRE)**^{12} 7338 3-8-12 72 StevieDonohoe 8 58
(Sir Mark Prescott) *t.k.h: chsd ldrs: nt clr run briefly and swtchd lft over 1f out: drvn 1f out: chsd wnr ins fnl f: no imp: hung rt towards fin* **2/7**^{1}

0602 **3** *1 3/4* **Red Willow**^{83} 5455 4-9-2 49 SamHitchcott 7 54
(J E Long) *led at stdy gallop: rdn and hdd ent fnl 2f: outpcd by wnr jst over 1f out: lost 2nd ins fnl f: styd on same pce* **16/1**

0 **4** *2 1/4* **Rustic Deacon**^{21} 7183 3-9-3 0 JimmyFortune 4 55
(W J Musson) *s.i.s: hld up in last pair: hdwy on outer bnd 2f out: hung lft fr over 1f out: wnt 4th ins fnl f: nvr threatened ldrs* **14/1**

5 *1/2* **Cabuchon (GER)** 3-9-3 0 TomQueally 1 54
(B J Curley) *prom early: hld up in midfield after 2f: outpcd 2f out: rdn and styd on same pce fr over 1f out* **7/1**^{3}

00 **6** *1/2* **Beseech (USA)**^{34} 6861 3-8-12 0 CathyGannon 3 48
(Miss J Feilden) *in tch in midfield: rdn over 2f out: outpcd 2f out: plugged on same pce and no threat to ldrs fr over 1f out* **66/1**

0 **7** *4* **Princess Runner**^{15} 7288 3-8-12 0 SteveDrowne 5 40
(J R Gask) *in tch in midfield: stmbld after 1f: rdn and struggling over 2f out: wl btn over 1f out* **20/1**

8 *1 3/4* **Quahadi (IRE)**^{30} 4-9-7 0 DaneO'Neill 6 41
(C Gordon) *dwlt: sn rcvrd: chsd ldr 9f out tl ent fnl 2f: swtchd lft wl over 1f out: wknd qckly over 1f out* **40/1**

0 **9** *2 1/4* **Harrys**^{9} 7381 3-9-3 0 JimmyQuinn 9 37
(P Howling) *s.i.s: a in rr: n.d* **66/1**

2m 8.06s (1.46) **Going Correction** +0.075s/f (Slow)
WFA 3 from 4yo 4lb **9** Ran SP% **127.3**
Speed ratings (Par 103): **97,95,93,91,91 91,87,86,84**
toteswingers:1&2 £1.80, 2&3 £3.30, 1&3 £6.40 CSF £8.86 TOTE £7.20: £1.40, £1.02, £3.40; EX 12.70 Trifecta £65.50 Pool: £507.76 - 5.73 winning units..
Owner Rupert Hambro **Bred** Killeen Castle Stud **Trained** Lambourn, Berks

FOCUS
A modest and uncompetitive maiden that was dominated by those with experience. Muddling form with the favourite again disappointing.
Rustic Deacon Official explanation: jockey said gelding hung left
Quahadi(IRE) Official explanation: jockey said gelding suffered interference turning in

7490 THREE BRIDGES AMATEUR RIDERS' H'CAP (DIV I) 1m 4f (P)
3:20 (3:20) (Class 5) (0-70,70) 3-Y-O+ £1,977 (£608; £304) Stalls Low

Form RPR

1040 **1** **Where's Susie**^{38} 6775 5-10-10 **66** MrSWalker 5 75
(M Madgwick) *hld up in midfield: clsd on ldrs 6f out: wnt 3rd over 4f out: rdn to ld ent fnl 2f: drvn and kpt on wl ins fnl f* **4/1**^{1}

-600 **2** *2* **Squad**^{21} 7167 4-10-1 **64** MrJCoffill-Brown$^{(7)}$ 11 69+
(S Dow) *stdd s: hld up in last trio: clsd on ldrs 6f out: hmpd 5f out: in tch whn nt clr run jst over 2f out tl over 1f out: r.o wl and edgd lft ins fnl f: wnt 2nd last strides* **11/1**

2504 **3** *hd* **Sir Boss (IRE)**^{25} 7101 5-10-7 **66** MissMMullineaux$^{(3)}$ 2 71
(M Mullineaux) *prom tl led 4f out: hdd ent fnl 2f: rdn wl over 1f out: styd on same pce and a hld after: lost 2nd last strides* **7/1**^{3}

4241 **4** *1/2* **James Pollard (IRE)**^{28} 7015 5-10-2 **63** (t) MrRJWilliams$^{(5)}$ 10 67+
(B J Llewellyn) *stdd and dropped in bhd after s: hdwy over 5f out: hdwy on inner ent fnl 2f: swtchd rt wl over 1f out: kpt on u.p ins fnl f: nvr gng pce to chal wnr* **12/1**

2600 **5** *2 1/4* **Winning Show**^{16} 4227 6-10-0 **59** (tp) MrTJCannon$^{(3)}$ 8 60
(C Gordon) *hld up off the pce in midfield: clsd and in tch 6f out: rdn and effrt ent fnl 2f: kpt on same pce u.p fr over 1f out* **9/1**

5221 **6** *7* **Lady Lam**^{15} 7286 4-10-5 **64** (t) MrMWall$^{(3)}$ 6 53
(S Kirk) *stdd and wnt rt s: hld up in midfield: clsd and in tch 6f out: rdn and chsd ldng pair wl over 1f out: no imp: wknd 1f out* **9/2**^{2}

2000 **7** *1 1/4* **Set To Go**^{23} 7125 3-9-2 **57** MrCVitler$^{(7)}$ 9 44
(Miss N A Lloyd-Beavis) *led for 1f: chsd ldrs after: wknd jst over 2f out* **66/1**

3602 **8** *1/2* **War Of The Roses (IRE)**^{118} 4279 7-10-11 **70** MrPCollington$^{(3)}$ 1 57
(R Brotherton) *hld up in rr: clsd and in tch 5f out: rdn and no hdwy bnd ent fnl 2f: wl btn over 1f out* **8/1**

0004 **9** *shd* **Jackson (BRZ)**^{13} 7315 8-9-9 **56** oh8 MrJNewman$^{(5)}$ 4 42
(R C Guest) *racd in midfield: dropped to rr 5f out: wl btn fnl 3f* **4/1**^{1}

5530 **10** *5* **Always De One**^{7} 7387 3-9-1 **56** oh8 (p) MissSBirkett$^{(7)}$ 7 34
(Miss J Feilden) *pushed rt and sltly hmpd s: rcvrd to ld after 1f: hdd ent fnl 2f: sn wknd* **33/1**

0/0- **11** *33* **Ede's**^{196} 7328 10-9-7 **56** oh11 MissLWilliams$^{(7)}$ 3 —
(P M Phelan) *w ldr tl lost pl qckly 5f out: sn wl bhd: t.o fnl 3f* **40/1**

2m 33.1s (0.10) **Going Correction** +0.075s/f (Slow)
WFA 3 from 4yo+ 6lb **11** Ran SP% **114.7**
Speed ratings (Par 103): **102,100,100,100,98 94,93,92,92,89 67**
toteswingers:1&2 £15.50, 2&3 £14.80, 1&3 £8.60 CSF £46.82 CT £298.07 TOTE £5.50: £1.50, £5.70, £2.00; EX 75.60 Trifecta £262.60 Part won. Pool of £354.91 - 0.42 winning units..
Owner Recycled Products Limited **Bred** Mrs L R Burrage **Trained** Denmead, Hants
■ Stewards' Enquiry : Mr J Coffill-Brown three-day ban: careless riding (Dec 20 & tbn)

FOCUS
A moderate amateur riders' handicap in which a quartet had established a sizeable advantage over the rest after half a mile, but most of them paid for it and the front pair had the race to themselves from the home turn. The winner rates a 4lb personal best.

7491 THREE BRIDGES AMATEUR RIDERS' H'CAP (DIV II) 1m 4f (P)
3:50 (3:50) (Class 5) (0-70,70) 3-Y-O+ £1,977 (£608; £304) Stalls Low

Form RPR

3664 **1** **William's Way**^{13} 7321 8-10-3 **64** (t) MrCMartin$^{(5)}$ 2 71
(I A Wood) *stdd s: hld up in last trio: hdwy 4f out: rdn to ld ent fnl 2f: hld on wl fnl 100yds* **13/2**^{3}

0142 **2** *shd* **Strike Force**^{2} 7467 6-10-4 **65** (t) MissALHutchinson$^{(5)}$ 9 72
(Miss Olivia Maylam) *stdd s: t.k.h: hld up wl in rr: hdwy on wd outside ent bnd 2f out: pushed along hands and heels fr over 1f out: ev ch ins fnl f: jst hld* **10/3**^{1}

5000 **3** *1* **The Wonga Coup (IRE)**^{183} 2200 3-9-1 **56** oh1 MissLWilliams$^{(7)}$ 6 61
(P M Phelan) *t.k.h: hld up in last trio: hdwy over 2f out: chsd ldrs and pushed along 1f out: n.m.r wl ins fnl f: kpt on* **25/1**

0242 **4** *1/2* **Larkrise Star**^{13} 7315 3-9-5 **60** MissECrossman$^{(7)}$ 5 65
(D K Ivory) *hld up in midfield: swtchd wd and hdwy 4f out: led 3f out: hdd ent fnl 2f: pushed along and styd on same pce fnl f* **7/2**^{2}

2366 **5** *1 3/4* **Relative Strength (IRE)**^{60} 6202 5-11-0 **70** (v) MrMarioBaratti 8 72
(S C Williams) *hld up towards rr: hdwy 4f out: rdn to chse ldng pair over 1f out: no imp ins fnl f* **7/2**^{2}

2000 **6** *1/2* **King Columbo (IRE)**^{21} 7184 5-10-3 **66** MissSBirkett$^{(7)}$ 4 67
(Miss J Feilden) *chsd ldr for 2f: steadily lost pl and last over 4f out: effrt and nt clr run on inner bnd 2f out: hdwy over 1f out: kpt on same pce ins fnl f* **25/1**

3300 **7** *2 3/4* **Vinces**^{13} 7323 6-10-7 **63** MrSWalker 1 60
(T D McCarthy) *in tch in midfield: rdn 3f out: stl in tch whn nt clr run and swtchd rt bnd ent fnl 2f: kpt on u.p fr over 1f out: nvr able to chal* **9/1**

3100 **8** *9* **Carr Hall (IRE)**^{15} 7286 7-10-4 **63** MrMJJSmith$^{(3)}$ 3 45
(A W Carroll) *stdd s: t.k.h: chsd ldr 9f out tl over 3f out: wknd ent fnl 2f* **17/2**

000- **9** *1/2* **Corlough Mountain**^{351} 7608 6-9-9 **56** oh11 MissMBryant$^{(5)}$ 10 37
(P Butler) *t.k.h: chsd ldrs tl wknd jst over 2f out* **66/1**

0000 **10** *1 1/2* **Lily Eva**^{33} 6905 4-9-7 **56** oh11 MrTHowell$^{(7)}$ 7 35
(D Donovan) *led tl 3f out: rdn and wknd jst over 2f out* **66/1**

2m 35.13s (2.13) **Going Correction** +0.075s/f (Slow)
WFA 3 from 4yo+ 6lb **10** Ran SP% **112.1**
Speed ratings (Par 103): **95,94,94,93,92 92,90,84,84,83**
toteswingers:1&2 £4.80, 2&3 £27.00, 1&3 £28.10 CSF £26.52 CT £501.50 TOTE £6.70: £1.90, £2.50, £10.60; EX 33.00 Trifecta £188.60 Part won. Pool of £254.98 - 0.10 winning units..
Owner Neardown Stables **Bred** Lewis Caterers **Trained** Upper Lambourn, Berks

FOCUS
A messy second division of this race in which the last three horses passing the post with a circuit left were the first three home. The winning time was over two seconds slower than division one but that is probably due to the fast early pace. The form makes sense.
T/Plt: £30.10 to a £1 stake. Pool of £42,540.28 - 1,028.93 winning tickets. T/Qpdt: £36.60 to a £1 stake. Pool of £4,355.91 - 88.00 winning tickets. SP

7461 WOLVERHAMPTON (A.W) (L-H)
Thursday, November 18

OFFICIAL GOING: Standard
Wind: Light behind Weather: Light rain

7493 BET PREMIER LEAGUE FOOTBALL - BETDAQ NURSERY 5f 216y(P)
4:10 (4:10) (Class 5) (0-75,75) 2-Y-O £2,590 (£770; £385; £192) Stalls Low

Form RPR

321 **1** **Insolenceofoffice (IRE)**^{17} 7269 2-9-5 **73** (p) GeorgeBaker 9 78
(Mrs A Duffield) *chsd ldrs: shkn up to ld and hung lft ins fnl f: rdn out* **5/1**^{2}

5224 **2** *1/2* **Its You Again**^{12} 7347 2-9-7 **75** (b) WilliamCarson 7 79
(M G Quinlan) *s.i.s: hdwy over 2f out: hung rt over 1f out: rdn and ev ch ins fnl f: unable qck towards fin* **13/2**

105 **3** *1 1/4* **Sacrosanctus**^{20} 7211 2-9-5 **73** IanMongan 12 73
(D Nicholls) *led early: chsd ldr tl led over 2f out: rdn over 1f out: hdd ins fnl f: styd on same pce* **16/1**

2100 **4** *4 1/2* **Restless Bay (IRE)**^{40} 6745 2-9-4 **72** (p) AdamKirby 2 58
(R Hollinshead) *s.i.s: hdwy over 2f out: rdn and hung lft over 1f out: no ex ins fnl f* **11/2**^{3}

5562 **5** *2* **Homeboy (IRE)**^{14} 7313 2-8-11 **65** (v) ChrisCatlin 1 45
(M P Tregoning) *chsd ldrs: rdn over 2f out: nt clr run over 1f out: hung lft and wknd ins fnl f* **4/1**^{1}

3235 **6** *1 3/4* **Imogen Louise (IRE)**^{32} 6954 2-9-0 **68** DaneO'Neill 5 43
(D Haydn Jones) *prom: rdn over 2f out: wknd over 1f out* **10/1**

636 **7** *3/4* **Veeb (IRE)**^{107} 4675 2-8-8 **62** JoeFanning 3 36
(M Johnston) *sn led: hdd over 2f out: hmpd and wknd over 1f out* **11/2**^{3}

606 **8** *1* **Bird In The Wind (USA)**^{29} 7021 2-8-11 **65** RichardKingscote 6 35
(R M Beckett) *hld up: nvr on terms* **10/1**

5000 **9** *1/2* **Safe Haven (IRE)**^{17} 7272 2-7-12 **52** CathyGannon 4 20
(A Bailey) *mid-div: sn pushed along: rdn and lost pl 1/2-way* **22/1**

246 **10** *6* **Hygrove Gal**^{17} 7268 2-8-13 **67** PaulMulrennan 10 17
(B Smart) *chsd ldrs: rdn over 2f out: wknd wl over 1f out* **33/1**

403 **11** *20* **Lady Mango (IRE)**^{17} 7269 2-8-9 **63** LukeMorris 8 —
(R A Harris) *hld up: rdn and wknd over 2f out: eased over 1f out: t.o* **12/1**

1m 15.38s (0.38) **Going Correction** +0.175s/f (Slow) **11** Ran SP% **119.8**
Speed ratings (Par 96): **104,103,101,95,93 90,89,88,87,79 53**
CSF £38.37 CT £492.66 TOTE £4.00: £1.10, £1.90, £6.40; EX 17.30.
Owner Middleham Park Racing XLIX **Bred** Gerard Kennedy **Trained** Constable Burton, N Yorks
■ Stewards' Enquiry : William Carson six-day ban: careless riding & excessive use of whip (Dec 2 - Dec 7)

FOCUS
They went a decent pace in this nursery and the first three pulled clear. The third sets the level.
NOTEBOOK
Insolenceofoffice(IRE) got off the mark on the seventh attempt when holding off a 70-rated rival at odds-on in a 5f maiden here last time. He travelled well just behind the pace with cheekpieces applied for a second time and found a sweeping run out widest of all to complete a double on the return to 6f. His profile has been consistent rather than progressive but he seems to have found some improvement since headgear has been applied and may be able to win again. He was reported to have lost a shoe which may explain why he edged left in the closing stages. (op 9-2)
Its You Again gave it a good try in second-time blinkers but was just outgunned. He is a quietly progressive half-brother to two 6f Polytrack winners and should be able to win a similar race. (op 9-2 tchd 4-1)
Sacrosanctus has a hit and miss profile but ran a solid race under a positive ride stepped up to 6f on debut for a new trainer.
Restless Bay(IRE) couldn't land a blow on the front three but his effort can be marked up a bit because he put a dent in his chance by starting slowly. (op 6-1)
Homeboy(IRE), a well-backed favourite, found a bit of trouble at a crucial stage but his effort seemed to be flattening out at the time, and he has not managed to build on his improved second in a visor at Kempton two weeks earlier. (op 6-1)
Veeb(IRE), a big market mover in the morning, was given an attacking ride on her first run for Mark Johnston after 107 days off but looked on the retreat when hampered early in the straight. (op 5-1 tchd 6-1)
Lady Mango(IRE) Official explanation: jockey said that the filly's bit slipped through her mouth

7494 BOOK NOW FOR BOXING DAY H'CAP — 5f 20y(P)
4:40 (4:40) (Class 5) (0-75,75) 3-Y-0+ — £2,590 (£770; £385; £192) Stalls Low

Form — RPR
0040 1 **Sir Geoffrey (IRE)**[22] 7180 4-9-5 **73**....(b) IanMongan 4 — 84
(D Nicholls) *led early: chsd ldr: rdn to ld ins fnl f: r.o* — **8/1**
6464 2 1 ½ **Cape Royal**[7] 7405 10-8-8 **62**....(bt) RichardKingscote 8 — 68
(J M Bradley) *sn led: hdd and unable qck ins fnl f* — **14/1**
6031 3 2 ¼ **Sloop Johnb**[13] 7326 4-9-4 **72**....(p) PaulMulrennan 10 — 70
(R A Fahey) *prom: rdn over 1f out: styd on* — **4/1**[3]
0661 4 ¾ **Perlachy**[21] 7194 6-8-10 **67**....(v) KellyHarrison(3) 2 — 62+
(D Shaw) *hld up: nt clr run 1/2-way: hdwy over 1f out: r.o: nt rch ldrs* **16/1**
3522 5 1 **Galpin Junior (USA)**[7] 7405 4-9-2 **70**.... LukeMorris 7 — 61
(Mrs R A Carr) *hld up: rdn 1/2-way: styd on u.p ins fnl f: nvr nrr* — **9/2**
241 6 ¾ **Angelo Poliziano**[42] 6700 4-9-4 **72**....(p) GeorgeBaker 1 — 61
(Mrs A Duffield) *prom: rdn 1/2-way: edgd lft fr over 1f out: no imp* — **10/3**[2]
0011 7 ¾ **Grand Stitch (USA)**[21] 7193 4-8-12 **71**....(v) NeilFarley(5) 3 — 57+
(D Carroll) *mid-div: rdn 1/2-way: nvr trbld ldrs* — **5/2**[1]
0006 8 1 ¼ **Ace Of Spies (IRE)**[8] 7399 5-9-1 **69**.... RobertWinston 5 — 50
(C R Dore) *hld up: no ch whn nt clr run ins fnl f: nvr trbld ldrs* — **28/1**
00 9 4 **Ridley Didley (IRE)**[21] 7194 5-8-11 **65**.... WilliamCarson 6 — 32
(N Wilson) *chsd ldrs: rdn 1/2-way: wknd over 1f out* — **33/1**
1006 10 3 ¼ **Yurituni**[14] 7320 3-9-7 **75**....(b) TomQueally 11 — 30
(Eve Johnson Houghton) *mid-div: rdn 1/2-way: sn wknd* — **20/1**
0460 11 nse **Steel City Boy (IRE)**[157] 3024 7-8-7 **61** oh1.... JoeFanning 12 — 16
(D Shaw) *s.i.s: a in rr* — **28/1**

62.10 secs (-0.20) **Going Correction** +0.175s/f (Slow) — 11 Ran SP% **128.1**
Speed ratings (Par 103): **108,105,102,100,99 98,96,94,88,83 83**
toteswingers:1&2 £17.90, 2&3 £21.50, 1&3 £6.90 CSF £117.33 CT £536.67 TOTE £8.70: £2.50, £6.10, £1.70; EX 103.00.
Owner Dixon, Howlett & The Chrystal Maze Ptn **Bred** P Rabbitte **Trained** Sessay, N Yorks
■ Stewards' Enquiry : William Carson two-day ban: careless riding (7 Dec)
FOCUS
A competitive handicap, involving four last-time-out winners. The first two dominated in a strongly run race and nothing else get involved. The winner is rated to his best for now.

7495 DINE IN THE HORIZONS RESTAURANT CLAIMING STKS — 1m 4f 50y(P)
5:10 (5:10) (Class 6) 3-Y-0 — £1,706 (£503; £252) Stalls Low

Form — RPR
1 **Humor Me Rene (USA)**[50] 6484 3-8-11 72.... MatthewDavies(3) 6 — 66
(George Baker) *hld up in tch: pushed along to chse ldr over 2f out: led over 1f out: styd on* — **1/2**[1]
0020 2 2 ¼ **Mary Helen**[8] 7387 3-8-4 51.... LiamJones 2 — 52
(W M Brisbourne) *s.i.s: hld up: hdwy over 2f out: rdn over 1f out: styd on to go 2nd nr fin: nt trble wnr* — **7/1**[3]
0300 3 nk **Half Sister (IRE)**[8] 7387 3-8-2 50....(b) NickyMackay 4 — 50
(M E Rimmer) *led over 4f: chsd ldr tl led again 3f out: rdn and hdd over 1f out: styd on same pce ins fnl f: lost 2nd nr fin* — **14/1**
5046 4 2 **Lauberhorn**[14] 7316 3-9-2 65....(b[1]) TomQueally 1 — 60
(Eve Johnson Houghton) *chsd ldrs: rdn over 2f out: hung lft over 1f out: styd on same pce* — **3/1**[2]
60 5 7 **Broughtons Bandit**[29] 7019 3-8-10 0 ow1.... StevieDonohoe 5 — 43
(W J Musson) *hld up: rdn and wknd over 2f out* — **25/1**
6000 6 38 **Little Buddy**[7] 7406 3-8-5 27.... AndrewHeffernan(3) 3 — —
(R J Price) *plld hrd: trckd ldr over 10f out: led over 7f out: hdd 3f out: sn wknd: t.o* — **66/1**

2m 44.78s (3.68) **Going Correction** +0.175s/f (Slow) — 6 Ran SP% **116.2**
Speed ratings (Par 98): **94,92,92,90,86 60**
CSF £5.34 TOTE £1.10: £1.02, £3.60; EX 5.40.
Owner M Khan X2 **Bred** Adrian P Hamman Jr Et Al **Trained** Moreton Morrell, Warwicks
FOCUS
An uncompetitive claimer run at a steady pace and rated around the runner-up to her recent best.

7496 BET IN RUNNING - BETDAQ NURSERY (DIV I) — 7f 32y(P)
5:40 (5:42) (Class 6) (0-60,60) 2-Y-0 — £1,364 (£403; £201) Stalls High

Form — RPR
640 1 **Magic Of The Sea (IRE)**[21] 7198 2-9-7 **60**.... ChrisCatlin 5 — 68+
(M Botti) *s.i.s: sn pushed along into mid-div: hdwy over 2f out: led over 1f out: r.o wl* — **9/4**[2]
0546 2 2 ½ **Empress Charlotte**[72] 5837 2-9-7 **60**.... TomQueally 12 — 62
(M L W Bell) *hld up: hdwy and hmpd over 2f out: rdn over 1f out: hung lft and styd on ins fnl f: no ch w wnr* — **2/1**[1]
440 3 ¾ **King Cobra (IRE)**[43] 6673 2-9-2 **55**....(v[1]) DaneO'Neill 8 — 55
(J W Hills) *a.p: rdn over 2f out: hung lft ins fnl f: styd on* — **5/1**[3]
0000 4 hd **Mrs Neat (IRE)**[8] 7394 2-8-13 **52**....(b[1]) JamesDoyle 1 — 52
(S Kirk) *sn pushed along in rr: hdwy over 5f out: rdn and hung lft over 1f out: styd on* — **20/1**
0000 5 2 ½ **Appyjack**[22] 7177 2-8-11 **50**....(t) LukeMorris 10 — 43
(A W Carroll) *sn outpcd: r.o ins fnl f: nrst fin* — **50/1**
0036 6 ¾ **Henrys Air**[2] 7469 2-9-3 **56**.... WilliamCarson 11 — 48
(D G Bridgwater) *mid-div: hdwy and hmpd over 2f out: rdn over 1f out: no ex fnl f* — **10/1**
0506 7 3 ½ **Sleeping Brave**[14] 7313 2-9-6 **59**.... StephenCraine 6 — 42
(J R Boyle) *s.s: in rr: rdn over 1f out: n.d* — **14/1**
0505 8 nk **Lovat Lane**[126] 4040 2-9-1 **54**.... CathyGannon 7 — 36
(Eve Johnson Houghton) *hld up: rdn over 2f out: nvr on terms* — **20/1**
0650 9 4 **Coedmor Boy**[43] 6673 2-8-8 **50**.... RussKennemore(3) 9 — 24
(J L Flint) *chsd ldr tl led over 2f out: rdn and hdd over 1f out: wknd fnl f* — **16/1**
0500 10 4 **Bankroller**[100] 4935 2-9-2 **55**.... RichardKingscote 3 — 18
(J G Portman) *chsd ldrs: rdn over 2f out: wknd over 1f out* — **16/1**
0065 11 2 **Bonniebridge**[7] 7400 2-8-11 **50**....(p) NickyMackay 2 — 8
(M E Rimmer) *chsd ldrs tl rdn and wknd over 1f out* — **20/1**
0030 12 5 **Finn's Rainbow**[73] 5818 2-9-4 **57**.... JoeFanning 4 — 2
(K A Ryan) *led over 4f: wknd over 1f out* — **8/1**

1m 31.98s (2.38) **Going Correction** +0.175s/f (Slow) — 12 Ran SP% **135.6**
Speed ratings (Par 94): **93,90,89,89,86 85,81,81,76,71 69,63**
toteswingers:1&2 £1.20, 2&3 £5.70, 1&3 £4.60 CSF £8.06 CT £24.19 TOTE £2.10: £1.10, £2.40, £3.00; EX 7.40.
Owner Mohammed Rashid **Bred** Rabbah Bloodstock Limited **Trained** Newmarket, Suffolk
■ Stewards' Enquiry : William Carson one-day ban: careless riding
FOCUS
A modest nursery involving 12 maidens but the two strong market leaders filled the first two places and could be improving types. The form is limited with the third and fourth the best guides to the level.
NOTEBOOK
Magic Of The Sea(IRE) was never involved behind a runaway Godolphin winner on her final maiden start but she attracted sustained support for this nursery debut and scored with plenty in hand after getting a dream run around the final bend. A half-sister to useful multiple 1m-1m2f winner Habalwatan, she has the potential for plenty of progress at this trip and a bit further and should be able to win more races. (op 7-2)
Empress Charlotte had a feasible excuse when losing a front shoe on nursery debut in September. She was sent off favourite in a bid to confirm her maiden promise and did really well to snatch second after being forced wide all the way from a horror draw. This well-connected filly rates better than the form implies and would be of strong interest in similar company next time. (op 11-4 tchd 3-1)
King Cobra(IRE) put in a more convincing effort stepped up to 7f with a first-time visor applied. (op 8-1 tchd 10-1)
Mrs Neat(IRE) was beaten 10l plus in three maidens and a nursery before this but she found a more dynamic response with blinkers applied on her Polytrack debut. Official explanation: jockey said that the filly hung both ways (op 16-1)
Appyjack showed very little in five previous starts but he did a bit of late work from some way back on debut for a new yard. (tchd 66-1)
Finn's Rainbow was keen and dropped away quickly on his first try beyond 6f. (op 15-2)

7497 BET IN RUNNING - BETDAQ NURSERY (DIV II) — 7f 32y(P)
6:10 (6:11) (Class 6) (0-60,60) 2-Y-0 — £1,364 (£403; £201) Stalls High

Form — RPR
6062 1 **Microlight**[8] 7394 2-9-2 **55**....(e) GrahamGibbons 9 — 59
(T D Easterby) *chsd ldr: rdn over 2f out: led over 1f out: styd on u.p* **9/4**[1]
3036 2 ½ **Three Scoops**[8] 7395 2-8-7 **51**....(t) BillyCray(5) 12 — 54
(D J S Ffrench Davis) *sn prom: rdn over 1f out: r.o: wnt 2nd nr fin* — **17/2**
006 3 ¾ **Century Dancer**[61] 6209 2-8-11 **50**.... JamesDoyle 4 — 51
(Miss Tor Sturgis) *s.i.s: sn pushed along in rr: hdwy over 1f out: r.o* — **11/1**
0000 4 ½ **Shutterbug**[24] 7118 2-9-1 **54**.... WilliamCarson 7 — 54
(S C Williams) *led: rdn: hung lft and hdd over 1f out: no ex wl ins fnl f: lost 2 pls nr fin* — **20/1**
500 5 nk **Les Landes (IRE)**[94] 5156 2-8-12 **54**.... SophieDoyle(3) 11 — 53
(J A Osborne) *s.i.s: in rr: r.o wl ins fnl f: nt rch ldrs* — **14/1**
5400 6 1 ¼ **Deva Le Deva (IRE)**[40] 6740 2-9-6 **59**.... RichardKingscote 6 — 55
(Tom Dascombe) *hld up: r.o ins fnl f: nt trble ldrs* — **16/1**
000 7 nk **Snow Trooper**[52] 6425 2-9-2 **55**.... SamHitchcott 5 — 50
(D K Ivory) *mid-div: hdwy 1/2-way: rdn over 1f out: styd on* — **20/1**
0000 8 3 ½ **Amore Et Labore**[2] 7471 2-8-4 **50**....(p) LukeRowe(7) 8 — 37
(S Kirk) *trckd ldrs: plld hrd: rdn over 1f out: wknd fnl f* — **25/1**
0550 9 3 **Melbury**[34] 6902 2-9-4 **57**.... JimmyQuinn 2 — 36
(P Howling) *hld up: nvr on terms* — **7/1**[3]
0500 10 2 **Amber Mist**[15] 7301 2-8-10 **49**.... LukeMorris 3 — 23
(David Pinder) *chsd ldrs: rdn 1/2-way: wknd over 1f out* — **18/1**
0050 11 3 ¼ **Special Endeavour (IRE)**[14] 7313 2-9-7 **60**.... GeorgeBaker 1 — 26
(W R Muir) *hld up: rdn 3f out: nvr on terms* — **8/1**
5003 12 3 ½ **Ajaafa**[14] 7313 2-9-7 **60**....(p) CathyGannon 10 — 18
(M J Attwater) *hld up: hdwy 1/2-way: sn rdn: wknd wl over 1f out* — **9/2**[2]

1m 31.9s (2.30) **Going Correction** +0.175s/f (Slow) — 12 Ran SP% **122.6**
Speed ratings (Par 94): **93,92,91,91,90 89,88,84,81,79 75,71**
CSF £22.07 CT £185.67 TOTE £3.50: £1.20, £2.50, £4.70; EX 24.80.
Owner Habton Farms **Bred** Newsells Park Stud **Trained** Great Habton, N Yorks
FOCUS
They pace was not very strong in the second division of this ordinary nursery. The form is limited and this is not a race to be with.
NOTEBOOK
Microlight pulled 6l clear of the third when showing improved form with eye-shields applied in a 1m Southwell nursery last week. A solid favourite, he got a good early position from a potentially troublesome draw and showed plenty of resilience to get by the long-time leader. He is progressing and should not go up much for this first win, but he may need a bit of time to recover from what looked a fairly tough race. (tchd 2-1 and 5-2)
Three Scoops ran a big race from a wide draw but couldn't quite get to the winner. She is an exposed 12-race maiden but may be able to get her timing right in a similar race. (op 9-1 tchd 8-1)
Century Dancer was a springer in the morning and flashed home to snatch third from a long way back on nursery debut. She has found a couple of jolts of improvement recently and shapes like a step up to 1m will suit. Official explanation: jockey said that the filly missed the break (op 10-1 tchd 12-1)
Shutterbug finished well beaten at 100-1 in three maidens and things got worse on her nursery debut on heavy ground last time. She had plenty to prove and was sent off at another biggish price, but put in a valiant bid switched to front-running tactics on AW debut. (op 12-1)
Les Landes(IRE) didn't show much in three quick-fire maiden runs in August, but he did some eye-catching late work out wide on this nursery debut back from 94 days off. (op 16-1)
Ajaafa worked his way into third after suffering early interference over 6f at Kempton last time, but he was keen out wide and weakened tamely stepped back up to 7f. (op 11-2)

7498 HOTEL & CONFERENCING AT WOLVERHAMPTON MAIDEN STKS — 7f 32y(P)
6:40 (6:40) (Class 5) 3-Y-0+ — £2,115 (£624; £312) Stalls High

Form — RPR
3-4 1 **Mr Emirati (USA)**[63] 6124 3-9-3 0.... PaulMulrennan 4 — 64+
(B Smart) *s.i.s: hld up: hdwy and hung lft fr over 1f out: rdn to ld wl ins fnl f* — **11/4**[3]

4 **2** 1 1/2 **Red Rhythm**[29] 7013 3-9-3 0 .... J-PGuillambert 5 61+
(L M Cumani) *plld hrd: led 6f out: rdn and hung rt fr over 1f out: hdd wl ins fnl f* **9/4**[2]

-000 **3** 5 **Tumbled Again**[170] 2633 3-9-3 44 .... NickyMackay 3 49
(M E Rimmer) *prom: outpcd over 2f out: styd on ins fnl f* **33/1**

4 2 3/4 **Gorgeous Goblin (IRE)** 3-8-9 0 .... AndrewHeffernan(3) 7 38
(D C Griffiths) *plld hrd and prom: chsd ldr 2f out: sn rdn: wknd ins fnl f* **25/1**

5 1 **American Smooth** 3-9-3 0 .... GeorgeBaker 2 40
(J Noseda) *chsd ldrs: pushed along 1/2-way: rdn and edgd lft over 1f out: wknd ins fnl f* **13/8**[1]

000 **6** 1 1/2 **Ettrick Mill**[27] 7070 4-9-1 45 .... (p) RussKennemore(3) 6 37
(J M Bradley) *led 1f: chsd ldr tl rdn over 2f out: wknd over 1f out* **33/1**

0500 **7** 3 1/2 **Swingle**[32] 6952 3-8-12 52 .... DaneO'Neill 1 24
(D Haydn Jones) *hld up: wknd over 2f out* **9/1**

0006 **8** 1 1/4 **Ariel Bender**[23] 7154 3-8-10 37 .... LeonnaMayor(7) 8 26
(Peter Grayson) *hld up: wknd 3f out* **33/1**

1m 31.15s (1.55) **Going Correction** +0.175s/f (Slow)
WFA 3 from 4yo 1lb **8** Ran SP% **118.2**
Speed ratings (Par 103): **98,96,90,87,86 84,80,79**
toteswingers:1&2 £1.10, 2&3 £28.00, 1&3 £17.90 CSF £9.43 TOTE £2.90: £1.10, £1.40, £28.50; EX 7.40.
Owner The Smart Emirati Partnership **Bred** Dr & Mrs Walter Zent & Tony Holmes **Trained** Hambleton, N Yorks

FOCUS
A modest maiden run at a very sedate pace. The proximity of the third limits the form.

7499 BET MULTIPLES - BETDAQ H'CAP 1m 141y(P)
7:10 (7:10) (Class 5) (0-75,74) 3-Y-O **£2,590** (£770; £385; £192) **Stalls** Low

Form RPR

0220 **1** **Slikback Jack (IRE)**[17] 7274 3-9-7 **74** .... IanMongan 4 83
(D Nicholls) *chsd ldr tl led over 3f out: rdn over 1f out: edgd lft ins fnl f: comf* **3/1**[3]

6030 **2** 2 3/4 **Abriachan**[15] 7298 3-8-10 **63** .... WilliamCarson 7 66
(M G Quinlan) *hld up in tch: chsd wnr over 2f out: sn rdn: styd on same pce ins fnl f* **3/1**[3]

4632 **3** nk **Lay Claim (USA)**[24] 7129 3-9-3 **70** .... (p) JamesDoyle 2 72
(A J McCabe) *trckd ldrs: rdn over 1f out: styd on same pce* **9/4**[2]

103 **4** 2 1/4 **Rubi Dia**[205] 1601 3-8-11 **64** .... JoeFanning 1 61
(M Johnston) *led: hdd over 3f out: sn rdn: no ex fr over 1f out* **2/1**[1]

000 **5** 13 **Kings Craic**[13] 7328 3-8-2 **60** oh15 .... NeilFarley(5) 5 27
(D Carroll) *hld up in tch: rdn and wknd over 2f out* **20/1**

4100 **U** **Khandaq (USA)**[41] 6709 3-9-7 **74** .... (t) PaulMulrennan 6 —
(V P Donoghue) *sing slowly whn rrd and uns rdr leaving stalls* **8/1**

1m 51.61s (1.11) **Going Correction** +0.175s/f (Slow) **6** Ran SP% **130.0**
Speed ratings (Par 102): **102,99,99,97,85** —
toteswingers:1&2 £2.20, 2&3 £1.80, 1&3 £1.20 CSF £14.82 TOTE £3.60: £1.30, £2.30.
Owner Brian Morton **Bred** Kilfrush Stud **Trained** Sessay, N Yorks

FOCUS
A fair handicap. They were tightly bunched off a steady pace for a long way before the winner seized the initiative over three furlongs out and made a successful dash for glory.The form is pretty weak rated around the runner-up to recent course form.
Slikback Jack(IRE) Official explanation: trainer's representative was unable to offer an explanation for the apparent improvement of form
T/Jkpt: £3,550.00 to a £1 stake. Pool of £10,000.00 - 2.00 winning tickets. T/Plt: £72.60 to a £1 stake. Pool of £69,243.94 - 695.80 winning tickets. T/Qpdt: £4.70 to a £1 stake. Pool of £10,903.27 - 1,693.15 winning tickets. CR

7493 WOLVERHAMPTON (A.W) (L-H)
Friday, November 19

OFFICIAL GOING: Standard
Wind: Almost nil Weather: Misty

7501 RACING START H'CAP (DIV I) 7f 32y(P)
4:15 (4:15) (Class 6) (0-60,60) 3-Y-O+ **£1,364** (£403; £201) **Stalls** High

Form RPR

3060 **1** **Saddlers Bend (IRE)**[213] 1443 4-9-1 **57** .... MatthewDavies(3) 6 66+
(George Baker) *hld up: hdwy 2f out: rdn to ld wl ins fnl f: r.o* **16/1**

505 **2** 1 1/4 **Ravi River (IRE)**[4] 7462 6-9-7 **60** .... (v) GeorgeBaker 7 66
(P D Evans) *a.p: chsd ldr over 4f out: chal 2f out: sn rdn: styd on same pce wl ins fnl f* **5/1**[2]

0304 **3** nk **South African Gold (USA)**[15] 7310 3-9-6 **60** .... (p) MickyFenton 9 65
(J M P Eustace) *led over 6f out: rdn over 1f out: hdd wl ins fnl f* **25/1**

3164 **4** 1/2 **Chookie Avon**[28] 7056 3-9-5 **59** .... (v[1]) JoeFanning 8 63
(V P Donoghue) *chsd ldrs: rdn over 1f out: styd on* **10/1**

1344 **5** 1/2 **Dancing Welcome**[8] 7401 4-9-0 **56** .... (b) RussKennemore(3) 1 58
(J M Bradley) *broke wl and led early: chsd ldrs: rdn and ev ch ins fnl f: no ex towards fin* **6/1**[3]

03 **6** 2 1/2 **Mr Lu**[20] 7241 5-9-6 **59** .... ChrisCatlin 5 55
(J S Goldie) *prom: rdn over 1f out: no ex fnl f* **9/2**[1]

0500 **7** 1 **Sairaam (IRE)**[14] 7336 4-9-4 **57** .... DaneO'Neill 4 50
(C Smith) *hld up: rdn over 1f out: nvr on terms* **14/1**

3510 **8** shd **Downhill Skier (IRE)**[9] 7390 6-9-6 **59** .... TomMcLaughlin 2 52
(W M Brisbourne) *hld up: rdn over 2f out: n.d* **15/2**

5000 **9** 2 1/4 **Diamond Daisy (IRE)**[28] 7068 4-9-1 **57** .... (p) AmyRyan(3) 3 44
(Mrs A Duffield) *s.s: hld up: rdn over 1f out: n.d* **8/1**

0035 **10** 1/2 **Bahamian Kid**[22] 7195 5-9-0 **60** .... (v) JackDuern(7) 10 45
(R Hollinshead) *hld up: hdwy over 2f out: edgd lft and wknd over 1f out* **13/2**

0600 **11** 7 **Ninth House (USA)**[76] 5768 8-9-6 **59** .... (t) RobertWinston 11 25
(Mrs R A Carr) *hdwy over 5f out: wknd over 1f out* **20/1**

1m 30.24s (0.64) **Going Correction** +0.075s/f (Slow)
WFA 3 from 4yo+ 1lb **11** Ran SP% **115.6**
Speed ratings (Par 101): **99,97,97,96,96 93,92,91,89,88 80**
CSF £92.61 CT £2007.89 TOTE £11.10: £2.40, £2.70, £6.40; EX 155.30.
Owner Mrs Christine Cone **Bred** J F Tuthill **Trained** Moreton Morrell, Warwicks

FOCUS
A modest handicap in which in-form runners were in the minority. The pace wasn't strong and most of the principals, the winner excepted, were close up throughout. The winner looks better than the bare form with the third possibly limiting things.

7502 RACING START H'CAP (DIV II) 7f 32y(P)
4:45 (4:45) (Class 6) (0-60,60) 3-Y-O+ **£1,364** (£403; £201) **Stalls** High

Form RPR

2400 **1** **Khajaaly (IRE)**[73] 5839 3-9-6 **60** .... JimmyQuinn 11 73
(Miss J Feilden) *hld up: hdwy over 2f out: shkn up to ld ins fnl f: readily* **25/1**

0006 **2** 1/2 **Suzhou**[11] 7376 3-9-4 **58** .... (v) CathyGannon 3 69
(D J Coakley) *chsd ldrs: led and edgd lft 2f out: rdn and hdd ins fnl f: styd on* **8/1**

0225 **3** 2 **Nicholas Pocock (IRE)**[3] 7468 4-9-7 **60** .... KierenFallon 4 66
(B Ellison) *hld up: hdwy over 1f out: sn hung lft: r.o: nt rch ldrs* **9/4**[1]

0000 **4** nk **Talent Scout (IRE)**[28] 7064 4-9-1 **54** .... GrahamGibbons 5 59
(T D Walford) *hld up: rdn over 2f out: hdwy over 1f out: r.o* **7/1**

1000 **5** 2 3/4 **Zeffirelli**[31] 7007 5-9-6 **59** .... FrannyNorton 8 57
(M Quinn) *sn pushed along and prom: rdn over 1f out: no ex ins fnl f* **50/1**

4305 **6** 1 1/4 **Namu**[7] 7426 7-9-1 **54** .... (p) AdamKirby 6 48
(Miss T Spearing) *hld up: hdwy over 1f out: no ex ins fnl f* **25/1**

0553 **7** nk **Just Jimmy (IRE)**[6] 7450 5-9-6 **59** .... (p) GeorgeBaker 2 53
(P D Evans) *chsd ldrs: hmpd over 2f out: wknd fnl f* **5/1**[3]

4400 **8** nk **Decency (IRE)**[36] 6864 3-9-6 **60** .... (v[1]) DaneO'Neill 1 53
(H J L Dunlop) *s.i.s: hld up: hdwy over 1f out: nt trble ldrs* **20/1**

4000 **9** 4 **Musical Script (USA)**[32] 6439 7-9-5 **58** .... (b) FrankieMcDonald 10 40
(Mouse Hamilton-Fairley) *trckd ldrs: racd keenly: rdn over 2f out: wknd over 1f out* **66/1**

6402 **10** 1 1/4 **My Name Is Bert**[11] 7377 4-9-4 **57** .... RobertWinston 12 36
(Lucinda Featherstone) *prom: rdn 1/2-way: wknd over 1f out* **9/2**[2]

-454 **11** 3 **Madame Boot (FR)**[16] 7298 3-9-3 **57** .... (p) TomQueally 9 27
(P J Makin) *hld up: a in rr* **8/1**

00 **12** 6 **Flyjack (USA)**[35] 6898 3-9-1 **58** .... AndrewHeffernan(3) 7 —
(Mrs L Williamson) *led: rdn and hdd 2f out: wkng whn hmpd over 1f out* **40/1**

1m 29.9s (0.30) **Going Correction** +0.075s/f (Slow)
WFA 3 from 4yo+ 1lb **12** Ran SP% **118.7**
Speed ratings (Par 101): **101,100,98,97,94 93,92,92,87,86 83,76**
Tote Swingers: 1&2 £43.80, 1&3 £5.90, 2&3 £5.30 CSF £201.98 CT £648.30 TOTE £52.90: £8.00, £3.10, £2.00; EX 360.60.
Owner Geegeez.co.uk **Bred** Barry Noonan And Denis Noonan **Trained** Exning, Suffolk

FOCUS
Another modest affair in which good recent form was thin on the ground, but in contrast to the first division, it was well run and most of the principals came from behind. The form is rated around the winner and third.
Musical Script(USA) Official explanation: jockey said gelding ran too freely.

7503 BET GRAND SLAM DARTS - BETDAQ MAIDEN AUCTION STKS 7f 32y(P)
5:15 (5:18) (Class 6) 2-Y-O **£1,706** (£503; £252) **Stalls** High

Form RPR

0 **1** **Islesman**[21] 7203 2-8-9 0 .... EddieAhern 8 70
(Mrs H S Main) *s.i.s: hld up: hdwy 1/2-way: led over 1f out: rdn out* **14/1**

2 nk **Fifth In Line (IRE)** 2-8-3 0 .... SophieDoyle(3) 5 66
(J A Osborne) *chsd ldrs: rdn and ev ch fr over 1f out: r.o* **50/1**

03 **3** 1 3/4 **Phase Shift**[20] 7242 2-8-6 0 .... DavidProbert 6 62
(W R Muir) *a.p: rdn over 2f out: styd on* **5/2**[2]

4 **4** 1/2 **Indian Arrow**[77] 5733 2-8-11 0 .... WilliamCarson 12 66
(J J Quinn) *s.i.s: in rr and rdn 1/2-way: r.o ins fnl f: nt rch ldrs* **33/1**

0 **5** 1 1/2 **Dunhoy (IRE)**[8] 7408 2-8-9 0 .... MickyFenton 10 60
(Stef Higgins) *s.i.s: bhd and rdn 1/2-way: r.o ins fnl f: nrst fin* **25/1**

3 **6** 1 **Unex Goya (IRE)**[31] 7002 2-8-10 0 .... MatthewDavies(3) 11 62
(George Baker) *prom: pushed along 1/2-way: rdn over 2f out: styd on same pce appr fnl f* **6/4**[1]

000 **7** 1 **Greenhead High**[8] 7408 2-8-9 0 .... J-PGuillambert 2 55
(P Howling) *led: rdn and hdd over 1f out: wknd insde fnl f* **100/1**

0 **8** shd **Crossword**[23] 7164 2-8-9 0 .... (b[1]) ChrisCatlin 4 55
(M Botti) *mid-div: pushed along 1/2-way: rdn and wknd over 1f out* **7/1**[3]

0 **9** 3/4 **Kambis**[23] 7163 2-8-11 0 .... KierenFallon 9 55
(L M Cumani) *s.i.s: shkn up on outer over 2f out: eased whn btn fnl f* **25/1**

10 1 **Georgey Girl** 2-8-4 0 .... JimmyQuinn 1 46+
(G A Swinbank) *s.s: a in rr* **10/1**

11 nse **Sir Randolf (IRE)** 2-8-11 0 .... JamesDoyle 7 53
(S Kirk) *chsd ldrs: rdn 1/2-way: wknd over 1f out* **10/1**

1m 31.37s (1.77) **Going Correction** +0.075s/f (Slow) **11** Ran SP% **119.5**
Speed ratings (Par 94): **92,91,89,89,87 86,85,84,84,82 82**
Tote Swingers: 1&2 £63.00, 1&3 £7.20, 2&3 £38.40 CSF £575.08 TOTE £24.20: £4.80, £20.70, £1.10; EX 646.70.
Owner Donald M Kerr **Bred** Barry Walters **Trained** Kingston Lisle, Oxon

FOCUS
A fair maiden run in thick fog. The gallop appeared to be a sensible one in the conditions. The third is rated close to her debut form.

NOTEBOOK
Islesman had made his debut at Newmarket in a better maiden than this and showed the benefit of that run with an improved performance, moving to the front quite smoothly turning in before battling on well. By Oratorio out of a Rainbow Quest mare, he'll be suited by further in time, but looks no more than a fair handicap prospect right now. (op 16-1)
Fifth In Line(IRE), a Kodiac filly with an ordinary pedigree that hadn't attracted much attention at the sales, shaped encouragingly on debut, never far away and keeping on well. Probably best kept around this trip for now, she seems likely to improve.
Phase Shift looked to hold good form claims and might still win one of these before long, but she was unsuited by the drop in trip as the race developed and needs a return to 1m. (tchd 2-1 and 3-1 in a place)
Indian Arrow looks to be taking more after his sire Sleeping Indian than his speedy dam, and was putting in some good late work. He'll improve again, and might be an interesting one for handicaps after another run.
Dunhoy(IRE) was poorly paced turning for home but stayed on in good fashion late and, being a half-brother to a 1m2f winner sired by a sprinter, probably has further improvement in him when tried over 1m.
Unex Goya(IRE), acquired for 17,000gns out of William Haggas' yard at the recent Horses-In-Training Sale, fared disappointingly for his new yard, starting to struggle even before the final turn. He's by a sire whose progeny tend to go well on Fibresand, however, and given he made a promising turf debut on soft ground, isn't one to give up on switched to that surface. (op 11-8 tchd 5-4 and 13-8)
Greenhead High might have blown his cover now as far as handicaps are concerned.
Crossword was once again short in the betting but presumably shows more at home than he has so far on the track, first-time blinkers having little effect here. (op 10-1 tchd 11-1)

Kambis needs one more run for a mark and looks something of a slow learner.
Georgey Girl Official explanation: jockey said filly was slow away.

7504 BACK & LAY AT BETDAQ H'CAP 1m 5f 194y(P)
5:45 (5:46) (Class 5) (0-70,70) 3-Y-0+ £2,007 (£597; £298; £149) Stalls Low

Form RPR
061 **1** **Jezza**[9] 7398 4-9-1 **57** 6ex StevieDonohoe 10 70
(V R A Dartnall) *hld up: hdwy and hmpd over 3f out: led 2f out: rdn and edgd lft ins fnl f: styd on* **10/1**
0-52 **2** *3* **Stormy Morning**[18] 7011 4-9-6 **62** DaneO'Neill 9 71
(Mrs Lawney Hill) *hld up: hdwy 6f out: rdn and ev ch 2f out: styd on same pce ins fnl f* **22/1**
5062 **3** *3 3/4* **Seaside Sizzler**[40] 6781 3-9-3 **67** (bt) JimCrowley 8 71
(R M Beckett) *hld up: drvn along 1/2-way: hdwy over 2f out: nt rch ldrs* **9/1**[3]
1051 **4** *3 3/4* **Mohawk Ridge**[23] 7176 4-9-10 **66** (p) GrahamGibbons 5 65
(M Dods) *chsd ldrs: led over 3f out: rdn and hdd 2f out: wknd fnl f* **16/1**
6011 **5** *7* **Naheell**[7] 7422 4-9-1 **64** JulieBurke(7) 13 53
(G Prodromou) *hld up: styd on appr fnl f: nvr on terms* **4/1**[2]
2 **6** *2 1/4* **Tenhoo**[175] 2500 4-8-10 **52** EddieAhern 3 38
(E J Alston) *hld up: hmpd 3f out: n.d* **9/1**[3]
5453 **7** *shd* **Starshine**[23] 7181 3-8-12 **62** SteveDrowne 2 47
(R Charlton) *hld up in tch: n.m.r 3f out: sn rdn and wknd* **12/1**
5420 **8** *15* **Light The City (IRE)**[46] 6631 3-8-4 **54** ChrisCatlin 7 18
(Mrs R A Carr) *chsd ldr tl rdn 4f out: wknd over 2f out: t.o* **33/1**
4360 **9** *8* **Weybridge Light**[18] 7270 5-9-1 **57** (v) AdamKirby 11 —
(M R Bosley) *hld up in tch: hmpd and wknd 3f out: t.o* **28/1**
5045 **10** *8* **Bushy Dell (IRE)**[23] 7167 5-9-1 **57** CathyGannon 1 —
(Miss J Feilden) *chsd ldrs: rdn over 4f out: wknd over 2f out: t.o* **14/1**
0305 **11** *6* **Faith Jicaro (IRE)**[18] 7275 3-8-12 **62** (b) LukeMorris 4 —
(N J Vaughan) *led: rdn and hdd over 3f out: wknd over 2f out: t.o* **25/1**
-212 **12** *111* **Kiama Bay (IRE)**[14] 7337 4-10-0 **70** KierenFallon 6 —
(J J Quinn) *hld up in tch: pushed along and lost pl over 5f out: sn bhd: t.o* **15/8**[1]

3m 3.52s (-2.48) **Going Correction** +0.075s/f (Slow)
WFA 3 from 4yo+ 8lb **12** Ran SP% **118.7**
Speed ratings (Par 103): **110,108,106,104,100 98,98,90,85,80 77,—**
Tote Swingers: 1&2 £21.60, 1&3 £15.60, 2&3 £43.00 CSF £215.63 CT £2051.49 TOTE £9.00: £6.00, £11.40, £2.80; EX 238.90.
Owner Under The Radar **Bred** C P Ranson **Trained** Brayford, Devon

FOCUS
A well-run contested affair on paper but it was run at a muddling gallop and a couple weren't seen to best advantage on account of trouble in running just as the race was beginning in earnest. The form is rated at face value with the third the best guide.
Kiama Bay(IRE) Official explanation: vet said gelding returned with a fibrillating heart.

7505 HOTEL & CONFERENCING AT WOLVERHAMPTON MAIDEN STKS 5f 216y(P)
6:15 (6:18) (Class 5) 3-4-Y-0 £2,007 (£597; £298; £149) Stalls Low

Form RPR
0030 **1** **Hidden Destiny**[7] 7426 3-9-3 55 TomQueally 7 71
(P J Makin) *mde all: rdn over 1f out: styd on* **12/1**[3]
20-2 **2** *1* **Opus Dei**[57] 6310 3-9-3 72 (p) IanMongan 1 68
(D Nicholls) *chsd ldrs: rdn over 2f out: styd on u.p* **1/2**[1]
005 **3** *1/2* **Crimson Queen**[121] 4251 3-8-12 57 JackMitchell 2 61
(R Brotherton) *chsd wnr: rdn over 2f out: styd on same pce ins fnl f* **25/1**
5354 **4** *1 3/4* **Luisa Tetrazzini (IRE)**[7] 7426 4-8-8 54 ow1 MarkCoumbe(5) 11 56
(D Bourton) *sn outpcd: hdwy over 1f out: edgd lft and styd on ins fnl f: nrst fin* **7/1**[2]
3662 **5** *2 3/4* **Ruler's Honour (IRE)**[23] 7166 3-9-0 55 (p) RobertLButler(3) 3 52
(T J Etherington) *prom: rdn over 2f out: wknd ins fnl f* **14/1**
6 *2* **Drumcliffe Dancer (IRE)**[120] 4311 3-8-7 60 KTO'Neill(5) 4 40
(W McCreery, Ire) *s.i.s: hld up: rdn over 2f out: nvr rchd ldrs* **7/1**[2]
0003 **7** *shd* **Jemimaville (IRE)**[16] 7300 3-8-12 47 (v) WilliamCarson 5 40
(G C Bravery) *hld up: rdn over 2f out: n.d* **25/1**
0003 **8** *2 1/2* **Cheshire Lady (IRE)**[4] 7461 3-8-12 47 (t) LiamJones 6 32
(W M Brisbourne) *mid-div: rdn over 2f out: wknd over 1f out* **20/1**
-000 **9** *1 3/4* **Orpen Lady**[84] 5471 4-8-9 42 AndrewHeffernan(3) 10 26
(J M Bradley) *mid-div: rdn over 2f out: sn wknd* **66/1**
10 *3/4* **Hyden (IRE)**[21] 7216 4-9-3 0 LukeMorris 12 29
(Thomas Gibney, Ire) *chsd ldrs: drvn along over 2f out: wknd wl over 1f out* **50/1**

1m 15.12s (0.12) **Going Correction** +0.075s/f (Slow) **10** Ran SP% **121.9**
Speed ratings (Par 103): **102,100,100,97,94 91,91,87,85,84**
Tote Swingers: 1&2 £3.10, 1&3 £11.90, 2&3 £7.80 CSF £18.70 TOTE £9.00: £1.30, £1.10, £6.90; EX 29.80.
Owner Mrs P J Makin **Bred** Newsells Park Stud **Trained** Ogbourne Maisey, Wilts

FOCUS
An uncompetitive maiden and something of a surprise result at the end of a steadily-run race in very poor visibility. The third is the best guide to the level.

7506 WOLVERHAMPTON-RACECOURSE.CO.UK APPRENTICE H'CAP 5f 216y(P)
6:45 (6:45) (Class 6) (0-52,52) 3-Y-0+ £1,706 (£503; £252) Stalls Low

Form RPR
0333 **1** **Cheery Cat (USA)**[11] 7380 6-8-12 **50** (v) MatthewCosham 12 67
(J Balding) *led early: chsd ldr tl led again over 2f out: rdn out* **7/2**[2]
0050 **2** *3 3/4* **Boy The Bell**[28] 7064 3-8-7 **50** JosephYoung(5) 2 55
(M Mullineaux) *s.i.s: hdwy 5f out: rdn over 1f out: styd on to go 2nd nr fin* **20/1**
405 **3** *nk* **Force To Spend**[15] 7314 3-8-6 **49** IanBurns(5) 7 53
(N P Littmoden) *chsd ldrs: rdn and edgd lft over 1f out: no ex ins fnl f: lost 2nd nr fin* **20/1**
3064 **4** *1/2* **Carnival Dream**[11] 7380 5-8-7 **50** (p) DavidSimmonson(5) 10 52
(H A McWilliams) *hld up: r.o u.p ins fnl f: nrst fin* **11/1**
5300 **5** *1/2* **Gilderoy**[8] 7402 3-8-9 **50** (b[1]) LucyBarry(3) 8 51
(D J S Ffrench Davis) *hld up: styd on ins fnl f: nvr nrr* **25/1**
6206 **6** *nk* **Abhainn (IRE)**[22] 7192 4-8-7 **50** ThomasBrown(5) 3 50
(B Palling) *sn led: hdd over 2f out: no ex ins fnl f* **11/1**
0006 **7** *hd* **Kheley (IRE)**[19] 7249 4-8-13 **51** MatthewLawson 13 50
(W M Brisbourne) *chsd ldrs: edgd lft 3f out: rdn over 1f out: no ex ins fnl f* **12/1**
6004 **8** *1 1/2* **Barraland**[2] 7477 5-8-11 **49** (v) NathanAlison 4 43
(George Baker) *trckd ldrs: nt clr run over 1f out: wknd ins fnl f* **8/1**[3]
4165 **9** *2* **Duke Of Rainford**[7] 7425 3-8-11 **52** ShaneBKelly(3) 5 40+
(M Herrington) *s.s: nvr on terms* **8/1**[3]
1040 **10** *11* **Commander Wish**[19] 7249 7-8-8 **51** VictoriaFletcher(5) 1 —
(Lucinda Featherstone) *hld up: bdly hmpd and rdr lost iron wl over 2f out: sn bhd* **8/1**[3]
560 **U** **Sorrel Point**[7] 7425 7-9-0 **52** (vt) NatashaEaton 9 —
(H J Collingridge) *hld up: hmpd and uns rdr wl over 2f out* **25/1**
5324 **F** **Shakespeare's Son**[37] 6847 5-9-0 **52** (p) SophieSilvester 6 —
(H J Evans) *prom tl fell wl over 2f out: fatally injured* **10/3**[1]

1m 15.41s (0.41) **Going Correction** +0.075s/f (Slow) **12** Ran SP% **120.2**
Speed ratings (Par 101): **100,95,94,93,93 92,92,90,87,73 —,—**
Tote Swingers: 1&2 £23.60, 1&3 £57.40, 2&3 £91.30 CSF £78.04 CT £1243.80 TOTE £4.00: £1.60, £1.50, £13.10; EX 141.40.
Owner The Cataractonium Racing Syndicate **Bred** K L Ramsay & Sarah K Ramsay **Trained** Scrooby, Notts

FOCUS
A very modest handicap but a trouble-fraught one with one faller and another brought down, though from could be seen through the murk only perhaps the fourth among the principals suffered any interference. The form is not entirely convincing, with the third the best guide.

7507 WOLVERHAMPTON HOLIDAY INN H'CAP 1m 4f 50y(P)
7:15 (7:29) (Class 2) (0-100,100) 3-Y-£8,705 (£2,605; £1,302; £651; £324) Stalls Low

Form RPR
4024 **1** **Tominator**[27] 7084 3-8-6 **88** GrahamGibbons 2 95
(R Hollinshead) *a.p: chsd ldr 2f out: rdn to ld over 1f out: edgd lft: styd on* **4/1**[2]
-030 **2** *1/2* **Moyenne Corniche**[27] 7100 5-9-5 **95** DaneO'Neill 3 101
(B Ellison) *led: rdn and hdd over 1f out: styd on* **12/1**
0-53 **3** *hd* **Pires**[48] 6562 6-9-3 **93** KierenFallon 6 99
(A J Martin, Ire) *hld up: hdwy over 1f out: sn rdn and edgd lft: r.o* **6/5**[1]
3001 **4** *7* **Mystery Star (IRE)**[22] 7196 5-9-10 **100** TomQueally 7 94
(M H Tompkins) *chsd ldr tl rdn over 2f out: styd on same pce appr fnl f* **6/1**[3]
5035 **5** *hd* **Nanton (USA)**[62] 6179 8-9-3 **93** ChrisCatlin 1 87
(J S Goldie) *chsd ldrs: rdn over 2f out: styd on same pce appr fnl f* **4/1**[2]
006 **6** *11* **Mister New York (USA)**[18] 6123 5-9-5 **95** (b) GeorgeBaker 4 72
(Noel T Chance) *hld up: rdn and wknd over 1f out* **28/1**

2m 38.11s (-2.99) **Going Correction** +0.075s/f (Slow)
WFA 3 from 5yo+ 6lb **6** Ran SP% **110.9**
Speed ratings (Par 109): **112,111,111,106,106 99**
Tote Swingers: 1&2 £5.40, 1&3 £1.30, 2&3 £2.90 CSF £44.87 TOTE £3.80: £2.50, £2.40; EX 55.40.
Owner Mrs Susy Haslehurst **Bred** Mrs S L Brimble **Trained** Upper Longdon, Staffs

FOCUS
A useful handicap, though one run at an ordinary tempo and that was probably the difference between victory and defeat as far as the runner-up was concerned. The form looks pretty ordinary, rated through the runner-up.

NOTEBOOK
Tominator came here on the back of two solid efforts, but his win here seemed to owe plenty to getting first run on the favourite and eventual third off the final bend, always looking just in command thereafter. That said, he was Listed placed as a 2yo, will still have some options this winter even after being reassessed (though his connections reportedly seem to favour a race at Deauville after Christmas) and ought to continue to give a good account. (op 11-2)
Moyenne Corniche has proved hard to predict this year but his new yard had gone to 30,000gns to secure him out of Michael Bell's yard at the recent Newmarket Sales and, while not obviously looking to have secured a bargain, at least on this evidence have something to work with. Soon out in front, he battled on better than might have been expected once headed, trying the trip for the first time on what was his AW debut. Probably running as well as he has all year, he is undoubtedly on a fair mark if his new yard can continue to coax him to put his best foot forward. (op 14-1 tchd 10-1)
Pires looked to hold good claims on his third in the Cambridgeshire but he can be counted a little unlucky, as he was denied a run when caught in a pocket on the home turn just when the leader was going for home. He was really starting to cut into that advantage close home and could make amends if kept to the surface this winter, but it's just as likely he'll go back hurdling now. (op 11-10 tchd Evens, 5-4 and 11-8 in a place)
Mystery Star(IRE) has won twice here before but was readily put in his place off his highest career mark yet, with the ordinary tempo back in trip also seeming not to suit. (op 13-2)
Nanton(USA) looked potentially well treated back on AW following a turf campaign at mostly higher levels this year. However, he was disappointing, dropping away tamely, and is perhaps in need of a break. (tchd 11-2)
Mister New York(USA) was again a long way below his best and is best watched for now. (op 20-1)

7508 BETDAQ - THE BETTING EXCHANGE H'CAP 1m 1f 103y(P)
7:45 (7:55) (Class 7) (0-50,50) 3-Y-0+ £1,364 (£403; £201) Stalls Low

Form RPR
3005 **1** **Iguacu**[29] 7039 6-8-11 **48** (p) MatthewDavies(3) 2 58
(George Baker) *s.i.s: hld up: hdwy over 2f out: rdn over 1f out: r.o to ld post* **9/1**
0500 **2** *hd* **Love In The Park**[50] 6518 5-9-1 **49** JackMitchell 13 59
(R Brotherton) *hld up: hdwy over 2f out: rdn to ld wl ins fnl f: hdd post* **12/1**
2343 **3** *1 3/4* **Al Rayanah**[22] 7199 7-9-2 **50** (p) KirstyMilczarek 7 56
(G Prodromou) *a.p: led over 2f out: rdn: edgd rt and hdd wl ins fnl f* **7/2**[1]
0042 **4** *1 1/2* **Escardo (GER)**[22] 7199 7-9-0 **48** WilliamCarson 6 51
(D G Bridgwater) *mid-div: hdwy 3f out: rdn over 1f out: styd on* **8/1**
2-00 **5** *nse* **Royal Island (IRE)**[16] 7299 8-9-2 **50** AdamKirby 4 53
(M G Quinlan) *mid-div: hdwy over 2f out: rdn over 1f out: no ex ins fnl f* **8/1**
2406 **6** *1 3/4* **Masterofceremonies**[22] 7200 7-9-2 **50** (v) TomMcLaughlin 1 49
(W M Brisbourne) *s.i.s: in rr: bhd and rdn 6f out: r.o ins fnl f: nvr nrr* **13/2**[2]
1060 **7** *1* **Ocean Of Peace (FR)**[19] 7251 7-9-1 **49** LukeMorris 10 46
(M R Bosley) *prom: chsd ldr over 3f out: rdn over 2f out: wknd ins fnl f* **10/1**
0000 **8** *2 1/2* **Mekong Miss**[7] 7429 4-8-13 **47** DaneO'Neill 8 39
(D Shaw) *hld up: nvr on terms* **20/1**
0000 **9** *3/4* **Wrecking Crew (IRE)**[29] 7043 6-9-2 **50** JamesMillman 3 40
(B R Millman) *prom: rdn over 3f out: wknd over 1f out* **11/1**
0300 **10** *3 1/4* **Bold Hawk**[28] 7070 4-8-9 **50** (tp) NathanAlison(7) 12 33
(Mrs C A Dunnett) *mid-div: rdn and wknd over 2f out* **50/1**
004 **11** *12* **Acropolis (IRE)**[22] 7199 9-9-0 **48** (p) KierenFallon 5 6
(A W Carroll) *chsd ldr tl led over 5f out: rdn and hdd over 2f out: wknd over 1f out* **7/1**[3]
000/ **12** *5* **Viking Rock (IRE)**[692] 7789 4-9-2 **50** TomQueally 9 —
(Matthew Salaman) *led: hdd over 5f out: wknd wl over 2f out* **16/1**

2m 2.61s (0.91) **Going Correction** +0.075s/f (Slow) **12** Ran SP% **118.0**
Speed ratings (Par 97): **98,97,96,94,94 93,92,90,89,86 76,71**
Tote Swingers: 1&2 £8.40, 1&3 £8.30, 2&3 £7.90 CSF £111.80 CT £454.34 TOTE £11.30: £2.10, £2.90, £1.90; EX 166.00.

Owner Derek & Cheryl Holder **Bred** Cheveley Park Stud Ltd **Trained** Moreton Morrell, Warwicks

FOCUS

Bottom-grade fare but competitive for the level and a close finish at the end of a well-run race. The form looks straightforward rated around the third and fourth to recent form.

T/Plt: £619.30 to a £1 stake. Pool of £74,250 - 87.51 winning tickets. T/Qpdt: £46.00 to a £1 stake. Pool of £10,562 - 169.60 winning tickets. CR

7509 - 7513a (Foreign Racing) - See Raceform Interactive

7431 DUNDALK (A.W) (L-H)

Friday, November 19

OFFICIAL GOING: Standard

7514a CROWNE PLAZA LEADING JOCKEY & TRAINER CHAMPIONSHIP H'CAP 2m (P)

8:30 (8:35) (60-90,86) 3-Y-O+ **£8,243** (£1,911; £836; £477)

RPR

1 **Herostatus**[19] 7252 3-9-0 83.......(b[1]) JMurtagh 1 91+
(M Johnston) *a.p: sn led: hdd after 4f: led again ent st: asserted over 1f out: styd on wl ins fnl f: comf* **6/4**[1]

2 4 **Hawk Flight (IRE)**[19] 7263 5-8-13 76....... GFCarroll(3) 2 79
(Miss Maura McGuinness, Ire) *trckd ldrs on inner: 5th 1/2-way: hdwy into 3rd 2f out: wnt 2nd u.p over 1f out: no imp on wnr and kpt on one pce* **7/1**[3]

3 1 3/4 **Champion Boy (IRE)**[19] 7263 4-8-11 71....... JAHeffernan 5 72
(J C Hayden, Ire) *in rr of mid-div on inner: 9th ent st: 6th on outer over 1f out: kpt on wl u.p ins fnl f* **7/1**[3]

4 shd **Total Victory (IRE)**[185] 2255 7-8-4 67....... ShaneFoley(3) 11 68
(C A Murphy, Ire) *towards rr: 10th appr st: 7th on outer over 1f out: kpt on wl ins fnl f* **16/1**

5 nk **Celendine**[35] 6910 3-9-3 86....... FMBerry 13 86
(John M Oxx, Ire) *mid-div: hdwy on outer into 4th appr st: sn rdn: no imp fr 1 1/2f out* **7/1**[3]

6 3 1/2 **Run With The Wind (IRE)**[54] 4217 4-8-5 65....... WMLordan 9 61
(Michael Hourigan, Ire) *trckd ldrs: 4th 1/2-way: rdn in 3rd early st: no ex u.p fr over 1f out* **9/1**

7 1 1/2 **Solo Performer (IRE)**[42] 6730 5-9-8 82....... DPMcDonogh 10 76
(H Rogers, Ire) *prom: plld hrd and led after 4f: hdd u.p ent st: sn no ex and wknd* **16/1**

8 2 **Alajan (IRE)**[19] 7263 4-9-3 84.......(bt) SHJames(7) 8 76
(William J Fitzpatrick, Ire) *chsd ldrs: 7th on inner 1/2-way: no ex fr under 2f out* **16/1**

9 22 **Summerlea (IRE)**[26] 5431 4-8-9 69.......(b) KJManning 6 35
(Eoin Griffin, Ire) *mid-div: 8th 1/2-way: no ex fr early st: wknd* **33/1**

10 shd **Are You The One (IRE)**[70] 5934 4-9-2 76....... CO'Donoghue 3 42
(Kieran Purcell, Ire) *trckd ldrs on inner: 3rd 1/2-way: drvn along and no ex ent st: sn wknd* **5/1**[2]

11 4 **Lord Chancellor (IRE)**[76] 5778 4-9-8 85.......(tp) BACurtis(3) 12 46
(Lee Smyth, Ire) *a towards rr: no ex fr early st: eased whn btn fr over 1f out* **33/1**

12 dist **All On Board (IRE)**[26] 4525 4-8-4 64....... DJMoran 4 —
(Paul Nolan, Ire) *a bhd: trailing fr 4f out: t.o* **33/1**

3m 23.73s (203.73)
WFA 3 from 4yo+ 9lb **12 Ran SP% 130.6**
CSF £13.94 CT £62.94 TOTE £2.70: £1.30, £2.30, £2.10; DF 17.40.
Owner Sheikh Hamdan Bin Mohammed Al Maktoum **Bred** Darley **Trained** Middleham Moor, N Yorks

NOTEBOOK

Herostatus showed the resolution displayed by most of the horses Mark Johnston has sent to Ireland during the autumn as he won without too many alarms. Always prominent, Johnny Murtagh was happy to take a lead to the top of the straight and, when he asked his mount to go and win his race, he responded well and poured it on from the front. He was never in danger. (op 5/4)
Hawk Flight(IRE) began to stay on from well over a furlong out and kept going to the line without making any impression on the winner. (op 7/1 tchd 13/2)
Champion Boy(IRE) came home well. (op 8/1 tchd 13/2)
Celendine pulled her way into a prominent position over half a mile out and one would have expected her to threaten from that point, but she hit something of a flat spot turning in and any headway she made from there was strictly at one pace. (op 8/1)
Run With The Wind(IRE) ◆ probably did a bit too much while being restrained for the first mile and a half, but he travelled strongly into the race turning into the straight and looked for a few strides as though he was going to make a real race of it with the favourite. He got a bit tired late on but looks an interesting one for maiden hurdles later on. (op 16/1 tchd 8/1)

7515 - 7516a (Foreign Racing) - See Raceform Interactive

7484 LINGFIELD (L-H)

Saturday, November 20

OFFICIAL GOING: Standard

Wind: Almost nil Weather: Overcast

7517 E B F LADBROKES SOUTH CHAMPIONS MAIDEN STKS 5f (P)

11:45 (11:45) (Class 5) 2-Y-O **£2,978** (£886; £442; £221) **Stalls** High

Form RPR

002 1 **Liberty Green (IRE)**[8] 7418 2-8-12 69....... JamesDoyle 6 68
(A J McCabe) *disp ld to over 1f out: sn hrd rdn and nt qckn: kpt on fnl f to ld nr fin* **3/1**[2]

04 2 nk **Crystallus (IRE)**[19] 7268 2-8-12 0....... JoeFanning 3 67
(Mrs A Duffield) *disp ld: narrow advantage over 1f out: worn down nr fin* **25/1**

4245 3 shd **Wolf Slayer**[76] 5785 2-8-12 73....... RichardKingscote 7 67
(Tom Dascombe) *chsd ldng pair: rdn wl over 1f out: clsd grad fnl f: nvr quite got there* **9/2**[3]

00 4 nk **Zeavola (IRE)**[9] 7408 2-8-12 0....... NeilChalmers 2 65
(A M Balding) *trckd ldng pair: gng strly 2f out: effrt against rail over 1f out: rdn and nt qckn fnl f* **28/1**

5 3 **Avon Supreme** 2-8-12 0....... ChrisCatlin 4 55+
(Miss Gay Kelleway) *a midfield: wnt 5th 2f out but nt on terms: shkn up and kpt on* **8/1**

5 6 3 1/2 **These Dreams**[18] 7279 2-8-12 0....... FrannyNorton 8 42
(R C Guest) *a abt same pl: outpcd fr 1/2-way: nvr on terms after* **50/1**

7 1 1/2 **Wealth Whispers (IRE)** 2-8-12 0....... LiamJones 5 37+
(P W D'Arcy) *dwlt: detached in last: pushed along and modest late prog* **16/1**

623 8 3 3/4 **Fettuccine (IRE)**[14] 7346 2-8-12 73....... JamieSpencer 10 23
(J Noseda) *forced to racd wd: sn struggling in rr and u.p: nvr a factor* **11/8**[1]

06 9 7 **Walshestown Lad (IRE)**[8] 7418 2-9-3 0....... LukeMorris 1 3
(R A Harris) *t.k.h: chsd ldng quartet: hrd rdn and wknd 2f out: t.o* **100/1**

59.90 secs (1.10) **Going Correction** +0.10s/f (Slow) **9 Ran SP% 112.5**
Speed ratings (Par 96): **95,94,94,93,89 83,81,75,63**
toteswingers: 1&2 £13.20, 1&3 £2.00, 2&3 £7.30 CSF £73.72 TOTE £3.20: £1.10, £6.00, £1.30; EX 52.70 Trifecta £309.70 Part won. Pool: £418.53 - 0.86 winning units..
Owner Mrs Linda Francis **Bred** Martin Francis Ltd **Trained** Averham Park, Notts

FOCUS

A modest maiden in which the principals were always handy and the front pair duelled for the lead from flag-fall. The winner is rated to recent course form.

NOTEBOOK

Liberty Green(IRE), officially rated 69 and narrowly beaten in a similar event over C&D eight days earlier, probably only needed to repeat that performance in order to take this. She showed a gritty attitude to force her head in front where it mattered, and is now likely to be given a break before being brought back over 6f. (tchd 7-2)
Crystallus(IRE) looked a difficult ride at Wolverhampton last time, but she did little wrong on this sharp turning track, battling for the lead throughout and keeping on to the end. She will have more options now that she can be handicapped. (op 20-1)
Wolf Slayer, rated 73, had some decent form to her name, especially when fifth behind four subsequent winners at York last time, but it was disappointing that she couldn't pick the front pair up in the home straight despite having every chance to do so. She is starting to run out of excuses. (op 6-1 tchd 13-2)
Zeavola(IRE), who had looked quirky in her first two starts, stayed on against the inside rail to record her best effort yet, though that has to be measured in the context of the race. She is another who now qualifies for a mark. (op 40-1)
Fettuccine(IRE) looked the one to beat after making the frame in a couple of recent turf maidens, but she struggled to go the pace and was being hard ridden in last place by halfway. Her rider reported that she was never travelling. Official explanation: jockey said filly was never travelling. (tchd 5-4 and 13-8 in a place)

7518 LADBROKES ARENA H'CAP (DIV I) 6f (P)

12:15 (12:16) (Class 6) (0-60,63) 3-Y-O+ **£1,706** (£503; £252) **Stalls** Low

Form RPR

6512 1 **Wooden King (IRE)**[15] 7334 5-9-5 60....... TomMcLaughlin 8 69
(M S Saunders) *trckd ldr: rdn to ld over 1f out: hrd pressed fnl f: hld on: all out* **3/1**[1]

6054 2 hd **Bollywood Style**[10] 7390 5-9-3 58....... LiamJones 11 67
(J R Best) *settled in last quartet on outer: rdn wl over 1f out: r.o fnl f: tk 2nd post* **12/1**

3121 3 nse **Rio Royale (IRE)**[20] 7249 4-9-5 60.......(p) JimCrowley 9 69
(Mrs A J Perrett) *trckd ldng pair: drvn to chal over 1f out: chsd wnr after: nt qckn and hld nr fin: lost 2nd post* **9/2**[2]

2306 4 hd **Chinese Democracy (USA)**[32] 7006 3-9-2 57.......(v) JamesDoyle 6 65
(P D Evans) *chsd ldrs: drvn 2f out: prog on inner to chal fnl f: nt qckn last 75yds* **12/1**

6600 5 hd **Charles Darwin (IRE)**[7] 7442 7-9-3 58....... FrannyNorton 7 65
(M Blanshard) *trckd ldrs: gng wl 2f out: rdn and nt qckn over 1f out: kpt on again ins fnl f: nvr gng to chal* **14/1**

003 6 1 1/2 **Clerical (USA)**[15] 7332 4-9-2 57.......(p) JamieSpencer 4 60
(R M H Cowell) *settled in midfield: nt clr run over 1f out: kpt on same pce fnl f: nvr able to chal* **8/1**

2000 7 nk **Sweet Avon**[10] 7390 3-9-4 59....... EddieAhern 12 61
(Matthew Salaman) *settled in midfield: shkn up 2f out: kpt on fr over 1f out: nvr rchd ldrs* **25/1**

3160 8 1 1/2 **Anjomarba (IRE)**[51] 6515 3-9-0 60.......(p) BillyCray(5) 5 57
(B R Johnson) *s.i.s: hld up in last quartet: pushed along 4f out: no prog tl kpt on fnl f* **14/1**

0500 9 1 1/4 **Poppy Golightly**[23] 7193 3-9-5 60....... GeorgeBaker 1 53
(R J Hodges) *trckd ldng trio on inner tl wknd over 1f out* **33/1**

204- 10 1/2 **One Oi**[472] 4645 5-9-2 57....... JoeFanning 2 48
(D W P Arbuthnot) *hld up in last quartet: shkn up over 1f out: no prog* **8/1**

0100 11 nse **Goodbye Cash (IRE)**[24] 7168 6-8-13 57....... AndrewHeffernan(3) 10 48
(R J Smith) *s.s: detached in last early: stl last 1f out: keeping on nr fin* **28/1**

3041 12 1 1/2 **Nollaig Shona (IRE)**[10] 7390 3-9-8 63....... KirstyMilczarek 3 49
(G Prodromou) *led to over 1f out: wknd rapidly* **11/2**[3]

1m 12.43s (0.53) **Going Correction** +0.10s/f (Slow) **12 Ran SP% 119.7**
Speed ratings (Par 101): **100,99,99,99,99 97,96,94,93,92 92,90**
toteswingers:1&2 £11.10, 2&3 £15.70, 1&3 £2.90 CSF £40.48 CT £164.41 TOTE £3.80: £1.10, £6.70, £1.70; EX 58.60 Trifecta £212.70 Part won. Pool: £287.55 - 0.62 winning units..
Owner Pat Hancock **Bred** Terence E Connelly **Trained** Green Ore, Somerset

FOCUS

A moderate sprint handicap and a typical Lingfield bunched finish. The form looks pretty solid rated around the placed horses.

7519 LADBROKES ARENA H'CAP (DIV II) 6f (P)

12:50 (12:54) (Class 6) (0-60,61) 3-Y-O+ **£1,706** (£503; £252) **Stalls** Low

Form RPR

0030 1 **Espy**[4] 7468 5-9-2 57....... AdamKirby 5 67
(I W McInnes) *trckd ldrs in 6th: effrt over 1f out: squeezed through rivals to ld last 150yds: pushed out: decisively* **14/1**

0025 2 1 **Loyal Royal (IRE)**[7] 7442 7-8-13 57.......(bt) RussKennemore(3) 10 64
(J M Bradley) *dwlt: t.k.h: hld up but rchd midfield after 2f: prog to press ldrs 2f out: drvn to chal and upsides 1f out: nt qckn* **9/1**

4653 3 3/4 **Laser Ruby**[10] 7391 3-9-6 61....... JimmyFortune 12 66+
(A M Balding) *stdd s: dropped in fr wd draw and hld up in last trio: pushed along and stdy prog 2f out: rdn ins fnl f: r.o to take 3rd last strides: too much to do* **8/1**[3]

1300 4 hd **Chjimes (IRE)**[15] 7331 6-9-5 60.......(p) KirstyMilczarek 11 64
(C R Dore) *trckd ldrs: effrt on inner over 1f out and cl enough: nt qckn fnl f* **11/1**

2160 5 3/4 **Silvee**[49] 6558 3-8-13 57....... KierenFox(3) 7 59
(J J Bridger) *trckd ldr: rdn to ld 2f out: hdd and fdd last 150yds* **10/1**

0530 6 1/2 **Athaakeel (IRE)**[4] 7468 4-9-5 60....... LukeMorris 4 60
(R A Harris) *s.v.s: latched on to bk of field after 2f: drvn and sme prog 2f out: kpt on u.p fnl f: nrst fin* **12/1**

3042 7 nse **Resplendent Alpha**[7] 7442 6-9-4 59.......(b) JimmyQuinn 8 59+
(P Howling) *stdd s and dropped in: hld up in last trio: rdn over 1f out: styd on: nvr rchd ldrs* **9/2**[1]

4112 8 1 **Bold Ring**[17] 7299 4-8-10 58....... JulieBurke(7) 6 55
(E J Creighton) *prom: drvn over 2f out: nt qckn over 1f out: wknd ins fnl f* **9/2**[1]

3005 **9** 1 **Teen Ager (FR)**[24] 7168 6-9-3 **58** TomMcLaughlin 2 51
(P Burgoyne) *t.k.h: n.m.r on inner over 4f out: effrt fr rr 2f out: no real prog* **25/1**

1500 **10** 2 1/4 **Thalia Grace**[72] 5898 3-9-2 **57** RobertHavlin 3 43
(L Montague Hall) *reluctant to enter stalls: led at mod pce to 2f out: wknd over 1f out* **25/1**

1260 **11** 3/4 **Fitz**[43] 6713 4-9-5 **60** RobertWinston 9 44
(Matthew Salaman) *racd wd in rr: rdn and no prog 2f out* **14/1**

3323 **12** 2 **Cwmni**[23] 7195 4-9-4 **59** DavidProbert 1 36
(B Palling) *taken down early: chsd ldrs: wkng whn n.m.r on inner over 2f out* **13/2**[2]

1m 13.2s (1.30) **Going Correction** +0.10s/f (Slow) **12** Ran SP% **117.0**
Speed ratings (Par 101): **95,93,92,92,91 90,90,89,88,85 84,81**
toteswingers: 1&2 £36.30, 1&3 £25.40, 2&3 £11.30 CSF £132.65 CT £1095.46 TOTE £19.40: £6.80, £4.20, £3.90; EX 180.50 TRIFECTA Not won..
Owner Keith Brown Properties (hull) Ltd **Bred** Miss Brooke Sanders **Trained** Catwick, E Yorks

FOCUS
Like the first division, a tight if moderate handicap and it took quite a time to get some of these loaded into the stalls. The winning time was 0.77 seconds slower than division one. The winner is rated to previous course form (in a seller), with the placed horses close to form.
Athaakeel(IRE) ◆ Official explanation: jockey said filly was slowly away.

7520 EVIE ROSE HECTOR INTRODUCTION (S) STKS 1m (P)
1:25 (1:26) (Class 6) 2-Y-O **£1,706** (£503; £252) **Stalls** High

Form RPR

004 **1** **A Little Bit Dusty**[5] 7464 2-8-8 60 (v[1]) KierenFox(3) 3 61
(W G M Turner) *mde all: racd lazily over 3f out and drvn: drew 3l clr over 2f out: hd high but maintained gallop: unchal* **8/1**

4422 **2** 2 1/4 **Ivan's A Star (IRE)**[4] 7471 2-8-11 57 (p) RobertWinston 6 56
(J S Moore) *hld up in tch: chsd wnr over 2f out: hanging lft and fnd nil u.p over 1f out* **9/4**[2]

1033 **3** 3 1/2 **Sir Lunchalott**[3] 7484 2-9-2 70 (b) LukeMorris 2 53
(J S Moore) *completely fluffed s and lft 6l: t.k.h and sn in tch: prog on outer to take 3rd 2f out: hrd rdn and fnd nil after* **7/4**[1]

0000 **4** 3 1/4 **Touch Of Red (USA)**[17] 7295 2-8-11 55 JimmyFortune 4 40
(R Hannon) *hld up in midfield: outpcd fr 3f out: n.d fnl 2f* **12/1**

0025 **5** nse **Bathwick Scanno (IRE)**[5] 7464 2-8-11 64 TomMcLaughlin 1 40
(P D Evans) *anticipated s but stl broke on terms: chsd wnr to over 2f out: wknd* **7/1**[3]

0000 **6** 3/4 **Talking Back**[50] 6542 2-8-11 48 TravisBlock 9 38
(S Kirk) *hld up in last trio: rdn 3f out: nvr on terms* **50/1**

6 **7** 3/4 **Littlepromisedland (IRE)**[18] 7279 2-8-3 0 AndrewHeffernan(3) 10 32
(R C Guest) *t.k.h: hld up in tch: rdn 3f out: sn btn* **20/1**

0640 **8** 2 3/4 **Lady On Top (IRE)**[10] 7392 2-8-3 50 SophieDoyle(3) 5 25
(Mrs P N Dutfield) *chsd ldrs tl wknd over 2f out* **25/1**

00 **9** 1 **Kitty Fisher**[19] 7271 2-8-6 0 SamHitchcott 7 23
(R J Hodges) *hld up in rr: rdn and struggling 3f out* **100/1**

1m 40.66s (2.46) **Going Correction** +0.10s/f (Slow) **9** Ran SP% **110.0**
Speed ratings (Par 94): **91,88,85,82,81 81,80,77,76**
toteswingers: 1&2 £3.50, 1&3 £3.20, 2&3 £1.80 CSF £24.27 TOTE £9.60: £3.40, £1.10, £1.10; EX 29.20 Trifecta £52.50 Pool: £531.65 - 7.49 winning units..There was no bid for the winner.
Owner T.O.C.S. Ltd **Bred** T O C S Limited **Trained** Sigwells, Somerset

FOCUS
By anyone's standards, this was a bad seller and they finished well spread out. The form is rated negatively around the second and sixth.

NOTEBOOK
A Little Bit Dusty was given a well-judged, front-running ride. His only real anxious moment came when the gelding was inclined to race rather lazily at around halfway and had to be shaken up, but he was kicked into a clear lead again rounding the home bend and was soon in no danger. The form is unlikely to add up to much, though. (op 6-1 tchd 5-1)
Ivan's A Star(IRE) had a bit to find with a few of these at the weights, but he has made the frame more often than not and did so again. However, he had every chance to pick the winner up had he been good enough and is becoming frustrating. (tchd 13-8)
Sir Lunchalott was just about best in at the weights even with his penalty, but he gave away a huge amount of ground after standing still as the stalls opened. The modest early pace enabled him to catch up fairly easily and he was then inclined to pull when back amongst the pack. He was still in with a chance turning for home, but he again gave the impression that he wasn't putting it all in and is not one to trust. Official explanation: jockey said gelding was slowly away. (op 5-2 tchd 11-4)
Touch Of Red(USA) is not among the best juveniles in Richard Hannon's stable. (op 10-1)

7521 LADBROKES SAFETY NET BET E B F FILLIES' H'CAP 1m (P)
2:00 (2:00) (Class 4) (0-85,84) 3-Y-O+ **£5,828** (£1,734; £866; £432) **Stalls** High

Form RPR

0053 **1** **Young Dottie**[93] 5237 4-8-4 **72** JemmaMarshall(5) 5 83
(P M Phelan) *trckd ldng trio: prog 2f out: shkn up to ld over 1f out: sn clr: readily* **11/1**

4334 **2** 2 3/4 **Valencha**[10] 7389 3-8-6 **71** JimmyQuinn 4 76
(H Morrison) *trckd ldr 2f: styd prom: rdn to chse wnr ins fnl f: r.o but no imp* **15/2**

0404 **3** 1 **Qalahari (IRE)**[26] 7114 4-9-1 **78** RobertWinston 2 82+
(D J Coakley) *s.i.s: hld up in last trio: nt clr run wl over 1f out: r.o fnl f to take 3rd last 75yds: no ch to threaten* **9/2**[2]

4065 **4** 1 3/4 **Seasonal Cross**[38] 6851 5-8-10 **73** JimCrowley 6 71
(S Dow) *s.i.s: rcvrd to chse ldr after 2f: rdn to ld over 2f out: edgd rt and hdd over 1f out: wknd* **7/1**

5103 **5** nk **Requisite**[3] 7488 5-8-13 **76** (v) JamesDoyle 1 74
(I A Wood) *hld up in last trio: rdn and effrt on outer over 1f out: one pce* **8/1**

0513 **6** 2 **Ray Of Joy**[18] 7289 4-9-7 **84** StephenCraine 8 77
(J R Jenkins) *t.k.h: hld up in last trio: shkn up and nt qckn over 1f out: no prog* **16/1**

1021 **7** 1 1/2 **Whispering Spirit (IRE)**[22] 7209 4-8-12 **78** (v) AmyRyan(3) 3 68
(Mrs A Duffield) *hld up in 5th: nt clr run wl over 1f out: effrt on inner after: no prog fnl f* **5/1**[3]

2341 **8** 1 1/4 **Song To The Moon (IRE)**[33] 6991 3-8-8 **76** (b) MatthewDavies(3) 7 63
(George Baker) *led to over 2f out: immediately btn* **9/4**[1]

1m 37.92s (-0.28) **Going Correction** +0.10s/f (Slow)
WFA 3 from 4yo+ 2lb **8** Ran SP% **115.2**
Speed ratings (Par 102): **105,102,101,99,99 97,95,94**
toteswingers: 1&2 £12.10, 1&3 £7.20, 2&3 £6.10 CSF £90.18 CT £428.93 TOTE £11.70: £3.10, £3.60, £1.80; EX 108.50 Trifecta £389.80 Part won. Pool: £526.79 - 0.62 winning units..
Owner Tony Smith **Bred** Tony J Smith **Trained** Epsom, Surrey

FOCUS
A fair fillies' handicap and a better pace than might have been expected. The principals all gave the inside rail a wide berth in the straight. The form is rated around the placed horses to their recent best.

7522 LADBROKES ODDS ON! CARD H'CAP 7f (P)
2:30 (2:32) (Class 2) (0-100,100) 3-Y-O+ **£9,714** (£2,890; £1,444; £721) **Stalls** Low

Form RPR

0300 **1** **Spirit Of Sharjah (IRE)**[36] 6888 5-9-4 **97** JoeFanning 13 106+
(Miss J Feilden) *hld up wl in rr: prog 2f out: clsng whn nt clr run and swtchd rt 1f out: squeezed through and urged into ld last 100yds: hld on* **10/1**

0000 **2** shd **Autumn Blades (IRE)**[49] 6564 5-9-2 **95** (v) DavidProbert 6 104
(A Bailey) *hld up in midfield: prog on outer over 1f out: drvn to chal and upsides 100yds out: jst hld* **8/1**[3]

1300 **3** 1 1/4 **Elna Bright**[70] 5950 5-9-2 **95** KierenFallon 7 100
(B R Johnson) *trckd ldng pair: effrt 2f out: drvn to ld 1f out: hdd and one pce last 100yds* **11/1**

0006 **4** 1 **Bravo Echo**[23] 7187 4-8-13 **92** LukeMorris 1 95
(M J Attwater) *t.k.h: trckd ldr: rdn to ld over 2f out: hdd and no ex 1f out* **10/1**

6515 **5** 1 **Docofthebay (IRE)**[14] 7348 6-9-2 **95** (b) IanMongan 2 95
(D Nicholls) *trckd ldng trio: rdn to chal over 1f out: nt qckn and wl hld ins fnl f* **4/1**[1]

5306 **6** nk **Yer Woman (IRE)**[18] 7289 3-8-12 **92** JimmyFortune 8 91
(R Hannon) *hld up in last pair: urged along 2f out: prog on wd outside over 1f out: styd on: nrst fin* **25/1**

020 **7** 1 1/2 **Noble Citizen (USA)**[56] 6349 5-9-2 **95** (be) EddieAhern 4 90
(D M Simcock) *trckd ldrs on inner: effrt and cl enough over 1f out: fdd ins fnl f* **5/1**[2]

1042 **8** 3/4 **Woodcote Place**[16] 7318 7-8-8 **87** RichardKingscote 5 80
(P R Chamings) *rrd stalls: hld up in rr: prog on inner over 1f out: nt pce to threaten fnl f* **8/1**[3]

2100 **9** 2 3/4 **Rulesn'regulations**[36] 6888 4-9-7 **100** GeorgeBaker 12 86
(Matthew Salaman) *wnt lft s: trckd ldrs: rdn 2f out: no prog over 1f out: sn wknd* **9/1**

4310 **10** 1/2 **Icelandic**[14] 7351 8-8-9 **88** (t) JamesDoyle 3 72
(F Sheridan) *trckd ldrs: rdn over 2f out: no prog over 1f out: wknd* **20/1**

650 **11** 4 1/2 **Mister Green (FR)**[158] 3050 4-8-13 **92** (be) StephenCraine 10 64
(D Flood) *sltly hmpd s: a towards rr: no prog 2f out: wl btn over 1f out* **20/1**

6101 **12** 3/4 **Malcheek (IRE)**[16] 7318 8-9-2 **95** DuranFentiman 14 65
(T D Easterby) *led at decent pce to over 2f out: sn wknd* **11/1**

1-06 **13** 7 **Champagne Style (USA)**[106] 4805 3-9-1 **95** (be) JamieSpencer 11 46
(R C Guest) *sltly hmpd s: nvr gng wl: a last* **33/1**

1m 23.39s (-1.41) **Going Correction** +0.10s/f (Slow)
WFA 3 from 4yo+ 1lb **13** Ran SP% **120.0**
Speed ratings (Par 109): **112,111,110,109,108 107,106,105,102,101 96,95,87**
toteswingers: 1&2 £16.70, 1&3 £19.30, 2&3 £24.60 CSF £83.64 CT £937.05 TOTE £13.90: £2.50, £3.70, £6.00; EX 70.80 Trifecta £579.90 Part won. Pool: £ 783.70- 0.40 winning units..
Owner A Dee **Bred** Mrs Kathleen Reynolds **Trained** Exning, Suffolk

FOCUS
A very strong handicap and they went a decent pace. Again the principals came wide down the home straight. The third and fourth set the level.

NOTEBOOK
Spirit Of Sharjah(IRE) was 8lb higher than when successful over C&D on his last visit back in April, though he was rated higher on turf in the summer. Given a hold-up ride, he travelled strongly into the race and his rider's skill in quickly switching him to his right when short of room a furlong out made the difference between victory and defeat. Having won this off 97, he may not find too many opportunities off a higher mark on the all-weather in the coming months. (op 7-1 tchd 13-2)
Autumn Blades(IRE) hasn't been in much form on turf recently, but he won four times on Polytrack last winter, including a couple around here. Held up before making his effort wide as usual, he may have been a touch unlucky as he had to hesitate for a stride when Elna Bright edged across him on the home bend and, given how narrowly he was beaten, it may have made the difference. He doesn't always convince with his attitude and was looking around him again here, but he has plenty of ability. (tchd 17-2)
Elna Bright ◆, 9lb higher than when winning this race last year, had failed to beat a rival in his last two starts, but this was a major return to form and he was in front entering the last furlong before being swamped on either side close to the line. (op 10-1 tchd 12-1)
Bravo Echo ◆, disappointing since showing good form on Polytrack at the start of the year, including around here, was another to bounce back to form and was in front turning in before getting run out of it from the furlong pole. He has been recovering from a back problem and this was certainly a big step back in the right direction. (op 12-1 tchd 14-1)
Docofthebay(IRE), making his debut for the trainer, came into this in decent form on turf, and he ran well here too having held every chance. His only all-weather win from five previous attempts came on Fibresand, but he has the ability to win a decent race on this surface. (op 9-2 tchd 5-1)
Yer Woman(IRE) ◆ had yet to conclusively prove that she stays this far and seemed to be ridden with that in mind, but she flashed home from the back of the field and looks worth another try over the trip. (op 20-1 tchd 16-1)
Noble Citizen(USA) has winning form on Polytrack, but he could never really make his presence felt and hasn't scored in over two years. (op 8-1 tchd 9-2)
Woodcote Place didn't run too badly considering he was fractious in the stalls beforehand and made his effort closer to the inside rail than the principals, but he is now 0-12 on the all-weather. Official explanation: jockey said gelding was fractious in the gates. (op 9-1)

7523 LADBROKES CHURCHILL STKS (LISTED RACE) 1m 2f (P)
3:05 (3:05) (Class 1) 3-Y-O+
£19,869 (£7,532; £3,769; £1,879; £941; £472) **Stalls** Low

Form RPR

5631 **1** **Nideeb**[10] 7384 3-8-12 101 ChrisCatlin 8 110
(C E Brittain) *trckd ldr after 2f: led wl over 1f out and qcknd: 2l clr ins fnl f: r.o* **10/3**[2]

0215 **2** 1 **Summit Surge (IRE)**[91] 5321 6-9-8 113 (t) KierenFallon 3 114+
(L M Cumani) *hld up disputing 5th: trapped on inner over 2f out: prog over 1f out: chsd wnr ins fnl f: r.o but no ch to chal* **5/4**[1]

4000 **3** 1 3/4 **Suits Me**[28] 7100 7-9-2 100 MickyFenton 4 105
(T P Tate) *led at varied pce: rdn and hdd wl over 1f out: one pce* **8/1**

0064 **4** 1/2 **Cumulus Nimbus**[21] 7237 3-8-12 95 JimmyFortune 7 104
(R Hannon) *dwlt: hld up disputing 5th: effrt over 2f out: nt qckn over 1f out: one pce after* **12/1**

0653 **5** 3 **Saphira's Fire (IRE)**[14] 7349 5-8-11 103 JimCrowley 1 93
(W R Muir) *hld up in last pair: effrt over 2f out: wl outpcd fr over 1f out* **7/1**[3]

-305 **6** 2 1/2 **Hidden Brief**[14] 7349 4-8-11 95 JamieSpencer 2 88
(M A Jarvis) *trckd ldrs: rdn 2f out: sn wknd on inner* **10/1**

0003 **7** 1 3/4 **Island Sunset (IRE)**[10] 7384 4-8-11 91................................ ShaneKelly 6 84
(W R Muir) *hld up in last pair: effrt over 2f out: wknd over 1f out* **40/1**

61 **8** 52 **Sweet Child O'Mine**[17] 7304 3-8-7 79............................ FrannyNorton 5 —
(R C Guest) *chsd ldr 2f: dropped away qckly 4f out and sn t.o: virtually p.u* **33/1**

2m 3.90s (-2.70) **Going Correction** +0.10s/f (Slow)
WFA 3 from 4yo+ 4lb **8** Ran SP% **113.3**
Speed ratings (Par 111): **114,113,111,111,109 107,105,64**
toteswingers: 1&2 £2.10, 1&3 £6.20, 2&3 £4.60 CSF £7.70 TOTE £4.00: £1.50, £1.50, £2.40; EX 8.90 Trifecta £45.50 Pool: £635.47- 10.31winning units..
Owner Saeed Manana **Bred** Rabbah Bloodstock Limited **Trained** Newmarket, Suffolk

FOCUS
Won last year by the subsequent Winter Derby winner Tranquil Tiger, this year's renewal of the Churchill Stakes didn't look the strongest, but Suits Me at least made sure it was run at a solid pace and the form looks sound, with the winner on the upgrade.

NOTEBOOK
Nideeb appeared to have plenty to find on these terms, but he had routed his three rivals in a Kempton conditions event last time on his all-weather debut in the style of a progressive colt. Always in a good position on the wide outside, he quickened up nicely after leading inside the last 2f and that enabled him to get first run on the favourite. He will probably now go for a 1m4f Listed event at Kempton next weekend before heading to Dubai. (op 11-4 tchd 5-2)
Summit Surge(IRE), a Group 2 winner on turf last seen finishing fifth in the Arlington Million, was using this race as a preparation for next month's Hong Kong Cup. A winner on the Dundalk Polytrack when trained by Ger Lyons, he was settled off the pace, but wasn't in a good position rounding the home bend. He stayed on well once in the clear, despite not being put under maximum pressure, but the winner had gained too much of an advantage. The stable had Presvis turned over at odds-on in this race last year before finishing third at Sha Tin, and connections will no doubt hope that this gelding can do even better. (op 15-8)
Suits Me came into this with a C&D record of 1-11, but he had finished runner-up six times including behind the likes of Gitano Hernando, Tranquil Tiger (twice), Re Barolo and Dansant. He set the early pace as usual, but the winner gave him little peace and he could only plug on once headed on the home bend. He remains without a win since February of last year. (tchd 13-2)
Cumulus Nimbus, making his all-weather debut, had plenty on at these weights but wasn't disgraced and ran on again after appearing to hang fire after turning in. Much may now depend on what this effort does to his handicap mark. (tchd 14-1)
Saphira's Fire(IRE), a regular in Group/Listed company on turf and sand since a successful racecourse debut on Polytrack, was marginally best in on these terms but she made very little impression from off the pace. She was reported to have run flat. Official explanation: trainer said mare ran flat. (op 6-1 tchd 8-1)
Hidden Brief, fresher than most following a light campaign on turf, was entitled to need the run at Doncaster a fortnight earlier but she failed to build on it and weakened tamely from the furlong pole. (op 8-1 tchd 11-1)
Island Sunset(IRE) started off the year in fine form on Polytrack, but she had over 9l to find with Nideeb on recent Kempton running and never got into the race at any stage. Like her stable companion, she was reported to have run flat. Official explanation: trainer said filly ran flat. (op 33-1)
Sweet Child O'Mine's saddle had slipped forward before they had reached halfway. Official explanation: jockey said saddle slipped. (tchd 28-1)

7524 LADBROKES.COM GOLDEN ROSE STKS (LISTED RACE) 6f (P)
3:40 (3:42) (Class 1) 3-Y-O+
£19,869 (£7,532; £3,769; £1,879; £941; £472) **Stalls** Low

Form RPR

1322 **1** **Hitchens (IRE)**[14] 7351 5-9-2 102................................ GrahamGibbons 9 109+
(T D Barron) *trckd ldrs on outer travelling smoothly: effrt to ld jst ins fnl f and rdr dropped whip: pushed out* **11/4**[1]

3-20 **2** 1 **Enact**[112] 4576 4-8-11 98.. KierenFallon 12 101+
(Sir Michael Stoute) *hld up last: prog over 1f out: r.o wl to take 2nd last 75yds: too much to do* **15/2**[3]

-015 **3** 1/2 **Brave Prospector**[42] 6735 5-9-2 104............................. JamieSpencer 7 104
(Jane Chapple-Hyam) *hld up in last quartet: prog on outer over 1f out: rdn and styd on fnl f: unable to chal* **5/1**[2]

1003 **4** hd **Rowe Park**[15] 7329 7-9-2 100... IanMongan 4 104
(Mrs L C Jewell) *hld up in midfield: prog 2f out: rdn to chal 1f out: styd on same pce after* **33/1**

4243 **5** 1 **Golden Desert (IRE)**[3] 7482 6-9-2 102............................ EddieAhern 11 104+
(R A Mills) *s.i.s: hld up in last trio: trying to make prog whn squeezed out ent fnl f: r.o wl nr fin* **9/1**

6006 **6** 1/2 **Arganil (USA)**[7] 7443 5-9-4 98...............................(b) ChrisCatlin 8 101
(K A Ryan) *trckd ldr after 2f: rdn to ld narrowly wl over 1f out: hdd & wknd jst ins fnl f* **25/1**

30 **7** nk **Angel's Pursuit (IRE)**[126] 4136 3-9-4 108..................... JimmyFortune 3 100
(R Hannon) *trckd ldrs: nt clr run and swtchd over 1f out: fdd ins fnl f* **16/1**

2031 **8** 1/2 **Little Garcon (USA)**[57] 6319 3-9-2 96................................ AdamKirby 6 96
(M Botti) *dwlt: hld up in last trio: drvn and effrt on inner over 1f out: sn no prog* **8/1**

5130 **9** 2 **Arabian Mirage**[36] 6887 4-8-11 97...................................... ShaneKelly 1 85
(B J Meehan) *nvr bttr than midfield on inner: rdn and no prog over 1f out* **14/1**

50 **10** 1 3/4 **Tweedy (IRE)**[14] 7355 3-8-11 0.. WMLordan 5 79
(Edward Lynam, Ire) *mde most to wl over 1f out: sn wknd* **15/2**[3]

502 **11** nk **Noverre To Go (IRE)**[22] 7217 4-9-2 97..................(t) RichardKingscote 2 83
(Tom Dascombe) *t.k.h: trckd ldr 2f: styd prom tl wknd on inner over 1f out* **9/1**

3600 **12** nk **Run For The Hills**[112] 4576 4-9-2 97............................ SteveDrowne 10 83
(R Charlton) *t.k.h: hld up towards rr on outer: wknd over 1f out* **20/1**

1m 11.04s (-0.86) **Going Correction** +0.10s/f (Slow) **12** Ran SP% **122.1**
Speed ratings (Par 111): **109,107,107,106,105 104,104,103,101,98 98,97**
toteswingers: 1&2 £4.80, 1&3 £4.70, 2&3 £5.90 CSF £23.59 TOTE £3.10: £1.10, £3.30, £2.10; EX 30.30 Trifecta £93.00 Pool: £16696.86 - 13.50winning units..
Owner Laurence O'Kane **Bred** Curragh Bloodstock Agency Ltd **Trained** Maunby, N Yorks

FOCUS
A strong line-up for the fourth running of the Golden Rose and a furiously run contest. There is a bit of doubt over the form with the fourth and sixth running their best races for some time, but it is worth taking at face value with the fifth close to this year's form.

NOTEBOOK
Hitchens(IRE), representing last year's winning stable, was beaten less than a length in Listed contests the last twice after 'winning' the race on the wrong side in the Ayr Gold Cup. Everything went his way here, though, as he travelled like a dream and was still on the bridle a furlong out. He quickened up well when asked and his jockey even had the luxury of sending his whip into orbit inside the last furlong. There are no firm plans for him. (op 9-2 tchd 5-1 in a place)
Enact, making her all-weather debut having not been seen since disappointing when favourite for the Stewards' Cup, had little choice than to be dropped in from the outside stall, but that meant she was trusting to luck and she had to weave her way through the field to make her effort. She finished well, but all too late. (op 13-2 tchd 8-1)
Brave Prospector, having only his fourth start of the year and making his all-weather debut, had a major chance on these terms and ran his race, finishing well down the outside to take third. He can win a race like this if persevered with. (op 11-2 tchd 9-2)
Rowe Park was entitled to need the run at Southwell earlier this month and stepped up from that, moving into contention from off the pace on the home turn and holding every chance a furlong out, but all ten of his career victories have come over the minimum, and the way he faded in the closing stages shows why.
Golden Desert(IRE) has been running consistently well since the summer and this was another good effort, especially as he was hampered when running on half a furlong from home, but he hasn't scored since September of last year. (tchd 15-2)
Arganil(USA), fifth in this last year, has won twice at this trip, but his best form has come over the minimum and again the sixth furlong seemed to find him out. (tchd 33-1)
Angel's Pursuit(IRE), best in at the weights, was racing for the first time since July but he was successful on his seasonal reappearance, so the absence shouldn't have been a problem. He had finished last in his only previous try on Polytrack, albeit at Group 3 level, and he still had a chance of a place when getting hampered over a furlong from home. (op 12-1)
Run For The Hills, making his all-weather debut on this first start since July following a wind operation, was reported to have been too keen. Official explanation: jockey said colt was too keen. (tchd 16-1)
T/Plt: £276.30 to a £1 stake. Pool: £40,641.20. 107.35 winning tickets. T/Qpdt: £51.00 to a £1 stake. Pool: £4,979.77. 72.20 winning tickets. JN

7501 WOLVERHAMPTON (A.W) (L-H)
Saturday, November 20

OFFICIAL GOING: Standard
Wind: Light against Weather: Overcast

7525 PHOSTERS H'CAP (DIV I) 5f 216y(P)
6:15 (6:17) (Class 5) (0-75,75) 3-Y-O+ **£1,942** (£578; £288; £144) **Stalls** Low

Form RPR

0320 **1** **Hulcote Rose (IRE)**[16] 7319 3-9-5 73................................ JamesDoyle 1 83
(S Kirk) *a.p: chsd ldr fnl f: r.o u.p to ld nr fin* **10/1**

0010 **2** hd **Devil You Know (IRE)**[9] 7405 4-8-13 67..................(t) RobertWinston 12 76
(M W Easterby) *chsd ldrs: led over 1f out: rdn and edgd rt ins fnl f: hdd nr fin* **11/1**

-235 **3** 2 1/4 **Dear Maurice**[8] 7421 6-9-5 73...................................(vt) TomMcLaughlin 4 75
(T B P Coles) *a.p: rdn over 1f out: styd on* **8/1**[3]

0510 **4** 1 1/4 **Dancing Freddy (IRE)**[9] 7405 3-9-2 70..........................(p) MickyFenton 2 68
(J G Given) *sn led: rdn and hdd over 1f out: styd on same pce ins fnl f* **22/1**

1415 **5** nk **Titus Gent**[16] 7320 5-9-5 73... KirstyMilczarek 11 70
(R A Harris) *rn out of stall 11 instead of scheduled stall 10: led early: chsd ldr tl rdn over 1f out: styd on same pce ins fnl f* **8/1**[3]

6353 **6** 1/2 **Emiratesdotcom**[7] 7441 4-8-9 63.. LukeMorris 9 58+
(J M Bradley) *hld up: drvn along 1/2-way: r.o ins fnl f: nrst fin* **6/1**[2]

6255 **7** 1 **Yankee Storm**[25] 7154 5-9-4 72....................................(v) JimmyQuinn 6 64
(H J Collingridge) *hld up in tch: rdn over 1f out: fnd nil* **9/1**

3500 **8** 3/4 **Defector (IRE)**[22] 7212 4-9-2 75.................................. MarkCoumbe(5) 7 65+
(D Bourton) *hld up: styd on ins fnl f: nvr nrr* **16/1**

1243 **9** shd **Ryedane (IRE)**[35] 6922 8-9-4 72.................................(b) DuranFentiman 13 61
(T D Easterby) *mid-div: drvn along 1/2-way: hdwy over 2f out: wknd over 1f out* **18/1**

0000 **10** 3 1/4 **Sarah's Art (IRE)**[22] 7212 7-9-6 74..................................(t) TomQueally 8 53
(Stef Higgins) *hld up: rdn over 1f out: nvr on terms* **9/1**

0100 **11** 1/2 **Rothesay Dancer**[21] 7239 7-8-8 65.............................. KellyHarrison(3) 10 42
(J S Goldie) *rn out of stall 10 instead of scheduled stall 11: hld up: a in rr* **50/1**

0131 **12** 6 **Forever's Girl**[15] 7331 4-9-0 75.................................... AdamCarter(7) 5 33
(G R Oldroyd) *broke wl enough: stmbld twice sn after s and lost pl: hdwy on outer over 2f out: wknd sn after* **3/1**[1]

00/0 **13** 17 **Benwilt Breeze (IRE)**[15] 7326 8-9-7 75.........................(t) DaneO'Neill 3 —
(C J Teague) *s.i.s: sme hdwy on ins over 2f out: sn wknd and eased: t.o* **50/1**

1m 14.4s (-0.60) **Going Correction** -0.05s/f (Stan) **13** Ran SP% **118.3**
Speed ratings (Par 103): **102,101,98,97,96 96,94,93,93,89 88,80,57**
toteswingers:1&2 £29.10, 2&3 £11.00, 1&3 £11.30 CSF £112.68 CT £956.76 TOTE £10.60: £4.10, £6.80, £2.80; EX 168.70.
Owner The Kathryn Stud **Bred** Ecurie Des Monceaux **Trained** Upper Lambourn, Berks
■ Stewards' Enquiry : Kelly Harrison one-day ban; entered wrong stall (4th Dec)
Kirsty Milczarek one-day ban; entered wrong stall (4th Dec)

FOCUS
An ordinary handicap in which not too many arrived here in top form and one in which the market leader disappointed. The gallop was sound and the winner raced centre to far side in the straight. The form is rated around the third.
Forever's Girl Official explanation: jockey said filly suffered interference shortly after start. Vet said filly had a cut to her right fore.
Benwilt Breeze(IRE) Official explanation: vet said gelding finished lame.

7526 PHOSTERS H'CAP (DIV II) 5f 216y(P)
6:45 (6:46) (Class 5) (0-75,75) 3-Y-O+ **£1,942** (£578; £288; £144) **Stalls** Low

Form RPR

0510 **1** **Ajara (IRE)**[22] 7209 4-8-8 62.. RichardKingscote 7 71
(Tom Dascombe) *led 1f: chsd ldr tl led again over 1f out: rdn out* **15/2**

5515 **2** 1 1/4 **Methaaly (IRE)**[7] 7446 7-8-13 74.................................(be) JosephYoung(7) 2 79
(M Mullineaux) *hdwy 5f out: chsd wnr over 1f out: sn rdn: styd on* **9/2**[2]

0063 **3** hd **Lastkingofscotland (IRE)**[8] 7421 4-9-4 72...............(b) RobertWinston 6 76
(C R Dore) *hld up in tch: racd keenly: rdn over 1f out: edgd lft: r.o* **6/1**[3]

0000 **4** 2 1/2 **Gwilym (GER)**[21] 7239 7-9-0 68.. DaneO'Neill 8 64
(D Haydn Jones) *chsd ldrs: rdn over 2f out: no ex fnl f* **16/1**

4640 **5** 1/2 **Kummel Excess (IRE)**[32] 6998 3-9-2 73................ MatthewDavies(3) 13 68+
(George Baker) *s.s: r.o u.p ins fnl f: nrst fin* **20/1**

0600 **6** 1/2 **Wigram's Turn (USA)**[36] 6904 5-9-7 75.............................. JimmyQuinn 1 68+
(M W Easterby) *s.i.s: hld up: r.o ins fnl f: nvr trbld ldrs* **7/1**

000 **7** 3/4 **Tenacestream (CAN)**[171] 2644 3-9-2 73......................... KierenFox(3) 9 64
(J R Best) *hld up: rdn over 1f out: kpt on: nvr trbld ldrs* **17/2**

-355 **8** 1/2 **Ballodair (IRE)**[166] 2815 3-8-11 72......................... GeorgeChaloner(7) 11 61+
(R A Fahey) *s.s: hld up: pushed along in rr: nvr on terms: styd on ins fnl f: nvr nrr* **16/1**

0054 **9** shd **Silver Wind**[60] 6274 5-8-13 70................................(v) AndrewHeffernan(3) 4 59
(A J McCabe) *prom: sn rdn along: wknd ins fnl f* **4/1**[1]

0020 **10** 5 **Wyatt Earp (IRE)**[34] 6962 9-9-5 73..................................(p) GregFairley 3 46
(P Salmon) *led 5f out: rdn and hdd over 1f out: wknd ins fnl f* **16/1**

3112 **11** *4 ½* **Monte Major (IRE)**[255] 848 9-8-3 **64**....................(v) ThomasWhite(7) 12 22
(D Shaw) *hld up: wknd over 2f out* **14/1**
1m 14.29s (-0.71) **Going Correction** -0.05s/f (Stan) **11** Ran SP% **116.3**
Speed ratings (Par 103): **102,100,100,96,96 95,94,93,93,86 80**
toteswingers:1&2 £10.20, 2&3 £10.20, 1&3 £7.10 CSF £40.74 CT £218.26 TOTE £12.00: £3.10, £2.60, £2.10; EX 62.10.
Owner Butt Scholes **Bred** Rozelle Bloodstock **Trained** Malpas, Cheshire

FOCUS
Division two of an ordinary handicap. Although the gallop was sound those held up could never land a blow and the winner came down the centre in the straight. The placed horses are rated close to recent form.

7527 EVENTMASTERS 25TH ANNIVERSARY (S) STKS 5f 216y(P)
7:15 (7:16) (Class 6) 2-Y-O **£1,706** (£503; £252) **Stalls** Low

Form RPR
5045 **1** **Whipphound**[16] 7309 2-8-12 66.................................... TomMcLaughlin 6 68
(W M Brisbourne) *a.p: rdn over 1f out: led and hung lft ins fnl f: r.o wl* **7/2**[1]
5460 **2** *3* **Magic Cross**[38] 6842 2-8-12 60.................................... NickyMackay 11 59
(P J McBride) *hdwy 4f out: led over 1f out: sn rdn: hdd and unable qck ins fnl f* **9/2**[2]
530 **3** *1 ¼* **Slatey Hen (IRE)**[140] 3686 2-8-7 64.................................... JimmyQuinn 8 50
(R A Fahey) *hld up in tch: rdn over 1f out: edgd lft and styd on to go 3rd nr fin: nt trble ldrs* **5/1**[3]
0630 **4** *¾* **Tony Hollis**[17] 7301 2-8-12 65.................................... JamesMillman 1 53
(B R Millman) *sn led: rdn and hdd over 1f out: no ex ins fnl f: lost 3rd nr fin* **7/1**
00 **5** *2 ½* **Irish Boy (IRE)**[19] 7272 2-8-12 0.................................... TravisBlock 2 46
(W J H Ratcliffe) *chsd ldrs: rdn over 2f out: wknd ins fnl f* **40/1**
5000 **6** *nse* **Granny Anne (IRE)**[36] 6902 2-8-0 49.......................... NatashaEaton(7) 13 40
(A Bailey) *sn outpcd: r.o ins fnl f: nvr nrr* **22/1**
6600 **7** *shd* **Scommettitrice (IRE)**[33] 6989 2-8-12 60.......................... LukeMorris 9 45
(R A Harris) *sn pushed along in rr: rdn over 1f out: hung rt ins fnl f: nvr on terms* **5/1**[3]
0620 **8** *1 ¼* **Cootehill Lass (IRE)**[21] 7224 2-8-7 68.......................... FrannyNorton 12 36
(G A Harker) *sn outpcd: styd on ins fnl f: nvr nrr* **13/2**
000 **9** *8* **Mrs Nisbett (IRE)**[158] 3058 2-8-4 45.................... AndrewHeffernan(3) 10 12
(A J McCabe) *chsd ldrs tl wknd over 1f out* **66/1**
10 *6* **Ice Angel** 2-8-8 0 ow1.................................... GrahamGibbons 5 —
(D Shaw) *s.s: outpcd* **16/1**
000 **11** *2* **Street Cred (IRE)**[38] 6842 2-8-7 10.................................... ChrisCatlin 4 —
(P Burgoyne) *s.i.s: outpcd* **100/1**
1m 15.38s (0.38) **Going Correction** -0.05s/f (Stan) **11** Ran SP% **114.7**
Speed ratings (Par 94): **95,91,89,88,85 84,84,83,72,64 61**
toteswingers:1&2 £2.80, 2&3 £5.20, 1&3 £5.20 CSF £18.13 TOTE £5.80: £2.80, £1.90, £1.50; EX 20.60.The winner was bought in for 6,500gns.
Owner Mark Brisbourne **Bred** Mrs B Skinner **Trained** Great Ness, Shropshire

FOCUS
A modest seller run at a decent gallop. The winner came down the centre in the straight and, although the form is limited, it is better than average and relaible for the grade.

NOTEBOOK
Whipphound, who attracted market support, proved suited by the drop into this company and ran up to his best to get off the mark at the fifth attempt, despite hanging left in front. He had a decent shout at the weights and this form isn't up to much, but he may be the type to win again for this yard. (op 9-2)
Magic Cross had a better chance at the weights in this company than in a Kempton claimer on her previous start, and she ran creditably at level weights against a rival that would have been conceding 6lb in a handicap. She's capable of picking up a small race on this surface. (op 5-1 tchd 4-1)
Slatey Hen(IRE) was fairly easy to back in the market after a near five-month break on this first run for her new trainer but who showed she retains ability on this all-weather debut. The drop back to 5f isn't likely to be an inconvenience and she should be placed to best advantage. (op 7-2)
Tony Hollis had a decent chance at the weights on this all-weather debut dropped in grade but, although not totally disgraced, he will have to raise his game if he is to get off the mark on this surface in the coming weeks. (op 6-1)
Scommettitrice(IRE)'s price contracted markedly but she never at any stage looked like justifying the support. Her record is one of inconsistency and she remains one to tread carefully with. (op 14-1 tchd 9-2)

7528 LARKSHILL ENGINEERING NURSERY 7f 32y(P)
7:45 (7:46) (Class 4) (0-85,77) 2-Y-O **£3,885** (£1,156; £577; £288) **Stalls** High

Form RPR
3031 **1** **My Lord**[12] 7378 2-9-4 **77**.................................... KierenFox(3) 9 81
(W G M Turner) *mde all: rdn over 1f out: jst hld on* **7/2**[2]
6603 **2** *½* **Planet Waves (IRE)**[28] 7085 2-9-7 **77**.......................... ChrisCatlin 6 80
(C E Brittain) *chsd ldrs: rdn over 2f out: edgd lft and r.o wl ins fnl f* **3/1**[1]
2025 **3** *1* **Fred Willetts (IRE)**[15] 7324 2-9-7 **77**.......................... TomMcLaughlin 2 77
(P D Evans) *s.i.s: sn pushed along in rr: r.o ins fnl f: nrst fin* **11/1**
014 **4** *½* **Geordie Iris (IRE)**[58] 6302 2-9-4 **74**.......................... JimmyFortune 8 73
(R Hannon) *chsd ldrs: rdn over 2f out: styd on* **7/1**
1004 **5** *nk* **Restless Bay (IRE)**[2] 7493 2-9-2 **72**.......................... AdamKirby 1 70
(R Hollinshead) *hld up: hdwy over 1f out: r.o: nt rch ldrs* **8/1**
0021 **6** *1* **Magic Stella**[21] 7240 2-9-5 **75**.......................... RobertWinston 7 71
(A P Jarvis) *chsd wnr over 5f out: rdn over 1f out: no ex ins fnl f* **11/2**[3]
0603 **7** *hd* **Point Du Jour (FR)**[12] 7379 2-9-4 **74**.......................... TomQueally 5 69
(I A Wood) *hld up: hdwy u.p over 1f out: edgd lft: styd on same pce ins fnl f* **12/1**
6355 **8** *6* **Cristaliyev**[10] 7395 2-8-10 **66**.......................... NickyMackay 4 47
(J R Boyle) *hld up in tch: rdn over 2f out: wknd over 1f out* **14/1**
2003 **9** *2 ½* **Golden Shine**[8] 7424 2-8-12 **75**.......................... JulieBurke(7) 3 50
(A Bailey) *hld up: rdn over 2f out: n.d* **16/1**
0040 **10** *3 ½* **Cerejeira (IRE)**[35] 6916 2-7-12 **54** oh5.......................... PaulQuinn 10 20
(E J Alston) *chsd ldrs tl rdn and wknd over 1f out* **66/1**
1m 29.56s (-0.04) **Going Correction** -0.05s/f (Stan) **10** Ran SP% **116.3**
Speed ratings (Par 98): **98,97,96,95,95 94,94,87,84,80**
CSF £14.39 CT £106.41 TOTE £5.00: £2.50, £1.50, £5.40; EX 12.60.
Owner Mrs M S Teversham **Bred** Mrs Monica Teversham **Trained** Sigwells, Somerset

FOCUS
A fair nursery but an ordinary gallop meant those held up were at a disadvantage. The winner raced close to the inside rail down the straight and the third is rated to form in a straightforward nursery.

NOTEBOOK
My Lord, who had beaten a subsequent winner in a C&D claimer earlier in the month, bettered that form from back in nursery company after being raised 3lb. He had the run of the race on a card that had favoured those up with the pace, but he may be capable of winning again on Polytrack when allowed to dominate. (op 4-1 tchd 9-2)
Planet Waves(IRE) ◆, who attracted support, had run well in a stronger nursery than this one on turf on his previous start and, although he ran up to his best on this AW debut, he left the strong impression that a stiffer overall stamina test over this trip or the return to 1m can see him win a race on Polytrack this winter. (op 4-1)
Fred Willetts(IRE) deserves plenty of credit as he fared easily the best of those that came from off the pace, and this was after making his ground on the wide outside. A stronger gallop would have suited but his overall record - one of inconsistency - suggests he wouldn't be one to place maximum faith in next time. (op 12-1)
Geordie Iris(IRE), having her first run in a nursery on artificial surfaces, failed to build on the form previously shown on this surface and on turf on her previous start but she will be worth another chance away from progressive sorts back over 1m. (op 13-2 tchd 15-2)
Restless Bay(IRE) hadn't been at his best since winning over 6f here in September but he left the impression he was a bit better than the bare form suggested in a race where the hold-up horses never figured. Whether this will be built on next time remains to be seen, though. (op 9-1 tchd 15-2)
Magic Stella was well placed given the way things unfolded back in nursery company but she failed to get home on this first run beyond sprint distances. The return to 6f may suit but she has little margin for error from her current mark. (op 5-1)

7529 D & G CONSULTANCY CLAIMING STKS 1m 141y(P)
8:15 (8:15) (Class 6) 3-Y-O+ **£1,706** (£503; £252) **Stalls** Low

Form RPR
1003 **1** **Cobo Bay**[12] 7382 5-9-6 78.......................................(b) RobertWinston 2 83
(C R Dore) *mde all: rdn clr over 1f out: styd on* **15/2**
5000 **2** *1 ¼* **Cyflymder (IRE)**[3] 7488 4-9-2 80.................................... JimmyFortune 4 76
(R Hannon) *prom: rdn over 1f out: styd on* **9/2**[2]
0300 **3** *hd* **Mastership (IRE)**[28] 7092 6-9-6 83.............................(v) JamieSpencer 8 80
(J J Quinn) *hld up: hdwy and nt clr run over 1f out: styd on* **6/1**[3]
-000 **4** *4* **Kildare Sun (IRE)**[133] 3911 8-8-13 68.............................(p) JimmyQuinn 6 63
(J Mackie) *chsd ldrs: rdn over 1f out: no ex ins fnl f* **40/1**
6030 **5** *1 ¼* **Dream Lodge (IRE)**[49] 6562 6-9-9 100.............................. JoeFanning 13 71
(R A Fahey) *prom: shkn up over 3f out: styng on same pce whn hung lft fr over 1f out* **8/11**[1]
6-06 **6** *nk* **Farleigh**[108] 4708 4-8-5 67.................................... ChrisCatlin 12 52
(George Baker) *hld up in tch: lost pl 7f out: n.d after* **40/1**
450 **7** *1 ¾* **Forbidden (IRE)**[5] 7467 7-8-11 61.............................(t) EddieAhern 11 54
(Daniel Mark Loughnane, Ire) *hld up: nvr on terms* **33/1**
5450 **8** *¾* **Shaluca**[21] 7239 3-8-7 62 ow2.................................... GrahamGibbons 3 51
(E S McMahon) *plld hrd and prom: chsd wnr over 2f out to over 1f out: sn wknd* **28/1**
4640 **9** *1 ¼* **Mojeerr**[35] 6915 4-8-7 48.......................................(v) AndrewHeffernan(3) 5 48
(A J McCabe) *hld up: rdn over 2f out: n.d* **80/1**
2436 **10** *½* **Saving Grace**[36] 6905 4-8-5 52.................................... FrannyNorton 7 42
(E J Alston) *chsd ldrs: rdn over 2f out: wknd wl over 1f out* **22/1**
1m 49.55s (-0.95) **Going Correction** -0.05s/f (Stan)
WFA 3 from 4yo+ 3lb **10** Ran SP% **119.0**
Speed ratings (Par 101): **102,100,100,97,96 95,94,93,92,92**
toteswingers:1&2 £4.30, 2&3 £3.30, 1&3 £4.90 CSF £39.07 TOTE £12.20: £3.00, £1.20, £1.40; EX 44.90.
Owner Patrick Wilmott **Bred** The C H F Partnership **Trained** Cowbit, Lincs

FOCUS
A wide variety of ability on show for this reasonable claimer but one in which the short-priced favourite disappointed. The gallop was an ordinary one and those held up again never figured. The winner raced close to the inside rail in the straight, and is rated around the best of his recent form.
Dream Lodge(IRE) Official explanation: jockey said gelding hung left.

7530 E B F CHERYL'S BIRTHDAY PARTY MAIDEN STKS 1m 141y(P)
8:45 (8:46) (Class 5) 2-Y-O **£2,978** (£886; £442; £221) **Stalls** Low

Form RPR
3 **1** **Boogie Shoes**[33] 6980 2-9-3 0.................................... JackMitchell 1 72+
(M A Jarvis) *a.p: chsd ldr over 2f out: led over 1f out: r.o wl* **13/8**[1]
0 **2** *3 ¼* **Praxios**[28] 7099 2-9-3 0.................................... KirstyMilczarek 7 65
(L M Cumani) *sn pushed along in rr: hdwy over 1f out: r.o to go 2nd post: no ch w wnr* **11/1**
5 **3** *shd* **Monicalew**[26] 7113 2-8-12 0.................................... AdamKirby 6 60
(W R Swinburn) *led: rdn and hdd over 1f out: styd on same pce ins fnl f: lost 2nd post* **11/1**
4 *2* **Spirit Of Grace** 2-8-12 0.................................... JamesDoyle 4 56
(A J McCabe) *a.p: rdn over 1f out: styd on same pce* **80/1**
3 **5** *nk* **Starstuded (IRE)**[16] 7312 2-8-12 0.................................... ShaneKelly 5 55
(W J Haggas) *chsd ldrs: rdn over 2f out: styd on same pce appr fnl f* **3/1**[2]
4 **6** *¾* **Duke Of Florence (IRE)**[17] 7302 2-9-3 0.......................... JimmyFortune 3 61+
(R Hannon) *hmpd s: hld up: r.o ins fnl f: nvr nr to chal* **5/1**[3]
0 **7** *nk* **Secoya**[40] 6803 2-8-12 0.................................... RichardKingscote 2 54
(R M Beckett) *wnt rt s: hld up in tch: racd keenly: rdn over 2f out: styd on same pce appr fnl f* **20/1**
8 *1 ½* **Potomac (IRE)** 2-9-3 0.................................... NickyMackay 9 55+
(J H M Gosden) *mid-div: rdn over 2f out: no imp* **12/1**
0 **9** *1* **Hopscotch**[21] 7232 2-8-12 0.................................... JamieSpencer 12 48
(M L W Bell) *chsd ldr over 6f out tl rdn over 2f out: wknd over 1f out* **25/1**
10 *½* **La Residenza** 2-8-12 0.................................... TomQueally 13 47
(J R Fanshawe) *hld up: pushed along over 3f out: a in rr* **33/1**
04 **11** *4 ½* **Romeo Montague**[24] 7178 2-9-3 0.................................... EddieAhern 11 42
(E A L Dunlop) *hld up: nvr on terms* **16/1**
12 *nk* **Omega Centauri** 2-8-12 0.................................... GrahamGibbons 10 37
(E S McMahon) *chsd ldrs tl rdn and wknd over 1f out* **50/1**
0 **13** *3 ¾* **River Avon**[58] 6308 2-9-0 0.................................... JamesSullivan(3) 8 34
(M W Easterby) *hld up: rdn 1/2-way: wknd 3f out* **100/1**
1m 51.17s (0.67) **Going Correction** -0.05s/f (Stan) **13** Ran SP% **125.7**
Speed ratings (Par 96): **95,92,92,90,89 89,89,87,86,86 82,82,78**
toteswingers:1&2 £6.00, 2&3 £7.60, 1&3 £7.80 CSF £22.01 TOTE £3.10: £2.00, £5.10, £5.20; EX 30.40.
Owner A D Spence **Bred** Haydock Park Stud **Trained** Newmarket, Suffolk

FOCUS
An ordinary maiden but an improved effort from the winner, who scored with plenty in hand. The winner raced towards the centre in the straight. The level of the form is fluid with improved efforts from the first two.

NOTEBOOK
Boogie Shoes ◆ was well supported and fully confirmed the promise shown on her debut at Pontefract last month, despite racing with the choke out, to win with plenty in hand on this all-weather debut. The step up to this trip suited, he is in good hands, has the physical scope for further improvement and should be able to hold his own over this trip once pitched into handicaps. (op 7-4 tchd 2-1)
Praxios ◆ had been soundly beaten behind a potentially smart sort at Newbury on his debut but fared a good deal better on this all-weather debut to fare easily the best of those held up. He'll be suited by the step up to 1m2f and, although he's capable of picking up an ordinary maiden, will be of most interest once qualified for a handicap mark. (op 12-1)

Monicalew had shown ability at an ordinary level on her debut, and she bettered that effort on a night where those right up with the pace were seen to very good effect. She too will be seen to best effect over further once handicapped. (op 16-1)
Spirit Of Grace, picked up cheaply by current connections at Doncaster earlier this month, showed a modicum of promise against more experienced rivals on this racecourse debut. She is entitled to improve for this experience and ordinary handicaps will be the way forward with her. (op 100-1)
Starstuded(IRE) failed to build on the form shown at Kempton on her debut, but left the impression that a much stiffer overall test of stamina would have been to her liking. She should do better over further in due course. (op 9-2 tchd 5-2)
Duke Of Florence(IRE) found this too much of a test of speed after his eyecatching run over this trip in heavy ground at Nottingham on his debut. He'll be one to bear in mind granted a suitable test next year. (tchd 13-2)

7531 EVENTMASTERS 25TH ANNIVERSARY H'CAP — 1m 4f 50y(P)
9:15 (9:15) (Class 6) (0-65,65) 3-Y-O+ — **£1,706** (£503; £252) **Stalls** Low

Form — RPR

4434 **1** **Straversjoy**[19] 7275 3-8-12 **59** .... LukeMorris 3 66+
(R Hollinshead) *hld up: hdwy over 2f out: rdn and edgd lft over 1f out: r.o to ld nr fin* **2/1**[1]

3253 **2** *hd* **Dubburg (USA)**[16] 7315 5-9-2 **57** .... StevieDonohoe 2 63+
(W J Musson) *hld up in tch: rdn over 2f out: r.o* **11/4**[2]

3200 **3** *nk* **Guga (IRE)**[5] 7467 4-9-4 **64** .... (p) RyanClark(5) 12 70
(J Mackie) *chsd ldrs: led over 2f out: rdn and hdd nr fin* **16/1**

0460 **4** *½* **Nayessence**[115] 4481 4-9-2 **60** .... (bt[1]) JamesSullivan(3) 9 65
(M W Easterby) *led: rdn and hdd over 2f out: styd on* **6/1**[3]

2062 **5** *1 ½* **Chincoteague (IRE)**[12] 7381 4-9-8 **63** .... ShaneKelly 1 66
(B J Meehan) *chsd ldrs: rdn over 3f out: styd on* **8/1**

0150 **6** *½* **Derby Desire (IRE)**[7] 7445 6-8-12 **56** .... SophieDoyle(3) 8 60+
(D Donovan) *hld up: hmpd over 2f out: hdwy u.p over 1f out: nt rch ldrs* **25/1**

-300 **7** *2* **Little Richard (IRE)**[19] 7275 11-8-13 **54** .... (p) AdamKirby 11 53
(M Wellings) *hld up: rdn over 1f out: nvr on terms* **25/1**

3046 **8** *nk* **Barbirolli**[25] 7149 8-8-3 **51** oh6 .... LauraPike(7) 7 49
(W B Stone) *hld up: effrt over 2f out: nvr nrr* **66/1**

-530 **9** *4 ½* **Horsley Warrior**[159] 3032 4-9-7 **62** .... GrahamGibbons 10 53
(E S McMahon) *mid-div: hdwy 5f out: wknd over 2f out* **28/1**

0520 **10** *4 ½* **Shoot The Pot (IRE)**[42] 6747 3-8-11 **58** .... JimmyQuinn 4 42
(J Mackie) *hmpd sn after s: hld up: rdn over 2f out: n.d* **16/1**

-150 **11** *1 ½* **Savaronola (USA)**[26] 7111 5-9-10 **65** .... TomQueally 6 46
(B J Curley) *prom: rdn over 2f out: sn edgd rt and wknd* **10/1**

036 **12** *6* **Heredias (GER)**[24] 7184 4-9-7 **62** .... TomMcLaughlin 5 34
(W M Brisbourne) *chsd ldrs: rdn over 3f out: wknd over 2f out* **12/1**

2m 42.56s (1.46) **Going Correction** -0.05s/f (Stan)
WFA 3 from 4yo+ 6lb — **12** Ran SP% **126.6**
Speed ratings (Par 101): **93,92,92,92,91 91,89,89,86,83 82,78**
toteswingers: 1&2 £1.20, 1&3 £13.60, 2&3 £10.20 CSF £7.64 CT £74.09 TOTE £3.40: £1.80, £2.20, £7.30; EX 8.80.
Owner E Bennion **Bred** Eric Bennion **Trained** Upper Longdon, Staffs
■ Stewards' Enquiry : Stevie Donohoe three-day ban; excessive use of whip (4th-6th Dec)

FOCUS
A modest handicap in which an ordinary gallop only picked up on the approach to the straight and the first four finished in a bit of a heap. The winner raced down the centre in the straight and the third and fourth are the best guides to the form.
Shoot The Pot(IRE) Official explanation: jockey said gelding suffered interference at start.
T/Plt: £151.00 to a £1 stake. Pool of £94,132.36 - 455.06 winning tickets. T/Qpdt: £13.00 to a £1 stake. Pool of £9,049.30 - 512.70 winning tickets. CR

6011 DORTMUND (R-H)
Saturday, November 20
OFFICIAL GOING: Turf: heavy

7532a RASHIT SHAYKHUTDINOV CUP (EX HESSEN-POKAL) (GROUP 3) (3YO+) (TURF) — 1m 2f
3:00 (12:00) 3-Y-O+
£28,318 (£9,734; £4,867; £2,654; £1,769; £1,327)

RPR

1 **Elle Shadow (IRE)**[48] 6613 3-8-10 0 .... AStarke 8 103+
(P Schiergen, Germany) *a.p and gng wl: trckd ldrs: smooth prog through fnl turn: shkn up in st to join ldrs 1 1/2f out: tk ld 1f out: r.o wl: drew clr: easily* **13/10**[1]

2 *1 ¼* **Keep Cool**[14] 7369 3-8-9 0 .... FilipMinarik 4 100
(Andreas Lowe, Germany) *towards rr under cover fr s: patiuently rdn ent st: produced ent fnl f: r.o wl to chse wnr home* **118/10**

3 *1 ¼* **Sun Society (GER)**[73] 5-8-9 0 .... AndreBest 7 94
(M Trybuhl, Germany) *bkmarker fr s: rdn early in st: sn picked up: qcknd wl to fin fastest of all ins fnl f* **32/1**

4 *2* **Durban Thunder (GER)**[28] 7102 4-9-3 0 .... NRichter 6 98
(T Mundry, Germany) *sent to ld fr s: set gd pce: led into st: r.o but hdd 1 1/2f out: r.o one pce* **9/5**[2]

5 *¾* **Falun (GER)**[28] 7102 4-9-1 0 .... (b) JiriPalik 2 95
(A Trybuhl, Germany) *racd in 5th fr s: threatened briefly on ins rail on fnl turn: no ex fnl 1 1/2f* **115/10**

6 *2* **Toughness Danon**[39] 4-8-13 0 .... EPedroza 5 89
(A Wohler, Germany) *settled in midfield: smooth prog arnd fnl turn: r.o in st: wknd 1 1/2f out* **42/10**[3]

7 *1 ¼* **Ordenstreuer (IRE)**[25] 4-9-1 0 .... StephanePasquier 3 89
(H-W Hiller, Germany) *racd in 3rd trcking ldrs: rdn arnd fnl turn: r.o wl early in st but qckly btn* **11/2**

2m 18.39s (138.39)
WFA 3 from 4yo+ 4lb — **7** Ran SP% **132.7**
WIN (incl. 10 euro stake): 23. PLACES: 11, 20, 63. SF: 223.
Owner Gestut Wittekindshof **Bred** Gestut Wittekindshof **Trained** Germany

1081 FONTAINEBLEAU
Monday, November 22
OFFICIAL GOING: Turf: very soft

7534a PRIX ZEDDAAN (LISTED RACE) (2YO) (TURF) — 6f
12:20 (12:00) 2-Y-O — **£24,336** (£9,734; £7,300; £4,867; £2,433)

RPR

1 **Captain Chop (FR)**[21] 7277 2-9-2 0 .... FlavienPrat 1 104
(D Guillemin, France) **37/10**[2]

2 *2* **Morache Music**[24] 7207 2-8-11 0 .... OlivierPeslier 13 93
(P J Makin) *amongst bkmarkers tl 1/2-way: stl wl off pce at 1/2-way: rdn 2f out: picked up wl: r.o strly u.p 1f out: nrest at fin* **58/10**[3]

3 *½* **Newcastle (FR)**[14] 2-8-8 0 .... JohanVictoire 12 89
(C Baillet, France) **12/1**

4 *1 ½* **Torentosa (FR)**[24] 7222 2-8-8 0 .... GregoryBenoist 8 84
(A De Royer-Dupre, France) **3/1**[1]

5 *hd* **My Delirium**[24] 7201 2-8-8 0 .... RichardKingscote 7 83
(R M Beckett) *prom bhd early ldrs fr s: rdn 1 1/2f out: styd on u.p fnl f* **27/1**

6 *1 ½* **Flying Scotsman (FR)**[14] 2-8-11 0 .... StephanePasquier 3 82
(J E Pease, France) **9/1**

7 *1 ½* **Passei (FR)**[29] 2-8-8 0 .... ThierryThulliez 11 74
(Mlle V Dissaux, France) **40/1**

8 *snk* **Moranda (FR)**[21] 7276 2-8-8 0 .... MaximeGuyon 4 74
(C Boutin, France) **43/1**

9 *nk* **Walk In Beauty (IRE)** 2-8-8 0 .... ThierryJarnet 2 73
(Robert Collet, France) **27/1**

10 *3* **Lips Poison (GER)**[29] 7108 2-8-8 0 .... (b) AHelfenbein 6 64
(Andreas Lowe, Germany) **13/2**

0 **Lone Cat (FR)**[29] 2-8-13 0 .... Pierre-CharlesBoudot 9 —
(Y De Nicolay, France) **23/1**

0 **Aglaia (IRE)**[24] 7222 2-8-8 0 .... ThomasHuet 10 —
(J E Pease, France) **39/1**

0 **Miyake (IRE)**[33] 2-8-8 0 .... IoritzMendizabal 5 —
(H Blume, Germany) **12/1**

1m 10.3s (70.30) — **13** Ran SP% **118.2**
WIN (incl. 1 euro stake): 4.70. PLACES: 1.90, 2.30, 3.10. DF: 18.10. SF: 38.80.
Owner Alain Chopard **Bred** A Chopard **Trained** France

NOTEBOOK
Morache Music raced towards the back of the field before making good progress in the closing stages, but he couldn't reel in the winner, who was handy throughout.
My Delirium, winner of a Newmarket maiden last time out, kept on for a creditable fifth on this step up in grade.

7468 SOUTHWELL (L-H)
Tuesday, November 23
OFFICIAL GOING: Standard
Wind: Fresh, behind. Weather: Bright and dry

7536 PAULHOWLINGRACING.CO.UK NOVICE STKS — 1m (F)
12:10 (12:10) (Class 5) 2-Y-O — **£2,072** (£616; £308; £153) **Stalls** Low

Form — RPR

4 **1** **Stansonnit**[27] 7172 2-9-0 0 .... PJMcDonald 1 83+
(G A Swinbank) *dwlt: hdwy to trck ldrs after 2f: smooth hdwy on inner to trck ldr 3f out: led on bit 2f out: shkn up appr fnl f: sn clr and styd on strly: readily* **8/1**

0051 **2** *5* **Imaginary World (IRE)**[26] 7197 2-8-11 70 .... JamesDoyle 3 69
(A J McCabe) *dwlt and sn rdn along after s: hdwy and cl up on outer after 1f: led over 3f out: rdn and hdd 2f out: drvn over 1f out: kpt on same pce* **11/4**[2]

3403 **3** *8* **Hoppy's Flyer (FR)**[27] 7172 2-8-9 80 .... GrahamGibbons 2 48
(P A Kirby) *led: pushed along 1/2-way: rdn and hdd over 3f out: drvn and wknd over 2f out* **3/1**[3]

01 **4** *7* **Spyder**[20] 7303 2-9-5 76 .... LukeMorris 4 42
(Jane Chapple-Hyam) *cl up: rdn along over 3f out: sn lost pl: bhd and eased fnl 2f* **6/5**[1]

1m 41.9s (-1.80) **Going Correction** -0.225s/f (Stan) — **4** Ran SP% **108.2**
Speed ratings (Par 96): **100,95,87,80**
CSF £28.02 TOTE £11.40; EX 30.10.
Owner The Twopin Partnership **Bred** R G Percival And Mrs A Lockhart **Trained** Melsonby, N Yorks

FOCUS
An uncompetitive novice event, but a potentially useful winner. The second ran to her mark.

NOTEBOOK
Stansonnit was beaten 15l over 1m on easy turf (10l behind Hoppy's Flyer) on debut, but he was noticeably green that day and did hint at ability. He was a different proposition this time, travelling well under a patient ride before easing to the front over a furlong out, still on the bridle, and then gradually drawing clear when asked. The winner's pedigree is a mix of speed and stamina, but he looks a middle-distance/stayer in the making. He showed a knee action and, incidentally, this was his sire's second winner on the Southwell Fibresand from just three runners. (op 15-2 tchd 7-1)
Imaginary World(IRE), a claiming winner on Polytrack for Ed McMahon in October, was recently sold to these connections for £9,200. She had her chance, but was ultimately no match for the winner, who's clearly much more progressive. (op 10-3 tchd 9-4)
Hoppy's Flyer(FR) could not be confirm recent Musselburgh placings with Stansonnit. She carried her head to one side in the straight and did not look happy, not taking to the surface and/or its kickback. (op 10-3)
Spyder was beaten almost as soon as he came off the bridle around the bend leaving the back straight. His maiden win was gained on heavy ground, but Fibresand is a different surface altogether. Official explanation: jockey said the gelding had no more to give (op 11-10 tchd 6-4)

7537 BOOK YOUR TICKETS ONLINE AT SOUTHWELL-RACECOURSE.CO.UK H'CAP (DIV I) — 5f (F)
12:40 (12:40) (Class 6) (0-58,58) 3-Y-O+ — **£1,364** (£403; £201) **Stalls** High

Form — RPR

6114 **1** **Fashion Icon (USA)**[27] 7170 4-8-12 **58** .... (b) ShaneBKelly(7) 11 74
(D O'Meara) *chsd ldrs towards stands' side: hdwy 2f out: rdn to chal over 1f out: led ent fnl f and kpt on strly* **12/1**

3144 **2** *3 ¼* **Ballarina**[37] 6965 4-9-2 **55** .... EddieAhern 10 59
(E J Alston) *sn led: rdn along wl over 1f out: drvn and hdd ent fnl f one pce* **6/1**[2]

5150 **3** 1 ¾ **Best One**[18] 7334 6-9-4 57 (b) LukeMorris 6 55
(R A Harris) *cl up: rdn along 2f out: drvn over 1f out and sn one pce* **8/1**[3]
4006 **4** ½ **Sharp Bullet (IRE)**[10] 7446 4-9-2 55 (b) GregFairley 8 51+
(Bruce Hellier) *sltly hmpd s: towards rr and swtchd lft after 1f: rdn 1/2-way: styd on fr over 1f out: nrst fin* **12/1**
5353 **5** shd **Black Baccara**[11] 7425 3-9-1 54 (v[1]) AdamKirby 1 50
(P S McEntee) *cl up: rdn along 2f out: drvn and edgd lft over 1f out: sn wknd* **8/1**[3]
6635 **6** ¾ **First Swallow**[18] 7334 5-9-5 58 (t) PJMcDonald 7 51
(D H Brown) *chsd ldrs: n.m.r and swtchd rt after 2f: rdn 2f out: sn drvn and one pce* **4/1**[1]
4005 **7** 1 **Fathey (IRE)**[12] 7402 4-8-11 50 MartinLane 12 40
(C Smith) *chsd ldrs: rdn along and outpcd after 1f: sn towards rr: drvn 2f out: kpt on appr fnl f: n.d* **14/1**
2000 **8** hd **Bertbrand**[15] 7380 5-8-9 48 (p) KirstyMilczarek 14 37
(I W McInnes) *towards rr and rdn along 1/2-way: drvn 2f out: sme hdwy appr fnl f: n.d* **66/1**
2045 **9** ½ **Errigal Lad**[88] 5496 5-9-5 58 (p) GrahamGibbons 5 45+
(J Balding) *midfield whn hmpd and lost pl after 1f: rdn along towards rr 1/2-way: hdwy over 1f out: nvr nr ldrs* **12/1**
0006 **10** 1 **Alsufooh (USA)**[28] 7155 3-8-11 50 PatrickMathers 9 33
(D Shaw) *sltly hmpd s: sn rdn along and a in rr* **80/1**
3530 **11** 2 **Imaginary Diva**[68] 6133 4-8-12 51 TomQueally 2 27
(G G Margarson) *midfield: rdn along and outpcd fr 1/2-way* **9/1**
505 **12** ½ **Bird Call (IRE)**[202] 1825 3-9-2 55 LNewman 3 29
(T D Barron) *sn rdn along and a in rr* **8/1**[3]
0000 **13** 4 **St Ignatius**[19] 7314 3-9-5 58 (b) ChrisCatlin 4 18
(K O Cunningham-Brown) *sn rdn along and a in rr* **18/1**

58.32 secs (-1.38) **Going Correction** -0.225s/f (Stan) **13** Ran SP% **115.4**
Speed ratings (Par 101): **102,96,94,93,93 91,90,89,89,87 84,83,77**
Tote Swingers:1&2:£9.40, 2&3:£13.10, 1&3:£19.40 CSF £79.45 CT £617.18 TOTE £13.10: £2.80, £2.60, £3.20; EX 44.90 TRIFECTA Not won..
Owner Trendy Ladies **Bred** Mr & Mrs Theodore Kuster **Trained** Nawton, N Yorks

FOCUS
Not a bad race for the grade, and the time was 0.52 seconds quicker than the second division. Those drawn high had the edge, which isn't always the case over this C&D. Improved form on the face of it from the winner.

7538 MARGARET RICE MEMORIAL MAIDEN STKS 1m 4f (F)
1:10 (1:10) (Class 5) 3-Y-O+ **£2,115** (£624; £312) **Stalls** Low

Form RPR
3402 **1** **Miniyamba (IRE)**[13] 7388 3-8-12 59 EddieAhern 5 64
(J L Dunlop) *trckd ldrs: smooth hdwy over 3f out: chal over 2f out: sn led: rdn and edgd lft over 1f out: sn clr* **7/4**[1]
2533 **2** 7 **Dandarrell**[12] 7407 3-9-3 53 GrahamGibbons 2 60
(Julie Camacho) *cl up: led after 1f: rdn along 3f out: drvn and hdd 2f out: chsd wnr tl no imp fnl f* **11/2**
3 5 **Odin's Raven (IRE)**[44] 6785 5-9-9 65 DaneO'Neill 1 50
(B Ellison) *led 1f: cl up on inner: ev ch 3f out: sn rdn and outpcd fnl 2f* **11/4**[2]
4 hd **Shouda (IRE)** 4-9-9 0 TomQueally 3 49
(B J Curley) *trckd ldrs: effrt over 3f out: rdn along over 2f out: drvn and one pce fr wl over 1f out* **12/1**
0545 **5** 24 **Penderyn**[20] 7304 3-8-12 50 AndreaAtzeni 7 —
(C Smith) *sn rdn along and a in rr* **33/1**
0000 **6** ¾ **Shanavaz**[28] 7147 4-9-4 34 (p) KirstyMilczarek 6 —
(C J Teague) *chsd ldrs: rdn along 5f out: sn wknd* **100/1**
5060 **7** 1 ½ **Ice Viking (IRE)**[27] 7181 3-9-3 56 (b) TomEaves 8 —
(J G Given) *prom: rdn along over 4f out: sn wknd* **4/1**[3]
0-6 **8** 30 **Countrycraft**[231] 1143 3-9-3 0 MickyFenton 4 —
(Miss S E Hall) *a in rr: bhd fnl 4f* **50/1**

2m 38.54s (-2.46) **Going Correction** -0.225s/f (Stan)
WFA 3 from 4yo+ 6lb **8** Ran SP% **112.0**
Speed ratings (Par 103): **99,94,91,90,74 74,73,53**
Tote Swingers:1&2:£1.60, 2&3:£2.50, 1&3:£1.70 CSF £11.42 TOTE £2.40: £1.70, £2.60, £1.02; EX 6.50 Trifecta £23.00 Pool £345.02 - 11.07 winning units..
Owner Benny Andersson **Bred** Swettenham Stud **Trained** Arundel, W Sussex

FOCUS
The first two finishers were rated in the 50s, and the time was 0.44 seconds slower than the later Class 5 handicap, so not form to dwell on. The winner did not need to be at her best.

7539 BET CHAMPIONS LEAGUE FOOTBALL H'CAP 6f (F)
1:40 (1:41) (Class 5) (0-75,75) 3-Y-O+ **£2,115** (£624; £312) **Stalls** Low

Form RPR
3033 **1** **Bonnie Prince Blue**[12] 7403 7-9-4 72 (be) DaneO'Neill 6 82
(B Ellison) *towards rr and rdn along after 2f: drvn 1/2-way: hdwy 2f out: chsd ldrs and edgd lft over 1f out: styd on wl u.p ins fnl f to ld nr fin* **11/2**[3]
0052 **2** ½ **Nadeen (IRE)**[13] 7399 3-9-7 75 GregFairley 7 83
(Michael Smith) *trckd ldrs: hdwy over 2f out: rdn to ld ent fnl f: sn drvn: hdd and no ex nr fin* **4/1**[1]
0104 **3** 2 ¼ **King's Wonder**[12] 7409 5-9-4 72 PJMcDonald 1 73
(Mrs R A Carr) *cl up on inner: hdwy to chal 2f out: sn rdn and ev ch tl drvn and one pce ins fnl f* **16/1**
1105 **4** 2 ½ **Kinigi (IRE)**[12] 7405 4-9-6 74 (b) LukeMorris 8 67
(R A Harris) *prom: rdn to ld 1 1/2f out: drvn and hdd ent fnl f: sn wknd* **10/1**
4144 **5** nse **Cardinal**[13] 7399 5-9-2 70 TomEaves 9 63
(R M H Cowell) *chsd ldrs: rdn along over 2f out: drvn wl over 1f out and kpt on same pce* **15/2**
0421 **6** ¾ **Conry (IRE)**[15] 7376 4-8-13 74 (e[1]) JulieBurke(7) 4 65
(Patrick Morris) *awkward and wnt lft s: towards rr tl styd on fnl 2f: n.d* **8/1**
0600 **7** ½ **Electioneer (USA)**[28] 7144 3-8-11 65 GrahamGibbons 14 54
(M W Easterby) *sltly hmpd s: in tch on outer: wd st: rdn to chse ldrs wl over 1f out: no imp fnl f* **25/1**
0645 **8** ¾ **Master Leon**[12] 7411 3-8-10 71 (v) AdamCarter(7) 3 58+
(B Smart) *dwlt and hmpd s: towards rr: swtchd rt to stands' rails and hdwy 2f out: sn rdn and n.d* **5/1**[2]
0004 **9** ½ **Amary (IRE)**[56] 6438 3-9-7 75 BarryMcHugh 11 60
(John A Harris) *in tch: rdn over 2f out: sn no imp* **33/1**
2100 **10** ¾ **Charles Parnell (IRE)**[13] 7399 7-8-11 65 ChrisCatlin 5 48
(S P Griffiths) *dwlt: a towards rr* **14/1**
0003 **11** nse **Johannesgray (IRE)**[28] 7144 3-9-1 72 MichaelO'Connell(3) 10 54
(D Nicholls) *led: rdn along over 2f out: drvn and hdd 1 1/2f out: sn wknd* **14/1**
650- **12** 7 **Flying Applause**[472] 4783 5-8-12 66 (b) JimmyQuinn 2 26
(S R Bowring) *midfield: rdn along 1/2-way: sn outpcd* **40/1**
4600 **13** 5 **Cut The Cackle (IRE)**[27] 7180 4-9-4 75 RobertLButler(3) 12 19
(P Butler) *a in rr* **66/1**
002- **14** 21 **Orchid Wing**[350] 7674 3-9-0 68 LNewman 13 —
(A G Foster) *wnt rt s: sn prom on outer: rdn along over 2f out: sn edgd rt and wknd* **20/1**

1m 14.72s (-1.78) **Going Correction** -0.225s/f (Stan) **14** Ran SP% **118.7**
Speed ratings (Par 103): **102,101,98,95,94 93,93,92,91,90 90,81,74,46**
Tote Swingers:1&2:£3.60, 2&3:£16.10, 1&3:£22.40 CSF £25.76 CT £347.45 TOTE £5.40: £1.90, £2.70, £7.00; EX 32.80 Trifecta £239.20 Part won. Pool £323.26 - 0.62 winning units..
Owner Koo's Racing Club **Bred** George Joseph Hicks **Trained** Norton, N Yorks

FOCUS
A fair handicap run at an overly strong pace. Straightforward form.
Orchid Wing Official explanation: jockey said the gelding hung right and lost his action; vet said gelding finished distressed

7540 PLAY GOLF BEFORE RACING CLAIMING STKS 7f (F)
2:10 (2:10) (Class 6) 2-Y-O **£1,706** (£503; £252) **Stalls** Low

Form RPR
0206 **1** **Endaxi Mana Mou**[13] 7393 2-8-1 65 KellyHarrison(3) 3 70+
(M G Quinlan) *dwlt: sn trcking ldrs: smooth hdwy 3f out: led over 2f out: rdn wl clr over 1f out: eased ins fnl f* **3/1**[2]
252 **2** 11 **Norton Girl**[12] 7404 2-8-6 60 WilliamCarson 6 43
(J J Quinn) *cl up: ev ch 3f out: rdn and outpcd 2f out: drvn and kpt on fnl f: no ch w wnr* **7/4**[1]
0003 **3** ¾ **Local Diktator**[12] 7404 2-9-1 45 (t) LukeMorris 1 50
(R A Harris) *trckd ldrs on inner whn n.m.r over 3f out: hdwy to chse wnr wl over 1f out: sn drvn and one pce* **14/1**[3]
4643 **4** 2 ¼ **Mary Boyle**[13] 7396 2-7-13 60 NeilFarley(5) 8 33
(A J McCabe) *trckd ldrs: hdwy on outer to ld 4f out: sddle slipped over 3f out: rdn and hdd 2f: sn btn* **7/4**[1]
00 **5** 8 **Hannah Cann**[13] 7392 2-7-10 38 ow1 LeonnaMayor(7) 4 11
(Peter Grayson) *a in rr* **100/1**
0000 **6** 4 ½ **Callipygos**[12] 7404 2-7-12 43 AndreaAtzeni 7 —
(P S McEntee) *led 2 1/2f: cl up tl rdn over 3f out and sn wknd* **50/1**
0000 **7** ¾ **Emperorsnewclothes (IRE)**[13] 7392 2-8-4 44 ow1..(v[1]) NeilChalmers 5 —
(M Appleby) *trckd ldrs: rdn along after 2f: in rr fr 1/2-way* **40/1**

1m 28.36s (-1.94) **Going Correction** -0.225s/f (Stan) **7** Ran SP% **109.8**
Speed ratings (Par 94): **102,89,88,86,76 71,70**
Tote Swingers:1&2:£2.20, 2&3:£2.00, 1&3:£4.20 CSF £7.94 TOTE £3.10: £2.00, £1.30; EX 10.90 Trifecta £30.50 Pool £694.36 - 16.84 winning units..Endaxi Mana Mou was claimed by George Prodromou for £5,000.
Owner Mrs J Quinlan **Bred** Plantation Stud **Trained** Newmarket, Suffolk

FOCUS
An uncompetitive claimer and the winner thrashed a modest field. The bare form is held down by the third.

NOTEBOOK
Endaxi Mana Mou, dropped in trip and grade, routed her six rivals. She can probably be competitive back in handicaps, but it would be unwise to get too carried away with this form seeing as she had 31lb in hand over the 45-rated third, and the fourth horse's saddle may have slipped forward. She was claimed for £5,000 by George Prodromou, who's had a few winners recently. (op 9-4)
Norton Girl, runner-up to an improver in a 6f seller here on her previous start, was unsuited by the step up in trip. She was a bit keen early and found little in the straight, only just confirming form from last time with Local Diktator. (op 13-8 tchd 11-8)
Local Diktator, 4lb worse off than when 4l behind Norton Girl last time, raced towards the often unfavoured inside rail in the straight. (op 20-1 tchd 22-1)
Mary Boyle, who was mounted on track and taken down early, is probably best excused as her saddle appeared to slip forward slightly and she ended up racing much too keenly. (op 9-4)

7541 BET ASIAN H'CAPS - BETDAQ HANDICAP 1m 4f (F)
2:40 (2:41) (Class 5) (0-75,72) 3-Y-O+ **£2,115** (£624; £312) **Stalls** Low

Form RPR
0501 **1** **Kingaroo (IRE)**[12] 7407 4-8-5 58 oh3 BillyCray(5) 4 66
(G Woodward) *mde all: pushed along 3f out: rdn over 2f out: drvn ent fnl f: kpt on wl* **9/2**[2]
0504 **2** 2 **Yossi (IRE)**[12] 7407 6-8-6 61 oh6 ow3 (be) SeanPalmer(7) 10 66
(R C Guest) *hld up: hdwy 4f out: trckd ldrs and n.m.r 3f out: effrt to chse wnr wl over 1f out: rdn and ch ins fnl f tl no ex last 100yds* **16/1**
061 **3** 6 **Hunters Belt (IRE)**[18] 7330 6-9-4 66 BarryMcHugh 6 61
(N Wilson) *hld up in rr: smooth hdwy on outer over 3f out: rdn to chse wnr 2f out: sn drvn and one pce* **7/2**[1]
3034 **4** 2 **Capable Guest (IRE)**[27] 7181 8-9-0 62 ChrisCatlin 2 54
(G M Moore) *in tch: hdwy to chse ldrs 4f out: rdn 3f out: drvn over 2f out and sn one pce* **5/1**[3]
2133 **5** 3 ½ **Affinity**[21] 7284 3-9-1 69 TomEaves 1 55
(J G Given) *chsd ldng pair: rdn along over 3f out: sn wknd* **11/2**
2236 **6** 2 ¼ **Amazing Blue Sky**[54] 6493 4-9-5 70 JamesSullivan(3) 8 53
(Mrs R A Carr) *trckd wnr: effrt to chal over 3f out: rdn wl over 2f out: sn wknd* **11/1**
3600 **7** 1 **General Tufto**[20] 7306 5-9-10 72 MartinLane 9 53
(C Smith) *a in rr* **14/1**
0030 **8** 16 **Knight's Victory (IRE)**[36] 6984 4-9-0 62 GregFairley 7 18
(Michael Smith) *in tch: hdwy to chse ldrs 1/2-way: rdn along over 4f out: sn drvn and wknd* **8/1**
1000 **9** 13 **Mme De Stael**[8] 7465 3-8-11 65 (b) StevieDonohoe 3 —
(Sir Mark Prescott) *ponied early to s: hld up: sme hdwy 1/2-way: rdn along wl over 4f out: sn wknd* **10/1**

2m 38.1s (-2.90) **Going Correction** -0.225s/f (Stan)
WFA 3 from 4yo+ 6lb **9** Ran SP% **113.5**
Speed ratings (Par 103): **100,98,94,93,91 89,88,78,69**
Tote Swingers:1&2:£8.90, 2&3:£15.00, 1&3:£3.80 CSF £71.21 CT £278.22 TOTE £6.50: £2.00, £5.10, £1.70; EX 68.20 TRIFECTA Not won..
Owner J Pownall **Bred** Kevin Walsh **Trained** Maltby, S Yorks
■ Stewards' Enquiry : Sean Palmer £140 fine: entered the parade ring after the signal to mount was called

FOCUS
A modest run handicap run at a good pace. Tricky form to assess with the first pair both out of the handicap but the winner could be better than the bare form.

7542 BOOK YOUR TICKETS ONLINE AT SOUTHWELL-RACECOURSE.CO.UK H'CAP (DIV II) 5f (F)
3:10 (3:10) (Class 6) (0-58,58) 3-Y-O+ **£1,364** (£403; £201) **Stalls** High

Form RPR
0020 **1** **Sleepy Blue Ocean**[88] 5485 4-9-2 55 LukeMorris 7 65
(J Balding) *dwlt: sn in tch: hdwy to chse ldrs 2f out: rdn to chal over 1f out: drvn ins fnl f: led last 75yds* **25/1**

3003 **2** *hd* **Guto**[28] 7155 7-8-11 **57**.................................. MatthewCosham(7) 9 66
(W J H Ratcliffe) *cl up: rdn to ld wl over 1f out: drvn ins fnl f whn rdr dropped whip: hdd and no ex last 75yds* **14/1**

4006 **3** *2* **Exceedingly Good (IRE)**[7] 7473 4-8-11 **50**.................. JimmyQuinn 14 52
(S R Bowring) *in tch towards stands' rail: hdwy wl over 1f out: sn rdn and styd on ins fnl f: nrst fin* **20/1**

0303 **4** *shd* **Cape Of Storms**[7] 7468 7-9-5 **58**..............................(b) PJMcDonald 5 59
(R Brotherton) *cl up: rdn 2f out and ev ch tl drvn and one pce ins fnl f* **11/2**[2]

4660 **5** *1 ¼* **Residency (IRE)**[18] 7328 4-9-2 **55**..................................(p) TomEaves 2 52
(B Smart) *in tch on wd outside: hdwy 2f out: rdn to chse ldrs over 1f out: kpt on same pce* **11/1**

2412 **6** *hd* **Desert Strike**[7] 7468 4-9-5 **58**.......................................(p) JamesDoyle 6 54
(A J McCabe) *chsd ldrs: rdn 2f out: sn drvn and one pce* **15/8**[1]

63 **7** *2* **Leahness (IRE)**[19] 7322 3-8-0 **46** oh1.........................(e[1]) JulieBurke(7) 3 35
(Patrick Morris) *in tch: rdn along 2f out: n.d* **14/1**

2030 **8** *shd* **Rio Sands**[55] 6464 5-8-9 **51**...............................(p) MichaelStainton(3) 4 40
(R M Whitaker) *midfield: effrt and sme hdwy 2f out: sn rdn and no imp appr fnl f* **9/1**

2000 **9** *½* **Mr Funshine**[28] 7154 5-9-1 **54**.. DaneO'Neill 13 41
(D Shaw) *awkward s: a towards rr* **20/1**

2606 **10** *hd* **Pocket's Pick (IRE)**[63] 6270 4-9-2 **58**.............(b) AndrewHeffernan(3) 11 44
(Jim Best) *led: rdn along 1/2-way: drvn and hdd wl over 1f out: sn wknd* **8/1**[3]

5U0 **11** *nk* **Lucky Art (USA)**[62] 6299 4-8-10 **52**.......................... JamesSullivan(3) 1 37
(Mrs R A Carr) *cl up: rdn along over 2f out: sn drvn and wknd over 1f out* **12/1**

0000 **12** *7* **Thoughtsofstardom**[13] 7390 7-8-11 **57**.................. LauraSimpson(7) 12 17
(P S McEntee) *dwlt: a in rr* **66/1**

6600 **13** *2 ¼* **Gleaming Spirit (IRE)**[6] 7477 6-8-10 **49**................(v) PatrickMathers 10 —
(Peter Grayson) *prom: rdn along after 1f: sn drvn and wknd: bhd fnl 2f* **100/1**

-500 **14** *nk* **Grand Palace (IRE)**[271] 694 7-8-13 **52**.........................(v) AdamKirby 8 3
(D Shaw) *a in rr* **18/1**

58.84 secs (-0.86) **Going Correction** -0.225s/f (Stan) **14** Ran SP% **121.8**
Speed ratings (Par 101): **97,96,93,93,91 91,87,87,86,86 86,74,71,70**
Tote Swingers:1&2:£53.50, 2&3:£52.60, 1&3:£49.80 CSF £330.52 CT £7177.44 TOTE £31.70: £10.40, £4.50, £9.40; EX 264.40 TRIFECTA Not won..
Owner Tykes And Terriers Racing Club **Bred** Exors Of The Late N Ahamad & P C Scott **Trained** Scrooby, Notts

FOCUS
The time was 0.52 seconds slower than the first division. Like in the other leg, a low draw was no help at all. The winner is rated back towards his best form.

7543 TRY BETDAQ FOR AN EXCHANGE AMATEUR RIDERS' H'CAP 1m (F)
3:40 (3:40) (Class 6) (0-60,60) 3-Y-O+ **£1,648** (£507; £253) **Stalls** Low

Form RPR

0064 **1** **Ubenkor (IRE)**[12] 7402 5-10-4 **55**................................ MrJNewman(5) 11 71
(M Herrington) *prom: hdwy to chse ldr 3f out: led 2f out: sn rdn clr: styd on strly* **5/1**[1]

6400 **2** *6* **Nevada Desert (IRE)**[32] 7062 10-10-2 **55**................. MrJMullaney(7) 13 57
(R M Whitaker) *hld up towards rr: hdwy on outer 3f out: rdn to chse wnr over 1f out: sn drvn and no imp* **12/1**

6456 **3** *1 ¼* **Bentley**[6] 7487 6-10-4 **55**..(b[1]) MrPPrince(5) 3 54
(B P J Baugh) *in tch: hdwy wl over 2f out: rdn wl over 1f out: kpt on fnl f* **9/1**

3506 **4** *1 ¾* **Kielty's Folly**[159] 3132 6-10-0 **53**.................... MissStefaniaGandola(7) 12 48
(B P J Baugh) *cl up on outer: effrt 3f out: rdn along over 2f out: sn one pce* **14/1**

1060 **5** *hd* **Know No Fear**[15] 7376 5-10-13 **59**.............................(p) MissEJJones 14 54
(A J Lidderdale) *hld up in tch: hdwy 2f out: sn rdn and no imp* **6/1**[3]

200 **6** *2 ½* **Angelena Ballerina (IRE)**[22] 7273 3-10-1 **56**..............(b[1]) MrLMichael(7) 1 45
(Karen George) *in rr: hdwy 1/2-way: n.m.r and swtchd rt 3f out: kpt on appr fnl f: nrst fin* **20/1**

5462 **7** *1 ¾* **Castle Myth (USA)**[12] 7401 4-10-7 **60**.......................... MissHBethell(7) 9 45
(B Ellison) *in rr: sme hdwy over 2f out: sn rdn and n.d* **11/2**[2]

4604 **8** *1 ¾* **Plenty O'Toole**[12] 7406 3-10-3 **58**.............................(p) MissDLenge(7) 6 39
(Mrs D J Sanderson) *led and set str pce: rdn along over 2f out: sn hdd & wknd* **12/1**

4000 **9** *½* **Ivestar (IRE)**[18] 7336 5-10-6 **57**...................(vt) MissCharlotteHolmes(5) 5 37
(B M R Haslam) *dwlt and towards rr: sme hdwy over 3f out: sn rdn and n.d* **25/1**

5000 **10** *2* **Daniel Thomas (IRE)**[27] 7184 8-10-7 **58**...................(t) MissMBryant(5) 7 33
(P Butler) *s.i.s: a in rr* **22/1**

0033 **11** *½* **We'll Deal Again**[18] 7328 3-10-12 **60**.............................. MissJCoward 4 34
(M W Easterby) *chsd ldr on inner: rdn along 3f out: sn wknd* **10/1**

6250 **12** *3 ¼* **Tasza (USA)**[20] 7305 3-10-7 **58**.................................. MrPCollington(5) 2 32
(A J McCabe) *chsd ldrs on inner: rdn along over 3f out: sn wknd* **7/1**

546- **13** *12* **Dudley Docker (IRE)**[351] 7668 8-10-7 **60**...................... MrJPearce(7) 8 —
(D C O'Brien) *chsd ldrs: rdn along 3f out: sn wknd* **22/1**

1m 42.52s (-1.18) **Going Correction** -0.225s/f (Stan)
WFA 3 from 4yo+ 2lb **13** Ran SP% **117.3**
Speed ratings (Par 101): **96,90,88,87,86 84,82,80,80,78 77,74,62**
Tote Swingers:1&2:£12.20, 2&3:£18.30, 1&3:£7.30. totesuper7: Win: Not won. Place: Not won. CSF £59.61 CT £544.42 TOTE £7.00: £2.70, £4.10, £3.10; EX 67.30 Trifecta £48.00 Pool £324.69 - 5.00 winning units..
Owner Stuart Herrington **Bred** Petra Bloodstock Agency Ltd **Trained** Cold Kirby, N Yorks

FOCUS
A moderate amateur riders' handicap and few were ever involved. The winner seemingly got back to something like his best form but the form is not convincing.
Tasza(USA) Official explanation: jockey said the filly was unsuited by the Fibresand surface
T/Jkpt: Not won. T/Plt: £170.90 to a £1 stake. Pool:£54,379.83. 232.20 winning tickets T/Qpdt: £5.10 to a £1 stake. Pool:£6,755.63. 972.20 winning tickets JR

7500 SAINT-CLOUD (L-H)
Tuesday, November 23

OFFICIAL GOING: Turf: heavy

7544a PRIX ISONOMY (LISTED RACE) (2YO) (TURF) 1m
1:10 (12:00) 2-Y-O **£24,336** (£9,734; £7,300; £4,867; £2,433)

RPR

1 **Whip And Win (FR)**[11] 2-8-8 0.................................... GregoryBenoist 2 97
(Robert Collet, France) **39/10**[3]

2 *1* **Nova Hawk**[12] 7415 2-8-8 0.. StephanePasquier 1 95
(Rod Collet, France) **17/2**

3 *¾* **Lustre (FR)**[28] 2-8-11 0.. Pierre-CharlesBoudot 6 96
(Y De Nicolay, France) **31/1**

4 *¾* **Stark Danon (FR)**[42] 6913 2-8-11 0............................ DominiqueBoeuf 5 95
(W Hickst, Germany) **14/5**[1]

5 *2 ½* **Celenza (FR)**[96] 5252 2-8-8 0.................................. AntoineHamelin 3 86
(A De Royer-Dupre, France) **11/1**

6 *½* **Eigelstein** 2-8-11 0.. AStarke 7 88
(P Schiergen, Germany) **3/1**[2]

7 *1 ½* **Barista (IRE)**[21] 7280 2-8-11 0.. OlivierPeslier 9 85
(M R Channon) *broke wl on outside: sn led: set stdy pce: led into st: sn rdn: hdd 2f out: no ex: grad wknd* **7/1**

8 *8* **Flinch Cat (FR)**[30] 2-8-11 0.. IoritzMendizabal 8 67
(J E Hammond, France) **20/1**

9 *4* **Zack Yield (FR)**[37] 6973 2-8-11 0..............................(b) MaximeGuyon 4 58
(A Lamotte D'Argy, France) **14/1**

1m 54.5s (7.00) **9** Ran SP% **117.6**
WIN (incl. 1 euro stake): 4.90. PLACES: 2.00, 2.60, 5.60. DF: 17.70. SF: 29.60.
Owner Mme C Wingtans & SC Famille Vidal **Bred** Mme C Wingtans & Sc Famille Vidal **Trained** Chantilly, France

NOTEBOOK
Barista(IRE) faded into seventh place having tried to make all the running.

7545a PRIX CERES (LISTED RACE) (3YO FILLIES) (TURF) 7f
1:40 (12:00) 3-Y-O **£24,336** (£9,734; £7,300; £4,867; £2,433)

RPR

1 **Courchevel (IRE)**[14] 3-8-11 0.. ThomasHuet 14 99
(Robert Collet, France) **2/1**[1]

2 *nk* **Agony And Ecstasy**[29] 7121 3-8-11 0...................... RichardKingscote 7 98
(R M Beckett) *sn led: maintained advantage into st: rdn 2f out: qcknd wl: wnt 2 l clr 1f out: r.o wl u.p fnl f: only hdd cl home* **31/1**

3 *¾* **Rada Angel (IRE)**[14] 3-8-11 0..(b) AlexisBadel 8 96
(Mme M Bollack-Badel, France) **12/1**

4 *1 ½* **Love Queen (IRE)**[33] 3-8-11 0.............................. StephanePasquier 3 93
(Mlle V Dissaux, France) **11/2**[2]

5 *½* **Akrivi (IRE)**[19] 3-8-11 0.. OlivierPeslier 9 91
(C Laffon-Parias, France) **9/1**

6 *½* **Asmaa (USA)**[158] 3-8-11 0.. TheoBachelot 6 90
(J E Hammond, France) **23/1**

7 *nse* **Diatribe**[23] 3-8-11 0.. DominiqueBoeuf 5 90
(W Baltromei, Germany) **28/1**

8 *snk* **So Long Malpic (FR)**[70] 3-8-11 0.................................. SylvainRuis 2 90
(T Lemer, France) **78/10**[3]

9 *¾* **Gold Harvest (FR)**[61] 6316 3-9-1 0........................ MickaelBarzalona 12 92
(Y De Nicolay, France) **48/1**

10 *6* **Katsya (FR)**[30] 3-8-11 0.. JohanVictoire 13 73
(J E Pease, France) **20/1**

0 **Absolute Music (USA)**[285] 514 3-8-11 0.................. IoritzMendizabal 4 —
(R M H Cowell) *racd in midfield: rdn bef st: no ex: grad fdd: eased ins fnl f* **10/1**

0 **Filly (FR)**[30] 3-8-11 0.. ThierryThulliez 1 —
(Mme C Head-Maarek, France) **42/1**

0 **Applique**[42] 3-8-11 0.. FabriceVeron 11 —
(H-A Pantall, France) **13/1**

0 **Mountain Rose (GER)**[114] 4640 3-8-11 0.................. MaximeGuyon 10 —
(Mario Hofer, Germany) **24/1**

1m 36.6s (4.40) **14** Ran SP% **117.9**
WIN (incl. 1 euro stake): 3.00. PLACES: 1.80, 6.90, 3.50. DF: 44.60. SF: 52.40.
Owner Peter Scherrer **Bred** Kilfrush And Waterside Studs **Trained** Chantilly, France

NOTEBOOK
Agony And Ecstasy enjoys these testing conditions and ran a sound race, just getting run out of it close home.
Absolute Music(USA) never really threatened.

7546a PRIX SOLITUDE (LISTED RACE) (3YO FILLIES) (TURF) 1m 2f
2:10 (12:00) 3-Y-O **£24,336** (£9,734; £7,300; £4,867; £2,433)

RPR

1 **Roche Ambeau (FR)**[45] 6761 3-8-11 0.................... YohannBourgois 12 —
(E Lellouche, France) **84/1**

2 *1 ½* **It's So You (USA)**[26] 3-8-11 0.. MaximeGuyon 7 —
(A Fabre, France) **43/10**[2]

3 *nse* **Diyaraka (FR)**[37] 3-8-11 0.. GregoryBenoist 14 —
(M Delzangles, France) **5/1**[3]

4 *3* **Jardaa**[30] 3-8-11 0.. DavyBonilla 1 —
(F Head, France) **17/2**

5 *1 ½* **Meduse Bleu**[119] 3-8-11 0.. TheoBachelot 2 —
(S Wattel, France) **30/1**

6 *hd* **Green China (FR)**[89] 3-8-11 0.................................... RaphaelMarchelli 8 —
(S Wattel, France) **19/1**

7 *2 ½* **Sarah Lynx (IRE)**[52] 6591 3-9-2 0................................ OlivierPeslier 5 —
(J E Hammond, France) **2/1**[1]

8 *2* **Good Hope (GER)**[37] 3-8-11 0.. AlexisBadel 15 —
(P Schiergen, Germany) **44/1**

9 *½* **Parade Militaire (IRE)**[63] 3-8-11 0.............................. SamuelFargeat 11 —
(E Lellouche, France) **95/1**

10 *½* **Homepage**[53] 6551 3-8-11 0..................................(p) StephanePasquier 13 —
(P Bary, France) **13/1**

0 **Heaven's Vault (IRE)**[10] 7455 3-9-2 0..........................(b[1]) FranckBlondel 4 —
(Robert Collet, France) **73/1**

0 **Titivation**[45] 6753 3-8-11 0.. DominiqueBoeuf 6 —
(M L W Bell) *sn prom bhd ldrs: wnt 4th at 1/2-way: hrd rdn 2f out: sn wknd* **29/1**

0 **Peinted Song (USA)**[89] 3-8-11 0.................................... IoritzMendizabal 10 —
(J-C Rouget, France) **13/1**

0 **Amazing Beauty (GER)**[23] 3-8-11 0.......................... MickaelBarzalona 9 —
(M Figge, Germany) **27/1**

0 **Ezalli (IRE)**[29] 7140 3-8-11 0.. WMLordan 3 —
(Edward Lynam, Ire) *racd towards rr on inner: mde prog bef st: sn rdn: no ex: fdd qckly* **32/1**

2m 28.4s (12.40) **15** Ran SP% **117.6**
WIN (incl. 1 euro stake): 85.30. PLACES: 12.40, 2.20, 2.20. DF: 127.70. SF: 366.60.
Owner Alain Maubert **Bred** A Maubert **Trained** Lamorlaye, France

NOTEBOOK
Titivation was a beaten horse soon after entering the straight.

[7476]KEMPTON (A.W) (R-H)
Wednesday, November 24

OFFICIAL GOING: Standard
Wind: Light, across Weather: Clear, cold

7547 KIA VENGA MEDIAN AUCTION MAIDEN STKS 5f (P)
4:05 (4:06) (Class 6) 3-5-Y-O **£1,637** (£483; £241) **Stalls** High

Form RPR

5200 **1** **Picansort**[11] 7439 3-9-3 62 (v[1]) JimmyQuinn 2 71+
(B R Johnson) *racd wd: hld up in 5th: prog to ld 1f out: shkn up and sn clr* **11/4**[2]

3302 **2** 3 ¾ **Papageno**[20] 7322 3-9-3 57 JimCrowley 3 58
(J R Jenkins) *chsd ldrs in 4th: rdn to cl whn wnr sailed by over 1f out: kpt on to take 2nd last strides* **5/2**[1]

0006 **3** nk **Mind The Monarch**[7] 7477 3-8-12 50 (v[1]) EddieAhern 4 51
(R A Teal) *led: over 2 l clr 2f out: hdd 1f out: nt qckn: lost 2nd last strides* **11/2**

4 1 **Break On Through**[33] 7076 3-8-5 0 KWDeOliveira(7) 7 48+
(J L Hassett, Ire) *s.i.s: in tch in 6th: effrt on inner over 1f out: urged along and one pce* **9/2**[3]

06 **5** 3 ¼ **Gessabelle**[30] 7131 3-8-13 42 ow1 (t) AdamKirby 1 37
(P S McEntee) *slowest away: rousted along to chse ldr after 1f to over 1f out: wknd qckly* **20/1**

630 **6** 2 ¾ **Crazy Parachute**[189] 2234 3-9-3 60 GeorgeBaker 5 31
(G L Moore) *hld up last: hanging lft bnd after 1f: lost tch 2f out: bhd after* **5/1**

0505 **7** 1 ¼ **Riggs (IRE)**[20] 7322 4-9-3 36 (b) PatrickMathers 6 27
(Peter Grayson) *chsd ldr 1f: rdn 1/2-way: wknd rapidly over 1f out* **66/1**

59.82 secs (-0.68) **Going Correction** -0.125s/f (Stan) 7 Ran SP% 111.7
Speed ratings (Par 101): **100,94,93,91,86 82,80**
Tote Swingers:1&2:£2.50, 2&3:£5.80, 1&3:£3.80 CSF £9.57 TOTE £5.50: £2.50, £1.80; EX 14.10.
Owner Peter Crate **Bred** Miss Brooke Sanders **Trained** Ashtead, Surrey

FOCUS
Several exposed performers in a really weak maiden in which the gallop was an ordinary one. The winner raced on the outside of the group before edging towards the inside rail late on. The form looks sound enough.
Riggs(IRE) Official explanation: jockey said gelding hung right

7548 RACING AT SKYSPORTS.COM H'CAP 1m 2f (P)
4:35 (4:37) (Class 5) (0-75,75) 3-Y-O+ **£2,286** (£675; £337) **Stalls** High

Form RPR

2054 **1** **All The Winds (GER)**[85] 5624 5-9-6 74 RussKennemore(3) 8 83
(S Lycett) *hld up last: rapid prog on wd outside fr 2f out: led jst ins fnl f: rdn clr* **20/1**

2004 **2** 1 ¾ **Negotiation (IRE)**[27] 7190 4-9-2 67 FrannyNorton 14 73
(M Quinn) *disp 2nd pl: rdn to ld over 1f out: hdd and one pce jst ins fnl f* **16/1**

1601 **3** ½ **Aurora Sky (IRE)**[24] 7253 4-9-4 69 J-PGuillambert 10 77+
(J Akehurst) *t.k.h early: restrained into midfield: trapped bhd rivals and dropped to last pair 2f out: gd prog fnl f: fin wl to take 3rd last strides* **16/1**

0000 **4** hd **Kidlat**[37] 6990 5-9-8 73 JoeFanning 4 77
(A Bailey) *led and sn crossed fr wd draw: rdn and hdd over 1f out: one pce* **20/1**

3425 **5** 2 ¼ **Green Wadi**[58] 6427 5-9-5 70 GeorgeBaker 13 70
(G L Moore) *trckd ldrs: effrt to dispute 3rd over 1f out: nt qckn after: outpcd* **5/1**[2]

1223 **6** 1 ½ **Nisaal (IRE)**[33] 7063 5-9-8 73 AdamKirby 12 70
(A W Carroll) *hld up in last pair: prog on inner over 1f out: tried to cl ent fnl f: fdd sn after* **8/1**[3]

0030 **7** ¾ **Dream In Waiting**[21] 7307 4-9-7 72 ShaneKelly 5 67
(B J Meehan) *hld up in last trio: dropped to last 2f out: hanging over 1f out: passed sme wkng rivals fnl f* **14/1**

0302 **8** ¾ **Silent Oasis**[27] 7190 4-9-2 67 TomQueally 7 61
(B G Powell) *hld up in last quartet: prog on inner wl over 1f out: cl enough ent fnl f: sn wknd* **8/1**[3]

0503 **9** nk **Buddy Holly**[42] 6554 5-9-6 71 MartinLane 6 64
(Mrs V M Jordan) *disp 2nd pl to wl over 1f out: wknd fnl f* **8/1**[3]

6606 **10** ¾ **Penchesco (IRE)**[23] 6091 5-9-6 71 JimCrowley 9 63
(Mrs A J Perrett) *nvr bttr than midfield: rdn and nt qckn 2f out: wknd fnl f* **9/2**[1]

6254 **11** shd **Veroon (IRE)**[16] 7382 4-9-10 75 (p) TomEaves 11 66
(J G Given) *chsd ldrs: rdn wl over 2f out: wknd over 1f out* **14/1**

4250 **12** 2 **Bullet Man (USA)**[33] 7053 5-9-10 75 JimmyQuinn 3 62
(R A Fahey) *pushed up to go prom on outer: rdn wl over 2f out: wknd wl over 1f out* **12/1**

2m 5.24s (-2.76) **Going Correction** -0.125s/f (Stan)
WFA 3 from 4yo+ 4lb 12 Ran SP% 110.5
Speed ratings (Par 103): **106,104,104,104,102 101,100,99,99,99 98,97**
Tote Swingers:1&2:£97.70, 2&3:£35.10, 1&3:£60.60 CSF £260.10 CT £3793.94 TOTE £30.40: £7.90, £7.70, £6.60; EX 184.20.
Owner Nicholls Family **Bred** Stall Tralopp **Trained** Clapton-on-the-Hill, Gloucs

FOCUS
Exposed performers in a run-of-the-mill handicap. The gallop was only a modest one and the winner came down the centre in the straight. Sound form.

7549 DIGIBET H'CAP 5f (P)
5:05 (5:07) (Class 4) (0-85,81) 3-Y-O+ **£3,885** (£1,156; £577; £288) **Stalls** High

Form RPR

3440 **1** **High Spice (USA)**[54] 6539 3-9-4 78 (p) JimCrowley 6 84
(R M H Cowell) *chsd ldrs: effrt on inner over 1f out: drvn to ld 1f out: styd on wl* **16/1**

2302 **2** 1 **Vhujon (IRE)**[20] 7314 5-9-2 76 CathyGannon 4 78
(P D Evans) *pushed along in 6th: effrt and looking for room over 1f out: styd on to take 2nd ins fnl f: unable to chal* **6/1**

3001 **3** ¾ **Love You Louis**[22] 7285 4-8-13 73 EddieAhern 1 74
(J R Jenkins) *trckd ldrs on outer: rdn and nt qckn 1f out: styd on to press for 2nd after* **7/2**[2]

416 **4** ¾ **Angelo Poliziano**[6] 7494 4-8-9 72 (p) AmyRyan(3) 3 69+
(Mrs A Duffield) *hld up last: effrt on wd outside bnd 2f out: rdn over 1f out: kpt on: nvr nr enough to chal* **11/2**

6105 **5** ¾ **Freddie's Girl (USA)**[20] 7319 3-9-3 77 TomQueally 7 71
(Stef Higgins) *led at fast pce: hdd 1f out: wknd* **9/2**[3]

0103 **6** ½ **Italian Tom (IRE)**[20] 7314 3-9-3 77 LukeMorris 5 70+
(R A Harris) *chsd ldrs: shkn up 2f out: nt qckn over 1f out: lost pl ent fnl f: no room after* **10/1**

2226 **7** ¾ **Excellent Show**[26] 7212 4-9-7 81 TomEaves 2 71
(B Smart) *chsd ldr: drvn over 1f out: nt qckn and sn lost 2nd: wknd fnl f* **5/2**[1]

59.30 secs (-1.20) **Going Correction** -0.125s/f (Stan) 7 Ran SP% 113.6
Speed ratings (Par 105): **104,102,101,100,98 98,96**
Tote Swingers:1&2:£15.00, 2&3:£2.10, 1&3:£7.20 CSF £104.80 TOTE £26.50: £9.30, £5.70; EX 111.30.
Owner Khalifa Dasmal **Bred** Dell Ridge Farm Llc **Trained** Six Mile Bottom, Cambs

FOCUS
Pretty ordinary form for the grade, but the gallop was sound. The winner made his ground close to the inside rail in the straight.
Freddie's Girl(USA) Official explanation: jockey said filly hung left
Italian Tom(IRE) Official explanation: jockey said colt was denied a clear run

7550 DIGIBET.COM MEDIAN AUCTION MAIDEN STKS (DIV I) 7f (P)
5:35 (5:36) (Class 6) 2-Y-O **£1,364** (£403; £201) **Stalls** High

Form RPR

4 **1** **Herminella**[20] 7311 2-8-12 0 DavidProbert 8 72
(W R Muir) *chsd ldr: drvn 2f out: clsd to ld 1f out: styd on* **4/1**[2]

40 **2** ½ **Isingy Red (FR)**[14] 7385 2-9-3 0 StephenCraine 2 76
(J R Boyle) *t.k.h early: trckd ldng trio: clsd 2f out: tried to chal over 1f out: chsd wnr ins fnl f: kpt on but a hld* **20/1**

5 **3** ¾ **Corsican Boy**[123] 4375 2-9-3 0 SteveDrowne 11 74+
(R Charlton) *s.s: hld up in 7th: wnt 5th over 2f out and plld to outer: drvn and styd on grad after: tk 3rd last 75yds: nvr gng pce to chal* **11/4**[1]

344 **4** 1 **Follow My Dream**[11] 7447 2-8-12 67 RobertHavlin 3 66
(J H M Gosden) *led: rdn 2f out: hdd 1f out: steadily fdd* **11/4**[1]

2254 **5** 1 **Enlightening (IRE)**[21] 7294 2-9-3 72 JimmyFortune 9 68
(R Hannon) *t.k.h early: trckd ldng pair: effrt 2f out: nt qckn over 1f out: fdd ins fnl f* **4/1**[2]

06 **6** 4 ½ **Lynchpin**[28] 7177 2-9-3 0 LukeMorris 10 57
(R A Harris) *chsd ldrs in 6th: rdn 1/2-way: sn outpcd: nvr on terms after* **66/1**

7 1 **Wodian (IRE)** 2-8-12 0 DaneO'Neill 5 49
(D R Lanigan) *dwlt: hld up in 9th: modest prog over 2f out: nvr on terms* **10/1**[3]

00 **8** 7 **Trust Me Boy**[14] 7386 2-9-0 0 NataliaGemelova(3) 4 36
(J E Long) *reluctant to enter stalls: dwlt: rcvrd to rch 5th 1/2-way: sn rdn: wknd over 2f out* **66/1**

9 nk **Algris** 2-9-3 0 StevieDonohoe 6 35
(Sir Mark Prescott) *s.s: sn detached in last: a bhd* **20/1**

00 **10** 1 **Seadream**[28] 7177 2-8-12 0 LeeNewnes(5) 7 33
(M D I Usher) *hld up in 8th: rdn and wknd over 2f out: sn bhd* **40/1**

1m 27.16s (1.16) **Going Correction** -0.125s/f (Stan) 10 Ran SP% 117.4
Speed ratings (Par 94): **88,87,86,85,84 79,78,70,69,68**
Tote Swingers:1&2:£10.10, 2&3:£15.60, 1&3:£3.10 CSF £82.68 TOTE £11.70: £2.40, £6.50, £1.50; EX 85.40.
Owner Dulverton Equine **Bred** Herminoe Partnership **Trained** Lambourn, Berks

FOCUS
No more than a fair maiden and one in which the gallop was a moderate one. The winner raced centre-to-far-side in the straight and the first five pulled clear.

NOTEBOOK
Herminella, ideally placed in a race run at a moderate gallop, fully confirmed debut promise and showed a good attitude to justify the market confidence. A more truly run race over this trip or the step up to 1m should see her in a better light and she should be able to better this bare form in handicaps. (op 11-2)
Isingy Red(FR), who had shown only moderate form in two outings, was another to race with the choke out in this muddling event but he turned in an improved showing, in the process leaving the impression he'd be more at home over 1m when stepped into ordinary handicap company. He's sure to win a race.
Corsican Boy ◆ came from further back than the first two but bettered the form he had shown on his debut at Newmarket. Ordinary handicaps, granted a stiffer test of stamina, will be the way forward with him in due course. (tchd 5-2 and 3-1 in a place)
Follow My Dream had shown improved form at Wolverhampton over this trip on her previous start but failed to build on that, despite being allowed a fairly easy time of it in front. This run underlined her vulnerability in this grade but she's capable of picking up a small race somewhere down the line. (op 3-1 tchd 7-2 in a place and 10-3 in places)
Enlightening(IRE), who had a good chance strictly on official ratings, is also starting to look exposed and he didn't really improve for the step up to this trip. He too should be able to pick up a weak race in this grade but he'll do well to win a handicap from his current 72 mark. (op 10-3)

7551 DIGIBET.COM MEDIAN AUCTION MAIDEN STKS (DIV II) 7f (P)
6:05 (6:06) (Class 6) 2-Y-O **£1,364** (£302; £302) **Stalls** High

Form RPR

5 **1** **Prince Of Burma (IRE)**[7] 7478 2-9-3 0 RobertHavlin 2 85+
(J H M Gosden) *hld up in midfield: shkn up to cl on ldrs 2f out: rdn to ld over 1f out: edgd rt but readily drew clr* **10/11**[1]

02 **2** 4 **Flying Power**[13] 7400 2-9-3 0 ChrisCatlin 4 74
(D R Lanigan) *chsd ldng pair: tk 2nd 2f out: urged along to chal over 1f out but wnr wnt by: plugged on* **10/3**[2]

03 **2** dht **Blue Maisey**[20] 7311 2-8-12 0 TomQueally 8 69
(Miss S L Davison) *s.s: hld up in last trio: shkn up over 2f out: prog over 1f out: styd on u.p fnl f* **9/2**[3]

4 3 ½ **Suspender Belt** 2-8-12 0 CathyGannon 6 60+
(J R Best) *hld up in last trio: shkn up over 2f out: prog jst over 1f out: styd on to take 4th last 75yds* **14/1**

5 1 ½ **Polish Sunset** 2-9-3 0 HayleyTurner 1 61
(Miss Amy Weaver) *s.s: wl off the pce in last: prog on inner fr 2f out: no hdwy fnl f: nt disgracd* **33/1**

0604 **6** nk **Irie Ute**[14] 7393 2-9-3 0 TravisBlock 10 61
(S Kirk) *chsd clr ldr: clsd and drvn to ld over 2f out: hdd over 1f out: wkng whn sltly hmpd ent fnl f* **12/1**

0000 **7** 4 **Bernie's Tune**[30] 7124 2-9-3 0 SamHitchcott 9 50
(J L Spearing) *chsd ldrs on inner: rdn 1/2-way: effrt over 2f out: wknd over 1f out* **66/1**

0 **8** 4 **Dixie Gwalia**[11] 7447 2-8-5 0 LauraPike(7) 3 34
(D M Simcock) *t.k.h: racd wd: chsd ldrs: wknd over 2f out* **50/1**

6000 **9** *13* **Miss Maudie (IRE)**[165] 2963 2-8-12 0 LukeMorris 5 1
(R A Harris) *tanked off in clr ld: hdd & wknd rapidly over 2f out: t.o* **66/1**

1m 25.97s (-0.03) **Going Correction** -0.125s/f (Stan) **9** Ran SP% **115.9**
Speed ratings (Par 94): **95,90,90,86,84 84,79,75,60**
Place: FP £1.10, BM £1.50; Exacta: POB/FP £2.40, POB/BM £3.30; CSF: POB/FP £2.01, POB/BM £2.65. Tote Swingers:1&FP:£1.80, 2&2:£1.80, 1&BM:£2.10 TOTE £3.10: £1.80.
Owner H R H Princess Haya Of Jordan **Bred** P Burns **Trained** Newmarket, Suffolk
■ Stewards' Enquiry : Robert Havlin two-day ban: careless riding (Dec 8-9)

FOCUS
Division two of the maiden and one lacking anything in the way of strength in depth. The gallop was a reasonable one and the winner raced in the centre in the straight.

NOTEBOOK
Prince Of Burma(IRE) had shaped with promise on his debut over this course-and-distance and duly bettered that effort to justify market support. He'll be equally at home over 1m and, although this wasn't a strong race, there should be more to come when he steps into handicap company. (op 5-4 after 7-4 in a place 13-8 in places tchd 11-8 in places)
Flying Power had shown improved form, despite hanging badly on his all-weather debut at Southwell and he probably ran to a similar level, despite carrying his head a shade high under pressure. He should have no problems with 1m and may do better in ordinary handicaps as he strengthens up next year. (op 7-2 tchd 3-1)
Blue Maisey failed to build on her previous course-and-distance promise (in front of Herminella, who took the first division) but she was far from disgraced and was another to leave the impression (backed up by pedigree) that a stiffer test of stamina would suit better. Ordinary handicaps will be the way forward with her. (op 7-2 tchd 3-1)
Suspender Belt, a half-sister to the in-form yard's Polytrack and turf winner Sonny G, hinted at ability without being unduly knocked about on this racecourse debut. She is entitled to improve for this experience but she will have to raise her game if she is to win in this grade.
Polish Sunset hinted at ability, despite her apparent greenness on this debut run for a yard that isn't renowned for debut winners in this grade. She should be wiser for the experience.

7552 DIGIBET CASINO NURSERY 7f (P)
6:35 (6:38) (Class 6) (0-65,65) 2-Y-O £1,637 (£483; £241) Stalls High

Form RPR
2603 **1** **May's Boy**[21] 7295 2-9-4 62 (p) DaneO'Neill 12 70+
(M D I Usher) *fractious preliminaries: racd freely: mde all: rdn clr fr 2f out: in n.d after* **4/1**[1]
0000 **2** *1 ½* **Sky Diamond (IRE)**[14] 7394 2-8-13 57 (b[1]) TomEaves 10 63+
(J G Given) *s.i.s: hld up in rr: only 9th and looking for room 2f out: gd prog and squeezed through jst over 1f out: r.o wl to take 2nd last 75yds: no ch of rching wnr* **25/1**
0303 **3** *2 ¾* **Robber Stone**[49] 6673 2-8-11 55 ChrisCatlin 6 51
(M R Channon) *chsd wnr: outpcd fr 2f out: no ch after: lost 2nd last 75yds* **14/1**
0533 **4** *1 ¼* **Night Witch (IRE)**[7] 7486 2-9-3 64 AlanCreighton[(3)] 4 57+
(E J Creighton) *hld up towards rr in abt 10th: rdn and prog over 2f out: wnt 4th over 1f out: hanging rt and nt on terms: plugged on* **9/2**[2]
0030 **5** *1* **Ajaafa**[6] 7497 2-8-13 60 (p) KierenFox[(3)] 9 50+
(M J Attwater) *hld up in midfield: rdn on outer over 2f out: nt qckn and no prog wl over 1f out: kpt on* **16/1**
045 **6** *shd* **Abadejo**[78] 5835 2-9-1 59 IanMongan 13 49
(J R Jenkins) *plld hrd: chsd ldng pair: no ch w wnr over 1f out: stl clr of rest ent fnl f: wknd last 100yds* **8/1**
000 **7** *1 ¼* **If What And Maybe**[29] 7152 2-9-1 59 AdamKirby 1 47+
(J Ryan) *s.i.s: dropped in fr wd draw and settled in last: shkn up over 2f out: no prog tl gd hdwy jst over 1f out: fin quite wl* **40/1**
4540 **8** *nk* **Roman Strait**[49] 6674 2-8-13 57 FrannyNorton 5 43
(M Blanshard) *trckd ldrs on outer: rdn over 2f out: sn outpcd: wknd fnl f* **10/1**
0000 **9** *¾* **Salaamie**[12] 7417 2-9-5 63 (b[1]) EddieAhern 11 48
(E A L Dunlop) *s.i.s: sn trckd ldrs: pushed along over 2f out: sing to lose pl whn sltly squeezed 1f out: fdd* **7/1**[3]
2046 **10** *1 ½* **Welsh Inlet (IRE)**[94] 5328 2-9-7 65 (t) NeilChalmers 3 45
(J J Bridger) *t.k.h: hld up in last pair: shuffled along and no real prog fnl 2f* **40/1**
000 **11** *3* **Theavonfilly**[28] 7163 2-9-1 59 JackMitchell 14 31
(R A Teal) *chsd ldrs: rdn over 2f out: wknd over 1f out* **10/1**
466 **12** *4* **Silver Age (IRE)**[76] 5894 2-8-10 61 RyanPowell[(7)] 2 23
(J S Moore) *racd wd: a in rr: struggling over 2f out* **8/1**
3004 **13** *3 ½* **Chilworth Lass (IRE)**[16] 7378 2-8-10 54 CathyGannon 8 7
(M R Channon) *a in rr on outer: wknd 2f out* **14/1**

1m 25.69s (-0.31) **Going Correction** -0.125s/f (Stan) **13** Ran SP% **119.0**
Speed ratings (Par 94): **96,94,91,89,88 88,87,86,85,84 80,76,72**
Tote Swingers:1&2:£35.10, 2&3:£64.60, 1&3:£8.40 CSF £109.07 CT £1277.99 TOTE £6.60: £2.20, £14.70, £2.10; EX 131.90.
Owner High Five Racing **Bred** John Richardson **Trained** Upper Lambourn, Berks

FOCUS
A moderate nursery but, although the gallop was reasonable, it proved difficult to make ground from off the pace. The winner raced close to the inside rail in the straight.

NOTEBOOK
May's Boy is an improved performer since the cheekpieces have been refitted and he showed a good attitude under a well-judged ride from his high draw over this shorter trip. He'll be up in the weights for this but should continue to go well if the headgear continues to have the desired effect. (tchd 9-2)
Sky Diamond(IRE) deserves a bit of credit as he fared easily the best of those that attempted to come from off the pace. However his overall level of form has a very patchy look to it and it remains to be seen whether this will be reproduced or built on next time.
Robber Stone, who reportedly finished sore on his previous start in early October, didn't fail through lack of stamina returned to this longer trip. He is less exposed than a couple of these but is going to have to raise his game to win a similar event from this mark. (op 12-1)
Night Witch(IRE) had shown promise on her two previous runs over 1m on Polytrack but and, although not disgraced, didn't look suited by this shorter trip. The return to that longer trip will suit and she should be able to pick up an ordinary event. (tchd 5-1)
Ajaafa isn't the most reliable and has yet to win but confirmed he stays this trip. He'll be 3lb lower in future but he doesn't look one to be placing too much faith in at present. (tchd 14-1)
Abadejo wasn't disgraced on this nursery and all-weather debut on this first run over 7f and first for nearly three months but he'll have to settle better than he did here if he is to progress and he may be worth another try back over 6f. (op 12-1)
If What And Maybe Official explanation: jockey said colt did not face the kickback

7553 CHRISTMAS PARTIES FROM £49 H'CAP 2m (P)
7:05 (7:06) (Class 4) (0-85,84) 3-Y-O+ £3,885 (£1,156; £577; £288) Stalls High

Form RPR
000 **1** **Morar**[191] 2181 4-9-1 69 IanMongan 8 81+
(Mrs L J Mongan) *hld up in tch: prog on outer to ld 2f out: sn qcknd clr: pushed out* **25/1**
1100 **2** *3 ½* **Phoenix Flight (IRE)**[25] 6797 5-10-0 82 JimCrowley 4 88
(H J Evans) *t.k.h: hld up in last: prog gng easily over 2f out: wnt 2nd over 1f out but wnr already wl gone: kpt on* **7/1**
0511 **3** *1 ½* **Blackmore**[14] 7388 3-8-6 69 CathyGannon 9 73
(Miss J Feilden) *prom: rdn 3f out: cl enough 2f out: sn outpcd: plugged on to take 3rd last 75yds* **7/2**[2]
0100 **4** *½* **Satwa Gold (USA)**[13] 7410 4-9-10 78 TomQueally 5 82
(Stef Higgins) *hld up in 7th: smooth prog over 2f out: no answer to wnr's burst sn after: wl btn 3rd over 1f out: fdd last 75yds* **13/2**[3]
2054 **5** *8* **Atlantic Tiger (IRE)**[28] 7173 3-9-7 84 JoeFanning 6 78
(M Johnston) *prom: disp ld after 5f to 2f out: folded tamely* **6/4**[1]
0 **6** *8* **Bedouin Bay**[62] 3-9-1 78 JamesDoyle 1 62
(A J McCabe) *prom: disp ld after 5f to 2f out: wknd rapidly* **16/1**
0063 **7** *9* **King Supreme (IRE)**[20] 7321 5-8-13 67 (v[1]) JimmyFortune 2 41
(R Hannon) *led 5f: styd prom tl wknd rapidly over 2f out* **8/1**
001- **8** *14* **Decision**[14] 6907 4-9-11 79 (t) DaneO'Neill 3 36
(Mrs Lawney Hill) *prog to trck ldrs after 6f: rdn 4f out: wknd 3f out: eased: t.o* **16/1**

3m 28.12s (-1.98) **Going Correction** -0.125s/f (Stan)
WFA 3 from 4yo+ 9lb **8** Ran SP% **114.8**
Speed ratings (Par 105): **99,97,96,96,92 88,83,76**
Tote Swingers:1&2:£14.20, 2&3:£7.30, 1&3:£11.70 CSF £188.24 CT £773.51 TOTE £26.80: £6.90, £2.00, £1.10; EX 123.80.
Owner Mrs P J Sheen **Bred** St Clare Hall Stud **Trained** Epsom, Surrey

FOCUS
A fair handicap but one in which the market leader disappointed. The gallop was an ordinary one until the favourite went on, and the winner came down the centre in the straight. The wform is rated around the runner-up and the winner is capable of better.

7554 SKYSPORTS.COM RACING H'CAP 7f (P)
7:35 (7:36) (Class 4) (0-80,80) 3-Y-O+ £3,885 (£1,156; £577; £288) Stalls High

Form RPR
2332 **1** **Fantasy Gladiator**[12] 7421 4-9-1 74 (p) JimmyQuinn 7 84
(R M H Cowell) *s.i.s: hld up wl in rr: gd prog on inner fr 3f out: led gng easily 2f out: rdn and styd on fnl f* **4/1**[2]
5034 **2** *2* **Kurtanella**[44] 6805 3-9-3 77 (b[1]) JimmyFortune 2 82
(R Hannon) *s.i.s: hld up in last trio: prog on inner over 2f out: chsd wnr over 1f out: kpt on but nvr able to chal* **25/1**
2351 **3** *1 ¼* **Ginger Grey (IRE)**[32] 7082 3-8-13 73 (b) DaneO'Neill 13 77+
(D O'Meara) *hld up in midfield: looking for room over 2f out: swtchd to outer wl over 1f out: styd on to take 3rd nr fin* **7/2**[1]
0620 **4** *½* **Breathless Kiss (USA)**[13] 7411 3-9-1 78 (b) AmyRyan[(3)] 9 78
(K A Ryan) *chsd ldrs on outer: rdn over 2f out: chsd ldng pair over 1f out: no imp: lost 3rd nr fin* **25/1**
4105 **5** *2* **Hazzard County (USA)**[32] 7091 6-9-0 80 LauraPike[(7)] 8 74
(D M Simcock) *hld up in rr: prog fr 3f out: clsng whn stopped in trcks and lost pl bdly 2f out: kpt on again fnl f: no ch* **12/1**
1002 **6** *1 ¾* **Chat De La Burg (USA)**[11] 7438 3-8-11 74 KierenFox[(3)] 4 64
(J R Best) *sn pushed along in midfield on outer: struggling over 2f out: kpt on again fnl f* **12/1**
0100 **7** *2 ½* **Besty**[86] 5606 3-9-1 75 TomEaves 11 58
(B Smart) *chsd ldng pair to jst over 2f out: steadily wknd* **10/1**
0600 **8** *1 ¼* **Al Gillani (IRE)**[20] 7319 5-9-2 75 GeorgeBaker 1 55
(J R Boyle) *chsd ldr to jst over 2f out: sn lost pl and btn* **25/1**
5060 **9** *1* **Spitfire**[25] 7238 5-9-7 80 StephenCraine 14 57
(J R Jenkins) *chsd ldrs: cl enough and rdn 2f out: wknd over 1f out* **12/1**
4046 **10** *shd* **Buxton**[12] 7421 6-8-11 70 (t) RobertHavlin 5 47
(R Ingram) *hld up in last trio: plenty to do whn asked for effrt 2f out: rn into trble over 1f out: no ch* **25/1**
4603 **11** *¾* **Tewin Wood**[13] 7411 3-9-0 74 (p) LukeMorris 10 49
(A Bailey) *chsd ldng pair to over 2f out: wknd over 1f out* **16/1**
5000 **12** *½* **Mambo Spirit (IRE)**[25] 7238 6-9-2 75 TomQueally 12 48
(Stef Higgins) *led at str pce to 2f out: wknd rapidly* **15/2**
0024 **13** *11* **Duplicity**[30] 7115 3-9-6 80 JimCrowley 6 24
(J G Given) *nvr bttr than midfield: shkn up in rr 3f out: sn bhd* **10/1**
024 **14** *26* **Chris's Ridge**[32] 7086 3-9-1 75 ShaneKelly 3 —
(B J Meehan) *hld up in rr: virtually rn off the crse bnd over 4f out to 3f out: continued t.o* **7/1**[3]

1m 24.07s (-1.93) **Going Correction** -0.125s/f (Stan)
WFA 3 from 4yo+ 1lb **14** Ran SP% **129.0**
Speed ratings (Par 105): **106,103,102,101,99 97,94,93,92,91 91,90,77,48**
Tote Swingers:1&2:£8.50, 2&3:£26.50, 1&3:£3.10 CSF £113.70 CT £395.94 TOTE £3.70: £1.30, £9.80, £1.10; EX 104.50.
Owner The Fantasy Fellowship **Bred** R S A Urquhart **Trained** Six Mile Bottom, Cambs

FOCUS
Mainly exposed sorts in a fair handicap. The good gallop suited those held up and the winner raced towards the centre in the straight. He recorded a length personal best.
Hazzard County(USA) Official explanation: jockey said gelding lost an off-fore shoe and was denied a clear run
Chris's Ridge Official explanation: jockey said gelding hung badly left
T/Plt: £488.50 to a £1 stake. Pool:£49,273.51. 73.62 winning tickets T/Qpdt: £34.30 to a £1 stake. Pool:£8,857.12. 191.00 winning tickets JN

7517 LINGFIELD (L-H)
Wednesday, November 24

OFFICIAL GOING: Standard
Wind: Moderate, half-against. Weather: bright, chilly

7555 ALL-WEATHER "HANDS AND HEELS" APPRENTICE SERIES H'CAP 7f (P)
12:00 (12:01) (Class 6) (0-58,58) 3-Y-O+ £2,047 (£604; £302) Stalls Low

Form RPR
0653 **1** **Marksbury**[22] 7288 3-9-3 57 NathanAlison 9 63
(J M P Eustace) *bhd: rdn and hdwy ent fnl 2f: stl plenty to do over 1f out: str run ins fnl f to ld last stride* **10/1**
0004 **2** *shd* **Ymir**[87] 5555 4-8-9 48 (vt) MatthewLawson 3 53
(M J Attwater) *led: rdn ent fnl 2f: kpt on wl fr over 1f out: hdd last stride* **16/1**
0664 **3** *hd* **Rainsborough**[11] 7438 3-8-10 55 LewisWalsh[(5)] 4 60
(S Curran) *pushed along after s: sn chsng ldng pair: rdn over 1f out: chsd ldr 1f out: kpt on ins fnl f* **10/1**
4003 **4** *1* **Young Simon**[11] 7440 3-9-1 55 (v) NatashaEaton 13 57
(G G Margarson) *stdd after s: hld up towards rr: hdwy on outer over 2f out: kpt on ins fnl f: nt rch ldrs* **33/1**

0002 **5** *nk* **Batchworth Blaise**[27] 7192 7-9-4 **57** .... RichardRowe 12 58
(E A Wheeler) *stdd s: hld up in detached last: hdwy on outer bnd ent fnl 2f: r.o wl ins fnl f: nt rch ldrs* **9/1**[3]

6506 **6** *shd* **Pab Special (IRE)**[35] 7023 7-8-7 **51** ....(v) HobieGill(5) 6 52
(B R Johnson) *sn chsng ldr: rdn and unable qck over 1f out: lost 2nd 1f out: styd on same pce after* **14/1**

3050 **7** *nse* **Lord Deevert**[102] 5076 5-8-11 **55** .... IanBurns(5) 10 56
(W G M Turner) *chsd ldrs: rdn and sltly outpcd wl over 2f out: kpt on again ins fnl f: nt pce to chal* **10/1**

0005 **8** *1* **Dilys Maud**[11] 7440 3-8-9 **49** .... MatthewCosham 1 47
(R Ingram) *chsd ldrs: rdn and outpcd wl over 2f out: rallied ent fnl f: kpt on but nt pce to chal* **40/1**

5/20 **9** *shd* **Dontforgeturshovel**[16] 7380 4-8-3 **47** .... ThomasBrown(5) 7 45
(J Pearce) *hld up towards rr: effrt wl over 1f out: kpt on but nvr gng pce to chal* **8/1**[2]

5405 **10** *nk* **Grey Boy (GER)**[112] 4700 9-8-10 **56** .... GeorgeDowning(7) 8 53
(A W Carroll) *stdd after s: hld up towards rr: hdwy on inner 2f out: kpt on same pce and no imp ins fnl f* **9/1**[3]

0542 **11** *¾* **Bollywood Style**[4] 7518 5-8-12 **58** .... DanielBlackett(7) 5 55
(J R Best) *hld up in midfield: n.m.r and swtchd rt over 1f out: kpt on same pce fr 1f out: btn whn n.m.r and eased wl ins fnl f* **5/2**[1]

0000 **12** *1* **Gifted Lady (IRE)**[165] 2964 3-9-1 **58** .... LucyBarry(3) 2 50
(P M Phelan) *s.i.s: sn rcvrd and in midfield: rdn and lost pl over 2f out: one pce and no threat to ldrs fnl 2f* **14/1**

0400 **13** *shd* **Crystallize**[35] 7023 4-8-3 **49** .... JackDuern(7) 11 41
(A B Haynes) *in tch in midfield on outer: pushed along over 4f out: lost pl and towards rr whn n.m.r wl over 1f out: plugged on same pce after* **20/1**

1m 25.81s (1.01) **Going Correction** +0.05s/f (Slow)
WFA 3 from 4yo+ 1lb **13** Ran SP% **116.3**
Speed ratings (Par 101): **96,95,95,94,94 94,94,92,92,92 91,90,90**
Tote Swingers:1&2:£26.80, 2&3:£30.50, 1&3:£8.90 CSF £152.38 CT £1693.34 TOTE £5.40: £1.50, £6.30, £3.80; EX 142.00 TRIFECTA Not won..
Owner Major M G Wyatt **Bred** Dunchurch Lodge Stud Company **Trained** Newmarket, Suffolk

FOCUS
A moderate handicap, and these mainly inexperienced apprentices were not allowed to use their whips. It was slower than the later claimer and the form looks weak.
Batchworth Blaise Official explanation: jockey said gelding moved poorly early stages

7556 BET IN RUNNING - BETDAQ H'CAP 6f (P)
12:30 (12:30) (Class 5) (0-70,70) 3-Y-O+ **£2,388** (£705; £352) **Stalls** Low

Form RPR

3354 **1** **Mango Music**[20] 7319 7-9-2 **65** .... IanMongan 6 73
(R A Fahey) *led: sn hdd: chsd ldr after tl led again over 2f out: kpt on wl u.p fnl f: hld on cl home* **7/2**[2]

4224 **2** *hd* **Riflessione**[11] 7441 4-9-7 **70** ....(b) JoeFanning 7 77
(R A Harris) *chsd ldrs: wnt 2nd over 2f out: rdn and edgd rt u.p fr over 1f out: no imp tl kpt on fnl 100yds: nt quite get up* **6/1**[3]

3532 **3** *½* **Tislaam (IRE)**[11] 7441 3-9-3 **69** ....(p) AndrewHeffernan(3) 11 74
(A J McCabe) *pushed along leaving stalls: in tch in midfield on outer: rdn and effrt wl over 1f out: kpt on u.p ins fnl f: nt quite rch ldrs* **6/1**[3]

6456 **4** *hd* **Highland Harvest**[11] 7441 6-9-2 **65** .... StevieDonohoe 9 70
(Jamie Poulton) *towards rr: effrt on outer bnd ent fnl 2f: swtchd lft over 1f out: kpt on wl ins fnl f: nt quite rch ldrs* **16/1**

1151 **5** *1* **Paphos**[27] 7192 3-8-10 **64** ....(v) RyanClark(5) 2 69+
(S C Williams) *bustled along leaving stalls: in tch in midfield: hdwy whn nt clr run and squeezed out jst over 2f out: rallied and hdwy u.p jst over 1f out: no imp fnl 100yds* **3/1**[1]

036 **6** *2 ½* **Clerical (USA)**[4] 7518 4-8-8 **57** ....(p) J-PGuillambert 4 51
(R M H Cowell) *sn bustled along: in tch: rdn and hdwy on inner wl over 1f out: no prog ent fnl f: wknd fnl 100yds* **10/1**

030 **7** *nse* **Pilgrim Dancer (IRE)**[14] 7399 3-8-8 **64** ....(be) JulieBurke(7) 8 57
(Patrick Morris) *in tch in midfield: lost pl and dropped towards rr over 2f out: rallied ent fnl f: kpt on but no threat to ldrs* **12/1**

2020 **8** *1* **White Shift (IRE)**[11] 7441 4-9-1 **67** .... KierenFox(3) 12 57
(P Howling) *stdd s: in rr: effrt on outer bnd ent fnl 2f: kpt on but nvr gng pce to trble ldrs* **25/1**

3 **9** *1 ½* **Boragh Jamal (IRE)**[111] 4754 3-9-4 **67** ....(b) ShaneKelly 10 52
(B J Meehan) *stdd after s: hld up towards rr: rdn and effrt over 2f out: no imp fr over 1f out* **20/1**

3006 **10** *1* **Sherjawy (IRE)**[11] 7442 6-9-4 **67** .... SamHitchcott 1 49
(Miss Z C Davison) *chsd ldrs: drvn 1/2-way: wknd u.p jst over 1f out* **16/1**

3-00 **11** *13* **Wellington Fair**[22] 7285 3-9-6 **69** .... AdamKirby 3 —
(Miss Tor Sturgis) *taken down early: dwlt: sn rcvrd and led: hdd over 2f out: fdd wl over 1f out: wl bhd and eased ins fnl f* **40/1**

1m 11.4s (-0.50) **Going Correction** +0.05s/f (Slow) **11** Ran SP% **115.4**
Speed ratings (Par 103): **105,104,104,103,102 99,99,97,95,94 77**
Tote Swingers:1&2:£4.60, 2&3:£3.20, 1&3:£3.30 CSF £23.73 CT £124.16 TOTE £5.00: £1.40, £1.30, £1.60; EX 27.80 Trifecta £43.40 Pool £178.30 - 3.04 winning units..
Owner Northumbria Leisure Ltd **Bred** A G Antoniades **Trained** Musley Bank, N Yorks

FOCUS
A modest sprint handicap in which few were ever seriously involved. It was a fair time for the grade and the form looks solid. The winner was still 10lb off her autumn turf form.

7557 BETDAQ.COM CLAIMING STKS 7f (P)
1:00 (1:00) (Class 6) 3-Y-O+ **£1,706** (£503; £252) **Stalls** Low

Form RPR

4300 **1** **Lend A Grand (IRE)**[28] 7168 6-8-13 58 .... IanMongan 1 71
(Miss Jo Crowley) *chsd ldrs: rdn and wanting to hang lft over 1f out: rdn along hands and heels ins fnl f: chsd ldr fnl 100yds: kpt on to ld last stride* **66/1**

4066 **2** *shd* **Everymanforhimself (IRE)**[18] 7352 6-9-3 86 ....(b) AmyRyan(3) 10 78
(K A Ryan) *hld up in midfield: rdn and effrt on inner jst over 2f out: rdn to ld ins fnl f: hdd last stride* **5/2**[2]

3 **3** *hd* **Caprio (IRE)**[68] 6167 5-9-3 80 .... MatthewDavies(3) 11 77+
(J R Boyle) *hld up towards rr: hdwy and rdn jst over 2f out: chsng ldrs and swtchd rt 1f out: str run ins fnl f: nt quite get up* **13/2**[3]

3200 **4** *¾* **Fishforcompliments**[18] 7352 6-9-6 81 .... BarryMcHugh 3 75
(R A Fahey) *awkward leaving stalls: sn in tch in midfield: rdn to chse ldrs 2f out: squeezed between horses ins fnl f: no ex and hld whn n.m.r nr fin* **10/1**

0060 **5** *1 ½* **Harlech Castle**[22] 7289 5-9-6 85 ....(b) StephenCraine 12 71
(J R Boyle) *pressed ldrs: rdn ent fnl 2f: led over 1f out tl hdd ins fnl f: wknd fnl 100yds* **25/1**

0415 **6** *1 ½* **Samarinda (USA)**[32] 7092 7-9-0 80 ....(p) MickyFenton 4 61
(Mrs P Sly) *led but harried thrght: rdn ent fnl 2f: hdd over 1f out: struggling and btn whn pushed lft ins fnl f* **2/1**[1]

2150 **7** *2 ¼* **Timeteam (IRE)**[34] 7033 4-8-11 75 .... JimmyFortune 6 52
(G L Moore) *in tch in midfield: rdn and outpcd whn wd bnd ent fnl 2f: one pce and no threat to ldrs after* **20/1**

0142 **8** *1* **Fault**[13] 7403 4-8-13 72 ....(t) TomQueally 14 51
(Stef Higgins) *t.k.h: hld up towards rr: rdn and effrt on outer bnd 2f out: nvr trbld ldrs* **11/1**

0540 **9** *nk* **Straight And Level (CAN)**[7] 7487 5-8-13 51 ....(v) KirstyMilczarek 7 50
(Miss Jo Crowley) *t.k.h early: in tch: rdn and unable qck jst over 2f out: no threat to ldrs fr over 1f out* **66/1**

0226 **10** *1 ½* **Hand Painted**[44] 6800 4-8-13 71 .... SteveDrowne 2 46
(P J Makin) *chsd ldrs: rdn and unable qck over 2f out: wknd ent fnl 2f* **12/1**

0-00 **11** *11* **Northern Champ (IRE)**[13] 7413 4-8-10 45 .... ChrisCatlin 13 14
(D Bourton) *dwlt: in tch towards rr tl rdn and dropped to last over 3f out: lost tch over 2f out* **150/1**

1m 24.57s (-0.23) **Going Correction** +0.05s/f (Slow)
WFA 3 from 4yo+ 1lb **11** Ran SP% **112.6**
Speed ratings (Par 101): **103,102,102,101,100 98,95,94,94,92 80**
Tote Swingers:1&2:£18.70, 2&3:£5.80, 1&3:£33.80 CSF £214.70 TOTE £53.40: £8.80, £1.70, £2.30; EX 206.60 TRIFECTA Not won..
Owner Mrs Liz Nelson **Bred** Pat McDonnell **Trained** Whitcombe, Dorset
■ Stewards' Enquiry : Barry McHugh two-day ban: careless riding (Dec 8-9)

FOCUS
A nightmare race to analyse, with a surprise winner who is rated back to his 2008/9 winter form. The time was only 0.24 seconds quicker than the earlier Class 6 handicap. Clearly the next seven finishers behind the winner all ran below their official marks.
Lend A Grand(IRE) Official explanation: trainer said, regarding apparent improvement in form, that the gelding became intimidated when attempting to make its challenge through horses previously, whereas, on this occasion, it was able to make its bid wide.

7558 EUROPEAN BREEDERS' FUND MAIDEN STKS (DIV I) 1m (P)
1:30 (1:30) (Class 5) 2-Y-O **£2,590** (£770; £385; £192) **Stalls** High

Form RPR

1 **Atraaf (IRE)** 2-9-3 0 .... RichardHills 12 81+
(M P Tregoning) *dwlt: sn chsng ldrs: rdn to chal 2f out: led over 1f out: r.o strly and drew wl clr ins fnl f: readily* **7/2**[3]

6 **2** *4 ½* **Layla's King**[21] 7302 2-9-3 0 .... StevieDonohoe 10 70
(Jane Chapple-Hyam) *chsd ldrs: pushed along to chse ldr over 3f out: led over 2f out: drvn and hdd over 1f out: nt pce of wnr ins fnl f* **3/1**[2]

3 *3* **Picture Of Lily** 2-8-12 0 .... JimCrowley 11 58+
(W J Knight) *s.i.s: hld up in rr: hdwy on outer over 2f out: no ch w ldrs but kpt on to go 3rd ins fnl f* **10/1**

05 **4** *¾* **Lady Gabrielle (IRE)**[27] 7198 2-8-12 0 .... HayleyTurner 3 56
(M L W Bell) *chsd ldr tl over 3f out: outpcd u.p over 2f out: one pce and no ch w ldrs fnl 2f* **14/1**

5 *½* **Dililah** 2-8-12 0 .... ShaneKelly 4 55
(W J Knight) *stdd after s: racd in midfield: rdn and outpcd over 2f out: no ch w ldrs and kpt on same pce fnl 2f* **18/1**

00 **6** *½* **Black Iceman**[42] 6843 2-9-3 0 ....(b[1]) MickyFenton 2 59
(J Pearce) *led: rdn and hdd over 2f out: clr in ldng trio ent fnl 2f: btn over 1f out: fdd ins fnl f* **100/1**

7 *1 ¾* **Monopolize** 2-9-3 0 .... TomQueally 1 57+
(H R A Cecil) *dwlt: rn green and sn niggled along in midfield: lost pl and dropped to rr over 2f out: wl btn after: pluged on ins fnl f* **9/4**[1]

8 *½* **More Than Enough (IRE)** 2-9-3 0 .... TomEaves 7 54
(R A Fahey) *dwlt: in tch in midfield: rdn and struggling over 2f out: wknd 2f out* **15/2**

9 *¾* **Jody Bear** 2-8-12 0 .... JackMitchell 9 47
(J G Portman) *s.i.s: rn green in rr: nvr trbld ldrs* **50/1**

10 *2 ½* **Grace And Beauty (IRE)** 2-8-9 0 .... RobertLButler(3) 8 41+
(B W Duke) *in tch towards rr: nt clr run and swtchd rt ent fnl 3f: sn struggling: wl btn fnl 2f* **66/1**

6 **11** *6* **Peals And Plaudits**[21] 7303 2-9-3 0 .... EddieAhern 5 33
(E A L Dunlop) *in tch in midfield: lost pl and dropped to rr over 2f out: wl bhd and eased fr wl over 1f out* **14/1**

1m 39.15s (0.95) **Going Correction** +0.05s/f (Slow) **11** Ran SP% **121.9**
Speed ratings (Par 96): **97,92,89,88,88 87,86,85,84,82 76**
Tote Swingers:1&2:£4.90, 2&3:£6.80, 1&3:£4.70 CSF £15.03 TOTE £4.30: £1.40, £1.10, £2.80; EX 23.50 Trifecta £68.50 Pool £250.04 - 2.70 winning units..
Owner Hamdan Al Maktoum **Bred** Shadwell Estate Company Limited **Trained** Lambourn, Berks

FOCUS
Not a strong maiden, but a promising winner in a time 0.49 seconds quicker than the second division. He should rate a fair bit higher than the bare form.

NOTEBOOK
Atraaf(IRE) ◆'s dam has now won with all seven of her offspring to have raced, and she was successful twice herself. This one is a brother to a couple of winners, notably the very useful handicapper Suruor. Interestingly, prior to this Marcus Tregoning was only 5-57 with juvenile newcomers in the last two seasons, and those to have won include the smart pair Finjaan and Rumoush, so clearly this colt, who drew nicely clear, is worth noting. (op 5-1 tchd 6-1)
Layla's King confirmed the promise he showed on testing ground on debut, but was no match for the useful-looking winner. (op 9-4)
Picture Of Lily, a 25,000gns sister to 1m-1m6f Flat/2m4f hurdle winner Doctor Scott, was one of five newcomers for William Knight spread over the two divisions. She kept on after a slow start and showed ability. (op 9-1)
Lady Gabrielle(IRE) was comfortably held, but is now qualified for a handicap mark. (op 12-1)
Dililah, a half-sister to 1m2f winner Primo Dillettante, should be all the better for this first experience. (op 14-1)
Monopolize is a half-brother to 7f-1m winner Intense, out of 1m3f-1m6f (Listed) winner Modesta, who is a half-sister to, among others, Oaks winner Reams Of Verse. However, he started slowly and ran in snatches, never at any stage looking likely to justify favouritism on debut. He's got a lot of learning to do. (op 3-1tchd 10-3 in places)
Peals And Plaudits was reported to have got unsettled in the stalls and was never travelling. Official explanation: jockey said gelding was unsettled in stalls and never travelled (op 16-1 tchd 8-1)

7559 EUROPEAN BREEDERS' FUND MAIDEN STKS (DIV II) 1m (P)
2:05 (2:05) (Class 5) 2-Y-O **£2,590** (£770; £385; £192) **Stalls** High

Form RPR

0 **1** **Club Oceanic**[14] 7385 2-9-3 0 .... GeorgeBaker 7 80+
(J Noseda) *chsd ldr: shkn up to join ldr over 2f out: rdn to ld wl over 1f out: hdd fnl 150yds: kpt on to ld again fnl 75yds: rdn out* **5/6**[1]

0 **2** *nk* **Durante Alighieri**[29] 7152 2-9-3 0 .... TomQueally 12 79+
(H R A Cecil) *chsd ldrs: rdn to chse ldng pair ent fnl 2f: wnt 2nd wl over 1f out: ev ch ent fnl f: led fnl 150yds tl hdd and no ex fnl 75yds* **8/1**

3 1 1/4 **Hawaafez** 2-8-12 0 .... RichardHills 1 71+
(M P Tregoning) *chsd ldrs: effrt ent fnl 2f: swtchd rt and rdn to chse ldng pair over 1f out: styd on same pce ins fnl f* **6/1**[2]

4 5 **Around The Clock (USA)** 2-9-3 0 .... JoeFanning 4 65+
(Mrs A J Perrett) *led tl rdn and hdd wl over 1f out: wknd ent fnl f* **7/1**[3]

5 6 **By Implication** 2-9-3 0 .... RobertHavlin 6 51
(J H M Gosden) *rn green and racd off the pce towards rr: sme hdwy but no ch w ldrs whn hung lft wl over 1f out* **14/1**

6 1/2 **Apple Dumpling** 2-8-12 0 .... WilliamCarson 11 48+
(S C Williams) *stdd s: racd wl off the pce in rr: sme hdwy into midfield over 2f out: nvr trbld ldrs* **66/1**

0 7 nk **Last Act (IRE)**[55] 6511 2-8-12 0 .... ChrisCatlin 3 44
(M R Hoad) *chsd ldng pair tl ent fnl 2f: wknd qckly over 1f out* **100/1**

8 1 1/4 **Mayfair Lad** 2-9-3 0 .... EddieAhern 5 46+
(E A L Dunlop) *racd off the pce in midfield: nvr trbld ldrs* **33/1**

9 1 1/2 **Passion Play** 2-8-12 0 .... JimmyFortune 9 38+
(W J Knight) *rn green and racd wl off the pce in midfield: n.d* **22/1**

10 1 1/4 **Runaway Tiger (IRE)** 2-9-0 0 .... KierenFox(3) 2 40
(P W D'Arcy) *dwlt: bhd: hdwy 3f out: wnt modest 6th ent fnl 2f: no hdwy and wknd over 1f out* **50/1**

11 4 1/2 **Unbeatable** 2-8-12 0 .... ShaneKelly 8 25
(W J Knight) *a wl off the pce towards rr: n.d* **40/1**

12 1 1/4 **Igitur** 2-8-12 0 .... JimCrowley 10 22
(W J Knight) *a wl bhd: lost tch over 2f out* **33/1**

1m 39.64s (1.44) **Going Correction** +0.05s/f (Slow) **12** Ran SP% **116.2**
Speed ratings (Par 96): **94,93,92,87,81 80,80,79,77,76 72,70**
Tote Swingers:1&2:£3.10, 2&3:£6.10, 1&3:£3.20 CSF £7.22 TOTE £1.80: £1.10, £3.10, £1.80; EX 9.90 Trifecta £24.30 Pool £546.67 - 16.63 winning units..
Owner Sir Robert Ogden **Bred** Card Bloodstock **Trained** Newmarket, Suffolk

FOCUS
A time 0.49 seconds slower than the first division suggests the bare form is no better than fair, but the race ought to produce winners. The first two both showed big improvement.

NOTEBOOK
Club Oceanic was extremely well backed but made hard work of this, needing strong pressure to get the better of the runner-up whose rider, in notable contrast to Baker, hardly went for the whip. The winner was clearly expected to step up a good deal on form from his debut effort at Kempton, when he ran green and was always behind, and he duly did so, but he only scrambled home after not travelling all that strongly. He should, though, get a workable handicap mark as a result. (op Evens tchd 11-10)

Durante Alighieri finished tailed off on debut at Yarmouth, presumably not handling testing ground, but he was a completely different proposition this time. He looked likely to win when ranging upsides Club Oceanic early in the straight, and even seemed to hit the front inside the final furlong. However, he received minimal whip pressure, which in fairness is understandable considering this was his first proper race, and was worried out of it. (op 9-1)

Hawaafez, who is out of a 1m6f winner, was relatively solid in the market considering there was such a well-backed favourite, and she showed plenty of ability following a slow start. This experience was need, and she'll surely stay well next year. (tchd 5-1)

Around The Clock(USA) ◆ took the eye on pedigree, being by promising first-season sire Bernardini out of a 1m1f Grade 1 winner in the US, and he cost $320,000. However, after leading for much of the way, he put up little resistance when challenged. Few Amanda Perrett 2-y-os win first-time out, and this run was needed, so expect significantly better next time. (op 14-1)

By Implication, a half-brother to a couple of Polytrack winners and closely related to smart 7f-1m winner Stronghold, was weak in the market and ran as though badly in need of the experience. (op 10-1)

Apple Dumpling is bred to win races and this was a promising enough introduction.

7560 BET CHAMPIONS LEAGUE FOOTBALL - BETDAQ H'CAP 1m (P)
2:40 (2:40) (Class 4) (0-85,85) 3-Y-O+ **£4,209** (£1,252; £625; £312) **Stalls** High

Form RPR

0000 **1** **Follow The Flag (IRE)**[33] 7062 6-8-9 **76** .... (v[1]) AndrewHeffernan(3) 10 85
(A J McCabe) *chsd ldrs: clsd over 2f out: rdn and ev ch over 1f out: led fnl 100yds: r.o wl* **9/1**

3302 **2** 3/4 **Duster**[25] 7238 3-9-3 **83** .... SteveDrowne 2 90
(H Morrison) *chsd ldr: clsd over 2f out: rdn and ev ch ent fnl 2f: led 1f out: hdd and no ex fnl 100yds* **8/1**

2000 **3** 1/2 **Santefisio**[27] 7187 4-9-5 **83** .... JimmyFortune 6 91+
(P J Makin) *in tch in midfield: effrt ent fnl 2f: nt clr run jst over 1f out: swtchd rt ins fnl f: r.o wl fnl 100yds: nt rch ldrs* **11/2**[2]

0434 **4** nk **Faithful Ruler (USA)**[25] 7227 6-9-1 **79** .... TomEaves 3 84+
(R A Fahey) *chsd ldrs: clsd over 2f out: drvn: n.m.r and edging rt over 1f out: kpt on wl fnl 75yds* **8/1**

-040 **5** nk **Final Verse**[21] 7306 7-8-11 **75** .... (be[1]) LukeMorris 11 79+
(Matthew Salaman) *t.k.h: hld up in rr: stl gng strly whn nt clr run jst over 2f out tl 1f out: hdwy jst ins fnl f: drvn and kpt on same pce fnl 75yds* **8/1**

3-00 **6** 3/4 **Gala Casino Star (IRE)**[179] 2532 5-9-0 **85** .... GeorgeChaloner(7) 9 88+
(R A Fahey) *hld up in tch: clsd over 2f out: nt clr run and edgd rt over 1f out: kpt on fnl 100yds: unable to chal* **40/1**

0005 **7** 1/2 **King's Colour**[20] 7318 5-9-5 **83** .... GeorgeBaker 7 85
(B R Johnson) *hld up in last trio: hdwy on outer over 2f out: chsd ldrs and rdn over 1f out: wknd ins fnl f* **6/1**[3]

0505 **8** nk **Den's Gift (IRE)**[27] 7187 6-9-6 **84** .... (b) AdamKirby 8 85
(C G Cox) *sn pushed along to ld: clr after 1f: rdn and pressed ent fnl 2f: hdd 1f out: wknd ins fnl f* **4/1**[1]

2343 **9** 1/2 **Saharia (IRE)**[55] 6503 3-9-2 **82** .... BarryMcHugh 1 82
(Ollie Pears) *hld up in last trio: effrt towards inner wl over 1f out: n.m.r and no prog ins fnl f* **11/2**[2]

0136 **10** 1 1/2 **Master Of Dance (IRE)**[22] 7283 3-8-11 **77** .... J-PGuillambert 5 73
(J G Given) *sn niggled along in midfield: effrt and rdn on inner over 1f out: no prog 1f out: wknd ins fnl f* **25/1**

05-0 **11** 9 **Humungous (IRE)**[28] 7182 7-9-2 **80** .... MickyFenton 12 56
(C R Egerton) *s.i.s: in tch in midfield on outer: rdn over 4f out: lost tch over 2f out* **40/1**

1m 37.0s (-1.20) **Going Correction** +0.05s/f (Slow)
WFA 3 from 4yo+ 2lb **11** Ran SP% **117.1**
Speed ratings (Par 105): **108,107,106,106,106 105,104,104,104,102 93**
Tote Swingers:1&2:£13.60, 2&3:£4.30, 1&3:£13.00 CSF £77.42 CT £444.28 TOTE £14.10: £3.10, £3.20, £2.70; EX 107.60 Trifecta £297.90 Part won. Pool £402.59 - 0.64 winning units..
Owner S Gillen **Bred** Martin Francis **Trained** Averham Park, Notts
■ Stewards' Enquiry : George Chaloner caution: careless riding.

FOCUS
A messy race with several not getting clear runs. The leader seemed to set a reasonable pace in a clear lead (time quicker than both divisions of the 2-y-o maiden), yet all bar Humungous were covered by just about 3l with half a furlong to run. Clearly a competitive handicap, but not strong form. The race is rated around the winner.

7561 RACING POST PRICEWISE EXTRA EXPERT TIPPING H'CAP (DIV I) 1m 2f (P)
3:15 (3:15) (Class 6) (0-65,65) 3-Y-O+ **£1,706** (£503; £252) **Stalls** Low

Form RPR

600 **1** **Lingfield Bound (IRE)**[27] 7190 3-9-5 **64** .... LukeMorris 12 72
(J R Best) *in tch in midfield: rdn and effrt ent fnl 2f: drvn to chse ldr ins fnl f: led fnl 75yds: styd on wl* **14/1**

401 **2** 3/4 **Room For A View**[22] 7288 3-9-1 **60** .... (v[1]) HayleyTurner 8 66
(M P Tregoning) *led: rdn ent fnl 2f: hrd drvn and hdd ins fnl f: styd on same pce towards fin* **9/2**[1]

0001 **3** 2 1/4 **Irish Jugger (USA)**[12] 7429 3-9-0 **59** .... JamesMillman 9 61
(B R Millman) *hld up towards rr: hdwy into midfield 6f out: chsd ldrs and rdn ent fnl 2f: styd on same pce fr over 1f out: wnt 3rd towards fin* **7/1**

0025 **4** 1/2 **Chaqueta**[72] 6039 3-9-1 **60** .... JackMitchell 14 61
(C F Wall) *chsd ldrs: rdn to chal and hld hd high ent fnl 2f: nt qckn u.p over 1f out: wknd ins fnl f: lost 3rd towards fin* **20/1**

4000 **5** 1 **Prohibition (IRE)**[23] 6428 4-9-10 **65** .... JimmyFortune 2 64
(G L Moore) *dwlt: sn rcvrd and chsd ldrs: rdn and effrt over 1f out: drvn and unable qck 1f out: styd on same pce after* **25/1**

3025 **6** hd **New Den**[267] 762 3-9-4 **63** .... StephenCraine 6 61
(J R Boyle) *chsd ldr: rdn and ev ch ent fnl 2f: wknd jst ins fnl f* **18/1**

56-0 **7** 1 **Suntrap**[22] 7288 3-9-6 **65** .... ShaneKelly 4 61
(W J Knight) *towards rr: rdn along 6f out: effrt and rdn over 2f out: no prog tl styd on ent fnl f: keeping on but no threat to ldrs whn wnt rt ins fnl f* **12/1**

5001 **8** 1 **Atacama Sunrise**[11] 7445 4-9-0 **62** .... JulieBurke(7) 11 56
(G Prodromou) *hld up in rr: rdn and hdwy wl over 1f out: plugged on ins fnl f: nvr trbld ldrs* **15/2**

342 **9** 2 1/2 **Collect Art (IRE)**[19] 7336 3-9-5 **64** .... StevieDonohoe 10 53
(A B Haynes) *t.k.h: hld up in last trio: nvr trbld ldrs* **13/2**[3]

2355 **10** 1 1/2 **Diamond Twister (USA)**[30] 7111 4-9-7 **65** .... KierenFox(3) 7 51
(J R Best) *chsd ldrs: struggling u.p over 2f out: wknd 2f out* **6/1**[2]

-000 **11** 2 1/4 **Weald Park (USA)**[22] 7286 4-9-2 **57** .... MickyFenton 13 39
(J Pearce) *hld up in last trio: rdn and effrt on outer ent fnl 3f: no prog and wl hld whn hung lft wl over 1f out* **33/1**

1100 **12** 2 1/2 **Usquaebach**[102] 5072 3-9-2 **61** .... IanMongan 3 38
(P M Phelan) *hld up in midfield: rdn and struggling wl over 2f out: wl btn fnl 2f* **14/1**

-00 **13** 2 **Aphrodite's Rock**[47] 6718 4-9-5 **60** .... (t) ChrisCatlin 5 33
(G D Blake) *in tch in midfield: rdn and struggling ent fnl 3f: wknd and wl btn over 1f out* **50/1**

2m 7.37s (0.77) **Going Correction** +0.05s/f (Slow)
WFA 3 from 4yo 4lb **13** Ran SP% **109.9**
Speed ratings (Par 101): **98,97,95,95,94 94,93,92,90,89 87,85,84**
Tote Swingers:1&2:£7.70, 2&3:£5.10, 1&3:£20.50 CSF £60.92 CT £364.23 TOTE £15.50: £4.90, £2.70, £2.80; EX 84.40 TRIFECTA Not won..
Owner Lingfield Park Owners Club **Bred** Mrs Mary Gallagher **Trained** Hucking, Kent

FOCUS
A modest handicap, but the time was 1.09 seconds quicker than the steadily run second division. The winner had slipped to a good mark.
Collect Art(IRE) Official explanation: jockey said gelding ran too freely in early stages

7562 RACING POST PRICEWISE EXTRA EXPERT TIPPING H'CAP (DIV II) 1m 2f (P)
3:45 (3:46) (Class 6) (0-65,65) 3-Y-O+ **£1,706** (£503; £252) **Stalls** Low

Form RPR

3251 **1** **Buona Sarah (IRE)**[7] 7476 3-8-12 **64** .... NathanAlison(7) 9 73+
(J R Boyle) *t.k.h: hld up in tch towards rr: plld out and gd hdwy to ld over 3f out: sn clr: pushed along hands and heels and hrd pressed jst ins fnl f: edgd rt but hld on wl fnl 100yds* **9/2**[2]

0003 **2** hd **The Wonga Coup (IRE)**[7] 7491 3-8-5 **55** .... JemmaMarshall(5) 10 64
(P M Phelan) *chsd ldrs: hdwy to chse clr wnr over 2f out: rdn and clsd over 1f out: drvn and ev ch ins fnl f: unable qck and hld fnl 100yds* **6/1**[3]

0532 **3** 2 1/4 **Bubbly Braveheart (IRE)**[22] 7286 3-9-2 **61** .... LukeMorris 1 65+
(A Bailey) *t.k.h: hld up in tch: nt clr run and lost pl over 2f out: swtchd rt wl over 1f out: rallied u.p jst over 1f out: styd on wl ins fnl f: unable to rch ldng pair* **3/1**[1]

1660 **4** 1/2 **Beat Up**[39] 6934 4-9-7 **62** .... JimmyFortune 14 65
(G D Blake) *hld up towards rr: rdn and hdwy ent fnl 2f: styd on ins fnl f: nt rch ldrs* **9/1**

100 **5** 1 1/4 **Jinto**[44] 6816 3-8-13 **65** .... JulieBurke(7) 13 66
(R M H Cowell) *in tch in midfield: rdn and outpcd by ldng pair over 2f out: kpt on same pce fr over 1f out* **16/1**

5450 **6** shd **Folio (IRE)**[47] 6718 10-9-10 **65** .... StevieDonohoe 7 65
(W J Musson) *hld up in rr: hdwy on outer wl over 1f out: styd on ins fnl f: nvr able to chal* **20/1**

5610 **7** 1/2 **Starburst**[62] 6314 5-9-2 **57** .... ChrisCatlin 5 56
(Miss Gay Kelleway) *in tch in midfield: rdn and outpcd over 2f out: styd on same pce and no threat to ldrs fr wl over 1f out* **16/1**

0-04 **8** 5 **Hits Only Cash**[168] 2880 8-9-5 **60** .... (p) MickyFenton 6 49
(J Pearce) *hld up in tch towards rr: rdn and effrt on inner jst over 2f out: nvr trbld ldrs* **12/1**

0200 **9** shd **Mister Bit (IRE)**[20] 7323 3-9-4 **63** .... HayleyTurner 12 52
(J R Best) *in tch towards rr: outpcd and dropped towards rr over 2f out: rdn and no prog wl over 1f out* **15/2**

-100 **10** nk **Orpen Arms (IRE)**[23] 7273 3-9-1 **60** .... BarryMcHugh 2 49
(R A Fahey) *in tch in midfield: rdn and outpcd over 2f out: wl btn wl over 1f out* **40/1**

40/ **11** 1 1/2 **Topenhall (IRE)**[32] 7829 9-9-2 **60** .... (t) MatthewDavies(3) 3 46
(B I Case) *led tl over 3f out: sn rdn and outpcd by wnr: wknd over 2f out: wl bhd over 1f out* **17/2**

4430 **12** 22 **King Of Connacht**[11] 7449 7-9-0 **58** .... KierenFox(3) 4 —
(M Wellings) *chsd ldr tl over 3f out: wknd wl over 2f out: wl bhd and eased ins fnl f* **20/1**

2m 8.46s (1.86) **Going Correction** +0.05s/f (Slow)
WFA 3 from 4yo+ 4lb **12** Ran SP% **121.2**
Speed ratings (Par 101): **94,93,92,91,90 90,90,86,86,85 84,67**
Tote Swingers:1&2:£6.90, 2&3:£4.60, 1&3:£4.30 CSF £31.68 CT £95.79 TOTE £8.30: £2.50, £2.50, £1.10; EX 32.60 Trifecta £135.40 Pool £232.51 - 1.27 winning units..
Owner Mrs Pippa Boyle **Bred** Peter J Doyle Bloodstock Ltd **Trained** Epsom, Surrey
■ Stewards' Enquiry : Nathan Alison two-day ban: careless riding (Dec 8-9)

FOCUS
They went a steady and uneven pace (time 1.09 seconds slower than first division) and those held up until the straight had no chance. The form makes some sense and there may be more to come from the winner.
T/Plt: £307.50 to a £1 stake. Pool:£41,210.65. 97.83 winning tickets T/Qpdt: £35.70 to a £1 stake. Pool:£4,457.84. 92.20 winning tickets SP

7525 WOLVERHAMPTON (A.W) (L-H)
Thursday, November 25

OFFICIAL GOING: Standard
Wind: Fresh across Weather: Overcast

7563 ENJOY THE PARTY PACK GROUP OFFER MEDIAN AUCTION MAIDEN STKS 5f 216y(P)
4:10 (4:11) (Class 6) 3-5-Y-O **£1,706** (£503; £252) **Stalls** Low

Form RPR
0502 **1** **Boy The Bell**6 7506 3-8-10 50 JosephYoung(7) 3 60
(M Mullineaux) *s.i.s: hdwy over 3f out: rdn to ld wl ins fnl f* **10/1**3
5603 **2** 3/4 **Dower Glen**34 7051 3-8-5 49 (v) ShirleyTeasdale(7) 11 53
(V P Donoghue) *sn led: rdn over 1f out: hdd wl ins fnl f* **16/1**
0064 **3** 1 1/4 **Lily Wood**82 5766 4-8-12 46 (p) WilliamCarson 7 49
(J W Unett) *mid-div: hdwy over 2f out: styd on* **16/1**
/065 **4** 1 **Woodwind**14 7409 5-8-12 56 JoeFanning 5 46
(D Shaw) *a.p: chsd ldr over 2f out: no ex ins fnl f* **11/1**
6533 **5** 1 **Laser Ruby**5 7519 3-8-12 61 (t) JimmyFortune 10 48
(A M Balding) *s.i.s: hld up: nt clr run over 1f out: shkn up and r.o ins fnl f: eased nr fin: nvr nr to chal* **2/5**1
02 **6** 2 **La Chemme**10 7461 4-8-12 0 LukeMorris 1 36
(R Hollinshead) *hld up: hdwy over 2f out: wknd ins fnl f* **10/1**3
0000 **7** 5 **Aim'Ees Star**109 4861 3-8-12 35 BarryMcHugh 4 20
(John A Harris) *sn pushed along in rr: nvr on terms* **100/1**
000 **8** 3 1/4 **Mighty Aphrodite**28 7192 3-8-12 57 CathyGannon 6 10
(Miss Olivia Maylam) *mid-div: sn pushed along: rdn and wknd over 1f out* **9/1**2
0-5 **9** 1 1/4 **Aurora Lights**10 7461 3-8-5 0 LauraBarry(7) 12 —
(R A Fahey) *broke wl enough: lost pl 5f out: sn in rr* **33/1**
/0-0 **10** 13 **Rose De Rita**167 2919 5-8-12 29 FrankieMcDonald 2 —
(L P Grassick) *led early: chsd ldr tl rdn and wknd over 2f out* **100/1**

1m 15.75s (0.75) **Going Correction** +0.075s/f (Slow) **10** Ran SP% **124.6**
Speed ratings (Par 101): **98,97,95,94,92 90,83,79,77,60**
toteswingers:1&2 £8.30, 2&3 £21.10, 1&3 £9.80 CSF £164.32 TOTE £10.90: £2.70, £2.90, £4.60; EX 174.80.
Owner M K P Turner **Bred** D J P Turner **Trained** Alpraham, Cheshire

FOCUS
A weak maiden with the highest official rating on show being a lowly 61. The gallop looked sound enough considering the limitations of the runners.
Laser Ruby Official explanation: trainer's rep said filly appeared unsuited by being fitted with the first-time tongue strap and being denied a clear run in straight
Mighty Aphrodite Official explanation: jockey said filly had no more to give

7564 BET ASHES CRICKET - BETDAQ CLAIMING STKS 5f 216y(P)
4:40 (4:41) (Class 6) 3-Y-O+ **£1,706** (£503; £252) **Stalls** Low

Form RPR
3005 **1** **Abbondanza (IRE)**14 7403 7-9-8 82 MichaelO'Connell(3) 10 90
(D Nicholls) *mde all: rdn over 1f out: styd on* **9/4**2
4034 **2** 3 **Spin Again (IRE)**92 5405 5-8-12 69 BillyCray(5) 7 72
(D Nicholls) *a.p: chsd wnr 2f out: sn rdn: styd on same pce ins fnl f* **5/1**3
0200 **3** 4 1/2 **Kersivay**20 7332 4-8-4 65 (v) MatthewCosham(7) 11 52
(P D Evans) *mid-div: hdwy over 2f out: rdn over 1f out: styd on same pce* **12/1**
0000 **4** 1 1/4 **Stonecrabstomorrow (IRE)**9 7468 7-8-8 55 MarkCoumbe(5) 8 50
(D Bourton) *hld up: hdwy over 1f out: nvr on terms* **33/1**
4155 **5** nk **Titus Gent**5 7525 5-9-3 73 KirstyMilczarek 4 53
(R A Harris) *w wnr tl rdn over 2f out: wknd ins fnl f* **15/8**1
-400 **6** 8 **Estonia**27 7207 3-8-0 50 LukeMorris 2 10
(M D Squance) *s.i.s: hld up: racd keenly: rdn over 2f out: n.d* **33/1**
0000 **7** 2 1/2 **Tag Team (IRE)**9 7473 9-8-7 47 (p) BarryMcHugh 6 9
(John A Harris) *chsd ldrs tl rdn and wknd over 2f out* **33/1**
3440 **8** hd **Excusez Moi (USA)**55 6537 8-9-3 85 PJMcDonald 5 18
(Mrs R A Carr) *s.i.s: hdwy over 2f out: sn rdn and wknd* **7/1**
6400 **9** 16 **Morgans Choice**55 6536 3-8-7 53 SamHitchcott 1 —
(J L Spearing) *chsd ldrs: rdn over 3f out: wknd over 2f out: t.o* **16/1**

1m 14.52s (-0.48) **Going Correction** +0.075s/f (Slow) **9** Ran SP% **117.1**
Speed ratings (Par 101): **106,102,96,94,93 83,79,79,58**
.Titus Gent was claimed by J. R. Gask for £8000\n\x\x
Owner Middleham Park Racing XXXI **Bred** M Nolan **Trained** Sessay, N Yorks
■ Stewards' Enquiry : Mark Coumbe caution: careless riding.

FOCUS
An uncompetitive claimer with a wide variety of abilities on show. The pace didn't look overly strong and little got into it from behind, but it was the pick of the four C/D times. The first two were the only ones to show their form.

7565 WOLVERHAMPTON-RACECOURSE.CO.UK NURSERY 5f 216y(P)
5:10 (5:10) (Class 3) (0-90,90) 2-Y-O **£4,983** (£1,491; £745; £372; £185) **Stalls** Low

Form RPR
156 **1** **Fifth Commandment (IRE)**27 7204 2-9-4 90 SophieDoyle(3) 5 91
(J A Osborne) *chsd ldr tl led over 2f out: shkn up and hung rt fr over 1f out: drvn out* **6/1**
0045 **2** shd **Restless Bay (IRE)**5 7528 2-8-3 72 (b1) LukeMorris 6 73
(R Hollinshead) *s.i.s: hld up: hdwy and edgd lft over 1f out: r.o u.p: jst failed* **4/1**2
1111 **3** 1/2 **Jack Smudge**31 7116 2-9-5 88 TomEaves 3 88
(J G Given) *chsd ldrs: sn pushed along: rdn to chse wnr over 1f out: hung rt ins fnl f: styd on: hmpd nr fin* **2/1**1
2333 **4** 1/2 **Owain (USA)**12 7444 2-8-12 81 CathyGannon 1 80
(C A Dwyer) *s.i.s: hld up: nt clr run fr over 2f out: hmpd wl over 1f out: swtchd lft and r.o ins fnl f: nt trble ldrs* **4/1**2
0062 **5** 1 3/4 **Lenjawi Pride**31 7127 2-8-8 77 RichardKingscote 4 70
(Tom Dascombe) *chsd ldrs: rdn over 1f out: hmpd ins fnl f: no ex* **9/2**3
010 **6** 36 **Miss Sinatra (IRE)**62 6317 2-8-9 78 ShaneKelly 2 —
(B J Meehan) *sn led: hung rt and hdd over 2f out: sn wknd and eased: t.o* **11/1**

1m 15.08s (0.08) **Going Correction** +0.075s/f (Slow) **6** Ran SP% **114.1**
Speed ratings (Par 100): **102,101,101,100,98 50**
toteswingers:1&2 £6.20, 2&3 £2.70, 1&3 £3.80 CSF £30.36 TOTE £7.80: £6.60, £1.80; EX 30.20.
Owner Durkan, Hearn, Pennick **Bred** Keatly Overseas Ltd **Trained** Upper Lambourn, Berks
■ Stewards' Enquiry : Cathy Gannon one-day ban: careless riding (Dec 9)

FOCUS
A fair nursery with little between the majority of the runners for most of the straight. The gallop looked no more than fair. Little looked well treated pre-race and the form is rated around the second and third.

NOTEBOOK
Fifth Commandment(IRE) is unbeaten in nurseries, adding this one to the more competitive affair at Newmarket she landed from a 6lb lower mark in the summer. She didn't have much in hand at the end having got first run to a degree but she took to the surface well back on it for the first time since her debut and her attitude suggests she'll be a feisty opponent if kept going through the winter. (op 9-2)
Restless Bay(IRE) presumably had the blinkers on in an attempt to sharpen him up early, but though he turned in a better effort than of late he was still slowly away and had to make his effort from a tricky position. His attitude rather than his current mark leaves him with little room for error. (op 5-1)
Jack Smudge was bidding for a five-timer off a mark 5lb higher than last time but perhaps that race lacked the strength one likes to see in a 0-90 and there looked to be no excuses here from a handy position on the home bend. (tchd 15-8 and 9-4)
Owain(USA) is proving rather frustrating but undoubtedly possesses the ability to win a nursery if things fall right. Once again a slow start put him on the back foot, and his problems were compounded when hampered on the home turn. A really strongly-run 6f seems likely to bring out the best in him. (op 5-1)
Lenjawi Pride was in the mix for a long way but was just beginning to fade when squeezed for room late in the day. She could do with a bit more respite from the assess. (tchd 5-1)
Miss Sinatra(IRE) stopped as if shot on her all weather debut/first run for two months. (op 10-1 tchd 9-1)

7566 BETDAQ THE BETTING EXCHANGE H'CAP 5f 216y(P)
5:40 (5:41) (Class 3) (0-95,93) 3-Y-O+ **£5,677** (£1,699; £849; £424; £211) **Stalls** Low

Form RPR
0115 **1** **Piscean (USA)**10 7466 5-9-7 93 GeorgeBaker 8 104+
(T Keddy) *hld up: hdwy and nt clr run over 1f out: rdn to ld wl ins fnl f* **6/1**3
0621 **2** 1 1/4 **Sutton Veny (IRE)**23 7289 4-9-2 88 SteveDrowne 10 95
(J R Gask) *a.p: rdn over 1f out: r.o* **6/1**3
0200 **3** nse **Waveband**56 6509 3-9-4 90 GrahamGibbons 2 97
(T D Barron) *w ldr tl led over 1f out: rdn and hdd wl ins fnl f* **12/1**
4202 **4** 3/4 **Edinburgh Knight (IRE)**12 7443 3-9-2 88 JimCrowley 11 92
(P W D'Arcy) *hld up: hdwy over 1f out: sn rdn: styd on same pce ins fnl f* **7/2**1
0440 **5** 1/2 **Sioux Rising (IRE)**33 7097 4-8-8 80 BarryMcHugh 13 83
(R A Fahey) *hld up: hdwy over 1f out: r.o: nt trble ldrs* **16/1**
0000 **6** 1/2 **Secret Asset (IRE)**33 7079 5-9-0 93 LewisWalsh(7) 6 94+
(Jane Chapple-Hyam) *s.i.s: hld up: hdwy on outer over 2f out: rdn over 1f out: styd on: nt trble ldrs* **11/2**2
-062 **7** hd **Cape Vale (IRE)**61 6358 5-8-9 84 ow1 MichaelO'Connell(3) 9 85
(D Nicholls) *led: rdn and hdd over 1f out: no ex ins fnl f* **9/1**
3100 **8** 1 1/4 **Esuvia (IRE)**19 7351 3-8-13 85 TomEaves 1 82
(B Smart) *chsd ldrs: rdn over 1f out: no ex ins fnl f* **20/1**
6500 **9** nk **One Way Or Another (AUS)**19 7352 7-8-10 82 (b1) CathyGannon 3 78
(J R Gask) *s.i.s: hld up: swtchd lft and hdwy over 1f out: nt rch ldrs* **6/1**3
0035 **10** 1 1/4 **Tourist**12 7443 5-8-12 84 DaneO'Neill 4 76
(D Shaw) *prom: rdn over 1f out: styd on same pce* **11/1**
0000 **11** nse **Onceaponatime (IRE)**10 7466 5-8-10 82 LukeMorris 5 73
(M D Squance) *hld up: hdwy 2f out: sn rdn: wknd wl ins fnl f* **33/1**
0000 **12** 10 **Niran (IRE)**14 7411 3-8-12 84 PJMcDonald 7 43
(Mrs R A Carr) *chsd ldrs: rdn over 2f out: wknd over 1f out* **50/1**

1m 14.83s (-0.17) **Going Correction** +0.075s/f (Slow) **12** Ran SP% **122.0**
Speed ratings (Par 107): **104,102,102,101,100 99,99,98,97,95 95,82**
toteswingers:1&2 £3.40, 2&3 £16.80, 1&3 £18.20 CSF £42.48 CT £435.19 TOTE £11.80: £3.60, £1.20, £7.70; EX 23.90.
Owner Andrew Duffield **Bred** Connie And John Iacuone **Trained** Newmarket, Suffolk
■ Stewards' Enquiry : Luke Morris two-day ban: careless riding (Dec 9-10)

FOCUS
A useful sprint handicap run at a good, if not overly strong, gallop. There didn't look to be any hard-luck stories and it should prove reliable form, although the winner's hold-up style is hard to pin down.

NOTEBOOK
Piscean(USA) has done all his winning at up to 5f but he'd never had an opportunity at 6f on the AW before and he made light of a 4lb higher mark than for his last win to confirm what an unlucky loser he was last time. Finding a clean run through on this occasion, he produced a good turn of foot in the straight to hit the front plenty soon enough, suggesting another small rise in the weights might not stop him in his current mood, though the idea apparently is to go to Dubai. (op 9-2)
Sutton Veny(IRE) had won impressively at Kempton ridden with more restraint than she often is and ran well off a 5lb higher mark with those tactics repeated after racing a little keenly early on. This was a good effort. (op 11-2 tchd 9-2)
Waveband ◆ has joined a yard adept with sprinters on all weather and she made a bold bid to follow up the win she achieved on her only previous visit here, faring easily the better of the pair that cut out the running. She has early toe in abundance, so might well be in line for a drop to 5f, and would be of interest if tried at that trip in the big handicap at Southwell on New Year's Day given the very good record of her sire's progeny on Fibresand. (op 10-1)
Edinburgh Knight(IRE) looked a big danger to all when making a promising move on the home turn but didn't quite have the pace of the more established sprinters that beat him and he shaped once again like a horse that wants 7f ideally. (op 3-1)
Sioux Rising(IRE) was pushed a bit wide on the home turn but she stayed on well on her all weather debut without being knocked about unduly and left the impression that she's nearing a mark from which she can win off, particularly as she is eligible to race in a much lower grade than this. (op 20-1 tchd 22-1)
Secret Asset(IRE) had AW form figures of 21 coming into this but he ended up widest of all after being slow to stride and he ran well enough to suggest he's in form. (op 10-1)
Cape Vale(IRE) might have needed this having not run since September, before which he rejoined his current yard. He's on a potentially dangerous mark now and looked to take well to the surface. (op 14-1)
One Way Or Another(AUS) ended up with a lot to do in first-time blinkers as the race was run and never landed a blow. (tchd 11-2 and 13-2)

Tourist wasn't able to build on a more encouraging run last time but might just be ticking over until running on Fibresand again.

7567 GREAT OFFERS AT WOLVERHAMPTON-RACECOURSE.CO.UK MAIDEN STKS 1m 141y(P)
6:10 (6:11) (Class 5) 2-Y-O £2,007 (£597; £298; £149) Stalls Low

Form RPR
2 1 **Crimson China (USA)**[43] 6843 2-9-3 0 ShaneKelly 8 81
(B J Meehan) *s.i.s: hld up: hdwy 5f out: led 1f out: rdn out* 10/11[1]
3 2 3 **Bow River Arch (USA)**[31] 7113 2-8-12 0 TomQueally 4 70
(J Noseda) *hld up: racd keenly: rdn over 2f out: hdwy over 1f out: r.o to go 2nd wl ins fnl f: no ch w wnr* 2/1[2]
2505 3 1 **Riot Police (USA)**[15] 7385 2-9-3 73 (b) RobertHavlin 10 73
(J H M Gosden) *led: rdn and hdd 1f out: styd on same pce* 12/1
302 4 ½ **Lexington Bay (IRE)**[20] 7325 2-9-3 73 TomEaves 1 72
(R A Fahey) *chsd ldr: rdn over 1f out: no ex ins fnl f* 8/1[3]
06 5 3¾ **Pretty Diamond (IRE)**[29] 7172 2-8-12 0 JoeFanning 7 59+
(M Johnston) *hdwy 6f out: rdn over 2f out: wknd ins fnl f* 40/1
60 6 1¾ **Round Turn (IRE)**[12] 7452 2-9-3 0 GrahamGibbons 5 60
(E S McMahon) *s.i.s: hld up: r.o ins fnl f: n.d* 50/1
7 ¾ **Bassett Road (IRE)** 2-9-3 0 RichardKingscote 6 59
(Tom Dascombe) *chsd ldrs: shkn up over 1f out: sn wknd* 25/1
8 nk **Double Duchess** 2-8-12 0 JimCrowley 2 53
(P W D'Arcy) *hld up: shkn up over 1f out: wknd ins fnl f* 50/1
54 9 hd **History Girl (IRE)**[71] 6070 2-8-12 0 GregFairley 3 53
(M Johnston) *prom: lost pl 6f out: sn bhd* 25/1

1m 51.55s (1.05) **Going Correction** +0.075s/f (Slow) 9 Ran SP% 118.6
Speed ratings (Par 96): **98,95,94,94,90 89,88,88,88**
toteswingers:1&2 £1.10, 2&3 £5.50, 1&3 £3.00 CSF £2.80 TOTE £2.20: £1.10, £1.10, £1.70; EX 3.10.
Owner Highbury Terrace Owners Club I **Bred** Plantation Stud/Silver Springs Stud Farm **Trained** Manton, Wilts
■ Stewards' Enquiry : Robert Havlin three-day ban: careless riding (Dec 9-11)

FOCUS
A fair maiden run at something of an uneven tempo. The third is the key to the level of the form.

NOTEBOOK
Crimson China(USA) took the step forward expected from his debut without impressing as anything particularly special, gradually going further clear in the last furlong as his superior ability came through. He's going to be at least as effective at 1m2f and handicaps will probably be the next stop. (op 8-11tchd Evens in places)
Bow River Arch(USA) ran a similar race to the one she had on her debut, steadily closing as the race went on and never nearer than at the finish. A half-sister to a winner at 1m2f, she will also be suited by that distance next year but can win a fillies' maiden if given another run at this sort of trip before the end of this year. (op 9-4)
Riot Police(USA) was given every chance to shed his maiden tag from the front with the blinkers retained but his current official rating of 73 still probably flatters him a bit and, one-paced, he was readily brushed aside. (op 16-1)
Lexington Bay(IRE) is related to some speedy animals but, as at Southwell last time, looks more of a galloper than anything else, tapped for toe early in the straight before keeping on again late. His dam won at 1m4f and he might need that trip early as a 3yo. (tchd 15-2)
Pretty Diamond(IRE) stepped up on her previous turf efforts albeit left behind once the race began in earnest turning for home and is now qualified for handicaps. (op 33-1)
Round Turn(IRE) was struggling a long way out dropped back again in trip before making some late headway but will fare better in handicaps.
Bassett Road(IRE), a half-brother to the useful 6f winner (including here) Gramercy, looks to have some substance to him and should do better, possibly back in trip for all that he might well have needed this debut after showing up well.
Double Duchess has a stamina-laden pedigree and will be seen to better effect over further next year, though this debut wasn't without promise, not knocked about.

7568 BETDAQ ON 0870 178 1221 H'CAP 1m 4f 50y(P)
6:40 (6:40) (Class 4) (0-85,85) 3-Y-O+ £3,594 (£1,069; £534; £266) Stalls Low

Form RPR
231 1 **Mongoose Alert (IRE)**[26] 7244 8-8-11 72 StevieDonohoe 12 82+
(W J Musson) *hld up: r.o to ld wl ins fnl f: readily* 10/1
0042 2 1½ **Cosimo de Medici**[14] 7410 3-9-1 82 (t) SteveDrowne 8 89
(H Morrison) *led over 10f out: rdn and hung lft over 1f out: hdd and unable qck wl ins fnl f* 4/1[1]
4213 3 1¾ **Realisation (USA)**[13] 7428 3-9-3 84 GregFairley 1 88
(M Johnston) *led: hdd over 10f out: chsd ldr: rdn over 2f out: styd on* 4/1[1]
1524 4 ½ **Beggar's Opera (IRE)**[14] 7410 3-9-1 82 (bt[1]) RobertHavlin 4 85
(J H M Gosden) *hld up in tch: rdn and hung lft over 1f out: styd on same pce ins fnl f* 5/1[2]
6131 5 ¾ **Pelham Crescent (IRE)**[20] 7337 7-9-4 79 DavidProbert 10 81
(B Palling) *hld up: hdwy over 1f out: styd on same pce ins fnl f* 13/2
1145 6 nse **Chookie Hamilton**[29] 7173 6-9-9 84 TomEaves 5 86+
(V P Donoghue) *hld up: hmpd 2f out: r.o ins fnl f: nt trble ldrs* 20/1
5200 7 3½ **Trip The Light**[33] 7084 5-9-3 85 (v) MarzenaJeziorek[(7)] 11 82
(R A Fahey) *chsd ldrs: rdn over 2f out: wknd over 1f out* 25/1
1001 8 ¾ **Ethics Girl (IRE)**[14] 7410 4-9-1 76 FrannyNorton 2 71
(John Berry) *prom: hung rt fr 1/2-way: chsd ldr 2f out: rdn whn nt clr run over 1f out: wknd ins fnl f* 6/1[3]
6364 9 2¾ **Brouhaha**[28] 7196 6-8-9 77 SoniaEaton[(7)] 9 68
(Tom Dascombe) *hood removed late: s.s: hld up: a in rr* 12/1
4266 10 4½ **Dylanesque**[26] 7243 3-9-0 81 JackMitchell 3 65
(M A Jarvis) *hld up: hdwy over 3f out: sn rdn: wknd wl over 1f out* 8/1

2m 40.6s (-0.50) **Going Correction** +0.075s/f (Slow)
WFA 3 from 4yo+ 6lb 10 Ran SP% 120.8
Speed ratings (Par 105): **104,103,101,101,101 100,98,98,96,93**
toteswingers:1&2 £9.70, 2&3 £2.70, 1&3 £8.00 CSF £51.70 CT £192.92 TOTE £11.80: £3.40, £2.40, £1.30; EX 97.90.
Owner Python Partners **Bred** D And Mrs Noonan **Trained** Newmarket, Suffolk

FOCUS
A fairly useful handicap but one run at steady gallop and potentially muddling form for all that the best horse at the weights emerged the winner. The form does make some sense though.
Cosimo de Medici Official explanation: jockey said gelding hung left
Brouhaha Official explanation: jockey said, regarding delay in removing blindfold and gelding being slowly away, she was unable to remove it but it became free on 2nd attempt.

7569 SPONSOR A RACE BY CALLING 01902 390000 H'CAP 1m 4f 50y(P)
7:10 (7:10) (Class 6) (0-60,60) 3-Y-O+ £1,706 (£503; £252) Stalls Low

Form RPR
1000 1 **Abulharith**[14] 7407 4-9-0 50 (p) LukeMorris 3 59
(R A Harris) *chsd ldr tl led over 2f out: rdn and hung lft ins fnl f: styd on gamely* 50/1
3042 2 ½ **Eagle Nebula**[21] 7321 6-9-10 60 HayleyTurner 4 68
(B R Johnson) *hld up in tch: racd keenly: rdn to chse wnr ins fnl f: edgd lft: styd on* 11/4[2]
3462 3 4½ **Tres Froide (FR)**[28] 7200 5-9-2 52 (p) GrahamGibbons 6 53
(N Tinkler) *a.p: rdn to chse wnr over 1f out tl wknd ins fnl f* 10/1[3]
53-0 4 1½ **Royal Max (IRE)**[27] 720 4-8-11 47 (t) JoeFanning 9 45
(Ian Williams) *led: rdn and hdd over 2f out: wknd ins fnl f* 11/10[1]
3000 5 7 **Little Richard (IRE)**[5] 7531 11-9-4 54 (p) AdamKirby 1 41
(M Wellings) *chsd ldrs: rdn over 2f out: wknd over 1f out* 14/1
0005 6 2¾ **Black Coffee**[56] 6518 5-9-8 58 ShaneKelly 11 41
(W M Brisbourne) *s.i.s: hdwy 5f out: rdn and wknd over 2f out* 25/1
000 7 1 **Sumner (IRE)**[7] 7315 6-9-7 57 (v) GeorgeBaker 7 38
(P D Evans) *s.s: hld up: and a in rr: rdn over 3f out: sn wknd* 25/1
4104 8 ½ **Frameit (IRE)**[10] 7465 3-9-4 60 (vt) TomEaves 2 40
(J G Given) *prom: rdn 1/2-way: wknd 3f out* 10/1[3]
6000 9 1¾ **Given A Choice (IRE)**[24] 7270 8-8-13 49 (p) MickyFenton 8 27
(J Pearce) *s.s: hld up: rdn over 3f out: sn wknd* 20/1
-123 10 24 **Fine Tolerance**[279] 621 4-9-7 57 DavidProbert 5 —
(Miss S L Davison) *hld up: rdn and wknd over 3f out: t.o* 12/1

2m 41.72s (0.62) **Going Correction** +0.075s/f (Slow)
WFA 3 from 4yo+ 6lb 10 Ran SP% 121.2
Speed ratings (Par 101): **100,99,96,95,91 89,88,88,87,71**
toteswingers:1&2 £25.30, 2&3 £24.00, 1&3 £4.50 CSF £186.02 CT £1570.65 TOTE £65.20: £15.50, £1.40, £2.00; EX 276.40.
Owner The Yes No Wait Sorries **Bred** Lakin Bloodstock And H And W Thornton **Trained** Earlswood, Monmouths

FOCUS
A weak finale with few of the field in top form and the favourite disappointing. The gallop wound up gradually and it was an advantage to race prominently.
Abulharith Official explanation: trainer had no explanation for the apparent improvement in form
Little Richard(IRE) Official explanation: trainer said gelding appeared unsuited by the Polytrack
T/Plt: £540.40 to a £1 stake. Pool of £75,960.11 - 102.60 winning tickets. T/Qpdt: £16.80 to a £1 stake. Pool of £14,237.43 - 623.60 winning tickets. CR

7555 LINGFIELD (L-H)
Friday, November 26

OFFICIAL GOING: Standard
Wind: virtually nil Weather: bright and cold

7570 SPIFFING CRABBIE'S ALCOHOLIC GINGER BEER (S) STKS 1m 4f (P)
12:50 (12:50) (Class 6) 3-Y-O+ £1,706 (£503; £252) Stalls Low

Form RPR
0-06 1 **Traphalgar (IRE)**[9] 7480 5-9-6 77 (vt[1]) GeorgeBaker 11 71
(P D Evans) *stdd s: hld up in last pair: hdwy on outer ent fnl 3f: chsd ldng pair ent fnl 2f: rdn to chal ent fnl f: led ins fnl f: pushed out* 10/3[2]
04 2 1 **Mezarat (ITY)**[16] 7397 5-9-11 70 (t) AndreaAtzeni 6 74
(S C Williams) *in tch: effrt to ld over 2f out: hrd pressed and rdn 2f out: hung rt u.p ent fnl f: hdd and one pce ins fnl f* 7/2[3]
0300 3 2¾ **Robby Bobby**[26] 7251 5-9-6 70 IanMongan 10 67
(Mrs L J Mongan) *hld up in rr: hdwy on outer 4f out: rdn to chal ent fnl 2f: stl pressing ldr but nt qckning whn squeezed out and snatched up ent fnl f: styd on same pce and no imp after* 9/4[1]
1/1- 4 1½ **Wyeth**[22] 668 6-9-6 68 (b) AmirQuinn 3 63
(G L Moore) *in tch: rdn and outpcd ent fnl 2f: chsd ldng trio and drvn over 1f out: kpt on fnl f* 5/1
0005 5 8 **Sea Tobougie**[9] 7476 3-8-2 45 RyanPowell[(7)] 4 45
(M D I Usher) *hld up in tch towards rr: hdwy wl over 2f out: sn rdn and outpcd: no ch w ldrs fr wl over 1f out* 20/1
0000 6 hd **Hatch A Plan (IRE)**[30] 7167 9-9-6 46 FrankieMcDonald 9 49
(Mouse Hamilton-Fairley) *hld up in tch in rr: stl gng wl in rr whn nt clr run bnd ent fnl 2f: no ch but kpt on fr over 1f out: nvr trbld ldrs* 66/1
0000 7 1 **All About You (IRE)**[29] 7200 4-9-6 50 KirstyMilczarek 8 48
(P Howling) *led and set stdy gallop: hdd and rdn over 2f out: wknd ent fnl 2f: wl btn over 1f out* 33/1
0050 8 1 **Pursestrings**[29] 6080 3-8-9 49 EddieAhern 1 41
(Mrs L J Mongan) *in tch tl rdn and struggling wl over 2f out: wl btn fnl 2f* 33/1
4050 9 9 **Cragganmore Creek**[113] 4765 7-9-6 38 (b) LukeMorris 7 32
(D Morris) *in tch: hdwy to chse ldr 8f out tl ent fnl 3f: sn wknd: wl btn fnl 2f* 33/1
6460 10 3½ **Oak Leaves**[43] 6871 3-8-9 45 RichardKingscote 5 21
(J G Portman) *dwlt: sn rcvrd and chsd ldrs: rdn and wknd over 2f out: wl btn and eased ent fnl f* 14/1
000 11 26 **Poesmulligan (IRE)**[14] 7419 4-9-3 0 (v[1]) RobertLButler[(3)] 2 —
(Mrs L C Jewell) *t.k.h: chsd ldr tl 8f out: styd prom tl lost pl u.p over 4f out: t.o fnl 2f* 66/1

2m 32.9s (-0.10) **Going Correction** 0.0s/f (Stan)
WFA 3 from 4yo+ 6lb 11 Ran SP% 116.0
Speed ratings (Par 101): **100,99,97,96,91 91,90,89,83,81 64**
Tote Swingers: 1&2 £3.10, 1&3 £2.80, 2&3 £2.40 CSF £14.19 TOTE £4.10: £1.50, £1.10, £1.70; EX 15.60 Trifecta £47.20 Pool: £258.56 - 4.05 winning units..There was no bid for the winner. Mezarat was claimed by Michael Gates for £6,000.
Owner Mrs I M Folkes **Bred** Deepwood Farm Stud **Trained** Pandy, Monmouths
■ Stewards' Enquiry : Andrea Atzeni three-day ban: careless riding (Dec 10-12)

FOCUS
A fair seller run at just a modest pace. The front three are fair types for the grade and the form is rated around the third.
All About You(IRE) Official explanation: jockey said gelding finished distressed

7571 BET ASHES CRICKET - BETDAQ H'CAP 5f (P)
1:25 (1:25) (Class 5) (0-70,70) 3-Y-O+ £2,388 (£705; £352) Stalls High

Form RPR
3213 1 **Stratton Banker (IRE)**[58] 6466 3-9-5 68 WilliamCarson 5 79+
(S C Williams) *in tch: swtchd rt and effrt bnd ent fnl 2f: r.o wl u.p to ld ins fnl f: rdn out* 1/1[1]
0304 2 1¼ **Fromsong (IRE)**[22] 7314 12-8-12 61 SamHitchcott 4 67
(D K Ivory) *taken down early: sn bustled along to chse ldrs: rdn and effrt on inner ent fnl 2f: led ins fnl f: sn hdd and styd on same pce fnl 75yds* 12/1
2500 3 2 **Wanchai Whisper**[24] 7285 3-8-12 64 (p) AndrewHeffernan[(3)] 8 63
(P R Hedger) *dwlt: bhd: rdn and effrt on outer bnd ent fnl 2f: styd on u.p ins fnl f: nvr able to chal* 12/1

4642 **4** hd **Cape Royal**[8] 7494 10-8-12 **61**..............................(bt) RichardKingscote 3 59
(J M Bradley) *sn pushed up to press ldr: rdn ent fnl 2f: led over 1f out tl ins fnl f: wknd fnl 100yds* **11/2**[3]

400 **5** hd **Triple Dream**[13] 7446 5-9-3 **69**..............................(p) RussKennemore(3) 6 66
(J M Bradley) *in tch: rdn 1/2-way: edgd lft u.p over 1f out: styd on same pce fnl f* **20/1**

01 **6** 1 3/4 **Clear Praise (USA)**[22] 7322 3-9-4 **67**.............................. HayleyTurner 10 74+
(S Dow) *taken down early: in tch on outer tl dropped in towards rr over 3f out: effrt towards inner and nt clr run over 1f out: keeping on whn nt clr run again and eased ins fnl f* **7/2**[2]

316 **7** 4 **Schoolboy Champ**[57] 6492 3-9-3 **66**.............................. JamieSpencer 7 43
(Patrick Morris) *dwlt: sn outpcd in rr: c wd and rdn bnd ent fnl 2f: n.d* **12/1**

0150 **8** 1 1/2 **Six Diamonds**[30] 7180 3-9-4 **70**..............................(p) RobertLButler(3) 2 41
(P Butler) *chsd ldrs: rdn and wknd 2f out: wl btn fnl f* **25/1**

0416 **9** 1/2 **Cloth Ears**[21] 7329 4-8-13 **62**.............................. RobertWinston 1 31
(P S McEntee) *led tl over 1f out: sn wknd* **25/1**

58.41 secs (-0.39) **Going Correction** 0.0s/f (Stan) 9 Ran SP% **123.1**
Speed ratings (Par 103): **103,101,97,97,97 94,87,85,84**
Tote Swingers: 1&2 £4.80, 1&3 £4.10, 2&3 £12.40 CSF £16.33 CT £102.17 TOTE £2.10: £1.10, £3.50, £2.60; EX 23.10 Trifecta £191.90 Part won. Pool: £259.45 - 0.34 winning units..
Owner James & Sarah **Bred** Pat Grogan **Trained** Newmarket, Suffolk

FOCUS
Just a modest sprint handicap, but a progressive winner. He and the sixth stood out against exposed rivals. The form is rated around the runner-up's recent efforts.

7572 LARKINS BREWERY OF CHIDDINGSTONE NURSERY 7f (P)
2:00 (2:01) (Class 5) (0-75,75) 2-Y-O **£2,729** (£806; £403) **Stalls** Low

Form RPR

0441 **1** **Podgies Boy (IRE)**[16] 7396 2-8-13 **67**.............................. KierenFallon 6 72
(R A Fahey) *in tch: chsd ldr over 2f out: rdn to ld wl over 1f out: r.o wl fnl f* **6/1**

0553 **2** 1 1/2 **Seeking Glory**[16] 7394 2-8-13 **67**.............................. EddieAhern 7 68
(E A L Dunlop) *hld up in tch in last pair: hdwy to chse ldrs and rdn ent fnl 2f: chsd wnr ins fnl f: no imp towards fin* **3/1**[2]

561 **3** 1 1/4 **My Vindication (USA)**[36] 7034 2-9-5 **73**.............................. JimmyFortune 4 71
(R Hannon) *t.k.h: w ldr tl led and edgd lft over 2f out: rdn and hdd wl over 1f out: styd on same pce fnl f* **9/4**[1]

51 **4** 1/2 **Poyle Judy**[43] 6866 2-9-7 **75**.............................. JimCrowley 3 71
(R M Beckett) *in tch in last trio: rdn and effrt to chse ldrs over 1f out: kpt on same pce and no imp fnl f* **4/1**[3]

064 **5** 3 3/4 **Foxtrot Golf (IRE)**[16] 7385 2-9-5 **73**.............................. LukeMorris 1 60
(P Winkworth) *trckd ldrs tl no clr run: hmpd and shuffled bk to rr over 2f out: swtchd rt and tried to rally jst over 2f out: hung lft u.p and no prog over 1f out* **8/1**

4016 **6** 2 **Reachtothestars (USA)**[39] 6988 2-9-2 **70**.............................. AdamKirby 5 52
(M G Quinlan) *t.k.h: hld up in tch: rdn and effrt jst over 2f out: nvr gng pce to trble ldrs* **11/1**

004 **7** 14 **Whipperoo (IRE)**[24] 7279 2-7-12 **55** oh7 ow3........ NataliaGemelova(3) 2 —
(Patrick Morris) *racd keenly: led tl hdd and bmpd over 2f out: sn wknd* **50/1**

1m 25.86s (1.06) **Going Correction** 0.0s/f (Stan) 7 Ran SP% **111.5**
Speed ratings (Par 96): **93,91,89,89,85 82,66**
Tote Swingers: 1&2 £3.70, 1&3 £2.30, 2&3 £2.00 CSF £23.05 TOTE £5.40: £2.50, £1.50; EX 23.00.
Owner G Devlin **Bred** Seamus Duffy **Trained** Musley Bank, N Yorks

FOCUS
A modest nursery, but it did feature some in-form types. The early pace was just modest (time nearly three seconds above standard). Reliable form, with steps up from the first two.

NOTEBOOK
Podgies Boy(IRE) was sensibly taken to the front by Kieren Fallon on the run before the turn into the straight. Gradually winding up the pace, the winner stayed on strongly to follow up his recent selling win, gained over 1m on Fibresand. The manner of this success owed much to the ride he was given, and a rise in the weights means he'll be no sure thing to complete the hat-trick in handicap company. (tchd 13-2)
Seeking Glory, ridden more patiently than when third over 1m on Fibresand last time, followed the winner into the straight, but that rival had clearly saved something. (op 4-1 tchd 11-4)
My Vindication(USA), a Brighton maiden winner in October, was well placed turning into the straight considering the lack of pace in the race, but then the winner kept him towards the far rail in the straight, which can't have helped. (op 5-2)
Poyle Judy, the winner of a weak Kempton maiden on her previous start, was unsuited by the lack of pace and took too long to pick up. (tchd 7-2 and 5-1)
Foxtrot Golf(IRE) lost his place when caught on heels on the run to the final bend and couldn't recover, with the pace hotting up at that point. (op 13-2)

7573 BET PREMIER LEAGUE FOOTBALL - BETDAQ H'CAP 6f (P)
2:35 (2:38) (Class 4) (0-85,84) 3-Y-O+ **£4,209** (£1,252; £625; £312) **Stalls** Low

Form RPR

0251 **1** **Wallis**[30] 7166 3-8-12 **75**.............................. KierenFallon 11 87+
(L M Cumani) *t.k.h: hld up in tch: hdwy to chse ldrs whn n.m.r and swtchd rt wl over 1f out: rdn to ld 1f out: r.o wl* **9/2**[1]

0002 **2** nk **Lujeanie**[22] 7320 4-9-2 **79**..............................(p) AdamKirby 7 90
(D K Ivory) *hld up towards rr: reminder over 2f out: swtchd rt wl over 1f out: hdwy jst over 1f out: pressed wnr fnl 100yds: unable qck and hld towards fin* **10/1**[3]

5152 **3** 2 3/4 **Methaaly (IRE)**[6] 7526 7-8-4 **74**..............................(be) JosephYoung(7) 1 76
(M Mullineaux) *trckd ldrs on inner: swtchd rt and effrt over 1f out: ev ch ent fnl f: nt pce of ldng pair fnl 100yds* **16/1**

1614 **4** 3/4 **Hatta Stream (IRE)**[9] 7488 4-9-2 **79**.............................. MickyFenton 5 79
(J Pearce) *in tch: rdn to chse ldng pair jst over 2f out: unable qck over 1f out: styd on same pce ins fnl f* **11/2**[2]

60-6 **5** 1 **Flash McGahon (IRE)**[42] 6906 6-8-13 **76**..............................(p) JamieSpencer 2 73
(John M Oxx, Ire) *stdd s: detached in last after 1f: rdn over 2f out: kpt on ins fnl f: nvr able to chal* **9/2**[1]

0104 **6** 3/4 **Evelyn May (IRE)**[39] 6981 4-9-1 **78**.............................. MichaelHills 6 72
(B W Hills) *chsd ldr: rdn and ev ch ent fnl 2f: led jst over 1f out: hdd ins fnl f: sn wknd* **14/1**

2160 **7** 9 **For Life (IRE)**[22] 7318 8-8-9 **75**.............................. NataliaGemelova(3) 3 44
(J E Long) *taken down early: led: rdn jst over 2f out: hdd jst over 1f out: sn btn: heavily eased ins fnl f* **33/1**

6501 **8** 3 1/2 **Pose (IRE)**[64] 6310 3-9-1 **78**.............................. RobertHavlin 8 32
(R Ingram) *in tch in midfield tl dropped to rr and rdn jst over 2f out: wknd wl over 1f out* **33/1**

6302 **9** 3 3/4 **Quasi Congaree (GER)**[22] 7319 4-9-2 **79**..............................(t) MartinLane 10 21
(I A Wood) *in tch on outer: rdn and lost pl whn rn v wd bnd 2f out: sn wl bhd* **12/1**

20RR **R** **Stefanki (IRE)**[59] 6438 3-9-1 **78**.............................. GeorgeBaker 4 —
(G L Moore) *ref to r: tk no part* **10/1**[3]

1m 10.9s (-1.00) **Going Correction** 0.0s/f (Stan) **10** Ran SP% **96.1**
Speed ratings (Par 105): **106,105,101,100,99 98,86,81,76,—**
Tote Swingers: 1&2 £5.50, 1&3 £4.60, 2&3 £9.80 CSF £32.86 CT £334.15 TOTE £3.20: £1.20, £3.50, £4.60; EX 39.00 Trifecta £188.40 Part won. Pool: £254.60 - 0.10 winning units..Anne Of Kiev was withdrawn. Price at time of withdrawal 10/3F. Rule 4 applies to all bets. Deduction - 20p in the pound.
Owner Fittocks Stud **Bred** Fittocks Stud **Trained** Newmarket, Suffolk
■ Stewards' Enquiry : Natalia Gemelova two-day ban: careless riding (Dec 10-11)

FOCUS
The race was weakened following the withdrawal of recent C&D winner Anne Of Kiev, who was set to go off favourite but got upset in the gates (100/30F, deduct 20p in the £ under R4). The first two produced steps up.

7574 BET TEST MATCH RUGBY - BETDAQ H'CAP 7f (P)
3:05 (3:08) (Class 3) (0-95,95) 3-Y-O+ **£7,771** (£2,312; £1,155; £577) **Stalls** Low

Form RPR

062 **1** **Arteus**[60] 6429 4-9-0 **88**..............................(b) JamieSpencer 12 96
(Jane Chapple-Hyam) *led: rdn ent fnl 2f: hrd drvn and edgd rt over 1f out: hdd ins fnl f: led again wl ins fnl f: drvn out* **8/1**

0633 **2** 3/4 **Seek The Fair Land**[22] 7318 4-8-10 **87**..............................(b) MatthewDavies(3) 4 93
(J R Boyle) *in tch: rdn and effrt on inner ent fnl 2f: drvn and ev ch ent fnl f: led ins fnl f: hdd and no ex wl ins fnl f* **16/1**

0002 **3** hd **Autumn Blades (IRE)**[6] 7522 5-9-7 **95**..............................(v) DavidProbert 3 100+
(A Bailey) *hld up in tch: n.m.r ent fnl 2f: hmpd and swtchd lft over 1f out: chsd ldrs ent fnl f: kpt on towards fin* **9/2**[2]

0041 **4** 3/4 **Lowther**[9] 7488 5-9-3 **91** 6ex..............................(be) RobertWinston 11 94
(A Bailey) *t.k.h: in tch in midfield on outer: effrt and rdn over 1f out: kpt on u.p ins fnl f* **3/1**[1]

1106 **5** 1/2 **Avon River**[22] 7318 3-8-11 **86**..............................(b) JimmyFortune 6 88
(R Hannon) *chsd wnr: rdn and edgd rt wl over 1f out: lost 2nd jst over 1f out: no ex fnl f* **16/1**

0140 **6** 1 3/4 **Curtains**[26] 7254 3-8-10 **85**.............................. HayleyTurner 7 82+
(S Dow) *hld up towards rr: hdwy and n.m.r ent fnl 2f: rdn and effrt whn hmpd and swtchd lft over 1f out: styd on same pce fnl f* **16/1**

0012 **7** 1 1/4 **Mister Laurel**[20] 7352 4-8-9 **83**..............................(b) EddieAhern 5 77+
(R A Fahey) *chsd ldrs tl wknd u.p over 1f out* **8/1**

0060 **8** 1/2 **Ceremonial Jade (UAE)**[14] 7430 7-9-7 **95**..................(vt[1]) AdamKirby 1 88
(M Botti) *in tch in midfield: swtchd rt and rdn wl over 1f out: styd on same pce and no real prog after* **14/1**

200 **9** 3/4 **Noble Citizen (USA)**[6] 7522 5-9-7 **95**..............................(be) MartinLane 8 86
(D M Simcock) *towards rr: rdn and effrt on outer over 2f out: styd on same pce fr over 1f out: nvr trbld ldrs* **14/1**

-000 **10** hd **Eolith**[32] 7114 3-8-6 **81** oh4..............................(v[1]) LukeMorris 9 71
(W J Knight) *hld up in rr: effrt and rdn whn nt clr run ent fnl 2f: swtchd ins wl over 1f out: styd on same pce after* **16/1**

3021 **11** nk **Lutine Bell**[15] 7411 3-9-3 **92**..............................(b) GeorgeBaker 10 81
(Mike Murphy) *hld up towards rr on outer: rdn over 1f out: styd on same pce and no real hdwy: nvr trbld ldrs* **13/2**[3]

60-2 **12** 1 1/2 **Viva Ronaldo (IRE)**[203] 1862 4-8-6 **83**.................. NataliaGemelova(3) 2 68
(R A Fahey) *v.s.a: wl detached in last: kpt on fnl 2f: n.d* **25/1**

1m 23.38s (-1.42) **Going Correction** 0.0s/f (Stan)
WFA 3 from 4yo+ 1lb 12 Ran SP% **119.4**
Speed ratings (Par 107): **108,107,106,106,105 103,102,101,100,100 100,98**
Tote Swingers: 1&2 £8.40, 1&3 £9.80, 2&3 £23.10 CSF £129.94 CT £660.52 TOTE £10.00: £2.80, £4.10, £1.80; EX 114.20 Trifecta £538.90 Part won. Pool: £728.26 - 0.76 winning units..
Owner Norcroft Park Stud **Bred** Norcroft Park Stud **Trained** Dalham, Suffolk

FOCUS
A good, competitive handicap. It looked to favour front runners as things got a bit messy in the straight. The fifth helps with the standard.

NOTEBOOK
Arteus had been off the track since finishing a good second to the improving Mac's Power over 6f at Kempton in September, but he was only 1lb higher and was a decisive winner under a positive ride. Clearly effective between 6f-7f, it wouldn't surprise to see him defy a rise. (op 15-2 tchd 13-2)
Seek The Fair Land, 1lb higher than when third over C&D on his previous start, stuck towards the usually unfavoured inside rail in the straight and was always being held. He's in good form, but was given a hard enough race. (tchd 12-1)
Autumn Blades(IRE), off the same mark as when runner-up over C&D last time, lost ground when short of room around the turn into the straight and, considering the beaten margin, he could be considered a little unlucky. (op 4-1)
Lowther was 1lb well in under the penalty picked up for a clear-cut C&D win the previous week, but he seemed to run a bit flat. He was a bit wide into the straight, but basically didn't pick up sufficiently. (op 7-2)
Avon River had the blinkers back on but couldn't reverse recent form with Seek The Fair Land, and perhaps 1m suits best. (op 28-1 tchd 33-1)
Curtains didn't have a great deal of room in the straight, but she did not look unlucky. (tchd 18-1)

7575 GALLEONS LAP MAIDEN STKS 1m 2f (P)
3:40 (3:40) (Class 5) 3-Y-O **£2,388** (£705; £352) **Stalls** Low

Form RPR

52 **1** **Albertus Pictor**[13] 7451 3-9-3 0.............................. LukeMorris 6 74+
(Sir Mark Prescott) *in tch in midfield: rdn along 5f out: hdwy on outer to chse ldr over 2f out: rdn to ld 2f out and sn clr w rival: rn green and edgd rt 1f out: kpt on to assert towards fin* **13/8**[1]

-342 **2** 1/2 **Loyaliste (FR)**[16] 7389 3-9-3 69.............................. JimmyFortune 1 73
(R Hannon) *chsd ldr tl rdn to ld over 2f out: hdd but clr w wnr 2f out: ev ch after tl no ex and hld towards fin* **11/4**[2]

0 **3** 5 **Strophic**[182] 2507 3-9-3 0.............................. JamieSpencer 7 63+
(G C Bravery) *hld up in tch in rr: swtchd rt and hdwy on outer wl over 1f out: wnt modest 3rd 1f out: kpt on fnl f* **20/1**

400 **4** 4 1/2 **Mr Maximas**[115] 4676 3-9-3 48.............................. GeorgeBaker 10 54
(B Palling) *hld up towards rr on outer: hdwy to chse ldrs over 2f out: outpcd by ldng pair and drvn ent fnl 2f: one pce and wl hld after* **50/1**

5404 **5** 1 1/2 **Scorn (USA)**[13] 7453 3-8-12 68.............................. RobertHavlin 3 46
(J H M Gosden) *hld up in tch: nt clr run ent fnl 2f: rdn and fnd little wl over 1f out: styd on same pce and no ch after* **11/2**

04 **6** 1/2 **Rustic Deacon**[9] 7489 3-9-3 0.............................. JamieMackay 5 50
(W J Musson) *hld up in tch in midfield: rdn and outpcd ent fnl 2f: no ch w ldrs fr wl over 1f out* **25/1**

06 **7** 1 3/4 **Maydream**[14] 7419 3-8-12 0.............................. SamHitchcott 4 42
(J C Fox) *chsd ldrs: rdn to chse ldng pair jst over 2f out: sn outpcd and wl btn wl over 1f out: wknd over 1f out* **66/1**

5545 **8** 1/2 **Mavalenta (IRE)**[65] 6290 3-8-12 67.............................. MichaelHills 2 41
(J W Hills) *chsd ldrs: struggling u.p over 2f out: wknd ent fnl 2f* **5/1**[3]

0 **9** ½ **Drivemode**[30] 7183 3-9-3 0 .... MickyFenton 8 45
(Dr J D Scargill) *a in rr: rdn and struggling over 2f out: wl btn fnl 2f* **100/1**

-002 **10** 44 **Hedgerow (IRE)**[72] 6077 3-8-12 50 .... JimCrowley 11 —
(D Bourton) *racd keenly: led and sn clr: hdd over 2f out: sn dropped out: t.o and eased fnl f* **20/1**

00 **11** 6 **Mororatorio (IRE)**[21] 7338 3-9-3 0 .... IanMongan 9 —
(Mrs D J Sanderson) *a in rr: taken wd 8f out: lost tch 3f out: t.o and eased fnl f* **100/1**

2m 6.00s (-0.60) **Going Correction** 0.0s/f (Stan) **11** Ran SP% **115.6**
Speed ratings (Par 102): **102,101,97,94,92 92,91,90,90,55 50**
Tote Swingers: 1&2 £2.50, 1&3 £6.30, 2&3 £7.70. totesuper7: Win: Not won. Place: £1,3272.00. CSF £5.54 TOTE £2.70: £1.20, £1.20, £5.40; EX 7.10 Trifecta £143.80 Pool: £898.22 - 4.62 winning units..
Owner Miss K Rausing **Bred** Miss K Rausing **Trained** Newmarket, Suffolk

FOCUS
A modest maiden, but it will be surprising if the winner doesn't progress well beyond this level. The fourth is the best guide to the form.
Rustic Deacon Official explanation: jockey said, regarding running and riding, that his orders were to sit mid-division and ensure that the gelding was settled, it showed signs of keenness early and he chose to drop back towards the rail, resulting in it settling well, he was then denied a run and unable to mount a challenge until he reached the straight, at which point he felt it run on at one pace and was giving his all under hands and heels.
Hedgerow(IRE) Official explanation: jockey said filly ran too free
Mororatorio(IRE) Official explanation: jockey said gelding hung left
T/Plt: £66.00 to a £1 stake. Pool of £59,197.78 - 620.77 winning tickets. T/Qpdt: £18.60 to a £1 stake. Pool of £5,495.30 - 217.60 winning tickets. SP

7563 WOLVERHAMPTON (A.W) (L-H)

Friday, November 26

OFFICIAL GOING: Standard (abandoned after race 4 (5.30) due to concerns over the surface)
Wind: Light half-behind Weather: Cloudy

7576 BET HENNESSY GOLD CUP - BETDAQ NURSERY (DIV I) 5f 20y(P)
4:00 (4:00) (Class 6) (0-60,66) 2-Y-O **£1,364** (£403; £201) **Stalls** Low

Form RPR

6606 **1** **Dunmore Boy (IRE)**[10] 7471 2-9-6 59 .... (p) JimmyQuinn 2 63
(R A Fahey) *a.p: chsd ldr over 1f out: led ins fnl f: edgd rt: rdn out* **8/1**[3]

6060 **2** 1 **Misty Morn**[15] 7404 2-9-1 54 .... FrannyNorton 8 54
(A D Brown) *s.i.s: hld up: hdwy over 1f out: rdn and r.o* **28/1**

3133 **3** 1 ¼ **Miss Toldyaso (IRE)**[14] 7423 2-9-0 56 .... KellyHarrison(3) 1 52
(M G Quinlan) *led: rdn and hdd ins fnl f: styd on same pce* **9/4**[2]

011 **4** nk **Shostakovich (IRE)**[10] 7469 2-9-8 66 6ex .... (p) RyanClark(5) 10 61+
(S Kirk) *mid-div: hung rt 1/2-way: r.o ins fnl f: nrst fin* **11/10**[1]

0060 **5** ½ **Bon Appetit**[14] 7423 2-9-7 60 .... PhillipMakin 3 53
(N Tinkler) *chsd ldr tl rdn over 1f out: styd on same pce* **16/1**

0005 **6** 2 ¾ **Molly Mylenis**[14] 7424 2-9-2 55 .... CathyGannon 9 38
(P D Evans) *mid-div: hdwy 1/2-way: rdn over 1f out: styd on same pce* **28/1**

05 **7** ¾ **Hannah Cann**[3] 7540 2-7-13 45 .... LeonnaMayor(7) 6 25
(Peter Grayson) *s.i.s: hld up: nvr on terms* **66/1**

003 **8** 4 ½ **Georgian Silver**[16] 7392 2-8-11 50 .... LNewman 4 14
(A G Foster) *chsd ldrs: rdn 1/2-way: wknd over 1f out* **18/1**

6626 **9** 2 **Shutupandrive**[14] 7423 2-8-6 45 .... (v) ChrisCatlin 7 2
(M D I Usher) *chsd ldrs tl wknd 1/2-way* **16/1**

62.92 secs (0.62) **Going Correction** -0.025s/f (Stan) **9** Ran SP% **114.9**
Speed ratings (Par 94): **94,92,90,89,89 84,83,76,73**
Tote Swingers: 1&2 £21.80, 1&3 £2.80, 2&3 £11.70 CSF £196.89 CT £669.20 TOTE £7.40: £1.80, £9.00, £1.10; EX 155.20.
Owner Tom Flaherty **Bred** Conor Murphy & Rathmore Stud **Trained** Musley Bank, N Yorks

FOCUS
A pretty weak nursery run at a decent pace. The form looks sound. It was very cold and the kickback seemed to be flying up.

NOTEBOOK
Dunmore Boy(IRE) looked a generally regressive nine-race maiden before this but he burst back to form dropped in trip with first-time cheekpieces applied. He was value for a bit more than the winning margin implies and could have some scope to go back up the ranks if the headgear continues to work. (op 10-1)
Misty Morn stayed on steadily against the far rail without really posing a threat. She has dropped to a fair mark but has been unpredictable and wayward at times since her Redcar maiden auction win in April. (op 22-1)
Miss Toldyaso(IRE) attacked from a good draw but couldn't repel the finishers. This was her third placed effort in a row since landing a 0-60 nursery at Kempton last month but she is creeping up the weights and is now 8lb higher than her sole win. (op 5-2 tchd 2-1)
Shostakovich(IRE) had blown his rivals away in two races on Fibresand over 6f since tried in cheekpieces. He was a hot favourite to defy a 10lb rise but was trapped out wide for most of the way and couldn't get into contention after not handling the final bend very well. This has to rate as a slightly disappointing hat-trick bid but there were mitigating circumstances and it is possible he could resume his progress next time. Official explanation: jockey said colt hung badly right (op 5-4 tchd Evens)
Bon Appetit was a bit too keen up with the pace and couldn't finish off the race as well as some others. She has a patchy 0-7 record and needs to settle better to make a big impact at this level.

7577 BET HENNESSY GOLD CUP - BETDAQ NURSERY (DIV II) 5f 20y(P)
4:30 (4:35) (Class 6) (0-60,60) 2-Y-O **£1,364** (£403; £201) **Stalls** Low

Form RPR

3344 **1** **Misscomplacent**[22] 7313 2-9-7 60 .... (b) PhillipMakin 4 67
(Mrs A Duffield) *chsd ldr tl led wl over 1f out: rdn out* **3/1**[1]

4602 **2** 1 ½ **Magic Cross**[6] 7527 2-9-7 60 .... NickyMackay 10 62
(P J McBride) *s.i.s: outpcd: hdwy over 1f out: r.o to go 2nd towards fin: no ch w wnr* **4/1**[3]

032 **3** ¾ **Till Dawn (IRE)**[37] 7016 2-9-3 56 .... JimmyQuinn 8 55
(A W Carroll) *hld up in tch: edgd lft over 3f out: rdn to chse wnr fnl f: styd on same pce: lost 2nd towards fin* **7/2**[2]

4000 **4** 6 **Beach Patrol (IRE)**[51] 6666 2-9-0 56 .... (b[1]) AlanCreighton(3) 3 33
(E J Creighton) *led: rdn and hdd wl over 1f out: wknd ins fnl f* **10/1**

4230 **5** 1 ¾ **Liberty Ess (IRE)**[88] 5581 2-9-1 54 .... (p) StephenCraine 1 25
(M Wigham) *prom: pushed along 1/2-way: hmpd sn after: wknd over 1f out* **7/1**

000 **6** ½ **False Promises**[25] 7268 2-8-6 45 .... PatrickMathers 5 14
(D Shaw) *sn pushed along in mid-div: no ch fr 1/2-way* **25/1**

0350 **7** 1 **Look'N'Listen (IRE)**[10] 7469 2-9-0 53 .... DuranFentiman 9 19
(A D Brown) *chsd ldrs: rdn 1/2-way: wknd over 1f out* **33/1**

0006 **8** 4 **Make My Mark (IRE)**[39] 6989 2-8-9 48 .... AndreaAtzeni 6 —
(Mrs V M Jordan) *prom: sn hung rt and pushed along: lost pl over 3f out: n.d after* **9/2**

5600 **9** ½ **Renesmee (IRE)**[25] 7268 2-8-6 45 .... ChrisCatlin 2 —
(Peter Grayson) *sn outpcd* **33/1**

000 **10** ½ **Zohan (IRE)**[83] 5763 2-7-13 45 .... (b[1]) LeonnaMayor(7) 7 —
(Peter Grayson) *in rr whn bdly hmpd over 3f out: sn bhd* **66/1**

62.90 secs (0.60) **Going Correction** -0.025s/f (Stan) **10** Ran SP% **118.2**
Speed ratings (Par 94): **94,91,90,80,78 77,75,69,68,67**
Tote Swingers: 1&2 £3.10, 1&3 £3.00, 2&3 £2.80 CSF £14.98 CT £44.89 TOTE £3.50: £1.10, £1.80, £1.30; EX 18.90.
Owner Roger K Lee **Bred** Park Farm Racing **Trained** Constable Burton, N Yorks
■ Stewards' Enquiry : Jimmy Quinn five-day ban: careless riding (Dec 10-14)

FOCUS
There was an inspection of the track due to the freezing conditions before this second race. Racing was allowed to go ahead and mostly exposed runners lined-up for the second division of this modest nursery. The pace was fast and the three market leaders pulled clear of the rest. The form is very modest, rated around the second and third.

NOTEBOOK
Misscomplacent probably did too much too soon in front at Kempton on her previous run. She was ridden with a bit more restraint switched back to 5f and got her timing right to get off the mark on the 12th attempt. Her rating may head back up to the mid 60s after this but she is a consistent type who finishes in the money more often than not and should continue to go well. (op 11-4 tchd 4-1)
Magic Cross deserves plenty of credit for getting as close as she did after a slow start from a wide draw. She is a fairly reliable and versatile 5f-7f performer who scored at Bath in August and could be a major force if things pan out better next time. (tchd 7-2 and 9-2)
Till Dawn(IRE) travelled well behind the leaders for a long way but couldn't find an extra gear in the closing stages. She has had plenty of chances but has been knocking on the door with improved efforts on her last two runs and her style suggests she might be worth another try at 6f. Official explanation: vet said filly had been struck into near-hind (op 3-1)
Beach Patrol(IRE) had made little impact in three runs for a new yard. His mark had dropped 6lb after his latest run and he put in a fair front-running effort with first-time blinkers replacing a visor but was still ultimately well held. (tchd 11-1)
Liberty Ess(IRE) was never competitive under a patient ride back from almost three months off. She has looked a short runner at times but is entitled to improve for this effort and is still unexposed in handicaps. (op 13-2 tchd 8-1)
Make My Mark(IRE) was a springer in the market but couldn't live with the early pace and finished well beaten on the return to 5f. (op 10-1)
Zohan(IRE) Official explanation: jockey said gelding had suffered interference in runing

7578 SPONSOR A RACE BY CALLING 01902 390000 MEDIAN AUCTION MAIDEN STKS 5f 216y(P)
5:00 (5:04) (Class 6) 2-Y-O **£1,706** (£503; £252) **Stalls** Low

Form RPR

64 **1** **What About You (IRE)**[15] 7408 2-9-3 0 .... (t) SteveDrowne 5 87+
(R A Fahey) *mde virtually all: rdn clr and edgd lft fr over 1f out: comf* **9/4**[2]

2242 **2** 5 **Its You Again**[8] 7493 2-9-3 75 .... TomQueally 4 71
(M G Quinlan) *a.p: chsd wnr over 2f out: sn rdn: edgd lft and no ex fnl f* **1/1**[1]

5 **3** 2 ¼ **Consistant**[15] 7408 2-9-3 0 .... JackMitchell 6 65
(B P J Baugh) *hld up: hdwy over 1f out: r.o to go 3rd ins fnl f: nvr nrr* **25/1**

455 **4** ¾ **Flash City (ITY)**[39] 6980 2-9-3 75 .... DaneO'Neill 11 62
(B Smart) *chsd ldrs: rdn and hung lft over 1f out: styd on same pce* **13/2**[3]

5 hd **Asfurah's Image**[81] 5822 2-8-12 0 .... ChrisCatlin 9 57
(M Botti) *prom: rdn over 2f out: styd on same pce appr fnl f* **16/1**

0 **6** 2 ¼ **Goal (IRE)**[20] 7346 2-9-3 0 .... StevieDonohoe 3 55+
(D C Griffiths) *s.i.s: rdn 1/2-way: styd on ins fnl f: nvr nrr* **66/1**

00 **7** ½ **Legal Heights (IRE)**[94] 5381 2-9-3 0 .... CathyGannon 7 54
(J M P Eustace) *sn pushed along and prom: rdn and wknd over 1f out* **80/1**

50 **8** 2 ¾ **Way Chief (FR)**[20] 7346 2-9-3 0 .... JimmyQuinn 1 45
(R A Fahey) *sn pushed along in rr: nvr on terms* **20/1**

0 **9** 2 ½ **Take Your Partner**[20] 7346 2-9-3 0 .... PhillipMakin 10 38
(K A Ryan) *hld up: a in rr* **33/1**

60 **10** ½ **Three Opera Divas**[13] 7448 2-8-12 0 .... GregFairley 12 31
(M Johnston) *prom: rdn over 2f out: wknd over 1f out* **40/1**

0 **11** 4 ½ **Jane's Legacy**[13] 7447 2-8-12 0 .... GrahamGibbons 8 18
(R Hollinshead) *chsd ldr tl rdn over 2f out: wknd over 1f out* **66/1**

0 **12** 7 **Fire Commander**[14] 7427 2-9-3 0 .... J-PGuillambert 2 —
(B P J Baugh) *sn pushed along in rr: bhd fr 1/2-way* **100/1**

1m 14.48s (-0.52) **Going Correction** -0.025s/f (Stan) **12** Ran SP% **119.2**
Speed ratings (Par 94): **102,95,92,91,91 88,87,83,80,79 73,64**
Tote Swingers: 1&2 £1.50, 1&3 £7.30, 2&3 £6.50 CSF £4.53 TOTE £3.60: £1.10, £1.50, £3.50; EX 6.20.
Owner Errigal Racing **Bred** Mrs Sandra McCarthy **Trained** Musley Bank, N Yorks

FOCUS
There was a runaway front-running winner in this minor maiden, showing decent form for the time of year. The standard looks solid and the form could be rated up to 7lb higher.

NOTEBOOK
What About You(IRE) ruined his chance by hanging badly left on debut before a slightly unlucky fourth with a tongue tie applied in a tight finish over C&D last time. He had a bit to find but displayed some raw running power and overwhelmed this field on his third start. There are sprint winners and chase winners on his dam's side, so it is hard to get to grips with his future trip requirements but at this stage he looks a horse with plenty of natural speed, and potential for further improvement. (op 2-1)
Its You Again is fairly exposed but had leading claims on his close second off 75 behind a reliable performer in a C&D nursery last week. He broke much better than he did last time and kept close tabs on the leader but couldn't land a blow when that rival cranked it up around the final turn. (op 6-5)
Consistant did a bit of late work from a long way back but was beaten further by the winner than he was over C&D on debut. He may remain vulnerable to better sorts in this grade but is a brother to 7f winner Digit and a half-brother to plenty of other winners, so should get more competitive when sent handicapping.
Flash City(ITY) held his head at a slight angle and didn't find a great deal for pressure on this AW debut. He has been fairly consistent in four starts but has a bit to prove to live up to his official rating of 75. (op 7-1 tchd 8-1)
Asfurah's Image, an ex-Irish performer, attracted a bit of support at biggish prices but couldn't make an impact dropped back to 6f on her AW debut for a new yard. (op 25-1)

7579 STAY AT THE WOLVERHAMPTON HOLIDAY INN MAIDEN STKS 1m 5f 194y(P)
5:30 (5:31) (Class 5) 3-Y-O+ **£2,007** (£597; £298; £149) **Stalls** Low

Form RPR

30-0 **1** **Masterful Act (USA)**[44] 6856 3-9-3 67 .... JackMitchell 6 70+
(E F Vaughan) *hld up in tch: led over 2f out: rdn clr fr over 1f out* **5/1**[3]

66-4 **2** 9 **Money Money Money**15 7413 4-9-6 57 .... JamesMillman 5 52
(B R Millman) *chsd ldrs: ev ch 2f out: styd on same pce* **11/1**
0623 **3** 6 **Joan D'Arc (IRE)**10 5208 3-8-9 65 .... KellyHarrison(3) 2 44
(M G Quinlan) *chsd ldrs: rdn over 2f out: sn wknd* **2/1**1
4 shd **Yeomanry**13 5-9-11 0 .... SaleemGolam 1 49
(Ian Williams) *prom: lost pl over 3f out: styd on ins fnl f* **10/1**
36 **5** ½ **Asterisk**24 7288 3-8-12 0 .... FrannyNorton 12 43
(John Berry) *prom: lost pl after 3f: hdwy over 4f out: rdn and ev ch over 2f out: wknd over 1f out* **9/1**
0 **6** 1 **Jingoism (USA)**91 5487 4-9-11 0 .... DaneO'Neill 8 47
(B Ellison) *pushed along in rr: hdwy over 6f out: wknd over 2f out* **40/1**
0 **7** ½ **Big Bad Boo**35 7069 4-9-4 0 .... AlexEdwards(7) 3 46
(J W Unett) *led: hdd over 4f out: wknd over 2f out* **66/1**
0006 **8** hd **Kargarann (IRE)**28 7213 3-9-3 42 .... ChrisCatlin 4 46
(Stef Higgins) *s.s: hld up: hdwy over 3f out: wknd 2f out* **33/1**
0 **9** 7 **Maccool (IRE)**14 7419 4-9-11 0 .... TomQueally 11 36
(B J Curley) *hld up: hdwy to ld over 4f out: rdn and hdd over 2f out: sn wknd* **28/1**
00 **10** 38 **Titanic Mill**21 7338 3-9-3 0 ....(b) CathyGannon 10 —
(N J Vaughan) *chsd ldrs tl rdn and wknd wl over 3f out: t.o* **80/1**
-222 **U** **Fashionable Gal (IRE)**9 7489 3-8-12 72 .... StevieDonohoe 7 —
(Sir Mark Prescott) *stmbld and uns rdr leaving stalls* **5/2**2

3m 9.58s (3.58) **Going Correction** -0.025s/f (Stan)
WFA 3 from 4yo+ 8lb **11** Ran SP% **117.6**
Speed ratings (Par 103): **88,82,79,79,79 78,78,78,74,52** —
Tote Swingers: 1&2 £9.70, 1&3 £5.00, 2&3 £6.80 CSF £55.75 TOTE £9.10: £3.10, £2.40, £1.02; EX 42.70.
Owner Hungerford Park Stud **Bred** Fiona Craig & Dermot Cantillon **Trained** Newmarket, Suffolk

FOCUS
A weak maiden but it was eventful. The favourite had a troubled run and was a bit laboured, while her main market rival slipped and unseated her rider at the start, which left the door open for a market springer to power clear for a comfortable win. The winner was entitled to win this on his 2yo form. There was more work on the track and another delay after this race and eventually the meeting was abondoned due to unsafe conditions.

7580 BETDAQ THE BETTING EXCHANGE CLAIMING STKS 5f 216y(P)
() (Class 6) 2-Y-O £

7581 BETDAQ ON 0870 178 1221 H'CAP 1m 141y(P)
() (Class 2) (0-100,) 3-Y-O+ £

7582 GREAT OFFERS AT WOLVERHAMPTON-RACECOURSE.CO.UK H'CAP 1m 4f 50y(P)
() (Class 5) (0-70,) 3-Y-O+ £

T/Plt: £5.00 to a £1 stake. Pool of £83,614 - 12,074.70 winning tickets. T/Qpdt: £2.00 to a £1 stake. Pool of £9,705 - 3,459.08 winning tickets. CR

7586 - 7588a (Foreign Racing) - See Raceform Interactive

7509 DUNDALK (A.W) (L-H)
Friday, November 26

OFFICIAL GOING: Standard

7589a CROWNE PLAZA LEADING JOCKEY & TRAINER CHAMPIONSHIP H'CAP 1m 4f (P)
9:00 (9:02) (60-90,88) 3-Y-O+ £8,243 (£1,911; £836; £477)

RPR
1 **Solo Performer (IRE)**7 7514 5-9-5 82 ....(b) ShaneFoley(3) 12 84+
(H Rogers, Ire) *hld up in rr: last into st: hdwy on outer 2f out: led under 1f out: kpt on wl u.p* **25/1**
2 nk **Redera (IRE)**20 7220 4-9-0 74 .... FMBerry 14 76
(A J Martin, Ire) *hld up towards rr: 11th on outer early st: hdwy under 2f out: led briefly over 1f out: 2nd and kpt on wl ins fnl f* **8/1**
3 2½ **Denny Crane**14 7435 4-9-8 82 .... WMLordan 1 80
(Edward Lynam, Ire) *mid-div: 7th on inner 1/2-way: prog 1 1/2f out: 3rd and kpt on ins fnl f* **7/2**2
4 nk **Home Secretary**14 7435 6-8-13 76 ....(t) BACurtis(3) 10 74
(Garvan Donnelly, Ire) *hld up towards rr: prog travelling wl under 2f out: 6th 1f out: rdn and kpt on* **6/1**3
5 1½ **Kalacan (IRE)**14 7435 4-9-4 78 .... JAHeffernan 3 73
(G M Lyons, Ire) *trckd ldrs in 6th: prog ent st: 3rd and chal 2f out: disp ld briefly 1 1/2f out: no ex fnl f* **16/1**
6 2½ **The Pier (IRE)**40 6971 4-10-0 88 .... WJLee 5 79
(Joseph G Murphy, Ire) *trckd ldrs in 5th: impr into 2nd on inner early st: no ex fr over 1f out: eased cl home* **9/1**
7 2½ **Hawk Flight (IRE)**7 7514 5-9-3 77 .... PJSmullen 9 64
(Miss Maura McGuinness, Ire) *hld up in tch: impr to chsd ldrs under 2f out: chal 1 1/2f out: no ex fr over 1f out* **10/1**
8 ¾ **Lovers Causeway (USA)**50 6698 3-9-3 83 ....(b) JoeFanning 13 69
(M Johnston) *led: rdn and strly pressed st: hdd 1 1/2f out: sn no ex* **3/1**1
9 ½ **Queen Andromache (USA)**22 3138 4-8-10 77 ....(p) SHJames(7) 11 62
(John Queally, Ire) *mid-div: 8th 1/2-way: one pce st* **50/1**
10 1¼ **Star Power (IRE)**20 7359 3-9-2 82 .... KJManning 8 65
(J S Bolger, Ire) *trckd ldr in 2nd: chal ent st: sn no ex and wknd* **7/1**
11 2½ **Bashkirov**42 6912 5-9-9 88 .... MHarley(5) 6 67
(Luke Comer, Ire) *prom: 3rd 1/2-way: wknd ent st* **33/1**
12 1½ **Grand Opera (IRE)**12 7139 7-9-5 79 ....(b) MCHussey 2 56
(Gordon Elliott, Ire) *in rr of mid-div: rdn and wknd 3f out* **50/1**
13 1½ **Wikaala (USA)**36 6549 5-9-10 84 ....(b) DPMcDonogh 7 58
(Gordon Elliott, Ire) *prom: 4th 4f out: wknd early st* **11/1**
P **Kevkat (IRE)**14 7435 9-9-0 79 .... JPO'Brien(5) 4 —
(Eoin Griffin, Ire) *hld up in tch: p.u injured bef 1/2-way* **16/1**

2m 28.81s (148.81)
WFA 3 from 4yo+ 6lb **14** Ran SP% **135.0**
CSF £234.04 CT £903.68 TOTE £64.90: £12.30, £2.80, £2.30; DF 860.40.
Owner Mrs Margot McGuinness **Bred** Peter J McGuinness **Trained** Ardee, Co. Louth

NOTEBOOK
Solo Performer(IRE) was on his best behaviour here and won under a very canny ride. Dropped in off a slow pace, he was nearly last turning in, but began to pick off his rivals on the outside one by one up the straight and kept on well inside the last. He's likely to return for a similar handicap on the final day of the season. Official explanation: vet said gelding was found to have burst a blood vessel post-race
Redera(IRE) was ridden in very similar fashion to the winner. He found plenty and was unlucky to find one too good for him. (op 12/1)
Denny Crane was ridden with restraint in mid-division and ran on inside the last furlong, but the first two had built up a fair bit of momentum and he just couldn't match it. (op 4/1)
Home Secretary does run well here, but can be frustrating. Nothing travelled better entering the straight, but his rider seemed at pains to keep him covered up for as long as possible. However, even when he saw daylight, he didn't pick up as it appeared he would.
Kalacan(IRE) ran another solid race without being good enough to win. He held a good position most of the way but proved a bit one-paced in the straight.
The Pier(IRE) moved up strongly to lead on the inside rail early in the straight, but faded inside the last. (op 8/1 tchd 10/1)
Lovers Causeway(USA) tried to make all, but raced keenly and faded quickly once headed early in the straight. (op 5/2)

7590 - (Foreign Racing) - See Raceform Interactive

7547 KEMPTON (A.W) (R-H)
Saturday, November 27

OFFICIAL GOING: Standard
Wind: nil Weather: dry, very cold

7591 WILLIAMHILL.COM H'CAP 1m 2f (P)
2:10 (2:10) (Class 2) (0-100,97) 3-Y-O+
£9,221 (£2,761; £1,380; £691; £344; £173) Stalls High

Form RPR
2201 **1** **Akhmatova**15 7420 3-8-10 87 .... WilliamBuick 6 98+
(G A Butler) *t.k.h: hld up wl in tch: rdn and effrt to chal jst over 1f out: led 1f out: kpt on wl: rdn out* **15/2**
0542 **2** nk **Right Step**35 7100 3-9-0 91 .... KierenFallon 8 100
(A P Jarvis) *hld up in tch in midfield: nt clr run wl over 1f out: effrt and rdn over 1f out: chsng ldrs whn pushed lft jst ins fnl f: chsd wnr fnl 100yds: r.o wl: nt quite rch wnr* **13/2**3
3 1 **Nice Style (IRE)**650 6459 5-9-6 93 .... SteveDrowne 9 100
(J R Gask) *stdd s: t.k.h: hld up in tch in last trio: hdwy 3f out: chsng ldrs whn nt clr run and swtchd lft jst ins fnl f: kpt on fnl 100yds: nt rch wnr* **20/1**
3651 **4** 1¼ **Tinshu (IRE)**28 7243 4-9-1 88 .... DaneO'Neill 1 93
(D Haydn Jones) *hld up wl in tch in midfield: rdn and effrt to chse ldrs whn pushed lft jst ins fnl f: styd on same pce and no imp fnl 100yds* **8/1**
241 **5** shd **Colour Scheme (IRE)**22 7338 3-8-10 87 ....(t) ShaneKelly 10 91
(B J Meehan) *t.k.h: chsd ldr: rdn to chal wl over 1f out: led jst over 1f out: sn hdd: wknd ins fnl f* **7/2**1
3005 **6** 1¾ **Mafeking (UAE)**25 7287 6-9-3 90 .... ChrisCatlin 4 91
(M R Hoad) *led: rdn wl over 1f out: hdd jst over 1f out: wknd ins fnl f* **16/1**
0432 **7** 2¾ **Baylini**15 7430 6-9-1 88 .... JamesDoyle 2 83
(J A Osborne) *t.k.h early: sn chsng ldng pair: rdn and effrt 2f out: wknd ent fnl f* **10/1**
032 **8** nk **Greylami (IRE)**25 7287 5-9-10 97 .... EddieAhern 7 92
(R A Mills) *stdd s: hld up in tch in last trio: rdn and effrt wl over 1f out: no real hdwy: n.d* **9/2**2
0060 **9** 3¼ **Yahrab (IRE)**178 2640 5-8-11 89 .... NeilFarley(5) 5 77
(D Carroll) *t.k.h: hld up in tch in last trio: rdn and outpcd ent fnl 2f: wl btn over 1f out* **8/1**
4610 **10** 13 **Dubai Crest**35 7100 4-8-13 86 .... TomQueally 3 48
(Mrs A J Perrett) *in tch: rdn over 3f out: dropped to rr u.p wl over 2f out: lost tch 2f out* **9/1**

2m 3.88s (-4.12) **Going Correction** -0.175s/f (Stan)
WFA 3 from 4yo+ 4lb **10** Ran SP% **117.5**
Speed ratings (Par 109): **109,108,107,106,106 105,103,103,100,90**
toteswingers:1&2:£10.70, 1&3:£24.00, 2&3:£34.00 CSF £56.02 CT £943.34 TOTE £8.00: £3.00, £1.50, £8.50; EX 53.10 Trifecta £340.90 Part won..
Owner Trevor C Stewart **Bred** Sunny Days Ltd **Trained** Newmarket, Suffolk
■ Stewards' Enquiry : Steve Drowne one-day ban: careless riding (Dec 11)

FOCUS
A decent handicap, run at a solid pace thanks to Mafeking who again didn't get home.

NOTEBOOK
Akhmatova had been raised 4lb after winning a Lingfield fillies' handicap a fortnight earlier, which meant she apparently had it to do to reverse earlier Wolverhampton form with Tinshu and Baylini, but races around the inner loop here rely on the contest panning out to advantage and, in that respect, she was given a peach of a ride. She travelled well behind the leaders and, when asked to go and win her race a furlong out, she was able to get first run on the hold-up horses. She now heads for a Listed race at Deauville on December 18. (op 5-1)
Right Step, the only AW debutant in the field, was given a waiting ride and wasn't helped by taking a nudge from Nice Style when staying on inside the last furlong. He was never quite going to get up and remains without a win since his second start at two, but he can put that right on this surface. (op 6-1)
Nice Style(IRE) ◆ was making his debut for the yard having not been seen since finishing runner-up in a Hereford maiden hurdle in February in his one outing for David Pipe. Another to be held up, he got a nice run through on the inside turning in and kept on well after being switched left. He has winning form on Polytrack and is worth watching with this run under his belt. (op 25-1 tchd 28-1)
Tinshu(IRE) was up 2lb for her narrow success at Wolverhampton last month. She ran on down the outside in the home straight and had her chance with no apparent excuses. (op 7-1)
Colour Scheme(IRE) was making his handicap debut after bolting up in an uncompetitive Wolverhampton maiden earlier this month. He was in the ideal position to pounce on the early leader, but no sooner had he done so over a furlong out than the winner arrived and he was swamped. He still has some scope. (tchd 4-1)
Baylini took a fair grip in a handy position early and found little off the bridle. She does look better at Lingfield. (op 9-1)
Greylami(IRE) was off a new career-high mark having been put up 4lb for his narrow defeat by the smart Ottoman Empire over C&D earlier this month, but he never got into the race at all. Official explanation: jockey said gelding ran flat (op 5-1 tchd 11-2 in a place)
Yahrab(IRE), formerly a smart performer for Clive Brittain, was making his debut for the yard on this first start since June, having lost his way for his former handler, but despite attracting market support he never looked like justifying it. (op 14-1)

7592 BEST ODDS GUARANTEED @ MOBILE.WILLIAMHILL.COM NURSERY 5f (P)
2:40 (2:40) (Class 5) (0-75,77) 2-Y-O £2,286 (£675; £337) Stalls High

Form RPR
3211 **1** **Insolenceofoffice (IRE)**9 7493 2-9-9 77 ....(p) GeorgeBaker 9 83
(Mrs A Duffield) *in tch: swtchd lft and effrt over 1f out: ev ch ent fnl f: kpt on wl ins fnl f to ld fnl 50yds* **5/2**1
0261 **2** nk **Crimson Cloud**15 7418 2-9-2 70 .... TomEaves 7 75
(R A Fahey) *sn led: rdn wl over 1f out: hrd pressed ent fnl f: kpt on wl tl hdd and no ex fnl 50yds* **5/2**1

The Form Book, Raceform Ltd, Compton, RG20 6NL

006 **3** *2* **Lisselton Cross**[23] 7309 2-8-1 **55**.. LukeMorris 6 53
(M R Bosley) *dwlt: in tch in rr: swtchd ins and effrt over 1f out: drvn to chse ldng pair ins fnl f: kpt on same pce after* **40/1**

053 **4** *3/4* **Sacrosanctus**[9] 7493 2-9-5 **73**.. IanMongan 1 68
(D Nicholls) *restless in stalls: wnt rt and bmpd rival s: in tch on outer: carried wd bnd 2f out: rdn and chsng ldrs whn pushed lft over 1f out: bmpd lft and pushed lft again 1f out: edgd rt and styd on same pce fnl f* **4/1**[2]

3206 **5** *1/2* **My Love Fajer (IRE)**[29] 7207 2-9-2 **70**.......................... KirstyMilczarek 8 63
(G Prodromou) *t.k.h: chsd ldrs: rdn and hung lft over 1f out: hung lft again and bmpd rival 1f out: styd on under pce after* **6/1**[3]

0600 **6** *2* **Dells Breezer**[85] 5720 2-8-3 **60**.. KierenFox(3) 5 49
(P M Phelan) *s.i.s: hld up in tch in rr: effrt and chsng whn squeezed out and hmpd over 1f out: one pce and no threat to ldrs after* **18/1**

232 **7** *3 1/2* **Johnny Hancocks (IRE)**[15] 7424 2-9-0 **75**........... MatthewCosham(7) 2 50
(P D Evans) *bmpd s: in tch on outer: pushed along 1/2-way: outpcd and n.m.r 2f out: sn wknd* **10/1**

4004 **8** *5* **Instructress**[15] 7424 2-9-0 **68**..(v[1]) EddieAhern 4 40
(R M H Cowell) *hung lft thrght: chsd ldr tl hung lft and wd bnd 2f out: struggling whn nt clr run and hmpd over 1f out: sn wl bhd* **16/1**

59.63 secs (-0.87) **Going Correction** -0.175s/f (Stan) **8** Ran SP% **114.1**
Speed ratings (Par 96): **99,98,95,94,93 90,84,76**
toteswingers:1&2:£2.00, 1&3:£10.20, 2&3:£13.30 CSF £8.59 CT £187.85 TOTE £3.30: £1.70, £1.90, £12.40; EX 8.70 Trifecta £88.50 Pool: £666.47 - 5.57 winning units..
Owner Middleham Park Racing XLIX **Bred** Gerard Kennedy **Trained** Constable Burton, N Yorks

FOCUS
A fair nursery, but quite rough race with a concertina effect starting with the winner being pulled out for his effort over a furlong from home. He continues on a roll, and the runner-up produced an improved effort.

NOTEBOOK
Insolenceofoffice(IRE) had the plum draw in his bid to complete the hat-trick off a 4lb higher mark and he broke well enough to get a nice lead from his main market rival. He had to be switched left in order to get past the hanging leader over a furlong out and caused problems for a few as he did, but despite the narrow margin he always looked likely to get there. (op 2-1)
Crimson Cloud, making her nursery debut after narrowly beating a subsequent winner in a Lingfield maiden a fortnight earlier, set out to make just about all but she gradually hung away from the inside rail once into the straight and was nailed close to the line. (op 9-4)
Lisselton Cross, making his nursery debut after showing little in two maidens and a claimer, all over 6f here, ran on up the inside rail to record his best effort yet. A small race can come his way, possibly back over further. (op 50-1)
Sacrosanctus had a 4lb pull for a near 2l beating by Insolenceofoffice over 6f at Wolverhampton nine days earlier, but whereas his old rival had the best of the draw here, he had the worst of it and, to make matters worse, he proved very restless in the stalls. He was carried very wide into the straight when trying to get closer and under the circumstances he did well to finish where he did, especially as he took two bumps from My Love Fajer in the closing stages. (op 5-1 tchd 11-2)
My Love Fajer(IRE) attracted market support and had his chance, but tended to hang about once into the straight. Official explanation: jockey said colt hung badly left (op 12-1)
Dells Breezer was dropping to the minimum trip for the first time after finishing unplaced in his first four starts. He was another to meet interference over a furlong out, but it didn't affect his chances of winning. Official explanation: jockey said gelding suffered interference in running (op 25-1)
Instructress raced freely in the first-time visor, but was beaten when getting badly hampered over a furlong from home. Official explanation: jockey said filly suffered interference in running

7593 WILLIAMHILL.COM HYDE STKS (LISTED RACE) 1m (P)
3:15 (3:22) (Class 1) 3-Y-O+

£14,483 (£14,483; £3,984; £1,986; £995; £499) **Stalls** High

Form RPR

3264 **1** **Riggins (IRE)**[73] 6089 6-9-2 **108**.. WilliamBuick 9 109
(Ed Walker) *hld up in tch in midfield: rdn and gd hdwy over 1f out: ev ch fnl 100yds: r.o wl u.p: jnd ldr on line* **4/1**[2]

4000 **1** *dht* **Fanunalter**[43] 6885 4-9-4 **105**.. AdamKirby 11 111
(M Botti) *hld up in tch: n.m.r on inner over 2f out: rdn and gd hdwy 2f out: drvn to ld ins fnl f: jnd on line* **9/1**

0132 **3** *3/4* **Beauchamp Viceroy**[10] 7482 6-9-2 **105**..........................(b) DaneO'Neill 8 107
(G A Butler) *broke v fast: led: rdn ent fnl 2f: kpt on wl tl hdd and no ex fnl 100yds* **7/2**[1]

6123 **4** *3/4* **Chapter And Verse (IRE)**[15] 7430 4-9-2 **94**.................. AndreaAtzeni 4 106
(Mike Murphy) *hld up towards rr: hdwy into midfield 1/2-way: chsd ldrs and rdn ent fnl 2f: kpt on same pce u.p fnl 100yds* **12/1**

4602 **5** *3/4* **The Cheka (IRE)**[28] 7234 4-9-2 **107**..............................(p) KierenFallon 3 104
(Eve Johnson Houghton) *chsd ldrs: rdn to chse ldr wl over 1f out tl ent fnl f: outpcd fnl 100yds* **9/2**[3]

5003 **6** *hd* **Viva Vettori**[28] 7233 6-9-2 **99**..(p) GeorgeBaker 2 103
(D R C Elsworth) *stdd after s: hld up in last trio: hdwy on outer over 2f out: rdn 1f out: kpt on ins fnl f: nt trble ldrs* **12/1**

2400 **7** *1* **Aldovrandi (IRE)**[56] 6570 3-9-0 **102**..................................(t) ChrisCatlin 5 101
(M Botti) *t.k.h: chsd ldr after 2f tl wl over 1f out: wknd u.p 1f out* **12/1**

0023 **8** *1 1/2* **Autumn Blades (IRE)**[1] 7574 5-9-2 **95**.........................(v) DavidProbert 7 98
(A Bailey) *t.k.h: hld up in tch: rdn and unable qck wl over 1f out: wknd 1f out* **10/1**

0006 **9** *nse* **Atlantic Story (USA)**[10] 7482 8-9-2 **106**................(bt) GrahamGibbons 6 98
(M W Easterby) *stdd after s: hld up in last trio: rdn and effrt whn n.m.r over 1f out: kpt on ins fnl f: nvr trbld ldrs* **10/1**

2100 **10** *4 1/2* **Marjury Daw (IRE)**[21] 7349 4-8-11 **85**.............................. TomEaves 10 82
(J G Given) *chsd ldr for 2f: chsd ldrs after tl wknd u.p ent fnl 2f* **66/1**

3540 **11** *2* **Street Power (USA)**[23] 7318 5-9-2 **88**.............................. SteveDrowne 1 83
(J R Gask) *stdd and dropped in bhd after s: hld up in rr: rdn jst over 2f out: no hdwy: n.d* **66/1**

1m 36.58s (-3.22) **Going Correction** -0.175s/f (Stan)
WFA 3 from 4yo+ 2lb **11** Ran SP% **114.6**
Speed ratings (Par 111): **109,109,108,107,106 106,105,104,104,99 97**WIN: Fanunalter £5.80, Riggins £2.80 PL: Fanunalter £3.10, Riggins £2.10, Beauchamp Viceroy £1.30. EX: F/R £18.90 R/F, £23.70 CSF: F/R £21.86, R/F £19.45. Trifecta: F/R/BV £106.00, R/F/BV £174.30.toteswingers: F&R £9.50, F&BV £8.30, R&BV £3.70. TOTE £0.0027: £Owner, £Dubai Thoroughbred Racing, £Bred, £Compagnia Generale S R LTrained Newmarket, Suffolk Trifecta £n Dead-heater Riggins was trainer Ed Walker's first ever runner. 1.
Owner Scuderia Rencati Srl **Bred** Azienda Agricola Francesca **Trained** Newmarket, Suffolk
■ Dead-heater Riggins was trainer Ed Walker's first ever runner.

FOCUS
The fourth running of this Listed event and, with the third horse making it is true test, they shaved 0.24 seconds off the course record set by Gentleman's Deal in February 2007. The result was in doubt right to the end and even the judge couldn't separate the front pair.

NOTEBOOK
Riggins(IRE), his trainer's first runner, was marginally best in at the weights and was successful on Polytrack in his first two career outings. He looked to have timed his effort down the outside just right and to the naked eye it seemed as though he had got up, but the photo proved otherwise. He is likely to join his rival in Dubai. (op 7-2)
Fanunalter, a winner over C&D on his only previous visit here, has found life tough (mostly in Group company) since winning a Doncaster Listed event in April, but the return to this level saw him back on the scoresheet. Having travelled well in mid-division, he looked likely to win outright when getting a nice run through on the inside after the cutaway, but having battled his way to the front he was joined on the line. He now heads for Dubai. (op 7-2)
Beauchamp Viceroy, just caught by the 116-rated Dream Eater over 7f here ten days earlier, has winning form over C&D and was ridden aggressively from the start. He kept on finding in front and wasn't worn down until around half a furlong from home. He deserves a change of luck. (op 4-1 tchd 5-1)
Chapter And Verse(IRE) picked up a nice prize when winning the London Mile Final over C&D in September, but this was a different ball game. Wide throughout, he kept on all the way to the line and this was a fine effort at the weights, but much will depend on whether this effort has spoilt his handicap mark. (op 14-1 tchd 11-1)
The Cheka(IRE), regularly placed in Group/Listed company and with a major chance at the weights, was the only AW debutant in the field. He looked a big danger a furlong from home, but then looked one-paced in the latter stages. (op 7-2)
Viva Vettori has gained all three career success here, two over this trip, including a similar event in February. With first-time cheekpieces replacing the blinkers, he was played late down the wide outside but didn't find as much as had seemed likely. (op 11-1)
Aldovrandi(IRE), twice placed in Listed company on turf after making a winning racecourse debut over C&D back in April, hasn't been at his best in recent outings but, although this was better, he could have done without taking such a keen hold early. (op 16-1)
Autumn Blades(IRE) hadn't enjoyed much luck in two recent handicaps at Lingfield, including the previous day, but he was up against it at this level and was comfortably shaken off. (op 11-1 tchd 8-1)

7594 WILLIAMHILL.COM WILD FLOWER STKS (LISTED RACE) 1m 4f (P)
3:50 (3:54) (Class 1) 3-Y-O+

£21,004 (£7,962; £3,984; £1,986; £995; £499) **Stalls** Centre

Form RPR

-164 **1** **Cheetah**[21] 7349 3-8-9 **96**.. KirstyMilczarek 7 103
(L M Cumani) *hld up in tch in midfield: hdwy to chse ldrs 4f out: rdn to ld wl over 1f out: edgd lft fnl f: hld on wl fnl 100yds* **6/1**[3]

6311 **2** *shd* **Nideeb**[7] 7523 3-9-2 **107**.. ChrisCatlin 10 110
(C E Brittain) *mostly chsd ldr: rdn jst over 2f out: ev ch ins fnl f: r.o wl: jst hld* **2/1**[1]

1335 **3** *2* **Status Symbol (IRE)**[24] 7297 5-9-6 **95**.......................... WilliamCarson 3 105
(G C Bravery) *in tch in last trio: hdwy into midfield 5f out: switching lft and trying to get out over 2f out: hdwy 2f out: chsd ldrs ent fnl f: keeping on same pce whn swtchd rt fnl 100yds* **33/1**

0355 **4** *1/2* **Nanton (USA)**[8] 7507 8-9-6 **90**.. JoeFanning 2 104
(J S Goldie) *stdd and dropped in bhd after s: hld up in last pair: rdn and effrt ent fnl 2f: running on whn swtchd rt jst ins fnl f: nt rch ldrs* **28/1**

5-06 **5** *2 3/4* **Apprimus (IRE)**[69] 6239 4-9-6 **98**..................................(t) WilliamBuick 9 100
(M Botti) *chsd ldrs tl led after 2f: hdd 7f out: rdn to ld again over 2f out: hdd wl over 1f out: wknd u.p 1f out* **16/1**

1523 **6** *1 3/4* **Dreamspeed (IRE)**[35] 7096 3-9-0 **105**.......................... JimmyFortune 12 97
(A M Balding) *in tch in midfield: swtchd lft and effrt jst over 2f out: drvn and no imp fr over 1f out* **9/4**[2]

3056 **7** *1/2* **Hidden Brief**[7] 7523 4-9-1 **95**.. TomQueally 5 91
(M A Jarvis) *in tch towards rr: swtchd rt and effrt u.p ent fnl 2f: drvn and no hdwy over 1f out* **25/1**

00-0 **8** *2* **Top Spin (IRE)**[101] 5225 3-9-0 **97**.. JAHeffernan 8 93
(John Joseph Murphy, Ire) *t.k.h: hld up in tch in midfield: rdn and effrt jst over 2f out: unable qck u.p and btn 2f out: no ch whn swtchd rt 1f out* **20/1**

-550 **9** *11* **Montbretia**[21] 7349 5-9-1 **93**.. EddieAhern 11 70
(Edward P Harty, Ire) *led for 2f: styd prom: rdn and unable qck whn pushed lft and hmpd over 2f out: lost pl and btn 2f out: eased ins fnl f* **66/1**

0504 **10** *8* **Man Of Iron (USA)**[24] 7297 4-9-6 **106**..........................(b) KierenFallon 6 62
(L M Cumani) *racd keenly: hdwy to chse ldr 8f out: led 7f out: sn clr: hdd over 2f out: sn fdd: wl bhd and eased ins fnl f* **6/1**[3]

500 **11** *22* **Mister Green (FR)**[7] 7522 4-9-6 **92**.......................... StephenCraine 4 —
(D Flood) *stdd s: hld up in rr: lost tch over 2f out: t.o* **66/1**

2000 **12** *21* **Munsef**[24] 7297 8-9-6 **102**.. StevieDonohoe 1 —
(Ian Williams) *in tch in midfield on outer: lost pl and dropped to rr over 3f out: sn lost tch: t.o and eased fnl 2f* **25/1**

2m 29.93s (-4.57) **Going Correction** -0.175s/f (Stan)
WFA 3 from 4yo+ 6lb **12** Ran SP% **120.4**
Speed ratings (Par 111): **108,107,106,106,104 103,102,101,94,88 74,60**
toteswingers:1&2:£3.90, 1&3:£26.10, 2&3:£13.00 CSF £17.43 TOTE £5.80: £1.70, £1.30, £7.70; EX 26.90 Trifecta £593.90 Pool: £1,099.62 - 1.37 winning units..
Owner Fittocks Stud **Bred** Fittocks Stud **Trained** Newmarket, Suffolk

FOCUS
Another Listed event being run for the fourth time and, like the preceding contest, a truly run race resulting in another course record.

NOTEBOOK
Cheetah, who hadn't been disgraced in Listed company the last twice and was having only her sixth start, was 1-1 on Polytrack having won a 1m2f maiden here in August. She travelled particularly well behind the leaders before being delivered with her effort a furlong out and, despite edging to her left, she refused to give in and had her head down where it mattered. She is in the sales and this will have enhanced her value. (tchd 13-2)
Nideeb, bidding for a Polytrack hat-trick after beating the 113-rated Summit Surge in the Churchill Stakes at Lingfield seven days earlier, was racing beyond 1m2f for the first time. Always close to the pace, he had every chance inside the last 2f and battled back gamely when headed. He certainly stayed the trip and will win more races. (tchd 15-8)
Status Symbol(IRE), one of the least exposed runners in the field having only made his racecourse debut in March, finished nearly 2l behind Man Of Iron when stepped up to Listed company over C&D earlier this month, but turned that form right around. He didn't have much room to play with over 2f from home, but still had every chance soon after and this big gelding continues to progress.
Nanton(USA) has won three times on Polytrack, but he is rated 13lb lower on sand than he is on grass and there is a good reason for that. He stayed on from well of the pace to snatch fourth, but never looked like winning. (op 25-1)
Apprimus(IRE), winner of a Listed event in Italy last year and fourth in the Derby Italiano, was making his AW debut on this first start for the yard. In and out of the lead at various stages of the contest, he was still there until fading from a furlong out but there was enough here for his new trainer to work on. (tchd 14-1)
Dreamspeed(IRE), making his AW debut after finishing a decent third in the Group 3 St Simon Stakes, could only stay on at one pace and the surface remains a question mark. (op 3-1)

Hidden Brief had nearly 9l to find with Nideeb on previous week's Lingfield running and fared little better, but she is now likely to be retired to the paddocks. (op 16-1 tchd 14-1)

Top Spin(IRE), returning from a three-month break, probably didn't help himself by taking a grip early. (op 25-1)

Man Of Iron(USA), marginally best in at the weights, has been mainly disappointing for his current yard since winning the Breeders' Cup Marathon for Aidan O'Brien a year ago. His rider set him alight before halfway and he held a clear lead rounding the home turn, but put up little resistance once headed over 2f from home. (op 8-1)

Munsef Official explanation: jockey said gelding hung left

7595 WILLIAM HILL WINTER FESTIVAL @ KEMPTON E B F MAIDEN STKS 6f (P)

4:20 (4:26) (Class 5) 2-Y-O £3,140 (£934; £467; £233) **Stalls High**

Form				RPR
4	1		**Guided Missile (IRE)**[29] 7201 2-8-12 0 JimmyFortune 6	69+
			(A M Balding) *racd in midfield: rdn and outpcd 3f out: rallied u.p over 1f out: chsd ldr ins fnl f: r.o wl to ld fnl 50yds* **5/4**[1]	
5	2	½	**Quality Art (USA)**[169] 2930 2-9-3 0 GeorgeBaker 8	73+
			(G L Moore) *stdd s: t.k.h: hdwy to chse ldr over 6f out: shkn up to ld over 1f out: cajoled along ins fnl f: hdd and nt qckn fnl 50yds* **16/1**	
044	3	hd	**Whistle On By**[21] 7346 2-9-3 75 RobertWinston 7	72
			(B W Hills) *chsd ldr tl over 6f out: styd chsng ldrs: outpcd u.p 2f out: rallied ins fnl f: keeping on wl towards fin* **8/1**[3]	
06	4	1 ½	**Steenbok (IRE)**[17] 7386 2-9-3 0 WilliamBuick 10	67
			(J H M Gosden) *t.k.h early: in tch: chsd ldrs and drvn wl over 1f out: styd on same pce ins fnl f* **8/1**[3]	
04	5	nk	**Captain Noble (IRE)**[61] 6425 2-9-3 0 SteveDrowne 1	68+
			(P J Makin) *stdd and dropped in bhd after s: hld up in rr: stl disputing last ent fnl 2f: gd hdwy and rdn over 1f out: kpt on ins fnl f and gng on at fin: nt rch ldrs* **16/1**	
	6	hd	**Logans Legend (IRE)** 2-9-3 0 WilliamCarson 4	68+
			(B W Hills) *hld up off the pce towards rr: rdn and gd hdwy wl over 1f out: kpt on ins fnl f: nt rch ldrs* **20/1**	
46	7	½	**Rambo Will**[48] 6778 2-9-3 0 JimmyQuinn 9	64
			(J R Jenkins) *led tl over 1f out: wknd ins fnl f* **25/1**	
5	8	nk	**Robin Hoods Bay**[10] 7485 2-9-3 0 DaneO'Neill 3	64+
			(E F Vaughan) *stdd and dropped in bhd after s: hld up towards rr: swtchd lft and effrt on outer ent fnl 2f: kpt on but nvr gng pce to trble ldrs* **10/1**	
	9	1	**Russian Affair** 2-9-3 0 JackMitchell 11	61
			(M A Jarvis) *dwlt: racd in midfield: rdn and effrt whn swtchd rt ent fnl 2f: styd on same pce and no imp over 1f out* **4/1**[2]	
00	10	¾	**Dysios (IRE)**[17] 7386 2-9-3 0 KierenFallon 5	58+
			(L M Cumani) *in tch: rdn and unable qck over 2f out: outpcd 2f out: one pce and no threat to ldrs fr over 1f out* **50/1**	
0	11	1	**Konstantin (IRE)**[95] 5381 2-9-3 0 ChrisCatlin 2	55
			(M P Tregoning) *s.i.s: sn pushed along and outpcd in rr: kpt on fr over 1f out: n.d* **66/1**	

1m 12.89s (-0.21) **Going Correction** -0.175s/f (Stan) **11** Ran SP% **119.6**
Speed ratings (Par 96): **94,93,93,91,90 90,89,89,88,87 85**
toteswingers:1&2:£7.20, 1&3:£3.90, 2&3:£12.30 CSF £24.74 TOTE £2.30: £1.20, £5.00, £1.70; EX 25.00 Trifecta £123.90 Pool: £1,079.95 - 6.45 winning units..
Owner J C Smith **Bred** Littleton Stud **Trained** Kingsclere, Hants

FOCUS
An uncompetitive maiden.

NOTEBOOK
Guided Missile(IRE) finished a very promising fourth of 15 on her Newmarket debut last month and probably didn't need to improve much on that to win this, but it took her a long time to wear down the runner-up and on this evidence she will appreciate another furlong. (tchd 6-5 and 11-8)

Quality Art(USA), a 105,000gns 2-y-o, hadn't been seen since finishing fifth of six on his Sandown debut in June. He travelled powerfully, if a little keenly in the early stages, before leading over a furlong from home, but he was collared close to the line as lack of a recent run began to tell. This effort suggests that he has he ability to win races and begin to recoup his purchase price. (op 20-1)

Whistle On By set the standard with a mark of 75 after finishing a fair fourth in maidens at Windsor and Doncaster. Never far away, he kept battling away despite coming off the bridle over 2f from home and provides the benchmark to the form.

Steenbok(IRE), in mid-division in a couple of 7f maidens including one here, again pulled hard despite the shorter trip and though he plugged on, he lacked the pace to land a blow. He is bred to need much further than this on pedigree and now gets a mark, but he doesn't look anything special. (op 11-1)

Captain Noble(IRE), a fair fourth of ten over C&D after blowing the start when last seen in September, stayed on steadily from off the pace and better can be expected now that he gets a mark. (op 14-1)

Robin Hoods Bay caught the eye of the stewards when a running-on fifth of 11 on his Lingfield debut ten days earlier and again suggested he is capable of better, especially once handicapped. (tchd 9-1 and 11-1)

Russian Affair, a half-brother to the useful sprinter Russian Epic and winning miler Russian Spirit, proved far too green to do himself justice. (tchd 9-2)

7596 BEST ODDS GUARANTEED @ MOBILE.WILLIAMHILL.COM MAIDEN STKS 1m (P)

4:50 (4:55) (Class 5) 3-Y-O+ £2,286 (£675; £337) **Stalls High**

Form				RPR
02	1		**Majestic Bright**[35] 7086 3-8-12 0 KierenFallon 6	65+
			(L M Cumani) *chsd ldr tl led 5f out: mde rest: nudged clr ent fnl 2f: hung lft fr over 1f out: kpt on: eased nr fin* **3/1**[2]	
	2	¾	**Private Joke** 3-9-3 0 WilliamBuick 4	66+
			(J H M Gosden) *chsd ldng pair: rdn and effrt over 2f out: chsd wnr over 1f out: styd on same pce and no real imp fnl f* **11/10**[1]	
	3	3 ¼	**Lady Rossetti** 3-8-5 0 KatiaScallan(7) 7	54+
			(M P Tregoning) *dwlt: rn green and pushed along in last trio: kpt on fr over 1f out: wnt 3rd ins fnl f: no threat to ldng pair* **33/1**	
00	4	¾	**Surprise Us**[37] 7043 3-9-3 0 (p) GeorgeBaker 2	57?
			(Mrs A Duffield) *broke v fast: led tl 5f out: chsd ldr tl over 1f out: wknd ent fnl f* **50/1**	
0	5	7	**Quahadi (IRE)**[10] 7489 4-9-5 0 DaneO'Neill 5	41
			(C Gordon) *dwlt: in tch in last trio: rdn and struggling over 2f out: wl btn over 1f out* **66/1**	
0	6	2 ½	**Dashwood**[35] 7086 3-9-3 0 WilliamCarson 8	35
			(G C Bravery) *dwlt: hld up in rr: hdwy to chse ldrs 1/2-way: rdn and wknd qckly over 2f out* **33/1**	
0-	7	19	**Countenance Divine**[392] 7182 3-8-12 0 RobertWinston 3	—
			(B W Hills) *plld hrd: chsd ldrs tl hung bdly lft and lost pl bnd 4f out: wl bhd and eased fnl 2f: t.o* **4/1**[3]	

1m 39.75s (-0.05) **Going Correction** -0.175s/f (Stan)
WFA 3 from 4yo 2lb **7** Ran SP% **102.0**
Speed ratings (Par 103): **93,92,89,88,81 78,59**
toteswingers:1&2:£1.10, 1&3:£4.40, 2&3:£5.50 CSF £5.22 TOTE £3.30: £1.30, £1.30; EX 4.70 Trifecta £18.50 Pool: £327.15 - 13.06 winning units..
Owner Brighton Farm Ltd **Bred** Aston House Stud **Trained** Newmarket, Suffolk

FOCUS
A moderate maiden weakened further when Handsome King was withdrawn having burst out the back of his stall riderless with the blindfold still on (7/1, deduct 10p in the £ under R4). Not form to dwell on.
Countenance Divine Official explanation: jockey said filly ran green

7597 WILLIAM HILL WINTER FESTIVAL @ KEMPTON H'CAP 1m (P)

5:20 (5:23) (Class 5) (0-75,75) 3-Y-O+ £2,286 (£675; £337) **Stalls High**

Form				RPR
4246	1		**Zebrano**[33] 7121 4-9-5 73 (b) JamesDoyle 11	87
			(A B Haynes) *bhd: hdwy on inner over 2f out: rdn to ld ent fnl f: r.o strly and drew clr fnl f: readily: rn wout declared eyeshield* **8/1**	
0050	2	3 ½	**Gallantry**[10] 7483 8-9-0 68 JimmyQuinn 5	74
			(P Howling) *hld up wl off the pce in rr: hdwy over 2f out: chsd ldrs and rdn over 1f out: nt pce of wnr fnl f but kpt on for 2nd ins fnl f* **25/1**	
2	3	nk	**Born To Excel**[108] 4978 4-9-6 74 JAHeffernan 9	79+
			(John Joseph Murphy, Ire) *chsd ldrs: wnt 2nd over 2f out: rdn to ld 2f out: hdd ent fnl f: sn no ch w wnr: lost 2nd ins fnl f* **10/1**	
3453	4	hd	**Al Jaadi**[44] 6864 3-8-10 66 DaneO'Neill 13	70
			(W Jarvis) *in tch: swtchd lft and effrt to press ldrs jst over 1f out: outpcd by wnr and styd on same pce fnl f* **14/1**	
3402	5	3 ¼	**Pittodrie Star (IRE)**[24] 7305 3-8-12 68 DavidProbert 6	65
			(A M Balding) *dwlt: bhd and sn pushed along towards rr: c wd over 2f out: styd on fnl f: nvr trbld ldrs* **11/2**[2]	
-051	6	½	**Tuxedo**[10] 7483 5-9-6 74 LukeMorris 12	70+
			(P W Hiatt) *in tch in midfield: nt clr run and shuffled bk over 2f out: swtchd lft and kpt on fr over 1f out but no ch w ldrs* **13/2**[3]	
4005	7	2	**Dichoh**[27] 7255 7-8-13 67 (v) ChrisCatlin 1	58
			(M Madgwick) *sn wl bhd in last pair: effrt on inner ent fnl 2f: swtchd lft ent fnl f: nvr trbld ldrs* **33/1**	
0050	8	3 ½	**Charlie Smirke (USA)**[33] 7115 4-9-7 75 GeorgeBaker 10	58
			(G L Moore) *hld up wl in rr: shkn up and effrt over 2f out: no prog and wl btn 2f out: nvr trbld ldrs* **16/1**	
0001	9	1 ¾	**Dinner Date**[25] 7290 8-8-13 74 (b) LucyBarry(7) 2	53
			(T Keddy) *racd in midfield: rdn and no hdwy over 2f out: wl btn fnl 2f* **16/1**	
-133	10	nk	**Round Won (USA)**[17] 7389 3-9-4 74 ShaneKelly 4	52
			(W J Knight) *chsd ldr tl over 2f out: sn wknd* **14/1**	
5034	11	¾	**Prince Of Thebes (IRE)**[15] 7421 9-9-2 73 KierenFox(3) 14	50
			(M J Attwater) *chsd ldrs: rdn 1/2-way: wknd ent fnl 2f* **8/1**	
32	12	1 ½	**Holiday Snap**[72] 6124 4-8-13 67 JimmyFortune 8	40
			(Mrs Mary Hambro) *led and sn clr: hdd 2f out: sn fdd and wl btn* **5/1**[1]	
0633	13	shd	**Lastkingofscotland (IRE)**[7] 7526 4-9-0 73 (v) AshleyMorgan(5) 3	46
			(C R Dore) *in tch: rdn and struggling over 3f out: wknd over 2f out* **14/1**	
0600	14	15	**Wise Dennis**[36] 7062 8-9-5 73 (t) MartinLane 7	12
			(A P Jarvis) *dwlt: a in rr: lost tch wl over 2f out: eased ins fnl f* **12/1**	

1m 36.94s (-2.86) **Going Correction** -0.175s/f (Stan)
WFA 3 from 4yo+ 2lb **14** Ran SP% **122.9**
Speed ratings (Par 103): **107,103,103,103,99 99,97,93,92,91 90,89,89,74**
toteswingers:1&2:£48.90, 1&3:£23.50, 2&3:£64.30 CSF £196.47 CT £2092.90 TOTE £12.90: £5.20, £10.40, £3.80; EX 368.60 TRIFECTA Not won..
Owner Caloona Racing **Bred** P R Attwater **Trained** Limpley Stoke, Bath

FOCUS
An ordinary handicap, but a strong pace set by the favourite. The race fell into the laps of the hold-up horses and the winning time was only 0.36 seconds slower than the earlier Listed event.
T/Plt: £20.20 to a £1 stake. Pool:£113,800.11 - 4,112.13 winning tickets T/Qpdt: £3.30 to a £1 stake. Pool:£6,834.47 - 1,498.40 winning tickets SP

7576 WOLVERHAMPTON (A.W) (L-H)

Saturday, November 27

OFFICIAL GOING: Standard changing to standard to slow after race 2 (6.20).
Racing was only given the go-ahead 25 minutes after the scheduled time of the opener.
Wind: Nil Weather: Frosty

7598 EUROPEAN BREEDERS' FUND MAIDEN STKS 5f 20y(P)

5:50 (5:51) (Class 5) 2-Y-O £2,978 (£886; £442; £221) **Stalls Low**

Form				RPR
0034	1		**Mr Optimistic**[15] 7423 2-9-3 62 BarryMcHugh 11	68
			(R A Fahey) *chsd ldr tl led over 1f out: sn rdn and hung rt: r.o* **9/1**	
042	2	1	**Crystallus (IRE)**[7] 7517 2-8-12 68 SamHitchcott 6	59
			(Mrs A Duffield) *chsd ldrs: rdn over 1f out: swtchd lft ins fnl f: r.o* **9/4**[2]	
00	3	nk	**Albany Rose (IRE)**[16] 7408 2-8-12 0 FrannyNorton 3	58
			(Rae Guest) *chsd ldrs: rdn over 1f out: r.o* **16/1**	
0535	4	½	**Silk Bounty**[15] 7423 2-9-3 63 TomEaves 4	62
			(J G Given) *led: rdn and hdd over 1f out: styd on same pce ins fnl f* **8/1**[3]	
00	5	7	**Ladydolly**[28] 7240 2-8-12 0 CathyGannon 1	31
			(R Brotherton) *sn outpcd: styd on fr over 1f out: nvr nrr* **66/1**	
0	6	¾	**Wealth Whispers (IRE)**[7] 7517 2-8-12 0 LiamJones 2	29
			(P W D'Arcy) *sn outpcd: styd on ins fnl f: nvr nrr* **33/1**	
42	7	3 ¾	**Missile Command (IRE)**[39] 6995 2-9-3 0 HayleyTurner 5	20
			(W J Haggas) *chsd ldrs: rdn 1/2-way: wknd over 1f out* **5/4**[1]	
	8	1 ¼	**Billyruben**[29] 7215 2-9-0 0 AmyRyan(3) 10	16
			(Daniel Mark Loughnane, Ire) *sn outpcd* **33/1**	
00	9	1 ¾	**Buon Compleanno (IRE)**[16] 7404 2-8-12 30 PaulQuinn 8	—
			(A Berry) *mid-div: sn pushed along and hung lft: wknd 1/2-way* **100/1**	
	10	4 ½	**Everybody Out** 2-9-3 0 GrahamGibbons 7	—
			(R Hollinshead) *s.s: outpcd* **33/1**	

63.37 secs (1.07) **Going Correction** +0.175s/f (Slow) **10** Ran SP% **113.5**
Speed ratings (Par 96): **98,96,95,95,83 82,76,74,71,64**
toteswingers:1&2:£3.90, 1&3:£13.50, 2&3:£8.20 CSF £28.16 TOTE £5.40: £1.40, £1.10, £7.10; EX 37.70.
Owner Frank Lenny Financial **Bred** C J Murfitt **Trained** Musley Bank, N Yorks
■ Stewards' Enquiry : Barry McHugh one-day ban: careless riding (Dec 11)

The Form Book, Raceform Ltd, Compton, RG20 6NL

FOCUS
The slow surface and excessive kick-back made it difficult to make ground from off the pace and the first four home were amongst the pace-setters from the off. The form is clearly limited but the time was good. A personal best from the winner.

NOTEBOOK
Mr Optimistic, rated just 62 and having his eighth start, took it up once in line for home and despite drifting right was always doing just enough. He looks a tough little customer. (op 8-1 tchd 10-1)

Crystallus(IRE), 25-1 when beaten a neck at Lingfield on her third start, has an official mark of 68. In receipt of the 5lb sex allowance, she could not get the better of the winner. (tchd 2-1)

Albany Rose(IRE), badly hampered when well beaten here on just her second start, seemed to turn in a much improved effort and this opens up the handicap route.

Silk Bounty, rated 63 and having his eighth start, took them along but is thoroughly exposed now.

Ladydolly, last on her two previous starts, did best of those coming from off the pace.

Wealth Whispers(IRE) still looks inexperienced and will be suited by a good deal further in time. (op 28-1)

Missile Command(IRE), turned over at odds-on on his first two starts, was in trouble at halfway and in the end was eased. His supporters must surely have lost faith now. (op 11-8 tchd 11-10)

7599 PLAY BINGO AT TOTESPORT.COM (S) STKS 1m 1f 103y(P)
6:20 (6:20) (Class 6) 3-Y-O+ **£1,535** (£453; £226) **Stalls** Low

Form				RPR
0033	**1**		**New Beginning (IRE)**[42] [6930] 6-9-3 60..................(p) GrahamGibbons 4 (J Mackie) *midfield: hdwy 2f out: r.o to ld 1f out: readily* **11/4**[2]	67+
1245	**2**	2 ½	**Sworn Tigress (GER)**[18] [1916] 5-8-13 76..........(b[1]) MatthewDavies(3) 10 (George Baker) *in rr: pushed along 4f out: hdwy on wd outside wl over 1f out: styd on ins fnl f to take 2nd cl home: no ch w wnr* **2/1**[1]	59
4110	**3**	hd	**High Five Society**[24] [7307] 6-8-12 73..........................(b) RyanClark(5) 6 (S R Bowring) *hld up: hdwy over 1f out: styd on ins fnl f: nt quite pce of ldrs* **9/2**[3]	60
4500	**4**	2	**Forbidden (IRE)**[7] [7529] 7-9-3 59..................................(tp) AdamKirby 13 (I W McInnes) *hld up: rdn and hdwy whn nt clr run and swtchd lft over 1f out: styd on ins fnl f: nt pce to rch ldrs* **9/1**	55
0062	**5**	nk	**Special Cuvee**[11] [7472] 4-9-3 56..................................(bt) CathyGannon 8 (Mrs A M Thorpe) *dwlt: hld up: hdwy 2f out: rdn over 1f out: one pce ins fnl f* **14/1**	55
26	**6**	1 ¾	**Tenhoo**[8] [7504] 4-9-3 52.. FrannyNorton 12 (E J Alston) *midfield: rdn 3f out: hdwy over 1f out: no ex ins fnl f* **6/1**	51
0006	**7**	1 ¼	**Jibrrya**[25] [7281] 3-8-11 50.. AmyRyan(3) 9 (D Nicholls) *prom: led over 6f out: kicked clr over 2f out: edgd rt and hdd 1f out: wknd ins fnl f* **33/1**	48
6320	**8**	4	**Magic Spirit**[23] [7315] 3-8-9 54.......................................(b) SamHitchcott 5 (Miss Suzy Smith) *trckd ldrs: rdn over 3f out: losing pl whn n.m.r 1f out: n.d after* **33/1**	35
000-	**9**	2 ¾	**Spares And Repairs**[538] [2746] 7-8-10 42................ NicolaJackson(7) 11 (R Hollinshead) *hld up: hdwy 2f out: no imp on ldrs: wknd over 1f out* **50/1**	34
-000	**10**	9	**Sams Spirit**[68] [6242] 4-9-0 42...............................(b) MichaelO'Connell(3) 1 (J A McShane) *racd keenly: trckd ldrs: wnt 2nd over 4f out: rdn over 3f out: wknd over 1f out* **66/1**	15
56/0	**11**	6	**Jack Jicaro**[90] [5560] 4-9-3 43.. NeilChalmers 3 (N J Vaughan) *racd keenly: led: hdd over 6f out: wknd 3f out* **66/1**	—
0-0	**12**	38	**Mon Mon (IRE)**[25] [7282] 3-8-9 0..(t) BarryMcHugh 7 (B Storey) *prom tl rdn and wknd over 3f out: sn wl bhd* **100/1**	—

2m 4.00s (2.30) **Going Correction** +0.175s/f (Slow)
WFA 3 from 4yo+ 3lb **12** Ran SP% **121.0**
Speed ratings (Par 101): **96,93,93,91,91 90,88,85,82,74 69,35**
toteswingers:1&2:£1.80, 1&3:£3.00, 2&3:£2.40 CSF £8.61 TOTE £4.80: £2.80, £1.10, £1.10; EX 11.50.The winner was sold to Richard Fahey for 6,000gns.
Owner Caroline Lawson and Sarah Underwood **Bred** Airlie Stud And Sir Thomas Pilkington **Trained** Church Broughton , Derbys

FOCUS
Plenty of deadwood in this seller. The winner didn't need to improve, with the second and third not at their best.

7600 PLAY BLACKJACK AT TOTESPORT.COM H'CAP 1m 1f 103y(P)
6:50 (6:51) (Class 4) (0-85,85) 3-Y-O+ **£3,626** (£1,079; £539; £269) **Stalls** Low

Form				RPR
0022	**1**		**West End Lad**[24] [7304] 7-8-10 **74**..........................(b) RussKennemore(3) 6 (S R Bowring) *trckd ldrs: rdn 3f out: r.o to ld ins fnl f: won gng away* **12/1**	86
5305	**2**	3 ¾	**Beetuna (IRE)**[22] [7337] 5-9-0 **75**.. SamHitchcott 3 (D Bourton) *midfield: hdwy gng wl 3f out: effrt to chal over 1f out: nt pce of wnr fnl 100yds* **7/2**[1]	79
0004	**3**	nk	**Kidlat**[3] [7548] 5-8-12 **73**... GrahamGibbons 5 (A Bailey) *prom: led over 3f out: hdd ins fnl f: styd on same pce ins fnl f* **4/1**[2]	76
1	**4**	nk	**Buaiteoir (FR)**[57] [6546] 4-9-1 **76**.. LiamJones 10 (P W D'Arcy) *hld up: hdwy 2f out: chalng fr 1f out: no ex fnl 75yds* **5/1**[3]	79
2410	**5**	½	**Urban Space**[10] [7488] 4-9-2 **77**.. CathyGannon 11 (C R Dore) *bhd: hdwy wl over 1f out: sn chsd ldrs: styd on same pce fnl 100yds* **18/1**	79
0441	**6**	½	**Kimberley Downs (USA)**[17] [7397] 4-8-11 **72**............. DuranFentiman 4 (N Wilson) *w ldr: pushed along and lost pl 4f out: sn u.p: one pce fr over 1f out* **14/1**	73
0031	**7**	1 ¾	**Cobo Bay**[7] [7529] 5-9-5 **80**..(b) HayleyTurner 8 (C R Dore) *racd keenly: midfield: hdwy 4f out: rdn and btn over 1f out* **13/2**	77
2052	**8**	2	**She's A Character**[19] [7382] 3-9-3 **81**..........................(p) BarryMcHugh 9 (R A Fahey) *hld up: struggling over 2f out: nvr on terms* **11/1**	74
0504	**9**	6	**Iron Out (USA)**[16] [7414] 4-9-1 **76**.. AdamKirby 7 (R Hollinshead) *midfield: rdn and wknd over 1f out* **14/1**	56
0100	**10**	7	**Hidden Glory**[38] [7012] 3-9-7 **85**.. TomEaves 2 (J G Given) *led: rdn and hdd over 3f out: wknd wl over 1f out* **12/1**	50

2m 1.94s (0.24) **Going Correction** +0.175s/f (Slow)
WFA 3 from 4yo+ 3lb **10** Ran SP% **114.5**
Speed ratings (Par 105): **105,101,101,101,100 100,98,96,91,85**
toteswingers:1&2:£9.10, 1&3:£9.80, 2&3:£2.80 CSF £52.87 CT £201.46 TOTE £12.30: £4.40, £3.00, £1.30; EX 86.20.
Owner K Nicholls **Bred** Keith Nicholls **Trained** Edwinstowe, Notts

FOCUS
A competitive 72-85 handicap and plenty in contention turning in but in the end a convincing winner. The form is rated around the second and third.

7601 PLAY ROULETTE AT TOTESPORT.COM (S) STKS 1m 141y(P)
7:20 (7:20) (Class 6) 3-Y-O+ **£1,535** (£453; £226) **Stalls** Low

Form				RPR
3426	**1**		**Majuro (IRE)**[60] [6447] 6-9-0 90.. AndreaAtzeni 3 (S C Williams) *trckd ldrs gng wl: led under 3f out: qcknd clr over 1f out: eased down ins fnl f* **2/7**[1]	91+
2342	**2**	10	**Orchard Supreme**[74] [6054] 7-9-5 84.............................. J-PGuillambert 1 (J Akehurst) *in tch: effrt 3f out: wnt 2nd and pushed along over 2f out: no ch w wnr fr over 1f out* **9/2**[2]	68
4406	**3**	hd	**Ella Grace (USA)**[12] [7467] 3-8-6 57..........................(b[1]) BarryMcHugh 11 (R A Fahey) *hld up: hdwy 3f out: rdn to chse ldrs over 2f out: sn no imp* **7/1**[3]	58
4360	**4**	6	**Saving Grace**[7] [7529] 4-9-0 50.. FrannyNorton 7 (E J Alston) *led: hdd over 3f out: wknd over 2f out* **12/1**	49
-000	**5**	17	**Old Firm**[82] [5821] 4-8-11 40.................................... MichaelO'Connell(3) 4 (J A McShane) *s.s: rcvrd to r w ldr after 1f: led over 3f out: sn hdd: wknd over 2f out* **50/1**	10
5650	**6**	19	**Kirkby's Gem**[43] [6897] 3-8-6 45..(b) PaulQuinn 9 (A Berry) *a struggling and bhd: nvr on terms* **40/1**	—
66-0	**7**	4 ½	**Chifah**[24] [7300] 3-8-3 49.. AndrewHeffernan(3) 2 (R J Price) *trckd ldrs: lost pl 5f out: struggling and bhd fnl 4f* **50/1**	—
0000	**8**	10	**Whispering Ridge**[16] [7413] 3-8-11 32............................(v) LiamJones 10 (M Wellings) *hld up in tch: rdn and hdd 3f out* **80/1**	—

1m 51.01s (0.51) **Going Correction** +0.175s/f (Slow)
WFA 3 from 4yo+ 3lb **8** Ran SP% **123.7**
Speed ratings (Par 101): **104,95,94,89,74 57,53,44**
toteswingers:1&2:£1.10, 1&3:£2.00, 2&3:£1.60 CSF £2.49 TOTE £1.10: £1.02, £1.20, £1.90; EX 2.70.The winner was bought in for 10,500gns.
Owner S Pecoraro **Bred** Tally-Ho Stud **Trained** Newmarket, Suffolk

FOCUS
The going was changed to standard to slow ahead of this seller, in which the first two stood out. The runner-up was below form and the winner is rated in line with this year's turf form.

7602 PLAY SLOTS AT TOTESPORT.COM MAIDEN STKS (DIV I) 7f 32y(P)
7:50 (7:57) (Class 5) 2-Y-O **£1,683** (£501; £250; £125) **Stalls** High

Form				RPR
3	**1**		**Rutland Boy**[15] [7427] 2-9-3 0... EddieAhern 9 (E A L Dunlop) *hld up: hdwy 3f out: rdn wl over 1f out: led ins fnl f: r.o wl and in command towards fin* **7/4**[1]	78
5	**2**	1 ¾	**School For Scandal (IRE)**[10] [7479] 2-9-3 0...................... GregFairley 3 (M Johnston) *prom: pushed along 3f out: outpcd over 1f out: swtchd rt ins fnl f: rallied to chse wnr towards fin: no imp* **5/2**[3]	74
2	**3**	1 ½	**Fifth In Line (IRE)**[8] [7503] 2-8-9 0.............................. SophieDoyle(3) 10 (J A Osborne) *racd keenly: prom: led 3f out: rdn and hdd ins fnl f: no ex fnl 75yds* **8/1**	65
00	**4**	1 ¼	**Pyrenean**[24] [7302] 2-8-12 0... TomEaves 6 (J G Given) *hld up: nt clr run over 2f out: sn pushed along: no imp on ldrs and one pce fnl f* **66/1**	62
00	**5**	2 ¾	**Certral**[14] [7448] 2-8-9 0... MatthewDavies(3) 1 (George Baker) *led: rdn 3f out: hdd 3f out: wknd ins fnl f* **2/1**[2]	55
3200	**6**	26	**Infectious (IRE)**[43] [6893] 2-8-12 60............................... GrahamGibbons 7 (Miss M E Rowland) *trckd ldrs: effrt 3f out: wknd 2f out* **50/1**	—

1m 31.64s (2.04) **Going Correction** +0.175s/f (Slow) **6** Ran SP% **112.8**
Speed ratings (Par 96): **95,93,91,89,86 57**
toteswingers:1&2:£1.10, 1&3:£1.40, 2&3:£1.60 CSF £6.60 TOTE £1.40: £1.10, £1.60; EX 6.40.
Owner Rutland Park Racing **Bred** Rabbah Bloodstock Limited **Trained** Newmarket, Suffolk

FOCUS
Racing continued after a lengthy inspection. Four were keen to lead and keep out of the kick-back so the pace was strong. The winner built on his promising debut, with improvement from the runner-up too.

NOTEBOOK
Rutland Boy, who achieved an RPR of 73 when runner-up on his debut here two weeks earlier, was happy to accept a lead. Making his effort widest of all, he went to the front travelling strongly and scored with something in hand. He should make a decent handicapper at three. (op 11-8 tchd 5-4)

School For Scandal(IRE), a handsome son of Pivotal, found himself outpaced going into the final turn. Pulled outside, he stayed on to snatch second spot in the closing stages. He will improve again and, likely to be better suited by a mile, he should take his maiden. (tchd 2-1)

Fifth In Line(IRE), 50-1 when runner-up here a week earlier, kicked for home two furlongs out but was only third best with no apparent excuse at the line. (op 5-1)

Pyrenean, stoutly bred on her dam's side, showed a lot more than on two back-end outings on turf. She looks the type to do better in handicaps next year. (op 50-1)

Certral, well beaten on his two starts, came in for market support but after racing bang in the firing line was beaten turning in. (op 7-2)

7603 PLAY SLOTS AT TOTESPORT.COM MAIDEN STKS (DIV II) 7f 32y(P)
8:20 (8:21) (Class 5) 2-Y-O **£1,683** (£501; £250; £125) **Stalls** High

Form				RPR
	1		**Coral Moon (IRE)** 2-8-12 0.. BarryMcHugh 7 (R A Fahey) *racd keenly: chsd ldr: str chal fr over 1f out: edgd rt ins fnl f: styd on to ld fnl stride* **9/2**[2]	82+
0	**2**	nk	**Arrow Storm (USA)**[93] [5453] 2-9-3 0......................... RichardKingscote 5 (Tom Dascombe) *led: rdn and hung rt whn hrd pressed ins fnl f: hdd fnl stride* **6/1**[3]	86+
5662	**3**	7	**Scented**[30] [7197] 2-8-12 72... EddieAhern 3 (W J Haggas) *chsd ldrs: rdn over 2f out and nt qckn: n.d to front pair after* **4/7**[1]	64
06	**4**	14	**Marie Du Plessis**[116] [4668] 2-8-12 0................................ GregFairley 9 (M Johnston) *chsd ldrs: pushed along over 3f out: sn wknd* **8/1**	30+
	5	1 ½	**Monadreen Dancer** 2-8-12 0.. AndreaAtzeni 8 (Daniel Mark Loughnane, Ire) *s.v.s: bhd: in tch w field 5f out: effrt over 3f out: wknd over 2f out* **25/1**	26+
	6	7	**Elegant Star (IRE)** 2-8-12 0.. WilliamCarson 6 (D Morris) *towards rr: pushed along over 3f out: sn lft bhd* **33/1**	9

1m 31.41s (1.81) **Going Correction** +0.175s/f (Slow) **6** Ran SP% **114.0**
Speed ratings (Par 96): **96,95,87,71,69 61**
toteswingers:1&2:£6.00, 1&3:£1.20, 2&3:£1.30 CSF £31.10 TOTE £10.00: £4.80, £1.80; EX 43.10.
Owner Sir Robert Ogden **Bred** Sir Robert Ogden **Trained** Musley Bank, N Yorks

■ Stewards' Enquiry : Barry McHugh two-day ban: used whip with excessive frequency (Dec 12-13)

FOCUS
A depleted field and two started slowly, one especially so. There was little depth but the front pair pulled clear and produced decent efforts. If anything the form could be underrated.

NOTEBOOK
Coral Moon(IRE), a newcomer out of a mare that finished runner-up in the Lancashire Oaks, was quite keen. Driven upsides once in line for home, she stayed on in very willing fashion to pull the prize out of the fire near the line. She has plenty of size but still looks weak and should make a useful performer over further next year. (op 5-1)
Arrow Storm(USA), who showed little on his debut on the all-weather at Lingfield in August, took them along and saw off the odds-on favourite before the final turn. He edged right and was chinned on the line. He can almost certainly go one better. (op 7-1 tchd 15-2)
Scented, beaten favourite in a claimer on her previous start, is rated 72. She found very little under pressure and ran nowhere near her official mark. (op 8-13)
Marie Du Plessis, having her third start, had shown very little in two outings on turf in the summer. She was under pressure a long way out and it remains to be seen if she is better than this in handicaps company at three. (op 15-2)
Monadreen Dancer showed a glimmer of ability before tiring after losing many lengths at the start.

7604 DINE IN THE HORIZONS RESTAURANT H'CAP (DIV I) 7f 32y(P)
8:50 (8:50) (Class 6) (0-55,55) 3-Y-0+ **£1,364** (£403; £201) **Stalls** High

Form RPR
0004 **1** **Talent Scout (IRE)**[8] 7502 4-9-0 **53**......................(b[1]) GrahamGibbons 10 62
(T D Walford) *chsd ldrs: wnt 2nd over 2f out: led over 1f out: edgd lft ins fnl f: rdn out and r.o* **7/2**[1]
0500 **2** *1 1/4* **Itsthursdayalready**[15] 7425 3-8-11 **51**............................... EddieAhern 2 57
(W M Brisbourne) *hld up: hdwy 3f out: n.m.r briefly 2f out: prog to take 2nd ins fnl f: styd on: nt rch wnr* **8/1**
0500 **3** *1 1/4* **Lord Deevert**[3] 7555 5-8-11 **55**......................................(p) RyanClark[(5)] 3 57
(W G M Turner) *chsd ldrs: effrt 3f out: nt qckn over 1f out: kpt on ins fnl f: nt quite pce of ldrs* **7/2**[1]
3400 **4** *1/2* **A Pocketful Of Rye (IRE)**[15] 7426 3-8-6 **49**.......... MichaelStainton[(3)] 1 50
(P Howling) *bhd: u.p 3f out: hdwy 2f out: styd on ins fnl f: nt pce to rch ldrs* **7/1**[2]
6045 **5** *1 1/4* **Stargazing (IRE)**[24] 7300 4-8-12 **54**......................(v) MatthewDavies[(3)] 8 51
(B J Meehan) *chsd ldr: led over 2f out: rdn and hdd over 1f out: no ex fnl 75yds* **7/2**[1]
6500 **6** *8* **December**[10] 7487 4-8-10 **49**......................................(vt) CathyGannon 11 25
(Mrs C A Dunnett) *led: clr to 3f out: hdd over 2f out: wknd wl over 1f out* **11/1**
0400 **7** *9* **Only A Game (IRE)**[15] 7425 5-9-1 **54**..............................(vt) AdamKirby 4 —
(I W McInnes) *bhd: rdn over 3f out: nvr on terms* **15/2**[3]
0530 **8** *4* **Magenta Strait**[15] 7426 3-8-8 **55**.................................... JackDuern[(7)] 12 —
(R Hollinshead) *missed break: a bhd* **25/1**

1m 30.99s (1.39) **Going Correction** +0.175s/f (Slow)
WFA 3 from 4yo+ 1lb 8 Ran SP% **114.2**
Speed ratings (Par 101): **99,97,96,95,94 85,74,70**
toteswingers:1&2:£5.10, 1&3:£3.70, 2&3:£5.40 CSF £32.63 CT £104.81 TOTE £6.20: £2.20, £1.10, £1.10; EX 34.80.
Owner John Stacey **Bred** Johnston King **Trained** Sheriff Hutton, N Yorks

FOCUS
Part one of a weak, low-grade 49-55 handicap run at a furious pace. The race is rated around the second and third.

7605 DINE IN THE HORIZONS RESTAURANT H'CAP (DIV II) 7f 32y(P)
9:20 (9:20) (Class 6) (0-55,55) 3-Y-0+ **£1,364** (£403; £201) **Stalls** High

Form RPR
0040 **1** **Shamarlane**[57] 6536 3-9-1 **55**..(p) CathyGannon 1 65
(Daniel Miley, Ire) *chsd ldrs: rdn to ld over 1f out: r.o wl and in command towards fin* **9/4**[1]
2125 **2** *2 1/4* **Join Up**[10] 7487 4-8-12 **54**... RossAtkinson[(3)] 4 58
(W M Brisbourne) *trckd ldrs: rdn over 1f out: wnt 2nd ins fnl f: styd on: nt trble wnr towards fin* **11/4**[2]
6043 **3** *1 1/2* **Olympic Dream**[31] 7161 4-8-13 **55**......................(p) MichaelO'Connell[(3)] 8 55
(M Herrington) *in tch: rdn 2f out: styd on ins fnl f: nt pce to chal ldrs ins fnl f* **5/1**[3]
4540 **4** *3/4* **Pie Poudre**[114] 4733 3-8-11 **51**..................................... GrahamGibbons 9 49
(R Brotherton) *hld up: hdwy to go prom 5f out: rdn and ev ch wl over 1f out: nt qckn ins fnl f: styd on same pce fnl 100yds* **20/1**
1600 **5** *shd* **Fair Bunny**[15] 7425 3-9-0 **54** ow1.......................................(b) AdamKirby 2 52
(A D Brown) *led: rdn and hdd over 1f out: no ex fnl 75yds* **9/1**
3205 **6** *2 1/4* **Novillero**[152] 3520 3-8-9 **49**.. LukeMorris 10 41
(J C Fox) *hld up: u.p 3f out: nvr able to chal* **17/2**
000 **7** *1* **Royal Envoy (IRE)**[15] 7425 7-8-5 **51**.............................. LauraSimpson[(7)] 5 40
(P Howling) *hld up: u.p over 2f out: nvr on terms w ldrs* **14/1**
6440 **8** *3* **Reddy To Star (IRE)**[14] 7450 3-9-0 **54**.......................(p) BarryMcHugh 7 35
(Julie Camacho) *chsd ldr: ev ch wl over 1f out: wknd ins fnl f* **16/1**

1m 31.08s (1.48) **Going Correction** +0.175s/f (Slow)
WFA 3 from 4yo+ 1lb 8 Ran SP% **111.9**
Speed ratings (Par 101): **98,95,93,92,92 90,89,85**
toteswingers:1&2:£2.20, 1&3:£2.90, 2&3:£3.60 CSF £8.12 CT £25.93 TOTE £3.20: £1.10, £2.50, £1.80; EX 11.60.
Owner Mark Connolly **Bred** John M Troy **Trained** Ashford, Co. Wicklow

FOCUS
Part two of the 49-55 handicap, but the pace was not as frenetic this time. A clear personal best from the winner.
T/Plt: £57.10 to a £1 stake. Pool:£85,903.62 - 1,096.718 winning tickets T/Qpdt: £30.70 to a £1 stake. Pool:£8,181.17 - 196.65 winning tickets DO

7591 KEMPTON (A.W) (R-H)
Sunday, November 28

OFFICIAL GOING: Standard
Wind: Light, half against Weather: Fine, cold

7607 BOXINGDAYRACES.CO.UK H'CAP 6f (P)
2:15 (2:15) (Class 7) (0-50,57) 3-Y-0+ **£1,364** (£403; £201) **Stalls** High

Form RPR
3331 **1** **Cheery Cat (USA)**[9] 7506 6-9-3 **57**......................(v) MatthewCosham[(7)] 4 65
(J Balding) *pressed ldr: rdn to ld over 1f out: drvn and kpt on fnl f* **2/1**[1]
00/0 **2** *1* **River Bounty**[25] 7299 5-9-3 **50**... KierenFallon 7 55
(A P Jarvis) *led: drvn and hdd over 1f out: kpt on same pce* **5/1**
-00 **3** *1* **Jonny Ebeneezer**[11] 7477 11-9-2 **49**......................(be) StephenCraine 10 51
(D Flood) *sn trckd ldng pair: poised to chal in bhd them over 1f out: rdn ent fnl f: fnd nil* **25/1**
0003 **4** *shd* **Song Of Praise**[31] 7192 4-9-3 **50**................................... FrannyNorton 5 52+
(M Blanshard) *hld up last: rdn and effrt over 2f out: grad clsd but nvr on terms* **5/2**[2]
0040 **5** *1 1/2* **Alana Banana (IRE)**[11] 7477 3-9-2 **49**.............................. JimCrowley 9 46
(J Akehurst) *chsd ldrs: rdn and outpcd wl over 2f out: tried to cl over 1f out: one pce fnl f* **9/2**[3]
4500 **6** *2 3/4* **Ballyvonane (USA)**[194] 2217 3-8-13 **49**.................. MichaelStainton[(3)] 3 37
(D C Griffiths) *in tch: outpcd and rdn sn after 1/2-way: effrt 2f out: wknd fnl f* **40/1**
0004 **7** *2* **Braddock (IRE)**[25] 7299 7-9-3 **50**......................................(t) ChrisCatlin 2 32
(K O Cunningham-Brown) *prom on outer 2f: last and struggling over 2f out* **16/1**

1m 12.59s (-0.51) **Going Correction** -0.125s/f (Stan) 7 Ran SP% **108.9**
Speed ratings (Par 97): **98,96,95,95,93 89,86**
Tote Swingers: 1&2 £2.70, 1&3 £6.10, 2&3 £8.30 CSF £11.19 CT £161.52 TOTE £2.60: £1.60, £2.30; EX 14.00 Trifecta £83.90 Pool: £460.45 - 4.06 winning units..
Owner The Cataractonium Racing Syndicate **Bred** K L Ramsay & Sarah K Ramsay **Trained** Scrooby, Notts

FOCUS
A moderate sprint handicap. The form is rated around the winner's latest Wolverhampton win.

7608 EUROPEAN BREEDERS' FUND MAIDEN FILLIES' STKS 6f (P)
2:45 (2:49) (Class 5) 2-Y-0 **£3,076** (£915; £457; £228) **Stalls** High

Form RPR
1 **Echo Ridge (IRE)** 2-9-0 0.. JimCrowley 7 75+
(R M Beckett) *chsd ldrs in 5th: pushed along bef 1/2-way: no imp tl picked up wl jst over 1f out: r.o to ld last 50yds* **7/2**[3]
0 **2** *3/4* **Fairy Familiar (USA)**[15] 7448 2-9-0 0........................... KierenFallon 5 74
(L M Cumani) *mde most: drvn over 1f out: styd on: hdd and outpcd last 50yds* **5/2**[2]
3 **3** *2* **Palais Glide**[11] 7485 2-9-0 0... JimmyFortune 12 67
(R Hannon) *pressed ldr to 2f out: one pce u.p over 1f out* **6/4**[1]
4 *2* **Encore View** 2-9-0 0.. DavidProbert 10 61+
(A M Balding) *s.i.s: sn chsd ldng pair: shkn up over 2f out: tried to cl over 1f out: fdd fnl f* **6/1**
0 **5** *2 1/2* **Heavenly Pursuit**[41] 6986 2-9-0 0............................... StephenCraine 11 54
(J R Boyle) *chsd ldng pair: shkn up over 2f out: tried to cl over 1f out: sn wknd* **40/1**
0 **6** *5* **Pink Sari**[11] 7485 2-9-0 0.. CathyGannon 8 39
(P J Makin) *dwlt: a off the pce in last trio: shkn up and no prog over 2f out* **66/1**
7 *4* **Radiant Dream** 2-9-0 0.. DaneO'Neill 9 27
(Pat Eddery) *dwlt and stdd s: hld up last: a wl off the pce* **8/1**
8 *11* **Ippi N Tombi (IRE)** 2-8-7 0.. AliceHaynes[(7)] 6 —
(P S McEntee) *reluctant to enter stalls: prom whn hung lft bnd 4f out to 3f out: bhd after: t.o* **100/1**

1m 13.0s (-0.10) **Going Correction** -0.125s/f (Stan) 8 Ran SP% **121.1**
Speed ratings (Par 93): **95,94,91,88,85 78,73,58**
Tote Swingers: 1&2 £3.00, 1&3 £2.20, 2&3 £2.40 CSF £13.59 TOTE £3.70: £1.60, £1.70, £1.10; EX 15.90 Trifecta £31.70 Pool: £666.37 - 15.55 winning units..
Owner J C Smith **Bred** Littleton Stud **Trained** Whitsbury, Hants

FOCUS
Some powerful connections were represented and this looked a fair fillies' maiden for the time of year. A nice start from thwe winner and the form is rated through the third.

NOTEBOOK
Echo Ridge(IRE), who is out of a 6f Listed winner, looks a pretty useful type. She came off the bridle around the bend into the straight, but showed a good attitude, gradually getting the idea to get on top late on. She had been due to make her debut back in July, so has been on the go for a while, but there should still be plenty of improvement to come. (op 11-4 tchd 4-1)
Fairy Familiar(USA), who didn't see her race out over 7f at Wolverhampton on her debut, stepped up on that form with a good effort behind quite a nice type. She should progress again. (op 4-1)
Palais Glide couldn't justify favouritism, but she still confirmed the promise she showed when third on her debut over this trip at Lingfield, and she can find an ordinary maiden. (op 15-8 tchd 2-1 and 9-4 in a place)
Encore View, who is out of a 7f winner, ran as though in need of the outing, but she showed ability. (op 8-1)
Heavenly Pursuit stepped up on the form she showed first time out at Windsor, but she's probably more of a handicap prospect. (op 33-1)

7609 WIN A KIA VENGA @ KEMPTON.CO.UK MEDIAN AUCTION MAIDEN STKS (DIV I) 1m (P)
3:20 (3:21) (Class 5) 2-Y-0 **£1,944** (£574; £287) **Stalls** High

Form RPR
5 **1** **Amerthyst**[48] 6804 2-8-12 0... DaneO'Neill 3 65
(Miss Jo Crowley) *hld up in rr: stdy prog to take 5th 3f out: rdn 2f out: styd on stoutly after: led last stride* **8/1**
0 **2** *shd* **Top Diktat**[18] 7385 2-9-3 0... KierenFallon 11 70
(Sir Michael Stoute) *led: narrowly hdd over 2f out: drvn ahd over 1f out: collared last stride* **5/1**[3]
3 *2 1/4* **Ringstead Bay (FR)** 2-9-3 0... JimCrowley 10 65
(R M Beckett) *chsd ldrs but sn pushed along: outpcd over 2f out: kpt on again to take 3rd wl ins fnl f* **10/1**
402 **4** *1 3/4* **Sylas Ings**[11] 7479 2-9-3 73.. IanMongan 2 61
(P M Phelan) *pressed ldr over 4f out: rdn to ld narrowly over 2f out: hdd over 1f out: wknd quite qckly fnl f* **11/2**
4 **5** *nk* **For What (USA)**[15] 7452 2-9-3 0.. ChrisCatlin 1 60
(D R Lanigan) *sn prom: chsd ldng pair over 3f out: drvn and no imp 2f out: fdd* **13/8**[1]
2000 **6** *1 3/4* **Alantina**[12] 7469 2-8-10 42...................................... DannyBrock[(7)] 4 56
(J R Jenkins) *pushed along in last after 3f: sme hdwy over 2f out: plugged on u.p: nrst fin* **100/1**
7 *nk* **Laser Blazer** 2-9-3 0.. DavidProbert 7 55
(Miss S L Davison) *s.i.s: wl in rr and pushed along: sme hdwy fr 3f out: rdn and kpt on: nrst fin* **66/1**
04 **8** *3 1/4* **Frederick William**[108] 5006 2-9-3 0................................ SteveDrowne 8 48+
(P J Makin) *t.k.h: trapped bhd wkng rival 1/2-way and dropped to rr: rdn and no prog 3f out* **9/2**[2]
00 **9** *5* **Phantom House**[25] 7302 2-8-10 0 ow1........................ RobertLButler[(3)] 6 32
(B W Duke) *sn pushed along: a in rr: bhd fnl 2f* **100/1**
4200 **10** *10* **Baileys Moneypenny**[20] 7379 2-8-12 70.........................(p) TomEaves 9 —
(J G Given) *chsd ldr over 3f: sn wknd rapidly: t.o* **25/1**

1m 39.55s (-0.25) **Going Correction** -0.125s/f (Stan) 10 Ran SP% **115.8**
Speed ratings (Par 96): **96,95,93,91,91 89,89,86,81,71**
Tote Swingers: 1&2 £6.20, 1&3 £9.30, 2&3 £8.60 CSF £46.81 TOTE £8.20: £1.70, £1.90, £2.60; EX 48.10 Trifecta £452.80 Pool: £783.32 - 1.28 winning units..
Owner Kilstone Limited **Bred** Mrs Sally Roberts **Trained** Whitcombe, Dorset

The Form Book, Raceform Ltd, Compton, RG20 6NL

FOCUS
An ordinary maiden, although the time was 0.74 seconds quicker than the following division. The first two improved but the form is limited.

NOTEBOOK
Amerthyst, who made the running on her debut at Salisbury, was ridden differently on this first try on Polytrack. She had ground to make up with 2f to go, but came with a sustained run down the outside to get up on the post. The extra furlong was clearly in her favour. (tchd 9-1)
Top Diktat improved on what he showed in a similar race over 7f here on his debut. After leading in the straight he battled on to to take the measure of the fourth horse, but was just pipped by the filly. A step up in trip will suit him and he should make a fair handicapper. (op 4-1)
Ringstead Bay(FR) comes from a good family in Germany and he made a pleasing debut, staying on nicely in the final furlong after sticking to the inside all the way. He will benefit from the experience. (tchd 9-1)
Sylas Ings set just a fair target with a BHA mark of 73, and probably ran below that level. He had every chance in the straight as he duelled with the runner-up but, just as he had in recent races over a furlong less, he did not see out his race well. His best trip remains open to conjecture. (tchd 9-2)
For What(USA) was fitted with a blindfold and Monty Roberts rug for stalls entry. Trapped wide from his outside stall, he was close enough in third place entering the straight but lacked the pace to get in a blow at the leaders. He did not build on his debut effort but the minor drop in trip was not ideal. (op 7-4 tchd 15-8)
Laser Blazer, who was withdrawn after misbehaving in the stalls on his intended debut, made late headway and will be suited by further, being out of a winner at 2m.
Frederick William was well supported on this AW debut, but he was hampered on the home turn and was never a factor. He is now qualified for handicaps. (op 15-2)

7610 WIN A KIA VENGA @ KEMPTON.CO.UK MEDIAN AUCTION MAIDEN STKS (DIV II) 1m (P)
3:50 (3:53) (Class 5) 2-Y-O **£1,944** (£574; £287) **Stalls** High

Form RPR
1 **Towering Storm** 2-9-3 0 StevieDonohoe 8 70+
(G A Butler) *v s.i.s and detached in last early: prog fr 1/2-way: rdn 2f out: clsd to ld last 100yds: readily* **20/1**
60 2 3/4 **If You Whisper (IRE)**[72] [6158] 2-9-3 0 GeorgeBaker 10 65
(Mike Murphy) *trckd ldrs: prog on inner over 2f out: rdn to ld over 1f out: hdd and outpcd last 100yds* **20/1**
05 3 nk **Dunhoy (IRE)**[9] [7503] 2-9-3 0 MickyFenton 9 64+
(Stef Higgins) *s.i.s: settled in rr: pushed along and prog on inner over 2f out: shkn up and styd on wl fnl f to take 3rd nr fin* **33/1**
52 4 1 1/4 **Sinfonico (IRE)**[18] [7386] 2-9-3 0 JimmyFortune 4 61
(R Hannon) *t.k.h: led at mod pce: jnd over 2f out: hdd over 1f out: nt qckn* **8/11**[1]
03 5 1 3/4 **Groomed (IRE)**[25] [7302] 2-9-3 0 EddieAhern 7 58
(W J Haggas) *prom: trckd ldr 1/2-way: chal and upsides over 2f out to wl over 1f out: fading whn sltly hmpd ins fnl f* **2/1**[2]
6 1 1/4 **Kristollini** 2-8-12 0 HayleyTurner 1 50
(W R Muir) *chsd ldrs: rdn over 2f out: no imp over 1f out: fdd* **40/1**
0 7 1/2 **Sir Randolf (IRE)**[9] [7503] 2-9-3 0 (t) JamesDoyle 6 53
(S Kirk) *sn restrained to last: pushed along 3f out: kpt on steadily fr over 1f out* **50/1**
0006 8 3 1/4 **Bodie**[12] [7470] 2-9-3 60 AdamKirby 5 46
(Mrs P Sly) *in tch in midfield: rdn over 2f out: steadily wknd* **66/1**
9 10 **Abysse** 2-8-12 0 JimCrowley 3 18
(R M Beckett) *sn pushed along in rr: last and wkng 3f out: t.o* **12/1**[3]
00 10 3 **Jam Maker**[120] [4595] 2-8-5 0 DannyBrock(7) 2 11
(J R Jenkins) *pressed ldr to 1/2-way: wknd rapidly: t.o* **100/1**

1m 40.29s (0.49) **Going Correction** -0.125s/f (Stan) 10 Ran SP% **118.3**
Speed ratings (Par 96): **92,91,90,89,87 86,86,82,72,69**
Tote Swingers: 1&2 £16.00, 1&3 £18.30, 2&3 £15.40 CSF £311.48 TOTE £26.80: £3.60, £2.80, £3.60; EX 208.50 Trifecta £1107.60 Part won. Pool: £1,496.80 - 0.80 winning units..
Owner Five Horses Ltd **Bred** Five Horses Ltd **Trained** Newmarket, Suffolk

FOCUS
A modest maiden run in a time was 0.74 seconds slower than the first division. Limited form off a slow pace, but the winner impressed and looks a likely improver. Minor personal bests from the next two.

NOTEBOOK
Towering Storm ◆ an gelded already half-brother to 1m Flat/2m4f-3m hurdle/chase winner Kristoffersen, attracted little market support but overcame greenness to make a winning debut. He lost several lengths with a slow start, but gradually recovered and moved into contention going well early in the straight. Although taking a while to pick up once asked, he got the idea in enough time and was nicely on top at the line. This isn't strong form, but he should get a workable handicap mark as a consequence and looks just the type to progress given time and distance. (op 16-1)
If You Whisper(IRE) was denied a clear run when well beaten in a weak Newmarket maiden when last seen in September, but he'd shown ability on debut and confirmed that initial promise this time. Handicaps are now an option. (op 16-1)
Dunhoy(IRE), upped in trip again, ran an encouraging race on his qualifying run for a mark. He was going on at the finish and is one to have on side in handicaps. (op 25-1)
Sinfonico(IRE) was well below the form he showed when runner-up over 7f here last time and proved unsuited by the step up in trip. (op 10-11 tchd Evens)
Groomed(IRE) was another to disappoint, running nowhere near the form he showed when third on heavy ground last time. Perhaps that latest run on a testing surface left its mark. (tchd 15-8)

7611 DIGIBET.COM H'CAP 1m (P)
4:20 (4:21) (Class 6) (0-65,69) 3-Y-O+ **£1,637** (£483; £241) **Stalls** High

Form RPR
5321 1 **Final Drive (IRE)**[13] [7467] 4-9-11 69 StevieDonohoe 5 81
(J Ryan) *hld up last in fiercely run r: gd prog fr 2f out: stormed through on inner to ld ent fnl f: sn clr: decisively* **10/3**[2]
0020 2 2 1/4 **Hip Hip Hooray**[48] [6794] 4-9-7 65 IanMongan 7 72
(L A Dace) *hld up wl in rr in strly run contest: rdn and prog on outer over 2f out: styd on to take 2nd last 150yds: no ch w wnr* **25/1**
0301 3 1 3/4 **Having A Ball**[81] [5867] 6-9-7 65 ChrisCatlin 8 68
(P D Cundell) *hld up wl in rr in strly run r: rdn and prog on outer over 2f out: kpt on to take 3rd ins fnl f* **12/1**
1200 4 nk **Provost**[72] [6165] 6-9-2 60 (b) GrahamGibbons 6 62
(M W Easterby) *hld up wl in rr in fast run r: prog on outer wl over 2f out: drvn and kpt on same pce fr over 1f out* **20/1**
3512 5 2 1/4 **Eastern Hills**[12] [7474] 5-9-1 62 (p) AndrewHeffernan(3) 12 59
(A J McCabe) *racd in 3rd and clr of rest in strly run contest: chsd ldr 1/2-way: rdn to ld 2f out: sitting duck for patiently rdn rivals over 1f out: hdd & wknd ent fnl f* **7/2**[3]
050 6 1 1/4 **Edgeworth (IRE)**[47] [6832] 4-9-5 63 GeorgeBaker 4 57
(B G Powell) *hld up in midfield: rdn over 2f out: tried to cl over 1f out but hanging: nt qckn* **6/1**
0564 7 nk **King's Caprice**[20] [7376] 9-9-6 64 (t) SamHitchcott 14 58
(J C Fox) *led at blistering pce: hdd 2f out: grad wknd* **25/1**
5323 8 1 1/4 **Bubbly Braveheart (IRE)**[4] [7562] 3-9-1 61 J-PGuillambert 9 53
(A Bailey) *chsd ldr to 1/2-way: sn u.p: wknd fr 2f out* **6/1**
5660 9 3 **Before The War (USA)**[112] [4867] 3-9-4 64 SteveDrowne 10 48
(J R Gask) *settled midfield: shkn up and lost pl over 2f out: n.d after* **33/1**
1045 10 1 1/2 **Valentino Swing (IRE)**[221] [1482] 7-9-0 65 HobieGill(7) 2 45
(M Appleby) *hld up wl in rr: sme promising hdwy over 2f out: folded tamely over 1f out* **50/1**
404 11 1/2 **Vezere (USA)**[26] [7288] 3-9-2 62 HayleyTurner 1 41
(S Dow) *chsd clr ldng trio: drvn wl over 2f out: wknd wl over 1f out* **33/1**
0053 12 1 **Serious Drinking (USA)**[15] [7453] 4-9-4 62 EddieAhern 13 39
(W R Swinburn) *chsd clr ldng trio: drvn over 2f out: sn wknd* **3/1**[1]
0000 13 2 **Twilight Star (IRE)**[27] [5075] 6-9-4 62 (b) DaneO'Neill 11 34
(R A Teal) *hld up in midfield: rdn over 2f out: sn wknd* **33/1**

1m 38.03s (-1.77) **Going Correction** -0.125s/f (Stan)
WFA 3 from 4yo+ 2lb 13 Ran SP% **129.8**
Speed ratings (Par 101): **103,100,99,98,96 95,94,93,90,89 88,87,85**
Tote Swingers: 1&2 £18.10, 1&3 £8.60, 2&3 £16.80 CSF £95.21 CT £950.17 TOTE £4.00: £1.50, £5.50, £3.50; EX 109.40 Trifecta £703.00 Part won. Pool: £950.10 - 0.42 winning units..
Owner Par 4 Racing **Bred** D Day & B Cantwell **Trained** Newmarket, Suffolk

FOCUS
A modest handicap run at an overly strong pace, and the first four were the last four turning in. The winner is on a high and posted a clear personal best.

7612 OFFICE CHRISTMAS PARTIES AT KEMPTON PARK H'CAP 1m 4f (P)
4:50 (4:53) (Class 3) (0-95,94) 3-Y-O+ **£6,281** (£1,869; £934; £466) **Stalls** Centre

Form RPR
5011 1 **Spensley (IRE)**[38] [7045] 4-8-12 80 KierenFallon 7 95+
(J R Fanshawe) *settled in 6th: prog 3f out: rdn to cl and led over 1f out: sn in command: nvr seriously threatened nr fin* **11/8**[1]
3161 2 1/2 **Iron Condor**[24] [7316] 3-8-2 76 LukeMorris 2 87
(J M P Eustace) *hld up in 10th: prog 3f out: swtchd lft and rdn jst over 2f out: styd on to take 2nd last 100yds: clsd on wnr fin but nvr gng to get there* **8/1**
1204 3 1 1/2 **Resentful Angel**[61] [6447] 5-9-5 87 AndreaAtzeni 9 96
(Pat Eddery) *awkward s: trckd ldng trio: wnt 3rd over 3f out: rdn to cl 2f out: clsd wnr over 1f out but sn outpcd: lost 2nd last 100yds* **6/1**[2]
0660 4 3 **Bow To No One (IRE)**[37] [7061] 4-8-13 81 DaneO'Neill 4 85
(A P Jarvis) *hld up in 8th: effrt over 3f out: kpt on to take 4th ins fnl f: n.d to ldng trio* **7/1**[3]
550/ 5 3 1/4 **Deadly Silence (USA)**[789] [6355] 5-8-10 78 SteveDrowne 3 77
(Dr J D Scargill) *hld up in 9th: dropped to last 3f out: couple of reminders arnd 2f out: pushed along after and kpt on quite encouragingly* **33/1**
0-11 6 nk **Alsadaa (USA)**[29] [500] 7-9-4 86 IanMongan 10 85
(Mrs L J Mongan) *led after 1f: stretched field fr 4f out: at least 3 l clr over 2f out: hdd & wknd over 1f out* **9/1**
4416 7 1 1/4 **Sequillo**[25] [7292] 4-8-13 81 JimmyFortune 8 78
(R Hannon) *awkward s: hld up in 7th: urged along and no prog over 2f out: wl btn after* **33/1**
0443 8 hd **Record Breaker (IRE)**[31] [7196] 6-8-11 86 (b) DCByrne(7) 1 82
(M Johnston) *sn pushed along in last: nvr gng wl: nvr a factor* **14/1**
0000 9 5 **Shadows Lengthen**[17] [7410] 4-9-6 88 GrahamGibbons 6 76
(M W Easterby) *mostly chsd ldng pair to over 3f out: wknd over 2f out* **25/1**
00 10 1/2 **Funday**[31] [7189] 4-9-1 83 ow1 GeorgeBaker 11 70
(G L Moore) *led 1f: mostly chsd ldr to over 2f out: wknd qckly* **16/1**
0100 11 3 3/4 **King Olav (UAE)**[27] [6562] 5-9-12 94 AdamKirby 5 75
(A W Carroll) *chsd ldng quartet: rdn over 4f out: wknd 3f out* **25/1**

2m 31.96s (-2.54) **Going Correction** -0.125s/f (Stan)
WFA 3 from 4yo+ 6lb 11 Ran SP% **116.1**
Speed ratings (Par 107): **103,102,101,99,97 97,96,96,93,92 90**
Tote Swingers: 1&2 £6.10, 1&3 £7.50, 2&3 £4.50 CSF £11.87 CT £49.78 TOTE £2.50: £1.10, £2.30, £2.00; EX 15.00 Trifecta £63.30 Pool: £940.26 - 10.98 winning units..
Owner Axom (XV) **Bred** Mount Coote Stud And M H Dixon **Trained** Newmarket, Suffolk

FOCUS
A good handicap and there was a useful winner, but it was not the strong-run race it might have been. The progressive winner looks better than the bare form, which has a solid look.

NOTEBOOK
Spensley(IRE) ◆ was completing a hat-trick of C&D victories. A 6lb rise for his latest win looked to have underestimated him seeing as he overcame trouble in running that day and nabbed a promising Sir Michael Stoute-trained runner, and so it proved. He was ridden closer to the pace this time, proving he's not a one-dimensional hold-up performer, but having quickened well to quickly seal the race over a furlong out, he soon idled and was in front sooner than ideal. He's significantly better than the winning margin indicates and can make further progress on Polytrack. Unfortunately there is not a race for him until the Rosebery here in early April. (op 13-8)
Iron Condor ◆ is flattered to get so close to the winner, but this was still a useful performance, the best of his career. This improver was 4lb higher than when winning over C&D last time, but showed this sort of mark is not beyond him. He won't always run into such a decent type. (op 15-2)
Resentful Angel ran well behind two improving runners on her return from a two-month break. (tchd 11-2)
Bow To No One(IRE) offered encouragement on her return to Polytrack. (op 8-1)
Deadly Silence(USA) ◆ caught the eye on his return from an absence of over two years. He was in an unpromising position turning into the straight and wasn't subjected to a hard ride, but he kept on nicely. Still lightly raced, this looked just the sort of performance he can improve from. (op 40-1)
Alsadaa(USA), back on the Flat after a couple of runs over hurdles, found this trip too short. He'd won his last two starts on the level at this track, but both of those wins were over 2m. (op 10-1 tchd 8-1)

7613 NAME A RACE FOR CHRISTMAS PRESENTS H'CAP (DIV I) 7f (P)
5:20 (5:24) (Class 6) (0-65,65) 3-Y-O+ **£1,364** (£403; £201) **Stalls** High

Form RPR
1406 1 **Leelu**[25] [7298] 4-9-2 60 CathyGannon 14 71
(D W P Arbuthnot) *mde all: clr over 2f out: drvn and styd on fr over 1f out* **15/2**[3]
R1 2 2 1/2 **Delaware Dancer (IRE)**[39] [7013] 3-9-3 62 SteveDrowne 8 66
(J R Gask) *s.s: hld up towards rr: prog through rivals over 2f out: chsd wnr over 1f out: kpt on but nvr able to chal* **8/1**
0032 3 1 1/4 **Sovereignty (JPN)**[25] [7298] 8-9-0 58 AdamKirby 6 59+
(D K Ivory) *hld up in midfield: looking for room over 2f out: prog over 1f out: styd on to take 3rd last strides* **11/2**[1]
0000 4 hd **Perfect Ch'I (IRE)**[15] [7439] 3-9-4 63 (b) DaneO'Neill 10 63
(I A Wood) *trckd ldrs: rdn over 2f out: kpt on same pce: no imp fnl f* **16/1**
3004 5 1 1/2 **Dvinsky (USA)**[11] [7483] 9-9-6 64 (b) JimmyQuinn 9 60
(P Howling) *firmly drvn fr s but unable to ld: chsd wnr to over 1f out: wknd fnl f* **9/1**

2103 **6** 1 **Annes Rocket (IRE)**[20] 7377 5-9-2 **63** RussKennemore(3) 4 57
(J C Fox) *hld up in last pair: pushed along and stdy prog over 2f out: nt pce to trble ldrs fnl f* **9/1**

0460 **7** 1 1/4 **Super Frank (IRE)**[15] 7439 7-9-3 **61** (b) IanMongan 3 51
(J Akehurst) *racd wd in rr: drvn over 2f out: no prog tl kpt on ins fnl f* **10/1**

0453 **8** 3/4 **Minortransgression (USA)**[89] 5648 3-9-5 **64** (t) GeorgeBaker 12 52
(P D Evans) *trckd ldrs on inner: rdn 2f out: steadily wknd fnl f* **13/2**[2]

5100 **9** 1 1/4 **Downhill Skier (IRE)**[9] 7501 6-8-13 **57** EddieAhern 13 42
(W M Brisbourne) *dwlt: wl in rr: prog into midfield on inner 2f out: no hdwy over 1f out: fdd* **10/1**

0050 **10** 1/2 **Teen Ager (FR)**[8] 7519 6-8-13 **57** ChrisCatlin 5 41
(P Burgoyne) *racd wd: trckd ldrs: lost pl and rdn over 2f out: sn btn* **33/1**

6020 **11** hd **Cawdor (IRE)**[29] 7241 4-9-4 **65** JamesSullivan(3) 2 48
(Mrs L Stubbs) *racd wd in rr: sn pushed along: wl btn over 2f out* **25/1**

6600 **12** 1 **First Service (IRE)**[53] 6671 4-9-0 **58** (b1) JimCrowley 11 38
(M J Attwater) *dwlt: t.k.h: hld up in last pair: effrt on inner over 2f out: wknd over 1f out* **15/2**[3]

4041 **13** hd **Sonny G (IRE)**[106] 5077 3-8-12 **60** KierenFox(3) 7 40
(J R Best) *t.k.h early: chsd ldng pair to over 2f out: wknd qckly* **16/1**

1m 24.45s (-1.55) **Going Correction** -0.125s/f (Stan)
WFA 3 from 4yo+ 1lb 13 Ran SP% **120.1**
Speed ratings (Par 101): **103,100,98,98,96 95,94,93,91,91 91,89,89**
Tote Swingers: 1&2 £11.40, 1&3 £4.10, 2&3 £7.80 CSF £66.75 CT £373.95 TOTE £9.90: £3.00, £3.30, £2.00; EX 85.80 Trifecta £428.50 Part won. Pool: £579.18 - 0.60 winning units..
Owner Philip Banfield **Bred** P Banfield **Trained** Compton, Berks

FOCUS
The first division of the 7f handicap looked an open affair but one horse dominated from the start. The time dipped under standard and was 0.51 seconds quicker than the second division. A clear personal best from the winner.

7614 NAME A RACE FOR CHRISTMAS PRESENTS H'CAP (DIV II) 7f (P)
5:50 (5:53) (Class 6) (0-65,65) 3-Y-0+ **£1,364** (£403; £201) **Stalls** High

Form RPR

0000 **1** **Nacho Libre**[23] 7331 5-9-0 **57** (b) GrahamGibbons 3 65
(M W Easterby) *pressed ldr: one of the first u.p wl over 2f out: persisted and forced ahd over 1f out: styd on wl* **8/1**[3]

2610 **2** 1 1/4 **Pipers Piping (IRE)**[15] 7439 4-9-4 **64** (v) MichaelStainton(3) 6 69
(P Howling) *hld up in midfield and racd wd: rdn over 2f out: prog over 1f out: styd on to take 2nd last 50yds* **12/1**

0556 **3** 1/2 **Kipchak (IRE)**[15] 7439 5-9-4 **61** (p) HayleyTurner 4 65
(C R Dore) *racd freely: led: hrd pressed over 2f out: hdd over 1f out: kpt on but lost 2nd last 50yds* **9/2**[2]

6360 **4** 1 1/4 **Rich Boy**[25] 7298 3-9-4 **62** (t) IanMongan 8 62
(Mrs L J Mongan) *pressed ldrs: drvn and cl up 2f out: one pce after* **20/1**

2213 **5** 1/2 **The Happy Hammer (IRE)**[15] 7439 4-9-6 **63** WilliamCarson 14 62
(Eugene Stanford) *dwlt: wl in rr: prog on inner fr over 2f out: kpt on fr over 1f out: nt pce to threaten* **5/2**[1]

0000 **6** 1 **Fine Ruler (IRE)**[32] 7168 6-9-1 **58** ow1 GeorgeBaker 7 55
(M R Bosley) *hld up in midfield: effrt whn chopped off over 2f out: kpt on same pce fr over 1f out* **20/1**

6046 **7** 1 3/4 **Poor Prince**[18] 7389 3-9-7 **65** AdamKirby 2 57
(Mrs A M Batchelor) *hld up last fr wdst draw: drvn and struggling over 2f out: modest late prog* **14/1**

5200 **8** 1/2 **Ede's Dot Com (IRE)**[144] 3777 6-8-13 **59** KierenFox(3) 13 49
(P M Phelan) *chsd ldrs: tried to chal 2f out: wknd fnl f* **11/1**

5000 **9** nse **Simple Rhythm**[18] 7391 4-9-0 **57** StevieDonohoe 12 47
(J Ryan) *pressed ldrs: rdn over 2f out: wknd over 1f out* **20/1**

3536 **10** 1 **Emiratesdotcom**[8] 7525 4-9-3 **63** RussKennemore(3) 9 50
(J M Bradley) *a towards rr: out of tch and struggling over 2f out* **8/1**[3]

4254 **11** 2 1/2 **Cactus King**[143] 3810 7-9-2 **62** RobertLButler(3) 10 43
(Jim Best) *nvr bttr than midfield: rdn wl over 2f out: sn lost pl and btn* **14/1**

3000 **12** 2 **Spirit Of Love (IRE)**[27] 7273 3-9-3 **61** StephenCraine 11 36
(M Wigham) *hld up in last trio: first one u.p: no prog* **20/1**

0P46 **13** 2 3/4 **Premier League**[15] 7451 3-9-1 **59** JimCrowley 5 27
(Miss J Feilden) *pressed ldng pair on outer: drvn wl over 2f out: sn wknd* **16/1**

1m 24.96s (-1.04) **Going Correction** -0.125s/f (Stan)
WFA 3 from 4yo+ 1lb 13 Ran SP% **123.3**
Speed ratings (Par 101): **100,98,98,96,96 94,92,92,92,91 88,85,82**
Tote Swingers: 1&2 £12.60, 1&3 £5.00, 2&3 £16.00 CSF £96.92 CT £375.09 TOTE £8.40: £3.30, £3.30, £2.30; EX 107.70 Trifecta £252.50 Pool: £590.49 - 1.73 winning units..
Owner Tri Nations Racing Syndicate **Bred** Lostford Manor Stud **Trained** Sheriff Hutton, N Yorks
■ Stewards' Enquiry : Hayley Turner one-day ban: failed to ride to draw (Dec 12)

FOCUS
A modest handicap where it proved beneficial to race up with the pace. The form is sound but limited.
T/Jkpt: Not won. T/Plt: £1,597.90 to a £1 stake. Pool of £140,533 - 64.20 winning tickets. T/Qpdt: £743.50 to a £1 stake. Pool of £9,848 - 9.80 winning tickets. JN

7267 TOKYO (L-H)
Sunday, November 28

OFFICIAL GOING: Turf: firm

7615a JAPAN CUP (GRADE 1) (3YO+) (TURF) 1m 4f
6:20 (12:00) 3-Y-O£1,689,613 (£672,969; £423,035; £252,996; £166,444)

RPR

1 1 3/4 **Rose Kingdom (JPN)**[35] 3-8-9 0 YutakaTake 6 121
(Kojiro Hashiguchi, Japan) *settled in 5th early: racd in 8th bk st: 5th 3f out and travelling wl on rail: swtchd outside appr 2f out: 4th whn sltly impeded ins fnl f: r.o wl u.p to take 2nd on line: fin 2nd: awrdd the r* **78/10**

2 **Buena Vista (JPN)**[28] 7267 4-8-9 0 ChristopheSoumillon 16 119
(Hiroyoshi Matsuda, Japan) *settled midfield fr s: smooth hdwy on outside appr 2f out: rdn 1 1/2f out: edgd lft and sltly impeded Rose Kingdom ins fnl f: r.o strly to ld 110yds out: pushed clr: fin 1st: disq and plcd 2nd* **9/10**[1]

3 nse **Victoire Pisa (JPN)**[56] 6612 3-8-9 0 MaximeGuyon 2 121
(Katsuhiko Sumii, Japan) *trckd ldr on rail: rdn and r.o 2f out: led over 1f out: kpt on u.p: hdd fnl 110yds: lost 2nd on line* **27/1**

4 3/4 **Jaguar Mail (JPN)**[28] 7267 6-9-0 0 (b) RyanMoore 8 119
(Noriyuki Hori, Japan) *w.w towards rr: 16th 2 1/2f out: sn mde hdwy on outside: styd on u.p to take 4th ins fnl 100yds: nvr nrr* **194/10**

5 nk **Pelusa (JPN)**[28] 7267 3-8-9 0 KatsumiAndo 7 119
(Kazuo Fujisawa, Japan) *settled in last: styd on fr 2f out: nrest at fin* **74/10**[3]

6 1/2 **Meisho Beluga (JPN)**[14] 7460 5-8-9 0 KenichiIkezoe 13 112
(Kaneo Ikezoe, Japan) *racd towards fnl 3rd: 3f out: 12th and r.o 2f out: nt qckn fnl 150yds: nvr able to threaten ldrs* **62/1**

7 nse **Oken Bruce Lee (JPN)**[49] 5-9-0 0 Christophe-PatriceLemaire 14 117
(Hidetaka Otonashi, Japan) *pushed along to go pce early stages: settled in rr: 17th 1/2-way: rdn ins fnl 3f: hdwy on outside appr 2f out: nt pce to chal* **148/10**

8 1 1/4 **Eishin Flash (JPN)**[63] 3-8-9 0 HiroyukiUchida 10 116
(Hideaki Fujiwara, Japan) *a.p (4th for much of r): 3rd 2 1/2f out: sn rdn: 4th ins fnl f: nt qckn u.str.p: wknd cl home* **113/10**

9 nse **Cirrus Des Aigles (FR)**[42] 6974 4-9-0 0 FranckBlondel 18 115
(Mme C Barande-Barbe, France) *w.w towards rr: kpt on fnl 1 1/2f u.str driving: nvr able to chal* **108/1**

10 1/2 **Joshua Tree (IRE)**[43] 6951 3-8-9 0 CO'Donoghue 12 115
(A P O'Brien, Ire) *w.w in midfield on ins: hdwy u.p to go 6th 1f out: unable qck and wknd fnl 110yds* **40/1**

11 3/4 **Dandino**[78] 5945 3-8-9 0 (b1) PaulMulrennan 3 114
(J G Given) *settled in in fnl 3rd on rail: effrt 2 1/2f out: no imp on ldrs* **130/1**

12 hd **Shingen (JPN)**[28] 7267 7-9-0 0 ShinjiFujita 4 113
(Hirofumi Toda, Japan) *broke wl and led: 1 1/2 l clr ins fnl 2f: hdd over 1f out: sn btn and wknd* **46/1**

13 1 1/2 **Mores Wells**[43] 6951 6-9-0 0 (b) SebastienMaillot 5 111
(R Gibson, France) *settled 10th: rdn and unable qck fr 2f out: nvr threatened* **98/1**

14 nk **Nakayama Festa (JPN)**[56] 6612 4-9-0 0 MasayoshiEbina 11 110
(Yoshitaka Ninomiya, Japan) *prom early: settled in 6th: travelling wl 3f out: sn rdn: nt qckn fr over 2f out: wknd appr fnl f* **67/10**[2]

15 1 1/2 **Timos (GER)**[42] 6974 5-9-0 0 OlivierPeslier 9 108
(T Doumen, France) *nvr plcd to chal* **119/1**

16 1 **Voila Ici (IRE)**[21] 7373 5-9-0 0 MircoDemuro 1 106
(Vittorio Caruso, Italy) *chsd ldrs on ins rail: disputing 4th 3f out: rdn and wknd ins fnl 2f* **66/1**

17 7 **Marinous (FR)**[56] 6612 4-9-0 0 DavyBonilla 17 95
(F Head, France) *racd keenly in midfield early: 9th 3f out: no imp: wknd fnl 2f* **86/1**

18 dist **Fifty Proof (CAN)**[43] 6951 4-9-0 0 JStein 15 —
(Ian Black, Canada) *prom (disp 2nd and 3rd much of the way): 4th 3f out: grad wknd fnl 2 1/2f* **89/1**

2m 25.2s (-0.30)
WFA 3 from 4yo+ 6lb 18 Ran SP% **125.3**
PARI-MUTUEL (all including 100 ypj stake): WIN 880; SHOW 200, 110, 530; DF 710; SF 1,880.
Owner Sunday Racing Co Ltd **Bred** Northern Farm **Trained** Japan

FOCUS
A ludicrous decision from the stewards robbed the 30th Japan Cup of a superstar winner.

NOTEBOOK
Rose Kingdom(JPN) did well to stay on for second considering he was short of room at a crucial stage and his performance, as well as the good run of Victoire Pisa, proved that the Japanese 3-y-o males are a good bunch. Snow Fairy demolished the country's top 3-y-o filly at Kyoto earlier in the month, but the colts are a different story. The winner had run well in defeat in all three legs of the Triple Crown.
Buena Vista(JPN) was clearly much the best horse, but she was demoted to second having slightly hampered the runner-up when swooping to the front inside the final furlong. The verdict from the stewards would have been understandable had Rose Kingdom not taken second spot seeing as that one's rider had to ever so slightly snatch up as the first-past-the-post edged into his path. But the interference made absolutely no difference to the result, indeed the beaten margin would still have been over a length had there been no trouble. However, for all that it was a ridiculous decision, Christophe Soumillon does have to take some responsibility. In the closing stages he continually used his whip on the right side, not correcting Buena Vista as she began to drift left. It's unfortunate that this controversial race will be remembered for the all the wrong reasons because Buena Vista proved herself a top-class filly.
Victoire Pisa(JPN), the Satsuki Sho (Japanese 2000 Guineas) winner, had been set too much to do when beaten just over 6l in the Arc, but this was his true running.
Joshua Tree(IRE), bidding to follow up his Canadian International win, wasn't good enough to get competitive.
Dandino didn't improve for blinkers and was not up to the level.
Nakayama Festa(JPN), who defeated Buena Vista in June (when much the fresher of the pair), had a tough race it the Arc when a game second to Workforce and clearly that effort has taken its toll. It was telling that his trainer was quoted beforehand as saying: "He doesn't misbehave like he used to at the stable - we're wondering if something is wrong with him."

7598 WOLVERHAMPTON (A.W) (L-H)
Monday, November 29

OFFICIAL GOING: Standard to slow
Wind: nil Weather: Frosty, fog final 4 races

7626 STAY AT THE WOLVERHAMPTON HOLIDAY INN H'CAP (FOR AMATEUR RIDERS) 1m 5f 194y(P)
2:10 (2:11) (Class 6) (0-65,65) 3-Y-0+ **£1,592** (£493; £246; £123) **Stalls** Low

Form RPR

0040 **1** **Taste The Wine (IRE)**[11] 6744 4-10-5 **60** MrRJWilliams(5) 4 67
(B J Llewellyn) *racd keenly: sddle slipped: hld up: hdwy 3f out: rdn to ld jst over 1f out: r.o ins fnl f: wl on top at fin* **12/1**

-503 **2** 1 1/4 **Private Equity (IRE)**[238] 1134 4-10-3 **53** MissGAndrews 11 58
(W Jarvis) *plld hrd: a.p: rdn whn chalng 1f out: nt qckn ins fnl f: hld by wnr towards fin* **11/4**[2]

-141 **3** 1 **Valantino Oyster (IRE)**[16] 4448 3-9-6 **55** MissCharlotteHolmes(5) 7 59+
(B M R Haslam) *trckd ldrs: rdn and outpcd over 2f out: rallied to chse ldrs over 1f out: styd on ins fnl f: gng on at fin* **14/1**

4 3/4 **Kammamuri (IRE)**[58] 5-11-0 **64** MrMarioBaratti 5 67+
(S C Williams) *midfield: pushed along over 3f out: rdn and hdwy over 1f out: styd on ins fnl f: clsng at fin: nt quite gng pce to get to ldrs* **5/1**[3]

605- **5** shd **King's Revenge**[17] 6342 7-10-7 **62** (b) MrOGarner(5) 12 64
(S Lycett) *completely missed break: rcvrd to go prom after 2f: led over 2f out: rdn and hdd jst over 1f out: no ex fnl 100yds* **11/2**

4341 **6** 2 1/4 **Straversjoy**[9] 7531 3-10-1 **62** MrStephenHarrison(3) 3 61
(R Hollinshead) *hld up: rdn and sme hdwy over 1f out: kpt on but no imp on ldrs ins fnl f* **9/4**[1]

400/ **7** 3 3/4 **Aberdeen Park**[382] 5474 8-9-5 **46** MrJEngland(5) 9 40
(P D Evans) *completely missed break: hld up: sn in tch w field but in rr: niggled along 4f out: nvr able to get on terms* **25/1**

The Form Book, Raceform Ltd, Compton, RG20 6NL

-454 **8** 1 ½ **Django Reinhardt**[11] 2894 4-9-11 **50** ow1 MrDavidTurner(3) 10 42
(Miss S L Davison) *set stdy pce: grad increased tempo fr over 4f out: rdn and hdd over 2f out: wknd over 1f out* **28/1**

00-0 **9** ½ **Corlough Mountain**[12] 7491 6-9-4 **45** (v¹) MissMBryant(5) 1 36
(P Butler) *hld up: struggling wl 2f out: nvr on terms* **66/1**

6233 **10** 4 ½ **Joan D'Arc (IRE)**[3] 7579 3-10-0 **65** MrLiamWard(7) 8 50
(M G Quinlan) *prom: pushed along 3f out: wknd 2f out: n.d whn n.m.r briefly wl over 1f out* **11/1**

3m 25.75s (19.75) **Going Correction** +0.275s/f (Slow)
WFA 3 from 4yo+ 8lb **10** Ran SP% **121.0**
Speed ratings (Par 101): **54,53,52,52,52 50,48,47,47,45**
toteswingers:1&2 £9.60, 2&3 £10.90, 1&3 £19.40 CSF £46.31 CT £489.30 TOTE £14.70: £5.30, £1.10, £3.80; EX 60.60 Trifecta £475.80 Part won. Pool of £643.08 - 0.17 winning units..
Owner Alan J Williams **Bred** Trevor Reilly **Trained** Fochriw, Caerphilly
■ Stewards' Enquiry : Mr David Turner two-day ban: careless riding (Dec 20,Jan 2)

FOCUS
The meeting survived a morning inspection, but the track was expected to ride on the slow side. The field only cantered around until going down the back straight for the final occasion, so clearly this is not form to trust.

7627 WOLVERHAMPTON-RACECOURSE.CO.UK (S) STKS 7f 32y(P)
2:45 (2:46) (Class 6) 3-Y-O+ **£1,535** (£453; £226) **Stalls** High

Form RPR

0206 **1** **I Confess**[47] 6853 5-9-4 64 (v) GeorgeBaker 6 67
(P D Evans) *led early: trckd ldrs after: chalng 2f out: rdn to ld jst ins fnl f: r.o: in command towards fin* **10/1**

1643 **2** 1 ¼ **Apache Ridge (IRE)**[14] 7462 4-9-10 64 (p) PhillipMakin 10 70
(K A Ryan) *a.p: led 2f out: sn rdn: hdd jst ins fnl f: no ex towards fin* **8/1³**

6052 **3** nk **Rebellious Spirit**[14] 7462 7-9-10 64 JamesDoyle 3 69
(S Curran) *in tch: pushed along over 2f out: effrt to chse ldrs over 1f out: sn edgd rt: styd on towards fin: nt quite gng pce to mount serious chal* **7/1²**

1 **4** 3 ¾ **The Big Haerth (IRE)**[14] 7462 4-9-10 77 (t) AndreaAtzeni 2 59
(S C Williams) *trckd ldrs: rdn over 1f out: one pce: nvr able to chal* **1/4¹**

440 **5** 2 ¼ **Landucci**[14] 7462 9-9-4 60 (p) LukeMorris 12 47
(S Curran) *midfield: rdn 2f out: one pce: no imp on ldrs* **25/1**

0030 **6** 6 **Cheshire Lady (IRE)**[10] 7505 3-8-12 47 (t) LiamJones 5 26
(W M Brisbourne) *towards rr: rdn 2f out: nvr on terms w ldrs* **50/1**

6050 **7** ½ **Lockantanks**[112] 4910 3-9-9 68 NeilChalmers 11 35
(M Appleby) *hdd 2f out: rdn and wknd over 1f out* **25/1**

6014 **8** 4 ½ **Fol Liam**[16] 7439 4-9-7 62 (p) AndrewHeffernan(3) 4 23
(A J McCabe) *s.i.s: a bhd: nvr on terms: b.b.v* **14/1**

1m 30.74s (1.14) **Going Correction** +0.275s/f (Slow)
WFA 3 from 4yo+ 1lb **8** Ran SP% **129.0**
Speed ratings (Par 101): **104,102,102,97,95 88,87,82**
toteswingers:1&2 £5.70, 2&3 £2.40, 1&3 £3.90 CSF £93.46 TOTE £12.60: £2.80, £1.80, £1.60; EX 68.00 Trifecta £682.30 Pool: £1226.45 - 1.33 winning units..There was no bid for the winner. The Big Haerth was subject to a friendly claim.
Owner J E Abbey **Bred** Gestut Sohrenhof **Trained** Pandy, Monmouths

FOCUS
A modest seller in which the well-backed favourite proved disappointing.
Fol Liam Official explanation: trainer said gelding bled from the nose

7628 BET EUROPA LEAGUE FOOTBALL - BETDAQ H'CAP 5f 20y(P)
3:20 (3:20) (Class 6) (0-65,65) 3-Y-O+ **£1,942** (£578; £288; £144) **Stalls** Low

Form RPR

5121 **1** **Wooden King (IRE)**[9] 7518 5-9-3 **61** LukeMorris 1 70
(M S Saunders) *a.p: rdn to ld over 1f out: strly pressed ins fnl f: stuck on gamely cl home* **7/2¹**

0301 **2** hd **Towy Boy (IRE)**[24] 7334 5-9-6 **64** (bt) CathyGannon 2 72
(I A Wood) *trckd ldrs: wnt 2nd 3f out: str chal ins fnl f: jst hld fnl strides* **4/1²**

5462 **3** 1 ¾ **The Tatling (IRE)**[16] 7446 13-9-3 **64** RussKennemore(3) 7 66
(J M Bradley) *midfield: effrt to chse ldrs over 1f out: kpt on ins fnl f: nt gng pce to chal front pair* **8/1³**

0352 **4** nk **Prince James**[24] 7332 3-9-7 **65** GrahamGibbons 4 66
(M W Easterby) *midfield: pushed along over 3f out: rdn and hdwy over 1f out: kpt on: nt quite gng pce of ldrs* **7/2¹**

2360 **5** 1 ¼ **Flaxen Lake**[24] 7334 3-8-13 **57** (tp) ChrisCatlin 10 53
(J M Bradley) *trckd ldrs: rdn over 1f out: kpt on same pce ins fnl f* **33/1**

6424 **6** nk **Cape Royal**[3] 7571 10-9-6 **64** (bt) RichardKingscote 5 59
(J M Bradley) *led: rdn and hdd over 1f out: no ex fnl 75yds* **8/1³**

500 **7** nk **Straboe (USA)**[74] 6110 4-9-6 **64** (v) WilliamCarson 8 58
(S C Williams) *outpcd: rdn over 1f out: hung lft and prog ins fnl f: styd on: nt gng pce to chal* **14/1**

1120 **8** 4 ½ **Monte Major (IRE)**[9] 7526 9-9-5 **63** (v) JimmyQuinn 3 41
(D Shaw) *outpcd: rdn over 1f out: nvr on terms* **8/1³**

2006 **9** 17 **Liberty Ship**[34] 7148 5-9-4 **62** (p) HayleyTurner 6 —
(Mark Buckley) *a outpcd and bhd: nvr on terms* **16/1**

62.88 secs (0.58) **Going Correction** +0.275s/f (Slow) **9** Ran SP% **113.3**
Speed ratings (Par 101): **106,105,102,102,100 99,99,92,65**
toteswingers:1&2 £2.80, 2&3 £7.40, 1&3 £6.10 CSF £17.13 CT £102.70 TOTE £4.70: £1.20, £2.10, £3.60; EX 15.20 Trifecta £65.50 Pool: £1006.92 - 11.36 winning units..
Owner Pat Hancock **Bred** Terence E Connelly **Trained** Green Ore, Somerset

FOCUS
The first four came into the race in good form and this was a fair sprint handicap for the grade.
Liberty Ship Official explanation: jockey said gelding never travelled

7629 SPONSOR A RACE BY CALLING 01902 390000 (S) STKS 1m 1f 103y(P)
3:50 (3:50) (Class 6) 2-Y-O **£1,535** (£453; £226) **Stalls** Low

Form RPR

3031 **1** **Sheila's Star (IRE)**[14] 7464 2-8-12 62 LukeMorris 1 60
(J S Moore) *trckd ldrs: pushed along under 4f out: wnt 2nd over 3f out: hrd at work whn ldr drew clr over 2f out: styd on for press over 1f out: led wl ins fnl f: kpt on whn on top at fin* **8/11¹**

0041 **2** ¾ **A Little Bit Dusty**[9] 7520 2-9-0 61 (v) KierenFox(3) 6 64
(W G M Turner) *a.p: led 4f out: kicked abt 6 l clr over 2f out: hrd rdn over 1f out: worn down wl ins fnl f: hld cl home* **4/1²**

2100 **3** 4 **Countrywide Flame**[26] 7296 2-9-3 58 (tp) PhillipMakin 2 56
(K A Ryan) *led: hdd 4f out: sn rdn wl outpcd over 2f out: kpt on u.p ins fnl f: no imp* **6/1³**

0005 **4** 3 ½ **Senor Sassi (USA)**[32] 7197 2-8-12 50 (p) JamesDoyle 3 44
(J S Moore) *bmpd s: hld up in rr: rdn over 3f out: tk mod 4th wl over 1f out: nvr a danger* **10/1**

0006 **5** 4 **Boogie Star**[14] 7464 2-8-5 53 (p) RyanPowell(7) 4 37
(J S Moore) *prom: lost pl over 3f out: outpcd and n.d after* **33/1**

00 **6** 9 **River Avon**[9] 7530 2-8-12 0 GrahamGibbons 7 20
(M W Easterby) *dwlt: sn in midfield: rdn along 7f out: wl outpcd over 3f out: wl btn* **50/1**

0000 **7** 11 **Bathwick Nero**[126] 4436 2-8-7 48 CathyGannon 5 —
(P D Evans) *hld up: u.p and bhd 4f out: nvr a danger* **25/1**

2m 6.08s (4.38) **Going Correction** +0.275s/f (Slow) **7** Ran SP% **110.0**
Speed ratings (Par 94): **91,90,86,83,80 72,62**
CSF £3.45 TOTE £1.60: £1.10, £2.20; EX 4.10.There was no bid for the winner.
Owner Ray Styles & J S Moore **Bred** Albert Conneally **Trained** Upper Lambourn, Berks
■ Stewards' Enquiry : Kieren Fox one-day ban: used whip with excessive frequency (Dec 13)

FOCUS
A moderate, uncompetitive seller.

NOTEBOOK
Sheila's Star(IRE) followed up her recent win gained in an extended 1m claimer. She needed all of this longer trip, though, and is going to want further. At the following auction she was retained without a bid.
A Little Bit Dusty was a good 5l clear turning into the straight, and touched 1.06 in-running, but he soon idled and was worn down. He won a Lingfield seller last time, but was behind Sheila's Star two starts back. (tchd 7-2)
Countrywide Flame did not improve for the fitting of cheekpieces and a tongue-tie. (op 5-1)
Senor Sassi(USA), a stable companion of the winner, offered little. (op 16-1 tchd 9-1)

7630 BET MULTIPLES - BETDAQ NURSERY (DIV I) 1m 141y(P)
4:20 (4:20) (Class 6) (0-65,65) 2-Y-O **£1,619** (£481; £240; £120) **Stalls** Low

Form RPR

0040 **1** **Urban Kode (IRE)**[46] 6868 2-8-4 **48** CathyGannon 11 56
(P D Evans) *midfield: rdn and hdwy over 1f out: led wl ins fnl f: r.o* **14/1**

6503 **2** 1 ¼ **Indian Wish (USA)**[41] 7004 2-8-13 **57** JamieSpencer 9 62
(M G Quinlan) *led: rdn over 1f out: edgd lft ins fnl f: sn hdd: hld cl home* **2/1¹**

5000 **3** 3 ¼ **Aquilifer (IRE)**[74] 6129 2-8-9 **53** J-PGuillambert 4 51
(W Jarvis) *trckd ldrs: rdn and nt qckn over 1f out: kpt on ins fnl f: nt gng pce to trble front pair* **33/1**

0052 **4** nk **Farmer's Wife**[14] 7464 2-9-1 **59** DavidProbert 10 57
(B J Llewellyn) *chsd ldr: rdn over 2f out: lost 2nd over 1f out: styd on same pce ins fnl f* **12/1**

006 **5** nse **Sammy Alexander**[32] 7186 2-9-6 **64** AndreaAtzeni 8 61
(D M Simcock) *racd keenly: in tch: rdn 2f out: nt qckn over 1f out: kpt on same pce ins fnl f* **10/1**

0621 **6** 2 ½ **Microlight**[11] 7497 2-9-2 **60** (e) GrahamGibbons 1 52
(T D Easterby) *chsd ldrs: rdn 3f out: keeping on u.p over 1f out: wknd fnl 100yds* **5/1²**

000 **7** shd **Shirocco Vice (IRE)**[17] 7427 2-8-1 **45** JimmyQuinn 12 37
(R A Fahey) *s.i.s: bhd: rdn and hdwy over 1f out: styd on: nt gng pce to trble ldrs* **7/1**

000 **8** nk **Titan Diamond (IRE)**[109] 4999 2-8-3 **47** HayleyTurner 7 38
(M D I Usher) *n.m.r s: hld up: pushed along over 3f out: kpt on ins fnl f: nvr able to trble ldrs* **66/1**

005 **9** nse **Dance For Livvy (IRE)**[117] 4709 2-8-10 **57** PatrickDonaghy(3) 2 48
(B M R Haslam) *midfield: rdn 3f out: sn wknd* **33/1**

5005 **10** 5 **Les Landes (IRE)**[11] 7497 2-8-10 **54** ChrisCatlin 5 35
(J A Osborne) *bmpd s: towards rr: rdn 4f out: nvr on terms* **11/2³**

16 **11** 8 **Brand Bob (IRE)**[19] 7396 2-9-4 **62** DaneO'Neill 3 46
(Miss Amy Weaver) *in tch: rdn and wknd over 2f out: eased whn wl btn ins fnl f: lame* **9/1**

0340 **12** 8 **Windsor Knights**[33] 7165 2-9-7 **65** (v¹) JamesDoyle 6 12
(A J Lidderdale) *hmpd whn n.m.r s: bhd: racd wd bk st: rdn over 3f out: nvr a danger: eased whn wl btn ins fnl f* **18/1**

1m 53.82s (3.32) **Going Correction** +0.275s/f (Slow) **12** Ran SP% **124.0**
Speed ratings (Par 94): **96,94,92,91,91 89,89,89,89,84 77,70**
toteswingers:1&2 £11.20, 2&3 £20.70, 1&3 £58.00 CSF £43.73 CT £987.76 TOTE £23.10: £4.70, £2.20, £11.90; EX 91.50 TRIFECTA Not won..
Owner Mrs I M Folkes **Bred** Nils Koop **Trained** Pandy, Monmouths

FOCUS
A weak nursery run in a time 0.44 seconds slower than the second division. There was no hanging about early on, but the pace looked to ease on the far side and the majority of those given waiting rides struggled.

NOTEBOOK
Urban Kode(IRE) got on top late on to gain his first success at the sixth time of asking. The step up in trip played much more to his strengths, but it was a decent effort considering he was drawn out wide and there was plenty to like about his attitude when under pressure. He ought to have more to offer. (op 16-1)
Indian Wish(USA) was again sent out in front and Jamie Spencer looked to have got the fractions just right as she was still going well turning for home. She spoilt her chance by drifting left when asked for an effort, though, and was reeled in late on. This was probably a missed opportunity, but she could be the sort to improve for a stiffer test and ought to find a race. (op 11-4 tchd 3-1)
Aquilifer(IRE) had the cheekpieces left off for this step back up from a seller and return from a 74-day break. This new surface suited and it rates his best effort so far, so he could get a bit closer next time out.
Farmer's Wife, only just denied in a C&D claimer a fortnight earlier, was again ridden positively and held every chance. She probably ran up to his previous level and helps to set the standard.
Sammy Alexander put up an eye-catching display on his nursery debut over a longer trip. He travelled nicely into contention, but still looked green under pressure and was getting there too late in the final furlong. (op 13-2)
Microlight had his chance off his 5lb higher mark, but was found out by the longer distance. Official explanation: vet said gelding lost a shoe (op 9-2 tchd 4-1 and 11-2)
Shirocco Vice(IRE) wasn't helped by being drawn on the outside and needed to be hard ridden from the start. She latched on to the pack on the back straight, but was in trouble as soon as the pace lifted again and her supporters knew their fate before the final bend. Better was clearly expected on this nursery debut off such a lowly mark, and perhaps she would be the sort to enjoy the deeper surface at Southwell where her sire already has a good record. (op 25-1)
Brand Bob(IRE) Official explanation: vet said gelding finished lame left-fore
Windsor Knights Official explanation: jockey said gelding suffered interference at start

7631 BET MULTIPLES - BETDAQ NURSERY (DIV II) 1m 141y(P)
4:50 (4:51) (Class 6) (0-65,65) 2-Y-O **£1,619** (£481; £240; £120) **Stalls** Low

Form RPR

0002 **1** **Sky Diamond (IRE)**[5] 7552 2-8-13 **57** (b) TomEaves 9 64
(J G Given) *prom: led over 3f out: strly pressed fr over 1f out: hung rt ins fnl f: r.o u.p in driving fin* **5/1³**

0340 **2** shd **Ivan Vasilevich (IRE)**[37] 7087 2-9-3 **61** JamieSpencer 11 68
(Jane Chapple-Hyam) *hld up: hdwy over 6f out: wnt 2nd 3f out: str chal fr over 1f out: bmpd whn upsides ins fnl f: r.o u.p in driving fin* **5/1³**

4222 **3** 2 ½ **Ivan's A Star (IRE)**[9] 7520 2-8-13 **57**...............(p) LukeMorris 7 59
(J S Moore) *midfield: hdwy over 2f out: lugged lft u.p fr over 1f out: styd on to take 3rd fnl 100yds: nt gng pce to rch front pair* **9/2**[2]

000 **4** ¾ **Desert Location**[32] 7185 2-9-5 **63**............... HayleyTurner 5 63
(M L W Bell) *prom: rdn over 2f out: nt qckn over 1f out: kpt on same pce ins fnl f* **10/3**[1]

0302 **5** 3 ¾ **Better Self**[72] 6209 2-9-1 **59**............... GeorgeBaker 1 51
(P D Evans) *prom: rdn over 2f out: one pce fr over 1f out* **8/1**

0000 **6** 1 ¼ **West Leake Melody**[17] 7417 2-8-9 **53**............... WilliamCarson 4 42
(B W Hills) *s.s: in rr: rdn over 1f out: kpt on ins fnl f: nt gng pce to trble ldrs* **16/1**

0604 **7** ½ **High Kickin**[19] 7394 2-8-11 **58**...............(p) AndrewHeffernan(3) 6 46
(A J McCabe) *hld up: hdwy into midfield 5f out: rdn 3f out: no imp on ldrs* **14/1**

0063 **8** nk **Century Dancer**[11] 7497 2-8-2 **51**............... BillyCray(5) 10 39
(Miss Tor Sturgis) *hld up: effrt 2f out: kpt on ins fnl f: nt gng pce to chal ldrs* **14/1**

0006 **9** 3 ½ **Torteval (IRE)**[35] 7124 2-8-1 **45**............... CathyGannon 3 25
(P D Evans) *hld up: struggling over 2f out: nvr on terms* **20/1**

3600 **10** 2 ½ **Joyously**[12] 7486 2-9-4 **65**............... RobertLButler(3) 2 40
(P Butler) *midfield: rdn and wknd over 3f out* **40/1**

505 **11** 1 ½ **Indian Dip**[77] 6027 2-8-4 **48**............... ChrisCatlin 8 20
(Matthew Salaman) *racd keenly: led: hdd over 3f out: rdn and wknd over 2f out* **40/1**

1m 53.38s (2.88) **Going Correction** +0.275s/f (Slow) 11 Ran SP% **114.6**
Speed ratings (Par 94): **98,97,95,95,91 90,90,89,86,84 83**
toteswingers:1&2 £5.80, 2&3 £4.70, 1&3 £4.40 CSF £28.77 CT £118.41 TOTE £4.30: £1.50, £1.50, £1.20; EX 32.70 Trifecta £140.60 Pool: £739.15 - 22.73 winning units..
Owner Peter Swann **Bred** David Bourke **Trained** Willoughton, Lincs
■ Stewards' Enquiry : Tom Eaves caution: careless riding; one-day ban: used whip with excessive frequency (Dec 13)
Jamie Spencer caution: careless riding; one-day ban: used whip with excessive frequency (Dec 13)

FOCUS
The time was 0.44 seconds quicker than the second division. The first two came close together on more than one occasion in the straight, but both runners were responsible for the trouble. A lengthy stewards' enquiry followed, but it would have been a major surprise were the placings reversed, and the correct decision was made.

NOTEBOOK
Sky Diamond(IRE), in second-time blinkers, was off the same mark as when runner-up over 7f at Kempton last time and proved suited by this longer trip. (op 4-1)
Ivan Vasilevich(IRE) received a bit of a bump from the winner late on, but he'd also wandered off a straight line himself, going left and making contact with Sky Diamond, so he couldn't be considered unlucky. (op 13-2)
Ivan's A Star(IRE) once again ruined his chance by hanging left. (op 6-1)
Desert Location, back up in trip on her nursery debut and sent off favourite, lacked a change of pace under pressure. (op 3-1 tchd 11-4)
Better Self, claimed for £6,000 after finishing runner-up in a 7f seller here in September, was entitled to need this after 72 days off and her stamina was unproven. (op 7-1 tchd 13-2)

7632 BOOK NOW FOR CHRISTMAS H'CAP 2m 119y(P)
5:20 (5:21) (Class 5) (0-75,74) 3-Y-0+ **£2,590** (£770; £385; £192) **Stalls** Low

Form RPR
1355 **1** **Leyte Gulf (USA)**[17] 7422 7-8-13 **59**............... DaneO'Neill 7 66+
(C C Bealby) *stdd s: hld up: hdwy 3f out: swtchd rt to chal over 1f out: styd on to ld ins fnl f: edgd lft towards fin: won gng away* **15/2**[3]

4301 **2** 1 ¼ **Dart**[14] 7465 6-9-8 **68**............... GeorgeBaker 8 73
(J Mackie) *led at stdy pce: hdd after 4f: remained prom: rdn to chal fr over 1f out: nt qckn fnl 75yds* **2/1**[2]

3-02 **3** nk **Master At Arms**[14] 7465 7-9-8 **68**............... JamieSpencer 1 73
(Daniel Mark Loughnane, Ire) *chsd ldrs: wnt 2nd 1/2-way: rdn to chal fr 3 out: ev ch tl kpt on same pce fnl 100yds* **7/4**[1]

0320 **4** 1 ¼ **Inside Knowledge (USA)**[19] 7398 4-8-4 **55** oh7............... BillyCray(5) 6 58
(G Woodward) *chsd ldr: led after 4f: strly pressed fr 3f out: hdd ins fnl f: no ex fnl 75yds* **16/1**

6641 **5** 5 **William's Way**[12] 7491 8-9-3 **66**...............(t) JamesSullivan(3) 3 63
(I A Wood) *hld up in midfield: effrt over 3f out: one pce and no imp fr over 1f out* **14/1**

051- **6** nk **Black Or Red (IRE)**[359] 7649 5-10-0 **74**............... JamesDoyle 2 71
(I A Wood) *racd keenly: hld up: rdn 2f out: no imp on ldrs* **10/1**

2202 **7** 6 **Hi Dancer**[31] 5364 7-9-2 **65**............... PatrickDonaghy(3) 4 55
(B M R Haslam) *in tch: pushed along 4f out: wknd over 3f out* **14/1**

3m 49.86s (8.06) **Going Correction** +0.275s/f (Slow)
WFA 3 from 4yo+ 9lb 7 Ran SP% **109.8**
Speed ratings (Par 103): **92,91,91,90,88 88,85**
toteswingers:1&2 £3.20, 2&3 £1.20, 1&3 £2.30 CSF £21.10 CT £34.72 TOTE £10.30: £4.70, £1.10; EX 26.20 Trifecta £23.90 Pool: £737.02 - 22.73 winning units..
Owner Robert Jenkinson **Bred** Paradigm Thoroughbred Inc **Trained** Barrowby, Lincs

FOCUS
As usual for a staying event on Polytrack, the pace was steady.

7633 TRY BETDAQ FOR AN EXCHANGE H'CAP 1m 1f 103y(P)
5:50 (5:50) (Class 6) (0-55,55) 3-Y-0+ **£1,942** (£578; £288; £144) **Stalls** Low

Form RPR
5002 **1** **Love In The Park**[10] 7508 5-9-0 **52**............... JackMitchell 12 59
(R Brotherton) *hld up in rr: hdwy 3f out: led over 1f out: kpt on wl and a doing enough towards fin* **3/1**[2]

2020 **2** nk **Herecomethegirls**[32] 7199 4-9-0 **52**...............(b) LukeMorris 11 58
(W G M Turner) *hld up: hdwy over 3f out: styng on whn n.m.r and hmpd 1f out: rcvrd to cl towards fin* **9/1**

0400 **3** 2 ¼ **Shark Man (IRE)**[40] 7019 3-9-0 **55**...............(v) AndreaAtzeni 3 56
(M Wigham) *led 1f: remained prom: chalng whn hung lft 1f out: kpt on same pce fnl 75yds* **16/1**

4563 **4** hd **Bentley**[6] 7543 6-8-10 **53**...............(b) NeilFarley(5) 7 54
(B P J Baugh) *trckd ldrs: rdn 3f out: effrt to chal on inner over 1f out: stl ev ch ins fnl f: no ex fnl 75yds* **11/2**[3]

0550 **5** ½ **Ruby Dazzler**[28] 7273 3-8-12 **53**...............(bt[1]) VinceSlattery 9 53
(S Lycett) *midfield: hdwy 4f out: rdn to chse ldrs 2f out: one pce ins fnl f* **25/1**

0002 **6** 1 ¾ **All Moving Parts (USA)**[17] 7429 3-9-0 **55**...............(v) JamesDoyle 10 51
(A J McCabe) *led after 1f: rdn 2f out: hung rt and hdd over 1f out: bmpd ins fnl f: wknd fnl 75yds* **15/8**[1]

055 **7** 15 **Spacecraft (IRE)**[16] 7451 3-8-11 **52**............... JimmyQuinn 4 17
(C N Kellett) *dwlt: hld up: struggling over 3f out: nvr on terms* **25/1**

50-3 **8** 17 **Carbon Print (USA)**[18] 2604 5-9-2 **54**............... JamieSpencer 13 —
(P R Webber) *prom: rdn 4f out: wknd over 3f out* **11/2**[3]

00-0 **9** 1 ¾ **Houda (IRE)**[229] 1302 3-8-11 **52**............... RichardKingscote 1 —
(J G Portman) *hld up: struggling 3f out: nvr on terms* **50/1**

2m 3.27s (1.57) **Going Correction** +0.275s/f (Slow)
WFA 3 from 4yo+ 3lb 9 Ran SP% **116.1**
Speed ratings (Par 101): **104,103,101,101,101 99,86,71,69**
toteswingers:1&2 £4.30, 2&3 £13.00, 1&3 £13.30. totesuper7: Win: Not won. Place: Not won. CSF £29.50 CT £372.17 TOTE £4.00: £1.70, £2.60, £5.90; EX 29.60 Trifecta £411.40 Part won. Pool of £1556.04 - 0.83 winning units..
Owner Arthur Clayton **Bred** New England Stud And Partners **Trained** Elmley Castle, Worcs

FOCUS
Mist restricted viewing around the bend into the straight. This was just a moderate handicap.
All Moving Parts(USA) Official explanation: jockey said gelding hung both ways
T/Jkpt: Not won. T/Plt: £191.90 to a £1 stake. Pool of £125,810.40 - 478.36 winning tickets. T/Qpdt: £7.10 to a £1 stake. Pool of £16,495.64 - 1,698.21 winning tickets. DO

7570 LINGFIELD (L-H)
Tuesday, November 30

OFFICIAL GOING: Standard
Wind: Almost nil. Weather: Overcast, snow flurries

7634 TANDRIDGE AMATEUR RIDERS' H'CAP 2m (P)
12:45 (12:47) (Class 6) (0-60,60) 3-Y-0+ **£1,977** (£608; £304) **Stalls** Low

Form RPR
000/ **1** **Brabazon (IRE)**[892] 3288 7-9-7 **46** oh1...............(bt) MrFMitchell(7) 7 62+
(Emmet Michael Butterly, Ire) *hld up in rr: smooth prog over 5f out: trckd ldr over 2f out: rdn to ld over 1f out: sn wl clr* **11/4**[1]

0-05 **2** 10 **Olivino (GER)**[70] 4328 9-10-0 **46** oh1............... MissIsabelTompsett 4 49
(B J Llewellyn) *hld up in midfield: n.m.r briefly 5f out: plenty to do whn prog over 3f out: kpt on wl to take 2nd ins fnl f: no ch w wnr* **11/2**[3]

4/52 **3** 1 ¾ **Zed Candy (FR)**[35] 7157 7-10-4 **53**......... MissPernillaHermansson(3) 14 54
(R Ford) *cl up: prog to join ldr after 7f: led 7f out to 5f out: chsd ldr to over 2f out: outpcd whn hmpd on inner over 1f out: kpt on to take 3rd nr fin* **12/1**

3600 **4** hd **Six Of Clubs**[191] 2361 4-9-9 **46** oh1...............(b) MrPPrince(5) 12 47
(W G M Turner) *hld up in midfield: prog 1/2-way: led 5f out: rdn and hdd over 1f out: wknd ins fnl f* **40/1**

0600 **5** nk **Pocket Too**[9] 7388 7-10-4 **55**...............(p) MrJBanks(5) 10 55
(Matthew Salaman) *sn lost prom pl: dropped to last pair 6f out: wl bhd 4f out: styd on u.p fr over 2f out: nrly snatched 3rd* **6/1**

600 **6** 8 **Jakeys Girl**[148] 3738 3-9-6 **54** ow3............... MissCPowell(7) 9 45
(P M Phelan) *hld up in midfield: sme prog on outer 6f out: wl outpcd in 6th 3f out: nvr on terms after* **25/1**

0536 **7** 4 **Delorain (IRE)**[20] 7388 7-9-8 **47** oh1 ow1...............(vt) MrMMarris(7) 1 33
(W B Stone) *led 2f: rdn in midfield 5f out: sn lft wl bhd* **6/1**

5300 **8** 3 **Always De One**[13] 7490 3-8-12 **46** oh1...............(p) MissSBirkett(7) 8 28
(Miss J Feilden) *prom: rdn in 5th 3f out: sn wknd* **25/1**

0660 **9** 7 **Jenny Soba**[28] 7284 7-9-11 **50**............... MrWFeatherstone(7) 3 24
(Lucinda Featherstone) *a in rr: dropped to last after 7f: lft wl bhd fr 5f out* **33/1**

00-0 **10** 3 ¼ **Coeur Brule (FR)**[12] 541 4-9-11 **46** oh1............... MrDavidTurner(3) 2 16
(Miss S L Davison) *prom: bmpd along fr 1/2-way: lost pl 5f out: sn no ch* **11/1**

0000 **11** ¾ **Zuwaar**[41] 5963 5-9-10 **47**...............(vt) MissMBryant(5) 13 16
(P Butler) *s.s and reluctant early: sn in tch: outpcd over 4f out: sn wknd* **40/1**

5005 **12** 18 **Swords**[56] 6662 8-9-7 **46** oh1............... MissSPeacock(7) 5 —
(R E Peacock) *led after 2f to 7f out: wknd 5f out: t.o: sddle slipped* **33/1**

0040 **13** 40 **Defence Of Realm (GER)**[13] 7476 3-10-2 **57**...............(p) MrSWalker 6 —
(George Baker) *hld up in midfield: rdn and wknd rapidly 5f out: wl t.o* **5/1**[2]

3m 24.67s (-1.03) **Going Correction** -0.025s/f (Stan)
WFA 3 from 4yo+ 9lb 13 Ran SP% **121.8**
Speed ratings (Par 101): **101,96,95,95,94 90,88,87,83,82 81,72,52**
Tote Swingers:1&2:£8.30, 2&3:£7.70, 1&3:£16.50 CSF £16.59 CT £159.26 TOTE £4.90: £2.50, £1.70, £2.10; EX 31.40 Trifecta £106.60 Part won. Pool £144.12 - 0.64 winning units..
Owner James Ferry **Bred** Dermot Cantillon And Forenaghts Stud **Trained** Letterkenny, Co Donegal
■ Emmet Butterly's first winner in Britain, and first Flat winner, and winning rider Freddie Mitchell's first ride under rules.
■ Stewards' Enquiry : Mr M Marris two-day ban: careless riding (tbn)

FOCUS
A very weak affair with eight racing from out of the handicap. It was run at an average pace and they were strung out with 4f to run and there was an easy winner.
Brabazon(IRE) Official explanation: trainer said, regarding apparent improvement in form, this was the gelding's first run since joining him four-five months ago, and has been freshened up by his training regime and gallops on the beach.
Swords Official explanation: jockey said saddle slipped

7635 MARSH GREEN CLAIMING STKS 5f (P)
1:15 (1:17) (Class 6) 3-Y-0+ **£1,706** (£503; £252) **Stalls** High

Form RPR
3004 **1** **Ebraam (USA)**[204] 1979 7-8-4 90............... JulieBurke(7) 2 82+
(Mike Murphy) *hld up in tch: trckd ldrs gng strly 2f out: effrt over 1f out: rdn and styd on wl enough to ld last strides* **13/2**

0146 **2** nk **Silaah**[50] 6799 6-9-2 83...............(p) MichaelO'Connell(3) 3 89
(D Nicholls) *cl up: led on inner 2f out and wnt for home: styd on fnl f: hdd last strides* **3/1**[2]

0504 **3** 1 ¼ **Lewyn**[15] 7466 3-8-9 82...............(t) FrannyNorton 4 75
(K A Ryan) *trckd ldrs on outer: rdn 2f out: styd on u.p to take 3rd nr fin* **4/1**[3]

5003 **4** ¾ **Wanchai Whisper**[4] 7571 3-8-2 64 ow1............... KierenFox(3) 1 68
(P R Hedger) *hld up in last trio: prog on inner 2f out: chsd ldng pair ins fnl f: one pce and lost 3rd nr fin* **20/1**

0114 **5** ½ **Matsunosuke**[17] 7443 8-9-3 100............... LukeMorris 6 78
(R A Harris) *hld up in last trio: urged along 2f out: nt qckn over 1f out: one pce after* **1/1**[1]

4506 **6** ½ **Brandywell Boy (IRE)**[26] 7319 7-8-2 72 ow2............... BillyCray(5) 5 66
(D J S Ffrench Davis) *sn pushed along in last: effrt on wd outside 2f out: kpt on same pce* **12/1**

5104 **7** nse **Dancing Freddy (IRE)**[10] 7525 3-8-11 70 ow3..(p) RussKennemore(3) 9 73
(J G Given) *mostly pressed ldr to jst over 1f out: wknd* **33/1**

-000 **8** 7 **The Magic Of Rio**[61] 6490 4-8-0 40 ow3...............(b) LeonnaMayor(7) 7 41
(Peter Grayson) *cl up tl wknd 2f out* **100/1**

The Form Book, Raceform Ltd, Compton, RG20 6NL

0000 9 7 **Hatman Jack (IRE)**[30] 7250 4-8-4 46....................(p) FrankieMcDonald 8 13
(B G Powell) *led to 2f out: wknd rapidly: t.o: b.b.v* **100/1**

58.23 secs (-0.57) **Going Correction** -0.025s/f (Stan) **9** Ran SP% **125.7**
Speed ratings (Par 101): **103,102,100,99,98 97,97,86,75**
Tote Swingers:1&2:£3.80, 2&3:£2.80, 1&3:£3.60 CSF £28.36 TOTE £5.70: £1.40, £1.10, £1.30; EX 26.00 Trifecta £113.30 Pool £790.61 - 5.16 winning units..Ebraam was claimed by Robert Bailey for £12,000. Lewyn was claimed by Horses First Racing Limited for £15,000. The Magic of Rio was claimed by P. D. Evans for £10,000.
Owner M Murphy **Bred** Shadwell Farm LLC **Trained** Westoning, Beds

FOCUS
There was a solid pace on in this interesting 5f claimer, which was run in a blizzard, and the form largely makes sense.
Hatman Jack(IRE) Official explanation: trainer said gelding bled from the nose

7636 BETDAQ.CO.UK NURSERY 1m (P)
1:45 (1:45) (Class 4) (0-85,82) 2-Y-O **£3,011** (£896; £447; £223) **Stalls** High

Form RPR
012 1 **Tullius (IRE)**[18] 7417 2-9-0 **75**.............................. LukeMorris 1 78
(P Winkworth) *hld up in 3rd: off the bridle after 3f: repsonded to press and wnt 2nd wl over 1f out: styd on to ld last 100yds* **7/4**[2]

0511 2 ½ **Piceno (IRE)**[95] 5490 2-9-2 **77**.............................. IanMongan 3 79
(D Nicholls) *pushed up to ld and styd wl away fr inner rail: drvn 2f out: hdd and nt qckn last 100yds* **6/4**[1]

01 3 2 ¾ **Islesman**[11] 7503 2-9-3 **78**.............................. JimmyFortune 4 74
(Mrs H S Main) *trckd ldr: rdn 2f out: nt qckn wl over 1f out and sn lost 2nd* **7/1**

1521 4 2 ¾ **Bilko Pak (IRE)**[13] 7484 2-9-7 **82**.............................. GeorgeBaker 2 71
(J G Given) *hld up last: cl enough on inner 2f out: wknd 1f out* **9/2**[3]

1m 37.9s (-0.30) **Going Correction** -0.025s/f (Stan) **4** Ran SP% **107.0**
Speed ratings (Par 98): **100,99,96,94**
CSF £4.67 TOTE £3.60; EX 5.30.
Owner Kennet Valley Thoroughbreds VI **Bred** Sc Archi Romani **Trained** Chiddingfold, Surrey

FOCUS
A very competitive nursery with three of the four being last-time-out winners, and the other having just lost out here on his previous outing. It was run at a fair enough pace with the snow again falling heavily, and the form looks sound.

NOTEBOOK
Tullius(IRE) ◆ had looked somewhat lazy when just held over 7f here 18 days earlier and things didn't look good for him here as he was the first off the bridle from around halfway. His in-form rider kept at him, however, and he just did enough to get on top near the finish. He has now won two of his three outings since switching to Polytrack, this extra furlong no doubt suited and he is the sort the handicapper could have trouble getting to grips with. With that in mind this lightly raced juvenile remains one to follow. (tchd 15-8)
Piceno(IRE) was purchased out of Luca Cumani's stable for 23,000gns last month after making it 2-2 since switching to nurseries. Making his AW debut, he was again sent to the front and got an uncontested lead. He kept on gamely as the challengers mounted and only just lost out to the progressive winner, so this rates a personal-best off his 6lb higher mark. (op 7-4 tchd 15-8)
Islesman had got off the mark at the second attempt at Wolverhampton 11 days earlier. His pedigree suggested the longer trip would suit and he travelled nicely into contention. He failed to see it out like the first pair, however, and appears to have begun life in this sphere on a tough mark. (op 5-1)
Bilko Pak(IRE), making his debut for new connections, was dropped 3lb for his claiming win here 13 days previously. He had stamina to prove for this extra furlong and ultimately looked a non-stayer at this stage of his career. (op 4-1)

7637 BETDAQ THE BETTING EXCHANGE H'CAP 1m (P)
2:15 (2:17) (Class 4) (0-80,80) 3-Y-O+ **£3,675** (£1,093; £546; £272) **Stalls** High

Form RPR
3211 1 **Final Drive (IRE)**[2] 7611 4-9-2 **75** 6ex.............................. EddieAhern 7 83
(J Ryan) *trckd ldrs: cl up 2f out: effrt to ld ent fnl f: sn hdd: styd on wl to regain ld last 75yds* **7/2**[2]

225 2 nk **Wilfred Pickles (IRE)**[122] 4598 4-9-4 **77**.............................. DaneO'Neill 8 84
(Miss Jo Crowley) *hld up in rr: prog gng easily wl over 1f out: swtchd ins and effrt to ld ins fnl f: fnd little and hdd last 75yds* **16/1**

0631 3 ¾ **Halsion Chancer**[18] 7421 6-9-2 **78**.............................. KierenFox(3) 5 83
(J R Best) *trckd ldrs: pushed along over 3f out: effrt u.p 2f out: styd on to take 3rd nr fin* **9/1**

0001 4 shd **Syrian**[17] 7438 3-9-0 **75**.............................. DavidProbert 1 80+
(Ian Williams) *s.s: t.k.h: hld up in last pair: stl last 2f out: weaved through fr jst over 1f out: styd on: nrst fin* **12/1**

3605 5 ½ **Thunderball**[24] 7352 4-9-1 **79**.............................. BillyCray(5) 4 83
(D Nicholls) *pressed ldr: rdn to ld jst over 2f out: hdd ent fnl f: fdd nr fin* **4/1**[3]

0062 6 ¾ **Elspeth's Boy (USA)**[13] 7488 3-9-2 **77**.............................. LukeMorris 9 79
(J R Best) *t.k.h: pressed ldng pair on outer: effrt 2f out: nrly upsides 1f out: fdd* **11/4**[1]

0531 7 1 **Young Dottie**[10] 7521 4-9-6 **79**.............................. IanMongan 11 79
(P M Phelan) *t.k.h: hld up in rr on outer: effrt over 2f out: one pce over 1f out* **13/2**

4600 8 2 ¼ **Salient**[18] 7421 6-8-11 **73**.............................. MatthewDavies(3) 6 68
(M J Attwater) *hld up in midfield: rdn and no prog over 2f out: wknd fnl f* **40/1**

230 9 1 ¾ **Waabel**[50] 6814 3-9-2 **77**.............................. JimmyFortune 3 68
(Jim Best) *led to jst 2f out: wknd fnl f* **33/1**

6400 10 ½ **Kavachi (IRE)**[36] 7121 7-9-7 **80**.............................. GeorgeBaker 2 70
(G L Moore) *trckd ldng pair on inner: rdn and wknd 2f out* **50/1**

1m 37.13s (-1.07) **Going Correction** -0.025s/f (Stan)
WFA 3 from 4yo+ 2lb **10** Ran SP% **113.1**
Speed ratings (Par 105): **104,103,102,102,102 101,100,98,96,96**
Tote Swingers:1&2:£8.80, 2&3:£14.90, 1&3:£6.30 CSF £54.69 CT £461.23 TOTE £6.20: £1.50, £4.80, £3.00; EX 61.00 Trifecta £559.60 Part won. Pool £756.33 - 0.50 winning units..
Owner Par 4 Racing **Bred** D Day & B Cantwell **Trained** Newmarket, Suffolk

FOCUS
A competitive handicap with four last-time-out winners in attendance. It was run at an ordinary pace, though, which resulted in lots of chances off the home turn and the overall form is worth treating with a little caution.

7638 BET ASHES CRICKET - BETDAQ H'CAP 1m 2f (P)
2:40 (2:44) (Class 4) (0-80,79) 3-Y-O **£3,675** (£1,093; £546; £272) **Stalls** Low

Form RPR
2164 1 **Dark Promise**[32] 7206 3-9-5 **77**.............................. JimmyFortune 5 89+
(M A Jarvis) *trckd ldr: led over 2f out: rdn 3 l clr over 1f out: idled bdly fnl f: drvn rt out* **8/13**[1]

0360 2 ½ **Fonterutoli (IRE)**[59] 6581 3-8-13 **71**.............................. DaneO'Neill 2 76
(R Ingram) *hld up last: effrt on inner over 2f out: shkn up to chse wnr over 1f out: clsng rapidly at fin* **20/1**

214 3 1 ¼ **Commerce**[30] 7253 3-8-9 **67**.............................. DavidProbert 3 70
(S Dow) *hld up bhd ldng pair: rdn to dipsute 2nd over 1f out: nt qckn* **5/1**[2]

3361 4 2 **Flag Of Glory**[75] 6122 3-9-1 **73**.............................. GeorgeBaker 4 72
(C F Wall) *led: tried to kick on over 3f out: hdd over 2f out: sn outpcd by wnr: lost 2nd and fdd over 1f out* **5/1**[2]

610 5 3 **Sweet Child O'Mine**[10] 7523 3-9-7 **79**.............................. FrannyNorton 1 72
(R C Guest) *t.k.h: hld up bhd ldng pair: outpcd and last over 2f out: n.d after* **8/1**[3]

2m 5.05s (-1.55) **Going Correction** -0.025s/f (Stan) **5** Ran SP% **111.1**
Speed ratings (Par 104): **105,104,103,102,99**
CSF £14.35 TOTE £1.90: £1.10, £9.70; EX 12.50.
Owner Lordship Stud **Bred** Lordship Stud **Trained** Newmarket, Suffolk

FOCUS
A modest 3-y-o handicap. The placed horses set the level.

7639 FELBRIDGE H'CAP (DIV I) 6f (P)
3:10 (3:12) (Class 6) (0-60,60) 3-Y-O+ **£1,706** (£503; £252) **Stalls** Low

Form RPR
3043 1 **South African Gold (USA)**[11] 7501 3-9-7 **60**.............(p) JackMitchell 10 67
(J M P Eustace) *trckd ldng trio: effrt 2f out: drvn to chal ins fnl f: led last strides* **13/2**[3]

2650 2 shd **Interchoice Star**[25] 7332 5-9-5 **58**..............................(p) GeorgeBaker 4 65
(R E Peacock) *trckd ldng pair: gng easily 2f out: rdn to ld on inner 1f out: kpt on: hdd last strides* **14/1**

1503 3 ½ **Best One**[7] 7537 6-9-4 **57**..............................(b) LukeMorris 8 62
(R A Harris) *hld up towards rr: rdn wl over 1f out: hanging and nt look keen: styd on u.p fnl f: tk 3rd last stride* **15/2**

0301 4 shd **Espy**[10] 7519 5-9-7 **60**.............................. FergusSweeney 5 65
(I W McInnes) *hld up in midfield: clsd on ldrs fr 2f out: drvn to chal ins fnl f: nt qckn* **4/1**[1]

0252 5 nk **Loyal Royal (IRE)**[10] 7519 7-9-1 **57**....................(bt) RussKennemore(3) 3 61
(J M Bradley) *s.i.s: hld up in midfield: rdn and looking for room over 1f out: cl up bhd ldrs fnl f but nvr really chal* **9/2**[2]

3400 6 3 ¼ **Mary's Pet**[20] 7391 3-9-7 **60**.............................. IanMongan 6 54
(J Akehurst) *trckd ldr: led over 2f out: hdd & wknd 1f out* **8/1**

6005 7 1 ¼ **Charles Darwin (IRE)**[10] 7518 7-9-5 **58**.............................. FrannyNorton 11 49
(M Blanshard) *hld up in rr and racd wd: shkn up wl over 1f out: no prog* **9/2**[2]

000 8 1 ½ **West Leake (IRE)**[20] 7391 4-9-3 **56**.............................. ChrisCatlin 1 42
(P Burgoyne) *hld up in midfield on inner: nt qckn 2f out: shkn up and wl btn over 1f out* **14/1**

0000 9 11 **Heliocentric**[14] 7475 3-9-2 **55**..............................(b[1]) DavidProbert 7 8
(B Palling) *dwlt: sn detached in last and nvr gng wl: t.o* **16/1**

000 10 nk **Flyjack (USA)**[11] 7502 3-8-13 **52**..............................(b) DaneO'Neill 2 4
(Mrs L Williamson) *led to over 2f out: wknd rapidly over 1f out: eased: t.o* **25/1**

1m 11.91s (0.01) **Going Correction** -0.025s/f (Stan) **10** Ran SP% **115.6**
Speed ratings (Par 101): **98,97,97,97,96 92,90,88,74,73**
Tote Swingers:1&2:£11.50, 2&3:£13.70, 1&3:£7.20 CSF £92.16 CT £715.39 TOTE £7.70: £2.40, £4.40, £1.90; EX 92.20 Trifecta £388.00 Part won. Pool £524.40 - 0.64 winning units..
Owner William Mocatta **Bred** Douglas S Arnold **Trained** Newmarket, Suffolk

FOCUS
This was wide open. It was run at a sound pace and the first five were very closely covered at the finish.

7640 FELBRIDGE H'CAP (DIV II) 6f (P)
3:40 (3:41) (Class 6) (0-60,60) 3-Y-O+ **£1,706** (£503; £252) **Stalls** Low

Form RPR
3445 1 **Dancing Welcome**[11] 7501 4-8-13 **55**.................(b) RussKennemore(3) 3 67
(J M Bradley) *pressed ldng pair: shkn up over 2f out: led wl over 1f out: sn clr: in n.d after* **15/2**

1213 2 3 ¼ **Rio Royale (IRE)**[10] 7518 4-9-7 **60**..............................(p) JimmyFortune 1 62
(Mrs A J Perrett) *pressed ldr to 2f out: sn outpcd: kpt on to take 2nd again ins fnl f* **11/4**[1]

3064 3 ½ **Chinese Democracy (USA)**[10] 7518 3-9-4 **57**..........(v) GeorgeBaker 10 58
(P D Evans) *hld up towards rr on outer: rdn wl over 1f out: styd on fnl f: tk 3rd fin* **9/2**[2]

0000 4 ¾ **Fayre Bella**[20] 7391 3-9-2 **55**.............................. FergusSweeney 12 54
(J Gallagher) *stdd s: hld up last of main gp: stl there gng easily 2f out: nt clr run sn after: rdn and r.o fnl f: nvr nr ldrs* **33/1**

6335 5 shd **Durgan**[17] 7441 4-9-4 **57**..............................(p) SteveDrowne 11 55
(Mrs L C Jewell) *settled in midfield: rdn wl over 1f out: nt qckn and no prog: kpt on last 75yds* **8/1**

0000 6 ½ **Bobs Dreamflight**[20] 7390 4-9-4 **57**..............................(b) SamHitchcott 6 54
(D K Ivory) *taken down early: led to wl over 1f out: steadily wknd* **12/1**

0020 7 ½ **Meydan Dubai (IRE)**[22] 7380 5-8-10 **52**.......................(b) KierenFox(3) 7 47
(J R Best) *hld up towards rr on inner: rdn 2f out: no prog and btn over 1f out* **11/2**[3]

0001 8 1 ½ **Pragmatist**[20] 7391 6-9-7 **60**.............................. JamesMillman 4 51
(B R Millman) *hld up bhd ldrs gng strly: rdn and no rspnse over 1f out: immediately btn* **10/1**

-010 9 ½ **Final Rhapsody**[30] 7249 4-9-1 **54**.............................. ChrisCatlin 2 43
(W J Musson) *sn trckd ldrs: rdn 2f out: disp 3rd briefly jst over 1f out: sn wknd* **16/1**

5306 10 3 **Athaakeel (IRE)**[10] 7519 4-9-7 **60**.............................. LukeMorris 5 40
(R A Harris) *rel to r: a t.o* **11/1**

1m 11.9s **Going Correction** -0.025s/f (Stan) **10** Ran SP% **117.0**
Speed ratings (Par 101): **99,94,94,93,92 92,91,89,88,84**
Tote Swingers:1&2:£5.30, 2&3:£3.50, 1&3:£6.00. totesuper7: Win: Not won. Place: £219.80. CSF £28.52 CT £107.99 TOTE £5.50: £1.40, £2.50, £2.80; EX 27.50 Trifecta £84.00 Pool £596.02 - 5.25 winning units..
Owner J M Bradley **Bred** The Hon Mrs E J Wills **Trained** Sedbury, Gloucs

FOCUS
The second division of the weak 6f handicap and another wide-open looking race.
Fayre Bella ◆ Official explanation: jockey said filly was denied a clear run

T/Jkpt: £42,576.30 to a £1 stake. Pool of £179,899.99. 3.00 winning tickets. T/Plt: £568.30 to a £1 stake. Pool of £100,259.90. 128.77 winning tickets. T/Qpdt: £67.70 to a £1 stake. Pool of £8,399.26. 91.69 winning tickets. JN

7536 SOUTHWELL (L-H)

Tuesday, November 30

OFFICIAL GOING: Standard to slow

Wind: Light, half-behind. Weather: wintry showers, misty, cold

7641 THANKS LOVELY DOREEN (S) STKS — 5f (F)

1:00 (1:00) (Class 6) 2-Y-O — £1,637 (£483; £241) Stalls High

Form				RPR
3044	1		**Je Suis Unrockstar**[14] 7469 2-8-12 55 (p) PJMcDonald 7 (D Nicholls) *mde all: drew clr fnl f: drvn out* 11/4[1]	60
0056	2	3 ½	**Molly Mylenis**[4] 7576 2-8-12 55 JamesDoyle 12 (P D Evans) *chsd ldrs stands' side: styd on to take 2nd jst ins fnl f* 16/1	47
61	3	2 ¼	**Hereseliie (IRE)**[147] 3757 2-8-12 55 GrahamGibbons 1 (T D Barron) *w wnr: wknd fnl f* 11/4[1]	39
60	4	¾	**Just For Leo (IRE)**[29] 7269 2-8-12 64 CathyGannon 4 (P D Evans) *chsd ldrs: wknd over 1f out* 3/1[2]	37
3020	5	1 ½	**Beyaz Villas**[59] 6569 2-8-12 68 PaulQuinn 5 (D Nicholls) *wnt lft s: outpcd and edgd lft over 2f out: kpt on fnl f: nvr on terms* 10/3[3]	31
00	6	2 ½	**Ngina**[19] 7408 2-8-7 0 PatrickMathers 9 (D Shaw) *s.i.s: sn chsng ldrs: hung lft and lost pl over 1f out* 66/1	17
000	7	1 ¼	**Mrs Nisbett (IRE)**[10] 7527 2-8-4 40 AndrewHeffernan(3) 11 (A J McCabe) *racd stands' side: in tch: outpcd over 2f out: no threat after* 33/1	13
00	8	8	**Likeable Lad**[61] 6500 2-8-9 0 JamesSullivan(3) 10 (Mrs R A Carr) *w ldrs stands' side: lost pl over 2f out: sn bhd* 50/1	—

61.24 secs (1.54) **Going Correction** +0.175s/f (Slow) 8 Ran SP% **113.7**

Speed ratings (Par 94): **94,88,84,83,81 77,75,62**

Tote Swingers:1&2:£8.00, 2&3:£7.20, 1&3:£2.00 CSF £44.61 TOTE £2.40: £1.02, £7.70, £1.10; EX 42.40.There was no bid for the winner.

Owner Paul J Dixon **Bred** Mrs Yvette Dixon **Trained** Sessay, N Yorks

FOCUS

The track saw 10mm of snow overnight, but had been worked through the night and racing went ahead without any problems. The course was expected to ride on the slow side and the time of this opener, over three seconds above standard, seemed to confirm that was the case. A moderate juvenile seller.

NOTEBOOK

Je Suis Unrockstar proved unsuited by a fast-run 6f around here last time and the drop back to a stiff 5f clearly suited. This was his first success at the tenth attempt and he seemed to run above his official mark of 55, so he should have more to offer at this distance. \n\x\x \bMolly Mylenis\p, trying Fibresand for the first time, had the same chance as the winner at the weights, but she was no match for that rival.\n (op 4-1)

Molly Mylenis, trying Fibresand for the first time, had the same chance as the winner at the weights, but she was no match for that rival. (op 14-1)

Hereseliie(IRE), off the track since winning a C&D seller in July (retained without a bid), made a respectable return. She should be sharper next time. (op 3-1 tchd 10-3)

Just For Leo(IRE), trying Fibresand for the first time, didn't run up to his official mark of 64. (tchd 11-4)

Beyaz Villas, the winner's stable companion, was never going on this first taste of Fibresand. (op 11-4 tchd 7-2)

7642 DOUG CLARKE'S 80TH BIRTHDAY CELEBRATIONS H'CAP — 1m 4f (F)

1:30 (1:30) (Class 5) (0-75,72) 3-Y-O+ — £2,183 (£644; £322) Stalls Low

Form				RPR
1502	1		**Maslak (IRE)**[38] 7101 6-9-10 72 WilliamCarson 6 (P W Hiatt) *trckd ldr: led 3f out: narrowly hdd 2f out: styd on strly to regain ld jst ins fnl f* 5/1	83
5042	2	2 ¼	**Yossi (IRE)**[7] 7541 6-8-3 58 oh6 (be) SeanPalmer(7) 5 (R C Guest) *dwlt: sn trcking ldrs: drvn 3f out: led narrowly 2f out: hdd jst ins fnl f: kpt on same pce* 10/3[2]	65
5011	3	4	**Kingaroo (IRE)**[7] 7541 4-8-11 62 6ex AndrewHeffernan(3) 3 (G Woodward) *led: qcknd over 4f out: hdd 3f out: one pce fnl 2f* 15/8[1]	63
6000	4	1	**General Tufto**[7] 7541 5-9-10 72 (b) PhillipMakin 4 (C Smith) *trckd ldrs: t.k.h: drvn over 3f out: one pce fnl 2f* 20/1	71
0444	5	½	**Dance For Julie (IRE)**[136] 2993 3-8-13 70 PatrickDonaghy(3) 2 (B M R Haslam) *hld up in rr: hdwy over 4f out: swtchd rt over 2f out: one pce* 10/1	68
222U	6	6	**Fashionable Gal (IRE)**[4] 7579 3-9-2 70 StevieDonohoe 1 (Sir Mark Prescott) *dwlt: t.k.h in rr: hdwy on outside over 4f out: drvn over 3f out: wknd end edgd lft over 1f out: eased towards fin* 4/1[3]	59

2m 44.68s (3.68) **Going Correction** +0.075s/f (Slow)

WFA 3 from 4yo+ 6lb 6 Ran SP% **108.4**

Speed ratings (Par 103): **90,88,85,85,84 80**

Tote Swingers:1&2:£3.70, 2&3:£1.10, 1&3:£4.00 CSF £20.26 TOTE £4.70: £1.80, £1.80; EX 22.90.

Owner Alan Swinburne **Bred** Shadwell Estate Company Limited **Trained** Hook Norton, Oxon

FOCUS

A modest handicap.

7643 KRIS & HELEN CLARK'S 4 YEAR ANNIVERSARY NURSERY — 7f (F)

2:00 (2:03) (Class 6) (0-60,60) 2-Y-O — £1,706 (£503; £252) Stalls Low

Form				RPR
6046	1		**Irie Ute**[6] 7551 2-9-7 60 JamesDoyle 2 (S Kirk) *trckd ldrs: hrd rdn 3f out: styd on to take narrow ld over 1f out: all out* 8/1[3]	66
0001	2	shd	**Geronimo Chief (IRE)**[20] 7393 2-9-5 58 PJMcDonald 12 (B M R Haslam) *led tl over 4f out: racd upsides: stuck on wl ins fnl f: jst hld* 3/1[1]	64
0402	3	nk	**Ace Master**[14] 7469 2-8-12 51 CathyGannon 1 (S R Bowring) *w ldr: led over 4f out: narrowly hdd over 1f out: hung lft: no ex fnl 75yds* 4/1[2]	56
0401	4	1 ¾	**Urban Kode (IRE)**[1] 7630 2-9-1 54 6ex JimmyQuinn 9 (P D Evans) *chsd ldrs: outpcd and lost pl over 3f out: kpt on fnl 2f* 3/1[1]	55
0006	5	2	**False Promises**[4] 7577 2-8-6 45 PatrickMathers 6 (D Shaw) *chsd ldrs: outpcd over 3f out: kpt on fnl 2f* 80/1	40
0406	6	½	**Miss Cosette (IRE)**[20] 7394 2-8-7 46 ow1 GrahamGibbons 11 (T D Barron) *chsd ldrs on outer: carried wd and lost pl over 4f out: kpt on fnl 2f* 9/1	40
000	7	1	**Fearless Poet (IRE)**[34] 7172 2-8-7 46 ow1 TomEaves 8 (B Smart) *s.i.s: outpcd over 3f out: kpt on fnl 2f: nvr a factor* 14/1	37
6434	8	9	**Mary Boyle**[7] 7540 2-9-4 60 AndrewHeffernan(3) 5 (A J McCabe) *gave problems in stalls: in tch: drvn 3f out: lost pl over 1f out: sn bhd* 11/1	28
4006	9	6	**Deva Le Deva (IRE)**[12] 7497 2-9-3 56 RichardKingscote 10 (Tom Dascombe) *chsd ldrs on outer: rn wd and lost pl over 4f out: eased whn bhd ins fnl f* 16/1	8
0006	10	36	**Iwantobreakfree**[36] 7118 2-8-6 45 WilliamCarson 3 (P D Evans) *s.s: in rr: bhd fnl 3f: sn eased: t.o* 28/1	—

1m 31.67s (1.37) **Going Correction** +0.075s/f (Slow) 10 Ran SP% **116.7**

Speed ratings (Par 94): **95,94,94,92,90 89,88,78,71,30**

Tote Swingers:1&2:£4.20, 2&3:£2.60, 1&3:£5.20 CSF £32.25 CT £114.36 TOTE £8.80: £2.40, £1.80, £2.70; EX 32.90.

Owner I A N Wight **Bred** Poulton Farm Stud **Trained** Upper Lambourn, Berks

■ Stewards' Enquiry : P J McDonald four-day ban: used whip with excessive frequency (Dec 14-17)

FOCUS

Another snow shower forced a delay, with the tractors having to go round again. A moderate but competitive nursery.

NOTEBOOK

Irie Ute had travelled well for a long way before fading into fourth behind Geronimo Chief over 1m around here on November 10 and this shorter trip helped him reverse form on 7lb better terms. The winner had subsequently been beaten on Polytrack, but the return to Fibresand suited and he benefited from a good, strong ride. (op 6-1 tchd 11-2)

Geronimo Chief(IRE) stayed on well for pressure, but struggled to peg back his old rival and this drop in trip, even on a particularly slow surface, slightly inconvenienced him. (op 10-3 tchd 7-2)

Ace Master, back up in trip, got stuck towards the inside rail late on, which is rarely the place to be at Southwell. This was a noteworthy effort relative to the grade. (op 9-2 tchd 11-2)

Urban Kode(IRE), penalised for winning over an extended 1m at Wolverhampton the previous day, found this an insufficient test of stamina. (op 4-1 tchd 11-4)

Deva Le Deva(IRE) Official explanation: jockey said filly never travelled

7644 ADAM WILKINSON HAPPY 50TH BIRTHDAY MAIDEN STKS — 1m (F)

2:30 (2:36) (Class 5) 2-Y-O — £2,183 (£644; £322) Stalls Low

Form				RPR
3024	1		**Lexington Bay (IRE)**[5] 7567 2-9-3 73 TomEaves 3 (R A Fahey) *sn drvn along to chse ldr: hrd rdn over 2f out: styd on to ld last 150yds: won gng away* 15/8[1]	73
0402	2	2	**Rath Maeve**[20] 7396 2-8-9 55 AndrewHeffernan(3) 4 (A J McCabe) *led: hdd jst ins fnl f: no ex* 16/1	63
04	3	1 ¼	**Dictate**[19] 7400 2-8-12 0 AshleyMorgan(5) 5 (M H Tompkins) *dwlt: sn drvn along: chsng ldrs 5f out: kpt on same pce fnl f: wknd nr fin* 2/1[2]	66
4455	4	15	**Entrance**[38] 7087 2-8-12 68 CathyGannon 1 (Miss J Feilden) *chsd ldrs: effrt over 3f out: outpcd over 2f out: wknd over 1f out: eased ins fnl f* 5/1[3]	26

1m 45.34s (1.64) **Going Correction** +0.075s/f (Slow) 4 Ran SP% **90.7**

Speed ratings (Par 96): **94,92,90,75**

CSF £15.14 TOTE £2.50; EX 11.30.

Owner Keith Denham & Tony Denham **Bred** Mrs Vanessa Hutch **Trained** Musley Bank, N Yorks

■ Honest Deal (5/1) was withdrawn after breaking out of the stalls. Deduct 15p in the £ under R4.

■ Stewards' Enquiry : Andrew Heffernan four-day ban: used whip with excessive frequency (Dec 14-17)

FOCUS

The snow shower continued, resulting in another delay, with four tractors harrowing the course before the off. The race was run in gloomy conditions, and by the time the runners reached the straight, the course was again covered in snow. Honest Deal had to be withdrawn after getting under the front of the stalls. This was a weak maiden.

NOTEBOOK

Lexington Bay(IRE), back on Fibresand, made hard work of getting off the mark at the fifth attempt. He needed to be driven along to take up a prominent position, and then took an age to get by the runner-up when under more vigorous driving, not really knuckling down. However, there may be more to come over further in handicaps if and when he's gelded, although his high knee action suggests he'll want a forgiving surface. (op 7-4 tchd 13-8 and 2-1)

Rath Maeve, runner-up to a subsequent nursery winner in a C&D seller on her previous start, enjoyed the run of the race and had her chance. (op 9-1)

Dictate ran to just a modest level, but handicaps are now an option. (op 5-2 tchd 15-8)

Entrance, bought out of Ed Dunlop's yard for 8,000gns in October, ran no sort of race on this switch to Fibresand. (op 15-2)

7645 COCO & LUIS AT DOUBLE MAIDEN STKS — 7f (F)

3:00 (3:01) (Class 5) 3-Y-O+ — £2,183 (£644; £322) Stalls Low

Form				RPR
6363	1		**Adam De Beaulieu (USA)**[14] 7473 3-9-3 61 (t) PhillipMakin 5 (B M R Haslam) *led: qcknd over 3f out: styd on u.p: eased nr fin* 13/8[2]	70
2330	2	2	**Turning Circle**[206] 1924 4-9-4 64 JoeFanning 6 (M Brittain) *chsd ldrs: wnt 2nd over 3f out: kpt on same pce: no imp* 11/4[3]	65
0-22	3	1 ¼	**Opus Dei**[11] 7505 3-9-3 71 PJMcDonald 1 (D Nicholls) *trckd ldrs: drvn 4f out: sn outpcd: wnt modest 3rd over 2f out: kpt on fnl f* 6/4[1]	62
0006	4	8	**Northumberland**[25] 7328 4-9-1 42 RobertLButler(3) 3 (M C Chapman) *w ldr: outpcd over 3f out: wknd 2f out* 80/1	41
00-0	5	2 ¼	**Towthorpe**[182] 2629 4-8-11 57 JohnCavanagh(7) 2 (M Brittain) *dwlt: sn chsng ldrs: drvn over 3f out: sn lost pl* 33/1	35
000	6	8	**Mighty Aphrodite**[5] 7563 3-8-5 57 (p) JamesRogers(7) 4 (Miss Olivia Maylam) *in rr: sn drvn along: lost tch 5f out: eased whn wl bhd clsng stages* 16/1	9

1m 30.31s (0.01) **Going Correction** +0.075s/f (Slow)

WFA 3 from 4yo 1lb 6 Ran SP% **114.8**

Speed ratings (Par 103): **102,99,98,89,86 77**

Tote Swingers:1&2:£1.60, 2&3:£1.70, 1&3:£1.40 CSF £6.81 TOTE £3.80: £2.10, £1.30; EX 6.90.

Owner E D Feather **Bred** Brian Kahn, Richard O'Neil Et Al **Trained** Middleham Moor, N Yorks

FOCUS

A modest, uncompetitive maiden.

7646 SOUTHWELL-RACECOURSE.CO.UK H'CAP — 1m (F)

3:30 (3:31) (Class 6) (0-65,65) 3-Y-O+ — £1,706 (£503; £252) Stalls Low

Form				RPR
3655	1		**Ingleby King (USA)**[31] 7230 4-8-7 51 oh1 GrahamGibbons 11 (T D Barron) *w ldr: chal over 2f out: led appr fnl f: drew away clsng stages* 4/1[3]	66
0641	2	1 ½	**Ubenkor (IRE)**[7] 7543 5-9-3 61 6ex TomEaves 10 (M Herrington) *led: narrowly hdd appr fnl f: styd on same pce* 2/1[1]	73
0452	3	10	**Olney Lass**[19] 7406 3-8-5 58 JamesRogers(7) 1 (Mike Murphy) *chsd ldrs: outpcd over 3f out: swtchd lft and styd on over 1f out: tk n.d 3rd jst ins fnl f* 11/1	47
5531	4	1	**Watch Chain (IRE)**[19] 7402 3-8-10 61 AshleyMorgan(5) 6 (M H Tompkins) *hld up towards rr: effrt 3f out: kpt on to take n.d 4th jst ins fnl f* 11/4[2]	47

3263 **5** 2 1/4 **Morocchius (USA)**22 6463 5-8-12 56........................(p) BarryMcHugh 12 37
(Julie Camacho) *trckd ldrs: effrt 3f out: sn rdn: one pce* **8/1**
0200 **6** 4 1/2 **Orpen Wide (IRE)**39 6890 8-8-10 57........................(bt) RobertLButler(3) 4 28
(M C Chapman) *in rr: reminders over 4f out: nvr on terms* **33/1**
6400 **7** 1 **Mojeerr**10 7529 4-8-4 51 oh1................................(v) AndrewHeffernan(3) 3 19
(A J McCabe) *sn pushed along in rr: sme hdwy over 3f out: nvr a factor* **20/1**
4/0- **8** 4 1/2 **Ryan's Rock**575 1741 5-8-7 51 oh1................................ AndreaAtzeni 9 9
(R J Price) *s.s: bhd fnl 3f* **66/1**
440 **9** 3/4 **Plenilune (IRE)**76 6077 5-8-7 51 oh5................................ JimmyQuinn 8 7
(M Brittain) *chsd ldrs: rdn 4f out: lost pl over 2f out* **33/1**
0006 **10** 3 3/4 **Flores Sea (USA)**103 5241 6-9-7 65................................ PhillipMakin 7 13
(Mrs R A Carr) *chsd ldrs: lost pl 3f out: sn bhd* **22/1**

1m 42.77s (-0.93) **Going Correction** +0.075s/f (Slow)
WFA 3 from 4yo+ 2lb **10** Ran SP% **115.9**
Speed ratings (Par 101): **107,105,95,94,92 87,86,82,81,77**
Tote Swingers:1&2:£3.00, 2&3:£4.20, 1&3:£5.70 CSF £11.61 CT £81.84 TOTE £4.40: £1.80, £1.10, £3.20; EX 15.00.
Owner Dave Scott **Bred** Glencrest Farm LLC **Trained** Maunby, N Yorks

FOCUS
Not for the first time on this snow-drenched card, it paid to race prominently. A moderate, uncompetitive handicap in which the first two finished clear.
T/Plt: £47.70 to a £1 stake. Pool of £81,801.76. 1,251.68 winning tickets. T/Qpdt: £10.30 to a £1 stake. Pool of £8,365.70. 598.20 winning tickets. WG

7048 DEAUVILLE (R-H)
Tuesday, November 30

OFFICIAL GOING: Fibresand: standard

7647a PRIX DE FONTENEROUX (CONDITIONS) (2YO COLTS & GELDINGS) (FIBRESAND) 7f 110y
12:05 (12:00) 2-Y-O **£15,044** (£6,017; £4,513; £3,008; £1,504)

RPR
1 **Uldiko (FR)**29 2-8-8 0................................(p) MatthieuAutier(6) 11 83
(Mme C Barande-Barbe, France) **37/10**2
2 1/2 **Lachlan Bridge (GER)**12 2-9-0 0................................ OlivierPeslier 4 82
(Y De Nicolay, France) **5/2**1
3 1 1/2 **Point Du Jour (FR)**10 7528 2-8-10 0................................ IoritzMendizabal 1 74
(I A Wood) *mid-div on rail: rdn bef st: swtchd to mid-trck: picked up wl 1 1/2f out: fin wl ins fnl 100yds* **11/1**
4 1 **Alphorn (FR)** 2-8-7 0................................ DominiqueBoeuf 9 69
(Y Barberot, France) **19/1**
5 1 1/2 **The Nought Man (FR)**29 2-9-0 0................................ MaximeGuyon 3 72
(J E Hammond, France) **11/1**
6 hd **Rudyard (IRE)**22 2-9-0 0................................(b) FranckBlondel 2 72
(J E Hammond, France) **63/10**
7 1 **Dejeuner D'Enfer (FR)** 2-8-10 0................................ AlexandreRoussel 6 65
(Mlle C Cardenne, France) **18/1**
8 nk **Pam (IRE)** 2-9-0 0................................ GregoryBenoist 8 69
(Robert Collet, France) **9/2**3
9 6 **Juliano (FR)** 2-7-13 0................................ JeremyBonin(8) 7 48
(J-L Pelletan, France) **53/1**
10 10 **Gatinello (FR)**17 2-8-10 0................................ MickaelBarzalona 5 27
(C Laffon-Parias, France) **22/1**

1m 30.6s (90.60) **10** Ran SP% **114.9**
WIN (incl. 1 euro stake): 4.70. PLACES: 1.70, 1.40, 2.70. DF: 7.80. SF: 16.20.
Owner Mme Corine Barande-Barbe **Bred** Mme S Langlois **Trained** France

NOTEBOOK
Point Du Jour(FR), who settled much better than has been the case, slightly lost his position from the inside draw, allowing the front two first run, but he kept on well for a place. He proved suited by the surface, which seemed to be riding on the slow side, and shaped as though he'll get further.

7648a PRIX BELLE DE NUIT (LISTED RACE) (3YO+ FILLIES & MARES) (FIBRESAND) 1m 4f
1:40 (12:00) 3-Y-O+ **£23,008** (£9,203; £6,902; £4,601; £2,300)

RPR
1 **Terre Du Vent (FR)**26 4-9-0 0................................ FabriceVeron 5 —
(Y De Nicolay, France) **30/1**
2 nk **Salontanzerin (GER)**30 5-9-0 0................................ MickaelBarzalona 16 —
(W Hickst, Germany) **16/1**
3 1 1/2 **Santa Biatra (FR)**17 4-9-0 0................................ GaetanMasure 12 —
(A Couetil, France) **9/1**2
4 snk **La Boum (GER)**19 7416 7-9-4 0................................ IoritzMendizabal 14 —
(Robert Collet, France) **14/5**1
5 1 1/2 **Seeking Solace**62 6486 3-8-8 0................................ MaximeGuyon 9 —
(A Fabre, France) **17/1**
6 snk **Para Elisa (IRE)** 4-9-0 0................................ JulienGrosjean 8 —
(Y Durepaire, Spain) **49/1**
7 snk **Indiana Wells (FR)**80 5980 3-8-8 0................................ FranckBlondel 10 —
(F Rohaut, France) **36/1**
8 shd **Next Dream (FR)** 3-8-8 0................................ Francois-XavierBertras 11 —
(F Rohaut, France) **18/1**
9 snk **Plume Rose**17 7457 3-8-8 0................................ RonanThomas 2 —
(Y De Nicolay, France) **22/1**
10 hd **Foundation Filly**62 6486 3-8-8 0................................ ThierryThulliez 15 —
(F Doumen, France) **11/1**3
0 **Fleur Enchantee (FR)**35 7160 6-9-4 0................................(p) OlivierPeslier 6 —
(P Van De Poele, France) **14/5**1
0 **La Poesie (GER)**59 4-9-0 0................................ DominiqueBoeuf 1 —
(W Baltromei, Germany) **26/1**
0 **Shany De Loriol (FR)**35 4-9-0 0................................ ThomasHuet 4 —
(C Provot, France) **59/1**
0 **Nezhenka**33 7189 3-8-8 0................................ Jean-BernardEyquem 13 —
(Sir Mark Prescott) *broke wl on outside and disp ld early: ld after 1f and sn swtchd to ins rail: pushed along and hdd over 2f out: sn wknd and bhd: eased appr fnl f* **28/1**
0 **Skia (FR)**37 3-8-8 0................................ JeromeClaudic 3 —
(C Laffon-Parias, France) **12/1**

2m 33.4s (153.40)
WFA 3 from 4yo+ 6lb **15** Ran SP% **116.5**
PARI-MUTUEL (all including 1 euro stakes): WIN 13.20 (coupled with Plume Rose) ; PLACE 8.30, 5.20, 3.30; DF 199.40; SF 387.20.
Owner Claude Lambert **Bred** Claude Lambert **Trained** France

7607 KEMPTON (A.W) (R-H)
Wednesday, December 1

OFFICIAL GOING: Standard
Wind: Strong, across Weather: Overcast, bitterly cold

7649 BOXINGDAYRACES.CO.UK ALL WEATHER "HANDS AND HEELS" APPRENTICE SERIES H'CAP 1m (P)
2:00 (2:00) (Class 7) (0-50,50) 3-Y-0+ **£1,364** (£403; £201) **Stalls High**

Form RPR
0400 **1** **Custard Cream Kid (IRE)**160 3370 4-8-8 49................ LauraBarry(5) 8 53
(R A Fahey) *sn settled in midfield: prog over 2f out: chal fnl f: kpt on to ld nr fin* **7/1**
6665 **2** hd **Djalalabad (FR)**194 2299 6-8-13 49................................(t) ShaneBKelly 12 53
(J Pearce) *hld up in rr: prog on outer over 2f out: led ins fnl f: hdd nr fin* **12/1**
0063 **3** shd **Devon Diva**20 7413 4-9-0 50................................ RichardRowe 2 53
(M Hill) *racd wd: sn prom: chal over 1f out: upsides ins fnl f: jst hld* **16/1**
40/3 **4** 3/4 **Kadouchski (FR)**315 228 6-8-7 48................................ HannahNunn(5) 1 50+
(John Berry) *settled in last pair: sn wl off the pce: styd on fr 2f out: nrst fin* **16/1**
2066 **5** 1/2 **Abhainn (IRE)**12 7506 4-8-9 48................................ ThomasBrown(3) 6 48
(B Palling) *chsd ldr: led over 1f out to ins fnl f: wknd nr fin* **9/1**
5400 **6** 1/2 **Straight And Level (CAN)**7 7557 5-8-9 50.......(v) CharlotteJenner(5) 14 49
(Miss Jo Crowley) *settled towards rr: no imp on ldrs 2f out: kpt on ins fnl f* **4/1**2
5000 **7** 1/2 **Lucky Diva**155 3526 3-8-8 50................................ LukeRowe(5) 13 48
(S Kirk) *hld up last: sn t.o: stl t.o over 2f out: r.o fr over 1f out: nrst fin* **16/1**
0042 **8** 1 1/4 **Ymir**7 7555 4-8-12 48................................(vt) MatthewLawson 9 43
(M J Attwater) *trckd ldng pair: lost pl 2f out: n.d ins fnl f* **7/2**1
0500 **9** 1 1/2 **Inquisitress**42 7023 6-8-12 48................................ MatthewCosham 10 40
(J J Bridger) *hld up: trckd ldrs in 6th fr 1/2-way: cl up 2f out: nt qckn over 1f out: wknd* **9/1**
2-00 **10** 2 1/2 **Daily Double**14 7487 4-8-9 50................................(v1) KirstenSmith(5) 3 36
(M R Bosley) *in tch: effrt on inner over 2f out: wknd over 1f out* **50/1**
300- **11** 1 1/2 **Brooksby**382 7392 4-8-11 50................................(b) LucyBarry(3) 7 33
(L A Dace) *led to over 1f out: wknd rapidly* **13/2**3

1m 41.5s (1.70) **Going Correction** +0.10s/f (Slow)
WFA 3 from 4yo+ 1lb **11** Ran SP% **115.4**
Speed ratings (Par 97): **95,94,94,93,93 92,92,91,89,87 85**
toteswingers:1&2: £8.50, 2&3: £11.00, 1&3: £18.80 CSF £86.17 CT £1320.77 TOTE £9.40: £3.80, £3.00, £4.50; EX 88.00 Trifecta £423.70 Part won. Pool of £572.63 - 0.10 winning units..
Owner L Milligan **Bred** Freddie Lynch **Trained** Musley Bank, N Yorks
■ Laura Barry's first winner under rules.

FOCUS
This looked competitive beforehand and it certainly turned out that way, with narrow margins separating the front three and those in behind coming home well bunched.

7650 RACING AT SKYSPORTS.COM CLAIMING STKS 1m (P)
2:30 (2:30) (Class 6) 2-Y-O **£1,637** (£483; £241) **Stalls High**

Form RPR
5256 **1** **Danzigs Grandchild (USA)**123 4578 2-7-11 68.......... RyanPowell(7) 6 63
(J S Moore) *hld up in last trio: prog 2f out: chsd ldr 1f out: shkn up to ld last 100yds* **6/4**1
4660 **2** nk **Silver Age (IRE)**7 7552 2-8-5 61................................(p) CathyGannon 4 63
(J S Moore) *t.k.h: pressed ldr after 1f: drvn over 3f out: responded to press to ld over 1f out: hdd last 100yds: kpt on* **11/1**
60 **3** 1 3/4 **Hackett (IRE)**61 6520 2-8-8 60................................ FrannyNorton 7 62
(M Quinn) *hld up last: pushed along over 3f out: prog u.p over 1f out: kpt on one pce ins fnl f* **12/1**
5014 **4** 1 1/4 **Skeleton (IRE)**20 7412 2-8-4 60................................(b) ChrisCatlin 3 55
(W J Haggas) *pushed up to ld after 100yds: asked to kick on over 2f out but no real rspnse: hdd and nt qckn over 1f out* **7/4**2
0540 **5** 2 **Blaze On By**28 7295 2-8-5 50 ow3................................ NeilChalmers 2 52
(J J Bridger) *hld up in abt 5th: rdn and no imp on ldrs 2f out* **28/1**
0600 **6** 1 3/4 **Stacey**16 7464 2-8-1 55................................ JimmyQuinn 1 44
(M Blanshard) *racd wd: prom: lost pl fr 3f out: struggling fnl 2f* **20/1**
0060 **7** 6 **Danube Dancer (IRE)**19 7417 2-8-2 60................................(b1) LukeMorris 5 31
(J S Moore) *led 100yds: styd prom: wknd rapidly over 1f out* **8/1**3

1m 41.2s (1.40) **Going Correction** +0.10s/f (Slow) **7** Ran SP% **111.7**
Speed ratings (Par 94): **97,96,94,93,91 89,83**
toteswingers:1&2: £4.20, 2&3: £7.40, 1&3: £3.20 CSF £17.97 TOTE £2.40: £1.10, £6.00; EX 23.70.Danzigs Grandchild was subject to a friendly claim.
Owner J S Moore **Bred** Ashleigh Stud, F Ramos And J Ramos **Trained** Upper Lambourn, Berks
■ Stewards' Enquiry : Cathy Gannon caution: used whip without giving gelding time to respond.

FOCUS
The duel between the front two in the market didn't develop.

NOTEBOOK
Danzigs Grandchild(USA) looked the pick on her turf efforts, moved well in behind the leaders and, having been switched, just had to be driven out to score by a comfortable neck. The step up to 1m suited her well and she may well show herself capable of winning outside this company. (op 13-8)
Silver Age(IRE), well held at this course on three previous visits, including when fancied for a 7f claimer in September, was a bit keen with the cheekpieces on for the first time, but the step up to 1m seemed to suit and he did really well considering he was badly in at the weights with the winner. Something similar should come his way. (op 10-1)
Hackett(IRE) had struggled in three 5f maidens, and it was no surprise to see him up his game dropped in grade/raised in distance, staying on late having taken a while to pick up.
Skeleton(IRE), winner of a course handicap off 53 two starts back (first-time blinkers), was disappointing at Wolverhampton last time and she again failed to meet with expectation on this drop in grade, finding little having made the running. Official explanation: jockey said filly hung left on bend (op 15-8)
Danube Dancer(IRE) was another to stop quickly, the first-time blinkers evidently not having the desired effect. (op 17-2)

7651 DIGIBET.COM MEDIAN AUCTION MAIDEN STKS 7f (P)
3:00 (3:04) (Class 5) 3-5-Y-O **£2,286** (£675; £337) **Stalls High**

Form RPR
6300 **1** **Jaldarshaan (IRE)**28 7305 3-8-12 64................................ TravisBlock 8 63
(W J H Ratcliffe) *dwlt and stdd s: t.k.h: hld up last: gd prog fr 2f out to ld ent fnl f: styd on wl* **6/1**

442 2 1 1/4 **Handsome King**29 7288 3-9-3 62 FergusSweeney 10 65
(J R Jenkins) *led: rdn over 2f out: hung lft over 1f out: hdd ent fnl f: kpt on* 5/2[1]

60 3 hd **Jo Boy**78 6060 3-9-3 0 AndreaAtzeni 2 64
(D M Simcock) *dwlt: hld up in last pair: prog over 2f out: rdn to chal over 1f out: nt qckn* 13/2

50 4 1 1/2 **Hippique**35 7166 3-8-12 0 JimmyFortune 9 55
(A M Balding) *prom: chsd wnr over 2f out: drvn to chal wl over 1f out: wknd ins fnl f* 7/2[2]

0030 5 3 **Jemimaville (IRE)**12 7505 3-8-12 47 (v) WilliamCarson 3 47
(G C Bravery) *hld up in rr: prog on outer over 2f out: nt qckn over 1f out: wknd ins fnl f* 20/1

06 6 3 3/4 **Some Yarn (IRE)**18 7440 3-9-3 0 (v) FrankieMcDonald 6 42
(Mrs L C Jewell) *t.k.h: pressed ldr to over 2f out: sn wknd* 100/1

2040 7 2 **Faithful Duchess (IRE)**63 6455 3-8-12 59 JamieSpencer 7 31
(E F Vaughan) *hld up in midfield: prog on inner over 2f out: no hdwy over 1f out: wknd* 9/2[3]

0003 8 1 1/2 **Tumbled Again**13 7498 3-9-3 48 NickyMackay 5 32
(M E Rimmer) *chsd ldrs: pushed along 1/2-way: wknd over 2f out* 33/1

2000 9 1 1/4 **Libertino (IRE)**150 3715 3-9-3 60 JimmyQuinn 4 29
(A W Carroll) *trckd ldng pair to 3f out: sn lost pl u.p and btn* 14/1

1m 27.81s (1.81) **Going Correction** +0.10s/f (Slow) 9 Ran SP% **112.0**
Speed ratings (Par 103): **93,91,91,89,86 81,79,77,76**
toteswingers:1&2: £3.10, 2&3: £4.50, 1&3: £5.90 CSF £20.37 TOTE £7.40: £2.80, £1.10, £3.00; EX 21.90 Trifecta £154.10 Pool: £775.11 - 3.72 winning units..
Owner T B Tarn **Bred** Ivan And Mrs Eileen Heanen **Trained** Newmarket, Suffolk

FOCUS
This was nothing more than a modest maiden.
Some Yarn(IRE) Official explanation: jockey said gelding hung left

7652 DIGIBET NURSERY 7f (P)
3:30 (3:36) (Class 4) (0-85,85) 2-Y-O £3,238 (£963; £481; £240) **Stalls** High

Form RPR
251 1 **Muntasib (USA)**49 6849 2-9-2 80 RichardHills 4 85+
(M P Tregoning) *t.k.h: trckd ldr: bmpd jst over 2f out: rallied over 1f out: rdn and styd on wl to ld last strides* 5/6[1]

0253 2 hd **Fred Willetts (IRE)**11 7528 2-8-13 77 (v[1]) JimmyFortune 3 78
(P D Evans) *led: rdn and veered lft jst over 2f out: hdd over 1f out: styd on again to ld last 100yds: hdd fnl strides* 5/1[3]

1132 3 3/4 **Dozy Joe**18 7444 2-9-7 85 DaneO'Neill 7 85
(I A Wood) *t.k.h: hld up in 3rd: effrt over 2f out: rdn to ld over 1f out: hdd and no ex last 100yds* 9/4[2]

0053 4 1 1/2 **Reginald Claude**19 7417 2-8-5 69 HayleyTurner 2 65
(M D I Usher) *hld up last: effrt on wd outside 2f out: cl enough 1f out: sn wknd* 9/1

1m 26.58s (0.58) **Going Correction** +0.10s/f (Slow) 4 Ran SP% **112.0**
Speed ratings (Par 98): **100,99,98,97**
CSF £5.63 TOTE £1.70; EX 6.40.
Owner Hamdan Al Maktoum **Bred** Branch Equine Llc **Trained** Lambourn, Berks

FOCUS
A decent nursery despite the defections.

NOTEBOOK
Muntasib(USA), who twice showed fair form on the Flat before winning a 7f Lingfield maiden in October, has a bit of size about him and was well backed at the head of the market, with a mark of 80 looking reasonable. He initially seemed in trouble when coming under pressure, but Richard Hills conjured a late run out of him to rescue the situation. On this evidence he's clearly in need of 1m and he can win again, with him not expected to go up too much for winning by such a narrow margin. (op 6-5 tchd 5-4 in a place)
Fred Willetts(IRE), whose only previous win had come in a seller, upped his game for the fitting of a first-time visor and found plenty for pressure, only to be nailed in the final strides.
Dozy Joe, 9lb higher than when winning a 6f course nursery in August, had finished second to a decent type over this trip at Lingfield on his latest start, but having got to the front his stamina appeared to ebb away close home. (op 2-1 tchd 5-2 in a place)
Reginald Claude still appeared to be going well enough turning in, but couldn't race on with the front three from 1f out.

7653 DIGIBET CASINO H'CAP 1m 4f (P)
4:00 (4:05) (Class 4) (0-85,82) 3-Y-O £3,885 (£1,156; £577) **Stalls** Centre

Form RPR
6225 1 **Valid Reason**20 7410 3-9-4 79 AdamKirby 5 87
(D K Ivory) *mde all: hrd rdn and drew clr over 1f out: styd on* 11/4[2]

1612 2 3 **Iron Condor**3 7612 3-9-1 76 LukeMorris 1 80
(J M P Eustace) *hld up last: moved up to chal over 2f out: sn rdn and nt qckn: one pce fr over 1f out* 10/11[1]

1130 3 8 **Gomrath (IRE)**179 2758 3-9-7 82 JimmyFortune 4 77
(M R Channon) *trckd wnr to over 2f out: wknd over 1f out* 11/4[2]

2m 36.93s (2.43) **Going Correction** +0.10s/f (Slow) 3 Ran SP% **105.7**
Speed ratings (Par 104): **95,93,87**
CSF £5.56 TOTE £3.50; EX 4.30.
Owner M J Yarrow **Bred** Juddmonte Farms Ltd **Trained** Radlett, Herts

FOCUS
Another small field and probably not form to get carried away with.

7654 KIA SPORTAGE H'CAP 6f (P)
4:30 (4:35) (Class 4) (0-85,84) 3-Y-O+ £3,885 (£1,156; £577; £288) **Stalls** High

Form RPR
5136 1 **Ray Of Joy**11 7521 4-9-7 84 FergusSweeney 4 91
(J R Jenkins) *hld up in 6th: prog 2f out to chse ldr over 1f out: rdn to ld last 100yds: kpt on* 9/1

6204 2 nk **Breathless Kiss (USA)**7 7554 3-9-1 78 (b) FrannyNorton 8 84
(K A Ryan) *jockey struggling w blindfold as stalls opened: misssed break: hld up last: plld out wd 2f out: gd prog jst over 1f out: wnt 2nd nr fin and clsd on wnr* 15/2

0-65 3 nk **Flash McGahon (IRE)**5 7573 6-8-13 76 (b) JamieSpencer 1 81
(John M Oxx, Ire) *t.k.h: trckd ldng pair: led over 2f out: edgd rt after: hdd and nt qckn last 100yds* 7/2[2]

3022 4 1 **Vhujon (IRE)**7 7549 5-8-13 76 CathyGannon 3 78
(P D Evans) *trckd ldrs: rdn and nt qckn 2f out: kpt on same pce after* 4/1[3]

30-3 5 1/2 **Dark Lane**16 7466 4-9-2 79 JimmyFortune 5 79
(R A Fahey) *pressed ldr: led briefly wl over 2f out: sltly hmpd over 1f out and lost 2nd: one pce after* 11/8[1]

0140 6 5 **Crown (IRE)**72 6253 3-9-6 83 IanMongan 9 67
(Miss Jo Crowley) *in tch: rdn wl over 2f out: steadily wknd* 12/1

6400 7 1 3/4 **Little Perisher**221 1511 3-8-7 70 ChrisCatlin 2 49
(Karen George) *led to wl over 2f out: steadily wknd* 16/1

1m 13.2s (0.10) **Going Correction** +0.10s/f (Slow) 7 Ran SP% **119.7**
Speed ratings (Par 105): **103,102,102,100,100 93,91**
toteswingers:1&2: £5.00, 2&3: £4.00, 1&3: £4.40 CSF £76.49 CT £286.47 TOTE £6.80: £2.50, £4.30; EX 41.90 Trifecta £757.70 Pool: £1023.92- 0.72 winning units..
Owner Robin Stevens **Bred** D R Tucker **Trained** Royston, Herts
■ Stewards' Enquiry : Jamie Spencer two-day ban: careless riding (Dec 15-16)

FOCUS
There was a decent pace on for this 6f handicap and it can be no coincidence that the first two home were at the back of the field through the early stages.
Flash McGahon(IRE) Official explanation: jockey said gelding hung right

7655 SKYSPORTS.COM RACING H'CAP (DIV I) 6f (P)
5:00 (5:08) (Class 6) (0-65,65) 3-Y-O+ £1,364 (£403; £201) **Stalls** High

Form RPR
0000 1 **Torres Del Paine**77 6085 3-9-3 61 (t) SamHitchcott 2 70
(J C Fox) *trckd ldrs on outer: rdn over 2f out: prog over 1f out: wnt 2nd ent fnl f: styd on to ld last 50yds* 20/1

0301 2 nk **Hidden Destiny**12 7505 3-9-7 65 FergusSweeney 10 73
(P J Makin) *led: edgd lft fr 2f out: kpt on but worn down last 50yds* 9/2[3]

0000 3 3/4 **C'Mon You Irons (IRE)**18 7441 5-9-1 62 (b) KierenFox(3) 9 68
(M R Hoad) *t.k.h: prom: drvn over 2f out: nt qckn and no imp over 1f out: styd on ins fnl f to take 3rd nr fin* 8/1

0120 4 1/2 **Namir (IRE)**79 6018 8-9-4 62 (vt) DaneO'Neill 3 66
(H J Evans) *hld up wl in rr: shkn up 2f out: swtchd lft jst over 1f out: styd on last 150yds: nrst fin* 25/1

0166 5 hd **Mack's Sister**21 7391 3-9-6 64 RobertHavlin 12 68
(D K Ivory) *prom: rdn over 2f out: nt qckn and no imp over 1f out: kpt on* 11/4[1]

0410 6 shd **Nollaig Shona (IRE)**11 7518 3-9-5 63 CathyGannon 5 66
(G Prodromou) *t.k.h: chsd ldr tl ent fnl f: wknd* 11/1

0643 7 nk **Chinese Democracy (USA)**1 7640 3-8-13 57 (v) AdamKirby 8 59
(P D Evans) *hld up in midfield: rdn 2f out: no prog over 1f out: kpt on ins fnl f* 4/1[2]

420 8 nk **Resplendent Alpha**11 7519 6-9-1 59 (b) JimmyQuinn 11 61
(P Howling) *dwlt: hld up wl in rr: effrt on inner over 2f out: no prog over 1f out: one pce* 15/2

0-00 9 2 1/2 **Moonlight Cass (IRE)**18 7442 3-9-4 62 (b[1]) SteveDrowne 4 56
(J R Gask) *t.k.h: hld up in tch: rdn over 2f out: no prog and btn over 1f out* 20/1

300 10 16 **Pilgrim Dancer (IRE)**7 7556 3-9-6 64 (v) JamieSpencer 6 —
(Patrick Morris) *dwlt: a last: wd and wl bhd in st: t.o* 8/1

1m 12.97s (-0.13) **Going Correction** +0.10s/f (Slow) 10 Ran SP% **120.5**
Speed ratings (Par 101): **104,103,102,101,101 101,101,100,97,76**
toteswingers:1&2: £17.90, 2&3 £9.70, 1&3: £24.90 CSF £108.84 CT £824.76 TOTE £24.20: £7.40, £3.30, £2.30; EX 239.00 TRIFECTA Not won..
Owner Mrs Sarah-Jane Fox **Bred** Deepwood Farm Stud **Trained** Collingbourne Ducis, Wilts

FOCUS
There wasn't much between the front eight at the line.
C'Mon You Irons(IRE) Official explanation: jockey said gelding hung left
Mack's Sister Official explanation: jockey said filly hung left

7656 SKYSPORTS.COM RACING H'CAP (DIV II) 6f (P)
5:30 (5:37) (Class 6) (0-65,64) 3-Y-O+ £1,364 (£403; £201) **Stalls** High

Form RPR
3601 1 **Liberty Trail (IRE)**19 7426 4-9-2 59 (p) GeorgeBaker 7 69+
(P D Evans) *chsd ldr: clsd to ld over 1f out: rdn clr* 11/4[1]

0366 2 2 **Clerical (USA)**7 7556 4-9-0 57 (p) J-PGuillambert 8 61
(R M H Cowell) *chsd clr ldng pair: effrt u.p to take 2nd fnl f: nvr able to chal* 11/2[3]

0045 3 2 1/4 **Dvinsky (USA)**3 7613 9-9-7 64 (b) JimmyQuinn 10 61
(P Howling) *blindfold off sltly late and dwlt: mostly in last pair tl effrt on inner over 2f out: one pce: snatched 3rd nr fin* 11/4[1]

404 4 1/2 **Doctor Hilary**21 7391 8-9-5 62 (v) ChrisCatlin 6 58
(M R Hoad) *pushed up to ld at str pce: hdd & wknd over 1f out* 4/1[2]

1605 5 4 1/2 **Silvee**11 7519 3-8-10 56 KierenFox(3) 5 38
(J J Bridger) *mostly in last pair: rdn and no prog 2f out* 7/1

3415 6 2 3/4 **Katy's Secret**181 2679 3-9-5 62 DaneO'Neill 2 36
(W Jarvis) *chsd ldng trio to 1/2-way: sn struggling* 14/1

1m 12.87s (-0.23) **Going Correction** +0.10s/f (Slow) 6 Ran SP% **107.9**
Speed ratings (Par 101): **105,102,99,98,92 89**
toteswingers:1&2:£3.50, 2&3: £3.40, 1&3: £1.90 CSF £16.55 CT £37.53 TOTE £3.00: £2.60, £3.80; EX 19.00 Trifecta £54.40 Pool: £611.117 - 8.31 winning units..
Owner Mrs B Grainger **Bred** Clougher Partnership **Trained** Pandy, Monmouths

FOCUS
This had cut up considerably more than the first division.
T/Jkpt: Not won. T/Plt: £784.80 to a £1 stake. Pool of £123,553.80 - 114.92 winning tickets. T/Qpdt: £81.10 to a £1 stake. Pool of £15,030.69 - 137.00 winning tickets. JN

7634 LINGFIELD (L-H)
Thursday, December 2
7657 Meeting Abandoned - Snow

7626 WOLVERHAMPTON (A.W) (L-H)
Thursday, December 2
OFFICIAL GOING: Standard to slow changing to slow after race 3 (5:00) changing to standard to slow after race 6 (6:30)
Wind: moderate 1/2 against Weather: wintry showers, cold

7663 BET ON ASHES AT TOTESPORT.COM APPRENTICE H'CAP 1m 141y(P)
4:00 (4:00) (Class 5) (0-70,81) 3-Y-O+ £2,007 (£597; £298; £149) **Stalls** Low

Form RPR
1422 1 **Strike Force**15 7491 6-9-5 67 (t) KierenFox 8 75
(Miss Olivia Maylam) *hld up: effrt over 2f out: led appr fnl f: kpt on wl* 15/8[1]

6112 2 1 **Inpursuitoffreedom**31 7273 3-9-1 70 JulieBurke(5) 2 76
(P J McBride) *trckd ldrs: t.k.h: chal appr fnl f: kpt on same pce fnl 100yds* 15/8[1]

5530 **3** 2 3/4 **Mighty Clarets (IRE)**[24] 7377 3-8-9 **66**.................. GeorgeChaloner(7) 1 66
(R A Fahey) *trckd ldrs: drvn and outpcd over 2f out: styd on fnl f: edgd lft and tk 3rd nr line* **6/1**[3]

0503 **4** 3/4 **Merrymadcap (IRE)**[42] 7038 8-9-1 **68**........................ RichardRowe(5) 3 67
(Matthew Salaman) *w ldr: led over 4f out: hdd appr fnl f: fdd and lost 3rd nr line* **12/1**

6000 **5** 3 1/4 **Justcallmehandsome**[47] 6935 8-8-11 **62**........................(v) BillyCray(3) 6 54
(D J S Ffrench Davis) *s.s: hdwy over 6f out: chsng ldrs 5f out: upsides over 3f out: wknd over 1f out* **9/2**[2]

0000 **6** 26 **Vanadium**[24] 7380 8-8-0 **55** oh10................................(p) KatiaScallan(7) 4 —
(A J Lidderdale) *led: hdd over 4f out: sn lost pl and bhd: t.o* **66/1**

1m 55.16s (4.66) **Going Correction** +0.50s/f (Slow)
WFA 3 from 4yo+ 2lb **6** Ran SP% **111.2**
Speed ratings (Par 103): **99,98,95,95,92 69**
toteswingers:1&2:£1.10, 1&3:£2.30, 2&3:£2.40 CSF £5.31 CT £14.58 TOTE £4.10: £2.70, £1.10; EX 5.40.
Owner Miss A L Hutchinson **Bred** Cheveley Park Stud Ltd **Trained** Newmarket, Suffolk

FOCUS
Although the early pace was steady, things picked up a bit once Vanadium got to the front, and that suited the first two in the betting, who were ridden with a little patience.
Justcallmehandsome Official explanation: jockey said gelding slipped leaving stalls

7664 STAY AT THE WOLVERHAMPTON HOLIDAY INN (S) STKS 1m 141y(P)
4:30 (4:31) (Class 6) 2-Y-O £1,619 (£481; £240; £120) Stalls Low

Form RPR

2223 **1** **Ivan's A Star (IRE)**[3] 7631 2-8-12 57..............................(p) LukeMorris 5 61
(J S Moore) *hld up in mid-div: drvn over 3f out: hdwy on outside over 2f out: wnt 2nd over 1f out: hung bdly lft: led and bmpd jst ins fnl f: rdn out* **11/2**[3]

6005 **2** 1 3/4 **Ad Vitam (IRE)**[22] 7394 2-8-12 42....................................(t) JamesDoyle 9 56
(S Kirk) *in rr: reminders over 4f out: hdwy over 2f out: styd on wl to take 2nd nr fin* **80/1**

0465 **3** 1 1/4 **Beating Harmony**[15] 7486 2-8-12 60........................ RichardKingscote 3 54
(Tom Dascombe) *in rr: drvn 7f out: kpt on fnl 2f: tk 3rd nr fin* **15/2**

0412 **4** hd **A Little Bit Dusty**[3] 7629 2-9-0 61..................................(v) KierenFox(3) 1 59
(W G M Turner) *led: drvn over 2f out: edgd rt: bmpd and hdd jst ins fnl f: wknd nr fin* **7/2**[2]

3055 **5** 1/2 **Mediplomat**[24] 7378 2-8-12 58...(t) ChrisCatlin 4 52
(M Botti) *trckd ldrs: drvn over 3f out: one pce over 1f out* **12/1**

363 **6** 3/4 **So Is She (IRE)**[48] 6901 2-8-3 66 ow3...........................(v) JulieBurke(7) 7 49
(A Bailey) *trckd ldrs: t.k.h: drvn 3f out: one pce whn hmpd jst ins fnl f* **3/1**[1]

54 **7** 4 1/2 **Bill Page (USA)**[20] 7427 2-8-12 0.................................... HayleyTurner 6 41
(D M Simcock) *hmpd and dropped bk to last sn after s: sn pushed along: nvr a factor* **3/1**[1]

6360 **8** 9 **Veeb (IRE)**[14] 7493 2-8-7 58.. GregFairley 2 17
(M Johnston) *dwlt: sn trcking ldrs: drvn 4f out: lost pl over 2f out: eased whn bhd ins fnl f* **17/2**

1m 55.01s (4.51) **Going Correction** +0.50s/f (Slow) **8** Ran SP% **118.8**
Speed ratings (Par 94): **99,97,96,96,95 95,91,83**
toteswingers:1&2:£16.50, 1&3:£6.00, 2&3:£18.90 CSF £279.46 TOTE £5.60: £1.40, £6.30, £3.80; EX 158.30.There was no bid for the winner.
Owner Ray Styles & J S Moore **Bred** Philip Hore Jnr **Trained** Upper Lambourn, Berks
■ Stewards' Enquiry : Luke Morris one-day ban: careless riding (Dec 16th)
Kieren Fox one-day ban: careless riding (Dec 16th)

FOCUS
They went an ordinary early pace in this seller.

NOTEBOOK
Ivan's A Star(IRE) is a pretty consistent sort and, although he hung left under pressure again, all the way up the straight, he had a fair bit in hand at the line. He was 5lb better off with A Little Bit Dusty compared with when he was beaten 2 1/4l by that rival at Lingfield two starts back, so was entitled to reverse that form. (tchd 5-1)
Ad Vitam(IRE), beaten double-figure distances by the winner in each of his previous seven starts, ran his best race so far, staying on from off the pace to be nearest at the finish. He looks like he'll be suited by stepping up in trip. (op 66-1)
Beating Harmony, dropping into a seller for the first time, did best of those who raced nearest the inside rail. There could be a bit better to come from him, although his current mark appears to flatter him. (tchd 8-1)
A Little Bit Dusty looked to have things under control for much of the race, appearing to do things easily on the front end, but he got tired approaching the final furlong and edged right under pressure, giving the winner a bump in the process, and in the end he was run out of the places. Not for the first time he proved he's not one to be backing at short odds in-running. (op 9-2)
So Is She(IRE) carried 3lb overweight, but that wasn't the difference between winning and losing – the filly simply pulled too hard early and as a result was never going to see out this longer trip. (op 5-2)
Bill Page(USA), weak in the betting on his third run for a mark, was squeezed out at the start, lost several lengths and was then chased along to make up the lost ground. Always towards the back, he never threatened to land a blow. (op 5-2)

7665 BET ON LIVE CRICKET AT TOTESPORT.COM H'CAP 7f 32y(P)
5:00 (5:01) (Class 4) (0-85,80) 3-Y-O+ £3,594 (£1,069; £534; £266) Stalls High

Form RPR

3201 **1** **Hulcote Rose (IRE)**[12] 7525 3-9-3 **76**.............................. JamesDoyle 8 85+
(S Kirk) *hld up in rr: hdwy over 2f out: swtchd outside over 1f out: r.o wl to ld last 50yds* **10/3**[1]

3062 **2** 1/2 **Tiradito (USA)**[21] 7411 3-9-5 **78**...................................(p) AndreaAtzeni 7 86
(M Botti) *trckd ldrs: t.k.h: effrt 2f out: upsides ins fnl f: no ex nr fin* **7/2**[2]

1530 **3** nk **Bawaardi (IRE)**[117] 4828 4-9-0 **80**.......................... MarzenaJeziorek(7) 1 87
(R A Fahey) *led 1f: t.k.h: trckd ldrs: effrt on ins to ld 1f out: hdd and no ex towards fin* **11/2**[3]

1035 **4** 2 1/2 **Requisite**[12] 7521 5-9-3 **76**..(v) CathyGannon 5 76
(I A Wood) *hld up in mid-div: effrt over 2f out: kpt on one pce over 1f out* **11/2**[3]

0002 **5** 1/2 **Cyflymder (IRE)**[12] 7529 4-8-13 **77**............................ MarkCoumbe(5) 4 76
(D Bourton) *led after 1f: hdd 1f out: wknd fnl 75yds* **7/2**[2]

1006 **6** hd **Chief Exec**[30] 7290 8-8-13 **72** ow1...................................... AdamKirby 3 71
(J R Gask) *dwlt: in rr: effrt over 2f out: nvr rchd ldrs* **10/1**

2260 **7** 5 **Weet A Surprise**[21] 7409 5-9-2 **75**..................................(v) LukeMorris 2 60
(J W Unett) *w ldrs: drvn to chal over 2f out: wknd over 1f out* **14/1**

1m 33.33s (3.73) **Going Correction** +0.50s/f (Slow) **7** Ran SP% **114.0**
Speed ratings (Par 105): **98,97,97,94,93 93,87**
toteswingers:1&2:£1.80, 1&3:£3.60, 2&3:£4.30 CSF £15.20 CT £60.94 TOTE £5.20: £1.40, £3.30; EX 9.40.
Owner The Kathryn Stud **Bred** Ecurie Des Monceaux **Trained** Upper Lambourn, Berks

FOCUS
The early pace was steady and a few raced keenly.

7666 PARADE RESTAURANT NURSERY 5f 216y(P)
5:30 (5:31) (Class 6) (0-65,66) 2-Y-O £1,619 (£481; £240; £120) Stalls Low

Form RPR

6022 **1** **Magic Cross**[6] 7577 2-8-10 **61**... JulieBurke(7) 2 65
(P J McBride) *dwlt: sn mid-div: hdwy to chse ldrs over 2f out: stmbld over 1f out: led 1f out: rdn out* **7/4**[1]

0004 **2** 3/4 **Shutterbug**[14] 7497 2-8-10 **54**...(t) DavidProbert 8 55
(S C Williams) *trckd ldrs: wnt 2nd 1f out: kpt on same pce* **9/2**[3]

4026 **3** 1 1/2 **Crazy In Love**[58] 6645 2-8-6 **53**.......................................(b) KierenFox(3) 9 49
(W G M Turner) *mid-div on outer: drvn over 3f out: sn wl outpcd: kpt on appr fnl f: tk 3rd ins fnl f* **12/1**

0661 **4** 1/2 **Bachelor Knight (IRE)**[33] 7224 2-9-7 **65**........................ BarryMcHugh 4 60
(Ollie Pears) *in rr: effrt over 2f out: sn chsng ldrs: kpt on fnl f* **7/2**[2]

054 **5** 3 1/4 **Pineapple Pete (IRE)**[120] 4691 2-9-0 **65**.................... DuilioDaSilva(7) 5 50+
(P F I Cole) *trckd ldr: t.k.h: led over 2f out: hdd 1f out: sn wknd* **5/1**

0366 **6** 4 **Henrys Air**[14] 7496 2-8-11 **55**...(v[1]) LukeMorris 6 28
(D G Bridgwater) *led: hdd over 2f out: wknd over 1f out* **11/1**

500 **7** 4 1/2 **Gekko (IRE)**[20] 7427 2-8-11 **55**..................................... StephenCraine 3 15
(Patrick Morris) *dwlt: hdwy 4f out: chsng ldrs over 2f out: sn lost pl* **9/1**

1m 18.86s (3.86) **Going Correction** +0.50s/f (Slow) **7** Ran SP% **119.5**
Speed ratings (Par 94): **94,93,91,90,86 80,74**
toteswingers:1&2:£2.20, 1&3:£6.00, 2&3:£6.20 CSF £10.74 CT £74.31 TOTE £2.60: £1.20, £4.60; EX 13.90.
Owner Peter Charter **Bred** J W P Clark **Trained** Newmarket, Suffolk

FOCUS
The going description was changed to slow before this race.

NOTEBOOK
Magic Cross overcame quite a bit to score. Although not badly away this time, she raced nearest the unfavoured rail until turning into the straight, at which point she was switched out and then stumbled. To her credit she maintained her challenge and kept on well for a deserved success. This is probably her best trip. (op 5-2)
Shutterbug, who shaped as though a drop back to 6f would suit on her previous start, wore a tongue-tie for the first time. Never far away and towards the outside, she was given every opportunity, but just came up a little short. There should still be improvement to come given her relative lack of experience. (tchd 5-1)
Crazy In Love was under heavy pressure on the turn into the straight, but she'd raced away from the fence throughout and came wide up the straight, and in the end posted her best AW effort so far. (op 20-1)
Bachelor Knight(IRE), having his first outing for his new stable, probably didn't have his chance helped by racing on the rail until the straight. (tchd 10-3)
Pineapple Pete(IRE), making his handicap debut, raced keenly in behind the leader and as a result he was always going to struggle to see his race out. (op 4-1)

7667 BET SP+ IN DECEMBER AT TOTESPORT.COM MAIDEN STKS 5f 216y(P)
6:00 (6:00) (Class 5) 2-Y-O £2,115 (£624; £312) Stalls Low

Form RPR

2453 **1** **Wolf Slayer**[12] 7517 2-8-12 68.................................. RichardKingscote 1 66+
(Tom Dascombe) *sn led: shkn up and qcknd wl over 1f out: drew clr jst ins fnl f: v readily* **8/11**[1]

0000 **2** 5 **Juarla (IRE)**[49] 6868 2-9-3 45... DavidProbert 4 50
(R A Harris) *led early: trckd ldrs: swtchd ins over 1f out: kpt on to take 2nd ins fnl f* **16/1**[3]

6032 **3** 1 **Lady Platinum Club**[21] 7408 2-8-5 67........................(p) AdamCarter(7) 5 42
(G R Oldroyd) *sn w wnr: rdn wl over 1f out: lost 2nd ins fnl f: wknd towards fin* **Evs**[2]

000 **4** 1 1/2 **Steel Rain**[31] 7272 2-9-3 38... CathyGannon 6 43
(Mrs N S Evans) *chsd ldrs: one pce fnl 2f* **66/1**

1m 17.79s (2.79) **Going Correction** +0.50s/f (Slow) **4** Ran SP% **115.3**
Speed ratings (Par 96): **101,94,93,91**
CSF £11.90 TOTE £2.10; EX 8.20.
Owner A Black & M Owen **Bred** Langton Stud **Trained** Malpas, Cheshire

FOCUS
The runner-up's performance puts the form in context.

NOTEBOOK
Wolf Slayer landed the odds in easy fashion, pulling nicely clear in the straight. Hopefully this will do her some good and she can build on it, as she'd looked fairly promising earlier in the year. (op 4-5 tchd 5-6 in places)
Juarla(IRE) is rated 45 so it wasn't a bad effort from him to finish second to a filly rated 23lb higher who was also in receipt of 5lb from him. However, the performance of the fourth suggests he ran pretty much close to his rating. (op 20-1 tchd 25-1)
Lady Platinum Club came into the race rated 1lb lower than the winner and clearly ran a long way below that level. She matched strides with her to the turn in, but was then soon left behind. Perhaps the slow surface didn't suit her. (op 6-5 tchd 5-4)
Steel Rain ran his best race to date, but that's not saying much. Official explanation: jockey said colt hung right (op 50-1)

7668 SP+ FOR BIGGER WINS AT TOTESPORT.COM H'CAP 5f 20y(P)
6:30 (6:30) (Class 5) (0-75,75) 3-Y-O+ £2,115 (£624; £312) Stalls Low

Form RPR

0061 **1** **Grudge**[19] 7446 5-9-3 **71**..(be) HayleyTurner 3 79
(C R Dore) *hood removed late: led 1f: chsd ldr: led appr fnl f: styd on u.p: hld on towards fin* **3/1**[1]

0313 **2** 1/2 **Sloop Johnb**[14] 7494 4-9-4 **72**.....................................(p) BarryMcHugh 6 78
(R A Fahey) *trckd ldrs: wnt 2nd and edgd lft appr fnl f: kpt on same pce fnl 75yds* **3/1**[1]

3621 **3** 1 **Fear Nothing**[90] 5726 3-9-4 **72**.. AdamKirby 7 75
(I W McInnes) *in rr: drvn and outpcd 3f out: hdwy over 1f out: kpt on to take 3rd ins fnl f* **10/1**[2]

164 **4** 1/2 **Angelo Poliziano**[8] 7549 4-9-4 **72**..................................(p) ChrisCatlin 2 76+
(Mrs A Duffield) *trckd ldrs: t.k.h: effrt over 2f out: swtchd rt and hmpd 1f out: kpt on clsng stages* **3/1**[1]

0110 **5** 2 1/4 **Grand Stitch (USA)**[14] 7494 4-8-12 **71**........................(v) NeilFarley(5) 5 64
(D Carroll) *chsd ldr: drvn to ld after 1f: hdd appr fnl f: wknd last 100yds* **3/1**[1]

1000 **6** 20 **Raimond Ridge (IRE)**[201] 2123 4-9-0 **68**........................ AndreaAtzeni 1 —
(D Shaw) *dwlt: in rr: bhd fnl 2f: t.o* **20/1**[3]

63.57 secs (1.27) **Going Correction** +0.50s/f (Slow) **6** Ran SP% **113.9**
Speed ratings (Par 103): **109,108,106,105,102 70**
toteswingers:1&2:£2.40, 1&3:£3.50, 2&3:£6.00 CSF £12.40 CT £77.02 TOTE £3.00: £1.10, £2.10; EX 13.10.
Owner Mrs Jennifer Marsh **Bred** D H Brailsford **Trained** Cowbit, Lincs

FOCUS
Quite a competitive little sprint handicap and it was run at a good gallop.

Raimond Ridge(IRE) Official explanation: jockey said gelding was slowly away and never travelled

7669 WOLVERHAMPTON-RACECOURSE.CO.UK H'CAP 1m 4f 50y(P)
7:00 (7:01) (Class 6) (0-60,59) 3-Y-O £1,535 (£453; £226) Stalls Low

Form RPR

0002 1 **Rhythm Stick**[22] 7387 3-9-1 **53**.. FrannyNorton 5 65+
(John Berry) *trckd ldrs: drvn 4f out: led 3f out: in command whn edgd rt ins fnl f* **4/7**[1]

4000 2 *5* **Port Hill**[22] 7387 3-9-0 **52**.. ShaneKelly 7 57
(W M Brisbourne) *trckd ldr: reminders 5f out: chsd wnr 3f out: one pce whn swtchd lft ins fnl f* **5/1**[2]

5-0P 3 *19* **Noverre Over There (IRE)**[71] 6287 3-9-5 **57**.................... AdamKirby 2 33
(Miss Olivia Maylam) *in rr: reminders after 3f: hdwy 7f out: outpcd over 3f out: wnt modest 3rd 2f out* **8/1**

3003 4 *18* **Half Sister (IRE)**[14] 7495 3-8-10 **48**..........................(bt) NickyMackay 8 —
(M E Rimmer) *led: hdd over 3f out: sn wknd: eased ins fnl f* **15/2**[3]

0400 5 *35* **Defence Of Realm (GER)**[2] 7634 3-8-12 **57**............(p) DavidKenny(7) 3 —
(George Baker) *dwlt: racd in last: hmpd and lost pl over 5f out: nt run on and sn bhd: t.o whn eased and virtually p.u 2f out* **11/1**

0000 6 *23* **Sue And Sue**[19] 7449 3-8-7 **45**.. CathyGannon 4 —
(G Woodward) *mid-div: reminders over 6f out: lost pl over 4f out: t.o whn eased 2f out: virtually p.u* **40/1**

2m 49.92s (8.82) **Going Correction** +0.50s/f (Slow) **6 Ran SP% 114.0**
Speed ratings (Par 98): **90,86,74,62,38 23**
toteswingers:1&2:£1.30, 1&3:£3.00, 2&3:£5.20 CSF £4.03 TOTE £1.70: £1.10, £2.00; EX 5.80.
Owner Red Furlongs Partnership **Bred** Mrs M L Parry & P M Steele-Mortimer **Trained** Newmarket, Suffolk

FOCUS
None of these had won a race before.
Sue And Sue Official explanation: jockey said filly had no more to give
T/Jkpt: £465.20 to a £1 stake. Pool:£23,590.44 - 36.00 winning tickets T/Plt: £26.40 to a £1 stake. Pool:£145,377.55 - 4,016.89 winning tickets T/Qpdt: £5.70 to a £1 stake. Pool:£15,207.36 - 1,949.62 winning tickets WG

7634 LINGFIELD (L-H)
Friday, December 3
7670 Meeting Abandoned - Snow

7663 WOLVERHAMPTON (A.W) (L-H)
Friday, December 3

OFFICIAL GOING: Standard to slow changing to slow after race 4 (4.15)
Wind: moderate 1/2 behind Weather: dry but cold, wintry showers race 8 onwards

7676 TONY MCCOY FOR BBC SPORTS PERSONALITY MEDIAN AUCTION MAIDEN STKS 5f 216y(P)
2:35 (2:35) (Class 6) 3-5-Y-O £1,706 (£503; £252) Stalls Low

Form RPR

0643 1 **Lily Wood**[8] 7563 4-8-12 **47**..(p) LiamJones 5 61
(J W Unett) *trckd ldrs: led over 2f out: rdn clr over 1f out* **13/8**[1]

6000 2 *8* **True Red (IRE)**[16] 7477 3-8-9 **46**..........................(b) AndrewHeffernan(3) 6 35
(Mrs N S Evans) *w ldr: led 4f out: hdd over 2f out: kpt on: no ch w wnr* **14/1**

630 3 *2 ½* **Leahness (IRE)**[10] 7542 3-8-5 **45**..............................(e) JulieBurke(7) 3 27
(Patrick Morris) *in rr: hdwy over 2f out: kpt on to take modest 3rd nr fin* **4/1**[3]

0060 4 *¾* **Ariel Bender**[15] 7498 3-8-10 **37**..............................(b) LeonnaMayor(7) 8 30
(Peter Grayson) *chsd ldrs: hung rt after 2f: outpcd and lost pl over 3f out: kpt on to take modest 3rd 1f out: lost 3rd nr line* **80/1**

6656 5 *6* **Rose Bed (IRE)**[54] 6773 3-8-12 **43**...................................... JackMitchell 1 —
(M G Quinlan) *in rr and sn drvn along: bhd fnl 3f* **5/1**

0000 6 *4* **Cheveyo (IRE)**[165] 3279 4-9-3 **47**..............................(v[1]) StephenCraine 2 —
(Patrick Morris) *hld up: smooth hdwy over 3f out: sn chsng ldrs: rdn and wknd 2f out* **3/1**[2]

65 7 *shd* **Gessabelle**[9] 7547 3-8-12 **42**..(bt[1]) CathyGannon 4 —
(P S McEntee) *led tl 4f out: lost pl 3f out* **14/1**

1m 18.77s (3.77) **Going Correction** +0.60s/f (Slow) **7 Ran SP% 114.3**
Speed ratings (Par 101): **98,87,84,83,75 69,69**
toteswingers:1&2:£4.20, 1&3:£2.10, 2&3:£8.20 CSF £26.44 TOTE £2.50: £1.10, £4.10; EX 20.20.
Owner Mrs Shirley Downes **Bred** Mrs Shirley Downes **Trained** Tedsmore Hall, Shropshire

FOCUS
The fact that the horse best in at the weights was officially rated 47 says it all about this maiden.

7677 VOTE FOR TONY MCCOY MAIDEN AUCTION STKS 1m 141y(P)
3:10 (3:10) (Class 6) 2-Y-O £1,706 (£503; £252) Stalls Low

Form RPR

053 1 **Dunhoy (IRE)**[5] 7610 2-8-12 **0**.. MickyFenton 4 77+
(Stef Higgins) *trckd ldrs: smooth hdwy 4f out: led on bit over 2f out: shkn up to go wl clr over 1f out: eased fnl 75yds: v easily* **8/15**[1]

00 2 *11* **Crossword**[14] 7503 2-8-9 **0**..(b) ChrisCatlin 1 49
(M Botti) *led: drvn over 3f out: hdd over 2f out: no ch w wnr* **9/2**[3]

0643 3 *2 ½* **Thank You Joy**[23] 7393 2-8-0 **60**.. DannyBrock(7) 3 42
(J R Jenkins) *trckd ldr: drvn over 3f out: one pce* **11/4**[2]

1m 59.17s (8.67) **Going Correction** +0.60s/f (Slow) **3 Ran SP% 110.1**
Speed ratings (Par 94): **85,75,73**
CSF £3.30 TOTE £1.40; EX 3.50.
Owner David Gilbert **Bred** Rossenarra Bloodstock Limited **Trained** Lambourn, Berks

FOCUS
With the field reduced to three, this moderate maiden was in danger of becoming tactical, but as it turned out they went a reasonable pace.

NOTEBOOK
Dunhoy(IRE), who had improved in each of his three previous runs, took a bit of a hold early but then settled nicely last of the three. Asked to get closer on the outside starting the final turn, he was set alight over 2f from and was soon in an unassailable lead. He extended his margin of superiority over Crossword from 2l in their previous meeting to 11l here, which suggests that he has stepped up again, and connections may look for a nursery for him now. (op 8-13)
Crossword tried to make all, but was left choking on the winner's dust from the 2f pole. He now gets a mark, but looks moderate. (op 5-1 tchd 11-2)
Thank You Joy, who had run more often than her two rivals added together, found nothing once off the bridle over 3f from home. She may be better on Fibresand. (tchd 5-2)

7678 PLAY BINGO AT TOTESPORT.COM APPRENTICE H'CAP 1m 1f 103y(P)
3:45 (3:45) (Class 6) (0-65,65) 3-Y-O+ £1,619 (£481; £240; £120) Stalls Low

Form RPR

0356 1 **The Winged Assasin (USA)**[37] 7162 4-9-1 **64**.............(t) LucyBarry(5) 6 72
(S Lycett) *hld up in mid-div: smooth hdwy over 4f out: led 3f out: drvn out* **13/2**

0605 2 *½* **Know No Fear**[10] 7543 5-8-10 **59**...............................(p) KatiaScallan(5) 3 66
(A J Lidderdale) *hld up in rr: hdwy on outside 3f out: edgd lft and chsd wnr over 1f out: no ex towards fin* **4/1**

2003 3 *10* **Guga (IRE)**[13] 7531 4-9-7 **65**..(p) RyanClark 5 51
(J Mackie) *trckd ldrs: drvn over 2f out: one pce* **3/1**[2]

5240 4 *1 ¾* **Stanley Rigby**[32] 7270 4-8-2 **51** oh6....................(b[1]) MarzenaJeziorek(5) 1 33
(R A Fahey) *dwlt: sn drvn along in last: hdwy on outside over 5f out: chsng ldrs over 2f out: one pce* **25/1**

41 5 *13* **Mr Emirati (USA)**[15] 7498 3-9-3 **63**...................................... AdamCarter 7 18
(B Smart) *trckd ldrs: t.k.h: drvn over 3f out: wnt 2nd 2f out: sn wknd: eased ins fnl f* **11/4**[1]

6214 6 *4 ½* **Catbells (IRE)**[29] 7316 3-9-0 **65**..................................(p) HobieGill(5) 2 11
(A Bailey) *led: hdd 3f out: lost pl 2f out* **7/2**[3]

2000 7 *5* **Tricky Situation**[43] 7045 4-9-1 **62**.............................(b[1]) ShaneBKelly(3) 4 —
(D H Brown) *dwlt: sn trcking ldrs: lost pl over 5f out: bhd fnl 3f* **12/1**

2m 7.34s (5.64) **Going Correction** +0.60s/f (Slow)
WFA 3 from 4yo+ 2lb **7 Ran SP% 118.8**
Speed ratings (Par 101): **98,97,88,87,75 71,67**
toteswingers:1&2:£6.60, 1&3:£4.90, 2&3:£3.70 CSF £34.21 CT £95.76 TOTE £7.00: £2.70, £3.80; EX 36.80.
Owner A R James **Bred** John T L Jones Jr & Bemak N V **Trained** Clapton-on-the-Hill, Gloucs

FOCUS
A moderate apprentice handicap run at a sound pace and the front pair pulled miles clear of the rest.
Mr Emirati(USA) Official explanation: trainer said, regarding running, that the gelding failed to stay the 1m 1 1/2f trip.

7679 SPONSOR A RACE BY CALLING 01902 390000 CLASSIFIED CLAIMING STKS 1m 141y(P)
4:15 (4:15) (Class 5) 3-Y-O+ £2,007 (£597; £298; £149) Stalls Low

Form RPR

0004 1 **Kildare Sun (IRE)**[13] 7529 8-8-8 **67**...........................(p) GrahamGibbons 7 68
(J Mackie) *trckd ldr: led over 2f out: strly chal fnl f: jst hld on* **9/2**

5404 2 *nse* **William Morgan (IRE)**[18] 7462 3-7-11 **63**................ JamesSullivan(3) 10 62
(R A Fahey) *trckd ldrs: pushed up to chal 2f out: kpt on fnl f: jst hld* **4/1**[3]

6013 3 *nk* **Fujin Dancer (FR)**[23] 7251 5-8-9 **70**...............................(p) JulieBurke(7) 4 75
(K A Ryan) *dwlt: hld up: hdwy over 5f out: wnt handy 3rd over 1f out: kpt on wl: no ex nr fin* **3/1**[2]

5005 4 *5* **Kumbeshwar**[18] 7467 3-9-0 **60**..(v[1]) PhillipMakin 9 64
(P D Evans) *hld up in midfield: effrt over 2f out: one pce* **14/1**

4 5 *¾* **The Lock Master (IRE)**[61] 6599 3-7-9 **70**.................... RyanPowell(7) 11 50
(M Appleby) *dwlt: hld up in rr: hdwy on outside to chse ldrs over 4f out: wknd 2f out* **8/1**

0 6 *8* **Pinsplitter (USA)**[17] 7474 3-8-0 **63**..............................(p) NickyMackay 5 29
(A J McCabe) *chsd ldrs: drvn over 3f out: lost pl 2f out* **28/1**

3041 7 *2 ¾* **April Fool**[17] 7472 6-8-8 **68**..(v) LukeMorris 6 29
(R A Harris) *led: hdd over 2f out: lost pl over 1f out* **11/4**[1]

1m 55.13s (4.63) **Going Correction** +0.60s/f (Slow)
WFA 3 from 4yo+ 2lb **7 Ran SP% 111.1**
Speed ratings (Par 103): **103,102,102,98,97 90,88**
toteswingers:1&2:£4.10, 1&3:£2.60, 2&3:£3.10 CSF £21.37 TOTE £5.70: £3.10, £2.20; EX 21.40.William Morgan was claimed by A. G. Juckes for £5,000.
Owner Mrs Barbara Woodworth **Bred** Gordan Woodworth **Trained** Church Broughton , Derbys

FOCUS
A moderate classified claimer and, with the pace slackening at halfway, a couple of these were inclined to pull. There was little between the front three at the line, but they pulled well clear of the rest.

7680 PLAY ROULETTE AT TOTESPORT.COM H'CAP 1m 141y(P)
4:45 (4:45) (Class 4) (0-85,84) 3-Y-O+ £3,594 (£1,069; £534; £266) Stalls Low

Form RPR

0000 1 **Spectait**[25] 7382 8-9-5 **82**.. GeorgeBaker 6 96+
(Jonjo O'Neill) *dwlt: hdwy to trck ldrs over 3f out: led 2f out: clr 1f out: idled and drvn out clsng stages* **4/1**[3]

1-63 2 *¾* **Dahaam**[77] 6151 3-9-1 **80**.. HayleyTurner 5 90
(D M Simcock) *hld up towards rr: effrt over 3f out: sn outpcd: hdwy to chse ldrs over 1f out: kpt on to take 2nd last stride* **9/2**

3011 3 *shd* **Elijah Pepper (USA)**[32] 7274 5-8-9 **72**.......................... GrahamGibbons 7 82
(T D Barron) *sn trcking ldrs: drvn 3f out: chsd wnr ins fnl f: lost 2nd line* **5/2**[1]

4344 4 *4 ½* **Faithful Ruler (USA)**[9] 7560 6-9-2 **79**............................... PhillipMakin 3 79
(R A Fahey) *in rr and sn drvn along: hdwy over 2f out: styd on fnl f: tk n.d 4th nr fin* **10/3**[2]

2201 5 *nk* **Slikback Jack (IRE)**[15] 7499 3-9-1 **80**.............................. IanMongan 2 79
(D Nicholls) *sn chsng ldrs: wnt 2nd 2f out: wknd fnl 100yds* **8/1**

0001 6 *17* **Opus Maximus (IRE)**[37] 7171 5-9-7 **84**............................ GregFairley 1 44
(M Johnston) *led: hdd over 4f out: lost pl 3f out: sn bhd* **16/1**

6006 7 *1 ¾* **Wigram's Turn (USA)**[13] 7526 5-8-12 **75**......................... JamieSpencer 10 31
(M W Easterby) *racd wd early: sn w ldr: led over 4f out: hdd over 2f out: sn wknd* **14/1**

1m 54.29s (3.79) **Going Correction** +0.60s/f (Slow)
WFA 3 from 4yo+ 2lb **7 Ran SP% 113.5**
Speed ratings (Par 105): **107,106,106,102,101 86,85**
toteswingers:1&2:£4.90, 1&3:£3.60, 2&3:£2.50 CSF £21.85 CT £52.61 TOTE £6.60: £3.30, £3.40; EX 31.10.
Owner John P McManus **Bred** Blyth Tait **Trained** Cheltenham, Gloucs

FOCUS
This wasn't a bad handicap at all and there was a solid early pace on resulting in a time 0.84 seconds faster than the claimer.

7681 WOLVERHAMPTON HOLIDAY INN MAIDEN FILLIES' STKS (DIV I) 7f 32y(P)
5:15 (5:16) (Class 5) 2-Y-O £1,683 (£501; £250; £125) Stalls High

Form RPR

0 1 **Dan's Martha**[65] 6459 2-8-11 **0**.................................... PatrickDonaghy(3) 4 71
(B M R Haslam) *dwlt: hld up in rr: hdwy over 4f out: chal over 2f out: led over 1f out: styd on strly: readily* **14/1**

5 **2** 2¼ **Psychic's Dream**[20] 7447 2-9-0 0................................ ChrisCatlin 2 65
(M Botti) *trckd ldr: led over 2f out: sn jnd and rdn: hdd over 1f out: kpt on same pce* **2/5**[1]

0 **3** 8 **Wodian (IRE)**[9] 7550 2-9-0 0................................ IanMongan 5 49
(D R Lanigan) *hld up in rr: hdwy u.p 3f out: wnt 3rd over 1f out: one pce: eased towards fin* **11/2**[2]

4 4½ **Yours** 2-9-0 0................................ PhillipMakin 6 34+
(K A Ryan) *dwlt: drvn to sn chse ldrs: rdn and lost pl 3f out: kpt on to take modest 4th clsng stages* **8/1**[3]

00 **5** 1 **Dixie Gwalia**[9] 7551 2-8-7 0................................ LauraPike(7) 3 32
(D M Simcock) *trckd ldrs: t.k.h: rdn and wknd 2f out* **33/1**

00 **6** 14 **Rattleyurjewellery**[50] 6874 2-8-7 0................................ PNolan(7) 1 —
(D H Brown) *led: hdd over 2f out: sn wknd and bhd* **40/1**

1m 34.73s (5.13) **Going Correction** +0.60s/f (Slow) 6 Ran SP% **110.0**
Speed ratings (Par 93): **94,91,82,77,76 60**
toteswingers:1&2:£1.70, 1&3:£2.20, 2&3:£1.30 CSF £19.70 TOTE £14.10: £5.10, £1.10; EX 26.60.
Owner D.G.O. Partnership **Bred** D G O Partnership **Trained** Middleham Moor, N Yorks

FOCUS
An ordinary looking maiden, and the slower of the two divisions by 0.89sec.

NOTEBOOK
Dan's Martha was beaten a long way on her debut in testing ground at Newcastle, but she wasn't unfancied that day and, despite once again missing the break and showing signs of inexperience, she came through from off the pace to run out a clear winner. She did carry her head a bit high, but that was probably just greenness, and there should be better to come from her. (op 10-1 tchd 9-1)
Psychic's Dream set the standard on her debut effort here last month and was sent off a short price. Although on the face of it this was disappointing, she might well have run to a similar level and was just unlucky to bump into a filly stepping up significantly on her debut run. (op 4-7 tchd 8-13)
Wodian(IRE) stayed on steadily from off the pace to take third, but never held out much hope of troubling the first two. She's likely to appreciate further in time. (op 13-2)
Yours is out of a mare whose only win came in a heavy ground maiden but who recorded her highest RPR at this track. She was beaten off leaving the back straight before staying on again for a poor fourth, and should could on plenty for this debut experience. (op 11-2)
Dixie Gwalia was keen early and raced on the slower ground next to the inside rail. (op 20-1)

7682 WOLVERHAMPTON HOLIDAY INN MAIDEN FILLIES' STKS (DIV II) 7f 32y(P)
5:45 (5:45) (Class 5) 2-Y-O **£1,683** (£501; £250; £125) **Stalls High**

Form RPR

1 **Ninita** 2-9-0 0................................ NickyMackay 1 73+
(M E Rimmer) *hld up in rr: hdwy and c outside over 2f out: led 1f out: styd on strly to qckn clr clsng stages* **50/1**

2 3¾ **Always Like This (IRE)** 2-9-0 0................................ AndreaAtzeni 5 64
(M Botti) *trckd ldrs: chal 1f out: hung lft and styd on same pce* **7/2**[3]

3 1¾ **Roman Flame**[49] 6908 2-9-0 0................................ FrannyNorton 4 60+
(M Quinn) *mde most: hdd 1f out: kpt on same pce* **1/1**[1]

6 **4** 3½ **Verrazano**[20] 7448 2-9-0 0................................ PhillipMakin 6 51
(K A Ryan) *sn w ldr: ev ch tl wknd jst ins fnl f* **11/4**[2]

0 **5** 6 **Omega Centauri**[13] 7530 2-9-0 0................................ GrahamGibbons 2 36
(E S McMahon) *chsd ldrs: effrt on ins 2f out: wknd fnl f* **18/1**

6 ¾ **Zareena** 2-9-0 0................................ CathyGannon 3 34
(P D Evans) *s.i.s: hld up in rr: drvn over 3f out: lost pl over 2f out* **16/1**

1m 33.84s (4.24) **Going Correction** +0.60s/f (Slow) 6 Ran SP% **112.0**
Speed ratings (Par 93): **99,94,92,88,81 81**
toteswingers:1&2:£7.70, 1&3:£4.00, 2&3:£1.20 CSF £212.29 TOTE £37.60: £19.80, £1.80; EX 80.70.
Owner Clive Dennett **Bred** Clive Dennett **Trained** Newmarket, Suffolk

FOCUS
There was a shock result in this maiden, which was run in a time 0.89sec quicker than the first division.

NOTEBOOK
Ninita, first foal of an unraced half-sister to numerous winners including Fair Trade and Island Sound, travelled pretty well in behind before being switched wide off the home turn and living up to her sire's name and storming home down the outside. She's bred to appreciate further in time and this surface, riding slower than standard, probably helped. (op 40-1)
Always Like This(IRE), who cost 110,000euros as a yearling and is out of a dual Group 3 winner, came there to have every chance early in the straight but just didn't see her race out as strongly as the winner. This surface may have been a little more testing than ideal, and she should be able to go one better soon. (op 4-1 tchd 5-1)
Roman Flame was the one to beat at the ratings but she tended not to find a great deal off the bridle in Ireland, and it was the same again here on her debut for her new stable. Her cause wasn't helped by being stuck on the rail the majority of way round, though. (tchd 11-10 and 11-8 in a place)
Verrazano, better away this time, took on the favourite up front and was beaten early in the straight. A more patient ride might suit in future. (tchd 5-2)

7683 PLAY BLACKJACK AT TOTESPORT.COM H'CAP 5f 216y(P)
6:15 (6:15) (Class 5) (0-70,70) 3-Y-O+ **£2,007** (£597; £298; £149) **Stalls Low**

Form RPR

1445 **1** **Cardinal**[10] 7539 5-9-7 **70**................................ HayleyTurner 2 86+
(R M H Cowell) *trckd ldrs: stdd and dropped to rr after 1f: shkn up 3f out: gd hdwy on outside 2f out: led jst ins fnl f: forged clr* **6/1**[3]

0000 **2** 4 **Norville (IRE)**[30] 7305 3-8-13 **62**................................(b[1]) CathyGannon 7 65
(P D Evans) *in rr-div: hdwy 3f out: chsng ldrs over 1f out: kpt on same pce fnl f* **16/1**

2242 **3** ½ **Riflessione**[9] 7556 4-9-7 **70**................................(v[1]) LukeMorris 8 71
(R A Harris) *led 1f: chsd ldrs: hung rt 2f out: styd on same pce fnl f* **11/2**[2]

3306 **4** 1½ **Desert Icon (IRE)**[28] 7332 4-8-9 **65**................................ AliceHaynes(7) 11 62
(D M Simcock) *w ldrs: led over 2f out: hdd jst ins fnl f: no ex* **16/1**

4126 **5** ½ **Desert Strike**[10] 7542 4-8-5 **61**................................(p) NoraLooby(7) 5 56
(A J McCabe) *trckd ldrs on inner: t.k.h: hmpd and lost pl 2f out: swtchd wd: kpt on ins fnl f* **12/1**

3550 **6** 5 **Ballodair (IRE)**[13] 7526 3-9-7 **70**................................ BarryMcHugh 3 49
(R A Fahey) *dwlt: in rr: hdwy on ins 2f out: nvr nr ldrs* **11/1**

0060 **7** nk **Ace Of Spies (IRE)**[15] 7494 5-9-4 **67**................................ LiamJones 10 45
(C R Dore) *trckd ldrs on outside: lost pl 1f out* **14/1**

226 **8** 3½ **Cavitie**[23] 7390 4-8-10 **62**................................ RussKennemore(3) 1 29
(Andrew Reid) *in tch: sme hdwy over 2f out: sn lost pl* **8/1**

0102 **9** 11 **Devil You Know (IRE)**[13] 7525 4-9-6 **69**................................(t) JamieSpencer 9 1
(M W Easterby) *led after 1f: hdd over 2f out: sn lost pl and bhd: eased* **11/8**[1]

1m 17.78s (2.78) **Going Correction** +0.60s/f (Slow) 9 Ran SP% **117.3**
Speed ratings (Par 103): **105,99,99,97,96 89,89,84,69**
toteswingers:1&2:£16.50, 1&3:£7.00, 2&3:£15.10 CSF £96.72 CT £563.69 TOTE £6.00: £1.70, £3.80, £1.90; EX 89.60.
Owner Mrs J May **Bred** The Queen **Trained** Six Mile Bottom, Cambs

FOCUS
They went pretty quick up front and that set things up for a closer.
Riflessione Official explanation: jockey said gelding hung right
Devil You Know(IRE) Official explanation: jockey said gelding became unruly in stalls

7684 PLAY SLOTS AT TOTESPORT.COM MAIDEN STKS 5f 20y(P)
6:45 (6:46) (Class 5) 3-Y-O+ **£2,007** (£597; £298; £149) **Stalls Low**

Form RPR

0053 **1** **Crimson Queen**[14] 7505 3-8-12 57................................ JackMitchell 2 65
(R Brotherton) *s.i.s: hdwy over 2f out: swtchd ins and styd on to ld over 1f out: hld on towards fin* **9/4**[1]

3630 **2** nk **Sparking**[28] 7328 3-8-12 60................................ GrahamGibbons 9 64
(T D Barron) *sn drvn along to chse ldrs: styd on to chse wnr fnl f: no ex towards fin* **11/4**[2]

052 **3** 4½ **Francis Albert**[16] 7477 4-8-10 52................................(v[1]) JosephYoung(7) 6 53
(M Mullineaux) *led: hdd over 1f out: hrd rdn and edgd rt: one pce* **3/1**[3]

00 **4** ½ **Spirit Of Dixie**[161] 3407 3-8-9 0................................ MichaelGeran(3) 8 46
(D Nicholls) *chsd ldrs on outer: kpt on same pce appr fnl f* **9/1**

5 6 **Spring Leap** 3-9-3 0................................ HayleyTurner 4 29+
(R M H Cowell) *dwlt: in rr: sn pushed along: bhd tl sme hdwy fnl 2f: will improve* **13/2**

0/0 **6** 1¾ **Red Rani**[18] 7461 5-8-12 0................................ ChrisCatlin 3 18
(R Hollinshead) *prom early: sn lost pl and in rr* **33/1**

-000 **7** 2 **Rightcar Dominic**[146] 3903 5-9-3 37................................(b) PatrickMathers 5 16
(Peter Grayson) *reminders after s: sn outpcd and in rr: bhd fnl 2f* **66/1**

4-00 **8** 6 **Charles Bear**[18] 7461 3-8-12 50................................ GregFairley 7 —
(Bruce Hellier) *chsd ldrs: lost pl over 1f out* **22/1**

65.07 secs (2.77) **Going Correction** +0.60s/f (Slow) 8 Ran SP% **114.6**
Speed ratings (Par 103): **101,100,93,92,82 80,76,67**
toteswingers:1&2:£1.40, 1&3:£2.20, 2&3:£2.20 CSF £8.55 TOTE £2.50: £1.10, £2.30, £1.30; EX 9.90.
Owner Arthur Clayton **Bred** Cheveley Park Stud Ltd **Trained** Elmley Castle, Worcs
■ Stewards' Enquiry : Joseph Young two-day ban: used whip with excessive force (Dec 17-18)

FOCUS
They went fast up front and that suited the more patiently ridden horses. The form is very moderate.

7685 SPONSOR A RACE BY CALLING 01902 390000 H'CAP 1m 1f 103y(P)
7:15 (7:15) (Class 6) (0-60,60) 3-Y-O **£1,535** (£453; £226) **Stalls Low**

Form RPR

304 **1** **Loyalty**[20] 7451 3-9-7 **60**................................(v) PatrickMathers 8 71
(D Shaw) *hld up in rr: hdwy to chse ldng pair 2f out: styd on on ins to ld jst ins fnl f: drvn out* **14/1**

-556 **2** ¾ **Professor John (IRE)**[29] 7323 3-9-5 **58**................................(v) GrahamGibbons 4 67
(I A Wood) *t.k.h: wnt 2nd over 2f out: edgd rt over 1f out: edgd lft and upsides ins fnl f: no ex towards fin* **15/2**

404 **3** 1¾ **Bizarrely (IRE)**[32] 7273 3-9-7 **60**................................ MickyFenton 5 66
(J Pearce) *t.k.h: sn trcking ldrs: led over 2f out: hdd jst ins fnl f: kpt on same pce* **10/1**

0013 **4** 6 **Irish Jugger (USA)**[9] 7561 3-9-6 **59**................................ JamesMillman 2 54
(B R Millman) *hld up in rr: hdwy over 4f out: sn chsng ldrs: wknd over 1f out* **3/1**[1]

550 **5** 3¾ **Mush Mir (IRE)**[149] 3786 3-9-2 **58**................................ MatthewDavies(3) 9 45
(J R Boyle) *trckd ldrs: led over 3f out: hdd over 2f out: wknd over 1f out* **9/2**[3]

1654 **6** 7 **Empress Leizu (IRE)**[18] 7467 3-9-3 **56**................................ HayleyTurner 3 30
(A W Carroll) *led 1f: chsd ldrs: drvn over 3f out: lost pl over 1f out* **9/2**[3]

524 **7** 2½ **Sennybridge**[42] 7069 3-9-7 **60**................................ EddieAhern 1 29
(J W Hills) *in rr: rdn over 2f out: nvr a factor* **4/1**[2]

0000 **8** 27 **Princess Of Troy (IRE)**[32] 7273 3-8-10 **49**................................ CathyGannon 6 —
(P D Evans) *t.k.h: led after 1f: hdd over 3f out: sn lost pl and bhd: eased fnl f: t.o* **40/1**

2m 6.66s (4.96) **Going Correction** +0.60s/f (Slow) 8 Ran SP% **111.3**
Speed ratings (Par 98): **101,100,98,93,90 83,81,57**
toteswingers:1&2:£8.30, 1&3:£10.90, 2&3:£6.30 CSF £107.29 CT £1075.54 TOTE £15.50: £4.70, £2.80, £1.10; EX 76.40.
Owner Mrs Lyndsey Shaw **Bred** Ecoutila Partnership **Trained** Sproxton, Leics

FOCUS
Quite a competitive race on paper.
Sennybridge Official explanation: jockey said filly ran flat
Princess Of Troy(IRE) Official explanation: jockey said filly had no more to give
T/Plt: £219.60 to a £1 stake. Pool:£158,616.91 - 527.04 winning tickets T/Qpdt: £38.60 to a £1 stake. Pool:£14,983.55 - 286.94 winning tickets WG

7649 KEMPTON (A.W) (R-H)
Saturday, December 4

OFFICIAL GOING: Standard
Wind: Almost Nil Weather: Overcast

7686 WILLIAMHILL.COM MAIDEN FILLIES' STKS 6f (P)
2:05 (2:05) (Class 5) 2-Y-O **£2,115** (£624; £312) **Stalls High**

Form RPR

1 **Swift Breeze** 2-9-0 0................................ LiamJones 6 70+
(W J Haggas) *cl up: chsd wnr over 2f out: sn chalng: looked hld fnl f tl drvn to ld nr fin* **11/2**[3]

33 **2** hd **Palais Glide**[6] 7608 2-9-0 0................................ JimmyFortune 7 69+
(R Hannon) *fly-jmpd s: led at modest pce: kicked on over 2f out: hd high and edgd rt fr over 1f out: maintained narrow ld tl hdd and nt qckn nr fin* **5/4**[1]

5 **3** 4 **Avon Supreme**[14] 7517 2-9-0 0................................ ChrisCatlin 5 57
(Miss Gay Kelleway) *rrd s and slowly away: sn in tch: prog on inner to chse ldng pair 2f out: outpcd over 1f out: kpt on* **11/4**[2]

5040 **4** nk **Fairy Tales**[45] 7017 2-9-0 44................................ NeilChalmers 1 56
(J J Bridger) *hld up in last: prog over 2f out: disp 3rd over 1f out: sn outpcd: plugged on* **50/1**

000 **5** 2¼ **Brandy Snap (IRE)**[141] 4095 2-9-0 0................................ FrankieMcDonald 2 50
(R Hannon) *racd wd: chsd ldrs: lost pl sn after 1/2-way: toiling in rr 2f out* **25/1**

00 **6** 2¾ **Bluberry**[17] 7485 2-9-1 0 ow1................................ GeorgeBaker 3 42
(G L Moore) *hld up in tch: pushed along over 2f out: sn outpcd* **10/1**

7 1 1/4 **Nahawand (USA)** 2-9-0 0 .... StephenCraine 4 37
(J R Boyle) *chsd ldr to over 2f out: sn wknd* **8/1**

1m 14.22s (1.12) **Going Correction** +0.075s/f (Slow) 7 Ran SP% **112.5**
Speed ratings (Par 93): **95,94,89,89,86 82,80**
Tote Swingers: 1&2 £1.10, 1&3 £3.90, 2&3 £1.70 CSF £12.40 TOTE £4.30: £1.70, £1.10; EX 11.70.
Owner Saif Ali **Bred** Rabbah Bloodstock Limited **Trained** Newmarket, Suffolk

FOCUS
Probably only an ordinary maiden, which was run at a modest early tempo.

NOTEBOOK
Swift Breeze, related to a couple of winners, is a good size and showed a likeable attitude once asked for maximum effort to win with a bit in hand. One would imagine that there is more to come from her. (op 4-1)
Palais Glide shaped well over C&D six-days previously and looked the one to beat on that performance. She got to the lead without too much of a problem but started to edge right inside the final furlong from a middle-of-the-course position, taking the winner with her towards the inside rail. While clearly not one to take a short price about, she should win a small contest during the winter. (tchd 6-4)
Avon Supreme showed some ability of her debut over 5f at Lingfield but didn't obviously progress here after starting slowly. (op 4-1)
Fairy Tales has an official mark of 44, which is slightly worrying with regards to how strong this form might be. There is no reason to think she didn't run up to her best. (op 40-1)
Brandy Snap(IRE), having her first try on Polytrack, had hardly beaten a rival in three previous outings (she finished lame on the last of those starts) so this didn't seem much better. (tchd 20-1)
Bluberry failed to make any impression but does at least have the opportunity to run in handicaps now. (op 9-1)
Nahawand(USA), half-sister to the very useful Dubai Miracle, was unraced for Ed Dunlop after costing $50,000 as a yearling and looked green under pressure once asked to quicken. (tchd 7-1)

7687 BEST ODDS GUARANTTED AT MOBILE.WILLIAMHILL.COM H'CAP 1m 3f (P)
2:40 (2:40) (Class 5) (0-75,75) 3-Y-O+ **£2,388** (£705; £352) **Stalls** High

Form RPR
4025 1 **Pittodrie Star (IRE)**[7] 7597 3-8-10 68 .... DavidProbert 1 78+
(A M Balding) *t.k.h: led at mod pce for 3f: trckd ldrs after: wnt 2nd over 2f out: edgd lft u.p but led jst ins fnl f: styd on wl* **4/1[2]**
3055 2 3 **Archie Rice (USA)**[19] 7463 4-8-11 65 .... RobertHavlin 2 70
(T Keddy) *s.s: sn in tch in rr: prog over 2f out: styd on same pce fnl f to take 2nd nr fin* **7/1[3]**
1 3 3/4 **Pertuis (IRE)**[17] 7489 4-9-4 72 .... JimmyQuinn 11 76
(H J L Dunlop) *s.i.s: sn prom: led after 3f: styd on inner and tried to kick on over 2f out: hdd and fdd jst ins fnl f* **7/1[3]**
0004 4 nk **Encircled**[34] 7252 6-9-7 75 .... FergusSweeney 3 78
(J R Jenkins) *hld up in rr: gng bttr than most whn prog over 2f out: drvn over 1f out: kpt on same pce after* **8/1**
4255 5 3/4 **Green Wadi**[10] 7548 5-9-1 69 .... GeorgeBaker 7 71
(G L Moore) *racd wd: hld up in tch: wnt prom over 3f out: rdn and nt qckn over 2f out: one pce after* **11/4[1]**
0220 6 3 1/4 **Watchmaker**[32] 7286 7-8-7 61 oh1 ....(p) SamHitchcott 6 57
(Miss Tor Sturgis) *hld up in rr: rdn over 3f out: no prog and btn over 2f out* **16/1**
4105 7 1 3/4 **Urban Space**[7] 7600 4-9-7 75 .... HayleyTurner 8 68
(C R Dore) *trckd ldr 2f: styd handy: drvn wl over 2f out: steadily wknd* **7/1[3]**
3111 8 2 **Talenti (IRE)**[17] 7480 7-9-4 72 ....(tp) StephenCraine 4 61
(D Flood) *trckd ldr after 3f tl over 2f out: wknd qckly over 1f out* **9/1**
434R 9 10 **Rare Malt (IRE)**[18] 6328 3-8-12 70 .... FrankieMcDonald 10 41
(M F Harris) *s.v.s: sn in tch in last: rdn over 3f out: wknd over 2f out: t.o* **25/1**

2m 21.87s (-0.03) **Going Correction** +0.075s/f (Slow)
WFA 3 from 4yo+ 4lb 9 Ran SP% **115.0**
Speed ratings (Par 103): **103,100,100,100,99 97,95,94,87**
Tote Swingers:1&2:£6.40, 1&3:£9.40, 2&3:£10.70 CSF £31.96 CT £189.52 TOTE £2.90: £1.10, £3.00, £1.70; EX 24.70 Trifecta £370.00 Pool: £880.08 - 1.76 winning units..
Owner Evan M Sutherland **Bred** Gary O'Reilly **Trained** Kingsclere, Hants

FOCUS
This isn't form to take seriously as the early fractions were slow and the pace didn't pick up until they started off down the back straight.

7688 WILLIAMHILL.COM H'CAP 1m (P)
3:10 (3:11) (Class 4) (0-80,80) 3-Y-O+ **£3,885** (£1,156; £577; £288) **Stalls** High

Form RPR
3321 1 **Fantasy Gladiator**[10] 7554 4-9-7 80 ....(p) JimmyQuinn 6 93
(R M H Cowell) *hld up in 5th off the pce: smooth prog over 2f out: led wl over 1f out: edgd lft but readily drew clr* **9/4[1]**
3013 2 3 1/2 **Having A Ball**[6] 7611 6-8-7 66 oh1 .... ChrisCatlin 7 71
(P D Cundell) *settled in last pair and wl off the pce: pushed along over 3f out: prog over 2f out: drvn to chse wnr over 1f out: kpt on but outpcd* **9/2[3]**
0520 3 1 **She's A Character**[7] 7600 3-9-6 80 ....(p) JimmyFortune 3 83
(R A Fahey) *slowest away but pushed up to chse ldng pair: clsd to ld briefly 2f out: outpcd fnl f but kpt on* **10/1**
3560 4 6 **Suffolk Punch (IRE)**[35] 7238 3-9-6 80 .... DavidProbert 8 69
(A M Balding) *chsd ldng pair: rdn over 2f out: wl outpcd and lft bhd fr over 1f out* **11/4[2]**
5-00 5 nk **Humungous (IRE)**[10] 7560 7-9-1 74 .... MickyFenton 2 62
(C R Egerton) *sn restrained in rr and wl bhd in last after 3f: pushed along 1/2-way: no rspnse whn rdn over 2f out* **16/1**
0310 6 9 **Cobo Bay**[7] 7600 5-9-7 80 ....(b) RobertWinston 5 48
(C R Dore) *led at str pce but sn hrd pressed: rdn over 3f out: hdd & wknd rapidly over 2f out: t.o* **15/2**
0543 7 3/4 **Blakey's Boy**[31] 7304 3-9-3 77 .... FrannyNorton 1 43
(H J L Dunlop) *sn pressed ldrs str pce: led briefly over 2f out and appeared to be gng strly: wknd rapidly over 1f out: t.o* **8/1**

1m 38.43s (-1.37) **Going Correction** +0.075s/f (Slow)
WFA 3 from 4yo+ 1lb 7 Ran SP% **113.5**
Speed ratings (Par 105): **109,105,104,98,98 89,88**
Tote Swingers:1&2:£2.20, 1&3:£4.90, 2&3:£8.40 CSF £12.53 CT £81.46 TOTE £3.60: £3.00, £2.00; EX 8.90 Trifecta £75.80 Pool: £725.49 - 7.08 winning units..
Owner The Fantasy Fellowship **Bred** R S A Urquhart **Trained** Six Mile Bottom, Cambs

FOCUS
The two leaders set a strong pace, so the form should be sound.

Blakey's Boy Official explanation: jockey said gelding stopped quickly

7689 WILLIAM HILL - HOME OF BETTING H'CAP 7f (P)
3:40 (3:41) (Class 2) (0-100,104) 3-Y-O+ **£9,066** (£2,697; £1,348; £673) **Stalls** High

Form RPR
00 1 **Angel's Pursuit (IRE)**[14] 7524 3-9-11 104 .... JimmyFortune 9 113
(R Hannon) *prom in chsng gp: clsd over 2f out: drvn to press ldr jst over 1f out: styd on gamely to ld last strides* **12/1**
6332 2 hd **Seek The Fair Land**[8] 7574 4-8-6 88 ....(b) MatthewDavies[(3)] 2 96
(J R Boyle) *chsd clr ldng pair: clsd over 2f out: rdn to ld over 1f out: kpt on fnl f: hdd last strides* **9/1**
0210 3 1 **Lutine Bell**[8] 7574 3-8-12 91 ....(b) MickyFenton 10 96+
(Mike Murphy) *t.k.h: hld up in last quartet: rdn and prog fr 2f out: styd on to take 3rd last 75yds: clsng at fin* **12/1**
3003 4 2 **Elna Bright**[14] 7522 5-9-2 95 .... JimmyQuinn 3 95
(B R Johnson) *hld up in midfield: rdn and prog towards inner 2f out: disp 3rd fnl f tl fdd last 75yds* **8/1**
5400 5 hd **Street Power (USA)**[7] 7593 5-8-8 87 .... RobertHavlin 11 86
(J R Gask) *s.i.s: hld up in midfield: rdn and prog on inner 2f out: disp 3rd fnl f: fdd last 75yds* **12/1**
0454 6 nk **Mia's Boy**[22] 7430 6-9-6 99 .... GeorgeBaker 7 98
(C A Dwyer) *hld up in last quartet: rdn and prog 2f out: kpt on same pce fnl f: n.d* **9/2[1]**
0230 7 2 1/2 **Autumn Blades (IRE)**[7] 7593 5-9-4 97 ....(v) DavidProbert 4 89
(A Bailey) *s.s: wl off the pce in last pair: u.p and struggling over 2f out: passed wkng rivals fnl f* **13/2[3]**
1140 8 2 1/4 **Rjeef (IRE)**[22] 7430 3-8-11 90 .... HayleyTurner 6 76
(D M Simcock) *prom in chsng gp: rdn to cl over 2f out: wknd over 1f out* **6/1[2]**
5000 9 1 **One Way Or Another (AUS)**[9] 7566 7-8-4 86 oh5 ....(b) KierenFox[(3)] 1 69
(J R Gask) *t.k.h: hld up in midfield: drvn over 2f out: wknd over 1f out* **20/1**
0621 10 2 3/4 **Arteus**[8] 7574 4-8-12 91 ....(b) RobertWinston 12 67+
(Jane Chapple-Hyam) *led at frntic pce but pressed: drew clr over 2f out: hdd & wknd rapidly over 1f out* **9/2[1]**
120- 11 7 **Art Scholar (IRE)**[441] 6104 3-8-11 90 .... FergusSweeney 5 47
(G L Moore) *a in last pair: lost tch 3f out: t.o* **33/1**
5000 12 1 1/2 **Mister Green (FR)**[7] 7594 4-8-2 86 oh1 ....(b) AmyScott[(5)] 8 39
(D Flood) *pressed ldr's frntic pce and clr of rest: wknd over 2f out: t.o* **33/1**

1m 23.83s (-2.17) **Going Correction** +0.075s/f (Slow) 12 Ran SP% **118.8**
Speed ratings (Par 109): **115,114,113,111,111 110,107,105,104,101 93,91**
Tote Swingers:1&2:£13.70, 1&3:£34.40, 2&3:£27.00 CSF £113.54 CT £1346.60 TOTE £10.80: £4.80, £4.00, £5.30; EX 153.40 Trifecta £1279.00 Part won. Pool: £775.11 - 3.72 winning units..
Owner Malih Lahej Al Basti **Bred** Hong Kong Breeders Club **Trained** East Everleigh, Wilts

FOCUS
A cracking handicap in which the well-fancied Arteus and outsider Mister Green appeared to go off too quickly. The former had a good draw for his usual running style, but set off at a pace he was unlikely to sustain, and was quickly swallowed up after holding a healthy lead on turning in.

NOTEBOOK
Angel's Pursuit(IRE) didn't shape too badly on his return to the AW last time in what looked a good race, but was trying 7f and handicap company for the first time here. Settled in midfield, he showed great tenacity under a strong drive to get his head in front just in time. (tchd 14-1)
Seek The Fair Land had chased home Arteus at Lingfield on his previous outing, so this was a big turnaround in form. He is a mainly consistent sort and was only mugged in the final strides. (tchd 8-1 and 10-1)
Lutine Bell slightly disappointed off a much higher mark on his second start for these connections after winning on his first outing for them. Keen under restraint in rear, he finished really well and did the best of those held up. (tchd 14-1)
Elna Bright, a place behind Autumn Blades last time when they met, had his chance but proved to be one paced. (op 7-1)
Street Power(USA) has a good record at this track but is no more than fairly treated.
Mia's Boy is an admirable sort who has run numerous good races throughout his career, but couldn't make any impression here after being held up. (tchd 4-1)
Autumn Blades(IRE) didn't make any impression. Official explanation: jockey said gelding was slowly away (op 15-2 tchd 6-1)
Rjeef(IRE) attracted some market support but was readily held. (op 8-1)

7690 BEST ODDS GUARANTEED AT MOBILE.WILLIAMHILL.COM MAIDEN STKS 1m 3f (P)
4:10 (4:10) (Class 5) 3-Y-O+ **£2,115** (£624; £312) **Stalls** High

Form RPR
6462 1 **Cast Of Stars (IRE)**[22] 7419 3-9-3 72 ....(b) GeorgeBaker 4 72+
(R M Beckett) *hld up in last pair: gng easily whn squeezed through to trck ldrs wl over 1f out: shkn up to ld jst ins fnl f: sn in command* **6/4[1]**
2 1 1/2 **Wade Farm Billy (IRE)**[28] 6-9-7 0 .... JimmyFortune 7 70
(G L Moore) *s.s: settled in last pair: rdn and prog on outer over 2f out: led over 1f out: hdd and outpcd jst ins fnl f* **8/1[3]**
2230 3 nk **Fascination (IRE)**[55] 6781 3-8-12 70 .... HayleyTurner 1 64+
(M L W Bell) *hld up in tch: nt clr run over 2f out: plld out and effrt wl over 1f out: styd on fnl f to take 3rd and cl on runner-up at fin* **9/4[2]**
0062 4 1 3/4 **Royal Etiquette (IRE)**[14] 3787 3-9-3 65 .... ChrisCatlin 3 66
(Mrs Lawney Hill) *t.k.h: hld up in rr: prog on outer to ld 2f out: hdd over 1f out: wknd ins fnl f* **12/1**
0 5 2 **Royal And Ancient (IRE)**[24] 6753 3-9-3 70 .... SamHitchcott 8 63
(M F Harris) *cl up on inner: lost pl 4f out: renewed effrt to chal 2f out: sn outpcd* **8/1[3]**
06 6 1/2 **Lady Willa (IRE)**[16] 5713 3-8-12 58 .... DavidProbert 6 57
(Mark Gillard) *led 1f: trckd ldr: upsides 2f out: sn btn* **16/1**
2230 7 14 **Moonbalej**[21] 1054 3-9-3 57 ....(v) FergusSweeney 2 40
(M F Harris) *led after 1f to 2f out: wknd rapidly: t.o* **16/1**
00/0 8 7 **Dancing Belle**[51] 6865 5-8-9 42 .... DannyBrock[(7)] 5 24
(J R Jenkins) *pressed ldrs tl wknd rapidly 2f out: t.o* **66/1**

2m 23.41s (1.51) **Going Correction** +0.075s/f (Slow)
WFA 3 from 5yo+ 4lb 8 Ran SP% **113.9**
Speed ratings (Par 103): **97,95,95,94,92 92,82,77**
Tote Swingers:1&2:£3.50, 1&3:£1.60, 2&3:£3.10 CSF £14.47 TOTE £2.30: £1.10, £2.60, £1.30; EX 18.50 Trifecta £30.20 Pool: £662.75 - 16.21 winning units..
Owner D P Barrie & M J Rees **Bred** Airlie Stud **Trained** Whitsbury, Hants

FOCUS
This was a weak contest, mainly full of horses that have had plenty of chances on the Flat and over Jumps. There was little pace throughout and the first two in the betting met trouble in running.

7691 WILLIAMHILL.COM NURSERY 7f (P)
4:40 (4:40) (Class 6) (0-65,65) 2-Y-O £1,535 (£453; £226) Stalls High

Form				RPR
605	1		**Amazon Twilight**[60] 6651 2-9-7 65 GeorgeBaker 3 (B R Johnson) hld up in last pair: shkn up and prog on outer over 2f out: led wl over 1f out: drvn out fnl f 7/2[2]	69+
6006	2	1	**Dells Breezer**[7] 7592 2-8-11 58 KierenFox(3) 6 (P M Phelan) plld hrd: hld up in last pair: prog over 2f out: rdn to chse wnr ins fnl f: kpt on but no imp 10/1	57
0006	3	1 1/4	**Magical Star**[64] 6521 2-8-6 50 FrankieMcDonald 4 (R Hannon) t.k.h: trckd ldng trio: prog to ld over 2f out: hdd wl over 1f out: one pce and lost 2nd ins fnl f 12/1	46
5050	4	1 1/4	**Lovat Lane**[16] 7496 2-8-8 52 ChrisCatlin 5 (Eve Johnson Houghton) hld up in 5th: outpcd over 2f out and dropped to last: kpt on again fnl f 33/1	45
5462	5	nk	**Empress Charlotte**[16] 7496 2-9-4 62 HayleyTurner 2 (M L W Bell) mde most to over 2f out: sn outpcd and btn 10/11[1]	54
0000	6	1/2	**Amore Et Labore**[16] 7497 2-8-2 46 (p) FrannyNorton 7 (S Kirk) trckd ldng pair to over 2f out: sn outpcd and btn 11/1	37
0050	7	6	**Les Landes (IRE)**[5] 7630 2-8-10 54 (p) FergusSweeney 1 (J A Osborne) chsd ldr to over 2f out: sn wknd 8/1[3]	29

1m 28.15s (2.15) **Going Correction** +0.075s/f (Slow) 7 Ran SP% **113.8**
Speed ratings (Par 94): **90,88,87,86,85 85,78**
Tote Swingers:1&2:£2.20, 1&3:£6.60, 2&3:£8.70 CSF £36.54 TOTE £3.60: £1.50, £3.10; EX 31.40.
Owner Mrs A M Upsdell & S J Townsend **Bred** Equine Breeding Ltd **Trained** Ashtead, Surrey
■ Stewards' Enquiry : Kieren Fox two-day ban: used whip with excessive frequency (Dec 18-19)

FOCUS
A moderate handicap.

NOTEBOOK
Amazon Twilight, making her handicap debut, showed a great attitude after travelling strongly towards the rear and won nicely. There is every chance she will get a bit further. Official explanation: trainer said, regarding apparent improvement in form, that this was the filly's first run on the all-weather and appreciated the drop in class. (op 9-2)
Dells Breezer, up 2f in distance, pulled really hard in rear and stayed on once in the clear. (op 12-1)
Magical Star, dropping in distance, travelled strongly into a prominent position but couldn't quicken when holding every chance. (op 16-1 tchd 20-1)
Lovat Lane hadn't run well in her two previous attempts in handicaps but stayed on down the middle of the course when in the clear.
Empress Charlotte was a beaten favourite last time from a wide draw at Wolverhampton but looked to have every chance in this company. Quickly away, she raced keenly and didn't seem to get home. (op 8-11 tchd 4-6)
Les Landes(IRE), with cheekpieces on for the first time, could be given a chance on his Wolverhampton performance last month but he dropped away quickly once under pressure. (tchd 15-2)
T/Jkpt: £7,100.00 to a £1 stake. Pool:£10,000.00 - 1.00 winning ticket T/Plt: £339.30 to a £1 stake. Pool:£139,754.20 - 300.60 winning tickets T/Qpdt: £39.80 to a £1 stake. Pool:£8,000.84 - 148.60 winning tickets JN

7641 SOUTHWELL (L-H)
Saturday, December 4

OFFICIAL GOING: Standard to slow
Wind: Virtually nil Weather: Bright but cold

7692 TOTEPLACEPOT WIN WITHOUT BACKING A WINNER MAIDEN AUCTION STKS 5f (F)
12:20 (12:20) (Class 6) 2-Y-O £1,619 (£481; £240; £120) Stalls High

Form				RPR
4	1		**Verus Decorus (IRE)**[24] 7392 2-8-1 0 JamesSullivan(3) 2 (Patrick Morris) cl up gng wl: led on bit wl over 1f out: in command whn eased wl ins fnl f: shkn up and kpt on towards fin 5/4[1]	55
4030	2	nk	**Silent Blessing**[24] 7392 2-8-11 60 (p) GrahamGibbons 3 (R M H Cowell) chsd ldrs and niggled along whn n.m.r and hmpd after 1f: rdn along 1/2-way: hdwy to chse wnr ent fnl f: sn drvn: edgd rt and kpt on 11/4[2]	59
0006	3	4	**Bigalo's Vera B**[23] 7404 2-8-6 40 DuranFentiman 6 (L A Mullaney) dwlt: sn chsng ldrs: rdn along 2f out: kpt on u.p fnl f 14/1	40
	4	1 1/2	**Mazovian (USA)** 2-8-9 0 ow3 RobertLButler(3) 5 (M C Chapman) dwlt: sn prom: led after 2f: rdn along 2f out and sn hdd: drvn over 1f out and grad wknd 9/1	40
00	5	1 3/4	**Sea Of Love (IRE)**[68] 6425 2-8-6 0 LukeMorris 8 (R A Harris) chsd ldrs: rdn along 1/2-way: sn wknd 14/1	28
050	6	1 3/4	**Hannah Cann**[8] 7576 2-8-4 36 (b1) NickyMackay 4 (Peter Grayson) chsd ldrs: rdn along 1/2-way: sn wknd 40/1	20
0006	7	1 1/2	**Mujapiste (IRE)**[24] 7392 2-8-1 45 (p) AndrewHeffernan(3) 7 (L A Mullaney) led 2f: cl up tl rdn 2f out and sn wknd 7/1[3]	14
0500	8	11	**Bold Deceiver**[120] 4788 2-8-4 33 (t) CathyGannon 1 (P S McEntee) towards rr: outpcd and bhd fr 1/2-way 40/1	—

61.45 secs (1.75) **Going Correction** +0.075s/f (Slow) 8 Ran SP% **111.8**
Speed ratings (Par 94): **89,88,82,79,76 74,71,54**
Tote Swingers: 1&2 £1.20, 1&3 £5.90, 2&3 £5.00 CSF £4.42 TOTE £4.20: £1.10, £1.10, £3.40; EX 3.10 Trifecta £28.40 Pool: £341.21 - 8.86 winning units..
Owner Jason Deaves **Bred** P Burns **Trained** Tarporley, Cheshire

FOCUS
Maidens don't come much worse than this, and the key was a similar event over C&D last month which featured four of this field.

NOTEBOOK
Verus Decorus(IRE) did best of the quartet in this field that met over C&D last month, finishing fourth of the 11 runners on debut, and she confirmed the form here. Always travelling well up with the pace, she seemed likely to win easily after taking it up 2f from home, but her rider took things rather too easily and she had to be shaken up near the line as the runner-up closed in. The form amounts to little, but she is entitled to improve again. (op 11-8)
Silent Blessing was probably not quite ready when last in that contest last month, but he had a decent chance on official ratings. With cheekpieces replacing the visor, he was fortunate not to come down when taking a broadside from Hannah Cann after a furlong which knocked him out of his stride, so the fact that he got so close may suggest he was unlucky. However, the winner had more in hand than the margin would suggest and he lacks the scope of the filly. (op 2-1 tchd 3-1)
Bigalo's Vera B, well beaten in three maidens and a seller, ran on past beaten horses to claim a remote third, but achieved little. (op 12-1)
Mazovian(USA), a half-brother to four winners including the high-class Folk, cost just £800 as a 2-y-o. He attracted market support, despite the 3lb overweight, and made much of the running to the 2f pole, but was then left behind. (op 14-1)

7693 EUROPEAN BREEDERS' FUND MAIDEN STKS 1m (F)
12:50 (12:51) (Class 5) 2-Y-O £3,139 (£926; £463) Stalls Low

Form				RPR
0	1		**Potomac (IRE)**[14] 7530 2-9-3 0 (p) NickyMackay 4 (J H M Gosden) cl up: led 1/2-way: pushed clr appr fnl f: easily 3/1[2]	82+
56	2	6	**Samarkand (IRE)**[21] 7452 2-9-3 0 LukeMorris 2 (Sir Mark Prescott) trckd ldrs: hdwy on inner to chse wnr 3f out: rdn over 2f out: drvn over 1f out and kpt on: no ch w wnr 8/1	69
02	3	1 3/4	**Frosty Friday**[18] 7470 2-8-12 0 GregFairley 7 (J R Jenkins) trckd ldrs: rdn along and outpcd over 3f out: kpt on u.p fr over 1f out: n.d 7/1[3]	59
52	4	nk	**School For Scandal (IRE)**[7] 7602 2-8-10 0 DCByrne(7) 1 (M Johnston) j.w but stdd sn after s: sn outpcd and pushed along in rr: hdwy over 3f out: rdn to chse ldrs whn hung rt 2f out: sn drvn and no imp 5/4[1]	63+
4042	5	8	**Phoenix Flame**[24] 7393 2-8-12 61 ShaneKelly 3 (A J McCabe) led to 1/2-way: cl up: rdn along 3f out: wkng whn sltly hmpd 2f out 7/1[3]	41
0	6	3/4	**More Than Enough (IRE)**[10] 7558 2-9-3 0 BarryMcHugh 5 (R A Fahey) in tch: hdwy to chse ldrs 1/2-way: rdn along 3f out: wkng whn sltly hmpd 2f out 20/1	44
0	7	16	**Gud Day (IRE)**[23] 7400 2-9-3 0 DuranFentiman 6 (Mrs D J Sanderson) prom: rdn along 1/2-way: sn wknd: bhd and eased fnl 2f 80/1	14

1m 44.68s (0.98) **Going Correction** +0.075s/f (Slow) 7 Ran SP% **111.6**
Speed ratings (Par 96): **98,92,90,89,81 81,65**
Tote Swingers: 1&2 £4.40, 1&3 £3.30, 2&3 £6.00 CSF £25.28 TOTE £4.00: £4.10, £1.80; EX 33.00.
Owner H R H Princess Haya Of Jordan **Bred** New England Stud Myriad Norelands **Trained** Newmarket, Suffolk

FOCUS
An uncompetitive maiden which took little winning with the favourite running so moderately.

NOTEBOOK
Potomac(IRE) was never a factor when eighth of 13 on his Wolverhampton debut last month, but his sire's progeny have a 25 per cent strike-rate here and he looked a different horse on this surface with the cheekpieces applied. He was always travelling well and, having taken over in front at halfway, pulled right away when shaken up inside the last furlong. He hasn't beaten much, but can probably improve again with this success under his belt. (op 5-1)
Samarkand(IRE), who shaped with some promise in his first two starts, was in vain pursuit of the winner over the last 2f, but he now gets a mark and is bred to appreciate much further than this. (op 17-2 tchd 15-2)
Frosty Friday probably ran into one when slammed 6l by a Godolphin hotpot over C&D last month, but that was still an improvement from her debut. She was making hard work of this from some way out and merely plugged on, but she also now gets a mark. (op 9-2)
School For Scandal(IRE), tried on Fibresand after showing ability in two 7f maidens on Polytrack, broke well enough but then seemed extremely reluctant to race and his rider had to work overtime to get him interested. He did plug on down the home straight despite hanging, but was never going to win and although he also now gets a mark, he should be treated with caution after this effort. (op 11-8 tchd 13-8)
Phoenix Flame set the standard with a mark of 61 having finished runner-up in a fair nursery over C&D last month. She made the early running, but was already out of it when bumped by the favourite 2f from home and just wasn't good enough. (tchd 13-2 and 8-1)

7694 TOTESWINGER THREE WAYS TO WIN H'CAP 1m 3f (F)
1:25 (1:25) (Class 5) (0-75,78) 3-Y-O+ £2,266 (£674; £337; £168) Stalls Low

Form				RPR
3400	1		**Jawaab (IRE)**[15] 6797 6-9-7 75 (e1) AndrewHeffernan(3) 7 (R C Guest) hld up: stdy hdwy 4f out: rdn to chse ldr over 1f out: sn drvn and styd on to ld wl ins fnl f 7/1	85
1034	2	1/2	**Rubi Dia**[16] 7499 3-8-8 63 GregFairley 3 (M Johnston) trckd ldrs: hdwy on inner to ld 3f out: rdn 2f out: drvn over 1f out: hdd and no ex wl ins fnl f 7/1	72
6323	3	2 1/2	**Lay Claim (USA)**[16] 7499 3-9-1 70 ShaneKelly 2 (A J McCabe) hld up towards rr: smooth hdwy on outer 3f out: chsd ldr 2f out: rdn and hung lft over 1f out: sn btn 7/1	75
4416	4	6	**Kimberley Downs (USA)**[7] 7600 4-9-6 71 TomEaves 8 (N Wilson) cl up: rdn along 4f out: drvn 3f out and sn wknd: fin 5th: plcd 4th 3/1[1]	67
3246	5	nk	**My Mate Mal**[151] 3764 6-9-3 68 BarryMcHugh 6 (W B Stone) led: rdn along and hdd 3f out: drvn over 2f out: wknd wl over 1f out: fin 6th: plcd 5th 10/1	63
5030	6	12	**Buddy Holly**[10] 7548 5-9-4 69 AndreaAtzeni 5 (Mrs V M Jordan) trckd ldrs: rdn along 4f out: drvn 3f out and sn wknd: fin 7th: plcd 6th 11/2[3]	45
5021	7	hd	**Maslak (IRE)**[4] 7642 6-9-6 78 6ex JamesRogers(7) 4 (P W Hiatt) chsd ldrs: pushed along and lost pl 1/2-way: rdn 4f out and sn bhd: fin 8th: plcd 7th 9/2[2]	54
0004	D	7	**General Tufto**[4] 7642 5-9-0 70 (b) BillyCray(5) 1 (C Smith) hld up: in rr and rdn along 1/2-way: drvn 4f out: plugged on u.p fnl 2f: nrst fin: fin 4th: disqualified - rdr failed to draw correct weight 12/1	66

2m 27.13s (-0.87) **Going Correction** +0.075s/f (Slow)
WFA 3 from 4yo+ 4lb 8 Ran SP% **112.8**
Speed ratings (Par 103): **106,105,103,94,94 85,85,98**
Tote Swingers: 1&2 £8.70, 1&3 £8.80, 2&3 £6.00 CSF £53.17 CT £353.95 TOTE £5.70: £1.20, £2.10, £2.60; EX 57.80 Trifecta £307.80 Part won. Pool: £415.95 - 0.64 winning units..
Owner L & D Interiors Ltd **Bred** Hascombe And Valiant Studs **Trained** Stainforth, S Yorks

FOCUS
An ordinary handicap, but they went a decent pace and the field were soon well spread out. However, two of those that helped force the issue ended up well beaten, which suggests they went off too quickly.
Maslak(IRE) Official explanation: trainer said, regarding running, that the race came too soon for the gelding following its run four days previously.

7695 BET TOTEPOOL TO SUPPORT YOUR SPORT H'CAP 1m 6f (F)
1:55 (1:55) (Class 5) (0-75,73) 3-Y-O+ £2,007 (£597; £298; £149) Stalls Low

Form				RPR
0100	1		**Sunny Spells**[79] 6132 5-8-7 57 RyanClark(5) 5 (Miss J Feilden) a.p: cl up 4f out: led 3f out: sn jnd and rdn: drvn wl over 1f out and kpt on gamely 7/2[2]	68

5343 **2** ½ **Stadium Of Light (IRE)**[19] 7465 3-8-10 **62** .... TomEaves 1 72
(B Ellison) *hld up in tch: smooth hdwy to trck ldrs over 4f out: chal 3f out: rdn and sltly outpcd wl over 1f out: drvn and rallied ins fnl f: no ex last 100yds* **5/2**[1]

22-6 **3** *14* **Grand Art (IRE)**[8] 4923 6-9-11 **73** ....(vt) AndrewHeffernan(3) 6 65
(Tim Vaughan) *hld up in rr: stdy hdwy over 4f out: rdn along over 3f out: drvn and kpt on same pce fnl 2f* **11/1**

0113 **4** 1 ½ **Kingaroo (IRE)**[4] 7642 4-8-10 **60** .... BillyCray(5) 4 50
(G Woodward) *led: rdn along 4f out: hdd 3f out and grad wknd* **9/2**[3]

40 **5** 2 ¼ **Mashdood (USA)**[23] 7061 4-9-9 **68** .... LukeMorris 7 55
(P W Hiatt) *chsd ldng pair: rdn along 1/2-way: sn lost pl and bhd fnl 4f* **11/1**

1040 **6** *nk* **Frameit (IRE)**[9] 7569 3-8-3 **58** ....(vt) JamesSullivan(3) 2 45
(J G Given) *prom: rdn along on inner 4f out: sn wknd* **12/1**

3513 **7** *15* **Ultimate Quest (IRE)**[14] 6416 5-9-6 **68** .... RobertLButler(3) 3 35
(M C Chapman) *a in rr: pushed along and outpcd after 4f: bhd fr 1/2-way* **11/2**

3m 10.45s (2.15) **Going Correction** +0.075s/f (Slow)
WFA 3 from 4yo+ 7lb **7 Ran SP% 108.7**
Speed ratings (Par 103): **96,95,87,86,85 85,76**
Tote Swingers: 1&2 £3.20, 1&3 £6.80, 2&3 £3.90 CSF £11.37 TOTE £4.40: £1.80, £1.50; EX 12.70.
Owner W E Enticknap **Bred** Whitsbury Manor Stud **Trained** Exning, Suffolk

FOCUS
An ordinary staying handicap, but again the pace seemed solid and there were some yawning gaps separating the runners behind the front pair.

7696 TOTEEXACTA YOUR BETTER VALUE FORECAST NURSERY 5f (F)
2:25 (2:25) (Class 4) (0-85,77) 2-Y-O **£3,238** (£963; £481; £240) **Stalls** High

Form RPR

4554 **1** **Flash City (ITY)**[8] 7578 2-9-3 **73** .... TomEaves 4 83+
(B Smart) *mde all: rdn wl over 1f out: styd on strly* **15/2**

0114 **2** 2 ¼ **Shostakovich (IRE)**[8] 7576 2-9-1 **71** ....(p) JamesDoyle 3 73+
(S Kirk) *trckd ldrs: hdwy 2f out: rdn and edgd lft over 1f out: sn drvn: carried hd high and edgd rt ins fnl f* **5/4**[1]

005 **3** 1 ½ **Irish Boy (IRE)**[14] 7527 2-7-12 **54** oh5 .... AndreaAtzeni 6 51
(W J H Ratcliffe) *chsd ldrs: rdn along 2f out: drvn over 1f out: kpt on same pce fnl f* **33/1**

0341 **4** *nk* **Mr Optimistic**[7] 7598 2-8-12 **68** .... BarryMcHugh 2 63
(R A Fahey) *t.k.h: hld up: hdwy on outer 2f out: rdn to chal wl over 1f out: sn edgd rt and one pce* **11/4**[2]

1344 **5** 2 ½ **Style And Panache (IRE)**[29] 7333 2-9-7 **77** .... CathyGannon 1 64
(P D Evans) *chsd ldrs: rdn along 2f out: drvn whn n.m.r and hmpd over 1f out: sn btn* **9/2**[3]

0040 **6** *9* **Instructress**[7] 7592 2-8-10 **66** ....(p) GrahamGibbons 5 23
(R M H Cowell) *cl up: rdn along 1/2-way: sn wknd* **20/1**

59.75 secs (0.05) **Going Correction** +0.075s/f (Slow) **6 Ran SP% 108.8**
Speed ratings (Par 98): **102,98,96,95,91 77**
Tote Swingers: 1&2 £2.50, 1&3 £15.10, 2&3 £5.10 CSF £16.38 TOTE £9.10: £5.50, £1.10; EX 20.80.
Owner Ceffyl Racing **Bred** G Riccioni Et Al **Trained** Hambleton, N Yorks

FOCUS
A fair nursery and the winner was impressive.

NOTEBOOK
Flash City(ITY) ◆ didn't improve for the switch to Polytrack last time, but it was a different story on his Fibresand debut. Quick from the stalls, he had to fight to hold off the challengers but was really sticking his neck out inside the final furlong and won going away. He is still unexposed and promises to be a bit better than this level. (op 6-1 tchd 10-1)
Shostakovich(IRE), a disappointing favourite over this trip at Wolverhampton last time after bolting up in two modest 6f contests here, had another 5lb rise to contend with. He didn't enjoy the smoothest of passages early, but had every chance to run the winner down inside the last 2f and just found his rival much too classy. A return to 6f will help, but he may also now be in the grip of the handicapper. (op 6-4 tchd 13-8)
Irish Boy(IRE), making his nursery debut from 5lb wrong after finishing unplaced in two maidens and a seller, plugged on to take third but it may be dangerous to take this effort at face value and more evidence is needed. (op 20-1)
Mr Optimistic, off the mark at the eighth attempt in a Wolverhampton maiden last time, met a spot of trouble after half a furlong and was forced to make his effort wide. He was close enough 2f out, but his effort soon flattened out and he doesn't look that well handicapped having been beaten off lower marks than this in a couple of nurseries before his recent win. (tchd 7-2)
Style And Panache(IRE), having her 15th start, ran really well on her racecourse debut over C&D in March when chasing home a rival now rated 102, but on this occasion she was already under pressure when getting messed about just after halfway. (op 4-1)

7697 TOTEPOOL A BETTER WAY TO BET H'CAP 6f (F)
2:55 (2:56) (Class 2) (0-100,92) 3-Y-O£9,335 (£2,794; £1,397; £698; £347) **Stalls** Low

Form RPR

0620 **1** **Cape Vale (IRE)**[9] 7566 5-8-12 **83** .... AdrianNicholls 4 93
(D Nicholls) *mde all: rdn wl over 1f out: drvn ins fnl f: hld on gamely towards fin* **9/1**

2302 **2** 1 ¼ **Imprimis Tagula (IRE)**[23] 7409 6-8-6 **84** ....(v) NatashaEaton(7) 3 91
(A Bailey) *trckd ldrs: effrt to chse wnr wl over 1f out and sn rdn: drvn ins fnl f and ev ch tl nt qckn towards fin* **13/2**[3]

0502 **3** *hd* **Love Delta (USA)**[29] 7329 3-9-7 **92** .... GregFairley 8 98
(M Johnston) *towards rr: hdwy on inner over 2f out: rdn to chse ldrs over 1f out: drvn ins fnl f and kpt on same pce* **3/1**[1]

5101 **4** *hd* **Ingleby Arch (USA)**[35] 7225 7-9-3 **88** .... PhillipMakin 1 93
(T D Barron) *trckd ldrs on inner: hdwy over 2f out: rdn wl over 1f out and ev ch tl drvn and one pce ins fnl f* **17/2**

0120 **5** ½ **Mister Laurel**[8] 7574 4-8-12 **83** ....(b) BarryMcHugh 5 87
(R A Fahey) *midfield: hdwy on inner 1/2-way: sn chsng ldrs: rdn over 1f out: drvn and kpt on same pce fnl f* **8/1**

0000 **6** ½ **Nightjar (USA)**[35] 7238 5-8-10 **88** .... JulieBurke(7) 11 90
(K A Ryan) *dwlt and towards rr: hdwy over 2f out: swtchd lft and rdn over 1f out: drvn and kpt on fnl f* **13/2**[3]

/000 **7** *2* **Alhaban (IRE)**[42] 7083 4-9-5 **90** .... LukeMorris 10 86
(R A Harris) *chsd ldrs: rdn along over 2f out: drvn wl over 1f out and grad wknd* **33/1**

0660 **8** 2 ½ **Great Charm (IRE)**[28] 7351 5-8-8 **79** ow1 .... ShaneKelly 6 68
(E J Alston) *chsd ldrs: effrt over 2f out: sn rdn and wknd over 1f out* **5/1**[2]

-030 **9** 3 ½ **Hard Rock City (USA)**[34] 7262 10-9-2 **92** .... NeilFarley(5) 2 70
(D Carroll) *t.k.h: hld up: a in rr* **25/1**

0605 **10** 1 ¼ **Harlech Castle**[10] 7557 5-8-9 **80** ....(b) TomEaves 7 55
(J R Boyle) *a towards rr* **8/1**

0312 **11** 3 ¼ **Earlsmedic**[44] 7033 5-8-10 **86** ....(e) RyanClark(5) 9 51
(S C Williams) *chsd ldrs on outer: rdn along over 2f out: sn wknd* **20/1**

1m 15.97s (-0.53) **Going Correction** +0.075s/f (Slow) **11 Ran SP% 122.6**
Speed ratings (Par 109): **106,104,104,103,103 102,99,96,91,90 85**
Tote Swingers: 1&2 £8.80, 1&3 £4.20, 2&3 £10.40 CSF £67.79 CT £226.87 TOTE £10.30: £3.60, £2.20, £2.70; EX 87.40 Trifecta £407.10 Pool: £27,820.83 - 50.56 winning units..
Owner Lady O'Reilly **Bred** Derek Veitch **Trained** Sessay, N Yorks

FOCUS
The first six horses home finished in a bit of a heap, but this was still a cracking sprint handicap and it was crucial to race up with the pace.

NOTEBOOK
Cape Vale(IRE) was without a win since September of last year, but was now 2lb lower. There was a question mark over his ability to handle the Fibresand at the first time of asking, but his style of running is well suited to this surface and it was a big help given the way the race panned out. Quick from the stalls, it was just a case of him keeping enough in reserve in order to hold off his rivals over the last couple of furlongs and he showed an admirable attitude. (tchd 11-1)
Imprimis Tagula(IRE), an eight-time course winner including five over this trip, was a stone lower than at the start of the year and this was as good a performance as he has shown here. He was always up there and had every chance against the stands' rail in the straight, but he could never get to the winner and had to be content with just snatching second near the line. He still has a race like this in him if avoiding unexposed types. (op 6-1 tchd 11-2)
Love Delta(USA), 3-5 here, including two wins over this trip, signalled a return to form when splitting higher-rated rivals in a 5f conditions event here last month. He didn't seem to be travelling that well early and gave himself a bit to do, but he ran on well towards the far side of the track, away from the other principals, and did best of those that tried to come from behind. (op 9-2)
Ingleby Arch(USA), a seven-time winner over C&D, was 20lb higher than when winning on turf at Ayr last time. His trainer had expressed reservations over the inside draw (3-60 over the past year) but he had every chance had he been good enough and he probably ran right up to form. (op 9-1 tchd 15-2)
Mister Laurel, still 6lb higher than when winning on his Polytrack debut at Wolverhampton last month, was encountering this surface for the first time. He stayed on well from off the pace in the second half of the contest, but has gained all four of his wins when ridden more positively, so he may be worth returning here with those tactics applied. (op 17-2)
Nightjar(USA) is on a long losing run, but he has a good record here and was 7lb lower than for his last visit back in February. Another to do all his best work late from well off the pace, he has won over this C&D but does look better over an extra furlong. (op 9-1)
Alhaban(IRE) ◆ has faced some very stiff tasks in his abbreviated career, but he ran well for a long way on this Fibresand/handicap debut and his shrewd yard are likely to find an opportunity for him, especially if dropping a few more pounds. (op 25-1)
Great Charm(IRE), 2-4 here but still 6lb higher than when successful over C&D a year ago, can have his performance upgraded a little as he was squeezed right out soon after exiting the stalls. (op 8-1)

7698 BET TOTEPOOL ON ALL UK RACING H'CAP 1m 3f (F)
3:25 (3:25) (Class 3) (0-95,86) 3-Y-O+
£6,044 (£1,810; £905; £452; £226; £113) **Stalls** Low

Form RPR

1000 **1** **Hidden Glory**[7] 7600 3-9-0 **83** .... JamesSullivan(3) 6 89
(J G Given) *hld up in rr: stdy hdwy 4f out: chsd ldrs over 2f out: rdn to chal over 1f out: led ent fnl f: drvn out* **25/1**

0422 **2** *nk* **Cosimo de Medici**[9] 7568 3-9-5 **85** ....(t) SteveDrowne 1 91
(H Morrison) *led 3f: cl up on inner: rdn to ld over 1f out: drvn and hdd ent fnl f: kpt on* **5/2**[1]

2100 **3** *1* **Daaweitza**[28] 7352 7-9-3 **79** ....(be) PhillipMakin 2 83
(B Ellison) *trckd ldng pair: effrt 3f out: rdn along 2f out: swtchd lft and drvn over 1f out: kpt on same pce* **8/1**

1645 **4** *2* **Proud Times (USA)**[37] 7196 4-9-10 **86** .... PJMcDonald 3 87
(G A Swinbank) *cl up: led after 3f: rdn along over 2f out: drvn and hdd over 1f out: kpt on same pce* **4/1**

2133 **5** *7* **Realisation (USA)**[9] 7568 3-8-10 **83** .... DCByrne(7) 4 73
(M Johnston) *trckd ldrs: hdwy over 3f out: rdn to chal on outer 2f out: sn drvn and wknd* **3/1**[2]

2360 **6** *5* **Red Jade**[28] 7350 5-9-9 **85** .... BarryMcHugh 7 67
(R A Fahey) *hld up: hdwy over 4f out: rdn along over 3f out and sn btn* **10/3**[3]

2m 26.55s (-1.45) **Going Correction** +0.075s/f (Slow)
WFA 3 from 4yo+ 4lb **6 Ran SP% 111.6**
Speed ratings (Par 107): **108,107,107,105,100 96**
Tote Swingers: 1&2 £2.60, 1&3 £91.10, 2&3 £2.00 CSF £85.60 TOTE £13.30: £10.70, £1.20; EX 92.70.
Owner Peter Swann **Bred** P Balding **Trained** Willoughton, Lincs

FOCUS
A decent handicap and the winning time was 0.58 seconds faster than the earlier lower-grade handicap.

NOTEBOOK
Hidden Glory was making his Fibresand debut on this second start for the yard, but tends to blow hot and cold, which explains his generous starting price. Having travelled well off the pace early, he maintained his effort to hit the front a furlong out and saw it out well. His new yard may have found the key to him, but it remains to be seen if he will reproduce this next time. Official explanation: trainer said, regarding apparent improvement in form, that it was the gelding's first run on the course and benefited from a change in tactics. (op 22-1 tchd 28-1)
Cosimo de Medici, edging up the weights after a couple of recent near-misses on Polytrack, was successful in a maiden here back in January on his only previous visit. He stays further, so was understandably given a positive ride, but was given no peace up front by Proud Times. To his credit, he kept battling back gamely when looking to be struggling, but the winner's challenge was one too many. He is proving most consistent on sand. (op 11-4 tchd 3-1)
Daaweitza has been inconsistent on turf lately, but he showed some decent form around here earlier in the year and attracted market support. He had every chance, but could only plug on after coming off the bridle 3f out. (op 11-1)
Proud Times(USA), 8lb higher than when winning over 1m4f here in August on his only previous visit, looked the one to beat starting up the home straight, but he then started to hang and was run out of it. (op 7-2)
Realisation(USA), closely matched with Cosimo de Medici on recent Wolverhampton running, was trying this surface for the first time and was close enough turning in, but his stride seemed to shorten dramatically inside the last 2f. (op 5-2)
Red Jade, making his AW debut and still 4lb above his last winning mark, was the first beaten but is due to go jumping soon. Official explanation: jockey said gelding never travelled (op 4-1 tchd 3-1)

T/Plt: £104.60 to a £1 stake. Pool:£107,301 - 748.41 winning tickets T/Qpdt: £19.30 to a £1 stake. Pool:£10,246 - 392.64 winning tickets JR

The Form Book, Raceform Ltd, Compton, RG20 6NL

[7676]WOLVERHAMPTON (A.W) (L-H)

Saturday, December 4

OFFICIAL GOING: Standard to slow

Wind: light /2 behind Weather: early rain, cold

7699 BET ON LIVE FOOTBALL AT TOTESPORT.COM H'CAP 7f 32y(P)

5:20 (5:20) (Class 5) (0-70,70) 3-Y-O+ **£2,007** (£597; £298; £149) **Stalls** High

Form				RPR
2162	1		**Lord Of The Dance (IRE)**[26] 7376 4-9-7 **70**...................... EddieAhern 2	77
			(W M Brisbourne) *in tch: effrt over 2f out: styd on to ld nr fin* **4/1**[1]	
5653	2	hd	**Just Timmy Marcus**[26] 7376 4-9-1 **64**.............................(b) JackMitchell 7	70
			(B P J Baugh) *trckd ldrs: led over 1f out: hdd towards fin* **4/1**[1]	
0500	3	¾	**Lockantanks**[5] 7627 3-9-5 **68**... NeilChalmers 10	73
			(M Appleby) *mid-div: effrt over 2f out: chsng ldrs over 1f out: nt clr run ins fnl f: swtchd lft and r.o nr fin* **66/1**	
0602	4	hd	**Violent Velocity (IRE)**[43] 7056 7-8-9 **65**.................... ShaneBKelly(7) 12	68
			(J J Quinn) *in tch: effrt over 2f out: styd on wl fnl f* **9/2**[2]	
6011	5	2 ½	**Liberty Trail (IRE)**[3] 7656 4-9-2 **65** 6ex......................(p) JamieSpencer 9	62
			(P D Evans) *fast away: led: hdd over 1f out: wknd ins fnl f* **5/1**[3]	
2001	6	1 ¼	**Peter's Gift (IRE)**[26] 7377 4-8-12 **64**................................(p) AmyRyan(3) 4	57
			(K A Ryan) *trckd ldrs: kpt on same pce appr fnl f: fdd fnl 75yds* **10/1**	
1323	7	1	**Lake Chini (IRE)**[21] 7446 8-8-10 **59**.......................(b) GrahamGibbons 11	50
			(M W Easterby) *in rr: sn drvn along: styd on fnl 2f: nt rch ldrs* **10/1**	
5500	8	2 ½	**Safwaan**[21] 7439 3-8-11 **60**.. JamieMackay 3	44
			(W J Musson) *s.i.s: in rr: sme hdwy 2f out: nvr on terms* **20/1**	
0000	9	7	**Lisahane Bog**[24] 7389 3-9-7 **70**..(p) DaneO'Neill 6	35
			(P R Hedger) *s.i.s: bhd and sn drvn along: nvr a factor: eased ins fnl f* **12/1**	
-000	10	2 ¼	**Dubai Legend**[21] 7442 4-8-10 **59**.............................(v[1]) DuranFentiman 8	18
			(N Wilson) *in rr-div: sme hdwy whn hmpd over 1f out: sn lost pl: eased whn bhd ins fnl f* **50/1**	
2000	11	9	**Spinning Ridge (IRE)**[164] 3309 5-9-6 **69**......................(p) JamesDoyle 1	4
			(R A Harris) *trckd ldrs: effrt over 2f out: wknd over 1f out: eased ins fnl f* **20/1**	

1m 31.42s (1.82) **Going Correction** +0.375s/f (Slow) **11** Ran SP% **113.7**

Speed ratings (Par 103): **104,103,102,102,99 98,97,94,86,83 73**

toteswingers:1&2:£3.10, 1&3:£31.10, 2&3:£43.20 CSF £18.26 CT £907.58 TOTE £5.50: £1.80, £1.30, £17.50; EX 18.20.

Owner D C Rutter & H Clewlow **Bred** Bridgewater Equine Ltd **Trained** Great Ness, Shropshire

FOCUS

An ordinary handicap in which they went a modest pace, giving those prominent an advantage.

7700 EUROPEAN BREEDERS' FUND MAIDEN STKS 7f 32y(P)

5:50 (5:52) (Class 5) 2-Y-O **£2,978** (£886; £442; £221) **Stalls** High

Form				RPR
3	1		**Acclamazing (IRE)**[137] 4233 2-9-3 0.................................... AdamKirby 6	74+
			(M Botti) *w ldr: chal over 1f out: styd on wl to ld towards fin* **15/8**[2]	
	2	½	**March On Beetroot** 2-9-3 0... JamieSpencer 4	73+
			(R M H Cowell) *in rr: hdwy on outside to join ldr 4f out: led over 1f out: edgd lft ins fnl f: hdd towards fin* **6/5**[1]	
6	3	6	**Royal Bonsai**[29] 7335 2-8-10 0.. ShaneBKelly(7) 8	56
			(J J Quinn) *chsd ldrs: drvn and outpcde 3f out: kpt on same pce to take modest 3rd ins fnl f* **20/1**	
0	4	1 ¼	**The Auctioneer (IRE)**[28] 7346 2-9-3 0........................... JamieMackay 1	53
			(W J Musson) *hld up in rr: outpcd and lost pl 3f out: kpt on fnl f* **33/1**	
	5	½	**Great Surprise** 2-9-3 0.. GrahamGibbons 3	52
			(R Hollinshead) *drvn to chse ldrs: wknd over 1f out* **12/1**	
	6	½	**Ana Emarati (USA)** 2-9-3 0... EddieAhern 7	51
			(E A L Dunlop) *s.s: hld up in rr: hdwy on ins over 2f out: wknd over 1f out* **8/1**[3]	
00	7	6	**Fire Commander**[8] 7578 2-9-3 0...................................... J-PGuillambert 5	40
			(B P J Baugh) *led: qckng 3f out: hdd over 1f out: sn wknd* **80/1**	
	8	½	**Speedy Joe** 2-9-3 0.. TomEaves 2	35
			(B Smart) *slowly away and swvd lft s: hdwy to chse ldrs over 3f out: lost pl over 1f out* **16/1**	

1m 35.65s (6.05) **Going Correction** +0.375s/f (Slow) **8** Ran SP% **113.9**

Speed ratings (Par 96): **80,79,72,71,70 70,63,62**

toteswingers:1&2:£1.10, 1&3:£6.60, 2&3:£9.10 CSF £4.34 TOTE £2.80: £1.10, £1.10, £3.20; EX 4.90.

Owner Giuliano Manfredini **Bred** Michael And John Fahy **Trained** Newmarket, Suffolk

FOCUS

They went a steady early pace. The bare form might not be that strong, but this was a relatively interesting maiden that ought to produce winners. Considering the gallop, the front two did well to pull clear.

NOTEBOOK

Acclamazing(IRE) improved on the form he showed when a well-beaten third in an ordinary 6f Yarmouth maiden on his only previous start back in July. He should progress again and looks a fair handicap prospect. (op 2-1 tchd 11-8)

March On Beetroot, a 30,000gns half-brother to, among others, 6f winner Silca Elegance, is out of a useful dual 5f winner (for this yard). The subject of a positive gallops report, he was well backed and only just failed to make a winning debut. Having sensibly made good headway down the back straight in this modestly run race, he got first run on the winner, but his inexperience told late on as he edged left onto the possibly unfavoured rail. He has scope and can progress into a useful type. (op 11-8 tchd 2-1)

Royal Bonsai, well held over C&D on his debut, raced further back than the front two and was outpaced when the gallop quickened leaving the back straight. He has ability, but looks one for handicaps. (op 16-1)

The Auctioneer(IRE) ◆ is very much one to note. Keen early, he was consequently poorly placed when the race got serious and had no chance, but he finished well, despite finding a bit of trouble. He has a bit of size and is bred to improve when stepped up in trip.

Great Surprise was well held on his debut. (op 16-1)

Ana Emarati(USA) can do better. He raced in an unpromising position following a slow start and stuck to the often unfavoured inside rail in the straight. (op 6-1)

7701 STAY AT THE WOLVERHAMPTON HOLIDAY INN (S) STKS 5f 216y(P)

6:20 (6:20) (Class 6) 3-Y-O+ **£1,535** (£453; £226) **Stalls** Low

Form				RPR
5101	1		**Ajara (IRE)**[14] 7526 4-9-1 67.. RichardKingscote 9	71
			(Tom Dascombe) *led tl over 3f out: led over 2f out: kpt on wl fnl f* **4/1**[3]	
0342	2	1	**Spin Again (IRE)**[9] 7564 5-9-6 68.................................. AdrianNicholls 10	73
			(D Nicholls) *w ldrs: drvn 3f out: upsides over 1f out: kpt on same pce ins fnl f* **3/1**[2]	
0350	3	nk	**Bahamian Kid**[15] 7501 5-8-7 58......................................(v) JackDuern(7) 5	66
			(R Hollinshead) *mid-div: hdwy over 2f out: wnt 3rd over 1f out: kpt on wl ins fnl f* **12/1**	
6450	4	3	**Master Leon**[11] 7539 3-9-6 69...(v) TomEaves 3	62
			(B Smart) *s.i.s: hdwy over 2f out: hung rt and kpt on fnl f: nvr nr to chal* **6/1**	
6432	5	1	**Apache Ridge (IRE)**[5] 7627 4-9-3 64...............................(p) AmyRyan(3) 2	59
			(K A Ryan) *chsd ldrs: rdn on ins over 1f out: hung lft and grad wknd* **11/4**[1]	
500	6	½	**Dickie Le Davoir**[79] 6110 6-8-7 57................................ SeanPalmer(7) 7	52
			(D Bourton) *in rr-div: drvn 3f out: styd on over 1f out: nvr nr ldrs* **20/1**	
0303	7	2 ¾	**Clear Ice (IRE)**[166] 3276 3-8-9 67.................................. MarkCoumbe(5) 6	43
			(D Bourton) *chsd ldrs: drvn 3f out: lost pl over 1f out* **16/1**	
0450	8	3	**Valentino Swing (IRE)**[6] 7611 7-8-13 65.......................... HobieGill(7) 4	39
			(M Appleby) *s.s: a in rr* **16/1**	
2003	9	8	**Kersivay**[9] 7564 4-8-13 62.....................................(v) MatthewCosham(7) 1	14
			(P D Evans) *sn chsng ldr: led over 3f out: hdd over 2f out: sn lost pl and bhd: eased ins fnl f* **18/1**	

1m 16.64s (1.64) **Going Correction** +0.375s/f (Slow) **9** Ran SP% **115.4**

Speed ratings (Par 101): **104,102,102,98,96 96,92,88,77**

toteswingers:1&2:£2.30, 1&3:£10.20, 2&3:£7.00 CSF £16.42 TOTE £4.10: £1.40, £1.10, £4.80; EX 10.10.The winner was bought in for 7,500gns. Spin Again was claimed by Mark Wellings for £6,000.

Owner Butt Scholes **Bred** Rozelle Bloodstock **Trained** Malpas, Cheshire

■ Stewards' Enquiry : Sean Palmer caution: used whip after the line.

FOCUS

A modest seller in which it paid to race prominently.

7702 40 LIVE FOOTBALL MARKETS AT TOTESPORT.COM H'CAP 5f 20y(P)

6:50 (6:50) (Class 4) (0-85,85) 3-Y-O+ **£3,594** (£1,069; £534; £266) **Stalls** Low

Form				RPR
1523	1		**Methaaly (IRE)**[8] 7573 7-8-4 **75**..............................(be) JosephYoung(7) 2	84
			(M Mullineaux) *in rr: effrt on outside wl over 1f out: r.o to ld post* **5/1**	
0401	2	hd	**Sir Geoffrey (IRE)**[16] 7494 4-9-1 **79**.................................(b) IanMongan 6	87
			(D Nicholls) *sn led: drvn 3 l clr appr fnl f: hdd post* **5/2**[1]	
2260	3	2 ¾	**Excellent Show**[10] 7549 4-9-1 **79**.. TomEaves 4	77
			(B Smart) *chsd ldrs: wnt 2nd over 1f out: edgd lft and kpt on same pce* **4/1**[3]	
4401	4	2 ¼	**High Spice (USA)**[10] 7549 3-9-4 **82**...........................(p) JamieSpencer 1	72
			(R M H Cowell) *s.i.s: hld up: hdwy 2f out: sn chsng ldrs: kpt on same pce: eased nr fin* **7/2**[2]	
3660	5	19	**Jargelle (IRE)**[92] 5734 4-9-7 **85**...................................... AdrianNicholls 7	—
			(D Nicholls) *racd wd: t.k.h: sn w ldrs: wknd over 1f out: eased ins fnl f* **11/2**	
0345	6	3	**Ingleby Star (IRE)**[103] 5356 5-8-9 **73**.......................(p) DuranFentiman 5	—
			(N Wilson) *led early: chsd ldrs: lost pl over 2f out: eased whn bhd* **12/1**	

62.98 secs (0.68) **Going Correction** +0.375s/f (Slow) **6** Ran SP% **110.5**

Speed ratings (Par 105): **109,108,104,100,70 65**

toteswingers:1&2:£2.80, 1&3:£2.40, 2&3:£3.20 CSF £17.30 TOTE £8.40: £3.40, £1.10; EX 15.00.

Owner Noel Racing **Bred** Scuderia Golden Horse S R L **Trained** Alpraham, Cheshire

FOCUS

Not particularly competitive with the field strung out behind the front two.

7703 BET ON THE ASHES AT TOTESPORT.COM MAIDEN STKS 1m 4f 50y(P)

7:20 (7:22) (Class 5) 3-Y-O+ **£2,007** (£597; £298; £149) **Stalls** Low

Form				RPR
-330	1		**Alubari**[44] 7042 3-9-3 71.. JamieSpencer 9	73+
			(D M Simcock) *hld up in rr: hdwy to join ldr after 3f: led over 6f out: hrd drvn and edgd rt over 1f out: styd on* **4/9**[1]	
	2	3	**Destiny Of A Diva** 3-8-12 0....................................... GrahamGibbons 8	64
			(R Hollinshead) *s.i.s: hdwy 5f out: chsd wnr 2f out: kpt on same pce fnl f* **22/1**	
3050	3	7	**Faith Jicaro (IRE)**[15] 7504 3-8-12 57.................................. LukeMorris 4	53
			(N J Vaughan) *chsd ldrs: wnt 2nd 3f out: one pce fnl 2f* **7/1**[3]	
0000	4	2 ¼	**Wrecking Crew (IRE)**[15] 7508 6-9-8 48...................(b[1]) JamesMillman 2	55?
			(B R Millman) *hld up in rr: hdwy 4f out: wknd over 1f out* **25/1**	
4	5	11	**Yeomanry**[8] 7579 5-9-8 0... SaleemGolam 3	38
			(Ian Williams) *chsd ldrs: lost pl over 5f out* **10/1**	
4	6	1	**No Rain (IRE)**[57] 6716 3-8-12 0...................................... PJMcDonald 6	32
			(G A Swinbank) *t.k.h: trckd ldrs: lost pl over 2f out* **13/2**[2]	
3456	7	nk	**Marafong**[26] 7381 3-9-3 42... J-PGuillambert 1	36
			(B P J Baugh) *hld up in midfield: lost pl 5f out: sn bhd* **40/1**	
00	8	26	**Big Bad Boo**[8] 7579 4-9-1 0.. AlexEdwards(7) 5	—
			(J W Unett) *led 3f: lost pl 4f out: sn bhd: t.o 2f out* **50/1**	
/50-	9	4 ½	**Sergeant Sharpe**[244] 918 5-9-3 52................................ MarkCoumbe(5) 7	—
			(D Bourton) *chsd ldrs: led after 3f: hdd over 6f out: lost pl over 3f out: t.o 2f out* **66/1**	

2m 45.98s (4.88) **Going Correction** +0.375s/f (Slow)

WFA 3 from 4yo+ 5lb **9** Ran SP% **118.3**

Speed ratings (Par 103): **98,96,91,89,82 81,81,64,61**

toteswingers:1&2:£8.60, 1&3:£2.00, 2&3:£42.60 CSF £19.06 TOTE £1.20: £1.10, £5.90, £1.20; EX 19.40.

Owner Dr Marwan Koukash **Bred** Pendley Farm **Trained** Newmarket, Suffolk

FOCUS

An uncompetitive maiden.

7704 WOLVERHAMPTON-RACECOURSE.CO.UK H'CAP 2m 119y(P)

7:50 (7:50) (Class 6) (0-65,65) 3-Y-O+ **£1,535** (£453; £226) **Stalls** Low

Form				RPR
2323	1		**Motirani**[40] 7117 3-9-1 **57**... MickyFenton 6	71
			(J Pearce) *hld up in rr: hdwy 6f out: led 3f out: styd on wl fnl f* **20/1**	
00/1	2	1 ½	**Brabazon (IRE)**[4] 7634 7-8-10 **51** 6ex...........................(bt) JulieBurke(7) 10	63
			(Emmet Michael Butterly, Ire) *hld up in rr: stdy hdwy over 5f out: chsd wnr over 2f out: rdn over 1f out: styd on same pce* **13/8**[1]	
0513	3	5	**Dubai Phantom (USA)**[47] 6983 3-9-9 **65**........................... HayleyTurner 9	71
			(D M Simcock) *dwlt and swtchd lft s: hld up in rr: hdwy over 3f out: wnt 3rd over 2f out: styd on same pce* **15/8**[2]	
32U5	4	9	**Pearl (IRE)**[12] 7388 6-9-0 **48**...................................(bt) CathyGannon 1	43
			(Mrs A M Thorpe) *dwlt: sn mid-div: hdwy 4f out: one pce fnl 2f* **20/1**	
6236	5	24	**Soundbyte**[22] 7422 5-10-0 **62**.. FergusSweeney 4	28
			(J Gallagher) *chsd ldrs: drvn over 5f out: lost pl over 2f out: eased over 1f out* **8/1**[3]	
4061	6	4 ½	**Lucas Pitt**[24] 7387 3-9-2 **58**.. DaneO'Neill 8	19
			(M J Scudamore) *mid-div: drvn 5f out: lost pl 3f out: sn bhd* **12/1**	

4604 7 17 **Nayessence**14 7531 4-9-12 60 (b) GrahamGibbons 5 —
(M W Easterby) *trckd ldr: led 7f out: hdd 3f out: sn lost pl: eased whn t.o over 1f out* 10/1
-340 8 21 **Trumpstoo (USA)**44 3552 4-9-7 55 (v1) BarryMcHugh 2 —
(R A Fahey) *reminders after s: chsd ldrs: lost pl over 4f out: sn bhd: t.o 2f out* 25/1
50/0 P **Hugo Quick**23 7407 6-8-11 45 (b1) SamHitchcott 3 —
(J L Spearing) *led: hdd 7f out: sn drvn and lost pl: hopelessly t.o 5f out: sn p.u: lame* 80/1

3m 46.22s (4.42) **Going Correction** +0.375s/f (Slow)
WFA 3 from 4yo+ 8lb **9 Ran SP% 115.4**
Speed ratings (Par 101): **104,103,100,96,85 83,75,65,—**
toteswingers:1&2:£7.90, 1&3:£7.50, 2&3:£1.20 CSF £51.34 CT £95.49 TOTE £18.50: £5.60, £1.02, £2.20; EX 75.80.
Owner Richard Ames **Bred** Scuderia San Pancrazio Sas **Trained** Newmarket, Suffolk
■ Stewards' Enquiry : Hayley Turner one-day ban: careless riding (Dec 18)

FOCUS
Unusually for a staying event on the Polytrack, the pace was quick. That, combined with a slow surface, made this a serious stamina test.
Hugo Quick Official explanation: vet said gelding finished lame behind

7705 BET ON LIVE CRICKET AT TOTESPORT.COM H'CAP (DIV I) 1m 141y(P)
8:20 (8:20) (Class 6) (0-60,59) 3-Y-0+ **£1,364** (£403; £201) **Stalls** Low

Form RPR
1252 1 **Join Up**7 7605 4-8-13 54 RossAtkinson(3) 10 64
(W M Brisbourne) *hld up in tch: dropped bk over 5f out: hdwy over 2f out: styd on to ld jst ins fnl f: kpt on wl* 9/2²
5101 2 1 ¾ **Cyril The Squirrel**21 7450 6-9-7 59 ChrisCatlin 9 65
(Karen George) *sn chsng ldrs: led over 1f out: hdd jst ins fnl f: no ex* 10/3¹
4003 3 4 ½ **Shark Man (IRE)**5 7633 3-9-1 55 (v) AndreaAtzeni 8 51
(M Wigham) *trckd ldrs: effrt over 2f out: kpt on one pce appr fnl f* 9/2²
0625 4 2 ¾ **Special Cuvee**7 7599 4-9-4 56 (bt) CathyGannon 5 45
(Mrs A M Thorpe) *sn drvn along in rr: hdwy over 2f out: nvr rchd ldrs* 12/1
5004 5 3 ½ **Lujano**21 7450 5-9-4 56 (b1) BarryMcHugh 3 37
(Ollie Pears) *led tl 3f out: wknd appr fnl f* 9/2²
00 6 1 **Mackintosh (IRE)**37 7199 4-8-10 48 LukeMorris 6 27
(Patrick Morris) *hld up in rr: stdy hdwy over 2f out: rdn over 1f out: sn wknd* 12/1
0020 7 5 **Hedgerow (IRE)**8 7575 3-8-7 52 ow2 MarkCoumbe(5) 2 19
(D Bourton) *hld up in rr: hdwy over 3f out: rdn and lost pl over 2f out* 28/1
0500 8 6 **Bobering**203 757 10-8-7 45 GrahamGibbons 7 —
(B P J Baugh) *chsd ldrs: lost pl over 2f out: sn bhd* 40/1
1644 9 1 **Chookie Avon**15 7501 3-9-5 59 (p) TomEaves 1 —
(V P Donoghue) *dwlt: t.k.h in mid-div: drvn 3f out: sn lost pl: eased whn bhd* 13/2³

1m 53.29s (2.79) **Going Correction** +0.375s/f (Slow)
WFA 3 from 4yo+ 2lb **9 Ran SP% 112.2**
Speed ratings (Par 101): **102,100,96,94,90 90,85,80,79**
toteswingers:1&2:£2.60, 1&3:£7.30, 2&3:£5.40 CSF £19.13 CT £69.11 TOTE £4.60: £1.10, £2.20, £3.00; EX 13.60.
Owner P R Kirk **Bred** A Reid **Trained** Great Ness, Shropshire

FOCUS
A moderate handicap, although the time was 1.04 seconds quicker than the second division.

7706 BET ON LIVE CRICKET AT TOTESPORT.COM H'CAP (DIV II) 1m 141y(P)
8:50 (8:50) (Class 6) (0-60,59) 3-Y-0+ **£1,364** (£403; £201) **Stalls** Low

Form RPR
340 1 **John Potts**160 1503 5-8-7 45 CathyGannon 5 53
(B P J Baugh) *s.i.s: in rr: hdwy on outer over 2f out: styd on to ld jst ins fnl f: drvn out* 9/1
5064 2 2 ¼ **Kielty's Folly**11 7543 6-9-0 52 JackMitchell 2 55
(B P J Baugh) *hld up in rr: hdwy over 2f out: led over 1f out: hdd jst ins fnl f: no ex* 3/1²
2100 3 hd **Katmai River (IRE)**23 7401 3-9-2 56 (v1) DaneO'Neill 4 58
(M D I Usher) *hld up in mid-div: hdwy 4f out: chsng ldrs on ins whn n.m.r over 1f out: kpt on last 100yds* 10/1
4 nk **Mount Hollow**31 5-9-2 59 (p) MarkCoumbe(5) 1 61
(D Bourton) *wl in rr: hdwy u.p over 2f out: styng on whn n.m.r and swtchd lft nr fin* 12/1
0041 5 1 ½ **Talent Scout (IRE)**7 7604 4-9-5 57 (b) GrahamGibbons 6 55
(T D Walford) *trckd ldrs: led 2f out: hung lft and sn hdd: n.m.r and eased cl home* 13/8¹
6006 6 11 **Penrod Ballantyne (IRE)**19 7462 3-9-3 57 LukeMorris 10 30
(Mike Hammond) *chsd ldrs: drvn over 3f out: upsides 2f out: hung lft and wknd over 1f out* 12/1
1000 7 3 ¼ **Orpen Arms (IRE)**10 7562 3-9-4 58 (b1) BarryMcHugh 3 23
(R A Fahey) *led: hdd 2f out: sn lost pl* 12/1
04-4 8 15 **She's My Rock (IRE)**320 216 3-8-10 50 JamesDoyle 8 —
(S Kirk) *chsd ldrs: drvn 3f out: sn lost pl and bhd* 13/2³

1m 54.33s (3.83) **Going Correction** +0.375s/f (Slow)
WFA 3 from 4yo+ 2lb **8 Ran SP% 118.6**
Speed ratings (Par 101): **97,95,94,94,93 83,80,67**
toteswingers:1&2:£5.20, 1&3:£9.40, 2&3:£4.80 CSF £37.65 CT £283.70 TOTE £13.00: £2.30, £1.30, £3.00; EX 43.10.
Owner Miss S M Potts **Bred** Miss S M Potts **Trained** Audley, Staffs
■ Stewards' Enquiry : Mark Coumbe one-day ban: careless riding (Dec 18)

FOCUS
The time was poor, being 1.04 seconds slower than the first division. There was a one-two for trainer Brian Baugh.
T/Plt: £16.80 to a £1 stake. Pool:£112,582.52 - 4,864.66 winning tickets T/Qpdt: £5.90 to a £1 stake. Pool:£9,901.19 - 1,235.11 winning tickets WG

7711 - 7714a (Foreign Racing) - See Raceform Interactive

7634 LINGFIELD (L-H)
Sunday, December 5

OFFICIAL GOING: Standard
Wind: nil Weather: dry, cold

7715 TOTEPLACEPOT MAIDEN AUCTION STKS 6f (P)
12:30 (12:32) (Class 6) 2-Y-0 **£1,706** (£503; £252) **Stalls** Low

Form RPR
2422 1 **Its You Again**9 7578 2-8-9 78 JackMitchell 1 71+
(M G Quinlan) *mde all: rdn and hung rt bnd 2f out: kpt on wl and a in command after* 1/2¹
02 2 1 ¼ **Justbookie Dot Com (IRE)**202 2183 2-8-11 0 JimmyFortune 6 69
(Louise Best) *stdd s: hld up in last: hdwy over 2f out: chsd wnr on inner wl over 1f out: hung rt over 1f out: styd on same pce fnl f* 8/1³
5022 3 2 ¼ **Buddy Miracle**31 7309 2-8-3 72 DavidProbert 3 54
(A M Balding) *in tch: rdn to chse ldng pair wl over 1f out: outpcd and btn ent fnl f* 11/4²
5000 4 11 **Bankroller**17 7496 2-8-9 50 HayleyTurner 4 27
(J G Portman) *chsd ldr tl wl over 1f out: sn wknd: fdd fnl f* 33/1
0 5 3 ¾ **Ippi N Tombi (IRE)**7 7608 2-8-4 0 ow1 ChrisCatlin 2 11
(P S McEntee) *awkward leaving stalls: chsd ldng pair tl 1/2-way: sn toiling and bhd* 100/1

1m 11.6s (-0.30) **Going Correction** -0.025s/f (Stan) **5 Ran SP% 108.4**
Speed ratings (Par 94): **101,99,96,81,76**
CSF £5.17 TOTE £1.50: £1.30, £2.40; EX 5.70.
Owner Brian Dick **Bred** Springcombe Park Stud **Trained** Newmarket, Suffolk

FOCUS
A weak maiden.

NOTEBOOK
Its You Again, well backed, won from the front in straightforward enough fashion on his eighth start. He looked a bit awkward going around the bend into the straight, giving the impression he wasn't fully concentrating, but he was still good enough, his chance helped by his main rival hanging. In fairness, his connections felt this track did not really suit and, set to be kept on the go, he's likely to stick to Kempton and Wolverhampton from now on. Whatever the case, though, there is still the option of gelding him. (op 5-6 tchd 10-11)
Justbookie Dot Com(IRE), gelded since finishing a closing second over 5f at Wolverhampton when last seen in May, was weak in the market and ruined his chance by hanging badly when first coming under pressure in the straight. Handicaps are now an option, and he clearly has ability, but he might be best watched next time. (op 7-1)
Buddy Miracle, runner-up in similar company at Kempton on her last two starts, raced keenly this time and failed to pick up for pressure. Not progressing, she's struggling to win a race, and while a drop back to 5f might help, she's not one to be following. (op 7-4)

7716 TOTESWINGER FLEXI BETTING H'CAP 1m 4f (P)
1:00 (1:01) (Class 7) (0-50,55) 3-Y-0+ **£1,774** (£523; £262) **Stalls** Low

Form RPR
0054 1 **Suhailah**23 7422 4-8-10 47 KierenFox(3) 15 55
(M J Attwater) *in tch: hdwy to chse ldr ent fnl 3f: led over 2f out: drvn clr over 1f out: styd on wl: drvn out* 7/1²
2260 2 2 **Rosewood Lad**131 4448 3-8-11 50 CathyGannon 14 55
(J S Moore) *in tch: rdn and effrt over 3f out: chsd wnr over 2f out: styd on same pce u.p fr over 1f out* 8/1³
0540 3 1 ¼ **Captain Cool (IRE)**41 7117 3-8-10 49 EddieAhern 10 52
(R Hannon) *in tch: hdwy to chse ldrs over 2f out: n.m.r briefly over 2f out: rdn and kpt on same pce fr wl over 1f out* 6/1¹
0505 4 nk **Tifoso (FR)**18 6032 5-8-13 47 (v) DaneO'Neill 1 50
(R C Guest) *t.k.h early: hld up in tch tl grad stdd bk and towards rr 8f out: hdwy towards outer and n.m.r over 2f out: rdn and effrt ent fnl 2f: kpt on same pce fr over 1f out* 7/1²
0460 5 nse **Barbirolli**15 7531 8-8-11 45 ChrisCatlin 16 47
(W B Stone) *in tch: effrt and rdn to chse ldrs ent fnl 2f: unable qck wl over 1f out: one pce and no threat to ldr after* 25/1
4300 6 hd **Carnac (IRE)**39 7181 4-8-9 50 (p) NoraLooby(7) 4 52
(A J McCabe) *stdd s: hld up in tch: hdwy ent fnl 3f: n.m.r over 2f out: nt clr run towards inner over 1f out: swtchd rt jst over 1f out: plugged on but nvr gng pce to threaten wnr* 8/1³
0405 7 hd **Our Kes (IRE)**22 7453 8-9-1 49 JimmyQuinn 7 53+
(P Howling) *stdd s: hld up in tch in midfield: nt clr run and swing to outer over 2f out: swtchd rt and effrt over 1f out: kpt on ins fnl f: nvr threatened ldrs* 7/1²
0006 8 2 ½ **Hatch A Plan (IRE)**9 7570 9-9-1 49 FrankieMcDonald 5 47
(Mouse Hamilton-Fairley) *hld up in tch: hdwy to trck ldrs over 2f out: rdn and unable qck 2f out: wknd ins fnl f* 40/1
5000 9 ½ **Fleur De'Lion (IRE)**179 2870 4-9-2 50 JamesDoyle 11 47
(S Kirk) *racd in last pair: rdn and effrt over 2f out: hung lft and no imp over 1f out: styd on same pce fnl f* 33/1
0001 10 hd **Abulharith**10 7569 4-9-7 55 (p) LukeMorris 2 52
(R A Harris) *chsd ldrs: gng wl over 2f out: nt clr run and shuffled bk over 1f out: swtchd rt and drvn 1f out: no imp fnl f* 10/1
0055 11 nk **Sea Tobougie**9 7570 3-8-1 45 RyanPowell(5) 12 41
(M D I Usher) *hld up in last pair: rdn and effrt jst over 2f out: plugged on ins fnl f: n.d* 25/1
0-00 12 1 ¾ **Colonel Henry**316 274 3-8-9 48 HayleyTurner 9 41
(S Dow) *in tch: rdn and struggling ent fnl 3f: wknd jst over 2f out* 25/1
000 13 4 **Prince Blue**33 7288 3-8-6 45 (b1) KirstyMilczarek 3 32
(G G Margarson) *dwlt: sn rcvrd and led: rdn and hdd over 2f out: wknd over 1f out* 33/1
540 14 7 **Sanctum**40 7157 4-9-2 50 SteveDrowne 13 —
(Dr J D Scargill) *t.k.h: hld up in rr tl swtchd rt and hdwy into midfield on outer 8f out: lost pl and dropped to rr wl over 3f out: lost tch over 2f out: eased ins fnl f* 14/1
00-0 15 3 ¼ **Brooksby**4 7649 4-9-2 50 (b) IanMongan 6 —
(L A Dace) *chsd ldr tl wl over 2f out: sn wknd: wl bhd and eased ins fnl f* 16/1

2m 32.77s (-0.23) **Going Correction** -0.025s/f (Stan)
WFA 3 from 4yo+ 5lb **15 Ran SP% 115.5**
Speed ratings (Par 97): **99,97,96,96,96 96,96,94,94,94 94,92,90,85,83**
toteswingers:1&2:£8.90, 1&3:£7.20, 2&3:£10.20 CSF £53.84 CT £357.09 TOTE £6.80: £2.30, £2.50, £2.10; EX 68.20 Trifecta £171.50 Part won. Pool: £231.82 - 0.10 winning units..
Owner Canisbay Bloodstock **Bred** Canisbay Bloodstock Ltd **Trained** Epsom, Surrey

FOCUS
They finished in a bunch behind the front two and this is weak form. A few of these found trouble.
Our Kes(IRE) Official explanation: jockey said mare was denied a clear run

7717 TOTETRIFECTA FLEXI BETTING APPRENTICE H'CAP 1m (P)
1:30 (1:31) (Class 6) (0-55,57) 3-Y-0+ **£2,047** (£604; £302) **Stalls** High

Form RPR
-005 1 **Royal Island (IRE)**16 7508 8-8-10 49 TobyAtkinson 3 57
(M G Quinlan) *hld up wl in tch in last trio: hdwy over 1f out: r.o wl u.p to ld fnl 75yds: rdn out* 8/1
2000 2 1 ¼ **Shared Moment (IRE)**20 7467 4-9-2 55 (p) AmyBaker 8 60
(J Gallagher) *s.i.s: in tch in rr: hdwy and nt clr run over 1f out tl ins fnl f: r.o wl u.p fnl 100yds: nvr gng to rch wnr* 25/1
243 3 nk **Ermyntrude**18 7487 3-8-11 54 DCByrne(3) 10 58
(P M Phelan) *prom: rdn to chse clr ldr over 2f out: lft w ev ch wl over 1f out: led over 1f out tl hdd and no ex fnl 75yds* 9/2¹

2521 **4** 1 1/2 **Join Up**[1] 7705 4-9-7 **54** 6ex.............. RossAtkinson 2 61
(W M Brisbourne) *hld up in tch: nt clr run over 2f out tl swtchd ins and effrt wl over 1f out: chsd ldr u.p ent fnl f: no ex fnl 100yds* **5/1**[2]

2662 **5** 1 1/4 **Fly By Nelly**[18] 7487 4-9-2 **55**.............. BillyCray 1 53
(M R Hoad) *dwlt: in tch in rr: hdwy on inner ent fnl 2f: swtchd rt and rdn wl over 1f out: styd on same pce and wl hld fnl f* **13/2**

0034 **6** nk **Young Simon**[11] 7555 3-8-10 **55**..............(v) NatashaEaton(5) 5 52
(G G Margarson) *stdd s: sn t.k.h and wl in tch: rdn and unable qck jst over 2f out: plugged on again but no threat to ldrs fnl f* **12/1**

0026 **7** shd **All Moving Parts (USA)**[6] 7633 3-8-10 **55**..............(b[1]) NoraLooby(5) 12 52+
(A J McCabe) *t.k.h: chsd ldrs on outer: nudged ahd ent fnl 3f: sn clr: rn v wd bnd 2f out: hdd over 1f out: continued edging rt and wknd 1f out* **11/2**[3]

6643 **8** 3/4 **Rainsborough**[11] 7555 3-8-12 **57**.............. LewisWalsh(5) 11 52
(S Curran) *in tch: drvn to chse ldrs jst over 2f out: wknd u.p 1f out* **9/1**

0056 **9** 1 1/4 **Ice Road Trucker (IRE)**[39] 7166 3-8-5 **48**.............. NathanAlison(3) 6 41
(J R Boyle) *t.k.h: chsd ldrs: jostling match w rival over 2f out: wknd u.p over 1f out* **9/1**

4002 **10** 4 **Queenie's Star (IRE)**[52] 6865 3-8-7 **52**.............. MatthewLawson(5) 7 35
(M J Attwater) *led tl ent fnl 3f: styd chsng ldrs but drvn over 2f out: wknd ent fnl f* **33/1**

5000 **11** 8 **The Grey One (IRE)**[39] 7168 7-8-11 **53**..............(p) RyanPowell(3) 9 18
(J M Bradley) *awkward leaving stalls and dwlt: sn rcvrd and hdwy on outer to ld over 6f out: hdd 3f out: wknd qckly over 2f out* **20/1**

3005 **12** 12 **Gilderoy**[16] 7506 3-8-5 **48**..............(b) JamesRogers(3) 4 —
(D J S Ffrench Davis) *prom tl lost pl qckly over 2f out: lost tch 2f out: t.o* **20/1**

1m 38.29s (0.09) **Going Correction** -0.025s/f (Stan)
WFA 3 from 4yo+ 1lb 12 Ran SP% **118.7**
Speed ratings (Par 101): **98,96,96,94,93 93,93,92,91,87 79,67**
toteswingers:1&2:£55.40, 1&3:£10.70, 2&3:£23.00 CSF £198.04 CT £1026.28 TOTE £11.20: £2.70, £8.40, £1.30; EX 336.00 TRIFECTA Not won..
Owner M T Neville **Bred** Mrs Bill O'Neill **Trained** Newmarket, Suffolk

FOCUS
The pace was good with the lead being contested, and then All Moving Parts, one of those towards the front-end, was driven along to take a clear advantage on the run to the final bend.

7718 TOTEEXACTA FLEXI BETTING NURSERY 7f (P)
2:00 (2:00) (Class 5) (0-75,74) 2-Y-O **£2,590** (£770; £385; £192) **Stalls** Low

Form RPR

4411 **1** **Podgies Boy (IRE)**[9] 7572 2-9-7 **74**.............. TomEaves 6 77
(R A Fahey) *t.k.h: in tch: rdn ent fnl 2f: carried rt bnd 2f out: hdwy u.p ins fnl f: led fnl 50yds: hld on wl* **4/1**[2]

0045 **2** shd **Palm Pilot (IRE)**[24] 7412 2-9-1 **68**.............. EddieAhern 4 71+
(E A L Dunlop) *t.k.h: hld up in tch in last trio: racd awkwardly and rdn ent fnl 2f: swtchd lft and drvn to chse ldrs ent fnl f: ev ch fnl 75yds: jst hld* **7/2**[1]

0144 **3** nk **Geordie Iris (IRE)**[15] 7528 2-9-7 **74**.............. DaneO'Neill 5 76
(R Hannon) *pressed ldr: rdn wl over 1f out: kpt on gamely u.p: led fnl 75yds: sn hdd and no ex towards fin* **7/2**[1]

3410 **4** 1/2 **Spartic**[85] 5969 2-9-6 **73**.............. JamesDoyle 2 74
(A J McCabe) *led: rdn ent fnl 2f: hrd pressed but battled on gamely u.p tl hdd fnl 75yds: no ex after* **9/2**[3]

0166 **5** 1 **Reachtothestars (USA)**[9] 7572 2-9-1 **68**.............. AdamKirby 3 66
(M G Quinlan) *stdd s: hld up in tch in rr: swtchd lft and effrt over 1f out: kpt on but no imp ins fnl f* **9/1**

222 **6** 1 1/4 **Piece Of Mind**[72] 6323 2-9-5 **72**.............. JimmyFortune 7 67
(R Hannon) *wl in tch in last trio: rdn and effrt over 1f out: styd on same pce and no imp after* **13/2**

004 **7** 3/4 **Cool Water Oasis**[18] 7485 2-9-0 **67**.............. AmirQuinn 1 60
(G L Moore) *t.k.h: chsd ldrs: rdn and edgd rt on bnd 2f out: drvn and unable qck over 1f out: wknd ent fnl f* **25/1**

1m 25.25s (0.45) **Going Correction** -0.025s/f (Stan) 7 Ran SP% **109.8**
Speed ratings (Par 96): **96,95,95,94,93 92,91**
toteswingers:1&2:£3.20, 1&3:£2.50, 2&3:£2.60 CSF £16.83 TOTE £3.30: £1.40, £2.60; EX 20.90.
Owner G Devlin **Bred** Seamus Duffy **Trained** Musley Bank, N Yorks

FOCUS
A fair nursery. The pace was just modest early on, but seemed to increase after a couple of furlongs or so.

NOTEBOOK
Podgies Boy(IRE) came under pressure well before the straight but kept responding and just got up to defy a 7lb rise for his recent C&D win, his third success on the bounce (sequence started in 1m Fibresand seller). He's likely to be forced up in grade once reassessed, but can find further improvement back over 1m. (op 7-2)
Palm Pilot(IRE) ◆ was reported by the vet to have coughed on her return at Wolverhampton on her previous start, but she posted a career-best this time. Her effort is all the more creditable seeing as she made her move against the inside rail in the straight, so rarely the quickest part of the track, and was also intimidated by a rival edging towards her path in the closing stages. (op 9-2)
Geordie Iris(IRE) won his maiden over an extended 1m and probably won't mind a return to further. (op 3-1)
Spartic, gelded since last seen in September, hung left under pressure when tired late on. Perhaps this was needed. (op 5-1)
Reachtothestars(USA), keen to post, got going too late in the race itself. (op 11-1)
Piece Of Mind offered little on her AW debut after 72 days off. Official explanation: jockey said filly finished lame (op 11-2 tchd 5-1)

7719 DRY HILL H'CAP 6f (P)
2:30 (2:30) (Class 4) (0-80,80) 3-Y-O+ **£3,885** (£1,156; £577; £288) **Stalls** Low

Form RPR

-260 **1** **Perfect Act**[199] 2247 5-9-5 **78**.............. DavidProbert 7 86
(A M Balding) *short of room and swtchd lft s: hld up towards rr: hdwy to chse ldrs over 2f out: rdn to ld over 1f out: hld on u.p nr fin: all out* **9/1**

4405 **2** nse **Sioux Rising (IRE)**[10] 7566 4-9-7 **80**..............(p) TomEaves 6 88
(R A Fahey) *chsd ldrs: rdn over 1f out: drvn and swtchd rt ins fnl f: r.o strly nr fin: jst failed* **9/2**[2]

0323 **3** shd **Even Bolder**[31] 7320 7-8-11 **73**.............. KierenFox(3) 10 81
(E A Wheeler) *stdd and swtchd lft s: hld up in rr: hdwy towards inner ent fnl 2f: rdn to chse ldrs over 1f out: ev ch ins fnl f: no ex cl home* **7/1**[3]

4020 **4** 1 1/2 **Ivory Silk**[31] 7320 5-8-12 **76**..............(b) TobyAtkinson(5) 8 79
(J R Gask) *short of room s and s.i.s: bhd: hdwy towards inner ent fnl 2f: styd on wl fnl f: nt rch ldrs* **14/1**

1055 **5** 1 1/4 **Freddie's Girl (USA)**[11] 7549 3-9-3 **76**.............. MickyFenton 2 75
(Stef Higgins) *led tl ent fnl 2f: stl ev ch tl wknd ins fnl f* **12/1**

0320 **6** 1/2 **Whiskey Junction**[24] 7405 6-8-13 **72**.............. ShaneKelly 4 69
(M Quinn) *chsd ldrs tl rdn to ld ent fnl 2f: hdd and edgd rt over 1f out: wknd fnl 100yds* **12/1**

0000 **7** 3/4 **Onceaponatime (IRE)**[10] 7566 5-9-4 **77**.............. LukeMorris 11 72
(M D Squance) *in tch in midfield: rdn along over 2f out: plugged on same pce u.p fr over 1f out* **25/1**

3110 **8** 3/4 **Efistorm**[30] 7326 9-8-13 **72**.............. RobertWinston 5 64
(C R Dore) *chsd ldrs on outer: wknd u.p wl over 1f out* **16/1**

-341 **9** 1/2 **Baby Dottie**[22] 7440 3-9-1 **74**.............. IanMongan 9 65
(P M Phelan) *in tch on outer: rdn and effrt over 1f out: no prog and kpt on same pce fnl f* **4/1**[1]

-033 **10** 1 1/4 **Comadoir (IRE)**[123] 4693 4-9-0 **73**.............. FergusSweeney 3 60
(Miss Jo Crowley) *chsd ldr tl over 2f out: wknd u.p over 1f out* **8/1**

0540 **11** 1 1/4 **Silver Wind**[15] 7526 5-8-9 **68**..............(b) JamesDoyle 12 51
(A J McCabe) *racd wd: sn pushed along: in tch tl dropped to rr ent fnl 2f: wl hld and edging lft over 1f out* **8/1**

1210 **12** 2 1/4 **Avonvalley**[22] 7442 3-8-9 **68**.............. RobbieFitzpatrick 1 44
(Peter Grayson) *s.i.s and sn rdn along: hdwy into midfield over 4f out: wknd over 1f out* **33/1**

1m 10.98s (-0.92) **Going Correction** -0.025s/f (Stan) 12 Ran SP% **117.6**
Speed ratings (Par 105): **105,104,104,102,101 100,99,98,97,96 94,91**
toteswingers:1&2:£9.60, 1&3:£15.10, 2&3:£5.80 CSF £48.80 CT £305.78 TOTE £9.00: £3.50, £1.60, £2.20; EX 45.50 TRIFECTA Not won..
Owner Dr Bridget Drew & Partners **Bred** Howard Barton Stud **Trained** Kingsclere, Hants

FOCUS
A competitive sprint handicap, and with several front-runners in the line-up, they unsurprisingly went a good pace.

7720 HAXTED H'CAP (DIV I) 5f (P)
3:00 (3:00) (Class 6) (0-60,60) 3-Y-O+ **£1,706** (£503; £252) **Stalls** High

Form RPR

1422 **1** **You'relikemefrank**[94] 5697 4-9-2 **55**..............(p) LukeMorris 7 65+
(J Balding) *chsd ldrs: effrt and edgd lft u.p 1f out: led jst ins fnl f: in command and pushed out fnl 100yds* **9/4**[2]

6660 **2** 1 1/4 **Spic 'n Span**[114] 5025 5-9-7 **60**..............(b) AndreaAtzeni 2 65
(R A Harris) *taken down early: sn led: rdn wl over 1f out: hdd jst ins fnl f: sn outpcd by wnr but kpt on for 2nd* **10/1**

0535 **3** 1/2 **Bluebok**[18] 7477 9-8-9 **48**..............(bt) RussKennemore 6 51
(J M Bradley) *sn chsng ldr: rdn and ev ch wl over 1f out: keeping on same pce whn hmpd sltly jst ins fnl f: no threat to wnr after but kpt on* **7/1**

400- **4** 3/4 **Chantilly Jewel (USA)**[359] 7710 5-8-12 **51**..............(v) EddieAhern 3 52
(R M H Cowell) *bhd: hdwy over 2f out: chsd ldrs and rdn over 1f out: one pce and no imp fnl f* **8/1**

3004 **5** 1 1/2 **Chjimes (IRE)**[15] 7519 6-9-6 **59**..............(p) RobertWinston 1 54
(C R Dore) *sn niggled along towards rr: rdn and outpcd wl over 1f out: no imp u.p after* **2/1**[1]

0000 **6** 2 3/4 **Silver Prelude**[22] 7446 9-9-6 **59**..............(t) JackMitchell 4 44
(S C Williams) *in tch in midfield: rdn and effrt 2f out: wknd 1f out* **11/2**[3]

0000 **7** 3/4 **Thoughtsofstardom**[12] 7542 7-9-1 **54**..............(be) ChrisCatlin 8 37
(P S McEntee) *broke wl: sn stdd and grad lost pl: bhd and rdn wl over 1f out: no prog* **16/1**

58.40 secs (-0.40) **Going Correction** -0.025s/f (Stan) 7 Ran SP% **118.1**
Speed ratings (Par 101): **102,100,99,98,95 91,90**
toteswingers:1&2:£3.50, 1&3:£3.20, 2&3:£4.20 CSF £25.84 CT £140.01 TOTE £3.80: £1.90, £6.30; EX 30.30 Trifecta £86.30 Pool: £654.51 - 5.61 winning units..
Owner Kate Barrett, Paul & David Clarkson **Bred** J R Mitchell **Trained** Scrooby, Notts
■ Stewards' Enquiry : Eddie Ahern three-day ban: weighed in 2lb overweight (Dec 20-21)

FOCUS
Only one progressive runner in this moderate sprint, You'relikemefrank.

7721 HAXTED H'CAP (DIV II) 5f (P)
3:30 (3:30) (Class 6) (0-60,59) 3-Y-O+ **£1,706** (£503; £252) **Stalls** High

Form RPR

4006 **1** **Estonia**[10] 7564 3-8-11 **49**.............. CathyGannon 10 59
(M D Squance) *taken down early: stdd s: t.k.h: hld up in rr: stl last wl over 1f out: hdwy ent fnl f: rdn and r.o strly to ld wl ins fnl f: sn in command* **25/1**

5206 **2** 1 **Edith's Boy (IRE)**[109] 5207 4-9-6 **58**.............. HayleyTurner 8 64
(S Dow) *chsd ldr tl led over 3f out: rdn wl over 1f out: drvn ins fnl f: hdd and nt pce of wnr wl ins fnl f* **5/1**[3]

0201 **3** 1/2 **Sleepy Blue Ocean**[12] 7542 4-9-7 **59**.............. LukeMorris 7 63
(J Balding) *in tch in last trio: hung rt and racd awkwardly bnd 4f out: hdwy ent fnl 2f: drvn to chse ldr jst over 1f out: ev ch ins fnl f: one pce fnl 75yds* **9/4**[1]

0200 **4** 1 3/4 **Ten Down**[150] 3818 5-9-0 **52**.............. AndreaAtzeni 1 50
(M Quinn) *broke wl and led: hdd over 3f out: chsd ldr after tl jst over 1f out: wknd ins fnl f* **12/1**

3535 **5** 1/2 **Black Baccara**[12] 7537 3-9-2 **54**.............. ChrisCatlin 3 50
(P S McEntee) *in tch: rdn and unable qck wl over 1f out: styd on same pce fnl f* **13/2**

4001 **6** nk **Bidruma**[18] 7477 3-9-1 **53**.............. DaneO'Neill 9 48
(Mike Murphy) *in tch: dropped in bhd 4f out: effrt and n.m.r over 1f out tl 1f out: drvn and styd on same pce after* **3/1**[2]

0000 **7** 2 **Brazilian Brush (IRE)**[182] 2791 5-8-2 **45**..............(bt) RyanPowell(5) 2 33
(J M Bradley) *chsd ldrs: drvn and unable qck wl over 1f out: wknd ent fnl f* **20/1**

4403 **8** 1 1/2 **Miss Polly Plum**[18] 7477 3-8-7 **48**..............(e) KellyHarrison(3) 5 30
(C A Dwyer) *in tch towards rr: rdn and no rspnse ent fnl 2f: wknd over 1f out* **8/1**

59.00 secs (0.20) **Going Correction** -0.025s/f (Stan) 8 Ran SP% **113.2**
Speed ratings (Par 101): **97,95,94,91,91 90,87,84**
toteswingers:1&2:£9.00, 1&3:£11.00, 2&3:£3.70 CSF £141.69 CT £400.51 TOTE £17.80: £4.90, £2.70, £1.30; EX 133.60 Trifecta £273.60 Pool: £539.86 - 1.46 winning units..
Owner Miss K Squance **Bred** Millsec Limited **Trained** Newmarket, Suffolk

FOCUS
The pace was strong, but a time 0.60 seconds slower than the first division suggests the early leaders were tired late on.

T/Jkpt: Not won.. T/Plt: £72.80 to a £1 stake. Pool:£86,306.39 - 864.98 winning tickets T/Qpdt: £35.40 to a £1 stake. Pool:£7,933.19 - 165.60 winning tickets SP

7715 LINGFIELD (L-H)

Monday, December 6

OFFICIAL GOING: Standard

Wind: virtually nil Weather: murky, very cold

7722 BET SP+ ON WEEKDAYS AT TOTESPORT.COM (S) STKS — 6f (P)

12:30 (12:35) (Class 6) 2-Y-O — £2,047 (£604; £302) **Stalls** Low

Form / RPR

5303 **1** **Slatey Hen (IRE)**[16] 7527 2-8-8 63 ow2 .... BarryMcHugh 5 — 61
(R A Fahey) *chsd ldng: effrt to ld wl over 1f out: kpt on wl u.p ins fnl f* **13/2**

5064 **2** ½ **Silence Is Bliss (IRE)**[35] 7271 2-9-2 74 .... (p) LukeMorris 9 — 68
(J S Moore) *hld up in tch towards rr: effrt whn n.m.r wl over 1f out: hdwy u.p and hanging lft ins fnl f: pressed wnr fnl 75yds: kpt on* **11/4**[1]

0050 **3** 1¼ **Honkers Bonkers**[24] 7417 2-8-11 67 .... (p) JamesDoyle 1 — 58
(A J McCabe) *awkward s: sn rcvrd and chsng ldng pair: rdn and effrt 2f out: ev ch and drvn ent fnl f: unable qck and btn fnl 100yds* **4/1**[2]

000 **4** 2¾ **Mi Sun Donk**[102] 5453 2-8-11 50 .... GregFairley 3 — 50
(B R Johnson) *led: rdn 2f out: hdd over 1f out: outpcd fnl f* **50/1**

0420 **5** nk **Soviet Spring (IRE)**[35] 7271 2-8-11 65 .... JimmyFortune 7 — 49
(A M Balding) *jostled after s: hld up in tch: rdn and nt qckn over 1f out: styd on same pce ins fnl f* **5/1**[3]

3033 **6** ½ **Robber Stone**[12] 7552 2-8-11 55 .... ChrisCatlin 2 — 47
(M R Channon) *t.k.h early: hld up wl in tch: rdn and nt qckn over 1f out: one pce and no imp fnl f* **4/1**[2]

60 **7** ½ **Go Maggie Go (IRE)**[35] 7268 2-8-6 0 .... CathyGannon 6 — 41
(K A Ryan) *t.k.h early: sn chsng ldr tl ent fnl 2f: wknd u.p ent fnl f* **16/1**

0004 **8** 1½ **Beach Patrol (IRE)**[10] 7577 2-8-4 53 .... (b) JulieBurke(7) 10 — 41
(E J Creighton) *in tch in rr: rdn and outpcd ent fnl 2f: plugged on same pce and no threat to ldrs after* **25/1**

00 **9** 27 **Bridget The Fidget**[19] 7485 2-8-6 0 .... NickyMackay 8 — —
(E J Creighton) *short of room after s: sn swtchd lft: a bhd: lost tch ent fnl 2f: t.o fnl f* **50/1**

1m 11.86s (-0.04) **Going Correction** -0.025s/f (Stan) — **9** Ran SP% **110.3**

Speed ratings (Par 94): **99,98,96,93,92 91,91,89,53**

toteswingers:1&2:£3.50, 1&3:£4.70, 2&3:£3.00 CSF £22.91 TOTE £8.50: £2.00, £1.60, £2.30; EX 25.70 Trifecta £55.40 Pool: £252.70 - 3.37 winning units..There was no bid or the winner.

Owner David W Armstrong **Bred** Shane Doyle **Trained** Musley Bank, N Yorks

FOCUS

A modest juvenile seller. The time and the fourth help set the level.

NOTEBOOK

Slatey Hen(IRE), third in a similar event at Wolverhampton on her debut for Richard Fahey following a break, built on that effort to become her trainer's 13th winner already since the start of the AW season. A straightforward individual, she may have run slightly above her official mark of 63 (carried 2lb overweight), and can win again in the right company. (op 9-2)

Silence Is Bliss(IRE), reported to have moved poorly in the closing stages last time, had cheekpieces back on and was dropped in trip. He was briefly denied a clear run early in the straight, but was in the open in enough time if good enough and basically just seemed to lack the winner's resolution. (op 10-3 tchd 5-2)

Honkers Bonkers, dropped in grade and trip, was well enough placed if good enough, but he didn't seem to run up to his official mark of 67. (op 7-2)

Mi Sun Donk may have run slightly above his official mark of 50 on this return from over three months off, so not a bad effort considering he stuck more towards the inside rail than most of these. (op 40-1)

Soviet Spring(IRE), reported to have run too free when a beaten favourite over 7f on his previous start, again failed to settle and did not pick up for pressure. He looks one to swerve. (tchd 11-2)

7723 BIGGER WINS WITH SP+ AT TOTESPORT.COM MEDIAN AUCTION MAIDEN STKS — 1m (P)

1:00 (1:05) (Class 6) 2-Y-O — £2,047 (£604; £302) **Stalls** High

Form / RPR

02 **1** **Reem Star**[23] 7447 2-8-12 0 .... EddieAhern 2 — 72+
(E A L Dunlop) *dwlt: hld up in tch: hdwy and swtchd rt on bnd 2f out: str run ins fnl f to ld towards fin: won gng away* **5/4**[1]

2 ½ **Aldedash (USA)** 2-9-3 0 .... IanMongan 1 — 76
(H R A Cecil) *chsd ldr: rdn and ev ch over 1f out: led jst ins fnl f: hdd and no ex towards fin* **9/2**[3]

03 **3** ¾ **Destiny Of Dreams**[36] 7248 2-8-12 0 .... DaneO'Neill 8 — 69
(Miss Jo Crowley) *chsd ldrs: rdn to chal 2f out: led ent fnl f: sn hdd: styd on same pce fnl 150yds* **3/1**[2]

4 2¾ **Palagonia** 2-9-3 0 .... GregFairley 3 — 68+
(M Johnston) *sn led: hrd pressed 2f out: rdn wl over 1f out: hdd ent fnl f: wknd fnl 150yds* **6/1**

00 **5** 3¾ **Bobby Dazzler (IRE)**[20] 7470 2-9-3 0 .... JamesDoyle 6 — 59
(S Kirk) *stdd s: hld up in tch in last: rdn and effrt on inner ent fnl 2f: outpcd and no ch w ldrs over 1f out* **66/1**

0006 **6** 2 **Alantina**[8] 7609 2-9-3 42 .... LukeMorris 5 — 55
(J R Jenkins) *hld up in tch: effrt u.p and hung rt on bnd 2f out: sn drvn and wknd* **40/1**

00 **7** 1¾ **Paradise Place**[19] 7479 2-8-12 0 .... (v¹) JamieSpencer 7 — 46
(J Noseda) *chsd ldr tl jst over 2f out: wknd qckly wl over 1f out: wl btn fnl f* **25/1**

00 **8** 4½ **Jacquotte (IRE)**[121] 4838 2-8-5 0 .... JulieBurke(7) 4 — 35
(E J Creighton) *in tch: swtchd rt and rdn over 2f out: sn lost pl: wl bhd out over 1f* **100/1**

1m 39.24s (1.04) **Going Correction** -0.025s/f (Stan) — **8** Ran SP% **110.7**

Speed ratings (Par 94): **93,92,91,89,85 83,81,77**

toteswingers:1&2:£2.50, 1&3:£1.70, 2&3:£2.60 CSF £6.67 TOTE £2.20: £1.10, £2.00, £1.10; EX 7.10 Trifecta £17.30 Pool: £332.57 - 14.19 winning units..

Owner Ahmed Ali **Bred** Newsells Park Stud Limited **Trained** Newmarket, Suffolk

FOCUS

The bare form looks no better than fair, but the race should produce some winners. The third and the sixth help set the level.

NOTEBOOK

Reem Star, an improved second over 7f at Wolverhampton last time, lost ground at the start and, having recovered into a challenging position, hit a flat a spot early in the straight. Being on the best part of the track late on surely helped, though, and she picked up well. There may be more to come. (op 9-4)

Aldedash(USA), a £35,000 half-brother to four winners, looked likely to take this when nipping through against the inside rail early in the straight. However, he continued to stick to the inside fence, which isn't always the place to be, and was caught late on. He's a tall, leggy individual and should progress into a useful type. (tchd 5-1)

Destiny Of Dreams seems to be going the right way. Her trainer expects the filly to make a better 3-y-o. (op 11-4 tchd 10-3)

Palagonia, who is out of a 1m6f winner, sister to Breeders' Cup Juvenile winner Action This Day, has scope. He ran green when coming under pressure and can do much better as he gains further experience. (op 7-2)

Bobby Dazzler(IRE) offered some encouragement and can now switch to handicaps.

7724 BET ON TONIGHT'S FOOTBALL AT TOTESPORT.COM H'CAP — 1m (P)

1:30 (1:37) (Class 5) (0-75,81) 3-Y-O+ — £2,729 (£806; £403) **Stalls** High

Form / RPR

2132 **1** **Blue Moon**[23] 7453 3-9-2 71 .... PhillipMakin 10 — 80+
(K A Ryan) *racd wl off the pce in midfield: clsd 3f out: hdwy u.p to chse ldrs over 1f out: edgd lft but r.o wl fnl f to ld on post* **11/1**

540 **2** nse **Copperwood**[19] 7483 5-8-13 67 .... DaneO'Neill 1 — 76
(M Blanshard) *chsd clr ldr: clsd over 2f out: drvn to ld 1f out: kpt on wl u.p tl hdd on post* **20/1**

111 **3** nse **Final Drive (IRE)**[6] 7637 4-9-13 81 12ex .... EddieAhern 2 — 90
(J Ryan) *prom in main gp: clsd on ldng pair wl over 2f out: drvn and pressed ldrs ent fnl f: ev ch fnl 100yds: jst hld* **7/1**

1011 **4** 2½ **Tevez**[77] 6260 5-9-6 74 .... CathyGannon 8 — 77+
(D Donovan) *racd wl off the pce in last trio: clsd but stl last 2f out: hdwy and swtchd lft jst ins fnl f: r.o wl fnl 100yds: nvr able to chal* **6/1**[3]

0500 **5** nse **Charlie Smirke (USA)**[9] 7597 4-9-4 72 .... GeorgeBaker 7 — 75
(G L Moore) *prom in main gp: clsd 3f out: rdn: fnd little and hung lft over 1f out: no imp fnl f* **12/1**

0405 **6** nk **Final Verse**[12] 7560 7-9-7 75 .... (be) LukeMorris 12 — 77
(Matthew Salaman) *stdd s: hld up wl off the pce in last trio: hdwy 3f out: midfield and drvn over 1f out: kpt on but no real imp ins fnl f* **5/1**[2]

0061 **7** 1½ **Kilburn**[36] 7255 6-9-6 74 .... (b) JamesDoyle 4 — 73
(A J Lidderdale) *racd keenly: led and sn clr: rdn and c towards centre wl over 1f out: hdd 1f out: wknd fnl 150yds* **13/2**

0014 **8** 3 **Syrian**[6] 7637 3-9-6 75 .... JamieSpencer 6 — 67
(Ian Williams) *stdd s: plld hrd: hld up wl off the pce in rr: hdwy on outer over 2f out: rdn: hung lft and sn btn wl over 1f out* **4/1**[1]

0340 **9** ½ **Prince Of Thebes (IRE)**[9] 7597 9-9-0 71 .... KierenFox(3) 5 — 62
(M J Attwater) *dwlt: racd wl off the pce in midfield: clsd on ldrs 3f out: rdn and struggling ent fnl 2f: wl btn fnl f* **8/1**

0460 **10** 1¼ **Buxton**[12] 7554 6-9-0 68 .... (t) RobertHavlin 9 — 56
(R Ingram) *prom in main gp: clsd on ldrs 3f out: rdn and wknd ent fnl 2f* **33/1**

10P6 **11** shd **Peadar Miguel**[25] 7411 3-9-3 72 .... AdamKirby 11 — 60
(M G Quinlan) *a wl off the pce towards rr: pushed along 4f out: clsd on ldrs 3f out: wknd u.p ent fnl 2f* **33/1**

1m 36.87s (-1.33) **Going Correction** -0.025s/f (Stan)

WFA 3 from 4yo+ 1lb — **11** Ran SP% **114.6**

Speed ratings (Par 103): **105,104,104,102,102 102,100,97,97,95 95**

toteswingers:1&2:£22.00, 1&3:£4.90, 2&3:£19.20 CSF £207.20 CT £1669.35 TOTE £9.10: £2.50, £7.20, £1.70; EX 105.60 Trifecta £383.40 Part won. Pool: £518.17 - 0.60 winning units..

Owner Guy Reed **Bred** Theakston Stud **Trained** Hambleton, N Yorks

FOCUS

Early leader Kilburn was soon allowed a sizeable advantage, and was chased by Copperwood, who was in turn clear of the remainder. As a consequence, it paid to be prominent in the main bunch. The front three crossed the line almost as one and this was clearly a really competitive handicap. Ordinary form, rated around the runner-up.

Syrian Official explanation: jockey said gelding ran flat

7725 LINGFIELDPARK.CO.UK CLAIMING STKS — 7f (P)

2:00 (2:05) (Class 6) 3-Y-O+ — £2,047 (£604; £302) **Stalls** Low

Form / RPR

33 **1** **Caprio (IRE)**[12] 7557 5-9-5 79 .... NickyMackay 7 — 75
(J R Boyle) *pressed ldr: rdn and ev ch over 1f out: drvn to ld ins fnl f: hld on wl* **9/2**[3]

0662 **2** nse **Everymanforhimself (IRE)**[12] 7557 6-9-5 80 .... (b) PhillipMakin 1 — 75
(K A Ryan) *t.k.h: wl in tch: effrt to press ldrs over 1f out: ev ch ins fnl f: jst hld* **9/4**[1]

2004 **3** ½ **Fishforcompliments**[12] 7557 6-9-5 77 .... BarryMcHugh 6 — 74
(R A Fahey) *led for 1f: trckd ldng pair after: effrt and rdn over 1f out: ev ch ins fnl f: unable qck towards fin* **5/1**

3350 **4** ½ **Avonrose**[59] 6709 3-8-9 75 .... GregFairley 10 — 62
(M Johnston) *led after 1f and crossed to rail: rdn over 1f out: hdd and one pce ins fnl f* **7/2**[2]

4000 **5** nk **Decency (IRE)**[17] 7502 3-8-6 58 .... LukeMorris 4 — 58
(H J L Dunlop) *hld up in tch towards rr: hdwy to chse ldrs over 1f out: nt clr run and swtchd rt jst ins fnl f: r.o: nt rch ldrs* **33/1**

0050 **6** hd **Dichoh**[9] 7597 7-9-0 65 .... (vt) AdamKirby 5 — 66
(M Madgwick) *hld up in tch towards rr: effrt and rdn over 1f out: drvn and r.o wl fnl 100yds: nt rch ldrs* **9/1**

0025 **7** nk **Batchworth Blaise**[12] 7555 7-8-9 57 .... KierenFox(3) 3 — 63
(E A Wheeler) *stdd s: hld up in tch in rr: gd hdwy on inner over 1f out: chsd ldrs ins fnl f: styd on same pce fnl 100yds* **16/1**

1500 **8** 1½ **Timeteam (IRE)**[12] 7557 4-8-10 73 ow1 .... JamieSpencer 9 — 57
(G L Moore) *v.s.a: t.k.h: hld up in tch in rr: effrt on outer bnd ent fnl 2f: no prog and btn ent fnl f* **14/1**

00 **9** 7 **Suttonia (IRE)**[20] 7473 4-8-5 41 .... ChrisCatlin 8 — 33
(Noel T Chance) *t.k.h: wl in tch tl rdn and wknd ent fnl 2f* **100/1**

1m 26.39s (1.59) **Going Correction** -0.025s/f (Stan) — **9** Ran SP% **114.3**

Speed ratings (Par 101): **89,88,88,87,87 87,86,85,77**

toteswingers:1&2:£2.80, 1&3:£3.40, 2&3:£3.40 CSF £14.85 TOTE £4.90: £1.30, £1.10, £1.20; EX 12.20 Trifecta £27.60 Pool: £523.03 - 13.99 winning units..

Owner M Khan X2 **Bred** P Rabbitte **Trained** Epsom, Surrey

■ Stewards' Enquiry : Chris Catlin one-day ban: used whip when out of contention (Dec 20)

FOCUS

A fair but rather muddling claimer. The fifth and seventh limit the form.

7726 40 LIVE FOOTBALL MARKETS AT TOTESPORT.COM H'CAP — 1m 4f (P)

2:30 (2:35) (Class 5) (0-70,67) 3-Y-O — £2,729 (£806; £403) **Stalls** Low

Form / RPR

5505 **1** **Mush Mir (IRE)**[3] 7685 3-8-12 58 .... (b¹) StephenCraine 2 — 71+
(J R Boyle) *mde all: clr and travelling strly over 2f out: in n.d fr wl over 1f out: eased ins fnl f* **13/2**

2402 **2** 5 **Sheila's Bond**[23] 7445 3-8-11 57 .... LukeMorris 3 — 59
(J S Moore) *hld up in tch: rdn 4f out: pressing for 2nd but no ch w wnr over 1f out: kpt on to go 2nd nr fin* **11/4**[2]

3 ½ **Indefinite Hope (ITY)**[86] 3-9-2 62 .... (t) AndreaAtzeni 1 — 63
(M Botti) *trckd ldrs: rdn and outpcd by wnr over 2f out: wnt modest 2nd 2f out: no imp: lost 2nd nr fin* **5/4**[1]

3032 **4** 3 ¾ **Florio Vincitore (IRE)**[19] 7476 3-9-4 **67**.................... AlanCreighton(3) 4 62
(E J Creighton) *awkward leaving stalls: t.k.h: chsd ldr: rdn over 3f out: outpcd by wnr and btn over 2f out: wknd ent fnl f* **4/1**[3]

0000 **5** 8 **Beneath**[12] 6753 3-9-4 **64**...(b1) PhillipMakin 5 46
(K A Ryan) *hld up in tch: rdn and no prog 3f out: wl btn 2f out: eased fnl f* **10/1**

2m 33.31s (0.31) **Going Correction** -0.025s/f (Stan) **5** Ran SP% **113.5**
Speed ratings (Par 102): **97,93,93,90,85**
CSF £24.99 TOTE £8.20: £4.40, £1.30; EX 28.50.
Owner M Khan X2 **Bred** Shadwell Estate Company Limited **Trained** Epsom, Surrey

FOCUS
The well-handicapped winner was allowed an easy lead and this form is a bit shaky.
Mush Mir(IRE) Official explanation: trainer said, regarding apparent improvement in form, that the gelding had benefited from the application of blinkers.

7727 HOLLOW LANE H'CAP (DIV 1) 1m 2f (P)
3:00 (3:05) (Class 6) (0-52,52) 3-Y-0+ **£1,706** (£503; £252) **Stalls** Low

Form RPR

0600 **1** **Ocean Of Peace (FR)**[17] 7508 7-8-12 **48**.................... FergusSweeney 3 56
(M R Bosley) *taken down early: hld up in midfield: rdn and effrt ent fnl f: qcknd to ld ins fnl f: edgd lft towards fin* **7/1**

5066 **2** 1 ¼ **Pab Special (IRE)**[12] 7555 7-9-0 **50**.............................(v) AdamKirby 1 55
(B R Johnson) *t.k.h: hld up in tch: effrt on inner 2f out: ev ch over 1f out: led jst ins fnl f: hdd and nt pce of wnr ins fnl f* **13/2**

-500 **3** ½ **Dawson Creek (IRE)**[177] 2965 6-9-1 **51**.......................... GregFairley 10 55
(L A Dace) *led: rdn wl over 1f out: battled on wl tl hdd ins fnl f: styd on same pce towards fin* **16/1**

2444 **4** nse **Little Meadow (IRE)**[46] 7038 3-8-10 **49**.................. CathyGannon 2 53
(Miss J Feilden) *in tch: trcking ldrs and nt clr run over 2f out tl 2f out: rdn to chse ldrs wl over 1f out: nt qckn u.p and styd on same pce fnl f* **11/2**[3]

0000 **5** 2 ¼ **Mouchez**[34] 7288 3-8-12 **51**.. SamHitchcott 4 50
(D K Ivory) *dwlt: towards rr: rdn along wl over 3f out: hdwy towards inner ent fnl 2f: kpt on but nvr gng pce to rch ldrs* **25/1**

0051 **6** ¾ **Iguacu**[17] 7508 6-8-9 **52**..(p) DavidKenny(7) 9 50
(George Baker) *s.i.s: hld up in rr: c wd and effrt over 1f out: kpt on fnl f: nvr trbld ldrs* **9/2**[2]

0656 **7** 1 **Primera Rossa**[21] 6450 4-8-10 **46** oh1................................ LukeMorris 8 42
(J S Moore) *chsd ldrs: rdn 4f out: wknd u.p over 1f out* **14/1**

0000 **8** ¾ **Lily Eva**[19] 7491 4-8-10 **46** oh1.................................... DavidProbert 12 40
(D Donovan) *w ldr: ev ch and rdn wl over 1f out: wknd ent fnl f* **20/1**

00-0 **9** 2 **Dalrymple (IRE)**[14] 6637 4-8-10 **46** oh1...................(t) FrankieMcDonald 6 36
(M Madgwick) *in tch in midfield: lost pl and rdn wl over 2f out: n.d fnl 2f* **66/1**

0000 **10** nk **On The Cusp (IRE)**[41] 7156 3-8-7 **46**.............................(p) ChrisCatlin 5 36
(P Butler) *t.k.h: hld up in tch towards rr: rdn and hung lft over 1f out: no prog* **16/1**

0060 **11** 6 **Binnion Bay (IRE)**[57] 6775 9-9-1 **51**...........................(b) NeilChalmers 7 29
(J J Bridger) *v.s.a: a towards rr: lost tch ent fnl 2f* **10/1**

005 **12** ½ **Western Eyes (IRE)**[37] 7244 3-8-13 **52**........................... ShaneKelly 11 29
(B J Meehan) *in tch in midfield: hdwy to chse ldrs 7f out: rdn and unable qck over 2f out: wknd wl over 1f out* **11/4**[1]

2m 6.68s (0.08) **Going Correction** -0.025s/f (Stan)
WFA 3 from 4yo+ 3lb **12** Ran SP% **123.7**
Speed ratings (Par 101): **98,97,96,96,94 94,93,92,91,90 86,85**
toteswingers:1&2:£10.90, 1&3:£22.20, 2&3:£21.20 CSF £53.44 CT £723.00 TOTE £13.20: £3.40, £3.60, £5.90; EX 54.30 Trifecta £393.40 Pool: £531.71 - 1.00 winning unit..
Owner Mrs Jean M O'Connor **Bred** Raoul Rousset **Trained** Chalfont St Giles, Bucks

FOCUS
A moderate handicap run in a time 2.15 seconds slower than the strongly run second division. It has been rated around the runner-up's recent form.

7728 HOLLOW LANE H'CAP (DIV II) 1m 2f (P)
3:30 (3:35) (Class 6) (0-52,52) 3-Y-0+ **£1,706** (£503; £252) **Stalls** Low

Form RPR

2060 **1** **Indian Violet (IRE)**[45] 7068 4-9-0 **50**............................ JamieGoldstein 5 62+
(Miss Sheena West) *t.k.h: hld up in midfield: hdwy to ld 2f out: clr and hung lft over 1f out: in command fnl f: comf* **8/1**

2265 **2** 2 ¼ **Mister Frosty (IRE)**[25] 7407 4-9-2 **52**........................ KirstyMilczarek 3 59
(G Prodromou) *hld up in midfield: clsd on ldrs 3f out: chsd ldrs and rdn over 2f out: chsd wnr jst over 1f out: kpt on but no imp on wnr fnl f* **5/1**[3]

4004 **3** 3 ½ **Mr Maximas**[10] 7575 3-8-12 **51**..................................... RobertWinston 11 51
(B Palling) *hld up in last pair: rdn and effrt on inner 2f out: no ch w wnr but kpt on u.p to go 3rd ins fnl f* **9/2**[2]

0050 **4** ¾ **Dilys Maud**[12] 7555 3-8-9 **48**.. RobertHavlin 8 47
(R Ingram) *racd in midfield: reminder 5f out: chsd ldrs and drvn ent fnl 2f: sn outpcd and no ch w wnr: plugged on ins fnl f* **16/1**

0624 **5** 1 ¾ **Mayfair's Future**[34] 7286 5-9-1 **51**...................................(p) EddieAhern 6 46
(J R Jenkins) *chsd ldng pair: clsd over 3f out: rdn to press ldrs ent fnl 2f: sn outpcd: wl hld fnl f* **3/1**[1]

060 **6** 1 ½ **Fastinthestraight (IRE)**[83] 6060 3-8-12 **51** ow1...........(p) DaneO'Neill 10 43
(J R Boyle) *hld up in rr: rdn wl over 2f out: no hdwy tl kpt on wl ins fnl f: n.d* **7/1**

600 **7** ¾ **Rosy Dawn**[76] 6273 5-8-10 **46** oh1.................................. GregFairley 7 37
(L A Dace) *led: rdn ent fnl 2f: sn hdd: sn outpcd by wnr: wknd jst over 1f out* **14/1**

006 **8** nse **Beseech (USA)**[19] 7489 3-8-13 **52**.................................. CathyGannon 9 42
(Miss J Feilden) *awkward leaving stalls and s.i.s: nvr travelling wl and a towards rr: rdn 4f out: sme hdwy ins fnl f: n.d* **9/1**

5000 **9** 1 **Inquisitress**[5] 7649 6-8-12 **48**.......................................(p) NeilChalmers 4 36
(J J Bridger) *hld up in midfield: hdwy 3f out: rdn and no hdwy ent fnl 2f: wknd over 1f out* **14/1**

0-00 **10** 3 ¼ **Corlough Mountain**[7] 7626 6-8-10 **49** oh1 ow3......(v) RobertLButler(3) 2 31
(P Butler) *chsd ldr tl 2f out: sn wknd* **40/1**

2m 4.53s (-2.07) **Going Correction** -0.025s/f (Stan)
WFA 3 from 4yo+ 3lb **10** Ran SP% **115.1**
Speed ratings (Par 101): **107,105,102,101,100 99,98,98,97,95**
toteswingers:1&2:£8.80, 1&3:£11.50, 2&3:£5.30. totesuper7: Win: Not won. Place: Not won. CSF £47.13 CT £203.44 TOTE £11.50: £4.10, £1.90, £1.60; EX 64.20 Trifecta £473.40 Pool: £831.66 - 1.30 winning units..
Owner Gerald West **Bred** James F Hanly **Trained** Falmer, E Sussex

FOCUS
They went an overly strong pace and the time was 2.05 seconds quicker than the first division, a fair time for the grade. The form has been rated slightly positively.
T/Jkpt: Not won. T/Plt: £130.00 to a £1 stake. Pool:£87,987.77 - 494.08 winning tickets T/Qpdt: £87.50 to a £1 stake. Pool:£6,190.90 - 52.30 winning tickets SP

7692 SOUTHWELL (L-H)
Monday, December 6

OFFICIAL GOING: Standard to slow
This Fibresand card, arranged at short notice, consisted of three Flat races followed by three bumpers.
Wind: Almost nil Weather: Sunny, cold

7729 TOTEPLACEPOT WIN WITHOUT BACKING A WINNER CLAIMING STKS 1m 4f (F)
12:50 (12:51) (Class 6) 3-Y-0+ **£1,706** (£503; £252) **Stalls** Low

Form RPR

4620 **1** **Castle Myth (USA)**[13] 7543 4-9-2 60..............................(be) TomEaves 6 65
(B Ellison) *hld up in last but in tch: stdy hdwy over 3f out: led on outside over 1f out: shkn up and drew clr fnl f* **6/1**[3]

0422 **2** 6 **Yossi (IRE)**[6] 7642 6-8-9 56.......................................(be) SeanPalmer(7) 2 56
(R C Guest) *dwlt: in tch: hdwy after 4f: led over 2f out to over 1f out: no ch w wnr fnl f* **7/4**[1]

4000 **3** 1 ¾ **Mojeerr**[6] 7646 4-8-12 50...(v) MichaelGeran(3) 4 52
(A J McCabe) *t.k.h: chsd ldr on ins: led over 3f out to over 2f out: sn outpcd* **18/1**

052 **4** 5 **Ravi River (IRE)**[17] 7501 6-9-5 61.............................. TobyAtkinson(5) 3 53
(B Ellison) *prom: drvn over 4f out: rallied: effrt over 2f out: wknd wl over 1f out* **7/1**

06 **5** 6 **Pinsplitter (USA)**[3] 7679 3-8-9 63.......................(p) AndrewHeffernan(3) 5 36
(A J McCabe) *led to over 3f out: rdn and wknd fr 2f out* **20/1**

5640 **6** 12 **A P Ling**[15] 2619 3-8-4 48.. FrannyNorton 7 9
(C N Kellett) *trckd ldrs: outpcd over 4f out: lost tch fr over 3f out: eased whn btn fnl 2f* **40/1**

2452 **7** 23 **Sworn Tigress (GER)**[9] 7599 5-8-12 73................. MatthewDavies(3) 1 —
(George Baker) *nvr gng wl: in tch: hrd rdn and struggling 5f out: eased whn no ch fnl 2f* **15/8**[2]

2m 46.03s (5.03) **Going Correction** +0.20s/f (Slow)
WFA 3 from 4yo+ 5lb **7** Ran SP% **110.4**
Speed ratings (Par 101): **91,87,85,82,78 70,55**
toteswingers:1&2:£1.40, 1&3:£15.10, 2&3:£6.40 CSF £15.77 TOTE £5.30: £2.80, £2.00; EX 15.60.
Owner Brian Ellison **Bred** Mr & Mrs Gerald J Stautberg **Trained** Norton, N Yorks

FOCUS
Temperatures reached -12c overnight and the track had to be worked continuously resulting in Standard to Slow going, described as 'very deep' by Tom Eaves aboard the first winner. This was a run-of-the-mill claimer run at a steady pace. The third limits the form.
Sworn Tigress(GER) Official explanation: jockey said mare never travelled

7730 TOTEEXACTA YOUR BETTER VALUE FORECAST H'CAP 6f (F)
1:20 (1:21) (Class 5) (0-70,69) 3-Y-0+ **£2,266** (£674; £337; £168) **Stalls** Low

Form RPR

0102 **1** **Takajan (IRE)**[20] 7473 3-8-6 61.................................. JamesRogers(7) 3 71+
(W M Brisbourne) *prom: effrt whn nt clr run over 1f out: swtchd rt and qcknd to ld ins fnl f: edgd lft: kpt on strly* **9/2**[2]

6053 **2** 2 ¼ **My One Weakness (IRE)**[25] 7402 3-8-4 55.........(be) JamesSullivan(3) 1 58
(B Ellison) *dwlt: sn prom on ins: effrt and ev ch over 1f out to ins fnl f: kpt on: nt pce of wnr* **11/2**

0600 **3** 1 ½ **Ace Of Spies (IRE)**[3] 7683 5-9-5 67.............................. HayleyTurner 5 65
(C R Dore) *cl up: led wl over 1f out to ins fnl f: kpt on same pce u.p* **8/1**

3311 **4** ½ **Cheery Cat (USA)**[8] 7607 6-8-9 64 6ex...............(v) MatthewCosham(7) 8 61+
(J Balding) *hld up in tch on outside: drvn and edgd towards ins rail fr 1/2-way: kpt on same pce fr over 1f out* **9/1**

5323 **5** ¾ **Tislaam (IRE)**[12] 7556 3-9-4 69...........................(p) AndrewHeffernan(3) 6 63
(A J McCabe) *prom on outside: rdn to dispute ld over 1f out: sn rdn and edgd lft: one pce fnl f* **5/1**[3]

0510 **6** nk **Gracie's Gift (IRE)**[44] 7093 8-9-2 64.....................(be1) GrahamGibbons 2 57
(R C Guest) *w ldr: led over 3f out to wl over 1f out: kpt on same pce ins fnl f* **6/1**

4150 **7** 7 **Double Carpet (IRE)**[66] 6536 7-8-5 56......................... RossAtkinson(3) 4 27
(G Woodward) *rrd s: bhd and sn drvn along: nvr on terms* **18/1**

3541 **8** 1 **Mango Music**[12] 7556 7-9-4 66.. TomEaves 7 34
(R A Fahey) *t.k.h: led to over 3f out: rdn and wknd fr over 2f out* **7/2**[1]

1m 17.2s (0.70) **Going Correction** +0.20s/f (Slow) **8** Ran SP% **113.1**
Speed ratings (Par 103): **103,100,98,97,96 95,86,85**
toteswingers:1&2:£3.30, 1&3:£14.00, 2&3:£18.60 CSF £28.67 CT £190.73 TOTE £3.60: £1.10, £2.80, £2.80; EX 29.40.
Owner Stephen Jones **Bred** His Highness The Aga Khan's Studs S C **Trained** Great Ness, Shropshire
■ Stewards' Enquiry : Graham Gibbons caution: allowed gelding to coast home with no assistance.
James Sullivan one-day ban: careless riding (Dec 20)

FOCUS
A competitive 55-69 sprint handicap and six of the eight runners were still in with a shout nearing the final furlong. The winner posted his best effort since he was a 2yo, and the runner-up ran to his recent form.

7731 TOTESWINGER THREE WAYS TO WIN H'CAP 1m (F)
1:50 (1:50) (Class 6) (0-60,60) 3-Y-0+ **£1,706** (£503; £252) **Stalls** Low

Form RPR

6551 **1** **Ingleby King (USA)**[6] 7646 4-9-4 56 6ex.................... GrahamGibbons 7 65
(T D Barron) *cl up: led centre 3f out: edgd lft and hrd pressed fr over 1f out: styd on wl u.p fnl f* **8/11**[1]

6001 **2** ½ **It's A Mans World**[25] 7401 4-8-8 51.................................. RyanPowell(5) 1 59
(Ian Williams) *prom gng wl on ins: hdwy to chal over 1f out: sn rdn: kpt on fnl f* **6/1**[2]

0040 **3** 2 ¾ **Royal Holiday (IRE)**[20] 7474 3-9-2 60........................ TobyAtkinson(5) 4 62
(B Ellison) *trckd ldrs gng wl: rdn over 2f out: edgd lft and outpcd over 1f out: kpt on fnl f* **11/1**

04-0 **4** 4 ½ **Gold Story**[233] 1394 3-8-5 47....................................... JamesSullivan(3) 5 39
(B Ellison) *hld up bhd ldng gp: effrt over 2f out: no imp fr over 1f out* **25/1**

0000 **5** 2 ¾ **Baraconti (IRE)**[25] 7401 3-8-13 52..................................(p) TomEaves 3 37
(Mrs R A Carr) *led cl to ins rail tl hdd 3f out: sn rdn: wknd over 1f out* **50/1**

0064 **6** ¾ **Northumberland**[6] 7645 4-8-4 45.............................. KellyHarrison(3) 9 29
(M C Chapman) *prom on outside: drvn and outpcd over 3f out: drifted lft u.p 2f out: sn no imp* **25/1**

0005 **7** 6 **Lord Lansing (IRE)**[25] 7406 3-8-9 48............................ FrannyNorton 10 18
(Mrs K Burke) *dwlt: sn in tch: rdn over 3f out: wknd fr 2f out* **16/1**

6600 **8** 2 1/4 **Raghdaan**[24] 7429 3-8-3 47 RyanClark(5) 11 12
(P W Hiatt) *cl up on outside: rdn over 3f out: wknd 2f out* **25/1**
400 **9** 6 **Ancient Times (USA)**[20] 7474 3-9-3 59 AndrewHeffernan(3) 12 10
(P A Kirby) *s.i.s: bhd and nvr gng wl: nvr on terms* **28/1**
4063 **10** hd **Ella Grace (USA)**[9] 7601 3-9-3 56 (b) PJMcDonald 6 —
(R A Fahey) *racd wd: sn drvn in rr: nvr on terms* **7/1**[3]
0000 **11** 20 **Hopefull Blue (IRE)**[221] 1635 4-8-7 45 HayleyTurner 2 —
(H J Evans) *bhd: struggling after 3f: rdr looked down and eased whn no ch fr 2f out* **66/1**

1m 46.15s (2.45) **Going Correction** +0.20s/f (Slow)
WFA 3 from 4yo 1lb 11 Ran SP% **117.3**
Speed ratings (Par 101): **95,94,91,87,84 83,77,75,69,69 49**
toteswingers:1&2:£3.00, 1&3:£3.80, 2&3:£7.60 CSF £4.64 CT £29.05 TOTE £1.70: £1.10, £2.10, £3.00; EX 6.40.
Owner Dave Scott **Bred** Glencrest Farm LLC **Trained** Maunby, N Yorks

FOCUS
A 45-60 handicap with an odds-on penalised favourite. He produced a small personal best and they came home well strung out. The form is rated around the third.

7722 LINGFIELD (L-H)
Tuesday, December 7

OFFICIAL GOING: Standard
Wind: virtually nil Weather: bright and cold

7732 TOTEPLACEPOT CLAIMING STKS 1m 2f (P)
12:50 (12:50) (Class 6) 3-Y-O+ £1,535 (£453; £226) Stalls Low

Form RPR
024 **1** **Officer In Command (USA)**[48] 7015 4-9-4 77 (b) JamesDoyle 2 77
(J S Moore) *dwlt: sn rcvrd and trckd ldrs: rdn ent fnl 2f: drvn to ld ent fnl f: kpt on wl u.p* **7/1**
3221 **2** 1 1/2 **Dream Of Fortune (IRE)**[37] 7251 6-9-4 68 (t) CathyGannon 9 74
(P D Evans) *hld up in tch: shkn up and nt clr run over 2f out: swtchd rt and hdwy over 1f out: nt clr run and swtchd rt jst ins fnl f: r.o to 2nd towards fin* **13/2**[3]
506 **3** nk **Edgeworth (IRE)**[9] 7611 4-8-12 63 (p) DaneO'Neill 1 68
(B G Powell) *hld up in last pair: hdwy over 2f out: chsd ldrs and hung lft over 1f out: kpt on ins fnl f* **14/1**
3422 **4** hd **Orchard Supreme**[10] 7601 7-9-0 80 J-PGuillambert 4 69
(J Akehurst) *t.k.h: hld up in midfield: hdwy on inner over 1f out: chsd ldrs and drvn jst ins fnl f: one pce fnl 100yds* **7/1**
5034 **5** nse **Merrymadcap (IRE)**[5] 7663 8-8-10 68 RussKennemore 6 65
(Matthew Salaman) *led: rdn over 2f out: hdd ent fnl f: no ex and lost 3 pls wl ins fnl f* **11/1**
2511 **6** nk **Buona Sarah (IRE)**[13] 7562 3-8-3 69 NathanAlison(7) 3 67
(J R Boyle) *stdd s: plld hrd: hld up towards rr: hdwy into midfield 5f out: gd hdwy to chse ldr over 2f out: rdn 2f out: no ex ins fnl f: wknd fnl 100yds* **4/1**[2]
6100 **7** nk **Starburst**[13] 7562 5-8-2 55 KierenFox(3) 5 59
(Miss Gay Kelleway) *hld up in midfield: nt clr run: hmpd and shuffled bk jst over 2f out: swtchd rt and rallied over 1f out: kpt on ins fnl f: unable to chal* **20/1**
0020 **8** 2 **Free Tussy (ARG)**[43] 7111 6-9-8 74 (bt) GeorgeBaker 10 72
(G L Moore) *stdd s: hld up in rr: swtchd wd and effrt wl over 1f out: kpt on ins fnl f: nvr threatened ldrs* **8/1**
3 **9** 1 3/4 **Too Late Jones (USA)**[24] 7438 3-8-7 0 ChrisCatlin 7 56
(M A Magnusson) *t.k.h: chsd ldr tl over 2f out: wkng whn hmpd over 1f out* **7/2**[1]
6 **10** 3 3/4 **Roilos (IRE)**[26] 7414 4-8-13 70 (t) TobyAtkinson(5) 8 57
(M Botti) *chsd ldrs tl over 2f out: wknd wl over 1f out* **16/1**

2m 6.00s (-0.60) **Going Correction** +0.025s/f (Slow)
WFA 3 from 4yo+ 3lb 10 Ran SP% **117.3**
Speed ratings (Par 101): **103,101,101,101,101 101,100,99,97,94**
toteswingers:1&2 £8.60, 2&3 £19.90, 1&3 £12.00 CSF £52.32 TOTE £8.80: £3.20, £2.30, £4.90; EX 49.60.Buona Sarah was claimed by Sheena West for £10,000.
Owner N Brunskill & J S Moore **Bred** Blooming Hills Inc **Trained** Upper Lambourn, Berks

FOCUS
A wide-open looking claimer. It was run at an uneven pace and there was a blanket finish for the places, so the form looks a bit shaky. It has been rated around the runner-up.
Free Tussy(ARG) Official explanation: jockey said the gelding was denied a clear run
Too Late Jones(USA) Official explanation: jockey said the gelding hung left

7733 E B F TOTESWINGER FLEXI BETTING MAIDEN FILLIES' STKS 1m (P)
1:20 (1:21) (Class 5) 2-Y-O £2,752 (£818; £409; £204) Stalls High

Form RPR
3 **1** **Hawaafez**[13] 7559 2-9-0 0 GeorgeBaker 4 75+
(M P Tregoning) *in tch: chsd ldrs over 2f out: rdn to ld over 1f out: styd on wl ins fnl f: comf* **8/11**[1]
2 2 **Baisse** 2-8-11 0 KellyHarrison(3) 2 70+
(H R A Cecil) *t.k.h: w ldrs early tl stdd bk into midfield after 1f: hdwy to chse ldrs on inner ent fnl 2f: rdn over 1f out: chsd wnr ins fnl f: kpt on: no imp on wnr* **5/1**[3]
4 **3** 2 1/2 **Al Khatma**[24] 7448 2-9-0 0 AdamKirby 9 64
(M Botti) *t.k.h: w ldr: rdn and ev ch wl over 1f out: hung lft and outpcd ins fnl f: dismntd after fin* **5/2**[2]
0 **4** 2 1/4 **Twin Soul (IRE)**[174] 3082 2-9-0 0 DavidProbert 5 59
(A M Balding) *stdd s: hld up wl in tch in rr: rdn: hung rt and outpcd bnd 2f out: rallied fnl f: styd on steadily: nvr trbld ldrs* **33/1**
0 **5** 3/4 **Igitur**[13] 7559 2-9-0 0 ShaneKelly 3 57
(W J Knight) *led: rdn and hrd pressed ent fnl 2f: hdd over 1f out: wknd ins fnl f* **66/1**
00 **6** 1 1/2 **Secoya**[17] 7530 2-9-0 0 RichardKingscote 6 55
(R M Beckett) *t.k.h: chsd ldrs after 1f tl wknd qckly ent fnl 2f* **16/1**
7 3 3/4 **Dune Island** 2-9-0 0 NeilChalmers 8 46
(J J Bridger) *v.s.a: in tch in rr after 1f: rdn and struggling over 2f out: wl btn over 1f out* **66/1**
0 **8** 1 3/4 **Jody Bear**[13] 7558 2-9-0 0 JackMitchell 7 41
(J G Portman) *t.k.h: chsd ldrs on outer tl lost pl over 2f out: wl bhd over 1f out* **66/1**
9 6 **Movingly (USA)** 2-9-0 0 WilliamBuick 1 27
(J H M Gosden) *dwlt: pushed along early: sn chsng ldrs: rdn and lost pl wl over 2f out: wl btn fnl 2f* **15/2**

1m 40.03s (1.83) **Going Correction** +0.025s/f (Slow) 9 Ran SP% **128.2**
Speed ratings (Par 93): **91,89,86,84,83 82,78,76,70**
toteswingers:1&2 £2.60, 2&3 £2.50, 1&3 £1.60 CSF £6.06 TOTE £2.60: £1.20, £1.50, £1.10; EX 7.10.
Owner Hamdan Al Maktoum **Bred** Shadwell Estate Co Ltd **Trained** Lambourn, Berks

FOCUS
An average fillies' maiden run at a steady early pace. Just fair form, but the winner made a pleasing start.

NOTEBOOK
Hawaafez ◆ built on her debut third over C&D 13 days previously, as was expected, and got off the mark with a ready effort. She travelled best of all and it was clear from 2f out she would take the beating. This daughter of Nayef still showed her inexperience when asked to win the race, so there really ought to be more to come and she should relish being faced with more of a test next year. Her trainer later said she will now be put away for a turf campaign. (op 11-10)
Baisse ◆, aboard whom Kelly Harrison was having her first ride for the yard, is a half-sister to the dual Group 3 winner Azmeel, who was also a debut winner over 7f at two. She too travelled kindly and, while ultimately put in her place by the winner, left the distinct impression she would come on sufficiently to win one of these on her next assignment. (op 9-2)
Al Khatma posted an encouraging debut effort over 7f at Wolverhampton last month and rates the benchmark. She spoilt her chance by running too keen early on, but that was down to the lack of pace and she can be rated a bit better than the bare form. Unfortunately she was dismounted after the finish, though, and was found to have finished lame behind so could be set for a spell on the sidelines. Official explanation: vet said filly finished lame behind (op 11-4)
Twin Soul(IRE) was last seen finishing out the back on her debut over 7f at Kempton in June. She got markedly outpaced as the race became serious, but stayed on very nicely once straightening up for home. Her pedigree strongly suggests a further step up in trip is required and she ought to have no trouble winning races as she matures. (op 25-1)
Igitur, a long way behind the winner on her debut, posted a more encouraging effort from the front and will be eligible for a mark after her next outing.
Secoya wasn't given a hard time when beaten off the home turn and, another who should peak over longer trips, is now qualified for nurseries. She was reported to have run too free. Official explanation: jockey said that the filly ran too freely
Movingly(USA), well bred, looked a likely sort on her debut for her leading stable, but she proved weak on the market and was far too green. She doesn't have that much scope, but will get further and surely leave this behind with further experience. (op 7-1)

7734 TOTEQUADPOT NURSERY 6f (P)
1:50 (1:50) (Class 4) (0-85,76) 2-Y-O £2,428 (£722; £361; £180) Stalls Low

Form RPR
3122 **1** **Forty Proof (IRE)**[25] 7423 2-9-7 76 (v) ShaneKelly 5 79
(W J Knight) *stdd s: hld up in last pair: hdwy to chse ldng pair ent fnl 2f: rdn to chal and hung lft ent fnl f: led wl ins fnl f: kpt on* **5/2**[2]
0021 **2** hd **Liberty Green (IRE)**[17] 7517 2-9-0 69 JamesDoyle 3 71
(A J McCabe) *w ldr: rdn to ld jst over 2f out: hrd pressed 1f out: hdd wl ins fnl f: unable qck nr fin* **10/3**
0460 **3** 3 1/2 **Welsh Inlet (IRE)**[13] 7552 2-8-8 63 NeilChalmers 1 55
(J J Bridger) *racd keenly: led for 1f: chsd ldrs after: swtchd rt over 1f out: nt gng pce of ldng pair ins fnl f* **20/1**
004 **4** 1 **Zeavola (IRE)**[17] 7517 2-8-10 65 DavidProbert 4 54
(A M Balding) *stdd and swtchd lft s: hld up in last pair: effrt to chse ldrs on inner and drvn over 1f out: outpcd ins fnl f* **9/4**[1]
0216 **5** 1 **Magic Stella**[17] 7528 2-9-6 75 DaneO'Neill 2 61
(A P Jarvis) *w ldr: led after 1f tl rdn and hdd jst over 1f out: wknd ins fnl f* **3/1**[3]

1m 12.42s (0.52) **Going Correction** +0.025s/f (Slow) 5 Ran SP% **112.2**
Speed ratings (Par 98): **97,96,92,90,89**
CSF £11.31 TOTE £2.30: £1.10, £1.90; EX 8.30.
Owner G Roddick **Bred** David Jamison Bloodstock And G Roddick **Trained** Patching, W Sussex

FOCUS
A moderate little nursery. There was a decent pace on and the first pair came well clear in a tight finish. The form is rated around the front pair.

NOTEBOOK
Forty Proof(IRE), a runner-up over 5f the last twice, gained a much-deserved success and got up with a bit more in hand than the bare margin suggests. He was given a well-judged ride from off the pace and, kept to the middle of the track off the home turn, was always just doing enough near the business end. Despite sporting a visor there is little wrong with his attitude and, now due to be put away for the year, he is open to further progression over this trip. (op 15-8)
Liberty Green(IRE) has improved since switching to Polytrack and got off the mark in a maiden over 5f here 17 days earlier. She deserves extra credit as she did plenty on the front end and still only just lost out, clearly getting the extra furlong. Compensation is probably not far off. (op 7-2 tchd 3-1)
Welsh Inlet(IRE), taken back off the solid early pace, was near last at the furlong marker. She kept on well down the centre when held, however, and this was a return to something like her best on her second outing for connections. (tchd 25-1)
Zeavola(IRE) was not far behind the runner-up here last time and was 4lb better off on this nursery debut, so it wasn't that surprising to see her come in for decent support. She never looked that happy after a sluggish start, though, and was held on the inside before stamina for the extra furlong really became an issue. (op 5-2 tchd 11-4)
Magic Stella, back down in trip, was well backed late on but she did too much on the front end and paid the price after turning for home. (op 9-2)

7735 TOTETRIFECTA FLEXI BETTING H'CAP 1m (P)
2:20 (2:21) (Class 3) (0-95,92) 3-Y-O+ £5,504 (£1,637; £818; £408) Stalls High

Form RPR
0056 **1** **Mafeking (UAE)**[10] 7591 6-9-3 88 ChrisCatlin 1 96
(M R Hoad) *t.k.h early: chsd ldr: rdn to chse ldr ent fnl 2f: outpcd wl over 1f out: styd on wl u.p ins fnl f to ld fnl 50yds* **15/2**
4320 **2** 1 **Baylini**[10] 7591 6-9-3 88 JamesDoyle 3 94+
(J A Osborne) *hld up in tch in midfield: effrt and rdn wl over 1f out: kpt on wl u.p ins fnl f: wnt 2nd towards fin* **5/2**[1]
2060 **3** 1/2 **Layline (IRE)**[45] 7083 3-9-4 90 AdamKirby 7 95
(M Botti) *stdd s: hld up in tch in rr: effrt on inner wl over 1f out: kpt on ins fnl f: snatched 3rd last stride* **4/1**[3]
5604 **4** shd **Suffolk Punch (IRE)**[3] 7688 3-8-8 80 (v) DavidProbert 2 85
(A M Balding) *led: rdn and qcknd clr wl over 1f out: drvn and tired ins fnl f: hdd and lost 3 pls fnl 50yds* **9/1**
2461 **5** 1/2 **Zebrano**[10] 7597 4-8-11 82 (b) RobertHavlin 8 85+
(A B Haynes) *stdd s: hld up in last pair: effrt and swtchd rt over 1f out: kpt on u.p ins fnl f* **11/2**
-021 **6** 1 3/4 **The Fifth Member (IRE)**[38] 7227 6-9-4 89 StephenCraine 5 88
(J R Boyle) *chsd ldr tl ent fnl 2f: rdn and unable qck wl over 1f out: styd on same pce ins fnl f* **7/2**[2]
0106 **7** 8 **Sarah Park (IRE)**[25] 7430 5-9-3 88 ShaneKelly 9 69
(B J Meehan) *chsd ldrs: rdn and struggling over 2f out: wl btn over 1f out* **12/1**

0000 **8** *15* **Big Bay (USA)**[25] 7430 4-8-7 85..................................(p) LewisWalsh(7) 6 32
(Jane Chapple-Hyam) *in tch: dropped in rr and pushed along over 4f out: rdn over 2f out: sn lost tch* **16/1**

1m 35.83s (-2.37) **Going Correction** +0.025s/f (Slow) course record
WFA 3 from 4yo+ 1lb **8** Ran SP% **121.5**
Speed ratings (Par 107): **112,111,110,110,109 108,100,85**
toteswingers:1&2 £5.20, 2&3 £4.70, 1&3 £7.60 CSF £28.44 CT £90.24 TOTE £13.10: £3.00, £1.30, £1.60; EX 29.60 Trifecta £112.90 Pool: £695.74 - 4.56 winning units..
Owner Mrs J E Taylor **Bred** Darley **Trained** Lewes, E Sussex

FOCUS
This fair handicap was another race run at something of an uneven pace and it proved hard to get seriously involved from off the speed. Ordinary form, with a bunch finish.

NOTEBOOK
Mafeking(UAE) bounced back to winning ways with a decent effort on this first outing over 1m since 2007. He wasn't able to dictate on this drop back in trip and hit a flat spot as the front-running Suffolk Punch kicked for home, but as that rival began to toil late on he found his full stride. He was always going to get up where it mattered and it was another deserved success for this consistent 6-y-o, but his profile dictates he is one to take on again next time. (op 7-1 tchd 13-2 and 8-1)
Baylini ◆, back down in trip, travelled kindly off the pace but was another caught out when the pace lifted around 3f out. Four of her five career wins have been over 1m2f and her turn isn't looking far off again. (op 9-2 tchd 5-1)
Layline(IRE) came in for solid support on this debut for new connections, who originally purchased him with a view to being a lead horse for their Group 1 winner Gitano Hernando. His best form had come in two out of three previous outings on the AW, including over C&D in July, but he has developed into a tricky sort and his usual blinkers were abandoned. He didn't find the race run to suit here and is capable of stepping up on this. (op 5-1 tchd 3-1)
Suffolk Punch(IRE), with the visor back on, dictated pretty much as he pleased and made a bold bid rounding the home turn. It looked as though he may have done enough passing the furlong marker, but although things may have been a little different had he kept away from the far rail, he was treading water near the finish. This was just his third outing on the AW and he should be capable of winning a race this winter, but he has to rate as somewhat flattered here. (op 8-1 tchd 10-1)
Zebrano, 9lb higher than when winning at Kempton ten days earlier, was found out by the way the race unfolded and should be given another chance. (op 5-1)
The Fifth Member(IRE) was 3lb higher for scoring at Ayr in October. He proved a bit free up with the early pace and was beat off the home turn. (op 10-3)

7736 TOTEEXACTA FLEXI BETTING H'CAP 1m 4f (P)
2:50 (2:50) (Class 4) (0-85,83) 3-Y-O+ **£2,914** (£867; £433; £216) **Stalls** Low

Form RPR
5431 **1** **Kiss A Prince**[40] 7190 4-9-4 76..(b) AdamKirby 9 84+
(D K Ivory) *stdd and dropped in bhd after s: hld up in tch in rr: gd hdwy on inner ent fnl 2f: rdn to ld over 1f out: styd on wl* **3/1**[1]
2 *3/4* **Al Amaan**[28] 5-8-12 70.. DavidProbert 8 76
(G L Moore) *t.k.h early: hld up in tch: effrt and swtchd rt over 1f out: hrd drvn and styd on wl ins fnl f: wnt 2nd fnl 50yds* **33/1**
06 **3** *3/4* **Bedouin Bay**[13] 7553 3-8-12 75... JamesDoyle 7 80
(A J McCabe) *t.k.h: chsd ldrs: rdn to chse ldr ent fnl 2f: ev ch over 1f out tl ins fnl f: styd on same pce fnl 150yds* **7/1**
114- **4** *3 1/2* **Benhego**[562] 1007 5-9-10 82... AmirQuinn 5 81
(G L Moore) *led tl over 6f out: clsd on ldr jst over 2f out: rdn and unable qck wl over 1f out: styd on same pce and hld ins fnl f* **16/1**
321 **5** *1 3/4* **Treacle Tart**[29] 7381 5-8-12 70.. RobertWinston 1 66
(P Charalambous) *t.k.h: hld up in tch in midfield: switching rt and effrt bnd 2f out: outpcd and no threat to ldrs fr over 1f out* **7/2**[2]
0013 **6** *1 1/4* **Rosco Flyer (IRE)**[34] 7292 4-9-4 76................................. DaneO'Neill 6 70
(R A Teal) *hld up in tch: rdn and effrt jst over 2f out: wknd wl over 1f out: wl hld ins fnl f* **5/1**[3]
1 **7** *1 1/2* **Humor Me Rene (USA)**[19] 7495 3-8-6 72............... MatthewDavies(3) 2 64
(George Baker) *hld up in tch: rdn and struggling whn wd bnd 2f out: wknd and wl hld whn hung lft over 1f out* **10/1**
-061 **8** *3/4* **Traphalgar (IRE)**[11] 7570 5-8-7 72..............................(vt) KevinLundie(7) 4 63
(P D Evans) *t.k.h: chsd ldr 9f out tl led over 6f out: sn clr: rdn and c bk to field jst over 2f out: hdd over 1f out: sn wknd* **20/1**
9 *4* **Battleoftrafalgar**[57] 6824 3-9-6 83.................................. NickyMackay 3 67
(M J Attwater) *chsd ldr tl 9f out: styd prom: rdn and struggling 4f out: bhd fnl 2f* **7/2**[2]

2m 32.21s (-0.79) **Going Correction** +0.025s/f (Slow)
WFA 3 from 4yo+ 5lb **9** Ran SP% **121.3**
Speed ratings (Par 105): **103,102,102,99,98 97,96,96,93**
toteswingers:1&2 £19.10, 2&3 £26.20, 1&3 £7.20 CSF £105.23 CT £662.98 TOTE £4.20: £1.40, £7.30, £2.30; EX 142.30.
Owner A Pryer **Bred** Baroness, Magnusson, Myriade, Redmyre **Trained** Radlett, Herts

FOCUS
A modest handicap and yet another race run at a muddling pace, so the form has not been rated too positively.
Humor Me Rene(USA) Official explanation: jockey said that the filly hung left

7737 TOTEPOOL A BETTER WAY TO BET H'CAP 7f (P)
3:20 (3:22) (Class 5) (0-75,74) 3-Y-O+ **£1,876** (£554; £277) **Stalls** Low

Form RPR
6003 **1** **Hinton Admiral**[20] 7483 6-9-0 70............................ MichaelStainton(3) 2 77
(P Howling) *a travelling strly: chsd ldr: rdn to chal jst over 1f out: led ins fnl f: r.o wl* **7/2**[2]
0114 **2** *1/2* **Tevez**[1] 7724 5-9-7 74...(p) CathyGannon 6 80+
(D Donovan) *hld up in last trio: rdn and hdwy ent fnl 2f: nt clr run and swtchd rt ent fnl f: rn wl ins fnl f: nt rch wnr* **5/2**[1]
2550 **3** *3/4* **Yankee Storm**[17] 7525 5-9-3 70.......................................(v) JimmyQuinn 7 74
(H J Collingridge) *bmpd s: chsd ldrs: shkn up and effrt ent fnl 2f: kpt on u.p ins fnl f* **9/2**[3]
1006 **4** *1/2* **Starwatch**[35] 7285 3-9-0 67.. NeilChalmers 4 69
(J J Bridger) *chsd ldrs: rdn along over 2f out: drvn over 1f out: kpt on same pce ins fnl f* **33/1**
6102 **5** *1* **Pipers Piping (IRE)**[9] 7614 4-8-4 64.......................(v) LauraSimpson(7) 1 64
(P Howling) *led: urged along over 1f out: hdd ins fnl f: no ex fnl 100yds* **14/1**
0002 **6** *3/4* **Nubar Boy**[27] 7391 3-8-9 62..(v) MartinLane 5 60
(P D Evans) *t.k.h: hld up in tch in midfield: rdn and unable qck over 1f out: edgd rt and styd on same pce ins fnl f* **9/1**
0000 **7** *1/2* **Sarah's Art (IRE)**[17] 7525 7-9-5 72...................................(t) AdamKirby 9 68
(Stef Higgins) *stdd and dropped in bhd after s: hld up in tch in last trio: effrt on outer bnd ent fnl 2f: styd in same pce fr over 1f out* **16/1**
0000 **8** *4* **Durham Town (IRE)**[141] 4206 3-8-10 63.............................. ChrisCatlin 8 48
(D K Ivory) *short of room s: hld up in last trio: rdn and effrt wl over 1f out: no prog and wl hld ent fnl f* **10/1**

4460 **9** *1/2* **Spinning Bailiwick**[47] 7047 4-9-0 67 ow1....................... GeorgeBaker 10 51
(G L Moore) *wnt lft s: hld up in tch in midfield: rdn and unable qck wl over 1f out: sn wknd* **11/2**
2160 **10** *3 1/4* **Tous Les Deux**[181] 2866 7-8-13 66................................... FergusSweeney 3 41
(Dr J R J Naylor) *taken down early: hld up in last trio: rdn and wknd wl over 1f out* **25/1**

1m 24.47s (-0.33) **Going Correction** +0.025s/f (Slow) **10** Ran SP% **122.8**
Speed ratings (Par 103): **102,101,100,100,98 98,97,92,92,88**
toteswingers:1&2 £4.30, 2&3 £5.10, 1&3 £7.80 totesuper7: Win: 2100.00. Place: £11.30. CSF £13.47 CT £42.66 TOTE £6.80: £2.70, £1.30, £1.40; EX 25.90.
Owner Rory Murphy **Bred** Gainsborough Stud Management Ltd **Trained** Newmarket, Suffolk

FOCUS
An ordinary handicap run at an average pace, and again it paid to race handily. The form is rated around the runner-up.
T/Jkpt: Not won. T/Plt: £81.30 to a £1 stake. Pool of £95,341.61 - 855.57 winning tickets. T/Qpdt: £24.80 to a £1 stake. Pool of £9,782.59 - 291.23 winning tickets. SP

7729 SOUTHWELL (L-H)
Tuesday, December 7

OFFICIAL GOING: Standard to slow (abandoned after race 3 due to freezing fog and poor visibility)
Wind: almost nil Weather: very cold, foggy

7738 HOSPITALITY AT SOUTHWELL RACECOURSE H'CAP (DIV I) 6f (F)
12:00 (12:02) (Class 6) (0-60,58) 3-Y-O+ **£1,364** (£403; £201) **Stalls** Low

Form RPR
3034 **1** **Cape Of Storms**[14] 7542 7-9-7 58..(b) TomEaves 2 68
(R Brotherton) *mde all: clr 2f out: styd on strly* **11/4**[1]
0060 **2** *3 1/4* **Sir Louis**[51] 6965 3-9-4 55.. PhillipMakin 8 55
(R A Fahey) *chsd ldrs thrght* **9/1**
5021 **3** *3/4* **Boy The Bell**[12] 7563 3-8-13 57...............................(e[1]) JosephYoung(7) 6 54+
(M Mullineaux) *off pce after 2f: hdwy over 2f out: styd on* **7/2**[2]
5000 **4** *2 3/4* **Memphis Man**[49] 7007 7-8-10 54........................... MatthewCosham(7) 1 42
(P D Evans) *s.s: in rr after 2f and over 2f out: nrst fin* **22/1**
0050 **5** *3/4* **Fathey (IRE)**[14] 7537 4-8-12 49.. AndreaAtzeni 10 35
(C Smith) *chsd ldrs: one pce fnl 2f* **13/2**
050 **6** *1/2* **Dispol Grand (IRE)**[40] 7195 4-9-3 57.............................. PaulPickard(3) 7 41
(P T Midgley) *chsng ldrs after 2f and over 2f out: wknd clsng stages* **10/1**
0506 **7** *1 1/2* **Liel**[51] 6952 4-9-4 55.. LukeMorris 5 35
(B J Meehan) *chsd ldrs: rdn and outpcd over 2f out* **6/1**[3]
4006 **8** *2 1/2* **Hart Of Gold**[29] 7380 6-8-3 47...(b) JakePayne(7) 4 19
(R A Harris) *chsd ldrs: wkng 2f out* **8/1**
0050 **9** *6* **Norse Warrior (USA)**[99] 5579 4-8-8 45.......................... RobbieFitzpatrick 3 —
(Peter Grayson) *reluctant to go to s: a bhd* **66/1**

1m 20.58s (4.08) **Going Correction** +0.725s/f (Slow) **9** Ran SP% **112.6**
Speed ratings (Par 101): **101,96,95,92,91 90,88,85,77**
toteswingers:1&2 £5.50, 2&3 £6.80, 1&3 £1.80 CSF £27.40 CT £87.44 TOTE £3.40: £1.40, £2.10, £1.30; EX 19.90 Trifecta £98.60 Pool: £140.10 - 98.60 winning units..
Owner Arthur Clayton **Bred** R J Turner **Trained** Elmley Castle, Worcs

FOCUS
Another bitterly cold night in which temperatures dipped to -15c. The track was worked again throughout the night and, not surprisingly, the Fibresand surface was on the slow side. Thick fog meant visibility was severely restricted. Mainly exposed performers in a moderate handicap in which very few arrived in peak form. The gallop seemed an ordinary one (6 seconds slower than Racing Post Standard) and the winner came down the centre in the straight. He is been rated to his best form of the past year.

7739 BET SP+ WITH TOTESPORT 0800 221221 NURSERY 5f (F)
12:30 (12:30) (Class 5) (0-75,79) 2-Y-O **£2,115** (£624; £312) **Stalls** High

Form RPR
221 **1** **Monsieur Jamie**[27] 7392 2-8-13 67....................................... GregFairley 4 70
(J R Jenkins) *w ldr: styd on to ld ins fnl f* **10/3**[2]
5541 **2** *3/4* **Flash City (ITY)**[3] 7696 2-9-4 79 6ex.............................. AdamCarter(7) 5 79
(B Smart) *led: hdd and no ex ins fnl f* **5/4**[1]
0053 **3** *4* **Irish Boy (IRE)**[3] 7696 2-7-12 52 oh3................................ AndreaAtzeni 2 38
(W J H Ratcliffe) *chsd ldng trio: styd on: nrst fin* **10/1**
2612 **4** *1* **Crimson Cloud**[10] 7592 2-9-7 75... TomEaves 1 57
(R A Fahey) *chsd ldrs: wknd over 1f out* **9/2**[3]
5354 **5** *hd* **Silk Bounty**[10] 7598 2-8-6 63..(p) JamesSullivan(3) 3 45
(J G Given) *sn drvn along and outpcd: nvr a threat* **6/1**

62.33 secs (2.63) **Going Correction** +0.375s/f (Slow) **5** Ran SP% **109.1**
Speed ratings (Par 96): **93,91,85,83,83**
CSF £7.82 TOTE £4.10: £1.60, £1.10; EX 8.70.
Owner Mark Goldstein & Stephen Pettman **Bred** Greg Parsons **Trained** Royston, Herts

FOCUS
Only five runners but a fair handicap in which all the field had been running creditably. The gallop was a reasonable one and the first two, who finished clear, raced towards the centre. The form makes sense as rated but is best treated with a degree of caution given the lack of visibility.

NOTEBOOK
Monsieur Jamie ◆ is a progressive sort who bettered the form of his maiden win to make it two wins from as many starts over this course-and-distance. There's room for further improvement, he should prove equally effective back over 6f and he should remain competitive after reassessment. (op 7-2 tchd 3-1)
Flash City(ITY) ◆ had created a good impression when winning his previous start over this course-and-distance and he ran creditably against a previous winner under his penalty (due to go up the same amount in future). He pulled clear of the remainder, is well worth a try on Polytrack and there are more races to be won with him. (op 11-10 tchd 6-4)
Irish Boy(IRE) had shown improved form over this course-and-distance when third to Flash City on his previous start and he was far from disgraced against a couple of progressive previous winners after again racing from out of the handicap. He shapes as though the return to 6f will suit and he's not one to write off yet. (op 11-1 tchd 12-1)
Crimson Cloud, the only filly in the field, had been progressing nicely on Polytrack but failed to reproduce the pick of that form on this Fibresand debut from this 5lb higher mark. Presumably the switch back to that quicker surface will now be on the cards and she will be worth another chance. (op 4-1)

Silk Bounty, with the cheekpieces fitted for the return to handicap company on this Fibresand debut, was never travelling with much fluency and failed to match his recent Polytrack form. The return to that surface could suit better but he doesn't look one to place too much faith in. (op 8-1)

7740 SP+ FOR BIGGER WINS AT TOTESPORT.COM H'CAP 5f (F)

1:00 (1:00) (Class 3) (0-95,92) 3-Y-O+ **£5,828** (£1,734; £866; £432) **Stalls** High

Form RPR

5023 **1** **Love Delta (USA)**[3] 7697 3-9-7 **92** .... GregFairley 6 105
(M Johnston) *slipped s and lost many l: gd hdwy stands' side 2f out: led jst ins fnl f: sn clr: v readily* **4/1**[2]

0331 **2** *5* **Bonnie Prince Blue**[14] 7539 7-8-4 **78** oh3 .... (be) JamesSullivan(3) 1 73
(B Ellison) *sn wl outpcd: hdwy on wd outside over 1f out: styd on to take n.d 2nd nr fin* **8/1**

1462 **3** *1 ¼* **Silaah**[7] 7635 6-8-10 **84** ow1 .... (p) MichaelO'Connell(3) 7 75
(D Nicholls) *w ldr: led and edgd bdly lft over 2f out: hdd jst ins fnl f: lost 2nd towards fin* **7/1**

6032 **4** *1* **Lenny Bee**[22] 7466 4-9-0 **92** .... PNolan(7) 2 79
(D H Brown) *w ldrs on outside: drvn 3f out: kpt on one pce* **5/1**[3]

6201 **5** *½* **Cape Vale (IRE)**[3] 7697 5-9-4 **89** 6ex .... AdrianNicholls 5 74
(D Nicholls) *led tl over 2f out: fdd ins fnl f* **5/2**[1]

0000 **6** *½* **Luscivious**[60] 6723 6-9-7 **92** .... (b) IanMongan 4 75
(D Nicholls) *w ldrs: drvn 3f out: fdd appr fnl f* **12/1**

0230 **7** *9* **Nickel Silver**[37] 7254 5-9-6 **91** .... (v) TomEaves 3 42
(B Smart) *w ldrs on outer: drvn 3f out: lost pl over 1f out: eased towards fin* **6/1**

60.36 secs (0.66) **Going Correction** +0.375s/f (Slow) 7 Ran SP% **110.8**
Speed ratings (Par 107): **109,101,99,97,96 95,81**
toteswingers:1&2 £4.20, 2&3 £6.80, 1&3 £7.10 CSF £32.76 TOTE £4.10: £2.00, £5.60; EX 33.60.
Owner Crone Stud Farms Ltd **Bred** Palides Investments N V Inc & Hair 'Em Corporation **Trained** Middleham Moor, N Yorks

FOCUS
A decent-quality handicap and a strong pace (almost 2 seconds quicker than the previous nursery) in the conditions saw the two that struggled to go the early pace come to the fore late on. The winner raced towards the stands side. Visibility was slightly better than for the two previous races but the remainder of the meeting was subsequently abandoned on safety grounds.

NOTEBOOK
Love Delta(USA) had finished third to Cape Vale over 6f here last weekend but comprehensively reversed placings with that rival over this shorter trip, despite losing many lengths after slipping at the start, in a race where the five that vied for the lead fell in a hole late on. He looks flattered by the winning margin given the way things panned out and will find life tough after reassessment if the handicapper takes this literally but he is bordering on smart on Fibresand and he will be worth a second look if turned out under a penalty returned to 7f (well worth another try at that trip) on Sunday. (op 10-3)
Bonnie Prince Blue ◆, 6lb higher than when scoring in a lesser grade over 6f on his previous visit to the track, wasn't disgraced considering this trip (even in a strongly run race) provided an insufficient test of stamina. The return to 6f will suit and this largely consistent sort, who stays 7f and acts on Polytrack, is capable of winning again from his proper mark (3lb out of handicap) this winter. (op 10-1 tchd 15-2)
Silaah fared the best (albeit narrowly) of those that helped to force a strong gallop on this Fibresand debut, despite hanging under pressure when hitting the front. This dual Polytrack winner is effective from 5f-7f, may not want to be in front as soon as he was here and he should be able to make amends in the coming months. (op 8-1)
Lenny Bee was easy to back near the off but ran creditably after racing up with the decent gallop on this Fibresand debut. He's a Polytrack winner and may be better suited to that surface but he's vulnerable to anything progressive or well-handicapped from his current mark in the low-90s. (op 7-2)
Cape Vale(IRE) had today's winner back in third when winning on his Fibresand debut last weekend but failed to build on that under his penalty returned to 5f in a race where the leaders went off too quickly in the deep conditions. However he'll be worth another chance on the surface over either sprint distance when it looks as though he will be able to dominate. (op 3-1)
Luscivious, having his first run after a short break and his first for a new stable, has been generally disappointing since making all over this course and distance in August and he was again below his best. He's high enough in the weights at present but is the type to win again when his current trainer finds the key to him. (op 11-1)
Nickel Silver, a real speedball, hadn't been at his best on his previous start in October and disappointed back on Fibresand, even allowing for the fact he was never going to be seen to best effect in this deep ground after being taken on for the lead. (op 8-1)

7741 BET ON TONIGHT'S FOOTBALL AT TOTESPORT.COM H'CAP 1m 6f (F)

() (Class 6) (0-60,) 3-Y-O+ £

7742 40 LIVE FOOTBALL MARKETS AT TOTESPORT.COM H'CAP 1m 3f (F)

() (Class 6) (0-65,) 3-Y-O+ £

7743 MEMBERSHIP AT SOUTHWELL GOLF CLUB CLASSIFIED CLAIMING STKS 6f (F)

() (Class 6) 3-Y-O+ £

7744 BOOK YOUR TICKETS ON LINE AT SOUTHWELL-RACECOURSE.CO.UK H'CAP 7f (F)

() (Class 6) (0-60,) 3-Y-O+ £

7745 HOSPITALITY AT SOUTHWELL RACECOURSE H'CAP (DIV II) 6f (F)

() (Class 6) (0-60,) 3-Y-O+ £

T/Plt: £4.20 to a £1 stake. Pool of £76132.89 - 1298.08 winning tickets. T/Qpdt: £1.70 to a £1 stake. Pool of £5189.71 - 2141.20 winning tickets. WG

7750 - 7753a (Foreign Racing) - See Raceform Interactive

7686 KEMPTON (A.W) (R-H)

Wednesday, December 8

OFFICIAL GOING: Standard
Wind: Moderate, against Weather: Fine, cold

7754 RACING AT SKYSPORTS.COM H'CAP 5f (P)

2:20 (2:20) (Class 5) (0-75,75) 3-Y-O+ **£2,286** (£675; £337) **Stalls** High

Form RPR

1265 **1** **Desert Strike**[5] 7683 4-8-7 **61** .... (p) NeilChalmers 10 70
(A J McCabe) *hld up bhd ldrs on inner: effrt to go 2nd ent fnl f: shkn up and fnd enough to ld last 100yds* **9/2**[2]

0013 **2** *¾* **Love You Louis**[14] 7549 4-9-5 **73** .... EddieAhern 8 79
(J R Jenkins) *led against rail: rdn over 1f out: hdd and nt qckn last 100yds* **7/2**[1]

41 **3** *1 ¼* **Danzoe (IRE)**[25] 7442 3-9-1 **72** .... KierenFox(3) 3 74
(Mrs C A Dunnett) *pushed along to chse ldrs: rdn to dispute 2nd over 1f out: one pce fnl f* **13/2**

0 **4** *hd* **Boragh Jamal (IRE)**[14] 7556 3-8-11 **65** .... (b) ShaneKelly 11 66+
(B J Meehan) *settled in last trio: looking for room over 1f out: prog fnl f: styd on wl nr fin* **11/2**[3]

5463 **5** *hd* **Lord Of The Reins (IRE)**[36] 7285 6-9-0 **68** .... TomEaves 2 68
(J G Given) *settled in last: prog on inner over 1f out: drvn and kpt on same pce fnl f* **6/1**

0266 **6** *hd* **Feelin Foxy**[23] 7466 6-9-4 **75** .... JamesSullivan(3) 4 74
(J G Given) *chsd ldrs and wdst of all: nt qckn wl over 1f out: one pce after* **13/2**

005 **7** *nk* **Triple Dream**[12] 7571 5-9-0 **68** .... (p) RussKennemore 7 66
(J M Bradley) *prom: rdn to chse ldr 2f out to 1f out: fdd nr fin* **14/1**

0151 **8** *7* **La Capriosa**[27] 7405 4-9-2 **75** .... BillyCray(5) 1 48
(D Nicholls) *sn rdn to stay in tch: wknd over 1f out* **14/1**

4160 **9** *4* **Cloth Ears**[12] 7571 4-8-7 **61** .... CathyGannon 6 20
(P S McEntee) *chsd ldr to 2f out: wknd rapidly over 1f out* **25/1**

59.55 secs (-0.95) **Going Correction** +0.025s/f (Slow) 9 Ran SP% **113.9**
Speed ratings (Par 103): **108,106,104,104,104 103,103,92,85**
toteswingers:1&2:£3.70, 1&3:£5.20, 2&3:£3.30 CSF £20.33 CT £101.05 TOTE £6.00: £1.70, £1.40, £1.40; EX 22.00.
Owner Mrs M J McCabe **Bred** Mrs Mary Rowlands **Trained** Averham Park, Notts

FOCUS
Three of the first four home in this moderate sprint handicap came from the top three stalls. Straightforward form.

7755 CHRISTMAS AT THE PANORAMIC MAIDEN AUCTION STKS 1m 2f (P)

2:50 (2:52) (Class 5) 2-Y-O **£2,286** (£675; £337) **Stalls** High

Form RPR

3402 **1** **Ivan Vasilevich (IRE)**[9] 7631 2-8-12 **61** .... ShaneKelly 7 70
(Jane Chapple-Hyam) *mde all: set stdy pce tl over 3f out: kpt on wl* **4/1**[3]

0 **2** *1 ¼* **Rosaria**[39] 7231 2-8-9 **0** .... EddieAhern 5 65
(R Hannon) *chsd wnr: rdn over 3f out: nt qckn fnl 2f* **8/1**

46 **3** *¾* **Duke Of Florence (IRE)**[18] 7530 2-9-0 **0** .... SteveDrowne 4 68
(R Hannon) *nvr gng wl: mostly 4th tl kpt on to take 3rd last 100yds* **5/2**[2]

22 **4** *nk* **Copper Canyon**[39] 7242 2-8-9 **0** .... FergusSweeney 6 63
(A B Haynes) *chsd ldng pair: rdn over 1f out: one pce and lost 3rd last 100yds* **6/4**[1]

5 *2 ¼* **Heavenly Music (IRE)** 2-8-7 **0** .... DavidProbert 1 57
(S Kirk) *hld up in last: rdn over 3f out: nvr on terms* **25/1**

6 *4 ½* **Larimar (IRE)** 2-8-10 **0** .... TomEaves 8 52
(Mrs A J Perrett) *dwlt: in tch tl 3f out: wknd* **12/1**

5405 **7** *nse* **Blaze On By**[7] 7650 2-8-6 **50** .... NeilChalmers 2 48
(J J Bridger) *t.k.h: hld up: wknd 3f out* **100/1**

2m 12.14s (4.14) **Going Correction** +0.025s/f (Slow) 7 Ran SP% **112.2**
Speed ratings (Par 96): **84,83,82,82,80 76,76**
toteswingers:1&2:£4.70, 1&3:£2.00, 2&3:£3.60 CSF £33.63 TOTE £5.00: £3.40, £4.80; EX 37.70.
Owner Chris Fahy **Bred** Liam Butler **Trained** Dalham, Suffolk

FOCUS
The winning time of the opening handicap suggested the track was riding quicker than of late. This ordinary juvenile maiden was run at an uneven pace and, with the winner making all, there wasn't much change in the order throughout. The winner built on his recent nursery form.

NOTEBOOK
Ivan Vasilevich(IRE) deservedly shed his maiden tag at the eighth attempt courtesy of being granted an uncontested lead. He quickened up when asked for an effort off the home turn, which caught his rivals out, and was always doing enough from then on. He was beaten a short head off his current mark when held up over 1m2f last time, but the positive tactics over this sharper test obviously did the trick. (op 3-1 tchd 11-4)
Rosaria ◆ was her trainer's second-string looking at the betting, but she showed the clear benefit of her Newmarket debut in October and posted a much-improved effort. She lacks a turn of foot and her pedigree strongly suggests a longer trip will be up her street, so she ought to be winning when faced with more of a test. (op 12-1)
Duke Of Florence(IRE) looked sure to enjoy this longer trip and was well supported. He went in snatches from a very early stage, however, and does look a lazy sort. Perhaps some headgear would sharpen him up, but this was just his third outing and he would've been seen to better effect off a stronger pace. He also now has the option of handicaps. (op 4-1 tchd 9-2)
Copper Canyon had finished runner-up on his two previous outings and looked to have found an ideal opportunity to go one better. He wasn't at all suited by the way the race unfolded, though, and he really needs an end-to-end gallop over this trip. Indeed, he ought to peak as he steps up in trip next year, and he does now qualify for a mark. (op 6-5)
Heavenly Music(IRE) proved distinctly green through the early parts. She did show ability when asked to close from 2f out, but rather flattened out inside the final furlong and this debut experience was much needed. She is another here that is bred to enjoy a stiffer test. (op 20-1)

7756 DIGIBET.COM H'CAP 1m 2f (P)

3:20 (3:24) (Class 4) (0-85,85) 3-Y-O+ **£3,885** (£1,156; £577; £288) **Stalls** High

Form RPR

0601 **1** **Franco Is My Name**[35] 7292 4-9-0 **81** .... KierenFox(3) 4 88+
(P R Hedger) *reluctant to enter stalls and restless in them: hld up: rdn and prog on outer 3f out: led over 1f out: idled bdly: jst hld on* **11/4**[1]

6100 **2** *shd* **Dubai Crest**[11] 7591 4-9-7 **85** .... ShaneKelly 7 91
(Mrs A J Perrett) *hld up: trckd ldrs 3f out: chal on inner fnl f: jst failed* **14/1**

0043 **3** *hd* **Kidlat**[11] 7600 5-8-9 **73** .... GrahamGibbons 11 79
(A Bailey) *mde most tl 2f out: kpt on wl: jst hld* **6/1**[3]

135 **4** *nk* **Reverend Green (IRE)**[208] 917 4-8-12 **76** .... SteveDrowne 5 81
(C J Down) *t.k.h: cl up: upsides over 1f out: nt qckn* **40/1**

0030 **5** *¾* **Stand Guard**[26] 7428 6-9-1 **79** .... DavidProbert 8 83
(P Howling) *hld up: prog to chse ldrs 2f out: kpt on: nvr able to chal* **13/2**

3552 **6** *½* **The Which Doctor**[51] 6990 5-9-7 **85** .... (p) GeorgeBaker 2 88
(J Noseda) *hld up: prog and prom 1/2-way: led 2f out tl over 1f out: fnd nil* **9/2**[2]

3200 **7** *6* **I'm In The Pink (FR)**[27] 2922 6-8-7 **71** oh1 .... (v1) CathyGannon 3 62
(P D Evans) *a in rr: outpcd over 2f out* **33/1**

0001 **8** *1* **Follow The Flag (IRE)**[14] 7560 6-8-12 **79** .... (p) AndrewHeffernan(3) 6 68
(A J McCabe) *t.k.h in rr: wknd over 2f out* **8/1**

9 *2* **Major Victory (SAF)**[144] 3-8-7 **84** .... ChrisCatlin 10 59
(Miss Gay Kelleway) *t.k.h: mostly 2nd tl 4f out: sn wknd* **10/1**

1000 **10** *3 ½* **Marjury Daw (IRE)**[11] 7593 4-9-7 **85** .... TomEaves 12 63
(J G Given) *prom tl 3f out: wknd* **20/1**

4160 **11** *10* **Sequillo**[10] 7612 4-9-3 **81**....(b) EddieAhern 1 39
(R Hannon) *restless in stalls: prom tl 4f out: wknd: t.o* **12/1**

2m 7.18s (-0.82) **Going Correction** +0.025s/f (Slow)
WFA 3 from 4yo+ 3lb **11** Ran SP% **117.2**
Speed ratings (Par 105): **104,103,103,103,102 102,97,96,95,92 84**
toteswingers:1&2:£6.80, 1&3:£5.50, 2&3:£11.30 CSF £43.05 CT £217.45 TOTE £3.80: £1.70, £4.40, £2.50; EX 43.90.
Owner P C F Racing Ltd **Bred** J J Whelan **Trained** Dogmersfield, Hampshire

FOCUS
This fair handicap was run at a sound pace and the first six came clear late on, being closely covered at the finish. The winner did not need to improve.

7757 DIGIBET CASINO MAIDEN STKS 6f (P)
3:50 (3:52) (Class 5) 3-Y-O+ **£2,286** (£675; £337) **Stalls** High

Form RPR
0 **1** **But Beautiful (IRE)**[222] 1659 3-8-12 0.... EddieAhern 6 63+
(R A Mills) *in tch: pushed along and no prog over 2f out: gd hdwy over 1f out: styd on wl to ld last 100yds* **12/1**

3355 **2** *1 1/4* **Durgan**[8] 7640 4-9-3 57....(p) SteveDrowne 4 64
(Mrs L C Jewell) *prom: rdn to chal and upsides over 1f out: outpcd last 100yds* **9/2**[3]

42 **3** *1/2* **Red Rhythm**[20] 7498 3-9-3 0.... J-PGuillambert 5 63
(L M Cumani) *plld hrd: led after 1f: hrd rdn over 1f out: hdd last 100yds: b.b.v* **10/11**[1]

3022 **4** *1 3/4* **Papageno**[14] 7547 3-9-3 56.... GeorgeBaker 9 57
(J R Jenkins) *cl up: rdn to dispute 2nd 2f out: one pce after* **7/1**

32-0 **5** *2 1/4* **Co Dependent (USA)**[182] 2866 4-9-3 67.... FergusSweeney 2 50
(J A Osborne) *sn trckd ldrs: prog to dispute 2nd over 2f out: nt qckn over 1f out: wknd* **4/1**[2]

0604 **6** *3 1/4* **Dancing Again**[25] 7440 4-8-9 42.... KierenFox(3) 7 34
(E A Wheeler) *led 1f: chsd ldr tl over 2f out: wknd* **33/1**

650 **7** *1* **Gessabelle**[5] 7676 3-8-5 42....(t) LauraSimpson(7) 1 31
(P S McEntee) *racd wd: nvr on terms* **100/1**

05 **8** *2* **Quahadi (IRE)**[11] 7596 4-9-3 0....(t) ChrisCatlin 8 30
(C Gordon) *a in rr: wknd over 2f out* **50/1**

9 *25* **Intriguing Look** 3-8-12 0.... IanMongan 3 —
(P M Phelan) *s.i.s: sn t.o* **25/1**

1m 12.99s (-0.11) **Going Correction** +0.025s/f (Slow) **9** Ran SP% **120.5**
Speed ratings (Par 103): **101,99,98,96,93 89,87,85,51**
toteswingers:1&2:£6.00, 1&3:£4.00, 2&3:£1.80 CSF £66.32 TOTE £24.30: £3.70, £1.10, £1.40; EX 74.80.
Owner B Ecclestone, J Humphreys, T G Mills **Bred** Gerrardstown House Stud **Trained** Headley, Surrey

FOCUS
A weak maiden, run at a fair enough pace and there were changing fortunes in the home straight. The form is rated around the runner-up and fourth.
Red Rhythm Official explanation: jockey said colt bled from the nose

7758 DIGIBET NURSERY 1m (P)
4:20 (4:22) (Class 5) (0-75,74) 2-Y-O **£2,286** (£675; £337) **Stalls** High

Form RPR
001 **1** **Angelic Upstart (IRE)**[37] 7272 2-9-7 **74**.... DavidProbert 5 78
(A M Balding) *hld up in tch: rdn over 2f out: prog to ld over 1f out: edgd lft: kpt on* **11/8**[1]

0162 **2** *3/4* **Azlaa**[21] 7486 2-9-5 **72**.... EddieAhern 2 74
(R Hannon) *trckd ldrs: hung lft bnd 4f out to 3f out: tried to chal over 2f out: rallied to press wnr fnl f: a hld* **3/1**[2]

0512 **3** *2 1/4* **Imaginary World (IRE)**[15] 7536 2-9-3 **70**.... JamesDoyle 8 67
(A J McCabe) *sn led: hdd over 1f out: one pce* **7/1**

3224 **4** *1/2* **Suddenly Susan (IRE)**[33] 7324 2-9-1 **68**.... IanMongan 7 64
(D Nicholls) *mostly pressed ldr: upsides 2f out: rdr dropped whip over 1f out: nt qckn over 1f out* **4/1**[3]

0050 **5** *3* **History Repeating**[21] 7486 2-7-9 **55**....(p) IanBurns(7) 6 44
(M D I Usher) *reminder after 3f: sn dropped to last: nvr on terms after* **20/1**

3004 **6** *2 3/4* **Oliver's Gold**[21] 7486 2-8-8 **61**.... JimmyQuinn 1 44
(Mrs A J Perrett) *dwlt: prog fr rr over 2f out: wknd over 1f out* **5/1**

2500 **7** *13* **Loves Theme (IRE)**[21] 7486 2-8-11 **64**.... J-PGuillambert 3 17
(A Bailey) *chsd ldrs tl 1/2-way: wknd rapidly over 3f out: t.o* **66/1**

1m 40.09s (0.29) **Going Correction** +0.025s/f (Slow) **7** Ran SP% **122.5**
Speed ratings (Par 96): **99,98,96,95,92 89,76**
toteswingers:1&2:£1.90, 1&3:£4.10, 2&3:£3.00 CSF £6.45 CT £22.56 TOTE £2.90: £2.40, £1.20; EX 8.80.
Owner Barry Burdett **Bred** Swordlestown Stud **Trained** Kingsclere, Hants

FOCUS
A modest nursery, run at routine pace and the form looks sound enough, rated around the second and third.

NOTEBOOK
Angelic Upstart(IRE), whose yard won this last year, had made it third time lucky on his AW debut last month and he followed up under top weight on this first start in handicap company. He was allowed to find his feet early and got involved turning for home. He took time to pick up under pressure, but eventually responded passing the furlong marker and was always doing enough when in front despite drifting left. He clearly needed every yard back over this extra furlong and looks the sort that could rate a fair bit higher yet. (op 6-4 tchd 2-1)
Azlaa was 3lb higher and again managed to find one too good, but once more shaped better than the bare form. She does travel well in her races, but wasn't helped by racing without cover and, having her first run at the course, didn't handle the final bend that well. The fact she still went close suggests she remains weighted to win again when things go more her way. Official explanation: jockey said filly hung left (op 10-3)
Imaginary World(IRE), another handicap debutante, came here in decent heart and held every chance. She just looks weighted to her best, but remains in good form and may be worth another go over a slightly stiffer test. (tchd 13-2 and 15-2)
Suddenly Susan(IRE) was well backed on this first outing since her new trainer took over the reigns at her stable. She posted a better run in defeat, but did just appear to find this trip stretching her stamina. (op 11-2)
Oliver's Gold got badly outpaced from the stalls and was never seriously in the hunt. He was beat a lot further here by Azlaa than was the case on his previous outing on 4lb worse terms and may need some form of headgear. (op 6-1)

7759 KIA VENGA H'CAP (DIV I) 1m 4f (P)
4:50 (4:53) (Class 6) (0-55,55) 3-Y-O+ **£1,364** (£403; £201) **Stalls** Centre

Form RPR
54-6 **1** **Covert Mission**[31] 210 7-9-3 **53**.... StevieDonohoe 9 63+
(P D Evans) *trckd ldrs: rdn and prog to ld wl over 1f out: styd on wl* **7/1**[3]

3626 **2** *2 3/4* **Dovedon Angel**[22] 7475 4-8-11 **50**.... KierenFox(3) 7 56
(Miss Gay Kelleway) *hld up in last pair: n.m.r 4f out: hdwy and nt clr run over 2f out: wnt 2nd fnl f: unable to chal* **9/2**[1]

2200 **3** *1 3/4* **Zelos Diktator**[34] 7315 4-9-5 **55**.... GeorgeBaker 12 58
(G L Moore) *hld up towards rr: prog 2f out: styd on to take 3rd ins fnl f* **5/1**[2]

6003 **4** *3/4* **Blackstone Vegas**[36] 7286 4-9-2 **52**....(v) GrahamGibbons 4 54
(D Shaw) *trckd ldr: led briefly 2f out: sn outpcd* **9/2**[1]

0516 **5** *3/4* **Iguacu**[2] 7727 6-8-13 **52**....(p) MatthewDavies(3) 11 57+
(George Baker) *stdd s: hld up in last pair: nt clr run over 2f out: styd on wl fnl f: nrst fin* **9/2**[1]

4P-0 **6** *2 1/2* **Nothing Is Forever (IRE)**[27] 331 6-8-13 **49**....(p) SteveDrowne 5 46
(L Corcoran) *led tl 2f out: wknd over 1f out* **8/1**

605 **7** *5* **Drummers Drumming (USA)**[23] 2694 4-9-4 **54**....(t) IanMongan 8 43
(C P Morlock) *a in rr: rdn and struggling 4f out* **20/1**

1230 **8** *nk* **Fine Tolerance**[13] 7569 4-9-5 **55**.... JimmyQuinn 10 43
(Miss S L Davison) *chsd ldng pair: rdn over 2f out: sn wknd* **16/1**

0000 **9** *1 3/4* **Fleur De'Lion (IRE)**[3] 7716 4-9-0 **50**.... JamesDoyle 1 36
(S Kirk) *chsd ldng trio: rdn over 2f out: sn wknd* **12/1**

/00- **10** *1* **Softly Killing Me**[630] 874 5-8-10 **46** oh1.... NeilChalmers 3 30
(B Forsey) *nvr on terms w ldrs: btn over 2f out* **40/1**

5505 **11** *8* **Ruby Dazzler**[9] 7633 3-8-12 **53**....(bt) VinceSlattery 2 24
(S Lycett) *t.k.h: hld up: rdn and wknd over 3f out* **12/1**

2m 34.4s (-0.10) **Going Correction** +0.025s/f (Slow)
WFA 3 from 4yo+ 5lb **11** Ran SP% **123.3**
Speed ratings (Par 101): **101,99,98,97,97 95,92,91,90,89 84**
toteswingers:1&2:£7.50, 1&3:£11.40, 2&3:£5.00 CSF £40.54 CT £178.08 TOTE £20.50: £4.60, £1.80, £1.90; EX 71.00.
Owner Lost Souls Racing **Bred** Mrs Marian Harding **Trained** Pandy, Monmouths
■ Stewards' Enquiry : Matthew Davies three-day ban: careless riding (Dec 22,26-27)

FOCUS
There was a fair pace on in this weak handicap and it was the quicker division. The first pair came nicely clear at the finish and the runner-up is rated back to her best.

7760 KIA VENGA H'CAP (DIV II) 1m 4f (P)
5:20 (5:23) (Class 6) (0-55,55) 3-Y-O+ **£1,364** (£403; £201) **Stalls** Centre

Form RPR
-060 **1** **Active Asset (IRE)**[41] 7200 8-9-2 **52**.... SteveDrowne 1 58
(D C Griffiths) *hld up in last: prog 2f out: styd on wl fnl f to ld last strides* **10/1**

5054 **2** *nk* **Tifoso (FR)**[3] 7716 5-8-8 **47**....(v) AndrewHeffernan(3) 8 53
(R C Guest) *pressed ldr: hrd rdn to ld 2f out: kpt on: hdd last strides* **10/3**[1]

3300 **3** *1 1/2* **Sunset Boulevard (IRE)**[50] 6999 7-9-4 **54**....(b) EddieAhern 6 58
(Jim Best) *hld up: smooth prog 3f out: chal gng wl 2f out: rdn over 1f out: fnd nil* **16/1**

0004 **4** *nk* **Ladies Dancing**[36] 2363 4-9-5 **55**.... FergusSweeney 5 58
(C J Down) *trckd ldng pair: nt qckn 2f out: kpt on again fnl f* **15/2**

0060 **5** *1 1/4* **Hatch A Plan (IRE)**[3] 7716 9-8-13 **49**.... FrankieMcDonald 2 50
(Mouse Hamilton-Fairley) *hld up in last trio: prog over 2f out: kpt on same pce fr over 1f out* **28/1**

6245 **6** *2* **Mayfair's Future**[2] 7728 5-9-1 **51**....(p) GeorgeBaker 3 49
(J R Jenkins) *hld up in last trio: effrt over 2f out: sn rdn and nt qckn* **5/1**[3]

1305 **7** *8* **Litenup (IRE)**[25] 7445 4-9-0 **53**.... KierenFox(3) 11 38
(Miss Gay Kelleway) *racd freely: led tl 2f out: wkng whn n.m.r over 1f out* **9/2**[2]

0055 **8** *19* **Storming Redd**[31] 6631 3-9-0 **55**....(tp) MickyFenton 9 10
(J M P Eustace) *pushed along in midfield 1/2-way: wknd 3f out: t.o* **13/2**

-400 **9** *2* **Set Em Up Mo**[245] 1160 4-8-10 **46** oh1....(v) CathyGannon 7 —
(M J Attwater) *chsd ldrs: rdn 5f out: wknd over 3f out: t.o* **33/1**

300 **10** *9* **Storms Over (USA)**[36] 7286 3-8-7 **48**.... JimmyQuinn 12 —
(B W Duke) *prom tl wknd rapidly over 3f out: t.o* **6/1**

2m 35.62s (1.12) **Going Correction** +0.025s/f (Slow)
WFA 3 from 4yo+ 5lb **10** Ran SP% **118.7**
Speed ratings (Par 101): **97,96,95,95,94 93,88,75,74,68**
toteswingers:1&2:£7.20, 1&3:£26.10, 2&3:£10.40. CSF £44.19 CT £544.23 TOTE £11.60: £3.00, £1.10, £7.40; EX 64.70.
Owner D W Noble **Bred** Rathasker Stud **Trained** Bawtry, S Yorks
■ Stewards' Enquiry : Andrew Heffernan four-day ban: used whip with excessive frequency down shoulder in the forehand (Dec 22,26-28)

FOCUS
The second and slower division of the 1m4f handicap and it looked the weaker. It was run at an average pace and there was a tight finish. The winner showed his best form since this time last year.
Storms Over(USA) Official explanation: jockey said gelding had no more to give

7761 SKYSPORTS.COM RACING H'CAP 7f (P)
5:50 (5:53) (Class 6) (0-55,61) 3-Y-O+ **£1,637** (£483; £241) **Stalls** High

Form RPR
2540 **1** **Sirjosh**[141] 4234 4-9-2 **55**.... CathyGannon 13 66
(D Donovan) *hld up in midfield: prog to ld main gp 2f out: overall ldr 1f out: styd on wl* **16/1**

0000 **2** *1 1/4* **Musical Script (USA)**[19] 7502 7-9-1 **54**....(b) ChrisCatlin 1 62
(Mouse Hamilton-Fairley) *hld up in last: gd prog on inner over 2f out: chsd wnr ins fnl f: styd on* **28/1**

5002 **3** *2 1/2* **Itsthursdayalready**[11] 7604 3-9-0 **53**.... EddieAhern 14 54
(W M Brisbourne) *chsd clr ldrs: chal w wnr over 2f out: wknd fnl f: clung on for 3rd* **11/2**[1]

6431 **4** *nk* **Lily Wood**[5] 7676 4-9-0 **53** 6ex....(p) WilliamCarson 12 53
(J W Unett) *hld up in rr: prog over 2f out: kpt on same pce fr over 1f out* **15/2**[3]

1000 **5** *nk* **Goodbye Cash (IRE)**[18] 7518 6-8-13 **55**.... AndrewHeffernan(3) 6 54
(R J Smith) *led at str pce: hung lft to nr side rail over 2f out: hdd and fdd 1f out* **16/1**

0005 **6** *nk* **Guildenstern (IRE)**[49] 7023 8-8-12 **51**.... JimmyQuinn 3 50
(P Howling) *hld up in last pair: prog over 2f out: kpt on: nvr rchd ldrs* **10/1**

4451 **7** *shd* **Dancing Welcome**[8] 7640 4-9-8 **61** 6ex....(b) RussKennemore 5 59
(J M Bradley) *sn pressed ldr: carried lft to nr side rail over 2f out: wknd fnl f* **6/1**[2]

6056 **8** *4 1/2* **Woodsley House (IRE)**[47] 7071 8-8-12 **51**.... NickyMackay 8 37
(M E Rimmer) *hld up in rr: no real prog over 2f out* **9/1**

0006 **9** *hd* **Replicator**[26] 7426 5-8-9 **53**....(e) RyanClark(5) 9 39
(P L Gilligan) *pressed ldng pair: carried lft to nr side rail over 2f out: upsides over 1f out: wknd* **16/1**

3006 **10** *nk* **Connor's Choice**[26] 7425 5-9-0 **53**.... HayleyTurner 11 38
(Andrew Turnell) *hld up in rr: rdn and no prog over 2f out* **12/1**

4050 **11** *2* **Grey Boy (GER)**[14] 7555 9-8-8 **54** GeorgeDowning(7) 4 33
(A W Carroll) *dwlt: nvr bttr than mid-div: wknd 2f out* **16/1**
6360 **12** *1 ¼* **Chateau Zara**[21] 7487 3-8-13 **52** (p) LukeMorris 7 28
(C G Cox) *chsd ldng trio: wknd over 2f out* **15/2**[3]
004 **13** *½* **Surprise Us**[11] 7596 3-9-2 **55** (p) GeorgeBaker 10 30
(Mrs A Duffield) *chsd ldrs: lost pl over 2f out: sn wknd* **8/1**

1m 25.48s (-0.52) **Going Correction** +0.025s/f (Slow) **13** Ran SP% **118.1**
Speed ratings (Par 101): **103,101,98,98,98 97,97,92,92,91 89,88,87**
toteswingers:1&2:£53.60, 1&3:£23.20, 2&3:£36.80. totesuper7: Win: Not won. Place: Not won. CSF £395.49 CT £2857.13 TOTE £18.90: £5.50, £14.70, £1.60; EX 369.60.
Owner River Racing **Bred** Mrs Clair Murphy **Trained** Newmarket, Suffolk

FOCUS
This low-grade handicap looked to be wide open. There was a strong pace on with the first three attaining a clear advantage, but the leader hung over to the stands' side after straightening for home and took the other two with him. The time was good for the grade and the form is rated slightly positively.
Replicator Official explanation: jockey said gelding hung left
T/Jkpt: Not won. T/Plt: £56.70 to a £1 stake. Pool:£108,170.56 - 1,392.23 winning tickets T/Qpdt: £8.90 to a £1 stake. Pool:£7,268.86 - 598.00 winning tickets JN

7732 LINGFIELD (L-H)
Wednesday, December 8

OFFICIAL GOING: Standard
Wind: medium, against Weather: overcast, cold

7762 BET SP+ WITH TOTESPORT 0800 221221 CLAIMING STKS 7f (P)
12:40 (12:41) (Class 6) 2-Y-O £1,706 (£503; £252) Stalls Low

Form RPR
0642 **1** **Silence Is Bliss (IRE)**[2] 7722 2-8-9 **74** RyanPowell(5) 2 71
(J S Moore) *trckd ldrs: swtchd ins and rdn to chal over 1f out: drvn to ld fnl 100yds: r.o wl* **4/1**[2]
0311 **2** *¾* **My Lord**[18] 7528 2-9-4 **81** KierenFox(3) 5 76
(W G M Turner) *led tl jst over 2f out: rdn to ld again wl over 1f out: hdd and unable qck fnl 100yds* **4/7**[1]
0333 **3** *½* **Sir Lunchalott**[18] 7520 2-9-0 **70** (b) LukeMorris 1 68
(J S Moore) *v.s.a and pushed along early: hdwy on inner over 1f out: hrd drvn and swtchd rt jst ins fnl f: kpt on: nt rch ldrs* **11/2**[3]
4 *hd* **Eternal Youth (IRE)**[47] 7074 2-8-9 **0** JakePayne(7) 4 69
(R A Harris) *stdd s: hld up in tch in last pair: hdwy to chse ldrs over 2f out: unable qck over 1f out: kpt on again fnl 100yds* **16/1**
0033 **5** *7* **Local Diktator**[15] 7540 2-8-12 **55** (t) AndreaAtzeni 6 47
(R A Harris) *chsd ldr: rdn to ld jst over 2f out tl wl over 1f out: sn hung lft and unable qck: wknd qckly 1f out: heavily eased towards fin* **50/1**
0000 **6** *3 ¼* **Theavonfilly**[14] 7552 2-8-5 **54** (p) MartinLane 3 32
(R A Teal) *in tch but sn niggled along: drvn 4f out: wknd jst over 2f out* **50/1**

1m 26.43s (1.63) **Going Correction** +0.075s/f (Slow) **6** Ran SP% **108.8**
Speed ratings (Par 94): **93,92,91,91,83 79**
toteswingers:1&2:£1.50, 1&3:£1.70, 2&3:£1.10 CSF £6.25 TOTE £3.90: £2.40, £1.10; EX 6.70.
Owner J S Moore **Bred** Mrs E Thompson **Trained** Upper Lambourn, Berks

FOCUS
An ordinary claimer. The first four finished in a bunch, but the time was respectable. The form is rated around the principals.

NOTEBOOK
Silence Is Bliss(IRE) was back up in grade after finishing runner-up in a 6f seller here two days earlier, and had not convinced at this trip in three previous tries. He had a live chance at the weights, though, and while his resolution has been questioned at times, there was little wrong with his attitude. (op 10-3)
My Lord was 1lb ahead of the winner on adjusted official figures. Bidding for a hat-trick on this first visit to Lingfield, he went out in front again and fought off the fifth horse's brief challenge on the home turn, but could not repel the winner. He ran his race with no apparent excuses, although Silence Is Bliss did edge into him slightly late on. (op 4-6)
Sir Lunchalott, the winner's stablemate, missed the break again before running on for pressure in the straight, without giving the impression that he was particularly enjoying himself. (op 6-1)
Eternal Youth(IRE), who was sold out of Dermot Weld's stable after winning a Dundalk nursery in October, was keen on the way to the start. Reportedly a nervous type, he hung up the straight and looked less than straightforward, but stayed on and performed creditably on the figures. (tchd 20-1)
Local Diktator, the stable second string, briefly looked a threat when nosing in front for a few strides on the crown of the final bend, but he hung from there and was soon on the retreat. He had a good deal to find on these terms. Official explanation: jockey said colt hung left

7763 FELBRIDGE (S) STKS 7f (P)
1:10 (1:11) (Class 6) 3-Y-O+ £1,706 (£503; £252) Stalls Low

Form RPR
34- **1** **Prize Point**[561] 2355 4-8-9 **69** MatthewDavies(3) 1 58
(J R Boyle) *racd keenly: sn led: rdn over 1f out: hrd drvn fnl f: jst hld on* **13/8**[2]
5003 **2** *nse* **Lord Deevert**[11] 7604 5-8-9 **54** KierenFox(3) 2 58
(W G M Turner) *in tch: rdn over 2f out: hdwy u.p 1f out: chsd wnr fnl 100yds: edgd lft but kpt on u.p and str chal nr fin: jst failed* **7/2**[3]
4050 **3** *1* **Boundless Applause**[22] 7468 4-8-7 **39** MartinLane 5 50
(I A Wood) *in tch: rdn and effrt ent fnl 2f: hdwy u.p to chse ldrs 1f out: kpt on same pce fnl 100yds* **66/1**
3604 **4** *1* **Rich Boy**[10] 7614 3-8-12 **62** (tp) IanMongan 9 52
(Mrs L J Mongan) *sn pushed along to chse ldr: jnd ldr over 2f out: drvn over 1f out: lost 2nd and no ex ins fnl f* **6/4**[1]
-060 **5** *1 ½* **Public Image**[56] 6853 4-8-7 **46** WilliamCarson 4 43
(Jamie Poulton) *dwlt: sn rcvrd to chse ldrs: rdn over 2f out: hrd drvn and pressed ldrs ent fnl f: no ex fnl 100yds* **25/1**
0304 **6** *2 ½* **Louisiade (IRE)**[202] 2257 9-8-9 **48** ow2 (p) MarkCoumbe(5) 10 44
(D Bourton) *sn niggled along in rr: rdn over 2f out: outpcd and btn jst over 1f out* **25/1**
0040 **7** *19* **Braddock (IRE)**[10] 7607 7-8-12 **50** (t) ChrisCatlin 6 —
(K O Cunningham-Brown) *in tch: dropped to rr and struggling over 2f out: lost tch wl over 1f out: b.b.v* **25/1**

1m 25.48s (0.68) **Going Correction** +0.075s/f (Slow) **7** Ran SP% **113.3**
Speed ratings (Par 101): **99,98,97,96,94 92,70**
toteswingers:1&2:£1.90, 1&3:£14.20, 2&3:£13.50 CSF £7.37 TOTE £2.30: £1.50, £2.00; EX 9.80 Trifecta £218.20 Pool: £648.81 - 2.20 winning units..There was no bid for the winner.
Owner M Khan X2 **Bred** Mrs B Skinner **Trained** Epsom, Surrey

FOCUS
An uncompetitive seller, and pretty weak form limited by the third. The winner was better than this in the past.
Braddock(IRE) Official explanation: jockey said gelding moved poorly and eased in straight; vet said gelding bled from the nose

7764 LINGFIELDPARK.CO.UK (S) STKS 5f (P)
1:40 (1:40) (Class 6) 3-Y-O+ £1,706 (£503; £252) Stalls High

Form RPR
5066 **1** **Brandywell Boy (IRE)**[8] 7635 7-9-4 **72** JamesDoyle 7 74
(D J S Ffrench Davis) *chsd ldng trio: rdn and hdwy ent fnl 2f: ev ch ent fnl f: kpt on gamely u.p to ld last stride* **3/1**[2]
0034 **2** *shd* **Wanchai Whisper**[8] 7635 3-8-10 **64** AndrewHeffernan(3) 8 68
(P R Hedger) *hld up towards rr: hdwy wl over 1f out: swtchd rt and rdn over 1f out: drvn to ld ins fnl f: kpt on u.p tl hdd last stride* **2/1**[1]
201 **3** *2* **Sharp Shoes**[35] 7300 3-9-4 **58** (p) SamHitchcott 10 66
(Mrs A Duffield) *taken down early: chsd ldr: rdn ent fnl 2f: led jst ins fnl f: sn hdd: outpcd fnl 100yds* **12/1**
3035 **4** *¾* **Decider (USA)**[285] 727 7-8-5 **60** (p) JakePayne(7) 3 57
(R A Harris) *chsd ldng pair: hung rt on bnd 2f out: rdn and effrt whn short of room and hmpd over 1f out: kpt on same pce ins fnl f* **16/1**
6602 **5** *1 ¼* **Spic 'n Span**[3] 7720 5-9-4 **60** (b) AndreaAtzeni 6 59
(R A Harris) *taken down early: led: shkn up ent fnl f: hdd jst ins fnl f: sn fdd* **7/2**[3]
0006 **6** *3 ¼* **Bobs Dreamflight**[8] 7640 4-9-4 **57** (b) AdamKirby 1 47
(D K Ivory) *a towards rr: rdn and no prog over 2f out: nvr trbld ldrs* **7/1**
3605 **7** *1* **Flaxen Lake**[9] 7628 3-9-4 **57** (tp) ChrisCatlin 9 44
(J M Bradley) *dwlt: racd wd and a towards rr: struggling over 2f out* **25/1**
040 **8** *15* **Flow Chart (IRE)**[97] 5697 3-8-12 **50** (b) RobbieFitzpatrick 5 —
(Peter Grayson) *dwlt: sn pushed along in rr: lost tch 2f out* **100/1**

58.85 secs (0.05) **Going Correction** +0.075s/f (Slow) **8** Ran SP% **111.5**
Speed ratings (Par 101): **102,101,98,97,95 90,88,64**
toteswingers:1&2:£1.90, 1&3:£5.70, 2&3:£5.40 CSF £8.89 TOTE £4.20: £1.10, £1.80, £2.80; EX 10.10 Trifecta £53.90 Pool: £795.42 - 10.92 winning units..There was no bid for the winner.
Owner P B Gallagher **Bred** Mountarmstrong Stud **Trained** Lambourn, Berks

FOCUS
The second seller on the card, this was run at a strong pace and the leaders fell away late on, setting it up for a couple of closers. The first two were the form pair going into it.
Decider(USA) Official explanation: jockey said gelding hung right on bend

7765 BIGGER WINS WITH SP+ AT TOTESPORT.COM H'CAP 1m 4f (P)
2:10 (2:10) (Class 5) (0-70,70) 3-Y-O+ £2,388 (£705; £352) Stalls Low

Form RPR
1313 **1** **Cozy Tiger (USA)**[187] 2723 5-9-10 **70** StevieDonohoe 1 78
(W J Musson) *in tch: hdwy to chse ldrs and nt clr run over 1f out: swtchd rt 1f out: rdn and r.o wl to ld towards fin* **12/1**
0552 **2** *½* **Archie Rice (USA)**[4] 7687 4-9-5 **65** JimmyQuinn 5 72
(T Keddy) *sn chsng ldrs: wnt 2nd over 4f out: rdn to ld over 1f out: kpt on u.p fnl f tl hdd and no ex towards fin* **13/2**
1215 **3** *1* **Bold Adventure**[195] 2476 6-9-1 **61** JamieMackay 2 66
(W J Musson) *led tl 10f out: led again 9f out tl rdn and hdd over 1f out: kpt on tl no ex and btn fnl 100yds* **33/1**
3665 **4** *3 ¼* **Relative Strength (IRE)**[21] 7491 5-9-8 **68** (t) AndreaAtzeni 10 68
(S C Williams) *hld up in last trio: rdn and hdwy on inner jst over 2f out: kpt on but no imp on ldrs fnl f* **6/1**[3]
0401 **5** *1 ½* **Where's Susie**[21] 7490 5-9-10 **70** JamieSpencer 9 68
(M Madgwick) *racd in midfield: hdwy and rdn over 2f out: chsd ldrs and unable qck u.p over 1f out: one pce and hld fnl f* **5/1**[2]
0422 **6** *nk* **Eagle Nebula**[13] 7569 6-9-3 **63** GeorgeBaker 12 60
(B R Johnson) *chsd ldrs: wnt 3rd 3f out: rdn and unable qck 2f out: wknd fnl f* **4/1**[1]
2424 **7** *1* **Larkrise Star**[21] 7491 3-8-9 **60** WilliamCarson 3 56
(D K Ivory) *in tch in midfield: rdn and unable qck wl over 1f out: one pce and no threat to ldrs fr over 1f out* **7/1**
6002 **8** *nk* **Squad**[21] 7490 4-9-5 **65** HayleyTurner 8 60
(S Dow) *stdd s: hld up in last trio: rdn 4f out: nt clr run 3f out: no prog u.p ent fnl 2f* **13/2**
6020 **9** *2 ½* **War Of The Roses (IRE)**[21] 7490 7-9-3 **70** JulieBurke(7) 11 61
(R Brotherton) *stdd s: hld up in rr: rdn 4f out: wd and no prog u.p on bnd ent fnl 2f: wl btn ent fnl f* **9/1**
1500 **10** *6* **Savaronola (USA)**[18] 7531 5-9-1 **61** TomQueally 7 43
(B J Curley) *stdd and dropped in bhd after s: hld up in last trio: rdn 4f out: effrt on outer over 2f out: wknd and btn wl over 1f out* **25/1**
6005 **11** *7* **Winning Show**[21] 7490 6-8-12 **58** ow1 (tp) IanMongan 6 28
(C Gordon) *sn chsng ldr tl led 10f out tl 9f out: chsd ldr after tl over 4f out: dropped to rr u.p 3f out: wl bhd fnl 2f* **18/1**

2m 32.22s (-0.78) **Going Correction** +0.075s/f (Slow)
WFA 3 from 4yo+ 5lb **11** Ran SP% **119.9**
Speed ratings (Par 103): **105,104,104,101,100 100,99,99,98,94 89**
toteswingers:1&2:£17.20, 1&3:£17.60, 2&3:£37.90 CSF £89.70 CT £2527.08 TOTE £17.10: £3.10, £3.40, £8.70; EX 79.30 Trifecta £314.00 Part won. Pool: £424.42 - 0.50 winning units..
Owner McHugh & Partners **Bred** Alan S Kline Et Al **Trained** Newmarket, Suffolk

FOCUS
A modest handicap, but it was an open race and the pace was sound. The form is rated slightly positively.
Relative Strength(IRE) Official explanation: jockey said, regarding running and riding, that his orders were, being drawn wide, he chose to drop into the pack and started to make his effort over 3f out, the gelding gave some response to pressure, but was unable to keep up with the first three who went away in the straight, at this stage he felt signs of reluctance and used his whip to ensure he held on to fourth.

7766 BET ON TONIGHT'S FOOTBALL AT TOTESPORT.COM H'CAP 7f (P)
2:40 (2:40) (Class 4) (0-85,86) 3-Y-O+ £3,885 (£1,156; £577; £288) Stalls Low

Form RPR
221 **1** **Norman Orpen (IRE)**[28] 7389 3-9-7 **80** JamieSpencer 6 91+
(Jane Chapple-Hyam) *stdd s: sn trcking ldrs: rdn and effrt jst over 1f out: r.o wl u.p to ld fnl 50yds* **10/11**[1]
0210 **2** *¾* **Whispering Spirit (IRE)**[18] 7521 4-9-5 **78** (v) SamHitchcott 2 85
(Mrs A Duffield) *chsd ldng pair: rdn and effrt on inner 2f out: led 1f out: kpt on u.p tl hdd and no ex fnl 50yds* **7/1**[2]
0354 **3** *1 ½* **Requisite**[6] 7665 5-9-3 **76** (v) MartinLane 4 79
(I A Wood) *stdd s: in tch towards rr: rdn and effrt over 1f out: styd on u.p ins fnl f: nt rch ldrs* **12/1**
2026 **4** *nk* **Headache**[30] 7377 5-8-11 **70** (bt) HayleyTurner 7 72
(B W Duke) *chsd ldr: rdn and ev ch ent fnl 2f tl ins fnl f: no ex fnl 100yds* **7/1**[2]
5503 **5** *½* **Yankee Storm**[1] 7737 5-8-11 **70** (v) MickyFenton 1 71
(H J Collingridge) *t.k.h: hld up in tch in midfield: rdn and effrt on inner over 1f out: styd on same pce and no imp ins fnl f* **10/1**

6000 **6** *1* **Salient**[8] 7637 6-9-0 **73**........(p) LukeMorris 3 71
(M J Attwater) *led: jnd and rdn ent fnl 2f: hdd 1f out: wknd ins fnl f* **15/2**[3]

0046 **7** *2* **Rapid Water**[60] 6739 4-9-1 **74**........ JimmyQuinn 5 67
(P Howling) *t.k.h: hld up in tch in last pair: rdn and no prog over 1f out: nvr trbld ldrs* **20/1**

2210 **8** *1 ½* **Dingaan (IRE)**[21] 7488 7-9-7 **80**........ RobbieFitzpatrick 9 69
(Peter Grayson) *sn niggled in last pair: rdn: edgd lft and no imp fr over 1f out: n.d* **25/1**

1m 25.18s (0.38) **Going Correction** +0.075s/f (Slow) **8** Ran SP% **114.5**
Speed ratings (Par 105): **100,99,97,97,96 95,93,91**
toteswingers:1&2:£2.00, 1&3:£2.70, 2&3:£6.50 CSF £7.84 CT £46.97 TOTE £2.20: £1.20, £2.00, £3.00; EX 8.80 Trifecta £55.30 Pool: £5,769.23 - 7.71 winning units..

Owner Gordon Li **Bred** Kevin Walsh **Trained** Dalham, Suffolk

FOCUS
A fair handicap. The pace seemed reasonable but the time was not particularly quick relative to the seller and the juvenile claimer over this trip. The bare form is only ordinary but the winner may do better again.

7767 40 LIVE FOOTBALL MARKETS AT TOTESPORT.COM MEDIAN AUCTION MAIDEN STKS 1m 2f (P)
3:10 (3:13) (Class 6) 3-5-Y-O **£1,706** (£503; £252) **Stalls** Low

Form RPR

6-00 **1** **Suntrap**[14] 7561 3-9-4 63........(v[1]) LukeMorris 2 73
(W J Knight) *chsd ldng pair: rdn to chal wl over 1f out: led over 1f out: drew clr fnl f: rdn out* **4/1**[3]

5-43 **2** *7* **Crystal Gale (IRE)**[211] 1992 3-8-13 67........ JamieSpencer 6 54
(W J Knight) *chsd ldr: rdn to ld wl over 1f out tl hdd over 1f out: nt pce of wnr fnl f* **7/2**[2]

4422 **3** *2 ½* **Handsome King**[7] 7651 3-9-4 64........ AdamKirby 4 54
(J R Jenkins) *in tch: rdn and fnd little over 2f out: plugged on same pce and no ch w wnr fnl f* **10/3**[1]

0256 **4** *1 ¾* **New Den**[14] 7561 3-9-4 61........(v) StephenCraine 5 51
(J R Boyle) *reminders sn after s: in tch: rdn again 4f out: drvn and struggling over 2f out: no ch fr wl over 1f out* **4/1**[3]

0 **5** *1* **Beyond Rubies**[47] 7069 3-8-13 0........ TomQueally 1 44
(H R A Cecil) *led tl wl over 1f out: btn ent fnl f: fdd fnl f* **8/1**

6 *27* **Cheyne Walk (USA)** 3-8-13 0........ HayleyTurner 3 —
(J Noseda) *v.s.a: sn rdn and nvr travelling in last: lost tch over 3f out: sn t.o* **9/2**

2m 6.72s (0.12) **Going Correction** +0.075s/f (Slow) **6** Ran SP% **114.6**
Speed ratings (Par 101): **102,96,94,93,92 70**
toteswingers:1&2:£3.90, 1&3:£3.50, 2&3:£1.50 CSF £18.76 TOTE £7.90: £4.90, £1.70; EX 21.70.

Owner Mrs B Sumner **Bred** Mrs B Sumner **Trained** Patching, W Sussex

FOCUS
A very moderate maiden. It was run at a decent pace and three of the runners were hard at work with half a mile to run. The winner is rated to the best view of his 2yo form, with the rest 10lb+ off.

7768 TANDRIDGE APPRENTICE H'CAP 1m (P)
3:40 (3:40) (Class 6) (0-62,61) 3-Y-O+ **£2,047** (£604; £302) **Stalls** High

Form RPR

5000 **1** **Mountrath**[34] 7323 3-9-1 **60**........(v[1]) AmyBaker 6 68
(B R Johnson) *t.k.h: led tl 5f out: chsd ldr after: rdn to chal over 1f out: led jst ins fnl f: hung lft u.p wout correction and hmpd rival wl ins fnl f: kpt on* **8/1**

6531 **2** *¾* **Marksbury**[14] 7555 3-8-12 **60**........ RyanClark[(3)] 9 66
(J M P Eustace) *in tch in midfield: effrt to chse ldrs 2f out: rdn wl over 1f out: kpt on u.p ins fnl f: wnt 2nd towards fin* **6/1**[3]

603 **3** *¾* **Eastern Gift**[23] 7467 5-9-0 **61**........ JulieBurke[(3)] 1 67+
(Miss Gay Kelleway) *in tch: effrt on inner u.p over 1f out: ev ch whn carried lft by wnr ins fnl f: eventually no room against rail and snatched up wl ins fnl f: sn lost 2nd and unable to rcvr* **7/2**[1]

4130 **4** *¾* **Yakama (IRE)**[182] 2876 5-8-5 **56**........(v) AliceHaynes[(7)] 10 59
(Mrs C A Dunnett) *stdd s: hld up in tch in rr: hdwy over 2f out: chsd ldrs and rdn ent fnl f: styd on same pce fnl 150yds* **20/1**

0500 **5** *1 ¼* **Teen Ager (FR)**[10] 7613 6-8-8 **57**........ MatthewCosham[(5)] 8 57
(P Burgoyne) *t.k.h: chsd ldr tl led 5f out: rdn and hdd jst ins fnl f: stl ev ch but looked btn whn sltly hmpd sn after: wknd fnl 100yds* **16/1**

4043 **6** *nk* **Bizarrely (IRE)**[5] 7685 3-8-12 **60**........(p) RyanPowell[(3)] 4 59
(J Pearce) *t.k.h: chsd ldrs: rdn and unable qck over 1f out: styd on same pce fnl f* **7/2**[1]

0001 **7** *3 ¾* **Sir Ike (IRE)**[21] 7487 5-8-13 **57**........(tp) AshleyMorgan 2 47
(W S Kittow) *hld up in tch towards rr: rdn and no real prog wl over 1f out: n.d* **9/2**[2]

2500 **8** *½* **Tasza (USA)**[15] 7543 3-8-11 **56**........ TobyAtkinson 3 45
(A J McCabe) *taken down early: in tch towards rr on outer: rdn and wknd ent fnl 2f* **8/1**

006 **9** *7* **Athboy Auction**[85] 6061 5-8-1 **50** oh5........(v) NatashaEaton[(5)] 7 23
(H J Collingridge) *stdd s: plld hrd: hld up in last pair: rdn and no hdwy ent fnl 2f: wl btn fnl f* **50/1**

6000 **10** *6* **First Service (IRE)**[10] 7613 4-8-9 **58**........(b) MatthewLawson[(5)] 5 17
(M J Attwater) *stdd s: t.k.h and sn chsng ldrs: rdn and lost pl over 2f out: bhd over 1f out* **12/1**

1m 38.36s (0.16) **Going Correction** +0.075s/f (Slow)
WFA 3 from 4yo+ 1lb **10** Ran SP% **119.4**
Speed ratings (Par 101): **102,101,100,99,98 98,94,93,86,80**
toteswingers:1&2:£8.50, 1&3:£5.10, 2&3:£4.50 CSF £56.81 CT £206.41 TOTE £10.40: £3.30, £1.20, £1.10; EX 65.70 Trifecta £568.80 Part won. Pool: £768.67 - 0.52 winning units..

Owner David Phelan **Bred** A G Antoniades **Trained** Ashtead, Surrey

■ Stewards' Enquiry : Amy Baker three-day ban: careless riding (Dec 22,26-27)

FOCUS
A low-grade handicap for apprentices, run at an ordinary pace. The third and fourth set the level.

T/Plt: £49.80 to a £1 stake. Pool:£82,926.46 - 1,213.74 winning tickets T/Qpdt: £21.40 to a £1 stake. Pool:£5,653.03 - 195.15 winning tickets SP

7769 - 7775a (Foreign Racing) - See Raceform Interactive

7647 DEAUVILLE (R-H)
Wednesday, December 8
OFFICIAL GOING: Fibresand: standard

7776a PRIX LYPHARD (LISTED RACE) (3YO+) (FIBRESAND) 1m 1f 110y
1:55 (12:00) 3-Y-O+ **£23,008** (£9,203; £6,902; £4,601; £2,300)

RPR

1 **Livandar (FR)**[48] 4-8-13 0........ RonanThomas 13 —
(P Van De Poele, France) **33/1**

2 *hd* **Le Roi Mage (IRE)**[20] 7500 5-8-13 0........ GregoryBenoist 16 —
(T Lallie, France) **9/1**

3 *1* **Lake Palace**[27] 7416 4-8-13 0........ Jean-BernardEyquem 14 —
(N Clement, France) **17/1**

4 *½* **Charybde En Scylla (FR)**[41] 3-8-11 0........ IoritzMendizabal 2 —
(Robert Collet, France) **19/1**

5 *nse* **Lowenherz (GER)**[20] 7500 6-8-13 0........ TonyPiccone 7 —
(H Billot, France) **76/1**

6 *shd* **Pallodio (IRE)**[55] 6881 5-9-5 0........ FabriceVeron 1 —
(J E Hammond, France) **4/1**[1]

7 *nk* **Russian Cross (IRE)**[75] 6344 5-9-2 0........(b) Pierre-CharlesBoudot 15 —
(A Fabre, France) **44/5**[3]

8 *snk* **Pont Des Arts (FR)**[55] 6881 6-9-2 0........ FredericSpanu 3 —
(A Scharer, Germany) **42/1**

9 *nk* **Usbeke (GER)**[20] 7500 4-8-13 0........(p) ThierryJarnet 18 —
(J-P Carvalho, Germany) **15/1**

10 *½* **Charlotte Point (USA)**[40] 4-8-9 0........ ThomasHuet 9 —
(J E Pease, France) **28/1**

0 **Willywell (FR)**[49] 8-8-13 0........ MathiasSautjeau 11 —
(J-P Gauvin, France) **22/1**

0 **Eire**[43] 6-8-9 0........ FabienLefebvre 16 —
(M Nigge, France) **21/1**

0 **Cool Star (FR)**[20] 7500 5-8-13 0........ RaphaelMarchelli 17 —
(A Bonin, France) **19/1**

0 **Aristote**[18] 7533 4-8-13 0........(b) Francois-XavierBertras 5 —
(P Van De Poele, France) **10/1**

0 **King Of Sydney (USA)**[192] 2576 4-8-13 0........ FlavienPrat 6 —
(Mario Hofer, Germany) **35/1**

0 **Beauchamp Xerxes**[26] 7430 4-9-2 0........ DaneO'Neill 12 —
(G A Butler) *broke wl: led briefly then settled bhd ldrs: 5th into st: rdn and ev ch ent fnl f: no ex: grad fdd* **75/1**

0 **Magic Moon (FR)**[101] 4-8-9 0........ SylvainRuis 10 —
(T Lemer, France) **44/5**[3]

0 **Rostrum (FR)**[122] 3-8-11 0........ MickaelBarzalona 8 —
(A Fabre, France) **13/2**[2]

1m 57.2s (117.20)
WFA 3 from 4yo+ 2lb **18** Ran SP% **117.6**
WIN (incl. 1 euro stake): 34.90. PLACES: 10.90, 3.60, 5.80. DF: 267.30. SF: 340.00.
Owner Christos Theodorakis **Bred** Haras De S A Aga Khan Scea **Trained** France

7754 KEMPTON (A.W) (R-H)
Thursday, December 9
OFFICIAL GOING: Standard
Wind: Virtually nil

7777 BOXINGDAYRACES.CO.UK CLAIMING STKS 5f (P)
4:00 (4:00) (Class 6) 2-Y-O **£1,637** (£483; £241) **Stalls** High

Form RPR

2320 **1** **Johnny Hancocks (IRE)**[12] 7592 2-8-9 74........ MartinLane 8 66
(P D Evans) *trckd ldr: led over 2f out: hrd rdn fr over 1f out: hld on all out* **7/4**[2]

0400 **2** *shd* **Majestic Ridge (IRE)**[50] 7016 2-8-8 52........(b[1]) WilliamCarson 9 65
(R A Harris) *in tch whn checked after 1f: sn trcking ldrs: chsd wnr ins fnl 2f: hung rt u.p fr over 1f out: clsng u.p thrght fnl f: jst failed* **20/1**

0404 **3** *2* **Fairy Tales**[5] 7686 2-8-4 44........ NeilChalmers 6 54
(J J Bridger) *chsd ldrs: one pce over 2f out: styd on again fr over 1f out: kpt on but nt trble ldng duo* **25/1**

6260 **4** *1 ¾* **Shutupandrive**[13] 7576 2-8-2 45........(v) JimmyQuinn 5 46
(M D I Usher) *s.i.s: in rr: hdwy fr 2f out: styd on same pce fnl f* **33/1**

0030 **5** *½* **Golden Shine**[19] 7528 2-8-0 72........ JulieBurke[(7)] 7 49
(A Bailey) *in tch: rdn 2f out: styd on same pce fnl f* **13/8**[1]

1333 **6** *¾* **Miss Toldyaso (IRE)**[13] 7576 2-8-4 56........ DavidProbert 2 43
(M G Quinlan) *s.i.s: in rr: wd into st: hung lft over 2f out: styd on fnl f* **11/2**[3]

0406 **7** *¾* **Instructress**[5] 7696 2-8-4 66........(p) FrannyNorton 1 40
(R M H Cowell) *in tch to 1/2-way* **10/1**

6660 **8** *1 ½* **Mini Bon Bon**[27] 7423 2-7-9 54........(p) JessicaSteven[(7)] 3 33
(A Bailey) *led tl hdd over 2f out: wknd ins fnl f* **33/1**

60.74 secs (0.24) **Going Correction** -0.025s/f (Stan) **8** Ran SP% **113.4**
Speed ratings (Par 94): **97,96,93,90,90 88,87,85**
Tote Swingers: 1&2 £3.90, 1&3 £5.70, 2&3 £6.50 CSF £38.18 TOTE £3.10: £1.70, £5.70, £2.60; EX 35.40.Johnny Hancocks was claimed by Mrs L. Stubbs for £6,000. Majestic Ridge was claimed by Nick Shutts for £5,000.
Owner Shropshire Wolves 3 **Bred** Mountarmstrong Stud **Trained** Pandy, Monmouths
■ Stewards' Enquiry : William Carson one-day ban: used whip with excessive frequency (Dec 26)

FOCUS
A few of these limit the form, notably the runner-up, third and fourth, and this was just a modest claimer.

NOTEBOOK
Johnny Hancocks(IRE) didn't run to his official mark of 74 seeing as he had 19lb in hand over the runner-up on the figures. His chance wasn't helped, though, by being hassled throughout by Mini Bon Bon, who dropped away. (op 6-4 tchd 11-8)
Majestic Ridge(IRE) was helped by first-time blinkers on his return from a 50-day break and ran to the sort of form he showed when fourth in a Wolverhampton maiden in September. (op 16-1 tchd 25-1)
Fairy Tales had her official rating bumped up to 55 after running fourth in a 6f maiden here five days earlier, but she didn't seem to reach that figure this time. (op 16-1)
Shutupandrive was one-paced under pressure and offered little. (op 25-1)
Golden Shine was most disappointing. She was just behind Johnny Hancocks at Wolverhampton on her penultimate start, and was best off at the weights this time, but she ran significantly below her official mark of 72. (op 3-1)

Miss Toldyaso(IRE), poorly drawn, raced much too wide throughout and is better than she showed. (op 9-2)

Instructress Official explanation: jockey said filly hung left

7778 WIN A KIA VENGA AT KEMPTON.CO.UK H'CAP 1m 2f (P)

4:30 (4:31) (Class 5) (0-70,70) 3-Y-0+ **£2,286** (£675; £337) **Stalls** High

Form			Horse	Jockey	RPR
6013	1		**Aurora Sky (IRE)**^{15} [7548] 4-9-7 **70**	AdamKirby 10	79
			(J Akehurst) *in tch: drvn and rapid hdwy fr 3f out to ld appr fnl 2f: strly chal thrght fnl f: hld on wl u.p*	**9/2**^{1}	
0042	2	*nk*	**Negotiation (IRE)**^{15} [7548] 4-9-5 **68**	FrannyNorton 9	76
			(M Quinn) *chsd ldrs: drvn to chse wnr ins fnl 2f: str chalkenge thrght fnl f: a jst hld*	**15/2**	
4506	3	*2 ¼*	**Folio (IRE)**^{15} [7562] 10-9-1 **64**	StevieDonohoe 6	68
			(W J Musson) *in rr: hdwy over 2f out: styd on u.p fnl f to take 3rd cl home but no imp on ldng duo*	**8/1**	
3003	4	*½*	**Robby Bobby**^{13} [7570] 5-9-2 **65**	IanMongan 14	68
			(Mrs L J Mongan) *chsd ldrs: rdn and styd to chse ldng duo fnl f: no imp and one pce into 4th cl home*	**11/1**	
0356	5	*1 ¼*	**Beaubrav**^{52} [6055] 4-9-5 **68**	(t) ChrisCatlin 3	68
			(M Madgwick) *in rr: hdwy ins fnl 2f: styd on strly fnl f: gng on cl home but nt rch ldrs*	**11/1**	
2414	6	*1*	**James Pollard (IRE)**^{22} [7490] 5-8-11 **63**	(t) AndrewHeffernan$^{(3)}$ 11	61+
			(B J Llewellyn) *in rr: hdwy 2f out: styng on whn nt clr run on ins and hmpd appr fnl f: kpt on again but nt rcvr*	**16/1**	
506	7	*¾*	**Dalhaan (USA)**^{24} [7465] 5-9-4 **67**	FrankieMcDonald 8	64+
			(L A Dace) *stdd s: hld up in rr: stdy hdwy fr 2f: nt clr run fr over 1f out and ins fnl f: styd on wl cl home under hand riding*	**33/1**	
5360	8	*½*	**Tuscan King**^{202} [2279] 3-9-3 **69**	(b) GeorgeBaker 4	65
			(P D Evans) *chsd ldrs: rdn over 2f out: sn outpcd*	**25/1**	
3-64	9	*hd*	**Gordy Bee (USA)**^{23} [7474] 4-9-3 **66**	(e) PaulEddery 2	61
			(R C Guest) *led tl hdd appr fnl 2f: btn whn hung rt over 1f out*	**8/1**	
1000	10	*½*	**Carr Hall (IRE)**^{22} [7491] 7-8-5 **61**	GeorgeDowning$^{(7)}$ 13	55
			(A W Carroll) *nvr beyond mid-div*	**40/1**	
43-5	11	*shd*	**Muzo (USA)**^{49} [7043] 4-9-6 **69**	SteveDrowne 7	63
			(C A Dwyer) *a towards rr*	**11/2**^{2}	
0302	12	*1 ¼*	**Abriachan**^{21} [7499] 3-8-11 **63**	JackMitchell 12	54
			(M G Quinlan) *in rr: rdn and hdwy to chse ldrs ins fnl 3f: one pce fr over 1f out*	**7/1**^{3}	
61-6	13	*½*	**Jenny Potts**^{209} [2080] 6-9-1 **69**	TobyAtkinson$^{(5)}$ 1	59
			(C J Down) *a towards rr*	**16/1**	
610	14	*19*	**Lytham (IRE)**^{190} [2645] 9-9-0 **63**	JimmyQuinn 5	15
			(A W Carroll) *plld hrd: sn chsng ldr: chal 7f out to 5f out: wknd rapidly 3f out*	**20/1**	

2m 8.09s (0.09) **Going Correction** -0.025s/f (Stan)
WFA 3 from 4yo+ 3lb **14** Ran SP% **122.5**
Speed ratings (Par 103): **98,97,95,95,94 93,93,92,92,92 92,91,90,75**
Tote Swingers: 1&2 £6.50, 1&3 £17.30, 2&3 £20.50 CSF £36.66 CT £270.38 TOTE £6.40: £2.30, £2.20, £4.50; EX 25.40.

Owner M Chandler **Bred** Roland Alder & Morton Bloodstock **Trained** Epsom, Surrey

■ Stewards' Enquiry : Andrew Heffernan one-day ban: careless riding (Jan 5)

FOCUS

It paid to be prominent. They went steady early, before the pace increased noticeably down the back straight when the often free-running Lytham took on Gordy Bee up front. Ordinary form, with the winner producing a length personal best.

Dalhaan(USA) ◆ Official explanation: jockey said, regarding running and riding, that his orders were to drop the gelding out and run on to the finish as best he can but, in the home straight, it was unable to get a clear run.

7779 CHRISTMAS AT THE PANORAMIC MEDIAN AUCTION MAIDEN STKS 7f (P)

5:00 (5:03) (Class 6) 2-Y-0 **£1,637** (£483; £241) **Stalls** High

Form			Horse	Jockey	RPR
	1		**Seeking Magic** 2-9-3 0	AdamKirby 2	68+
			(C G Cox) *t.k.h: trckd ldrs: wnt 2nd 2f out: drvn to ld over 1f out: styd in strly fnl f*	**2/1**^{2}	
00	2	*2 ½*	**Take Your Partner**^{13} [7578] 2-9-3 0	PhillipMakin 5	61+
			(K A Ryan) *broke wl: chsd ldrs early tl bdly outpcd and bhd after 3f: stl plenty to do whn styd on fr over 1f out: kpt on wl fnl f to take 2nd fnl strides: no ch w wnr*	**10/1**	
00	3	*shd*	**Konstantin (IRE)**^{12} [7595] 2-9-3 0	JackMitchell 3	61+
			(M P Tregoning) *led 1f: styd trcking ldr: led over 2f out: sn hdd: outpcd by wnr fnl f: lost 2nd last strides*	**8/1**^{3}	
06	4	*2 ¾*	**Stirling Bridge**^{55} [6882] 2-9-3 0	SteveDrowne 1	54
			(W Jarvis) *led after 1f: hdd over 2f out: wknd over 1f out*	**4/5**^{1}	
0	5	*11*	**Bedibyes**^{22} [7485] 2-8-12 0	RussKennemore 4	20
			(N R Mitchell) *reluctant to load: a struggling in rr*	**50/1**	

1m 26.27s (0.27) **Going Correction** -0.025s/f (Stan) **5** Ran SP% **111.1**
Speed ratings (Par 94): **97,94,94,90,78**
CSF £19.95 TOTE £2.70: £1.30, £3.20; EX 16.40.

Owner The Seekers **Bred** R, J D & M R Bromley Gardner **Trained** Lambourn, Berks

FOCUS

A moderate maiden won by the only newcomer in the line-up.

NOTEBOOK

Seeking Magic ◆ had a sheepskin noseband fitted and was keener than ideal early on, but he was professional once asked for his challenge. This 35,000gns purchase is bred to stay well, being a half-brother to quite useful 1m7f scorer Grey Mystique, out of a 1m4f winner, so it's encouraging he was able to win over 7f at two. He ought to get a workable handicap mark and should progress. (tchd 5-2)

Take Your Partner dropped away to a detached last turning into the straight, but credit to his rider, who was really persistent, and the colt ran on to take an unlikely second, despite being inclined to hang right. It would probably be unwise to get carried away seeing as the leaders weren't going particularly fast late on, and he's not that big, but handicaps are now an option. (tchd 9-1 and 11-1)

Konstantin(IRE) ◆, who hinted at ability over 6f here on his second start, was unsuited by the step up in trip but again offered encouragement. Bred to make a decent sprinter, he's one to keep in mind now he's qualified for an official mark. (op 9-1)

Stirling Bridge, upped in trip after 55 days off, failed to build on the form he showed in a couple of 6f Newmarket maidens. However, he's a scopey type who looks very much a 3-y-o prospect and can yet do a lot better. Handicaps are now an option. (op 10-11 tchd evens in places)

7780 STUDENT RACING MAGAZINE MAIDEN AUCTION STKS 1m (P)

5:30 (5:31) (Class 6) 2-Y-0 **£1,637** (£483; £241) **Stalls** High

Form			Horse	Jockey	RPR
022	1		**Flying Power**^{15} [7551] 2-8-11 71	ChrisCatlin 3	74
			(D R Lanigan) *trckd ldrs: drvn and styd on fr over 1f out to ld fnl 120yds: kpt on wl*	**5/2**^{1}	
2250	2	*nk*	**Nothing To Hide (IRE)**^{68} [6555] 2-8-12 75	JamesDoyle 5	74
			(D J S Ffrench Davis) *led: rdn 2f out: kpt on u.p: hdd fnl120yds: no ex cl home*	**7/2**^{3}	
033	3	*1 ½*	**Phase Shift**^{20} [7503] 2-8-4 66	JamesRogers$^{(7)}$ 2	70
			(W R Muir) *chsd ldr: rdn over 2f out: chal between horses over 1f out: wknd fnl 120yds*	**13/2**	
	4	*2*	**Cecile De Volanges** 2-8-7 0	DavidProbert 6	61
			(Miss Tor Sturgis) *chsd ldrs: rdn over 2f out: wknd over 1f out*	**33/1**	
00	5	*3 ½*	**Sir Randolf (IRE)**^{11} [7610] 2-9-0 0	(t) TravisBlock 8	60
			(S Kirk) *in rr: rdn over 3f out: no imp*	**9/1**	
032	6	*1 ¾*	**Blue Maisey**^{15} [7551] 2-8-6 71	JimmyQuinn 1	48
			(Miss S L Davison) *chsd ldrs tl pushed along and no prog over 2f out: wknd wl over 1f out*	**11/4**^{2}	
00	7	*2 ½*	**Last Act (IRE)**^{15} [7559] 2-8-7 0	WilliamCarson 7	43
			(M R Hoad) *s.i.s: a towards rr*	**50/1**	
0	8	*hd*	**Mayfair Lad**^{15} [7559] 2-9-1 0	EddieAhern 4	51
			(E A L Dunlop) *s.i.s: a in rr*	**14/1**	

1m 39.98s (0.18) **Going Correction** -0.025s/f (Stan) **8** Ran SP% **112.4**
Speed ratings (Par 94): **98,97,96,94,90 88,86,86**
Tote Swingers: 1&2 £2.10, 1&3 £3.60, 2&3 £3.80 CSF £11.12 TOTE £3.60: £1.10, £1.10, £3.60; EX 11.70.

Owner Saif Ali **Bred** Rabbah Bloodstock Limited **Trained** Newmarket, Suffolk

FOCUS

An ordinary maiden. The pace seemed just modest for much of the way.

NOTEBOOK

Flying Power had fared best of those handy despite finding 7f too short when runner-up around here on his previous start and proved suited by the step up in trip. He would have preferred a stronger pace to run at, and once again carried his head awkwardly, giving the impression he's got his own ideas, but he was persuaded to go through with his effort under a determined Chris Catlin. If he can mature mentally, perhaps he'll cope with a likely rise in the weights, but he's still probably best watched next time. (op 11-4 tchd 3-1)

Nothing To Hide(IRE) was well ridden from the front and had every chance, albeit he was a bit keen. This was a pleasing after a 68-day break. He really should be up to winning a similar race this winter. (op 4-1 tchd 9-2)

Phase Shift kept tabs on Nothing To Hide throughout but was one-paced under pressure and didn't really see her race out. She seems caught between two trips at the moment, having found 7f too sharp last time. (op 11-2 tchd 7-1)

Cecile De Volanges, a 5,000gns first foal of a 1m4f winner, made a pleasing debut, keeping on well for pressure in the straight. She should improve and looks to have inherited more stamina from the dam's side of her pedigree than speed from the sire.

Sir Randolf(IRE) might do better over further in handicaps. (tchd 10-1 and 8-1 in places)

Blue Maisey, although flattered to have dead-heated with Flying Power over 7f here last time, should have fared better. She raced keenly without any cover and found little. (tchd 9-4 and 10-3 in a place)

7781 KIA VENGA H'CAP 2m (P)

6:00 (6:01) (Class 4) (0-85,82) 3-Y-0+ **£3,885** (£1,156; £577; £288) **Stalls** High

Form			Horse	Jockey	RPR
0053	1		**High On A Hill (IRE)**^{35} [7316] 3-8-10 **72**	JamesDoyle 2	81
			(S Kirk) *trckd ldr: led ins fnl 3f: hrd drvn and styd on wl fnl f*	**15/2**	
-003	2	*2 ¼*	**Spring Jim**^{20} [7061] 9-10-0 **82**	GeorgeBaker 8	88
			(J R Fanshawe) *hld up in rr but in tch: hdwy 3f out: chsd wnr 2f out: no imp fnl f but hld on wl for 2nd*	**5/2**^{1}	
1456	3	*hd*	**Chookie Hamilton**^{14} [7568] 6-10-0 **82**	TomEaves 6	88
			(V P Donoghue) *s.i.s: sn chsng ldrs: rdn over 2f out: rallied and kpt on to press for 2nd fnl f but no imp on wnr: no ex and dropped to 3rd cl home*	**11/1**	
1004	4	*1 ¾*	**Satwa Gold (USA)**^{15} [7553] 4-9-8 **76**	AdamKirby 4	80
			(Stef Higgins) *hld up in rr: hdwy over 2f out: kpt on but nvr gng pce to get into contention*	**4/1**^{3}	
1124	5	*9*	**Sinbad The Sailor**^{52} [1273] 5-9-4 **75**	(v) MatthewDavies$^{(3)}$ 5	68
			(George Baker) *led tl hdd ins fnl 3f: wknd over 2f out*	**10/1**	
0001	6	*3 ¼*	**Morar**^{15} [7553] 4-9-9 **77**	IanMongan 1	66
			(Mrs L J Mongan) *hld up in rr: hdwy on outside 3f out: nvr rchd ldrs and wknd u.p over 2f out*	**11/4**^{2}	
0000	7	*12*	**Highly Regal (IRE)**^{20} [7114] 5-9-10 **78**	(b) EddieAhern 3	53
			(R A Teal) *in rr but in tch tl wknd rapidly over 2f out*	**25/1**	
531/	8	*13*	**Crimson Monarch (USA)**^{1148} [6275] 6-8-11 **65**	ChrisCatlin 7	24
			(P W Hiatt) *chsd ldrs tl rdn and wknd 4f out*	**20/1**	

3m 29.86s (-0.24) **Going Correction** -0.025s/f (Stan)
WFA 3 from 4yo+ 8lb **8** Ran SP% **113.0**
Speed ratings (Par 105): **99,97,97,96,92 90,84,78**
Tote Swingers: 1&2 £4.60, 1&3 £15.20, 2&3 £6.80 CSF £26.00 CT £205.57 TOTE £7.70: £1.70, £1.10, £4.00; EX 37.20.

Owner Seahorse Five & Tim Pearson **Bred** Dominic Fagan **Trained** Upper Lambourn, Berks

FOCUS

The pace set by Sinbad The Sailor was just ordinary and the form is a bit muddling, placed around the second and third.

7782 BOOK FOR BOXING DAY ON 0844 579 3008 H'CAP 6f (P)

6:30 (6:32) (Class 4) (0-85,83) 3-Y-0+ **£3,885** (£1,156; £577; £288) **Stalls** High

Form			Horse	Jockey	RPR
6144	1		**Hatta Stream (IRE)**^{13} [7573] 4-9-2 **78**	MickyFenton 5	84
			(J Pearce) *t.k.h and disp ld at mod pce 2f: racd in 2nd fr 4f out: drvn and narrow ld ins fnl f: hld on all out*	**7/2**^{3}	
3020	2	*shd*	**Quasi Congaree (GER)**^{13} [7573] 4-9-3 **79**	(t) GeorgeBaker 7	85
			(I A Wood) *trckd ldrs off mod early pce: drvn and styd on wl fnl f: clsng on wnr fnl 120yds: not quite get up*	**8/1**	
2042	3	*hd*	**Breathless Kiss (USA)**^{8} [7654] 3-9-1 **77**	(b) PhillipMakin 2	82
			(K A Ryan) *disp ld off mod pce tl led after 2f: rdn 2f out: hdd ins fnl f: styd chalng: lost cl 2nd fnl 120yds but stl ev ch tl no ex cl home*	**4/1**	
0022	4	*¾*	**Lujeanie**^{13} [7573] 4-9-7 **83**	(p) AdamKirby 3	86
			(D K Ivory) *trckd ldrs off mod early pce: drvn and styd on to chal ins fnl f: nt quite get on terms: no ex cl home*	**11/4**^{2}	

2131 **5** ½ **Stratton Banker (IRE)**[13] 7571 3-8-12 **74**.................... WilliamCarson 1 75+
(S C Williams) *plld hrd and disp ld off mod early pce: styd chsng ldrs: rdn over 2f out: styd on same pce fnl f* **9/4**[1]

1m 13.69s (0.59) **Going Correction** -0.025s/f (Stan) **5** Ran SP% **110.8**
Speed ratings (Par 105): **95,94,94,93,92**
CSF £28.12 TOTE £4.80: £4.20, £5.10; EX 32.70.
Owner Macniler Racing Partnership **Bred** T W Bloodstock Ltd **Trained** Newmarket, Suffolk

FOCUS
They went no pace at all through the first half of the contest (time 0.94 seconds slower than following 46-50 handicap) and this is not form to trust at all. They finished in a bunch.

7783 KEMPTON.CO.UK APPRENTICE H'CAP 6f (P)
7:00 (7:00) (Class 7) (0-50,50) 3-Y-O+ **£1,364** (£403; £201) **Stalls** High

Form RPR

0063 **1** **Mind The Monarch**[15] 7547 3-9-0 **50**.............................(v) RyanPowell 9 56
(R A Teal) *chsd ldrs: drvn to take slt ld jst ins fnl f: hld on wl* **14/1**

0060 **2** ½ **Kheley (IRE)**[20] 7506 4-8-13 **49**.................................. JamesRogers 12 53
(W M Brisbourne) *trckd ldrs: hdwy fr 2f out: drvn to chse wnr ins fnl f: styd on wl but a jst hld* **7/2**[1]

4053 **3** *hd* **Force To Spend**[20] 7506 3-8-13 **49**...................................... RyanClark 7 53
(N P Littmoden) *towards rr: hdwy fr 2f out: fin wl fnl f to take 3rd cl home: nt quite rch ldng duo* **6/1**[3]

0000 **4** ½ **Spoof Master (IRE)**[27] 7426 6-8-13 **49**...........................(t) JulieBurke 10 51
(J Pearce) *chsd ldr: led ins fnl 3f: rdn over 2f our: hdd jst insde fnl f: styd rt there tl no ex cklose home* **5/1**[2]

6055 **5** 1 **Cane Cat (IRE)**[43] 7166 3-8-5 **48**..........................(t) GeorgeDowning(7) 8 47+
(A W Carroll) *in rr: hdwy whn hmpd 2f out: styd on wl fnl f: nt rch ldrs* **20/1**

6032 **6** *nk* **Dower Glen**[14] 7563 3-8-7 **50**............................(v) ShirleyTeasdale(7) 1 48
(V P Donoghue) *sn in tch: chsd ldrs over 2f out: one pce whn edgd lft clsng stages* **8/1**

/0-6 **7** ½ **Lend A Light**[26] 7449 4-8-11 **50**................................... RichardRowe(3) 2 46+
(P J Hobbs) *s.i.s: in rr: hdwy over 1f out: kpt on fnl f: nt rch ldrs* **11/1**

0050 **8** 2 ¼ **Gilderoy**[4] 7717 3-8-7 **48**.. LucyBarry(5) 3 37
(D J S Ffrench Davis) *s.i.s: in rr tl styd on fr over 1f out* **12/1**

4402 **9** *hd* **Cocktail Party (IRE)**[31] 7380 4-8-9 **48**......................... AlexEdwards(3) 6 37
(J W Unett) *in tch: rdn and no imp fr over 2f out* **7/1**

0000 **10** 12 **Suhayl Star (IRE)**[22] 7477 6-8-9 **48**.......................... MatthewCosham(3) 4 —
(P Burgoyne) *chsd ldrs tl wknd over 2f out* **20/1**

-003 **11** 1 **Jonny Ebeneezer**[11] 7607 11-8-8 **49**.....................(b) KatiaScallan(5) 11 —
(D Flood) *led tl hdd ins fnl 3f: wknd over 2f out* **14/1**

1m 12.75s (-0.35) **Going Correction** -0.025s/f (Stan) **11** Ran SP% **115.7**
Speed ratings (Par 97): **101,100,100,99,98 97,97,94,93,77 76**
Tote Swingers: 1&2 £6.60, 1&3 £10.20, 2&3 £5.80 CSF £61.56 CT £335.18 TOTE £27.80: £6.60, £1.10, £3.20; EX 115.50.
Owner Alan Cotton **Bred** J Morton **Trained** Ashtead, Surrey

FOCUS
A very moderate sprint handicap run at a good pace. It is hard to view the form positively.
T/Jkpt: £19,237.70 to a £1 stake. Pool:£67,738.73 - 2.50 winning tickets T/Plt: £282.10 to a £1 stake. Pool:£98,623.22 - 255.14 winning tickets T/Qpdt: £33.70 to a £1 stake. Pool:£9,067.16 - 199.10 winning tickets ST

7699 WOLVERHAMPTON (A.W) (L-H)
Thursday, December 9

OFFICIAL GOING: Standard to slow
Wind: moderate 1/2 behind Weather: fine and sunny, cold

7784 BIGGER WINS WITH SP+ AT TOTESPORT.COM CLAIMING STKS 5f 20y(P)
1:45 (1:45) (Class 6) 3-Y-O+ **£1,706** (£503; £252) **Stalls** Low

Form RPR

0041 **1** **Ebraam (USA)**[9] 7635 7-9-7 **88**....................................... AndreaAtzeni 3 82+
(R A Harris) *trckd ldrs: wnt 2nd 2f out: led 1f out: pushed out: readily* **6/5**[1]

1100 **2** 1 ¼ **Efistorm**[4] 7719 9-9-2 **72**... KierenFox(3) 2 76
(C R Dore) *chsd ldrs: swtchd ins over 1f out: edgd rt and kpt on to take 2nd clsng stages* **4/1**[2]

4623 **3** 1 **The Tatling (IRE)**[10] 7628 13-8-11 **64**......................... RussKennemore 9 64
(J M Bradley) *chsd ldrs: n.m.r and checked after 2f: wnt 2nd jst ins fnl f: kpt on same pce* **5/1**[3]

2100 **4** *hd* **Avonvalley**[4] 7719 3-8-10 **68**.. RobbieFitzpatrick 5 63
(Peter Grayson) *sn drvn along in rr: hdwy on outside over 2f out: styd on wl ins fnl f* **25/1**

1040 **5** ¾ **Dancing Freddy (IRE)**[9] 7635 3-8-13 **70**......................(p) MickyFenton 7 63
(J G Given) *sn w ldr: led over 3f out: hdd 1f out: wknd towards fin* **4/1**[2]

0000 **6** 2 ¾ **Brazilian Brush (IRE)**[4] 7721 5-8-7 **43**.................(bt) KirstyMilczarek 6 47?
(J M Bradley) *led: hdd over 3f out: wknd over 1f out* **66/1**

1200 **7** 1 ½ **Monte Major (IRE)**[10] 7628 9-8-0 **61**...........................(v) SoniaEaton(7) 1 42
(D Shaw) *a in rr: pushed along 3f out: nvr a factor* **10/1**

63.01 secs (0.71) **Going Correction** +0.30s/f (Slow) **7** Ran SP% **116.6**
Speed ratings (Par 101): **106,104,102,102,100 96,94**
Tote Swingers: 1&2 £2.20, 1&3 £2.40, 2&3 £3.60 CSF £6.62 TOTE £2.20: £1.20, £2.00; EX 6.10 Trifecta £16.20 Pool: £750.29 - 34.14 winning units..
Owner Robert & Nina Bailey **Bred** Shadwell Farm LLC **Trained** Earlswood, Monmouths

FOCUS
A muddling claimer with the form anchored by the sixth.

7785 BET SP+ AT TOTESPORT 0800 221 221 NURSERY 7f 32y(P)
2:15 (2:16) (Class 6) (0-65,65) 2-Y-O **£1,706** (£503; £252) **Stalls** High

Form RPR

3025 **1** **Better Self**[10] 7631 2-8-7 **58**..................................... MatthewCosham(7) 7 68
(P D Evans) *s.i.s: drvn on outside to improve over 3f out: chsng ldrs 2f out: led appr fnl f: drew clr* **5/1**[3]

0021 **2** 4 **Sky Diamond (IRE)**[10] 7631 2-9-4 **62**..........................(b) MickyFenton 8 62
(J G Given) *sn w ldr: led over 3f out: hdd over 1f out: styd on same pce* **7/4**[1]

461 **3** 3 **Irie Ute**[9] 7643 2-9-6 **64**.. JamieSpencer 5 57
(S Kirk) *trckd ldrs: wnt 2nd over 2f out: led briefly over 1f out: edgd lft and wknd fnl 75yds* **9/4**[2]

6614 **4** *nk* **Bachelor Knight (IRE)**[7] 7666 2-9-4 **65**.................... JamesSullivan(3) 3 57
(Ollie Pears) *trckd ldrs: t.k.h: stdd and dropped to rr after 2f: hdwy over 2f out: sn chsng ldrs: kpt on towards fin* **6/1**

6000 **5** 2 ¼ **Joyously**[10] 7631 2-9-0 **61**.. RobertLButler(3) 6 47
(P Butler) *s.i.s: hdwy over 4f out: chsng ldrs over 2f out: one pce over 1f out* **25/1**

4500 **6** 18 **River Blade**[116] 5111 2-8-3 **50**... KierenFox(3) 1 —
(W M Brisbourne) *s.s: drvn along in rr: bhd whn eased ins fnl f* **20/1**

0600 **7** 10 **Danube Dancer (IRE)**[8] 7650 2-8-12 **56**.................(b) FergusSweeney 4 —
(J S Moore) *sn led: hdd over 3f out: lost pl over 2f out: bhd whn eased fnl f* **14/1**

0506 **8** 24 **Hannah Cann**[5] 7692 2-8-1 **45**... NickyMackay 2 —
(Peter Grayson) *led early: trckd ldrs: t.k.h: drvn and lost pl over 3f out: bhd whn eased over 1f out: t.o* **100/1**

1m 31.36s (1.76) **Going Correction** +0.30s/f (Slow) **8** Ran SP% **114.4**
Speed ratings (Par 94): **101,96,93,92,90 69,58,30**
Tote Swingers: 1&2 £1.50, 1&3 £3.40, 2&3 £1.30 CSF £13.98 CT £24.56 TOTE £3.50: £1.50, £1.10, £1.40; EX 14.70 Trifecta £45.90 Pool: £706.94 - 11.38 winning units..
Owner Mrs Sally Edwards **Bred** Miss K Rausing **Trained** Pandy, Monmouths

FOCUS
A modest nursery but the early pace looked strong.

NOTEBOOK
Better Self couldn't live with the front-runners early but came with a strong run down the middle of the course in the home straight. Behind the runner-up last time at this course over further, she had clearly benefited for that run, which had come after a 72-day break, and she reversed the form to gain a first victory.
Sky Diamond(IRE) travelled powerfully into the lead but became one-paced as soon as pressure was applied. The drop in trip possibly didn't help. (tchd 13-8 and 15-8 in places)
Irie Ute, a narrow winner at Southwell on his previous start, was, like Sky Diamond, quite keen in the leading bunch, which may have counted against him in the latter stages. (op 5-2 tchd 11-4)
Bachelor Knight(IRE) sat in behind in the early stages, close to the inside rail, before finding very little once asked to go after the first three.
Joyously, who was behind both Sky Diamond and Better Self last time, chased the leaders but couldn't quicken in the home straight.
Hannah Cann Official explanation: jockey said filly had no more to give

7786 TOTESPORT.COM HOME OF POOL BETTING MAIDEN STKS 1m 141y(P)
2:45 (2:45) (Class 5) 3-Y-O+ **£2,590** (£770; £385; £192) **Stalls** Low

Form RPR

2 **1** **Private Joke**[12] 7596 3-9-3 0.. NickyMackay 2 73+
(J H M Gosden) *stdd s: hdwy on outside to trck ldrs 5f out: drvn to ld over 2f out: styd on wl fnl f* **1/5**[1]

2 1 ¼ **D'Artagnan (SAF)**[131] 3-8-4 80..................................... KierenFox(3) 4 60
(Miss Gay Kelleway) *t.k.h: trckd ldrs: drvn and upsides over 2f out: kpt on same pce ins fnl f* **4/1**[2]

0000 **3** 9 **Flyjack (USA)**[9] 7639 3-9-0 47.............................(p) PatrickDonaghy(3) 3 49
(Mrs L Williamson) *hld up in rr: hdwy to trck ldrs over 3f out: wnt modest 3rd over 1f out* **33/1**

06 **4** 4 ½ **Jingoism (USA)**[13] 7579 4-9-2 0................................ JamesSullivan(3) 6 39
(B Ellison) *s.i.s: towards rr: reminders after s and over 3f out: chsng ldrs over 2f out: sn wl outpcd: kpt on to take modest 4th last 100yds* **18/1**[3]

00-0 **5** 3 ¾ **Edge End**[28] 7125 6-8-12 45.. JosephYoung(7) 5 30
(Mrs L Williamson) *t.k.h: led: racd wd: hdd over 2f out: wknd over 1f out* **80/1**

0000 **6** 16 **Rightcar Dominic**[6] 7684 5-9-5 37........................... RobbieFitzpatrick 1 —
(Peter Grayson) *chsd ldrs: drvn over 4f out: lost pl 3f out: sn bhd: eased last 150yds* **100/1**

1m 55.99s (5.49) **Going Correction** +0.30s/f (Slow)
WFA 3 from 4yo+ 2lb **6** Ran SP% **113.8**
Speed ratings (Par 103): **87,85,77,73,70 56**
Tote Swingers: 1&2 £1.10, 1&3 £3.80, 2&3 £2.50 CSF £1.48 TOTE £1.30: £1.10, £1.50; EX 1.50.
Owner H R H Princess Haya Of Jordan **Bred** Whatton Manor Stud **Trained** Newmarket, Suffolk

FOCUS
The first pair came clear in this weak maiden. The winner looks sure to do better and the poor third sets the standard.

7787 PLAY BLACKJACK AT TOTESPORT.COM H'CAP 1m 141y(P)
3:20 (3:20) (Class 6) (0-55,55) 3-Y-O+ **£1,706** (£503; £252) **Stalls** Low

Form RPR

5634 **1** **Bentley**[10] 7633 6-9-1 **52**..(b) GrahamGibbons 2 61
(B P J Baugh) *mde all: drvn over 2f out: edgd lft ins fnl f: all out* **5/1**[2]

0260 **2** *nk* **All Moving Parts (USA)**[4] 7717 3-9-2 **55**......................(b) ShaneKelly 12 63
(A J McCabe) *hld up towards rr: hdwy on outer 4f out: wnt 2nd over 1f out: styd on ins fnl f: jst hld* **13/2**

3 **3** 1 ¼ **Odin's Raven (IRE)**[16] 7538 5-9-1 **55**......................... JamesSullivan(3) 4 60
(B Ellison) *chsd ldrs: chsd wnr 3f out: styd on to take 3rd towards fin* **6/1**[3]

0051 **4** *nk* **Royal Island (IRE)**[4] 7717 8-8-12 **49**............................ JamieSpencer 11 54
(M G Quinlan) *hld up in rr: smooth hdwy on wd outside to trck ldrs over 2f out: rdn over 1f out: no ex last 100yds* **2/1**[1]

5300 **5** 4 ½ **Dane Cottage**[51] 7003 3-8-4 **50**............................... MatthewCosham(7) 13 44
(P D Evans) *hld up in rr: hdwy over 5f out: sn trcking ldrs: wknd over 1f out* **33/1**

4001 **6** 1 ½ **Custard Cream Kid (IRE)**[8] 7649 4-8-7 **51**................... LauraBarry(7) 6 42
(R A Fahey) *mid-div: effrt over 2f out: sn outpcd: kpt on ins fnl f* **16/1**

7 *nk* **Celtic Life (IRE)**[48] 7077 4-8-10 **47**............................(t) AndreaAtzeni 10 37
(Miss Amy Weaver) *chsd ldrs: wknd over 1f out* **8/1**

0002 **8** 3 ¼ **Shared Moment (IRE)**[4] 7717 4-9-1 **55**........................(p) AmyRyan(3) 3 38
(J Gallagher) *s.i.s: mid-div: effrt over 2f out: lost pl over 1f out* **6/1**[3]

3000 **9** 5 **Bold Hawk**[20] 7508 4-8-7 **47**.......................................(tp) KierenFox(3) 9 18
(Mrs C A Dunnett) *chsd ldrs: drvn over 3f out: wknd 2f out* **66/1**

0000 **10** ¾ **Daniel Thomas (IRE)**[16] 7543 8-9-1 **55**..................(p) RobertLButler(3) 7 25
(P Butler) *s.s: a towards rr* **20/1**

0000 **11** *nk* **Ivestar (IRE)**[16] 7543 5-9-0 **54**................................(t) PatrickDonaghy(3) 8 23
(B M R Haslam) *mid-div: drvn over 2f out: sn lost pl* **16/1**

1m 53.15s (2.65) **Going Correction** +0.30s/f (Slow)
WFA 3 from 4yo+ 2lb **11** Ran SP% **124.0**
Speed ratings (Par 101): **100,99,98,98,94 93,92,89,85,84 84**
Tote Swingers: 1&2 £4.20, 1&3 £4.90, 2&3 £6.60 CSF £39.16 CT £208.81 TOTE £6.80: £2.30, £3.10, £1.60; EX 34.80 Trifecta £258.70 Pool: £1,031.52 - 2.95 winning units..
Owner The Flying Spur Racing Partnership **Bred** Paul Blows And Jenny Hall **Trained** Audley, Staffs

FOCUS
A moderate handicap. The winner made all and is rated to his autumn best.
Celtic Life(IRE) Official explanation: jockey said gelding hung left

7788 PLAY ROULETTE AT TOTESPORT.COM H'CAP 1m 1f 103y(P)
3:50 (3:50) (Class 5) (0-70,70) 3-Y-O+ **£2,590** (£770; £385; £192) **Stalls** Low

Form RPR

5303 **1** **Mighty Clarets (IRE)**[7] 7663 3-8-6 **64**...................... GeorgeChaloner(7) 7 74
(R A Fahey) *racd wd: hdwy to ld 7f out: kpt on wl fnl f: all out* **12/1**

3041 **2** *hd* **Loyalty**[6] 7685 3-9-0 **65**..(v) PatrickMathers 6 75
(D Shaw) *chsd ldrs: drvn over 2f out: sn chsng wnr: chalng whn hung lft ins fnl f: jst hld* **7/2**[3]

2253 **3** 6 **Nicholas Pocock (IRE)**[20] 7502 4-8-8 60..............(b[1]) JamesSullivan(3) 4 57
(B Ellison) *hld up in rr: hdwy over 2f out: wnt n.d 3rd over 1f out* **10/3**[2]
0406 **4** 1 ½ **Penang Cinta**[34] 7337 7-9-2 65.. StephenCraine 5 59
(P D Evans) *hld up in rr: hdwy to trck ldrs over 6f out: outpcd over 2f out: kpt on fnl f* **33/1**
0041 **5** 2 **Kildare Sun (IRE)**[6] 7679 8-9-4 67............................(p) GrahamGibbons 2 57
(J Mackie) *trckd ldrs: effrt 3f out: lost pl over 1f out* **7/1**
4221 **6** 2 **Strike Force**[7] 7663 6-9-4 70...(t) KierenFox(3) 3 55+
(Miss Olivia Maylam) *hld up in rr: effrt on ins over 2f out: no ch whn hmpd and swtchd rt 1f out* **11/4**[1]
-600 **7** 6 **Etruscan (IRE)**[66] 6639 5-8-13 62.................................... SamHitchcott 1 35
(C Gordon) *led over 2f: chsd ldrs: drvn over 2f out: lost pl and edgd lft over 1f out* **11/2**

2m 4.68s (2.98) **Going Correction** +0.30s/f (Slow)
WFA 3 from 4yo+ 2lb **7** Ran SP% **110.5**
Speed ratings (Par 103): **98,97,92,91,89 87,82**
Tote Swingers: 1&2 £3.90, 1&3 £2.70, 2&3 £5.00 CSF £49.93 TOTE £14.20: £4.40, £2.30; EX 57.30.
Owner The Matthewman Partnership **Bred** Ellesmere Bloodstock Ltd **Trained** Musley Bank, N Yorks
■ George Chaloner's first winner.
■ Stewards' Enquiry : Sam Hitchcott one-day ban: careless riding (Dec 26)

FOCUS
A modest handicap domintated by the first pair. The winner set a steady pace. There is a chance the form is better than this, but also that the race fell apart behind the front two.

7789 PLAY BINGO AT TOTESPORT.COM H'CAP 1m 4f 50y(P)
4:20 (4:22) (Class 6) (0-60,62) 3-Y-O **£1,706** (£503; £252) **Stalls** Low

Form RPR
0002 **1** **Port Hill**[7] 7669 3-9-1 50.. ShaneKelly 4 57
(W M Brisbourne) *led: drvn over 2f out: edgd rt fnl f: jst hld on* **11/4**[2]
1413 **2** *shd* **Valantino Oyster (IRE)**[10] 7626 3-9-3 55................ PatrickDonaghy(3) 7 62
(B M R Haslam) *trckd ldrs: wnt 2nd over 6f out: drvn over 3f out: styd on fnl f: forced rt: jst hld* **6/4**[1]
2604 **3** 3 ¾ **Bring Sweets (IRE)**[57] 6183 3-8-12 50....................... JamesSullivan(3) 1 51
(B Ellison) *hld up: stdy hdwy over 2f out: wnt 3rd over 1f out: kpt on one pce* **5/1**[3]
-0P3 **4** 6 **Noverre Over There (IRE)**[7] 7669 3-9-1 53..................... KierenFox(3) 6 44
(Miss Olivia Maylam) *hld up in rr: hdwy to trck ldrs after 3f: drvn over 4f out: wknd fnl f* **9/1**
1000 **5** 12 **Miss Whippy**[29] 7387 3-8-11 46.................................... KirstyMilczarek 2 18
(P Howling) *trckd wnr: drvn 3f out: thrashed tail and lost pl wl over 1f out* **6/1**
6000 **6** 20 **Penshurst Lad (IRE)**[15] 6921 3-8-10 45...................(t) FergusSweeney 5 —
(R T Phillips) *dwlt: in rr: reminders over 5f out: lost pl over 3f out: sn bhd: eased ins fnl f: t.o* **33/1**

2m 45.06s (3.96) **Going Correction** +0.30s/f (Slow) **6** Ran SP% **110.6**
Speed ratings (Par 98): **98,97,95,91,83 70**
Tote Swingers: 1&2 £1.60, 1&3 £2.10, 2&3 £2.60 CSF £7.05 TOTE £4.40: £1.80, £1.40; EX 8.20.
Owner Derek & Mrs Marie Dean **Bred** M E Hughes **Trained** Great Ness, Shropshire
■ Stewards' Enquiry : Patrick Donaghy two-day ban: used whip with excessive frequency (Dec 26-27)

FOCUS
A weak handicap. The winner is rated close to his latest level.
T/Plt: £18.30 to a £1 stake. Pool:£109,344.48 - 4,358.36 winning tickets T/Qpdt: £12.90 to a £1 stake. Pool:£5,896.50 - 337.28 winning tickets WG

7776 DEAUVILLE (R-H)
Thursday, December 9
OFFICIAL GOING: Fibresand: standard

7800a PRIX LUTHIER (LISTED RACE) (3YO+) (FIBRESAND) 7f 110y
1:55 (12:00) 3-Y-O+ **£23,008** (£9,203; £6,902; £4,601; £2,300)

RPR
1 **Polytechnicien (USA)**[21] 7500 4-8-11 0.................. MickaelBarzalona 3 —
(A Fabre, France) **93/10**
2 3 **As De Trebol (USA)**[459] 5709 4-8-11 0........................ JulienGrosjean 13 —
(M Delcher-Sanchez, Spain) **10/1**
3 ½ **Chopastair (FR)**[58] 6914 9-8-11 0.................... Jean-BernardEyquem 4 —
(T Lemer, France) **43/10**[1]
4 ½ **Desertar (FR)**[51] 4-8-11 0.................................. Francois-XavierBertras 6 —
(D De Watrigant, France) **7/1**[3]
5 1 ½ **Slickly Royal (FR)**[75] 6384 6-9-1 0............................. GregoryBenoist 8 —
(P Demercastel, France) **13/1**
6 *hd* **Amazing Beauty (GER)**[16] 7546 3-8-8 0........................ TonyPiccone 14 —
(M Figge, Germany) **51/1**
7 1 ½ **Dam D'Augy (FR)**[66] 6640 5-8-11 0............................(b) ThierryJarnet 11 —
(Mlle S-V Tarrou, France) **20/1**
8 *nse* **Le Big (GER)**[17] 7535 6-9-1 0...................................... Jean-MichelBreux 7 —
(U Stoltefuss, Germany) **19/1**
9 ¾ **Polarix**[75] 6384 4-8-11 0.......................................(p) FabriceVeron 10 —
(H-A Pantall, France) **9/1**
10 2 **Beauchamp Viceroy**[12] 7593 6-8-11 0...............................(b) DaneO'Neill 9 —
(G A Butler) *broke smartly to ld fr s: rdn bef st: hdd 1 1/2f out: r.o u.p: no ex fnl f: fdd* **5/1**[2]
0 **Salut L'Africain (FR)**[17] 7535 5-9-1 0.............................(p) ThomasHuet 2 —
(Robert Collet, France) **19/1**
0 **Entre Deux Eaux (FR)**[17] 7535 4-8-8 0......................... IoritzMendizabal 1 —
(Robert Collet, France) **13/1**
0 **Mary's Precedent (FR)**[21] 7500 4-8-8 0...................... MorganDelalande 5 —
(C Lerner, France) **38/1**
0 **Kite Hunter (IRE)**[123] 4888 3-9-4 0.................................. StefanieHofer 15 —
(Mario Hofer, Germany) **31/1**
0 **Gold Harvest (FR)**[16] 7545 3-8-11 0........................ Pierre-CharlesBoudot 12 —
(Y De Nicolay, France) **22/1**

1m 27.1s (87.10) **15** Ran SP% **117.8**
WIN (incl. 1 euro stake): 10.30. PLACES: 3.20, 3.40, 1.90. DF: 79.60. SF: 218.30.
Owner Wertheimer & Frere **Bred** Wertheimer & Frere **Trained** Chantilly, France

7738 SOUTHWELL (L-H)
Friday, December 10
OFFICIAL GOING: Standard to slow changing to standard after race 1 (11.20).
Wind: Virtually nil Weather: Cloudy but dry

7801 TOTEPLACEPOT WIN WITHOUT BACKING A WINNER (S) STKS 1m (F)
11:20 (11:20) (Class 6) 2-Y-O **£1,489** (£443; £221; £110) **Stalls** Low

Form RPR
0065 **1** **Boogie Star**[11] 7629 2-8-6 53...(p) RyanPowell(5) 6 63
(J S Moore) *hld up in tch: hdwy wl over 2f out: sn cl up: rdn to ld over 1f out: clr whn edgd rt ins fnl f* **18/1**
2231 **2** 3 ¾ **Ivan's A Star (IRE)**[8] 7664 2-9-2 57.............................(p) CathyGannon 4 59
(J S Moore) *trckd ldr: led wl over 2f out: sn rdn: hdd and drvn over 1f out: sn one pce* **1/1**[1]
4066 **3** 5 **Miss Cosette (IRE)**[10] 7643 2-8-7 45 ow1.................. GrahamGibbons 5 39
(T D Barron) *trckd ldng pair: hdwy and cl up over 3f out: rdn and ch over 2f out: drvn over 1f out and sn one pce* **5/1**[3]
0050 **4** 2 ¾ **Carver County (IRE)**[30] 7396 2-8-6 41........................(p) RyanClark(5) 3 36
(Miss M E Rowland) *chsd ldrs: rdn along and outpcd 3f out: styd on u.p appr fnl f* **66/1**
6040 **5** 4 **High Kickin**[11] 7631 2-8-3 58................................(v) AndrewHeffernan(3) 8 22
(A J McCabe) *trckd ldrs on outer: hdwy and cl up over 3f out: rdn wl over 2f out and sn btn* **7/2**[2]
5050 **6** 4 **Indian Dip**[11] 7631 2-8-3 48.. KierenFox(3) 7 13
(Matthew Salaman) *dwlt and in rr: rdn along 1/2-way: nvr a factor* **25/1**
0 **7** 3 **Algris**[16] 7550 2-8-11 0.. StevieDonohoe 2 11
(Sir Mark Prescott) *s.i.s: sn rdn along: a bhd* **8/1**
00 **8** 1 ½ **Evelyns Diamond**[27] 7452 2-8-6 0 ow3.......................... PaulPickard(3) 1 5
(P T Midgley) *led: rdn along and hdd wl over 2f out: sn drvn and wknd* **66/1**

1m 47.35s (3.65) **Going Correction** +0.35s/f (Slow) **8** Ran SP% **112.1**
Speed ratings (Par 94): **95,91,86,83,79 75,72,71**
Tote Swingers: 1&2:£3.60, 1&3:£5.20, 2&3:£1.80 CSF £35.51 TOTE £20.30: £5.50, £1.02, £1.40; EX 29.10 Trifecta £120.70 Pool: £182.78 - 1.12 winning units..There was no bid for the winner
Owner Ray Styles & J S Moore **Bred** Mrs J A Chapman & Mrs Shelley Dwyer **Trained** Upper Lambourn, Berks

FOCUS
The going was changed to standard after this poor seller was run.

NOTEBOOK
Boogie Star, apparently the lesser-fancied of the Stan Moore-trained pair, came from off the pace to see out his race better than his stable companion. The switch to Fibresand clearly made a huge difference to him. (op 16-1)
Ivan's A Star(IRE), the only previous winner in the line-up, finished clear of the rest but found his stablemate, who was trying the surface for the first time, improving past him. (op 6-4)
Miss Cosette(IRE), whose rider put up 1lb overweight, is probably more at home over slightly shorter. (tchd 9-2)
Carver County(IRE) faced a stiff task at the weights and did as well as could be expected. (op 40-1)
High Kickin, who was down in class and had the visor back on, was weak in the market beforehand and there were unusually large amounts on the lay side in the place market in running, despite her appearing to travel well on the bend. She found little for pressure in the straight. (op 3-1)

7802 EUROPEAN BREEDERS' FUND MAIDEN STKS 7f (F)
11:50 (11:50) (Class 5) 2-Y-O **£3,139** (£926; £463) **Stalls** Low

Form RPR
2 **1** **Swimsuit**[46] 7123 2-8-12 0.. JackMitchell 3 67+
(M A Jarvis) *led over 2f: cl up: rdn to ld over 2f out: jnd wl over 1f out and sn drvn: edgd lft ent fnl f: styd on* **4/9**[1]
054 **2** 3 ½ **Szabo's Destiny**[24] 7470 2-9-3 65.. TomEaves 6 63
(J G Given) *cl up on outer: rdn along: edgd lft and outpcd 2f out: drvn over 1f out: kpt on ins fnl f: tk 2nd nr fin* **6/1**[3]
4 **3** *nk* **Mazovian (USA)**[6] 7692 2-9-0 0.................................. RobertLButler(3) 4 63
(M C Chapman) *trckd ldrs: smooth hdwy on inner over 2f out: rdn to chal wl over 1f out and ev ch tl drvn and one pce ent fnl f: lost 2nd nr fin* **28/1**
44 **4** 9 **Indian Arrow**[21] 7503 2-9-3 0... PhillipMakin 1 40
(J J Quinn) *cl up on inner: led over 4f out: rdn and hdd wl over 2f out: sn drvn and wknd* **7/2**[2]
6 **5** 16 **Elegant Star (IRE)**[13] 7603 2-8-12 0................................ WilliamCarson 5 —
(D Morris) *dwlt: sn rdn along in rr: bhd fr 1/2-way* **100/1**

1m 34.11s (3.81) **Going Correction** +0.35s/f (Slow) **5** Ran SP% **110.2**
Speed ratings (Par 96): **92,88,87,77,59**
CSF £3.77 TOTE £1.40: £1.40, £1.50; EX 3.70.
Owner Stephen Dartnell **Bred** Mrs S J Walker **Trained** Newmarket, Suffolk

FOCUS
A weak maiden.

NOTEBOOK
Swimsuit got off the mark at the second attempt in fairly workmanlike fashion. A half-sister to a winner over this C&D, she coped with the surface fairly well while still showing signs of inexperience, so it's likely there's better to come from her. (op 1-2)
Szabo's Destiny didn't find the drop back to 7f playing to his strengths, but he was staying on nicely at the finish and will appreciate a return to 1m. (op 7-1 tchd 15-2)
Mazovian(USA), stepping up 2f in distance, travelled best of all and looked a big danger early in the straight, but he didn't deliver under pressure and was eventually run out of second place. He's bred for this surface and a drop back to 6f could see him off the mark.
Indian Arrow, debuting on Fibresand, failed to run up to the level he showed at Wolverhampton last time. He needed this for a mark and will be of more interest back on Polytrack. (tchd 4-1)

7803 TOTESWINGER THREE WAYS TO WIN NURSERY 6f (F)
12:20 (12:20) (Class 5) (0-75,75) 2-Y-O **£2,115** (£624; £312) **Stalls** Low

Form RPR
0625 **1** **Lenjawi Pride**[15] 7565 2-9-7 75................................ RichardKingscote 7 82
(Tom Dascombe) *trckd ldrs: hdwy 3f out: rdn to chse ldr wl over 1f out: drvn to chal ins fnl f: kpt on to ld nr fin* **4/1**[3]
0300 **2** *shd* **Finn's Rainbow**[22] 7496 2-8-1 55.. FrannyNorton 8 62
(K A Ryan) *sn led: rdn 2f out: drvn over 1f out: jnd ins fnl f: hdd and no ex towards fin* **6/1**
0452 **3** 7 **Restless Bay (IRE)**[15] 7565 2-9-3 74..........................(be) PaulPickard(3) 1 60
(R Hollinshead) *in tch: hdwy over 2f out: rdn to chse ldrs whn hung lft and rt over 1f out: drvn and kpt on same pce fnl f* **4/1**[3]

504 **4** *shd* **Cheylesmore (IRE)**[60] 6811 2-8-12 **66**..........................[1] WilliamCarson 3 52
(S C Williams) *pushed along in rr and outpcd 1/2-way: rdn and hdwy on inner over 1f out: kpt on ins fnl f* **7/2**[2]

600 **5** *3/4* **Three Opera Divas**[14] 7578 2-8-2 **56**................................ NickyMackay 6 39
(M Johnston) *cl up: rdn along wl over 2f out: drvn wl over 1f out and sn wknd* **14/1**

2301 **6** *3/4* **Rowan Spirit (IRE)**[30] 7395 2-9-6 **74**.......................... GrahamGibbons 5 55
(W M Brisbourne) *cl up: effrt wl over 2f out: sn rdn and ev ch tl drvn and wknd over 1f out* **5/2**[1]

1m 17.68s (1.18) **Going Correction** +0.35s/f (Slow) **6** Ran SP% **111.7**
Speed ratings (Par 96): **106,105,96,96,95 94**
Tote Swingers:1&2: £4.40, 1&3:£1.90, 2&3:£5.20 CSF £26.92 CT £98.89 TOTE £5.20: £1.80, £4.00; EX 28.30 Trifecta £93.00 Pool: £253.99 - 2.02 winning units..

Owner A G D Lenjawi **Bred** Mill House Stud **Trained** Malpas, Cheshire

■ Stewards' Enquiry : Franny Norton two-day ban: used whip with excessive frequency (Dec 26-27)

FOCUS

Two pulled clear in this weakly contested nursery. The winner was finally back to his spring form.

NOTEBOOK

Lenjawi Pride just edged the photo with Finn's Rainbow. Runner-up in a novice race on her previous start here and hampered last time out, she finally took advantage of a slide in the weights, but whether she'll be able to cope with a return to a higher mark remains to be seen. (op 3-1)

Finn's Rainbow was given a positive ride, led them into the straight and battled on well, only to be run down close home. This was a return to form from him on his first try on this surface, and on this evidence there's a race to be won with him on Fibresand. (op 7-1)

Restless Bay(IRE) just came out on top in the minor battle for third. A regular at Wolverhampton, he didn't seem to run to his best on this different surface. (tchd 9-2)

Cheylesmore(IRE) ◆, another trying this surface for the first time, was returning from a two-month break and debuting in a handicap. He was struggling out the back for much of the race but kept on nicely next to the unfavoured inside rail in the straight, and it wouldn't be a surprise if there's a good deal better to come from him. (op 13-2)

Rowan Spirit(IRE) was found out by a 5lb rise for his recent C&D win in an ordinary race. Official explanation: trainer had no explanation for the poor form shown (op 9-4 tchd 2-1)

7804 TOTEEXACTA YOUR FLEXIBLE FORECAST H'CAP 1m (F)

12:55 (12:55) (Class 5) (0-75,74) 3-Y-O+ **£2,115** (£624; £312) **Stalls** Low

Form RPR

5125 **1** **Eastern Hills**[12] 7611 5-8-6 **62**.............................(p) AndrewHeffernan(3) 1 72
(A J McCabe) *trckd ldr: cl up 1/2-way: led wl over 2f out: rdn over 1f out: kpt on wl fnl f* **3/1**[2]

6240 **2** *2* **Miss Bootylishes**[54] 6963 5-9-2 **74**................................... AmyBaker(5) 5 79
(A B Haynes) *trckd ldrs: effrt 2f out: n.m.r and swtchd lft over 1f out: rdn to chse wnr ins fnl f: no imp* **6/1**[3]

6412 **3** *2 3/4* **Ubenkor (IRE)**[10] 7646 5-8-11 **64**................................ TomEaves 3 63
(M Herrington) *led: rdn along 3f out and sn hdd: drvn 2f out: grad wknd appr fnl f* **10/11**[1]

0044 **4** *hd* **General Tufto**[6] 7694 5-9-0 **70**...(b) KierenFox(3) 2 68
(C Smith) *chsd ldrs: rdn along over 3f out: drvn 2f out: sn one pce* **10/1**

6024 **5** *2* **Violent Velocity (IRE)**[6] 7699 7-8-5 **65**........................ ShaneBKelly(7) 4 59
(J J Quinn) *chsd ldrs: rdn along on outer 2f out: sn outpcd* **10/1**

1m 46.05s (2.35) **Going Correction** +0.35s/f (Slow) **5** Ran SP% **109.9**
Speed ratings (Par 103): **102,100,97,97,95**
CSF £19.71 TOTE £3.80: £2.30, £2.10; EX 24.90.

Owner Charles Wentworth **Bred** Azienda Agricola Patrizia **Trained** Averham Park, Notts

FOCUS

A modest handicap where the runner-up set the standard.

7805 TOTEPOOL A BETTER WAY TO BET H'CAP 2m (F)

1:30 (1:30) (Class 6) (0-60,59) 3-Y-O+ **£1,569** (£463; £231) **Stalls** Low

Form RPR

6004 **1** **Six Of Clubs**[10] 7634 4-8-9 **45**...(b) KierenFox(3) 11 53
(W G M Turner) *hld up: stdy hdwy to trck ldrs 6f out: effrt to chal over 2f out: led wl over 1f out and sn rdn: kpt on wl u.p fnl f* **13/2**[3]

/523 **2** *1/2* **Zed Candy (FR)**[10] 7634 7-9-6 **53**.................................. J-PGuillambert 1 61
(R Ford) *trckd ldrs: hdwy 4f out: cl up 3f out: rdn to dispute ld 2f out: drvn and ev ch over 1f out tl no ex ins fnl f* **5/1**[1]

0233 **3** *3* **Davana**[24] 7475 4-8-8 **48**...(p) MatthewCosham(7) 5 52
(W J H Ratcliffe) *a cl up: effrt to ld 3f out: sn rdn and jnd: drvn and hdd wl over 1f out: kpt on same pce* **5/1**[1]

0344 **4** *4 1/2* **Capable Guest (IRE)**[17] 7541 8-9-12 **59**........................ PJMcDonald 7 58
(G M Moore) *a.p: effrt and ev ch 3f out: rdn over 2f out: sn edgd lft and wknd over 1f out* **8/1**

0-00 **5** *hd* **Diktalina**[15] 7149 4-8-6 **46**.. JulieBurke(7) 2 44
(Mrs A M Thorpe) *chsd ldrs: rdn along 4f out: drvn 3f out and grad wknd* **10/1**

6460 **5** *dht* **Free Falling**[31] 6273 4-8-12 **45**..................................(v) RichardKingscote 3 43
(A J Lidderdale) *led: rdn along 4f out: drvn and hdd 3f out: grad wknd* **28/1**

6436 **7** *17* **Go Amwell**[18] 6132 7-8-13 **46**..(v) GregFairley 6 24
(J R Jenkins) *s.i.s: a in rr* **11/2**[2]

0406 **8** *8* **Frameit (IRE)**[6] 7695 3-9-3 **58**...(vt) TomEaves 12 26
(J G Given) *prom on outer: cl up 1/2-way: rdn along 4f out: wknd 3f out* **20/1**

50-0 **9** *21* **Mister Pete (IRE)**[23] 1113 7-9-0 **54**.............................(p) ShaneBKelly(7) 9 —
(C Grant) *a towards rr: bhd and outpcd over 5f out: t.o fnl 3f* **9/1**

-030 **10** *20* **Bateau Bleu**[111] 4945 3-9-4 **59**......................................(v) PhillipMakin 10 —
(B M R Haslam) *hld up in tch: hdwy on outer 1/2-way: chsd ldrs 6f out: rdn along 4f out: sn wknd and bhd whn eased fnl 2f* **11/2**[2]

00/0 **11** *30* **Little Lily Morgan**[45] 7149 7-8-9 **45**................................ PaulPickard(3) 8 —
(R Bastiman) *a in rr: bhd fr 1/2-way: t.o fnl 3f* **100/1**

3m 51.5s (6.00) **Going Correction** +0.35s/f (Slow)
WFA 3 from 4yo+ 8lb **11** Ran SP% **116.8**
Speed ratings (Par 101): **99,98,97,95,94 94,86,82,71,61 46**
Tote Swingers: 1&2 £8.30, 1&3 £9.50, 2&3 £3.70. CSF £38.07 CT £177.66 TOTE £6.80: £2.50, £2.30, £1.80; EX 43.70 Trifecta £245.70 Pool: £332.10 - 0.94 winning units..

Owner Gongolfin **Bred** R V Young **Trained** Sigwells, Somerset

FOCUS

The early pace wasn't that strong in this ordinary staying event, and so the usual bottomless stamina normally associated with winners over 2m here might not have been needed. The fornt pair are rated up a few pounds on their latest form.

Go Amwell Official explanation: jockey said gelding never travelled

7806 MEMBERSHIP AT SOUTHWELL GOLF CLUB H'CAP 1m 4f (F)

2:05 (2:05) (Class 6) (0-65,64) 3-Y-O+ **£1,569** (£463; £231) **Stalls** Low

Form RPR

0342 **1** **Rubi Dia**[6] 7694 3-9-1 **63**... AndrewHeffernan(3) 8 73+
(K M Prendergast) *hld up in tch: hdwy 4f out: rdn to ld over 2f out: drvn and edgd rt over 1f out: kpt on gamely fnl f* **9/4**[1]

0022 **2** *1* **Shifting Gold (IRE)**[24] 7475 4-9-0 **57**...........................(b) AmyRyan(3) 7 65
(K A Ryan) *a.p: cl up on outer 4f out: rdn over 2f out: drvn and ev ch over 1f out: kpt on same pce fnl f* **9/2**[3]

2422 **3** *1 1/2* **Mediterranean Sea (IRE)**[30] 7398 4-9-7 **61**................ StephenCraine 5 67
(J R Jenkins) *hld up in tch: stdy hdwy 4f out: effrt whn n.m.r and sltly outpcd 3f out: rdn to chse ldng pair 2f out: sn drvn and kpt on same pce fnl f* **3/1**[2]

1355 **4** *7* **Greenbelt**[28] 506 9-9-0 **54**.. PJMcDonald 2 49
(G M Moore) *cl up: led 1/2-way: rdn over 3f out: hdd over 2f out: sn drvn and grad wknd* **22/1**

0000 **5** *30* **Lava Steps (USA)**[30] 7397 4-9-3 **57**............................... MickyFenton 3 —
(P T Midgley) *a in rr: rdn along over 4f out: outpcd and bhd fnl 3f* **50/1**

0514 **6** *4* **Mohawk Ridge**[21] 7504 4-9-10 **64**...................................(p) PhillipMakin 1 —
(M Dods) *led to 1/2-way: cl up tl rdn along over 3f out and sn wknd* **9/2**[3]

0001 **7** *18* **Ramora (USA)**[24] 7475 4-9-1 **60**.................................... KylieManser(5) 6 —
(Miss Olivia Maylam) *trckd ldrs: hdwy on inner and cl up 1/2-way: rdn along 4f out: sn wknd* **7/1**

2m 44.7s (3.70) **Going Correction** +0.35s/f (Slow)
WFA 3 from 4yo+ 5lb **7** Ran SP% **110.9**
Speed ratings (Par 101): **101,100,99,94,74 72,60**
Tote Swingers: 1&2 £3.00, 1&3 £2.70, 2&3 £2.60. CSF £11.94 CT £28.06 TOTE £2.90: £1.50, £2.80; EX 11.90 Trifecta £20.50 Pool: £737.13 - 26.48 winning units..

Owner K M Prendergast **Bred** Castlemartin Stud And Skymarc Farm **Trained** Matlon, N Yorks

■ Stewards' Enquiry : Andrew Heffernan one-day ban: used whip with excessive frequency (Jan 6)

FOCUS

A moderate handicap, but the winner is relatively unexposed and can do better. The third ran to his latest form.

7807 SOUTHWELL-RACECOURSE.CO.UK APPRENTICE H'CAP (DIV I) 5f (F)

2:40 (2:40) (Class 6) (0-55,55) 3-Y-O+ **£1,364** (£403; £201) **Stalls** High

Form RPR

0602 **1** **Kheley (IRE)**[1] 7783 4-8-7 **49**.. JamesRogers(3) 8 62
(W M Brisbourne) *a.p: rdn to chse ldr over 1f out: drvn and styd on ins fnl f to ld last 100yds* **11/2**

0000 **2** *1/2* **Thoughtsofstardom**[5] 7720 7-9-1 **54**.............................. TobyAtkinson 2 65
(P S McEntee) *sn led: rdn wl over 1f out: drvn ins fnl f: hdd and no ex last 100yds* **18/1**

0000 **3** *5* **Mr Funshine**[17] 7542 5-9-0 **53**... AshleyMorgan 7 46
(D Shaw) *towards rr: rdn along 1/2-way: hdwy over 1f out: styd on fnl f: nrst fin* **5/1**[3]

000 **4** *nk* **Figaro Flyer (IRE)**[40] 7249 7-8-13 **52**................................ DeanHeslop 1 44
(P Howling) *midfield: rdn along 1/2-way: n.d* **11/2**

0064 **5** *3/4* **Sharp Bullet (IRE)**[17] 7537 4-8-10 **54**..............(b) MatthewCosham(5) 10 43
(Bruce Hellier) *cl up: reminders 1/2-way: rdn wl over 1f out and grad wknd* **7/2**[1]

0050 **6** *3* **Lets Move It**[184] 2879 3-8-4 **46** oh1.................................(v) RyanClark(3) 5 24
(D Shaw) *chsd ldrs: rdn along 2f out: sn wknd* **16/1**

4220 **7** *3/4* **Best Known Secret (IRE)**[24] 7468 4-8-4 **48**.............. RichardRowe(5) 3 24
(C C Bealby) *chsd ldrs: rdn along 2f out: sn wknd* **4/1**[2]

1000 **8** *4* **Darcy's Pride (IRE)**[24] 7473 6-8-11 **55**.......................... ShaneBKelly(5) 4 16
(P T Midgley) *rrd s: a in rr* **15/2**

0604 **9** *5* **Ariel Bender**[7] 7676 3-8-2 **46** oh1...............................(b) LeonnaMayor(5) 9 —
(Peter Grayson) *a in rr: bhd fr 1/2-way* **66/1**

60.41 secs (0.71) **Going Correction** +0.275s/f (Slow) **9** Ran SP% **114.1**
Speed ratings (Par 101): **105,104,96,95,94 89,88,82,74**
Tote Swingers: 1&2 £18.00, 1&3 £7.40, 2&3 £19.20. CSF £95.58 CT £526.81 TOTE £6.70: £2.70, £6.30, £1.90; EX 69.40 Trifecta £403.10 Pool: £577.46 - 1.06 winning units..

Owner W M Clare **Bred** Matt Gilsenan **Trained** Great Ness, Shropshire

FOCUS

A weak handicap, but the quicker of the two divisions by 1.16sec. The front pair were both on good marks.

Darcy's Pride(IRE) Official explanation: jockey said mare missed the break

7808 SOUTHWELL-RACECOURSE.CO.UK APPRENTICE H'CAP (DIV II) 5f (F)

3:15 (3:15) (Class 6) (0-55,55) 3-Y-O+ **£1,364** (£403; £201) **Stalls** High

Form RPR

2000 **1** **Your Gifted (IRE)**[45] 7148 3-8-13 **55**...........................(e[1]) JulieBurke(3) 4 62
(Patrick Morris) *trckd ldrs: smooth hdwy to ld wl over 1f out: pushed clr ins fnl f* **10/1**

6605 **2** *1 1/2* **Residency (IRE)**[17] 7542 4-8-12 **54**...............................(p) AdamCarter(3) 8 56
(B Smart) *chsd ldrs: rdn along 1/2-way: hdwy wl over 1f out: squeezed through and drvn to chse wnr ins fnl f: no imp* **9/4**[1]

4560 **3** *3/4* **Hold On Tiger (IRE)**[41] 7225 3-8-6 **52**.................(p) ShirleyTeasdale(7) 9 51
(V P Donoghue) *chsd ldrs: rdn along wl over 1f out: kpt on u.p fnl f* **8/1**

5005 **4** *1 1/2* **Southwark Newshawk**[165] 3516 3-8-0 **46** oh1.........(p) AliceHaynes(7) 6 40
(Mrs C A Dunnett) *cl up: rdn along and sltly outpcd 2f out: styng on whn n.m.r and swtchd lft over 1f out: sn one pce* **20/1**

5355 **5** *1 1/4* **Black Baccara**[5] 7721 3-9-1 **54**.....................................(tp) TobyAtkinson 2 43
(P S McEntee) *sn led: rdn 2f out: sn hdd and drvn: edgd rt over 1f out: wknd ins fnl f* **9/2**[2]

0040 **6** *nk* **Sophie's Beau (USA)**[46] 7131 3-8-8 **50**...................... JamesRogers(3) 3 38
(M C Chapman) *s.i.s and bhd tl sme late hdwy* **9/2**[2]

050 **7** *1 1/2* **Lieu Day Louie (IRE)**[46] 7132 3-8-7 **46** oh1.................... DeanHeslop 7 29
(N Wilson) *prom: rdn along over 2f out: sn drvn and wknd* **18/1**

5000 **8** *1 3/4* **Grand Palace (IRE)**[17] 7542 7-8-10 **49**........................(v) AshleyMorgan 1 26
(D Shaw) *racd wd: outpcd and bhd fr 1/2-way* **13/2**[3]

0000 **9** *2 1/2* **Albaher**[45] 7154 4-8-2 **46** oh1..(b) LeonnaMayor(5) 5 14
(Peter Grayson) *a in rr: outpcd and bhd fr 1/2-way* **50/1**

61.57 secs (1.87) **Going Correction** +0.275s/f (Slow) **9** Ran SP% **112.7**
Speed ratings (Par 101): **96,93,92,90,88 87,85,82,78**
Tote Swingers: 1&2 £5.20, 1&3 £10.30, 2&3 £5.90. CSF £31.90 CT £191.61 TOTE £9.80: £3.50, £1.30, £2.10; EX 32.00 Trifecta £229.50 Pool: £589.27 - 1.90 winning units..

Owner L Walsh **Bred** Rathasker Stud **Trained** Tarporley, Cheshire

FOCUS

The winning time was much worse than the first division (1.16sec slower), but the winner did it cosily. Weak form, rated around the runner-up.

T/Plt: £61.60 to a £1 stake. Pool:£38,096.71 - 450.89 winning tickets. T/Qpdt: £41.60 to a £1 stake. Pool:£4,774.52 - 84.80 winning tickets. JR

7784 WOLVERHAMPTON (A.W) (L-H)

Friday, December 10

OFFICIAL GOING: Standard

Wind: Fresh behind Weather: Overcast

7809 WOLVERHAMPTON-RACECOURSE.CO.UK NURSERY 5f 20y(P)

3:45 (3:47) (Class 6) (0-65,65) 2-Y-O £1,457 (£433; £216; £108) Stalls Low

Form				RPR
003	1		**Albany Rose (IRE)**[13] 7598 2-9-2 60 SteveDrowne 2 *(Rae Guest) mde all: rdn clr over 1f out: jst hld on* 9/2[3]	66
0063	2	nk	**Lisselton Cross**[13] 7592 2-8-11 55 FergusSweeney 5 *(M R Bosley) a.p: rdn to chse wnr over 1f out: r.o* 12/1	60
505	3	5	**Koha (USA)**[179] 3034 2-8-12 56 AdamKirby 4 *(D K Ivory) hld up: hdwy over 1f out: sn rdn: edgd rt and styd on same pce* 4/1[2]	43
04	4	¾	**Just For Leo (IRE)**[10] 7641 2-9-3 64 (b[1]) JamesSullivan(3) 6 *(P D Evans) chsd wnr tl rdn over 1f out: wknd fnl f* 25/1	48
005	5	¾	**Ladydolly**[13] 7598 2-8-4 48 CathyGannon 1 *(R Brotherton) s.i.s: sme hdwy over 1f out: sn wknd* 33/1	30
441	6	3	**Misscomplacent**[14] 7577 2-9-7 65 (b) GeorgeBaker 8 *(Mrs A Duffield) hld up in tch: rdn and wknd over 1f out* 5/2[1]	36
0545	7	½	**Pineapple Pete (IRE)**[8] 7666 2-9-7 65 TomQueally 7 *(P F I Cole) prom: pushed along 1/2-way: rdn and wknd over 1f out* 6/1	34

63.18 secs (0.88) **Going Correction** +0.20s/f (Slow) 7 Ran SP% 95.5

Speed ratings (Par 94): **100,99,91,90,89 84,83**

Tote Swingers: 1&2 £6.30, 1&3 £3.20, 2&3 £5.70. CSF £36.43 CT £120.36 TOTE £5.00: £2.00, £3.80; EX 35.10.

Owner E P Duggan **Bred** Blue Bloodstock Ltd **Trained** Newmarket, Suffolk

■ Even Stevens (4/1) was withdrawn on veterinary advice. R4 applies, deduct 20p in the £.

FOCUS

Times suggest the surface was on the slow side. A modest nursery, but the front two pulled clear in a time 0.84 seconds quicker than the promising Two Certainties recorded in the following older-horse maiden.

NOTEBOOK

Albany Rose(IRE) ◆, having her first start outside maiden company, built on her recent C&D third. She showed good speed from the off, and although hassled by the free-running Just For Leo, sustained her effort to the line, despite hanging left, after going a couple of lengths clear early in the straight. She can defy a rise. (tchd 5-1)

Lisselton Cross ◆, an improved third in a similar race at Kempton last time, confirmed he's going the right way, finishing well clear of the rest. He should win a similar race.

Koha(USA), a smartly bred filly, offered some encouragement after 179 days off the track. (op 13-2)

Just For Leo(IRE), blinkered for the first time, was keen to post and didn't settle in the race itself. (op 20-1 tchd 16-1)

Ladydolly started slowly and was outpaced for most of the way before making the briefest of efforts at the top of the straight. (op 28-1)

Misscomplacent, 5lb higher than when winning over C&D on her previous start, raced wide throughout and found nothing. (op 11-4 tchd 3-1)

Pineapple Pete(IRE), keen early, is going the wrong way. (op 7-2)

7810 PLAY BINGO AT TOTESPORT.COM MEDIAN AUCTION MAIDEN STKS 5f 20y(P)

4:15 (4:15) (Class 6) 3-5-Y-O £1,706 (£503; £252) Stalls Low

Form				RPR
00	1		**Two Certainties**[237] 1393 3-9-3 0 WilliamCarson 3 *(S C Williams) s.i.s: outpcd: hdwy over 1f out: r.o u.p to ld nr fin* 10/1	65+
004	2	½	**Spirit Of Dixie**[7] 7684 3-8-9 0 MichaelGeran(3) 7 *(D Nicholls) chsd ldrs: rdn to ld ins fnl f: hdd nr fin* 6/1	58
0400	3	½	**Faithful Duchess (IRE)**[9] 7651 3-8-12 59 (b[1]) ShaneKelly 5 *(E F Vaughan) sn pushed along in rr: hdwy over 3f out: rdn and ev ch ins fnl f: styd on same pce* 11/4[1]	57
2300	4	1 ¼	**Gower Sophia**[45] 7148 3-8-12 48 CathyGannon 2 *(R A Harris) led 1f: chsd ldrs: rdn over 1f out: styd on same pce ins pce fnl f* 9/2[2]	52
0000	5	¾	**Libertino (IRE)**[9] 7651 3-9-3 60 (b) EddieAhern 9 *(A W Carroll) prom: rdn 1/2-way: styd on same pce fnl f* 8/1	54
-000	6	2 ¼	**Charles Bear**[7] 7684 3-8-5 50 DanielleMooney(7) 6 *(Bruce Hellier) led 4f out: rdn over 1f out: hdd & wknd ins fnl f* 33/1	41
5353	7	¾	**Sally's Swansong**[249] 1112 4-8-12 50 DuranFentiman 8 *(E J Alston) mid-div: sn pushed along: styd on same pce appr fnl f* 5/1[3]	39
4060	8	¾	**Elle Est**[157] 3758 3-8-12 58 TomQueally 10 *(E J Alston) s.i.s: nvr on terms* 12/1	36
560-	9	¾	**My Best Man**[477] 5184 4-9-3 53 AdamKirby 11 *(A W Carroll) hld up: n.d* 10/1	38

64.02 secs (1.72) **Going Correction** +0.20s/f (Slow) 9 Ran SP% 115.7

Speed ratings (Par 101): **94,93,92,90,89 85,84,83,82**

Tote Swingers: 1&2 £8.10, 1&3 £6.00, 2&3 £3.50. CSF £68.79 TOTE £11.20: £3.40, £1.80, £1.50; EX 85.90.

Owner A Simpson, M Kerr-Dineen & D Shekells **Bred** Old Mill Stud Ltd And Oomswell Ltd **Trained** Newmarket, Suffolk

FOCUS

A weak maiden run in a poor time (0.84 seconds slower than earlier 0-65 nursery), but an interesting winner. The form is a bit dubious, rated around the fourth.

7811 NAME A RACE TO ENHANCE YOUR BRAND CLAIMING STKS 5f 216y(P)

4:45 (4:45) (Class 6) 2-Y-O £1,706 (£503; £252) Stalls Low

Form				RPR
0451	1		**Whipphound**[20] 7527 2-9-0 69 ShaneKelly 8 *(W M Brisbourne) hld up: hdwy to ld over 1f out: edgd lft: drvn out* 11/4[2]	73
366	2	1	**Arowana (IRE)**[23] 7485 2-8-0 64 (b[1]) CathyGannon 4 *(W J Haggas) hld up in tch: rdn and edgd lft over 1f out: sn ev ch: styd on* 9/2[3]	56
3031	3	3 ¾	**Slatey Hen (IRE)**[4] 7722 2-7-11 63 JamesSullivan(3) 1 *(R A Fahey) prom: rdn whn hmpd and lost pl over 1f out: kpt on to go 3rd wl ins fnl f* 5/6[1]	45
5	4	1 ¾	**Monadreen Dancer**[13] 7603 2-8-12 0 EddieAhern 5 *(Daniel Mark Loughnane, Ire) s.i.s: hdwy over 1f out: nvr trbld ldrs* 33/1	52
0	5	nse	**Una Vita Pius (IRE)**[28] 7427 2-8-0 0 JamieMackay 9 *(P L Gilligan) racd keenly: led 5f out: rdn and hdd over 1f out: wknd ins fnl f* 66/1	39
4055	6	nse	**Glenns Princess**[24] 7469 2-8-1 48 ow3 (b) FrannyNorton 3 *(R A Fahey) s.i.s: hld up: hdwy over 1f out: sn rdn: wknd fnl f* 16/1	40
	7	¾	**Sailing North (USA)** 2-8-9 0 WilliamCarson 2 *(R A Harris) sn led: hdd 5f out: rdn and wknd over 1f out* 40/1	46
000	8	½	**Scommettitrice (IRE)**[20] 7527 2-7-12 58 (p) NickyMackay 6 *(R A Harris) prom: rdn over 2f out: wkng whn hmpd over 1f out* 20/1	33
6304	9	29	**Tony Hollis**[20] 7527 2-8-3 60 DavidProbert 7 *(B R Millman) chsd ldrs: rdn and hung rt fr over 3f out: wknd over 2f out* 10/1	—

1m 16.83s (1.83) **Going Correction** +0.20s/f (Slow) 9 Ran SP% 126.0

Speed ratings (Par 94): **95,93,88,86,86 86,85,84,45**

Tote Swingers: 1&2 £3.00, 1&3 £2.00, 2&3 £3.10. CSF £16.79 TOTE £4.30: £1.70, £1.10, £1.10; EX 20.70.

Owner Mark Brisbourne **Bred** Mrs B Skinner **Trained** Great Ness, Shropshire

■ Stewards' Enquiry : Cathy Gannon one-day ban: careless riding (Dec 26)

FOCUS

A modest claimer and they didn't seem to go that quick early.

NOTEBOOK

Whipphound was a bit keen early and came wide into the straight, but he still readily followed up his recent C&D selling success, proving more resolute than the runner-up. He seemed to run above his official mark of 69 and is better than this level. (tchd 9-4)

Arowana(IRE), blinkered for the first time on this drop in grade, went left under pressure and did not look straightforward. (op 13-2)

Slatey Hen(IRE), a recent Lingfield selling winner but behind Whipphound at that level over C&D on November 20, lost her chance when squeezed out by the runner-up over 1f out, although she would have had a job to trouble the winner. (op Evens tchd 5-4and 11-8 in places)

Monadreen Dancer showed little in a 7f maiden here on her debut, but her connections didn't want to lose her cheaply, setting her claiming price at £12,000, and she showed ability after a slow start.

Una Vita Pius(IRE) was a bit keen and ran to only a moderate level.

7812 PLAY BLACKJACK AT TOTESPORT.COM H'CAP 7f 32y(P)

5:15 (5:19) (Class 6) (0-65,64) 3-Y-O+ £1,706 (£503; £252) Stalls High

Form				RPR
4001	1		**Khajaaly (IRE)**[21] 7502 3-9-7 64 CathyGannon 2 *(Miss J Feilden) chsd ldrs: nt clr run over 2f out: rdn to ld ins fnl f: r.o* 3/1[1]	73+
5563	2	nk	**Kipchak (IRE)**[12] 7614 5-9-4 61 (p) HayleyTurner 4 *(C R Dore) chsd ldr: rdn to ld over 1f out: hdd ins fnl f: r.o* 7/2[3]	69
1500	3	1 ¾	**Double Carpet (IRE)**[4] 7730 7-8-10 56 RossAtkinson(3) 8 *(G Woodward) chsd ldrs: rdn and ev ch over 1f out: styd on same pce ins fnl f* 25/1	59
1000	4	¾	**Downhill Skier (IRE)**[12] 7613 6-9-0 57 EddieAhern 6 *(W M Brisbourne) hld up: hdwy over 1f out: styd on same pce fnl f* 10/1	58
6532	5	2	**Just Timmy Marcus**[6] 7699 4-9-7 64 (b) JackMitchell 10 *(B P J Baugh) hld up: hdwy over 1f out: sn rdn: no ex ins fnl f* 10/3[2]	60
0026	6	hd	**Nubar Boy**[3] 7737 3-9-5 62 GeorgeBaker 1 *(P D Evans) hld up: rdn over 1f out: nvr on terms* 9/2	57
00-0	7	shd	**Alpha Tauri (USA)**[241] 1270 4-9-2 64 (t) BillyCray(5) 9 *(F Sheridan) led: rdn and hdd over 1f out: wknd ins fnl f* 12/1	59
0006	8	2 ¾	**Fine Ruler (IRE)**[12] 7614 6-9-0 57 FergusSweeney 3 *(M R Bosley) s.i.s: hld up: a in rr* 14/1	45

1m 31.1s (1.50) **Going Correction** +0.20s/f (Slow) 8 Ran SP% 115.8

Speed ratings (Par 101): **99,98,96,95,93 93,93,90**

Tote Swingers: 1&2 £3.10, 1&3 £15.30, 2&3 £11.30. CSF £13.95 CT £218.78 TOTE £4.30: £1.90, £1.40, £6.90; EX 12.30.

Owner Geegeez.co.uk **Bred** Barry Noonan And Denis Noonan **Trained** Exning, Suffolk

FOCUS

A modest but competitive handicap run at a good pace. The winner backed up his latest C&D form.

7813 PLAY ROULETTE AT TOTESPORT.COM NURSERY 1m 141y(P)

5:45 (5:46) (Class 6) (0-60,58) 2-Y-O £1,706 (£503; £252) Stalls Low

Form				RPR
0000	1		**Snow Trooper**[22] 7497 2-9-3 54 SamHitchcott 3 *(D K Ivory) chsd ldrs: drvn along over 3f out: r.o u.p to ld wl ins fnl f* 12/1	61
0004	2	1 ½	**Mrs Neat (IRE)**[22] 7496 2-9-1 52 (b) JamesDoyle 8 *(S Kirk) a.p: chsd ldr over 3f out: led over 2f out: rdn clr over 1f out: hdd wl ins fnl f* 7/1[3]	56
1003	3	3 ¼	**Countrywide Flame**[11] 7629 2-9-7 58 (tp) PhillipMakin 11 *(K A Ryan) hld up: hdwy over 4f out: rdn over 3f out: styd on to go 3rd nr fin* 4/1[2]	55
0060	4	½	**Torteval (IRE)**[11] 7631 2-8-8 45 (v[1]) CathyGannon 2 *(P D Evans) led: rdn and hdd over 2f out: wknd ins fnl f* 14/1	41
5032	5	1	**Indian Wish (USA)**[11] 7630 2-9-6 57 StevieDonohoe 4 *(M G Quinlan) hld up: rdn over 3f out: styd on: nt trble ldrs* 6/5[1]	51
0000	6	8	**Titan Diamond (IRE)**[11] 7630 2-8-10 47 HayleyTurner 6 *(M D I Usher) hld up: hdwy over 5f out: rdn and wknd over 2f out* 20/1	24
000	7	½	**Seadream**[16] 7550 2-8-6 50 (p) RachealKneller(7) 13 *(M D I Usher) s.i.s: nvr nrr* 33/1	26
0630	8	½	**Century Dancer**[11] 7631 2-9-0 51 DavidProbert 9 *(Miss Tor Sturgis) chsd ldr tl rdn over 3f out: wknd wl over 1f out* 12/1	26
0006	9	1 ¾	**Talking Back**[20] 7520 2-8-9 46 SteveDrowne 1 *(S Kirk) prom: lost pl over 6f out: wknd over 3f out* 20/1	17
0054	10	1 ¼	**Senor Sassi (USA)**[11] 7629 2-8-8 50 (p) RyanPowell(5) 5 *(J S Moore) sn pushed along in rr: rdn and wknd over 2f out* 14/1	19

1m 52.94s (2.44) **Going Correction** +0.20s/f (Slow) 10 Ran SP% 119.1

Speed ratings (Par 94): **97,95,92,92,91 84,83,83,81,80**

Tote Swingers: 1&2 £13.30, 1&3 £9.20, 2&3 £4.40. CSF £92.73 CT £410.46 TOTE £12.90: £2.90, £2.50, £1.20; EX 46.60.

Owner K B Taylor **Bred** Ashridge Farm Stud **Trained** Radlett, Herts

FOCUS

They finished strung out in this uncompetitive nursery.

NOTEBOOK

Snow Trooper found 7f too short around here last time and proved suited by this longer trip. He came under pressure before the runner-up, but stuck on well to take advantage when that one idled. Official explanation: trainer said, regarding apparent improvement in form, that the colt appeared to benefit from being raced over a longer trip. (op 11-1)

Mrs Neat(IRE) travelled best and looked all over the winner when going clear entering the straight, but she soon begun to hang left and idle. She had been reported to have hung both ways when a staying-on fourth over 7f here last time and is not straightforward, but she clearly has the ability win a similar race. Maybe waiting tactics and/or back a return to shorter will help. (tchd 13-2 and 15-2)

Countrywide Flame, well beaten in a seller over slightly further around here last time, ran okay without improving for the drop in trip. (op 9-2)

Torteval(IRE) ran a bit better than of late in a first-time visor. (op 16-1)

Indian Wish(USA) was desperately disappointing, running nowhere near the form she showed when runner-up over C&D off this mark last time. She was due to go up 5lb. (tchd 11-8)

7814 STAY AT THE WOLVERHAMPTON HOLIDAY INN H'CAP 1m 1f 103y(P)
6:15 (6:17) (Class 6) (0-60,60) 3-Y-O+ £1,706 (£503; £252) Stalls Low

Form				RPR
0514	1		**Esteem Lord**[27] 7445 4-9-3 56 ... AdamKirby 8 (D K Ivory) *hld up in tch: rdn over 1f out: r.o to ld nr fin* 7/4[1]	66+
0000	2	½	**Lucky Diva**[9] 7649 3-8-9 50 ... DavidProbert 9 (S Kirk) *chsd ldr tl led over 2f out: sn rdn: hdd nr fin* 14/1	59
0056	3	¾	**Black Coffee**[15] 7569 5-9-2 55 ... ShaneKelly 5 (W M Brisbourne) *hld up: hdwy over 4f out: rdn over 1f out: r.o* 25/1	63
5562	4	nk	**Professor John (IRE)**[7] 7685 3-9-3 58 ...(v) GrahamGibbons 13 (I A Wood) *a.p: racd keenly: rdn over 1f out: unable qck towards fin* 7/2[2]	65
	5	1	**Sligo All Star**[14] 7585 5-8-7 46 oh1 ... FrannyNorton 3 (Thomas McLaughlin, Ire) *hld up: outpcd 3f out: hdwy over 1f out: swtchd rt nr fin: r.o: nt rch ldrs* 66/1	51+
0254	6	1 ¾	**Chaqueta**[16] 7561 3-9-4 59 ... JackMitchell 12 (C F Wall) *hld up: hdwy over 3f out: rdn and hung lft fr over 1f out: nt run on* 8/1	60
5004	7	6	**Forbidden (IRE)**[13] 7599 7-9-4 57 ...(tp) TomEaves 2 (I W McInnes) *chsd ldrs: rdn over 2f out: wknd over 1f out* 16/1	46
-536	8	¾	**Dr Valentine (FR)**[25] 7282 4-9-7 60 ... GeorgeBaker 11 (Mrs A Duffield) *sn led: rdn and hdd over 2f out: wknd over 1f out* 12/1	47
2206	9	1	**Watchmaker**[6] 7687 7-9-7 60 ...(p) SamHitchcott 6 (Miss Tor Sturgis) *hld up: rdn over 2f out: sn wknd* 8/1	45
3501	10	9	**Star Addition**[56] 6905 4-9-4 57 ... RobertWinston 4 (E J Alston) *s.i.s: rdn over 2f out: a in rr* 15/2[3]	23
0360	11	1 ½	**Heredias (GER)**[20] 7531 4-9-5 58 ... EddieAhern 7 (W M Brisbourne) *prom: rdn over 2f out: sn wknd* 18/1	21

2m 4.40s (2.70) **Going Correction** +0.20s/f (Slow)
WFA 3 from 4yo+ 2lb 11 Ran SP% **123.4**
Speed ratings (Par 101): **96,95,94,94,93 92,86,86,85,77 75**
Tote Swingers: 1&2 £10.40, 1&3 £14.20, 2&3 £47.30. CSF £31.65 CT £491.81 TOTE £4.20: £1.40, £6.10, £4.60; EX 46.50.
Owner Bill Brown & Ian Brown **Bred** G Davey & Exors Of The Late J Davey **Trained** Radlett, Herts

FOCUS
The pace slowed significantly down the back straight and those handy were at an advantage. The bare form is a bit shaky due to the muddling nature of the race.

7815 PLAY SLOTS AT TOTESPORT.COM H'CAP 1m 4f 50y(P)
6:45 (6:45) (Class 3) (0-95,94) 3-Y-O+ £5,677 (£1,699; £849; £424; £211) Stalls Low

Form				RPR
5410	1		**Lovers Causeway (USA)**[14] 7589 3-8-6 79 ...(b) GregFairley 8 (M Johnston) *mde all: clr 8f out: rdn over 1f out: hld on* 6/1	90
4222	2	½	**Cosimo de Medici**[6] 7698 3-8-12 85 ...(t) RobertWinston 7 (H Morrison) *hld up: hdwy over 2f out: rdn to chse wnr over 1f out: sn hung lft: kpt on* 7/2[2]	95
1142	3	1 ¾	**Denton (NZ)**[37] 7292 7-9-4 86 ...(t) TomQueally 6 (J R Gask) *hld up: hdwy u.p over 1f out: sn hung lft: r.o* 11/1	93+
1051	4	2 ¼	**Captain John Nixon**[28] 7428 3-8-13 86 ... EddieAhern 3 (Pat Eddery) *chsd wnr: rdn over 2f out: styd on same pce appr fnl f* 5/2[1]	89
3	5	1 ¼	**Nice Style (IRE)**[13] 7591 5-9-12 94 ... SteveDrowne 5 (J R Gask) *hld up in tch: racd keenly: rdn over 2f out: styd on same pce* 4/1[3]	95
4033	6	½	**Camps Bay (USA)**[29] 7410 6-8-7 78 ... JamesSullivan(3) 1 (B Ellison) *hld up: hdwy over 2f out: sn rdn: styd on same pce* 5/1	79
01-0	7	13	**Decision**[16] 7553 4-8-8 76 ... ChrisCatlin 9 (Mrs Lawney Hill) *chsd ldrs: pushed along 5f out: wknd over 2f out* 33/1	56
1150	8	13	**That'll Do Nicely (IRE)**[21] 5408 7-8-8 76 ... TomEaves 10 (N G Richards) *prom: rdn over 3f out: wknd over 2f out: t.o* 25/1	35
6/0-	9	19	**Fight Club (GER)**[13] 6480 9-9-11 93 ... StevieDonohoe 4 (B J Llewellyn) *s.i.s: hld up: rdn and wknd over 3f out: t.o* 28/1	22

2m 40.37s (-0.73) **Going Correction** +0.20s/f (Slow)
WFA 3 from 4yo+ 5lb 9 Ran SP% **120.3**
Speed ratings (Par 107): **110,109,108,107,106 105,97,88,75**
Tote Swingers: 1&2 £5.80, 1&3 £9.90, 2&3 £7.40. CSF £28.02 CT £231.83 TOTE £8.30: £1.60, £1.20, £3.00; EX 30.00.
Owner Crone Stud Farms Ltd **Bred** Skara Glen Stables **Trained** Middleham Moor, N Yorks

FOCUS
A good handicap. The winner enjoyed an uncontested lead and is rated in line with the best view of his recent C&D win.

NOTEBOOK
Lovers Causeway(USA), allowed an uncontested lead, made all at a fair pace. He was a beaten favourite at Dundalk last time, but was only 4lb higher than when winning over C&D two starts back, and presumably the handicapper had a re-think, as this gelding was due to be 3lb higher in future. This was a game effort, but everything went his way. (op 11-2 tchd 13-2)
Cosimo de Medici made his move in just enough time, but his head carriage was awkward and he wouldn't go by the winner, filling second spot for the fourth consecutive race. (op 5-1 tchd 11-2)
Denton(NZ) was set too much to do. Perhaps connections were concerned about his stamina, but he ended up giving the winner far too much of a start. (op 9-1)
Captain John Nixon, up 6lb for a recent C&D win, was a bit keen to post and could have settled better in the race itself. He was one-paced under pressure. (op 3-1 tchd 7-2)
Nice Style(IRE) ran okay without building on the form he showed on his return from a long absence over 1m2f at Kempton. He didn't really prove his stamina. (op 7-2 tchd 3-1)
T/Plt: £131.90 to a £1 stake. Pool:£90,780.38 - 502.20 winning tickets. T/Qpdt: £18.00 to a £1 stake. Pool:£10,615.60 - 436.00 winning tickets. CR

7769 DUNDALK (A.W) (L-H)
Friday, December 10

OFFICIAL GOING: Standard

7816a CROWNE PLAZA RACE & STAY PACKAGE RACE 7f (P)
6:00 (6:00) 3-Y-O+ £10,075 (£2,336; £1,022; £584)

			RPR
1		**Webbow (IRE)**[56] 6888 8-9-3 ... FMBerry 5 (B Ellison) *chsd ldr: 2nd 1/2-way: rdn to chal 1 1/2f out: led over 1f out: kpt on wl fnl f* 13/2	84
2	2 ½	**Anam Chara (IRE)**[2] 7772 4-9-0 95 ... JPO'Brien(5) 4 (Andrew Oliver, Ire) *led: rdn and chal 1 1/2f out: hdd over 1f out: no ex ins fnl f and disp 2nd: kpt on same pce: jst hld 2nd* 9/4[1]	79
3	shd	**Rambling Dancer (IRE)**[2] 7771 6-9-4 72 ... SMGorey(3) 2 (Mrs Valerie Keatley, Ire) *chsd ldrs: 4th 1/2-way: rdn 2f out: 3rd 1 1/2f out: kpt on to dispute 2nd fnl f: jst hld for 2nd* 8/1	81
4	6	**Finicius (USA)**[34] 7358 6-9-7 105 ...(t) JMurtagh 7 (Eoin Griffin, Ire) *hld up towards rr: hdwy in 5th 2f out: rdn and no imp 1 1/2f out: kpt on one pce* 11/4[3]	65
5	1	**Quinmaster (USA)**[21] 7513 8-9-0 102 ... GFCarroll(3) 6 (M Halford, Ire) *chsd ldr: 3rd 1/2-way: rdn 2f out: no ex in 4th 1 1/2f out: kpt on one pce* 5/2[2]	58
6	21	**Cooke's Bar (IRE)**[42] 7216 3-8-9 ... MCHussey 3 (Noel Lawlor, Ire) *settled bhd ldrs: rdn in 5th 1/2-way: no imp and wknd ent st* 50/1	—
7	24	**Sacred Aria**[14] 7590 3-8-4 70 ...(b[1]) KTO'Neill(5) 1 (Daniel O'Gorman, Ire) *a towards rr: wknd bef st* 40/1	—

1m 23.05s (83.05) 7 Ran SP% **114.9**
CSF £21.76 TOTE £5.70: £3.10, £2.10; DF 21.00.
Owner Wentdale Limited **Bred** Joe O'Callaghan **Trained** Norton, N Yorks

FOCUS
The jockeys reported the ground as slower than normal for the venue, although the recorded time suggested otherwise. The form is rated through the third.

NOTEBOOK
Webbow(IRE) appeared to have plenty to do at the weights but managed to win for the first time in three years. Racing for the first time on an all-weather surface since winning over 7f at Southwell in 2006, he ran out a comfortable winner after racing prominently and going to the front a furlong and a half out. This was his first start since joining Brian Ellison and he has a couple of placed efforts in decent turf handicaps to his name this season. (op 13/2 tchd 6/1)
Anam Chara(IRE) could find no extra when tackled and headed by the winner. (op 9/4 tchd 2/1)
Rambling Dancer(IRE) tracked the leaders and was third and clear of the rest from a furlong and a half out. He kept on and just missed out on second spot.
Finicius(USA), rated 105 and four from five at this track before this race, had been well beaten here on his previous start. Dropping back in trip, he was held up before failing to make any impression from 2f out. (op 10/3 tchd 7/2)
Quinmaster(USA), without a win since scoring over 1m here just over two years ago, held sound claims on official ratings but, after tracking the leaders and holding third spot heading into the straight, he was soon done with. (op 2/1 tchd 11/4)

7823a HORSE RACING RETURNS TO DUNDALK ON 25TH MARCH 2011 H'CAP 1m 4f (P)
9:25 (9:25) 3-Y-O+ £12,367 (£3,615; £1,712; £570)

			RPR
1		**Denny Crane**[14] 7589 4-8-9 82 ... WMLordan 2 (Edward Lynam, Ire) *in rr of mid-div: hdwy in 9th 2f out: rdn into 5th 1f out: kpt on wl fnl f to ld last strides* 4/1[2]	82+
2	hd	**Dark Prospect**[5] 7753 5-9-6 96 ... GFCarroll(3) 3 (Noel Meade, Ire) *chsd ldrs: 5th 1/2-way: impr to go 2nd 2f out: rdn to ld over 1 1/2f out: strly pressed fr 1f out: kpt on wl: hdd last strides* 7/1	96
3	shd	**Bravely Fought (IRE)**[2] 7775 5-9-12 99 ... KJManning 1 (Sabrina J Harty, Ire) *mid-div: 7th 1/2-way: hdwy into 3rd 2f out: rdn to chal in 2nd over 1f out: kpt on fnl f: no ex cl home: fin 4th: plcd 3rd* 20/1	99
4	1	**Herostatus**[21] 7514 3-9-1 93 ...(b) JMurtagh 4 (M Johnston) *chsd ldrs: 3rd 1/2-way: rdn in 4th 2f out: swtchd 1f out: no ex ins fnl f: kpt on same pce: fin 5th: plcd 4th* 10/3[1]	91
5	¾	**Solo Performer (IRE)**[5] 7753 5-8-11 87 ...(b) ShaneFoley(3) 7 (H Rogers, Ire) *hld up towards rr: late hdwy fr 2f out: rdn into 7th 1f out: kpt on same pce fnl f: fin 6th: plcd 5th* 12/1	84
6	1 ¼	**Home Secretary**[5] 7753 6-8-9 85 ...(t) BACurtis(3) 9 (Garvan Donnelly, Ire) *hld up towards rr: hdwy into 8th 2f out: rdn into 6th 1f out: no imp and kpt on one pce: fin 7th: plcd 6th* 13/2[3]	80
7	5 ½	**Redera (IRE)**[14] 7589 4-7-11 77 ... SHJames(7) 14 (A J Martin, Ire) *in rr of mid-div: rdn into 7th 2f out: no ex over 1f out: kpt on one pce: fin 8th: plcd 7th* 12/1	63
8	4	**The Pier (IRE)**[14] 7589 4-9-0 87 ... WJLee 10 (Joseph G Murphy, Ire) *mid-div: rdn into 6th 2f out: no ex over 1f out: fin 9th: plcd 8th* 20/1	67
9	¾	**Gargano (IRE)**[6] 7712 5-7-13 77 ... KTO'Neill(5) 13 (Ms Joanna Morgan, Ire) *chsd ldr: 2nd 1/2-way: rdn in 3rd 3f out: sn no ex and wknd: fin 10th: plcd 9th* 16/1	56
10	2 ½	**Bashkirov**[14] 7589 5-8-12 85 ... SeamieHeffernan 8 (Luke Comer, Ire) *led: rdn and hdd over 2f out: no ex and wknd: fin 11th: plcd 10th* 33/1	60
11	3 ½	**London Bridge**[5] 7751 4-8-8 81 ... MCHussey 6 (Noel Meade, Ire) *chsd ldrs: 6th 1/2-way: rdn and wknd over 2f out: fin 12th: plcd 11th* 16/1	50
12	23	**Grand Admiral (USA)**[90] 5977 4-9-7 99 ... JPO'Brien(5) 11 (A P O'Brien, Ire) *mid-div: hdwy into 7th 5f out: rdn and wknd over 3f out: fin 13th: plcd 12th* 15/2	31
D	nk	**Moyenne Corniche**[21] 7507 5-9-10 97 ... FMBerry 12 (B Ellison) *chsd ldrs: 4th 1/2-way: rdn to ld over 2f out: hdd over 1 1/2f out: cl 3rd 1f out: kpt on fnl f: no ex cl home: fin 3rd: disqualified and plcd last (rdr weighed in late)* 8/1	97
P		**Keeptheboatafloat (USA)**[477] 5186 4-8-7 80 ... DJMoran 5 (Mrs A M O'Shea, Ire) *a towards rr: p.u 1/2-way* 33/1	—

2m 29.21s (149.21)
WFA 3 from 4yo+ 5lb 14 Ran SP% **134.3**
CSF £34.97 CT £534.66 TOTE £5.80: £2.50, £3.00, £6.80; DF 31.70.
Owner Edward Lynam **Bred** P T Tellwright **Trained** Dunshaughlin, Co Meath
■ Gary Carroll, narrowly beaten in this last race of the season, shares the Irish apprentice title with Ben Curtis & Joseph O'Brien.

NOTEBOOK
Denny Crane confirmed his improvement with a strong-finishing run which saw him get up in the last few strides. Rated 72 when he won a handicap over just short of 1m3f here last month, he went up 10lb for his win in a conditions event over this course and trip and had subsequently run third off that revised mark which he raced off here. (op 9/2 tchd 7/2)
Dark Prospect was 4lb higher than when running second to Home Secretary over a slightly shorter trip here five days previously. Always close up, he was sent to the front under 2f out and kept on well for pressure only to be collared close home. A winner over hurdles, he should do well when reverting. (op 15/2)
Bravely Fought(IRE) had run second over almost 1m3f here two days previously. He got into contention early in the straight and had every chance from over 1f out in what turned into a four-horse photo finish.
Herostatus, down 4f in trip and up 10lb in the weights since winning over 2m here last month, tracked the leaders in a race run at a good pace and kept on for pressure before and after being switched 1f out without quite getting on terms. (op 3/1)
Home Secretary, penalised for his win from Dark Prospect over just short of 1m3f here five days previously, was held up before closing and trying to get into contention early in the straight. He kept on but was never able to mount a serious challenge. (op 15/2)

Moyenne Corniche raced close up and got to the front early in the straight. Headed under 2f out, he stuck to his task but was disqualified from third place when his rider weighed in 6lb light. It transpired that the horse had been fractious when being saddled and that the lead cloth had been left off in error. (op 17/2)
T/Jkpt: Not won. T/Plt: @542.10. Pool of @24,956.25 - 34 winning units. II

7820 - 7855a (Foreign Racing) - See Raceform Interactive

[7762]LINGFIELD (L-H)
Saturday, December 11

OFFICIAL GOING: Standard
This card, consisting of an AW bumper and six Flat races, replaced the scheduled jumps card which was frozen off.
Wind: Almost nil Weather: Overcast

7824 AERIAL SERVICES H'CAP (DIV I) 6f (P)
12:25 (12:25) (Class 6) (0-60,60) 3-Y-O+ **£1,364** (£403; £201) **Stalls** Low

Form RPR
4600 **1** **Super Frank (IRE)**[13] 7613 7-9-6 59................(b) IanMongan 8 68
(J Akehurst) *led after 1f: kicked more than 2 l clr 2f out: drvn out ins fnl f* **11/4**[1]
4510 **2** *1 ¼* **Dancing Welcome**[3] 7761 4-9-7 60................(b) RichardKingscote 9 65
(J M Bradley) *chsd wnr after 2f: rdn wl over 2f out: tried to cl ins fnl f: a hld* **11/4**[1]
200 **3** *2 ½* **Resplendent Alpha**[10] 7655 6-9-5 58................(v[1]) JamesDoyle 2 55
(A J Lidderdale) *hld up in last pair: plenty to do whn effrt over 2f out: prog w hd high over 1f out: tk 3rd ins fnl f: no imp* **9/2**[3]
3000 **4** *hd* **Pilgrim Dancer (IRE)**[10] 7655 3-9-2 58................(p) RossAtkinson(3) 5 54
(Patrick Morris) *rdn in last pair after 2f: no prog tl styd on strly fr over 1f out: nrly snatched 3rd* **16/1**
5006 **5** *1 ¾* **Ballyvonane (USA)**[13] 7607 3-8-6 48 ow1............ MichaelStainton(3) 6 39
(D C Griffiths) *hld up bhd ldrs: rdn to chse clr ldng pair over 1f out: no imp: fdd last 100yds* **25/1**
000 **6** *5* **Suttonia (IRE)**[5] 7725 4-8-0 46 oh1................ RichardRowe(7) 4 21
(Noel T Chance) *led 1f: sn lost pl: rdn over 3f out: no ch over 2f out* **33/1**
0000 **7** *1 ¼* **Rightcar**[99] 5730 3-8-9 48................(b) RobbieFitzpatrick 10 19
(Peter Grayson) *prom on outer: disp 2nd fr 4f out to jst over 2f out: wknd rapidly* **66/1**
6430 **8** *1* **Chinese Democracy (USA)**[10] 7655 3-9-3 56................(v) GeorgeBaker 3 24
(P D Evans) *in tch: rdn over 2f out: no prog on inner wl over 1f out: sn wknd rapidly* **3/1**[2]

1m 12.13s (0.23) **Going Correction** +0.075s/f (Slow) **8** Ran SP% **110.7**
Speed ratings (Par 101): **101,99,96,95,93 86,85,83**
toteswingers:1&2 £2.10, 2&3 £1.80, 1&3 £3.10 CSF £9.80 CT £29.35 TOTE £5.10: £1.60, £1.10, £1.60; EX 11.40.
Owner Mrs S Sheldon **Bred** A Butler **Trained** Epsom, Surrey

FOCUS
Few counted in this low-grade sprint handicap, which concerned only the first two in the straight. Very modest form, rated around the runner-up.
Chinese Democracy(USA) Official explanation: jockey said filly ran flat

7825 WATCH UK & IRISH RACING AT CORAL.CO.UK (S) STKS 1m 2f (P)
1:00 (1:00) (Class 6) 3-Y-O+ **£1,569** (£463; £231) **Stalls** Low

Form RPR
4224 **1** **Orchard Supreme**[4] 7732 7-9-7 80................(v) J-PGuillambert 2 63
(J Akehurst) *hld up: prog 3f out: rdn to chse ldr 2f out: narrow ld jst over 1f out: urged along and hld on* **5/4**[1]
065 **2** *nk* **Pinsplitter (USA)**[5] 7729 3-9-0 57................(p) JamesDoyle 4 58
(A J McCabe) *led: drvn and hdd jst over 1f out: kpt on wl ins fnl f: a jst hld* **14/1**
0040 **3** *nse* **Forbidden (IRE)**[1] 7814 7-9-3 57................(tp) DaneO'Neill 3 58
(I W McInnes) *trckd ldng pair: wnt 2nd 4f out to 2f out: drvn to chal over 1f out: fnd nil* **11/2**[3]
0323 **4** *3* **Sovereignty (JPN)**[13] 7613 8-9-7 58................ AdamKirby 1 56
(D K Ivory) *plld hrd: hld up: effrt to dispute 2nd over 2f out: sn rdn and nt qckn: wl hld after* **3/1**[2]
000 **5** *6* **Transfer**[100] 5689 5-9-3 62................(t) IanMongan 5 40
(C P Morlock) *chsd ldr to 4f out: last and u.p over 2f out: sn no ch* **11/2**[3]

2m 6.82s (0.22) **Going Correction** +0.075s/f (Slow)
WFA 3 from 5yo+ 3lb **5** Ran SP% **106.9**
Speed ratings (Par 101): **102,101,101,99,94**
CSF £17.11 TOTE £2.10: £1.20, £5.70; EX 13.20.There was no bid for the winner.
Owner Mrs I Marshall **Bred** Mrs M H Goodrich **Trained** Epsom, Surrey
■ Stewards' Enquiry : James Doyle three-day ban: used whip with excessive frequency with giving gelding time to respond (Dec 26-28)

FOCUS
Not the most competitive of sellers on paper, but it was run at a sound pace and produced a close finish. The form is a bit dubious and the winner did not even need to match his recent level.
Forbidden(IRE) Official explanation: jockey said gelding hung left
Sovereignty(JPN) Official explanation: jockey said gelding ran too free and hung right

7826 STEVE ABBOTT MEMORIAL H'CAP 6f (P)
1:35 (1:35) (Class 3) (0-95,92) 3-Y-O+ **£5,677** (£1,699; £849; £424; £211) **Stalls** Low

Form RPR
0006 **1** **Secret Asset (IRE)**[16] 7566 5-9-7 92................ GeorgeBaker 4 104
(Jane Chapple-Hyam) *trckd ldng trio: prog on outer 2f out: pushed into ld last 150yds: v decisive* **15/8**[1]
4052 **2** *1 ¾* **Sioux Rising (IRE)**[6] 7719 4-8-9 80................(p) JackMitchell 2 86
(R A Fahey) *chsd ldng pair: rdn over 2f out: clsd to ld over 1f out: hdd last 150yds: styd on: easily outpcd* **11/4**[2]
0224 **3** *3* **Vhujon (IRE)**[10] 7654 5-8-7 78 oh2................ LukeMorris 5 75
(P D Evans) *trckd ldng trio: rdn and effrt on inner 2f out: nt qckn over 1f out: tk 3rd ins fnl f* **12/1**
4451 **4** *½* **Cardinal**[8] 7683 5-8-7 78................ HayleyTurner 1 73
(R M H Cowell) *chsd ldr to wl over 1f out: sn btn* **4/1**[3]
4302 **5** *2 ¼* **Billy Red**[41] 7254 6-9-0 85................(b) FergusSweeney 3 73
(J R Jenkins) *led at str pce and sn 3 l clr: hdd & wknd over 1f out* **7/1**
2100 **6** *3 ¾* **Dingaan (IRE)**[3] 7766 7-8-9 80................ RobbieFitzpatrick 6 56
(Peter Grayson) *sn rdn in 6th: nvr on terms and no prog* **33/1**
20-0 **7** *2 ¼* **Art Scholar (IRE)**[7] 7689 3-9-0 85................ AmirQuinn 7 54
(G L Moore) *a last: rdn and struggling sn after 1/2-way* **25/1**

1m 10.88s (-1.02) **Going Correction** +0.075s/f (Slow) **7** Ran SP% **108.4**
Speed ratings (Par 107): **109,106,102,102,99 94,91**
CSF £6.34 TOTE £2.50: £1.20, £2.50; EX 7.10.
Owner Simon Pierpoint & Paul Salisbury **Bred** Mrs C Hartery **Trained** Dalham, Suffolk

FOCUS
A decent handicap run at a sound pace and in a time over a second quicker than the earlier 46-60 handicap. The winner matched his turf best and the form should prove sound.

NOTEBOOK
Secret Asset(IRE) was delivered down the centre of the track for a smooth victory. A class act on his day who was Group 3-placed in the summer, he had hinted that he was on the way back when returned to this surface at Wolverhampton last time and was able to run off a pound lower here. There is a similar race for him back here at the end of the month. (op 9-4 tchd 7-4)
Sioux Rising(IRE) raced off the same mark as when just failing to get up here six days earlier. She raced less lazily in the retained cheekpieces but her turn in the lead proved all too brief. (op 9-4 tchd 3-1)
Vhujon(IRE) was well held by the first two, but he is a reliable sort and this was a solid run from 2lb out of the weights. (op 11-1)
Cardinal went up 8lb to a career-high 78 for his recent impressive Wolverhampton win, having begun the year officially rated 52. He was well enough positioned from his inside stall turning in but was soon held. (op 9-2)
Billy Red was held up when second to subsequent scorer Piscean over 5f last time, but reverted to trailblazing tactics here and could not hold on in the straight. (op 13-2)
Dingaan(IRE) has shown nothing in three starts for this yard now. (op 25-1)
Art Scholar(IRE) has given no encouragement in two runs on this surface after more than a year off. (op 14-1)

7827 AERIAL SERVICES H'CAP (DIV II) 6f (P)
2:10 (2:11) (Class 6) (0-60,60) 3-Y-O+ **£1,364** (£403; £201) **Stalls** Low

Form RPR
4006 **1** **Mary's Pet**[11] 7639 3-9-5 58................ J-PGuillambert 3 67
(J Akehurst) *mde all: rdn over 1f out: edgd rt ins fnl f: jst hld on* **10/1**[3]
0045 **2** *hd* **Chjimes (IRE)**[6] 7720 6-9-6 59................(b[1]) HayleyTurner 4 67
(C R Dore) *mistimed s: t.k.h in last pair: prog fr 2f out: str run fnl f: wnt 2nd nr fin and clsd on wnr: jst failed* **9/2**[2]
2525 **3** *½* **Loyal Royal (IRE)**[11] 7639 7-9-4 57................(bt) RichardKingscote 9 64
(J M Bradley) *t.k.h: trckd ldng pair: chsd wnr over 3f out: hrd rdn and nt qckn over 1f out: lost 2nd nr fin* **9/2**[2]
6504 **4** *¾* **Dualagi**[41] 7250 6-9-2 55................ GeorgeBaker 7 59
(M R Bosley) *hld up in 5th: effrt on outer 2f out: nt qckn over 1f out: kpt on fnl f: nvr able to chal* **4/1**[1]
3014 **5** *1 ¼* **Espy**[11] 7639 5-9-7 60................ AdamKirby 6 60
(I W McInnes) *trckd ldng trio: wnt 3rd 1/2-way: rdn and nt qckn wl over 1f out: fdd nr fin* **4/1**[1]
640 **6** *5* **Masteeat (USA)**[187] 2812 3-8-5 47................ KellyHarrison(3) 10 31
(Miss Olivia Maylam) *free to post: racd wd in 6th: rdn and btn 2f out* **20/1**
5042 **7** *¾* **Lordsbury Pride (USA)**[41] 7249 3-8-11 53................(v) KierenFox(3) 8 35
(J R Best) *chsd wnr to over 3f out: sn lost pl and btn* **9/2**[2]
6303 **8** *1 ¼* **Leahness (IRE)**[8] 7676 3-8-4 46 oh1................ RossAtkinson(3) 2 24
(Patrick Morris) *a in last pair: struggling sn after 1/2-way* **33/1**

1m 11.98s (0.08) **Going Correction** +0.075s/f (Slow) **8** Ran SP% **111.3**
Speed ratings (Par 101): **102,101,101,100,98 91,90,89**
toteswingers:1&2 £1.90, 2&3 £3.40, 1&3 £9.00 CSF £51.54 CT £226.50 TOTE £10.90: £3.00, £1.60, £2.10; EX 71.90.
Owner Mrs I Marshall **Bred** Green Pastures Farm **Trained** Epsom, Surrey
■ Stewards' Enquiry : J-P Guillambert one-day ban: careless riding (Dec 26)

FOCUS
A moderate event run in a time slightly quicker than division one. Several of these had met here in recent weeks. The winner produced a small personal best.

7828 £150 WELCOME BONUS AT GALACASINO.CO.UK H'CAP 1m 2f (P)
2:45 (2:46) (Class 2) (0-100,98) 3-Y-O+
£8,723 (£2,612; £1,306; £653; £326; £163) **Stalls** Low

Form RPR
0030 **1** **Island Sunset (IRE)**[21] 7523 4-8-3 87................ JamesRogers(7) 6 94
(W R Muir) *trckd ldr: rdn and nt qckn wl over 1f out: looked hld after: styd on wl ins fnl f: led last strides* **6/1**
1-00 **2** *nk* **Distinctive Image (USA)**[295] 627 5-9-2 93................ DaneO'Neill 4 100
(G A Butler) *led: wound pce up fr 4f out: looked likely to hold on 1f out: collared last strides* **7/2**[2]
3202 **3** *nk* **Baylini**[4] 7735 6-8-11 88................ JamesDoyle 7 94+
(J A Osborne) *hld up last: prog on outer over 2f out: hrd rdn over 1f out: styd on: nvr quite got there* **7/4**[1]
0001 **4** *nk* **Hidden Glory**[7] 7698 3-8-2 85................ KellyHarrison(3) 2 90+
(J G Given) *hld up in 5th: looking for room on inner 2f out: prog 1f out: styd on wl last 100yds: nrst fin* **11/2**[3]
0305 **5** *1 ½* **Dream Lodge (IRE)**[21] 7529 6-9-7 98................ FergusSweeney 1 100
(R A Fahey) *trckd ldng pair: rdn and nt qckn wl over 1f out: sn lost pl and btn* **8/1**
5040 **6** *½* **Chalice Welcome**[25] 6797 7-8-7 84 oh4................ HayleyTurner 5 85
(N B King) *hld up in 4th: rdn 2f out: nt qckn over 1f out: n.d ins fnl f* **16/1**

2m 6.22s (-0.38) **Going Correction** +0.075s/f (Slow)
WFA 3 from 4yo+ 3lb **6** Ran SP% **105.2**
Speed ratings (Par 109): **104,103,103,103,102 101**
toteswingers:1&2 £2.70, 2&3 £1.10, 1&3 £2.70 CSF £23.45 TOTE £7.60: £3.50, £1.90; EX 25.40.
Owner Mrs J M Muir **Bred** Rathasker Stud **Trained** Lambourn, Berks
■ Pertuis (10/1) was withdrawn (restless in stalls). Deduct 5p in the £ under R4.
■ Stewards' Enquiry : Kelly Harrison caution: careless riding.

FOCUS
A good handicap, but it was not run at a true pace and they finished in a heap. The time compared unfavourably to that of the earlier seller and this is muddling form.

NOTEBOOK
Island Sunset(IRE) has faced stiffer tasks than this in recent races, contesting Listed events on four of her last five starts. She was ridden closer to the pace than she was on her last two outings, and conjured up a strong run to collar the leader near the line. The aim is to try and gain some black type for her. (op 11-2 tchd 9-2)
Distinctive Image(USA) failed to acclimatise to Dubai in the early part of the year and niggling problems have kept him off the track since. Normally held up, he dictated the pace on this drop in trip before gradually winding things up. He was just collared, but this was a pleasing return to action. (op 6-1)
Baylini, fourth here earlier in the week, finished well down the outside but could have done with a truer test at this trip. She is a pretty consistent mare. (op 13-8 tchd 6-4 and 2-1)
Hidden Glory went up just 2lb for last week's Southwell win, but that put him on a career-high mark. Held up, he attempted to improve on the inside in the straight but only really found his stride when pulled off the rail late on. (op 13-2 tchd 7-1 and 5-1)
Dream Lodge(IRE) showed more than in a claimer last time but continues to operate below his best. (op 7-1 tchd 10-1)

Chalice Welcome, returning from a stint over hurdles, was 4lb out of the weights and running over a trip short of his optimum. (op 10-1)

7829 GET BEST ODDS GUARANTEED AT CORAL.CO.UK H'CAP 1m (P)
3:20 (3:21) (Class 6) (0-55,56) 3-Y-O+ £1,535 (£453; £226) Stalls High

Form RPR
0601 1 **Indian Violet (IRE)**[5] 7728 4-9-3 56 6ex........ JamieGoldstein 4 66
(Miss Sheena West) *sn trckd ldrs: prog to go 2nd 2f out: rdn to ld 1f out: sn in command* 5/2[1]
04-0 2 1 ½ **One Oi**[21] 7518 5-9-2 55........ GeorgeBaker 8 61
(D W P Arbuthnot) *t.k.h: hld up towards rr: lost pl 3f out but stl gng wl: prog 2f out: rdn over 1f out: styd on to take 2nd last 50yds* 11/2[3]
2602 3 ½ **All Moving Parts (USA)**[2] 7787 3-9-1 55........(b) JamesDoyle 12 60
(A J McCabe) *dwlt: hld up last fr wdst draw: prog on outer fr 3f out: drvn over 1f out: styd on to take 3rd last strides* 7/2[2]
0005 4 hd **Goodbye Cash (IRE)**[3] 7761 6-9-2 55........ JackMitchell 10 60
(R J Smith) *broke wl: led: drvn and hdd 1f out: one pce* 11/1
3000 5 1 **Isabella Romee (IRE)**[30] 7401 4-8-2 48........ LewisWalsh(7) 11 50
(Jane Chapple-Hyam) *pressed ldr to 2f out: bmpd along and one pce fr over 1f out* 14/1
0560 6 shd **Ice Road Trucker (IRE)**[6] 7717 3-8-1 48........ NathanAlison(7) 6 50
(J R Boyle) *prom: rdn and effrt on inner 2f out: one pce fr over 1f out* 20/1
0020 7 nk **Queenie's Star (IRE)**[6] 7717 3-8-12 52........ RobbieFitzpatrick 7 53
(M J Attwater) *hld up in last pair: stl there over 2f out: prog over 1f out: styd on thrght fnl f: nvr rchd ldrs* 50/1
8 ¾ **Sopran Nad (ITY)**[297] 6-8-8 47........(t) WilliamCarson 5 47
(S C Williams) *hld up wl in rr: stl there 2f out: pushed along and prog into midfield over 1f out: kpt on in one pce ins fnl f* 10/1
0032 9 2 ¾ **Lord Deevert**[3] 7763 5-8-12 54........(p) KierenFox(3) 1 47
(W G M Turner) *dwlt: nvr beyond midfield: pushed along 3f out: no prog* 8/1
5065 10 ½ **Transfixed (IRE)**[51] 7037 3-8-11 51........ J-PGuillambert 9 43
(P D Evans) *racd wd: hld up in midfield: no prog over 2f out: wknd over 1f out* 16/1
-000 11 8 **Aphrodite's Rock**[17] 7561 4-9-1 54........(bt[1]) DaneO'Neill 3 28
(G D Blake) *dwlt: hld up in midfield: rdn over 2f out: sn wknd rapidly: eased* 33/1
5006 12 15 **Eclipsed (USA)**[45] 7161 3-8-8 48........(t) LukeMorris 2 —
(J R Best) *prom: rdn bef 1/2-way: sn wknd: t.o* 40/1

1m 38.33s (0.13) **Going Correction** +0.075s/f (Slow)
WFA 3 from 4yo+ 1lb 12 Ran SP% 119.4
Speed ratings (Par 101): **102,100,100,99,98 98,98,97,94,94 86,71**
toteswingers:1&2 £2.90, 2&3 £5.30, 1&3 £2.50 CSF £15.76 CT £49.19 TOTE £2.80: £1.10, £3.00, £1.40; EX 23.80 Trifecta £37.30 Pool: £721.66 - 14.30 winning units..
Owner Gerald West **Bred** James F Hanly **Trained** Falmer, E Sussex

FOCUS
A very moderate handicap, run at a sound pace. The form looks solid enough.
Transfixed(IRE) Official explanation: jockey said filly lost its action
Eclipsed(USA) Official explanation: jockey said gelding hung left
T/Plt: £171.40 to a £1 stake. Pool of £67,905.75 - 289.11 winning tickets. T/Qpdt: £38.10 to a £1 stake. Pool £5,655.75 - 109.60 winning tickets. JN

7801 SOUTHWELL (L-H)
Saturday, December 11

OFFICIAL GOING: Standard
Wind: Virtually nil Weather: Bright and dry

7830 BET ON TOTESCOOP6 AT TOTESPORT.COM E B F MAIDEN STKS 1m (F)
12:00 (12:00) (Class 5) 2-Y-O £2,978 (£886; £442) Stalls Low

Form RPR
45 1 **For What (USA)**[13] 7609 2-9-3 0........ ChrisCatlin 2 79
(D R Lanigan) *trckd ldr: pushed along 3f out: hdwy on inner and cl up 2f out: rdn to ld jst over 1f out: clr ins fnl f* 7/4[2]
6342 2 7 **Oversteer (USA)**[28] 7452 2-9-3 77........(b) NickyMackay 5 63
(J H M Gosden) *set stdy pce: qcknd over 3f out: jnd and rdn 2f out: drvn and hdd jst over 1f out: sn one pce* 4/7[1]
60 3 10 **Peals And Plaudits**[17] 7558 2-9-3 0........ EddieAhern 3 40
(E A L Dunlop) *in rr: pushed along after 2f: rdn 1/2-way: outpcd and bhd fnl 3f* 25/1[3]

1m 44.88s (1.18) **Going Correction** +0.225s/f (Slow) 3 Ran SP% 103.9
Speed ratings (Par 96): **103,96,86**
CSF £3.07 TOTE £2.50; EX 3.20.
Owner Niarchos Family **Bred** Flaxman Holdings Limited **Trained** Newmarket, Suffolk

FOCUS
A poor turnout for this maiden, and each of the three runners were trying this surface for the first time.

NOTEBOOK
For What(USA) had a bit to find with Oversteer strictly on their form from Wolverhampton last month, but he was making his racecourse debut that day and, while he didn't build on that performance at Kempton last time, the greater test of stamina on this switch to Fibresand clearly suited him better than the John Gosden-trained colt. (op 2-1 tchd 11-8)
Oversteer(USA) ran a better race in the first-time blinkers last time out, and the headgear was retained on this switch to Fibresand. He perhaps did a bit too much in front as he didn't find much for pressure in the straight and the winner saw the trip out much better. (op 1-2 tchd 8-11)
Peals And Plaudits was struggling throughout and looks of very moderate ability. He is eligible for a mark now, though. (op 16-1)

7831 BET ON TODAY'S FOOTBALL AT TOTESPORT.COM NURSERY 1m (F)
12:35 (12:35) (Class 6) (0-65,64) 2-Y-O £2,047 (£604; £302) Stalls Low

Form RPR
0000 1 **Fearless Poet (IRE)**[11] 7643 2-8-2 45........(p) MartinLane 5 48
(B Smart) *dwlt: sn cl up on outer: effrt to chal 2f out: sn rdn: kpt on to ld ent fnl f: sn edgd rt: jst hld on* 10/1
000 2 hd **Investment World (IRE)**[72] 6497 2-8-2 45........ FrannyNorton 8 48
(M Johnston) *swtchd lft after s and hld up in rr: hdwy and swtchd rt to chse ldrs wl over 2f out: drvn to chal ent fnl f: styng on and ev ch whn n.m.r towards fin* 16/1
0205 3 2 **Bernisdale**[25] 7471 2-9-0 57........ PJMcDonald 7 55
(G M Moore) *led: rdn along wl over 2f out: drvn and edgd lft over 1f out: hdd and edgd rt ent fnl f: no ex* 25/1
4014 4 1 ¾ **Urban Kode (IRE)**[11] 7643 2-8-12 55........ CathyGannon 6 49
(P D Evans) *hld up towards rr: hdwy 3f out: rdn to chse ldrs wl over 1f out: drvn and no imp appr fnl f* 5/2[2]
0012 5 2 ¼ **Geronimo Chief (IRE)**[11] 7643 2-9-4 61........ PhillipMakin 1 50
(B M R Haslam) *prom: effrt 3f out: rdn wl over 1f out and ch tl drvn and wknd appr fnl f* 13/8[1]
000 6 2 **Jay Jays Joy**[86] 6111 2-8-2 45........ NickyMackay 4 30
(T D Barron) *prom: rdn along 3f out: drvn over 2f out and grad wknd* 6/1[3]
0065 7 1 **False Promises**[11] 7643 2-8-2 45........(v[1]) PatrickMathers 2 28
(D Shaw) *dwlt: sn prom on inner: cl up over 3f out: sn rdn and wknd over 2f out* 28/1
4022 8 9 **Rath Maeve**[11] 7644 2-9-4 64........ AndrewHeffernan(3) 3 27
(A J McCabe) *sn pushed along: a towards rr* 17/2

1m 46.92s (3.22) **Going Correction** +0.225s/f (Slow) 8 Ran SP% 113.7
Speed ratings (Par 94): **92,91,89,88,85 83,82,73**
toteswingers:1&2 £15.80, 2&3 £16.90, 1&3 £8.70 CSF £149.05 CT £3814.22 TOTE £9.00: £3.00, £3.50, £5.30; EX 154.00 TRIFECTA Not won..
Owner The Smart Fear Not Partnership **Bred** Messrs N McSweeney & Jeff O'Callaghan **Trained** Hambleton, N Yorks

FOCUS
With the market leaders below their best the form looks pretty questionable.

NOTEBOOK
Fearless Poet(IRE) was slowly away and struggled to get competitive over 7f here on his handicap debut, but he had cheekpieces on this time and didn't lose too much ground at the start. The extra furlong really played to his strengths, but he was winning from 5lb out of the handicap so can expect a fair hike in the weights now, which could hold him back. Official explanation: trainer's rep said, regarding apparent improvement in form, that the colt benefited by being ridden more prominently in a poor race. (op 14-1 tchd 16-1)
Investment World(IRE), also running from 5lb out of the handicap, hadn't shown much in three maiden starts, but he's a half-brother to four winners and, returning from a break, ran a much better race on his handicap debut. Having started off on a basement mark, there's probably better to come from him. (op 14-1)
Bernisdale could only finish in mid-division in a seller over 7f here last time, but she was always in the front rank this time and put up an improved effort. (op 16-1)
Urban Kode(IRE) was in the kickback and struggled to make an impression from off the pace. (tchd 2-1)
Geronimo Chief(IRE) ended up more towards the inside rail in the straight, which is rarely the place to be. (op 9-4)

7832 40 LIVE FOOTBALL MARKETS AT TOTESPORT.COM (S) STKS 1m (F)
1:10 (1:10) (Class 6) 3-Y-O+ £1,569 (£463; £231) Stalls Low

Form RPR
4042 1 **William Morgan (IRE)**[8] 7679 3-9-0 61........ VinceSlattery 5 57
(A G Juckes) *trckd ldrs: hdwy 2f out: swtchd lft and rdn over 1f out: styd on to ld last 100yds: drvn out* 9/4[2]
240 2 ½ **Crocodile Bay (IRE)**[80] 6296 7-9-4 57........ AndrewHeffernan(3) 2 62
(D Bourton) *trckd ldrs: hdwy 3f out: chal over 2f out: rdn to ld wl over 1f out: drvn ent fnl f: hdd and no ex last 100yds* 9/2[3]
0030 3 2 **Tumbled Again**[10] 7651 3-9-0 48........(b) NickyMackay 1 51
(M E Rimmer) *cl up on inner: led 3f out: sn rdn and hdd wl over 1f out: drvn and ev ch tl one pce ins fnl f* 16/1
4300 4 4 ½ **Vogarth**[27] 4897 6-8-12 46........ RobertLButler(3) 6 41
(M C Chapman) *cl up: rdn along wl over 2f out: drvn: edgd lft and wknd over 1f out* 10/1
6003 5 4 ½ **Starry Mount**[24] 7476 3-9-0 64........(b[1]) PhillipMakin 4 31
(A B Haynes) *led: rdn along and hdd 3f out: drvn over 2f out and sn wknd* 2/1[1]
3046 6 1 **Louisiade (IRE)**[3] 7763 9-8-10 48........(p) MarkCoumbe(5) 3 28
(D Bourton) *in tch: rdn along over 3f out: sn wknd* 8/1
60 7 13 **Lord's Seat**[122] 4951 3-9-0 42........ FrannyNorton 7 —
(A Berry) *a bhd* 33/1

1m 46.06s (2.36) **Going Correction** +0.225s/f (Slow)
WFA 3 from 6yo+ 1lb 7 Ran SP% 111.3
Speed ratings (Par 101): **97,96,94,90,85 84,71**
CSF £12.10 TOTE £3.60: £1.90, £1.70; EX 15.30.There was no bid for the winner.
Owner Whispering Winds **Bred** R P Ryan **Trained** Abberley, Worcs

FOCUS
An ordinary seller.

7833 GET LIVE FOOTBALL STATS AT TOTESPORT.COM H'CAP 1m (F)
1:45 (1:45) (Class 6) (0-65,62) 3-Y-O+ £1,706 (£503; £252) Stalls Low

Form RPR
2140 1 **D'Urberville**[37] 7323 3-9-6 62........ EddieAhern 6 72
(J R Jenkins) *trckd ldng pair: smooth hdwy to chse ldr 3f out: led 2f out: rdn wl over 1f out: drvn ins fnl f and kpt on wl* 5/2[1]
4530 2 ½ **Minortransgression (USA)**[13] 7613 3-9-6 62........ StevieDonohoe 3 71
(P D Evans) *in tch: hdwy 3f out: rdn to chse ldrs 2f out: drvn to chal over 1f out and ev ch tl no ex wl ins fnl f* 7/2[2]
0016 3 10 **Custard Cream Kid (IRE)**[2] 7787 4-8-3 51........ LauraBarry(7) 4 37
(R A Fahey) *trckd ldrs on inner: hdwy wl over 2f ouit: rdn to chse wnr wl over 1f out: sn drvn and wknd ins fnl f* 4/1[3]
0005 4 1 ¾ **Baraconti (IRE)**[5] 7731 3-8-10 52........(p) TomEaves 1 34
(Mrs R A Carr) *led: rdn along 3f out: hdd 2f out: sn drvn and grad wknd* 12/1
0034 5 7 **Half Sister (IRE)**[9] 7669 3-8-6 48 oh1........(bt) NickyMackay 2 14
(M E Rimmer) *chsd wnr: rdn along over 3f out: sn wknd* 12/1
5036 6 6 **Spread Boy (IRE)**[46] 7144 3-9-2 58........ FrannyNorton 7 —
(A Berry) *a in rr: rdn along over 3f out: sn outpcd and bhd* 11/2
0010 7 11 **Atacama Sunrise**[17] 7561 4-9-7 62........ KirstyMilczarek 5 —
(G Prodromou) *a in rr: rdn along over 3f out: sn outpcd and bhd* 8/1

1m 44.39s (0.69) **Going Correction** +0.225s/f (Slow)
WFA 3 from 4yo 1lb 7 Ran SP% 112.7
Speed ratings (Par 101): **105,104,94,92,85 79,68**
toteswingers:1&2 £2.40, 2&3 £3.70, 1&3 £2.50 CSF £11.02 TOTE £2.40: £1.10, £3.30; EX 12.30.
Owner Smart K Syndicate **Bred** Llety Stud **Trained** Royston, Herts

FOCUS
Two came clear in this handicap.
Spread Boy(IRE) Official explanation: jockey said gelding didn't face the kickback

7834 CHAPPO'S 21ST BIRTHDAY MAIDEN STKS 1m 4f (F)
2:20 (2:20) (Class 5) 3-4-Y-O £2,388 (£705; £352) Stalls Low

Form RPR
3233 1 **Lay Claim (USA)**[7] 7694 3-9-3 69........(e[1]) ShaneKelly 2 75+
(A J McCabe) *hld up in tch: smooth hdwy 4f out: led wl over 2f out and sn wl clr: eased last 100yds* 11/10[1]
2 3 **Truly Magnificent (USA)**[118] 3-8-9 0........ RobertLButler(3) 5 57
(B W Duke) *chsd ldrs: rdn along and sltly outpcd over 3f out: sn drvn and kpt on fnl 2f: no ch w wnr* 14/1

00 3 2 3/4 **Zakeeta (IRE)**[28] 1358 3-8-12 0 EddieAhern 7 53
(O Sherwood) *trckd ldrs: hdwy and cl up 1/2-way: rdn to ld briefly 3f out: sn hdd: drvn and outpcd fnl 2f: lost remote 2nd ins fnl f* 2/1[2]
4 4 15 **Shouda (IRE)**[18] 7538 4-9-8 0 TomQueally 6 34
(B J Curley) *led: rdn along 4f out: hdd over 3f out and sn wknd* 9/2[3]
00 5 22 **Drivemode**[15] 7575 3-9-3 0 MickyFenton 3 —
(Dr J D Scargill) *a in rr: rdn along and outpcd fr 1/2-way: bhd fnl 3f* 33/1
0500 6 12 **Solo Choice**[199] 1113 4-9-8 44 KirstyMilczarek 8 —
(I W McInnes) *a in rr: rdn along and bhd fr 1/2-way* 50/1
000 7 30 **Titanic Mill**[15] 7579 3-9-0 0 (b) AndrewHeffernan(3) 4 —
(N J Vaughan) *prom: rdn along and lost pl after 4f: sn bhd and t.o fnl 4f* 80/1

2m 44.85s (3.85) **Going Correction** +0.225s/f (Slow)
WFA 3 from 4yo 5lb 7 Ran SP% **111.9**
Speed ratings (Par 103): **96,94,92,82,67 59,39**
toteswingers:1&2 £3.60, 2&3 £5.10, 1&3 £1.10 CSF £17.21 TOTE £2.30: £1.10, £4.50; EX 15.40 Trifecta £55.70 Pool: £406.80 - 5.40 winning units..
Owner Abdul Rahman Al Jasmi **Bred** George Strawbridge Et Al **Trained** Averham Park, Notts

FOCUS
An uncompetitive maiden.

7835 TONY MCCOY FOR BBC SPORTS PERSONALITY H'CAP 7f (F)
2:55 (3:01) (Class 6) (0-55,54) 3-Y-O+ £1,569 (£463; £231) Stalls Low

Form RPR
3500 1 **Clever Omneya (USA)**[200] 2419 4-8-9 47 FrannyNorton 6 64
(J R Jenkins) *led over 2f: cl up tl led again 2f out: rdn clr appr fnl f: readily* 9/1
0514 2 5 **Royal Island (IRE)**[2] 7787 8-8-11 49 TomQueally 10 53
(M G Quinlan) *hld up towards rr: wd st: hdwy on outer over 2f out: rdn to chse wnr over 1f out: sn drvn: edgd lft and no imp* 10/3[1]
0000 3 1/2 **Jonnie Skull (IRE)**[25] 7474 4-9-1 53 (vt) NickyMackay 8 55
(M D Squance) *in tch: hdwy over 2f out: sn rdn: kpt on ins fnl f* 5/1[2]
5536 4 1/2 **Norcroft**[30] 7402 8-8-2 45 (p) RyanClark(5) 14 46
(Mrs C A Dunnett) *prom: effrt 2f out: sn rdn and one pce appr fnl f* 12/1
0433 5 3/4 **Olympic Dream**[14] 7605 4-9-2 54 (p) TomEaves 7 53
(M Herrington) *trckd ldrs on inner: hdwy 3f out: rdn 2f out: drvn and wknd over 1f out* 7/1
3004 6 1/2 **Novastasia (IRE)**[25] 7473 4-8-7 45 (b) SamHitchcott 3 43
(D K Ivory) *cl up on inner: led over 4f out: rdn along 3f out: hdd 2f out: sn drvn and grad wknd* 11/2[3]
5400 7 3 1/2 **Dancing Wave**[122] 4939 4-8-0 45 JackDuern(7) 12 33
(M C Chapman) *cl up: rdn along 3f out: sn wknd* 40/1
506- 8 10 **Cullybackey (IRE)**[197] 7533 5-8-7 45 (b) FrankieMcDonald 2 —
(John A Harris) *dwlt: a bhd* 66/1
1426 9 1 **Mushy Peas (IRE)**[41] 7250 3-8-13 51 CathyGannon 1 —
(P D Evans) *a towards rr* 11/2[3]
000 10 nk **Polemica (IRE)**[29] 7426 4-8-6 49 (t) BillyCray(5) 13 —
(F Sheridan) *dwlt: a in rr* 12/1
000 11 20 **Miss Flash Dancer**[106] 5486 4-9-0 52 ChrisCatlin 9 —
(C C Bealby) *a in rr: bhd fnl 3f* 20/1

1m 30.09s (-0.21) **Going Correction** +0.225s/f (Slow) 11 Ran SP% **117.1**
Speed ratings (Par 101): **110,104,103,103,102 101,97,86,85,84 61**
toteswingers:1&2 £10.00, 2&3 £4.30, 1&3 £8.60 CSF £38.35 CT £170.52 TOTE £11.50: £3.10, £1.50, £2.30; EX 44.70 Trifecta £326.90 Part won. Pool of £441.80 - 0.63 winning units..
Owner Fhad Al Harthi **Bred** Lantern Hill Farm Llc **Trained** Royston, Herts

FOCUS
A moderate handicap.
Mushy Peas(IRE) Official explanation: jockey said gelding had no more to give

7836 PLAY GOLF BEFORE RACING AT SOUTHWELL H'CAP 1m 4f (F)
3:30 (3:30) (Class 5) (0-75,71) 3-Y-O+ £2,388 (£705; £352) Stalls Low

Form RPR
6-16 1 **Dontpaytheferryman (USA)**[27] 331 5-8-3 57 oh5 ShaneBKelly(7) 4 66
(B Ellison) *trckd ldr: led 4f out: rdn 2f out: jnd and drvn 1f out: hld on gamely towards fin* 2/1[2]
0024 2 3/4 **Trachonitis (IRE)**[26] 7463 6-9-7 68 ShaneKelly 1 76
(J R Jenkins) *hld up in rr: hdwy on bit over 3f out: chal wd 2f out: edgd lft and disp ld over 1f out: shkn up ins fnl f: sn drvn and one pce last 75yds* 13/8[1]
2000 3 12 **Eton Fable (IRE)**[118] 5118 5-9-10 71 (p) TravisBlock 5 60
(W J H Ratcliffe) *led: rdn along 4f out: sn hdd and outpcd fnl 2f* 5/1[3]
/05- 4 3 1/4 **Black Tor Figarro (IRE)**[655] 668 5-8-10 57 oh2 CathyGannon 3 40
(B W Duke) *trckd ldrs: hdwy to chse ldng pair 4f out: rdn 3f out and sn outpcd* 10/1
10 5 23 **Dosti**[255] 1060 3-8-12 67 MatthewDavies(3) 2 14
(Tim Vaughan) *chsd ldrs: rdn along over 4f out: lost pl over 3f out and sn bhd* 8/1

2m 44.41s (3.41) **Going Correction** +0.225s/f (Slow)
WFA 3 from 5yo+ 5lb 5 Ran SP% **108.3**
Speed ratings (Par 103): **97,96,88,86,71**
CSF £5.44 TOTE £2.40: £4.00, £1.10; EX 4.00.
Owner Koo's Racing Club **Bred** Rojan Farms **Trained** Norton, N Yorks

FOCUS
This was fought out by the two at the head of the market.
T/Plt: £1,136.40 to a £1 stake. Pool of £51,374.10 - 33.00 winning tickets. T/Qpdt: £6.40 to a £1 stake. Pool of £5,909.63 - 679.02 winning tickets. JR

7809 WOLVERHAMPTON (A.W) (L-H)
Saturday, December 11

OFFICIAL GOING: Standard
Wind: Light across Weather: Cloudy

7837 PLAY BINGO AT TOTESPORT.COM H'CAP 7f 32y(P)
6:20 (6:21) (Class 5) (0-70,70) 3-Y-O+ £2,007 (£597; £298; £149) Stalls High

Form RPR
6325 1 **Sunset Kitty (USA)**[24] 7483 3-9-4 67 AdamKirby 3 81
(W R Swinburn) *mid-div: pushed along over 4f out: hdwy over 1f out: edgd rt 1f out: rdn to ld ins fnl f: r.o* 11/4[2]
5003 2 2 3/4 **Lockantanks**[7] 7699 3-9-5 68 NeilChalmers 9 75
(M Appleby) *hld up: hdwy over 1f out: r.o* 10/1
5640 3 1 3/4 **King's Caprice**[13] 7611 9-8-13 62 SamHitchcott 4 64
(J C Fox) *led early: chsd ldr: rdn 1/2-way: styd on same pce ins fnl f* 9/1
5325 4 1 **Just Timmy Marcus**[1] 7812 4-9-2 65 (b) JackMitchell 8 65
(B P J Baugh) *dwlt: hld up: hdwy over 2f out: rdn over 1f out: no ex ins fnl f* 5/1[3]
0-14 5 1 3/4 **Taurakina**[29] 7425 4-9-3 66 ChrisCatlin 1 61
(M Botti) *led over 6f out: clr 1/2-way: rdn over 1f out: hdd & wknd ins fnl f* 5/2[1]
0223 6 3/4 **Cat Hunter**[74] 6438 3-9-7 70 LukeMorris 5 63
(R A Harris) *prom: rdn over 2f out: wknd fnl f* 13/2
1420 7 nk **Fault**[17] 7557 4-9-7 70 (t) MickyFenton 7 62
(Stef Higgins) *hld up: rdn over 1f out: styd on ins fnl f: nvr on terms* 14/1
21-6 8 4 **Goddess Of Light (IRE)**[6] 7747 3-9-7 70 SeamieHeffernan 2 51
(Daniel Mark Loughnane, Ire) *chsd ldrs: rdn over 2f out: wknd over 1f out* 28/1
6000 9 11 **Cut The Cackle (IRE)**[18] 7539 4-9-3 69 RobertLButler(3) 6 21
(P Butler) *mid-div: rdn 4f out: sn wknd* 50/1

1m 29.44s (-0.16) **Going Correction** +0.175s/f (Slow) 9 Ran SP% **116.4**
Speed ratings (Par 103): **107,103,101,100,98 97,97,92,80**
toteswingers:1&2:£7.20, 1&3:£5.50, 2&3:£14.10 CSF £30.77 CT £221.01 TOTE £5.00: £2.10, £3.10, £5.20; EX 34.90.
Owner Cool Cats **Bred** Mckee Stables Inc **Trained** Aldbury, Herts

FOCUS
A modest handicap and one run at a reasonable gallop. The winner raced centre-to-far-side in the straight.

7838 WOLVERHAMPTON-RACECOURSE.CO.UK MAIDEN STKS 7f 32y(P)
6:50 (6:50) (Class 5) 3-Y-O+ £2,007 (£597; £298; £149) Stalls High

Form RPR
0/ 1 **John Veale (USA)**[7] 7707 4-9-3 72 (t) EddieAhern 6 77+
(Thomas McLaughlin, Ire) *chsd ldr tl led 2f out: sn rdn clr: eased nr fin* 4/9[1]
04 2 7 **Penbryn (USA)**[36] 7338 3-9-3 0 J-PGuillambert 2 55
(N P Littmoden) *s.i.s: hld up: pushed along 1/2-way: rdn over 2f out: styd on to go 2nd wl ins fnl f: no ch w wnr* 7/2[2]
026 3 1 1/2 **La Chemme**[16] 7563 4-8-12 49 ChrisCatlin 1 46
(R Hollinshead) *led: rdn and hdd 2f out: sn outpcd* 14/1
6- 4 3/4 **Marshal Plat Club**[395] 7331 3-8-12 0 RobertWinston 3 44
(A Bailey) *plld hrd and prom: rdn over 2f out: edgd lft and styd on same pce fr over 1f out* 8/1[3]

1m 31.46s (1.86) **Going Correction** +0.175s/f (Slow) 4 Ran SP% **109.3**
Speed ratings (Par 103): **96,88,86,85**
CSF £2.35 TOTE £1.30; EX 2.10.
Owner T McLaughlin **Bred** Crown's Way Farm Et Al **Trained** Rathmullan, Co Donegal

FOCUS
A thoroughly uncompetitive maiden in which the proximity of the 49-rated third says much about the worth of the form. The gallop was only fair and the winner came down the centre in the straight.

7839 PLAY BLACKJACK AT TOTESPORT.COM CLAIMING STKS 1m 1f 103y(P)
7:20 (7:20) (Class 5) 2-Y-O £2,007 (£597; £298; £149) Stalls Low

Form RPR
0144 1 **Skeleton (IRE)**[10] 7650 2-8-0 60 (b) CathyGannon 6 57
(W J Haggas) *hld up in tch: rdn to ld and hung lft ins fnl f: r.o* 7/2[2]
03 2 1 **Oratouch (IRE)**[26] 7464 2-8-10 0 ChrisCatlin 8 65
(M Botti) *hld up: hdwy over 1f out: r.o to go 2nd post: nt rch wnr* 6/1
4653 3 hd **Beating Harmony**[9] 7664 2-8-5 58 (p) RichardKingscote 4 60
(Tom Dascombe) *led: rdn over 1f out: hdd and unable qck ins fnl f: lost 2nd post* 7/2[2]
0311 4 1 1/2 **Sheila's Star (IRE)**[12] 7629 2-8-6 62 LukeMorris 3 58
(J S Moore) *chsd ldr 2f: remained handy: rdn over 2f out: styd on same pce ins fnl f* 11/4[1]
0000 5 3 **Blade Pirate**[42] 7236 2-8-5 45 KirstyMilczarek 5 51
(J Ryan) *racd keenly: prom: chsd ldr over 6f out: rdn and hung rt fr over 1f out: no ex ins fnl f* 66/1
535 6 nk **Polly Holder (IRE)**[42] 7242 2-8-2 65 FrannyNorton 2 48
(A Bailey) *hld up: rdn over 2f out: nvr on terms* 4/1[3]
0255 7 1/2 **Bathwick Scanno (IRE)**[21] 7520 2-8-7 57 MartinLane 1 52
(P D Evans) *prom: pushed along over 5f out: wknd over 1f out* 18/1
00 8 3/4 **Jane's Legacy**[15] 7578 2-8-10 0 GrahamGibbons 7 53
(R Hollinshead) *s.i.s: hld up: a in rr* 40/1

2m 3.91s (2.21) **Going Correction** +0.175s/f (Slow) 8 Ran SP% **114.6**
Speed ratings (Par 96): **97,96,95,94,91 91,91,90**
toteswingers:1&2 £4.40, 1&3 £2.40, 2&3 £6.10 CSF £24.81 TOTE £4.00: £1.80, £3.40, £1.40; EX 25.20.Skeleton was claimed by P. D. Evans for £5,000
Owner Raymond Tooth **Bred** Darley **Trained** Newmarket, Suffolk

FOCUS
A modest claimer run at just an ordinary gallop. The winner edged towards the far rail in the closing stages.

NOTEBOOK
Skeleton(IRE), who had a good chance at the weights on this first run over this trip, travelled strongly for a long way and did enough to notch her second win on Polytrack. She doesn't look entirely straightforward but now joins David Evans and is the type to win again. (op 4-1 tchd 9-2 in places)
Oratouch(IRE) has improved with every outing and posted her best effort over this first run at the trip, in the process reversing previous placings with Sheila's Star. She's now qualified for a mark, is in good hands and should be placed to best advantage. (op 11-2)
Beating Harmony, tried in cheekpieces, had the run of the race and ran creditably on this first run over this longer trip. He has had a few chances and he did have the rub of things here so it remains to be seen whether this can be built on next time. (tchd 4-1)
Sheila's Star(IRE) looked to have good claims in this company but wasn't at her very best and couldn't reverse recent placings with Oratouch over this trip. However she was far from disgraced and should continue to give a good account. (op 4-1)
Blade Pirate, a very moderate and inconsistent maiden, wasn't totally disgraced in the face of a stiff task but looked anything like a straightforward proposition. (op 100-1)
Polly Holder(IRE) failed to improve in the anticipated manner for this first outing over this trip but she isn't fully exposed and will probably be worth another chance granted a stiffer test, especially when the market speaks more favourably. (op 7-2)

7840 TONY MCCOY FOR BBC SPORTS PERSONALITY H'CAP 1m 4f 50y(P)
7:50 (7:50) (Class 6) (0-60,58) 3-Y-O+ £1,619 (£481; £240; £120) Stalls Low

Form RPR
0211 1 **Alternative Choice (USA)**[132] 4620 4-9-10 58 GeorgeBaker 1 65+
(N P Littmoden) *hld up: hdwy over 2f out: rdn to ld wl ins fnl f: r.o* 9/2[2]
0010 2 3/4 **Abulharith**[6] 7716 4-9-7 55 (p) LukeMorris 10 61
(R A Harris) *led: rdn over 2f out: sn edgd rt: hdd wl ins fnl f* 10/1

1506 **3** 3/4 **Derby Desire (IRE)**[21] 7531 6-9-6 **54** .... CathyGannon 9 59
(D Donovan) *hld up: hdwy over 4f out: outpcd over 3f out: rallied over 1f out: r.o* **13/2**

0034 **4** *nk* **Blackstone Vegas**[3] 7759 4-9-4 **52** .... (v) PatrickMathers 4 57
(D Shaw) *hld up in tch: rdn over 1f out: r.o* **11/2**[3]

44-4 **5** *nse* **Dot's Delight**[25] 6021 6-9-0 **48** .... ChrisCatlin 5 52
(M G Rimell) *mid-div: racd keenly: rdn over 2f out: r.o* **10/1**

4323 **6** 3/4 **Amical Risks (FR)**[83] 4781 6-9-10 **58** .... TomEaves 6 61
(Ollie Pears) *s.i.s: hld up: hdwy over 6f out: rdn over 2f out: styd on same pce ins fnl f* **4/1**[1]

0625 **7** 1 1/2 **Motarjm (USA)**[19] 6314 6-9-5 **53** .... (t) MickyFenton 2 54
(J Pearce) *prom: rdn to chse ldr 2f out: edgd rt and no ex ins fnl f* **6/1**

060 **8** *nk* **Maydream**[15] 7575 3-8-8 **47** .... SamHitchcott 8 47
(J C Fox) *chsd ldr tl over 6f out: rdn over 2f out: styd on same pce fnl f* **40/1**

20/0 **9** 1/2 **Acknowledgement**[91] 5959 8-9-7 **55** .... (b) StevieDonohoe 7 54
(J L Spearing) *prom: racd keenly: chsd ldr over 6f out tl rdn 2f out: no ex fnl f* **7/1**

0550 **10** 7 **Spacecraft (IRE)**[12] 7633 3-8-11 **50** .... FrannyNorton 3 38
(C N Kellett) *hld up: pushed along 6f out: rdn and wknd over 2f out* **50/1**

000- **11** 5 **Almowj**[506] 4220 7-8-4 **45** .... JackDuern(7) 11 25
(G H Jones) *hld up: a in rr: rdn and wknd over 2f out* **100/1**

2m 45.71s (4.61) **Going Correction** +0.175s/f (Slow)
WFA 3 from 4yo+ 5lb **11** Ran SP% **117.3**
Speed ratings (Par 101): **91,90,90,89,89 89,88,88,87,83 79**
toteswingers:1&2 £7.00, 1&3 £5.90, 2&3 £15.10 CSF £48.51 CT £293.89 TOTE £4.60: £1.60, £2.70, £5.00; EX 53.10.
Owner A A Goodman **Bred** Gainesway Thoroughbreds Ltd **Trained** Newmarket, Suffolk

FOCUS
A moderate handicap run at a modest gallop. The winner came down the centre in the straight.

7841 PLAY ROULETTE AT TOTESPORT.COM H'CAP 5f 216y(P)
8:20 (8:20) (Class 5) (0-75,75) 3-Y-O+ **£2,007** (£597; £298; £149) **Stalls** Low

Form RPR

3524 **1** **Prince James**[12] 7628 3-8-8 **65** .... JamesSullivan(3) 6 75
(M W Easterby) *a.p: chsd ldr over 1f out: rdn to ld ins fnl f: r.o* **5/1**[3]

0000 **2** 1/2 **Sarah's Art (IRE)**[4] 7737 7-9-4 **72** .... (t) AdamKirby 2 80+
(Stef Higgins) *mid-div: hdwy over 2f out: rdn over 1f out: r.o* **4/1**[1]

2666 **3** 1 3/4 **Feelin Foxy**[3] 7754 6-9-7 **75** .... TomEaves 1 78
(J G Given) *trckd ldrs: racd keenly: rdn over 1f out: styd on same pce ins fnl f* **15/2**

1054 **4** 1/2 **Kinigi (IRE)**[18] 7539 4-8-12 **73** .... (b) JakePayne(7) 3 74
(R A Harris) *led: rdn over 1f out: hdd and no ex ins fnl f* **8/1**

60 **5** 1/2 **Schoolboy Champ**[15] 7571 3-8-11 **65** .... LukeMorris 5 65
(Patrick Morris) *prom: rdn 1/2-way: styd on same pce appr fnl f* **33/1**

0500 **6** 1 **Dametime (IRE)**[61] 6820 4-9-7 **75** .... SeamieHeffernan 12 71
(Daniel Mark Loughnane, Ire) *chsd ldr over 4f out tl rdn over 1f out: no ex fnl f* **8/1**

4315 **7** 3/4 **Emerald Girl (IRE)**[166] 3505 3-8-13 **74** .... GeorgeChaloner(7) 7 68+
(R A Fahey) *s.i.s: in rr: styd on ins fnl f: nvr nrr* **12/1**

6000 **8** 1/2 **Electioneer (USA)**[18] 7539 3-8-9 **63** .... GrahamGibbons 9 55
(M W Easterby) *mid-div: rdn over 2f out: styd on u.p: nvr on terms* **9/2**[2]

5000 **9** 4 1/2 **Northern Dare (IRE)**[148] 4090 6-9-6 **74** .... StevieDonohoe 4 52
(R A Fahey) *sn outpcd* **13/2**

0006 **10** 1 1/4 **Raimond Ridge (IRE)**[9] 7668 4-8-11 **65** .... PatrickMathers 11 39
(D Shaw) *s.i.s: sn outpcd* **66/1**

1m 15.18s (0.18) **Going Correction** +0.175s/f (Slow) **10** Ran SP% **114.3**
Speed ratings (Par 103): **105,104,102,101,100 99,98,97,91,90**
toteswingers:1&2 £4.60, 1&3 £9.00, 2&3 £7.40 CSF £24.77 CT £151.13 TOTE £5.20: £1.70, £1.20, £4.10; EX 26.40.
Owner A Saha **Bred** A C M Spalding **Trained** Sheriff Hutton, N Yorks

FOCUS
Exposed performers in an ordinary handicap. The gallop was a reasonable one but those held up could never land a blow. The winner raced centre-to-far-side in the straight.

7842 PLAY SLOTS AT TOTESPORT.COM H'CAP 1m 141y(P)
8:50 (8:50) (Class 4) (0-85,84) 3-Y-O+ **£3,594** (£1,069; £534; £266) **Stalls** Low

Form RPR

113 **1** **Final Drive (IRE)**[5] 7724 4-9-0 **77** .... StevieDonohoe 6 92+
(J Ryan) *hld up: hdwy over 2f out: led over 1f out: shkn up and r.o wl: readily* **6/4**[1]

110 **2** 4 **Miami Gator (IRE)**[85] 6144 3-8-11 **76** .... (v) LukeMorris 2 80
(Mrs K Burke) *led: rdn and hdd over 1f out: styd on same pce* **9/2**[3]

1621 **3** 1 1/2 **Lord Of The Dance (IRE)**[7] 7699 4-8-9 **72** .... EddieAhern 5 73
(W M Brisbourne) *hld up in tch: rdn over 2f out: styd on same pce appr fnl f* **9/2**[3]

0030 **4** 1/2 **Unbreak My Heart (IRE)**[49] 7100 5-9-7 **84** .... PhillipMakin 4 84
(R A Fahey) *chsd ldr tl rdn over 1f out: no ex fnl f* **3/1**[2]

0240 **5** 24 **Duplicity**[17] 7554 3-8-13 **78** .... TomEaves 1 23
(J G Given) *chsd ldrs tl rdn and wknd over 2f out* **17/2**

1m 50.69s (0.19) **Going Correction** +0.175s/f (Slow)
WFA 3 from 4yo+ 2lb **5** Ran SP% **111.9**
Speed ratings (Par 105): **106,102,101,100,79**
toteswingers:1&2 £5.20 CSF £8.75 TOTE £2.90: £3.20, £1.10; EX 9.60.
Owner Par 4 Racing **Bred** D Day & B Cantwell **Trained** Newmarket, Suffolk

FOCUS
A fair handicap but one run at just a steady gallop. The winner, who won with plenty in hand, made his ground in the centre in the straight.
T/Plt: £144.20 to a £1 stake. Pool £106,169.46 - 537.17 winning tickets T/Qpdt: £34.30 to a £1 stake. Pool £8,477.56 - 182.48 winning tickets CR

7830 SOUTHWELL (L-H)
Sunday, December 12

OFFICIAL GOING: Standard
Wind: moderate 1/2 behind Weather: fine but cold

7843 BET TODAY'S FOOTBALL AT TOTESPORT.COM MAIDEN STKS 6f (F)
12:45 (12:46) (Class 5) 2-Y-O **£2,655** (£790; £394; £197) **Stalls** Low

Form RPR

64 **1** **Verrazano**[9] 7682 2-8-12 0 .... PhillipMakin 9 66
(K A Ryan) *led tl over 4f out: drvn and outpcd over 3f out: styd on to ld last 100yds* **4/1**[2]

60 **2** 1 1/4 **Elusive Love (IRE)**[121] 5053 2-9-3 0 .... GregFairley 11 67
(M Johnston) *w ldrs: led over 4f out: hdd 3f out: led 1f out: hdd and no ex fnl 100yds* **5/1**[3]

0 **3** *shd* **Speedy Joe**[8] 7700 2-9-3 0 .... TomEaves 7 67
(B Smart) *sn chsng ldrs on outer: effrt over 2f out: upsides and hung lft over 1f out: kpt on same pce last 100yds* **16/1**

0302 **4** 2 3/4 **Silent Blessing**[8] 7692 2-9-3 60 .... (p) GrahamGibbons 2 59
(R M H Cowell) *sn w ldrs: led 3f out: hdd 1f out: wknd fnl 100yds* **11/2**

0006 **5** 1 1/2 **Granny Anne (IRE)**[22] 7527 2-8-5 47 .... NatashaEaton(7) 5 49
(A Bailey) *in rr: kpt on fnl 2f: nt rch ldrs* **33/1**

50 **6** 1 1/4 **Robin Hoods Bay**[15] 7595 2-9-3 0 .... DavidProbert 4 50
(E F Vaughan) *dwlt: in rr: kpt on fnl 2f: nvr nr ldrs* **10/3**[1]

066 **7** 3 1/4 **Lynchpin**[18] 7550 2-9-3 58 .... LukeMorris 3 41
(R A Harris) *chsd ldrs: drvn over 3f out: hung rt and lost pl over 1f out* **14/1**

00 **8** 1 **Oh What's Occuring**[30] 7424 2-8-9 0 .... KellyHarrison(3) 6 33
(T T Clement) *in rr: sme hdwy 2f out: nvr a factor* **100/1**

0435 **9** 2 3/4 **Sapphire Girl**[149] 4083 2-8-5 68 .... LauraBarry(7) 8 24
(R A Fahey) *w ldrs: lost pl 2f out* **5/1**[3]

10 3 **She Deals** 2-8-9 0 .... PaulPickard(3) 10 15
(P T Midgley) *chsd ldrs on outer: wknd 2f out* **40/1**

11 11 **Musical Leap** 2-9-3 0 .... SamHitchcott 1 —
(S A Harris) *s.s: in rr: sme hdwy over 2f out: sn lost pl and bhd* **80/1**

1m 16.53s (0.03) **Going Correction** -0.075s/f (Stan) **11** Ran SP% **112.0**
Speed ratings (Par 96): **96,94,94,90,88 86,82,81,77,73 58**
toteswingers:1&2: £3.70, 2&3: £14.60, 1&3: £9.00 CSF £22.65 TOTE £5.40: £2.40, £3.00, £6.10; EX 24.00 Trifecta £158.20 Pool: £466.26 - 2.18 winning units..
Owner Guy Reed **Bred** G Reed **Trained** Hambleton, N Yorks

FOCUS
The jockeys were convinced that the track was riding a little quicker than at recent meetings. A weak maiden in which the first four pulled clear to battle it out in the straight. The first four are all likely improvers.

NOTEBOOK
Verrazano raced closer to the inside of the track in the straight than the other principals and, after being brought under pressure some way out, eventually hit the front inside the last half-furlong. Her first two starts had been over 7f and she will not mind a return to that trip on this evidence. (tchd 7-2 and 9-2)
Elusive Love(IRE) ran creditably on this sand debut and briefly nosed in front in the final furlong, but changed his legs and was cut down. He is now eligible for a handicap mark. (tchd 11-2)
Speedy Joe started slowly on his debut and wasn't the best away here. He was staying on at the end and the return to 7f will benefit him. (op 14-1)
Silent Blessing showed pace and had his chance, before being eased late on when held. He has yet to conclusively prove his stamina for this trip. (op 6-1 tchd 13-2)
Granny Anne(IRE) plugged on from the rear on this Fibresand bow, but is probably flattered by this seemingly improved showing.
Robin Hoods Bay, who had shown ability on Polytrack, was slow to break once again and made just moderate late progress. (op 4-1 tchd 3-1)
Sapphire Girl was clearly best in among those with BHA ratings, but after chasing the pace on her debut on this surface she dropped right away. (op 9-2 tchd 4-1)

7844 GET LIVE FOOTBALL STATS AT TOTESPORT.COM CLAIMING STKS 7f (F)
1:15 (1:15) (Class 6) 3-Y-O+ **£1,706** (£503; £252) **Stalls** Low

Form RPR

3504 **1** **Avonrose**[6] 7725 3-8-10 75 .... GregFairley 2 74
(M Johnston) *sn chsng ldrs: hung lft and styd on to ld last 100yds* **7/1**[2]

4261 **2** 1 1/4 **Majuro (IRE)**[15] 7601 6-9-0 90 .... RyanClark(5) 8 79
(S C Williams) *w ldrs: led over 2f out: hung rt and hdd last 100yds: no ex* **2/5**[1]

4504 **3** 1 1/4 **Master Leon**[8] 7701 3-8-12 67 .... (p) TomEaves 11 69
(B Smart) *chsd ldrs on outer: rdn over 2f out: kpt on same pcen ins fnl f* **20/1**

0026 **4** 1 1/4 **Chat De La Burg (USA)**[18] 7554 3-9-3 73 .... KierenFox(3) 7 74
(J R Best) *led tl over 3f out: led 3f out tl over 2f out: wknd last 75yds* **14/1**

0016 **5** 1 1/2 **Opus Maximus (IRE)**[9] 7680 5-9-3 80 .... AdrianNicholls 1 67
(M Johnston) *sn chsng ldrs: kpt on one pce fnl 2f* **9/1**[3]

0144 **6** *hd* **Toby Tyler**[26] 7472 4-8-6 60 .... (v) PaulPickard(3) 6 58
(P T Midgley) *s.i.s: hld up in rr: swtchd ins over 4f out: effrt over 2f out: sn chsng ldrs: wknd last 100yds* **33/1**

0040 **7** 1/2 **Amary (IRE)**[19] 7539 3-8-3 69 .... JulieBurke(7) 3 58
(John A Harris) *dwlt: in rr: effrt on outside over 2f out: kpt on ins fnl f* **33/1**

1000 **8** 3 **Masked Dance (IRE)**[36] 7352 3-9-7 80 .... (b[1]) PhillipMakin 5 61
(K A Ryan) *w ldrs: led over 3f out: sn hdd: wknd over 1f out: eased ins fnl f* **18/1**

402 **9** 6 **Crocodile Bay (IRE)**[1] 7832 7-8-7 57 ow3 .... (b) MarkCoumbe(5) 12 35
(D Bourton) *chsd ldrs on outer: lost pl over 4f out: sme hdwy 3f out: sn wknd* **25/1**

1m 28.25s (-2.05) **Going Correction** -0.075s/f (Stan) **9** Ran SP% **120.3**
Speed ratings (Par 101): **108,106,105,103,102 101,101,97,90**
toteswingers:1&2: £2.30, 2&3:£3.80, 1&3: £5.70 CSF £10.29 TOTE £8.10: £1.10, £1.30, £2.70; EX 16.00 Trifecta £313.30 Pool: £486.90 - 1.15 winning units..Avonrose was claimed by Derek Shaw for £10,000.
Owner Around The World Partnership **Bred** Mrs Mary Taylor **Trained** Middleham Moor, N Yorks

FOCUS
A fair claimer run in a good time compared with the later handicap. The third and fourth are the key to the form.
Crocodile Bay(IRE) Official explanation: trainer said race came too soon for gelding

7845 40 LIVE FOOTBALL MARKETS AT TOTESPORT.COM H'CAP 1m (F)
1:45 (1:45) (Class 5) (0-70,67) 3-Y-O **£2,266** (£674; £337; £168) **Stalls** Low

Form RPR

0030 **1** **Steed**[27] 7467 3-8-4 **57** .... (p) JulieBurke(7) 5 65
(K A Ryan) *s.i.s: hld up: hdwy on outer over 3f out: chal over 1f out: led last 100yds: all out* **8/1**

415 **2** *shd* **Mr Emirati (USA)**[9] 7678 3-9-3 **63** .... TomEaves 3 70
(B Smart) *hld up: hdwy over 3f out: chal over 1f out: hrd rdn and edgd rt ins fnl f: jst failed* **9/2**[3]

45 **3** 1 1/2 **The Lock Master (IRE)**[9] 7679 3-9-6 **66** .... NeilChalmers 8 70
(M Appleby) *hld up in rr: hdwy on outer to ld over 3f out: carried hd high and hdd last 100yds: no ex* **12/1**

335 **4** 10 **Lean Machine**[32] 7389 3-9-4 **64** .... LukeMorris 2 45
(R A Harris) *hld up: hdwy on inner to trck ldrs over 4f out: n.m.r over 3f out: lost pl over 1f out* **11/2**

4523 **5** 1/2 **Olney Lass**[12] 7646 3-8-3 **56** .... JamesRogers(7) 1 36
(Mike Murphy) *w ldrs: drvn over 3f out: wknd 2f out* **7/2**[2]

0104 **6** ¾ **Buzz Bird**[159] 3759 3-9-7 67.. GrahamGibbons 4 45
(T D Barron) *led 1f: sn drvn along: lost pl over 4f out: hung lft and bhd fnl 2f* **5/2**[1]

6200 **7** 16 **Saigon Kitty (IRE)**[45] 7191 3-8-8 57................................ KierenFox(3) 6 —
(J R Best) *led after 1f tl over 3f out: lost pl over 2f out: sn bhd* **14/1**

005 **8** 12 **Pont De Nuit**[105] 5560 3-8-7 56.................................... KellyHarrison(3) 7 —
(Miss Tracy Waggott) *chsd ldrs: t.k.h: lost pl over 2f out: sn bhd* **25/1**

1m 41.55s (-2.15) **Going Correction** -0.075s/f (Stan) 8 Ran SP% **113.7**
Speed ratings (Par 102): **107,106,105,95,94 94,78,66**
toteswingers:1&2: £6.60, 2&3: £10.30, 1&3: £7.60 CSF £43.22 CT £434.53 TOTE £8.60: £3.30, £1.40, £4.50; EX 46.60 TRIFECTA Not won..
Owner Mrs J Ryan **Bred** Rosyground Stud **Trained** Hambleton, N Yorks

FOCUS
A very moderate handicap, but it was sound run. The first three drew a long way clear but this is not form to get too excited about. The winner is rated back to his debut form.
Buzz Bird Official explanation: jockey said filly hung left throughout

7846 FREE RACING POST FORM AT TOTESPORT.COM H'CAP 7f (F)
2:15 (2:17) (Class 2) (0-100,98) 3-Y-£10,092 (£3,020; £1,510; £755; £376) **Stalls** Low

Form RPR

1010 **1** **Malcheek (IRE)**[22] 7522 8-9-7 95................................ DuranFentiman 11 106
(T D Easterby) *w ldrs on outer: led over 2f out: hld on wl* **25/1**

0006 **2** ¾ **Nightjar (USA)**[8] 7697 5-8-7 88.. JulieBurke(7) 8 97
(K A Ryan) *hld up in mid-div: hdwy on outer over 2f out: chal over 1f out: no ex clsng stages* **4/1**[1]

5303 **3** 3 ¼ **Bawaardi (IRE)**[10] 7665 4-8-4 81 oh1........................ JamesSullivan(3) 9 81
(R A Fahey) *mid-div: hdwy to chse ldrs over 2f out: kpt on same pce appr fnl f* **11/1**

0101 **4** 2 ½ **Salerosa (IRE)**[31] 7403 5-8-8 82..................................(p) SamHitchcott 12 75
(Mrs A Duffield) *bhd and swtchd lft after s: in rr: hdwy on outside over 2f out: styd on ins fnl f* **11/1**

0133 **5** shd **Trans Sonic**[28] 7283 7-8-7 88....................................(b) ShaneBKelly(7) 2 81
(D O'Meara) *w ldrs: led over 4f out: hdd over 3f out: kpt on same pce appr fnl f* **8/1**[3]

0043 **6** 1 ¼ **Fishforcompliments**[6] 7725 6-8-7 81 oh4..............(p) GrahamGibbons 7 71
(R A Fahey) *gave problems in stalls: w ldrs: kpt on same pce over 1f out* **16/1**

0231 **7** ¾ **Love Delta (USA)**[5] 7740 3-9-10 98 6ex........................... GregFairley 4 86
(M Johnston) *mid-div: lost pl over 3f out: sn drvn along: hdwy on wd outside over 2f out: nvr nr ldrs* **9/2**[2]

3022 **8** ½ **Imprimis Tagula (IRE)**[8] 7697 6-8-3 84..................(v) NatashaEaton(7) 5 70
(A Bailey) *w ldrs: led over 3f out: hdd over 2f out: wknd appr fnl f* **4/1**[1]

1014 **9** 4 ½ **Ingleby Arch (USA)**[8] 7697 7-9-0 88.............................. PhillipMakin 6 62
(T D Barron) *led tl over 4f out: lost pl over 2f out* **8/1**[3]

-006 **10** 2 **Gala Casino Star (IRE)**[18] 7560 5-8-3 84..................... LauraBarry(7) 3 53
(R A Fahey) *s.i.s: in rr: bhd fnl 2f* **33/1**

0-20 **11** 2 ½ **Viva Ronaldo (IRE)**[16] 7574 4-8-9 83.............................. TomEaves 1 45
(R A Fahey) *s.i.s: sn chsng ldrs: lost pl over 2f out* **20/1**

1m 28.21s (-2.09) **Going Correction** -0.075s/f (Stan) 11 Ran SP% **114.5**
Speed ratings (Par 109): **108,107,103,100,100 99,98,97,92,90 87**
toteswingers:1&2: £17.60, 2&3: £10.90, 1&3: £26.50 CSF £117.37 CT £883.78 TOTE £25.50: £9.80, £2.30, £4.10; EX 129.90 Trifecta £691.40 Part won. Pool: £934.42 - 0.64 winning units..
Owner Habton Farms **Bred** Carrigbeg Stud **Trained** Great Habton, N Yorks

FOCUS
Quite a valuable handicap, run at a brisk pace, and fairly solid form, but the time was not that quick. The first two came towards the stands' side of the track and finished clear.

NOTEBOOK
Malcheek(IRE) ◆ had never run at Southwell before but has a fine record on Polytrack, and on this evidence will prove just as good on this surface. Always close to the pace on the outside, travelling nicely, he took it up in the straight and won a shade readily. Opportunities may be limited for him back here but he is one to keep on the right side. Official explanation: trainer's rep said, regarding apparent improvement in form, that the gelding was better suited by being ridden with more restraint. (tchd 22-1)
Nightjar(USA) turned around recent 6f course form with three of these opponents. He travelled well before delivering his challenge out widest, but was always just being held by the winner. Sound run though it was, it took his losing sequence to 21. His rider, who might have pulled her stick through sooner, is now set to take a break until February in order to preserve her claim, which has just been reduced to 5lb. (op 7-2 tchd 9-2)
Bawaardi(IRE) was no match for the first pair in the straight, but that was no disgrace and this was a solid effort from a pound out of the weights on his Fibresand debut. (tchd 10-1)
Salerosa(IRE), winner of a C/D claimer on her last start a month ago, was dropped in from her outside stall before staying on for fourth in the straight. She remains in good heart. (op 14-1)
Trans Sonic, whose most recent run was over hurdles, ran creditably on this return to his favourite venue. He remains 6lb above his last winning mark. (tchd 15-2)
Fishforcompliments, another of the Fahey contingent, had cheekpieces back on for this Fibresand debut. He became stirred up in the stalls but seemed to give his running. (tchd 18-1)
Love Delta(USA)'s penalty for his wide-margin win over 5f here took him to a career-high mark, but his record at the track made him a major player. He disappointed, though, soon outpaced in rear, and looking set to finish right out the back before running past rivals late on. Another go at this trip may prove worthwhile. Official explanation: trainer's rep had no explanation for the poor form shown (op 7-2)
Imprimis Tagula(IRE) finished ahead of three of these rivals when runner-up to Cape Vale over 6f here last time, and is perhaps most effective at that trip. (op 9-2)
Ingleby Arch(USA) has done all his winning over 6f, but was beaten too early for this longer trip to be solely to blame. (op 10-1)

7847 MEMBERSHIP OF SOUTHWELL GOLF CLUB H'CAP 6f (F)
2:45 (2:47) (Class 5) (0-70,70) 3-Y-O+ **£2,266** (£674; £337; £168) **Stalls** Low

Form RPR

1 **1** **Benato The Great (IRE)**[58] 6896 4-9-2 65..................... AdrianNicholls 6 79+
(D Nicholls) *gave problems loading: t.k.h: led tl over 4f out: led 2f out: wandered: edgd lft and kpt on wl towards fin* **9/2**[2]

2651 **2** 2 **Desert Strike**[4] 7754 4-8-10 66 6ex..........................(p) NoraLooby(7) 5 74
(A J McCabe) *t.k.h: sn trcking ldrs: swtchd lft over 2f out: kpt on same pce ins fnl f* **6/1**

3440 **3** hd **Punching**[108] 5454 6-9-7 70.. PhillipMakin 7 77
(C R Dore) *w ldrs: hrd rdn over 1f out: kpt on same pce* **11/2**[3]

6003 **4** 1 ¼ **Ace Of Spies (IRE)**[6] 7730 5-9-1 64........................... KirstyMilczarek 4 67
(C R Dore) *wnt lft s: w ldrs: led 3f out: hdd 2f out: kpt on same pce ins fnl f* **6/1**

0205 **5** 2 **Rubenstar (IRE)**[29] 7439 7-8-12 61............................. CathyGannon 3 58
(Patrick Morris) *n.m.r sn after s: hld up in rr: sme hdwy over 2f out: hung lft: nvr a threat* **12/1**

1021 **6** ½ **Takajan (IRE)**[6] 7730 3-8-11 67 6ex............................. JamesRogers(7) 2 62
(W M Brisbourne) *wnt rt s: trckd ldrs: effrt over 2f out: wknd over 1f out* **2/1**[1]

0003 **7** hd **Jonnie Skull (IRE)**[1] 7835 4-8-7 56 oh3..........................(vt) LukeMorris 8 51
(M D Squance) *in rr: effrt over 2f out: nvr threatened* **18/1**

460 **8** 8 **Misaro (GER)**[139] 4430 9-9-7 70.......................................(b) DavidProbert 1 39
(R A Harris) *w ldrs: led over 4f out tl 3f out: hung lft sn lost pl* **28/1**

1m 16.07s (-0.43) **Going Correction** -0.075s/f (Stan) 8 Ran SP% **111.9**
Speed ratings (Par 103): **99,96,96,94,91 91,90,80**
toteswingers:1&2: £4.90, 2&3: £5.70, 1&3: £2.80 CSF £30.04 CT £148.19 TOTE £5.50: £1.50, £1.90, £1.40; EX 32.40 Trifecta £31.30 Pool: £1410.38 - 33.25 winning units..
Owner Nicholls Family **Bred** Glending Bloodstock **Trained** Sessay, N Yorks
■ Stewards' Enquiry : Adrian Nicholls caution: careless riding.

FOCUS
A reasonable race for the grade but the time was ordinary. The unexposed winner has more to offer.
Misaro(GER) Official explanation: jockey said gelding hung left

7848 TONY MCCOY FOR BBC SPORTS PERSONALITY H'CAP 1m 4f (F)
3:15 (3:15) (Class 6) (0-60,62) 3-Y-O **£1,706** (£503; £252) **Stalls** Low

Form RPR

5332 **1** **Dandarrell**[19] 7538 3-9-3 52.. GrahamGibbons 5 60
(Julie Camacho) *hld up: hdwy to trck ldrs 7f out: chal over 4f out: led over 2f out: drvn rt out* **15/8**[1]

2602 **2** 1 **Rosewood Lad**[7] 7716 3-9-1 50.. CathyGannon 8 56
(J S Moore) *w ldrs: led 5f out: hdd over 2f out: styd on same pce ins fnl f* **9/4**[2]

000 **3** 3 ¼ **Jasmin Rai**[179] 3080 3-8-13 55.. JulieBurke(7) 6 56
(D Donovan) *hld up in tch: effrt over 3f out: one pce fnl 2f* **25/1**

3053 **4** 9 **Lalika**[32] 7387 3-9-6 55.. LukeMorris 4 41
(C G Cox) *led: hdd 5f out: sn rdn: wknd 2f out* **4/1**[3]

6030 **5** 2 **Annelko**[32] 7388 3-9-1 50.. PhillipMakin 1 33
(A B Haynes) *trckd ldrs: drvn 6f out: wknd 2f out* **11/1**

0445 **6** 16 **Chichina (USA)**[136] 4519 3-8-7 45.............................. JamesSullivan(3) 3 3
(Miss Tracy Waggott) *chsd ldrs: sn drvn along: lost pl over 7f out: sn bhd: t.o 3f out* **16/1**

0550 **7** 14 **Sea Tobougie**[7] 7716 3-8-10 45.. DavidProbert 2 —
(M D I Usher) *dwlt: in rr: drvn 6f out: lost pl over 4f out: t.o 3f out: eased over 1f out* **12/1**

2m 41.61s (0.61) **Going Correction** -0.075s/f (Stan) 7 Ran SP% **111.3**
Speed ratings (Par 98): **94,93,91,85,83 73,63**
toteswingers:1&2: £1.60, 2&3: £7.80, 1&3 £6.20 CSF £5.93 CT £67.38 TOTE £2.50: £1.10, £2.40; EX 6.00 Trifecta £93.50 Pool: £609.09 - 4.82 winning units..
Owner W F Frewen & J Waller **Bred** Peter Onslow **Trained** Norton, N Yorks

FOCUS
A maiden handicap in all but name. The pace was solid enough and the first two came clear up the straight. The front three basically ran to form.
T/Plt: £147.10 to a £1 stake. Pool of £131,069.24 - 650.28 winning tickets. T/Qpdt: £45.30 to a £1 stake. Pool of £10,330.09 - 168.46 winning tickets. WG

PISA (R-H)
Sunday, December 12

OFFICIAL GOING: Turf: soft

7849a PREMIO JOSE' ROMERO (MAIDEN) (2YO) (TURF) 7f 110y
1:30 (12:00) 2-Y-O **£4,424** (£1,946; £1,061; £530)

RPR

1 **Perica** 2-9-2 0.. DPerovic 6 —
(D Pajic, Salvador) **99/10**

2 ¾ **Lowawatha**[67] 6675 2-9-2 0.. APolli 12 —
(M G Quinlan) *broke wl to trck ldrs on outside for 4f: bdly hmpd 2 1/2f out whn forced v wd ent st: hrd rdn to recoup lost grnd: str hdwy fnl f to go cl: unlucky* **9/5**[1]

3 1 **Dubai Caffe** 2-8-13 0.. SSulas 4 —
(P L Giannotti, Italy) **10/3**[2]

4 5 **Ceroli (IRE)** 2-9-2 0.. SLandi 9 —
(Cristiana Signorelli, Italy) **172/10**

5 hd **I'm A Cracker (IRE)** 2-8-13 0.................................. DaisakuMatsuda 17 —
(D Gambarota, Italy) **100/1**

6 3 ¾ **Solleone (USA)** 2-8-13 0.. GSanna 8 —
(Luca De Maria, Italy) **49/1**

7 snk **Debejki** 2-8-13 0.. ZIlic 5 —
(D Pajic, Salvador) **99/10**

8 2 ½ **Millet (FR)** 2-8-13 0.. ASanna 13 —
(E Galli, Italy) **33/1**

9 nse **Ager Hadrianus (ITY)** 2-9-2 0............................. PierantonioConvertino 11 —
(E Galli, Italy) **30/1**

10 1 ¾ **Polvius (ITY)** 2-8-13 0.. UmbertoRispoli 7 —
(S Botti, Italy) **41/5**

11 1 ¼ **Trait D'Union** 2-9-2 0.. NPinna 3 —
(S Botti, Italy) **17/5**[3]

12 2 **Monte Rughe (IRE)** 2-8-13 0...................................... MKolmarkaj 1 —
(M Gasparini, Italy) **28/1**

13 9 **Mister Langan (IRE)** 2-9-2 0...................................... DarioVargiu 14 —
(B Grizzetti, Italy) **23/4**

14 2 **Destination Paris** 2-8-13 0.. MSanna 2 —
(D Pajic, Salvador) **54/1**

15 3 ¾ **Principe Caspian (ITY)** 2-9-2 0..................................(b) MDiaz 15 —
(R Pecoraro, Italy) **34/1**

16 8 ½ **Good Light** 2-8-9 0.. GMarcelli 10 —
(Camilla Trapassi, Italy) **65/1**

17 4 **Tito Lucrezio (ITY)** 2-8-13 0...................................... GVirdis 16 —
(M Gasparini, Italy) **28/1**

1m 30.3s (90.30) 17 Ran SP% **153.3**
WIN (incl. 1 euro stake): 10.85 (Perica coupled with Debejki). PLACES: 2.82, 1.56, 1.79. DF: 42.75.
Owner Surcin Ergela K K **Bred** Cheveley Park Stud **Trained** Slovakia

NOTEBOOK
Lowawatha, an unlucky loser, had shown he handles soft ground on his previous start at Nottingham.

7850a PREMIO CRITERIUM DI PISA (LISTED RACE) (2YO) (TURF) 7f 110y
2:30 (12:00) 2-Y-O **£24,778** (£10,902; £5,946; £2,973)

RPR
1 **Silver Ocean (USA)**[51] 7065 2-8-11 0 .... CDemuro 15 —
(M G Quinlan) *broke wl: racd mid-div on outer after 1f: prog to go 4th after 3f: lost grnd ent st whn edgd lft: hrd rdn 2f out: gd hdwy to chal for ld 1 1/2f out: wnt 2 l clr ent fnl f: rdn out t* **83/10**
2 2¾ **Master Fitz (ITY)**[59] 2-9-2 0 .... MickaelBarzalona 13 —
(G Botti, Italy) **2/1**[1]
3 3 **Red Roof**[77] 2-8-8 0 .... GMarcelli 19 —
(D Gambarota, Italy) **30/1**
4 nk **Bit Of Chocolate**[77] 2-8-11 0 .... SLandi 2 —
(R Brogi, Italy) **29/4**
5 shd **Gold Sprinter (IRE)** 2-8-11 0 .... DarioVargiu 8 —
(B Grizzetti, Italy) **145/20**
6 2¼ **Profumo D'Irlanda (IRE)** 2-8-11 0 .... EFumi 17 —
(R Monaco, Italy) **103/20**[2]
7 2¾ **Demi Gallant (ITY)**[161] 2-8-8 0 .... CFiocchi 5 —
(R Menichetti, Italy) **115/10**
8 ½ **Antinoo (IRE)**[217] 2-8-11 0 .... MTellini 1 —
(Cristiano Davide Fais, Italy) **189/10**
9 hd **Rien A Faire (IRE)** 2-8-11 0 .... PierantonioConvertino 7 —
(M Marcialis, Italy) **129/10**
10 shd **Bellucci (GER)** 2-8-11 0 .... MSanna 12 —
(P L Giannotti, Italy) **30/1**
11 ¾ **King's Omaha (IRE)**[84] 2-8-11 0 .... SDiana 11 —
(A Peraino, Italy) **51/1**
12 ¾ **Schliemann (ITY)** 2-8-11 0 .... GBietolini 9 —
(G Di Chio, Italy) **61/10**[3]
13 2½ **Capitano Knox (IRE)** 2-8-11 0 .... SUrru 3 —
(Laura Grizzetti, Italy) **199/10**
14 2 **Alaska Trip (IRE)** 2-8-11 0 .... UmbertoRispoli 10 —
(S Botti, Italy) **10/1**
15 2½ **Jabot (ITY)** 2-8-11 0 .... SSulas 6 —
(M Marcialis, Italy) **67/1**
16 ¾ **Olmo On Line (USA)**[36] 2-8-11 0 .... LManiezzi 16 —
(R Menichetti, Italy) **115/10**
17 3 **Pretium Sceleris**[134] 2-8-11 0 .... NPinna 14 —
(S Botti, Italy) **84/1**
18 3 **Provide (IRE)**[53] 2-8-11 0 .... (b) SMulas 18 —
(D Gambarota, Italy) **30/1**
19 2½ **Heliaster Re (ITY)** 2-8-11 0 .... (b) APolli 4 —
(V Cangiano, Italy) **80/1**

1m 28.9s (88.90) **19** Ran SP% **156.3**
WIN (incl. 1 euro stake): 9.28. PLACES: 3.08, 1.87, 16.44. DF: 16.00.
Owner Paolo Benedetti **Bred** Sun Valley Farm **Trained** Newmarket, Suffolk

NOTEBOOK
Silver Ocean(USA) had no problem with the trip and ran out an emphatic winner, giving his trainer a Listed winner on his birthday.

1568 SHA TIN (R-H)
Sunday, December 12

OFFICIAL GOING: Turf: good

7851a CATHAY PACIFIC HONG KONG VASE (GROUP 1) (3YO+) (TURF) 1m 4f
6:00 (12:00) 3-Y-0+ **£634,844** (£245,027; £111,376; £63,643; £36,595; £22,275)

RPR
1 **Mastery**[39] 7297 4-9-0 0 .... FrankieDettori 2 120
(Saeed Bin Suroor) *a.p (3rd for much of the way) and t.k.h: wnt 2nd over 3f out: swtchd off rail to chal ldr appr 2f out: led ins fnl 2f: sn clr: kpt on strly* **19/5**[2]
2 2½ **Redwood**[57] 6951 4-9-0 0 .... MichaelHills 6 116
(B W Hills) *settled in 5th on rail: lost a couple of pls 4f out: pushed along 3f out and r.o: 3rd 2f out: kpt on wl u.p fnl f: no ch w wnr* **11/1**
3 ½ **Americain (USA)**[40] 7291 5-9-0 0 .... GeraldMosse 9 115+
(A De Royer-Dupre, France) *settled in midfield: 6th over 4f out: outpcd and 9th over 2f out: styd on fnl 1 1/2f: nt pce to chal: nrest at fin* **11/10**[1]
4 1¼ **Jaguar Mail (JPN)**[14] 7615 6-9-0 0 .... (b) CraigAWilliams 7 113
(Noriyuki Hori, Japan) *settled towards rr: hdwy on rail ins fnl 2f: styd on u.p fnl f: nvr plcd to chal* **9/1**
5 1 **Jakkalberry (IRE)**[35] 7373 4-9-0 0 .... (t) Christophe-PatriceLemaire 12 112+
(E Botti, Italy) *settled towards rr: 12th and c wdst of all bnd appr fnl 2f: styd on u.p: nvr nrr* **89/1**
6 nk **King Dancer (IRE)**[28] 4-9-0 0 .... (p) DouglasWhyte 4 111
(S Woods, Hong Kong) *racd in midfield: 8th 4f out: hdwy to go 4th 2f out: kpt on at same pce* **30/1**
7 nk **Mighty High (FR)**[28] 4-9-0 0 .... JeffLloyd 1 111
(J Moore, Hong Kong) *qckly away and led: hdd ins fnl 2f: unable qck: no ex ins fnl f* **35/1**
8 2 **Viva Pataca**[21] 8-9-0 0 .... DarrenBeadman 13 107
(J Moore, Hong Kong) *chsd ldrs: 6th ins fnl 2f: unable qck* **15/1**
9 2½ **Indian Days**[56] 6977 5-9-0 0 .... AlanMunro 8 103
(J G Given) *hld up: bhd whn rdn and n.m.r ins fnl 2f: nvr in contention* **209/1**
10 3¾ **Crystal Capella**[57] 6928 5-8-10 0 .... RyanMoore 10 93
(Sir Michael Stoute) *trckd ldr racing keenly early: dropped to 3rd over 3f out: rdn 2 1/2f out: wknd fnl 2f* **56/10**[3]
11 ½ **Winchester (USA)**[36] 7366 5-9-0 0 .... (b) OlivierPeslier 3 97
(Christophe Clement, U.S.A) *a bhd: no imp fnl 2f* **29/1**
12 4 **Mr Medici (IRE)**[40] 7291 5-9-0 0 .... HWLai 14 90
(L Ho, Hong Kong) *settled towards rr: nvr plcd to chal* **37/1**
13 42 **Board Meeting (IRE)**[47] 7160 4-8-10 0 .... (b) AnthonyCrastus 11 —
(E Lellouche, France) *hld up: a bhd: t.o* **131/1**

2m 27.69s (-0.51)
WFA 3 from 4yo+ 5lb **13** Ran SP% **122.5**
PARI-MUTUEL (all including HK$10 stake): WIN 48.00; PLACE 17.00, 28.00, 13.00; DF 226.00.
Owner Godolphin **Bred** Darley **Trained** Newmarket, Suffolk

FOCUS
An open-looking contest for this valuable prize and the pace appeared to be strong early before it slackened for a while down the back straight. Aidan O'Brien's Joshua Tree\p was withdrawn in the morning after being found to be lame in his right front leg. With the horse he beat in the Canadian International finishing second, connections must wonder what might have been.

NOTEBOOK
Mastery was given a brilliant tactical ride by Frankie Dettori, as he had his mount well positioned from the outset before pushing on at a crucial stage of the race to gain a winning advantage. The winner of the 2009 St Leger, and an honourable fifth in this year's Dubai World Cup, stamina was never going to be a concern and he held on comfortably once in the clear. It appears that he will remain in training next season and be aimed towards the Sheema Classic during the spring.

Redwood has enjoyed a fine year, which started back in April, and had won twice over 1m4f, once at Grade 1 level. Well placed just in behind, he stayed on in good style but could make no impression on Mastery after that rival had poached a lead. He can develop into a top world traveller if kept in training, and races in America could be decent opportunities for him next summer. Long-term, the Breeders' Cup Turf looks a target.

Americain(USA), the Melbourne Cup winner, is not short of speed but his rider felt that his chance was compromised by the lack of pace in the middle of the race. He kept on well but the winner was gone by the time he was out in the clear. His trainer said afterwards that the Japan Cup could be the race for him next year.

Jaguar Mail(JPN), third and fourth in this race previously, ran well in the Japan Cup and again here after not having a great deal of room up the inside rail. He was doing his best work late on and once again shaped like a horse that would be of some interest if taken to Flemington next year for the Melbourne Cup.

Jakkalberry(IRE), who didn't have much to find with Mastery on their clash in the 2009 Derby Italiano, sat in last for much of the race and could not get involved after sweeping wide into the home straight. He may have played a bigger part had he raced closer to the leaders.

King Dancer(IRE), a four-time winner since moving to race in Hong Kong from Alan Swinbank's (raced as Uramazin in Great Britain), won the Hong Kong Derby Trial earlier this year and ran respectably here before his effort flattened out in the latter stages.

Mighty High(FR), who raced as Berouni in France, had won a couple of handicaps in Hong Kong and was a confirmed front-runner, so it was not a big surprise to see him dominating. He did a good job of setting the race up and kept on well when joined and passed.

Viva Pataca, who won the Audemars Piguet QE II Cup in April, had not been disgraced over different trips since but was one paced in this after having every chance.

Indian Days, just behind Jakkalberry when last on the racecourse, was making up some ground in the home straight when appearing to be squeezed for room. He can be rated a few lengths better than his final position, especially as his jockey also reported that his mount sat down as the stalls opened.

Crystal Capella came here much fresher than most but almost certainly ruined her chance by pulling far too hard just behind the leader, as she had nothing left once the tempo increased. Connections reported that she found the ground too quick, and didn't let herself down on it.

Winchester(USA) hadn't been right-handed since his days in Ireland, and was a little disappointing without his usual lasix to race on.

Mr Medici(IRE) put up two fair efforts in Australia when sent for an attempt on the Melbourne Cup, but was disappointing back in Hong Kong. The jockey felt the going was too firm for his mount.

Board Meeting(IRE)'s trainer had a fine record in this race (2 wins and 2 places) but his runner showed no signs of improving on that, as she was the first beaten. She was reported to have had a medial quarter crack in her right-fore hoof with some associated infection a few days before the contest, and had been fitted with Heart-Bar plates in front to relieve pressure on the hoof.

7852a CATHAY PACIFIC HONG KONG SPRINT (GROUP 1) (3YO+) (TURF) 6f
6:40 (12:00) 3-Y-0+ **£634,844** (£245,027; £111,376; £63,643; £36,595; £22,275)

RPR
1 **J J The Jet Plane (SAF)**[147] 6-9-0 0 .... PStrydom 8 125
(M Houdalakis, South Africa) *racd in 4th: hdwy on outside 1 1/2f out: cl 3rd 1f out: r.o strly to ld on line* **179/10**
2 shd **Rocket Man (AUS)**[21] 5-9-0 0 .... FCoetzee 6 124
(Patrick Shaw, Singapore) *broke wl and settled in 3rd: rdn appr fnl 1 1/2f: r.o to ld narrowly ins fnl f: ct on line* **18/5**[2]
3 ¾ **Sacred Kingdom (AUS)**[21] 7-9-0 0 .... (t) BrettPrebble 2 122
(P F Yiu, Hong Kong) *settled in 5th fr the off: 6th 2f out: swtchd ins and r.o to go 4th 1f out: r.o wl u.p: no ex fnl 50yds* **7/5**[1]
4 ¾ **Let Me Fight (IRE)**[21] 3-9-0 0 .... DarrenBeadman 11 120
(J Moore, Hong Kong) *racd in 6th: styd on u.p fnl f* **13/1**
5 nk **Ortensia (AUS)**[36] 5-8-10 0 .... (bt) CraigAWilliams 5 115
(Tony Noonan, Australia) *settled towards rr: 9th appr 2f out: r.o u.p fnl f: nvr able to chal* **33/1**
6 ½ **Kingsgate Native (IRE)**[77] 6390 5-9-0 0 .... RyanMoore 1 117
(Sir Michael Stoute) *settled in midfield on rail: 5th and ev ch appr fnl 2f: sn rdn: swtchd outside and r.o 1f out: nt qckn fnl 100yds* **99/1**
7 nk **Lucky Nine (IRE)**[21] 3-9-0 0 .... GeraldMosse 12 116
(C Fownes, Hong Kong) *in rr: last appr 2f out: r.o wl fr over 1f out: nrest at fin* **22/5**[3]
8 ¾ **Little Bridge (NZ)**[21] 4-9-0 0 .... (t) ZacPurton 3 114
(C S Shum, Hong Kong) *bhd tl hdwy fnl f: nvr plcd to chal* **87/10**
9 shd **Dim Sum**[21] 6-9-0 0 .... (v[1]) ODoleuze 9 113
(J Moore, Hong Kong) *pushed along to ld: hdd ins fnl f: no ex: wknd last 50yds* **60/1**
10 nk **Green Birdie (NZ)**[70] 7-9-0 0 .... DouglasWhyte 7 112
(C Fownes, Hong Kong) *nvr in contention* **26/1**
11 1¼ **Joy And Fun (NZ)**[176] 3192 7-9-0 0 .... (p) TyeAngland 13 108
(D Cruz, Hong Kong) *hld up towards rr: nvr a factor* **161/1**
12 ¾ **Cerise Cherry (SAF)**[21] 5-9-0 0 .... (b) FrankieDettori 10 —
(D Cruz, Hong Kong) *racd in middle of field: rdn 2f out: no imp: wknd fnl f* **46/1**
13 1¼ **One World (AUS)**[21] 6-9-0 0 .... (t) JeffLloyd 14 102
(J Moore, Hong Kong) *missed break and 4 l adrift of next runner: a in rr: nvr a factor* **35/1**
14 1½ **Ultra Fantasy (AUS)**[70] 8-9-0 0 .... (bt) HWLai 4 97
(P F Yiu, Hong Kong) *chsd ldr: 2nd and rdn 2f out: nt qckn: wknd fnl f* **35/1**

68.84 secs (68.84) **14** Ran SP% **122.3**
PARI-MUTUEL (all including HK$10 stake): WIN 188.50; PLACE 56.00, 15.00, 11.50; DF 328.50.
Owner H S N Du Preez, C F Strydom et al **Bred** Mrs P J Devine **Trained** South Africa

FOCUS
As usual a top-class sprint, one of the best run this year.

NOTEBOOK

J J The Jet Plane(SAF) claimed a somewhat surprising but well-earned victory. He was largely disappointing during a spell in Britain in 2009, not going on from a Listed-race success, and third in the July Cup being just about the pick of his achievements, but clearly that wasn't his true form. Previously a high-class performer in South Africa (also won a Group 3 in Dubai), he had won both his starts in Grade 1 company since returning there this year, the latter by a wide margin. That form was difficult to equate, but this performance indisputably proved him to be one of the best sprinters in the world. Having tracked Rocket Man in fourth, he took a while to get by that one in the straight, but he grabbed him in the final strides. It remains to be seen where he goes next, but presumably Dubai, where he'd have the option of the Al Quoz Sprint (won the race in 2009) or the Golden Shaheen on Tapeta, will be considered, and the International Sprint in Singapore is another obvious potential target.

Rocket Man(AUS) is the nearly horse of these major sprints, this being the fourth time he's been narrowly beaten into second in an international event. He was on his toes beforehand but not sweating and ran a tremendous race. Having sat in third, he took up the running just inside the final 200m and looked to be doing enough. He gamely saw off Sacred Kingdom's challenge and seemed to be holding J J The Jet Plane, but that rival found extra in the final strides and denied him in agonising fashion. He's likely to be aimed at Dubai again next season and could bid to improve on this year's second placing in the Golden Shaheen.

Sacred Kingdom(AUS) suffered a life-threatening bout of colic earlier in the year, but he looked as good as ever when winning a Group 3 handicap on his return in October. However, he was then slightly below par in the trial for this and failed to make the required improvement. He made his bid towards the inside rail but simply couldn't get by Rocket Man. Chasing his third success in the race, this was still a good performance, but his best days now look behind him.

Let Me Fight(IRE), a Carlisle maiden winner for Alan Swinbank last year when named Ask Frank, ran a terrific race for one so young. He has the potential to be high class.

Ortensia(AUS) ran on from a long way back but the line came too soon.

Kingsgate Native(IRE) continued the poor record of European runners (now 0-39). He lacked the acceleration of some of these but kept on and ran respectably.

Lucky Nine(IRE) ruined his chance with a slow start but finished well, indeed he had the quickest closing sectional.

One World(AUS) often takes a while to get going and completely blew the start this time. He had dead-heated with Rocket Man (when getting 5lb) in the trial, but was never going this time.

7853a CATHAY PACIFIC HONG KONG MILE (GROUP 1) (3YO+) (TURF) 1m

7:50 (12:00) 3-Y-0+

£725,536 (£280,031; £127,287; £57,279; £57,279; £25,457)

			RPR
1		**Beauty Flash (NZ)**[21] 5-9-0 0 .....(t) GeraldMosse 14 (A S Cruz, Hong Kong) *broke wl on wd outside: trckd ldr: pushed along to ld 1 1/2f out: r.o wl u.p fnl f* **91/10**	119
2	¾	**Royal Bench (IRE)**[71] 6593 3-8-13 0 ..... OlivierPeslier 12 (Robert Collet, France) *hld up towards rr: 12th appr 2f out: hdwy u.p ins fnl 1 1/2f: styd on wl fnl f to take 2nd cl home* **23/1**	117+
3	½	**Sahpresa (USA)**[21] 5-8-10 0 .....(t) Christophe-PatriceLemaire 9 (Rod Collet, France) *settled in midfield: 8th 3f out: 5th and gng wl 2f out: rdn 1 1/2f out: r.o to go 2nd over 100yds out: nt qckn fnl 50yds* **67/10**[3]	112
4	nk	**A Shin Forward (USA)**[21] 5-9-0 0 ..... YasunariIwata 8 (Masato Nishizono, Japan) *hld up: 9th and rdn ins fnl 2f: styd on u.p fnl f: grabbed share of 4th on line: nrest at fin* **41/5**	115
4	dht	**Rajsaman (FR)**[42] 7266 3-8-13 0 ..... DavyBonilla 6 (F Head, France) *prom in 3rd racing freely: settled in 4th after 2f: kpt on fnl 1 1/2f* **70/1**	115
6	¾	**Thumbs Up (NZ)**[21] 6-9-0 0 ..... BrettDoyle 11 (C Fownes, Hong Kong) *hld up: disputing 9th whn rdn 3f out: hdwy u.p to be 6th ins fnl f: no ex* **27/10**[2]	114
7	shd	**Sight Winner (NZ)**[21] 7-9-0 0 .....(b[1]) DouglasWhyte 10 (J Size, Hong Kong) *set stdy pce tl hdd 1 1/2f out: no ex* **46/1**	113
8	nk	**Dream Eater (IRE)**[25] 7482 5-9-0 0 .....(t) JimmyFortune 1 (A M Balding) *w.w in fnl 3rd: hdwy on rail to go 7th 2f out: nt qckn fnl f* **109/1**	113
9	nk	**Chater Way**[21] 4-9-0 0 .....(b) WCMarwing 4 (D E Ferraris, Hong Kong) *chsd ldrs: 3rd 3f out: nt qckn fr 1 1/2f out:* **43/5**	112
10	1 ½	**Good Ba Ba (USA)**[21] 8-9-0 0 .....(t) ODoleuze 7 (C W Chang, Hong Kong) *hld up: mde sme hdwy 2 1/2f out: nt qcknd fnl 1 1/2f: n.d* **25/1**	109
11	shd	**Fellowship (NZ)**[21] 8-9-0 0 .....(t) ZacPurton 3 (P O'Sullivan, Hong Kong) *nvr beyond mid-div: rdn and btn over 1 1/2f out* **24/1**	108
12	shd	**Beethoven (IRE)**[36] 7364 3-8-13 0 .....(v) CO'Donoghue 5 (A P O'Brien, Ire) *a bhd: n.d* **59/1**	108
13	shd	**Paco Boy (IRE)**[36] 7364 5-9-0 0 ..... RyanMoore 13 (R Hannon) *settled towards rr on outside: last and c wdst of all fnl bnd appr 2f out: sn pushed along: no imp* **2/1**[1]	108

1m 34.79s (0.09)

WFA 3 from 4yo+ 1lb **13** Ran SP% **122.7**

PARI-MUTUEL (all including HK$10 stake): WIN 100.50; PLACE 26.50, 77.00, 23.50; DF 1,535.50.

Owner Kwok Siu Ming **Bred** Windsor Park Stud Ltd **Trained** Hong Kong

FOCUS

An already below average running of the Mile was weakened further when one of the leading fancies, Able One, was withdrawn at the start after being found to be lame on his left hind leg. The pace was a bit stop-start, quickening mid-race and then slowing again before the final dash.

NOTEBOOK

Beauty Flash(NZ) stepped up significantly on the form he showed when well held by Able One in the C&D trial. He managed to get a good position from his wide draw and stayed on strongly to record a career-best performance. According to connections he could race in Dubai next year.

Royal Bench(IRE) is a rapidly improving colt, this performance bettering the bare form of his success in the Group 2 Prix Daniel Wildenstein on Arc weekend. He raced much further back than the winner and came wide into the straight, but finished really strong, recording the quickest closing sectional.

Sahpresa(USA), the dual Sun Chariot winner, loomed up going well early in the straight and looked a big threat to the winner, but her effort flattened out late on.

Rajsaman(FR), a bit keen early, hit a flat spot early in the straight and took too long to pick up. Still, this was a fine effort and he looks up to the class.

A Shin Forward(USA), who had Sahpresa behind when winning the Mile Championship at Kyoto last time, produced a sustained finishing effort in the straight, but he was never quite getting there.

Thumbs Up(NZ) proved a bit disappointing and there didn't seem to be any excuses.

Dream Eater(IRE) isn't quite up to this level, but wasn't beaten far and ran well.

Good Ba Ba(USA), winner of this race for the last three years, couldn't pick up sufficiently after racing wide. He isn't the force of old.

Beethoven(IRE) was a surprise winner of the Dewhurst last season, but he's been well exposed this year as short of top class and was out of his depth.

Paco Boy(IRE) had been due to retire to stud after his fast-finishing fourth (didn't cope with going left-handed) in the Breeders' Cup Mile, but came here for one last run. Stall 13 shouldn't have been too much of a handicap (winner and runner-up drawn in double figures) with a long run to the first bend, but Ryan Moore failed to get him tucked in and the colt was wide throughout, noticeably so into the straight. He had no chance of winning under such circumstances, but whatever, he was below par and probably found this one run too many in a long season.

7854a CATHAY PACIFIC HONG KONG CUP (GROUP 1) (3YO+) (TURF) 1m 2f

8:30 (12:00) 3-Y-0+

£906,921 (£350,039; £159,108; £90,692; £52,505; £31,821)

			RPR
1		**Snow Fairy (IRE)**[28] 7460 3-8-7 0 ..... RyanMoore 8 (E A L Dunlop) *hld up: 12th 2f out: r.o strly ins fnl 1 1/2f to ld last 25yds* **6/4**[1]	116+
2	nk	**Irian (GER)**[28] 4-9-0 0 .....(t) BrettPrebble 2 (J Moore, Hong Kong) *racd in midfield: 8th 2 1/2f out: hdwy over 1 1/2f out: r.o wl u.p and led fnl half f: hdd last 25yds* **53/10**	119
3	1 ¼	**Packing Winner (NZ)**[28] 8-9-0 0 ..... ODoleuze 6 (L Ho, Hong Kong) *pushed along to ld: hdd fnl half f: no ex* **67/1**	117
4	shd	**Vision D'Etat (FR)**[57] 6925 5-9-0 0 ..... OlivierPeslier 7 (E Libaud, France) *w.w towards rr: jst one bhd him and upsides wnr appr 2f out: kpt on u.p last 300yds: nvr nrr* **51/10**[3]	116
5	nk	**Planteur (IRE)**[70] 6612 3-8-11 0 ..... FrankieDettori 10 (E Lellouche, France) *settled in 6th: travelling wl 2f out: rdn appr fnl 1 1/2f: disputing 3rd 1f out: unable qck u.p last f* **11/1**	116
6	nk	**Super Satin (NZ)**[28] 5-9-0 0 .....(b) DouglasWhyte 1 (C Fownes, Hong Kong) *racd in 5th: disputing 3rd fnl 110yds: unable qck* **21/1**	115
7	shd	**Cirrus Des Aigles (FR)**[14] 7615 4-9-0 0 ..... FranckBlondel 13 (Mme C Barande-Barbe, France) *sn trcking ldr: 2nd and pressing ldr 2f out: nt qckn ins fnl f* **45/1**	115
8	½	**Stacelita (FR)**[70] 6613 4-8-10 0 ..... Christophe-PatriceLemaire 12 (J-C Rouget, France) *a.p (4th for much of the way): 3rd and ev ch ins fnl 2f: nt qckn u.p fnl f* **12/1**	110
9	¾	**Reggane**[57] 6950 4-8-10 0 .....(t) GeraldMosse 11 (A De Royer-Dupre, France) *last: rdn ins fnl 2 1/2f: styd on ins fnl f: n.d* **44/1**	108
10	shd	**Super Pistachio (IRE)**[28] 4-9-0 0 .....(t) FCoetzee 9 (A S Cruz, Hong Kong) *chsd ldng pair tl nt qckn 2f out: wknd fnl f* **29/1**	112
11	nk	**Sri Putra**[57] 6925 4-9-0 0 .....(b) PhilipRobinson 3 (M A Jarvis) *nvr beyond mid-div* **113/1**	112
12	nk	**Glass Harmonium (IRE)**[57] 6925 4-9-0 0 .....(t) CraigAWilliams 4 (Sir Michael Stoute) *a towards rr: no imp fnl 2f* **136/1**	111
13	1	**Collection (IRE)**[28] 5-9-0 0 ..... DarrenBeadman 5 (J Moore, Hong Kong) *nvr rchd chalng position: bhd fnl 2f* **42/10**[2]	109

2m 2.96s (1.56)

WFA 3 from 4yo+ 3lb **13** Ran SP% **122.9**

PARI-MUTUEL (all including HK$10 stake): WIN 25.00; PLACE 13.00, 21.00, 127.00; DF 98.50.

Owner Anamoine Limited **Bred** Windflower Overseas Holdings Inc **Trained** Newmarket, Suffolk

FOCUS

A field full of top-class performers produced a tremendously close finish, possibly because the field was stacked up. The whole field finished in a heap passing the winning post, casts doubt on the form.

NOTEBOOK

Snow Fairy(IRE), who produced a truly stunning performance, has enjoyed a tremendous season, and became only the second 3-y-o to take this contest. With the pace not a true one it looked of some concern that she had virtually all of her rivals in front of her heading into the home straight (Ryan Moore said afterwards he thought they had no chance turning in) but, once again, she produced an electrifying turn of foot and surged to the front in the dying strides. Ed Dunlop reported that she stays in training and there ought to be plenty of options for her worldwide as well as at home. If one knew for certain she had any chance of handling the surface, the Dubai World Cup is a race well within her capabilities, as there is a distinct lack of depth at that trip, and it's difficult to name too many horses worldwide she couldn't live with at the distance, using Vision D'Etat as a guide.

Irian(GER), the 2009 German Guineas winner, had been mainly disappointing in Hong Kong until being gelded, but bounced right back to something like his best with success in the Cathay Pacific Jockey Club Cup last time, in which he had Packing Winner, Super Satin, Collection and Super Pistachio behind. Ridden in a similar style to that day, he made his bid at what looked the right time but was mugged in the final stages.

Packing Winner(NZ), who had been well beaten in the Vase the previous year, set the pace and stacked the field up down the back straight. He did enough to hang on for third despite being an outsider.

Vision D'Etat(FR) has an excellent record at this distance and took last year's renewal in good style from Collection, even after a late injury scare. Positioned just in front of Snow Fairy early, he looked to be undone by the quickening pace and couldn't lengthen in the same style as the winner, while still doing enough to finish a closing fourth. He now reportedly heads into retirement.

Planteur(IRE) showed classy form throughout 2010 in France between 1m2.5f-1m4f, and finished a respectable seventh (before being disqualified) in the Arc behind Workforce. Trying a fast surface and new jockey for the first time, he once again appeared to race freely under restraint, which didn't help him get home. If kept in training at four, which it seems he will be, he should add to his victories, but will probably need a pacemaker to help him, especially if running in small-field contests in France.

Super Satin(NZ), this year's Hong Kong Derby winner (Super Pistachio and Irian behind), had blinkers back on and looked a little unlucky to not finish even closer, as he got locked away on the inside over 300 metres out. He didn't really quicken once in the clear but would have got first run had the gaps appeared.

Cirrus Des Aigles(FR) ran a cracker in the Vase last year in, what at the time, looked a solid contest, although subsequent performances have spoilt that illusion a touch. Twice a winner in France this season, he ran well again after his performance in the Japan Cup, and is a thoroughly consistent performer.

Stacelita(FR), the 2009 Prix De Diane winner, was difficult to fault this season on her performances at mainly the highest level, especially the Group 1 success at Deauville, where she had Reggane behind. Well placed turning in, she was one paced after holding every chance, and her jockey felt she didn't handle the going.

Reggane landed a Grade 1 in Canada on her previous outing (Christophe Soumillon rode that day) but was never likely to get involved here after sitting last, in what looked a stop-start gallop. This run is best forgiven.

Super Pistachio(IRE), better known to the British racing public as Westphalia, who was with Aidan O'Brien back in 2008/9, was another to be well placed before fading.

Sri Putra hugged the inside rail but couldn't pick up as strongly as others around him when his rider asked for more. Philip Robinson was pleased with the effort and appeared to indicate that the horse will be kept in training next year at the post-race interviews.

Glass Harmonium(IRE) didn't show a lot with a tongue-tie and noseband tried this time, and now heads off to be trained in Australia.

Collection(IRE), runner-up to Vision D'Etat in this last season, was disappointingly turned over in a race last month at odds of 1-2 and put up a lacklustre performance here. It was reported to the vet the previous day that he was mildly lame in his right front leg, but the vet passed him to race on the morning of the race.

7837 WOLVERHAMPTON (A.W) (L-H)

Monday, December 13

OFFICIAL GOING: Standard

Wind: Light across Weather: Overcast

7856 ALL WEATHER "HANDS AND HEELS" APPRENTICE SERIES H'CAP (RACING EXCELLENCE INITIATIVE) 1m 1f 103y(P)

2:15 (2:16) (Class 5) (60-92,78) 3-Y-O+ £2,266 (£674; £337; £168) Stalls Low

Form RPR

3561 **1** **The Winged Assasin (USA)**[10] 7678 4-8-12 **67**..........(t) LucyBarry(3) 8 74
(S Lycett) *chsd ldrs: led 1/2-way: shkn up over 1f out: r.o* **4/1**[3]

2533 **2** *hd* **Nicholas Pocock (IRE)**[4] 7788 4-8-8 **60**.......................... ShaneBKelly 5 66
(B Ellison) *hld up: hdwy over 2f out: r.o wl: jst failed* **7/2**[2]

2212 **3** *hd* **Dream Of Fortune (IRE)**[6] 7732 6-9-2 **68**............(bt) MatthewCosham 7 74
(P D Evans) *a.p: swtchd lft over 1f out: shkn up and ev ch ins fnl f: r.o* **5/1**

0221 **4** *nk* **Star Links (USA)**[5] 7771 4-9-4 **73**...............................(b[1]) JakePayne(3) 4 78
(S Donohoe, Ire) *dwlt: hld up: hdwy over 3f out: ev ch ins fnl f: r.o* **8/1**

2500 **5** *5* **My Sister**[61] 6856 3-8-2 **59**.. RachealKneller(3) 3 54
(M D I Usher) *chsd ldr: shkn up over 1f out: no ex ins fnl f* **33/1**

51 **6** *12* **Mush Mir (IRE)**[7] 7726 3-8-8 **62** 6ex..............................(b) NathanAlison 1 32
(J R Boyle) *led to 1/2-way: sn pushed along: wknd over 2f out* **7/4**[1]

1050 **7** *2 ½* **Urban Space**[9] 7687 4-9-7 **73**....................................... MatthewLawson 2 37
(C R Dore) *sn bhd: pushed along over 3f out: wknd over 2f out* **14/1**

2m 3.68s (1.98) **Going Correction** +0.30s/f (Slow)

WFA 3 from 4yo+ 2lb **7 Ran SP% 116.0**

Speed ratings (Par 103): **103,102,102,102,97 87,85**

toteswingers:1&2 £3.10, 2&3 £2.20, 1&3 £3.80 CSF £18.92 CT £71.03 TOTE £4.50: £2.80, £1.70; EX 22.80 Trifecta £91.30 Pool: £493.23 - 3.56 winning units..

Owner A R James **Bred** John T L Jones Jr & Bemak N V **Trained** Clapton-on-the-Hill, Gloucs

■ Stewards' Enquiry : Jake Payne seven-day ban: used whip in contravention of race conditions (Dec 28,Jan 1,3,5-7,9)

FOCUS

The pace slowed when the disappointing favourite Mush Mir dropped away down the back straight. There was a bunch finish and the form looks modest.

Mush Mir(IRE) Official explanation: trainer's rep had no explanation for the poor form shown

7857 WOLVERHAMPTON HOLIDAY INN (S) STKS 7f 32y(P)

2:45 (2:45) (Class 6) 2-Y-O £1,535 (£453; £226) Stalls High

Form RPR

3132 **1** **Takeaway**[26] 7484 2-9-0 78.. MatthewDavies(3) 9 64
(J R Boyle) *hld up: hdwy 2f out: rdn to ld and hung lft over 1f out: r.o* **10/11**[1]

0304 **2** *½* **Neytiri**[27] 7471 2-8-7 55.. RichardKingscote 1 53
(R M Beckett) *chsd ldrs: led wl over 1f out: sn rdn and hdd: styd on* **8/1**

3350 **3** *1 ¼* **Arabella Fenella**[32] 7404 2-8-7 55...............................(p) HayleyTurner 4 50
(R M H Cowell) *hld up in tch: rdn over 1f out: hung rt ins fnl f: styd on* **25/1**

5 **4** *hd* **Asfurah's Image**[17] 7578 2-8-7 0.. ChrisCatlin 10 49+
(M Botti) *hld up in tch: racd keenly: hung rt over 2f out: rdn over 1f out: swtchd lft: r.o* **7/2**[2]

0006 **5** *1* **Amore Et Labore**[9] 7691 2-8-12 45..............................(p) JamesDoyle 6 52
(S Kirk) *a.p: rdn over 2f out: styd on* **50/1**

0000 **6** *hd* **Bathwick Nero**[14] 7629 2-8-7 46.. CathyGannon 5 47
(P D Evans) *hld up: drvn along 1/2-way: r.o ins fnl f: nrst fin* **50/1**

0263 **7** *2 ¼* **Crazy In Love**[11] 7666 2-8-3 51 ow1..............................(b) RyanClark(5) 8 42
(W G M Turner) *chsd ldrs: rdn and ev ch wl over 1f out: no ex ins fnl f* **16/1**

206 **8** *1 ¼* **Red Gold And Green (IRE)**[69] 6646 2-8-12 64........... AdrianNicholls 7 43
(D Nicholls) *led: rdn and hung rt over 2f out: hdd wl over 1f out: wknd ins fnl f* **13/2**[3]

00 **9** *½* **Algris**[3] 7801 2-8-12 0.. StevieDonohoe 2 42
(Sir Mark Prescott) *s.s: hdwy over 5f out: rdn and lost pl over 3f out: n.d after* **33/1**

0060 **10** *3 ¼* **Iwantobreakfree**[13] 7643 2-8-12 41..............................(v[1]) MartinLane 11 34
(P D Evans) *s.i.s: sn pushed along in rr: hdwy over 4f out: rdn and wknd wl over 1f out: hung lft ins fnl f* **66/1**

1m 33.93s (4.33) **Going Correction** +0.30s/f (Slow) **10 Ran SP% 117.1**

Speed ratings (Par 94): **87,86,85,84,83 83,80,79,78,75**

toteswingers:1&2 £2.60, 2&3 £13.40, 1&3 £8.70 CSF £8.86 TOTE £1.70: £1.10, £1.70, £5.20; EX 9.60 Trifecta £72.90 Pool: £624.67 - 6.34 winning units..There was no bid for the winner.

Owner M Khan X2 **Bred** Redhill Bloodstock Limited **Trained** Epsom, Surrey

FOCUS

They didn't seem to go that quick in this modest seller. Weak form, with the winner well below his level from earlier in the year.

NOTEBOOK

Takeaway had upwards of 9lb in hand on official figures and did what was required. He failed to run to his official mark of 78, but was waited with on a track that seemed to be favouring those racing prominently, and then idled once in front after going wide into the straight. (tchd 5-6 and Evens)

Neytiri, beaten in sellers the last twice, plugged on in a manner that suggests she might get 1m. Officially rated 55, she looks to set the standard. (op 10-1 tchd 11-1)

Arabella Fenella, upped in trip and tried in cheekpieces, seemed to travel okay, but she failed to pick up for pressure after having to be switched early in the straight. (op 20-1)

Asfurah's Image did not improve for the step up to 7f and only looked to run to a mark in the 50s. She ran as though a stronger pace would have suited better. (op 4-1)

Amore Et Labore was hampered early in the straight, but he wasn't picking up sufficiently at the time. Still, he ran above his official mark of 45.

7858 BET TOTEPOOL AT TOTESPORT.COM MAIDEN STKS 5f 20y(P)

3:20 (3:20) (Class 5) 2-Y-O £2,266 (£674; £337; £168) Stalls Low

Form RPR

223 **1** **Steps (IRE)**[31] 7418 2-9-2 74... JackMitchell 3 75
(M A Jarvis) *mde all: pushed clr over 1f out: styd on* **5/4**[2]

52 **2** *1 ¾* **Quality Art (USA)**[16] 7595 2-9-2 0.................................. GeorgeBaker 9 69+
(G L Moore) *trckd ldrs: racd keenly: rdn to chse wnr over 1f out: hung lft: r.o* **10/11**[1]

0535 **3** *2 ¾* **Pizzarra**[38] 7333 2-8-8 58... JamesSullivan(3) 11 54
(J G Given) *hld up: r.o ins fnl f: wnt 3rd nr fin: nvr nrr* **16/1**[3]

30 **4** *1* **Mandy's Hero**[177] 3204 2-9-2 0...................................... StevieDonohoe 5 55
(Ian Williams) *chsd wnr: rdn 1/2-way: no ex ins fnl f* **20/1**

5 *3 ¾* **Doesn't Care (IRE)** 2-8-9 0.................................. GeorgeChaloner(7) 4 42
(R A Fahey) *sn outpcd: r.o ins fnl f: nvr nrr* **25/1**

0 **6** *1 ¼* **Inde Country**[37] 7346 2-8-11 0... LukeMorris 1 32
(N J Vaughan) *prom: rdn 1/2-way: wknd over 1f out* **66/1**

6 **7** *1* **Zareena**[10] 7682 2-8-11 0.. CathyGannon 6 29
(P D Evans) *sn pushed along and a in rr* **40/1**

000 **8** *1* **Renesmee (IRE)**[17] 7577 2-8-11 31.....................(b[1]) RobbieFitzpatrick 8 25
(Peter Grayson) *mid-div: rdn and wknd 1/2-way* **100/1**

0 **9** *2* **Layla's Princess**[219] 1930 2-8-11 0.................................. EddieAhern 2 18
(Ian Williams) *chsd ldrs: rdn 1/2-way: wknd over 1f out* **33/1**

U **Pickled Pumpkin** 2-9-2 0..(b[1]) HayleyTurner 7 —
(Miss Olivia Maylam) *swvd rt and uns rdr sn after s* **50/1**

63.56 secs (1.26) **Going Correction** +0.30s/f (Slow) **10 Ran SP% 121.1**

Speed ratings (Par 96): **101,98,93,92,86 84,82,81,77,—**

toteswingers:1&2 £1.20, 2&3 £3.50, 1&3 £2.20 CSF £2.64 TOTE £1.90: £1.10, £1.10, £3.30; EX 2.80 Trifecta £16.60 Pool: £630.84 -28.06 winning units..

Owner Michael Hill **Bred** Eamon Beston **Trained** Newmarket, Suffolk

FOCUS

An uncompetitive juvenile maiden. The form makes sense, with the time and the eighth offering perspective. The winner found a length on his preious form.

NOTEBOOK

Steps(IRE) got a bit unbalanced on the downhill run when dropped to this trip for the first time at Lingfield on his previous start according to connections, and the combination of this flatter track and being allowed an easy lead on a track favouring pace clearly suited. He was never seriously challenged and Jack Mitchell didn't have to use his whip. The winner lacks scope, but is a straightforward type and should be competitive in handicaps over this distance. (tchd Evens and 11-8)

Quality Art(USA) was unsuited by the drop back to 5f, failing to build on his recent second over 6f at Kempton, although the way the track was riding, appearing to favour those racing prominently, might not have helped. (op Evens tchd 5-4)

Pizzarra plugged on after being set a lot to do, but she would be better off in handicap company.

Mandy's Hero, having his first start since leaving Richard Fahey and returning from a 177-day break, ran to just a modest level but is entitled to come on for the outing. Handicaps are now an option. (op 16-1)

Doesn't Care(IRE) needed the experience but made modest late progress. (op 33-1)

7859 BIGGER WINS WITH SP+ AT TOTESPORT.COM H'CAP (DIV I) 5f 20y(P)

3:50 (3:50) (Class 6) (0-60,61) 3-Y-O+ £1,364 (£403; £201) Stalls Low

Form RPR

013 **1** **Sharp Shoes**[5] 7764 3-9-5 **58**......................................(p) SamHitchcott 12 75
(Mrs A Duffield) *mde virtually all: edgd lft over 3f out: drvn clr ins fnl f* **10/1**

00-4 **2** *4 ½* **Chantilly Jewel (USA)**[8] 7720 5-8-12 **51**....................(v) HayleyTurner 9 52
(R M H Cowell) *chsd ldrs: rdn over 1f out: styd on same pce* **12/1**

0001 **3** *1* **Your Gifted (IRE)**[3] 7808 3-8-13 **55**.........................(e) RossAtkinson(3) 5 52
(Patrick Morris) *hld up: hmpd over 3f out: hdwy over 1f out: no imp ins fnl f* **11/1**

0000 **4** *1 ¼* **Stolt (IRE)**[52] 7051 6-9-4 **60**.. JamesSullivan(3) 10 53
(Mrs L Stubbs) *chsd rdn and hung lft fr over 1f out: no ex* **13/2**[3]

4221 **5** *hd* **You'relikemefrank**[8] 7720 4-9-8 **61** 6ex..........................(p) LukeMorris 2 53
(J Balding) *trckd wnr: plld hrd: hmpd wl over 3f out: rdn over 1f out: hung lft and no ex ins fnl f* **13/8**[1]

3103 **6** *2 ½* **Almaty Express**[31] 7426 8-9-1 **54**...................................(b) MartinLane 7 37
(J R Weymes) *mid-div: rdn 1/2-way: n.d* **6/1**[2]

6050 **7** *1 ¼* **Flaxen Lake**[5] 7764 3-9-2 **55**......................................(bt[1]) CathyGannon 11 33
(J M Bradley) *hld up: rdn 1/2-way: n.d* **12/1**

0506 **8** *shd* **Lets Move It**[3] 7807 3-8-7 **46** oh1..............................(v) PatrickMathers 3 24
(D Shaw) *sed fr wrong stall: in rr and rdn 1/2-way: n.d* **50/1**

0-20 **9** *3 ¼* **Sir Don (IRE)**[31] 7426 11-9-0 **53**.................................(tp) StevieDonohoe 6 19
(Mrs D J Sanderson) *chsd ldrs: rdn 1/2-way: sn wknd* **20/1**

5050 **10** *5* **Riggs (IRE)**[19] 7547 4-8-8 **47** oh1 ow1....................(b) RobbieFitzpatrick 1 —
(Peter Grayson) *hld up: sme hdwy u.p over 1f out: sn wknd* **150/1**

0501 **R** **Pinball (IRE)**[35] 7380 4-8-13 **52**.....................................(b) PhillipMakin 4 —
(Mrs L Williamson) *sed fr wrong stall: rrd s: tk no part* **17/2**

63.01 secs (0.71) **Going Correction** +0.30s/f (Slow) **11 Ran SP% 116.4**

Speed ratings (Par 101): **106,98,97,95,94 90,88,88,83,75 —**

toteswingers:1&2 £14.20, 2&3 £10.80, 1&3 £10.60 CSF £120.63 CT £1367.81 TOTE £9.30: £2.20, £4.10, £3.90; EX 140.60 TRIFECTA Not won..

Owner T P McMahon and D McMahon **Bred** Mrs Mary Rowlands **Trained** Constable Burton, N Yorks

■ Stewards' Enquiry : Sam Hitchcott two-day ban: careless riding (Dec 27-28)
Patrick Mathers one-day ban: started from wrong stall (Dec 27)

FOCUS

The time was 0.43 seconds quicker than the second division. The form is rated around the time and it is worth crediting the winner with improvement.

Stolt(IRE) Official explanation: jockey said gelding hung left in home straight

Sir Don(IRE) Official explanation: jockey said gelding hung right in home straight

7860 BIGGER WINS WITH SP+ AT TOTESPORT.COM H'CAP (DIV II) 5f 20y(P)

4:20 (4:21) (Class 6) (0-60,60) 3-Y-O+ £1,364 (£403; £201) Stalls Low

Form RPR

2013 **1** **Sleepy Blue Ocean**[8] 7721 4-9-6 **59**...............................(p) LukeMorris 7 68
(J Balding) *a.p: chsd ldr 1/2-way: rdn to ld over 1f out: r.o* **10/3**[2]

5353 **2** *1 ¾* **Bluebok**[8] 7720 9-8-9 **48**...(bt) RussKennemore 5 51
(J M Bradley) *led: hdd over 3f out: n.m.r 2f out: rdn and ev ch over 1f out: styd on same pce ins fnl f* **4/1**[3]

1442 **3** *1 ¼* **Ballarina**[20] 7537 4-9-2 **55**.. EddieAhern 6 53
(E J Alston) *led over 3f out: rdn and hdd over 1f out: no ex ins fnl f* **11/4**[1]

00 **4** *hd* **Radiator Rooney (IRE)**[38] 7334 7-8-12 **54**...................... AmyRyan(3) 2 51
(Patrick Morris) *hld up: nt clr run 1/2-way: swtchd lft and hdwy over 1f out: r.o* **16/1**

0645 **5** *hd* **Sharp Bullet (IRE)**[3] 7807 4-9-1 **54**..........................(p) PatrickMathers 4 51
(Bruce Hellier) *chsd ldrs: rdn over 1f out: r.o* **15/2**

2-50 **6** *2 ¾* **Grace And Virtue (IRE)**[129] 4811 3-8-13 **52**.................. ShaneKelly 10 39
(S Donohoe, Ire) *hld up: r.o ins fnl f: nvr nrr* **33/1**

500 **7** *½* **Tyrannosaurus Rex (IRE)**[46] 7195 6-9-4 **57**................... PhillipMakin 8 42
(D Shaw) *hld up: rdn over 1f out: n.d* **8/1**

0003 **8** *2 ¼* **Mr Funshine**[3] 7807 5-9-0 **53**.. DaneO'Neill 11 30
(D Shaw) *chsd ldrs: rdn 1/2-way: wknd over 1f out* **10/1**

0000 **9** *½* **Albaher**[3] 7808 4-8-0 **46** oh1..(b) LeonnaMayor(7) 3 21
(Peter Grayson) *dwlt: a in rr* **100/1**

0-00 **10** *13* **Egyptian Lord**[312] 402 7-8-8 **47** oh1 ow1..............(b) RobbieFitzpatrick 1 —
(Peter Grayson) *mid-div: rdn 1/2-way: sn wknd* **66/1**

63.44 secs (1.14) **Going Correction** +0.30s/f (Slow) **10** Ran SP% **113.0**
Speed ratings (Par 101): **102,99,97,96,96 92,91,87,86,66**
toteswingers:1&2 £3.90, 2&3 £3.20, 1&3 £2.50 CSF £16.40 CT £40.01 TOTE £6.10: £2.30, £1.30, £1.10; EX 16.80 Trifecta £38.60 Pool: £783.74 -15.01 winning units..
Owner Tykes And Terriers Racing Club **Bred** Exors Of The Late N Ahamad & P C Scott **Trained** Scrooby, Notts

FOCUS
The time was 0.43 seconds slower than the first division. Straightforward form for the grade.

7861 BET ON TONIGHT'S FOOTBALL AT TOTESPORT.COM H'CAP 1m 5f 194y(P)
4:50 (4:51) (Class 5) (0-75,75) 3-Y-0+ **£2,104** (£626; £312; £156) **Stalls** Low

Form RPR
0611 **1** **Jezza**[24] 7504 4-9-4 **65**.. StevieDonohoe 3 76+
(V R A Dartnall) *hld up in tch: led wl over 2f out: clr over 1f out: eased nr fin* **9/4**[1]

0003 **2** *2 1/4* **Houston Dynimo (IRE)**[28] 7463 5-9-8 **69**......................... PhillipMakin 7 74
(N G Richards) *hld up: hdwy over 1f out: r.o to go 2nd nr fin: nt trble wnr* **9/1**

3162 **3** *1 1/4* **Carlton Scroop (FR)**[28] 7463 7-9-8 **69**........................... AndreaAtzeni 2 72
(A W Carroll) *a.p: rdn to chse wnr over 2f out: styd on: lost 2nd nr fin* **8/1**

0010 **4** *1 1/2* **Ethics Girl (IRE)**[18] 7568 4-10-0 **75**................................ FrannyNorton 4 76
(John Berry) *hld up: hdwy over 2f out: rdn over 1f out: no ex ins fnl f* **6/1**[3]

-522 **5** *1* **Stormy Morning**[24] 7504 4-9-3 **64**...................................... ChrisCatlin 5 67+
(Mrs Lawney Hill) *prom: nt clr run and lost pl wl over 2f out: n.d after* **9/2**[2]

3204 **6** *2* **Inside Knowledge (USA)**[14] 7632 4-8-9 **56** oh6.............. MartinLane 6 53
(G Woodward) *chsd ldr tl rdn 3f out: wknd over 1f out* **28/1**

3551 **7** *3* **Leyte Gulf (USA)**[14] 7632 7-9-0 **61**................................ DaneO'Neill 8 54
(C C Bealby) *dwlt: hld up: rdn over 2f out: sn wknd* **9/2**[2]

0450 **8** *15* **Bushy Dell (IRE)**[24] 7504 5-8-9 **56** oh4............................ CathyGannon 1 28
(Miss J Feilden) *led: rdn and hdd wl over 2f out: sn wknd* **10/1**

3m 9.26s (3.26) **Going Correction** +0.30s/f (Slow) **8** Ran SP% **115.1**
Speed ratings (Par 103): **102,100,100,99,98 97,95,87**
toteswingers:1&2 £4.80, 2&3 £9.50, 1&3 £4.10 CSF £23.94 CT £138.30 TOTE £3.00: £1.10, £5.60, £2.50; EX 24.70 Trifecta £105.60 Pool: £806.97 - 5.65 winning units..
Owner Under The Radar **Bred** C P Ranson **Trained** Brayford, Devon

FOCUS
A modest handicap. The winner continues to progress and was value for extra, with the form rated around the second and third.
Leyte Gulf(USA) Official explanation: trainer said gelding had colic post-race

7862 TONY MCCOY FOR BBC SPORTS PERSONALITY MEDIAN AUCTION MAIDEN STKS 1m 141y(P)
5:20 (5:20) (Class 6) 3-5-Y-0 **£1,706** (£503; £252) **Stalls** Low

Form RPR
2-20 **1** **Midnight Strider (IRE)**[136] 4547 4-9-5 65.............(t) RichardKingscote 3 56+
(Tom Dascombe) *a.p: rdn to ld 1f out: r.o: readily* **6/5**[2]

3 **2** *1 3/4* **Lady Rossetti**[16] 7596 3-8-12 0.. ChrisCatlin 1 47
(M P Tregoning) *chsd ldrs: rdn and ev ch 1f out: styd on same pce* **1/1**[1]

/0-0 **3** *3/4* **Ryan's Rock**[13] 7646 5-9-5 47.. AndreaAtzeni 6 50
(R J Price) *chsd ldr tl led over 2f out: rdn and hdd 1f out: styd on same pce* **14/1**

2044 **4** *3 1/4* **Farmers Dream (IRE)**[30] 7449 3-8-12 54............................ EddieAhern 7 38
(J L Spearing) *hld up: hdwy over 3f out: rdn over 1f out: hung lft and no ex ins fnl f* **5/1**[3]

6/00 **5** *nk* **Jack Jicaro**[16] 7599 4-9-5 39... LukeMorris 4 42
(N J Vaughan) *s.s: rdn over 2f out: hung lft over 1f out: n.d* **33/1**

6 **6** *8* **Maitre 'D**[184] 2981 3-9-3 0... CathyGannon 5 23
(C N Kellett) *hld up in tch: rdn and wknd 2f out* **25/1**

6-00 **7** *17* **Chifah**[16] 7601 3-8-12 44..(v[1]) JamesDoyle 2 —
(R J Price) *led: rdn and hdd over 2f out: sn wknd* **33/1**

600 **8** *2 3/4* **Bluegrass Gal (USA)**[28] 7461 4-8-11 25.................. PatrickDonaghy[(3)] 8 —
(Mrs L Williamson) *hld up: rdn and wknd over 3f out* **50/1**

1m 54.93s (4.43) **Going Correction** +0.30s/f (Slow)
WFA 3 from 4yo+ 2lb **8** Ran SP% **130.5**
Speed ratings (Par 101): **92,90,89,86,86 79,64,61**
toteswingers:1&2 £1.10, 2&3 £7.10, 1&3 £5.20 CSF £3.21 TOTE £1.30: £1.02, £1.20, £3.40; EX 3.10 Trifecta £25.60 Pool: £863.38 - 24.95 winning units..
Owner Owen Promotions Limited **Bred** Jim McDonald **Trained** Malpas, Cheshire

FOCUS
A weak maiden run in a time 1.84 seconds slower than the following Class 6 handicap. It was slowly run and there was little positive to say about the form.

7863 40 LIVE FOOTBALL MARKETS AT TOTESPORT.COM H'CAP 1m 141y(P)
5:50 (5:51) (Class 6) (0-55,58) 3-Y-0+ **£1,706** (£503; £252) **Stalls** Low

Form RPR
5404 **1** **Pie Poudre**[16] 7605 3-8-10 **50**..(p) JackMitchell 5 57
(R Brotherton) *hld up: hdwy 3f out: rdn over 1f out: styd on to ld nr fin* **8/1**

3506 **2** *nk* **Director General (USA)**[42] 7273 3-9-1 **55**......................(b) PhillipMakin 8 62+
(Julie Camacho) *hld up in tch: nt clr run over 2f out: rdn over 1f out: r.o* **9/1**

6341 **3** *hd* **Bentley**[4] 7787 6-9-6 **58** 6ex..(b) GrahamGibbons 1 64
(B P J Baugh) *chsd ldr: led 7f out: rdn over 1f out: hdd nr fin* **5/1**[3]

1003 **4** *nk* **Katmai River (IRE)**[9] 7706 3-9-1 **55**...........................(v) SteveDrowne 12 60
(M D I Usher) *chsd ldrs: rdn and ev ch fr over 1f out: styd on* **15/2**

0640 **5** *1 1/2* **Fortunate Bid (IRE)**[104] 5636 4-8-10 **51**................ JamesSullivan[(3)] 11 53+
(Mrs L Stubbs) *hld up: racd keenly: hdwy over 1f out: r.o* **33/1**

0202 **6** *1 1/4* **Herecomethegirls**[14] 7633 4-9-2 **54**...............................(b) LukeMorris 3 53
(W G M Turner) *chsd ldrs: rdn over 1f out: styd on same pce ins fnl f* **9/2**[2]

0653 **7** *6* **Zarius**[32] 7401 3-9-1 **55**... GeorgeBaker 10 40
(C F Wall) *prom: rdn over 1f out: sn wknd* **6/1**

020 **8** *1/2* **The Bay Bandit**[133] 4665 3-9-1 **55**..................................... ShaneKelly 9 39
(S Donohoe, Ire) *led: hdd 7f out: chsd ldr: rdn and ev ch over 2f out: wknd ins fnl f* **7/2**[1]

0000 **9** *4 1/2* **Bold Hawk**[4] 7787 4-8-9 **47**..(vt) AdrianNicholls 2 21
(Mrs C A Dunnett) *sn pushed along in rr: n.d* **50/1**

0536 **10** *1 1/2* **Rigid**[40] 6848 3-8-11 **51**... JamesDoyle 6 21
(A W Carroll) *s.i.s: sn rcvrd into mid-div: rdn over 2f out: sn wknd* **16/1**

3065 **11** *3* **The Graig**[200] 2456 6-8-13 **51**...(t) EddieAhern 13 14
(J R Holt) *hld up: rdn and wknd over 2f out* **28/1**

1m 53.09s (2.59) **Going Correction** +0.30s/f (Slow)
WFA 3 from 4yo+ 2lb **11** Ran SP% **118.5**
Speed ratings (Par 101): **100,99,99,99,97 96,91,91,87,85 83**
toteswingers:1&2 £1.10, 2&3 £7.10, 1&3 £5.20. totesuper7: Win: Not won. Place: £308.80. CSF £77.30 CT £408.91 TOTE £6.20: £1.80, £4.20, £1.50; EX 95.30 TRIFECTA Not won..
Owner Bredon Hill Racing Club **Bred** Peter Holmes **Trained** Elmley Castle, Worcs

FOCUS
A moderate but competitive handicap. The form is somehwat muddling, but has been rated at face value.
Fortunate Bid(IRE) Official explanation: jockey said gelding was denied a clear run
T/Jkpt: £1,775.00 to a £1 stake. Pool £10,000.00 - 4.00 winning tickets. T/Plt: £54.50 to a £1 stake. Pool of £90,493.91 - 1,210.15 winning tickets. T/Qpdt: £7.80 to a £1 stake. Pool of £9,385.49 - 884.84 winning tickets. CR

7843 SOUTHWELL (L-H)
Tuesday, December 14

OFFICIAL GOING: Standard
Wind: Virtually nil Weather: Overcast and damp, moderate visibility

7864 TOTEPLACEPOT NURSERY 6f (F)
12:25 (12:25) (Class 6) (0-60,55) 2-Y-0 **£1,569** (£463; £231) **Stalls** Low

Form RPR
4061 **1** **Even Stevens**[55] 7017 2-8-12 **51**.. BillyCray[(5)] 8 66
(D Nicholls) *sn led: rdn clr 2f out: shkn up ins fnl f and kpt on wl* **5/1**[3]

3002 **2** *3 3/4* **Finn's Rainbow**[4] 7803 2-9-7 **55**.. PhillipMakin 7 59
(K A Ryan) *trckd ldrs on outer: hdwy wl over 2f out: rdn to chse wnr wl over 1f out: drvn and hung lft appr fnl f: sn no imp* **7/4**[1]

4023 **3** *5* **Ace Master**[14] 7643 2-9-0 **53**.. RyanClark[(5)] 3 42
(S R Bowring) *hld up towards rr: effrt and n.m.r over 2f out: sn swtchd rt and rdn wl over 1f out: kpt on to take 3rd ins fnl f: n.d* **5/2**[2]

0002 **4** *1* **Juarla (IRE)**[12] 7667 2-9-2 **50**.. LukeMorris 5 36
(R A Harris) *chsd ldrs: rdn along over 2f out: drvn wl over 1f out: sn one pce: lost 3rd ins fnl f* **14/1**

5056 **5** *1 3/4* **Ridgeway Hawk**[150] 4129 2-9-6 **54**..............................(v[1]) DaneO'Neill 6 35
(M D I Usher) *dwlt: hdwy to chse ldrs over 3f out: rdn wl over 2f out: grad wknd* **33/1**

0562 **6** *8* **Molly Mylenis**[14] 7641 2-9-3 **51**.. StevieDonohoe 1 8
(P D Evans) *sn chsng wnr on inner: rdn along 1/2-way: sn wknd* **33/1**

0533 **7** *2 1/4* **Irish Boy (IRE)**[7] 7739 2-9-1 **49**.. TravisBlock 4 —
(W J H Ratcliffe) *prom: rdn along bef 1/2-way: sn lost pl and bhd fnl 2f* **13/2**

0000 **8** *3/4* **Bernie's Tune**[20] 7551 2-9-0 **48** ow2.. AdamKirby 2 —
(J L Spearing) *a towards rr: rdn along 1/2-way: bhd fnl 2f* **33/1**

1m 16.06s (-0.44) **Going Correction** -0.075s/f (Stan) **8** Ran SP% **110.4**
Speed ratings (Par 94): **99,94,87,86,83 73,70,69**
toteswingers:1&2:£2.50, 1&3:£2.90, 2&3:£2.00 CSF £13.14 CT £24.58 TOTE £7.00: £1.30, £1.70, £1.20; EX 13.50 Trifecta £16.80.
Owner Paul J Dixon **Bred** Mrs Yvette Dixon **Trained** Sessay, N Yorks

FOCUS
A weak nursery with the top weight rated just 55. The first pair came clear and the form looks solid for the track.

NOTEBOOK
Even Stevens, put up 1lb for his narrow success in a 5f Kempton nursery last time, was having his first start for his new trainer and his first on Fibresand, though he had apparently worked on the track. Quickly away, he basically ran his rivals into the ground and never looked in much danger of being caught. He would be hard to beat if taking up his entry over 5f here on Friday. (tchd 6-1 and 7-1 in a place)
Finn's Rainbow, narrowly beaten in a fast-run nursery over C&D four days earlier when the third horse was 7l away, was able to race off the same mark. He tried hard to bridge the gap to the winner and pulled clear of the rest, but was inclined to carry his head to one side and hang in behind the winner from the furlong pole. (op 11-8)
Ace Master, placed in a couple of nurseries here last month, plugged on from the rear to take a remote third and may benefit from a return to 7f. (op 100-30)
Juarla(IRE), making his Fibresand debut after finishing a well-beaten second of four in a Wolverhampton maiden last time, was handy enough early but came under strong pressure a fair way out and was easily seen off. (op 16-1)
Ridgeway Hawk, visored for the first time on this return from five months off, missed the break and was caught out wide throughout. At least the outing should have brought him on.

7865 TOTEEXACTA CLAIMING STKS 1m 3f (F)
12:55 (12:56) (Class 6) 3-Y-0+ **£1,569** (£463; £231) **Stalls** Low

Form RPR
0054 **1** **Kumbeshwar**[11] 7679 3-9-1 60....................................(v) StevieDonohoe 4 78
(P D Evans) *trckd ldng pair on inner: reminders 5f out: hdwy to chse ldr 4f out: led 3f out: rdn clr wl over 1f out: styd on* **9/1**

2000 **2** *4 1/2* **Trip The Light**[19] 7568 5-9-2 82..............................(v) GeorgeChaloner[(7)] 6 74
(R A Fahey) *trckd ldr: rdn along and outpcd 4f out: hdwy on inner to chse ldr over 2f out: sn drvn and no imp fnl f* **1/1**[1]

6201 **3** *nk* **Castle Myth (USA)**[8] 7729 4-8-0 60..........................(be) ShaneBKelly[(7)] 2 58
(B Ellison) *hld up and bhd: stdy hdwy 4f out: rdn to chse ldng pair wl over 1f out: eased and no imp ins fnl f* **4/1**[3]

3/12 **4** *7* **Scary Movie (IRE)**[27] 7480 5-8-7 73.. RobertWinston 3 46
(D J Coakley) *chsd ldrs: rdn along over 3f out: drvn over 2f out and sn wknd* **3/1**[2]

0000 **5** *3* **Look Officer (USA)**[48] 7167 4-8-3 46 ow2....................(b) RyanClark[(5)] 5 42
(Miss M E Rowland) *led: rdn along 4f out: hdd 3f out and sn wknd* **50/1**

0-00 **6** *30* **Owls FC (IRE)**[79] 186 4-8-5 27.. KellyHarrison[(3)] 7 —
(M C Chapman) *in tch on outer: pushed along after 3f: rdn along 1/2-way: sn outpcd and bhd: t.o fnl 3f* **200/1**

2m 27.21s (-0.79) **Going Correction** -0.075s/f (Stan)
WFA 3 from 4yo+ 4lb **6** Ran SP% **107.5**
Speed ratings (Par 101): **99,95,95,90,88 66**
toteswingers:1&2:£2.10, 1&3:£2.10, 2&3:£1.80 CSF £17.09 TOTE £10.40: £4.80, £1.10; EX 18.30.
Owner G E Amey **Bred** G E Amey **Trained** Pandy, Monmouths
■ Stewards' Enquiry : Shane B Kelly 10-day ban: failed to take all reasonable and permissible measures to obtain best possible placing (Dec 28-Jan 6)

FOCUS
An uncompetitive claimer, but run at a fair pace. Tricky to rate with the winner back to something like his best but the rest 10lb+ off.
Castle Myth(USA) Official explanation: jockey said, regarding running and riding, that his orders were to settle the gelding towards rear, make up ground down the back straight and finish in the best possible place; trainer's rep said she was unaware of the trainer's instructions.

7866 TOTEQUADPOT H'CAP 5f (F)
1:25 (1:25) (Class 4) (0-85,83) 3-Y-0+ **£3,594** (£1,069; £534; £266) **Stalls** High

Form RPR
4012 **1** **Sir Geoffrey (IRE)**[10] 7702 4-9-4 **80**..(b) IanMongan 2 94
(D Nicholls) *cl up: led 1/2-way: rdn over 1f out: kpt on strly* **5/1**[3]

4623 **2** 2 ¼ **Silaah**[7] 7740 6-9-7 **83**..........(p) AdrianNicholls 1 89
(D Nicholls) *dwlt: sn trcking ldrs: hdwy to chse wnr wl over 1f out: rdn and kpt on fnl f* **10/3**[1]
3132 **3** 2 ¼ **Sloop Johnb**[12] 7668 4-8-10 **72**..........(p) BarryMcHugh 3 70
(R A Fahey) *trckd ldrs: hdwy 2f out: sn rdn and kpt on fnl f* **9/2**[2]
1436 **4** 1 ½ **Colorus (IRE)**[33] 7405 7-8-2 **71** ow1..........(v) MatthewCosham(7) 4 64
(W J H Ratcliffe) *in tch: swtchd lft after 1f: rdn along over 2f out: kpt on u.p fnl f: nrst fin* **14/1**
403 **5** ¾ **Equuleus Pictor**[33] 7405 6-8-13 **75**.......... AdamKirby 6 65
(J L Spearing) *sn led: pushed along and hdd 1/2-way: sn rdn and wknd wl over 1f out* **8/1**
0000 **6** ½ **Onceaponatime (IRE)**[9] 7719 5-9-1 **77**.......... LukeMorris 7 65
(M D Squance) *chsd ldrs: rdn along over 2f out: sn one pce* **22/1**
1510 **7** 1 ¾ **La Capriosa**[6] 7754 4-8-8 **75**.......... BillyCray(5) 8 57
(D Nicholls) *prom: rdn along over 2f out: sn drvn and wknd* **8/1**
0611 **8** nk **Grudge**[12] 7668 5-8-11 **73**..........(be) RobertWinston 9 54
(C R Dore) *chsd ldrs: rdn along over 2f out: sn wknd* **10/1**
5225 **9** ½ **Galpin Junior (USA)**[26] 7494 4-8-7 **72**.......... JamesSullivan(3) 5 51
(Mrs R A Carr) *chsd ldrs: rdn along and lost pl after 1 1/2f: bhd fr 1/2-way* **11/1**
0350 **10** 4 ½ **Tourist**[19] 7566 5-9-6 **82**.......... DaneO'Neill 10 45
(D Shaw) *rrd s: a bhd* **12/1**

58.82 secs (-0.88) **Going Correction** +0.10s/f (Slow) **10** Ran SP% **116.3**
Speed ratings (Par 105): **111,107,103,101,100 99,96,96,95,88**
toteswingers:1&2:£3.60, 1&3:£5.10, 2&3:£3.50 CSF £21.96 CT £79.11 TOTE £6.60: £2.10, £2.20, £1.60; EX 19.50 Trifecta £124.00.
Owner Dixon, Howlett & The Chrystal Maze Ptn **Bred** P Rabbitte **Trained** Sessay, N Yorks

FOCUS
A fair sprint handicap and normal service was resumed with the race dominated by low-drawn horses. The time was good compared with the lesser race later. The winner recorded a personal best, in a race rated through his stablemate the runner-up.

7867 TOTESUPER7 H'CAP 1m (F)
1:55 (1:56) (Class 4) (0-85,85) 3-Y-O+ £3,594 (£1,069; £534; £266) Stalls Low

Form RPR
6013 **1** **Nazreef**[38] 7352 3-9-7 **85**..........(t) TravisBlock 10 104
(H Morrison) *chsd ldrs: pushed along and hdwy on outer over 3f out: led 2f out: sn clr: eased ins fnl f: v easily* **5/4**[1]
0010 **2** 11 **Follow The Flag (IRE)**[6] 7756 6-9-2 **79**..........(v) JamesDoyle 8 73
(A J McCabe) *in tch: hdwy 3f out: sn rdn and styd on appr fnl f: no ch w wnr* **7/1**[3]
2036 **3** ¾ **Elusive Fame (USA)**[40] 7314 4-9-1 **78**..........(b) GregFairley 2 70
(M Johnston) *chsd ldng pair on inner: rdn along over 2f out: drvn wl over 1f out: kpt on same pce* **11/1**
1554 **4** nk **Ours (IRE)**[41] 7304 7-9-6 **83**..........(p) BarryMcHugh 1 74
(John A Harris) *s.i.s and bhd: wd st: hdwy on outer wl over 1f out: sn rdn and styd on ins fnl f: nrst fin* **20/1**
6055 **5** hd **Thunderball**[14] 7637 4-8-10 **78**..........(b) BillyCray(5) 5 69
(D Nicholls) *led: rdn along 3f out: hdd 2f out: sn drvn and wknd fnl f* **9/2**[2]
0 **6** nse **Major Victory (SAF)**[6] 7756 3-8-10 **84**.......... DavidProbert 4 65
(Miss Gay Kelleway) *in tch: hdwy to chse ldrs 3f out: rdn over 2f out: sn drvn and kpt on same pce* **25/1**
0221 **7** 4 **West End Lad**[17] 7600 7-9-4 **81**..........(b) DaneO'Neill 9 63
(S R Bowring) *in tch: rdn along 1/2-way: sn outpcd and bhd* **8/1**
0040 **8** 13 **Street Devil (USA)**[29] 1395 5-8-7 **70** oh2..........(p) GrahamGibbons 3 22
(F J Brennan) *chsd ldr: cl up 3f out: sn rdn and wknd over 2f out* **16/1**
41- **9** ½ **Revelator (IRE)**[61] 7079 3-8-6 **77**.......... HobieGill(7) 6 27
(A J McCabe) *in tch: rdn along over 3f out: sn outpcd and bhd* **50/1**
-242 **10** 30 **Capricornus (USA)**[18] 1061 3-9-0 **78**.......... AdrianNicholls 7 —
(Ferdy Murphy) *swtchd wd and rdn along after 1f: a in rr: bhd fnl 3f* **33/1**

1m 42.39s (-1.31) **Going Correction** -0.075s/f (Stan)
WFA 3 from 4yo+ 1lb **10** Ran SP% **114.0**
Speed ratings (Par 105): **103,92,91,90,90 90,86,73,73,43**
toteswingers:1&2:£3.50, 1&3:£5.00, 2&3:£10.30 CSF £9.49 CT £67.45 TOTE £2.30: £1.20, £2.60, £2.20; EX 10.60 Trifecta £58.70.
Owner Deborah Collett & M J Watson **Bred** M J Watson **Trained** East Ilsley, Berks

FOCUS
This looked a competitive handicap on paper and it was run at a decent pace, but it was turned into a one-horse race by Nazreef. He is unlikely to match this figure elsewhere.
Street Devil(USA) Official explanation: jockey said gelding moved poorly
Capricornus(USA) Official explanation: jockey said colt never travelled

7868 GB GROUP IDENTITY MANAGEMENT H'CAP 5f (F)
2:25 (2:26) (Class 5) (0-70,70) 3-Y-O+ £2,115 (£624; £312) Stalls High

Form RPR
0000 **1** **Incomparable**[56] 6998 5-9-5 **68**..........(bt) IanMongan 4 79
(D Nicholls) *a.p: effrt 2f out: led over 1f out: rdn ins fnl f and kpt on wl* **7/2**[1]
2423 **2** 1 ¼ **Riflessione**[11] 7683 4-9-7 **70**..........(b) SeamieHeffernan 10 76
(R A Harris) *led: rdn 2f out: edgd rt and drvn over 1f out: sn hdd: kpt on* **8/1**
0030 **3** ½ **Johannesgray (IRE)**[21] 7539 3-9-7 **70**..........(be[1]) AdrianNicholls 3 74
(D Nicholls) *chsd ldrs: rdn along and edgd lft 2f out: styd on u.p fnl f* **11/2**[3]
614 **4** ¾ **Perlachy**[26] 7494 6-9-1 **67**..........(v) KellyHarrison(3) 5 69
(D Shaw) *prom: rdn along 2f out: drvn over 1f out and kpt on same pce* **14/1**
2001 **5** shd **First Blade**[49] 7155 4-8-11 **65**..........(b) RyanClark(5) 1 66
(S R Bowring) *chsd ldrs on outer: rdn along wl over 1f out: sn one pce* **6/1**
1141 **6** ¾ **Fashion Icon (USA)**[21] 7537 4-8-9 **65**..........(b) ShaneBKelly(7) 2 63
(D O'Meara) *chsd ldrs: rdn along and n.m.r 2f out: sn one pce* **4/1**[2]
0032 **7** 1 ½ **Guto**[21] 7542 7-8-11 **60**.......... AndreaAtzeni 11 53
(W J H Ratcliffe) *chsd ldrs: rdn along 2f out: sn drvn and wknd over 1f out* **8/1**
4600 **8** 7 **Steel City Boy (IRE)**[26] 7494 7-8-9 **58**.......... GrahamGibbons 12 26
(D Shaw) *a towards rr* **33/1**
3456 **9** ¾ **Ingleby Star (IRE)**[10] 7702 5-9-7 **70**..........(p) RobertWinston 7 35
(N Wilson) *chsd ldrs: rdn along over 2f out: sn wknd* **25/1**
3400 **10** ¾ **Eviction (IRE)**[139] 4478 3-9-1 **64**..........(b) AdamKirby 9 26
(Miss M E Rowland) *dwlt: outpcd and bhd fr 1/2-way* **40/1**
0556 **11** nk **Royal Blade (IRE)**[33] 7409 3-8-9 **58**.......... PatrickMathers 6 19
(A Berry) *sn outpcd: bhd fr 1/2-way* **22/1**

60.52 secs (0.82) **Going Correction** +0.10s/f (Slow) **11** Ran SP% **114.4**
Speed ratings (Par 103): **97,95,94,93,92 91,89,78,76,75 75**
toteswingers:1&2:£5.80, 1&3:£5.90, 2&3:£6.80 CSF £29.41 CT £152.30 TOTE £5.10: £1.90, £2.20, £1.30; EX 34.80 Trifecta £309.80.
Owner Paul J Dixon & Brian Morton **Bred** Mrs Yvette Dixon **Trained** Sessay, N Yorks
■ Stewards' Enquiry : Seamie Heffernan one-day ban: used whip down shoulder in the forehand (Dec 28)

FOCUS
Another sprint handicap in which apart from the runner-up, those who raced centre-to-far-side were favoured. The winning time was 1.7 seconds slower than the earlier Class 4 handicap over the same trip. The winner is rated back to something like his best.
Ingleby Star(IRE) Official explanation: trainer's rep said gelding had a breathing problem; jockey said gelding hung left

7869 PLAY GOLF BEFORE RACING AT SOUTHWELL MEDIAN AUCTION MAIDEN STKS 6f (F)
2:55 (2:57) (Class 6) 3-5-Y-O £1,569 (£463; £231) Stalls Low

Form RPR
6- **1** **Broughtons Day**[486] 5029 3-9-3 0.......... StevieDonohoe 2 68
(W J Musson) *trckd ldrs: hdwy on outer over 2f out: led wl over 1f out: rdn ins fnl f: kpt on* **11/8**[1]
4003 **2** ½ **Faithful Duchess (IRE)**[4] 7810 3-8-12 57..........(b) ShaneKelly 7 61
(E F Vaughan) *trckd ldrs: smooth hdwy on wd outside over 2f out: trckd wnr on bit over 1f out: swtchd lft ent fnl f: shkn up and nt run on last 100yds* **7/2**[2]
4 **3** 3 ½ **King Bertolini (IRE)**[50] 7129 3-9-3 0.......... PatrickMathers 3 55
(A Berry) *towards rr and rdn along 1/2-way: kpt on u.p fnl 2f: nrst fin* **25/1**
4 **4** 4 ½ **Gorgeous Goblin (IRE)**[26] 7498 3-8-12 0.......... RobertWinston 1 35
(D C Griffiths) *trckd ldng pair on inner: hdwy and ev ch 2f out: sn rdn and wknd over 1f out* **6/1**[3]
0600 **5** nk **Elle Est**[4] 7810 3-8-12 58.......... GrahamGibbons 6 34
(E J Alston) *led: rdn along wl over 2f out: hdd wl over 1f out: sn wknd* **12/1**
500 **6** 7 **Gessabelle**[6] 7757 3-8-7 38.......... TobyAtkinson(5) 5 12
(P S McEntee) *blind removed late and s.i.s: a in rr* **20/1**
-060 **7** 1 ¾ **Champagne All Day**[39] 7328 4-9-0 38.......... MichaelStainton(3) 8 11
(S P Griffiths) *cl up: rdn along wl over 2f out: sn wknd* **22/1**
0006 **8** 1 **Sue And Sue**[12] 7669 3-8-9 21..........(p) RossAtkinson(3) 9 —
(G Woodward) *v s.i.s: a in rr* **66/1**

1m 18.17s (1.67) **Going Correction** -0.075s/f (Stan) **8** Ran SP% **100.8**
Speed ratings (Par 101): **85,84,79,73,73 63,61,60**
toteswingers:1&2:£1.70, 1&3:£6.10, 2&3:£3.90 CSF £4.37 TOTE £1.90: £1.10, £1.10, £6.20; EX 5.10 Trifecta £56.00.
Owner Broughton Thermal Insulation **Bred** Broughton Bloodstock **Trained** Newmarket, Suffolk
■ Sally's Swansong (13/2) was withdrawn after trying to break out of the stalls. Deduct 10p in the £ under R4.

FOCUS
This was a weak maiden and all bar one of the field decided to come centre-to-stands' side up the home straight. The time was poor and the form is rated loosely around the runner-up.

7870 TONY MCCOY FOR BBC SPORTS PERSONALITY H'CAP 7f (F)
3:25 (3:26) (Class 6) (0-65,65) 3-Y-O+ £1,569 (£463; £231) Stalls Low

Form RPR
0-00 **1** **Alpha Tauri (USA)**[4] 7812 4-9-6 **64**..........(t) JamesDoyle 7 77
(F Sheridan) *mde all: rdn and qcknd clr wl over 1f out: kpt on strly* **20/1**
34 **2** 6 **This Ones For Eddy**[99] 5817 5-9-1 **59**.......... LukeMorris 10 56
(J Balding) *trckd ldrs: hdwy to chse wnr over 2f out: sn rdn and kpt on fnl f: no ch w wnr* **7/2**[2]
0012 **3** nk **It's A Mans World**[8] 7731 4-8-2 **51**.......... RyanPowell(5) 4 47
(Ian Williams) *midfield: hdwy on outer and wd st: sn rdn to chse ldrs 2f out: drvn: edgd lft and no imp appr fnl f* **13/8**[1]
1446 **4** hd **Toby Tyler**[2] 7844 4-9-2 **60**..........(v) MickyFenton 8 55
(P T Midgley) *dwlt and in rr: hdwy 2f out: swtchd rt and rdn over 1f out: styd on ins fnl f: nrst fin* **12/1**
0034 **5** nk **Ace Of Spies (IRE)**[2] 7847 5-9-6 **64**.......... HayleyTurner 3 59
(C R Dore) *in tch on inner: hdwy to chse ldrs over 2f out: sn rdn and kpt on same pce* **15/2**[3]
0406 **6** 4 ½ **Sophie's Beau (USA)**[4] 7808 3-8-4 **51** oh1.......... KellyHarrison(3) 13 33
(M C Chapman) *chsd wnr: rdn along over 2f out: sn drvn and grad wknd* **50/1**
0505 **7** 4 **Fathey (IRE)**[7] 7738 4-8-8 **52** oh2 ow1.......... RobbieFitzpatrick 12 24
(C Smith) *chsd ldrs: rdn along wl over 2f out: grad wknd* **50/1**
0000 **8** 1 **Ponting (IRE)**[33] 7401 4-8-10 **57**.......... PaulPickard(3) 11 26
(P T Midgley) *bmpd and pushed wd after 1f: hdwy into midfield over 2f out: sn rdn and n.d* **33/1**
500- **9** ¾ **Fools Gold**[510] 4202 5-9-7 **65**.......... GrahamGibbons 1 32
(R C Guest) *a towards rr* **15/2**[3]
1000 **10** ¾ **Charles Parnell (IRE)**[21] 7539 7-9-4 **62**.......... AdrianNicholls 5 27
(S P Griffiths) *dwlt: sn chsng ldrs: rdn along wl over 2f out: sn wknd* **20/1**
0060 **11** 3 ½ **Scruffy Skip (IRE)**[48] 7162 5-9-2 **60**..........(v) DavidProbert 9 15
(Mrs C A Dunnett) *a towards rr* **25/1**
0060 **12** 3 ½ **Flores Sea (USA)**[14] 7646 6-9-1 **62**.......... JamesSullivan(3) 2 —
(Mrs R A Carr) *a in rr* **33/1**

1m 28.94s (-1.36) **Going Correction** -0.075s/f (Stan) **12** Ran SP% **114.7**
Speed ratings (Par 101): **104,97,96,96,96 91,86,85,84,83 79,75**
toteswingers:1&2:£12.50, 1&3:£9.80, 2&3:£2.70 CSF £81.66 CT £182.68 TOTE £31.80: £6.80, £1.90, £1.10; EX 146.60 Trifecta £566.80.
Owner Frank Sheridan **Bred** Flaxman Holdings Ltd **Trained** Averham Park, Notts

FOCUS
A moderate handicap lacking depth, but another race that developed into a one-horse contest. The winner was seemingly back to his best.
Flores Sea(USA) Official explanation: jockey said gelding did not face the kickback
T/Plt: £11.00 to a £1 stake. Pool £57,323.74 - 3,775.56 winning tickets T/Qpdt: £6.50 to a £1 stake. Pool £5,920.60 - 667.70 winning tickets JR

7777 KEMPTON (A.W) (R-H)
Wednesday, December 15

OFFICIAL GOING: Standard
Wind: Light, half against Weather: Very overcast, drizzly

7871 RACING AT SKYSPORTS.COM MEDIAN AUCTION MAIDEN STKS 6f (P)
3:55 (3:57) (Class 6) 2-Y-O £1,637 (£483; £241) Stalls High

Form RPR
0 **1** **Pippa's Gift**[41] 7309 2-9-3 0.......... HayleyTurner 8 71
(W R Muir) *dwlt: sn trckd ldrs: wnt 2nd wl over 2f out: hrd rdn over 1f out: styd on to ld last 100yds* **7/1**

23 **2** ¾ **Fifth In Line (IRE)**[18] 7602 2-8-12 0 FergusSweeney 7 64
(J A Osborne) *pressed ldr: led 1/2-way: shkn up and looked in command over 1f out: wilted and hdd last 100yds* **13/8**[1]
3 1 **Circuitous** 2-9-3 0 TomQueally 4 66+
(P F I Cole) *awkward s: rn green in last: stl there 2f out: rdn and gd prog over 1f out: styd on to take 3rd last 50yds: nrst fin* **7/2**[2]
000 **4** 2 **Greenhead High**[26] 7503 2-9-3 62 J-PGuillambert 3 60
(Jane Chapple-Hyam) *chsd ldrs: wd bnd 3f out: sn rdn: wnt 3rd briefly ins fnl f: one pce* **20/1**
5333 **5** 1 **Regal Bullet (IRE)**[29] 7469 2-9-3 56 SamHitchcott 1 57
(D K Ivory) *in tch: drvn and effrt over 2f out: disp 3rd briefly 1f out: fdd* **11/2**
6 1¾ **Litotes** 2-8-7 0 JemmaMarshall(5) 6 47
(M J Attwater) *settled in 7th: prog on inner to dispute 3rd 2f out to 1f out: wknd* **50/1**
460 **7** 3½ **Rambo Will**[18] 7595 2-9-3 68 JimmyQuinn 2 41
(J R Jenkins) *in tch: rdn to dispute 3rd 2f out tl wknd over 1f out* **5/1**[3]
00 **8** 21 **Hey Mambo**[75] 6520 2-8-12 0 SteveDrowne 5 —
(R Ingram) *led to 1/2-way: wknd rapidly 2f out: t.o* **80/1**

1m 13.12s (0.02) **Going Correction** +0.025s/f (Slow) **8** Ran SP% **112.8**
Speed ratings (Par 94): **100,99,97,95,93 91,86,58**
toteswingers:1&2:£3.50, 1&3:£3.90, 2&3:£2.10 CSF £18.34 TOTE £10.60: £2.70, £1.10, £1.50; EX 23.60.
Owner Perspicacious Punters Racing Club **Bred** M P Graham **Trained** Lambourn, Berks

FOCUS
No strength to this ordinary maiden. The gallop was no more than fair and the winner edged towards the far rail in the closing stages. The runner-up and those down the field set the level.

NOTEBOOK
Pippa's Gift, who reportedly split a pastern in summer, was fairly easy to back but showed a good attitude and stepped up a fair way on the form he showed over course-and-distance on his debut to take this ordinary event. He'll prove equally effective over 7f, has a bit of physical scope and may do better in run-of-the-mill handicaps. (op 8-1 tchd 10-1)
Fifth In Line(IRE), the well-backed market leader, had the run of the race against the inside rail and seemed to give it her best shot dropped in trip. The handicap route is an option but she doesn't have much in the way of physical presence and she really needs to settle better if she is to progress. (tchd 2-1 in a place)
Circuitous ◆, who was fairly easy in the market, was too green to do himself justice on this racecourse debut. Half-brothers Seradim (very useful) and Circumvent (smart) were better over further and this one is more than capable of picking up a similar race granted a more suitable test of stamina with this experience behind him. (op 11-4 tchd 4-1)
Greenhead High, having his first run for a new trainer, doesn't look as good as his 62-rating suggests but, while he probably ran as well as he ever has done, he's likely to remain vulnerable in this grade and will have to improve to win a handicap from this mark. (op 14-1)
Regal Bullet(IRE) was nibbled at in the market but he had his limitations firmly exposed. He has had a few chances but the return to modest handicap company is likely to provide him with his best chance of success. (op 15-2 tchd 5-1)
Hey Mambo Official explanation: jockey said filly had no more to give

7872 DIGIBET MEDIAN AUCTION MAIDEN STKS 7f (P)
4:25 (4:26) (Class 6) 3-5-Y-O **£1,637** (£483; £241) **Stalls** High

Form RPR
504 **1** **Hippique**[14] 7651 3-8-12 56 (v[1]) DavidProbert 2 63
(A M Balding) *in tch: prog towards inner over 2f out: drvn to ld ins fnl f: sn nrly a l clr: jst hld on* **7/1**[3]
0 **2** nse **Dazzled**[198] 2603 3-8-12 0 [1] HayleyTurner 5 62
(J R Fanshawe) *chsd ldrs: rdn over 2f out: wnt 2nd and chal over 1f out: nt qckn jst ins fnl f: styd on again nr fin: jst failed* **7/1**[3]
32P5 **3** 2 **Resuscitator (USA)**[54] 7069 3-9-3 70 (p) EddieAhern 6 62
(Mrs H S Main) *led: rdn over 2f out: hdd and no ex ins fnl f* **4/1**[2]
4 2½ **Little Luxury (IRE)**[11] 7707 3-8-12 64 (v[1]) SeamieHeffernan 10 50
(Edward Lynam, Ire) *wl plcd bhd ldrs: rdn to chal wl over 1f out: sn nt qckn: wknd fnl f* **6/4**[1]
56 **5** ½ **Officer Lily (USA)**[154] 4028 3-8-12 0 LukeMorris 7 49
(J R Best) *sn rdn to stay in tch towards rr: kpt on fnl 2f: nrst fin* **16/1**
0 **6** 1½ **Kassiodor (GER)**[34] 7406 3-9-3 0 TomQueally 3 50
(B J Curley) *trckd ldr: shkn up 3f out: lost 2nd and fdd over 1f out* **33/1**
055 **7** 7 **Flying Cherry (IRE)**[43] 7288 3-8-12 51 FergusSweeney 11 26
(Miss Jo Crowley) *prom: rdn to dispute 2nd over 2f out: sn lost pl and wknd* **11/1**
0 **8** 1¾ **Bianco Boy (USA)**[249] 1222 3-9-0 0 KierenFox(3) 1 26
(J R Best) *dwlt: sn drvn in rr: nvr gng wl: bhd fnl 2f* **12/1**
00 **9** nse **Epsom Girl**[55] 7043 3-8-13 0 ow1 IanMongan 8 22
(P M Phelan) *sn detached in last: nvr a factor* **20/1**
/0-0 **10** 9 **Fiveonthreeforjd**[324] 291 5-9-3 40 TravisBlock 9 —
(W J H Ratcliffe) *s.s: a in last pair: t.o* **50/1**

1m 26.03s (0.03) **Going Correction** +0.025s/f (Slow) **10** Ran SP% **116.6**
Speed ratings (Par 101): **100,99,97,94,94 92,84,82,82,72**
toteswingers:1&2:£6.60, 1&3:£3.70, 2&3:£3.80 CSF £54.10 TOTE £10.00: £1.60, £3.20, £1.10; EX 31.70.
Owner Trebles Holford Thoroughbreds **Bred** Trebles Holford Farm Thoroughbreds **Trained** Kingsclere, Hants

FOCUS
A weak maiden and one in which the market leaders proved disappointing. The gallop was an ordinary one and the winner raced centre-to-far-side in the closing stages. The first two are rated up around 8lb.

7873 EUROPEAN BREEDERS' FUND KIA SPORTAGE MAIDEN STKS 1m (P)
4:55 (4:56) (Class 5) 2-Y-O **£3,076** (£915; £457; £228) **Stalls** High

Form RPR
2 **1** **Yaseer (IRE)**[53] 7099 2-9-3 0 GeorgeBaker 6 83+
(M P Tregoning) *hld up in midfield: prog over 2f out: stl looked green but pushed into ld over 1f out: qckly asserted* **4/6**[1]
2 2½ **Energizing** 2-9-3 0 JimmyFortune 7 74+
(R Hannon) *trckd ldrs: swtchd ins and effrt jst over 2f out: tried to chal over 1f out: kpt on but no ch w wnr* **50/1**
524 **3** 1½ **School For Scandal (IRE)**[11] 7693 2-9-3 71 KierenFallon 1 71
(M Johnston) *racd wd: pressed ldng pair: pushed along over 3f out: nt qckn and lost pl 2f out: shkn up and kpt on to take 3rd nr fin* **8/1**[3]
02 **4** ¾ **Silenzio**[35] 7385 2-9-3 0 RyanMoore 5 69
(R Hannon) *led to over 3f out: drvn into narrow ld again over 2f out: hdd over 1f out: wknd ins fnl f* **4/1**[2]
0 **5** 1¼ **Holcombe Boy**[68] 6712 2-9-3 0 StevieDonohoe 8 66
(J Pearce) *w ldr: led over 3f out: drvn and hdd over 2f out: wknd jst over 1f out* **12/1**
6 2½ **Rasheed** 2-9-3 0 TomQueally 4 60
(J H M Gosden) *in tch in rr: pushed along over 4f out and rn green: lft bhd over 2f out: kpt on* **14/1**
7 ½ **Ilissos (USA)** 2-9-3 0 ShaneKelly 3 59
(J Noseda) *in tch in rr: pushed along fr 1/2-way: lft bhd over 2f out: plugged on* **33/1**
0 **8** 3½ **Laser Blazer**[17] 7609 2-9-3 0 JimmyQuinn 10 51
(Miss S L Davison) *t.k.h: trckd ldrs: cl up 3f out: wknd over 2f out* **66/1**
9 3 **Area Fifty One** 2-9-3 0 NickyMackay 9 44
(J H M Gosden) *sn dropped to last and drvn: nvr a factor* **25/1**
10 ¾ **Star Danser** 2-9-3 0 SteveDrowne 2 43
(T Keddy) *s.s: sn in tch in rr: wknd over 2f out* **80/1**

1m 39.98s (0.18) **Going Correction** +0.025s/f (Slow) **10** Ran SP% **116.9**
Speed ratings (Par 96): **100,97,96,95,94 91,91,87,84,83**
toteswingers:1&2:£7.40, 1&3:£2.70 , 2&3:£10.10 CSF £62.78 TOTE £2.00: £1.10, £4.10, £1.70; EX 26.10.
Owner Hamdan Al Maktoum **Bred** Shadwell Estate Company Limited **Trained** Lambourn, Berks

FOCUS
A fair maiden for the track and the winner looks a useful prospect at least. The gallop was an ordinary one and the winner raced down the centre. The third helps with the standard.

NOTEBOOK
Yaseer(IRE) ◆, no match for a very exciting prospect on his debut at Newbury, faced nothing of that calibre this time and probably did not have to improve too much to win in decisive fashion on this all-weather debut. He should have no problems with 1m2f, is open to plenty of improvement and appeals strongly as the type to win more races. (tchd evens in places and 10-11 in a place)
Energizing, a 24,000gns first foal of a maiden claiming winner (on Polytrack), was no match for the ready winner but nevertheless shaped with promise on this racecourse debut, despite his big odds. He is entitled to come on for this experience and should be able to pick up a small race in due course. (op 40-1)
School For Scandal(IRE), who underlined his vulnerability in this grade but who seemed to give it his best shot on this return to Polytrack and he looks the best guide to this form. He should be able to pick up an ordinary handicap. He looks well worth a try over 1m2f. (tchd 9-1)
Silenzio, who finished a fair way behind the winner after his saddle slipped on his debut, had shown fair form on Polytrack on his next start and probably ran to a similar level this time after enjoying the run of the race. He should be able to win a small race. (tchd 7-2)
Holcombe Boy bettered the form shown at Wolverhampton on his debut but the best of him is unlikely to be seen until he steps into ordinary handicap company. (tchd 10-1)
Rasheed, in the same ownership as the winner, has a stack of winners from 1m-1m4f in his pedigree but he only hinted at ability after proving easy to back in the market. He should be able to step up on these bare facts in due course. (tchd 16-1)
Ilissos(USA) is out of a prolific winner in the US/Chile but was too green to do himself justice on this racecourse debut. He should do better with time.

7874 DIGIBET CASINO H'CAP 1m (P)
5:25 (5:25) (Class 6) (0-60,60) 3-Y-O **£1,637** (£483; £241) **Stalls** High

Form RPR
0651 **1** **Zafeen's Pearl**[54] 7070 3-9-0 53 SamHitchcott 5 64
(D K Ivory) *led after 1f: mde rest: drvn clr wl over 1f out: in n.d after* **8/1**
0062 **2** 3½ **Suzhou**[26] 7502 3-9-7 60 (v) CathyGannon 7 63
(D J Coakley) *plld hrd: chsd wnr after 2f: hrd rdn 2f out: no imp after: kpt on fnl f* **9/2**[2]
3-00 **3** nk **Valkov**[58] 6992 3-9-4 60 KierenFox(3) 8 62
(E A Wheeler) *pushed along in midfield after 2f: u.p and wd bnd 3f out: sn dropped to rr: styd on wl fr over 1f out: tk 3rd nr fin* **20/1**
5606 **4** nk **Ice Road Trucker (IRE)**[4] 7829 3-8-6 48 (p) MatthewDavies(3) 4 49
(J R Boyle) *prom: rdn sn after 1/2-way: struggling to hold pl over 2f out: kpt on to take 3rd briefly ins fnl f* **12/1**
0005 **5** 2 **Decency (IRE)**[9] 7725 3-9-5 58 LukeMorris 1 55
(H J L Dunlop) *v awkwardly away and lost several l: sn in tch in rr: prog 3f out: rdn to dispute 2nd over 1f out: wknd ins fnl f* **16/1**
6 ¾ **Haveahaarth (IRE)**[10] 7752 3-9-4 57 6ex (tp) TomQueally 10 52
(Michael Butler, Ire) *trckd ldrs: rdn over 2f out: nt qckn wl over 1f out: wknd fnl f* **7/2**[1]
1000 **7** hd **Usquaebach**[21] 7561 3-9-6 59 IanMongan 6 54
(P M Phelan) *led 1f: lost pl after 2f: drvn and tried to rally on inner 2f out: wknd fnl f* **7/1**
4130 **8** nk **Ting Ting (USA)**[58] 6993 3-9-6 59 (t) GeorgeBaker 11 53
(J R Boyle) *settled in last trio: shkn up 2f out: no imp on ldrs: kpt on* **8/1**
1401 **9** ¾ **Denton Ryal**[36] 4761 3-9-4 57 JamieGoldstein 9 49
(Miss Sheena West) *settled in last pair: bandage worked loose fr 1/2-way: rdn and struggling 3f out* **10/1**
5312 **10** 4 **Marksbury**[7] 7768 3-9-0 60 NathanAlison(7) 3 43
(J M P Eustace) *racd wd: hld up in rr: effrt and v wd bnd 3f out: lost grnd and sn wknd* **11/2**[3]

1m 39.74s (-0.06) **Going Correction** +0.025s/f (Slow) **10** Ran SP% **117.9**
Speed ratings (Par 98): **101,97,97,96,94 94,93,93,92,88**
toteswingers:1&2:£8.50, 1&3:£58.10, 2&3:£21.40 CSF £44.46 CT £705.61 TOTE £11.50: £3.60, £2.40, £6.20; EX 51.70.
Owner John Reddington **Bred** Mr And Mrs L Baker **Trained** Radlett, Herts

FOCUS
A moderate handicap and one run at just a steady early gallop. The winner raced towards the centre in the straight. The form has been taken at face value.
Marksbury Official explanation: jockey said filly ran flat

7875 SUNBURY STKS (LISTED RACE) 7f (P)
5:55 (5:57) (Class 1) 3-Y-O+
£21,004 (£7,962; £3,984; £1,491; £1,491; £499) **Stalls** High

Form RPR
3001 **1** **Spirit Of Sharjah (IRE)**[25] 7522 5-9-4 100 JimmyQuinn 2 111+
(Miss J Feilden) *dropped in fr wd draw and hld up last: daring run against rail and gd prog 2f out: sustained effrt to ld ins fnl f: pushed out* **20/1**
2202 **2** 1 **Mosqueras Romance**[48] 7188 4-8-11 102 AdamKirby 10 101
(M Botti) *dwlt: hld up in midfield: prog on inner 2f out: drvn to chal fnl f: kpt on to take 2nd last strides* **8/1**
2640 **3** shd **Duff (IRE)**[60] 6923 7-9-2 110 (v) KJManning 6 106
(Edward Lynam, Ire) *pressed ldr: drvn to ld wl over 1f out: hdd and one pce ins fnl f* **11/2**[3]
0060 **4** 1 **Atlantic Story (USA)**[18] 7593 8-9-2 103 (bt) GrahamGibbons 7 103
(M W Easterby) *settled in 9th: shkn up over 2f out: no prog whn n.m.r over 1f out: styd on stoutly last 150yds: nrst fin* **25/1**
01 **4** dht **Angel's Pursuit (IRE)**[11] 7689 3-9-4 108 JimmyFortune 9 105
(R Hannon) *trckd ldng quartet: shkn up over 2f out: nvr quite pce to threaten but kpt on wl fnl f* **3/1**[1]
-202 **6** hd **Enact**[25] 7524 4-8-11 98 RyanMoore 11 98+
(Sir Michael Stoute) *hld up in midfield: prog on inner 2f out: tried to chal fnl f: hld whn n.m.r last 100yds: lost pl nr fin* **7/2**[2]

The Form Book, Raceform Ltd, Compton, RG20 6NL

3230 **7** *hd* **Beauchamp Viceroy**[6] 7800 6-9-2 104..........................(p) DaneO'Neill 3 102
(G A Butler) *hld up in last quartet and racd wd: shkn up over 2f out: prog jst over 1f out: kpt on fnl f: nvr able to chal* **14/1**

0000 **8** *nk* **Alhaban (IRE)**[11] 7697 4-9-2 87..........................(t) LukeMorris 13 101?
(R A Harris) *chsd ldng trio: reminders 1/2-way: struggling to hold pl after but kpt on same pce u.p* **66/1**

5155 **9** *1 1/2* **Docofthebay (IRE)**[25] 7522 6-9-2 94..........................(b) IanMongan 4 97
(D Nicholls) *racd wd: hld up in 6th: drvn over 2f out: hanging and nt qckn: wl hld fnl f: eased nr fin* **10/1**

0153 **10** *1/2* **Brave Prospector**[25] 7524 5-9-2 104..........................(t) GeorgeBaker 1 96
(Jane Chapple-Hyam) *hld up last quartet: nvr much room whn looking for room fr over 2f out: nvr on terms* **10/1**

6210 **11** *2* **Arteus**[11] 7689 4-9-2 91..........................(b) ShaneKelly 12 91
(Jane Chapple-Hyam) *led to wl over 1f out: wknd rapidly fnl f* **33/1**

0066 **12** *3* **Arganil (USA)**[25] 7524 5-9-4 98.......................... PhillipMakin 14 85
(K A Ryan) *settled in last quartet: brief effrt on inner over 2f out: sn rdn and struggling* **50/1**

0410 **13** *2 3/4* **Navajo Chief**[81] 6349 3-9-2 102.......................... KierenFallon 5 75
(A P Jarvis) *pressed ldng pair tl wknd over 2f out* **20/1**

1m 24.24s (-1.76) **Going Correction** +0.025s/f (Slow) **13** Ran SP% **118.3**
Speed ratings (Par 111): **111,109,109,108,108 108,108,107,106,105 103,99,96**
toteswingers:1&2:£19.80, 1&3:£19.00, 2&3:£8.70 CSF £160.83 TOTE £18.90: £5.30, £1.70, £3.10; EX 249.30.
Owner A Dee **Bred** Mrs Kathleen Reynolds **Trained** Exning, Suffolk

FOCUS
Several smart performers in a good-quality Listed event. The gallop in the first half of the race was only an ordinary one and the winner raced against the inside rail in the closing stages. He is rated better than ever.

NOTEBOOK
Spirit Of Sharjah(IRE) is at the top of his game and showed a striking turn of foot after being held up in a race run at just an ordinary gallop. He'd have been even better suited by a more truly run race and, although he would have been interesting in Dubai, he'll reportedly take in a Listed event at Deauville early next month before being put away for the winter. (op 16-1)
Mosqueras Romance is a smart performer who was fairly easy to back near the off but showed she was equally effective over 7f as over the 1m trip she was just beaten over in Listed company at Lingfield last month. She should be able to pick up a similar event up to 1m on synthetics. (op 6-1)
Duff(IRE), the highest rated of these and who won this race two years ago, had the run of the race and ran creditably back on a synthetic surface with the visor again fitted. He's also a smart sort on turf at up to 1m and, although he is fully exposed, he would be of interest if sent to Dubai next month. (op 9-2)
Atlantic Story(USA) hasn't been at his best since winning over this trip at Lingfield in January but he fared a bit better back over this trip. However he's the type that invariably needs things to fall just right and he'll have to show a bit more before he's a solid betting proposition in this grade. (tchd 28-1)
Angel's Pursuit(IRE), fresh from a career-best effort over course-and-distance in handicap company, got a good tow into the race and ran creditably back in Listed company. The way he travelled through this race suggested he'd be worth another try over 6f in this grade on this surface. (tchd 28-1)
Enact seems to stay this trip and isn't fully exposed on Polytrack but, although far from disgraced, left the impression that the step back to 6f in a race run at more of an end-to-end gallop would suit her ideally. (op 3-1)
Beauchamp Viceroy stays further so a muddling race over this trip was never going to see him in his most favourable light. He should be able to step up on these bare facts granted a more suitable test of stamina. (op 16-1 tchd 18-1)
Docofthebay(IRE)'s rider reported he hung right. Official explanation: jockey said gelding hung right (op 16-1)

7876 DIGIBET.COM H'CAP 1m 4f (P)
6:25 (6:25) (Class 4) (0-85,84) 3-Y-O **£3,885** (£1,156; £577; £288) **Stalls** Centre

Form RPR

1611 **1** **New Code**[60] 6933 3-8-7 **70**.......................... FergusSweeney 3 81+
(G L Moore) *hld up last: swift move 2f out to ld jst over 1f out: hung rt but sn drvn clr* **15/2**

0251 **2** *4* **Pittodrie Star (IRE)**[11] 7687 3-8-12 **75**.......................... DavidProbert 6 80
(A M Balding) *t.k.h: trckd ldng pair: rdn and nt qckn over 2f out: kpt on again fnl f to take 2nd nr fin* **9/4**[1]

3602 **3** *nk* **Fonterutoli (IRE)**[15] 7638 3-8-10 **73**.......................... DaneO'Neill 4 78
(R Ingram) *hld up in 5th: prog on inner over 2f out: rdn to ld briefly over 1f out: sn outpcd: lost 2nd nr fin* **16/1**

1434 **4** *1/2* **Lyric Poet (USA)**[42] 7293 3-9-0 **77**..........................(t) WilliamCarson 5 81
(G C Bravery) *hld up in 4th: rdn and nt qckn over 2f out: plugged on again fnl f* **7/2**[2]

5244 **5** *3* **Beggar's Opera (IRE)**[20] 7568 3-9-4 **81**..........................(bt) NickyMackay 2 80
(J H M Gosden) *trckd ldr: rdn to ld over 2f out: hdd & wknd over 1f out* **5/1**[3]

2251 **6** *1 3/4* **Valid Reason**[14] 7653 3-9-7 **84**.......................... AdamKirby 1 80
(D K Ivory) *led: kicked on over 3f out: drvn and hdd over 2f out: wknd over 1f out* **7/2**[2]

2m 34.94s (0.44) **Going Correction** +0.025s/f (Slow) **6** Ran SP% **109.5**
Speed ratings (Par 104): **99,96,96,95,93 92**
toteswingers:1&2:£2.10, 1&3:£7.40, 2&3:£7.20 CSF £23.54 TOTE £5.40: £4.40, £1.40; EX 13.80.
Owner Mrs Elizabeth Kiernan **Bred** Foursome Thoroughbreds **Trained** Lower Beeding, W Sussex

FOCUS
A fair handicap but one in which the gallop was no more than fair until picking up early in the straight. The winner drifted to the far rail late on but did it well and can rate higher. The second and third set the standard.

7877 SKYSPORTS.COM RACING CLASSIFIED STKS 6f (P)
6:55 (6:56) (Class 6) 3-Y-O+ **£1,637** (£483; £241) **Stalls** High

Form RPR

6055 **1** **Silvee**[14] 7656 3-8-11 54.......................... KierenFox(3) 3 55
(J J Bridger) *mde all: rdn 2f out: kpt on steadily and a holding on* **13/2**

0305 **2** *1 1/4* **Jemimaville (IRE)**[14] 7651 3-9-0 47..........................(v) WilliamCarson 6 51
(G C Bravery) *hld up in 5th: gng strly 1/2-way: rdn and nt qckn 2f out: kpt on same pce to take 2nd ins fnl f* **12/1**

4000 **3** *3/4* **Fiancee (IRE)**[37] 7380 4-9-0 49..........................(b) JackMitchell 7 49
(R Brotherton) *rdn in last trio after 2f: u.p after: kpt on fnl 2f to take 3rd wl ins fnl f* **9/2**[3]

0006 **4** *nk* **Suttonia (IRE)**[4] 7824 4-9-0 41.......................... TravisBlock 9 48
(Noel T Chance) *trckd ldng trio: rdn and nt qckn on inner over 2f out: kpt on again fnl f* **33/1**

0004 **5** *3/4* **Fayre Bella**[15] 7640 3-9-0 54.......................... FergusSweeney 10 45
(J Gallagher) *hld up in last trio: gng strly 1/2-way: pushed along and no prog 2f out: reminders and styd on fnl f: nvr nr ldrs* **4/1**[2]

P460 **6** *1/2* **Premier League**[17] 7614 3-9-0 55.......................... JimmyQuinn 4 44
(Miss J Feilden) *chsd wnr to over 3f out and over 2f out tl ins fnl f: wknd* **7/1**

4260 **7** *hd* **Mushy Peas (IRE)**[4] 7835 3-9-0 51..........................(v[1]) CathyGannon 8 43
(P D Evans) *plld hrd: swtchd shaply lft sn after s and rapid prog to trck wnr: hung lft and lost pl over 2f out: n.d fnl f* **5/2**[1]

3555 **8** *5* **Black Baccara**[5] 7808 3-8-9 54..........................(p) TobyAtkinson(5) 5 27
(P S McEntee) *hmpd sn after s: nvr gng wl in last rest of way* **9/1**

1m 14.23s (1.13) **Going Correction** +0.025s/f (Slow) **8** Ran SP% **113.2**
Speed ratings (Par 101): **93,91,90,89,88 88,88,81**
toteswingers:1&2:£5.80, 1&3:£5.20, 2&3:£11.40 CSF £77.60 TOTE £8.00: £2.10, £3.00, £1.20; EX 54.10.
Owner Mr & Mrs K Finch **Bred** Mr And Mrs K Finch **Trained** Liphook, Hants

FOCUS
A moderate classified event. The early gallop was an ordinary one and those held up were at a disadvantage. The winner raced centre-to-far side in the straight and the form is a big doubt over the form.
Mushy Peas(IRE) Official explanation: jockey said gelding ran too free
T/Plt: £68.10 to a £1 stake. Pool £69,330.91 - 742.70 winning units T/Qpdt: £24.30 to a £1 stake. Pool £6,285.72 - 191.00 winning units JN

7824 LINGFIELD (L-H)
Wednesday, December 15

OFFICIAL GOING: Standard
Wind: Light, across Weather: murky, cold

7878 BET SP+ WITH TOTESPORT 0800 221221 CLASSIFIED CLAIMING STKS 1m 2f (P)
12:05 (12:05) (Class 6) 3-Y-O+ **£1,774** (£523; £262) **Stalls** Low

Form RPR

063 **1** **Edgeworth (IRE)**[8] 7732 4-8-7 60..........................(p) FergusSweeney 2 68
(B G Powell) *stdd s: t.k.h: hld up in rr: switching to outer and effrt 2f out: hdwy and hung lft over 1f out: str run but stl edging lft ins fnl f: led on post* **8/1**[3]

2123 **2** *shd* **Dream Of Fortune (IRE)**[2] 7856 6-8-13 68..........................(bt) TomQueally 4 74+
(P D Evans) *t.k.h: hld up in tch in midfield: hdwy over 2f out: w ldr gng wl over 1f out: pushed into ld 1f out: drvn fnl 100yds: hdd on post* **2/1**[1]

0040 **3** *3/4* **Quanah Parker (IRE)**[34] 7403 4-9-0 69.......................... MichaelStainton(3) 7 76
(R M Whitaker) *in tch in midfield: effrt over 2f out: rdn to chse ldrs over 1f out: wnt 2nd ins fnl f tl fnl 75yds: keeping on same pce and hld whn nt clr run and eased nr fin* **18/1**

0506 **4** *3 1/4* **Dichoh**[9] 7725 7-8-13 65..........................(v) AdamKirby 3 66
(M Madgwick) *stdd s: rdn along early: in rr: stdy hdwy over 3f out: effrt and rdn on inner wl over 1f out: one pce and no imp fnl f* **10/1**

0345 **5** *1/2* **Merrymadcap (IRE)**[8] 7732 8-8-5 65.......................... LukeMorris 12 57
(Matthew Salaman) *chsd ldrs tl wnt 2nd 6f out: led over 3f out: rdn ent fnl 2f: hdd 1f out: sn outpcd and wl hld fnl 100yds* **11/1**

0504 **6** *2 1/4* **Turjuman (USA)**[28] 7480 5-8-13 69.......................... StevieDonohoe 1 60
(W J Musson) *s.i.s: bhd and rdn along early: clsd and in tch 7f out: rdn along over 3f out: kpt on but no threat to ldrs fr over 1f out* **9/1**

3230 **7** *1 1/2* **Bubbly Braveheart (IRE)**[17] 7611 3-8-0 62.......................... AndreaAtzeni 11 47
(A Bailey) *in tch: rdn to chse ldr wl over 2f out tl over 1f out: wknd fnl f* **10/3**[2]

/500 **8** *nse* **Vintage Quest**[77] 6472 8-8-3 42..........................(p) CathyGannon 5 47
(D Burchell) *in tch towards rr: rdn and unable qck whn n.m.r wl over 1f out: one pce and n.d after* **100/1**

0324 **9** *1/2* **Florio Vincitore (IRE)**[9] 7726 3-8-10 67.......................... ShaneKelly 9 56
(E J Creighton) *led tl 7f out: chsd ldrs after: rdn over 2f out: wknd over 1f out* **16/1**

0033 **10** *6* **Guga (IRE)**[12] 7678 4-8-9 64..........................(b) DavidProbert 6 40
(J Mackie) *chsd ldr for 1f: steadily lost pl: rdn and struggling 4f out: wl bhd fr wl over 1f out* **11/1**

5003 **11** *3/4* **Dawson Creek (IRE)**[9] 7727 6-8-9 51.......................... GregFairley 8 39
(L A Dace) *in tch: rdn to chse ldng pair 3f out: wknd qckly over 1f out* **50/1**

060 **12** *25* **Annie Bonita**[43] 7288 3-8-4 48.......................... ChrisCatlin 10 —
(P R Hedger) *t.k.h: chsd ldr after 1f tl led 7f out: hdd over 3f out: lost pl qckly over 2f out: t.o fnl f* **40/1**

2m 4.07s (-2.53) **Going Correction** +0.025s/f (Slow)
WFA 3 from 4yo+ 3lb **12** Ran SP% **119.8**
Speed ratings (Par 101): **111,110,110,107,107 105,104,104,103,99 98,78**
toteswingers:1&2:£4.20, 1&3:£34.10, 2&3:£10.20 CSF £24.41 TOTE £8.50: £2.00, £1.40, £6.00; EX 28.80 Trifecta £175.40 Part won. Pool £237.06 - 0.82 winning units..Bubbly Braveheart was claimed by P. Wheatley for £5,000.
Owner K Rhatigan **Bred** Yvonne & Gerard Kennedy **Trained** Upper Lambourn, Berks

FOCUS
A fair claimer, and the time was good, being just above standard and 1.37 seconds quicker than the later slowly run Class 4 handicap. The form is best judged around the first two.

7879 EBF BIGGER WINS WITH SP+ 0800 221221 MAIDEN FILLIES' STKS 7f (P)
12:35 (12:38) (Class 5) 2-Y-O **£3,070** (£906; £453) **Stalls** Low

Form RPR

5 **1** **Birdolini**[48] 7185 2-9-0 0.......................... FergusSweeney 12 71+
(A King) *s.i.s: hld up towards rr: gd hdwy on outer over 2f out: chsd ldr over 1f out: led 1f out: kpt on wl ins fnl f* **9/2**[2]

0 **2** *3/4* **Sottovoce**[193] 2749 2-9-0 0.......................... HayleyTurner 14 69
(S Dow) *chsd ldr: rdn along 4f out: led u.p ent fnl 2f: hdd 1f out: kpt on wl but a hld fnl f* **25/1**

3 *1 3/4* **Links Drive Lady** 2-9-0 0.......................... NickyMackay 9 64+
(M E Rimmer) *s.i.s: hld up towards rr: gd hdwy between horses jst over 1f out: chsd ldng pair and edgd lft ins fnl f: kpt on* **33/1**

540 **4** *1 1/4* **Close To The Edge (IRE)**[116] 5301 2-9-0 65.......................... JamesDoyle 13 61
(A J McCabe) *t.k.h early: hld up in tch towards rr: rdn and effrt towards outer ent fnl 2f: chsd ldrs 1f out: styd on same pce and no imp after* **12/1**

5 *1 3/4* **Snowy Peak** 2-9-0 0..........................(t) EddieAhern 5 56+
(J Noseda) *hld up in tch towards rr: pushed along and n.m.r over 2f out: hdwy over 1f out: styd on steadily ins fnl f: nvr trbld ldrs* **11/2**[3]

3624 **6** *nk* **Fenella Fudge**[54] 7049 2-9-0 77.......................... TomQueally 1 56
(J G Given) *in tch: hdwy to chse ldng pair 3f out: nt clr run ent fnl 2f: rdn and unable qck over 1f out: one pce and wl hld fnl f* **7/2**[1]

7 *1 1/2* **Go On The Badger** 2-9-0 0.......................... KirstyMilczarek 6 52
(J A R Toller) *sn chsng ldrs: rdn over 2f out: wknd u.p over 1f out* **16/1**

03 **8** *nk* **Wodian (IRE)**[12] 7681 2-9-0 0 DaneO'Neill 3 51+
(D R Lanigan) *hld up towards rr: effrt on inner and nt clr run ent fnl 2f: hdwy over 1f out: styd on same pce ins fnl f: nvr trbld ldrs* **20/1**

4 **9** *3/4* **Encore View**[17] 7608 2-9-0 0 DavidProbert 10 49
(A M Balding) *in tch: rdn and unable qck whn short of room 2f out: wknd u.p over 1f out* **7/2**[1]

00 **10** *1/2* **Tymismoni (IRE)**[121] 5147 2-8-11 0 KierenFox(3) 7 48+
(B R Johnson) *in tch in last trio: rdn and effrt ent fnl 2f: kpt on same pce fr over 1f out: nvr trbld ldrs* **50/1**

11 *1 1/4* **Katherine Parr** 2-9-0 0 JackMitchell 11 44
(P W Chapple-Hyam) *restless in stalls: rn green in last trio: nvr trbld ldrs* **14/1**

00 **12** *3/4* **Elusive Diva (IRE)**[51] 7113 2-9-0 0 ShaneKelly 2 48+
(E J Creighton) *in tch in midfield: effrt and rdn to chse ldrs jst over 2f out: styng on same pce and looking hld whn nt clr run and shuffled bk towards rr over 1f out: nt rcvr and switching rt ins fnl f* **100/1**

4 **13** *1 1/4* **Suspender Belt**[21] 7551 2-9-0 0 CathyGannon 4 39
(J R Best) *led tl rdn and hdd ent fnl 2f: wknd qckly over 1f out* **12/1**

0 **14** *3/4* **Nahawand (USA)**[11] 7686 2-8-11 0 MatthewDavies(3) 8 37
(J R Boyle) *in tch: rdn and unable qck jst over 2f out: wkng whn nt clr run and hmpd jst over 1f out: wl btn fnl f* **33/1**

1m 25.52s (0.72) **Going Correction** +0.025s/f (Slow) **14** Ran SP% **123.4**
Speed ratings (Par 93): **96,95,93,91,89 89,87,87,86,85 84,83,82,81**
toteswingers:1&2:£36.00, 1&3:£42.90, 2&3:£154.00 CSF £124.62 TOTE £5.10: £2.50, £13.30, £9.70; EX 195.90 TRIFECTA Not won..

Owner Mrs Robert Langton **Bred** Mrs Robert Langton **Trained** Barbury Castle, Wilts

FOCUS

The bare form looks just ordinary, although the time was fractionally quicker than the following maiden for juvenile colts and geldings. The winner can rate higher but the form is limited by a few down the field.

NOTEBOOK

Birdolini ◆ showed plenty of ability when fifth from the widest draw over C&D on her debut and she more than confirmed that promise after a 48-day break. Again poorly drawn, she was slowest away and raced well off the pace through the early stages. She was then forced to make her ground out wide, but produced a sustained challenge. It's fair to argue she's better than the bare result and could be useful. (op 7-2 tchd 5-1)

Sottovoce showed nothing on her only previous start in a 6f turf maiden here back in June, but this was a fair performance. She raced up with the pace throughout but kept on well. There should be improvement to come. (op 66-1)

Links Drive Lady, a 1,500gns first foal of a triple 7f Polytrack winner (all at Wolverhampton), raced a long way back towards the inside rail after missing the break, but she stayed on nicely, showing plenty of ability.

Close To The Edge(IRE), retuning from 116 days off, travelled well to a point but was one-paced under pressure and didn't fully see out this trip. A half-sister to, among others, smart Polytrack sprinter Qadar, she could do better in handicaps over shorter. (op 20-1)

Snowy Peak ◆, a half-sister to ill-fated Royal Lodge winner/2,000 Guineas 2nd Snow Ridge, made an encouraging debut and will know a lot more next time. Fitted with a tongue-tie, she was outpaced turning into the straight and dropped back to just about last, but she finished well. A step up in trip should suit. (op 7-2)

Fenella Fudge found little for pressure on her return from a 54-day break and is going the wrong way. (op 4-1 tchd 100-30)

Wodian(IRE) didn't get the clearest of runs into the straight and then made her bid against the often unfavoured inside rail. She could do better now handicaps are an option. (tchd 16-1)

Encore View failed to build on the form she showed when a modest fourth on her debut over 6f at Kempton. (op 9-2 tchd 100-30)

7880 EBF POWER2000.COM MAIDEN STKS 7f (P)

1:05 (1:10) (Class 5) 2-Y-O **£3,070** (£906; £453) **Stalls** Low

Form RPR

2 **1** **March On Beetroot**[11] 7700 2-9-0 0 ShaneKelly 6 76+
(R M H Cowell) *stdd s: t.k.h: hld up in tch: hdwy to trck ldrs 3f out: pressed ldr ent fnl 2f: pushed ahd ins fnl f: comf* **4/9**[1]

035 **2** *1* **Kingscroft (IRE)**[135] 4645 2-9-0 68 GregFairley 4 71
(M Johnston) *led: clr 4f out: pressed and rdn ent fnl 2f: kpt on wl tl hdd and unable qck fnl 100yds* **5/1**[2]

04 **3** *4* **The Auctioneer (IRE)**[11] 7700 2-9-0 0 JamieMackay 7 61+
(W J Musson) *in tch in midfield: rdn and outpcd by ldng pair over 1f out: no threat to ldrs after: kpt on to go 3rd wl ins fnl f* **25/1**

30 **4** *3/4* **Ezzles (USA)**[137] 4599 2-9-0 0 TomQueally 5 59
(P F I Cole) *t.k.h: chsd ldrs: rdn and effrt ent fnl 2f: outpcd by ldng pair over 1f out: one pce and wl hld fnl f: lost 3rd wl ins fnl f* **9/1**[3]

0 **5** *3* **Icebuster**[28] 7479 2-9-0 0 JamesMillman 2 51+
(B R Millman) *in tch in last pair: effrt and rdn over 2f out: n.m.r and swtchd ins wl over 1f out: sn wknd* **33/1**

5 **6** *1 3/4* **Polish Sunset**[21] 7551 2-9-0 0 HayleyTurner 8 46
(Miss Amy Weaver) *chsd ldr tl jst over 2f out: sn wknd u.p* **10/1**

7 *21* **Alston** 2-9-0 0 CathyGannon 1 —
(D W P Arbuthnot) *s.i.s: rn green in rr: rdn ent fnl 4f: lost tch qckly over 2f out: eased fnl f: t.o* **16/1**

1m 25.6s (0.80) **Going Correction** +0.025s/f (Slow) **7** Ran SP% **117.7**
Speed ratings (Par 96): **96,94,90,89,86 84,60**
toteswingers:1&2:£1.50, 1&3:£5.50, 2&3:£7.60 CSF £3.40 TOTE £1.50: £1.10, £2.50; EX 3.10 Trifecta £28.10 Pool £479.78 - 12.61 winning units..

Owner G S Shropshire **Bred** West Dereham Abbey Stud **Trained** Six Mile Bottom, Cambs

FOCUS

An uncompetitive maiden, it was steadily run and the time was 0.08 seconds slower than the earlier fillies' version. The form is taken at face value and not sure to work out, but the winner and third have plenty of potential.

NOTEBOOK

March On Beetroot ◆ readily confirmed the promise he showed when runner-up (clear of remainder) on his debut over this trip at Wolverhampton. A scopey type, he travelled with noticeable ease and, still green when asked for his effort, had more to spare than the margins suggest. It remains to be seen what his optimum trip will be, as although by Cape Cross, his dam was a successful sprinter and he's certainly not short of speed. He could be very useful as he matures both mentally and physically and is likely to be put away now. (op 4-6 tchd 2-5)

Kingscroft(IRE), upped in trip and trying Polytrack for the first time after a 135-day break, had his chance under a positive ride, but he bumped into a potentially decent sort. (op 7-2)

The Auctioneer(IRE) ◆ very much caught the eye keeping on from a long way back behind March On Beetroot at Wolverhampton last time, and this performance was equally promising. He would surely have finished closer had he been more vigorously ridden and is now qualified for a mark. Bred to improve over middle-distances next year, he's a fine handicap prospect. (op 20-1)

Ezzles(USA), upped a couple of furlongs in trip after 137 days off, didn't see his race out. He's entitled to come on for this and may do better over sprint trips in handicaps. (op 8-1)

7881 BET ON TONIGHT'S FOOTBALL AT TOTESPORT.COM H'CAP 1m 2f (P)

1:40 (1:41) (Class 4) (0-85,85) 3-Y-O+ **£3,885** (£1,156; £577; £288) **Stalls** Low

Form RPR

1641 **1** **Dark Promise**[15] 7638 3-9-1 82 JimmyFortune 1 92+
(M A Jarvis) *mde all: rdn and clr over 1f out: in command fnl f: rdn out* **6/4**[1]

5526 **2** *3/4* **The Which Doctor**[7] 7756 5-9-7 85 (p) GeorgeBaker 7 90
(J Noseda) *hld up in tch: rdn and effrt over 1f out: chsd wnr ins fnl f: kpt on wl but nvr able to chal wnr* **7/2**[2]

6001 **3** *1 3/4* **Lingfield Bound (IRE)**[21] 7561 3-8-4 71 oh1 LukeMorris 5 73
(J R Best) *in tch in midfield: rdn and effrt over 2f out: chsd wnr over 1f out: kpt on same pce after: lost 2nd ins fnl f* **16/1**

12- **4** *1 3/4* **Farleigh House (USA)**[47] 6830 6-9-5 83 HayleyTurner 3 81
(N B King) *hld up in last pair: hdwy ent fnl f: kpt on: nt pce to trble wnr* **25/1**

1002 **5** *1/2* **Dubai Crest**[7] 7756 4-9-7 85 ShaneKelly 6 82
(Mrs A J Perrett) *t.k.h early: hld up in tch: rdn and effrt on inner ent fnl 2f: one pce and no imp fnl f* **7/1**[3]

0050 **6** *2 1/2* **King's Colour**[21] 7560 5-9-4 82 AdamKirby 4 74
(B R Johnson) *chsd ldr: rdn ent fnl 2f: lost 2nd over 1f out: wknd fnl f* **8/1**

0305 **7** *shd* **Stand Guard**[7] 7756 6-9-1 79 JimmyQuinn 8 71
(Jane Chapple-Hyam) *chsd ldrs: effrt u.p on outer bnd 2f out: wknd ent fnl f* **9/1**

063 **8** *3* **Bedouin Bay**[8] 7736 3-8-8 75 JamesDoyle 2 61
(A J McCabe) *dwlt: sn pushed along and rcvrd to chse ldrs: rdn over 2f out: wknd u.p over 1f out* **12/1**

2m 5.37s (-1.23) **Going Correction** +0.025s/f (Slow)
WFA 3 from 4yo+ 3lb **8** Ran SP% **113.3**
Speed ratings (Par 105): **105,104,103,101,101 99,99,96**
toteswingers:1&2:£2.50, 1&3:£6.80, 2&3:£8.50 CSF £6.51 CT £55.73 TOTE £2.10: £1.10, £1.80, £5.20; EX 7.40 Trifecta £48.20 Pool £611.00 - 9.37 winning units.

Owner Lordship Stud **Bred** Lordship Stud **Trained** Newmarket, Suffolk

FOCUS

A fair handicap run at a slow gallop with the winner given an easy time in front. He is unexposed and capable of better still.

7882 MORE LIVE FOOTBALL BETTING AT TOTESPORT.COM H'CAP (DIV I) 6f (P)

2:15 (2:15) (Class 6) (0-55,55) 3-Y-O+ **£1,706** (£503; £252) **Stalls** Low

Form RPR

5044 **1** **Dualagi**[4] 7827 6-9-2 55 GeorgeBaker 11 64
(M R Bosley) *broke fast and crossed to rail: mde all: rdn clr ent fnl f: in command after: eased nr fin* **4/1**[1]

0004 **2** *1 3/4* **Memphis Man**[8] 7738 7-8-8 54 MatthewCosham(7) 2 57
(P D Evans) *hld up in midfield: effrt u.p over 1f out: r.o u.p to go 2nd fnl 75yds: no threat to wnr* **11/1**

4004 **3** *nk* **A Pocketful Of Rye (IRE)**[18] 7604 3-8-6 48 MichaelStainton(3) 8 50
(Jane Chapple-Hyam) *hld up in last trio: rdn and effrt wl over 1f out: r.o u.p ins fnl f: wnt 3rd towards fin: no threat to wnr* **5/1**[2]

0100 **4** *1* **Final Rhapsody**[15] 7640 4-8-13 52 StevieDonohoe 10 51
(W J Musson) *bhd: kpt on wl u.p ins fnl f: wnt 4th towards fin: nvr trbld ldrs* **8/1**

035 **5** *1/2* **Metropolitan Chief**[45] 7249 6-8-12 51 LukeMorris 7 49
(P Burgoyne) *sn chsng ldr: rdn and pressed ldr over 1f out: outpcd 1f out and wl hld fnl 150yds: lost 3 pls fnl 75yds* **8/1**

0560 **6** *1/2* **Woodsley House (IRE)**[7] 7761 8-8-12 51 NickyMackay 4 47
(M E Rimmer) *chsd ldrs: rdn ent fnl 2f: outpcd jst over 1f out: plugged on same pce and no ch w wnr ins fnl f* **8/1**

0631 **7** *shd* **Mind The Monarch**[6] 7783 3-8-6 50 (v) RyanPowell(5) 1 46
(R A Teal) *chsd ldrs: rdn and effrt over 1f out: hrd rdn and unable qck ent fnl f: one pce and no ch w wnr fnl 150yds* **4/1**[1]

1104 **8** *1* **Bubbly Bellini (IRE)**[11] 7709 3-8-13 55 (p) MatthewDavies(3) 3 48
(Lee Smyth, Ire) *hld up in last trio: rdn and hdwy on inner over 1f out: no imp u.p ins fnl f* **6/1**[3]

0000 **9** *4* **Albaher**[2] 7860 4-8-8 47 oh1 ow1 (b) RobbieFitzpatrick 5 27
(Peter Grayson) *in tch in midfield: rdn and struggling jst over 2f out: wknd over 1f out* **66/1**

-600 **10** *8* **Auburn Place**[176] 3291 3-9-0 53 (v[1]) DaneO'Neill 9 —
(D Shaw) *in tch in midfield on outer: rdn and struggling over 2f out: wknd wl over 1f out: wl btn and eased ins fnl f* **16/1**

1m 11.98s (0.08) **Going Correction** +0.025s/f (Slow) **10** Ran SP% **120.0**
Speed ratings (Par 101): **100,97,97,95,95 94,94,93,87,77**
toteswingers:1&2:£8.10, 1&3:£4.60, 2&3:£8.30 CSF £50.86 CT £233.03 TOTE £4.20: £1.10, £4.80, £2.20; EX 42.60 Trifecta £320.70 Part won. Pool £433.38 - 0.20 winning units..

Owner Inca Financial Services **Bred** B Burrough **Trained** Chalfont St Giles, Bucks

FOCUS

The time was 0.25 seconds slower than the second division. The winner is rated to her best form in the last two years.

Auburn Place Official explanation: jockey said filly moved poorly

7883 MORE LIVE FOOTBALL BETTING AT TOTESPORT.COM H'CAP (DIV II) 6f (P)

2:50 (2:50) (Class 6) (0-55,55) 3-Y-O+ **£1,706** (£503; £252) **Stalls** Low

Form RPR

042 **1** **Mr Skipiton (IRE)**[33] 7426 5-9-2 55 LiamJones 11 65
(B J McMath) *racd off the pce in midfield: rdn and hdwy ent fnl 2f: chal 1f out: led ins fnl f: kpt on wl* **7/2**[1]

000 **2** *1/2* **Grand Honour (IRE)**[95] 5962 4-8-12 51 StevieDonohoe 7 59
(Jane Chapple-Hyam) *sn outpcd in last: hdwy over 1f out: r.o wl u.p ins fnl f: nvr quite getting to wnr* **7/2**[1]

0054 **3** *shd* **Goodbye Cash (IRE)**[4] 7829 6-8-9 55 JamesRogers(7) 1 63
(R J Smith) *chsd ldrs: rdn and effrt on inner 2f out: led jst ins fnl f: hdd and one pce ins fnl f: lost 2nd nr fin* **5/1**[2]

6605 **4** *1 1/2* **Royal Box**[27] 7377 3-8-8 52 (p) RyanClark(5) 6 55
(D Burchell) *chsd ldr tl over 2f out: stl ev ch and rdn over 1f out: one pce and btn ins fnl f* **7/1**[3]

0000 **5** *3/4* **West Leake (IRE)**[15] 7639 4-9-1 54 LukeMorris 3 55
(P Burgoyne) *chsd ldrs: hdwy to chal whn hung rt bnd 2f out: rdn to ld 1f out: sn hdd: wknd ins fnl f* **14/1**

6040 **6** *1/2* **Ariel Bender**[5] 7807 3-8-8 47 oh1 ow1 (b) RobbieFitzpatrick 8 46
(Peter Grayson) *sn pushed along in last trio: hdwy and styng on whn nt clr run and swtchd rt ins fnl f: kpt on fnl 100yds: nt rch ldrs* **66/1**

0300 **7** *nk* **Rio Sands**[22] 7542 5-8-8 50 MichaelStainton(3) 9 48
(R M Whitaker) *in tch: rdn and unable qck ent fnl 2f: no imp ent fnl f* **10/1**

0002 **8** *1 3/4* **Thoughtsofstardom**[5] 7807 7-8-10 54 TobyAtkinson(5) 5 46
(P S McEntee) *led: rdn wl over 1f out: hdd 1f out: wknd fnl f* **8/1**

0000 **9** *3 1/2* **Grand Palace (IRE)**[5] 7808 7-8-10 49 (v) DaneO'Neill 2 30
(D Shaw) *racd off the pce in midfield: rdn and struggling ent fnl 2f: no prog and wl hld fr over 1f out* **14/1**

0420 **10** *1/2* **Lordsbury Pride (USA)**[4] 7827 3-8-11 53 (v) KierenFox(3) 10 33
(J R Best) *sn rdn along in last trio: nvr trbld ldrs* **7/1**[3]

1m 11.73s (-0.17) **Going Correction** +0.025s/f (Slow) **10** Ran SP% **121.1**
Speed ratings (Par 101): **102,101,101,99,98 97,97,94,90,89**
toteswingers:1&2:£4.10, 1&3:£4.60, 2&3:£7.40 CSF £15.95 CT £64.36 TOTE £3.70: £1.10, £2.30, £2.50; EX 21.80 Trifecta £50.10 Pool £374.05 - 5.52 winning units.
Owner Steve & Ros Chaplin-Brown **Bred** Darragh O'Reilly **Trained** Newmarket, Suffolk

FOCUS
The time was 0.25 seconds quicker than the first division. The sixth is a bit of a doubt but the form makes sense around the front four.
Rio Sands Official explanation: jockey said gelding was denied a clear run

7884 PLAY BINGO AT TOTESPORT.COM APPRENTICE H'CAP 1m 4f (P)
3:25 (3:25) (Class 5) (60-92,75) 3-Y-O+ **£2,388** (£705; £352) **Stalls** Low

Form RPR

5522 **1** **Archie Rice (USA)**[7] 7765 4-8-10 **66** RyanClark(5) 6 72+
(T Keddy) *t.k.h: chsd ldrs tl settled in front 10f out: mde rest: rdn and qcknd clr over 1f out: in n.d fnl f: eased towards fin* **11/4**[2]

2555 **2** *3 1/2* **Green Wadi**[11] 7687 5-8-10 **68** ChelseyBanks(7) 7 65+
(G L Moore) *t.k.h: hld up in last pair: effrt on inner wl over 1f out: no ch w wnr but kpt on to go 2nd ins fnl f* **6/1**[3]

521 **3** *1 1/4* **Albertus Pictor**[19] 7575 3-8-12 **73** RosieJessop(5) 1 68+
(Sir Mark Prescott) *stdd s: t.k.h: hld up in tch: chsd ldrs and n.m.r jst over 2f out: sn rdn and outpcd: no ch w wnr 1f out: kpt on again towards fin* **8/11**[1]

000 **4** *1/2* **Rosy Dawn**[9] 7728 5-8-10 **61** oh16 MartinLane 3 55?
(L A Dace) *t.k.h: led tl 10f out: chsd ldrs after tl rdn and nt pce of wnr over 1f out: 2nd and wl hld 1f out: lost 2 pls wl ins fnl f* **33/1**

0034 **5** *2* **Robby Bobby**[6] 7778 5-8-7 **65** CharlotteJenner(7) 2 56
(Mrs L J Mongan) *mostly chsd ldr tl rdn: outpcd by wnr and lost 2nd over 1f out: n.d fnl f* **13/2**

31-0 **6** *17* **Lord Chancellor (IRE)**[10] 7753 4-9-5 **70** (tp) MatthewDavies 4 34
(Lee Smyth, Ire) *w ldrs for 2f: stdd and in tch in last pair 9f out: rdn along and no rspnse wl over 3f out: wknd ent fnl 2f* **20/1**

2m 34.87s (1.87) **Going Correction** +0.025s/f (Slow)
WFA 3 from 4yo+ 5lb **6** Ran SP% **119.9**
Speed ratings (Par 103): **94,91,90,90,89 77**
toteswingers:1&2:£2.20, 1&3:£1.40, 2&3:£2.30 CSF £20.74 CT £23.21 TOTE £4.00: £1.80, £1.90; EX 14.90 Trifecta £33.30 Pool £876.72 - 19.42 winning units..
Owner Andrew Duffield **Bred** Baltusrol Thoughbreds Llc Et Al **Trained** Newmarket, Suffolk
■ Stewards' Enquiry : Chelsey Banks eight-day ban: failed to take all reasonable and permissable measures to obtain best possible placing (Dec 29-Jan 5)

FOCUS
The pace, dictated by the winner from an early stage, was slow (time over five seconds above standard), and both the runner-up and third-placed were poorly ridden, so this is form to treat with caution. The winner was value for 6l but did not need to be at his best, and the fourth limits the form.
Green Wadi Official explanation: jockey said, regarding running and riding, that her orders were to ensure the gelding got cover in order to help it settle and to improve from 4f out, but it became stuck in a pocket until straightening for home at which point she allowed it to stride out; trainer's rep said the gelding is a "bridle horse" who tends not to respond to strong pressure; vet said gelding was found to be two-three tenths lame right-fore.
Lord Chancellor(IRE) Official explanation: jockey said gelding made a noise
T/Plt: £54.60 to a £1 stake. Pool:£40,148.28 - 535.91 winning tickets T/Qpdt: £3.90 to a £1 stake. Pool:£4,797.24 - 893.60 winning tickets SP

7871 KEMPTON (A.W) (R-H)
Thursday, December 16

OFFICIAL GOING: Standard
Wind: Strong across Weather: Sleet turning to snow

7885 WELCOME TO SEABET.COM H'CAP 7f (P)
4:00 (4:01) (Class 7) (0-50,53) 3-Y-O+ **£1,364** (£403; £201) **Stalls** High

Form RPR

2630 **1** **Aqua Vitae (IRE)**[50] 7161 3-9-3 50 CathyGannon 2 58
(Miss Tor Sturgis) *in rr: stl last on bnd ins fnl 3f: hdwy and n.m.r on ins over 2f out: rapid hdwy over 1f out to ld jst ins fnl f: r.o strly* **33/1**

0030 **2** *1 3/4* **Jonny Ebeneezer**[7] 7783 11-9-2 49 (be) JamesDoyle 11 52
(D Flood) *chsd ldrs: rdn to chal appr fnl f: chsd wnr sn after: no imp whn hung rt fnl 50yds* **50/1**

0555 **3** *1/2* **Cane Cat (IRE)**[7] 7783 3-9-1 48 (t) AdamKirby 4 52+
(A W Carroll) *hld up in rr: nt clr run ins fnl 2f: styng on whn hmpd fnl 50yds: swtchd rt: r.o but nt rcvr* **25/1**

0-60 **4** *1/2* **Lend A Light**[7] 7783 4-9-3 50 DaneO'Neill 5 51
(P J Hobbs) *s.i.s: in rr tl stdy hdwy fr over 2f out: r.o ins fnl f: no imp whn hung lft fnl 50yds* **11/2**[2]

000 **5** *nk* **Polemica (IRE)**[5] 7835 4-9-2 49 (bt) JimmyQuinn 14 49
(F Sheridan) *s.i.s: sn in tch: drvn and qcknd to chal appr fnl f: one pce fnl 120yds* **16/1**

2056 **6** *shd* **Novillero**[19] 7605 3-9-1 48 SamHitchcott 8 49+
(J C Fox) *s.i.s: in rr: hdwy whn checked wl over 1f out: styng on whn hmpd fnl 50yds: nt rcvr* **20/1**

0034 **7** *2* **Song Of Praise**[18] 7607 4-9-3 50 SteveDrowne 10 44
(M Blanshard) *in tch: rdn and effrt to chse ldrs over 2f out: wknd ins fnl f* **12/1**

2500 **8** *hd* **Kenswick**[148] 4249 3-9-3 50 (v[1]) AndreaAtzeni 13 44
(Pat Eddery) *chsd ldrs: wnt 2nd 3f out: slt ld appr fnl f: hdd sn after: wknd fnl f: btn whn n.m.r fnl 50yds* **14/1**

0000 **9** *1 3/4* **Suhayl Star (IRE)**[7] 7783 6-9-1 48 GeorgeBaker 6 37
(P Burgoyne) *led after 1f: sn clr: stl traveling wl 2f out: wknd and hdd appr fnl f* **40/1**

0420 **10** *1/2* **Ymir**[15] 7649 4-9-3 50 (vt) RobbieFitzpatrick 9 37
(M J Attwater) *racd towards outside: outpcd* **10/1**

5001 **11** *1/2* **Clever Omneya (USA)**[5] 7835 4-9-6 53 6ex EddieAhern 7 39
(J R Jenkins) *chsd ldrs: rdn and wknd over 1f out* **5/4**[1]

000 **12** *1 1/2* **Royal Envoy (IRE)**[19] 7605 7-8-13 49 MichaelStainton(3) 1 31
(Jane Chapple-Hyam) *racd wd: a outpcd* **9/1**[3]

0004 **13** *3/4* **Stonecrabstomorrow (IRE)**[21] 7564 7-8-12 50 (b) MarkCoumbe(5) 3 30
(R C Guest) *s.i.s: outpcd* **33/1**

0263 **14** *10* **La Chemme**[5] 7838 4-9-2 49 FergusSweeney 12 2
(R Hollinshead) *led 1f: styd chsng ldr to 3f out: wknd wl over 2f out* **16/1**

1m 26.63s (0.63) **Going Correction** -0.025s/f (Stan) **14** Ran SP% **123.9**
Speed ratings (Par 97): **95,93,92,91,91 91,89,88,86,86 85,84,83,71**
toteswingers:1&2:£97.30, 1&3:£42.70, 2&3:£41.00 CSF £1152.03 CT £35032.18 TOTE £51.20: £13.80, £15.30, £7.70; EX 1182.10.
Owner David Redvers **Bred** Miss Mary Davison **Trained** Upper Lambourn, Berks
■ Stewards' Enquiry : Dane O'Neill one-day ban: careless riding (Dec 30)

FOCUS
The pace was overly strong, courtesy of the free-running Suhayl Star. The winner is rated to her handicap best and the form seems fairly sound.
Stonecrabstomorrow(IRE) Official explanation: jockey said gelding ran too free

7886 BET BIG, WIN BIG AT SEABET.COM CLAIMING STKS 7f (P)
4:30 (4:30) (Class 6) 2-Y-O **£1,637** (£483; £241) **Stalls** High

Form RPR

6602 **1** **Silver Age (IRE)**[15] 7650 2-8-7 63 (p) CathyGannon 4 67
(J S Moore) *trckd ldng duo: wnt 2nd ins fnl 3f: drvn to ld 2f out: pushed out fnl f: readily* **11/4**[3]

0645 **2** *1* **Foxtrot Golf (IRE)**[20] 7572 2-8-4 73 JamesRogers(7) 3 68
(P Winkworth) *led after 1f: rdn and hdd 2f out: rallied and styd on ins fnl f but a readily hld* **6/4**[1]

4 **3** *3/4* **Eternal Youth (IRE)**[8] 7762 2-9-3 0 (p) SeamieHeffernan 1 72
(R A Harris) *racd in 4th: hdwy to take 3rd over 2f out: rdn and styd on thrght fnl f but nvr gng pce to rch ldng duo* **10/1**

3333 **4** *9* **Sir Lunchalott**[8] 7762 2-8-13 70 JamesDoyle 2 45
(J S Moore) *led 1f: chsd ldr tl ins fnl 3f: sn btn* **2/1**[2]

1m 26.7s (0.70) **Going Correction** -0.025s/f (Stan) **4** Ran SP% **109.1**
Speed ratings (Par 94): **95,93,93,82**
CSF £7.33 TOTE £3.80; EX 14.30.
Owner South London Sisters Syndicate **Bred** Brendan Corbett **Trained** Upper Lambourn, Berks

FOCUS
A modest, uncompetitive juvenile claimer won in straightforward fashion.

NOTEBOOK
Silver Age(IRE) gained his first success at the sixth attempt. He could be competitive in ordinary handicaps. (tchd 3-1)
Foxtrot Golf(IRE) was best off at the weights, but he clearly ran well below his official rating of 73 seeing as he had 6lb in hand over the winner. (tchd 13-8)
Eternal Youth(IRE) had plenty to find with the front two on these terms (16lb with the winner), so clearly this was a creditable effort. (op 7-1)
Sir Lunchalott had finished just ahead of Eternal Youth on his previous start, but he ran a lazy race without his usual blinkers this time, needing to be niggled before the straight and finding little for pressure. Presumably headgear will be back on next time. (op 9-4 tchd 5-2)

7887 WINNERS WELCOME AT SEABET.COM MEDIAN AUCTION MAIDEN STKS 1m 4f (P)
5:00 (5:01) (Class 6) 3-5-Y-O **£1,637** (£483; £241) **Stalls** Centre

Form RPR

0504 **1** **Dilys Maud**[10] 7728 3-8-12 48 (b[1]) RobertHavlin 3 56
(R Ingram) *trckd ldrs: qcknd to ld wl over 2f out: drvn and kpt on strly fnl f* **20/1**

0000 **2** *1 1/2* **Astrodiva**[30] 7475 4-9-3 52 JimmyQuinn 4 54
(M H Tompkins) *in tch: hdwy 3f out: drvn to chse wnr over 2f out: styd on u.p ins fnl f: no imp on wnr* **8/1**

0503 **3** *1 1/2* **Faith Jicaro (IRE)**[12] 7703 3-8-12 53 NeilChalmers 8 51
(N J Vaughan) *in rr: hdwy 3f out: tk 3rd over 2f out: styd on thrght fnl f but no imp on ldng duo* **7/1**[3]

06 **4** *2 1/2* **Etoile Filante (IRE)**[35] 7413 3-8-12 0 SteveDrowne 6 47
(J R Gask) *in rr: rdn and styd on towards outside over 2f out: no imp on ldrs fnl f* **20/1**

5 **5** *5* **Cabuchon (GER)**[29] 7489 3-9-3 0 TomQueally 7 44
(B J Curley) *led tl hdd wl over 2f out: wknd appr fnl f* **3/1**[2]

0030 **6** *7* **Kitty Koo (IRE)**[40] 6871 3-8-12 42 AdamKirby 2 28
(A W Carroll) *chsd ldrs: drvn along 7f out and 5f out: wknd ins fnl 3f* **50/1**

-432 **7** *1* **Crystal Gale (IRE)**[8] 7767 3-8-12 67 (v[1]) ShaneKelly 1 26
(W J Knight) *chsd ldr: rdn and effrt ins fnl 3f: sn no imp and wknd qckly sn after* **11/8**[1]

8 *1* **Ocean Treasure (IRE)** 3-8-12 0 DavidProbert 5 25
(E F Vaughan) *slowly away: green and a in rr* **11/1**

2m 36.47s (1.97) **Going Correction** -0.025s/f (Stan)
WFA 3 from 4yo 5lb **8** Ran SP% **110.5**
Speed ratings (Par 101): **92,91,90,88,85 80,79,79**
toteswingers:1&2:£13.70, 1&3:£8.60, 2&3:£6.50 CSF £157.45 TOTE £27.90: £4.90, £3.40, £2.10; EX 120.30.
Owner The Stargazers **Bred** Sharon Ingram **Trained** Epsom, Surrey

FOCUS
The front two in the market disappointed and the respective official ratings of the first three finishers (48 beat 52 and 53) confirms this was an extremely moderate maiden. The winner was seemingly back to her early maiden form.
Kitty Koo(IRE) Official explanation: jockey said filly never travelled

7888 ASIAN FOOTBALL BETTING EXPLAINED NURSERY 1m (P)
5:30 (5:30) (Class 6) (0-65,65) 2-Y-O **£1,637** (£483; £241) **Stalls** High

Form RPR

540 **1** **Bill Page (USA)**[14] 7664 2-9-2 **60** AndreaAtzeni 10 64
(Mrs V M Jordan) *mde virtually all: hrd pressed fr ins fnl 2f: stl strly chal thrght fnl f: edgd lft fnl 100yds: hld on gamely* **7/1**[3]

0042 **2** *nk* **Mrs Neat (IRE)**[6] 7813 2-8-9 **53** ow1 (b) JamesDoyle 6 56
(S Kirk) *chsd ldrs: edgd lft over 1f out: drvn and qcknd to chal between horses ins fnl f: pushed lft fnl 100yds: styd on wl: jst hld* **3/1**[1]

0003 **3** *shd* **Aquilifer (IRE)**[17] 7630 2-8-8 **52** J-PGuillambert 7 55
(W Jarvis) *chsd ldrs: drvn and str chal fr over 1f out: stl upsides thrght fnl f: pushed lft fnl 100yds: kpt on wl: jst failed* **16/1**

0212 **4** *1 1/4* **Sky Diamond (IRE)**[7] 7785 2-9-4 **62** (b) TomQueally 2 62
(J G Given) *chsd ldrs: styng on whn hmpd over 1f out: swtchd rt and styd on again ins fnl f* **3/1**[1]

000 **4** *dht* **Blue Cossack (IRE)**[126] 5006 2-8-1 **45** DavidProbert 11 45
(M D I Usher) *chsd ldrs: rdn and upsides 2f out: outpcd ins fnl f* **80/1**

0005 **6** *2 1/4* **Brandy Snap (IRE)**[12] 7686 2-8-9 **53** SteveDrowne 8 48
(R Hannon) *s.i.s: in rr: hdwy over 2f out: styd on fnl f: nvr gng pce to trble ldrs* **33/1**

0005 **7** *hd* **Joyously**[7] 7785 2-9-0 **61** RobertLButler(3) 9 56
(P Butler) *in rr: rdn and styd on fnl 2f: nvr rchd ldrs* **50/1**

4023 **8** 2 1/4 **Dr Darcey**[43] 7296 2-8-13 **57** ... DaneO'Neill 3 46
(R Hannon) *chsd ldrs: rdn over 3f out: outpcd over 2f out: sme prog again fnl f* **9/2**[2]

0046 **9** 3/4 **Oliver's Gold**[8] 7758 2-9-3 **61** ... (b[1]) JimmyQuinn 5 49
(Mrs A J Perrett) *s.i.s: in rr: hdwy and rdn over 2f out: wknd sn after* **8/1**

0005 **10** 2 1/4 **Appyjack**[28] 7496 2-8-2 **46** ... (t) CathyGannon 4 28
(A W Carroll) *racd towards outside: rdn 3f out: nvr bttr then mid-div* **20/1**

006 **11** 5 **Black Iceman**[22] 7558 2-9-7 **65** ... (b) MickyFenton 1 36
(J Pearce) *t.k.h: chsd ldrs 5f* **33/1**

064 **12** 5 **Marie Du Plessis**[19] 7603 2-8-8 **52** ... AdrianNicholls 12 11
(M Johnston) *early spd: bhd fr 1/2-way* **16/1**

1m 41.15s (1.35) **Going Correction** -0.025s/f (Stan) **12** Ran SP% **117.4**
Speed ratings (Par 94): **92,91,91,90,90 88,87,85,84,82 77,72**
toteswingers:1&2:£8.20, 1&3:£16.10, 2&3:£12.70 CSF £26.79 CT £330.41 TOTE £10.80: £4.40, £1.20, £3.10; EX 52.70.
Owner Colin Davey **Bred** Brereton C Jones & B Ned Jones **Trained** Quainton, Bucks
■ Stewards' Enquiry : Andrea Atzeni two-day ban: careless riding (Dec 30-31)

FOCUS
This race was run in a driving snow shower. A modest nursery and the winner set a slow pace.

NOTEBOOK
Bill Page(USA) showed ability in maidens on his first two starts for David Simcock, but left that yard after a poor effort in selling company last time. Well drawn for his nursery debut, he was allowed a soft lead and then proved much more resolute than the runner-up when joined. He can remain competitive. (op 8-1 tchd 9-1 and 10-1 in a place)
Mrs Neat(IRE) carried 1lb overweight but it made no difference to the result. She had thrown away a winning opportunity by hanging left and idling in front over slightly further at Wolverhampton a week earlier, and although waited with this time, she again didn't seem to be giving everything for pressure. Admittedly a stronger-run race might have suited better, but she was still produced with every chance before again being inclined to edge left under pressure, and came close together with Sky Diamond. Her asset is her cruising speed and she may be capable of winning a race back over 7f, but she's not one to trust. (op 10-3)
Aquilifer(IRE) was well placed considering how the race unfolded but was worried out of it. (op 14-1)
Sky Diamond(IRE) Official explanation: jockey said gelding suffered interference in running (op 66-1)
Blue Cossack(IRE), gelded since last seen in August, offered some encouragement on this handicap debut. (op 66-1)
Dr Darcey was disappointing. (op 11-2)

7889 IN-RUNNING BETTING AT SEABET.COM H'CAP (DIV I) 1m (P)
6:00 (6:00) (Class 5) (0-70,70) 3-Y-O+ **£1,944** (£574; £287) **Stalls** High

Form RPR
2300 **1** **Jodawes (USA)**[253] 1168 3-8-10 **60** ... SteveDrowne 10 71
(J R Best) *trckd ldrs: led ins fnl 2f: drvn and styd on wl fnl f* **25/1**

0200 **2** 2 1/4 **Expensive Problem**[64] 6851 7-9-7 **70** ... GeorgeBaker 4 76
(R J Smith) *s.i.s: hld up in rr: gd hdwy fr 2f out: chsd wnr ins fnl f: kpt on but no imp* **7/1**

0004 **3** 1 1/4 **Perfect Ch'I (IRE)**[18] 7613 3-8-12 **62** ... (b) CathyGannon 11 65
(I A Wood) *t.k.h: in tch 1/2-way: hdwy over 2f out: chsd wnr over 1f out: no imp and lost 2nd ins fnl f* **8/1**

4534 **4** 1/2 **Al Jaadl**[19] 7597 3-9-2 **66** ... J-PGuillambert 6 68
(W Jarvis) *trckd ldrs: effrt and n.m.r ins fnl 2f: hdwy to chse ldrs over 1f out: edgd rt u.p: wknd nr fin* **4/1**[2]

0000 **5** hd **Lisahane Bog**[12] 7699 3-9-3 **67** ... (e[1]) DaneO'Neill 8 69
(P R Hedger) *s.i.s: in rr: hdwy over 1f out: styd on fnl f: no rch ldrs* **10/1**

0132 **6** 2 **Having A Ball**[12] 7688 6-9-2 **65** ... ChrisCatlin 5 62
(P D Cundell) *in rr tl drvn and hdwy on outside over 1f out: kpt on cl home: nvr a threat* **7/2**[1]

5231 **7** 2 **Sunrise Lyric (IRE)**[132] 4775 3-9-0 **64** ... EddieAhern 7 56
(P F I Cole) *slowly ito stride: t.k.h in rr: hdwy over 2f out: sn chsng ldrs on ins: wknd over 1f out* **6/1**[3]

4445 **8** 1/2 **Merals Choice**[286] 805 3-8-7 **57** ... NickyMackay 9 48
(J R Boyle) *led tl hdd & wknd ins fnl 2f* **33/1**

1042 **9** 3/4 **Piquante**[29] 7483 4-9-2 **68** ... KellyHarrison(3) 3 57
(N Tinkler) *in tch: pushed along 2f out: nvr gng pce to get into contention: wknd over 1f out* **6/1**[3]

6020 **10** hd **Gazboolou**[29] 7483 6-8-12 **68** ... JamesRogers(7) 2 57
(David Pinder) *chsd ldrs tl wknd over 1f out* **12/1**

0000 **11** nk **Spinning Ridge (IRE)**[12] 7699 5-9-4 **67** ... (p) DavidProbert 1 55
(R A Harris) *chsd ldr tl over 2f out: sn wknd* **50/1**

1m 38.94s (-0.86) **Going Correction** -0.025s/f (Stan)
WFA 3 from 4yo+ 1lb **11** Ran SP% **119.9**
Speed ratings (Par 103): **103,100,99,99,98 96,94,94,93,93 93**
toteswingers:1&2:£35.40, 1&3:£26.70, 2&3:£10.80 CSF £192.51 CT £1588.57 TOTE £41.90: £7.70, £4.40, £2.80; EX 453.20.
Owner Stephen Fisher & John Ball **Bred** Mcdowell Farm **Trained** Hucking, Kent

FOCUS
A modest handicap run in a time 0.12 seconds quicker than the second division. Sound form, with a clear personal best from the winner.
Al Jaadl Official explanation: jockey said filly was denied a clear run

7890 IN-RUNNING BETTING AT SEABET.COM H'CAP (DIV II) 1m (P)
6:30 (6:30) (Class 5) (0-70,69) 3-Y-O+ **£1,944** (£574; £287) **Stalls** High

Form RPR
0502 **1** **Gallantry**[19] 7597 8-9-7 **69** ... JimmyQuinn 2 79+
(Jane Chapple-Hyam) *in tch: trckd ldrs: hdwy to ld ins fnl 2f: pushed clr fnl f: readily* **5/1**[2]

0202 **2** 2 1/4 **Hip Hip Hooray**[18] 7611 4-9-5 **67** ... IanMongan 5 72
(L A Dace) *towards rr: hdwy fr 3f out: ev ch ins fnl 2f: outpcd by wnr fnl f* **10/1**

0300 **3** 2 1/2 **Aflaam (IRE)**[46] 7255 5-9-3 **65** ... SeamieHeffernan 8 64
(R A Harris) *led 4f: styd w ldr and led again over 2f out: hdd ins fnl 2f: outpcd by ldng duo fnl f but kpt on wl for 3rd* **12/1**

1624 **4** 1 1/2 **Tilsworth Glenboy**[43] 7305 3-9-6 **69** ... GeorgeBaker 10 65
(J R Jenkins) *in rr: stdy hdwy to trck ldrs fr 2f out: sn rdn: fnd no ex fnl f* **6/1**

3234 **5** hd **Sovereignty (JPN)**[5] 7825 8-8-10 **58** ... SamHitchcott 6 53
(D K Ivory) *broke wl: stdd in tch: hdwy to chse ldrs 2f out: wknd fnl f* **11/2**[3]

0662 **6** 3 **Posy Fossil (USA)**[49] 7191 3-9-0 **63** ... (tp) DavidProbert 9 51
(S C Williams) *chsd ldrs: rdn 3f out: wknd fr 2f out* **12/1**

0000 **7** 1 1/4 **Very Well Red**[73] 6629 7-8-7 **55** oh1 ... WilliamCarson 4 41
(P W Hiatt) *chsd ldrs: rdn over 3f out: wknd over 2f out* **20/1**

1150 **8** 2 1/4 **Astrodonna**[30] 7474 5-9-4 **66** ... TomQueally 3 46
(M H Tompkins) *rdn 3f out: a towards rr* **12/1**

2021 **9** nk **Ice Cool Lady (IRE)**[43] 7298 3-9-5 **68** ... (v) EddieAhern 7 48
(W R Swinburn) *chsd ldrs tl rdn and wknd rapidly wl over 2f out* **9/4**[1]

640- **10** 3 1/2 **Rossatron**[581] 2004 4-9-1 **63** ... SteveDrowne 11 35
(J R Gask) *t.k.h: w ldr tl led 4f out: hdd & wknd over 2f out* **14/1**

1m 39.06s (-0.74) **Going Correction** -0.025s/f (Stan)
WFA 3 from 4yo+ 1lb **10** Ran SP% **120.7**
Speed ratings (Par 103): **102,99,97,95,95 92,91,89,88,85**
toteswingers:1&2:£6.70, 1&3:£11.00, 2&3:£17.90 CSF £56.20 CT £596.98 TOTE £7.00: £2.60, £2.80, £4.60; EX 34.70.
Owner The Circle Bloodstock I Limited **Bred** Cheveley Park Stud Ltd **Trained** Dalham, Suffolk

FOCUS
Another race to be run in a heavy snow shower. This was an uncompetitive handicap and the time was 0.12 seconds slower than the first division. The form is rated around the runner-up.

7891 BEST ASIAN MARKETS AT SEABET.COM NURSERY 6f (P)
7:00 (7:01) (Class 3) (0-95,88) 2-Y-O **£5,504** (£1,637; £818; £408) **Stalls** High

Form RPR
1330 **1** **Loki's Revenge**[68] 6734 2-8-13 **80** ... SteveDrowne 9 84
(W Jarvis) *trckd ldrs: qcknd over 1f out to ld jst ins fnl f: sn rdn: r.o strly: won gng away* **7/1**[3]

1221 **2** 1 1/4 **Forty Proof (IRE)**[9] 7734 2-9-1 **82** 6ex ... (v) ShaneKelly 4 82
(W J Knight) *in rr: hdwy but hd to one side over 1f out: qcknd between horses ins fnl f and styd on wl to take 2nd cl home but no imp on wnr* **11/1**

0534 **3** nk **Sacrosanctus**[19] 7592 2-8-6 **73** ... JimmyQuinn 10 72
(D Nicholls) *trckd ldr: led ins fnl 2f: sn hrd drvn hdd jst ins fnl f and outpcd by wnr: lost 2nd cl home* **4/1**[2]

4523 **4** 1 1/4 **Restless Bay (IRE)**[6] 7803 2-8-7 **74** ... (b) SamHitchcott 1 69
(R Hollinshead) *in rr: hdwy over 1f out: styd on ins fnl f but nvr a threat* **33/1**

142 **5** 1/2 **Shostakovich (IRE)**[12] 7696 2-8-4 **71** ... (tp) ChrisCatlin 11 65
(S Kirk) *chsd ldrs: rdn over 2f out: wknd ins fnl f* **9/1**

1443 **6** 1 **Geordie Iris (IRE)**[11] 7718 2-8-7 **74** ... DavidProbert 7 65
(R Hannon) *chsd ldrs tl rdn and outpcd over 2f out: styd on again ins fnl f* **8/1**

1113 **7** nk **Jack Smudge**[21] 7565 2-9-7 **88** ... TomQueally 12 78
(J G Given) *led tl hdd ins fnl 2f: wknd fnl f* **3/1**[1]

0212 **8** 1/2 **Liberty Green (IRE)**[9] 7734 2-8-2 **69** ... MartinLane 8 57
(A J McCabe) *chsd ldrs: rdn over 2f out: wknd fnl f* **8/1**

0135 **9** 1 **Roman Dancer (IRE)**[95] 5987 2-8-8 **75** ... FergusSweeney 2 60
(J Gallagher) *outpcd most of way* **33/1**

1 **10** 1/2 **Lady Prodee**[34] 7424 2-8-1 **68** ... CathyGannon 5 52
(W G M Turner) *chsd ldrs: rdn over 2f out: wknd appr fnl f* **16/1**

3230 **11** 12 **New Latin (IRE)**[43] 7294 2-8-7 **74** ... AdrianNicholls 3 22
(M Johnston) *slowly away: a wl bhd* **16/1**

3460 **12** 2 3/4 **Belle Bayardo (IRE)**[54] 7080 2-9-7 **88** ... SeamieHeffernan 6 28
(R A Harris) *in rr: hung bdly lft and off crse bnd 3f out: no ch after* **40/1**

1m 12.49s (-0.61) **Going Correction** -0.025s/f (Stan) **12** Ran SP% **118.1**
Speed ratings (Par 100): **103,101,100,99,98 97,96,96,94,94 78,74**
toteswingers: 1&2 £13.10, 1&3 £10.60, 2&3 £8.50 CSF £80.09 CT £357.33 TOTE £10.50: £3.50, £2.10, £1.80; EX 111.80.
Owner Dr J Walker **Bred** The Athenians **Trained** Newmarket, Suffolk

FOCUS
The top weight was rated 7lb below the ceiling of 95 and this was an ordinary nursery for the class.

NOTEBOOK
Loki's Revenge, a dual winner over slightly shorter on turf in August, returned from a 68-day break with a career-best performance. He looks the type to go on improving. (op 10-1)
Forty Proof(IRE), 2lb wrong under the penalty picked up for his Lingfield win, was dropped in from his low draw, resulting in the winner get first run. He stayed on, but didn't totally convince with his attitude, carrying his head to one side when looking for a clear run. Still, this was another useful effort. (op 12-1 tchd 10-1)
Sacrosanctus raced up with the pace and seemed to have every chance, but he simply didn't see his race out as well as the front two, both of whom are improving. (op 5-1)
Restless Bay(IRE) had the worst draw but was soon tucked away towards the inside. He couldn't muster the required speed, but kept on and this was a respectable effort.
Shostakovich(IRE) ran with credit, but his best form is on Fibresand. (op 11-2)
Jack Smudge was just behind Restless Bay when his winning sequence came to an end last time, ran as though he's now had enough for the time being.
Lady Prodee Official explanation: jockey said filly had no more to give
Belle Bayardo(IRE) Official explanation: jockey said gelding hung left

7892 VIP SERVICE AT SEABET.COM H'CAP 7f (P)
7:30 (7:33) (Class 5) (0-75,75) 3-Y-O+ **£2,286** (£675; £337) **Stalls** High

Form RPR
0062 **1** **Chilli Green**[33] 7439 3-9-1 **69** ... DaneO'Neill 11 83+
(J Akehurst) *trckd ldr: led wl over 1f out: drvn clr fnl f* **9/2**[2]

1025 **2** 3 **Pipers Piping (IRE)**[9] 7737 4-8-8 **65** ... (v) MichaelStainton(3) 9 71
(Jane Chapple-Hyam) *chsd ldrs: rdn 2f out: styd on to chse wnr fnl 70yds but nvr any ch* **6/1**[3]

3543 **3** 3/4 **Requisite**[8] 7766 5-9-7 **75** ... (b[1]) MartinLane 6 79
(I A Wood) *in rr but in tch: rdn and hdwy on outside over 1f out: styd on to take 3rd nr fin but nvr any ch w wnr* **15/2**

3001 **4** 1/2 **Jaldarshaan (IRE)**[15] 7651 3-8-10 **64** ... TravisBlock 5 67+
(W J H Ratcliffe) *stdd s: hld up in rr: hdwy over 1f out: styd on ins fnl f: nt pce to rch ldng trio* **12/1**

1515 **5** 1/2 **Paphos**[22] 7556 3-8-10 **64** ... (v) DavidProbert 4 65
(S C Williams) *led: rdn over 2f out: hdd wl over 1f out: wknd and lost 4 pls fnl 70yds* **4/1**[1]

0516 **6** 1/2 **Tuxedo**[19] 7597 5-9-6 **74** ... WilliamCarson 12 74
(P W Hiatt) *chsd ldrs: rdn over 2f out: outpcd wl over 1f out: styd on again fnl 120yds* **4/1**[1]

000 **7** 1 3/4 **Tenacestream (CAN)**[26] 7526 3-9-4 **72** ... LiamJones 7 67
(J R Best) *in rr: rdn over 2f out: nvr gng pce to rch ldrs* **25/1**

0264 **8** 1/2 **Headache**[8] 7766 5-8-13 **70** ... (bt) RobertLButler(3) 3 64
(B W Duke) *chsd ldrs: rdn 3f out: btn ins fnl 2f* **12/1**

3060 **9** 3 1/4 **Tudor Prince (IRE)**[155] 4024 6-9-0 **68** ... AdamKirby 2 53
(A W Carroll) *outpcd most of way* **25/1**

1204 **10** 5 **Namir (IRE)**[15] 7655 8-8-8 **62** ... (vt) FergusSweeney 1 34
(H J Evans) *led to post: slowly away: a in rr* **14/1**

0000 **11** 1/2 **Cut The Cackle (IRE)**[5] 7837 4-9-1 **69** ... RobbieFitzpatrick 10 39
(P Butler) *a outpcd* **50/1**

1m 24.62s (-1.38) **Going Correction** -0.025s/f (Stan) **11** Ran SP% **115.9**
Speed ratings (Par 103): **106,102,101,101,100 100,98,97,93,88 87**
toteswingers: 1&2 £7.00, 2&3 £8.20, 1&3 £6.40 CSF £30.58 CT £198.51 TOTE £6.40: £2.00, £1.70, £2.90; EX 31.30.
Owner Peter M Crane **Bred** P M Crane **Trained** Epsom, Surrey

FOCUS
A modest handicap, but it was competitive and the time was good for the grade. The form is rated around the second and the winner is on the up.
T/Plt: £20,798.40 to a £1 stake. Pool:£48,434.81 - 1.70 winning tickets T/Qpdt: £253.30 to a £1 stake. Pool:£10,341.27 - 30.20 winning tickets ST

7864 SOUTHWELL (L-H)

Thursday, December 16

OFFICIAL GOING: Standard
Wind: Moderate across Weather: Overcast and showers

7893 BET SP+ IN DECEMBER AT TOTESPORT.COM MAIDEN AUCTION STKS 7f (F)
12:30 (12:31) (Class 6) 2-Y-O £1,706 (£503; £252) Stalls Low

Form RPR
602 1 **If You Whisper (IRE)**[18] 7610 2-8-8 78 MartinLane 3 72
(Mike Murphy) *s.i.s: sn trcking ldrs: hdwy on outer 3f out: rdn to ld wl over 1f out: edgd rt over 1f out: hdd ent fnl f: drvn and rallied wl to ld last 100yds* 4/6[1]
43 2 1 **Mazovian (USA)**[6] 7802 2-8-4 0 KellyHarrison(3) 2 68
(M C Chapman) *trckd ldrs: smooth hdwy on outer over 2f out: chal over 1f and sltly hmpd: rdn to ld ent fnl f: sn drvn: hdd and no ex last 100yds* 5/1[3]
54 3 3 3/4 **Woop Woop (IRE)**[42] 7309 2-8-5 0 ChrisCatlin 5 57
(Stef Higgins) *chsd ldr: hdwy 3f out: led over 2f out: sn rdn and hdd wl over 1f out: sn one pce* 5/2[2]
05 4 22 **Ippi N Tombi (IRE)**[11] 7715 2-7-11 0 RyanPowell(5) 1 —
(P S McEntee) *blind removed late and s.i.s: hdwy on inner to chse ldrs after 2f: rdn along 3f out: sn wknd* 100/1
5000 5 3/4 **Bold Deceiver**[12] 7692 2-8-3 28 (t) WilliamCarson 4 —
(P S McEntee) *led: rdn along 3f out: sn hdd & wknd* 100/1
1m 30.25s (-0.05) **Going Correction** -0.05s/f (Stan) 5 Ran SP% **107.2**
Speed ratings (Par 94): **98,96,92,67,66**
CSF £4.28 TOTE £1.70: £1.10, £2.60; EX 5.10.
Owner Phil Woods **Bred** Mrs Vanessa Hutch **Trained** Westoning, Beds

FOCUS
Effectively this was a three-runner maiden, and a moderate one at that.

NOTEBOOK
If You Whisper(IRE), just ahead of a subsequent winner when runner-up at Kempton last time, moved readily to the front soon after turning in and, although sternly challenged a furlong out, he saw the trip out better than the runner-up. He will probably be given a break now and return in the spring. He still has a bit of scope. (op 4-5 tchd 5-6 and 10-11 in a place)
Mazovian(USA), in the frame in a couple of modest maidens here, slipstreamed the favourite starting up the home straight and looked a big danger when pulled out over a furlong from home, but as was the case here last time the seventh furlong seemed to find him out. He now gets a mark and could be interesting over 6f here.
Woop Woop(IRE) showed ability in a couple of 6f Kempton maidens, but she was the first of the big three off the bridle and didn't get home. Perhaps the surface didn't suit her. (op 2-1)
Ippi N Tombi(IRE) Official explanation: jockey said when he tried to remove blindfold it had been caught on bridle leaving filly slowly away.

7894 BIGGER WINS WITH SP+ AT TOTESPORT.COM NURSERY 5f (F)
1:00 (1:01) (Class 6) (0-60,60) 2-Y-O £2,047 (£604; £302) Stalls High

Form RPR
0441 1 **Je Suis Unrockstar**[16] 7641 2-9-2 60 (p) BillyCray(5) 4 68
(D Nicholls) *prom: led 2f out: rdn over 1f out: styd on strly* 11/4[1]
6240 2 2 **Rylee Mooch**[68] 6740 2-9-3 56 (e[1]) MartinLane 9 57
(R C Guest) *cl up: effrt 2f out: sn rdn and ev ch tl drvn and one pce ent fnl f* 8/1
41 3 1/2 **Verus Decorus (IRE)**[12] 7692 2-9-0 56 JamesSullivan(3) 2 55
(Patrick Morris) *dwlt and wnt lft s: hdwy and in tch 1/2-way: effrt on outer 2f out: rdn to chse ldrs over 1f out: sn drvn and edgd rt: one pce fnl f* 3/1[2]
3600 4 hd **Veeb (IRE)**[14] 7664 2-9-1 54 GregFairley 6 52
(M Johnston) *midfield: hdwy 2f out: swtchd rt and rdn to chse ldrs wl over 1f out: drvn and kpt on ins fnl f* 10/1
5626 5 3 **Molly Mylenis**[2] 7864 2-8-5 51 MatthewCosham(7) 5 38
(P D Evans) *in tch: hdwy to chse ldrs 2f out: sn rdn and no imp* 22/1
060 6 4 1/2 **Walshestown Lad (IRE)**[26] 7517 2-8-11 50 (b[1]) ChrisCatlin 7 21
(R A Harris) *slt ld: rdn along 1/2-way: sn hdd and grad wknd* 40/1
000 7 3/4 **William Wainwright (IRE)**[75] 6569 2-8-8 47 HayleyTurner 8 16
(Mrs A Duffield) *dwlt and sn rdn along in rr: sme hdwy whn hung rt 2f out: nvr a factor* 7/1
4002 8 4 **Majestic Ridge (IRE)**[7] 7777 2-8-13 52 (v[1]) StevieDonohoe 11 —
(P D Evans) *hld up: a in rr* 5/1[3]
305 9 1 1/2 **Liberty Ess (IRE)**[20] 7577 2-8-13 52 (b[1]) GrahamGibbons 12 —
(M Wigham) *chsd ldrs: rdn along 1/2-way: sn wknd* 20/1
0060 10 13 **Mujapiste (IRE)**[12] 7692 2-8-6 45 (tp) DuranFentiman 10 —
(L A Mullaney) *chsd ldrs: rdn along bef 1/2-way: sn outpcd and bhd* 100/1
0000 11 1/2 **Miss Maudie (IRE)**[22] 7551 2-8-6 45 (b[1]) WilliamCarson 3 —
(R A Harris) *cl up: rdn along after 1 1/2f: sn lost pl and bhd fr 1/2-way* 50/1
59.88 secs (0.18) **Going Correction** -0.10s/f (Stan) 11 Ran SP% **115.5**
Speed ratings (Par 94): **94,90,90,89,84 77,76,70,67,46 46**
toteswingers:1&2:£5.30, 1&3:£2.10, 2&3:£7.70 CSF £23.39 CT £70.98 TOTE £3.00: £1.30, £2.50, £1.20; EX 25.80 Trifecta £82.60 Pool £246.76 - 2.21 winning units..
Owner Paul J Dixon **Bred** Mrs Yvette Dixon **Trained** Sessay, N Yorks

FOCUS
A moderate if competitive nursery and five of the 11 runners were in new or different headgear for the first time. Those drawn low once again mainly held the advantage.

NOTEBOOK
Je Suis Unrockstar, off the mark at the tenth attempt in a C&D seller last month, probably didn't need to improve much from that in order to follow up here. He wasn't best away, but was soon cruising in behind the leaders and, once taking it up over 2f out, the race was in the bag. He should find other opportunities back here. (op 5-2 tchd 3-1)
Rylee Mooch, tried in an eyeshield, was running in his first race here but had worked a couple of times on the track. He was never far away from his high draw and kept on right to the line. There is a race like this in him. (op 7-1)
Verus Decorus(IRE), making her nursery debut after winning a weak C&D maiden, blew her chance with a tardy start so did well to finish as close as she did. She still has a bit of scope. (op 7-2 tchd 4-1)
Veeb(IRE) ran on late despite racing closer to the nearside rail than ideal in the closing stages, but has basically become disappointing. (op 8-1)
Molly Mylenis, 31/2l behind Je Suis Unrockstar in that C&D seller last month, had every chance but might have been expected to have got closer to the winner considering she was 9lb better off. (op 25-1)
William Wainwright(IRE), making his nursery and AW debuts after finishing well beaten in three turf maidens over much further, attracted market support but he was struggling soon after the gates opened. (op 14-1)

7895 BET ON ASHES AT TOTESPORT.COM H'CAP 1m (F)
1:30 (1:31) (Class 5) (0-75,75) 3-Y-O+ £2,251 (£664; £332) Stalls Low

Form RPR
0444 1 **General Tufto**[6] 7804 5-9-1 68 (b) MartinLane 3 78
(C Smith) *hld up in rr: pushed along 3f out: swtchd lft and hdwy 2f out: rdn to chal over 1f out: kpt on to ld ins fnl f: drvn out* 7/1
4123 2 2 **Ubenkor (IRE)**[6] 7804 5-8-7 65 BillyCray(5) 6 70
(M Herrington) *led after 1f: rdn 2f out: drvn over 1f out: hdd ins fnl f: no ex last 75yds* 7/2[3]
-223 3 2 **Opus Dei**[16] 7645 3-8-11 68 MichaelGeran(3) 4 68
(D Nicholls) *prom: rdn along and outpcd over 2f out: sn drvn: kpt on ins fnl f* 11/4[1]
2402 4 1 1/2 **Miss Bootylishes**[6] 7804 5-9-4 74 AmyBaker(3) 2 71
(A B Haynes) *led 1f: a.p: effrt over 2f out and ev ch tl rdn and wknd ent fnl f* 6/1
1360 5 1 3/4 **Master Of Dance (IRE)**[22] 7560 3-9-4 75 JamesSullivan(3) 5 68
(J G Given) *chsd ldrs: hdwy on outer to chse ldr 3f out: rdn over 2f out: sn drvn and wknd* 9/1
-640 6 12 **Gordy Bee (USA)**[7] 7778 4-8-13 66 (be[1]) GrahamGibbons 1 31
(R C Guest) *chsd ldrs on inner: rdn along 3f out: drvn over 2f out and sn wknd* 3/1[2]
1m 42.32s (-1.38) **Going Correction** -0.05s/f (Stan)
WFA 3 from 4yo+ 1lb 6 Ran SP% **110.7**
Speed ratings (Par 103): **104,102,100,98,96 84**
toteswingers:1&2:£2.60, 1&3:£3.50, 2&3:£1.80 CSF £30.38 TOTE £9.30: £3.50, £2.70; EX 31.80.
Owner Phil Martin & Trev Sleath **Bred** Hascombe And Valiant Studs **Trained** Temple Bruer, Lincs

FOCUS
An ordinary handicap which began in a snowstorm and the six runners were still tightly packed passing the 2f pole. The winner is rated back to something like his best.
Gordy Bee(USA) Official explanation: jockey said gelding became upset in stalls

7896 BET ON LIVE CRICKET AT TOTESPORT.COM MAIDEN STKS 1m 3f (F)
2:00 (2:00) (Class 5) 3-Y-O+ £2,115 (£624; £312) Stalls Low

Form RPR
3432 1 **Stadium Of Light (IRE)**[12] 7695 3-9-3 65 BarryMcHugh 5 72
(B Ellison) *trckd ldrs: hdwy to trck ldr 4f out: rdn to chal 2f out: drvn over 1f out: slt ld jst ins fnl f: kpt on u.p* 11/8[1]
2303 2 nk **Fascination (IRE)**[12] 7690 3-8-12 67 HayleyTurner 9 66
(M L W Bell) *a.p: cl up 1/2-way: led over 4f out: jnd and rdn 2f out: drvn over 1f out: hdd ins fnl f: rallied u.p and ev ch tl no ex towards fin* 9/4[2]
2 3 4 1/2 **Destiny Of A Diva**[12] 7703 3-8-12 0 GrahamGibbons 2 58
(R Hollinshead) *trckd ldrs: hdwy 4f out: cl up on inner over 2f out: sn rdn to chal and ev ch tl drvn and one pce ent fnl f* 5/1[3]
4 8 **Bold Warning**[59] 6-9-7 0 GregFairley 6 49
(A M Hales) *towards rr: hdwy 4f out: in tch and rdn 3f out: sn no imp* 100/1
45 5 4 1/2 **Yeomanry**[12] 7703 5-9-7 0 MartinLane 7 41
(Ian Williams) *dwlt and bhd: rdn along 1/2-way: styd on fnl 3f: nvr a factor* 20/1
0004 6 1 1/4 **Wrecking Crew (IRE)**[12] 7703 6-9-7 48 (b) JamesMillman 8 39
(B R Millman) *chsd ldrs on outer: rdn along 4f out: drvn and outpcd fnl 3f* 50/1
0646 7 1 1/2 **Northumberland**[10] 7731 4-9-4 42 KellyHarrison(3) 1 36
(M C Chapman) *chsd ldrs: rdn along 5f out: drvn over 3f out and sn outpcd* 80/1
8 3 **Ancailinoir (IRE)** 3-8-9 0 JamesSullivan(3) 3 26
(J G Given) *dwlt: a in rr* 20/1
9 shd **Bullring (FR)**[132] 4-9-7 0 WilliamCarson 11 30
(P D Niven) *dwlt: hdwy and prom after 2f: led 1/2-way: rdn along and hdd over 4f out: sn wknd* 66/1
0003 10 8 **Mojeerr**[10] 7729 4-9-4 48 (v) MichaelGeran(3) 4 16
(A J McCabe) *led: pushed along and hdd 1/2-way: sn wknd* 25/1
5 11 30 **Donny Briggs**[195] 2697 5-9-7 0 (t) DuranFentiman 10 —
(T D Easterby) *dwlt: a in rr: bhd and eased fnl 3f* 16/1
2m 27.43s (-0.57) **Going Correction** -0.05s/f (Stan)
WFA 3 from 4yo+ 4lb 11 Ran SP% **114.5**
Speed ratings (Par 103): **100,99,96,90,87 86,85,83,83,77 55**
toteswingers:1&2:£1.30, 1&3:£2.50, 2&3:£2.90 CSF £3.97 TOTE £2.40: £1.20, £1.10, £1.30; EX 4.50 Trifecta £14.00 Pool £265.57 - 24.48 winning units..
Owner Dan Gilbert & Mark Lawrence **Bred** Rabbah Bloodstock Limited **Trained** Norton, N Yorks
■ Stewards' Enquiry : Kelly Harrison caution: careless riding.
Hayley Turner one-day ban: used whip with excessive frequency (Dec 30)

FOCUS
Another race run in driving snow. Only three counted in this moderate maiden according to the market and the trio had the race to themselves over the last half-mile.

7897 TONY MCCOY FOR BBC SPORTS PERSONALITY CLAIMING STKS 1m (F)
2:30 (2:30) (Class 6) 3-4-Y-O £1,706 (£503; £252) Stalls Low

Form RPR
2421 1 **Diggeratt (USA)**[41] 7327 4-8-12 79 MatthewDavies(3) 4 75
(George Baker) *trckd ldr: pushed along over 3f out: hdwy and cl up over 2f out: led wl over 1f out and sn rdn: drvn and hung rt ins fnl f: kpt on towards fin* 1/2[1]
4321 2 1 **Lakeman (IRE)**[47] 7229 4-8-10 65 (be) BarryMcHugh 2 68
(B Ellison) *led: rdn along over 2f out: hdd and drvn wl over 1f out: rallied ins fnl f: no ex last 75yds* 5/2[2]
0035 3 4 **Starry Mount**[5] 7832 3-8-4 64 AmyBaker(3) 3 57
(A B Haynes) *hld up in rr: hdwy on outer 3f out: rdn to chse wnr over 1f out: sn drvn: edgd lft and one pce appr fnl f* 10/1[3]
4000 4 12 **Briary Mac**[94] 6039 3-7-5 51 RichardRowe(7) 1 20
(P A Pritchard) *prom on inner: rdn along over 3f out: sn wknd* 33/1
1m 44.85s (1.15) **Going Correction** -0.05s/f (Stan)
WFA 3 from 4yo 1lb 4 Ran SP% **107.3**
Speed ratings (Par 101): **92,91,87,75**
CSF £1.96 TOTE £1.40; EX 1.90.
Owner George Baker & Partners **Bred** Hobby Horse Farm Inc **Trained** Moreton Morrell, Warwicks

FOCUS
An uncompetitive claimer run in a relatively slow time. The form is rated around the runner-up.

7898 CAPTAIN COGHILL'S H'CAP 1m 4f (F)
3:00 (3:00) (Class 5) (0-70,68) 3-Y-0+ **£2,115** (£624; £312) **Stalls** Low

Form RPR
2323 **1** **Rosewin (IRE)**51 7149 4-9-0 **60** ... JamesSullivan(3) 6 69
(Ollie Pears) *in tch: trckd ldrs 1/2-way: pushed along 4f out: hdwy 3f out: rdn to chal 2f out: led wl over 1f out: kpt on strly fnl f* **7/2**3
0 **2** 3 ¾ **Not Til Monday (IRE)**44 7284 4-9-10 **67** ... GregFairley 5 70
(J R Jenkins) *cl up: effrt 3f out and ev ch tl rdn and edgd lft and outpcd over 1f out: swtchd lft and drvn ins fnl f: kpt on to take 2nd towards fin* **3/1**2
3321 **3** *shd* **Dandarrell**4 7848 3-8-10 **58** 6ex ... GrahamGibbons 4 61
(Julie Camacho) *trckd ldng pair: hdwy to ld over 4f out: rdn over 2f out: drvn and hdd wl over 1f out: kpt on same pce* **13/8**1
2466 **4** *27* **My Mate Mal**12 7694 6-9-9 **66** ... BarryMcHugh 3 26
(W B Stone) *led: pushed along and hdd over 4f out: rdn over 3f out and sn wknd* **9/2**
-000 **5** *8* **Number One Guy**132 4796 3-9-6 **68** ... RussKennemore 1 15
(P A Kirby) *chsd ldrs: rdn along over 4f out: sn wknd* **14/1**
2m 39.66s (-1.34) **Going Correction** -0.05s/f (Stan)
WFA 3 from 4yo+ 5lb 5 Ran SP% **110.2**
Speed ratings (Par 103): **102,99,99,81,76**
CSF £14.16 TOTE £3.50: £1.30, £2.10; EX 14.50.
Owner Major P H K Steveney **Bred** E A Bourke M R C V S **Trained** Norton, N Yorks

FOCUS
An ordinary handicap and the pace looked reasonable. The winner is rated up 3lb on this year's form.

7899 HOSPITALITY AT SOUTHWELL RACECOURSE H'CAP 1m (F)
3:30 (3:31) (Class 6) (0-60,60) 3-Y-0+ **£1,706** (£503; £252) **Stalls** Low

Form RPR
1346 **1** **Exopuntia**35 7401 4-8-11 **49** ... GregFairley 1 62
(Miss J Feilden) *trckd ldrs on inner: hdwy 3f out: led over 2f out: rdn clr over 1f out: kpt on* **7/2**2
0123 **2** 2 ¾ **It's A Mans World**2 7870 4-8-8 **51** ... RyanPowell(5) 3 57
(Ian Williams) *hld up in tch: hdwy on inner wl over 2f out: rdn to chse wnr wl over 1f out: drvn and no imp fnl f* **11/4**1
4623 **3** *6* **Tres Froide (FR)**21 7569 5-8-13 **51** ...(p) GrahamGibbons 7 44
(N Tinkler) *trckd ldrs: hdwy on outer 3f out: rdn to chse ldrs over 2f out: drvn and one pce fr wl over 1f out* **7/2**2
06 **4** ½ **Mackintosh (IRE)**12 7705 4-8-4 **45** ...(e1) JamesSullivan(3) 2 37
(Patrick Morris) *cl up on outer: effrt 3f out: sn rdn and wknd wl over 1f out* **14/1**
0403 **5** *5* **Royal Holiday (IRE)**10 7731 3-9-2 **60** ... TobyAtkinson(5) 4 40
(B Ellison) *hld up: a towards rr* **9/2**3
0000 **6** *2* **Lily Eva**10 7727 4-8-3 **46** ow1 ...(v1) BillyCray(5) 6 21
(D Donovan) *cl up: led 3f out: rdn and hdd over 2f out: sn wknd* **33/1**
1023 **7** ½ **Red Skipper (IRE)**30 5439 5-9-0 **57** ... DeanHeslop(5) 5 31
(N Wilson) *led: rdn along and hdd 3f out: sn wknd* **15/2**
1m 42.99s (-0.71) **Going Correction** -0.05s/f (Stan)
WFA 3 from 4yo+ 1lb 7 Ran SP% **110.7**
Speed ratings (Par 101): **101,98,92,91,86 84,84**
toteswingers:1&2:£2.20, 1&3:£2.60, 2&3:£2.30 CSF £12.63 TOTE £4.00: £1.60, £2.70; EX 14.90.
Owner John W Ford **Bred** J W Ford **Trained** Exning, Suffolk

FOCUS
A weak handicap run in deteriorating visibility and the front pair pulled well clear. The winner posted a clear personal best.
T/Plt: £17.50 to a £1 stake. Pool:£44,117.35 - 1,835.17 winning tickets T/Qpdt: £8.60 to a £1 stake. Pool:£2,784.34 - 238.80 winning tickets JR

7893 SOUTHWELL (L-H)
Friday, December 17

OFFICIAL GOING: Standard to slow
Wind: Fresh behind Weather: Bright and cold

7906 TOTEPLACEPOT WIN WITHOUT BACKING A WINNER CLAIMING STKS 6f (F)
12:05 (12:05) (Class 6) 3-Y-0+ **£1,569** (£463; £231) **Stalls** Low

Form RPR
4403 **1** **Punching**5 7847 6-8-12 70 ... HayleyTurner 2 79
(C R Dore) *cl up on inner: led 1/2-way: rdn wl over 1f out: drvn ins fnl f and hld on wl towards fin* **9/2**3
0051 **2** *nk* **Abbondanza (IRE)**22 7564 7-9-0 82 ... AdrianNicholls 10 80
(D Nicholls) *a cl up: effrt to chal 2f out: sn rdn and ev ch tl drvn ins fnl f and no ex towards fin* **5/2**1
6050 **3** *1* **Harlech Castle**13 7697 5-8-9 77 ...(b) MatthewDavies(3) 1 75
(J R Boyle) *midfield: rdn along and sltly outpcd over 3f out: hdwy and swtchd rt 2f out: sn rdn and styd on strly ins fnl f: nrst fin* **8/1**
0000 **4** 1 ¼ **Masked Dance (IRE)**5 7844 3-9-3 80 ...(b) PhillipMakin 9 76
(K A Ryan) *chsd ldrs on outer: hdwy over 2f out: sn rdn and ch tl drvn and one pce ent fnl f* **14/1**
0411 **5** *3* **Ebraam (USA)**8 7784 7-9-2 88 ... AndreaAtzeni 7 65
(R A Harris) *trckd ldrs: hdwy on inner wl over 2f out: rdn to chse ldrs wl over 1f out: sn drvn and btn* **10/3**2
0216 **6** 1 ¼ **Takajan (IRE)**5 7847 3-8-7 61 ... JamesRogers(7) 3 59
(W M Brisbourne) *chsd ldrs: rdn along over 2f out: sn one pce* **8/1**
4000 **7** *hd* **Dancing Wave**6 7835 4-7-11 45 ... RyanPowell(5) 4 47
(M C Chapman) *led: hdd 1/2-way: sn rdn along and grad wknd fnl 2f* **100/1**
0300 **8** 2 ½ **Hard Rock City (USA)**13 7697 10-8-12 90 ... NeilFarley(5) 5 54
(D Carroll) *a towards rr* **15/2**
0420 **9** *7* **Baby Judge (IRE)**53 7132 3-8-0 45 ... JackDuern(7) 8 21
(M C Chapman) *a in rr* **100/1**
0000 **10** *8* **Bertbrand**24 7537 5-8-7 47 ...(p) KirstyMilczarek 6 —
(I W McInnes) *chsd ldrs: rdn along 1/2-way: sn wknd* **150/1**
1m 19.36s (2.86) **Going Correction** +0.475s/f (Slow) 10 Ran SP% **113.1**
Speed ratings (Par 101): **99,98,97,95,91 89,89,86,77,66**
toteswingers: 1&2 £2.90, 1&3 £8.60, 2&3 £5.30. CSF £15.67 TOTE £3.60: £1.10, £1.20, £2.60; EX 17.60 Trifecta £104.50 Pool: £238.70 - 1.69 winning units..
Owner Liam Breslin **Bred** Cheveley Park Stud Ltd **Trained** Cowbit, Lincs
■ Stewards' Enquiry : Hayley Turner one-day ban: used whip with excessive force (Dec 31)

FOCUS
Times suggest the surface was riding on the slow side. The proximity of 45-rated Dancing Wave suggests a few of these ran below their official marks, and the form pair were not at their best, but this was still a fair claimer. The winner is rated back to his best.
Bertbrand Official explanation: jockey said gelding was unsuited by the standard to slow Fibresand

7907 TOTEEXACTA THE BETTER VALUE FORECAST FILLIES' MEDIAN AUCTION MAIDEN STKS 1m (F)
12:35 (12:35) (Class 5) 2-Y-O **£2,115** (£624; £312) **Stalls** Low

Form RPR
5334 **1** **Night Witch (IRE)**23 7552 2-9-0 65 ... JimmyQuinn 4 66
(E J Creighton) *trckd ldng pair: hdwy 2f out: shkn up and led appr fnl f: sn rdn clr: readily* **9/2**3
023 **2** 3 ¾ **Frosty Friday**13 7693 2-9-0 66 ... GregFairley 3 58
(J R Jenkins) *led 1f: cl up tl led again wl over 2f out and sn rdn: drvn over 1f out: hdd appr fnl f: sn edgd lft and one pce* **6/4**2
0333 **3** 1 ¾ **Phase Shift**8 7780 2-8-7 73 ... JamesRogers(7) 1 54
(W R Muir) *cl up: led after 1f: rdn along and hdd wl over 2f out: drvn and ev ch tl wknd appr fnl f* **11/10**1
000 **4** *30* **Jacquotte (IRE)**11 7723 2-9-0 0 ... KirstyMilczarek 2 —
(E J Creighton) *chsd ldrs on inner: rdn along over 3f out: sn outpcd and bhd* **50/1**
1m 49.46s (5.76) **Going Correction** +0.475s/f (Slow) 4 Ran SP% **107.8**
Speed ratings (Par 93): **90,86,84,54**
CSF £11.56 TOTE £4.00; EX 8.00.
Owner Martin Bourke **Bred** M And P Associates **Trained** Wormshill, Kent

FOCUS
A modest, uncompetitive fillies' maiden, and the time was slow, being 3.52 seconds off the later Class 6 handicap for 3yos.

NOTEBOOK
Night Witch(IRE) proved suited by the step back up to 1m and switch to Fibresand, finding plenty after travelling best. She seemed to run a little way above her official mark of 65. (tchd 4-1 and 5-1)
Frosty Friday is exposed as modest. She may well want a lot further in time. (tchd 13-8)
Phase Shift had looked a suspect stayer at this trip on Polytrack, and the switch to Fibresand only put the emphasis even more on stamina. (tchd Evens and 6-5 and 5-4 in a place)

7908 ARCHER ELECTRICAL NURSERY 5f (F)
1:10 (1:10) (Class 4) (0-85,83) 2-Y-O **£3,043** (£905; £452; £226) **Stalls** High

Form RPR
0611 **1** **Even Stevens**3 7864 2-7-7 **57** 6ex ... NeilFarley(5) 1 79+
(D Nicholls) *cl up: led 1/2-way: rdn and qcknd clr over 1f out: readily* **5/4**1
211 **2** *6* **Monsieur Jamie**10 7739 2-8-11 **73** 6ex ... GregFairley 2 70
(J R Jenkins) *chsd ldng pair: hdwy 2f out: sn rdn: styd on ins fnl f: no ch w wnr* **7/2**3
5412 **3** ¾ **Flash City (ITY)**10 7739 2-9-3 **79** ... PhillipMakin 5 73
(B Smart) *led: hdd 1/2-way and sn pushed along: rdn wl over 1f out and sn one pce* **5/2**2
2111 **4** *2* **Insolenceofoffice (IRE)**20 7592 2-9-7 **83** ...(p) GeorgeBaker 4 70
(Mrs A Duffield) *chsd ldrs: pushed along 1/2-way: sn rdn along and outpcd fr wl over 1f out* **6/1**
59.10 secs (-0.60) **Going Correction** -0.15s/f (Stan) 4 Ran SP% **109.5**
Speed ratings (Par 98): **98,88,87,84**
CSF £5.92 TOTE £2.20; EX 6.70.
Owner Paul J Dixon **Bred** Mrs Yvette Dixon **Trained** Sessay, N Yorks

FOCUS
Only four runners, but they all came into the race in good form.

NOTEBOOK
Even Stevens recorded a quick time considering the track was riding slow. He had got off the mark on his final start for Jeremy Glover in a Polytrack nursery over this trip before a much-improved performance when winning on his Fibresand debut (dam won on the surface) over 6f here three days earlier. Dropped back in trip, he thrashed some in-form rivals, taking this in the manner of at least a 70-rated performer, although he will have to prove himself as good elsewhere. (op 11-8 tchd 6-4)
Monsieur Jamie, like the winner, came into this bidding for a hat-trick under a penalty, but he was clearly nowhere near as well handicapped as Even Stevens. (tchd 4-1)
Flash City(ITY) couldn't reverse recent C&D placings with Monsieur Jamie, but was well clear of the fourth. (tchd 9-4)
Insolenceofoffice(IRE) had won his last three starts on Polytrack, but is clearly not the same horse on Fibresand. (tchd 7-1)

7909 TOTEPOOL A BETTER WAY TO BET H'CAP 1m 3f (F)
1:45 (1:45) (Class 5) (0-70,71) 3-Y-O **£2,115** (£624; £312) **Stalls** Low

Form RPR
3004 **1** **Miereveld**52 7147 3-8-7 **53** oh7 ...(be) JimmyQuinn 4 59
(B Ellison) *trckd ldrs: hdwy over 2f out: rdn to ld over 1f out: drvn and hung lft ins fnl f: kpt on* **4/1**3
0003 **2** 3 ¼ **Jasmin Rai**5 7848 3-8-9 **55** ... CathyGannon 3 55
(D Donovan) *trckd ldrs: hdwy 1/2-way and sn cl up: rdn to ld over 2f out: drvn and hdd over 1f out: kpt on same pce fnl f* **13/2**
0412 **3** 1 ¼ **Loyalty**8 7788 3-9-5 **65** ...(v) PatrickMathers 1 63
(D Shaw) *trckd ldng pair on inner: hdwy wl over 2f out and sn cl up: rdn and ev ch wl over 1f out tl drvn and one pce ent fnl f* **5/4**1
0604 **4** ½ **Maison Brillet (IRE)**49 5353 3-9-7 **67** ... RobertHavlin 2 64
(C Drew) *hld up in rr: hdwy 3f out and sn pushed along: rdn to chse ldrs 2f out: drvn and n.m.r ent fnl f: sn no imp* **16/1**
3 **5** *14* **Indefinite Hope (ITY)**11 7726 3-9-2 **62** ...(t) AndreaAtzeni 5 45
(M Botti) *led: rdn along over 3f out: hdd over 2f out: sn wknd and eased* **11/4**2
2m 33.88s (5.88) **Going Correction** +0.475s/f (Slow) 5 Ran SP% **110.3**
Speed ratings (Par 102): **97,94,93,93,83**
toteswinger: 1&2 £10.30. CSF £27.44 TOTE £4.50: £2.00, £2.00; EX 31.30.
Owner J D Cotterill **Bred** St Clare Hall Stud **Trained** Norton, N Yorks

FOCUS
A weak handicap, and with the pace steady on this slow surface, the final time was poor. The winner was 7lb wrong but has not had many chances, and the favourite was below his Polytrack form.
Indefinite Hope(ITY) Official explanation: jockey said filly stopped quickly and had no more to give

7910 RICHARD MATTHEWS 40TH BIRTHDAY NURSERY 7f (F)
2:20 (2:20) (Class 6) (0-60,64) 2-Y-O **£1,569** (£463; £231) **Stalls** Low

Form RPR
0065 **1** **Granny Anne (IRE)**5 7843 2-8-8 **47** ... CathyGannon 2 56
(A Bailey) *chsd ldrs: rdn along 1/2-way: hdwy on inner over 2f out: rdn to ld wl over 1f out: clr ent fnl f: rdn out* **5/1**

2522 **2** 5 **Norton Girl**[24] 7540 2-9-2 **55** WilliamCarson 6 51
(J J Quinn) *trckd ldrs: hdwy over 2f out: rdn wl over 1f out: kpt on to take 2nd ins fnl f* **7/2**[3]

0251 **3** 1 1/2 **Better Self**[8] 7785 2-9-4 **64** 6ex MatthewCosham(7) 7 56
(P D Evans) *in rr and pushed along 1/2-way: hdwy on wd outside to chse ldrs over 2f out: sn rdn and edgd lft: kpt on u.p fnl f* **9/4**[1]

0001 **4** 1 **Fearless Poet (IRE)**[6] 7831 2-8-12 **51** 6ex (p) MartinLane 3 41
(B Smart) *sn pushed along and cl up after 1f: led briefly 1/2-way: hdd 3f out and sn rdn: drvn 2f out and sn one pce* **10/3**[2]

0335 **5** 3/4 **Local Diktator**[9] 7762 2-9-2 **55** (t) AndreaAtzeni 5 43
(R A Harris) *prom: hdwy to ld 3f out: rdn over 2f out: drvn and hdd wl over 1f out: sn wknd* **16/1**

004 **6** 3 3/4 **Pyrenean**[20] 7602 2-9-7 **60** J-PGuillambert 4 39
(J G Given) *t.k.h and led early: styd prom: rdn along 3f out: sn drvn and edgd lft: wknd fnl f* **8/1**

0650 **7** 1 **False Promises**[6] 7831 2-8-7 **46** ow1 (v) RobbieFitzpatrick 1 22
(D Shaw) *sn cl up on inner: led after 1f: rdn along and hdd 1/2-way: sn wknd* **28/1**

1m 34.65s (4.35) **Going Correction** +0.475s/f (Slow) **7** Ran SP% **113.2**
Speed ratings (Par 94): **94,88,86,85,84 80,79**
toteswingers: 1&2 £3.80, 1&3 £3.70, 2&3 £1.80. CSF £22.29 TOTE £6.60: £2.90, £1.80; EX 25.50.
Owner H Herne **Bred** Mrs J A Dene **Trained** Newmarket, Suffolk

FOCUS
A moderate nursery run in a slow time, 2.13 seconds off the later 0-55 classified event for older horses.

NOTEBOOK
Granny Anne(IRE) was well suited by the step back up in trip and improved on her recent fifth in a 6f maiden here, gaining her first success at the tenth attempt. She was off the bridle well before the straight, and then once in line for the finish she stuck to the so often unfavoured inside rail, but clearly there was no problem with that part of the track this time. She won well, but this certainly isn't form to get carried away with. Official explanation: trainer said, regarding apparent improvement in form, that the filly appeared suited by the longer trip and drop in class. (op 9-2)
Norton Girl plugged on at the one pace, but she was comfortably held and doesn't look a strong stayer at this trip. (op 9-2)
Better Self had struggled to go the pace before staying on well when improving to win a better race than this on Polytrack last time, but she again failed to apply herself early and this Fibresand surface patently didn't suit as well. Official explanation: jockey said filly resented kickback (op 11-4)
Fearless Poet(IRE), penalised for a recent win over 1m here, had to be niggled along early to take up a prominent position, but he only responded to a point and was back in trouble soon enough. It seems the drop in trip did not suit. (op 3-1 tchd 7-2)
Local Diktator again went left under pressure and offered little. Official explanation: jockey said colt hung left in straight (op 14-1)

7911 TOTESWINGER THREE WAYS TO WIN CLASSIFIED STKS 7f (F)
2:55 (2:55) (Class 6) 3-Y-O+ **£1,489** (£443; £221; £110) **Stalls** Low

Form RPR
4335 **1** **Olympic Dream**[6] 7835 4-8-9 54 (p) BillyCray(5) 5 60
(M Herrington) *towards rr and pushed along 1/2-way: gd hdwy to join ldrs over 2f out: rdn to ld 1 1/2f out: drvn and edgd rt over 1f out: kpt on* **3/1**[2]

023 **2** 1 1/4 **Itsthursdayalready**[9] 7761 3-8-7 53 JamesRogers(7) 4 57
(W M Brisbourne) *trckd ldrs: hdwy and ev ch 2f out: sn rdn and sltly hmpd over 1f out: drvn and kpt on ins fnl f* **11/4**[1]

2303 **3** 1 1/2 **Hambleton**[36] 7406 3-8-7 55 (p) AdamCarter(7) 8 53
(B Smart) *trckd ldrs on outer: hdwy and cl up 1/2-way: rdn to ld 2f out: sn drvn and hdd 1 1/2f out: edgd rt over 1f out: kpt on same pce* **7/2**[3]

0602 **4** 8 **Sir Louis**[10] 7738 3-9-0 55 PhillipMakin 6 31
(R A Fahey) *dwlt: sn chsng ldrs on outer: rdn along over 2f out: sn drvn and one pce* **9/2**

5050 **5** 6 **Fathey (IRE)**[3] 7870 4-9-0 49 RobbieFitzpatrick 1 15
(C Smith) *sn rdn along to chse ldrs on inner: lost pl over 3f out and sn bhd* **16/1**

2200 **6** 3 1/4 **Best Known Secret (IRE)**[7] 7807 4-9-0 48 (b1) RussKennemore 7 —
(C C Bealby) *sn led: rdn along 3f out: hdd 2f out and sn wknd* **8/1**

00-3 **7** 13 **Teeraha (IRE)**[334] 213 3-8-9 44 RyanClark(5) 3 —
(Miss M E Rowland) *prom: rdn along after 3f: sn lost pl and bhd* **22/1**

1m 32.52s (2.22) **Going Correction** +0.475s/f (Slow) **7** Ran SP% **113.4**
Speed ratings (Par 101): **106,104,102,93,86 83,68**
toteswingers: 1&2 £2.20, 1&3 £2.80, 2&3 £3.10. CSF £11.50 TOTE £3.70: £1.90, £2.10; EX 14.10 Trifecta £35.60 Pool: £671.90 - 13.93 winning units..
Owner Stuart Herrington **Bred** H Hurst **Trained** Cold Kirby, N Yorks
■ Stewards' Enquiry : Billy Cray one-day ban: careless riding (Dec 31)

FOCUS
A really moderate race full of infrequent winners and maidens. Not form to rate positively.

7912 TONY MCCOY FOR BBC SPORTS PERSONALITY H'CAP 1m (F)
3:30 (3:31) (Class 6) (0-65,68) 3-Y-O **£1,569** (£463; £231) **Stalls** Low

Form RPR
1401 **1** **D'Urberville**[6] 7833 3-9-10 **68** 6ex AdrianNicholls 4 75
(J R Jenkins) *cl up: led over 4f out: rdn 2f out: drvn appr fnl f and styd on gamely* **2/1**[2]

4-04 **2** 1 3/4 **Gold Story**[11] 7731 3-8-7 **51** oh4 JimmyQuinn 6 54
(B Ellison) *hld up: hdwy 1/2-way: rdn along over 3f out: hdwy to chse wnr 2f out: sn rdn and ev ch tl drvn and one pce ins fnl f* **9/2**[3]

5000 **3** 1 1/2 **Verluga (IRE)**[23] 6168 3-9-0 **58** DuranFentiman 5 58
(T D Easterby) *cl up: rdn along on outer and sltly outpcd 2f out: drvn and kpt on fnl f* **16/1**

2600 **4** 1/2 **Stef And Stelio**[53] 7128 3-9-2 **60** CathyGannon 2 58
(G A Butler) *sn led: hdd over 4f out: cl up: rdn 2f out and ev ch tl drvn and one pce appr fnl f* **12/1**

3631 **5** 7 **Adam De Beaulieu (USA)**[17] 7645 3-9-7 **65** (t) PhillipMakin 3 47
(B M R Haslam) *chsd ldrs: rdn along on inner 2f out: sn drvn and btn* **15/8**[1]

0310 **6** 8 **Cuckoo Rock (IRE)**[34] 7445 3-8-13 **57** (p) MartinLane 1 21
(J G Portman) *chsd ldrs: rdn along over 3f out: sn outpcd and bhd fnl 2f* **8/1**

1m 45.94s (2.24) **Going Correction** +0.475s/f (Slow) **6** Ran SP% **111.0**
Speed ratings (Par 98): **107,105,103,103,96 88**
toteswingers: 1&2 £2.40, 1&3 £6.10, 2&3 £6.70. CSF £11.09 TOTE £2.70: £1.20, £3.20; EX 10.80.
Owner Smart K Syndicate **Bred** Llety Stud **Trained** Royston, Herts

FOCUS
A moderate handicap with a disappointing favourite. The winner built on his good C&D record and a 6lb personal bestr from the second.
Adam De Beaulieu(USA) Official explanation: trainer had no explanation for the poor form shown

T/Plt: £456.30 to a £1 stake. Pool:£56,352.80 - 90.15 winning tickets. T/Qpdt: £51.70 to a £1 stake. Pool:£7,391.87 - 105.70 winning tickets. JR

7856 WOLVERHAMPTON (A.W) (L-H)
Friday, December 17

OFFICIAL GOING: Standard to slow (last race (6.50) abandoned due to unsafe ground)
Wind: Fresh across, becoming almost nil race 4 onwards Weather: Fine

7913 BIGGER WINS WITH SP+ AT TOTESPORT.COM MEDIAN AUCTION MAIDEN FILLIES' STKS 5f 216y(P)
2:05 (2:07) (Class 6) 2-Y-O **£1,706** (£503; £252) **Stalls** Low

Form RPR
4324 **1** **Malpas Missile (IRE)**[106] 5682 2-9-0 78 RichardKingscote 7 68+
(Tom Dascombe) *mde all: rdn over 1f out: edgd lft: r.o wl* **1/4**[1]

00 **2** 5 **Boushra**[34] 7447 2-9-0 0 JamesDoyle 5 53
(S Kirk) *chsd ldrs: rdn over 1f out: styd on same pce: wnt 2nd post* **33/1**

0 **3** nse **Miss Firefox**[41] 7345 2-9-0 0 LukeMorris 4 53
(N J Vaughan) *chsd wnr: rdn over 2f out: no ex ins fnl f* **8/1**[3]

0044 **4** 3 1/4 **Zeavola (IRE)**[10] 7734 2-9-0 65 DavidProbert 1 43
(A M Balding) *unruly prior to the s: chsd ldrs: rdn over 1f out: wknd fnl f* **4/1**[2]

00 **5** 9 **Layla's Princess**[4] 7858 2-9-0 0 StevieDonohoe 6 16
(Ian Williams) *hld up: hdwy on outer over 2f out: wknd over 1f out* **16/1**

56 **6** 1 1/2 **These Dreams**[27] 7517 2-8-11 0 RossAtkinson(3) 2 12
(R C Guest) *prom: pushed along and lost pl over 3f out: wknd over 2f out* **20/1**

60 **7** 1 **Zareena**[4] 7858 2-9-0 0 TomQueally 8 9
(P D Evans) *hld up: rdn and wknd over 2f out* **25/1**

00 **8** 3/4 **Buon Compleanno (IRE)**[20] 7598 2-9-0 27 BarryMcHugh 3 —
(A Berry) *mid-div: rdn 1/2-way: wknd over 2f out* **100/1**

1m 17.05s (2.05) **Going Correction** +0.35s/f (Slow) **8** Ran SP% **129.5**
Speed ratings (Par 91): **100,93,93,88,76 74,73,72**
toteswingers: 1&2 £9.00, 1&3 £1.70, 2&3 £11.40. CSF £25.71 TOTE £1.20: £1.02, £8.20, £2.10; EX 23.00.
Owner A Black & M Owen **Bred** Honora Corridan And Mrs Mary Murphy **Trained** Malpas, Cheshire

FOCUS
A modest fillies' median auction maiden dominated by the long odds-on favourite. Nothing got into the race from off the pace.

NOTEBOOK
Malpas Missile(IRE) returned from a 106-day absence to take this in facile fashion. Pushed up to lead after a furlong, she kicked clear rounding the home bend and ran right away from some very modest rivals. She didn't need to run up to her official rating to win this, but had been competitive off marks in the 70s when last seen in nursery company. She is likely to be put away now. (tchd 2-7)
Boushra stepped up on her two previous starts (well-beaten at this course) without ever threatening the winner. Settled nicely in behind the pace, she ran on to just grab second on the line. She'll be eligible for handicaps after this.
Miss Firefox was ridden positively in the early stages and kept on despite coming under heavy pressure with 3f to run. She is bred to appreciate 1m+ in time and should be noted when stepped up in trip once qualified for handicaps. (op 14-1)
Zeavola(IRE) was the big disappointment of the race, getting worked up in the preliminaries and finding absolutely nothing once coming under pressure in the race itself. She seems reticent to channel her concentration to racing and is one to avoid. (op 3-1)
Layla's Princess made a short-lived move around the outside with 3f to run. She is another now qualified for handicaps.

7914 WOLVERHAMPTON HOLIDAY INN MAIDEN STKS 7f 32y(P)
2:40 (2:40) (Class 5) 2-Y-O **£2,007** (£597; £298; £149) **Stalls** High

Form RPR
0 **1** **Bassett Road (IRE)**[22] 7567 2-9-3 0 RichardKingscote 3 80
(Tom Dascombe) *chsd ldr: rdn to ld over 1f out: hung rt ins fnl f: styd on u.p* **8/13**[1]

060 **2** nk **Cloud Illusions (USA)**[55] 7098 2-8-12 83 EddieAhern 5 75
(Mrs H S Main) *hld up: hdwy on outside 1/2-way: ev ch fr over 1f out: edgd lft: rdn wl ins fnl f: r.o* **85/40**[2]

06 **3** 10 **Goal (IRE)**[21] 7578 2-9-3 0 StevieDonohoe 2 55
(D C Griffiths) *led: rdn and hung rt over 2f out: hdd over 1f out: wknd fnl f* **8/1**[3]

4 39 **Big City Boy (IRE)** 2-9-3 0 AdamKirby 1 —
(P S McEntee) *s.i.s: sn chsng ldrs: rdn and lost pl over 4f out: sn wl bhd: t.o* **25/1**

1m 31.24s (1.64) **Going Correction** +0.35s/f (Slow) **4** Ran SP% **108.9**
Speed ratings (Par 96): **104,103,92,47**
CSF £2.19 TOTE £1.80; EX 2.40.
Owner Mrs Sam Dascombe **Bred** Michael Mullins **Trained** Malpas, Cheshire

FOCUS
They went a brisk gallop in this ordinary juvenile maiden.

NOTEBOOK
Bassett Road(IRE), a half-brother to smart 6f performer Gramercy, had shown early pace before weakening late on when well beaten over the extended 1m here on his racecourse debut last month. Suited by the drop back to 7f, he made his challenge with 2f to run and kept on gamely to the line, despite hanging right in the last 100 yards. He is quite a scopey sort and has the makings of a decent 3-y-o handicapper, with a step back up in trip likely to suit as he matures. (tchd 4-6)
Cloud Illusions(USA) had not been disgraced in Listed company when last seen at Newbury in October. Despite slightly fluffing the start, she travelled effortlessly into contention and looked to have the race sewn up before just being ground down in the dying stages. Eddie Ahern appeared keen to avoid using his whip and whether that was overconfidence, or that the filly doesn't respond to it, is hard to know. She should be able to pick up a similar contest. (op 2-1 tchd 9-4)
Goal(IRE) had been slowly away on his two previous starts over 6f, but there was no messing about here. He stretched the field right out down the back straight and developed a lead of over three lengths at one stage. It soon became apparent, though, that he was a sitting duck to the market principals once they turned into the home straight. (op 11-1 tchd 7-1)

7915 CALL TOTESPORT 0800 221221 FOR SP+ H'CAP 7f 32y(P)
3:15 (3:16) (Class 4) (0-85,84) 3-Y-O+ **£3,594** (£1,069; £534; £266) **Stalls** High

Form
2011 **1** **Hulcote Rose (IRE)**[15] 7665 3-9-2 **79** JamesDoyle 7 97+
(S Kirk) *a.p: chsd ldr over 2f out: shkn up to ld ins fnl f: r.o wl: eased nr fin* **11/4**[1]

1-10 **2** 5 **Striker Torres (IRE)**[317] 393 4-8-9 **72** (v) GrahamGibbons 10 76
(G R Oldroyd) *led: clr over 2f out: rdn over 1f out: hdd and no ex ins fnl f* **7/1**

0040 **3** ¾ **Mr Macattack**[114] 5407 5-9-7 **84**.............................(t) RichardKingscote 5 86+
(Tom Dascombe) *hld up: r.o ins fnl f: nvr trbld ldrs* **15/2**

3033 **4** *nk* **Bawaardi (IRE)**[5] 7846 4-9-3 **80**... EddieAhern 3 81
(R A Fahey) *hld up: hdwy 1/2-way: rdn over 1f out: styd on same pce* **4/1**[2]

3430 **5** 1 ¼ **Saharia (IRE)**[23] 7560 3-9-4 **81**.. BarryMcHugh 4 79
(Ollie Pears) *chsd ldrs: rdn 1/2-way: styd on same pce fnl 2f* **17/2**

2102 **6** 4 ½ **Whispering Spirit (IRE)**[9] 7766 4-8-12 **78**...................(v) AmyRyan(3) 9 64
(Mrs A Duffield) *chsd ldrs tl rdn and wknd over 1f out* **13/2**[3]

0214 **7** 1 ¼ **Solar Spirit (IRE)**[45] 7283 5-8-9 **79**.............................. ShaneBKelly(7) 6 61
(J J Quinn) *chsd ldr tl rdn over 2f out: wknd over 1f out* **8/1**

2200 **8** 2 ¼ **Ocean Legend (IRE)**[35] 7430 5-9-7 **84**.............................. AdamKirby 2 60
(A W Carroll) *broke wl: sn stdd and lost pl: n.d after* **16/1**

0204 **9** *nk* **Ivory Silk**[12] 7719 5-8-13 **76**..(b) SteveDrowne 12 51
(J R Gask) *s.i.s: hld up: rdn 1/2-way: a in rr* **25/1**

231- **10** ½ **Qaraaba**[431] 6730 3-9-3 **80**.. TomQueally 11 54
(Seamus Durack) *hld up: rdn over 2f out: sn wknd* **10/1**

1m 30.17s (0.57) **Going Correction** +0.35s/f (Slow) 10 Ran SP% **124.7**
Speed ratings (Par 105): **110,104,103,103,101 96,95,92,92,91**
toteswingers: 1&2 £7.20, 1&3 £7.20, 2&3 £11.60. CSF £24.41 CT £137.45 TOTE £4.70: £1.80, £2.70, £3.50; EX 41.60.
Owner The Kathryn Stud **Bred** Ecurie Des Monceaux **Trained** Upper Lambourn, Berks

FOCUS
A competitive handicap won in impressive fashion by a 3-y-o filly distinctly on the upgrade. Fair form with a clear personal best from the progressive winner.

7916 BET ON THE ASHES AT TOTESPORT.COM NURSERY 1m 141y(P)
3:45 (3:45) (Class 4) (0-85,85) 2-Y-O £3,238 (£963; £481; £240) Stalls Low

Form RPR

4503 **1** **Swift Alhaarth (IRE)**[62] 6936 2-8-4 **68**............................... GregFairley 1 76
(M Johnston) *chsd ldr tl led over 2f out: rdn over 1f out: jnd ins fnl f: styd on gamely* **11/2**[3]

0531 **2** 3 ¼ **Dunhoy (IRE)**[14] 7677 2-8-13 **77**....................................... MickyFenton 8 78
(Stef Higgins) *hld up: hdwy over 2f out: rdn and ev ch ins fnl f: styd on same pce* **13/2**

2532 **3** 2 ¼ **Fred Willetts (IRE)**[16] 7652 2-9-1 **79**........................... StevieDonohoe 3 75
(P D Evans) *chsd ldrs: rdn 1/2-way: no ex fnl f* **10/1**

4021 **4** 1 ¼ **Ivan Vasilevich (IRE)**[9] 7755 2-8-7 **71** 6ex......................... ShaneKelly 5 65
(Jane Chapple-Hyam) *chsd ldrs: rdn over 3f out: outpcd over 2f out: styd on u.p ins fnl f* **6/1**

5112 **5** ½ **Piceno (IRE)**[17] 7636 2-9-0 **78**... IanMongan 7 71
(D Nicholls) *pushed along to ld: rdn and hdd over 2f out: wknd fnl f* **5/2**[1]

01 **6** 16 **Potomac (IRE)**[13] 7693 2-9-7 **85**...................................(p) NickyMackay 4 44
(J H M Gosden) *hld up: hdwy over 3f out: rdn and wknd over 2f out* **3/1**[2]

0021 **7** 10 **Malice Or Mischief (IRE)**[30] 7486 2-8-11 **78**................. KierenFox(3) 9 16
(A W Carroll) *sn drvn along in rr: wknd over 3f out: t.o* **12/1**

0500 **8** 1 ¼ **Arctic Reach**[53] 7124 2-7-12 **62** oh9................................... DavidProbert 6 —
(G D Blake) *hld up: rdn 1/2-way: sn wknd: t.o* **50/1**

1m 52.74s (2.24) **Going Correction** +0.35s/f (Slow) 8 Ran SP% **115.3**
Speed ratings (Par 98): **104,101,99,98,97 83,74,73**
toteswingers: 1&2 £7.10, 1&3 £5.60, 2&3 £7.50. CSF £41.13 CT £350.08 TOTE £5.30: £1.70, £2.70, £2.90; EX 40.50.
Owner Dr Marwan Koukash **Bred** Mrs Joan Murphy **Trained** Middleham Moor, N Yorks

FOCUS
A strong gallop in this competitive nursery.

NOTEBOOK
Swift Alhaarth(IRE) ◆, having his first start in handicap company having been placed in a C&D maiden 62 days ago, shadowed the pacesetter to the home straight before hitting the front when that rival weakened. He faced a concerted challenge until pulling away inside the last 100 yards. A strapping gelding, he should continue to improve and is likely to stay further. (op 5-1)
Dunhoy(IRE) had bolted up in a three-runner C&D maiden here a fortnight ago, and looked likely to follow up in handicap company when sweeping round the outside of the field rounding the home bend. However, the energy expended making that move probably softened him up for the renewed effort of the winner. He has a race in him off this mark and also has the scope to make a 3-y-o. (op 7-1 tchd 6-1)
Fred Willetts(IRE) stuck on gamely up the rail without ever looking like winning. He remains winless in handicap company and needs some respite from the assessor. (op 8-1)
Piceno(IRE), the market-leader, crossed over from his wide draw to lead and set a strong gallop in this competitive nursery. He had cried enough with 2f to run though. (op 3-1 tchd 7-2)
Potomac(IRE) had improved on a modest debut effort here to win a Southwell maiden last time out, but he ran poorly and is probably best suited to the Fibresand. (op 7-2)

7917 RINGSIDE CONFERENCE SUITE - 700 THEATRE STYLE H'CAP (DIV I) 1m 141y(P)
4:20 (4:22) (Class 7) (0-50,50) 3-Y-O+ £1,364 (£403; £201) Stalls Low

Form RPR

020 **1** **No Complaining (IRE)**[52] 7153 3-8-11 **49**......................... TomQueally 1 61
(B J Curley) *trckd ldrs: rdn to ld over 1f out: sn hung rt: r.o* **5/2**[1]

0002 **2** 2 ¼ **Lucky Diva**[7] 7814 3-8-11 **49**.. DavidProbert 4 58+
(S Kirk) *chsd ldrs: nt clr run over 1f out: r.o to go 2nd wl ins fnl f: nt trble wnr* **5/2**[1]

3433 **3** ½ **Al Rayanah**[28] 7508 7-9-0 **50**...(p) KirstyMilczarek 5 56
(G Prodromou) *dwlt: hld up: hdwy over 2f out: rdn to chse wnr over 1f out: edgd rt: styd on same pce and lost 2nd wl ins fnl f* **9/2**[2]

0644 **4** 4 ½ **Carnival Dream**[28] 7506 5-8-13 **49**.............................(p) PatrickMathers 9 45
(H A McWilliams) *trckd ldr tl led wl over 1f out: sn rdn and hdd: wknd ins fnl f* **16/1**

0005 **5** ½ **Isabella Romee (IRE)**[6] 7829 4-8-5 **48**......................... LewisWalsh(7) 10 42
(Jane Chapple-Hyam) *hld up: rdn over 2f out: r.o ins fnl f: nvr nrr* **17/2**

0-03 **6** 4 ½ **Ryan's Rock**[4] 7862 5-8-11 **47**.. JamesDoyle 2 31
(R J Price) *led: rdn and edgd rt over 2f out: hdd wl over 1f out: sn wknd* **13/2**[3]

0000 **7** *hd* **Barton Bounty**[21] 6189 3-8-4 **45**................................. JamesSullivan(3) 3 29
(P D Niven) *hld up: rdn 1/2-way: hdwy over 2f out: wknd over 1f out* **40/1**

05/6 **8** 12 **Shipboard Romance (IRE)**[36] 3032 5-8-9 **45**.................(t) ChrisCatlin 8 —
(M G Rimell) *mid-div: sn pushed along: lost pl over 6f out: wknd over 3f out* **20/1**

000- **9** 27 **Lambrini Lace (IRE)**[353] 7869 5-8-6 **45**...............(p) PatrickDonaghy(3) 6 —
(Mrs L Williamson) *hld up: racd keenly: hdwy over 6f out: rdn and wknd over 2f out* **40/1**

1m 53.98s (3.48) **Going Correction** +0.35s/f (Slow)
WFA 3 from 4yo+ 2lb 9 Ran SP% **114.7**
Speed ratings (Par 97): **98,96,95,91,91 87,86,76,52**
toteswingers: 1&2 £3.00, 1&3 £3.90, 2&3 £2.20. CSF £8.22 CT £24.84 TOTE £4.80: £2.00, £1.50, £1.10; EX 13.00.
Owner P A Byrne **Bred** Epona Bloodstock Ltd **Trained** Newmarket, Suffolk

FOCUS
A very modest handicap notable for one thing, a successful Barney Curley gamble. It was faster than division II but still muddling. The winner recorded a 10lb personal best.

7918 RINGSIDE CONFERENCE SUITE - 700 THEATRE STYLE H'CAP (DIV II) 1m 141y(P)
4:50 (4:50) (Class 7) (0-50,50) 3-Y-O+ £1,364 (£403; £201) Stalls Low

Form RPR

01 **1** **John Potts**[13] 7706 5-8-9 **48**.. KellyHarrison(3) 4 55
(B P J Baugh) *trckd ldrs: racd keenly: led over 1f out: sn rdn: r.o* **7/2**[1]

0000 **2** *nk* **On The Cusp (IRE)**[11] 7727 3-8-8 **46**...............................(p) ChrisCatlin 5 52
(P Butler) *plld hrd: led 7f out: rdn and hdd over 1f out: r.o* **18/1**

6043 **3** 2 **Bring Sweets (IRE)**[8] 7789 3-8-12 **50**................................. DaneO'Neill 9 52+
(B Ellison) *hld up: hdwy over 1f out: r.o: wnt 3rd wl ins fnl f: nt rch ldrs* **4/1**[2]

0 **4** *nk* **Celtic Life (IRE)**[8] 7787 4-8-11 **47**..................................(t) TomQueally 8 48
(Miss Amy Weaver) *a.p: chsd ldr over 5f out: rdn over 1f out: styd on same pce ins fnl f* **6/1**[3]

4050 **5** 2 ¼ **Our Kes (IRE)**[12] 7716 8-8-13 **49**............................... SeamieHeffernan 1 45
(Jane Chapple-Hyam) *hld up in tch: rdn over 2f out: styd on same pce fnl f* **4/1**[2]

0633 **6** 2 ¼ **Devon Diva**[16] 7649 4-9-0 **50**... KirstyMilczarek 3 41
(M Hill) *led: hdd 7f out: chsd ldrs: rdn over 2f out: wknd fnl f* **15/2**

0003 **7** 1 **Flyjack (USA)**[8] 7786 3-8-6 **47**.............................(p) PatrickDonaghy(3) 10 35
(Mrs L Williamson) *hld up: hdwy over 3f out: rdn and wknd over 1f out* **22/1**

0500 **8** 1 ½ **Mullitovermaurice**[35] 7429 4-8-6 **45**......................(vt[1]) RossAtkinson(3) 2 30
(Patrick Morris) *hld up: rdn over 3f out: hdwy over 2f out: wkng whn hung lft over 1f out* **12/1**

4-40 **9** 23 **She's My Rock (IRE)**[13] 7706 3-8-11 **49**............................ JamesDoyle 6 —
(S Kirk) *hld up in tch: rdn over 3f out: sn wknd: t.o* **14/1**

0006 **10** 67 **Penshurst Lad (IRE)**[8] 7789 3-8-9 **47** ow2..................(b[1]) SteveDrowne 7 —
(R T Phillips) *s.s: a t.o* **50/1**

1m 56.11s (5.61) **Going Correction** +0.35s/f (Slow)
WFA 3 from 4yo+ 2lb 10 Ran SP% **114.2**
Speed ratings (Par 97): **89,88,86,86,84 82,81,80,60,—**
toteswingers: 1&2 £22.60, 1&3 £2.30, 2&3 £16.30. CSF £66.32 CT £266.31 TOTE £2.80: £1.10, £8.20, £1.20; EX 85.00.
Owner Miss S M Potts **Bred** Miss S M Potts **Trained** Audley, Staffs

FOCUS
A very modest event light on in-form horses and it was very steadily run to boot, meaning a prominent position was an advantage. It was slower than the first division and the form is muddling.

7919 BET ON LIVE CRICKET AT TOTESPORT.COM H'CAP (DIV I) 1m 1f 103y(P)
5:20 (5:20) (Class 6) (0-65,70) 3-Y-O+ £1,706 (£503; £252) Stalls Low

Form RPR

1011 **1** **Querido (GER)**[34] 7449 6-9-6 **61**....................................(t) GeorgeBaker 5 75+
(G Brown) *trckd ldrs: a gng wl: n.m.r and led 2f out: sn clr: comf* **5/4**[1]

0021 **2** 4 **Love In The Park**[18] 7633 5-9-1 **56**................................... JackMitchell 3 62
(R Brotherton) *hld up in tch: rdn to chse wnr fnl f: no imp* **11/4**[2]

0043 **3** 2 ¾ **Mr Maximas**[11] 7728 3-8-8 **51**....................................... RobertWinston 2 51
(B Palling) *chsd ldr: rdn and ev ch 2f out: hung lft over 1f out: no ex fnl f* **8/1**

34 **4** ½ **Chichen Daawe**[35] 7429 4-8-11 **52**..................................(p) DaneO'Neill 4 51
(B Ellison) *led: rdn and hdd 2f out: sn btn* **11/2**[3]

0100 **5** 2 ¼ **Atacama Sunrise**[6] 7833 4-9-7 **62**............................... KirstyMilczarek 6 56
(G Prodromou) *hld up: hdwy 2f out: rdn and wknd over 1f out* **12/1**

-040 **6** 8 **Hits Only Cash**[23] 7562 8-9-3 **58**...................................(p) MickyFenton 7 36
(J Pearce) *hld up: drvn along over 3f out: wknd over 2f out* **12/1**

2m 6.69s (4.99) **Going Correction** +0.35s/f (Slow)
WFA 3 from 4yo+ 2lb 6 Ran SP% **113.0**
Speed ratings (Par 101): **91,87,85,84,82 75**
toteswingers: 1&2 £1.40, 1&3 £2.00, 2&3 £3.40. CSF £4.93 TOTE £2.40: £1.60, £1.10; EX 4.10.
Owner Miss Emma Wettern **Bred** Gestut Brummerhof **Trained** East Garston, Berks

FOCUS
An uncompetitive race turned into something of a procession by the well-handicapped winner. Once again the pace was steady. The form is rated through the third and the winner may have more to offer.

7920 BET ON LIVE CRICKET AT TOTESPORT.COM H'CAP (DIV II) 1m 1f 103y(P)
5:50 (5:50) (Class 6) (0-65,62) 3-Y-O+ £1,706 (£503; £252) Stalls Low

Form RPR

0563 **1** **Black Coffee**[7] 7814 5-9-0 **55**.......................................(b[1]) ShaneKelly 5 63
(W M Brisbourne) *hld up: hdwy to chse ldr over 2f out: rdn over 1f out: swtchd rt ins fnl f: r.o u.p to ld post* **3/1**[3]

033 **2** *hd* **Eastern Gift**[9] 7768 5-9-4 **62**..................................(p) KierenFox(3) 6 70
(Miss Gay Kelleway) *rn in snatches in rr: hdwy to ld over 2f out: rdn and edgd lft ins fnl f: hdd post* **11/4**[2]

0050 **3** 13 **Una Pelota (IRE)**[113] 5457 4-9-5 **60**......................... RichardKingscote 3 40+
(Tom Dascombe) *trckd ldrs: nt clr run and lost pl over 2f out: nt rcvr* **2/1**[1]

50 **4** 18 **Non Tiscordardime**[7] 7818 3-8-11 **54**............................(tp) TomQueally 2 —
(Niall Moran, Ire) *led: rdn and hdd over 2f out: sn wknd: t.o* **7/1**

-130 **5** 16 **Bestowed**[312] 467 5-9-2 **62**.......................................(v) DeanHeslop(5) 4 —
(P D Evans) *chsd ldr: rdn and ev ch over 2f out: sn wknd: t.o* **7/1**

2m 5.56s (3.86) **Going Correction** +0.35s/f (Slow)
WFA 3 from 4yo+ 2lb 5 Ran SP% **110.0**
Speed ratings (Par 101): **96,95,84,68,54**
toteswinger: 1&2 £5.40. CSF £11.51 TOTE £4.50: £1.30, £2.00; EX 8.40.
Owner Derek & Mrs Marie Dean **Bred** Mrs M Campbell-Andenaes **Trained** Great Ness, Shropshire

FOCUS
Only five runners but an eventful race not properly conveyed by the bare result. The gallop wasn't a bad one considering the size of the field. The first two are rated in line with recent form.

7921 TONY MCCOY FOR BBC SPORTS PERSONALITY H'CAP (DIV I) 1m 4f 50y(P)
6:20 (6:20) (Class 6) (0-65,64) 3-Y-O+ £1,535 (£453; £226) Stalls Low

Form RPR

0021 **1** **Rhythm Stick**[15] 7669 3-9-1 **60**.. FrannyNorton 7 72+
(John Berry) *mde all: rdn 2f out: styd on wl* **5/4**[1]

-161 **2** 1 ½ **Dontpaytheferryman (USA)**[6] 7836 5-8-11 **58** 6ex..... ShaneBKelly(7) 5 66
(B Ellison) *trckd ldrs: plld hrd: wnt 2nd 5f out: rdn over 2f out: styd on same pce ins fnl f* **15/8**[2]

303- **3** 9 **First Spirit**[39] 3588 4-8-13 **53**... LukeMorris 3 47
(R Dickin) *hld up: rdn over 4f out: wknd over 2f out* **22/1**

4605 **4** 2 ¾ **Barbirolli**[12] 7716 8-8-10 **50** oh5....................................... BarryMcHugh 4 39
(W B Stone) *prom: rdn over 3f out: wknd over 2f out* **20/1**

0115 **5** *60* **Naheell**[28] 7504 4-9-10 **64** KirstyMilczarek 1 —
(G Prodromou) *chsd wnr 7f: sn rdn: wknd over 1f out: virtually p.u ins fnl f: dismntd after crossing the line* **3/1**[3]

2m 47.16s (6.06) **Going Correction** +0.35s/f (Slow)
WFA 3 from 4yo+ 5lb **5** Ran SP% **113.3**
Speed ratings (Par 101): **93,92,86,84,44**
toteswinger: 1&2 £2.70. CSF £4.06 TOTE £2.10: £1.80, £1.60; EX 4.30.
Owner Red Furlongs Partnership **Bred** Mrs M L Parry & P M Steele-Mortimer **Trained** Newmarket, Suffolk

FOCUS
The two last-time-out winners came clear in an uncompetitive race run at a steady pace for the most part. Another personal best from the winner, who had an easy lead.

7922 TONY MCCOY FOR BBC SPORTS PERSONALITY H'CAP (DIV II) 1m 4f 50y(P)
() (Class 6) (0-65,) 3-Y-0+ £

T/Plt: £50.30 to a £1 stake. Pool:£82,052.19 -1,190.43 winning tickets. T/Qpdt: £28.60 to a £1 stake. Pool:£9,038.27 - 233.40 winning tickets. CR

7878 LINGFIELD (L-H)
Saturday, December 18
7923 Meeting Abandoned - Frost and snow

7906 SOUTHWELL (L-H)
Saturday, December 18
OFFICIAL GOING: Standard to slow
Wind: Almost nil Weather: Bright and clear, very cold

7931 TOTEPLACEPOT NURSERY 6f (F)
12:30 (12:30) (Class 5) (0-70,66) 2-Y-O **£2,388** (£705; £352) **Stalls** Low

Form RPR
6061 **1** **Dunmore Boy (IRE)**[22] 7576 2-8-12 65 (p) GeorgeChaloner(7) 2 68
(R A Fahey) *t.k.h: trckd ldr: led over 1f out: edgd lft: rdn and hld on wl fnl f* **8/1**

4411 **2** *nk* **Je Suis Unrockstar**[2] 7894 2-9-1 66 6ex (p) BillyCray(5) 1 68
(D Nicholls) *t.k.h: led to over 1f out: rallied: kpt on fnl f: hld towards fin* **8/11**[1]

6144 **3** *2 1/4* **Bachelor Knight (IRE)**[9] 7785 2-8-13 62 JamesSullivan(3) 4 57
(Ollie Pears) *prom: outpcd and hung lft over 2f out: kpt on fnl f: nt rch first two* **10/3**[2]

0313 **4** *3 3/4* **Slatey Hen (IRE)**[8] 7811 2-9-4 64 BarryMcHugh 3 48
(R A Fahey) *trckd ldrs: rdn over 2f out: edgd rt and wknd over 1f out* **5/1**[3]

1m 21.04s (4.54) **Going Correction** +0.525s/f (Slow) **4** Ran SP% **108.8**
Speed ratings (Par 96): **90,89,86,81**
CSF £14.81 TOTE £9.90; EX 13.10.
Owner Tom Flaherty **Bred** Conor Murphy & Rathmore Stud **Trained** Musley Bank, N Yorks

FOCUS
The temperature dropped to -5°C overnight and the surface was given as standard to slow. This looked a little more competitive than the odds suggested.

NOTEBOOK
Dunmore Boy(IRE) broke his maiden at Wolverhampton last time out and, while that came over 5f, he'd done enough racing over 7f-1m earlier in the campaign to suggest the step up to 6f wouldn't be a problem. Returning to Fibresand having disappointed on his previous visit was a concern, but he coped well with the surface this time and his stamina eventually saw him through.
Je Suis Unrockstar had yet to prove himself over this trip. Chasing a hat-trick following a couple of wins over the minimum trip, he took them along for most of the race, but just couldn't see off the persistent Dunmore Boy and was eventually outstayed. It still wasn't a bad effort under his penalty, however. (op 5-6 tchd 10-11)
Bachelor Knight(IRE) is a heavy ground winner over this trip and it was possible to make a case for him improving for the switch to this testing surface. Racing widest round the turn, the first two got away from him somewhat, but he was putting in some good work at the finish, and with this experience behind him he should be capable of finding a race here, either over this distance or 7f. (op 11-4)
Slatey Hen(IRE) was below her best on her Fibresand debut and is probably better suited to the Polytrack. (op 6-1)

7932 TOTESWINGER H'CAP 1m 3f (F)
1:00 (1:00) (Class 5) (0-75,75) 3-Y-O+ **£2,388** (£705; £352) **Stalls** Low

Form RPR
0541 **1** **Kumbeshwar**[4] 7865 3-8-5 66 6ex (v) ShaneBKelly(7) 5 77+
(P D Evans) *t.k.h: trckd ldr: led over 4f out: hung lft and kpt on strly fnl 2f* **1/1**[1]

2013 **2** *5* **Castle Myth (USA)**[4] 7865 4-8-10 60 (be) BarryMcHugh 4 62
(B Ellison) *s.i.s: sn trckd clr ldng pair: outpcd over 4f out: rallied and wnt 2nd over 2f out: kpt on fnl f: nt rch wnr* **11/4**[2]

0003 **3** *3 3/4* **Eton Fable (IRE)**[7] 7836 5-9-1 68 (p) PaulPickard(3) 6 63
(W J H Ratcliffe) *dictated modest gallop: rdn and hdd over 4f out: outpcd fnl 2f* **9/1**

0010 **4** *4 1/2* **Ramora (USA)**[8] 7806 4-8-6 59 MatthewDavies(3) 1 46
(Miss Olivia Maylam) *hld up: shortlived effrt over 3f out: sn rdn and no imp* **14/1**

4441 **5** *12* **General Tufto**[2] 7895 5-9-8 72 6ex (b) MartinLane 2 38
(C Smith) *hld up: pushed along over 3f out: sn struggling: t.o* **6/1**[3]

2m 33.84s (5.84) **Going Correction** +0.525s/f (Slow)
WFA 3 from 4yo+ 4lb **5** Ran SP% **107.6**
Speed ratings (Par 103): **99,95,92,89,80**
CSF £3.71 TOTE £2.30: £1.70, £1.10; EX 3.70.
Owner G E Amey **Bred** G E Amey **Trained** Pandy, Monmouths

FOCUS
A modest handicap rated around the second and third.
General Tufto Official explanation: trainer said race came too soon for gelding

7933 BET TOTEPOOL AT TOTESPORT.COM CLAIMING STKS 1m 4f (F)
1:35 (1:35) (Class 6) 3-Y-O+ **£2,047** (£604; £302) **Stalls** Low

Form RPR
0336 **1** **Camps Bay (USA)**[8] 7815 6-9-8 76 BarryMcHugh 5 86
(B Ellison) *hld up bhd ldng gp: pushed along over 4f out: gd hdwy on outside to ld over 2f out: hung lft and sn rdn wl clr: kpt up to work fnl f* **6/5**[1]

4222 **2** *21* **Yossi (IRE)**[12] 7729 6-8-8 56 ow1 (be) SeanPalmer(7) 4 50
(R C Guest) *dwlt: sn in tch: stdy hdwy to chse (clr) wnr over 1f out: no imp* **15/2**[3]

0030 **3** *2 3/4* **Mojeerr**[2] 7896 4-8-12 48 (e[1]) NeilChalmers 6 43
(A J McCabe) *prom: effrt and rdn 3f out: no imp fr 2f out* **66/1**

4211 **4** *1* **Diggeratt (USA)**[2] 7897 4-9-4 79 (p) MatthewDavies(3) 2 50
(George Baker) *cl up gng wl: ev ch 3f out: sn rdn: outpcd whn edgd lft and lost 2nd over 1f out* **7/4**[2]

5045 **5** *1 3/4* **Dunaskin (IRE)**[72] 6699 10-9-4 57 (b) MartinLane 3 45
(R C Guest) *led after 2f: rdn and hdd over 2f out: sn wknd* **14/1**

5360 **6** *2* **Aldaado (IRE)**[57] 7055 4-8-13 58 PaulPickard(3) 7 40
(P T Midgley) *sn pushed along in rr: struggling 4f out: no ch whn hung lft 2f out* **66/1**

4644 **7** *29* **Baggsy (IRE)**[27] 7381 3-8-2 48 AndreaAtzeni 1 —
(Miss J Feilden) *led 2f: cl up: rdn over 4f out: wknd 3f out: eased whn no ch fnl 2f* **14/1**

2m 46.97s (5.97) **Going Correction** +0.525s/f (Slow)
WFA 3 from 4yo+ 5lb **7** Ran SP% **109.9**
Speed ratings (Par 101): **101,87,85,84,83 82,62**
Tote Swingers: 1&2 £2.10, 1&3 £6.20, 2&3 £6.00 CSF £10.22 TOTE £3.00: £1.10, £2.20; EX 8.90.Camps Bay (USA) was claimed by C. R. Dore for £8,000.
Owner Keith Hanson & Steve Catchpole **Bred** Kidder,Cole,Marnakos,Graves & Beck **Trained** Norton, N Yorks

FOCUS
On paper this looked a two-horse race, and with Diggeratt not getting home on this slower than standard surface, after a two-day break, that left the way clear for Camps Bay to win by a wide margin.
Baggsy(IRE) Official explanation: jockey said filly had no more to give

7934 BET ON TOTESCOOP6 AT TOTESPORT.COM H'CAP 6f (F)
2:05 (2:05) (Class 4) (0-85,83) 3-Y-O+ **£3,885** (£1,156; £577; £288) **Stalls** Low

Form RPR
6622 **1** **Everymanforhimself (IRE)**[12] 7725 6-9-2 78 (b) PhillipMakin 4 90
(K A Ryan) *trckd ldrs: led wl over 1f out: sn rdn: hdd ins fnl f: rallied gamely to regain ld cl home* **5/1**[3]

6232 **2** *hd* **Silaah**[4] 7866 6-9-4 83 (p) MichaelO'Connell(3) 5 94
(D Nicholls) *stdd in tch: t.k.h: smooth hdwy over 2f out: led gng wl ins fnl f: sn rdn: outbattled and hdd cl home* **9/4**[1]

5035 **3** *4* **Yankee Storm**[10] 7766 5-8-8 70 (v) KirstyMilczarek 3 68
(H J Collingridge) *t.k.h: w ldr: rdn 2f out: kpt on same pce fnl f* **7/1**

3312 **4** *3/4* **Bonnie Prince Blue**[11] 7740 7-9-2 78 (be) MartinLane 6 74
(B Ellison) *t.k.h: hld up in tch: effrt over 2f out: no imp over 1f out* **3/1**[2]

5400 **5** *4* **Silver Wind**[13] 7719 5-8-0 69 oh3 (p) HobieGill(7) 7 52
(A J McCabe) *racd wd: slt ld to wl over 1f out: sn rdn: wknd appr fnl f* **33/1**

0303 **6** *5* **Johannesgray (IRE)**[4] 7868 3-8-3 70 (be) BillyCray(5) 8 37
(D Nicholls) *wnt rt s: bhd on outside: struggling over 3f out: sn btn* **11/2**

0-35 **7** *shd* **Dark Lane**[17] 7654 4-9-2 78 BarryMcHugh 1 45
(R A Fahey) *prom: drvn 1/2-way: wknd fnl 2f* **10/1**

1m 18.14s (1.64) **Going Correction** +0.525s/f (Slow) **7** Ran SP% **112.4**
Speed ratings (Par 105): **110,109,104,103,98 91,91**
Tote Swingers: 1&2 £2.50, 2&3 £4.20 CSF £16.08 CT £76.75 TOTE £4.60: £3.00, £2.10; EX 16.10.
Owner J Duddy B McDonald & A Heeney **Bred** Denis McDonnell **Trained** Hambleton, N Yorks

FOCUS
A competitive sprint handicap which looked sure to go the way of Silaah when he came there cruising approaching the final furlong (touched 1.02 in-running), but once let down he didn't find as much as had looked likely and in the end was worn down by Everymanforhimself. The surface was slow and the form may not work out, but the form is taken at face value with the winner to this year's turf best.

7935 TOTESPORT.COM H'CAP 7f (F)
2:40 (2:41) (Class 3) (0-95,94) 3-Y-O+ **£6,476** (£1,927; £963; £481) **Stalls** Low

Form RPR
0062 **1** **Nightjar (USA)**[6] 7846 5-9-1 88 PhillipMakin 10 98
(K A Ryan) *prom: hdwy to ld 2f out: sn rdn: hrd pressed fnl f: hld on gamely* **2/1**[1]

1550 **2** *hd* **Docofthebay (IRE)**[3] 7875 6-9-7 94 (p) IanMongan 3 103
(D Nicholls) *sn pushed along towards rr: stdy hdwy 1/2-way: effrt over 1f out: ev ch and edgd rt ins fnl f: kpt on: jst hld* **9/2**[2]

1335 **3** *3* **Trans Sonic**[6] 7846 7-8-8 88 ShaneBKelly(7) 1 89
(D O'Meara) *trckd ldrs: effrt and ev ch over 2f out: kpt on same pce over 1f out* **25/1**

1014 **4** *1 1/4* **Salerosa (IRE)**[6] 7846 5-8-9 82 (p) MartinLane 7 80
(Mrs A Duffield) *t.k.h: hld up on outside: effrt over 2f out: no imp over 1f out* **10/1**

0102 **5** *2 3/4* **Follow The Flag (IRE)**[4] 7867 6-8-4 80 oh1 (v) AndrewHeffernan(3) 6 71
(A J McCabe) *sn drvn in rr: struggling 1/2-way: styd on fnl f: nvr rchd ldrs* **20/1**

3322 **6** *2* **Seek The Fair Land**[14] 7689 4-9-1 91 (v[1]) MatthewDavies(3) 2 76
(J R Boyle) *in tch: drvn and outpcd over 3f out: no imp fr 2f out* **17/2**

1000 **7** *1 1/4* **Something (IRE)**[91] 6175 8-9-2 92 MichaelO'Connell(3) 8 74
(D Nicholls) *hld up on outside: stdy hdwy gng wl over 2f out: rdn wl over 1f out: no further imp* **22/1**

0555 **8** *1 1/2* **Thunderball**[4] 7867 4-8-2 80 oh2 (b) BillyCray(5) 4 58
(D Nicholls) *sn rdn to ld: hdd 2f out: sn lost pl* **7/1**[3]

0334 **9** *3 3/4* **Bawaardi (IRE)**[1] 7915 4-8-4 80 JamesSullivan(3) 9 48
(R A Fahey) *in tch: drvn and outpcd 1/2-way: nvr dnagerous after* **10/1**

0522 **10** *2 1/2* **Sioux Rising (IRE)**[7] 7826 4-8-9 82 (p) BarryMcHugh 5 43
(R A Fahey) *trckd ldrs: rdn along 1/2-way: wknd over 2f out* **7/1**[3]

1m 32.37s (2.07) **Going Correction** +0.525s/f (Slow) **10** Ran SP% **118.2**
Speed ratings (Par 107): **109,108,105,103,100 98,97,95,91,88**
Tote Swingers: 1&2 £3.30, 1&3 £7.90, 2&3 £14.20 CSF £10.45 CT £177.11 TOTE £4.50: £1.90, £2.90, £7.40; EX 15.10.
Owner Hambleton Racing Ltd XIV **Bred** Derry Meeting Farm & London Thoroughbred Services **Trained** Hambleton, N Yorks
■ Stewards' Enquiry : Ian Mongan caution: careless riding.

FOCUS
A decent handicap. The winner set the standard on his C&D second and the runner-up ran his best race for a couple of years.

NOTEBOOK
Nightjar(USA) clearly relishes his trips to this track and really knows how to battle as well. The runner-up was a persistent challenger inside the final furlong, but he kept sticking his neck out and gained his fourth C&D success. He will return here for a 1m handicap on New Year's Day, a race in which he was second last year. (op 5-2)

Docofthebay(IRE), whose only previous outing at this course had yielded a win, wore cheekpieces instead of blinkers. Towards the rear early, he made his way between rivals rounding the home bend before going down narrowly to a course specialist. Edging right inside the final furlong may have cost him victory but, bizarrely, he made the same movement when landing his maiden here back in 2006. (op 6-1)
Trans Sonic is another who enjoys Fibresand, and he kept on well after racing prominently. The Handicapper, however, appears to have his measure for now. (op 20-1)
Salerosa(IRE) kept on after being held up to claim fourth, but never threatened to get any closer. (op 11-1)
Follow The Flag(IRE) needed pushing along as soon as the stalls opened but did pass some tiring rivals in the latter stages. (op 16-1)
Seek The Fair Land, with a visor on for the first time, travelled strongly under restraint but failed to quicken from 3f out. (op 13-2)
Something(IRE), absent since mid-September, was friendless in the betting and didn't get seriously involved after racing towards the rear and wide. That said, the effort wasn't without promise. (op 16-1)
Thunderball, who raced in the same colours as the runner-up, went off in front, setting a decent pace, but was unable to sustain his effort from well over 2f out. (op 8-1)
Bawaardi(IRE) dropped right out and might have found this coming too quick after finishing fourth the previous day at Wolverhampton. (op 14-1)
Sioux Rising(IRE) was trying Fibresand for the first time but gave no indication that she enjoyed the experience. (op 8-1 tchd 6-1)

7936 BET ON THE ASHES AT TOTESPORT.COM H'CAP 6f (F)
3:15 (3:15) (Class 6) (0-65,65) 3-Y-O+ £2,047 (£604; £302) Stalls Low

Form				RPR
0345	1		**Ace Of Spies (IRE)**[4] 7870 5-9-7 65 KirstyMilczarek 6 (C R Dore) *trckd ldrs: rdn to ld wl over 1f out: kpt on strly fnl f* **7/4**[1]	75
5400	2	4 ½	**Bel Cantor**[32] 7474 7-9-2 60 (v) AndreaAtzeni 3 (W J H Ratcliffe) *sn rdn to ld: hdd wl over 1f out: kpt on same pce fnl f* **9/4**[2]	56
4325	3	2	**Apache Ridge (IRE)**[14] 7701 4-9-7 65 (b) PhillipMakin 9 (K A Ryan) *prom: rdn and outpcd over 2f out: edgd lft and rallied over 1f out: sn no imp* **3/1**[3]	55
6000	4	3	**Fyodorovich (USA)**[32] 7473 5-8-7 47 oh6 (v) NeilChalmers 1 (A J McCabe) *dwlt: bhd and sn outpcd: sme late hdwy: nvr on terms* **18/1**	31
0000	5	1	**Darcy's Pride (IRE)**[8] 7807 6-8-6 53 (b[1]) PaulPickard(3) 8 (P T Midgley) *w ldr: drvn over 2f out: wknd over 1f out* **10/1**	30
0065	6	20	**Ballyvonane (USA)**[7] 7824 3-8-7 54 oh5 ow3 (e[1]) MichaelStainton(3) 2 (D C Griffiths) *in tch: sn drvn along: struggling 1/2-way: sn btn: t.o* **16/1**	—

1m 19.49s (2.99) **Going Correction** +0.525s/f (Slow) 6 Ran SP% 112.4
Speed ratings (Par 101): **101,95,92,88,87 60**
Tote Swingers: 1&2 £1.90, 2&3 £1.20 CSF £5.98 CT £9.73 TOTE £2.80: £1.20, £1.30; EX 7.40.
Owner Mrs Louise Marsh **Bred** Gainsborough Stud Management Ltd **Trained** Cowbit, Lincs

FOCUS
Ordinary fare.
T/Plt: £127.40 to a £1 stake. Pool:£155,182 - 888.74 winning tickets. T/Qpdt: £9.30 to a £1 stake. Pool:£16,324 - 1,296.04 winning tickets. RY

7885 KEMPTON (A.W) (R-H)
Sunday, December 19
7937 Meeting Abandoned - Frozen track

7913 WOLVERHAMPTON (A.W) (L-H)
Monday, December 20
7943 Meeting Abandoned - Frozen track

7931 SOUTHWELL (L-H)
Tuesday, December 21

OFFICIAL GOING: Standard to slow
Wind: Light across Weather: Overcast

7952 BET SP+ FOR BIGGER WINS AT TOTESPORT.COM H'CAP (DIV I) 5f (F)
12:35 (12:35) (Class 6) (0-60,66) 3-Y-O+ £2,590 (£770; £385; £192) Stalls High

Form				RPR
6052	1		**Residency (IRE)**[11] 7808 4-8-8 54 (p) AdamCarter(7) 10 (B Smart) *sn pushed along in rr: hdwy u.p over 1f out: hung lft and led nr fin* **8/1**	62
354	2	nk	**Decider (USA)**[13] 7764 7-9-7 60 (p) LukeMorris 5 (R A Harris) *trckd ldrs: rdn over 1f out: led ins fnl f: edgd rt and hdd nr fin* **12/1**	67
0000	3	1 ¼	**The Magic Of Rio**[21] 7635 4-8-7 46 oh1 CathyGannon 3 (P D Evans) *disp ld tl def advantage over 3f out: rdn over 1f out: hdd ins fnl f: stayaing on same pce whn hmpd nr fin* **5/1**[2]	48
0000	4	shd	**Dancing Wave**[4] 7906 4-8-2 46 oh1 RyanPowell(5) 7 (M C Chapman) *sn outpcd: hdwy over 1f out: r.o* **33/1**	48
0020	5	1 ¾	**Thoughtsofstardom**[6] 7883 7-8-11 55 TobyAtkinson(5) 6 (P S McEntee) *disp ld tl over 3f out: chsd ldr: rdn over 1f out: no ex ins fnl f* **5/1**[2]	51
2000	6	2	**Monte Major (IRE)**[12] 7784 9-9-5 58 (v) DaneO'Neill 11 (D Shaw) *sn pushed along in rr: rdn 1/2-way: kpt on ins fnl f: nvr nrr* **28/1**	47
1650	7	3 ¾	**Duke Of Rainford**[32] 7506 3-8-8 50 BillyCray(3) 1 (M Herrington) *pushed along in rr early: hdwy over 3f out: rdn over 1f out: wknd fnl f* **14/1**	25
523	8	2 ¼	**Francis Albert**[18] 7684 4-8-6 52 (b) JosephYoung(7) 8 (M Mullineaux) *chsd ldrs: rdn over 3f out: wknd wl over 1f out* **16/1**	19
6666	9	4	**Bombay Mist**[116] 5477 3-8-4 46 oh1 (e) JamesSullivan(3) 9 (R C Guest) *in tch: sn pushed along: wknd 1/2-way* **66/1**	—
001	10	1	**Alpha Tauri (USA)**[7] 7870 4-9-6 66 6ex (t) NoraLooby(7) 4 (F Sheridan) *prom: hmpd 4f out: rdn 1/2-way: wknd wknd wl over 1f out* **5/2**[1]	—
40-	11	¾	**Silk Slippers**[11] 7818 3-9-6 59 KierenFallon 2 (John Joseph Murphy, Ire) *prom: rdn over 3f out: sn wknd* **6/1**[3]	—

63.37 secs (3.67) **Going Correction** +0.80s/f (Slow) 11 Ran SP% 115.4
Speed ratings (Par 101): **102,101,99,99,96 93,87,83,77,75 74**
Tote Swingers: 1&2 £7.70, 1&3 £5.70, 2&3 £10.10 CSF £96.28 CT £538.78 TOTE £6.40: £1.80, £3.50, £2.10; EX 45.50 TRIFECTA Not won..
Owner B Smart **Bred** Tally-Ho Stud **Trained** Hambleton, N Yorks
■ Stewards' Enquiry : Luke Morris one-day ban: careless riding (Jan 4)
Adam Carter one-day ban: careless riding (Jan 4)

FOCUS
This time it was the high numbers who were favoured, with stall ten providing the winner of both divisions. The time was 0.29 seconds faster than the second division.
Alpha Tauri(USA) Official explanation: jockey said gelding never travelled

7953 BET SP+ FOR BIGGER WINS AT TOTESPORT.COM H'CAP (DIV II) 5f (F)
1:05 (1:06) (Class 6) (0-60,60) 3-Y-O+ £2,590 (£770; £385; £192) Stalls High

Form				RPR
5060	1		**Lets Move It**[8] 7859 3-8-7 46 oh1 (v) RobbieFitzpatrick 10 (D Shaw) *sn outpcd: hdwy to chse ldr over 1f out: rdn to ld wl ins fnl f* **66/1**	55
013	2	1 ¾	**Your Gifted (IRE)**[8] 7859 3-8-13 59 (e) AdamCarter(7) 11 (Patrick Morris) *s.i.s: sn prom: led 1/2-way: clr over 1f out: rdn and hdd wl ins fnl f* **13/2**	62
6021	3	4 ½	**Kheley (IRE)**[11] 7807 4-8-6 52 JamesRogers(7) 7 (W M Brisbourne) *chsd ldrs: rdn 1/2-way: no ex fnl f* **7/4**[1]	39
0320	4	5	**Guto**[7] 7868 7-9-0 60 MatthewCosham(7) 6 (W J H Ratcliffe) *chsd ldrs: rdn and lost pl 1/2-way: n.d after* **5/1**[2]	29
0054	5	hd	**Southwark Newshawk**[11] 7808 3-8-7 46 oh1 (p) DavidProbert 1 (Mrs C A Dunnett) *chsd ldrs: rdn 1/2-way: wknd over 1f out* **20/1**	14
0030	6	2 ¼	**Mr Funshine**[8] 7860 5-8-13 52 DaneO'Neill 3 (D Shaw) *s.i.s: outpcd* **11/1**	12
5033	7	nk	**Best One**[21] 7639 6-9-4 57 (b) LukeMorris 2 (R A Harris) *s.i.s: hdwy 4f out: rdn 1/2-way: wknd over 1f out* **11/2**[3]	16
4066	8	½	**Sophie's Beau (USA)**[7] 7870 3-8-10 49 CathyGannon 4 (M C Chapman) *s.i.s: outpcd* **12/1**	—
0042	9	6	**Spirit Of Dixie**[11] 7810 3-8-13 55 MichaelGeran(3) 9 (D Nicholls) *chsd ldrs: rdn and lost pl over 3f out: sn bhd* **8/1**	—
0006	10	½	**Charles Bear**[11] 7810 3-8-0 46 oh1 (p) DanielleMooney(7) 5 (Bruce Hellier) *led to 1/2-way: wknd over 1f out* **66/1**	—

63.66 secs (3.96) **Going Correction** +0.80s/f (Slow) 10 Ran SP% 116.6
Speed ratings (Par 101): **100,97,90,82,81 78,77,76,67,66**
Tote Swingers: 1&2 £76.30, 1&3 £33.60, 2&3 £5.30 CSF £450.85 CT £1089.96 TOTE £67.00: £13.90, £3.20, £1.50; EX 1106.00 TRIFECTA Not won..
Owner Mrs Lyndsey Shaw **Bred** Derek Shaw **Trained** Sproxton, Leics
■ Robbie Fitzpatrick's first winner since his recent return from a three-year ban.
■ Stewards' Enquiry : Danielle Mooney one-day ban: careless riding (Jan 4)

FOCUS
The time was 0.29 seconds slower than the first division. Again, a high draw was a big advantage.
Lets Move It Official explanation: trainer said, regarding apparent improvement in form, that the gelding appeared to appreciate a return to its preferred surface of Fibresand.

7954 E B F BET SP+ WITH TOTESPORT 0800 221 221 MAIDEN STKS 7f (F)
1:35 (1:36) (Class 5) 2-Y-O £3,626 (£1,079; £539; £269) Stalls Low

Form				RPR
636	1		**So Is She (IRE)**[19] 7664 2-8-12 66 CathyGannon 6 (A Bailey) *chsd ldrs: outpcd over 5f out: hdwy 2f out: rdn to ld 1f out: styd on wl* **11/2**[2]	71
432	2	3	**Mazovian (USA)**[5] 7893 2-9-0 0 RobertLButler(3) 4 (M C Chapman) *hld up: hdwy over 2f out: chal 1f out: sn rdn and fnd nil* **13/2**[3]	68
	3	6	**Songjiang** 2-9-3 0 RobertHavlin 1 (J H M Gosden) *s.s: reminders and hdwy over 5f out: rdn over 2f out: wknd over 1f out* **8/1**	53+
002	4	1 ½	**Take Your Partner**[12] 7779 2-9-3 60 (b[1]) PhillipMakin 2 (K A Ryan) *sn led: hdd over 5f out: chsd ldr tl led again 3f out: rdn: hdd & wknd 1f out* **13/2**[3]	49+
0542	5	4	**Szabo's Destiny**[11] 7802 2-9-0 65 JamesSullivan(3) 3 (J G Given) *chsd ldrs: rdn over 4f out: wknd 3f out* **12/1**	39
602	6	14	**Elusive Love (IRE)**[9] 7843 2-9-3 0 KierenFallon 8 (M Johnston) *led over 5f out: hdd 3f out: rdn and wknd 2f out* **1/1**[1]	4
	7	10	**Depden (IRE)** 2-9-3 0 DavidProbert 5 (R J Price) *s.s: outpcd: t.o* **50/1**	—

1m 37.84s (7.54) **Going Correction** +0.925s/f (Slow) 7 Ran SP% 112.8
Speed ratings (Par 96): **93,89,82,81,76 60,49**
Tote Swingers: 1&2 £5.30, 1&3 £5.40, 2&3 £2.80 CSF £39.07 TOTE £8.20: £4.10, £2.20; EX 45.90 Trifecta £225.40 Pool: £825.58 - 2.71 winning units..
Owner Allan McNamee **Bred** Bayview Properties Ltd **Trained** Newmarket, Suffolk

FOCUS
Four horses traded at odds-on in running, and the obvious conclusion is the pace was much too fast, with the surface riding particularly deep (time nearly ten seconds above standard). The race rather fell apart and the winner is rated back towards his best.

NOTEBOOK
So Is She(IRE) was too keen when beaten in a Polytrack seller last time, but she proved suited by the switch to Fibresand and was well placed considering how the race unfolded. She didn't apply herself early, needing reminders, but the leaders came back to her in the straight and she stayed on best to get off the mark at the 12th attempt. This isn't form to trust. (op 7-1 tchd 8-1 and 5-1)
Mazovian(USA) once again travelled well before not quite seeing his race out. However, considering the surface was so testing, there can be no doubt he stays this trip. (op 6-1 tchd 11-2)
Songjiang, a 20,000gns brother to useful miler Tiger Reigns, ran green throughout and needed the experience. (op 6-1)
Take Your Partner, who didn't apply himself midway through the contest at Kempton last time, was much sharper in first-time blinkers, but he went too fast. Having travelled strongly into the straight (touched 1.28 in running), he got very tired late on and had a hard race. (op 6-1)
Elusive Love(IRE), runner-up over 6f here last time, was unproven over this trip and went much too fast. Even so, he could have been expected to last a little longer in front, but was beaten at the top of the straight after trading at 1.35 in running. Official explanation: trainer's rep had no explanation for the poor form shown (op 6-5)

7955 BET TOTEPOOL AT TOTESPORT.COM H'CAP 1m (F)
2:05 (2:05) (Class 4) (0-85,91) 3-Y-O+ £4,776 (£1,410; £705) Stalls Low

Form				RPR
0131	1		**Nazreef**[7] 7867 3-9-13 91 6ex (t) TravisBlock 3 (H Morrison) *s.i.s: hdwy over 6f out: rdn over 3f out: chsd ldr over 1f out: styd on u.p to ld wl ins fnl f* **30/100**[1]	103
4005	2	½	**Snow Bay**[56] 7146 4-8-13 79 MichaelGeran(3) 4 (D Nicholls) *led: edgd rt over 2f out: rdn over 1f out: hdd wl ins fnl f* **11/1**	90
1025	3	5	**Follow The Flag (IRE)**[3] 7935 6-9-2 79 (v) NeilChalmers 1 (A J McCabe) *sn pushed along in rr: rdn over 3f out: styd on ins fnl f: wnt 3rd nr fin: nt trble ldrs* **25/1**	79
0363	4	hd	**Elusive Fame (USA)**[7] 7867 4-9-1 78 (b) KierenFallon 2 (M Johnston) *chsd ldrs: rdn over 3f out: edgd rt and no ex fnl f: lost 3rd nr fin* **9/1**[3]	77

41-0 **5** *13* **Revelator (IRE)**[7] 7867 3-8-6 **77**........ HobieGill(7) 8 46
(A J McCabe) *chsd ldr: rdn over 2f out: wknd over 1f out* **100/1**

2-12 **6** *12* **Xilerator (IRE)**[94] 6197 3-9-3 **84**........ MichaelO'Connell(3) 5 26
(D Nicholls) *chsd ldrs: rdn over 3f out: sn wknd: t.o* **7/1**[2]

1m 50.26s (6.56) **Going Correction** +0.925s/f (Slow)
WFA 3 from 4yo+ 1lb **6** Ran SP% **112.6**
Speed ratings (Par 105): **104,103,98,98,85 73**
Tote Swingers: 1&2 £2.50, 1&3 £3.20, 2&3 £7.70 CSF £4.91 CT £31.20 TOTE £1.30: £1.20, £3.30; EX 5.50 Trifecta £40.00 Pool: £707.49 - 13.08 winning units..Ours was withdrawn. Price at time ofwithdrawal 16/1. Rule 4 does not apply.
Owner Deborah Collett & M J Watson **Bred** M J Watson **Trained** East Ilsley, Berks

FOCUS
A good handicap.

7956 BET TOTEPOOL ON 0800 221 221 H'CAP 7f (F)
2:35 (2:35) (Class 5) (0-70,76) 3-Y-0+ **£3,885** (£1,156; £577; £288) **Stalls** Low

Form RPR

0223 **1** **Dubai Hills**[41] 7399 4-8-9 **65**........ AdamCarter(7) 4 81
(B Smart) *sn led: clr over 1f out: hung rt ins fnl f: easily* **9/4**[1]

453 **2** *13* **The Lock Master (IRE)**[9] 7845 3-9-3 **66**........ NeilChalmers 1 47
(M Appleby) *s.s: bhd: hdwy to go 2nd 1f out: no ch w wnr* **8/1**

200 **3** *6* **Fault**[10] 7837 4-9-5 **68**........(t) MickyFenton 9 33
(Stef Higgins) *hld up: hdwy over 2f out: rdn to chse wnr over 1f out: sn wknd* **15/2**

0400 **4** *1 1/4* **Amary (IRE)**[9] 7844 3-9-6 **69**........ BarryMcHugh 5 30
(John A Harris) *hld up: rdn 1/2-way: n.d* **20/1**

0016 **5** *3 3/4* **Peter's Gift (IRE)**[17] 7699 4-9-0 **63**........(p) PhillipMakin 2 14
(K A Ryan) *chsd ldrs: rdn over 3f out: wknd wl over 1f out* **13/2**[3]

4031 **6** *2 1/4* **Punching**[4] 7906 6-9-6 **76** 6ex........ MatthewCosham(7) 7 21
(C R Dore) *trckd wnr: rdn over 2f out: wknd wl over 1f out* **15/2**

1251 **7** *5* **Eastern Hills**[11] 7804 5-9-3 **66**........(p) GrahamGibbons 3 —
(A J McCabe) *chsd ldrs: rdn over 2f out: sn wknd* **3/1**[2]

0004 **8** *2 1/4* **Fyodorovich (USA)**[3] 7936 5-8-7 **56** oh11........(v) DavidProbert 8 —
(A J McCabe) *s.i.s: sn prom: rdn 1/2-way: sn wknd* **25/1**

1m 32.77s (2.47) **Going Correction** +0.925s/f (Slow) **8** Ran SP% **112.4**
Speed ratings (Par 103): **122,107,100,98,94 92,86,83**
Tote Swingers: 1&2 £5.70, 1&3 £4.10, 2&3 £9.80 CSF £20.19 CT £114.25 TOTE £2.70: £1.30, £2.10, £1.90; EX 25.70 Trifecta £122.00 Pool: £712.53 - 4.32 winning units..
Owner Mrs F Denniff **Bred** A S Denniff **Trained** Hambleton, N Yorks

FOCUS
Just a modest handicap, but a very useful performance from Dubai Hills.
Eastern Hills Official explanation: jockey said gelding had no more to give

7957 SOUTHWELL GOLF CLUB H'CAP 1m 6f (F)
3:05 (3:05) (Class 6) (0-65,66) 3-Y-0+ **£2,266** (£674; £337; £168) **Stalls** Low

Form RPR

0460 **1** **Juwireya**[44] 5963 3-9-1 **58**........(v) WilliamCarson 2 66
(P W Hiatt) *led: rdn and hung rt over 2f out: hdd over 1f out: sn led again: hung lft ins fnl f: styd on u.p* **25/1**

3231 **2** *nk* **Rosewin (IRE)**[5] 7898 4-9-13 **66** 6ex........ JamesSullivan(3) 5 74
(Ollie Pears) *prom: lost pl after 3f: hdwy over 7f out: chsd wnr over 4f out: hung lft and hit rails over 3f out: rdn and hung rt over 2f out: led briefly over 1f out: hung lft ins fnl f: kpt on* **3/1**[1]

0222 **3** *7* **Shifting Gold (IRE)**[11] 7806 4-9-5 **58**........(p) AmyRyan(3) 1 56
(K A Ryan) *prom: chsd wnr 10f out: rdn over 5f out: outpcd over 3f out: styd on to go 3rd ins fnl f* **3/1**[1]

-066 **4** *1 1/4* **Beau Fighter**[36] 7101 5-9-12 **62**........(p) FergusSweeney 4 58
(G L Moore) *hld up in tch: rdn over 3f out: styd on same pce fnl 2f* **6/1**[3]

2333 **5** *4* **Davana**[11] 7805 4-8-4 **47**........ MatthewCosham(7) 8 38
(W J H Ratcliffe) *chsd ldr 4f: pushed along 8f out: sn lost pl: n.d after* **4/1**[2]

3554 **6** *18* **Greenbelt**[11] 7806 9-9-2 **52**........ PhillipMakin 9 18
(G M Moore) *chsd ldrs: rdn over 4f out: wknd over 3f out* **16/1**

00/0 **7** *32* **Aberdeen Park**[22] 7626 8-8-9 **45**........(p) CathyGannon 7 —
(P D Evans) *s.s: a wl bhd: t.o* **11/1**

0/0- **8** *48* **The Buck (IRE)**[8] 6217 7-9-9 **64**........ BrianToomey(5) 6 —
(John Joseph Murphy, Ire) *hld up: pushed along over 8f out: sn wl bhd: t.o* **7/1**

3m 23.05s (14.75) **Going Correction** +0.925s/f (Slow)
WFA 3 from 4yo+ 7lb **8** Ran SP% **114.8**
Speed ratings (Par 101): **94,93,89,89,86 76,58,30**
Tote Swingers: 1&2 £7.90, 1&3 £10.00, 2&3 £3.00 CSF £99.58 CT £300.81 TOTE £23.20: £6.50, £1.90, £1.50; EX 101.50 Trifecta £528.20 Pool: £728.18 - 1.02 winning units..
Owner Mrs Rosemary Gasson **Bred** Shadwell Estate Company Limited **Trained** Hook Norton, Oxon

FOCUS
A moderate handicap.

7958 HAPPY CHRISTMAS H'CAP 1m 4f (F)
3:35 (3:38) (Class 6) (0-60,72) 3-Y-0+ **£2,590** (£770; £385; £192) **Stalls** Low

Form RPR

5411 **1** **Kumbeshwar**[3] 7932 3-10-0 **72** 12ex........(v) MatthewCosham(7) 10 88
(P D Evans) *led over 10f out: clr fr 8f out: hung rt over 1f out: easily* **9/4**[2]

1010 **2** *13* **Short Supply (USA)**[26] 7181 4-9-7 **53**........ GrahamGibbons 13 51
(T D Walford) *dwlt: sn drvn along to go prom: chsd wnr over 5f out: outpcd fr over 3f out* **12/1**

3006 **3** *1* **Carnac (IRE)**[16] 7716 4-9-4 **50**........(p) NeilChalmers 7 46
(A J McCabe) *hld up: hdwy over 5f out: rdn over 3f out: styd on same pce* **12/1**

2222 **4** *10* **Yossi (IRE)**[3] 7933 6-9-3 **56**........(be) SeanPalmer(7) 9 38
(R C Guest) *hld up: hdwy over 3f out: nvr trbld ldrs* **15/2**[3]

0303 **5** *shd* **Mojeerr**[3] 7933 4-8-9 **48**........(e) HobieGill(7) 1 30
(A J McCabe) *hld up: rdn over 2f out: nvr on terms* **16/1**

6050 **6** *17* **Cruise Control**[40] 7125 4-9-1 **47**........ DavidProbert 2 —
(R J Price) *mid-div: hdwy over 4f out: rdn and wknd over 3f out: t.o* **66/1**

4355 **7** *2 1/2* **Whaston (IRE)**[25] 7401 5-8-13 **48**........ JamesSullivan(3) 12 —
(Miss P Robson) *hld up: sme hdwy over 5f out: sn wknd: t.o* **10/1**

6300 **8** *1* **Lean Burn (USA)**[26] 2361 4-8-13 **45**........ CathyGannon 11 —
(B D Leavy) *edgd rt s: hld up: hdwy 6f out: rdn over 4f out: wknd sn after: t.o* **2/1**[1]

4560 **9** *50* **Marafong**[17] 7703 3-8-8 **45**........ WilliamCarson 4 —
(B P J Baugh) *mid-div: drvn along 7f out: wknd over 5f out: t.o* **33/1**

0102 **10** *9* **Abulharith**[10] 7840 4-9-10 **56**........(p) LukeMorris 5 —
(R A Harris) *led: hdd over 10f out: rdn and edgd let over 5f out: wknd over 4f out: eased: t.o* **28/1**

0P34 **11** *2 1/2* **Noverre Over There (IRE)**[12] 7789 3-8-13 **50**........ DaneO'Neill 6 —
(Miss Olivia Maylam) *chsd ldrs: rdn and wknd over 5f out: t.o* **40/1**

5360 **12** *dist* **Dr Valentine (FR)**[11] 7814 4-9-10 **56**........ MickyFenton 3 —
(Mrs A Duffield) *prom: nt clr run and lost pl over 5f out: sn bhd: virtually p.u: t.o* **33/1**

2m 51.01s (10.01) **Going Correction** +0.925s/f (Slow)
WFA 3 from 4yo+ 5lb **12** Ran SP% **119.5**
Speed ratings (Par 101): **103,94,93,87,86 75,73,73,39,33 32,—**
Tote Swingers: 1&2 £9.20, 1&3 £7.80, 2&3 £13.90 CSF £28.45 CT £276.26 TOTE £3.30: £1.40, £2.80, £2.90; EX 41.50 Trifecta £337.40 Pool: £971.24 - 2.13 winning units..
Owner G E Amey **Bred** G E Amey **Trained** Pandy, Monmouths
■ Stewards' Enquiry : Luke Morris one-day ban: careless riding (Jan 4)

FOCUS
A modest handicap.
Abulharith Official explanation: jockey said gelding stopped quickly
Dr Valentine(FR) Official explanation: trainer said gelding had a breathing problem
T/Plt: £141.90 to a £1 stake. Pool £87,331.28 - 449.02 winning units T/Qpdt: £29.10 to a £1 stake. Pool £7,749.02 - 196.70 winning units CR

7951 DEAUVILLE (R-H)
Tuesday, December 21

OFFICIAL GOING: Fibresand: standard

7959a PRIX DE RABODANGES (CONDITIONS) (3YO COLTS & GELDINGS) (FIBRESAND) 1m 1f 110y
9:00 (12:00) 3-Y-O **£10,619** (£4,247; £3,185; £2,123; £1,061)

RPR

1 **Titus Bere (FR)**[51] 3-8-11 0........(b) ThierryJarnet 5 —
(Y Barberot, France) **9/2**[3]

2 *3* **Professor John (IRE)**[11] 7814 3-9-2 0........ RonanThomas 11 —
(I A Wood) *racd in midfield fr s: rdn and gd prog early in st: r.o u.p fnl f: wnt 2nd fnl 50yds* **11/2**

3 *nk* **Saristan (FR)**[12] 3-8-11 0........ MichaelPoirier 4 —
(A De Royer-Dupre, France) **43/10**[2]

4 *2* **Tall Chief (IRE)**[13] 3-9-2 0........ MickaelBarzalona 2 —
(Mlle V Dissaux, France) **7/1**

5 *1/2* **Kepresh (FR)**[177] 3-8-6 0........(b) MathieuTavaresDaSilva(5) 6 —
(H-A Pantall, France) **17/1**

6 *1 1/2* **Boreal D'Evaille (FR)** 3-8-11 0........ SamuelFargeat 9 —
(S Morineau, France) **25/1**

7 *1* **Anzas (IRE)**[98] 3-9-2 0........ GregoryBenoist 1 —
(R Gibson, France) **4/1**[1]

8 *4* **Mezzotinto (FR)**[225] 3-9-2 0........ FabriceVeron 7 —
(H-A Pantall, France) **15/2**

9 *2 1/2* **Rolling Sea** 3-8-11 0........ StefanieHofer 8 —
(Frau S Weis, Germany) **32/1**

10 *1 1/2* **Highland Fighter (GER)**[186] 3-8-11 0........ Pierre-CharlesBoudot 3 —
(H-W Hiller, Germany) **33/1**

0 **Mathurino (FR)**[227] 3-8-11 0........ ThomasHuet 10 —
(H Billot, France) **31/1**

2m 0.20s (120.20) **11** Ran SP% **115.2**
WIN (incl. 1 euro stake): 6.90. PLACES: 2.30, 2.30, 2.20. DF: 23.00. SF: 21.60.
Owner Ecurie Camacho Courses **Bred** S N C Regnier & San Gabriel Inv Inc **Trained** France

NOTEBOOK
Professor John(IRE), without a visor this time, ran a good race. He got a bit too far back to challenge the winner, but stayed on nicely for second, continuing his good recent run of form.

7885 KEMPTON (A.W) (R-H)
Wednesday, December 22

OFFICIAL GOING: Standard
Wind: Moderate, against Weather: Very overcast

7960 BOXINGDAYRACES.CO.UK MAIDEN STKS 5f (P)
3:55 (3:57) (Class 5) 3-5-Y-O **£2,286** (£675; £337) **Stalls** High

Form RPR

2-05 **1** **Co Dependent (USA)**[14] 7757 4-9-3 64........ FergusSweeney 4 61
(J A Osborne) *hld up in 7th: plenty to do over 1f out: pushed along and gd prog on outer after: wnt 2nd last 75yds: rdn to ld fnl strides* **5/1**[3]

45- **2** *hd* **Mosa Mine**[404] 7365 3-8-9 60........ MichaelStainton(3) 6 55
(Jane Chapple-Hyam) *cl up on inner: wnt 2nd 2f out: swtchd lft over 1f out: edgd lft w hd at awkward angle after: kpt on to ld last 100yds: hdd fnl strides* **7/2**[2]

6-4 **3** *1* **Marshal Plat Club**[11] 7838 3-8-12 0........ AdamKirby 9 51
(A Bailey) *led: drvn 2f out: edgd lft over 1f out: hdd and no ex last 100yds* **8/1**

06 **4** *3/4* **Dashwood**[25] 7596 3-9-3 0........ WilliamCarson 3 54
(G C Bravery) *chsd ldrs: pushed along 1/2-way: nt clr run wl over 1f out: rdn and kpt on fnl f: nvr able to chal* **66/1**

3552 **5** *3/4* **Durgan**[14] 7757 4-9-3 60........(p) SteveDrowne 1 51
(Mrs L C Jewell) *chsd ldrs and racd wd: rdn and nt qckn over 1f out: one pce after* **3/1**[1]

5 **6** *nk* **Spring Leap**[19] 7684 3-9-3 0........ JimmyQuinn 7 50
(R M H Cowell) *s.i.s: settled in last: drvn and prog over 1f out: one pce ins fnl f* **12/1**

0006 **7** *1 1/2* **Rightcar Dominic**[13] 7786 5-8-10 34........ LeonnaMayor(7) 8 45?
(Peter Grayson) *pushed along in last pair over 3f out: drvn and effrt on inner over 1f out: sn no prog: fdd ins fnl f* **100/1**

3004 **8** *5* **Gower Sophia**[12] 7810 3-8-12 50........(b) LukeMorris 5 22
(R A Harris) *pressed ldng pair to wl over 1f out: wknd rapidly* **12/1**

0224 **9** *3 1/2* **Papageno**[14] 7757 3-9-3 56........ NickyMackay 2 14
(J R Jenkins) *racd wd: mostly chsd ldr to 2f out: wknd rapidly* **5/1**[3]

60.98 secs (0.48) **Going Correction** +0.025s/f (Slow) **9** Ran SP% **111.0**
Speed ratings (Par 103): **97,96,95,93,92 92,89,81,76**
toteswingers: 1&2 £4.00, 1&3 £7.30, 2&3 £5.80. CSF £21.47 TOTE £4.90: £2.00, £2.10, £4.50; EX 18.50.
Owner Dr Geraldine O'Sullivan **Bred** Daniel M Ryan **Trained** Upper Lambourn, Berks
■ Stewards' Enquiry : Jimmy Quinn caution: careless riding.

FOCUS
A weak maiden featuring a disputed lead.

7961 WIN A KIA VENGA AT KEMPTON.CO.UK H'CAP 5f (P)
4:25 (4:25) (Class 4) (0-85,81) 3-Y-0+ £3,885 (£1,156; £577; £288) Stalls High

Form RPR
0423 1 **Breathless Kiss (USA)**[13] 7782 3-9-4 **78**......(b) KierenFallon 7 87
(K A Ryan) dwlt and hmpd s: pushed along in last: gd prog on inner over 1f out: shkn up and shot between rivals to ld last 75yds **10/3**[1]
2243 2 ¾ **Vhujon (IRE)**[11] 7826 5-9-2 **76**...... StevieDonohoe 6 82
(P D Evans) mostly in 7th: rdn and prog over 1f out: styd on wl to take 2nd nr fin: no ch w wnr **13/2**[3]
6110 3 nk **Grudge**[8] 7866 5-8-13 **73**......(be) AdamKirby 3 78
(C R Dore) chsd ldng pair: no imp over 1f out: lost 3rd jst ins fnl f: kpt on last 75yds **8/1**
0132 4 ½ **Love You Louis**[14] 7754 4-9-1 **75**...... FergusSweeney 5 78
(J R Jenkins) pressed ldr: clr of rest whn rdn into narrow ld over 1f out: hdd & wknd last 75yds **7/2**[2]
5043 5 ½ **Lewyn**[22] 7635 3-9-7 **81**......(t) SteveDrowne 10 82
(J R Gask) wnt lft s: led: drvn and hdd over 1f out: stl pressing ldr ins fnl f: wknd last 75yds **13/2**[3]
1002 6 nk **Efistorm**[13] 7784 9-8-9 **72**...... AmyRyan(3) 9 72
(C R Dore) sltly hmpd s: chsd ldng trio: rdn and no imp over 1f out: wl hld whn short of room nr fin **8/1**
0040 7 nk **Kylladdie**[41] 7411 3-8-12 **72**...... JimmyQuinn 1 71
(S Gollings) dropped in fr wd draw: settled in last pair: drvn over 1f out: one pce and limited prog **20/1**
036 8 1 **Italian Tom (IRE)**[28] 7549 3-9-2 **76**...... LukeMorris 8 71
(R A Harris) dwlt and sltly hmpd s: chsd ldrs in 6th: u.p fr 1/2-way: no prog and btn over 1f out **14/1**
5213 9 2 **Elhamri**[48] 7319 6-8-7 **74**...... NoraLooby(7) 2 62
(C R Dore) racd wd: chsd ldrs: no prog over 1f out: sn wknd **14/1**

60.00 secs (-0.50) **Going Correction** +0.025s/f (Slow) 9 Ran SP% **112.3**
Speed ratings (Par 105): **105,103,103,102,101 101,100,99,95**
toteswingers: 1&2 £5.00, 1&3 £7.50, 2&3 £11.30. CSF £24.31 CT £156.95 TOTE £4.90: £1.90, £1.50, £2.60; EX 23.30.
Owner Mrs Angie Bailey **Bred** Don Mattox & Pam Mattox **Trained** Hambleton, N Yorks

FOCUS
Once again the leaders went off too quick, and the principals came from the back.

7962 DIGIBET.COM MEDIAN AUCTION MAIDEN STKS 7f (P)
4:55 (4:56) (Class 6) 2-Y-0 £1,637 (£483; £241) Stalls High

Form RPR
53 1 **Corsican Boy**[28] 7550 2-9-3 0...... SteveDrowne 8 77
(R Charlton) dwlt: chsd ldrs: prog 1/2-way: wnt 2nd over 2f out: rdn and sustained chal fnl f: jst prevailed **5/4**[1]
620 2 nse **Les Verguettes (IRE)**[72] 6796 2-8-12 69...... MickyFenton 9 72
(Stef Higgins) led: jnd 1f out: battled on wl: jst pipped **15/2**[3]
543 3 3 **Woop Woop (IRE)**[6] 7893 2-8-12 0...... AdamKirby 5 64
(Stef Higgins) rrd s: sn chsd ldrs: outpcd in 5th wl over 2f out: kpt on fr over 1f out to take 3rd ins fnl f **20/1**
2502 4 nk **Nothing To Hide (IRE)**[13] 7780 2-9-3 75...... DaneO'Neill 3 68
(D J S Ffrench Davis) chsd ldr to over 2f out: sn outpcd by ldng pair: lost 3rd ins fnl f **5/2**[2]
05 5 ¾ **Holcombe Boy**[7] 7873 2-9-3 0...... StevieDonohoe 2 66
(J Pearce) s.i.s: sn off the pce in 8th: shkn up over 2f out: styd on encouragingly fnl f **8/1**
6 1 ¼ **Too Many Questions (IRE)** 2-9-3 0...... CathyGannon 4 63
(P D Evans) rn green in 7th: sme prog over 2f out: tried to cl on ldrs over 1f out: fdd fnl f **50/1**
7 3 ¼ **Revolutionary** 2-9-3 0...... FergusSweeney 6 55
(J A Osborne) s.s: rn green in last: nvr a factor **25/1**
06 8 ½ **Wealth Whispers (IRE)**[25] 7598 2-8-12 0...... LiamJones 7 48
(P W D'Arcy) chsd ldng pair: pushed along 1/2-way: outpcd over 2f out: wknd fnl f **16/1**
6 9 27 **Ana Emarati (USA)**[18] 7700 2-9-3 0...... KierenFallon 1 —
(E A L Dunlop) chsd ldng trio: hung bdly lft bnd fr 4f out: v wd 3f out and lost all ch: t.o **16/1**

1m 25.96s (-0.04) **Going Correction** +0.025s/f (Slow) 9 Ran SP% **118.2**
Speed ratings (Par 94): **101,100,97,97,96 94,91,90,59**
toteswingers: 1&2 £3.20, 1&3 £7.80, 2&3 £11.50. CSF £11.76 TOTE £2.40: £1.30, £3.20, £2.30; EX 12.80.
Owner R A Pegum **Bred** Bloomsbury Stud **Trained** Beckhampton, Wilts

FOCUS
A fair maiden and pretty solid maiden form for the time of year.

NOTEBOOK
Corsican Boy eventually wore down the leader to get off the mark at the third attempt. He can expect a mark in the high 70s on the back of this, but is bred to improve as he steps up in trip - 1m2f plus should suit him next year - so there's plenty of scope for him to take advantage of a mark like that over a more suitable distance. (op 6-4 tchd 7-4 in places)
Les Verguettes(IRE) ran well here two starts back but was very disappointing on her return visit last time. She clearly wasn't herself that day, but this was a return to form and, having made most of the running, she was only just beaten on the nod. It was a brave effort, one for which she will pay with a hike in the ratings. However, a repeat of this would be good enough to win most AW maidens during the winter. (op 13-2)
Woop Woop(IRE) promises to do better when upped to 1m. (tchd 16-1)
Nothing To Hide(IRE) tracked the leader but was beaten off early in the straight. The drop in trip didn't help him, but he's becoming exposed. (op 3-1)
Holcombe Boy looked to be going nowhere fast at the top of the straight, but he picked up nicely in the closing stages. Handicaps might offer better opportunities. (tchd 9-1)
Ana Emarati(USA) hung left in the straight. Official explanation: jockey said colt hung left in home straight (op 12-1)

7963 DIGIBET CASINO H'CAP 1m 4f (P)
5:25 (5:27) (Class 5) (0-75,76) 3-Y-0 £2,286 (£675; £337) Stalls Centre

Form RPR
503 1 **Kitty Wells**[40] 7419 3-9-5 **68**...... KierenFallon 5 85
(L M Cumani) settled in 3rd: pushed up to ld narrowly on outer over 2f out: shkn up and forged clr fr over 1f out **13/8**[2]
6111 2 6 **New Code**[7] 7876 3-9-13 **76** 6ex...... FergusSweeney 1 83
(G L Moore) hld up in last: prog on inner to chal wl over 2f out: outpcd by wnr fr over 1f out **10/11**[1]
2564 3 5 **New Den**[14] 7767 3-8-11 **60**......(v) NickyMackay 2 59
(J R Boyle) led to over 8f out: rdn over 4f out: dropped to last whn short of room over 2f out: tk modest 3rd over 1f out **12/1**
0032 4 6 **The Wonga Coup (IRE)**[28] 7562 3-8-4 **58**...... JemmaMarshall(5) 3 47
(P M Phelan) plld way up to ld over 8f out: hdd & wknd over 2f out **6/1**[3]

2m 36.39s (1.89) **Going Correction** +0.025s/f (Slow) 4 Ran SP% **112.5**
Speed ratings (Par 102): **94,90,86,82**
toteswinger: 1&2 £2.30. CSF £3.67 TOTE £2.60; EX 4.00.
Owner S Stuckey **Bred** Fittocks Stud **Trained** Newmarket, Suffolk

FOCUS
Just the four runners, and a tactical affair seemed in prospect, but in the event New Den took them along at a fair pace early and then The Wonga Coup pulled himself to the front and ensured the race was a proper enough test at the trip.

7964 DIGIBET CLAIMING STKS 1m (P)
5:55 (5:55) (Class 6) 3-Y-0 £1,637 (£483; £241) Stalls High

Form RPR
6030 1 **Tewin Wood**[28] 7554 3-8-8 72...... LiamJones 2 68
(A Bailey) mde virtually all: kicked on fr 2f out: clr 1f out: unchal **5/1**[2]
3020 2 2 **Abriachan**[13] 7778 3-8-11 62......(p) WilliamCarson 4 66
(M G Quinlan) hld up in last trio: swtchd out wd over 2f out: prog over 1f out: styd on to take 2nd last 100yds: no ch to chal **13/2**
6 3 ½ **Haveahaarth (IRE)**[7] 7874 3-8-5 57 ow2...... TobyAtkinson(5) 3 64
(M G Quinlan) hld up in last trio: prog over 2f out: chsd wnr 1f out: kpt on but lost 2nd last 100yds **20/1**
1155 4 2 **Sabatini (IRE)**[63] 7019 3-8-9 70 ow1...... MickyFenton 6 58
(J Pearce) trckd ldrs in 5th: rdn and nt qckn 2f out: brief effrt 1f out: sn nt qckn **7/2**[1]
354 4 dht **Lean Machine**[10] 7845 3-8-11 64...... LukeMorris 7 60
(R A Harris) chsd wnr to 1/2-way and 2f out to 1f out: wknd **11/2**[3]
0-00 6 3 ¼ **Art Scholar (IRE)**[11] 7826 3-9-1 77......(p) AmirQuinn 8 57
(G L Moore) t.k.h: trckd ldng trio: cl enough over 2f out: sn rdn and nt qckn: wknd over 1f out **10/1**
0000 7 2 **Durham Town (IRE)**[15] 7737 3-8-9 60...... JimmyQuinn 9 46
(D K Ivory) hld up in 6th: swtchd ins and effrt over 2f out: sn no prog: wknd over 1f out **10/1**
3600 8 ¾ **Tuscan King**[13] 7778 3-8-13 67......(b) StevieDonohoe 5 48
(P D Evans) slowest away but pushed up to go prom: chsd wnr 1/2-way to 2f out: edgd lft and wknd **6/1**
5050 9 1 **Wishformore (IRE)**[39] 7438 3-8-6 63...... CathyGannon 1 39
(J S Moore) hld up and sn last: rdn 1/2-way: no prog **10/1**

1m 40.29s (0.49) **Going Correction** +0.025s/f (Slow) 9 Ran SP% **113.9**
Speed ratings (Par 98): **98,96,95,93,93 90,88,87,86**
toteswingers: 1&2 £7.70, 1&3 £33.30, 2&3 £29.60. CSF £36.85 TOTE £5.50: £1.40, £2.20, £7.50; EX 46.90.Tewin Wood was claimed by P D Evans for £5,000.
Owner The Perle d'Or Partnership **Bred** Perle D'Or Partnership **Trained** Newmarket, Suffolk

FOCUS
A pretty competitive claimer on paper.
Sabatini(IRE) Official explanation: jockey said filly hung left
Wishformore(IRE) Official explanation: jockey said filly hung right

7965 RACING AT SKYSPORTS.COM H'CAP 1m (P)
6:25 (6:26) (Class 4) (0-85,85) 3-Y-0 £3,885 (£1,156; £577; £288) Stalls High

Form RPR
211 1 **Norman Orpen (IRE)**[14] 7766 3-9-6 **84**...... KierenFallon 2 94
(Jane Chapple-Hyam) settled in 4th: pushed along fr 3f out: wnt in pursuit of clr ldr wl over 1f out: drvn and clsd fnl f to ld last 75yds **5/4**[1]
1065 2 ¾ **Avon River**[26] 7574 3-9-7 **85**......(b) DaneO'Neill 1 93
(R Hannon) led at decent pce: drew more than 2 l clr wl over 1f out: styd on: collared last 75yds **9/2**[3]
0622 3 3 ¾ **Tiradito (USA)**[20] 7665 3-9-1 **79**......(p) AndreaAtzeni 6 78
(M Botti) t.k.h: hld up in 5th: shkn up over 2f out: kpt on to take 3rd ins fnl f: n.d **11/2**
-224 4 ¾ **Khanivorous**[306] 617 3-9-0 **78**...... StephenCraine 4 76
(J R Boyle) mostly chsd ldr to wl over 1f out: steadily fdd **12/1**
21 5 1 ¼ **Private Joke**[13] 7786 3-8-11 **75**...... NickyMackay 5 70
(J H M Gosden) mostly pressed ldng pair to 2f out: steadily wknd over 1f out **11/4**[2]
4- 6 8 **Jungle Bay**[71] 3-9-7 **85**...... JimmyQuinn 3 61
(Jane Chapple-Hyam) settled in last: pushed along over 2f out: sn lft bhd **20/1**

1m 39.01s (-0.79) **Going Correction** +0.025s/f (Slow) 6 Ran SP% **117.1**
Speed ratings (Par 104): **104,103,99,98,97 89**
toteswingers: 1&2 £1.80, 1&3 £2.50, 2&3 £3.50. CSF £7.91 TOTE £2.20: £1.10, £5.30; EX 8.70.
Owner Gordon Li **Bred** Kevin Walsh **Trained** Dalham, Suffolk

FOCUS
A decent handicap.

7966 SKYSPORTS.COM RACING H'CAP 1m (P)
6:55 (6:56) (Class 6) (0-65,65) 4-Y-0+ £1,637 (£483; £241) Stalls High

Form RPR
4-02 1 **One Oi**[11] 7829 5-8-12 **56**...... LiamKeniry 12 66
(D W P Arbuthnot) chsd ldng pair: wnt 2nd over 3f out: clsd to ld over 1f out: hdd u.p last 100yds: rallied to ld again fnl strides **8/1**
0252 2 hd **Pipers Piping (IRE)**[6] 7892 4-9-4 **65**......(v) MichaelStainton(3) 10 75
(Jane Chapple-Hyam) t.k.h: hld up bhd ldrs: prog over 2f out: produced to chal fnl f: cajoled into ld last 100yds: gave up and hdd fnl strides **5/1**[2]
5632 3 3 ¾ **Kipchak (IRE)**[12] 7812 5-9-6 **64**......(p) KirstyMilczarek 9 65
(C R Dore) led at gd pce and sn at least 3 l clr: hdd over 1f out: sn no ch w ldng pair but kpt on for 3rd **7/1**
3003 4 2 **Aflaam (IRE)**[6] 7890 5-9-7 **65**......(t) LukeMorris 8 61
(R A Harris) sn in midfield: u.p fr 3f out: plugged on fnl 2f: nvr gng pce to threaten **8/1**
5141 5 nk **Esteem Lord**[12] 7814 4-9-1 **59**...... AdamKirby 4 55
(D K Ivory) hld up towards rr: prog on inner over 2f out: tried to cl on ldrs over 1f out: sn no imp **3/1**[1]
0020 6 1 ¾ **Shared Moment (IRE)**[13] 7787 4-8-8 **55**......(p) AmyRyan(3) 5 47
(J Gallagher) s.s: last early: rdn and sme prog over 2f out: no imp over 1f out **25/1**
6011 7 2 ¼ **Indian Violet (IRE)**[11] 7829 4-9-3 **61**...... JamieGoldstein 7 47
(Miss Sheena West) chsd clr ldr to over 3f out: steadily wknd fnl 2f **5/1**[2]
-460 8 10 **Marmooq**[342] 162 7-9-5 **63**...... RobbieFitzpatrick 3 26
(M J Attwater) a wl in rr: u.p sn after 1/2-way: no ch over 2f out **50/1**
6652 9 9 **Djalalabad (FR)**[21] 7649 6-8-4 **51** oh2......(t) BillyCray(3) 2 —
(J Pearce) led to s: racd wd: chsd ldrs: rdn 1/2-way: sn dropped out: t.o **25/1**
4200 10 15 **Play Up Pompey**[251] 1318 8-8-4 **51** oh6...... KierenFox(3) 6 —
(J J Bridger) s.i.s: a wl in rr: in trble bef 1/2-way: t.o **50/1**

The Form Book, Raceform Ltd, Compton, RG20 6NL

5120 **11** *36* **Cheddar George**[49] 7298 4-9-4 **62**................................ JackMitchell 13 —
(P W Chapple-Hyam) *trckd ldrs: wknd v rapidly 3f out: wl t.o: lame* **11/2**[3]
1m 38.59s (-1.21) **Going Correction** +0.025s/f (Slow) **11** Ran SP% **120.1**
Speed ratings (Par 101): **107,106,103,101,100 99,96,86,77,62 26**
toteswingers: 1&2 £9.00, 1&3 £5.20, 2&3 £5.40. CSF £47.36 CT £244.71 TOTE £6.70: £2.20, £2.40, £3.70; EX 56.40.
Owner Saxon Gate Partnership **Bred** Mrs Margaret H Goodrich **Trained** Compton, Berks

FOCUS
An open-looking handicap run at a fair gallop.
Esteem Lord Official explanation: vet said gelding lost its right-fore shoe
Cheddar George Official explanation: jockey said gelding was lame behind
T/Plt: £164.80 to a £1 stake. Pool £92,313.33 - 408.74 winning units. T/Qpdt: £28.60 to a £1 stake. Pool £9,994.26 - 258.00 winning units. JN

7878 LINGFIELD (L-H)
Wednesday, December 22

OFFICIAL GOING: Standard
Wind: Nil Weather: Dry and cold

7967 BET TOTEPOOL TO SUPPORT YOUR SPORT H'CAP 2m (P)
12:35 (12:35) (Class 6) (0-65,65) 3-Y-0+ **£2,047** (£604; £302) **Stalls** Low

Form RPR
100 **1** **Coda Agency**[168] 3780 7-9-12 **63**.. LiamKeniry 8 71
(D W P Arbuthnot) *chsd ldrs: hdwy to ld over 3f out: rdn ent fnl 2f: kpt on wl u.p fnl f* **10/1**
3231 **2** *3/4* **Motirani**[18] 7704 3-9-3 **62**.. MickyFenton 2 69
(J Pearce) *in tch: hdwy over 3f out: rdn to chse wnr ent fnl 2f: styd on same pce u.p and a hld fnl f* **11/4**[1]
005- **3** *nse* **Kahfre**[36] 7064 3-9-6 **65**...(be[1]) DavidProbert 7 72
(G L Moore) *in tch: rdn and hdwy to chse ldrs wl over 2f out: drvn to press ldrs ins fnl f: kpt on same pce towards fin* **15/2**
2365 **4** *4* **Soundbyte**[18] 7704 5-9-9 **60**... FergusSweeney 5 62
(J Gallagher) *t.k.h: hld up wl in tch in last trio: hdwy to chse ldrs on inner whn nt clr run bnd over 1f out: drvn over 1f out: wknd fnl 100yds* **14/1**
2040 **5** *hd* **Gandalf**[86] 6427 8-10-0 **65**.. DaneO'Neill 10 67
(Miss Amy Weaver) *hld up in tch in rr: hdwy and nt clr run on outer ent fnl 3f: chsd ldrs and drvn over 1f out: wknd ins fnl f* **16/1**
5133 **6** *1 1/4* **Dubai Phantom (USA)**[18] 7704 3-9-5 **64**............................ MartinLane 3 65
(D M Simcock) *wnt lft s and s.i.s: in tch towards rr: rdn and effrt over 2f out: plugged on u.p ins fnl f: nvr gng pce to trble ldrs* **3/1**[2]
4060 **7** *2* **Frameit (IRE)**[12] 7805 3-8-10 **55**...................................(vt) FrannyNorton 13 53
(J G Given) *hld up in tch towards rr: rdn and struggling 4f out: outpcd and bhd over 2f out: rallied u.p over 1f out: styd on fnl f but no ch w ldrs* **14/1**
-030 **8** *8* **Cossack Prince**[261] 748 5-9-10 **61**................................... IanMongan 14 50
(Mrs L J Mongan) *chsd ldrs tl led over 5f out: hdd and rdn over 3f out: wknd jst over 2f out* **33/1**
262- **9** *1/2* **Screaming Brave**[27] 5872 4-9-4 **55**..........................(t) JamieGoldstein 11 43
(Miss Sheena West) *hld up in tch towards rr: gd hdwy on outer to chse ldrs wl over 2f out: rdn and struggling ent fnl 2f: sn wknd* **11/2**[3]
/0-0 **10** *18* **The Buck (IRE)**[1] 7957 7-9-13 **64**.................................(b[1]) StephenCraine 4 30
(John Joseph Murphy, Ire) *t.k.h: hld up in tch tl hdwy to press ldr over 4f out tl over 3f out: wknd over 2f out: eased fr over 1f out* **25/1**
066 **11** *12* **Lady Willa (IRE)**[18] 7690 3-8-11 **56**................................. NeilChalmers 6 8
(Mark Gillard) *led tl 11f out: styd w ldr tl over 5f out: dropped to rr u.p 4f out: lost tch 3f out: t.o fnl 2f* **40/1**
0 **12** *15* **Waldsee (GER)**[25] 7147 5-9-3 **54**....................................... LukeMorris 9 —
(S Curran) *w ldr tl led 11f out: hdd over 5f out: wknd qckly wl over 3f out: t.o fnl 2f* **50/1**
3m 28.39s (2.69) **Going Correction** +0.25s/f (Slow)
WFA 3 from 4yo+ 8lb **12** Ran SP% **118.3**
Speed ratings (Par 101): **103,102,102,100,100 99,98,94,94,85 79,72**
toteswingers: 1&2 £6.00, 1&3 £16.00, 2&3 £4.20. CSF £36.55 CT £225.67 TOTE £13.20: £4.00, £2.00, £2.30; EX 25.30 Trifecta £235.00 Part won. Pool: £317.70 - 0.10 winning units..
Owner Banfield, Thompson **Bred** Baydon House Stud **Trained** Compton, Berks

FOCUS
The early pace wasn't strong in this moderate staying handicap and plenty still has a chance running to the final bend.
Frameit(IRE) Official explanation: jockey said gelding suffered interference in runing
The Buck(IRE) Official explanation: jockey said gelding lost its action 2f out

7968 EDENBRIDGE APPRENTICE H'CAP 1m 2f (P)
1:05 (1:07) (Class 6) (0-65,65) 3-Y-0+ **£2,047** (£604; £302) **Stalls** Low

Form RPR
0000 **1** **Lord Theo**[37] 7467 6-9-0 **59**.. RyanClark(3) 4 71
(N P Littmoden) *s.i.s: hld up in tch: hdwy and rdn to chse ldrs ent fnl 2f: led over 1f out: r.o wl and drew clr fnl 100yds: rdn out* **9/2**[1]
2146 **2** *3* **Catbells (IRE)**[19] 7678 3-8-12 **62**..........................(p) NatashaEaton(5) 12 68
(A Bailey) *fly-jmpd leaving stalls and s.i.s: hld up towards rr: gd hdwy on outer to ld over 2f out: rdn and hdd over 1f out: nt pce of wnr ins fnl f: kpt on* **8/1**
4256 **3** *2* **Lunar River (FR)**[39] 7445 7-8-7 **52**..............................(t) JamesRogers(3) 6 54
(David Pinder) *chsd ldrs: rdn to chse ldr jst over 2f out: outpcd u.p fnl f* **5/1**[2]
5063 **4** *3 1/4* **Derby Desire (IRE)**[11] 7840 6-8-12 **54**................................. BillyCray 9 50
(D Donovan) *hld up in tch: rdn to chse ldrs jst over 2f out: outpcd and btn jst over 1f out* **5/1**[2]
365 **5** *hd* **Asterisk**[26] 7579 3-8-6 **58**.. HannahNunn(7) 5 53
(John Berry) *hld up in tch in last trio: outpcd over 2f out: rallied and hdwy 1f out: kpt on wl ins fnl f: nvr trbld ldrs* **6/1**
5254 **6** *6* **Until The Man (IRE)**[35] 7476 3-9-6 **65**.......................(p) MarcGoldstein 7 48
(Jim Best) *t.k.h: chsd ldrs: wknd u.p jst over 2f out: wl btn ent fnl f* **12/1**
6052 **7** *nse* **Know No Fear**[19] 7678 5-9-0 **61**..................................(p) LucyBarry(5) 2 44
(A J Lidderdale) *t.k.h: chsd ldr tl led 7f out: clr over 4f out: hdd over 2f out: wknd qckly wl over 1f out* **11/2**[3]
013- **8** *2 3/4* **My Les**[54] 6918 4-9-2 **63**.. MatthewLawson(5) 3 41
(Jim Best) *chsd ldrs: wnt 2nd over 4f out: rdn and clsd on ldr ent fnl 3f: wknd over 2f out: wl btn over 1f out* **14/1**
0000 **9** *nk* **Usquaebach**[7] 7874 3-8-11 **59**..................................... NathanAlison(3) 13 36
(P M Phelan) *in tch: n.m.r over 2f out: sn rdn and wknd jst over 2f out: wl btn over 1f out* **11/1**

6/00 **10** *36* **Sweet Seville (FR)**[161] 748 6-8-0 **49** oh4................ JessicaSteven(7) 1 —
(T T Clement) *led tl 7f out: chsd ldr tl over 4f out: sn lost pl and bhd: t.o fnl 2f* **33/1**
2m 8.15s (1.55) **Going Correction** +0.25s/f (Slow)
WFA 3 from 4yo+ 3lb **10** Ran SP% **117.9**
Speed ratings (Par 101): **103,100,99,96,96 91,91,89,88,60**
toteswingers: 1&2 £9.80, 1&3 £7.30, 2&3 £9.00. CSF £41.17 CT £188.68 TOTE £5.00: £1.90, £3.00, £1.70; EX 49.20 Trifecta £191.80 Pool: £331.77 - 1.28 winning units..
Owner Mrs Karen Graham **Bred** Mike Perkins **Trained** Newmarket, Suffolk

FOCUS
A moderate apprentice handicap, but a dramatic race with the front pair both having a problem with blindfolds at the start. Each lost ground, but the leaders must have gone off too quick as the pair slowest away dominated the finish.

7969 TOTEPOOL OUR PROFITS STAY IN RACING MAIDEN STKS 1m (P)
1:35 (1:36) (Class 5) 3-Y-0+ **£2,388** (£705; £352) **Stalls** High

Form RPR
2 **1** **D'Artagnan (SAF)**[13] 7786 3-8-5 75................................. KierenFox(3) 6 63
(Miss Gay Kelleway) *mde all: set stdy gallop tl rdn and clr ent fnl 2f: in command over 1f out: comf* **2/5**[1]
042 **2** *3 3/4* **Penbryn (USA)**[11] 7838 3-9-3 69... LukeMorris 5 64
(N P Littmoden) *t.k.h: chsd wnr: rdn and nt qckn over 2f out: one pce u.p and wl hld by wnr fr over 1f out* **7/2**[2]
003- **3** *2 1/2* **Abigails Angel**[396] 7482 3-8-5 52................................ NathanAlison(7) 4 53
(B R Johnson) *t.k.h: hld up in tch: outpcd ent fnl 2f: pushed along and wnt 3rd ent fnl f: no threat to wnr* **12/1**
4 *5* **Diplomatic (IRE)** 5-9-4 0.. CathyGannon 1 47
(M D Squance) *s.i.s: t.k.h: hld up in tch: hdwy to chse ldrs over 5f out: rdn over 2f out: wknd jst over 2f out: wl hld fr over 1f out* **8/1**[3]
066 **5** *1/2* **Some Yarn (IRE)**[21] 7651 3-9-3 45..............................(p) SteveDrowne 2 45
(Mrs L C Jewell) *stdd after s: hld up in tch: rdn and outpcd ent fnl 2f: wl hld whn hung rt u.p over 1f out* **50/1**
1m 41.44s (3.24) **Going Correction** +0.25s/f (Slow)
WFA 3 from 4yo+ 1lb **5** Ran SP% **114.4**
Speed ratings (Par 103): **93,89,86,81,81**
toteswinger: 1&2 £2.50. CSF £2.35 TOTE £2.00: £1.70, £1.10; EX 2.40.
Owner H M K Al Mehairi **Bred** Yellow Star Stud **Trained** Exning, Suffolk

FOCUS
A moderate older-horse maiden and with some of these looking quirky, the form is suspect.
Abigails Angel Official explanation: jockey said filly ran too free
Diplomatic(IRE) Official explanation: jockey said gelding hung left

7970 MARRIOTT BREATHE SPA H'CAP 1m (P)
2:05 (2:06) (Class 2) (0-100,99) 3-Y-0+ **£9,066** (£2,697; £1,348; £673) **Stalls** High

Form RPR
131 **1** **Final Drive (IRE)**[11] 7842 4-8-10 **87** ow1..................... StevieDonohoe 3 96
(J Ryan) *stdd after s: hld up in tch in last pair: rdn and effrt ent fnl 2f: hdwy on outer over 1f out: rdn to ld fnl 100yds: r.o wl* **13/2**
0414 **2** *nk* **Lowther**[26] 7574 5-8-10 **92**...(be) SladeO'Hara(5) 7 100
(A Bailey) *stdd after s: t.k.h: hld up in tch: effrt and nt clr run briefly wl over 1f out: sn swtchd rt and hdwy: ev ch ins fnl f: r.o but hld towards fin* **5/1**
0561 **3** *2 1/4* **Mafeking (UAE)**[15] 7735 6-9-0 **91**... IanMongan 6 94
(M R Hoad) *led: set stdy gallop tl rdn and qcknd jst over 2f out: drvn over 1f out: hdd fnl 100yds: sn outpcd* **7/2**[2]
2024 **4** *1 1/4* **Audemar (IRE)**[53] 7243 4-8-13 **90**................................ AndreaAtzeni 8 90
(E F Vaughan) *t.k.h: chsd ldr: rdn jst over 2f out: drvn and unable qck over 1f out: one pce and btn ins fnl f* **9/2**
4000 **5** *3 1/2* **Aldovrandi (IRE)**[25] 7593 3-9-7 **99**....................................(t) AdamKirby 5 91
(M Botti) *stdd after s: t.k.h and sn chsng ldrs: rdn and unable qck ent fnl 2f: wknd u.p 1f out* **11/4**[1]
3211 **6** *4* **Fantasy Gladiator**[18] 7688 4-8-10 **87**...........................(p) JimmyQuinn 1 70
(R M H Cowell) *dwlt: sn rcvrd to chse ldrs and t.k.h: rdn and unable qck on inner ent fnl 2f: wknd over 1f out* **4/1**[3]
0660 **7** *3/4* **The Scorching Wind (IRE)**[130] 5067 4-8-9 **91**.............(t) RyanClark(5) 9 72
(S C Williams) *t.k.h: hld up in tch on outer: wknd u.p over 1f out* **25/1**
1m 38.23s (0.03) **Going Correction** +0.25s/f (Slow)
WFA 3 from 4yo+ 1lb **7** Ran SP% **120.9**
Speed ratings (Par 109): **109,108,106,105,101 97,96**
toteswingers: 1&2 £4.80, 1&3 £3.70, 2&3 £4.40. CSF £41.28 CT £135.41 TOTE £9.20: £4.60, £2.50; EX 38.50 Trifecta £214.90 Pool: £647.74 - 2.23 winning units..
Owner Par 4 Racing **Bred** D Day & B Cantwell **Trained** Newmarket, Suffolk

FOCUS
A decent handicap, but a modest early pace puts a small question mark against the reliability of the form.

NOTEBOOK
Final Drive(IRE) had won four of his last five starts, but was up against much better rivals and the market vibes were negative. However, after having been dropped out early, he was brought with a withering run widest of all in the home straight and his momentum got him home just in front. He was off a 10lb higher mark here including the 1lb overweight, so is obviously improving at a rate of knots and there is no telling how much further he can go. He may reappear at Wolverhampton next Wednesday. (op 9-2 tchd 4-1 and 7-1)

Lowther, up another 1lb, travelled well behind the leaders and may have hit the front for a stride half a furlong from home until collared by the winner. He has been racing over shorter trips for more than a year, but has winning form at 1m and stamina wasn't an issue here. (tchd 9-2 and 11-2 in places)

Mafeking(UAE), raised 3lb for his recent C&D success, was allowed his own way out in front and tried to quicken off the home bend, but was worn down half a furlong from home. This was another sound effort. (tchd 3-1 and 4-1 in a place)

Audemar(IRE), whose four career wins have all come on Polytrack, was always in a good position behind the leader and had every chance, but couldn't quicken in the straight. He remains on a career-high mark. (op 11-2 tchd 6-1)

Aldovrandi(IRE), making his handicap debut and racing outside of Pattern company for the first time since making a successful racecourse debut at Kempton in April, attracted good market support, but having raced keenly early he didn't find much off the bridle after turning in and this was disappointing. (op 5-1)

Fantasy Gladiator, 7lb higher in his bid for a hat-trick, missed the break then race keenly when back in touch, and then tried to make his final effort tight against the inside rail. He has run well here, but looks especially effective at Kempton. Official explanation: trainer's rep had no explanation for the poor form shown (op 5-1 tchd 7-1)

7971 TOTEPOOL RACING'S BIGGEST SUPPORTER H'CAP 6f (P)
2:35 (2:36) (Class 4) (0-85,85) 3-Y-0+ £3,885 (£1,156; £577; £288) Stalls Low

Form RPR
1651 1 **Anne Of Kiev (IRE)**[48] 7319 5-9-6 84 (t) SteveDrowne 2 96
(J R Gask) *chsd ldng pair: rdn and qckndt to ld jst ins fnl f: r.o wl: rdn out* 3/1[1]

6663 2 1 ¾ **Feelin Foxy**[11] 7841 6-8-10 74 FrannyNorton 6 80
(J G Given) *taken down early: led: rdn ent fnl 2f: hdd jst ins fnl f: kpt on same pce after* 10/1

3025 3 shd **Billy Red**[11] 7826 6-9-7 85 (b) FergusSweeney 8 91
(J R Jenkins) *fly-jmpd leaving stalls: chsd ldr: ev ch and rdn over 1f out: kpt on same pce u.p ins fnl f* 7/1

2601 4 hd **Perfect Act**[17] 7719 5-9-3 81 DavidProbert 9 86
(A M Balding) *t.k.h: hld up in tch: hdwy to chse ldrs and n.m.r over 1f out tl jst ins fnl f: kpt on same pce u.p after* 4/1[3]

6330 5 ½ **Lastkingofscotland (IRE)**[25] 7597 4-8-8 72 (b) KirstyMilczarek 12 75
(C R Dore) *in tch in last trio: effrt to chse ldrs jst over 1f out: nt clr run ins fnl f: nvr able to chal* 15/2

0460 6 hd **Rapid Water**[14] 7766 4-8-8 72 JimmyQuinn 3 75
(Jane Chapple-Hyam) *s.i.s: hld up in tch in last pair: effrt and rdn wl over 1f out: styd on same pce fnl f* 15/2

1012 7 hd **Vintage (IRE)**[83] 6501 6-9-1 79 IanMongan 4 81
(J Akehurst) *chsd ldrs: rdn and unable qck over 1f out: one pce and no threat to wnr fnl f* 10/3[2]

0006 8 1 ¼ **Onceaponatime (IRE)**[8] 7866 5-8-11 75 LukeMorris 7 73
(M D Squance) *hld up in tch in midfield: rdn and effrt jst over 2f out: wknd u.p over 1f out* 20/1

1006 9 1 ¾ **Dingaan (IRE)**[11] 7826 7-8-10 74 RobbieFitzpatrick 10 67
(Peter Grayson) *stdd s: hld up in rr: effrt on outer ent fnl 2f: no real hdwy: n.d* 33/1

0000 10 5 **Mister Green (FR)**[18] 7689 4-9-2 80 StephenCraine 1 57
(D Flood) *hld up in tch in midfield: rdn and unable qck ent fnl 2f: sn wknd* 33/1

1m 11.97s (0.07) **Going Correction** +0.25s/f (Slow) 10 Ran SP% **123.8**
Speed ratings (Par 105): **109,106,106,106,105 105,105,103,101,94**
toteswingers: 1&2 £12.10, 1&3 £3.60, 2&3 £11.90. CSF £35.60 CT £203.71 TOTE £4.70: £1.90, £3.00, £2.20; EX 48.50 Trifecta £257.70 Pool: £459.79 - 1.32 winning units..
Owner P Bamford **Bred** Deerfield Farm **Trained** Sutton Veny, Wilts

FOCUS
A fair sprint handicap and although the pace looked solid enough, the first four were always handy.
Feelin Foxy Official explanation: jockey said filly hung right throughout
Lastkingofscotland(IRE) Official explanation: jockey said gelding was denied a clear run
Rapid Water Official explanation: jockey said gelding was slowly away

7972 TOTEPOOL A BETTER WAY TO BET H'CAP (DIV I) 6f (P)
3:05 (3:07) (Class 6) (0-60,60) 3-Y-0+ £1,706 (£503; £252) Stalls Low

Form RPR
1600 1 **Anjomarba (IRE)**[32] 7518 3-9-3 59 BillyCray(3) 3 69
(B R Johnson) *chsd ldr tl rdn to ld over 1f out: r.o wl fnl f: rdn out* 12/1

5253 2 1 ½ **Loyal Royal (IRE)**[11] 7827 7-9-4 57 (bt) LiamKeniry 7 62
(J M Bradley) *t.k.h: chsd ldrs: chsd wnr and rdn 1f out: fnd little and no imp fnl f* 9/2[2]

0002 3 ½ **Musical Script (USA)**[14] 7761 7-9-4 57 (b) DaneO'Neill 4 60
(Mouse Hamilton-Fairley) *hld up in tch: hdwy on inner 2f out: drvn to chse ldrs over 1f out: one pce and no imp fnl f* 6/1

5335 4 1 ¼ **Laser Ruby**[27] 7563 3-9-7 60 DavidProbert 6 59
(A M Balding) *hld up in tch in midfield: rdn and unable qck over 1f out: one pce and no threat to wnr after* 4/1[1]

0145 5 nse **Espy**[11] 7827 5-9-7 60 RobbieFitzpatrick 5 59
(I W McInnes) *in tch: rdn and effrt to chse ldrs over 1f out: wknd fnl 100yds* 8/1

0060 6 1 **Replicator**[14] 7761 5-8-12 51 (e) JamieMackay 11 47
(P L Gilligan) *in tch on outer: rdn and unable qck over 1f out: one pce and wl hld fnl f* 14/1

000 7 1 ¼ **Vertumnus**[40] 7429 3-8-10 49 (be[1]) MartinLane 8 41
(N P Littmoden) *stdd s: t.k.h: hld up in last trio: short of room and hmpd 4f out: no prog u.p over 1f out* 22/1

04 8 hd **Radiator Rooney (IRE)**[9] 7860 7-8-8 54 JamesRogers(7) 1 45
(Patrick Morris) *stdd s: hld up in last trio: effrt on inner over 1f out: no hdwy and wl hld fnl f* 8/1

0004 9 ½ **Spoof Master (IRE)**[13] 7783 6-8-10 49 (t) MickyFenton 2 39
(J Pearce) *led tl rdn and hdd over 1f out: wkng whn short of room ins fnl f* 11/1

0003 10 hd **The Magic Of Rio**[1] 7952 4-8-7 46 oh1 CathyGannon 9 35
(P D Evans) *stdd s: t.k.h: hld up in rr: rdn and no hdwy over 1f out: n.d* 5/1[3]

1m 12.41s (0.51) **Going Correction** +0.25s/f (Slow) 10 Ran SP% **118.4**
Speed ratings (Par 101): **106,104,103,101,101 100,98,98,97,97**
toteswingers: 1&2 £10.90, 1&3 £9.30, 2&3 £4.40. CSF £66.37 CT £365.19 TOTE £8.60: £2.50, £2.20, £3.00; EX 85.20 Trifecta £405.90 Part won. Pool: £548.60 - 0.85 winning units..
Owner Suresh Sivagnanam **Bred** Tally-Ho Stud **Trained** Ashtead, Surrey

FOCUS
A moderate first division of the 46-60 sprint handicap.
The Magic Of Rio Official explanation: jockey said filly ran too free

7973 TOTEPOOL A BETTER WAY TO BET H'CAP (DIV II) 6f (P)
3:35 (3:36) (Class 6) (0-60,60) 3-Y-0+ £1,706 (£503; £252) Stalls Low

Form RPR
0452 1 **Chjimes (IRE)**[11] 7827 6-9-7 60 (b) KirstyMilczarek 11 69
(C R Dore) *wnt lft and stdd s: t.k.h: hld up in last trio: hdwy to chse ldrs wl over 1f out: led 1f out: in command fnl 100yds: r.o wl: comf* 2/1[1]

5102 2 1 ¼ **Dancing Welcome**[11] 7824 4-9-7 60 (b) LiamKeniry 2 65
(J M Bradley) *led: set stdy gallop tl rdn and qcknd ent fnl 2f: hdd 1f out: nt pce of wnr after: kpt on* 11/4[2]

0533 3 1 ½ **Force To Spend**[13] 7783 3-8-6 50 RyanClark(5) 6 50
(N P Littmoden) *w ldr: rdn ent fnl 2f: ev ch tl outpcd jst ins fnl f: wl hld fnl 100yds* 15/2

0042 4 1 ¼ **Memphis Man**[7] 7882 7-8-8 54 MatthewCosham(7) 7 50
(P D Evans) *taken down early: stdd s: t.k.h: hld up in tch in last trio: rdn and effrt over 1f out: swtchd rt 1f out: r.o fnl 100yds: nvr trbld ldrs* 8/1

3662 5 hd **Clerical (USA)**[21] 7656 4-9-4 57 (p) AndreaAtzeni 4 53
(R M H Cowell) *t.k.h: hld up wl in tch: effrt u.p 2f out: drvn and no hdwy over 1f out: wknd 1f out* 7/2[3]

40-0 6 2 ½ **Silk Slippers**[1] 7952 3-9-6 59 (b[1]) StephenCraine 5 47
(John Joseph Murphy, Ire) *chsd ldrs: rdn and nt qckn wl over 1f out: sn wknd* 14/1

0406 7 1 **Ariel Bender**[7] 7883 3-8-7 46 oh1 (b) RobbieFitzpatrick 10 30
(Peter Grayson) *stdd s: t.k.h: hld up in last trio: hdwy to chse ldrs 1/2-way: hung rt and lost pl bnd ent fnl 2f: sn wknd* 33/1

1m 14.47s (2.57) **Going Correction** +0.25s/f (Slow) 7 Ran SP% **114.7**
Speed ratings (Par 101): **92,90,88,86,86 83,81**
toteswingers: 1&2 £2.30, 1&3 £3.70, 2&3 £3.90. toteSuper 7: WIN: Not won. PLACE: 94.60 - 4 winning units. CSF £7.77 CT £32.35 TOTE £3.60: £1.70, £2.00; EX 6.90 Trifecta £36.60 Pool: £773.61 - 15.60 winning units..
Owner Sean J Murphy **Bred** Morgan O'Flaherty **Trained** Cowbit, Lincs

FOCUS
No great pace on here and the winning time was more than two seconds slower than the first division.
T/Jkpt: Not won. T/Plt: £80.30 to a £1 stake. Pool £85,719.40 - 779.02 winning units. T/Qpdt: £11.30 to a £1 stake. Pool £6,481.23 - 422.90 winning units. SP

7959 DEAUVILLE (R-H)
Wednesday, December 22
OFFICIAL GOING: Fibresand: standard

7974a PRIX SOLEIL (CONDITIONS) (2YO COLTS & GELDINGS) (FIBRESAND) 1m 1f 110y
11:15 (12:00) 2-Y-0 £15,044 (£6,017; £4,513; £3,008; £1,504)

RPR
1 **Varadero (IRE)** 2-8-10 0 Pierre-CharlesBoudot 10 —
(Y De Nicolay, France) 98/10

2 hd **Burj Alzain (IRE)**[35] 7481 2-9-0 0 AnthonyCrastus 7 —
(G A Butler) *racd in 4th tl qckning smoothly to take ld early in st: sn wnt clr: rdn fnl 100yds: ct almost on line* 6/4[1]

3 8 **Brainstormer (FR)**[63] 2-8-8 0 (p) TheoBachelot(6) 12 —
(M Nigge, France) 12/1

4 nk **Giantrio (IRE)**[13] 2-8-10 0 SylvainRuis 3 —
(Rod Collet, France) 9/1

5 nk **Reves De Printemps (FR)**[39] 7454 2-9-0 0 TonyPiccone 4 —
(J Reynier, France) 13/1

6 nk **Tixto (FR)** 2-8-10 0 (b) MickaelBarzalona 9 —
(J-L Pelletan, France) 51/1

7 shd **Happy Monster (FR)**[105] 2-8-3 0 StevanBourgois(7) 1 —
(Robert Collet, France) 14/1

8 ¾ **Point Du Jour (FR)**[22] 7647 2-8-10 0 RonanThomas 5 —
(I A Wood) *broke wl to ld: rdn early in st: hdd 1 1/2f out: rdn but no ex fnl 150yds* 53/10[2]

9 8 **Adiamondforhelen (IRE)** 2-8-10 0 ThomasHuet 6 —
(E J O'Neill, France) 24/1

10 3 **Milord Des Aigles (FR)** 2-8-10 0 FranckBlondel 2 —
(Mme C Barande-Barbe, France) 17/2[3]

0 **Soeurchichi (FR)** 2-8-7 0 MichaelMartinez 11 —
(J-M Lefebvre, France) 67/1

0 **Crack Chichi (FR)** 2-8-7 0 MorganDelalande 8 —
(M Seror, France) 60/1

1m 59.1s (119.10) 12 Ran SP% **116.2**
WIN (incl. 1 euro stake): 10.80. PL: 2.90, 1.60, 3.10. DF: 12.30. SF: 39.70.
Owner Aleyrion Bloodstock Ltd **Bred** Aleyrion Bloodstock Ltd **Trained** France

NOTEBOOK
Varadero(IRE) ◆, by Dalakhani out of a 1m2f Listed winner, looked a smart colt on debut, finishing strongly to deny a very useful type, with the pair clear.
Burj Alzain(IRE), the winner of his first two starts over 1m at Kempton, a maiden and a nursery (off 77), travelled really well but maybe went to the front too soon and was just caught. Still, he was a long way clear of the rest and this was probably another step forward and he's probably not far off pattern class.
Point Du Jour(FR) seems to be settling better now, but didn't match for the form he showed when third in a similar event over an extended 7f here last time. He led into the straight, but gradually faded and looked a non-stayer.

7974 DEAUVILLE (R-H)
Thursday, December 23
OFFICIAL GOING: Fibresand: standard

7975a PRIX DU VEXIN NORMAND (CONDITIONS) (2YO) (FIBRESAND) 6f 110y
12:15 (12:00) 2-Y-0 £12,831 (£5,132; £3,849; £2,566; £1,283)

RPR
1 **Venetien (FR)**[15] 2-9-2 0 (b) RonanThomas 2 —
(R Gibson, France) 14/5[1]

2 2 **King David (FR)**[14] 2-9-2 0 SebastienMaillot 13 —
(M Boutin, France) 21/1

3 snk **Dozy Joe**[22] 7652 2-9-2 0 FranckBlondel 11 —
(I A Wood) *racd midfield towards outer: rdn early in st to chse ldr: qcknd wl to go 2nd 1f out: r.o wl: lost 2nd cl home* 58/10[3]

4 2 **Jo Speedy (IRE)**[23] 2-8-9 0 ThierryJarnet 5 —
(Mlle S-V Tarrou, France) 14/1

5 ¾ **Bearheart (IRE)**[14] 2-8-13 0 ThomasHuet 8 —
(E J O'Neill, France) 13/1

6 snk **Madly In Love (FR)**[23] 2-8-13 0 FlavienPrat 10 —
(J-L Gay, France) 78/10

7 2 **Kanotier (FR)**[14] 2-9-2 0 AlexisBadel 4 —
(Mme M Bollack-Badel, France) 15/1

8 ¾ **Lady Jak (FR)**[6] 2-8-13 0 FabriceVeron 6 —
(J-V Toux, France) 17/1

9 shd **Singapore Smile (FR)**[44] 2-8-9 0 WilliamsSaraiva(4) 14 —
(Mlle V Dissaux, France) 46/1

10 ½ **Pepito Grillo**[14] 2-9-2 0 (b[1]) SylvainRuis 9 —
(L A Urbano-Grajales, France) 24/1

0 **Passei (FR)**[23] 2-8-13 0 AnthonyCrastus 7 —
(Mlle V Dissaux, France) 13/1

0 **Veulettes (IRE)**[101] 2-8-6 0.. MickaelBarzalona 3 —
(Y De Nicolay, France) **38/1**
0 **Militante (IRE)**[124] 5322 2-8-13 0........................ Pierre-CharlesBoudot 1 —
(Y De Nicolay, France) **5/1**[2]
0 **Abandon (FR)** 2-8-6 0... MorganDelalande 12 —
(C Plisson, France) **69/1**
1m 17.3s (77.30) **14** Ran SP% **116.5**
WIN (incl. 1 euro stake): 3.80. PLACES: 1.80, 5.60, 2.30. DF: 50.00. SF: 59.10.
Owner Mme Erik Soderberg **Bred** Haras Du Quesnay **Trained** Lamorlaye, France

NOTEBOOK
Dozy Joe had no chance with the easy winner, but he picked up well early in the straight and looked set to finish a good second, only to tire late on. Trips beyond 6f seem to stretch him and he should do better back over shorter.

7913 WOLVERHAMPTON (A.W) (L-H)
Sunday, December 26
7976 Meeting Abandoned - Frost

7952 SOUTHWELL (L-H)
Monday, December 27
OFFICIAL GOING: Standard to slow
Wind: Moderate across Weather: Overcast

7982 BET TOTEPOOL ON ALL UK RACING NURSERY 6f (F)
12:10 (12:11) (Class 5) (0-75,73) 2-Y-O **£2,217** (£654; £327) **Stalls** Low

Form RPR
425 **1** **Shostakovich (IRE)**[11] 7891 2-9-4 **70**........................(tp) TravisBlock 1 75
(S Kirk) *sn led: rdn over 2f out: drvn and hung rt ins fnl f: kpt on* **6/1**[1]
0000 **2** ¾ **William Wainwright (IRE)**[11] 7894 2-7-12 **50** oh3......... NickyMackay 3 53
(Mrs A Duffield) *trckd ldrs on inner: hdwy to chse wnr over 2f out: sn rdn and hung rt wl over 1f out: drvn and kpt on ins fnl f* **33/1**
6004 **3** ¾ **Veeb (IRE)**[11] 7894 2-8-2 **54**.. JimmyQuinn 7 55
(M Johnston) *in tch: hdwy on outer to chse ldrs over 2f out: rdn over 1f out: kpt on u.p ins fnl f: nrst fin* **7/1**[2]
4322 **4** 7 **Mazovian (USA)**[6] 7954 2-9-1 **70**.............................. RobertLButler(3) 6 50
(M C Chapman) *hld up towards rr: sme hdwy on inner over 2f out: sn no imp* **9/1**[3]
5234 **5** ¾ **Restless Bay (IRE)**[11] 7891 2-9-7 **73**...........................(b) LukeMorris 2 50
(R Hollinshead) *cl up: rdn over 2f out: drvn wl over 1f out: sn hung rt and wknd* **9/1**[3]
1665 **6** 9 **Reachtothestars (USA)**[22] 7718 2-9-1 **67**........................ AdamKirby 4 17
(M G Quinlan) *chsd ldrs: rdn along wl over 2f out: sn wknd* **22/1**
061 **7** 10 **Winning Draw (IRE)**[140] 4890 2-8-9 **61**........................ MickyFenton 8 —
(P T Midgley) *chsd ldrs: rdn along and wd st: sn outpcd and bhd* **18/1**
1m 22.37s (5.87) **Going Correction** +0.875s/f (Slow) **7** Ran SP% **59.3**
Speed ratings (Par 96): **95,94,93,83,82 70,57**
toteswingers:1&2:£17.40, 1&3:£1.50, 2&3:£20.30 CSF £44.22 CT £153.32 TOTE £3.70: £1.80, £12.10; EX 55.00 Trifecta £89.80 Part won. Pool £121.47 - 0.84 winning units..
Owner Dr J Wilson & S Kirk **Bred** Marchwood Aggregates **Trained** Upper Lambourn, Berks

7983 BET TOTEPOOL ON ALL IRISH RACING (S) STKS 5f (F)
12:45 (12:45) (Class 6) 2-Y-O **£1,706** (£503; £252) **Stalls** High

Form RPR
613 **1** **Hereselllie (IRE)**[27] 7641 2-8-12 55.......................... GrahamGibbons 13 64
(T D Barron) *racd nr stands' rail: qckly away: mde all: rdn appr fnl f and kpt on wl* **9/2**[1]
3545 **2** 1 ¾ **Silk Bounty**[20] 7739 2-8-12 63... MickyFenton 2 58
(J G Given) *a cl up in centre: rdn and ev ch wl over 1f out: edgd rt and drvn appr fnl f: kpt on same pce* **5/1**[2]
044 **3** 3 ¾ **Just For Leo (IRE)**[17] 7809 2-8-5 60................(v) MatthewCosham(7) 10 44
(P D Evans) *a.p: rdn along 2f out: drvn over 1f out and kpt on same pce* **15/2**
0602 **4** ½ **Misty Morn**[31] 7576 2-8-12 57... JimmyQuinn 5 42
(A D Brown) *s.i.s: in rr and swtchd lft after 1f: rdn along 1/2-way: hdwy to chse ldrs over 1f out: sn drvn and kpt on ins fnl f: nrst fin* **6/1**
063 **5** ¾ **Bigalo's Vera B**[23] 7692 2-8-7 45.................................. DuranFentiman 3 35
(L A Mullaney) *stmbld s and sn rdn along to chse ldrs: drvn wl over 1f out and kpt on same pce* **25/1**
063 **6** 4 **Goal (IRE)**[10] 7914 2-9-0 60 ow2.. AdamKirby 4 27
(D C Griffiths) *chsd ldrs: rdn along over 2f out: grad wknd* **8/1**
6600 **7** ½ **Mini Bon Bon**[18] 7777 2-8-5 52..................................(p) NatashaEaton(7) 7 24
(A Bailey) *outpcd and towards rr: swtchd lft and sme hdwy wl over 1f out: n.d* **33/1**
4350 **8** nk **Sapphire Girl**[15] 7843 2-8-7 60... ChrisCatlin 12 17
(R A Fahey) *in tch: rdn along and outpcd 1/2-way: n.d* **14/1**
2060 **9** 1 ¾ **Red Gold And Green (IRE)**[14] 7857 2-8-9 60.................. BillyCray(3) 8 16
(D Nicholls) *chsd ldrs: rdn along bef 1/2-way: sn outpcd* **11/2**[3]
6045 **10** 1 ¾ **Key To The Motion (IRE)**[105] 6035 2-8-7 45.......... RobbieFitzpatrick 6 —
(P T Midgley) *dwlt and wnt rt s: bhd and swtchd lft to far rail after 1f: nvr a factor* **40/1**
0606 **11** 1 ¾ **Walshestown Lad (IRE)**[11] 7894 2-8-12 46..................(b) LukeMorris 9 —
(R A Harris) *chsd ldrs: rdn along 1/2-way: sn wknd* **66/1**
005 **12** 10 **Layla's Princess**[10] 7913 2-8-7 40...................................... GregFairley 1 —
(Ian Williams) *chsd ldrs: rdn along 1/2-way: sn drvn and wknd* **7/1**
0000 **13** 12 **Miss Maudie (IRE)**[11] 7894 2-8-7 30......................(be) WilliamCarson 11 —
(R A Harris) *a in rr: outpcd and bhd fr 1/2-way* **100/1**
64.67 secs (4.97) **Going Correction** +0.70s/f (Slow) **13** Ran SP% **118.3**
Speed ratings (Par 94): **88,85,79,78,77 70,70,69,66,63 61,45,25**
toteswingers:1&2:£4.60, 1&3:£9.90, 2&3:£9.70 CSF £25.46 TOTE £4.30: £1.30, £2.10, £2.90; EX 26.80 Trifecta £356.10 Pool £606.34 - 1.26 winning units..The winner was sold to M C Chapman for 4,750gns.
Owner D Pryde & J Cringan **Bred** E Byrne & C Roker **Trained** Maunby, N Yorks

7984 BET ON TONIGHT'S FOOTBALL AT TOTESPORT.COM CLAIMING STKS 5f (F)
1:15 (1:16) (Class 6) 3-Y-O+ **£1,706** (£503; £252) **Stalls** High

Form RPR
4364 **1** **Colorus (IRE)**[13] 7866 7-8-5 70....................................(v) WilliamCarson 4 —
(W J H Ratcliffe) *mde all: rdn wl over 1f out: drvn ins fnl f: hld on wl towards fin* **3/1**[2]
604- **2** shd **Soopacal (IRE)**[641] 965 5-8-11 68...................................... GregFairley 7 —
(M Herrington) *cl up: rdn wl over 1f out: drvn ins fnl f and ev ch tl nt qckn nr fin* **20/1**
1323 **3** 2 ¾ **Sloop Johnb**[13] 7866 4-8-13 72..(p) JackMitchell 9 —
(R A Fahey) *dwlt: pushed along and swtchd lft after 1f: rdn and hdwy to chse ldrs wl over 1f out: drvn and no imp fnl f* **5/2**[1]
000 **4** 2 **Where's Reiley (USA)**[52] 7326 4-8-4 75....................... DeanHeslop(5) 5 —
(T D Barron) *prom: rdn along and sltly outpcd over 2f out: kpt on u.p fnl f* **12/1**
2130 **5** shd **Elhamri**[5] 7961 6-8-13 74.. HayleyTurner 1 —
(C R Dore) *chsd ldrs on outer: effrt 2f out: sn rdn and edgd rt over 1f out: sn one pce* **6/1**
1145 **6** 2 ¾ **Matsunosuke**[27] 7635 8-9-7 100.. LukeMorris 2 —
(R A Harris) *chsd ldrs: rdn along 2f out: sn drvn and btn wl over 1f out* **7/2**[3]
-000 **7** ½ **Egyptian Lord**[14] 7860 7-8-8 30.............................(b) RobbieFitzpatrick 8 —
(Peter Grayson) *chsd ldrs: rdn along bef 1/2-way: sn outpcd* **100/1**
3036 **8** 3 ¼ **Johannesgray (IRE)**[9] 7934 3-8-2 69...........................(be) BillyCray(3) 3 —
(D Nicholls) *dwlt: towards rr and pushed along after 1f: swtchd lft to wd outside 1/2-way: sn rdn and n.d* **17/2**
0405 **9** 3 ½ **Dancing Freddy (IRE)**[18] 7784 3-8-5 67.........................(p) JimmyQuinn 6 —
(J G Given) *n.m.r sn after s and sn pushed along: a in rr* **14/1**
62.41 secs (2.71) **Going Correction** +0.70s/f (Slow) **9** Ran SP% **120.7**
Speed ratings (Par 101): **106,105,101,98,98 93,92,87,82**
toteswingers:1&2:£9.00, 1&3:£2.30, 2&3:£10.20 CSF £63.17 TOTE £4.10: £1.30, £6.10, £1.80; EX 73.50 Trifecta £274.70 Pool £1,255.05 - 3.38 winning units..Dancing Freddy was claimed by S Arnold for £6,000.
Owner J Sheard & W J S Ratcliffe **Bred** M Ervine **Trained** Newmarket, Suffolk

7985 MORE LIVE FOOTBALL BETTING AT TOTESPORT.COM H'CAP 1m 3f (F)
1:50 (1:50) (Class 5) (0-75,75) 3-Y-O+ **£2,217** (£654; £327) **Stalls** Low

Form RPR
1612 **1** **Dontpaytheferryman (USA)**[10] 7921 5-8-7 **61**........... DeanHeslop(5) 3 —
(B Ellison) *pushed along on inner to trck ldrs after 1f: hdwy to ld 4f out: rdn clr wl over 2f out: kpt on: easily* **5/2**[1]
0104 **2** 14 **Ramora (USA)**[9] 7932 4-8-10 **59** oh2................................ HayleyTurner 7 —
(Miss Olivia Maylam) *hld up in tch: hdwy over 3f out: rdn to chse wnr wl over 2f out: sn drvn and no imp* **25/1**
0056 **3** 2 ¼ **Jack Dawkins (USA)**[54] 7306 5-8-13 **65**............................ BillyCray(3) 5 —
(D Nicholls) *hld up: hdwy over 3f out: rdn to chse ldng pair wl over 2f out: sn drvn and kpt on same pce* **11/1**
5040 **4** 5 **Iron Out (USA)**[30] 7600 4-9-10 **73**...................................... AdamKirby 1 —
(R Hollinshead) *trckd ldrs: hdwy 4f out: rdn along 3f out: sn drvn and outpcd fnl 2f* **16/1**
4664 **5** 7 **My Mate Mal**[11] 7898 6-9-1 **64**.. JimmyQuinn 4 —
(W B Stone) *prom: rdn along over 4f out: wknd 3f out* **20/1**
1610 **6** 1 ¾ **City Stable (IRE)**[168] 3965 5-9-5 **68**.............................. JamieMackay 9 —
(M Wigham) *hld up in rr: sme hdwy on inner wl over 2f out: nvr a factor* **10/1**[3]
0242 **7** 1 ¼ **Trachonitis (IRE)**[16] 7836 6-9-7 **70**.................................. GregFairley 6 —
(J R Jenkins) *hld up: a in rr* **11/4**[2]
4500 **8** 20 **Helieorbea**[42] 5530 4-8-11 **60**... GrahamGibbons 2 —
(A D Brown) *led: hdd and pushed along 4f out: drvn and wknd over 3f out* **28/1**
3605 **9** 3 ½ **Master Of Dance (IRE)**[11] 7895 3-9-6 **73**......................... MickyFenton 8 —
(J G Given) *chsd ldrs on outer: rdn along 4f out: wknd over 3f out* **33/1**
2331 **10** 5 **Lay Claim (USA)**[16] 7834 3-9-8 **75**....................................(e) ShaneKelly 10 —
(A J McCabe) *hld up towards rr: sme hdwy 4f: rdn along over 3f out: nvr a factor* **11/4**[2]
2m 33.47s (5.47) **Going Correction** +0.875s/f (Slow)
WFA 3 from 4yo+ 4lb **10** Ran SP% **120.2**
Speed ratings (Par 103): **115,104,103,99,94 93,92,77,75,71**
toteswingers:1&2:£10.60, 1&3:£8.10, 2&3:£35.60 CSF £73.62 CT £606.49 TOTE £3.90: £1.60, £4.20, £3.10; EX 62.60 Trifecta £816.60 Part won. Pool £1,103.60 - 0.50 winning units..
Owner Koo's Racing Club **Bred** Rojan Farms **Trained** Norton, N Yorks

7986 PLAY GOLF BEFORE RACING AT SOUTHWELL H'CAP 1m (F)
2:25 (2:26) (Class 6) (0-60,60) 3-Y-O+ **£1,706** (£503; £252) **Stalls** Low

Form RPR
3413 **1** **Bentley**[14] 7863 6-9-5 **58**.. KellyHarrison 10 —
(B P J Baugh) *midfield: hdwy on outer 3f out: chsd ldrs 2f out: rdn to ld appr fnl f: sn edgd lft: styd on strly* **8/1**
3461 **2** 4 ½ **Exopuntia**[11] 7899 4-9-3 **56**... GregFairley 4 —
(Miss J Feilden) *sn prom: led after 2f: rdn over 2f out: drvn and hdd appr fnl f: kpt on same pce* **9/4**[1]
2-30 **3** 1 ½ **Almahaza (IRE)**[54] 7298 6-9-7 **60**.. AdamKirby 6 —
(A J Chamberlain) *in tch: hdwy over 3f out: rdn to chse ldrs over 2f out: drvn and one pce appr fnl f* **6/1**[3]
0360 **4** 2 ¼ **Positivity**[245] 1575 4-9-1 **54**... JimmyQuinn 3 —
(B Smart) *in tch: hdwy 3f out: rdn over 2f out: sn drvn and one pce* **12/1**
344 **5** 1 ½ **Chichen Daawe**[10] 7919 4-8-6 **50**.................................. DeanHeslop(5) 12 —
(B Ellison) *towards rr: hdwy wl over 2f out: sn rdn and kpt on appr fnl f: nrst fin* **10/1**
0003 **6** nse **Verluga (IRE)**[10] 7912 3-9-2 **56**.................................(b) DuranFentiman 13 —
(T D Easterby) *midfield: hdwy to chse ldrs 3f out: rdn over 2f out: sn drvn and one pce* **8/1**
0642 **7** ¾ **Kielty's Folly**[23] 7706 6-8-12 **51**.................................... GrahamGibbons 11 —
(B P J Baugh) *prom: chsd ldng pair 3f out: hdwy to chal over 2f out: drvn and wknd over 1f out* **11/2**[2]
2006 **8** 1 **Orpen Wide (IRE)**[5] 7646 8-8-13 **55**.........................(t) RobertLButler(3) 2 —
(M C Chapman) *chsd ldrs on inner: rdn along and lost pl 1/2-way: swtchd wd wl over 1f out and sme late hdwy* **33/1**
00 **9** 7 **Ancient Times (USA)**[21] 7731 3-9-1 **55**.......................... RussKennemore 9 —
(P A Kirby) *a in rr* **66/1**

0163 10 1 3/4 **Custard Cream Kid (IRE)**16 7833 4-8-11 **50**............(b1) JackMitchell 8 —
(R A Fahey) *prom: cl up 1/2-way: rdn along 3f out: wknd 2f out* **12/1**
06 11 6 **Masteeat (USA)**16 7827 3-8-6 **46** oh1.............................. ChrisCatlin 5 —
(Miss Olivia Maylam) *cl up: pushed along and lost pl bef 1/2-way: in rr fnl 3f* **50/1**
0602 12 3/4 **Mississippian (IRE)**58 7229 6-8-13 **52**........................ LukeMorris 7 —
(Mrs R Dobbin) *s.i.s: a in rr* **16/1**
/50- 13 16 **Wogan's Sister**584 2246 5-9-6 **59**............................ MickyFenton 1 —
(P T Midgley) *led 2f: rdn along and lost pl 1/2-way: bhd and eased fnl 2f* **33/1**

1m 50.32s (6.62) **Going Correction** +0.875s/f (Slow)
WFA 3 from 4yo+ 1lb 13 Ran SP% **122.4**
Speed ratings (Par 101): **101,96,95,92,91 91,90,89,82,80 74,73,57**
toteswingers:1&2:£5.40, 1&3:£8.30, 2&3:£4.40 CSF £26.39 CT £126.18 TOTE £7.80: £1.90, £1.10, £2.40; EX 27.20 Trifecta £42.00 Pool £1,015.23 - 17.86 winning units..
Owner The Flying Spur Racing Partnership **Bred** Paul Blows And Jenny Hall **Trained** Audley, Staffs

7987 PLAY GOLF AT SOUTHWELL IN 2011 MAIDEN STKS 6f (F)
3:00 (3:01) (Class 5) 3-Y-0+ **£2,217** (£654; £327) **Stalls** Low

Form RPR
2233 1 **Opus Dei**11 7895 3-9-0 66.............................(p) BillyCray(3) 4 —
(D Nicholls) *dwlt: sn pushed along and outpcd in rr: hdwy 1/2-way: sn rdn: drvn to chse ldr wl over 1f out: led jst ins fnl f: kpt on* **2/5**1
0032 2 4 1/2 **Faithful Duchess (IRE)**13 7869 3-8-12 55..................(b) ShaneKelly 1 —
(E F Vaughan) *trckd ldr: hdwy on bit to ld over 2f out: shkn up over 1f out: sn put hd in air and hdd jst ins fnl f: one pce* **5/2**2
6565 3 12 **Rose Bed (IRE)**24 7676 3-8-12 43...........................(b) JackMitchell 2 —
(M G Quinlan) *led: rdn along 3f out: hdd over 2f out and sn outpcd* **25/1**3
0/06 4 33 **Red Rani**24 7684 5-8-12 37.................................. ChrisCatlin 3 —
(R Hollinshead) *cl up: rdn along after 2f: sn outpcd and bhd fnl 3f* **40/1**

1m 21.26s (4.76) **Going Correction** +0.875s/f (Slow) 4 Ran SP% **106.3**
Speed ratings (Par 103): **103,97,81,37**
CSF £1.56 TOTE £1.40; EX 1.60.
Owner Brian Morton **Bred** Countess De La Warr **Trained** Sessay, N Yorks

7988 DOROTHY DIXON BIRTHDAY CELEBRATION H'CAP 1m (F)
3:35 (3:35) (Class 5) (0-75,75) 3-Y-0+ **£2,217** (£654; £327) **Stalls** Low

Form RPR
1020 1 **El Dececy (USA)**45 7421 6-9-5 **73**..........................(p) AdamKirby 6 —
(J Balding) *led: rdn and qcknd clr wl over 2f out: drvn over 1f out: kpt on gamely ins fnl f* **9/2**3
0244 2 2 **Pool Of Knowledge (FR)**69 6152 4-9-4 **75**............ BillyCray(3) 2 —
(D Nicholls) *dwlt and in rr: hdwy on inner 3f out: rdn over 2f out: chsd wnr wl over 1f out: drvn and kpt on ins fnl f* **9/1**
5302 3 3/4 **Minortransgression (USA)**16 7833 3-8-3 **65**....(t) MatthewCosham(7) 8 —
(P D Evans) *chsd ldrs on outer: wd st to stands' rail: rdn to chse wnr 2f out: sn drvn and kpt on same pce appr fnl f* **9/4**1
2540 4 11 **Ilie Nastase (FR)**40 7488 6-9-7 **75**......................... HayleyTurner 5 —
(C R Dore) *towards rr: pushed along over 3f out: hdwy over 2f out: sn rdn and nvr nr ldrs* **4/1**2
4415 5 5 **General Tufto**9 7932 5-9-5 **73**.........................(b) RobbieFitzpatrick 4 —
(C Smith) *in rr: pushed along 1/2-way: sme hdwy over 2f out: sn rdn and n.d* **7/1**
0-50 6 4 1/2 **Mangham (IRE)**51 7352 5-8-13 **74**................................ PNolan(7) 7 —
(D H Brown) *prom: chsd wnr 1/2-way: rdn 3f out and sn wknd* **20/1**
0060 7 7 **Wigram's Turn (USA)**24 7680 5-9-4 **72**.................. GrahamGibbons 1 —
(M W Easterby) *trckd ldrs on inner: rdn 3f out: sn wknd* **12/1**
6423 8 25 **High Rolling**140 4898 3-8-6 **61**............................ DuranFentiman 3 —
(T D Easterby) *chsd ldrs: rdn along over 3f out: sn wknd: bhd and eased fnl 2f* **7/1**

1m 50.48s (6.78) **Going Correction** +0.875s/f (Slow)
WFA 3 from 4yo+ 1lb 8 Ran SP% **116.4**
Speed ratings (Par 103): **101,99,98,87,82 77,70,45**
toteswingers:1&2:£7.50, 1&3:£3.20, 2&3:£5.70 CSF £44.79 CT £115.16 TOTE £4.80: £1.60, £2.70, £1.70; EX 46.60 Trifecta £132.60 Pool £1,830.13 - 10.21 winning units.
Owner Brian Morton & Willie McKay **Bred** Shadwell Farm LLC **Trained** Scrooby, Notts

T/Jkpt: £1,421.30 to a £1 stake. Pool £44,041.67 - 22 winning tickets T/Plt: £15.20 to a £1 stake. Pool £187,721.58 - 8,962.33 winning tickets T/Qpdt: £6.90 to a £1 stake. Pool £18,846.64 - 2,004.94 winning tickets JR

7967 LINGFIELD (L-H)
Tuesday, December 28

OFFICIAL GOING: Standard
Wind: Nil Weather: Foggy

7989 BET ON TODAY'S FOOTBALL AT TOTESPORT.COM APPRENTICE (S) STKS 1m (P)
11:30 (11:30) (Class 6) 3-Y-0+ **£2,047** (£604; £302) **Stalls** High

Form RPR
3444 1 **Faithful Ruler (USA)**25 7680 6-8-10 78..............(p) GeorgeChaloner(5) 2 —
(R A Fahey) *trckd ldr: led wl over 2f out: sn drew rt away: pushed out* **30/100**1
0601 2 7 **Saddlers Bend (IRE)**39 7501 4-9-2 61............................ DavidKenny 3 —
(George Baker) *hld up in tch: effrt on inner over 2f out: kpt on to take modest 2nd last 100yds* **6/1**2
0320 3 2 **Lord Deevert**17 7829 5-8-12 54........................ MatthewLawson(3) 5 —
(W G M Turner) *s.s: in tch and racd wd: reminder 5f out: prog to chse wnr over 2f out: sn lft bhd: lost modest 2nd last 100yds* **20/1**
0605 4 2 1/4 **Public Image**20 7763 4-8-7 46..................................... LucyBarry(3) 6 —
(Jamie Poulton) *hld up in tch: pushed along and outpcd over 2f out: plugged on to take 4th nr fin* **50/1**
0662 5 1/2 **Pab Special (IRE)**22 7727 7-8-10 51...........................(v) HobieGill(5) 4 —
(B R Johnson) *hld up in tch: gng bttr than most 3f out: sn outpcd: rdn and no rspnse over 1f out* **12/1**3
4000 6 13 **Ana Moutabahi**201 2906 3-9-6 68..............................(b1) JamesRogers 7 —
(Jim Best) *s.i.s: rousted along to ld: hdd wl over 2f out: sn wknd rapidly: t.o* **33/1**
0600 7 5 **Avow (USA)**56 7290 3-9-6 56...(b) RyanClark 1 —
(J J Bridger) *sn last: nvr gng wl: bhd fr 1/2-way: t.o* **40/1**

1m 38.75s (0.55) **Going Correction** +0.075s/f (Slow)
WFA 3 from 4yo+ 1lb 7 Ran SP% **111.0**
Speed ratings (Par 101): **100,93,91,88,88 75,70**
Tote Swingers: 1&2 £1.40, 1&3 £1.70, 2&3 £3.10 CSF £2.14 TOTE £1.20: £1.10, £2.00; EX 1.80.The winner was sold to Ron Harris for £8,600.
Owner George Murray **Bred** WinStar Farm LLC **Trained** Musley Bank, N Yorks

FOCUS
An uncompetitive seller. The gallop was a steady one and the winner raced against the far rail in the straight.

7990 EBF MORE LIVE FOOTBALL BETTING AT TOTESPORT.COM MAIDEN STKS 7f (P)
12:05 (12:08) (Class 5) 2-Y-0 **£3,139** (£926; £463) **Stalls** Low

Form RPR
6 1 **The Tichborne (IRE)**41 7479 2-9-3 0.............................. JackMitchell 5 80
(R A Teal) *trckd ldrs on outer: shkn up to ld 2f out: rdn clr 1f out: pushed out last 100yds* **16/1**
2 2 3 1/2 **Lady Rosamunde**54 7311 2-8-12 0................................ HayleyTurner 3 66
(M P Tregoning) *hld up in 6th: urged along to chse ldrs over 2f out: hd high and nt qckn wl over 1f out: kpt on to take 2nd nr fin* **8/11**1
3 3 3/4 **Links Drive Lady**13 7879 2-8-12 0................................ NickyMackay 4 64
(M E Rimmer) *trckd ldrs: rdn over 2f out: sn outpcd: swtchd rt and kpt on fnl f* **7/1**3
402 4 hd **Isingy Red (FR)**34 7550 2-9-3 76.................................... GeorgeBaker 2 68
(J R Boyle) *led to 2f out: sn outpcd by wnr u.p: lost 2 pls nr fin* **9/2**2
5 4 **Tornado Force (IRE)** 2-9-3 0... LukeMorris 7 58+
(J S Moore) *dwlt: rn green in last: pushed along over 4f out: outpcd fr 3f out: kpt on fnl f* **11/1**
0425 6 8 **Phoenix Flame**24 7693 2-8-12 61...................................... ShaneKelly 6 32
(A J McCabe) *w ldr to 2f out: sn wknd* **20/1**
6 7 1/2 **Apple Dumpling**34 7559 2-8-12 0.................................. SteveDrowne 1 31
(S C Williams) *cl up on inner tl wknd 3f out: n.m.r sn after: t.o* **28/1**
8 41 **Fantale** 2-8-5 0 .... MatthewCosham(7) 8 —
(P D Evans) *dwlt: t.k.h early in rr: rdn 4f out: wknd rapidly 3f out: wl t.o* **100/1**

1m 25.05s (0.25) **Going Correction** +0.075s/f (Slow) 8 Ran SP% **112.0**
Speed ratings (Par 96): **101,97,96,95,91 82,81,34**
Tote Swingers: 1&2 £3.90, 1&3 £8.60, 2&3 £1.80 CSF £27.31 TOTE £20.60: £3.70, £1.10, £1.90; EX 37.10 Trifecta £208.90 Pool: £432.07 - 1.53 winning units..
Owner Chris Simpson & Mick Waghorn **Bred** Ms Alyson Flower And Chris Simpson **Trained** Ashtead, Surrey

FOCUS
No more than a fair form and one in which and ordinary gallop only really picked up turning for home. The winner edged from the centre towards the far side in the closing stages.

NOTEBOOK
The Tichborne(IRE) was nibbled at in the market and stepped up a good deal on the form he showed on his debut at Kempton last month. He's the type physically that may have a bit of further improvement in him, and it will be interesting to see what the handicapper makes of this. (tchd 14-1)
Lady Rosamunde, the well-backed market leader, had shaped with a good deal of promise in a race that had thrown up winners on her debut at Kempton, but failed to build on that effort in a race that didn't exactly play to her strengths. This half-sister to Oaks runner-up Meeznah, who still looked green, will be suited by the step up to 1m and is capable of making amends granted a more suitable test. (op 4-5 tchd 5-6, Evens in places and 4-6 in places)
Links Drive Lady was easy in the market and probably ran to a similar level as the one she showed on her debut over this C&D earlier this month. She's likely to remain vulnerable to the more progressive or better types in this grade but should do better upped to 1m once qualified for a handicap mark. (op 13-2 tchd 8-1)
Isingy Red(FR) had shown improved form when in front of a subsequent winner over this trip at Kempton on his previous start but failed to build on that effort after racing with the choke out. He has had a few chances and, while he's capable of picking up an uncompetitive race in this grade, he'll have to improve to defy his current mark of 76 in handicaps. (tchd 4-1)
Tornado Force(IRE) ◆, a 67,000gns third foal of a dam who won over 1m4f in France, was far from disgraced despite his obvious greenness on this racecourse debut after attracting support. He will be better for this experience, should appreciate the step up to 1m and looks capable of picking up an ordinary event at some point. (op 16-1 tchd 10-1)
Phoenix Flame again had her limitations firmly exposed returned to Polytrack. She has had a few chances and is going to remain vulnerable against the more progressive sorts in this type of event. (tchd 25-1)

7991 ZENDRILL SCAFFOLDING H'CAP (DIV I) 7f (P)
12:35 (12:37) (Class 6) (0-65,65) 3-Y-0+ **£1,706** (£503; £252) **Stalls** Low

Form RPR
4600 1 **Buxton**22 7724 6-9-7 **65**...(t) RobertHavlin 11 —
(R Ingram) *stdd s fr wd draw: hld up in last trio: plenty to do whn effrt on outer over 2f out: drvn and gd prog over 1f out: styd on wl to ld last strides* **9/2**2
5064 2 hd **Dichoh**13 7878 7-9-5 **63**...(p) GeorgeBaker 7 —
(M Madgwick) *prom: chsd clr ldr 1/2-way: drvn over 2f out: clsd to chal 1f out: kpt on but outpcd last strides* **4/1**1
2055 3 nk **Rubenstar (IRE)**16 7847 7-9-2 **60**.. LiamKeniry 1 —
(Patrick Morris) *trckd ldrs: prog to go 3rd over 2f out: cajoled along to cl and led last 150yds: hdd and nt qckn last strides* **7/1**
0055 4 nk **Decency (IRE)**13 7874 3-8-13 **57**.. LukeMorris 4 —
(H J L Dunlop) *hld up in midfield: prog 2f out: clsd on ldrs ins fnl f: nt qckn last 100yds* **11/1**
2040 5 2 1/2 **Namir (IRE)**12 7892 8-9-3 **61**...(vt) DaneO'Neill 10 —
(H J Evans) *hld up in midfield: drvn and no prog over 2f out: n.d after: kpt on ins fnl f* **16/1**
0250 6 nk **Batchworth Blaise**22 7725 7-8-12 **59**............................ KierenFox(3) 6 —
(E A Wheeler) *stdd s: hld up in last trio: rdn over 2f out: kpt on fnl f but nvr on terms* **13/2**
0002 7 nse **Norville (IRE)**25 7683 3-8-11 **62**...................(b) MatthewCosham(7) 5 —
(P D Evans) *t.k.h: trckd ldng trio: rdn over 2f out: nt qckn and hld over 1f out: plugged on* **6/1**3
0000 8 1/2 **Spinning Ridge (IRE)**12 7889 5-9-6 **64**.....................(b) DavidProbert 9 —
(R A Harris) *dwlt: rousted up to ld after 1f: clr 1/2-way: stl 3 l up over 1f out: hdd & wknd rapidly last 150yds* **9/1**
2310 9 4 1/2 **Sunrise Lyric (IRE)**12 7889 3-8-13 **64**........................ DuilioDaSilva(7) 2 —
(P F I Cole) *s.s: hld up towards rr on inner: effrt over 2f out: no prog over 1f out: wknd* **14/1**
0000 10 1/2 **Spirit Of Love (IRE)**30 7614 3-9-0 **58**.......................... WilliamCarson 8 —
(M Wigham) *a in last trio and nvr gng wl: detached over 2f out* **16/1**

The Form Book, Raceform Ltd, Compton, RG20 6NL

0000 **11** *9* **Cut The Cackle (IRE)**[12] 7892 4-9-4 **65**..................... RobertLButler[(3)] 3 —
(P Butler) *led 1f: chsd ldr to 1/2-way: wknd rapidly: t.o* **50/1**

1m 24.89s (0.09) **Going Correction** +0.075s/f (Slow) 11 Ran SP% **117.0**
Speed ratings (Par 101): **102,101,101,101,98 97,97,97,92,91 81**
Tote Swingers: 1&2 £7.70, 1&3 £9.20, 2&3 £18.80 CSF £22.73 CT £127.77 TOTE £6.90: £2.40, £1.40, £2.70; EX 29.70 Trifecta £87.80 Pool: £301.45 - 2.54 winning units..
Owner Peter J Burton **Bred** Sharon Ingram **Trained** Epsom, Surrey

FOCUS
A modest yet open handicap featuring exposed sorts. An ordinary gallop picked up after 2f and the winner came down the centre in the straight.

7992 ZENDRILL SCAFFOLDING H'CAP (DIV II) 7f (P)
1:10 (1:12) (Class 6) (0-65,65) 3-Y-0+ £1,706 (£503; £252) Stalls Low

Form RPR
4564 **1** **Highland Harvest**[34] 7556 6-9-6 **64**..................................... IanMongan 1 —
(Jamie Poulton) *t.k.h: hld up bhd ldrs on inner: looking for room over 2f out: prog wl over 1f out: hrd rdn and kpt on to ld ins fnl f* **13/2**[3]

2061 **2** *hd* **I Confess**[29] 7627 5-9-6 **64**..........................(b) GeorgeBaker 9 —
(P D Evans) *trckd ldr after 2f: led jst over 2f out gng strly: hrd rdn over 1f out: nt qckn and hdd ins fnl f: styd on* **9/2**[1]

6000 **3** *1 1/4* **Fivefold (USA)**[41] 7483 3-9-7 **65**.................................... J-PGuillambert 8 —
(J Akehurst) *trckd ldrs: rdn 2f out: cl enough but nt qckn over 1f out: kpt on* **5/1**[2]

0004 **4** *3/4* **Pilgrim Dancer (IRE)**[17] 7824 3-8-9 **56**.................(p) JamesSullivan[(3)] 6 —
(Patrick Morris) *rousted along early in rr: prog fr 1/2-way: clsd on ldrs 2f out: one pce fnl f* **16/1**

0000 **5** *1/2* **Shaded Edge**[68] 7047 6-9-0 **58**... LiamKeniry 7 —
(D W P Arbuthnot) *dwlt: hld up in last trio: rdn 3f out: prog on inner over 1f out: styd on: nvr threatened* **7/1**

5401 **6** *hd* **Sirjosh**[20] 7761 4-9-0 **61**.. BillyCray[(3)] 5 —
(D Donovan) *dwlt: hld up in last trio and off the pce: rdn 1/2-way and no prog: styd on u.p fr over 1f out* **7/1**

5000 **7** *2 1/4* **Safwaan**[24] 7699 3-8-13 **57**... JamieMackay 10 —
(W J Musson) *dwlt: wl off the pce in last and nt gng wl: passed wkng rivals fr over 1f out* **20/1**

2000 **8** *2 1/4* **El Libertador (USA)**[153] 4488 4-9-2 **60**.......................... SteveDrowne 2 —
(J R Gask) *hld up towards rr: clsd on ldng gp over 2f out: shkn up and wknd qckly over 1f out* **9/1**

533 **9** *shd* **Catching Zeds**[64] 7129 3-9-5 **63**.. DavidProbert 4 —
(Ian Williams) *cl up bhd ldrs: stl there 2f out: rdn and wknd qckly over 1f out* **17/2**

6626 **10** *1 1/2* **Posy Fossil (USA)**[12] 7890 3-9-4 **62**...............................(v) AdamKirby 3 —
(S C Williams) *chsd ldr 2f: styd cl up tl wknd rapidly wl over 1f out* **16/1**

2546 **11** *3 3/4* **Until The Man (IRE)**[6] 7968 3-9-7 **65**...........................(b) GregFairley 11 —
(Jim Best) *pushed up to ld fr wd draw: set gd pce: hdd & wknd rapidly jst over 2f out* **16/1**

1m 24.9s (0.10) **Going Correction** +0.075s/f (Slow) 11 Ran SP% **116.1**
Speed ratings (Par 101): **102,101,100,99,98 98,96,93,93,91 87**
Tote Swingers: 1&2 £4.70, 1&3 £8.80, 2&3 £5.10 CSF £35.35 CT £162.30 TOTE £8.00: £2.60, £2.10, £1.90; EX 30.70 Trifecta £149.00 Pool: £408.84 - 2.03 winning units..
Owner J Wotherspoon **Bred** John Wotherspoon **Trained** Telscombe, E Sussex

FOCUS
Division two of a modest handicap. The gallop was a reasonable one and the winner raced close to the inside rail throughout.

7993 DRY HILL H'CAP 6f (P)
1:40 (1:43) (Class 2) (0-100,100) 3-Y-0+ £9,325 (£2,774; £1,386; £692) Stalls Low

Form RPR
2024 **1** **Edinburgh Knight (IRE)**[33] 7566 3-8-9 **88**......................... LiamJones 4 —
(P W D'Arcy) *hld up in last trio: prog on outer 2f out: str run fr over 1f out to ld last 50yds* **15/2**[3]

2322 **2** *1* **Silaah**[10] 7934 6-8-8 **87** oh1 ow1..............................(p) DaneO'Neill 7 —
(D Nicholls) *led: drvn more than 2 l clr over 1f out: wknd and hdd last 50yds* **6/1**[2]

0063 **3** *hd* **Five Star Junior (USA)**[92] 6429 4-8-10 **92**............... JamesSullivan[(3)] 1 —
(Mrs L Stubbs) *hld up in 8th: squeezed through and prog 2f out: drvn and styd on wl fnl f: nvr quite able to chal* **14/1**

0061 **4** *1/2* **Secret Asset (IRE)**[17] 7826 5-9-7 **100**............................... GeorgeBaker 5 —
(Jane Chapple-Hyam) *hld up in midfield: gng wl enough over 2f out: drvn and nt qckn over 1f out: styd on again ins fnl f: clsng at fin* **9/4**[1]

1151 **5** *hd* **Piscean (USA)**[33] 7566 5-9-4 **97**.. ShaneKelly 9 —
(T Keddy) *hld up in last trio: stl in last pair over 2f out: storming run on outer fr over 1f out: fin wl: too much to do* **6/1**[2]

6212 **6** *1 1/2* **Sutton Veny (IRE)**[33] 7566 4-8-9 **88**............................... SteveDrowne 3 —
(J R Gask) *cl up: rdn to chse ldr 2f out tl insde fnl f: wknd* **8/1**

0253 **7** *1/2* **Billy Red**[6] 7971 6-8-7 **86** oh1.....................................(b) FergusSweeney 8 —
(J R Jenkins) *chsd ldrs: wnt 3rd wl over 1f out: no imp u.p: wknd fnl f* **16/1**

0660 **8** *3* **Arganil (USA)**[13] 7875 5-9-3 **96**......................................(p) ChrisCatlin 10 —
(K A Ryan) *chsd ldr to 2f out: sn wknd* **14/1**

0000 **9** *3/4* **Alhaban (IRE)**[13] 7875 4-8-11 **90**.......................................(t) LukeMorris 11 —
(R A Harris) *chsd ldrs: lost pl u.p over 2f out: wl btn after* **20/1**

2310 **10** *3/4* **Love Delta (USA)**[16] 7846 3-9-6 **99**.................................... GregFairley 6 —
(M Johnston) *a in last trio: struggling over 2f out: no ch after* **14/1**

-000 **11** *1* **Tornadodancer (IRE)**[18] 7820 7-8-9 **88**.........................(v) HayleyTurner 2 —
(T G McCourt, Ire) *chsd ldrs on inner: lost pl over 2f out: steadily wknd after* **25/1**

1m 10.61s (-1.29) **Going Correction** +0.075s/f (Slow) 11 Ran SP% **116.7**
Speed ratings (Par 109): **111,109,109,108,108 106,105,101,100,99 98**
Tote Swingers: 1&2 £8.00, 1&3 £23.60, 2&3 £14.20 CSF £51.65 CT £635.47 TOTE £7.60: £2.30, £1.50, £4.50; EX 65.20 Trifecta £523.40 Part won. Pool: £707.41 - 0.30 winning units..
Owner Knights Racing **Bred** New England Stud Myriad Norelands **Trained** Newmarket, Suffolk

FOCUS
A good-quality handicap and one run at a reasonable gallop. The winner came down the centre in the straight and the runner-up, who raced against the inside rail, confirmed that part of the track was no slower than anywhere else.

NOTEBOOK
Edinburgh Knight(IRE) ◆, who had been running creditably since being gelded, found himself in a race where things panned out ideally, and he did enough to notch his first win since the spring. He's a very useful sort with bags of physical scope and will remain of interest over this trip in similar company after reassessment, when a good gallop looks likely. (op 7-1)
Silaah, 4lb higher than when just touched off at Southwell, was ridden much more forcefully this time and ran as well as he ever has done. He is worth a try over 5f on this surface irrespective of tactics but, although he's clearly capable of picking up a similar event from this sort of mark, he doesn't really appeal as one to be taking too short a price about.
Five Star Junior(USA), twice a winner on turf this year, again ran creditably from a mark in the 90s on Polytrack. He's clearly very useful but is likely to remain vulnerable against the better handicapped or more progressive types on this surface from that current mark. (tchd 12-1 and 16-1)
Secret Asset(IRE) attracted plenty of market support and ran creditably after being raised a fairly harsh-looking 8lb for his victory in a slightly lesser grade on his previous start. He'll have to raise his game to win a similarly competitive handicap from this mark. (op 3-1)
Piscean(USA) has progressed into a very useful hold-up handicapper on Polytrack, and he was far from disgraced from this 4lb higher mark in this slightly stronger grade after a short break. He should continue to give a good account when an end-to-end gallop is on the cards. (tchd 13-2)
Sutton Veny(IRE) is a fairly reliable yardstick who finished a similar distance behind Piscean as she had done on her previous start at Wolverhampton. She should continue to give a good account over sprint distances on Polytrack.
Billy Red, who has recent form that tied in with Secret Asset and Piscean, was nibbled at in the market and was far from disgraced on only his second start in this 0-100 grade. He'll be of more interest against more exposed sorts back in lesser company. (op 22-1)

7994 BET ON THE ASHES AT TOTESPORT.COM MAIDEN STKS 1m (P)
2:15 (2:16) (Class 5) 3-Y-0+ £2,729 (£806; £403) Stalls High

Form RPR
30-3 **1** **Talayeb**[171] 3911 5-9-4 68.. HayleyTurner 3 —
(M P Tregoning) *hld up in 3rd: clsd to ld narrowly wl over 1f out: pushed along firmly to assert ins fnl f* **4/6**[1]

0500 **2** *1 1/4* **Wishformore (IRE)**[6] 7964 3-8-12 63..............................(p) LiamKeniry 1 —
(J S Moore) *chsd clr ldr: clsd to chal 2f out: pressed wnr after tl no ex ins fnl f* **7/1**[3]

5 **3** *4 1/2* **American Smooth**[40] 7498 3-9-3 0...............................(v[1]) GeorgeBaker 2 —
(J Noseda) *hld up last: rdn and no rspnse wl over 2f out: struggling after: tk 3rd ins fnl f* **9/4**[2]

0002 **4** *4* **On The Cusp (IRE)**[11] 7918 3-9-0 47.......................(p) RobertLButler[(3)] 4 —
(P Butler) *sn led and clr: c bk to field over 2f out: hdd & wknd wl over 1f out* **16/1**

1m 39.68s (1.48) **Going Correction** +0.075s/f (Slow)
WFA 3 from 5yo 1lb 4 Ran SP% **109.1**
Speed ratings (Par 103): **95,93,89,85**
CSF £5.86 TOTE £1.60; EX 4.10.
Owner Hamdan Al Maktoum **Bred** Highfield Stud Ltd **Trained** Lambourn, Berks

FOCUS
A modest and uncompetitive maiden run in deteriorating (visibility) conditions. The gallop seemed fair and the winner raced centre to far side in the straight.

7995 BET ON LIVE CRICKET AT TOTESPORT.COM H'CAP (DIV I) 1m 2f (P)
2:50 (2:51) (Class 6) (0-60,60) 3-Y-0+ £1,706 (£503; £252) Stalls Low

Form RPR
046 **1** **Rustic Deacon**[32] 7575 3-9-0 **56**....................................... JamieMackay 4 —
(W J Musson) *a gng wl: trckd ldrs: prog on outer to ld wl over 1f out: clr fnl f: easily* **10/3**[1]

4040 **2** *2 1/4* **Vezere (USA)**[30] 7611 3-9-2 **58**....................................... HayleyTurner 10 —
(S Dow) *chsd ldng pair to 2f out: sn u.p: styd on to take 2nd ins fnl f: no ch w wnr* **22/1**

1012 **3** *nk* **Cyril The Squirrel**[24] 7705 6-9-7 **60**................................. ChrisCatlin 3 —
(Karen George) *hld up in 9th: looking for room fr over 3f out but finding little tl 1f out: drvn and kpt on to take 3rd ins fnl f* **7/2**[2]

6001 **4** *2* **Ocean Of Peace (FR)**[22] 7727 7-8-12 **51**.............. FergusSweeney 9 —
(M R Bosley) *hld up in 8th: drvn and no prog over 2f out: kpt on fnl f to take 4th nr fin* **13/2**[3]

-205 **5** *nk* **Home**[61] 6021 5-9-0 **53** ow1.. AdamKirby 7 —
(B G Powell) *chsd ldrs and racd wd: rdn fr 1/2-way but styd in tch: outpcd fr 2f out: plugged on* **10/1**

22-5 **6** *1/2* **Capacity (IRE)**[20] 7774 3-8-6 **55**.................................(v) CTKeane[(7)] 2 —
(T G McCourt, Ire) *hld up in 7th: prog on inner 3f out: chsd wnr over 1f out tl ins fnl f: wknd* **16/1**

0436 **7** *1/2* **Bizarrely (IRE)**[20] 7768 3-9-4 **60**................................... MickyFenton 12 —
(J Pearce) *rrd bdly s: last tl over 3f out: rdn and in tch at bk of main gp over 2f out: effrt on inner over 1f out: sn no prog* **8/1**

6625 **8** *1 3/4* **Fly By Nelly**[23] 7717 4-9-2 **55**... SteveDrowne 5 —
(M R Hoad) *hld up in 10th: rdn over 4f out: stl in tch at bk of main gp over 2f out: sn lft bhd* **8/1**

-003 **9** *2* **Valkov**[13] 7874 3-9-0 **59**... KierenFox[(3)] 6 —
(E A Wheeler) *chsd ldr: rdn 4f out: lost 2nd and wknd 2f out* **17/2**

0652 **10** *1 1/4* **Pinsplitter (USA)**[17] 7825 3-9-1 **57**..............................(p) ShaneKelly 13 —
(A J McCabe) *drvn to ld fr wd draw: hdd & wknd qckly wl over 1f out* **14/1**

2000 **11** *24* **Play Up Pompey**[6] 7966 8-8-7 **46** oh1................................ LukeMorris 1 —
(J J Bridger) *chsd ldng trio to 4f out: wknd rapidly: t.o* **50/1**

2m 6.10s (-0.50) **Going Correction** +0.075s/f (Slow)
WFA 3 from 4yo+ 3lb 11 Ran SP% **119.3**
Speed ratings (Par 101): **105,103,102,101,101 100,100,98,97,96 77**
Tote Swingers: 1&2 £22.80, 1&3 £4.30, 2&3 £14.00 CSF £78.30 CT £278.35 TOTE £4.70: £1.90, £5.60, £1.70; EX 161.60 Trifecta £390.40 Part won. Pool: £527.62 - 0.65 winning units..
Owner Mrs Rita Brown **Bred** P V Jackson **Trained** Newmarket, Suffolk

FOCUS
Division one of a moderate handicap. The gallop was an ordinary one and the easy winner came down the centre in the straight.

7996 BET ON LIVE CRICKET AT TOTESPORT.COM H'CAP (DIV II) 1m 2f (P)
3:25 (3:27) (Class 6) (0-60,60) 3-Y-0+ £1,706 (£503; £252) Stalls Low

Form RPR
5165 **1** **Iguacu**[20] 7759 6-8-13 **52**...(p) DaneO'Neill 13 —
(George Baker) *s.i.s: bustled up to trck ldng pair: dashed into ld 3f out: drvn over 1f out: hld on* **7/1**

2563 **2** *nk* **Lunar River (FR)**[6] 7968 7-8-6 **52**..........................(t) JamesRogers[(7)] 6 —
(David Pinder) *trckd ldng trio: wl plcd whn pce lifted 3f out: effrt 2f out: styd on fnl f to press wnr: a jst hld* **7/1**

450 **3** *1/2* **Carter**[61] 7199 4-8-10 **49**... DavidProbert 12 —
(Ian Williams) *led at slow pce for 2f: w ldr after to 3f out: sn rdn: kpt on to try to chal fnl f: a hld* **11/4**[1]

6- **4** *nk* **No Trimmings (IRE)**[18] 7819 4-8-7 **53**......................(bt) CTKeane[(7)] 2 —
(Gerard Keane, Ire) *t.k.h: hld up wl in rr in slowly run r: poorly plcd whn pce lifted 3f out: 9th 2f out: prog on inner after: drvn and styd on: nt rch ldrs* **16/1**

0065 **5** *shd* **Dancing Poppy**[116] 5730 3-8-4 **46**.................................. HayleyTurner 10 —
(R A Farrant) *trckd ldng quartet: outpcd whn pce lifted 3f out but bttr plcd than most: kpt on again fnl f: a hld* **33/1**

022 **6** *3/4* **Sheila's Bond**[22] 7726 3-9-1 **57**.....................................(p) LukeMorris 5 —
(J S Moore) *led after 2f and maintained slow pce: hdd 3f out: sn outpcd and drvn: kpt on same pce over 1f out* **5/1**[2]

3003 **7** 2 ½ **Sunset Boulevard (IRE)**[20] [7760] 7-9-1 **54**..................(b) SteveDrowne 3 52
(Jim Best) *hld up in last trio in slowly run r: poorly plcd whn pce lifted 3f out: nt clr run 2f out: styd on fnl f: no ch to be involved* **13/2**[3]

3005 **8** ½ **Dane Cottage**[19] [7787] 3-8-6 **48**.................... ChrisCatlin 8 45
(P D Evans) *hld up in midfield: outpcd in midfield over 2f out: no hdwy over 1f out* **20/1**

0010 **9** ¾ **Sir Ike (IRE)**[20] [7768] 5-9-4 **57**..(tp) ShaneKelly 4 53
(W S Kittow) *hld up in midfield: outpcd on inner wl over 2f out: no prog over 1f out* **16/1**

030 **10** ½ **Pedasus (USA)**[70] [6999] 4-9-4 **57**.................................... WilliamCarson 9 52
(R A Harris) *hld up in last trio in slowly run r: poorly plcd whn pce lifted 3f out: styd on fnl f: no ch to be involved* **20/1**

3000 **11** *shd* **Vinces**[41] [7491] 6-9-7 **60**.. SteveDrowne 14 54
(T D McCarthy) *hld up last in slowly run event: poorly plcd whn pce lifted 3f out: pushed along and kpt on: no ch to be involved* **12/1**

1300 **12** 1 **Ting Ting (USA)**[13] [7874] 3-8-9 **58**...........................(t) NathanAlison(7) 11 50
(J R Boyle) *dwlt: hld up towards rr: prog on outer over 3f out: rchd midfield over 2f out but rdn: wknd over 1f out* **16/1**

6000 **13** ½ **Etruscan (IRE)**[19] [7788] 5-9-6 **59**...................................(v¹) LiamKeniry 7 50
(C Gordon) *hld up in rr in slowly run r: outpcd and rdn wl over 2f out: no prog* **20/1**

0406 **14** 2 **Hits Only Cash**[11] [7919] 8-9-2 **55**....................................(p) MickyFenton 1 42
(J Pearce) *plld hrd: hld up towards rr: rdn and no prog over 2f out: wknd fnl f* **33/1**

2m 11.12s (4.52) **Going Correction** +0.075s/f (Slow) **14** Ran SP% **127.2**
WFA 3 from 4yo+ 3lb
Speed ratings (Par 101): **84,83,83,83,83 82,80,80,79,79 78,78,77,76**
Tote Swingers: 1&2 £9.40, 1&3 £6.60, 2&3 £4.80 CSF £54.41 CT £172.31 TOTE £9.80: £3.20, £2.90, £1.70; EX 58.30 Trifecta £356.80 Part won. Pool: £482.16 - 0.94 winning units..
Owner Derek & Cheryl Holder **Bred** Cheveley Park Stud Ltd **Trained** Moreton Morrell, Warwicks

FOCUS
A moderate and open handicap run at just a steady gallop. The winner came down the centre in the straight and the first six finished in a bit of a heap.
T/Plt: £29.60 to a £1 stake. Pool:£55,477 - 1,365.12 winning tickets. T/Qpdt: £25.00 to a £1 stake. Pool:£4,954 - 146.10 winning tickets. JN

7960 KEMPTON (A.W) (R-H)

Wednesday, December 29

OFFICIAL GOING: Standard
Wind: Virtually nil Weather: Misty, dry

7997 RACING AT SKYSPORTS.COM NURSERY 5f (P)
4:20 (4:20) (Class 5) (0-75,73) 2-Y-O £2,286 (£675; £337) Stalls High

Form RPR

10 **1** **Lady Prodee**[13] [7891] 2-8-8 **63**.. KierenFox(3) 12 71+
(W G M Turner) *trckd ldrs gng wl: rdn and effrt over 1f out: led ent fnl f: in command fnl 150yds: pushed out: comf* **15/2**

0422 **2** 1 ½ **Crystallus (IRE)**[32] [7598] 2-8-13 **65**................................ SamHitchcott 9 68
(Mrs A Duffield) *bustled along leaving stalls: in tch in midfield: hdwy u.p over 1f out: chsd wnr ins fnl f: kpt on but no imp on wnr* **16/1**

343 **3** ¾ **Sacrosanctus**[13] [7891] 2-9-7 **73**...................................... AdamKirby 2 73
(D Nicholls) *towards rr: effrt and drvn wl over 1f out: styd on wl u.p ins fnl f: nt rch ldrs* **3/1**[1]

4603 **4** ½ **Welsh Inlet (IRE)**[22] [7734] 2-8-10 **62**............................... NeilChalmers 7 61
(J J Bridger) *chsd ldrs: rdn and hung rt wl over 1f out: swtchd lft over 1f out: styd on same pce fnl f* **20/1**

0632 **5** 1 **Lisselton Cross**[19] [7809] 2-8-8 **60**............................ KirstyMilczarek 11 55
(M R Bosley) *in tch in midfield: rdn: swtchd lft and sltly outpcd over 1f out: kpt on again ins fnl f: nt pce to threaten ldrs* **4/1**[2]

5353 **6** *shd* **Pizzarra**[16] [7858] 2-8-6 **58**.. FrannyNorton 1 55+
(J G Given) *s.i.s: hld up in last pair: nt clr run and swtchd lft jst over 1f out: r.o wl fnl 100yds: nvr trbld ldrs* **20/1**

4112 **7** *nk* **Je Suis Unrockstar**[11] [7931] 2-9-2 **68**..................(p) DaneO'Neill 8 62
(D Nicholls) *taken down early: s.i.s: nt clr run on inner wl over 1f out tl 1f out: kpt on fnl 150yds: nvr trbld ldrs* **9/2**[3]

3336 **8** ½ **Miss Toldyaso (IRE)**[20] [7777] 2-8-3 **55**........................ DavidProbert 10 47
(M G Quinlan) *led: rdn and hdd ent fnl f: sn wknd* **12/1**

3662 **9** ½ **Arowana (IRE)**[19] [7811] 2-8-10 **62**.....................................(b) LiamJones 5 52
(W J Haggas) *taken down early: t.k.h: hld up wl in tch: rdn and nt qckn over 1f out: styd on same pce fnl f* **20/1**

0031 **10** 4 **Albany Rose (IRE)**[19] [7809] 2-9-0 **66**................................ SteveDrowne 4 41
(Rae Guest) *w ldr tl wknd 2f out: wl btn fnl f* **7/1**

5450 **11** 7 **Pineapple Pete (IRE)**[19] [7809] 2-8-8 **60**.......................... ChrisCatlin 3 10
(P F I Cole) *w ldrs: rn wd bnd after 1f: lost pl qckly 2f out: sn lost tch* **33/1**

60.60 secs (0.10) **Going Correction** -0.025s/f (Stan) **11** Ran SP% **118.2**
Speed ratings (Par 96): **98,95,94,93,92 91,91,90,89,83 72**
toteswingers:1&2:£11.60, 1&3:£8.10, 2&3:£7.50 CSF £112.14 CT £449.20 TOTE £10.60: £4.30, £5.20, £1.10; EX 96.60.
Owner Mrs M S Teversham **Bred** Mrs Monica Teversham **Trained** Sigwells, Somerset

FOCUS
Plenty of in-form horses in an open if routine nursery. As usual at this trip here, it was an advantage to race close to the pace as well as the inside rail. The third and fourth set a solid level for the form.

NOTEBOOK
Lady Prodee left her debut nursery form at 6f here last time behind her, reversing form with Sacrosanctus in the process, seeming suited by the drop back in trip. She was helped to a degree by a good tactical position as the race developed, but she still put a seal on things quickly and probably has more improvement in her. (op 13-2)
Crystallus(IRE) fared well on her nursery debut, in a similar position to the winner turning for home but unable to match that one's turn of foot. She was keeping on well at the end and won't mind a return to 6f. (op 11-1 tchd 10-1)
Sacrosanctus ◆ can be rated better than the result and it's only a matter of time before he wins another race. As it did over this C&D two runs ago, a wide draw badly hindered his chance but he finished his race with such a flourish that he would surely have gone very close drawn nearer the rail. (op 4-1 tchd 9-2)
Welsh Inlet(IRE) proved suited by the return to 5f but she had no excuses as the race developed and didn't impress with her head carriage. Official explanation: jockey said that the filly hung right in the home straight
Lisselton Cross took an age to get going kept more towards the inside. Official explanation: jockey said the colt was hampered leaving the stalls (op 11-2 tchd 6-1)
Pizzarra is another better than the result suggests as she was poorly placed turning for home and then went for a run towards the inside before finally making her challenge wide. She seemed to finish with some running in her, but she's also looked a short runner before and might be the type that needs things to fall right. (tchd 25-1)
Je Suis Unrockstar was another to take an age to get going kept more towards the inside. Official explanation: jockey said the gelding was hampered leaving the stalls (op 5-1 tchd 4-1)
Arowana(IRE) Official explanation: jockey said that filly was denied a clear run
Pineapple Pete(IRE) Official explanation: jockey said the gelding hung left on the bend

7998 WISHING ALL OUR CUSTOMERS A HAPPY NEW YEAR H'CAP 5f (P)
4:50 (4:50) (Class 4) (0-85,84) 3-Y-O+ £3,885 (£1,156; £577; £288) Stalls High

Form RPR

6632 **1** **Feelin Foxy**[7] [7971] 6-8-11 **74**.. FrannyNorton 4 85
(J G Given) *taken down early: mde all: rdn and r.o wl fnl f* **7/2**[2]

4115 **2** 1 ¼ **Ebraam (USA)**[12] [7906] 7-9-7 **84**.. LukeMorris 3 91
(R A Harris) *chsd wnr tl over 3f out: rdn to chse wnr again ent fnl f: styd on same pce and a hld after* **10/1**

1103 **3** ¾ **Grudge**[7] [7961] 5-8-10 **73**.......................................(be) KirstyMilczarek 2 77
(C R Dore) *taken down early: in tch in midfield: pushed along 1/2-way: drvn over 1f out: kpt on ins fnl f: no threat to wnr* **13/2**

2432 **4** *nk* **Vhujon (IRE)**[7] [7961] 5-8-13 **76**... DaneO'Neill 5 79
(P D Evans) *hld up in last pair: effrt over 1f out: drvn and styd on fnl 150yds: nvr trbld ldrs* **3/1**[1]

0435 **5** ½ **Lewyn**[7] [7961] 3-9-4 **81**...(t) SteveDrowne 7 82
(J R Gask) *in tch: bustled along 1/2-way: styd on same pce u.p fr over 1f out* **6/1**

131 **6** 1 ½ **Sharp Shoes**[16] [7859] 3-8-7 **70** oh1..............................(p) SamHitchcott 1 66
(Mrs A Duffield) *dwlt: sn rcvrd: chsd wnr over 3f out tl ent fnl f: wknd fnl 150yds* **5/1**[3]

4014 **7** 1 ½ **High Spice (USA)**[25] [7702] 3-9-4 **81**...........................(p) J-PGuillambert 6 71
(R M H Cowell) *hld up in last pair: effrt and rdn over 1f out: no prog 1f out: wknd ins fnl f* **7/1**

59.72 secs (-0.78) **Going Correction** -0.025s/f (Stan) **7** Ran SP% **113.1**
Speed ratings (Par 105): **105,103,101,101,100 98,95**
toteswingers:1&2:£7.00, 1&3:£5.60, 2&3:£8.70 CSF £36.09 TOTE £5.70: £3.10, £4.10; EX 36.40.
Owner Peter Swann **Bred** Bearstone Stud **Trained** Willoughton, Lincs

FOCUS
A fair handicap full of in-form runners but a potentially muddling result given that the gallop wasn't as strong as seemed likely beforehand.
Grudge Official explanation: jockey said the gelding reared in the stalls and she lost an iron as the gates opened

7999 EUROPEAN BREEDERS' FUND MAIDEN STKS 6f (P)
5:20 (5:20) (Class 5) 2-Y-O £3,140 (£934; £467; £233) Stalls High

Form RPR

0 **1** **Mi Regalo**[230] [2048] 2-9-3 0.. DavidProbert 6 76+
(A M Balding) *chsd ldr: rdn jst over 2f out: sustained effrt u.p to ld fnl 100yds: gng away at fin* **7/2**[1]

232 **2** 1 ¾ **Fifth In Line (IRE)**[14] [7871] 2-8-12 68........................... FergusSweeney 7 66
(J A Osborne) *led: rdn jst over 1f out: hdd fnl 100yds: no ex* **4/1**[2]

6 **3** 1 **Too Many Questions (IRE)**[7] [7962] 2-9-3 0..................... DaneO'Neill 5 68
(P D Evans) *chsd ldng trio: rdn and effrt to chse ldng pair wl over 1f out: styd on same pce fnl f* **9/2**[3]

043U **4** 3 **Barnet Fair**[76] [6878] 2-9-0 74.. KierenFox(3) 3 59+
(R C Guest) *racd wl off the pce in last trio: rdn and hdwy ent fnl 2f: kpt on to go 4th ins fnl f: nvr trbld ldrs* **7/2**[1]

5 ½ **Trojan Rocket (IRE)** 2-9-3 0.. KirstyMilczarek 9 58+
(G Prodromou) *s.i.s: c wd and sme hdwy ent fnl 2f: styd on but nvr any threat to ldrs* **40/1**

35 **6** 2 **Kassaab**[229] [2068] 2-9-3 0... SteveDrowne 2 52
(J R Gask) *chsd ldng trio: rdn and unable qck over 2f out: wknd u.p wl over 1f out* **12/1**

53 **7** 3 **Consistant**[33] [7578] 2-9-3 0... JackMitchell 1 43
(B P J Baugh) *racd in midfield: rdn and unable qck over 2f out: wknd 2f out: wl btn fnl f* **7/1**

5 **8** 5 **Doesn't Care (IRE)**[16] [7858] 2-9-3 0.................................. ChrisCatlin 8 28
(R A Fahey) *sltly hmpd s and s.i.s: bhd: pushed along and outpcd over 2f out: wl btn fnl 2f* **12/1**

9 6 **Pharoh Jake** 2-9-3 0... NeilChalmers 4 10
(J J Bridger) *v.s.a: rn green and a in rr* **66/1**

1m 13.47s (0.37) **Going Correction** -0.025s/f (Stan) **9** Ran SP% **114.4**
Speed ratings (Par 96): **96,93,92,88,87 85,81,74,66**
toteswingers:1&2:£3.10, 1&3:£4.60, 2&3:£4.00 CSF £17.44 TOTE £7.10: £3.00, £1.10, £1.80; EX 19.60.
Owner Mick and Janice Mariscotti **Bred** R J Turner **Trained** Kingsclere, Hants

FOCUS
A modest maiden in which the first two were prominent throughout. The winner looks a bit better than the average maiden winner for the time of year.

NOTEBOOK
Mi Regalo was having first run since May, since when he has been gelded, but he clearly lacked nothing in fitness as he ran down the runner-up to win with something in hand. For all this form doesn't amount to much, he's entitled to improve again and looks the sort that might be able to pick up a handicap either at this trip or 7f given that the handicapper can't be too hard on him. (op 3-1 tchd 4-1)
Fifth In Line(IRE) had shown a fair level of form on all her starts and probably did so again, soon out in front and not needing any excuses. There's nothing wrong with her attitude and she can win one of these before long, possibly back against her own sex. (op 3-1)
Too Many Questions(IRE) attracted support during the day and duly improved on his debut. That said, he didn't quite have the pace to really impose himself at this shorter trip and will be suited by a return to 7f. He looks to have some size about him and can improve again. (op 5-1)
Barnet Fair promised to be suited by the return to this trip but never threatened after racing rustily early on his first run for nearly three months. He's not one to write off yet, for all his current official rating looks on the high side. (op 9-2)
Trojan Rocket(IRE), the first foal of a sprint maiden, hails from a yard that get few first-time-out winners but he shaped with some promise, staying on well from a modest position turning for home.
Kassaab was having his first run since May and leaving Noel Wilson. For all he didn't shape with much promise, he left the impression the race was needed badly and he might be the type that will do better now he is handicapped. (op 14-1)
Consistant needed this for a mark but didn't run his race. He'd given the impression prior to this that he is in need of a longer trip. (op 15-2 tchd 13-2)
Pharoh Jake Official explanation: jockey said that the gelding was slowly away

8000 DIGIBET SPORTS BETTING MAIDEN STKS (DIV I) 1m (P)
5:50 (5:52) (Class 5) 2-Y-O £1,944 (£574; £287) Stalls High

Form RPR

6 **1** **Rasheed**[14] [7873] 2-9-3 0.. NickyMackay 6 75
(J H M Gosden) *sn led: rdn and qcknd clr 2f out: edgd lft u.p ins fnl f: pressed and hld on fnl 50yds* **9/4**[1]

2 ½ **Crafty Roberto** 2-9-3 0 GregFairley 8 75+
(B J Meehan) *s.i.s: rn green in rr: hdwy on outer over 2f out: kpt on wl u.p to chse clr wnr ins fnl f: pressed wnr fnl 50yds: no imp after* **12/1**

06 3 1 **Medaille D'Or**[46] 7447 2-8-12 0 JackMitchell 10 67
(M A Jarvis) *t.k.h: hld up wl in tch: rdn and outpcd by wnr ent fnl 2f: rallied u.p ins fnl f: kpt on* **11/2**

5 4 1 ¾ **Aussie Dollar (IRE)**[64] 7152 2-9-3 0 LiamKeniry 1 68
(A M Balding) *chsd wnr: rdn and nt pce of wnr ent fnl 2f: kpt on same pce fr over 1f out: lost 2 pls ins fnl f* **9/2**[3]

00 5 5 **Delagoa Bay (IRE)**[62] 7198 2-8-12 0 DaneO'Neill 9 51
(S Kirk) *racd in last trio: rdn and no hdwy over 2f out: no ch w ldrs but kpt on fr over 1f out* **50/1**

6 1 ¼ **Thymesthree (IRE)** 2-8-12 0 IanMongan 5 49+
(C F Wall) *dwlt: hld up in last trio: rdn and sme hdwy ent fnl 2f: sn no hdwy and wl hld over 1f out* **16/1**

7 ½ **Dance To Destiny** 2-8-13 0 ow1 AdamKirby 12 48
(P S McEntee) *t.k.h: hld up in midfield: rdn and unable qck over 2f out: wknd wl over 1f out* **16/1**

4 8 3 **Cecile De Volanges**[20] 7780 2-8-12 0 DavidProbert 11 41
(Miss Tor Sturgis) *chsd ldrs: rdn ent fnl 3f: wknd u.p jst over 2f out* **12/1**

5 9 ½ **Flying Phoenix**[135] 5160 2-8-12 0 EddieAhern 7 39
(W J Haggas) *stdd after s: sn t.k.h and hdwy to chse ldrs: rdn and wknd over 2f out* **4/1**[2]

10 3 **Mountain Myst** 2-9-3 0 HayleyTurner 4 38
(W R Muir) *in tch on outer tl rdn and dropped to rr over 3f out: lost tch over 2f out* **20/1**

1m 41.13s (1.33) **Going Correction** -0.025s/f (Stan) **10** Ran SP% **118.2**
Speed ratings (Par 96): **92,91,90,88,83 82,82,79,78,75**
toteswingers:1&2:£3.90, 1&3:£3.40, 2&3:£9.10 CSF £32.37 TOTE £2.30: £1.70, £2.30, £1.90; EX 38.60.
Owner Hamdan Al Maktoum **Bred** Miss K Rausing And Mrs S M Rogers **Trained** Newmarket, Suffolk
■ Stewards' Enquiry : Greg Fairley one-day ban: used whip with excessive frequency and down the shoulder

FOCUS
No more than a fair maiden, limited by some of those down the field. It wasn't strongly run and the runner-up shaped very well all things considered. The winner was another to do well from the front end on this card.

NOTEBOOK
Rasheed was much stronger in the market here than on his debut two weeks back and turned in a much improved effort, soon to the fore and pulling out more when challenged having looked to be dossing in front. More a galloper than anything else, he doesn't impress as much more than a middling handicapper right now, and looks the type that will always need plenty of use making of. His action is one usually associated with plenty of give in the ground. (op 5-1)
Crafty Roberto ◆, who is out of a well-related 1m2f winner, was unlucky not to have made a winning debut and should have little trouble going one better. He wasn't making any impression on the winner close home but considering he fluffed the start and was poorly placed and running green on the home turn he did well anyway to get as close as he did. He'll be well suited by 1m2f in time. (op 11-1)
Medaille D'Or was more settled here and turned in her best effort. She's qualified for handicaps now and is another that will be suited by an extra 2f. (op 4-1)
Aussie Dollar(IRE) confirmed the promise he had shown in the mud at Yarmouth in October without impressing as anything out of the ordinary. That said, this was only his second run and he might do better as he gains experience. (op 4-1)
Delagoa Bay(IRE) had shown very little in his two races to date but deserves some credit here given that he was poorly placed on the home turn. This run will have blown his cover in so far as handicaps are concerned. (op 66-1)
Thymesthree(IRE), by Galileo and first foal of a 6f AW winner, never really threatened but shaped with some promise, keeping on. Newcomers from her stable usually need their first run and she can do better.
Dance To Destiny has an ordinary pedigree and is from a yard that get few 2yo winners but she was nibbled at in the market and didn't look devoid of ability. (op 25-1)
Cecile De Volanges went backwards from her recent fourth over C&D. (op 8-1)
Flying Phoenix, who'd split a couple of subsequent winners when fifth in Yarmouth maiden on debut in August, promised to be well suited by this step up to 1m but was struggling early in the straight. (tchd 7-2)

8001 DIGIBET SPORTS BETTING MAIDEN STKS (DIV II) 1m (P)
6:20 (6:23) (Class 5) 2-Y-O £1,944 (£574; £287) Stalls High

Form RPR

2 1 **Energizing**[14] 7873 2-9-3 0 DaneO'Neill 5 77+
(R Hannon) *dwlt: sn rcvrd and chsng ldrs: rdn and qcknd to ld 2f out: sn clr: r.o wl: comf* **4/6**[1]

5433 2 3 ¾ **Woop Woop (IRE)**[7] 7962 2-8-13 62 ow1 AdamKirby 7 64
(Stef Higgins) *hld up in tch in midfield: swtchd lft and forced way out over 2f out: kpt on wl u.p to go 2nd ins fnl f: no ch w wnr* **7/1**[3]

3 ½ **Art History (IRE)** 2-9-3 0 GregFairley 1 67+
(M Johnston) *sn chsng ldr: rdn: rn green and racd awkwardly over 2f out: chsd clr wnr over 1f out: no imp: lost 2nd ins fnl f* **9/2**[2]

5425 4 1 ¼ **Szabo's Destiny**[8] 7954 2-9-3 68 FrannyNorton 4 64
(J G Given) *broke wl: chsd ldrs: rdn and unable qck whn swtchd lft 2f out: kpt on same pce after* **33/1**

06 5 ½ **More Than Enough (IRE)**[25] 7693 2-9-3 0 JackMitchell 9 64+
(R A Fahey) *hld up towards rr: rdn and n.m.r jst over 2f out: edging rt and hdwy over 1f out: kpt on but no ch w wnr* **40/1**

04 6 ½ **Twin Soul (IRE)**[22] 7733 2-8-12 0 LiamKeniry 8 57+
(A M Balding) *t.k.h: hld up in rr: rdn and hdwy over 1f out: kpt on ins fnl f: nvr trbld ldrs* **14/1**

7 nk **Khaki (IRE)** 2-8-12 0 EddieAhern 12 56+
(Miss Tor Sturgis) *in tch in midfield: rdn and unable qck jst over 2f out: kpt on same pce and no ch w wnr fr over 1f out* **40/1**

6 8 ¾ **Kristollini**[31] 7610 2-8-12 0 HayleyTurner 2 55
(W R Muir) *led tl rdn and hdd 2f out: sn outpcd by wnr: lost 2nd over 1f out: wknd 1f out* **12/1**

00 9 1 ¼ **Diverting**[60] 7231 2-8-12 0 SteveDrowne 3 52
(W Jarvis) *in tch: rdn whn pushed lft and lost pl jst over 2f out: n.d after* **14/1**

0 10 ¾ **Scarborough Lily**[42] 7478 2-8-12 0 FergusSweeney 10 50
(E F Vaughan) *hld up in rr: hdwy and nt clr run ent fnl 2f: swtchd rt and hdwy wl over 1f out: wknd fnl f* **66/1**

0 11 3 ½ **Dune Island**[22] 7733 2-8-12 0 NeilChalmers 11 42
(J J Bridger) *s.i.s: a towards rr: rdn and hdwy jst over 2f out: sn wknd* **100/1**

1m 42.0s (2.20) **Going Correction** -0.025s/f (Stan) **11** Ran SP% **122.0**
Speed ratings (Par 96): **88,84,83,82,82 81,81,80,79,78 74**
toteswingers:1&2:£2.30, 1&3:£2.00, 2&3:£3.50 CSF £6.21 TOTE £1.40: £1.10, £1.20, £1.50; EX 5.40.
Owner Ben CM Wong **Bred** Star Pointe Ltd & Partners **Trained** East Everleigh, Wilts

FOCUS
The second division of the maiden and won by the better long-term prospect despite the winning time being slower. The fourth limits the level of the form.

NOTEBOOK
Energizing, who'd finished ahead of a 71-rated rival when second at big odds over C&D on debut, had no trouble going one better in what was probably a weaker race, travelling strongly behind the leaders until quickening clear in good fashion. AW maiden winners at this time of year don't tend to be assessed highly by the official handicapper, and it might be that he'll get underestimated. He looks potentially quite useful. (tchd 4-5 and 10-11 in a place)
Woop Woop(IRE) had been running as if this step up in trip would suit and she seemed to run her best race yet for all she was never a threat to the winner. This effort will probably result in her handicap mark being revised upwards. (op 15-2)
Art History(IRE), a 170,000 guinea yearling and a half-brother to a Listed 1m winner in France, was far to green to do himself justice but showed a decent attitude to stick on for third. He looks to have some physical presence about him and is the type that could improve substantially next time. (op 5-1 tchd 7-2)
Szabo's Destiny was having his first try on Polytrack and wasn't discredited but he's shaped for some time now as if this trip is a bare minimum for him.
More Than Enough(IRE) hadn't been a threat in maidens so far and wasn't again here but was noted putting in some late work and can go handicapping now on an upward curve. Out of a Sadler's Wells mare, he will be suited by a stiffer test. (tchd 33-1)
Twin Soul(IRE) ◆ is now qualified for a mark and will be an interesting runner in that sphere. Better than the result suggested last time, she left the impression once again here not knocked about that the race didn't get to the bottom of her and she's one to keep an eye on when her stamina is tested more. (op 12-1)
Khaki(IRE), a half-sister to 7f Group 3 winner An Tadh, shaped with some promise on her debut without being given a hard time and is entitled to improve.
Kristollini looked a likely improver like most second time out from her yard but she finished her race tamely having been allowed the run of things in front.

8002 DIGIBET.COM CLAIMING STKS 6f (P)
6:50 (6:51) (Class 5) 2-Y-O £2,286 (£675; £337) Stalls High

Form RPR

1114 1 **Insolenceofoffice (IRE)**[12] 7908 2-8-13 83 (p) SamHitchcott 5 80+
(Mrs A Duffield) *chsd ldng pair: shkn up and swtchd lft over 2f out: rdn and qcknd to ld over 1f out: clr ins fnl f: r.o wl* **8/13**[1]

3134 2 2 **Slatey Hen (IRE)**[11] 7931 2-8-2 62 LukeMorris 4 63
(R A Fahey) *broke wl: sn stdd and racd in last pair: effrt and swtchd ins 2f out: drvn to chse wnr jst over 1f out: kpt on but no imp fnl f* **15/2**

4511 3 1 ¾ **Whipphound**[19] 7811 2-9-3 78 EddieAhern 1 73
(W M Brisbourne) *hld up in tch in last pair: rdn and effrt 2f out: kpt on u.p to go 3rd ins fnl f: no ch w wnr* **6/1**[3]

0223 4 3 **Buddy Miracle**[24] 7715 2-8-8 72 DavidProbert 3 55
(A M Balding) *racd freely: sn led: hdd and rdn over 1f out: sn outpcd by wnr: lost 2nd jst over 1f out: wknd fnl f* **9/2**[2]

5 2 ¾ **Braehead (IRE)**[68] 7074 2-8-13 0 DaneO'Neill 2 52
(P D Evans) *t.k.h: chsd ldr tl jst over 2f out: wknd wl over 1f out* **20/1**

1m 13.52s (0.42) **Going Correction** -0.025s/f (Stan) **5** Ran SP% **110.9**
Speed ratings (Par 96): **96,93,91,87,83**
CSF £6.01 TOTE £1.20: £1.02, £3.40; EX 7.30.Insolenceofoffice was the subject of a friendly claim. Slatey Hen was claimed by S. Arnold for £4,000.
Owner Middleham Park Racing XLIX **Bred** Gerard Kennedy **Trained** Constable Burton, N Yorks

FOCUS
An uncompetitive claimer that went the way the official ratings suggested it would. The standard is solid and possibly worth a length more.

NOTEBOOK
Insolenceofoffice(IRE) had been on a roll in maidens/nurseries before a substandard run on Fibresand last time but he had an outstanding chance at the weights dropped in grade and won readily. His mark won't go up for this and he'll continue to be a force back in handicaps on this surface. (tchd 4-6)
Slatey Hen(IRE) has had excuses the last twice and ran well on unfavourable terms. She ought to be up to winning another seller. (op 8-1)
Whipphound came here having won his last two but his new official rating of 78 looked on the high side for one that had landed only a seller and a claimer and so it proved, never a threat. He's going to find life tough in handicaps. (op 13-2)
Buddy Miracle continues a maiden and didn't help herself by running too freely through the early stages. (op 5-1)
Braehead(IRE), an Irish import having his first run since leaving Paul Deegan, probably isn't good enough anyway to win a race like this on these terms but he left the impression he just needed his first start for two months. His new yard do well with these types and he can be expected to find his level soon. (tchd 16-1)

8003 DIGIBET H'CAP 1m 4f (P)
7:20 (7:22) (Class 4) (0-85,85) 3-Y-0+ £3,885 (£1,156; £577; £288) Stalls Centre

Form RPR

0002 1 **Trip The Light**[15] 7865 5-9-3 78 (v) JackMitchell 5 92
(R A Fahey) *hld up in tch: swtchd lft and effrt wl over 1f out: drvn to chal ins fnl f: led fnl 75yds: drvn out* **9/1**

6011 2 1 **Franco Is My Name**[21] 7756 4-9-8 83 DaneO'Neill 12 95
(P R Hedger) *in tch: wnt 2nd 2f out: rdn to ld and edgd lft u.p ins fnl f: sn hdd and no ex* **3/1**[1]

4532 3 5 **Sing Sweetly**[47] 7420 3-9-3 83 EddieAhern 7 87
(G A Butler) *led after 1f: rdn and fnd ex ent fnl 2f: hdd: hmpd and snatched up ins fnl f: nt rcvr and wl btn after* **7/2**[3]

6404 4 2 ¼ **Addwaitya**[60] 6276 5-9-2 77 IanMongan 4 77
(Mrs L J Mongan) *sn detached in last: rdn over 4f out: styd on u.p fnl f: nvr trbld ldrs* **12/1**

6122 5 shd **Iron Condor**[28] 7653 3-8-12 78 LukeMorris 2 78
(J M P Eustace) *hld up wl off the pce in rr: rdn and effrt over 2f out: kpt on u.p fnl f: nvr trbld ldrs* **10/3**[2]

2425 6 1 ½ **Peace Corps**[100] 6257 4-9-0 75 (vt) StephenCraine 9 73
(J R Boyle) *chsd ldrs: rdn ent fnl 3f: chsd ldr briefly jst over 2f out: unable qck u.p whn pushed lft wl over 1f out: sn outpcd and wl hld 1f out* **16/1**

2-4 7 3 ¼ **Farleigh House (USA)**[14] 7881 6-9-8 83 HayleyTurner 6 76
(N B King) *hld up wl off the pce in rr: rdn and effrt on inner 2f out: no hdwy over 1f out: wknd ent fnl f* **12/1**

0-12 8 3 **Bariolo (FR)**[300] 785 6-8-10 71 oh1 TravisBlock 3 59
(Noel T Chance) *hld up off the pce towards rr: hdwy into midfield 4f out: rdn and no hdwy over 2f out: wl btn over 1f out* **16/1**

2/ 9 1 ½ **Pat's Legacy (USA)**[291] 4-9-0 75 J-PGuillambert 11 60
(F J Brennan) *t.k.h: led for 1f: chsd ldr after: rdn over 3f out: lost 2nd jst over 2f out: wknd over 1f out: eased ins fnl f* **25/1**

0406 10 6 **Chalice Welcome**[18] 7828 7-9-5 80 GeorgeBaker 8 56
(N B King) *stdd s: hld up in rr: hdwy into midfield over 4f out: wknd u.p over 2f out* **25/1**

0210 **11** *2 1/4* **Maslak (IRE)**[25] 7694 6-9-1 **76**........ ChrisCatlin 10 48
(P W Hiatt) *racd in midfield: dropped to rr and rdn over 3f out: wl bhd fnl 2f* **25/1**

2m 32.64s (-1.86) **Going Correction** -0.025s/f (Stan)
WFA 3 from 4yo+ 5lb **11** Ran SP% **119.0**
Speed ratings (Par 105): **105,104,101,99,99 98,96,94,93,89 87**
toteswingers:1&2:£5.20, 1&3:£18.00, 2&3:£2.50 CSF £35.78 CT £112.67 TOTE £11.40: £4.10, £1.40, £2.20; EX 53.00.
Owner The Matthewman One Partnership **Bred** Darley **Trained** Musley Bank, N Yorks
■ Stewards' Enquiry : Dane O'NeillM two-day ban: careless riding (Jan 12-13)

FOCUS
An interesting handicap. It was well run for the most part but even so, nothing managed to get involved from off the pace.
Addwaitya Official explanation: jockey said that the gelding was never travelling

8004 SKYSPORTS.COM RACING H'CAP 6f (P)
7:50 (7:51) (Class 5) (0-75,75) 3-Y-O+ **£2,286** (£675; £337) **Stalls** High

Form RPR
016 **1** **Clear Praise (USA)**[33] 7571 3-8-13 **67**........ HayleyTurner 11 79
(S Dow) *hld up towards rr: rdn and effrt ent fnl 2f: hdwy u.p over 1f out: led ins fnl f: r.o strly to draw clr towards fin* **9/2**[1]

2001 **2** *2 1/4* **Picansort**[35] 7547 3-8-13 **67**........(v) JimmyQuinn 6 72
(B R Johnson) *chsd ldrs: rdn to chal over 1f out: led ins fnl f: sn hdd and nt pce of wnr* **6/1**[3]

5506 **3** *nse* **Ballodair (IRE)**[26] 7683 3-8-13 **67**........ JackMitchell 12 72
(R A Fahey) *in tch: rdn and n.m.r ent fnl 2f: swtchd lft wl over 1f out: kpt on u.p fnl f* **12/1**

0000 **4** *2* **Best Trip (IRE)**[79] 6800 3-8-13 **67**........ DavidProbert 7 65
(R C Guest) *chsd ldrs: rdn and effrt on inner 2f out: led ent fnl f tl ins fnl f: wknd fnl 75yds* **12/1**

6000 **5** *1/2* **Al Gillani (IRE)**[35] 7554 5-9-4 **72**........(tp) GeorgeBaker 5 69
(J R Boyle) *hld up in tch in midfield: rdn and unable qck 2f out: kpt on again ins fnl f: no threat to ldrs* **15/2**

0400 **6** *nk* **Kylladdie**[7] 7961 3-9-4 **72**........ EddieAhern 4 68
(S Gollings) *hld up in rr: rdn and effrt over 2f out: nt clr run over 1f out: kpt on fnl f: nvr able to chal* **20/1**

2040 **7** *hd* **Ivory Silk**[12] 7915 5-9-7 **75**........(b) SteveDrowne 2 70
(J R Gask) *s.i.s: bhd: rdn over 2f out: styd on ins fnl f: nvr trbld ldrs* **14/1**

4232 **8** *3/4* **Riflessione**[15] 7868 4-9-2 **70**........(b) ChrisCatlin 9 63
(R A Harris) *led: rdn 2f out: hdd ent fnl f: sn wknd* **11/2**[2]

6512 **9** *1* **Desert Strike**[17] 7847 4-8-7 **68**........(p) NoraLooby[(7)] 10 58
(A J McCabe) *stdd s: t.k.h: hld up in tch towards rr: rdn and no hdwy ent fnl 2f* **8/1**

1555 **10** *1 1/4* **Titus Gent**[34] 7564 5-9-1 **69**........ AdamKirby 1 55
(J R Gask) *chsd ldr: rdn to chal wl over 1f out: wknd ent fnl f* **14/1**

4635 **11** *4* **Lord Of The Reins (IRE)**[21] 7754 6-8-13 **67**........ FrannyNorton 3 40
(J G Given) *awkward leaving stalls: t.k.h: hld up in midfield: rdn and wknd over 2f out* **10/1**

1m 12.19s (-0.91) **Going Correction** -0.025s/f (Stan) **11** Ran SP% **113.3**
Speed ratings (Par 103): **105,102,101,99,98 98,97,96,95,93 88**
toteswingers:1&2:£6.70, 1&3:£17.30, 2&3:£11.50 CSF £29.51 CT £305.03 TOTE £6.60: £3.00, £2.70, £5.60; EX 26.70.
Owner Chua, Moore, Goalen & Warner **Bred** Juddmonte Farms Inc **Trained** Epsom, Surrey
■ Stewards' Enquiry : Eddie Ahern two-day ban: careless riding (Jan 12-13)
David Probert one-day ban: careless riding (Jan 12)

FOCUS
An interesting sprint handicap run at a sound pace. Both the first two look progressive and several in behind promise to be of interest soon too.
Desert Strike Official explanation: jockey said that the gelding suffered interference in running
T/Plt: £45.70 to a £1 stake. Pool £80,529.21 - 1,284.83 winning units T/Qpdt: £4.20 to a £1 stake. Pool £8,740.92 - 1,519.68 winning units SP

7913 WOLVERHAMPTON (A.W) (L-H)
Wednesday, December 29

OFFICIAL GOING: Standard to slow
Wind: Light against Weather: Foggy

8005 BET TOTEPOOL ON ALL UK RACING H'CAP 5f 20y(P)
1:25 (1:26) (Class 5) (0-75,75) 3-Y-O+ **£2,007** (£597; £298; £149) **Stalls** Low

Form RPR
1011 **1** **Ajara (IRE)**[25] 7701 4-8-13 **67**........ RichardKingscote 12 75
(Tom Dascombe) *chsd ldrs: rdn over 1f out: led ins fnl f: r.o* **13/2**[3]

0266 **2** *nk* **Jigajig**[71] 6998 3-8-12 **69**........ AmyRyan[(3)] 3 76
(K A Ryan) *led: rdn and hdd ins fnl f: r.o* **11/1**

0001 **3** *2* **Incomparable**[15] 7868 5-9-3 **71**........(bt) IanMongan 6 71
(D Nicholls) *s.i.s: hdwy over 3f out: rdn over 1f out: styd on same pce ins fnl f* **7/2**[1]

0660 **4** *hd* **Garstang**[191] 3261 7-9-2 **70**........(b) LukeMorris 4 69
(J Balding) *s.i.s: hdwy 1/2-way: rdn over 1f out: hung lft and r.o ins fnl f* **16/1**

0000 **5** *1 1/4* **Electioneer (USA)**[18] 7841 3-8-8 **62** ow1........ GrahamGibbons 5 57
(M W Easterby) *hld up: r.o ins fnl f: nvr nrr* **12/1**

0026 **6** *nk* **Efistorm**[7] 7961 9-9-4 **72**........ HayleyTurner 13 66
(C R Dore) *prom: lost pl over 3f out: hdwy 1/2-way: edgd lft and r.o ins fnl f: nt trble ldrs* **14/1**

6213 **7** *nk* **Fear Nothing**[27] 7668 3-9-2 **70**........ GregFairley 1 62
(I W McInnes) *chsd ldrs: rdn over 1f out: no ex fnl f* **8/1**

5410 **8** *hd* **Mango Music**[23] 7730 7-8-12 **66**........ JimmyQuinn 8 58
(R A Fahey) *mid-div: rdn over 1f out: r.o: nt trble ldrs* **6/1**[2]

0050 **9** *hd* **Absa Lutte (IRE)**[128] 5368 7-9-0 **75**........(t) JosephYoung[(7)] 7 66
(M Mullineaux) *s.i.s: hld up: racd keenly: nt clr run over 1f out: nvr nrr* **25/1**

0555 **10** *nk* **Freddie's Girl (USA)**[24] 7719 3-9-7 **75**........ MickyFenton 2 65
(Stef Higgins) *chsd ldr tl rdn over 1f out: wknd ins fnl f* **9/1**

3012 **11** *2 3/4* **Towy Boy (IRE)**[30] 7628 5-9-0 **68**........(bt) JamesDoyle 11 48
(I A Wood) *s.i.s: hld up: rdn over 1f out: nvr on terms* **15/2**

5460 **12** *3 1/4* **Sir Loin**[292] 869 9-8-4 **61** oh16........(v) AmyBaker[(3)] 9 29
(J Gallagher) *chsd ldrs tl rdn and wknd over 1f out* **100/1**

62.54 secs (0.24) **Going Correction** +0.30s/f (Slow) **12** Ran SP% **116.1**
Speed ratings (Par 103): **110,109,106,106,104 103,103,102,102,101 97,92**
toteswingers:1&2:£18.30, 1&3:£3.70, 2&3:£11.20 CSF £74.49 CT £295.80 TOTE £6.80: £2.00, £4.10, £1.50; EX 115.10 Trifecta £232.60 Part won..
Owner Butt Scholes **Bred** Rozelle Bloodstock **Trained** Malpas, Cheshire

FOCUS
On a damp, foggy day the going was reported as standard to slow. A wide open 61-75 sprint handicap.
Towy Boy(IRE) Official explanation: jockey said gelding missed the break

8006 WOLVERHAMPTON-RACECOURSE.CO.UK MAIDEN STKS 7f 32y(P)
2:00 (2:01) (Class 5) 3-Y-O+ **£2,007** (£597; £298; £149) **Stalls** High

Form RPR
1 **Amica (SAF)**[260] 3-8-3 **84**........ JimmyQuinn 4 60+
(Miss Gay Kelleway) *s.i.s: sn prom: chsd ldr 5f out: led on bit over 2f out: drvn out* **5/6**[1]

5002 **2** *3/4* **Wishformore (IRE)**[1] 7994 3-8-7 **63**........(p) RyanPowell[(5)] 1 67
(J S Moore) *chsd ldr 2f: remained handy: chsd wnr over 1f out: sn rdn: r.o* **7/4**[2]

6005 **3** *13* **Elle Est**[15] 7869 3-8-12 **45**........ GrahamGibbons 7 32
(E J Alston) *hld up: hdwy 1/2-way: rdn and wknd wl over 1f out* **10/1**[3]

000 **4** *1 1/4* **Boxer Shorts**[62] 7199 4-8-10 **45**........(t) JosephYoung[(7)] 3 34
(M Mullineaux) *prom: rdn and wknd over 2f out* **40/1**

0000 **5** *10* **Warrior Nation (FR)**[57] 7290 4-9-3 **33**........ VinceSlattery 5 —
(A J Chamberlain) *s.s: a in rr: wknd 3f out* **50/1**

0-05 **6** *1 1/4* **Edge End**[20] 7786 6-9-3 **43**........(p) MickyFenton 6 —
(Mrs L Williamson) *led: rdn and hdd over 2f out: wknd wl over 1f out* **25/1**

1m 32.44s (2.84) **Going Correction** +0.30s/f (Slow) **6** Ran SP% **108.3**
Speed ratings (Par 103): **95,94,79,77,66 65**
toteswingers:1&2:£1.80, 1&3:£1.90, 2&3:£1.20 CSF £2.24 TOTE £2.00: £1.10, £1.10; EX 2.60.
Owner H M K Al Mehairi **Bred** Oldlands Stud **Trained** Exning, Suffolk

FOCUS
An uncompetitive maiden which as the betting suggested, developed into a match.

8007 BET TOTEPOOL ON TODAY'S IRISH RACING H'CAP 2m 119y(P)
2:35 (2:35) (Class 4) (0-85,83) 3-Y-O+ **£3,594** (£1,069; £534; £266) **Stalls** Low

Form RPR
0104 **1** **Ethics Girl (IRE)**[16] 7861 4-9-5 **73**........(t) RobertHavlin 4 81
(John Berry) *prom: lost pl over 3f out: hdwy over 1f out: rdn to ld and hung lft ins fnl f: styd on* **8/1**

1002 **2** *3/4* **Phoenix Flight (IRE)**[35] 7553 5-10-0 **82**........ GeorgeBaker 3 89
(H J Evans) *hld up: racd keenly: hdwy over 3f out: led over 1f out: rdn: edgd lft and hdd ins fnl f: styd on* **11/2**

0531 **3** *4 1/2* **High On A Hill (IRE)**[20] 7781 3-9-0 **76**........ JamesDoyle 2 78
(S Kirk) *a.p: chsd ldr 1/2-way: rdn over 2f out: ev ch over 1f out: no ex ins fnl f* **11/4**[2]

3361 **4** *hd* **Camps Bay (USA)**[11] 7933 6-9-10 **78**........ HayleyTurner 7 79
(C R Dore) *hld up: hdwy over 7f out: pushed along over 5f out: styd on same pce fnl f* **4/1**[3]

4101 **5** *nse* **Lovers Causeway (USA)**[19] 7815 3-9-7 **83**........(b) GregFairley 5 84
(M Johnston) *led: rdn over 2f out: edgd lft and hdd over 1f out: styd on same pce* **9/4**[1]

4563 **6** *10* **Chookie Hamilton**[20] 7781 6-9-7 **82**........ ShirleyTeasdale[(7)] 1 71
(V P Donoghue) *chsd ldr to 1/2-way: remained handy tl rdn and wknd over 1f out* **10/1**

3m 45.98s (4.18) **Going Correction** +0.30s/f (Slow)
WFA 3 from 4yo+ 8lb **6** Ran SP% **113.0**
Speed ratings (Par 105): **102,101,99,99,99 94**
toteswingers:1&2:£5.80, 1&3:£3.90, 2&3:£2.20 CSF £50.14 TOTE £10.80: £4.80, £1.80; EX 36.90.
Owner The 1997 Partnership **Bred** Newsells Park Stud **Trained** Newmarket, Suffolk

FOCUS
A modest stayers' handicap run at a sound gallop and in the end the first two came clear.

8008 STAY AT THE WOLVERHAMPTON HOLIDAY INN H'CAP 1m 1f 103y(P)
3:10 (3:10) (Class 5) (0-70,70) 3-Y-O+ **£2,007** (£597; £298; £149) **Stalls** Low

Form RPR
3031 **1** **Mighty Clarets (IRE)**[20] 7788 3-8-11 **69**........ GeorgeChaloner[(7)] 6 76
(R A Fahey) *chsd ldrs: shkn up to ld 1f out: r.o* **10/1**

2216 **2** *shd* **Strike Force**[20] 7788 6-9-2 **70**........(t) TobyAtkinson[(5)] 8 77
(Miss Olivia Maylam) *hld up in tch: rdn and swtchd lft over 1f out: ev ch ins fnl f: r.o* **14/1**

1665 **3** *nse* **Adoyen Spice**[57] 7286 3-8-4 **58**........ BillyCray[(3)] 3 65
(Mike Murphy) *s.i.s: hld up: rdn over 2f out: hung lft and r.o wl ins fnl f* **12/1**

5611 **4** *1 1/2* **The Winged Assasin (USA)**[16] 7856 4-8-12 **68**........(t) LucyBarry[(7)] 9 72
(S Lycett) *a.p: led 2f out: hdd 1f out: styd on same pce* **4/1**[2]

0001 **5** *shd* **Lord Theo**[7] 7968 6-8-5 **59**........ RyanClark[(5)] 7 63
(N P Littmoden) *hld up: hdwy over 2f out: rdn over 1f out: styd on* **5/2**[1]

1232 **6** *nk* **Dream Of Fortune (IRE)**[14] 7878 6-9-5 **68**........(bt) GeorgeBaker 2 71
(P D Evans) *stdd s: hld up: hdwy 2f out: nt clr run over 1f out: swtchd lft: sn rdn: no imp nr fin* **4/1**[2]

5631 **7** *2 1/2* **Black Coffee**[12] 7920 5-8-8 **57** ow1........(b) ShaneKelly 1 55
(W M Brisbourne) *hld up: rdn over 1f out: r.o ins fnl f: nvr nrr* **12/1**

1500 **8** *3* **Astrodonna**[13] 7890 5-9-1 **64**........ JimmyQuinn 4 55
(M H Tompkins) *hld up in tch: rdn over 2f out: wknd fnl f* **20/1**

-201 **9** *hd* **Midnight Strider (IRE)**[16] 7862 4-9-2 **65**........(t) RichardKingscote 10 56
(Tom Dascombe) *led 6f: ev ch 2f out: wknd fnl f* **6/1**[3]

0415 **10** *22* **Kildare Sun (IRE)**[20] 7788 8-9-2 **65**........(p) GrahamGibbons 5 10
(J Mackie) *chsd ldr tl led 3f out: rdn and hdd 2f out: wknd over 1f out: eased ins fnl f* **16/1**

2m 4.57s (2.87) **Going Correction** +0.30s/f (Slow)
WFA 3 from 4yo+ 2lb **10** Ran SP% **124.6**
Speed ratings (Par 103): **99,98,98,97,97 97,94,92,92,72**
toteswingers:1&2:£21.00, 1&3:£18.60, 2&3:£17.70 CSF £149.61 CT £1722.02 TOTE £14.10: £3.70, £3.70, £5.30; EX 94.20 Trifecta £380.50 Pool of £591.33 - 1.15 winning units..
Owner The Matthewman Partnership **Bred** Ellesmere Bloodstock Ltd **Trained** Musley Bank, N Yorks

FOCUS
A modest but highly competitive handicap and there were five abreast 2f from home.
Dream Of Fortune(IRE) Official explanation: jockey said gelding was denied a clear run
Kildare Sun(IRE) Official explanation: jockey said gelding stopped quickly

8009 BET ON TONIGHT'S FOOTBALL AT TOTESPORT.COM H'CAP 1m 1f 103y(P)
3:40 (3:40) (Class 2) (0-100,100) 3-Y-O+ **£8,705** (£2,605; £1,302; £651; £324) **Stalls** Low

Form RPR
311 **1** **Final Drive (IRE)**[7] 7970 4-8-13 **92** 6ex........ JamieSpencer 6 105
(J Ryan) *hld up: hdwy over 2f out: shkn up to ld over 1f out: hung lft and sn clr* **15/8**[1]

0301 **2** *2* **Island Sunset (IRE)**[18] 7828 4-8-2 **88** JamesRogers(7) 8 97
(W R Muir) *hld up: hdwy over 2f out: hung lft and r.o ins fnl f: nt trble wnr* **16/1**

0001 **3** *2* **Spectait**[26] 7680 8-8-9 **88** RichardKingscote 11 93
(Jonjo O'Neill) *hld up: hdwy over 2f out: nt clr run sn after: rdn and hung lft over 1f out: styd on* **8/1**[3]

002 **4** *1* **Distinctive Image (USA)**[18] 7828 5-9-0 **93** ShaneKelly 10 96
(G A Butler) *a.p: rdn and ev ch over 1f out: styd on same pce fnl f* **11/1**

0003 **5** *nk* **Suits Me**[39] 7523 7-9-7 **100** MickyFenton 4 102
(T P Tate) *chsd clr ldr tl led over 2f out: rdn and hdd over 1f out: no ex ins fnl f* **8/1**[3]

1234 **6** *3/4* **Chapter And Verse (IRE)**[32] 7593 4-9-7 **100** BarryMcHugh 9 100
(Mike Murphy) *hld up: hdwy over 1f out: nt trble ldrs* **13/2**[2]

0603 **7** *1 1/2* **Layline (IRE)**[22] 7735 3-8-9 **90** JimmyQuinn 1 87
(Miss Gay Kelleway) *hld up: hdwy over 2f out: nt clr run sn after: no ex fnl f* **9/1**

0260 **8** *11* **Thunderstruck**[210] 2640 5-8-4 **86** oh1 (p) BillyCray(3) 12 60
(D Nicholls) *led and sn clr tl rdn over 3f out: hdd over 2f out: wknd over 1f out* **28/1**

3055 **9** *2 1/2* **Dream Lodge (IRE)**[18] 7828 6-9-3 **96** (v) GeorgeBaker 3 65
(R A Fahey) *chsd ldrs tl rdn and wknd wl over 2f out* **16/1**

2351 **10** *12* **Fastnet Storm (IRE)**[47] 7430 4-8-9 **88** GrahamGibbons 7 32
(T P Tate) *chsd ldrs: rdn over 2f out: wknd sn after* **9/1**

1400 **11** *5* **Scamperdale**[110] 5913 8-8-11 **90** WilliamCarson 2 23
(B P J Baugh) *chsd ldrs: rdn over 2f out: wknd over 1f out* **20/1**

2m 0.76s (-0.94) **Going Correction** +0.30s/f (Slow)
WFA 3 from 4yo+ 2lb 11 Ran SP% **118.6**
Speed ratings (Par 109): **116,114,112,111,111 110,109,99,97,86 82**
toteswingers:1&2:£7.10, 1&3:£4.80, 2&3:£18.60 CSF £36.39 CT £204.22 TOTE £2.30: £1.10, £4.00, £2.70; EX 39.00 Trifecta £177.70 Pool of £518.93 - 2.16 winning units..
Owner Par 4 Racing **Bred** D Day & B Cantwell **Trained** Newmarket, Suffolk
■ Stewards' Enquiry : Barry McHugh two-day ban; careless riding (12th-13th Jan)

FOCUS
A valuable 86-100 handicap run at a furious pace.

NOTEBOOK
Final Drive(IRE) ◆, winner of five of his last six starts, is the find of the all-weather winter season so far. Penalised 6lb for his neck Lingfield success, he ran here off a mark of 92 having opened his account from just 55 a year ago. Ridden as usual from off the pace by Jamie Spencer - aboard his only mount of the day - he came sweeping round the field on the wide outside on the final turn and, despite a tendency to edge left, he came clear. It remains to be seen how many opportunities he will have in the New Year but he certainly looks capable of taking a Listed race at some stage. (op 5-2)
Island Sunset(IRE) had won on her handicap debut at Lingfield two weeks previously. She stayed on in willing fashion from off the pace but the winner had flown. She would have appreciated a stiffer test. (op 14-1)
Spectait, raised 6lb after his success here, had the hood removed very late and found himself in a poor position. He kept on from the final turn but is something of a moody individual who appreciates a break between races. (op 10-1)
Distinctive Image(USA), runner-up at Lingfield after an absence of ten months, found this trip on the sharp side but did not help his rider by tending to hang left. (op 9-1 tchd 12-1)
Suits Me was unable to dominate but regained the lead on the home turn. He was swallowed up coming to the final furlong and seems better suited by Lingfield. The question is will there be opportunities for him there in the New Year? (op 7-1)
Chapter And Verse(IRE), anchored in last, never entered the argument and was another who tended to hang under pressure. (op 7-1)
Thunderstruck, having his first outing for this yard, had the worst of the draw but his young rider was determined to lead. Clear entering the back stretch, he did well to last in front as long as he did after setting a suicidal pace. (op 33-1)
Dream Lodge(IRE) Official explanation: jockey said gelding hung left-handed throughout

8010 40 LIVE FOOTBALL MARKETS AT TOTESPORT.COM H'CAP 1m 4f 50y(P)
4:10 (4:10) (Class 6) (0-65,64) 3-Y-O+ £1,706 (£503; £252) Stalls Low

Form RPR
3416 **1** **Straversjoy**[30] 7626 3-9-2 **61** GrahamGibbons 10 69
(R Hollinshead) *hld up: hdwy over 4f out: rdn to ld ins fnl f: r.o* **5/1**[3]

2111 **2** *hd* **Alternative Choice (USA)**[18] 7840 4-9-8 **62** GeorgeBaker 6 70
(N P Littmoden) *hld up: hdwy over 2f out: rdn and ev ch ins fnl f: r.o* **9/4**[1]

3236 **3** *2 1/4* **Amical Risks (FR)**[18] 7840 6-9-4 **58** BarryMcHugh 1 62
(Ollie Pears) *hld up: pushed along 4f out: hdwy over 2f out: rdn over 1f out: no ex wl ins fnl f* **10/1**

5225 **4** *1/2* **Stormy Morning**[16] 7861 4-9-10 **64** RichardKingscote 7 68
(Mrs Lawney Hill) *chsd ldrs: led 2f out: sn rdn: hdd ins fnl f: styd on same pce* **4/1**[2]

2532 **5** *hd* **Dubburg (USA)**[39] 7531 5-9-4 **58** JamieMackay 4 61
(W J Musson) *s.i.s: hld up: hdwy u.p over 1f out: nt rch ldrs* **5/1**[3]

0021 **6** *2* **Port Hill**[20] 7789 3-8-9 **54** ShaneKelly 9 54
(W M Brisbourne) *led: rdn and hdd 2f out: no ex fnl f* **16/1**

0634 **7** *2 3/4* **Derby Desire (IRE)**[7] 7968 6-8-7 **54** PNolan(7) 2 50
(D Donovan) *hld up in tch: rdn over 2f out: wknd fnl f* **10/1**

0002 **8** *shd* **Astrodiva**[13] 7887 4-8-12 **52** JimmyQuinn 5 48
(M H Tompkins) *chsd ldrs: rdn over 3f out: wknd fnl f* **22/1**

31/0 **9** *7* **Crimson Monarch (USA)**[20] 7781 6-9-6 **60** WilliamCarson 3 44
(P W Hiatt) *prom: rdn and wknd over 2f out* **33/1**

0330 **10** *1* **Guga (IRE)**[14] 7878 4-9-3 **62** RyanClark(5) 8 45
(J Mackie) *chsd ldrs: rdn over 3f out: wknd over 2f out* **18/1**

2m 44.73s (3.63) **Going Correction** +0.30s/f (Slow)
WFA 3 from 4yo+ 5lb 10 Ran SP% **120.7**
Speed ratings (Par 101): **99,98,97,97,96 95,93,93,89,88**
toteswingers:1&2:£3.60, 1&3:£10.30, 2&3:£7.60; ToteSuper7: Win: Not won Place: Not won. CSF £17.28 CT £112.20 TOTE £6.20: £1.90, £1.40, £4.10; EX 20.60 Trifecta £322.90 Pool of £1047.56 - 2.40 winning units..
Owner E Bennion **Bred** Eric Bennion **Trained** Upper Longdon, Staffs

FOCUS
A low-grade finale run at a sound pace.
T/Plt: £383.60 to a £1 stake. Pool of £84,289.54 - 160.40 winning tickets T/Qpdt: £139.70 to a £1 stake. Pool of £6,686.34 - 35.40 winning tickets. CR

7997 KEMPTON (A.W) (R-H)
Thursday, December 30

OFFICIAL GOING: Standard
Wind: Almost nil Weather: Murky

8011 JUMP RACING ON 15TH JANUARY NURSERY 6f (P)
4:10 (4:10) (Class 6) (0-65,65) 2-Y-O £1,637 (£483; £241) Stalls High

Form RPR
064 **1** **Stirling Bridge**[21] 7779 2-9-2 **60** (b1) SteveDrowne 5 77+
(W Jarvis) *awkward s: swtchd to inner and hld up in 8th: prog on outer over 2f out: hung bdly lft to nr side rail over 1f out: led ins fnl f: romped clr* **9/2**[2]

2402 **2** *6* **Rylee Mooch**[14] 7894 2-9-0 **58** (e) DavidProbert 7 57
(R C Guest) *pressed ldr: rdn to ld wl over 1f out: hdd and outpcd ins fnl f* **8/1**

4531 **3** *1/2* **Wolf Slayer**[28] 7667 2-9-7 **65** RichardKingscote 8 63
(Tom Dascombe) *mde most: drvn and hdd wl over 1f out: outpcd fnl f* **7/4**[1]

030 **4** *hd* **Lady Mango (IRE)**[42] 7493 2-9-5 **63** LukeMorris 10 60
(R A Harris) *chsd ldrs in 7th: rdn over 2f out: no prog tl styd on wl last 150yds* **33/1**

4600 **5** *nk* **Rambo Will**[15] 7871 2-9-6 **64** FergusSweeney 3 60
(J R Jenkins) *spd fr wd draw to press ldrs: rdn and nt qckn over 2f out: sn lost pl: styd on again fnl f* **33/1**

443 **6** *nk* **Just For Leo (IRE)**[3] 7983 2-9-2 **60** (v) StevieDonohoe 12 55
(P D Evans) *rousted along to be prom on inner: rdn over 2f out: no imp over 1f out: fdd ins fnl f* **14/1**

4043 **7** *1 1/2* **Fairy Tales**[21] 7777 2-8-11 **55** NeilChalmers 11 46
(J J Bridger) *trckd ldrs in 5th: effrt over 2f out: cl enough over 1f out: fdd fnl f* **20/1**

0040 **8** *hd* **Cool Water Oasis**[25] 7718 2-9-6 **64** GeorgeBaker 9 54
(G L Moore) *dwlt: chsd ldrs on inner in 6th: shkn up and nt qckn 2f out: one pce and no imp after* **14/1**

3530 **9** *3/4* **Cathcart Castle**[66] 7118 2-9-2 **60** ChrisCatlin 6 48
(M R Channon) *sn in last pair: rdn and hanging wl over 2f out: no prog but kpt on ins fnl f* **6/1**[3]

4205 **10** *hd* **Soviet Spring (IRE)**[24] 7722 2-8-11 **62** ThomasBrown(7) 4 49
(A M Balding) *dwlt: wl in rr: u.p fr over 2f out: no real prog* **16/1**

300 **11** *hd* **City Legend**[122] 5587 2-9-6 **64** (bt1) JamesDoyle 2 51
(A J McCabe) *sn wl bhd in last pair: reminders 1/2-way: no prog but kpt on ins fnl f* **25/1**

002 **12** *4 1/2* **Boushra**[13] 7913 2-9-2 **60** LiamKeniry 1 33
(S Kirk) *dwlt: a wl in rr: struggling over 2f out: wknd over 1f out* **20/1**

1m 13.05s (-0.05) **Going Correction** +0.05s/f (Slow) 12 Ran SP% **118.4**
Speed ratings (Par 94): **102,94,93,93,92 92,90,90,89,88 88,82**
toteswingers:1&2:£4.50, 1&3:£3.80, 2&3:£2.80 CSF £37.03 CT £85.58 TOTE £4.70: £1.30, £2.20, £1.60; EX 38.50.
Owner Dr J Walker **Bred** Mrs W H Gibson-Fleming **Trained** Newmarket, Suffolk

FOCUS
Only one previous winner in a moderate nursery but a much-improved effort from the winner. The gallop was reasonable and the winner drifted to the stands rail after the intersection.

NOTEBOOK
Stirling Bridge disappointed over 7f here on his previous start but showed much-improved form in first-time blinkers on this nursery debut to justify the market support, despite drifting to the stands side late on. While he may not be straightforward, he'll be of obvious interest if turned out under a penalty, especially at one of the left-handed all-weather tracks. (op 13-2)
Rylee Mooch ◆, with the headgear again fitted, had the run of the race and seemed to give it his best shot back up in trip returned to Polytrack. He looks a decent guide to the worth of this form and should be able to pick up a small race away from progressive sorts. (op 15-2)
Wolf Slayer, dropped 3lb for winning an uncompetitive maiden on her previous start, was far from disgraced on this nursery debut. She has plenty of foot and won't be inconvenienced by the drop back to the minimum distance. (tchd 13-8 and 15-8 in a place)
Lady Mango(IRE)'s bit reportedly slipped when well beaten on her nursery debut on her previous start and she duly fared a good deal better, despite looking less than straightforward under pressure. She is worth a try over 7f but may not be one for maximum faith.
Rambo Will bettered the form shown over this course-and-distance on his previous start on this nursery debut and he also shaped (backed up by pedigree) as though the step up to 7f would be more to his liking. (op 25-1)
Just For Leo(IRE), who continues to edge down the weights, had the run of the race back over this longer trip and wasn't disgraced but a record of no wins from 14 starts shows he's not the best betting proposition around. (op 12-1)

8012 HAPPY NEW YEAR FROM KEMPTON PARK CLAIMING STKS 7f (P)
4:40 (4:40) (Class 6) 2-Y-O £1,637 (£483; £241) Stalls High

Form RPR
1321 **1** **Takeaway**[17] 7857 2-8-7 75 NickyMackay 3 66+
(J R Boyle) *dwlt: hld up in last trio: wd bnd 3f out: gd prog to ld 2f out: idled and drvn out* **13/8**[1]

2054 **2** *nk* **Captain Dimitrios**[78] 6842 2-8-13 75 StevieDonohoe 8 71
(P D Evans) *trckd ldrs: looking for room over 2f out: swtchd lft over 1f out: rn to take 2nd ins fnl f: clsng fin* **7/2**[2]

0350 **3** *1 1/4* **Mossgorda (IRE)**[119] 5682 2-9-0 62 MichaelGeran(3) 5 72
(Mrs K Burke) *pressed ldr to 2f out: drvn to chse wnr over 1f out: one pce and lost 2nd ins fnl f* **16/1**

3334 **4** *2 3/4* **Sir Lunchalott**[14] 7886 2-8-3 70 (b) CathyGannon 2 51
(J S Moore) *trckd ldrs: drvn and ch over 1f out: wknd* **10/1**[3]

0336 **5** *2 1/4* **Robber Stone**[24] 7722 2-8-5 55 ChrisCatlin 6 47
(M R Channon) *ld to over 2f out: wknd over 1f out* **10/1**[3]

6452 **6** *1 1/4* **Foxtrot Golf (IRE)**[14] 7886 2-8-3 70 (b1) LukeMorris 4 42
(P Winkworth) *dwlt: plld hrd: hld up bhd ldrs: rdn over 2f out: sn btn* **7/2**[2]

3503 **7** *shd* **Arabella Fenella**[17] 7857 2-7-12 53 (p) DavidProbert 7 36
(R M H Cowell) *dwlt: a in last trio: no prog over 2f out* **20/1**

6000 **8** *1/2* **Danube Dancer (IRE)**[21] 7785 2-7-8 50 ow1 RyanPowell(5) 1 36
(J S Moore) *s.s: detached in last: nvr a factor* **50/1**

1m 27.64s (1.64) **Going Correction** +0.05s/f (Slow) 8 Ran SP% **113.3**
Speed ratings (Par 94): **92,91,90,87,84 83,82,82**
toteswingers:1&2:£2.10, 1&3:£4.30, 2&3:£7.30 CSF £7.20 TOTE £1.40: £1.02, £2.80, £7.30; EX 8.90.
Owner M Khan X2 **Bred** Redhill Bloodstock Limited **Trained** Epsom, Surrey
■ Stewards' Enquiry : Michael Geran one-day ban: careless riding (Jan 13)

FOCUS
An ordinary claimer in which the two market leaders came to the fore late on. The gallop was a moderate one and the winner raced centre-to-far side in the closing stages.

NOTEBOOK

Takeaway had a good chance at the weights and did enough, despite edging right late on, in a race where he very much got first run on the runner-up. Things went his way here but he's a fair sort in this grade and should be able to add to his tally this winter. (op 6-4 tchd 7-4)

Captain Dimitrios, a leading player at the weights, is a fairly reliable yardstick who ran creditably back up in trip after a break of nearly three months and was arguably unlucky not to collect as he was denied room as the winner got first run. He is capable of making amends in similar company.

Mossgorda(IRE), having his all-weather debut and first run for four months, ran well in the face of a stiff task. However he was well placed in a race run at just an ordinary gallop and it is to be hoped the handicapper doesn't take this bare form at face value. (tchd 20-1)

Sir Lunchalott, who had a decent chance at the weights, fared better than he had at this course on his previous start with his usual headgear refitted but, while a stronger gallop would have suited, he didn't look to be giving his rider maximum assistance and he remains one to tread carefully with. (op 8-1)

Robber Stone was nibbled at in the market but ran with the choke out and had his limitations exposed in the face of a stiff task. He'll be better off in ordinary handicaps but is starting to look exposed. (op 16-1)

8013 01932 753518 - BISTRO IN THE PANORAMIC H'CAP — 2m (P)

5:10 (5:11) (Class 5) (0-70,70) 3-Y-O+ — **£2,286** (£675; £337) **Stalls** High

Form — RPR

060 **1** **Dalhaan (USA)**[21] 7778 5-9-11 **67** ..... IanMongan 12 — 76
(L A Dace) *dwlt: sn trckd ldrs: prog to ld 2f out: drvn clr fr over 1f out* **11/1**

6022 **2** *4 1/2* **Rosewood Lad**[18] 7848 3-8-2 **52** ..... CathyGannon 7 — 56
(J S Moore) *hld up and sn towards rr: prog fr 3f out: rdn to go 2nd over 1f out: no ch w wnr* **5/1**[3]

3565 **3** *1 1/4* **Beaubrav**[21] 7778 4-9-11 **67** ..... (t) ChrisCatlin 4 — 70
(M Madgwick) *settled midfield: hrd rdn wl over 2f out: styd on fr over 1f out to take 3rd nr fin* **12/1**

02 **4** *nk* **Not Til Monday (IRE)**[14] 7898 4-9-9 **65** ..... DavidProbert 6 — 67
(J R Jenkins) *pressed ldr: rdn to ld briefly jst over 2f out: outpcd over 1f out: fdd* **8/1**

2-63 **5** *3/4* **Grand Art (IRE)**[26] 7695 6-9-9 **70** ..... (vt) DeanHeslop(5) 9 — 71
(Tim Vaughan) *dwlt: hld up in last trio: drvn and wdst of all bnd 3f out: kpt on u.p fnl 2f: no ch* **33/1**

5510 **6** *nk* **Leyte Gulf (USA)**[17] 7861 7-9-5 **61** ..... LiamKeniry 11 — 62
(C C Bealby) *dwlt and stdd s: t.k.h: hld up in last pair: stdy prog over 2f out stl on bridle: clsd on plcd horses over 1f out: sn shkn up and folded tamely* **8/1**

0/30 **7** *1* **Rock 'N' Roller (FR)**[14] 1690 6-9-13 **69** ..... GeorgeBaker 5 — 69
(G L Moore) *settled in rr: effrt on inner over 2f out: one pce and no imp over 1f out: fdd* **25/1**

05-4 **8** *nk* **Black Tor Figarro (IRE)**[19] 7836 5-8-11 **53** ..... J-PGuillambert 10 — 52
(B W Duke) *cl up on inner: drvn to try to chal over 2f out: wknd over 1f out* **50/1**

1336 **9** *hd* **Dubai Phantom (USA)**[8] 7967 3-9-0 **64** ..... MartinLane 2 — 63
(D M Simcock) *dwlt: wl in rr: prog on outer 5f out: drvn over 3f out: fdd fnl 2f* **4/1**[2]

1001 **10** *8* **Sunny Spells**[26] 7695 5-9-1 **62** ..... RyanClark(5) 3 — 51
(S C Williams) *restless stalls: prom: rdn over 3f out: sn wknd* **12/1**

0005 **11** *5* **Judgethemoment (USA)**[166] 4147 5-9-12 **68** ..... EddieAhern 8 — 51
(Jane Chapple-Hyam) *led at mod pce: tried to wind it up over 3f out: hdd jst over 2f out: wknd and eased: t.o* **3/1**[1]

3m 32.08s (1.98) **Going Correction** +0.05s/f (Slow)
WFA 3 from 4yo+ 8lb — **11** Ran SP% **116.4**
Speed ratings (Par 103): **97,94,94,93,93 93,92,92,92,88 86**
toteswingers:1&2:£17.80, 1&3:£28.30, 2&3:£13.00 CSF £63.57 CT £680.32 TOTE £15.50: £4.90, £1.10, £6.30; EX 114.30.
Owner Copped Hall Farm & Stud **Bred** Shadwell Farm LLC **Trained** Five Oaks, W Sussex

FOCUS
A modest handicap but a modest that slowed further before halfway means this bare form isn't entirely reliable. A couple of the market leaders disappointed and the winner came down the centre in the straight.
Judgethemoment(USA) Official explanation: trainer said, regarding running, that the gelding curled up when it was crowded.

8014 GREATTIME.KEMPTON@THEJOCKEYCLUB.CO.UK H'CAP — 7f (P)

5:40 (5:42) (Class 5) (0-70,70) 3-Y-O+ — **£2,286** (£675; £337) **Stalls** High

Form — RPR

0005 **1** **Lisahane Bog**[14] 7889 3-9-3 **66** ..... (be) FergusSweeney 12 — 75
(P R Hedger) *s.i.s: hld up in last quartet: prog on inner over 2f out: sustained effrt against rail to ld last 150yds: a holding on* **11/2**[3]

5032 **2** *nk* **Could It Be Magic**[166] 4155 3-9-3 **69** ..... (b) KierenFox(3) 4 — 77
(W G M Turner) *chsd ldrs in 5th: rdn 1/2-way: prog u.p over 1f out: r.o to take 2nd last 75yds and cl on wnr fin* **20/1**

0032 **3** *1 1/4* **Lockantanks**[19] 7837 3-9-5 **68** ..... GeorgeBaker 10 — 73
(M Appleby) *trckd ldng trio: prog on inner to ld wl over 1f out: hdd and one pce last 150yds* **9/2**[2]

0064 **4** *1 3/4* **Starwatch**[23] 7737 3-9-4 **67** ..... NeilChalmers 7 — 67
(J J Bridger) *chsd ldrs in 6th: pushed along 1/2-way: nt qckn u.p over 2f out: renewed effrt over 1f out: kpt on* **16/1**

2135 **5** *hd* **The Happy Hammer (IRE)**[32] 7614 4-9-0 **63** ..... WilliamCarson 9 — 63
(Eugene Stanford) *chsd ldng pair: rdn and cl enough 2f out: steadily outpcd after* **6/1**

0066 **6** *3/4* **Chief Exec**[28] 7665 8-9-7 **70** ..... LukeMorris 1 — 68
(J R Gask) *rrd s: wl off the pce in last and nt gng wl: styd on fr over 1f out: nrst fin* **25/1**

0P60 **7** *nk* **Peadar Miguel**[24] 7724 3-9-5 **68** ..... AdamKirby 3 — 65
(M G Quinlan) *hit side of stalls s: hld up in 11th: pushed along over 2f out: styng on whn nt clr run over 1f out to ins fnl f: nvr nr ldrs* **16/1**

2640 **8** *shd* **Headache**[14] 7892 5-9-2 **68** ..... (t) RobertLButler(3) 8 — 64
(B W Duke) *chsd ldrs in 7th: rdn bef 3f out: lost pl and struggling over 2f out* **16/1**

6403 **9** *1* **King's Caprice**[19] 7837 9-8-12 **61** ..... SamHitchcott 6 — 55
(J C Fox) *led at decent pce: hdd jst over 2f out: wknd jst over 1f out* **20/1**

2522 **10** *1 3/4* **Pipers Piping (IRE)**[8] 7966 4-8-13 **65** ..... (v) MichaelStainton(3) 2 — 54
(Jane Chapple-Hyam) *nt that wl away: a in rr on outer: drvn and effrt over 2f out: sn no prog: eased whn btn* **5/2**[1]

0043 **11** *1* **Perfect Ch'I (IRE)**[14] 7889 3-8-13 **62** ..... (b) MartinLane 14 — 48
(I A Wood) *racd keenly: pressed ldr: led jst over 2f out to wl over 1f out: wknd* **10/1**

4500 **12** *3* **Valentino Swing (IRE)**[26] 7701 7-8-10 **59** ..... DavidProbert 5 — 37
(M Appleby) *dwlt: a in rr: u.p and no prog over 2f out: wknd over 1f out* **40/1**

1m 25.29s (-0.71) **Going Correction** +0.05s/f (Slow) — **12** Ran SP% **119.0**
Speed ratings (Par 103): **106,105,104,102,102 101,100,100,99,97 96,92**
toteswingers:1&2:£19.90, 1&3:£10.50, 2&3:£15.10 CSF £115.49 CT £547.24 TOTE £6.70: £1.20, £7.70, £1.30; EX 108.70.
Owner P C F Racing Ltd **Bred** J J Whelan **Trained** Dogmersfield, Hampshire

FOCUS
A modest handicap run at a reasonable gallop. The winner raced hard against the inside rail in the closing stages.
Peadar Miguel Official explanation: jockey said gelding was denied a clear run

8015 DIGIBET H'CAP — 1m 4f (P)

6:10 (6:11) (Class 6) (0-65,65) 3-Y-O — **£1,637** (£483; £241) **Stalls** High

Form — RPR

6044 **1** **Maison Brillet (IRE)**[13] 7909 3-9-7 **65** ..... (p) RobertHavlin 8 — 76
(C Drew) *stdd s: hld up in last pair in strly run r: stdy prog fr over 2f out gng easily: pushed along over 1f out: led ins fnl f: rdn clr* **25/1**

0334 **2** *2 1/4* **Wasara**[66] 7117 3-9-1 **59** ..... FergusSweeney 9 — 66
(Miss Amy Weaver) *hld up towards rr: rdn and gd prog on outer to ld over 1f out: hdd and outpcd ins fnl f* **10/3**[2]

0134 **3** *1* **Irish Jugger (USA)**[27] 7685 3-9-1 **59** ..... JamesMillman 10 — 64
(B R Millman) *t.k.h: hld up in midfield: nt clr run on inner over 2f out: prog sn after: wnt 3rd fnl f but readily outpcd* **9/1**

6600 **4** *4* **Before The War (USA)**[32] 7611 3-9-2 **60** ..... SteveDrowne 1 — 59
(J R Gask) *dwlt: hld up in last pair: u.p and gng nowhere 4f out: styd on past wkng rivals fnl 2f* **12/1**

3240 **5** *2 3/4* **Florio Vincitore (IRE)**[15] 7878 3-9-4 **65** ..... AlanCreighton(3) 4 — 60
(E J Creighton) *led at decent pce: kicked on 4f out: hdd & wknd over 1f out* **16/1**

0060 **6** *2 1/4* **Beseech (USA)**[24] 7728 3-8-7 **51** oh3 ..... CathyGannon 11 — 42
(Miss J Feilden) *hld up towards rr: pushed along over 3f out: no prog and struggling 2f out* **10/1**

5403 **7** *3/4* **Captain Cool (IRE)**[15] 7716 3-8-2 **51** oh2 ..... (b) RyanPowell(5) 7 — 41
(R Hannon) *trckd ldr 4f: wnt 2nd again briefly 2f out: sn wknd* **14/1**

0534 **8** *shd* **Lalika**[18] 7848 3-8-9 **53** ..... LukeMorris 6 — 43
(C G Cox) *v.s.a and lost abt 8 l: t.k.h and rapid prog to go 2nd 8f out to 2f out: wknd rapidly* **8/1**[3]

3032 **9** *1* **Fascination (IRE)**[14] 7896 3-9-7 **65** ..... GeorgeBaker 5 — 53
(M L W Bell) *t.k.h early: wl in tch: prog to trck ldng trio 1/2-way: rdn over 2f out: fnd nil and sn dropped out* **7/4**[1]

105 **10** *1/2* **Dosti**[19] 7836 3-9-7 **65** ..... (v[1]) NickyMackay 3 — 52
(Tim Vaughan) *t.k.h: trckd ldrs: rdn over 2f out: sn wknd* **16/1**

2m 36.01s (1.51) **Going Correction** +0.05s/f (Slow) — **10** Ran SP% **119.6**
Speed ratings (Par 98): **96,94,93,91,89 87,87,87,86,86**
toteswingers:1&2:£10.50, 1&3:£24.40, 2&3:£6.40 CSF £109.85 CT £842.05 TOTE £33.70: £6.90, £1.10, £2.60; EX 171.40.
Owner C Drew **Bred** Liam Webb **Trained** Rampton, Cambs
■ Trainer Clive Drew's first winner for more than four years.

FOCUS
A very ordinary handicap run in which the market leader disappointed. The gallop was modest to the straight and the winner came down the centre in the closing stages.
Dosti Official explanation: jockey said gelding ran flat

8016 RACING AT SKYSPORTS.COM H'CAP — 6f (P)

6:40 (6:41) (Class 4) (0-85,90) 3-Y-O+ — **£3,885** (£1,156; £577; £288) **Stalls** High

Form — RPR

6014 **1** **Perfect Act**[8] 7971 5-9-3 **81** ..... DavidProbert 7 — 91
(A M Balding) *t.k.h: hld up in 5th: looking for room 2f out: gap appeared and rdn to ld 1f out: sn clr* **9/2**[2]

6511 **2** *2 1/4* **Anne Of Kiev (IRE)**[8] 7971 5-9-12 **90** 6ex ..... (t) SteveDrowne 2 — 93
(J R Gask) *pressed ldr to over 1f out: styd on to take 2nd again ins fnl f: no ch w wnr* **9/4**[1]

00-0 **3** *nk* **Diriculous**[62] 7212 6-9-5 **83** ..... EddieAhern 3 — 85
(R A Mills) *hld up in 4th on outer: rdn and nt qckn over 1f out: kpt on to take 3rd ins fnl f* **10/1**

6221 **4** *1/2* **Everymanforhimself (IRE)**[12] 7934 6-9-3 **81** ..... (b) ShaneKelly 1 — 81
(K A Ryan) *hld up in last pair: stl last over 1f out: swtchd lft and rt after: styd on: no ch* **7/1**

4324 **5** *nk* **Vhujon (IRE)**[1] 7998 5-8-12 **76** ..... StevieDonohoe 6 — 75
(P D Evans) *led to 1f out: wknd* **6/1**

0202 **6** *nk* **Quasi Congaree (GER)**[21] 7782 4-9-1 **79** ..... (t) MartinLane 8 — 77
(I A Wood) *trckd ldng pair: wnt 2nd over 1f out and sn chalng: upsides ent fnl f: wknd* **7/1**

1361 **7** *3 3/4* **Ray Of Joy**[29] 7654 4-9-7 **85** ..... FergusSweeney 4 — 71
(J R Jenkins) *t.k.h: hld up in last pair: effrt on inner 2f out: no prog over 1f out: wknd and eased* **11/2**[3]

1m 13.07s (-0.03) **Going Correction** +0.05s/f (Slow) — **7** Ran SP% **112.7**
Speed ratings (Par 105): **102,99,98,97,97 97,92**
toteswingers:1&2:£2.20, 1&3:£12.30, 2&3:£5.50 CSF £14.62 CT £93.26 TOTE £4.20: £2.50, £1.50; EX 16.80.
Owner Dr Bridget Drew & Partners **Bred** Howard Barton Stud **Trained** Kingsclere, Hants

FOCUS
A useful handicap but one in which the pace wasn't overly strong for a sprint. The winner raced centre-to-far side in the closing stages.
Ray Of Joy Official explanation: jockey said filly was denied a clear run

8017 SKYSPORTS.COM H'CAP — 7f (P)

7:10 (7:10) (Class 4) (0-85,85) 3-Y-O+ — **£3,885** (£1,156; £577; £288) **Stalls** High

Form — RPR

1055 **1** **Hazzard County (USA)**[36] 7554 6-8-9 **80** ..... LauraPike(7) 9 — 90
(D M Simcock) *hld up in 5th and off the pce: prog to go 2nd 2f out: clsd gng easily 1f out: nudged along to ld last 100yds* **8/1**

0621 **2** *1 3/4* **Chilli Green**[14] 7892 3-8-11 **75** ..... SamHitchcott 6 — 80
(J Akehurst) *trckd ldng pair at str pce and clr of rest after 3f: lft in ld wl over 2f out: hrd rdn over 1f out: hdd and outpcd last 100yds* **11/8**[1]

5166 **3** *3* **Tuxedo**[14] 7892 5-8-9 **73** ..... (b[1]) LukeMorris 7 — 70
(P W Hiatt) *chsd ldng trio: outpcd and rdn 1/2-way: effrt to dispute 2nd over 2f out: one pce u.p after* **13/2**[3]

4005 **4** *2 3/4* **Street Power (USA)**[26] 7689 5-9-7 **85** ..... SteveDrowne 3 — 75
(J R Gask) *awkward s: hld up in last pair and wl off the pce: rdn and effrt over 2f out: one pce and no imp over 1f out* **4/1**[2]

1205 **5** *2* **Mister Laurel**[26] 7697 4-9-5 **83** ..... (b) JackMitchell 1 — 67
(R A Fahey) *t.k.h: hld up in last pair and wl off the pce: rdn and effrt over 2f out: hung rt over 1f out: no prog after* **8/1**

5010 **6** 26 **Pose (IRE)**[34] 7573 3-8-12 **76** FergusSweeney 2 —
(R Ingram) *hld up in 6th: shkn up and no prog over 2f out: wknd rapidly: t.o* **40/1**

110 **7** 2 **Global Village (IRE)**[68] 7091 5-8-12 **81** RyanClark(5) 5 —
(Michael Blake) *pressed ldr's furious pce: hung lft bnd 3f out: wknd rapidly: t.o* **9/1**

0060 **8** 3 **Gala Casino Star (IRE)**[18] 7846 5-9-4 **82** BarryMcHugh 10 —
(R A Fahey) *blasted off in front but pressed: edgd lft bnd 3f out: sn hdd & wknd rapidly: t.o* **16/1**

1m 24.57s (-1.43) **Going Correction** +0.05s/f (Slow) **8** Ran SP% **116.0**
Speed ratings (Par 105): **110,108,104,101,99 69,67,63**
toteswingers:1&2:£4.00, 1&3:£5.00, 2&3:£3.20 CSF £19.78 CT £78.43 TOTE £7.40: £2.10, £1.20, £1.20; EX 29.30.
Owner Khalifa Dasmal **Bred** Cho, Llc **Trained** Newmarket, Suffolk

FOCUS
A fair handicap but a strong gallop teed things up for the winner, who came down the centre in the straight.
T/Plt: £111.10 to a £1 stake. Pool:£73,656.30 - 483.54 winning tickets T/Qpdt: £59.50 to a £1 stake. Pool:£8,922.43 - 110.80 winning tickets JN

7989 LINGFIELD (L-H)
Thursday, December 30

OFFICIAL GOING: Standard
Wind: nil Weather: dry, overcast

8018 EAST GRINSTEAD CLAIMING STKS 1m 2f (P)
12:35 (12:35) (Class 6) 3-4-Y-O **£2,047** (£604; £302) **Stalls** Low

Form RPR

0050 **1** **Lord Lansing (IRE)**[24] 7731 3-8-7 47 LukeMorris 5 63
(Mrs K Burke) *hld up in tch: hdwy wl over 2f out: rdn and ev ch ent fnl 2f: led narrowly ent fnl f: hung rt u.p ins fnl f: hld on wl* **50/1**

0631 **2** *shd* **Edgeworth (IRE)**[15] 7878 4-8-9 63 (p) FergusSweeney 1 62
(B G Powell) *stdd after s: hld up in tch in last: rapid hdwy on outer to ld over 2f out: rdn and clr w wnr 2f out: hdd ent fnl f: carried rt ins fnl f: a jst hld* **11/10**[1]

0422 **3** 6 **Negotiation (IRE)**[21] 7778 4-9-6 72 FrannyNorton 3 61
(M Quinn) *led tl hdd and rdn over 2f out: outpcd 2f out: 3rd and wl hld over 1f out* **7/4**[2]

3000 **4** 5 **Ting Ting (USA)**[2] 7996 3-8-2 58 (t) NickyMackay 2 36
(J R Boyle) *chsd ldng pair tl rdn and outpcd over 2f out: wl btn over 1f out* **16/1**

0500 **5** 9 **Urban Space**[17] 7856 4-9-3 72 KirstyMilczarek 6 30
(C R Dore) *chsd ldr tl over 2f out: sn outpcd u.p: wl bhd fnl 2f* **5/1**[3]

2m 8.94s (2.34) **Going Correction** +0.225s/f (Slow)
WFA 3 from 4yo 3lb **5** Ran SP% **108.5**
Speed ratings (Par 101): **99,98,94,90,82**
CSF £104.41 TOTE £30.70: £11.70, £1.10; EX 107.50.
Owner Mrs Elaine M Burke **Bred** C J Wall **Trained** Middleham Moor, North Yorks

FOCUS
Little strength in depth to an uncompetitive claimer run at a steady pace.

8019 BIGGER WINS WITH SP+ AT TOTESPORT.COM (S) STKS 6f (P)
1:05 (1:06) (Class 6) 3-Y-O+ **£2,047** (£604; £302) **Stalls** Low

Form RPR

3060 **1** **Athaakeel (IRE)**[30] 7640 4-9-1 58 (b[1]) CathyGannon 8 66
(R A Harris) *v.s.a: early reminder and rdn after s: tagged on to field: travelling strly over 3f out: str run u.p on outer over 1f out: led ins fnl f: sn clr: r.o strly* **20/1**

003 **2** 3 **Waterloo Dock**[47] 7442 5-9-6 62 FrannyNorton 4 61
(M Quinn) *led: rdn and pressed jst over 1f out: hdd and nt pce of wnr ins fnl f: hld on for 2nd* **5/1**[3]

6001 **3** *hd* **Super Frank (IRE)**[19] 7824 7-9-6 63 (b) IanMongan 5 61
(J Akehurst) *dwlt: bustled along early: sn rcvrd and in tch: rdn and effrt over 2f out: drvn to press ldr and hung lft 1f out: styd on one pce u.p fnl f* **15/8**[1]

0543 **4** 1 ¾ **Goodbye Cash (IRE)**[15] 7883 6-8-8 57 JamesRogers(7) 2 50
(R J Smith) *nudged along in last pair early: hdwy ent fnl f: kpt on under hands and heels fnl 100yds: nvr trbld ldrs* **10/1**

3253 **5** *hd* **Apache Ridge (IRE)**[12] 7936 4-9-6 63 (p) ChrisCatlin 1 55
(K A Ryan) *t.k.h: hld up wl in tch: rdn and effrt over 1f out: fnd little: wknd fnl f* **6/1**

0330 **6** 2 ¾ **Best One**[9] 7953 6-9-6 57 (b) LukeMorris 6 46
(R A Harris) *chsd ldr after 2f: rdn and nt qckn over 1f out: wknd ins fnl f* **20/1**

3451 **7** ¾ **Ace Of Spies (IRE)**[12] 7936 5-9-6 70 KirstyMilczarek 3 43
(C R Dore) *chsd ldr for 2f: styd handy: n.m.r on inner bnd ent fnl 2f: wknd u.p over 1f out* **7/2**[2]

1455 **8** ¾ **Espy**[8] 7972 5-9-6 60 RobbieFitzpatrick 7 41
(I W McInnes) *t.k.h: chsd ldrs on outer: wknd u.p over 1f out* **12/1**

1m 12.55s (0.65) **Going Correction** +0.225s/f (Slow) **8** Ran SP% **114.3**
Speed ratings (Par 101): **104,100,99,97,97 93,92,91**
toteswingers:1&2:£19.20, 1&3:£9.80, 2&3:£3.40 CSF £116.09 TOTE £21.70: £4.70, £1.40, £1.40; EX 138.20 Trifecta £415.40 Pool of £701.79 - 1.25 winning units..There was no bid for the winner.
Owner Drag Star On Swan **Bred** Shadwell Estate Company Limited **Trained** Earlswood, Monmouths

FOCUS
A fair seller in which the field were well bunched to the home turn.

8020 BET SP+ WITH TOTESPORT 0800 221 221 NURSERY 6f (P)
1:35 (1:36) (Class 4) (0-85,84) 2-Y-O **£3,885** (£1,156; £577; £288) **Stalls** Low

Form RPR

3301 **1** **Loki's Revenge**[14] 7891 2-9-7 **84** SteveDrowne 3 90
(W Jarvis) *chsd ldrs: wnt 2nd and swtchd rt 2f out: hung lft u.p over 1f out: r.o wl u.p fnl f to ld towards fin* **6/4**[1]

2231 **2** *nk* **Steps (IRE)**[17] 7858 2-9-0 **77** JackMitchell 1 82
(M A Jarvis) *led: rdn and qcknd ent fnl 2f: hrd pressed ent fnl f: kpt on gamely tl hdd and no ex nr towards fin* **9/4**[2]

01 **3** 3 **Pippa's Gift**[15] 7871 2-8-5 **75** JamesRogers(7) 4 71
(W R Muir) *in tch: rdn and effrt over 1f out: chsd ldng pair ins fnl f: no imp* **13/2**

004 **4** 2 **Greenhead High**[15] 7871 2-8-2 **65** JimmyQuinn 6 55
(Jane Chapple-Hyam) *chsd ldr tl 2f out: sn rdn and sltly hmpd ent st: outpcd and wl hld fr over 1f out* **16/1**

0106 **5** ½ **Miss Sinatra (IRE)**[35] 7565 2-8-12 **75** (b[1]) LiamJones 2 64
(B J Meehan) *awkward leaving stalls and s.i.s: in tch in last pair: effrt on inner 2f out: chsd ldrs u.p ent fnl f: wknd fnl 100yds* **33/1**

2212 **6** 1 **Forty Proof (IRE)**[14] 7891 2-9-6 **83** (v) ShaneKelly 5 69
(W J Knight) *stdd s: hld up in last pair: c wd and effrt wl over 1f out: fnd little u.p and wl hld 1f out* **11/2**[3]

1m 12.94s (1.04) **Going Correction** +0.225s/f (Slow) **6** Ran SP% **108.3**
Speed ratings (Par 98): **102,101,97,94,94 92**
toteswingers:1&2:£1.50, 1&3:£2.50, 2&3:£2.80 CSF £4.65 TOTE £2.70: £1.80, £1.50; EX 5.10.
Owner Dr J Walker **Bred** The Athenians **Trained** Newmarket, Suffolk

FOCUS
A two-horse race according to the betting and that's how it panned out. The pace wasn't strong.

NOTEBOOK
Loki's Revenge looked to have a good chance up just 4lb from his ready win over an in-form field last time, and almost certainly improved again, just getting up after spotting the runner-up a couple of lengths into the straight. He left the impression he'd have won more easily granted a stronger pace, and probably has more to give, though his rating seems likely to ensure that opportunities on AW will soon start to dry up. (op 15-8)
Steps(IRE) was given every chance as the race developed but couldn't hold on despite getting first run on the eventual winner turning for home. This was his best effort yet and he seems equally effective at 5f and 6f. (op 2-1)
Pippa's Gift wasn't discredited on his nursery debut but didn't threaten all the same, and a mark of 75 for winning a weak maiden at Kempton last time is almost certainly too high. (op 6-1 tchd 11-2 and 7-1)
Greenhead High looks another on a stiffish mark at present but almost certainly isn't a sprinter anyway and will be better off returned to 7f. (tchd 18-1)
Miss Sinatra(IRE) fared better tried in headgear but she's not progressed and doesn't appeal as a betting proposition right now. (op 25-1)
Forty Proof(IRE) was closely matched with the winner on Kempton running last time but didn't give his running or impress with his head carriage when hanging early in the straight. (op 5-1 tchd 6-1)

8021 BET TOTEPOOL AT TOTESPORT.COM MAIDEN STKS 1m 2f (P)
2:10 (2:11) (Class 5) 3-Y-O **£2,729** (£806; £403) **Stalls** Low

Form RPR

1 **Necessity**[37] 3-9-3 0 GeorgeBaker 2 70
(S Dow) *stdd s: hld up in last pair: smooth hdwy on outer 3f out: trckd ldr wl over 1f out: led on bit ent fnl f: hung lft but sn in command: easily* **5/2**[1]

544 **2** 1 ¾ **Lean Machine**[8] 7964 3-9-3 62 (p) LukeMorris 4 66
(R A Harris) *t.k.h: led: rdn jst over 2f out: hdd 1f out: sn no ch w wnr: kpt on for 2nd* **5/1**

- **3** 1 ½ **Rulbin Realta** 3-8-13 0 ow1 IanMongan 6 59
(P M Phelan) *chsd ldrs: rdn to chse ldr ent fnl 3f tl wl over 1f out: outpcd u.p over 1f out: plugged on ins fnl f to go 3rd nr fin* **20/1**

32 **4** *hd* **Lady Rossetti**[17] 7862 3-8-12 0 CathyGannon 1 58
(M P Tregoning) *hld up in tch: rdn and effrt to chse ldrs over 1f out: outpcd and btn 1f out: lost 3rd nr fin* **7/2**[2]

5033 **5** ½ **Faith Jicaro (IRE)**[14] 7887 3-8-12 50 NeilChalmers 3 57
(N J Vaughan) *chsd ldr tl over 7f out: lost pl and dropped to last pair over 2f out: swtchd rt ent fnl 2f: hung lft u.p over 1f out: no ch but kpt on ins fnl f* **8/1**

0624 **6** 2 ½ **Royal Etiquette (IRE)**[26] 7690 3-9-3 64 ChrisCatlin 8 57
(Mrs Lawney Hill) *t.k.h: chsd ldr over 7f out tl over 2f out: wknd over 1f out* **9/2**[3]

7 4 **Majestueux (USA)**[60] 3-9-3 62 SteveDrowne 7 49
(M R Hoad) *dwlt: pushed along early: towards rr: hdwy into midfield 5f out: struggling u.p over 2f out: wl btn over 1f out* **11/1**

00 **8** *nk* **Harrys**[43] 7489 3-9-3 0 JimmyQuinn 5 48
(Jane Chapple-Hyam) *s.i.s: a in rr: rdn and struggling 3f out: n.d* **33/1**

2m 10.2s (3.60) **Going Correction** +0.225s/f (Slow) **8** Ran SP% **112.8**
Speed ratings (Par 102): **94,92,91,91,90 88,85,85**
toteswingers:1&2:£3.40, 1&3:£12.30, 2&3:£11.80 CSF £14.84 TOTE £3.50: £1.80, £1.80, £4.60; EX 18.10 Trifecta £465.50 Part won. Pool of £629.08 - 0.43 winning units..
Owner Paul G Jacobs **Bred** Juddmonte Farms Ltd **Trained** Epsom, Surrey

FOCUS
Weak form in a very modest maiden, but the winner won well and can rate higher. Once again, the gallop was on the steady side.

8022 ASHURST WOOD H'CAP 1m (P)
2:45 (2:45) (Class 4) (0-85,85) 3-Y-O+ **£3,885** (£1,156; £577; £288) **Stalls** High

Form RPR

1321 **1** **Blue Moon**[24] 7724 3-8-9 **74** FrannyNorton 3 83
(K A Ryan) *trckd ldng pair: effrt to chal between horse ent fnl f: edgd rt but r.o wl to ld wl ins fnl f* **7/2**[1]

102 **2** *nk* **Miami Gator (IRE)**[19] 7842 3-8-11 **76** (v) LukeMorris 8 84
(Mrs K Burke) *chsd ldr: rdn and ev ch over 2f out: drvn to ld over 1f out: kpt on wl tl hdd and no ex wl ins fnl f* **6/1**[3]

06 **3** 1 ½ **Major Victory (SAF)**[16] 7867 3-8-4 **81** KierenFox(3) 4 77
(Miss Gay Kelleway) *taken down early: in tch in midfield: rdn 4f out: outpcd and drvn ent fnl 2f: rallied and styd on ins fnl f: nvr gng pce to chal ldng pair* **25/1**

5021 **4** 1 **Gallantry**[14] 7890 8-8-10 **74** JimmyQuinn 7 77
(Jane Chapple-Hyam) *stdd after s: hld up in last trio: rdn and effrt ent fnl 2f: no real hdwy tl kpt on ins fnl f: nvr able to chal* **7/2**[1]

2002 **5** ¾ **Expensive Problem**[14] 7889 7-8-1 **72** ow1 JamesRogers(7) 9 73
(R J Smith) *t.k.h: chsd ldng trio: rdn and unable qck ent fnl 2f: no threat to ldrs and styd on same pce fr over 1f out* **12/1**

1142 **6** 1 ½ **Tevez**[23] 7737 5-8-12 **76** CathyGannon 5 73
(D Donovan) *in tch in last trio: rdn and no hdwy ent fnl 2f: kpt on same pce fr over 1f out: nvr trbld ldrs* **4/1**[2]

6000 **7** 1 **Pegasus Again (USA)**[148] 4690 5-9-7 **85** IanMongan 6 80
(R A Mills) *led: rdn and qcknd over 2f out: hdd over 1f out: wknd fnl f* **10/1**

5203 **8** *shd* **She's A Character**[26] 7688 3-9-0 **79** (p) BarryMcHugh 1 74
(R A Fahey) *dwlt: nudged along and nvr looked happy in rr: rdn: racd awkwardly and no hdwy wl over 1f out* **20/1**

0/50 **9** 3 ¼ **Levera**[61] 6534 7-9-5 **83** FergusSweeney 2 70
(A King) *in tch in midfield: rdn and dropped to rr over 2f out: wl btn over 1f out* **8/1**

1m 37.81s (-0.39) **Going Correction** +0.225s/f (Slow)
WFA 3 from 5yo+ 1lb **9** Ran SP% **115.2**
Speed ratings (Par 105): **110,109,108,107,106 104,103,103,100**
toteswingers:1&2:£5.50, 1&3:£15.10, 2&3:£17.50 CSF £24.73 CT £453.16 TOTE £4.00: £1.60, £1.90, £6.40; EX 24.50 Trifecta £246.00 Pool of £891.00 - 2.68 winning units..
Owner Guy Reed **Bred** Theakston Stud **Trained** Hambleton, N Yorks

FOCUS
An interesting handicap containing plenty of in-form horses but it wasn't as strongly run as seemed likely beforehand given two front runners were in opposition, and it proved difficult to come from behind.

8023 BET TOTEPOOL ON 0800 221 221 H'CAP (DIV I) 7f (P)
3:20 (3:20) (Class 6) (0-55,55) 3-Y-O+ £1,706 (£503; £252) Stalls Low

Form RPR

0000 1 **Bishopbriggs (USA)**[112] 5897 5-9-1 **54**.............................. AdamKirby 1 70
(M G Quinlan) *led tl over 5f out: chsd ldr tl rdn to ld again over 2f out: rdn clr ent fnl 2f: clr and in n.d fr over 1f out: drvn out* **11/4**[1]

1304 2 4 ½ **Yakama (IRE)**[22] 7768 5-8-13 **55**..................................(v) KierenFox(3) 11 59
(Mrs C A Dunnett) *v.s.a: in rr: hdwy 4f out: kpt on u.p over 1f out: chsd clr wnr ins fnl f: no imp* **7/1**

0043 3 1 ½ **A Pocketful Of Rye (IRE)**[15] 7882 3-8-6 **48**.......(p) MichaelStainton(3) 4 48
(Jane Chapple-Hyam) *chsd ldrs: rdn and nt pce of wnr ent fnl 2f: wnt 2nd but no ch w wnr ent fnl f: no imp and lost 2nd ins fnl f* **4/1**[2]

60 4 ½ **Masteeat (USA)**[3] 7986 3-8-7 **46** oh1......................... KirstyMilczarek 10 44
(Miss Olivia Maylam) *s.i.s: sn in tch on outer: rdn and outpcd ent fnl 2f: no threat to wnr and styd on same pce fr over 1f out* **40/1**

0346 5 ½ **Young Simon**[25] 7717 3-9-1 **54**...(v) IanMongan 5 51
(G G Margarson) *t.k.h: chsd ldrs: rdn to chse ldr over 2f out: sn outpcd and no ch w wnr over 1f out: lost 2nd ent fnl f: one pce* **5/1**[3]

-000 6 1 **Daily Double**[29] 7649 4-8-7 **46**......................................(v) FrannyNorton 3 40
(M R Bosley) *in tch towards rr: effrt u.p on inner over 1f out: no real hdwy: nvr trbld ldrs* **22/1**

0024 7 ¾ **On The Cusp (IRE)**[2] 7994 3-8-8 **47**......................(b) RobbieFitzpatrick 9 39
(P Butler) *racd freely: sn chsng ldr: led over 5f out tl over 2f out: sn rdn and outpcd: wknd 2f out* **10/1**

0503 8 1 ¾ **Boundless Applause**[22] 7763 4-8-7 **46** oh1...................... MartinLane 8 34
(I A Wood) *hld up in tch in midfield: short of room and lost pl bnd 2f out: n.d after* **14/1**

060 9 ½ **Athboy Auction**[22] 7768 5-8-7 **46** oh1.............................. JimmyQuinn 6 32
(H J Collingridge) *s.i.s: a in rr: n.d* **25/1**

0605 10 1 ½ **Cavalry Guard (USA)**[63] 7192 6-8-4 **46**.......................(b) AmyBaker(3) 7 28
(T D McCarthy) *chsd ldrs tl wknd 2f out: wl btn ent fnl f* **25/1**

5005 11 1 ¾ **Teen Ager (FR)**[22] 7768 6-9-2 **55**.................................. WilliamCarson 2 33
(P Burgoyne) *s.i.s: a bhd: n.d: burst blood vessel* **15/2**

1m 25.65s (0.85) **Going Correction** +0.225s/f (Slow) 11 Ran SP% **117.8**
Speed ratings (Par 101): **104,98,97,96,96 94,94,92,91,89 87**
toteswingers:1&2:£5.90, 1&3:£5.90, 2&3:£4.90 CSF £21.34 CT £78.66 TOTE £4.90: £2.20, £2.30, £1.40; EX 34.00 Trifecta £238.60 Pool of £615.86 - 1.91 winning units..

Owner Maurice Kirby **Bred** Sycamore Hall Farm Llc **Trained** Newmarket, Suffolk

FOCUS
Modest fare. The winner was never far off the steady pace and had little trouble landing something of a gamble.

8024 BET TOTEPOOL ON 0800 221 221 H'CAP (DIV II) 7f (P)
3:50 (3:50) (Class 6) (0-55,55) 3-Y-O+ £1,706 (£503; £252) Stalls Low

Form RPR

0000 1 **Tell Halaf**[75] 6930 3-9-1 **54**.. AdamKirby 7 61
(M G Quinlan) *t.k.h: hld up in midfield: nt clr run and shuffled bk ent fnl 2f: rdn and qcknd to chal 1f out: r.o wl under hands and heels to ld fnl 100yds: comf* **9/4**[1]

5364 2 ½ **Norcroft**[19] 7835 8-8-4 **46** oh1...(p) KierenFox(3) 8 52
(Mrs C A Dunnett) *in tch towards rr: rdn and effrt over 2f out: hdwy u.p to ld 1f out: hdd fnl 100yds: r.o but a hld by wnr after* **15/2**[3]

0064 3 3 ½ **Suttonia (IRE)**[15] 7877 4-8-7 **46**.. JimmyQuinn 1 43
(Noel T Chance) *led: rdn ent fnl 2f: hdd 1f out: nt pce of ldng pair ins fnl f: hld on for 3rd fnl f* **14/1**

0000 4 hd **Suhayl Star (IRE)**[14] 7885 6-8-7 **46**................................ WilliamCarson 9 42
(P Burgoyne) *t.k.h: hld up in tch: rdn and effrt to chal 2f out: ev ch and hung lft over 1f out: outpcd fnl f* **8/1**

0340 5 nk **Song Of Praise**[14] 7885 4-8-10 **49**.................................... FrannyNorton 4 44
(M Blanshard) *t.k.h: chsd ldrs: rdn ent fnl 2f: outpcd by ldng pair jst ins fnl f: one pce and wl hld after* **8/1**

0000 6 ½ **Royal Envoy (IRE)**[14] 7885 7-8-6 **48** ow1................ MichaelStainton(3) 3 42
(Jane Chapple-Hyam) *chsd ldr tl ent fnl 2f: keeping on same pce whn n.m.r over 1f out: no threat to ldng pair and one pce fnl f* **9/1**

4-53 7 shd **Strategic Mover (USA)**[332] 369 5-8-12 **54**...........(t) RobertLButler(3) 11 48
(P Butler) *s.i.s: hld up in last trio: effrt and hung lft whn rdn over 1f out: kpt on fnl 100yds: nvr trbld ldrs* **16/1**

1004 8 ¾ **Final Rhapsody**[15] 7882 4-8-13 **52**.................................... MickyFenton 10 44
(W J Musson) *hld up towards rr: rdn and effrt ent fnl 2f: kpt on same pce u.p fnl f: nvr trbld ldrs* **6/1**[2]

0060 9 1 ½ **Fine Ruler (IRE)**[20] 7812 6-9-2 **55**.............................. RussKennemore 5 43
(M R Bosley) *chsd ldrs on outer: wknd u.p wl over 1f out* **12/1**

-400 10 ½ **She's My Rock (IRE)**[13] 7918 3-8-7 **46** oh1................... JamieMackay 2 32
(S Kirk) *chsd ldrs: rdn wl over 1f out: wknd ent fnl f* **25/1**

040- 11 4 **Quick Single (USA)**[395] 7588 4-8-6 **50** ow2............(v) TobyAtkinson(5) 6 25
(P S McEntee) *a in rr: rdn and struggling 3f out: bhd fnl 2f* **50/1**

1m 27.46s (2.66) **Going Correction** +0.225s/f (Slow) 11 Ran SP% **115.1**
Speed ratings (Par 101): **93,92,88,88,87 87,87,86,84,84 79**
toteswingers:1&2:£3.40, 1&3:£9.10, 2&3:£14.80. ToteSuper7: Win: Not won Place: £945.70. CSF £18.49 CT £195.06 TOTE £3.30: £1.10, £1.70, £5.00; EX 21.10 Trifecta £163.90 Pool of £961.76 - 4.34 winning units..

Owner Level Par Racing **Bred** Baron F Von Oppenheim **Trained** Newmarket, Suffolk

FOCUS
Not many in-form horses in a very modest finale, but another gambled-on winner from the same yard that landed a touch in the previous race, and one with similarly undistinguished recent form figures. Once again, the gallop wasn't strong

T/Plt: £60.50 to a £1 stake. Pool:£62,892.07 - 757.83 winning tickets T/Qpdt: £25.00 to a £1 stake. Pool:£6,030.00 - 178.40 winning tickets SP

8025 - (Foreign Racing) - See Raceform Interactive

8018 LINGFIELD (L-H)
Friday, December 31

OFFICIAL GOING: Standard
Wind: nil Weather: dry, overcast

8030 AMELIA BUTLER'S 100TH BIRTHDAY MEDIAN AUCTION MAIDEN STKS 7f (P)
12:00 (12:01) (Class 6) 2-Y-O £2,047 (£604; £302) Stalls Low

Form RPR

0602 1 **Cloud Illusions (USA)**[14] 7914 2-8-12 77.......................... EddieAhern 1 73
(Mrs H S Main) *dwlt: sn chsng ldr: rdn and ev ch ent fnl 2f: looked hld: gamely sustained chal ins fnl f to ld towards fin* **5/4**[2]

6202 2 nk **Les Verguettes (IRE)**[9] 7962 2-8-12 69......................... MickyFenton 2 72
(Stef Higgins) *led: qcknd clr w wnr ent fnl 2f: edgd rt ent fnl f: rdn ins fnl f: hdd and no ex towards fin* **11/10**[1]

6 3 8 **Litotes**[16] 7871 2-8-9 0.. KierenFox(3) 3 51
(M J Attwater) *pressed ldrs tl rdn and outpcd ent fnl 2f: wl btn 1f out* **33/1**

320 4 nk **Littleportnbrandy (IRE)**[207] 2819 2-8-12 76.............. StevieDonohoe 5 50
(P D Evans) *niggled along in last pair: rdn 3f out: drvn and outpcd ent fnl 2f: wl btn 1f out* **15/2**[3]

4 5 12 **Big City Boy (IRE)**[14] 7914 2-9-3 0......................... RobbieFitzpatrick 4 24
(P S McEntee) *s.i.s: in tch but sn niggled along in rr: rdn and wknd enterng fnl 2f: wl bhd fnl f* **100/1**

1m 27.12s (2.32) **Going Correction** +0.175s/f (Slow) 5 Ran SP% **107.8**
Speed ratings (Par 94): **93,92,83,83,69**
CSF £2.78 TOTE £2.00: £1.10, £1.40; EX 2.90.

Owner Wetumpka Racing **Bred** John C Oxley **Trained** Kingston Lisle, Oxon

FOCUS
There were not many runners but they went a decent pace and the two market leaders dominated this maiden.

NOTEBOOK
Cloud Illusions(USA) seemed to show marked improvement when seventh in a 7f Newbury Listed race in October before a narrow defeat behind an odds-on shot in a four-runner Wolverhampton maiden. This 77-rated half-sister to a 1m/1m1f US stakes winner set the standard and showed a good attitude to run down her main market rival close home. She will be given a break now but her profile is generally progressive and she could do well in 1m handicaps next season. (tchd 11-8)
Les Verguettes(IRE) battled valiantly when beaten a nose in a slightly weaker 7f Kempton maiden last time. She was given another positive ride and it looked like she was in control for most of the straight but she was just reeled in after touching 1.03 in running. This was her third very narrow defeat in five starts but she looks a willing customer and the form of this run would be good enough to win most AW maidens during the winter. (op Evens tchd 6-5 in places)
Litotes, sixth of eight in a 6f Kempton maiden on her recent debut, raced keenly out wide and was left behind when the pace quickened turning in. (op 25-1)
Littleportnbrandy(IRE) showed promise when placed in a pair of Windsor maidens in April but was reported to have moved poorly when well beaten at the same track on her last run in June. She attracted a bit of support but was laboured back from 207 days off. This run should sharpen her up but her current mark of 76 looks on the high side for what she has achieved and she could prove tough to place. (op 11-1)
Big City Boy(IRE) was tailed off behind Cloud Illusions on his debut this month and it was a similar story here.

8031 BET TOTEPOOL TO SUPPORT YOUR SPORT NURSERY 7f (P)
12:30 (12:30) (Class 6) (0-65,65) 2-Y-O £2,047 (£604; £302) Stalls Low

Form RPR

5400 1 **Roman Strait**[37] 7552 2-8-11 **55**...................................... FrannyNorton 8 61
(M Blanshard) *hld up in last trio: swtchd rt wl over 1f out: str run on outer ent fnl f: led fnl 75yds: sn in command: r.o strly* **10/1**

4332 2 1 ¼ **Woop Woop (IRE)**[2] 8001 2-9-4 **62**...................................... AdamKirby 6 65
(Stef Higgins) *in tch in midfield: effrt on inner 2f out: drvn and ev ch 1f out: led fnl 100yds: sn hdd and nt gng pce of wnr* **5/2**[1]

5000 3 ¾ **Loves Theme (IRE)**[23] 7758 2-9-1 **59**......................... J-PGuillambert 4 60
(A Bailey) *sn pushed along to ld: rdn and hdd ent fnl 2f: drvn ahd again 1f out tl hdd and no ex fnl 100yds* **50/1**

6064 4 ½ **Moorland Boy**[104] 6209 2-9-0 **58**................................... FergusSweeney 9 58
(J A Osborne) *t.k.h: chsd ldr: rdn to ld narrowly 2f out: hdd 1f out: wknd u.p fnl 100yds* **20/1**

0604 5 ½ **Torteval (IRE)**[21] 7813 2-8-1 **45**..................................(b[1]) CathyGannon 7 43
(P D Evans) *hld up towards rr: hdwy on outer to chse ldrs over 2f out: rdn ent fnl 2f: pressed ldrs and drvn ent fnl f: outpcd fnl 150yds* **8/1**

5500 6 ¾ **Not So Bright (USA)**[70] 7050 2-8-11 **55**........................ DavidProbert 11 53
(D Donovan) *stdd and swtchd lft after s: hld up in rr: rdn and sltly hmpd wl over 1f out: kpt on ins fnl f: nvr trbld ldrs* **13/2**[3]

005 7 nk **Sir Randolf (IRE)**[22] 7780 2-9-7 **65**...............................(t) TravisBlock 1 62
(S Kirk) *chsd ldrs: rdn over 2f out: unable qck u.p whn nt clr run ent fnl f: one pce and n.d after* **7/2**[2]

03 8 1 ½ **Hackett (IRE)**[30] 7650 2-9-4 **62**... EddieAhern 5 54
(M Quinn) *in tch in midfield: rdn and unable qck over 1f out: wknd 1f out* **8/1**

006 9 ½ **Bluberry**[27] 7686 2-8-13 **57**.. LiamKeniry 10 48
(G L Moore) *stdd after s: t.k.h: hld up towards rr: rdn and no imp over 1f out: nvr trbld ldrs* **20/1**

0056 10 1 ½ **Brandy Snap (IRE)**[15] 7888 2-8-2 **51**.......................... RyanPowell(5) 3 38
(R Hannon) *chsd ldrs: rdn ent fnl 4f: lost pl u.p jst over 2f out: wl btn ent fnl f* **14/1**

6300 11 3 **Century Dancer**[21] 7813 2-8-5 **49**...................................... ChrisCatlin 2 28
(Miss Tor Sturgis) *stdd after s: t.k.h: hld up in rr: effrt on inner 2f out: wknd jst over 1f out* **20/1**

1m 26.34s (1.54) **Going Correction** +0.175s/f (Slow) 11 Ran SP% **118.4**
Speed ratings (Par 94): **98,96,95,95,94 93,93,91,91,89 85**
toteswingers:1&2: £6.30, 2&3: £26.20, 1&3: £35.70 CSF £33.75 CT £1229.87 TOTE £14.50: £4.00, £1.50, £9.70; EX 41.90 TRIFECTA Not won..

Owner J M Beever **Bred** J M Beever **Trained** Upper Lambourn, Berks

FOCUS
An ordinary nursery. Most of the runners were exposed and the field had not managed a win between them in a total of 60 starts. The pace was fair but they finished in a bunch behind the winner.

NOTEBOOK
Roman Strait had been beaten at least eight lengths in each of his five previous starts in maidens and nurseries, but it was a different story this time as he found a powerful run out wide to score with something in hand. He is unexposed at this trip on Polytrack and may be capable of further progress. (op 12-1)

Woop Woop(IRE) looked on an attractive mark on her two recent placed efforts in 7f/1m Kempton maidens, the latest 48 hours earlier. A solid favourite for this nursery debut, she battled well to get to the front before being mowed down by a faster finisher. She seems to be steadily improving and should be able to win a similar race. (tchd 11-4)
Loves Theme(IRE) lost her form after going close in a 6f York fillies' maiden in May but she has dropped 15lb in the weights since then and looked revived under a forcing ride dropped back to 7f.
Moorland Boy ran creditably, particularly as he raced keenly up with the pace. He looks a tricky ride and is 0-8 but could find a jolt of improvement if something clicks and he settles better. (tchd 22-1)
Torteval(IRE) did a bit better dropped in trip with first-time blinkers replacing a visor but was still ultimately well held. (op 10-1)
Not So Bright(USA) was not progressing when last seen in October but there was some promise on this return for a new yard after a gelding operation. (op 11-1 tchd 12-1)
Sir Randolf(IRE), a market mover in the morning, ran into some traffic problems in the closing stages and rates a bit better than the finishing position implies. (op 4-1)

8032 TOTEPOOL OUR PROFITS STAY IN RACING (S) STKS 1m 4f (P)
1:00 (1:00) (Class 6) 3-Y-O+ **£2,047** (£604; £302) **Stalls** Low

Form RPR
2311 **1** **Mongoose Alert (IRE)**[36] 7568 8-9-8 81 StevieDonohoe 5 71
(W J Musson) *chsd ldr: jnd ldr over 4f out: rdn ent fnl 2f: led over 1f out: edgd lft and drew clr ins fnl f: comf* **1/2**[1]
1110 **2** *4* **Talenti (IRE)**[27] 7687 7-9-8 69 (t) DaneO'Neill 4 65
(D Flood) *in tch: rdn over 2f out: outpcd by ldng pair wl over 1f out: kpt on to go 2nd ins fnl f: no ch w wnr* **5/1**[2]
610 **3** *2* **Traphalgar (IRE)**[24] 7736 5-9-8 69 (vt) GeorgeBaker 1 62
(P D Evans) *led and set slow gallop: qcknd ent fnl 3f: drvn and hdd over 1f out: btn jst ins fnl f: lost 2nd ins fnl f* **6/1**[3]
3241 **4** *1 3/4* **Mustajed**[223] 2337 9-9-8 69 JamesMillman 6 59
(B R Millman) *hld up in tch in rr: rdn wl over 2f out: outpcd ent fnl 2f: wl hld after: plugged on again ins fnl f* **12/1**
4050 **5** *1/2* **Sir Haydn**[147] 4804 10-8-11 43 DannyBrock(7) 2 54?
(J R Jenkins) *t.k.h: chsd ldrs: rdn and outpcd over 2f out: n.d fr over 1f out: plugged on again ins fnl f* **66/1**

2m 45.63s (12.63) **Going Correction** +0.175s/f (Slow) **5 Ran SP% 106.8**
Speed ratings (Par 101): **64,61,60,58,58**
CSF £3.09 TOTE £1.50: £1.10, £2.10; EX 2.60.The winner was bought by Jim Best for 9,800gns.
Owner Python Partners **Bred** D And Mrs Noonan **Trained** Newmarket, Suffolk

FOCUS
They went a very slow pace early on in this seller but the hot favourite coped well with the potential perils of a tactical affair and surged clear.

8033 TOTEPOOL RACING'S BIGGEST SUPPORTER H'CAP 7f (P)
1:30 (1:30) (Class 4) (0-80,80) 3-Y-O+ **£4,209** (£1,252; £625; £312) **Stalls** Low

Form RPR
0002 **1** **Sarah's Art (IRE)**[20] 7841 7-9-2 75 (t) AdamKirby 1 82
(Stef Higgins) *hld up in tch in last trio: rdn and hdwy ent fnl f: r.o wl u.p ins fnl f to ld towards fin* **13/2**[3]
0353 **2** *nk* **Yankee Storm**[13] 7934 5-8-9 68 (v) JimmyQuinn 4 74
(H J Collingridge) *chsd ldr: rdn and sltly outpcd wl over 1f out: rallied u.p and ev ch ins fnl f: no ex towards fin* **8/1**
0506 **3** *shd* **King's Colour**[16] 7881 5-9-7 80 (v[1]) GeorgeBaker 7 86
(B R Johnson) *t.k.h: hld up in tch in midfield: hdwy to chse ldrs 2f out: drvn over 1f out: ev ch ins fnl f: no ex towards fin* **11/4**[2]
6044 **4** *1/2* **Suffolk Punch (IRE)**[24] 7735 3-9-6 79 (v) DavidProbert 5 84
(A M Balding) *led: rdn and qcknd wl over 1f out: edgd lft u.p over 1f out: hdd wl ins fnl f: lost 2 pls towards fin* **9/4**[1]
4600 **5** *hd* **Spinning Bailiwick**[24] 7737 4-8-7 66 oh1 FergusSweeney 8 70
(G L Moore) *stdd s: hld up in tch in rr: rdn and effrt on outer 2f out: kpt on ins fnl f: nt rch ldrs* **25/1**
300 **6** *2* **Waabel**[31] 7637 3-9-1 74 IanMongan 2 73
(Jim Best) *t.k.h: chsd ldrs: rdn over 1f out: styd on same pce after* **7/1**
5000 **7** *1* **Desert Dreamer (IRE)**[160] 4354 9-9-0 73 StevieDonohoe 6 69
(P D Evans) *taken down early: s.i.s: a bhd: kpt on ins fnl f: nvr trbld ldrs* **33/1**
31 **8** *2* **Caprio (IRE)**[25] 7725 5-9-6 79 NickyMackay 9 70
(J R Boyle) *chsd ldrs: rdn and unable qck over 2f out: wknd over 1f out* **8/1**

1m 26.28s (1.48) **Going Correction** +0.175s/f (Slow) **8 Ran SP% 112.3**
Speed ratings (Par 105): **98,97,97,96,96 94,93,91**
toteswingers:1&2: £4.30, 2&3: £5.40, 1&3: £3.40 CSF £54.63 CT £175.96 TOTE £6.50: £2.00, £1.50, £1.30; EX 29.90 Trifecta £54.80 Pool: £677.26 - 9.14 winning units..
Owner ownaracehorse.co.uk (Shefford) **Bred** Newtownbarry House Stud **Trained** Lambourn, Berks

FOCUS
A competitive handicap. The pace was fair but there was a tight five-way finish.

8034 IN MEMORY OF BARRY COURT (THE JUDGE) H'CAP (DIV I) 6f (P)
2:00 (2:01) (Class 6) (0-65,65) 3-Y-O+ **£1,706** (£503; £252) **Stalls** Low

Form RPR
2532 **1** **Loyal Royal (IRE)**[9] 7972 7-8-13 57 (bt) LiamKeniry 3 64
(J M Bradley) *t.k.h: trckd ldrs: wnt 3rd stl travelling strly 2f out: rdn ins fnl f: drvn fnl 100yds and r.o to ld towards fin* **5/1**[3]
3505 **2** *nk* **Caramelita**[51] 7391 3-9-5 63 FergusSweeney 5 69
(J R Jenkins) *in tch in midfield: swtchd lft and effrt over 1f out: rdn to ld ins fnl f: hdd and no ex towards fin* **14/1**
2600 **3** *3/4* **Mushy Peas (IRE)**[16] 7877 3-8-7 51 oh1 (v) CathyGannon 11 55
(P D Evans) *taken down early: in tch in midfield: rdn along over 2f out: hdwy u.p over 1f out: swtchd lft jst ins fnl f: r.o: nt rch ldrs* **14/1**
3114 **4** *1/2* **Cheery Cat (USA)**[25] 7730 6-8-11 62 (v) MatthewCosham(7) 6 64
(J Balding) *led: rdn ent fnl 2f: hdd ins fnl f: no ex fnl 75yds* **8/1**
0005 **5** *1/2* **West Leake (IRE)**[16] 7883 4-8-9 53 WilliamCarson 10 53
(P Burgoyne) *hld up towards rr: effrt and nt clr run over 1f out: sn swtchd rt: r.o wl ins fnl f: nt rch ldrs* **16/1**
0431 **6** *1* **South African Gold (USA)**[31] 7639 3-9-4 62 (p) JackMitchell 8 59
(J M P Eustace) *chsd ldr after 1f: ev ch and rdn jst over 2f out: wknd u.p ins fnl f* **4/1**[1]
5000 **7** *shd* **Poppy Golightly**[41] 7518 3-9-0 58 RichardKingscote 2 55
(R J Hodges) *chsd ldr for 1f: styd chsng ldrs: rdn wl over 1f out: styng on same pce and btn whn hmpd ins fnl f* **28/1**
0441 **8** *1* **Dualagi**[16] 7882 6-9-2 60 GeorgeBaker 7 54
(M R Bosley) *chsd ldrs: rdn and unable qck ent fnl 2f: wknd over 1f out* **9/2**[2]
0200 **9** *hd* **White Shift (IRE)**[37] 7556 4-9-4 65 MichaelStainton(3) 1 58
(Jane Chapple-Hyam) *hld up in last trio: rdn and effrt over 1f out: kpt on ins fnl f: nvr trbld ldrs* **14/1**
6400 **10** *1* **Pippbrook Ministar**[88] 6638 3-9-7 65 StephenCraine 4 55
(J R Boyle) *in tch in midfield: effrt u.p and no hdwy wl over 1f out: no threat to ldrs ins fnl f* **20/1**
000 **11** *nk* **Tyrannosaurus Rex (IRE)**[18] 7860 6-8-10 54 DaneO'Neill 9 43
(D Shaw) *stdd and dropped in bhd after s: a in rr: nvr trbld ldrs* **20/1**
2P53 **12** *1 3/4* **Resuscitator (USA)**[16] 7872 3-9-7 65 EddieAhern 12 48
(Mrs H S Main) *a towards rr: reminders and no rspnse over 3f out: n.d* **15/2**

1m 12.68s (0.78) **Going Correction** +0.175s/f (Slow) **12 Ran SP% 116.6**
Speed ratings (Par 101): **101,100,99,98,98 96,96,95,95,93 93,91**
toteswingers:1&2: £12.80, 2&3: £27.50, 1&3: £16.80 CSF £69.43 CT £937.11 TOTE £5.90: £2.10, £4.30, £4.90; EX 89.10 Trifecta £321.70 Part won. Pool of £434.79 - 0.43 winning units..
Owner JMB Racing.co.uk **Bred** J F Tuthill **Trained** Sedbury, Gloucs

FOCUS
A modest handicap.

8035 IN MEMORY OF BARRY COURT (THE JUDGE) H'CAP (DIV II) 6f (P)
2:30 (2:31) (Class 6) (0-65,65) 3-Y-O+ **£1,706** (£503; £252) **Stalls** Low

Form RPR
0266 **1** **Nubar Boy**[21] 7812 3-9-2 60 (v) StevieDonohoe 11 68
(P D Evans) *hld up in last pair: rdn and hdwy ent fnl f: str run to ld last strides* **9/1**
0004 **2** *hd* **Speak The Truth (IRE)**[66] 7154 4-8-11 58 (p) MatthewDavies(3) 10 65
(J R Boyle) *chsd ldrs: rdn ent fnl 2f: kpt on u.p to ld fnl 75yds: hdd and no ex last strides* **10/1**
0020 **3** *1/2* **Norville (IRE)**[3] 7991 3-9-4 62 (b) CathyGannon 9 67
(P D Evans) *chsd ldr: rdn and ev ch ent fnl 2f: led jst ins fnl f: edgd lft u.p: hdd and no ex fnl 75yds* **15/2**
1022 **4** *nk* **Dancing Welcome**[9] 7973 4-9-4 62 (b) LiamKeniry 3 66
(J M Bradley) *in tch in midfield: effrt on inner and n.m.r ent fnl f: kpt on fnl 100yds* **9/2**[3]
40 **5** *1/2* **Radiator Rooney (IRE)**[9] 7972 7-8-3 52 RyanPowell(5) 4 55
(Patrick Morris) *t.k.h: hld up towards rr: rdn and hdwy over 1f out: chsng ldrs and styng on whn nt clr run fnl 100yds: sn swtchd rt: nt rcvr* **16/1**
421 **6** *shd* **Mr Skipiton (IRE)**[16] 7883 5-9-1 59 LiamJones 7 62
(B J McMath) *racd in midfield: rdn over 2f out: kpt on u.p to chse ldrs ins fnl f: no imp wl ins fnl f* **4/1**[2]
600 **7** *3/4* **Misaro (GER)**[19] 7847 9-9-7 65 (b) DavidProbert 12 65
(R A Harris) *led: rdn ent fnl 2f: hdd jst ins fnl f: wknd towards fin* **20/1**
4521 **8** *1 1/2* **Chjimes (IRE)**[9] 7973 6-9-7 65 (b) KirstyMilczarek 6 60
(C R Dore) *stdd s: t.k.h: hld up in last pair: rdn and effrt over 1f out: kpt on: nvr gng pce to rch ldrs* **3/1**[1]
0551 **9** *3/4* **Silvee**[16] 7877 3-8-7 54 KierenFox(3) 8 47
(J J Bridger) *chsd ldrs: rdn over 2f out: edgd lft u.p ent fnl f: wknd ins fnl f* **16/1**
355 **10** *1 3/4* **Metropolitan Chief**[16] 7882 6-8-7 51 oh1 WilliamCarson 5 38
(P Burgoyne) *stdd and awkward leaving stalls: hld up towards rr: effrt on outer wl over 1f out: no hdwy* **33/1**
1600 **11** *1 1/2* **Tous Les Deux**[24] 7737 7-9-6 64 FergusSweeney 1 47
(Dr J R J Naylor) *in tch in midfield: rdn and lost pl over 2f out: bhd ent fnl f* **33/1**

1m 12.45s (0.55) **Going Correction** +0.175s/f (Slow) **11 Ran SP% 116.4**
Speed ratings (Par 101): **103,102,102,101,101 100,99,97,96,94 92**
toteswingers:1&2 £11.10, 2&3: £12.40, 1&3: £10.20 CSF £92.40 CT £517.54 TOTE £9.80: £2.80, £3.10, £3.10; EX 51.80 Trifecta £412.60 Part won. Pool of £557.58 - 0.63 winning units..
Owner Phil Slater **Bred** Low Ground Stud **Trained** Pandy, Monmouths

FOCUS
The second division of a low-grade handicap. The leaders went off fast and the winner came from a long way back.

8036 TOTEPOOL A BETTER WAY TO BET H'CAP (DIV I) 5f (P)
3:00 (3:01) (Class 6) (0-65,65) 3-Y-O+ **£1,706** (£503; £252) **Stalls** High

Form RPR
2215 **1** **You'relikemefrank**[18] 7859 4-9-3 61 (p) GrahamGibbons 7 73
(J Balding) *chsd ldr: rdn to ld over 1f out: clr ins fnl f: r.o wl: comf* **15/8**[1]
6233 **2** *2* **The Tatling (IRE)**[22] 7784 13-9-5 63 RussKennemore 9 68
(J M Bradley) *in tch in midfield: effrt and rdn ent fnl 2f: chsd clr wnr jst ins fnl f: kpt on: a hld* **13/2**
0205 **3** *2 1/2* **Thoughtsofstardom**[10] 7952 7-8-10 54 ChrisCatlin 3 50
(P S McEntee) *chsd ldrs: rdn wl over 1f out: styd on same pce and wl hld ins fnl f* **11/2**[3]
000 **4** *3/4* **Straboe (USA)**[32] 7628 4-9-4 62 (v) WilliamCarson 8 55
(S C Williams) *s.i.s: hld up in rr: effrt and carried wd bnd 2f out: kpt on ins fnl f: nvr trbld ldrs* **9/2**[2]
-051 **5** *hd* **Co Dependent (USA)**[9] 7960 4-9-7 65 FergusSweeney 1 58
(J A Osborne) *stdd s: hld up in rr: effrt on inner over 1f out: kpt on u.p fnl f: nvr threatened wnr* **11/2**[3]
0060 **6** *nk* **Raimond Ridge (IRE)**[20] 7841 4-9-1 59 PatrickMathers 2 51
(D Shaw) *bhd: rdn 3f out: drvn over 1f out: kpt on fnl f: nvr gng pce to trble ldrs* **12/1**
0000 **7** *1 1/2* **Mythical Blue (IRE)**[113] 5876 4-8-9 60 LeonnaMayor(7) 5 46
(Peter Grayson) *s.i.s: a towards rr: nvr trbld ldrs* **40/1**
0000 **8** *3 1/2* **Louie's Lad**[16] 7314 4-8-5 52 oh6 ow1 KierenFox(3) 10 26
(J J Bridger) *chsd ldrs: rdn and hung rt bnd 2f out: sn wknd* **25/1**
6000 **9** *nse* **Gleaming Spirit (IRE)**[38] 7542 6-8-7 51 oh5 (v) RobbieFitzpatrick 4 24
(Peter Grayson) *sn rdn along to ld: rdn and hdd over 1f out: sn wknd* **66/1**

59.64 secs (0.84) **Going Correction** +0.175s/f (Slow) **9 Ran SP% 112.5**
Speed ratings (Par 101): **100,96,92,91,91 90,88,82,82**
toteswingers:1&2: £3.70, 2&3: £4.40, 1&3: £3.00 CSF £13.91 CT £55.77 TOTE £2.70: £1.20, £2.20, £1.80; EX 14.80 Trifecta £38.80 Pool of £898.87 - 17.14 winning units..
Owner Kate Barrett, Paul & David Clarkson **Bred** J R Mitchell **Trained** Scrooby, Notts

FOCUS
A minor handicap but the favourite did the job in good style to defy a career-high mark.

8037 TOTEPOOL A BETTER WAY TO BET H'CAP (DIV II) 5f (P)
3:30 (3:31) (Class 6) (0-65,63) 3-Y-O+ **£1,706** (£503; £252) **Stalls** High

Form RPR
0061 **1** **Estonia**[26] 7721 3-8-12 54 CathyGannon 1 62
(M D Squance) *taken down early: stdd after s: hld up in rr: hdwy into midfield over 2f out: rdn and chsd wnr ins fnl f: r.o wl to ld fnl 50yds: sn in command* **11/2**[3]
2062 **2** *1* **Edith's Boy (IRE)**[26] 7721 4-9-4 60 GeorgeBaker 2 64
(S Dow) *led: sn rdn 1f out: hdd fnl 50yds: sn btn* **5/2**[1]
542 **3** *3/4* **Decider (USA)**[10] 7952 7-9-6 62 (p) DavidProbert 6 64
(R A Harris) *taken down early: chsd ldrs: rdn and no hdwy jst over 2f out: styd on u.p to go 3rd ins fnl f: kpt on fnl 75yds* **9/2**[2]

3042 **4** *2* **Fromsong (IRE)**[35] 7571 12-9-7 **63**..............................(p) SamHitchcott 9 58
(D K Ivory) *taken down early: outpcd in rr: kpt on u.p fr over 1f out: nt rch ldrs* **8/1**

0030 **5** *1/2* **The Magic Of Rio**[9] 7972 4-8-7 **49** oh3.............................. MartinLane 8 42
(P D Evans) *racd in midfield: rdn and struggling 1/2-way: kpt on u.p ins fnl f* **8/1**

0006 **6** *nk* **Silver Prelude**[26] 7720 9-8-13 **55**..............................(t) WilliamCarson 3 47
(S C Williams) *sn bustled along to chse clr ldr: rdn wl over 1f out: no imp: lost 2nd and wknd jst ins fnl f* **14/1**

3532 **7** *nk* **Bluebok**[18] 7860 9-8-7 **49** oh1..............................(bt) RichardKingscote 5 40
(J M Bradley) *chsd ldrs: rdn and no hdwy jst over 2f out: styd on same pce and no threat to ldrs after* **15/2**

1004 **8** *2* **Avonvalley**[22] 7784 3-9-6 **62**.............................. RobbieFitzpatrick 4 45
(Peter Grayson) *s.i.s: a in rr: rdn and no hdwy whn hmpd bnd 2f out* **16/1**

0000 **9** *10* **Albaher**[16] 7882 4-8-0 **49** oh4..............................(b) LeonnaMayor(7) 10 —
(Peter Grayson) *s.i.s: bhd: lost tch 2f out* **66/1**

58.86 secs (0.06) **Going Correction** +0.175s/f (Slow) **9** Ran SP% **110.2**
Speed ratings (Par 101): **106,104,103,100,99 98,98,95,79**
toteswingers:1&2: £3.40, 2&3: £3.70, 1&3: £4.00 CSF £18.16 CT £61.94 TOTE £7.20: £2.10, £1.10, £2.20; EX 14.10 Trifecta £63.20 Pool of £850.82 - 9.95 winning units..
Owner Miss K Squance **Bred** Millsec Limited **Trained** Newmarket, Suffolk

FOCUS

This second division of a minor sprint handicap was run at a brutal pace but not many got into it. T/Plt: £77.50 to a £1 stake. Pool of £59,984.25 - 564.72 winning tickets. T/Qpdt: £39.30 to a £1 stake. Pool of £5,457.55 - 102.75 winning tickets. SP

INDEX TO FLAT RACING

Horses are shown in alphabetical order; the trainer's name follows the name of the horse. The figures to the right are current master ratings for all-weather and turf; the all-weather rating is preceded by the letter 'a'.Underneath the horse's name is its age, colour and sex in abbreviated format e.g. 6 b g indicates the horse is six-years-old, bay in colour, and a gelding.The descriptive details are followed by the race numbers of the races in which it has taken part in chronological order; a superscript figure indicates its finishing position in that race (brackets indicate it was the winner of the race).

Aahaykid (IRE) *P D Deegan* a80 101
4 ch g Intikhab(USA) —Trust In Luck (IRE) (Nashwan (USA))
511a[14] 610a[13]

Aah Haa *Nicholas Gifford* a53 52
5 b g King's Best(USA) —Snowtop (Thatching)
588[11] 763[4] 3263[4] 3983[8]

Aaim To Prosper (IRE) *Brian Meehan* a79 95
6 br g Val Royal(FR) —Bint Al Balad (IRE) (Ahonoora)
1902[3] ◆ 2541[6] 3050[3] 3447[8] 4320[2] 5080[8] 6352[3] (6926)

Aajel (USA) *Marcus Tregoning* a77 110
6 gr g Aljabr(USA) —Awtaan (USA) (Arazi (USA))
1615[2] 2345[6] 3195[2] 3695[6]

Aalsmeer *Karen George* a62 92
3 b f Invincible Spirit(IRE) —Flower Market (Cadeaux Genereux)
1870[10] 4251[3] 5960[3] 6466[11] 6773[3] 6931[2] 7194[5] 7446[11]

Aalya (IRE) *Peter Chapple-Hyam* a7 66
3 b f Peintre Celebre(USA) —Weqaar (USA) (Red Ransom (USA))
1386[6] 2050[8] 2924[4] 3626[7] 5679[3] 6065[3] 6623[6] 6921[6] 7388[12]

Aamaaq *A Al Raihe* a93 93
7 b g Danehill(USA) —Alabaq (USA) (Riverman (USA))
413a[9]

Aaman (IRE) *Edward Vaughan* a81 77
4 gr h Dubai Destination(USA) —Amellnaa (IRE) (Sadler's Wells (USA))
198[2] (331) (376) 409[7] 2464[10] 4223[5] 4765[8] 5813[9] 6538[2] (6921)

Aattash (IRE) *Mick Channon* a95 105
3 b g Clodovil(IRE) —Mothers Footprints (IRE) (Maelstrom Lake)
1666[4] 2250[2] (2692) (3351) 4504[5] (5121) (5511) 6193[18] 6355[6] 6659[4]

Abadejo *John Jenkins* a49 50
2 b c Acclamation—Silvereine (FR) (Bering)
4396[7] 5085[4] 5835[5] 7552[6]

Abandon (FR) *C Plisson*
2 b f King's Best(USA) —Abime (USA) (Woodman (USA))
7975a[0]

Abaton *Vittorio Caruso* 104
4 b h Dansili—Guntakal (IRE) (Night Shift (USA))
2576a[10]

Abayaan *Jane Chapple-Hyam* a81 82
4 gr g Sadler's Wells(USA) —Showdown (Darshaan)
1013[4] 1655[6] 2549[3] 2975[3] 4125[3] 4785[6] 5788[14] 7101[8]

Abbakhan (IRE) *John Dunlop* 67
2 gr c Dalakhani(IRE) —Agnetha (GER) (Big Shuffle (USA))
6196[8] 6689[14]

Abbashiva (GER) *T Mundry* a92 108
5 b h Tiger Hill(IRE) —Abba (GER) (Goofalik (USA))
412a[4] 818a[9] 1251a[5] (2559a) 3934a[4] 4888a[2]

Abbeyside *Paul Cole* a96 109
4 b h Danehill Dancer(IRE) —Trois Graces (USA) (Alysheba (USA))
1664[5]

Abbondanza (IRE) *David Nicholls* a90 104
7 b g Cape Cross(IRE) —Ninth Wonder (USA) (Forty Niner (USA))
740[5] 883[10] 1042[2] 1862[11] (1968) (2453) (3120) (3226) (3400) 3595[3] 4354[12] 7171[7] 7403[5] (7564) 7906[2]

Abdicate (IRE) *Richard Fahey* 73
2 b f Cape Cross(IRE) —Lady Salsa (IRE) (Gone West (USA))
5509[4] ◆

Abeer (USA) *Ed Dunlop* a64 45
2 ch f Shamardal(USA) —Ekleel (IRE) (Danehill (USA))
5692[14] 6248[6] 6796[7]

Aberdeen Park *David Evans* a40 60
8 gr m Environment Friend—Michelee (Merdon Melody)
7626[7] 7957[7]

Abergavenny *Mark Johnston* a64 93
3 b g Dubai Destination(USA) —Welsh Dawn (Zafonic (USA))
340[6] ◆ (421) (3737) 4376[2] 4504[6] 4841[8] 5286[2] ◆ 5913[4] ◆ 6185[2]

Abergeldie (USA) *Sir Michael Stoute* 68
2 b f Street Cry(IRE) —Camlet (Green Desert (USA))
5488[3] 6155[11]

Abfabfong (IRE) *Martin Bosley* a36 44
5 b g Dr Fong(USA) —Flatter (IRE) (Barathea (IRE))
316[11]

Abhainn (IRE) *Bryn Palling* a50 64
4 ch g Hawk Wing(USA) —Grannys Reluctance (IRE) (Anita's Prince)
1762[11] 2246[13] 2589[8] 3254[5] ◆ 4326[8] 5077[6] 6024[2] ◆ 6864[8] 7192[6] 7506[6] 7649[5]

Abhar (USA) *John Best* a81 72
3 b g Essence Of Dubai(USA) —Jocey's Dance (USA) (Seattle Dancer (USA))
9[2] 933[8] 1261[11] 2906[4] 3160[2] 3390[9] (3739) 4058[7] 4491[4] 5384[2] 5891[2] 6430[3] 6851[3] 7042[3]

Abidhabidubai *John Quinn* 66
2 b f Dubai Destination(USA) —Madamoiselle Jones (Emperor Jones (USA))
1421[2] 2813[3]

Abigails Angel *Brett Johnson* a53 19
3 br f Olden Times—Make Ready (Beveled (USA))
7969[3]

A Big Sky Brewing (USA) *David Barron* a78 66
6 b g Arch(USA) —Runalpharun (USA) (Thunder Rumble (USA))
129[9]

Ability N Delivery *Michael J Browne* a72 69
5 gr g Kyllachy—Tryptonic (FR) (Baryshnikov (AUS))
5990[3] 7334[4]

Abjer (FR) *Clive Brittain* a71 104
2 b c Singspiel(IRE) —Fine And Mellow (FR) (Lando (GER))
4568[5] 4838[4] (6036) (6737) 7265a[10]

Able Master (IRE) *Jeremy Gask* 111
4 b g Elusive City(USA) —Foresta Verde (USA) (Green Forest (USA))
1326[7] 1955a[9] 2344[5] 3193[25] 6175[8] ◆ 6752[16]

Above All *William Haggas* a68 71
2 b c Nayef(USA) —Anyaas (IRE) (Green Desert (USA))
5751[3] 6442[2] 7150[6]

Above Average (IRE) *Lee Freedman* 109
4 b h High Chaparral(IRE) —Crystal Valkyrie (IRE) (Danehill (USA))
7368a[5]

Above Limits (IRE) *David Simcock* a75 99
3 b f Exceed And Excel(AUS) —Cin Isa Luv (USA) (Private Account (USA))
2545[17] 2972[3] 4185a[2] 5250[12] 6238a[3] 6976a[6]

Above The Stars *Richard Fahey* 79
2 b f Piccolo—Swindling (Bahamian Bounty)
(1294)

A Boy Named Suzi *Mark Rimmer* a73 68
2 b g Medecis—Classic Coral (USA) (Seattle Dancer (USA))
4803[8] 5718[2] 7444[5]

Abraham Lincoln (IRE) *Ronald Harris* a68 100
6 b g Danehill(USA) —Moon Drop (Dominion)
1295[10] 1727[22] 2280[2] 2657[2] ◆ 2748[11] 3578[6] 3850[7] 4401[13] 5632[4] 5787[9] 5884[14] 6368[4]

Abrasive (IRE) *William Haggas* 81
3 b c Rock Of Gibraltar(IRE) —Independence (Selkirk (USA))
2115[2] ◆

Abriachan *Michael Quinlan* a66 77
3 b g Celtic Swing—Cape Finisterre (IRE) (Cape Cross (IRE))
1279[9] 5524[14] 5964[6] 6370[9] 6934[3] 7298[7] 7499[2] 7778[12] 7964[2]

Absa Lutte (IRE) *Michael Mullineaux* a85 87
7 b m Darnay—Zenana (IRE) (Lucky Guest)
307[4] (384) 578[6] (1445) 1691[4] 2136[5] 2327[6] 2954[2] 4378[7] 4684[12] 5054[5] 5368[8] 8005[9]

Absent Pleasure (USA) *Doug Watson* a83 95
4 b h Elusive Quality(USA) —Delighted (IRE) (Danehill (USA))
437a[8]

Absinthe (IRE) *Walter Swinburn* a84 101
4 b g King's Best(USA) —Triple Try (IRE) (Sadler's Wells (USA))
1156[3] (4758) (5375) 6562[13]

Absolute Music (USA) *Robert Cowell* a54 99
3 b f Consolidator(USA) —Allegro Lady (USA) (Souvenir Copy (USA))
333a[9] 514a[13] 7545a[0]

Abtasaamah (USA) *Saeed Bin Suroor* a85 80
2 b f Distorted Humor(USA) —Fleet Lady (USA) (Avenue Of Flags (USA))
4844[2] ◆ (6658) ◆ 6927[10]

Abu Dubai (IRE) *Jeremy Glover* a65 60
4 b m Kheleyf(USA) —Boudica (IRE) (Alhaarth (IRE))
1771[9] 2299[10] 2920[3] (3238) 3503[4] 3978[7] 4485[4] 4897[2]

Abulharith *Ronald Harris* a60 68
4 b g Medicean—Limuru (Salse (USA))
(4279) 5011[9] 6314[10] 7407[9] (7569) 7716[10] 7840[2] 7958[10]

Abu Wathab *Peter Chapple-Hyam* 65
3 b g Nayef(USA) —Fleeting Rainbow (Rainbow Quest (USA))
1824[5] 2255[12] 2684[8] 3607[3] 4212[3]

Abydos *Barney Curley* a51 83
6 b g King's Best(USA) —Polska (USA) (Danzig (USA))
7200[5] 7407[10]

Abysse *Ralph Beckett* a23
2 b f Gulch(USA) —Grand Opening (IRE) (Desert King (IRE))
7610[9]

Abzolutely (IRE) *David O'Meara* a35 69
2 ch f Chineur(FR) —Solo Symphony (IRE) (Fayruz)
4149[5] 4451[2] 4896[3] 5221[10] 5418[3] (5640) 6030[9] 6900[11] 7174[7]

Academy (IRE) *Sir Michael Stoute* 79
2 br c Montjeu(IRE) —Rock The Casbah (FR) (Lavirco (GER))
6504[2] ◆ 7179[5]

Academy Blues (USA) *David Nicholls* a95 94
5 bb g Fusaichi Pegasus(USA) —Lover's Talk (CAN) (Vice Regent (CAN))
907[3] (1115) (1152) (1361) 1826[2] 1857[2] 4617[5] 4894[5] 6178[10] 6357[4] 6721[18]

Academy Gigsnreels (USA) *Seamus Fahey* a61 67
5 bb g Rahy(USA) —Eloquent Minister (USA) (Deputy Minister (CAN))
409[10] 429[6] 983[12]

Acambo (GER) *David Pipe* 43
9 gr g Acambaro(GER) —Artic Lady (FR) (No Pass No Sale)
4467[19]

Accamelia *Chris Fairhurst* a65 60
4 br m Shinko Forest(IRE) —Bo' Babbity (Strong Gale)
1485[10] 1804[8] 2393[14] 4982[4] 5816[4] 6246[7] 6464[2] 6896[4] 7300[2] (7468)

Acclamation (USA) *Donald Warren* a109 113
4 b h Unusual Heat(USA) —Winning In Style (USA) (Silveyville (USA))
4417a[6]

Acclamatory *Stuart Williams* a60 59
2 b f Royal Applause—Degree (Warning)
6153[12] 7021[5] 7478[6]

Acclamazing (IRE) *Marco Botti* a74 63
2 b c Acclamation—Pearl Egg (IRE) (Mukaddamah (USA))
4233[3] (7700)

Accompanist *T G McCourt* a76 66
7 b g Pivotal—Abscond (USA) (Unbridled (USA))
173[3] (220) 5408[5] 7078a[2]

According *Nicky Henderson* 86
4 gr g Dalakhani(IRE) —Amaryllis (IRE) (Sadler's Wells (USA))
2549[5]

Accord Secret (FR) *J-C Rouget* a80 98
4 b h Okawango(USA) —Super Vite (USA) (Septieme Ciel (USA))
(1055a)

Accountable *Brendan Powell* a52 57
3 b c Avonbridge—Fair Compton (Compton Place)
2841[6] 4300[2] 5077[13] 5670[5] 6054[11]

Account Closed *Michael Easterby* a37 26
3 bb f Gentleman's Deal(IRE) —Forest Of Love (Charnwood Forest (IRE))
782[10] 894[8] 1057[9] 3207[9] 4893[8] 5299[11]

Ace Master *Roy Bowring* a55 43
2 ch g Ballet Master(USA) —Ace Maite (Komaite (USA))
6465[14] 6675[4] 7150[7] 7469[2] 7643[3] 7864[3]

Ace Of Spies (IRE) *Conor Dore* a78 78
5 br g Machiavellian(USA) —Nadia (Nashwan (USA))
(1723) 2378[5] 3120[3] (3534) 4084[2] 4431[5] (4895) 5327[3] 5647[5] 6057[11] 7180[9] 7326[7] 7399[6] 7494[8] 7683[7] 7730[3] 7847[4] 7870[5] (7936) 8019[7]

Achalas (IRE) *Heather Main* a59 39
2 b g Statue Of Liberty(USA) —Princess Of Iona (IRE) (Fasliyev (USA))
6497[6] 6844[7] 7099[10]

Acheekyone (IRE) *Brian Meehan* a93 70
7 b g Indian Ridge—Tafrah (IRE) (Sadler's Wells (USA))
2339[8] 3558[7] 4206[8]

Achinora *M G Mintchev* 78
2 b f Sleeping Indian—Via Borghese (USA) (Seattle Dancer (USA))
7108a[10]

Achromatic *Walter Swinburn* a58 53
4 gr g Green Desert(USA) —Pericardia (Petong)
13[4] 131[8] 1262[9] 1635[10] 2636[10] 5704[12]

Aciano (IRE) *Brian Meehan* a87 74
2 b g Kheleyf(USA) —Blue Crystal (IRE) (Lure (USA))
4096[13] 4490[4] 5047[4] 5587[8] (6249) 6560[26]

Acknowledgement *John Spearing* a53 77
8 b g Josr Algarhoud(IRE) —On Request (IRE) (Be My Guest (USA))
5959[8] 7840[9]

Acol *George Foster* 43
3 ch g Domedriver(IRE) —Bridge Pal (First Trump)
2072[9] 2501[7] 3073[8] 3501[5] 4061[7] 4951[7] 5336[5] 5738[4]

Acoma (USA) *David M Carroll* a110 114
5 b m Empire Maker(USA) —Aurora (USA) (Danzig (USA))
5320a[7] 7344a[5]

Acquainted *B W Hills* 96
3 b f Shamardal(USA) —Love Everlasting (Pursuit Of Love)
1820[2] (2244) 3101[11] 4347[7] 5938[7]

Acquaviva *Eve Johnson Houghton* 63
3 ch f Medicean—Amazing Bay (Mazilier (USA))
1872[9] 2249[3] 2408[2] 2584[8] 6638[7] 7013[6]

Acropolis (IRE) *Tony Carroll* a63 101
9 b g Sadler's Wells(USA) —Dedicated Lady (IRE) (Pennine Walk)
164[5] 237[3] 420[4] 6450[9] 7023[9] 7199[4] 7508[11]

Across The Rhine (USA) *Tracey Collins* a97 107
4 ch g Cuvee(USA) —Seductive Smile (USA) (Silver Hawk (USA))
413a[7] 626a[7] 710a[8] 6006a[3]

Across The Sands *Christopher Kellett* a60
4 b g Oasis Dream—Well Beyond (IRE) (Don't Forget Me)
561[3] 727[7] (1234)

Across The Sea (USA) *Tom Tate* 61
3 rg g Giant's Causeway(USA) —Trust Your Heart (USA) (Relaunch (USA))
1572[3]

Acrosstheuniverse (USA) *Jeremy Gask* a60
4 bb m Forestry(USA) —Belong To Lassie (USA) (Belong To Me (USA))
14[10] 531[9] 866[10]

Acrostic *Luca Cumani* a99 112
5 ch g Tobougg(IRE) —Royal Dream (Ardkinglass)
2057[4] 3069[8] 3692[2] 4537[14] 5247[2] 6349[7]

Acting Elegant *David Evans* a19 52
3 b f Needwood Blade—Diamond Vanessa (IRE) (Distinctly North (USA))
1796[15]

Acting Happy (USA) *Richard Dutrow Jr* a110
3 bb f Empire Maker(USA) —I Ain't Bluffing (USA) (Pine Bluff (USA))
7344a[6]

Acting Zippy (USA) *William Bennett* a102 102
5 ch g City Zip(USA) —Stormack (USA) (Future Storm (USA))
6759a[6]

Action Chope (FR) *D Guillemin* 96
2 b f Muhaymin(USA) —Free Track (FR) (Solid Illusion (USA))
4884a[4]

Action Girl *Robert Cowell* a58 61
5 gr m Act One—Mohican Girl (Dancing Brave (USA))
2419[9] 2874[7] 4932[5]

Actionmax (TUR) *B Dag* 94
5 ch m River Special(USA) —Harbinger (TUR) (Lockton)
5782a[6]

Activate *Michael Bell* a86 97
3 b g Motivator—Princess Manila (CAN) (Manila (USA))
(1624) 2079[2] 2869[3] 4751[5] (5747) (6131)

Active Asset (IRE) *David C Griffiths* a62 62
8 ch g Sinndar(IRE) —Sacristy (Godswalk (USA))
1296[8] 6890[6] 7200[7] (7760)

Act Of Faith (IRE) *Jamie Osborne*
2 b f Exceed And Excel(AUS) —Nawaji (USA) (Trempolino (USA))
6118[11] 6697[8]

Act Of Kalanisi (IRE) *Mark Johnston* a85 88
4 b g Kalanisi(IRE) —Act Of The Pace (IRE) (King's Theatre (IRE))
2395[4] 2857[11] 3402[3] 3772[3] 4686[2] 4846[6] 5443[2] (5612) 5996[9] 6397[3] (6750) 6926[18]

Act Of Love (IRE) *David Marnane* a72 81
2 b f Acclamation—Piaf (Pursuit Of Love)
6230a[9] 6727a[7]

Act Three *Mouse Hamilton-Fairley* a52 64
6 br m Beat Hollow—Rada's Daughter (Robellino (USA))
1262[2] 1759[5] 2691[7] 3760[11] 4426[7]

Acute (IRE) *Brian Meehan* a66 66
2 ch g Medicean—Pretty Sharp (Interrex (CAN))
5263[12] 5717[5] 6087[5] 6471[13] 6978[16]

Adamantina *Vittorio Caruso* 103
2 b f Diktat—Royal Hawk (IRE) (Wolfhound (USA))
(6975a)

Adam De Beaulieu (USA) *Ben Haslam* a70 61
3 b g Broken Vow(USA) —Gambling Champ (USA) (Fabulous Champ (USA))
267[3] 374[2] 815[3] 933[9] 1070[2] 1514[7] 2274[8] 6371[8] 6713[6] 7082[3] 7331[6] 7473[3] (7645) 7912[5]

Adam's Return (IRE) *W T Farrell* a50 79
4 b g Fath(USA) —Sally Anne (ITY) (Scenic)
5129a[10]

Adaria *David C Griffiths* 40
2 ch f Sleeping Indian—Isle Of Flame (Shirley Heights)
6046[6]

Addahab (USA) *Saeed Bin Suroor* a73 71
3 b f Rock Hard Ten(USA) —Compassionate (USA) (Housebuster (USA))
2047[6] 7253[6]

Added Attraction (FR) *R Laplanche* a39 63
6 ch m Kendor(FR) —Spring Morning (FR) (Ashkalani (IRE))
273a[0]

Addictive Dream (IRE) *Walter Swinburn* a89 94
3 ch g Kheleyf(USA) —Nottambula (IRE) (Thatching)
(936) 2052[2] ◆ (3085) 4204[3] 4858[2] 5966[4]

Addikt (IRE) *James Evans* a13 82
5 b h Diktat—Frond (Alzao (USA))
5039[9] 6372[11]

Addock And Egg *Tom Dascombe* 65
2 b c Danbird(AUS) —Luanshya (First Trump)
1517[8] 2312[5] (Dead)

Address Unknown *D K Weld* a87 106
3 b g Oasis Dream—Return (USA) (Sadler's Wells (USA))
1414a[5] 1951a[2]

Addwaitya *Laura Mongan* a84 86
5 br g Xaar—Three White Sox (Most Welcome)
(1645) 2284[3] 2467[9] 3581[5] 4019[2] 4579[6] 4859[4] 5311[9] 6276[4] 8003[4]

Adelina Patti *Walter Swinburn* 57
2 b f Leporello(IRE) —Camerlata (Common Grounds)
3590[7]

Aden Gulf (IRE) *P Schiergen* a76 86
4 b h Medicean—Aglow (Spinning World (USA))
1055a[6]

Adiamondforhelen (IRE) *E J O'Neill*
2 b c Motivator—Maho (IRE) (Efisio)
7974a[9]

Adjami (IRE) *John Harris* 47
9 b g Entrepreneur—Adjriyna (Top Ville)
2604[7]

Adlington *Richard Fahey* 70
2 b g Dansili—Kiralik (Efisio)
4089[3] 4447[3] 4821[5] 5595[6]

Admin (IRE) *Ralph Beckett* a82 77
3 ch g Namid—Night Rhapsody (IRE) (Mujtahid (USA))
1584[6] 2179[6] 2840[12] (3276)

Admirable Duchess *Dominic Ffrench Davis* a69 76
3 gr f Compton Place—Smart Hostess (Most Welcome)
2320[2] 2648[4] 3277[2] 3952[2] (4531) 4998[3] 6284[2]

Admirable Duque (IRE) *Dominic Ffrench Davis* a83 79
4 b g Selkirk(USA) —Stunning (USA) (Nureyev (USA))
395[2] 526[2] (620) 811[7] 1472[6] 1690[6] 2341[6] 2821[2] 3688[5] 4101[3] 4657[3] (5443) 5591[9]
Admirable Spirit *Richard Hannon* 89
2 b f Invincible Spirit(IRE) —Demi Voix (Halling (USA))
(3590) ◆ 4305[6] 5293[2] 5965[3]
Admiral Alex (USA) *L Blusiewicz* a67 87
3 ch c Afleet Alex(USA) —Madam Lagonza (USA) (Kingmambo (USA))
5544a[11]
Admiral Barry (IRE) *Eoin Griffin* a74 99
5 b g Kalanisi(IRE) —Kart Star (IRE) (Soviet Star (USA))
6926[27]
Admiral Bond (IRE) *Geoffrey Oldroyd* a69 45
5 ch g Titus Livius(FR) —Where's Charlotte (Sure Blade (USA))
178[2] 271[2] 726[9]
Admiral Breese *Reg Hollinshead* a54 59
3 b g Halling(USA) —Covet (Polish Precedent (USA))
2619[10] 3113[2] 6517[2]
Admiral Cochrane (IRE) *William Jarvis* a88 62
3 b g Noverre(USA) —Michelle Hicks (Ballad Rock)
(136) (149) 772[5] 1086[13] 1315[18] 4699[9] 6799[8] 7092[6]
Admiral Dundas (IRE) *Kim Bailey* a84 84
5 b g Noverre(USA) —Brandish (Warning)
2467[7]
Admiral Rodney *Pam Sly* a53 51
3 b c Erhaab(USA) —Bromeigan (Mtoto)
1627[8] 2231[7] 6115[9] 6525[10] 6871[3] 7213[U]
Admiral Sandhoe (USA) *Amanda Perrett* a70 74
4 ch g Diesis—Dancing Sea (USA) (Storm Cat (USA))
1637[9] 2246[8] 2727[9] 3056[10]
Admirals Way *Christopher Kellett* a61 37
5 ch g Observatory(USA) —Dockage (CAN) (Riverman (USA))
10[10] 193[9] 295[10] 388[12] 1172[13] 1470[11] 1723[8] 2263[6] 2788[2] 3338[9] 3911[10]
Admire The View (IRE) *David Lanigan* a62 89
3 ch f Dubawi(IRE) —Miss Honorine (IRE) (Highest Honor (FR))
1480[6] 2242[6] 2892[12] (3434) (3806) 4296[6] 5222[6]
Admission *Michael Bell* 103
3 b g Azamour(IRE) —Eve (Rainbow Quest (USA))
(1127) 1354[3] ◆ 2070[2] 5136a[8] 5949[7] 6203[14] 7100[8]
Adone (IRE) *Sir Michael Stoute* 66
2 br g Araafa(IRE) —Athene (IRE) (Rousillon (USA))
5491[7] ◆ 5916[6]
Adonise (TUR) *Y Demir* 102
4 b h Bin Ajwaad(IRE) —Lady Willpower (TUR) (Tagula (IRE))
5804a[6]
Adorabella (IRE) *Simon Earle* a71 77
7 b m Revoque(IRE) —Febrile (USA) (Trempolino (USA))
5180[13]
Adorable Choice (IRE) *Tom Dascombe* a72
2 b f Choisir(AUS) —Burnin' Memories (USA) (Lit De Justice (USA))
5721[4] ◆ 6230a[20] (7185)
Adorna (GER) *J Hirschberger* 63
3 b f Tiger Hill(IRE) —Astilbe (GER) (Monsun (GER))
6409a[8]
Adostern (GER) *P Lacroix* a56 64
6 gr h Sternkoenig(IRE) —Adora (GER) (Danehill (USA))
332a[3]
Adoyen Spice *Mike Murphy* a65 26
3 ch f Doyen(IRE) —Ariadne (GER) (Kings Lake (USA))
768[12] 950[9] 1504[10] 3478[9] 4479[6] (5869) ◆ 6080[6] 6669[6] 7286[5] 8008[3]
A Dream Come True *Dai Burchell* a57 64
5 b m Where Or When(IRE) —Katy Ivory (IRE) (Night Shift (USA))
467[11]
Ad Value (IRE) *Alan Swinbank* 52
2 b g Ad Valorem(USA) —Sopran Marida (IRE) (Darshaan)
2577[5] 3058[9] 5602[4] 6300[3]
Advanced *Kevin Ryan* a96 109
7 b g Night Shift(USA) —Wonderful World (GER) (Dashing Blade)
740[4] 1008[17] 1400[3] 1900[12] 3869[9] 4358[11] 4576[8] 5095[9] 5526[2] 6175[4] 6349[11] 6721[15] 7060[15] 7348[13]
Adventure Story *Richard Hannon* 72
3 ch f Bold Edge—Birthday Venture (Soviet Star (USA))
2824[7] 3154[5] 4754[6] 5262[12] 5809[9] 6466[8] 6656[5]
Advertise *Andrew Balding* 81
4 br g Passing Glance—Averami (Averti (IRE))
1737[2] 2053[5] 3168[5] 3558[3] (4382) 5287[2] 6444[10]
Advertisement (USA) *Jeremy Noseda* a81 80
3 bb c Mr Greeley(USA) —Banner (USA) (A.P. Indy (USA))
1381[7] 1766[2] 2852[2] 4385[2] 4679[4] (5153)
Ad Vitam (IRE) *Sylvester Kirk* a56 41
2 ch c Ad Valorem(USA) —Love Sonnet (Singspiel (IRE))
1263[7] 3269[9] 3624[14] 3769[6] 4678[12] 4967[7] 7394[5] 7664[2]
Adzing (IRE) *Ronald Harris* a19 42
2 b c Ad Valorem(USA) —Zingari (Groom Dancer (USA))
2687[11] 3106[7] 4447[12] 5630[13] 6795[12] 6953[9] 7197[8]
Aegean Destiny *John Mackie* a56 67
3 b f Beat Hollow—Starlist (Observatory (USA))
133[4] 1601[2] 2219[4] 2704[4] 5093[2] 5923[5] 6650[2] 7307[4]
Aegean King *Michael Wigham* a64 55
4 b g Falbrav(IRE) —Aegean Dream (IRE) (Royal Academy (USA))
1508[4] 3294[7] 4227[6] 5208[7] 6187[8]
Aegean Shadow *Henry Cecil* a82 84
4 ch m Sakhee(USA) —Noble View (USA) (Distant View (USA))
(2331) ◆ (2783) ◆ 3262[4] ◆ 3806[5]
Aerial Acclaim (IRE) *Clive Cox* 78
2 b c Acclamation—Stratospheric (Slip Anchor)
4577[3] ◆ 6149[6]
Aerodynamic (IRE) *Pat Eddery* 93
3 b g Oratorio(IRE) —Willowbridge (IRE) (Entrepreneur)
1781[4] 2324[11] 3481[3] 5917[8] 6467[2] (6771) 6990[4]
Aeroplane *David Evans* a108 84
7 b h Danehill Dancer(IRE) —Anita At Dawn (IRE) (Anita's Prince)
109[2] 163[2] 204[2] 266[5] 278[3] 299[8] 365[5] 4924[7] 5388[9]
Aestival *Sir Mark Prescott Bt* a44 83
4 b g Falbrav(IRE) —Summer Night (Nashwan (USA))
2303[3] ◆ (2488) ◆ (2636) ◆ (2690) 4252[2] 4737[5] 6091[12] 6552[6]
Aetos *Marcus Tregoning* a92 61
3 b g Royal Applause—Hagwah (USA) (Dancing Brave (USA))
843[3] (1222)
Afaara (IRE) *Amanda Perrett* a31 63
2 b f Araafa(IRE) —Pompey Girl (Rainbow Quest (USA))
5829[9] 6635[3] 6859[6] 7295[12]
Affinity *James Given* a75 72
3 b f Sadler's Wells(USA) —Kalinka (IRE) (Soviet Star (USA))
1451[4] 2092[3] 4229[2] (6166) 6631[3] 7284[3] 7541[5]
Affirmable *J W Hills* 62
3 b f Doyen(IRE) —Bella Bellisimo (IRE) (Alzao (USA))
2180[7] ◆ 2812[4] 3522[4] 4046[4] 4728[3] 5653[6] 6020[6]
Affirmatively *Tony Carroll* a53 51
5 b m Diktat—Circlet (Lion Cavern (USA))
368[10] 499[12] 1179[8] 1235[9] 1775[8] 2456[7] 3254[11] 3377[8]
Affordable (IRE) *Sheena West* a30 61
3 b g Johannesburg(USA) —Nan Scurry (FR) (Danehill (USA))
1844[12] 2143[4] 2840[10] 3530[6] 5867[11] 6024[14]
Afkar (IRE) *Clive Brittain* 82
2 b c Invincible Spirit(IRE) —Indienne (IRE) (Indian Ridge)
2486[2] ◆
Aflaam (IRE) *Ronald Harris* a77 81
5 br g Dubai Destination(USA) —Arjuzah (IRE) (Ahonoora)
29[3] ◆ (256) 367[3] (487) 588[6] 752[9] 975[7] 1323[8] 3558[5] 4108[7] 4265[4] 4548[3] 5115[9] 5634[2] 5852[3] 6260[10] 6558[3] 7012[11] 7255[9] 7890[3] 7966[4]
Afleet Again (USA) *Robert E Reid Jr* a112
3 rg c Afleet Alex(USA) —Lucky Again (USA) (Wild Again (USA))
824a[10] 4643a[5] 5544a[4]
Afleet Express (USA) *James Jerkens* a124
3 bb c Afleet Alex(USA) —Expanse (USA) (Distant View (USA))
4613a[3] (5544a)
African Blues *Dominic Ffrench Davis* a13 41
7 ch g College Chapel—Pearl Dawn (IRE) (Jareer (USA))
369[11] 704[8]
African Cheetah *Reg Hollinshead* a84 80
4 ch h Pivotal—Miss Queen (USA) (Miswaki (USA))
1975 430[P]
African Wave (USA) *John Gosden* 74
3 b c Elusive Quality(USA) —Sahara Star (Green Desert (USA))
1029[2] 5487[4]
Afrikanos (FR) *F-X De Chevigny* a71 69
2 b g Johannesburg(USA) —Hill Of Grace (Desert Prince (IRE))
4565a[5]
Afsare *Luca Cumani* a91 112
3 b c Dubawi(IRE) —Jumaireyah (Fairy King (USA))
1769[2] ◆ (2128) (2738) ◆ (3104)
Afsoun (FR) *Neil King* 96
8 b g Kahyasi—Afragha (IRE) (Darshaan)
7208[3]
After The Show *Rae Guest* a69 64
9 b g Royal Applause—Tango Teaser (Shareef Dancer (USA))
(344) 896[6] 1711[9]
Afton View (IRE) *Phil McEntee* a34 64
5 gr g Clodovil(IRE) —Moonlight Partner (IRE) (Red Sunset)
6119[7]
Agapanthus (GER) *Barney Curley* a75 79
5 b g Tiger Hill(IRE) —Astilbe (GER) (Monsun (GER))
(1961) (2685) 3319[9] 4804[5] 5563[7] 6091[5] 6832[11]
Agent Archie (USA) *John Best* a84 87
3 b c Smart Strike(CAN) —Dans La Ville (CHI) (Winning (USA))
(1608) (2254) 3105[15] 3824[14] 6904[5] 7293[6]
Agent Secret (IRE) *F Rohaut* a87 107
4 b h Pyrus(USA) —Ron's Secret (Efisio)
(4276a) 5107a[7] 7102a[5]
Age Of Aquarius (IRE) *A P O'Brien* a83 122
4 b h Galileo(IRE) —Clara Bow (FR) (Top Ville)
1859[2] 2571a[2] 3102[2] 4506[P]
Age Of Reason (UAE) *Saeed Bin Suroor* a108 113
5 b g Halling(USA) —Time Changes (USA) (Danzig (USA))
(418a) 712a[2] 2345[10] 7297[3]
Ager Hadrianus (ITY) *E Galli*
2 b c Blu Air Force(IRE) —Ava Gavenser (FR) (Bluebird (USA))
7849a[9]
Aggbag *Tony Carroll* a60 59
6 b g Fath(USA) —Emaura (Dominion)
1193[8] 3132[4] 3521[6] 4987[5] 5767[8] 5877[6]
Agglestone Rock *Philip Kirby* a67 73
5 b g Josr Algarhoud(IRE) —Royalty (IRE) (Fairy King (USA))
1012[3]
Aghadoe (IRE) *Andrew Balding* 87
3 b g Danehill Dancer(IRE) —Regal Star (Sadler's Wells (USA))
4593[4] 5121[3]
Aglaia (IRE) *J E Pease* a52 91
2 gr f Invincible Spirit(IRE) —Latona (FR) (Kendor (FR))
5137a[6] 7534a[0]
Agnes Champ (FR) *M Boutin* a65 78
4 b g Agnes Kamikaze(JPN) —Antilles (IRE) (Danehill (USA))
560a[8]
Agnes Love *John Akehurst* a64 27
4 gr m Piccolo—Erracht (Emarati (USA))
185[9] 242[3] 525[11] 4790[10]
Agony And Ecstasy *Ralph Beckett* a80 98
3 ch f Captain Rio—Agony Aunt (Formidable (USA))
(1761) 4472[6] 6556[5] 7121[2] 7545a[2]
Agricultural *Lucy Normile* a41 53
4 b g Daylami(IRE) —Rustic (IRE) (Grand Lodge (USA))
815[10] 1103[6] 1576[9] 2208[5]
Ahaazeeg *John Dunlop* a61 73
3 ch g Sakhee(USA) —Russian Ruby (FR) (Vettori (IRE))
5001[5] 5610[4] 6079[3] 6678[5]
Ahlaain (USA) *David Simcock* 97
2 b c Bernstein(USA) —Brocatelle (Green Desert (USA))
2932[11] 3219[4] 3991[2] (4691) 5257[3] 6507[5]
Ahla Wasahl *David Simcock* a105 102
4 br m Dubai Destination(USA) —In Full Cry (USA) (Seattle Slew (USA))
439a[11] 711a[6] 1693[7] 1908[6]
Ahlawy (IRE) *Frank Sheridan* a86 83
7 gr g Green Desert(USA) —On Call (Alleged (USA))
176[4] 429[2] 565[4] 1631[3] (1907) 2243[4] 3283[6] 4652[6] (5237) 5736[7] 6185[9] 6701[12] (6904) 7251[8] 7382[8]
Ahmedy (IRE) *John Quinn* a80 76
7 b g Polish Precedent(USA) —Nawaji (USA) (Trempolino (USA))
220[4] 756[3] 1398[3] 2941[4] 5333[2]
Ahtoug *Mahmood Al Zarooni* a91 79
2 b c Byron—Cherokee Rose (IRE) (Dancing Brave (USA))
1905[2] 2498[3] (3658) 4262[4] (6900) ◆
Ahwahnee *Ralph Beckett* a44 44
3 ch f Compton Place—Tahara (IRE) (Caerleon (USA))
4385[6]
Aiboa (IRE) *L A Urbano-Grajales* 107
4 ch m King Charlemagne(USA) —Spirit of Hope (IRE) (Danehill Dancer (IRE))
6640a[0]
Aichi (AUS) *Saeed Bin Suroor* a100 108
5 b g Strategic(AUS) —Nagoya (AUS) (Quest For Fame)
336a[9] 606a[12] 707a[9] 822a[10]
Aigrette Garzette (IRE) *P Schiergen* 100
2 b f Peintre Celebre(USA) —Aigrette (USA) (Gone West (USA))
7108a[2]
Aikenite (USA) *Todd Pletcher* a111 83
3 bb c Yes It's True(USA) —Silverlado (USA) (Saint Ballado (CAN))
2137a[10] 4613a[7] 7365a[8]
Ailsa Craig (IRE) *Edwin Tuer* a66 82
4 b m Chevalier(IRE) —Sharplaw Destiny (IRE) (Petardia)
1926[11] 2392[4] (3022) (3317) 4450[3] 5096[4] (5638) 6361[9] 7062[13]
Aim'Ees Star *John Harris* a26 22
3 ch f Trade Fair—Star Cast (IRE) (In The Wings)
849[9] 1878[12] 2174[9] 2879[12] 3359[15] 3685[11] 4861[9] 7563[7]
Aine's Delight (IRE) *Andy Turnell* a17 67
4 b m King's Best(USA) —Gentle Thoughts (Darshaan)
1141[8] 2080[11] 3040[8] 6518[7]
Aintgottaname *Murty McGrath* a48
3 b f Trade Fair—Emouna (Cadeaux Genereux)
1059[8] 2231[11] 2780[8]
Ain't Talkin' *Michael Attwater* a40 8
4 ch g Zaha(CAN) —Royal Ivy (Mujtahid (USA))
2419[10] 7023[11] 7191[8]
Air Chief Marshal (IRE) *A P O'Brien* a103 112
3 b c Danehill Dancer(IRE) —Hawala (IRE) (Warning)
2353a[10] 3489a[12] (4160a) ◆ 4457[11] 6009a[6] 6350[8] 6617a[3]
Air Crew (USA) *R Menichetti* 101
3 b c Pollard's Vision(USA) —Crystal Bull (USA) (Holy Bull (USA))
1418a[4] 1945a[7] 7372a[10]
Airedale Lad (IRE) *Noel Wilson* a42 36
9 b g Charnwood Forest(IRE) —Tamarsiya (USA) (Shahrastani (USA))
5019[9]
Air Of Grace (IRE) *Mahmood Al Zarooni* 35
2 gr c Dalakhani(IRE) —Star On Stage (Sadler's Wells (USA))
6635[8]
Airspace (IRE) *M Halford* a74 92
4 bb g Kheleyf(USA) —Peace In The Park (IRE) (Ahonoora)
4180a[11] 5127a[13]
Air Support (USA) *Claude McGaughey III* 106
2 b c Smart Strike(CAN) —Gaze (USA) (Danzig (USA))
7360a[9]
Aizavoski (IRE) *E Lellouche* 113
4 b h Monsun(GER) —Arlesienne (IRE) (Alzao (USA))
1856a[3] 3099a[2] 4038a[4] 6974a[5]
Ajaafa *Michael Attwater* a54 68
2 b g Araafa(IRE) —Cloridja (Indian Ridge)
3020[3] 3665[5] 4645[8] 4967[2] 5434[2] 5818[2] 6130[5] 6745[10] 7040[7] 7313[3] 7497[12] 7552[5]
Ajaan *Henry Cecil* 105
6 br h Machiavellian(USA) —Alakananda (Hernando (FR))
1821[16] 5220[5] 5743[8] 6201[6] (6621) 6926[25]
Ajara (IRE) *Tom Dascombe* a75 65
4 b m Elusive City(USA) —My-Lorraine (IRE) (Mac's Imp (USA))
1238[10] 1588[6] 2310[5] 2751[5] 3637[7] 5809[7] 6330[8] 6537[5] (7064) 7209[12] (7526) (7701) (8005)
Ajeeb (USA) *David Simcock* a72 72
2 b c Harlan's Holiday(USA) —Fair Settlement (USA) (Easy Goer (USA))
5985[3] 6742[2] ◆
Ajjaadd (USA) *Ted Powell* a78 77
4 b g Elusive Quality(USA) —Millstream (USA) (Dayjur (USA))
(538) 806[7] (2196) 2973[2] ◆ 4961[10] 5368[4] 5855[10] (6440) 6998[3] 7285[5]
Ajla (IRE) *Richard Hannon* 36
2 b f Exceed And Excel(AUS) —Yukon Hope (USA) (Forty Niner (USA))
4595[11]
Ajman (IRE) *Evan Williams* a70 67
5 b g Orpen(USA) —Grand Madam (Grand Lodge (USA))
584[9]
Ajool (USA) *Paul D'Arcy* a58 72
3 ch f Aljabr(USA) —Tamgeed (USA) (Woodman (USA))
1654[9] 2842[5] (3285) 4381[4] 5541[9] 5887[8] 6632[10] 6992[8] 7273[12] 7445[3] 7487[11]
Akamon *Ed Dunlop* a66 63
3 ch f Monsun(GER) —Akanta (GER) (Wolfhound (USA))
1431[9] 1934[6] 2619[6] 3238[5] 4022[9] 4763[3] (5550) 6080[4] 6527[5]
Akarlina (FR) *N Clement* 103
4 gr m Martaline—Akaralda (FR) (Akarad (FR))
(6344a) 6950a[6]
Akbabend *Mark Johnston* a88 89
4 b g Refuse To Bend(IRE) —Akdariya (IRE) (Shirley Heights)
974[4] 2739[4] 2996[9] 4147[2] 4671[3] 5070[2] 5922[8] 6715[6]
Akdarena *J S Bolger* 113
3 b f Hernando(FR) —Akdariya (IRE) (Shirley Heights)
957a[4] (2037a) 2711[5] 3467a[3] 4178a[6] 5016a[5]
Akhmatova *Gerard Butler* a98 82
3 b f Cape Cross(IRE) —Maganda (IRE) (Sadler's Wells (USA))
2998[5] (3484) (4134) ◆ 4389[2] ◆ 5096[6] 5727[2] 6199[12] 6428[3] 6701[2] 7090[2] 7243[7] (7420) (7591)
Akinoshirabe (JPN) *Luca Cumani* a98 84
3 b f Shamardal(USA) —Autumn Melody (FR) (Kingmambo (USA))
1881[4] ◆ (2463) 3298[5] ◆ (7293) ◆
Akmal *John Dunlop* 112
4 ch g Selkirk(USA) —Ayun (USA) (Swain (IRE))
1382[13] 1615[7] (2469) 3102[11] 5218[7] 6929[4]
Akrias (USA) *Luca Cumani* 36
2 b c Lemon Drop Kid(USA) —Prevail (USA) (Danzig (USA))
7303[10]
Akrivi (IRE) *C Laffon-Parias* 91
3 ch f Tobougg(IRE) —Halland Park Lass (IRE) (Spectrum (IRE))
7545a[5]
Aktia (IRE) *Luca Cumani* a64 95
3 b f Danehill Dancer(IRE) —La Gandilie (FR) (Highest Honor (FR))
(2886) ◆ (3606) 4476[3] (5008) 6199[8]
Akula (IRE) *Mark H Tompkins* 66
3 ch c Soviet Star(USA) —Danielli (IRE) (Danehill (USA))
2250[6] 5146[9] 5631[4] 6132[7]
Akzar (IRE) *John M Oxx* 101
3 ch c Selkirk(USA) —Alaiyda (USA) (Shahrastani (USA))
4769a[2]
Al Aasifh (IRE) *Saeed Bin Suroor* 104
2 b c Invincible Spirit(IRE) —Urgele (FR) (Zafonic (USA))
1728[3] (2882) ◆ 3100[9] (4097) 5347a[10] 6531[7]
Alacity (IRE) *Neville Bycroft* 64
4 b m Elusive City(USA) —Minamala (IRE) (Desert King (IRE))
3879[7] 4342[6] (4672) 5023[9] 5422[12] 6880[15]
Alaghiraar (IRE) *Emma Lavelle* a62 84
6 b g Act One—Tarsheeh (USA) (Mr Prospector (USA))
25[9]
Alaia (IRE) *John M Oxx* 81
3 b f Sinndar(IRE) —Alasana (IRE) (Darshaan)
4631a[11]
Alainmaar (FR) *Michael Jarvis* 116
4 b g Johar(USA) —Lady Elgar (IRE) (Sadler's Wells (USA))
(1474) ◆ (1911)
Alajan (IRE) *William J Fitzpatrick* a76 82
4 b g Alhaarth(IRE) —Alasha (IRE) (Barathea (IRE))
6971a[16] 7514a[8]
Alajana (GER) *J-P Carvalho* 68
2 b f Sinndar(IRE) —Arlekinada (Lycius (USA))
6407a[5]
Alajmal (USA) *Mark Johnston* 65
2 b c First Samurai(USA) —Alattrah (USA) (Shadeed (USA))
4477[6] ◆ 5857[3]

Alakhan (IRE) *Ian Williams* a76 82
4 gr g Dalakhani(IRE) —Alte Kunst (IRE) (Royal Academy (USA))
1117[5]
Al Amaan *Gary Moore* a78 72
5 b g Nayef(USA) —Siobhan (Generous (IRE))
7736[2]
Alana Banana (IRE) *John Akehurst* a53 3
3 b f Invincible Spirit(IRE) —Aquiform (Cadeaux Genereux)
3171[10] 6329[12] 6665[4] 7477[10] 7607[5]
Al Andalyya (USA) *David Lanigan* 67
2 ch f Kingmambo(USA) —Kushnarenkovo (Sadler's Wells (USA))
2330[5] 2749[4] 3386[9]
Alantina *John Jenkins* a56 38
2 b g Diktat—Maddie's A Jem (Emperor Jones (USA))
2041[2] 4208[7] 5047[14] 7469[9] 7609[6] 7723[6]
Al Aqabah (IRE) *Brian Gubby* a68 59
5 ch m Redback—Snow Eagle (IRE) (Polar Falcon (USA))
2643[4] 3330[5] 4134[11] 5541[4] 6671[4] (7168)
Al Arab (BRZ) *A Cintra Pereira* a106
5 b h Redattore(BRZ) —Ocala Sales (BRZ) (Choctaw Ridge (USA))
(412a) 798a[10]
Alareen (USA) *Saeed Bin Suroor* a64 64
2 b f Selkirk(USA) —Innuendo (IRE) (Caerleon (USA))
5066[4] ◆ 7113[4] 7312[2]
Alaskan Spirit (IRE) *Ann Duffield* 95
2 b c Kodiac—Alexander Phantom (IRE) (Soviet Star (USA))
(3665) 4332[4] (4948) 5532[2] 5880[6]
Alaska Trip (IRE) *S Botti*
2 b c Refuse To Bend(IRE) —De Puntillas (Distant Relative)
7850a[14]
Alazan (IRE) *Philip Hobbs* 92
4 ch g Dubai Destination(USA) —Marion Haste (IRE) (Ali-Royal (IRE))
(6091) 7084[2]
Alazeyab (USA) *A Al Raihe* a107 106
4 b h El Prado(IRE) —Itnab (Green Desert (USA))
517a[9] 610a[11] 710a[3] (817a)
Albaasil (IRE) *Sir Michael Stoute* 63
2 b c Dansili—Wrong Key (IRE) (Key Of Luck (USA))
3602[2]
Albacocca *Sir Mark Prescott Bt* a50 60
3 gr f With Approval(CAN) —Ballymac Girl (Niniski (USA))
(4235) ◆ 4519[4]
Albaher *Peter Grayson* a40 58
4 b g Oasis Dream—Dance Sequence (USA) (Mr Prospector (USA))
595[5] 789[8] 899[7] 6119[10] 7154[10] 7808[9] 7860[9] 7882[9] 8037[9]
Albany Rose (IRE) *Rae Guest* a66 27
2 br f Noverre(USA) —Teide Lady (Nashwan (USA))
6954[12] 7408[11] 7598[3] (7809) ◆ 7997[10]
Albaqaa *Richard Fahey* a103 106
5 ch g Medicean—Basbousate Nadia (Wolfhound (USA))
885[3] 1008[7] (1274) 1697[8] 2608[3] 3144[7] 3921[15]
Albeed *John Dunlop* 77
3 b f Tiger Hill(IRE) —Ayun (USA) (Swain (IRE))
1394[9] 3155[6] 4301[2] (5058) 5612[2] 6132[10] 6955[2]
Alben Star (IRE) *Richard Fahey* 95
2 b g Clodovil(IRE) —Secret Circle (Magic Ring (IRE))
(3498) (6139) 6719[6]
Albero Di Giuda (IRE) *Frank Sheridan* a64 61
5 b m Clodovil(IRE) —All Away (IRE) (Glow (USA))
178[3] (264) (369) 531[5] 836[6] 1534[11] 1884[12] 2184[6] 2720[3] ◆ 2791[2] 3762[8] 3979[3] 4244[2] 4342[2] 4559[4] 4895[7] 5920[4] 6025[5] 6643[5]
Albert Bridge *Ralph Beckett* 69
2 gr c Hernando(FR) —Alvarita (Selkirk (USA))
6474[7] 7178[3]
Albertine Rose *Eric Alston* a72 87
4 gr m Namid—Barathiki (Barathea (IRE))
432[9]
Albertus Pictor *Sir Mark Prescott Bt* a81
3 gr g Selkirk(USA) —Albanova (Alzao (USA))
143[5] 7451[2] (7575) ◆ 7884[3] ◆
Al Biruni (USA) *Saeed Bin Suroor* a50
2 ch c Kingmambo(USA) —Ebaraya (IRE) (Sadler's Wells (USA))
7335[7]
Alburj (USA) *D K Weld* 87
3 b g Dynaformer(USA) —Rumansy (USA) (Theatrical)
3145[11]
Al Burkaan (IRE) *Ed Dunlop* 76
2 bb g Medicean—Lone Look (Danehill (USA))
2630[3]
Alcalde *Mark Johnston* 95
4 b g Hernando(FR) —Alexandrine (IRE) (Nashwan (USA))
1282[3] 1720[8] 2276[4] 2976[2] 3456[5]
Alcohuaz (CHI) *Lennart Reuterskiold Jr* a102 108
5 b g Merchant Of Venice(USA) —Giverny (CHI) (Hussonet (USA))
2019a[2] 4122[6] (6640a) 7278a[2]
Alcomo (BRZ) *Eduardo Caramori* a111
7 b h Rainbow Corner—Amazing Singer (BRZ) (Tokatee (USA))
335a[10] 632a[12] 706a[7] 7339a[5]
Alcopop (AUS) *Jake Stephens* 118
6 b g Jeune—Iota Of Luck (AUS) (Blevic (AUS))
6947a[11]
Aldaado (IRE) *Paul Midgley* a37 78
4 b g Alhaarth(IRE) —Zobaida (IRE) (Green Desert (USA))
1426[8] 1867[5] 2451[3] 2766[6] 7055[12] 7933[6]
Al Dafa (USA) *Gordon Elliott* a54 78
3 ch g Kingmambo(USA) —Crimson Conquest (USA) (Diesis)
815[6] 1362[8] (2221) 2702[3] 3039[4] 3606[3] 6730a[12]
Aldedash (USA) *Henry Cecil* a76
2 b c Aldebaran(USA) —Hawzah (Green Desert (USA))
7723[2]
Aldermoor (USA) *Stuart Williams* 94
4 b g Tale Of The Cat(USA) —Notting Hill (BRZ) (Jules (USA))
1032[16] 2322[4] 3224[2] 3389[9] 3619[5] 5068[8] 5495[13] 6963[15] 7352[18]
Aldo *Alastair Lidderdale* a71 69
3 b c Lucky Owners(NZ) —Chaperone (Shaamit (IRE))
2755[7] 3766[4] ◆ 4661[6] 5367[9] 6212[6]
Aldorable *Roger Teal* a41 59
3 ch f Starcraft(NZ) —Aldora (Magic Ring (IRE))
1075[6] 1796[13] 2418[12] 2675[14] 3210[5] 6638[11] 7288[13] 7476[7]
Aldovrandi (IRE) *Marco Botti* a102 106
3 b c Cape Cross(IRE) —Rasana (Royal Academy (USA))
(1083) 2159a[14] 2471[3] 3460[2] ◆ 5554[4] 6147[14] 6570[7] 7593[7] 7970[5]
Aldwick Bay (IRE) *Richard Hannon* a76 77
2 b c Danehill Dancer(IRE) —Josie Doocey (IRE) (Sadler's Wells (USA))
3000[7] 3735[8] 5608[4] 6386[12] (6810) 7165[4]
Aleatricis *John Quinn* a31 88
5 bg g Kingmambo(USA) —Alba Stella (Nashwan (USA))
2031[10] 2739[3]
Alemaratiya *David Simcock* a33
2 b f Dalakhani(IRE) —Marannatha (IRE) (Pursuit Of Love)
7164[6]
Alensgrove (IRE) *Paul Midgley* a25 62
2 ch f Byron—Unicamp (Royal Academy (USA))
1510[4] ◆ 4116[4] 4650[2] 5644[5] 6071[9] 7124[12]
Aleqa *Chris Wall* 76
3 b f Oasis Dream—Vanishing Point (USA) (Caller I.D. (USA))
1966[8] 2340[4] 2834[3] ◆ 3434[3] 3816[4] (4237) 4588[4] (5205) 6197[9]
Aleron (IRE) *John Quinn* a47 69
12 b g Sadler's Wells(USA) —High Hawk (Shirley Heights)
41[6]
Alexandros *Saeed Bin Suroor* 119
5 ch h Kingmambo(USA) —Arlette (IRE) (King Of Kings (IRE))
(417a) 801a[2] 1025a[14] 2707[2] 4418a[3] 6529[5] 7234[8]
Alexs Rainbow (USA) *John Gallagher* a55 60
2 b f Silver Deputy(CAN) —Swirling Sky (USA) (Sky Classic (CAN))
1375[12] 1773[3] 2251[7] 5301[16] 6513[3] 6866[10]
Alfalevva *Mick Channon* a56 59
3 b g Piccolo—Evanesce (Lujain (USA))
3359[3] 3597[6] 4337[16]
Al Farahidi (USA) *Mark Johnston* a92 98
3 b g Seeking The Gold(USA) —Banksia (Marju (IRE))
825[2] (950) ◆ 1279[11] 1781[3] 2324[2] 2713[10] 3103[19] 4358[17] 5143[3] 5731[11] 6002[7] (6620) 6960[8]
Alfie Tupper (IRE) *Jim Boyle* a78 67
7 ch g Soviet Star(USA) —Walnut Lady (Forzando)
12[2] ◆ 83[2] 202[8] 868[2] (929)
Alfonso The Wise (IRE) *Jeremy Noseda* a82 79
3 b c Galileo(IRE) —Dalawara (IRE) (Top Ville)
1268[3] 1581[5] 5860[2] 6283[4] 6678[4] 7045[4]
Alfouzy *Michael Jarvis* a62 55
2 b f Red Ransom(USA) —Kartuzy (JPN) (Polish Precedent (USA))
6154[6] 6843[4]
Alfraamsey *Mick Channon* a46 75
2 b g Fraam—Evanesce (Lujain (USA))
1541[2] ◆ 1871[3] 2127[3] 2312[2] 2990[4] (3365) 3749[4] 4129[5] 4539[6] 4955[7] 5483[8] 6052[6] 6300[10] 6694[7]
Alfred Nobel (IRE) *A P O'Brien* a98 112
3 b c Danehill Dancer(IRE) —Glinting Desert (IRE) (Desert Prince (IRE))
2353a[3]
Alfredtheordinary *Mick Channon* a67 63
5 b g Hunting Lion(IRE) —Solmorin (Fraam)
34[4] 131[3] 390[2] 541[3] 753[2] 969[2] 1078[2] 1225[4] 1591[8] 1922[5] 2201[3] 2433[5] 2894[3] 3473[4] 3783[7] 4213[3] 5585[5]
Alfresco *John Best* a91 83
6 b g Mtoto—Maureena (IRE) (Grand Lodge (USA))
359[6] 487[7] (672) 1428[3] 1767[6] (2592) 3373[2] 3401[12] 4662[3] 5005[3] 5750[15]
Alf Tupper *Lee Smyth* a73 51
7 b g Atraf—Silvery (Petong)
289[4] 348[7] 467[4] 724[5] 868[11]
Al Furat (USA) *David Lanigan* a44 40
2 b g El Prado(IRE) —No Frills (IRE) (Darshaan)
3631[12] 3991[9] 5892[8]
Al Gillani (IRE) *Jim Boyle* a91 71
5 b g Monashee Mountain(USA) —Whisper Dawn (IRE) (Fasliyev (USA))
4930[9] 5995[6] 6798[7] 7319[8] 7554[8] 8004[5]
Algris *Sir Mark Prescott Bt* a42
2 gr g Domedriver(IRE) —Ballymac Girl (Niniski (USA))
7550[9] 7801[7] 7857[9]
Algurayn (IRE) *George Prodromou* a49 61
2 ch c Kheleyf(USA) —Majborah (IRE) (Entrepreneur)
3602[5] 3991[4] 4437[9] 5374[7] 5701[10] 7272[7] 7378[10]
Alhaban (IRE) *Ronald Harris* a101 76
4 gr g Verglas(IRE) —Anne Tudor (IRE) (Anabaa (USA))
6147[13] 6735[14] 7083[7] 7697[7] ◆ 7875[8] 7993[9]
Alhamark (IRE) *F Foresi* a67 58
7 b g Mark Of Esteem(IRE) —Alharir (USA) (Zafonic (USA))
304a[9]
Alhaprince (IRE) *F Seguin* a73
6 b h Desert Prince(IRE) —Alharir (USA) (Zafonic (USA))
559a[2]
Alhaque (USA) *Gary Moore* a70 83
4 ch g Galileo(IRE) —Safeen (USA) (Storm Cat (USA))
179[3]
Al Hazim (CAN) *J-L Pelletan* 101
2 b c Anabaa(USA) —Fantastic Women (USA) (Henbane (USA))
5799a[4]
Alhena (IRE) *Kevin Ryan* a40 54
3 b f Alhaarth(IRE) —Mail Boat (Formidable (USA))
793[5] 1201[6]
Alhoni *John Quinn* 56
2 ch f Needwood Blade—Cashel Kiss (Bishop Of Cashel)
2391[5] 2848[3] 3058[2] 3175[2] 4241[3] 4554[3] 5020[3] 5682[5]
Alhoralhora (IRE) *James Given* 40
2 b f Kodiac—Villa Nova (IRE) (Petardia)
3686[8] 4543[10] 5602[16]
Alhudhud (USA) *Kevin Morgan* a24
4 b g Swain(IRE) —Wasnah (USA) (Nijinsky (CAN))
6499[8] 7022[10]
Alianthus (GER) *J Hirschberger* 110
5 b h Hernando(FR) —Allure (GER) (Konigsstuhl (GER))
2559a[2] 3251a[5] 3934a[9] 4888a[3] (6408a) (6791a) 7266a[2]
Alice Alleyne (IRE) *Sir Michael Stoute* a79 90
3 b f Oasis Dream—Vas Y Carla (USA) (Gone West (USA))
2120[12] 3373[4] 3790[3] 4593[5] (5521) 6319[13]
Alice Cullen *Walter Swinburn* a65 63
3 b f Bertolini(USA) —Albavilla (Spectrum (IRE))
1504[3] 2004[5] 2398[9] 3268[8] 3852[6] 4775[8]
Alighieri (FR) *Mme M-C Naim* 23
2 b c Vettori(IRE) —Premiraza (FR) (Nombre Premier)
5251a[7]
Alioonagh (USA) *Nick Littmoden* a70 48
3 ch f Giant's Causeway(USA) —Alidiva (Chief Singer)
4697[5] 5395[5] 5925[5]
Alis Aquilae (IRE) *Tim Etherington* a71 83
4 b g Captain Rio—Garnock Academy (USA) (Royal Academy (USA))
(3663) 4148[6] 7093[4]
A Little Bit Dusty *Bill Turner* a64 70
2 ch g Needwood Blade—Dusty Dazzler (IRE) (Titus Livius (FR))
3035[3] 3399[2] 4208[6] 5256[11] 5701[5] 6129[8] 7296[7] 7464[4] (7520) 7629[2] 7664[4]
A Little Warm (USA) *Anthony Dutrow* a118
3 b c Stormin Fever(USA) —Minidar (USA) (Alydar (USA))
(4613a) 5544a[5]
Al Jaadl *William Jarvis* a70 69
3 b f Shamardal(USA) —Three Wishes (Sadler's Wells (USA))
1881[5] ◆ 2674[6] 3259[5] 4735[3] ◆ 5384[4] 5891[5] 6864[3] 7597[4] 7889[4]
Al Janadeirya *David Lanigan* 56
2 b f Oasis Dream—Elegant Times (IRE) (Dansili)
2088[5]
Al Joza *Clive Brittain* a64 70
3 b f Dubawi(IRE) —Avila (Ajdal (USA))
2516[5] (3479)
Al Kazeem *Roger Charlton* 87
2 b c Dubawi(IRE) —Kazeem (Darshaan)
6689[5] ◆ (7094)
Al Khaleej (IRE) *David Simcock* a101 108
6 b g Sakhee(USA) —Mood Swings (IRE) (Shirley Heights)
413a[4] 626a[3] 3146[17] 3692[13] 4473[2] ◆ (4843) 5948[5]
Al Khali (USA) *William Mott* a84 111
4 b r Medaglia D'Oro(USA) —Maya (USA) (Capote (USA))
6951a[4] 7366a[7]
Alkhataaf (USA) *John Dunlop* 83
3 b g Green Desert(USA) —Elrafa Ah (USA) (Storm Cat (USA))
1731[4] 2122[3] 2892[2] (3397) 4398[7]
Al Khatma *Marco Botti* a69
2 ch f Haafhd—Al Afreata (Bering)
7448[4] ◆ 7733[3]
Al Khawarezmi *Cecil Ross* 57
3 b g Shamardal(USA) —Mrs Ting (USA) (Lyphard (USA))
4563a[6]
Al Khimiya (IRE) *Steve Woodman* a75 70
3 b f Van Nistelrooy(USA) —Golden Flyer (FR) (Machiavellian (USA))
934[6] 1061[5] 1850[8] 2342[7] (2871) 3154[6] 3441[4] 4308[5] 5145[P]
All About Jack *Gerald Ham*
6 b g Cigar—Dorothea Sharp (IRE) (Foxhound (USA))
18[8]
All About Timing (IRE) *J T Gorman* a74 78
5 b g Val Royal(FR) —Albula (FR) (Anabaa (USA))
6730a[7]
All About You (IRE) *Paul Howling* a74 84
4 b g Mind Games—Expectation (IRE) (Night Shift (USA))
294[9] 485[5] 676[11] 853[9] 975[8] 1128[7] 1238[7] 2188[12] 2789[7] 3521[10] 7200[10] 7570[7]
All Action (USA) *Henry Cecil* 93
3 ch c Storm Cat(USA) —Wandesta (Nashwan (USA))
1386[2] ◆ 2043[4] 2507[4] (6557)
Allanit (GER) *Barney Curley* a54 103
6 b g Tiger Hill(IRE) —Astilbe (GER) (Monsun (GER))
4719[7] 5180[10] 5959[5] 7167[12]
Allannah Abu *Sir Mark Prescott Bt* a77 91
3 b f Dubawi(IRE) —Alexandrine (IRE) (Nashwan (USA))
2909[6] 3522[2] (4017) (4211) (4301) 6074[2] 6519a[6] 7374a[3]
All Annalena (IRE) *Lucy Wadham* 101
4 b m Dubai Destination(USA) —Alla Prima (IRE) (In The Wings)
1693[9] 4143[10] 4841[4] 5387[3] (6361) 7349[U]
Alleesky (FR) *W J Cargeeg*
8 b h Sky Lawyer(FR) —Vallee D'Aube (FR) (Baillamont (USA))
221a[0]
Allegorio (FR) *Tom Dascombe* a44 60
2 b c One Cool Cat(USA) —Escouades (FR) (General Assembly (USA))
4089[9] 5137a[7] 5251a[4]
Allegrissimo (IRE) *Clive Cox* a33 56
2 ch f Redback—Operissimo (Singspiel (IRE))
1879[8] 2358[5] 2638[6]
Allesson (FR) *N Clement* 86
3 ch c Ransom O'War(USA) —Anna Of Russia (GER) (Acatenango (GER))
4039a[7]
Allez Bailey (FR) *W Walton* a83 75
4 b g Orpen(USA) —Herba Buena (FR) (Fabulous Dancer (USA))
560a[3] 743a[0]
Allez Les Bleus (FR) *Mme J Bidgood* a81 74
2 b f Layman(USA) —Atlantique (IRE) (Alzao (USA))
4274a[5] 5137a[5]
Allez Leulah (IRE) *Mark Johnston* 36
2 b f Cape Cross(IRE) —Kootenay (IRE) (Selkirk (USA))
7001[8] 7325[9]
Allez Wonder (AUS) *Bart Cummings* 111
5 b m Redoute's Choice(AUS) —Luna Tudor (AUS) (Military Plume (NZ))
6
All Guns Firing (IRE) *Declan Carroll* a68 75
4 b g High Chaparral(IRE) —Lili Cup (FR) (Fabulous Dancer (USA))
18[2] 246[5] (457) 835[5] 1296[13] 6832[15] 7230[8] 7475[5]
All Honesty *William Knight* a44
2 b f Medicean—Al Joudha (FR) (Green Desert (USA))
7185[12]
Allied Powers (IRE) *Michael Bell* a70 115
5 b h Invincible Spirit(IRE) —Always Friendly (High Line)
1382[12] (1856a) (2803a) 4164a[5] 5806a[5] 6410a[7]
All In A Paddy *Ed McMahon* a50
2 ch g With Approval(CAN) —Fervent Fan (IRE) (Soviet Lad (USA))
5156[9] 5924[6] 6712[11]
All I Want *Andreas Lowe* a57 78
3 ch f King's Best(USA) —Alla Prima (IRE) (In The Wings)
5805a[8]
All Moving Parts (USA) *Alan McCabe* a63 60
3 bb g Forest Camp(USA) —Smooth Player (USA) (Bertrando (USA))
1178[7] 1630[5] 1970[2] 2633[13] 6026[9] 6287[10] 7429[2] 7633[6] 7717[7] 7787[2] 7829[3]
All On Board (IRE) *Paul Nolan* a73 66
4 b g Docksider(USA) —Thakhayr (Sadler's Wells (USA))
7514a[12]
Alloro *Alan Kirtley* a23 51
6 ch g Auction House(USA) —Minette (Bishop Of Cashel)
1424[6] (2085) 2430[4] 2765[5] 3122[13]
Allperksonice *Mark Gillard* a8
7 b m Executive Perk—Double Chimes (Efisio)
179[8]
All Right Now *Sylvester Kirk* a40
3 b g Night Shift(USA) —Cookie Cutter (IRE) (Fasliyev (USA))
236[6] 484[8] 1158[12]
All Silent (AUS) *Grahame Begg* 119
7 b g Belong To Me(USA) —Lisheenowen (AUS) (Semipalatinsk (USA))
1021a[5]
All The Evil (IRE) *Brian Meehan* a66 62
2 ch c Exceed And Excel(AUS) —Mezzanine (Sadler's Wells (USA))
3915[9] 4962[4] 5178[3] 5675[7] 6162[8] 6694[5]
All The Nines (IRE) *Deborah Sanderson* a90 86
4 b m Elusive City(USA) —Sagaing (Machiavellian (USA))
1770[2] 2113[12] (2475) (3083)
Alltherightmoves (IRE) *Eve Johnson Houghton* a49 30
2 b f Namid—Russian Countess (USA) (Nureyev (USA))
2319[13] 2958[9] 3260[4] 5581[12]
All The Winds (GER) *Shaun Lycett* a83 83
5 ch g Samum(GER) —All Our Luck (GER) (Spectrum (IRE))
2845[2] 4306[13] 5084[5] 5624[4] (7548)
Allumeuse (USA) *Andrew Balding* a59
2 rg f Rockport Harbor(USA) —Atlantic Frost (USA) (Stormy Atlantic (USA))
5892[7]
Allure D'Amour (USA) *Todd Pletcher* 90
2 ch f Giant's Causeway(USA) —Salut D'Amour (IRE) (Danehill Dancer (IRE))
7340a[13]
Alluring Star *Michael Easterby* a37 47
2 b f Gentleman's Deal(IRE) —Alustar (Emarati (USA))
6360[7] 7057[14] 7335[10]
All Ways To Rome (FR) *H-A Pantall* a80 91
6 b g Slickly(FR) —Always On Time (Lead On Time (USA))
(272a) 458a[4]
All We Know *Terry Clement* a14 26
3 b g Green Desert(USA) —Anniversary (Salse (USA))
1447[4] 6661[6]

Allybar (IRE) *Mahmood Al Zarooni* a121 112
4 ch h King's Best(USA) —Irika (USA) (Irish River (FR))
(435a) (609a) 800a[4] 1027a[3] 3068[11] 4390[3]

All You Need (IRE) *Reg Hollinshead* a56 58
6 b g Iron Mask(USA) —Choice Pickings (IRE) (Among Men (USA))
70[7] 195[2] 249[3] 264[7] 530[10] 4606[5] 4936[11] 6577[9]

Almaasah (USA) *Saeed Bin Suroor* a58
2 b f Street Cry(IRE) —Bedazzle (USA) (Dixieland Band (USA))
7311[5] ◆

Almadaa *David Marnane* a67 59
3 b g Exceed And Excel(AUS) —Masaader (USA) (Wild Again (USA))
4563a[7]

Al Madina (IRE) *Bryan Smart* 95
2 b f Noverre(USA) —Tasha's Dream (USA) (Woodman (USA))
(3316) 4356[7] 4842[4] 5245[11] 5910[2] 6737[7]

Almaguer *M Boutin* a69 71
8 b g Spectrum(IRE) —Cerita (IRE) (Wolfhound (USA))
(221a) 332a[5]

Almahaza (IRE) *Adrian Chamberlain* a72 56
6 b g Alzao(USA) —Morna's Moment (USA) (Timeless Moment (USA))
857[3] ◆ 7298[13] 7986[3] ◆

Almail (USA) *F Head* 105
4 b h Swain(IRE) —Khassah (Green Desert (USA))
6974a[7]

Almajd (IRE) *M Al Muhairi* a72 60
5 b h Marju(IRE) —Irish Valley (USA) (Irish River (FR))
628a[11] 710a[14]

Almarmooq (USA) *John Gosden* a70 73
3 bb c Dynaformer(USA) —Tuscoga (USA) (Theatrical)
5258[4] 6313[4]

Almatlaie (USA) *James Unett* a55 35
4 b m Elusive Quality(USA) —Hachiyah (IRE) (Generous (IRE))
195[10] 249[2] ◆ 523[4] 567[4] 794[7] 854[11]

Almaty Express *John Weymes* a65 54
8 b g Almaty(IRE) —Express Girl (Sylvan Express)
462[9] 525[9] 778[9] 967[3] 1234[5] 2186[6] 2213[6] 2720[4] (3357) 3979[6] 4244[10] 4516[7] 4559[5] 5362[4] 6119[3] (6206) 7018[7] 7426[3] 7859[6]

Al Mayasah (IRE) *David Simcock* 61
2 b f Shamardal(USA) —Mia Mambo (USA) (Affirmed (USA))
6825[4]

Almiqdaad *Michael Jarvis* 108
4 b g Haafhd—Etizaaz (USA) (Diesis)
1333[2] 1831[5] 3672[4] 4455[4] 5188[8] 6193[15]

Almiranta *Sir Mark Prescott Bt* a68
3 gr f Galileo(IRE) —Alvarita (Selkirk (USA))
2478[3]

Almowj *George Jones* a24 38
7 b g Fasliyev(USA) —Tiriana (Common Grounds)
7840[11]

Al Muheer (IRE) *David Nicholls* a106 110
5 b g Diktat—Dominion Rose (USA) (Spinning World (USA))
818a[11] 1662[4] 2100[11] 3069[12] 3692[16] 4358[8] ◆ 4537[6] ◆ 5247[16]

Almutaham (USA) *James Moffatt* 57
3 bb c Dynaformer(USA) —Forest Lady (USA) (Woodman (USA))
1521[4] 2248[8] 3639[3] 5437[8] 6114[12]

Al Muthanaa *William Haggas* 86
3 ch g Pivotal—Mail The Desert (IRE) (Desert Prince (IRE))
4146[2] ◆ 5065[2] (5603) 6467[3]

Alnaseem (USA) *Michael Easterby* a53 37
3 bb f Nayef(USA) —Elrehaan (Sadler's Wells (USA))
1355[12] 3333[8] 5925[6] 6454[5] 7161[4] 7429[5]

Alnitak (USA) *Bent Olsen* 97
9 br h Nureyev(USA) —Very True (USA) (Proud Truth (USA))
2195a[6] 4641a[5] 5350a[7]

Alnwick *Peter Cundell* a84 83
6 b g Kylian(USA) —Cebwob (Rock City)
500[4] 811[6] 3780[3] 4141[6] 5144[2] 5996[6]

Aloneinthestreet (USA) *Mark Johnston* a66 41
2 b g Street Cry(IRE) —Crown Of Jewels (USA) (Half A Year (USA))
5717[4] 6087[9] 7020[9]

Along The Nile *Keith Reveley* 54
8 b g Desert Prince(IRE) —Golden Fortune (Forzando)
1199[4]

Alo Pura *D Selvaratnam* a102 102
6 b m Anabaa(USA) —Rubies From Burma (USA) (Forty Niner (USA))
416a[5] 707a[3]

Alotago (IRE) *David Nicholls* a41 46
3 ch f Tagula(IRE) —Batool (USA) (Bahri (USA))
475[6] 507[3]

Alpacco (IRE) *Sandie Kjaer Nortoft* a91 100
8 b g Desert King(IRE) —Albertville (GER) (Top Ville)
(2195a) 2637a[11] 4641a[10]

Alpen Glen *John Berry* a71 97
4 ch m Halling(USA) —Anne D'Autriche (IRE) (Rainbow Quest (USA))
4603[14] 5115[11] 5611[9] 6372[12]

Alphacino *Ben Haslam* a47 66
3 b g Hunting Lion(IRE) —Fading Away (Fraam)
247[4] 702[6] 1465[6] ◆ 1753[8] 2273[5]

Alpha Delta Whisky *John Gallagher*
2 ch g Intikhab(USA) —Chispa (Imperial Frontier (USA))
5808[10]

Alpha Tauri (USA) *Frank Sheridan* a80 77
4 b g Aldebaran(USA) —Seven Moons (JPN) (Sunday Silence (USA))
1270[13] 7812[7] (7870) 7952[10]

Alphorn (FR) *Y Barberot* a69
2 b c Vatori(FR) —Vallee De Joux (FR) (Welkin (CAN))
7647a[4]

Alqaahir (USA) *Paddy Butler* a76 66
8 b h Swain(IRE) —Crafty Example (USA) (Crafty Prospector (USA))
202[10] 294[2] 367[4] (496) 695[4] 853[5] (1322) 1914[10] 2236[3] 3330[4] 3782[5] 4681[3] 5254[5] 5867[12]

Al Qasi (IRE) *A Al Raihe* a78 101
7 b h Elnadim(USA) —Delisha (Salse (USA))
515a[11] 606a[7]

Alrafid (IRE) *Gary Moore* a63 4
11 ch g Halling(USA) —Ginger Tree (USA) (Dayjur (USA))
237[2] 4202[9]

Al Rannan *Ed Dunlop* a59 61
2 ch c Nayef(USA) —Oshiponga (Barathea (IRE))
4247[12] 4747[5] 5385[5] ◆ 6059[6] 6717[5] 7004[14] 7295[9]

Al Raqi *Bryan Smart* 7
2 b c Beat Hollow—Merewood (USA) (Woodman (USA))
4899[10]

Alrasm (IRE) *Michael Jarvis* a107 105
3 b g Acclamation—New Deal (Rainbow Quest (USA))
1182[2] (1823) 2543[4] 3104[14] 6123[2] ◆ 6355[8]

Al Rayanah *George Prodromou* a59 60
7 b m Almushtarak(IRE) —Desert Bloom (FR) (Last Tycoon)
1193[6] 1507[2] 2636[7] 2966[5] 3263[5] 3690[7] 4236[3] 5159[6] 5560[2] 5704[3] 6061[4] 7199[3] 7508[3] 7917[3]

Already Basking (CAN) *Paul Cole* 49
2 ch c More Than Ready(USA) —Basking (USA) (Alydar (USA))
5546[6] 5954[6] 6795[13]

Alright Chuck *Peter Hiatt* 51
6 b g Petoski—Snowline (Bay Express)
2023[9] 2388[9] 3309[3] 3690[6] 4168[6]

Alsace Lorraine (IRE) *James Fanshawe* 107
5 b m Giant's Causeway(USA) —Mer De Corail (IRE) (Sadler's Wells (USA))
(1899) 3067[4] ◆ 4319[3] (4957) 6007a[8] 6561[10]

Alsadaa (USA) *Laura Mongan* a91 77
7 b g Kingmambo(USA) —Aljawza (USA) (Riverman (USA))
(232) (500) 7612[6]

Alsadeek (IRE) *Doug Watson* a110 73
5 b g Fasliyev(USA) —Khulan (USA) (Bahri (USA))
416a[9] 628a[9]

Alsahil (USA) *Micky Hammond* a91 76
4 ch h Diesis—Tayibah (IRE) (Sadler's Wells (USA))
175[5] 553[12] 1006[18] 3319[14] 3750[6] 5638[9] 6116[11] (6306) 6754[6] 7061[17]

Alsalwa (IRE) *Kevin Prendergast* a93 86
3 b f Nayef(USA) —Ros The Boss (IRE) (Danehill (USA))
6907a[2]

Al Samha (USA) *J Barton* a73 78
5 b h Elusive Quality(USA) —Dubian (High Line)
338a[10]

Alseraaj (USA) *Ian Williams* a53 71
5 ch m El Prado(IRE) —Barzah (IRE) (Darshaan)
347[8]

Al Shababiya (IRE) *David Simcock* a75 68
3 b f Dubawi(IRE) —Multaka (USA) (Gone West (USA))
1538[6] (2189) 3074[7] 4211[5] (5653) 6373[2] 6955[7]

Al Sharood *Mahmood Al Zarooni* 86
2 b f Shamardal(USA) —Massomah (USA) (Seeking The Gold (USA))
1901[7] (2505) 3141[18]

Alshazah *Rod Millman* a75 63
2 b g Haafhd—Mountain Law (USA) (Mountain Cat (USA))
3000[12] 5006[6] 5892[5] 6498[3]

Al Shemali *A Al Raihe* a115 121
6 ch h Medicean—Bathilde (IRE) (Generous (IRE))
517a[5] (629a) 800a[6] (1025a) 2154a[3]

Alspritza *Chris Wall*
2 b f Bahamian Bounty—Spritzeria (Bigstone (IRE))
6465[16] 7201[15]

Alston *David Arbuthnot*
2 ch c Cadeaux Genereux—Chetwynd (IRE) (Exit To Nowhere (USA))
7880[7]

Alsufooh (USA) *Derek Shaw* a40 60
3 ch f Haafhd—Dufoof (USA) (Kingmambo (USA))
1278[7] 1753[6] 2274[10] 6741[11] 7018[10] 7155[6] 7537[10]

Alta Fedelta *Vittorio Caruso* 103
4 b m Oasis Dream—Infiel (Luge)
(1419a) 1944a[2] 6765a[5] 7370a[7]

Altair Star (IRE) *P Schiergen* 99
3 b c Kris Kin(USA) —Aglow (Spinning World (USA))
3719a[7] 5671a[6] 7102a[9]

Alternative Choice (USA) *Nick Littmoden* a70 59
4 b g Grand Slam(USA) —Northern Fleet (USA) (Afleet (CAN))
612[3] ◆ 771[8] 989[8] 2230[9] 2636[8] 3278[2] (3967) (4620) (7840) ◆ 8010[2]

Altimatum (USA) *Paul Cole* a64 74
4 ch g Rahy(USA) —Aldiza (USA) (Storm Cat (USA))
1323[4] 1636[10] 1763[3] 2012[11] 2645[6] 2894[13] 3323[4] 3758[8]

Altos Reales *Michael Scudamore* a56 48
6 b m Mark Of Esteem(IRE) —Karsiyaka (IRE) (Kahyasi)
228[F] 1207[3]

Alubari *David Simcock* a73 76
3 b g Tiger Hill(IRE) —Why So Silent (Mill Reef (USA))
5832[3] ◆ 6356[3] 7042[8] (7703)

Alverta (AUS) *Paul Messara* 119
7 ch m Flying Spur(AUS) —Grilse (USA) (Rahy (USA))
( ) 3192[14] 3870[3] 4885a[7]

Alwaary (USA) *John Gosden* a75 120
4 b g Dynaformer(USA) —Tabrir (IRE) (Unfuwain (USA))
6533[4] 6925[10]

Al Wasef (USA) *Jim Goldie* 64
5 b g Danzig(USA) —Widady (USA) (Gone West (USA))
2433[3] 2859[6] 3164[8] 4644[13] 4824[10] 5213[13]

Always Baileys (IRE) *Pam Ford* a69 71
7 ch g Mister Baileys—Dubiously (USA) (Jolie Jo (USA))
5635[8] 7071[10]

Always Be True (IRE) *David Wachman* 98
4 b m Danehill Dancer(IRE) —Doctrine (Barathea (IRE))
4630a[7]

Always Dazzling *Mark Johnston* a50 66
3 ch f Cadeaux Genereux—Woodlass (USA) (Woodman (USA))
(1648) 2005[11] 2329[5] 2628[10] 3371[8] 3993[3] 4438[4] 4850[6] 5598[2] 5820[10]

Always De Man (IRE) *Mark Johnston* a49 22
2 b c Lucky Story(USA) —Yes Virginia (USA) (Roanoke (USA))
5352[8] 6712[8] 6891[12] 7197[7]

Always De One *Julia Feilden* a53 56
3 b f Fruits Of Love(USA) —Yes Virginia (USA) (Roanoke (USA))
372[2] 564[3] 762[4] 904[4] 1461[5] 1982[7] 2333[5] 2878[5] 7039[3] 7387[9] 7490[10] 7634[8]

Always Dixie (IRE) *Andrew Crook* a57 59
3 b f Lucky Story(USA) —Jerre Jo Glanville (USA) (Skywalker (USA))
216[8] 475[2] 1298[9] 1810[5] 2273[7] 2620[11] 4337[14] 4448[4] 4800[5] (4980) 5423[2] 5653[2] 5923[8] (6183) 6262[4] 7475[13]

Always Gunner *Jimmy O'Reilly* 61
4 b g Mujahid(USA) —Westcourt Ruby (Petong)
6896[2]

Always Like This (IRE) *Marco Botti* a64
2 br f Cape Cross(IRE) —Jazz Princess (IRE) (Bahhare (USA))
7682[2]

Always Roses *Chris Bealby* a36 29
3 ch f Generous(IRE) —Arcady (Slip Anchor)
5058[11]

Always The Lady *Clive Cox* 81
2 ch f Halling(USA) —Hector's Girl (Hector Protector (USA))
5829[2] ◆

Always The Sun *Patrick Leech* a59 51
4 b m Intikhab(USA) —Dane Dancing (IRE) (Danehill (USA))
211[10] 316[3] 410[10] 669[RR]

Alyarf (USA) *B W Hills* 109
4 b h Dixie Union(USA) —Tabheej (IRE) (Mujtahid (USA))
1519[5]

Alyshakeys (DEN) *Wido Neuroth* a88 90
3 ch f Sendawar(IRE) —Alamea (IRE) (Ela-Mana-Mou)
1250a[10] (4526a)

Al Zir (USA) *Saeed Bin Suroor* 111
3 b c Medaglia D'Oro(USA) —Bayou Plans (USA) (Bayou Hebert (USA))
1699[9] 2746[5] 5853[3] 6885[4]

Amanda Carter *Richard Fahey* a82 92
6 b m Tobougg(IRE) —Al Guswa (Shernazar)
224[6] 3618[6] 4389[10] 4891[9] 6050[4] 6397[7] 6984[15]

Amarak *F Head* 87
3 b g War Chant(USA) —America (IRE) (Arazi (USA))
5136a[3] 5800a[5]

Amarama (IRE) *V Bariamoglou* 86
5 br m Fraam—Amarapura (FR) (Common Grounds)
5782a[9]

Amare *T Mundry* 98
3 b f Hernando(FR) —Amore (GER) (Lando (GER))
4640a[12] 5345a[5] 6011a[11] 6763a[5]

Amarilou (FR) *C Boutin* a57 68
2 gr f Slickly(FR) —Amarige (FR) (Lesotho (USA))
5622a[10]

Amary (IRE) *John Harris* a87 82
3 b f Acclamation—Amistad (GER) (Winged Love (IRE))
(772) 945[11] 1663[8] 2815[9] 4137[8] 5524[11] 6438[4] 7539[9] 7844[7] 7956[4]

Amazing Amoray (IRE) *David Barron* 49
2 b c Tagula(IRE) —Amistad (GER) (Winged Love (IRE))
3087[11]

Amazing Beauty (GER) *M Figge* a84 85
3 ch f Bahamian Bounty—Amidala (GER) (Monsagem (USA))
5739a[8] 6409a[6] 7546a[0] 7800a[6]

Amazing Blue Sky *Ruth Carr* a50 80
4 b g Barathea(IRE) —Azure Lake (USA) (Lac Ouimet (USA))
857[8] 1013[10] 1484[10] 1925[10] 4546[2] 4781[2] 5355[2] 6050[3] 6493[6] 7541[6]

Amazing King (IRE) *Philip Kirby* a68 77
6 b g King Charlemagne(USA) —Kraemer (USA) (Lyphard (USA))
1807[8] 2277[5] (3166) (3403) 5243[2] 5868[6]

Amazingreyce *O Brennan* a45
5 gr m Rainbow High—Lightning Belle (Belfort (FR))
7338[6]

Amazing Star (IRE) *Declan Carroll* a86 81
5 b g Soviet Star(USA) —Sadika (IRE) (Bahhare (USA))
5500[3] (6366) ◆

Amazon Twilight *Brett Johnson* a69 66
2 b f Librettist(USA) —My Way (IRE) (Marju (IRE))
5488[6] 6278[7] 6651[5] (7691)

Amba *Derek Shaw* a17 18
4 ch m Hold That Tiger(USA) —Gal Gloria (PR) (Tralos (USA))
3766[8]

Amber May *Simon West*
7 b m Mark Of Esteem(IRE) —June Brilly (IRE) (Fayruz)
598[4]

Amber Mist *David Pinder* a50 58
2 b f Haafhd—Miss Adelaide (IRE) (Alzao (USA))
2963[6] 3509[8] 4029[6] 5675[9] 6209[5] 7017[10] 7301[10] 7497[10]

Amber Moon *Ann Stokell* a60 49
5 ch m Singspiel(IRE) —Merewood (USA) (Woodman (USA))
40[6] 88[5] 229[7] 347[5] 503[5] 603[3] 780[3] 786[4] 918[7] 1142[8]

Amber Ridge *Brian Baugh* a41 56
5 b g Tumbleweed Ridge—Amber Brown (Thowra (FR))
211[13] 347[11] 2299[13] 2625[9] 3502[9] 4156[13]

Amber Sunset *Dave Morris* a69 79
4 b m Monsieur Bond(IRE) —Quantum Lady (Mujadil (USA))
312[5] 615[11] (2419) 2643[5] 4236[4] (4502) 5174[4] 5499[8] (5889) 6274[7] 6558[2] ◆ 7209[9] 7421[11]

Ambrogina *Marco Botti* a66 47
3 b f Osorio(GER) —Oh Bej Oh Bej (IRE) (Distinctly North (USA))
(38) 247[3] 3761[10] 4427[8]

Am Brose (USA) *J-M Capitte* a66 75
11 ch g Nureyev(USA) —Madame Premier (USA) (Raja Baba (USA))
207a[0] 303a[8]

Ambrose Princess (IRE) *Michael Scudamore* a60 75
5 b m Chevalier(IRE) —Mark One (Mark Of Esteem (IRE))
2810[2] 3241[3] (4026) 4467[5]

A Media Luz (FR) *Y Fouin* 101
3 b f Johann Quatz(FR) —Immensement (FR) (Garde Royale)
1496a[2] 1946a[6] 3015a[6]

Ameer (IRE) *Saeed Bin Suroor* 106
3 b g Monsun(GER) —Ailette (Second Set (IRE))
1310[2] 1945a[10] 2543[5]

Ameliana *Michael Quinlan* a33
2 ch f Doyen(IRE) —Homeward (IRE) (Kris)
5701[9] 7271[10]

Amelia's Surprise *Michael Bell* 29
2 b f Ad Valorem(USA) —Salagama (IRE) (Alzao (USA))
6878[10]

Amenable (IRE) *David Nicholls* a96 94
3 b g Bertolini(USA) —Graceful Air (IRE) (Danzero (AUS))
884[6] 1376[5] 2112[5] 2762[3] 3949[5] (4288) (4684) (5606) 6142[26]

Amends (USA) *John Best* a66 63
3 b g Trippi(USA) —Day Of Atonement (USA) (Devil His Due (USA))
843[6] 1766[8] 2441[7] 3788[2] ◆ 4056[7] 4586[3] 5072[2] 6993[15] 7323[10]

Americain (USA) *A De Royer-Dupre* 125
5 b h Dynaformer(USA) —America (IRE) (Arazi (USA))
3099a[5] (4566a) (5349a) (7032a) (7291a) 7851a[3]

Americaine Cat (FR) *J-V Toux* 81
2 b f American Post—Cat's Pearl (FR) (Enrique)
5226a[7]

American Agent (USA) *Paul Cole* a58
3 b c Eavesdropper(USA) —Storm Season (USA) (Storm Cat (USA))
128[9] 276[7]

American Light *David Simcock* a76 71
4 b g Statue Of Liberty(USA) —Break Of Dawn (USA) (Mt. Livermore (USA))
208[2]

American Lion (USA) *Eoin Harty* a111
3 b c Tiznow(USA) —Storm Tide (USA) (Storm Cat (USA))
1714a[11]

American Mail (FR) *T Doumen* a67 65
4 b h American Post—Shamo (Green Desert (USA))
690a[0]

American Nizzy (FR) *Y De Nicolay* a77 100
3 b f American Post—Quietude (USA) (Woodman (USA))
1746a[5]

American Smooth *Jeremy Noseda* a62
3 b c Oasis Dream—Two Step (Mujtahid (USA))
7498[5] 7994[3]

American Spin *Luke Dace* a82 82
6 ch g Groom Dancer(USA) —Sea Vixen (Machiavellian (USA))
500[7] 688[3]

Amerthyst *Jo Crowley* a65 56
2 b f Doyen(IRE) —Seeking Utopia (Wolfhound (USA))
6804[5] (7609)

Amethyst Dawn (IRE) *Tim Easterby* 94
4 gr m Act One—A L'Aube (IRE) (Selkirk (USA))
1396[4] 1751[8] 2850[2] (3107) 3438[8] 3659[3] 4404[2] 4847[4] (5199) 5510[8] 6003[5] 6367[2] (6709) (6963) 7227[2]

Amhran (IRE) *Brian Meehan* a73
2 b c Songandaprayer(USA) —Ra Hydee (USA) (Rahy (USA))
4695[2]

Amica (SAF) *Gay Kelleway* a60
3 ch f Silvano(GER) —Light Fandango (SAF) (Cordoba I (USA))
(8006)

Amical Risks (FR) *Ollie Pears* a62 65
6 bl g Take Risks(FR) —Miss High (FR) (Concorde Jr (USA))
661[2] (813) 875[2] 1012[4] 1462[3] 2995[8] 4190[4] 4246[3] 4582[2] 4781[3] 7840[6] 8010[3]

Amico Fritz (GER) *H-A Pantall* a80 114
4 b h Fasliyev(USA) —Arctic Appeal (IRE) (Ahonoora)
(560a) (1081a) 1955a[3] (2805a) 3192[5] 4885a[15] (5573a) 6608a[19] 6949a[10]

Amicolini *Karen George*
2 ch f Bertolini(USA) —Justbetweenfriends (USA) (Diesis)
1793[15]
Amir Pasha (UAE) *Micky Hammond* a58 71
5 br g Halling(USA) —Clarinda (IRE) (Lomond (USA))
1150[3] ◆ 1424[8] 1803[3] 2533[2] 2881[2] 3122[9] 3535[3] (3600) 4174[2] (4781) 4945[3] 5215[5] 5642[7] 5681[6] 6306[5]
Amistress *Eve Johnson Houghton* a35 55
2 b f Kalanisi(IRE) —Atwirl (Pivotal)
2677[8] 3296[13] 4254[6] 5660[11] 6302[2] (6412) 6979[4]
Amitola (IRE) *David Barron* 96
3 ch f Choisir(AUS) —Emly Express (IRE) (High Estate)
2960[5] 5088[4] ◆ 6000[7] (6509) 6887[3]
Amity (IRE) *Mark Johnston* a56 64
3 ch f Nayef(USA) —Follow My Lead (Night Shift (USA))
3258[5] 3620[4] 3924[7] 4189[5] (4482) 4931[5] 5648[6]
Amjad *Simon West* 37
13 ch g Cadeaux Genereux—Babita (Habitat)
6648[13]
Amno Dancer (IRE) *Mark H Tompkins* a60 71
3 b g Namid—Special Dancer (Shareef Dancer (USA))
1608[6] 2620[9]
A Moment With You (IRE) *K Borgel* a68 70
2 b f Redback—Alexander Capetown (IRE) (Fasliyev (USA))
5063a[3]
Amor De Pobre (CHI) *J Barton* a107
5 b g Stuka(USA) —Angel De Furia (CHI) (Stagecraft)
1027a[13]
Amore Et Labore *Sylvester Kirk* a52 16
2 bg c Ivan Denisovich(IRE) —In The Highlands (Petong)
1845[11] 3767[5] 4131[14] 6542[7] 7088[8] 7471[7] 7497[8] 7691[6] 7857[5]
Amor Patrice *Les Hall* 32
2 b c Ransom O'War(USA) —Sweet Stormy (IRE) (Bluebird (USA))
7203[11]
Amosite *John Jenkins* a72 73
4 b m Central Park(IRE) —Waterline Dancer (IRE) (Danehill Dancer (IRE))
1595[2] ◆ 2123[5] 2635[9]
Amoureuse *Declan Carroll* 51
3 b f Needwood Blade—Good Health (Magic Ring (IRE))
1468[4] ◆ 2217[11] 2432[2] 3030[11] (4649) 5211[3] 5548[5] 6492[9] 6644[4]
Amour Propre *Henry Candy* 119
4 ch g Paris House—Miss Prim (Case Law)
1700[9] 3047[8] 4505[12]
Amoya (GER) *P Schiergen* 90
3 b f Royal Dragon(USA) —Arkona (GER) (Aspros (GER))
4640a[16]
Amroth *David Evans* a28 56
4 b m Rock Of Gibraltar(IRE) —Gwen John (USA) (Peintre Celebre (USA))
1756[2] 2232[3] 2337[10] 2586[8]
Amtaar *Clive Brittain* a67 53
3 b f Nayef(USA) —Emerald Fire (Pivotal)
889[2]
Amun Ra (USA) *Jeremy Gask* a33
2 bb c E Dubai(USA) —Pocketbrook (USA) (Montbrook (USA))
6308[8]
Amwell Brave *John Jenkins* a57 50
9 b g Pyramus(USA) —Passage Creeping (IRE) (Persian Bold)
539[8] 660[5]
Amwell House *John Jenkins* a53 27
5 gr g Auction House(USA) —Amwell Star (USA) (Silver Buck (USA))
656[9] 1078[5] 1437[15]
Amwell Pinot *Alan Bailey* 91
2 ch c Dubawi(IRE) —Kartajana (Shernazar)
(2312) 3049[3] 3872[2] 4135[2] 4550[3] 5392[3]
Amylyn *John Holt* a35 40
3 b f Starcraft(NZ) —Skirt Around (Deploy)
2390[7] 3116[12] 4200[6] 4765[13] 6871[11]
Amy Thorpe *O Brennan* a35 45
3 b f Danbird(AUS) —Nunthorpe (Mystiko (USA))
6896[6] 7461[4]
Anacopa (USA) *Mahmood Al Zarooni* a91 91
3 b f Arch(USA) —Awaamir (Green Desert (USA))
2401[8] 2718[8] (3266) 3995[2] 5096[2] ◆ 5329[3] 6090[5] 6430[2]
Anadolu (IRE) *Tracey Collins* 95
2 b f Statue Of Liberty(USA) —Afto (USA) (Relaunch (USA))
2828a[5] (3939a) 6734[9]
Ana Emarati (USA) *Ed Dunlop* a64
2 b c Forestry(USA) —Triple Edition (USA) (Lear Fan (USA))
7700[6] 7962[9]
Anagram *James Given* a65 47
4 b m Efisio—Saint Ann (USA) (Geiger Counter (USA))
3768[11]
Anam Chara (IRE) *Andrew Oliver* a94 94
4 gr m Soviet Star(USA) —Adelaide Pearl (USA) (Skip Away (USA))
4524a[2] 5774a[15] 6597a[9] 7816a[2]
Ana Moutabahi *Jim Best* a67 49
3 b c Anabaa(USA) —Runaway Venus (USA) (Runaway Groom (CAN))
(283) 686[4] 1307[8] 1582[10] 2906[11] 7989[6]
Ananda Kanda (USA) *Brian Ellison* a56 75
3 bb f Hero's Tribute(USA) —Roja (USA) (L'Enjoleur (CAN))
1571[6] 2033[15]
Ana Style (FR) *P Demercastel* a84 85
2 b f Anabaa Blue—European Style (FR) (Ezzoud (IRE))
7008a[8] 7276a[8]
Anasy (USA) *Gay Kelleway* a39
4 b m Gone West(USA) —Blue Moon (FR) (Lomitas)
1983[10] 2303[12]
Anawin (FR) *F Chappet* a72 69
2 b f Meshaheer(USA) —Star Dancing (Danehill Dancer (IRE))
4275a[7]
Anaya *David Bourton* a67 70
3 b f Tobougg(IRE) —Nacho Venture (FR) (Rainbow Quest (USA))
2005[12] 2379[3] 2792[6] 6165[10] 6696[3] 7161[5]
Ancailinoir (IRE) *James Given* a27
3 b f Azamour(IRE) —Lassie's Gold (USA) (Seeking The Gold (USA))
7896[8]
Ancestral Dream *Andrew Reid*
3 ch g Dubai Destination(USA) —B Beautiful (IRE) (Be My Guest (USA))
2812[9] 4258[8] 4330[9]
Anchorage Boy (USA) *Amy Weaver* a51 54
3 b g Southern Image(USA) —Alaskan Winter (USA) (Gulch (USA))
118[7] 279[4] 1422[7]
Ancien Regime (IRE) *Saeed Bin Suroor* a97 107
5 b g King's Best(USA) —Sadalsud (IRE) (Shaadi (USA))
2563[10] 4576[28] 5731[10]
Ancient Cross *Michael Easterby* a73 96
6 b g Machiavellian(USA) —Magna Graecia (IRE) (Warning)
2205[4] 2532[2] 3107[2] 3619[2] 4370[4] 5043[5] 5884[3] 6142[5] 6739[2] 7060[5]
Ancient Egypt *Annelie Larsson* a76 43
8 b g Singspiel(IRE) —Nekhbet (Artaius (USA))
2019a[6]
Ancient Greece *George Baker* a58 77
3 b g Pivotal—Classicism (USA) (A.P. Indy (USA))
1127[13] 2585[6] 3258[2] 4259[7] (4718) 5456[7]
Ancient Times (USA) *Philip Kirby* a75 23
3 bb g Smart Strike(CAN) —Histoire Sainte (FR) (Kendor (FR))
381[3] ◆ 664[5] 949[3] 1046[3] 2994[12] 3508[8] 4433[4] 5272[8] 7474[12] 7731[9] 7986[9]
Andaman Sunset *John Spearing* a47 74
5 b h Red Ransom(USA) —Miss Amanpuri (Alzao (USA))
576[6]
Anddante (IRE) *Tim Easterby* 74
2 b g Antonius Pius(USA) —Lady Digby (IRE) (Petorius)
1294[8] 2138[3] 2498[6] 3222[5] 5498[5]
Andhaar *Steve Gollings* a85 81
4 b g Bahri(USA) —Deraasaat (Nashwan (USA))
1013[5] 1398[5] 1751[4]
Andorn (GER) *Philip Kirby* a59 74
6 b h Monsun(GER) —Anthyllis (GER) (Lycius (USA))
1427[10] 2109[10] (2833) (3109) 3496[2] (4854) (5420) (5687)
Andrasta *Shaun Harris* a45 61
5 b m Bertolini(USA) —Real Popcorn (IRE) (Jareer (USA))
2791[10] 3605[6] 4047[8] 4324[11]
Andrei Roublev (USA) *D Windrif* 70
9 b g Woodman(USA) —Albertine (FR) (Irish River (FR))
742a[9]
Anduril *Declan Carroll* a52 39
9 ch g Kris—Attribute (Warning)
75[5] 199[6] 521[4] 1801[8]
Aneedah (IRE) *John Gosden* 94
2 b f Invincible Spirit(IRE) —Fairy Of The Night (IRE) (Danehill (USA))
5691[2] 6559[4] ◆ (7000) 7235[4]
Aneel *Jeremy Noseda* 85
3 b c Danehill Dancer(IRE) —Marula (IRE) (Sadler's Wells (USA))
2507[9] 5610[3] 6115[4] 6557[3] 7062[4]
Angaric (IRE) *Bryan Smart* a63 72
7 ch g Pivotal—Grannys Reluctance (IRE) (Anita's Prince)
194[2] 269[10] 464[5] 773[9] 912[4] (3900) 4605[3] (5482) 6110[10] 7468[13]
Angelena Ballerina (IRE) *Karen George* a70 79
3 ch f Indian Haven—Nom Francais (First Trump)
776[5] 978[9] 1542[7] 3765[9] (4249) 4534[6] 4988[3] 5768[2] 6212[10] 7273[11] 7543[6]
Angelica Z (ARG) *A Al Raihe* a62 39
4 br m Thunder Gulch(USA) —Nut Case (ARG) (Perfect Parade (USA))
333a[8]
Angelic Upstart (IRE) *Andrew Balding* a78 60
2 b c Singspiel(IRE) —Rada (IRE) (Danehill (USA))
6196[11] 6689[9] ◆ (7272) (7758)
Angel Of Fashion (IRE) *Peter Charalambous* a60 76
3 b f Invincible Spirit(IRE) —Vanitycase (IRE) (Editor's Note (USA))
1399[10] 1651[3] 2203[4] (2624) 3371[4] 3610[2] 4250[4] 4717[3] 5417[4] 6168[10]
Angel Of Harlem (FR) *E J O'Neill* 88
2 b f Holy Roman Emperor(IRE) —Music Express (FR) (Compton Place)
7008a[6] 7276a[3]
Angelofthenorth *Colin Teague* 53
8 b m Tomba—Dark Kristal (IRE) (Gorytus (USA))
2213[8] 3075[3] 4516[11] 5212[7] 6644[9] 6708[8] 7170[6]
Angelo Poliziano *Ann Duffield* a77 74
4 ch g Medicean—Helen Sharp (Pivotal)
1805[3] 2301[8] 2695[6] 3119[7] 3321[4] ◆ (3623) 3711[3] 5477[2] 6299[4] (6700) 7494[6] 7549[4] 7668[4]
Angel's Pursuit (IRE) *Richard Hannon* a113 111
3 ch c Pastoral Pursuits—Midnight Angel (Machiavellian (USA))
(2075) 2537[4] 2999[3] 4136[8] 7524[7] (7689) 7875[4]
Angels Quest *Tony Carroll* a56 63
5 b m Piccolo—Tamara (Marju (IRE))
282[14] 486[9] 691[2] 940[P]
Angie's Nap (USA) *Phil McEntee* a66 60
3 ch f Lion Heart(USA) —Magick Top (USA) (Topsider (USA))
72[3]
Angle Knight (USA) *Brian Meehan* 52
2 b g Arch(USA) —Safeen (USA) (Storm Cat (USA))
1597[5] 1845[8] 2493[11] 4967[5]
Angle Of Attack (IRE) *Alan Brown* a64 52
5 b g Acclamation—Travel Spot Girl (Primo Dominie)
69[3] 234[2] 569[3] 773[8] 860[2] 1068[6] 1270[7] 1569[10] 1813[8] 6464[16] 6848[8] 7132[9]
Anglezarke (IRE) *Richard Fahey* 107
4 br m Acclamation—Welsh Mist (Damister (USA))
1545[3] 2030[10] 2326[7] 5120[7] 5512[4] 5742[4] 6194[15] 6265[4] 6508[5] 7079[6] 7351[17]
Angus Newz *Michael Quinn* a64 100
7 ch m Compton Place—Hickleton Lady (IRE) (Kala Shikari)
1174[4] 1545[6] 1727[3] 2563[9] 2877[2] 3415[5] 3629[10] 4105[2] 4440[5] 4892[4] 5054[4] (5528) 5632[2] 6064[9] 6509[10] 7329[5] 7466[9]
Anhar (USA) *Saeed Bin Suroor* 103
3 bb g Kingmambo(USA) —Because (IRE) (Sadler's Wells (USA))
1702[5] (3670) 4461[10] 5217[9] 6387[U]
Anice Stellato (IRE) *Ralph Beckett* 93
4 br m Dalakhani(IRE) —Summer Spice (IRE) (Key Of Luck (USA))
2044[6] 2703[7] 5444[6]
Animate Bio (JPN) *Koji Maki* 106
3 ch f Zenno Rob Roy(JPN) —Regenbogen (JPN) (French Deputy (USA))
7460a[15]
Animator *Martin Hill* a46 75
5 b g Act One—Robsart (IRE) (Robellino (USA))
7089[8] 7410[9]
Anis Etoile *John Berry* a52 53
5 b m Helissio(FR) —French Spice (Cadeaux Genereux)
1521[7] 1847[8] 2994[6] 4915[5] 5179[11]
Anjomarba (IRE) *Brett Johnson* a69 80
3 b f Tillerman—Golden Charm (IRE) (Common Grounds)
(17) 276[2] (370) 424[3] 702[3] 826[5] (1444) 1642[3] 1994[4] (2722) 3276[6] 3685[3] 4298[3] (5075) 5897[6] 6515[7] 7518[8] (7972)
Anking (GER) *S Smrczek* 87
3 b f Konigstiger(GER) —A Winning Dream (GER) (Law Society (USA))
1250a[7]
Anmar (USA) *Mahmood Al Zarooni* a111 112
4 ch g Rahy(USA) —Ranin (Unfuwain (USA))
(436a) ◆ 799a[5] 1026a[11]
An Mhi (IRE) *Ms Joanna Morgan* a56 57
5 ch g Namid—Minstrels Folly (USA) (The Minstrel (CAN))
7200[4]
Annabelle's Charm (IRE) *Luca Cumani* a77 104
5 ch m Indian Ridge—Kylemore (IRE) (Sadler's Wells (USA))
1725[5] 2355a[3]
Annacaboe (IRE) *Dean Ivory* a49 44
3 b f Footstepsinthesand—Alexandria (IRE) (Irish River (FR))
768[11] 1165[6] 1795[7] 2398[11]
Anna Fontenail *Rod Millman* a58
2 gr f Proclamation(IRE) —Nina Fontenail (FR) (Kaldounevees (FR))
7478[7] ◆
Annalika *Bill Ratcliffe* 25
2 b f King's Best(USA) —Anapola (GER) (Polish Precedent (USA))
2041[3] 2701[7] 6092[12]
Annambo *Andrew Reid* a66 63
10 ch g In The Wings—Anna Matrushka (Mill Reef (USA))
2013[6] 2645[3] 3278[10] 3967[6] 4227[12]
Anna Salai (USA) *Mahmood Al Zarooni* 110
3 b f Dubawi(IRE) —Anna Palariva (IRE) (Caerleon (USA))
(1566a) 2370a[2] 3143[7]
Anna's Boy *Alan Berry* a36 48
3 ch g Reel Buddy(USA) —Simianna (Bluegrass Prince (IRE))
2185[9] 2438[8] 3073[6] 3666[4] 6077[7] 6966[9] 7171[11]
Annelko *Andrew Haynes* a33 55
3 b c Sulamani(IRE) —Creeking (Persian Bold)
1393[7] 2390[6] 4764[11] 5289[3] 7388[13] 7848[5]
Anne Of Kiev (IRE) *Jeremy Gask* a96 87
5 b m Oasis Dream—Top Flight Queen (Mark Of Esteem (IRE))
345[5] 578[3] 935[4] 1192[2] 1580[7] 2113[4] ◆ (2399) 2635[6] 7041[5] ◆ (7319) (7971) 8016[2]
Annes Rocket (IRE) *Jimmy Fox* a68 66
5 b h Fasliyev(USA) —Aguilas Perla (IRE) (Indian Ridge)
1350[7] 2053[6] 2456[6] 3131[10] (3338) 4308[2] 4488[9] 4870[7] 6371[5] 6713[2] (6903) 7162[7] 7377[3] 7613[6]
Annia Galeria (IRE) *Chris Dwyer* a54 55
3 b f Antonius Pius(USA) —Jay Gee (IRE) (Second Set (IRE))
111[6] 265[6] 343[3] 471[6] 619[7] 831[4] 988[5] 1187[4] 1444[3] 1774[3] 2217[3] 3372[4] 3637[5] 4720[3] 4998[4] (5152) 5417[2] 5715[5] 6206[11]
Annibale Caro *Jim Goldie* a58 66
8 b g Mtoto—Isabella Gonzaga (Rock Hopper)
2761[3] 3166[3] 4648[8]
Annie Bonita *Peter Hedger* a50 44
3 b f Umistim—Orpen Annie (IRE) (Orpen (USA))
2718[10] 7086[6] 7288[9] 7878[12]
Annie Moyles *Christopher Kellett* 24
4 b m Makbul—So Generous (Young Generation)
2003[12] 2290[10] 2600[6] 3360[10] 3910[8]
Annie The Doc *Anna Newton-Smith* a17 69
5 b m Nayef(USA) —Susquehanna Days (USA) (Chief's Crown (USA))
1768[7]
Announce *A Fabre* 104
3 ch f Selkirk(USA) —Hachita (USA) (Gone West (USA))
(4037a) (5138a) 6591a[8]
Annuity (IRE) *William Knight* a33 54
3 ch g Beat Hollow—Anna Simona (GER) (Slip Anchor)
5493[5] 5842[7] 6499[11]
A Nod And A Wink (IRE) *Shaun Lycett* a44 53
6 b m Raise A Grand(IRE) —Earth Charter (Slip Anchor)
667[5] 854[10]
Anoint *William Haggas* 81
2 b g Pivotal—Pious (Bishop Of Cashel)
7346[2]
Another Character (USA) *Mark Usher* 26
3 bb c Giant's Causeway(USA) —Mambo Halo (USA) (Southern Halo (USA))
3593[9] 4792[P]
Another Citizen (IRE) *Tim Easterby* 76
2 b g Byron—Royal Rival (IRE) (Marju (IRE))
3923[5] 4368[10] (6102)
Another For Joe *Jim Goldie* 55
2 b g Lomitas—Anna Kalinka (GER) (Lion Cavern (USA))
6569[9] 7049[5]
Another Jayjay (IRE) *M Halford* a76 75
9 br g Grand Lodge(USA) —Huraymila (IRE) (Darshaan)
7078a[13] (Dead)
Another Laugh *B W Hills* a69 76
2 ch g Where Or When(IRE) —Jane Jubilee (IRE) (Mister Baileys)
4954[3] 5657[5] 5871[2] 6634[4]
Another Magic Man (USA) *John Best* a72 74
3 bb c Chief Seattle(USA) —Georgia Anna (USA) (Stutz Blackhawk (USA))
1876[3] 2289[4] 2702[5] 2888[6] (3387) 3899[4] 4057[7] 5968[9] 6632[5] 6854[7] 7019[8] 7046[12]
Another True Story *Z Koplik* a58 67
6 b h Piccolo—Lost In Lucca (Inchinor)
4183a[3]
Another Try (IRE) *Alan Jarvis* a73 83
5 b g Spinning World(USA) —Mad Annie (USA) (Anabaa (USA))
287[4] 552[3] 767[5] 1641[4] 2331[2] 2504[6] 3037[5] 3815[2] (4836) 5238[2] (5838) 7352[12]
Another Wise Kid (IRE) *Paul Midgley* 65
2 b g Whipper(USA) —Romancing (Dr Devious (IRE))
1359[6] ◆ 2832[9] 3658[8] 6111[3]
Ans Bach *D Selvaratnam* a83 84
7 b g Green Desert(USA) —Bezzaaf (Machiavellian (USA))
438a[8]
Ansells Pride (IRE) *Bryan Smart* a73 84
7 b g King Charlemagne(USA) —Accounting (Sillery (USA))
451[2] 1202[3] 1395[5] 1628[7] 2524[2] 2850[6] 3284[9] 4796[6] 5732[8]
Ansiei (ITY) *L Polito* 107
3 b c Highest Honor(FR) —Albiatra (USA) (Dixieland Band (USA))
1945a[2] 7373a[13]
An Tadh (IRE) *G M Lyons* a93 87
7 b g Halling(USA) —Tithcar (Cadeaux Genereux)
1091a[9]
Antara (GER) *Saeed Bin Suroor* 117
4 b m Platini(GER) —Auenpracht (GER) (General Assembly (USA))
(2744) 3067[3] 4575[3] 5348a[2] 6613a[11] 7109a[2]
Antarctic Desert (IRE) *Kevin Ryan* 74
3 b g Green Desert(USA) —Arctic Silk (Selkirk (USA))
1362[10] 1868[2] 2393[3] 3148[3] 3539[U]
Antares World (USA) *Steve Specht* a102 107
3 bb f Decarchy(USA) —Alashir's World (USA) (Spinning World (USA))
5351a[4]
Anthemion (IRE) *Jean McGregor* a48 53
13 ch g Night Shift(USA) —New Sensitive (Wattlefield)
2454[9] 2670[2] 2859[4] 3147[9] 3531[8] 4644[14] 4824[8]
Anthology *Bryan Smart* 81
4 b g Haafhd—Annapurna (IRE) (Brief Truce (USA))
4652[9]
Antigone (FR) *K Borgel* a71 66
5 b m Invincible Spirit(IRE) —Courtenay (Vettori (IRE))
207a[F]
Antigua Sunrise (IRE) *Richard Fahey* 86
4 b m Noverre(USA) —Staff Approved (Teenoso (USA))
1379[8] (1629) 2096[4] 2761[2] 2976[5] 4389[5] 5217[8] (5790) 6361[3]
Antinoo (IRE) *Cristiano Davide Fais* 74
2 ch c Footstepsinthesand—Amorada (FR) (Kendor (FR))
7850a[8]
Antinori (IRE) *Mahmood Al Zarooni* a104 104
4 b g Fasliyev(USA) —Albavilla (Spectrum (IRE))
419a[3] (706a) 2710[5] 3144[11]
Antipas (IRE) *Mrs K Burke* a10 14
2 b f Antonius Pius(USA) —Miss Beverley (Beveled (USA))
2623[9] 5020[7] 6307[12]
Ant Music (IRE) *J S Moore* a66 66
3 b g Antonius Pius(USA) —Day Is Dawning (IRE) (Green Forest (USA))
9[3] 283[2] (399) 524[6] 633[4] 760[3] 977[2] ◆ 1582[7] 2049[7] 2279[7] 2414[7]
Antoella (IRE) *Philip Kirby* a39 51
3 gr f Antonius Pius(USA) —Bella Estella (GER) (Sternkoenig (IRE))
1392[13] 1989[7] 2412[9] 6336[9] 7330[5]
Anton Dolin (IRE) *John Dunlop* 59
2 ch g Danehill Dancer(IRE) —Ski For Gold (Shirley Heights)
4096[14] 4856[6] 5857[5] 7004[4] ◆
Antoniola (IRE) *Tim Easterby* 83
3 b g Antonius Pius(USA) —Balliamo (IRE) (Royal Academy (USA))
1334[5] 2110[7] 2979[6] 3451[4] 4394[10] 4647[2] 6105[12]

Antonios (IND) *S Shah* a88
5 b h Glory Of Dancer—Twin Star (IND) (Portroe (USA))
513a[6] ◆
Any Day (IRE) *M Ramadan* a67 70
3 b f Kheleyf(USA) —Daylight Ahead (IRE) (Tenby)
333a[13]
Any Given Moment (IRE) *David Simcock* a51 67
4 b g Alhaarth(IRE) —Shastri (USA) (Alleged (USA))
1283[2] (1759) 2907[9] (4223) 6132[2] 6621[3]
Any Odds (IRE) *John Ryan* 16
2 b f Traditionally(USA) —Coeur De La Mer (IRE) (Caerleon (USA))
6532[12]
Anzas (IRE) *R Gibson* a63 99
3 b c Anabaa(USA) —Lake Baino (Highest Honor (FR))
819a[7] 7959a[7]
Aoife Alainn (IRE) *M Guarnieri* 117
3 ch f Dr Fong(USA) —Divine Secret (Hernando (FR))
3495a[4] (7109a)
Apace (IRE) *Sir Michael Stoute* a71 80
2 b f Oasis Dream—Much Faster (IRE) (Fasliyev (USA))
3590[4] ◆ 4029[3] (5324) 6317[7] 6559[20]
Apache Kid (IRE) *David Simcock* a69 66
3 b g Antonius Pius(USA) —She's The Tops (Shernazar)
1450[10] 2321[4] 2909[2] 3564[2] 4235[4] 4764[4] 5625[9]
Apache Moon *Roger Curtis* a61
4 ch g Monsieur Bond(IRE) —Mighty Squaw (Indian Ridge)
147[3] 301[5] 496[13] 836[10]
Apache Ridge (IRE) *Kevin Ryan* a70 77
4 ch g Indian Ridge—Seraphina (IRE) (Pips Pride)
1929 2875 508[8] 1653[3] 1869[4] 2504[5] (2578) 3107[9] 3664[3] 4084[3] 4857[4] (5299) 6078[6] 6537[4] 7462[3] 7627[2] 7701[5] 7936[3] 8019[5]
Apache Warrior *George Moore* 70
3 b g Westerner—Aldevonie (Green Desert (USA))
5603[2] 5815[5]
Apapane (JPN) *Sakae Kunieda* 110
3 b f King Kamehameha(JPN) —Salty Bid (USA) (Salt Lake (USA))
7460a[3]
Apazine (USA) *John Gosden* a64 70
2 bb f Storm Cat(USA) —Fanzine (USA) (Cozzene (USA))
2223[5] 2505[9] 2958[3] 3386[5] 3871[8] 6162[5] 6901[6]
Apex *Martin Hill* a74 69
9 ch g Efisio—Royal Loft (Homing)
1543[7] 2024[5] 2411[4] 3079[9] 4382[4] 4620[7]
Aphrodisia *Ian Williams* a81 86
6 b m Sakhee(USA) —Aegean Dream (IRE) (Royal Academy (USA))
931[6] ◆ 1156[4] (1379) 1629[6] 4389[3] 5217[14] 6427[3] 6797[8]
Aphrodite's Rock *Gavin Blake* a34 69
4 ch m Falbrav(IRE) —Comtesse Noire (CAN) (Woodman (USA))
5959[7] 6718[10] 7561[13] 7829[11]
A P Ling *Christopher Kellett* a53 31
3 b f Antonius Pius(USA) —Spain (Polar Falcon (USA))
33[5] 279[6] 564[4] 2619[11] 7729[6]
A Pocketful Of Rye (IRE) *Jane Chapple-Hyam* a68 67
3 b f Acclamation—Rye (IRE) (Charnwood Forest (IRE))
1275[7] 1505[2] 1753[7] 2215[7] 2634[10] 3030[10] 3637[9] 4210[2] 4760[6] 5379[3] 5730[4] 6931[11] 7426[9] 7604[4] 7882[3] 8023[3]
Apollo D'Negro (IRE) *Clive Cox* a65 73
2 b c Fasliyev(USA) —Special One (Aragon)
4396[3] 6146[4] 6575[2] 6849[6]
Apotheosis *Conor Dore* a71 73
5 ch g Dr Fong(USA) —Carradale (Pursuit Of Love)
3619 467[9] 808[6]
Appalachian Trail (IRE) *Noel Wilson* a93 104
9 b g Indian Ridge—Karinski (USA) (Palace Music (USA))
862[4] 883[6] 920[3]
Apparel (IRE) *Ed Dunlop* a57
2 b f Cape Cross(IRE) —Independence (Selkirk (USA))
7198[4]
Appel Au Maitre (FR) *Wido Neuroth* 114
6 ch h Starborough—Rotina (FR) (Crystal Glitters (USA))
(1420a) 2195a[3] 5132a[2] 6017a[3]
Applaude *Richard Guest* a68 75
5 b g Royal Applause—Flossy (Efisio)
1919[13] 2388[3] 2600[3] (2859) 3131[7] 3683[4] 4082[4] (4173) (4514) 4852[3] 5213[6] 5436[10] 6037[5] 6298[8]
Appleby Fair *David Barron* 38
3 gr g Paris House—Gypsy Fair (Compton Place)
5097[5] ◆ 5514[5] 5816[6]
Appledore (IRE) *Tony Newcombe* a52 7
3 b g Act One—Memo (Groom Dancer (USA))
551[6] ◆ 815[11] 1268[14] 3788[13]
Apple Dumpling *Stuart Williams* a48
2 b f Haafhd—Divina Mia (Dowsing (USA))
7559[6] 7990[7]
Applique *H-A Pantall* 63
3 ch f Halling(USA) —Needlecraft (IRE) (Mark Of Esteem (IRE))
7545a[0]
Apprehend (AUS) *Tony Vasil* 105
5 ch g Hold That Tiger(USA) —Regal Touch (NZ) (Touching Wood (USA))
7032a[9]
Apprimus (IRE) *Marco Botti* a100 103
4 b g Trans Island—Athlumney Dancer (Shareef Dancer (USA))
1540a[7] 6239a[6] 7594[5]
Approve (IRE) *William Haggas* 112
2 b c Oasis Dream—Wyola (USA) (Sadler's Wells (USA))
1901[3] ◆ (2245) 2743[4] ◆ (3100) 3823[4] 4419a[3] (5219) 5943[2] 6531[3] 7277a[8]
Appyjack *Tony Carroll* a43 59
2 b c Royal Applause—Petrikov (IRE) (In The Wings)
3961[13] 4954[8] 5465[11] 6162[9] 7177[15] 7496[5] 7888[10]
Apres Vous (IRE) *A Fabre*
3 b c Monsun(GER) —Mandamou (GER) (Ela-Mana-Mou)
6014a[6]
Aprication (IRE) *John Weymes* 40
2 b g Captain Rio—Countess Bankes (Son Pardo)
2202[8] 2498[10] 3087[12] 4899[8] 5434[13]
April Fool *Ronald Harris* a75 79
6 ch g Pivotal—Palace Affair (Pursuit Of Love)
6581[10] (6794) 6991[3] 7255[8] 7403[4] (7472) 7679[7]
April The Second *Richard Price* a40 56
6 b g Tomba—Little Kenny (Warning)
244[9] 463[8]
Apticanti (USA) *B W Hills* 50
2 b f Aptitude(USA) —Musicanti (USA) (Nijinsky (CAN))
3871[10]
Apt Son (USA) *Francis Ennis* a5 65
5 b g Aptitude(USA) —Jungle Sun (USA) (Private Terms (USA))
7015[7]
Apurna *John Harris* 22
5 ch m Rock Of Gibraltar(IRE) —Dance Lesson (In The Wings)
2600[9] 3684[7] 4986[11]
Aqmaar *E Charpy* a87 95
6 b h Green Desert(USA) —Hureya (USA) (Woodman (USA))
438a[9]
Aquapark *Ray Craggs* a23
4 b g Shinko Forest(IRE) —Waterpark (Namaqualand (USA))
1813[10]
Aquarian Spirit *Richard Fahey* 86
3 b g Fantastic Light(USA) —Notable Lady (IRE) (Victory Note (USA))
1518[4] 2117[8] 2607[3] 2758[13] 3824[9] 4603[10] 5394[3] 5759[2] 6366[5]
Aquarius Star (IRE) *Pat Eddery* a80 83
3 ch f Danehill Dancer(IRE) —Easter Heroine (IRE) (Exactly Sharp (USA))
1260[9] 2516[2] 2893[5] 4134[3] ◆ (5266) 5972[7] 6698[6]
Aqua Vitae (IRE) *Tor Sturgis* a60 58
3 ch f Camacho—Baileys Cream (Mister Baileys)
980[5] 1275[8] 1605[4] 1971[6] 2699[4] 3030[5] 3534[8] 5379[2] 5730[6] 6865[3] 7161[14] (7885)
Aquilifer (IRE) *William Jarvis* a58 50
2 b g Holy Roman Emperor(IRE) —Sassy Bird (USA) (Storm Bird (CAN))
3459[11] 4691[5] 5523[9] 5837[10] 6129[10] 7630[3] 7888[3]
Arabella Fenella *Robert Cowell* a53 46
2 b f Araafa(IRE) —Hyde Hall (Barathea (IRE))
5466[7] 6369[3] 6658[3] 6899[5] 7404[11] 7857[3] 8012[7]
Arabian Flame (IRE) *Seamus Fahey* a48 74
4 b g King's Best(USA) —Frappe (IRE) (Inchinor)
405[9] 430[6]
Arabian Gleam *Jeremy Noseda* a89 118
6 b h Kyllachy—Gleam Of Light (IRE) (Danehill (USA))
4160a[6] 4885a[12] 5946[12]
Arabian History (USA) *Saeed Bin Suroor* 77
3 b c Kingmambo(USA) —Weekend In Seattle (USA) (Seattle Slew (USA))
6876[5]
Arabian Jewel *David Simcock* 44
3 b f Kheleyf(USA) —Lady Liesel (Bin Ajwaad (IRE))
4966[8] 5395[8]
Arabian Mirage *Brian Meehan* a102 96
4 b m Oasis Dream—Bathilde (IRE) (Generous (IRE))
1899[11] 3063[2] (3681) 4378[5] (5154) ◆ 5952[3] 6887[9] 7524[9]
Arabian Pearl (IRE) *Peter Chapple-Hyam* a70 83
4 b m Refuse To Bend(IRE) —Intercede (Pursuit Of Love)
1361[4] 1754[2] 2129[5] ◆ (2601) 2959[4] 4440[2] 5495[4] 5937[13] 6887[8] 7238[19]
Arabian Pride *David Simcock* a58 80
3 b g Cadeaux Genereux—Noble Peregrine (Lomond (USA))
6253[12]
Arabian Spirit *Richard Fahey* a96 92
5 b g Oasis Dream—Royal Flame (IRE) (Royal Academy (USA))
2142[3] 2580[7] 2937[7] 4093[3] (5407) 6105[2] 6510[3] 6960[6] 7227[3]
Arabian Star (IRE) *Mick Channon* 79
2 b c Green Desert(USA) —Kassiopeia (IRE) (Galileo (IRE))
2493[5] 2715[2] 3000[4] 3449[6] (4623) 5234[4] 5597[3] 5947[2]
Arab League (IRE) *Richard Price* 82
5 b g Dubai Destination(USA) —Johnny And Clyde (USA) (Sky Classic (CAN))
3127[2] 3588[4] 3896[4] (5011) 5788[7] 6201[11] 6516[2] 6926[29] 7061[16]
Arachnophobia (IRE) *Pat Eddery* a88 81
4 b g Redback—La Mata (IRE) (Danehill Dancer (IRE))
580[4] (779) 1219[13] 1767[10] 2472[10] 3083[10] ◆ 4354[9] 4598[4] 5142[12] 5834[5] 7091[10]
Aragall (GER) *George Baker* a63 69
5 gr g Black Sam Bellamy(IRE) —A J Bear (USA) (Slew City Slew (USA))
3520[4] (3684) 3954[2]
Arakan Ridge (IRE) *Ronald Harris*
2 b c Arakan(USA) —Vida Bandida (IRE) (Alhaarth (IRE))
2867[11]
Arakette (IRE) *Andrew Haynes* a33 27
3 b f Arakan(USA) —Etiquette (Law Society (USA))
6415[8] 6716[7] 7069[8]
Arakova (IRE) *Matthew Salaman* a44
2 b f Araafa(IRE) —Blast (USA) (Roar (USA))
3260[7] 3778[9] 4254[10]
Aramid (IRE) *B W Hills* a38 56
2 b g Aussie Rules(USA) —Bollicina (USA) (Woodman (USA))
2077[9] 2384[6] 4622[10] 6695[9]
Aranel (IRE) *M Delcher-Sanchez* a100 97
4 ch h Hawk Wing(USA) —Antinnaz (IRE) (Thatching)
339a[2] 606a[3]
Arashi *Lucinda Featherstone* a71 73
4 b g Fantastic Light(USA) —Arriving (Most Welcome)
(1520) 2583[8] 2821[9] 3203[5] 3613[4] 4070[6] 4945[2] 5591[2] 6322[7] 6754[10]
Arashone *John Weymes* 47
2 b f Araafa(IRE) —Shoshone (Be My Chief (USA))
4368[12] 4645[11] 5332[4] 6294[6]
Arasin (IRE) *P Bary* 109
3 ch c Footstepsinthesand—Arazena (USA) (Woodman (USA))
1565a[7] 5574a[3] 6219a[7]
Arazan (IRE) *John M Oxx* 94
4 b h Anabaa(USA) —Asmara (USA) (Lear Fan (USA))
6006a[4]
Arbiter (IRE) *Jarlath P Fahey* a40 53
3 b c Camacho—Rite Of Spring (Niniski (USA))
7401[11]
Arcadian Dream (IRE) *Edward Lynam* a92 76
3 b g King's Best(USA) —Mac Melody (IRE) (Entrepreneur)
3489a[9]
Arcano (IRE) *Brian Meehan* 116
3 b c Oasis Dream—Tariysha (IRE) (Daylami (IRE))
1385[3] 4569[5]
Arc De Triomphe (GER) *J Morin* a51 99
8 b h Big Shuffle(USA) —Alepha (Celestial Storm (USA))
2446a[8]
Archers Road (IRE) *David Barron* 99
3 b g Titus Livius(FR) —Somoushe (IRE) (Black Minnaloushe (USA))
(1860) 3891[8] 4541[4] 5742[7] 6364[9] 6706[2] 6918[7] ◆
Arch Event *Tony Carroll* a44
5 ch m Umistim—Arch Angel (IRE) (Archway (IRE))
290[8] 389[8]
Archie Rice (USA) *Tom Keddy* a79 90
4 b g Arch(USA) —Gold Bowl (USA) (Seeking The Gold (USA))
987[7] 1306[10] 2093[3] 2506[6] 2685[3] 2937[18] (3512) 4019[5] 4594[5] 4907[5] 5311[10] 5852[7] 6202[3] 6639[11] 7045[5] 7463[5] 7687[2] 7765[2] (7884)
Archilini *Matt Sheppard* a45 18
5 b g Bertolini(USA) —Dizzy Knight (Distant Relative)
5023[10]
Architrave *Sir Mark Prescott Bt* a73 71
3 ch g Hernando(FR) —White Palace (Shirley Heights)
2252[5] 2697[3] 3772[4]
Arch Support (USA) *Gary Contessa* 92
2 bb f Arch(USA) —Two Ninety Jones (USA) (Sir Harry Lewis (USA))
7340a[12]
Arch Walker (IRE) *Jedd O'Keeffe* 68
3 ch g Choisir(AUS) —Clunie (Inchinor)
1402[7] 1706[11] 2426[8] (3228) 4703[4] 5422[6] 6040[4] 6295[12] 7144[8]
Arc Light (IRE) *Mahmood Al Zarooni* 81
2 b c Shamardal(USA) —Banakill (FR) (Funambule (USA))
4803[5] 5263[3] 5916[7]
Arcodoro (USA) *Eric J Guillot* a90 95
4 bb h Medaglia D'Oro(USA) —Northern Gulch (USA) (Gulch (USA))
5780a[6]
Arco Felice (USA) *Keith Goldsworthy*
3 b c Giant's Causeway(USA) —Better Than Honour (USA) (Deputy Minister (CAN))
5971[15]
Arctic (IRE) *Tracey Collins* 114
3 gr c Shamardal(USA) —Shawanni (Shareef Dancer (USA))
3486a[10] 6608a[5] 7278a[8]
Arctic Cat (IRE) *Alan Swinbank* 52
2 b g Oratorio(IRE) —Ivy Queen (IRE) (Green Desert (USA))
2990[9] 3705[5]
Arctic Cosmos (USA) *John Gosden* a93 122
3 b c North Light(IRE) —Fifth Avenue Doll (USA) (Marquetry (USA))
(1460) 2079[3] (2869) ◆ 3142[2] 4456[3] ◆ (5945)
Arctic Feeling (IRE) *Richard Fahey* a85 99
2 ch g Camacho—Polar Lady (Polar Falcon (USA))
(1066) 1359[2] 3100[8] 3611[2] (4797) 5221[6] 5907[9] (6141) 6734[6]
Arctic Lynx (IRE) *John Best* a83 70
3 b g One Cool Cat(USA) —Baldemara (FR) (Sanglamore (USA))
900[4] (6060) 6739[12] 6812[8] 7093[2] (7441) ◆
Arctic Maiden *Willie Musson* a61 49
2 br f Iceman—Eglantine (IRE) (Royal Academy (USA))
6153[14] 6866[5] 7484[5]
Arctic Mirage *Michael Blanshard* 74
2 b g Iceman—Marysienka (Primo Dominie)
2819[6] 3269[4] (4323) 4783[5] 5472[3] 6690[7] 6988[10]
Arctic Myth (USA) *Brendan Duke* a62 62
2 b c North Light(IRE) —Art Critic (USA) (Fusaichi Pegasus (USA))
5924[5] 6149[9] 6653[2]
Arctic Reach *Gavin Blake* a54 43
2 b g Phoenix Reach(IRE) —Arctic Queen (Linamix (FR))
2677[9] 3209[9] 3832[12] 6333[5] 6717[10] 7124[8] 7916[8]
Arctic Wings (IRE) *Tony Carroll* a55 64
6 b g In The Wings—Arctic Hunt (IRE) (Bering)
7181[6]
Ardent *John Gosden* 84
3 b f Pivotal—Polish Romance (USA) (Danzig (USA))
4339[7] (5065) ◆ 6113[9] 6509[8]
Ardent Prince *Andrew Haynes* a52 4
7 b g Polar Prince(IRE) —Anthem Flight (USA) (Fly So Free (USA))
847[9] 976[12] 2299[11]
Ardesia (IRE) *Tina Jackson* 32
6 b g Red Sunset—Lowtown (Camden Town)
4900[9]
Ardha (USA) *H-A Pantall* 77
3 b f Elusive Quality(USA) —Dance Trick (USA) (Diesis)
6406a[4]
Ardlui (IRE) *Henry Candy* 41
2 b c Galileo(IRE) —Epping (Charnwood Forest (IRE))
7302[9]
Ardmaddy (IRE) *Gary Moore* a62 57
6 b g Generous(IRE) —Yazmin (IRE) (Green Desert (USA))
121[6] 309[2] 463[4]
Ardour (IRE) *Richard Hannon* 92
2 b c Danehill Dancer(IRE) —Lovers Walk (USA) (Diesis)
3961[2] (4384) (5234) 6156[2]
Area Fifty One *John Gosden* a44
2 b c Green Desert(USA) —Secret History (USA) (Bahri (USA))
7873[9]
Areeda (IRE) *Clive Brittain* a77 73
3 b f Refuse To Bend(IRE) —Raindancing (IRE) (Tirol)
(624) 807[3] 1018[5] 1908[7]
Areef (IRE) *Michael Bell* a51
2 b f Kheleyf(USA) —Sanpala (Sanglamore (USA))
6712[7] 7210[5]
Areeg (IRE) *Alan Berry* 47
3 b f Doyen(IRE) —Total Aloof (Groom Dancer (USA))
3728[10] 4194[5] 4651[11] 4826[7] 5046[2] 5410[8] 5600[5] 6103[17] 6490[7] 6643[9]
Areopagitica *John Flint* a55 57
2 ch f Reel Buddy(USA) —Elegia Prima (Mon Tresor)
3332[10] 5373[2] 6307[4] 6770[10] 7066[6]
Ares Flight (IRE) *P Bary* 93
2 ch f Hernando(FR) —Visions On Space (IRE) (Lure (USA))
5133a[5]
Are You The One (IRE) *Kieran Purcell* a42 75
4 b g Alhaarth(IRE) —Sand Pigeon (Lammtarra (USA))
7514a[10]
Arganil (USA) *Kevin Ryan* a113 109
5 ch g Langfuhr(CAN) —Sherona (USA) (Mr Greeley (USA))
(163) 737[4] (948) ◆ 1700[11] 2135[6] 3489a[7] 5127a[5] 5944[6] 6177[25] 7079[21] 7443[6] 7524[6] 7875[12] 7993[8]
Argaum (IRE) *Walter Swinburn* a82 76
3 ch g Medicean—Poppy Carew (IRE) (Danehill (USA))
1189[3] 4571[3] ◆ 5858[3] 6331[9] 7045[3]
Argentine (IRE) *George Foster* a84 84
6 b g Fasliyev(USA) —Teller (ARG) (Southern Halo (USA))
(74) 172[5] 4513[5] 4798[6] 5198[11] 5356[11] 5734[10] 5920[7] 6031[6] 6103[2] ◆ 6245[3] 6492[8] 6700[8] 6714[8] 7405[12]
Argocat (IRE) *Paul Cole* 87
2 b c Montjeu(IRE) —Spirit Of South (AUS) (Giant's Causeway (USA))
6149[8] 6473[4] (6883)
Aria Di Festa (IRE) *B Grizzetti* 103
4 b m Orpen(USA) —Alarme Belle (Warning)
1419a[15]
Ariel Bender *Peter Grayson* a46 44
3 gr g Needwood Blade—Wandering Stranger (Petong)
5423[12] 5990[7] 6392[10] 6931[10] 7154[6] 7498[8] 7676[4] 7807[9] 7883[6] 7973[7]
Ari Gold (IRE) *Tom Dascombe* 63
2 b g Motivator—Holy Nola (USA) (Silver Deputy (CAN))
5263[8]
Aris (IRE) *P J Prendergast* 89
2 b f Danroad(AUS) —Cumbres (FR) (Kahyasi)
6005a[3] ◆ 6784a[10]
Arisea (IRE) *James Moffatt* a48 41
7 b m Cape Cross(IRE) —Castelfranca (IRE) (Scenic)
18[3] 186[2] 331[8] 506[7] 3669[5]
Aristeia *Richard Hannon* a61 64
2 b f Invincible Spirit(IRE) —Presto Vento (Air Express (IRE))
6247[8] 6442[5] ◆ 6688[4] ◆
Aristote *P Van De Poele* a88 96
4 ch h Domedriver(IRE) —Abime (USA) (Woodman (USA))
7776a[0]
Arizona High *Andrew Balding* a54
2 ch g Phoenix Reach(IRE) —Floriana (Selkirk (USA))
7248[6]
Arizona Jewel *Henry Cecil* 73
2 b f Dansili—Rainbow Lake (Rainbow Quest (USA))
7000[3] ◆
Arizona John (IRE) *John Mackie* a88 90
5 b g Rahy(USA) —Preseli (IRE) (Caerleon (USA))
1513[13] 2133[2] 2705[5] (3239) ◆ 3889[6] 4376[3] 4943[9] 5638[5] (6185) 7084[13] 7428[4]
Arjemis *Christopher Wilson* 69
4 b m Hunting Lion(IRE) —Kungfu Kerry (Celtic Swing)
2504[9] (2698) (3076) 3551[4] 3774[4] 4285[4]

Arkas *Christopher Wilson*
4 b m Rambling Bear—Adar Jane (Ardar)
2658[9] 3179[5] 3776[8] 4484[8]
Arken Lad *Desmond Donovan* a61 67
3 b g Arakan(USA) —Object Of Vertu (FR) (Kendor (FR))
370[4] 425[6] 550[3] 851[5] 1181[2] 1347[8] 1604[6] 2234[11]
Arlequin *James Bethell* a79 98
3 b c Rock Of Gibraltar(IRE) —Fairy Dance (IRE) (Zafonic (USA))
(548a) 741a[6] 1330[6] (2033) 2742[9] 3824[3] 4570[3] 5188[5] 6355[5] 7084[8]
Armagnac Rebel *Simon Burrough*
2 b g Grape Tree Road—Charm Offensive (Zieten (USA))
3326[12]
Arma Mani (IRE) *B Grizzetti* 95
2 b c One Cool Cat(USA) —Icy Love (Pursuit Of Love)
6762a[8]
Armoise *Marco Botti* 64
2 b f Sadler's Wells(USA) —Di Moi Oui (Warning)
7057[7]
Army Of Stars (IRE) *Jamie Osborne* a81 49
4 ch h Kyllachy—Land Army (IRE) (Desert Style (IRE))
253[5] 758[3] 915[2] (1304) 1492[8] 2415[10] 3777[2] (4024) 4662[10] 5852[16] 6085[2] 6503[5] 6801[5] 7047[7]
Army Scout (USA) *J-C Rouget* a97
3 b c Giant's Causeway(USA) —Volga (IRE) (Caerleon (USA))
927a[3]
Arniecoco *Emma McWilliam* a59
5 b g Dr Fong(USA) —Groovy (Shareef Dancer (USA))
2870[13]
Arnie Guru *Michael Attwater* a48 56
3 ch g Ishiguru(USA) —Who Goes There (Wolfhound (USA))
980[8] 1873[12] 2200[7] 2753[11]
Aroundthebay *Harry Dunlop* a86 84
4 b m Diktat—Bayleaf (Efisio)
981[8] 1516[10] 2284[9] 2808[5] 3557[10]
Around The Clock (USA) *Amanda Perrett* a65
2 bb c Bernardini(USA) —Plenty Of Light (USA) (Colony Light (USA))
7559[4] ◆
Arowana (IRE) *William Haggas* a59
2 b f Kodiac—Bali Royal (King's Signet (USA))
6995[3] ◆ 7088[6] 7485[6] 7811[2] 7997[9]
Arrivaderci *Richard Whitaker* a50
2 b f Kyllachy—Arrivato (Efisio)
7392[2]
Arriva La Diva *Linda Perratt* 70
4 ch m Needwood Blade—Hillside Girl (IRE) (Tagula (IRE))
2278[2] ◆ 3064[7] (3711) 4047[4] 4516[3] ◆ (4799) 4982[7] 5502[5] (5735) 6031[12] 7175[8]
Arrivederla (IRE) *Harry Dunlop* a86 86
4 b m Acclamation—Alwiyda (USA) (Trempolino (USA))
1625[6] 2885[10] 4924[3] 5739a[11] 6366[11]
Arrow Storm (USA) *Tom Dascombe* a86
2 bb g Sunday Break(JPN) —Sugars For Nanny (USA) (Brocco (USA))
5453[10] 7603[2]
Arry's Orse *Bryan Smart* a89 72
3 b c Exceed And Excel(AUS) —Georgianna (IRE) (Petardia)
(392) ◆ 6570[9]
Artesium *Patrick Morris* a59 27
4 ch g Haafhd—Multicolour (Rainbow Quest (USA))
86[2] 403[9]
Arteus *Jane Chapple-Hyam* a96 94
4 b g Fantastic Light(USA) —Enchanted (Magic Ring (IRE))
3083[9] (3833) 5068[12] 5731[6] 6429[2] (7574) 7689[10] 7875[11]
Art Gallery *David Thompson* a42 41
6 ch g Indian Ridge—Party Doll (Be My Guest (USA))
6649[11]
Art History (IRE) *Mark Johnston* a67
2 gr c Dalakhani(IRE) —What A Picture (FR) (Peintre Celebre (USA))
8001[3]
Arthur's Edge *Bryn Palling* a105 103
6 b g Diktat—Bright Edge (Danehill Dancer (IRE))
(916) 1007[6] 2119[9]
Artica (GER) *T Mundry* 99
3 gr f Pentire—Astica (GER) (Surumu (GER))
1250a[6] 4035a[4] 6765a[8]
Artic Rose (IRE) *Stuart Williams* a68 59
2 b f Antonius Pius(USA) —Positano Princess (Tobougg (IRE))
2391[4] 2631[2] 2905[2] 3603[7]
Artimino *I Mohammed* a95 89
6 b g Medicean—Palatial (Green Desert (USA))
511a[7] 626a[11]
Art Machine (USA) *Sir Mark Prescott Bt* a65 49
3 ch f Sky Mesa(USA) —Grazia (Sharpo)
5648[5]
Art Man *James Frost* a87 58
7 b g Dansili—Persuasion (Batshoof)
1736[8] 6054[7]
Art Market (CAN) *Jo Crowley* a72 69
7 ch g Giant's Causeway(USA) —Fantasy Lake (USA) (Salt Lake (USA))
(135) 696[4] 1224[10] 3056[2] 4308[13] 5077[3]
Art Of War (SAF) *M F De Kock* a94
6 b g Kahal—Cariad (SAF) (Northern Guest (USA))
337a[7] 441a[6] 632a[6]
Artreju (GER) *Paddy Butler* a68 63
7 ch g Perugino(USA) —Art Of Easter (GER) (Dashing Blade)
685[5] 854[12] 984[10]
Art Scholar (IRE) *Gary Moore* a57 93
3 b g Pyrus(USA) —Marigold (FR) (Marju (IRE))
7689[11] 7826[7] 7964[6]
Artsu *Michael Dods* a67 83
5 b g Bahamian Bounty—War Shanty (Warrshan (USA))
1365[6] 2453[3] (3075) 3529[3] 4060[7] 5197[6]
Art Thief *Sylvester Kirk* 37
2 b g Catcher In The Rye(IRE) —Eurolink Sundance (Night Shift (USA))
7201[9]
Aruna (USA) *J E Pease* 104
3 b f Mr Greeley(USA) —Surya (USA) (Unbridled (USA))
1566a[4] 2373a[6]
Asaab (IRE) *Clive Brittain* 57
3 b f Refuse To Bend(IRE) —Shalev (GER) (Java Gold (USA))
3620[6]
As Brave As You (IRE) *Brian Ellison* a50 39
3 b g Hawk Wing(USA) —Scanno's Choice (IRE) (Pennine Walk)
717[6] 909[5] 1830[4] 1989[10]
Ascot Glory (IRE) *S Wattel* a82 103
3 b f Kheleyf(USA) —Lake Victoria (IRE) (Lake Coniston (IRE))
926a[7] 1196a[5]
As De Trebol (USA) *M Delcher-Sanchez* a92 92
4 gr h Tapit(USA) —Adelphi (USA) (Danzig (USA))
7800a[2]
Asfurah's Image *Marco Botti* a57 65
2 br f Diktat—Asfurah (USA) (Dayjur (USA))
7578[5] 7857[4]
Ashalanda (FR) *A De Royer-Dupre* 115
4 gr m Linamix(FR) —Ashaninka (USA) (Woodman (USA))
953a[7]
Ashbrittle *Ralph Beckett* 97
3 b g Rainbow Quest(USA) —Caesarea (GER) (Generous (IRE))
1735[2] ◆ (4062) 5989[3] (7061) ◆
Asheerah *Kevin Prendergast* a79 78
2 b f Shamardal(USA) —Adaala (USA) (Sahm (USA))
7256a[3]
Ashgrove Nell (IRE) *Daniel Mark Loughnane* a43 60
2 b f Ad Valorem(USA) —Pennycairn (Last Tycoon)
6161[7]
A Shin Forward (USA) *Masato Nishizono* a62 119
5 bb h Forest Wildcat(USA) —Wake Up Kiss (USA) (Cure The Blues (USA))
7853a[4]
Ashiyla (FR) *A De Royer-Dupre* 112
3 b f Rock Of Gibraltar(IRE) —Asharna (IRE) (Darshaan)
6013a[4]
Ashkalara *Stuart Howe* 71
3 b f Footstepsinthesand—Asheyana (IRE) (Soviet Star (USA))
2587[8] 3001[7] 3628[3] 4492[3] (4988) (5988) 6361[12] 6807[6]
Ashram (IRE) *Saeed Bin Suroor* a108 113
4 ch g Indian Haven—Tara's Girl (IRE) (Fayruz)
3455[6] 3893[4] (5609) 6147[6] 7083[2]
Ashva (USA) *Michael Dods* 76
2 b c Quiet American(USA) —Pondicherry (USA) (Sir Wimborne (USA))
5277[9] ◆ 6293[3]
Ask *Sir Michael Stoute* 124
7 b h Sadler's Wells(USA) —Request (Rainbow Quest (USA))
3102[5]
Askar Tau (FR) *Marcus Tregoning* a106 115
5 b g Montjeu(IRE) —Autriche (IRE) (Acatenango (GER))
1615[8] 5909[7] 6607a[5]
Askaud (IRE) *Jeremy Glover* a68 78
2 b f Iffraaj—Tarabaya (IRE) (Warning)
3517[2] (4899) 5490[2]
Ask Dan (IRE) *Michael Dods* a59 66
4 b g Refuse To Bend(IRE) —Bush Cat (USA) (Kingmambo (USA))
1270[11] 1887[7] 1928[4] 2207[11]
Ask Jack (USA) *Joseph G Murphy* a89 103
6 ch g Mt. Livermore(USA) —Moll (USA) (Criminal Type (USA))
(4463a) 5774a[5]
Ask Jenny (IRE) *Patrick Morris* a65 67
8 b m Marju(IRE) —Waltzing Matilda (Mujtahid (USA))
1166[6] 1595[10] (2278) 2396[2] 2485[3] 2751[3] 3057[6] 3356[4] 3623[5] (3722) 4209[3] 5368[7]
Ask The Butler *M Al Muhairi* 108
6 b g Dansili—Heronetta (Halling (USA))
419a[12]
Ask The Oracle *Hughie Morrison* a69
4 ch g Where Or When(IRE) —Delphic Way (Warning)
(166) 509[3]
Aslana (IRE) *P Schiergen* 103
3 b f Rock Of Gibraltar(IRE) —Alte Kunst (IRE) (Royal Academy (USA))
1715a[9] 2404a[5] (3236a) (4035a) 5139a[6] 5739a[3] 6765a[9]
Asmaa (USA) *J E Hammond* 90
3 b f Canadian Frontier(USA) —Da River Hoss (USA) (River Special (USA))
7545a[6]
A Southside Boy (GER) *Jim Goldie* 12
2 b g Samum(GER) —Anthurium (GER) (Hector Protector (USA))
6104[4] 6566[15]
Aspantau (IRE) *Marcus Tregoning* 52
2 b g Encosta De Lago(AUS) —Jabali (FR) (Shirley Heights)
2932[6]
Aspectoflove (IRE) *Saeed Bin Suroor* a103 111
4 b m Danetime(IRE) —Rose Vibert (Caerleon (USA))
439a[2] 711a[2] 1693[4] 2744[5] 3067[7] (6346) 6765a[2] (7188)
Aspectus (IRE) *Jamie Osborne* a101 112
7 ch h Spectrum(IRE) —Anna Thea (IRE) (Turfkonig (GER))
415a[11] 610a[4] 2651[6] 3956[2] 4537[8] 4816[10] 5950[11] 6312[12] 6877[12]
Aspirational (IRE) *Bryn Palling* a58 52
4 ch g Rainbow Quest(USA) —Londonnetdotcom (IRE) (Night Shift (USA))
1755[9] 2023[5] 2360[3] 3128[7] 4992[4] 5585[10]
Aspro Mavro (IRE) *John Gosden* a77 84
4 b g Spartacus(IRE) —Alexia Reveuse (IRE) (Dr Devious (IRE))
1011[3] (1132) 1780[5]
Asraab (IRE) *Saeed Bin Suroor* 95
3 b c Oasis Dream—Alexander Queen (IRE) (King's Best (USA))
4963[2] ◆
Assahab (GER) *U Stech* 96
7 ch h Lando(GER) —Akasha (GER) (Dashing Blade)
2806a[7]
Assam (GER) *Carmen Bocskai* a75 35
8 b h Big Shuffle(USA) —Arbarine (GER) (Aspros (GER))
207a[10]
Asserdoun (FR) *R Crepon* a44 52
10 ch g Cardoun(FR) —Assermara (FR) (Assert)
281a[9]
Assertion *Mel Brittain* 52
2 gr c Proclamation(IRE) —Cantina (Tina's Pet)
2936[10] 4392[5] 4941[16] 6674[17]
Asset (IRE) *Saeed Bin Suroor* a107 119
7 b g Marju(IRE) —Snow Peak (Arazi (USA))
437a[3] 710a[2] 1021a[10] 3460[5] 4126[5] 5609[6]
Asterales *Willie Musson* a57 49
3 b f Royal Applause—Shalimar (IRE) (Indian Ridge)
1278[14] 1620[10] 2478[9] 3171[9] 4134[10] 5923[6] 6574[6] 7156[12] 7387[4]
Asterisk *John Berry* a55 69
3 b f Fantastic Light(USA) —Sydney Star (Machiavellian (USA))
6655[3] 7288[6] 7579[5] 7968[5]
Asterrlini (IRE) *Clive Brittain* a60 53
3 b f Refuse To Bend(IRE) —Alithini (IRE) (Darshaan)
758[5] 864[6]
Aston Boy *Michael Blanshard* a48 22
5 ch g Dr Fong(USA) —Hectic Tina (Hector Protector (USA))
2361[10] 2676[11] 2955[12] 4676[13] 4990[8]
Astonishment (IRE) *F Nass* a76 96
3 b c Desert Style(IRE) —Lucky Norwegian (IRE) (Almutawakel)
414a[12] 510a[8] 819a[6]
Astound *David Evans* a74 70
3 ch f Pivotal—Sensation (Soviet Star (USA))
4679[3] 5209[4] 5445[4] 6122[4] 6668[3] (6937) 6993[7]
Astral Flower *Sir Michael Stoute* a74 77
3 b f Kalanisi(IRE) —Arum Lily (USA) (Woodman (USA))
2011[2] 2704[3] 3789[2] 4493[2] 5380[2] 6079[2] 6499[5] 7282[3]
Astrodiva *Mark H Tompkins* a58 77
4 b m Where Or When(IRE) —Astromancer (USA) (Silver Hawk (USA))
6832[7] 7101[7] 7323[7] 7475[11] 7887[2] 8010[8]
Astrodonna *Mark H Tompkins* a75 78
5 ch m Carnival Dancer—Mega (IRE) (Petardia)
1430[5] 2024[10] 2580[4] 3854[7] 4236[5] 4763[9] 5391[9] (6062) (6479) 7063[5] 7474[8] 7890[8] 8008[8]
Astroleo *Mark H Tompkins* a54 54
4 ch g Groom Dancer(USA) —Astrolove (IRE) (Bigstone (IRE))
1283[4] 2302[2] 2907[7] 4765[5] 7398[9]
Astrolibra *Mark H Tompkins* a65 61
6 b m Sakhee(USA) —Optimistic (Reprimand)
1012[8]
Astrologue *K Borgel* a47 57
5 b g Anabaa(USA) —Chantereine (USA) (Trempolino (USA))
559a[9]
Astromagick *Mark H Tompkins* 55
2 b f Rainbow Quest(USA) —Astrocharm (IRE) (Charnwood Forest (IRE))
6154[11] 6618[4]
Astromoon *Mark H Tompkins* 65
3 b f Beat Hollow—Astromancer (USA) (Silver Hawk (USA))
1607[4] 4545[9] 5666[7]
Astronomer's Dream *Edward Vaughan* a62 63
3 ch f Galileo(IRE) —Danehill's Dream (IRE) (Danehill (USA))
279[3] 308[5] 2909[5] 3444[15]
Astronomical (IRE) *Reg Hollinshead* a69 71
8 b g Mister Baileys—Charm The Stars (Roi Danzig (USA))
3360[4] 3617[2] (4070) 5019[10] 5549[8] 6213[8] 6538[13]
Astrophysical Jet *Ed McMahon* 114
3 b f Dubawi(IRE) —Common Knowledge (Rainbow Quest (USA))
1918[7] 2326[2] 2978[6] (3828) 4505[3] ◆ (5569a) (6194) ◆
Astrovenus *Mark H Tompkins* a9 55
3 ch f Tobougg(IRE) —Astrolove (IRE) (Bigstone (IRE))
1777[4] 4557[9] 5173[4] 6272[3] 7388[11]
Atabaas Allure (FR) *Chris Gordon* a82 85
4 b m Alhaarth(IRE) —Atabaa (FR) (Anabaa (USA))
4055[7]
Atacama Sunrise *George Prodromou* a72 70
4 b m Desert Sun—Top Of The Morning (Keen)
83[5] 202[4] 261[4] 623[3] 675[3] 814[2] 929[3] 1208[3] 1318[5] (1606) 2013[5] 2477[2] 3179[3] 3787[5] 6452[9] 7190[10] (7445) 7561[8] 7833[7] 7919[5]
Atakora (IRE) *Amanda Perrett* a57 58
3 b f King's Best(USA) —Orinoco (IRE) (Darshaan)
1261[9] 2780[4]
Atasari (IRE) *J S Bolger* 109
3 b f Whipper(USA) —Azra (IRE) (Danehill (USA))
1312[8] 1952a[2] 2370a[12] 2912a[8] 4463a[17]
Ateeb *Ed Dunlop* a79 69
4 b g Red Ransom(USA) —Design Perfection (USA) (Diesis)
5367[3] 5959[2] 6331[3] 6797[5] 7044[9]
At First Sight (GER) *Frau E Mader* 85
3 b f Azamour(IRE) —Aberdeen (GER) (Polish Precedent (USA))
6238a[6]
At First Sight (IRE) *A P O'Brien* 117
3 ch c Galileo(IRE) —Healing Music (FR) (Bering)
1414a[2] 1951a[3] 2746[2] 3142[4] 3491a[5]
Athaakeel (IRE) *Ronald Harris* a69 47
4 b m Almutawakel—Asaafeer (USA) (Dayjur (USA))
851[8] 968[10] 1072[7] 1239[4] 1457[3] 1928[10] 2409[5] (3762) 4255[7] 4431[10] 5698[11] 5920[9] 6330[5] 7336[3] 7468[14] 7519[6] ◆ 7640[10] (8019)
Athania (IRE) *J S O Arthur* a62 69
4 ch m Fath(USA) —Xania (Mujtahid (USA))
3748a[RR]
Athboy Auction *Hugh Collingridge* a53 52
5 b m Auction House(USA) —Thabeh (Shareef Dancer (USA))
(847) ◆ 940[3] 1170[14] 2298[6] 3115[5] 3526[8] 4071[6] 4715[11] 5271[8] 6061[6] 7768[9] 8023[9]
Athenian Garden (USA) *Henry Cecil* a69 70
3 b f Royal Academy(USA) —Webee (USA) (Kingmambo (USA))
1278[4] 1619[6]
Athwaab *Michael Quinlan* a76 73
3 b f Cadeaux Genereux—Ahdaaf (USA) (Bahri (USA))
111[2] 222[3] 277[3] (577) 901[9] (1057) (1187) 1511[4] 2046[6] 5652[7] 6057[12] 6523[6] 6858[8]
Atia *Jonathan Portman* a34 67
2 b f Royal Applause—Chrysalis (Soviet Star (USA))
1577[13] 2223[6] 2951[3] 4872[9] 6052[8]
Atila Sher Danon (GER) *W Hickst* a80 91
4 b h Sholokhov(IRE) —Art Of Easter (GER) (Dashing Blade)
441a[10] 632a[10]
Atlaal (USA) *Michael Jarvis* 81
3 ch g Speightstown(USA) —Deputy Maiden (USA) (Deputy Minister (CAN))
1913[15]
Atlantic Beach *David O'Meara* 82
5 ch g Kyllachy—Amused (Prince Sabo)
1366[3] ◆ 1924[11] 2144[2] 2982[6] (3321) (3660) 4118[9] 5069[11] 5480[9] 5735[2] 5999[6] 6140[2] 7169[6] 7281[3]
Atlantic Cycle (IRE) *K J Condon* a81 93
3 ch f Stormy Atlantic(USA) —Cycle Of Life (USA) (Spinning World (USA))
1091a[7] 1545[5]
Atlantic Dancer (GER) *A Schennach* a34 86
7 b g Starborough—Arousal (GER) (Goofalik (USA))
461a[8]
Atlantic Sport (USA) *P Schiergen* 111
5 b h Machiavellian(USA) —Shy Lady (FR) (Kaldoun (FR))
1251a[9] 2559a[10] 4122[5] 5573a[5]
Atlantic Story (USA) *Michael Easterby* a113 96
8 bb g Stormy Atlantic(USA) —Story Book Girl (USA) (Siberian Express (USA))
108[2] ◆ (204) 2940[10] 3446[13] 3919[9] 4413[10] 7482[6] 7593[9] 7875[4]
Atlantic Tiger (IRE) *Mark Johnston* a87 91
3 b g Tiger Hill(IRE) —Summertime Legacy (Darshaan)
484[3] ◆ 618[2] ◆ (734) (1452) ◆ 2252[3] 3878[2] 4815[8] 6352[5] 7173[4] 7553[5]
Atlantis Star *Saeed Bin Suroor* a108 102
3 b c Cape Cross(IRE) —Ladeena (IRE) (Dubai Millennium)
(6123) 6761a[3]
Atlas Shrugged (IRE) *Clive Cox* 45
2 bb c Red Ransom(USA) —Kalambara (IRE) (Bluebird (USA))
7099[8]
Atomic Rain (USA) *Saeed Bin Suroor* a107
4 b h Smart Strike(CAN) —Paradise Pond (USA) (Cox's Ridge (USA))
607a[12]
Atoned (USA) *Neil J Howard* a102 96
5 bb h Repent(USA) —Amidst (USA) (Icecapade (USA))
7339a[8]
Atraaf (IRE) *Marcus Tregoning* a81
2 b c Intikhab(USA) —Kismah (Machiavellian (USA))
(7558) ◆
Atta Boy Roy (USA) *Valorie Lund* a118 104
5 b h Tribunal(USA) —Irish Toast (USA) (Synastry (USA))
7361a[10]
Attainable *Jim Old* a62 17
4 bb m Kalanisi(IRE) —Balleta (USA) (Lyphard (USA))
1160[10] 3294[11] 4327[14]
Attracted To You (IRE) *Richard Hannon* 86
2 b f Hurricane Run(IRE) —Haute Volta (FR) (Grape Tree Road)
4471[6] ◆ (5078)
Attrition *Andrew Reid* 50
3 b g Selkirk(USA) —Barsine (IRE) (Danehill (USA))
2548[9] 2903[5] 4222[5] 6643[3] 7170[8]
At Wits End *James Toller* a75 80
4 b g Orpen(USA) —Pagan Princess (Mujtahid (USA))
1780[4] 2934[7] 3782[4] 5375[6] 6288[8]
Auburn Lady *Alan Brown* 57
2 ch f Tobougg(IRE) —Carati (Selkirk (USA))
4650[7] 4940[6] 5509[9] 5998[8] 6294[11] 6891[14]
Auburn Place *Derek Shaw* a47 51
3 ch f Compton Place—Barboukh (Night Shift (USA))
985[6] 1278[13] 3291[13] 7882[10]
Audacious *Sir Michael Stoute* 87
2 b g Motivator—Flash Of Gold (Darshaan)
4803[11] 5878[4] 6676[4]

Audacity Of Hope *Jeremy Noseda* 104
3 b c Red Ransom(USA) —Aliena (IRE) (Grand Lodge (USA))
1311[4] 1699[17] 3103[6] 4642a[2]

Audemar (IRE) *Edward Vaughan* a97 90
4 ch g Exceed And Excel(AUS) —Bathe In Light (USA) (Sunshine Forever (USA))
(231) ◆ 553[7] 635[3] ◆ 1006[8] 1617[5] 2124[2] 2708[12] 6312[2] 7243[4] 7970[4]

Auden (USA) *Mahmood Al Zarooni* 81
2 b c Librettist(USA) —Moyesii (USA) (Diesis)
5047[2] 5651[3] (6504)

Auendon (GER) *Uwe Ostmann* 73
3 b g Doyen(IRE) —Auengunst (GER) (Waky Nao)
(6487a)

Aughcarra (IRE) *Harry Chisman* a58 54
5 b g High Chaparral(IRE) —Pearly Brooks (Efisio)
4327[8] 4990[6] 5625[10] 5963[14]

Augustus John (IRE) *Roy Brotherton* a78 73
7 gr g Danehill(USA) —Rizerie (FR) (Highest Honor (FR))
(293) (529) 888[3] 996[3]

Aujiang (GER) *P Schiergen* 92
3 b f Royal Dragon(USA) —Anna Maria (GER) (Night Shift (USA))
5739a[7]

Auld Arty (FR) *Jo Crowley* a77 72
4 bb g Dansili—Provisoire (USA) (Gone West (USA))
552[9] 802[7]

Auld Burns *Richard Hannon* 94
2 gr c Pastoral Pursuits—Crackle (Anshan)
(3472) 4355[4] 6200[6] 6560[6]

Aultcharn (FR) *Brian Meehan* a77 79
3 b g Kyllachy—Nuit Sans Fin (FR) (Lead On Time (USA))
1450[2] 4699[7] 5150[2] 6701[6] 6904[13]

A. U. Miner (USA) *Clark Hanna* a106
5 bb h Mineshaft(USA) —Clerical Etoile (ARG) (The Watcher (USA))
7339a[3]

Aureate *Brian Forsey* a95 82
6 ch g Jade Robbery(USA) —Anne D'Autriche (IRE) (Rainbow Quest (USA))
526[3] 756[7] 974[8] 1357[10] 2182[9]

Aurivorous *Jonjo O'Neill* a7 58
2 ch f Reel Buddy(USA) —Vax Rapide (Sharpo)
1972[12] 2687[6] 3029[3] 5720[12]

Aurora Lights *Richard Fahey* a30
3 ch f Fantastic Light(USA) —Sweet Revival (Claude Monet (USA))
7461[5] 7563[9]

Aurora Sky (IRE) *John Akehurst* a79 75
4 gr m Hawk Wing(USA) —To The Skies (USA) (Sky Classic (CAN))
1530[7] 2236[7] 2643[10] 2966[4] 3781[4] 4295[5] 5072[3] (5457) (5959) 6427[6] 6846[10] (7253) 7548[3] (7778)

Aurorian (IRE) *Richard Hannon* a83 91
4 b g Fantastic Light(USA) —Aurelia (Rainbow Quest (USA))
(1579) 1783[2] 2747[10] 3633[3] 4334[6] 4933[2] 5788[4] 6423[4]

Aussie Blue (IRE) *Richard Whitaker* a75 73
6 b g Bahamian Bounty—Luanshya (First Trump)
1426[15] 1628[4] 1926[18] 2382[9] 4173[3] 4485[6] 4804[8] (5271) 5767[6] (6116) 6580[2] 6935[6] 7128[12]

Aussie Dollar (IRE) *Andrew Balding* a68 49
2 b c Dansili—Spectacular Show (IRE) (Spectrum (IRE))
7152[5] 8000[4]

Australia Day (IRE) *Paul Webber* a98 106
7 gr g Key Of Luck(USA) —Atalina (FR) (Linamix (FR))
2710[10] 3194[4] 3633[2] 4455[5] 5307[9]

Austria (GER) *R Crepon* 66
5 b m Second Set(IRE) —Aica (GER) (Big Shuffle (USA))
273a[0]

Auteur (USA) *Barbara J Minshall* 96
4 b g El Prado(IRE) —Camella (USA) (Housebuster (USA))
6237a[11]

Authentic Act (IRE) *Martin Todhunter* 59
6 ch g Pivotal—All In All (Halling (USA))
1801[3] 6187[13]

Autocracy *Eric Alston* a69 63
3 b g Green Desert(USA) —Imperial Bailiwick (IRE) (Imperial Frontier (USA))
1347[7] 1784[5] 2442[4] 3030[12] 3205[7] 4649[8]

Auto Mac *Neville Bycroft* 38
2 b g Auction House(USA) —Charlottevalentina (IRE) (Perugino (USA))
6047[9]

Autonomy (IND) *B Chenoy* a87 95
5 b g Razeen(USA) —All Heart (IND) (Steinbeck (USA))
517a[7] 820a[11]

Autumn Blades (IRE) *Alan Bailey* a104 103
5 ch g Daggers Drawn(USA) —September Tide (IRE) (Thatching)
71[3] (278) (286) 358[3] 537[2] 635[7] 885[6] 944[2] 1085[9] 1662[5] (1857) 2311[3] 2539[8] 2971[10] 3869[18] 6564[9] 7522[2] 7574[3] 7593[8] 7689[7]

Autumn Harvest *Geoffrey Harker* 78
6 b g Beat Hollow—Welsh Autumn (Tenby)
3750[4] 4196[7] 4671[4] 5786[9]

Autumn Morning (IRE) *David Evans* a25 49
4 b m Danetime(IRE) —Soviet Maid (IRE) (Soviet Star (USA))
3983[7] 4434[13]

Autumn Riches *Mark Johnston* 93
3 ch g Pivotal—Harvest Festival (IRE) (Dubai Millennium)
4028[3] ◆ (4414) 4828[7] (5540) 6096[5] 6447[9] 6749[16]

Ava Doll *John Jenkins* a12 18
3 b f Statue Of Liberty(USA) —Foolish Gift (FR) (Barathea (IRE))
2909[12]

Avalon Bay *Pat Eddery* a62 26
2 b c Avonbridge—Feeling Blue (Missed Flight)
2867[6] 3785[6] 4228[4] 4696[2] 5365[6] 5720[5] 6271[11] 6867[2] 7313[5]

Avaricious *Chris Wall* 40
3 b f Avonbridge—First Tarf (Primo Dominie)
1685[8] 2297[7] 3765[11]

Avatar Day (USA) *R Menichetti* 99
2 b c Afleet Alex(USA) —Investagain (USA) (Salt Lake (USA))
3253a[2]

Ave *Roger L Attfield* a88 109
4 b m Danehill Dancer(IRE) —Anna Amalia (IRE) (In The Wings)
5320a[8] 7460a[16]

Avec Moi *Christine Dunnett* a48 48
3 b f Reset(AUS) —Pardon Moi (First Trump)
1605[9] 4969[15] 5395[10] 5645[4] 6285[10]

Aven Mac (IRE) *Neville Bycroft* 48
4 ch m Indian Haven—Anamara (IRE) (Fairy King (USA))
18[11]

Avenuesnalleyways (IRE) *Ralph Beckett* a89 96
3 b g Bertolini(USA) —Princess Mood (GER) (Muhtarram (USA))
(24) (1453) ◆ 1658[5] 2170[3] (3876) 5143[6]

Averoo *Michael Squance* a61 82
5 br g Averti(IRE) —Roo (Rudimentary (USA))
(1924) 2462[10] (2719) (2982) ◆ 3216[7] 4536[20] 5082[7]

Averroes (IRE) *Clive Cox* 97
3 ch c Galileo(IRE) —Shapely (USA) (Alleged (USA))
1502[3] ◆ 1823[2] 2226[8] 4573[4] 5511[3] 6654[2]

Avertis *Stef Higgins* a84 84
5 b g Averti(IRE) —Double Stake (USA) (Kokand (USA))
837[12] 1634[6] (4057) 5834[7]

Avertor *Roger Charlton* a87 87
4 b g Oasis Dream—Avessia (Averti (IRE))
1349[9] 4090[3] 5495[2] 5966[5] 6776[10] 7212[3] 7488[6]

Avertuoso *Bryan Smart* a77 75
6 b g Averti(IRE) —First Musical (First Trump)
1988[15] 4047[6] 4737[3] 5760[8] (6490) (6643) 6880[5] 7169[8]

Aviate *Henry Cecil* a80 111
3 b f Dansili—Emplane (USA) (Irish River (FR))
(1613) (2029) 2711[6] 6007a[5] 6561[5] 7160a[4]

Avid Kale *Marco Botti* a72 72
2 gr c Keltos(FR) —Lake Diva (Dockside (USA))
4741[6] 5156[2] ◆ 5724[4] 7151[2] 7379[2]

Aviso (GER) *Barney Curley* a76 75
6 b g Tertullian(USA) —Akasma (GER) (Windwurf (GER))
587[8] 941[10] (1130) 3412[9] (4108) 5050[6] 5561[5] 6289[5] (6581) 7421[10]

Avitus *Micky Hammond* 63
4 gr g Monsieur Bond(IRE) —Top (Shirley Heights)
1920[6] 2421[10] 2625[2] 3177[2] 3552[3] (4120) 4411[10] 4708[2] 5515[2] 6297[6]

Avoir Choisi (IRE) *Noel Wilson* a74 68
4 ch g Choisir(AUS) —Dolara (IRE) (Dolphin Street (FR))
1467[9] 1717[9]

Avon Castle *Ronald Harris* a60 41
3 b f Avonbridge—Castellina (USA) (Danzig Connection (USA))
147[5] 425[8] 5113[6] 6454[8]

Avon Causeway *Milton Bradley* a18 39
2 ch f Avonbridge—Giant Leap (Giant's Causeway (USA))
4095[17] 4678[11] 5029[14] 6769[13]

Avoncharm *Mel Brittain* 26
2 b f Avonbridge—Be My Charm (Polish Precedent (USA))
4451[11]

Avoncreek *Brian Baugh* a43 55
6 b g Tipsy Creek(USA) —Avondale Girl (IRE) (Case Law)
531[4] 694[8] 2381[7] 2647[5] 2854[4] 3254[7] 3556[7] 4487[8] 5169[3] 5579[8] 5906[4] 6189[6] 6494[7]

Avon Ferry *Andrew Haynes*
3 b f Avonbridge—I'm Connected (USA) (Palmister (USA))
7069[12]

Avongate *Ronald Harris* a55 78
3 b g Avonbridge—Palacegate Episode (IRE) (Drumalis)
1140[7] 1584[9] 2320[4] 2648[10] 3154[10] 4284[6] 5764[9]

Avon Lady *James Fanshawe* a81 81
3 b f Avonbridge—Delightful Rhythm (USA) (Diesis)
2652[6] 3268[5] (4236) 4847[3] 5396[2] (5896)

Avonlini *Brian Baugh* a33 55
4 b m Bertolini(USA) —Avondale Girl (IRE) (Case Law)
270[8] 532[6] 693[9] 1923[11] 2297[6] 2535[3] 3026[7] 3526[3] 4155[5] 4486[9] 5175[2] 5586[2] 6025[12]

Avonmore Star *Richard Hannon* a75 93
2 b c Avonbridge—Pooka's Daughter (IRE) (Eagle Eyed (USA))
1764[3] ◆ (2319) 3476[2] (3913) 4458[5] 4903[2] 6477[2] 6636[5]

Avon River *Richard Hannon* a93 85
3 ch g Avonbridge—Night Kiss (FR) (Night Shift (USA))
1018[8] 1453[4] 1761[3] (2398) (2644) 3334[10] 7318[6] 7574[5] 7965[2]

Avon Rock *Alastair Lidderdale* a33 55
3 b g Avonbridge—Big Pink (IRE) (Bigstone (IRE))
4430[12] 4861[6] 5379[8] 5469[11] 5765[7]

Avonrose *Mark Johnston* a77 86
3 b f Avonbridge—Loveleaves (Polar Falcon (USA))
1487[4] 1718[5] 2110[4] 3063[7] 3508[3] 3973[2] (4322) 4603[3] 4950[3] 5737[5] 6709[7] 7725[4] (7844)

Avonside (IRE) *John Bridger* a56 61
3 ch g Avonbridge—Loch Fyne (Ardkinglass)
1057[7] 1259[2] 1870[6] 2682[11] 3561[8]

Avon Supreme *Gay Kelleway* a55
2 ch f Avonbridge—Fredora (Inchinor)
7517[5] 7686[3]

Avontuur (FR) *Ruth Carr* a55 76
8 ch g Kabool—Ipoh (FR) (Funambule (USA))
867[7] 1365[2] 1509[8] 1802[2] 2206[4] 5424[5] 5601[4] 5760[2] 6310[8]

Avonvalley *Peter Grayson* a65 75
3 b f Avonbridge—Piper's Ash (USA) (Royal Academy (USA))
1140[5] 1546[6] 2052[8] 2688[5] (3966) 4761[3] 5557[5] 6656[4] (6996) 7148[2] (7281) 7442[10] 7719[12] 7784[4] 8037[8]

Avow (USA) *John Bridger* a68 70
3 b g Mingun(USA) —Knoosh (USA) (Storm Bird (CAN))
122[6] 233[2] 343[4] 550[4] (826) 932[7] 1057[3] (1237) 1449[5] 3567[6] 4398[8] 5027[11] 5182[7] 5557[9] 5898[2] 6456[7] 6741[6] 6996[7] 7290[7] 7989[7]

Avrilo *Malcolm Saunders* a58 75
4 ch m Piccolo—Arctic High (Polar Falcon (USA))
1799[3] 2021[8] (2229) 2332[2] (2485) (2751) 2954[4] 3299[2] 3440[2] 3818[8]

Await The Dawn (USA) *A P O'Brien* 114
3 b c Giant's Causeway(USA) —Valentine Band (USA) (Dixieland Band (USA))
(5772a) ◆

Award Ceremony (IRE) *D K Weld* a96 98
5 b g Green Desert(USA) —Ripple Of Pride (IRE) (Sadler's Wells (USA))
6597a[8] 6907a[8]

Awatuki (IRE) *Jim Boyle* a87 61
7 b g Distant Music(USA) —Itkan (IRE) (Marju (IRE))
25[12] 200[4] 314[3] 395[7] 588[9]

Awe Inspiring (IRE) *A P O'Brien* a75 92
3 b f Montjeu(IRE) —Nuriva (USA) (Woodman (USA))
2711[10] 3101[8] 4178a[5] 4631a[6]

Awesome Act (USA) *Jeremy Noseda* a106 114
3 ch c Awesome Again(CAN) —Houdini's Honey (USA) (Mr Prospector (USA))
(824a) 1097a[3] 1714a[19]

Awesome Asset (USA) *Jeremy Noseda* 39
2 b f Awesome Again(CAN) —Authorized Staff (USA) (Relaunch (USA))
3411[10] 7034[8]

Awesome Feather (USA) *Stanley I Gold* a117
2 b f Awesome Of Course(USA) —Precious Feather (USA) (Gone West (USA))
(7342a)

Awesome Gem (USA) *Craig Dollase* a116 114
7 ch g Awesome Again(CAN) —Piano (USA) (Pentelicus (USA))
5577a[10] 7339a[6]

Awinnersgame (IRE) *Jeremy Noseda* a93 108
4 b g Kyllachy—Polish Descent (IRE) (Danehill (USA))
416a[6] 626a[10]

A Word Apart (IRE) *D K Weld* 86
2 b g Desert Style(IRE) —Lady Luck (IRE) (Kris)
5975a[9]

Awsaal *John Dunlop* 103
3 b c Nayef(USA) —Design Perfection (USA) (Diesis)
1314[3] (1735) (2323) ◆

Awzaan *Mark Johnston* 118
3 br c Alhaarth(IRE) —Nufoos (Zafonic (USA))
1699[15] 5741[3] 6147[3] 6529[9]

Axiom *Luca Cumani* a81 110
6 ch g Pivotal—Exhibitor (USA) (Royal Academy (USA))
336a[10] 626a[13] 3069[28] 3869[14] 5068[5] ◆ (5516) 6349[18] 7348[18]

Ayaarah (IRE) *Michael Jarvis* a68 43
2 b f Cape Cross(IRE) —La Jwaab (Alhaarth (IRE))
4595[9] 6248[4]

Ayam Zainah *Mick Channon* a59 50
3 ch f Pivotal—Ya Hajar (Lycius (USA))
1355[10] 2180[10] 2718[13] 3788[8] 4733[4] 5326[9] 5730[2] 5926[4] 6847[2] 7161[2]

Aye Aye Digby (IRE) *Jim Boyle* 98
5 b g Captain Rio—Jane Digby (IRE) (Magical Strike (USA))
1903[15] 3578[4] 4536[11] 4995[9] 5551[4]

Ayun Tara (FR) *X Nakkachdji* a100 105
3 gr f Martaline—Annee De La Femme (IRE) (Common Grounds)
514a[2] 2158a[8] 2801a[9]

Azaday (IRE) *Chris Wall* a75 76
3 b f Azamour(IRE) —Generous Lady (Generous (IRE))
1643[5] 1970[3] 4212[2] ◆ 4552[2] ◆ 5654[2] ◆ 6290[4] 6856[7]

Azameera (IRE) *Clive Cox* 78
2 b f Azamour(IRE) —Claustra (FR) (Green Desert (USA))
(5691) 6156[7]

Azarra (IRE) *C Lerner* 79
2 b f Green Tune(USA) —I C Cindy (USA) (Gallapiat (USA))
5252a[10]

Azimuth (USA) *Jeremy Noseda* a83 76
3 bb c Giant's Causeway(USA) —Zoe Montana (USA) (Seeking The Gold (USA))
1769[3] 2335[2] 3038[4] 4107[3] 5026[3]

Azizi *William Haggas* a100 99
3 b g Haafhd—Harayir (USA) (Gulch (USA))
1083[2] 1703[12] 3103[25]

Azlaa *Richard Hannon* a74 70
2 b f Dubawi(IRE) —Veiled Beauty (USA) (Royal Academy (USA))
3590[8] 5633[4] 6155[9] (6695) ◆ 6902[6] 7486[2] 7758[2]

Azlak (USA) *Clive Brittain* a80 88
3 ch c Shamardal(USA) —Nasaieb (IRE) (Fairy King (USA))
698[2] (805) (1189) 2254[13] (2515) (2816)

Azmeel *John Gosden* 111
3 b c Azamour(IRE) —Best Side (IRE) (King's Best (USA))
(1498) (1858) 2746[10] 4420a[9]

Aznavour (IRE) *John M Oxx* a58 89
3 b g Azamour(IRE) —Cadence (Cadeaux Genereux)
1786a[6] 4630a[11] 6597a[13]

Azrael *Alan McCabe* 91
2 b c Makbul—Fontaine Lady (Millfontaine)
3433[4] 4318[3] (4856) (6156) 7095[6]

A Z Warrior (USA) *Bob Baffert* a112
2 bb f Bernardini(USA) —Carson Jen (USA) (Carson City (USA))
7342a[12]

Azygous *G P Kelly* a70 55
7 ch g Foxhound(USA) —Flag (Selkirk (USA))
2849[2] 3287[10] 3977[U] 4672[11] 4942[13] 5513[13] 6073[8] 7148[11]

Azzoom (IRE) *Clive Brittain* a55 78
2 br f Cadeaux Genereux—Prancing (Prince Sabo)
4103[2] 5719[7]

Azzurra Du Caprio (IRE) *Ben Haslam* 79
2 ch f Captain Rio—Dunbrody (FR) (Jeune Homme (USA))
1749[3] (1964) 3596[2] 4242[5] 5187[2] (5476) 5882[6] 6619[8]

Baahama (IRE) *A Fabre* 106
3 b f Anabaa(USA) —Silver Rain (FR) (Rainbow Quest (USA))
1946a[4] (6551a) 7160a[5]

Baba Ghanoush *Michael Attwater* a45 11
8 ch m Zaha(CAN) —Vrennan (Suave Dancer (USA))
847[7]

Bab Al Bahrain (USA) *R Bouresly* a101 90
6 br h Kingmambo(USA) —Honfleur (IRE) (Sadler's Wells (USA))
630a[11] 710a[13]

Bab Al Salam (USA) *Saeed Bin Suroor* a108 99
4 b h Seeking The Gold(USA) —Encandiladora (ARG) (Equalize (USA))
335a[6] 513a[12]

Babayigit (TUR) *Z B Cinar* a89
6 b h Royal Abjar(USA) —Prima Facie (Primo Dominie)
5781a[7]

Babe Maccool (IRE) *David Pipe* a43 66
8 ch g Giant's Causeway(USA) —Kotama (USA) (Shahrastani (USA))
6699[7]

Babich Bay (IRE) *F J Brennan* 61
2 b g Captain Rio—Ibtihal (IRE) (Hamas (IRE))
1136[6] 5372[3] 5936[5]

Babilu *Dai Burchell* a65 65
5 ch m Lomitas—Creeking (Persian Bold)
1768[2] 5272[6] 5722[8] 6744[8]

Ba Bonanza *Mick Channon*
3 b g High Chaparral(IRE) —In Your Dreams (IRE) (Suave Dancer (USA))
803[P]

Babycakes (IRE) *Michael Bell* a90 91
3 b f Marju(IRE) —Dark Rosaleen (IRE) (Darshaan)
979[5] 1537[2] (1982) 2219[2] 2843[3] (5972) 6361[6] 7420[3]

Baby Dottie *Pat Phelan* a77 68
3 ch f Dr Fong(USA) —Auntie Dot Com (Tagula (IRE))
2416[3] 2871[4] (7440) 7719[9]

Baby Driver *Howard Johnson* 60
2 gr g Proclamation(IRE) —Renee (Wolfhound (USA))
2654[12] 3528[2] 4240[5] 6027[2]

Baby Is Here (IRE) *Dominic Ffrench Davis* a20 46
4 br m Namid—Attymon Lill (IRE) (Marju (IRE))
7[13]

Baby Judge (IRE) *Michael Chapman* a53 58
3 ch g Captain Rio—Darling Clementine (Lion Cavern (USA))
17[5] 43[3] 188[4] 574[7] 782[7] 1469[4] 1605[8] 2132[11] 2385[8] 2617[5] 2876[6] 3682[7] 3972[4] 4761[2] 7132[11] 7906[9]

Babyla *A Fabre* a79 97
4 gr m Linamix(FR) —Labour Of Love (USA) (Silver Deputy (CAN))
3099a[6] 7457a[3]

Babylonian *Mark Johnston* a48 70
3 b f Shamardal(USA) —Evil Empire (GER) (Acatenango (GER))
856[5]

Baby Queen (IRE) *Brian Baugh* a40 68
4 b m Royal Applause—Kissing Time (Lugana Beach)
2310[9] 2751[DSQ] 3687[7] 3908[2] 4041[6] 4672[10]

Baby Rock *Chris Wall* 60
5 b g Selkirk(USA) —Vanishing Point (USA) (Caller I.D. (USA))
2875[7] 3510[2] 4234[12]

Baby Strange *Derek Shaw* a91 98
6 gr g Superior Premium—The Manx Touch (IRE) (Petardia)
1349[7] (2992) 4085[5] 4685[6] 4832[6] 5154[2] 5702[5] (5884) 6175[20] 6539[5] 6799[4] 7060[17] 7289[5]

Bacarrita (FR) *L A Urbano-Grajales* a80 80
5 b m Marathon(USA) —Congostena (IRE) (Dr Devious (IRE))
560a[0] 690a[10]

Bachelor Knight (IRE) *Ollie Pears* a60 66
2 b g Bachelor Duke(USA) —Labetera (Lujain (USA))
1331[3] ◆ 1646[3] (2139) (3598) 3925[5] 4429[4] 5269[3] 5602[7] 5921[6] 6891[6] (7224) 7666[4] 7785[4] 7931[3]

Backbord (GER) *Lucy Wadham* 71
8 b g Platini(GER) —Bukowina (GER) (Windwurf (GER))
2938[7] 4467[20]

Back For Tea (IRE) *Tom Dascombe* a50 46
2 b g Redback—Jasmine Pearl (IRE) (King Of Kings (IRE))
3459[9] 3785[8] 4247[8] 4890[6] 5483[6]

Back Hunting (USA) *Gianluca Bietolini* 98
3 b c Put It Back(USA) —Huntingland (USA) (Dove Hunt (USA))
1418a[3] 7372a[11]

Back On *Patrick Leech* a39 46
3 b g Reset(AUS) —Teal Flower (Pivotal)
581[5] 655[7] 1449[6]

Backtalk (USA) *Thomas Amoss* a104
3 ch c Smarty Jones(USA) —Apasionata Sonata (USA) (Affirmed (USA))
1714a[20]

Back To Paris (IRE) *Philip Kirby* a49 78
8 b g Lil's Boy(USA) —Alisco (IRE) (Shalford (IRE))
19[8] 1570[5] 1801[4] 2142[6] *3967[10]* 4170[2] 4481[4] 5364[8]

Bad Cigar (IRE) *F Costello* a30 64
2 b c Big Bad Bob(IRE) —Corridora Slew (ARG) (Corridor Key (USA))
4175a[11]

Baddam *Ian Williams* 94
8 b g Mujahid(USA) —Aude La Belle (FR) (Ela-Mana-Mou)
1798[5] 3195[12] 4467[8]

Badeel (USA) *Saeed Bin Suroor* a77 74
2 b c El Prado(IRE) —Hasheema (IRE) (Darshaan)
6036[2] *(6843)*

Badguy (IRE) *O Valachovic* 73
3 b c Spartacus(IRE) —Bound To Glitter (USA) (Boundary (USA))
4420a[10]

Badiat Alzaman (IRE) *Ed Dunlop* a95 90
4 b m Zamindar(USA) —Fair Weather (IRE) (Marju (IRE))
1725[8] 1899[13] *5702[8]*

Ba Dreamflight *Hughie Morrison* a52 58
5 b g Noverre(USA) —Aunt Tate (Tate Gallery (USA))
898[5]

Badster (IRE) *Nicholas Gifford* a40
5 b g Ashley Park(IRE) —Petale De Rose (IRE) (Roselier (FR))
803[7]

Bagamoyo *James Fanshawe* a91 105
3 b c Acclamation—Queen Of Silk (IRE) (Brief Truce (USA))
1701[2] ◆ 2545[7] 3791[2] 4536[7] 5088[6]

Bagber *P Monteith* a82 82
4 b g Diktat—Torcross (Vettori (IRE))
6650[8] (7053) 7228[6]

Baggsy (IRE) *Julia Feilden* a52 41
3 b f Statue Of Liberty(USA) —Nisibis (In The Wings)
206[4] 589[6] 2333[6] 2724[4] 3113[6] 7003[4] *7381[4] 7933[7]*

Bagutta Sun *Barry Leavy* a31 76
4 b m Diktat—Valhalla Moon (USA) (Sadler's Wells (USA))
1333[U] 1519[7] 2314[5] 2703[6] 3203[7] 3388[4] 3960[10] 6328[7] *6578[10]*

Bahama Baileys *Chris Dwyer* 50
5 ch g Bahamian Bounty—Baileys Silver (USA) (Marlin (USA))
1129[9] 1443[3] ◆ 1884[7] 1958[3] 2808[7] 3993[6] 4435[5]

Bahamian Ballet *Ed McMahon* a70 78
8 ch g Bahamian Bounty—Plie (Superlative)
3114[5] (3687) 4452[7] 5356[8] 6073[11] *6700[3]*

Bahamian Bolt *Robin Bastiman* a30 36
3 ch g Bahamian Bounty—Feeling Blue (Missed Flight)
699[8] 1425[7]

Bahamian Box *T Larriviere* a85 95
3 b c Bahamian Bounty—Bible Box (IRE) (Bin Ajwaad (IRE))
741a[4]

Bahamian Jazz (IRE) *Robin Bastiman* 74
3 ch g Bahamian Bounty—Nandy's Cavern (Lion Cavern (USA))
1425[5] 1991[7] 3091[2] 3808[4] 4714[9] 5214[4] 6040[7] 6897[14]

Bahamian Kid *Reg Hollinshead* a76 76
5 b g Bahamian Bounty—Barachois Princess (USA) (Barachois (CAN))
214[2] 431[4] 750[7] 924[7] 1276[3] *4910[7]* 5906[9] *6164[9] 6713[7] 6898[3] 7195[5]* ◆ 7501[10] 7701[3]

Bahamian Lad *Reg Hollinshead* a87 82
5 b g Bahamian Bounty—Danehill Princess (IRE) (Danehill (USA))
905[5] 1192[9] 1653[6] 2113[6] (2646) 2982[8] 3389[2] 3898[5] (4558) 5290[3] *5647[11] 6799[11]*

Bahamian Music (IRE) *Richard Fahey* a86 86
3 b f Bahamian Bounty—Strings (Unfuwain (USA))
2110[8] 2737[6] 3208[4] 3806[4] 4520[2] (5056) 5529[U] 6361[4] *7253[2]*

Bahamian Sunset *Richard Fahey* 79
2 b f Bahamian Bounty—Jalissa (Mister Baileys)
2623[3] (3945) 4578[4] 5476[5] 6325[9]

Bahati (IRE) *Jonathan Portman* 99
3 ch f Intikhab(USA) —Dawn Chorus (IRE) (Mukaddamah (USA))
1384[8] 2120[5] 2565[2] 3375[2] 4145[8] 5114[7] ◆ 5694[5] 6346[4] 7097[2]

Bahatoo *X Thomas-Demeaulte* 45
3 b c Bahamian Bounty—And Toto Too (Averti (IRE))
450a[7]

Bahceli (IRE) *Richard Hannon* 88
2 gr g Mujadil(USA) —Miss Shaan (FR) (Darshaan)
(1626) (2032) 4097[4] 5245[9] 5880[19]

Bahiano (IRE) *Clive Brittain* a76 81
9 ch g Barathea(IRE) —Trystero (Shareef Dancer (USA))
908[9]

Bahkov (IRE) *Andy Turnell* a59 63
4 ch g Bahamian Bounty—Petrikov (IRE) (In The Wings)
234[8] 353[12] 1437[11] 1771[4] 2441[4]

Bahri Beat (IRE) *John Norton*
2 b g Bahri(USA) —Optimal Quest (IRE) (Septieme Ciel (USA))
7471[8]

Bahri Sheen (IRE) *John Best* a71 67
2 b c Bahri(USA) —Kama's Wheel (Magic Ring (IRE))
4871[2] 5277[8] *5865[5]* 6988[11]

Baibars (USA) *Gerard Butler* a51 75
3 bb c Gone West(USA) —Mombasa (USA) (Dynaformer (USA))
2507[5] 2994[11] 3754[5] *4230[8] 5958[10]*

Bailadeira *Tim Etherington* 33
2 bb f Intikhab(USA) —Sainte Gig (FR) (Saint Cyrien (FR))
7057[16] 7345 [10]

Baila Me (GER) *Saeed Bin Suroor* a106 105
5 b m Samum(GER) —Bandeira (GER) (Law Society (USA))
(7189)

Baileys Agincourt *Mark Johnston*
2 ch g Beat Hollow—Numberonedance (USA) (Trempolino (USA))
7302[13]

Baileys Cacao (IRE) *Richard Hannon* 100
4 b m Invincible Spirit(IRE) —Baileys Cream (Mister Baileys)
2387[4] 4137[5]

Baileys Moneypenny *James Given* a57 75
2 b f Monsieur Bond(IRE) —Baileys Silver (USA) (Marlin (USA))
5156[8] 5761[4] 6293[2] 6920[11] *7379[7] 7609[10]*

Baileys Vision *Chris Dwyer* a56 68
3 b f Kyllachy—Southern Psychic (USA) (Alwasmi (USA))
1048[9] 2042[11] 2566[13] 2962[12] *3759[6]*

Baine (FR) *F Rohaut* 114
3 b f Country Reel(USA) —Benzolina (IRE) (Second Empire (IRE))
2158a[2]

Baisse *Henry Cecil* a70
2 b f High Chaparral(IRE) —Best Side (IRE) (King's Best (USA))
7733[2] ◆

Bajan Bear *Michael Blanshard* 67
2 ch g Compton Place—Bajan Rose (Dashing Blade)
2839[16] 3362[3] 4116[2] 5099[4] 6465[7]

Bajan Bullet *David Evans* a64 71
2 gr f With Approval(CAN) —Khaladja (IRE) (Akarad (FR))
1043[3] ◆ 1173[2] 1256[4] 2007[2] 2358 [6] 4615[8] 5389[8] 5630[3] 6129[9]

Bajan Flash *David Nicholls* 73
3 gr g Bahamian Bounty—Molly Moon (IRE) (Primo Dominie)
1100[3] ◆ 1464[3] 1706[10] 2700[8] 5064[9] 5411[2] 6832[9]

Bajan Pride *Paul Midgley* a67 71
6 b g Selkirk(USA) —Spry (Suave Dancer (USA))
7[3] 169[5] (248) 354[4] 467[8] 541[7] 918[9] 1148[2] (1507) 1576[2] 1922[4] 2337[2] (3025) (3610) 3973[4] 4411[11] 4514[2] 4985[7] 5241[3] 5596[10]

Bajan Tryst (USA) *Kevin Ryan* a103 105
4 bb g Speightstown(USA) —Garden Secrets (USA) (Time For A Change (USA))
(350) 528[2] 887[9] 2745[18] *3261[2]* 4180a[3] 4510[2] *(5127a)* 5944[2] *7073a[5]*

Ba Jetstream *F Jordan* a36 52
3 b g Monsieur Bond(IRE) —Merch Rhyd-Y-Grug (Sabrehill (USA))
387[5] 581[9] 870[6] 1259[7]

Bakongo (IRE) *Michael Bell* a78 73
3 b f Cape Cross(IRE) —Badawi (USA) (Diesis)
1356[4] ◆ *(1538) 2479[5]* 4098[8] 5056[7] *6122[3] (6718) 7042[11]*

Bakoura *John Dunlop* a68 80
2 b f Green Desert(USA) —Bunood (IRE) (Sadler's Wells (USA))
2505[5] 3392[2] 4299[2] 5882[5] *7185[4]*

Balance On Time (IRE) *Linda Perratt* 45
4 b m Imperial Ballet(IRE) —Balance The Books (Elmaamul (USA))
6033[9] 6242[8] 7171[8] 7229[8]

Balatoma (IRE) *Marcus Tregoning* a65 74
3 b f Mr Greeley(USA) —Honfleur (IRE) (Sadler's Wells (USA))
1355[9] 2050[6] 2974[5] *4698[6]* (5258) 5988[2] 6623[9]

Balcarce Nov (ARG) *Tom Tate* a101 110
5 br h Romanov(IRE) —Rosada Fitz (ARG) (Fitzcarraldo (ARG))
175[3] 412a[5] 610a[3] 818a[6] 1708[3] 2057[3] 2651[2] 3069[18] 5247[7] 5948[7] 6180[10] 6749[15]

Balcombe (FR) *Tom Tate* a18
3 b c Danehill Dancer(IRE) —Lady Of St Kilda (Mark Of Esteem (IRE))
381[6]

Baldemar *Richard Fahey* a93 99
5 b g Namid—Keen Melody (USA) (Sharpen Up)
1032[4] *1206[5]* ◆ 1423[6] 2100[2] 2748[7] 3446[11] 4085[9] 4391[8] 4653[3] 6142[23] 6776[4]

Balducci *Andrew Balding* a80 105
3 b c Dansili—Miss Meltemi (IRE) (Miswaki Tern (USA))
950[3] (1308) 1703[2] ◆ (2324) 3103[12] 5948[10] 6806[2] 7234[3]

Balerina (FR) *K Borgel* 93
3 b f Della Francesca(USA) —Santa Marina (FR) (Kendor (FR))
952a[7]

Balius (IRE) *Saeed Bin Suroor* a120 120
7 b h Mujahid(USA) —Akhla (USA) (Nashwan (USA))
4390[8] 5090[2]

Balkan Knight *David Elsworth* 104
10 b g Selkirk(USA) —Crown Of Light (Mtoto)
1382[15] 1615[9] 2116[7] 2469[6] 3195[15]

Ballade De La Mer *George Foster* a51 53
4 b m Ishiguru(USA) —Riviere Rouge (Forzando)
2214[9] 2833[3] 3078[5] 3901[5] (4511) (4825) 5202[4] *6373[6]* 7176[5] *7398[4]*

Ballarina *Eric Alston* a59 62
4 b m Compton Place—Miss Uluwatu (IRE) (Night Shift (USA))
4672[3] ◆ 4799[4] 5097[3] (5816) 6246[4] 6965[4] *7537[2] 7860[3]*

Balletlou (IRE) *John Best* 79
3 b f Peintre Celebre(USA) —For Freedom (IRE) (King Of Kings (IRE))
(3477) ◆ 4360[8] 5008[10]

Ballinargh Boy *R D Wylie* 51
2 b g Royal Applause—Can Can Lady (Anshan)
5298[10] 6046[5] 6365[8]

Ballinargh Girl (IRE) *R D Wylie* 73
2 b f Footstepsinthesand—Rack And Ruin (IRE) (King's Best (USA))
3204[2] (4083) 4592[5] 4831[5] 5547[6]

Ballinteni *Gay Kelleway* a68 91
8 b g Machiavellian(USA) —Silabteni (USA) (Nureyev (USA))
2472[11] 2934[11] (4170) 4713[3] 5311[6] 5756[4] *6288[4]*

Ballista (IRE) *Tom Dascombe* 94
2 b g Majestic Missile(IRE) —Ancient Secret (Warrshan (USA))
(2540) ◆ 3476[3] ◆ 4138[13] 6568[3] 6751[7]

Ballistic (USA) *John Gosden*
2 b c War Chant(USA) —Morena Park (Pivotal)
7248[U]

Ballivor (IRE) *W T Farrell* a76 91
7 b g Marju(IRE) —Delphinus (Soviet Star (USA))
3487a[12] 5571a[22]

Ballodair (IRE) *Richard Fahey* a72 78
3 b g Antonius Pius(USA) —Vision Of Dreams (Efisio)
1523[3] 2069[5] 2815[5] *7526[8] 7683[6] 8004[3]*

Ballyday (IRE) *Frederick Watson*
8 b g Oscar(IRE) —Malbay Sunrise (IRE) (Religiously (USA))
7282[11]

Ballyhaunis *W P Mullins* 86
5 b g Daylami(IRE) —Ballet (Sharrood (USA))
3492a[5]

Ballyvonane (USA) *David C Griffiths* a55 44
3 b g Strong Hope(USA) —Wild Light (USA) (Tabasco Cat (USA))
678[8] 745[5] (831) 988[4] 1057[5] 1162[12] 2217[16] *7607[6] 7824[5] 7936[6]*

Balthazaar's Gift (IRE) *Clive Cox* a56 119
7 b h Xaar—Thats Your Opinion (Last Tycoon)
3192[7] 3870[8] 4457[5] (5946) 6949a[12]

Baltic Ben (USA) *Eve Johnson Houghton* 60
3 b g Johannesburg(USA) —Baltic Dip (IRE) (Benny The Dip (USA))
1912[8] 2131[3]

Baltimore Clipper (USA) *Paul Cole* a73 84
3 b g Mizzen Mast(USA) —Resounding Grace (USA) (Thunder Gulch (USA))
1624[5] 1976[3] 2782[2] 3273[4] 3593[3] 3820[2] (4341) 6448[7] *6698[9]*

Baltimore Jack (IRE) *Tim Walford* a66 79
6 b g Night Shift(USA) —Itsibitsi (IRE) (Brief Truce (USA))
1520[2] 1751[9] 2349[7] 3203[3] (3690) 4198[5] 4522[7] 6029[3] *6543[7]*

Baltimore Patriot (IRE) *Roger Curtis* a67 63
7 b g Tiger Hill(IRE) —Berenice (Groom Dancer (USA))
3[4] 322[2] 409[3] 1816a[2]

Balwearie (IRE) *Linda Perratt* 62
9 b g Sesaro(USA) —Eight Mile Rock (Dominion)
3166[4] 3499[5] (3709) 4190[7] 4953[6] 5336[2] 6032[8] 6242[5]

Balzarine *Colin Teague* a48 40
4 ch m Auction House(USA) —Worsted (Whittingham (IRE))
1966[10] 2629[10] 3075[5] 3903[9]

Banana Republic (IRE) *Paul Cole* a74 71
3 ch g Danehill Dancer(IRE) —Elite Guest (IRE) (Be My Guest (USA))
2115[4] 2717[8] 3414[5] 4344[10] 4793[11]

Banco Busto (IRE) *Stuart Howe* a14 32
3 b f Chineur(FR) —Banco Solo (Distant Relative)
2050[9] 2409[6]

Bandanaman (IRE) *Alan Swinbank* a64 66
4 b g Danehill Dancer(IRE) —Band Of Angels (IRE) (Alzao (USA))
897[4] 1071[6] 1150[9] 3669[2] 4604[6] 5119[8]

Bandear (IRE) *Clive Brittain* a58 63
3 b f Royal Applause—Royals Special (IRE) (Caerleon (USA))
856[6] 1048[7] 1205[5] 2619[8]

Banderille (IRE) *E Lellouche* 90
3 b f Red Ransom(USA) —Buenos Aires (IRE) (Rainbow Quest (USA))
3720a[7]

Bandstand *Bryan Smart* a80
4 b g Royal Applause—Incise (Dr Fong (USA))
301[2] 751[4]

Bangalore Gold (IRE) *David Marnane* a80 97
4 b g Elusive City(USA) —Tenny's Gold (IRE) (Marju (IRE))
3146[16]

Banimpire (IRE) *J S Bolger* 92
2 br f Holy Roman Emperor(IRE) —My Renee (USA) (Kris S (USA))
6005a[5] 6401a[7]

Bankable (IRE) *H J Brown* 118
6 b h Medicean—Dance To The Top (Sadler's Wells (USA))
(631a) 1025a[2]

Bankroller *Jonathan Portman* a27 55
2 b g Indesatchel(IRE) —Easy Feeling (IRE) (Night Shift (USA))
2077[11] 3112[5] *3785[12]* 4935[9] *7496[10] 7715[4]*

Banks And Braes *Richard Hannon* a78 74
3 b c Red Ransom(USA) —Bonnie Doon (IRE) (Grand Lodge (USA))
106[2] 634[5] 1973[3] 2438[2] (2953)

Banna Boirche (IRE) *M Halford* a103 84
4 b g Lucky Owners(NZ) —Ziet D'Alsace (FR) (Zieten (USA))
3487a[9] *6597a[4] (6907a) 7217a[3]*

Bannaby (FR) *M Delcher-Sanchez* 114
7 ch h Dyhim Diamond(IRE) —Trelakari (FR) (Lashkari)
3102[4] 6016a[7]

Banned (USA) *Thomas F Proctor* a69 107
2 b c Kitten's Joy(USA) —Cardinalli (USA) (Capote (USA))
7360a[5]

Banquet (IRE) *Tim Walford* 57
5 ch g Dr Fong(USA) —Barbera (Barathea (IRE))
3600[8] 4946[4] 5336[7]

Bansha (IRE) *Alan Bailey* a51 47
4 b g Indian Haven—Cha Cha (IRE) (Charnwood Forest (IRE))
331[9] 470[7] 503[3] 661[11] 1536[5]

Baoli *Luca Cumani* a65 66
3 b f Dansili—Thorntoun Piccolo (Groom Dancer (USA))
1795[5] *2336[2] (2753) 4134[2]* (5173) 5812[5] 7038[10]

Baptist (USA) *Andrew Balding* 89
2 bb c Tapit(USA) —Twist A Lime (USA) (Copelan (USA))
(6190) 6737[5]

Baqaat (USA) *Ed Dunlop* 70
2 bb f Alhaarth(IRE) —Hachiyah (IRE) (Generous (IRE))
4844[10] ◆ 5691[5]

Baraaya (IRE) *William Haggas* 70
2 ch f Dalakhani(IRE) —Sayedati Eljamilah (USA) (Mr Prospector (USA))
4595[4]

Baracas (FR) *Eoin Griffin* a74 82
5 b g Miesque's Son(USA) —Sara Baras (IRE) (Turtle Island (IRE))
3492a[13]

Barack (IRE) *Francis Ennis* a91 101
4 b g Pyrus(USA) —Morna's Fan (FR) (Lear Fan (USA))
1408a[2] 5571a[11] 5774a[2] 6783a[9]

Baraconti (IRE) *Ruth Carr* a51 71
3 b g Barathea(IRE) —Continuous (IRE) (Darshaan)
1804[4] 2886[7] 4344[12] 6463[7] *7401[12] 7731[5] 7833[4]*

Baralaka *Sir Mark Prescott Bt* a92 95
3 ch g Barathea(IRE) —Shakalaka Baby (Nashwan (USA))
3443[3] (5380) (5679) *5922[4]* 6654[5]

Baransky *Mahmood Al Zarooni* 82
2 b c Green Desert(USA) —Mount Elbrus (Barathea (IRE))
3452[5] ◆ 3794[2] 4263[3] 5085[2]

Barastar *Nigel Tinkler* a43 56
3 b g Sampower Star—Barachois Princess (USA) (Barachois (CAN))
422[8] 698[11] 2132[10] 2503[7] 2838[9] 3153[6] 3532[7] 3907[4] 4210[13]

Barataria *Robin Bastiman* a78 76
8 ch g Barathea(IRE) —Aethra (USA) (Trempolino (USA))
1115[15] 1653[13] 2451[5] 3500[7] 4439[6] 4987[8]

Barathea Dancer (IRE) *Roger Teal* a74 74
2 b f Barathea(IRE) —Showering (Danehill (USA))
3349[7] 4096[7] 5587[4] *5961[2]* ◆ 6555[3] 7236[5] *7481[7]*

Barbadine (USA) *David Wachman* a91 91
3 bb f Giant's Causeway(USA) —Damson (IRE) (Entrepreneur)
5568a[6] *7358a[7]*

Barbarian *Alan Brown* a69 73
4 b g Noverre(USA) —Love In The Mist (USA) (Silver Hawk (USA))
291[5] 3758[9] 4407[12] 4648[3] 4945[9]

Barbecue Eddie (USA) *Doug Watson* a106 94
6 br g Stormy Atlantic(USA) —The Green Owl (USA) (Carson City (USA))
(438a) 607a[5] 797a[7]

Barberhoney *John Jenkins* a48 52
3 ch f Sulamani(IRE) —Maddie's A Jem (Emperor Jones (USA))
1431[7] 1782[7] 3484[5] 4774[6] *5729[5] 6847[11]*

Barbieri (IRE) *Jeremy Gask* a70 90
2 ch f Encosta De Lago(AUS) —Glenmara (USA) (Known Fact (USA))
4658[11] *6286[3] (6666)* 7204[5]

Barbirolli *William Stone* a55 58
8 b g Machiavellian(USA) —Blushing Barada (USA) (Blushing Groom (FR))
130[3] 210[10] 539[6] 661[10] 1262[3] 1635[3] *1984[6]* 2302[7] 2529[4] 2811[8] 5625[3] 6022[7] *6662[4]* 7149[6] 7531[8] 7716[5] 7921[4]

Barefoot Lady (IRE) *Richard Fahey* 97
2 b f Footstepsinthesand—Lady Angharad (IRE) (Tenby)
(4981) ◆ (5850) 6176[3] 6751[2]

Bariolo (FR) *Noel Chance* a74 72
6 b g Priolo(USA) —La Bardane (FR) (Marignan (USA))
(660) 785[2] 8003[8]

Barista (IRE) *Mick Channon* a62 85
2 b g Titus Livius(FR) —Cappuccino (IRE) (Mujadil (USA))
1066[6] 1389[8] 3678[3] (4067) 4578[7] 4677[3] 5187[5] 5476[3] 5745[8] 5856[4] *6081[5]* 6412[2] *6695[5]* 6875[9] (7124) (7280) 7544a[7]

Barking (IRE) *Richard Hannon* a63 72
2 b c Bahri(USA) —Pivot D'Amour (Pivotal)
1541[7] 4423[2] 4743[2] *5381[3]* 6086[4] 6445[10] 6954[7]

Barkston Ash *Eric Alston* 70
2 b g Kyllachy—Ae Kae Ae (USA) (King Of Kings (IRE))
2540[3] 3204[5] 3897[5] 4388[7]

Barlaman (USA) *Clive Brittain* a72 69
3 ch c Langfuhr(CAN) —Party Circuit (USA) (Kingmambo (USA))
382[3] 596[4] 783[5] 933[4] 2491[4] *3325[6]* (3525)

Barliffey (IRE) *Denis Coakley* a73 78
5 b g Bahri(USA) —Kildare Lady (IRE) (Indian Ridge)
1617[7] 2233[4] 3404[4] 4794[2] 5679[2] *7044[4] 7275[6]*

Barndeh (IRE) *T G McCourt* a54 56
7 b g Marju(IRE) —Sweetest Thing (IRE) (Prince Rupert (FR))
7275[8]

Barnet Fair *Richard Guest* a71 63
2 br g Iceman—Pavement Gates (Bishop Of Cashel)
5298[12] 6111[4] ◆ *6666[3]* ◆ 6878[U] *7999[4]*

Barney McGrew (IRE) *Michael Dods* a93 112
7 b g Mark Of Esteem(IRE) —Success Story (Sharrood (USA))
707a[10] 822a[7] 1007[5] ◆ 1326[5] 1727[23] 3193[24] (3445) 4136[9] 5183[14] 5744[11] 6177[20]

Barney Rebel (IRE) *B W Hills* 74
2 b c Holy Roman Emperor(IRE) —Opera Ridge (FR) (Indian Ridge)
4460^5 ◆ 6200^{12}

Barnmore *Peter Hedger* a68 32
2 b c Royal Applause—Veronica Franco (Darshaan)
7099^{13} 7386^5 ◆

Barnstorm *Mark Johnston* a57 61
3 b g Exceed And Excel(AUS) —Caribbean Star (Soviet Star (USA))
1153^5 ◆ 1425^6 1586^5 ◆ 2221^7 2700^{12} 3073^4 3387^{10} 3706^7

Barodine *Ron Hodges* a64 59
7 ch g Barathea(IRE) —Granted (FR) (Cadeaux Genereux)
354^2 (407) 540^6 665^4 795^3 940^2 1078^{12} 1980^8 2167^4 2337^7 2691^6 2955^{10} 7200^9

Baron De'L (IRE) *Edward P Harty* a78 97
7 ch g In The Wings—Lightstorm (IRE) (Darshaan)
1247a^8

Barons Spy (IRE) *Richard Price* a84 84
9 b g Danzero(AUS) —Princess Accord (USA) (D'Accord (USA))
1688^{10} 2091^6 2592^5 3373^9 3850^3 (5809) 5995^2 6256^6 7014^6

Barony (IRE) *Lee Smyth* a1
4 ch g Swift Gulliver(IRE) —Musical Flyer (IRE) (Prince Of Birds (USA))
31^8

Barouda (FR) *J-M Beguigne* 111
3 ch f My Risk(FR) —Baroudia (FR) (Kaldoun (FR))
1566a^7 2158a^7 2801a^{11}

Barq (IRE) *Saeed Bin Suroor* a97 86
3 br c Green Desert(USA) —Zaeema (Zafonic (USA))
4238^2 (5007) 5627^2 5964^4 (6253) 6798^2

Barraland *George Baker* a49 52
5 b g Compton Place—Dance Land (IRE) (Nordance (USA))
2213^{11} 2669^7 2756^8 3356^7 3990^3 ◆ 4605^7 4822^3 5331^{10} 5405^2 6644^6 6847^8 7409^8 7477^4 ◆ 7506^8

Barra Raider *Roger Fisher* 54
3 b g Avonbridge—Baileys Silver (USA) (Marlin (USA))
1705^6 2131^8 4407^7 5336^6 6183^3

Barrel Of Fun (IRE) *Jim Best* a66 82
4 b g Sadler's Wells(USA) —Mabrova (Prince Mab (FR))
803^3

Barren Brook *Michael Easterby* 85
3 b g Beat Hollow—Carinthia (IRE) (Tirol)
3207^8 (3554) 4288^2 (4865) ◆ 6105^6 6142^{20} 6620^3 6963^8

Barreq (USA) *Bryan Smart* a79 59
3 b c Proud Citizen(USA) —The Wrong Face (USA) (Marlin (USA))
4339^5

Barring Decree (IRE) *F Dunne* a94 104
5 b m Dalakhani(IRE) —Barring Order (IRE) (Barathea (IRE))
5568a^{10}

Barry Crockett (IRE) *Lisa Williamson* 66
2 b g Modigliani(USA) —Great Morning (IRE) (Galileo (IRE))
5900^7 6293^{15} 7427^{12}

Barshiba (IRE) *David Elsworth* a84 114
6 ch m Barathea(IRE) —Dashiba (Dashing Blade)
(1898) 2538^4 3191^3 (3671) 4575^6 5248^6 6928^4

Barton Bounty *Peter Niven* a29 51
3 b g Bahamian Bounty—Tenebrae (IRE) (In The Wings)
4339^8 4556^{10} 5065^{10} 5758^{11} 6189^7 7917^7

Barwick *Mark H Tompkins* 75
2 b c Beat Hollow—Tenpence (Bob Back (USA))
4803^{13} 5294^5 ◆ 5900^2

Basalt (IRE) *Tim Pitt* a84 61
6 b g Rock Of Gibraltar(IRE) —Sniffle (IRE) (Shernazar)
2659^8

Baschar *M G Mintchev* 105
3 b c Starcraft(NZ) —Belle Et Deluree (USA) (The Minstrel (CAN))
3018a^3 4184a^{17} 5804a^5 6239a^4 7103a^5

Bashir Biyoum Zain (IRE) *P D Deegan* a89 82
3 b g Green Desert(USA) —Alshamatry (USA) (Seeking The Gold (USA))
5127a^{10}

Bashkirov *Luke Comer* a98 87
5 ch h Galileo(IRE) —Tina Heights (Shirley Heights)
2709^8 7589a^{11} 7823a^{10}

Basilica *Rod Millman* 78
2 ch g Zafeen(FR) —Thicket (Wolfhound (USA))
1793^4 4954^{11} (5835) 6445^{13}

Basiliko (USA) *Ron Hodges* a30 50
7 ch g Fusaichi Pegasus(USA) —Shootforthestars (USA) (Seattle Slew (USA))
4042^8

Basle *Gay Kelleway* a74 81
3 b f Trade Fair—Gibaltarik (IRE) (Jareer (USA))
1269^5 (1842) 3328^7 4583^5 4892^3 (5388) 6000^3 6487a^0 6772^{10}

Basra (IRE) *Jo Crowley* a84 82
7 b g Soviet Star(USA) —Azra (IRE) (Danehill (USA))
239^7 637^3 2093^6 3863^8 6851^9 7190^7

Bassett Road (IRE) *Tom Dascombe* a80
2 ch g Byron—Topiary (IRE) (Selkirk (USA))
7567^7 (7914)

Batchworth Blaise *Eric Wheeler* a67 53
7 b g Little Jim—Batchworth Dancer (Ballacashtal (CAN))
318^4 367^7 656^8 (1171) 1737^7 2053^8 (2417) 2596^{12} 2967^3 3323^7 4260^7 4681^8 7192^2 7555^5 7725^7 7991^6

Bateau Bleu *Ben Haslam* a58 66
3 b g Auction House(USA) —Fresh Look (IRE) (Alzao (USA))
3978^8 4708^3 4945^8 7805^{10}

Bated Breath *Roger Charlton* 111
3 b c Dansili—Tantina (USA) (Distant View (USA))
(1425) ◆ (2815) ◆ (3673) ◆ 5088^3 5526^4

Bateleur *Mick Channon* a45 72
6 b g Fraam—Search Party (Rainbow Quest (USA))
1547^6 1869^8 2246^5 2590^{12} 3057^5 (3200) 3497^9 3534^7 3914^7 4130^3 4283^4 4589^8 4875^4 5112^3 5169^4 5714^2 6295^5 6421^3 6741^{10}

Batgirl *John Berry* a56 71
3 ch f Mark Of Esteem(IRE) —Serriera (FR) (Highest Honor (FR))
1586^3 2042^{15} 2879^7 (3907) 4588^3 5614^{11} (6098) 6992^9

Bathwick Bear (IRE) *David Evans* 99
2 b g Kodiac—Bayleaf (Efisio)
(1136) ◆ (1359) 1819^2 2525^4 4138^{16} 4539^7 5094^3 5221^4 (5604) 5907^{10} 6230a^3

Bathwick Freeze *David Evans* a44 52
2 b f Iceman—Society Rose (Saddlers' Hall (IRE))
1577^{11} 1999^5 2245^8 4429^5

Bathwick Nero *David Evans* a47 41
2 b f Numerous(USA) —Sierra (FR) (Anabaa (USA))
1793^{12} 2022^9 2245^7 4436^7 7629^7 7857^6

Bathwick Quest (IRE) *Brendan Powell* 26
6 b m Barathea(IRE) —Ninth Quest (USA) (Quest For Fame)
6415^9

Bathwick Scanno (IRE) *David Evans* a57 62
2 b g Aptitude(USA) —Hundred Year Flood (USA) (Giant's Causeway (USA))
5269^6 5701^4 6209^{11} 7118^9 7177^2 7464^5 7520^5 7839^7

Bathwick Siesta *Jonathan Portman* 44
2 br g Dr Fong(USA) —Light Dreams (Fantastic Light (USA))
2839^{12} 3106^{11} 5255^{13} 5373^9

Bathwick Xaara *Jonathan Portman* a61 73
3 br f Xaar—Anapola (GER) (Polish Precedent (USA))
933^{11} 2919^3 3336^2 3866^7 4234^3 4529^4 4730^4 4989^2 5898^{12} (6656) 6812^3

Battenberg *Amy Weaver* a27 33
2 ch f Iceman—Cragreen (Green Desert (USA))
1603^8 2631^5 3035^{13} 3784^6

Battery Power *Mark H Tompkins* a71 54
2 b f Royal Applause—Missouri (Charnwood Forest (IRE))
4844^{11} 6070^8 6521^3 (7394)

Battimoore (IRE) *Ian McInnes* a52 52
4 b m Beckett(IRE) —Silver Spoon (IRE) (College Chapel)
249^4 320^{12} 388^8 591^{13} 721^{10}

Battle Honour *Henry Candy* a64 82
3 b g Mark Of Esteem(IRE) —Proserpine (Robellino (USA))
2128^2 ◆ 3766^6 4521^2 5150^3

Battlemaiden (IRE) *Mark Johnston* a80 83
3 br f Shamardal(USA) —Kirk (Selkirk (USA))
(1571) 2466^6 3320^2 3830^7 4593^{11} 5199^8 6167^6

Battle Of Britain *Mahmood Al Zarooni* 72
2 b c Invincible Spirit(IRE) —Laramie (USA) (Gulch (USA))
2007^3 2621^3 3053^2 3536^2 4111^6

Battle Of Hastings *Jeff Mullins* a113 114
4 b g Royal Applause—Subya (Night Shift (USA))
5577a^4

Battleoftrafalgar *Michael Attwater* a80 80
3 b c Galileo(IRE) —Pink Stone (FR) (Bigstone (IRE))
7736^9

Battle Planner (USA) *Valentine Donoghue* a84 86
4 b h War Chant(USA) —The Administrator (USA) (Afleet (CAN))
7173^7

Battleship Grey *Dean Ivory* a33
3 gr g Cape Town(IRE) —Think It Over (IRE) (Bijou D'Inde)
1878^{14} 2968^{14} 5668^8 6255^{14} 7161^{11}

Battle Study (IRE) *Alan McCabe* a49 66
3 b g Fath(USA) —Osprey Point (IRE) (Entrepreneur)
1029^7 1362^4 1649^5 1992^2 2438^6 2704^5 3113^4 3975^4 4344^{11} 4522^5 5159^8 5455^4 5550^4 5758^9

Bauer (IRE) *Luca Cumani* a47 110
7 gr g Halling(USA) —Dali's Grey (Linamix (FR))
5696^5 6148^4

Baunagain (IRE) *Peter Chapple-Hyam* a81 92
5 b g No Excuse Needed—Manuka Honey (Mystiko (USA))
2119^{13} 2508^{12} 3037^7 3373^{11} 3833^6

Bavarian Nordic (USA) *Ann Duffield* a80 79
5 b g Barathea(IRE) —Dubai Diamond (Octagonal (NZ))
1996^8 3090^3 3588^5 3764^3 4405^9 4781^6 4891^8

Bavarian Princess (USA) *Ralph Beckett* 58
2 b f Invincible Spirit(IRE) —Lileagh (IRE) (Sadler's Wells (USA))
5078^8 5692^9

Bavarica *Julia Feilden* a84 80
8 b m Dansili—Blue Gentian (USA) (Known Fact (USA))
202^7 284^4 (426) 752^4 (871) 903^8 1161^6 1379^9 2081^3 2349^5 2511^4 (2894) 3912^2 4657^2 5071^3 5591^8 6322^{14}

Bawaab (USA) *Saeed Bin Suroor* a76 71
2 bb c Street Cry(IRE) —Her She Kisses (CAN) (Dehere (USA))
4263^5 (5178) ◆ 6160^8

Bawaardi (IRE) *Richard Fahey* a87 86
4 b g Acclamation—Global Trend (Bluebird (USA))
(29) 151^5 4394^3 ◆ 4828^{12} 7665^3 7846^3 7915^4 7935^9

Baxter (IRE) *J W Hills* a46 43
3 b g Kheleyf(USA) —Victoria Lodge (IRE) (Grand Lodge (USA))
1211^7 1694^9 1870^{11} 2480^{13} 3291^{10} 3820^6

Baybshambles (IRE) *Ron Barr* 77
6 b g Compton Admiral—Payvashooz (Ballacashtal (CAN))
1366^{11} 1805^5 1988^4 2818^8 3551^7 3775^4 4171^7 4555^8 4704^8 5499^9 5601^6

Baycat (IRE) *Jonathan Portman* a50 92
4 b g One Cool Cat(USA) —Greta D'Argent (IRE) (Great Commotion (USA))
1346^{11} 2414^9

Bay Knight (IRE) *K J Condon* a87 101
4 b g Johannesburg(USA) —Sabeline (IRE) (Caerleon (USA))
(4180a) 5774a^8 5944^5 6783a^{10}

Baylini *Jamie Osborne* a96 83
6 gr m Bertolini(USA) —Bay Of Plenty (FR) (Octagonal (NZ))
205^2 252^7 (360) 536^7 697^4 863^4 1015^4 1220^8 2044^4 2339^3 ◆ 2823^4 3217^2 3457^7 3846^5 4108^4 (4261) 4579^8 6447^{12} 7012^4 7243^3 7430^2 7591^7 7735^2 ◆ 7828^3

Bay Of Fires (IRE) *David O'Meara* 76
2 b f Iffraaj—No Tippling (IRE) (Unblest)
2238^3 (2832) 3141^{15} (4013) 4592^{15} 5882^{15} 6647^3 6920^5

Bay Swallow (IRE) *Patrick J Flynn* a68 68
4 b m Daylami(IRE) —Starlight Smile (USA) (Green Dancer (USA))
7078a^5

Bay Willow (IRE) *Mark Johnston* 107
3 b g Singspiel(IRE) —Tree House (USA) (Woodman (USA))
1475^4 1757^2 2115^3 (2390) 3105^4 ◆ (3492a) 3873^2 (4400) 5273^{14} 6387^4

Bazergan (IRE) *Clive Brittain* a96 94
5 b g Machiavellian(USA) —Lunda (IRE) (Soviet Star (USA))
1474^{12} 3121^8 3239^6

Bazroy (IRE) *David Evans* a98 88
6 b g Soviet Star(USA) —Kunucu (IRE) (Bluebird (USA))
862^3 1049^5 1301^7

Beach Babe *Jonathan Portman* a50 61
2 b f Zafeen(FR) —Beechnut (IRE) (Mujadil (USA))
4021^8 5006^{10} 5583^5 6411^7

Beachfire *John Gosden* a76 102
3 ch c Indian Haven—Maine Lobster (USA) (Woodman (USA))
(1590) ◆ 2225^3 ◆ (2969) (3697) (4504) ◆

Beach Patrol (IRE) *Edward Creighton* a66 57
2 b g Antonius Pius(USA) —Slip Ashore (IRE) (Slip Anchor)
1017^2 1136^9 1389^5 1764^4 2139^4 4274a^8 6442^{13} 6666^7 7577^4 7722^8

Beachwood Bay *Roger Curtis* 7
2 b g Tobougg(IRE) —The Terrier (Foxhound (USA))
2210^7

Beacon Hill (IRE) *John Gosden* 62
2 b c Shamardal(USA) —Alegranza (IRE) (Lake Coniston (IRE))
2319^6 2621^5 7002^6

Beacon Lodge (IRE) *Clive Cox* 117
5 b h Clodovil(IRE) —Royal House (FR) (Royal Academy (USA))
1531^5 1974^4 4166a^2

Be A Devil *William Muir* a82 78
3 ch g Dubai Destination(USA) —Devil's Imp (IRE) (Cadeaux Genereux)
1913^9 2644^3 3081^4 3612^3 4058^4 ◆ 4956^7

Beagle Boy (IRE) *A Wohler* a79 88
3 b c American Post—Heronetta (Halling (USA))
2405a^7 6408a^6

Be A Good Lady *Paul Midgley* a35 49
2 b f Goodricke—Lady Double U (Sheikh Albadou)
1065^6 ◆ 1421^5 6111^7 6658^6 7301^9 7404^4

Be Amazing (IRE) *David Lanigan* a69 2
2 b f Refuse To Bend(IRE) —Snow Peak (Arazi (USA))
5047^{15} 5841^7 ◆ 6118^3

Bea Menace (USA) *Paul Cole* a90 83
4 b m Mizzen Mast(USA) —Questonia (Rainbow Quest (USA))
3565^{10}

Bean Uasal (IRE) *John M Oxx* a71 85
4 b m Oasis Dream—Catch The Blues (IRE) (Bluebird (USA))
5571a^{16}

Bea Remembered *Francis Ennis* 97
3 b f Doyen(IRE) —Leinster Mills (IRE) (Doyoun)
4312a^3

Bearheart (IRE) *E J O'Neill* a75 58
2 b c Aragorn(IRE) —Guana (FR) (Sillery (USA))
3805^6 4254^3 5156^3 5837^9 6426^3 7975a^5

Bear Tobouggie *Alan Swinbank* 73
3 b f Tobougg(IRE) —Brave Bear (Bold Edge)
(1119) 1571^5 6003^6 6183^7

Beat Baby (IRE) *Michael Scudamore* a77 92
3 ch g Johannesburg(USA) —Najiya (Nashwan (USA))
(1868) 3065^{12} (4171) 5250^{14} 6000^8 7488^9

Beating Harmony *Tom Dascombe* a60 53
2 b g Beat Hollow—Heart's Harmony (Blushing Groom (FR))
4208^8 5047^{10} 6307^7 6500^4 7324^6 7486^5 7664^3 7839^3

Beat Of The Blues *Andrew Balding* 32
2 b g Beat Hollow—Skies Are Blue (Unfuwain (USA))
7094^{12}

Beatrice Aurore (IRE) *John Dunlop* 83
2 b f Danehill Dancer(IRE) —Mondschein (Rainbow Quest (USA))
5691^8 (6155)

Beat Route *Michael Attwater* a69 64
3 ch g Beat Hollow—Steppin Out (First Trump)
1067^7 340^4 484^5 680^3 949^4 (1060) 2321^8 2869^7 4360^7 4698^3 5180^6 5869^4 (6526) 6781^4

Beat The Bell *David Barron* a98 92
5 b g Beat All(USA) —Bella Beguine (Komaite (USA))
761^3 ◆ (987) 1206^6 (1428) 1516^6 (1641) 2364^2 3401^7 5734^4 ◆ 6142^7 (6706)

Beat The Rush *Julie-Ann Camacho* 91
3 b g Tobougg(IRE) —Rush Hour (IRE) (Night Shift (USA))
1299^2 (1630) 2323^4 (3123) 4153^2 6754^{12}

Beat The Shower *Peter Niven* a46 76
4 b g Beat Hollow—Crimson Shower (Dowsing (USA))
(3989) (4785) 5788^6 6397^2 7284^5

Beat Up *Gavin Blake* a67 67
4 b g Beat Hollow—Whitgift Rose (Polar Falcon (USA))
1877^8 2643^8 3323^3 ◆ (4913) 5367^6 6718^6 6934^{10} 7562^4

Beaubahhare (FR) *J-P Delaporte* 65
5 b g Bahhare(USA) —Offense Vive (USA) (Sharpen Up)
1056a^6

Beaubrav *Michael Madgwick* a76 66
4 b g Falbrav(IRE) —Wavy Up (IRE) (Brustolon)
(1225) 1623^9 2360^7 (2966) 3862^8 4426^8 4780^3 5457^5 6055^6 7778^5 8013^3

Beauchamp Viceroy *Gerard Butler* a110 84
6 ch g Compton Admiral—Compton Astoria (USA) (Lion Cavern (USA))
(109) 441a^8 610a^2 818a^5 946^7 (1085) 6123^3 7482^2 7593^3 7800a^{10} 7875^7

Beauchamp Wizard *Gerard Butler* a62 67
5 b h Compton Admiral—Compton Astoria (USA) (Lion Cavern (USA))
1322^6 1637^{10} 2643^{13} 2790^7 5559^5 5867^6 6125^7

Beauchamp Xenia *Henry Candy* a58 69
4 b m Compton Admiral—Beauchamp Jade (Kalaglow)
2341^7 2923^7

Beauchamp Xerxes *Gerard Butler* a103 106
4 ch g Compton Admiral—Compton Astoria (USA) (Lion Cavern (USA))
334a^{13} 517a^6 629a^{12} (2318) 2707^5 3144^{10} 3455^5 4537^{16} 7233^2 7430^7 7776a^0

Beauchamp Xiara *Henry Candy* a71 77
4 b m Compton Admiral—Beauchamp Buzz (High Top)
2081^4 2602^8 2956^5 3268^2 3821^3 4422^3 5146^2 7044^7 7307^8

Beauchamp Yorker *Henry Candy* 94
3 ch c Compton Admiral—Compton Astoria (USA) (Lion Cavern (USA))
4750^7

Beau Fighter *Gary Moore* a58 80
5 b g Tobougg(IRE) —Belle De Jour (Exit To Nowhere (USA))
5994^{10} 6554^6 7101^6 7957^4 ◆

Beau Marchand (FR) *Mlle Y Vollmer* 66
6 b g Marchand De Sable(USA) —Divine (GER) (Wauthi (GER))
1056a^{10}

Beaumont's Party (IRE) *Richard Hannon* a71 82
3 b g High Chaparral(IRE) —Miss Champagne (FR) (Bering)
2888^3 3297^5 3680^5 (4335) 5050^2 5919^2 6780^4

Beautiful Lando (FR) *Heather Main* 33
2 bb g Lando(GER) —Beautiful Baroness (USA) (Fortunate Prospect (USA))
5204^5 5626^7 6279^{10}

Beautiful One *Tim McCarthy* 60
3 b f Doyen(IRE) —Dodona (Lahib (USA))
3266^5 4028^5 4874^P

Beauty Flash (NZ) *A S Cruz* 119
5 ch g Golan(IRE) —Wychwood Rose (NZ) (Volksraad)
(7853a)

Beauty Pageant (IRE) *Ed McMahon* 63
3 ch f Bahamian Bounty—My American Beauty (Wolfhound (USA))
1966^3 2441^2 (3125)

Beaver Patrol (IRE) *Eve Johnson Houghton* a109 87
8 ch g Tagula(IRE) —Erne Project (IRE) (Project Manager)
2119^{11} 2532^3 2926^7 3401^{11} 4057^4 4905^6 (5652) 6780^7 7238^5

Bebopalula (IRE) *B W Hills* a65 79
3 gr f Galileo(IRE) —Pearl Bright (FR) (Kaldoun (FR))
(484) (1578) 1909^4 2758^{14} 3298^7

Becausewecan (USA) *Mark Johnston* a101 99
4 b g Giant's Causeway(USA) —Belle Sultane (USA) (Seattle Slew (USA))
947^2 1015^5 1151^3 1724^{10} 3194^{14} 3447^{13} 4320^5 4461^6 4817^5 5278^3 ◆ 5743^{13} 6181^3 6362^5 6565^3 6754^9 7130^2 7337^{10}

Beckermet (IRE) *Ruth Carr* a93 99
8 b g Second Empire(IRE) —Razida (IRE) (Last Tycoon)
537^5 1219^{12} 1672^3 2086^3 2532^7 2736^{14} 4370^7 4795^4 5197^3 5496^2 6048^{11}

Beck's Bolero (IRE) *Jamie Osborne* a18 58
4 ch g Haafhd—Prealpina (IRE) (Indian Ridge)
3442^9 4912^7 5233^2 5664^{11} 6023^9

Becqu Adoree (FR) *Luca Cumani* 109
4 b m Nombre Premier—L'Etoile La Lune (IRE) (Groom Dancer (USA))
2538^8 3031^9 4143^6 4624^4 6946a^7

Becuille (IRE) *Brian Meehan* a76 73
5 b m Redback—Danz Danz (Efisio)
2823^{10} 3036^5 5039^2 6372^3 6578^5

Bedarra Boy *David Arbuthnot* a56 57
4 ch g Needwood Blade—Roonah Quay (IRE) (Soviet Lad (USA))
1983^3 (2361) 2811^2 3267^7 6120^3 6373^{11}

Bed Fellow (IRE) *P Monteith* a65 66
6 b g Trans Island—Moonlight Partner (IRE) (Red Sunset)
2433^2 2858^6 3147^8 3707^{11} 3905^2 4189^2 4374^5 (4824) 5241^2 5737^{11} 6243^8

Bedibyes *Richard Mitchell* a42
2 b f Sleeping Indian—Aunt Sadie (Pursuit Of Love)
7485^{10} 7779^5

Bedloe's Island (IRE) *Neville Bycroft* a34 75
5 b g Statue Of Liberty(USA) —Scenaria (IRE) (Scenic)
6073^3 6572^7 6965^2 7180^{11}

Bedouin Bay *Alan McCabe* a80 72
3 b g Dubai Destination(USA) —Sahara Sonnet (USA) (Stravinsky (USA))
5136a^7 7553^6 7736^3 ◆ 7881^8

Bedouin Princess (IRE) *Lucinda Featherstone* a43 53
3 b f Desert Prince(IRE) —Poulkovo (IRE) (Sadler's Wells (USA))
3766[11] 4874[6] *5270[4]* 5812[7] 6415[10] *6696[7] 7462[8]*

Beer Flush (IRE) *Jedd O'Keeffe* 61
2 ch c Intikhab(USA) —Viola Royale (IRE) (Royal Academy (USA))
3665[9] 4368[3] 5594[7] 6471[8] 6875[3] *7393[10]*

Bees River (IRE) *Jim Goldie* a63 61
4 b m Acclamation—Notley Park (Wolfhound (USA))
3497[7] 3711[4] 3903[7]

Bee Sting *Lisa Williamson* a96 27
6 b g Selkirk(USA) —Desert Lynx (IRE) (Green Desert (USA))
6091[10]

Bee Stinger *Peter Hedger* a81 89
8 b g Almaty(IRE) —Nest Egg (Prince Sabo)
32[3]

Beethoven (IRE) *A P O'Brien* a111 118
3 b c Oratorio(IRE) —Queen Titi (IRE) (Sadler's Wells (USA))
3048[6] 4469[4] (5016a) 5775a[4] 6350[4] *6548a[6]* 7364a[10] 7853a[12]

Beetuna (IRE) *David Bourton* a82 82
5 b g Statue Of Liberty(USA) —High Atlas (Shirley Heights)
6543[4] 6832[5] ◆ 6984[3] 7062[10] *7337[5] 7600[2]*

Be Fair (USA) *D Wayne Lukas* a104
4 bb m Exchange Rate(USA) —Go Donna Go (USA) (Wild Again (USA))
1242a[3]

Before The War (USA) *Jeremy Gask* a59 67
3 ch g El Corredor(USA) —Adrenalin Running (USA) (A.P. Indy (USA))
2603[5] 3607[6] 4335[6] 4867[10] *7611[9] 8015[4]*

Beggar's Opera (IRE) *John Gosden* a85
3 b c Singspiel(IRE) —Hannda (IRE) (Dr Devious (IRE))
755[3] ◆ *(928) 6872[5] 7252[2] 7410[4] 7568[4] 7876[5]*

Beginnings (USA) *D Smaga* 82
2 b f Aptitude(USA) —Birthplace (USA) (King Of Kings (IRE))
5252a[3]

Behest *David Bridgwater* 44
5 b m Rainbow Quest(USA) —Keyboogie (USA) (Lyphard (USA))
1432[8] 1757[10] 1932[12] 2489[7] 2676[5] 2952[10] 4734[4] 4946[10]

Behkabad (FR) *J-C Rouget* 125
3 b c Cape Cross(IRE) —Behkara (IRE) (Kris)
(1985a) 2802a[4] (4039a) (6014a) 6612a[4] 7366a[3]

Behtarini (IRE) *John M Oxx* a87 84
3 b g Dalakhani(IRE) —Behkiyra (IRE) (Entrepreneur)
3492a[6]

Beidh Tine Anseo (IRE) *Lucinda Russell* 92
4 b g Rock Of Gibraltar(IRE) —Siamsa (USA) (Quest For Fame)
6493[5]

Be Invincible (IRE) *B W Hills* 94
3 b c Invincible Spirit(IRE) —Lupulina (CAN) (Saratoga Six (USA))
1352[9] 2253[9] 2888[2] (4660) 5188[3] 5638[11] 6534[13]

Be Kind *Karen George* a41 45
4 b m Generous(IRE) —Aquavita (Kalaglow)
2952[6] 4328[9]

Bel Cantor *Bill Ratcliffe* a88 84
7 b h Largesse—Palmstead Belle (IRE) (Wolfhound (USA))
115[2] 192[12] 250[3] 299[4] 474[2] (573) 737[6] 859[4] 1332[3] 1423[8] 1826[11] 2877[5] 3389[12] 3753[8] 4105[5] 4413[7] 4684[6] 4894[8] 5528[8] 6110[6] 6515[5] 7006[4] 7399[10] 7474[7] 7936[2]

Belgian Bill *George Baker* 93
2 b c Exceed And Excel(AUS) —Gay Romance (Singspiel (IRE))
2701[2] (3433) 5525[2] 6507[6]

Belgique (IRE) *Richard Hannon* a85 78
3 b f Compton Place—Liege (IRE) (Night Shift (USA))
1355[4] 1542[3] 2180[2] (3738) 4548[5] *(5031)* 6090[10] *6291[2]*

Belgooree *James Given* a11 53
3 b f Haafhd—Ziggy Zaggy (Diktat)
1393[5] 2425[14]

Believe In A. P. (USA) *Richard Dutrow Jr* a104 84
2 bb f A.P. Indy(USA) —I Believe In You (USA) (Pleasant Tap (USA))
7342a[4]

Believe It Or Not (IRE) *J S Moore* a70 76
2 b c Diamond Green(FR) —Yomalo (IRE) (Woodborough (USA))
2594[10] (3034) 3630[5] 4111[7] 5301[7] 5856[8] *6745[4]*

Belinsky (IRE) *Nigel Tinkler* a70 75
3 b g Compton Place—Westwood (FR) (Anabaa (USA))
1709[5] (2215) 2815[7] 3436[9] 4091[9] 4865[7] 6226[4] 6679[11]

Bella Cara (FR) *M Boutin* a61 73
2 b f Bernebeau(FR) —La Kador (FR) (Kadounor (FR))
5063a[6]

Bella Charlie (IRE) *Michael Quinlan* a61
3 b c Pyrus(USA) —Beseeching (IRE) (Hamas (IRE))
134[6] 346[8]

Bellaetta *Amy Weaver*
4 ch m Beat Hollow—Julietta Mia (USA) (Woodman (USA))
82[8]

Bella Fighetta *Ollie Pears* a38 11
4 b m Bertolini(USA) —My Girl (Mon Tresor)
88[7]

Bella Nemica *Edward Creighton* a33 31
2 b f Iceman—Bella Helena (Balidar)
6161[9] 6441[14] *6849[10]*

Bella Noir *Mrs K Burke* 79
3 b f Kyllachy—Lady Broughton (IRE) (Grand Lodge (USA))
(5487) 7097[14]

Bella Nueva (FR) *F Rohaut* a67 73
4 b m Indian Rocket—Besca Nueva (FR) (Lesotho (USA))
690a[4]

Bella Platina (GER) *U Stoltefuss* 97
6 ch m Platini(GER) —Burgberg Lady (Fleetwood (IRE))
3236a[11]

Bella's Story *Jim Goldie* 35
4 b m Lucky Story(USA) —Harrken Heights (IRE) (Belmez (USA))
4706[10] 5439[9]

Bella Swan *Walter Swinburn* a97 98
3 ch f Leporello(IRE) —Lydia Maria (Dancing Brave (USA))
1082[2] 1613[3] 2224[5] 3375[7] 3694[5] 4145[3] 4819[5] *5731[5]*

Belle Aumone (FR) *S Jesus* a80 86
2 b f Miesque's Son(USA) —Salut Simone (FR) (Simon Du Desert (FR))
2917a[6] 3307a[4]

Belle Bayardo (IRE) *Ronald Harris* a77 94
2 b g Le Vie Dei Colori—Heres The Plan (IRE) (Revoque (IRE))
1136[8] *1319[3]* ◆ 2407[2] 2680[5] 3087[4] *(3784)* (3849) *4228[5]* (4278) 4903[6] 5850[3] 5965[4] 6627[6] 7080[8] *7891[12]*

Belle Boleyn *Chris Wall* a60 59
3 b f Tobougg(IRE) —Belle De Jour (Exit To Nowhere (USA))
2899[4] 4115[5] 4874[5] 5653[4] ◆ 6065[10] *6525[2]* ◆ *7117[6]*

Belle Des Airs (IRE) *Ralph Beckett* a91 91
4 ch m Dr Fong(USA) —Belle Reine (King Of Kings (IRE))
1481[3] 2929[11] 3579[2] 3851[3]

Bellemere *Michael Easterby* 71
2 b f Ad Valorem(USA) —Five Lakes (USA) (Coronado's Quest (USA))
1749[7] 2693[7] 2980[5] 3923[7] (5042) 5483[2] 6139[11]

Belle Noverre (IRE) *Shaun Harley* a78 84
6 b m Noverre(USA) —Belle Etoile (FR) (Lead On Time (USA))
(3074) (5213)

Belle Park *Karen George* a61 61
3 b f Hamairi(IRE) —Cape Siren (Warning)
9[5] 594[5] 745[8] (993) 2418[3] 2722[5] 3129[10] *4430[11]* 4733[2] (4987) 5469[6] *5766[5]* 6125[2] 6335[9] 6937[11]

Belle Royale (IRE) *Mark Brisbourne* a61 93
2 b f Val Royal(FR) —Kahyasi Moll (IRE) (Brief Truce (USA))
1360[2] 1603[2] *1981[2]* 2130[6] (2591) 3141[22] 3859[2] 4544[2] (4615) (4783) (5293) 5882[13] 5901[7] 6627[4]

Belles Beau *Reg Hollinshead* a53
3 b f Fraam—Victory Flip (IRE) (Victory Note (USA))
267[2]

Belles Boudier *Gary Woodward* a15 16
2 b f Needwood Blade—Bahamian Belle (Bahamian Bounty)
4981[7] *6309[10]* 6569[11] *7396[9]*

Belle Zorro *Michael Bell* a56 47
3 br f Dr Fong(USA) —Special Beat (Bustino)
6816[7] *7117[2]*

Bellini Rose (IRE) *Jeremy Gask* a65
3 b f Bertolini(USA) —Prospectress (USA) (Mining (USA))
6997[11]

Bellini Surprise *Alan Jarvis* a12
3 ch f Sulamani(IRE) —Beleza (IRE) (Revoque (IRE))
1621[12]

Bell Island *Lady Herries* a83 77
6 b g Dansili—Thermal Spring (Zafonic (USA))
1169[3] 1931[3] 2810[5]

Bellomi (IRE) *Alan Juckes* a75 94
5 gr g Lemon Drop Kid(USA) —Reina Blanca (Darshaan)
1457[7]

Bell's Ocean (USA) *John Ryan* a68 72
3 b f Proud Citizen(USA) —Golden Train (USA) (Slew O'Gold (USA))
357[5] 809[11] 1362[12] 1605[6] 2634[7] 2879[9] 3271[5] 3413[7] (3666) 3911[6] *4133[4]* 4337[11] *(4687)* 5050[4] *5384[5]* 5494[6] *6452[6]*

Bellucci (GER) *P L Giannotti*
2 ch c Desert Prince(IRE) —Baila (Lando (GER))
7850a[10]

Below Zero (IRE) *Mark Johnston* a78 98
3 b g Shamardal(USA) —Chilly Start (IRE) (Caerleon (USA))
1500[3] 1687[4] 1865[3] 2545[8] 2862[4] (3429) 3791[14] 4819[5] 5292[12] 5903[4] 6175[23] 6357[3] 6564[10] 7014[2] *7289[11]*

Beltanus (GER) *T Potters* 104
6 ch h Tertullian(USA) —Brighella (GER) (Lomitas)
1251a[3] 2559a[11]

Belvidera *Tony Carroll* 20
4 b m Golden Snake(USA) —Satiric (IRE) (Doyoun)
2674[11] 3176[12] 3960[15] 6415[11] 6637[6] *6855[11]*

Be My Spy *Peter Salmon* 35
2 b f Monsieur Bond(IRE) —Star Sign (Robellino (USA))
3805[7] 4048[9] 4447[10] 5066[14] 6036[9] 6293[11]

Benamy Boy *Neville Bycroft* 31
4 ch g First Trump—Carol Again (Kind Of Hush)
1119[7] 2994[10] 3754[9]

Benandonner (USA) *Mike Murphy* a102 103
7 ch g Giant's Causeway(USA) —Cape Verdi (IRE) (Caerleon (USA))
108[9] 278[2] 635[2] 1006[17] *1085[12]* 1383[13] 2472[9] 3334[2] 3585[2] *(4030)* 4459[4] 4816[3] 6391[10]

Benato The Great (IRE) *David Nicholls* a79 67
4 b g Acclamation—Teodora (IRE) (Fairy King (USA))
(6896) *(7847)*

Benbaun (IRE) *Kevin Ryan* a109 120
9 b g Stravinsky(USA) —Escape To Victory (Salse (USA))
1024a[6] 2157a[2] 2325[8] 3486a[9] 5569a[11]

Ben Chorley *David Evans* a23 93
6 gr g Inchinor—Arantxa (Sharpo)
1006[4] 1837[10]

Bencoolen (IRE) *David Nicholls* a53 99
5 b g Daylami(IRE) —Jakarta (IRE) (Machiavellian (USA))
1333[5] 2423[3] 2977[12] 4459[13] 4579[5] (4943) 5529[10] 6106[6] (6396) 6877[3]

Bendigedig *Sylvester Kirk* a53 60
2 b f Indesatchel(IRE) —Four Legs Good (IRE) (Be My Guest (USA))
1577[14] 1930[12] *2677[7]* 3288[4] 3864[6] *4429[7] 4788[3] 5268[2] 5365[8] 5863[8]* 6072[11] *6369[5]* 7016[5] 7378[6]

Beneath *Kevin Ryan* a81 83
3 b g Dansili—Neath (Rainbow Quest (USA))
755[2] (922) ◆ 1734[4] 2125[3] 2607[4] *3519[7]* 5300[7] 5747[12] *6122[8]* 6753[14] *7726[5]*

Benedict Spirit (IRE) *John Flint* a87 82
5 b g Invincible Spirit(IRE) —Kathy Caerleon (IRE) (Caerleon (USA))
383[2] 430[3] 546[3] 636[3] (756) (811) 888[5] 1069[6] 1684[4] 1798[6] 4817[7]

Benfleet Boy *Brendan Powell* a54 77
6 gr g Fasliyev(USA) —Nicely (IRE) (Bustino)
6322[12]

Benhego *Gary Moore* a81 76
5 ch g Act One—Sadaka (USA) (Kingmambo (USA))
7736[4]

Benidorm *Alan McCabe* a43 62
2 b g Bahamian Bounty—Famcred (Inchinor)
5546[4] ◆ *6498[7]* 6919[4] 7178[6]

Benjamin (FR) *L A Urbano-Grajales* a78 79
5 b g Highest Honor(FR) —Mia's Baby (USA) (Rahy (USA))
(5378a)

Bennelong *Giles Bravery* a81 71
4 b g Bahamian Bounty—Bundle Up (USA) (Miner's Mark (USA))
231[8] 487[6] 749[5] 837[11] 943[8] 6851[12] 7128[14]

Bennie Blue (SAF) *A Al Raihe* a90 89
8 ch h Rich Man's Gold(USA) —Biloxi Blue (SAF) (Al Mufti (USA))
334a[7] 419a[10]

Benny The Bear *Linda Perratt* 61
3 ch g Rambling Bear—Mitchelland (Namaqualand (USA))
5214[3] ◆ 5686[7] 7051[4] 7225[5]

Benozzo Gozzoli *Hughie Morrison* a62 62
4 ch g Medicean—Star Precision (Shavian)
1446[3] ◆ 2445[5] *3760[3]*

Bentley *Brian Baugh* a73 55
6 b g Piccolo—April Lee (Superpower)
328[6] 464[9] 562[2] 789[3] 968[3] 1585[9] 2698[3] 2896[11] 3027[4] 3322[2] 4606[4] *5267[12]* 5535[5] 5820[9] 6054[5] 6375[2] 6578[6] 6937[4] 7068[5] 7487[6] 7543[3] 7633[4] (7787) 7863[3] (7986)

Benwilt Breeze (IRE) *Colin Teague* a58 46
8 b g Mujadil(USA) —Image Of Truce (IRE) (Brief Truce (USA))
7326[12] 7525[13]

Beowulf (FR) *P Bary* 86
2 ch c Layman(USA) —Belga Wood (USA) (Woodman (USA))
4036a[4]

Berberana (IRE) *Tim Easterby* a78 82
2 b f Acclamation—Barbera (GER) (Night Shift (USA))
(3756) 4934[5] 5301[3] 5745[2] 6139[7] 6568[16] (7174)

Berbice (IRE) *Linda Perratt* a81 74
5 gr g Acclamation—Pearl Bright (FR) (Kaldoun (FR))
696[3] 2399[5] 2840[8] 3716[4] 3892[4] 4510[15] *5027[7]* 5477[3] 5732[3] 6108[5] 6394[3] 6710[6] 7056[7] 7169[4] 7225[3]

Bere Davis (FR) *David Evans* a31 80
5 gr g Verglas(IRE) —Zerelda (Exhibitioner)
1241[10] 1396[10] 1673[8] 2109[7] 2488[3] 2596[5] 3291[11] 4681[7] 4897[3]

Berg Bahn (IRE) *G M Lyons* a100 101
3 b f Big Bad Bob(IRE) —Ski For Me (IRE) (Barathea (IRE))
514a[3] 709a[4] 3071[11] (3571a) 5351a[6]

Bergo (GER) *Gary Moore* 109
7 b g Silvano(GER) —Bella Figura (USA) (Surumu (GER))
2116[5] (3195) 5517[2] 6926[28]

Bergonzi (IRE) *Howard Johnson* a78 85
6 ch g Indian Ridge—Lady Windley (Baillamont (USA))
2276[2] 3060[6] (3772) (4671) 5788[10]

Beringoer (FR) *T Larriviere* a86 65
7 ch g Bering—Charmgoer (USA) (Nureyev (USA))
281a[2]

Berling (IRE) *John Dunlop* 99
3 gr c Montjeu(IRE) —Danaskaya (IRE) (Danehill (USA))
(1448) (2079) ◆ 3105[5] 3670[4] 4470[9] 5273[12]

Bermondsey Bob (IRE) *John Spearing* a14 68
4 b g Trans Island—Tread Softly (IRE) (Roi Danzig (USA))
1884[11] 2589[4] 2896[2] 3292[2] (3556) 3734[5] 4244[4] 4936[4] 5175[3] (5714) 6421[11] 6515[3] 6679[2] 7007[2] 7125[11]

Bermuda Rye (IRE) *A Al Raihe* a75 81
5 b h Cape Cross(IRE) —Alleluia Tree (IRE) (Royal Academy (USA))
415a[9]

Bernie's Moon (USA) *Brian Meehan* 58
3 bb f Bernstein(USA) —Moonstar (USA) (Kingmambo (USA))
2564[6] 3272[5] 3738[10]

Bernie's Tune *John Spearing* a50 43
2 b g Indesatchel(IRE) —Sweet Patoopie (Indian Ridge)
3332[8] 3832[11] 4587[9] 5613[7] 7124[10] *7551[7] 7864[8]*

Bernie The Bolt (IRE) *Andrew Balding* a50 102
4 br g Milan—Chaparral Lady (IRE) (Broken Hearted)
1821[13] 3447[11] (4817) 5220[17]

Bernisdale *George Moore* a55 65
2 ch f Bertolini(USA) —Carradale (Pursuit Of Love)
2832[14] 3536[4] 4862[5] 5682[10] 6569[2] 6891[15] *7471[5] 7831[3]*

Bernix *Nigel Tinkler* a68 58
8 gr g Linamix(FR) —Bernique (USA) (Affirmed (USA))
470[6] ◆ *(1239) (1508)* 2240[4] 3502[8] 5244[5] *6718[11] 7068[9]*

Berriedale *Ann Duffield* a14 54
4 ch m Fraam—Carradale (Pursuit Of Love)
2006[7] 2303[7]

Berry Hill Lass (IRE) *John O'Shea* a60 39
6 b m Alhaarth(IRE) —Gold Mist (Darshaan)
3560[7]

Berrymead *Ann Stokell* a52 61
5 br m Killer Instinct—Mill End Quest (King's Signet (USA))
125[6] 264[3] 530[6] 721[4] 1112[5]

Berrynarbor *Tony Newcombe* a41 57
5 b m Tobougg(IRE) —River Art (USA) (Irish River (FR))
228[10]

Berry Pomeroy *Liam Grassick*
5 ch g Fantastic Light(USA) —Compton Emerald (IRE) (Bluebird (USA))
2279[11]

Bert And Ernie *Mick Channon* 34
2 b c Bertolini(USA) —Walnut Grove (Forzando)
2839[18] 3035[10] 3678[6] 4241[11]

Bertbrand *Ian McInnes* a62 52
5 b g Bertolini(USA) —Mi Amor (IRE) (Alzao (USA))
69[8] 249[11] 320[10] 403[3] 569[7] 726[3] 866[6] 1154[5] *1235[8]* 1569[11] 1885[15] 1968[2] 2381[11] 7300[7] 7380[12] 7537[8] 7906[10]

Bertie Blu Boy *Paul Green* 18
2 b g Central Park(IRE) —Shaymee's Girl (Wizard King)
7303[13]

Bertie Buckle (IRE) *Jeremy Gask* a52
3 b g Bertolini(USA) —Buckle (IRE) (Common Grounds)
127[6] 329[2] 455[4] 581[10]

Bertie Smalls *Mark H Tompkins* a51 51
4 b g Xaar—Largo (IRE) (Selkirk (USA))
396[9] 611[4] 2023[U] 2655[10] 3263[13]

Bertie Southstreet *Jimmy O'Reilly* a73 76
7 bb g Bertolini(USA) —Salvezza (IRE) (Superpower)
2695[8] 3064[5] 3615[2] 4047[5] (4435) 4717[2] (4938)

Bertiewhittle *David Barron* 64
2 ch g Bahamian Bounty—Minette (Bishop Of Cashel)
4896[12] 6301[4] 6878[4] 7224[2]

Bertoliver *Stuart Williams* a85 92
6 b g Bertolini(USA) —Calcavella (Pursuit Of Love)
905[10] 1471[3] 2054[13] 2136[12] (2745) 3430[6] 5589[7] 5967[7]

Beseech (USA) *Julia Feilden* a46 14
3 rg f Maria's Mon(USA) —Concert Hall (USA) (Stravinsky (USA))
5366[12] 6861[9] *7489[6] 7728[8] 8015[6]*

Beshairt *Dai Burchell* a46 40
6 b m Silver Wizard(USA) —Irja (Minshaanshu Amad (USA))
5445[5]

Beso (IRE) *Luca Cumani* a68
2 ch f Medicean—Olivia Grace (Pivotal)
7021[4] ◆ *7447[3]*

Bessie Lou (IRE) *Michael Joseph Fitzgerald* a53 73
4 b m Montjeu(IRE) —Almond Mousse (FR) (Exit To Nowhere (USA))
4045[2] *4134[6]*

Best Be Careful (IRE) *Mark Usher* a57 64
2 b f Exceed And Excel(AUS) —Precautionary (Green Desert (USA))
3331[3] 3686[3] (4363) 4688[4] 6769[4] *7211[4]*

Best Catch (USA) *John Best* a32
3 b g Western Pride(USA) —Majestical (USA) (Garthorn (USA))
5842[8] 6124[9] 6313[9]

Bestdressed (USA) *John W Sadler* a104 98
6 rg g Lit De Justice(USA) —Undressed (USA) (Black Tie Affair)
3935a[7]

Best In Class *Stuart Williams* a80 71
4 gr g Best Of The Bests(IRE) —Third Party (Terimon)
480[10] 676[13] 975[12] 1530[12] 2013[7]

Best Intent *Michael Jarvis* 75
3 ch f King's Best(USA) —Hydro Calido (USA) (Nureyev (USA))
1882[4] 2463[3] 3347[3] 4294[3] (5209) 5918[6]

Best Joking (GER) *W Hefter* 102
5 ch m Big Shuffle(USA) —Bergwelt (GER) (Solarstern (FR))
1081a[5] 2157a[10] 3425a[0]

Best Known Secret (IRE) *Chris Bealby* a52 50
4 b m Captain Rio—Secret Justice (USA) (Lit De Justice (USA))
2535[8] 3111[9] 4251[6] 4982[3] 5485[11] 6643[4] *7131[2] 7328[2] 7468[7] 7807[7] 7911[6]*

Best Of Broadway (IRE) *David Lanigan* a55 51
3 b g King's Best(USA) —Broadway Hit (Sadler's Wells (USA))
1325[8] 1581[14] 1851[8] *2792[3] 3564[5]* 4235[5] *5864[3]*

Best One *Ronald Harris* a63 73
6 ch g Best Of The Bests(IRE) —Nasaieb (IRE) (Fairy King (USA))
112[3] 132[4] 525[7] 1068[5] 1146[2] 1583[4] 1979[9] 2021[2] *2721[6]* 2779[7] 3052[6] 3516[4] (3979) 4256[10] 4326[4] 4778[3] 5176[4] 5990[2] 6270[2] 6536[2] 6956[5] (7018) 7250[5] 7334[10] 7537[3] 7639[3] 7953[7] 8019[6]

Bestowed *David Evans* a68 58
5 b g Kyllachy—Granted (FR) (Cadeaux Genereux (IRE))
(75) 298[3] 467[7] 7920[5]

Best Prospect (IRE) *Michael Dods* a87 83
8 b g Orpen(USA) —Bright Prospect (USA) (Miswaki (USA))
1011^7 2937^{13} 4290^3 6181^9 6832^3 ◆ 7053^7 (7228)

Best Trip (IRE) *Richard Guest* a75 28
3 b g Whipper(USA) —Tereed Elhawa (Cadeaux Genereux)
(147) 478^3 ◆ 783^7 2170^8 5964^8 6800^{11} 8004^4 ◆

Besty *Bryan Smart* a76 81
3 ch g Compton Place—Petrovna (IRE) (Petardia)
1750^8 2099^{10} 2426^2 2815^2 3024^8 (3904) 4369^{10} 5606^9 7554^7

Betfair Lady (ITY) *M Manili*
5 b m Daggers Drawn(USA) —Imco Trendy (IRE) (Sri Pekan (USA))
273a^0

Bethlehem (IRE) *Hughie Morrison* a58 53
3 b g Oratorio(IRE) —Bumble (Rainbow Quest (USA))
971^5 1268^{12} 1432^7 2412^{13} 3564^9 3723^7 4230^3 5289^7

Bethrah (IRE) *D K Weld* 110
3 br f Marju(IRE) —Reve D'Iman (FR) (Highest Honor (FR))
(1952a) (2370a) 5773a^5

Bet Noir (IRE) *Tony Carroll* a62 64
5 b m King's Best(USA) —Ivowen (USA) (Theatrical)
13^7 295^7

Betrothed (IRE) *T Stack* 71
2 b f Oratorio(IRE) —Ring The Relatives (Bering)
6784a^6

Betteras Bertie *Mel Brittain* a63 72
7 gr g Paris House—Suffolk Girl (Statoblest)
2512^5 3508^2 4119^{15} 4602^{11} 5641^5 6116^{12} 7128^3

Better Be Blue (IRE) *Tony Carroll* a47 65
3 b f Big Bad Bob(IRE) —Ginger Lily (IRE) (Lucky Guest)
288^7 534^3 1158^{13} 1795^{14} 2487^6 3852^9 4113^4

Better Offer (IRE) *Amy Weaver* 66
2 ch c Bahamian Bounty—Yaky Romani (IRE) (Victory Note (USA))
3550^9 4221^9 4759^3 5675^{10} 6059^7

Better Self *David Evans* a68 64
2 b f With Approval(CAN) —Alter Ego (Alzao (USA))
3550^7 4240^8 4668^3 5682^7 6209^2 ◆ 7631^5 (7785) 7910^3

Between Dreams *Andy Turnell* a19
7 br m Silver Wizard(USA) —I Have A Dream (SWE) (Mango Express)
7251^{12} 7451^7

Beverly Hill Billy *Sandra Forster* a81 19
6 b g Primo Valentino(IRE) —Miss Beverley (Beveled (USA))
7171^{10}

Bewdley *Ray Peacock* a39 39
5 b m Best Of The Bests(IRE) —Garota De Ipanema (FR) (Al Nasr (FR))
3132^{10} 3557^5 4366^{11} 5905^8

Bewitched (IRE) *Charles O'Brien* a81 112
3 gr f Dansili—Abbatiale (FR) (Kaldoun (FR))
(2537) ◆ 3197^3 3571a^6 (4269a) 4882a^3 (6009a) (6735) ◆

Beyaz Villas *David Nicholls* a31 64
2 b g Ishiguru(USA) —Ante Futura (FR) (Suave Dancer (USA))
2376^8 3058^4 3625^2 3923^3 4242^8 4512^2 6569^{13} 7641^5

Beyeh (IRE) *Clive Brittain* 70
2 b f King's Best(USA) —Cradle Rock (IRE) (Desert Sun)
(3281) 5257^5

Beyond (IRE) *Jeremy Noseda* a81
3 ch g Galileo(IRE) —Run To Jane (IRE) (Doyoun)
31^3 (340) ◆ (830)

Beyonda Dream *Lucinda Featherstone* a34
4 b m And Beyond(IRE) —Richenda (Mister Baileys)
6933^{12}

Beyond Desire *Michael Jarvis* 103
3 b f Invincible Spirit(IRE) —Compradore (Mujtahid (USA))
(2326) 2912a^2 5120^8 6194^{13} 6887^5

Beyond Rubies *Henry Cecil* a47
3 b f Zamindar(USA) —Idma (Midyan (USA))
7069^{10} 7767^5

Bianca De Medici *Hughie Morrison* a77 75
3 b f Medicean—Tremiere (FR) (Anabaa (USA))
4425^3 4906^3 5872^2 (6540) 7046^7 7421^7

Biancarosa (IRE) *B Grizzetti* 98
3 b f Dalakhani(IRE) —Rosa Di Brema (ITY) (Lomitas)
1252a^6

Bianco Boy (USA) *John Best* a58
3 rg g Roman Ruler(USA) —Sterling Cat (USA) (Event Of The Year (USA))
1222^9 7872^8

Biaraafa (IRE) *Michael Bell* 72
2 b f Araafa(IRE) —Bianca Nera (Salse (USA))
4474^3 (5160) 5998^5 ◆ 6920^6

Biarritz (SAF) *M F De Kock* a103 109
7 b h Count Dubois—Corlia's Bid (AUS) (Polish Patriot (USA))
798a^9

Biased *M Delzangles* 103
4 ch m Haafhd—Pas D'Heure (IRE) (Arazi (USA))
1792a^6 2403a^5 5320a^9

Bibiana Bay *Ben Case* a41 35
3 b f Leporello(IRE) —Polisonne (Polish Precedent (USA))
128^{11} 583^{11} 1782^6

Bible Belt (IRE) *Mrs John Harrington* 103
2 br f Big Bad Bob(IRE) —Shine Silently (IRE) (Bering)
6401a^3

Bicksta *Paul Midgley* a54 54
4 b m Haafhd—Premiere Dance (IRE) (Loup Solitaire (USA))
7^5 19^5 (142)

Bidable *Bryn Palling* a62 75
6 b m Auction House(USA) —Dubitable (Formidable (USA))
2362^7 2920^4 (3131) 3683^5 (3853) 4681^2 5584^7 6023^2 6629^9 6958^5 7214^7

Bideeya (USA) *Clive Brittain* a57 67
3 bb f Dubawi(IRE) —Menhoubah (USA) (Dixieland Band (USA))
978^3 3434^2 3739^{10} 4482^4 6930^{10} 7006^{14}

Bid For Glory *Hugh Collingridge* a74 63
6 ch h Auction House(USA) —Woodland Steps (Bold Owl)
294^5 485^3 588^3 814^9 5272^7 5753^P

Bid For Gold *Jedd O'Keeffe* a36 78
6 b g Auction House(USA) —Gold And Blue (IRE) (Bluebird (USA))
1030^{14} 1276^7 1869^6 2206^7 2817^6 4063^7 5064^6 5357^7 5482^4 6110^3 ◆ 6491^5 7125^5

Bidruma *Mike Murphy* a58 58
3 b f Numerous(USA) —Go Polar (Polar Falcon (USA))
2249^4 3125^4 3620^5 4250^6 5031^{11} 5670^4 5898^9 7064^7 (7477) 7721^6

Bigalo's Laura B (IRE) *Lawrence Mullaney* 53
2 ch f Needwood Blade—Rash (Pursuit Of Love)
3392^7 3770^4 4150^3 4934^9 5602^{11} 6294^2

Bigalo's Princessa *Lawrence Mullaney* a19 19
2 b f Kyllachy—Emouna (Cadeaux Genereux)
7142^7 7400^7

Bigalo's Vera B *Lawrence Mullaney* a40 32
2 b f Ishiguru(USA) —Maid For Running (Namaqualand (USA))
2376^{12} 5099^9 6892^7 7404^6 7692^3 7983^5

Big Audio (IRE) *Saeed Bin Suroor* 103
3 b c Oratorio(IRE) —Tarbela (IRE) (Grand Lodge (USA))
2471^6 4504^{13} 5292^8

Big Bad Boo *James Unett* a46
4 b g Almutawakel—Forever Loved (Deploy)
7069^{11} 7579^7 7703^8

Big Bay (USA) *Jane Chapple-Hyam* a96 87
4 b g Horse Chestnut(SAF) —Takipy (USA) (Persian Bold)
1383^{23} 1697^{16} 2971^{15} 7233^9 7430^9 7735^8

Big Boom *Michael Quinn* a45 72
5 ch g Cadeaux Genereux—Kastaway (Distant Relative)
1130^4 1998^{11} 5238^7 5386^{10} 6133^2 6679^4 7005^7 7155^5

Big Bound (USA) *B Al Subaie* a80 103
4 b h Grand Slam(USA) —Golden Cat (USA) (Storm Cat (USA))
706a^{14}

Big Brown Tsar (FR) *M Delzangles*
4 b g Machiavellian Tsar(FR) —Big Brown Eyes (FR) (Saumarez)
1055a^0

Big City Boy (IRE) *Phil McEntee* a24
2 b g Tamarisk(IRE) —Cuddles (IRE) (Taufan (USA))
7914^4 8030^5

Big Creek (IRE) *B Grizzetti* 94
3 b c Galileo(IRE) —Baranja (USA) (St Jovite (USA))
1945a^8 2802a^{20}

Big Drama (USA) *David Fawkes* a122
4 bb h Montbrook(USA) —Riveting Drama (USA) (Notebook (USA))
5779a^2 (7361a)

Big Eric *David Evans* a38
3 b g Bollin Eric—Rose Hill (Sabrehill (USA))
31^7 206^7 484^{11}

Bigern *Michael Mullineaux* a9
3 b g Firebreak—Lady Boxer (Komaite (USA))
5065^{11} 6696^{10}

Big Hunter (FR) *E Kurdu* 80
3 ch c Green Tune(USA) —Ashley River (Ashkalani (IRE))
6791a^7

Big Issue (IRE) *Richard Hannon* 102
2 b c Dubawi(IRE) —Improvise (Lend A Hand)
4460^2 ◆ (4954) 5567a^3 5831^2 (6475) 6733^3 7095^5

Big Nige (IRE) *Jeff Pearce* a67 55
4 br g Mull Of Kintyre(USA) —Queen's Quest (Rainbow Quest (USA))
82^3 260^3 429^5 586^7

Big Noise *Dr Jon Scargill* a96 99
6 b h Lake Coniston(IRE) —Mitsubishi Video (IRE) (Doulab (USA))
1900^5 3172^5 3681^4 4358^{19} 6888^{26}

Big Robert *P D Deegan* a104 99
6 b h Medicean—Top Flight Queen (Mark Of Esteem (IRE))
1247a^7 1954a^5 4463a^{10} 5571a^{23}

Big Sur *Tom Keddy* a61 61
4 ch g Selkirk(USA) —Bombazine (IRE) (Generous (IRE))
1591^9 2299^9 4439^8 4969^2 5271^3 (5864) 7005^8

Big Wave Bay (IRE) *Alan Jarvis* a69 67
3 b c Alamshar(IRE) —Lady Pahia (IRE) (Pivotal)
1158^2 2501^4 3039^3 4719^5 5656^9 6144^{12}

Big Whitfield *Michael Dods* a51 62
4 b g Tobougg(IRE) —Natalie Jay (Ballacashtal (CAN))
1179^{10} 1808^3 2274^{12} 2764^8 3369^9

Big Zaf *Paul Midgley* 7
2 bb g Zafeen(FR) —Raasors Edge (Ajraas (USA))
5594^{11}

Bijou Dan *George Moore* a49 71
9 ch g Bijou D'Inde—Cal Norma's Lady (IRE) (Lyphard's Special (USA))
1150^7 2814^4 3772^5

Bikini Babe (IRE) *Mark Johnston* a106 102
3 b f Montjeu(IRE) —Zeiting (IRE) (Zieten (USA))
514a^5 709a^2 1498^3 2029^5 2711^7 3101^{10} 4347^6 4612a^2 5138a^5 5538^4 5938^6 6886^5 7358a^3

Bilash *Reg Hollinshead* 70
3 rg c Choisir(AUS) —Goldeva (Makbul)
1511^{14} 1878^2 2114^2 2309^4 3393^8 3808^3 5390^7 6466^2 6773^2

Bilbaray (IRE) *Bill Ratcliffe*
4 b m Fath(USA) —Last Shaambles (IRE) (Shaamit (IRE))
3511^9

Bilidn *Clive Brittain* 50
2 b f Tiger Hill(IRE) —Brightest Star (Unfuwain (USA))
3392^6 4203^9

Bilko Pak (IRE) *James Given* a88 86
2 b c Barathea(IRE) —Vale View (FR) (Anabaa (USA))
1309^5 (1429) 2918^2 (3327) 4138^{23} 5187^{13} (5921) 6842^5 7378^2 (7484) 7636^4

Billberry *Stuart Williams* a77 69
5 gr g Diktat—Elderberry (Bin Ajwaad (IRE))
110^4 (317) 657^3 802^2 981^6 1224^3 1634^5 2383^4 2750^4 3129^6 4839^4 5087^2 5557^4 6098^4 6800^{12} 7046^{11}

Billie Jean *B W Hills* a67 47
3 b f Bertolini(USA) —Factice (USA) (Known Fact (USA))
111^4 471^7 1175^4

Billionaire Boy (IRE) *Patrick Morris* a47 51
3 b g Acclamation—Shalwell (IRE) (Shalford (IRE))
4340^6 4584^4 5438^4 6246^8 6931^6 7322^4

Bill Page (USA) *Mrs V M Jordan* a65
2 ch c Proud Citizen(USA) —Da River Hoss (USA) (River Special (USA))
6712^5 7427^4 7664^7 (7888)

Bill's Story *Mick Channon* a55 53
3 b f Lucky Story(USA) —Heavenly Goddess (Soviet Star (USA))
3738^6 4307^6 4997^7 5669^6 6540^9 6865^7

Billy Boy Blue (IRE) *J E Hammond* a79 78
3 b c Whipper(USA) —Holy Norma (Nashwan (USA))
1195a^8

Billy Budd (IRE) *S Botti* 98
2 b c Shamardal(USA) —Baranja (USA) (St Jovite (USA))
6762a^3

Billy Dane (IRE) *Finbar Murtagh* a77 96
6 b g Fayruz—Lomalou (IRE) (Lightning Dealer)
1006^9 1708^2 1889^6 2423^4 3206^8 3667^7 3920^9 4603^5 5407^{10} 5737^4 5789^5

Billyonair *W De Best-Turner* a16
3 ch g Auction House(USA) —Westmead Tango (Pursuit Of Love)
2121^{11}

Billy One Punch *George Foster* a72 75
8 b g Mark Of Esteem(IRE) —Polytess (IRE) (Polish Patriot (USA))
4188^9 4585^{12} 6396^8

Billy Red *John Jenkins* a92 81
6 ch g Dr Fong(USA) —Liberty Bound (Primo Dominie)
192^8 (250) 345^4 (535) 722^8 2563^{11} 3216^5 3578^7 4043^5 (4693) 5528^4 5678^3 7033^{12} 7254^2 7826^5 7971^3 7993^7

Billyruben *Daniel Mark Loughnane* a57 22
2 ch g Bertolini(USA) —River Crossing (Zafonic (USA))
7598^8

Billys Flyer (IRE) *Evan Williams* 35
5 b g Sinndar(IRE) —Beeper The Great (USA) (Whadjathink (USA))
2004^{10}

Billy Simmonds *Julia Feilden* a30
5 b g Man Among Men(IRE) —Lizzie Simmonds (IRE) (Common Grounds)
667^7 912^{11} 1129^{11}

Bin End *Michael Bell* a83 89
4 b g King's Best(USA) —Overboard (IRE) (Rainbow Quest (USA))
1069^5

Binglybonglyboo *Lawrence Mullaney* 62
4 b g Elmaamul(USA) —Sabotini (Prince Sabo)
3595^{10} 4403^7 4866^5

Binnion Bay (IRE) *John Bridger* a61 57
9 b g Fasliyev(USA) —Literary (Woodman (USA))
13^9 124^5 184^7 261^{12} (656) 847^5 970^{10} (1591) 3160^{13} 3338^3 3783^{11} 4621^7 5962^6 6775^9 7727^{11}

Bin Shamardal (IRE) *B W Hills* a74 79
3 b c Shamardal(USA) —Lonely Ahead (USA) (Rahy (USA))
950^4 ◆ (1485) 1969^4 2863^6 3708^4 4491^7 5304^3 5887^9

Bint Alakaaber (IRE) *John Jenkins* a61
2 b f Elusive City(USA) —Lady Of Pleasure (IRE) (Marju (IRE))
5719^5

Bintalwaadi *Ed Dunlop* a83 93
3 b f Barathea(IRE) —Al Durrah (USA) (Darshaan)
(1589) 2898^2 4030^8 5524^5 6346^8 7097^{11}

Bint Doyen *Clive Brittain* a82 79
3 br f Doyen(IRE) —Zonda (Fabulous Dancer (USA))
840^2 1082^6 2224^7

Binthere Dunthat *Michael Bell* a77
3 b f Bahamian Bounty—Bijou A Moi (Rainbow Quest (USA))
453^2 624^2 (793)

Bint Mazyouna *Mick Channon* a63 65
2 ch f Cadeaux Genereux—Resistance Heroine (Dr Fong (USA))
4471^7 5147^9 5441^5 5961^3

Bint Modelliste *D Gambarota* 71
2 b f Refuse To Bend(IRE) —Modelliste (Machiavellian (USA))
6975a^8

Bint Nas (IRE) *Mick Channon* 56
2 b f Clodovil(IRE) —Molomo (Barathea (IRE))
6688^5

Biographical (USA) *John Gosden* a77 71
2 bb c Dynaformer(USA) —Tell It (USA) (Storm Cat (USA))
5582^3 (6211) 6471^{15}

Biondetti (USA) *Mahmood Al Zarooni* a98 105
2 b c Bernardini(USA) —Lyphard's Delta (USA) (Lyphard (USA))
(4803) (5751) (6762a) 7363a^4

Bird Call (IRE) *David Barron* a53
3 b f Danbird(AUS) —Paradise Eve (Bahamian Bounty)
699^5 ◆ 886^7 1825^5 7537^{12}

Bird In The Wind (USA) *Ralph Beckett* a60 44
2 b f Henny Hughes(USA) —Go For It Lady (USA) (Mr Prospector (USA))
5719^6 6441^9 7021^6 7493^8

Birdolini *Alan King* a71
2 ch f Bertolini(USA) —Bird Over (Bold Edge)
7185^5 ◆ (7879) ◆

Bird On The Wire *Bill Turner* a55 36
3 gr f Compton Place—Pomponette (USA) (Rahy (USA))
1456^6 2000^{14} 2217^9

Birdwatcher (IRE) *Mark Johnston*
2 ch c Cadeaux Genereux—Dancing Feather (Suave Dancer (USA))
6811^{12} 7385^{14}

Birkside *Linda Perratt* a67 82
7 ch g Spinning World(USA) —Bright Hope (IRE) (Danehill (USA))
1098^4 1199^3 1539^3 2672^2 3166^2

Bishopbriggs (USA) *Michael Quinlan* a70 46
5 ch g Victory Gallop(CAN) —Inny River (USA) (Seattle Slew (USA))
(193) ◆ (351) ◆ 684^8 869^9 1063^{10} 1300^{10} 1929^9 4130^{12} 4789^7 5897^{12} (8023)

Bishop Rock (USA) *Nigel Tinkler* a29 30
4 b g Vicar(USA) —Rhumba Rage (USA) (Nureyev (USA))
6269^{12} 6905^9

Bishops Moon *Michael Quinlan* 43
2 b f Araafa(IRE) —Shirley Moon (IRE) (Montjeu (IRE))
1256^7 4103^8 4436^6

Bit Of Bling *Jeremy Noseda* a1
3 b f Dansili—Bling Bling (IRE) (Indian Ridge)
1661^{12}

Bit Of Chocolate *R Brogi* 94
2 b c Motivator—Lady Coquette (SWE) (Mujadil (USA))
7850a^4

Bitter Fortune (USA) *Jeremy Noseda* a67 76
3 b c More Than Ready(USA) —Cataballerina (USA) (Tabasco Cat (USA))
2754^3 3523^2 4069^3 4660^4

Bitter Honey *Eric Alston* a53 62
3 b f Reset(AUS) —Piccolo Cativo (Komaite (USA))
717^7 991^4 2426^9

Bivouac (UAE) *Alan Swinbank* a84 65
6 b g Jade Robbery(USA) —Tentpole (USA) (Rainbow Quest (USA))
(720) (1493) (1828) ◆ 1996^5 3764^8 4686^4 (5646) 6715^2 7130^4

Bizarrely (IRE) *Jeff Pearce* a66 67
3 b g Antonius Pius(USA) —Diamond Field (USA) (Mr Prospector (USA))
4238^3 4763^5 4971^3 ◆ 5656^7 6212^4 6993^{11} 7273^4 7685^3 7768^6 7995^7

Black Annis Bower *Michael Easterby* 74
2 b f Proclamation(IRE) —Bow Bridge (Bertolini (USA))
3274^{12} 4336^7 5196^5 5418^5 (5998) 6325^6 7174^2 (7301)

Black Baccara *Phil McEntee* a56 65
3 b f Superior Premium—Areish (IRE) (Keen)
2046^5 2566^{11} 3171^{11} 3606^{11} 4210^3 4435^3 4720^4 4861^5 7018^5 7064^3 7331^5 7425^3 7537^5 7721^5 7808^5 7877^8

Black Cadillac (IRE) *Andrew Balding*
2 br c Kheleyf(USA) —Desert Design (Desert King (IRE))
6532^{17}

Black Coffee *Mark Brisbourne* a63 67
5 br g Vettori(IRE) —In The Woods (You And I (USA))
2894^{10} 3294^3 4781^7 5437^7 6051^8 6213^{11} 6518^5 7569^6 7814^3 (7920) 8008^7

Black Crystal (USA) *Robert Collet* 93
4 b m Elusive Quality(USA) —Watership Crystal (IRE) (Sadler's Wells (USA))
742a^{11}

Black Dahlia *Jeremy Glover* a98 91
5 br m Dansili—South Rock (Rock City)
553^2 885^{11} 1084^{10} 3448^7 3969^4 4287^4

Blackdown Boy *Rod Millman* 75
3 b g Sampower Star—Shielaligh (Aragon)
1731^2 2164^3 (3511) 4109^7

Black Draft *Brian Forsey* a52 41
8 bb g Josr Algarhoud(IRE) —Tilia (Primo Dominie)
10^4 146^3 976^3 1235^7 1771^7

Black Eagle (IRE) *A bin Huzaim* a104 107
4 b h Cape Cross(IRE) —Shimna (Mr Prospector (USA))
417a^4 632a^{13} 801a^7

Black Falcon (IRE) *John Harris* a61 62
10 ch g In The Wings—Muwasim (USA) (Meadowlake (USA))
90^4 (113) 244^{10} 377^5 6660^7 7397^6 7475^7

Black Iceman *Jeff Pearce* a59
2 bl g Iceman—Slite (Mind Games)
6159^{18} 6843^9 7558^6 7888^{11}

Black Jacari (IRE) *Philip Kirby* 86
5 b g Black Sam Bellamy(IRE) —Amalia (IRE) (Danehill (USA))
1720^7 3402^2

Blackleyf (IRE) *Tom Dascombe* a65 60
2 br g Kheleyf(USA) —Cuca Vela (USA) (Devil's Bag (USA))
3310^U 3721^6 4096^{12} 4543^5 5720^4 6163^5 6500^{RR}

Black Mambazo (IRE) *L Riccardi* 116
5 b h Statue Of Liberty(USA) —Rich Gift (Cadeaux Genereux)
2157a^4 2804a^9 6976a^8 7459a^{13}

Blackmore *Julia Feilden* a76 57
3 b g Rainbow Quest(USA) —Waki Music (USA) (Miswaki (USA))
2244^4 6313^8 6861^5 (7321) (7388) ◆ 7553^3

Black Moth (IRE) *Brian Meehan* a96 103
2 b c Invincible Spirit(IRE) —Tshusick (Dancing Brave (USA))
2474[3] (2687) 3100[11] (3611) 4097[7] 4787[2] 5221[7] 5604[3] 5907[4]

Black N Brew (USA) *John Best* a83 78
4 b g Milwaukee Brew(USA) —Natural Glow (USA) (Siphon (BRZ))
485[6] 1530[2] 2685[7] 3317[15] (4488) 5264[9] 5866[3] 6444[7]

Black Or Red (IRE) *Ian Wood* a79 71
5 b g Cape Cross(IRE) —Gentle Thoughts (Darshaan)
7632[6]

Black Out (GER) *W Figge* 106
5 ch h Second Set(IRE) —Bella Vista (GER) (Konigsstuhl (GER))
743a[0]

Black Quartz (FR) *A P O'Brien* 104
3 b c Danehill Dancer(IRE) —Mirina (FR) (Pursuit Of Love)
1038a[5]

Black Raja (USA) *R Menichetti* 88
2 b f Aragorn(IRE) —Mambo Princess (USA) (Kingmambo (USA))
6975a[10]

Black Snowflake (USA) *Mahmood Al Zarooni* a89 97
3 b c Elusive Quality(USA) —Black Escort (USA) (Southern Halo (USA))
414a[5] 819a[4] 1313[8] 2324[3] 3103[24]

Black Spirit (USA) *Clive Cox* 108
3 b c Black Minnaloushe(USA) —L'Extra Honor (USA) (Hero's Honor (USA))
1703[10] (3692) 4420a[5] 5135a[3] 5853[4] 6219a[6]

Blackstone Vegas *Derek Shaw* a61 63
4 ch g Nayef(USA) —Waqood (USA) (Riverman (USA))
32[4] 409[8] 665[5] 813[2] 865[2] (1984) 2610[7] 2880[2] 3110[6] 5663[9] 5864[8] 7286[3] 7759[4] 7840[4]

Black Tor Figarro (IRE) *Brendan Duke* a55 67
5 b g Rock Of Gibraltar(IRE) —Will Be Blue (IRE) (Darshaan)
7836[4] 8013[8]

Blade *Mark Brisbourne* a43 54
2 ch g Needwood Blade—Ellina (Robellino (USA))
5924[9] 6268[9] 6743[10]

Blade Pirate *John Ryan* a51 51
2 ch g Needwood Blade—CC Canova (Millkom)
1603[10] 2561[4] 2873[9] 3269[11] 4499[8] 4716[7] 5365[9] 6129[14] 6795[10] 6859[11] 7236[7] 7839[5]

Blades Harmony *Ed McMahon* a57
3 b g Needwood Blade—Yabint El Sham (Sizzling Melody)
253[4] 473[4] 784[6] 991[5] 1456[5] 2000[15]

Blagueuse (IRE) *E Lellouche* 92
3 b f Statue Of Liberty(USA) —Bright Sky (IRE) (Wolfhound (USA))
4773a[0]

Blaise Tower *Andrew Haynes* a78 82
4 ch g Fantastic Light(USA) —Blaise Castle (USA) (Irish River (FR))
3995[6] 5375[9]

Blake Dean *Ben Haslam* 65
2 b g Halling(USA) —Antediluvian (Air Express (IRE))
5762[9] 6001[3] 6268[6]

Blakeshall Diamond *David Bourton* a26 47
5 gr m Piccolo—Hi Hoh (IRE) (Fayruz)
6119[9]

Blakey's Boy *Harry Dunlop* a42 85
3 b g Hawk Wing(USA) —Divine Grace (IRE) (Definite Article)
1497[7] 2117[10] 2927[5] 3916[4] 7304[3] 7688[7]

Blame (USA) *Albert M Stall Jr* a131
4 b h Arch(USA) —Liable (USA) (Seeking The Gold (USA))
(4855a) 6586a[2] (7367a)

Blanche Dubawi (IRE) *Michael Quinlan* a74 80
2 b f Dubawi(IRE) —Dixie Belle (Diktat)
5719[2] ◆ (6892)

Blast Furnace (IRE) *Peter Chapple-Hyam* 71
3 b f Sadler's Wells(USA) —Race The Wild Wind (USA) (Sunny's Halo (CAN))
1356[5] 2890[6] 4845[9]

Blaze Brightly (IRE) *Mrs John Harrington* a84 94
3 b f Big Bad Bob(IRE) —Kristal's Paradise (IRE) (Bluebird (USA))
4524a[15]

Blaze Of Fire *M F De Kock* a88 99
4 b g Bering—Flamenco Red (Warning)
605a[9] 706a[12]

Blaze Of Thunder (IRE) *Alan Swinbank* 78
2 ch g Ad Valorem(USA) —Palatine Dancer (IRE) (Namid)
3087[5] (3624) 4388[6] 4948[2] 5637[6] 6139[6]

Blaze On By *John Bridger* a51 56
2 ch f Firebreak—Yanomami (USA) (Slew O'Gold (USA))
2358 [10] 3399[5] 3625[4] 4623[12] 5373[5] 6081[4] 7295[8] 7650[5] 7755[7]

Blazing Apostle (IRE) *Christine Dunnett* a51
2 ch f Redback—Salonika Sky (Pursuit Of Love)
5160[15] 5721[6]

Blazing Buck *Tony Carroll* a30 74
4 ch g Fraam—Anapola (GER) (Polish Precedent (USA))
6454[11]

Blazing Desert *John Quinn* 79
6 b g Beat All(USA) —Kingsfold Blaze (Mazilier (USA))
2244[3] 2697[6] 3176[3] 3709[2] ◆ (4266) ◆ 5497[2] 5940[5]

Blazing Field *Clive Cox* 17
2 ch f Halling(USA) —Autumn Wealth (IRE) (Cadeaux Genereux)
6468[10]

Blek (FR) *E Lellouche* 112
5 gr h Chichicastenango(FR) —Exande (FR) (Exit To Nowhere (USA))
(1748a) 2375a[3] (4038a) 5349a[3] 6607a[8] 7110a[5]

Blessed Biata (USA) *William Haggas* a63 91
2 b f Mr Greeley(USA) —June Moon (IRE) (Sadler's Wells (USA))
5719[4] ◆ 6559[6] ◆ 7098[9]

Blessed Luck (IRE) *S Botti* 102
3 b f Rock Of Gibraltar(IRE) —Pinky Mouse (IRE) (Machiavellian (USA))
2575a[8] 3495a[8]

Blessed Place *Dominic Ffrench Davis* a43 64
10 ch g Compton Place—Cathedra (So Blessed)
1166[12] 1534[10] 1799[12] 2186[10] 2720[7] 3255[3] 3687[9] (4099) 4343[6] 4659[8]

Bless You *Henry Candy* 63
2 b f Bahamian Bounty—Follow Flanders (Pursuit Of Love)
7123[3]

Blind Luck (USA) *Jerry Hollendorfer* a120
3 ch f Pollard's Vision(USA) —Lucky One (USA) (Best Of Luck (USA))
7344a[2]

Blind Stag (IRE) *Paul Midgley* a48 58
2 b c Majestic Missile(IRE) —Floralia (Auction Ring (USA))
1331[5] 1749[9] 2522[6] 2836[7] 3757[4] 4150[2] 4367[6] 5602[13]

Bling (FR) *C Ferland* a92 92
3 b c Kingsalsa(USA) —Bricoleuse (USA) (A.P. Indy (USA))
1195a[5]

Blinka Me *Alex Hales* a54 65
3 b c Tiger Hill(IRE) —Easy To Love (USA) (Diesis)
1145[3] (1778) 2175[3] 2650[2] 4493[6] 5260[6]

Blissful Moment (USA) *Sir Michael Stoute* 96
3 bb g Dynaformer(USA) —Arabian Spell (IRE) (Desert Prince (IRE))
3428[3] (4205) 5118[7] (6074) ◆

Blitzed *Gary Moore* a79 79
3 b g Fantastic Light(USA) —Broken Peace (USA) (Devil's Bag (USA))
2812[3] 3443[2] 4360[10] 4964[5] 5367[2] (5842)

Blizzard Blues (USA) *Henry Cecil* 104
4 ch h Mr Greeley(USA) —Blush Damask (USA) (Green Dancer (USA))
1382[6] 2116[9] 5080[7] 5949[4] 6388[7]

Block Party *David Simcock* a85 86
4 b g Dansili—Mylania (Midyan (USA))
1088[9] 1306[9] 2328[7] 2872[10] 3389[11]

Bloodsweatandtears *William Knight* 79
2 b c Barathea(IRE) —Celestial Princess (Observatory (USA))
3794[7] (4437) 5310[4]

Bloody Sunday (FR) *M Boutin* 31
2 b f Soave(GER) —Deltichope (FR) (Sin Kiang (FR))
4274a[7]

Blow Hole (USA) *Alison Thorpe* a76 14
5 ch g Mr Greeley(USA) —Nevis (USA) (Cox's Ridge (USA))
148[11]

Blowing Bubbles (USA) *Brian Meehan* a72
2 ch f Songandaprayer(USA) —Ms Versatality (USA) (Opening Verse (USA))
6451[11] 6697[3] 6869[4] 7065[5]

Blown It (USA) *Jim Goldie* a74 80
4 bb g More Than Ready(USA) —Short Shadow (USA) (Out Of Place (USA))
5480[11] 6103[14] 6140[8] 6492[10] 7239[9]

Blow Up (IRE) *R Menichetti* 99
3 ch c Daggers Drawn(USA) —Miss Buffy (Polar Falcon (USA))
1945a[11]

Blu Basic (IRE) *M Planard*
4 ch g Fath(USA) —Margin Call (IRE) (Tirol)
207a[0]

Bluberry *Gary Moore* a54 4
2 b f Kyllachy—Stormy Monday (Cadeaux Genereux)
6882[12] 7485[7] 7686[6] 8031[9]

Blu Constellation (ITY) *Vittorio Caruso* 119
2 b c Orpen(USA) —Stella Celtica (ITY) (Celtic Swing)
(3253a) (7277a)

Blue Again *Walter Swinburn* a70 68
3 b f Leporello(IRE) —Forever Blue (Spectrum (IRE))
1278[11] 1661[3] 2342[6] 2871[5] 3441[6] 4248[4] 5010[3]

Blue And Gold (FR) *C Lerner* a92 95
4 ch m Spinning World(USA) —Blue Story (FR) (Gold Away (IRE))
2778a[6] 3704a[11]

Blue Angel (IRE) *Richard Hannon* a75 105
3 b f Oratorio(IRE) —Blue Cloud (IRE) (Nashwan (USA))
1613[2] 1899[8] 4319[7] 4540[4] 5305[4] 5883[3] 6351[2] 6923[12]

Blue Aura (IRE) *Brendan Powell* a55 66
7 b g Elnadim(USA) —Absent Beauty (IRE) (Dancing Dissident (USA))
1596[7] 1929[10] 2596[10] 2866[7] (3254) 3556[3] 4478[12] 4875[7]

Blue Avon *Richard Fahey* 56
3 b f Avonbridge—Blue Nile (IRE) (Bluebird (USA))
1104[7] 1465[9] 2132[9]

Blue Bajan (IRE) *Andy Turnell* a98 113
8 b g Montjeu(IRE) —Gentle Thoughts (Darshaan)
266[2]

Bluebaru *Peter Salmon* 13
4 b g Bahamian Bounty—Gina Of Hithermoor (Reprimand)
4414[6] 4673[6]

Blueberry Fizz (IRE) *John Ryan* a26
2 b f Kheleyf(USA) —Miss Poppets (Polar Falcon (USA))
7231[19] 7385[11]

Bluebird Chariot *Milton Bradley* a40 33
7 b g Bluebird(USA) —Boadicea's Chariot (Commanche Run)
1507[10] 2023[11]

Bluebok *Milton Bradley* a69 67
9 ch g Indian Ridge—Blue Sirocco (Bluebird (USA))
77[3] 132[3] 351[9] 525[2] 774[3] 967[6] 1583[5] 2021[14] 2186[9] 2721[5] 6665[3] 7477[5] 7720[3] 7860[2] 8037[7]

Blue Bunting (USA) *Mahmood Al Zarooni* 99
2 gr f Dynaformer(USA) —Miarixa (FR) (Linamix (FR))
4595[2] (5066) (7235)

Blue Cayenne (FR) *Mlle S-V Tarrou* a73 103
5 b m Anabaa Blue—Nakiya (FR) (Kendor (FR))
1081a[8]

Blue Celeste *Richard Phillips* a36 13
4 b m Sakhee(USA) —Ellie Ardensky (Slip Anchor)
308[9]

Blue Charm *Ian McInnes* a67 73
6 b g Averti(IRE) —Exotic Forest (Dominion)
465[5] 668[10] 855[10] 1305[5] 1508[8] 1628[3] 2643[9] 2850[5] 3124[6] 4700[11] 4939[10] 5331[9] 5962[8] 6024[6]

Blue Cossack (IRE) *Mark Usher* a51 12
2 b g Ivan Denisovich(IRE) —Biasca (Erhaab (USA))
2887[13] 4695[12] 5006[14] 7888[4]

Blue Cross Boy (USA) *Adrian McGuinness* a51 51
5 gr g Sunday Break(JPN) —Introducer (USA) (Cozzene (USA))
530[8]

Blue Dazzler (IRE) *Amanda Perrett* 72
2 b g Dalakhani(IRE) —Lady Ragazza (IRE) (Bering)
2077[6] 2547[6] 6473[8] 6809[5]

Blue Deer (IRE) *Mick Channon* 70
2 b c Bahamian Bounty—Jaywick (UAE) (Jade Robbery (USA))
6019[3] 6436[2]

Blue Destination *Philip McBride* 78
2 b c Dubai Destination(USA) —Bluebelle (Generous (IRE))
4803[6] 7172[2]

Blue Eyed Eloise *B J McMath* a64 48
8 b m Overbury(IRE) —Galix (FR) (Sissoo)
868[3] 5011[10]

Bluegrass Gal (USA) *Lisa Williamson* a9
4 ch m Cape Canaveral(USA) —Reigning Princess (USA) (Storm Boot (USA))
5514[6] 7328[13] 7461[8] 7862[8]

Bluegrass Lion (USA) *Lisa Williamson* 50
4 bb g Volponi(USA) —Exactly Dixie (USA) (Dixie Brass (USA))
6915[13] 7157[11] 7327[8] 7429[12]

Blue Ivy *Chris Fairhurst* 45
2 b f Blue Dakota(IRE) —Matilda Peace (Namaqualand (USA))
1879[6]

Blue Jack *Tom Dascombe* a84 113
5 b g Cadeaux Genereux—Fairy Flight (IRE) (Fairy King (USA))
(1353) ◆ 1700[3] ◆ 2325[7] 3047[9] (3895) 5569a[13] 6608a[14]

Blue Lyric *Luca Cumani* a79 70
3 b f Refuse To Bend(IRE) —Powder Blue (Daylami (IRE))
35[4] 366[3] 4847[8] 5396[6] 5887[5] 7114[7] 7411[7]

Blue Maiden *Philip McBride* 110
3 b f Medicean—Bluebelle (Generous (IRE))
1312[2] 1726[9] 2370a[11] 3071[2]

Blue Maisey *Sam Davison* a69 31
2 b f Monsieur Bond(IRE) —Blue Nile (IRE) (Bluebird (USA))
6802[12] 7311[3] 7551[2] 7780[6]

Blue Mamba *Reg Hollinshead* 56
3 b f Bollin Eric—Maradata (IRE) (Shardari)
3437[8]

Blue Monday *Roger Charlton* a104 111
9 b g Darshaan—Lunda (IRE) (Soviet Star (USA))
2716[5]

Blue Moon *Kevin Ryan* a83 77
3 gr f Trade Fair—Sunningdale (IRE) (Indian Ridge)
894[3] 997[4] 3091[7] 4374[2] 5766[3] 6144[6] 6541[2] (7273) 7305[3] 7453[2] (7724) (8022)

Blue Neptune *David Evans* a65 54
3 ch g Compton Place—Centre Court (Second Set (IRE))
111[7] 209[3] 343[2] 662[7] (886) 962[2] 1057[6] 1444[4] 1667[10] 1784[8] 2217[13] 2291[8] 2485[8]

Blue Noodles *Jim Best* a72 72
4 b g Reset(AUS) —Gleam Of Light (IRE) (Danehill (USA))
1492[11] 2188[9] 2409[3] 2624[5] 3580[2] 4053[3] 4857[5] (6452)

Blue Nymph *John Quinn* a91 82
4 ch m Selkirk(USA) —Blue Icon (Peintre Celebre (USA))
252[6] 2031[8] 2513[4] 2975[10] 4393[7] 4785[7]

Blue Panis (FR) *F Chappet* a82 113
3 b c Panis(USA) —Rhapsody In Blue (FR) (Bering)
3016a[2] 5574a[5]

Blue Ronnie (IRE) *Ben Haslam* 17
2 b g Majestic Missile(IRE) —Amoras (IRE) (Hamas (IRE))
6457[4] 6894[16]

Blue Rum (IRE) *Alan Kirtley* a30 51
3 b g Pyrus(USA) —Secret Combe (IRE) (Mujadil (USA))
6966[11]

Blues Ballad *S Seemar* a94 67
6 br g Singspiel(IRE) —Balisada (Kris)
610a[5]

Blues Buddy *Mark Allen*
3 b f Dubai Destination(USA) —Swift Spring (FR) (Bluebird (USA))
928[6]

Blues Forever (IRE) *David Evans* a60 54
3 b g Oratorio(IRE) —Swiss Roll (IRE) (Entrepreneur)
274[5] 374[7] 473[5] ◆ 664[2] 775[5] 1887[3] 2250[8]

Blues Jazz *John McShane* a49 36
4 b g Josr Algarhoud(IRE) —Belle Of The Blues (IRE) (Blues Traveller (IRE))
5816[7] 5925[8] 6710[11]

Blues Music (IRE) *B W Hills* a74 85
3 ch c Indian Ridge—Sportsticketing (IRE) (Spectrum (IRE))
374[4] ◆ 634[3] 930[2] ◆ (2496) 2927[3] 3351[7] 4758[2] 5592[4] 6447[15] 6753[17]

Blue Sparkle (IRE) *Mme J Bidgood* a60 61
3 b f Acclamation—Westlife (IRE) (Mind Games)
2342[13] 2844[15] 6487a[6]

Blue Spartan (IRE) *Charlie Mann* 64
5 gr g Spartacus(IRE) —Bridelina (FR) (Linamix (FR))
2821[11]

Blue Spinnaker (IRE) *Michael Easterby* a51 76
11 b g Bluebird(USA) —Suedoise (Kris)
(1028) 1177[2] 1296[2] 2204[3] 2937[3] 3613[9] 6297[9] 6935[9] 7306[10]

Blue Tango (IRE) *Amanda Perrett* a77 73
4 ch h Noverre(USA) —It Takes Two (IRE) (Alzao (USA))
771[3] (1226) 1440[2] 1636[2] 1961[6] 2966[11] (4227) 4694[3] 5680[5] 6774[6] 7089[5]

Blue Tiger's Eye (IRE) *Saeed Bin Suroor* a86 75
2 bb g Motivator—Bush Cat (USA) (Kingmambo (USA))
5523[2] (6053) 6870[3]

Blue Vinney *Marcus Tregoning* 40
2 b c Proclamation(IRE) —Easy Mover (IRE) (Bluebird (USA))
3961[9] 5709[U]

Blue Zealot (IRE) *Michael Bell* 59
3 b f Galileo(IRE) —Massada (Most Welcome)
1881[8] 2180[8] 2425[11] 4236[7] 4774[3] 5414[6] 5923[11] 7039[12]

Blue Zephyr *David C Griffiths* a64 55
3 br g Pastoral Pursuits—Pippa's Dancer (IRE) (Desert Style (IRE))
257[2] ◆ 362[3] 936[9] 1058[3] 1436[3] 1594[6] 1994[3] 2787[2] 3276[5] 3966[9] 6332[11] 6672[3] 7161[8] 7328[9]

Blushing Dreamer (IRE) *Natalie Lloyd-Beavis* a23
4 ch m Frenchmans Bay(FR) —Second Dream (IRE) (Second Set (IRE))
571[7]

Blushing Maid *Stuart Howe* a63 65
4 br m Namid—Music Maid (IRE) (Inzar (USA))
1234[9] 1477[9] 2589[13] 4283[11]

Bluster (FR) *Robert Collet* 107
4 b g Indian Rocket—Tell Me Why (FR) (Distant Relative)
1081a[2] 2157a[5] 4773a[10] 6012a[2] 6608a[16] 7278a[0]

Boa *Reg Hollinshead* a60 66
5 b m Mtoto—Maradata (IRE) (Shardari)
563[8] 872[3] 963[7] 1296[6] 1489[2] 1920[10]

Board Meeting (IRE) *E Lellouche* 111
4 b m Anabaa(USA) —Bright Moon (USA) (Alysheba (USA))
2374a[8] 5348a[3] 6613a[8] (7160a) 7851a[13]

Boastful (IRE) *Mahmood Al Zarooni* 60
2 gr f Clodovil(IRE) —Vanity (IRE) (Thatching)
2330[3]

Bobby Dazzler (IRE) *Sylvester Kirk* a59 30
2 b g Refuse To Bend(IRE) —Just My Hobby (Kris)
6874[10] 7470[10] 7723[5]

Bobbyow *Bryn Palling* 59
2 b c Bertolini(USA) —Brooklyn's Sky (Septieme Ciel (USA))
2621[6] 6465[13] 6954[11] 7142[6] 7301[4]

Bobbyscot (IRE) *P D Deegan* a65 104
3 b c Alhaarth(IRE) —Sogno Verde (IRE) (Green Desert (USA))
2367a[2]

Bobby Smith (IRE) *Michael Quinlan* a59 45
2 ch c Elnadim(USA) —Elhareer (IRE) (Selkirk (USA))
1065[7] 1319[5] 1794[3]

Bobering *Brian Baugh* a41 43
10 b g Bob's Return(IRE) —Ring The Rafters (Batshoof)
353[8] 541[5] 590[8] 757[11] 7705[8]

Bob Goes Electric (IRE) *John Best* a54 39
3 b c Camacho—Gracious Gretclo (Common Grounds)
759[6] 900[6] 1316[6]

Bob Le Beau (IRE) *Mrs John Harrington* a103 90
3 br g Big Bad Bob(IRE) —Shine Silently (IRE) (Bering)
7358a[2]

Bobs Dreamflight *Dean Ivory* a67 72
4 b g Royal Applause—Millybaa (USA) (Anabaa (USA))
393[9] 502[6] 658[6] 869[7] 1166[2] 1300[3] 1595[9] 1929[14] 2964[2] ◆ 3052[5] 4255[4] (4875) 5698[5] 6523[8] 6812[9] 6987[7] 7162[8] 7390[10] 7640[6] 7764[6]

Bob Stock (IRE) *Willie Musson* a67 67
4 b g Dubai Destination(USA) —Red Rita (IRE) (Kefaah (USA))
256[10] 518[9] 855[7] 1170[4] 2188[7] 3279[4] (3783) 4427[10] 5271[11] 5897[11] 6671[11]

Bobtail (FR) *F Rohaut* 71
7 b g Dyhim Diamond(IRE) —Bengalie (FR) (Lesotho (USA))
560a[0]

Boccalino (GER) *H-A Pantall* 98
2 b c Iron Mask(USA) —Bella Monica (GER) (Big Shuffle (USA))
4275a[2] 5226a[2] 6044a[3] 6760a[6] 7277a[0]

Bodie *Pam Sly* a51 51
2 ch c Iceman—Saida Lenasera (FR) (Fasliyev (USA))
4110[10] 4856[8] 5498[11] 7470[6] 7610[8]

Boga (IRE) *Ron Hodges* a47 53
3 b f Invincible Spirit(IRE) —Miznapp (Pennekamp (USA))
1168[8] 1456[11] 1814a[2] 2000[11] (2584) 5876[11] 6952[9] 7300[16]

Bogside Dancer *John Harris* 33
8 b g Groom Dancer(USA) —Madame Crecy (USA) (Al Nasr (FR))
5635[7] 6335[11] 6472[13]

Bogside Theatre (IRE) *George Moore* a32 84
6 b m Fruits Of Love(USA) —Royal Jubilee (IRE) (King's Theatre (IRE))
1101[3] 1525[6] 2938[8]

Bogue Chitto (USA) *Ian Howard* a79 109
6 ch g Crafty Prospector(USA) —Zurita (USA) (Storm Bird (CAN))
6949a[8]

Bogula (IRE) *Ann Duffield* 61
4 b m Tagula(IRE) —Bobbydazzle (Rock Hopper)
1113[16] 2430[8]

Bohemian Melody *Marco Botti* a100 89
3 b g Desert Sun—Chamonis (USA) (Affirmed (USA))
692[2] (980) 1480[2] 2970[2] 3886[4] ◆ (4231) ◆ 5143[2] ◆ 6429[4]

Boho Chic *George Baker* a67 69
4 b m Kyllachy—Summer Lightning (IRE) (Tamure (IRE))
(595) 967[2] 1300[5] 1482[4] 1547[11] 2196[3] 2485[5]

Bojangles Andrews *Tim Pitt* 49
3 b g Avonbridge—Polished Up (Polish Precedent (USA))
4864[11]

Bolagio *Gabriele Miliani* 55
2 b c Librettist(USA) —Lady Poison (IRE) (Charnwood Forest (IRE))
3253a[6]

Bolanderi (USA) *Andy Turnell* a78 80
5 ch g Seeking The Gold(USA) —Lilium (Nashwan (USA))
255[3] ◆ 485[4] 2411[5] 3036[7] 3862[6] 4227[7] 5840[8]

Bold Adventure *Willie Musson* a67 65
6 ch g Arkadian Hero(USA) —Impatiente (USA) (Vaguely Noble)
198[8] 584[6] (874) 1273[2] (1459) 2476[5] 7765[3]

Bold Argument (IRE) *Nerys Dutfield* a56 74
7 ch g Shinko Forest(IRE) —Ivory Bride (Domynsky)
2246[16] 3474[8] 3734[6] 4936[6] 6421[10]

Bold Bidder *Kevin Ryan* 86
2 b f Indesatchel(IRE) —Quiz Show (Primo Dominie)
2493[10] 2861[6] (3315) (3986) ◆ 4138[2] 4458[11] 6141[8] 6530[11]

Bold Bomber *Paul Green* a51 51
4 b g Kyllachy—Latina (IRE) (King's Theatre (IRE))
2629[12] 7071[9] 7213[11]

Bold Cross (IRE) *Edward Bevan* a75 87
7 b g Cape Cross(IRE) —Machikane Akaiito (IRE) (Persian Bold)
2328[6] 2705[4] 3117[4] 3581[4] 3894[6] 4044[5] 4382[9] 4859[8] 5115[3] 5786[8] 6260[5] 6444[9] 6581[7]

Bold Deceiver *Phil McEntee* a37 14
2 b f Proclamation(IRE) —Naivety (Machiavellian (USA))
1017[9] 1066[7] 1324[11] 1632[5] 3992[7] 4788[7] 7692[8] 7893[5]

Bold Diktator *Richard Whitaker* a83 68
8 b g Diktat—Madam Bold (Never So Bold)
2512[7] 2875[2] 3438[3] 4404[11]

Bold Diva *Tony Carroll* a66 36
5 ch m Bold Edge—Trina's Pet (Efisio)
312[12] 498[13] 693[8] 794[2] (838) 918[2] 1170[3] 1304[5] 1885[6] 1998[9] (3280) 3768[6] 4428[5] 4987[9] 5766[11] 6455[8]

Bold Hawk *Christine Dunnett* a50 27
4 b g Mujahid(USA) —Girl Next Door (Local Suitor (USA))
2010[9] 2258[7] 3518[3] 4591[12] 7070[8] 7508[10] 7787[9] 7863[9]

Bold Indian (IRE) *Mike Sowersby* a58 60
6 b g Indian Danehill(IRE) —Desert Gift (Green Desert (USA))
1208[6] 1503[13] 4170[7] 6269[3] 7149[11]

Boldinor *Martin Bosley* a58 63
7 b g Inchinor—Rambold (Rambo Dancer (CAN))
(495) 694[6] (2779) 3292[8] (4071) 4478[11] 5169[6] 5714[U]

Boldly Go *Richard Hannon* a28
3 ch g Bold Edge—Level Pegging (IRE) (Common Grounds)
6496[10] 6815[0] 7288[14]

Bold Marc (IRE) *Mrs K Burke* a76 86
8 b g Bold Fact(USA) —Zara's Birthday (IRE) (Waajib)
1374[15] 1513[16] 1707[8] 2531[5] 2864[4] 3595[2] 3905[5] 4394[12] 5357[9] 6117[2] 6375[7] 6915[4] 7306[4]

Bold Ring *Edward Creighton* a64 62
4 ch m Bold Edge—Floppie Disk (Magic Ring (IRE))
658[3] 828[6] 961[10] 1642[2] 1843[4] 2010[2] 2385[3] 3292[12] 4298[8] 6848[4] (7191) (7250) 7299[2] 7519[8]

Bold Rose *Mark Usher* a62 67
4 ch m Bold Edge—Bowden Rose (Dashing Blade)
135[3] 225[5] 3971[0] 615[5] 673[4]

Bold Tie *Richard Hannon* a71 82
4 ch g Bold Edge—Level Pegging (IRE) (Common Grounds)
2247[3] 2622[10] 2846[3] 3779[6] 4662[2]

Bold Warning *Alex Hales* a50
6 b g Erhaab(USA) —Celandine (Warning)
7896[4]

Bollin Andrew *Tim Easterby* a24 46
3 b c Bollin Eric—Bollin Roberta (Bob's Return (IRE))
1145[5] 5423[9]

Bollin Dolly *Tim Easterby* 86
7 ch m Bien Bien(USA) —Bollin Roberta (Bob's Return (IRE))
1379[4] 1629[3] (2142) 2579[10] 3089[2] 3416[4] (3679) 4389[9] 4841[6] 5638[10]

Bollin Felix *Tim Easterby* 93
6 br g Generous(IRE) —Bollin Magdalene (Teenoso (USA))
1151[6] 2541[8] 2938[4] 3588[6] (4086) 4846[5] 6181[5] 6362[2] ◆ 7173[3]

Bollin Freddie *Alan Lockwood* a53 69
6 ch g Golden Snake(USA) —Bollin Roberta (Bob's Return (IRE))
1296[12] 1576[8] 2500[7] (3110) (3370) 7184[8] 7330[6]

Bollin Greta *Tim Easterby* a47 76
5 bb m Mtoto—Bollin Zola (Alzao (USA))
1655[5] 1925[7] 2243[6] 3090[2] 4117[5] 4604[4] 4983[4] 5790[4] 6224[6] (6895) 7284[2] 7410[6]

Bollin Harry *Tim Easterby* 52
2 br c Val Royal(FR) —Bollin Dolly (Bien Bien (USA))
3222[9] 7179[10]

Bollin Hugo *Tim Easterby*
2 b c Bollin Eric—Bollin Roberta (Bob's Return (IRE))
4682[10]

Bollin Judith *Tim Easterby* a51 76
4 br m Bollin Eric—Bollin Nellie (Rock Hopper)
2549[7] 3367[3] 4125[6] 4656[4] (5681) 6109[3] 6516[6] 6750[3] 6983[4] 7226[2]

Bollin Julie *Tim Easterby* 49
3 b f Bollin Eric—Bollin Nellie (Rock Hopper)
6356[7]

Bollin Ruth *Donald Whillans* 22
8 gr m Silver Patriarch(IRE) —Bollin Roberta (Bob's Return (IRE))
4582[12]

Bollywood Style *John Best* a66 65
5 b m Josr Algarhoud(IRE) —Dane Dancing (IRE) (Danehill (USA))
14[2] ◆ 318[5] 442[3] 486[4] (614) 684[7] 844[9] 1171[5] 1224[9] 1443[4] 1929[4] 2246[2] 2490[6] 2809[9] 3322[5] 7390[4] 7518[2] 7555[11]

Bolodenka (IRE) *Richard Fahey* a86 93
8 b g Soviet Star(USA) —My-Lorraine (IRE) (Mac's Imp (USA))
196[2] 837[8] 1474[8] 1684[7] 1990[5] 2328[8] 2377[4] 2760[4] 3616[2] 4154[6] 4522[2] 4849[3] 5098[4] 5596[6] 6029[6]

Boltcity (FR) *J-C Rouget* a93 103
3 b c Elusive City(USA) —Combloux (USA) (Southern Halo (USA))
1195a[4] 2159a[7]

Bombadero (IRE) *John Dunlop* a76 82
3 b c Sadler's Wells(USA) —Fantasy Girl (IRE) (Marju (IRE))
1268[6] ◆ 1847[2] 2281[2] 3256[4] 4827[4] 5665[2] 6359[2] 6661[3] 6861[2]

Bombardino (IRE) *George Prodromou*
3 b g Pivotal—Magnolia Lane (IRE) (Sadler's Wells (USA))
7003[11]

Bombay Mist *Richard Guest* a37 48
3 b f Rambling Bear—Paris Mist (Paris House)
784[4] 906[8] 3277[8] 4194[9] 4406[6] 4516[6] 5410[6] 5477[6] 7952[9]

Bomber Brown (IRE) *Peter Chapple-Hyam* a78 79
4 b g Pyrus(USA) —Secret Of Gold (IRE) (Peintre Celebre (USA))
1749 1169[6]

Bomber Command (USA) *J W Hills* a90 71
7 b g Stravinsky(USA) —Parish Manor (USA) (Waquoit (USA))
1618[6] 2080[14] 2596[2] 3036[6] 3565[12] 4354[17]

Bo McGinty (IRE) *Richard Fahey* a80 85
9 ch g Fayruz—Georges Park Lady (IRE) (Tirol)
138[4] 165[2] 431[6] 601[2] 716[2] 774[2] 869[4] 899[4] 1068[7] 1234[2] 1366[4] 1547[3] 1988[10] 2073[5]

Bona Fortuna *Sir Mark Prescott Bt* a50 80
3 ch g Mark Of Esteem(IRE) —Time Honoured (Sadler's Wells (USA))
(2460) (2673) (2704)

Bonamassa *Michael Attwater* a48
3 b g Sulamani(IRE) —Anastasia Venture (Lion Cavern (USA))
4840[6] 5380[10] 6454[13] 7117[13]

Bon Appetit *Nigel Tinkler* a57 44
2 b f Exceed And Excel(AUS) —Welcome Band (Dixieland Band (USA))
1510[7] 1986[5] 6566[9] 6893[8] 7269[6] 7423[8] 7576[5]

Bondage (IRE) *James Fanshawe* a69 75
3 b g Whipper(USA) —Shamah (Unfuwain (USA))
1608[5] 2175[4] 2909[3] (5631) 6166[6] (6829)

Bond City (IRE) *Geoffrey Oldroyd* a94 94
8 b g Trans Island—Where's Charlotte (Sure Blade (USA))
(1332) 2465[12] 2992[9] 3969[7] 4684[8] 5601[5] 6367[8] 6701[11] (7063)

Bonded (IRE) *Brian Meehan* a75 72
3 b g Oasis Dream—Lovealoch (IRE) (Lomond (USA))
1448[4] 4522[6] 4898[4] 6467[8] 6692[7]

Bonded Spirit *Kate Walton* 11
2 b g Monsieur Bond(IRE) —Country Spirit (Sayf El Arab (USA))
2420[7] 3315[11] 4150[14]

Bond Fastrac *Geoffrey Oldroyd* a53 93
3 b g Monsieur Bond(IRE) —Kanisfluh (Pivotal)
2028[7] 2542[6] 3446[10] 3731[9] 4288[9]

Bond Together *Ray Peacock* a50 50
3 ch g Monsieur Bond(IRE) —My Bonus (Cyrano De Bergerac)
3515[10]

Bonfire Knight *John Quinn* a71 90
3 b g Red Ransom(USA) —Attune (Singspiel (IRE))
1487[3] ◆ 2117[4] ◆ 2758[10] 2979[2] 4570[2] 5511[2] 5913[8]

Bon Grain (FR) *M bin Shafya* a66 108
5 br h Muhtathir—Such Is Life (FR) (Akarad (FR))
609a[10] 800a[14]

Bonheurs Art (IRE) *B W Hills* 74
3 b f Acclamation—Anneliina (Cadeaux Genereux)
1137[3] (1890) 2565[3] 3270[2] 4091[7] 4714[7] 5809[4]

Bonita Star *Mick Channon* a69 80
2 b f Beat Hollow—Catch (USA) (Blushing Groom (FR))
4508[6] 5049[5] 5369[7] (6070) 6563[12] 6784a[9]

Bonjour Bongee *Alan McCabe* a58 58
2 ch g Monsieur Bond(IRE) —Bond Babe (Forzando)
1686[12] 2059[9] 2384[8] 4614[8] 4984[8] 5667[2] 6035[10] 6072[3] 6435[14] 6576[8] 6902[4] 7301[7]

Bonne Millie *Richard Fahey* 38
2 b f Compton Place—Bonne Etoile (Diesis)
3658[10] 3971[6] 4451[12]

Bonnie Bea *Ben Case* a49 25
4 b m Royal Applause—Boojum (Mujtahid (USA))
4676[8] 5457[10]

Bonnie Brae *George Margarson* a59 76
3 b f Mujahid(USA) —Skara Brae (Inchinor)
1278[8] 1959[4] 2221[6] 2634[4] (2879) 4209[4]

Bonniebridge *Mark Rimmer* a40 52
2 b f Avonbridge—Marie La Rose (FR) (Night Shift (USA))
3209[5] 3769[7] 4437[8] 5709[6] 7400[5] 7496[11]

Bonnie Charlie *William Haggas* a76 109
4 ch g Intikhab(USA) —Scottish Exile (IRE) (Ashkalani (IRE))
1700[8] ◆ 3445[3] ◆ 4085[14] 4569[3] 5068[10] 6175[18] 6349[26] 6749[11]

Bonnie Prince Blue *Brian Ellison* a85 83
7 ch g Tipsy Creek(USA) —Heart So Blue (Dilum (USA))
207a[2] (303a) 560a[6] 851[3] 905[4] 1366[5] ◆ 1650[2] 1923[3] 3317[9] 4060[2] 4084[4] 4685[3] 5601[8] 5999[3] 7403[3] (7539) 7740[2] ◆ 7934[4]

Bon Spiel *Chris Gordon* a78 90
6 b g Singspiel(IRE) —L'Affaire Monique (Machiavellian (USA))
946[13] 3050[16] 3873[8] 4266[5] 5084[7] 5888[6]

Boo *James Unett* a75 56
8 b g Namaqualand(USA) —Violet (IRE) (Mukaddamah (USA))
174[2] 255[6] 565[2] 752[6] 2864[8] 4932[7]

Boogie Dancer *Stuart Howe* a59 68
6 b m Tobougg(IRE) —Bolero (Rainbow Quest (USA))
98[5] 184[8] 529[7] 770[8]

Boogie Diva *Jane Chapple-Hyam* 85
3 b f Tobougg(IRE) —Distant Diva (Distant Relative)
(4662) 5205[4] 5884[11] 6198[13]

Boogie Down (IRE) *Walter Swinburn* 40
2 ch f Tobougg(IRE) —Enrichetta (IRE) (Primo Dominie)
3590[10] 4203[11] 4741[7]

Boogie Shoes *Michael Jarvis* a72 68
2 b g Bertolini(USA) —Space Time (FR) (Bering)
6980[3] ◆ (7530) ◆

Boogie Star *J S Moore* a62 53
2 b c Tobougg(IRE) —Donyana (Mark Of Esteem (IRE))
4716[8] 5006[8] 6414[10] 7177[11] 7464[6] 7629[5] (7801)

Boogie Waltzer *Stuart Williams* a79 77
3 b f Tobougg(IRE) —Upping The Tempo (Dunbeath (USA))
(111) (167) 363[2] 783[2] 1175[2] 1390[3] (1784) (2320) 3350[3] 3561[3] (4892) 5528[6] 6739[4] 7041[7]

Bookend *D Smaga* a90 89
6 b g Dansili—Roupala (USA) (Vaguely Noble)
5109a[4]

Bookiebasher Babe (IRE) *Michael Quinn* a74 69
5 b m Orpen(USA) —Jay Gee (IRE) (Second Set (IRE))
398[6] 715[11] 893[8] 1179[4] 1591[10] 1995[8] 2172[8] 3263[3] 3765[6] 4213[4] 5159[7] 5455[3]

Bookiesindex Boy *John Jenkins* a77 55
6 bb g Piccolo—United Passion (Emarati (USA))
306[4] 462[5] 601[4] 723[9] (913) 1131[6] 1320[2] 2809[4] 3052[3] 3761[2] 4239[5] 4895[2] 5647[13] 6310[11]

Bookiesindex Girl (IRE) *John Jenkins* a66 42
3 b f Rakti—Distant Valley (Distant Relative)
104[2] (329) 566[5] 4025[14] 7439[14]

Book Keeper *Mahmood Al Zarooni* a61 67
2 b c Oasis Dream—Turning Leaf (IRE) (Last Tycoon)
4054[6] 4499[3] 4993[8] 6162[6]

Book Of Music (IRE) *S Seemar* a83 87
7 b g Sadler's Wells(USA) —Novelette (Darshaan)
415a[8] 605a[11]

Book Smart (IRE) *Gay Kelleway* 28
3 b c Chevalier(IRE) —Vasanta (IRE) (Indian Ridge)
6773[9] 7153[10]

Boom And Bust (IRE) *Marcus Tregoning* a70 74
3 b g Footstepsinthesand—Forest Call (Wolfhound (USA))
4425[7] (4906) 5662[7] 6276[5] 6958[2]

Boom Boom (TUR) *M H Esin* a102
4 b h Distant Relative—Sun Child (USA) (Beau Genius (CAN))
5781a[3]

Boomtown Kat *Karen George*
6 b g Double Trigger(IRE) —Storm Kitten (IRE) (Catrail (USA))
3563[13]

Boragh Jamal (IRE) *Brian Meehan* a71 71
3 b f Namid—Danccini (IRE) (Dancing Dissident (USA))
1977[13] 2588[9] 2679[6] 3515[9] (3561) 4349[4] 4754[3] 7556[9] 7754[4] ◆

Borasco (USA) *David Barron* a83 91
5 ch m Stormy Atlantic(USA) —Seek (USA) (Devil's Bag (USA))
40[2] ◆ (398) ◆ 451[8]

Border Abby *Rae Guest* 40
2 ch f Selkirk(USA) —Perfect Solution (IRE) (Entrepreneur)
6803[11] 7152[6]

Border Fox *Peter Salmon* a50 59
7 b g Foxhound(USA) —Vado Via (Ardross)
622[9] 838[5] 918[6] 1507[5] 2343[10]

Borderlescott *Robin Bastiman* a105 121
8 b g Compton Place—Jeewan (Touching Wood (USA))
1700[2] 2325[3] 3047[3] 3895[3] (4505) 5276[6] 5744[8]

Border Owl (IRE) *Peter Salmon* a69 76
5 b g Selkirk(USA) —Nightbird (IRE) (Night Shift (USA))
668[5] (787) 908[7] 1508[7] 2580[3] 3391[8] (3732) 4093[9] 5071[8] 7063[8] 7474[6]

Border Patrol *Roger Charlton* 115
4 b g Selkirk(USA) —Ffestiniog (IRE) (Efisio)
1531[7] 3017a[8]

Border Tale *James Moffatt* a44 59
10 b g Selkirk(USA) —Likely Story (IRE) (Night Shift (USA))
2765[4]

Boreal D'Evaille (FR) *S Morineau* a60
3 b c Timboroa—Cardounteller (FR) (Cardoun (FR))
7959a[6]

Born A Dancer (IRE) *J W Hills* a37 54
3 b f Danehill Dancer(IRE) —Born Beautiful (USA) (Silver Deputy (CAN))
849[8] 9931[0] 1205[10]

Born To Be King (USA) *D Selvaratnam* a87 85
4 b h Storm Cat(USA) —Quarter Moon (IRE) (Sadler's Wells (USA))
412a[11]

Born To Excel *John Joseph Murphy* a79 81
4 b g Exceed And Excel(AUS) —Reem One (IRE) (Rainbow Quest (USA))
3257[2] 7597[3]

Born To Frill *Lynn Siddall* 27
5 b m Muhtarram(USA) —Superfrills (Superpower)
1777[5] 2463[10]

Born To Perform *Alan Swinbank* 66
5 b g Theatrical—My Hansel (USA) (Hansel (USA))
1113[2] 1424[4] 1803[6]

Borug (USA) *Saeed Bin Suroor* a89 77
2 b c Kingmambo(USA) —Marienbad (FR) (Darshaan)
(4490) 5257[6] 5947[9] (6670)

Borysthene (FR) *J-C Rouget* 94
2 ch c Zamindar(USA) —Eve's Garden (FR) (Boundary (USA))
4036a[2] 5323a[5]

Bosambo *Alan Swinbank* 59
2 b g King's Best(USA) —Roseum (Lahib (USA))
5040[8] 5814[5]

Bosamcliff (IRE) *David Evans* a79 79
5 b m Daylami(IRE) —L'Animee (Green Tune (USA))
202[3] 280[7] 330[2] 400[2] (719) 6224[7] 6639[7]

Boschka (SLO) *Zuzana Kubovicova*
4 b m Global Player—Bodkin (Reference Point)
4183a[2]

Boss Hog *Paul Midgley* a73 55
5 b g Key Of Luck(USA) —Dania (GER) (Night Shift (USA))
39[4] 144[8] 297[4] 377[6] 598[3]

Boss's Destination *Alan Swinbank* a76 84
3 b g Dubai Destination(USA) —Blushing Sunrise (USA) (Cox's Ridge (USA))
1706[5] 2033[5] (2767) 3123[2] 3519[6]

Bossy Kitty *Nigel Tinkler* 78
3 gr f Avonbridge—Between The Sticks (Pharly (FR))
1376[9] 1656[3] 2426[5] 2768[7] 3243[9] 3436[7] 4109[3] 4349[3] 4567[5] ◆ 4703[6] 6073[7] 6466[7] ◆ 6879[5]

Boston Blue *William Knight* a66 89
3 b g Halling(USA) —City Of Gold (IRE) (Sadler's Wells (USA))
1581[12] 2321[2] (2924) 3123[3] 3909[3] 4470[6] 5747[5] 5996[3] 6448[2]

Boston Court (IRE) *Brian Meehan* 40
2 b g Tomba—Chiffon (Polish Precedent (USA))
6443[14] 6748[10]

Bosun Breese *David Barron* a61 82
5 b g Bahamian Bounty—Nellie Melba (Hurricane Sky (AUS))
192[7] 1320[4] 1711[5] 2534[10] 2982[17] (3205) 3584[11] 3902[8] 4343[4] 4452[10] (5123) 6303[8] 6572[10] 7175[7] 7239[6]

Botanique (FR) *M Pimbonnet* a96 96
4 ch g Panis(USA) —Dhaunasing (FR) (Sin Kiang (FR))
458a[8]

Botanist *Sir Michael Stoute* 85
3 b g Selkirk(USA) —Red Camellia (Polar Falcon (USA))
5004[8] 6510[9] ◆

Botham (USA) *Jim Goldie* a58 71
6 bb g Cryptoclearance(USA) —Oval (USA) (Kris S (USA))
1717[4] 2206[10] 2671[7] 2856[6] 3534[2] 3900[2] 4064[2] 4515[9] 4947[5] 5406[6] 6107[6] 6243[3] 6495[3] 7054[U] 7230[3]

Both Ends Burning (IRE) *John Wainwright* 31
3 ch f Choisir(AUS) —Giadamar (IRE) (Be My Guest (USA))
2425[13] 3972[7] 4944[5] 5550[9]

Bothy *Brian Ellison* a81 91
4 ch g Pivotal—Villa Carlotta (Rainbow Quest (USA))
1829[7] 2976[12] 6565[6] 7084[9]

Bottega (USA) *M Delcher-Sanchez* 98
3 ch c Mineshaft(USA) —Sun Is Up (JPN) (Sunday Silence (USA))
1985a[8]

Bottomless Wallet *Frederick Watson* 48
9 ch m Titus Livius(FR) —Furry Dance (USA) (Nureyev (USA))
6915[14] 7282[10] 7472[7]

Boucheron *Richard Fahey* a14 75
5 b m Galileo(IRE) —Rainbow Lyrics (IRE) (Rainbow Quest (USA))
3319[8] 3974[7] 6724[4] 7101[5] 7321[7]

Bougainvilia (IRE) *Richard Hannon* a77 90
3 b f Bahamian Bounty—Temple Street (IRE) (Machiavellian (USA))
(2718) ◆ 3217[9] 4148[3] 4424[2] 4837[2] 5182[3] 5528[9]

Bouggatti *William Jarvis* a65 65
2 b g Tobougg(IRE) —Western Sal (Salse (USA))
4716[9] 5047[9] 5523[11] 6059[2] ◆ 6717[2]

Bouggie Daize *Clive Cox* a56 64
4 b m Tobougg(IRE) —Milly's Lass (Mind Games)
2919[5] 4833[5] 5557[7] 6898[9]

Bouguereau *Peter Chapple-Hyam* 52
5 b h Alhaarth(IRE) —Blessed Honour (Ahonoora)
3632[P] 5291[11]

Bould Mover *F J Brennan* a51 111
3 b g Kyllachy—Maugwenna (Danehill (USA))
3047[5] 3691[3]

Bouncy Bouncy (IRE) *Michael Bell* a51 58
3 ch f Chineur(FR) —Wunderbra (IRE) (Second Empire (IRE))
4251[9] 4966[7] 5395[9] (6018) 6329[8] 6880[3] 7154[3]

Boundaries *Tim Easterby* 82
2 b c Indesatchel(IRE) —On The Brink (Mind Games)
1389[4] 1930[9] 3665[2] 3985[4] 4367[2] 4599[2] 4831[2] 5196[4] 5531[4] (5733) 6030[4] (6354) 6719[9]
Bound By Honour (SAF) *Gary Moore* a101 100
7 b g Rambo Dancer(CAN) —Child Of Grace (SAF) (Only A Pound)
81[6] 536[13]
Boundless Applause *Ian Wood* a50 54
4 b m Royal Applause—Liberty Bound (Primo Dominie)
145[7] 369[10] 1884[13] 3948[14] 4790[7] 5559[4] 6826[12] 7131[5] 7468[8] 7763[3] 8023[8]
Boundless Prospect (USA) *David Evans* a74 71
11 b g Boundary(USA) —Cape (USA) (Mr Prospector (USA))
76[6] (190) 327[2] (456)
Boundless Spirit *David Nicholls* 88
2 b g Invincible Spirit(IRE) —Bye Bold Aileen (IRE) (Warning)
1359[5] ◆ (2068) (2525) 3051[13] 4138[20] 4831[8] 6139[12]
Bounty Box *Chris Wall* 107
4 b m Bahamian Bounty—Bible Box (IRE) (Bin Ajwaad (IRE))
1918[5] 2508[4] (3415) 3875[4] 4616[4] (5120) 5952[5] 6390[6]
Bounty Quest *Doug Watson* a90 66
8 b g Fasliyev(USA) —Just Dreams (Salse (USA))
606a[6]
Bourbon Bay (USA) *Neil Drysdale* a97 108
4 b g Sligo Bay(IRE) —Coral Necklace (USA) (Conquistador Cielo (USA))
(1435a)
Bourne *Luca Cumani* a78 87
4 gr g Linamix(FR) —L'Affaire Monique (Machiavellian (USA))
(1883) ◆ (7062) ◆
Bournefree (IRE) *Sylvester Kirk* a43
2 b f Tiger Hill(IRE) —Ceannanas (IRE) (Magical Wonder (USA))
2078[12] 6211[6] 6500[10]
Bourse (IRE) *George Foster* a68 66
5 b g Dubai Destination(USA) —Quarter Note (USA) (Danehill (USA))
4374[6] 4824[4] 5331[8] 5439[5]
Boushra *Sylvester Kirk* a53
2 ch f Redback—Esdaraat (Pivotal)
6575[8] 7447[11] 7913[2] 8011[12]
Bouzy *Peter Winkworth* a54 57
2 rg f Proclamation(IRE) —Ambonnay (Ashkalani (IRE))
3295[10] 4029[5] 4999[3] 5452[10] 6081[7] 6868[11]
Bow Beaver (USA) *Howard Johnson* 93
3 b g Vindication(USA) —Miss Carolina (USA) (Unbridled (USA))
(1865) 3893[6]
Bowdler's Magic *Mark Johnston* a79 97
3 b g Hernando(FR) —Slew The Moon (ARG) (Kitwood (USA))
2315[2] 2758[5] 3105[18] (3427) 3670[2] 4092[2] (4304) ◆ 4470[10] 4815[5] 5273[7] 5747[8] 6387[6] 7173[2]
Bowermaster (USA) *Mahmood Al Zarooni* 79
2 b c Invincible Spirit(IRE) —Muneera (USA) (Green Dancer (USA))
3452[2] 3794[3] 4755[5] 5849[11] 6809[3] 6978[P]
Bowmaker *Mark Johnston* a88 85
3 b g Dubawi(IRE) —Viola Da Braccio (IRE) (Vettori (IRE))
4893 ◆ 1352[6] 6002[6]
Bow River Arch (USA) *Jeremy Noseda* a70
2 b f Arch(USA) —Bow River Gold (Rainbow Quest (USA))
7113[3] 7567[2]
Bowsers Brave (USA) *Marcus Tregoning* a79 66
4 ch g Dixieland Band(USA) —Hazimah (USA) (Gone West (USA))
1260[13] 1450[3] ◆ 1844[10] 2685[11]
Bow To No One (IRE) *Alan Jarvis* a89 93
4 b m Refuse To Bend(IRE) —Deadly Buzz (IRE) (Darshaan)
1472[8] 1902[2] 2976[11] 3843[2] ◆ 4461[12] 4817[6] 6352[6] 7061[8] 7612[4]
Boxer Shorts *Michael Mullineaux* a47 13
4 b g Puissance—Lady Boxer (Komaite (USA))
31[6] 667[6] 849[7] 2378[13] 5875[14] 7070[10] 7199[13] 8006[4]
Boxeur Des Rues (USA) *William Haggas* a73 92
2 b c Smart Strike(CAN) —Marseille Express (USA) (Caerleon (USA))
(5718) ◆
Boxing Day *Bent Olsen* 90
3 b c Galileo(IRE) —Special Oasis (Green Desert (USA))
4641a[9]
Box Of Frogs (IRE) *Alan McCabe* a20 57
2 b f One Cool Cat(USA) —Absolute Pleasure (Polar Falcon (USA))
1879[4] 2286[2] 2623[8] 3175[10] 3757[7] 4241[7]
Boy Blue *Peter Salmon* a51 87
5 b r Observatory(USA) —Rowan Flower (IRE) (Ashkalani (IRE))
1754[5] 3107[8] 4119[3] 4450[9]
Boy Dancer (IRE) *John Quinn* a46 65
7 ch g Danehill Dancer(IRE) —Mary Gabry (IRE) (Kris)
290[7] 457[5]
Boy Racer (IRE) *Colin Teague* a67 26
5 br g Singspiel(IRE) —Gombay Girl (USA) (Woodman (USA))
2629[9] 4173[9] 4482[8]
Boys At Tosconova (USA) *Richard Dutrow Jr* a115
2 bb c Officer(USA) —Little Bonnet (USA) (Coronado's Quest (USA))
7363a[2]
Boy The Bell *Michael Mullineaux* a68 67
3 b g Choisir(AUS) —Bella Beguine (Komaite (USA))
85[2] 253[3] 2309[3] 2628[5] 3151[4] 3372[3] 3682[5] 4559[6] 4861[U] 5548[9] 5697[10] 5906[7] 6896[5] 7064[11] 7506[2] (7563) 7738[3]
Brabazon (IRE) *Emmet Michael Butterly* a63 4
7 b g In The Wings—Azure Lake (USA) (Lac Ouimet (USA))
(7634) 7704[2]
Brace Of Doves *Donald Whillans* a55 54
8 b g Bahamian Bounty—Overcome (Belmez (USA))
2454[12]
Bradbury (IRE) *James Bethell* a38 71
2 ch g Redback—Simonaventura (IRE) (Dr Devious (IRE))
1886[5] 3964[9] 4013[2] 4899[7] 5682[2] 6505[9] 6978[9]
Braddock (IRE) *K O Cunningham-Brown* a73 70
7 b g Pivotal—Sedna (FR) (Bering)
4430[13] 5764[11] 6864[9] 7299[4] 7607[7] 7763[7]
Bradford (IRE) *Eve Johnson Houghton* a47 72
3 b g Pyrus(USA) —Lypharden (IRE) (Lyphard's Special (USA))
2025[8]
Brad's Luck (IRE) *Michael Blanshard* a55 62
4 ch g Lucky Story(USA) —Seymour (IRE) (Eagle Eyed (USA))
1980[5] 2363[2] 2810[4] 3127[4] 3819[3] 4362[4]
Braehead (IRE) *David Evans* a80 52
2 b g Ivan Denisovich(IRE) —Poppy's Song (Owington)
8002[5]
Brae Hill (IRE) *Richard Fahey* a74 103
4 b g Fath(USA) —Auriga (Belmez (USA))
1857[4] ◆ (2311) 3146[18] 3869[11] 4617[2] 5292[6] 5774a[12] 6363[15] 6564[3] 6752[7]
Braille *Tim Walford* 59
5 b g Bahamian Bounty—Branston Gem (So Factual (USA))
1391[6] 2213[4] ◆ 2504[4] 2849[14] 3774[7] 4605[4] (4868) 5422[13] 5599[11]
Brainstormer (FR) *M Nigge* a68
2 b c Limnos(JPN) —La Deviniere (IRE) (Nashamaa)
7974a[3]
Bramalea *Brendan Duke* a70 91
5 b m Whitmore's Conn(USA) —Aster (IRE) (Danehill (USA))
280[8] 546[5] 777[11] 2690[2] 3314[7] 3865[4] (4958) (5115) 5260[2] 5591[5] 5888[3] (6322) 6929[6]
Brampour (IRE) *J-C Rouget* 89
3 b g Daylami(IRE) —Brusca (USA) (Grindstone (USA))
5136a[2]
Bramshaw (USA) *Amanda Perrett* a87 90
3 rg c Langfuhr(CAN) —Milagra (USA) (Maria's Mon (USA))
5662[3] ◆ 5968[2] 6321[8] 6888[28]
Bramshill Lady (IRE) *Pat Eddery* 68
3 rg f Verglas(IRE) —Jinx Johnson (IRE) (Desert King (IRE))
2000[10] 2587[4] (3514)
Brananx (USA) *Kevin Ryan* 56
3 b c Red Ransom(USA) —Shady Reflection (USA) (Sultry Song (USA))
1029[5] ◆ 1335[5] 2501[6]
Brand Bob (IRE) *Amy Weaver* a37 63
2 b g Big Bad Bob(IRE) —Brandina (IRE) (Lil's Boy (USA))
(7177) 7396[6] 7630[11]
Brandy Alexander *Richard Hannon* 59
2 b g Invincible Spirit(IRE) —Valhalla Moon (USA) (Sadler's Wells (USA))
4421[6] 5032[7] ◆ 5294[9]
Brandy Butter *David Pipe* a54 57
4 ch g Domedriver(IRE) —Brand (Shareef Dancer (USA))
140[7] 2169[2] 2363[5]
Brandy Snap (IRE) *Richard Hannon* a49 33
2 b f Hennessy(USA) —Natural Skill (USA) (Aptitude (USA))
1972[13] 2330[7] 4095[18] 7686[5] 7888[6] 8031[10]
Brandywell Boy (IRE) *Dominic Ffrench Davis* a79 81
7 b g Danetime(IRE) —Alexander Eliott (IRE) (Night Shift (USA))
2166[4] 2622[5] (2954) (3474) (3892) 4148[7] 4625[5] 5285[4] 5915[10] 6280[4] 6446[5] 6998[8] 7319[6] 7635[6] (7764)
Brannagh (USA) *Jeremy Noseda* a84 88
3 ch c Hennessy(USA) —Green Room (USA) (Theatrical)
1450[6] (1959) 2466[4] (3394) ◆ 4296[4] ◆ 4849[5] 6167[8] 6321[7]
Brasingaman Eric *S Wynne* a51 43
3 b g Bollin Eric—Serene Pearl (IRE) (Night Shift (USA))
2290[11]
Bravalto *Bryan Smart* a65 59
4 b h Falbrav(IRE) —Bunty Boo (Noalto)
189[3]
Brave Battle *Richard Hannon* a69 69
2 b g Compton Place—War Shanty (Warrshan (USA))
3459[10] 5465[4] 5886[5] 6308[7] 6740[3] (6995) 7347[10]
Brave Bugsy (IRE) *Michael Appleby* a60 61
7 b g Mujadil(USA) —Advancing (IRE) (Ela-Mana-Mou)
2169[5] (2363) 2810[7] 4042[6] 5420[8]
Brave Decision *Robert Cowell* a68 53
3 gr g With Approval(CAN) —Brave Vanessa (USA) (Private Account (USA))
128[6] 385[11] 1995[4] 2414[3] 2878[2] 3413[10] 3758[11]
Brave Dream *Kevin Ryan* a73 72
2 b g Sleeping Indian—Aimee's Delight (Robellino (USA))
2420[4] 2649[4] 3658[5] 4111[3] 4388[2] ◆ 5092[4] (5352) 5745[4] 6311[2] 6619[4]
Brave Enough (USA) *Mikael Magnusson* a62 22
3 b g Yes It's True(USA) —Courageous (USA) (Kingmambo (USA))
106[4] 1601[10] 2906[10]
Brave Ghurka *Sylvester Kirk* a59 66
3 b g Bahamian Bounty—Wondrous Maid (GER) (Mondrian (GER))
1873[13] 2584[7] 2962[10] 3788[5] 4202[6]
Braveheart Move (IRE) *Jonjo O'Neill* a78 102
4 b g Cape Cross(IRE) —Token Gesture (IRE) (Alzao (USA))
4100[12] 5004[4] 5743[3]
Bravely (IRE) *Tim Easterby* a62 81
6 b g Rock Of Gibraltar(IRE) —Raghida (IRE) (Nordico (USA))
1650[11] 2136[11] 2528[7] 2883[8] 3321[8] 3879[6] 4192[11] 4706[8] (5817) 6103[3] 6398[6] 6965[14] 7468[4]
Bravely Fought (IRE) *Sabrina J Harty* a99 101
5 b g Indian Ridge—Amazing Tale (Shareef Dancer (USA))
7823a[3]
Brave Mave *Jane Chapple-Hyam* a83 74
5 gr m Daylami(IRE) —Baalbek (Barathea (IRE))
42[4] 420[8]
Brave Prospector *Jane Chapple-Hyam* a101 110
5 b h Oasis Dream—Simply Times (USA) (Dodge (USA))
2100[7] (6063) 6735[5] 7524[3] 7875[10]
Brave Talk *Sylvester Kirk* a66
3 ch g Avonbridge—Zyzania (Zafonic (USA))
340[3] ◆ 551[2] ◆ 677[4] 872[10] 1735[11] 2333[9]
Brave Tiger (IRE) *Stuart Williams* a56 33
2 b g Shamardal(USA) —Designed (Zamindar (USA))
2895[6] 4599[12] 4856[10] 5581[6] (5862) ◆ 6035[6] 6867[8] 7017[3]
Bravo Belle (IRE) *Terry Caldwell* a23
3 b f Bertolini(USA) —Dazilyn Lady (USA) (Zilzal (USA))
7462[9]
Bravo Blue (IRE) *Terry Caldwell* a18 6
3 b f Mark Of Esteem(IRE) —Fantazia (Zafonic (USA))
1143[8] 2274[11] 2724[8]
Bravo Bravo *Mick Channon* 61
3 b g Sadler's Wells(USA) —Top Table (Shirley Heights)
4661[14] 5001[6] (5522) (5666) 6132[5] 6272[4] 6955[4]
Bravo Echo *Michael Attwater* a100 94
4 b g Oasis Dream—Bold Empress (USA) (Diesis)
150[2] ◆ 358[2] ◆ (944) 1085[4] 1900[16] 2595[14] 5731[8] 6204[12] 7187[6] 7522[4] ◆
Bravo Tango *David Arbuthnot* a8 8
3 b g Bold Edge—My Dancer (IRE) (Alhaarth (IRE))
1222[10] 1872[10] 3276[10]
Brazilian Beauty *Kevin Prendergast* 84
3 b f Galileo(IRE) —Braziliz (USA) (Kingmambo (USA))
4178a[13]
Brazilian Brush (IRE) *Milton Bradley* a60 32
5 ch g Captain Rio—Ejder (IRE) (Indian Ridge)
14[7] (69) 112[2] 146[9] 296[10] 368[8] 568[9] 1236[9] 1884[8] 2791[9] 7721[7] 7784[6]
Breakheart (IRE) *Andrew Balding* a71 98
3 b g Sakhee(USA) —Exorcet (FR) (Selkirk (USA))
(2334) (3196) ◆ 3824[2] 4321[2] ◆ 4830[7] 6193[5] ◆ 6562[14]
Break On Through *J L Hassett* a77 56
3 ch f Dr Fong(USA) —Lady Gin (USA) (Saint Ballado (CAN))
7547[4]
Break Serve (USA) *Walter Swinburn* a75
3 ch c Grand Slam(USA) —Oonagh (USA) (Wild Again (USA))
1450[4] ◆ 2335[3] ◆
Breathless Kiss (USA) *Kevin Ryan* a87 84
3 b f Roman Ruler(USA) —Crusading Miss Cox (USA) (Crusader Sword (USA))
(478) 577[3] 7833 ◆ 1052[3] 1399[8] 2450[2] 3023[2] 3361[4] 4287[6] 4647[7] 5421[6] 5896[2] 7411[10] 7554[4] 7654[2] 7782[3] (7961)
Breathless Storm (USA) *Tom Tate* 76
2 ch c Storm Cat(USA) —Takesmybreathaway (USA) (Gone West (USA))
1686[5] (2138) 3872[10]
Breedj (IRE) *Clive Brittain* a68 86
2 b f Acclamation—Kildare Lady (IRE) (Indian Ridge)
1660[3] 2095[2]
Breezed Well (IRE) *James McAuley* a44 61
3 b g Pyrus(USA) —Full Traceability (IRE) (Ron's Victory (USA))
4563a[14]
Breezolini *Richard Whitaker* 75
2 br f Bertolini(USA) —African Breeze (Atraf)
4896[8] 5298[8] 5640[3] 6075[3] (6264) 6719[2]
Brenda Duke *Jonathan Portman* a52 42
3 ch f Bachelor Duke(USA) —Fiina (Most Welcome)
22[2] 283[6] 372[5] 534[4]
Brendan's Gift *Brendan Powell*
2 b f Phoenix Reach(IRE) —Digyourheelsin (IRE) (Mister Lord (USA))
4021[13] 4299[9]
Bret Maverick (IRE) *Brian Baugh* a30 57
6 b g Josr Algarhoud(IRE) —Shady Street (USA) (Shadeed (USA))
1981[0]
Breton Star *David Simcock* 58
2 b g Medicean—Wannabe Grand (IRE) (Danehill (USA))
5049[12] 6127[5] 6831[12]
Brett Vale (IRE) *Peter Hedger* a91 91
4 br g Sinndar(IRE) —Pinta (IRE) (Ahonoora)
1544[6] 1902[15] (2228) 3566[9] 3843[13] 4597[8] 5035[9]
Brevity (USA) *Brian Meehan* 101
2 b f Street Cry(IRE) —Cut Short (USA) (Diesis)
4471[4] ◆ (4921) (5693)
Brewers Boy *Rod Millman* 67
3 ch g Compton Place—Manila Selection (USA) (Manila (USA))
4385[5] 5007[4] 6773[4] 7013[2]
Brezza Di Mare (IRE) *Brian Meehan* a26 53
2 b g Rainbow Quest(USA) —Sea Picture (IRE) (Royal Academy (USA))
5718[9] 6689[12]
Briannsta (IRE) *John E Long* a58 56
8 b g Bluebird(USA) —Nacote (IRE) (Mtoto)
829[6] 1167[8] 2008[4] 2234[9] 2965[8] 3526[7] 4789[4] 5075[8]
Brian Sprout *John Weymes* a28 52
2 ch c Zafeen(FR) —Ducal Diva (Bahamian Bounty)
2836[3] 3365[6] 6309[8]
Briary Mac *Peter Pritchard* a20 65
3 b f Royal Applause—Red May (IRE) (Persian Bold)
3599[6] 3924[5] 4172[4] 4864[7] 5501[7] 6039[7] 7897[4]
Bribon (FR) *Todd Pletcher* a117 114
7 ch g Mark Of Esteem(IRE) —Rowat Arazi (Arazi (USA))
5779a[6]
Brick Red *Andrew Balding* a90 97
3 ch g Dubawi(IRE) —Duchcov (Caerleon (USA))
4963[8] (5383) 6321[3] (6391) 6749[8] (7233)
Bridgefield (USA) *Mahmood Al Zarooni* 81
2 ch c Speightstown(USA) —Treysta (USA) (Belong To Me (USA))
6532[3] (7058)
Bridge Of Fermoy (IRE) *Daniel Christopher O'Brien* a76 60
5 b g Danetime(IRE) —Banco Solo (Distant Relative)
3961[0]
Bridge Of Gold (USA) *Mikael Magnusson* a109 110
4 br h Giant's Causeway(USA) —Lady Doc (USA) (Doc's Leader (USA))
(205) 512a[8] 706a[9] 5220[3] ◆
Bridge Of Peace *J-Y Artu* 81
3 b f Anabaa(USA) —Hope Town (FR) (Sillery (USA))
3015a[9]
Bridgetown (USA) *Kenneth McPeek* 115
3 ch c Speightstown(USA) —Ellesmere (USA) (Tabasco Cat (USA))
6949a[5] 7362a[4]
Bridget The Fidget *Edward Creighton* a44 6
2 b f Avonbridge—Long Tall Sally (IRE) (Danehill Dancer (IRE))
2561[7] 7485[9] 7722[9]
Bridle Belle *Richard Fahey* 88
2 b f Dansili—River Belle (Lahib (USA))
(4338) 5849[9] (6174) 6505[4]
Brierty (IRE) *Declan Carroll* a83 88
4 b m Statue Of Liberty(USA) —Bridelina (FR) (Linamix (FR))
223[7] 431[3] 750[3] 924[2] 1192[3] 1688[2] 1888[3] 2136[2] 2327[11] (3879) 4090[2] 4345[5] 4583[2] 5069[4]
Brigadoon *William Jarvis* a70 72
3 b g Compton Place—Briggsmaid (Elegant Air)
1392[6] 1973[7] 4793[2] 5266[4] ◆ 5679[6]
Brigantin (USA) *A Fabre* 100
3 ch c Cozzene(USA) —Banyu Dewi (GER) (Poliglote)
2557a[2] (5800a) 6590a[6]
Bright Applause *Gary Moore* a57 67
2 b c Royal Applause—Sadaka (USA) (Kingmambo (USA))
3349[8] 4131[4] 4437[4] 4736[4] 5626[6] 6500[5]
Bright Dictator (IRE) *James Given* 45
2 b f Diktat—Me (Green Desert (USA))
2740[9] 4048[8] 4517[4] 5644[8] 6300[6] 6891[13]
Bright Horizon *A P O'Brien* a89 100
3 b c Galileo(IRE) —Kissogram (Caerleon (USA))
3105[12] 3491a[10] 7339a[11]
Brightia Pulse (JPN) *Osamu Hirata* 112
5 b m Daitaku Riva(JPN) —Storm Sunday (USA) (Storm Bird (CAN))
7460a[8]
Bright Sparky (GER) *Michael Easterby* a58 54
7 ch g Dashing Blade—Braissim (Dancing Brave (USA))
41[4] 470[2] (661) 1984[4] 6121[3] 6373[5] 7145[8]
Brilliana *David Lanigan* a75 89
4 b m Danehill Dancer(IRE) —Streak Of Silver (USA) (Dynaformer (USA))
6990[7] 7206[8]
Brilliant Disguise *Ben Haslam*
2 b f Kyllachy—Dance Sequel (Selkirk (USA))
5092[11]
Bring It Back (FR) *Y Fertillet* 70
6 ch m Wathik(USA) —Danemara (FR) (Fabulous Dancer (USA))
281a[7]
Bring Sweets (IRE) *Brian Ellison* a52 53
3 b g Firebreak—Missperon (IRE) (Orpen (USA))
1392[8] 1970[8] 2503[13] 2838[7] 4864[2] 5361[6] 5927[8] 6183[4] 7789[3] 7918[3]
Brink *Tim Pitt* a47 64
3 b f Powerscourt—Fonage (Zafonic (USA))
1571[7] 2499[3] 3662[6] 6966[4] 7328[5]
Brinscall *Julie-Ann Camacho* a64 69
3 b f Lucky Story(USA) —Happy Lady (FR) (Cadeaux Genereux)
1593[7] 2296[8] 2834[15]
Brisant (GER) *R Suerland* 107
8 br g Goofalik(USA) —Beresina (Surumu (GER))
2574a[2]
Brisbane (IRE) *Dianne Sayer* 70
3 b g Kheleyf(USA) —Waroonga (IRE) (Brief Truce (USA))
5337[8] 5819[13]
Bristol Delauriere (FR) *Natalie Lloyd-Beavis* a30 23
6 b g Epistolaire(IRE) —Shenedova (FR) (Hellios (USA))
8031[0] 1183[4] 2169[7]
British Sea Power (IRE) *Jeremy Gask* a52 40
3 b g Barathea(IRE) —Shannon Dore (IRE) (Turtle Island (IRE))
1137[6] 1490[4] 1769[11]
Broad Meaning *D K Weld* 100
4 b g Oasis Dream—Avoidance (USA) (Cryptoclearance (USA))
3487a[16] 5774a[18]
Broadway Dancer *Richard Fahey* a69 69
3 b f Fantastic Light(USA) —Stage School (USA) (Sunday Silence (USA))
3733[3] 4601[2] 5270[2] 5607[6] (6244) 6816[5] 7078a[7]

Brockfield *Mel Brittain* 72
4 ch h Falbrav(IRE) —Irish Light (USA) (Irish River (FR))
1116[2] (1177) 1296[3] 1807[5] 1925[11] 2941[12] 4781[4]

Broctune Papa Gio *Keith Reveley* 54
3 b g Tobougg(IRE) —Fairlie (Halling (USA))
1119[9] 1271[8] 1971[2] 2503[3] 3073[7] 5821[2] 7153[9]

Brody's Boy *Gary Moore* 51
3 ch g Tumbleweed Ridge—Raffelina (USA) (Carson City (USA))
2340[6] 2925[8] 4248[8] 5077[10] 5650[7] 6862[10]

Broken Belle (IRE) *J W Hills* 25
2 b f Clodovil(IRE) —Lady Express (IRE) (Soviet Star (USA))
2223[9]

Bromhead (USA) *Kevin Morgan* a73 60
4 ch g Johannesburg(USA) —Caramel Queen (NZ) (Turbulent Dancer (USA))
113[4] 314[6] 1134[10]

Bronze Beau *Linda Stubbs* a64 84
3 ch g Compton Place—Bella Cantata (Singspiel (IRE))
1104[8] 1825[3] 3181[2] (3903) 3988[3] (4169) 4567[2] 4703[2] (5600) 5956[2] 6245[5]

Bronze Cannon (USA) *Gary Moore* a95 122
5 br h Lemon Drop Kid(USA) —Victoria Cross (IRE) (Mark Of Esteem (IRE))
6089[3]

Bronze Dancer (IRE) *Brian Storey* 20
8 b g Entrepreneur—Scrimshaw (Selkirk (USA))
5203[7]

Bronze Prince *Saeed Bin Suroor* a82
3 b c Oasis Dream—Sweet Pea (Persian Bold)
6321[14]

Brooklands Bay (IRE) *John Weymes* a75 67
3 b g Pyrus(USA) —Brooklands Time (IRE) (Danetime (IRE))
33[2] ◆ 428[4] 2033[8] 2816[5] 4092[5] 4618[5] 5093[4] 5738[5] 6122[10]

Brooklyn Spirit *Alison Batchelor* a46 73
4 ch g Cadeaux Genereux—Serengeti Bride (USA) (Lion Cavern (USA))
1579[5] 2975[9] 3847[5] 4141[7] 6055[12] 7445[11]

Brooksby *Luke Dace* a72 68
4 b m Diktat—Lovely Lyca (Night Shift (USA))
7649[11] 7716[15]

Brootommity (IRE) *Noel Wilson* 45
3 b f Azamour(IRE) —Polyandry (IRE) (Pennekamp (USA))
1203[5] 1528[5] 2244[8]

Broox (IRE) *E J O'Neill* 111
2 b c Xaar—Miss Brooks (Bishop Of Cashel)
4419a[2] 5347a[4] (6044a) 7277a[9]

Brother Cha (IRE) *Michael Quinlan* a84 88
4 ch g Indian Ridge—Sun On The Sea (IRE) (Bering)
1306[2] ◆ 1933[3] 2508[9]

Brother In Arms (USA) *Kelly Breen* a76
2 ch c Yes It's True(USA) —She's A Rebel Too (USA) (Two Punch (USA))
6756a[6]

Broughton Beck (IRE) *Roger Fisher* a58 54
4 ch g Distant Music(USA) —Mauras Pride (IRE) (Cadeaux Genereux)
7282[5]

Broughtons Bandit *Willie Musson* a43 44
3 b g Kyllachy—Broughton Bounty (Bahamian Bounty)
6652[6] 7019[13] 7495[5]

Broughtons Day *Willie Musson* a66 50
3 b g Mujahid(USA) —Rainy Day Song (Persian Bold)
(7869)

Broughtons Dream *Willie Musson* a31 61
4 b m Kyllachy—Broughton Bounty (Bahamian Bounty)
2678[8] 3765[10] 5559[3] (6860)

Broughtons Paradis (IRE) *Willie Musson* a61 71
4 b m Royal Applause—Amankila (IRE) (Revoque (IRE))
771[10] 1177[8] 1478[8] 2013[2] 2560[5] 3040[2] 3268[3] 4329[2] 4804[3] 5051[5]

Broughtons Point *Willie Musson* a60 74
4 b m Falbrav(IRE) —Glowing Reference (Reference Point)
420[5] 539[5] (777) 865[3] 1053[3] (1283) 1849[4] 2476[4] 2907[3] 3780[4] (3996) (4719) 5612[3] 7061[9]

Broughtons Silk *Alistair Whillans* a46 60
5 b m Medicean—Soviet Cry (Soviet Star (USA))
3369[11] 3948[8] 4820[5] 5331[5] 5406[2] 5821[13] 7229[3]

Broughtons Swinger *Willie Musson* a58 71
3 b f Celtic Swing—Pachanga (Inchinor)
533[8] 633[5] 812[5] 2189[6] (2620) 2909[7] 4764[5] (5611) 6959[11]

Brouhaha *Tom Dascombe* a90 87
6 b g Bahhare(USA) —Top Of The Morning (Keen)
231[11] 480[8] 2173[6] (2821) 3432[4] 3847[2] 4405[14] 5757[6] 6312[3] 6797[6] 7196[4] 7568[9]

Brown Panther *Tom Dascombe* a69
2 b c Shirocco(GER) —Treble Heights (IRE) (Unfuwain (USA))
(7400)

Brown Pete (IRE) *Paul W Flynn* a76 45
2 bb c Aussie Rules(USA) —Banba (IRE) (Docksider (USA))
6727a[10]

Brunelleschi *Patrick Gilligan* a81 86
7 ch g Bertolini(USA) —Petrovna (IRE) (Petardia)
737[8] 1044[10] 1428[14] 2123[11] 4431[9] 4806[11]

Brunston *Roger Charlton* 94
4 gr g High Chaparral(IRE) —Molly Mello (GER) (Big Shuffle (USA))
(1383) 1697[9] 2317[8] 3633[6] 6562[26] 7100[3] 7350[10]

Brusco *A Wohler* 102
4 b h Rock Of Gibraltar(IRE) —Blaze Of Colour (Rainbow Quest (USA))
4012a[2] 6011a[3] 6607a[6]

Brushed Aside *D K Weld* a77 92
3 b f Oasis Dream—Avoidance (USA) (Cryptoclearance (USA))
3489a[2] 4269a[11]

Brushing *Mark H Tompkins* 105
4 ch m Medicean—Seasonal Blossom (IRE) (Fairy King (USA))
1128[2] ◆ 1426[2] 2256[4] (2579) (3319) 4830[6] (5249) 5881[8] 6320[5] 6928[12]

Brynfa Boy *Paul D'Arcy* a77 83
4 b g Namid—Funny Girl (IRE) (Darshaan)
(241) ◆ 806[2] 1266[4] ◆ 2094[2] 2301[3] 2973[5] 3417[2] 3892[6] (4292) 4961[7]

Buachaill Dona (IRE) *David Nicholls* a101 109
7 b g Namid—Serious Contender (IRE) (Tenby)
1400[4] (1573) 1822[10] 2100[10] 3406[11] (Dead)

Buaiteoir (FR) *Paul D'Arcy* a82 60
4 b g Mineshaft(USA) —Witching Hour (FR) (Fairy King (USA))
(5129a) 7600[4]

Bubbelas *John Quinn* 71
3 b f Pastoral Pursuits—Arctic High (Polar Falcon (USA))
2215[13] 2702[13] 3243[5] 3668[7]

Bubber (IRE) *Richard Fahey* a49 42
3 b f Westerner—Bubble N Squeak (IRE) (Catrail (USA))
2132[8] 2438[7]

Bubble Chic (FR) *G Botti* 106
2 b c Chichicastenango(FR) —Bubble Back (FR) (Grand Lodge (USA))
6973a[2] 7456a[2]

Bubble Zack (FR) *D Prod'Homme* a76 76
3 ch g Muhtathir—Bubble Back (FR) (Grand Lodge (USA))
547a[2]

Bubbly Bellini (IRE) *Lee Smyth* a76 73
3 b g Mull Of Kintyre(USA) —Gwapa (IRE) (Imperial Frontier (USA))
168[2] (276) (3276) 6207[9] 7193[4] 7882[8]

Bubbly Braveheart (IRE) *Alan Bailey* a70 67
3 b g Cape Cross(IRE) —Infinity (FR) (Bering)
279[2] (422) (564) 830[5] 964[6] 1261[3] 1666[5] 3171[6] 3390[12] 4022[11] 4439[7] 6020[5] 7068[3] ◆ 7286[2] 7562[3] 7611[8] 7878[7]

Bubses Boy *Paul Howling* a60 61
4 ch g Needwood Blade—Welcome Home (Most Welcome)
130[6] 411[9] 622[5] 1606[5]

Buccellati *Tony Noonan* 117
6 ch h Soviet Star(USA) —Susi Wong (IRE) (Selkirk (USA))
6947a[16] 7291a[20]

Bucephalus (IRE) *Maurice Barnes* a62 69
6 b g Montjeu(IRE) —Flyleaf (FR) (Persian Bold)
1907[6] 2133[7]

Buckie Boy (IRE) *Jim Goldie* a86 78
4 b g Bahri(USA) —Woodren (USA) (Woodman (USA))
3198[6] 3807[5] 4656[6]

Buckie Massa *J S O Arthur* a79 80
6 ch g Best Of The Bests(IRE) —Up On Points (Royal Academy (USA))
2162a[3]

Buckland (IRE) *Brian Meehan* a79 84
2 b g Oratorio(IRE) —Dollar Bird (IRE) (Kris)
4622[3] ◆ 5032[3] 5892[2] 6386[3] 6670[6] 7036[4]

Budai (GER) *W Hickst* 116
4 b g Dai Jin—Bejaria (GER) (Konigsstuhl (GER))
5107a[2] (5542a) 6592a[2]

Buddhist Monk *Dagmar Geissmann* a79 91
5 b g Dr Fong(USA) —Circle Of Light (Anshan)
461a[9]

Budding Daffodil *William Knight* a53 71
3 b f Reel Buddy(USA) —Jezadil (IRE) (Mujadil (USA))
2255[7] 2674[7] 3443[6] 4764[2]

Buddy Holly *Mrs V M Jordan* a87 84
5 b g Reel Buddy(USA) —Night Symphonie (Cloudings (IRE))
25[7] 565[6] 765[2] 1011[5] (2093) 2173[3] 2685[8] 4579[13] 5611[5] 5991[7] 6554[3] 7548[9] 7694[6]

Buddy Miracle *Andrew Balding* a67 72
2 ch f Reel Buddy(USA) —Sukuma (IRE) (Highest Honor (FR))
2687[7] 4622[5] 4954[5] 5613[3] 6086[5] 6317[11] 7088[2] 7309[2] 7715[3] 8002[4]

Buddy Twosocks *Simon West* 47
2 ch c Reel Buddy(USA) —Via Dolorosa (Chaddleworth (IRE))
5352[7]

Budva *Hughie Morrison* a74 60
3 b g Kylian(USA) —Danlu (USA) (Danzig (USA))
2792[5] (4683) 5058[13] 5646[3] ◆ 6955[5] 7397[2]

Buena Vista (JPN) *Hiroyoshi Matsuda* 122
4 bb m Special Week(JPN) —Biwa Heidi (JPN) (Caerleon (USA))
1026a[2] 7615a[2]

Buen Rumbero (USA) *Francisco Castro* a68
4 ch g City Zip(USA) —Knoosh (USA) (Storm Bird (CAN))
2019a[8]

Buffering *A Fabre* a78 89
3 b f Beat Hollow—Mooring (Zafonic (USA))
5981a[2] 6551a[8]

Buffett *Luca Cumani* a81 81
3 b c Bertolini(USA) —Batik (IRE) (Peintre Celebre (USA))
1448[5] (1973) 2386[2] 3081[2] 3697[5] 4571[5]

Bugaku *Sir Michael Stoute* a94 91
5 b g Montjeu(IRE) —Bryony Brind (IRE) (Kris)
(1282) 1837[7] 2934[2] 3873[9] 4306[8]

Bugsy's Boy *George Baker* a72 77
6 b g Double Trigger(IRE) —Bugsy's Sister (Aragon)
500[8] 874[4] (6775)

Bullet Man (USA) *Richard Fahey* a62 94
5 br g Mr Greeley(USA) —Silk Tapestry (USA) (Tank's Prospect (USA))
1474[6] 1889[5] 2314[2] 2865[10] 4450[6] 5436[4] 6223[2] 6780[5] 7053[9] 7548[12]

Bullet Train *Henry Cecil* 113
3 b c Sadler's Wells(USA) —Kind (IRE) (Danehill (USA))
1354[2] ◆ (1910) 2746[12] 3142[6] 5538[5] 6281[5]

Bull Five *Nick Littmoden* a68
3 b g Intikhab(USA) —Digamist Girl (IRE) (Digamist (USA))
4840[2] 5380[3]

Bulliciosa (USA) *M Pimbonnet* 98
2 b f Successful Appeal(USA) —Bailonguera (ARG) (Southern Halo (USA))
4275a[3] 6044a[5]

Bull Market (IRE) *M S Tuck* a74 36
7 b g Danehill(USA) —Paper Moon (IRE) (Lake Coniston (IRE))
383[9] 4910[11] 5868[14] 6669[13]

Bullring (FR) *Peter Niven* a60
4 ch g Green Tune(USA) —Capework (USA) (El Gran Senor (USA))
7896[9]

Bullwhip (IRE) *John Gosden* 103
3 b c Whipper(USA) —Flaming Song (IRE) (Darshaan)
(1029) ◆ 1385[5] 1834[6] 2971[6] 4144[7] 4750[6] (5524) ◆ 5950[8] 6564[7] 6960[5]

Bumbling Bertie *Andrew Balding* 42
2 b g Bertolini(USA) —Putuna (Generous (IRE))
5582[12] 6159[10] 6859[9]

Bunce (IRE) *Richard Hannon* 82
2 b c Good Reward(USA) —Bold Desire (Cadeaux Genereux)
1517[4] 1686[2] 2561[2] 2930[3] 3624[15] 5785[2] (5992) (6627)

Bungie *Jennie Candlish* a48 35
6 gr g Forzando—Sweet Whisper (Petong)
3028[11]

Bungur (FR) *R Gibson* a65 43
2 b c Holy Roman Emperor(IRE) —Marion (IRE) (Doyoun)
4565a[6]

Buona Sarah (IRE) *Jim Boyle* a73 66
3 ch f Bertolini(USA) —Midnight Partner (IRE) (Marju (IRE))
1048[4] (1209) 1476[6] 1696[2] 2619[3] 2820[3] 3404[2] 3789[5] (7476) (7562) 7732[6]

Buon Compleanno (IRE) *Alan Berry* 24
2 b f Tagula(IRE) —Matetsi (IRE) (Wagon Limit (USA))
2272[8] 2693[9] 3625[6] 4241[9] 7404[10] 7598[9] 7913[8]

Burdlaz (IRE) *Mahmood Al Zarooni* a103 99
5 ch h Indian Ridge—Babalu (IRE) (Doyoun)
513a[3] 820a[8] 1911[4]

Bureaucrat *Milton Harris* a71 96
8 b g Machiavellian(USA) —Lajna (Be My Guest (USA))
205[8]

Burghley *Michael Bell* a78 86
3 b g Shamardal(USA) —Badminton (Zieten (USA))
(128) 884[7] 1834[3] 2090[4] 3886[5] 4699[6] 5861[5] 6805[11]

Burj Alzain (IRE) *Gerard Butler* a86
2 b c Marju(IRE) —Bahareeya (USA) (Riverman (USA))
(7164) (7481) ◆ 7974a[2]

Burj Hatta (USA) *Saeed Bin Suroor* 74
2 bb c Kingmambo(USA) —Vadahilla (FR) (Danehill (USA))
3452[4]

Burma Gold (IRE) *P Schiergen* 101
3 ch c Java Gold(USA) —Bougainvillea (GER) (Acatenango (GER))
4164a[6] 6011a[2] (7103a)

Burma Rock (IRE) *Luca Cumani* a84 79
4 b g Danehill Dancer(IRE) —Burmese Princess (USA) (King Of Kings (IRE))
4652[8] 5311[11] 5919[12] 6252[4] 6449[7] 7111[6]

Burnbrake *Les Hall* a63 52
5 b g Mujahid(USA) —Duena (Grand Lodge (USA))
1323[9] 2417[10] 3263[6] 4591[4] (6454)

Burnem Green *Alan Bailey* a43 28
2 b f Librettist(USA) —Lambeth Belle (USA) (Arazi (USA))
4759[8] 5147[11] 5381[9] 5667[8]

Burnett (IRE) *Saeed Bin Suroor* 83
3 b c Dynaformer(USA) —Secret Garden (IRE) (Danehill (USA))
5387[8] 6185[5]

Burning Thread (IRE) *Tim Etherington* a38 93
3 b g Captain Rio—Desert Rose (Green Desert (USA))
1685[2] (2437) (2972) 5851[9]

Burns Night *Geoffrey Harker* a77 83
4 ch g Selkirk(USA) —Night Frolic (Night Shift (USA))
1361[7] ◆ 1669[6] 2850[8] 4515[12] (4796)

Burnt Cream *Bryan Smart* a49 63
3 b f Exceed And Excel(AUS) —Basbousate Nadia (Wolfhound (USA))
2741[4] 3228[7] 5152[5]

Burn The Breeze (IRE) *Mlle H Van Zuylen* a91 110
5 b m Beat Hollow—Madiyla (Darshaan)
5108a[3]

Burnwynd Boy *John McShane* 87
5 b g Tobougg(IRE) —Cadeau Speciale (Cadeaux Genereux)
71[7] 5480[12] 5601[11] 5734[11] 6103[8] 6245[8] 6491[6]

Bursary (CAN) *Mark Johnston* a43 77
3 b c Elusive Quality(USA) —Rare Opportunity (USA) (Danzig Connection (USA))
2220[3] 2564[9] 3733[2] 4483[7]

Burst Of Applause (IRE) *Michael Quinlan* a60
2 b f Royal Applause—Lake Nipigon (Selkirk (USA))
5865[10] 6866[12] 7309[9]

Burst Of Stardust *Bryn Palling* 41
2 ch f Peintre Celebre(USA) —Ymlaen (IRE) (Desert Prince (IRE))
5441[7]

Bury The Hatchet (IRE) *Alan Swinbank*
4 gr g Sesaro(USA) —Royal Myth (USA) (Sir Ivor (USA))
4893[10]

Bushman *David Simcock* a82 115
6 gr g Maria's Mon(USA) —Housa Dancer (FR) (Fabulous Dancer (USA))
(1974) (2707) 4390[2] 5186[9] 6350[7]

Bush Master *Jim Boyle* a70 68
3 b g Hunting Lion(IRE) —Patandon Girl (IRE) (Night Shift (USA))
1784[9] 3510[10]

Bushwhacker (AUS) *William Muir* a70 68
5 b g Statue Of Liberty(USA) —Tortola (AUS) (West Point (AUS))
5514[2] 5810[2] 6310[5] 6746[2] 6931[3]

Bushy Dell (IRE) *Julia Feilden* a73 91
5 br m King Charlemagne(USA) —Nisibis (In The Wings)
224[5] 375[3] 786[5] 910[7] 6744[4] 7167[5] 7504[10] 7861[8]

Business As Usual *Michael Jarvis* a87 101
3 b g Invincible Spirit(IRE) —Lesgor (USA) (Irish River (FR))
2028[4] (2544) ◆

Business Bay (USA) *Edward Vaughan* a64 64
3 bb g Salt Lake(USA) —Jeweled Lady (USA) (General Meeting (USA))
1460[3] 2011[5] 2401[9] 3564[7] 5155[7] 5522[9]

Business Class (BRZ) *Marjorie Fife* a70 64
5 b g Thignon Lafre(BRZ) —Dioner (BRZ) (Rotioner (BRZ))
814[7] 2187[11] 2788[7]

Businessmoney Judi *Rod Millman* a55 63
4 ch m Kirkwall—Cloverjay (Lir)
1851[6] 2921[5] 3347[5] 5011[11] 5382[8]

Busker (USA) *Mahmood Al Zarooni* a79 80
2 ch c Street Cry(IRE) —Adonesque (IRE) (Sadler's Wells (USA))
4110[6] 4549[2] 4909[2] 5718[7]

Bussa *David Evans* 81
2 b g Iceman—Maid To Dance (Pyramus (USA))
2048[8] 2540[4] (2895) 4544[4] 5245[18] 5830[4]

Bussell Along (IRE) *Stef Higgins* a58 58
4 b m Mujadil(USA) —Waaedah (USA) (Halling (USA))
803[4] 1478[10] 1976[5] 2487[2] 2691[5] 2923[4] 4689[5] 5148[4] 5813[7]

But Beautiful (IRE) *Robert Mills* a63
3 ch f Pivotal—Sweet Firebird (IRE) (Sadler's Wells (USA))
1659[11] (7757) ◆

Bute Street *Ron Hodges* a67 64
5 b g Superior Premium—Hard To Follow (Dilum (USA))
2923[8] (4676) (4991) 5625[7] (6121) 6373[3]

Buthelezi (USA) *John Gosden* 94
2 bb c Dynaformer(USA) —Ntombi (USA) (Quiet American (USA))
4803[2] (5392) ◆ (5947) 6505[11]

Butterfly Flip (FR) *J-P Perruchot* a47 43
6 b m Cardoun(FR) —Barisha (FR) (Baryshnikov (AUS))
207a[8] 303a[0] 459a[10] 559a[0]

Butterfly Hill (FR) *P Bary* 83
2 b f Kingsalsa(USA) —Luna Hill (FR) (Danehill (USA))
7276a[6]

Button Moon (IRE) *Ian Wood* a67 84
2 ch f Compton Place—Portelet (Night Shift (USA))
2048[3] ◆ 2376[2] 2638[3] 4138[24] 5284[4] 5527[2] 5880[12] 6157[9] 6419[7]

Buxfizz (USA) *Robert Mills* a85 79
2 b g Elusive Quality(USA) —Argentina (USA) (Storm Cat (USA))
4490[8] ◆ 4838[6] (6634) (7066) 7236[8]

Buxted (IRE) *Robert Mills* a108 106
4 b h Dynaformer(USA) —Bintalreef (USA) (Diesis)
(179) ◆ (447) (903) 1382[5] 2375a[6] 5749[8] 6929[3]

Buxton *Roger Ingram* a77 86
6 b g Auction House(USA) —Dam Certain (IRE) (Damister (USA))
1877[10] 2187[5] (2490) ◆ 2783[5] 3033[6] 3579[6] 4057[8] 4308[3] 5157[2] 5652[4] 6085[9] 7241[4] 7421[6] 7554[10] 7724[10] (7991)

Buy On The Red *David Nicholls* a73 78
9 b g Komaite(USA) —Red Rosein (Red Sunset)
138[7] 562[6]

Buzz Bird *David Barron* a72 50
3 b f Danbird(AUS) —Ashtaroute (USA) (Holy Bull (USA))
455[2] ◆ 574[2] ◆ 1394[7] (1495) 1970[11] (2787) 3238[9] 3759[4] 7845[6]

Buzz Law (IRE) *Mrs K Burke* 68
2 b g Fasliyev(USA) —Buzz Two (IRE) (Case Law)
2693[8] 2939[7] 4167[5] (4801) 5490[5] 5784[3] 6386[7]

Buzzword *Mahmood Al Zarooni* 115
3 b c Pivotal—Bustling (Danehill (USA))
1699[14] 2159a[4] 2746[8] 3142[3] (4184a) 5804a[3]

Byblos *Warren Greatrex* a68 62
5 ch g Tobougg(IRE) —My Girl (Mon Tresor)
677[2] 842[8] 1087[5] 3348[8] 3848[8]

By Command *Gerald Ham* a73 75
5 b g Red Ransom(USA) —Rafha (Kris)
144[6] (540) ◆ 752[2] 855[6] 965[3] (1129) 1926[17] 2392[3] 2527[7] 3022[10] 3518[2] 3768[10] 7307[10]

By Implication *John Gosden* a51
2 br c Cacique(IRE) —Insinuate (USA) (Mr Prospector (USA))
7559[5]

Byrd In Hand (IRE) *John Bridger* a61 70
3 b g Fasliyev(USA) —Military Tune (IRE) (Nashwan (USA))
2401[6] 2925[4] 4205[6] 4905[8] 6197[10] 6527[6] 6999[3] 7316[7]

By Request *Sir Mark Prescott Bt* 60
4 b m Giant's Causeway(USA) —Approach (Darshaan)
2463[7]

Byron Bay *Robert Johnson* a64 73
8 b g My Best Valentine—Candarela (Damister (USA))
7128[13] 7401[13]

Byron Bear (IRE) *Paul Midgley* 43
2 b g Byron—Paulas Pride (Pivotal)
4089[7] 5040[11] 5595[8]

Byronic (IRE) *Clive Cox* 91
2 b g Byron—Lear's Crown (USA) (Lear Fan (USA))
3310[2] ◆ (3735) 5525[3] 5849[2]

Byrony (IRE) *Richard Hannon* a87 79
2 ch f Byron—Saphire (College Chapel)
1972[6] 2163[6] 3562[4] (4020) (4331) (5177) 6317[12] (6845)

Byword *A Fabre* 126
4 ch h Peintre Celebre(USA) —Binche (USA) (Woodman (USA))
(1716a) 2374a[2] (3068) 5186[3] 6015a[4]

Cabal *Sir Michael Stoute* a72 83
3 br f Kyllachy—Secret Flame (Machiavellian (USA))
1164[2] 1777[2] (2702) ◆ 3661[3] 4491[2] 5149[6]

Cabaret (IRE) *A P O'Brien* 106
3 b f Galileo(IRE) —Witch Of Fife (USA) (Lear Fan (USA))
2029[7] 2711[12] 3101[9]

Cabimas *P Schiergen* 102
3 b c King's Best(USA) —Casanga (IRE) (Rainbow Quest (USA))
7457a[2]

Cabuchon (GER) *Barney Curley* a52
3 b c Fantastic Light(USA) —Catella (GER) (Generous (IRE))
7489[5] 7887[5]

Cactus King *Jim Best* a61 47
7 b g Green Desert(USA) —Apache Star (Arazi (USA))
80[4] 1318[2] 3442[5] 3810[4] 7614[11]

Cadeau For Maggi *H-A Pantall* a90 106
5 ch h Cadeaux Genereux—Maggi For Margaret (Shavian)
304a[2] (549a) 743a[3] 4122[3] 4526a[11]

Cadeaux Fax *Rod Millman* a72 66
5 ch g Largesse—Facsimile (Superlative)
1304[6] 1762[5] 2383[9] 3558[8]

Cadeaux Pearl *Richard Hannon* 90
2 b c Acclamation—Anneliina (Cadeaux Genereux)
2715[5] 3805[2] (4303) 5221[13]

Cadmium Loch *Reg Hollinshead* a51 50
2 b g Needwood Blade—Vermilion Creek (Makbul)
6514[8] 6712[6] 7065[7]

Cadore (IRE) *Peter Chapple-Hyam* 76
2 b c Hurricane Run(IRE) —Mansiya (Vettori (IRE))
4550[6] 6127[2] 6514[2]

Cadre (IRE) *Saeed Bin Suroor* a79 104
5 b g King's Best(USA) —Desert Frolic (IRE) (Persian Bold)
419a[5]

Caesar's Song (IRE) *Patrick O Brady* 86
5 b g Singspiel(IRE) —Caesarea (GER) (Generous (IRE))
2571a[3]

Cafe Elektric *Sir Mark Prescott Bt* a87 92
2 ch c Pivotal—Shanghai Lily (IRE) (King's Best (USA))
(2486) ◆ 2918[3] 4928[4] (6104) 6553[2]

Cafe Mystique (IRE) *P Vovcenko* a65
4 b g Celtic Swing—Roseanna (FR) (Anabaa (USA))
458a[11]

Cafe Racer (IRE) *M bin Shafya* a76 105
4 b h Royal Applause—Metisse (USA) (Kingmambo (USA))
339a[14] 434a[11]

Cailin Coillteach *Andrew Oliver* a61 65
2 b f Woodman(USA) —Kathy's Rocket (USA) (Gold Legend (USA))
7256a[10]

Cairanne *Tom Keddy* 26
2 b f High Chaparral(IRE) —Celestial Choir (Celestial Storm (USA))
6092[11] 6881[13]

Cairnsmore *Mark Johnston* a93 101
4 b g Singspiel(IRE) —Dunloskin (Selkirk (USA))
(308) 536[11] 1015[10] 1831[4] (2282) 2608[11]

Cai Shen (IRE) *Richard Hannon* 91
2 ch c Iffraaj—Collada (IRE) (Desert Prince (IRE))
4622[8] (5263) (5690)

Calabaza *Michael Attwater* a21 32
8 ch g Zaha(CAN) —Mo Stopher (Sharpo)
4308[14] 4790[9] 5169[7] 5557[11]

Calaf *Jane Chapple-Hyam* 74
2 b c Dubai Destination(USA) —Tarandot (IRE) (Singspiel (IRE))
6126[2] 7058[9]

Calahonda *Paul D'Arcy* a81 81
4 ch m Haafhd—Californie (IRE) (Rainbow Quest (USA))
1265[13] 1883[12] (2477) 3036[2] 3565[11] 4804[6] 5391[7] 5866[8] 6372[13] 6633[12]

Calatrava Cape (IRE) *John Dunlop* 106
3 b f Cape Cross(IRE) —Pershaan (IRE) (Darshaan)
(3170) 3414[2] 5008[2] 5747[6] (6199) 7206[2]

Calbuco (FR) *B Dutruel* a93 90
6 b g Kendor(FR) —Pennegale (IRE) (Pennekamp (USA))
2446a[7]

Calculating (IRE) *Mark Usher* a83 71
6 b g Machiavellian(USA) —Zaheemah (USA) (El Prado (IRE))
173[2] 224[2] 352[2] 401[2] 811[2] 938[4] 1069[3] 1454[4] 1798[2] 2228[3] 2814[8] (4686) 5296[4] 5443[4] 5922[5] 6693[11] 7067[6] 7181[5]

Calculus Affair (IRE) *Jeremy Noseda* a73
3 b c Trans Island—Where's Charlotte (Sure Blade (USA))
381[2]

Caldercruix (USA) *Tom Tate* 96
3 ch g Rahy(USA) —Al Theraab (USA) (Roberto (USA))
(1649) (1969) 2562[2] 3824[18] 5188[15] 6106[4] 6567[10] 6749[19]

Caldermud (IRE) *John Best* a74 78
3 ch g Chineur(FR) —Dalal (Cadeaux Genereux)
1661[6] 3154[2] 4031[5] 4714[6] 5073[9]

Caledonia Prince *F J Brennan* 37
2 b g Needwood Blade—Granuaile O'Malley (IRE) (Mark Of Esteem (IRE))
4247[10] 5385[9] 6053[10]

Caledonia Princess *F J Brennan* a74 83
4 b m Kyllachy—Granuaile O'Malley (IRE) (Mark Of Esteem (IRE))
1337[9] 2849[15] (3958) (4424) (4904) 5526[8] 5966[7] 6446[9]

Calfraz *Micky Hammond* 34
8 bb g Tamure(IRE) —Pas De Chat (Relko)
1424[5]

Calico Bay (IRE) *Alan McCabe* a27
2 b c Whipper(USA) —Caribbean Escape (Pivotal)
6333[10]

California Flag (USA) *Brian Koriner* 123
6 rg g Avenue Of Flags(USA) —Ultrafleet (USA) (Afleet (CAN))
1021a[3] 7362a[8]

Calina Salsa (FR) *Y Barberot* a87 84
3 b f Kingsalsa(USA) —Lacina (Nashwan (USA))
926a[2]

Calipatria *John Gosden* a74 83
3 ch f Shamardal(USA) —Golden Silca (Inchinor)
4340[2] ◆ 4697[3] (5265) ◆ 5972[3] 6361[14]

Calley Ho *Linda Stubbs* a70 41
4 b g Kyllachy—Lucayan Belle (Cadeaux Genereux)
2854[7] 3286[10] 3900[6]

Callie's Angel *Bryn Palling* a44 64
2 b c Piccolo—Oriel Girl (Beveled (USA))
4909[7] 5385[4] 6019[6] (6628) 7394[8]

Callipygos *Phil McEntee* a43 21
2 b f Largesse—En Grisaille (Mystiko (USA))
1065[3] 1324[10] 4960[13] 6646[10] 6884[8] 7021[9] 7404[7] 7540[6]

Callisto Light *Walter Swinburn* 44
3 ch f Medicean—Luminda (IRE) (Danehill (USA))
2890[10]

Callisto Moon *F J Brennan* a69 88
6 b g Mujahid(USA) —Nursling (IRE) (Kahyasi)
1544[4] (1798) 3050[20] 4405[13] 5788[13] 6715[9]

Call It On (IRE) *Mark H Tompkins* 91
4 ch g Raise A Grand(IRE) —Birthday Present (Cadeaux Genereux)
2027[11]

Call Of Duty (IRE) *Dianne Sayer* a52 72
5 br g Storming Home—Blushing Barada (USA) (Blushing Groom (FR))
1150[10] 1717[6] 1983[5] 2207[5] 2583[2] 3022[3] 3357[2] 3502[3] 3774[2] 4404[3] (4644) 4985[3] 5819[11] 6267[2] 6492[4]

Call The Law (IRE) *Pam Sly* a39 51
4 b m Acclamation—Savvy Shopper (USA) (Stravinsky (USA))
3287[7] 4071[3] 4559[6]

Call To Arms (IRE) *Mark Johnston* a82 80
3 br g Shamardal(USA) —Requesting (Rainbow Quest (USA))
(655) 1584[P] 2170[7] 2599[6] 3394[3] 4065[3] 4602[2]

Call To Reason (IRE) *Jeremy Noseda* 91
3 ch f Pivotal—Venturi (Danehill Dancer (IRE))
(5493) 5993[4] 7238[3] ◆

Calm And Serene (USA) *Rae Guest* a32 47
3 b f Quiet American(USA) —Charm Away (USA) (Silver Charm (USA))
1782[8] 2675[11] 3443[10] 3662[5] 4027[6]

Calm Bay (IRE) *H Rogers* a93 93
4 b g Medecis—Queen Sigi (IRE) (Fairy King (USA))
1091a[5] 3489a[18] 5127a[7] 7073a[6] 7217a[14]

Calmdownmate (IRE) *Ruth Carr* a80 85
5 b g Danehill Dancer(IRE) —Lady Digby (IRE) (Petorius)
380[6] 601[14] 832[6] 892[6] 1072[2] 1147[5] 1491[4] 2791[5] 3763[12] 4895[5]

Calming Influence (IRE) *Mahmood Al Zarooni* a118 98
5 b h King's Best(USA) —Idilic Calm (IRE) (Indian Ridge)
440a[4] (610a) 798a[3] (1022a) 3046[9]

Calormen *Alan Juckes* a46 59
2 b c Imperial Dancer—Queen Of Narnia (Hunting Lion (IRE))
1073[2] ◆ 1180[8] 1463[2] 2300[2] 3678[8] 5581[11] 7177[4] 7396[5]

Calrissian (GER) *Fredrik Reuterskiold* a96 109
6 ch g Efisio—Centaine (Royal Academy (USA))
434a[8] 604a[5] 822a[4] 3425a[7] (6406a)

Calvados Blues (FR) *Mahmood Al Zarooni* a109 112
4 ch h Lando(GER) —Persian Belle (Machiavellian (USA))
609a[3] 821a[5] 1025a[10] 6123[7]

Calvero (FR) *Mlle Valerie Boussin* a63 77
3 b g Sabiango(GER) —La Bastoche (IRE) (Kaldoun (FR))
6487a[0]

Calypso Bay (IRE) *Jonjo O'Neill* a56 83
4 b g Galileo(IRE) —Poule De Luxe (IRE) (Cadeaux Genereux)
1088[16] 1430[6]

Calypso Girl (IRE) *Alex Hales* a34 59
4 gr m Verglas(IRE) —Clochette (IRE) (Namaqualand (USA))
995[11] 2263[12]

Calypso Magic (IRE) *Howard Johnson* 79
2 gr g Aussie Rules(USA) —Calypso Dancer (FR) (Celtic Swing)
2210[6] 3945[2] 5210[2] 5814[2] 6566[2]

Calypso Star (IRE) *Richard Hannon* a80 79
3 ch c Exceed And Excel(AUS) —Reematna (Sabrehill (USA))
(1061) 1317[2] 1433[5] 1975[7] 2869[10] 3039[7] (3413) 3853[4] (4133) 4383[2] 5254[2] 5540[7]

Calzaghe (IRE) *Jim Best* a70 75
6 ch g Galileo(IRE) —Novelette (Darshaan)
182[4] 1160[3] 1283[5] 2455[3] (3819)

Camache Queen (IRE) *Denis Coakley* a73 56
2 b f Camacho—Alinda (IRE) (Revoque (IRE))
2867[5] 5835[4] ◆ (6161)

Camacho Flyer (IRE) *Paul Midgley* a27 69
3 b g Camacho—Despondent (IRE) (Broken Hearted)
1483[5] 2217[12] 2768[6] 3228[10]

Camberley Two *Roger Charlton* 29
2 bg c Invincible Spirit(IRE) —Diamond Line (FR) (Linamix (FR))
5916[9] 7099[15]

Cambina (IRE) *T Stack* 89
2 ch f Hawk Wing(USA) —Await (IRE) (Peintre Celebre (USA))
6005a[2]

Came Back (IRE) *Ann Stokell* a86 63
7 ch g Bertolini(USA) —Distant Decree (USA) (Distant View (USA))
223[13] 380[7] 504[7] 892[8]

Camelia Rose (FR) *J-C Rouget* 97
2 b f Oratorio(IRE) —Solaz (IRE) (Galileo (IRE))
(5622a)

Camerooney *Brian Ellison* a64 97
7 b g Sugarfoot—Enkindle (Relkino)
(7) (169) 248[3] (1374) 1672[2] (2293) (3318) (3448) 5292[7] 6180[7] 6562[5] 6888[3] 7348[19]

Camill (IRE) *P Kalas* 106
6 b g Monsun(GER) —Classic Light (IRE) (Classic Secret (USA))
6239a[5]

Camilla Grey (IRE) *Camilla Trapassi* 61
3 gr f Clodovil(IRE) —La Captive (IRE) (Selkirk (USA))
1713a[15]

Camira (IRE) *Edward P Harty* a82 82
5 br m Namid—Yanni (IRE) (Pennekamp (USA))
4524a[9]

Camomile *Tracy Waggott* 26
4 b m Xaar—Pretty Davis (USA) (Trempolino (USA))
3774[9]

Campaigner *J W Hills* a41 53
3 b c Dansili—Rosapenna (IRE) (Spectrum (IRE))
134[8]

Campanologist (USA) *Saeed Bin Suroor* a102 118
5 b h Kingmambo(USA) —Ring Of Music (Sadler's Wells (USA))
(799a) 1026a[9] 2152a[4] 3019a[3] (4164a) (5132a) 6148[3] 7291a[16]

Campos (IRE) *T Stack* 76
2 b c Oratorio(IRE) —Queens Head (King's Best (USA))
(4668)

Camps Bay (USA) *Conor Dore* a85 99
6 b g Cozzene(USA) —Seewillo (USA) (Pleasant Colony (USA))
1274[13] 1684[5] 2031[17] 6181[4] 7061[10] 7337[3] 7410[3] 7815[6] (7933) 8007[4]

Canada Fleet (CAN) *Ed Dunlop* 52
2 rg g Afleet Alex(USA) —Marieval (USA) (El Prado (IRE))
2547[7] 3112[7] 3577[6]

Canadian Ballet (USA) *Linda Rice* a68 107
5 ch m City Zip(USA) —Canadian Flagship (USA) (Northern Flagship (USA))
7362a[14]

Canadian Danehill (IRE) *Robert Cowell* a87 99
8 b g Indian Danehill(IRE) —San Jovita (CAN) (St Jovite (USA))
2[5] 172[6] 212[6] 432[5] 578[5] 4401[19] 5069[12] 6064[8] 6374[10] 6700[10] 7193[7] 7331[8] 7446[8]

Canaveral *Brian Meehan* 62
2 bb g Cape Cross(IRE) —Tarneem (USA) (Zilzal (USA))
5629[11] 6279[5]

Can Can Star *Tony Carroll* a89 86
7 br h Lend A Hand—Carrie Can Can (Green Tune (USA))
341[3] 7428[8]

Candilejas *Roger Curtis* a63 47
4 br m Diktat—Nacho Venture (FR) (Rainbow Quest (USA))
326[6] 470[8]

Candleshoe (IRE) *Richard Hannon* 73
3 b f Danehill Dancer(IRE) —Keepers Dawn (IRE) (Alzao (USA))
1476[3] ◆ (1775) 2587[2] 2888[14]

Candotoo (IRE) *Jeremy Noseda* a32 70
3 b f Cape Cross(IRE) —Leopard Hunt (USA) (Diesis)
1621[10] 2255[6] 2860[5] ◆ 3376[3]

Candyfloss Girl *Harry Dunlop* a77 65
3 b f Intikhab(USA) —Annatalia (Pivotal)
483[2] (689) 809[8] 1191[2] 1913[13] 3085[7] 3830[8] 4529[3] 5010[9] 5875[12] 6330[10]

Candys Girl *Michael Bell* 77
2 b f Bertolini(USA) —Sweet Cando (IRE) (Royal Applause)
4317[5] 5196[2] 5885[3] 6919[5]

Cane Cat (IRE) *Tony Carroll* a53 59
3 bb f One Cool Cat(USA) —Seven Wonders (USA) (Rahy (USA))
5715[6] 5898[11] 6665[5] 7166[5] 7783[5] 7885[3]

Canford Cliffs (IRE) *Richard Hannon* 130
3 b c Tagula(IRE) —Mrs Marsh (Marju (IRE))
1385[2] 1699[3] (2354a) (3048) (4469)

Canna (IRE) *B W Hills* 75
2 b c High Chaparral(IRE) —Brave Madam (IRE) (Invincible Spirit (IRE))
6532[4]

Cannon Bolt (IRE) *Robin Bastiman* 41
2 b c Chineur(FR) —Prime Time Girl (Primo Dominie)
6264[9] 6704[8] 6980[6]

Cansili Star *Michael Jarvis* 102
3 b g Dansili—Canis Star (Wolfhound (USA))
(1872) (2713) 3429[2] 4509[12] (5442) 6319[12]

Cantabilly (IRE) *Ron Hodges* a67 54
7 b g Distant Music(USA) —Cantaloupe (Priolo (USA))
1587[7] 1756[8]

Cantonese Cat (IRE) *Brian Meehan* 56
2 b c Tiger Hill(IRE) —Hsi Wang Mu (IRE) (Dr Fong (USA))
2932[12] 3219[8] 4131[9] 4962[6] 5807[8]

Cantor *John Gosden* a22
2 b c Iceman—Choir Mistress (Chief Singer)
7248[11]

Caol Ila (IRE) *James Given* a55 52
3 b f Invincible Spirit(IRE) —Pink Cashmere (IRE) (Polar Falcon (USA))
167[5] 906[6] 1118[10] 1456[9]

Capable Guest (IRE) *George Moore* a71 81
8 bb g Cape Cross(IRE) —Alexander Confranc (IRE) (Magical Wonder (USA))
(2013) 2341[10] 2694[3] 4656[3] 5642[3] 6114[9] 6895[3] 7181[4] 7541[4] 7805[4]

Capacity (IRE) *T G McCourt* a59 75
3 b g Cape Cross(IRE) —Carry On Katie (USA) (Fasliyev (USA))
7273[5] 7995[6]

Capa Cruz (IRE) *Ronald Harris* 41
2 b c Cape Cross(IRE) —Madame Arcati (IRE) (Sinndar (IRE))
1794[5] 1978[9] 2687[10] 5581[15]

Capaill Liath (IRE) *B W Hills* 87
2 gr g Iffraaj—Bethesda (Distant Relative)
2493[4] 2895[2] (3269) 3887[6] 5245[16] 6191[7] (6386)

Capall Dorcha *John Holt* 29
2 bl g Needwood Blade—Harriet (IRE) (Grand Lodge (USA))
1389[10] 1704[4] 4409[8] 4678[9]

Capeability (IRE) *Mick Channon* a77 91
4 b g Cape Cross(IRE) —Mennetou (IRE) (Entrepreneur)
291[2] 468[4] 1133[6] 2362[4] 3160[6] 3500[9]

Cape Blanco (IRE) *A P O'Brien* 127
3 ch c Galileo(IRE) —Laurel Delight (Presidium)
(2056) 2802a[10] (3491a) 4359[2] (5775a) 6612a[13]

Cape Classic (IRE) *William Haggas* a71 32
2 b c Cape Cross(IRE) —Politesse (USA) (Barathea (IRE))
7201[11] ◆ 7479[3]

Capecover (NZ) *Patrick Payne* 109
8 b g Cape Cross(IRE) —Set Up (NZ) (Zabeel (NZ))
7368a[2]

Cape Dollar (IRE) *Sir Michael Stoute* 104
2 b f Cape Cross(IRE) —Green Dollar (IRE) (Kingmambo (USA))
2505[3] (3296) ◆ 5519[3] (6927) ◆

Cape D'Or (IRE) *J L Hassett* a56 75
3 b g Cape Cross(IRE) —Sombreffe (Polish Precedent (USA))
1314[10]

Cape Dutch (IRE) *Mahmood Al Zarooni* 86
3 b c Cape Cross(IRE) —Rosia (IRE) (Mr Prospector (USA))
2043[10] 6876[2]

Cape Kimberley *Tony Newcombe* a77 67
3 b g Arakan(USA) —Etoile Volant (USA) (Silver Hawk (USA))
1584[3] ◆ 2656[9] 4684[11] 5027[3] 5388[2] 5852[4] ◆ 7241[7]

Capellanus (IRE) *E J O'Grady* 87
4 b g Montjeu(IRE) —Secret Dream (IRE) (Zafonic (USA))
6971a[12]

Cape Martin (IRE) *Gianluca Bietolini* 100
8 b g Polish Precedent(USA) —Clara House (Shirley Heights)
742a[7]

Cape Melody *Hughie Morrison* a78 79
4 b m Piccolo—Cape Charlotte (Mon Tresor)
1779[5] 2342[8] (2957) 3115[2] 3845[5] 4145[7] 4836[4] 5768[4] 6208[3] 6714[2] ◆ 6987[U]

Cape Of Dance (IRE) *Mark Johnston* 69
2 b f Cape Cross(IRE) —Nesaah's Princess (Sinndar (IRE))
4782[5] (5210)

Cape Of Storms *Roy Brotherton* a68 24
7 b g Cape Cross(IRE) —Lloc (Absalom)
20[10] 243[3] 402[9] 839[5] 961[12] 1491[3] 1929[16] 7468[3] 7542[4] ◆ (7738)

Cape Quarter (USA) *William Haggas* a65 65
4 b g Elusive Quality(USA) —June Moon (IRE) (Sadler's Wells (USA))
2133[5] 2750[8] 3262[3] 3777[8] 4260[4] 5039[3] 5959[3] 6573[8] 6718[3]

Cape Rambler *Henry Candy* 80
2 ch g Pastoral Pursuits—Cape Charlotte (Mon Tresor)
3332[6] 4110[3] 6882[3] 7119[2]

Capercaillie (USA) *Mark Johnston* 90
3 ch f Elusive Quality(USA) —Silent Eskimo (USA) (Eskimo (USA))
4569[4] 4819[3] 5088[10] 5694[7] 6113[14]

Cape Rock *William Knight* a92 88
5 b g Cape Cross(IRE) —Wildwood Flower (Distant Relative)
1625[4] 2091[3] (2872) 3083[4] 3796[7] 4459[8] 5264[14] 5997[4]

Cape Royal *Milton Bradley* a71 87
10 b g Prince Sabo—Indigo (Primo Dominie)
185[6] 306[3] 402[3] 810[3] 967[7] 1915[3] 2001[4] 2622[3] (3119) 3474[3] 3809[3] 4041[5] 4292[2] 4625[3] 4961[2] (5151) (5589) 5966[6] 6064[6] 6446[4] 7193[6] 7405[4] 7494[2] 7571[4] 7628[6]

Cape To Rio (IRE) *Richard Hannon* 103
2 b c Captain Rio—Misaayef (USA) (Swain (IRE))
(1256) (2177) 2468[3] 4097[2] 5245[14] 6734[5] 7080[4]

Cape Vale (IRE) *David Nicholls* a93 93
5 b g Cape Cross(IRE) —Wolf Cleugh (IRE) (Last Tycoon)
3489a[17] 5127a[6] 6358[2] 7566[7] (7697) 7740[5]

Cape Velvet (IRE) *Mme J Bidgood* a71 71
6 b m Cape Cross(IRE) —Material Lady (IRE) (Barathea (IRE))
690a[0]

Capitaine Courage (IRE) *F Doumen* a89 108
5 ch g Bering—Four Green (FR) (Green Tune (USA))
953a[6] 6344a[8]

Capital Attraction (USA) *Henry Cecil* a106 91
3 ch g Speightstown(USA) —Cecilia's Crown (USA) (Chief's Crown (USA))
(2335) ◆ 5370[3] 5741[8]

Capitano Knox (IRE) *Laura Grizzetti*
2 ch c Halling(USA) —Purple Haze (IRE) (Spectrum (IRE))
7850a[13]

Capone (IRE) *F J Brennan* a94 79
5 b g Daggers Drawn(USA) —Order Of The Day (USA) (Dayjur (USA))
4832[11]

Cappiwino (USA) *Saeed Bin Suroor* a63
3 b g Soto(USA) —Slow And Steady (USA) (Malibu Moon (USA))
510a[10]

Capponi (IRE) *Mark Johnston* a100 111
3 ch c Medicean—Nawaiet (USA) (Zilzal (USA))
(930) ◆ 2261[2] ◆ (3667) (3920) 4504[9] 5247[12] (5948) 6562[10]

Capricorn Run (USA) *Alan McCabe* a106 103
7 bb g Elusive Quality(USA) —Cercida (USA) (Copelan (USA))
413a[11] 606a[8] 883[11]

Capricornus (USA) *Ferdy Murphy* a80
3 ch c Rahy(USA) —Silent Partner (USA) (Capote (USA))
136[2] 268[4] 1061[2] 7867[10]

Caprio (IRE) *Jim Boyle* a89 85
5 ch g Captain Rio—Disarm (IRE) (Bahamian Bounty)
16[7] (214) 405[3] (481) 902[2] 981[3] 1625[10] (2668) 3120[2] 3226[7] 4053[5] 5027[4] 6167[3] 7557[3] (7725) 8033[8]

Captain Bellamy (USA) *Hughie Morrison* 44
2 ch g Bellamy Road(USA) —Thesky'sthelimit (USA) (Northern Prospect (USA))
6159[17] 6689[16] 6953[7]

Captain Bertie (IRE) *B W Hills* 84
2 ch c Captain Rio—Sadika (IRE) (Bahhare (USA))
4096[3] ◆ 4577[2] (5900)

Captain Bluebird (IRE) *Desmond Donovan* a61 61
3 gr g Captain Rio—Dolly Blue (IRE) (Pennekamp (USA))
236[4] 371[6] 782[8] 1155[2] 1491[6] 4406[12] 4989[7] 5697[3] 6133[11] 6330[3] 6746[6] 6847[5]

Captain Brilliance (USA) *Jeremy Noseda* 108
5 ch h Officer(USA) —Bloomin Genius (USA) (Beau Genius (CAN))
2651[4] 3869[8]

Captain Brown *Sir Mark Prescott Bt* 71
2 b g Lomitas—Nicola Bella (IRE) (Sadler's Wells (USA))
6436[4] 6894[2]

Captain Carey *Malcolm Saunders* a99 96
4 b g Fraam—Brigadiers Bird (IRE) (Mujadil (USA))
916[4] (1506) (2280) 2940[6] (3261) 4180a[5] 4685[4] 4814[4]

Captain Chop (FR) *D Guillemin* 106
2 b c Indian Rocket—Hatane Chope (FR) (Sin Kiang (FR))
2917a[4] 3718a[4] 4637a[2] 5347a[7] 6760a[2] 7277a[5] (7534a)

Captain Clint (IRE) *Mark H Tompkins* a32 48
3 b g Captain Rio—Lake Poopo (IRE) (Persian Heights)
1606[3] 1989[5] 2675[13] 3213[8] 4113[3] 4761[5]

Captain Coke (IRE) *Michael Jarvis* a74 87
3 b c Fath(USA) —Akariyda (IRE) (Salse (USA))
(2639) (3174) (3417) ◆ 5309[2] ◆ 5855[5]

Captain Cool (IRE) *Richard Hannon* a60 66
3 ch g Captain Rio—Aiaie (Zafonic (USA))
118[2] 183[4] 589[4] 677[3] 762[2] 1060[5] 1264[2] (1394) 1578[2] (1880) 2248[4] 2650[6] 3564[11] 4327[9] 5653[5] 6816[4] 7117[8] 7716[3] 8015[7]

Captain Cornelius (IRE) *Joss Saville* 58
3 b g Captain Rio—Bolas (Unfuwain (USA))
1572[4] 2083[5] 4348[8] 5642[11]

Captain Dancer (IRE) *B W Hills* a5 88
4 ch g Danehill Dancer(IRE) —Rain Flower (IRE) (Indian Ridge)
1030[8] 1361[2] ◆ 2885[8] 5937[3] (6327) 6677[2] 6807[2]

Captain Dimitrios *David Evans* a72 74
2 b g Dubai Destination(USA) —Tripti (IRE) (Sesaro (USA))
2163[8] 2677[3] 3058[3] 3596[5] (3864) 4066[2] 4331[5] 4615[2] 5472[2] 6191[8] 6325[5] 6842[4] 8012[2]

Captain Dunne (IRE) *Tim Easterby* a107 108
5 b g Captain Rio—Queen Bodicea (IRE) (Revoque (IRE))
1573[2] 2135[2] 2745[12] (3406) 3674[7] 3895[2] 4191[11] 4505[7] 5183[5] 5512[3] 5851[4] 6265[2] (6663)

Captain Flack *James Toller* a61 54
4 ch g Lucky Story(USA) —Au Contraire (Groom Dancer (USA))
584[10] 842[7] 982[12]

Captain Imperial (IRE) *Robin Bastiman* a68 71
4 b g Captain Rio—Imperialist (IRE) (Imperial Frontier (USA))
426[12] 705[5] 838[6] 1204[5] 2273[6] 2779[5] 3948[7]

Captain James Cook *A P O'Brien* a88 65
3 b c Montjeu(IRE) —Pink Cristal (Dilum (USA))
1910[P] (Dead)

Captain John Nixon *Pat Eddery* a90 76
3 b c Beat Hollow—Leaping Flame (USA) (Trempolino (USA))
1165[11] 1442[9] 2121[8] (2853) (3055) (3444) (3564) 4334[7] 7090[5] (7428) 7815[4]

Captain Kallis (IRE) *Dominic Ffrench Davis* a63 64
4 ch g Captain Rio—Alicedale (USA) (Trempolino (USA))
351[4] 504[4] 556[5] 674[8] 763[7] 839[3] (912) 1072[3] 1534[4] 1799[2] 2021[6] 2719[4] 2809[3] 3299[6] 4326[9] 4589[9] 5262[11] 5377[9] 6018[8] 6270[9] 6952[3] 7132[2]

Captain Kolo (IRE) *Tim Easterby* 76
2 b g Captain Rio—Patsy Grimes (Beveled (USA))
6045[3] (6646) 6916[3]

Captain Loui (IRE) *Dai Burchell* a66 59
2 gr g Verglas(IRE) —Miss Corinne (Mark Of Esteem (IRE))
2138[6] 2493[8] 2785[2] 4059[3] (4436) ◆ 4848[10] (5269) 5837[4] 6694[2] 7066[5] 7395[4]

Captain Macarry (IRE) *John Quinn* a96 94
5 ch g Captain Rio—Grannys Reluctance (IRE) (Anita's Prince)
1006[14] 1900[27] 2971[14] 3796[15] 4306[4] 5287[11] 6922[2] ◆

Captain Noble (IRE) *PETER Makin* a68 52
2 b c Captain Rio—Noble Nova (Fraam)
6145[9] 6425[4] 7595[5]

Captain Oats (IRE) *Pam Ford* a54 54
7 b g Bahhare(USA) —Adarika (Kings Lake (USA))
4620[9] 4987[12]

Captain Peachey *P Monteith* 44
4 b g Pursuit Of Love—Dekelsmary (Komaite (USA))
4947[10] 5732[7] 6029[8]

Captain Ramius (IRE) *Kevin Ryan* a97 96
4 b g Kheleyf(USA) —Princess Mood (GER) (Muhtarram (USA))
1349[6] 2992[12] 4085[8] 5154[7] (5903) 6178[5] 6357[7] 6907a[5] 7348[8]

Captainrisk (IRE) *Christine Dunnett* a76 76
4 b g Captain Rio—Helderberg (USA) (Diesis)
2399[11] 2635[8] 3062[9]

Captain Royale (IRE) *Tracy Waggott* a61 83
5 ch g Captain Rio—Paix Royale (Royal Academy (USA))
3977[12] 4244[11] 4706[12] 5045[2] (5485) 5599[7] 5999[2] (6492) 6962[9] (6981) 7180[8]

Captain Scooby *Richard Whitaker* 79
4 b g Captain Rio—Scooby Dooby Do (Atraf)
1524[12] 2578[8] (4372) 4834[8] 5198[3] 6073[2] (6245) 6572[4] 6981[9]

Captain Sharpe *Harry Dunlop* a37 68
2 ch c Tobougg(IRE) —Helen Sharp (Pivotal)
2245[11] 3832[9] 4587[4] 5659[11] 6129[7] 6859[3] 7034[3]

Captain Tony (IRE) *Matthew Salaman* a40
3 ch g Captain Rio—Curtistown (IRE) (Elbio)
24[9] 362[5] 962[8]

Captain Webb *E Charpy* a99 100
5 br h Storming Home—Criquette (Shirley Heights)
419a[9] 605a[3] 706a[4]

Captivator *James Fanshawe* a77 70
3 gr f Motivator—Cashew (Sharrood (USA))
2632[2] ◆ 3586[9] 4697[4] ◆ 5925[2]

Caraboss *Sir Michael Stoute* 73
2 b f Cape Cross(IRE) —Fairy Godmother (Fairy King (USA))
5692[4]

Caracal *Gordon Elliott* a73 67
3 b g Dubai Destination(USA) —Desert Lynx (IRE) (Green Desert (USA))
583[2] 3180[5] 3531[7] 3899[6] 4439[2] 4585[4] 5925[4]

Cara Carmela *Stuart Williams* a17
2 gr f Compton Place—Carmela Owen (Owington)
5914[10] 7418[9]

Caracciola (GER) *Nicky Henderson* 101
13 b g Lando(GER) —Capitolina (FR) (Empery (USA))
2345[9] 3195[4] 4506[8]

Caracortado (USA) *Michael Machowsky* a106
3 ch g Cat Dreams(USA) —Mons Venus (CAN) (Maria's Mon (USA))
2137a[7]

Caramelita *John Jenkins* a71 72
3 b f Deportivo—Apple Of My Eye (Fraam)
483[3] 683[2] 744[3] 900[3] (1075) 1347[10] 1640[2] 2679[4] 4833[3] 5562[3] 5890[5] 6656[7] 7391[5] 8034[2]

Caramella Brownie *Tim Easterby* 57
2 b f Le Vie Dei Colori—Rabarama (Xaar)
3106[8] 6569[5] 7123[8] 7279[9]

Caranbola *Mel Brittain* a65 77
4 br m Lucky Story(USA) —Ladywell Blaise (IRE) (Turtle Island (IRE))
935[6] 1365[7] 2504[7] (4199) 4558[6] 4712[9] (4982) (5513)

Cara's Request (AUS) *David Nicholls* a55 89
5 gr g Urgent Request(IRE) —Carahill (AUS) (Danehill (USA))
1361[11] 2451[7] 4515[6] (5357) 5634[4] 6108[3] (6394) (6917) 7146[2] (7283)

Carata (FR) *C Boutin* a39 62
2 b f Country Reel(USA) —Lyphard's Dream (IRE) (Lyphard (USA))
5226a[0]

Carazam (IRE) *T Stack* a88 90
3 b c Azamour(IRE) —Carallia (IRE) (Common Grounds)
3466a[5] 5772a[10]

Carbon Print (USA) *Paul Webber* 60
5 ch g Johannesburg(USA) —Caithness (USA) (Roberto (USA))
2604[3] 7633[8]

Carcinetto (IRE) *David Evans* a98 102
8 b m Danetime(IRE) —Dolphin Stamp (IRE) (Dolphin Street (FR))
108[4] 204[3] 278[6] 324[3] 537[4] 553[5] 635[4] 740[3] 790[5] 883[5] 921[6] 944[5] 1084[6] 1481[5] 1519[2] 1672[10] 1857[6] 2311[10] 2508[10] 2651[5] 3063[9] 3431[3] 3830[6] 3894[8] 4489[2] 4860[5] 5114[11]

Cardiff Boy (USA) *Brian Meehan* a70
3 b c Fusaichi Pegasus(USA) —April Starlight (USA) (Storm Bird (CAN))
782[4]

Cardinal *Robert Cowell* a86 79
5 ch h Pivotal—Fictitious (Machiavellian (USA))
674[3] 773[11] 836[4] 2790[3] 2965[2] 4237[3] 4715[4] (5162) 5379[5] 6515[4] (6812) 6880[4] 7399[4] 7539[5] (7683) 7826[4]

Carefree Smile (IRE) *D K Weld* a88 85
4 b m Invincible Spirit(IRE) —Frippet (IRE) (Ela-Mana-Mou)
6910a[8]

Caribbean Coral *Andrew Haynes* a73 70
11 ch g Brief Truce(USA) —Caribbean Star (Soviet Star (USA))
1805[2] 2166[7] 2294[6] 2809[6] 3052[4] 3293[5] 3717[5] 3727[7] 3993[2] 4298[5]

Carimo (IRE) *W Walton* a63 82
6 b h Fasliyev(USA) —Barnabas (ITY) (Slip Anchor)
273a[6]

Carioca (IRE) *Marco Botti* a78 107
3 br f Rakti—Cidaris (IRE) (Persian Bold)
(978) (1252a) 2098[2] 2801a[6] 3720a[8] 5114[5] 5883[4] 6351[12]

Cark *David C Griffiths* a50 36
12 b g Farfelu—Precious Girl (Precious Metal)
4047[16]

Carlcol Girl *Christine Dunnett* a4 46
3 b f Where Or When(IRE) —Capstick (JPN) (Machiavellian (USA))
4971[8] 5656[11]

Carlitos Spirit (IRE) *Ian McInnes* a81 84
6 ch g Redback—Negria (IRE) (Al Hareb (USA))
23[9] 285[10] 1030[7] 1426[9] 1530[9] 1754[11] 3124[8] 3610[3] 3948[3] (4082) (4198) 4579[11] 4939[4] 5545[4] 6116[5] ◆ 6267[4] 6462[6] 6984[10] 7063[9]

Carlix (FR) *J-L Gay* a48 57
8 gr g Linamix(FR) —Carlitta (USA) (Olympio (USA))
1056a[0]

Carlton House (USA) *Sir Michael Stoute* 95
2 b c Street Cry(IRE) —Talented (Bustino)
6474[2] ◆ (7099) ◆

Carlton Scroop (FR) *Tony Carroll* a73 72
7 ch g Priolo(USA) —Elms Schooldays (Emarati (USA))
612[2] (771) 1303[4] (1655) 1916[6] 2199[3] 2723[6] 3221[10] 3522[6] 4070[10] 4681[5] (5663) 5770[2] 6314[3] (6669) 7044[6] 7463[2] 7861[3]

Carmela Maria *Mike Sowersby* a68 64
5 b m Medicean—Carmela Owen (Owington)
4174[5] 5119[12]

Carmenero (GER) *Conor Dore* a74 74
7 b g Barathea(IRE) —Claire Fraser (USA) (Gone West (USA))
129[4] (194) 269[2] 373[11] 451[6] 579[7] 747[5] 1147[7] 1270[6] 1914[6] 2490[4] 2896[4] 3279[9]

Carnaby Street (IRE) *Richard Hannon* a98 105
3 b c Le Vie Dei Colori—Prodigal Daughter (Alhaarth (IRE))
1221[3] 1985a[7] 3103[23] 5275[8] 5854[7] 5950[4] ◆ (6564) 6806[4]

Carnac (IRE) *Alan McCabe* a60 72
4 gr g Dalakhani(IRE) —Traou Mad (IRE) (Barathea (IRE))
1176[9] 1655[7] 1925[4] 2349[9] 2941[15] 3221[8] 5770[5] 6033[4] 6373[4] 6855[3] 7039[9] 7181[14] 7716[6] 7958[3]

Carnival Dream *Hugh McWilliams* a58 57
5 b m Carnival Dancer—Reach The Wind (USA) (Relaunch (USA))
193[3] 269[9] 404[9] 1235[5] 1722[4] 2184[7] 2671[6] 3322[8] 3409[10] 4486[3] 4868[2] 5535[9] 5817[3] 6329[11] 7051[6] 7380[4] 7506[4] 7917[4]

Carnival Time (IRE) *Clive Cox* a47 51
3 ch g Captain Rio—Latest (IRE) (Bob Back (USA))
3587[4] 4289[7] 4992[11] 5467[6] 6021[8] 6579[6]

Carnivore *David Barron* a83 83
8 ch g Zafonic(USA) —Ermine (IRE) (Cadeaux Genereux)
150[3] 292[6] 779[5] 1306[4] 2241[10] 3659[8] 4450[8] 5287[6] 7006[8]

Carnivore (USA) *Joseph W Delozier III* a92
3 ch c Giant's Causeway(USA) —Biogio's Rose (USA) (Polish Numbers (USA))
1097a[5]

Carolina Cherry (IRE) *Amy Weaver* a24
3 b f Antonius Pius(USA) —Lady Abigail (IRE) (Royal Academy (USA))
550[7] 766[7] 962[7]

Carousel *Ralph Beckett* 41
2 b f Pivotal—Supereva (IRE) (Sadler's Wells (USA))
6804[7] 7231[16]

Carragold *Mel Brittain* a56 58
4 b g Diktat—Shadow Roll (IRE) (Mark Of Esteem (IRE))
139[8] 1575[7] 4707[4] 6076[3]

Carraiglawn (IRE) *J S Bolger* a68 112
3 b c Rock Of Gibraltar(IRE) —Affianced (IRE) (Erins Isle)
3491a[6]

Carrauntoohil (IRE) *Amy Weaver* a39 51
2 b f Marju(IRE) —Tashyra (IRE) (Tagula (IRE))
3222[8] 5829[13] 6844[9]

Carr Hall (IRE) *Tony Carroll* a62 72
7 b g Rossini(USA) —Pidgeon Bay (IRE) (Perugino (USA))
162[2] (969) 1225[8] 1520[3] (1756) 2081[7] 7286[8] 7491[8] 7778[10]

Carrick A Rede (IRE) *Clive Cox* 66
2 b c Footstepsinthesand—Intricate Design (Zafonic (USA))
6443[5]

Carrie's Magic *David Barron* a36 73
3 b f Kyllachy—Carrie Pooter (Tragic Role (USA))
699[6] 1275[3] (1966) 2628[3] 3151[2] 3751[6]

Carrignavar (USA) *Ralph Beckett* 88
2 br f Tale Of The Cat(USA) —Wendy Vaala (USA) (Dayjur (USA))
5441[3] ◆ (5914) 6751[3]

Carter *Ian Williams* a65 63
4 b g Reset(AUS) —Cameo Role (GER) (Acatenango (GER))
1539[2] 1980[11] 2597[4] 3032[3] 3560[4] 3894[5] 4156[8] 4752[9] 5272[4] 5770[4] 6905[5] 7199[11] 7996[3]

Cartesio (USA) *J-M Lefebvre* a58 60
6 b g War Chant(USA) —Roseboom (USA) (Affirmed (USA))
221a[5]

Carver County (IRE) *Mandy Rowland* a38 18
2 b g Desert Style(IRE) —Chaska (Reprimand)
3274[7] 3756[11] 4240[10] 6294[8] 6964[5] 7396[7] 7801[4]

Casa Battlo (FR) *Robert Collet* a84 91
3 b g Green Tune(USA) —Victoria Royale (FR) (Garde Royale)
1254a[7]

Casamento (IRE) *M Halford* 121
2 ch c Shamardal(USA) —Wedding Gift (FR) (Always Fair (USA))
5975a[2] (6403a) (7081)

Casela Park (IRE) *Eamon Tyrrell* a82 80
5 ch g Elnadim(USA) —Taormina (IRE) (Ela-Mana-Mou)
4704[6] 4796[4]

Cashel Bay (USA) *Luke Comer* a41 47
12 b g Nureyev(USA) —Madame Premier (USA) (Raja Baba (USA))
7213[4]

Cashelgar (IRE) *D K Weld* 116
4 b g Anabaa(USA) —Tropical Barth (IRE) (Peintre Celebre (USA))
5772a[6]

Cashpoint *Anthony Middleton* a89
5 b g Fantastic Light(USA) —Cashew (Sharrood (USA))
355[2] (669) (947) 1220[11]

Cash Refund (USA) *Steve Margolis* a116
4 b g Petionville(USA) —Swept Away (USA) (Mystery Storm (USA))
7361a[8]

Casino Night *Linda Perratt* a52 78
5 ch m Night Shift(USA) —Come Fly With Me (Bluebird (USA))
1467[10] 1717[10] 2084[6] 2766[5] 3074[5] 3707[8] 4752[4] 5215[10] 5244[4] (6243) 6462[5] (6495) 6710[3] 7053[10] 7228[5]

Casper's Touch (USA) *Kenneth McPeek* a59 95
2 bb c Touch Gold(USA) —Lizzy Cool (USA) (Saint Ballado (CAN))
3190[3]

Cassidy K *David Thompson* 55
3 ch f Zafeen(FR) —Alizar (IRE) (Rahy (USA))
1362[9] 1526[8]

Cassique Lady (IRE) *Lucy Wadham* a85 103
5 b m Langfuhr(CAN) —Palacoona (FR) (Last Tycoon)
2538[7] 3031[2] 3671[6] 4507[13]

Caster Sugar (USA) *Richard Hannon* a56 87
4 b m Cozzene(USA) —Only Royale (IRE) (Caerleon (USA))
1379[7] 1780[7] 2243[7] 3031[8] 3679[4]

Castle Bar Sling (USA) *T J O'Mara* a80 92
5 b g Diesis—Lady Of The Woods (USA) (Woodman (USA))
1408a[13] 3487a[8] 4463a[13] 5571a[20]

Castleburg *Gary Moore* a67 48
4 b m Johannesburg(USA) —Castellina (USA) (Danzig Connection (USA))
137[7] 238[2] 318[3] 615[7] 673[2] 808[3] (931) 1305[7] 2235[5] 2409[4]

Castlebury (IRE) *Ruth Carr* 69
5 b g Spartacus(IRE) —La Vie En Rouge (IRE) (College Chapel)
2421[11] 2694[2] 3552[6] 4015[7] 4484[5] 4863[2] 6076[8] 6298[9]

Castle Kirk (IRE) *Pat Phelan* 22
2 b c Oratorio(IRE) —Sunlit Silence (IRE) (Green Desert (USA))
3035[8] 3326[13]

Castlemorris King *Michael Chapman* 59
2 br c And Beyond(IRE) —Brookshield Baby (IRE) (Sadler's Wells (USA))
5049[10] 5943[5] 6305[6] 7004[8]

Castle Myth (USA) *Brian Ellison* a67 65
4 bb g Johannesburg(USA) —Castlemania (CAN) (Bold Ruckus (USA))
255[P] 328[4] (379) (491) 715[2] 893[7] 1114[2] 1293[6] 1771[5] 1995[3] (5821) 6267[5] 6463[4] 7122[6] 7401[2] 7543[7] (7729) 7865[3] 7932[2]

Castles In The Air *Richard Fahey* a95 109
5 b g Oasis Dream—Dance Parade (USA) (Gone West (USA))
(1423) 1900[20] 3146[12] 3674[3] (4358) 4576[11] 5275[10] 6177[17] 6349[6]

Cast Of Stars (IRE) *Ralph Beckett* a79 67
3 b g Nayef(USA) —Scarpe Rosse (IRE) (Sadler's Wells (USA))
3917[7] 4227[2] ◆ 4965[6] 6427[4] 7043[6] 7419[2] (7690)

Casual Garcia *Mark Gillard* a56 72
5 gr g Hernando(FR) —Frosty Welcome (USA) (With Approval (CAN))
3195[16] 4042[5] 4223[7]

Casual Glimpse *Richard Hannon* 98
2 b c Compton Place—Glimpse (Night Shift (USA))
(1695) 2743[5] (3826) 5219[8] 6507[7]

Catalan Bay (AUS) *Jeremy Gask* a82 81
6 b m Rock Of Gibraltar(IRE) —Kim Angel (AUS) (Serheed (USA))
1361[12] 1797[7] 2233[6]

Catalinas Diamond (IRE) *Brendan Duke* 86
2 b f One Cool Cat(USA) —Diamondiferous (USA) (Danzig (USA))
2358[2] 2616[3] 3070[5] ◆ 3906[4] 4356[11]

Catalpa Sail (IRE) *D K Weld* a78 86
2 b g Modigliani(USA) —Briland (IRE) (Namid)
6230a[12] 7135a[8]

Catalyze *Andrew Balding* a57 90
2 b c Tumblebrutus(USA) —Clarita Dear (CHI) (Hussonet (USA))
3785[4] (5006) 5849[3] 6733[4]

Catawollow *Richard Guest* a39 52
3 b f Beat Hollow—Catalonia (IRE) (Catrail (USA))
993[8] 1495[9] 2221[8] (2503) 3238[4] 5411[8] 5479[3] 5819[9]

Catbells (IRE) *Alan Bailey* a70 74
3 ch f Rakti—Moonbi Ridge (IRE) (Definite Article)
1050[4] 1275[6] 1861[7] 3055[8] 4061[6] 4329[4] 4453[3] 6495[11] 6747[6] 6860[2] (7038) 7316[4] 7678[6] 7968[2]

Catch A Cloud *James Moffatt* 65
4 b g Catcher In The Rye(IRE) —Overcast (IRE) (Caerleon (USA))
1459[12]

Catchafallingstar *A P O'Brien* 70
3 b f Montjeu(IRE) —Half Glance (Danehill (USA))
4631a[10]

Catchanova (IRE) *Eve Johnson Houghton* a62 71
3 b g Catcher In The Rye(IRE) —Head For The Stars (IRE) (Head For Heights)
1582[5] 2168[4] 2620[5] 3478[2] 3957[2] 4756[3] 4994[4] (5689) 5877[2] 6413[5] 6991[5]

Cat Chat (FR) *P Azzopardi* 100
10 ch g Starborough—Udina (Unfuwain (USA))
332a[0]

Catcher Of Dreams (IRE) *George Foster* a62 52
4 b g Catcher In The Rye(IRE) —No Islands (Lomond (USA))
1717[13] 2208[6] 2500[12] 3147[2] 3758[12] 4707[7] 6029[7] 7230[10]

Catching Zeds *Ian Williams* a65
3 b f Lucky Story(USA) —Perfect Poppy (Shareef Dancer (USA))
5028[5] 5658[3] 7129[3] 7992[9]

Catch Light *Amanda Perrett* 34
2 b f Shirocco(GER) —Bright Spells (USA) (Alleged (USA))
5692[17]

Catchmeifyoucan (FR) *Andy Turnell* a61 60
4 b g Marju(IRE) —Catch Us (FR) (Selkirk (USA))
1172[14] 1737[11] 2360[9] 2653[10]

Categorical *Keith Reveley* a69 55
7 b g Diktat—Zibet (Kris)
6895[8] 7145[6]

Cat Fire (IRE) *Kevin Prendergast* 82
2 b f One Cool Cat(USA) —Filimeala (IRE) (Pennekamp (USA))
2828a[4]

Catfish (IRE) *Gay Kelleway* 79
2 bb f One Cool Cat(USA) —Castellane (FR) (Danehill (USA))
(3871) 4356[10]

Cathcart Castle *Mick Channon* a60 68
2 b g Imperial Dancer—Stephanie's Mind (Mind Games)
2819[4] 3399[4] 3657[4] 4955[6] 5389[4] 5675[4] 6220[3] 6426[5] 7035[3] 7118[11] 8011[9]

Cathedral Spires *Howard Johnson* 77
2 b g Intikhab(USA) —Munakashah (IRE) (Machiavellian (USA))
2980[3] 3550[2] (4336) 5301[5] 6184[3]

Catherineofaragon (IRE) *A P O'Brien* a80 79
2 b f Holy Roman Emperor(IRE) —Monevassia (USA) (Mr Prospector (USA))
2828a[6]

Catherines Call (IRE) *Desmond Donovan* a77 75
3 b f Captain Rio—It's Academic (Royal Academy (USA))
(1259) (1505) (1640) 2120[14] 2475[10] 4968[7] 5205[6] 5769[2] 6207[3] 6577[3]

Catholic Hill (USA) *Mark Gillard* a59 48
5 rg g Pleasant Tap(USA) —Celestial Bliss (USA) (Relaunch (USA))
282[13] 390[4] 969[8] 1193[13] 1225[11] 2676[4] 3473[5] 4992[7]

Cat Hunter *Ronald Harris* a74 75
3 b f One Cool Cat(USA) —Eoz (IRE) (Sadler's Wells (USA))
2042[13] 2871[6] 3001[3] 3464[3] 3739[7] 5391[2] 5677[2] 6438[3] 7837[6]

Cat Island *Mark H Tompkins* 58
2 b f Bahamian Bounty—Dolls House (Dancing Spree (USA))
4759[6] 6058[5] 6722[5]

Cativo Cavallino *John E Long* a71 68
7 ch g Bertolini(USA) —Sea Isle (Selkirk (USA))
1596[4] 2009[4] 2331[6] (3262) 4255[3] 4929[5] 5561[4] 6292[4] (6851)

Cat Junior (USA) *Brian Meehan* a116 116
5 bb h Storm Cat(USA) —Luna Wells (IRE) (Sadler's Wells (USA))
440a[5] 630a[5] (798a) 1022a[9] 1531[4] 3046[8] 4457[2] 5081[2] 5946[6] 6923[2]

Cat Melody (FR) *B Dutruel* a64 79
2 ch f Hurricane Cat(USA) —Sabmalody (FR) (Riche Mare (FR))
6589a[3]

Cat O' Nine Tails *Mark Johnston* 82
3 b f Motivator—Purring (USA) (Mountain Cat (USA))
1809[4] 2244[2] 2697[4] 3532[4] 4120[10] (4557) (5333) 5747[9] (6028) 6224[11]

Cat Six (USA) *Tom Gretton* a25 21
6 b m Tale Of The Cat(USA) —Hurricane Warning (USA) (Thunder Gulch (USA))
7213[7]

Caucus *Hughie Morrison* 106
3 b c Cape Cross(IRE) —Maid To Perfection (Sadler's Wells (USA))
(2281) 3105[3] ◆ 3822[3] 5517[3] 6590a[8]

Caudillo (GER) *Dr A Bolte* 106
7 b h Acatenango(GER) —Corsita (Top Ville)
2574a[4] 4012a[4] 6011a[7] 7103a[4]

Cause For Applause (IRE) *Ray Craggs* a56 42
4 b m Royal Applause—Polyandry (IRE) (Pennekamp (USA))
7[12]

Cavaliere (FR) *M Cesandri* 98
4 b m Traditionally(USA) —Lavandou (Sadler's Wells (USA))
1792a[8] 6519a[7]

Cavalry Guard (USA) *Tim McCarthy* a58 57
6 ch g Officer(USA) —Leeward City (USA) (Carson City (USA))
124[6] 234[4] 444[8] 498[7] 614[6] 976[11] 7192[5] 8023[10]

Cavalryman *Saeed Bin Suroor* a114 125
4 b h Halling(USA) —Silversword (FR) (Highest Honor (FR))
800a[7] 1026a[5] 2709[5] 3068[12] 5186[4] ◆ 5806a[3] 6612a[8] 6977a[3]

Cavendish Road (IRE) *Nicky Vaughan* a74 76
4 b g Bachelor Duke(USA) —Gronchi Rosa (IRE) (Nashwan (USA))
543[7] 2240[6] 3022[9] 4366[2] 4839[8] (5710) 6267[9] 6543[10] 6958[7] 7063[7]

Cavitie *Andrew Reid* a71 55
4 b g Teofilio(IRE) —Kirriemuir (Lochnager)
896[4] ◆ (1072) 1477[2] 2186[2] 3763[2] 4431[4] 5025[4] (5267) 5920[2] ◆ 6898[2] 7390[6] 7683[8]

Cawdor (IRE) *Linda Stubbs* a75 83
4 b g Kyllachy—Dim Ots (Alhijaz)
26[6] (1722) 1968[4] 2668[2] 4084[6] 6371[7] 6491[2] 7241[9] 7613[11]

Cawthorne *Michael Easterby* a4
4 b g Mark Of Esteem(IRE) —Oh Whataknight (Primo Dominie)
7244[8]

Cayman Fox *Linda Perratt* a70 77
5 ch m Cayman Kai(IRE) —Kalarram (Muhtarram (USA))
2669[5] 3064[9] 3533[5] 4373[15] 5362[2] ◆ (5477) ◆ (5599) 6031[4] 6245[7] 6706[5] 7169[9]

Caymans (AUS) *Saeed Bin Suroor* 55
5 b g Secret Savings(USA) —Easy Out (AUS) (Anabaa (USA))
7304[6]

Cayo *Mark Johnston* 2
3 ch g Danroad(AUS) —Caysue (Cayman Kai (IRE))
1927[14] 2083[6]

Ceannline (IRE) *J S Bolger* a80 86
4 b m Lil's Boy(USA) —Scarpetta (USA) (Seattle Dancer (USA))
3492a[11]

Cecile De Volanges *Tor Sturgis* a61
2 ch f Kheleyf(USA) —Fyvie (Grand Lodge (USA))
7780[4] 8000[8]

Cecina Marina *Kate Walton* a20 52
7 b m Sugarfoot—Chasetown Cailin (Suave Dancer (USA))
1576[11] 1801[9]

Ceffyl Gwell *Richard Hannon* 73
2 b c Compton Place—Corinium (IRE) (Turtle Island (IRE))
4871[9] 6196[7] 6626[2] 6811[2] 7345[5]

Ceilidh House *Ralph Beckett* 103
3 ch f Selkirk(USA) —Villa Carlotta (Rainbow Quest (USA))
1909[3] ◆ 2711[13] 5249[9] 5553[8] (7349)

Celani *Andy Turnell* a74 59
2 b f Jelani(IRE) —Celandine (Warning)
6451[2] 6804[3] 7427[5]

Celebrian *Walter Swinburn* a64 41
3 b f Fasliyev(USA) —Triplemoon (USA) (Trempolino (USA))
2189[3] 2619[7]

Celebrissime (IRE) *F Head* 110
5 ch g Peintre Celebre(USA) —Ring Beaune (USA) (Bering)
2374a[7] 4166a[4]

Celebrity *Richard Hannon* 84
2 b f Pivotal—Dance Solo (Sadler's Wells (USA))
3296[8] (4095)

Celendine *John M Oxx* a86 86
3 b f Oratorio(IRE) —Affaire D'Amour (Hernando (FR))
(1336) 6910a[4] 7514a[5]

Celenza (FR) *A De Royer-Dupre* 86
2 b f Dansili—Celebre Vadala (FR) (Peintre Celebre (USA))
5252a[2] 7544a[5]

Celestial Flyer (IRE) *G M Lyons* 45
2 b c Balmont(USA) —Pearly Gates (IRE) (Night Shift (USA))
4175a[13]

Celestial Girl *Hughie Morrison* a76 73
3 b f Dubai Destination(USA) —Brightest Star (Unfuwain (USA))
238[4] 381[4] 1437[2] 1796[5] (3714) (3983) 5172[5] 5812[2] 6290[2] (6527) 6846[4]

Celestial Tryst *George Moore* 74
3 b f Tobougg(IRE) —Celestial Welcome (Most Welcome)
1334[9] 2656[11] 3062[12] 6243[10] 6897[3] 7082[10]

Celestyna *Henry Cecil* a64
2 b f Observatory(USA) —Mysterix (IRE) (Linamix (FR))
6309[3]

Celimene (IRE) *C Lerner* 114
4 b m Dr Fong(USA) —Lunassa (FR) (Groom Dancer (USA))
1255a[3] 1747a[4] 2403a[2] 3494a[4] 5348a[6]

Celtic Anu *Patrick Morris* 27
2 b g Marju(IRE) —Shohrah (IRE) (Giant's Causeway (USA))
1704[5] 2239[9] 2667[6]

Celtic Celeb (IRE) *F Doumen* 113
3 ch c Peintre Celebre(USA) —Gaelic Bird (FR) (Gay Mecene (USA))
1567a[4] 2160a[2] 2802a[17] (6590a) 7110a[2]

Celtic Change (IRE) *Michael Dods* a47 91
6 br g Celtic Swing—Changi (IRE) (Lear Fan (USA))
1513[5] (1990) 2204[2] 2835[3] 4450[2] 6105[8] 6567[8] 6904[10]

Celtic Commitment *Simon Dow* a70 68
4 gr g Mull Of Kintyre(USA) —Grey Again (Unfuwain (USA))
971[2] 1302[5]

Celtic Dane (IRE) *Kevin Prendergast* a80 93
6 b g Danetime(IRE) —Quelle Celtique (FR) (Tel Quel (FR))
3492a[9] 6971a[6]

Celtic Dragon *David Evans* a83 69
5 b g Fantastic Light(USA) —Zanzibar (IRE) (In The Wings)
2961[13] 3522[3] 3865[8] 4202[2] 4657[11] 5115[8]

Celticello (IRE) *Michael Quinlan* a74 72
8 bb g Celtic Swing—Viola Royale (IRE) (Royal Academy (USA))
5591[6] 5828[3]

Celtic Life (IRE) *Amy Weaver* a49 48
4 gr g Celtic Swing—Night Life (IRE) (Night Shift (USA))
7787[7] 7918[4]

Celtic Lynn (IRE) *Michael Dods* 83
5 br m Celtic Swing—Sheryl Lynn (Miller's Mate)
1808[2] 2524[6] 3320[5] 4287[7] 5598[6] 6460[4] 7056[9]

Celtic Ransom *J W Hills* a64 62
3 b g Red Ransom(USA) —Welsh Valley (USA) (Irish River (FR))
1209[2] 1796[2] 2189[2] 2619[4] 3957[4]

Celtic Sixpence (IRE) *Michael Quinlan* a73 74
2 b f Celtic Swing—Penny Ha'Penny (Bishop Of Cashel)
4702[2] 5558[2] 6161[2] (6778)

Celtic Soprano (IRE) *P D Deegan* 93
5 b m Celtic Swing—Midnight Glimmer (IRE) (Dr Devious (IRE))
1560a[6] 4081a[7] 6786a[3]

Celtic Sovereign (IRE) *Michael Quinlan* a84
4 b g Celtic Swing—Penny Ha'Penny (Bishop Of Cashel)
259[2] ◆ 580[P]

Celtic Step *Alan Kirtley* a67 81
6 br g Selkirk(USA) —Inchiri (Sadler's Wells (USA))
1926[9] (2788) 4119[10] 5486[8] 5819[5] 6462[7]

Celtic Sultan (IRE) *Tom Tate* a94 97
6 b g Celtic Swing—Farjah (IRE) (Charnwood Forest (IRE))
1219[6] 1688[8] 2428[2] 2736[9] (3150) 3619[9] 4371[10] 5702[3] 6178[3]

Celtic Warrior (IRE) *John Harris* 34
7 b g Celtic Swing—Notable Dear (ITY) (Last Tycoon)
1919[12] 2006[10]

Celtic Wolf (FR) *E Charpy* a90 100
5 b g Loup Solitaire(USA) —Rose Of Tralee (FR) (Kendor (FR))
513a[8] 821a[11]

Cemgraft *Paddy Butler* a52 56
9 b m In The Wings—Soviet Maid (IRE) (Soviet Star (USA))
1983[11]

Census (IRE) *Richard Hannon* 80
2 b c Cacique(IRE) —Slieve (Selkirk (USA))
5985[7] 6473[2] (6953)

Centennial (IRE) *Jonjo O'Neill* 101
5 gr h Dalakhani(IRE) —Lurina (IRE) (Lure (USA))
2116[6] 4320[9] 5220[18] 6630[3] 7084[14]

Centigrade (IRE) *William Haggas* 89
3 gr g Verglas(IRE) —American Queen (FR) (Fairy King (USA))
1781[5]

Centime *Brian Meehan* 73
3 b f Royal Applause—Argent Du Bois (USA) (Silver Hawk (USA))
2401[2] (2901) 3268[4] 4098[4] 4626[5]

Central Bank (IRE) *Mark Johnston*
3 ch g Pivotal—Siringas (IRE) (Barathea (IRE))
1335[12]

Central City (USA) *Ronny Werner* a72 116
4 b h City Place(USA) —Apache Dancer (USA) (Alphabet Soup (USA))
7362a[2]

Centre Stage *George Margarson* 42
2 b g Fasliyev(USA) —Purple Rain (IRE) (Celtic Swing)
7201[8]

Centurio *Roger Charlton* 79
3 b c Pivotal—Grain Of Gold (Mr Prospector (USA))
(3173)

Century Dancer *Tor Sturgis* a51 30
2 b f Trade Fair—Be Bop Aloha (Most Welcome)
4029[9] 5835[9] 6209[6] 7497[3] 7631[8] 7813[8] 8031[11]

Ceodora (GER) *J-P Perruchot* a74 77
5 b m Efisio—Caerosa (Caerleon (USA))
(207a) 303a[5] 560a[0]

Ceoil An Aith (IRE) *Mark Johnston* 81
4 b m Accordion—Lady In Pace (Burslem)
2767[3] 3116[4] ◆ 3776[2] 4655[2] (5022) 5444[3] 5788[9]

Cereal Killer (IRE) *Richard Hannon* a42 74
3 br c Xaar—Snap Crackle Pop (IRE) (Statoblest)
1589[7] 2089[10] (2279) 2888[10] 3739[4] 4426[9] 6255[5]

Cerejeira (IRE) *Eric Alston* a17 46
2 b f Exceed And Excel(AUS) —Camassina (IRE) (Taufan (USA))
2286[4] 2936[7] 3070[18] 6323[4] 6916[10] 7528[10]

Ceremonial Jade (UAE) *Marco Botti* a109 62
7 b g Jade Robbery(USA) —Talah (Danehill (USA))
108[8] 412a[8] 626a[12] 817a[12] 1085[7] 1206[7] 5370[6] 7430[8] 7574[8]

Cerise Cherry (SAF) *D Cruz* 108
5 ch h Goldkeeper(USA) —Cherry Girl (ZIM) (Pochard (ARG))
7852a[12]

Cerito *Jim Boyle* a88 69
4 ch g Bahamian Bounty—Pascali (Compton Place)
992[5] 1691[6] 2657[13] 2872[12] 6523[5] 6987[9] 7122[7] 7442[8]

Ceroli (IRE) *Cristiana Signorelli*
2 b c Alamshar(IRE) —Salon Des Refuses (IRE) (Nordance (USA))
7849a[4]

Certral *George Baker* a60 50
2 b f Iffraaj—Craigmill (Slip Anchor)
6954[9] 7448[9] ◆ 7602[5]

Cerveza *C Laffon-Parias* 83
2 ch f Medicean—Kalindi (Efisio)
7383a[9]

Cesare *James Fanshawe* a99 121
9 b g Machiavellian(USA) —Tromond (Lomond (USA))
(4050) 5274[8]

C'Est La Guerre (NZ) *Robert Hickmott* 118
6 b g Shinko King(IRE) —La Magnifique (NZ) (Kampala)
6946a[6]

Ceto *Phil McEntee* a60
3 b f Tobougg(IRE) —Natural Grace (Zamindar (USA))
180[7] 313[2] 392[6] 473[2]

Chabal (IRE) *Saeed Bin Suroor* 116
3 b c Galileo(IRE) —Vagary (IRE) (Zafonic (USA))
1498[DSQ] 2056[4] 4805[2]

Chachamaidee (IRE) *Henry Cecil* 106
3 b f Footstepsinthesand—Canterbury Lace (USA) (Danehill (USA))
(2098) 3143[12] 4319[2] 5305[5]

Chadford *Tim Walford* 57
2 b g Trade Fair—Quiz Time (Efisio)
1749[5] 2376[10] 2832[12] 4935[8] 5818[3] 6300[2] 7004[P]

Chadwell Spring (IRE) *Julia Feilden* a68 74
4 b m Statue Of Liberty(USA) —Cresalin (Coquelin (USA))
1034[6] 1440[7] 1875[10] 2714[11] 3683[9] 4591[5]

Chagal (IRE) *Kevin Ryan* 49
2 b c Whipper(USA) —Quivala (USA) (Thunder Gulch (USA))
4650[6] 5040[7] 5814[8] 7177[13]

Chain Lightning *Richard Hannon* 83
2 ch c Hurricane Run(IRE) —Sachet (USA) (Royal Academy (USA))
3631[11] 4054[2] 6190[2] (6473)

Chain Of Events *Neil King* a76 79
3 ch g Nayef(USA) —Ermine (IRE) (Cadeaux Genereux)
1010[4] 1310[15] (3176) 4106[4] 4594[2] ◆ 5091[5] 6288[5] 7044[10] 7293[8]

Chain Of Office *William Haggas* a39 71
3 ch f Mark Of Esteem(IRE) —Lady Mayor (Kris)
3413[9] 3759[5]

Chalice Welcome *Neil King* a88 74
7 b g Most Welcome—Blue Peru (IRE) (Perugino (USA))
(12) 220[2] 676[8] (1169) (1348) 1960[5] 2739[8] 6449[4] 6797[13] 7828[6] 8003[10]

Chamberlain Bridge (USA) *W Bret Calhoun* 121
6 b g War Chant(USA) —Shes Got Class (USA) (Trempolino (USA))
(7362a)

Chambers (IRE) *Eric Alston* a56 62
4 b g Green Desert(USA) —Court Lane (USA) (Machiavellian (USA))
1723[10] 2274[2] 3396[11] (3539) 3855[12] 4670[7] 5500[2] 5732[5] 6917[9]

Champagne All Day *Simon Griffiths* a9 29
4 ch g Timeless Times(USA) —Miss Ceylon (Brief Truce (USA))
4340[9] 4853[6] 7328[12] 7869[7]

Champagne D'Oro (USA) *Eric J Guillot* a115
3 b f Medaglia D'Oro(USA) —Champagne Glow (USA) (Saratoga Six (USA))
7341a[4]

Champagne Fizz (IRE) *Jo Crowley* a60 61
4 gr m King Charlemagne(USA) —Silver Moon (Environment Friend)
282[11] 771[4] 1478[6] 2870[2] 5180[5] 6454[2]

Champagne Floozie *Jimmy Fox* a24
7 ch m Fleetwood(IRE) —On Request (IRE) (Be My Guest (USA))
1451[8]

Champagnelifestyle *B W Hills* 96
3 b f Montjeu(IRE) —White Rose (GER) (Platini (GER))
1820[3] 2711[9] 3671[9]

Champagne Princess *Phil McEntee*
2 b f Avonbridge—Flying Visitor (Magic Ring (IRE))
5717[10] 6058[9] 6308[11]

Champagne Style (USA) *Richard Guest* a80 100
3 ch g Lion Heart(USA) —Statute (USA) (Verzy (CAN))
3104[15] 4805[6] 7522[13]

Champain Sands (IRE) *Eric Alston* a61 64
11 b g Green Desert(USA) —Grecian Bride (IRE) (Groom Dancer (USA))
1717[5] 2382[10] 2864[6] 3391[11] 3538[3] 4119[11] 4602[7] 5499[2] 5756[5]

Champion Boy (IRE) *J C Hayden* a72 70
4 b g Val Royal(FR) —Strina (IRE) (Indian Ridge)
7514a[3]

Champ Pegasus (USA) *Richard E Mandella* 119
4 b h Fusaichi Pegasus(USA) —Salt Champ (ARG) (Salt Lake (USA))
7366a[2]

Chandrayaan *John E Long* a65 62
3 ch g Bertolini(USA) —Muffled (USA) (Mizaaya)
766[5] 933[6] 1058[12] 1594[5] 2049[3] 2633[8] 3325[8] 4300[7] 4791[9] 5559[7]

Changing The Guard *Richard Fahey* a87 91
4 b g King's Best(USA) —Our Queen Of Kings (Arazi (USA))
2027[6] 2435[2] 2608[6] 3239[3] 3627[5] 4100[4] 4455[2] 5307[12] 6193[9] 7287[4]

Chaninbar (FR) *Milton Harris* a39
7 b g Milford Track(IRE) —Logicia (FR) (Homme De Loi (IRE))
162[8]

Channel Crossing *Richard Ford* a42 54
8 b g Deploy—Wave Dancer (Dance In Time (CAN))
(2604) 2811[7]

Channel Squadron (IRE) *Henry Cecil* 86
3 b c Sadler's Wells(USA) —Caladira (IRE) (Darshaan)
(2974) ◆

Chanrossa (IRE) *Ed Dunlop* a69 62
4 b m Galileo(IRE) —Palacoona (FR) (Last Tycoon)
182[3] (390)

Chantilly Dancer (IRE) *Michael Quinn* a47 51
4 b m Danehill Dancer(IRE) —Antiguan Jane (Shirley Heights)
2299[4] 3264[8] 4236[9] 5039[7] 7037[9]

Chantilly Jewel (USA) *Robert Cowell* a56 60
5 b m Century City(IRE) —Betty's Star (USA) (Pentelicus (USA))
7720[4] 7859[2]

Chantilly Pearl (USA) *James Given* a68 69
4 bb m Smart Strike(CAN) —Cataballerina (USA) (Tabasco Cat (USA))
1883[5] 2516[3] 3950[5] 4546[4] 4913[7] 5636[2] 6298[4] 6890[2] 7054[5]

Chantilly Tiffany *John Gosden* a98 104
6 ch m Pivotal—Gaily Royal (IRE) (Royal Academy (USA))
1084[3] 4957[8]

Chaotic (IRE) *T Hogan* 57
4 b g Montjeu(IRE) —Inchoate (Machiavellian (USA))
6242[10]

Chaperno (USA) *Saeed Bin Suroor* a95 93
3 br c More Than Ready(USA) —Timeless Forest (USA) (Forestry (USA))
510a[12]
Chapter And Verse (IRE) *Mike Murphy* a106 94
4 gr g One Cool Cat(USA) —Beautiful Hill (IRE) (Danehill (USA))
1088[2] 1533[6] 2472[8] 3117[2] 5087[6] (5750) 6204[2] ◆ 7430[3] 7593[4] 8009[6]
Chapter Nine (IRE) *J G Coogan* a79 77
4 b g Expelled(USA) —Abbey Ever After (Glenstal (USA))
6730a[10]
Chaqueta *Chris Wall* a61 56
3 b f High Chaparral(IRE) —New Design (IRE) (Bluebird (USA))
3220[7] 4114[8] 5395[2] 6039[5] 7561[4] 7814[6]
Chardonnay *Alan Swinbank* a73 63
3 br f Piccolo—Icy (Mind Games)
2502[7] 2884[11] 5353[6]
Chardonnay Star (IRE) *Colin Teague* a22 38
3 b f Bertolini(USA) —Coup De Coeur (IRE) (Kahyasi)
2258[8] 2792[9] 4407[8] 5361[8] 6077[10]
Charging Indian (IRE) *Paul Midgley* a83 66
4 b g Chevalier(IRE) —Kathy Tolfa (IRE) (Sri Pekan (USA))
42[3] (330) (400) (509)
Charity Fair *Alan Berry* 48
3 ch f Bahamian Bounty—Be Most Welcome (Most Welcome)
1971[13] 2296[9] 3948[9] 4374[4] 4822[5] 6026[11] 7229[10]
Charles Bear *Bruce Hellier* a53
3 br f Needwood Blade—Zamyatina (IRE) (Danehill Dancer (IRE))
6966[14] 7461[9] 7684[8] 7810[6] 7953[10]
Charles Camoin (IRE) *Sylvester Kirk* 77
2 b c Peintre Celebre(USA) —Birthday (IRE) (Singspiel (IRE))
5033[5] 5985[4] (7179)
Charles Darwin (IRE) *Michael Blanshard* a70 70
7 ch g Tagula(IRE) —Seymour (IRE) (Eagle Eyed (USA))
961[2] 1300[8] (1595) 2896[7] 3373[3] 3584[13] 4662[6] 4875[6] 5076[6] 5764[6] 6310[10] 7442[9] 7518[5] 7639[7]
Charles Fosterkane *John Best* a77 52
2 bl c Three Wonders(USA) —Retainage (USA) (Polish Numbers (USA))
5724[2] 6159[5] 6844[5] (7379) ◆
Charles Parnell (IRE) *Simon Griffiths* a78 71
7 b g Elnadim(USA) —Titania (Fairy King (USA))
(20) 380[2] 602[6] 2589[5] 3761[7] 4244[7] 5920[5] 6370[5] 6515[2] (7051) 7241[8] 7399[9] 7539[10] 7870[10]
Charleston Lady *Ralph Beckett* a75
2 b f Hurricane Run(IRE) —Dance Lively (USA) (Kingmambo (USA))
6451[4] ◆ (7113)
Charlie Be (IRE) *Nerys Dutfield* a24 44
5 ch g King Charlemagne(USA) —Miriana (IRE) (Bluebird (USA))
1592[8]
Charlie Cool *Ruth Carr* a82 101
7 ch h Rainbow Quest(USA) —Tigwa (Cadeaux Genereux)
1011[4] 1669[4] 1889[8] (2133) (2423) 2835[2] (3121) 3692[9] 3920[3] 4537[17] 4830[9] 5188[11] 5786[4] 6296[3] 6567[2] 6749[5]
Charlie Delta *Ronald Harris* a67 57
7 b g Pennekamp(USA) —Papita (IRE) (Law Society (USA))
251[5] 481[3] 532[7] 614[9] 4936[13] 5267[9] (6078) 6329[3] 6455[5] 6741[7] 7195[6] 7332[9]
Charlie Green (IRE) *Paul Green* a33 19
5 b g Traditionally(USA) —Saninka (IRE) (Doyoun)
2285[11]
Charlie Smirke (USA) *Gary Moore* a83 73
4 b g Gulch(USA) —Two Altazano (USA) (Manzotti (USA))
202[2] 262[2] 385[2] (587) ◆ 943[4] (1047) 1645[4] 2080[5] 2714[8] 6091[13] 6701[5] 7115[10] 7597[8] 7724[5]
Charlie Tipple *Tim Easterby* 90
6 b g Diktat—Swing Of The Tide (Sri Pekan (USA))
1117[8] 1513[7] 3318[15] 5098[9]
Charlietoo *Edward Bevan* a53 54
4 b g King Charlemagne(USA) —Ticcatoo (IRE) (Dolphin Street (FR))
2590[14] 3132[5] 3556[8] 4071[5] 4857[3] 5579[6] 5927[10]
Charlotte Point (USA) *J E Pease* a88 90
4 b m Distorted Humor(USA) —Skygusty (USA) (Skywalker (USA))
1084[7] 1265[12] 1899[14] 7776a[10]
Charlottesometimes (USA) *David Simcock* a45 48
3 bb f Dehere(USA) —Alexander Charlote (IRE) (Titus Livius (FR))
43[6] 213[6] 305[6]
Charmaxjoanne *Ben Haslam* a46 48
3 ch f Lucky Story(USA) —Dance Of The Swans (IRE) (Try My Best (USA))
993[4] 1469[10]
Charminamix (IRE) *W McCreery* a88 89
7 gr g Linamix(FR) —Cheeky Charm (USA) (Nureyev (USA))
3487a[14]
Charming Man *Mahmood Al Zarooni* a72 75
3 b g Pivotal—Mythical Girl (USA) (Gone West (USA))
2290[6] 3116[6] 3754[3] 6427[7]
Charming Woman (IRE) *Vittorio Caruso* 103
3 b f Invincible Spirit(IRE) —Sospel (Kendor (FR))
1419a[8] (1944a) 5802a[8] 6976a[2] 7459a[6]
Charpoy Cobra *James Toller* a61 62
3 b f Mark Of Esteem(IRE) —Duena (Grand Lodge (USA))
1537[6] 2189[12] 2906[3] 3606[5] 4335[9] 4969[8] 6054[6] 6499[6] 7117[9]
Charybde En Scylla (FR) *Robert Collet* a93 81
3 ch c Muhtathir—Desir De Mai (FR) (Cardoun (FR))
7776a[4]

Chasing Halos (USA) *A Fabre* 105
3 b c Elusive Quality(USA) —Ballado's Halo (USA) (Saint Ballado (CAN))
3016a[6]
Chasing Pirates *Rae Guest* 11
2 ch f Bahamian Bounty—Amorette (King's Best (USA))
4716[12]
Chasse Coeur *Andrew Balding* a59 67
3 ch f Dr Fong(USA) —Royal Patron (Royal Academy (USA))
2842[8] 3738[4] 4840[3] 5380[4] 5811[3] 6517[6] 6959[13]
Chatanoogachoochoo *Martin Hill* a65 69
5 ch m Piccolo—Taza (Persian Bold)
101[6]
Chat De La Burg (USA) *John Best* a77 81
3 ch g Johannesburg(USA) —Catsuit (USA) (Sir Cat (USA))
3401[8] 3779[11] 4531[4] 4836[2] (5677) 6197[8] 7114[8] 7438[2] 7554[6] 7844[4]
Chat De Soie (IRE) *J S Moore* a43 63
3 b f Barathea(IRE) —Margay (IRE) (Marju (IRE))
1433[8] 2935[10] 4988[9] 5414[13] 6054[9] 7191[10]
Chateau Galliard (IRE) *Terry Clement* a23
4 bb g Xaar—Chalosse (Doyoun)
4697[13] 5493[11] 6696[11]
Chateauneuf (IRE) *Mark Brisbourne* a54 56
4 b m Marju(IRE) —Night Eyes (IRE) (Night Shift (USA))
3223[4] 3669[10] 4328[11] 4854[10] 5202[2] 5564[12] 6120[8]
Chateau Zara *Clive Cox* a53 62
3 b f Zaha(CAN) —Glensara (Petoski)
2387 592[5] 762[6] 1178[2] 1392[3] 1977[4] 2398[7] 2844[9] 5877[4] 6863[6] 7037[3] 7305[6] 7487[8] 7761[12]
Chater Way *D E Ferraris* 113
4 b g Oasis Dream—Singed (Zamindar (USA))
7853a[9]
Chaussini *James Toller* 81
3 b f Dubawi(IRE) —Miss Chaussini (IRE) (Rossini (USA))
2565[4] 3375[8] 4145[9]
Cheam Forever (USA) *Roger Charlton* a77 80
4 b g Exchange Rate(USA) —Many Charms (USA) (St Jovite (USA))
1265[9] 1625[7] 2024[8] 2823[9] 3558[4] 4119[2] ◆ 4690[7]
Cheap Street *Jonathan Portman* a59 66
6 ch g Compton Place—Anneliina (Cadeaux Genereux)
1884[10]
Checklist (USA) *Todd Pletcher* a93
4 b h Gone West(USA) —Yearly Report (USA) (General Meeting (USA))
5779a[9]
Check The Anchor (IRE) *Nigel Tinkler* 43
3 ch g Observatory(USA) —Fleet River (USA) (Riverman (USA))
5550[10]
Cheddar George *Peter Chapple-Hyam* a68 63
4 ch g Pivotal—Grandalea (Grand Lodge (USA))
2334[8] 2900[3] 3586[10] 4547[6] 4968[5] (6671) ◆ 7006[2] 7298[10] 7966[11]
Cheeky Chilli *Irene J Monaghan* a36 56
5 b m Olden Times—Promissory (Caerleon (USA))
3147[10]
Cheeky Wee Red *Richard Fahey* 50
2 ch f Pastoral Pursuits—Swynford Elegance (Charmer)
4941[15] 5352[5]
Cheerfully *John Gosden* a50 68
3 gr f Sadler's Wells(USA) —Light Of Morn (Daylami (IRE))
3563[9] 4114[3] 4552[7]
Cheers *Richard Hannon* 54
2 b f Haafhd—Ziggy Zaggy (Diktat)
2839[6] ◆ 3959[6] 4203[14]
Cheers Big Ears (IRE) *Richard Price* a56 54
4 gr g Kheleyf(USA) —Grey Galava (Generous (IRE))
1782[5]
Cheers For Thea (IRE) *Tim Easterby* a93 92
5 gr m Distant Music(USA) —Popiplu (USA) (Cozzene (USA))
715[9] (873) 1426[7] (2207) 2429[5] (3320) 3830[3] 4287[2] 4603[2] (4849) 5605[4] 6167[2] 6395[P]
Cheery Cat (USA) *John Balding* a67 56
6 bb g Catienus(USA) —Olinka (USA) (Wolfhound (USA))
116[2] 296[4] 569[6] (773) 968[7] 1236[5] 2184[9] 2698[6] 4285[11] 5482[3] 7249[3] 7380[3] (7506) (7607) 7730[4] 8034[4]
Cheetah *Luca Cumani* a103 98
3 b f Tiger Hill(IRE) —Kassiyra (IRE) (Kendor (FR))
(5366) 6095[6] 7349[4] (7594)
Chef *Andrew Balding* 79
2 b c Selkirk(USA) —Ego (Green Desert (USA))
(6802) ◆
Chelsea Morning (USA) *B W Hills* a72 81
3 ch f Giant's Causeway(USA) —Binya (GER) (Royal Solo (IRE))
1620[5] 2981[3] 4115[2] (4655) 5444[4] 6251[5]
Chenin (IRE) *Peter Grayson* a41
4 b m Statue Of Liberty(USA) —Baltic Beach (IRE) (Polish Precedent (USA))
208[7]
Chenonceau (IRE) *Ed Dunlop* a9
2 b f Fasliyev(USA) —Isengard (USA) (Cobra King (USA))
7248[9]
Cheque Book *B W Hills* 72
2 b f Araafa(IRE) —Black Belt Shopper (IRE) (Desert Prince (IRE))
(3386)
Cherokee Lord (USA) *Charlie Livesay* 106
3 b g Sir Cherokee(USA) —Sequins N'Lace (USA) (Mari's Book (USA))
5319a[4]
Cherrego (USA) *Bryn Palling* a40 30
2 ch f Borrego(USA) —My Cherie (USA) (Woodman (USA))
7303[11] 7427[6]

Cherri Fosfate *Declan Carroll* a52 67
6 b g Mujahid(USA) —Compradore (Mujtahid (USA))
1276[9] 1628[10] 1923[7] 2392[9] 5155[2] 5331[7] (5515) 5635[4] 6328[5]
Cherry Bee *Mark Johnston* 74
3 b f Acclamation—Norfolk Lavender (CAN) (Ascot Knight (CAN))
4450[5] 4823[7] 5096[3] 5479[6] (5758) 6003[7] 6395[6] 6753[11]
Cherryblossommiss (USA) *John W Sadler* a95
5 rg m Langfuhr(CAN) —Bodhavista (USA) (Pass The Tab (USA))
3044a[6]
Cheshire Lady (IRE) *Mark Brisbourne* a52 41
3 b f Marju(IRE) —Kiris World (Distant Relative)
624[9] 849[6] 1205[2] 1456[3] 1605[11] 5730[8] 6848[10] 7461[3] 7505[8] 7627[6]
Cheshire Rose *Alex Hales* a67 64
5 ch m Bertolini(USA) —Merch Rhyd-Y-Grug (Sabrehill (USA))
103[7] 271[6] 402[10] 477[7]
Chesnut Coffee *David Simcock* 66
2 ch f Nayef(USA) —Culture Queen (King's Best (USA))
5066[8] 6154[8] 6770[4]
Chester Deelyte (IRE) *Lisa Williamson* a46 52
2 b f Desert Style(IRE) —Bakewell Tart (IRE) (Tagula (IRE))
1292[7] 1835[9] 3126[4] 3770[2] 3986[3] 4451[10] 6645[11] 7017[4] 7268[8]
Chestival (IRE) *Patrick Morris* a25 49
2 b f Acclamation—Inspectors Choice (IRE) (Spectrum (IRE))
2605[3] 2951[10] 3897[U] 4083[4] 5000[11] 5863[5]
Cheveton *Richard Price* a106 104
6 ch g Most Welcome—Attribute (Warning)
1353[7] 2346[16] 2992[10] 3629[8] 4191[3] 4904[7] 5183[6] 5528[5] 5966[2] (6142) (6364) ◆ 7079[4] 7351[14]
Cheveyo (IRE) *Patrick Morris* a73 62
4 br g Celtic Swing—La Catalane (IRE) (Marju (IRE))
1509[10] 1722[5] 1923[9] 2278[9] 2629[7] 3056[7] 3279[8] 7676[6]
Cheviot (USA) *Reginald Roberts* a70 93
4 b g Rahy(USA) —Camlet (Green Desert (USA))
850[6] 1962[2] 2532[5] 7217a[12]
Chevise (IRE) *Ralph Beckett* a74 76
2 b f Holy Roman Emperor(IRE) —Lipica (IRE) (Night Shift (USA))
3331[4] 3913[2] 4293[2] 5099[3] (5865) 6842[2] (7040)
Chewdeh (USA) *John Dunlop* 52
2 bb f Cape Cross(IRE) —Jaish (USA) (Seeking The Gold (USA))
4095[14]
Cheyenne Chant *David O'Meara* a50 57
3 ch f Singspiel(IRE) —Apache Song (USA) (Dynaformer (USA))
2336[9] 3506[9] 4015[3] 5058[7] (5423) (5738) 6038[10]
Cheyenne Red (IRE) *Michael Dods* a57 75
4 br g Namid—Red Leggings (Shareef Dancer (USA))
1869[5] ◆ 2528[4] ◆ 2671[2] 4192[10] 4834[3] 4952[10] 6492[3] 7051[11]
Cheylesmore (IRE) *Stuart Williams* a52 64
2 b g Kodiac—Hemaca (Distinctly North (USA))
3439[5] 6458[7] 6811[4] 7803[4] ◆
Cheyne Walk (USA) *Jeremy Noseda*
3 b f Royal Academy(USA) —Lady Liberty (NZ) (Noble Bijou (USA))
7767[6]
Cheyrac (FR) *X Nakkachdji* 103
4 gr m Smadoun(FR) —One Way (FR) (Exit To Nowhere (USA))
439a[4] 1111a[4]
Chez Vrony *Dave Morris* a43 60
4 b g Lujain(USA) —Polish Abbey (Polish Precedent (USA))
1127[14] 6826[3] 7122[5]
Chi (TUR) *A Ozgen* 100
4 ch m Unaccounted For(USA) —Agas Joy (TUR) (Agam (FR))
5782a[7]
Chia (IRE) *Derek Haydn Jones* a65 66
7 ch m Ashkalani(IRE) —Motley (Rainbow Quest (USA))
(36) 261[13]
Chibcha (IRE) *Kevin Prendergast* a69 80
4 b m High Chaparral(IRE) —Chica Roca (USA) (Woodman (USA))
1408a[12]
Chibchan (IRE) *Mahmood Al Zarooni* a26 60
2 b c Exceed And Excel(AUS) —Cunas (USA) (Irish River (FR))
4110[4] 4477[5] 5040[10] 6694[11]
Chiberta King *Andrew Balding* 104
4 b g King's Best(USA) —Glam Rock (Nashwan (USA))
1724[2] ◆ (2126) 3447[10] ◆ 3922[7] 5908[13] 6387[7] 6889[9]
Chicamia *Michael Mullineaux* a41 55
6 b m Kyllachy—Inflation (Primo Dominie)
2701[0] 7911[0] 9691[2] (2382) 3147[11] 3502[7] 4454[10]
Chicane *William Haggas* a63 72
3 b f Motivator—Wosaita (Generous (IRE))
2478[8] 3157[3] 4120[5] 4557[4] 4972[4] 5467[3] 6336[7] (6816)
Chica Whopa (IRE) *Richard Hannon* 87
3 b f Oasis Dream—Just Ice (Polar Falcon (USA))
(2842) 3790[11] 4905[3] 5149[2] 5524[7]
Chicaya (FR) *F Vermeulen* 74
6 b m Kaldounevees(FR) —Peaceful Paradise (Turtle Island (IRE))
690a[2]
Chichen Daawe *Brian Ellison* a54 56
4 b m Daawe(USA) —Chichen Itza (Shareef Dancer (USA))
1489[4] 1920[13] 2516[4] 3147[4] 5331[3] 6076[2] 7071[3] 7429[4] 7919[4] 7986[5]

Chichi (IRE) *Tom Dascombe* a41 60
3 b f Tomba—Chiffon (Polish Precedent (USA))
4521[5] 4925[5] 5812[8]
Chichina (USA) *Tracy Waggott* a37 52
3 b f Afleet Alex(USA) —St Aye (USA) (Nureyev (USA))
2503[8] 3614[4] 4017[4] 4519[5] 7848[6]
Chicken Momo *Arnfinn Lund* a70 98
4 b g Pyrus(USA) —Italian Affair (Fumo Di Londra (IRE))
4526a[8]
Chico Del Sol (FR) *J Rossi* a72 75
5 b g Divine Light(JPN) —Lady Flasheart (FR) (Wolfhound (USA))
690a[0]
Chiefdom Prince (IRE) *Sir Michael Stoute* 80
3 b c Dansili—Jouet (Reprimand)
1325[5] ◆ 7183[2]
Chief Exec *Jeremy Gask* a81 54
8 br g Zafonic(USA) —Shot At Love (IRE) (Last Tycoon)
696[5] 867[3] 1063[6] 1238[8] 5454[3] (6085) 6503[12] 7091[7] 7290[6] 7665[6] 8014[6]
Chief Of Men *Denis Coakley* 69
2 b c Sleeping Indian—Hidden Meaning (Cadeaux Genereux)
4384[4] 6436[7]
Chief Red Cloud (USA) *Mrs K Burke* a76 76
4 bb g Cherokee Run(USA) —Pertuisane (Zamindar (USA))
1152[7] (1585) 2187[2] 2512[2] 3317[7] 4119[12] 4602[4] (5641) 6112[4] 6581[4]
Chief Storm Eagle (IRE) *Marco Botti* 47
3 b c Montjeu(IRE) —Glass Slipper (IRE) (Danehill (USA))
4069[10] 5057[6] 5414[12] 6098[3]
Chieftan *Sir Michael Stoute*
2 ch c Halling(USA) —Salydora (FR) (Peintre Celebre (USA))
4550[8]
Chifah *Richard Price* a36 45
3 b f Choisir(AUS) —Danifah (IRE) (Perugino (USA))
7300[15] 7601[7] 7862[7]
Chik's Dream *C Roberts* 11
3 ch g Dreams End—Chik's Secret (Nalchik (USA))
6470[11]
Child Bride *Paul Cole* 75
2 b f Invincible Spirit(IRE) —Cultured Pearl (IRE) (Lammtarra (USA))
(1603) 5284[3] 5527[9] 5882[7] 6258[3] 6563[7] 6920[2]
Child Of Our Time (IRE) *Peter Chapple-Hyam* a21 73
3 b f Oratorio(IRE) —Shariyfa (FR) (Zayyani)
4397[5] 4997[4] 5391[3] 5942[8] 6336[11] 6864[7]
Chill (IRE) *Luca Cumani* 74
2 b c Diamond Green(FR) —Time To Relax (IRE) (Orpen (USA))
6158[6] (6626) ◆
Chilled *Sir Michael Stoute* 65
2 b g Iceman—Irresistible (Cadeaux Genereux)
5491[6]
Chilledtothebone *Linda Stubbs* a68 64
2 ch g Iceman—Spanish Craft (IRE) (Jareer (USA))
4645[7] 6138[4] (6425)
Chillianwallah *James Unett* a11
2 ch g Primo Valentino(IRE) —Spark Up (Lahib (USA))
6899[7]
Chillie Peppar *George Prodromou* a49 49
2 b c Araafa(IRE) —Obsessive (USA) (Seeking The Gold (USA))
5717[8] 6092[7] 6425[7] 7004[7] 7201[13]
Chilli Green *John Akehurst* a83 67
3 b f Desert Sun—Jade Pet (Petong)
1694[5] 2227[5] 2968[11] 6801[9] 7209[6] 7439[2] (7892) 8017[2] ◆
Chill Out Charley *John Bridger* 6
3 b g Cyrano De Bergerac—We're Joken (Statoblest)
4835[8] 5470[8] 5557[12]
Chilly Filly (IRE) *Mark Johnston* a69 97
4 b m Montjeu(IRE) —Chill Seeking (USA) (Theatrical)
4117[2] (4290) 4711[2] (4933) ◆ 5217[10] 5743[5] 5908[3] 6493[2] 6736[8]
Chilworth Lad *Mick Channon* 101
2 b g Diktat—Dowhatjen (Desert Style (IRE))
1695[2] (1901) 2468[2] 3051[5] 3488a[4] 4468[4] 5094[2] 5604[5] 5880[7]
Chilworth Lass (IRE) *Mick Channon* a57 57
2 b f Imperial Dancer—Inching (Inchinor)
1972[11] 2642[6] 2905[3] 3864[8] 4554[2] (4788) 5020[2] 5560[3] 6082[7] 6891[16] 7378[4] 7552[13]
Chinchon (IRE) *C Laffon-Parias* 115
5 b h Marju(IRE) —Jarama (IRE) (Hector Protector (USA))
(953a) 1747a[6] 2803a[4] 6015a[6] 6951a[6]
Chincoteague (IRE) *Brian Meehan* a66 71
4 b m Daylami(IRE) —Blue Water (USA) (Bering)
2231[4] 2597[9] 3360[2] 3917[6] 4734[2] 5179[10] 7011[6] 7381[2] 7531[5]
Chinese Democracy (USA) *David Evans* a64 66
3 b f Proud Citizen(USA) —Double's Lass (USA) (Mr. Leader (USA))
1162[6] 1437[8] 1643[3] 2049[2] 2296[4] 2588[5] 3002[7] 3161[5] 3525[2] 3771[4] (4130) 4324[9] 4365[3] 4739[5] 4922[5] 5037[5] 6168[4] 6226[2] 6439[3] 6541[8] 7006[6] 7518[4] 7640[3] 7655[7] 7824[8]
Chinese Wall (IRE) *D Guillemin* 104
2 b f Aussie Rules(USA) —Ganar El Cielo (Ashkalani (IRE))
4275a[4] (5226a) 6044a[2] 6760a[5]
Chinese White (IRE) *D K Weld* 116
5 gr m Dalakhani(IRE) —Chiang Mai (IRE) (Sadler's Wells (USA))
2369a[3] (3467a)
Chink Of Light *Andrew Balding* a83 99
3 ch g Dr Fong(USA) —Isle Of Flame (Shirley Heights)
(677) 904[2] ◆ 1138[2] 1833[3] 3145[6] 4461[13]

Chin'n Tonic (IRE) *Alan Swinbank* 78
2 ch g Chineur(FR) —Terra Nova (Polar Falcon (USA))
3316[8] (4368) 5597[6] 6230a[7]

Chinook Wind (IRE) *B W Hills* 72
2 b f Encosta De Lago(AUS) —Dedicated Lady (IRE) (Pennine Walk)
3871[7] 5692[3] 6092[13]

Chip N Pin *Tim Easterby* 35
6 b m Erhaab(USA) —Vallauris (Faustus (USA))
2500[10]

Chiqueta (FR) *C Gourdain* 67
2 gr f Take Risks(FR) —Attendrissante (USA) (Cresta Rider (USA))
7009a[7]

Chiswick Bey (IRE) *Richard Fahey* 89
2 b g Elusive City(USA) —Victoria Lodge (IRE) (Grand Lodge (USA))
(1009) 2525[2] 3049[10] (4367) 5245[3] 5880[11] 6568[10]

Chjimes (IRE) *Conor Dore* a84 79
6 b g Fath(USA) —Radiance (IRE) (Thatching)
119[6] 275[5] 806[4] 848[5] (1167) 1482[6] 1979[2] (2234) 3516[3] 4428[7] 7331[10] 7519[4] 7720[5] 7827[2] (7973) 8035[8]

Choc'A'Moca (IRE) *Declan Carroll* 60
3 b g Camacho—Dear Catch (IRE) (Bluebird (USA))
1178[4] 1469[2] 1753[10] 2834[11] (3501) 4344[7] 4674[6] 5024[8] 6466[6] ◆ 6643[2] 6897[8] 7052[3] 7154[2] 7300[9]

Chock A Block (IRE) *Saeed Bin Suroor* a94 109
4 gr h Dalakhani(IRE) —Choc Ice (IRE) (Kahyasi)
2593[8] 4500[2] 5291[4] 5853[6] 6720[5] 7384[2]

Chocolate Caramel (USA) *Richard Fahey* a77 72
8 b g Storm Creek(USA) —Sandhill (BRZ) (Baynoun)
190[2] 910[3] 1069[8] 1689[4] 2495[4] (2694) 3282[2] 4015[8] 4511[6] 4825[5] 5119[7] 5437[2] 6109[6] 6744[5] 6915[11] 7465[5]

Chocolate Cookie (IRE) *Mandy Rowland* a66 72
3 b f Desert Style(IRE) —Back At De Front (IRE) (Cape Cross (IRE))
698[8] 809[12] 1602[7] 1982[6] 2634[9] 6865[12]

Choctaw Nation *Malcolm Jefferson* 66
6 b g Sadler's Wells(USA) —Space Quest (Rainbow Quest (USA))
3122[3]

Choice *Sir Michael Stoute* 70
3 b f Azamour(IRE) —Poise (IRE) (Rainbow Quest (USA))
2767[4]

Chokidar (IRE) *Jeremy Glover* 77
2 b g Sleeping Indian—Lola Sapola (IRE) (Benny The Dip (USA))
5053[4] 5531[2] 6047[2]

Chokurei (IRE) *Clive Cox* 64
2 b f Bertolini(USA) —Catch Us (FR) (Selkirk (USA))
4203[6] 6441[7]

Chookie Avon *Valentine Donoghue* a63 64
3 ch g Avonbridge—Lady Of Windsor (IRE) (Woods Of Windsor (USA))
2296[7] 3710[4] 6189[3] 6494[3] (6710) 6897[6] 7056[4] 7501[4] 7705[9]

Chookie Hamilton *Valentine Donoghue* a88 88
6 ch g Compton Place—Lady Of Windsor (IRE) (Woods Of Windsor (USA))
2243[9] 3198[4] 6224[5] (6397) (6707) 6895[4] 7173[5] 7568[6] 7781[3] 8007[6]

Choose Me (IRE) *Kevin Prendergast* a76 106
4 ch m Choisir(AUS) —Hecuba (Hector Protector (USA))
2355a[7] 4877a[4] 6007a[3] 6379a[6] 7358a[12]

Choose The Moment *Eve Johnson Houghton* 68
2 b f Choisir(AUS) —Enclave (USA) (Woodman (USA))
4753[2] 5255[2] 5755[2]

Choose Wisely (IRE) *Kevin Ryan* 101
2 ch c Choisir(AUS) —Right After Moyne (IRE) (Imperial Ballet (IRE))
1359[10] 1800[3] (2202) 2917a[5] 4458[3] 5221[5] 5639[3] 5850[5]

Choparlas (FR) *M Boutin* 79
8 gr g Verglas(IRE) —Rayonne (Sadler's Wells (USA))
560a[0]

Chopastair (FR) *T Lemer* a91 111
9 b g Astair(FR) —Very Sol (FR) (Solicitor (FR))
7800a[3]

Chopouest (FR) *A Spanu* 98
3 b c Indian Rocket—Free Track (FR) (Solid Illusion (USA))
4885a[11] 6012a[13] 6608a[21]

Choral *Richard Hannon* a77 72
2 b f Oratorio(IRE) —Sierra (Dr Fong (USA))
3509[6] 5078[5] 5369[2] 6154[4] 6634[2] 7036[2] 7232[2]

Choral Festival *John Bridger* a73 69
4 b m Pivotal—Choirgirl (Unfuwain (USA))
182[5] 309[5] 612[5] 660[4] 770[3] 1077[5] 1756[7] 2337[6] 2645[2] 3040[3] 3294[5] 3513[3] 3862[7] 4201[2] (4422) 4873[5] 5536[3] 5994[7] 6639[3] 6959[12]

Choreography *Jim Best* a48 77
7 ch g Medicean—Stark Ballet (USA) (Nureyev (USA))
1637[5] 2783[4] (3057) 3289[7]

Chosen Character (IRE) *Tom Dascombe* 72
2 b g Choisir(AUS) —Out Of Thanks (IRE) (Sadler's Wells (USA))
4123[4] 4702[4] 5761[3]

Chosen Forever *Geoffrey Oldroyd* a89 79
5 b g Choisir(AUS) —Forever Bond (Danetime (IRE))
(174) ◆ 255[2] (430) ◆ 790[9] 1378[9] 1684[6] 2093[7] 2937[2] 4093[2] 4849[6] 5641[6]

Chosen One (IRE) *Ruth Carr* a66 76
5 ch g Choisir(AUS) —Copious (IRE) (Generous (IRE))
20[12] 378[4] 601[8] 778[10] 1072[6] (1923) (2213) (2528) 2818[5] 3201[5] 3321[9] 4199[4] (4542) ◆ 4712[3] 5198[6] 5513[6]

Chris's Jem *John Jenkins* a60 58
4 b m Makbul—Royal Orchid (IRE) (Shalford (IRE))
4234[13]

Chris's Ridge *Brian Meehan* a76 21
3 gr g Indian Ridge—Dundel (IRE) (Machiavellian (USA))
5150[9] 6496[2] 7086[4] 7554[14]

Christian Love (ITY) *R Menichetti* 89
3 b c Tout Seul(IRE) —Nicol Love (ITY) (Nicolotte)
1945a[12]

Christine's Gold (IRE) *Eric Alston* 30
2 b f Acclamation—Twinberry (IRE) (Tagula (IRE))
5117[9] 5785[9] 6045[6]

Christmas Aria (IRE) *Simon Dow* 68
2 b c Oratorio(IRE) —Christmas Cracker (FR) (Alhaarth (IRE))
4131[8] 5074[3] 5651[6]

Christmas Carnival *Brian Meehan* a72 90
3 ch g Cadeaux Genereux—Ellebanna (Tina's Pet)
1381[4] 2603[3] 3207[5] (4112) (4784) 5529[4]

Christmas Coming *David Elsworth* a69 67
3 b c Cape Cross(IRE) —Aunty Rose (IRE) (Caerleon (USA))
274[4] 484[2] 734[2] 1486[3] 2510[7]

Christmas Light *David O'Meara* 81
3 b f Zafeen(FR) —Arabian Dancer (Dansili)
3612[4] (3924) 4389[6] 4750[5] 5222[7] 5759[5] 6753[15] 6917[8]

Christophers Quest *Natalie Lloyd-Beavis* a69 54
5 b g Forzando—Kaprisky (IRE) (Red Sunset)
1920[5] 2676[6] 5457[9] 5813[5] 6275[7]

Christopher Wren (USA) *John Best* a60 97
3 ch c D'Wildcat(USA) —Ashley's Coy (USA) (Country Pine (USA))
1476[11] (2289) ◆ 3105[6] ◆ (3594) ◆ 4815[7] 5273[3]

Chrysanthemum (IRE) *David Wachman* 104
2 b f Danehill Dancer(IRE) —Well Spoken (IRE) (Sadler's Wells (USA))
(6005a) ◆ (6401a)

Chushka *Bryan Smart* 74
3 ch f Pivotal—Ravine (Indian Ridge)
1100[2] 1488[3] 2502[5] 3061[6] (4155) 5409[3] 6040[11] 6879[13]

Cian Rooney (IRE) *Ann Duffield* 73
3 b g Camacho—Exponent (USA) (Exbourne (USA))
2768[10] 4193[10] 4654[7]

Cigalas *Jean McGregor* 67
5 ch g Selkirk(USA) —Langoustine (AUS) (Danehill (USA))
1204[3] 1575[8] 1717[8] 5213[12] 5437[10] 6187[14]

Cilium (IRE) *Andrew Oliver* a80 89
4 b m War Chant(USA) —Venturi (Danehill Dancer (IRE))
4631a[8]

Cill Rialaig *Hughie Morrison* a78 102
5 gr m Environment Friend—Pang Valley Girl (Rock Hopper)
1474[4] 2747[2] (3194) 4143[5]

Cils Blancs (IRE) *Bryan Smart* a49 63
4 b m Barathea(IRE) —Immortelle (Arazi (USA))
2211[5] ◆ 4082[6] 5379[11] 6460[9]

Cima De Pluie *B Grizzetti* 95
3 b g Singspiel(IRE) —Grey Way (USA) (Cozzene (USA))
1945a[15] 7103a[3]

Cima De Triomphe (IRE) *B Grizzetti* 110
5 gr h Galileo(IRE) —Sopran Londa (IRE) (Danehill (USA))
1540a[4] 6239a[2] 6592a[7] 6977a[9] 7373a[16]

Cinderella *Lucinda Featherstone* a18 12
3 ch f Zafeen(FR) —Flighty Dancer (Pivotal)
2903[9] 3125[11] 7461[6]

Cinderkamp *Edward Vaughan* a77 69
2 b c Kyllachy—Topkamp (Pennekamp (USA))
1986[6] 5160[6] 5523[10] 6086[6] ◆ (6645) (6868)

Cinq Heavens (IRE) *Tom Dascombe* a23 47
2 b g Chevalier(IRE) —Prime Site (IRE) (Burslem)
2474[9] 3126[6] 3712[3] 4967[8]

Cinta *Marco Botti* a68 58
2 b f Monsun(GER) —Night Year (IRE) (Jareer (USA))
6155[13] 6651[8] 7185[3]

Circuitous *Paul Cole* a66
2 b c Fasliyev(USA) —Seren Devious (Dr Devious (IRE))
7871[3] ◆

Circumvent *Paul Cole* a95 113
3 ch g Tobougg(IRE) —Seren Devious (Dr Devious (IRE))
1567a[3] 2056[5] (3824) 4456[8] 5135a[5] 6179[3] 6562[16]

Circus Act *Mahmood Al Zarooni* 38
2 b c Cape Cross(IRE) —Carry On Katie (USA) (Fasliyev (USA))
7303[8]

Circus Girl (IRE) *Ralph Beckett* a56 83
3 ch f Bertolini(USA) —Blew Her Top (USA) (Blushing John (USA))
(1431) 2256[3] 2843[7] 4265[5] 5972[10]

Circus Star (USA) *Brian Meehan* a66 66
2 b g Borrego(USA) —Picadilly Circus (USA) (Fantastic Fellow (USA))
6159[4] 6844[6] 7248[7]

Cirrus Des Aigles (FR) *Mme C Barande-Barbe* a112 120
4 b g Even Top(IRE) —Taille De Guepe (FR) (Septieme Ciel (USA))
5107a[3] (6592a) 6974a[2] 7615a[9] 7854a[7]

Citadella *David Simcock* 65
3 b f Exceed And Excel(AUS) —City Maiden (USA) (Carson City (USA))
4966[6] 5395[6] 5986[3]

Citizenship *Ian Williams* a73 81
4 b g Beat Hollow—Three More (USA) (Sanglamore (USA))
2857[3] 4055[4] 4619[9] 5286[6]

Citrus Star (USA) *Chris Wall* 107
3 b g Broken Vow(USA) —Twist A Lime (USA) (Copelan (USA))
1687[3] 2713[4] (4509) 5911[6] 6349[24] 6888[8]

City Dancer (IRE) *David Nicholls* a89 99
4 b m Elusive City(USA) —Calypso Dancer (FR) (Celtic Swing)
1670[4] 2431[5] 2745[6] ◆ 3197[2] ◆ 3875[8] 5589[4]

City For Conquest (IRE) *John Harris* a42 55
7 b m City On A Hill(USA) —Northern Life (IRE) (Distinctly North (USA))
1112[8] 1598[8] 1885[8] 2263[11] 3615[8] 3976[6] 4234[5] 4478[7] 4869[8] 5482[8]

City Gossip (IRE) *Mandy Rowland* a64 50
3 b f Shinko Forest(IRE) —Lady At War (Warning)
5[4] 122[7] 454[3] 574[8] 1536[6] 2962[16]

City Ground (USA) *Michael Jarvis* a77 86
3 bb g Orientate(USA) —Magnet (USA) (Seeking The Gold (USA))
2706[2] 2968[2] ◆ 3586[3] 4146[4] (5270) (6276)

City Legend *Alan McCabe* a50 66
2 b c Lucky Story(USA) —Urban Calm (Cadeaux Genereux)
4421[3] 5298[7] 5587[10] 8011[11]

City Of The Kings (IRE) *Geoffrey Harker* a83 101
5 b g Cape Cross(IRE) —Prima Volta (Primo Dominie)
1889[7] 2423[6] 4154[9] (4652) 4849[2] 5098[2] 5605[16] 6749[12] 6960[4] 7227[11]

Cityscape *Roger Charlton* 124
4 ch h Selkirk(USA) —Tantina (USA) (Distant View (USA))
1383[4] ◆ 1614[2] (5741) (6529)

City Stable (IRE) *Michael Wigham* a77 67
5 b g Machiavellian(USA) —Rainbow City (IRE) (Rainbow Quest (USA))
261[5] ◆ 2006[2] 2302[5] (3028) 3324[6] ◆ (3760) 3965[10] 7985[6]

City Style (USA) *Mahmood Al Zarooni* 107
4 ch g City Zip(USA) —Brattothecore (CAN) (Katahaula County (CAN))
2344[4] 2651[3] 5516[4] 7083[9]

City Vaults Girl (IRE) *Richard Fahey* 76
3 b f Oratorio(IRE) —Uriah (GER) (Acatenango (GER))
2033[13] (2516) 3613[6] 4573[16] 5300[9]

Claddagh *Mark Johnston* a60 49
3 b g Dubai Destination(USA) —Ring Of Love (Magic Ring (IRE))
371[4]

Claimant (IRE) *Miss J R Tooth* a68 46
3 b g Acclamation—Between The Winds (USA) (Diesis)
2754[2] 4022[12]

Clairvoyance (IRE) *John Gosden* a93 100
3 b f Shamardal(USA) —Crystal View (IRE) (Imperial Ballet (IRE))
(979) 1082[4] 1899[5] 2712[7] 3071[13] 3375[5]

Clanachy *George Foster* 37
4 b m Kyllachy—Antonia's Dream (Clantime)
1569[8] 2213[13] 4064[8] 4516[8]

Clare Glen (IRE) *Mrs Sarah Dawson* a65 76
4 b m Sakhee(USA) —Desert Grouse (USA) (Gulch (USA))
(4327)

Clare Harrier (IRE) *Alan Berry* 57
3 ch g Medecis—Assafiyah (IRE) (Kris)
1425[12] 1890[6] 3227[2] 3507[4] 3808[6] 4127[15] 5214[6] 5419[6] 6186[P]

Claremont (IRE) *Mahmood Al Zarooni* 113
4 b h Sadler's Wells(USA) —Mezzo Soprano (USA) (Darshaan)
516a[4] ◆ 799a[6] 1382[3] 1698[3] (2116) 3191[10]

Claret'N'Blue (USA) *Brian Meehan* a75 78
2 bb c El Prado(IRE) —High Humidity (USA) (Petionville (USA))
4550[5] 5746[4] 6088[3] 6743[3] 7066[3]

Clarietta *John Dunlop* a97 97
3 b f Shamardal(USA) —Claxon (Caerleon (USA))
1082[3] 5553[9] 6095[2] 6551a[10] 6886[11] 7349[14]

Clarinette (IRE) *Ralph Beckett* 25
2 ch f Dalakhani(IRE) —Caborig (IRE) (Entrepreneur)
5829[11]

Clarke Lane (USA) *Michael Jarvis* 83
2 b c Giant's Causeway(USA) —Wonder Lady Anne L (USA) (Real Quiet (USA))
(1905) 2514[2] 3190[11] 5525[7]

Clasp *Doug Watson* a98 98
8 ch g Singspiel(IRE) —Embrace Me (Nashwan (USA))
334a[9] 513a[9] 629a[4]

Classical Air *John Dunlop* 16
2 b f Dubai Destination(USA) —Claxon (Caerleon (USA))
6155[16]

Classically (IRE) *Hughie Morrison* a84 84
4 b g Indian Haven—Specifically (USA) (Sky Classic (CAN))
4023[8] 4382[11] 4910[5] (5367) (5958) 6449[6]

Classical Piece (USA) *Deborah Sanderson* a68 52
3 b g Brahms(USA) —Nueva (USA) (Jade Hunter (USA))
1298[10] 1619[10]

Classical World (USA) *Torben Christensen* a87 93
5 rg g El Prado(IRE) —Tethkar (Machiavellian (USA))
2195a[4] 4641a[7]

Classic Angel (GER) *Y De Nicolay* 87
3 b f Samum(GER) —Classic Cara (GER) (Nikos)
1946a[7]

Classic Blade (IRE) *Doug Watson* a98 93
4 b h Daggers Drawn(USA) —Queen Bodicea (IRE) (Revoque (IRE))
416a[10] 604a[10] 822a[8]

Classic Blue (IRE) *Ian Williams* a60 43
6 b m Tagula(IRE) —Palace Blue (IRE) (Dara Monarch)
(80) 497[5]

Classic Colori (IRE) *Tom Dascombe* a101 100
3 b g Le Vie Dei Colori—Beryl (Bering)
(945) 1083[4] 2159a[15] 2707[9] 5247[9] 6203[5] 6877[16]

Classic Contours (USA) *John Quinn* 77
4 b g Najran(USA) —What's Up Kittycat (USA) (Tabasco Cat (USA))
1150[6] 1671[7] 2277[6] 3552[5] 4246[9] 7147[10]

Classic Descent *Ruth Carr* a85 74
5 b g Auction House(USA) —Polish Descent (IRE) (Danehill (USA))
350[6] 508[7] 907[6] 1152[5] 1426[13] 1808[5] 2700[4] 2850[DSQ] 3022[2] 3180[2] 3595[4] 3732[2] 3911[4] 4119[6] 4823[10] 5244[9] 5641[9]

Classic Gem (IRE) *Tom Dascombe* a39 38
2 br f Diamond Green(FR) —Undercover (Grand Lodge (USA))
1541[9] 2347[6] 6118[8] 6891[17]

Classic Hero (GER) *H-W Hiller* a81 85
3 b c Konigstiger(GER) —Classic Queen (GER) (Greinton)
2802a[19]

Classic Punch (IRE) *David Elsworth* a109 107
7 b g Mozart(IRE) —Rum Cay (USA) (Our Native (USA))
1529[5] 2096[15] 2640[2] 3456[2] (4376) 5090[4] 5749[3] 6889[6] 7297[8]

Classic Summer (GER) *Andreas Lowe* a74 87
4 ch m Pentire—Classic Queen (GER) (Greinton)
3236a[10]

Classic Vintage (USA) *Amanda Perrett* 103
4 b g El Prado(IRE) —Cellars Shiraz (USA) (Kissin Kris (USA))
1274[4] 1724[6] 2317[2] 3194[13] 4461[7] 6889[7] 7084[3] 7350[4]

Classic Voice (IRE) *Richard Hannon* a71 62
2 b c Oratorio(IRE) —Pearly Brooks (Efisio)
5006[9] 5651[4] 5914[5] 6311[6] 6513[8] 6875[6] (7087)

Class Is Class (IRE) *Sir Michael Stoute* 116
4 b g Montjeu(IRE) —Hector's Girl (Hector Protector (USA))
1724[7] 2096[13] (2593) 4829[2] 5539[4]

Classlin *Jim Goldie* 52
3 b f Bertolini(USA) —Class Wan (Safawan)
1667[9] 2291[6] 2449[2] 3200[6] 3410[3] 3710[9] 3946[8] 4194[6] 4826[6] 5410[9] 6103[10]

Classofsixtythree (USA) *Gary Contessa* a93
4 b m Include(USA) —Rambling Rose (USA) (Blush Rambler (USA))
5578a[5]

Claude Carter *Alistair Whillans* 20
6 b g Elmaamul(USA) —Cruz Santa (Lord Bud)
3901[11]

Clayton Flick (IRE) *Andrew Haynes* a57 45
3 b g Kheleyf(USA) —Mambodorga (USA) (Kingmambo (USA))
43[4] 168[4] 288[8] 372[3] 542[2] 670[4] 1394[12] 2359[8] 2418[10] 3640[9]

Clear Ice (IRE) *David Bourton* a74 64
3 gr g Verglas(IRE) —Mynu Girl (IRE) (Charnwood Forest (IRE))
17[3] 886[4] 962[3] 1181[8] 1237[2] 1491[2] 1750[4] 1994[2] 2203[7] 2668[3] 2879[8] 3276[3] 7701[7]

Clearing House *John Ryan* a46 50
5 ch g Zamindar(USA) —Easy Option (IRE) (Prince Sabo)
3168[10] 3982[6] 4213[2] 4308[11] 4498[4] 4969[7] 5159[10] 6439[11]

Clearing Sky (IRE) *Jim Boyle* a28 62
9 gr m Exploit(USA) —Litchfield Hills (USA) (Relaunch (USA))
145[10] 498[14] 694[10]

Clearly Cryptonite (USA) *Tim Pitt* a41 50
3 rg g El Prado(IRE) —Coconut Girl (USA) (Cryptoclearance (USA))
2627[10] 5065[8] 5419[5] 6579[8]

Clear Praise (USA) *Simon Dow* a79
3 b g Songandaprayer(USA) —Pretty Clear (USA) (Mr Prospector (USA))
6496[9] (7322) 7571[6] ◆ (8004) ◆

Clear Reef *Jane Chapple-Hyam* a90 88
6 b h Hernando(FR) —Trinity Reef (Bustino)
4334[8] 4597[6] 5378a[2] 5991[4]

Clear Sailing *Patrick Leech* a83 51
7 b g Selkirk(USA) —Welsh Autumn (Tenby)
19[2] (105) (200) (314) 871[2] 938[6]

Clerical (USA) *Robert Cowell* a61 61
4 b g Yes It's True(USA) —Clerical Etoile (ARG) (The Watcher (USA))
234[12] 397[9] 576[8] 2876[4] 3263[9] (3993) (4234) (4487) 5557[8] 6295[11] 7332[3] 7518[6] 7556[6] 7656[2] 7973[5]

Cleveland *Reg Hollinshead* a68 57
8 b g Pennekamp(USA) —Clerio (Soviet Star (USA))
39[5]

Clever Man *Mick Channon* 65
2 b c Librettist(USA) —Lindesberg (Doyoun)
3459[6] 4221[7] 4743[4] 6182[5]

Clever Omneya (USA) *John Jenkins* a64 36
4 ch m Toccet(USA) —Clever Empress (Crafty Prospector (USA))
145[3] (320) 388[4] 691[3] 976[5] 1129[10] 2419[8] (7835) 7885[11]

Click And Go (IRE) *P F McEnery* a32 31
2 b f Kodiac—Sticky Fingers (IRE) (Dr Devious (IRE))
6726a[12]

Cliffords Reprieve *Eric Wheeler* 46
2 b g Kheleyf(USA) —Bijan (IRE) (Mukaddamah (USA))
6514[14] 6688[8] 6986[7]

Clifton Bridge *Ralph Beckett* a82 79
3 b g Avonbridge—Ambitious (Ardkinglass)
(277) 1315[9] 3892[5] 4625[9] 6253[7] 6799[10]

Clifton Encore (USA) *Tom Dascombe* 15
3 b f War Chant(USA) —Theatrical Pause (USA) (Theatrical)
3816[6] 4661[13]

Climate (IRE) *David Evans* a63 36
11 ch g Catrail(USA) —Burishki (Chilibang)
131[10] 290[6] 353[11] 410[11]

Climaxfortackle (IRE) *Derek Shaw* a52 57
2 b f Refuse To Bend(IRE) —Miss Asia Quest (Rainbow Quest (USA))
4089[11] 4748[4] 5301[13] 5660[7] 5882[16]

Clinical *Sir Mark Prescott Bt* 85
2 gr f Motivator—Doctor's Glory (USA) (Elmaamul (USA))
(4048) 4842[6]

Clipthorne *Ollie Pears* 71
2 gr f Ivan Denisovich(IRE) —Dim Ofan (Petong)
(2693) 3611[4] 6184[8] 6619[11]

Clockmaker (IRE) *John Gosden* a95 94
4 b g Danetime(IRE) —Lady Ingabelle (IRE) (Catrail (USA))
1127[2] ◆ 1450[7] 2872[2] ◆ (3565) 5264[15] 5750[4] 6204[5] 6447[5]

Clondinnery (IRE) *G M Lyons* a82 104
2 b c Choisir(AUS) —Grand Lili (Linamix (FR))
954a[3] 3488a[3]

Cloneylass (IRE) *Mrs John Harrington* 90
2 b f Verglas(IRE) —Consensus (IRE) (Common Grounds)
3939a[3]

Close To The Edge (IRE) *Alan McCabe* a64 67
2 b f Iffraaj—Iktidar (Green Desert (USA))
2936[5] 3658[4] 5301[15] 7879[4]

Cloth Ears *Phil McEntee* a63 43
4 b m Fraam—Estimada (Mark Of Esteem (IRE))
5658[10] 6638[4] (6931) 7329[6] 7571[9] 7754[9]

Cloud Fire (IRE) *Kevin Prendergast* a67 74
4 b m Refuse To Bend(IRE) —Flying Millie (IRE) (Flying Spur (AUS))
5129a[3]

Cloud Hawk (IRE) *T J O'Mara* 50
2 b f Hawk Wing(USA) —Grey Clouds (Cloudings (IRE))
7256a[7]

Cloud Illusions (USA) *Heather Main* a75 79
2 rg f Smarty Jones(USA) —Ilusoria (USA) (Maria's Mon (USA))
4658[9] 5147[6] 7098[7] 7914[2] (8030)

Cloud Rock *Peter Chapple-Hyam* a75 84
2 b c Tiger Hill(IRE) —Tambourin (Halling (USA))
(5204) 6149[4] 6850[4]

Cloud's End *William Haggas* a74 82
3 b f Dubawi(IRE) —Kangra Valley (Indian Ridge)
(3441) 4847[5] 5205[7]

Cloudy City (USA) *Mark Johnston* a77 81
3 bb g Giant's Causeway(USA) —Mambo Slew (USA) (Kingmambo (USA))
781[5] 2935[12] 3519[2] 3772[2] 4026[4] 5333[6] 5922[6] 6416[9]

Cloudy Start *Jamie Osborne* a108 108
4 b g Oasis Dream—Set Fair (USA) (Alleged (USA))
1377[5] 1664[3] 2020a[9] 5370[4] 5879[9] 6123[4] 6877[8]

Clowance *Roger Charlton* 114
5 b m Montjeu(IRE) —Freni (GER) (Sternkoenig (IRE))
1382[11] (7096) 7373a[10]

Cluain Alainn (IRE) *Ian Williams* a84 77
4 b g Dalakhani(IRE) —Josh's Pearl (IRE) (Sadler's Wells (USA))
947[5] 1156[8] 2031[11] 2934[12]

Club Oceanic *Jeremy Noseda* a80
2 b c Cape Cross(IRE) —My Lass (Elmaamul (USA))
7385[9] (7559)

Club Tahiti *Tony Carroll* a9 90
4 b m Hernando(FR) —Freni (GER) (Sternkoenig (IRE))
3031[10] 4322[9] 5149[10] 5972[9] 6444[8] 7182[4] 7306[3] 7474[13]

Clueless *Brian Storey* a33 34
8 b g Royal Applause—Pure (Slip Anchor)
4648[11]

Clumber Place *Richard Guest* a64 80
4 ch m Compton Place—Inquirendo (USA) (Roberto (USA))
1928[3] 2429[6] 2875[6] 3061[7] 3854[4] 4342[3] 4515[10] (5598) (5905) (6460) (7238)

C'Mon You Irons (IRE) *Mark Hoad* a80 85
5 b g Orpen(USA) —Laissez Faire (IRE) (Tagula (IRE))
1580[6] 3037[15] 4662[11] (5027) 5388[7] 6078[7] 6812[15] 7093[9] 7441[10] 7655[3]

Cnocandancer (IRE) *T Stack* 80
3 ch f Danehill Dancer(IRE) —Dancing Diva (FR) (Sadler's Wells (USA))
2370a[15]

Coachlight *John Dunlop* 71
2 b c Cape Cross(IRE) —Spotlight (Dr Fong (USA))
3915[4] 4755[6] 5676[3] 6810[7] 7059[8]

Coal Miner (IRE) *Ruth Carr* a40
3 b g Chineur(FR) —Rose Vibert (Caerleon (USA))
784[5] 894[5] 997[10]

Coastal Bequest (IRE) *Sir Michael Stoute* a30 24
2 br g Cape Cross(IRE) —Gift Range (IRE) (Spectrum (IRE))
6092[14] 6742[8]

Coasting *Amanda Perrett* 99
5 b g Cape Cross(IRE) —Sweeping (Indian King (USA))
(2091) 2971[5] 3692[11] 4473[7] 5950[12]

Coax *Mark Johnston* a62 71
2 b g Red Ransom(USA) —True Glory (IRE) (In The Wings)
6626[4] 7223[3] 7478[8]

Cobbs Quay *John Gosden* 82
2 b c Danehill Dancer(IRE) —Rave Reviews (IRE) (Sadler's Wells (USA))
5440[2] 6560[12]

Cobo Bay *Conor Dore* a91 99
5 b g Primo Valentino(IRE) —Fisher Island (IRE) (Sri Pekan (USA))
197[7] 408[3] (851) (1049) 1408a[3] 1708[6] 1826[8] 2141[3] (3021) 4023[13] 5142[6] (5233) 5753[8] 7182[14] 7382[3] (7529) 7600[7] 7688[6]

Cochabamba (IRE) *Roger Teal* a80 103
2 ch f Hurricane Run(IRE) —Bolivia (USA) (Distant View (USA))
(3785) 4305[2] 5519[2] 6528[6] 6927[2]

Cockney (IRE) *Mark Johnston* 76
3 b c Theatrical—Cumulate (USA) (Gone West (USA))
2812[2] 3077[2] 3355[2] 3953[P]

Cockney Class (USA) *Brian Meehan* 98
3 rg g Speightstown(USA) —Snappy Little Cat (USA) (Tactical Cat (USA))
1706[3] (2090) 3461[15] 3791[16] 6709[3] 6885[6]

Cockney Colonel (USA) *Edward Creighton* a21 18
3 bb g Dixie Union(USA) —Kristina's Wish (USA) (Smart Strike (CAN))
424[6] 744[8] 1259[6]

Cocktail Charlie *Tim Easterby* 97
2 b g Danbird(AUS) —Royal Punch (Royal Applause)
(1331) 2032[2] 2757[2] ◆ 5604[4]

Cocktail Party (IRE) *James Unett* a56 54
4 b m Acclamation—Irish Moss (USA) (Irish River (FR))
178[4] 271[4] 368[6] 477[3] 561[10] 726[7] 4938[6] 5580[4] 6952[4] 7300[10] 7380[2] 7783[9]

Cocohatchee *Pat Phelan* 74
2 b c Avonbridge—Chilly Cracker (Largesse)
1256[2] 2680[4] 3811[2] 5033[3] (5328) 5880[18] 6191[6] 6690[4]

Coconut Ice *Tom Dascombe* a62 73
2 ch f Bahamian Bounty—Winter Ice (Wolfhound (USA))
1359[3] ◆ 1527[2] 1819[5] 3353[4] 3596[6] (3817) 4124[7] 6030[2] 6445[9] 6769[7] 7040[4]

Coda Agency *David Arbuthnot* a71 55
7 b g Agnes World(USA) —The Frog Lady (IRE) (Al Hareb (USA))
263[4] (748) 1160[8] (1768) 3084[10] 3780[11] (7967)

Codemaster *Henry Candy* 95
2 b c Choisir(AUS) —Verbal Intrigue (USA) (Dahar (USA))
4384[2] (5523) ◆ 6568[2]

Code Of War (USA) *A De Royer-Dupre* a85 91
4 b h Mutakddim(USA) —Code Nine Six (USA) (Cure The Blues (USA))
6147[9]

Co Dependent (USA) *Jamie Osborne* a61 39
4 ch g Cozzene(USA) —Glowing Breeze (USA) (Southern Halo (USA))
2866[10] 7757[5] (7960) 8036[5]

Codigo De Honor (ARG) *B Al Subaie* a104
6 b h Honour And Glory(USA) —Miner Classic (USA) (Mining (USA))
610a[9] 710a[5]

Codoor (GER) *P Schiergen* 96
3 b c Sabiango(GER) —Codera (GER) (Zilzal (USA))
6011a[6]

Coedmor Boy *John Flint* a46 47
2 b g Leporello(IRE) —Denise Best (IRE) (Goldmark (USA))
4477[9] 4909[6] 5895[5] 6673[10] 7496[9]

Coeur (USA) *David Arbuthnot*
2 rg f Aeneas(USA) —Siber Runner (USA) (Siberian Summer (USA))
4208[9]

Coeur Brule (FR) *Sam Davison* a39 41
4 b g Polish Summer—Sally's Cry (FR) (Freedom Cry)
541[8] 7634[10]

Coeur Courageux (FR) *W De Best-Turner* a59 39
8 b g Xaar—Linoise (FR) (Caerwent)
986[7] 1167[6]

Coeur De Lionne (IRE) *Ed Dunlop* a92 84
6 b g Invincible Spirit(IRE) —Lionne (Darshaan)
252[2] 620[5]

Coeur Loyal (CHI) *Saeed Bin Suroor* a82 57
4 b g Dance Brightly(CAN) —L'Eclipse (CHI) (Smooth Performance (USA))
414a[8] 819a[12]

Coeus *Sir Mark Prescott Bt* a87
2 gr g Ishiguru(USA) —Lady Georgia (Arazi (USA))
2413[3] (2677) 3327[3]

Cognomen (IRE) *V T O'Brien* 64
3 b g Antonius Pius(USA) —Imposition (UAE) (Be My Guest (USA))
4563a[9]

Coiled Spring *Amanda Perrett* a57 74
4 b g Observatory(USA) —Balmy (Zafonic (USA))
1847[6] 2845[7] 4102[4] 4386[7] 4804[7] 5840[4] 6669[8]

Coin Box *Mahmood Al Zarooni* a69 39
2 b f Dubai Destination(USA) —Small Change (IRE) (Danzig (USA))
5841[8] 6894[6]

Coin From Heaven (IRE) *Richard Fahey* 83
3 b f Invincible Spirit(IRE) —Capital Gain (FR) (Bluebird (USA))
1917[7] 2450[5] 3731[8] 4865[5] 6461[2] 6879[6] 7082[4] 7283[14]

Coin Of The Realm (IRE) *Gary Moore* a78 104
5 b g Galileo(IRE) —Common Knowledge (Rainbow Quest (USA))
(1472) 2747[4]

Colamandis *Hugh McWilliams* a57 53
3 b f Lucky Story(USA) —Merry Mary (Magic Ring (IRE))
2496[7] 2837[7] 3407[5] 4018[5] 4649[7] 5041[4] 5815[4] 6332[5]

Cold Quest (USA) *Linda Perratt* a86 63
6 b g Seeking The Gold(USA) —Polaire (IRE) (Polish Patriot (USA))
1204[9] 2293[3] 2433[6] 2670[4] 3164[3] 3500[6] 4082[5] 4188[10] (5331) 5732[4] 6026[6]

Cold Secret *David Elsworth* a23 41
2 ch c Iceman—Dance Sequence (USA) (Mr Prospector (USA))
2638[9] 3000[10]

Cold Turkey *Gary Moore* a83 98
10 bb g Polar Falcon(USA) —South Rock (Rock City)
676[12] 842[4] (982) 1160[2]

Colebrooke *Mark Johnston* 68
2 b g Shamardal(USA) —Shimna (Mr Prospector (USA))
5033[9] 5762[3] 5985[6] 6777[3] 7085[13]

Coleorton Choice *Reg Hollinshead* a73 86
4 ch h Choisir(AUS) —Tayovullin (IRE) (Shalford (IRE))
1032[12] 1516[9] 1888[5] 2883[3] 3584[6] 4345[12] 5154[10] 5297[2] 5495[10] 6256[7] 6358[13] 6625[8]

Colepeper *Mark Johnston* a98 104
3 b c Cape Cross(IRE) —Autumn Wealth (IRE) (Cadeaux Genereux)
2542[3] 2898[5] 3867[7] 5030[2] (5416) 5854[3] 6180[2] 6349[13] 6562[19]

Colinca's Lad (IRE) *Peter Charalambous* a46 64
8 b g Lahib(USA) —Real Flame (Cyrano De Bergerac)
3168[7] (4715) 4969[3] 6125[10]

Collateral Damage (IRE) *Tim Easterby* a92 102
7 b g Orpen(USA) —Jay Gee (IRE) (Second Set (IRE))
1008[16] 1708[7] 2057[6] 2835[6] 3366[2] 3692[10] 4828[10] 5605[6] 6178[6]

Collect Art (IRE) *Andrew Haynes* a69 73
3 b g Footstepsinthesand—Night Scent (IRE) (Scenic)
915[9] 1029[13] 1450[11] (2418) (2634) (2876) 3171[8] 4255[9] 4475[5] 5299[4] 6413[3] 7037[4] 7336[2] 7561[9]

Collection (IRE) *J Moore* 122
5 b g Peintre Celebre(USA) —Lasting Chance (USA) (American Chance (USA))
1568a[6] 7854a[13]

Collesano (IRE) *R Biondi* 98
3 ch c Pearl Of Love(IRE) —Mother's Hope (IRE) (Idris (IRE))
1418a[6]

Collingwood (IRE) *T M Walsh* a87 86
8 br g Machiavellian(USA) —Almaaseh (IRE) (Dancing Brave (USA))
4180a[6] 6907a[7] 7217a[8]

Colloquial *Henry Candy* a90 95
9 b g Classic Cliche(IRE) —Celia Brady (Last Tycoon)
1902[8] 3050[15] (3634) (4320) 4817[3]

Colombian (IRE) *John Gosden* 79
2 bg c Azamour(IRE) —Clodora (FR) (Linamix (FR))
6190[3] ◆

Colonel Carter (IRE) *Brian Meehan* 89
3 br g Danehill Dancer(IRE) —Pina Colada (Sabrehill (USA))
(1381) (2110)

Colonel Flay *Nerys Dutfield* a72 79
6 ch g Danehill Dancer(IRE) —Bobbie Dee (Blakeney)
2228[8] 3475[5] 5011[6] 5722[3]

Colonel Henry *Simon Dow* a46
3 br g Imperial Dancer—Spark Of Life (Rainbows For Life (CAN))
106[8] 274[7] 7716[12]

Colonel Mak *David Barron* 106
3 br g Makbul—Colonel's Daughter (Colonel Collins (USA))
1315[15] 1917[4] 2978[9] 3619[7] 3886[7] 4369[2] (5390) (6175) ◆ 6752[17]

Colonel Percy (IRE) *Mark Johnston*
2 ch c Danehill Dancer(IRE) —Elite Guest (IRE) (Be My Guest (USA))
6293[14]

Colonel Sherman (USA) *Philip Kirby* a66 54
5 bb h Mr Greeley(USA) —Spankin 'n Fannin (USA) (Lear Fan (USA))
36[6] ◆ 410[2] 1188[2] (1303) 1919[3] 7275[11]

Colonial (IRE) *A Fabre* 106
3 b c Cape Cross(IRE) —Elizabeth Bay (USA) (Mr Prospector (USA))
2778a[2] 5802a[4] 7266a[9]

Colony (IRE) *M Al Subouse* a93 99
5 b h Statue Of Liberty(USA) —Funoon (IRE) (Kris)
335a[7] 512a[9]

Colorado Gold *Paul Cole* a77 85
2 ch c Dubawi(IRE) —Yanka (USA) (Blushing John (USA))
1389[9] 1793[2] 2238[5] 2680[6] (3362) 4550[2] 5133a[7] 6088[4] 6870[6]

Colorus (IRE) *Bill Ratcliffe* a84 77
7 b g Night Shift(USA) —Duck Over (Warning)
2[7] 349[5] (492) 520[3] 736[6] 832[3] (1146) 1445[4] 1710[4] 2528[9] 2954[5] 3211[6] 3474[5] 4415[6] 4518[2] 4659[6] 4938[7] 5915[12] 6064[5] (6284) 6858[4] 7326[3] 7405[6] 7866[4] (7984)

Colourful Move *Pat Murphy* a67 63
5 b h Rainbow Quest(USA) —Flit (USA) (Lyphard (USA))
164[14] 420[3] 584[5] 982[3]

Colourful Past (USA) *Mahmood Al Zarooni* 56
2 ch f Street Cry(IRE) —Loving Claim (USA) (Hansel (USA))
2286[3] 2740[7]

Colour Scheme (IRE) *Brian Meehan* a91 86
3 ch c Peintre Celebre(USA) —Lipica (IRE) (Night Shift (USA))
1387[2] ◆ 6815[4] (7338) 7591[5]

Colour Vision (FR) *Mark Johnston* 80
2 gr g Rainbow Quest(USA) —Give Me Five (GER) (Monsun (GER))
5049[11] (5498) 5947[12] 6555[8]

Columba's Boy *Dean Ivory* a5 9
2 b g Avonbridge—Mirasol Princess (Ali-Royal (IRE))
3035[11] 3757[9]

Columbus Circle (JPN) *Futoshi Kojima* 106
4 bb m White Muzzle—Manhattan Fizz (JPN) (Sunday Silence (USA))
7460a[6]

Colzium *Mark H Tompkins* a29 39
2 b g Zafeen(FR) —Mild Deception (IRE) (Glow (USA))
5160[14] 6158[16] 7400[6]

Comadoir (IRE) *Jo Crowley* a81 76
4 ch g Medecis—Hymn Of The Dawn (USA) (Phone Trick (USA))
1044[8] 3980[3] 4693[3] 7719[10]

Come And Go (UAE) *Alan Swinbank* 86
4 b g Halling(USA) —Woven Silk (USA) (Danzig (USA))
1513[6] (1926) 2133[3] 2580[6] 3150[5] 3537[3] 4652[7] 5098[8] 5756[7]

Come Back To Me (FR) *J-Y Artu* 79
2 b f My Risk(FR) —Santander (FR) (Saint Andrews (FR))
4884a[5]

Comedy Act *Sir Mark Prescott Bt* a41 93
3 b g Motivator—Comic (IRE) (Be My Chief (USA))
2221[5] (2501) (2619) 3335[3] 3724[2] (4092) 4827[2] 5273[10] 7061[2]

Comedy Hall (USA) *Mark Johnston* a84 94
3 b c Valid Expectations(USA) —Comedy At The Met (USA) (Metfield (USA))
1315[17] 1523[5] 1917[6] 2260[8] 2815[6] 3599[5]

Come On Buckers (IRE) *Edward Creighton* a62 59
4 ch g Fath(USA) —Deerussa (IRE) (Jareer (USA))
829[7] 2008[5] 2385[5] 2721[9] 3292[13] 5927[9] 6025[2] 6119[5]

Come On Eileen (IRE) *Richard Guest* a15 23
2 b f Diamond Green(FR) —Lady Taverner (Marju (IRE))
5239[7] 6844[10] 7400[8]

Come On Safari (IRE) *Peter Winkworth* a73 78
3 b g Antonius Pius(USA) —Calypso Dancer (FR) (Celtic Swing)
2253[10]

Come On The Irons (USA) *Brian Meehan* a60
2 ch c Birdstone(USA) —Spa (USA) (Strodes Creek (USA))
5893[7] 6333[4]

Cometh *Nick Littmoden* a36 70
2 b f Iceman—Ennobling (Mark Of Esteem (IRE))
3411[11] 4253[8] 4802[2] ◆ (5675) (6130) 6317[9] 7151[4]

Commanche Luke *C Roberts* 42
7 b g Commanche Run—Dawn O'Er Kells (IRE) (Pitskelly)
4912[9] 5148[7]

Commanche Raider (IRE) *Michael Dods* 80
3 b g Tale Of The Cat(USA) —Alsharq (IRE) (Machiavellian (USA))
2069[9] (2768) 3151[6] 4091[4] 4288[6]

Commander Cave (USA) *E Charpy* a97 72
5 b g Tale Of The Cat(USA) —Royal Shyness (Royal Academy (USA))
412a[6] 710a[6]

Commander Veejay *B S Rothwell* 44
2 ch g Piccolo—Poly Blue (IRE) (Thatching)
4116[10] 4241[4] 4747[6] 5020[10]

Commander Wish *Lucinda Featherstone* a52 80
7 ch g Arkadian Hero(USA) —Flighty Dancer (Pivotal)
368[12] 866[8] 1391[10] 2073[3] 2581[8] 3205[8] 3286[8] 3615[10] 4071[7] 4478[9] 5906[8] (6679) 6739[15] 7007[4] 7249[8] 7506[10]

Commandingpresence (USA) *John Bridger* a55 59
4 bb m Thunder Gulch(USA) —Sehra (USA) (Silver Hawk (USA))
14[8] 103[8] 146[4] 319[2] 495[3] 615[6] 829[5] 931[8] 1762[9] 2229[3] 2719[9] 3299[5] 3717[4] 3979[8] 4589[6] 5076[2] 5471[2] 5714[7] 6025[4] 6672[2] 6956[9]

Command Marshal (FR) *Michael Scudamore* a59 66
7 b g Commands(AUS) —Marsakara (IRE) (Turtle Island (IRE))
198[11] 3084[11] 3896[3]

Commando Scott (IRE) *Declan Carroll* a72 75
9 b g Danetime(IRE) —Faye (Monsanto (FR))
3584[10] 4121[8] 4192[6] 4547[5] (5067) 5357[5] (5499) 5789[6] 6107[3] 6394[4]

Commemoration Day (IRE) *Gary Moore* 64
9 b g Daylami(IRE) —Bequeath (USA) (Lyphard (USA))
1849[6]

Commended *B W Hills* 80
2 b c Royal Applause—Granted (FR) (Cadeaux Genereux)
6145[8] 6722[2] 7201[2]

Commerce *Simon Dow* a70 57
3 b f Trade Fair—Well Away (IRE) (Sadler's Wells (USA))
5842[2] (6716) 7253[4] 7638[3]

Commercial (IRE) *Jamie Osborne* a62 30
2 br g Kodiac—Call Collect (IRE) (Houmayoun (FR))
1845[10] 2238[11] 5465[14] 6309[6] 6694[12]

Commissionaire *John Gosden* 87
3 b c Medicean—Appointed One (USA) (Danzig (USA))
1500[4] 2562[8] 2969[7]

Common Touch (IRE) *Richard Fahey* 81
2 ch c Compton Place—Flying Finish (FR) (Priolo (USA))
(4392) 5784[4]

Communicator *Michael Bell* 74
2 b c Motivator—Goodie Twosues (Fraam)
7202[4] ◆

Complete Frontline (GER) *John Weymes* a60 57
5 ch g Tertullian(USA) —Carola Rouge (Arazi (USA))
347[12]

Complexion *Sir Michael Stoute* a71 67
2 b f Hurricane Run(IRE) —Ithaca (USA) (Distant View (USA))
6248[2] 7057[6]

Complicate *Andrew Reid* a38 46
2 b f Storming Home—Gentle Irony (Mazilier (USA))
3517[10] 4658[8] 5147[7] 5660[12] 6153[16] 6635[9]

Compton Blue *Richard Hannon* a52 81
4 b g Compton Place—Blue Goddess (IRE) (Blues Traveller (IRE))
(2024) 2339[4] 3863[14] 4322[5] 5540[9] (5833) 6780[11] 7182[11]

Compton Lad *Donal Nolan* a11 37
7 b g Compton Place—Kintara (Cyrano De Bergerac)
2212[6] 2669[10]

Compton Lass *Brendan Powell* 21
2 br f Compton Place—Susquehanna Days (USA) (Chief's Crown (USA))
3029[9] 3310[7] 4299[8]

Compton Micky *O Brennan* a40 35
9 ch g Compton Place—Nunthorpe (Mystiko (USA))
7131[3] 7376[11]

Compton Park *William Knight* a73 65
3 ch c Compton Place—Corps De Ballet (IRE) (Fasliyev (USA))
1164[4] 1659[3] 2393[4] (6696)

Comptonspirit *Brian Baugh* a66 79
6 ch m Compton Place—Croeso Cynnes (Most Welcome)
1112[3] 1391[11] 2581[3] (3024) 3255[2] (3637) (4043) 4415[3] 4982[2] (5198) 5513[9] 5809[3]

Compton Way *B W Hills* 62
3 b c Compton Place—Never Away (Royal Applause)
2841[9] 3350[8] 3511[2] 3726[5]

Comrade Bond *Mark H Tompkins* a61 62
2 ch g Monsieur Bond(IRE) —Eurolink Cafe (Grand Lodge (USA))
1603[4] 2059[10] 2867[3] 3288[5] 4111[5] 5862[6] 6072[15]

Comrade Cotton *John Ryan* a65 62
6 b g Royal Applause—Cutpurse Moll (Green Desert (USA))
1012[15] 1193[10] 1262[5] 1478[7] 2636[3] 2676[9]

Con Artist (IRE) *Saeed Bin Suroor* a83 100
3 b c Invincible Spirit(IRE) —Hoodwink (IRE) (Selkirk (USA))
(3481) 4100[2] 4757[2]

Concealing *A Fabre* 93
2 b f Dansili—Revealing (Halling (USA))
5226a[4]

Conceptual Art *Michael Bell* a61
3 b c Haafhd—Hasty Words (IRE) (Polish Patriot (USA))
1589[3] 2258[3] 2755[4]

Conciliatory *Rae Guest* a84 83
3 gr f Medicean—Condoleezza (USA) (Cozzene (USA))
2334[6] 3407[4] (4697) (5222) 5662[5] 6556[6]

Concorde Kiss (USA) *Sylvester Kirk* a51
3 b f Harlan's Holiday(USA) —Saraa Ree (USA) (Caro)
216[10] 279[7]

Concurrence (USA) *Mark Johnston* a51 53
3 b c Elusive Quality(USA) —Balanchine (USA) (Storm Bird (CAN))
1164[8] 1804[6]

Condor (DEN) *Soren Jensen* 90
5 b g Kendor(FR) —Liberty (DEN) (Kris)
4641a[6] 6017a[10]

Conduct (IRE) *Sir Michael Stoute* 100
3 gr g Selkirk(USA) —Coventina (IRE) (Daylami (IRE))
(5971) ◆ (6447) ◆

Conducting *Brian Meehan* a75 78
2 b c Oratorio(IRE) —Aiming (Highest Honor (FR))
6146[8] (6704) 7317[5]

Confessional *Tim Easterby* a92 100
3 b g Dubawi(IRE) —Golden Nun (Bishop Of Cashel)
1399[2] 1860[3] (2260) 2545[3] 3218[3] 3673[5] 4541[2] 4685[2] 5250[10] (5742) 5944[9] 7079[12]

Confide In Me *John Akehurst* a63 66
6 b g Medicean—Confidante (USA) (Dayjur (USA))
256[6]

Confidentiality (IRE) *Michael Wigham* a91 81
6 b m Desert Style(IRE) —Confidential (Generous (IRE))
239[3] 360[3] 536[10] 738[5] 790[4] 863[5] 921[3] 990[3] 1084[11]

Confident Warrior (IRE) *Jeff Pearce* 50
5 b g Viking Ruler(AUS) —Fluent (Polar Falcon (USA))
2297[9]

Confront *Sir Michael Stoute* a95 119
5 b g Nayef(USA) —Contiguous (USA) (Danzig (USA))
1025a[13] 1531[6] 3632[7] 4359[6] 5274[5] 5590[4]

Confrontation *David Simcock* a61 63
3 b f War Chant(USA) —Billiard (Kirkwall)
1504[5] 2227[8] 2925[10] 5891[4] 6934[9]

Confuchias (IRE) *Jeremy Gask* a109 94
6 b h Cape Cross(IRE) —Schust Madame (IRE) (Second Set (IRE))
580[3] 887[8] 1032[17] 1491[5]

Conjecture *Robin Bastiman* a37 66
8 b g Danzig(USA) —Golden Opinion (USA) (Slew O'Gold (USA))
187[7] 368[9] 423[7] 839[9] 2779[11]

Conjuror's Bluff *Richard Hannon* 66
2 b c Tiger Hill(IRE) —Portmeirion (Polish Precedent (USA))
6635[6] 6953[3] 7178[12]

Connor's Choice *Andy Turnell* a70 66
5 b g Bertolini(USA) —Susan's Dowry (Efisio)
2246[14] 2647[6] 3056[6] 3556[13] 4130[11] 4936[10] 5586[3] 6713[8] 7195[11] 7425[6] 7761[10]

Cono (IRE) *Tracy Waggott*
2 b g Librettist(USA) —Lilyfoot (IRE) (Sanglamore (USA))
1331[11] 4241[13]

Cono Zur (FR) *Ruth Carr* 76
3 b g Anabaa(USA) —Alaskan Idol (USA) (Carson City (USA))
1969[7] 2863[8] (3597) 3972[2] 4483[5] 4866[2] 5353[5] 5596[7]

Conquest (IRE) *M Al Muhairi* a84 114
6 b g Invincible Spirit(IRE) —Aguinaga (IRE) (Machiavellian (USA))
707a[12]

Conquisto *Steve Gollings* a60 94
5 ch g Hernando(FR) —Seal Indigo (IRE) (Glenstal (USA))
2976[16]

Conry (IRE) *Patrick Morris* a80 89
4 ch g Captain Rio—Altizaf (Zafonic (USA))
1006[19] 5290[10] 6167[7] 6851[11] 7146[4] 7283[2] (7376) 7539[6]

Consider Yourself (USA) *Michael Bell* a76 74
3 rg f Afleet Alex(USA) —Champagne Royale (USA) (French Deputy (USA))
1260[7] 2042[12] 3055[5]

Consistant *Brian Baugh* a65
2 b g Reel Buddy(USA) —Compact Disc (IRE) (Royal Academy (USA))
7408[5] 7578[3] 7999[7]

Constant Contact *Andrew Balding* 93
3 b g Passing Glance—Floriana (Selkirk (USA))
(1781) 2742[11] 3824[13]

Constant Craving *Clive Cox* 70
3 b f Pastoral Pursuits—Addicted To Love (Touching Wood (USA))
(6815)

Consul General *N Al Mandeel* a110 101
6 b h Selkirk(USA) —West Dakota (USA) (Gone West (USA))
338a[3] 630a[3] 818a[3] 1022a[13]

Consult *Sir Mark Prescott Bt* a57 55
3 ch g Dr Fong(USA) —Merle (Selkirk (USA))
2792[2] 3996[3] 4200[5] 5923[3] 6649[6]

Contat (GER) *P Vovcenko* 113
7 br h Diktat—Conga (Robellino (USA))
(1955a) 2805a[3] 4122[7] 4888a[7] 5573a[2]

Contemplate *Dr Jon Scargill* a28 59
4 ch m Compton Place—Billie Blue (Ballad Rock)
1958[5] 3458[3] 6025[11]

Contented (IRE) *Linda Jewell* a49 63
8 b g Orpen(USA) —Joyfullness (USA) (Dixieland Band (USA))
135[9] 242[5] 319[9] 615[4] 691[6]

Contest (IRE) *C Theodorakis* a115 111
6 b h Danehill Dancer(IRE) —Mala Mala (IRE) (Brief Truce (USA))
1081a[9]

Contract Caterer (IRE) *Andrew Balding* 99
3 b c Azamour(IRE) —Nawaji (USA) (Trempolino (USA))
1330[4] 2033[3] 3105[7] ◆ 3824[6] 4470[3] 6203[3]

Contrada *Jim Old* a59 21
5 b g Medicean—Trounce (Barathea (IRE))
4328[10] 4676[9]

Contradiktive (IRE) *Jim Boyle* a37 52
4 b g Diktat—Additive (USA) (Devil's Bag (USA))
1503[10] 2604[2] 3294[2] ◆ 3608[3]

Contredanse (IRE) *Luca Cumani* a73 111
3 bl f Danehill Dancer(IRE) —Ahdaab (USA) (Rahy (USA))
(1582) (2047) ◆ (2575a) 4575[5] 5346a[2] 6950a[4]

Control Chief *Ralph Beckett* 63
2 b g Medicean—Sahara Rose (Green Desert (USA))
3631[9] 6200[13] 6827[7]

Converre *Gerard Butler* a51 51
3 b f Noverre(USA) —Conquestadora (Hernando (FR))
2998[10] 3275[8] 3766[7] 4289[5] 4764[9] 5738[6] 6094[8]

Converti *Simon Burrough* a57 55
6 b g Averti(IRE) —Conquestadora (Hernando (FR))
6051[5]

Conveyance (USA) *Bob Baffert* a112
3 rg c Indian Charlie(USA) —Emptythetill (USA) (Holy Bull (USA))
1714a[15]

Convince (USA) *John Flint* a64 67
9 ch g Mt. Livermore(USA) —Conical (Zafonic (USA))
297[3] 348[8] 451[7] 5377[5] 5580[2] 5875[5] 6261[7]

Convitezza *Mike Sowersby* 29
4 b m Domedriver(IRE) —Condoleezza (USA) (Cozzene (USA))
3776[7] 4168[8] 4866[8]

Convocation (USA) *James Jerkens* a111
4 b h Pulpit(USA) —Shade Dance (USA) (Nureyev (USA))
5780a[4]

Cooke's Bar (IRE) *Noel Lawlor* a31
3 b f Invincible Spirit(IRE) —St Clair Star (Sallust)
7816a[6]

Cookie Crumbles (IRE) *Chris Wall* a76 76
3 ch f Bahamian Bounty—Diaspora (IRE) (Kris)
1654[2] 4115[8] 4521[4] 5122[6] 5833[10] 6935[3]

Cookie Galore *Jeremy Glover* a58 51
3 ch f Monsieur Bond(IRE) —Ginger Cookie (Bold Edge)
(788) 1163[6] 1605[10] 2185[5] 2698[5] 2962[8] 3763[8] 4109[9] 4674[10] 5055[9]

Cool Art (IRE) *John Wainwright* a80 57
4 b g One Cool Cat(USA) —Fee Faw Fum (IRE) (Great Commotion (USA))
1651[5] 1812[4] 2010[3] 2378[6] 3062[8] 3538[11] 4014[7]

Cool Baranca (GER) *P Monteith* 79
4 b m Beat Hollow—Cool Storm (IRE) (Rainbow Quest (USA))
3202[3] 3627[8] 4094[3] 4585[8] 4823[8] 6223[3] 7055[8]

Cool Coal Man (USA) *Nicholas Zito* a110
5 b h Mineshaft(USA) —Coral Sea (USA) (Rubiano (USA))
7365a[4]

Cool Contest (IRE) *R Brogi* 94
3 b f One Cool Cat(USA) —Love Contest (IRE) (Love The Groom (USA))
1419a[11]

Coole Dodger (IRE) *Brian Ellison* a44 61
5 ch g Where Or When(IRE) —Shining High (Shirley Heights)
1115[8] 1296[4] 1891[9] 2527[8] 2655[4] 2851[5] 3180[4] 4082[2] 4939[5] 5244[7] 5596[5]

Coolella (IRE) *John Weymes* a45 57
3 gr f Verglas(IRE) —Tianella (GER) (Acatenango (GER))
1201[2] 2209[2] 2380[6] 3161[4] 3501[4] 4649[5] 5337[3] 5926[8] 6579[9]

Cool Hand Jake *PETER Makin* a87 65
4 b g Storming Home—Monawara (IRE) (Namaqualand (USA))
4023[7] 5716[5] 6252[11] 6701[13]

Cool In The Shade *Paul Midgley* 46
2 b f Pastoral Pursuits—Captain Margaret (Royal Applause)
2832[8] 3237[4] 4338[9] 5818[6]

Cool Judgement (IRE) *Michael Jarvis* 101
5 b g Peintre Celebre(USA) —Sadinga (IRE) (Sadler's Wells (USA))
5387[7] 6131[5]

Cool Kitten (IRE) *William Knight* a30 62
3 b f One Cool Cat(USA) —Zoom Lens (IRE) (Caerleon (USA))
(1643) 2359[5] 3002[11] 3788[6] 4439[5] (4969) 5559[9] 7192[9]

Cool Land (IRE) *Ronald Harris* a53
2 b g One Cool Cat(USA) —Land Ahead (USA) (Distant View (USA))
4323[10] 5269[5] 5701[8] 6500[6] 6711[6] 6867[6] 7210[7]

Cool Luke *Alan Swinbank* a61 42
2 b g Piccolo—Icy (Mind Games)
6047[8] 7335[3]

Coolminx (IRE) *Richard Fahey* 96
3 b f One Cool Cat(USA) —Greta D'Argent (IRE) (Great Commotion (USA))
2437[2] 2978[15] 4369[4] 5088[5] 6000[2] ◆ 6142[12] 7079[19]

Coolnaharan (IRE) *Lee Smyth* a65 58
10 b g Blues Traveller(IRE) —Alma Assembly (General Assembly (USA))
427[7] 469[6] 666[4] 757[6] (Dead)

Coolree Pearl (IRE) *Andrew Haynes* 45
2 b f Mujadil(USA) —Amount (Salse (USA))
1794[6] 2022[8] 2300[5] 2905[4] 3992[3]

Coolree Star (IRE) *Jeremy Glover* a82 76
3 ch g Kheleyf(USA) —Amount (Salse (USA))
117[2] 310[3] 550[5] 766[2] 1086[14] 3904[4] 4121[10] 4662[9] 4834[9] 5409[5] 6330[2] 6515[15] 6996[4]

Cool Star (FR) *A Bonin* 100
5 ch h Starborough—Valverda (USA) (Irish River (FR))
7776a[0]

Cool Strike (UAE) *Andrew Balding* a67 96
4 b g Halling(USA) —Velour (Mtoto)
1544[2] ◆ 2096[12] 2509[4] 3198[8] 3955[3] 5035[3] 5591[15] 6202[5]

Cool The Heels (IRE) *Emma Lavelle* a58 59
5 b g Catcher In The Rye(IRE) —Alinea (USA) (Kingmambo (USA))
1763[13]

Cool Water Oasis *Gary Moore* a60 40
2 b f Elnadim(USA) —Creek Dancer (Josr Algarhoud (IRE))
6278[8] 7123[12] 7485[4] 7718[7] 8011[8]

Cool Wind (IRE) *Mahmood Al Zarooni* a68 39
2 ch f Shirocco(GER) —Golden Anthem (USA) (Lion Cavern (USA))
5369[8] 6071[8]

Coombeshead Lass *John Gallagher* a35
3 ch f Best Of The Bests(IRE) —Riyma (IRE) (Dr Fong (USA))
677[8]

Coordinated Cut (IRE) *Michael Bell* 112
3 b c Montjeu(IRE) —Apache Star (Arazi (USA))
(1310) ◆ 2056[3] 2746[7] 3491a[7]

Cootehill Lass (IRE) *Geoffrey Harker* a36 62
2 b f Ivan Denisovich(IRE) —Heat Alert (USA) (Valid Expectations (USA))
4338[10] 6459[6] 6893[2] 7224[7] 7527[8]

Copex *Kevin Ryan* 35
2 ch f Compton Place—May Light (Midyan (USA))
1360[6] 1463[6]

Copperbeech (IRE) *Saeed Bin Suroor* a101 99
4 b m Red Ransom(USA) —Aynthia (USA) (Zafonic (USA))
4347[5] 5249[3] 7189[4] 7349[12]

Copper Canyon *Andrew Haynes* a68 71
2 ch c Haafhd—Deep Ravine (USA) (Gulch (USA))
5626[2] ◆ 7242[2] 7755[4]

Copper Dock (IRE) *T G McCourt* a100 87
6 b g Docksider(USA) —Sundown (Polish Precedent (USA))
2563[5] 3489a[22] 5127a[8] 6597a[10] 6907a[10] 7217a[6]

Copper King *Tor Sturgis* a60 44
6 ch g Ishiguru(USA) —Dorissio (IRE) (Efisio)
160[2] (388) 614[7]

Copper Penny *David Lanigan* a79 79
3 b f Dansili—Makara (Lion Cavern (USA))
1431[2] ◆ 1881[2] (2434) 3361[7] 4850[5] 5896[7] 6266[9] 6580[3] 6851[6]

Copper Sovereign *Gary Brown* a18 18
8 ch g Compton Place—Lady Kitty (Petong)
470[12]

Copperwood *Michael Blanshard* a77 68
5 ch g Bahamian Bounty—Sophielu (Rudimentary (USA))
(486) (844) 1064[4] (1224) 1509[2] 1877[5] 2750[6] 3262[2] 3851[6] 4024[3] 4260[3] 5634[3] 6085[5] 7047[4] 7483[9] 7724[2]

Copt Hill *Tracy Waggott*
2 b g Avonbridge—Lalique (IRE) (Lahib (USA))
6457[7]

Coracle *Jeremy Glover* 58
2 b g Fasliyev(USA) —Cora Pearl (IRE) (Montjeu (IRE))
4110[11] 5404[7] 6268[7]

Coral Creek (IRE) *M J Grassick* a80 78
6 b m Invincible Spirit(IRE) —Antapoura (IRE) (Bustino)
873[5]

Coral Moon (IRE) *Richard Fahey* a82
2 b f Dubai Destination(USA) —Flying Wanda (Alzao (USA))
(7603)

Coral Shores *Peter Hiatt* a62 69
5 b m Carnival Dancer—Leading Role (Cadeaux Genereux)
162[7] 244[8] 457[8] 4740[7]

Corconte (FR) *S Kobayashi* a79 98
5 b h Sagacity(FR) —Joie De Rose (FR) (Procida (USA))
6593a[7]

Corcovada (IRE) *V Luka Jr* 96
3 ch f Captain Rio—Misty Mountain (IRE) (Namaqualand (USA))
5139a[10] 6765a[7]

Cordell (IRE) *Jim Best* a98 70
5 b g Fasliyev(USA) —Urgele (FR) (Zafonic (USA))
1128[9] 1457[5] 1634[4] 3054[3] 3715[5]

Cordiality *Pat Murphy* a51 56
3 b g Kingsalsa(USA) —Peace (Sadler's Wells (USA))
118[5] 775[8] 1264[7]

Coreliev (IRE) *F Rossi* a83 77
3 b f Fasliyev(USA) —Coremis (FR) (Bering)
926a[4]

Corky Dancer *P Monteith* 60
5 b g Groom Dancer(USA) —Cita Verda (FR) (Take Risks (FR))
4062[8] 4407[4] 5122[8] 6028[5] 6397[6]

Corlough Mountain *Paddy Butler* a50 66
6 ch g Inchinor—Two Step (Mujtahid (USA))
7491[9] 7626[9] 7728[10]

Cornakill (USA) *Kevin Prendergast* a79 97
3 b f Stormin Fever(USA) —It's Heidi's Dance (USA) (Green Dancer (USA))
1952a[4]

Corneille (FR) *J-L Gay* a57 64
5 b h Daliapour(IRE) —Hollandia (FR) (Saumarez)
281a[0]

Cornish Beau (IRE) *Mark H Tompkins* a69 76
3 ch g Pearl Of Love(IRE) —Marimar (IRE) (Grand Lodge (USA))
(1422) 4751[9] 5266[6] 6424[3]

Cornish Quest *Mark H Tompkins* 67
2 ch g Needwood Blade—Persuasion (Batshoof)
2598[4] 5006[3] 5626[5] 6130[4] 6859[4]

Cornus *Alan McCabe* a80 91
8 ch g Inchinor—Demerger (USA) (Distant View (USA))
165[3] 328[3] 505[3] 844[6] 961[6] (1276) (1470) 1641[2] 1802[7] 2113[8] 2206[2] 2592[4] 2647[2] 2957[6] (3065) (3401) (3753) 3919[6] 4413[9] 4551[7] 4832[13] 4995[8] 5495[8] 5884[6] 6198[11] 6256[5] 6358[5]

Coronata (ITY) *P A Picchi* 95
4 b m Guys And Dolls—Corona Ferrea (Sri Pekan (USA))
5108a[10]

Corporal Maddox *Henry Cecil* 105
3 b g Royal Applause—Noble View (USA) (Distant View (USA))
1616[2] 2075[6] 2537[5]

Corran Ard (IRE) *Tim Vaughan* a56 89
9 b g Imperial Ballet(IRE) —Beeper The Great (USA) (Whadjathink (USA))
600[6] 827[6] 994[5]

Corredor Sun (USA) *Nigel Twiston-Davies* a45 67
4 b g El Corredor(USA) —Cozzie Maxine (USA) (Cozzene (USA))
1931[4] 2341[12]

Correlandie (USA) *Jeremy Gask* 23
3 ch f El Corredor(USA) —I'm An Issue (USA) (Cox's Ridge (USA))
2174[11] 2842[10]

Corres (IRE) *David Elsworth* a73 73
3 b g Peintre Celebre(USA) —Kesh Kumay (IRE) (Danehill (USA))
385[7] 618[3] ◆ 1010[3] 1132[3] 2079[4] 2908[7] 3170[3] 6079[4]

Corrib (IRE) *Bryn Palling* a54 56
7 b m Lahib(USA) —Montana Miss (IRE) (Earl Of Barking (IRE))
411[10] 479[8] 666[2] 854[6] 1507[9] 3128[5] (3559) 4434[3] 4992[3] 5585[3] 5704[4] 5873[2] 6860[5] 7199[8]

Corr Point (IRE) *Jamie Osborne* a77 74
3 b g Azamour(IRE) —Naazeq (Nashwan (USA))
(2175) 2439[2] 3444[2] (3639) (4362) 5382[3] 5752[P] 6424[5] 7067[5]

Corsica (IRE) *Mark Johnston* a89 119
3 b c Cape Cross(IRE) —Cedar Sea (IRE) (Persian Bold)
(1299) (1666) ◆ (2070) 2758[3] ◆ 3145[4] (3822) 4456[5] 5945[3]

Corsican Boy *Roger Charlton* a77 55
2 gr g Tobougg(IRE) —Madiyla (Darshaan)
4375[5] 7550[3] ◆ (7962)

Corsicanrun (IRE) *Richard Fahey* 75
2 ch c Medicean—Castara Beach (IRE) (Danehill (USA))
5762[2] (6268)

Corton Charlemagne (IRE) *Rae Guest* a63 77
4 b m King Charlemagne(USA) —Teller (ARG) (Southern Halo (USA))
2094[12] 2751[7]

Corvette *John Jenkins* a63 53
2 b f Araafa(IRE) —Clipper (Salse (USA))
5489[6] 6247[7] 7312[6]

Cosimo de Medici *Hughie Morrison* a95 50
3 b g Medicean—Wish (Danehill (USA))
(73) (183) ◆ 5868[12] 6447[14] 7090[4] 7410[2] 7568[2] 7698[2] 7815[2]

Cosmic Moon *Richard Fahey* 72
2 b f Doyen(IRE) —Cosmic Case (Casteddu)
(5294) 6174[7] 6920[7]

Cosmic Orbit *Roger Curtis* a9 56
3 b g Royal Applause—Susquehanna Days (USA) (Chief's Crown (USA))
1335[9] 2480[10]

Cosmic Sun *Richard Fahey* 102
4 b g Helissio(FR) —Cosmic Case (Casteddu)
2541[10] 3198[7] 3877[4] 4619[4] 5278[13] 5591[12] (6181) 6493[7] 6926[30]

Cosmoledo (FR) *C Biancheri* 54
10 ch g Apple Tree(FR) —Tonic Stream (FR) (Bering)
281a[0]

Cossack Prince *Laura Mongan* a64 73
5 b g Dubai Destination(USA) —Danemere (IRE) (Danehill (USA))
148[7] 497[3] 748[9] 7967[8]

Cote D'Argent *Chris Down* 73
7 b g Lujain(USA) —In The Groove (Night Shift (USA))
1756[4] (2023) 2897[9] 3127[6] 3917[4] 4386[5]

Cotillion *Ian Williams* 94
4 b g Sadler's Wells(USA) —Riberac (Efisio)
1757[6] 2860[2] 3090[5] (4125) 4846[4] 5743[7] 6131[2] 6926[19]

Cotswold Village (AUS) *Michael Appleby* a32 75
4 b f Hawk Wing(USA) —Scenic Bold Dancer (AUS) (Scenic)
(3258) 3853[2] 4533[4]

Cottam Donny *Mel Brittain* 27
2 ch g Doyen(IRE) —Northern Bird (Interrex (CAN))
4702[9] 6458[10] 7058[17]

Cottam Stella *Mel Brittain* 49
2 br f Diktat—Flower Breeze (USA) (Rahy (USA))
4981[4] 5785[10] 6075[9]

Cottonfields (USA) *Heather Main* a68 57
4 rg g Maria's Mon(USA) —Known Romance (USA) (Known Fact (USA))
2417[4] 3968[2] 4428[3] 4700[10] 5254[11]

Cotton Grass *Mark H Tompkins* 52
2 b f Medicean—Astromancer (USA) (Silver Hawk (USA))
7001[7] 7232[13]

Cotton King *Tobias B P Coles* a68 50
3 b g Dubawi(IRE) —Spinning The Yarn (Barathea (IRE))
5209[6] 5493[7] 5815[6] (6314) 7181[13]

Cotton Mill *William Jarvis* 92
3 b g Tiger Hill(IRE) —Mill Line (Mill Reef (USA))
2507[8] (3795) 4805[5] 6423[5] ◆

Cotton Spirit *Richard Fahey* 69
2 ch g Araafa(IRE) —Truly Bewitched (USA) (Affirmed (USA))
2882[6] 3316[2] 4346[7] 5404[5] 6184[4] 6471[7] 6979[7]

Could It Be Magic *Bill Turner* a77 71
3 b c Dubai Destination(USA) —Lomapamar (Nashwan (USA))
1842[3] 2296[5] 2587[9] 3062[3] 4155[2] 8014[2]

Councellor (FR) *Stef Higgins* a97 79
8 b g Gilded Time(USA) —Sudden Storm Bird (USA) (Storm Bird (CAN))
231[5] 324[2] 769[7] 1430[9]

Count Bertoni (IRE) *Steve Gollings* a60 76
3 b g Bertolini(USA) —Queen Sceptre (IRE) (Fairy King (USA))
625[7] (1921) 2898[6] 3661[5] 4128[5] 4742[5]

Count Ceprano (IRE) *Jeff Pearce* a71 75
6 b g Desert Prince(IRE) —Camerlata (Common Grounds)
442[6] 499[8] 613[4] 1171[2] 1772[9] 2419[4] 2596[9] 3323[6] (3862) (4213) (4481) 5071[7]

Countenance Divine *B W Hills* 66
3 ch f Pivotal—Sundari (IRE) (Danehill (USA))
7596[7]

Count Encosta (AUS) *John P Thompson* 105
4 b g Encosta De Lago(AUS) —Sovereign Countess (AUS) (Sovereign Red (NZ))
7032a[6]

Countermarch *Richard Hannon* 68
2 b f Selkirk(USA) —Day Of Reckoning (Daylami (IRE))
7346[5]

Countess Cheval (IRE) *Ben Haslam* 50
2 b f Chevalier(IRE) —Alexander Nitelady (IRE) (Night Shift (USA))
3118[11] 3550[6] 6264[10]

Countess Comet (IRE) *Ralph Beckett* a84 84
3 b f Medicean—Countess Sybil (IRE) (Dr Devious (IRE))
(2585) ◆ 3594[7] 4360[9] 5008[5] 5753[7] 6422[2] ◆ 7253[3]

Countess Ellen (IRE) *Jeremy Gask* a60 66
2 b f Fasliyev(USA) —Princess Ellen (Tirol)
2251[6] 2616[4] 5895[4]

Count Of Anjou (USA) *Richard Hannon* a76 78
3 bb c Lion Heart(USA) —Woodmaven (USA) (Woodman (USA))
1308[3] 1659[2]

Count Of Tuscany (USA) *Charles Egerton* a78 77
4 b g Arch(USA) —Corsini (Machiavellian (USA))
4530[3] 5144[5]

Countrycraft *Sally Hall* a37 32
3 b g Pastoral Pursuits—Turn Back (Pivotal)
1143[6] 7538[8]

Country Road (IRE) *Tony Carroll* a81 74
4 b g Montjeu(IRE) —Souffle (Zafonic (USA))
917[4] 1208[5] 2941[7] 3405[4] 3978[3] 4453[7] 4945[4] (5765) 6331[2] 6829[2] 7089[4] (7463)

Country Waltz *Mick Channon* a52 63
2 b f Pastoral Pursuits—Elegant Dance (Statoblest)
2358[11] 3029[7] 3310[4] 5412[4] 6052[3] (6258) 6674[16] 6740[6] (6989) 7116[7]

Countrywide City (IRE) *Alan Coogan* a64 18
4 b g Elusive City(USA) —Handy Station (IRE) (Desert Style (IRE))
4776[8] 5422[14]

Countrywide Flame *Kevin Ryan* a63 54
2 b g Haafhd—Third Party (Terimon)
2540[5] 3528[3] 4336[6] 4984[2] (5659) 6082[9] 7296[10] 7629[3] 7813[3]

Courageous (IRE) *David Nicholls* 101
4 ch g Refuse To Bend(IRE) —Bella Bella (IRE) (Sri Pekan (USA))
1032[11] 1423[3] 1727[13] 2657[9] 3919[4] 4510[8] 5742[3] ◆ 6142[2]

Courageous Cat (USA) *William Mott* 121
4 b h Storm Cat(USA) —Tranquility Lake (USA) (Rahy (USA))
1025a[9] 6759a[3]

Courchevel (IRE) *Robert Collet* a72 99
3 b f Whipper(USA) —Choc Ice (IRE) (Kahyasi)
(7545a)

Court Applause (IRE) *William Muir* a47 51
2 b c Royal Applause—Forever Blue (Spectrum (IRE))
6190[13] 6497[7]

Court Canibal *M Delzangles* 112
5 b h Montjeu(IRE) —Pas D'Heure (IRE) (Arazi (USA))
953a[5] 1255a[2] 1747a[8] 3045a[2] 4276a[6] 5107a[5]

Court Circle *Sir Michael Stoute* 80
3 ch c Pivotal—Noble Lady (Primo Dominie)
1581[9] 2507[6] (3038)

Court Drinking (USA) *John Best* a54
3 ch c Alke(USA) —Royal Forum (USA) (Open Forum (USA))
655[4] 758[4] 1168[11]

Court Princess *George Baker* a68 35
7 b m Mtoto—Fairfields Cone (Celtic Cone)
2218[6] 2659[9] 3324[12]

Court Vision (USA) *Richard Dutrow Jr* a110 122
5 bb h Gulch(USA) —Weekend Storm (USA) (Storm Bird (CAN))
(6237a) 7364a[5]

Court Wing (IRE) *Richard Price* a52 58
4 b m Hawk Wing(USA) —Nicely (IRE) (Bustino)
1062[6] 1437[13] 2232[6] 2955[13] 4765[6] 5873[5] 6660[2] 7039[6] (7157) 7407[6]

Covert Mission *David Evans* a63 56
7 b m Overbury(IRE) —Peg's Permission (Ra Nova)
210[6] (7759)

Coxwain (IRE) *Mark Johnston* a61 40
3 b c Exceed And Excel(AUS) —Coxwold (USA) (Cox's Ridge (USA))
321[10] 533[7] 915[7] 1048[2]

Cozy Tiger (USA) *Willie Musson* a80 70
5 gr g Hold That Tiger(USA) —Cozelia (USA) (Cozzene (USA))
179[2] ◆ (246) 835[3] (1980) 2723[3] (7765) ◆

C P Joe (IRE) *Paul Green* a55 64
2 br g One Cool Cat(USA) —Trinity Fair (Polish Precedent (USA))
3624[7] 4123[11] 4240[7] 4783[6] 6695[7] 6875[10]

Crabbies Bay *Lisa Williamson* 23
2 b f Indesatchel(IRE) —Multi-Sofft (Northern State (USA))
3072[4]

Crabbies Gold (IRE) *Lisa Williamson* 32
2 ch g Sleeping Indian—Sharpe's Lady (Prince Des Coeurs (USA))
6240[6]

Crack Chichi (FR) *M Seror*
2 gr g Chichicastenango(FR) —Une Etoile (FR) (Take Risks (FR))
7974a[0]

Crackentorp *Tim Easterby* a91 99
5 b g Generous(IRE) —Raspberry Sauce (Niniski (USA))
1151[7] 2096[2] 2541[3] 2976[3] ◆ 3447[12] 3877[3] 4393[9] 5217[13] 5743[4] 6362[8] 7084[11]

Cracking Lass (IRE) *Richard Fahey* 100
3 b f Whipper(USA) —Lady From Limerick (IRE) (Rainbows For Life (CAN))
1310[5] ◆ 2029[6] 2800a[9] 3368[7] 6355[4] (6654) 7350[20]

Crafty Roberto *Brian Meehan* a75
2 ch g Intikhab(USA) —Mowazana (IRE) (Galileo (IRE))
8000[2] ◆

Cragganmore Creek *Dave Morris* a48 46
7 b g Tipsy Creek(USA) —Polish Abbey (Polish Precedent (USA))
90[2] 228[9] 470[4] 1071[7] 2786[5] 4765[15] 7570[9]

Craicajack (IRE) *Edward Creighton* a62 45
3 ch g Avonbridge—Rash Gift (Cadeaux Genereux)
1590[4] 1870[8] 2334[9] 7111[9] 7184[11] 7474[14]

Craicattack (IRE) *Sharon Watt* a70 76
3 ch g Arakan(USA) —Jack-N-Jilly (IRE) (Anita's Prince)
366[5] (594) 772[7] 932[3] (1449) 1594[2] 2415[4] 4031[10] 5197[5] 5424[12] 7403[12]

Craighall *David Simcock* 64
3 b f Dubawi(IRE) —Craigmill (Slip Anchor)
1932[6] 2891[4] 5056[4] 6959[14]

Crazy Bold (GER) *Tony Carroll* a49 44
7 ch g Erminius(GER) —Crazy Love (GER) (Presto)
539[4] 816[6]

Crazy Chris *Bryn Palling* a83 83
5 b m Ishiguru(USA) —Ellopassoff (Librate)
375[2] 546[8] (2823) 3130[2]

Crazy Gracie (IRE) *Julia Feilden* a39
4 b m Beckett(IRE) —Miss Hoofbeats (Unfuwain (USA))
599[6]

Crazy In Love *Bill Turner* a52 54
2 ch f Bertolini(USA) —Fission (Efisio)
1043[6] 1223[6] 1794[2] 2139[6] 2591[3] 3757[6] 4067[4] 5000[12] 6072[2] 6645[6] 7666[3] 7857[7]

Crazy Parachute *Gary Moore* a64 58
3 b g Bahamian Bounty—Shersha (IRE) (Priolo (USA))
1222[6] ◆ 1639[3] 2234[10] 7547[6]

Cream Of Esteem *Robert Johnson* a11 45
8 b g Mark Of Esteem(IRE) —Chantilly (FR) (Sanglamore (USA))
139[7]

Credential *John Harris* a58 51
8 b g Dansili—Sabria (USA) (Miswaki (USA))
5565[7] 6472[14]

Credit Swap *Michael Wigham* a84 99
5 b g Diktat—Locharia (Wolfhound (USA))
1383[15] 1837[8] 4399[6] 4943[12] (6097) 6391[3] 6510[4] ◆ (6562)

Creevy (IRE) *Sylvester Kirk* a51 55
3 b f Trans Island—Kilbride Lass (IRE) (Lahib (USA))
217[4] 279[5] 372[4] 422[11] 475[4]

Crespo Crispado (SPA) *C Boutin* a75 82
2 b c Dubawi(IRE) —Azzuri (GER) (Big Shuffle (USA))
2917a[10]

Cresta Run (GER) *C Von Der Recke* 70
2 b c Ransom O'War(USA) —Cara Dilis (USA) (El Prado (IRE))
6589a[4]

Creyente (IRE) *S Wattel* 92
2 ch f Delfos(IRE) —Yafoul (USA) (Torrential (USA))
(6589a) 7456a[6]

Crianza *Nigel Tinkler* a49 56
4 ch m Polish Precedent(USA) —Red To Violet (Spectrum (IRE))
2463[11] 2899[7] (3227) 3434[10] 4706[15] 5482[6] 5820[11]

Crick Court (FR) *D De Waele*
2 b c Cricket Ball(USA) —Crackcourt (FR) (Crack Regiment (USA))
7009a[0]

Crimea (IRE) *David Nicholls* a67 95
4 b g Kheleyf(USA) —Russian Countess (USA) (Nureyev (USA))
2327[13] 2745[14] 3201[6] ◆ (3529) 3828[5] 4243[10] 4510[3] 4536[5]

Crimson China (USA) *Brian Meehan* a81
2 b c Giant's Causeway(USA) —Parisian Affair (USA) (Mr Greeley (USA))
6843[2] ◆ (7567)

Crimson Cloud *Richard Fahey* a75 67
2 ch f Kyllachy—Calamanco (Clantime)
4896[9] 6646[2] 7065[6] (7418) 7592[2] 7739[4]

Crimson Empire (USA) *Bryan Smart* a34 60
3 b f Empire Maker(USA) —Crimson Palace (SAF) (Elliodor (FR))
4340[4] 5122[4] 6244[3] 6930[11]

Crimson Fern (IRE) *Malcolm Saunders* a96 98
6 ch m Titus Livius(FR) —Crimada (IRE) (Mukaddamah (USA))
948[10] 1206[13]

Crimson Flame (IRE) *Sean Curran* a56 73
7 b g Celtic Swing—Wish List (IRE) (Mujadil (USA))
130[2] 199[2] 228[6] 479[10] 590[9]

Crimson King (IRE) *Terry Clement* a89
9 ch g Pivotal—Always Happy (Sharrood (USA))
4684[13]

Crimson Knot (IRE) *Alan Berry* 79
2 b f Red Ransom(USA) —Green Minstrel (FR) (Green Tune (USA))
1668[5] 2210[2] 3163[2] 3897[3] 4580[5] 4797[2] (5239) 5639[5] 6030[5] 6354[2] 6705[2] 7174[3]

Crimson Mitre *J Jay* a77 67
5 b h Bishop Of Cashel—Pink Champagne (Cosmonaut)
42[6]

Crimson Monarch (USA) *Peter Hiatt* a44 75
6 b g Red Ransom(USA) —Tolltally Light (USA) (Majestic Light (USA))
7781[8] 8010[9]

Crimson Queen *Roy Brotherton* a65 54
3 ch f Red Ransom(USA) —Rainbow Queen (Rainbow Quest (USA))
2899[10] 3635[7] 4251[5] 7505[3] (7684)

Crinan Classic *Clive Cox* a53 10
3 b g Fraam—Black And Amber (Weldnaas (USA))
1211[5] 2122[9]

Crindegun (FR) *P Khozian* a91 99
4 ch h Divine Light(JPN) —Kitty D'Argos (FR) (Ecossais (FR))
640a[2]

Cripsey Brook *Keith Reveley* 59
12 ch g Lycius(USA) —Duwon (IRE) (Polish Precedent (USA))
2464[8] 2610[9]

Crisp (USA) *John W Sadler* a105 102
3 bb f El Corredor(USA) —Cat's Fair (USA) (Sir Cat (USA))
5351a[5]

Cristaliyev *Jim Boyle* a68 68
2 b c Fasliyev(USA) —Desert Cristal (IRE) (Desert King (IRE))
4960[4] 5328[2] 5657[6] 6575[3] 6666[5] 7395[5] 7528[8]

Criterion *Ian Williams* a60 81
5 b g Dr Fong(USA) —Film Script (Unfuwain (USA))
330[5] 6538[9]

Critical Moment (USA) *B W Hills* 110
3 b c Aptitude(USA) —Rouwaki (USA) (Miswaki (USA))
1327[3] 1833[7] 3104[5] (3827) (4574) 5274[7]

Critical Path (IRE) *Andrew Balding* a72 86
4 b m Noverre(USA) —Elemental (Rudimentary (USA))
2256[6] (2922) (4594) 5553[6] 6199[5] 7206[6]

Croce Rossa (IRE) *Jim Boyle* a51 31
2 ch f Golan(IRE) —Van De Cappelle (IRE) (Pivotal)
5841[10] 6161[10] 7256a[12]

Crocodile Bay (IRE) *David Bourton* a65 62
7 b g Spectrum(IRE) —Shenkara (IRE) (Night Shift (USA))
1148[5] 1492[6] 1998[6] 2383[2] (2670) 3062[4] 3132[3] 3690[5] (3768) 3855[4] 4189[6] 4428[8] 4602[10] 4795[6] 5159[2] 5439[4] 6296[8] 7832[2] 7844[9]

Crocodile Canyon (NZ) *Howie Mathews* 88
6 b g Jahafil—The Stranger (NZ) (Omnicorp (NZ))
6946a[10]

Crocus Rose *Harry Dunlop* a81 85
4 b m Royal Applause—Crodelle (IRE) (Formidable (USA))
1544[5] 2975[2] 3634[6] 4125[8] (5070) 5908[10] 6808[4] 7061[4]

Croeso Cusan *John Spearing* a46 76
5 b m Diktat—Croeso Croeso (Most Welcome)
1177[7] 2788[6] 2880[5] (3132) 3377[3] 3905[7] 4488[4] (4680) 4988[6] 6023[6] (6633) 6991[7]

Croeso Mawr *John Spearing* 53
4 ch m Bertolini(USA) —Croeso-I-Cymru (Welsh Captain)
2249[6] 3125[6] 3952[3]

Croeso Ynol *James Evans* 50
4 ch m Medicean—Croeso Croeso (Most Welcome)
2874[11] 4681[11] 4959[7] 5326[8] 5473[4] 5990[6] 6025[8]

Croft Bridge *Philip Kirby* a27 48
3 ch g Avonbridge—Aahgowangowan (IRE) (Tagula (IRE))
6133[10] 6392[7]

Croisultan (IRE) *Liam McAteer* a83 108
4 ch g Refuse To Bend(IRE) —Zoudie (Ezzoud (IRE))
1246a[3] 2570a[3] 4160a[5] 4882a[8] 6009a[2] 6617a[4] 7351[6]

Croix Rouge (USA) *Ralph Smith* a67 57
8 b g Chester House(USA) —Rougeur (USA) (Blushing Groom (FR))
25[6] 120[5] 282[4] 309[4] 383[7] 5216[3] 5625[4] 6502[7]

Cromwellian *Mick Channon* a18
3 b g Tobougg(IRE) —Bint Alajwaad (IRE) (Fairy King (USA))
2011[11] 2333[8]

Cronsa (GER) *S Botti* 101
3 b f Martino Alonso(IRE) —Croa (IRE) (Alzao (USA))
1252a[2] 1713a[2] 2575a[4] 3495a[5] 7109a[8]

Croon *Andy Turnell* a13 47
8 b g Sinndar(IRE) —Shy Minstrel (USA) (The Minstrel (CAN))
3560[10]

Crosby Jemma *Mike Sowersby* 30
6 ch m Lomitas—Gino's Spirits (Perugino (USA))
2610[11]

Crossbill *Y Fertillet* a71 71
7 b g Cape Cross(IRE) —Nightbird (IRE) (Night Shift (USA))
559a[4]

Crossbow Creek *Mark Rimell* a89 81
12 b g Lugana Beach—Roxy River (Ardross)
5996[12]

Cross Culture (IRE) *Andrew Balding* 74
2 b c Cape Cross(IRE) —Margay (IRE) (Marju (IRE))
4263[11] 5629[4] 6158[3]

Cross Examination (USA) *Mahmood Al Zarooni* a72
2 b f Dixie Union(USA) —Crossover (Cape Cross (IRE))
6247[2] 6451[6]

Cross Key (IRE) *Richard Fahey* 69
3 b f Trans Island—Cayman Sunrise (IRE) (Peintre Celebre (USA))
(3073) 3601[3]

Cross Of Lorraine (IRE) *Chris Grant* a38 72
7 b g Pivotal—My-Lorraine (IRE) (Mac's Imp (USA))
1813[2] 2263[8] 2850[11] 3534[6] (4014) (4373) 4644[11] 5422[9] 5760[5] 6398[5] 6965[9] 7170[5]

Cross Section (USA) *Edward Vaughan* a71 57
4 bb m Cape Cross(IRE) —Demure (Machiavellian (USA))
38[3] 194[11]

Cross The Boss (IRE) *Ben Haslam* a66 62
3 b g Cape Cross(IRE) —Lady Salsa (IRE) (Gone West (USA))
267[4] 374[5] ◆ 1392[14] 1971[3] 2503[9] (6335) ◆ 6935[5] ◆

Cross The Creek (IRE) *David Lanigan* a4
2 ch c Shirocco(GER) —Wivenhoe (UAE) (Timber Country (USA))
5893[11]

Cross The Line (IRE) *Alan Jarvis* a78 71
8 b g Cape Cross(IRE) —Baalbek (Barathea (IRE))
975[6]

Crossword *Marco Botti* a54
2 b g Cape Cross(IRE) —Foxilla (IRE) (Foxhound (USA))
7164[8] 7503[8] 7677[2]

Crowded House *B Cecil* a116 110
4 ch h Rainbow Quest(USA) —Wiener Wald (USA) (Woodman (USA))
417a[2] ◆ 609a[2] 1027a[9] 1532[4] 3191[6] 3825[7] 4417a[4] 5577a[2] 6237a[4]

Crown (IRE) *Jo Crowley* a88 88
3 b f Royal Applause—Bolivia (USA) (Distant View (USA))
1376[7] 2120[11] (3779) 5182[4] 6253[11] 7654[6]

Crown Choice *Walter Swinburn* a104 98
5 b g King's Best(USA) —Belle Allemande (CAN) (Royal Academy (USA))
1219[2] ◆ (1481) 1900[10] 2508[3] (2971) ◆ 3869[4] ◆ 4358[16]

Crowned Supreme (IRE) *Liam McAteer* 40
2 b g Balmont(USA) —Best Dancing (GER) (Keos (USA))
6919[8] 7223[5]

Crown Prosecutor (IRE) *Brian Meehan* 107
2 b c Exceed And Excel(AUS) —Miss Brief (IRE) (Brief Truce (USA))
(2594) (3476) ◆ 4468[6] 5219[2] 6192[3]

Crown Ridge (IRE) *Mick Channon* 60
2 b g Oratorio(IRE) —Don't Care (IRE) (Nordico (USA))
2111[4] 2427[4] 2763[4] 3035[2] 3625[3] 4150[5] 4678[3] 5111[5] 5412[5] 6674[5] 6891[7] (7035)

Crucis Abbey (IRE) *James Unett* a70 57
2 b g Acclamation—Golden Ribes (USA) (Charismatic (USA))
4941[6] 5418[6] 5763[3] 6311[4] 6628[5] 7240[3]

Cruise Control *Richard Price* a54 54
4 b g Piccolo—Urban Dancer (IRE) (Generous (IRE))
301[6] 433[5] 540[3] 795[7] 1305[4] 1737[4] 2596[4] 2874[6] 5875[9] 6716[5] 7125[8] 7958[6]

Cruiser *William Muir* 85
2 b c Oasis Dream—Good Girl (IRE) (College Chapel)
4622[6] 4960[2] 5527[4] (6046) 6560[15]

Cruise Racer (IRE) *Patrick Morris* 19
2 gr g Aussie Rules(USA) —Ash Moon (IRE) (General Monash (USA))
3770[5] 7268[13]

Cruise Tothelimit (IRE) *Patrick Morris* a60 76
2 b c Le Vie Dei Colori—Kiva (Indian Ridge)
1066[8] 4432[3] (4782) 5472[7] 6325[8]

Crunched *Michael Bell* a72 77
3 b g Dubai Destination(USA) —Amica (Averti (IRE))
964[3] 1189[6] 1582[12] 2250[3] (2993) 3689[2]

Crushing (IRE) *Julie-Ann Camacho* a53 66
3 b g Kheleyf(USA) —Filmgame (IRE) (Be My Guest (USA))
1461[6] 1970[13] 2962[9]

Cry Alot Boy *Kevin Morgan* a81 79
7 ch g Spinning World(USA) —Intellectuelle (Caerleon (USA))
231[4] 480[7] 676[5] 1512[9]

Cry Fury *Roger Charlton* 66
2 b c Beat Hollow—Cantanta (Top Ville)
6883[11]

Crying Lightening (IRE) *Peter Chapple-Hyam* 102
2 b f Holy Roman Emperor(IRE) —Auction Room (USA) (Chester House (USA))
(2616) ◆ 3141[6] 4305[3] 4842[2] 5322a[4]

Cry Of Freedom (USA) *Mark Johnston* a78 99
4 b g Street Cry(IRE) —Tustarta (USA) (Trempolino (USA))
635[10] 769[9] 981[7]

Cry Of Liberty (IRE) *L Riccardi* 85
3 b f Statue Of Liberty(USA) —Martine Bellis (ITY) (Darshaan)
1419a[7] 6976a[9]

Crystal B Good (USA) *John Best* a34 58
4 bb m Successful Appeal(USA) —Unbridled Run (USA) (Unbridled (USA))
8[11] 674[11] 1642[6] 1914[12]

Crystal Capella *Sir Michael Stoute* a75 120
5 b m Cape Cross(IRE) —Crystal Star (Mark Of Esteem (IRE))
(6928) ◆ 7851a[10]

Crystal Celebre (IRE) *Henry Candy* a64 72
4 b g Peintre Celebre(USA) —Top Crystal (IRE) (Sadler's Wells (USA))
4205[9] 4893[7] 5860[3] 6427[12]

Crystal Etoile *Sir Michael Stoute* 78
2 b f Dansili—Crystal Star (Mark Of Esteem (IRE))
6150[6] ◆

Crystal Feather *Edward Vaughan* a59 67
4 ch m Monsieur Bond(IRE) —Prince's Feather (IRE) (Cadeaux Genereux)
1028[5] 1172[2] 2259[6] 2625[4] 3238[11]

Crystal Gal (IRE) *Kevin Prendergast* 103
3 b f Galileo(IRE) —Park Crystal (IRE) (Danehill (USA))
1036a[3] 2370a[7] 3467a[6] 4178a[10]

Crystal Gale (IRE) *William Knight* a70 71
3 gr f Verglas(IRE) —Mango Groove (IRE) (Unfuwain (USA))
1537[4] 1992[3] 7767[2] 7887[7]

Crystal Glass *Tim Easterby* a40
3 b g Exceed And Excel(AUS) —Cumbrian Crystal (Mind Games)
886[6] 1456[13]

Crystallize *Andrew Haynes* a64 69
4 b g Bertolini(USA) —Adamas (IRE) (Fairy King (USA))
2187[7] 2727[5] 3056[3] 3280[7] 3762[9] 4586[2] 4715[8]
5077[15] 5711[4] 6956[13] 7023[8] 7555[13]

Crystallus (IRE) *Ann Duffield* a68 24
2 b f Diamond Green(FR) —Lominda (IRE) (Lomond (USA))
6980[8] 7268[4] 7517[2] 7598[2] 7997[2]

Crystal Reign (IRE) *Mrs A Corson* a71 74
5 b g Noverre(USA) —Crystal Springs (IRE) (Kahyasi)
1816a[6]

Crystal Set (IRE) *Andrew Haynes* 26
2 gr g Verglas(IRE) —Bayletta (IRE) (Woodborough (USA))
1541[8] 2022[11] 2905[7]

C. S. Silk (USA) *Dale Romans* a105 113
4 bb m Medaglia D'Oro(USA) —Remember The Day (USA) (Settlement Day (USA))
6757a[2]

Cuando Cuanto (FR) *B Goudot* a80 69
6 ch g Chelsea Manor—Embraze Moi (FR) (Vacarme (USA))
690a[5]

Cuban (FR) *J-P Delaporte* a64 53
7 b g Ski Chief(USA) —If Only (FR) (Highest Honor (FR))
1056a[8]

Cuban Piece (IRE) *Tom Dascombe* a71 63
2 b g Azamour(IRE) —Naazeq (Nashwan (USA))
4263[7] 5676[6] 6211[3]

Cuban Quality (USA) *Tom Dascombe* 68
2 bb c Elusive Quality(USA) —Russian Lullaby (IRE) (Galileo (IRE))
3433[7] 4054[4] 4614[7] 5675[5]

Cubism *Milton Harris* a68 65
4 b g Sulamani(IRE) —Diagonale (IRE) (Darshaan)
4990[2]

Cuckoo Rock (IRE) *Jonathan Portman* a54 62
3 b g Refuse To Bend(IRE) —Ringmoor Down (Pivotal)
1432[6] 1977[8] 2460[5] 3739[6] 4733[3] 5414[10] 5729[3]
(7156) 7445[10] 7912[6]

Cuddly *Robert Cowell* 14
2 b f Royal Applause—Smooch (Inchinor)
5640[6]

Cul A Dun (IRE) *John Joseph Murphy* a76 90
4 b g Soviet Star(USA) —Omanah (USA) (Kayrawan (USA))
6910a[10]

Cullofane (IRE) *Patrick Martin* a51 67
5 b m Bold Fact(USA) —Rose Tinted (Spectrum (IRE))
5129a[9]

Cullybackey (IRE) *John Harris* a41 52
5 ch m Golan(IRE) —Leitrim Lodge (IRE) (Classic Music (USA))
7835[8]

Cult Classic (IRE) *Richard Hannon* 78
2 ch c Choisir(AUS) —Fashion Guide (IRE) (Bluebird (USA))
2887[4] 3452[P]

Cultivar *B W Hills* 88
3 b c Xaar—New Orchid (USA) (Quest For Fame)
1029[4] 1824[2] (2290) 2979[7] (3857) 4504[14]

Cultural Desert *Ralph Beckett* 74
2 b g Footstepsinthesand—Border Minstral (IRE) (Sri Pekan (USA))
5255[6] 6153[3] 7201[3]

Cultured Pride (IRE) *Richard Hannon* 80
3 ch f King's Best(USA) —Cultured Pearl (IRE) (Lammtarra (USA))
2253[3] 2510[5] 3158[2] 3464[2]

Cumbrian Knight (IRE) *Malcolm Jefferson* a67 53
12 b g Presenting—Crashrun (Crash Course)
15[4]

Cumulus Nimbus *Richard Hannon* a104 101
3 ch c Muhtathir—Supreme Talent (Desert King (IRE))
(1846) ◆ 2471[8] 3103[14] 3827[5] (4106) 4504[4]
5307[4] 5529[12] 6193[7] 7100[6] 7237[4] 7523[4]

Cunning Act *Jonathan Portman* 68
2 ch g Act One—Saffron Fox (Safawan)
5582[11] 6196[9] 6634[3]

Cunning Plan (IRE) *Peter Chapple-Hyam* a45 51
3 ch g Bachelor Duke(USA) —Madamaa (IRE) (Alzao (USA))
1694[10] 6865[5] 7156[6]

Cup Cake (FR) *B Dutruel* a60 63
3 ch f Bahhare(USA) —Territorial (Selkirk (USA))
548a[4]

Cupid's Glory *Gary Moore* a80 80
8 b g Pursuit Of Love—Doctor's Glory (USA) (Elmaamul (USA))
200[2] (383) 637[4] 765[3] 929[4] 1156[9] 1318[3]
4132[6]

Curacao *Amanda Perrett* a82 85
4 br g Sakhee(USA) —Bourbonella (Rainbow Quest (USA))
1161[3] 1690[2] 2228[4] 3634[4] (4147) 4467[13] 5144[6]

Cure For Sale (ARG) *Raja Malek* a94 108
6 ch m Not For Sale(ARG) —Key Cure (USA) (Cure The Blues (USA))
6757a[8]

Curious Ciara (IRE) *Anthony Mulholland*
3 b f Val Royal(FR) —Morgan Le Fay (Magic Ring (IRE))
5359[4]

Curlew (IRE) *Chris Down* a73 30
4 b g Cape Cross(IRE) —Billbill (USA) (Storm Cat (USA))
2334[2] 6056[10] 7307[11]

Curtains *Simon Dow* a82 91
3 b f Dubawi(IRE) —Voile (IRE) (Barathea (IRE))
(1436) 2712[8] 6198[7] (6438) 6887[4] 7254[7] 7574[6]

Custard Cream Kid (IRE) *Richard Fahey* a50 55
4 b g Statue Of Liberty(USA) —Diniesque (Rainbow Quest (USA))
1967[10] 2382[4] 2859[7] 3370[11] (7649) 7787[6]
7833[3] 7986[10]

Custom House (IRE) *Richard Hannon* a80 80
2 b g Tale Of The Cat(USA) —L'Acajou (CAN) (Gulch (USA))
3844[4] ◆ 4142[2] (5892) 6386[11]

Cut And Thrust (IRE) *Mark Wellings* a78 62
4 b g Haafhd—Ego (Green Desert (USA))
393[2] 552[4] 747[8] 1238[3] 2188[3] 2959[10] 7046[4] ◆
7377[7]

Cuthbert (IRE) *William Jarvis* a78 74
3 ch g Bertolini(USA) —Tequise (IRE) (Victory Note (USA))
107[4] (268) 366[4] 4260[5] 5968[5] 6800[13] 7488[14]

Cutlass Bay (UAE) *Saeed Bin Suroor* a110 119
4 b h Halling(USA) —Dunnes River (USA) (Danzig (USA))
(1255a) (1747a) 2369a[5] 5186[7] 5781a[2] 6606a[6]

Cuts Both Ways (USA) *Paul Cole* a25 52
3 b g Johannesburg(USA) —Wise Investor (USA) (Belong To Me (USA))
1264[9]

Cut The Cackle (IRE) *Paddy Butler* a79 81
4 b m Danetime(IRE) —Alexander Anapolis (IRE) (Spectrum (IRE))
1770[5] 2601[7] 3037[8] 3400[3] (3777) 6085[12]
6374[8] 6637[4] 6858[6] 6985[11] 7180[15] 7539[13]
7837[9] 7892[11] 7991[11]

Cutting Comments *Patrick Holmes* 67
4 b g Acclamation—Razor Sharp (Bering)
1364[7] ◆ 2144[6] ◆ 3946[7] 4285[9] 6189[8] 6295[16]

Cwmni *Bryn Palling* a64 66
4 b m Auction House(USA) —Sontime (Son Pardo)
(423) 773[3] 1547[2] 1843[3] 2246[10] 3556[2] 4130[14]
4478[5] 5267[3] 5875[3] 6952[2] 7195[3] 7519[12]

Cwm Rhondda (USA) *Peter Chapple-Hyam* a16 81
5 b m Gulch(USA) —Frayne (USA) (Red Ransom (USA))
2256[2] 2685[12] 4376[7]

Cyber Star *James Fanshawe* 65
2 b f King's Best(USA) —Spectral Star (Unfuwain (USA))
7001[5]

Cyflymder (IRE) *David Bourton* a88 99
4 b g Mujadil(USA) —Nashwan Star (IRE) (Nashwan (USA))
358[6] 2595[7] 2971[12] 3483[5] 4459[15] 5495[16]
7488[7] 7529[2] 7665[5]

Cygnet *Luca Cumani* 90
4 b g Dansili—Ballet Princess (Muhtarram (USA))
1600[9] ◆ 2044[9] 3627[9]

Cygnet Committee (IRE) *John Wainwright* 54
3 gr f Kheleyf(USA) —Forest Light (IRE) (Rainbow Quest (USA))
1651[7] 1971[4] 2379[6] 2838[4] 3601[5] 3728[5]

Cyril The Squirrel *Karen George* a67 56
6 b g Cyrano De Bergerac—All Done (Northern State (USA))
(2955) 3314[5] (4434) 4914[9] (7450) 7705[2]
7995[3]

Daa'lman *Clive Brittain* a59
2 b f Dansili—Sauterne (Rainbow Quest (USA))
4021[6] 7020[6]

Daas Rite (IRE) *Kevin Ryan* a79 77
2 b g Byron—Sweet Surrender (IRE) (Pennekamp (USA))
1066[3] 1292[5] (2391) 2939[9] 5701[2] (5894)
6174[3] (6453)

Daaweitza *Brian Ellison* a84 89
7 ch g Daawe(USA) —Chichen Itza (Shareef Dancer (USA))
837[3] (897) ◆ 1031[6] 1272[11] 1493[2] 1996[3]
2395[2] 2608[9] 2976[8] 3319[12] 3450[8] 5533[2] (6112)
6567[9] 7352[9] 7698[3]

Dabbers Ridge (IRE) *Ian McInnes* a83 83
8 b h Indian Ridge—Much Commended (Most Welcome)
1115[9] (1293) (1754) 2937[19] 3521[3] (3968)
4354[3] (4713) 5510[3] 6112[3] 6366[5] 7182[15]

Da Bomber (IRE) *James Unett* a53 41
5 b g Tagula(IRE) —Talahari (IRE) (Roi Danzig (USA))
3131[13] 3520[10]

Daboos (USA) *Marcus Tregoning* a80 77
3 b g Mr Greeley(USA) —Touch Love (USA) (Not For Love (USA))
(3816) 6430[4] ◆ 7012[9]

Daddyow *Bryn Palling* 28
2 b g Indesatchel(IRE) —Generous Share (Cadeaux Genereux)
6827[11]

Daddy's Gift (IRE) *Richard Hannon* a91 84
4 b m Trans Island—Lady Corduff (IRE) (Titus Livius (FR))
1076[3] 1438[5] 1580[14] 2331[8] 2823[13] 3557[4]
(4298) 4857[2] 5388[3] 5555[6] 6479[5] (6864) 7037[6]

Dads Amigo *David Brown* 83
2 b c Bertolini(USA) —Pip's Way (IRE) (Pips Pride)
(1749) 2514[5] 3364[3] 7059[4] ◆

Dafeef *Saeed Bin Suroor* 110
3 b c Medicean—Almahab (USA) (Danzig (USA))
(1732) 2546[4] 3591[2] 4140[2] (5088) 5526[3] 6063[2]

Daffodil Walk (IRE) *P D Deegan* a78 85
4 b m Captain Rio—Majestic Launch (Lear Fan (USA))
1676a[13]

Daffydowndilly *Hughie Morrison* a67 76
2 b f Oasis Dream—Art Eyes (USA) (Halling (USA))
6150[5] 6559[19] 7294[3] 7485[2]

Dagda Mor (ITY) *S Botti* 97
3 b c Martino Alonso(IRE) —Bagnolese (ITY) (Cape Cross (IRE))
4185a[3] 6238a[7] 6976a[7]

Dahaam *David Simcock* a89 85
3 b g Red Ransom(USA) —Almansoora (USA) (Bahri (USA))
5086[6] 6151[3] 7680[2] ◆

Dahindar (IRE) *Edward Lynam* a98 89
5 b g Invincible Spirit(IRE) —Daftara (IRE) (Caerleon (USA))
3487a[10]

Daily Double *Martin Bosley* a40 60
4 gr g Needwood Blade—Coffee To Go (Environment Friend)
5962[12] 7487[9] 7649[10] 8023[6]

Daisy Brown *Nigel Tinkler* 48
3 b f Exceed And Excel(AUS) —Hazy Heights (Shirley Heights)
2962[14] 3393[10] 3663[10]

Daisy Dolittle *John Holt* a34
3 b f Tagula(IRE) —Misty Cay (IRE) (Mujadil (USA))
2478[12] 3275[11] 4018[8]

Dajen *David Simcock* a79 87
4 b h Kyllachy—Eau Rouge (Grand Lodge (USA))
84[2] 285[6] (853) (925) (1128) 2885[9] (3956)
5415[6] 6205[11]

Dakiyah (IRE) *Laura Mongan* a90 88
6 b m Observatory(USA) —Darariyna (IRE) (Shirley Heights)
25[13] 2996[5] 3329[4] 4933[3] 5002[2] 6808[3] 7120[2]
7252[3]

Dakota Phone (USA) *Jerry Hollendorfer* a119 107
5 b g Zavata(USA) —World Of Gold (USA) (Spinning World (USA))
5577a[3] (7365a)

Dalanoni (IRE) *James Fanshawe* 4
3 gr g Dalakhani(IRE) —Winona (IRE) (Alzao (USA))
5376[8] 6313[P] (Dead)

Dalarna (GER) *W Hickst* 95
2 b f Dashing Blade—Daily Mail (GER) (Konigsstuhl (GER))
7108a[5]

Dalghar (FR) *A De Royer-Dupre* a105 117
4 gr h Anabaa(USA) —Daltawa (IRE) (Miswaki (USA))
(2778a) 3046[5] 4457[3] 5802a[2] 6390[2] 7278a[3]

Dalhaan (USA) *Luke Dace* a76 75
5 b g Fusaichi Pegasus(USA) —Khazayin (USA) (Bahri (USA))
1484[7] 2495[5] 7252[7] 7465[6] 7778[7] ◆ (8013)

Dallas Legend (IRE) *John Ryan* a11 30
2 ch f Halling(USA) —Legend House (FR) (Grand Lodge (USA))
3029[8] 3411[12] 3778[11] 4103[10] 4554[13]

D'Allziance (IRE) *Jonjo O'Neill* a34 54
4 ch m Masterful(USA) —Allzi (USA) (Zilzal (USA))
3727[8] 4256[8] 5055[3] 6025[9]

Dalradian (IRE) *William Knight* a100 85
4 b g Dansili—Aethra (USA) (Trempolino (USA))
(536) ◆ (740) ◆ 946[8] 1383[7] 1697[11]

Dalrymple (IRE) *Michael Madgwick* a41 53
4 ch g Daylami(IRE) —Dallaah (Green Desert (USA))
6637[9] 7727[9]

Daltaban (FR) *Peter Salmon* a32 48
6 ch g Rainbow Quest(USA) —Daltaiyma (IRE) (Doyoun)
1803[11] 2343[7] 2694[6]

Damascus Symphony *James Bethell* 63
2 b f Pastoral Pursuits—Syrian Queen (Slip Anchor)
2461[6] 2813[6] 4368[2] 4948[4] 5597[8] 6647[9] 6920[8]

Dam D'Augy (FR) *Mlle S-V Tarrou* a84 100
5 ch m Bernebeau(FR) —Cardamome (FR) (Cardoun (FR))
3425a[2] 4165a[3] 6012a[8] 6640a[0] 7800a[7]

Dametime (IRE) *Daniel Mark Loughnane* a81 81
4 b m Danetime(IRE) —Fee Eria (FR) (Always Fair (USA))
(1588) 1903[9] 2696[5] 4524a[13] 6113[11] 7841[6]

Damien (IRE) *B W Hills* a98 107
4 gr h Namid—Miss Shaan (FR) (Darshaan)
1007[4] 1400[2] 2030[7] 3193[23] 4391[6] 5183[12]
5911[4] 6177[11] 6752[2] 7348[9]

Damietta (USA) *Mark Johnston* a77 74
3 b f More Than Ready(USA) —Dixie Eyes Blazing (USA) (Gone West (USA))
1210[4] 1453[5] 2289[8] 3074[4] 3530[4]

Damika (IRE) *Richard Whitaker* a97 103
7 ch g Namid—Emly Express (IRE) (High Estate)
1423[11] 1672[6] (2134) (2465) 3446[12] 3619[6]
4085[2] 4391[14] 4832[3] (5095) 5911[15] 6177[23]
6363[9] 6888[25]

Danadana (IRE) *Luca Cumani* a72 72
2 b c Dubawi(IRE) —Zeeba (IRE) (Barathea (IRE))
6334[5] 6827[3]

Dananna (IRE) *Timothy Doyle* 34
2 b f Ivan Denisovich(IRE) —Dame Noir (IRE) (Alzao (USA))
7256a[17]

Danbrook (IRE) *C W Thornton*
2 ch g Danroad(AUS) —Pip'n Judy (IRE) (Pips Pride)
6566[16]

Dan Buoy (FR) *Richard Guest* a64 75
7 b g Slip Anchor—Bramosia (Forzando)
(76) 114[2] 575[5] 701[3] 982[14] (1273) 1424[2]
2060[11] 2814[2] 3241[6] 4433[8] 6114[2] (6983)

Dance And Dance (IRE) *Edward Vaughan* a91 99
4 b g Royal Applause—Caldy Dancer (IRE) (Soviet Star (USA))
(1862) ◆ 2311[2] 3146[23] 5702[6] (6510)

Dance East *Jeremy Noseda* 99
3 b f Shamardal(USA) —Russian Dance (USA) (Nureyev (USA))
1329[2] (1991) (3271) 3867[3] (4472) 5114[4] 6346[13]

Dance For Julie (IRE) *Ben Haslam* a66 74
3 b f Redback—Dancing Steps (Zafonic (USA))
934[8] 1571[4] 2502[4] 2993[4] 7642[5]

Dance For Livvy (IRE) *Ben Haslam* a47 53
2 br f Kodiac—Dancing Steps (Zafonic (USA))
2990[12] 3665[8] 4709[5] 7630[9]

Danceintothelight *Micky Hammond* a60 71
3 gr g Dansili—Kali (Linamix (FR))
1119[4] 1464[7] 1810[7] 2724[3] 3113[3] 3755[3] 4017[2]
4410[5] 4656[5] 5093[3] 5423[4] 5534[4] (6187) 6650[4]
7145[2]

Dance On By (IRE) *A P O'Brien* 89
3 b f Sadler's Wells(USA) —Kasora (IRE) (Darshaan)
1820[6] 2037a[8] 4178a[14]

Dancerella *David Elsworth* 55
2 b f Norse Dancer(IRE) —Cinder's Prize (Sinndar (IRE))
5488[4] 6804[10]

Dancer's Legacy *Jim Boyle* a67 58
5 ch g Nayef(USA) —Blond Moment (USA) (Affirmed (USA))
1636[7] 2198[12]

Dances With Words (IRE) *Rodney Farrant* a56 52
2 b g Mujadil(USA) —Lyric Dances (FR) (Sendawar (IRE))
3961[11] 4587[5] 5865[11]

Dance Tempo *Hughie Morrison* 80
3 b g Dansili—Musical Twist (USA) (Woodman (USA))
3173[5] 3593[2] 4330[6] 6115[7]

Dance The Star (USA) *Ed Dunlop* a97 92
5 b g Dynaformer(USA) —Dance The Slew (USA) (Slew City Slew (USA))
81[5] (252) 447[4] 697[2] 947[3] 1020[4] 4594[8]
5723[9] 6202[2] 6450[2]

Dance To Destiny *Phil McEntee* a48
2 ch f Carnival Dancer—Java Dawn (IRE) (Fleetwood (IRE))
8000[7]

Dance To My Tune (CAN) *Jerry Hollendorfer* a103 100
6 ch m Stravinsky(USA) —Bandore (USA) (Forty Niner (USA))
4887a[5]

Dance With Chance (IRE) *Walter Swinburn* a47 40
3 b f Kalanisi(IRE) —Persian Lass (IRE) (Grand Lodge (USA))
1504[8] 2336[11] 2909[8]

Danceyourselfdizzy (IRE) *Richard Hannon* 67
2 b c Danehill Dancer(IRE) —Gamra (IRE) (Green Desert (USA))
4954[7] 6146[5] 6474[9] 6988[4]

Dancing Again *Eric Wheeler* a34 41
4 ch m Reel Buddy(USA) —Batchworth Breeze (Beveled (USA))
4364[8] 4835[5] 5377[11] 5580[8] 6025[6] 6773[7] 7440[4]
7757[6]

Dancing All Night *Mick Channon* 53
2 b f Iceman—Sociable (Danehill (USA))
6628[4] 6859[10]

Dancing Belle *John Jenkins* a29 46
5 b m Fasliyev(USA) —May Ball (Cadeaux Genereux)
6865[11] 7690[8]

Dancing Cavalier (IRE) *Reg Hollinshead* a49 29
2 ch g Halling(USA) —El Tigress (GER) (Tiger Hill (IRE))
6628[6] 7242[6] 7335[9]

Dancing David (IRE) *Brian Meehan* 108
3 b c Danehill Dancer(IRE) —Seek Easy (USA) (Seeking The Gold (USA))
1327[2] ◆ 1858[2] 2802a[9] 5185[8] 5741[5]

Dancing Dude (IRE) *Mark Johnston* a60 72
3 ch g Danehill Dancer(IRE) —Wadud (Nashwan (USA))
963[4] 1103[2] ◆ 1380[2] (1572) 2101[5] 3105[11]
3634[7]

Dancing Dynamite (GER) *H-W Hiller*
2 b c Auenadler(GER) —Donatio (IRE) (Royal Academy (USA))
7277a[0]

Dancing Freddy (IRE) *James Given* a76 83
3 b g Chineur(FR) —Majesty's Dancer (IRE) (Danehill Dancer (IRE))
1656[5] 1836[4] 2260[6] 2599[7] 2824[6] 3436[6] 4406[2]
4567[4] 5600[3] 5890[8] 6466[5] (7052) 7405[10] 7525[4]
7635[7] 7784[5] 7984[9]

Dancing Jest (IRE) *Rae Guest* a19 69
6 b m Averti(IRE) —Mezzanine (Sadler's Wells (USA))
(2233) 3416[7] 3862[3] 4860[3]

Dancing Maite *Roy Bowring* a83 89
5 ch g Ballet Master(USA) —Ace Maite (Komaite (USA))
1185[4] 1516[4] 2113[3] 2736[13] 3216[3] 3876[17] (4431)

Dancing Poppy *Rodney Farrant* a56 58
3 b f Kyllachy—Broughtons Motto (Mtoto)
2359[7] 2956[10] 3291[8] 3978[12] 4281[6] 5730[5] 7996[5]

Dancing Queen (IRE) *Mikael Magnusson* a80 71
3 ch f Danehill Dancer(IRE) —Elauyun (IRE) (Muhtarram (USA))
5238[5] 5866[2] 6852[8] 7111[3]

Dancing Rain (IRE) *William Haggas* 71
2 ch f Danehill Dancer(IRE) —Rain Flower (IRE) (Indian Ridge)
7000[2]

Dancing Red Devil (IRE) *Paul Green* 76
3 b f Desert Style(IRE) —Mannsara (IRE) (Royal Academy (USA))
3430[9] 3856[4] 4091[3] 4670[5] ◆ 4858[4] 5421[3]

Dancing Storm *Stuart Kittow* a56 66
7 b m Trans Island—Stormswell (Persian Bold)
4676[2] 5468[2] 6021[3] ◆ 6639[5] 6959[9]

Dancing Sword *Dai Burchell* a65 67
5 b g Groom Dancer(USA) —Kristina (Kris)
938[3] 1303[7] 3278[4] 4223[P]

Dancing Tara *David Evans* 59
2 b f Chevalier(IRE) —Prayer (IRE) (Rainbow Quest (USA))
1375[11] 1773[2] 1999[7] 3386[8] 4802[6] 5630[8]

Dancing Wave *Michael Chapman* a48 65
4 b m Baryshnikov(AUS) —Wavet (Pursuit Of Love)
20[11] 603[6] 1928[5] 2698[4] 4373[8] 4939[14] 7835[7] 7906[7] 7952[4]

Dancing Welcome *Milton Bradley* a67 57
4 b m Kyllachy—Highland Gait (Most Welcome)
498[4] 614[2] ◆ 937[6] 4324[12] 4428[6] 4987[10] 5271[10] 5704[10] 5927[2] ◆ (6119) 6455[3] 6671[4] 7401[4] 7501[5] (7640) 7761[7] 7824[2] 7973[2] 8035[4]

Dancing With Fire *Desmond Donovan* a33 34
2 b f Halling(USA) —Emerald Fire (Pivotal)
1764[5] 1981[6] 2139[5] 2631[4] 3992[6] 4788[6] 6902[11] 7124[11]

Dancourt (IRE) *Saeed Bin Suroor* a75 98
4 b h Cadeaux Genereux—Stage Struck (IRE) (Sadler's Wells (USA))
419a[7]

Dandarrell *Julie-Ann Camacho* a61 62
3 b g Makbul—Dress Design (IRE) (Brief Truce (USA))
1685[7] 2380[7] 3758[3] 5479[2] 6297[5] 7156[3] 7407[3] 7538[2] (7848) 7898[3]

Danderek *Richard Fahey* a86 86
4 ch g Fantastic Light(USA) —Maureena (IRE) (Grand Lodge (USA))
1[6] 433[2] (941) ◆ (1241) 1512[3] 1867[2]

Dandino *James Given* 116
3 br c Dansili—Generous Diana (Generous (IRE))
(1116) (1657) (2742) ◆ (3105) 4456[2] 5945[8] 7615a[11]

Dandy Boy (ITY) *David Marnane* a102 109
4 b h Danetime(IRE) —Fleet Of Light (Spectrum (IRE))
(1900) 3069[21] 4160a[3] 5016a[2] 6089[6]

Dane Cottage *David Evans* a64 68
3 ch f Beat Hollow—Lady Soleas (Be My Guest (USA))
545[3] 728[2] 858[3] 1460[7] 2175[6] 2460[4] (3113) 3264[3] 3513[9] (3640) 3954[3] 4046[3] 4618[8] 4728[4] 5636[6] 6326[3] 6571[5] 6637[3] 6829[7] 7003[9] 7787[5] 7996[8]

Danedream (GER) *P Schiergen* 101
2 b f Lomitas—Danedrop (IRE) (Danehill (USA))
5323a[3] 6609a[6] 7108a[3]

Danehill Dazzler (IRE) *J S O Arthur* a77 80
8 b m Danehill Dancer(IRE) —Finnegans Dilemma (IRE) (Marktingo)
(2162a)

Danehill Deb *Ben De Haan* a9 24
2 ch f Bertolini(USA) —Dance To The Blues (IRE) (Danehill Dancer (IRE))
1073[7] 1375[10] 3126[10] 7016[10]

Danehill's Pearl (IRE) *Tom Dascombe* 103
4 b m Danehill Dancer(IRE) —Mother Of Pearl (IRE) (Sadler's Wells (USA))
957a[5] ◆ 3031[7] 4276a[7]

Danehillsundance (IRE) *David Brown* a91 87
6 b g Danehill Dancer(IRE) —Rosie's Guest (IRE) (Be My Guest (USA))
1669[5] (1752) 1990[6] 2579[2] (3283) 3889[9] 4450[7]

Danehill Sunset (IRE) *B W Hills* a74 78
3 ch c Danehill Dancer(IRE) —Waratah (IRE) (Entrepreneur)
825[4] 1870[3] 3635[3] 5007[3] 5288[2] 6124[6] (6624)

Dane Julia (SAF) *Lee Freedman* 105
7 b m Caesour(USA) —Precious Julia (AUS) (Danehill (USA))
[10]

Daneside (IRE) *W G Harrison* a34 53
3 b g Danehill Dancer(IRE) —Sidecar (IRE) (Spectrum (IRE))
4113[5] 4718[5] 5073[10] 5361[4] 5479[8]

Danger Mulally *Andrew Balding* a77 67
3 b g Governor Brown(USA) —Glittering Image (IRE) (Sadler's Wells (USA))
(33) 386[2] 5286[8] 5859[7] 6289[4]

Dangerous Illusion (IRE) *Michael Quinn* 45
2 bl f Statue Of Liberty(USA) —Miss Dangerous (Komaite (USA))
7002[9] 7207[5]

Dangerous Midge (USA) *Brian Meehan* 121
4 b h Lion Heart(USA) —Adored Slew (USA) (Seattle Slew (USA))
(1378) ◆ 2096[6] 3194[6] (3672) 5220[8] (6148) (7366a)

Daniel Defoe (USA) *Sir Michael Stoute* 60
4 ch g Smart Strike(CAN) —Dear Daughter (Polish Precedent (USA))
1380[6] 3038[7]

Daniella De Bruijn (IRE) *Andrew Haynes* a68 74
3 b f Orpen(USA) —Ardent Lady (Alhaarth (IRE))
1537[9] 1982[9]

Daniel Thomas (IRE) *Paddy Butler* a76 71
8 b g Dansili—Last Look (Rainbow Quest (USA))
348[5] 1628[5] 2167[5] 2602[4] 2894[7] 3508[6] 5867[2] 6165[5] 6288[7] 6669[12] 7184[12] 7543[10] 7787[10]

Dani's Girl (IRE) *Pat Phelan* a85 83
7 bb m Second Empire(IRE) —Quench The Lamp (IRE) (Glow (USA))
232[6] 688[5] 1020[6] 4266[6] 5235[4]

Danish Art (IRE) *Michael Easterby* a76 77
5 b g Danehill Dancer(IRE) —Lady Ounavarra (IRE) (Simply Great (FR))
838[9] 995[7]

Danish Pastry *Hughie Morrison* a49
2 b f Dansili—Foodbroker Fancy (IRE) (Halling (USA))
7312[5]

Danish Rebel (IRE) *George Charlton* a49 67
6 b g Danetime(IRE) —Wheatsheaf Lady (IRE) (Red Sunset)
2295[4]

Danny's Choice *Ralph Beckett* a62 87
3 ch f Compton Place—Pie High (Salse (USA))
2283[4] 2822[5] 3225[3] 4204[8] 6198[9] 6440[5] 6998[10]

Danrose *Ray Craggs*
3 b f Danroad(AUS) —Miss Fleurie (Alzao (USA))
6298[12]

Dansant *Gerard Butler* a101 113
6 b h Dansili—La Balagna (Kris)
(5109a) 5781a[4] 6548a[7] 7297[7]

Dan's Heir *Wilf Storey* a56 63
8 b g Dansili—Million Heiress (Auction Ring (USA))
(2533) 4604[2] 4900[6] 6921[11] 7145[4]

Dansico *Y Durepaire* 107
3 b c Dansili—Chicodove (In The Wings)
2160a[4]

Dansili Dancer *Clive Cox* a113 105
8 b g Dansili—Magic Slipper (Habitat)
(1015) ◆ 1382[9] 2096[7] 3462[5] 5307[11] (7297)

Dansilver *Tony Carroll* a64 67
6 b g Dansili—Silver Gyre (IRE) (Silver Hawk (USA))
6120[7] 6502[2] 6855[2]

Dan's Martha *Ben Haslam* a71
2 b f Tagula(IRE) —Piedmont (UAE) (Jade Robbery (USA))
6459[7] (7681)

Dantari (IRE) *Evan Williams* a63 65
5 b g Alhaarth(IRE) —Daniysha (IRE) (Doyoun)
621[6]

Danube (IRE) *Henry Cecil* a56 58
3 b f Montjeu(IRE) —Darabela (IRE) (Desert King (IRE))
1705[7] 4229[7] 6525[7]

Danube Dancer (IRE) *J S Moore* a60 69
2 b f Balmont(USA) —Green Danube (USA) (Irish River (FR))
1660[6] (1999) 2397[8] 4592[12] 5452[6] 7417[10] 7650[7] 7785[7] 8012[8]

Danum Dancer *Neville Bycroft* a68 62
6 ch g Allied Forces(USA) —Branston Dancer (Rudimentary (USA))
2849[8] 4244[9] 4833[7] 5599[5] 5855[15] 6464[3] 6679[9] 6880[2] 6965[5]

Danvilla *Paul Webber* a72 52
3 b f Dansili—Newtown Villa (Spectrum (IRE))
4874[7] 5366[7] 6290[8] (7315) 7422[2]

Danzig Fox *Michael Mullineaux* a57 57
5 b g Foxhound(USA) —Via Dolorosa (Chaddleworth (IRE))
3122[11]

Danzigs Grandchild (USA) *J S Moore* a64 66
2 b f Anabaa(USA) —Millie's Choice (IRE) (Taufan (USA))
2358[7] 3296[5] 3832[2] 4247[5] 4578[6] (7650)

Danzoe (IRE) *Christine Dunnett* a78 77
3 br g Kheleyf(USA) —Fiaba (Precocious)
1280[2] 1604[2] 2301[4] 2648[2] 2931[3] 3174[6] 3463[2] 4248[9] 4553[6] 4858[5] (5368) 5562[4] (7442) 7754[3]

Da Paolino (FR) *D Prod'Homme* a66 80
3 b g Enrique—Tora Tune (FR) (Green Tune (USA))
547a[5]

Daphne Du Maurier (IRE) *Ed McMahon* a6 34
3 b f Arakan(USA) —Butter Knife (IRE) (Sure Blade (USA))
209[7]

Da Ponte *Pat Eddery* 73
2 b c Librettist(USA) —Naharnook (Fantastic Light (USA))
1930[5] (3209) 4331[4] 5187[6]

Da'Quonde (IRE) *Bryan Smart* 24
2 br f Pivotal—Bobcat Greeley (USA) (Mr Greeley (USA))
2936[9]

Darajaat (USA) *Marcus Tregoning* a85 97
2 bb f Elusive Quality(USA) —Misterah (Alhaarth (IRE))
5078[2] ◆ (5719) 6317[2] 6734[3]

Daraqala (FR) *Paul Murphy*
4 b m Loup Solitaire(USA) —Distale (USA) (Trempolino (USA))
17

Dara Tango (FR) *Mlle S-V Tarrou* a75 100
3 b c Lando(GER) —Dara Dancer (Batshoof)
1254a[4] 1947a[8]

Darcey *Amy Weaver* a80 77
4 ch m Noverre(USA) —Firozi (Forzando)
1641[5] 2009[12] 2331[7] 3061[2] 3309[7] 3830[5] 4237[2] (5698) 6371[4] (6714) 7046[6] ◆ 7209[2]

Darcy's Pride (IRE) *Paul Midgley* a63 61
6 bb m Danetime(IRE) —Cox's Ridge (IRE) (Indian Ridge)
1112[10] 1569[9] 2582[6] 2818[2] 3286[2] 3615[5] 3976[9] 4342[5] 4415[4] 4869[7] 5817[5] 6110[5] (7132) 7300[14] 7402[13] 7473[8] 7807[8] 7936[5]

Daredevil Dan *Mark H Tompkins* 74
4 b g Golden Snake(USA) —Tiempo (King Of Spain)
1133[2] ◆ 1427[3]

Dare It And Smile (USA) *David Simcock* a65 59
2 bb f Bandini(USA) —Grin And Dare It (USA) (Exploit (USA))
6019[4] 6521[2]

Darej (USA) *William Haggas* a84 80
2 ch c Speightstown(USA) —Hi Lili (USA) (Silver Deputy (CAN))
(4759) 5751[2]

Darfour *Martin Hill* a52 58
6 b g Inchinor—Gai Bulga (Kris)
124[10] 1983[4]

Dariana (AUS) *Bart Cummings* 110
4 b f Redoute's Choice(AUS) —Beldarian (IRE) (Last Tycoon)
6947a[18]

Daring Dream (GER) *Jim Goldie* a65 78
5 ch g Big Shuffle(USA) —Daring Action (Arazi (USA))
1673[6] 2206[5] 2451[2] 2670[3] ◆ (3149) 3531[4] 3708[3] (4602) 5213[4] 5407[3] 5852[8] 6108[2] 7063[4] 7227[8]

Dariole (FR) *P Bary* 108
3 b f Highest Honor(FR) —Dzinigane (FR) (Exit To Nowhere (USA))
(1496a) 2373a[7] 6013a[6] 6613a[9]

Darizi (FR) *J-C Rouget* 101
3 gr c Daylami(IRE) —Darakiyla (IRE) (Last Tycoon)
1567a[6] 2557a[7]

Dark And Dangerous (IRE) *Peter Winkworth* a55 58
2 b g Cacique(IRE) —Gilah (IRE) (Saddlers' Hall (IRE))
6087[7] 6843[6] 7386[9]

Dark Dune (IRE) *Tim Easterby* 68
2 b g Diamond Green(FR) —Panpipes (USA) (Woodman (USA))
1886[4] 2498[14] 3281[4] 3657[2] 4984[5] 5597[10] 6300[11]

Dark Energy *Michael Scudamore* a63 59
6 br g Observatory(USA) —Waterfowl Creek (IRE) (Be My Guest (USA))
2811[3] 4042[3] 4386[4] 5722[6]

Dark Eyes (IRE) *Denis Coakley* a83 83
3 b f Camacho—Sherkova (USA) (State Dinner (USA))
1480[4] 1850[7] 3361[6] 5031[9] 5454[10]

Dark Gem *Simon West* 14
3 br f Makbul—Giffoine (Timeless Times (USA))
3728[7] 4673[5]

Dark Lane *Richard Fahey* a83 86
4 b g Namid—Corps De Ballet (IRE) (Fasliyev (USA))
7466[3] 7654[5] 7934[7]

Dark Moment *Ollie Pears* 79
4 gr g Spartacus(IRE) —Dim Ofan (Petong)
2531[9] 3076[2] 3409[2] 3664[2] 4063[8] 4602[9] 5043[8] 5486[6] 5852[9] 6295[10] 6826[2] 7122[8]

Dark Promise *Michael Jarvis* a92 86
3 b f Shamardal(USA) —La Sky (IRE) (Law Society (USA))
5038[2] (6115) 7062[6] 7206[4] (7638) (7881) ◆

Dark Prospect *Noel Meade* a96 91
5 b g Nayef(USA) —Miss Mirasol (Sheikh Albadou)
7823a[2]

Dark Ranger *Tim Pitt* a64 70
4 br g Where Or When(IRE) —Dark Raider (IRE) (Definite Article)
34[8] 361[6] 588[5] (3128) 3369[5] 3894[4] ◆ 5072[9] (5636)

Dark Secret *Jeremy Gask* 78
2 b g Oasis Dream—Princess Miletrian (IRE) (Danehill (USA))
(6145)

Dark Shines *Rod Millman* 20
3 ch g Exceed And Excel(AUS) —Reaf (In The Wings)
3258[7] 4069[14]

Dark Times (IRE) *Mrs K Burke* a26 48
2 b f Statue Of Liberty(USA) —Tafilah (Foxhound (USA))
1510[11] 2420[5] 3058[5] 4150[12] 5434[6] 6891[11] 7404[5]

Darley Sun (IRE) *Saeed Bin Suroor* a61 111
4 b h Tiger Hill(IRE) —Sagamartha (Rainbow Quest (USA))
2469[3] 3102[9] 5220[12] 5909[6] 6621[2]

Darling Buds *Kevin Ryan* a52
3 b f Reel Buddy(USA) —Its Another Gift (Primo Dominie)
127[9] 213[9]

Darling Story (FR) *J-C Rouget* 96
2 b f Nombre Premier—Gondwana (FR) (Hours After (USA))
(5252a)

Dar Re Mi *John Gosden* 120
5 b m Singspiel(IRE) —Darara (Top Ville)
(1026a) 3693[4]

Dar Said *D Camuffo* 89
4 ch h Sulamani(IRE) —Edwardian Era (Bering)
1943a[6]

Darshonin *Jeremy Noseda* a74 61
3 ch g Pivotal—Incheni (IRE) (Nashwan (USA))
180[4] 274[2] 356[2]

Dart *John Mackie* a73 49
6 br m Diktat—Eilean Shona (Suave Dancer (USA))
(3) 41[2] 835[4] 6933[3] 7181[15] (7465) 7632[2]

D'Artagnan (SAF) *Gay Kelleway* a63
3 gr g Count Dubois—Russian Nature (SAF) (Russian Fox (USA))
7786[2] ◆ (7969)

D'Artagnans Dream *Gavin Blake* a65 57
4 b g Cyrano De Bergerac—Kairine (IRE) (Kahyasi)
2645[13] 3214[9] 4257[13]

Darwin Star *Dean Ivory* a65 66
2 gr f Aussie Rules(USA) —Fine Lady (Selkirk (USA))
1429[3] 1930[4] 2338[9] 2642[4] 3331[2] 3959[5] 4040[4] 6308[4] 6666[4] 7040[5]

Daryainur (IRE) *F J Brennan* a38 34
3 br f Auction House(USA) —Maylan (IRE) (Lashkari)
2115[9] 2820[5] 6527[10] 6955[8]

Daryakana (FR) *A De Royer-Dupre* 115
4 ch m Selkirk(USA) —Daryaba (IRE) (Night Shift (USA))
2403a[3] 3494a[3] 4359[4] 6015a[5]

Dashing Beauty (IRE) *Michael Quinlan* a74 71
4 ch m Daggers Drawn(USA) —Near The End (Shirley Heights)
2535[7] (2903) 3289[4] 3980[3] 4255[2] 4704[12]

Dashing Doc (IRE) *David Elsworth* a43 83
3 ch g Dr Fong(USA) —Dashiba (Dashing Blade)
2544[7] 3039[9] 3963[8] 4381[2] 4621[2] (4740) 5084[4] 5918[11]

Dashing Eddie (IRE) *Kevin Ryan* a51 40
2 b c Dubawi(IRE) —Step Too Far (USA) (Cozzene (USA))
7058[13] 7302[10] 7452[7]

Dashwood *Giles Bravery* a54
3 b c Pivotal—Most Charming (FR) (Darshaan)
7086[9] 7596[6] 7960[4]

Date With Destiny (IRE) *Richard Hannon* 93
2 b f George Washington(IRE) —Flawlessly (FR) (Rainbow Quest (USA))
(3861) ◆ 5519[6] 6927[5]

Daudet (GER) *H Blume* a76 50
6 b h Dashing Blade—Diasprina (GER) (Aspros (GER))
273a[0] 459a[2]

Dauntsey Park (IRE) *Tor Sturgis* a60 44
3 ch g Refuse To Bend(IRE) —Shauna's Honey (IRE) (Danehill (USA))
1977[11] 2480[2] 2753[10]

Dauphine (IRE) *Andrew Balding* 71
2 b f Doyen(IRE) —Papillon De Bronze (IRE) (Marju (IRE))
7303[3]

Davana *Bill Ratcliffe* a54 42
4 b m Primo Valentino(IRE) —Bombay Sapphire (Be My Chief (USA))
326[3] 503[10] 599[4] 700[3] 1071[2] 1283[10] 5564[9] 6660[5] 6933[9] 7330[2] 7398[3] 7475[3] 7805[3] 7957[5]

Dave In Dixie (USA) *John W Sadler* a108
3 bb c Dixie Union(USA) —Risk (USA) (Wavering Monarch (USA))
2776a[10]

Davids City (IRE) *Geoffrey Harker* a53 32
6 b g Laveron—Irelands Own (IRE) (Commanche Run)
506[6] 2430[6]

Davids Mark *John Jenkins* a63 55
10 b g Polar Prince(IRE) —Star Of Flanders (Puissance)
103[5] 319[3] 495[2] 721[6]

Dawnbreak (USA) *Saeed Bin Suroor* a71 86
3 ch f Distorted Humor(USA) —Dawn Princess (USA) (Polish Numbers (USA))
333a[7]

Dawn Eclipse (IRE) *T G McCourt* a80 89
5 b m Acclamation—Prima (Primo Dominie)
4269a[6] 5127a[11]

Dawnhill (GER) *John Quinn* a68 11
6 b g Tiger Hill(IRE) —Dateline (GER) (Surumu (GER))
563[5] 889[6] 1117[11]

Dawn Storm (IRE) *John Spearing* a56
5 ch g City On A Hill(USA) —Flames (Blushing Flame (USA))
41[9] 186[8] 1459[6] 1828[9]

Dawson Creek (IRE) *Luke Dace* a56 47
6 ch g Titus Livius(FR) —Particular Friend (Cadeaux Genereux)
969[5] 1301[8] 2965[10] 7727[3] 7878[11]

Dayia (IRE) *Jeff Pearce* a97 99
6 b m Act One—Masharik (IRE) (Caerleon (USA))
1736[5] (2541) 3050[4] 3566[3] 4393[3] 5909[9] 6926[24] (7457a)

Daylami Dreams *John Harris* a60 72
6 gr g Daylami(IRE) —Kite Mark (Mark Of Esteem (IRE))
4252[4] 4933[5] 5646[5]

Day Of The Eagle (IRE) *Luca Cumani* 97
4 b g Danehill Dancer(IRE) —Puck's Castle (Shirley Heights)
(2129) ◆ (2736) ◆ 3146[25] 3920[10] 4843[5]

Days Ahead (IRE) *Eoin Doyle* a65 71
3 ch g Kheleyf(USA) —Hushaby (IRE) (Eurobus)
(4563a)

Days Of Summer (IRE) *Ralph Beckett* a78 81
2 b f Bachelor Duke(USA) —Pharaoh's Delight (Fairy King (USA))
4203[8] (5453) 6176[9]

Days Of Thunder (IRE) *Rob Summers* a26 21
5 b g Choisir(AUS) —Grazina (Mark Of Esteem (IRE))
429[8]

Daytime Dreamer (IRE) *Martin Todhunter* a67 73
6 b g Diktat—Tuppenny (Salse (USA))
(4246) 4511[5] 5019[2] 5355[5]

Dazakhee *Paul Midgley* a62 65
3 ch f Sakhee(USA) —Ziya (IRE) (Lion Cavern (USA))
(717) 1298[3] 1753[3] 2379[2] 2702[4] 3390[3] 5942[5]

Dazeen *Paul Midgley* a46 70
3 b g Zafeen(FR) —Bond Finesse (IRE) (Danehill Dancer (IRE))
783[8] 919[5] 1104[3] 1511[9] 1750[9] 2834[2] 3387[4] 4127[5] 4647[6] 4989[3] 5353[3] 5636[3] 5906[2]

Dazinski *Mark H Tompkins* 93
4 ch g Sulamani(IRE) —Shuheb (Nashwan (USA))
(1525) 3843[7] 4393[2] ◆ 5278[10] 6201[13] 6423[3] 6926[13]

Dazzled *James Fanshawe* a62 54
3 b f Starcraft(NZ) —Morning After (Emperor Jones (USA))
2603[7] 7872[2]

Dazzle The Crowd (IRE) *John Gosden* a79 70
3 b f Montjeu(IRE) —Goncharova (USA) (Gone West (USA))
4397[4] ◆ 5902[3] *6250[2]* 7206[7]

Dazzling Begum *Jeff Pearce* a60 61
5 br m Okawango(USA) —Dream On Me (Prince Sabo)
140[5] (411) 621[10] 813[5] 942[7] 1194[8] 1635[5] *1980[3]* 2302[3] (2811) 3403[3] (3641) 4070[2] 4780[5] 5180[4] 5468[4] 6213[6] 6538[8]

Dazzling Day *Kevin Prendergast* a78 95
3 b f Hernando(FR) —Dazzling Dancer (Nashwan (USA))
2037a[7] 6379a[11]

Dazzling Diamond *B W Hills* 72
2 ch c Compton Place—Zing (Zilzal (USA))
6146[6] ◆ 6626[3]

Dazzling Light (UAE) *Jim Goldie* a69 86
5 bb m Halling(USA) —Crown Of Light (Mtoto)
1101[5] 1629[2] 2096[5] (2313) 2857[6] ◆ 3368[6] 3873[7] 4393[8] 5217[2] 5790[3] 6181[6] 6926[7]

Dazzling Valentine *Alan Bailey* a68 67
2 b f Oratorio(IRE) —Bedazzling (IRE) (Darshaan)
3219[6] 3386[4] *4021[4]* 4437[6] 4614[6] 5374[5] *5699[3]* 6138[3] *(6521) 6745[9] 7066[8]*

Deacon Blues *James Fanshawe* 99
3 b g Compton Place—Persario (Bishop Of Cashel)
1376[3] ◆ 1917[2] (2877) 3791[8] ◆ 4333[2] 5088[2] 5944[3] 6319[11]

Deadly Encounter (IRE) *Richard Fahey* 89
4 br g Lend A Hand—Cautious Joe (First Trump)
(1030) 1672[9] 3150[7] 3448[6] 4394[11] 5242[11] 5937[7] 6394[12] 7056[11]

Deadly Secret (USA) *Richard Fahey* 95
4 b g Johannesburg(USA) —Lypink (USA) (Lyphard (USA))
1990[3] 2708[14] 3366[7] 4371[4] *4894[12]* 5435[9] 6107[5] 6710[7] 7054[8]

Deadly Silence (USA) *Dr Jon Scargill* a77 88
5 b g Diesis—Mill Guineas (USA) (Salse (USA))
7612[5] ◆

Dead Womans Pass (IRE) *Noel Wilson* 40
3 b f High Chaparral(IRE) —Pedicure (Atticus (USA))
1528[6]

Deal Clincher *M McDonagh* a7 50
4 b m Reset(AUS) —Princess Of Garda (Komaite (USA))
3950[8]

Dean Iarracht (IRE) *Tracy Waggott* a60 69
4 b g Danetime(IRE) —Sirdhana (Selkirk (USA))
1103[7] 1887[5] 2207[3] 2583[4] 3025[3] 3369[2] (3614) 4410[6] 4582[5] (6269) (6890) 7228[8]

Dean's Kitten (USA) *Michael J Maker* a111 111
3 ch c Kitten's Joy(USA) —Summer Theatre (USA) (Ide (USA))
1714a[14] 5319a[5]

Dean Swift *Brian Meehan* 84
2 b c Dansili—Magical Romance (IRE) (Barathea (IRE))
6254[4] 7202[2]

Dear Maurice *Tobias B P Coles* a83 91
6 b g Indian Ridge—Shamaiel (IRE) (Lycius (USA))
6523[2] 7093[3] 7421[5] 7525[3]

Deauville Flyer *Tim Easterby* 100
4 b g Dubai Destination(USA) —Reaf (In The Wings)
1484[5] ◆ (2031) (2938) ◆ 3447[5] 3922[3] 5278[7] 6926[14] ◆

Deauville Post (FR) *Richard Hannon* a81 89
3 b c American Post—Loyola (FR) (Sicyos (USA))
949[2] 1314[2] (1515) 2252[7] 5273[16] *6872[2]*

Debejki *D Pajic*
2 b c Where Or When(IRE) —Dream Again (Medicean)
7849a[7]

Debussy (IRE) *John Gosden* a110 122
4 b h Diesis—Opera Comique (FR) (Singspiel (IRE))
631a[9] *800a[10]* (1832) 3068[7] 4390[4] (5321a) 6925[3] 7366a[5]

Decadence *Eric Alston* a24 41
2 b f Singspiel(IRE) —Penny Cross (Efisio)
6353[5] *7335[12]*

December *Christine Dunnett* a61 63
4 b g Oasis Dream—Winter Solstice (Unfuwain (USA))
983[7] 1133[5] *1305[3] 1585[3]* 2010[8] *2417[6] 2870[6] 3214[5] 3566[12] 7487[10] 7604[6]*

December Draw (IRE) *William Knight* a105 98
4 br g Medecis—New York (IRE) (Danzero (AUS))
239[2] (637) 790[2] (921) 1016[3] 1665[5] 2444[6] 3069[9] 4455[8]

Decency (IRE) *Harry Dunlop* a63 69
3 b f Celtic Swing—Siem Reap (USA) (El Gran Senor (USA))
(1163) 1643[2] 2200[5] *2480[6]* 2879[3] (3336) 3677[6] 4589[3] 4744[4] *5669[4] 6292[9]* 6864[14] *7502[8] 7725[5] 7874[5]* 7991[4]

Decent Fella (IRE) *Andrew Balding* a73 91
4 b g Marju(IRE) —Mac Melody (IRE) (Entrepreneur)
2508[6] ◆ 4358[10] 5068[9] 6205[2] 6888[9]

Deceptive *Roger Charlton* a36 26
2 b f Red Ransom(USA) —Fleeting Memory (Danehill (USA))
6843[7] 7094[13]

Dechiper (IRE) *Robert Johnson* a35 75
8 bb g Almutawakel—Safiya (USA) (Riverman (USA))
2085[9] 2500[11] 2765[6] 3370[4] 4511[3] ◆ 4900[5] 5203[5] 5687[9]

Decibel *Kevin Ryan* a53 54
6 ch g Zamindar(USA) —Xaymara (USA) (Sanglamore (USA))
563[6] 718[5] 2131[5] 2533[6] 3028[10]

Decider (USA) *Ronald Harris* a69 50
7 ch g High Yield(USA) —Nikita Moon (USA) (Secret Hello (USA))
79[3] 306[7] 462[3] 727[5] 7764[4] *7952[2] 8037[3]*

Decimate *Andrew Reid* 38
2 br g Teofilio(IRE) —Kirriemuir (Lochnager)
1263[5] ◆

Decimus Meridius (IRE) *Howard Johnson* 60
3 ch g Danehill Dancer(IRE) —Simaat (USA) (Mr Prospector (USA))
1866[5] 5215[11]

Deciphering Dreams (USA) *Richard Dutrow Jr* 103
2 b c Freud(USA) —Plinking (USA) (Talkin Man (CAN))
7360a[11]

Decision *Lawney Hill* a56 88
4 b g Royal Applause—Corinium (IRE) (Turtle Island (IRE))
7553[8] 7815[7]

Decorative (IRE) *Michael Jarvis* 99
3 b f Danehill Dancer(IRE) —Source Of Life (IRE) (Fasliyev (USA))
(2898) 5305[6] 6830[5]

Decree Absolute (USA) *Miss J R Tooth* a57 71
3 bb g Orientate(USA) —Midriff (USA) (Naevus (USA))
1602[3] 2888[12] *3768[4]* 4383[5] *4700[12] 5271[12]*

Dee Cee Elle *Dai Burchell* a55 50
6 b m Groom Dancer(USA) —Missouri (Charnwood Forest (IRE))
2476[3] 3324[13] 3965[8]

Deejan (IRE) *Bryn Palling* a57 65
5 b m Oscar(IRE) —Boleree (IRE) (Mandalus)
2921[6] *3563[8] 4258[6]* 4990[4] (5468) *6373[12]* 7147[6]

Deely Plaza *Jeremy Glover* a69 68
3 b g Compton Place—Anchorage (IRE) (Slip Anchor)
1070[5] 1514[3] 1776[9] 2162a[5] 2624[6] 2919[11] 5357[14] 6255[15] *7023[14]*

Deem (IRE) *J Barton* a92 117
5 gr m Dalakhani(IRE) —Hijaz (IRE) (Sadler's Wells (USA))
(711a) 1026a[4]

Deep And Blue (USA) *J-C Rouget* a64 82
3 b f Toccet(USA) —Catty (USA) (Storm Cat (USA))
5981a[7]

Deep Applause *Michael Dods* 63
2 b g Royal Applause—Deep Deep Blue (Hernando (FR))
3316[5] 5594[4] 6138[9] 6978[10]

Deep South *Mahmood Al Zarooni* a92 92
2 b c Red Ransom(USA) —Dash To The Top (Montjeu (IRE))
(3326) ◆ 4355[5] *4928[3]* 5392[5] *6670[5]*

Defector (IRE) *David Bourton* a82 67
4 b g Fasliyev(USA) —Rich Dancer (Halling (USA))
123[2] 259[6] 1933[10] *2872[5]* 3604[4] *3970[5]* 4501[8] *5027[2] (6207) 6310[3] 6501[5] 7092[12]* 7212[9] 7525[8]

Defence Council (IRE) *Howard Johnson* 81
2 b c Kheleyf(USA) —Miss Gally (IRE) (Galileo (IRE))
2138[2] 2577[2] (3087) 3504[4] 4367[4] 5021[5] 5547[4] 6916[7]

Defence Of Duress (IRE) *Tom Tate* 79
2 b c Motivator—Ultra Finesse (USA) (Rahy (USA))
5040[4] 6036[3] (6873)

Defence Of Realm (GER) *George Baker* a60 54
3 ch g Paolini(GER) —Diktion (GER) (Sendawar (IRE))
1485[8] 2899[8] *3275[7]* ◆ 3829[8] *6871[4] 7476[8] 7634[13] 7669[5]*

Deferto Delphi *Finbar Murtagh* 51
3 ch g Mark Of Esteem(IRE) —Delphic Way (Warning)
4646[5] 5487[5] 6186[6]

Defi (IRE) *Donal Nolan* a75 49
8 b g Rainbow Quest(USA) —Danse Classique (IRE) (Night Shift (USA))
1719[10] 3706[9] 4585[11]

Definightly *Roger Charlton* 113
4 b g Diktat—Perfect Night (Danzig Connection (USA))
(1692) 2992[8] 4832[14] (5551) (5952) ◆ 6175[16] 6783a[2] (7278a) 7459a[9]

Definite Honey *Milton Bradley* 22
4 ch m Baryshnikov(AUS) —By Definition (IRE) (Definite Article)
682[10] 1543[9]

Degly Bo (IRE) *Peter Chapple-Hyam* a47 62
2 b c Araafa(IRE) —Frond (Alzao (USA))
2677[4] 3832[5] 4499[4]

Deha (TUR) *E Sengel* 95
4 gr h Mountain Cat(USA) —Tajarib (IRE) (Last Tycoon)
5803a[8]

Deirdre *John Gosden* a70 101
3 b f Dubawi(IRE) —Dolores (Danehill (USA))
1384[6] 1613[4] 2224[3] 2889[8]

Dejeuner D'Enfer (FR) *Mlle C Cardenne* a65
2 ch g Layman(USA) —Amazing Story (FR) (Cricket Ball (USA))
7647a[7]

Delagoa Bay (IRE) *Sylvester Kirk* a51 21
2 b f Encosta De Lago(AUS) —Amory (GER) (Goofalik (USA))
6770[15] *7198[9] 8000[5]*

Delaney's Dream *David Nicholls* 70
2 gr g Distant Music(USA) —Kilmovee (Inchinor)
6891[3] ◆ 7142[4] (7279)

Delaware Dancer (IRE) *Jeremy Gask* a66 64
3 b f Danehill Dancer(IRE) —Labrusca (Grand Lodge (USA))
5153[RR] (7013) *7613[2]*

Delegator *Saeed Bin Suroor* 123
4 b h Dansili—Indian Love Bird (Efisio)
(6147) 6923[4] 7364a[8]

Delek (IRE) *Jonathan Portman* a58 41
4 b m Marju(IRE) —Dangle (IRE) (Desert Style (IRE))
6903[11]

Delia Eria (IRE) *E J O'Neill* 76
3 b f Zamindar(USA) —Flow Beau (Mtoto)
5805a[10]

Deliberation (IRE) *Ollie Pears* 63
2 b g Antonius Pius(USA) —Pursuit Of Truth (USA) (Irish River (FR))
7142[3] ◆

Delightful Mary (USA) *Mark Casse* a107
2 ch f Limehouse(USA) —Deputy's Delight (USA) (French Deputy (USA))
7342a[3]

Delira (IRE) *Jonathan Portman* a56 63
2 b f Namid—Singing Millie (Millfontaine)
2338[6] 2951[2] 3295[12] 4729[2] *5720[7]* 6259[6]

Della'Alba (IRE) *M Halford* a83 79
3 ch f Namid—Oriane (Nashwan (USA))
7073a[8] 7217a[10]

Della Barba (CHI) *J Barton* a105
4 b h Della Francesca(USA) —Barbera (CHI) (Hussonet (USA))
608a[3] 796a[2] 1023a[8]

Dellarte (FR) *L A Urbano-Grajales* 93
2 b g Della Francesca(USA) —Arletta (USA) (Quest For Fame)
6589a[0]

Dells Breezer *Pat Phelan* a57 60
2 ch g Kheleyf(USA) —Here To Me (Muhtarram (USA))
4695[9] 4871[6] 5204[8] *5720[10] 7592[6] 7691[2]*

Del Mar (FR) *Y Fouin*
4 gr g Highest Honor(FR) —Divination (FR) (Groom Dancer (USA))
221a[0]

Delorain (IRE) *William Stone* a54 53
7 b g Kalanisi(IRE) —Lady Nasrana (FR) (Al Nasr (FR))
15[9] 186[6] 506[3] (584) 1113[3] 1283[8] *1459[5]* 1849[11] *6933[5] 7213[3] 7388[6]* 7634[7]

Delphi Dream *Hughie Morrison* a55
2 b f Oasis Dream—Delphic Way (Warning)
6248[8]

Delta Sky (IRE) *Amy Weaver* a57 57
3 ch f Refuse To Bend(IRE) —Delta Blues (IRE) (Digamist (USA))
283[4] 597[6] 977[9]

Deluxe (USA) *A Fabre* 111
3 b f Storm Cat(USA) —Hasili (IRE) (Kahyasi)
2373a[2] 3015a[4] 7160a[8]

Delvita (FR) *J-V Toux* 106
6 gr m Pinmix(FR) —Very Very Nice (IRE) (Soviet Star (USA))
2804a[4] (3425a) 4165a[6] 6012a[12]

Demeanour (USA) *Lars Bexell* a79 75
4 ch m Giant's Causeway(USA) —Akuna Bay (USA) (Mr Prospector (USA))
(7374a)

Demi Gallant (ITY) *R Menichetti* 57
2 b f Democratic Deficit(IRE) —Suave Gallant (USA) (Suave Prospect (USA))
7850a[7]

Democrate *S Seemar* a81 113
5 b h Dalakhani(IRE) —Aiglonne (USA) (Silver Hawk (USA))
605a[12]

Demo Jo *Michael Wigham* a28 45
4 gr m Auction House(USA) —Demolition Jo (Petong)
872[7] 1302[12]

Demolition *Richard Fahey* a86 99
6 ch g Starborough—Movie Star (IRE) (Barathea (IRE))
871[3] ◆ *1015[12]* 2977[4] 3672[2] 3921[3] 5220[16] 6193[4] 6720[4]

Demonstrative (USA) *Mark Johnston* a88 79
3 b g Elusive Quality(USA) —Loving Pride (USA) (Quiet American (USA))
(524) ◆ *625[2]* ◆ *792[2]* 1297[4] 3450[6]

Dendor *A Dickman* a16 63
6 b g Warningford—Dolphin Dancer (Dolphin Street (FR))
716[7]

Denices Moonlight *Mark Johnston* a44 63
2 b c Monsun(GER) —Denice (Night Shift (USA))
2932[13] 4187[5] *4682[5]* 6810[9]

Denison Flyer *Lawrence Mullaney* 51
3 b g Tobougg(IRE) —Bollin Victoria (Jalmood (USA))
4556[8] 4939[13] 5303[14]

Denny Crane *Edward Lynam* a82 71
4 b g Red Ransom(USA) —Fleeting Rainbow (Rainbow Quest (USA))
7589a[3] (7823a)

Den's Gift (IRE) *Clive Cox* a96 89
6 rg g City On A Hill(USA) —Romanylei (IRE) (Blues Traveller (IRE))
231[2] 324[6] 672[3] 943[5] 1088[7] (1767) 2971[8] *4030[5] 5750[7] 7187[5]* 7560[8]

Denton (NZ) *Jeremy Gask* a93 91
7 b g Montjeu(IRE) —Melora (NZ) (Sir Tristram)
3203[6] *3781[3]* ◆ (4546) (4804) 5475[4] *7292[2] 7815[3]*

Denton Ryal *Sheena West* a54 59
3 b f Trade Fair—My Valentina (Royal Academy (USA))
889[8] 1127[11] 1643[7] *2336[7]* 2633[4] 2909[4] 3055[3] (3478) 3714[4] 4236[8] (4761) *7874[9]*

Deny *Sir Michael Stoute* a59 67
2 ch g Mr Greeley(USA) —Sulk (IRE) (Selkirk (USA))
5491[11] 6190[4] *7112[6]*

Deo Valente (IRE) *Milton Bradley* a67 43
5 b g Dubai Destination(USA) —Pack Ice (USA) (Wekiva Springs (USA))
6773[11]

Depden (IRE) *Richard Price*
2 ch g Captain Rio—Attribute (Warning)
7954[7]

Deportista *John Pickering* a49 14
4 ch m Deportivo—Wadenhoe (IRE) (Persian Bold)
1067[3] 1188[5] 1507[12]

Deportment *Stuart Williams* 88
4 b m Barathea(IRE) —Tina Heights (Shirley Heights)
1176[4] 2155a[7] 5517[6] 6565[14]

Deputy Darling (CAN) *Michael J Maker* a84
4 b m Service Stripe(USA) —Classy Little Bing (USA) (Binalong (USA))
7371a[5]

Derbaas (USA) *A Al Raihe* a105 105
4 b h Seeking The Gold(USA) —Sultana (USA) (Storm Cat (USA))
438a[12] 610a[6] 713a[6]

Derby Desire (IRE) *Desmond Donovan* a60 61
6 b m Swallow Flight(IRE) —Jaldi (IRE) (Nordico (USA))
4298[7] 5209[3] *6671[13]* (7039) 7157[5] *7445[9] 7531[6] 7840[3] 7968[4] 8010[7]*

Derecho *Clive Cox* a68 65
3 gb f Monsun(GER) —Niner's Home (USA) (Forty Niner (USA))
1621[3] 1882[8] *3080[8] 4134[7]*

Derison (USA) *P Monfort* a82 91
8 b g Miesque's Son(USA) —Devolli (Saumarez)
207a[3] 303a[2] 459a[4]

De Roberto (IRE) *F Holcak* 98
7 gr g Barathea(IRE) —Bridelina (FR) (Linamix (FR))
4183a[6]

Dervis Aga (TUR) *S Mutlu* a111
5 b h Unaccounted For(USA) —Mesitas (GER) (Surumu (GER))
(5781a)

Derwisch (IRE) *A Wohler* 101
4 ch g Aeskulap(GER) —Distella (GER) (Big Shuffle (USA))
5542a[5] 7102a[11]

Descarado (NZ) *Gai Waterhouse* 119
4 b g High Chaparral(IRE) —Karamea Lady (NZ) (Lord Ballina (AUS))
(6947a) 7291a[P]

Descaro (USA) *David O'Meara* a64 77
4 gr g Dr Fong(USA) —Miarixa (FR) (Linamix (FR))
3613[8] 4120[2] 4453[6] (5642) (6143) 6750[5] 7061[6]

Desdichas (FR) *T Mercier* a35
5 gr m Astair(FR) —Nada Es Amor (IRE) (Zafonic (USA))
460a[7]

Desertar (FR) *D De Watrigant* a101 95
4 b h Zamindar(USA) —Desert Melody (FR) (Green Desert (USA))
7800a[4]

Desert Auction (IRE) *Richard Hannon* a70 88
3 b g Desert Style(IRE) —Double Gamble (Ela-Mana-Mou)
1913[7] 2324[12] 3271[7]

Desert Bump *Edward Vaughan* a70
4 b m Medicean—Greenfly (Green Desert (USA))
225[6] 920[7]

Desert Creek (IRE) *Sir Michael Stoute* a87 98
4 ch g Refuse To Bend(IRE) —Flagship (Rainbow Quest (USA))
1383[22] *1665[6]* 3692[5] 4828[5] ◆ 5516[2] 5950[5] 6721[19]

Desert Destiny *Chris Grant* a7 71
10 b g Desert Prince(IRE) —High Savannah (Rousillon (USA))
834[4]

Desert Dreamer (IRE) *David Evans* a85 88
9 b g Green Desert(USA) —Follow That Dream (Darshaan)
150[7] 214[4] 1672[11] 1862[10] 2247[9] 2885[5] 3389[8] 4044[7] 4354[16] *8033[7]*

Desert Dust *Giles Bravery* a49 48
7 b g Vettori(IRE) —Dust (Green Desert (USA))
306[7] 495[10]

Desert Emerald (USA) *David Simcock* a54
3 bb g Mr Greeley(USA) —Anita Madden (USA) (Arch (USA))
3563[11]

Desert Fairy *James Unett* a54 46
4 b m Tobougg(IRE) —Regal Fairy (IRE) (Desert King (IRE))
227[4] 354[6] 479[3] 599[2] 816[7] 1919[11] 3032[8] 3684[3] 4070[7] 4514[8]

Desert Falls *Richard Whitaker* a66 84
4 b g Pyrus(USA) —Sally Traffic (River Falls)
1707[9] 2086[9] 2524[8] 2877[8] 3435[10] 4285[6] 4706[6] *5267[5]* 5496[4] *6125[5] 6672[9]* 6864[2] *7195[2] 7376[9]*

Desert Forest (IRE) *Howard Johnson* 73
3 b g Desert Style(IRE) —Minehostess (IRE) (Shernazar)
(2296) 3161[8] 3771[6]

Desert Hawk *Paul Howling* a55 60
9 b g Cape Cross(IRE) —Milling (IRE) (In The Wings)
331[4] 463[3] 590[4] ◆ *661[7] 898[6]*

Desert Hunter (IRE) *Micky Hammond* a54 64
7 b g Desert Story(IRE) —She-Wolff (IRE) (Pips Pride)
1813[3] 2207[2] 2382[2] 3022[8] (3508) 4119[4] 5641[3] 5688[7] 6117[6]

Desert Icon (IRE) *David Simcock* a69 86
4 b g Desert Style(IRE) —Gilded Vanity (IRE) (Indian Ridge)
1580[10] 2247[5] 2926[11] 3845[7] 4551[6] 5076[4] 5473[2] 5995[3] ◆ 6280[3] *6800[8] 7332[6] 7683[4]*

Desert Kiss *Walter Swinburn* a92 95
5 b m Cape Cross(IRE) —Kiss And Don'Tell (USA) (Rahy (USA))
1088[3] 1383[5] *1767[3]* (2703) (3388) 3921[11] 4830[13]

Desert Law (IRE) *Andrew Balding* a76 88
2 b c Oasis Dream—Speed Cop (Cadeaux Genereux)
5381[2] ◆ 6192[7] (6882) ◆

Desert Liaison *Jeremy Noseda* 66
3 b f Dansili—Toffee Nosed (Selkirk (USA))
1127[4] 1431[6] 3289[8]

Desert Location *Michael Bell* a63 56
2 b f Dubai Destination(USA) —Film Script (Unfuwain (USA))
6468[8] 6859[7] *7185[7] 7631[4]*

Desert Mile (IRE) *Ollie Pears* a80 76
7 b m Desert Style(IRE) —Maiskaya (IRE) (Mark Of Esteem (IRE))
211[3] 757[7]

Desert Myth (USA) *Sir Michael Stoute* 110
3 b c Smart Strike(CAN) —Colonella (USA) (Pleasant Colony (USA))
(1314) 1910[5] 4068[2] 4574[2] 5741[4]

Desert Ocean (IRE) *G Collet* a91 100
6 b g Desert Sun—Skerray (Soviet Star (USA))
560a[4] 5802a[5] 6640a[8]

Desert Party (USA) *Saeed Bin Suroor* a118
4 b h Street Cry(IRE) —Sage Cat (USA) (Tabasco Cat (USA))
(797a) 1022a[11]

Desert Phantom (USA) *David Simcock* 98
4 b h Arch(USA) —Junkinthetrunk (USA) (Top Account (USA))
1353[5] 2119[10] 2940[7] 6063[3] 6256[2] 6364[10]

Desert Poppy (IRE) *Walter Swinburn* a78 96
3 b f Oasis Dream—Flanders (IRE) (Common Grounds)
(3736) 4625[2] (5037) 5442[5] 6509[6]

Desert Pride *Stuart Kittow* a65 64
5 b g Desert Style(IRE) —Dalu (IRE) (Dancing Brave (USA))
1171[7] 1477[3] 1799[13] 2589[6] 2919[4] 3510[3]

Desert Recluse (IRE) *Pat Eddery* a97 98
3 ch c Redback—Desert Design (Desert King (IRE))
(589) (775) ◆ (904) 1299[3] 1880[3] (2252) (2976) 3843[6] 4320[4] 5273[11] 6352[2] 7196[2]

Desert Sage *Ralph Beckett* 91
3 ch f Selkirk(USA) —Prairie Flower (IRE) (Zieten (USA))
2076[4] ◆ (2921) 4178a[7] 5273[8] 6199[6] 6535[3]

Desert Sea (IRE) *David Arbuthnot* a103 103
7 b g Desert Sun—Sea Of Time (USA) (Gilded Time (USA))
1821[6] 3447[3] 5220[6] 5908[14]

Desert Shine (IRE) *Michael Bell* 76
2 b f Green Desert(USA) —Star Express (Sadler's Wells (USA))
6511[2] 6803[2]

Desert Strike *Alan McCabe* a74 77
4 b g Bertolini(USA) —Mary Jane (Tina's Pet)
1391[5] 1598[2] 1799[6] 2229[5] 3308[5] 3763[6] 3966[3] 4542[6] 5697[6] 6206[2] 7132[4] (7425) 7468[2] 7542[6] 7683[5] (7754) 7847[2] 8004[9]

Desert Vision *Michael Easterby* a94 84
6 b g Alhaarth(IRE) —Fragrant Oasis (USA) (Rahy (USA))
480[3] 1378[12] 2084[4] 2937[6] 3450[7] 5723[5] 6449[3] 7414[2] ◆

Deslaya (IRE) *Henry Cecil* a48 52
2 b f Green Desert(USA) —Behlaya (IRE) (Kahyasi)
6651[7] 7185[10]

Desperate Dan *Andrew Haynes* a79 83
9 b g Danzero(AUS) —Alzianah (Alzao (USA))
349[2] (750) 810[5] 1583[6] (1965) 2689[7] (3994) 4043[2] (4776) 5212[4] 7033[13]

Dessert Flower (IRE) *F Poulsen*
3 b f Intikhab(USA) —Division Bell (Warning)
6487a[0]

Destination Paris *D Pajic*
2 b c Dubai Destination(USA) —Kyle Rhea (In The Wings)
7849a[14]

Destination Place (IRE) *Maria Rita Salvioni* 94
4 ch m Dubai Destination(USA) —Pleasure Place (IRE) (Compton Place)
6765a[15]

Destiny Blue (IRE) *Jamie Osborne* a67 79
3 b g Danehill Dancer(IRE) —Arpege (IRE) (Sadler's Wells (USA))
1912[7] ◆ 2697[11] 5710[4] (6061) ◆ (6297) ◆ 6692[2] 7042[12]

Destiny Of A Diva *Reg Hollinshead* a72
3 b f Denounce—Royal Fontaine (IRE) (Royal Academy (USA))
7703[2] ◆ 7896[3]

Destiny Of Dreams *Jo Crowley* a69 61
2 b f Dubai Destination(USA) —Valjarv (IRE) (Bluebird (USA))
6803[7] 7248[3] 7723[3]

Destiny Rules *John Berry* 36
3 br f Endoli(USA) —Up The Order (Forzando)
4601[7] 5665[7] 6183[8]

Destiny's Dancer *Ben Haslam* a50 62
3 b f Dubai Destination(USA) —Cybinka (Selkirk (USA))
(998) 1394[5] 1461[8] 1970[5] 2132[4] 2838[2] ◆ 3073[2] 4648[2]

Destinys Dream (IRE) *Tracy Waggott* 92
5 b m Mull Of Kintyre(USA) —Dream Of Jenny (Caerleon (USA))
1398[9] ◆ 1655[3] 1807[2] (1925) 2276[3] (2395) 3060[3] 3432[2] (4389) 5249[7] 6185[3]

Desuetude (AUS) *Saeed Bin Suroor* a100 107
5 gr g Strategic(AUS) —Martella (AUS) (Unbridled's Song (USA))
336a[U] 437a[6] 626a[8] 818a[10]

Detailedassessment *Bryan Smart* 24
2 b f Avonbridge—Lady Eberspacher (IRE) (Royal Abjar (USA))
4286[8] 6071[10]

Detonator (IRE) *M Al Muhairi* a107 105
5 b g Fantastic Light(USA) —Narwala (Darshaan)
627a[8]

Deutschland (USA) *W P Mullins* a91 105
7 b g Red Ransom(USA) —Rhine Valley (USA) (Danzig (USA))
3195[11]

Deva Le Deva (IRE) *Tom Dascombe* a55 63
2 b f Acclamation—Margaux Dancer (IRE) (Danehill Dancer (IRE))
3392[8] 3729[5] 4286[4] 6264[8] 6740[11] 7497[6] 7643[9]

Devastation *John Gosden* 82
2 b f Montjeu(IRE) —Attraction (Efisio)
6468[2] ◆ (7057)

Develop U *Bill Turner* a40 36
3 b g Mutazayid(IRE) —Verdura (Green Desert (USA))
5[7]

Dever Dream *William Haggas* a97 110
3 b f Medicean—Sharplaw Venture (Polar Falcon (USA))
(2174) (2679) (2868) 3375[3] (4145) 5120[2] ◆ (5883) (6887)

Deveze (IRE) *J W Hills* a19 39
2 b f Kyllachy—La Caprice (USA) (Housebuster (USA))
5466[9] 6419[8] 6811[8] 7268[9]

Devilfishpoker Com *Shaun Harris* a48 51
6 ch g Dr Fong(USA) —Midnight Allure (Aragon)
3496[10] 6120[9]

Devilish Lips (GER) *Andreas Lowe* 99
3 b f Konigstiger(GER) —Djidda (GER) (Lando (GER))
1250a[5] 1715a[6] 2404a[6] 3236a[3] 5739a[10]

Devil May Care (USA) *Todd Pletcher* a116 115
3 b f Malibu Moon(USA) —Kelli's Ransom (USA) (Red Ransom (USA))
1714a[10]

Devil To Pay *Alan King* 84
4 b g Red Ransom(USA) —My Way (IRE) (Marju (IRE))
1357[2] 1690[3] 2228[5]

Devil You Know (IRE) *Michael Easterby* a76 86
4 b g Elusive City(USA) —Certainly Brave (Indian Ridge)
2113[13] 2696[6] 6208[8] 6664[12] (7162) 7405[9] 7525[2] ◆ 7683[9]

Devon Delight *Robert Cowell* a23 9
2 b f Araafa(IRE) —To Grace (IRE) (Barathea (IRE))
6469[11] 7126[8]

Devon Diva *Martin Hill* a51 15
4 b m Systematic—General Jane (Be My Chief (USA))
691[12] 1303[10] 1542[8] 1797[11] 3559[12] 6696[6] 7413[3] 7649[3] 7918[6]

Devoted (IRE) *Ralph Beckett* 76
2 gr f Dalakhani(IRE) —Wavertree Girl (IRE) (Marju (IRE))
(5520) ◆ 6160[6]

Devoted To You (IRE) *A P O'Brien* a91 104
3 b f Danehill Dancer(IRE) —Alleged Devotion (USA) (Alleged (USA))
957a[2] ◆ 1726[15] 6007a[9] 6379a[4] 7266a[7]

Dew Reward (IRE) *Eve Johnson Houghton* a45 63
2 b g Aussie Rules(USA) —Shariyfa (FR) (Zayyani)
3332[13] 3577[5] 4253[7] 4802[11] 5709[3] (5807) 6411[4] 6471[11] 6717[13]

Dffar (IRE) *Clive Brittain* 79
2 b c Shamardal(USA) —Deveron (USA) (Cozzene (USA))
2547[5] (3395)

Dhaafer *Alan King* a51 74
3 b g Nayef(USA) —Almurooj (Zafonic (USA))
2128[5] 2548[8] 2899[2] 7043[7]

Dhaamer (IRE) *John Gosden* a71 94
3 ch g Dubai Destination(USA) —Arjuzah (IRE) (Ahonoora)
3220[2] ◆ (4840) (5918) 6565[7]

Dhan Dhana (IRE) *William Haggas* a76 79
3 b f Dubawi(IRE) —Kylemore (IRE) (Sadler's Wells (USA))
(4746) 4944[6] (5654) ◆ 6166[4] 7042[7]

Dhania (IRE) *Chris Gordon* a70 73
4 b g Gulch(USA) —Novograd (USA) (Gentlemen (ARG))
2361[3] 2489[2] 2691[3]

Dhaular Dhar (IRE) *Jim Goldie* a93 106
8 b h Indian Ridge—Pescara (IRE) (Common Grounds)
1006[15] 1900[11] 5435[5] (5736) 6180[8] 6709[6]

Dherghaam (IRE) *Ed Dunlop* a85 98
3 b g Exceed And Excel(AUS) —Alnasreya (IRE) (Machiavellian (USA))
1222[2] (1804) (2348) 3103[26]

Dhhamaan (IRE) *Ruth Carr* a58 61
5 b g Dilshaan—Safe Care (IRE) (Caerleon (USA))
(530) 567[5] 753[3] 1304[2] (1813) 2211[4] 2726[9] 3280[10] (3774) 4197[5] 4704[7] 5357[6] 5732[9] 6188[7]

Diableside (FR) *Y Durepaire* a81 99
4 b g Diableneyev(USA) —Karnatika (FR) (Kendor (FR))
1111a[6]

Diablo Dancer *Tim Walford* 65
2 b f Zafeen(FR) —Faithful Beauty (IRE) (Last Tycoon)
1879[3]

Dialogue *Geoffrey Harker* a89 75
4 b g Singspiel(IRE) —Zonda (Fabulous Dancer (USA))
5357[12] 6117[5]

Diamond Affair (IRE) *Michael Quinlan* a61 56
3 b f Namid—Subtle Affair (IRE) (Barathea (IRE))
5206[8] 5726[8] 6285[9]

Diamond Blade *Tim Easterby* a73 68
4 ch g Needwood Blade—Branston Gem (So Factual (USA))
1147[2] 1524[6] 5920[8] 6572[11]

Diamond Bob *Ed Dunlop* 5
2 b g Diamond Green(FR) —Songsheet (Dominion)
6474[10]

Diamond Boy (FR) *F Doumen* a67 102
4 b h Mansonnien(FR) —Gold Or Silver (FR) (Glint Of Gold)
4566a[9]

Diamond Charlie (IRE) *Simon Dow* 77
2 br c Diamond Green(FR) —Rosy Lydgate (Last Tycoon)
2245[4] 2680[3] 3310[3] (4743) 5992[4]

Diamond City (IRE) *Deborah Sanderson* a27 44
2 b g Diamond Green(FR) —Easter Girl (Efisio)
6128[8] 6742[9]

Diamond Daisy (IRE) *Ann Duffield* a53 76
4 b m Elnadim(USA) —Charlotte's Dancer (Kris)
3063[6] 3508[5] 3876[15] 4394[16] 7068[7] 7501[9]

Diamond Duchess (IRE) *David Lanigan* a75 92
3 ch f Dubawi(IRE) —Tarakana (USA) (Shahrastani (USA))
1362[3] 2042[3] (2935) (6691) 7053[4]

Diamond Geezah (IRE) *B W Hills* 91
2 b c Diamond Green(FR) —Lanark Belle (Selkirk (USA))
1009[4] ◆ 1389[2] 1835[4] 3051[8] (3705) 4539[2] 5245[6] 5912[3]

Diamondgeezer Luke (IRE) *Patrick Morris* a48 68
3 b g War Chant(USA) —Banquise (IRE) (Last Tycoon)
2289[9] 2587[7] 3957[5] 4127[4] 4408[6] 5271[13] 6243[7] 7005[10]

Diamond Johnny G (USA) *Edward Creighton* a77 77
3 b g Omega Code(USA) —My Dancin Girl (USA) (Sun War Dancer (USA))
445[2] 489[4] 807[6] 1345[2] 1599[2] (1639) 2807[4] 2972[6] 3417[4] (3856) 4541[11] 5309[7] 5417[5]

Diamond Laura *Doug Watson* a78 85
3 gr f Lucky Story(USA) —Erracht (Emarati (USA))
333a[6] 514a[14]

Diamond Max (GER) *Manfred Hofer* 92
3 b g Big Shuffle(USA) —Diamond Sun (Primo Dominie)
6487a[0]

Diamond MM (IRE) *Alan Swinbank* a45
4 b m Sakhee(USA) —Equity Princess (Warning)
4893[6]

Diamond Penny (IRE) *Paul Cole* a68 86
2 b g Diamond Green(FR) —Penny Fan (Nomination)
3326[5] 3832[4] 4346[2] (5047) 5690[2] 6174[4]

Diamond Sunrise (IRE) *Noel Wilson* a46
2 b f Diamond Green(FR) —Sunrise (IRE) (Sri Pekan (USA))
7279[8] 7392[5]

Diamond Surprise *Roger Curtis* a70 59
4 b m Mark Of Esteem(IRE) —Lucky Dip (Tirol)
602[8]

Diamond Twister (USA) *John Best* a74 72
4 b h Omega Code(USA) —King's Pact (USA) (Slewacide (USA))
588[8] 1225[2] 1645[2] 1883[7] 2285[10] 3911[9] 4201[6] 4361[2] (4793) 5208[5] 5457[4] 5680[2] 6289[3] 6472[5] 7111[5] 7561[10]

Diamond Vine (IRE) *Ronald Harris* a50 79
2 b c Diamond Green(FR) —Glasnas Giant (Giant's Causeway (USA))
2163[4] 2687[4] 3053[7] 4066[6] 4277[3] (4678) 5111[3] 5874[2] 6426[10] (6769) 6916[2] 7347[8]

Diam Queen (GER) *Luca Cumani* a87 93
3 b f Lando(GER) —Dance Solo (Sadler's Wells (USA))
1330[11] 2889[6]

Diane's Choice *Gay Kelleway* a61 63
7 ch m Komaite(USA) —Ramajana (USA) (Shadeed (USA))
(146) 235[6] 499[6] (674) 693[4] 961[4] 1131[4]

Diapason (IRE) *Tom Dascombe* a79 76
4 b m Mull Of Kintyre(USA) —Suaad (IRE) (Fools Holme (USA))
(125) 225[3] 2475[8] 3505[3] ◆ 3947[8] 4988[10]

Diatribe *W Baltromei* 95
3 b f Tertullian(USA) —Diacada (GER) (Cadeaux Genereux)
1715a[11] 6409a[3] 7545a[7]

Dibir (FR) *J-C Rouget* a88 89
3 gr c Shamardal(USA) —Diasilixa (FR) (Linamix (FR))
3933a[9]

Dicey Affair *Gary Moore* a65 58
4 b m Medicean—Lucky Dice (Perugino (USA))
135[2] 320[6] 423[11]

Dichoh *Michael Madgwick* a82 67
7 b g Diktat—Hoh Dancer (Indian Ridge)
230[3] 342[2] 827[3] 929[7] 1301[2] 2167[8] 2415[3] 3054[4] 3338[4] 4366[3] 4870[4] 5866[9] 6479[8] 7255[5] 7597[7] 7725[6] 7878[4] 7991[2]

Dickie Le Davoir *David Bourton* a62 82
6 b g Kyllachy—Downeaster Alexa (USA) (Red Ryder (USA))
243[2] 296[8] 325[2] 404[4] 442[10] 1270[12] 2184[13] 2206[3] 2504[3] 2671[4] 2817[2] 3129[5] 3216[9] 3753[7] 4084[5] 4285[2] 4404[8] 4478[2] (4947) 5048[5] 5242[10] 6110[12] 7701[6]

Dickie's Lad (IRE) *Kevin Ryan* 58
2 b c Diamond Green(FR) —Shadow Mountain (Selkirk (USA))
6878[5]

Dick Turpin (IRE) *Richard Hannon* 124
3 b c Arakan(USA) —Merrily (Sharrood (USA))
(1385) 1699[2] 2159a[2] 3048[2] (3719a) 5186[5] 6611a[3]

Dictate *Mark H Tompkins* a69 69
2 ch g Araafa(IRE) —Navajo Love Song (IRE) (Dancing Brave (USA))
7203[7] 7400[4] 7644[3]

Dictionary *William Haggas* 23
2 ch c Zamindar(USA) —She Is Zen (FR) (Zieten (USA))
5085[6]

Diddums *Phil McEntee* a65 71
4 b g Royal Applause—Sahara Shade (USA) (Shadeed (USA))
1374[4] 325[8] 462[10] 555[6] ◆ 674[9] 693[6] 1131[3] 1391[13]

Diego (GER) *T Mundry* 86
2 b c High Chaparral(IRE) —Dea (GER) (Shareef Dancer (USA))
5740a[6]

Diescentric (USA) *Henry Cecil* 92
3 b c Diesis—Hawzah (Green Desert (USA))
(1325) 2045[4]

Dies Solis *Valentine Donoghue* 67
3 ch c Exceed And Excel(AUS) —Rose Of America (Brief Truce (USA))
2209[6] (3393) 3710[2] 4193[6] 6103[6] 6295[15]

Dig Deep (IRE) *John Quinn* a79 86
8 b g Entrepreneur—Diamond Quest (Rainbow Quest (USA))
16[6] 342[5] 379[7]

Diggeratt (USA) *George Baker* a86 77
4 rg m Maria's Mon(USA) —Miss Exhilaration (USA) (Gulch (USA))
4555[3] ◆ 4796[3] 5357[2] 5906[5] 6289[2] 6718[4] 6992[2] (7327) ◆ (7897) 7933[4]

Digital (BRZ) *A Cintra Pereira* a80
4 b h Romarin(BRZ) —Dites Moi (BRZ) (Choctaw Ridge (USA))
510a[7] 710a[11]

Dikanta *Alan Berry* 8
2 b c Diktat—Frascati (Emarati (USA))
6919[9] 7345 [14]

Diktalina *Alison Thorpe* a55 56
4 b m Diktat—Oiselina (FR) (Linamix (FR))
5940[8] 7149[9] 7805[5]

Dikta Melody (FR) *P Demercastel* 80
3 b f Diktat—Desert Melody (FR) (Green Desert (USA))
6487a[9]

Diktatorship (IRE) *Jennie Candlish* a54 50
7 b g Diktat—Polka Dancer (Dancing Brave (USA))
411[8]

Dililah *William Knight* a55
2 b f Auction House(USA) —Jezadil (IRE) (Mujadil (USA))
7558[5]

Dilli Dancer *Gavin Blake* a54 64
5 b m Dansili—Cup Of Kindness (USA) (Secretariat (USA))
2419[6] 2779[10] 3727[11]

Dilys Maud *Roger Ingram* a59 49
3 b f Auction House(USA) —Dam Certain (IRE) (Damister (USA))
1872[8] 2334[5] 3125[9] 4025[12] 5669[9] 7440[5] 7555[8] 7728[4] (7887)

Dimaire *Derek Haydn Jones* a64 64
3 b f Kheleyf(USA) —Dim Ots (Alhijaz)
1205[4] 1456[2] 1760[7] 2185[3] 2892[3] 3279[3] 4922[4]

Diman Waters (IRE) *Eric Alston* 86
3 br g Namid—Phantom Waters (Pharly (FR))
1104[2] ◆ (1511) 1860[2] 2099[2] 2862[6] 3856[2] 4349[2] 5309[3]

Dimashq *Paul Midgley* a33 59
8 b m Mtoto—Agwaas (IRE) (Rainbow Quest (USA))
1467[3] 1891[8] 2560[9] 3614[6] 3978[4] 4511[4] 4980[3] 5019[3] 5364[9] 6033[8] 6915[9]

Dimension *James Fanshawe* a77 63
2 b c Medicean—Palatial (Green Desert (USA))
5893[4] 6569[4]

Dim Sum *J Moore* 116
6 b g Kyllachy—Heckle (In The Wings)
7852a[9]

Dingaan (IRE) *Peter Grayson* a89 86
7 b g Tagula(IRE) —Boughtbyphone (Warning)
(580) 943[11] 1306[3] 2339[9] 3033[5] 3888[8] (4489) 5768[3] 6439[2] 7092[2] (7314) 7488[8] 7766[8] 7826[6] 7971[9]

Dingle View (IRE) *David Evans* 106
2 b f Mujadil(USA) —Livius Lady (IRE) (Titus Livius (FR))
1136[4] (1375) (1733) 4388[3] (4831) 5226a[3] (5567a) 6568[6]

Dinkie Short *Ben De Haan* a51 61
3 b g Reset(AUS) —Spring Sunrise (Robellino (USA))
762[8]

Dinkum Diamond (IRE) *Henry Candy* 107
2 b c Aussie Rules(USA) —Moving Diamonds (Lomitas)
(2048) ◆ (2468) 3100[6] 5276[7] ◆ 5907[2] 6734[4]

Dinkys Diamond (IRE) *Brian Ellison* 54
3 b g Modigliani(USA) —Along Came Molly (Dr Fong (USA))
1572[9] 1810[9]

Dinner Date *Tom Keddy* a81 64
8 ch g Groom Dancer(USA) —Misleading Lady (Warning)
23[4] 123[3] 580[2] 696[2] 981[2] 2298[4] 2653[7] 3079[7] 5142[4] ◆ 5866[10] 6449[10] 7115[9] (7290) 7597[9]

Diocese (USA) *Sir Michael Stoute* 21
2 b g Pulpit(USA) —Dalisay (IRE) (Sadler's Wells (USA))
5491[15]

Diocleziano (USA) *R Menichetti* a94 99
5 b h Barkerville(USA) —Essie's Maid (USA) (Linkage (USA))
1712a[2] 2576a[6]

Diodoros (FR) *C Laffon-Parias* a93 80
4 ch g High Chaparral(IRE) —Light Quest (USA) (Quest For Fame)
5109a[3]

Diplomasi *Clive Brittain* a65 50
2 b c Iceman—Piper's Ash (USA) (Royal Academy (USA))
1009[14] 2389[8] 6159[6] (6717) 6901[7]

Diplomatic (FR) *Mme C Head-Maarek* 59
3 ch g Numerous(USA) —Dalna (FR) (Anabaa (USA))
6487a[0]

Diplomatic (IRE) *Michael Squance* a47
5 b g Cape Cross(IRE) —Embassy (Cadeaux Genereux)
7969[4]

Dirakh Shan *Luca Cumani* a68 65
3 b g Kyllachy—Mi Amor (IRE) (Alzao (USA))
2564[15] 4521[6] 5028[2] 5700[4] 6023[10] 6580[5]

Dirar (IRE) *Gordon Elliott* a99 111
5 b g King's Best(USA) —Dibiya (IRE) (Caerleon (USA))
(3198) (5220) 5909[5]

Direct Answer (USA) *Sir Michael Stoute* 84
3 b c Dynaformer(USA) —Proud Fact (USA) (Known Fact (USA))
1912[2] ◆ 2684[4] 2974[2]

Director General (USA) *Julie-Ann Camacho* a62 61
3 b g Bernstein(USA) —Champagne Royal (USA) (Jeblar (USA))
1336[10] 1648[4] 2837[3] 3755[5] 5758[13] 7273[6] 7863[2]

Director's Dream (IRE) *Peter Winkworth* 54
2 gr f Act One—Najayeb (USA) (Silver Hawk (USA))
6770[11]

Directorship *Patrick Chamings* 94
4 br g Diktat—Away To Me (Exit To Nowhere (USA))
1530[3] 2339[2] 2683[2] 3796[8] 5264[2] 6204[3] 6562[20] 7233[4]

Diriculous *Robert Mills* a88 90
6 b g Diktat—Sheila's Secret (IRE) (Bluebird (USA))
7212[7] 8016[3]

Discanti (IRE) *Tim Easterby* a58 92
5 ch g Distant Music(USA) —Gertie Laurie (Lomond (USA))
1363[4] ◆ 1710[2] (1888) 2134[3] 2346[12] 3065[7] 3178[6] 3919[2] 4413[4] 4942[2] 5302[6] 5787[10] 6723[7]

Disclose *A Fabre* 94
3 b f Dansili—Revealing (Halling (USA))
5139a[7]

Disco Des *Chris Grant*
2 b g Desert Style(IRE) —Jubilee Treat (USA) (Seeking The Gold (USA))
2763[6]

Disco Doll *Gavin Blake* a45
2 b f Diktat—Cookie Cutter (IRE) (Fasliyev (USA))
1660[8] 2641[7]

Discoteca *Andrew Balding* 72
2 b c Nayef(USA) —Blaenavon (Cadeaux Genereux)
6087[3] 6473[3]

Discovery Bay *Roger Charlton* 72
2 b c Dansili—Rainbow's Edge (Rainbow Quest (USA))
6190[5] 6873[3]

Discreetly Mine (USA) *Todd Pletcher* a124
3 b c Mineshaft(USA) —Pretty Discreet (USA) (Private Account (USA))
1714a[13]

Dishdasha (IRE) *Alison Thorpe* a81 74
8 b g Desert Prince(IRE) —Counterplot (IRE) (Last Tycoon)
2411[3] 4399[7] 5679[10]

Dispol Diva *Paul Midgley* a47 67
4 b m Deportivo—Kingston Rose (GER) (Robellino (USA))
897[7] 1012[9] 1489[11] 2424[4] 2655[2] 3122[10] 3282[3] 4015[4] 4410[9] 4656[9] 6662[3]

Dispol Grand (IRE) *Paul Midgley* a58 74
4 b g Raise A Grand(IRE) —Hever Rosina (Efisio)
(1154) 1363[6] 1524[11] 2528[11] 3119[5] 5356[9] 6073[14] 6741[5] 7195[12] 7738[6]

Dispol Kabira *David Thompson* 55
3 b f Kheleyf(USA) —Abir (Soviet Star (USA))
1651[8] 1970[9] 2209[4] 2273[2] (2380) 2700[9] 3073[10] 3501[6] 3668[4] 3759[12] 4674[8] 4864[8] 5201[8] 5423[13]

Dispol Keasha *Paul Midgley* 74
3 ch f Kheleyf(USA) —Easy Mover (IRE) (Bluebird (USA))
1399[4] 1656[7] 2099[11] 3225[5]

Dispol Kylie (IRE) *Kate Walton* a46 72
4 b m Kheleyf(USA) —Professional Mom (USA) (Spinning World (USA))
1112[2] 1365[9] 2087[3] 2626[3] 2849[9] 3064[2] 3622[7] 5599[2] 6103[4] 6572[12]

Dispol Snapper (IRE) *Paul Midgley* 51
2 b c Whipper(USA) —Laylati (IRE) (Green Desert (USA))
1294[9] 1626[7] 2111[5] 2605[5] 3058[6] 3281[6] 4241[6] 4554[7]

Distant Florin *Mark Rimmer*
5 b m Medicean—Sunday Night (GER) (Bakharoff (USA))
181[0] 3477[10]

Distant Memories (IRE) *Tom Tate* 116
4 b g Falbrav(IRE) —Amathia (IRE) (Darshaan)
1274[2] (2977) 4139[2] 4829[3] (5539) 6592a[3]

Distant Sun (USA) *Linda Perratt* a89 75
6 b g Distant View(USA) —The Great Flora (USA) (Unaccounted For (USA))
1200[11] 2756[7] 3076[3] ◆ 3201[4] 3321[3] (3533) 4060[4] 4513[3] 4952[8] 5048[10] 5212[5] 5480[8] 6103[15] 6140[11] 6708[4] 7051[14] 7169[5]

Distant Vision (IRE) *Hugh McWilliams* a40 54
7 br m Distant Music(USA) —Najeyba (Indian Ridge)
2378[3] 2582[8] 2669[6] 3409[8] 3903[4]

Distant Waters *Alan Jarvis* a49 61
3 gr f Lomitas—Silent Waters (Polish Precedent (USA))
1358[8] 1782[2] 5366[10] 5958[9] 7168[6] 7315[11]

Di Stefano *David Nicholls* a72 96
3 b g Bahamian Bounty—Marisa (GER) (Desert Sun)
1499[7] 2090[6] 2545[15] 2815[4] 3270[4] 3731[7] 4837[3] 6303[4] 6998[5] 7144[2] 7320[7]

Distinctive *Bryan Smart* 104
3 b f Tobougg(IRE) —Blue Azure (USA) (American Chance (USA))
1312[6] 1726[5] 2912a[3] 3571a[4] ◆ 5351a[9]

Distinctive Image (USA) *Gerard Butler* a101 84
5 b g Mineshaft(USA) —Dock Leaf (USA) (Woodman (USA))
335a[13] 627a[9] 7828[2] 8009[4]

Distinguish (IRE) *Mark Johnston* a46 68
2 ch f Refuse To Bend(IRE) —Colourful Cast (IRE) (Nashwan (USA))
6353[4] 6726a[9] 7112[8]

Disturbia (IRE) *J W Hills* a40 36
2 b f Dubai Destination(USA) —Eoz (IRE) (Sadler's Wells (USA))
5029[13] 5691[16]

Divertimenti (IRE) *Roy Bowring* a74 85
6 b g Green Desert(USA) —Ballet Shoes (IRE) (Ela-Mana-Mou)
69[4] 402[11] 531[2] 568[6] 723[8] 1236[4] 1884[2] 2699[2] ◆ 2957[3] 3762[3] (4285) 4869[5] (4936) (5760) 6198[3] (6985) 7352[20]

Diverting *William Jarvis* a52 60
2 b f Nayef(USA) —Tawny Way (Polar Falcon (USA))
6883[13] 7231[10] 8001[9]

Divinatore *James Moffatt* a64 65
4 b g Sakhee(USA) —Divina Mia (Dowsing (USA))
282[7] 400[5] 1520[5] 2445[3] 3127[5] 7465[7]

Divine Call *William Haggas* a84 83
3 b c Pivotal—Pious (Bishop Of Cashel)
1661[8] 2903[3] 6655[2] ◆ (7129)

Divine Force *Michael Wigham* a85 64
4 b g Bertolini(USA) —Malcesine (IRE) (Auction Ring (USA))
78[3] (129) ◆ (223) ◆ (259) ◆ 432[3] 502[4] 779[3] 902[8] 1192[10] 1580[12] 2458[4]

Divine Rule (IRE) *Hughie Morrison* a67 58
2 br g Cacique(IRE) —Island Destiny (Kris)
5718[5] 6249[4] 6634[6]

Divine Spirit *Michael Dods* a63 79
9 b g Foxhound(USA) —Vocation (IRE) (Royal Academy (USA))
1391[9] 1923[6] 2528[12] 2849[10] 3287[5] 3977[5] 4373[3] ◆ 5485[4] 5599[4] 5817[9] 6490[3]

Divine White *Gerry Enright* a62 44
7 ch m College Chapel—Snowy Mantle (Siberian Express (USA))
10[6] 319[10] 638[7]

Divinite Green (IRE) *Peter Chapple-Hyam* 72
2 b c Diamond Green(FR) —Divinite (USA) (Alleged (USA))
6883[9]

Dixie Gwalia *David Simcock* a48
2 b f Tobougg(IRE) —Dixieanna (Night Shift (USA))
7447[10] 7551[8] 7681[5]

Dixie Land Band *Andrew Haynes* a31 29
2 b f Diktat—Spring Mood (FR) (Nashwan (USA))
6770[14] 7198[10]

Dixie Music (IRE) *A P O'Brien* 102
4 b h Montjeu(IRE) —Dixielake (IRE) (Lake Coniston (IRE))
1247a[4] 1789a[4] 2369a[6] 2709[9] 4877a[2]

Dixi Heights *Jim Boyle* a50 58
3 b f Golan(IRE) —Ninfa Of Cisterna (Polish Patriot (USA))
1593[9] 2418[7] 2634[8]

Diyaraka (FR) *M Delzangles* 88
3 gr f Clodovil(IRE) —Diamonaka (FR) (Akarad (FR))
7546a[3]

Dizziness (USA) *Roger Charlton* a58 62
3 b f Stormy Atlantic(USA) —Danzante (USA) (Danzig (USA))
1164[3] 1504[7]

Djalalabad (FR) *Jeff Pearce* a56 53
6 b m King's Best(USA) —Daraydala (IRE) (Royal Academy (USA))
229[6] 249[7] 320[8] 389[6] 791[9] 1130[5] 1301[6] 1633[6] 2008[6] 2299[5] 7649[2] 7966[9]

Django (SWE) *Jessica Long* a75 96
7 b g Acatenango(GER) —Praeriens Drottning (SWE) (Elmaamul (USA))
(4641a)

Django Reinhardt *Sam Davison* a42 54
4 b g Tobougg(IRE) —Alexander Ballet (Mind Games)
2337[4] 2714[5] 2894[4] 7626[8]

Djumama (IRE) *Andreas Lowe* 102
2 b f Aussie Rules(USA) —Western Sky (Barathea (IRE))
(7108a)

Dobravany (IRE) *Kevin Morgan* a56 60
6 b g Danehill Dancer(IRE) —Eadaoin (USA) (King Of Kings (IRE))
100[3] 353[4] 479[2] 622[7]

Doc Hay (USA) *Paul Cole* a71 66
3 bb g Elusive Quality(USA) —Coherent (USA) (Danzig (USA))
6638[6] (6746) 7052[4] 7239[4]

Docofthebay (IRE) *David Nicholls* a103 101
6 ch g Docksider(USA) —Baize (Efisio)
1708[8] 2057[5] 2472[7] 3069[17] 4030[6] 4859[6] 5993[2] (6178) ◆ 6357[6] 6721[5] (6888) 7348[5] 7522[5] 7875[9] 7935[2]

Doctor Hilary *Mark Hoad* a67 71
8 b g Mujahid(USA) —Agony Aunt (Formidable (USA))
351[6] (532) 789[5] 1258[7] 2178[6] (2964) 3463[5] 4099[3] 4659[2] 4961[6] 5614[4] 6812[7] 7391[4] 7656[4]

Doctor Of Music (IRE) *Bryan Smart* a44 43
4 ch g Dr Fong(USA) —Sublime Beauty (USA) (Caerleon (USA))
389[10] 503[8] 718[8]

Doctor Parkes *Eric Alston* 93
4 b g Diktat—Lucky Parkes (Full Extent (USA))
1822[8] 2134[2] 2431[8] 2992[3] 3753[6] 4798[4] 5069[2] 5734[7] 5941[7]

Doctor's Cave *K O Cunningham-Brown* a80 61
8 b g Night Shift(USA) —Periquitum (Dilum (USA))
4427[12] 5586[8]

Doctor Zhivago *Mark Johnston* a87 93
3 b g Shamardal(USA) —Balalaika (Sadler's Wells (USA))
(522) ◆ 1310[13] 2117[3] 2742[12] 3824[19]

Dodaa (USA) *Noel Wilson* a61 61
7 b g Dayjur(USA) —Ra'A (USA) (Diesis)
7231[0] 896[9]

Doesn't Care (IRE) *Richard Fahey* a42
2 gr c Shamardal(USA) —Senegal (IRE) (Grand Lodge (USA))
7858[5] 7999[8]

Doganhan (TUR) *A Sivgin* 23
4 b h Strike The Gold(USA) —Iles (GER) (Acatenango (GER))
5804a[9]

Doggerbank (IRE) *T Mundry* 93
4 b m Oasis Dream—Discreet Brief (IRE) (Darshaan)
2155a[2]

Dogs May Bark *Peter Chapple-Hyam* 86
2 b c Iceman—Arruhan (IRE) (Mujtahid (USA))
(7202)

Dohasa (IRE) *I Mohammed* a109 109
5 b g Bold Fact(USA) —Zara's Birthday (IRE) (Waajib)
607a[13] 822a[3] 1021a[16]

Doku (TUR) *D Ergin* a97
4 b m Ocean Crest(USA) —Irish Victory (IRE) (Danehill (USA))
5781a[5]

Dolcetto (IRE) *Alan King* a77 82
5 b m Danehill Dancer(IRE) —Rutledge (IRE) (Entrepreneur)
(2586) ◆ (3268) 4134[4] 5611[3] 6152[7]

Dolcezza (IRE) *Brian Meehan* a54 58
2 ch f Dr Fong(USA) —Wedding Cake (IRE) (Groom Dancer (USA))
4595[8] 5369[10] 5691[9] 6081[6] 6411[12] 6936[7]

Dolled Up (IRE) *Robert Collet* 111
3 b f Whipper(USA) —Belle De Cadix (IRE) (Law Society (USA))
1566a[9] 2158a[9] 2804a[8]

Dolly Ann *George Prodromou* a25
3 ch f Namid—Kalanda (Desert King (IRE))
7310[8]

Dolly Colman (IRE) *Andrew Haynes* a20 2
2 bg f Diamond Green(FR) —Absolutely Cool (IRE) (Indian Ridge)
5626[13] 6711[8]

Dolly Parton (IRE) *David Nicholls* 79
2 b f Tagula(IRE) —Batool (USA) (Bahri (USA))
1510[5] 1668[2] (2130) 3059[7] (3625) 4578[14]

Dolly Royal (IRE) *Robert Johnson* a36 62
5 b m Val Royal(FR) —Roos Rose (IRE) (Grand Lodge (USA))
1722[3] 2463[9] 2791[8] 2854[5] (3407) 5598[9] 6003[4] 6460[2]

Dolly Will Do *Neil Mulholland* a44 44
3 b f Bahamian Bounty—Desert Flower (Green Desert (USA))
104[6] 265[7] 387[3] 581[4] 788[8] 3727[10] 4733[9] 4989[16] 7310[5]

Dolphina (USA) *Henry Cecil* a77 80
3 ch f Kingmambo(USA) —Sea Of Showers (USA) (Seattle Slew (USA))
2674[2] 4114[2] 4893[2] 5366[3] 5953[7] (6415)

Dolphin Rock *David Barron* a86 88
3 b g Mark Of Esteem(IRE) —Lark In The Park (IRE) (Grand Lodge (USA))
(1362) 1718[2] 2261[3] (2863) 3857[2] 4750[2] 5904[3] 6534[9] 7227[5]

Dolphin's Dream *Brian Meehan* a41 54
3 b f Medicean—Arriving (Most Welcome)
1329[12] 1621[8] 2890[8] 3444[13]

Dominant (IRE) *Michael Jarvis* 87
2 bl c Cacique(IRE) —Es Que (Inchinor)
(6278) 6560[8]

Domination *Hughie Morrison* a83 88
3 b g Motivator—Soliza (IRE) (Intikhab (USA))
1299[4] (2893) 3335[2] ◆ 4092[3] 5727[3]

Dominator *Alan Swinbank* 87
2 b g Motivator—Subya (Night Shift (USA))
(4821)

Dominium (USA) *Jeremy Gask* a76
3 b g E Dubai(USA) —Sudenlylastsummer (USA) (Rinka Das (USA))
362[2] (900) 1086[6] 1453[3]

Domino Dancer (IRE) *Jim Best* a71 75
6 b g Tagula(IRE) —Hazarama (IRE) (Kahyasi)
(3787) 4132[2] 5840[12]

Domino Effect (IRE) *Howard Johnson* 51
2 bb g Diamond Green(FR) —Lypharden (IRE) (Lyphard's Special (USA))
3162[5] 3657[6] 4368[11] 6979[12]

Domino Play (FR) *R Avial Lopez*
3 b c Panis(USA) —Lady Domino (FR) (Second Empire (IRE))
450a[0]

Do More Business (IRE) *Pat Phelan* a64 67
3 b g Dubai Destination(USA) —Tokyo Song (USA) (Stravinsky (USA))
1058[8] (1316) 1873[10] 2868[6] 3567[4]

Donair *Paul Cole* a54 42
3 ch c Nayef(USA) —Darwinia (GER) (Acatenango (GER))
1766[9] 2336[10] 3055[9] 6093[11] 6330[7] 6522[14]

Donaldson (GER) *Jonjo O'Neill* a91 75
8 b g Lando(GER) —Daytona Beach (GER) (Konigsstuhl (GER))
536[14] 697[6] 888[8] 1062[3] 2044[10] 4100[13] 4520[9]

Don Bosco (FR) *D Smaga* 99
3 ch c Barathea(IRE) —Perfidie (IRE) (Monsun (GER))
3933a[4] 6761a[4]

Don Carlos (GER) *A P O'Brien* a101 104
3 b c Galileo(IRE) —Dapprima (GER) (Shareef Dancer (USA))
1310[11] 1910[6]

Doncaster Rover (USA) *David Brown* a84 114
4 b g War Chant(USA) —Rebridled Dreams (USA) (Unbridled's Song (USA))
1326[3] 2030[4] 2539[2] 3455[3] 4136[4] 4616[6] (5526) 5744[7] 6735[7] 7351[3]

Donegal (USA) *Robert Alan Hennessy* a92 101
5 b g Menifee(USA) —Vickey's Echo (CAN) (Clever Trick (USA))
2571a[6]

Dongola (IRE) *Peter Winkworth* a49 13
3 b f Xaar—Laura Margaret (Persian Bold)
4840[5] 5366[11] 6080[7] 6526[9] 7388[8]

Donna Elvira *Richard Hannon* a11 78
3 b f Doyen(IRE) —Impatiente (USA) (Vaguely Noble)
2585[3] 2921[2] 4330[3] 5008[8] 5444[5] 6781[5]

Donny Briggs *Tim Easterby* a66 66
5 b g Orpen(USA) —Passionate Pursuit (Pursuit Of Love)
2697[5] 7896[11]

Don Pele (IRE) *Ronald Harris* a78 75
8 b g Monashee Mountain(USA) —Big Fandango (Bigstone (IRE))
137[5] 242[4] 328[5] 505[2] (556) 839[4] 896[10] 961[11] 1166[8] 1443[10] 1979[7] 2234[2] 2589[3] 2964[8]

Don Pietro *F J Brennan* a77 74
7 b g Bertolini(USA) —Silver Spell (Aragon)
6958[9]

Don Renato (CHI) *J Barton* a93
7 ch h Edgy Diplomat(USA) —Tabla Redonda (CHI) (Braka (USA))
607a[11] 798a[12]

Don't Call Me (IRE) *Bryan Smart* a70 96
3 ch g Haafhd—Just Call Me (NZ) (Blues Traveller (IRE))
(915) ◆ 1649[2] 2110[6] (3612) (3949) (4357) 5511[10] 6318[4] 6567[6]

Dontforgetursh ovel *Jeff Pearce* a45 50
4 b h Josr Algarhoud(IRE) —Peggys Rose (IRE) (Shalford (IRE))
7155[2] 7380[10] 7555[9]

Don't Hurry Love (IRE) *Tim Pitt* 50
3 b f High Chaparral(IRE) —Queen Margrethe (Grand Lodge (USA))
4863[7] 7145[10]

Dontpaytheferryman (USA) *Brian Ellison* a83 57
5 ch g Wiseman's Ferry(USA) —Expletive Deleted (USA) (Dr Blum (USA))
(90) 331[6] (7836) 7921[2] (7985)

Don't Tell Mary (IRE) *Tom Dascombe* 97
3 b f Starcraft(NZ) —Only In Dreams (Polar Falcon (USA))
2404a[8] 3790[10] 5694[10]

Dontuwishitwereso *Paul D'Arcy* a62 43
4 b g Kyllachy—Prospering (Prince Sabo)
(21) 86[4] 518[7]

Don Velez (ARG) *J Barton* a103
5 b h Ride The Rails(USA) —Vacancy Girl (ARG) (Bold Forli (USA))
632a[2]

Doon Kalal (IRE) *Marcus Tregoning* a49 92
3 b g Dubai Destination(USA) —Muwajaha (Night Shift (USA))
5026[5] (5623) (6282)

Dora Explora *Linda Jewell* a11 47
6 br m Vettori(IRE) —Fredora (Inchinor)
2811[9] 3403[7] 4361[4] 6905[11]

Dorback *Henry Candy* 95
3 ch g Kyllachy—Pink Supreme (Night Shift (USA))
1499[3]

Dorden *Noel Wilson*
3 gr f Paris House—Dolphin Dancer (Dolphin Street (FR))
7406[11]

Dordogne (IRE) *Mark Johnston* 93
2 bb c Singspiel(IRE) —Riberac (Efisio)
(6279) ◆ 6884[3]

Doric Echo *Charlie Morlock* a32 75
4 b g Bertolini(USA) —Latour (Sri Pekan (USA))
3036[10] 3557[7] 6479[11]

Doric Lady *James Toller* a89 89
5 b m Kyllachy—Tanasie (Cadeaux Genereux)
1727[15] 3261[5] 3828[11] 4685[10] 5393[4] 6064[3] (6446) 6887[6] 7351[13]

Dorothy's Dancing (IRE) *Gary Moore* a35 35
2 b f Acclamation—Segoria (IRE) (Shinko Forest (IRE))
4658[13] 5074[7] 5667[7]

Dortmund *Mahmood Al Zarooni* 81
2 b c Dubawi(IRE) —Zacheta (Polish Precedent (USA))
2493[2] 2887[2] 3449[5] 5049[4] 5546[3]

Dos Lunas (USA) *John Glenney* a92 94
2 ch f Hennessy(USA) —Mi Luna Nueva (USA) (El Prado (IRE))
7340a[9]

Dosti *Tim Vaughan* a66
3 ch g Zamindar(USA) —Justbetweenfriends (USA) (Diesis)
(551) ◆ 1060[7] 7836[5] 8015[10]

Dot's Delight *Mark Rimell* a51 51
6 b m Golden Snake(USA) —Hotel California (IRE) (Last Tycoon)
6021[4] ◆ 7840[5]

Dotty Darroch *Robin Bastiman* 57
2 b f Ad Valorem(USA) —Sensible Idea (Dr Fong (USA))
2210[3] 2873[5] 3665[6] 4451[7] 5042[6] 5434[10] 5733[2] 6645[5] 7224[4]

Douala *P Schiergen* 95
3 b f Dubawi(IRE) —Desca (GER) (Cadeaux Genereux)
5739a[4]

Double Bill (USA) *Paul Cole* a68 74
6 bb g Mr Greeley(USA) —Salty Perfume (USA) (Salt Lake (USA))
78[2] 287[2]

Double Carpet (IRE) *Gary Woodward* a63 65
7 b g Lahib(USA) —Cupid Miss (Anita's Prince)
1234[13] 2721[2] 3763[11] 4285[5] 5697[4] (6133) 6329[5] 6536[9] 7730[7] 7812[3]

Double Dealer *Mahmood Al Zarooni* a77 80
2 b c Dubawi(IRE) —Infiel (Luge)
5491[3] 5893[3] 6301[7] (6777)

Double Duchess *Paul D'Arcy* a61
2 b f Val Royal(FR) —Ti Adora (IRE) (Montjeu (IRE))
7567[8]

Double Fortune *Jamie Poulton* a66 49
3 b f Singspiel(IRE) —Four-Legged Friend (Aragon)
979[3] 1358[10] 2754[6] 3155[7]

Double Up (SWE) *Bo Neuman* a74
5 b m Funambule(USA) —Ginger (SWE) (Diaghlyphard (USA))
7374a[4]

Double Whammy *Jamie Poulton* 64
4 b g Systematic—Honor Rouge (IRE) (Highest Honor (FR))
3780[12] 6775[4]

Doubnov (FR) *Ian Williams* a79 58
7 gr g Linamix(FR) —Karmitycia (FR) (Last Tycoon)
174[3] 323[4] (488) (600) 714[2] 888[6] 994[4] 1357[8] 2285[8] 2752[4]

Douchkette (FR) *John Berry* a58 56
4 b m Califet(FR) —Douchka (FR) (Fijar Tango (FR))
1301[4] 1591[6] 2414[2] 2487[4] 5155[5]

Douze Points (IRE) *Joseph G Murphy* a78 93
4 b g Redback—Grade A Star (IRE) (Alzao (USA))
3489a[15] 5571a[10] 5774a[3]

Dove Cottage (IRE) *Stuart Kittow* a65 79
8 b g Great Commotion(USA) —Pooka (Dominion)
1579[7] 2411[6] 2996[7] 3860[10] 4327[10] 4794[4] 5625[2] 5991[10]

Dovedon Angel *Gay Kelleway* a56 56
4 b m Winged Love(IRE) —Alexander Star (IRE) (Inzar (USA))
13 130[4] 407[12] 599[3] 2302[4] 2676[3] (3267) 4174[4] 4734[3] 5663[6] 7039[2] 7475[6] 7759[2]

Dovedon Diva *Tom Keddy* 50
3 b f Generous(IRE) —Alexander Star (IRE) (Inzar (USA))
1029[8] 1522[8] 5379[13] 6098[11]

Dovedon Earl *Tom Keddy* a59 49
4 b g Millkom—Syrian Flutist (Shaamit (IRE))
179[4] 316[9] 983[8] 1283[6] 3221[7] 4441[6] 4765[12] 5164[6]

Dower Glen *Valentine Donoghue* a59 65
3 b f Camacho—Aimee's Delight (Robellino (USA))
619[2] 936[6] 1104[4] 1468[2] 1667[3] 2291[4] 2449[6] 3167[6] 6246[5] 6392[6] 6490[9] 7051[3] 7563[2] 7783[6]

Downhill Skier (IRE) *Mark Brisbourne* a65 69
6 ch g Danehill Dancer(IRE) —Duchy Of Cornwall (USA) (The Minstrel (CAN))
3280[11] 3763[7] 4232[3] 4789[10] 4936[3] 5267[4] 5614[2] 5906[3] 6456[5] (7007) 7390[9] 7501[8] 7613[9] 7812[4]

Downtoobusiness *Karen George* a51 40
3 b g Desert Sun—Mariette (Blushing Scribe (USA))
2675[15]

Downtown Boy (IRE) *Tom Tate* 60
2 br g Kheleyf(USA) —Uptown (IRE) (Be My Guest (USA))
2498[15] 3222[6] 4089[5] 5021[3] 5818[11] 6978[8]

Doyenne Dream *James Eustace* 56
3 b f Doyen(IRE) —Cribella (USA) (Robellino (USA))
1607[2]

Dozy Joe *Ian Wood* a86 82
2 b c Sleeping Indian—Surrey Down (USA) (Forest Wildcat (USA))
3332[12] (4221) (4696) 7347[3] 7444[2] 7652[3] 7975a[3]

Dragonera *Ed Dunlop* 66
2 b f Doyen(IRE) —Time Will Show (FR) (Exit To Nowhere (USA))
6154[9] 6468[7] 6873[5]

Dragonessa (IRE) *Bryn Palling* a42 57
3 b f Red Ransom(USA) —Principessa (Machiavellian (USA))
1760[5] 2000[12] 2962[3]

Dragon Slayer (IRE) *John Harris* a68 77
8 ch g Night Shift(USA) —Arandora Star (USA) (Sagace (FR))
1883[13] 2314[7] 3391[2] 3894[7] 4520[10] 4852[4] 5545[9] 6472[6] 7184[9]

Dramatic Jewel (USA) *Lucinda Russell* a65 64
4 b g Diesis—Seeking The Jewel (USA) (Seeking The Gold (USA))
5437[6] 6109[9] 6242[3] 6495[7]

Drawing Board *Kevin Ryan* 101
2 b c Pastoral Pursuits—Grand Design (Danzero (AUS))
(1517) (2082) 3504[2] 4355[7] 4903[5] 6139[2]

Drawn Free (IRE) *William Knight* a44
2 b g Tagula(IRE) —Mayfair (Green Desert (USA))
4253[6]

Drawnfromthepast (IRE) *Jamie Osborne* a101 74
5 ch g Tagula(IRE) —Ball Cat (FR) (Cricket Ball (USA))
(2689) 3461[12] 3845[8] 4401[5] 4536[24] 5308[3] 5967[11] (6374) (6539) 7014[3]

Drawn Gold *Reg Hollinshead* a68 67
6 b g Daggers Drawn(USA) —Gold Belt (IRE) (Bellypha)
2560[4] 3028[3] (3475)

Dr Darcey *Richard Hannon* a60 58
2 b g Dr Fong(USA) —Ballet (Sharrood (USA))
2932[8] 3842[4] 4499[7] 6810[2] 7296[3] 7888[8]

Dreamacha *Stuart Williams* a70 68
3 b f Oasis Dream—Machaera (Machiavellian (USA))
313[7] 1075[3] 3484[7] 4970[3] 5650[3] (6025) (6329) 6656[2] 7442[4]

Dream Achieved *B W Hills* 66
2 b c Oasis Dream—Achieve (Rainbow Quest (USA))
4318[5]

Dream Ahead (USA) *David Simcock* 125
2 b c Diktat—Land Of Dreams (Cadeaux Genereux) (4110) ◆ (5347a) (6531) 6924[5]

Dream Catcher (FR) *David Nicholls* a87 94
2 gr g Della Francesca(USA) —Gallopade (FR) (Kendor (FR))
3718a[6] 6737[8]

Dream Champion *A J Martin* a76 74
7 b g Fraam—Forest Fantasy (Rambo Dancer (CAN))
4467[11]

Dream Dream Dream (IRE) *K M Prendergast* a3 53
3 b f Oasis Dream—Egoli (USA) (Seeking The Gold (USA))
6905[12]

Dream Eater (IRE) *Andrew Balding* a103 119
5 gr h Night Shift(USA) —Kapria (FR) (Simon Du Desert (FR))
2539[3] 3046[3] 3888[3] 4469[5] 5009[6] 5803a[2] 6923[11] (7482) 7853a[8]

Dream Esteem *David Pipe* a9 66
5 b m Mark Of Esteem(IRE) —City Of Angels (Woodman (USA))
120[10]

Dream Express (IRE) *David Thompson* a73 76
5 b g Fasliyev(USA) —Lothlorien (USA) (Woodman (USA))
8[4] 135[8] 486[11] 773[2] 961[3] 1642[4] 2184[8] 2589[12] 3538[10] 3775[7] 4487[7] 4605[2] 4869[11] 5535[4] 5817[8] 7199[9] 7380[4]

Dream Huntress *J W Hills* a65 64
4 ch m Dubai Destination(USA) —Dream Lady (Benny The Dip (USA))
83[8]

Dream In Blue *Jeremy Glover* a73 49
5 b g Oasis Dream—Blue Birds Fly (Rainbow Quest (USA))
(42) 114[3] 377[4] 456[2] 700[2] 833[2] 1028[14]

Dream In Waiting *Brian Meehan* a79 81
4 b m Oasis Dream—Lady In Waiting (Kylian (USA))
2256[11] 2705[11] 6691[3] 7307[7] 7548[7]

Dream Lodge (IRE) *Richard Fahey* a99 111
6 ch g Grand Lodge(USA) —Secret Dream (IRE) (Zafonic (USA))
1570[2] 2539[7] 2977[3] 3921[8] 4390[6] 4830[10] 6180[3] 6562[29] 7529[5] 7828[5] 8009[9]

Dream Number (IRE) *William Muir* a65 72
3 ch f Fath(USA) —Very Nice (Daylami (IRE))
1168[7] 1593[8] 2892[7] 3336[7] 3677[4] 4031[7] 4744[3] 4861[2] (5206) 5588[6] 6421[6] 6772[4] 7194[4] 7390[3]

Dream Of Fortune (IRE) *David Evans* a79 72
6 b g Danehill Dancer(IRE) —Tootling (IRE) (Pennine Walk)
383[3] 586[5] 1684[8] 1840[7] 2182[5] 2388[8] 2966[7] 3079[5] (4132) 5367[4] 5840[2] 6054[10] 6165[8] 6450[3] 6718[2] 6934[2] (7251) 7732[2] 7856[3] 7878[2] 8008[6]

Dream Of Olwyn (IRE) *James Given* a65 75
5 b m Nayef(USA) —Jam (IRE) (Arazi (USA))
2602[5] 3950[10] 4546[9] 5563[3] 6328[4] 6984[11]

Dream On Buddy (IRE) *B W Hills* a80 80
3 b f Oasis Dream—My Renee (USA) (Kris S (USA))
(533) ◆ (934) 1159[4] 1582[4] 2652[8] 4784[6] 5236[2] 5758[2] 6266[2] 6813[6] 7274[4]

Dream Peace (IRE) *Robert Collet* a82 94
2 b f Dansili—Truly A Dream (IRE) (Darshaan)
4884a[7]

Dream Pedlar (AUS) *Troy Blacker* 103
6 br g West Quest(CAN) —Unamah (AUS) (Top Avenger (AUS))
6946a[4] 7368a[4]

Dream Risk (FR) *Kate Walton* 60
4 b m Dream Well(FR) —Lovarisk (FR) (Take Risks (FR))
1380[8] 2085[5] 3760[12] (5203) 6921[10]

Dreams Of Glory *Ron Hodges* a43 38
2 ch c Resplendent Glory(IRE) —Pip's Dream (Glint Of Gold)
3555[9] 4838[10] 5651[7] 6769[6]

Dreamspeed (IRE) *Andrew Balding* a97 108
3 b c Barathea(IRE) —Kapria (FR) (Simon Du Desert (FR))
(1473) 1945a[5] 6533[2] 7096[3] 7594[6]

Dream Spinner *John Dunlop* a68 76
3 b g Royal Applause—Dream Quest (Rainbow Quest (USA))
1433[2] 1880[2] (2650) 3909[6] 4493[4] 5679[8] 6290[12]

Dreamwalk (IRE) *Roger Curtis* a86 85
4 b g Bahri(USA) —Celtic Silhouette (FR) (Celtic Swing)
25[3] 352[4] 500[5] 974[3] 1161[9]

Dreamweaving (IRE) *Nigel Tinkler* 49
2 b f Sleeping Indian—Wicked (Common Grounds)
1331[6] 2059[13] 5298[14] 6301[10] 6878[11]

Dream Win *Brian Ellison* a79 79
4 b h Oasis Dream—Wince (Selkirk (USA))
1434 3781[0] 1395[7] (1967) 2625[6] 3279[2] ◆ (3520) 4261[2] (5533)

Dressing Room (USA) *Mark Johnston* 69
2 b g Dixie Union(USA) —Green Room (USA) (Theatrical)
5032[5] 5404[4] 6514[3]

Dress Up (IRE) *Sylvester Kirk* 78
2 b f Noverre(USA) —Lisfannon (Bahamian Bounty)
1577[2] (1835) 3070[8] 4138[5] 6445[7] 7204[8]

Dr Faustus (IRE) *Doug Watson* a91 91
5 gr g Sadler's Wells(USA) —Requesting (Rainbow Quest (USA))
419a[4] 627a[6]

Dr Finley (IRE) *Jeff Pearce* a69 75
3 ch g Dr Fong(USA) —Farrfesheena (USA) (Rahy (USA))
864[4] 1182[4] 1880[4] 2650[5] 2924[5] 4259[3] 4545[3] 6816[3]

Dr Green (IRE) *Richard Hannon* 90
2 b c Diamond Green(FR) —Tikitano (IRE) (Dr Fong (USA))
1845[2] ◆ 2239[3] 2594[3] (3459) 3844[3]

Drift And Dream *Chris Wall* 93
3 b f Exceed And Excel(AUS) —Sea Drift (FR) (Warning)
2046[4] (2931) 3436[3] (4754) 5967[4] ◆

Drifting Gold *Clive Cox* a77 81
6 ch m Bold Edge—Driftholme (Safawan)
3114[9] 3527[4] 3958[4]

Drill Sergeant *Mark Johnston* 111
5 br g Rock Of Gibraltar(IRE) —Dolydille (IRE) (Dolphin Street (FR))
1176[7] 1529[3] 1698[4] 2096[11] 3194[10]

Drinking Buddy *David Thompson* 54
3 ch g Reel Buddy(USA) —Tancred Arms (Clantime)
1362[13] 6188[13]

Drivemode *Dr Jon Scargill* a45 26
3 b g Domedriver(IRE) —Miss Prism (Niniski (USA))
7183[9] 7575[9] 7834[5]

Driven By Success (USA) *Todd Pletcher* a108
5 ch g Precise End(USA) —Afleet Closer (CAN) (Afleet (CAN))
6582a[5]

Drizzi (IRE) *Jeff Pearce* a70 72
9 b g Night Shift(USA) —Woopi Gold (IRE) (Last Tycoon)
724[2] 770[2] (983) 1303[3]

Dr Light (IRE) *M A Peill* a52 37
6 b g Medicean—Allumette (Rainbow Quest (USA))
3110[7] 3370[7] 4070[9]

Dr Livingstone (IRE) *Charles Egerton* a90 95
5 b g Dr Fong(USA) —Radhwa (FR) (Shining Steel)
5970[10] 6565[5]

Dr Mathias *David Evans* a63 68
3 b g Dubai Destination(USA) —Herminoe (Rainbow Quest (USA))
698[6] 977[4] 2409[7] 2650[7]

Dr Noverre (IRE) *Kevin Ryan* 73
2 ch c Noverre(USA) —Zuniga's Date (USA) (Diesis)
2667[2] ◆ (3072)

Droit Devant (FR) *D Prod'Homme* 84
2 b f Bernebeau(FR) —Lettre A France (USA) (Lear Fan (USA))
3307a[3]

Drombeg Dawn (IRE) *A J McNamara* 88
4 b m Orpen(USA) —Dawn's Sharp Shot (IRE) (Son Of Sharp Shot (IRE))
4463a[5] 5571a[12]

Dromore (IRE) *Andrew Balding* a91 83
3 ch g Traditionally(USA) —Try To Catch Me (USA) (Shareef Dancer (USA))
(1317) 1624[2] 2117[12] 2869[4] 3781[2] 4573[3] 5371[6] 6283[3]

Drop The Hammer *David O'Meara* a22 67
4 b m Lucky Story(USA) —Paperweight (In The Wings)
1113[14] 1803[2] 2464[6] 3552[2] (4174) 4246[5] 4854[7] 6109[5] (6649) 6895[11] 7145[5]

Drosselmeyer (USA) *William Mott* a116
3 ch c Distorted Humor(USA) —Golden Ballet (USA) (Moscow Ballet (USA))
(2776a)

Drovetti (AUS) *S Burridge* 105
6 b g Mossman(AUS) —Clareta (AUS) (Pauillac (AUS))
2154a[9]

Droxford (USA) *Jamie Osborne* a46 51
2 ch g Orientate(USA) —Dixiehunt (USA) (Dixieland Band (USA))
4695[11] 5413[6] 5924[7] 6411[9]

Dr Red Eye *Jeremy Glover* 61
2 ch c Dr Fong(USA) —Camp Fire (IRE) (Lahib (USA))
3020[5]

Drubinca *Stuart Williams* a52 44
3 b g Dubai Destination(USA) —Racina (Bluebird (USA))
698[12] 870[4] 1163[9] 6076[12] 6848[9]

Drumadoon (IRE) *John Dunlop* 36
2 b c Hawk Wing(USA) —Lady Taufan (IRE) (Taufan (USA))
4741[8] 5413[7] 6473[7]

Drumcliffe Dancer (IRE) *W McCreery* a40 58
3 ch f Footstepsinthesand—Tea Service (USA) (Atticus (USA))
7505[6]

Drumcomie *Jim Goldie* 12
3 b f Supreme Sound—Rhinefield Lass (Bijou D'Inde)
3148[8]

Drumfire (IRE) *Eoin Griffin* 115
6 b g Danehill Dancer(IRE) —Witch Of Fife (USA) (Lear Fan (USA))
4081a[2]

Drum Major (IRE) *Jim Best* a59 73
5 b g Sadler's Wells(USA) —Phantom Gold (Machiavellian (USA))
509[6] 676[6] 983[6] 2811[6] 3214[4]

Drummer Boy *Peter Winkworth* 57
2 ch g Haafhd—Largo (IRE) (Selkirk (USA))
4254[11] 5582[6] 6279[8]

Drummers Drumming (USA) *Charlie Morlock* a54 51
4 b g Stroll(USA) —Afleet Summer (USA) (Afleet (CAN))
1302[6] 2231[8] 2694[5] 7759[7]

Drumpellier (IRE) *Simon West* a55 62
3 ch f Rakti—Early Memory (USA) (Devil's Bag (USA))
519[3] 906[11] 1118[2] 1468[5] 2962[2] 3167[5] 3393[6] 3710[5] (4651) 5422[4] 5599[9] 5999[5] 6392[3] 6880[14] 7170[9]

Drunken Sailor (IRE) *Luca Cumani* a109 117
5 b g Tendulkar(USA) —Ronni Pancake (Mujadil (USA))
(335a) ◆ (627a) 820a[5] 2593[3] 3447[2] ◆ 3922[2] (5517) 7032a[11] 7368a[10]

Dr Valentine (FR) *Ann Duffield* a54 73
4 ch g Dr Fong(USA) —Red Roses Story (FR) (Pink (FR))
754[5] 834[3] 7282[6] 7814[8] 7958[12]

Dr Wintringham (IRE) *Karen George* a75 83
4 b m Monsieur Bond(IRE) —Shirley Collins (Robellino (USA))
11[9] 853[6] 1141[4] 1762[3] 2417[2] 2727[6] (2920) (3130) 3830[4] 4533[2] 5114[9] 5919[6] 6430[7] 7122[2] 7403[11]

Dualagi *Martin Bosley* a64 64
6 b m Royal Applause—Lady Melbourne (IRE) (Indian Ridge)
296[6] 693[7] 1236[3] 2026[5] 2589[7] 2779[6] ◆ 3292[6] 3526[4] (4744) 5010[6] 5714[5] 6455[7] 7250[4] 7827[4] (7882) 8034[8]

Dualite (IRE) *John Dunlop* 45
2 ch f Dubawi(IRE) —Morality (Elusive Quality (USA))
3871[11] 4753[4]

Dubai Affair *Hughie Morrison* a71 60
2 b f Dubawi(IRE) —Palace Affair (Pursuit Of Love)
2616[9] 3000[5] 4590[3] 5000[5] ◆ (5365) 5725[6]

Dubai Bounty *Gerard Butler* a75 87
3 ch f Dubai Destination(USA) —Mary Read (Bahamian Bounty)
1159[3] 1448[3] ◆ 3995[3] (4619)

Dubai Caffe *P L Giannotti*
2 ch f Dubai Destination(USA) —Crimson Topaz (Hernando (FR))
7849a[3]

Dubai Celebration *Jedd O'Keeffe* 83
2 b g Dubai Destination(USA) —Pretty Poppy (Song)
1292[6] 2376[4] (3204) 4388[8] 5245[17] 7347[12]

Dubai Creek (IRE) *Donald McCain* a67 50
4 b g Cape Cross(IRE) —Humilis (IRE) (Sadler's Wells (USA))
166[2] ◆ 246[2]

Dubai Crest *Amanda Perrett* a91 90
4 b g Dubai Destination(USA) —On The Brink (Mind Games)
1780[6] 2467[4] ◆ 2747[6] (6428) 7100[15] 7591[10] 7756[2] 7881[5]

Dubai Dynamo *Ruth Carr* a100 106
5 b g Kyllachy—Miss Mercy (IRE) (Law Society (USA))
474[5] 722[3] ◆ (850) 887[5] 1030[3] 1117[6] 1397[3] 1672[3] 1708[5] (2086) 2141[2] 2311[8] (2508) 3146[15] 3366[6] 3869[15] 4816[9] 5068[7] 5605[14] 6296[6] 6312[5] 6577[6] 6749[17]

Dubai Gem *Jamie Poulton* a59 66
4 b m Fantastic Light(USA) —Reflectance (Sadler's Wells (USA))
593[8] 1177[9] 1849[8] 2597[8] 3160[8] 3962[5] 4680[4] 5655[8]

Dubai Glory *Ed Dunlop* a59 63
2 b f Dubai Destination(USA) —Rosse (Kris)
3082[8] 3657[3] 4447[5] 5256[8] 5961[5] 6471[6] 7296[6]

Dubai Hills *Bryan Smart* a89 70
4 b g Dubai Destination(USA) —Hill Welcome (Most Welcome)
4192[9] 4834[2] 5601[7] 6492[2] 7051[2] 7399[3] (7956) ◆

Dubai Legend *Noel Wilson* a22 77
4 ch m Cadeaux Genereux—Royal Future (IRE) (Royal Academy (USA))
5598[7] 6108[10] 7442[12] 7699[10]

Dubai Majesty (USA) *W Bret Calhoun* a119 108
5 bb m Essence Of Dubai(USA) —Great Majesty (USA) (Great Above (USA))
(7341a)

Dubai Media (CAN) *Ed Dunlop* a95 83
3 b f Songandaprayer(USA) —Forty Gran (USA) (El Gran Senor (USA))
1329[5] 2120[2] ◆ 3071[8] 3924[2] (4835) (5454) 6253[3] 6509[5]

Dubai Miracle (USA) *David Simcock* a85 95
3 ch g Consolidator(USA) —East Cape (USA) (Mr Prospector (USA))
608a[11] 819a[8] 945[12] 2738[3] 3104[12] 3824[15] 4500[4] 6312[6] 6556[4]

Dubai Moon (USA) *Mahmood Al Zarooni* a73
2 ch f Malibu Moon(USA) —Fun Crowd (USA) (Easy Goer (USA))
3082[3]

Dubai Moonlight *Jane Chapple-Hyam* a48 38
3 b f Domedriver(IRE) —Moon Is Up (USA) (Woodman (USA))
728[3] 978[7] 1329[11]

Dubai Phantom (USA) *David Simcock* a71 70
3 b g Arch(USA) —Sharp Apple (USA) (Diesis)
1830[5] 2924[8] 5164[5] (5963) 6983[3] 7704[3] 7967[6] 8013[9]

Dubai Prince (IRE) *D K Weld* 111
2 b c Shamardal(USA) —Desert Frolic (IRE) (Persian Bold)
(7135a) ◆

Dubai Queen (USA) *Luca Cumani* a73
2 b f Kingmambo(USA) —Zomaradah (Deploy)
6796[6] ◆ 7185[2]

Dubai Set *Richard Hannon* a63 92
3 ch g Reset(AUS) —Bint Makbul (Makbul)
1732[5] 2544[6] 2969[9] 3579[3] 3916[3] 4264[8]

Dubai's Touch *Mark Johnston* a72 103
6 b h Dr Fong(USA) —Noble Peregrine (Lomond (USA))
1008[19] 1085[14]

Dubara Reef (IRE) *Paul Green* a42 73
3 ch g Dubawi(IRE) —Mamara Reef (Salse (USA))
1100[5] 1461[4] 1989[3] (2606) 2853[4] ◆ 3626[6] (4519) 5119[6] 5420[6] (6038) (6359) 6750[8] (7284)

Dubarshi *Jo Crowley* a83 32
2 b g Dubawi(IRE) —Asheyana (IRE) (Soviet Star (USA))
2887[12] 4838[3] 6053[4] (6497) (7317)

Dubawi Dancer *William Haggas* a38 40
2 ch f Dubawi(IRE) —Adees Dancer (Danehill Dancer (IRE))
5488[5] 6092[10] 6248[11]

Dubawi Gold *Michael Dods* 104
2 b c Dubawi(IRE) —Savannah Belle (Green Desert (USA))
(2427) 2743[2] 3100[10] 5219[11] 5850[4] (6733) 7081[9]

Dubawi Gulf *Ed Dunlop* a49 79
2 b f Dubawi(IRE) —Sea Angel (Nashwan (USA))
4048[2] 4508[2] ◆ 5324[2] 6200[14] 6521[5]

Dubawi King *Nigel Tinkler* 64
3 b g Dubawi(IRE) —Laughing Girl (USA) (Woodman (USA))
2131[6] 2606[3] 2853[2] (3532) 4087[4] 4519[2] 5058[5] (5534) 5738[3] 6038[5] 6623[5]

Dubawi Phantom *David Simcock* 105
3 ch g Dubawi(IRE) —Anna Amalia (IRE) (In The Wings)
1327[4] 1910[2] 3491a[9] 4456[9]

Dubburg (USA) *Willie Musson* a66 69
5 ch g Johannesburg(USA) —Plaisir Des Yeux (FR) (Funambule (USA))
4433[10] 6213[3] 6314[2] 6669[5] 7315[3] 7531[2] 8010[5]

Dublin (USA) *D Wayne Lukas* a115
3 ch c Afleet Alex(USA) —Classy Mirage (USA) (Storm Bird (CAN))
1714a[7] 2137a[5]

Duchess Dora (IRE) *John Quinn* 99
3 b f Tagula(IRE) —Teodora (IRE) (Fairy King (USA))
(1499) 1860[4] 2058[3] 2972[4] 4191[4] 5250[3] 5944[12] 6364[12] 6918[5] 7079[17]

Duchess Of Foxland (IRE) *Mark L Fagan* a71 101
3 br f Medecis—Itsanothergirl (Reprimand)
1036a[2] 1787a[3] 6007a[10]

Dudley *Jonathan Portman* a46 51
3 ch g Compton Place—Just A Glimmer (Bishop Of Cashel)
4989[10] 6255[3] 6522[10] 7153[6] 7328[4]

Dudley Docker (IRE) *Daniel Christopher O'Brien* a50 75
8 b g Victory Note(USA) —Nordic Abu (IRE) (Nordico (USA))
7543[13]

Due Date (USA) *Steve Margolis* 110
5 gr h El Prado(IRE) —Hidden Assets (USA) (Mt. Livermore (USA))
7362a[6]

Duel (IRE) *Vittorio Caruso*
2 ch c Shamardal(USA) —River Hill (ITY) (Danehill (USA))
(7264a)

Duellist *Mark Johnston* a91 87
3 b c Dubawi(IRE) —Satin Flower (USA) (Shadeed (USA))
128[2] (267) 596[5] 934[2] 1018[3] (1086) 1497[5] 2002[4] 2713[7] 3172[3] 3696[8]

Duff (IRE) *Edward Lynam* a106 117
7 b g Spinning World(USA) —Shining Prospect (Lycius (USA))
1954a[4] 2570a[2] 3489a[10] 4160a[2] 4882a[6] 5946[4] 6923[8] 7875[3]

Duke Of Burgundy (FR) *Jennie Candlish* 74
7 b g Danehill(USA) —Valley Of Gold (FR) (Shirley Heights)
1357[12]

Duke Of Florence (IRE) *Richard Hannon* a68 65
2 b g Medicean—Bonheur (IRE) (Royal Academy (USA))
7302[4] ◆ 7530[6] 7755[3]

Duke Of Normandy (IRE) *Brian Baugh* a50 52
4 gr g Refuse To Bend(IRE) —Marie De Bayeux (FR) (Turgeon (USA))
2477[8] 2874[8] 3360[8] 3960[4] 4912[11] 5636[10]

Duke Of Rainford *Michael Herrington* a58 52
3 gr g Bahamian Bounty—Night Haven (Night Shift (USA))
215[5] (265) 619[3] 662[2] 831[3] 919[4] 1118[12] 1535[2] 2217[8] 2582[3] 3228[6] 3287[6] 3966[8] 4406[5] 4651[3] 5152[6] 5548[2] 5957[4] 6392[4] (6665) 7018[6] 7425[5] 7506[9] 7952[7]

Duke Of Touraine (IRE) *Ben Haslam* a71 37
5 gr g Linamix(FR) —Miss Mission (IRE) (Second Empire (IRE))
2937[17]

Dukes Art *James Toller* a89 90
4 b h Bachelor Duke(USA) —Creme Caramel (USA) (Septieme Ciel (USA))
1625[5] (2683) 3172[7] 3565[4] 4306[7]

Dul Ar An Ol (IRE) *John C McConnell* a76 81
9 b g Perugino(USA) —Sprint For Gold (USA) (Slew O'Gold (USA))
3487a[20]

Dulce Domum *Andrew Haynes* a57 49
4 b m Dansili—Enclave (USA) (Woodman (USA))
(898) 1071[8] 1635[12] 2302[6] 2610[4] 3352[6] 3760[7] 4991[8]

Dulcie *Mark H Tompkins* a78 84
4 b m Hernando(FR) —Dulcinea (Selkirk (USA))
2938[3] ◆ 5996[8] 6750[4]

Dumbarton (IRE) *Sir Michael Stoute* 65
2 br c Danehill Dancer(IRE) —Scottish Stage (IRE) (Selkirk (USA))
5629[6]

Dunaden (FR) *Y Fouin* a75 97
4 b h Nicobar—La Marlia (FR) (Kaldounevees (FR))
494a[4] 742a[8]

Dunaskin (IRE) *Richard Guest* a81 84
10 b g Bahhare(USA) —Mirwara (IRE) (Darshaan)
190[3] 327[3] 456[3] 600[3] (700) (834) 2897[4] 4449[5] 4891[7] 6213[4] 6699[5] 7933[5]

Dunboyne Express (IRE) *Kevin Prendergast* 112
2 b c Shamardal(USA) —Love Excelling (FR) (Polish Precedent (USA))
(4176a) 7081[5]

Duncan *John Gosden* 123
5 b g Dalakhani(IRE) —Dolores (Danehill (USA))
1898[2] 3191[2] 4535[4] (6015a) 6612a[15]

Duneen Dream (USA) *Nikki Evans* a54 45
5 ch g Hennessy(USA) —T N T Red (USA) (Explosive Red (CAN))
210[9] 816[2] (995) 3559[6] 4327[13]

Dune Island *John Bridger* a46
2 b f Compton Admiral—Desert Island Disc (Turtle Island (IRE))
7733[7] 8001[11]

Dunelight (IRE) *Clive Cox* a110 109
7 ch h Desert Sun—Badee'A (IRE) (Marju (IRE))
440a[7] 631a[10] 823a[6] (883) 1377[3] 1900[21] 3893[2] 4457[10] 6147[7]

Dune Raider (USA) *David Evans* a57 83
9 b g Kingmambo(USA) —Glowing Honor (USA) (Seattle Slew (USA))
322[6]

Dunfishin (IRE) *M S Tuck* a4
3 ch g Chineur(FR) —Sisal (IRE) (Danehill (USA))
667[8] 980[13] 1760[13]

Dungannon *Andrew Balding* a77 97
3 b g Monsieur Bond(IRE) —May Light (Midyan (USA))
1731[5] (2164) 2868[3] 4398[2] (4742) 6319[2]

Dunhoy (IRE) *Stef Higgins* a78
2 ch c Goodricke—Belle Of The Blues (IRE) (Blues Traveller (IRE))
7408[8] 7503[5] 7610[3] (7677) 7916[2]

Dunmore Boy (IRE) *Richard Fahey* a68 65
2 ch c Iffraaj—Night Club (Mozart (IRE))
2855[3] 3316[4] 3897[4] 5021[4] 5354[7] 6163[6] 6694[6] 6978[7] 7471[6] (7576) (7931)

Dunn'o (IRE) *Clive Cox* a100 102
5 b g Cape Cross(IRE) —Indian Express (Indian Ridge)
1085[2] 1533[3] 1857[8] 2472[3] 3692[3] 4816[8] 5556[2] 6089[5]

Duo Victorieux (FR) *T Larriviere* a63 85
3 b c Victory Note(USA) —Spring Morning (FR) (Ashkalani (IRE))
548a[3]

Du Plessis *Brian Ellison* a17 40
3 b g Kyllachy—Shrink (Mind Games)
1878[11] 2787[7]

Duplicity *James Given* a95 95
3 b g Cadeaux Genereux—Artful (IRE) (Green Desert (USA))
945[10] 1019[3] 1315[12] 2972[7] ◆ 3696[10] 5442[6] 5966[10] 6358[11] 6771[2] 7115[4] 7554[13] 7842[5]

Duquesa (IRE) *David Evans* a65 61
2 b f Intikhab(USA) —Love Of Silver (USA) (Arctic Tern (USA))
4517[6] 5441[6] 6286[8] (6674) ◆ 6868[2] 7087[9] 7118[3]

Durante Alighieri *Henry Cecil* a79
2 b c Galileo(IRE) —Puce (Darshaan)
7152[12] 7559[2]

Durban Thunder (GER) *T Mundry* a84 102
4 ch h Samum(GER) —Donna Alicia (GER) (Highland Chieftain)
(7102a) 7532a[4]

D'Urberville *John Jenkins* a75 55
3 b g Auction House(USA) —Laser Crystal (IRE) (King's Theatre (IRE))
134[3] 302[2] 455[6] 1495[2] (2336) 3055[7] 4931[3] 5869[2] (6287) 6856[4] 7323[12] (7833) (7912)

Durgan *Linda Jewell* a68 68
4 b g Dansili—Peryllys (Warning)
110[9] 285[4] 356[4] 587[11] 5623[8] 6455[6] 6956[3] 7250[3] 7441[5] 7640[5] 7757[2] 7960[5]

Durham Express (IRE) *Michael Dods* a34 74
3 b g Acclamation—Edwina (IRE) (Caerleon (USA))
2494[2] 3277[7] 3599[8] 6299[9] (6461) 6879[12] 7225[4]

Durham Town (IRE) *Dean Ivory* a68 62
3 b g Arakan(USA) —Southern Spectrum (IRE) (Spectrum (IRE))
(692) 2702[10] 3325[7] 4022[10] 4206[9] 7737[8] 7964[7]

During The War (USA) *Chris Dwyer* a45 67
3 b g Lion Heart(USA) —Carson's Star (USA) (Carson City (USA))
133[7] 283[9]

Dust Cloud (IRE) *Peter Winkworth* 30
2 gr g Verglas(IRE) —For Freedom (IRE) (King Of Kings (IRE))
5582[13] 6279[11]

Duster *Hughie Morrison* a90 88
3 b g Pastoral Pursuits—Spring Clean (FR) (Danehill (USA))
1873[2] (2807) 3401[9] 5838[3] 6274[3] 6798[11] 7238[2] 7560[2]

Dusty Bluebells (IRE) *J S Moore* 54
2 ch f Le Vie Dei Colori—Flying Ridge (IRE) (Indian Ridge)
5372[5]

Dusty Spirit *Bill Turner* a78 75
3 b g Invincible Spirit(IRE) —Dusty Dazzler (IRE) (Titus Livius (FR))
901[2] 1052[2] 1546[4] 2287[8] 2824[10] 3400[5]

Dutiful *Mick Channon* a76 74
3 ch g Dubawi(IRE) —Pelagia (IRE) (Lycius (USA))
1392[10] 2200[2] 2503[4] (3363) 3755[2] 4479[4] (4779) 5238[6] 5887[6] 6336[2] (Dead)

Duty Free (IRE) *James Moffatt* a71 74
6 b g Rock Of Gibraltar(IRE) —Photographie (USA) (Trempolino (USA))
1807[7] 2285[3]

Dux Scholar *Sir Michael Stoute* 105
2 b c Oasis Dream—Alumni (Selkirk (USA))
4550[4] ◆ 5392[2] ◆ (5871) 6737[3] 7095[2]

Dvinsky (USA) *Paul Howling* a82 74
9 b g Stravinsky(USA) —Festive Season (USA) (Lypheor)
26[3] 102[4] 192[5] 325[3] (364) 579[4] 678[2] 924[4] 986[5] 1063[3] 1276[5] (2246) 2635[4] 3463[3] 3855[7] 4130[9] (4255) 4777[2] 5174[5] 5768[7] 6078[3] 6164[7] 6524[6] 6854[3] 6997[7] 7391[10] 7483[4] 7613[5] 7656[3]

Dwilano (GER) *N Sauer* 102
7 ch h Silvano(GER) —Dwings (IRE) (In The Wings)
7457a[10]

Dylanesque *Michael Jarvis* a86 89
3 b f Royal Applause—Ventura Highway (Machiavellian (USA))
2682[2] 3790[6] 4483[2] 5199[4] 5972[2] 6430[6] 7243[6] 7568[10]

Dynamic Air (USA) *John Gosden* 42
3 b c Dynaformer(USA) —Polaire (IRE) (Polish Patriot (USA))
2684[11]

Dynamic Drive (IRE) *Walter Swinburn* a81 92
3 b g Motivator—Biriyani (IRE) (Danehill (USA))
1268[5] 1912[4] ◆ 2386[7] 5918[9] 6427[2] (6781) ◆ (6957)

Dynamic Idol (USA) *Mikael Magnusson* a78 70
3 bb c Dynaformer(USA) —El Nafis (USA) (Kingmambo (USA))
1735[4] 3563[3] 4062[4]

Dynamic Saint (USA) *Doug Watson* a85 64
7 b g Sweetsouthernsaint(USA) —Le Nat (USA) (Dynaformer (USA))
436a[9]

Dynamo Dave (USA) *Mark Usher* a54 53
5 b g Distorted Humor(USA) —Nothing Special (CAN) (Tejabo (CAN))
135[6] 249[9] 318[9] 614[4] 847[10] 1443[7] 1633[9] 2589[10] 3132[7] 3338[8] 4283[8] 4776[6] 5075[6]

Dynaslew (USA) *Seth Benzel* 108
4 bb m Dynaformer(USA) —Slew's Final Answer (USA) (Seattle Slew (USA))
6757a[6]

Dynasty *A P O'Brien* a84 103
3 b c Danehill Dancer(IRE) —Dash To The Top (Montjeu (IRE))
1786a[2] 2354a[8]

Dyna Waltz *John Gosden* a77 105
3 b f Dynaformer(USA) —Valentine Waltz (IRE) (Be My Guest (USA))
1312[9] (1909) 5881[12] 6320[4]

Dysios (IRE) *Luca Cumani* a58
2 b c Invincible Spirit(IRE) —Hataana (USA) (Robellino (USA))
7112[9] 7386[11] 7595[10]

Dzesmin (POL) *Richard Fahey* a64 85
8 b g Professional(IRE) —Dzakarta (POL) (Aprizzo (IRE))
220[9] 1398[13]

Eager To Bow (IRE) *Patrick Chamings* a67 71
4 b g Acclamation—Tullawadgeen (IRE) (Sinndar (IRE))
499[3] 693[2] 1171[3] (1441) 2198[2] (3056) (4232) 5174[2] 5555[2] 6023[4] 6864[5]

Eagle Falls (AUS) *David Hayes* a109 116
5 br g Hussonet(USA) —Desina (AUS) (Desert King (IRE))
1024a[5] ◆

Eagle Mountain *M F De Kock* a101 124
6 b h Rock Of Gibraltar(IRE) —Masskana (IRE) (Darshaan)
630a[2]

Eagle Nebula *Brett Johnson* a68 55
6 ch g Observatory(USA) —Tarocchi (USA) (Affirmed (USA))
4433[3] 5180[7] 7167[4] 7321[2] 7569[2] 7765[6]

Earl Of Fire (GER) *W Baltromei* 113
5 ch g Areion(GER) —Evry (GER) (Torgos)
1955a[8] 2559a[9] (3934a) 5649a[2] 6764a[9]

Earl Of Leitrim (IRE) *Brian Meehan* 102
2 ch c Johannesburg(USA) —Mambo Halo (USA) (Southern Halo (USA))
4221[5] ◆ (6465) (7080)

Earlsmedic *Stuart Williams* a96 89
5 ch g Dr Fong(USA) —Area Girl (Jareer (USA))
177[6] 212[5] 307[5] ◆ 1332[16] 2399[15] 3401[13] 5048[9] 6040[3] (6421) 7033[2] 7697[11]

Earl Wild (IRE) *Howard Johnson* 83
2 b c Kodiac—Canoe Cove (IRE) (Grand Lodge (USA))
3498[2] 3897[2] (4402) 4797[3] (6030)

Early Applause *B W Hills* 78
2 b c Royal Applause—Early Evening (Daylami (IRE))
1309[6] 2547[8] 4346[4] 5947[3] 6505[5]

Earth Symbol (JPN) *Yoshitada Munakata* 98
5 b m Tokai Teio(JPN) —Triple Time (JPN) (Real Shadai (USA))
7460a[14]

Eastern Anthem (IRE) *Mahmood Al Zarooni* 120
6 b h Singspiel(IRE) —Kazzia (GER) (Zinaad)
1026a[6]

Eastern Aria (UAE) *Mark Johnston* a87 114
4 b m Halling(USA) —Badraan (USA) (Danzig (USA))
1665[7] 1956a[4] 3144[13] (4143) (4507) ◆ 5108a[4] (5881) 7368a[7]

Eastern Gift *Gay Kelleway* a74 79
5 ch g Cadeaux Genereux—Dahshah (Mujtahid (USA))
256[2] 814[5] 1323[6] 1440[8] 2383[3] 3168[2] 3412[6] 3690[2] (3911) 4108[11] 4690[6] 5391[6] 5852[15] 7467[3] 7768[3] 7920[2]

Eastern Hills *Alan McCabe* a72 76
5 b g Dubai Destination(USA) —Rainbow Mountain (Rainbow Quest (USA))
2382[8] 2864[10] 3061[9] 3610[7] 5864[6] (6077) 6335[3] 6633[3] 6922[5] (7125) 7474[2] 7611[5] (7804) 7956[7]

Eastern Magic *Reg Hollinshead* a59 71
3 b g Observatory(USA) —Inchtina (Inchinor)
2603[4] 3275[6] 4521[7] 7184[3]

Eastern Paramour (IRE) *Rod Millman* 86
5 b m Kris Kin(USA) —Hishi Lover (USA) (Pleasant Colony (USA))
2674[3] 3477[3] (4294) (5084) 6151[7] 6691[9]

Eastwell Smiles *Richard Phillips* a63 60
6 gr g Erhaab(USA) —Miss University (USA) (Beau Genius (CAN))
1758[4] 4990[7]

Easydoesit (IRE) *Desmond Donovan* a40 21
2 b g Iffraaj—Fawaayid (USA) (Vaguely Noble)
6514[13] 6743[9] 7152[9]

Easy Over (IRE) *Ed McMahon* 65
2 ch c Dr Fong(USA) —Desert Alchemy (IRE) (Green Desert (USA))
4543[4] ◆

Easy Target (FR) *Gary Moore* a90 89
5 ch g Danehill Dancer(IRE) —Aiming (Highest Honor (FR))
4133[6] 4489[7]

Easy Terms *Rod Millman* 74
3 b f Trade Fair—Effie (Royal Academy (USA))
1137[4] 1431[3] 2718[6] 2998[2] 3628[5] 5038[3] 5872[4] 5986[4] 6476[4] 6829[4] 7015[5]

Easy Ticket (IRE) *David Brown* 97
2 ch c Kheleyf(USA) —Lady Joshua (IRE) (Royal Academy (USA))
3199[2] ◆ (4116) 4851[2] (5745) 6191[3] 6751[5]

Easy Wonder (GER) *Ian Wood* a51 49
5 b m Royal Dragon(USA) —Emy Coasting (USA) (El Gran Senor (USA))
160[6] 234[3] 320[7] 390[7] 470[10] 576[5] 682[9] 795[8] 847[12] 1771[10] 2010[7] 2257[7] 2875[4] 3291[7] 3338[6] 3524[6] 3715[3] 3982[8] 4439[3] 4763[8] 4969[4] 5159[3] 5326[10] 5655[7] 6098[7]

Eavesdropper *Mahmood Al Zarooni* 91
3 br c Singspiel(IRE) —Echoes In Eternity (IRE) (Spinning World (USA))
(1912) ◆ 2226[6] 2738[5]

Eaves Lane (IRE) *Richard Fahey* 66
2 b f Whipper(USA) —Cape Columbine (Diktat)
6071[5] ◆ 6360[4]

Ebiayn (FR) *Alan King* a82 79
4 b g Monsun(GER) —Drei (USA) (Lyphard (USA))
(971) 3512[6] 4101[5] 4657[7] 4694[5]

Ebony Boom (IRE) *Gary Moore* a77 77
3 b g Boreal(GER) —Elegant As Well (IRE) (Sadler's Wells (USA))
1302[2] 1735[3] 2252[6] (2782) 4573[13]

Ebony Cat (IRE) *B P Galvin* a45 58
3 bb f One Cool Cat(USA) —Kariyh (USA) (Shadeed (USA))
4563a[4]

Ebony Song (USA) *Jeremy Noseda* a65 72
2 bb g Songandaprayer(USA) —Thiscatsforcaryl (USA) (Storm Cat (USA))
4803[12] 5453[8] (6019) 6870[4] 7035[5]

Ebraam (USA) *Ronald Harris* a105 92
7 b g Red Ransom(USA) —Futuh (USA) (Diesis)
108[10] 212[4] 358[7] 446[5] 528[4] 737[7] 887[3] 1206[12] 1580[9] 1979[4] (7635) (7784) 7906[5] 7998[2]

Ebtihaj *Richard Hannon* a48
2 br f Trade Fair—Bint Makbul (Makbul)
7112[7]

Ebur Mac *Neville Bycroft*
6 ch g Abou Zouz(USA) —Nishara (Nishapour (FR))
2994[15]

Echo Dancer *Trevor Wall* a74 62
4 br g Danehill Dancer(IRE) —Entail (USA) (Riverman (USA))
1508[11]

Echoes Rock (GER) *Doug Watson* a71 108
7 b g Tiger Hill(IRE) —Evening Breeze (GER) (Surumu (GER))
440a[8] 610a[10] 823a[10]

Echo Ridge (IRE) *Ralph Beckett* a75
2 b f Oratorio(IRE) —Lochridge (Indian Ridge)
(7608)

Echos Of Motivator *Ronald Harris* a67 21
2 ch c Motivator—Echo River (USA) (Irish River (FR))
3769[5] 4131[12] 5156[7] 5659[14] 6334[6]

Eclair De Lune (GER) *Ronald McAnally* 108
4 b m Marchand De Sable(USA) —Elegante (GER) (Acatenango (GER))
(5320a) 7343a[6]

Eclipsed (USA) *John Best* a48 15
3 ch g Proud Citizen(USA) —Kamareyah (IRE) (Hamas (IRE))
655[5] 5839[8] 6522[13] 7161[6] 7829[12]

Ecliptic (USA) *Mahmood Al Zarooni* 104
2 ch c Kingmambo(USA) —Indy Five Hundred (USA) (A.P. Indy (USA))
2547[2] (2932) 3868[2]

Ecological (IRE) *Rune Haugen*
2 b c Intikhab(USA) —Ecco Mi (IRE) (Priolo (USA))
7099[18]

Edas *Tom Cuthbert* a74 75
8 b g Celtic Swing—Eden (IRE) (Polish Precedent (USA))
2492[6] 2976[14] 3502[5] 4405[7] 5530[8] 6032[3] 7054[2]

Eddie Dowling *Milton Harris* a54 22
5 b g High Chaparral(IRE) —Dans Delight (Machiavellian (USA))
3348[12]

Eddie Jock (IRE) *S Seemar* a99 100
6 ch g Almutawakel—Al Euro (FR) (Mujtahid (USA))
337a[5] 513a[7] 708a[5]

Edelweiss *Richard Fahey* 60
3 b f Royal Applause—Flying Wanda (Alzao (USA))
5122[3]

Eden Nights (USA) *John Gosden* a52 65
3 bb f Mr Greeley(USA) —So Spirited (USA) (Favorite Trick (USA))
1431[5] ◆ 2180[6] 2478[11] 2901[U]

Ede's *Pat Phelan* a32
10 ch g Bijou D'Inde—Ballagarrow Girl (North Stoke)
7490[11]

Ede'Sajolygoodfelo *Pat Phelan*
2 b c Exceed And Excel(AUS) —For Love (USA) (Sultry Song (USA))
6635[11]

Ede's Dot Com (IRE) *Pat Phelan* a66 63
6 b g Trans Island—Kilkee Bay (IRE) (Case Law)
1064[5] 1305[2] 1737[9] 3777[12] 7614[8]

Edge Closer *Richard Hannon* a111 106
6 b g Bold Edge—Blue Goddess (IRE) (Blues Traveller (IRE))
2030[8] 2400[3] 3193[8] 3461[5] 3674[5] 4136[7] 4576[15] 6735[16]

Edge End *Lisa Williamson* a50 61
6 ch g Bold Edge—Rag Time Belle (Raga Navarro (ITY))
7125[15] 7786[5] 8006[6]

Edgefour (IRE) *Ben Case* a50 41
6 b m King's Best(USA) —Highshaan (Pistolet Bleu (IRE))
1931[6]

Edgewater (IRE) *John Akehurst* a88 88
3 b g Bahamian Bounty—Esteemed Lady (IRE) (Mark Of Esteem (IRE))
1019[2] ◆ 1315[7] 1913[5] 3088[7] 3578[9] 4231[3] 4930[3] 5390[6] 5754[8] 6253[5] 6478[6] 6780[3] 7115[6] 7414[7]

Edgeworth (IRE) *Brendan Powell* a68 79
4 b g Pyrus(USA) —Credibility (Komaite (USA))
1265[4] 1618[4] 2339[7] 2823[6] 4108[10] 4498[5] 6832[13] 7611[6] 7732[3] (7878) 8018[2]

Edin Burgher (FR) *Terry Clement* a36 46
9 br g Hamas(IRE) —Jaljuli (Jalmood (USA))
248[6] 682[5]

Edinburgh Knight (IRE) *Paul D'Arcy* a99 85
3 b g Selkirk(USA) —Pippas Song (Reference Point)
(583) ◆ (884) 1327[9] 1616[7] 5030[7] 5383[4] 6253[2] 7079[13] 7443[2] ◆ 7566[4] (7993) ◆

Edith's Boy (IRE) *Simon Dow* a74 70
4 ch g Trans Island—My Ramona (Alhijaz)
241[6] 806[10] 2639[7] 3211[5] 3818[2] 4292[10] 5207[6] 7721[2] 8037[2]

Edition *Jeremy Gask* a66 71
3 b g Bahamian Bounty—Sumingasedit (IRE) (Peintre Celebre (USA))
392[8] 1260[3] 1766[5] 2398[2] 2863[7] 3739[5] 4289[4] 6632[6] 7015[3]

Edmaaj (IRE) *B W Hills* 77
2 ch c Intikhab(USA) —Lady Angola (USA) (Lord At War (ARG))
4490[2] ◆ 5277[5] 5936[2]

Ed's A Red *Alan Berry* 28
3 b f Auction House(USA) —Gracious Imp (USA) (Imp Society (USA))
2535^{9} 3354^{5}

Eduardo *Jedd O'Keeffe* a60 54
2 b g Beat Hollow—Cuyamaca (IRE) (Desert King (IRE))
2384^{11} 3769^{4} 4682^{3} 5389^{8} 6300^{5} 7004^{5}

Educated Son *William Muir* a65 61
2 br g Diktat—Spring Sunrise (Robellino (USA))
3832^{8} 4587^{3} 5170^{8} 6695^{3} 7210^{2} 7295^{4}

Edward Whymper *Mark H Tompkins* a69 64
3 ch g Bahamian Bounty—Sosumi (Be My Chief (USA))
3606^{10} (7003)

Eeny Mac (IRE) *Neville Bycroft* 55
3 ch g Redback—Sally Green (IRE) (Common Grounds)
1118^{5} 1298^{4} 1753^{4} 1970^{10} 4151^{4} 4898^{9} 6076^{7}

Effervesce (IRE) *Sir Michael Stoute* a46 81
3 ch f Galileo(IRE) —Royal Fizz (IRE) (Royal Academy (USA))
1501^{6} 3266^{3} 4117^{3} 4618^{2} (5902) 6361^{7}

Efficiency *Michael Blanshard* a66 73
4 b m Efisio—Trounce (Barathea (IRE))
587^{5} 855^{9} 931^{9} 1225^{13} 1763^{14}

Effigy *Henry Candy* a80 86
6 b g Efisio—Hymne D'Amour (USA) (Dixieland Band (USA))
1841^{4} 2284^{2} 2991^{5} 3737^{5} 4501^{6} 5287^{4} 5833^{3} 6444^{3} ◆ 6958^{3}

Efidium *Neville Bycroft* a54 69
12 b g Presidium—Efipetite (Efisio)
2851^{10} 4168^{5} 4897^{14}

Efisio Princess *John E Long* a73 72
7 br m Efisio—Hardiprincess (Keen)
892^{4} (2790) 3761^{4}

Efistorm *Conor Dore* a76 88
9 b g Efisio—Abundance (Cadeaux Genereux)
(1266) 2681^{12} 3474^{7} 4245^{5} 4625^{4} 4942^{3} (5262) (5628) 7326^{10} 7719^{8} ◆ 7784^{2} 7961^{6} 8005^{6}

Efrosini *Alan McCabe*
2 b f Phoenix Reach(IRE) —Lady Soleas (Be My Guest (USA))
6071^{11}

Egmarey (IRE) *David Lanigan* a74 71
3 bb f Oasis Dream—Qui Liz (USA) (Benny The Dip (USA))
2998^{4} 3437^{7} 4069^{9} 4705^{2} 5113^{4} 5607^{3} 6166^{2} (6578)

Egon (IRE) *W Hickst* 101
4 ch h Groom Dancer(USA) —Ernanda (GER) (Hernando (FR))
4012a^{5} 6011a^{9}

Egorr Redfeer *Paul Midgley* a49
3 b g Grand Slam(USA) —Tobaranama (IRE) (Sadler's Wells (USA))
533^{9} 670^{7} 1887^{12}

Egyptian Lord *Peter Grayson* a49 57
7 ch g Bold Edge—Calypso Lady (IRE) (Priolo (USA))
243^{9} 402^{13} 7860^{10} 7984^{7}

Egyptology (IRE) *Mark Johnston* a63 63
3 ch g Shamardal(USA) —Golden Digger (USA) (Mr Prospector (USA))
366^{7} 698^{13}

Eigelstein *P Schiergen* 88
2 b c Dubawi(IRE) —Estefania (GER) (Acatenango (GER))
7544a^{6}

Eightdaysaweek *Alan McCabe* a65 51
4 b m Montjeu(IRE) —Figlette (Darshaan)
42^{5}

Eightfold Path (USA) *P Bary* 106
3 b c Giant's Causeway(USA) —Divine Proportions (USA) (Kingmambo (USA))
5576a^{7}

Eight Hours *Richard Fahey* a68 63
3 b g Bahamian Bounty—Alchimie (IRE) (Sri Pekan (USA))
(519) 782^{6} 1584^{11} 1968^{7} 2203^{5} 2787^{4} 3276^{12}

Eijaaz (IRE) *Geoffrey Harker* a40 69
9 b g Green Desert(USA) —Kismah (Machiavellian (USA))
1801^{2} 2218^{3} (4015) (4484) (4673) 6032^{6} 6297^{3} 6650^{6} (6915) 7284^{12} 7475^{9}

Eilean Eeve *George Foster* a27 16
4 b m And Beyond(IRE) —Yeveed (IRE) (Wassl)
7170^{7}

Eilean Mor *Jim Goldie* 68
2 ch g Ishiguru(USA) —Cheviot Heights (Intikhab (USA))
3163^{4} 3498^{7} 4512^{3} 5042^{2} 5434^{3} 5818^{9} 6220^{2} 6619^{5} 7050^{4} 7224^{5}

Eire *M Nigge* a103 98
6 ch m Medicean—Mavourneen (USA) (Dynaformer (USA))
953a^{4} 1792a^{10} 7776a^{0}

Eirnin (IRE) *A P O'Brien* 75
2 ch f Galileo(IRE) —Litani River (USA) (Irish River (FR))
6401a^{9}

Eishin Flash (JPN) *Hideaki Fujiwara* 119
3 bb c King's Best(USA) —Moonlady (GER) (Platini (GER))
7615a^{8}

Eisteddfod *Paul Cole* a91 111
9 ch g Cadeaux Genereux—Ffestiniog (IRE) (Efisio)
108^{12} 204^{4} 1662^{8}

Ejeed (USA) *Zoe Davison* a69 60
5 b g Rahy(USA) —Lahan (Unfuwain (USA))
(145) (234) 552^{5} ◆ 1063^{4} 1304^{4} 1779^{3} 2009^{6} 2866^{8} 2964^{3}

Ejteyaaz *Richard Fahey* 86
3 b g Red Ransom(USA) —Camaret (IRE) (Danehill (USA))
2058^{9} 2466^{2} 2979^{4} 3427^{4} 3878^{4} 5121^{4} ◆ 6355^{9} 6753^{2}

Ekin *P Riccioni* 101
5 b g Mujahid(USA) —Eye To Eye (Exit To Nowhere (USA))
1944a^{5} 6238a^{4} 6976a^{5}

Ekstreme (NZ) *Bryce Revell* 106
5 b m Ekraar(USA) —Cashcade (NZ) (Anziyan (USA))
14

Ektibaas *B W Hills* 71
2 ch c Haafhd—Aspen Leaves (USA) (Woodman (USA))
4803^{7}

Ektimaal *Ed Dunlop* a86 78
7 ch g Bahamian Bounty—Secret Circle (Magic Ring (IRE))
292^{2}

Ela Gonda Mou *Peter Charalambous* a29 70
3 ch f Where Or When(IRE) —Real Flame (Cyrano De Bergerac)
4805^{4} 5842^{6}

Ela Gorrie Mou *Peter Charalambous* a51 83
4 b m Mujahid(USA) —Real Flame (Cyrano De Bergerac)
1775^{3} ◆ 2262^{6} (3036) 3457^{4} ◆ 3962^{3} 4137^{7}

El Amarillista (ARG) *J Barton* a80
4 br h Mutakddim(USA) —Potra Amazona (ARG) (Potrillon (ARG))
414a^{10} 608a^{14} 797a^{12}

Eland Ally *Tom Tate* 71
2 b g Striking Ambition—Dream Rose (IRE) (Anabaa (USA))
2498^{4} 3365^{3} 4368^{5} 4701^{3} 5637^{3} 6878^{3}

Elas Diamond *Jeremy Noseda* 97
2 gb f Danehill Dancer(IRE) —Ela Athena (Ezzoud (IRE))
6154^{2} ◆ (6874) 7235^{2}

El Cambio (AUS) *Mahmood Al Zarooni* a101 112
6 br g Commands(AUS) —Chaparra (AUS) (Canny Lad (AUS))
515a^{3} ◆ 822a^{11} 2400^{7}

El Cuerpo E L'Alma (USA) *G Botti* 36
2 b f Harlan's Holiday(USA) —Fabulist (USA) (Devil's Bag (USA))
7383a^{8}

Eldaafer (USA) *Diane Alvarado* a107 104
5 bb g A.P. Indy(USA) —Habibti (USA) (Tabasco Cat (USA))
(7339a)

Eldalil *Sir Michael Stoute* a61 103
3 br f Singspiel(IRE) —White House (Pursuit Of Love)
(1329) 3101^{2} ◆ 4178a^{11} 5249^{6} 6886^{13}

El Dececy (USA) *John Balding* a82 86
6 b g Seeking The Gold(USA) —Ashraakat (USA) (Danzig (USA))
1366^{6} 1653^{10} 2381^{3} 2854^{2} 3149^{2} ◆ 5067^{2} (5406) 5732^{11} 6664^{2} 7421^{12} (7988)

El Diego (IRE) *Jeremy Gask* a63 66
6 b g Sadler's Wells(USA) —Goncharova (USA) (Gone West (USA))
1783^{9} 2243^{8}

El Dorado (JPN) *H Takaoka* 106
6 b g Stay Gold(JPN) —White Leap (JPN) (White Muzzle)
2154a^{8}

Eleanora Duse (IRE) *Sir Michael Stoute* a79 115
3 b f Azamour(IRE) —Drama Class (IRE) (Caerleon (USA))
1334^{2} ◆ 2029^{3} (2889) 5248^{3} (6007a) 6928^{10}

Electioneer (USA) *Michael Easterby* a64 80
3 b g Elusive Quality(USA) —Secret Charm (IRE) (Green Desert (USA))
4558^{3} ◆ 4654^{5} 4942^{7} ◆ 5484^{9} 6073^{9} ◆ 6664^{6} 6981^{12} 7144^{7} 7539^{7} 7841^{8} 8005^{5}

Electra Star *William Haggas* a75 76
2 b f Shamardal(USA) —Ascot Cyclone (USA) (Rahy (USA))
4095^{3} 4508^{7} 7198^{2}

Electric City (IRE) *Michael Quinlan* a61 73
3 b f Elusive City(USA) —Accell (IRE) (Magical Wonder (USA))
884^{11} 1061^{8} 1810^{8} 2503^{11} 3055^{6} 3951^{2} 4249^{7} 4687^{7} 5423^{5} 5653^{9}

Electric Feel *Marco Botti* 103
3 b f Firebreak—Night Gypsy (Mind Games)
2546^{5} 3143^{13} 5120^{5} 5883^{5} 6351^{3} 6887^{7}

Electric Warrior (IRE) *Conor Dore* a92 92
7 b g Bold Fact(USA) —Dungeon Princess (IRE) (Danehill (USA))
297^{8}

Electric Waves (IRE) *Ed McMahon* 105
2 ch f Exceed And Excel(AUS) —Radiant Energy (IRE) (Spectrum (IRE))
1577^{4} 2202^{2} (3029) (4124) (5036) ◆ 5907^{7} (6734)

Electrolyser (IRE) *Clive Cox* a90 115
5 gr h Daylami(IRE) —Iviza (IRE) (Sadler's Wells (USA))
1615^{3} 4506^{2} 5218^{4} 5909^{10}

Elegant Dancer (IRE) *Paul Green* 53
3 ch f Choisir(AUS) —Sofistication (IRE) (Dayjur (USA))
1465^{2} ◆ 1753^{9} 1971^{8} 3205^{5} 3387^{8} 3677^{9} 4127^{7} 6574^{8} 7300^{6}

Elegant Muse *Walter Swinburn* a67 72
2 b f Fraam—Georgianna (IRE) (Petardia)
2338^{3} 7021^{7} 7408^{3}

Elegant Star (IRE) *Dave Morris* a9
2 b f Where Or When(IRE) —So Elegant (IRE) (Bahhare (USA))
7603^{6} 7802^{5}

Elevate Bobbob *Alan Berry* a29
4 b g Observatory(USA) —Grandma Lily (IRE) (Bigstone (IRE))
503^{14}

Elfaaten (USA) *Marcus Tregoning* 14
2 bb c Forestry(USA) —Thaminah (USA) (Danzig (USA))
7094^{16}

Elfine (IRE) *Harry Dunlop* 63
2 b f Invincible Spirit(IRE) —Donnelly's Hollow (IRE) (Docksider (USA))
6651^{6} ◆ 6953^{2}

El Hadji (CZE) *Ivan Kub*
8 g Glenstal(USA) —Emlah (USA) (Elmaamul (USA))
4183a^{8}

Elhamri *Conor Dore* a80 71
6 bb g Noverre(USA) —Seamstress (IRE) (Barathea (IRE))
3958^{9} 4041^{8} 4518^{7} 5176^{2} 6284^{3} 6368^{2} 6700^{5} 6932^{2} (6997) 7319^{3} 7961^{9} 7984^{5}

Elie Shore *Ben Haslam* a49 46
3 b f Tobougg(IRE) —Mitsuki (Puissance)
1461^{12}

Elijah Pepper (USA) *David Barron* a81 74
5 ch g Crafty Prospector(USA) —Dovie Dee (USA) (Housebuster (USA))
171^{3} 2578^{6} (2817) 2982^{12} 3216^{4} 3855^{2} ◆ 4515^{7} 5067^{3} 5407^{2} 5737^{3} 6116^{8} (6935) (7274) 7680^{3}

Elisheba (FR) *F Doumen* a76 91
3 b f Okawango(USA) —Art Fair (FR) (Fairy King (USA))
926a^{9}

Elite Land *Brian Ellison* a71 74
7 b g Namaqualand(USA) —Petite Elite (Anfield)
173^{4} 2285^{2} 5549^{7} 6224^{9} 7145^{3}

Eliza Doolittle *Nick Littmoden* a64 59
4 b m Royal Applause—Green Supreme (Primo Dominie)
3280^{5} 4232^{8} 4427^{5}

Eljowzah (IRE) *Clive Brittain* 47
2 b f Acclamation—Express Logic (Air Express (IRE))
2505^{7}

Elkhorn *Julie-Ann Camacho* a34 60
8 b g Indian Ridge—Rimba (USA) (Dayjur (USA))
1885^{9} 2381^{2} 3027^{5} 5045^{4} 5535^{6} 5817^{10} 7468^{11}

Elkmait *Clive Brittain* a38 80
2 b f Trade Fair—Rich Dancer (Halling (USA))
2223^{3} 2641^{8} 3583^{3} (4233) 4842^{8} 5880^{20} 6563^{15}

Ella *Alan Swinbank* a96 96
6 b m Pivotal—Flossy (Efisio)
1151^{2} 1829^{2} 5387^{5} 5879^{5} 7084^{17}

Ella Grace (USA) *Richard Fahey* a61 65
3 bb f Broken Vow(USA) —Shy Swan (USA) (Nureyev (USA))
4188^{6} 4867^{5} 5550^{2} 6266^{4} 6747^{4} 6993^{8} 7467^{6} 7601^{3} 7731^{10}

Ella Woodcock (IRE) *Eric Alston* a76 71
6 b g Daggers Drawn(USA) —Hollow Haze (USA) (Woodman (USA))
29^{5} (543) 725^{3} 855^{4} 1028^{10} 1396^{3} 1426^{3} 1513^{11} 2204^{4}

Ellbeedee (IRE) *Michael Jarvis* a66 75
3 b f Dalakhani(IRE) —Tochar Ban (USA) (Assert)
1932^{2} 2860^{8} 3428^{2} 4134^{8} (4874)

Elle Est *Eric Alston* a36 58
3 ch f Zafeen(FR) —Shafaq (USA) (Dayjur (USA))
1335^{4} 1648^{7} 2706^{6} 3758^{14} 7810^{8} 7869^{5} 8006^{3}

Ellemujie *Dean Ivory* a89 96
5 b g Mujahid(USA) —Jennelle (Nomination)
1265^{6} 1617^{6} (2506) 2934^{9} 4051^{2} 4594^{7} 5753^{4} 5913^{7} 6447^{10} (7044) 7292^{4}

Elleno (IRE) *F & L Camici* 88
6 b h Celtic Swing—El Gran Love (USA) (El Gran Senor (USA))
1712a^{5}

Ellen Vannin (IRE) *Eve Johnson Houghton* a54 58
3 ch f Tagula(IRE) —Felin Special (Lyphard's Special (USA))
1280^{7} 2879^{6} 3333^{5} 3507^{3} 4210^{9} (4692) 5169^{8} 5580^{7} 6255^{6} 6956^{4}

Elle Shadow (IRE) *P Schiergen* 105
3 b f Shamardal(USA) —Elle Danzig (GER) (Roi Danzig (USA))
2372a^{3} 3943a^{2} 4640a^{2} (5671a) 6613a^{6} (7532a)

El Libertador (USA) *Jeremy Gask* a73 74
4 bb g Giant's Causeway(USA) —Istikbal (USA) (Kingmambo (USA))
315^{3} 487^{5} 587^{9} 1047^{6} 1520^{8} 2167^{6} 2726^{2} 3280^{2} 3768^{7} 4308^{8} 4488^{11} 7992^{8}

Ellie In The Pink (IRE) *Alan Jarvis* a4 51
2 ch f Johannesburg(USA) —Stravinia (USA) (Stravinsky (USA))
2642^{9} 3861^{7} 4317^{10}

Ellies Image *Brian Baugh* a24 66
3 b f Lucky Story(USA) —Crown City (USA) (Coronado's Quest (USA))
1392^{12} (2274) 2834^{4} 3387^{6} (3775) 4127^{16} (4674) 5024^{14}

Ellie's Prince *Simon Burrough*
7 b g Baryshnikov(AUS) —Princess Imp (Impecunious)
922^{9}

Ellikan (IRE) *Nick Littmoden* 38
2 b f Exceed And Excel(AUS) —Ikan (IRE) (Sri Pekan (USA))
6263^{6}

Elliptical (USA) *Gerard Butler* a88 104
4 b g Arch(USA) —Citidance Missy (USA) (Citidancer (USA))
1088^{13} 1388^{2} 1697^{2} 1846^{4} 2977^{13} (4579) 5307^{5} ◆ 6193^{2} ◆ 6562^{25}

Elliwan *Michael Easterby* a65 36
5 b g Nayef(USA) —Ashbilya (USA) (Nureyev (USA))
2583^{10}

El Maachi *David Evans* 71
2 b g Librettist(USA) —Tatanka (IRE) (Lear Fan (USA))
4263^{6} 4899^{3} 5676^{7}

Elmaam *William Haggas* 73
2 ch f Nayef(USA) —Almahab (USA) (Danzig (USA))
7231^{3}

El Mansour (USA) *Clive Cox* 76
2 ch c Rahy(USA) —La Vida Loca (IRE) (Caerleon (USA))
3000^{6} 3631^{4} 5582^{2} 6160^{2} 6414^{3}

Elmfield Giant (USA) *Richard Fahey* a82 78
3 ch g Giant's Causeway(USA) —Princess Atoosa (USA) (Gone West (USA))
2072^{3} 2515^{4} (3451) 4496a^{5} 5641^{4} 5942^{7} 6543^{3} 7042^{2} 7293^{5}

El Miracle (SWE) *Ole Larsen* 72
4 b g Funambule(USA) —L'Arc De Ciel (FR) (Bay Comeau (FR))
4641a^{11}

El Muqbil (IRE) *Brian Meehan* 87
2 b c Medicean—Tariysha (IRE) (Daylami (IRE))
3794^{4} ◆ 5277^{2} 6883^{2}

Elna Bright *Brett Johnson* a101 93
5 b g Elnadim(USA) —Acicula (IRE) (Night Shift (USA))
(108) (365) 739^{3} 944^{10} 5950^{13} 7522^{3} ◆ 7689^{4}

Elnawin *Richard Hannon* a106 109
4 b h Elnadim(USA) —Acicula (IRE) (Night Shift (USA))
1014^{2} 1353^{2} 1700^{5} 1906^{3} 2536^{6} 2999^{2} 3486a^{3} (4105)

El Passos (IRE) *Roger Curtis* a42
6 b g Imperial Ballet(IRE) —Hever Golf Lady (Dominion)
963^{11}

El Potro *John Holt* a48 62
8 b g Forzando—Gaelic Air (Ballad Rock)
178^{7} 264^{6} 668^{9}

Elrasheed *John Dunlop* 65
2 b c Red Ransom(USA) —Ayun (USA) (Swain (IRE))
5049^{7}

Elshabakiya (IRE) *Clive Brittain* 82
2 b f Diktat—Amalie (IRE) (Fasliyev (USA))
2251^{2} 2616^{2}

Elsie Jo (IRE) *Michael Wigham* a56 23
4 b m Catcher In The Rye(IRE) —Joy St Clair (IRE) (Try My Best (USA))
3064^{15} 3605^{7} 3993^{11}

Elsie's Orphan *Patrick Chamings* a72 60
3 br f Pastoral Pursuits—Elsie Plunkett (Mind Games)
3125^{2} 5206^{4} (5668) 6524^{4} 6812^{11}

Elsie's Star *Tim Easterby*
2 gr f Proclamation(IRE) —Elsie Hart (IRE) (Revoque (IRE))
2461^{9}

Elspeth's Boy (USA) *John Best* a88 74
3 bb c Tiznow(USA) —Miss Waki Club (USA) (Miswaki (USA))
1699^{19} 2542^{7} 3081^{7} 7091^{6} 7488^{2} 7637^{6}

El Suacillo (IRE) *D Camuffo* 89
3 br c Invincible Spirit(IRE) —Max Almabrouka (USA) (Hennessy (USA))
1944a^{12} 4185a^{5}

Eltheeb *John Dunlop* a75 76
3 gr c Red Ransom(USA) —Snowdrops (Gulch (USA))
(1696) 2717^{3} 4546^{8} 5266^{5} 5858^{6} 6856^{3}

El Torbellino (IRE) *David O'Meara* 78
2 b f Chineur(FR) —Deeday Bay (IRE) (Brave Act)
4554^{4} ◆ 4899^{4} 5509^{6} 5784^{2} 5947^{5} (6457)

Elusive Art (IRE) *David Marnane* a67 67
3 b f Elusive City(USA) —Ink Pot (USA) (Green Dancer (USA))
4563a^{2}

Elusive Award (USA) *Andrew Oliver* a99 90
3 b g Elusive Quality(USA) —Victoria Cross (IRE) (Mark Of Esteem (IRE))
1414a^{7} 1786a^{7}

Elusive Diva (IRE) *Edward Creighton* a48
2 b f Elusive City(USA) —Wonders Gift (Dr Devious (IRE))
6520^{7} 7113^{10} 7879^{12}

Elusive Fame (USA) *Mark Johnston* a89 68
4 b g Elusive Quality(USA) —Advancing Star (USA) (Soviet Star (USA))
16^{2} 115^{6} 245^{2} 572^{8} 908^{2} 1306^{7} 1826^{3} (1997) 2524^{9} 3391^{12} 3565^{14} 3969^{9} 4684^{9} 4894^{2} 5142^{13} 5647^{3} 7314^{6} ◆ 7867^{3} 7955^{4}

Elusive Hawk (IRE) *Barney Curley* a83 78
6 b g Noverre(USA) —Two Clubs (First Trump)
(4717) 6198^{16} 7033^{6}

Elusive Love (IRE) *Mark Johnston* a66 52
2 b c Elusive City(USA) —Love Ridot (IRE) (Fruits Of Love (USA))
4702^{6} 5053^{7} 7843^{2} 7954^{6}

Elusive Pimpernel (USA) *John Dunlop* 116
3 bb c Elusive Quality(USA) —Cara Fantasy (IRE) (Sadler's Wells (USA))
(1327) ◆ 1699^{5}

Elusive Prince *David Barron* a75 71
2 b g Storming Home—Ewenny (Warrshan (USA))
5433^{3} 6264^{3} 6899^{2}

Elusive Ridge (IRE) *H Rogers* a88 81
4 b g Elusive City(USA) —Woodwing (USA) (Indian Ridge)
6971a^{13}

Elusive Ronnie (IRE) *Roger Teal* a65 48
4 b g One Cool Cat(USA) —Elusive Kitty (USA) (Elusive Quality (USA))
110^{3} (137) 312^{7} 325^{9} 614^{10} (659) 1166^{9} 1300^{11} 2198^{15} 2417^{8} 3211^{4} 3510^{7}

Elusive Sue (USA) *Richard Fahey* 78
3 bb f Elusive Quality(USA) —Show Me The Stage (USA) (Slew The Surgeon (USA))
1487^{2} 2140^{6} 3320^{3} 3919^{11} 5199^{3} 5789^{15} 7146^{9}

Elusive Trader (USA) *Ralph Beckett* a75 74
3 bb c Elusive Quality(USA) —Kumari Continent (USA) (Kris S (USA))
2052^{5} ◆ 2892^{8}

Elusive Vine (IRE) *Ronald Harris* a48 24
2 b f Elusive City(USA) —Red Eagle (IRE) (Eagle Eyed (USA))
2358^{12} 3517^{8} 5269^{4} 5583^{9} 5701^{7} 6795^{6} 7378^{7}

Elusive Warrior (USA) *Alan McCabe* a77 46
7 b g Elusive Quality(USA) —Love To Fight (CAN) (Fit To Fight (USA))
(39) (144) 191^{2} 508^{5} 572^{9} 907^{5} 1492^{5} 1653^{15} 3761^{3} 4684^{5} 4895^{6} 5647^{2} ◆ (6664) 7128^{7} 7403^{10}

Elusive Wave (IRE) *J-C Rouget* 118
4 b m Elusive City(USA) —Multicolour Wave (IRE) (Rainbow Quest (USA))
1716a^{5} 3017a^{4} 4639a^{3} (5574a) 6593a^{5}

Elusivity (IRE) *Brian Meehan* a66 65
2 b g Elusive City(USA) —Tough Chic (IRE) (Indian Ridge)
2882[7] 3624[6] 5523[5] 6810[5] ◆ *7272[3]*

El Viento (FR) *Richard Fahey* 90
2 ch g Compton Place—Blue Sirocco (Bluebird (USA))
3658[2] 4116[9] 5301[9] (5785) 5880[16] 6568[8] (6916)

Elvira Delight (IRE) *Jeremy Noseda* a65
2 b f Desert Style(IRE) —Entente Cordiale (IRE) (Ela-Mana-Mou)
7294[5]

Elvira Madigan *Andrew Balding* a71 75
3 b f Sakhee(USA) —Santa Isobel (Nashwan (USA))
2935[4] 3889[3] *4698[9]* 5467[4] 6480[8] *7022[7]*

Elyaadi *John Queally* a76 100
6 b m Singspiel(IRE) —Abyaan (IRE) (Ela-Mana-Mou)
3050[2] 5220[11]

Elysian Heights (IRE) *Jeremy Noseda* 49
2 b g Galileo(IRE) —Ziffany (Taufan (USA))
5594[8] 6128[6] 6365[5]

Elzaam (AUS) *Michael Jarvis* 111
2 b c Redoute's Choice(AUS) —Mambo In Freeport (USA) (Kingmambo (USA))
(2059) 3049[2] 3823[3] 7095[3]

Embalo (BRZ) *Doug Watson* a64
5 ch g Boatman(USA) —Shirley Purple (BRZ) (Purple Mountain (USA))
606a[9]

Embarkation *James Fanshawe* a33 50
3 ch g Medicean—Embark (Soviet Star (USA))
1769[13] 3413[11] 3640[3]

Embezzle *Roger Charlton* 43
2 b g Sadler's Wells(USA) —Trick (IRE) (Shirley Heights)
5440[5] 5857[6] 6279[9]

Embra (IRE) *Tim Etherington* a64 58
5 b g Monashee Mountain(USA) —Ivory Turner (Efisio)
2582[5] ◆ 2849[5] 3409[11] 4373[13] 5023[7] 5485[2] *6329[6]* 6464[5] *(6848)* *7018[3]* *7390[5]*

Embsay Crag *Kate Walton* 88
4 b g Elmaamul(USA) —Wigman Lady (IRE) (Tenby)
1013[2] 1378[2] 1863[3] 2513[5] 3432[7]

Emeebee *Willie Musson* a80 79
4 b g Medicean—Broughtons Motto (Mtoto)
1185[9] *1509[5]* *2236[10]* 2823[12] 3412[5] *3970[6]* *5157[U]* *7255[2]*

Emerald Commander (IRE) *Saeed Bin Suroor* 116
3 b c Pivotal—Brigitta (IRE) (Sadler's Wells (USA))
3016a[3] (3703a) 4420a[7] (5649a) 6593a[3]

Emerald Fields (IRE) *Robert Collet* 71
2 b f Whipper(USA) —Shamdiyna (IRE) (Machiavellian (USA))
5622a[8]

Emerald Girl (IRE) *Richard Fahey* a68 77
3 b f Chineur(FR) —Faypool (IRE) (Fayruz)
2242[4] 2815[3] (3023) 3505[5] *7841[7]*

Emerald Glade (IRE) *Tim Easterby* 72
3 b f Azamour(IRE) —Woodland Glade (Mark Of Esteem (IRE))
1810[2] 2438[5] 3390[8] (4648) (5093) 6225[5] 6623[4]

Emerald Ring (IRE) *David Wachman* a90 90
2 ch f Johannesburg(USA) —Inkling (USA) (Seeking The Gold (USA))
2828a[2] 3421a[5]

Emerald Royal *Edward Creighton* a30
2 b c Royal Applause—Bakhtawar (IRE) (Lomitas)
7178[11] *7478[10]*

Emeralds Spirit (IRE) *John Weymes* a19 67
3 b f Rock Of Gibraltar(IRE) —Spiritual Air (Royal Applause)
1495[5] 1866[3] 2838[10] 3153[7] 3728[8] (4337) 4864[5] 4898[2] 5758[8] (6494) 6710[2] 7056[6]

Emerald Wilderness (IRE) *Robert Cowell* a106 97
6 b g Green Desert(USA) —Simla Bibi (Indian Ridge)
334a[6] *512a[5]* *708a[4]* *821a[2]*

Emerging Artist (FR) *Mark Johnston* 100
4 b g Dubai Destination(USA) —Picture Princess (Sadler's Wells (USA))
2860[4] (3256) 3877[2] (4100) 4461[5] 4818[2] 5291[7] 5949[6]

Emil (DEN) *Ole Larsen* a90 85
6 b g Cajun Cadet—Elysian Fields (IRE) (Marju (IRE))
4526a[6]

Emilio Largo *Ralph Beckett* 64
2 b g Cadeaux Genereux—Gloved Hand (Royal Applause)
2048[5]

Eminem (GER) *N Sauer* 105
6 ch g Samum(GER) —Enigma (GER) (Sharp Victor (USA))
1420a[6]

Emirate Isle *Brian Storey* 57
6 b g Cois Na Tine(IRE) —Emmajoun (Emarati (USA))
1574[7] 2382[13] 2670[9] 6393[6] 6648[7] (7147)

Emirates Champion *Saeed Bin Suroor* a103 104
4 b h Haafhd—Janaat (Kris)
436a[2] ◆ *(605a)* 3921[13]

Emiratesdotcom *Milton Bradley* a69 61
4 b g Pivotal—Teggiano (IRE) (Mujtahid (USA))
2590[3] 2919[7] 3556[9] (3727) 4283[6] (5586) *(5926)* 6421[5] 6515[6] *6713[3]* *7162[5]* *7441[3]* *7525[6]* *7614[10]*

Emirates Dream (USA) *Saeed Bin Suroor* 105
3 b c Kingmambo(USA) —My Boston Gal (USA) (Boston Harbor (USA))
2160a[7] 4068[3] 4470[15] (5556) 6562[31] 7233[6]

Emirates Gold (IRE) *E Charpy* a66 102
7 b h Royal Applause—Yara (IRE) (Sri Pekan (USA))
440a[6]

Emirates Hills *Edward Vaughan* 73
3 b f Dubawi(IRE) —Starstone (Diktat)
1709[6] 2398[10]

Emma Jean Lass (IRE) *David Evans* a67 61
3 b f Choisir(AUS) —Enlisted (IRE) (Sadler's Wells (USA))
9[7] *159[4]* *276[9]*

Emma's Gift (IRE) *Julia Feilden* 96
2 gr f Aussie Rules(USA) —Rose Of Mooncoin (IRE) (Brief Truce (USA))
1324[4] ◆ 1603[3] (2022) 3141[5] 4097[6] 4592[4] 4842[9]

Emma's Secrets *Derek Shaw* a27 48
5 bb m Fraam—Hopping Higgins (IRE) (Brief Truce (USA))
1345[4] 4234[10] 4938[4] 5055[8] 5535[7]

Emmeline Pankhurst (IRE) *Julia Feilden* a24 51
2 b f Marju(IRE) —Mango Groove (IRE) (Unfuwain (USA))
2389[7] 6884[6] *7164[7]*

Emmpat (IRE) *C F Swan* a91 94
12 b g Bigstone(IRE) —Nordic Abu (IRE) (Nordico (USA))
6730a[P] (Dead)

Emmrooz *D Selvaratnam* a106 106
5 b g Red Ransom(USA) —Nasmatt (Danehill (USA))
607a[7] *713a[13]*

Emmy Darling (USA) *Doug O'Neill* a90 102
4 ch m Graeme Hall(USA) —Dance Delight (USA) (Colonial Affair (USA))
6603a[5]

Emperor Hadrian (IRE) *A P O'Brien* 98
2 b g Holy Roman Emperor(IRE) —Gilded Edge (Cadeaux Genereux)
954a[7] ◆ 3100[7] 3868[4] 4880a[4] 5567a[4]

Emperorsnewclothes (IRE) *Michael Appleby* a37 27
2 gr c Holy Roman Emperor(IRE) —On Air (USA) (Cozzene (USA))
5921[13] 6628[7] 6953[12] *7392[7]* *7540[7]*

Emperor's Princess (FR) *Richard Hannon* a68 62
2 b f Holy Roman Emperor(IRE) —Elanaaka (Lion Cavern (USA))
5692[8] *6247[6]* 6468[6]

Emperor's Well *Michael Easterby* a53 54
11 ch g First Trump—Catherines Well (Junius (USA))
3520[7] 3538[6] 3978[9] 4454[5] 4644[3] 4985[12] *5767[4]* *5927[7]* 6296[11]

Empires Choice (NZ) *Bart Cummings* 108
7 b h Redoute's Choice(AUS) —Rosie's Star (NZ) (Star Way)
6946a[13]

Empire Seeker (USA) *Heather Main* a53 60
5 br g Seeking The Gold(USA) —Lady From Shanghai (USA) (Storm Cat (USA))
164[7]

Empire Storm (GER) *A Wohler* 97
3 b c Storming Home—Emy Coasting (USA) (El Gran Senor (USA))
5671a[2]

Empirico (FR) *David Marnane* a86 77
4 b g Oasis Dream—Esprit Libre (Daylami (IRE))
6142[22]

Empowering (IRE) *A P O'Brien* a84 46
2 b f Encosta De Lago(AUS) —Blue Cloud (IRE) (Nashwan (USA))
7256a[8]

Empress Charlotte *Michael Bell* a62 55
2 b f Holy Roman Emperor(IRE) —Charlotte O Fraise (IRE) (Beat Hollow)
3411[9] 3906[5] 4421[4] 5837[6] *7496[2]* *7691[5]*

Empress Leizu (IRE) *Tony Carroll* a64 51
3 b f Chineur(FR) —Silk Point (IRE) (Barathea (IRE))
1775[5] 3739[11] 4325[10] *5155[4]* *(6574)* *6930[6]* *7117[5]* *7467[4]* *7685[6]*

Empress Royal *Michael Dods* 66
2 b f Royal Applause—Akhira (Emperor Jones (USA))
1879[5] 3549[4] 4149[4] (6035) 6645[8]

Emulous *D K Weld* 108
3 b f Dansili—Aspiring Diva (USA) (Distant View (USA))
5016a[3] (6617a) ◆

Enabling (IRE) *Richard Hannon* a90 90
2 b c High Chaparral(IRE) —Joyful (IRE) (Green Desert (USA))
3794[10] 4856[3] 5413[2] (5857) 6149[3] *6850[2]*

Enact *Sir Michael Stoute* a98 104
4 b m Kyllachy—Constitute (USA) (Gone West (USA))
1727[2] 4576[24] *7524[2]* *7875[6]*

Enak (ARG) *Saeed Bin Suroor* a110
4 br h Orpen(USA) —Enfeite (ARG) (Roy (USA))
510a[9] *796a[3]* *1023a[4]*

Enchanted Evening (IRE) *D K Weld* 93
4 b m High Chaparral(IRE) —Glen Kate (Glenstal (USA))
2355a[4] 5568a[12]

Enchanting Smile (FR) *Alan McCabe* 70
3 b f Rakti—A Thousand Smiles (IRE) (Sadler's Wells (USA))
1010[8] 1380[4] 3176[5] ◆ 3662[2]

Encircled *John Jenkins* a86 92
6 b m In The Wings—Ring Of Esteem (Mark Of Esteem (IRE))
636[4] *888[4]* *1161[2]* *5753[9]* *6428[8]* *7044[11]* *7252[4]* *7687[4]*

Encompassing (IRE) *A P O'Brien* a54 99
3 b g Montjeu(IRE) —Sophisticat (USA) (Storm Cat (USA))
1858[5] 2354a[13] 3048[9] 4469[7]

Encore Une Annee *Ralph Beckett* a78 77
2 b f Hernando(FR) —Eternelle (Green Desert (USA))
6442[4] 7057[3] ◆ *(7325)*

Encore Un Fois *B W Hills* 50
2 br c Val Royal(FR) —Factice (USA) (Known Fact (USA))
6532[9] ◆

Encore View *Andrew Balding* a61
2 b f Oasis Dream—Aricia (IRE) (Nashwan (USA))
7608[4] *7879[9]*

Endaxi Mana Mou *Michael Quinlan* a74 41
2 bb f Araafa(IRE) —Lake Nyasa (IRE) (Lake Coniston (IRE))
4587[7] *6118[2]* *6451[9]* *7393[6]* *(7540)*

Enderby Spirit (GR) *Bryan Smart* 108
4 gr g Invincible Spirit(IRE) —Arctic Ice (IRE) (Zafonic (USA))
1400[5] 2400[8] 3108[2] 3674[4] 4085[12] 5911[16] 7060[3] 7351[11]

End Of The Affair (IRE) *V C Ward* a71 90
6 ch m Indian Ridge—Blend Of Pace (IRE) (Sadler's Wells (USA))
1560a[7]

Endorser *William Muir* a54
2 ch c Le Vie Dei Colori—Cinciallegra (Royal Applause)
4096[17] 4436[12] *4682[4]* 5373[11] 5389[11]

Energizing *Richard Hannon* a77
2 b c Zamindar(USA) —Maria Bonita (IRE) (Octagonal (NZ))
7873[2] *(8001)*

En Fuego *Peter Chapple-Hyam* 78
3 b c Firebreak—Yanomami (USA) (Slew O'Gold (USA))
2122[P] 5493[8] (5839) 6197[13] 6805[7]

Engaging *Peter Cundell* a58
4 b m Oasis Dream—Dialing Tone (USA) (Distant View (USA))
768[5] *931[10]*

England (IRE) *Nick Littmoden* a59 55
3 b g Bertolini(USA) —Radha (Bishop Of Cashel)
638[3] *788[7]* 2221[14]

Engulf (IRE) *William Haggas* a73 84
3 b g Danehill Dancer(IRE) —All Embracing (IRE) (Night Shift (USA))
1381[6] 2121[2] 2762[2] 3397[2] 5419[2] *6056[4]*

Enjoyment *Michael Bell* 63
3 b f Dansili—Have Fun (Indian Ridge)
5474[9]

Enjoy The Moment *Jamie Osborne* 91
7 b g Generous(IRE) —Denial (Sadler's Wells (USA))
3050[12] 4467[17]

Enlightening (IRE) *Richard Hannon* a69 76
2 b c Elusive City(USA) —Mono Star (IRE) (Soviet Star (USA))
4263[10] 5651[2] 6145[2] 6675[5] *7294[4]* *7550[5]*

Enlist *Brendan Powell* a69 40
6 b g Beat Hollow—Dawna (Polish Precedent (USA))
941[9] 1077[7] *1226[11]* 2198[11]

Enora (GER) *T Mundry* 106
3 ch f Noverre(USA) —Enrica (Niniski (USA))
(4640a) 6013a[11]

Enriched (USA) *Doug O'Neill* a104 112
5 bb g High Brite(USA) —Li'l Ms. Leonard (USA) (Nostalgia's Star (USA))
4417a[3] 6759a[5]

Enrichment *Harry Dunlop* 19
2 b f Iffraaj—Prospering (Prince Sabo)
1256[6] 1793[13]

Ensaya (IRE) *M Delzangles* 90
3 b f Alhaarth(IRE) —Ebatana (IRE) (Rainbow Quest (USA))
6519a[3]

Ensign's Trick *Mark Brisbourne* a26 23
6 b m Cayman Kai(IRE) —River Ensign (River God (USA))
2590[15] 2965[9] 4342[9] 4606[11] 5331[12]

Ensnare *Ann Duffield* a81 71
5 b g Pivotal—Entrap (USA) (Phone Trick (USA))
151[6] 7306[13]

Entangle *Arnfinn Lund* a82 90
4 b m Pivotal—Entwine (Primo Dominie)
2020a[4] 5350a[2]

Enthusing (IRE) *David Elsworth* 77
2 b c Noverre(USA) —Catatonic (Zafonic (USA))
3034[2] 4379[2] 5053[2] (6146) 6989[4]

Entitled *Sir Michael Stoute* a81 82
3 ch f Pivotal—Noble One (Primo Dominie)
3738[2] 4414[2] 4874[2] *(7310)* ◆

Entrance *Julia Feilden* a69 66
2 ch f Iceman—Enrapture (USA) (Lear Fan (USA))
5829[4] *6247[4]* *6711[5]* *7087[5]* *7644[4]*

Entre Deux Eaux (FR) *Robert Collet* a83 108
4 gr m Ange Gabriel(FR) —Goutte D'Eau (FR) (Vacarme (USA))
7800a[0]

Enzio (GER) *N Milliere* a88 103
4 ch g Next Desert(IRE) —Elle Diva (GER) (Big Shuffle (USA))
(1251a) 1716a[8]

Eolith *William Knight* a83 85
3 ch f Pastoral Pursuits—Evening Guest (FR) (Be My Guest (USA))
6252[7] 6510[15] *7114[9]* *7574[10]*

Epernay *Ian Williams* 61
3 b f Tiger Hill(IRE) —Riberac (Efisio)
4114[9] 4661[7] 5150[6] 5942[6]

Ephigenie (IRE) *T Mundry* 97
4 b m Groom Dancer(USA) —Enrica (Niniski (USA))
5345a[6] 6763a[4]

Epic (IRE) *Mark Johnston* a75 89
3 b g Celtic Swing—Needwood Epic (Midyan (USA))
203[3] *840[3]* 1608[8] 2422[5] 2816[7] 3390[7] 3750[7] (4289) 4520[7] (4953) (5215) (5858) 6074[7] 6565[13] *7084[7]*

Epsom Girl *Pat Phelan* a42
3 ch f Haafhd—Largo (IRE) (Selkirk (USA))
6499[9] *7043[9]* *7872[9]*

Epsom Salts *Pat Phelan* a78 84
5 b g Josr Algarhoud(IRE) —Captive Heart (Conquistador Cielo (USA))
1087[3] 1579[8] 2228[2] 2975[4] 3843[11] 6201[7] *7044[12]*

Equiano (FR) *B W Hills* 124
5 b h Acclamation—Entente Cordiale (IRE) (Ela-Mana-Mou)
(1326) (1700) 2325[2] (3047) 3870[2] 5276[12]

Equine Science *Gavin Blake* a61 31
3 b g Lucky Owners(NZ) —Miles (Selkirk (USA))
4697[6] 5150[8] *5842[5]* *6452[10]*

Equinity *Jeff Pearce* a63 52
4 b m Ishiguru(USA) —Notable Lady (IRE) (Victory Note (USA))
8[6] *146[2]* *251[3]* *(319)* *391[4]* *555[7]* *(968)* *1166[10]* 1642[5] 2010[6] 2234[4] 3510[8] 3762[6] 4430[10] 4790[6] 6329[2] 7425[2]

Equuleus Pictor *John Spearing* a93 94
6 br g Piccolo—Vax Rapide (Sharpo)
2[4] 1295[13] 2681[9] 2940[8] 3736[8] 4243[4] 4625[7] 5528[7] 6064[4] 7180[4] *7326[8]* *7405[3]* *7866[5]*

Equus Ferus (IRE) *Ms Joanna Morgan* a79 62
2 b c Noverre(USA) —Kibarague (Barathea (IRE))
6726a[2]

Eradicate (IRE) *Nicky Henderson* 103
6 b g Montjeu(IRE) —Coyote (Indian Ridge)
2469[7] 3194[16]

Ercolini (IRE) *F Rodriguez Puertas* 98
3 b f Pyrus(USA) —Bajan Belle (IRE) (Efisio)
2801a[7] 5139a[8]

Erdeli (IRE) *Tim Vaughan* a71 62
6 b g Desert Prince(IRE) —Edabiya (IRE) (Rainbow Quest (USA))
4691[1] 4327[3] *(4915)* 5260[10]

Erebus (IRE) *Sylvester Kirk* a64 76
3 b c Fasliyev(USA) —Velvet Slipper (Muhtafal (USA))
1760[3] (2408) 3914[8] 4248[3] 4398[3] 4754[2] (5614) 6461[8] *7093[5]*

Erfaan (USA) *Julie-Ann Camacho* a27 66
3 bb g Forest Camp(USA) —Look For Good (USA) (Unbridled's Song (USA))
399[5] 2114[4] 5816[5] 6896[15] *7064[12]*

Ergo (FR) *James Moffatt* a71 76
6 b h Grand Lodge(USA) —Erhawah (Mark Of Esteem (IRE))
1458[7] 1867[4]

Ericaceous *Christine Dunnett*
3 b f Bollin Eric—Sealed Orders (Bustino)
2674[12]

Erinjay (IRE) *Michael Wigham* a85 66
4 b g Bachelor Duke(USA) —Quinella (Generous (IRE))
(367) ◆ *430[4]* *487[4]* 1617[10]

Ermine Grey *Tony Carroll* a63 68
9 gr g Wolfhound(USA) —Impulsive Decision (IRE) (Nomination)
656[5] *853[7]* 1028[7] 1179[2] *1193[2]* *1763[4]* 2922[10] 3130[7] *3783[10]* 4681[6]

Ermyn Express *Pat Phelan* a66 63
3 b f Selkirk(USA) —Aymara (Darshaan)
1582[14] 4626[7] 5593[5] 6633[8] 6991[2] *(7323)* *7445[8]*

Ermyn Lodge *Pat Phelan* a83 87
4 br g Singspiel(IRE) —Rosewood Belle (USA) (Woodman (USA))
(1454) (1902) 3159[8] (6352)

Ermyntrude *Pat Phelan* a58 57
3 bb f Rock Of Gibraltar(IRE) —Ruthie (Pursuit Of Love)
3788[7] 4621[9] (5171) 5414[4] 6862[2] *7323[4]* *7487[3]* *7717[3]*

Ernmoor *Andrew Price* a51 34
8 b g Young Ern—Linpac North Moor (Moorestyle)
2012[9] 2604[8] 2874[9] 3360[9]

Errigal Lad *John Balding* a45 88
5 ch g Bertolini(USA) —La Belle Vie (Indian King (USA))
2113[18] 2883[11] 3120[4] 3809[8] 4234[2] 4706[11] 4868[4] 5496[5] *7537[9]*

Erroll (SWE) *Patrick Wahl* a63 98
4 ch h King Charlemagne(USA) —Trisha (SWE) (Brief Truce (USA))
2020a[7]

Ertikaan *Michael Jarvis* 94
3 b g Oasis Dream—Aunty Mary (Common Grounds)
2121[7] 2564[3] 3220[3] (3621) 4264[2] 4858[3] 6321[4]

Ertiyaad *Sir Michael Stoute* a78 70
3 b f Sakhee(USA) —Asawer (IRE) (Darshaan)
3437[4] 4115[6] *6166[3]* *6698[5]*

Erythrina (IRE) *Brendan Powell* a16 48
2 b f Elnadim(USA) —Louve Heureuse (IRE) (Peintre Celebre (USA))
3861[11] 4299[7] 5032[8] *5660[14]* 7177[10]

Esaar (USA) *B W Hills* 83
3 b g Mr Greeley(USA) —Al Desima (Emperor Jones (USA))
1308[6] 4238[5]

Escala *Michael Squance* a45 67
2 b f Diktat—Starbeck (IRE) (Spectrum (IRE))
6058[8] *6575[6]* 6748[3] 7098[11] *7470[8]*

Escape Artist *Tim Easterby* 56
3 gr g Act One—Free At Last (Shirley Heights)
2606[2] 2853[6] 3626[5] (4200) 5534[5] 6648[4]

Escape Route (USA) *S Seemar* a103 103
6 b g Elusive Quality(USA) —Away (USA) (Dixieland Band (USA))
(511a) *707a[5]*

Escardo (GER) *David Bridgwater* a66 51
7 b g Silvano(GER) —Epik (GER) (Selkirk (USA))
746[4] *852[6]* *1241[9]* *1462[9]* 1771[6] 2006[11] *2788[9]* 3787[7] *7071[4]* *7199[2]* *7508[4]*

Escholido (IRE) *B W Hills* 77
2 b c Noverre(USA) —Midnight Partner (IRE) (Marju (IRE))
4396[2] 4902[3] 5886[2] (6635)

Eseej (USA) *Peter Hiatt* a82 78
5 ch g Aljabr(USA) —Jinaan (USA) (Mr Prospector (USA))
282[2] *323[3]* *(857)* *897[3]* 1077[4] 1277[4] 1484[9] *1828[8]* *1996[6]* *3781[6]* *4019[7]* 5180[2] 5828[6] 6427[8]

Eshoog (IRE) *Clive Brittain* 77
2 b f Kyllachy—Catherine Wheel (Primo Dominie)
2397[5] 3590[3] 4095[4]

Eshtyaaq *Marcus Tregoning* a74 73
3 b c Mark Of Esteem(IRE) —Fleet Hill (IRE) (Warrshan (USA))
1479[2] 2011[3]

Eskendereya (USA) *Todd Pletcher* a126 86
3 ch c Giant's Causeway(USA) —Aldebaran Light (USA) (Seattle Slew (USA))
(1097a)

Eskimo (IRE) *A P O'Brien* 99
2 b c Galileo(IRE) —Dietrich (USA) (Storm Cat (USA))
3190[8] 6347[4]

Esoterica (IRE) *Jim Goldie* 97
7 b g Bluebird(USA) —Mysterious Plans (IRE) (Last Tycoon)
1708[12] 2100[3] 3146[22] 3448[3] 3619[3] 4085[11] 5787[11] 6178[9]

Especially Special (IRE) *Peter Grayson* a67 72
4 b m Exceed And Excel(AUS) —Super Trouper (FR) (Nashwan (USA))
119[9] (Dead)

Espero (IRE) *Linda Perratt* a85 82
4 b g Celtic Swing—Zota (IRE) (Barathea (IRE))
1513[8] 2428[7] 3318[8] 3708[2] 3987[3] 4371[9] 5407[5] 5737[10] 6105[11] 6709[8]

Espirita (FR) *E Lellouche* 108
2 b f Iffraaj—Belle Esprit (Warning)
(4884a) (7008a)

Espiritu (FR) *Saeed Bin Suroor* a103 107
4 b g Dansili—Red Bravo (USA) (Red Ransom (USA))
441a[2] 627a[5]

Espoir City (JPN) *Akio Adachi* a123
5 ch h Gold Allure(JPN) —Eminent City (JPN) (Brian's Time (USA))
7367a[10]

Esprit De Midas *Kevin Ryan* a88 97
4 b g Namid—Spritzeria (Bigstone (IRE))
286[7] 474[4] 1332[2] 2657[10] 3178[9] 4085[7] 4370[3] ◆ 4894[6] 5197[2] (6048) 6357[12] 6721[10] 7060[2] ◆

Espy *Ian McInnes* a73 75
5 b g Piccolo—Running Glimpse (IRE) (Runnett)
27[5] 391[2] (562) 678[7] 789[9] 4942[10] 5513[5] 5764[4] 6295[13] 6456[8] 6741[3] 7468[10] (7519) 7639[4] 7827[5] 7972[5] 8019[8]

Essexbridge *Richard Hannon* a73 82
3 b c Avonbridge—Aonach Mor (Anabaa (USA))
1582[9] 1973[2] 2079[8] 3697[4] 4758[4] 5529[13] 6202[8] (6257) 6637[2]

Estate *David Pipe* a70 80
8 b g Montjeu(IRE) —Fig Tree Drive (USA) (Miswaki (USA))
173[5] 293[5] 529[5] 874[3]

Esteem Lord *Dean Ivory* a66 69
4 ch g Mark Of Esteem(IRE) —Milady Lillie (IRE) (Distinctly North (USA))
552[7] 975[11] 1172[12] 1304[7] 2235[3] 2419[7] 2596[15] 3323[10] 3786[5] (7023) ◆ 7445[4] ◆ (7814) 7966[5]

Esteem Machine (USA) *David Evans* a83 91
6 b g Mark Of Esteem(IRE) —Theme (IRE) (Sadler's Wells (USA))
695[7]

Estejo (GER) *R Rohne* 111
6 b h Johan Cruyff—Este (GER) (The Noble Player (USA))
1540a[2] 3019a[5] 5804a[7] 6764a[10] 7373a[3]

Estephe (IRE) *T Stack* a73 87
4 b m Sadler's Wells(USA) —Tarascon (IRE) (Tirol)
1247a[10]

Estonia *Michael Squance* a62 36
3 b f Exceed And Excel(AUS) —Global Trend (Bluebird (USA))
6931[4] 7166[9] 7207[9] 7564[6] (7721) (8037)

Estourah (IRE) *Saeed Bin Suroor* 73
2 b c Dalakhani(IRE) —Canouan (IRE) (Sadler's Wells (USA))
6831[3] ◆ 7099[3]

Estrela Anki (BRZ) *P Bary* 96
5 b m Thignon Lafre(BRZ) —Marne La Coquette (BRZ) (Effervescing (USA))
418a[10] 711a[8]

Esuvia (IRE) *Bryan Smart* a82 94
3 b f Whipper(USA) —Aoife (IRE) (Thatching)
(1104) ◆ 1399[5] 2140[2] ◆ 2656[3] (3599) 6113[15] 7351[12] 7566[8]

Etarre (IRE) *Pam Sly* a68 60
2 br f Giant's Causeway(USA) —Speedy Sonata (USA) (Stravinsky (USA))
5078[7] 6248[3] 6469[7]

Etched (USA) *Kiaran McLaughlin* a124
5 ch h Forestry(USA) —Unbridled Elaine (USA) (Unbridled's Song (USA))
7367a[6]

Eternal Instinct *Jim Goldie* 79
3 b f Exceed And Excel(AUS) —Glenhurich (IRE) (Sri Pekan (USA))
2450[3] 4583[6] 5335[7] 5409[4] 6221[8]

Eternal Ruler (IRE) *Alan Swinbank* 74
2 b g Aussie Rules(USA) —Villafranca (IRE) (In The Wings)
(7049)

Eternal Youth (IRE) *Ronald Harris* a69 60
2 ch g Intikhab(USA) —Endless Peace (IRE) (Russian Revival (USA))
7762[4] 7886[3]

Ethics Girl (IRE) *John Berry* a81 81
4 b m Hernando(FR) —Palinisa (FR) (Night Shift (USA))
3217[7] 3679[2] 4306[5] 4737[4] 5243[3] (5757) 6199[10] 7045[7] (7410) 7568[8] 7861[4] (8007)

Etoile Filante (IRE) *Jeremy Gask* a47
3 br f Key Of Luck(USA) —Callisto (IRE) (Darshaan)
7086[7] 7413[6] 7887[4]

Eton Fable (IRE) *Bill Ratcliffe* a63 84
5 b g Val Royal(FR) —Lina Story (Linamix (FR))
1960[6] 2513[2] 4334[9] 4737[7] 5118[10] 7836[3] 7932[3]

Eton Forever (IRE) *Michael Jarvis* a96 95
3 b g Oratorio(IRE) —True Joy (IRE) (Zilzal (USA))
1387[6] (1769) 2542[2] 3696[5]

Eton Rifles (IRE) *Howard Johnson* 101
5 b g Pivotal—Maritsa (IRE) (Danehill (USA))
2657[4] 4371[8] 4843[13] 6142[6] 6570[2] 6721[2] 7348[2]

Etruscan (IRE) *Chris Gordon* a55 79
5 b g Selkirk(USA) —Maddelina (IRE) (Sadler's Wells (USA))
2181[6] 6091[11] 6639[8] 7788[7] 7996[13]

Ettrick Mill *Milton Bradley* a37 45
4 ch g Selkirk(USA) —Milly-M (Cadeaux Genereux)
2004[7] 2298[9] 3374[10] 7070[11] 7498[6]

Eucharist (IRE) *Richard Hannon* a90 98
2 b f Acclamation—Satin Rose (Lujain (USA))
1577[7] 2251[4] (2680) 3482[3] (4228) (4578) (5882) ◆

Eurasian *David Simcock* a37 62
3 b c Oasis Dream—Habariya (IRE) (Perugino (USA))
5116[6] 5665[8] 6876[13] 7117[12]

European Dream (IRE) *Richard Fahey* a77 90
7 br g Kalanisi(IRE) —Tereed Elhawa (Cadeaux Genereux)
205[7] 6106[7]

Euroquip Boy (IRE) *Michael Scudamore* a9 53
3 b g Antonius Pius(USA) —La Shalak (IRE) (Shalford (IRE))
1450[12] 2003[8] 2441[5]

Euston Square *David Nicholls* a83 77
4 b g Oasis Dream—Krisia (Kris)
1099[12] 1707[10] 2428[4] 3876[7] 4579[12] 5510[5] 6108[4] 6366[3]

Evading Tempete *F Rohaut* a95 110
3 b f Dubai Destination(USA) —Late Summer (USA) (Gone West (USA))
(926a) 1196a[2] (1713a) 3143[5] 5139a[5] 5782a[2]

Evaporation (FR) *C Laffon-Parias* a90 107
3 b f Red Ransom(USA) —Polygreen (FR) (Green Tune (USA))
1566a[10] 2801a[3] 4639a[6] 5802a[3]

Evaso Nice *Desmond Donovan* a34 38
2 b f Iceman—Avanindra (Zamindar (USA))
2642[7] 2963[9]

Evelyn May (IRE) *B W Hills* a81 80
4 b m Acclamation—Lady Eberspacher (IRE) (Royal Abjar (USA))
1770[3] ◆ 2094[4] 2626[7] (4090) 6256[11] 6981[4] 7573[6]

Evelyns Diamond *Paul Midgley* a34
2 b f Act One—Warning Belle (Warning)
7325[8] 7452[12] 7801[8]

Even Bolder *Eric Wheeler* a82 81
7 ch g Bold Edge—Level Pegging (IRE) (Common Grounds)
241[4] (345) 431[8] 736[7] 1691[2] 2592[6] 3474[11] 3892[9] 4401[14] 4961[4] 5262[3] 5915[6] 6440[10] 6739[3] 6998[2] 7320[3] 7719[3]

Evening Dress *Mark Johnston* 59
2 ch f Medicean—Miss Hawai (FR) (Peintre Celebre (USA))
1597[6] 2448[5] 3392[5]

Evening In (IRE) *Paul Midgley* 49
2 b f Balmont(USA) —By Candlelight (IRE) (Roi Danzig (USA))
4150[4] 4554[9] 4848[7]

Evening Jewel (USA) *James Cassidy* a115 110
3 b f Northern Afleet(USA) —Jewel Of The Night (USA) (Giant's Causeway (USA))
(5351a) 7341a[3]

Evening Sunset (GER) *Michael Quinlan* a62 69
4 b m Dansili—Evening Promise (Aragon)
1395[4] 1797[5]

Evens And Odds (IRE) *David Nicholls* a111 110
6 ch g Johannesburg(USA) —Coeur De La Mer (IRE) (Caerleon (USA))
1007[7] 1326[4] 1906[7] 3193[17] 3869[12] (4576) 6177[18] 6570[4]

Even Stevens *David Nicholls* a79 52
2 br g Ishiguru(USA) —Promised (IRE) (Petardia)
6045[4] 6458[8] 6675[6] (7017) (7864) (7908)

Everaard (USA) *Kate Walton* a70 69
4 ch g Lion Heart(USA) —Via Gras (USA) (Montbrook (USA))
1028[15] 3600[7]

Ever Cheerful *Andrew Haynes* a68 47
9 b g Atraf—Big Story (Cadeaux Genereux)
442[8] 615[8] 845[9] 3763[4] 4130[5] 4790[4] 6672[6] 7192[4] 7299[6]

Evergreen Forest (IRE) *Alastair Lidderdale* 62
2 ch g Haafhd—Inaaq (Lammtarra (USA))
6149[10]

Evergrey (FR) *C Boutin* a73 77
5 gr m Verglas(IRE) —Eretria (USA) (Dynaformer (USA))
690a[3]

Ever Roses *Paul Midgley* a48 54
2 br f Pastoral Pursuits—Eljariha (Unfuwain (USA))
1375[5] ◆ 1646[5] 2130[11] 3770[7] 4409[7] 5483[3] 6034[7] 6658[4]

Ever So Bold *William Muir* a69 64
3 b g Reset(AUS) —Bold Byzantium (Bold Arrangement)
2725[3] 3259[7]

Everybody Knows *Jo Crowley* a84 96
5 b g King's Best(USA) —Logic (Slip Anchor)
(1430)

Everybody Out *Reg Hollinshead*
2 b g Striking Ambition—Nanna (IRE) (Danetime (IRE))
7598[10]

Everymanforhimself (IRE) *Kevin Ryan* a101 105
6 b g Fasliyev(USA) —Luisa Demon (IRE) (Barathea (IRE))
278[4] (537) 944[8] 2748[15] 3146[9] 3869[16] 4576[21] 5095[13] 5292[11] 5884[17] 6142[4] 6363[7] 7143[6] 7352[6] 7557[2] 7725[2] (7934) 8016[4]

Eviction (IRE) *Mandy Rowland* a67 56
3 b g Kheleyf(USA) —La Belle Katherine (USA) (Lyphard (USA))
1029[15] 2722[3] 3276[4] 3970[10] 4478[8] 7868[10]

Evident Pride (USA) *Brett Johnson* a93 73
7 b g Chester House(USA) —Proud Fact (USA) (Known Fact (USA))
25[4] 341[5]

Exceedingly Bold *Gay Kelleway* a59 89
3 b g Exceed And Excel(AUS) —Grey Pearl (Ali-Royal (IRE))
1687[5] 2028[9] 2348[5] 5524[13] 5838[11] 6701[10]

Exceedingly Good (IRE) *Roy Bowring* a52 58
4 ch m Exceed And Excel(AUS) —Ikan (IRE) (Sri Pekan (USA))
836[5] 912[9] 1391[14] (2647) 3287[3] 3763[5] 3976[4] 6679[14] 7300[13] 7473[6] 7542[3]

Exceedingthestars *Michael Squance*
3 b f Exceed And Excel(AUS) —Starbeck (IRE) (Spectrum (IRE))
5668[10]

Exceed Power *David Simcock* a60 58
3 ch f Exceed And Excel(AUS) —Israar (Machiavellian (USA))
104[4] 215[3] 265[2] 581[2] (619) 831[6] 1140[3] 1390[7] 1774[8] 2584[2] 3561[7]

Exceedthewildman *J S Moore* a85 73
3 b c Exceed And Excel(AUS) —Naomi Wildman (USA) (Kingmambo (USA))
107[3] 136[4] (203) 240[2] (386) 686[2] (840) 973[6] 2117[13] 2479[6] 4815[9] 5728[6] 6841[3]

Excel Bolt *Bryan Smart* 101
2 ch c Exceed And Excel(AUS) —Dearest Daisy (Forzando)
(2210) ◆ (2757) ◆ 3100[3]

Excelebration (IRE) *Marco Botti* 90
2 b c Exceed And Excel(AUS) —Sun Shower (IRE) (Indian Ridge)
2216[4] (2701) (4332)

Excelerate (IRE) *Edward Lynam* a90 100
7 b g Mujadil(USA) —Perle D'Irlande (FR) (Top Ville)
5571a[7] 5774a[11] 6617a[10]

Excellence (IRE) *Karen George* 18
2 b f Exceed And Excel(AUS) —Aphra Benn (IRE) (In The Wings)
4474[12]

Excellent Aim *Jane Chapple-Hyam* a30 71
3 b c Exceed And Excel(AUS) —Snugfit Annie (Midyan (USA))
1308[7] 1878[3] 2564[7] 4063[11] 6812[12] 7019[11]

Excellent Day (IRE) *Mick Channon* a68 75
3 b f Invincible Spirit(IRE) —Tosca (Be My Guest (USA))
1487[6] 2120[7] 2502[2] 3001[8] 4325[6] (4475) 5041[3] 5145[2] 5383[8] 5896[9] 6164[6]

Excellent Guest *George Margarson* 93
3 b g Exceed And Excel(AUS) —Princess Speedfit (FR) (Desert Prince (IRE))
1279[7] 2287[2] 2545[2] 3103[22] 3791[11] 4440[8] 6198[4] (6321)

Excellent Show *Bryan Smart* a89 82
4 ch m Exceed And Excel(AUS) —Quiz Show (Primo Dominie)
172[2] 250[2] 492[2] 7212[6] 7549[7] 7702[3]

Excellent Thought *Paul Howling* a74 71
3 b f Exceed And Excel(AUS) —Amiata (Pennekamp (USA))
3174[9] 4031[6] 4553[5] 5588[8] 5810[4] 6186[3] 6541[11]

Excellent Vision *Bryan Smart* a34 73
3 b c Exceed And Excel(AUS) —Classic Vision (Classic Cliche (IRE))
894[7]

Excellerator (IRE) *George Baker* a98 98
4 ch m Exceed And Excel(AUS) —Amsicora (Cadeaux Genereux)
2326[3] 2929[6] 3629[6] 5154[3] 5903[6] 7187[10]

Excelling (IRE) *PETER Makin* a66 82
3 b f Exceed And Excel(AUS) —Nojoom (IRE) (Alhaarth (IRE))
6368[6] 6996[6]

Excello *Malcolm Saunders* a87 95
2 b f Exceed And Excel(AUS) —Muffled (USA) (Mizaaya)
2176[9] (2638) 3051[3] 3482[4] 5036[10]

Excelsior Academy *Brian Meehan* a75 86
4 b g Montjeu(IRE) —Birthday Suit (IRE) (Daylami (IRE))
3955[2] 4467[18]

Exceptionally (NZ) *Terry & Karina O'Sullivan* 107
4 bb f Ekraar(USA) —Sahayb (NZ) (Zabeel (NZ))
7032a[3] 7368a[6] 7458a[2]

Exchange *William Haggas* 63
2 b g Kheleyf(USA) —Quantum Lady (Mujadil (USA))
4142[7] 4499[6] 5160[8]

Exciting Life (IRE) *T Kluczynski* 94
2 b c Titus Livius(FR) —Puerto Oro (IRE) (Entrepreneur)
7277a[4]

Excusez Moi (USA) *Ruth Carr* a58 100
8 b g Fusaichi Pegasus(USA) —Jiving (Generous (IRE))
1295[15] 2657[12] 2992[17] 3446[3] 3619[4] 4653[4] 6537[10] 7564[8]

Exearti *Alan McCabe* a67
3 b f Exceed And Excel(AUS) —Graffiti Girl (IRE) (Sadler's Wells (USA))
141[5] 370[7]

Exemplary *Mark Johnston* a86 91
3 b g Sulamani(IRE) —Epitome (IRE) (Nashwan (USA))
680[2] 1138[3] (1518) 6282[5] 6797[9] 7053[14]

Exhibition (IRE) *Francisco Castro* a97 101
5 b g Invincible Spirit(IRE) —Moonbi Ridge (IRE) (Definite Article)
2019a[3] 4526a[9]

Existentialist *Andrew Price* a61 79
3 b f Exceed And Excel(AUS) —Owdbetts (IRE) (High Estate)
1390[8] 1760[10]

Exit Smiling *Paul Midgley* a85 91
8 ch g Dr Fong(USA) —Away To Me (Exit To Nowhere (USA))
837[7] (1117) 1333[4] 1708[9] 2141[4] 2835[10] 4112[4] 5098[7] 5605[2] 5919[8] 6367[6]

Exodus *A P O'Brien* 92
2 b c Montjeu(IRE) —Spacecraft (USA) (Distant View (USA))
7456a[4]

Exopuntia *Julia Feilden* a62 55
4 b m Sure Blade(USA) —Opuntia (Rousillon (USA))
2874[4] 3238[10] 4213[5] 4763[7] (5560) 6062[3] 7005[4] 7401[6] (7899) 7986[2]

Expansion (USA) *Steven Asmussen* 111
5 b h Maria's Mon(USA) —La Sylphide (SWI) (Barathea (IRE))
6236a[9]

Expensive Legacy *Natalie Lloyd-Beavis* a51 56
3 ch f Piccolo—American Rouge (IRE) (Grand Lodge (USA))
542[8] 760[4] 6080[13]

Expensive Problem *Ralph Smith* a77 73
7 b g Medicean—Dance Steppe (Rambo Dancer (CAN))
27[8] 84[3] (262) 361[5] 487[8] 1323[5] (1875) 2236[5] 3079[6] 4057[10] 5716[2] 6289[8] 6851[10] 7889[2] 8022[5]

Experimentalist *Hughie Morrison* a67 55
2 b g Monsieur Bond(IRE) —Floppie (FR) (Law Society (USA))
6474[5] 6828[6] 7164[4]

Explorator (IRE) *George Baker* a56 89
3 b c Whipper(USA) —Certainly Brave (Indian Ridge)
1872[7] (3788) ◆ (4027) (4156) 4381[3] 6813[9]

Expose *William Haggas* a76 74
2 ch c Compton Place—Show Off (Efisio)
6146[3] (6308) 7347[6]

Expressionist *Mark Johnston* 63
3 b c Motivator—Deeply (IRE) (Darshaan)
3312[4]

Extracurricular (USA) *Steve Gollings* a62 48
4 ch m Thunder Gulch(USA) —Frans Lass (USA) (Shanekite (USA))
1507[8]

Extra Power (IRE) *Mick Channon* 82
2 b c Acclamation—Vintage Escape (IRE) (Cyrano De Bergerac)
2077[5] 2448[2] (2930) 3826[5] 4138[19] 4615[6]

Extraterrestrial *Richard Fahey* a105 106
6 b g Mind Games—Expectation (IRE) (Night Shift (USA))
885[4] 1008[5] 1383[6] 1857[10] 2708[7] 3921[14] 4463a[16] 5247[10] 6180[9] 6749[7] 7121[9]

Extremely So *Philip McBride* a64 68
4 ch m Kyllachy—Antigua (Selkirk (USA))
989[6] 1194[11] 4441[4] 4765[4] 5681[3] (6065) 6213[9]

Extreme Warrior (IRE) *David Lanigan* 83
3 ch g Dubawi(IRE) —Extreme Beauty (USA) (Rahy (USA))
2969[8]

Eye For The Girls *Mick Channon* 59
4 ch g Bertolini(USA) —Aunt Ruby (USA) (Rubiano (USA))
1130[2] 1812[9] 2053[9] 2876[3] 2965[7] 3338[2] 3914[3] 4130[10] 4959[6] (5362) 5579[4] 6679[10] 7007[7]

Eye Of Eternity *Rae Guest* a25 62
3 b f Oratorio(IRE) —Eyeq (IRE) (Cadeaux Genereux)
2335[10] 2632[12] (3264) 3607[2] 3821[2] 4746[7] 5171[3] 5664[3] 5877[5] 6862[6]

Eye Of The Tiger (GER) *J Hirschberger* 113
5 b h Tiger Hill(IRE) —Evening Breeze (GER) (Surumu (GER))
(1956a) 2574a[3]

Eyes Like A Hawk (IRE) *Jedd O'Keeffe* 61
4 br m Diktat—Mexican Hawk (USA) (Silver Hawk (USA))
1179[11] 1813[6] 2207[10] 2382[12]

Eyes On *Philip McBride* a58 64
2 b f Diktat—Almost Amber (USA) (Mt. Livermore (USA))
4474[11] 4759[4] 5160[3] 5682[3] ◆ 6695[6]

Eyesore *Shaun Harris* a32
4 b m Reel Buddy(USA) —Segretezza (IRE) (Perugino (USA))
142[5] 457[10]

Eywa *William Jarvis* a48 60
3 ch f Mark Of Esteem(IRE) —Engulfed (USA) (Gulch (USA))
583[7] 950[7] 1127[7] 2005[3] 2634[5] 3171[4] 3982[7] 4475[2]

Ezalli (IRE) *Edward Lynam* 93
3 b f Cape Cross(IRE) —Ezilla (IRE) (Darshaan)
7546a[0]

Ezdeyaad (USA) *Alan Swinbank* 98
6 b g Lemon Drop Kid(USA) —August Storm (USA) (Storm Creek (USA))
1272[12] 1513[4] (1672) 1802[6] (2241) (2885) (3206) 3585[6] 5292[13] 5605[17] 5736[9]

Ezra Church (IRE) *David Barron* a35 77
3 br g Viking Ruler(AUS) —Redrightreturning (Diktat)
1336[4] 1991[2] 2609[2] 2981[4] 3285[2] 6696[5] 6966[7]

E Z's Gentleman (USA) *Bob Baffert* a112 93
5 b r Yankee Gentleman(USA) —Tensie's Pro (USA) (Distinctive Pro (USA))
(3935a)

Ezzles (USA) *Paul Cole* a59 53
2 bb c Speightstown(USA) —Paris Glory (USA) (Honour And Glory (USA))
4303[3] 4599[8] 7880[4]

Fabiana *Andreas Lowe* 110
4 ch m Ashkalani(IRE) —Fox Croft (FR) (Bustino)
4035a[3] 4639a[4] 5649a[3] 6408a[7]

Fabiello *Tom Dascombe* a67 77
2 b c Indesatchel(IRE) —Beauty (IRE) (Alzao (USA))
3274[10] 3767[2] 4568[3] (4747) 4911[3] 5699[5] 6647[10] 6979[14]

Fabled Dancer (IRE) *Eric Alston* 48
4 ch g Choisir(AUS) —Age Of Fable (IRE) (Entrepreneur)
2421[13] 2881[7] 3207[7]

Fabulous Fong (IRE) *S Labate*
5 ch m Dr Fong(USA) —Queen Of Fairies (IRE) (Fairy King (USA))
273a[0]

Face East (USA) *Alan Berry* 15
2 b c Orientate(USA) —Yes Honey (USA) (Royal Academy (USA))
6138[13] 6488[6]

Face Reality (USA) *Richard Hannon* 87
2 ch f More Than Ready(USA) —Tivadare (FR) (Distant View (USA))
(6441) 7098[4] 7235[7]

Face The Future *Michael Dods* a58 58
2 b c Green Desert(USA) —Bird Key (Cadeaux Genereux)
4187[8] 5595[4] 6046[7] 6717[11] 6891[10] (7471)

Face The Problem (IRE) *B W Hills* 105
2 b c Johannesburg(USA) —Foofaraw (USA) (Cherokee Run (USA))
2077[4] (3961) (4388) (4600) ◆ 5221[8] 5907[8]

Face Value *Brian Meehan* a68 54
2 b g Tobougg(IRE) —Zia (GER) (Grand Lodge (USA))
6158[13] 6498[4] 7163[5] ◆

Fact *Amanda Perrett* a37
3 b f American Post—Fetish (Dancing Brave (USA))
6056[9]

Factum (USA) *A P O'Brien* a87 95
2 b c Storm Cat(USA) —Starry Dreamer (USA) (Rubiano (USA))
6403a[4] 6560[13]

Fadela Style (FR) *F Rossi* 99
3 b f Desert Style(IRE) —Tounsi (FR) (Sendawar (IRE))
3720a[2]

Fadhaa (IRE) *B W Hills* 67
2 b c Bahri(USA) —Weqaar (USA) (Red Ransom (USA))
7058[6]

Fadhb Ar Bith (IRE) *John Harris* a74 86
5 b g Tagula(IRE) —Teodora (IRE) (Fairy King (USA))
1492[3] 1997[4] 3107[4] 4121[2] (4404)

Failasoof (USA) *B W Hills* a79
2 bb c Dynaformer(USA) —Curriculum (USA) (Danzig (USA))
7112[3]

Faint Perfume (AUS) *Bart Cummings* 112
4 b f Shamardal(USA) —Zona (AUS) (Zabeel (NZ))
[9] 6947a[17] 7368a[9]

Fair Breeze *Richard Phillips* 51
3 b f Trade Fair—Soft Touch (IRE) (Petorius)
5265[7] 5839[4] 6814[8]

Fair Bunny *Alan Brown* a67 65
3 b f Trade Fair—Coney Hills (Beverley Boy)
2426[10] 2700[10] 3243[6] 4109[5] 4406[7] (5044) 5817[6] 6461[7] 7425[7] 7605[5]

Fair Dame (IRE) *Nerys Dutfield*
2 b f Fasliyev(USA) —Dame Portia (IRE) (Approach The Bench (IRE))
2407[10] 3156[7]

Fair Flair (IRE) *Pal Jorgen Nordbye* 70
6 ch m Fruits Of Love(USA) —Percision Vision (IRE) (Eagle Eyed (USA))
4526a[7]

Fairlie Dinkum *Bryan Smart* 71
2 b f Tobougg(IRE) —Fairlie (Halling (USA))
4368[7] (5332) 6184[5] 6513[7] 6979[5]

Fair Nella *Jonathan Portman* a59 62
3 b f Trade Fair—Zanella (IRE) (Nordico (USA))
422[3] 551[4] 677[5] 760[5]

Fair Passion *Derek Shaw* a83 52
3 b f Trade Fair—United Passion (Emarati (USA))
(699) (919) ◆ 1281[7] 6374[3] ◆ 6539[3] 6739[11] 7041[3] 7285[2] 7405[8]

Fairplaytomyself *Peter Hiatt* a52 37
5 ch m Ballet Master(USA) —Over The Moon (Beveled (USA))
7[9]

Fair Spin *Micky Hammond* 57
10 ch g Pivotal—Frankie Fair (IRE) (Red Sunset)
(1424) 5119[5] 6114[3] 6648[3] 6983[6]

Fair Trade *David Elsworth* 113
3 ch g Trade Fair—Ballet (Sharrood (USA))
(1387) 1699[10] 3104[8] 3827[2] 5009[4] 6195[3] 6529[3]

Fair Value (IRE) *Simon Dow* 36
2 b f Compton Place—Intriguing Glimpse (Piccolo)
6811[9]

Fairy Familiar (USA) *Luca Cumani* a74
2 b f Smart Strike(CAN) —Arabian Spell (IRE) (Desert Prince (IRE))
7448[8] 7608[2]

Fairy Flight (USA) *William Knight* a75 71
3 bb f Fusaichi Pegasus(USA) —La Barberina (USA) (Nijinsky (CAN))
1666[2] 2893[8] 3626[8] 4259[6] 4972[6] 5664[12]

Fairyhall *B Grizzetti* 92
2 b c Halling(USA) —Fairy Sensazione (Fairy King (USA))
6762a[5] 7264a[3]

Fairy Oasis *B Grizzetti* 82
3 b f Oasis Dream—Fairy Sensazione (Fairy King (USA))
1252a[5]

Fairy Promises (USA) *Pat Eddery* 77
3 ch f Broken Vow(USA) —Fairy Glade (USA) (Gone West (USA))
1658[6] 2618[13]

Fairy Shoes *Richard Fahey* a51 77
3 b f Kyllachy—Calamanco (Clantime)
1275[2] 1622[5] (2212)

Fairys In A Storm (IRE) *Alan Lockwood* 37
3 gr f Choisir(AUS) —Fidra (IRE) (Vettori (IRE))
7472[6]

Fairy Tales *John Bridger* a53 34
2 ch f Monsieur Bond(IRE) —True Magic (Magic Ring (IRE))
2413[9] 2963[10] 3439[4] 4423[5] 5412[7] 5863[4] 7017[9] 7686[4] 7777[3] 8011[7]

Faited To Pretend (IRE) *Marco Botti* a70 70
3 b f Kheleyf(USA) —Lady Moranbon (USA) (Trempolino (USA))
(985) 1453[9] 2679[3] 2904[4] 4430[5] 6078[4] 6853[2]

Faithful Duchess (IRE) *Edward Vaughan* a67 68
3 b f Bachelor Duke(USA) —Portelet (Night Shift (USA))
1362[5] 2274[5] 2875[5] 3515[2] 4031[3] 4789[2] 5267[10] 6060[4] 6455[11] 7651[7] 7810[3] 7869[2] 7987[2]

Faithful One (IRE) *David Lanigan* a91 88
3 b f Dubawi(IRE) —Have Faith (IRE) (Machiavellian (USA))
1329[4] (1659) 2170[2] 2475[2] 3217[3] 3890[4] 4956[2] (5662) 7188[10]

Faithful Ruler (USA) *Richard Fahey* a90 94
6 bb g Elusive Quality(USA) —Fancy Ruler (USA) (Half A Year (USA))
6[4] 4450[4] 5098[3] ◆ 5736[3] 6105[10] 6630[4] 6960[3] 7227[4] 7560[4] 7680[4] (7989)

Faith Jicaro (IRE) *Nicky Vaughan* a68 76
3 b f One Cool Cat(USA) —Wings To Soar (USA) (Woodman (USA))
2290[4] 2901[6] 3606[9] 3857[3] 4282[5] 4618[4] 5115[10] 6165[7] 6578[3] 7167[7] 7275[5] 7504[11] 7703[3] 7887[3] 8021[5]

Fajer Al Kuwait *George Prodromou* a48 24
2 b c Byron—Sweetypie (IRE) (Golan (IRE))
4233[8] 5160[13] 6869[5]

Fakhuur *Clive Brittain* 56
2 b f Dansili—Halska (Unfuwain (USA))
3411[7]

Falakee *Peter Chapple-Hyam* a74 41
3 b c Sakhee(USA) —Sakhya (IRE) (Barathea (IRE))
(1165) 1658[7]

Falasteen (IRE) *Richard Fahey* a72 93
3 ch g Titus Livius(FR) —Law Review (IRE) (Case Law)
(1184) 1860[6] 2260[7] 2978[11] 3430[7] 3856[8] 5290[12] (5678) 6048[8] 6364[15] 6985[10]

Falcativ *I Mohammed* a100 101
5 b g Falbrav(IRE) —Frottola (Muhtarram (USA))
629a[9]

Falcharge *B Grizzetti* 90
4 b g Falbrav(IRE) —Polar Charge (Polar Falcon (USA))
1712a[4]

Falcon Rock (IRE) *Simon Callaghan* a78 101
5 bb g Hawk Wing(USA) —Champaka (IRE) (Caerleon (USA))
1435a[4]

Falcon's Tribute (IRE) *Peter Salmon* 56
8 b m Beneficial—Early Storm (IRE) (Glacial Storm (USA))
1153[7] 2434[10]

Falcun *Luca Cumani* a33 20
3 b g Danehill Dancer(IRE) —Fanofadiga (IRE) (Alzao (USA))
2334[10] 5376[6] 5971[14]

Faldal *Gay Kelleway* a6 85
4 br m Falbrav(IRE) —Tidal (Bin Ajwaad (IRE))
1034[4] 1379[10]

Falkland Flyer (IRE) *Mick Channon* a74 74
2 b c Johannesburg(USA) —Tree Chopper (USA) (Woodman (USA))
2687[3] 2882[2] (3162) 3395[2] 3844[6] 4539[5] 4851[6] 5637[8] 5894[2] 6184[7] 6690[5] 6902[2] 7035[2]

Fallen Idol *John Gosden* a82 107
3 b c Pivotal—Fallen Star (Brief Truce (USA))
(1497) (2471) 3016a[5] 4829[4]

Falling Angel *Paul Cole* a77 77
3 b f Kylian(USA) —Belle Ile (USA) (Diesis)
3866[6] 4250[2] (5145) 5541[10]

False Promises *Derek Shaw* a39 17
2 b g Piccolo—Park Star (Gothenberg (IRE))
4890[8] 5298[13] 7268[11] 7577[6] 7643[5] 7831[7] 7910[7]

Falun (GER) *A Trybuhl* a97 101
4 ch h Pentire—Fortunata (GER) (Daun (GER))
5542a[7] 6606a[3] 7102a[7] 7532a[5]

Fama Mac *Neville Bycroft* 65
3 b g Fraam—Umbrian Gold (IRE) (Perugino (USA))
6115[11] 6966[2] 7183[6]

Fame And Glory *A P O'Brien* 131
4 b h Montjeu(IRE) —Gryada (Shirley Heights)
1247a[3] (1789a) (2369a) (2709) (4877a) 6612a[5]

Fame Is The Spur *J W Hills* a66 77
3 ch f Motivator—Subya (Night Shift (USA))
1620[6] 2225[5] 3954[5] (4381) 4996[8] 6122[11]

Family Story (FR) *J-J Napoli* a58 72
5 b m Gold Away(IRE) —Cadline (FR) (Cardoun (FR))
690a[0]

Famous (IRE) *A P O'Brien* 104
3 gr f Danehill Dancer(IRE) —Starlight Dreams (USA) (Black Tie Affair)
1036a[10] 1787a[2] 2370a[13] 3143[8] 4630a[3]

Famous Name *D K Weld* 122
5 b h Dansili—Fame At Last (USA) (Quest For Fame)
(1954a) (4312a) 5775a[6] 6237a[7]

Famous Warrior (IRE) *Kevin Prendergast* a100 101
3 b g Alhaarth(IRE) —Oriental Fashion (IRE) (Marju (IRE))
1038a[3] 1414a[4]

Fan Club *Ruth Carr* a23 41
6 ch g Zamindar(USA) —Starfan (USA) (Lear Fan (USA))
493[5] 700[4]

Fancy Point (USA) *William Phipps* a70 96
2 ch f Point Given(USA) —Fancy Clancy (USA) (Rahy (USA))
7340a[10]

Fancy Star *B W Hills* a63 55
3 b c Starcraft(NZ) —Lorien Hill (IRE) (Danehill (USA))
692[4] 2754[5] 3714[7]

Fancy Vivid (IRE) *Sir Michael Stoute* a69
3 b f Galileo(IRE) —Starchy (Cadeaux Genereux)
1769[6] 2473[3]

Fandango Boy *J P Broderick* a76 63
9 b g Victory Note(USA) —Dancing Chimes (London Bells (CAN))
259[8] 405[7] 543[5] 715[5] 925[7] 5129a[8]

Fanditha (IRE) *Luca Cumani* a86 92
4 ch m Danehill Dancer(IRE) —Splendid (IRE) (Mujtahid (USA))
2703[5] 5002[3] 5529[8] 5994[2] 6447[2] 6886[14]

Fanny May *Denis Coakley* 91
2 b f Nayef(USA) —Sweet Wilhelmina (Indian Ridge)
(2749) 3190[5] 4611a[4] 6407a[4]

Fantale *David Evans* a10
2 ch f Arakan(USA) —Question (USA) (Coronado's Quest (USA))
7990[8]

Fantasia *Jonathan Sheppard* 115
4 b m Sadler's Wells(USA) —Blue Symphony (Darshaan)
6757a[4]

Fantastic Cuix (FR) *Luca Cumani* a72 83
3 gr f Fantastic Light(USA) —Cuixmala (FR) (Highest Honor (FR))
1501[10] 2011[4] 2893[3] ◆ 4117[7]

Fantastic Favour *Jedd O'Keeffe* 62
3 b g Fantastic Light(USA) —Dixie Favor (USA) (Dixieland Band (USA))
1116[9] 1627[6] 2425[10] 3506[7] 4120[9] 5216[9] 5423[14]

Fantastico Roberto (IRE) *Todd Pletcher* 103
3 ch c Refuse To Bend(IRE) —Fantastic Account (Fantastic Light (USA))
4642a[7]

Fantastic Sam (IRE) *Kate Walton* 55
3 ch f Redback—Jellybeen (IRE) (Petardia)
1654[11] 2143[5] 2463[8] 3506[8]

Fantastic Storm *Robin Bastiman* 45
3 b g Fantastic Light(USA) —Answered Prayer (Green Desert (USA))
3077[5] 4655[3] 5303[9] 6472[7] 7147[9]

Fantastic Strike (IRE) *Mark Johnston* a79 80
3 b g Noverre(USA) —Hariya (IRE) (Shernazar)
3537[7] 5244[6] 5549[2] 5868[7] 6554[4] (6872) 7090[6]

Fantastic Times *Mel Brittain*
4 b g Fantastic Light(USA) —Goodnight Kiss (Night Shift (USA))
1119[10]

Fantasy Explorer *John Quinn* a96 72
7 b g Compton Place—Zinzi (Song)
1032[13] 1206[9] 1727[19]

Fantasy Fighter (IRE) *John Quinn* a81 54
5 b g Danetime(IRE) —Lady Montekin (Montekin)
119[5] 404[6] 2790[4] 3200[5] 3615[3] 4717[4] 4789[3] 5267[2] (5764) (5920) 6167[9] 6374[6]

Fantasy Free (USA) *A C Avila* a103
5 bb g Free House(USA) —Cat Ballado (USA) (Saint Ballado (CAN))
3935a[6]

Fantasy Fry *Hughie Morrison* 70
2 b g Avonbridge—Footlight Fantasy (USA) (Nureyev (USA))
2621[7] 3053[4] 3721[2] (4277) 4783[4] 5354[3] 5874[6]

Fantasy Gladiator *Robert Cowell* a92 79
4 b g Ishiguru(USA) —Fancier Bit (Lion Cavern (USA))
2877[4] 3845[4] 4333[6] 4684[3] 4894[3] 5561[2] 5838[2] 6501[3] 7092[3] 7421[2] (7554) (7688) ◆ 7970[6]

Fantasy King (FR) *P Demercastel* a75 77
5 b h Kingsalsa(USA) —My Fantasy (IRE) (Desert King (IRE))
273a[0] 332a[8]

Fantasy Ride *Jeff Pearce* a60 58
8 b g Bahhare(USA) —Grand Splendour (Shirley Heights)
(130) 420[6] 612[P]

Fantino *John Mackie* a79 76
4 b g Shinko Forest(IRE) —Illustre Inconnue (USA) (Septieme Ciel (USA))
2109[11] 3032[4] (3617) (3865) 5035[7] (5922) 6423[6]

Fanunalter *Marco Botti* a111 113
4 b g Falbrav(IRE) —Step Danzer (IRE) (Desert Prince (IRE))
885[2] (1377) ◆ 2576a[4] 3455[4] 5009[8] 5741[7] 6885[7] (7593)

Faraday's Fancy (IRE) *Anna Newton-Smith* a38
4 b m Tagula(IRE) —Brunswick (Warning)
985[10] 1260[11] 1659[13] 2965[15]

Fardyieh *Clive Brittain* a80 77
3 b f King's Best(USA) —Injaaz (Sheikh Albadou)
2416[10] 3612[7] 4255[11] 5205[2] 5561[8] 6800[4]

Fareej (USA) *Saeed Bin Suroor* a92 90
3 b c Kingmambo(USA) —Adonesque (IRE) (Sadler's Wells (USA))
510a[14] 4106[7] 4470[7] 4815[4] 5371[7]

Fareer *Ed Dunlop* 112
4 ch g Bahamian Bounty—Songsheet (Dominion)
1531[8] (2057) 3069[11] 3888[6]

Fareham Town *Sylvester Kirk* a58
3 ch f Cape Town(IRE) —Fareham (Komaite (USA))
104[7] 213[7] 265[9]

Fares (IRE) *Doug Watson* a79 88
6 b g Mark Of Esteem(IRE) —Iftitan (USA) (Southern Halo (USA))
413a[13]

Far Far Away (FR) *B Barbier* 62
2 ch c Machiavellian Tsar(FR) —Fleur De Mad (FR) (Maiymad)
5251a[6]

Far From Old (IRE) *Michael Bell* a99 101
7 b g Vettori(IRE) —Jabali (FR) (Shirley Heights)
1724[13] 2126[9] 2509[7]

Farhh *Saeed Bin Suroor* 92
2 b c Pivotal—Gonbarda (GER) (Lando (GER))
(4375)

Farleigh *George Baker* a52 74
4 b m Trans Island—Medway (IRE) (Shernazar)
284[10] 4708[6] 7529[6]

Farleigh House (USA) *Neil King* a89 88
6 b g Lear Fan(USA) —Verasina (USA) (Woodman (USA))
7881[4] 8003[7]

Farlow (IRE) *Ralph Beckett* a69 54
2 ch g Exceed And Excel(AUS) —Emly Express (IRE) (High Estate)
4954[10] 5657[4]

Farmer Palmer *Louise Best* a36
3 b g Gleaming(IRE) —Annalena (IRE) (Ela-Mana-Mou)
1766[13] 2335[7] 2754[9] 4200[9] 5330[7]

Farmers Dream (IRE) *John Spearing* a52 60
3 b f Antonius Pius(USA) —Beucaire (IRE) (Entrepreneur)
4280[3] 4534[9] 5171[2] 5710[8] 6862[4] 7449[4] 7862[4]

Farmers Glory *Alan Swinbank* 55
3 b g Mujahid(USA) —Action De Grace (USA) (Riverman (USA))
1991[6] 3176[6] 4062[7] 4545[11]

Farmers Surprise *James Evans*
3 b f Fraam—Adaptable (Groom Dancer (USA))
2414[10] 2921[9] 3442[11]

Farmer's Wife *Bernard Llewellyn* a57 31
2 b f Bertolini(USA) —Lady Mayor (Kris)
6247[12] 6512[7] 7271[5] 7464[2] 7630[4]

Farmers Wish (IRE) *John Spearing* a78 80
3 b f Val Royal(FR) —Farmers Swing (IRE) (River Falls)
1453[10] 2283[6] 2904[2] 3115[11] 3638[2] 4424[6] 4922[6] 5327[5] 5614[5]

Farncombe (IRE) *Michael Scudamore* a66 68
4 ch m Where Or When(IRE) —Promenade (Primo Dominie)
429[4] 497[2] 611[6] 827[4] 929[8] 970[4] 3032[2] 3983[6] 4361[3] 4992[5] 5585[6]

Farrel (IRE) *B Grizzetti* 106
5 b g Fruits Of Love(USA) —Folcungi (IRE) (Mukaddamah (USA))
(6238a) 6976a[3] 7370a[8] 7459a[8]

Far View (IRE) *J W Hills* a57 51
3 b g Oasis Dream—Night Mirage (USA) (Silver Hawk (USA))
5007[7] 5658[4] 6168[6] 6421[8] 6903[6] 7153[11]

Fascination (IRE) *Michael Bell* a67 74
3 ch f Galileo(IRE) —Dolydille (IRE) (Dolphin Street (FR))
1501[4] 3116[2] 3754[2] 5209[2] 6415[3] 6781[7] 7690[3] 7896[2] 8015[9]

Fasette *Mark H Tompkins* 59
3 b f Fasliyev(USA) —Londonnet (IRE) (Catrail (USA))
1127[8] 1278[12] 2633[9] (2878) 3113[8] 4718[6] 5161[4]

Fashionable Gal (IRE) *Sir Mark Prescott Bt* a68 73
3 b f Galileo(IRE) —Fashion (Bin Ajwaad (IRE))
3620[2] 7338[2] 7489[2] 7579[U] 7642[6]

Fashion Flow *Henry Cecil* 57
3 ch f Danehill Dancer(IRE) —Verasina (USA) (Woodman (USA))
1355[7]

Fashion Icon (USA) *David O'Meara* a74 64
4 ch m Van Nistelrooy(USA) —Los Altos (USA) (Robin Des Pins (USA))
569[12] 860[6] 1068[2] 1154[3] 1391[4] 1569[5] 2849[13] 3287[4] 3615[6] 3977[4] (4047) 4672[4] 5055[10] 5502[6] (6644) (7148) 7170[4] (7537) ◆ 7868[6]

Fashion Lady (IRE) *Chris Wall* 41
3 b f Montjeu(IRE) —No Quest (IRE) (Rainbow Quest (USA))
4661[12] 5376[9]

Fashion Tycoon (IRE) *Milton Harris* a42 57
3 ch f Chineur(FR) —Fern Tycoon (IRE) (College Chapel)
2227[7] 2968[13] 4053[7] 4791[10] 4989[5] 5469[12] 6862[7]

Fasliyanne (IRE) *Kevin Ryan* a52 68
3 b m Fasliyev(USA) —Happy Memories (IRE) (Thatching)
344[7] 472[5] 1154[2] 1569[3] 2213[5] 2396[3] 2582[2] 3024[3] 3497[4] 3977[7] 4947[6] 5299[8] 5422[9]

Fastada (IRE) *Jonathan Portman* 68
2 b f Holy Roman Emperor(IRE) —Mellow Park (IRE) (In The Wings)
2338[15] 4103[4] 5006[13] 5389[3] 6875[8]

Fastback (IRE) *Ralph Beckett* 91
4 ch m Singspiel(IRE) —Glen Rosie (IRE) (Mujtahid (USA))
2685[5] 3513[2] (4046) (5329) 5553[2]

Fastest Magician (USA) *Jeremy Noseda* a79
2 ch g Johannesburg(USA) —Houdini's Honey (USA) (Mr Prospector (USA))
(7485)

Fast Freddie *Mrs A Malzard* a76 46
6 b g Agnes World(USA) —Bella Chica (IRE) (Bigstone (IRE))
(1814a) (2161a) (3748a)

Fastinthestraight (IRE) *Jim Boyle* a43 18
3 b g Catcher In The Rye(IRE) —La Colombari (ITY) (Lomond (USA))
5028[8] 5658[6] 6060[10] 7728[6]

Fastnet Storm (IRE) *Tom Tate* a95 96
4 br g Rock Of Gibraltar(IRE) —Dreams (Rainbow Quest (USA))
1272[10] 1837[9] 2241[3] 3121[7] 3796[14] 4570[8] 4943[4] 5638[2] 6304[3] 7121[5] (7430) 8009[10]

Fast Samurai (USA) *David Simcock* 54
2 ch c First Samurai(USA) —Lady Blockbuster (USA) (Silent Screen (USA))
5085[3]

Fast Shot *Tim Easterby* a51 60
2 b g Fasliyev(USA) —Final Pursuit (Pursuit Of Love)
1806[6] 2292[4] 3756[6] 4580[3] 4935[5]

Fatal Bullet (USA) *Reade Baker* a118 110
5 b g Red Bullet(USA) —Sararegal (CAN) (Regal Classic (CAN))
6949a[3]

Fatanah (IRE) *Marcus Tregoning* a74 103
3 b f Green Desert(USA) —Wijdan (USA) (Mr Prospector (USA))
(1501) 2076[2] 3101[6] 3632[9] 4957[6]

Fateh Field (USA) *A bin Huzaim* a78 104
5 b g Distorted Humor(USA) —Too Cool To Fool (USA) (Foolish Pleasure (USA))
511a[11]

Fathey (IRE) *Charles Smith* a44 69
4 ch g Fath(USA) —Christoph's Girl (Efisio)
1574[3] 1812[3] 2207[8] 2880[7] 3284[3] 3534[4] 3774[5] 4939[3] 5326[4] 6098[8] 7064[10] 7402[5] 7537[7] 7738[5] 7870[7] 7911[5]

Fathom Five (IRE) *Chris Wall* 102
6 b g Fath(USA) —Ambria (ITY) (Final Straw)
(1471) 2745[7] 3629[7] 4814[7] 5589[5] 6256[3] 6918[4]

Fathsta (IRE) *David Simcock* a96 107
5 b g Fath(USA) —Kilbride Lass (IRE) (Lahib (USA))
108[5] 177[7] 365[4] 887[13] 1192[5] 1349[4] 1862[4] 2327[3] 3389[7] 4440[3] 4832[9] (5297) 5950[2] 6049[2] 6357[2] (6752)

Fault *Stef Higgins* a76 76
4 b g Bahamian Bounty—Trundley Wood (Wassl)
924[5] 1063[7] 1224[4] 1322[3] (1543) 1637[6] 2024[9] 2236[11] 2920[8] 3212[6] 3400[6] 4298[4] (4857) (5325) 5838[10] (6439) 6826[4] 7403[2] 7557[8] 7837[7] 7956[3]

Faustina *Amy Weaver*
3 b f Antonius Pius(USA) —Purple Rain (IRE) (Celtic Swing)
2564[14] 2878[7]

Favouring (IRE) *Michael Chapman* a43 32
8 ch g Fayruz—Peace Dividend (IRE) (Alzao (USA))
39[6] 87[8] 187[5] 297[7] 571[5] 3610[11]

Favourite Girl (IRE) *Tim Easterby* 99
4 b m Refuse To Bend(IRE) —Zuccini Wind (IRE) (Revoque (IRE))
1332[4] 1650[5] 2140[5] (2534) 2940[2] (3373) (3622) (4191) 5095[11] 5742[6] 6175[22] 6918[2] 7079[15]

Favours Brave *Tim Easterby* a72 73
4 b g Galileo(IRE) —Tuning (Rainbow Quest (USA))
2995[6] 3669[6]

Fawley Green *William Muir* a80 77
3 b g Shamardal(USA) —Wars (IRE) (Green Desert (USA))
1842[2] 2052[9] 2824[8] 3638[5] 4206[6] 4588[2] 5205[5] 5968[6] 6057[3] 6524[2] 6714[13]

Fayre Bella *John Gallagher* a54 71
3 ch f Zafeen(FR) —Hollybell (Beveled (USA))
(1137) 1842[4] 2140[7] 6280[8] 6656[15] 7162[10] 7391[11] 7640[4] ◆ 7877[5]

Fazbee (IRE) *Paul D'Arcy* a83 85
4 b m Fasliyev(USA) —Kelpie (IRE) (Kahyasi)
192[3] (275) ◆ 544[2] 828[7] 1641[6] 2415[2] 2678[2] 2904[3] 3510[6]

Fazza *David Arbuthnot* a74 71
3 ch g Sulamani(IRE) —Markievicz (IRE) (Doyoun)
136[3] 311[3] 3270[6] 4588[6] 5031[5] 5769[7] 6370[10] 7046[8]

Fearchar (IRE) *Paul W Flynn* a25 59
3 ch g Governor Brown(USA) —Bajan Girl (IRE) (Pips Pride)
6290[11]

Fear Factor (IRE) *Gerard Butler* 37
3 b g Invincible Spirit(IRE) —Fa E Desfa (Nashwan (USA))
3621[5] 4906[10] 5603[8] 6061[7] 6638[12]

Fearless Poet (IRE) *Bryan Smart* a48 36
2 b c Byron—Fear Not (IRE) (Alzao (USA))
6001[9] 6293[7] 7172[9] 7643[7] (7831) 7910[4]

Fear Nothing *Ian McInnes* a76 75
3 ch g Exceed And Excel(AUS) —Galatrix (Be My Guest (USA))
2099[5] 2442[3] 2741[3] 3277[3] 3834[6] 4908[2] (5726) 7668[3] 8005[7]

Feathered Crown (FR) *Henry Cecil* a53 91
4 ch g Indian Ridge—Attractive Crown (USA) (Chief's Crown (USA))
1388[5] (2173) 2506[2] 2996[2]

Feather Falls (USA) *Mahmood Al Zarooni* 62
2 ch f Henny Hughes(USA) —Merrill Gold (USA) (Gold Fever (USA))
2958[5]

Featherweight (IRE) *B W Hills* a82 85
4 ch m Fantastic Light(USA) —Dancing Feather (Suave Dancer (USA))
1783[8] 2509[5] 3566[6] 4125[9] 5008[9]

Federal Reserve *Michael Madgwick* a46 34
3 ch g Central Park(IRE) —Attlongglast (Groom Dancer (USA))
1590[9] 2359[10] 2753[6] 3213[5] 3960[12] 4689[10]

Feed The Goat (IRE) *Amy Weaver* 31
3 ch g Choisir(AUS) —Charming Victoria (IRE) (Mujadil (USA))
3226[10] 3666[5] 4113[7]

Feelin Foxy *James Given* a88 87
6 b m Foxhound(USA) —Charlie Girl (Puissance)
1363[12] 1710[5] 1827[2] 2346[4] 2940[3] 3197[5] 3622[4] 3947[4] 4510[14] 5054[2] 5435[6] 7466[6] 7754[6] 7841[3] 7971[2] (7998)

Feeling (IRE) *Dai Burchell* a46 45
6 b g Sadler's Wells(USA) —La Pitie (USA) (Devil's Bag (USA))
753[9] 5536[9] 6051[4] 7397[7]

Feeling Fragile (IRE) *Pat Eddery* a72 62
3 b g Fasliyev(USA) —Boutique (Selkirk (USA))
1546[5] ◆ 2052[10] 2385[6] 3510[5] 4053[6]

Feeling Fresh (IRE) *Paul Green* a58 78
5 b h Xaar—Oh'Cecilia (IRE) (Scenic)
(3391) (3664) 3855[8] 4071[9] (4833) 4910[8] 5424[7] 6048[3] 6366[10] 7283[7]

Feel The Heat *Bryan Smart* 79
3 ch c Firebreak—Spindara (IRE) (Spinning World (USA))
2114[3] 2517[3] (2609) 3215[6]

Feel The Magic (IRE) *Sylvester Kirk* a47
3 b f Cadeaux Genereux—Triple Green (Green Desert (USA))
(104) 213[8] 288[F] (Dead)

Feet Of Fury *Ian Williams* a67 62
4 b m Deportivo—Fury Dance (USA) (Cryptoclearance (USA))
1503[4] 2006[9] 2299[8] (2727) 3279[10] 3783[12] 3968[5] 4547[7] 7023[7] 7402[2]

Felicia *John E Long* a51 49
5 b m Diktat—Gracia (Linamix (FR))
827[5] 1078[3] 1591[7] 3214[10] 4132[5] 5457[8]

Fellowship (NZ) *P O'Sullivan* 120
8 b g O'Reilly(NZ) —Mystical Flight (NZ) (Danzalion (USA))
7853a[11]

Felsham *Henry Candy* a71 80
3 br c Kyllachy—Border Minstral (IRE) (Sri Pekan (USA))
(1546) 2283[8] 3779[8] 4204[5] 4754[5]

Felt *James Given* a18
2 b f Tiger Hill(IRE) —Cashmere (Barathea (IRE))
7057[17] 7447[12]

Fencing Master *A P O'Brien* a86 114
3 b c Oratorio(IRE) —Moonlight Dance (USA) (Alysheba (USA))
1699[7] 2354a[10] 3104[6] 4456[4]

Fenella Fudge *James Given* a56 85
2 b f Rock Hard Ten(USA) —Rahcak (IRE) (Generous (IRE))
4048[3] 4508[3] 5910[6] 6512[2] 7049[4] 7879[6]

Fenella Rose *P Vovcenko* a71 73
3 b f Compton Place—Xtrasensory (Royal Applause)
5573a[12]

Fenners (USA) *Michael Easterby* a66 57
7 ch g Pleasant Tap(USA) —Legal Opinion (IRE) (Polish Precedent (USA))
2500[14]

Fennica (USA) *John Gosden* a63 43
2 b f Empire Maker(USA) —Stellaria (USA) (Roberto (USA))
6443[12] 6843[3]

Fen Spirit (IRE) *John Gosden* a83 75
4 b m Invincible Spirit(IRE) —Irinatinvidio (Rudimentary (USA))
223[3] 350[3]

Ferdoos *Michael Jarvis* a86 107
3 b f Dansili—Blaze Of Colour (Rainbow Quest (USA))
(5026) (5989) ◆ 6320[2] ◆

Fernando Torres *Nick Littmoden* a72 68
4 b g Giant's Causeway(USA) —Alstemeria (IRE) (Danehill (USA))
1875[11] 3330[10] 4024[9] 5897[14] 6515[14] 6854[4]

Ferney Boy *Alan Swinbank* a56 56
4 b g Courteous—Jendorcet (Grey Ghost)
815[7] 963[5] 1203[3] 1467[8] 2765[7] 4683[11]

Fern House (IRE) *Alan Berry* a54 46
8 b g Xaar—Certain Impression (USA) (Forli (ARG))
2294[7] 2581[9] 2699[9] 3027[8]

Ferris Wheel (IRE) *Paul Cole* a76 71
3 b f One Cool Cat(USA) —Saffron Crocus (Shareef Dancer (USA))
1269[3] 1709[8] 2170[6] 2644[10] 3350[6] 3972[6]

Ferruccio (IRE) *James Fanshawe* 40
2 br g Marju(IRE) —Unreal (Dansili)
6153[17] 6514[10]

Fervent Prince *A bin Huzaim* a93 91
5 b g Averti(IRE) —Maria Theresa (Primo Dominie)
630a[12]

Fetching *B W Hills* a55 78
3 b f Zamindar(USA) —Esplanade (Danehill (USA))
1329[9] 1861[4]

Fettuccine (IRE) *Jeremy Noseda* a23 75
2 b f Invincible Spirit(IRE) —Capannacce (IRE) (Lahib (USA))
3482[6] 7002[2] 7346[3] 7517[8]

Feuergott (GER) *Ian Williams* a46
4 br g Eden Rock(GER) —Francisca (GER) (Lagunas)
5925[7] 6454[7] 6662[10]

Fever Tree *PETER Makin* a60 62
3 b f Trade Fair—Spielbound (Singspiel (IRE))
1589[5] ◆ 3002[9] 4280[2] 4791[4] 6522[7]

Few Are Chosen (IRE) *Tracey Collins* 86
4 ch m Sulamani(IRE) —Much Commended (Most Welcome)
4463a[15]

Fiancee (IRE) *Roy Brotherton* a49 53
4 b m Pivotal—Name Of Love (IRE) (Petardia)
1620[9] 2231[9] 3968[7] 4324[4] 4987[13] 7023[13] 7380[8] 7877[3]

Fibs And Flannel *Tim Easterby* 79
3 ch g Tobougg(IRE) —Queens Jubilee (Cayman Kai (IRE))
1298[2] (1488) (1718) 2002[7] 6961[6] 7283[12]

Fictional Account (IRE) *V C Ward* a90 106
5 ch m Stravinsky(USA) —Romantic Venture (IRE) (Indian Ridge)
(6388)

Fidler Bay *Henry Candy* 70
4 b g Falbrav(IRE) —Fiddle-Dee-Dee (IRE) (Mujtahid (USA))
1757[13] 2632[4] 4133[10]

Fiefdom (IRE) *Ian McInnes* a80 77
8 br g Singspiel(IRE) —Chiquita Linda (IRE) (Mujadil (USA))
965[8] 1171[8] 1628[8] 2454[2] 2850[4] 3147[7]

Field Commission (CAN) *Daniel J Vella* a109 115
5 ch h Service Stripe(USA) —Tearfull Moment (USA) (Schossberg (CAN))
6949a[4]

Field Day (IRE) *Brian Meehan* 109
3 br f Cape Cross(IRE) —Naval Affair (IRE) (Last Tycoon)
2652[2] (3918) (4319) ◆ 5139a[2] 6613a[4]

Fielder (IRE) *Jonathan Portman* a27 18
5 b g Catcher In The Rye(IRE) —Miss Garuda (Persian Bold)
7398[10]

Fieldgunner Kirkup (GER) *David Barron* 74
2 b g Acclamation—Fire Finch (Halling (USA))
4116[3] 5092[3] (6980)

Field Of Dream *Luca Cumani* 109
3 b c Oasis Dream—Field Of Hope (IRE) (Selkirk (USA))
2045[5] (2546) 3066[5] 4574[3] 5274[9] 6885[11]

Field Of Miracles (IRE) *John Gosden* 71
2 b f Galileo(IRE) —Landmark (USA) (Arch (USA))
7232[4] ◆

Fiery Lad (IRE) *Luca Cumani* a103 114
5 b g Mull Of Kintyre(USA) —Forget Paris (IRE) (Broken Hearted)
436a[8] 821a[7] 946[12] (2710) 3144[9] 3672[3] ◆

Fifth Ave *Jamie Osborne* a80 81
2 b f Avonbridge—Cozette (IRE) (Danehill Dancer (IRE))
1577[6] (1793) 2095[3] 2397[4] 2757[3] 2950[3] 3327[2] 3476[4] (5140) 5882[14] 6445[4] 6636[2] 6842[8]

Fifth Commandment (IRE) *Jamie Osborne* a91 89
2 b f Holy Roman Emperor(IRE) —Via Milano (FR) (Singspiel (IRE))
1660[4] 1972[2] 2338[10] 2749[2] (2951) ◆ 4138[8] (4592) (4903) 5293[5] 7204[6] (7565)

Fifth Dimension (IRE) *Jamie Osborne* a72 73
2 b c Acclamation—Sail With The Wind (Saddlers' Hall (IRE))
(3767) 5699[4] 6059[3] 6453[6] (6901)

Fifth In Line (IRE) *Jamie Osborne* a67
2 b f Kodiac—Surrender To Me (USA) (Royal Anthem (USA))
7503[2] 7602[3] 7871[2] 7999[2]

Fifty Cents *Milton Harris* a65 68
6 ch g Diesis—Solaia (USA) (Miswaki (USA))
672[9] 867[9] 994[3] 1208[4] 2477[7] 2714[2]

Fiftyfourth Street *PETER Makin* a57 71
4 ch g Central Park(IRE) —Retaliator (Rudimentary (USA))
3440[8] 4225[7] 6773[10]

Fifty Moore *Jedd O'Keeffe* 73
3 b g Selkirk(USA) —Franglais (GER) (Lion Cavern (USA))
1029[3] 1706[2] 2852[7] 4750[9] 5487[2] 6356[8] 6624[10]

Fifty Proof (CAN) *Ian Black* 110
4 ch g Whiskey Wisdom(CAN) —Phi Beta (USA) (Horatius (USA))
6236a[2] 6951a[5] 7615a[18]

Figaro *William Haggas* 70
2 ch g Medicean—Chorist (Pivotal)
6532[6] 7058[5] ◆

Figaro Flyer (IRE) *Paul Howling* a75 64
7 b g Mozart(IRE) —Ellway Star (IRE) (Night Shift (USA))
185[3] 431[4] 601[10] 806[5] 913[8] 1482[8] (2186) 2639[8] 3761[6] 4256[5] 4839[9] 5267[6] 5697[7] 6455[12] 6956[7] 7249[7] 7807[4]

Fight Club (GER) *Bernard Llewellyn* a22 33
9 b h Lavirco(GER) —Flaming Song (IRE) (Darshaan)
7815[9]

Fighter Boy (IRE) *David Barron* a76 106
3 b g Rock Of Gibraltar(IRE) —In My Life (IRE) (Rainbow Quest (USA))
453[4] 751[3] (889) ◆ 1313[2]

Fight For You (IRE) *John Norton*
3 b g Antonius Pius(USA) —Amiela (FR) (Mujtahid (USA))
5815[13]

Fighting Brave (USA) *A P O'Brien* a97 102
3 br c Storm Cat(USA) —Get Lucky (USA) (Mr Prospector (USA))
1038a[4] 2367a[5]

Fighting Johan (GER) *G Raveneau* a71 95
6 b g Johan Cruyff—Fireglow (FR) (Glow (USA))
461a[2]

Fighting Talk (IRE) *Mark Johnston* 59
3 ch c Shamardal(USA) —Slap Shot (IRE) (Lycius (USA))
2441[8]

Fight Or Flight *Brendan Powell*
3 b f Mark Of Esteem(IRE) —My Preference (Reference Point)
7438[10]

Fight The Chance (IRE) *Mick Channon* 92
2 b g Elusive City(USA) —Blue Daze (Danzero (AUS))
2887[5] 3332[3] 3624[2] (4142) 4903[4] (5295)

Figli Fanesi (IRE) *Vittorio Caruso* 85
2 b c Tiger Hill(IRE) —Fanofadiga (IRE) (Alzao (USA))
7456a[9]

Figo (GER) *P Lefevre* 62
10 ch g Peintre Celebre(USA) —Flamingo Queen (GER) (Surumu (GER))
1056a[7]

Fikrah *Daniel Mark Loughnane* a55 59
5 ch m Medicean—Justbetweenfriends (USA) (Diesis)
3950[9]

File And Paint (IRE) *J S Bolger* a58 76
2 b f Chevalier(IRE) —Have A Heart (IRE) (Daggers Drawn (USA))
6726a[5]

Filibuster *Chris Wall* 40
3 b g Tobougg(IRE) —Blinding Mission (IRE) (Marju (IRE))
3374[8] 4146[5] 4679[11]

Fillibeg (IRE) *Richard Fahey* a55 34
3 b f Chevalier(IRE) —Alexander Capetown (IRE) (Fasliyev (USA))
523[3] 793[4] 1504[6] 1811[8]

Filligree (IRE) *Rae Guest* a90 93
5 b m Kyllachy—Clunie (Inchinor)
2134[6] 2689[2] ◆ 3178[7] 3445[6] 3845[10] 6113[7] 6429[10]

Filly (FR) *Mme C Head-Maarek* a64 97
3 b f Marchand De Sable(USA) —Private Quest (USA) (Quest For Fame)
7545a[0]

Film Festival (USA) *Brian Ellison* a72 81
7 ch g Diesis—To Act (USA) (Roberto (USA))
1115[10] 1574[2] 1883[8] 2295[5] 2705[9] (3552) 4015[2] (4405) 4708[8]

Film Score (USA) *Mahmood Al Zarooni* 105
3 b g Street Cry(IRE) —Soundtrack (CAN) (Lear Fan (USA))
(2507) 3104[4] 4456[F] (Dead)

Film Set (USA) *F Vermeulen* a91 92
4 b h Johar(USA) —Dippers (USA) (Polish Numbers (USA))
304a[7] 743a[8]

Filun *Anthony Middleton* a70 65
5 b g Montjeu(IRE) —Sispre (FR) (Master Willie)
1226[3] 2870[9] 3128[3] 3641[2] 3984[3] 4227[8] 4794[3] 5289[5] 6022[3]

Fimias (IRE) *Luca Cumani* a68 65
2 bb c Aussie Rules(USA) —Miss Lacey (IRE) (Diktat)
5053[6] 5453[6] 5763[4] 6426[4] 6875[4] 7035[6]

Final Drive (IRE) *John Ryan* a105 63
4 b g Viking Ruler(AUS) —Forest Delight (IRE) (Shinko Forest (IRE))
1322[4] 1653[7] 5560[6] 6061[3] 6581[6] 6794[5] 7298[3] ◆ 7323[2] (7467) (7611) (7637) 7724[3] (7842) ◆ (7970) (8009) ◆

Final Flash (GER) *Zuzana Kubovicova*
4 g Tertullian(USA) —Flying Wings (IRE) (Monsun (GER))
4183a[7]

Final Flashback (IRE) *Patrick J Flynn* a85 86
5 ch g Singspiel(IRE) —Early Memory (USA) (Devil's Bag (USA))
4463a[7] 6730a[5] 6971a[2]

Final Frame *Lucinda Featherstone*
3 ch g And Beyond(IRE) —Argostoli (Marju (IRE))
4912[10]

Final Liberation (FR) *Sir Mark Prescott Bt* a44 37
2 b g Sinndar(IRE) —Hispalis (IRE) (Barathea (IRE))
6743[11] 7152[13] 7303[9] 7470[9]

Final Ovation (IRE) *John Quinn* 71
3 b g Acclamation—Last Gasp (Barathea (IRE))
1483[2] 1987[2]

Final Rhapsody *Willie Musson* a54 59
4 b m Royal Applause—Rivers Rhapsody (Dominion)
6133[9] (6956) 7249[9] 7640[9] 7882[4] 8024[8]

Final Salute *Bryan Smart* a61 59
4 b g Royal Applause—Wildwood Flower (Distant Relative)
1366[9] ◆ 1924[15] 2207[12] 2854[3] 3357[4] 5357[11] 5688[4] 7131[10] (7473)

Final Try *Paddy Butler* a29 35
3 ch g Baryshnikov(AUS) —Scotland Bay (Then Again)
2755[10] 3272[11] 4364[9] 5379[12]

Final Turn *Henry Candy* a52 64
3 b g Kyllachy—Eveningperformance (Night Shift (USA))
1878[4] 2215[6] 2931[7] 4284[9] 5726[6]

Final Verse *Matthew Salaman* a87 78
7 b g Mark Of Esteem(IRE) —Tamassos (Dance In Time (CAN))
151[7] 6852[4] 7306[12] 7560[5] 7724[6]

Final Victory *Andrew Balding* a86 93
4 ch g Generous(IRE) —Persian Victory (IRE) (Persian Bold)
1472[2] ◆ (2317) 3194[12] 3672[6] 6387[8] 6808[6]

Financial Times (USA) *Stef Higgins* a74 63
8 b g Awesome Again(CAN) —Investabull (USA) (Holy Bull (USA))
905[9] 987[6] 1192[8] 1321[7] 1799[10] 2001[5]

Finch Flyer (IRE) *Gary Moore* a48 62
3 ch g Indian Ridge—Imelda (USA) (Manila (USA))
1796[8] 2336[8] 3155[5] 4958[3] 5414[3] (6020)

Fine And Dandie (IRE) *David Nicholls* a50 12
3 b g Bertolini(USA) —Jazz Baby (IRE) (Fasliyev (USA))
301[4] 453[6] 784[3] 906[13] 1118[14] 3286[11] 3410[7]

Fine Art Dealer (IRE) *Gary Moore* 66
2 b c Oasis Dream—Horatia (IRE) (Machiavellian (USA))
4577[6] (Dead)

Finefrenzyrolling (IRE) *Mrs K Burke* 32
2 ch f Refuse To Bend(IRE) —Oasis Star (IRE) (Desert King (IRE))
5531[11]

Fine Lace (IRE) *Dominic Ffrench Davis* a62 67
3 b f Barathea(IRE) —Fine Detail (IRE) (Shirley Heights)
2620[3] 3444[10] 4545[4] 4991[2] 5666[2] 6084[5] (6517)

Finellas Fortune *George Moore* 61
5 b m Elmaamul(USA) —Fortune's Filly (Nomination)
2697[12] 3176[8] 3754[6] 4604[11] 5681[2] 6114[4] 6649[5] 6895[14]

Fine Ruler (IRE) *Martin Bosley* a66 70
6 b g King's Best(USA) —Bint Alajwaad (IRE) (Fairy King (USA))
11[4] 262[10] 496[7] 663[8] 7168[7] 7614[6] 7812[8] 8024[9]

Fine Sight *Gerard Butler* a84 86
3 b g Cape Cross(IRE) —Daring Aim (Daylami (IRE))
1834[9] 2742[5] 3594[3] 6904[3] 7130[5] 7428[6]

Fine Silk (USA) *Michael Quinlan* a70 69
4 ch m Rahy(USA) —Meiosis (USA) (Danzig (USA))
225[2] 317[6] 392[3] 624[6] 828[5] 1639[2] 1843[2] 2094[11] 2751[4] 3111[5] 3338[11]

Finest Reserve (IRE) *Mick Channon* 90
3 b c Royal Applause—Red Bandanna (IRE) (Montjeu (IRE))
1335[2] 1658[3] (2510) 3196[4] 3867[6] 4573[11] 5083[2] 5300[4] 5993[3] 6467[4]

Fine Style (IRE) *Michael Bell* 55
2 ch c Pivotal—Hidden Hope (Daylami (IRE))
4803[14] 5413[4]

Fine Threads *B W Hills* 71
2 b f Barathea(IRE) —Pink Cristal (Dilum (USA))
6512[3] (7223)

Fine Tolerance *Sam Davison* a62 57
4 b m Bertolini(USA) —Sashay (Bishop Of Cashel)
(199) 228[2] 621[3] 7569[10] 7759[8]

Finicius (USA) *Eoin Griffin* a88 103
6 b g Officer(USA) —Glorious Linda (FR) (Le Glorieux)
4312a[4] 5774a[6] 7358a[10] 7816a[4]

Finjaan *Marcus Tregoning* 114
4 b h Royal Applause—Alhufoof (USA) (Dayjur (USA))
1021a[8] 4457[7] 5081[7] 6147[5]

Finnker (IRE) *John Quinn* 58
2 b c Kodiac—Finnine (USA) (Zafonic (USA))
2701[5] 3222[7] 6111[8]

Finn's Rainbow Kevin Ryan a68 55
2 ch c Iffraaj—Aptina (USA) (Aptitude (USA))
2474[4] 2990[11] 3658[7] 4948[3] 5818[12] 7496[12] 7803[2] 7864[2]
Finoon (IRE) Saeed Bin Suroor 91
2 ch f Pivotal—Fibou (USA) (Seeking The Gold (USA))
(5558) 6176[10]
Finsbury Linda Perratt a65 71
7 gr g Observatory(USA) —Carmela Owen (Owington)
1673[4] 1967[7] 2172[3] 2377[2] (2583) 2858[5] 3531[2] 3582[6] 4088[3] 4514[6] 4949[2] 5213[8] 5737[7] 6029[5] 6243[9] 6396[5] 7054[10] 7171[3]
Finzi Contini (FR) Tim Vaughan a74 44
6 gr g Kaldounevees(FR) —Rainbird (Rainbow Quest (USA))
3559[11] 3848[7] 4990[9]
Fireback Andrew Balding a76 95
3 b g Firebreak—So Discreet (Tragic Role (USA))
1589[2] (1913) 3103[9] (3791) 4509[11] 4819[6] 5911[8]
Firebet (IRE) Saeed Bin Suroor a112 112
4 b h Dubai Destination(USA) —Dancing Prize (IRE) (Sadler's Wells (USA))
629a[2] 820a[3]
Fire Commander Brian Baugh a40
2 b g Firebreak—Spectrum Queen (IRE) (Spectrum (IRE))
7427[11] 7578[12] 7700[7]
Fire Crystal Mick Channon a46 51
2 b f High Chaparral(IRE) —Bint Alajwaad (IRE) (Fairy King (USA))
5078[10] 5954[5] 6209[7] 7177[3]
Fire Fighter (IRE) Sir Mark Prescott Bt a50 46
2 b c Tiger Hill(IRE) —Firecrest (IRE) (Darshaan)
6333[7] 6569[8] 6827[10]
Fireflash (IRE) Nigel Tinkler 37
3 b c Noverre(USA) —Miss Langkawi (Daylami (IRE))
4156[7] 5058[10] 5423[11]
Fire Flyer (FR) J C Napoli a69
7 ch g Priolo(USA) —Flyer (FR) (Highest Honor (FR))
559a[3]
Firehawk David Evans a60 61
3 b g Firebreak—Distinctly Blu (IRE) (Distinctly North (USA))
1437[3] 1815a[4] (2248) ◆ 2893[7] 3730[3] 4545[10] 5923[2] 6747[3] 7039[10]
Fire King Andrew Haynes a61 65
4 b g Falbrav(IRE) —Dancing Fire (USA) (Dayjur (USA))
2198[6] 2955[6] 3291[2] 3715[2] (3982) (4738) 5159[5] 5710[2] 7037[8]
Fire N'Brimstone Mouse Hamilton-Fairley a47 41
2 b g Firebreak—Ellovamul (Elmaamul (USA))
6145[11] 6688[9] 7163[9]
Fire Raiser Andrew Balding a61 65
3 b g Firebreak—Mara River (Efisio)
1731[8] 2480[4] 3002[4] 3739[2] 3954[6] 4700[6] 5664[6] 6527[8] (6863)
Firetrap Ann Duffield a47 61
3 b g Firebreak—Amber Mill (Doulab (USA))
1209[6] 1465[7] 3322[7] 3710[8] 3903[5]
Firsaan (IRE) John Norton 46
4 b g Haafhd—Walayef (USA) (Danzig (USA))
909 1576[13] 2388[7] 2902[11] 3128[13] 4015[12]
First Battalion (IRE) Sir Michael Stoute 67
2 b g Sadler's Wells(USA) —Mubkera (IRE) (Nashwan (USA))
6092[9] 6831[4] 7202[10]
First Bay (IRE) Keith Goldsworthy 83
4 b g Hawk Wing(USA) —Montmartre (IRE) (Grand Lodge (USA))
2443[5]
First Blade Roy Bowring a73 69
4 ch g Needwood Blade—Antonias Melody (Rambo Dancer (CAN))
1391[8] 2187[9] 2698[8] 4427[2] 5634[12] 6110[7] (7155) 7868[5]
First Cat Richard Hannon a65 91
3 b g One Cool Cat(USA) —Zina La Belle (Mark Of Esteem (IRE))
1502[13] 1734[7] 2253[2] 2515[3] 2933[3] 3867[2] 4377[2] 4963[5] 6205[3] 6391[4] 6805[3] 7233[10]
First City David Simcock 106
4 b m Diktat—City Maiden (USA) (Carson City (USA))
1693[5] 1899[2] 2387[2] 2744[8] (4137) 5114[10] 5554[2] 6351[4]
First Class Favour (IRE) Tim Easterby 80
2 b f Exceed And Excel(AUS) —Lamh Eile (IRE) (Lend A Hand)
1375[3] ◆ (1800) 2436[7] 3163[3] 4600[4] (5021) 5187[12] 5547[5] 5939[4] (6184) 6647[2] (6920)
First Coming B J McMath 60
6 ch g Best Of The Bests(IRE) —Arriving (Most Welcome)
6470[6]
First Dude (USA) Dale Romans a118
3 b c Stephen Got Even(USA) —Run Sarah Run (USA) (Smart Strike (CAN))
2137a[2] 2776a[3] 4643a[3] 5544a[3] 7367a[8] ◆
First Fandango J W Hills 85
3 b c Hernando(FR) —First Fantasy (Be My Chief (USA))
1393[3] ◆ 1757[7] 2168[2] 2717[5] 3273[3] 3953[3] 4493[3] (5116) 5858[2] 6437[2]
First In Command (IRE) Daniel Mark Loughnane a74 88
5 b g Captain Rio—Queen Sigi (IRE) (Fairy King (USA))
2327[8] 6421[2] ◆ 6714[3]
First In The Queue (IRE) Sylvester Kirk a84 83
3 b g Azamour(IRE) —Irina (IRE) (Polar Falcon (USA))
1330[8] 1657[7] 1973[6] 2587[5] 2888[11] 4201[5] 4563a[11] (5664) 6266[3] (6692) 7012[7]
Firstknight Tom Dascombe a65 64
2 b c Kyllachy—Wedding Party (Groom Dancer (USA))
4934[7] ◆ 5527[10] 6520[4]
First Mohican Henry Cecil 77
2 ch c Tobougg(IRE) —Mohican Girl (Dancing Brave (USA))
(7150)
First Order Ann Stokell a90 87
9 b g Primo Dominie—Unconditional Love (IRE) (Polish Patriot (USA))
20[8] 275[12] 462[4] 520[4] 601[9] 723[4] 778[6] 896[2] 1147[8] 5599[12]
First Post (IRE) Derek Haydn Jones a77 86
3 b g Celtic Swing—Consignia (IRE) (Definite Article)
(381) 781[2] 1657[8] 2398[4] 3297[U] (3863) 4322[2] (5264) 5918[3] 6813[3]
First Pressing John Berry 51
2 b f Bertolini(USA) —Lady Donatella (Last Tycoon)
1686[10] 2022[10]
First Service (IRE) Michael Attwater a69 60
4 ch g Intikhab(USA) —Princess Sceptre (Cadeaux Genereux)
2236[12] 3330[7] 4024[4] 4260[6] 4839[6] 6210[7] 6671[7] 7613[12] 7768[10]
First Spirit Robin Dickin a51 56
4 ch m First Trump—Flaming Spirt (Blushing Flame (USA))
7921[3]
First Swallow David Brown a68 66
5 ch g Bahamian Bounty—Promise Fulfilled (USA) (Bet Twice (USA))
504[3] 601[3] 832[5] 3623[3] 3977[2] 4373[6] 6880[6] 7148[3] 7334[5] 7537[6]
First Term Malcolm Saunders a16 59
3 b f Acclamation—School Days (Slip Anchor)
1329[10] 1760[9] 2000[4] ◆ 2844[16] 5469[P] 6903[10]
First Time (GER) Karin Suter 103
7 br m Silvano(GER) —First Wings (IRE) (In The Wings)
461a[11]
First To Call PETER Makin a74 29
6 ch g First Trump—Scarlett Holly (Red Sunset)
996[4] 3294[10]
Fishforcompliments Richard Fahey a79 102
6 b g Royal Applause—Flyfisher (USA) (Riverman (USA))
3317[2] 3876[2] 4354[6] 5480[2] 5685[3] 5789[2] 6357[9] 7352[17] 7557[4] 7725[3] 7846[6]
Fists And Stones Mick Channon 81
2 b g Distant Music(USA) —Keeping The Faith (IRE) (Ajraas (USA))
4460[8] 4954[2] 5886[4]
Fit The Cove (IRE) H Rogers a88 92
10 b g Balla Cove—Fit The Halo (Dance In Time (CAN))
1408a[11]
Fityaan B W Hills a79 77
2 b g Haafhd—Welsh Diva (Selkirk (USA))
3826[4] 5453[2] 6301[5]
Fitz Matthew Salaman a67 56
4 b g Mind Games—Timoko (Dancing Spree (USA))
1772[5] 3132[8] 3783[13] (5379) 5897[2] 6210[6] 6713[9] 7519[11]
Fitz Flyer (IRE) Bryan Smart a104 103
4 b g Acclamation—Starry Night (Sheikh Albadou)
2[3] 1007[3] 1400[7] 2400[4] 2526[4] 3674[6] 7329[4]
Fitzolini Alan Brown a63 46
4 b g Bertolini(USA) —Coney Hills (Beverley Boy)
290[3] 705[2] ◆ 857[6] 1575[10] 2789[3] 3370[10] (4591) 4913[6]
Fitzwarren Alan Brown a51 49
9 b g Presidium—Coney Hills (Beverley Boy)
99[5] 295[3] 795[5] 939[2] 1296[9] 2500[9] 3369[12] 4454[2]
Fiulin Evan Williams a94 107
5 ch g Galileo(IRE) —Fafinta (IRE) (Indian Ridge)
1821[14]
Five Bells (IRE) Mick Channon 39
3 ch f Rock Of Gibraltar(IRE) —Gold Mist (Darshaan)
1356[11] 1735[9]
Fivefold (USA) John Akehurst a81 81
3 bb c Hennessy(USA) —Calming (USA) (Wild Again (USA))
(180) 1913[4] ◆ 2253[11] 2682[3] 3579[12] 4264[4] 5031[4] 5495[15] 6280[6] 6798[6] 7091[13] 7320[9] 7483[11] 7992[3]
Five Gold Rings (IRE) F J Brennan a63 45
4 ch m Captain Rio—Metisse (IRE) (Indian Ridge)
501[10] 5077[11] 5580[6]
Five Hearts Mark H Tompkins 68
2 b f Bertolini(USA) —Light Hand (Star Appeal)
7231[5] ◆
Fiveonthreeforjd Bill Ratcliffe a32
5 br g Compton Admiral—Patrician Fox (IRE) (Nicolotte)
291[7] 7872[10]
Five Star Junior (USA) Linda Stubbs a99 99
4 b g Five Star Day(USA) —Sir Harriett (USA) (Sir Harry Lewis (USA))
434a[6] 628a[6] 887[4] 1206[8] 1688[4] 2119[5] (2431) 3178[2] 3406[10] 3828[2] (4148) 4536[6] 4937[2] 5308[10] 5787[14] 6265[6] 6429[3] 7993[3]
Five To Five Tom Tate
2 b g Librettist(USA) —Fiveofive (IRE) (Fairy King (USA))
3118[13]
Five Two Gavin Patrick Cromwell a58 59
7 ch g Mark Of Esteem(IRE) —Queen's Gallery (USA) (Forty Niner (USA))
5129a[13]
Fix The Rib (IRE) Gary Moore a76
7 b g Dr Massini(IRE) —Hot Curry (IRE) (Beau Sher)
308[2]
Flag Officer Saeed Bin Suroor a85
2 b c Dubai Destination(USA) —Dusty Answer (Zafonic (USA))
6334[2] ◆ (6711) (7165)
Flag Of Glory Chris Wall a79 73
3 b g Trade Fair—Rainbow Sky (Rainbow Quest (USA))
(1796) 2089[5] 2993[3] 3739[3] 4710[6] (6122) 7638[4]
Flambeau Henry Candy 104
3 b f Oasis Dream—Flavian (Catrail (USA))
(2122) 3415[3] ◆ 4145[2] 5120[3] 7083[3]
Flame Of Gibraltar (IRE) Henry Cecil a93 103
4 b m Rock Of Gibraltar(IRE) —Spirit Of Tara (IRE) (Sadler's Wells (USA))
2538[5] 4507[11]
Flameoftheforest (IRE) C F Swan a82 87
3 b c Danehill Dancer(IRE) —Coralita (IRE) (Night Shift (USA))
4496a[2] 5571a[17]
Flamestone Andrew Price a56 52
6 b g Piccolo—Renee (Wolfhound (USA))
145[8] 691[8] 862[6] 940[5] 984[2] 1305[11]
Flaming Blaze P C Haslam a38 34
4 b g Tobougg(IRE) —Catch The Flame (USA) (Storm Bird (CAN))
407[9] 470[11]
Flamingo Fantasy (GER) W Hickst 114
5 ch h Fantastic Light(USA) —Flamingo Road (GER) (Acatenango (GER))
1956a[5]
Flaneur Tim Easterby 87
3 b g Chineur(FR) —Tatanka (IRE) (Lear Fan (USA))
1376[13] 1709[2] 2069[2] (2287) 3088[2] 3436[4] 3731[6] 4369[7] 5390[2] 5606[5] (6000) 6962[8]
Flannel (IRE) James Fanshawe a58 68
4 gr g Clodovil(IRE) —La Captive (IRE) (Selkirk (USA))
186[5] 246[3] 355[7] (Dead)
Flapper (IRE) J W Hills a76 76
4 b m Selkirk(USA) —Pure Spin (USA) (Machiavellian (USA))
3330[3] ◆ 3782[8] 4472[5] 4847[6] 5689[5] 6085[3] 6479[9]
Flash City (ITY) Bryan Smart a83 68
2 b g Elusive City(USA) —Furnish (Green Desert (USA))
4409[4] 5092[5] 6980[5] 7578[4] (7696) ◆ 7739[2] ◆ 7908[3]
Flash Dance (IRE) H-A Pantall 101
4 ch m Zamindar(USA) —Resquilleuse (USA) (Dehere (USA))
3704a[4] 4885a[9] 5802a[6] 6409a[2]
Flash Forward Chris Wall
2 gr c Haafhd—Regrette Rien (USA) (Unbridled's Song (USA))
6465[17]
Flash McGahon (IRE) John M Oxx a81 81
6 b g Namid—Astuti (IRE) (Waajib)
187[6] 7573[5] 7654[3]
Flashy Max Jedd O'Keeffe a50 33
5 b g Primo Valentino(IRE) —Be Practical (Tragic Role (USA))
3369[8]
Flattery Charles O'Brien a67 67
4 b m Dansili—Azur (IRE) (Brief Truce (USA))
7078a[3]
Flaxen Lake Milton Bradley a71 68
3 b g Sampower Star—Cloudy Reef (Cragador)
527[2] 662[5] (962) 1784[7] 2648[7] 2784[3] 3030[13] 4284[7] 5152[2] 5957[3] 6536[6] 7334[11] 7628[5] 7764[7] 7859[7]
Flaxton (UAE) Mel Brittain a41 46
5 b h Halling(USA) —Yasmeen Valley (USA) (Danzig Connection (USA))
7472[5]
Fleet Captain Kevin Ryan 69
2 b c Compton Place—Mrs Brown (Royal Applause)
2216[9] 2980[6] 3498[6] (5434) 6220[7] 6719[13]
Fleeting Echo Richard Hannon a82 98
3 b f Beat Hollow—Sempre Sorriso (Fleetwood (IRE))
2884[3] (3158) 3790[9] 4264[3] (5082) 6351[6] 6776[7] 7097[4]
Fleeting Glance (IRE) Brian Meehan 72
3 b f Cape Cross(IRE) —Speech Room (USA) (Gulch (USA))
2998[11] (3620) 6090[7]
Fleeting Moment (IRE) Patrick Martin a71 73
5 b g Oasis Dream—Snippets (IRE) (Be My Guest (USA))
7078a[8]
Fleeting Spirit (IRE) Jeremy Noseda a109 122
5 b m Invincible Spirit(IRE) —Millennium Tale (FR) (Distant Relative)
3192[4] ◆ 3870[5]
Fleeting Star (USA) Jeremy Noseda a78 83
4 rg m Exchange Rate(USA) —Disperse A Star (USA) (Dispersal (USA))
3037[14] 3417[6] 3845[9]
Fleeting Tiger John Dunlop 40
2 b c Tiger Hill(IRE) —Fleeting Rainbow (Rainbow Quest (USA))
5033[10] 6474[11] 6953[10]
Fleetwoodsands (IRE) Ollie Pears a74 59
3 b g Footstepsinthesand—Litchfield Hills (USA) (Relaunch (USA))
1114[8] 2203[2] 3027[3] (3515) 3975[14] (6168) 6541[6]
Fleur De'Lion (IRE) Sylvester Kirk a67 57
4 ch m Lion Heart(USA) —Viburnum (USA) (El Gran Senor (USA))
1454[6] 1623[11] 2165[5] 2230[10] 2676[7] 2870[12] 7716[9] 7759[9]
Fleur Enchantee (FR) P Van De Poele a97 109
6 b m Marchand De Sable(USA) —Mademoiselle Fleur (FR) (River Mist (USA))
1792a[5] 5348a[4] 6613a[3] 7160a[5] 7648a[0]
Fleurissimo John Gosden a23 80
4 ch m Dr Fong(USA) —Agnus (IRE) (In The Wings)
3781[11]
Flic Flac (IRE) D K Weld a79 79
2 ch f Bahamian Bounty—Polite Reply (IRE) (Be My Guest (USA))
954a[4]
Flight Lieutenant Jane Chapple-Hyam 37
2 ch c Officer(USA) —Frambroise (Diesis)
4379[7]
Flight Wise Richard Mitchell a51
6 b g Riverwise(USA) —Madame Poulet (Gold Dust)
685[9] 803[9] 1042[6]
Flighty Fellow (IRE) Olivia Maylam a62 48
10 ch g Flying Spur(AUS) —Al Theraab (USA) (Roberto (USA))
261[6] 411[12] (541) 665[7] 685[7] 920[5] 3124[9] 3783[8] 4434[9]
Flighty Frances (IRE) David Elsworth a74 80
3 ch f Camacho—Moon Diamond (Unfuwain (USA))
1257[3] ◆ (1504) 1850[6] 2120[6] 3217[6] 5086[4] 5494[3] 6652[2] 6841[6]
Flinch Cat (FR) J E Hammond a70 79
2 b c One Cool Cat(USA) —Flinch (Zafonic (USA))
7544a[8]
Flinty Richard Hannon 53
2 b c Cape Cross(IRE) —Favourita (Diktat)
4549[11] 5676[4] 6443[8]
Flipando (IRE) David Barron a108 103
9 b g Sri Pekan(USA) —Magic Touch (Fairy King (USA))
(528) 885[10] 1206[2] ◆ 1727[8] 1900[8] ◆ 2311[6] (2748) 3489a[11] 5787[13] 5911[12] 6177[21] 6888[23] 7187[8] 7443[3]
Flip Flop (IRE) B W Hills a78 87
3 b f Footstepsinthesand—Dame Alicia (IRE) (Sadler's Wells (USA))
1703[8] ◆ 2737[5] 3271[3] 5383[7] 6090[9] 6800[7]
Flipping Stuart Kittow a78 84
3 br g Kheleyf(USA) —Felona (Caerleon (USA))
3857[5] 4698[8] 5300[8] 5993[5] (6632) (7305)
Floating Angel (USA) John Best 36
3 bb f Alke(USA) —Relic Notebook (USA) (Notebook (USA))
1355[13] 1882[10] 2121[9]
Flockton Tobouggie Michael Easterby 48
4 b g Tobougg(IRE) —Johnson's Point (Sabrehill (USA))
1801[6] 2131[4] 2343[8]
Flodden (USA) Paul Cole a57 75
2 ch g Henny Hughes(USA) —Dundrummin' (USA) (Gone West (USA))
3794[8] 4375[2] 5277[4] 6249[6] 6779[5]
Flo Motion (IRE) J W Hills 53
2 b f Sadler's Wells(USA) —Darling (Darshaan)
6770[12]
Flood Plain John Gosden 92
2 b f Orpen(USA) —Delta (Zafonic (USA))
(6804) ◆ 7098[2] 7340a[14]
Floor Show Noel Wilson 86
4 ch g Bahamian Bounty—Dancing Spirit (IRE) (Ahonoora)
1102[5] 1650[3] 2086[5] 2534[6] 2982[7] 4345[4] 4850[10] 5480[10] 6723[11]
Flora's Pride Keith Reveley 60
6 b m Alflora(IRE) —Pennys Pride (IRE) (Pips Pride)
1113[8] 6890[9] 7147[2]
Flora Trevelyan Walter Swinburn a85 105
4 b m Cape Cross(IRE) —Why So Silent (Mill Reef (USA))
1899[4] (2472) 3752[4] 4319[6] 5305[3] 5883[13]
Florentine Ruler (USA) Henry Cecil a68 86
3 b g Medicean—Follow That Dream (Darshaan)
1335[3] ◆ (2143) ◆ 2562[4]
Flores Sea (USA) Ruth Carr a76 80
6 ch g Luhuk(USA) —Perceptive (USA) (Capote (USA))
6[7] 508[4] (571) 787[3] 895[3] 1051[8] 1115[3] (1492) 1826[4] 1997[5] 3518[9] 3765[8] 4547[10] 5241[6] 7646[10] 7870[12]
Florestans Match Ralph Beckett a63 83
2 ch f Medicean—Fidelio's Miracle (USA) (Mountain Cat (USA))
3000[3] 3590[2] 4317[2] 4921[2] 6286[4]
Floridita (USA) Mark Johnston a29 25
3 ch f Fusaichi Pegasus(USA) —Rose Of Zollern (IRE) (Seattle Dancer (USA))
776[8] 5057[8] 5366[13]
Florio Vincitore (IRE) Edward Creighton a80 81
3 b g High Chaparral(IRE) —Salome's Attack (Anabaa (USA))
1221[5] 5143[8] 5647[8] 6992[10] 7290[3] 7438[9] 7474[3] 7476[2] 7726[4] 7878[9] 8015[5]
Flotate (USA) Jane Chapple-Hyam a55 4
3 bb f Orientate(USA) —Flo Jo (USA) (Graustark)
977[6] 1209[4]
Flotation (USA) B W Hills 74
3 bb f Chapel Royal(USA) —Storm Dove (USA) (Storm Bird (CAN))
2974[3] ◆ (3428) 5083[7]
Flouncing (IRE) William Haggas a77 79
3 b f Barathea(IRE) —Man Eater (Mark Of Esteem (IRE))
1257[5] (1490) 2178[3] 2871[3] 3174[5] 3677[5] 3751[4] (4342) 4503[2] 5037[2] 5890[2] 6487a[4]
Flow Chart (IRE) Peter Grayson a74 67
3 b g Acclamation—Free Flow (Mujahid (USA))
4[3] 141[2] 370[3] 454[2] 826[4] 932[4] 1237[7] 3988[4] 5697[11] 7764[8]
Flower F Rohaut a81 73
5 ch m Zamindar(USA) —Time For Tea (IRE) (Imperial Frontier (USA))
303a[3]
Flower Fairy (USA) John Gosden a74 69
3 b f Dynaformer(USA) —Santolina (USA) (Boundary (USA))
4661[2] (5141)
Flower Haven Victor Dartnall a53 28
8 b m Dr Fong(USA) —Daisy May (In The Wings)
4683[9]
Flowers In Spring (FR) D Selvaratnam a31 85
3 br f Country Reel(USA) —Wadayama (GER) (Surumu (GER))
709a[8]
Flowing Cape (IRE) Reg Hollinshead a97 87
5 b g Cape Cross(IRE) —Jet Lock (USA) (Crafty Prospector (USA))
108[11] 177[2] 299[6] 528[8] 722[6] 1423[13] 1688[12] 2172[4] 2477[5] 2705[3] (2959) 3117[3] ◆ 3318[10] 3681[2] 3969[3] 4354[7] 5068[4] 5703[5] 6312[7] 6577[4]

Fluster (USA) *Mark Johnston*
4 ch m Street Cry(IRE) —Bluster (USA) (Storm Cat (USA))
1116[10]

Flute Magic *Rod Millman* a44 72
4 b g Piccolo—Overcome (Belmez (USA))
976[9] 1067[4]

Fluter Phil *Roger Ingram*
3 b g Piccolo—Figura (Rudimentary (USA))
4926[5] 5842[10]

Fluvial (IRE) *Mahmood Al Zarooni* a74 76
2 ch f Exceed And Excel(AUS) —Flamanda (Niniski (USA))
(4741) 5721[3] 6259[5] 7035[11]

Fly By Nelly *Mark Hoad* a66 66
4 b m Compton Place—Dancing Nelly (Shareef Dancer (USA))
11[5] 101[3] 318[6] 2383[7] 2967[5] 4232[6] 4987[2] 5689[6] 6335[6] 7487[2] 7717[5] 7995[8]

Fly By White (IRE) *Richard Hannon* a72 73
2 ch f Hawk Wing(USA) —Le Montrachet (Nashwan (USA))
4021[9] 4587[2] 5029[3] 5807[2] ◆ 6471[9] (6859)

Fly Down (USA) *Nicholas Zito* a124
3 ch c Mineshaft(USA) —Queen Randi (USA) (Fly So Free (USA))
2776a[2] 4613a[5] 5544a[2] 6586a[3] 7367a[3]

Flyinflyout *Sheena West* a56 72
3 b f Fath(USA) —Hana Dee (Cadeaux Genereux)
1696[4] 2248[9] 2753[5] 3263[2] 3788[11] 4280[7]

Flying Applause *Roy Bowring* a28 80
5 b g Royal Applause—Mrs Gray (Red Sunset)
7539[12]

Flying Arch (USA) *Luca Cumani* a69 66
2 b f Arch(USA) —Proud Tradition (USA) (Seeking The Gold (USA))
5324[6] 7002[4] 7427[2]

Flying Blue (FR) *R Martin Sanchez* a55 85
5 b h Fly To The Stars—Viking's Cove (USA) (Miswaki (USA))
460a[5]

Flying Cherry (IRE) *Jo Crowley* a52
3 ch f Medecis—Fly With Wings (IRE) (In The Wings)
5028[9] 5658[5] 7288[5] 7872[7]

Flying Cloud (IRE) *Saeed Bin Suroor* 113
4 b m Storming Home—Criquette (Shirley Heights)
2055[3] 3467a[2] 4507[5] 5248[5] 5539[3] 6095[7] 7373a[11]

Flying Cross (IRE) *John Gosden* 113
3 b c Sadler's Wells(USA) —Ramruma (USA) (Diesis)
5976a[3] ◆ 7110a[9]

Flying Destination *William Knight* a89 89
3 ch g Dubai Destination(USA) —Fly For Fame (Shaadi (USA))
(1393) 2386[5] 2927[4] 3581[2] (4306) 4996[7] 5918[7] 6449[2]

Flying Doctor *Elliott Cooper* a36 36
7 b g Mark Of Esteem(IRE) —Vice Vixen (CAN) (Vice Regent (CAN))
3669[7]

Flying Gazebo (IRE) *J S Moore* a44 55
4 b g Orpen(USA) —Grand Summit (IRE) (Grand Lodge (USA))
124[7]

Flying Phoenix *William Haggas* a39 56
2 b f Phoenix Reach(IRE) —Rasmalai (Sadler's Wells (USA))
5160[5] ◆ 8000[9]

Flying Power *David Lanigan* a74 9
2 b g Dubai Destination(USA) —Rah Wa (USA) (Rahy (USA))
7152[10] 7400[2] 7551[2] (7780)

Flying Scotsman (FR) *J E Pease* 83
2 b c Kyllachy—Icechigasus (USA) (Fusaichi Pegasus (USA))
7534a[6]

Flying Silks (IRE) *Jeremy Gask* a68 76
4 b g Barathea(IRE) —Future Flight (Polar Falcon (USA))
1508[3] 2527[4] 2864[2] (4119) 4522[8] 5287[5] 6112[10]

Flying Squad (UAE) *Milton Harris* a75 52
6 b g Jade Robbery(USA) —Sandova (IRE) (Green Desert (USA))
1478[5] 2955[5]

Flying Statesman (USA) *Richard Fahey* 95
3 b g Johannesburg(USA) —Insomnie (USA) (Seattle Slew (USA))
5854[11] 6363[4] ◆ 7060[21]

Flying Trump *Robert Cowell*
3 b f First Trump—Cold Blow (Posse (USA))
6470[13]

Flying Valentino *Ian Williams* a77 83
6 b m Primo Valentino(IRE) —Flying Romance (IRE) (Flying Spur (AUS))
3117[6] 3765[2] 4053[2] 4949[3] 5867[8]

Flyjack (USA) *Lisa Williamson* a70 67
3 b g Johannesburg(USA) —Let Fly (USA) (Flying Paster (USA))
6713[11] 6898[11] 7502[12] 7639[10] 7786[3] 7918[7]

Flynn's Boy *Rae Guest* 70
2 ch g Tobougg(IRE) —Bukhoor (IRE) (Danehill (USA))
7119[3]

Fly Silca Fly (IRE) *Mick Channon* a77 83
3 b f Hawk Wing(USA) —Nevis Peak (AUS) (Danehill (USA))
1279[5] 1663[4] 2283[3] (2565) 3088[6] 3790[5] 4378[9] 4865[6] 5052[5] 5442[7] 6438[2] 6887[13] 7033[5]

Focail Maith *John Ryan* a82 71
2 b c Oratorio(IRE) —Glittering Image (IRE) (Sadler's Wells (USA))
4254[8] 4549[7] 5047[7] 6411[5] (7151) 7295[2] 7317[3] 7481[6]

Focal *Sir Michael Stoute* 65
2 b f Pivotal—Coy (IRE) (Danehill (USA))
4595[6]

Fochabers *Roger Charlton* a61 44
3 b g Dr Fong(USA) —Celtic Cross (Selkirk (USA))
1975[9]

Foghorn Leghorn *Peter Chapple-Hyam* a79 93
2 ch c Medicean—Dance Away (Pivotal)
1686[3] 2048[2] 2468[5] 2743[6] (4590) 5221[9] (5939) 6354[5] 6531[5]

Fol Hollow (IRE) *David Nicholls* a93 103
5 b g Monashee Mountain(USA) —Constance Do (Risk Me (FR))
916[7] ◆ 1206[3] 1295[4] 1471[4] 1822[3] 2054[14] (2135) 2748[2] ◆ 3406[5] 4401[18] 4814[8] 5512[10] 5944[20] 6364[4] 6706[10]

Folio (IRE) *Willie Musson* a72 63
10 b g Perugino(USA) —Bayleaf (Efisio)
383[8] 2080[10] 2602[2] 3416[5] 4102[5] 4873[4] 5565[5] 6718[7] 7562[6] 7778[3]

Folk Tune (IRE) *John Quinn* 80
7 b h Danehill(USA) —Musk Lime (USA) (Private Account (USA))
1151[5] 5118[4] 6185[7] 6750[10]

Fol Liam *Alan McCabe* a74 61
4 b g Observatory(USA) —Tide Of Fortune (Soviet Star (USA))
(867) 1238[2] 1374[10] 2678[3] 3033[7] 3518[8] 3765[4] 5545[12] 5768[6] 6371[9] (6853) 7439[4] 7627[8]

Follow My Dream *John Gosden* a68 67
2 ch f Kyllachy—Follow A Dream (USA) (Gone West (USA))
6803[3] 7123[4] 7447[4] 7550[4]

Follow On *Maurice Barnes* a72 28
8 b h Barathea(IRE) —Handora (IRE) (Hernando (FR))
4511[11] 5019[12]

Follow The Dream *Karen George* a67 57
7 b m Double Trigger(IRE) —Aquavita (Kalaglow)
554[9] 7481[11] 6933[8] 7213[8]

Follow The Flag (IRE) *Alan McCabe* a87 93
6 ch g Traditionally(USA) —Iktidar (Green Desert (USA))
(16) 115[3] 245[5] 405[6] 725[4] 943[3] 1645[3] (1684) 1925[5] (2044) 2444[2] 2608[5] 3239[2] 3585[3] 3796[3] 4376[5] 4570[5] 4943[7] 5913[10] 6252[12] 6534[8] 6724[7] 7062[8] (7560) 7756[8] 7867[2] 7935[5] 7955[3]

Follow The Sun (IRE) *Peter Niven* a52 61
6 br g Tertullian(USA) —Sun Mate (IRE) (Miller's Mate)
4946[6] 5530[12] 6051[2] 6518[6] 7475[10]

Folly Bridge *Roger Charlton* 96
3 b f Avonbridge—Jalissa (Mister Baileys)
1315[10] (1917) 2545[12] (3790) 4378[3] 5694[3]

Folly Drove *Jonathan Portman* a68 62
2 b f Bahri(USA) —Zoena (Emarati (USA))
2594[7] 3296[12] 4095[10] 5837[8] (6694)

Fol Pickle *David Nicholls* 62
2 b g Val Royal(FR) —Branston Gem (So Factual (USA))
2693[6] 4241[10]

Fongoli *Brendan Powell* a52 55
4 b m Dr Fong(USA) —Darmagi (IRE) (Desert King (IRE))
90[6] 420[11]

Fong's Alibi *J S Moore* a74 66
4 b m Dr Fong(USA) —Alchemy (IRE) (Sadler's Wells (USA))
586[2] 685[2]

Fonnie (IRE) *Rae Guest* 56
2 ch f Barathea(IRE) —Top Row (Observatory (USA))
6628[2]

Fonterutoli (IRE) *Roger Ingram* a78 73
3 gr g Verglas(IRE) —Goldendale (IRE) (Ali-Royal (IRE))
(1210) ◆ 1876[5] 3271[4] 4058[8] 5661[3] 6093[6] 6581[9] 7638[2] 7876[3]

Fontley *Eve Johnson Houghton* 100
3 b f Sadler's Wells(USA) —Horatia (IRE) (Machiavellian (USA))
1502[14] (2253) (2933) 3694[2] 5307[14] 6346[7]

Foolin Myself *D Selvaratnam* a105 98
5 b g Montjeu(IRE) —Friendlier (Zafonic (USA))
630a[13]

Foolish Ambition (GER) *David Wachman* 94
3 b f Danehill Dancer(IRE) —Foolish Act (IRE) (Sadler's Wells (USA))
1786a[5]

Foolproof (IRE) *John Joseph Murphy* a84 84
2 ch c King's Best(USA) —Reasonably Devout (CAN) (St Jovite (USA))
2352a[8] 4880a[6] 6727a[5]

Fools Gold *Richard Guest* a57 43
5 b g Ishiguru(USA) —Sally Green (IRE) (Common Grounds)
7870[9]

Foot Perfect (IRE) *David Marnane* a37 84
2 b f Footstepsinthesand—Lupine (IRE) (Lake Coniston (IRE))
2828a[7] 3421a[6]

Footsie (IRE) *James Given* a37 65
3 b f Footstepsinthesand—Marlene-D (Selkirk (USA))
2564[12] 3662[7] 4408[4] 5058[9] 5423[6] 6080[10]

Footsteppy (IRE) *S Wattel* a77 101
2 b f Footstepsinthesand—Final Opinion (IRE) (King's Theatre (IRE))
5137a[3] 7008a[2]

Footstepsofspring (FR) *Willie Musson* a84 89
3 b g Footstepsinthesand—Moon West (USA) (Gone West (USA))
1701[13] 2545[13] 3270[5] 4333[8] 4806[10] 6292[8] 7007[5]

Forbidden (IRE) *Ian McInnes* a76 74
7 ch g Singspiel(IRE) —Fragrant Oasis (USA) (Rahy (USA))
6165[4] 6930[5] 7467[7] 7529[7] 7599[4] 7814[7] 7825[3]

Forced Opinion (USA) *Kevin Morgan* a61 47
5 gr h Distant View(USA) —Kinetic Force (USA) (Holy Bull (USA))
666[7] 942[12] 2874[12]

Force Freeze (USA) *Doug Watson* a109 105
5 br g Forest Camp(USA) —Antifreeze (USA) (It's Freezing (USA))
(437a) 797a[8] 1024a[9]

Force Group (IRE) *Mark H Tompkins* a72 78
6 b g Invincible Spirit(IRE) —Spicebird (IRE) (Ela-Mana-Mou)
3294[6]

Force Of Habit *D K Weld* a78 69
4 br g Dalakhani(IRE) —Bedside Story (Mtoto)
(7078a)

Force To Spend *Nick Littmoden* a56 50
3 b f Reset(AUS) —Mon Petit Diamant (Hector Protector (USA))
683[3] 1825[10] 2174[6] 2584[4] ◆ 2931[8] 3515[7] 4281[3] 5927[4] 6863[10] 7314[5] 7506[3] 7783[3] 7973[3]

Foreign Investment (IRE) *David Evans* a66 72
4 ch m Desert Prince(IRE) —Muneera (USA) (Green Dancer (USA))
675[8] 868[9] 1585[5] 1762[7] 3982[9]

Foreign King (USA) *Seamus Mullins* a59 66
6 b g Kingmambo(USA) —Foreign Aid (USA) (Danzig (USA))
4099[9] (6502) 7388[4]

Foreign Rhythm (IRE) *Ron Barr* 68
5 ch m Distant Music(USA) —Happy Talk (IRE) (Hamas (IRE))
1965[2] 2278[6] 3287[2] 3711[2] 4606[3] (4869) 5123[5] 5760[6] 6040[5] 6295[6] 6464[7] (6965)

Forest Crown *Ralph Beckett* a98 98
3 b f Royal Applause—Wiener Wald (USA) (Woodman (USA))
1850[2] (2652) 4137[6] 5114[3] 6346[5] 7188[3]

Forest Dane *Mrs N Smith* a78 72
10 b g Danetime(IRE) —Forest Maid (Thatching)
2719[10] (3292) 3980[5]

Forest Legend (USA) *Victoria Oliver* a102 102
2 b f Forest Camp(USA) —Silver Comic (USA) (Silver Hawk (USA))
7340a[4]

Forest Runner *Saeed Bin Suroor* 81
3 b c Pivotal—Tiriana (Common Grounds)
4107[2] 5057[3]

Foreteller *D Smaga* 107
3 b c Dansili—Prophecy (IRE) (Warning)
1985a[4] 3016a[8] 5574a[6] 6219a[9]

Forethought *Paul Howling* a35 64
3 b f Lujain(USA) —Flourish (Selkirk (USA))
2501[5] 4764[7] 6080[11]

Forever Fong *John Weymes* a1
3 ch f Dr Fong(USA) —Always On My Mind (Distant Relative)
545[8]

Forever Hope *Tim Walford* 68
3 b f Mark Of Esteem(IRE) —Polar Dancer (Polar Falcon (USA))
3924[3] 4521[3] 4853[7] 6116[7]

Forever's Girl *Geoffrey Oldroyd* a82 66
4 b m Monsieur Bond(IRE) —Forever Bond (Danetime (IRE))
601[5] 869[3] 1112[6] 4606[2] 4799[3] (5535) 5920[3] 6295[2] 6700[9] (6898) 7239[3] (7331) 7525[12]

Forever Together (USA) *Jonathan Sheppard* a110 119
6 rg m Belong To Me(USA) —Constant Companion (USA) (Relaunch (USA))
7343a[6]

Forever Vienna *Howard Johnson* 33
2 b g Proclamation(IRE) —Alizar (IRE) (Rahy (USA))
3058[10] 3770[3] 4195[7]

Forget (IRE) *Jamie Poulton* a54 44
3 b f Tiger Hill(IRE) —Wajina (Rainbow Quest (USA))
1844[13]

Forgotten Army (IRE) *Mark H Tompkins* a54 71
3 b c Arakan(USA) —Brioney (IRE) (Barathea (IRE))
2033[4] 2816[6] 5456[5] 6065[12] 6290[10] 6999[7]

Forgotten Voice (IRE) *Jeremy Noseda* a116 115
5 b g Danehill Dancer(IRE) —Asnieres (USA) (Spend A Buck (USA))
338a[2] 798a[7] 1022a[5] 3069[7] 3888[5] 4457[12]

Forjatt (IRE) *Michael Jarvis* 100
2 b g Iffraaj—Graceful Air (IRE) (Danzero (AUS))
(2649) 4049[2] (4934) ◆ 5880[10] 6568[11]

Fork Handles *Mick Channon* 98
2 b f Doyen(IRE) —Natalie Jay (Ballacashtal (CAN))
(2286) ◆ 4305[4] ◆ 4842[7] 5322a[3] 6348[4]

Fork Lightning (USA) *Sir Mark Prescott Bt* a65 87
3 gr f Storm Cat(USA) —Last Second (IRE) (Alzao (USA))
2473[7] 2755[6] 4339[2] (4997) 5981a[4] 7349[11]

Forks *Bryan Smart* 66
3 ch g Fraam—Balinsky (IRE) (Skyliner)
1335[8] 1648[3] 4556[3] 4951[4]

For Life (IRE) *John E Long* a82 79
8 b g Bachir(IRE) —Zest (USA) (Zilzal (USA))
1044[2] 1641[3] 1963[6] 2750[2] (4260) 4930[6] 7318[9] 7573[7]

Formal Demand *Edward Vaughan* 65
2 b c Invincible Spirit(IRE) —Lady High Havens (IRE) (Bluebird (USA))
3602[3] 4110[2]

Formidable Girl (USA) *Kevin Ryan* a54 59
2 bb f Roman Ruler(USA) —Gracility (USA) (Known Fact (USA))
4029[8] 4508[11] 6161[6]

Formidable Guest *Jeff Pearce* a80 25
6 b m Dilshaan—Fizzy Treat (Efisio)
12[3] ◆ (162) 282[5] (375) (565) 725[2] 765[4] 1015[9] 1346[7] 3079[8] 3781[9] 4019[4] 4433[7] 5155[3] 5663[11]

Formosina (IRE) *Jeremy Noseda* 112
2 b c Footstepsinthesand—Scarlett Rose (Royal Applause)
2078[3] ◆ (2990) (3488a) ◆ 3868[6] 6192[2] 6560[3]

Formulation (IRE) *Hughie Morrison* a68 78
3 b g Danehill Dancer(IRE) —Formal Approval (USA) (Kingmambo (USA))
1387[9] 1766[6] 2684[5] 3155[3] 6243[2] 6543[6] 7090[8]

Forrest Flyer (IRE) *Jim Goldie* 78
6 b g Daylami(IRE) —Gerante (USA) (Private Account (USA))
2295[2] (3152) 3709[3] 4190[2] 5070[3] 5278[5] 6143[4] 6397[8]

Forshour *Ed McMahon* a62 62
3 ch g Forzando—Sharoura (Inchinor)
1753[11] 3279[6] 3758[7] 4337[13]

Forsyth *Alan Swinbank* a58 72
3 ch g Pursuit Of Love—Forsythia (Most Welcome)
815[5] 1271[2] 2083[3] 2816[4] 4062[6]

Forte Dei Marmi *Luca Cumani* a64 116
4 b g Selkirk(USA) —Frangy (Sadler's Wells (USA))
(1388) 2027[4] (2608) ◆ 3921[12] (5307) ◆ (6193) ◆

Fortezza *Alan McCabe* a53 52
4 b m Efisio—Donna Anna (Be My Chief (USA))
242[8] ◆ 499[7] 1884[4] 2257[3] 2629[2] 2726[4] 2896[9] 3458[5]

Fort Hastings (IRE) *Mario Hofer* 92
2 b c Aragorn(IRE) —Peaceful Love (GER) (Dashing Blade)
5740a[3]

For That Reason (IRE) *Michael Quinlan*
2 b c Medicean—Jamrah (IRE) (Danehill (USA))
1389[11]

Fortina's Boy (USA) *Walter Swinburn* a63 56
4 ch g Mr Greeley(USA) —Really Quick (USA) (In Reality (USA))
1235[11] 1928[13]

Fortunate Bid (IRE) *Linda Stubbs* a58 74
4 ch g Modigliani(USA) —Mystery Bid (Auction Ring (USA))
1396[6] 1575[6] 2382[3] 2850[7] 3597[4] 4644[12] 4897[6] 5331[4] 5636[8] 7863[5]

Fortunateencounter (FR) *John Gosden* a32 76
2 b f Muhtathir—Tashtiyana (IRE) (Doyoun)
6155[4] 7113[9]

Fortuni (IRE) *Sir Mark Prescott Bt* a96 101
4 b g Montjeu(IRE) —Desert Ease (IRE) (Green Desert (USA))
2096[14] (2747) 5220[15] 5908[11] 6437[5]

Forty Proof (IRE) *William Knight* a82 74
2 b c Invincible Spirit(IRE) —Cefira (USA) (Distant View (USA))
4142[6] ◆ 4622[7] 4960[3] 5785[4] 6419[3] (6954) 7333[2] 7423[2] (7734) 7891[2] 8020[6]

Forty Thirty (IRE) *Sheena West* a66 57
4 b g Poliglote—Ciena (FR) (Gold Away (IRE))
3723[8] 6860[11]

Forum Magnum (USA) *A Fabre* a72 97
3 b c Elusive Quality(USA) —French Bid (AUS) (Anabaa (USA))
1610a[5] 2159a[12]

Forward Feline (IRE) *Bryn Palling* a74 62
4 b m One Cool Cat(USA) —Ymlaen (IRE) (Desert Prince (IRE))
29[7] 373[3] 486[2] 587[3] 853[8] 965[10] 4910[3] 5897[10] 6210[4]

For What (USA) *David Lanigan* a79
2 ch c Mingun(USA) —Cuanto Es (USA) (Exbourne (USA))
7452[4] ◆ 7609[5] (7830)

Forzarzi (IRE) *Hugh McWilliams* a49 60
6 b g Forzando—Zarzi (IRE) (Suave Dancer (USA))
2187[8] 2583[7] 2864[12] 3205[4] 3948[12] 4487[3] 4869[6] 5496[3] 5821[11]

Fossgate *James Bethell* a60 60
9 ch g Halling(USA) —Peryllys (Warning)
5687[10]

Foundation Filly *F Doumen* a83 96
3 ch f Lando(GER) —Fureau (GER) (Ferdinand (USA))
952a[8] 2800a[4] 4037a[5] 7648a[10]

Four Kicks (IRE) *J S Moore* 63
4 b m Pyrus(USA) —Dynamo Minsk (IRE) (Polish Precedent (USA))
1437[4] 1633[2] (1922) (2201) 2360[4] 2488[2]

Fourlanends *Noel Wilson* 30
3 ch g Dubawi(IRE) —Nova Cyngi (USA) (Kris S (USA))
6876[16] 7129[8]

Four Nations (USA) *Amanda Perrett* a60 60
2 ch g Langfuhr(CAN) —Kiswahili (Selkirk (USA))
2887[8] 5263[11] 5724[9] ◆

Fourpenny Lane *Ms Joanna Morgan* a101 101
5 b m Efisio—Makara (Lion Cavern (USA))
439a[7] 630a[6] 713a[7] 957a[7] 4630a[6] ◆

Four Quartets (GER) *Derek Shaw* 39
4 b g Tiger Hill(IRE) —Four Roses (IRE) (Darshaan)
1450[14] 2994[9] 3116[9] 4070[11] 4211[7]

Four Star General (IRE) *Henry Cecil* 60
4 b h Danehill Dancer(IRE) —Teslemi (USA) (Ogygian (USA))
4572[7] 5860[4]

Fourth Generation (IRE) *Alan Swinbank* a82 79
3 ch g Kris Kin(USA) —Merewood Lodge (IRE) (Grand Lodge (USA))
3766[2] ◆ (4407) 5371[2] 6397[9]

Foxhaven *Patrick Chamings* a79 88
8 ch g Unfuwain(USA) —Dancing Mirage (IRE) (Machiavellian (USA))
1388[3] 1783[7] 3329[6] (5034) 5591[11] 5991[6] (6639)

Fox Hunt (IRE) *Mark Johnston* 107
3 ch g Dubawi(IRE) —Kiltubber (IRE) (Sadler's Wells (USA))
(4661) 5736[4] 5970[4] ◆ 6355[2] ◆

Foxtrot Alpha (IRE) *Peter Winkworth* a71 68
4 b m Desert Prince(IRE) —Imelda (USA) (Manila (USA))
1797[4] 2299[7] 2967[8] 4232[5] (4959) (5326) 6024[3] 6656[8]

Foxtrot Bravo (IRE) *Sam Davison* a62 59
4 b g Noverre(USA) —Standcorrected (Shareef Dancer (USA))
99[7] 126[3] 2291[0] 540[7] 2781[3] 3291[3] 3338[5] 3524[3] 3984[2] 4780[8] 5468[5] 5873[7] 6637[5] 7039[11]

Foxtrot Charlie *Peter Winkworth* a73 68
4 b g Lucky Story(USA) —Holy Smoke (Statoblest)
2080[16] 2966[13]

Foxtrot Golf (IRE) *Peter Winkworth* a68 38
2 b g Diamond Green(FR) —Tides (Bahamian Bounty)
2839[15] 6994[6] 7385[4] 7572[5] 7886[2] 8012[6]

Foxy Music *Eric Alston* a74 94
6 b g Foxhound(USA) —Primum Tempus (Primo Dominie)
(2622) 3675[2] 4372[7] (5941) 6364[13]

Foxy's Mint *Richard Hannon* 39
2 b f Tobougg(IRE) —Fred's Dream (Cadeaux Genereux)
2680[12] 3209[10] 3864[10]

Fraam Lea *Andrew Price*
4 b m Fraam—Castanet (Pennekamp (USA))
2921[10]

Frameit (IRE) *James Given* a65 64
3 b g Antonius Pius(USA) —Delisha (Salse (USA))
421[4] 484[4] 664[3] 928[3] 1433[6] 1578[3] 1975[8] 2333[3] 2606[5] (3213) 3564[4] 3724[4] 3960[4] (6525) 6747[8] 7465[4] 7569[8] 7695[6] 7805[8] 7967[7]

Frances Stuart (IRE) *Andrew Balding* a71 83
3 b f King's Best(USA) —Higher Love (IRE) (Sadler's Wells (USA))
1694[6] 2478[2] (2998) 3918[2]

Francis Albert *Michael Mullineaux* a57 57
4 b g Mind Games—Via Dolorosa (Chaddleworth (IRE))
4047[15] 4938[10] 5240[2] 5502[4] 5876[10] 6206[7] 6931[5] 7477[2] 7684[3] 7952[8]

Franciscan *Luca Cumani* a56 62
2 b c Medicean—Frangy (Sadler's Wells (USA))
4803[17] 6092[5] 6465[3] ◆ 6902[5] 7151[3]

Francis Walsingham (IRE) *Hughie Morrison* a76 76
4 b g Invincible Spirit(IRE) —Web Of Intrigue (Machiavellian (USA))
2166[5] 3037[12] 3205[10] 3687[2]

Franco Is My Name *Peter Hedger* a95 78
4 b g Namid—Veronica Franco (Darshaan)
(282) (588) ◆ (676) 1161[5] 1780[8] 2467[10] 2640[10] 3512[7] 6428[6] 6797[7] (7292) (7756) 8003[2] ◆

Frank Crow *Nigel Tinkler* 39
7 b g Josr Algarhoud(IRE) —Belle De Nuit (IRE) (Statoblest)
1114[5]

Frankel *Henry Cecil* 127
2 b c Galileo(IRE) —Kind (IRE) (Danehill (USA))
(5049) ◆ (5912) ◆ (6347) ◆ (6924)

Frankie Falco *Giuseppe Fierro* a7 39
4 br h Bollin Eric—Marsh Marigold (Tina's Pet)
1183[3] 1380[9] 1520[10] 6921[14]

Franki J *Desmond Donovan* a56 77
3 ch f Barathea(IRE) —Whassup (FR) (Midyan (USA))
4408[5] 4775[7] (4970) 5730[3] 6574[5] (7006) (7153)

Frankish Dynasty (GER) *Paul Cole* 66
2 b c Holy Roman Emperor(IRE) —Fantastic Belle (IRE) (Night Shift (USA))
2715[4] 2980[10] 3459[5] 3721[5] 4688[5]

Frank Street *Eve Johnson Houghton* a59 72
4 ch g Fraam—Pudding Lane (IRE) (College Chapel)
2053[10] 2331[3] 2646[5] 3510[4] (3910) 4383[3] 4793[6] 6452[3] 6992[7]

Frantic Storm (GER) *W Hickst* 102
4 b h Nayef(USA) —Flamingo Road (GER) (Acatenango (GER))
2574a[5]

Frantz De Galais (FR) *Y Fouin* 74
4 ch g Trempolino(USA) —Exceptionnel Lady (FR) (Vertical Speed (FR))
5378a[4]

Fratazz *S Botti* 99
5 b h Pivotal—Lorne Lady (Local Suitor (USA))
(1712a)

Fratellino *Alan McCabe* a97 101
3 ch c Auction House(USA) —Vida (IRE) (Wolfhound (USA))
945[5] 1315[6] 1499[2] 2058[7]

Fravashi (AUS) *Saeed Bin Suroor* a106 118
5 bb h Falbrav(IRE) —Angelic Smile (AUS) (Dehere (USA))
631a[5] 798a[8] 1021a[2] 3192[23] 4136[5] 5275[3]

Freckenham (IRE) *Michael Bell* a74 65
2 ch f Exceed And Excel(AUS) —Farrfesheena (USA) (Rahy (USA))
1999[3] 3053[3] 4029[2] 4592[8] 5720[2]

Fred Archer (IRE) *David Marnane* 85
2 b c Iffraaj—Fairy Contessa (IRE) (Fairy King (USA))
5567a[9]

Freda's Rose (IRE) *O Brennan* a29 51
6 b m Rossini(USA) —African Scene (IRE) (Scenic)
2902[6]

Freddie's Girl (USA) *Stef Higgins* a82 62
3 bb f More Than Ready(USA) —Carib Gal (USA) (Awesome Again (CAN))
38[2] 180[6] (257) 357[2] (483) 807[2] 901[7] 3561[5] 4031[4] 4424[7] 4930[2] 5454[2] 6253[4] 6501[6] (6998) 7093[8] 7319[5] 7549[5] 7719[5] 8005[10]

Frederick William *PETER Makin* a48 62
2 b c Tobougg(IRE) —Bisaat (USA) (Bahri (USA))
4490[9] 5006[4] 7609[8]

Fred Lalloupet *D Smaga* 101
3 b c Elusive City(USA) —Firm Friend (IRE) (Affirmed (USA))
6012a[7] 6640a[4] 7278a[9]

Fred Willetts (IRE) *David Evans* a80 77
2 b g Noverre(USA) —Intaglia (GER) (Lomitas)
1517[10] 1930[13] 2111[2] 2882[3] 3426[5] 4935[6] (5602) 5849[5] 5901[2] 6900[10] 6988[2] 7324[5] 7528[3] 7652[2] 7916[3]

Free Agent *Richard Hannon* 112
4 b g Dr Fong(USA) —Film Script (Unfuwain (USA))
3462[4] (3922) 4506[4] (5696) 6388[2]

Free Art *P D Deegan* a83 89
2 b c Iffraaj—Possessive Artiste (Shareef Dancer (USA))
3645a[3] 4175a[6]

Free As A Lark *Chris Wall* 70
3 b f Oratorio(IRE) —Regal Magic (IRE) (Sadler's Wells (USA))
1882[7] ◆ 2632[2] 4028[4] 4762[8] 5664[5] 6298[2]

Freedom Fire (IRE) *Gary Moore* a69 65
4 b g Alhaarth(IRE) —Feel Free (IRE) (Generous (IRE))
98[3] 261[2] (316) 588[4] 770[7] 1763[2] 1961[4]

Freedom Pass (USA) *James Toller* a53 56
3 b f Gulch(USA) —Bold Desire (Cadeaux Genereux)
1870[12] 2564[8] 4237[4] 5206[3] 5898[10] 7161[10]

Freedom Trail *David Elsworth* a54 60
2 b f Bertolini(USA) —Film Buff (Midyan (USA))
2176[7] 2547[10] 2813[5] 5527[11] 6867[5]

Free Falling *Alastair Lidderdale* a48 53
4 ch m Selkirk(USA) —Free Flying (Groom Dancer (USA))
13[6] 263[13] 376[3] 463[6] 898[7] (2489) 2952[5] 3290[3] 3819[5] 4026[3] 4780[6] 5179[4] 5564[6] 6273[7] 7805[5]

Freeforaday (USA) *John Best* a94 103
3 ch c Freefourinternet(USA) —All My Yesterdays (USA) (Wild Again (USA))
1701[11] 2316[4] 3066[4] 3869[19] 4509[6] 4574[5] 5009[9] 5247[15]

Free For All (IRE) *Sylvester Kirk* 82
3 br c Statue Of Liberty(USA) —Allegorica (IRE) (Alzao (USA))
(1257)

Free Grain *John Dunlop* 60
3 b f Sakhee(USA) —All Grain (Polish Precedent (USA))
1393[9] 2051[10] 2908[5]

Freehand (USA) *Mahmood Al Zarooni* 61
2 b c Kingmambo(USA) —Portrayal (USA) (Saint Ballado (CAN))
3219[11] 4940[3] 5413[5] 6082[10]

Free Judgement (USA) *J S Bolger* a98 117
3 b c Vindication(USA) —South Bay Cove (CAN) (Fusaichi Pegasus (USA))
1038a[6] (1786a) 2354a[2] 3066[7] 4160a[7]

Free Tussy (ARG) *Gary Moore* a84 77
6 b g Freelancer(USA) —Perlada (ARG) (Cipayo (ARG))
25[5] 341[4] 480[6] 697[3] 1062[4] 1348[7] 6428[12] 6699[2] 7111[8] 7732[8]

Free Winner (IRE) *B Grizzetti* 95
2 b c Oratorio(IRE) —Freedom (GER) (Second Empire (IRE))
3253a[4]

Freja (IRE) *Bent Olsen* a40
3 br f Singspiel(IRE) —La Belle Simone (IRE) (Grand Lodge (USA))
7374a[10]

Fremen (USA) *David Nicholls* a90 88
10 ch g Rahy(USA) —Northern Trick (USA) (Northern Dancer (CAN))
(862) (1098) (1587) (1839) (2208) (2760) 3021[3] 5545[2] (6029) (6296) 7171[6]

Freminius (GER) *W Baltromei* 107
6 bb h Erminius(GER) —Freixenet (GER) (Big Shuffle (USA))
3017a[6] 4888a[5] 6408a[4]

Fremont (IRE) *Richard Hannon* 101
3 b c Marju(IRE) —Snow Peak (Arazi (USA))
1311[5] 1703[9]

French Applause (IRE) *Tom Tate* 78
4 b g Royal Applause—A Ma Guise (USA) (Silver Hawk (USA))
1374[14] 2142[4] 2739[7] 3090[6] 3617[5] 4546[7] 5408[8] 6296[10] 7214[9]

French Art *Nigel Tinkler* a71 75
5 ch g Peintre Celebre(USA) —Orange Sunset (IRE) (Roanoke (USA))
1395[3] (1628) 1926[6] 2392[5] 2823[8] 3514[4] 3911[8] 4119[5] 4354[4] ◆ 4968[4] 5756[8] 6794[7]

French Fantasy *Hughie Morrison* a49 61
3 ch f Cadeaux Genereux—Footlight Fantasy (USA) (Nureyev (USA))
1760[2] 3727[15] 4109[4] 4920[3] 5535[2] 7013[7]

French Hollow *Tim Fitzgerald* a71 71
5 b g Beat Hollow—Campaspe (Dominion)
355[4] 585[2] 1357[5] 4604[3] 4983[6] 6114[7] 6895[6] 7284[6]

French Navy *A Fabre* 108
2 b c Shamardal(USA) —First Fleet (USA) (Woodman (USA))
(6218a) 7265a[5]

French Seventyfive *Tim Walford* 63
3 b g Pursuit Of Love—Miss Tun (Komaite (USA))
1394[8] 1971[5] 2503[6] 2838[12] 3614[8]

French Wind *Pat Eddery* a54
3 b g Cadeaux Genereux—Blast (USA) (Roar (USA))
527[8] 683[4] 2896[12]

Frequency *Amy Weaver* a73 70
3 br g Starcraft(NZ) —Soundwave (Prince Sabo)
1165[3] 1402[2] 2197[2] 2892[4] 5162[5] (5494) 6255[13] 6741[11] 6997[2]

Freya's Flight (IRE) *Kevin Ryan* a44 55
4 ch m Viking Ruler(AUS) —Polish Saga (Polish Patriot (USA))
290[9] 398[7]

Fricoteiro (ARG) *Niels Petersen* 91
7 ch h Lode(USA) —Fricote (USA) (Ogygian (USA))
2195a[7] 4641a[8]

Friend Or Foe (USA) *John C Kimmel* a115
3 ch c Friends Lake(USA) —Unbridled Star (USA) (Unbridled (USA))
4613a[4] 5544a[6]

Friends Hope *Roger Curtis* a80 83
9 ch m Docksider(USA) —Stygian (USA) (Irish River (FR))
(327) 521[3] 600[4]

Frill A Minute *Lynn Siddall* a14 26
6 b m Lake Coniston(IRE) —Superfrills (Superpower)
2852[10] 4064[6] 5214[5] 5482[10]

Frisbee *David Thompson* a64 72
6 b m Efisio—Flying Carpet (Barathea (IRE))
1365[4] 1719[5] 1924[2]

Frognal (IRE) *Ruth Carr* a80 89
4 b g Kheleyf(USA) —Shannon Dore (IRE) (Turtle Island (IRE))
859[6] 1030[19] 1332[10] 1516[8] 1688[7] ◆ 2275[6] 2534[3] 2982[16] 3409[5] 3553[4] 3664[6] 3809[2] ◆ (4452) 4942[11] 5069[9] 5290[7] 5855[11] 6501[10]

Fromsong (IRE) *Dean Ivory* a76 69
12 b g Fayruz—Lindas Delight (Batshoof)
79[5] 119[2] 241[2] 306[6] 501[2] 616[4] 806[3] (899) 1044[6] 1320[3] 3358[2] 4047[11] 4255[10] 5025[5] 5377[7] 6292[3] 6880[13] 7314[4] ◆ 7571[2] 8037[4]

Fromthebeginning *David Elsworth* a68 56
4 b g Lomitas—Zacchera (Zamindar (USA))
2414[6]

Front House (IRE) *M F De Kock* a103 111
5 b m Sadler's Wells(USA) —Adjalisa (IRE) (Darshaan)
417a[6] 821a[10]

Frontline Boy (IRE) *Mrs K Burke* a52 70
3 b g One Cool Cat(USA) —Diamant (IRE) (Bigstone (IRE))
1201[4] 2329[4] 2722[7] 3685[2] 3904[5] 5162[9] 5299[12]

Frontline Girl (IRE) *Mrs K Burke* 77
4 b m Fath(USA) —Ellistown Lady (IRE) (Red Sunset)
1926[12] 2764[4] 3434[8] (3948) 4188[2] (5486) 6367[5] 7063[6]

Frontline Phantom (IRE) *Mrs K Burke* a38 66
3 b g Noverre(USA) —Daisy Hill (Indian Ridge)
1336[7] 1927[8] 2258[6] 2702[8] 3520[9] 4061[4] (4408) 5266[3] 5607[4] 6225[6] 7054[7]

Front Rank (IRE) *Dianne Sayer* a52 56
10 b g Sadler's Wells(USA) —Alignment (IRE) (Alzao (USA))
376[8] 1113[5] 3122[8] 5364[3]

Frosty Friday *John Jenkins* a62
2 b f Storming Home—Seasonal Blossom (IRE) (Fairy King (USA))
7311[8] 7470[2] 7693[3] 7907[2]

Frosty Secret (USA) *M F De Kock* a105 91
6 br h Put It Back(USA) —Secret From Above (USA) (Great Above (USA))
336a[5] 434a[3] (604a) 822a[5]

Frosty's Gift *Jimmy Fox* a46 17
6 ch m Bold Edge—Coughlan's Gift (Alnasr Alwasheek)
3264[12]

Frozen Fire (GER) *M F De Kock* 114
5 b h Montjeu(IRE) —Flamingo Sea (USA) (Woodman (USA))
417a[8] 516a[8] 712a[7] 799a[8]

Frozen Over *Stuart Kittow* a27
2 b g Iceman—Pearly River (Elegant Air)
6995[5]

Frozen Power (IRE) *Mahmood Al Zarooni* a106 106
3 b c Oasis Dream—Musical Treat (IRE) (Royal Academy (USA))
414a[2] 608a[2] (819a) 1023a[5] (2405a) 3719a[5] 4888a[8] 5803a[9]

Fuego Dreamer *John Holt* a14
3 b g Firebreak—Mays Dream (Josr Algarhoud (IRE))
1490[9]

Fuisse (FR) *Mme C Head-Maarek* 120
4 b h Green Tune(USA) —Funny Feerie (FR) (Sillery (USA))
(3017a) (4166a) 5134a[4] (5801a) 6925[7]

Fujin Dancer (FR) *Kevin Ryan* a75 86
5 ch g Storming Home—Badaayer (USA) (Silver Hawk (USA))
32[2] 174[7] 1241[3] (1395) 1669[2] (1717) 1990[4] 2608[4] 3283[7] 3667[9] 4484[2] (4795) (4939) 5213[5] 5360[2] 5545[6] 6107[8] (6223) 7251[3] 7679[3]

Fulfilment (IRE) *Willie Musson* a58 50
4 ch m Alhaarth(IRE) —Noble Dane (IRE) (Danehill (USA))
1188[3] 1755[4] 3324[7]

Fulford *Mel Brittain* a65 56
5 ch g Elmaamul(USA) —Last Impression (Imp Society (USA))
69[5] 296[3] (403) ◆ 569[2] 704[2] 839[2] 892[3] 1276[8] 1366[7] 1813[5] 2263[7] 4706[16]

Fulgur *Luca Cumani* 85
2 b c High Chaparral(IRE) —Selebela (Grand Lodge (USA))
5491[2] 6159[3] (6689)

Fullandby (IRE) *Tim Etherington* a105 105
8 b g Monashee Mountain(USA) —Ivory Turner (Efisio)
1007[8] 1353[10] 2992[16] 4191[6] 4832[4] 5095[12] 6178[11] 6363[8] 7289[8] 7351[10]

Full Footage *Roger Charlton* 52
2 b f Lando(GER) —Widescreen (USA) (Distant View (USA))
5691[12]

Full Of Hope (IRE) *A P O'Brien* a66 90
3 b f Invincible Spirit(IRE) —Tathkara (USA) (Alydar (USA))
1787a[8] 1952a[7] 2370a[18] 2912a[5]

Full Speed (GER) *Alan Swinbank* a95 89
5 b g Sholokhov(IRE) —Flagny (FR) (Kaldoun (FR))
572[5] (917) ◆ 1274[14]

Full Steam *A Fabre* a79 97
3 b f Oasis Dream—Western Appeal (USA) (Gone West (USA))
2158a[10]

Full Title (IRE) *Reginald Roberts* a79 79
7 b g Desert Sun—Rusti La Russe (Rusticaro (FR))
6907a[12]

Full Toss *David Evans* a101 88
4 b g Nayef(USA) —Spinning Top (Alzao (USA))
81[4] 205[4] 252[4] 266[3] 360[6] ◆ (408) 447[3] 536[6] 885[9] 946[10] 1008[15] 1208[2]

Full Victory (IRE) *Rodney Farrant* a66 75
8 b g Imperial Ballet(IRE) —Full Traceability (IRE) (Ron's Victory (USA))
1179[3] 2024[2] 2167[2] 2362[6] 2885[7] 3765[3] 4201[10] 5237[8] 5287[3] 5584[3] 6165[12] 6633[4] 7128[8] 7449[3]

Fully Armed (IRE) *Rae Guest* 28
2 ch f Indian Haven—Madame Marjou (IRE) (Marju (IRE))
6628[9] 7001[9]

Ful Of Grace (IRE) *James Frost* 56
6 b m Marju(IRE) —Mitawa (IRE) (Alhaarth (IRE))
7315[13]

Fun Affair (USA) *John Gosden* a85 56
3 b f Distorted Humor(USA) —Caressing (USA) (Honour And Glory (USA))
5395[3] ◆ (5925)

Funday *Gary Moore* a86 90
4 b m Daylami(IRE) —Morina (USA) (Lyphard (USA))
5970[9] 7189[11] 7612[10]

Funky Lady (USA) *Richard Hannon* 81
3 b f El Corredor(USA) —Anja (IRE) (Indian Ridge)
(1355) ◆

Funky Munky *Alistair Whillans* a36 71
5 b g Talaash(IRE) —Chilibang Bang (Chilibang)
2864[11] 3905[8] 4582[13] 5244[10] 5820[13] 6571[9] 7230[2] 7402[12]

Furiosa (IRE) *Edward Creighton* a21 45
2 b f Captain Rio—Proud Myth (IRE) (Mark Of Esteem (IRE))
2638[8] 3858[5] 4274a[9] 6666[9]

Furmigadelagiusta *Richard Fahey* a95 111
6 ch h Galileo(IRE) —Sispre (FR) (Master Willie)
1031[5] 2469[8]

Furthest Land (USA) *Michael J Maker* a120 101
5 br g Smart Strike(CAN) —Flagrant (USA) (Rahy (USA))
1027a[14]

Fury *William Haggas* 101
2 gb c Invincible Spirit(IRE) —Courting (Pursuit Of Love)
(6196) (6560) ◆

Fusaichi Flyer (USA) *Roger Charlton* a66
3 bb g Fusaichi Pegasus(USA) —Songbook (Singspiel (IRE))
490[4] 762[9] 830[4]

Future Gem *Noel Wilson* a36 69
4 b m Bertolini(USA) —Georgianna (IRE) (Petardia)
1276[11] 1524[13] 2790[6] 3064[14] 4064[5] 4559[7] 4706[7] 4947[7] 5599[3] 6464[13] 6643[11]

Future Generation (IRE) *G M Lyons* a80 62
2 b f Hurricane Run(IRE) —Posterity (IRE) (Indian Ridge)
7256a[5]

Future Impact (IRE) *P D Deegan* a73 74
2 b g Kheleyf(USA) —Daring Imp (IRE) (Mac's Imp (USA))
954a[6]

Future Regime (IRE) *Patrick Morris* a57 32
3 b f Xaar—Sadalsud (IRE) (Shaadi (USA))
85[5] 689[7] 998[9] 4680[5] 5469[9] 5711[6] 6077[11]

Futurism *Richard Hannon* a68 53
2 b c Bertolini(USA) —Pastel (Lion Cavern (USA))
3000[9] 3326[11] 4902[7] 5659[3] 5969[6]

Fuzzy Cat *David Barron* a68 68
4 b g Nayef(USA) —Curfew (Marju (IRE))
296[2] (569) 1300[4] 1723[5] (1885) 2008[3] 2647[3] 2896[8] 3761[9] 4285[10] 6189[4] 6398[7] 7007[12]

Fuzzypeg (IRE) *James Fanshawe* 64
3 ch f Motivator—Nibbs Point (IRE) (Sure Blade (USA))
2994[8] 3242[4] 4115[7] (4765) (5564) 6132[8]

Fyodorovich (USA) *Alan McCabe* a31 57
5 b g Stravinsky(USA) —Omnia (USA) (Green Dancer (USA))
1813[4] 2010[4] 2381[9] 3538[7] 3610[6] 3976[10] 7131[7] 7473[9] 7936[4] 7956[8]

Gabby's Brother (IRE) *M Oppo*
2 b c Ashkalani(IRE) —Paola Quatraro (Cure The Blues (USA))
7264a[8]

Gabby's Golden Gal (USA) *Bob Baffert* a115
4 bb m Medaglia D'Oro(USA) —Gabriellina Giof (Ashkalani (IRE))
7341a[10]

Gabriel's Hill (USA) *Seth Benzel* a105 98
6 b h A.P. Indy(USA) —Lailani (Unfuwain (USA))
7339a[2]

Gabriel's Spirit (IRE) *Joseph Quinn* a8 56
3 b g Invincible Spirit(IRE) —Over Rating (Desert King (IRE))
5267[13]

Gadobout Dancer *Declan Carroll* 60
3 b f Tobougg(IRE) —Delta Tempo (IRE) (Bluebird (USA))
1887[10] 3226[9] (4707) 4951[2] (5361)

Gaily Noble (IRE) *Andrew Haynes* a95 96
4 b g One Cool Cat(USA) —Dream Genie (Puissance)
(394) 508[6] 769[2] (943) 1455[5] 2708[4] 3334[3] 4455[15] 4924[4] 5605[9] 6205[7]

Gainsborough's Art (IRE) *Chris Down* a63 22
5 ch g Desert Prince(IRE) —Cathy Garcia (IRE) (Be My Guest (USA))
2361[11]

Gainsboroughs Best (IRE) *William Haggas* a45 66
2 b f Invincible Spirit(IRE) —Catherinofaragon (USA) (Chief's Crown (USA))
5558[6] 5841[12] 6511[3] 6920[10]

Gakalina (IRE) *Jeremy Noseda* a82 77
3 ch f Galileo(IRE) —Ramona (Desert King (IRE))
1356[10] 6250[4] 6661[2] (6861) 7189[12]

Gala Casino Star (IRE) *Richard Fahey* a89 93
5 ch g Dr Fong(USA) —Abir (Soviet Star (USA))
2241[9] 2532[8] 7560[6] ◆ 7846[10] 8017[8]

Galactic Star *A Al Raihe* a82 103
7 ch h Galileo(IRE) —Balisada (Kris)
418a[13] 513a[10] 706a[10]

Gala Evening *Jim Old* a101 101
8 b g Daylami(IRE) —Balleta (USA) (Lyphard (USA))
(1020) 1139[2] 2126[2] 6926[26]

Galatian *Rod Millman* 83
3 ch g Traditionally(USA) —Easy To Imagine (USA) (Cozzene (USA))
2931[6] 3350[4] (4861) (5956)

Galaxidi *F Head* 107
3 b f High Chaparral(IRE) —Trexana (Kaldoun (FR))
2373a[4]

Gale Green *Henry Candy* 73
3 b f Galileo(IRE) —Anna Of Brunswick (Rainbow Quest (USA))
2051[9] 2890[4]

Galikova (FR) *F Head* 103
2 b f Galileo(IRE) —Born Gold (USA) (Blushing Groom (FR))
6609a[5]

Galileo's Choice (IRE) *D K Weld* 104
4 b g Galileo(IRE) —Sevi's Choice (USA) (Sir Ivor (USA))
1789a[3]

Galiotto (IRE) *Chris Wall* a55 67
4 b g Galileo(IRE) —Welsh Motto (USA) (Mtoto)
(1635) 2232[2] 3348[5] 5625[8] 6538[6]

Galivant (IRE) *J W Hills* 51
2 bb f Galileo(IRE) —Valdara (Darshaan)
6154[10]

Galizani (AUS) *John P Thompson* 92
4 b f Galileo(IRE) —Zahani (AUS) (Zabeel (NZ))
7368a[13]

Gallagher *Brian Meehan* a104 108
4 ch g Bahamian Bounty—Roo (Rudimentary (USA))
413a[3] 626a[6] 817a[5] 3193[10] 3869[10] 4358[6] ◆ 4843[12] 5516[8] 5950[6] 6349[19] 6888[16]

Gallant Eagle (IRE) *Sylvester Kirk* a84 81
3 ch g Hawk Wing(USA) —Generous Gesture (IRE) (Fasliyev (USA))
1086[2] 1352[11] 1761[2] 2225[4] ◆ 2742[10] 6813[8] 7012[5]

Gallant Lady (AUS) *Lee Freedman* 99
4 ch f Galileo(IRE) —Dalzing (AUS) (Blazing Sword (AUS))
7032a[12]

Gallantry *Jane Chapple-Hyam* a84 89
8 b g Green Desert(USA) —Gay Gallanta (USA) (Woodman (USA))
231[3] ◆ 315[4] 394[4] 672[4] (749) 867[6] 981[5] 1088[15] 1306[6] 5716[8] 6430[8] 6800[9] 7115[7] 7290[5] 7483[7] 7597[2] (7890) 8022[4]

Gallego *Richard Price* a49 75
8 br g Danzero(AUS) —Shafir (IRE) (Shaadi (USA))
1779[9] 2204[7] 2602[6] 2714[6] 3323[11] 4382[3] 4620[2] 4958[6] 5689[3] 6375[6] 6479[6]

Galley Slave (IRE) *Michael Chapman* a62 10
5 b g Spartacus(IRE) —Cimeterre (IRE) (Arazi (USA))
2874[13]

Gallic Star (IRE) *Mick Channon* 104
3 b f Galileo(IRE) —Oman Sea (USA) (Rahy (USA))
1313[7] 1729[6] 2800a[5] 3101[3] 4624[5] 4957[2] 5346a[6] 6950a[7]

Galloping Queen (IRE) *Mick Channon* 89
2 b f Refuse To Bend(IRE) —Rouge Noir (USA) (Saint Ballado (CAN))
2861[3] ◆ 3421a[4] 4135[3] 4862[3] 5583[2] 6222[3]

Galpin Junior (USA) *Ruth Carr* a79 88
4 ch g Hennessy(USA) —Reluctant Diva (Sadler's Wells (USA))
1688[13] 2534[8] 3551[8] 4060[3] (4245) 4712[6] 5198[5] 5513[4] 6140[9] 6303[3] 6572[5] 7281[2] 7405[2] 7494[5] 7866[9]

Galtymore Lad *Mick Channon* 106
2 b c Indesatchel(IRE) —Right Answer (Lujain (USA))
1263[12] 1749[4] (1986) (2514) 3049[7] 4355[2] 5245[2] 5880[2] (6477) 7080[3]

Gamedor (FR) *Gary Moore* a42 68
5 ch g Kendor(FR) —Garmeria (FR) (Kadrou (FR))
4794[6]

Game Lad *Tim Easterby* a28 87
8 b g Mind Games—Catch Me (Rudimentary (USA))
1030[10] 1374[3] 1707[11] (1808) 2086[8] (2205) 2462[3] 3448[5] 3619[8] 3876[10] 4370[2] 5043[9] 5435[4] 5937[12] 6366[8] 6963[4] 7143[11] 7352[11]

Game On Dude (USA) *Bob Baffert* a112
3 bb c Awesome Again(CAN) —Worldly Pleasure (USA) (Devil His Due (USA))
2776a[4]

Gamesmanship *John Dunlop*
2 b c Beat Hollow—Artful (IRE) (Green Desert (USA))
3915[11]

Gamesters Lady *Jim Best* a66 63
7 br m Almushtarak(IRE) —Tycoon Tina (Tina's Pet)
(622) ◆ 1635[7] 3967[2]

Ganache (IRE) *Patrick Chamings* a52 51
8 ch g Halling(USA) —Granted (FR) (Cadeaux Genereux)
1477[11] 2235[6] 2965[3] 4428[10] 6024[5]

Gan Amhras (IRE) *J S Bolger* 119
4 b g Galileo(IRE) —All's Forgotten (USA) (Darshaan)
1247a[9] 4630a[9]

Gandalf *Amy Weaver* a77 73
8 b g Sadler's Wells(USA) —Enchant (Lion Cavern (USA))
764[3] 4226[2] 5179[7] 5722[4] 6427[11] 7967[5]

Ganesa *Marco Botti* a10 41
2 b c Oasis Dream—Guntakal (IRE) (Night Shift (USA))
4960[12] 5763[11]

Gap Princess (IRE) *Geoffrey Harker* a79 97
6 b m Noverre(USA) —Safe Care (IRE) (Caerleon (USA))
1152[4] (2275) 3065[5] (3551) 3919[3] 4583[4] (4653) ◆ 5242[2] ◆ 5302[9] 6175[7] 6721[9]

Garafena *Richard Lee* a69 59
7 b m Golden Snake(USA) —Eclipsing (IRE) (Baillamont (USA))
3641[4] 3848[2] 4327[6] 4676[5] 5813[6]

Garde Cotiere (USA) *Jeremy Noseda* a94 63
2 b c Giant's Causeway(USA) —Amonita (Anabaa (USA))
6532[8] (6850)

Gardening Leave *Andrew Balding* 104
3 b c Selkirk(USA) —Misty Waters (IRE) (Caerleon (USA))
1354[5] (1702)

Garden Party *T J Bougourd* a79 72
6 b g Green Desert(USA) —Tempting Prospect (Shirley Heights)
1817a[3]

Gargano (IRE) *Ms Joanna Morgan* a79 72
5 b g Galileo(IRE) —Tudor Loom (Sallust)
(121) (280) 400[6] 636[2] 871[7] 1101[13] 1690[7] 7823a[9]

Garnica (FR) *David Nicholls* a84 99
7 gr g Linamix(FR) —Gueridia (IRE) (Night Shift (USA))
272a[2] 304a[0] 549a[2] 640a[3] 743a[7]

Garstang *John Balding* a84 69
7 ch g Atraf—Approved Quality (IRE) (Persian Heights)
74[6] 172[8] 345[6] 2883[6] 3261[7] 8005[4] ◆

Garth Mountain *Amanda Perrett* 72
3 b c Rock Of Gibraltar(IRE) —One Of The Family (Alzao (USA))
5116[5]

Gartsherrie *Paul Midgley* 47
2 gr f Proclamation(IRE) —Shining Oasis (IRE) (Mujtahid (USA))
1198[3] 3163[6] 3498[8] 4150[13]

Gaselee (USA) *Rae Guest* a75 96
4 b m Toccet(USA) —Vingt Et Une (FR) (Sadler's Wells (USA))
1454[2] 1849[2] 2659[4] 2938[11] 6480[4] 6693[8] (7181) 7457a[4]

Gasolina (FR) *C Gourdain* 54
2 b f Goldneyev(USA) —Aquae (FR) (Tel Quel (FR))
7009a[10]

Gatamalata (IRE) *Joseph G Murphy* 96
2 b f Spartacus(IRE) —Ardent Lady (Alhaarth (IRE))
3421a[2] 4879a[6] 5570a[8]

Gatinello (FR) *C Laffon-Parias* a27
2 b c Lando(GER) —Tiyi (FR) (Fairy King (USA))
7647a[10]

Gavriel (USA) *G Botti* 87
2 gr c Tale Of The Cat(USA) —Angry Reply (USA) (Grand Slam (USA))
7009a[2] (7383a)

Gayego (USA) *Saeed Bin Suroor* a121
5 bb h Gilded Time(USA) —Devils Lake (USA) (Lost Code (USA))
515a[2] ◆ 1024a[8] 3935a[3] 7365a[3]

Gay Gallivanter *John Gosden* a46 73
2 b f Iceman—Gallivant (Danehill (USA))
3562[10] 4962[2] 5583[3]

Gay Mirage (GER) *Michael Jarvis* a69 71
3 b f Highest Honor(FR) —Geminiani (IRE) (King Of Kings (IRE))
1271[5] 1451[2] 2175[2] 7022[6] 7282[7]

Gazamali (IRE) *James Evans* a48 55
3 b g Namid—Frond (Alzao (USA))
930[9] 1164[10] 2780[6] 3030[2] 3975[6]

Gazboolou *David Pinder* a79 72
6 b g Royal Applause—Warning Star (Warning)
552[5] 767[8] 1064[2] 1238[4] 1625[2] 2053[2] 3129[2] 4024[10] 4488[3] 6085[7] 6801[6] 7046[9] 7241[2] 7483[8] 7889[10]

Gearbox (IRE) *Harry Dunlop* a63 63
4 br g Tillerman—Persian Empress (IRE) (Persian Bold)
2255[11] 2812[5] 4327[12] 5011[8] 5663[2] 6213[7] 6535[2] 6841[4] 7089[6]

Geblah (IRE) *David Simcock* a39 66
2 b f Green Desert(USA) —Cedar Sea (IRE) (Persian Bold)
4747[4] ◆ 6770[7] 7198[8]

Gee Ceffyl Bach *Gary Woodward* a4 41
6 b m Josr Algarhoud(IRE) —Miletrian Cares (IRE) (Hamas (IRE))
2726[10] 5545[13] 5821[10] 6062[6]

Gee Dee Nen *Gary Moore* a95 89
7 b g Mister Baileys—Special Beat (Bustino)
4467[15]

Gee Major *Nicky Vaughan* a31 60
3 b g Reset(AUS) —Polly Golightly (Weldnaas (USA))
3275[9] 4280[5] (4534) (4733) 5201[4] 5711[5]

Geesala (IRE) *Kevin Ryan* 85
2 ch f Barathea(IRE) —Shivaree (Rahy (USA))
(1421) 2095[4] (2436) 2828a[8] 5525[9] 5880[21] 6647[6]

Geezers Colours *John Weymes* a70 79
5 b g Fraam—Konica (Desert King (IRE))
181[4] 464[4] 663[2]

Gekko (IRE) *Patrick Morris* a43 49
2 b g Iffraaj—Acidanthera (Alzao (USA))
4396[5] 6126[8] 7427[7] 7666[7]

Geminus (IRE) *Jedd O'Keeffe* 33
2 b g Choisir(AUS) —Macca Luna (IRE) (Kahyasi)
6222[7] 6894[14]

Gemma's Delight (IRE) *James Unett* a64 62
3 gr f Clodovil(IRE) —Duckmore Bay (IRE) (Titus Livius (FR))
288[5] 527[9] 1205[8] 1774[6] 2000[3] 2584[3] 3030[4] (3855) 4515[3] 4988[5] 5906[6] 6261[12] 7064[2]

Gems *Harry Dunlop* a50
3 b f Haafhd—Megdale (IRE) (Waajib)
592[6] 755[5] 872[6] 1461[10] 2250[12] 2678[11]

Gemstone (IRE) *A P O'Brien* 85
2 b f Galileo(IRE) —Kincob (USA) (Kingmambo (USA))
4077a[7] 4879a[8] 6005a[6] (6784a)

Gene Autry (USA) *Richard Hannon* 106
3 bb g Zavata(USA) —Total Acceptance (USA) (With Approval (CAN))
1776[2] ◆ 2242[2] ◆ 2545[5] (3270) 3791[3] 4509[3] 4819[2]

Generale (IRE) *Frank Sheridan* a38
2 b g Needwood Blade—Harvest Gold (IRE) (Goldmark (USA))
5269[10] 5701[11] 6307[10]

General Eliott (IRE) *Paul Cole* a73 112
5 b g Rock Of Gibraltar(IRE) —Marlene-D (Selkirk (USA))
1533[5] 2977[11] 3431[5] 5264[12] 5556[5] 6097[7] 6780[2]

General Quarters (USA) *Thomas R McCarthy* a118 118
4 rg h Sky Mesa(USA) —Ecology (USA) (Unbridled's Song (USA))
5321a[7]

General Synod *Richard Hannon* 76
2 b c Invincible Spirit(IRE) —New Assembly (IRE) (Machiavellian (USA))
5033[2] ◆ 5916[5]

General Tufto *Charles Smith* a81 81
5 b g Fantastic Light(USA) —Miss Pinkerton (Danehill (USA))
40[3] 169[4] 245[4] (298) 400[3] 451[2] 509[5] (715) 787[4] 837[6] 1374[8] 1494[3] 1751[2] 2093[5] (2523) 2937[12] 3283[4] 3613[3] 4196[6] 5786[12] 7306[14] 7541[7] 7642[4] 7694[DSQ] 7804[4] (7895) 7932[5] 7988[5]

Generous Genella *Julia Feilden* a48 29
2 b f Cape Cross(IRE) —Gombay Girl (USA) (Woodman (USA))
4747[7] 6155[15] 6866[13]

Generous Lad (IRE) *Andrew Haynes* a60 48
7 b g Generous(IRE) —Tudor Loom (Sallust)
1591[3] ◆ 2012[7] 4912[6] 5072[DSQ] 5840[5] 6121[4] 6314[7]

Generous Pursuit *Phil McEntee*
2 b f Pursuit Of Love—Not So Generous (IRE) (Fayruz)
6884[9] 7152[14]

Genes Of A Dancer (AUS) *Michael Appleby* a40 56
4 ch g Galileo(IRE) —Jugah's Dancer (AUS) (Jugah (USA))
3256[6] 3593[7] 4257[6] 5260[5] 5631[7]

Geneva Geyser (GER) *James Eustace* a75 93
4 b g One Cool Cat(USA) —Genevra (IRE) (Danehill (USA))
2031[16] 2314[9] (3688) 3737[2] 5307[13] 6096[4] 6447[11]

Genius Beast (USA) *Mahmood Al Zarooni* 89
2 b c Kingmambo(USA) —Shawanda (IRE) (Sinndar (IRE))
5049[3] 5878[3] (6365)

Genki (IRE) *Roger Charlton* a53 114
6 ch g Shinko Forest(IRE) —Emma's Star (ITY) (Darshaan)
1727[4] 3193[6] ◆ (3674) 4576[23] 5744[3] 6177[4] 6735[2]

Genovesa (GER) *C Von Der Recke* 91
3 b f Ransom O'War(USA) —Ginza (GER) (Acatenango (GER))
1250a[11] 1715a[10]

Gentle Guru *Richard Phillips* a75 75
6 b m Ishiguru(USA) —Soft Touch (IRE) (Petorius)
380[3] 602[4] 1258[9]

Gentle Lord *Tom Dascombe* 80
2 b c Ishiguru(USA) —Soft Touch (IRE) (Petorius)
4622[4] 5301[2] (6047)

Gentleman Is Back (USA) *John Gosden* a79
2 bb c Johannesburg(USA) —Torros Straits (USA) (Boundary (USA))
5718[4] ◆ (6334) 7379[4]

Gentoo (FR) *A Lyon* a94 113
6 b g Loup Solitaire(USA) —Ifni (FR) (Bering)
5109a[2] (6016a) (6607a) (7110a)

Geoffdaw *Sheena West* a74 67
5 b g Vettori(IRE) —Talighta (USA) (Barathea (IRE))
390[3] 539[9]

Geojimali *Jim Goldie* a82 67
8 ch g Compton Place—Harrken Heights (IRE) (Belmez (USA))
1869[9] 2453[6] 3409[3] 4063[6] 4192[7] 4404[6] 4704[9] 4824[5] 5486[3] 6108[6] 6494[2] 7056[8]

Geordie Iris (IRE) *Richard Hannon* a76 71
2 b f Elusive City(USA) —Tiger Desert (GER) (Desert King (IRE))
4962[8] (5699) 6302[4] 7528[4] 7718[3] 7891[6]

Geordie Joe *John Weymes*
2 ch c Avonbridge—Quick Flight (Polar Falcon (USA))
5595[10] 5814[9]

George Adamson (IRE) *Alan Swinbank* a55 80
4 b g Where Or When(IRE) —Tactile (Groom Dancer (USA))
1490[5] 1717[2] 2207[4] (2500) (2766) 2851[2] 3405[3] (4656) 4953[3] 5757[3] 6754[8]

George Baker (IRE) *George Baker* a63 78
3 b g Camacho—Petite Maxine (Sharpo)
4248[5] 6168[5] 6452[4] 6937[3]

George Benjamin *David Nicholls* a75 82
3 b g Trade Fair—Unchain My Heart (Pursuit Of Love)
1993[2] 2702[14] (4018) 4646[3] 6107[2] 6394[2] 6622[3] 6800[10]

Georgebernardshaw (IRE) *David Simcock* a81 108
5 b g Danehill Dancer(IRE) —Khamseh (Thatching)
1904[4] 2539[5] 3460[4] 3893[5] 5554[5] 5952[4] 6363[16]

Georges Lane *Richard Fahey* 88
2 b g Diamond Green(FR) —Corps De Ballet (IRE) (Fasliyev (USA))
(3805)

George Thisby *Rod Millman* a70 78
4 b g Royal Applause—Warning Belle (Warning)
1580[11] 2129[8] 2646[3] 3463[6] 3863[12] (5473) 6085[8] 6421[9] 6991[10]

George Woolf *Alan McCabe* a69 58
2 b g Iceman—Beading (Polish Precedent (USA))
1626[6] 2990[7] 4254[4] 5177[4]

Georgey Girl *Alan Swinbank* a44
2 b f Doyen(IRE) —Thrasher (Hector Protector (USA))
7503[10]

Georgian Silver *George Foster* a46 33
2 ch f Auction House(USA) —Proud Titania (IRE) (Fairy King (USA))
3498[10] 6916[11] 7392[3] 7576[8]

Georgina Bailey (IRE) *Alan McCabe* 43
2 ch f Iffraaj—Baileys First (IRE) (Alzao (USA))
2389[6] 2740[8] 3237[7] 7197[9]

Germanico (IRE) *C Laffon-Parias* 76
2 b c Holy Roman Emperor(IRE) —Tartouche (Pursuit Of Love)
7009a[5]

Geronimo Chief (IRE) *Ben Haslam* a63 50
2 b g Sleeping Indian—Portorosa (USA) (Irish River (FR))
4941[12] 5531[9] 5814[7] (7393) 7643[2] 7831[5]

Gertmegalush (IRE) *John Harris* a78 83
3 b g One Cool Cat(USA) —Aiming Upwards (Blushing Flame (USA))
596[3] ◆ 884[10] 1191[7] 3436[5] 3753[3] 4288[7] 4714[5] 4858[6] 6540[11] 6879[6]

Gertrude Bell *John Gosden* a76 104
3 ch f Sinndar(IRE) —Sugar Mill (FR) (Polar Falcon (USA))
(1358) (1820) 2711[4] 3101[7]

Gessabelle *Phil McEntee* a46 49
3 b f Largesse—Palmstead Belle (IRE) (Wolfhound (USA))
2651[7] 2878[8] 3415[6] 3827[9] 4720[5] 4760[3] 4998[2] 5162[10] 6060[8] 6285[4] 6773[8] 7131[6] 7547[5] 7676[7] 7757[7] 7869[6]

Getabuzz *Tim Easterby* 47
2 b g Beat Hollow—Ailincala (IRE) (Pursuit Of Love)
6894[4]

Getaway (GER) *J Hirschberger* 124
7 b h Monsun(GER) —Guernica (Unfuwain (USA))
1956a[2] 3019a[2]

Getcarter *Richard Hannon* a83 91
4 b h Fasliyev(USA) —Pourquoi Pas (IRE) (Nordico (USA))
1088[8] (1580) 1903[5] 2595[8] 2748[12] 3346[6] 4904[6] 5495[6] 5750[8] 6252[5] 7114[5]

Get Stormy (USA) *Thomas Bush* 114
4 b h Stormy Atlantic(USA) —Foolish Gal (USA) (Kiri's Clown (USA))
6759a[4] 7364a[11]

Ghazwah *Richard Fahey* a78 74
3 b f Shamardal(USA) —Bahja (USA) (Seeking The Gold (USA))
(301) (596) 926a[8]

Gheed (IRE) *Kevin Morgan* a61 50
5 b m Cape Cross(IRE) —Hareer (Anabaa (USA))
(98) 309[14] 969[7] 1226[5] 1489[10] 4763[6] 5565[2]

Ghimaar *Nicky Henderson* a73 99
5 b g Dubai Destination(USA) —Charlecote (IRE) (Caerleon (USA))
3050[4] ◆ (4467)

Ghost (IRE) *B W Hills* 82
3 b g Invincible Spirit(IRE) —Alexander Phantom (IRE) (Soviet Star (USA))
(4340) 5524[15]

Ghost Dancer *Milton Bradley* a69 76
6 ch g Danehill Dancer(IRE) —Reservation (IRE) (Common Grounds)
1547[12] 2246[7] 2647[9] 3254[14] 4875[9] 4936[9] 5875[11] 5920[10] 6672[11]

Ghostwing *John Gallagher* a97 94
3 gr g Kheleyf(USA) —Someone's Angel (USA) (Runaway Groom (CAN))
1019[4] 1315[14] 1836[8] (2283) 2862[7] 4118[12] 4231[2] 4536[12] 4904[5] 5787[16] 6429[11]

Ghufa (IRE) *Jeff Pearce* a77 77
6 b g Sakhee(USA) —Hawriyah (USA) (Dayjur (USA))
1012[5] 1262[8] (1462) 1623[6] 2230[2] (2285) ◆ 2597[3] (2881) 3221[2] (3294) 3618[5] 4094[2] 4597[4] 4907[6] 6055[10] 6846[6] 7275[3]

Giant Oak (USA) *Chris Block* a113 109
4 ch h Giant's Causeway(USA) —Crafty Oak (USA) (Crafty Prospector (USA))
7339a[4]

Giantrio (IRE) *Rod Collet* a69
2 ch c Shamardal(USA) —Apperella (Rainbow Quest (USA))
7974a[4]

Giants Play (USA) *Sir Michael Stoute* a98 84
3 b f Giant's Causeway(USA) —Playful Act (IRE) (Sadler's Wells (USA))
2050[3] 4341[3] (6250) 6797[4] 7189[3]

Giant Strides *David Evans* a59
4 b m Xaar—Brandish (Warning)
31[4] 226[7]

Gibraltar Applied (IRE) *F & L Camici* 91
5 ch h Rock Of Gibraltar(IRE) —Warranty Applied (USA) (Monteverdi)
1943a[5]

Gibraltar Lass (USA) *Hugh Collingridge* a48 28
3 ch f Concerto(USA) —Mango Lassie (USA) (Montreal Red (USA))
9[8] 2702[12] 3677[10] 4908[6] 6656[12] 7288[8]

Gifted Apakay (USA) *Ed Dunlop* a74 82
3 ch f Leroidesanimaux(BRZ) —Sentimental Gift (USA) (Green Dancer (USA))
1317[4] 1876[4] 2256[7] 3171[3] 3806[3] ◆ 4335[2] (5041) 5833[2] 6204[10] 6771[6]

Gifted Lady (IRE) *Pat Phelan* a50 61
3 gr f Bahri(USA) —Zest (USA) (Zilzal (USA))
978[10] 1581[10] 2401[7] 2964[7] 7555[12]

Gift Of Love (IRE) *David Elsworth* 70
3 b f Azamour(IRE) —Spot Prize (USA) (Seattle Dancer (USA))
4906[2] ◆ 5971[4] 6814[2] 6993[5]

Gilderoy *Dominic Ffrench Davis* a53 51
3 b g Compton Place—Lola Sapola (IRE) (Benny The Dip (USA))
2684[14] 3759[8] 4133[11] 4692[2] 4989[9] 5650[5] 5926[3] 6996[8] 7402[7] 7506[5] 7717[12] 7783[8]

Gile Na Greine (IRE) *J S Bolger* a84 113
3 b f Galileo(IRE) —Scribonia (IRE) (Danehill (USA))
1726[3] ◆ 2370a[17] 3143[2] 3793[6] 5773a[6]

Gilt Edge Girl *Clive Cox* a102 114
4 ch m Monsieur Bond(IRE) —Tahara (IRE) (Caerleon (USA))
992[2] (1545) (2912a) 3875[3] 4505[9] 5573a[3] 6194[6] (6608a)

Gimli's Rock (IRE) *Mrs John Harrington* a67 90
4 b g Rock Of Gibraltar(IRE) —Beltisaal (FR) (Belmez (USA))
3492a^{2} (6971a)

Ginga Dude (NZ) *Graeme Boyd* 116
7 ch g Istidaad(USA) —Clatitude (NZ) (Clay Hero (AUS))
(6946a) 7458a^{4}

Ginger Bazouka (FR) *P Demercastel* 95
3 b f Okawango(USA) —Cedar Springs (IRE) (Sadler's Wells (USA))
1496a^{6}

Ginger Grey (IRE) *David O'Meara* a77 77
3 gr g Bertolini(USA) —Just In Love (FR) (Highest Honor (FR))
(443) 582^{4} 1168^{5} 1488^{2} 1594^{3} ◆ 2235^{8} 2566^{9} 3297^{2} 3580^{3} 5494^{5} (7082) 7554^{3}

Ginger Jack *Mark Johnston* a88 98
3 ch g Refuse To Bend(IRE) —Coretta (IRE) (Caerleon (USA))
(385) ◆ (617) ◆ 2324^{7} 2737^{3} 2933^{6} 3206^{6} (3585) (3987) ◆ 4357^{9} 5759^{3} 6391^{6}

Ginger Jalapeno *Edward Bevan*
4 ch m Tobougg(IRE) —Hello Sweety (Shaamit (IRE))
3518^{10} 4069^{15}

Ginger's Lad *Michael Easterby* a47
6 ch g Elmaamul(USA) —Chadwick's Ginger (Crofthall)
456^{6}

Ginger Ted (IRE) *Richard Guest* a35 93
3 ch g Fath(USA) —Estertide (IRE) (Tagula (IRE))
1184^{3} (2069) 2862^{5} 3215^{7} 4192^{2} 4806^{6} 5048^{6} 5390^{3} (5601) 6142^{27} 6962^{10} 7207^{2}

Ginobili (IRE) *Andrew Reid* a65 94
4 b g Fasliyev(USA) —Imperial Graf (USA) (Blushing John (USA))
1074^{2} 1267^{2} 1428^{5} 3463^{8} 5377^{12} 6208^{7} 6455^{10} 6932^{8}

Gio Ponti (USA) *Christophe Clement* a127 123
5 b h Tale Of The Cat(USA) —Chipeta Springs (USA) (Alydar (USA))
1027a^{4} 5321a^{2} (6759a) ◆ 7364a^{2}

Giotto (IRE) *Nick Littmoden* 25
2 b c Shamardal(USA) —Otelcalifomi (USA) (Gulch (USA))
6882^{10}

Girolamo (USA) *Saeed Bin Suroor* a122
4 bb h A.P. Indy(USA) —Get Lucky (USA) (Mr Prospector (USA))
5779a^{5} (6582a) 7361a^{11}

Gitano Hernando *Marco Botti* a123 120
4 ch h Hernando(FR) —Gino's Spirits (Perugino (USA))
(738) ◆ 1027a^{6} ◆ (6548a) ◆ 6925^{4}

Giulia Vis (IRE) *F Santella* 78
3 b f Altieri—Vis Et Robur (Pursuit Of Love)
1713a^{9}

Giulietta Da Vinci *Steve Woodman* a63 70
3 b f Mujahid(USA) —Gennie Bond (Pivotal)
932^{2} 1593^{4} 1873^{11} 2416^{11} 3479^{4} 4025^{8} 5555^{8} 5712^{3} 6024^{7} 6522^{5} 6862^{8} 7438^{8}

Give It To Me (FR) *Mario Hofer* a40 45
2 ch f Dashing Blade—Gobhana (IRE) (Spinning World (USA))
7009a^{0}

Given A Choice (IRE) *Jeff Pearce* a62 46
8 b g Trans Island—Miss Audimar (USA) (Mr. Leader (USA))
5367^{7} 5635^{6} 5840^{6} 6328^{8} 6999^{8} 7270^{9} 7569^{9}

Givenn *Ms J S Doyle* a30
6 b m Tomba—Bedford Falls (Mind Games)
585^{11} 655^{8} 758^{9} 1068^{10} 1167^{12}

Give Your Verdict (USA) *Sir Michael Stoute* 93
3 b g Arch(USA) —Remediate (USA) (Miswaki (USA))
1844^{4} 2842^{2} ◆ 3272^{2} 4028^{2} (4521) (5917)

Givine (FR) *B De Montzey* 98
3 gr f Blackdoun(FR) —Viguerie (FR) (Double Bed (FR))
1566a^{11}

Glacial *Edward Vaughan* a78 64
3 b g Cape Cross(IRE) —Silver Bracelet (Machiavellian (USA))
1325^{7} 1769^{5} ◆ 2496^{4}

Glad Sky *W Gulcher* 100
4 b g Big Shuffle(USA) —Glady Sum (GER) (Surumu (GER))
1955a^{6} 7370a^{3}

Gladstone (IRE) *William Haggas* 60
2 b g Dansili—Rockerlong (Deploy)
6883^{14}

Glady Romana (GER) *W Baltromei* 90
3 b f Doyen(IRE) —Glady Sum (GER) (Surumu (GER))
3943a^{6} 4640a^{13} 6409a^{4}

Glamorous Emma (IRE) *G Botti* 60
2 b f Byron—Golden Land (FR) (Octagonal (NZ))
7009a^{9}

Glamorous Spirit (IRE) *Ronald Harris* a105 104
4 b m Invincible Spirit(IRE) —Glamorous Air (IRE) (Air Express (IRE))
212^{9} 307^{3} 384^{4} 578^{2} (736) 948^{2} ◆ 2745^{11} 3197^{4} (3486a) 3895^{8} 4505^{14} 5569a^{15}

Glanusk *Ralph Beckett* a70 76
2 b c Dansili—Palinisa (FR) (Night Shift (USA))
4954^{4} ◆ 5893^{6} 6465^{8}

Glan Y Mor (IRE) *Tony Carroll* a44 47
3 b f Mark Of Esteem(IRE) —Molly Mello (GER) (Big Shuffle (USA))
624^{4} 793^{8} 3263^{12} 4992^{8} 5584^{12} 6527^{12} 6826^{8}

Glas Burn *Jonathan Portman* 92
2 b f Avonbridge—Dunya (Unfuwain (USA))
6441^{6} (6986) 7204^{4}

Glass Harmonium (IRE) *Sir Michael Stoute* 116
4 gr h Verglas(IRE) —Spring Symphony (IRE) (Darshaan)
(1532) 2470^{3} 3068^{6} 6925^{6} 7854a^{12}

Glass Mountain (IRE) *James Fanshawe* 27
2 gr g Verglas(IRE) —Exotic Mix (FR) (Linamix (FR))
6626^{7}

Gleaming Silver (IRE) *G M Lyons* a73 77
4 gr m Dalakhani(IRE) —Green Lassy (FR) (Green Tune (USA))
5129a^{11}

Gleaming Spirit (IRE) *Peter Grayson* a55 30
6 b g Mujadil(USA) —Gleam (Green Desert (USA))
178^{11} 271^{7} (477) 659^{6} 899^{6} 4435^{9} 7477^{11} 7542^{13} 8036^{9}

Glenavon *Amanda Perrett* a48 44
2 b g Nayef(USA) —Corndavon (USA) (Sheikh Albadou)
2887^{11} 6414^{7} 6795^{7}

Glencadam Gold (IRE) *Henry Cecil* 77
2 b c Refuse To Bend(IRE) —Sandrella (IRE) (Darshaan)
6676^{2} ◆ (6894)

Glendaragh (IRE) *Kevin Prendergast* 82
2 b c Ad Valorem(USA) —Happy Flight (IRE) (Titus Livius (FR))
6230a^{14}

Glen Lass *Jeff Pearce* a64 59
3 ch f Zafeen(FR) —Welcome Aboard (Be My Guest (USA))
(133) 305^{3} 422^{4} 589^{3} 775^{7} (1264)

Glenluji *Jim Goldie* 69
5 b g Lujain(USA) —Glenhurich (IRE) (Sri Pekan (USA))
2454^{7} 2854^{8} (3147) 3357^{5} (3500) 4082^{3} (4188) 4796^{5} 5407^{6} 5737^{6} 6108^{8}

Glen Molly (IRE) *B W Hills* 96
4 b m Danetime(IRE) —Sonorous (IRE) (Ashkalani (IRE))
1397^{6} 4358^{9} 4617^{12}

Glenmuir (IRE) *John Quinn* a46 75
7 b g Josr Algarhoud(IRE) —Beryl (Bering)
1117^{7} 1426^{6} 1802^{5} 2524^{7} 3438^{6} 4119^{7} 5819^{3} 6117^{3} 6462^{2} 7063^{2} 7306^{5}

Glenns Princess *Richard Fahey* a40 64
2 b f Needwood Blade—Ryan's Quest (IRE) (Mukaddamah (USA))
1292^{4} 1527^{3} 4645^{9} 5334^{4} 5630^{12} 6072^{5} 7469^{5} 7811^{6}

Glenridding *James Given* a77 92
6 b g Averti(IRE) —Appelone (Emperor Jones (USA))
1361^{5} 1707^{12} 1926^{8} 2531^{2} 3061^{13} 3391^{5} 3553^{8} 3855^{3} (4428) (4555) 5157^{8} 5499^{11} (5937) 6372^{5} (6558) 7143^{2} 7274^{7} 7488^{11}

Glen's Diamond *Richard Fahey* 87
2 b g Intikhab(USA) —Posta Vecchia (USA) (Rainbow Quest (USA))
4543^{3} ◆ (5196) (5525) ◆

Glen Shiel (USA) *Mark Johnston* a67 91
3 ch g Whywhywhy(USA) —Staffin (Salse (USA))
2069^{6} (2450) 3085^{5} 3401^{2} ◆ 3579^{8} (4104) 4413^{3} ◆ 4509^{4} 4843^{6} ◆ 5242^{3} 5435^{2} 5716^{P}

Glitter Bug (IRE) *Mark Johnston* a12
2 b g Oasis Dream—Aethra (USA) (Trempolino (USA))
2427^{7} 3072^{5} 3528^{5} 7016^{9} 7394^{10}

Global *Brian Ellison* a77 88
4 ch g Bahamian Bounty—Tuppenny Blue (Pennekamp (USA))
3317^{13} 3973^{5} 6534^{12}

Global City (IRE) *Saeed Bin Suroor* a105 107
4 b h Exceed And Excel(AUS) —Victory Peak (Shirley Heights)
(416a) (628a) 817a^{6} 3674^{8} 4616^{9} 6241^{3} 7482^{7}

Global Guest *Sean Curran* a52 71
6 b g Piccolo—By Arrangement (IRE) (Bold Arrangement)
229^{9} 4797^{7} 5914^{4}

Global Magic (GER) *A Wohler* 87
2 b f Lando(GER) —Goonda (Darshaan)
7108a^{7}

Global Recovery (IRE) *J S Bolger* a61 67
3 b g El Corredor(USA) —Altarejos (IRE) (Vettori (IRE))
7078a^{9}

Global Strategy *Oliver Sherwood* a43 67
7 b g Rainbow Quest(USA) —Pleasuring (Good Times (ITY))
15^{8} 376^{9}

Global Village (IRE) *Michael Blake* a89 68
5 b g Dubai Destination(USA) —Zelding (IRE) (Warning)
(668) (1350) (1509) 7091^{8} 8017^{7}

Gloria De Campeao (BRZ) *P Bary* a122 122
7 b h Impression(ARG) —Audacity (BRZ) (Clackson (BRZ))
(338a) 800a^{2} (1027a) 2154a^{2}

Glorified *David Wachman* a83 85
3 ch f Danehill Dancer(IRE) —Olivia Grace (Pivotal)
2912a^{6}

Glorious Noah (JPN) *Yoshito Yahagi* a110 101
4 bb h Precise End(USA) —Love Robbery (JPN) (Jade Robbery (USA))
1022a^{4}

Glor Na Mara (IRE) *J S Bolger* 113
2 b c Leroidesanimaux(BRZ) —Sister Angelina (USA) (Saint Ballado (CAN))
4176a^{4} 4880a^{2} ◆ 5316a^{2} 5567a^{2} 5975a^{5} 6924^{3}

Glorybe (GER) *Chris Bealby* a44
4 ch m Monsun(GER) —Glorosia (FR) (Bering)
575^{6}

Gloucester *Michael Scudamore* a71 80
7 b g Montjeu(IRE) —Birdlip (USA) (Sanglamore (USA))
2845^{5} 3576^{7}

Glow Star (SAF) *Gary Moore* a93 94
6 ch g Muhtafal(USA) —Arctic Glow (SAF) (Northern Guest (USA))
286^{9}

Glyn Ceiriog *George Baker* 67
2 b f Hawk Wing(USA) —Ceiriog Valley (In The Wings)
5583^{7} 6469^{3}

Gnr Steamtrain (IRE) *Richard Fahey* 46
2 b c Oratorio(IRE) —Undercover Glamour (USA) (Kingmambo (USA))
6324^{5} 6704^{9}

Go *Richard Hannon* a54 57
2 b g Royal Applause—Kind Of Light (Primo Dominie)
4396^{6} 5871^{5} 6158^{10} 6498^{6} 6988^{12}

Goal (IRE) *David C Griffiths* a55 49
2 b c Mujadil(USA) —Classic Lin (FR) (Linamix (FR))
7346^{11} 7578^{6} 7914^{3} 7983^{6}

Go Alone (IRE) *Alan Swinbank* a40 72
4 b g Elusive City(USA) —Ya Ya (IRE) (Royal Academy (USA))
1396^{12} 1722^{6}

Go Amwell *John Jenkins* a61 60
7 b g Kayf Tara—Daarat Alayaam (IRE) (Reference Point)
554^{8} 1273^{6} 4223^{4} 5666^{3} 6132^{6} 7805^{7}

Gobama *J W Hills* a83 95
3 br f Dr Fong(USA) —Chine (Inchinor)
1159^{9} 1619^{3} (2042) 2652^{4} (3063) 3457^{5} 4137^{2} 5222^{2} 6346^{16} 7188^{11}

Go Country (FR) *P Schiergen* 99
3 b c Country Reel(USA) —Gerone (FR) (Saumarez)
1564a^{4} 2405a^{8}

Goddess Of Light (IRE) *Daniel Mark Loughnane* a73 70
3 b f Chineur(FR) —Blues Over (IRE) (Sri Pekan (USA))
2287^{6} 7837^{8}

Godfreyson (IRE) *A Trybuhl* a66 66
5 b g Viking Ruler(AUS) —Monzitta (GER) (Monsun (GER))
1056a^{9}

Godfrey Street *Tony Newcombe* a81 80
7 ch g Compton Place—Tahara (IRE) (Caerleon (USA))
138^{6} 402^{7}

Go Directa (GER) *Y Fertillet* 66
7 ch g Big Shuffle(USA) —Greese (Mukaddamah (USA))
273a^{0}

Go Forth North (USA) *A C Avila* 98
3 ch f North Light(IRE) —Witch Tradition (USA) (Holy Bull (USA))
6604a^{8}

Go Go Green (IRE) *David Brown* a82 96
4 b g Acclamation—Preponderance (IRE) (Cyrano De Bergerac)
1423^{7} 2940^{4} ◆ 3435^{9} 4118^{10} 4942^{8}

Going French (IRE) *F J Brennan* a71 69
3 ch g Frenchmans Bay(FR) —Easy Going (Hamas (IRE))
625^{8} 4284^{4} 4529^{6} 5206^{6} 6026^{13}

Going Gaga (IRE) *Michael Mulvany* 74
2 b c Mujadil(USA) —Carrozzina (Vettori (IRE))
6230a^{11}

Gojeri (IRE) *Michael Jarvis* a80 88
3 ch g Choisir(AUS) —Lady Elysees (USA) (Royal Academy (USA))
1050^{5} 2868^{2} ◆ 3085^{4} (4860) 5917^{3} 6620^{4}

Golconde Mine (IRE) *J Van Handenhove* a57 73
8 b m Alamo Bay(USA) —Grenouillere (USA) (Alysheba (USA))
221a^{10} 332a^{0}

Golda Go *Paul Midgley*
2 ch f Rambling Bear—Water Well (Sadler's Wells (USA))
1800^{7} 2848^{8}

Goldarover (IRE) *Noel Meade* a66 75
3 b g Fasliyev(USA) —Glamadour (IRE) (Sanglamore (USA))
4563a^{16}

Gold Bubbles (USA) *J S Bolger* 106
3 b f Street Cry(IRE) —Well Revered (USA) (Red Ransom (USA))
1787a^{11} 2029^{2}

Gold Crusher (USA) *Julie-Ann Camacho* a64 57
3 b g Johannesburg(USA) —Compressed (USA) (Green Forest (USA))
1425^{10} 2329^{6} 4151^{5} 4649^{6}

Golden Alchemist *Mark Usher* a49 57
7 ch g Woodborough(USA) —Pure Gold (Dilum (USA))
748^{5}

Golden Aria (IRE) *Richard Hannon* 79
3 b f Rakti—Yellow Trumpet (Petong)
1850^{9}

Golden Arrow (IRE) *E Charpy* a108 97
7 b h Danehill(USA) —Cheal Rose (IRE) (Dr Devious (IRE))
632a^{9}

Golden Blaze *James Moffatt* 69
2 ch c Iceman—Astrolove (IRE) (Bigstone (IRE))
2577^{4} 2667^{4} 3705^{6} 4242^{4} 4701^{4} 5597^{11} 5947^{6} 6174^{2} 6386^{2} 7059^{5}

Golden Clou (FR) *P Demercastel* a104 97
4 ch m Kendor(FR) —Glaoutchka (FR) (Glaieul (USA))
742a^{10}

Golden Compass *Giles Bravery* a34
2 ch f Sakhee(USA) —Northern Bows (Bertolini (USA))
2474^{7} 6849^{11}

Golden Creek (USA) *Ralph Beckett* a71 57
2 b c Seeking The Gold(USA) —Oyster Bay (USA) (Saint Ballado (CAN))
3842^{3} ◆ 4432^{2} (5643)

Golden Delicious *Hughie Morrison* 83
2 ch f Cadeaux Genereux—Playgirl (IRE) (Caerleon (USA))
(6688) 7098^{12}

Golden Desert (IRE) *Robert Mills* a101 109
6 b g Desert Prince(IRE) —Jules (IRE) (Danehill (USA))
1727^{18} 1900^{9} 3193^{5} ◆ 3461^{3} 6349^{4} 6888^{2} 7060^{4} 7482^{3} 7524^{5}

Golden Destiny (IRE) *PETER Makin* a56 108
4 ch m Captain Rio—Dear Catch (IRE) (Bluebird (USA))
1545^{2} 1918^{11} 3875^{10} 4401^{12} 4814^{2} 5742^{2} 6194^{2} ◆ 6887^{11}

Golden Dixie (USA) *Ronald Harris* a66 76
11 ch g Dixieland Band(USA) —Beyrouth (USA) (Alleged (USA))
116^{6} 242^{10}

Golden Dynamic (IRE) *E Galli* 75
6 b h Danetime(IRE) —Golden Vizcaya (USA) (Alydeed (CAN))
7459a^{11}

Golden Future *Peter Niven* a48 61
7 b g Muhtarram(USA) —Nazca (Zilzal (USA))
720^{5} 3122^{2} 4410^{8} (4800) 5336^{3} 6187^{11}

Golden Games (IRE) *Daniel Christopher O'Brien* a19 67
4 b m Montjeu(IRE) —Ski For Gold (Shirley Heights)
120^{9} 1446^{5}

Golden Gates (IRE) *Ann Duffield* 66
3 b g Key Of Luck(USA) —Golden Anthem (USA) (Lion Cavern (USA))
1010^{12} 2143^{9}

Golden Hinde *Mark Johnston* 80
2 b c Red Ransom(USA) —Treacle (USA) (Seeking The Gold (USA))
4167^{4} ◆ 4460^{4} (5546)

Golden Joker (IRE) *F Boccardelli* a80 110
6 ch h Shinko Forest(IRE) —Westside Girl (USA) (Way West (FR))
7459a^{7}

Golden Penny *Michael Dods* a80 81
5 b g Xaar—Dog Rose (SAF) (Fort Wood (USA))
129^{8}

Golden Prospect *Miss J R Tooth* a68 66
6 b g Lujain(USA) —Petonellajill (Petong)
8^{3} 135^{10} 270^{6} (1078) 1179^{9} 1636^{4} 2360^{5} 3787^{4} 6860^{9}

Golden Ramon (IRE) *B Grizzetti* 89
3 ch f Captain Rio—Solid Golden (USA) (Mountain Cat (USA))
1419a^{16} 1713a^{14} 4185a^{10} 6976a^{4} 7459a^{14}

Golden Ratio (IRE) *Jeremy Gask* a58 41
3 b f Noverre(USA) —Golden Opinion (USA) (Slew O'Gold (USA))
527^{5} 849^{2} 1211^{3} 2005^{7} 2480^{5} 2886^{9} 3520^{6}

Golden Rock (IRE) *Roger Charlton* a73 77
4 ch g Rock Of Gibraltar(IRE) —Sister Golden Hair (IRE) (Glint Of Gold)
1440^{6} 1875^{2} (2167) 3130^{8} 3725^{4} 4860^{4}

Golden Shaheen (IRE) *Mark Johnston* a90 99
3 b g Invincible Spirit(IRE) —Cheeky Weeky (Cadeaux Genereux)
2815^{8} ◆ 3448^{9} 3876^{8} (4369) 4995^{7} 5703^{3} 6357^{5} 6721^{14}

Golden Shine *Alan Bailey* a65 83
2 b f Royal Applause—Branston Jewel (IRE) (Prince Sabo)
1324^{3} ◆ (1773) 2074^{5} 3482^{2} 4138^{22} 4592^{11} 7424^{3} 7528^{9} 7777^{5}

Golden Spikes (USA) *Richard Dutrow Jr* a91
5 b h Seeking The Gold(USA) —A P Interest (USA) (A.P. Indy (USA))
6582a^{7}

Golden Stamp (IRE) *A Peraino* 86
3 ch c Captain Rio—Golden Lively (USA) (Lively One (USA))
1418a^{10}

Golden Stream (IRE) *Sir Michael Stoute* 109
4 b m Sadler's Wells(USA) —Phantom Gold (Machiavellian (USA))
1326^{6} 1908^{2} 3067^{5} 4540^{2} 5081^{5} 6923^{14}

Golden Sword *Jane Chapple-Hyam* 120
4 b h High Chaparral(IRE) —Sitara (Salse (USA))
517a^{11} 799a^{3} 1026a^{14} 4535^{8} 5080^{4} 5517^{5} 5938^{5}

Golden Taurus (IRE) *J W Hills* 73
2 b c Danehill Dancer(IRE) —Nadwah (USA) (Shadeed (USA))
2319^{10} 2930^{4} 3498^{5} 4262^{3} 4578^{9} 5261^{8}

Golden Tempest (IRE) *Walter Swinburn* a82 79
2 b f Clodovil(IRE) —Honey Storm (IRE) (Mujadil (USA))
3509^{3} 4203^{3} 4729^{3} (5720) ◆ 6317^{4} 6670^{4} 7165^{2}

Golden Tiger *Tom Tate* a69 20
3 br g Kyllachy—Roxy (Rock City)
399^{3} 782^{3} 2863^{11}

Golden Tirol (GER) *T Kluczynski* 97
4 bb h Is Tirol(IRE) —Goldglockchen (GER) (Big Shuffle (USA))
1251a^{4} 1955a^{11}

Goldenveil (IRE) *Richard Fahey* 83
2 b f Iffraaj—Line Ahead (IRE) (Sadler's Wells (USA))
3705^{3} (4187) 6104^{2} 7059^{7}

Golden Waters *Eve Johnson Houghton* a30 72
3 b f Dubai Destination(USA) —Faraway Waters (Pharly (FR))
1501^{5} 1909^{5} 2893^{12} 4022^{13}

Golden Whip (GER) *W Hickst* 105
3 b f Seattle Dancer(USA) —Genevra (IRE) (Danehill (USA))
3236a^{5} (5739a)

Gold Express *P J O'Gorman* a87 88
7 b g Observatory(USA) —Vanishing Point (USA) (Caller I.D. (USA))
3083^{3} ◆ 3796^{13}

Gold Gleam (USA) *Jeremy Noseda* a63 65
3 ch c Forest Wildcat(USA) —Spinner (USA) (Conquistador Cielo (USA))
1825^{4} 2174^{4} 2741^{2} 3111^{6} 3994^{6} 5816^{8}

Gold Harvest (FR) *Y De Nicolay* a87 100
3 gr f Kaldounevees(FR) —Last Harvest (FR) (Kahyasi)
1746a^{3} 7545a^{9} 7800a^{0}

Goldikova (IRE) *F Head* 131
5 b m Anabaa(USA) —Born Gold (USA) (Blushing Groom (FR))
(2374a) (3046) (4639a) 5134a^{2} (6611a) ◆ (7364a)

Gold Mine *Andrew Balding* 42
2 b c Diktat—Memsahib (Alzao (USA))
6689[15]

Gold Party *Kevin McAuliffe* a66 56
3 ch c Bahamian Bounty—West River (USA) (Gone West (USA))
73[2] 136[6] 240[4] 524[4]

Gold Pearl (USA) *Stuart Williams* a74 85
2 bb c Henny Hughes(USA) —Gold Pattern (USA) (Slew O'Gold (USA))
2649[2] (4902) 5219[9] 6191[4] 7116[4]

Gold Post *P D Deegan* 78
2 b c Alhaarth(IRE) —Far Post (USA) (Defensive Play (USA))
6230a[13]

Gold Ring *Mark Gillard* a46 51
10 ch g Groom Dancer(USA) —Indubitable (Sharpo)
2752[6] 3967[11] 4226[5]

Gold Rock (FR) *Tony Carroll* a59 90
5 b g Anabaa(USA) —Golden Sea (FR) (Saint Cyrien (FR))
847[4] 939[8] 1171[12] 1958[8]

Gold Rules *Luca Cumani* a87 93
3 ch g Gold Away(IRE) —Raphaela (FR) (Octagonal (NZ))
(1307) ◆ 2002[3] (2607) 3824[11] 5511[13]

Goldschatz (NZ) *S Gray* 101
7 br g Pins(AUS) —Centri Belle (NZ) (Centaine (AUS))
2154a[10]

Gold Sprinter (IRE) *B Grizzetti*
2 ch c Gold Sphinx(USA) —Laissez Faire (USA) (Talinum (USA))
7850a[5]

Gold Story *Brian Ellison* a56 48
3 ch g Lucky Story(USA) —Incatinka (Inca Chief (USA))
1394[14] 7731[4] 7912[2]

Goldtara (FR) *Mme J Bidgood* a69 75
2 ch f Gold Away(IRE) —Diatara (FR) (Sillery (USA))
5063a[2]

Gold Trail (AUS) *Gary Portelli* 114
6 b g Hussonet(USA) —Trail Of Gold (AUS) (Danewin (AUS))
3047[10]

Goldtrek (USA) *Roger Charlton* a62 83
3 b f Medallist(USA) —Traipse (USA) (Digression (USA))
1392[4] 1977[6] (2675) (3522) (3789) 5008[6] 5858[5]

Goldwaki (GER) *A Fabre* 113
3 b c Dalakhani(IRE) —Gold Round (IRE) (Caerleon (USA))
(3014a) 4039a[4] 5575a[5] 6590a[4]

Gold Water (AUS) *Gai Waterhouse* 111
5 b m Choisir(AUS) —Float (USA) (Devil's Bag (USA))
2

Golestan Palace (IRE) *Luca Cumani* 55
2 b c Galileo(IRE) —Danse Spectre (IRE) (Spectrum (IRE))
6831[10] 7302[8]

Goliaths Boy (IRE) *Richard Fahey* 93
4 ch g Medecis—Green Belt (FR) (Tirol)
(1202)

Go Maggie Go (IRE) *Kevin Ryan* a52 28
2 b f Kheleyf(USA) —Born To Glamour (Ajdal (USA))
2111[6] 7268[10] 7722[7]

Gomez Adams (IRE) *P Demercastel* 99
3 b c Green Tune(USA) —Linamox (FR) (Linamix (FR))
1567a[7]

Gomrath (IRE) *Mick Channon* a78 87
3 b c Lomitas—Diner De Lune (IRE) (Be My Guest (USA))
(949) (1466) 2323[3] 2758[11] 7653[3]

Go Nani Go *Bryan Smart* 88
4 b g Kyllachy—Go Between (Daggers Drawn (USA))
3435[3] 4171[5] 4653[9]

Gone Fighting (FR) *Y De Nicolay* a62 61
2 b f Iron Mask(USA) —Gone Fishing (IRE) (Cadeaux Genereux)
7009a[8] 7383a[0]

Gone Hunting *Jeff Pearce* a78 81
4 b g Hunting Lion(IRE) —Arasong (Aragon)
102[7] 214[3] 481[4] 767[3] 1482[3] 2235[7] 2678[7] 6330[4] 6537[6]

Gone'N'Dunnett (IRE) *Christine Dunnett* a58 50
11 b g Petardia—Skerries Bell (Taufan (USA))
2196[8] 5559[10]

Gone Shopping (FR) *Y De Nicolay* a41 79
3 ch f Muhtathir—Gone Fishing (IRE) (Cadeaux Genereux)
6551a[11]

Good Again *Gerard Butler* a86 99
4 ch m Dubai Destination(USA) —Good Girl (IRE) (College Chapel)
334a[12] 1899[10] 3752[5] 4378[6] 4816[4] 5114[6] 5736[5] 6312[11]

Good Ba Ba (USA) *C W Chang* 121
8 b g Lear Fan(USA) —Elle Meme (USA) (Zilzal (USA))
1025a[8] 7853a[10]

Good Boy Jackson *Kevin Ryan* a23 67
2 b c Firebreak—Fisher Island (IRE) (Sri Pekan (USA))
4187[3] 4682[7] 5332[3] 6457[2]

Good Buy Dubai (USA) *Edward Creighton* a63 62
4 gr g Essence Of Dubai(USA) —Sofisticada (USA) (Northern Jove (CAN))
1262[10] 1478[13] 7315[12]

Goodbye Cash (IRE) *Ralph Smith* a66 66
6 b m Danetime(IRE) —Jellybeen (IRE) (Petardia)
11[2] 27[3] (101) (181) 225[4] 284[3] 317[5] 442[7] 593[6] 673[5] 1441[10] 1815a[5] 2235[9] 3323[2] (3524) 3968[3] 4232[11] 4589[10] 5077[7] 6023[8] (6672) 7037[10] 7168[9] 7518[11] 7761[5] 7829[4] 7883[3] 8019[4]

Good Bye Day *Tim Easterby* 31
3 b f Presidium—All On (Dunbeath (USA))
5022[6] 5303[10] 6298[10]

Good Control (AUS) *Pat Lee* a105 101
5 b g Fasliyev(USA) —Change Of Control (AUS) (Marauding (NZ))
336a[4] 604a[6] 707a[2] 817a[8]

Goodenough Magic *George Foster* 4
4 b m Lend A Hand—Rekindled Flame (IRE) (Kings Lake (USA))
4082[8] 4486[11]

Good Faith *George Moore* 33
2 b g Sleeping Indian—Femme Femme (USA) (Lyphard (USA))
1359[11] 3087[14] 6001[7] 6457[8] 6894[9]

Good For All (IRE) *I Bugattella* 84
3 b c Intikhab(USA) —Peralta (IRE) (Green Desert (USA))
1418a[8]

Good Hope (GER) *P Schiergen* 100
3 b f Seattle Dancer(USA) —Giralda (IRE) (Tenby)
5805a[4] 7546a[8]

Goodison Goal (IRE) *Patrick Morris* a51 48
3 b f Trade Fair—Chantilly (FR) (Sanglamore (USA))
1163[8] 1469[7]

Goodison Park *George Foster* a15 57
3 ch f Big Shuffle(USA) —Perfect Dream (Emperor Jones (USA))
2673[5] 3153[4] 4582[9] 4823[11] 5216[7] 6707[6] 7398[8]

Good Light *Camilla Trapassi*
2 b f Tobougg(IRE) —Constant Delight (Never So Bold)
7849a[16]

Goodlukin Lucy *Pat Eddery* a71 83
3 ch f Supreme Sound—Suka Ramai (Nashwan (USA))
1010[2] (1103) 1452[5] 2869[11] 3298[9] (6832) 7042[9] 7349[15]

Goodmanyourself *Paul Midgley* 42
2 b g Dubawi(IRE) —Frazzled (USA) (Prized (USA))
2936[8] 3222[11] 3874[6]

Good Morning Dubai (IRE) *Brian Meehan* a60 69
2 b f Dubawi(IRE) —Min Asl Wafi (IRE) (Octagonal (NZ))
1972[4] 2251[5] 3029[2] 3658[6] 4696[7] 5472[8]

Goodness *Sir Michael Stoute* 65
2 ch c Cadeaux Genereux—Dayrose (Daylami (IRE))
7094[4]

Good Shot Noreen (IRE) *T Stack* 23
2 ch f Sleeping Indian—Much Commended (Most Welcome)
7256a[14]

Good Society *Alex Fracas* 57
2 b f Holy Roman Emperor(IRE) —Society (IRE) (Barathea (IRE))
5252a[9]

Good Star (FR) *B Dutruel* a55 78
4 ch m Bad As I Wanna Be(IRE) —Arctic Starry (FR) (Star Maite (FR))
1055a[0]

Good Time Sue (IRE) *Ms M Dowdall Blake* a91 93
6 b m Commander Collins(IRE) —Poppy Lewis (IRE) (Paris House)
1408a[7] 2355a[5]

Good Timin' *David Brown* a40 56
2 b c Royal Applause—Record Time (Clantime)
4432[8] 4782[3] 5523[13]

Goodwood Maestro *John Dunlop* a71 84
3 b g Piccolo—Madurai (Chilibang)
1913[8] 2682[9] 4204[12] 4541[12] 5005[6] 5890[7] 6997[9]

Goodwood Starlight (IRE) *Sheena West* a56 90
5 br g Mtoto—Starring (FR) (Ashkalani (IRE))
1077[2] 2181[3] 2506[5] 3319[5] (4055) 5035[4] 5727[7] 6437[6]

Goodwood Treasure *John Dunlop* 76
2 ch f Bahamian Bounty—Lalectra (King Charlemagne (USA))
2223[2] (3156) 3913[3] 4578[12] 5856[6] 6435[13]

Googlette (IRE) *Edward Vaughan* a85 85
2 b f Exceed And Excel(AUS) —Jayzdoll (IRE) (Stravinsky (USA))
2505[2] ◆ (6796)

Googoobarabajagal (IRE) *Stuart Kittow* 54
4 b g Almutawakel—Shamah (Unfuwain (USA))
1758[8] 2691[4]

Goolagong (IRE) *Ralph Beckett* a67 77
3 b f Giant's Causeway(USA) —Maroochydore (IRE) (Danehill (USA))
979[2] 1654[7] 2342[3] 2956[4] (3680) 4104[6] 4502[4]

Go On Ahead (IRE) *John Coombe* a57 63
10 b g Namaqualand(USA) —Charm The Stars (Roi Danzig (USA))
228[5] 661[5]

Go On The Badger *James Toller* a52
2 b f Bachelor Duke(USA) —Swissmatic (Petong)
7879[7]

Gooseberry Bush *PETER Makin* a38 66
3 b f Tobougg(IRE) —Away To Me (Exit To Nowhere (USA))
5010[4] 5668[4]

Goose Green (IRE) *Ron Hodges* a64 69
6 b g Invincible Spirit(IRE) —Narbayda (IRE) (Kahyasi)
1225[5] 1508[10] 1636[3] 1961[3] 2233[9] 2690[6] 3404[5] 4756[9] 5115[12] 6125[12]

Gordon Flash *Richard Hannon* a67 72
3 ch c Alhaarth(IRE) —Goslar (In The Wings)
1778[2] ◆ 1975[3] 2321[3] 2924[6] 4259[4] 5536[2]

Gordon Road (IRE) *Michael Quinlan* a63 63
4 b g Amilynx(FR) —Celtic Smiles (IRE) (Nucleon (USA))
585[3] ◆ 669[3] 963[3] 2093[8] 2894[15]

Gordonsville *Jim Goldie* a81 91
7 b g Generous(IRE) —Kimba (USA) (Kris S (USA))
1101[8] 1525[5] 1720[2] 2126[4]

Gordy Bee (USA) *Richard Guest* a70 71
4 b g More Than Ready(USA) —Honoria (USA) (Danzig (USA))
7307[6] 7474[4] 7778[9] 7895[6]

Gorgeous Goblin (IRE) *David C Griffiths* a38
3 b f Lujain(USA) —Tama (IRE) (Indian Ridge)
7498[4] 7869[4]

Gosforth Park *Mel Brittain* a58 61
4 ch h Generous(IRE) —Love And Kisses (Salse (USA))
2259[4] 4120[7] (4946)

Gospel Spirit *John Jenkins* a47
5 b g Cool Jazz—Churchtown Spirit (Town And Country)
18[9] 308[8] 479[0]

Gothic Chick *Amy Weaver* a20 65
2 br f Araafa(IRE) —Entail (USA) (Riverman (USA))
3657[11] 4286[10] 6512[4] 7151[6] 7395[8]

Gotlandia (FR) *Y De Nicolay* a76 106
3 b f Anabaa(USA) —Grenade (FR) (Bering)
1566a[2] 2801a[10]

Gotta Have Her (USA) *Jenine Sahadi* a97 113
6 b m Royal Academy(USA) —Winnowing (USA) (Rahy (USA))
6757a[3]

Gottcher *David Barron* 67
2 b g Fasliyev(USA) —Danalia (IRE) (Danehill (USA))
3204[6] 4599[3] 4896[10] 6986[6]

Gouranga *Tony Carroll* a14 11
7 b m Robellino(USA) —Hymne D'Amour (USA) (Dixieland Band (USA))
90[7] 186[9]

Gouray Girl (IRE) *Walter Swinburn* a89 102
3 b f Redback—Brillano (FR) (Desert King (IRE))
5154[4] 5521[2] ◆ 6113[5] ◆ 6319[9] (7097)

Govenor Eliott (IRE) *Alan Lockwood* a45 41
5 ch g Rock Of Gibraltar(IRE) —Lac Dessert (USA) (Lac Ouimet (USA))
113[10] 3286[9] 3610[9] 4014[8]

Govenor General (IRE) *Jeremy Noseda* a4 57
2 b c Araafa(IRE) —Requested Pleasure (IRE) (Rainbow Quest (USA))
4695[13] 6127[6] 6560[27]

Govinda (USA) *A Wohler* 103
3 bb c Pulpit(USA) —Garden In The Rain (FR) (Dolphin Street (FR))
(4122) 6406a[2]

Gower *Richard Price* a51 60
6 b g Averti(IRE) —Alashaan (Darshaan)
30[5] 70[8] 368[7]

Gower Diva *David Nicholls* 38
3 b f Sakhee(USA) —Fine Arts (Cadeaux Genereux)
1425[9] 1685[10] 4340[8] 5548[13]

Gower Rules (IRE) *Mark Usher* a40 63
2 br g Aussie Rules(USA) —Holy Norma (Nashwan (USA))
2163[9] 2819[9] 3209[2] 3767[9] 4111[4] 5256[10] 5389[7] 6412[8]

Gower Sophia *Ronald Harris* a64 60
3 b f Captain Rio—Hollow Quaill (IRE) (Entrepreneur)
167[7] 1118[3] 1468[8] 2217[10] 4169[5] 4651[2] 5548[3] 6464[10] 7148[10] 7810[4] 7960[8]

Gra Adhmhar (IRE) *George Prodromou* a72 65
3 b g Mull Of Kintyre(USA) —Enya (Orpen (USA))
592[4] 864[2] ◆ 1590[7] 2025[7] 3275[3] 4058[10] 5073[5] 5867[10] 7005[11] 7191[11]

Grace And Beauty (IRE) *Brendan Duke* a41
2 b f Diamond Green(FR) —Balliamo (IRE) (Royal Academy (USA))
7558[10]

Graceandgratitude *Stuart Williams* a52
3 b f Royal Applause—Shararah (Machiavellian (USA))
215[9] 265[5]

Grace And Virtue (IRE) *S Donohoe* a60 73
3 b f Statue Of Liberty(USA) —One For Fun (Unfuwain (USA))
2449[5] 4516[12] 7860[6]

Graceful Descent (FR) *Jim Goldie* a74 84
5 b m Hawk Wing(USA) —Itab (USA) (Dayjur (USA))
2429[2] 2703[4] ◆ 3074[3] 3618[4] (3901) 4405[2] 4619[6] 5215[2] (5363) 6224[3] (6493) 7173[6]

Gracelightening *Paul Green* a61 64
2 b f Reset(AUS) —Monica Geller (Komaite (USA))
2725[9]

Grace O'Malley (IRE) *D K Weld* 101
4 b m Refuse To Bend(IRE) —Lionne (Darshaan)
1560a[3] 2037a[3] (3007a) 3671[5]

Gracie May *Reg Hollinshead* 46
3 ch f Grape Tree Road—Sequin Slippers (IRE) (Revoque (IRE))
2900[6] 3586[12] 4069[8] 4522[11] 4857[7]

Gracie's Games *Richard Price* a52 62
4 b m Mind Games—Little Kenny (Warning)
69[6] 189[5] 264[10] 389[11] (4760) (5055) 5473[3] 5876[7] 5990[5] 6656[3] 7154[9]

Gracie's Gift (IRE) *Richard Guest* a70 70
8 b g Imperial Ballet(IRE) —Settle Petal (IRE) (Roi Danzig (USA))
20[6] 86[6] 270[3] 668[7] (839) 1585[4] 2263[2] 2646[2] (2791) 4895[3] 5386[4] 5647[7] 6210[5] (6491) 7093[12] 7730[6]

Gracious Melange *Marco Botti* a84
3 b f Medicean—Goodness Gracious (IRE) (Green Desert (USA))
1159[2] ◆ 4699[8]

Gramercy (IRE) *Michael Bell* a82 105
3 b g Whipper(USA) —Topiary (IRE) (Selkirk (USA))
1352[3] ◆ 1732[7] 2713[6] 3845[2] (4091) (4819) 5088[8] 6349[P] 6752[18]

Gramm *G P Kelly* a66 11
7 b g Fraam—Beacon Silver (Belmez (USA))
3119[12] 7147[15]

Grams And Ounces *Amy Weaver* a62 80
3 b g Royal Applause—Ashdown Princess (IRE) (King's Theatre (IRE))
2702[9] 3582[2] (3951) 4289[2] (5051) (5624) 6447[16]

Granakey (IRE) *Ian Williams* a54
7 b m Key Of Luck(USA) —Grand Morning (IRE) (King Of Clubs)
389[3] 503[2] 518[5] 1148[6]

Grandad Bill (IRE) *Jim Goldie* a47 66
7 ch g Intikhab(USA) —Matikanehanafubuki (IRE) (Caerleon (USA))
7054[4]

Grandad Mac *Jane Chapple-Hyam* 54
2 b c Invincible Spirit(IRE) —No Rehearsal (FR) (Baillamont (USA))
7202[7]

Grand Admiral (USA) *A P O'Brien* a94 97
4 b h Giant's Causeway(USA) —Myth (USA) (Ogygian (USA))
3466a[3] 4877a[3] 7823a[12]

Grand Adventure (USA) *Mark Frostad* 112
4 bb h Grand Slam(USA) —Val Marie (USA) (Coronado's Quest (USA))
6237a[8] 6949a[2] 7362a[9]

Grand Art (IRE) *Tim Vaughan* a71 79
6 b g Raise A Grand(IRE) —Mulberry River (IRE) (Bluebird (USA))
4923[6] 7695[3] 8013[5]

Grand Bay (USA) *Jonjo O'Neill* a71 58
9 b g Coronado's Quest(USA) —Buckeye Gal (USA) (Good Counsel (USA))
5011[12]

Grand Diamond (IRE) *Jim Goldie* a68 74
6 b g Grand Lodge(USA) —Winona (IRE) (Alzao (USA))
1669[3] 3202[2] 3499[4] 3707[2] 3950[6] 4823[4] 5244[2] 5408[4] (5436) 5852[6]

Grand Duchy *Mahmood Al Zarooni* a67 78
2 b c Medicean—Pazzazz (IRE) (Green Desert (USA))
4940[2] 5498[3] 6092[6] 6513[2] 7280[3]

Grande Caiman (IRE) *Geoffrey Harker* a65 80
6 ch g Grand Lodge(USA) —Sweet Retreat (Indian Ridge)
4489[4] 5034[5] 7327[3] 7397[3]

Grand Hombre (USA) *R Bouresly* a99 92
10 br g Grand Slam(USA) —Santona (CHI) (Winning (USA))
511a[13]

Grand Honour (IRE) *Jane Chapple-Hyam* a68 60
4 gr g Verglas(IRE) —Rosy Dudley (IRE) (Grand Lodge (USA))
151[10] 317[4] 373[4] 587[7] 696[8] 845[3] 937[9] 1304[8] 2299[6] 2967[7] 5545[10] 5962[9] 7883[2]

Grand Lucius (FR) *D Guillemin* a68 88
3 b g Baroud D'Honneur(FR) —Khayriya (FR) (Valanour (IRE))
450a[6]

Grand Mary (IRE) *Paul Cole* 43
3 ch f Kyllachy—Magic Sister (Cadeaux Genereux)
3210[7] 3677[12]

Grandmas Dream *Giles Bravery* a72 84
2 b f Kyllachy—Sabina (Prince Sabo)
2330[4] 3141[10] 3959[2] 4474[4] 5748[4] 6796[5]

Grand Minstrel (IRE) *P J Lally* a39 48
6 ch m Ashkalani(IRE) —Blushing Minstrel (IRE) (Nicholas (USA))
726[5]

Grand Nordique (USA) *N Clement* 68
4 b h Grand Slam(USA) —Miss Firefly (USA) (Salt Lake (USA))
1055a[0]

Grand Opera (IRE) *Gordon Elliott* a90 81
7 b g City On A Hill(USA) —Victoria's Secret (IRE) (Law Society (USA))
6910a[6] 7589a[12]

Grand Palace (IRE) *Derek Shaw* a61 39
7 b g Grand Lodge(USA) —Pocket Book (IRE) (Reference Point)
112[5] 312[11] 694[9] 7542[14] 7808[8] 7883[9]

Grand Palais (IRE) *C Lerner* 70
4 b g Dr Fong(USA) —Siksikawa (Mark Of Esteem (IRE))
1055a[5]

Grand Piano (IRE) *Andrew Balding* a60 62
3 b g Arakan(USA) —Stately Princess (Robellino (USA))
1590[5] 3635[6]

Grand Stitch (USA) *Declan Carroll* a78 71
4 b g Grand Slam(USA) —Lil Sister Stich (USA) (Seattle Bound (USA))
1153[3] 1804[9] 2206[11] 4415[8] 4670[9] 6210[11] (6536) (7193) ◆ 7494[7] 7668[5]

Grand Vent (IRE) *A Fabre* 99
2 b c Shirocco(GER) —Housa Dancer (FR) (Fabulous Dancer (USA))
6702a[3]

Grand Vista *Gary Moore* a67 82
6 b g Danehill(USA) —Revealing (Halling (USA))
259[RR] 3580[6]

Grand Vizier (IRE) *Chris Wall* a91 74
6 b g Desert Style(IRE) —Distant Decree (USA) (Distant View (USA))
231[7] 1455[8] 1767[13] 4969[5] 5555[3] (6024) 6864[4]

Grand Zafeen *Mick Channon* a84 80
3 ch f Zafeen(FR) —Majestic Desert (Fraam)
1765[5] 2112[9] 2824[11] (3313) 3677[3] 4109[2] (4297) 4529[2] 5501[4] (6524) 6772[7]

Granite Girl *Philip McBride* a67 81
3 b f Kyllachy—Native Ring (FR) (Bering)
1278[5] ◆ 2042[5] 2725[3] 3606[2] 3821[6] (4626) 4971[2] 5511[11] 6199[9]

Granny Anne (IRE) *Alan Bailey* a56 53
2 ch f Redback—Krayyalei (IRE) (Krayyan)
4451[6] 4549[9] 5523[6] 6102[5] 6139[8] 6435[11] 6902[10] 7527[6] 7843[5] (7910)

Granny McPhee *Alan Bailey* a72 86
4 b m Bahri(USA) —Allumette (Rainbow Quest (USA))
469[5] 588[2] (666) 675[5] 925[6] 941[7] 1440[3] (1636) (3040) 3388[2] 3679[5] (3894) 4334[3] 4619[7]

Granski (IRE) *D M Fogarty* a56 68
4 b g Alhaarth(IRE) —Purple Haze (IRE) (Spectrum (IRE))
842[10]

Granston (IRE) *James Bethell* a99 93
9 gr g Revoque(IRE) —Gracious Gretclo (Common Grounds)
1378[2] 1889[3] (2276) 4818[7] 5638[3] 6185[6] 6877[11] 7084[19]

Grant Me A Wish *Simon Griffiths*
4 ch g Timeless Times(USA) —Baby Be (Bold Arrangement)
3663[11] 5097[7]

Gran Yago (IRE) *C Delcher-Sanchez* a58 71
6 b h Fasliyev(USA) —Prickly Pearl (IRE) (Lahib (USA))
460a[4]

Graylyn Ruby (FR) *Robin Dickin* a70 74
5 b g Limnos(JPN) —Nandi (IRE) (Mujadil (USA))
121[12] 282[6] 2023[2] 2341[3] 2923[3] (3324) 4141[9] 5179[9] 5382[7]

Graymalkin (IRE) *M bin Shafya* a83 83
3 br g Singspiel(IRE) —Pearl Grey (Gone West (USA))
510a[13]

Graysland *Philip Kirby* 43
4 gr m Silver Patriarch(IRE) —Celtic Island (Celtic Swing)
1113[4]

Grazeon Again (IRE) *John Quinn* 67
2 b c Diamond Green(FR) —Saviolo (Rossini (USA))
3550[8] 4116[5] 4447[9] 5298[6] 5784[9] 6294[5]

Grazeon Gold Blend *John Quinn* 87
7 ch g Paris House—Thalya (Crofthall)
4943[13] 6112[5] ◆ 6573[5]

Great Acclaim *James Fanshawe* 56
2 b g Acclamation—Pearl Bright (FR) (Kaldoun (FR))
4379[5]

Great Bounder (CAN) *Michael Blake* a62 58
4 bb g Mr Greeley(USA) —Jo Zak (USA) (Vilzak (USA))
110[7] 248[2] 295[2] 2419[11] 2955[4] 3559[9] 3967[3]

Great Charm (IRE) *Eric Alston* a81 87
5 b g Orpen(USA) —Briery (IRE) (Salse (USA))
4684[10] (5290) 5903[5] 6142[9] 6358[6] 6962[6] 7351[9] 7697[8]

Great Hawk (USA) *F Nass* a74 106
7 b g El Prado(IRE) —Laser Hawk (USA) (Silver Hawk (USA))
441a[13] 605a[14]

Great Intrigue (IRE) *J S Moore* a38 67
3 b g Azamour(IRE) —Bakewell Tart (IRE) (Tagula (IRE))
582[5] 2340[3] 2892[9] 3816[7] 4529[7]

Great Knight (IRE) *John Joseph Hanlon* a63 40
5 b g Acclamation—Wild Vintage (USA) (Alysheba (USA))
251[6] 270[4] 569[13]

Great Shot *Sylvester Kirk* 59
2 b c Marju(IRE) —Highland Shot (Selkirk (USA))
6473[5] ◆ 7094[8]

Great Show *Ronald Harris*
3 ch f Choisir(AUS) —Maple Branch (USA) (Stravinsky (USA))
7183[10] 7310[9]

Great Surprise *Reg Hollinshead* a52
2 ch g Hernando(FR) —Moment (Nashwan (USA))
7700[5]

Greatwallofchina (USA) *A P O'Brien* a92 88
5 b h Kingmambo(USA) —Dietrich (USA) (Storm Cat (USA))
6597a[2]

Grebe Huppe (FR) *F Chappet* 72
5 b g Fly To The Stars—Eclat De Cristal (FR) (Funambule (USA))
207a[0]

Grecian Goddess (IRE) *John Ryan* a60 69
2 b f Kris Kin(USA) —Grecian Air (FR) (King's Best (USA))
4844[7] 5488[2] 6154[5] 6866[6] 7163[6]

Greek Islands (IRE) *Mahmood Al Zarooni* a75 75
2 b c Oasis Dream—Serisia (FR) (Exit To Nowhere (USA))
2138[5] 2621[2] 3112[2] 4020[2] 4911[6] 6647[8]

Greek Renaissance (IRE) *E Charpy* a86 77
7 b g Machiavellian(USA) —Athene (IRE) (Rousillon (USA))
511a[9]

Greek Secret *Jimmy O'Reilly* a62 63
7 b g Josr Algarhoud(IRE) —Mazurkanova (Song)
132[6] 1391[RR] 1598[6] 2849[6] (3605) 3976[12] 4239[3] 4487[4] 4869[10] 5123[8] 6299[7] 6455[4] 7334[8]

Greeley Bright (USA) *James Given* a59 58
3 b f Mr Greeley(USA) —Lady Nicholas (USA) (Nicholas (USA))
1622[4] 1966[4] 2434[8] 3181[5]

Greeley's Qik Chic (USA) *George Baker* 31
3 b f Mr Greeley(USA) —Chaste (USA) (Cozzene (USA))
2180[13] 2674[9]

Green Agenda *Mark Johnston* a80 81
4 b g Anabaa(USA) —Capistrano Day (USA) (Diesis)
1128[6] 1494[5] 1808[6] 2451[4] 2859[9] 3538[2]

Green Apple *PETER Makin* a63
2 b f Needwood Blade—Scarlett Ribbon (Most Welcome)
7240[4]

Greenapple Martini (CAN) *Michael Mattine* a53
4 b m Medaglia D'Oro(USA) —Trishyde Slew (USA) (Seattle Slew (USA))
7371a[8]

Green Army *Mick Channon* 46
3 b g Sulamani(IRE) —Dowhatjen (Desert Style (IRE))
5148[6] 5603[9] 6183[6] 6517[5]

Greenbank Destiny *Peter Hedger*
4 b m Tobougg(IRE) —Sea Isle (Selkirk (USA))
7043[13]

Greenbelt *George Moore* a61 56
9 b g Desert Prince(IRE) —Emerald (USA) (El Gran Senor (USA))
42[7] (139) 244[3] 401[5] 506[5] 7806[4] 7957[6]

Greenbelt Star *Mrs John Harrington* 78
4 ch g Generous(IRE) —Dusty Shoes (Shareef Dancer (USA))
6971a[8]

Green Birdie (NZ) *C Fownes* 122
7 b g Catbird(AUS) —Mrs Squillionaire (AUS) (Last Tycoon)
7852a[10]

Green China (FR) *S Wattel* a79 79
3 b f Green Tune(USA) —China Moon (USA) (Gone West (USA))
7546a[6]

Green Coast (IRE) *Doug Watson* a115 95
7 b h Green Desert(USA) —Oriental Fashion (IRE) (Marju (IRE))
339a[4] 511a[4] (626a) 798a[2] 1022a[2]

Green Community (USA) *Edward Vaughan* a66 62
3 rg f El Prado(IRE) —Dreams (USA) (Silver Hawk (USA))
1392[7] 1537[7] 3390[5] 3758[2] 4156[4] 5072[8] 5873[9] 6863[7]

Green Dandy (IRE) *E J O'Neill* a83 100
3 b f Green Desert(USA) —Hawas (Mujtahid (USA))
5739a[5]

Green Destiny (IRE) *William Haggas* a65 93
3 b g Marju(IRE) —Mubkera (IRE) (Nashwan (USA))
1769[7] (3586) (7121) ◆

Green Earth (IRE) *Pat Phelan* a79 75
3 b g Cape Cross(IRE) —Inchyre (Shirley Heights)
772[2] 934[3] 1189[2] 1317[3] 1969[6] 2225[9] 5456[8] 5866[7] 6851[2] (7019) 7251[2] 7438[5]

Green Energy *Amanda Perrett* a50 60
3 b g Rainbow Quest(USA) —Carambola (IRE) (Danehill (USA))
1912[6] 2248[5] 2924[7] 3444[6] 4301[3] (4780) 5653[10]

Green For Luck (IRE) *Steve Gollings* 64
3 b c Key Of Luck(USA) —Kasota (IRE) (Alzao (USA))
1992[5] 2221[4] 2633[2] 3975[5] 4864[3] 4898[10]

Greenhead High *Jane Chapple-Hyam* a59 25
2 b g Statue Of Liberty(USA) —Artistry (Night Shift (USA))
6532[13] 7058[14] 7408[13] 7503[7] 7871[4] 8020[4]

Green Lagonda (AUS) *David Evans* a61 75
8 gr g Crown Jester(AUS) —Fidelis (AUS) (John's Hope (AUS))
1266[7] 1428[11] 3308[4] 3527[5] 3736[6] 3958[5] 4041[9] 5176[6] 5876[6] 6270[7] 6284[4] 6536[4] 6956[8]

Green Lightning (IRE) *Mark Johnston* 90
3 b g Montjeu(IRE) —Angelic Song (CAN) (Halo (USA))
1033[4] 1518[3] (2125) 5273[6] 5757[8] 6050[7]

Green Manalishi *Kevin Ryan* a109 102
9 b g Green Desert(USA) —Silca-Cisa (Hallgate)
737[2] 1091a[8] 1822[12] 2759[8] 3406[9] 3753[9] 4440[7] 4558[11] 4942[4] 5297[6] 6368[3] 6987[4]

Green Moon (IRE) *Harry Dunlop* 108
3 b c Montjeu(IRE) —Green Noon (FR) (Green Tune (USA))
(1521) (2117) ◆ (2543) ◆ 3142[5] 4829[8] 6195[5]

Greenore Gordon *Malcolm Saunders* a22 15
3 ch g Namid—Approaching Storm (IRE) (Entrepreneur)
849[10] 1535[7] 4989[P]

Green Park (IRE) *Declan Carroll* a101 97
7 b g Shinko Forest(IRE) —Danccini (IRE) (Dancing Dissident (USA))
71[6] 172[4] 250[6] 1363[2] ◆ 1711[3] 2134[9] 2275[2] 2534[7] 2696[4] 2982[14] 3321[6] 3430[2] 3898[2] 4118[3] 4345[6] 4798[2] 4942[12] 5154[5] 5297[3] (6358) (6625) (6798) 6918[12]

Green Passion (USA) *Mark Johnston* a43 51
4 bb g Forestry(USA) —Date Stone (USA) (Forty Niner (USA))
1296[14] 1520[6] 2527[13] 3177[5] 3520[8]

Green Pastures (IRE) *Howard Johnson* 57
2 b g Diamond Green(FR) —Continuous (IRE) (Darshaan)
2498[13] 3665[7] 4447[8]

Green Pearl (IRE) *Ralph Beckett* a69 70
2 b g Green Desert(USA) —Kinnaird (IRE) (Dr Devious (IRE))
3472[5] 4871[3] 5465[8] 6163[3]

Green Poppy *Bryan Smart* a34 62
4 b m Green Desert(USA) —Vimy Ridge (FR) (Indian Ridge)
(2629) 2849[16] 3497[8] 3977[10] 4486[10]

Green Pride *G Martin* a49 67
7 b g Piccolo—Little Greenbird (Ardkinglass)
304a[0]

Green Ridge (FR) *J Van Handenhove* 95
3 b f Green Tune(USA) —Baino Ridge (FR) (Highest Honor (FR))
3720a[9]

Green Rock (FR) *Mme M Bollack-Badel* a80 102
3 b c Green Tune(USA) —Pyramid Painter (IRE) (Peintre Celebre (USA))
1947a[3] 2802a[12] 3703a[4]

Green Secret *Alan McCabe* a52 8
3 b f Green Desert(USA) —Kiralik (Efisio)
843[7] 1275[9]

Greensward *Brian Meehan* a91 92
4 b g Green Desert(USA) —Frizzante (Efisio)
1618[7] 2399[2] (5157) 5903[3] 6888[6] 7238[4]

Green Tango (FR) *P Van De Poele* a95 106
7 ch h Majorien—Miss Bonfosse (FR) (Hard Leaf (FR))
1748a[3] 2375a[4] 3099a[3] 4566a[5] 5349a[6] 6016a[6]

Green Velvet *PETER Makin* a66 64
5 b m Iron Mask(USA) —Scarlett Ribbon (Most Welcome)
1166[3] 1547[5] 2026[3] 2751[2] 3527[2] 4256[2] 5695[5]

Green Wadi *Gary Moore* a81 78
5 b g Dansili—Peryllys (Warning)
4758[9] 5375[3] 5679[4] 5868[2] 6427[5] 7548[5] 7687[5] 7884[2]

Green With Envy (IRE) *George Baker* a59 51
2 br c Diamond Green(FR) —Merci (IRE) (Cadeaux Genereux)
3517[9] 5630[2] 6209[3] 6717[12]

Gremlin *Dai Burchell* a78 49
6 b g Mujahid(USA) —Fairy Free (Rousillon (USA))
756[4] 871[5] (938) (1053) 1357[9]

Grenane (IRE) *Mrs A Malzard* a63 62
7 b g Princely Heir(IRE) —Another Rainbow (IRE) (Rainbows For Life (CAN))
1815a[3]

Grenso (ITY) *S Botti* 97
3 b c Martino Alonso(IRE) —Green Reew (IRE) (Sikeston (USA))
1944a[6] 4185a[7]

Grethel (IRE) *Alan Berry* a35 52
6 b m Fruits Of Love(USA) —Stay Sharpe (USA) (Sharpen Up)
3122[6] 3352[7] 4454[8] 6051[11]

Grey Boy (GER) *Tony Carroll* a70 75
9 gr g Medaaly—Grey Perri (Siberian Express (USA))
84[6] 317[8] 367[8] 442[5] 1772[2] 2965[11] 3131[2] 3323[12] 3783[5] 4232[4] 4366[9] 4700[5] 7555[10] 7761[11]

Grey Bunting *B W Hills* a60 89
3 gr c Oasis Dream—Ribbons And Bows (IRE) (Dr Devious (IRE))
1581[2] (2627) 3337[2] 4100[3] 4470[13] 5273[9] 6152[10]

Grey Command (USA) *Mel Brittain* a73 58
5 gr g Daylami(IRE) —Shmoose (IRE) (Caerleon (USA))
(131) (354) ◆ (427) ◆ 469[9] 752[3] 941[8] 1398[15] 1576[6] 4156[5] 4656[7] 4945[7] 5515[7] 6306[6]

Grey Crystal *Mel Brittain* 7
4 gr m Tamayaz(CAN) —Mother Corrigan (IRE) (Paris House)
4339[12] 5097[6] 5514[7]

Greyfriarschorista *Mark Johnston* a101 107
3 ch g King's Best(USA) —Misty Heights (Fasliyev (USA))
31[2] (206) (311) (406) 945[2] 1699[18] 2471[5] 3103[3] 3692[12] 3886[8] 5247[13] 5879[6]

Greyfriars Drummer *Mark Johnston* 54
2 ch c Where Or When(IRE) —Loveleaves (Polar Falcon (USA))
6676[7]

Grey Gauntlet *Roger Ingram*
3 gr g Cape Town(IRE) —Its All Too Much (Chaddleworth (IRE))
1302[13] 4257[14]

Grey Granite (IRE) *William Jarvis* a80 84
4 gr g Dalakhani(IRE) —Royal Ballerina (IRE) (Sadler's Wells (USA))
1783[4] 2975[6] 3329[5] 4086[5] 5243[4] 5611[8]

Greylami (IRE) *Robert Mills* a101 98
5 gr g Daylami(IRE) —Silent Crystal (USA) (Diesis)
1474[15] 2640[7] (3889) 4321[4] 5307[7] 5723[3] 7287[2] 7591[8]

Grey Steel (IRE) *Denis P Quinn* a9 54
2 gr g Namid—Pride Of Pendle (Grey Desire)
5808[8] 6369[10]

Greystoke Prince *Michael Squance* a57 52
5 gr g Diktat—Grey Princess (IRE) (Common Grounds)
10[7] 124[9] 2198[10] 2414[8] 2875[9] 3168[8] 3608[5]

Griffin Point (IRE) *William Muir* 46
3 b f Tagula(IRE) —Lady Corduff (IRE) (Titus Livius (FR))
6420[4]

Griraz (FR) *J-L Dubord* a81 92
5 gr g Nombre Premier—Niraz (FR) (Nikos)
742a[6]

Gris De Gris (IRE) *A De Royer-Dupre* a109 117
6 gr h Slickly(FR) —Deesse Grise (FR) (Lead On Time (USA))
(1111a) 1716a[2]

Grissom (IRE) *Tim Easterby* 85
4 b g Desert Prince(IRE) —Misty Peak (IRE) (Sri Pekan (USA))
1200[4] ◆ 2431[11] 3165[3] ◆ 3430[5] ◆ 3584[4] 5855[2] 6358[3] 6625[5] 6985[2] (7169)

Grit (IRE) *Brendan Powell* a63 70
5 gr g Clodovil(IRE) —Lisa's Pride (IRE) (Pips Pride)
83[12] 294[7]

Gritstone *Richard Fahey* 87
3 b g Dansili—Cape Trafalgar (IRE) (Cape Cross (IRE))
1119[3] 1652[2] 2289[3] (3531) 4943[3] ◆ 5511[4] 6203[4] 6677[7]

Grizedale (IRE) *Michael Attwater* a60 48
11 ch g Lake Coniston(IRE) —Zabeta (Diesis)
145[9] 234[9] 320[4] 388[6] 499[11] 691[10] 763[10]

Groomed (IRE) *William Haggas* a63 73
2 b c Acclamation—Enamoured (Groom Dancer (USA))
6532[7] 7302[3] 7610[5]

Groove Master *Alan King* 57
3 b g Tobougg(IRE) —Magic Mistress (Magic Ring (IRE))
4052[6] 4519[6] 5467[9]

Gross Prophet *Alastair Lidderdale* a75 82
5 b g Lujain(USA) —Done And Dusted (IRE) (Up And At 'Em)
1579[13] 2080[4] 3160[12] (5039) (5254) 5624[2] 6288[6] 6832[12]

Group Captain *Alex Fracas* a92 96
8 b g Dr Fong(USA) —Alusha (Soviet Star (USA))
1056a[3]

Group Leader (IRE) *John Jenkins* a50 67
4 ch g Noverre(USA) —Stem The Tide (USA) (Proud Truth (USA))
1134[2] 1493[5] 2810[9]

Group Therapy *Jeremy Noseda* a72 113
5 ch g Choisir(AUS) —Licence To Thrill (Wolfhound (USA))
(3108) ◆ 3691[2] 4505[2] 5851[3] 6194[8]

Grove View Star *Patrick Morris* a65 57
5 ch g Auction House(USA) —Gracious Imp (USA) (Imp Society (USA))
2955[15]

Grudge *Conor Dore* a81 80
5 b g Timeless Times(USA) —Envy (IRE) (Paris House)
165[4] 349[4] 462[2] (520) 913[4] (1147) 1506[2] 1710[9] 2001[2] 2622[12] (3211) 3440[3] 5262[4] 5647[6] 5915[14] 7180[16] 7326[6] (7446) (7668) 7866[8] 7961[3] 7998[3]

Grumeti *Michael Bell* 62
2 b g Sakhee(USA) —Tetravella (IRE) (Groom Dancer (USA))
5629[10] 6159[9] 6689[7] ◆

Gtaab *Paul Webber* a65 32
4 b g Cape Cross(IRE) —Nabadhaat (USA) (Mr Prospector (USA))
6322[9]

Guards Chapel *Luca Cumani* 15
2 b g Motivator—Intaaj (IRE) (Machiavellian (USA))
6092[15] 7094[17]

Gud Day (IRE) *Deborah Sanderson* a20
2 gr g Aussie Rules(USA) —Queen Al Andalous (IRE) (King's Best (USA))
7400[10] 7693[7]

Guertino (IRE) *Colin Teague* a64 72
5 ch g Choisir(AUS) —Isana (JPN) (Sunday Silence (USA))
1365[8] 1524[10] 1719[6] 2263[4] 2791[6] 3022[5] 4403[11]

Guest Book (IRE) *Mark Johnston* 93
3 b g Green Desert(USA) —Your Welcome (Darshaan)
5510[4] ◆ 5904[6] 6556[2] ◆

Guest Connections *David Nicholls* a41 75
7 b g Zafonic(USA) —Llyn Gwynant (Persian Bold)
913[7] 1270[4] 1869[2] 1965[4] 2206[8] 2381[8] 2671[9] 2854[6] 3809[9] 4060[8]

Guga (IRE) *John Mackie* a70 69
4 b g Rock Of Gibraltar(IRE) —Attitre (FR) (Mtoto)
1756[12] 2259[5] 2600[2] (2880) (3179) 3314[6] 3910[4] 4863[3] 5636[5] 6298[3] 6937[2] 7128[10] 7467[8] 7531[3] 7678[3] 7878[10] 8010[10]

Guided Missile (IRE) *Andrew Balding* a69 64
2 b f Night Shift(USA) —Exorcet (FR) (Selkirk (USA))
7201[4] ◆ (7595)

Guilded Warrior *Stuart Kittow* a96 96
7 b g Mujahid(USA) —Pearly River (Elegant Air)
(1185) 1857[11] 2971[11] (3483) 4224[5] 4995[4] 5903[8] 6327[8] 7121[10]

Guildenstern (IRE) *Paul Howling* a68 57
8 b g Danetime(IRE) —Lyphard Abu (IRE) (Lyphard's Special (USA))
124[4] 234[6] (498) 704[7] 968[2] 1305[6] 1534[5] 1813[9] 2187[6] 2726[4] 3768[2] 4428[11] 5926[7] 6847[9] 7023[5] 7761[6]

Guinea Seeker *Tim Easterby* a36 64
2 b g Mujadil(USA) —Nefeli (First Trump)
1517[13] 3536[5] 3767[10] 5354[8] 5755[4] 6264[5] 6645[2] 6705[6]

Guipago (CAN) *Analisa M Delmas* a104 99
4 ch h My Way Only(CAN) —Cherokee Chick (USA) (Cherokee Fellow (USA))
6236a[6]

Guiseppe Verdi (USA) *Tor Sturgis* a65 57
6 ch g Sky Classic(CAN) —Lovington (USA) (Afleet (CAN))
2611[11] 2645[11] 3214[11]

Guisho (IRE) *Brian Meehan* 75
2 b c Iffraaj—Jorghinia (FR) (Seattle Slew (USA))
7203[4] ◆

Gulbank (IRE) *Jeremy Noseda*
2 gr c Kyllachy—Bunditten (IRE) (Soviet Star (USA))
4110[12]

Gulf Coast *Tim Walford* a65 62
5 ch g Dubai Destination(USA) —Lloc (Absalom)
1296[7] 1576[5] 2500[6] 2655[5] 4246[7] (4410) 4648[4] 5333[5]

Gulf Of Aqaba (USA) *David Pipe* a1 60
4 bb g Mr Greeley(USA) —Ocean Jewel (USA) (Alleged (USA))
139[9]

Gulf President *Tim Vaughan* a63 74
4 b g Polish Precedent(USA) —Gay Minette (IRE) (Peintre Celebre (USA))
(3290) 3560[8]

Gulf Punch *Milton Harris* a56 57
3 b f Dubawi(IRE) —Fruit Punch (IRE) (Barathea (IRE))
998[8] 1209[5] 1264[5] 1461[7] 2780[7]

Gumnd (IRE) *James Bethell* a82 86
3 b g Selkirk(USA) —Surval (IRE) (Sadler's Wells (USA))
634[2] (755) 1083[6] 1473[4] 1846[2] 2324[16] 2544[11] 2970[9] 7228[9]

Gunalt Joy *Michael Easterby* a52 38
2 b f Blue Dakota(IRE) —Lawless Bridget (Alnasr Alwasheek)
4941[9] 5640[4] 6075[8] 6263[4] 6645[13] 7268[2] 7423[9]

Gunalt Penny Sweet *Michael Easterby* 23
2 b f Blue Dakota(IRE) —La Corujera (Case Law)
1749[10] 1986[8] 2376[9] 2693[11] 5644[7]

Gundaroo *John Dunlop* 67
3 b f Oasis Dream—Encore My Love (Royal Applause)
1640[5] 2197[3] 2588[4] 6024[10] 6864[16]

Gunner Lindley (IRE) *B W Hills* 99
3 ch c Medicean—Lasso (Indian Ridge)
1732[2] 2324[6] 2898[4] 4509[5] 6510[2] (6749)

Gunslinger (FR) *Michael Scudamore* a80 81
5 b g High Chaparral(IRE) —Gamine (IRE) (High Estate)
2821[7] 4023[14]

Guppy's Girl (IRE) *Sam Davison* a48 36
3 b f Fantastic Light(USA) —Ninth Quest (USA) (Quest For Fame)
5455[5] 5765[5] 6637[8]

Guto *Bill Ratcliffe* a74 78
7 b g Foxhound(USA) —Mujadilly (Mujadil (USA))
165[6] 380[5] 472[3] 504[2] 601[7] 1147[9] 1337[6] 1915[13] 2622[6] 3064[12] 5562[2] ◆ 6018[2] 6270[3] 6464[9] 7007[11] 7155[3] 7542[2] 7868[7] 7953[4]

Gwenhwyfar (IRE) *C Boutin* a57 86
2 b f Cacique(IRE) —Grosgrain (USA) (Diesis)
5252a[5] (7009a) 7383a[5]

Gwenllian (IRE) *Ian Williams* a65 58
3 b f Royal Dragon(USA) —Desiraka (Kris)
2478[4] 3275[4] 4201[9] 5585[11] 6937[7] 7161[9]

Gwilym (GER) *Derek Haydn Jones* a76 78
7 b g Agnes World(USA) —Glady Rose (GER) (Surumu (GER))
2399[12] 2689[5] 2973[3] (3037) 4662[4] 5151[4] 5262[2] 5809[8] 5915[7] 6280[9] 7239[7] 7526[4]

Gwynedd (IRE) *Ed McMahon* 70
3 b f Bertolini(USA) —Bethesda (Distant Relative)
4248[10]

Gypsy Boy (USA) *F J Brennan* a68 64
3 bb g Dixie Union(USA) —Think Fast (USA) (Crafty Prospector (USA))
2925[7] 3525[5] 3831[7]

Gypsy Carnival *Ralph Beckett* 80
3 b f Trade Fair—Czarna Roza (Polish Precedent (USA))
(5986) ◆ 6467[6]

Gypsy Highway (IRE) *D Smaga* 90
2 b f High Chaparral(IRE) —Rose Gypsy (Green Desert (USA))
5622a[2] 7276a[2]

Gypsy Jazz (IRE) *Ann Stokell* a49 66
3 b f Antonius Pius(USA) —Dawn's Folly (IRE) (Bluebird (USA))
1514[8] 7207[7] 7304[8]

Gypsy Legend (IRE) *Sylvester Kirk* a51 48
2 b f Dr Fong(USA) —Generous Gesture (IRE) (Fasliyev (USA))
5029[10] 5583[8] 6307[9] 7177[5] 7396[8]

Gypsy Style *Kate Walton* 54
3 gr f Desert Style(IRE) —Gentle Gypsy (Junius (USA))
2517[9] 5057[9] 5487[3] 6460[13]

Gypsy's Warning (SAF) *H Graham Motion* 104
5 b m Mogok(USA) —Gypsy Queen (SAF) (Royal Chalice (SAF))
5320a[3] 6604a[3]

Gyrate *Jeremy Glover* a23
3 b g Lujain(USA) —Discoed (Distinctly North (USA))
1143[7]

Haadeeth *Marcus Tregoning* a81 86
3 b g Oasis Dream—Musical Key (Key Of Luck (USA))
945[8] 1376[6] 3696[6] 4387[6] 4930[8] 6253[10]

Haafhd Sharp *Michael Quinlan* 52
3 b f Haafhd—Miss Adelaide (IRE) (Alzao (USA))
1966[6] 2517[6] 2903[8] 4210[12]

Haajes *Paul Midgley* a96 94
6 ch g Indian Ridge—Imelda (USA) (Manila (USA))
1032[9] 1332[8] 1888[6] 2534[5] 2657[7] 3675[3] (3902) 4118[4] 4372[3] 5183[4] 5742[5] 6142[18] 6364[5] (6723)

Haasem (USA) *John Jenkins* a60 49
7 b g Seeking The Gold(USA) —Thawakib (IRE) (Sadler's Wells (USA))
194[6] 442[12] 1437[7] 1633[13] 2417[7] 2636[9] 3263[11]

Haatheq (USA) *John Dunlop* a95 95
3 b c Seeking The Gold(USA) —Alshadiyah (USA) (Danzig (USA))
(1522) (2170) 2737[2] 3886[3] 4357[7]

Habaayib *Ed Dunlop* 108
3 b f Royal Applause—Silver Kestrel (USA) (Silver Hawk (USA))
1384[2] 1726[8] 5883[11] 6351[10]

Habshan (USA) *Chris Wall* a87 87
10 ch g Swain(IRE) —Cambara (Dancing Brave (USA))
1617[4] 2683[9] 3438[2] 4322[4] 4905[5] 5919[10]

Hacienda (IRE) *Mark Johnston* a91 102
3 br g Kheleyf(USA) —Hartstown House (IRE) (Primo Dominie)
(374) ◆ (1487) ◆ 1786a[4] 2324[5] 3196[3] (3354) 3692[17] 4144[4] 4358[20] 5759[4] 6510[14]

Hackett (IRE) *Michael Quinn* a61 57
2 b c Hawk Wing(USA) —Khudud (Green Desert (USA))
4590[5] 4960[6] 6520[9] 7650[3] 8031[8]

Hades (IRE) *Tim Easterby* 68
3 b g Antonius Pius(USA) —Lady Lucre (IRE) (Last Tycoon)
2393[6] 4556[6] 4853[4] 5479[7] 6144[2] 6462[3] 6897[11]

Hadrian's Waltz (IRE) *David Wachman* a72 73
2 b f Holy Roman Emperor(IRE) —Dance To The Top (Sadler's Wells (USA))
6784a[5] ◆

Haf (IRE) *Peter Grayson*
3 b f Iron Mask(USA) —Lady Peculiar (CAN) (Sunshine Forever (USA))
997[12] 1187[7] 1240[4]

Hafawa (IRE) *Mark Johnston* 102
3 b f Intikhab(USA) —Banaadir (USA) (Diesis)
1312[5] 1693[2] 2098[4]

Haigh Hall *Richard Fahey* 70
4 ch m Kyllachy—Miss Meltemi (IRE) (Miswaki Tern (USA))
1099[8] ◆ 1650[6]

Hail Bold Chief (USA) *Alan Swinbank* a55 79
3 b g Dynaformer(USA) —Yanaseeni (USA) (Trempolino (USA))
1464[8] 1804[10] 2242[7] 3091[6] 3530[2] 3708[8] 4337[3] (4867) 5300[3] (5479) (6266) 6753[8]

Hail Promenader (IRE) *B W Hills* a81 89
4 b h Acclamation—Tribal Rite (Be My Native (USA))
1265[2] 1617[9] 2683[12] 4459[9]

Hail The King (USA) *Roger Curtis* 8
10 gr g Allied Forces(USA) —Hail Kris (USA) (Kris S (USA))
3589[6]

Hail Tiberius *Tim Walford* 76
3 b g Iktibas—Untidy Daughter (Sabrehill (USA))
1119[5] 1927[4] 2290[2] 2816[9] 4341[4] 4867[8] 6074[9] 6832[4] 7307[5]

Hairspray *Mick Channon* a87 88
3 ch f Bahamian Bounty—Quickstyx (Night Shift (USA))
1384[7] 1701[10] 2283[7] 3361[5] (3815) 4204[10] (5182) 6000[6] 6319[16] 7097[10]

Hairstyle *Sir Michael Stoute* 63
2 b f Dansili—Quiff (Sadler's Wells (USA))
6770[6]

Hairy Maclary *Tim Easterby* 54
3 b g Tobougg(IRE) —Pearl Venture (Salse (USA))
3176[10] 3554[5] 3733[5] 4344[8] 5201[5] 5758[12] 6896[7]

Hajjaan (USA) *John Dunlop* 84
3 b c Mr Greeley(USA) —Danzig Island (USA) (Danzig (USA))
5839[2] (6655)

Hajoum (IRE) *Mark Johnston* a102 102
4 b h Exceed And Excel(AUS) —Blue Iris (Petong)
2280[5] (2532) 2736[11] 3146[4] 3448[8] 3681[7] 4358[14] 4843[8] (5702) (5950) 6175[15] 6363[6] (6597a) 6888[15]

Haka (USA) *Christophe Clement* a107 84
4 b m Dynaformer(USA) —Juke (USA) (Mr Prospector (USA))
7371a[4]

Haka Dancer (USA) *Philip Kirby* a52 46
7 b g War Chant(USA) —Safe Return (USA) (Mr Prospector (USA))
18[4] 166[6] 246[4] 411[6] 1983[6] 2533[7] 3223[6] 3496[7] 6076[6]

Hakuna Matata *Brian Ellison* 73
3 b g Dubai Destination(USA) —Green Song (FR) (Green Tune (USA))
(6966)

Haldibari (IRE) *Shaun Lycett* a45 57
6 b g Kahyasi—Haladiya (IRE) (Darshaan)
1768[6] 3804[2] 4362[3]

Halfsin (IRE) *Marco Botti* a78 82
2 b g Haafhd—Firesteed (IRE) (Common Grounds)
5717[3] ◆ 6159[2] 6676[3] 7452[3]

Half Sister (IRE) *Mark Rimmer* a50 67
3 b f Oratorio(IRE) —Fifty Five (IRE) (Lake Coniston (IRE))
1431[4] 1581[13] 2042[14] 4762[6] 5050[9] 6020[4] 6526[7] 6652[3] 7003[8] 7387[11] 7495[3] 7669[4] 7833[5]

Half Truth (IRE) *Mahmood Al Zarooni* 73
2 gr f Verglas(IRE) —Millennium Tale (FR) (Distant Relative)
2861[7] (3310) 4129[3]

Halicarnassus (IRE) *Mick Channon* a111 114
6 b h Cape Cross(IRE) —Launch Time (USA) (Relaunch (USA))
337a[2] (516a) 799a[P] 1382[10] 1698[5] 2369a[4] 2716[8] 3144[15] 5274[10] 5804a[4] 6148[7] 6389[4] 6977a[8]

Halifax (IRE) *Mark Johnston* a53
2 ch c Halling(USA) —Lady Zonda (Lion Cavern (USA))
6844[8]

Haljaferia (UAE) *David Elsworth* a82 84
4 ch g Halling(USA) —Melisendra (FR) (Highest Honor (FR))
1484[8] 2109[5] (2560) 2845[4] (3502) 4019[3] 4405[10]

Halkin (USA) *F Nass* a97 78
8 br h Chester House(USA) —Estala (Be My Guest (USA))
339a[10] 511a[10]

Halla San *Richard Fahey* a91 102
8 b g Halling(USA) —St Radegund (Green Desert (USA))
1176[3] 1525[3] 1821[3] 3447[18]

Hallelujah *James Fanshawe* 76
2 b f Avonbridge—My Golly (Mozart (IRE))
(7002)

Hallie's Comet (IRE) *D K Weld* a79 102
4 b m One Cool Cat(USA) —Secretariat's Tap (USA) (Pleasant Tap (USA))
4524a[5]

Hallingdal (UAE) *John Bridger* a85 77
5 b m Halling(USA) —Saik (USA) (Riverman (USA))
151[8]

Halling Gal *Evan Williams* a49 76
4 b m Halling(USA) —Saik (USA) (Riverman (USA))
239[13]

Hallo Heart (IRE) *R Betti*
2 b c Invincible Spirit(IRE) —Hail Kris (USA) (Kris S (USA))
7264a[4]

Hallstatt (IRE) *John Mackie* a77 83
4 ch g Halling(USA) —Last Resort (Lahib (USA))
586[3] 871[4] 1013[7] 1398[7] 1655[4] (1916) 2313[4] 2975[11] 3398[3] 5070[6] 5549[6] 6213[2] 6538[10]

Hal Of A Lover *Richard Fahey* 63
2 b c Halling(USA) —Latent Lover (IRE) (In The Wings)
3805[5] 4240[6] 5099[7] 6300[12] 6695[11]

Halowin *J-V Toux* a78 69
2 b c Beat Hollow—Hoh My Darling (Dansili)
4565a[3]

Halsion Chancer *John Best* a86 81
6 b g Atraf—Lucky Dip (Tirol)
535[2] ◆ 657[4] 761[5] 987[2] 1258[4] (1530) 2129[6] 2339[5] 2683[4] 3317[8] 4265[6] 5264[10] 5919[7] 6252[6] 7190[3] (7421) 7637[3]

Halyard (IRE) *Walter Swinburn* a74 69
3 b g Halling(USA) —Brindisi (Dr Fong (USA))
1143[5] 1448[7] 1975[5] 2321[6] 5146[3] (5656) 6290[9]

Hamazing Destiny (USA) *D Wayne Lukas* a118
4 b h Salt Lake(USA) —Ms Proud Destiny (USA) (Artax (USA))
7361a[2]

Hambledon Hill *Paul Burgoyne* a64 75
4 ch g Selkirk(USA) —Dominica (Alhaarth (IRE))
552[11] 802[4] 969[6] 1188[11]

Hambleton *Bryan Smart* a53 59
3 b g Monsieur Bond(IRE) —Only Yours (Aragon)
4853[3] 5214[2] 5359[3] 6896[9] 7406[3] 7911[3]

Hamilcar Barca (FR) *G Collet*
4 b g Bahhare(USA) —Grazia Bella (Green Desert (USA))
304a[0]

Hamish McGonagall *Tim Easterby* 112
5 b g Namid—Anatase (Danehill (USA))
1295[3] 1822[2] (2346) (2759) 3108[3] 3691[4] 4401[6] (5183) 5569a[4] 6194[4] 6508[4]

Hamlool (IRE) *Clive Brittain* 80
2 b c Red Ransom(USA) —Chelsea Rose (IRE) (Desert King (IRE))
2887[3]

Hamloola *William Haggas* a79 89
3 b f Red Ransom(USA) —Dusty Answer (Zafonic (USA))
4697[2] (5395) ◆ 5896[5] (6395)

Hammer *Alison Thorpe* a56 75
5 b g Beat Hollow—Tranquil Moon (Deploy)
121[7] 813[7] 875[5]

Hammer Home (USA) *Brian Meehan* a45 75
2 b c Awesome Again(CAN) —Alicita My Love (USA) (Birdonthewire (USA))
3805[3] (4379) 5874[5] 6667[5]

Hamoody (USA) *David Nicholls* 95
6 ch g Johannesburg(USA) —Northern Gulch (USA) (Gulch (USA))
1423[14] 2054[9] 2465[10] 3065[4] 3401[10] (4510) 4536[13]

Hampstead Heath (IRE) *David Marnane* a73 70
5 gr g Daylami(IRE) —Hedera (USA) (Woodman (USA))
7078a[11]

Hampton Court *Seamus Mullins* a62 46
5 ch g King's Best(USA) —Rafting (IRE) (Darshaan)
164[3] 584[4]

Hanbelation (USA) *Edward Vaughan* a49 68
3 bb f Malibu Moon(USA) —Baldellia (FR) (Grape Tree Road)
1504[9] 1966[2] 2628[11] 2871[13]

Handel's Messiah (IRE) *Michael Bell* 5
2 bg c Oratorio(IRE) —Silver Pursuit (Rainbow Quest (USA))
4375[7]

Handicraft (IRE) *Mark Johnston* a48 44
2 ch f Halling(USA) —Luana (Shaadi (USA))
5369[11] 6436[6] 7000[7] 7296[3] ◆

Hand Painted *PETER Makin* a77 82
4 b g Lend A Hand—Scarlett Holly (Red Sunset)
3373[5] 3815[4] 4777[5] 5838[9] 6280[2] 6524[2] 6800[6] 7557[10]

Handsinthemist (IRE) *Anthony Mulholland* a67 57
5 b m Lend A Hand—Hollow Haze (USA) (Woodman (USA))
243[6] 402[8] 569[9] 716[5] 3711[6] 5362[7]

Handsome Cross (IRE) *Willie Musson* a77 77
9 b g Cape Cross(IRE) —Snap Crackle Pop (IRE) (Statoblest)
185[2] ◆ 306[2] 431[2] 616[2] (687) 935[2]

Handsome Devil *E Lellouche* 109
3 b c Footstepsinthesand—Acqua Verde (King's Best (USA))
1947a[2] 2802a[8]

Handsome Falcon *Richard Fahey* a86 86
6 b g Kyllachy—Bonne Etoile (Diesis)
1272[9] 1752[2] 2133[8] 2835[7] 3318[11] 3659[4] 3973[7]

Handsome Hawk (IRE) *Wido Neuroth* a95 91
4 b g Hawk Wing(USA) —She Is Zen (FR) (Zieten (USA))
1251a[10] 2020a[8] 5350a[5]

Handsome Jack (IRE) *Robert Mills* a82 82
2 b g Iffraaj—Alexanders Way (FR) (Persian Heights)
3326[6] ◆ (3769) 5830[2] ◆ (6059) 6453[2] 6670[8]

Handsome King *John Jenkins* a67 60
3 ch g Lucky Story(USA) —Samar Qand (Selkirk (USA))
6655[4] 7183[4] 7288[2] 7651[2] 7767[3]

Hannah Cann *Peter Grayson* a29
2 b f Indesatchel(IRE) —Bullion (Sabrehill (USA))
1463[8] 2677[11] 5269[12] 7392[8] 7540[5] 7576[7] 7692[6] 7785[8]

Hannah Hawk *Lucinda Featherstone* a4 29
3 b f Hawk Wing(USA) —Regal Portrait (IRE) (Royal Academy (USA))
2473[12] 2860[14] 3207[10] 4340[11] 5155[9] 6526[10] 6624[8]

Hannicean *Ian Williams* a76 78
6 ch g Medicean—Hannah's Music (Music Boy)
(294) 565[7] 852[2] 1348[8]

Hanoverian Baron *Tony Newcombe* a85 100
5 b g Green Desert(USA) —Josh's Pearl (IRE) (Sadler's Wells (USA))
1474[2] ◆ (2096) ◆ 3672[9] (4321) 5307[2] 5908[16]

Hansinger (IRE) *Cathrine Erichsen* a89 103
5 b g Namid—Whistfilly (First Trump)
4526a[4]

Hansomis (IRE) *Bruce Mactaggart* 72
6 b m Titus Livius(FR) —Handsome Anna (IRE) (Bigstone (IRE))
1575[4] 2206[9] 2378[2] 2581[6] 3022[6] 4706[3] 5406[3] 5821[4] 6108[7] 6221[6]

Hanson'D (IRE) *Kevin Ryan* a89 100
3 ch c Pivotal—Dinka Raja (USA) (Woodman (USA))
945[6] 1311[7] 4140[4] 4805[3] 5188[18]

Happy Anniversary (IRE) *Deborah Sanderson* a52 87
4 b m Intikhab(USA) —Happy Story (IRE) (Bigstone (IRE))
1117[2] 1383[12] 1933[8] 2885[2] 2991[4]

Happy Clapper (CAN) *Michael J Doyle* a75 100
3 rg f Awesome Again(CAN) —Phil's Pill (USA) (Cozzene (USA))
7371a[7]

Happy Dubai (IRE) *A Al Raihe* a99 77
3 ch c Indian Ridge—Gentle Wind (USA) (Gentlemen (ARG))
510a[3]

Happy Fleet *Roger Curtis* a64
7 b m Beat All(USA) —Fleeting Affair (Hotfoot I)
179[6] 308[3] 468[6] 748[2] ◆ 7388[7]

Happy Monster (FR) *Robert Collet*
2 b c Xaar—Armama (Linamix (FR))
7974a[7]

Happy Mood *Gary Moore* a35 59
3 b f Piccolo—Love And Kisses (Salse (USA))
1501[7] 2401[10] 2901[7] 3444[12]

Happy The Man (IRE) *Tim Easterby* 38
3 b g Kyllachy—Jazan (IRE) (Danehill (USA))
2706[8] 3091[10] 3397[4] 4485[13] 5097[4]

Happy Today (USA) *Brian Meehan* 83
2 b c Gone West(USA) —Shy Lady (FR) (Kaldoun (FR))
4803[4] (5582)

Happy Zero (AUS) *J Moore* 121
6 br g Danzero(AUS) —Have Love (AUS) (Canny Lad (AUS))
3192[22]

Haralan (IRE) *John M Oxx* 102
4 b g Sinndar(IRE) —Haratila (IRE) (Marju (IRE))
2571a[P] (Dead)

Harald Bluetooth (IRE) *David Simcock* a97 94
5 b h Danetime(IRE) —Goldthroat (IRE) (Zafonic (USA))
4596[3] 5948[9]

Harare *Richard Price* a69 66
9 b g Bahhare(USA) —Springs Eternal (Salse (USA))
565[9] 668[2] 753[7] 867[2] 1051[9] 1238[5] 1762[8] 2596[11] (3032) 3582[5] 3860[8] 4327[5] 4676[6]

Harbinger *Sir Michael Stoute* 135
4 b h Dansili—Penang Pearl (FR) (Bering)
(1382) (1859) (3191) ◆ (4359)

Harcas (IRE) *Martin Todhunter* 63
8 b g Priolo(USA) —Genetta (Green Desert (USA))
1803[8] 3223[8] 3989[3] 4825[2] 5681[5] 6187[12] 6649[9]

Hard Ball *Michael Quinn* a57 51
4 b g Pivotal—Miss Pinkerton (Danehill (USA))
142[6] 270[2] 296[5] 568[3] 838[11] 1129[7]

Hard Bargain (IRE) *Denis Coakley* a67 72
2 b g Refuse To Bend(IRE) —Super Gift (IRE) (Darshaan)
2839[3] 4131[6] 4999[2] 5865[9]

Hard Life (IRE) *M Oppo* 100
3 ch f Peintre Celebre(USA) —Golden Fortune (Forzando)
1713a[16]

Hard Rock City (USA) *Declan Carroll* a86 93
10 b g Danzig(USA) —All The Moves (USA) (A.P. Indy (USA))
5774a[7] 6597a[3] 6907a[11] 7697[9] 7906[8]

Hareem (IRE) *William Muir* a59 27
6 b g King's Best(USA) —Knight's Place (IRE) (Hamas (IRE))
3760[10] 4686[8] 4915[4] 5289[6]

Harlan's Ruby (USA) *Kenneth McPeek* a107 90
2 b f Harlan's Holiday(USA) —Smiling Eyes (USA) (Saint Ballado (CAN))
7342a[8]

Harlech Castle *Jim Boyle* a95 84
5 b g Royal Applause—Ffestiniog (IRE) (Efisio)
(71) (474) 3919[14] 4894[13] 5551[6] 7289[12] 7557[5] 7697[10] 7906[3]

Harlequin Girl *Terry Clement*
2 ch f Where Or When(IRE) —Lauren Louise (Tagula (IRE))
6058[10]

Harlequinn Danseur (IRE) *David Evans* a45 57
5 b g Noverre(USA) —Nassma (IRE) (Sadler's Wells (USA))
1459[11] 1635[9]

Harlestone Times (IRE) *John Dunlop* 94
3 b g Olden Times—Harlestone Lady (Shaamit (IRE))
4306[10] (5994) (6437)

Harley Fern *Terry Clement* a25 47
4 b m Primo Valentino(IRE) —Its All Relative (Distant Relative)
2249[9] 3507[5] 4760[11]

Harmonious (USA) *John Shirreffs* 111
3 bb f Dynaformer(USA) —Jade Tree (USA) (Storm Cat (USA))
5351a[2] 7343a[10]

Haroldini (IRE) *John Balding* a71 16
8 b g Orpen(USA) —Ciubanga (IRE) (Arazi (USA))
895[5] 1148[7]

Harriers Call (IRE) *J C Hayden* a85 103
5 b m Atraf—Bow Harrier (IRE) (Sri Pekan (USA))
1408a[5] 1787a[9] 5568a[5] 6786a[9]

Harriet's Girl *Mrs K Burke* 86
4 ch m Choisir(AUS) —Harriet (IRE) (Grand Lodge (USA))
2328[2] (2512) 3206[2] 3667[8] 4603[7] 5533[3] (6105) 6395[4] 7182[9]

Harrison George (IRE) *Richard Fahey* a73 114
5 b g Danetime(IRE) —Dry Lightning (Shareef Dancer (USA))
1008[9] (1272) (2344) 2707[8] (4126) 4412[3] 5274[6] 5946[11] (6570) 6923[10]

Harrison's Cave *A P O'Brien* a76 74
2 b c Galileo(IRE) —Sitara (Salse (USA))
4175a[9]

Harris Tweed *William Haggas* a64 117
3 b g Hernando(FR) —Frog (Akarad (FR))
(1528) ◆ 2125[2] (2758) ◆ 3822[2] 5185[7] (5938) (6506) ◆

Harris Tweed (NZ) *Murray & Bjorn Baker* 118
5 b g Montjeu(IRE) —Sally (NZ) (Prized (USA))
6947a[2] 7291a[5]

Harry Hunt *Cecil Ross* a70 73
3 b g Bertolini(USA) —Qasirah (IRE) (Machiavellian (USA))
7306[2]

Harry Luck (IRE) *Henry Candy* 73
2 b g Red Ransom(USA) —Tara Gold (IRE) (Royal Academy (USA))
3459[2] 3961[3] 4856[4]

Harry Patch *Michael Jarvis* a87 99
4 b g Lujain(USA) —Hoh Dancer (Indian Ridge)
4832[2] ◆ (5393) ◆ 7079[11] 7348[3]

Harrys *Jane Chapple-Hyam* a47
3 b g Desert Sun—Emerald Angel (IRE) (In The Wings)
7381[8] 7489[9] 8021[8]

Harry Up *Andrew Reid* a67 65
9 ch g Piccolo—Faraway Lass (Distant Relative)
1979[5] 2310[10] 3958[8] 7193[10] 7446[12]

Harsh But Fair *Michael Easterby* a43 20
4 br g Sakhee(USA) —Royal Distant (USA) (Distant View (USA))
5303[13] 6244[6] 6313[6]

Hartforth *James Bethell* a49 62
2 ch g Haafhd—St Edith (IRE) (Desert King (IRE))
3923[9] 4668[7] 6070[11] 6891[2] 7272[6]

Harting Hill *Marcus Tregoning* a72 66
5 b g Mujahid(USA) —Mossy Rose (King Of Spain)
(499) 696[6] 965[5] 1304[3] 2009[7] 2643[2] 2866[2] 3777[3] 4700[3] 5559[2] (5897) 6580[7] 6801[7] 7162[2] 7290[2] 7483[6]

Hart Of Gold *Ronald Harris* a58 59
6 b g Foxhound(USA) —Bullion (Sabrehill (USA))
70[3] 135[4] 195[6] 234[5] 423[2] 694[7] 773[4] 860[5] 1235[4] 2021[4] 2590[5] 2779[9] 2840[9] 3292[10] 3526[10] 4790[2] 5075[2] 5586[4] 5875[13] 7300[12] 7380[6] 7738[8]

Hartshead *Tracy Waggott* a84 74
11 b g Machiavellian(USA) —Zalitzine (USA) (Zilzal (USA))
4404[10] 5486[9] 5821[5] 6269[11]

Harvest Dancer (IRE) *Brian Meehan* 84
3 ch c Danehill Dancer(IRE) —Autumnal (IRE) (Indian Ridge)
1308[2] (1844)

Hasay *P Schiergen* 93
3 ch f Lomitas—Saralea (FR) (Sillery (USA))
5805a[2] 6551a[6]

Hassadin *Andrew Haynes* a48 54
4 ch g Reset(AUS) —Crocolat (Croco Rouge (IRE))
90[3] 1758[3] 2907[2] 3324[8] 4765[14]

Hasty Katie (IRE) *J S Bolger* a71 78
2 b f Whipper(USA) —Hasanat (Night Shift (USA))
4879a[9]

Hatch A Plan (IRE) *Mouse Hamilton-Fairley* a56 60
9 b g Vettori(IRE) —Fast Chick (Henbit (USA))
100[11] 479[12] 576[2] 746[5] 791[4] 970[8] 1318[6] 1507[6] 2080[12] 2360[10] 2894[12] 7167[11] 7570[6] 7716[8] 7760[5]

Hathaway (IRE) *Mark Brisbourne* a51 59
3 ch f Redback—Finty (IRE) (Entrepreneur)
104[3] 134[5] 288[6] 475[8] 1777[3] (2132) 3073[5] 3387[5] 3852[8] 4337[6]

Hatman Jack (IRE) *Brendan Powell* a64 32
4 ch g Bahamian Bounty—Mary Hinge (Dowsing (USA))
137[9] 344[8] 674[4] 967[10] 5471[9] 6018[10] 7250[12] 7635[9]

Hattan (IRE) *M Al Muhairi* a108 99
8 ch h Halling(USA) —Luana (Shaadi (USA))
630a[8] 708a[3] 821a[12]

Hatta Stream (IRE) *Jeff Pearce* a85 75
4 b g Oasis Dream—Rubies From Burma (USA) (Forty Niner (USA))
950[8] 1260[4] 1659[5] 2399[8] 2877[6] 5157[6] 5495[12] 5698[2] 6057[4] (6515) 6812[6] (7093) 7488[4] 7573[4] (7782)

Hatton Flight *Andrew Balding* a89 93
6 b g Kahyasi—Platonic (Zafonic (USA))
1898[5] 3240[4] 4818[6] 5949[10]

Haunting *Linda Perratt* 16
4 b m Beat Hollow—Broken Spectre (Rainbow Quest (USA))
1721[5]

Havane Smoker *J-C Rouget* 106
2 ch c Dubawi(IRE) —Ballet Ballon (USA) (Rahy (USA))
6218a[2] 7265a[7]

Havant *Sir Michael Stoute* 103
2 b f Halling(USA) —Louella (USA) (El Gran Senor (USA))
(5489) (6528)

Haveahaarth (IRE) *Michael Quinlan* a64 42
3 b g Alhaarth(IRE) —Castelletto (Komaite (USA))
7874[6] 7964[3]

Having A Ball *Peter Cundell* a73 54
6 b g Mark Of Esteem(IRE) —All Smiles (Halling (USA))
496[2] 676[9] 975[2] 1172[11] 1323[3] 1772[6] 3862[4] 4488[10] 5039[3] 5142[8] (5867) 7611[3] 7688[2] 7889[6]

Havre De Grace (USA) *Anthony Dutrow* a116
3 b f Saint Liam(USA) —Easter Bunnette (USA) (Carson City (USA))
7344a[3]

Hawaafez *Marcus Tregoning* a75
2 b f Nayef(USA) —Merayaat (IRE) (Darshaan)
7559[3] (7733) ◆

Hawaana (IRE) *Gay Kelleway* a85 90
5 b g Bahri(USA) —Congress (IRE) (Dancing Brave (USA))
394[3] 480[4] 765[7] 1051[5] 1883[3] 2240[2] 2492[3] 3203[2] 3688[2] 4152[4] (4737)

Hawawi *David Lanigan* 62
2 b c Motivator—Abide (FR) (Pivotal)
7152[3]

Hawdyerwheesht *Mark Johnston* a74 80
2 b g Librettist(USA) —Rapsgate (IRE) (Mozart (IRE))
5040[5] 5294[4] (5886) ◆ 6568[20] 7165[6]

Hawkeshead *William Haggas* 53
3 b c Rainbow Quest(USA) —Ciboure (Norwick (USA))
2974[11]

Hawkeyethenoo (IRE) *Jim Goldie* a48 102
4 b g Hawk Wing(USA) —Stardance (USA) (Rahy (USA))
(1363) ◆ (1727) 2745[2] 3489a[3] 4085[13] (4391) 6177[15] 6752[13]

Hawk Flight (IRE) *Miss Maura McGuinness* a79 74
5 b g Hawk Wing(USA) —Rapid Action (USA) (Quest For Fame)
7514a[2] 7589a[7]

Hawk Junior (IRE) *Patrick Morris* 8
4 b g Hawk Wing(USA) —Naughty Nell (Danehill Dancer (IRE))
2653[9] 4582[14]

Hawk Moth (IRE) *John Spearing* a68 62
2 b g Hawk Wing(USA) —Sasimoto (USA) (Saratoga Six (USA))
2873[3] 3971[5] 4871[4] (6162) 6453[3] 7151[5]

Hawk Mountain (UAE) *John Quinn* 90
5 b g Halling(USA) —Friendly (USA) (Lear Fan (USA))
1720[5] 2541[9] 2938[12] (5278) 6926[11]

Hawridge King *Stuart Kittow* a65 85
8 b g Erhaab(USA) —Sadaka (USA) (Kingmambo (USA))
1544[3] 1902[7] 2549[4] 3127[3] (4386) 5788[11] 7208[5]

Hawridge Knight *Rod Millman* 48
2 ch g Peintre Celebre(USA) —Desiraka (Kris)
4577[9] 6514[11] 6874[7]

Hawridge Star (IRE) *Stuart Kittow* a42 81
8 b g Alzao(USA) —Serenity (Selkirk (USA))
(1077) 5996[2] 6480[5] (7208)

Hayaku (USA) *Ralph Beckett* a47 54
2 b f Arch(USA) —Promptly (IRE) (Lead On Time (USA))
6053[8] 6559[17]

Hayek *William Jarvis* a75 62
3 b g Royal Applause—Salagama (IRE) (Alzao (USA))
4025[2] 4344[9] 4931[8] 6093[4] 7006[10]

Haylaman (IRE) *Ed Dunlop* a73
2 b g Diamond Green(FR) —Schonbein (IRE) (Persian Heights)
5724[5] (6542)

Hayley Cropper *David Nicholls* 66
2 ch f Bertolini(USA) —Lavender Dancer (Tragic Role (USA))
2202[3] 2623[5] (2836) (3058) 3596[10]

Hayley's Girl *S W James* a39 38
4 b m Deportivo—Eurolink Artemis (Common Grounds)
1167[11]

Haynesfield (USA) *Steven Asmussen* a125
4 ch h Speightstown(USA) —Nothing Special (CAN) (Tejabo (CAN))
4855a[4] (6586a) 7367a[11]

Hayri Baba (TUR) *E Sengel* 83
4 b h Distant Relative—Rettin (TUR) (Down The Flag (USA))
5803a[10]

Hayzoom *Peter Chapple-Hyam* 88
3 b c Anabaa(USA) —Green Swallow (FR) (Green Tune (USA))
(1757) 2254[4] 3105[13] 4751[2] 5259[6] 5747[7] 6448[4]

Hazarafa (IRE) *John M Oxx* a71 99
3 gr f Daylami(IRE) —Hazariya (IRE) (Xaar)
(6786a)

Hazelrigg (IRE) *Tim Easterby* a78 96
5 b g Namid—Emma's Star (ITY) (Darshaan)
1366[10] 1924[7] 2113[5] ◆ 2578[3] 3024[2] 3119[3] 3356[2] (3675) 4090[6] 4372[2] 4542[3] 5198[4] 5513[3] (5855) (6140) 6364[3] 6918[14]

Hazita *Jeremy Gask* a7
3 b f Singspiel(IRE) —Hazaradjat (IRE) (Darshaan)
274[9]

Hazy Ridge *Michael Madgwick*
2 b f Compton Place—Hazy (Vettori (IRE))
2749[12] 3332[14] 5147[15]

Hazytoo *PETER Makin* a70 76
6 ch g Sakhee(USA) —Shukran (Hamas (IRE))
802[6] (2846) 3777[5] ◆ 6085[4]

Hazzard County (USA) *David Simcock* a90 81
6 ch g Grand Slam(USA) —Sweet Lexy May (USA) (Danzig (USA))
231[6] 360[7] ◆ 637[6] 769[8] 1914[2] 2443[2] 3036[4] 4501[7] 5716[4] (5964) 6503[7] 7091[5] 7554[5] (8017)

Headache *Brendan Duke* a76 73
5 b g Cape Cross(IRE) —Romantic Myth (Mind Games)
21[3] (269) (318) 442[4] 668[3] 1063[5] 1323[7] 1914[4] (2187) 3033[3] 3734[2] 4024[8] 7047[2] 7377[6] 7766[4] 7892[8] 8014[8]

Head Down *Martin Bosley* a80 80
4 b g Acclamation—Creese (USA) (Diesis)
200[7] 1877[9] 2643[12] 3131[6]

Head First *William Jarvis* a76 77
4 b m Dansili—Break Point (Reference Point)
131[7] (295) 466[2] ◆ 675[2] 1034[2] ◆

Headford View (IRE) *James Halpin* a92 98
6 b m Bold Fact(USA) —Headfort Rose (IRE) (Desert Style (IRE))
5571a[25]

Head Hunted *David Simcock* a61 75
3 b g Dubai Destination(USA) —Tropical Breeze (IRE) (Kris)
825[6] 922[6] 1778[4] 2908[2] 4259[5] 4545[2] (5164) 5996[4] 6750[9]

Heading To First *Paddy Butler* a70 73
3 b g Sulamani(IRE) —Bahirah (Ashkalani (IRE))
664[4] 830[2] 1059[4] 1608[4] (3117) 3594[6] 6289[10]

Head Of Steam (USA) *Mme C Head-Maarek* 102
3 ch c Mizzen Mast(USA) —Summer Mist (USA) (Miswaki (USA))
1610a[6]

Head To Head (IRE) *Alan Brown* a61 40
6 gr g Mull Of Kintyre(USA) —Shoka (FR) (Kaldoun (FR))
112[7] (178) 344[9] 525[10] 3286[5] 3763[13] 4244[8]

Hear Hear *David Lanigan* a51
3 gr f With Approval(CAN) —Hertha (Hernando (FR))
4697[7]

Heart Attack (FR) *G Martin* a74 88
4 b h Double Heart(FR) —Indefinite (FR) (Definite Article)
272a[4] 458a[7] 549a[3]

Heart Beat Song *Ed Dunlop* 52
2 b c Cape Cross(IRE) —Polly Perkins (IRE) (Pivotal)
6442[9]

Heartbreak *Richard Fahey* a73 74
2 b c Iffraaj—Romantic Myth (Mind Games)
3353[3] 3964[3] 4645[4] 4941[7] (5683) (6489) 6705[5]

Heart Breaker (FR) *M Boutin* a55 50
3 b c American Post—Hierarchie (FR) (Sillery (USA))
548a[5]

Heart Felt *Richard Hannon* a45 65
2 b f Beat Hollow—Name Of Love (IRE) (Petardia)
5691[15] 6469[5] 6770[8] 7296[8]

Hear The Roar (IRE) *Jim Boyle* 88
3 b g High Chaparral(IRE) —Talbiya (IRE) (Mujtahid (USA))
2632[6] (2925) 3813[2] 6096[2]

Hearthstead Dream *Gordon Elliott* a66 73
9 ch g Dr Fong(USA) —Robin Lane (Tenby)
4467[16]

Heart In Motion (IRE) *Mick Channon* a69 59
2 b f Mujadil(USA) —Valluga (IRE) (Ashkalani (IRE))
6161[3] 6369[8] 6802[6]

Heart Of Dubai (USA) *Micky Hammond* a69 50
5 b g Outofthebox(USA) —Diablo's Blend (USA) (Diablo (USA))
1427[5] 1922[9] 4854[3] 5203[4] 5687[5]

Heart Of Hearts *Henry Cecil* a69 86
3 b f Oasis Dream—Shirley Valentine (Shirley Heights)
2507[3] ◆ 2921[3] (3593) 4360[3] 5858[4] 6282[2] 6698[8]

Heart Of Tuscany *Jonathen de Giles* a58 58
4 b m Falbrav(IRE) —Zarma (FR) (Machiavellian (USA))
1755[12] 3128[15]

Hearts Of Fire *Pat Eddery* 119
3 b c Firebreak—Alexander Ballet (Mind Games)
1699[13] 3048[3] ◆ 3719a[4] 5009[5] 6350[6]

Heatherbird *William Jarvis* 67
2 b f Shamardal(USA) —Bronwen (IRE) (King's Best (USA))
6651[4]

Heathyards Junior *Alan McCabe* a73 40
4 b g Beat All(USA) —Heathyards Lady (USA) (Mining (USA))
(126) 255[8] 715[4] 857[4] 910[2] 1012[17] 1526[6] 2259[7] 4686[9]

Heathyards Pride *Reg Hollinshead* a87 74
10 b g Polar Prince(IRE) —Heathyards Lady (USA) (Mining (USA))
1069[7] (2182) 2313[7] (2786)

Heaven Forbid *James Fanshawe* a61 73
3 b f Pivotal—Red Heaven (Benny The Dip (USA))
1127[3] ◆ 1882[9] 2473[8] 2993[2] ◆

Heavenly Dawn *Sir Michael Stoute* 84
3 ch f Pivotal—Heavenly Ray (USA) (Rahy (USA))
1654[4] (2180) 3298[4]

Heavenly Music (IRE) *Sylvester Kirk* a55
2 b f Oratorio(IRE) —Treca (IRE) (Darshaan)
7755[5]

Heavenly Pursuit *Jim Boyle* a54 17
2 b f Pastoral Pursuits—Stylish Clare (IRE) (Desert Style (IRE))
6986[9] 7608[5]

Heavenly Song (IRE) *Sylvester Kirk* 61
2 b f Oratorio(IRE) —Lochangel (Night Shift (USA))
5078[6] 5691[13]

Heaven's Vault (IRE) *Robert Collet* 93
3 b f Hernando(FR) —Neutrina (IRE) (Hector Protector (USA))
1946a[3] 3015a[8] 6551a[7] 7546a[0]

Hecton Lad (USA) *John Best* a51 24
3 bb g Posse(USA) —Foxy Queen (USA) (Fit To Fight (USA))
5623[7] 6079[6] 7381[5]

Hector Spectre (IRE) *Nikki Evans* a71 64
4 gr g Verglas(IRE) —Halicardia (Halling (USA))
12[6] 162[6] 868[8] 1194[10] 2360[2] 2922[5] 3314[8] 4914[4] 7449[2]

Heddwyn (IRE) *Marcus Tregoning* 94
3 b g Bahri(USA) —Penny Rouge (IRE) (Pennekamp (USA))
(1268) 1730[2] 7121[3] ◆

Hedgerow (IRE) *David Bourton* a32 55
3 b f Azamour(IRE) —Miss Childrey (IRE) (Dr Fong (USA))
1971[10] 2380[9] 6077[2] 7575[10] 7705[7]

Hedonist (IRE) *Jeremy Gask* a58 62
3 ch g Encosta De Lago(AUS) —Coral Strand (Indian Ridge)
1137[7] 4521[9] 5303[5] 5869[10] 6525[6] 6993[12]

Heedas *L Riccardi* 104
4 gr h Lomitas—Heed The Way (USA) (Rahy (USA))
3019a[7]

Heezararity *Stuart Kittow* 56
2 b g Librettist(USA) —Extremely Rare (IRE) (Mark Of Esteem (IRE))
6443[7] ◆

Heidikly (FR) *B De Montzey* 82
2 gr f Slickly(FR) —Hier Deja (FR) (Neverneyev (USA))
7276a[7]

Hekatompylos (FR) *Mme Pia Brandt* 97
5 b g Black Sam Bellamy(IRE) —Dansia (GER) (Lavirco (GER))
3099a[8]

Helaku (IRE) *Richard Hannon* 58
3 b c Rakti—Saibhreas (IRE) (Last Tycoon)
1381[11] 2412[3] 2675[8]

Helen Of Toy *Brendan Powell* a16 34
2 b f Phoenix Reach(IRE) —Toy Girl (IRE) (Cadeaux Genereux)
1073[5] 1324[9] 1660[9] 5718[10] 5894[P]

Heliaster Re (ITY) *V Cangiano*
2 b c Moscow Ballet(IRE) —Halesia Carolina (USA) (Diesis)
7850a[19]

Helieorbea *Alan Brown* a73 76
4 b g Reset(AUS) —Rendition (Polish Precedent (USA))
4196[4] 4481[5] 5215[8] 5530[11] 7985[8]

Heligoland *Tony Newcombe* a46 34
3 b f Trade Fair—Fine Frenzy (IRE) (Great Commotion (USA))
5[5] 216[9]

Heliocentric *Bryn Palling* a64 50
3 ch g Galileo(IRE) —Yding (IRE) (Danehill (USA))
583[5] 889[5] 1387[13] 1757[8] 2620[10] 6794[11] 7475[12] 7639[9]

Heliodor (USA) *Richard Hannon* a107 110
4 b h Scrimshaw(USA) —Playing Footsie (USA) (Valiant Nature (USA))
903[3] 1016[6] 1724[3] 2116[4] 4500[3] 5749[7] 6281[3]

Helipad (FR) *F-X De Chevigny* a72 81
4 b g Green Tune(USA) —High Living (USA) (Diesis)
560a[0]

Helium (FR) *Nicholas Gifford* a41
5 b g Dream Well(FR) —Sure Harbour (SWI) (Surumu (GER))
771[9]

Hellbender (IRE) *Sylvester Kirk* a86 69
4 ch g Exceed And Excel(AUS) —Desert Rose (Green Desert (USA))
292[5] 580[6] 2719[12] 2872[8] 3779[10] 4430[6] 4839[2] 4910[2] 5326[2] 5711[3] 5964[2] 6664[5] 6991[6] (7047)

Helleborine *Mme C Head-Maarek* 112
2 b f Observatory(USA) —New Orchid (USA) (Quest For Fame)
(4611a) (5899a) 6609a[2]

Hellenio *Michael Quinlan* a54 61
3 b g Cape Cross(IRE) —Llia (Shirley Heights)
4210[7] 4970[2] 5159[4] 5560[4] 6062[7]

Hello Fuji *L A Urbano-Grajales* 96
2 b f Dansili—Ziya (IRE) (Lion Cavern (USA))
5322a[5]

Hello Morning (FR) *E Charpy* a92 88
5 gr h Poliglote—Hello Molly (FR) (Sillery (USA))
441a[4] 627a[4]

Hello Tomorrow (USA) *David Lanigan* a64 66
2 b f Forest Wildcat(USA) —Never Gone (USA) (Gone West (USA))
4595[10] 5324[4] 5841[9]

Helping Hand (IRE) *Reg Hollinshead* a33 55
5 b g Lend A Hand—Cardinal Press (Sharrood (USA))
(3286) 3727[6] 3977[8] 4559[11] 5580[5] 6206[13]

Helpmeronda *Mark Brisbourne* a46 61
4 b m Medicean—Lady Donatella (Last Tycoon)
199[10] 354[10] 545[7] 776[6] 979[7]

Hel's Angel (IRE) *Ann Duffield* a71 84
4 b m Pyrus(USA) —Any Dream (IRE) (Shernazar)
(2277) (3060) 3432[5] 4055[3] 4859[2] 5181[5] 5888[5] 6677[6]

Hemera (USA) *Mark Johnston* a72
3 rg f Maria's Mon(USA) —North Cork (USA) (Doneraile Court (USA))
973[7] 1307[7]

Hendersyde (USA) *Walter Swinburn* a91 96
5 ch g Giant's Causeway(USA) —Cimmaron Lady (USA) (Grand Slam (USA))
5922[7] (6797)

Hen Night (IRE) *David Wachman* a91 107
3 b f Danehill Dancer(IRE) —Twice The Ease (Green Desert (USA))
1952a[3] (4630a) 5773a[4] 6561[9]

Henry Bond *Shaun Harris* 5
2 ch g Monsieur Bond(IRE) —Decatur (Deploy)
3106[12] 4247[11] 6676[10]

Henry Chettle (IRE) *David C Griffiths* 32
2 ch g Iffraaj—Nipitinthebud (USA) (Night Shift (USA))
2701[8] 5546[7] 5878[15]

Henry Havelock *Chris Grant* 58
3 ch c Noverre(USA) —Burmese Princess (USA) (King Of Kings (IRE))
1572[5] 1992[7] 2606[7] 3506[3] 4200[7] 4545[7] 4854[13] 5216[11]

Henry Morgan *Bryan Smart* 67
3 ch c Bahamian Bounty—Hill Welcome (Most Welcome)
3397[3] (4584) (5211)

Henrys Air *David Bridgwater* a68 48
2 b g Piccolo—Humble Gift (Cadeaux Genereux)
1517[12] 1930[7] 2474[2] 2785[3] 3106[9] 5453[9] 5862[8] 7211[7] 7395[3] 7469[6] 7496[6] 7666[6]

Henry San (IRE) *Alan King* 74
3 ch g Exceed And Excel(AUS) —Esclava (USA) (Nureyev (USA))
5266[9]

Henrys Gift (IRE) *Michael Dods* 46
2 b g Titus Livius(FR) —Xania (Mujtahid (USA))
5196[7]

Herbert Crescent *Ollie Pears* a64 75
5 b g Averti(IRE) —With Distinction (Zafonic (USA))
567[7] 976[4] 984[4]

Herculean *William Haggas* a86 101
3 b g Sakhee(USA) —Someone Special (Habitat)
4207[5] ◆ (4893) (5475) ◆ (6362) ◆

Herculian Prince (NZ) *Gai Waterhouse* 114
5 b g Yamanin Vital(NZ) —Sea Island (NZ) (Woodman (USA))
6947a[9]

Here Comes Ben (USA) *Charles Lopresti* a122 91
4 bb h Street Cry(IRE) —Chasetheragingwind (USA) (Dayjur (USA))
(5779a) 7365a[11]

Herecomethegirls *Bill Turner* a58 46
4 b m Falbrav(IRE) —Always On My Mind (Distant Relative)
1756[10] 2006[12] 3263[8] 4775[5] 4913[2] ◆ 5704[7] 7071[2] 7199[10] 7633[2] 7863[6]

Heredias (GER) *Mark Brisbourne* a55 66
4 b g Lomitas—Happy Gini (USA) (Ginistrelli (USA))
173[7] 6518[3] 7184[6] 7531[12] 7814[11]

Hereford Boy *Dean Ivory* a84 76
6 ch g Tomba—Grown At Rowan (Gabitat)
(23) (315) 394[2] 749[8] 1030[18] 1088[14] 1625[12]

Heresellie (IRE) *David Barron* a64 32
2 b f Clodovil(IRE) —Special Dissident (Dancing Dissident (USA))
2605[6] (3757) 7641[3] (7983)

Here To Eternity (USA) *Peter Chapple-Hyam* 20
2 bb f Stormy Atlantic(USA) —Heat Of The Night (Lear Fan (USA))
4517[7]

Hermes *Ralph Beckett* 76
2 b c Observatory(USA) —Parisette (Dansili)
6635[2] ◆

Herminella *William Muir* a72
2 b f Lucky Story(USA) —Herminoe (Rainbow Quest (USA))
7311[4] (7550)

Hermoun (FR) *X Nakkachdji* 102
4 b h Septieme Ciel(USA) —Hermine (FR) (Kaldoun (FR))
6344a[3]

Hernando's Boy *Keith Reveley* 61
9 b g Hernando(FR) —Leave At Dawn (Slip Anchor)
7284[8]

Hernando Torres *Michael Easterby* a53 58
2 b g Iffraaj—Espana (Hernando (FR))
2785[4] 3274[9] 3756[10] 6674[2] 7224[6]

Heroes *Jim Boyle* a84 81
6 b g Diktat—Wars (IRE) (Green Desert (USA))
787[7] 966[6]

Hero From Zero (IRE) *Brian Meehan* a8 63
2 b c Invincible Spirit(IRE) —Truly Generous (IRE) (Generous (IRE))
3961[6] 4549[8] 4954[9] 5659[13] 6875[16] 7035[4]

Heroic Lad *Andrew Haynes* a39 48
5 ch g Arkadian Hero(USA) —Erith's Chill Wind (Be My Chief (USA))
90[8]

Heron Bay *Peter Bowen* a103 99
6 b g Hernando(FR) —Wiener Wald (USA) (Woodman (USA))
4817[10]

Herostatus *Mark Johnston* a91 76
3 ch g Dalakhani(IRE) —Desired (Rainbow Quest (USA))
4572[8] 6115[6] 6313[2] 6661[5] 7043[2] (7252) (7514a) 7823a[4]

Herotozero (IRE) *Gerard O'Leary* a72 49
6 b g Mull Of Kintyre(USA) —Free To Trade (IRE) (Royal Academy (USA))
2639[11]

Herrera (IRE) *Richard Fahey* a63 76
5 b m High Chaparral(IRE) —Silk (IRE) (Machiavellian (USA))
1751[7]

Herschel (IRE) *Gary Moore* a78 75
4 br g Dr Fong(USA) —Rafting (IRE) (Darshaan)
394[8] 990[2] 1346[5] 4055[6]

He'Sahit (FR) *Peter Hedger* a14
2 b g Strike Out(IRE) —Lucky Us (IRE) (Fayruz)
6500[12] 6842[11] 7424[8]

He's A Humbug (IRE) *Jimmy O'Reilly* a68 74
6 b g Tagula(IRE) —Acidanthera (Alzao (USA))
171[6] 1270[4] 1653[11] 2698[7] 2817[4] 3061[10] 4234[4] 4868[7] 4936[2] 5045[6]

He's Got Rhythm (IRE) *David Marnane* a87 91
5 b g Invincible Spirit(IRE) —Kathy Jet (USA) (Singspiel (IRE))
6597a[7] 6907a[6]

He's Invincible *Brian Meehan* a73 64
3 b g Invincible Spirit(IRE) —Adamas (IRE) (Fairy King (USA))
(1619) 2644[9] 6197[7] 6692[10] 7047[10]

He's The Star (IRE) *David Evans* a41 62
2 b c Ad Valorem(USA) —Divine Quest (Kris)
1793[8] 2022[3] 2687[9] 2939[13] 4429[6] (4554) 5020[8]

Hettie Hubble *David Thompson* 53
4 ch m Dr Fong(USA) —White Rabbit (Zilzal (USA))
1574[10] 1804[7] 2273[3] 2382[6] 2671[5] 3147[12] 3597[3] 3900[4] 4172[7] 4581[8] 6261[11]

Heureux (USA) *Jens Erik Lindstol* 93
7 b g Stravinsky(USA) —Storm West (USA) (Gone West (USA))
4526a[2]

Hevelius *Walter Swinburn* 97
5 b g Polish Precedent(USA) —Sharp Terms (Kris)
1472[9] 2509[6] 3159[2] 3843[5] 4320[3] 4817[8] 5492[4] 6131[3] 6808[9]

Hey Mambo *Roger Ingram* a3 31
2 b f Bertolini(USA) —Upping The Tempo (Dunbeath (USA))
5914[9] 6520[10] 7871[8]

Hibaayeb *Saeed Bin Suroor* 109
3 b f Singspiel(IRE) —Lady Zonda (Lion Cavern (USA))
1726[16] 2373a[3] (3101) 4178a[15] 4640a[7] 5248[7] (6604a) 7343a[8]

Hibba (USA) *Marcus Tregoning* a65 70
3 bb f Sahm(USA) —Nuzooa (USA) (A.P. Indy (USA))
5116[4] 6250[5] 7022[3]

Hi Dancer *Ben Haslam* a55 73
7 b g Medicean—Sea Music (Inchinor)
910[6] 2060[8] 2610[10] 3352[2] 3535[2] 4604[9] 5364[2] 7632[7]

Hidden *Brian Meehan* 68
4 b g Hernando(FR) —For More (FR) (Sanglamore (USA))
1432[4] 1705[3] 3754[8] 5011[7] 5666[6] 6132[9]

Hidden Brief *Michael Jarvis* a91 97
4 b m Barathea(IRE) —Hazaradjat (IRE) (Darshaan)
1031[3] 1274[9] 7349[5] 7523[6] 7594[7]

Hidden Destiny *PETER Makin* a73 30
3 ch g Bahamian Bounty—Cayetana's Raid (USA) (Rahy (USA))
6638[10] 7013[8] 7166[3] 7426[7] (7505) 7655[2]

Hidden Fire *David Elsworth* a74 80
3 b f Alhaarth(IRE) —Premier Prize (Selkirk (USA))
(1661) (3962) 5083[5] 5972[4]

Hidden Glory *James Given* a90 87
3 b g Mujahid(USA) —Leominda (Lion Cavern (USA))
1657[4] 2002[6] 2927[2] 3697[3] 4056[6] 4758[3] 5375[8] 5918[8] (6430) 6701[7] 7012[10] 7600[10] (7698) 7828[4]

Hidden Valley *Andrew Balding* 48
2 b f Haafhd—Spurned (USA) (Robellino (USA))
6779[3]

Hierarch (IRE) *David Flood* a70 73
3 b g Dansili—Danse Classique (IRE) (Night Shift (USA))
1581[7] 3635[2] 4056[5] 4335[7] 5051[7] 5494[4] 6164[4] 6413[2] (6854) 7019[7] 7190[5] 7251[4]

Higenius *Dai Burchell* a26
3 b g Auction House(USA) —I'm Sophie (IRE) (Shalford (IRE))
744[7] 997[11] 1505[7] 2279[10]

Higgy's Ragazzo (FR) *Richard Hannon* a43 85
3 b g Sinndar(IRE) —Super Crusty (IRE) (Namid)
1502[10] 2079[9] 2869[12] 3414[3] 3594[4] 3917[2] (5146) 5456[4] 5953[3] 6813[5]

High Ambition *Richard Fahey* a37 84
7 b g High Estate—So Ambitious (Teenoso (USA))
2739[6] 3060[2] ◆ 3319[7] 4348[9]

High Avon *Dean Ivory* a49 56
2 b g Avonbridge—High Finale (Sure Blade (USA))
3459[7] 4110[7] 4960[7] 6673[8] 7017[8]

High Award (IRE) *T Stack* 98
2 b c Holy Roman Emperor(IRE) —Tarascon (IRE) (Tirol)
(954a) 2352a[4] (2743) 3488a[5]

High Class (FR) *C Gourdain* 82
2 b f High Yield(USA) —Millefiori (USA) (Machiavellian (USA))
3307a[5]

High Class Lady *Walter Swinburn* a37 65
2 b f Royal Applause—Lekka Ding (IRE) (Raise A Grand (IRE))
4474[5] 4960[10] 5466[8] 6673[2] ◆ 7313[9]

High Class Problem (IRE) *Daniel Christopher O'Brien* a2 71
7 b g Mozart(IRE) —Sarah-Clare (Reach)
540[12] 1078[10] 2235[12]

Highcliffe *Richard Hannon* a55 51
2 ch f Bertolini(USA) —Galapagar (USA) (Miswaki (USA))
3295[9] 3861[12] 5006[12] 5660[2] 6081[3] 6500[7]

High Constable *Roger Charlton* a89 96
3 b g Shamardal(USA) —Abbey Strand (USA) (Shadeed (USA))
(31) ◆ 1352[2] ◆

High Dee Jay (IRE) *Dai Burchell* 51
5 b g High Chaparral(IRE) —Brogan's Well (IRE) (Caerleon (USA))
4912[12]

Highest *John Gosden* 67
2 b f Dynaformer(USA) —Solaia (USA) (Miswaki (USA))
6154[13] 6469[4]

Highest Bid (USA) *Michael Jarvis* 50
2 ch f Monsun(GER) —Geminiani (IRE) (King Of Kings (IRE))
6651[9]

High Fallutin (IRE) *Eve Johnson Houghton* a14 35
2 b f Ad Valorem(USA) —Top Brex (FR) (Top Ville)
3832[10] 6521[10]

High Five Society *Roy Bowring* a64 77
6 b g Compton Admiral—Sarah Madeline (Pelder (IRE))
469[2] 4522[4] (4932) (5635) 7307[12] 7599[3]

High Heeled (IRE) *John Gosden* a81 120
4 b m High Chaparral(IRE) —Uncharted Haven (Turtle Island (IRE))
2709[3] 3494a[7] 5108a[2] 6013a[8] 6591a[2] 6928[8]

High Holborn (IRE) *David Pipe* a14 67
3 b g Danehill Dancer(IRE) —Wedding Morn (IRE) (Sadler's Wells (USA))
1178[8] 1522[7] 3564[10] 4689[12]

High Importance (USA) *A J Martin* a81 81
3 b g Arch(USA) —Music Lane (USA) (Miswaki (USA))
1240[3] 1542[2] 1934[3] 2242[3] 3212[5] 3539[3] (3716) 6910a[7]

High Jinx (IRE) *James Fanshawe* 64
2 b c High Chaparral(IRE) —Leonara (GER) (Surumu (GER))
7179[4]

High Kickin *Alan McCabe* a60 48
2 ch f Noverre(USA) —Grateful (Generous (IRE))
1421[7] 2216[6] 2740[10] 5924[3] 6471[12] 6717[6] 6978[14] 7394[4] 7631[7] 7801[5]

Highkingofireland *John Weymes* 71
4 br g Danehill Dancer(IRE) —Lucky Date (IRE) (Halling (USA))
1177[5] ◆ 1920[2] 2421[3] 3950[3]

Highland Bridge *David Elsworth* a65 29
3 b g Avonbridge—Reciprocal (IRE) (Night Shift (USA))
(321) 698[7] 1261[10] 1619[5] 2566[12] 3413[12]

Highland Cadett *Rod Millman* a59 56
3 ch g Putra Sandhurst(IRE) —Highland Rossie (Pablond)
533[11] 670[5] 825[5] 2248[7] 2620[6] 3002[6] 3723[6] 4552[5] 4991[7]

Highland Fighter (GER) *H-W Hiller* a41 68
3 ch c Samum(GER) —Honni By (IRE) (Be My Guest (USA))
7959a[10]

Highland Glen *Saeed Bin Suroor* a106 102
4 b g Montjeu(IRE) —Daring Aim (Daylami (IRE))
(512a) 2345[8] 3454[5] 4711[5] 7287[6]

Highland Harvest *Jamie Poulton* a72 82
6 b g Averti(IRE) —Bee One (IRE) (Catrail (USA))
275[10] 325[4] 501[7] 2458[2] 2719[7] 3057[2] (3527) 4292[9] 4510[16] 4777[6] 5652[6] 6439[4] 6858[5] 7441[6] 7556[4] (7992)

Highland Homestead *Mark Hoad* a69 66
5 b g Makbul—Highland Rossie (Pablond)
611[7]

Highland Jewel (IRE) *Clive Cox* a64 55
3 b f Azamour(IRE) —Raysiza (IRE) (Alzao (USA))
2478[6] ◆ 2871[12] 3582[7]

Highland Knight (IRE) *Andrew Balding* a86 93
3 b g Night Shift(USA) —Highland Shot (Selkirk (USA))
2564[2] (2755) 3867[5] 4357[6] 4750[3] 5917[6] 6534[5]

Highland Legacy *Michael Bell* a72 95
6 ch g Selkirk(USA) —Generous Lady (Generous (IRE))
1101[4] 1736[2] 2975[7] ◆ 3566[11] 4125[5] 4686[5] 7061[12]

Highland Love *Jedd O'Keeffe* a67 64
5 b g Fruits Of Love(USA) —Diabaig (Precocious)
1920[12] 2421[6] (2851) 3110[3] 4752[5] 5515[10] (6375) 6937[8]

Highland Park (IRE) *Sir Michael Stoute* 82
3 ch c Pivotal—Highland Gift (IRE) (Generous (IRE))
6115[3] ◆ 6876[7]

Highland Quaich *David Elsworth* a84 72
3 ch g Compton Place—Bee One (IRE) (Catrail (USA))
(366) ◆ 1018[7] 6204[13] 7033[8] 7114[3]

Highland River *Aytach Mehmet Sadik* a63 55
4 b g Indian Creek—Bee One (IRE) (Catrail (USA))
88[2] 210[8] (244) 330[6] 457[2] 575[3] 720[7] 1053[4] 1983[12]

Highland Warrior *Paul Midgley* a62 78
11 b g Makbul—Highland Rowena (Royben)
1099[2] (1200) ◆ 1364[2] 2073[9] 3879[5] 4090[12] 4513[2] 5240[3] 5528[10] 6031[2] (6398) 7175[2]

Highlife Dancer *Mick Channon* 74
2 br g Imperial Dancer—Wrong Bride (Reprimand)
3577[3] 3832[6] (4208) 6475[2] 6690[6] 7085[10]

High Link (FR) *X Thomas-Demeaulte* 93
3 b g High Yield(USA) —Sante De Fer (FR) (Shining Steel)
3933a[7]

Highly Acclaimed *Ann Duffield* a44 49
4 b m Acclamation—Ebba (Elmaamul (USA))
1149[10]

Highly Composed *T Stack* 95
2 b f Oratorio(IRE) —Kanisfluh (Pivotal)
4077a[4]

Highly Regal (IRE) *Roger Teal* a91 85
5 b g High Chaparral(IRE) —Regal Portrait (IRE) (Royal Academy (USA))
(1088) 1618[3] 2124[5] 2640[12] 3334[7] 4030[4] 4459[18] 5750[9] 6252[13] 7114[10] 7781[7]

High Office *Richard Fahey* a82 90
4 b g High Chaparral(IRE) —White House (Pursuit Of Love)
(1203) 2204[6] 2766[4] (3203) 4400[5] 5355[6] (6096) 6304[4] 7292[5]

High On A Hill (IRE) *Sylvester Kirk* a81 80
3 b g Val Royal(FR) —Blue Kestrel (IRE) (Bluebird (USA))
1059[2] (1433) 1975[2] 2323[8] 5953[10] 6359[7] 7044[5] 7316[3] (7781) 8007[3]

High On The Hog (IRE) *John Dunlop* 69
2 b c Clodovil(IRE) —Maraami (Selkirk (USA))
2319[9] 3288[3] 3981[4] 5234[2] 5709[4] 7035[9]

High Ransom *Michael Jarvis* a72 73
3 b f Red Ransom(USA) —Shortfall (Last Tycoon)
1356[9] 2585[5] ◆ 3626[2] 4230[4] 6955[6]

High Resolution *Linda Perratt* a53 87
3 ch g Haafhd—Individual Talents (USA) (Distant View (USA))
1718[6] 2209[3] 2380[8] 3073[3] 3161[2] 3530[3] 3668[3] (4061) (4088) (4585) 5213[7] 5408[3] 7053[6] 7227[6]

High Rolling *Tim Easterby* 66
3 b g Fantastic Light(USA) —Roller Girl (Merdon Melody)
1422[8] 1652[3] 1989[2] 3506[6] 4120[4] 4602[2] 4898[3] 7988[8]

High Ruler (USA) *A P O'Brien* 104
2 b c Mr Greeley(USA) —Lady Carla (Caerleon (USA))
4310a[2] 5316a[4] 5975a[6]

High Samana *Ralph Beckett* a47 51
2 b g High Chaparral(IRE) —Kirkby Belle (Bay Express)
6689[13] 7163[10]

High Spice (USA) *Robert Cowell* a84 84
3 b f Songandaprayer(USA) —Erin Moor (USA) (Holy Bull (USA))
2287[9] 3218[6] (3311) 4016[3] 4654[4] 4901[4] 6539[7] (7549) 7702[4] 7998[7]

High Standing (USA) *William Haggas* a87 117
5 b g High Yield(USA) —Nena Maka (Selkirk (USA))
(2536) 3192[19] 4136[2] 4885a[3] 5946[5] 6923[6]

High Table (IRE) *Tom Dascombe* a35
2 b g High Chaparral(IRE) —Inner Strength (FR) (Take Risks (FR))
6334[9]

High Treason (USA) *John C McConnell* a69 71
8 ch g Diesis—Fabula Dancer (USA) (Northern Dancer (CAN))
521[5]

High Twelve (IRE) *John Gosden* a106 102
3 b g Montjeu(IRE) —Much Faster (IRE) (Fasliyev (USA))
1310[4] 2045[2] 2324[14] 3103[10] 5030[3] (6312) 6562[12]

High Voltage *Mrs J L Le Brocq* 53
9 ch g Wolfhound(USA) —Real Emotion (USA) (El Prado (IRE))
1814a[4]

Highway (IRE) *Francisco Castro* a96 82
7 b g King's Theatre(IRE) —Havinia (Habitat)
2020a[3]

Highway Magic (IRE) *Alan Jarvis* a33 20
4 ch g Rainbow Quest(USA) —Adultress (IRE) (Ela-Mana-Mou)
2388[11]

High Window (IRE) *G P Kelly* a47 21
10 b g King's Theatre(IRE) —Kayradja (IRE) (Last Tycoon)
4047[10] 4285[12] 4986[10] 6644[7]

Hi Ho Ron *David Brown* 64
2 b g Tobougg(IRE) —Hi Ho Silca (Atraf)
1686[11] 2068[3] 2654[5] 4984[10]

Hikaru Amaranthus (JPN) *Yasuo Ikee* 112
4 ch m Agnes Tachyon(JPN) —Star Mie (USA) (A.P. Indy (USA))
7460a[5]

Hilbre Court (USA) *Brian Baugh* a81 56
5 br g Doneraile Court(USA) —Glasgow's Gold (USA) (Seeking The Gold (USA))
23[7] 174[10] 245[6] 466[6] 715[10] 3131[11] 3377[4] 3911[7] 4488[7] 4987[11] 5767[7] 6165[11] 7071[5] 7128[2]

Hilbre Point (USA) *Nicky Vaughan* 61
4 b g Giant's Causeway(USA) —Lady Carla (Caerleon (USA))
468[9] 777[12]

Hill Of Clare (IRE) *George Jones* a17 51
8 gr m Daylami(IRE) —Sarah-Clare (Reach)
4681[12]

Hill Of Miller (IRE) *Rae Guest* a72 75
3 b g Indian Ridge—Roshani (IRE) (Kris)
667[4] 856[7] 1181[3] 1259[3] 1760[4] 2459[5] 2566[6] 2844[7] 3113[7] 3993[5] 4151[7]

Hilltop Alchemy *John Jenkins* a29 22
4 ch g Zaha(CAN) —Saferjel (Elmaamul (USA))
2263[10] 4213[7] 4969[10]

Hilltop Artistry *John Jenkins* a44 65
4 b g Polish Precedent(USA) —Hilltop (Absalom)
2643[11] 4108[13] 4763[10] 6062[5] 7487[12]

Hilltop Legacy *John Jenkins* a31 53
7 b m Danzig Connection(USA) —Hilltop (Absalom)
499[10] 1130[8] 2257[9] 4969[14]

Hill Tribe *Richard Guest* a73 71
3 b f Tiger Hill(IRE) —Morning Queen (GER) (Konigsstuhl (GER))
1620[3] 2717[6] 4786[6] 7069[2] 7453[8] 7476[6]

Hillview Boy (IRE) *Jim Goldie* 104
6 bb g Bishop Of Cashel—Arandora Star (USA) (Sagace (FR))
1724[4] (2071) 3672[14] 3921[4] 5220[9]

Himalya (IRE) *Jeremy Noseda* a106 117
4 b g Danehill Dancer(IRE) —Lady Miletrian (IRE) (Barathea (IRE))
2100[8] 2563[2] 3146[2] 3445[2] 4358[3] 5081[4] 5554[3] 5946[3] 6390[4] 6923[9]

Himba *Nicholas Gifford* a54 64
7 b g Vettori(IRE) —Be My Wish (Be My Chief (USA))
764[2] 982[13]

Hindu Kush (IRE) *Robert Mills* a75 108
5 b g Sadler's Wells(USA) —Tambora (Darshaan)
1139[3] 1357[3] 1863[5] 2313[8] 3588[9] 5272[3]

Hi Note *Mick Channon* a52 33
2 b f Acclamation—Top Tune (Victory Note (USA))
4729[5] 5626[8] 6425[6] 6868[10] 7296[9]

Hint Of Honey *Tony Newcombe* a57 21
4 ch m King Charlemagne(USA) —Jugendliebe (IRE) (Persian Bold)
705[10] 1503[7] 1919[14]

Hinton Admiral *Paul Howling* a77 77
6 b g Spectrum(IRE) —Shawanni (Shareef Dancer (USA))
1583[3] 1979[8] 2235[4] (2678) 4024[12] (4430) 4836[6] 5454[7] 7319[9] 7483[3] (7737)

Hip Hip Hooray *Luke Dace* a75 72
4 ch m Monsieur Bond(IRE) —Birthday Belle (Lycius (USA))
27[4] 256[8] 284[2] 383[6] 685[3] 804[2] 931[3] (1063) 1304[12] 1779[4] 2233[7] 2596[13] 3040[9] (4756) 5149[8] 5664[9] 6452[2] 6794[10] 7611[2] 7890[2]

Hippique *Andrew Balding* a63
3 b f Bertolini(USA) —Elemental (Rudimentary (USA))
6496[5] ◆ 7166[7] 7651[4] (7872)

Hippodrome (IRE) *John Harris* a31 74
8 b g Montjeu(IRE) —Moon Diamond (Unfuwain (USA))
2786[6] 5564[8]

Hiram (FR) *S Cerulis* a72 70
5 ch h Septieme Ciel(USA) —Bonnie And Howard (USA) (Fly So Free (USA))
273a[7]

Hiresh (IRE) *Mario Vincis* 80
3 b c Redback—Polissena (IRE) (Perugino (USA))
7372a[8]

His Grace (IRE) *Andrew Haynes* a58 73
2 gr g Proclamation(IRE) —Little Miss Gracie (Efisio)
4131[10] 4759[2] 5160[2] 5453[5] 6626[5]

Hi Shinko *Rod Millman* a71 89
4 b g Shinko Forest(IRE) —Up Front (IRE) (Up And At 'Em)
1516[11] 2024[7] 2783[6] 3289[6] 3813[3] 4995[10] (5238) (5627) 5834[2]

Hi Spec (IRE) *Mandy Rowland* a55 49
7 b m Spectrum(IRE) —Queen Of Fibres (IRE) (Scenic)
211[4] 320[3] (389) 591[5] 854[9] 984[9] 5560[3] 6188[10]

History Girl (IRE) *Mark Johnston* a53 65
2 b f Hernando(FR) —City Of Gold (IRE) (Sadler's Wells (USA))
5332[5] 6070[4] 7567[9]

History Repeating *Mark Usher* a58 53
2 b f Singspiel(IRE) —Annapurna (IRE) (Brief Truce (USA))
4568[7] (4967) 5837[12] 6412[10] 7296[5] 7486[9] 7758[5]

Hitchens (IRE) *David Barron* a106 110
5 b g Acclamation—Royal Fizz (IRE) (Royal Academy (USA))
3489a[23] 4391[7] 4576[14] 5095[6] ◆ (5787) 6177[3] 7073a[2] 7351[2] (7524)

Hitches Dubai (BRZ) *Geoffrey Harker* 70
5 ch g A Good Reason(BRZ) —Orquidea Vermelha (BRZ) (Lucence (USA))
913[11] 1805[8] 3357[7] 3615[4] ◆ (3977) 4373[9] 4452[8] 5123[7] 6040[10]

Hits Only Cash *Jeff Pearce* a67 64
8 b g Inchinor—Persian Blue (Persian Bold)
2093[10] 2880[4] 7562[8] 7919[6] 7996[14]

Hits Only Jude (IRE) *Declan Carroll* a85 71
7 gr g Bold Fact(USA) —Grey Goddess (Godswalk (USA))
16[8] 508[2] (703) 859[3] 1152[2] 1270[3] 1628[2] 1926[15] 1997[2] 2392[12] 6710[9] 6917[5] 7125[3] 7403[7]

Hit The Switch *Patrick Morris* a69 69
4 b g Reset(AUS) —Scenic Venture (IRE) (Desert King (IRE))
(40) 298[7]

Hobbesian War *Tom Tate* 25
2 b g Danehill Dancer(IRE) —Bold Classic (USA) (Pembroke (USA))
4089[12] 6293[9] 6964[6] 7301[11]

Hobson *Eve Johnson Houghton* a70 79
5 b g Choisir(AUS) —Educating Rita (Emarati (USA))
1543[5] (1762) 2531[6] 3212[8] 3604[3] 4065[5] 5838[8] 7376[4]

Hogmaneigh (IRE) *Jim Goldie* a106 102
7 b g Namid—Magical Peace (IRE) (Magical Wonder (USA))
2759[12] 5944[21] 6175[24]

Hoh Hoh Hoh *Richard Price* a83 111
8 ch g Piccolo—Nesting (Thatching)
212[8] 446[6] 639[3] 916[9] 1471[9] 2745[16] 3430[10] 4401[15] 5967[10] 6374[12]

Hokoumah (USA) *Saeed Bin Suroor* a79 72
2 b c Elusive Quality(USA) —Silca's Sister (Inchinor)
3274[2] 3961[4] (5895)

Holbeck Ghyll (IRE) *Andrew Balding* a97 77
8 ch g Titus Livius(FR) —Crimada (IRE) (Mukaddamah (USA))
1471[8]

Holberg (UAE) *Saeed Bin Suroor* a112 117
4 b h Halling(USA) —Sweet Willa (USA) (Assert)
(2716) ◆ 3825[5] 5749[2] (6281) 7291a[6]

Holcombe Boy *Jeff Pearce* a66
2 b g Intikhab(USA) —Lady Lindsay (IRE) (Danehill Dancer (IRE))
6712[9] 7873[5] 7962[5]

Holden Eagle *Tony Newcombe* a62 79
5 b h Catcher In The Rye(IRE) —Bird Of Prey (IRE) (Last Tycoon)
2240[5] 6846[12]

Hold Me Back (USA) *William Mott* a120 103
4 bb h Giant's Causeway(USA) —Restraint (USA) (Unbridled's Song (USA))
5577a[8] 6586a[4]

Hold On Tiger (IRE) *Valentine Donoghue* a54 74
3 b g Acclamation—Our Juliette (IRE) (Namid)
1104[5] 1869[13] 3200[8] 3599[9] 4826[4] 5410[5] 6490[6] 7225[8] 7808[3]

Hold The Aces *John Joseph Murphy* a73 83
2 ch g Singspiel(IRE) —Katina (USA) (Danzig (USA))
6403a[7]

Hold The Bucks (USA) *Mrs A Malzard* a73 63
4 b g Hold That Tiger(USA) —Buck's Lady (USA) (Alleged (USA))
105[6] 200[5] 426[10] 586[4] (685) 780[10] 827[7] 929[6] (1815a) 2162a[4]

Hold The Star *Ann Stokell* a65 51
4 b m Red Ransom(USA) —Sydney Star (Machiavellian (USA))
38[6] 85[4] 235[5]

Holiday Cocktail *John Quinn* a64 69
8 b g Mister Baileys—Bermuda Lily (Dunbeath (USA))
565[5] 1012[6] 1427[4] 2851[9] 3950[4] 4411[2] 4708[7] 6051[9]

Holiday Snap *Mary Hambro* a75 70
4 ch m American Post—High Summer (USA) (Nureyev (USA))
5474[3] ◆ 6124[2] 7597[12]

Holkham *Nick Littmoden* a50 33
3 ch g Beat Hollow—Spring Sixpence (Dowsing (USA))
134[9] 217[5] 329[5]

Hollins *Micky Hammond* 89
6 b g Lost Soldier(USA) —Cutting Reef (IRE) (Kris)
(2060) 3195[9] 4467[6] 5278[11] 5492[6]

Hollow Green (IRE) *David Evans* a77 88
4 b m Beat Hollow—Three Greens (Niniski (USA))
785[4] 1011[2] ◆ 1282[4] (1783) 1837[3] 2282[6] 3388[5] 5444[7] 6131[4] 6516[8] 7101[13]

Hollow Jo *John Jenkins* a72 49
10 b g Most Welcome—Sir Hollow (USA) (Sir Ivor (USA))
(312) 325[4] 501[9] (658)

Hollow Tree *Andrew Balding* 73
2 b c Beat Hollow—Hesperia (Slip Anchor)
5582[8] 6159[7] 6689[3] 7059[9]

Hollyhocks (IRE) *Valentine Donoghue* 46
2 ch f Ad Valorem(USA) —Desert Blues (IRE) (Desert Prince (IRE))
1864[4] 2210[5] 6240[8]

Holly Rose (FR) *Robert Collet* a70 67
2 ch f Sevres Rose(IRE) —Hollyhead (FR) (Green Tune (USA))
5063a[8]

Hollywood Kiss (GER) *A Wohler* 110
3 ch c Paolini(GER) —Hollywood Love (GER) (Lomitas)
4420a[3]

Holy Arrangement (IRE) *Patrick Morris* 28
2 b f Holy Roman Emperor(IRE) —Queen Of Palms (IRE) (Desert Prince (IRE))
3549[6] 4402[7]

Holyfield Warrior (IRE) *Ralph Smith* a64 48
6 b g Princely Heir(IRE) —Perugino Lady (IRE) (Perugino (USA))
256[7] 603[7] 1078[11] 1225[10] 2232[5] 2636[4] 2955[9] 3263[7] 3521[4] 3967[5] 4434[8] 4689[8]

Holy Mackerel (IRE) *Mick Channon* a54 60
2 b c Cape Cross(IRE) —Sparky's Song (Electric)
5263[14] 5582[5] 5871[4] 6411[3] 6717[7]

Holyrood *T G McCourt* a75 87
4 b g Falbrav(IRE) —White Palace (Shirley Heights)
3492a[15]

Home *Brendan Powell* a58 56
5 b g Domedriver(IRE) —Swahili (IRE) (Kendor (FR))
995[2] 1193[11] 6021[5] 7995[5]

Home Advantage *Roger Charlton* a92 85
3 b c Beat Hollow—Houseproud (USA) (Riverman (USA))
1460[6] 1589[6] (2168) (3376) (3724) 4380[4] (5868) ◆ (6251)

Home Before Dark *Richard Whitaker* a39 29
4 b g Bertolini(USA) —Compton Girl (Compton Place)
2624[7] 3610[12]

Homeboy (IRE) *Marcus Tregoning* a63 62
2 b g Camacho—Berenica (IRE) (College Chapel)
4871[8] 5255[5] 6293[5] 6878[6] 7313[2] 7493[5]

Homeboykris (USA) *Richard Dutrow Jr* a113
3 b g Roman Ruler(USA) —One Last Salute (USA) (Salutely (USA))
1714a[16]

Home Office *Mark Johnston* a81 73
2 b c Nayef(USA) —Humility (Polar Falcon (USA))
6443[15] 6704[2] (7335)

Homepage *P Bary* 92
3 b f Dansili—Condition (Deploy)
6551a[5] 7546a[10]

Home Secretary *Garvan Donnelly* a81 77
6 b g Machiavellian(USA) —Darrery (Darshaan)
6730a[4] 7589a[4] 7823a[6]

Home Sweet Home (GER) *David Simcock* a48
3 ch f Traditionally(USA) —Homing Instinct (Arctic Tern (USA))
3768[8] 4475[9]

Honest Broker (IRE) *Mark Johnston* a76 83
3 b g Trade Fair—Kashra (IRE) (Dancing Dissident (USA))
73[4] (809) 1168[4] 1488[5] (3325) 4197[2] 4515[8] 4795[2] (5360) 5919[3] 6112[6]

Honest Buck *Kate Walton* 54
3 ch g Chineur(FR) —Noble Penny (Pennekamp (USA))
2425[7]

Honest Strike (USA) *Henry Cecil* a88 79
3 b c Smart Strike(CAN) —Honest Lady (USA) (Seattle Slew (USA))
3563[7] 4330[5] 6313[3] (6661)

Honeymead (IRE) *Richard Fahey* 84
2 b f Pivotal—Camaret (IRE) (Danehill (USA))
(2577) 3141[14] 5187[9] 5882[8] (6563) 7085[5]

Honey Of A Kitten (USA) *D K Weld* 78
2 b g Kitten's Joy(USA) —Sweet Baby Jane (USA) (Kingmambo (USA))
4175a[8]

Hong Kong Island (IRE) *George Foster* 74
3 br g Alhaarth(IRE) —Three Owls (IRE) (Warning)
1100[7] 1464[6] 1868[6] 3597[8] 5411[7] 6032[2] (6393) 6707[3] 7176[2]

Honimiere (IRE) *Alan Swinbank* a99 103
4 b m Fasliyev(USA) —Sugar (Hernando (FR))
1016[4] 1725[2] 2055[4] 3031[6] 3368[3] 4143[4] 5249[4] 6095[11]

Honkers Bonkers *Alan McCabe* a63 58
2 b g Val Royal(FR) —Amerissage (USA) (Rahy (USA))
5160[9] 5761[7] 6849[5] 7417[8] 7722[3]

Honneur Supreme (FR) *Y Barberot* 85
2 b f Baroud D'Honneur(FR) —Un Petit Tour (FR) (Double Bed (FR))
6589a[5]

Honorable Endeavor *Edward Vaughan* a63 61
4 b g Law Society(USA) —Lilac Dance (Fabulous Dancer (USA))
164[2] 1849[5] 2302[8] 2907[8] 4362[5] 4745[4] 5179[6] 5722[9] 5963[5] 6775[8]

Honor Breeze (USA) *Louise Best*
2 ch f Honor Glide(USA) —Blue Missy (USA) (Swain (IRE))
5724[11] 7408[12]

Honourable Knight (IRE) *Mark Usher* 70
2 b c Celtic Swing—Deemeh (IRE) (Brief Truce (USA))
1351[8] 1793[3] (2839) 4331[3] 4801[8] 5490[7]

Honoured (IRE) *Sir Mark Prescott Bt* a59 67
3 ch g Mark Of Esteem(IRE) —Traou Mad (IRE) (Barathea (IRE))
3153[2] ◆ 5414[2] 6526[3] 6747[10]

Hoodie (IRE) *Saeed Bin Suroor* a43 46
3 ch c Street Cry(IRE) —Something Mon (USA) (Maria's Mon (USA))
4205[8] 5026[8]

Hoof It *Michael Easterby* 106
3 b g Monsieur Bond(IRE) —Forever Bond (Danetime (IRE))
1298[8] (1750) (2099) (2494) 2978[13] 3856[5] ◆ 5250[7] 5911[18] 6364[2] (7079)

Hoofprintinthesnow *Amanda Perrett* 43
2 b c Footstepsinthesand—Spring Snowdrop (IRE) (Danehill Dancer (IRE))
6442[12]

Hooligan Sean *Henry Candy* a58 77
3 ch g Ishiguru(USA) —Sheesha (USA) (Shadeed (USA))
2842[4] 3511[6] 4146[3] 5677[6] 6056[8]

Hooray *Sir Mark Prescott Bt* a113 117
2 b f Invincible Spirit(IRE) —Hypnotize (Machiavellian (USA))
(2641) 3141[8] 3792[3] 5036[6] (5246) (5748) (6530)

Hoot (IRE) *Saeed Bin Suroor* a81 80
2 b c Invincible Spirit(IRE) —Roslea Lady (IRE) (Alhaarth (IRE))
3624[10] 5074[2] ◆ (5381) 5901[5]

Hopefull Blue (IRE) *James Evans* a47
4 b m High Chaparral(IRE) —Misbelief (Shirley Heights)
356[8] 585[9] 803[8] 1635[11] 7731[11]

Hope Of An Angel (IRE) *Niall Moran* a72 82
2 b f Intikhab(USA) —Faleh (USA) (Silver Hawk (USA))
6401a[6] 6784a[7]

Hope Road *Andrew Haynes* a53 76
6 ch g Sakhee(USA) —Bibliotheque (USA) (Woodman (USA))
186[4] 777[10]

Hopes And Fears (IRE) *M Al Muhairi* a57 80
5 b h Captain Rio—Saibhreas (IRE) (Last Tycoon)
706a[13]

Hope She Does (USA) *Linda Jewell* a44 50
3 ch f Johannesburg(USA) —Flirting (USA) (Pleasant Colony (USA))
985[8] 1870[5] 2755[11] 3479[9] 4791[14]

Hoppy's Flyer (FR) *Philip Kirby* a60 82
2 b f Country Reel(USA) —Madeleine's Blush (USA) (Rahy (USA))
1331[8] 1510[3] 2641[4] 3386[2] 4884a[3] 5252a[4] 5622a[9] 7172[3] 7536[3]

Hopscotch *Michael Bell* a48 28
2 br f Pivotal—Bonnie Doon (IRE) (Grand Lodge (USA))
7232[16] 7530[9]

Horatio Carter *Michael Smith* 99
5 b g Bahamian Bounty—Jitterbug (IRE) (Marju (IRE))
1397[9] 3448[2] 4370[5] 5068[6] 5302[11] 6357[8] 6962[11]

Horseradish *Michael Bell* a76 101
3 b g Kyllachy—Lihou Island (Beveled (USA))
(1279) 1701[3] (1836) (6049) 6363[3] 6888[7] (7348)

Horsewithnoname (IRE) *T G McCourt* a62 62
3 b g Daylami(IRE) —City Zone (IRE) (Zafonic (USA))
5411[5]

Horsley Warrior *Ed McMahon* a67 66
4 b g Alhaarth(IRE) —Polish Lake (Polish Precedent (USA))
787[5] 1172[3] 3032[9] 7531[9]

Hortensia (IRE) *Mick Channon* a78 81
2 b f Holy Roman Emperor(IRE) —Snippets (IRE) (Be My Guest (USA))
1375[4] 1626[2] (2088) 3141[19] 3583[2] 3859[4] 4696[4] 5140[2] (5358) 5639[4] 5921[2] 6307[2]

Hortensis *Tim Easterby* 63
2 ch f Iceman—Anthos (GER) (Big Shuffle (USA))
2654[4] 3087[6] 3550[3] 4242[3] 4480[2] 6182[3] 6719[14] 6892[5] 7118[5] 7347[11]

Hosanna *J Barclay* a67 56
4 b m Oasis Dream—Rada's Daughter (Robellino (USA))
1200[10] 1569[14] 1869[10] 2293[2] 2454[8] 2854[11] 3164[4] 3357[9] 3706[2] 3948[2] 3990[5] 4515[13] 4824[9] 5405[8]

Hosiba (GER) *R Rohne* 94
3 b f Black Sam Bellamy(IRE) —Hosina (GER) (Goofalik (USA))
3495a[3]

Hot Cha Cha (USA) *Phillip A Sims* a103 113
4 bb m Cactus Ridge(USA) —Reduced Sentence (USA) (Broad Brush (USA))
5320a[2] 7343a[5]

Hotfoot *John Berry* 58
3 ch f Desert Sun—Heneseys Leg (Sure Blade (USA))
3738[11] 4425[6] 4997[6] 5414[11]

Hotgrove Boy *George Foster* 44
3 b g Tobougg(IRE) —Tanwir (Unfuwain (USA))
1145[9] 1971[12] 2673[8] 3148[7] 4408[8]

Hotham *Noel Wilson* a85 101
7 b g Komaite(USA) —Malcesine (IRE) (Auction Ring (USA))
1032[5] 1423[10] 1688[11] 2465[3] 2759[13] (2940) 3406[3] 3489a[13] (3919) 5183[13] 5944[17] 6175[13] 6918[13] 7079[18]

Hot Prospect *Michael Jarvis* 116
3 b c Motivator—Model Queen (USA) (Kingmambo (USA))
1310[3] 1910[3] 2746[9] 3824[5] (4830) 5539[2] 6281[4] 7096[6]

Hot Pursuits *Hughie Morrison* a75 83
3 br f Pastoral Pursuits—Perfect Partner (Be My Chief (USA))
1546[3] ◆ 4531[2] (5285)

Hot Rod Mamma (IRE) *Dianne Sayer* a42 59
3 ch f Traditionally(USA) —Try The Air (IRE) (Foxhound (USA))
1118[9] 3027[7] 3710[7] 4337[9] 4408[7] (5024) 5820[2] 6644[3]

Hot Six (BRZ) *P Bary* a102 104
5 gr h Burooj—Babysix (USA) (With Approval (CAN))
419a[2] 605a[10] 5575a[10]

Hot Spark *John Akehurst* a73 88
3 b c Firebreak—On The Brink (Mind Games)
751[2] 1190[3] 1401[3] 1991[4] (2112) 2394[6] 2884[2] 3394[4] 3731[4] (4593) 4995[5] 5524[2]

Hot Spice *John Dunlop* 65
2 b g Kodiac—Harlestone Lady (Shaamit (IRE))
5836[5] 6278[10] 6827[6]

Hot Toddie *James Given* a9 32
2 b f Firebreak—Bebe De Cham (Tragic Role (USA))
6566[8] 6894[10] 7309[10]

Houda (IRE) *Jonathan Portman* a31 48
3 ch f Trans Island—Islandagore (IRE) (Indian Ridge)
1302[11] 7633[9]

Hounds Ditch *Eve Johnson Houghton* a60 60
3 b g Avonbridge—Pudding Lane (IRE) (College Chapel)
1661[9] 2164[4] 2408[6] 2903[6] 3359[6] 3685[6] 4249[6] 5585[9]

Houngun (USA) *Dennis J Manning* 70
3 ch c Tiger Ridge(USA) —Chaposa (USA) (Wild Event (USA))
4642a[5]

House Point *Stuart Williams* 57
3 b f Pivotal—Lighthouse (Warning)
2003[7] 3091[9] 5631[9] 6460[3] 6860[13] 7005[5] 7153[7]

House Red (IRE) *B W Hills* a74 71
3 b g Antonius Pius(USA) —Cindy's Star (IRE) (Dancing Dissident (USA))
218[2] 382[2]

Houston Dynimo (IRE) *Nicky Richards* a76 47
5 b g Rock Of Gibraltar(IRE) —Quiet Mouse (USA) (Quiet American (USA))
255[4] (546) 852[4] 996[2] 6109[11] 6573[7] 7055[10] 7463[3] 7861[2]

Hovering Hawk (IRE) *B W Hills* a38
3 b f Hawk Wing(USA) —Cause Celebre (IRE) (Peintre Celebre (USA))
106[9]

Howards Prince *Donal Nolan* a6 22
7 gr g Bertolini(USA) —Grey Princess (IRE) (Common Grounds)
1723[11] 2213[12] 2669[11]

Ho Ya Mal (IRE) *Ed Dunlop* a77
2 ch c Shamardal(USA) —Ridotto (Salse (USA))
(7427) ◆

Hubble Space *Marco Botti* a56
3 ch f Observatory(USA) —Double Stake (USA) (Kokand (USA))
5[3] 168[5]

Hucking Hero (IRE) *Tim Vaughan* a76 73
5 b g Iron Mask(USA) —Selkirk Flyer (Selkirk (USA))
(612)

Huckle Duckle (IRE) *Phil McEntee* a19
2 b f Chineur(FR) —Flash And Dazzle (IRE) (Bertolini (USA))
1017[11] 1065[8] 1324[12] 6058[11] 6884[10] 6995[6] 7396[10]

Hudoo *Saeed Bin Suroor* a70 72
3 ch f Halling(USA) —Zarara (USA) (Manila (USA))
2219[5]

Hudson Steele (USA) *Todd Pletcher* 101
3 bb g Johannesburg(USA) —Strike The Sky (USA) (Smart Strike (CAN))
(4642a)

Huff And Puff *Amanda Perrett* a75 79
3 b g Azamour(IRE) —Coyote (Indian Ridge)
(1479) 2079[5]

Hugely Exciting *J S Moore* a65
2 b c Bahamian Bounty—Princess Louise (Efisio)
7186[5]

Hugo Quick *John Spearing* a52 49
6 b g Zaha(CAN) —Skedaddle (Formidable (USA))
7407[12] 7704[P]

Hujaylea (IRE) *M Halford* a87 104
7 b g Almutawakel—Red Eagle (IRE) (Eagle Eyed (USA))
(5571a) (5774a)

Hulcote Rose (IRE) *Sylvester Kirk* a97 74
3 b f Rock Of Gibraltar(IRE) —Siksikawa (Mark Of Esteem (IRE))
(1537) 2042[6] 3628[4] 3866[8] 5083[4] 5713[4] 5896[4] 6291[7] 6479[3] 6879[2] 7319[7] (7525) (7665) (7915) ◆

Humble And Hungry (USA) *Ignacio Correas IV* a85 105
2 b c Limehouse(USA) —Cukee (USA) (Langfuhr (CAN))
7360a[8]

Humdrum *Richard Hannon* 82
2 b f Dr Fong(USA) —Spinning Top (Alzao (USA))
3296[11] 5147[2] ◆ 5441[2] (6353) 6563[2] ◆ (7059)

Humidor (IRE) *George Baker* 94
3 b g Camacho—Miss Indigo (Indian Ridge)
1731[6] (2114) 2822[2] ◆ 3311[2] (5417) (6280) (6739)

Humor Me Rene (USA) *George Baker* a66 78
3 bb f Kitten's Joy(USA) —Star Of Humor (USA) (Distorted Humor (USA))
(7495) 7736[7]

Humourous (IRE) *Brian Storey* 46
8 b g Darshaan—Amusing Time (IRE) (Sadler's Wells (USA))
2765[9]

Humungous (IRE) *Charles Egerton* a67 87
7 ch g Giant's Causeway(USA) —Doula (USA) (Gone West (USA))
7182[13] 7560[11] 7688[5]

Hung Parliament (FR) *Tom Dascombe* a80 107
2 b c Numerous(USA) —Sensational Mover (USA) (Theatrical)
4135[4] 4565a[2] (5133a) 5799a[2]

Huntdown (USA) *Saeed Bin Suroor* 111
4 ch h Elusive Quality(USA) —Infinite Spirit (USA) (Maria's Mon (USA))
6147[4] 6735[6]

Hunters Belt (IRE) *Noel Wilson* a70 73
6 b g Intikhab(USA) —Three Stars (Star Appeal)
468[7] 718[2] 1103[3] 2285[9] 2941[2] 3709[4] 4781[8] 6109[13] 7176[6] (7330) 7541[3]

Hunter's Light (IRE) *Saeed Bin Suroor* a76
2 ch c Dubawi(IRE) —Portmanteau (Barathea (IRE))
7478[2]

Hunterview *David Pipe* a96 98
4 ch g Reset(AUS) —Mount Elbrus (Barathea (IRE))
6736[11]

Huntingfortreasure *Michael Dods* 77
3 b g Pastoral Pursuits—Treasure Trove (USA) (The Minstrel (CAN))
(1927) 2466[5] 6105[7] 6467[9] 6984[14]

Hunting Tartan *John Gosden* 92
3 b c Oasis Dream—Delta (Zafonic (USA))
1732[6] 2028[6] 3429[5]

Hunting Tower (SAF) *M F De Kock* a107 112
8 ch g Fort Wood(USA) —Stirrup Cup (SAF) (Royal Chalice (SAF))
338a[9] 440a[9] 607a[8] 708a[6] 823a[5]

Hunza Dancer (IRE) *John Gosden* 75
2 b f Danehill Dancer(IRE) —Hawala (IRE) (Warning)
7001[3]

Hurakan (IRE) *David Evans* a79 53
4 gr g Daylami(IRE) —Gothic Dream (IRE) (Nashwan (USA))
151[4] 239[4] (497) (746) (827) 841[2]

Hurlingham *Michael Easterby* a77 81
6 b g Halling(USA) —Society (IRE) (Barathea (IRE))
1398[6] ◆ 1883[6] 2579[8] 3060[4] 4656[2] 5363[4] 5631[2] 5888[7] 6650[9] 7228[4]

Hurricane Guest *George Margarson* 9
2 ch g Hurricane Run(IRE) —Figlette (Darshaan)
6618[12] 6653[3]

Hurricane Havoc (IRE) *J S Bolger* 90
2 b f Hurricane Run(IRE) —Cheeky Madam (IRE) (Night Shift (USA))
6784a[3] 6927[6]

Hurricane Hymnbook (USA) *Willie Musson* a83 81
5 b g Pulpit(USA) —April Squall (USA) (Summer Squall (USA))
1625[9] 3083[8] 5142[10] 6252[10] 6701[9] 7182[10] 7483[10]

Hurricane Ike (USA) *John W Sadler* a110
3 bb c Graeme Hall(USA) —Parental Uproar (USA) (Future Storm (USA))
7365a[9]

Hurricane Lady (IRE) *Walter Swinburn* a70
2 b f Hurricane Run(IRE) —Yaria (IRE) (Danehill (USA))
6451[7] ◆ 6994[3] 7448[2]

Hurricane Spear *Gary Moore* 39
2 ch g Hurricane Run(IRE) —Sarissa (USA) (Diesis)
4577[8] 5676[8]

Hurricane Spirit (IRE) *John Best* a88 97
6 b g Invincible Spirit(IRE) —Gale Warning (IRE) (Last Tycoon)
1306[5] 1767[5] 3083[5] 3565[5]

Hurricane Thomas (IRE) *Richard Fahey* a61 64
6 b g Celtic Swing—Viola Royale (IRE) (Royal Academy (USA))
3028[5] 3122[7] 3684[2] 3978[5] (4453) 4511[2] 5019[8] 5530[4] 6269[7] 6518[14] 6890[14] (7184) 7323[9]

Hurtle Myrtle (AUS) *Matthew A Smith* 105
4 b f Dane Shadow(AUS) —Ravenswood (AUS) (Woodman (USA))
5

Hustle (IRE) *Gay Kelleway* a85 91
5 ch g Choisir(AUS) —Granny Kelly (USA) (Irish River (FR))
1428[9] 1779[7] 2123[7] 2750[3] (3458) 4108[14] 4438[6] 5235[7] 6164[8] 6713[4]

Huwayit (IRE) *Clive Brittain* a60
2 ch f Dalakhani(IRE) —Matin De Tempete (FR) (Cardoun (FR))
3562[7]

Huygens *Denis Coakley* a98 95
3 b g Zafeen(FR) —Lindfield Belle (IRE) (Fairy King (USA))
(1018) ◆ 1497[3] ◆ 2324[8] 4144[5] 5970[5]

Huzzah (IRE) *B W Hills* a89 105
5 b g Acclamation—Borders Belle (IRE) (Pursuit Of Love)
1008[11] 1383[17] 1900[6] ◆ 2595[10] 2971[4] 4224[6] 4459[11] 6204[6] 7012[8]

Hyades (USA) *B Cecil* a96 108
4 b h Aldebaran(USA) —Lingerie (Shirley Heights)
4417a[5]

Hyde Lea Flyer *Ed McMahon* a84 48
5 b g Hernando(FR) —Sea Ridge (Slip Anchor)
668[6]

Hyden (IRE) *Thomas Gibney* a53
4 br g Mull Of Kintyre(USA) —Katies Crown (IRE) (Royal Abjar (USA))
7505[10]

Hydrant *Peter Salmon* a73 76
4 b g Haafhd—Spring (Sadler's Wells (USA))
352[3] 468[2] (718) 1751[5] 2579[3] 3499[3] 3860[5]

Hygrove Gal *Bryan Smart* a31 68
2 b f Auction House(USA) —Vida (IRE) (Wolfhound (USA))
6111[2] ◆ 6646[4] 7268[6] 7493[10]

Hymnsheet *Sir Michael Stoute* a91 86
3 b f Pivotal—Choir Mistress (Chief Singer)
2076[5] 5723[4] 6251[6]

Hyperspace *Henry Cecil* a67
3 b f Dansili—Spacecraft (USA) (Distant View (USA))
1621[5]

Hypnosis *Noel Wilson* a70 84
7 b m Mind Games—Salacious (Sallust)
2431[3] 2756[5] 2940[11] 3622[3] 4243[7] 5855[14] 6708[7] 7193[3] 7446[4]

Hypnotic Gaze (IRE) *John Mackie* a77 72
4 b g Chevalier(IRE) —Red Trance (IRE) (Soviet Star (USA))
144[7] 298[2] 543[3] 715[6] 994[2] (4433) 4719[4] 5765[3]

Hypnotist (UAE) *Clive Brittain* a74 73
4 b g Halling(USA) —Poised (USA) (Rahy (USA))
393[10] 808[2] 907[7] 3124[11] 3524[7]

Hypnotized (USA) *Michael Bell* a92 97
3 b c Elusive Quality(USA) —Delighted (IRE) (Danehill (USA))
(1480) 1703[4] 2225[2] ◆ 3103[17] ◆ 5030[6] 6318[7]

Iasia (GR) *Jane Chapple-Hyam* a70 97
4 b m One Cool Cat(USA) —Alanis (Warning)
3890[7] 4849[4] 6167[10]

Ibbetson (USA) *Alison Thorpe* a71 65
5 bb g Street Cry(IRE) —Object Of Virtue (USA) (Partners Hero (USA))
120[7] 148[10]

Ibn Bajjah (FR) *Saeed Bin Suroor* a80
2 b c King's Best(USA) —Grecian Slipper (Sadler's Wells (USA))
(7470)

Ibn Battuta (USA) *M Al Muhairi* a104 114
5 ch h Seeking The Gold(USA) —Sulk (IRE) (Selkirk (USA))
631a[3] 801a[4] 1025a[7]

Ibn Hiyyan (USA) *Mark Johnston* a73 60
3 rg g El Prado(IRE) —Lovely Later (USA) (Green Dancer (USA))
1067[2] (1145)

Ibn Khaldun (USA) *Saeed Bin Suroor* 100
5 ch h Dubai Destination(USA) —Gossamer (Sadler's Wells (USA))
631a[8] 801a[8]

Ibrox (IRE) *Alan Brown* a76 73
5 b g Mujahid(USA) —Ling Lane (Slip Anchor)
3[3] 5646[7]

Ibsaar *William Haggas* 76
2 gr g Red Ransom(USA) —Mosquera (GER) (Acatenango (GER))
4614[5] 5594[3] (5936) 6386[6]

Ice Angel *Derek Shaw*
2 b f Iceman—Someone's Angel (USA) (Runaway Groom (CAN))
7527[10]

Iceblast *Michael Easterby* 76
2 b g Iceman—Medici Princess (Medicean)
6722[3] ◆ 7346[6]

Ice Blue *P Bary* 112
3 b c Dansili—Winter Solstice (Unfuwain (USA))
(1947a) 2802a[7] 4039a[8]

Ice Box (USA) *Nicholas Zito* a119
3 ch c Pulpit(USA) —Spice Island (USA) (Tabasco Cat (USA))
1714a[2] 2776a[8] 4643a[6] 5544a[8]

Icebuster *Rod Millman* a51
2 ch g Iceman—Radiate (Sadler's Wells (USA))
7479[8] 7880[5]

Ice Cold Bex *Philip McBride* 71
2 ch c Iceman—Musica (Primo Dominie)
4142[5] 4549[5] 5204[2]

Ice Cool Lady (IRE) *Walter Swinburn* a72 72
3 gr f Verglas(IRE) —Cafe Creme (IRE) (Catrail (USA))
1453[7] 1934[5] 2491[5] 3212[9] 5669[7] 6168[2] 6540[10] 7037[2] (7298) 7890[9]

Ice Diva *Paul D'Arcy* a71 83
3 gb f Verglas(IRE) —La Coqueta (GER) (Kris)
1159[6] 1608[2] ◆ (2219) 4098[2] 4571[7] 5096[5]

Ice Empress (IRE) *A P O'Brien* a72 74
3 gr f Danehill Dancer(IRE) —Moon Festival (Be My Guest (USA))
1036a[8] 4178a[12]

Ice Girl *Michael Easterby* 54
2 b f Iceman—Descriptive (IRE) (Desert King (IRE))
2939[15] 5785[7] 6034[9] 6264[7]

Icelady *Robert Cowell* 43
2 b f Iceman—Nursling (IRE) (Kahyasi)
5160[12] 5558[3] 6058[7] 7118[7] 7393[9]

Icelandic *Frank Sheridan* a87 107
8 b g Selkirk(USA) —Icicle (Polar Falcon (USA))
1662[9] 2119[7] 4832[15] 6327[10] 6625[4] 6962[3] (7143) 7351[8] 7522[10]

Ice Magic *Mark H Tompkins* a61 59
2 b c Iceman—Naomi Wildman (USA) (Kingmambo (USA))
2621[4] 4346[9] 5178[4] 6059[4] 6810[8]

Iceman George *Giles Bravery* a65 67
6 b g Beat Hollow—Diebiedale (Dominion)
457[7] 720[13] 1478[4] (2006) (2303) 3608[2] 4102[7] 6669[3]

Ice Nelly (IRE) *Hughie Morrison* a58 57
2 b f Iceman—Dancing Nelly (Shareef Dancer (USA))
6802[7] 7163[4] 7470[3]

Ice Road Trucker (IRE) *Jim Boyle* a55 40
3 ch g Bertolini(USA) —Bye Bold Aileen (IRE) (Warning)
5658[9] 5971[11] 6638[5] 7166[6] 7717[9] 7829[6] 7874[4]

Ice Trooper *Linda Stubbs* 73
2 b g Iceman—Out Like Magic (Magic Ring (IRE))
1986[4] 2522[2] 2832[5] 4336[2] (4512)

Ice Viking (IRE) *James Given* a68 77
3 b g Danehill Dancer(IRE) —Maddelina (IRE) (Sadler's Wells (USA))
1310[14] 1422[3] 1830[3] 2620[7] 2935[2] 4128[2] 4618[3] 4786[2] 5631[5] 6225[8] 6816[6] 7181[16] 7538[7]

Icon Dream (IRE) *David Wachman* 105
3 b g Sadler's Wells(USA) —Silver Skates (IRE) (Slip Anchor)
1414a[6] 1833[2] 2367a[4] 3145[10] 4829[6] 5772a[5] 6736[9]

I Confess *David Evans* a85 83
5 br g Fantastic Light(USA) —Vadsagreya (FR) (Linamix (FR))
123[5] 275[6] 393[3] 487[3] 587[2] 1877[6] 3391[3] 4133[3] 4260[9] 5325[2] 6439[12] 6853[6] (7627) 7992[2]

Icy Blue *Richard Whitaker* 70
2 b g Iceman—Bridal Path (Groom Dancer (USA))
4480[6] 5117[6] 5546[5] 6325[3] 6704[4] 6919[2] 7172[5] 7347[5]

Idealism *John Gosden* 76
3 b g Motivator—Fickle (Danehill (USA))
1386[5]

Idiom (IRE) *Mahmood Al Zarooni* 82
2 ch f Iffraaj—Alexander Confranc (IRE) (Magical Wonder (USA))
2088[4] (2461) 3141[21] 3872[9] 6317[10]

Idle Power (IRE) *Jim Boyle* a71 79
12 b g Common Grounds—Idle Fancy (Mujtahid (USA))
486[12] 696[7] 1076[6]

Idol Deputy (FR) *Mark Usher* a45
4 gr g Silver Deputy(CAN) —Runaway Venus (USA) (Runaway Groom (CAN))
815[9] 889[10] 1536[10] 2337[12]

I Dreamed A Dream *Dean Ivory* a24
2 b f Tobougg(IRE) —Janaah (In The Wings)
2641[9] 3035[14] 3562[13]

I Feel Fine *Alan Kirtley* a46 35
7 ch m Minster Son—Jendorcet (Grey Ghost)
923[6] 1273[7] 1801[10] 2085[7]

If I Had Him (IRE) *George Baker* a70 59
6 b g City Honours(USA) —Our Valentine (IRE) (Be My Native (USA))
1983[2] ◆ (2302) (2476) 6933[4]

If I Were A Boy (IRE) *Dominic Ffrench Davis* a78 83
3 b f Invincible Spirit(IRE) —Attymon Lill (IRE) (Marju (IRE))
33[3] 2079[11] 3963[7] (4056) 4422[2] 4573[10] 5728[8] 6438[7] 6556[7] 6957[9]

If Only *Dave Morris* a61 60
4 ch g Monsieur Bond(IRE) —La Belle Dominique (Dominion)
1534[9] 2299[12] 2678[10] 5169[5] 5388[4] 5715[3] 6133[4] 6672[4]

If Per Chance (IRE) *M Halford* a88 96
5 b g Danetime(IRE) —Zafaraya (IRE) (Ashkalani (IRE))
1408a[10] 4463a[4]

If What And Maybe *John Ryan* a47 57
2 ch c Needwood Blade—Pink Champagne (Cosmonaut)
6092[16] 6504[10] 7152[8] 7552[7]

If You Knew Suzy *Ron Barr* a67 56
5 b m Efisio—Sioux (Kris)
21[10] 113[7]

If You Whisper (IRE) *Mike Murphy* a72 49
2 b g Iffraaj—Little Whisper (IRE) (Be My Guest (USA))
5717[6] ◆ 6158[14] 7610[2] (7893)

Igitur *William Knight* a57
2 ch f Nayef(USA) —Vrennan (Suave Dancer (USA))
7559[12] 7733[5]

Ignatieff (IRE) *Linda Stubbs* 84
3 b g Fasliyev(USA) —Genial Jenny (IRE) (Danehill (USA))
1399[7] 1656[4] 2179[2] 2822[3] (3225) 4541[8] 4901[3] 5335[9]

Igneous *David Thompson* a30 47
4 ch g Lucky Story(USA) —Double Top (IRE) (Thatching)
5821[8] 6037[10]

Ignore *Ruth Carr* a31 41
3 b g Bertolini(USA) —Amalie (IRE) (Fasliyev (USA))
699[11] 858[6] 915[8] 1118[11] 3228[3] 3988[5]

Ignore The Advice (IRE) *J S Moore* a52 52
2 b g Chevalier(IRE) —Golden Charm (IRE) (Common Grounds)
3785[9] 4323[8] 4528[3] 5000[10] 5667[3] 6072[9]

Igotim *Paul Burgoyne* a40 36
4 b g Umistim—Glistening Silver (Puissance)
234[13]

I Got Music *Keith Reveley* 49
3 gr f Silver Patriarch(IRE) —I Got Rhythm (Lycius (USA))
1116[8] 1271[7] 1572[7] 2606[8] 6038[8] 6649[3]

I Got You Babe (IRE) *Richard Guest* 59
2 gr f Clodovil(IRE) —Duck Over (Warning)
4702[10] 6075[5] 6488[3] 6892[4] 7347[7]

Igoyougo *Geoffrey Harker* 83
4 b g Millkom—Club Oasis (Forzando)
(1710) 2136[6] 2431[7] 4090[10]

Iguacu *George Baker* a61 58
6 b g Desert Prince(IRE) —Gay Gallanta (USA) (Woodman (USA))
2230[4] 2604[4] 2870[3] 3128[8] 6662[8] 7039[5] (7508) 7727[6] 7759[5] (7996)

Iguazu Falls (USA) *M bin Shafya* a65 93
5 ch g Pivotal—Anna Palariva (IRE) (Caerleon (USA))
416a[11] 606a[11]

I Hate To Lose (USA) *Philip McBride* a59
2 b f Medaglia D'Oro(USA) —My Alibi (USA) (Sheikh Albadou)
6451[8]

Ihavenotime (IRE) *Mick Channon* 69
2 ch f Refuse To Bend(IRE) —Finnmark (Halling (USA))
4844[13] 5170[5] 5633[3] 5857[2] 6302[5] 6809[10]

Ijaaza (USA) *Ed Dunlop* 37
3 b f Storm Cat(USA) —Sierra Madre (FR) (Baillamont (USA))
5265[6]

Il Battista *Alan McCabe* a85 69
2 b g Medicean—Peace (Sadler's Wells (USA))
2701[6] 3112[3] 4447[4] 4993[4] (5644) 5901[6] 7324[2] 7444[4]

Ildiko (USA) *Sir Mark Prescott Bt* a63 41
3 b f Yes It's True(USA) —Eternity (Suave Dancer (USA))
4134[9] 4972[8] 6290[14] 7003[5]

Il Divo (GER) *A Wohler* 100
5 bb h Dashing Blade—Independent Miss (GER) (Polar Falcon (USA))
1420a[4] 3251a[6]

Il Fenomeno (ITY) *B Grizzetti* 101
4 b h Denon(USA) —Fabulous Charm (ITY) (Fabulous Dancer (USA))
(1943a) 6239a[7]

Il Forno *Ian Williams* a69 77
3 b g Exceed And Excel(AUS) —Fred's Dream (Cadeaux Genereux)
208[3] (313) 702[4] 886[2] 1058[7] 1511[3] (1604) 3276[11]

Ilie Nastase (FR) *Conor Dore* a90 93
6 b g Royal Applause—Flying Diva (Chief Singer)
(230) 359[3] 466[3] (623) 749[3] ◆ 827[2] 1088[11] 1219[5] 1481[4] 1767[7] 2124[6] 3083[11] 3565[6] 4024[7] 4713[2] 5050[3] 5237[2] 5624[5] 7274[4] 7488[10] 7988[4]

Ilissos (USA) *Jeremy Noseda* a59
2 b c Mineshaft(USA) —Ema Bovary (CHI) (Edgy Diplomat (USA))
7873[7]

Ilkley *Michael Easterby* 44
3 b f Fantastic Light(USA) —Zakuska (Zafonic (USA))
2899[5] 3238[7] 5423[P] 7149[12]

Illandrane (IRE) *Ed Dunlop* 75
2 b f Cape Cross(IRE) —Lalindi (IRE) (Cadeaux Genereux)
6155[14] 6559[15]

Illawalla *Hugh McWilliams* 28
2 b g Indesatchel(IRE) —Adorable Cherub (USA) (Halo (USA))
2376[11] 2832[15] 6075[12] 6458[9]

I'Lldoit *James Evans* a56 16
3 br g Tamayaz(CAN) —Club Oasis (Forzando)
894[6] 1222[8] 6536[11] 6865[6]

Illicit *John Holt* a65 33
5 b g Oasis Dream—Daring Miss (Sadler's Wells (USA))
1078[8] 1492[10]

Illmindu (IRE) *Rod Millman* a47 51
2 gr f Exceed And Excel(AUS) —Alphilda (Ezzoud (IRE))
4517[5] 5466[6] 5763[6] 6259[8] 6697[5]

Illo (GER) *J Hirschberger* 105
4 b h Tertullian(USA) —Iora (GER) (Konigsstuhl (GER))
3251a[3] 5542a[6] 6606a[2]

Illuminative (USA) *Zoe Davison* a74 70
4 b g Point Given(USA) —Pretty Clear (USA) (Mr Prospector (USA))
1430[4] 1579[10] 2081[8] 2414[4] 4227[9] 4498[8] 5172[7]

Illustrious Blue *William Knight* a110 117
7 bb h Dansili—Gipsy Moth (Efisio)
516a[9] 820a[9] 903[4] 1220[3] (1615) 2469[4] 3695[2] (4506) 5218[5] 7291a[9]

Illustrious Forest *John Mackie* 59
2 ch c Shinko Forest(IRE) —Illustre Inconnue (USA) (Septieme Ciel (USA))
4755[7] 5498[6] 6159[8]

Illustrious Prince (IRE) *Jeremy Noseda* a88 86
3 b g Acclamation—Sacred Love (IRE) (Barathea (IRE))
(1164) 3215[5] 4104[5] 4929[7] 6197[3] (6501) 6798[9]

I Love Me *Andrew Balding* 102
2 b f Cape Cross(IRE) —Garanciere (FR) (Anabaa (USA))
(6200) 6559[5] 6927[3] ◆

Il Portico *Mick Channon* a61 62
3 b g Zafeen(FR) —Diddymu (IRE) (Revoque (IRE))
(1054) 1422[6] 1866[2] 2412[12] 2909[10] 3532[3] 3820[3] 4328[8] 4745[3] 5534[2] 5923[4]

I'm A Cracker (IRE) *D Gambarota*
2 b c Elusive City(USA) —Cherry Chase (IRE) (Red Sunset)
7849a[5]

I'm A Dreamer (IRE) *David Simcock* 103
3 b f Noverre(USA) —Summer Dreams (IRE) (Sadler's Wells (USA))
(1278) (1850) ◆ (3217) ◆ 4319[5] ◆ 6346[3] ◆

Imaginary Diva *George Margarson* a55 60
4 b m Lend A Hand—Distant Diva (Distant Relative)
3994[8] (4659) 5377[3] 5562[5] 5876[3] 6133[8] 7537[11]

Imaginary World (IRE) *Alan McCabe* a69 39
2 b f Exceed And Excel(AUS) —Plutonia (Sadler's Wells (USA))
3964[8] 4286[7] 4909[8] 5602[10] 6795[5] (7197) 7536[2] 7758[3]

Imagination (IRE) *Richard Brabazon* a69
3 b f Marju(IRE) —Height Of Fantasy (IRE) (Shirley Heights)
7244[2] (7451)

Imbongi (SAF) *M F De Kock* a115 120
6 ch g Russian Revival(USA) —Garden Verse (SAF) (Foveros)
438a[2] 631a[2] (823a) 1025a[3]

Ime Not Bitter *Bill Moore* a47 10
2 b g Needwood Blade—Gymcrak Flyer (Aragon)
6045[7] 6365[10] 6712[10]

I'm Frank *Alan Swinbank* 68
4 ch g Medicean—Poiana (Pivotal)
1100[6] 1485[4] 1721[3] 2392[8] 3025[10]

I'm In The Pink (FR) *David Evans* a79 80
6 b g Garuda(IRE) —Ahwaki (FR) (River Mist (USA))
220[5] 300[4] 1077[3] 1863[2] 2314[8] 2922[7] 7756[7]

Imjin River (IRE) *Mark H Tompkins* a79 75
3 b g Namid—Lady Nasrana (FR) (Al Nasr (FR))
1279[10] 2099[3] 2599[5] 3174[7]

Immacolata (IRE) *Alan Berry*
2 gr f Aussie Rules(USA) —Mujadilly (Mujadil (USA))
2292[6] 4123[13] 5640[8] 7172[11]

Immaculate Red *C Roberts* a35 54
7 ch g Woodborough(USA) —Primula Bairn (Bairn (USA))
354[11]

Immortal Verse (IRE) *Robert Collet* 94
2 b f Pivotal—Side Of Paradise (IRE) (Sadler's Wells (USA))
5899a[2]

Immovable (USA) *Mikael Magnusson* 64
3 b g Rock Of Gibraltar(IRE) —Passive Action (USA) (Double Negative (USA))
4307[10] 4661[8] 4906[7] ◆ 5670[9]

Imogen Louise (IRE) *Derek Haydn Jones* a43 69
2 gr f Verglas(IRE) —Strina (IRE) (Indian Ridge)
2440[4] 5147[3] 5808[2] 6259[3] 6954[5] 7493[6]

Im Ova Ere Dad (IRE) *Don Cantillon* a82 87
7 b g Second Empire(IRE) —Eurolink Profile (Prince Sabo)
245[3] ◆

Imperial Delight *Henry Candy* a57 86
3 b g Royal Applause—Playgirl (IRE) (Caerleon (USA))
1663[7] (2197) (2682) 3696[4] 6478[12] 6805[2]

Imperial Djay (IRE) *Ruth Carr* a66 45
5 b g Dilshaan—Slayjay (IRE) (Mujtahid (USA))
794[5] 866[4] 1050[3] (1236) ◆ 1509[6] (1812) 2188[8] 2381[4] (2531) 2764[2] (3062) 3150[2] 3396[7] 4394[4] 4598[6] 4850[3] 5043[2] 6625[11]

Imperial Fong *David Elsworth* a49 50
2 b f Dr Fong(USA) —Chine (Inchinor)
7232[11] 7479[7]

Imperial Guest *George Margarson* 101
4 ch g Imperial Dancer—Princess Speedfit (FR) (Desert Prince (IRE))
(1438) 2563[8] 3146[3] 3869[13] 4358[7] ◆ 4843[3] 5393[5] 5911[2] 6349[3] 6888[4]

Imperial House *Ronald Harris* a73 67
4 b h Imperial Dancer—Cotton House (IRE) (Mujadil (USA))
(78) 2223[8] 464[10] 695[6] 1595[3] 1923[14] 3966[7] 4839[11] 5027[8]

Imperialistic Diva (IRE) *Tim Easterby* 99
2 ch f Haafhd—Imperialistic (IRE) (Imperial Ballet (IRE))
2238[2] 2448[4] (2936) 3453[3] 4356[4] 5246[5] 5880[15] 6563[4]

Imperial Look *Ed McMahon* a54 66
2 b c Royal Applause—Look Here's Carol (IRE) (Safawan)
3274[6] 3756[5] 4432[7] (5389) 6717[8]

Imperial Pirouette *Mick Channon* 39
2 b f Imperial Dancer—Canadian Capers (Ballacashtal (CAN))
4921[6] 5885[5] 6150[P]

Imperial Skylight *Mick Channon* a68 58
4 gr g Imperial Dancer—Sky Light Dreams (Dreams To Reality (USA))
135[7] 320[2] 388[5] 530[2] 567[8] 763[8] 976[8] 1114[7]

Imperial Waltzer *George Moore* 55
2 gr g Imperial Dancer—Sky Light Dreams (Dreams To Reality (USA))
1073[6] 1360[3] 1806[9] 4701[10] 5020[6]

Imperial Warrior *Hughie Morrison* a57 71
3 ch g Imperial Dancer—Tribal Lady (Absalom)
1476[9] 1873[4] 2844[6] 4589[11] 5891[7] 6522[12]

Imperium *Jean-Rene Auvray* a62 65
9 b g Imperial Ballet(IRE) —Partenza (USA) (Red Ransom (USA))
100[10] 229[5] 591[3] 691[9]

Imposing *Sir Michael Stoute* 111
4 b h Danehill Dancer(IRE) —On Fair Stage (IRE) (Sadler's Wells (USA))
(2027) 3194[2] 3921[6]

Impossible Time (CAN) *Roger L Attfield* a103 94
5 b m Not Impossible(IRE) —Classiest Carat (CAN) (Pleasant Colony (USA))
7371a[2]

Impressible *Stuart Williams* a52 96
4 b m Oasis Dream—Imperial Bailiwick (IRE) (Imperial Frontier (USA))
1545[8] 1918[8] 2536[4] 3197[9] 5851[8] 6406a[7]

Impressioniste (IRE) *Luke Comer* a27 81
3 ch c Peintre Celebre(USA) —Al Amlah (USA) (Riverman (USA))
1057[8] 1594[7] 5661[8]

Imprimis Tagula (IRE) *Alan Bailey* a104 83
6 b g Tagula(IRE) —Strelitzia (IRE) (Bluebird (USA))
108[6] 299[2] ◆ 358[8] 528[9] 1206[11] 1662[7] (2123) 3037[13] 3389[5] 3898[4] ◆ (4063) 4394[7] 4440[6] 4617[10] 4685[9] 5154[6] 5435[7] 5703[6] 6577[2] 6625[2] 7033[3] 7289[10] 7409[2] 7697[2] 7846[8]

Improper (USA) *Mouse Hamilton-Fairley* a23 33
4 b g Northern Afleet(USA) —Bare It Properly (USA) (Proper Reality (USA))
6637[11]

Impulse Dancer *John Bridger*
2 b f Bertolini(USA) —Galatrix (Be My Guest (USA))
2048[10] 2594[15]

I'm Steppin' It Up (USA) *Anthony Pecoraro* a87 95
2 ch c Congrats(USA) —Cindy Woo Who (USA) (Thunder Gulch (USA))
6756a[3]

I'm Super Too (IRE) *Alan Swinbank* 80
3 b g Fasliyev(USA) —Congress (IRE) (Dancing Brave (USA))
1297[2] 1969[2] 2315[4] 2935[6] (3355) 3661[6] 4483[6]

Imvula (AUS) *Saeed Bin Suroor* a101 104
6 br g Rock Of Gibraltar(IRE) —African Rain (AUS) (Woodman (USA))
334a[4] 512a[14]

In A Fortnight *Hugh Collingridge* a49
3 ch g Indian Haven—Taskone (Be My Chief (USA))
671[3] 971[6]

Inagh River *Richard Hannon* a50 79
2 b f Fasliyev(USA) —Bolshaya (Cadeaux Genereux)
1510[8] (1879) 2074[2] 2436[6] 3849[2] 4332[5] 4592[10] 5140[5]

In Babylon (GER) *Tom Dascombe* a63 47
2 b c Oasis Dream—Ice Dream (GER) (Mondrian (GER))
6333[2] ◆ 6704[6]

Inca Blue *Tim Easterby* 53
2 ch g Indian Haven—Gold And Blue (IRE) (Bluebird (USA))
6293[12] 6566[7] 6748[6] 7124[9]

Inca Chief *Ann Duffield* a35 48
2 b c Sleeping Indian—Queen Of Havana (USA) (King Of Kings (IRE))
3767[11] 6365[9] 6894[3]

Inca Princess (IRE) *A P O'Brien* 80
2 b f Holy Roman Emperor(IRE) —Miletrian (IRE) (Marju (IRE))
4879a[7]

Incendo *James Fanshawe* a86 86
4 ch g King's Best(USA) —Kindle (Selkirk (USA))
1348[3] 2031[14] 2975[5] ◆ 3329[3] (4252) 5035[6] 5991[9]

Inch Lodge *Debbie Mountain* a73 66
8 ch h Grand Lodge(USA) —Legaya (Shirley Heights)
(1763)

Inchmarlow (IRE) *Terry Caldwell* a43 29
7 b g Cape Cross(IRE) —Glenstal Priory (Glenstal (USA))
3021[6] 3207[12] 3374[9] 4014[11]

Inchnadamph *Tim Fitzgerald* a60 93
10 b g Inchinor—Pelf (USA) (Al Nasr (FR))
2814[6] 3367[4] 3896[7]

Incomparable *David Nicholls* a83 87
5 ch g Compton Place—Indian Silk (IRE) (Dolphin Street (FR))
345[3] 535[4] 1364[3] 1710[7] 2094[6] 2626[4] 2973[10] 3114[8] 6303[10] 6998[9] (7868) 8005[3]

Incy Wincy *Milton Bradley* a39 31
4 b g Zahran(IRE) —Miss Money Spider (IRE) (Statoblest)
4914[10]

Inde Country *Nicky Vaughan* a32 6
2 b f Indesatchel(IRE) —Countrywide Girl (IRE) (Catrail (USA))
7346[15] 7858[6]

Indefinite Hope (ITY) *Marco Botti* a63
3 b f Ekraar(USA) —Ricredes (IRE) (Night Shift (USA))
7726[3] 7909[5]

Indiana Gal (IRE) *Patrick Martin* a99 101
5 b m Intikhab(USA) —Genial Jenny (IRE) (Danehill (USA))
439a[8] 632a[11] 957a[6] 2037a[2] 2355a[2] 3007a[6] 4631a[7] 4769a[3] 5772a[4] 6379a[9] 7358a[6]

Indian Arrow (FR) *F Doumen*
2 b c More Than Ready(USA) —Indian View (GER) (Spectrum (IRE))
7009a[0]

Indian Arrow *John Quinn* a66 43
2 b c Sleeping Indian—Hillside Girl (IRE) (Tagula (IRE))
5733[4] 7503[4] 7802[4]

Indiana Wells (FR) *F Rohaut* a84 88
3 b f Sadler's Wells(USA) —Clara Bow (FR) (Top Ville)
7648a[7]

Indian Ballad (IRE) *Ed McMahon* a75 83
2 b g Oratorio(IRE) —Cherokee Stream (IRE) (Indian Ridge)
1905[4] 2882[4] 3624[11] (4040) 4927[2] (5354) (5874) (6719)

Indian Breeze (GER) *J Hirschberger* 105
3 b f Monsun(GER) —Indian Jewel (GER) (Local Suitor (USA))
(5805a) 6790a[4] 7160a[7]

Indian Chant (USA) *A Al Raihe* a85
7 ch g Suggest(USA) —Icy Luck (USA) (Ice Age (USA))
515a[8]

Indian City (FR) *J-M Capitte* a68 61
6 ch g City On A Hill(USA) —Mary Linda (Grand Lodge (USA))
273a[2]

Indian Dance (USA) *Lawrence E Murray* a105 90
4 b g Indian Charlie(USA) —Darlin's Band (USA) (Dixieland Band (USA))
5780a[5]

Indian Days *James Given* a105 117
5 ch h Daylami(IRE) —Cap Coz (IRE) (Indian Ridge)
1474[5] 2027[2] 2593[4] 3144[6] 3921[7] (4455) (5804a) 6977a[6] 7851a[9]

Indian Dip *Matthew Salaman* a41 44
2 b f Sleeping Indian—Illeana (GER) (Lomitas)
1043[9] 1999[8] 3035[5] 5581[14] 6027[5] 7631[11] 7801[6]

Indian Emperor (IRE) *Michael Jarvis* a71 69
2 b g Araafa(IRE) —Soft (USA) (Lear Fan (USA))
6365[4] 6827[4] (7408)

Indian Ghyll (IRE) *Roger Teal* a46 67
4 ch h Indian Haven—Arzachena (FR) (Grand Lodge (USA))
1302[8] 1847[3] 2255[13] 2845[8] 3576[6]

Indian Giver *Hugh McWilliams* 66
2 b f Indesatchel(IRE) —Bint Baddi (FR) (Shareef Dancer (USA))
2577[7] 2861[8] 4089[8] 4645[2] 5352[2] 5595[3] 6034[10] (6459) 7050[3]

Indian Haze (IRE) *Daniel Mark Loughnane* a37 44
4 br m Indian Haven—Hollow Haze (USA) (Woodman (USA))
539[10]

Indian Jack (IRE) *Alan Bailey* a80 73
2 ch g Indian Haven—Almaviva (IRE) (Grand Lodge (USA))
5878[9] 6748[P] 7302[2] (7478)

Indian Maj (FR) *J Suarez Paniagua*
3 ch c Indian Rocket—Lady Model (FR) (Sendawar (IRE))
450a[0]

Indian Narjes *Mick Channon* a67 67
2 b f Sleeping Indian—Flora Burn (UAE) (Jade Robbery (USA))
1838[2] 2176[6] 2677[2] 3053[5]

Indian Shuffle (IRE) *Jonathan Portman* a66 70
2 b g Sleeping Indian—Hufflepuff (IRE) (Desert King (IRE))
3269[12] 3767[7] 4528[2] 5808[3] 6271[7] 6769[3] 6989[10] 7088[4] 7392[10]

Indian Skipper (IRE) *Richard Guest* a90 88
5 b g Indian Danehill(IRE) —Rosy Lydgate (Last Tycoon)
(150) 163[3] 286[13] ◆ 350[2] 365[3] 446[2] 492[4] 635[11] 902[9] 1516[2] 1727[20] 2134[7] 2327[2] 2524[4] 2856[2] 3065[9] (3178) 3681[6] 3753[5] 4413[6] 5510[13]

Indian Trail *David Nicholls* a74 93
10 ch g Indian Ridge—Take Heart (Electric)
1295[5] 1471[6] ◆ 2136[3] 2346[5] 2745[8] 3165[8] 3828[8] 4510[5] 5290[9] 5855[3] 6140[6]

Indian Valley (USA) *Rae Guest* a73 80
3 b f Cherokee Run(USA) —Shade Dance (USA) (Nureyev (USA))
1538[2] 2042[4] 2725[5] 5648[2] (6093) 6476[3] (6622) 7019[4]

Indian Violet (IRE) *Sheena West* a66 73
4 b g Indian Ridge—Violet Spring (IRE) (Exactly Sharp (USA))
1575[9] 1967[6] 2274[7] 3131[5] 3500[8] 4173[2] 4374[10] 6495[6] 7068[8] (7728) (7829) 7966[7]

Indian Wish (USA) *Michael Quinlan* a62 59
2 bb f Indian Charlie(USA) —Sister Girl (USA) (Conquistador Cielo (USA))
3082[7] 4338[6] 5651[5] 6081[10] 7004[3] 7630[2] 7813[5]

Indieslad *Ann Duffield* 79
2 b c Indesatchel(IRE) —Sontime (Son Pardo)
4336[3] 4896[2] ◆ 5245[8] 5531[3] (6075)

Indigo Ink *Amy Weaver* a30 54
3 b f Rock Of Gibraltar(IRE) —Blue Indigo (FR) (Pistolet Bleu (IRE))
22[5]

Indigo Sands (IRE) *Alan Berry* 3
2 b g Tagula(IRE) —Bella Vie (IRE) (Sadler's Wells (USA))
7142[9] 7279[10]

Indigo Way *Brian Meehan* 100
2 b g Encosta De Lago(AUS) —Artistic Blue (USA) (Diesis)
2078[7] (4568) (5830) 6505[2] (7236)

Indiracer (IRE) *Alan Bailey* a22 59
2 ch f Indian Haven—Discotheque (USA) (Not For Love (USA))
4471[8] 5147[5] 5373[6] 5894[8] 6673[11]

Indochina *Mark Johnston* 79
3 b g Sulamani(IRE) —Lane County (USA) (Rahy (USA))
3618[2]

Indomito (GER) *P Vovcenko* 105
4 b h Areion(GER) —Insola (GER) (Royal Solo (IRE))
2805a[2] 3704a[8] 4526a[3] 4885a[8] 5573a[8] 7372a[4]

Indy Driver *Matthew Salaman* a84 82
5 ch g Domedriver(IRE) —Condoleezza (USA) (Cozzene (USA))
239[5] 394[P]

Infanta (IRE) *Mahmood Al Zarooni* 65
3 b f Cape Cross(IRE) —Maria Isabella (USA) (Kris)
1881[7] 2463[4] 3039[11]

Infectious (IRE) *Mandy Rowland* 61
2 b f Mujadil(USA) —Common Cause (Polish Patriot (USA))
3204[11] 4149[3] 4981[2] 5602[14] 6893[10] 7602[6]

Infinity World *Geoffrey Oldroyd* a57 46
3 b f Lucky Story(USA) —Musical Refrain (IRE) (Dancing Dissident (USA))
127[10] 1465[10] 2787[5] 3086[11]

In Footlights (USA) *Saeed Bin Suroor* 83
4 b h Elusive Quality(USA) —Triple Act (USA) (Theatrical)
2683[13] 5685[8]

Informed Decision (USA) *Jonathan Sheppard* a121
5 rg m Monarchos(USA) —Palangana (USA) (His Majesty (USA))
7341a[7]

Ingenue *Paul Howling* a55 59
4 b m Hernando(FR) —I Do (Selkirk (USA))
15[11] 2218[5] 3804[3]

Ingleby Arch (USA) *David Barron* a98 84
7 b g Arch(USA) —Inca Dove (USA) (Mr Prospector (USA))
299[7] 573[6] 887[12] 1332[5] (1491) 6962[7] (7225) 7697[4] 7846[9]

Ingleby Exceed (IRE) *David Barron* 64
2 ch f Exceed And Excel(AUS) —Mistress Twister (Pivotal)
2130[4] 3059[8] (4480) 5483[4] 5998[4] 6220[5]

Ingleby King (USA) *David Barron* a66 61
4 bb g Doneraile Court(USA) —Smart Lady Too (USA) (Clever Trick (USA))
2114[6] 2393[12] 2852[6] 4485[8] 5045[3] 5821[3] 6125[6] 6890[5] 7230[5] (7646) (7731)

Ingleby Lady *David Barron* 102
4 ch m Captain Rio—Petra Nova (First Trump)
(2100) 2759[3] 3193[9] 4391[17] 4576[25]

Ingleby Spirit *Richard Fahey* a79 91
3 b g Avonbridge—Encore Du Cristal (USA) (Quiet American (USA))
1657[3] 2117[9] 2758[12] 4504[11] 5086[2] 6327[2] (6813)

Ingleby Star (IRE) *Noel Wilson* a77 81
5 b g Fath(USA) —Rosy Scintilla (IRE) (Thatching)
165[5] (462) 750[2] 1099[7] 1200[2] 1722[2] (2073) 2294[5] 2431[9] 2756[2] 3165[7] 4452[3] 4712[4] 5356[5] 7702[6] 7868[9]

Inheritor (IRE) *Bryan Smart* a91 87
4 b g Kheleyf(USA) —Miss Devious (IRE) (Dr Devious (IRE))
197[11] 2423[7] 3150[8] 5510[7] 6503[4] 6904[12] 7274[11]

Inimitable Romanee (USA) *Amanda Perrett* 76
2 gr f Maria's Mon(USA) —Cellars Shiraz (USA) (Kissin Kris (USA))
5691[4] ◆ (6770)

Inler (IRE) *Brian Meehan* 110
3 br c Red Ransom(USA) —Wedding Gift (FR) (Always Fair (USA))
1699[16] 2075[5] 6570[6] (7083)

Inlovingmemory (IRE) *Maurice Barnes* 62
3 bg f Dubai Destination(USA) —Oiselina (FR) (Linamix (FR))
1010[11] 1203[4] 1469[8]

In My Secret Life (IRE) *C M De Petra* 75
3 b f Spartacus(IRE) —Sticky Fingers (IRE) (Dr Devious (IRE))
2575a[9]

Inner Angel *Roger Teal* a70 63
3 ch f Motivator—Sea Angel (Nashwan (USA))
2674[5] 3581[7] 5366[6] 6452[13]

Inn For The Dancer *Jimmy Fox* a53 20
8 b g Groom Dancer(USA) —Lady Joyce (FR) (Galetto (FR))
228[8] 590[6] 661[6]

Innocuous *David Simcock* a82 93
3 b g Zafeen(FR) —Talah (Danehill (USA))
1460[2] (1993) ◆ 2933[4] (4224) ◆ 5556[4] 6327[11]

Inpursuitoffreedom *Philip McBride* a76 76
3 b f Pastoral Pursuits—Quilt (Terimon)
1132[7] 1973[5] 2702[6] 3171[7] 3413[6] (7005) (7205) 7273[2] 7663[2]

Inqaath (IRE) *Sir Michael Stoute* 87
3 ch g Mr Greeley(USA) —Sparkle Of Stones (FR) (Sadler's Wells (USA))
(2220) 3354[3]

Inquisitress *John Bridger* a56 56
6 b m Hernando(FR) —Caribbean Star (Soviet Star (USA))
160[4] 229[4] 389[4] 479[4] 591[9] 2198[5] 2488[4] (2781) 3264[7] (3715) 3982[3] 4591[8] 4690[9] 5962[5] 6848[7] 7023[10] 7649[9] 7728[9]

Inshaallah *James Given* a48 49
3 ch g Doyen(IRE) —Lake Diva (Docksider (USA))
1970[6] 4687[10]

Inside *Richard Fahey* 61
2 b f Iron Mask(USA) —Only Alone (USA) (Rahy (USA))
4702[3] ◆ 5352[3] 6240[3] 6777[5]

Inside Knowledge (USA) *Gary Woodward* a58 55
4 rg g Mizzen Mast(USA) —Kithira (Danehill (USA))
4290[5] 4683[14] 6571[10] 6915[7] 7157[3] 7270[2] 7398[7] 7632[4] 7861[6]

Inside Story (IRE) *Conor Dore* a70 74
8 b g Rossini(USA) —Sliding (Formidable (USA))
34[5] ◆ 113[2] 244[6] 353[7] 377[3] 493[3]

Inside Track (IRE) *David Evans* a73 78
3 b g Bertolini(USA) —True Crystal (IRE) (Sadler's Wells (USA))
5[2] (168) 452[2] 782[5] 909[2] 1070[7] 2886[11]

Insieme (IRE) *Marco Botti* 71
2 b f Barathea(IRE) —Rasana (Royal Academy (USA))
6469[6] 7000[4]

Insolenceofoffice (IRE) *Ann Duffield* a83 74
2 b c Kodiac—Sharp Diversion (USA) (Diesis)
2420[3] 5683[2] 6182[2] 6369[2] 6705[3] 6980[2] (7269) (7493) (7592) 7908[4] (8002)

Inspector (TUR) *A Sivgin* 111
6 b h Bin Ajwaad(IRE) —Pandora (GER) (Platini (GER))
5804a[8]

Inspirina (IRE) *Richard Ford* a75 86
6 b g Invincible Spirit(IRE) —La Stellina (IRE) (Marju (IRE))
1177[6] 1631[4] 1961[2] (2199) 3090[4] (3432) 3860[2] 4405[5] 4996[6] (5235) 6437[8] 6990[8]

Instance *Jeremy Noseda* a74
2 b f Invincible Spirit(IRE) —Hannda (IRE) (Dr Devious (IRE))
(7021)

Instant Recall (IRE) *M Al Muhairi* a93 103
9 ch g Indian Ridge—Happy Memories (IRE) (Thatching)
434a[7] 515a[6] 707a[11]

Instructress *Robert Cowell* a59 73
2 b f Diktat—Two Step (Mujtahid (USA))
3029[6] (3509) 3925[4] 4592[14] 5089[4] 6271[8] 7211[8] 7424[4] 7592[8] 7696[6] 7777[7]

Intapeace (IRE) *Francis Ennis* a88 94
3 b f Intikhab(USA) —Magical Peace (IRE) (Magical Wonder (USA))
4524a[12]

Intarsia (GER) *M Munch* 101
3 ch f Pentire—Iphianassa (GER) (Selkirk (USA))
5805a[13]

Intavac Boy *Simon Griffiths* a13 29
9 ch g Emperor Fountain—Altaia (FR) (Sicyos (USA))
113[9]

Integral (GER) *R Rohne* 106
6 b h Lando(GER) —Incenza (GER) (Local Suitor (USA))
2576a[7]

Integria *Venetia Williams* a74 67
4 b g Intikhab(USA) —Alegria (Night Shift (USA))
2922[4] 3581[8]

Interactif (USA) *Todd Pletcher* a106 115
3 b c Broken Vow(USA) —Broad Pennant (USA) (Broad Brush (USA))
2776a[6]

Interakt *Mick Channon* 69
3 b f Rakti—Amelie Pouliche (FR) (Desert Prince (IRE))
1178[6] 1486[5] (2459) 3297[8] 3525[3] 3866[3] 4058[2] 4324[7] 4735[8] 5677[5]

Interchoice Star *Ray Peacock* a71 58
5 b g Josr Algarhoud(IRE) —Blakeshall Girl (Piccolo)
(30) 193[5] (251) 351[12] 562[5] 727[2] 869[6] 3556[12] 3908[4] 4430[2] 4834[6] 4936[5] 7332[8] 7639[2]

Interdiamonds *Mark Johnston* a81 81
4 b m Montjeu(IRE) —Interpose (Indian Ridge)
1398[10] 1655[2] 1863[10] 4923[2] 5200[P] (Dead)

Interest Free *Tim Easterby* 54
3 b f Kyllachy—Holly Hayes (IRE) (Alzao (USA))
1890[4] 2212[3] 2628[6] 3027[6]

Internationaldebut (IRE) *Paul Midgley* a89 98
5 b g High Chaparral(IRE) —Whisper Light (IRE) (Caerleon (USA))
1030[2] 1202[2] 1423[2] 1900[18] 2532[6] 2736[15] 3919[5] 4617[4] ◆ 5754[3] ◆ 5937[9] 6142[16] 6721[7] 6985[3] 7146[10]

Intersky Charm (USA) *Sue Bradburne* a73 71
6 ch g Lure(USA) —Catala (USA) (Northern Park (USA))
1098[5] 1199[5] 6029[9] 6242[6]

Intersky Music (USA) *Jonjo O'Neill* 52
7 b g Victory Gallop(CAN) —Resounding Grace (USA) (Thunder Gulch (USA))
1758[5]

Inter Vision (USA) *A Dickman* a96 83
10 b g Cryptoclearance(USA) —Fateful (USA) (Topsider (USA))
1711[6] 1924[10] 2211[8] 2504[10]

Intigra (GER) *T Mundry* 93
4 b m Tiger Hill(IRE) —Incenza (GER) (Local Suitor (USA))
4122[8]

Intimar (IRE) *Ralph Smith* a26 37
4 b m Intikhab(USA) —Genetta (Green Desert (USA))
101[8]

Intimate Whisper *Henry Candy* 43
4 ch m Where Or When(IRE) —Lola Mora (Nearly A Hand)
2921[7]

Intiqaal (IRE) *Ed Dunlop*
3 b g Tiger Hill(IRE) —Pride In Me (Indian Ridge)
6124[10]

Intombi *Alan McCabe* 28
2 b f Val Royal(FR) —Western Bowl (USA) (Gone West (USA))
6469[10] 6873[10]

Into The Light *Ed McMahon* a68 71
5 b g Fantastic Light(USA) —Boadicea's Chariot (Commanche Run)
220[8] 4426[5] 4946[2] 5765[2] 6829[6]

Into The Wind *Rod Millman* 57
3 ch f Piccolo—In The Stocks (Reprimand)
3333[9] 3738[8] 4364[4] 5689[P]

Into Wain (USA) *David Simcock* a99 95
3 b g Eddington(USA) —Serene Nobility (USA) (His Majesty (USA))
206[2] (433) ◆ (680) (1138) ◆ 2125[4] 3014a[6] 5291[8] 6251[2]

Intriguing Look *Pat Phelan*
3 b f Avonbridge—Intriguing Glimpse (Piccolo)
7757[9]

Introvert (IRE) *Mahmood Al Zarooni* a73 87
2 b c Iffraaj—Isana (JPN) (Sunday Silence (USA))
3219[2] 3631[3] (4253) 5310[2] 6088[2] 6870[10]

Intrusion *Richard Fahey* 75
2 b f Indesatchel(IRE) —Waterfowl Creek (IRE) (Be My Guest (USA))
3204[4] 3550[3] 4059[2] 4580[2] 5092[2] (5433) 5882[9] 6563[11]

Invent *Sir Mark Prescott Bt* a63 41
2 b g Dansili—Fantasize (Groom Dancer (USA))
6334[7] 6634[10] 6831[13] 7179[7]

Investment World (IRE) *Mark Johnston* a50
2 b c Akbar(IRE) —Superb Investment (IRE) (Hatim (USA))
5099[10] 5587[12] 6497[10] 7831[2]

Invigilator *Harry Dunlop* a51 42
2 b c Motivator—Midpoint (USA) (Point Given (USA))
4096[11] 4384[7] 6249[8]

Invincibility (IRE) *Simon Dow* a81 73
3 b g Invincible Spirit(IRE) —Wonders Gift (Dr Devious (IRE))
5026[2] 5623[4] 5971[9]

Invincible Ash (IRE) *M Halford* a102 105
5 b m Invincible Spirit(IRE) —Fully Fashioned (IRE) (Brief Truce (USA))
1091a[6] 1406a[5] 1676a[7] 2353a[7] 2912a[7] (3489a) 5569a[6] (7073a)

Invincible Force (IRE) *Paul Green* a70 99
6 b g Invincible Spirit(IRE) —Highly Respected (IRE) (High Estate)
1708[4] 1857[7] 2311[4] 2992[18] 6363[12] 7243[8]

Invincible Lad (IRE) *Eric Alston* a98 93
6 b g Invincible Spirit(IRE) —Lady Ellen (Horage)
2346[10] 2536[7] 2681[4] ◆ 2940[5] 3828[3] 4118[5] 4685[5] 5308[5] 5855[6] 6358[12] 6739[9]

Invincible Prince (IRE) *Ralph Beckett* a81 86
3 b g Invincible Spirit(IRE) —Forest Prize (Charnwood Forest (IRE))
2002[5] 2510[4] (3557)

Invincible Ridge (IRE) *Richard Hannon* 95
2 b c Invincible Spirit(IRE) —Dani Ridge (IRE) (Indian Ridge)
4902[2] ◆ (5372) (6191) 6734[8] 7080[5]

Invincible Son (IRE) *E Sogutlu* 112
4 b h Orpen(USA) —Safe Exit (FR) (Exit To Nowhere (USA))
5803a[5]

Invincible Soul (IRE) *Richard Hannon* 103
3 b c Invincible Spirit(IRE) —Licorne (Sadler's Wells (USA))
1497[6] 1781[2] 2002[2] 3103[2] 3827[3] 4504[3]

Invisible Man *Saeed Bin Suroor* a97 111
4 ch h Elusive Quality(USA) —Eternal Reve (USA) (Diesis)
2124[4] 2472[4] (3069) 4537[2] 5803a[6] 7482[5]

Invitee *Ed Dunlop* 71
3 ch f Medicean—Party Doll (Be My Guest (USA))
2658[4] 3266[4] 3829[5] 4290[4] 4971[5]

Inxile (IRE) *David Nicholls* a108 111
5 b g Fayruz—Grandel (Owington)
948[4] (1007) 2030[6] 2536[5] 6194[5] 6640a[0]

In Your Time *Sir Michael Stoute* a37 50
3 b f Dalakhani(IRE) —Not Before Time (IRE) (Polish Precedent (USA))
2115[8] 4229[10]

Ionaguru *Barry Leavy* 37
5 b m Ishiguru(USA) —Morts Little Hen (Henbit (USA))
1521[5] 1932[13] 2290[9]

Ippi N Tombi (IRE) *Phil McEntee* a11
2 b f Captain Rio—Xema (Danehill (USA))
7608[8] 7715[5] 7893[4]

Ipswich Lad *Andrew Balding* a78 72
3 ch g Halling(USA) —Poised (USA) (Rahy (USA))
(1302) 1823[5] 6872[4]

Iptkaar (USA) *Clive Brittain* a69 72
3 br f Dixie Union(USA) —Low Tolerance (USA) (Proud Truth (USA))
922[2] 1060[6] 4236[6] 4479[8] 5391[5] 5541[11] 6937[5]

Irelandisuperman *David Nicholls* 51
2 b g Bertolini(USA) —Isidor (IRE) (Desert King (IRE))
3536[7] 4187[12] 4848[4] 5602[17]

Irian (GER) *J Moore* 119
4 br g Tertullian(USA) —Iberi (GER) (Rainbow Quest (USA))
7854a[2]

Irie Ute *Sylvester Kirk* a65 61
2 b c Sleeping Indian—Prends Ca (IRE) (Reprimand)
2077[14] 2319[12] 3209[6] ◆ 5256[12] 7393[4] 7551[6] (7643) 7785[3]

Irini (GER) *H J Groschel* 103
4 ch m Areion(GER) —Ircanda (GER) (Nebos (GER))
(6763a)

Irish Bay (IRE) *Luke Comer* a32 52
7 b g Brief Passing(IRE) —Echo Bay (IRE) (Barry's Run (IRE))
591[12]

Irish Boy (IRE) *Bill Ratcliffe* a51
2 b g Desert Millennium(IRE) —Shone Island (IRE) (Desert Sun)
7065[8] 7272[9] 7527[5] 7696[3] 7739[3] 7864[7]

Irish Cat (IRE) *Robert Collet* a83 101
3 b f One Cool Cat(USA) —Babacora (IRE) (Indian Ridge)
1566a[8]

Irish Chope (FR) *C Boutin* a62 89
2 b f Indian Rocket—Via Appia (FR) (Exit To Nowhere (USA))
2917a[9] 4611a[7]

Irish Eyes *Jedd O'Keeffe* 60
3 b g Mark Of Esteem(IRE) —Diabaig (Precocious)
1706[6] 2863[12] 3451[6] 4052[7] 4944[8]

Irish Field (IRE) *J W Hills* 113
2 b c Dubawi(IRE) —Turkana Girl (Hernando (FR))
3718a[2] (4419a) 5347a[5] 6531[4]

Irish Heartbeat (IRE) *Richard Fahey* 102
5 b g Celtic Swing—She's All Class (USA) (Rahy (USA))
(1006) 1383[10] 4085[6] 4537[15] 5571a[6] (5911) 6175[5] 6752[3]

Irish Jugger (USA) *Rod Millman* a65 68
3 ch g Johannesburg(USA) —Jinny's Gold (USA) (Gold Fever (USA))
1602[4] 3325[10] 3739[9] 6903[9] (7429) 7561[3] 7685[4] 8015[3]

Irish Legend (IRE) *Bernard Llewellyn* 31
10 b g Sadler's Wells(USA) —Wedding Bouquet (Kings Lake (USA))
2169[6]

Irish Lights (AUS) *David Hayes* 104
4 b f Fastnet Rock(AUS) —Aspen Falls (USA) (Hennessy (USA))
12

Irish Music (IRE) *Alan Jarvis* a66 62
5 b g Namid—Kelly's Tune (Alhaarth (IRE))
364[3] 699[3] 914[6] 1642[7]

Irish Queen (FR) *H-A Pantall* 93
4 b m Speedmaster(GER) —Intention (GER) (Nebos (GER))
4566a[8]

Irish Song (FR) *A Couetil* 97
3 ch f Singspiel(IRE) —Irish Order (USA) (Irish River (FR))
6590a[5]

Iron Condor *James Eustace* a87 74
3 b g Tobougg(IRE) —Coh Sho No (Old Vic)
1422[2] 1880[5] 2252[9] 3376[8] 4698[2] 5164[3] (6290) 6781[6] (7316) 7612[2] ◆ 7653[2] 8003[5]

Iron Green (FR) *Heather Main* a56 54
2 b g Iron Mask(USA) —Love For Ever (FR) (Kaldoun (FR))
4695[6] 6278[5] 6802[10]

Iron Man Of Mersey (FR) *Tony Carroll* a39 54
4 b g Poliglote—Miss Echo (Chief Singer)
847[11] 1172[9] 4731[5] 5585[12]

Iron Max (IRE) *Lisa Williamson* a21 46
4 b g Iron Mask(USA) —Starisa (IRE) (College Chapel)
531[10] 1072[8] 1154[14]

Iron Out (USA) *Reg Hollinshead* a87 84
4 b g Straight Man(USA) —Fit Fighter (USA) (Fit To Fight (USA))
197[8] 266[7] 1512[12] 1600[3] 1831[8] 2173[9] 2937[11] 3283[5] 7306[11] 7414[4] 7600[9] 7985[4]

Iron Range (IRE) *Ed McMahon* 85
2 b c Clodovil(IRE) —Islandagore (IRE) (Indian Ridge)
(6488)

Irons On Fire (USA) *Brian Meehan* a73
2 ch g Tale Of The Cat(USA) —One And Twenty (USA) (Honour And Glory (USA))
6334[4] (6742)

Iron Step *Ed Dunlop* 45
2 gr c Dubawi(IRE) —Giorgia Rae (IRE) (Green Desert (USA))
6779[4] 7036[8]

Iron Velvet (USA) *Mark Johnston* a53 78
3 b g Dubawi(IRE) —Not For Turning (USA) (Deputy Minister (CAN))
1052[5]

Isabella Grey *Kevin Ryan* 91
4 gr m Choisir(AUS) —Karsiyaka (IRE) (Kahyasi)
1081a[11] 2057[10]

Isabella Romee (IRE) *Jane Chapple-Hyam* a50 57
4 gr m Bahri(USA) —Silver Clasp (IRE) (Linamix (FR))
4657[9] 5655[2] 6077[3] 6269[13] 7037[7] 7401[7] 7829[5] 7917[5]

Isabella's Fancy *Tony Newcombe* a57 45
5 br m Captain Rio—Princess Of Spain (King Of Spain)
7[11]

Isabel's Pet *Karen George* a20
4 b m Lucky Story(USA) —Perle D'Azur (Mind Games)
979[9]

Isander (USA) *F Chappet* a41 66
5 b h Grand Slam(USA) —Let Fly (USA) (Flying Paster (USA))
303a[0] 559a[10]

Isantha (GER) *T Mundry* 101
3 b f Dai Jin—Iaskre (GER) (Slip Anchor)
2575a[3] 4640a[14]

I Scream (IRE) *David Elsworth* a52 28
2 b f Iceman—Fun Time (Fraam)
1972[16] 2413[4] 2839[14] 3295[13]

Ishbelle *Ralph Beckett* 92
2 gb f Invincible Spirit(IRE) —Belle Reine (King Of Kings (IRE))
3686[2] ◆ (4149) (4872) ◆ 5693[7]

Ishe Mac *Neville Bycroft* 84
4 b m Ishiguru(USA) —Zacinta (USA) (Hawkster (USA))
1707[14] 4287[10] 4850[9] 6113[10] 6917[10]

Ishetoo *Ollie Pears* 102
6 b g Ishiguru(USA) —Ticcatoo (IRE) (Dolphin Street (FR))
1008[10] 1295[14] 2054[11] 2465[7] 3406[4] 4118[7] 4558[7] 4942[6] 5302[15] 6723[5] ◆ 6981[7]

Ishiadancer *Eric Alston* a89 93
5 b m Ishiguru(USA) —Abaklea (IRE) (Doyoun)
465[6] (544) 739[5] 850[2] 1030[13] 1519[4] 1918[4] 2326[5] 3489a[8] 3893[3] 4832[12] 5120[9] 5609[4] 6113[13]

Ishibee (IRE) *John Bridger* a54 54
6 b m Ishiguru(USA) —Beauty (IRE) (Alzao (USA))
613[6]

Ishikawa (IRE) *Alan King* 36
2 b g Chineur(FR) —Nautical Light (Slip Anchor)
3961[14] 6953[11] 7178[8]

Ishipink *Ron Hodges* a43 40
3 gr f Ishiguru(USA) —Christmas Rose (Absalom)
1187[5] 1535[3] 1774[7] 2584[5] 3255[9]

Ishitaki (ARG) *Saeed Bin Suroor* a94
4 br m Interprete(ARG) —Nice Watch (ARG) (The Watcher (USA))
514a[7]

Ishraaqat *Marcus Tregoning* a64 79
3 ch f Singspiel(IRE) —Elshamms (Zafonic (USA))
1621[7] 2718[3] (4397) 5329[4] 6090[11]

Ishtar Gate (USA) *Paul Cole* a52 83
3 bb c Gone West(USA) —Sometime (IRE) (Royal Academy (USA))
1518[5] 2348[7] 2644[11] 3297[4] 4335[3] 5891[8] 6413[9]

Isingy Red (FR) *Jim Boyle* a76
2 ch c Chichicastenango(FR) —Loving Smile (FR) (Sillery (USA))
6995[4] 7385[8] 7550[2] 7990[4]

Isis Song (IRE) *Joseph G Murphy* 77
2 ch f Singspiel(IRE) —Baize (Efisio)
4077a[8]

Isitcozimcool (IRE) *Don Cantillon* a73 42
5 b g Shinko Forest(IRE) —Hazarama (IRE) (Kahyasi)
(503) (591) ◆ 705[13]

Isitfridayyet (IRE) *James Given* 50
2 bb c Diamond Green(FR) —Stella Del Mattino (USA) (Golden Gear (USA))
2932[14] 3175[4]

Island Chief *Michael Easterby* a70 79
4 b g Reel Buddy(USA) —Fisher Island (IRE) (Sri Pekan (USA))
704[6] 895[2] 1098[3] 1149[5] 1293[7] 1995[7] 4581[2] (4822) (4897) 5530[15] 6296[9] 6571[4] 6922[7] 7146[6] 7283[8]

Island Dreams (USA) *Sir Michael Stoute* 72
3 b f Giant's Causeway(USA) —Camanoe (USA) (Gone West (USA))
2050[4] ◆

Island Home *Brian Meehan* 69
4 b m Act One—Island Race (Common Grounds)
3062[5] 3592[11]

Island Legend (IRE) *Milton Bradley* a74 57
4 b g Trans Island—Legand Of Tara (USA) (Gold Legend (USA))
1915[8] 2229[7] 2639[2] 3255[6] 3994[7] 4256[3] (5025) 5368[2] 6700[4] 7194[3] 7285[4]

Island Rhapsody *Andrew Balding* a73 71
3 ch f Bahamian Bounty—Lovely Lyca (Night Shift (USA))
980[4] (1622) 7097[13] 7207[3]

Island Sunset (IRE) *William Muir* a97 92
4 ch m Trans Island—Islandagore (IRE) (Indian Ridge)
(593) ◆ (990) 1084[4] 1665[4] 3368[8] 6886[10] 7349[9] 7384[3] 7523[7] (7828) 8009[2]

Isle De Maurice *Gary Moore* a68 52
8 b g Sinndar(IRE) —Circe's Isle (Be My Guest (USA))
263[9] (420) 748[4]

Isle Of Ellis (IRE) *Ron Barr* a39 37
3 b g Statue Of Liberty(USA) —Fable (Absalom)
301[7] 782[9] 2143[7] 4485[10] 5535[12] 5819[10] 6076[9]

Isle Of Giant's (USA) *B Cecil* a108
5 b g Giant's Causeway(USA) —Oshima (USA) (Mr Prospector (USA))
5577a[7]

Islesman *Heather Main* a78 65
2 b g Oratorio(IRE) —Purple Vision (Rainbow Quest (USA))
7203[8] (7503) 7636[3]

Isobar (GER) *Luca Cumani* a86 81
4 b h Monsun(GER) —Ice Dream (GER) (Mondrian (GER))
3038[8] 4069[12] 4414[3] 5208[2] (5811) 6428[2] ◆ 6808[12]

Isolate *Hughie Morrison* a68 80
2 gb f Verglas(IRE) —Nirvana (Marju (IRE))
5692[10] 6247[5] (6651) 7235[8]

Isontonic (IRE) *Paul Midgley* a17 18
2 b f Kodiac—Bishop's Lake (Lake Coniston (IRE))
4512[4] 4890[7] 5268[9]

Isphahan *Andrew Balding* a77 88
7 b g Diktat—Waltzing Star (IRE) (Danehill (USA))
2683[11] 3863[15]

I Spy Baileys *James Given* a38
3 b f Starcraft(NZ) —Debby (USA) (Woodman (USA))
5270[5] 5815[10]

Issabella Gem (IRE) *Clive Cox* 84
3 b f Marju(IRE) —Robin (Slip Anchor)
1501[2] ◆ 2076[6] 2890[3] 4470[12] 5259[4] 5953[4] 6361[2] 7206[5]

Istidlaal *Sir Michael Stoute* 76
3 ch c Singspiel(IRE) —On A Soapbox (USA) (Mi Cielo (USA))
1757[12] 3116[3] 3909[5] 4792[2] 5747[10]

Istiqdaam *Michael Easterby* a80 77
5 b g Pivotal—Auspicious (Shirley Heights)
23[3] 245[10] 394[9] 749[4] 1152[3] 2696[7] 2982[4] 3876[5] 4704[11] 5510[8] 5789[13] 6370[11]

Istishaara (USA) *John Dunlop* 76
2 b f Kingmambo(USA) —Itnab (Green Desert (USA))
3411[6] ◆ 4048[5] (6468)

Italian Dame *James Turner* a31 35
4 b m Bertolini(USA) —Soyalang (FR) (Alydeed (CAN))
6464[15] 7132[10] 7468[9]

Italian Tom (IRE) *Ronald Harris* a80 80
3 b c Le Vie Dei Colori—Brave Cat (IRE) (Catrail (USA))
117[4] 310[2] 478[5] 766[8] 1140[6] 1584[10] (5309) 5855[16] 7314[3] 7549[6] 7961[8]

Italian Wizard (ITY) *P A Picchi* 84
3 b g Spirit Of Desert(IRE) —Harley Street (ITY) (Roi Danzig (USA))
1945a[9]

Itcanbedone Again (IRE) *James Unett* a30 47
11 b g Sri Pekan(USA) —Maradata (IRE) (Shardari)
353[9] 521[6]

Ithinkbest *Sir Michael Stoute* a91 94
4 b g King's Best(USA) —Monturani (IRE) (Indian Ridge)
1697[12] 2472[2] 2683[3] 3667[2] 4617[7] 6204[9]

Itlaaq *John Dunlop* a89 97
4 b g Alhaarth(IRE) —Hathrah (IRE) (Linamix (FR))
(2865) 5955[7]

It's A Date *Alan King* a80 91
5 b g Kyllachy—By Arrangement (IRE) (Bold Arrangement)
1161[7] (1736) 6808[5] 7208[6]

It's A Deal (IRE) *Peter Winkworth* a58 58
3 b f Indian Haven—Gold And Blue (IRE) (Bluebird (USA))
(1795) 2336[4] 2953[6] 4991[10]

It's A Mans World *Ian Williams* a59 65
4 b g Kyllachy—Exhibitor (USA) (Royal Academy (USA))
2053[12] 2410[5] 2876[10] 5579[7] 5927[6] 6125[8] 6860[7] (7401) 7731[2] 7870[3] 7899[2]

Its Beyond Me *Finbar Murtagh* 36
6 ch g And Beyond(IRE) —Hand On Heart (IRE) (Taufan (USA))
1149[8] 1801[11] 3021[4] 3775[9]

It's Dubai Dolly *Alastair Lidderdale* a71 79
4 ch m Dubai Destination(USA) —Betrothal (IRE) (Groom Dancer (USA))
266[8] 480[11] 1133[3] 2093[11] 5611[4] 5972[6] 6959[7]

It's Freezing (IRE) *Mrs John Harrington* a77 67
2 b c High Chaparral(IRE) —Freezing Love (USA) (Danzig (USA))
6560[19]

It's Josr *Ian Wood* a58 55
5 b g Josr Algarhoud(IRE) —It's So Easy (Shaadi (USA))
3028[6] 3641[3] 4156[10]

It's Midnight (USA) *P Bary* 95
3 b f Shamardal(USA) —Witching Hour (FR) (Fairy King (USA))
5139a[DSQ]

It's So You (USA) *A Fabre* 88
3 b f Empire Maker(USA) —You (USA) (You And I (USA))
7546a[2]

It's Tea Time (USA) *George R Arnold II* a107 91
3 b f Dynaformer(USA) —Prof. McGonagall (USA) (Storm Cat (USA))
7344a[4]

Itsthursdayalready *Mark Brisbourne* a72 75
3 b g Exceed And Excel(AUS) —Succinct (Hector Protector (USA))
35[7] 366[6] 625[3] 1058[6] 2215[12] 3030[6] 3393[5] 3685[9] 3966[4] 4651[6] 5438[3] 5898[3] 6329[7] 7064[5] 7250[8] 7425[9] 7604[2] 7761[3] 7911[2]

Itsy Bitsy *Willie Musson* a47 37
8 b m Danzig Connection(USA) —Cos I Do (IRE) (Double Schwartz)
4620[8]

Its You Again *Michael Quinlan* a79 75
2 b g Avonbridge—Summer Lightning (IRE) (Tamure (IRE))
1806[3] 2413[5] 6778[2] 7142[2] 7347[4] 7493[2] 7578[2] (7715)

Ittirad (USA) *Michael Jarvis* 74
2 b c Dubai Destination(USA) —Noushkey (Polish Precedent (USA))
7178[2]

It Tiz (USA) *Mark Glatt* a100 96
3 bb f Tiznow(USA) —Star Of The Woods (USA) (Woodman (USA))
5351a[8]

Itum *Christine Dunnett* 29
3 ch g Bahamian Bounty—Petomi (Presidium)
6060[9]

Itwasonlyakiss (IRE) *J W Hills* a46 78
3 b f Exceed And Excel(AUS) —Reem One (IRE) (Rainbow Quest (USA))
1425[13] 1639[4] 2197[6] 2931[5] 3480[6]

Itzakindamagic (IRE) *Mark Johnston* a58 72
2 b f Indian Haven—Nom Francais (First Trump)
3985[5] 5196[6] 5924[4] (6302) 6978[4] 7324[7]

Ivanov (IRE) *Willie Musson* a34 34
2 ch g Beat Hollow—Indy's Princess (USA) (A.P. Indy (USA))
5269[11] 5630[9] 5894[7]

Ivan's A Star (IRE) *J S Moore* a64 64
2 b g Ivan Denisovich(IRE) —Try The Air (IRE) (Foxhound (USA))
1017[7] 1136[3] 1319[2] 1793[9] 2300[3] 4436[5] 4623[10] 4967[4] 5373[4] 5659[4] 6082[2] 7471[2] 7520[2] 7631[3] (7664) 7801[2]

Ivan Vasilevich (IRE) *Jane Chapple-Hyam* a70 66
2 b c Ivan Denisovich(IRE) —Delisha (Salse (USA))
4379[6] 4743[3] 5156[11] 5837[3] ◆ 6412[4] 7087[8] 7631[2] (7755) 7916[4]

I've Got The Fever (USA) *John Terranova II* a74
3 ch c Stephen Got Even(USA) —Music Fever (USA) (Gold Fever (USA))
824a[7]

Iver Bridge Lad *John Ryan* a104 111
3 b c Avonbridge—Fittonia (FR) (Ashkalani (IRE))
1311[6] 1616[5] 2978[2] 3461[6] 3791[5] 4391[16] 4576[9] 5088[7] 5744[10] 6063[4] 6319[3] 6564[2] 6735[4] 7060[9] 7348[4] 7482[4]

Ivestar (IRE) *Ben Haslam* a58 66
5 b g Fraam—Hazardous (Night Shift (USA))
327[5] 476[2] 2629[8] (2854) 3124[4] 4644[7] 4986[8] 7336[9] 7543[9] 7787[11]

Ivory Lace *Steve Woodman* a71 81
9 b m Atraf—Miriam (Forzando)
11[6] 673[7] 931[3] ◆ 1224[11] 1634[9] 2714[4] 3160[5] 3821[7] 4579[14] 5713[2] 6023[3] 6864[6] 6992[3] 7439[12]

Ivory Land (FR) *A De Royer-Dupre* 109
3 ch c Lando(GER) —Ivory Coast (FR) (Peintre Celebre (USA))
1254a[3] 2160a[3] 2802a[11] 4039a[6] 6590a[2]

Ivory Pegasus (AUS) *Robert Price* 99
5 b m Fusaichi Pegasus(USA) —Red Ivory (AUS) (Ivory Way (USA))
15

Ivory Silk *Jeremy Gask* a92 84
5 b m Diktat—Ivory's Joy (Tina's Pet)
212[2] 639[2] 948[8] 1266[6] 5154[8] 5731[4] 6374[11] 6812[2] 7320[8] 7719[4] 7915[9] 8004[7]

Ivy And Gold *Alan Berry* 4
2 b c Bertolini(USA) —Free Spirit (IRE) (Caerleon (USA))
6045[8]

Iwantobreakfree *David Evans* a34 35
2 b c Firebreak—Nee Lemon Left (Puissance)
3961[12] 4599[10] 6278[11] 7118[6] 7643[10] 7857[10]

Izaaj (USA) *M bin Shafya* a95 62
3 ch c Giant's Causeway(USA) —Miss Coronado (USA) (Coronado's Quest (USA))
510a[4] 796a[4] 1023a[9]

Izalia (FR) *F Rossi* 92
2 b f Iron Mask(USA) —Tarabela (FR) (Johann Quatz (FR))
(7276a)

Izshelegal (USA) *Terry Knight* a92
2 rg f Maria's Mon(USA) —Unkatzable (USA) (A.P. Indy (USA))
7342a[9]

Iztaccihuatl *Michael Scudamore* a58
2 br f Iceman—Three White Sox (Most Welcome)
1017[3]

Izzet *Mark H Tompkins* 55
2 b g Cadeaux Genereux—Asbo (Abou Zouz (USA))
3169[6] 4716[10] 6268[8] 7004[10]

Izzi Mill (USA) *Paul D'Arcy* a70 73
4 rg m Lemon Drop Kid(USA) —Lets Get Cozzy (USA) (Cozzene (USA))
284[9] 398[5] 793[6] 937[11] 5562[7] 6847[6]

Izzi Top *John Gosden* 81
2 b f Pivotal—Zee Zee Top (Zafonic (USA))
7057[2] ◆

Jaahiz (IRE) *Richard Hannon* 80
2 b c Noverre(USA) —Band (USA) (Northern Dancer (CAN))
3000[2] 3433[2] (3923) 4138[18] 5187[15]

Jaaryah (IRE) *Michael Jarvis* a90 88
2 ch f Halling(USA) —Albahja (Sinndar (IRE))
(3562) 6670[3] 7085[4]

Jaasoos (IRE) *D Selvaratnam* a100 103
6 ch g Noverre(USA) —Nymphs Echo (IRE) (Mujtahid (USA))
339a[9] 628a[3]

Jabot (ITY) *M Marcialis*
2 b g Daro Sopran(GER) —Jackie (ITY) (Horage)
7850a[15]

Jackaroo (IRE) *A P O'Brien* 96
2 b c Galileo(IRE) —Ardbrae Lady (Overbury (IRE))
3190[7]

Jack Bell (IRE) *Alan Swinbank*
3 ch g Rock Of Gibraltar(IRE) —Slip Ashore (IRE) (Slip Anchor)
1890[7]

Jack Dawkins (USA) *David Nicholls* a57 101
5 b g Fantastic Light(USA) —Do The Mambo (USA) (Kingmambo (USA))
2423[8] 2835[12] 5098[11] 5638[12] 6367[12] 6984[5] ◆ 7306[6] 7985[3] ◆

Jackday (IRE) *Tim Easterby* 73
5 b g Daylami(IRE) —Magic Lady (IRE) (Bigstone (IRE))
1891[2] (2295)

Jackie Kiely *Roy Brotherton* a63 60
9 ch g Vettori(IRE) —Fudge (Polar Falcon (USA))
139[5] (470) 720[2] 1755[5] 3028[9] 4992[12] 7475[4]

Jack Jicaro *Nicky Vaughan* a42 19
4 b g Mind Games—Makeover (Priolo (USA))
5560[8] 7599[11] 7862[5]

Jack Junior (USA) *David Nicholls* a90 73
6 b g Songandaprayer(USA) —Ra Hydee (USA) (Rahy (USA))
(273a)

Jack Luey *Lawrence Mullaney* a63 72
3 b g Danbird(AUS) —Icenaslice (IRE) (Fayruz)
2768[3] 3751[2] (4406) (5046) 6879[4] 6985[8]

Jack My Boy (IRE) *David Evans* a81 100
3 b g Tagula(IRE) —Bobanlyn (IRE) (Dance Of Life (USA))
1086[4] 1281[5] 1376[2] (1523) (1701) 2545[14] 5442[2] 5944[22]

Jack O'Lantern *Richard Fahey* a39 76
3 b g Shamardal(USA) —Bush Cat (USA) (Kingmambo (USA))
1100[4] 1706[4] 2143[6] 2702[7] 3148[4] 3680[10]

Jack Rackham *Bryan Smart* a77 75
6 ch g Kyllachy—Hill Welcome (Most Welcome)
(325) 859[5]

Jack Smudge *James Given* a88 82
2 bb c One Cool Cat(USA) —Forever Fine (USA) (Sunshine Forever (USA))
3945[4] 5117[3] (5418) (6086) (6619) (7116) 7565[3] 7891[7]

Jackson (BRZ) *Richard Guest* a49 73
8 ch g Clackson(BRZ) —More Luck (BRZ) (Baynoun)
3750[8] 4154[10] 5852[13] 7315[4] 7490[9]

Jackson Bend (USA) *Nicholas Zito* a118
3 ch c Hear No Evil(USA) —Sexy Stockings (USA) (Tabasco Cat (USA))
1097a[2] 1714a[12] 2137a[3]

Jack's Revenge (IRE) *George Baker* a40 43
2 br c Footstepsinthesand—Spirit Of Age (IRE) (Indian Ridge)
3555[6] 4254[9] 6118[9]

Jackstown Road (IRE) *David Elsworth* a11
2 b c Lemon Drop Kid(USA) —Midris (IRE) (Namid)
7386[12] 7479[9]

Jacobs Son *Robert Mills* a75 79
2 ch g Refuse To Bend(IRE) —Woodwin (IRE) (Woodman (USA))
2932[9] 3452[6] 4254[2] 4682[2] 5256[2] 6809[2]

Jaconet (USA) *David Barron* a111 98
5 ch m Hussonet(USA) —Radiant Rocket (USA) (Peteski (CAN))
(737) 948[3] 2054[2] 2135[5] 2745[17] 3875[6] 7073a[10]

Jacqueline Quest (IRE) *Henry Cecil* 111
3 b f Rock Of Gibraltar(IRE) —Coquette Rouge (IRE) (Croco Rouge (IRE))
1312[7] 1726[2] 3143[3] 4540[5]

Jacquotte (IRE) *Edward Creighton* a40
2 b f Alhaarth(IRE) —Siskin (IRE) (Royal Academy (USA))
4299[10] 4838[8] 7723[8] 7907[4]

Jade *Ollie Pears* 75
2 b f Cadeaux Genereux—Ashdown Princess (IRE) (King's Theatre (IRE))
5298[4] 6034[4] (6301)

Jade Express (IRE) *Daniel Mark Loughnane* a50 55
3 b f Captain Rio—Leopardess (IRE) (Ela-Mana-Mou)
6937[9]

Jadhwah *Marcus Tregoning* 17
2 b f Nayef(USA) —Dhelaal (Green Desert (USA))
5871[9]

Jaguar Mail (JPN) *Noriyuki Hori* 121
6 b h Jungle Pocket(JPN) —Haya Beni Komachi (JPN) (Sunday Silence (USA))
7615a[4] 7851a[4]

Jahanara (IRE) *Richard Hannon* a66 66
2 b f Exceed And Excel(AUS) —Silversword (FR) (Highest Honor (FR))
4317[8] 6248[5] 6697[6]

Jake The Snake (IRE) *Tony Carroll* a93 83
9 ch g Intikhab(USA) —Tilbrook (IRE) (Don't Forget Me)
286[4] 502[2] 657[2] 902[5] (981) (1306) 1625[8] 2129[9] 3083[2] 4030[7] 4354[14]

Jakeys Girl *Pat Phelan* a45 47
3 b f Dubai Destination(USA) —Rosewood Belle (USA) (Woodman (USA))
3038[6] 3272[10] 3738[9] 7634[6]

Jakkalberry (IRE) *E Botti* 122
4 b h Storming Home—Claba Di San Jore (IRE) (Barathea (IRE))
(1540a) 2152a[6] (3019a) 5186[6] 6977a[5] 7373a[5] 7851a[5]

Jakor (ITY) *M Marcialis* 104
4 b h Orpen(USA) —Jackie (ITY) (Horage)
6238a[2] (6976a) 7459a[4]

Jaldarshaan (IRE) *Bill Ratcliffe* a67 67
3 b f Fath(USA) —Jaldini (IRE) (Darshaan)
5493[6] 6815[3] 7013[9] 7305[11] (7651) 7892[4]

Jalil (USA) *Saeed Bin Suroor* a92 87
6 br h Storm Cat(USA) —Tranquility Lake (USA) (Rahy (USA))
609a[6]

Jalors (IRE) *Mark Johnston* a67 74
2 b g Invincible Spirit(IRE) —Julie Jalouse (USA) (Kris S (USA))
6268[2] 6457[6] 6849[3]

Jamaayel *Kevin Prendergast* a77 93
3 b f Shamardal(USA) —Walayef (USA) (Danzig (USA))
1787a[6]

Jamaica Grande *Terry Clement* a49 66
2 ch c Doyen(IRE) —Mary Sea (FR) (Selkirk (USA))
2561[6] 2990[8] 3169[7] 3784[4] 3874[4] 4129[2] 4332[6] 4600[7] 4851[9] 6311[11] 6667[7] 6870[11] 6884[7] 7002[8] 7207[4] 7395[9]

Jamaican Bolt (IRE) *Bryan Smart* 78
2 b c Pivotal—Chiming (IRE) (Danehill (USA))
7345 [2]

Jamarjo (IRE) *Steve Gollings* a55 58
3 b g Marju(IRE) —Athlumney Lady (Lycius (USA))
1992[6] 2189[10]

Jambo Bibi (IRE) *Richard Hannon* a72 65
2 b f Iffraaj—Nouveau Riche (IRE) (Entrepreneur)
1660[2] 1764[2] 2642[3] 3260[2] 3959[7] 4802[5] 5412[3] 5894[3] 7301[8]

Jameel (USA) *Saeed Bin Suroor* a70
2 b c Monsun(GER) —Maids Causeway (IRE) (Giant's Causeway (USA))
7386[3]

Jameela Girl *Robert Cowell* a54 83
2 ch f Haafhd—Peach Sorbet (IRE) (Spectrum (IRE))
3260[6] 3778[6] 4149[2] (5000) ◆ (5261) 5639[2]

James Barrymore *Miss J R Tooth* a69 68
3 b g Fraam—Nine Red (Royal Applause)
3030[8] 3525[8] 4791[7] 5075[5]

James Junior *Peter Niven* 38
4 ch g Tobougg(IRE) —Celts Dawn (Celtic Swing)
700[6] 2655[9]

James Pollard (IRE) *Bernard Llewellyn* a66 62
5 ch g Indian Ridge—Manuetti (IRE) (Sadler's Wells (USA))
289[6] 496[10] 591[6] 791[6] 939[7] 995[8] 1239[10] 1839[6] 2955[7] 3264[2] 3559[3] 3954[8] 4657[6] 5828[4] 6472[2] 6905[4] (7015) 7490[4] 7778[6]

Jamesway (IRE) *Richard Fahey* a85 89
2 b g Camacho—Charlene Lacy (IRE) (Pips Pride)
(1065) 2757[6] (3059) 3630[3] 4138[12] 4831[4] 5295[3] 5939[2] 6141[7] 6568[12]

Jamhoori *Clive Brittain* 60
2 b c Tiger Hill(IRE) —Tanasie (Cadeaux Genereux)
2319[7] 2932[3] 3631[6]

Jam Maker *John Jenkins* a16 14
2 b f Diktat—Jawwala (USA) (Green Dancer (USA))
1879[9] 4595[12] 7610[10]

Jammy Shot (GER) *A Wohler* 100
3 ch c Samum(GER) —Jumble (Desert Prince (IRE))
4184a[20]

J'Amour Dance *Colin Teague* 20
3 ch g Rambling Bear—Kigema (IRE) (Case Law)
3111[11] 3507[6]

Jamr *Saeed Bin Suroor* a70
2 b c Singspiel(IRE) —Never Enough (GER) (Monsun (GER))
7452[5]

Jane Blue (FR) *W Walton* 98
5 b g Indian Rocket—Rastella (FR) (Funambule (USA))
304a[0]

Jane's Gift *John Akehurst* a28
3 b f Josr Algarhoud(IRE) —Robanna (Robellino (USA))
7086[10]

Jane's Legacy *Reg Hollinshead* a53
2 b f Needwood Blade—Victory Flip (IRE) (Victory Note (USA))
7447[9] 7578[11] 7839[8]

Janet's Delight *Sean Curran* a32 41
5 b m Erhaab(USA) —Ishona (Selkirk (USA))
816[8]

Janet's Pearl (IRE) *Ann Duffield* a70 69
2 ch f Refuse To Bend(IRE) —Sassari (IRE) (Darshaan)
4187[7] 4447[2] 4668[2] 5332[2] 5699[2] (6027)

Janicellaine (IRE) *B W Hills* 72
2 b f Beat Hollow—Danielli (IRE) (Danehill (USA))
(6511)

Janie's Encore *Malcolm Jefferson*
5 ch m Muhtarram(USA) —Janie-O (Hittite Glory)
5815[11]

Jan Mayen *Mark Johnston* a60
4 b m Halling(USA) —Simianna (Bluegrass Prince (IRE))
98[2] ◆ 226[4] 551[5] 868[10]

Janood (IRE) *Saeed Bin Suroor* 100
2 b c Medicean—Alluring Park (IRE) (Green Desert (USA))
(4549) ◆ (5079) 5975a[8] 6560[9]

Jan Smuts (IRE) *Brian Meehan* a27 41
2 b g Johannesburg(USA) —Choice House (USA) (Chester House (USA))
5032[10] 5718[8]

Jan Vermeer (IRE) *A P O'Brien* 119
3 b c Montjeu(IRE) —Shadow Song (IRE) (Pennekamp (USA))
(2367a) 2746[4] 3491a[3] 4039a[3]

Jaq's Sister *Michael Blanshard* a49
4 b m Bertolini(USA) —Polly Golightly (Weldnaas (USA))
390[10]

Jardaa *F Head* 98
3 ch f Pivotal—Filfilah (Cadeaux Genereux)
7546a[4]

Jardim (BRZ) *Eduardo Caramori* a104
4 rg h Ski Champ(USA) —Copacabana Beach (BRZ) (Midnight Tiger (USA))
414a[6] 608a[5] 796a[13] 4855a[6]

Jardina (GER) *P Schiergen* 95
2 b f Shirocco(GER) —Juvena (GER) (Platini (GER))
(6407a)

Jargelle (IRE) *David Nicholls* a6 103
4 b m Kheleyf(USA) —Winter Tern (USA) (Arctic Tern (USA))
1353[9] 1670[5] 2135[3] ◆ 3165[6] 5335[6] 5734[8] 7702[5]

Jaridh (USA) *Saeed Bin Suroor* a77
2 b c Bernardini(USA) —Mansfield Park (Green Desert (USA))
6211[2] ◆ 6742[3] 7112[10]

Jaroslaw (SAF) *David Simcock* a102
7 b g Jallad(USA) —Dacha (SAF) (Russian Fox (USA))
334a[3] 629a[6] 821a[8]

Jarrow (IRE) *Mark Johnston* a96 93
3 ch g Shamardal(USA) —Wolf Cleugh (IRE) (Last Tycoon)
(901) 1376[11] 1834[4] 2090[2] 2316[9] 3178[5] 3578[5] 3791[17] 4653[11] 5606[7] 6204[8] 6438[9] 6904[2]

Jasmeno *Hughie Morrison* 79
3 b f Catcher In The Rye(IRE) —Jasmick (IRE) (Definite Article)
1431[8] 2901[9] 3514[6] 4046[2] 4676[7] (5289) (5625) 6774[8]

Jasmin Rai *Desmond Donovan* a55
3 b f Doyen(IRE) —Ella's Wish (IRE) (Bluebird (USA))
1538[8] 2473[10] 3080[12] 7848[3] 7909[2]

Jawaab (IRE) *Richard Guest* a85 84
6 ch g King's Best(USA) —Canis Star (Wolfhound (USA))
1907[4] 2243[3] (2739) 3265[3] 3847[4] 4400[10] 6797[14] (7694)

Jawal *Clive Brittain* a66
3 ch c Motivator—Merewood (USA) (Woodman (USA))
667[3] ◆ 825[7]

Jawhar (IRE) *William Haggas* 50
2 ch g Halling(USA) —Kawn (Cadeaux Genereux)
7201[7] ◆

Jaycito (USA) *Mike Mitchell* a107
2 b c Victory Gallop(CAN) —Night Edition (CAN) (Ascot Knight (CAN))
7363a[7]

Jay Jays Joy *David Barron* a47 17
2 b g Diktat—Agrippina (Timeless Times (USA))
5418[10] 5763[8] 6111[9] 7831[6]

Jay's Treaty (USA) *Mark Johnston* a26 71
3 rg g Maria's Mon(USA) —J J'sdream (USA) (Glitterman (USA))
1694[3] 1959[2] 2425[3] 3363[5] 3970[12] 4548[7]

Jazacosta (USA) *Jo Crowley* a66 74
4 ch g Dixieland Band(USA) —Dance With Del (USA) (Sword Dance)
975[3] 1304[9] 2198[16]

Jazrawy *Alan McCabe* a60 59
8 b g Dansili—Dalila Di Mare (IRE) (Bob Back (USA))
113[3] 331[11] 377[2] 521[2] 600[5]

Jazz Age (IRE) *Jeremy Glover* a59 68
3 b g Shamardal(USA) —Tender Is Thenight (IRE) (Barathea (IRE))
33[7] 218[4]

J. B.'s Thunder (USA) *Albert M Stall Jr* a115 110
2 b c Thunder Gulch(USA) —Rebridled Dreams (USA) (Unbridled's Song (USA))
7363a[9]

Jealousy Defined (IRE) *Nigel Tinkler* 50
2 ch f Redback—Defined Feature (IRE) (Nabeel Dancer (USA))
1986[7] 2654[8] 2939[11] 4554[8] 4848[5] 4967[3] 5602[15] 6129[6]

Jeangeorges (IRE) *Patrick J Flynn* a65 68
4 b g Noverre(USA) —Appetina (Perugino (USA))
7078a[4]

Jeannie (IRE) *Nick Littmoden* a44 28
4 b m Acclamation—Saraluna (IRE) (Mark Of Esteem (IRE))
14[11] 242[11] 567[6] 753[10] 1441[14]

Jeannie Galloway (IRE) *Richard Fahey* 92
3 b f Bahamian Bounty—Housekeeper (IRE) (Common Grounds)
2112[6] (2762) 3947[2] 4524a[10] (5242) 6142[25]

Jebel Tara *Alan Brown* a71 83
5 b g Diktat—Chantilly (FR) (Sanglamore (USA))
114[5]

Jedi *Sir Michael Stoute* a92 105
4 ch g Pivotal—Threefold (USA) (Gulch (USA))
1220[4] ◆ (1863) 2857[4] 4461[2] ◆ 5291[3] 5908[2] 7096[4]

Jeer (IRE) *Michael Easterby* a83 84
6 ch g Selkirk(USA) —Purring (USA) (Mountain Cat (USA))
(202) 352[5] (852) (1062) 2060[5] 2349[8] 2937[10] 3688[4] 4051[4] 5868[11] 7337[11]

Jeeran *Clive Brittain* 74
2 b c Acclamation—Savvy Shopper (USA) (Stravinsky (USA))
3112[8] 5085[5] 6504[6] 7036[9]

Jehanbux (USA) *Richard Hannon* 85
2 b c Giant's Causeway(USA) —Harlan Honey (USA) (Silver Hawk (USA))
3631[2] ◆ 4318[4] (4755) 5310[3] 6160[3] 6505[6]

Jelyvator *Alex Hales* a65 45
2 b g Motivator—Camcorder (Nashwan (USA))
3785[11] 6211[4] 6514[9]

Jembatt (IRE) *Edward Lynam* a76 94
3 ch g Captain Rio—Silly Imp (IRE) (Imperial Frontier (USA))
3489a[25] 5774a[17]

Jemima Nicholas *William Haggas* 56
3 b f Compton Place—Spritzeria (Bigstone (IRE))
2297[2] ◆ 3407[2] 4584[5] 5163[7] 7006[13]

Jemimaville (IRE) *Giles Bravery* a51 65
3 b f Fasliyev(USA) —Sparkling Isle (Inchinor)
1329[8] 2221[12] 2906[6] 4687[12] 4762[7] 7005[13] 7155[9] 7300[3] 7505[7] 7651[5] 7877[2]

Jeninsky (USA) *Rae Guest* a83 95
5 ch m Stravinsky(USA) —Don't Ruffle Me (USA) (Pine Bluff (USA))
2595[11] 2971[9] 4617[9] 5052[3] 5416[3] 5834[6] 6558[10]

Jennerous Blue *Dean Ivory* a55 51
3 b f Generous(IRE) —Jennelle (Nomination)
118[3] 254[5] 2753[8] 3055[10] 4765[3] 5058[3] 5963[4] 6273[3] 6871[5] (7213)

Jenny Dawson (IRE) *John Berry* a35 35
4 b m Catcher In The Rye(IRE) —Dream Of Jenny (Caerleon (USA))
3484[10] 4207[7] 4840[7] 5380[9] 7157[12]

Jenny Potts *Chris Down* a70 74
6 b m Robellino(USA) —Fleeting Vision (IRE) (Vision (USA))
2080[6] 7778[13]

Jenny Soba *Lucinda Featherstone* a50 63
7 b m Observatory(USA) —Majalis (Mujadil (USA))
2511[8] 2902[4] 3032[5] 4174[3] 4673[2] (5202) 5289[4] 5813[8] 6051[10] 6416[6] 6915[6] 7284[9] 7634[9]

Jenny's Pride (IRE) *John Harris* a53 53
4 ch m Fath(USA) —Softly (IRE) (Grand Lodge (USA))
7[8] 503[6] 995[10] 1114[3] 7125[14]

Jenny's So Great (CAN) *Gregory De Gannes* a86 97
3 b f Greatness(USA) —Jenny's Search (USA) (Lost Soldier (USA))
6235a[6]

Jeremiah (IRE) *Jonathan Portman* a65 72
4 ch g Captain Rio—Miss Garuda (Persian Bold)
1637[3] 2279[3] 3160[9] 3783[2]

Jerrazzi (IRE) *Gary Moore* a75 88
2 bb c Kodiac—Sharadja (IRE) (Doyoun)
(4960) 5537[2] 6667[4]

Jesse James (IRE) *Jeremy Gask* a84 91
4 b g King's Best(USA) —Julie Jalouse (USA) (Kris S (USA))
769[5] 1272[5] 1841[7] 2284[4] 2926[10] 3389[13]

Jessica Ashton *John Gallagher* 26
2 ch f Monsieur Bond(IRE) —Feathergrass (IRE) (Fasliyev (USA))
6849[12] 7177[12]

Jessica Is Back (USA) *Martin D Wolfson* a107
6 ch m Put It Back(USA) —Jessica's Halo (USA) (Jolie's Halo (USA))
7341a[9]

Jessica Wigmo *Tony Carroll* a63 50
7 b m Bahamian Bounty—Queen Of Shannon (IRE) (Nordico (USA))
319[4] 388[2] 495[7] 694[5] 866[11] 976[13] 1884[15]

Je Suis Unrockstar *David Nicholls* a69 56
2 b g Monsieur Bond(IRE) —Discoed (Distinctly North (USA))
4599[11] 4890[3] 5298[9] 6035[12] 6072[4] 6645[3] 6674[8] 7016[4] 7469[4] (7641) (7894) 7931[2] 7997[7]

Jet Away *Henry Cecil* 111
3 b c Cape Cross(IRE) —Kalima (Kahyasi)
3586[5] (4028) ◆ (4757) ◆ 5590[2] 6720[6]

Jet Express (SAF) *A Al Raihe* a109 107
8 b g Jet Master(SAF) —Outback Romance (SAF) (Sharp Romance (USA))
609a[8] 713a[4] 798a[4] 1022a[14]

Jetfire *Paul Cole* a77 79
2 b f American Post—Saristar (Starborough)
2641[2] 3082[4] 3562[3] 4338[3] (5063a)

Jet Set Woman (IRE) *R Menichetti* 89
3 ch f Indian Haven—Groupetime (USA) (Gilded Time (USA))
1713a[6]

Jetta Joy (IRE) *Ann Duffield* a45 35
5 b m Hawk Wing(USA) —Woopi Gold (IRE) (Last Tycoon)
2659[11] 5515[8] 5765[6] 6076[5]

Jeu De Roseau (IRE) *Chris Grant* a57 66
6 b g Montjeu(IRE) —Roseau (Nashwan (USA))
(2765) 3223[5] (4900) 5497[5]

Jeu De Vivre (IRE) *Mark Johnston* a58 60
2 b f Montjeu(IRE) —In My Life (IRE) (Rainbow Quest (USA))
7057[9] 7223[4] 7447[7]

Jewelled *J W Hills* a68 79
4 b m Fantastic Light(USA) —Danemere (IRE) (Danehill (USA))
545[2] 673[8] 1141[6] 1797[9] (2362) 2956[9] (3309) 4044[2] 4533[3] 5237[5] 5833[11]

Jewelled Dagger (IRE) *Jim Goldie* a82 88
6 b g Daggers Drawn(USA) —Cappadoce (IRE) (General Monash (USA))
1669[9] 2452[2] 3317[10] 3708[7] 3987[4] 4823[6] 5436[6]

Jewellery (IRE) *James Fanshawe* a56 63
3 b f King's Best(USA) —Eilean Shona (Suave Dancer (USA))
1932[9] 2390[8] 3829[2] 4764[6] 5260[9] 5811[2] 6373[10] 6871[6] 7117[10]

Jezza *Victor Dartnall* a79 59
4 br g Pentire—Lara (GER) (Sharpo)
539[3] 942[2] 1207[5] (1755) 4913[10] 7068[6] (7398) ◆ (7504) (7861)

Jibaal (IRE) *Mark Johnston* a73 72
2 b g Acclamation—Maid To Order (IRE) (Zafonic (USA))
2059[5] 3199[3] 3945[7] 5637[4] ◆ 6130[3] (6902)

Jibouti (IRE) *Clive Brittain* a54
2 b c Exceed And Excel(AUS) —Treble Seven (USA) (Fusaichi Pegasus (USA))
1017[8] 3326[10]
Jibrrya *David Nicholls* a48 80
3 b g Motivator—Takarna (IRE) (Mark Of Esteem (IRE))
1182[7] 3481[4] 4377[6] 5241[8] 6144[13] 6540[7] 6826[7] 7281[6] 7599[7]
Jigajig *Kevin Ryan* a76 75
3 ch g Compton Place—Eau Rouge (Grand Lodge (USA))
998[4] (1456) 1667[2] (2185) (2291) 2449[4] 3167[3] (3277) 3731[3] 3834[3] 4343[7] 4654[3] 5424[11] 5600[2] 6714[6] 6998[6] 8005[2]
Jiggalong *Jim Best* a55 62
4 ch m Mark Of Esteem(IRE) —Kalamansi (IRE) (Sadler's Wells (USA))
1841[0] 479[9] (539) 590[7] 1262[7] 1606[2] 2303[6] 2489[8]
Jim Martin *Donal Nolan* a72 60
5 b g Auction House(USA) —Folly Finnesse (Joligeneration)
1098[9]
Jimmy Ryan (IRE) *Tim McCarthy* 65
9 b g Orpen(USA) —Kaysama (FR) (Kenmare (FR))
2808[6] 3818[6] 6270[5]
Jimmy Styles *Clive Cox* 110
6 ch g Inchinor—Inya Lake (Whittingham (IRE))
2353a[9] 2999[4] 3193[20] 4576[10] 6177[12] 6349[9] 6735[13]
Jimmy The Poacher (IRE) *Ed McMahon* a59 84
3 gr g Verglas(IRE) —Danish Gem (Danehill (USA))
1522[2] 1921[6] 2834[6] 3387[3] 3680[3] (4248) 4714[3] (5501)
Jimwil (IRE) *Michael Dods* a35 77
4 b g One Cool Cat(USA) —Vulnerable (Hector Protector (USA))
1653[8] 1967[8] 2624[RR]
Jingoism (USA) *Brian Ellison* a47
4 b g Empire Maker(USA) —Pert Lady (USA) (Cox's Ridge (USA))
5487[10] 7579[6] 7786[4]
Jinksy Minx *Suzy Smith* a43 18
3 b f Piccolo—Medway (IRE) (Shernazar)
2585[8] 3002[13] 4132[8]
Jinky *Mick Channon* a63 88
2 b g Noverre(USA) —Aries (GER) (Big Shuffle (USA))
5453[4] 5835[3] 6146[2] 6465[2] 6568[7] 6882[2] (7119)
Jinn And Tinick *Tony Carroll* 29
4 b m Kadastrof(FR) —Modesty Forbids (Formidable (USA))
3038[10] 4069[16]
Jinto *Robert Cowell* a66 70
3 ch g Halling(USA) —Sweet Willa (USA) (Assert) (4764) 6065[8] 6816[11] 7562[5]
Jira *Clive Brittain* a94 96
3 b f Medicean—Time Saved (Green Desert (USA))
945[4] 1310[6] 1713a[5] 2744[6] 4140[6] 5088[9]
Jiroft (ITY) *M Marcialis* 100
3 b c Blu Air Force(IRE) —Dexia (ITY) (Indian Ridge)
6238a[5] 7459a[3]
Jivry *Henry Candy* 79
3 ch f Generous(IRE) —Jadidh (Touching Wood (USA))
(4114) 5083[6]
J J The Jet Plane (SAF) *M Houdalakis* a80 125
6 b g Jet Master(SAF) —Majestic Guest (SAF) (Northern Guest (USA))
(7852a)
Joan D'Arc (IRE) *Michael Quinlan* a50 70
3 b f Invincible Spirit(IRE) —Prakara (IRE) (Indian Ridge)
2782[3] 4330[7] 4572[6] 4972[2] 5208[3] 7579[3] 7626[10]
Joanna (IRE) *J-C Rouget* 116
3 b f High Chaparral(IRE) —Secrete Marina (IRE) (Mujadil (USA))
(1196a) 2158a[3] (2801a) (3704a) 4885a[2] 6611a[5]
Joan's Legacy *Jimmy Fox* a32 51
3 b f Piccolo—CC Canova (Millkom)
387[7] 745[11] 2359[12] 2588[7] 3052[7]
Jobe (USA) *Kevin Ryan* a69 96
4 b g Johannesburg(USA) —Bello Cielo (USA) (Conquistador Cielo (USA))
1032[15] 2134[10]
Jobekani (IRE) *Lisa Williamson* a61 64
4 b g Tagula(IRE) —Lyca Ballerina (Marju (IRE))
354[8] 433[6] 4168[7]
Jo Boy *David Simcock* a64 17
3 b c Royal Applause—Bad Kitty (USA) (Mt. Livermore (USA))
980[6] 6060[11] 7651[3]
Jo'Burg (USA) *Jimmy O'Reilly* a75 97
6 b g Johannesburg(USA) —La Martina (Atraf)
2044[5] (2467) (2934) 3889[2] 4455[9] 5307[6] (5786) 6562[7] 6877[2] 7350[15]
Jocheski (IRE) *Tony Newcombe* a58 63
6 b g Mull Of Kintyre(USA) —Ludovica (Bustino)
2645[5] 3084[9]
Jodawes (USA) *John Best* a71
3 bb g Burning Roma(USA) —Venetian Peach (USA) (Desert Wine (USA))
443[2] 583[3] 934[7] 1168[12] (7889)
Jodi (ARG) *M F De Kock* a96 37
4 br m Matty G(USA) —Joying (ARG) (Roy (USA))
333a[5] 709a[5]
Jody Bear *Jonathan Portman* a47
2 b f Joe Bear(IRE) —Colins Lady (FR) (Colonel Collins (USA))
7558[9] 7733[8]
Joe Jo Star *Richard Fahey* a58 81
8 b g Piccolo—Zagreb Flyer (Old Vic)
2941[11]
Joe Junior *Gay Kelleway* 62
2 b g Royal Applause—Mindfulness (Primo Dominie)
1612[7] 2486[4] 2873[2]

Joe Le Taxi (IRE) *Mark Johnston* a44 56
2 ch g Johannesburg(USA) —Attasliyah (IRE) (Marju (IRE))
6102[8] 6498[8] 7279[3]
Joe Louis (ARG) *J Barton* a111 94
7 br h Lode(USA) —Jolie Caresse (USA) (Septieme Ciel (USA))
800a[9]
Joe Packet *Jonathan Portman* a66 103
3 ch g Joe Bear(IRE) —Costa Packet (IRE) (Hussonet (USA))
1061[6] 1442[4] 2052[3] (2919) (3216) (3845) ◆ 4551[4] 4819[7] 5390[4] (5966) 6319[5] 6508[7]
Joe Rua (USA) *John Ryan* a41 53
3 bb g Johannesburg(USA) —Red Tulle (USA) (A.P. Indy (USA))
118[6] 1606[6] 3170[7] 3273[6] 5058[8] 5164[10]
Joe Strummer (IRE) *Michael Bell* 44
2 b c Librettist(USA) —Post Modern (USA) (Nureyev (USA))
7303[7]
Johanan (FR) *F-X De Chevigny* a85 102
4 b g Canyon Creek(IRE) —Josapha (FR) (Tropular)
272a[8] 560a[2]
Johanna Dee (USA) *Dr Jon Scargill*
4 b m Johannesburg(USA) —School Of Deelites (USA) (Afternoon Deelites (USA))
1606[7]
Johannes (IRE) *Richard Fahey* a72 105
7 b g Mozart(IRE) —Blue Sirocco (Bluebird (USA)) (2054) 2346[13] 3193[13] 4576[13] 5095[10] 5944[11] 6177[19] 6918[3] ◆ 7079[8]
Johannesgray (IRE) *David Nicholls* a73 79
3 gr g Verglas(IRE) —Prepare For War (IRE) (Marju (IRE))
(1153) ◆ 1836[10] 2656[7] 6879[11] 7144[3] 7539[11] 7868[3] 7934[6] 7984[8]
Johannes Mozart (IRE) *F & L Camici* 109
4 ch h Spinning World(USA) —Nicolitta (IRE) (Nicolotte)
1540a[3] 2152a[5]
John Biscuit (IRE) *Andrew Balding* 80
2 ch c Hawk Wing(USA) —Princess Magdalena (Pennekamp (USA))
(5587)
Johnmanderville *Tony Carroll* a82 82
4 b g Kheleyf(USA) —Lady's Walk (IRE) (Charnwood Forest (IRE))
565[8] 779[2] 873[10] 1202[5] 1513[12] 2133[6] 3782[7]
Johnny Castle *John Gosden* a76 80
2 b c Shamardal(USA) —Photogenic (Midyan (USA))
4263[2] ◆ 4755[2] 6053[2]
Johnnycometomamie (FR) *U Suter* a88 89
3 gr g One Cool Cat(USA) —Aifa (Johann Quatz (FR))
6487a[5]
Johnny Hancocks (IRE) *David Evans* a74 78
2 b g Kodiac—Taisho (IRE) (Namaqualand (USA))
1017[6] 1632[3] 1886[3] 1978[4] 3035[6] 3598[4] (3770) 4124[6] 4600[8] 4688[2] 5000[2] 5365[5] 5863[2] (5987) 6271[2] 6435[12] 6900[5] 7211[2] 7333[3] 7424[2] 7592[7] (7777)
John Potts *Brian Baugh* a59 1
5 b g Josr Algarhoud(IRE) —Crown City (USA) (Coronado's Quest (USA))
199[4] 410[3] 622[4] 1503[8] (7706) (7918)
Johnston's Kiwi (IRE) *Eric Alston* a42 30
7 ch g Selkirk(USA) —Zilayah (USA) (Zilzal (USA))
3207[11] 3518[7]
Johnstown Lad (IRE) *Daniel Mark Loughnane* a86 84
6 b g Invincible Spirit(IRE) —Pretext (Polish Precedent (USA))
1963[2] 2689[10] 7217a[13]
John Terry (IRE) *Amanda Perrett* a95 97
7 b g Grand Lodge(USA) —Kardashina (FR) (Darshaan)
2051[1]
John Veale (USA) *Thomas McLaughlin* a77 77
4 b g Strong Hope(USA) —Soccory (USA) (Tricky Creek (USA))
(7838)
Joinedupwriting *Richard Whitaker* a60 66
5 b g Desert Style(IRE) —Ink Pot (USA) (Green Dancer (USA))
2208[3] 2421[5] 2625[10] 4156[3] 4411[6] 6298[7] 6375[3] 6669[11] 6860[12] 7055[9]
Join Up *Mark Brisbourne* a64 58
4 b g Green Desert(USA) —Rise (Polar Falcon (USA))
36[3] 124[3] 295[5] 353[3] 665[10] 757[3] 795[2] 847[2] 939[10] 4434[2] 4932[2] 5158[3] 5271[6] 5704[11] 5962[4] 6335[5] 6905[2] 7023[2] (7071) 7450[2] 7487[5] 7605[2] (7705) 7717[4]
Jolah *Clive Brittain* a66 75
2 b f Oasis Dream—Fanny's Fancy (Groom Dancer (USA))
2330[6] 3082[5] 4595[7] 5856[3] (6435) 6734[13]
Jolie Jioconde (IRE) *Edward Lynam* a63 94
2 b f Marju(IRE) —Jioconda (IRE) (Rossini (USA))
4310a[3]
Jolie's Shinju (JPN) *H Takaoka* 108
5 b m Jolie's Halo(USA) —Endearing Quality (USA) (Danzig (USA))
2154a[6]
Joli Haven (IRE) *Ms H McVittie* a33 45
4 ch m Indian Haven—Game Leader (IRE) (Mukaddamah (USA))
2161a[7]
Jolly Cooper *Mike Murphy* a40
7 gr m Silver Patriarch(IRE) —Party Treat (IRE) (Millfontaine)
1797 355[8] 563[7]
Jolly Ranch *Tony Newcombe* a59 44
4 gr m Compton Place—How Do I Know (Petong)
79[7] 3255[11]
Jolly Roger (IRE) *Neville Bycroft* 74
3 b g Oratorio(IRE) —Chalice Wells (Sadler's Wells (USA))
6262[6] (6571)

Jolly Snake (IRE) *Gerard O'Leary* a83 59
2 br c Elusive City(USA) —Satin Cape (IRE) (Cape Cross (IRE))
2352a[7]
Jollywood (IRE) *Richard Hannon* a67 79
2 bb f Holy Roman Emperor(IRE) —Save The Table (USA) (Tale Of The Cat (USA))
(2163) (2950) 3453[7] 5987[3] 6870[7]
Jonelha *Paul D'Arcy* a70 62
2 b f Kyllachy—Trump Street (First Trump)
4658[5] 5092[10] 5453[3] 5865[4] 6264[4]
Jonnie Skull (IRE) *Michael Squance* a72 74
4 b g Pyrus(USA) —Sovereign Touch (IRE) (Pennine Walk)
16[4] 115[5] 170[3] 317[7] 367[9] 451[5] 552[10] 802[DSQ] 892[5] (907) 1130[7] 1441[9] 1633[8] 5964[11] 7005[9] 7336[10] 7474[9] 7835[3] 7847[7]
Jonny Ebeneezer *David Flood* a52 66
11 b g Hurricane Sky(AUS) —Leap Of Faith (IRE) (Northiam (USA))
7250[11] 7477[7] 7607[3] 7783[11] 7885[2]
Jonny Lesters Hair (IRE) *Tim Easterby* a71 88
5 b g Danetime(IRE) —Jupiter Inlet (IRE) (Jupiter Island)
1673[2] 2211[3] 2392[2] (2580) 3317[6] 3627[2] (4152) 4652[4] (4943) 5736[8]
Jonny Mudball *Tom Dascombe* a100 111
4 b h Oasis Dream—Waypoint (Cadeaux Genereux)
1032[6] ◆ 1727[21] 2316[2] 2992[2] (3446) ◆ 4576[2] ◆ 6177[5]
Jonny No Eyebrows *Paul Leech* a50
3 br g Auction House(USA) —She's Expensive (IRE) (Spectrum (IRE))
4475[RR]
Jord (IRE) *Jeremy Glover* a65 53
6 b m Trans Island—Arcevia (IRE) (Archway (IRE))
36[7] 129[3] 194[7] 269[8] 464[2] 562[7] 845[5]
Jordan's Light (USA) *David Evans* a56 65
7 rg g Aljabr(USA) —Western Friend (USA) (Gone West (USA))
120[6] ◆ 309[8] 813[6] 2361[6] 2489[6] 2691[9]
Jordaura *John Holt* a82 92
4 br g Primo Valentino(IRE) —Christina's Dream (Spectrum (IRE))
1185[5] 1617[2] ◆ 2241[2] 2708[9] 3366[4] 4154[5] 4322[3] 4828[6] 5702[4] 6780[15] 7121[7]
Jordy Y (USA) *Wayne Catalano* a106
2 ch f Congrats(USA) —Debt Free (USA) (Fly So Free (USA))
7342a[10]
Joseph Henry *David Nicholls* a81 100
8 b g Mujadil(USA) —Iris May (Brief Truce (USA))
1006[11] 1397[4] 1857[5] 2205[8] 2657[3] 2992[4] 3224[3] 3446[5] (4536) 5302[8] 5787[4] 6175[9] 6721[4] 7060[20]
Josephine Malines *John Flint* a33 56
6 b m Inchinor—Alrisha (IRE) (Persian Bold)
7015[2]
Joseph Lister *John Gosden* a87 87
3 b g Nayef(USA) —Logic (Slip Anchor)
1735[6] 2860[3] 4257[2] (4751) 5259[3] 6359[4] 7067[2]
Joshua Tree (IRE) *A P O'Brien* 115
3 b c Montjeu(IRE) —Madeira Mist (IRE) (Grand Lodge (USA))
5185[3] 5945[5] (6951a) 7615a[10]
Josiah Bartlett (IRE) *Ian Williams* a62 58
4 b g Invincible Spirit(IRE) —Princess Caraboo (IRE) (Alzao (USA))
10[3] 269[6] 388[3] 498[11] 530[5] 665[5] 865[5]
Josie's Dream (IRE) *F J Brennan* 39
2 b g Tau Ceti—Gallery Breeze (Zamindar (USA))
3112[6]
Jo Speedy (IRE) *Mlle S-V Tarrou* a62
2 gr c Verglas(IRE) —Lorientaise (IRE) (Xaar)
7975a[4]
Josr's Magic (IRE) *Peter Hedger* a72 52
6 b g Josr Algarhoud(IRE) —Just The Trick (USA) (Phone Trick (USA))
3323[5] 3783[3] 4227[3] (5072) 5663[3] 5958[2] (6289) 6846[5] 7111[4]
Joss Stick *Luke Dace* a69 60
5 b g Josr Algarhoud(IRE) —Queen's College (IRE) (College Chapel)
1638[7] 2178[8] 3292[11] 3308[8] 3979[9] 4778[6] 5075[4] 5471[7] 5557[6] 6024[11] 6439[8]
Jossy Johnston (IRE) *Eric Alston* a47 58
2 ch g Captain Rio—Darzao (IRE) (Alzao (USA))
1686[9] 1905[7] 2785[5]
Jounce (USA) *John Gosden* a59
3 ch f Gone West(USA) —Shoogle (USA) (A.P. Indy (USA))
978[8]
Jovial (IRE) *Denis Coakley* a65 48
3 b g Sakhee(USA) —Baalbek (Barathea (IRE))
2754[8] 3635[9] 4425[11] 5330[4] 6527[3] 6574[2] (6999) ◆ (7117)
Joviality *John Gosden* 72
2 b f Cape Cross(IRE) —Night Frolic (Night Shift (USA))
7232[3] ◆
Joy And Fun (NZ) *D Cruz* 120
7 b g Cullen(AUS) —Gin Player (NZ) (Defensive Play (USA))
(1021a) 3192[13] 7852a[11]
Joyeaux *Ollie Pears* a63 68
8 b m Mark Of Esteem(IRE) —Divine Secret (Hernando (FR))
1988[11] 2849[12] 5485[12] 5926[10] 6490[8]
Joyful Victory (CAN) *Anthony Dutrow* a101
2 rg f Tapit(USA) —Wild Lucy Black (USA) (Wild Again (USA))
7342a[5]
Joyously *Paddy Butler* a69 78
2 ch f Needwood Blade—Lambadora (Suave Dancer (USA))
1263[13] (1794) 2082[2] 2397[3] 2630[2] (2918) 5246[8] 5745[13] 6130[6] 6307[8] (6500) 6845[3] 6979[6] 7165[7] 7486[8] 7631[10] 7785[5] 7888[7]
Jozafeen *Robin Bastiman* 65
3 ch f Zafeen(FR) —Faithful Beauty (IRE) (Last Tycoon)
2503[2] 3628[7] 4374[9] (5201)

J P's Gusto (USA) *David Hofmans* a113
2 b r Successful Appeal(USA) —Call Her Magic (USA) (Caller I.D. (USA))
7363a[6]
Juarla (IRE) *Ronald Harris* a57 3
2 ch c Tagula(IRE) —Jersey Lillie (IRE) (Hector Protector (USA))
4999[9] 6118[7] 6308[9] 6868[8] 7667[2] 7864[4]
Jubail (IRE) *Alan King* 80
3 ch g Redback—Daneville (IRE) (Danetime (IRE))
2900[4] 3272[3] 3963[5] (4479) 4956[5] 5994[5]
Jubilant Lady (USA) *Bryan Smart* a51 41
3 bb f Aptitude(USA) —Traverse City (USA) (Halo (USA))
3207[14] 5380[5] 5902 [6] 6494[10] 6716[9] 7166[10]
Jubilant Note (IRE) *Gordon Elliott* a68 58
8 b g Sadler's Wells(USA) —Hint Of Humour (USA) (Woodman (USA))
1207[4]
Jucebabe *John Upson* a17 18
7 b m Zilzal(USA) —Jucea (Bluebird (USA))
2809[10] 3292[15]
Judd Street *Eve Johnson Houghton* a107 110
8 b g Compton Place—Pudding Lane (IRE) (College Chapel)
434a[9] 604a[8] (822a) 1021a[6] 2030[12] 2536[3] 2999[8] 3193[26] 3891[7]
Judgement *John Gosden* a69
2 ch f Medicean—Virtuosity (Pivotal)
7185[8] 7448[3]
Judge 'n Jury *Ronald Harris* a85 108
6 ch g Pivotal—Cyclone Connie (Dr Devious (IRE))
1353[3] 2054[5] 2745[4] 3108[6] 3486a[11] 4401[16] 4814[9] 5183[2] 5308[2] ◆ 5569a[8] 5944[18] 6608a[8] 6918[15] 7079[9] 7254[8]
Judgethemoment (USA) *Jane Chapple-Hyam* a51 102
5 br g Judge T C(USA) —Rachael Tennessee (USA) (Matsadoon (USA))
1902[13] 2126[11] 2814[7] 4147[5] 8013[11]
Judiciary (IRE) *Mahmood Al Zarooni* a82 82
3 b g Invincible Spirit(IRE) —Theory Of Law (Generous (IRE))
(2101) 2607[5] 3450[4] 3807[3] 5953[6]
Judicious *Sir Michael Stoute* 54
3 ch c Pivotal—Virtuous (Exit To Nowhere (USA))
2684[7] 6356[6]
Juicy Pear (IRE) *Michael Bell* a76 72
3 b g Pyrus(USA) —Cappadoce (IRE) (General Monash (USA))
592[2] 754[3] (858) 1018[9] 2089[8] 2617[2] 3759[7]
Jukebox Jury (IRE) *Mark Johnston* 120
4 gr h Montjeu(IRE) —Mare Aux Fees (Kenmare (FR))
1026a[15] (1698) 2709[7] 3191[9] 4164a[4]
Juliano (FR) *J-L Pelletan* a48
2 gr g Enrique—My Vanessa (FR) (Medaaly)
7647a[9]
Julienas (IRE) *Walter Swinburn* a99 90
3 b g Cape Cross(IRE) —Dora Carrington (IRE) (Sri Pekan (USA))
(4425) ◆ 5264[5] 5917[2] (6449) 7100[10]
Julie's Love *Manfred Hofer* 73
2 ch f Ad Valorem(USA) —Skimmia (Mark Of Esteem (IRE))
6589a[2]
Juliet Capulet (IRE) *A P O'Brien* a85 86
2 b f Holy Roman Emperor(IRE) —Royal Ballerina (IRE) (Sadler's Wells (USA))
2059[7] 2828a[3] 3141[13] 6005a[8] 6401a[11] 6727a[4]
Julius Geezer (IRE) *Tom Dascombe* 94
2 b g Antonius Pius(USA) —Victoria's Secret (IRE) (Law Society (USA))
954a[10] 1309[4] (1819) 5221[3] 6141[9]
Jul's Lad (IRE) *Declan Carroll* a68 67
4 b g Modigliani(USA) —Woodenitbenice (USA) (Nasty And Bold (USA))
(70) 351[8] 836[8]
July Days (IRE) *David Marnane* a79 83
4 b m Exceed And Excel(AUS) —Tocade (IRE) (Kenmare (FR))
4524a[6]
Jumbajukiba *Mrs John Harrington* 112
7 b g Barathea(IRE) —Danseuse Du Soir (IRE) (Thatching)
1246a[4] 6006a[6] 6617a[9] 6783a[5]
Jumbo Vision (USA) *Daniel Mark Loughnane* a57 52
3 ch g Pollard's Vision(USA) —Ujane (USA) (Theatrical)
6168[8]
Jumeirah Palm (USA) *David Simcock* a62 47
3 rg f Distorted Humor(USA) —Zoftig (USA) (Cozzene (USA))
768[3] 971[3] 2180[12]
Jungle Bay *Jane Chapple-Hyam* a74 97
3 b c Oasis Dream—Dominica (Alhaarth (IRE))
7965[6]
Junior *David Pipe* a93 100
7 ch g Singspiel(IRE) —For More (FR) (Sanglamore (USA))
(3050) 4467[2]
Juniper Prince *Gerry Enright*
4 ch g Haafhd—Clara Vale (IRE) (In The Wings)
3559 1157[7] 4792[8]
Junket *Dr Jon Scargill* 79
3 b f Medicean—Gallivant (Danehill (USA))
6060[3] ◆ (6638) 7082[2]
Jupiter Fidius *Kate Walton* 78
3 b g Haafhd—Kyda (USA) (Gulch (USA))
1334[3] 1658[8] 2422[7] 2863[10] 3612[9] (3972) 4646[2] 5353[2] 5484[3] 6266[7] 6897[2] 7082[13]
Juquehy (FR) *P Chatelain* 60
5 gr m Verglas(IRE) —Madame Westwood (IRE) (Don't Forget Me)
332a[0]
Just As Well (USA) *Jonathan Sheppard* a95 119
7 bb h A.P. Indy(USA) —No Matter What (USA) (Nureyev (USA))
5321a[8]

Justazippy *Alan McCabe* a54 65
3 b f Where Or When(IRE) —Theatre Lady (IRE) (King's Theatre (IRE))
5971[10] 6499[7] 6876[9]

Just Beware *Zoe Davison* 46
8 b m Makbul—Bewails (IRE) (Caerleon (USA))
660[6]

Just Bond (IRE) *Geoffrey Oldroyd* a90 89
8 b g Namid—Give Warning (IRE) (Warning)
197[3] 405[4] 725[6] 863[7] (1513) 1990[2] 2241[5] 2835[11] 3408[4] 3537[5] 5685[7]

Justbookie Dot Com (IRE) *Louise Best* a69 44
2 ch g Fath(USA) —Dream On Deya (IRE) (Dolphin Street (FR))
1930[10] 2183[2] 7715[2]

Just Call Me Dave (USA) *Lisa Williamson* a19 45
4 b g Gneiss(USA) —Proud Future (USA) (Proud Birdie (USA))
2072[10] 2433[9]

Justcallmehandsome *Dominic Ffrench Davis* a77 67
8 ch g Handsome Ridge—Pearl Dawn (IRE) (Jareer (USA))
29[6] 84[5] 259[4] 315[6] 405[5] 587[10] 790[10] 873[4] 925[2] 1051[4] (1238) 1458[8] 3054[5] 3970[11] 5655[6] 6372[7] 6718[8] 6935[8] 7663[5]

Just Dan *David Thompson* a53 43
4 b g Best Of The Bests(IRE) —Scapavia (FR) (Alzao (USA))
1071[10]

Justenuffhumor (USA) *Saeed Bin Suroor* 119
5 b h Distorted Humor(USA) —Justenuffheart (USA) (Broad Brush (USA))
631a[6] 801a[5] 1025a[15]

Just Five (IRE) *Michael Dods* a85 80
4 b g Olmodavor(USA) —Wildsplash (USA) (Deputy Minister (CAN))
908[3] (1494) 1826[6] 3107[7] 4403[8] 4949[4] 5596[2] (7122) 7403[8]

Just For Leo (IRE) *David Evans* a59 68
2 b g Camacho—Coppelia (IRE) (Mac's Imp (USA))
1331[4] 1597[3] 1835[8] 2216[3] 2440[2] 4677[4] 5021[6] 6568[22] 6954[6] 7269[7] 7641[4] 7809[4] 7983[3] 8011[6]

Just For Mary *Daniel Mark Loughnane* a68 88
6 b g Groom Dancer(USA) —Summer Dance (Sadler's Wells (USA))
1091a[10] 1874[5] 4180a[10] 6739[7] 7466[10]

Justice Walk (IRE) *Miss J R Tooth* 41
2 ch c Exceed And Excel(AUS) —True Joy (IRE) (Zilzal (USA))
6634[8]

Just Jenda (USA) *Cindy Jones* a108
4 ch m Menifee(USA) —Liberty School (USA) (Pine Bluff (USA))
1242a[4]

Just Jimmy (IRE) *David Evans* a67 65
5 b g Ashkalani(IRE) —Berkeley Hall (Saddlers' Hall (IRE))
129[7] 348[6] 373[6] 4681[9] 5877[3] 6133[3] 6370[3] 6581[5] 6632[7] 6934[5] 7336[5] 7450[3] 7502[7]

Just Like Silk (USA) *Gerard Butler* a78 90
4 b g Elusive Quality(USA) —Ocean Silk (USA) (Dynaformer (USA))
2976[17] 3566[10] 3787[3]

Just Lille (IRE) *Ann Duffield* a99 98
7 b m Mull Of Kintyre(USA) —Tamasriya (IRE) (Doyoun)
1151[8] 1378[10] 1752[4] 2031[13] (2761) (2857) 3194[9] 3752[6] 4507[8] 6304[5] 6715[3] 7189[13]

Just Mandy (IRE) *Richard Fahey* a63 64
3 ch f Noverre(USA) —Unicamp (Royal Academy (USA))
453[3] 624[3] 784[2] (909) 977[5]

Just My Girl *Patrick Leech* a41
3 b f Antonius Pius(USA) —Corniche Quest (IRE) (Salt Dome (USA))
1620[11] 2011[12] 2564[16] 2787[9]

Just Nod (IRE) *Ruth Carr* 33
4 b m Deploy—Summerhill Special (IRE) (Roi Danzig (USA))
5022[5] 5478[6] 5636[11] 6262[8]

Justonefortheroad *Richard Fahey* a73 95
4 b g Domedriver(IRE) —Lavinia's Grace (USA) (Green Desert (USA))
(2451) 3366[5] 3920[6] 4459[12] 5386[2] (5737) ◆ 6178[4] (6721) 7348[15]

Just Rob *Ian Williams* a85 90
5 b g Robellino(USA) —Scapavia (FR) (Alzao (USA))
224[4] (1690) 3588[7]

Just Sam (IRE) *Ron Barr* a61 79
5 b m Mull Of Kintyre(USA) —Strawberry Sands (Lugana Beach)
1754[3] (2504) 2578[5] 3065[13] 3224[5] 3854[9] 4171[2] 4558[5] 5424[6] 5684[8] 6040[12]

Just Say Please *Dean Ivory* a51
3 ch f Needwood Blade—Roonah Quay (IRE) (Soviet Lad (USA))
392[7] 583[6] 843[8] 1162[11] 1495[10]

Just That (SLO) *M Weiss*
5 b m Capri—Just Me (FR) (El Badr)
461a[5]

Just The Tonic *Marjorie Fife* a55 69
3 ch f Medicean—Goodwood Blizzard (Inchinor)
2185[4] 2628[4] (2834) 3061[8] (3771) 4898[11] 5421[RR]

Just Timmy Marcus *Brian Baugh* a72 61
4 ch g Ishiguru(USA) —Grandads Dream (Never So Bold)
285[8] 373[8] 467[5] 2864[3] ◆ 4119[8] 4644[4] 4986[6] 5766[2] 6210[2] 6370[6] 6713[5] 6934[6] ◆ 7214[5] 7376[3] 7699[2] 7812[5] 7837[4]

Just Zak *O Brennan* a54 34
5 b g Superior Premium—Goodbye Millie (Sayf El Arab (USA))
5303[11] 7069[6] 7338[7]

Jutland *Mark Johnston* 98
3 b g Halling(USA) —Dramatique (Darshaan)
1362[2] ◆ 1502[6] 2253[6] 2969[3] (3265) (3581) 4470[8] 5188[4] 5475[3] 6106[5] 6355[11]

Juwireya *Peter Hiatt* a66 69
3 b f Nayef(USA) —Katayeb (IRE) (Machiavellian (USA))
2051[8] 2585[4] 3116[11] 3593[6] 4557[7] 5164[4] 5522[6] 5963[8] (7957)

Kaballero (GER) *Steve Gollings* a48 49
9 ch g Lomitas—Keniana (IRE) (Sharpo)
804[4] 918[8] 1172[5] 1293[13]

Kachgai (IRE) *Y De Nicolay* a100 108
7 b g Kaldounevees(FR) —Toujours Juste (FR) (Always Fair (USA))
5576a[2] 6640a[2]

Kachiri (IRE) *Peter Grayson* a1
2 b f Noverre(USA) —Eltihaab (USA) (Danzig (USA))
5268[7]

Kadabra (IRE) *F & L Camici* 95
3 b f Dubawi(IRE) —Windy Britain (Mark Of Esteem (IRE))
1713a[4]

Kader Firtinasi (TUR) *M Tekdemir* a56
6 b h Distant Relative—Nevres (TUR) (Barnato (USA))
5781a[8]

Kadoodd (IRE) *Mick Channon* 73
2 b c Motivator—Briery (IRE) (Salse (USA))
6473[6] 6779[2] 7236[6]

Kadouchski (FR) *John Berry* a53 42
6 b g Ski Chief(USA) —Douchka (FR) (Fijar Tango (FR))
228[3] 7649[4]

Kagera *B Grizzetti* 92
2 b f Halling(USA) —Baila Salsa (IRE) (Barathea (IRE))
6975a[4]

Kagura (USA) *G Henrot* a91 100
2 b f Vindication(USA) —Miss Emma (IRE) (Key Of Luck (USA))
5137a[2]

Kahfre *Gary Moore* a72 55
3 ch g Peintre Celebre(USA) —Minerva (IRE) (Caerleon (USA))
7967[3]

Kaiasedie (IRE) *David Nicholls*
3 b g Desert Style(IRE) —Silver Arrow (USA) (Shadeed (USA))
1402[10]

Kaifi (IRE) *Clive Brittain* 36
2 b f Dansili—Easter Fairy (USA) (Fusaichi Pegasus (USA))
2749[7] 3237[5] 5558[7]

Kai Mook *Olivia Maylam* a75 65
3 gb f Littletown Boy(USA) —Beenaboutabit (Komaite (USA))
3361[9] 5541[12] 5866[13] 6371[10]

Kaitlins Joy (IRE) *Patrick Martin* a89 91
5 b m Mark Of Esteem(IRE) —Cieladeed (USA) (Shadeed (USA))
4463a[9]

Kajima *Richard Hannon* a96 89
3 b g Oasis Dream—Mambo Mistress (USA) (Kingmambo (USA))
1168[3] (1476) ◆ (1934) 2713[3] 3271[2] (5030) 6888[29]

Kakapuka *Anabel L M King* a52 80
3 br c Shinko Forest(IRE) —No Rehearsal (FR) (Baillamont (USA))
(1547) ◆ 1750[3] 2599[3] 2928[3] (3436) 4091[10] 4865[8]

Kakatosi *Andrew Balding* a107 103
3 br g Pastoral Pursuits—Ladywell Blaise (IRE) (Turtle Island (IRE))
2122[2] ◆ (2968) (3696) (4264) (5143) 6349[12]

Kalacan (IRE) *G M Lyons* a81 82
4 br g Kalanisi(IRE) —Lovelyst (IRE) (Machiavellian (USA))
6730a[3] 7589a[5]

Kalahaag (IRE) *Richard Hannon* 84
2 ch f Iffraaj—Verbania (IRE) (In The Wings)
4095[9] ◆ (4508) 5490[3] 6157[5] 6559[14]

Kalahari Desert (IRE) *Richard Whitaker* a57 64
3 b g Captain Rio—Sally Traffic (River Falls)
1750[7] 2834[10] 4406[4] 4703[3] 5548[7] 6696[8] 7052[7]

Kalahari Gold (IRE) *Doug Watson* a108 110
5 ch g Trans Island—Neat Shilling (IRE) (Bob Back (USA))
417a[5] 626a[4] 823a[2] 1022a[6]

Kalamill (IRE) *Shaun Lycett* 79
3 b g Kalanisi(IRE) —Desert Pageant (IRE) (Desert King (IRE))
2281[5] 3116[8] 5260[3]

Kal Barg *D Selvaratnam* a104 87
5 b g Medicean—Persian Air (Persian Bold)
(441a) 632a[4] 706a[3] (821a)

Kaldoun Kingdom (IRE) *Richard Fahey* a47 111
5 b g King's Best(USA) —Bint Kaldoun (IRE) (Kaldoun (FR))
(1032) 2526[3] 3193[15] 4391[2] 4576[22] 6177[7] 6752[10] 7351[5]

Kalendar Girl (IRE) *Willie Musson* 53
2 b f Motivator—Kalanda (Desert King (IRE))
6158[8]

Kaleo *Simon Dow* a9 86
6 ch g Lomitas—Kazoo (Shareef Dancer (USA))
3814[2] 4996[P] 6450[10] 6552[7]

Kalgoolie *Rae Guest* a49 40
2 b f Aussie Rules(USA) —Kilbride (Selkirk (USA))
4695[7] 5170[7]

Kali (GER) *Mme M Bollack-Badel* 103
3 b f Areion(GER) —Kahlua (GER) (Dashing Blade)
(1715a) 2801a[2] 7266a[10]

Kalidoun (FR) *T Larriviere* a73
3 b g Kouroun(FR) —Vangeline (FR) (Vaguely Pleasant (FR))
547a[3]

Kalkan Bay *Jedd O'Keeffe* a72 71
2 b g Pastoral Pursuits—Gibraltar Bay (IRE) (Cape Cross (IRE))
3433[9] 3657[5] 4447[6] (4984) 5597[7] 5947[10] 6745[3] 7280[6]

Kalk Bay (IRE) *William Haggas* a94 89
3 b g Hawk Wing(USA) —Politesse (USA) (Barathea (IRE))
4107[4] ◆ (4679) (5086) ◆ 6002[3] (6659) ◆

Kalla *J Hirschberger* 107
4 b m Monsun(GER) —Kittiwake (Barathea (IRE))
5345a[10]

Kalleidoscope *Mick Channon* 74
2 ch f Pivotal—Brush Strokes (Cadeaux Genereux)
2223[7] 4338[5] (5509)

Kalligal *Roger Ingram* a53 57
5 br m Kyllachy—Anytime Baby (Bairn (USA))
538[4] 674[10] 768[9] 984[12] 1437[10] 1633[12] 4776[7] 5209[5]

Kalypso King (USA) *Sylvester Kirk* a51 98
3 ch c Giant's Causeway(USA) —Kalypso Katie (IRE) (Fairy King (USA))
2226[9] 2999[9] 4357[11] 5030[9] 6780[16] 7090[10] 7483[12]

Kamanja (UAE) *Michael Attwater* a59 40
4 b m Red Ransom(USA) —Nasmatt (Danehill (USA))
80[6]

Kambis *Luca Cumani* a54
2 b g Tobougg(IRE) —Queen Tomyra (IRE) (Montjeu (IRE))
7163[11] 7503[9]

Kameruka *R Pritchard-Gordon* a96 86
4 ch m Auction House(USA) —Love Letters (Pursuit Of Love)
6409a[5] 7188[5]

Kames Park (IRE) *Richard Guest* a79 86
8 b g Desert Sun—Persian Sally (IRE) (Persian Bold)
120[3] 282[3] 430[2] (526) 620[2] 756[5] 871[6] (888) 1348[5] (1484) 1720[9] 2031[5] 2343[3] 2739[5] 2857[10] 3060[5] (3282) 3807[2] 4348[3] 5070[5] 5549[5] 5757[7] 6393[4] 7089[2] 7337[8] 7480[3]

Kammaan *David Peter Nagle* a67 81
4 b m Diktat—Qasirah (IRE) (Machiavellian (USA))
5129a[4]

Kammamuri (IRE) *Stuart Williams* a67
5 b g Kalanisi(IRE) —Speedybird (IRE) (Danehill (USA))
7626[4]

Kamphora (IRE) *Terry Clement*
5 b m Desert Style(IRE) —Bobanvi (Timeless Times (USA))
1932[16] 2415[12]

Kanace *Ann Duffield* a56 50
3 ch g Pastoral Pursuits—Pendulum (Pursuit Of Love)
1796[3] 7338[10]

Kanaf (IRE) *Ed Dunlop* a88 96
3 b g Elnadim(USA) —Catcher Applause (Royal Applause)
(1599) 2090[3] 2960[4] 3436[2] 4398[4] (4930) (5967) ◆ 6319[14]

Kannon *Alan McCabe* a60 69
5 b m Kyllachy—Violet (IRE) (Mukaddamah (USA))
7[10] 88[3] 248[5]

Kanotier (FR) *Mme M Bollack-Badel* 77
2 b c Daliapour(IRE) —Knout (FR) (Kendor (FR))
7975a[7]

Kansai Spirit (IRE) *John Gosden* a94 102
4 ch g Sinndar(IRE) —Daanat Nawal (Machiavellian (USA))
2860[7] 3764[5] ◆ (4257) (5035) ◆ (5743)

Kaolak (USA) *John Ryan* a95 99
4 bb h Action This Day(USA) —Cerita (USA) (Magesterial (USA))
335a[5] 441a[12] 903[7] 1008[18] 1697[13] 2322[8] 2934[3] 3239[P] 3633[7]

Kaptain Kirkup (IRE) *Michael Dods* 107
3 ch c Captain Rio—Aquatint (Dansili)
1315[11] (2028) 2712[4] 3066[10] 4126[7] 5911[13] 6721[11]

Karafuse (IRE) *Tim Easterby* 51
2 ch f Refuse To Bend(IRE) —Prakara (IRE) (Indian Ridge)
2239[10] 2939[14] 3175[3] 4150[8] 4554[5] 5020[4]

Karaka Jack *Mark Johnston* a91 93
3 ch g Pivotal—Mauri Moon (Green Desert (USA))
1310[8] 1497[2] 1703[7] 2835[9] 3334[6] 3867[9] 4828[17] 6205[12] 6430[9] 6984[7]

Karam Albaari (IRE) *John Jenkins* a76 106
2 b c King's Best(USA) —Lilakiya (IRE) (Dr Fong (USA))
(5657) 5943[4] 7081[6]

Karasiyra (IRE) *John M Oxx* 99
3 ch f Alhaarth(IRE) —Kerania (IRE) (Daylami (IRE))
1036a[4] 3007a[2] 4631a[5] 6786a[7]

Karate (IRE) *Mark Johnston* a68 70
2 ch g Exceed And Excel(AUS) —La Belle Katherine (USA) (Lyphard (USA))
6046[2] 6309[4] 6666[8] 6989[2] ◆ 7224[8]

Karate Queen *Ron Barr* a57 43
5 b m King's Best(USA) —Black Belt Shopper (IRE) (Desert Prince (IRE))
2629[4] 2854[12] 3538[15] 4486[6] 4605[5] 4868[11] 5024[9] 5545[8] 6037[8] 6077[5]

Kardyls Hope (IRE) *Jarlath P Fahey* a78 82
4 b m Fath(USA) —Elite Hope (USA) (Moment Of Hope (USA))
4524a[3]

Karens Legacy (IRE) *Ian McInnes* 15
2 ch f Exceed And Excel(AUS) —Stardance (USA) (Rahy (USA))
5761[9] 6293[10]

Kargali (IRE) *Luke Comer* a109 105
5 gr h Invincible Spirit(IRE) —Karliyka (IRE) (Last Tycoon)
(1246a) 2118[7] 4463a[14] 6009a[9] 6611a[10]

Kargarann (IRE) *Stef Higgins* a46 49
3 b g Danehill Dancer(IRE) —Romancia (USA) (Woodman (USA))
3635[8] 4385[7] 5007[6] 6080[12] 6454[9] 6871[7] 7213[6] 7579[8]

Karky Schultz (GER) *James Eustace* a59 67
5 gr g Diktat—Kazoo (Shareef Dancer (USA))
121[9] (1262) 6065[9] 6775[3]

Karmarouge (IRE) *B S Rothwell* 17
2 b f Croco Rouge(IRE) —Karmafair (IRE) (Always Fair (USA))
5066[13]

Kartica *P Demercastel* 98
3 b f Rainbow Quest(USA) —Cayman Sunset (IRE) (Night Shift (USA))
1566a[6] 2801a[4] 7416a[3]

Kasbah Bliss (FR) *F Doumen* a78 117
8 b g Kahyasi—Marital Bliss (FR) (Double Bed (FR))
1748a[2] 2375a[2] 3102[6] 6016a[5] 6607a[3]

Kashimin (IRE) *Alan Swinbank* a82 85
5 b g Kyllachy—Oh So Misty (Teenoso (USA))
4170[5] 4403[4] 4822[2] 4949[5]

Kashmina *Sheena West* a67 70
5 ch m Dr Fong(USA) —Lady Melbourne (IRE) (Indian Ridge)
1636[5] 2488[5] 2811[4] 3040[6]

Kashmiriana (IRE) *Luca Cumani* a31 65
3 ch f Rainbow Quest(USA) —Thermopylae (Tenby)
5038[6] 5832[5] 6313[7]

Kassaab *Jeremy Gask* a52 67
2 br c Kyllachy—Aconite (Primo Dominie)
1668[3] 2068[5] 7999[6]

Kassiodor (GER) *Barney Curley* a50
3 b g Tiger Hill(IRE) —Kitcat (GER) (Monsun (GER))
7406[12] 7872[6]

Kataragama *Kate Walton* a68 67
4 b m Hawk Wing(USA) —Torrealta (In The Wings)
1116[4] 1489[5] 2109[3]

Katchmore (IRE) *Michael Blanshard* a65 65
3 br g Catcher In The Rye(IRE) —One For Me (Tragic Role (USA))
450a[2] 698[4] 1582[13] 2935[9] 7286[13]

Katehari (IRE) *Andrew Balding* a64 75
3 b f Noverre(USA) —Katariya (IRE) (Barathea (IRE))
1269[7] 1582[6] 2342[11] 2871[7]

Katell (IRE) *Linda Stubbs* 91
2 br g Statue Of Liberty(USA) —Procession (Zafonic (USA))
(3971) 4934[2] 5184[5] 5850[2]

Katerini (FR) *F Head* 90
2 b f Cacique(IRE) —Chanteleau (USA) (A.P. Indy (USA))
4637a[5]

Kate Skate *Gay Kelleway* a61 67
3 ch f Mark Of Esteem(IRE) —Saristar (Starborough)
3907[5] 4365[8] 4651[7] (5686) 5890[4] 6996[2] (7154)

Katherine Parr *Peter Chapple-Hyam* a44
2 ch f Haafhd—Kristina (Kris)
7879[11]

Kathindi (IRE) *Neil King* a69 57
3 ch g Pearl Of Love(IRE) —Turfcare Flight (IRE) (Mujadil (USA))
183[3] (305) 482[5] 564[2] 964[8] 1264[3] 3002[8] 3640[4] 3960[7] 7003[10]

Kathlatino *Micky Hammond* 73
3 b f Danbird(AUS) —Silver Rhythm (Silver Patriarch (IRE))
1804[3] 2425[2] 2837[4] 3601[4] 4117[4] 4867[7] 6225[9]

Kathleen Cox (IRE) *Niall Moran* a28 31
5 ch m Alhaarth(IRE) —Gintilgalla (IRE) (Grand Lodge (USA))
2765[10]

Kathleen Frances *Mark H Tompkins* 84
3 b f Sakhee(USA) —Trew Class (Inchinor)
1314[9] 2255[9] (2909) (4972) (5953) 6754[3]

Kathleen Kennet *Martin Bosley* a55 40
10 b m Turtle Island(IRE) —Evaporate (Insan (USA))
289[2] 389[7] 663[7] 1042[5] 1437[9] 2678[9]

Kathmanblu (USA) *Kenneth McPeek* 107
2 b f Bluegrass Cat(USA) —Abba Gold (USA) (Devil's Bag (USA))
7340a[3]

Katiesister *Jim Goldie* 56
2 b f Librettist(USA) —College Maid (IRE) (College Chapel)
5334[6] 5785[8] 6138[7] 6979[10]

Katie The Hatter (IRE) *Mike Murphy* a48
4 b m Celtic Swing—Kathleen's Dream (USA) (Last Tycoon)
950[10]

Katla (IRE) *J F Grogan* 106
2 b f Majestic Missile(IRE) —Bratislava (Dr Fong (USA))
6401a[5] (6751) 7277a[3]

Katmai River (IRE) *Mark Usher* a60 63
3 b g Choisir(AUS) —Katavi (USA) (Stravinsky (USA))
4679[10] 5153[2] 5658[7] 6255[2] (6657) 7006[11] 7401[9] 7706[3] 7863[4]

Katsya (FR) *J E Pease* a76 87
3 b f Sinndar(IRE) —Labyrinth (FR) (Exit To Nowhere (USA))
7545a[10]

Katy's Secret *William Jarvis* a66 55
3 b f Mind Games—Katy O'Hara (Komaite (USA))
1222[3] 1640[4] (1994) 2679[5] 7656[6]

Kaua'i Girl *Ann Duffield* 65
2 ch f Dubawi(IRE) —Sara Mana Mou (Medicean)
6071[7] ◆ 6268[4] 6459[3] 6920[9] 7412[6]

Kavachi (IRE) *Gary Moore* a70 95
7 b g Cadeaux Genereux—Answered Prayer (Green Desert (USA))
1474[7] 1846[5] 2472[5] 2977[8] 3456[4] 3889[8] 4459[6] ◆ (5003) 5540[6] 5994[4] 6780[14] 7121[8] 7637[10]

Kayaan *Pam Sly* a67 56
3 br g Marju(IRE) —Raheefa (USA) (Riverman (USA))
2220[8] 2632[7] 3587[7] 5656[3] ◆ (6080) 6623[7] 7167[8]

Kaya Belle (GER) *T Mundry* 78
3 b f Lando(GER) —Kahina (GER) (Warning)
3943a[9]

Kayf Aramis *Nigel Twiston-Davies* a66 94
8 b g Kayf Tara—Ara (Birthright)
6201[9] 6926[17]

Kay Gee Be (IRE) *William Jarvis* a96 99
6 b g Fasliyev(USA) —Pursuit Of Truth (USA) (Irish River (FR))
1085[3] 1900[14] 2508[5] 3366[3] (3846) 4459[17] 5264[4] 6204[7] 6510[8]

Kazbow (IRE) *Luca Cumani* a79 92
4 b g Rainbow Quest(USA) —Kasota (IRE) (Alzao (USA))
1609[2] 2014[2] (2495) (3398)

Kazzene (USA) *F Chappet* a80 87
3 b g Cozzene(USA) —Coconut Willamina (USA) (Pleasant Colony (USA))
2557a[5]

Keenes Day (FR) *Mark Johnston* a99 100
5 gr g Daylami(IRE) —Key Academy (Royal Academy (USA))
2126[10] 3566[2] 3843[9] 4320[7] (4983) 6352[9]

Keenes Royale *Ralph Beckett* a78 63
3 b f Red Ransom(USA) —Kinnaird (IRE) (Dr Devious (IRE))
(118) (254) (482) 1138[6] 2869[6] 3909[4] 5646[6]

Keep Cool *Andreas Lowe* 100
3 b c Starcraft(NZ) —Kirov (Darshaan)
1745a[2] 2406a[4] 4184a[16] 5671a[4] 7532a[2]

Keep Dancing (IRE) *Ron Barr* a63 73
4 b m Distant Music(USA) —Miss Indigo (Indian Ridge)
2087[8] 3064[16]

Keep Discovering (IRE) *E Charpy* a77 85
5 b g Oasis Dream—Side Of Paradise (IRE) (Sadler's Wells (USA))
441a[7]

Keep It Cool (IRE) *P F O'Donnell* a70 74
6 ch g Spinning World(USA) —Sudden Stir (USA) (Woodman (USA))
2571a[5]

Keep Silent *John Berry* a31 30
3 gr f Largesse—Not A Word (Batshoof)
1976[9] 3213[7]

Keeptheboatafloat (USA) *Mrs A M O'Shea* a90 85
4 b g Fusaichi Pegasus(USA) —The Perfect Life (IRE) (Try My Best (USA))
7823a[P]

Keertana (USA) *Thomas F Proctor* 109
4 bb m Johar(USA) —Motokiks (USA) (Storm Cat (USA))
7343a[3]

Keisha (FR) *C Laffon-Parias* 60
2 b f Green Tune(USA) —Alyzea (IRE) (King Charlemagne (USA))
7383a[6]

Kelinni (IRE) *Amanda Perrett* a75
2 b c Refuse To Bend(IRE) —Orinoco (IRE) (Darshaan)
5724[7] ◆ (6118)

Kellys Eye (IRE) *David Brown* 101
3 b g Noverre(USA) —Limit (IRE) (Barathea (IRE))
1750[2] 2069[3] (2426) (2656) (3088) 3791[7] 4536[18] ◆ 4653[8] 6175[19] 6319[4] 6776[9] 7060[8] ◆

Kelty In Love (FR) *T Larriviere* a86 100
3 b f Keltos(FR) —Ever In Love (FR) (Neverneyev (USA))
926a[6] 1610a[11]

Kendalewood *Tim Walford* 58
4 b g Viking Ruler(AUS) —Wilsonic (Damister (USA))
1705[4] 2424[8] 3552[9]

Kenmour (FR) *P Demercastel* a78 91
3 gr c Azamour(IRE) —Marie De Ken (FR) (Kendor (FR))
3703a[6]

Kensei (IRE) *Ralph Beckett* a77 81
3 ch g Peintre Celebre(USA) —Journey Of Hope (USA) (Slew O'Gold (USA))
1734[3] 2089[6] (2684) 4573[14] 5266[8] 6807[5]

Ken's Girl *Stuart Kittow* a64 82
6 ch m Ishiguru(USA) —There's Two (IRE) (Ashkalani (IRE))
1258[11] 1775[7] (2342) 3001[4] 3592[4] 4324[10] 4680[2] 5149[3] (5541) 6629[2] 7182[3]

Kensington (IRE) *Alan McCabe* a73 71
9 b g Cape Cross(IRE) —March Star (IRE) (Mac's Imp (USA))
285[2] 373[10] 465[2] 602[3] 779[6] 1374[16] 1509[4] 4910[9] 5634[5] 6110[2] 6679[12] 6812[4] 7033[4] 7399[8]

Kenswick *Pat Eddery* a57 58
3 b f Avonbridge—The Jotter (Night Shift (USA))
826[3] 1048[6] 1293[2] 1505[4] 1795[4] 2172[2] 2414[5] 4133[7] 4249[9] 7885[8]

Kentish (USA) *Jane Chapple-Hyam* a37
3 bb c Storm Cat(USA) —Apple Of Kent (USA) (Kris S (USA))
5668[6]

Kentish Dream *F Chappet* a79 53
4 b h Oasis Dream—Danella (FR) (Highest Honor (FR))
304a[0]

Kentmere (IRE) *Paul Webber* a70
9 b g Efisio—Addaya (IRE) (Persian Bold)
164[9] 322[3] 554[2] 4686[7]

Kenton Street *Michael J Browne* a67 64
5 ch g Compton Place—Western Applause (Royal Applause)
7336[4]

Kenyan Cat *George Baker* a66 71
3 br f One Cool Cat(USA) —Nairobi (FR) (Anabaa (USA))
2588[11] 3677[8] 4344[4] 4762[5] 5271[5] 5770[3] (6094) (6518) 6993[3] ◆ 7184[2]

Kepler's Law *Sir Mark Prescott Bt* 43
2 b g Galileo(IRE) —Tina Heights (Shirley Heights)
6514[12] 6676[9] 6874[9] 7036[6]

Kepresh (FR) *H-A Pantall* a76 75
3 b g Bahhare(USA) —Miss Balines (FR) (Grape Tree Road)
7959a[5]

Kerashan (IRE) *A Al Raihe* a66 86
8 b g Sinndar(IRE) —Kerataka (IRE) (Doyoun)
512a[11]

Keratiya (FR) *J-C Rouget* 105
2 b f Iron Mask(USA) —Kerasha (FR) (Daylami (IRE))
(3718a) 5347a[9] 5907[6] 7277a[0]

Kerchak (USA) *William Jarvis* a81 82
3 b g Royal Academy(USA) —Traude (USA) (River Special (USA))
1269[4] 2025[5] 2682[8] (3155) 3581[3] 4360[5] 5084[2] 5868[3] 6781[3]

Kerdem (IRE) *Patrick Payne* 102
7 b g Rainbow Quest(USA) —Kermiyana (IRE) (Green Desert (USA))
7032a[15]

Keredari (IRE) *John M Oxx* 107
3 b c Oasis Dream—Kerataka (IRE) (Doyoun)
2354a[6] 6617a[2] 7266a[5]

Kermiyan (FR) *J-C Rouget* a85 94
3 b c Green Desert(USA) —Kerasha (FR) (Daylami (IRE))
5576a[6]

Kerno (IRE) *P Monfort* a94 95
6 b g Invincible Spirit(IRE) —Waking Redhead (USA) (Miswaki (USA))
304a[5] 549a[4] 743a[6]

Kerrys Requiem (IRE) *Mick Channon* a86 96
4 b m King's Best(USA) —Moonlight Wish (IRE) (Peintre Celebre (USA))
1076[2] 1438[2] 1692[4] 1862[8] 2140[4] 2327[7] (2929) 3505[4] 3850[8] 4145[10] 4536[14] 4930[7] 5285[6] 5521[4]

Kersivay *David Evans* a79 73
4 b g Royal Applause—Lochmaddy (Selkirk (USA))
192[4] 373[7] 668[4] (767) 808[7] 1366[12] 1428[2] 7093[11] 7332[11] 7564[3] 7701[9]

Kevkat (IRE) *Eoin Griffin* a81 75
9 br g Dushyantor(USA) —Diamond Display (IRE) (Shardari)
6910a[3] 7589a[P]

Key Breeze *Kevin Ryan* a71 63
3 b g Exceed And Excel(AUS) —Cayman Sound (Turtle Island (IRE))
1511[11] 2762[5] 3151[8] 3515[8] 4061[5] (4951) 5361[3] (6336) ◆ 6540[5]

Key Impeller *Ollie Pears* 41
2 b g Bertolini(USA) —Latch Key Lady (USA) (Tejano (USA))
1749[8] 2832[16]

Key Lago (IRE) *Michael Dods* a75 70
2 b c Kheleyf(USA) —Up On Points (Royal Academy (USA))
2448[6] 3756[3] 5418[4] ◆ (6369) 6900[3]

Key Light (IRE) *J W Hills* a73 75
3 b f Acclamation—Eva Luna (IRE) (Double Schwartz)
(1269) 2120[13] 2565[5] 3328[6] 3958[2] 4424[3] 5037[6] 6057[9] 6772[9] 7377[10]

Key Of Fortune (IRE) *Jennie Candlish* a57 52
4 b m Key Of Luck(USA) —Alaynia (IRE) (Hamas (IRE))
410[8]

Key Partners (IRE) *Roger Curtis* a34 64
9 b g Key Of Luck(USA) —Teacher Preacher (IRE) (Taufan (USA))
470[9] 724[7]

Keys Of Cyprus *David Nicholls* a26 91
8 ch g Deploy—Krisia (Kris)
(1707) 2885[3] 3121[6] 3920[13] 3987[2] 4459[19] 5098[5] 5605[3] 6105[4] 6510[12] 7143[4]

Key To Love (IRE) *Adrian Chamberlain* a47 27
4 b m Key Of Luck(USA) —Ski For Me (IRE) (Barathea (IRE))
4987[15]

Key To The Motion (IRE) *Paul Midgley* 49
2 b f Kheleyf(USA) —Rustle In The Wind (Barathea (IRE))
1597[7] 2873[8] 3686[6] 4195[8] 5042[4] 6035[5] 7983[10]

Key West (IRE) *John Gosden* 64
2 ch g Kheleyf(USA) —Quinzey (JPN) (Carnegie (IRE))
2547[15] 4499[5] 4759[5] 5644[6]

Kfar Sama (FR) *D Guillemin* a64 81
2 b f Okawango(USA) —Ginger Twist (Most Welcome)
2917a[7]

K'Gari (USA) *Brian Ellison* a55 40
4 ch g Fusaichi Pegasus(USA) —To Act (USA) (Roberto (USA))
15[10] 764[5]

Khajaaly (IRE) *Julia Feilden* a73 70
3 b g Kheleyf(USA) —Joyfullness (USA) (Dixieland Band (USA))
1127[5] 1659[7] 2242[5] 2587[14] 3212[4] 3683[2] 4705[4] 5367[10] 5839[9] (7502) (7812)

Khaki (IRE) *Tor Sturgis* a56
2 b f Key Of Luck(USA) —Tithcar (Cadeaux Genereux)
8001[7]

Khaleeji *J W Hills* a78 66
2 b c Kyllachy—Fly In Style (Hernando (FR))
6145[5] 6697[2] 7065[2]

Khandaq (USA) *Valentine Donoghue* 77
3 b g Gulch(USA) —Jadarah (USA) (Red Ransom (USA))
1336[9] 1927[3] 3586[4] (6186) 6394[11] 6709[10] 7499[U]

Khanivorous *Jim Boyle* a80 59
3 b g Dubai Destination(USA) —Bright Edge (Danehill Dancer (IRE))
366[2] 490[2] 617[4] 7965[4]

Khateer *Clive Brittain* a67
3 ch c Shamardal(USA) —Polly Perkins (IRE) (Pivotal)
997[7] 7086[5] 7244[3]

Khattaab (USA) *B W Hills* 94
3 bb c Dixie Union(USA) —Jemima (Owington)
2537[8]

Khawatim *J-C Rouget* 103
2 b c Intikhab(USA) —Don't Tell Mum (IRE) (Dansili)
4637a[3] 6760a[4]

Khawlah (IRE) *Saeed Bin Suroor* 91
2 b f Cape Cross(IRE) —Villarrica (USA) (Selkirk (USA))
5692[2] ◆ (6154) 6528[3]

Khazara *David Evans* 33
3 ch f Starcraft(NZ) —Mystery Lot (IRE) (Revoque (IRE))
2998[13] 4534[10]

Kheley (IRE) *Mark Brisbourne* a67 72
4 b m Kheleyf(USA) —Namesake (Nashwan (USA))
79[2] 125[2] 306[8] 349[3] 462[7] 556[4] 678[3] 778[5] 896[5] 968[4] 1112[8] 1234[4] 1588[3] 1929[2] 2186[4] 2726[7] 2957[8] 7018[11] 7249[6] 7506[7] 7783[2] (7807) 7953[3]

Khelino (IRE) *Rodger Sweeney* a74 80
2 b f Kheleyf(USA) —Special Park (USA) (Trempolino (USA))
3421a[7]

Khelwa (FR) *R Gibson* 88
3 b f Traditionally(USA) —Khaliyna (IRE) (Danehill (USA))
5139a[11] 5981a[3] 6551a[9]

Kheskianto (IRE) *Michael Chapman* a52 64
4 b m Kheleyf(USA) —Gently (IRE) (Darshaan)
21[6] 34[9] 171[5] 1653[14] 1928[6] 2383[8] 3120[5] 3538[8] 3610[5] 4897[10] 4939[7] 6077[4]

Kheya (IRE) *George Moore* 64
2 b f Kheleyf(USA) —Monarchy (IRE) (Common Grounds)
1331[9] 2292[2] 2693[5] 3163[5] 6646[9] 7301[12]

Kheylide (IRE) *Daniel Christopher O'Brien* a57 72
4 ch g Kheleyf(USA) —Jayzdoll (IRE) (Stravinsky (USA))
1595[12]

Khor Dubai (IRE) *A bin Huzaim* a109 103
4 b h Kheleyf(USA) —Dievotchkina (IRE) (Bluebird (USA))
337a[11] 413a[8] 713a[8]

Khor Sheed *Luca Cumani* 102
2 ch f Dubawi(IRE) —Princess Manila (CAN) (Manila (USA))
2861[2] (3453) ◆ 4842[3] (6157) 6530[10]

Khun John (IRE) *Willie Musson* a67 66
7 b g Marju(IRE) —Kathy Caerleon (IRE) (Caerleon (USA))
868[12] (1134) 2723[8]

Kialoskar (IRE) *T Lemer* 66
2 b f Refuse To Bend(IRE) —Romea (Muhtarram (USA))
7009a[6]

Kiama Bay (IRE) *John Quinn* a81 74
4 b g Fraam—La Panthere (USA) (Pine Bluff (USA))
6297[2] ◆ (7054) 7337[2] 7504[12]

Kian's Delight *Jedd O'Keeffe* 56
2 b g Whipper(USA) —Desert Royalty (IRE) (Alhaarth (IRE))
6070[13] 6566[4]

Kickahead (USA) *Ian Williams* a62 65
8 b g Danzig(USA) —Krissante (USA) (Kris)
13[5] 130[5] (198) 1980[6]

Kid Charlemagne (IRE) *Warren Greatrex* 99
7 b g King Charlemagne(USA) —Albertville (GER) (Top Ville)
1851[2] 3195[7] 4506[6] 5492[7]

Kidlat *Alan Bailey* a85 87
5 b g Cape Cross(IRE) —Arruhan (IRE) (Mujtahid (USA))
837[4] ◆ 873[3] 943[6] 1011[6] (1051) (1156) 1513[2] 1780[10] 2241[8] 2314[4] 3121[9] 3318[16] 6797[10] 6990[11] 7548[4] 7600[3] 7756[3] ◆

Kidnapping (IRE) *S Botti* 117
3 b c Intikhab(USA) —Claba Di San Jore (IRE) (Barathea (IRE))
1945a[6] 6014a[3]

Kielder (IRE) *David Barron* 73
3 ch g Shinko Forest(IRE) —Ctesiphon (USA) (Arch (USA))
1890[2] 2517[5] 3227[5] (3507) 4647[8] 5484[6] 6571[6]

Kielty's Folly *Brian Baugh* a60 49
6 gr g Weet-A-Minute(IRE) —Three Sweeties (Cruise Missile)
7[7] 290[5] 499[4] 540[2] 753[8] 1193[4] 1507[4] 1998[3] 2417[5] 2727[7] 3132[6] 7543[4] 7706[2] 7986[7]

Kieron's Dream (IRE) *Jedd O'Keeffe* 46
2 b g Araafa(IRE) —Mount Street (IRE) (Pennekamp (USA))
6268[10] 6894[5] 7346[12]

Kilburn *Alastair Lidderdale* a78 79
6 b g Grand Lodge(USA) —Lady Lahar (Fraam)
1374[11] (2596) 3036[3] 3782[9] (4206) 4579[7] 5287[9] 5866[12] 5919[11] 6852[6] (7255) 7724[7]

Kildare Sun (IRE) *John Mackie* a74 73
8 b g Desert Sun—Megan's Dream (IRE) (Fayruz)
2392[11] 2705[7] 3911[12] 7529[4] (7679) 7788[5] 8008[10]

Kilk *Tony Newcombe* a14 61
2 b f Striking Ambition—Bathwick Alice (Mark Of Esteem (IRE))
4675[2] 5466[5] 6248[12]

Kilkenny Bay *William Jarvis* a57 21
4 b m Tobougg(IRE) —Miss Arizona (IRE) (Sure Blade (USA))
925[5] 1591[13]

Killing Moon (USA) *Kevin Ryan* a42 71
3 ch g Pleasantly Perfect(USA) —Luia (USA) (Forty Niner (USA))
385[9] 784[7] 1336[5] 1753[2] 2132[2] 2296[2] 3161[3] (3530)

Killusty Fancy (IRE) *Dominic Ffrench Davis* a67 70
3 b g Refuse To Bend(IRE) —Crafty Fancy (IRE) (Intikhab (USA))
1977[14] (2792) 4965[3] 5467[8] 5953[8]

Kilmanseck *Eve Johnson Houghton* a68 68
3 b g Royal Applause—Corndavon (USA) (Sheikh Albadou)
1347[2] 1619[7] 2618[9] 3350[7] 3771[5] 4700[9] 4775[9]

Kilo Alpha *Mme C Head-Maarek* 99
3 b f King's Best(USA) —Anasazi (IRE) (Sadler's Wells (USA))
5139a[9]

Kilt Rock (IRE) *Richard Guest* a72 77
3 ch g Giant's Causeway(USA) —Eliza (USA) (Mt. Livermore (USA))
1347[3] 1619[2] 1873[3] 3831[3] 4555[2] 4898[8] (5421) 5500[4]

Kimberley Downs (USA) *Noel Wilson* a75 90
4 gr g Giant's Causeway(USA) —Fountain Lake (USA) (Vigors (USA))
1151[9] 1689[5] 2938[13] 3588[8] 4190[5] 4825[8] (5244) 5436[8] 7171[4] 7327[4] (7397) 7600[6] 7694[4]

Kimble (FR) *N Leenders* a88 102
8 b g Jimble(FR) —Kipartira (FR) (Magwal (FR))
5109a[5] 6016a[3]

Kims Rose (IRE) *John Flint* a32 59
7 br m Desert Prince(IRE) —Pinta (IRE) (Ahonoora)
211[11] 499[13]

Kindest *Chris Wall* 92
4 b m Cadeaux Genereux—Star Profile (IRE) (Sadler's Wells (USA))
1933[11] (2937) ◆ 3627[4] 4152[2] 4841[5] 5994[3] (6204) 6510[10]

Kind Heart *Donald McCain* a77 77
4 b m Red Ransom(USA) —Portorosa (USA) (Irish River (FR))
3860[7]

Kindlelight Blue (IRE) *Nick Littmoden* a76 71
6 gr g Golan(IRE) —Kalimar (IRE) (Bigstone (IRE))
200[3]

Kindlelight Sun (JPN) *Nick Littmoden* a71
4 br g King Kamehameha(JPN) —Nicer (IRE) (Pennine Walk)
(355) ◆

Kingaroo (IRE) *Gary Woodward* a65 50
4 b g King Charlemagne(USA) —Lady Naomi (USA) (Distant View (USA))
1148[3] 1503[12] 2257[6] 2788[4] 4522[9] 5515[5] 7327[7] (7407) (7541) 7642[3] 7695[4]

Kingarrick *Eve Johnson Houghton* 74
2 ch g Selkirk(USA) —Rosacara (Green Desert (USA))
4096[6] 4460[6] (5608) 6505[10]

King Bertolini (IRE) *Alan Berry* a53
3 b c Bertolini(USA) —Bareilly (USA) (Lyphard (USA))
7129[4] 7869[3]

King Bling (IRE) *Sylvester Kirk* a43 51
2 b g Camacho—No Hard Feelings (IRE) (Alzao (USA))
2077[12] 2839[13] 4131[7] 5256[7] 5659[10] 5837[7] 6129[11] 7017[7] 7088[7]

King Canute (IRE) *Neil Mulholland* a59 59
6 b g Danehill(USA) —Mona Stella (USA) (Nureyev (USA))
389[2] (691) 845[4] 1148[9] 1305[9]

King Cobra (IRE) *J W Hills* a55 50
2 ch c Bachelor Duke(USA) —Remedy (Pivotal)
3964[10] 4423[4] 5328[4] 6673[15] 7496[3]

King Columbo (IRE) *Julia Feilden* a67 75
5 ch g King Charlemagne(USA) —Columbian Sand (IRE) (Salmon Leap (USA))
1128[8] 2009[10] 2714[3] 3168[3] 3412[3] 4108[6] 4382[7] 5254[4] 5593[2] 5905[10] 6261[15] 7184[10] 7491[6]

King Dancer (IRE) *S Woods* 116
4 ch h Danehill Dancer(IRE) —Uriah (GER) (Acatenango (GER))
7851a[6]

King David (FR) *M Boutin* a65 99
2 b c Iffraaj—Azucar (IRE) (Desert Prince (IRE))
5133a[3] 5799a[5] 6218a[4] 7975a[2]

Kingdom Of Fife *Sir Michael Stoute* 114
5 b g Kingmambo(USA) —Fairy Godmother (Fairy King (USA))
1328[7] 1832[5] 3144[3] 4139[5] 4535[6] 5538[6]

Kingdom Of Light *Howard Johnson* 102
3 gr g Exceed And Excel(AUS) —Silver Chime (Robellino (USA))
2346[14] 2978[16] (4118)

Kingdom Of Munster (IRE) *Richard Fahey* a41 93
3 b g Danehill Dancer(IRE) —Kitty O'Shea (Sadler's Wells (USA))
1019[7] 1315[19] 1834[11] 4153[5] 4545[8] 4925[3] 5942[2] 6269[14] 6359[3] 6650[3]

King Ferdinand *Andrew Balding* 71
2 b c Tobougg(IRE) —Spanish Gold (Vettori (IRE))
6153[7] 6748[4]

King Fernando *P Beaumont* a8 44
7 gr g Silver Patriarch(IRE) —Kastelruth (Midyan (USA))
139[10] 244[12]

King Fingal (IRE) *John Quinn* 85
5 b g King's Best(USA) —Llia (Shirley Heights)
1277[2] (1751) 2084[3] 2435[3] 2976[13] 4943[10] 6677[8]

Kingfisher Blue (IRE) *Jamie Osborne* a54 53
2 b g Majestic Missile(IRE) —Queenfisher (Scottish Reel)
4460[10] 5808[6] 6369[6] 6769[11]

King In Waiting (IRE) *J Hetherton* a63 68
7 b g Sadler's Wells(USA) —Ballerina (IRE) (Dancing Brave (USA))
1424[3] 2060[3] 2659[3]

King Jock (USA) *Tracey Collins* a85 107
9 b g Ghazi(USA) —Glen Kate (Glenstal (USA))
412a[9] 630a[7] (1408a) 1954a[2] 2570a[4] 3069[23] 5016a[4]

King Kenny *Mrs A Malzard* a78 44
5 ch g Lomitas—Salanka (IRE) (Persian Heights)
2162a[2]

King Kurt (IRE) *Kevin Ryan* 70
2 b g Holy Roman Emperor(IRE) —Rutledge (IRE) (Entrepreneur)
3624[9] 4477[3] 4709[6] 5849[12] 6979[11]

King Of Aquitaine (IRE) *Kevin Ryan* a80 80
2 b c Holy Roman Emperor(IRE) —Plume Rouge (Pivotal)
1905[6] 3118[2] (3449) 4066[3] 5094[5] 5745[9] 6184[11] (6795)

King Of Aran (IRE) *M J Grassick* a78 73
3 bb g Val Royal(FR) —Innishmore (IRE) (Lear Fan (USA))
6336[4]

King Of Cassis *Bill Turner* 63
2 b g Statue Of Liberty(USA) —Douce Maison (IRE) (Fools Holme (USA))
1793[5] 1957[4] 2407[5] 2631[3] 2939[8] 4150[10]

King Of Connacht *Mark Wellings* a64 63
7 b g Polish Precedent(USA) —Lady Melbourne (IRE) (Indian Ridge)
294[4] 396[4] 469[3] 7449[7] 7562[12]

King Of Dixie (USA) *William Knight* a111 112
6 ch g Kingmambo(USA) —Dixie Accent (USA) (Dixieland Band (USA))
(1614) 2318[4] 3888[7]

King Of Eden (IRE) *Eric Alston* 86
4 b g Royal Applause—Moonlight Paradise (USA) (Irish River (FR))
(1569) 1915[4] ◆ (2381) (2671) (3584) 4345[3] 5480[6] 5789[7]

King Of Jazz (IRE) *Richard Hannon* 79
2 b c Acclamation—Grand Slam Maria (FR) (Anabaa (USA))
2077[2] ◆ 2547[3]

King Of Legend (IRE) *Dave Morris* a70 59
6 b g King Charlemagne(USA) —Last Quarry (Handsome Sailor)
75[6]

King Of Reason *David Simcock* a68 99
3 b g King's Best(USA) —Sheer Reason (USA) (Danzig (USA))
1694[2] 2288[2] 3103[5] ◆ (3713) 4144[3] ◆ (4924)

King Of Rhythm (IRE) *Declan Carroll* a62 66
7 b g Imperial Ballet(IRE) —Sharadja (IRE) (Doyoun)
21[7] 194[9] 354[9] 757[8] 6269[16] 6518[15]

King Of Rome (IRE) *M F De Kock* a106 114
5 b g Montjeu(IRE) —Amizette (USA) (Forty Niner (USA))
334a[2] (419a) ◆ 627a[2] 799a[12]

King Of Swords (IRE) *Nigel Tinkler* a54 81
6 b g Desert Prince(IRE) —Okey Dorey (IRE) (Lake Coniston (IRE))
1337[7] 1524[9] 1710[6] 1988[7] 2528[8] 2818[9] 3687[6] 3908[3] 4343[3] 4415[2] 4452[5] (4712) 5123[3] 5513[10]

King Of Sydney (USA) *Mario Hofer* 111
4 b h Diesis—Padmore (USA) (French Deputy (USA))
1251a[7] 1747a[7] 2576a[8] 7776a[0]

King Of The Beers (USA) *T J Bougourd* a68 54
6 rg g Silver Deputy(CAN) —Pracer (USA) (Lyphard (USA))
1816a[5]

King Of The Celts (IRE) *Tim Easterby* 76
2 b g Celtic Swing—Flamands (IRE) (Sadler's Wells (USA))
2990[3] 3874[2] 4346[3] 6070[2]

King Of The Desert (IRE) *Ed Dunlop* a60 64
2 b c Librettist(USA) —Amandian (IRE) (Indian Ridge)
4228[3] 4871[5] 5453[7] 6162[10]

King Of The Moors (USA) *David Bourton* a55 76
7 b g King Of Kings(IRE) —Araza (USA) (Arazi (USA))
(1396) 1752[3] 2328[5] 2523[4] 2991[10] 3130[3] 3732[6] 3973[6] 4088[5] 5213[10] 5407[7] 5436[3] 6029[2] 6396[3] 7171[2] 7251[6]

King Of The Ring *John M Oxx* 76
2 b g Indesatchel(IRE) —Razzle (IRE) (Green Desert (USA))
4175a[5]

King Of The Titans (IRE) *Patrick Gilligan* a40 30
7 b g Titus Livius(FR) —She's The Tops (Shernazar)
4348[6] 7043[10]

King Of Wands *John Gosden* 114
4 b g Galileo(IRE) —Maid To Treasure (IRE) (Rainbow Quest (USA))
(1529) 2716[4] (3695) 5218[3]

King Of Windsor (IRE) *Ralph Beckett* a84 95
3 b g Intikhab(USA) —Kismah (Machiavellian (USA))
2517[2] (3148) 3867[4] 4357[2] 5662[6] 6391[9]

King Olav (UAE) *Tony Carroll* a98 93
5 ch g Halling(USA) —Karamzin (USA) (Nureyev (USA))
(480) (697) 1015[2] 1220[9] (1960) 2747[12] 6562[35] 7612[11]

Kings Ace (IRE) *Alan Berry* a60 62
4 b g King's Best(USA) —Full Cream (USA) (Hennessy (USA))
187[3] 297[2] 328[7] 836[7] 895[4]

Kings Aphrodite *Gay Kelleway* a33 42
3 gr g Reset(AUS) —Arctic Queen (Linamix (FR))
812[6] 861[6] 1181[9]

King's Approach (IRE) *Ronald Harris* a60 73
3 gr g Fasliyev(USA) —Lady Georgina (Linamix (FR))
1842[7] 2215[8] 2648[9] 2868[7] 3313[4] 3525[4] 3982[10] 4300[4] 4534[7] 4791[2] 5171[4] 5669[10] 6522[11] 6865[4]

Kings Arms *Michael Easterby* 33
2 ch g Needwood Blade—Silent Tribute (IRE) (Lion Cavern (USA))
3449[7] 3874[7] 4346[12] 5630[15] 6027[6] 6294[7]

Kings Bayonet *Henry Cecil* a80 85
3 ch g Needwood Blade—Retaliator (Rudimentary (USA))
2479[4] 5383[9] 5917[7] 6274[2] ◆ 6805[6]

King's Caprice *Jimmy Fox* a66 78
9 ch g Pursuit Of Love—Palace Street (USA) (Secreto (USA))
(1258) 1692[6] 2415[8] 2840[5] 3863[10] 6444[12] 6812[5] 7241[6] 7376[4] 7611[7] 7837[3] 8014[9]

King's Chorister *Finbar Murtagh* a61 60
4 ch g King's Best(USA) —Chorist (Pivotal)
4648[10]

King's Colour *Brett Johnson* a90 88
5 b g King's Best(USA) —Red Garland (Selkirk (USA))
3172[8] (3813) 4354[11] 6205[9] 6510[13] 7318[5] 7560[7] 7881[6] 8033[3]

King's Counsel (IRE) *David O'Meara* a41 65
4 ch g Refuse To Bend(IRE) —Nesaah's Princess (Sinndar (IRE))
1296[5] (2625) 3149[4] 4168[3]

Kings Craic *Declan Carroll* a27 24
3 b g Compton Place—Syzygy (IRE) (Entrepreneur)
1401[9] 6896[13] 7328[11] 7499[5]

Kingscroft (IRE) *Mark Johnston* a71 71
2 b g Antonius Pius(USA) —Handsome Anna (IRE) (Bigstone (IRE))
4123[7] 4379[3] 4645[5] 7880[2]

Kingsdale Orion (IRE) *Brian Ellison* a82 85
6 bb g Intikhab(USA) —Jinsiyah (USA) (Housebuster (USA))
300[2] 917[2] 1101[14] 1398[2] 2031[7] 3319[3] 3974[10]

Kings Destiny *Michael Jarvis* a111 108
4 b g Dubai Destination(USA) —Jalousie (IRE) (Barathea (IRE))
(1665) 2710[7] 4139[7] 5307[8] 5970[2] 6179[6] (6738)

Kingsdine (IRE) *Malcolm Saunders* a72 83
3 b c King's Best(USA) —Lunadine (FR) (Bering)
964[7] 1209[3] 1795[2] (2359) (2844) 3297[3] ◆ 3970[2] (4325)

King's Fable (USA) *Karen George* a51 65
7 b g Lear Fan(USA) —Fairy Fable (IRE) (Fairy King (USA))
942[10]

Kingsfort (USA) *Saeed Bin Suroor* 117
3 bb c War Chant(USA) —Princess Kris (Kris)
6570[5] (7234)

Kings Gambit (SAF) *Tom Tate* 116
6 ch g Silvano(GER) —Lady Brompton (SAF) (Al Mufti (USA))
(1333) 1832[4] 2637a[5] 3144[2] 3921[2] ◆ 5274[3] 6179[2] 6720[2]

Kingsgate Castle *Gay Kelleway* a68 65
5 b g Kyllachy—Ella Lamees (Statoblest)
501[4] 658[4] 810[4] 912[10]

Kingsgate Choice (IRE) *John Best* a76 97
3 b c Choisir(AUS) —Kenema (IRE) (Petardia)
2052[11] (2442) ◆ (2822) ◆ 3791[15] 5250[5] 5966[11]

Kingsgate Native (IRE) *Sir Michael Stoute* 123
5 b g Mujadil(USA) —Native Force (IRE) (Indian Ridge)
(2325) 3047[6] 3870[4] 5276[9] 5744[4] 6390[3] 7852a[6]

King's Head (IRE) *Linda Perratt* a96 77
7 b g King's Best(USA) —Ustka (Lomond (USA))
1512[7] 2243[5] 2761[5] 3202[6] 3901[3] 4405[15] 5215[9]

King's Icon (IRE) *Michael Wigham* a72 63
5 b g King's Best(USA) —Pink Sovietstaia (FR) (Soviet Star (USA))
262[9] 427[4] 665[2] 757[2] (814) 853[2] 1241[5] 2602[9]

King's Jester (IRE) *Lee Smyth* a59 56
8 b g King's Best(USA) —Scent Of Success (USA) (Quiet American (USA))
(211) 353[6] 665[9] 753[6] 939[4] 2454[3] 3147[6] 4188[7] 6213[12]

Kings Maiden (IRE) *James Moffatt* a65 68
7 b m King's Theatre(IRE) —Maidenhair (IRE) (Darshaan)
1207[7]

Kingsmaite *Roy Bowring* a74 34
9 b g Komaite(USA) —Antonias Melody (Rambo Dancer (CAN))
465[7] 1239[9] 1884[9] 2653[6] 5634[8] 6125[11]

King's Majesty (IRE) *Tim Pitt* a69 61
8 b g King's Best(USA) —Tiavanita (USA) (J O Tobin (USA))
5420[9]

King's Masque *Bernard Llewellyn* a80 85
4 b g Noverre(USA) —Top Flight Queen (Mark Of Esteem (IRE))
941[5] (994) 1241[2] (1840) (2411) 2922[2] 3265[2] 3894[3] 4399[4] (4859) 5591[3]

King's Miracle (IRE) *Jeremy Gask* a46
4 ch m King's Best(USA) —Pretty Sharp (Interrex (CAN))
145[5] 229[12]

Kings 'n Dreams *Dean Ivory* a66 78
3 b g Royal Applause—Last Dream (IRE) (Alzao (USA))
1269[8] 1619[4] 2566[15] 3393[2] (4109) 4398[5] 5495[5] ◆ 6198[12] 6879[8]

Kings Of Leo *Jim Boyle* a70 83
3 b f Compton Place—Mrs Brown (Royal Applause)
111[5] 2179[7] 2784[4] 3293[8]

King's Omaha (IRE) *A Peraino* 89
2 ch c King's Best(USA) —Lady Elysees (USA) (Royal Academy (USA))
3253a[5] 7850a[11]

Kings On The Roof *Patrick Leech* a13 49
4 b g King Charlemagne(USA) —Stylish Clare (IRE) (Desert Style (IRE))
845[10] 4234[9] 5565[4] 5680[7] 6062[9]

King's Parade *Sir Michael Stoute* a65 72
3 b c Dynaformer(USA) —Bay Tree (IRE) (Daylami (IRE))
1182[6] 2079[10]

Kings Point (IRE) *David Nicholls* a89 82
9 b h Fasliyev(USA) —Rahika Rose (Unfuwain (USA))
2377[6] 2760[3] 3180[3] 3537[8] 4093[8] 4514[4] 4986[3] 5406[4] 5499[4] 6026[5] 6396[6]

King's Realm (IRE) *Sir Mark Prescott Bt* a70 52
3 ch g King's Best(USA) —Sweet Home Alabama (IRE) (Desert Prince (IRE))
6527[11] (6855) 7067[7]

King's Revenge *Shaun Lycett* a64 65
7 br g Wizard King—Retaliator (Rudimentary (USA))
7626[5]

King's Sabre *David Bourton* a66 67
4 ch g King's Best(USA) —Lightsabre (Polar Falcon (USA))
378[9] 499[9] 789[7] 845[8] 912[6] 1170[6] 1812[2] 1885[3] 2263[9] 2385[4] 2624[4] (2874) 3226[2] 3284[5] 3597[2] 3610[4] 3973[9] 4403[5] 4581[4] 4866[4] 5357[13] 5499[5] 5867[7] 6296[2] 6452[7] 6853[10]

King's Salute (USA) *Mark Johnston* a97 68
4 b g Kingmambo(USA) —Imperial Gesture (USA) (Langfuhr (CAN))
447[2] 697[7]

King's Song (IRE) *Sir Michael Stoute* a79 84
4 ch h Indian Ridge—Alleluia (Caerleon (USA))
1161[8] 1579[2] 1783[6]

King's Starlet *Hughie Morrison* a87 95
4 b m King's Best(USA) —Brightest Star (Unfuwain (USA))
2326[9] 3752[8]

Kingston Acacia *Andrew Balding* a73 79
3 br f King Of Roses(AUS) —Derartu (AUS) (Last Tycoon)
(1593) (2005) 2713[8] 3375[9] 5896[8] 6291[6] 7209[10]

Kingston Folly *Andrew Haynes* a55
3 gr g Septieme Ciel(USA) —Napapijri (FR) (Highest Honor (FR))
189[7] 677[9] 7387[6]

Kings Topic (USA) *Andrew Haynes* a70 53
10 ch g Kingmambo(USA) —Topicount (USA) (Private Account (USA))
390[6] 611[5] 685[4] 791[3] 1226[8] 1507[11] 3214[8] 4132[3]

Kings Troop *Alan King* a70 90
4 ch g Bertolini(USA) —Glorious Colours (Spectrum (IRE))
3160[3] 3589[2] (4295) 5084[3] (5888) 6283[2] 7084[12]

King Supreme (IRE) *Richard Hannon* a76 88
5 b g King's Best(USA) —Oregon Trail (USA) (Gone West (USA))
251[0] 5084[6] 5286[3] 5679[7] 6480[7] 7190[6] 7321[3] 7553[7]

King's Vintage (IRE) *Thomas Mullins* 80
3 b f King's Best(USA) —Vintage Tipple (IRE) (Entrepreneur)
4178a[8]

Kingswinford (IRE) *David Evans* a80 85
4 b g Noverre(USA) —Berenica (IRE) (College Chapel)
1076[5] 1149[2] 1374[9] 1779[2] 1933[4] (2009) 2339[6] (2840) 3396[8] 5082[6]

King's Wonder *Ruth Carr* a87 97
5 ch g King's Best(USA) —Signs And Wonders (Danehill (USA))
1423[5] ◆ 2748[9] 3578[3] 3845[3] 4536[10] 5242[8] (5496) 6537[9] 7409[4] 7539[3]

King Torus (IRE) *Richard Hannon* 114
2 b c Oratorio(IRE) —Dipterous (IRE) (Mujadil (USA))
(2384) 3190[4] (3868) (4468) 6610a[7]

King Zeal (IRE) *Barry Leavy* a56 86
6 b g King's Best(USA) —Manureva (USA) (Nureyev (USA))
893[9] 1193[7] 1507[3] 2006[4] (2653) (2902) 3559[8] (4094) 4752[2] 5071[6] (6328) 6724[2] 7062[7]

Kinian (USA) *John Best* 55
3 ch g Langfuhr(CAN) —Back It Up (USA) (Mt. Livermore (USA))
1442[8] 2003[6] 4422[8]

Kinigi (IRE) *Ronald Harris* a77 79
4 gr m Verglas(IRE) —Kamalame (USA) (Souvenir Copy (USA))
116[4] 235[4] 296[7] 2965[6] 3086[5] 3518[4] 3763[9] 4430[8] 4789[5] 5579[2] (5715) (5876) 6455[2] (6741) (6858) 7033[9] 7405[5] 7539[4] 7841[4]

Kinkeel (IRE) *Tony Carroll*
11 b g Hubbly Bubbly(USA) —Bubbly Beau (Beau Charmeur (FR))
186[11]

Kinky Afro (IRE) *J S Moore* a84 99
3 b f Modigliani(USA) —Feet Of Flame (USA) (Theatrical)
(159) 448[5] (490) (792) 973[4] 1250a[2] 1715a[5] 2543[6] 3071[5] 3467a[8] 4472[3] 5114[2] 5782a[3]

Kinlochrannoch *Ben Haslam* 79
2 b f Kyllachy—Guermantes (Distant Relative)
4402[4] 5640[2] (6263)

Kinsale King (USA) *Carl O'Callaghan* a123 119
5 bb g Yankee Victor(USA) —Flaming Mirage (USA) (Woodman (USA))
(1024a) 3192[3] 3870[12] 7361a[7]

Kinsya *Mark H Tompkins* a86 88
7 ch g Mister Baileys—Kimono (IRE) (Machiavellian (USA))
231[10] 394[11] 2937[8] 5852[12]

Kinyras (IRE) *Sir Michael Stoute* 74
2 ch c Peintre Celebre(USA) —Amathusia (Selkirk (USA))
4263[4] 6414[4] ◆

Kipchak (IRE) *Conor Dore* a79 82
5 bb g Soviet Star(USA) —Khawafi (Kris)
144[4] (342) 465[4] (747) 802[5] 1044[7] 1149[6] 1458[4] 1634[7] 1995[2] 2524[5] 2896[10] 3777[7] 4260[8] (4366) (4586) 4690[5] 5157[5] 5866[4] 6372[9] 7332[5] 7399[5] 7439[6] 7614[3] 7812[2] 7966[3]

Kipling (FR) *Rod Collet* a66 77
6 gr g Kaldounevees(FR) —Racoon (FR) (Be My Guest (USA))
332a[4]

Kirkby's Gem *Alan Berry* 49
3 b f Firebreak—Just A Gem (Superlative)
1155[6] 1468[7] 1987[5] 3181[4] 3903[6] 4406[9] 4674[5] 5041[5] 6039[6] 6186[5] 6897[7] 7601[6]

Kirkie (USA) *Tim Pitt* a68 27
5 bb g Gulch(USA) —Saleela (USA) (Nureyev (USA))
227[8]

Kirklees (IRE) *Saeed Bin Suroor* a121 119
6 b h Jade Robbery(USA) —Moyesii (USA) (Diesis)
6179[4] 6720[3] 7237[6]

Kirkum (IRE) *Diana Weeden*
5 b g Selkirk(USA) —Jumilla (USA) (El Gran Senor (USA))
1705[8] 4258[9] 4893[11]

Kirsty's Boy (IRE) *J S Moore* a72 78
3 ch g Tagula(IRE) —Mayfair (Green Desert (USA))
136[5] (424) (633) 1842[5] 2049[4] 2415[7] 2617[3]

Kirstys Lad *Michael Mullineaux* a58 59
8 b g Lake Coniston(IRE) —Killick (Slip Anchor)
36[4] 131[6] 211[2] 227[2] (353) 407[3] 666[6] 753[4] 854[4] 940[8] 995[9]

Kirthill (IRE) *Luca Cumani* 77
2 b c Danehill Dancer(IRE) —Kirtle (Hector Protector (USA))
7058[2] ◆

Kissable (IRE) *Kevin Prendergast* 110
2 b f Danehill Dancer(IRE) —Kitty O'Shea (Sadler's Wells (USA))
4077a[3] ◆ 5570a[3]

Kiss A Prince *Dean Ivory* a84 72
4 b g Fraam—Prancing (Prince Sabo)
1530[5] 2236[6] 2821[8] 3330[2] 3782[2] 4488[6] (4839) 5142[11] 5964[5] 6479[4] 6852[3] (7190) (7736)

Kiss Doll (IRE) *C Lerner* a22 39
2 gr f Verglas(IRE) —King's Doll (IRE) (King's Best (USA))
5137a[8]

Kissing Clara (IRE) *J S Moore* a63 67
2 b f Elusive City(USA) —Purepleasureseeker (IRE) (Grand Lodge (USA))
1577[10] 2338[12] 2457[3] 3106[2] 3636[2] 4286[2] 4623[9] 4736[2] 5204[3] 6070[3] 6412[5] 6795[4] 7088[3] (7271)

Kiss Mine (USA) *David Vance* 105
4 bb m Mineshaft(USA) —Kiss The Devil (USA) (Kris S (USA))
6757a[7]

Kiss My Tiara (IRE) *Brian Meehan* 47
2 b f High Chaparral(IRE) —Blushing Away (USA) (Blushing Groom (FR))
5047[11] 5691[14]

Kiss N Kick *Lucinda Featherstone*
4 b g And Beyond(IRE) —Silent Angel (Petong)
6115[12]

Kiss 'n Tell *Gary Moore* a47 2
4 ch m Sakhee(USA) —Time For Tea (IRE) (Imperial Frontier (USA))
226[6] 356[5]

Kiss Senora (FR) *A Bonin* a60 66
6 gr m Chichicastenango(FR) —Bonne Bosq (FR) (Kaldoun (FR))
690a[0]

Kite Hunter (IRE) *Mario Hofer* 103
3 ch c Muhtathir—Miss Chryss (IRE) (Indian Ridge)
1564a[2] 2405a[2] 3934a[U] 4888a[9] 7800a[0]

Kite Wood (IRE) *Saeed Bin Suroor* 121
4 b h Galileo(IRE) —Kite Mark (Mark Of Esteem (IRE))
(2375a) 3102[7] 5080[6] 5976a[7]

Kithonia (FR) *Henry Cecil* 95
3 b f Sadler's Wells(USA) —Ratukidul (FR) (Danehill (USA))
2889[5] 3822[6] 6552[3]

Kitty Fisher *Ron Hodges* a23
2 b f Kyllachy—Alzianah (Alzao (USA))
6954[16] 7271[11] 7520[9]

Kitty Kiernan *J S Bolger* 104
3 b f Pivotal—Alstemeria (IRE) (Danehill (USA))
2353a[8] 3571a[7] 4269a[7]

Kitty Koo (IRE) *Tony Carroll* a50 42
3 ch f Dr Fong(USA) —Jesting (Muhtarram (USA))
326[5] 551[7] 768[10] 4992[10] 5869[8] 6517[3] 6871[9] 7887[6]

Kitty Wells *Luca Cumani* a85 61
3 b f Sadler's Wells(USA) —Kithanga (IRE) (Darshaan)
2891[5] 3795[10] 7419[3] ◆ (7963)

Kiwi Bay *Michael Dods* a88 100
5 b g Mujahid(USA) —Bay Of Plenty (FR) (Octagonal (NZ))
1006[5] ◆ 1272[4] 2086[7] (2835) 3146[21] 3920[5] 4570[7] 6178[8] (6567) 6749[10] 7348[7]

Kladester (USA) *Michael Herrington* a61 42
4 ch g Van Nistelrooy(USA) —Longing To Dance (USA) (Nureyev (USA))
269[4] 704[4] 853[3] 925[4] 1492[4] 2788[3] 3284[8] 3968[6] 4897[8] 6672[8] 7401[10]

Klammer *Jane Chapple-Hyam* 105
2 b c Exceed And Excel(AUS) —Aymara (Darshaan)
(1351) ◆ (2127) ◆ 3049[5] 3868[3] (5323a) 6347[2] (7095)

Kleio *Henry Cecil* a59 70
3 b f Sadler's Wells(USA) —Colza (USA) (Alleged (USA))
1451[6] 2092[4]

Klynch *Ruth Carr* a76 87
4 b g Kyllachy—Inchcoonan (Emperor Jones (USA))
432[6] ◆ 848[3] 1192[11] 1650[10] 1924[5] 2113[17] 2578[2] 2817[8] 3200[7] 4063[5] 4486[6] 4670[4] 5299[5] 5688[3] 6026[4] 6110[4] 6494[6]

Knavesmire (IRE) *Mel Brittain* 69
4 b m One Cool Cat(USA) —Caribbean Escape (Pivotal)
1030[15] 1361[13] 5601[12]

Kneesy Earsy Nosey *Ann Stokell* a51 34
4 ch m Compton Place—Evie Hone (IRE) (Royal Academy (USA))
491[4] 1114[6]

Knight Eagle (IRE) *Kevin Prendergast* a44 99
3 b g Night Shift(USA) —Heart's Desire (IRE) (Royal Applause)
6971a[7]

Knightfire (IRE) *Walter Swinburn* a78 51
3 b g Invincible Spirit(IRE) —The Castles (IRE) (Imperial Ballet (IRE))
43[2] 247[2] 809[6] (991) 1280[5] (1584) 2868[4] 3567[9] 5454[8] 6208[4] 6714[10] 7255[11]

Knightly Escapade *John Dunlop* 69
2 ch g Sakhee(USA) —Queen Of Iceni (Erhaab (USA))
6504[8] ◆

Knight's Victory (IRE) *Michael Smith* a53 71
4 b g Cape Cross(IRE) —Diminuendo (USA) (Diesis)
3750[5] 4152[6] 4481[2] 5118[9] 6297[8] 6571[3] 6984[9] 7541[8]

Knockdolian (IRE) *Roger Charlton* a70 70
3 b g Montjeu(IRE) —Doula (USA) (Gone West (USA))
1387[10] 2717[7] 3170[6] 6669[2] 7275[7]

Knock Stars (IRE) *Patrick Martin* a88 91
2 b f Soviet Star(USA) —Knockatotaun (Spectrum (IRE))
7073a[4]

Knock Three Times (IRE) *Wilf Storey* a36 51
4 b m Hernando(FR) —Tawoos (FR) (Rainbow Quest (USA))
1891[5] 2430[3] 3669[3] 3989[7] 4825[6] 5202[3] 5687[8]
Knotgarden (IRE) *James Fanshawe* 70
4 b m Dr Fong(USA) —Eilean Shona (Suave Dancer (USA))
3437[5] (4207) 4804[12] 5563[5] 6065[5]
Knot In Wood (IRE) *Richard Fahey* a113 115
8 b g Shinko Forest(IRE) —Notley Park (Wolfhound (USA))
2999[7] 3193[4] 3445[4] 4576[18] 5095[16] 6177[6] 6241[4] 6752[14] 7060[6]
Knowledgeable *Bryn Palling* a4 48
3 b g Reset(AUS) —Belle's Edge (Danehill Dancer (IRE))
3291[12] 3957[7] 4989[6] 5469[10] 5700[7]
Know No Fear *Alastair Lidderdale* a72 49
5 b g Primo Valentino(IRE) —Alustar (Emarati (USA))
108 (103) ◆ 195[3] (242) 285[3] 351[5] 404[8] 4366[7] 5377[10] 5471[6] 5926[2] 6025[10] 6853[5] (7128) 7168[8] 7336[6] 7376[8] 7543[5] 7678[2] 7968[7]
Knox Overstreet *Mick Channon* a57 57
2 b g Indesatchel(IRE) —Charlie Girl (Puissance)
2887[10] 3472[3] 3832[7] 4802[12] 7295[5]
Knudstrup Noble (IRE) *Phil McEntee*
2 b c Whipper(USA) —Noble Dane (IRE) (Danehill (USA))
2561[8] 2905[9] 3602[9]
Kochanski (IRE) *John Weymes* a58 59
4 ch m King's Best(USA) —Ascot Cyclone (USA) (Rahy (USA))
130[9] 2529[5]
Kodiac Star (IRE) *Jamie Osborne* a37 63
2 b f Kodiac—Grade A Star (IRE) (Alzao (USA))
1957[5] 2358 [3] 2457[4] 2963[7] 3864[9] 4363[7] 4788[4]
Kodibelle (IRE) *Tim Easterby* 52
2 b f Kodiac—Caribelle (Mark Of Esteem (IRE))
1704[7] 2139[3] 2391[7] 4241[2] 4554[12] 4848[8] 5602[9]
Kodicil (IRE) *Tim Walford* 46
2 b g Kodiac—Miss Caoimhe (IRE) (Barathea (IRE))
2498[11] 5762[4] 6070[10] 6978[13]
Koha (USA) *Dean Ivory* a43 56
2 b f Medaglia D'Oro(USA) —Puzzled Look (USA) (Gulch (USA))
2176[5] 2505[10] 3034[5] 7809[3]
Kojak (IRE) *Richard Hannon* 81
2 b c Kodiac—Face The Storm (IRE) (Barathea (IRE))
1901[U] 2022[2] 2687[5] (3053) 4138[21] 4934[6] 6200[9] 6435[6]
Koka Fast (FR) *Mrs A Malzard*
8 ch g Start Fast(FR) —Kaly Flight (FR) (Great Palm (USA))
1817a[4]
Kokkokila *Lady Herries* a56 66
6 b m Robellino(USA) —Meant To Be (Morston (FR))
3780[7] 5260[7] 5963[7]
Kokojo (IRE) *Brendan Powell* a66 65
2 ch f Majestic Missile(IRE) —Drawing Room (IRE) (Grand Lodge (USA))
2176[3] 2963[3] 3686[5] 5365[2] 5863[3] 6086[8] 6867[3]
Kolokol (IRE) *D Prod'Homme* 104
3 b c Statue Of Liberty(USA) —Hecterine (IRE) (Hector Protector (USA))
1610a[10] 2157a[3] 2804a[7] 3425a[9] 4773a[9]
Komreyev Star *Ray Peacock* a45 49
8 b g Komaite(USA) —L'Ancressaan (Dalsaan)
503[13] 1772[10] 2410[6] 2789[9]
Kona Coast *John Gosden* a88 96
3 b g Oasis Dream—Macadamia (IRE) (Classic Cliche (IRE))
796a[11] 945[13] 1310[16] 1703[3] 3103[16] 4377[3] 4593[6]
Konig Bernard (FR) *W Baltromei* 106
4 b h Touch Down(GER) —Kween (GER) (Surumu (GER))
1111a[7] 3017a[9] 5649a[9]
Konig Concorde (GER) *C Sprengel* 106
5 b g Big Shuffle(USA) —Kaiserin (GER) (Ile De Bourbon (USA))
1251a[11] 4888a[10] (7370a)
Konstantin (IRE) *Marcus Tregoning* a61
2 b c Balmont(USA) —Manuka Magic (IRE) (Key Of Luck (USA))
5381[11] 7595[11] 7779[3] ◆
Koo And The Gang (IRE) *Brian Ellison* a69 66
3 b g Le Vie Dei Colori—Entertain (Royal Applause)
1104[U] 3371[3] 4127[9] 4898[6] 5304[4] 5641[7]
Kookie *Ron Barr* 49
3 b f Makbul—Breakfast Creek (Hallgate)
1966[9] 4342[8] 4864[9] 6039[4] 6460[5] 6643[10]
Koraleva Tectona (IRE) *Pat Eddery* a61 79
5 b m Fasliyev(USA) —Miss Teak (USA) (Woodman (USA))
4260[11] 6629[12] 7047 [12]
Korngold *John Dunlop* 62
2 b c Dansili—Eve (Rainbow Quest (USA))
4096[9] 6442[11] 7058[10]
Kourdo (FR) *J Parize* 71
2 b c Double Heart(FR) —Sea Launch (FR) (Neverneyev (USA))
5251a[5]
Kreem *A Fabre* 101
2 b c Hurricane Run(IRE) —En Public (FR) (Rainbow Quest (USA))
6973a[3] 7456a[7]
Kristalette (IRE) *Walter Swinburn* a89 63
3 ch f Leporello(IRE) —Kristal Bridge (Kris)
4114[5] 5366[2] (6079)
Kristallo (GER) *Paul Webber* a65 65
5 ch g Lando(GER) —Key West (GER) (In The Wings)
164[12] (322) (554) 1087[4]
Kristen Jane (USA) *Linda Perratt* 53
3 ch f Forest Wildcat(USA) —British Columbia (Selkirk (USA))
1201[8] 1667[5] 2291[5] 2432[9] 3167[7] 3529[5] 3903[3] 3988[2] 4584[3] 4947[9] 5410[RR] 6392[9] 6490[5]

Kristollini *William Muir* a55
2 b f Bertolini(USA) —Lady Kris (IRE) (Kris)
7610[6] 8001[8]
Kristopher James (IRE) *Mark Brisbourne* a58 58
4 ch g Spartacus(IRE) —Ela Alethia (Kris)
1984[11] 2303[11]
Kronful *Michael Jarvis* a61 73
3 b f Singspiel(IRE) —Albahja (Sinndar (IRE))
1268[4] (1809) 6543[8]
Krymian *Sir Michael Stoute* a82 62
3 gr g Bahamian Bounty—Kryena (Kris)
1442[5] 2261[7] 3271[8]
Krypton Factor *Sir Mark Prescott Bt* a46 100
2 b g Kyllachy—Cool Question (Polar Falcon (USA))
2474[5] (2667) 4111[2] (4262) 4851[8] (5547) (5856) (5965) 6141[2] 6568[3]
Krysanthe *Michael Blanshard* a26 50
3 b f Kyllachy—Aegean Magic (Wolfhound (USA))
2841[7] 3336[9] 4280[8]
Ksenia (ITY) *R Menichetti* 87
2 bb f Tejano Run(USA) —Essie's Link (USA) (Cherokee Colony (USA))
6762a[7] 6975a[5]
Kuala Limper (IRE) *David Elsworth* a76 24
2 b c Royal Applause—Mandolin (IRE) (Sabrehill (USA))
5893[10] 6532[11] 7020[2] 7385[3]
Kuantan Two (IRE) *Paul Cole* a64 44
3 ch g Bertolini(USA) —Guaranda (Acatenango (GER))
2860[9] 3116[10] 3443[5] 4327[15]
Kuanyao (IRE) *PETER Makin* a76 49
4 b g American Post—Nullarbor (Green Desert (USA))
(3604) (3914) (6198)
Kublahara (IRE) *Andrew Balding* a54 54
2 b f Pulpit(USA) —Kisses For Me (IRE) (Sadler's Wells (USA))
7232[9] 7478[9]
Kumbeshwar *David Evans* a95 81
3 b g Doyen(IRE) —Camp Fire (IRE) (Lahib (USA))
884[4] 1033[6] 1334[6] 1776[7] 5524[12] 6223[5] 6438[11] 7214[8] 7467[5] 7679[4] (7865) (7932) (7958)
Kummel Excess (IRE) *George Baker* a75 76
3 ch f Exceed And Excel(AUS) —Ipanema Beach (Lion Cavern (USA))
689[2] ◆ (856) 1147[10] 2599[4] 6310[6] 6466[4] 6998[7] 7526[5]
Kurtanella *Richard Hannon* a83 85
3 bb f Pastoral Pursuits—Aconite (Primo Dominie)
1732[8] 2682[6] 2970[5] 3592[3] 4250[3] 4387[5] 5383[11] 5834[3] 6805[4] 7554[2]
Kurtiniadis (IRE) *S Kulak* 108
7 b h Mujahid(USA) —Fiddler's Moll (IRE) (Dr Devious (IRE))
5803a[7]
Kwami Biscuit *Geoffrey Harker* 46
3 ch g Clerkenwell(USA) —Singer On The Roof (Chief Singer)
3282[5] 4200[8] 4897[13]
Kwik Lightening *Ben Haslam* 35
2 b g Avonbridge—Runs In The Family (Distant Relative)
5531[12] 5755[8] 6182[9]
Kwik Time *Robin Bastiman* 7
2 b c Avonbridge—Never Away (Royal Applause)
6111[10] 6748[11] 6980[10]
Kyber *Jim Goldie* a27 52
9 ch g First Trump—Mahbob Dancer (IRE) (Groom Dancer (USA))
1671[8] 2214[8] 3496[4] 3989[5] 4825[9] 6707[8]
Kyle (IRE) *Conor Dore* a77 86
6 ch g Kyllachy—Staylily (IRE) (Grand Lodge (USA))
78[4] 223[6] 317[3] 486[8] 1147[6] 1596[11] 2790[F]
Kyleene *Mark Usher* a78 74
4 b m Kyllachy—Mrs Nash (Night Shift (USA))
1509[9] 1933[13] 2262[5] 2866[6] 3514[7]
Kyle Of Bute *Brian Baugh* a61 68
4 ch g Kyllachy—Blinding Mission (IRE) (Marju (IRE))
1177[12] 1520[4] 1919[7] 2602[3] 3177[3] 3582[4] (3978) 4454[4] 5272[5] 5530[10] 6269[9]
Kyllachy Spirit *Brett Johnson* 72
2 b g Kyllachy—Cartuccia (IRE) (Doyoun)
4318[7] 4755[4] 5954[4]
Kyllachy Star *Richard Fahey* a98 100
4 b g Kyllachy—Jaljuli (Jalmood (USA))
739[6] 944[7] 1085[11] 2971[3] 3585[5] (4617) 5292[4] 5571a[2] 5903[2] 6349[8] 7348[12]
Kyllachy Storm *Ron Hodges* a71 79
6 b g Kyllachy—Social Storm (USA) (Future Storm (USA))
1074[4] (1300) 1547[9] 2166[3] 2364[3] 2592[2] 2689[6] 3463[4] 3474[4] 3851[5] 5005[4] 5112[6] 5875[8] 6515[13]
Kylladdie *Steve Gollings* a76 80
3 ch g Kyllachy—Chance For Romance (Entrepreneur)
596[2] 807[4] 901[5] (1175) (1765) 2260[9] 6723[16] 7144[4] 7411[9] 7961[7] 8004[6]
Kyncraighe (IRE) *Alastair Lidderdale* a44 72
2 b g Kyllachy—Brighella (Sadler's Wells (USA))
2022[5] 2680[9] 3555[2] 4221[4] 4578[13] 5613[8] 6086[9] 6271[12] 6810[10] 7379[6] 7469[7]
Kyoatee Kilt *Paul Cole* a54 37
3 ch c Kyllachy—Oatey (Master Willie)
118[8] 4325[12] 4778[7] 5650[8]
Kyzer Chief *Ron Barr* 74
5 b g Rouvres(FR) —Payvashooz (Ballacashtal (CAN))
1337[2] 1524[5] 2144[10] 2669[9] 3119[9] 3976[3] 4047[2] 4452[11] 4672[5]
Laafet *Kevin Morgan* a76 76
5 b g Royal Applause—Golden Way (IRE) (Cadeaux Genereux)
1511[1]
Laafhd *Tony Newcombe* a27 23
2 ch f Haafhd—Lady In Colour (IRE) (Cadeaux Genereux)
5385[10] 6249[10]

Laaheb *Michael Jarvis* a118 118
4 b g Cape Cross(IRE) —Maskunah (IRE) (Sadler's Wells (USA))
1532[3] 2593[2] (3454) 5080[2] (5749) (6389)
Laajooj (IRE) *Michael Jarvis* a75
2 b c Azamour(IRE) —Flanders (IRE) (Common Grounds)
7112[5]
Laa Rayb (USA) *D Selvaratnam* a105 116
6 b g Storm Cat(USA) —Society Lady (USA) (Mr Prospector (USA))
710a[4] 798a[11]
Laatafreet (IRE) *Saeed Bin Suroor* a83
2 ch c Singspiel(IRE) —Cerulean Sky (IRE) (Darshaan)
6844[2]
La Bacouetteuse (FR) *George Foster* a28 61
5 b g Miesque's Son(USA) —Toryka (Vettori (IRE))
3901[4] 4407[3] 5303[8] ◆ 6033[3] 6397[5] 6921[9] 7229[5] 7407[8]
Labarinto *Sir Michael Stoute* 81
2 b c Dansili—Tarocchi (USA) (Affirmed (USA))
4549[6] 5263[4] (6514)
Labore *Marco Botti* a81 70
2 b g Bertolini(USA) —Hoh Intrepid (IRE) (Namid)
5892[9] 6569[3] 7034[2] (7412)
La Boum (GER) *Robert Collet* a91 117
7 b m Monsun(GER) —La Bouche (GER) (In The Wings)
(494a) 953a[3] 1255a[5] 1792a[3] 2403a[6] 5108a[6] 5575a[3] 6591a[5] 7160a[2] 7416a[2] 7648a[4]
Labretella (IRE) *Shaun Harris* a51 51
3 b f Bahamian Bounty—Known Class (USA) (Known Fact (USA))
1495[7] 2633[12] 3759[10] 4249[11] 4707[6]
La Capriosa *David Nicholls* a81 78
4 ch m Kyllachy—La Caprice (USA) (Housebuster (USA))
431[7] 504[5] 601[6] 767[11] 896[7] 967[4] (1068) (1112) 1337[5] (1827) 3902[5] 4243[5] 4510[10] 4892[2] 5356[7] 5855[9] 6073[13] 6572[2] 6700[7] 6965[10] (7175) 7326[5] (7405) 7754[8] 7866[7]
La Chassotte (FR) *Gerard O'Leary* a58 94
3 b f Until Sundown(USA) —River Trebor (USA) (Myrakalu (FR))
6971a[10]
La Chemme *Reg Hollinshead* a46
4 b m Ishiguru(USA) —Smartie Lee (Dominion)
7244[9] 7461[2] 7563[6] 7838[3] 7885[14]
Lachlan Bridge (GER) *Y De Nicolay* a82 78
2 b c Dubawi(IRE) —Lady Zorreghuietta (FR) (Anabaa (USA))
7647a[2]
La Columbina *James Evans* a60 49
5 ch m Carnival Dancer—Darshay (FR) (Darshaan)
174[8] 897[5] 1591[5] 5813[4] 6934[11]
La Concorde (FR) *Sir Michael Stoute* a71 78
3 b f Sadler's Wells(USA) —La Leuze (IRE) (Caerleon (USA))
2043[8] 2994[2] ◆ 4330[2] 5445[3] (7419)
Laconicos (IRE) *William Stone* a64 68
8 ch g Foxhound(USA) —Thermopylae (Tenby)
1226[4] 1462[2] 1980[2] 2341[9] 2870[7] 3028[7] 4102[2] 4621[4] 4804[2]
Laddies Poker Two (IRE) *Jeremy Noseda* a85 114
5 gr m Choisir(AUS) —Break Of Day (USA) (Favorite Trick (USA))
(3193) ◆
La De Two (IRE) *Saeed Bin Suroor* a83 113
4 ch h Galileo(IRE) —Firecrest (IRE) (Darshaan)
(3877) 5696[2] 7096[5]
Ladiesandgentlemen (IRE) *R Feligioni* 98
3 b c Celtic Swing—Flying Flag (IRE) (Entrepreneur)
1945a[13]
Ladies Are Forever *Geoffrey Oldroyd* 105
2 b f Monsieur Bond(IRE) —Forever Bond (Danetime (IRE))
(2522) ◆ 3070[3] (6568)
Ladie's Choice (IRE) *M J Tynan* a63 101
2 b f Choisir(AUS) —Lady Portia (IRE) (College Chapel)
5907[11] 7073a[12]
Ladies Dancing *Chris Down* a69 52
4 b g Royal Applause—Queen Of Dance (IRE) (Sadler's Wells (USA))
105[5] 309[3] 1462[8] 1763[11] 2230[7] 2363[4] 7760[4]
La Diosa (IRE) *Mrs S Lamyman* a60 43
4 b m Dansili—El Divino (IRE) (Halling (USA))
289[8] 663[9]
La Divina (IRE) *Sir Michael Stoute* a24
3 b f Sadler's Wells(USA) —Hellenic (Darshaan)
3080[10]
Lady Aline *T Clout* 73
4 b m Kyllachy—Waif (Groom Dancer (USA))
1055a[2]
Lady Amakhala *George Moore* 68
2 b f Val Royal(FR) —Isla Negra (IRE) (Last Tycoon)
2654[6] 4821[2] 5509[8] 6302[3]
Ladyanne (IRE) *Sylvester Kirk* 89
2 ch f Redback—Gillipops (IRE) (Xaar)
(1930) 3141[16] 5693[8] 5965[2] 6317[5] 6528[4] 7098[8]
Lady Anthracite *Bryan Smart* 42
3 b f Makbul—Crystal Canyon (Efisio)
2706[5] 3227[7]
Lady Areia (GER) *H J Groschel* 86
4 bb m Areion(GER) —Lady Anna (GER) (Acatenango (GER))
5739a[9] 6406a[9]
Lady Artemisia (IRE) *Marco Botti* a95 103
4 b m Montjeu(IRE) —Crimson Glory (Lycius (USA))
1379[2] 2703[2] 3031[3] 4143[3] 4624[6] 6320[8] 7189[5]
Lady Barastar (IRE) *Walter Swinburn* a58 64
2 b f Barathea(IRE) —Stariya (IRE) (Soviet Star (USA))
4021[10] 5724[8] 6770[5]
Lady Berta *Richard Hannon* a54 62
3 b f Bertolini(USA) —Lady Links (Bahamian Bounty)
2998[8] 3333[4] ◆ 3924[4] 4297[3] 5960[4]

Lady Bluesky *Alistair Whillans* 72
7 gr m Cloudings(IRE) —M N L Lady (Polar Falcon (USA))
2864[9] 5437[4] ◆ (6033) 6397[4] (6648) (7226)
Lady Brickhouse *Michael Squance* a52 47
3 b f Choisir(AUS) —Music Maid (IRE) (Inzar (USA))
43[5] 167[2] 215[2] 387[6] 471[3] 619[4] 699[10] 998[7] 1205[3] 1456[4] 3515[5] 4970[7] 5645[2] 6062[4] 6579[4] 7156[11] 7381[7]
Lady Bridget *B W Hills* a58 70
2 b f Hawk Wing(USA) —Change Partners (IRE) (Hernando (FR))
6155[8] 6770[3] 7010[2] 7486[6]
Lady Brookie *Peter Grayson* 78
2 br f Makbul—Miss Brookie (The West (USA))
1009[2] 1136[5] (1360) 2095[6] 3986[2] 4388[9] 4831[7]
Lady Cavendish (IRE) *Alan Bailey* a54 49
3 ch f Indian Haven—Madame Marjou (IRE) (Marju (IRE))
302[7]
Lady Champagne *Julia Feilden* a52
4 b m Zaha(CAN) —Slavonic Dance (Muhtarram (USA))
1[4] 3551[0]
Lady Chaparral *Michael Dods* 65
3 b f High Chaparral(IRE) —La Sylphide (Rudimentary (USA))
4115[3]
Lady Chloe *Philip Kirby* 60
2 b f Noverre(USA) —Iwunder (IRE) (King's Best (USA))
5066[12] 5509[7] 5878[12]
Lady Christie *Michael Blanshard* a35 33
3 b f Tobougg(IRE) —Atnab (USA) (Riverman (USA))
1059[9] 1796[16] 4925[4] 5467[10]
Lady Compton *Robin Bastiman* 42
3 ch f Compton Place—Bright Spells (Salse (USA))
2217[15] 3359[16]
Lady Darshaan (IRE) *J S Moore* a89 107
3 b f High Chaparral(IRE) —Diary (IRE) (Green Desert (USA))
1726[10] 2370a[6] 2889[4] 3694[3] 7188[9]
Lady Deanie (IRE) *Bryn Palling* 60
2 ch f Noverre(USA) —Darling Deanie (IRE) (Sinndar (IRE))
5985[9] 7123[5]
Lady Del Sol *Geoffrey Oldroyd* 78
2 b f Monsieur Bond(IRE) —Villa Del Sol (Tagula (IRE))
1964[2] (2623) 3364[4] 4851[4] 5187[10] (6891)
Lady Di (GER) *Jean De Roualle* 90
6 b m Samum(GER) —Lots Of Love (GER) (Java Gold (USA))
1056a[5]
Ladydolly *Roy Brotherton* a39
2 b f Kyllachy—Lady Pekan (Sri Pekan (USA))
6697[10] 7240[8] 7598[5] 7809[5]
Lady Eclair (IRE) *Mark Johnston* a72 102
4 b m Danehill Dancer(IRE) —Bex (USA) (Explodent (USA))
922[4] (1451) ◆ 2014[4] (2445) (2672) 2857[2] ◆ 3198[3] (3367) (3588) (3955) 4467[4] 4817[4] (5291) 5743[9] 5908[4] 6929[7]
Lady Ellice *Phil McEntee* a49 32
2 b f Iceman—Optimise (IRE) (Danehill (USA))
5160[11] 5721[7] 6161[8]
Lady Excel (IRE) *B S Rothwell* 73
4 b m Exceed And Excel(AUS) —Material Lady (IRE) (Barathea (IRE))
4939[8]
Lady Excellentia (IRE) *Andrew Haynes* a12 58
2 gr f Exceed And Excel(AUS) —Cayman Sunrise (IRE) (Peintre Celebre (USA))
1256[5] 1541[4] 1838[3] 2163[7] 5871[7] 6673[9] 7295[13]
Lady Florence *Alan Coogan* a60 79
5 gr m Bollin Eric—Silver Fan (Lear Fan (USA))
1293[12] 2198[13] 2456[2] 3715[8] (4308) 4502[2] (4735) 5087[7] (5174) 5652[3] 6439[6]
Lady Gabrielle (IRE) *Michael Bell* a56
2 b f Dansili—Zither (Zafonic (USA))
6532[15] 7198[5] 7558[4]
Lady Gar Gar *Geoffrey Oldroyd* 66
2 ch f Monsieur Bond(IRE) —Triple Tricks (IRE) (Royal Academy (USA))
2990[6] 3874[3] (6569) 7059[6]
Lady Goodricke *Mark Brisbourne*
2 ch f Goodricke—Seren Teg (Timeless Times (USA))
5294[10]
Lady Hestia (USA) *Marcus Tregoning* a49 80
5 b m Belong To Me(USA) —Awtaan (USA) (Arazi (USA))
(1689) ◆ (2165) 3955[4] (5497) 6929[8]
Lady Hetherington *Gary Brown* a58 29
3 b f Kyllachy—Silver Top Hat (USA) (Silver Hawk (USA))
484[9] 788[4] 998[6] 4692[8] 4733[8]
Lady Intrigue (IRE) *Richard Fahey* 39
2 b f Hurricane Run(IRE) —Intriguing (IRE) (Fasliyev (USA))
6704[7]
Lady Jak (FR) *J-V Toux* 83
2 b f American Post—Lady Angele (FR) (Ski Chief (USA))
2917a[8] 3718a[7] 5226a[10] 7975a[8]
Lady Jane Digby *Mark Johnston* a101 112
5 b m Oasis Dream—Scandalette (Niniski (USA))
2071[5] 2470[6] (3031) 3368[2] 3671[3] (4418a)
Lady Kent (IRE) *Jim Boyle* a78 74
4 b m Danetime(IRE) —Winning Note (IRE) (Victory Note (USA))
3936 5934 ◆ (673) 931[7] 1482[7] (2415) 2840[3] 3262[7] 4053[4] 5713[5] 6164[2] 6854[6] 7209[8]
Lady Kildare (IRE) *Jedd O'Keeffe* a62 68
2 br f Bachelor Duke(USA) —Teodora (IRE) (Fairy King (USA))
2130[5] 2693[3] 3549[2] 4896[6] 6030[3] 7269[2]
Lady Kingston *John Weymes* 11
4 ch m Kyllachy—Ash Moon (IRE) (General Monash (USA))
2971[0]

Lady L (IRE) *David Wachman* 68
3 b f Danehill Dancer(IRE) —Lilissa (IRE) (Doyoun)
4563a^{17}

Lady Lam *Sylvester Kirk* a70 66
4 b m Slip Anchor—Tamara (Marju (IRE))
(984) 1193^{9} 1772^{7} 1958^{2} (2456) 3524^{2} *3783^{4}* 3862^{10} (4361) 4746^{3} *4913^{5}* 6022^{5} 6518^{2} *6846^{2} (7286) 7490^{6}*

Lady Longcroft *Jeff Pearce* a61 61
5 ch m Tobougg(IRE) —Top Of The Morning (Keen)
131^{12} 457^{9} 685^{6}

Lady Luachmhar (IRE) *Richard Fahey* 91
4 b m Galileo(IRE) —Radhwa (FR) (Shining Steel)
1907^{3} 2513^{3} 4086^{2} 5278^{9} 5757^{2} 6181^{7}

Lady Lube Rye (IRE) *Noel Wilson* 65
3 b f Catcher In The Rye(IRE) —Lady Lucia (IRE) (Royal Applause)
1511^{10} 2432^{10} 3161^{9}

Lady Lupus (IRE) *A P O'Brien* 104
3 b f High Chaparral(IRE) —Lady Icarus (Rainbow Quest (USA))
957a^{8} 2037a^{5} 3007a^{5} 4178a^{3} 5976a^{5} 6379a^{5} 6786a^{4}

Lady Lynette (AUS) *Robert Smerdon* 110
6 br m Ladoni—Queen's Own (AUS) (Coronation Day (AUS))
8

Lady Mango (IRE) *Ronald Harris* a64 45
2 ch f Bahamian Bounty—Opera (Forzando)
6697^{4} 6954^{8} *7269^{3} 7493^{11} 8011^{4}*

Lady Marmelade (ITY) *D Ducci* a82 85
7 b m Diktat—Ridge Reef (IRE) (Indian Ridge)
1419a^{6} 1944a^{11}

Lady Mickataine (USA) *M J Grassick* a61 65
4 b m Speightstown(USA) —Ivy Leaf (IRE) (Nureyev (USA))
(875)

Lady Morganna (IRE) *Gay Kelleway* a59 62
2 b f Diamond Green(FR) —Lucky Flirt (USA) (Gulch (USA))
1324^{7} 2007^{6} *2867^{2}* 3106^{4} 3362^{4} *3769^{2} 4020^{3}* 4716^{11} 5389^{10}

Lady Norlela *B S Rothwell* a33 60
4 b m Reset(AUS) —Lady Netbetsports (IRE) (In The Wings)
1801^{7} 4015^{6} 4246^{11} 4669^{4} 4945^{10} 6915^{2} 7149^{2}

Lady Of Garmoran (USA) *Paul Cole* a60 61
3 bb f Mr Greeley(USA) —Poetically (CAN) (Silver Deputy (CAN))
1639^{5} 3738^{12} (4280) 4534^{2} 4774^{2} 5171^{6} *5656^{8} 6672^{12} (6865) 7191^{4}*

Lady Of The Desert (USA) *Brian Meehan* 121
3 ch f Rahy(USA) —Queen's Logic (IRE) (Grand Lodge (USA))
1384^{3} 2158a^{5} 3143^{6} 5744^{2} (6390) 6608a^{2}

Lady Of The Knight (IRE) *Hugh McWilliams* 13
2 b f Chevalier(IRE) —Temptation Island (IRE) (Spectrum (IRE))
3624^{16} 4862^{7} 5594^{12}

Lady On Top (IRE) *Nerys Duffield* a52 52
2 b f Oratorio(IRE) —Ascot Lady (IRE) (Spinning World (USA))
1319^{7} 1793^{11} 2407^{6} 3636^{4} *7392^{9} 7520^{8}*

Lady Pacha *Tim Pitt* 44
3 b f Dubai Destination(USA) —St Radegund (Green Desert (USA))
1866^{4} 2606^{10} 2853^{9}

Lady Paris (IRE) *Bryan Smart* 79
2 b f Invincible Spirit(IRE) —Quecha (IRE) (Indian Ridge)
6034^{3} ◆ (6323) 6719^{4} ◆ 7174^{6}

Lady Pattern (IRE) *Paul D'Arcy* a67 79
3 gr f Verglas(IRE) —Patteness (FR) (General Holme (USA))
2120^{4} 2342^{2} 2652^{3}

Lady Pilot *Jim Best* a74 62
8 b m Dansili—Mighty Flyer (IRE) (Mujtahid (USA))
164^{11} 263^{3} 376^{6}

Lady Platinum Club *Geoffrey Oldroyd* a65 69
2 ch f Monsieur Bond(IRE) —Bond Platinum Club (Pivotal)
1359^{4} ◆ 1686^{8} 2095^{5} 2461^{3} 3596^{4} 4544^{5} 4783^{3} 5196^{3} 5998^{6} *6902^{7} 7210^{3} 7408^{2} 7667^{3}*

Lady Prodee *Bill Turner* a71
2 b f Proclamation(IRE) —Dee-Lady (Deploy)
(7424) ◆ *7891^{10} (7997)*

Lady Rosamunde *Marcus Tregoning* a70
2 gr f Maria's Mon(USA) —String Quartet (IRE) (Sadler's Wells (USA))
7311^{2} 7990^{2}

Lady Rossetti *Marcus Tregoning* a57
3 ch f Reset(AUS) —Cottage Maid (Inchinor)
7596^{3} 7862^{2} 8021^{4}

Lady Royale *Geoffrey Oldroyd* 81
2 ch f Monsieur Bond(IRE) —Bond Royale (Piccolo)
1375^{6} 1986^{2} 2436^{2} 2832^{4} 3365^{5} 3658^{3} (3925) 4388^{4} 4797^{4} 5850^{6}

Lady's Art (FR) *S Wattel* a64 65
4 gr m Verglas(IRE) —Calithea (IRE) (Marju (IRE))
1055a^{4}

Lady Slippers (IRE) *Harry Dunlop* a17 61
3 ch f Royal Academy(USA) —Woodland Orchid (IRE) (Woodman (USA))
2844^{11} 4492^{7} 5456^{6} *6335^{10}*

Lady's Locket (IRE) *Andrew Oliver* 71
2 b f Fasliyev(USA) —Heart's Desire (IRE) (Royal Applause)
7256a^{11}

Lady Springbank (IRE) *P D Deegan* 102
3 gr f Choisir(AUS) —Severa (GER) (Kendor (FR))
(1036a) 2370a^{14}

Lady's Purse *H-A Pantall* 104
3 b f Doyen(IRE) —Jetbeeah (IRE) (Lomond (USA))
(2800a) 3493a^{3} 6013a^{10} 7160a^{0} 7416a^{10}

Lady Titticaca *Ron Hodges* 13
2 br f Striking Ambition—Sunrise Girl (King's Signet (USA))
6954^{14} *7269^{12}*

Lady Valiant *Ralph Beckett* a63
3 ch f Dr Fong(USA) —Protectorate (Hector Protector (USA))
1589^{9}

Lady Vivien *David Brown* a69 56
4 b m Kyllachy—Elsie Plunkett (Mind Games)
2186^{5} 2581^{5} 3064^{11} 3338^{10} 3976^{8}

Lady Vyrnwy (IRE) *Richard Fahey* a36 49
3 b f Bertolini(USA) —Cannikin (IRE) (Lahib (USA))
1685^{9} 1966^{7} 2380^{3} 2834^{12} 3501^{7}

Lady Willa (IRE) *Mark Gillard* a66 64
3 b f Footstepsinthesand—Change Partners (IRE) (Hernando (FR))
7684 1601^{7} *1982^{5}* 2844^{3} ◆ 5254^{13} 5713^{6} *7690^{6} 7967^{11}*

Laffraaj (IRE) *Pat Eddery* a7 55
2 br c Iffraaj—Have Fun (Indian Ridge)
3281^{5} 4247^{9} 5204^{4} 5626^{12} *7164^{10}*

La Fortunata *Mike Murphy* a74 88
3 b f Lucky Story(USA) —Phantasmagoria (Fraam)
2822^{7} 3211^{7} *3561^{2}* 4291^{2} (4567) (4837) 5250^{2} 5589^{2} 6256^{9}

Lagalp (GER) *P Schiergen* 101
3 b f Galileo(IRE) —La Dane (IRE) (Danehill (USA))
4640a^{4} 6790a^{8}

Lagan Lullaby *Neil Mulholland*
2 gr f Goodricke—Due To Me (Compton Place)
2358 ^{13}

Lago Indiano (IRE) *Peter Fahey* a75 76
3 b c Namid—My Potters (USA) (Irish River (FR))
900^{2} 1211^{2} 1475^{3} 2025^{4} 2892^{6} 3404^{6} *6937^{12}*

Lahaleeb (IRE) *Paul D'Arcy* 115
4 b m Redback—Flames (Blushing Flame (USA))
801a^{6} 1025a^{6} 2154a^{7} 3793^{8} 6561^{7} 6950a^{8}

Laid Bare *Nerys Dutfield* a33
3 b f Barathea(IRE) —Lady Eberspacher (IRE) (Royal Abjar (USA))
5380^{8} 6084^{6}

Lairy (IRE) *Milton Harris* a47 56
3 ch g Fath(USA) —Akebia (USA) (Trempolino (USA))
1676

Laish Ya Hajar (IRE) *Paul Webber* a64 79
6 ch g Grand Lodge(USA) —Ya Hajar (Lycius (USA))
3416^{8} 4101^{2} 4873^{7}

Lajidaal (USA) *Marcus Tregoning* 81
3 b c Dynaformer(USA) —Tayibah (IRE) (Sadler's Wells (USA))
(3754) 4933^{7} 5747^{15}

La Joie De Vivre (USA) *R Gibson* 73
2 b c During(USA) —Creme De La Creme (FR) (Vettori (IRE))
6589a^{8}

La Kalam *Michael Jarvis* a16 50
3 ch f Dubawi(IRE) —Jathaabeh (Nashwan (USA))
5986^{5} *6496^{11}*

Lake Chini (IRE) *Michael Easterby* a64 71
8 b g Raise A Grand(IRE) —Where's The Money (Lochnager)
836^{9} 937^{5} 1236^{12} (2582) 3026^{4} 3615^{9} 4064^{4} 4706^{2} (5045) 6679^{3} 7225^{2} *7446^{3}* ◆ *7699^{7}*

Lakeman (IRE) *Brian Ellison* a72 77
4 b g Tillerman—Bishop's Lake (Lake Coniston (IRE))
1117^{12} 1374^{5} 1990^{8} 2705^{10} 4372^{4} 4833^{11} 5241^{7} 5486^{5} 5819^{4} 6029^{4} 6269^{10} 6462^{4} 6890^{3} 7055^{2} (7229) *7897^{2}*

Lake Ontario (USA) *A P O'Brien* 89
2 b c Johannesburg(USA) —Dreamy Maiden (USA) (Meadowlake (USA))
5184^{4}

Lake Palace *N Clement* a93 102
4 ch m Nayef(USA) —Lia (IRE) (Desert King (IRE))
6519a^{5} 7416a^{4} *7776a^{3}*

Lakota *Jeremy Glover* 27
2 br f Sleeping Indian—Deep End (USA) (Lord Avie (USA))
3971^{9}

Lalika *Clive Cox* a58 57
3 b f Soviet Star(USA) —Lalique (IRE) (Lahib (USA))
1358^{9} 5265^{3} 5971^{8} *6287^{5} 7387^{3} 7848^{4} 8015^{8}*

La Maddalena (FR) *F-X De Chevigny* a61 63
5 b m Kahyasi—Sweet Contralto (Danehill (USA))
281a^{3}

Lamasaas (USA) *B W Hills* 76
2 b g Henny Hughes(USA) —Quick Feet (USA) (Dynaformer (USA))
4221^{6} 4709^{2} 6882^{4}

Lamborgino (FR) *J Parize* 66
7 gr h Silvano(GER) —Lamboghina (GER) (Alkalde (GER))
5378a^{9}

Lambrini Lace (IRE) *Lisa Williamson* a33 65
5 b m Namid—Feather 'n Lace (IRE) (Green Desert (USA))
7917^{9}

Lamh Albasser (USA) *A bin Huzaim* a39 96
3 ch g Mr Greeley(USA) —Madame Boulangere (Royal Applause)
414a^{14}

L'Ami Louis (IRE) *Henry Candy* 48
2 b g Elusive City(USA) —Princess Electra (IRE) (Lake Coniston (IRE))
6748^{8}

Lamino (GER) *P Vovcenko* 90
4 br h Tertullian(USA) —Limaga (Lagunas)
5542a^{8}

Lamool (GER) *Mario Hofer* 106
3 bb c Mamool(IRE) —Linara (GER) (Windwurf (GER))
1745a^{5} 2406a^{5} 3014a^{5} 4184a^{5} 6011a^{10}

Lamps *Brian Meehan* 65
3 b g Dynaformer(USA) —Conspiring (USA) (Grand Slam (USA))
1581^{8} 2974^{6} 3593^{8}

Lancelot (FR) *J-M Beguigne* 105
3 b c Bahri(USA) —Lunata (IRE) (Marju (IRE))
6219a^{4}

Lancetto (FR) *James J Hartnett* a55 71
5 b g Dubai Destination(USA) —Lanciana (IRE) (Acatenango (GER))
3492a^{7}

Land And Sea *B W Hills* a67 72
3 b f Beat Hollow—Stormy Channel (USA) (Storm Cat (USA))
5038^{10} 5474^{2} 5872^{3} 6815^{2} *(7406)*

Land Bank *Tim Easterby* 41
2 bg g Iceman—Southern Psychic (USA) (Alwasmi (USA))
3222^{10} 3657^{14} 4368^{13} 5020^{11}

Land Hawk (IRE) *Jeff Pearce* a75 67
4 br g Trans Island—Heike (Glenstal (USA))
1128^{5} *1323^{2} 1508^{6} 2236^{2} 2866^{5}* 3168^{12}

Land Of Plenty (IRE) *Jamie Poulton* a46 40
3 b f Azamour(IRE) —Bring Plenty (USA) (Southern Halo (USA))
118^{4} 254^{4} 2753^{9} 3442^{8} 3820^{4} 4202^{7} 4295^{7}

Landowner *A bin Huzaim* a89 89
3 b c Shamardal(USA) —Rentless (Zafonic (USA))
796a^{10}

Landucci *Sean Curran* a72 69
9 b g Averti(IRE) —Divina Luna (Dowsing (USA))
1585^{2} 1839^{2} 2172^{7} *2643^{3} 3518^{U} 4427^{7}* 5325^{4} *7162^{4} 7462^{7} 7627^{5}*

Lanfranc (FR) *M Gentile* a70 84
7 ch g Lahint(USA) —Lespois (Sicyos (USA))
303a^{10} 559a^{7}

Langen Voraus (GER) *Henry Cecil* 63
4 b m Tiger Hill(IRE) —Luttje Lage (GER) (Acatenango (GER))
1521^{3}

Langley *A Wohler* 90
3 b c Trempolino(USA) —Late Night (GER) (Groom Dancer (USA))
1745a^{6} 2406a^{6}

Lang Shining (IRE) *Jamie Osborne* a86 104
6 ch g Dr Fong(USA) —Dragnet (IRE) (Rainbow Quest (USA))
1008^{20} 1282^{7} *1829^{8}* 2760^{5} (3431) (3580) (3814) 4489^{5} 4579^{9} 5034^{2} 5233^{3} (5455) *(6054) (6450)* 6926^{23} *7251^{5}*

Laokoon (GER) *Mario Hofer* a76 83
5 b g Areion(GER) —Little Movie Star (Risk Me (FR))
207a^{7} 303a^{4}

La Pantera *Richard Hannon* a80 82
3 b f Captain Rio—Pantita (Polish Precedent (USA))
1761^{10} 2342^{9}

Lapina (IRE) *Anthony Middleton* a69 64
6 ch m Fath(USA) —Alpina (USA) (El Prado (IRE))
1980^{4} 2341^{11} *3278^{8}*

La Poesie (GER) *W Baltromei* 94
4 b m Pentire—L'Heure Bleue (IRE) (Kendor (FR))
7648a^{0}

La Polka *Mark Gillard* a41 66
4 ch m Carnival Dancer—Indubitable (Sharpo)
982^{10} 4223^{8}

La Residenza *James Fanshawe* a47
2 ch f Medicean—Ice Palace (Polar Falcon (USA))
7530^{10}

Largem *John Jenkins* a61 28
4 b g Largesse—Jem's Law (Contract Law (USA))
983^{10} 1194^{2} 2232^{7} 2811^{10}

Large Scotch *Paul Green* 46
3 b f Trade Fair—Brandish (Warning)
3428^{6} 4069^{13} 4407^{9}

Larimar (IRE) *Amanda Perrett* a49
2 ch g Selkirk(USA) —Campbellite (Desert Prince (IRE))
7755^{6}

Laristan (FR) *J-C Rouget* a88 98
3 gr c Sinndar(IRE) —Laxlova (FR) (Linamix (FR))
1254a^{6}

Larkrise Star *Dean Ivory* a66 56
3 b f Where Or When(IRE) —Katy Ivory (IRE) (Night Shift (USA))
618^{4} 768^{2} 1061^{4} 1590^{3} 1982^{8} 2844^{10} *3564^{3}* (3960) *6080^{8} 6526^{2} 6999^{4}* 7315^{2} 7491^{4} 7765^{7}

LA Rocket (AUS) *Dale Sutton* 120
6 ch g Rock Of Gibraltar(IRE) —La Bella Dama (NZ) (Desert Sun)
7458a^{5}

La Rogerais (FR) *T Doumen* a68 71
5 gr m Verglas(IRE) —La Legende (FR) (Desert Prince (IRE))
303a^{9}

Laser Blazer *Sam Davison* a55
2 b c Zafeen(FR) —Sashay (Bishop Of Cashel)
7609^{7} 7873^{8}

Lasercutter (IRE) *Peter Grayson*
2 b g One Cool Cat(USA) —San Luis Rey (Zieten (USA))
1978^{10}

Laser Ruby *Andrew Balding* a66 61
3 b f Compton Place—Lighted Way (Kris)
2841^{4} 3333^{6} *6285^{5} 7391^{3} 7519^{3}* ◆ *7563^{5} 7972^{4}*

Lasse (GER) *P Vovcenko* a65 72
7 b g Hamond(GER) —Liberia (GER) (Pentathlon)
690a^{7}

Last Act (IRE) *Mark Hoad* a44 6
2 gr f Act One—Laissez Faire (IRE) (Tagula (IRE))
6511^{10} *7559^{7} 7780^{7}*

Last Destination (IRE) *Nigel Tinkler* 72
2 b g Dubai Destination(USA) —Maimana (IRE) (Desert King (IRE))
1749^{2} 2522^{4} (3106) 4049^{3} 5947^{11} 6619^{9} 6978^{15}

Lastkingofscotland (IRE) *Conor Dore* a78 81
4 b g Danehill Dancer(IRE) —Arcade (Rousillon (USA))
444^{2} 587^{4} (804) 1047^{2} 1224^{5} (1642) 2009^{3} 2331^{4} 2409^{2} 2624^{3} *3779^{4} 3970^{3}* 4308^{4} 4522^{3} (4690) 5540^{5} 6260^{8} 7182^{8} 7382^{6} 7421^{3} 7526^{3} 7597^{13} 7971^{5}

Last Of The Ravens *John Coupland* a19
3 b f Zaha(CAN) —Eccentric Dancer (Rambo Dancer (CAN))
72^{4} 329^{6}

L'Astre De Choisir (IRE) *Walter Swinburn* a71 43
2 ch c Choisir(AUS) —Starring (FR) (Ashkalani (IRE))
5372^{8} *5893^{5} 6309^{2} 6870^{9}*

Lastroarofdtiger (USA) *John Weymes* a78 54
4 b g Cherokee Run(USA) —Innocent Affair (IRE) (Night Shift (USA))
466^{10}

Lastroseofsummer (IRE) *Rae Guest* a72 68
4 ch m Haafhd—Broken Romance (IRE) (Ela-Mana-Mou)
421^{6} 777^{3} 2476^{10} 2897^{3} (3221) 3475^{3} 4266^{3} ◆ 4719^{3} *5646^{2} 5963^{9}*

Last Sovereign *Jimmy O'Reilly* a86 88
6 b g Pivotal—Zayala (Royal Applause)
747^{2} ◆ *(902) 1088^{5}* 1862^{5} 3226^{8} (3898) 4598^{3} 5043^{7} 5297^{7} 6198^{10} *6503^{6}* 7146^{7}

Last Three Minutes (IRE) *Sir Michael Stoute* a89 98
5 b g Val Royal(FR) —Circe's Isle (Be My Guest (USA))
1831^{2}

Las Verglas Star (IRE) *Richard Fahey* a69 72
2 gr g Verglas(IRE) —Magnificent Bell (IRE) (Octagonal (NZ))
1009^{13} (1198) 3598^{9} 4544^{3} 5310^{6} 6220^{9} 6619^{7} 7118^{2} *7296^{2}*

Latansaa *Marcus Tregoning* a82 82
3 b g Indian Ridge—Sahool (Unfuwain (USA))
1381^{3} *1769^{4}*

Late Debate (USA) *J S Bolger* 65
2 br c Successful Appeal(USA) —Saintly Hertfield (USA) (Saint Ballado (CAN))
4175a^{10}

Latent Light (USA) *Ed Dunlop* 66
3 b c North Light(IRE) —Little Buckles (CAN) (Buckley Boy (USA))
1381^{10} 1976^{10} 2255^{8} 3155^{9}

Laterly (IRE) *Steve Gollings* a96 96
5 b g Tiger Hill(IRE) —La Candela (GER) (Alzao (USA))
6877^{15}

Lathaat *John Dunlop* 68
3 bb f Dubai Destination(USA) —Khulood (USA) (Storm Cat (USA))
2227^{3} ◆ 2603^{6} 3258^{4} 4364^{3} 5113^{5} 5713^{7} 6966^{8}

Latigo Shore (USA) *Nicholas Zito* a108
3 b c Malibu Moon(USA) —Carson's Vanity (USA) (Carson City (USA))
6582a^{6}

Latin Connection (IRE) *Lee Smyth* a32
4 b g Soviet Star(USA) —Via Verbano (IRE) (Caerleon (USA))
349^{7} 721^{7}

Latin Lashes (USA) *Richard Hannon* a72 71
2 bb f Stormy Atlantic(USA) —Magnificentaproval (USA) (Distant View (USA))
4658^{2} ◆ 5074^{4} *(6286)* 6989^{3}

Latin Love (IRE) *David Wachman* 108
4 ch m Danehill Dancer(IRE) —Ho Hi The Moon (IRE) (Be My Guest (USA))
957a^{3} 1787a^{5} 2355a^{8} 6235a^{2}

La Tournesol (GER) *R Rohne* 93
5 ch m Samum(GER) —La Bouche (GER) (In The Wings)
4566a^{2}

La Toya J (IRE) *Roger Curtis* a59
3 b f Noverre(USA) —Bevel (USA) (Mr Prospector (USA))
233^{9} 574^{4} 768^{6} 977^{7}

Lauberhorn *Eve Johnson Houghton* a75 75
3 b g Dubai Destination(USA) —Ski Run (Petoski)
1157^{3} 1578^{9} *(2333)* 2953^{2} (3506) 3807^{4} *4230^{5}* 5858^{7} 6424^{4} *7316^{6} 7495^{4}*

Laudatory *Walter Swinburn* a92 89
4 b g Royal Applause—Copy-Cat (Lion Cavern (USA))
1006^{7} 1430^{2} 1837^{4} 2467^{5} 2821^{6} 3632^{8} 4996^{3} 5311^{2} 6447^{8}

Laughing Boy (IRE) *W P Mullins* a43 85
4 b g Montjeu(IRE) —Mala Mala (IRE) (Brief Truce (USA))
5591^{7}

Laughing Jack *Michael Bell* 78
2 b c Beat Hollow—Bronzewing (Beldale Flutter (USA))
6883^{5}

Laughing Lashes (USA) *Mrs John Harrington* 111
2 gr f Mr Greeley(USA) —Adventure (USA) (Unbridled's Song (USA))
4077a^{2} (4879a) ◆ 5570a^{2}

Laugh Or Cry *PETER Makin* a66 76
2 br c Firebreak—Turkish Delight (Prince Sabo)
2867^{4} 3269^{5} 5465^{2} *5865^{8}* 6445^{11} *7400^{3}*

Laugia *John Jenkins* 43
2 b f Iceman—Rare Cross (IRE) (Cape Cross (IRE))
2176^{10} 2963^{8} 3906^{9}

Launchpad *Luca Cumani* a65 80
3 ch g Starcraft(NZ) —Revival (Sadler's Wells (USA))
5493^{10} *5842^{3}* 6470^{2} (6814)

Laura Land *Mark Brisbourne* a46 48
4 b m Lujain(USA) —Perdicula (IRE) (Persian Heights)
1983^{7} 3128^{12} 3639^{5} 3848^{4} 4279^{6} *4683^{3}* 5289^{8} 5564^{11}

Laura's Lady (IRE) *Alan Swinbank* 57
4 b m Namid—Catapila (USA) (Tactical Cat (USA))
7230^{6}

Laureldeans Best (IRE) *Richard Fahey* a65 66
4 b m King's Best(USA) —Vanishing River (USA) (Southern Halo (USA))
166^{3} 330^{3} 485^{7} 780^{2} 1204^{2} 1396^{9}

Laurel Guerreiro (JPN) *Mitsugu Kon* a110 117
6 bb h King Halo(JPN) —Big Tenby (JPN) (Tenby)
1024a^{4}

Laurie Grove (IRE) *T G Mills* a85 85
4 b g Danehill Dancer(IRE) —Fragrant (Cadeaux Genereux)
200^{6}

Lava Lamp (GER) *Geoffrey Harker* 78
3 b g Shamardal(USA) —La Felicita (Shareef Dancer (USA))
2884[10] 3390[11] 4017[6] 4200[4] (4669) (5119) ◆ 6983[2]

Lava Steps (USA) *Paul Midgley* a74 59
4 b g Giant's Causeway(USA) —Miznah (IRE) (Sadler's Wells (USA))
764 719[4] 910[5] 1398[12] 1807[10] 2218[8] 3901[8] 7397[9] 7806[5]

La Vecchia Scuola (IRE) *Jim Goldie* a39 102
6 b m Mull Of Kintyre(USA) —Force Divine (FR) (L'Emigrant (USA))
1821[15] 2313[2] 3447[6] 4393[4] (5118) 5291[6] 5908[7] ◆ 6493[3] 6926[2] 7350[22]

Laverre (IRE) *Tim Easterby* a37 69
3 b f Noverre(USA) —Ladood (Unfuwain (USA))
1336[3] 1528[2] 1927[6] 2993[7] 3376[5] 3730[2] 4752[7] 6212[11]

La Verte Rue (USA) *Mrs A Malzard* a49 65
4 b m Johannesburg(USA) —Settling In (USA) (Green Desert (USA))
5866[11]

Lawaaheb (IRE) *Tim Walford* a51 2
9 b g Alhaarth(IRE) —Ajayib (USA) (Riverman (USA))
3804[5]

Law Of Attraction (IRE) *Jeremy Gask* a75 48
3 b g Invincible Spirit(IRE) —Karatisa (IRE) (Nishapour (FR))
1622[2] 2919[8] 3325[3] 3759[3] 4547[9] 5383[10] 5769[3] 6164[3] 6541[9] 6664[7]

Law Of The Jungle (IRE) *Tom Dascombe* a66 74
4 b m Catcher In The Rye(IRE) —Haut Volee (Top Ville)
139[4] 210[7] 316[4]

Law Of The Range *Marco Botti* 88
3 b f Alhaarth(IRE) —Mountain Law (USA) (Mountain Cat (USA))
1278[3] 1654[10] 1882[5] (3628) 4389[8] 5394[5] (6090)

Lawspeaker *A Fabre* 108
3 b c Singspiel(IRE) —Forum Floozie (NZ) (Danasinga (AUS))
(2557a) 4039a[5] 6590a[9]

Law To Himself (IRE) *Alan Swinbank* 77
3 b g Rakti—Samhat Mtoto (Mtoto)
1485[3] (2425) 3451[3] 4153[4] 5121[9] 5942[4] 6753[6]

Layali Al Andalus *Saeed Bin Suroor* 109
3 b c Halling(USA) —Lafite (Robellino (USA))
2070[4] 5590[5] 6195[4] 6749[14]

Layali Al Arab (IRE) *Saeed Bin Suroor* a80 60
2 b c Cape Cross(IRE) —Easy Option (IRE) (Prince Sabo)
4447[7] (5156) 6184[9]

Lay Claim (USA) *Alan McCabe* a76 80
3 bb c Seeking The Gold(USA) —Promptly (IRE) (Lead On Time (USA))
2110[3] 2682[5] 3713[2] 4385[3] 5769[4] 6057[6] 6638[3] 7129[2] 7499[3] 7694[3] (7834) 7985[10]

Layla Jamil (IRE) *Mick Channon* 76
2 b f Exceed And Excel(AUS) —Guana Bay (Cadeaux Genereux)
3871[4] 4317[3] 5078[3] 5882[11]

Layla's Boy *John Mackie* a74 77
3 ch g Sakhee(USA) —Gay Romance (Singspiel (IRE))
889[7] 1059[3] 1515[2] 1666[3] 2315[5] 3428[4] 5607[7] 6623[12] 6895[15]

Layla's Dancer *Richard Fahey* 83
3 b c Danehill Dancer(IRE) —Crumpetsfortea (IRE) (Henbit (USA))
1297[3] 1658[4] 3949[3] 4619[3] ◆ 4751[3] 5511[12] 5904[8] 6355[7] 6753[12] 7053[13]

Layla's Hero (IRE) *David Simcock* a93 105
3 b g One Cool Cat(USA) —Capua (USA) (Private Terms (USA))
927a[4] 2537[6] 2712[6] 3429[7] 4750[4] 5416[2] 5854[6] 6321[5]

Layla's King *Jane Chapple-Hyam* a70 62
2 b c Dubawi(IRE) —Top Jem (Damister (USA))
7302[6] ◆ 7558[2]

Layla's Lad (USA) *David Simcock* a59
3 b c Dixieland Band(USA) —Requesting More (USA) (Norquestor (CAN))
35[5] 233[7] 582[3] 805[7] 904[6]

Layla's Lexi *Ian Williams* a68 73
3 b f Reset(AUS) —Tricoteuse (Kris)
894[2] (1514) 2042[2] 2288[3] (3390) 3857[4] 4618[6] 5096[7] 5654[6] 6054[3] 6257[2] 6856[12]

Layla's Princess *Ian Williams* a18 17
2 ch f Bahamian Bounty—Antonia's Choice (Music Boy)
1930[16] 7858[9] 7913[5] 7983[12]

Layline (IRE) *Gay Kelleway* a96 92
3 b g King's Best(USA) —Belle Reine (King Of Kings (IRE))
3103[15] 4030[2] ◆ 4473[8] 5703[2] 6312[8] 6806[6] 7083[8] 7735[3] 8009[7]

Lay Time *Andrew Balding* 69
2 b f Galileo(IRE) —Time Saved (Green Desert (USA))
5692[5]

La Zamora *David Barron* a84 91
4 b m Lujain(USA) —Love Quest (Pursuit Of Love)
1363[8] 1710[11] 1827[4] (2262) 3150[6] 3830[9] (4345) 5884[18] (6221)

La Zona (IRE) *Wido Neuroth* a78 78
4 b m Singspiel(IRE) —Reine De Neige (Kris)
7374a[2]

Leadenhall Lass (IRE) *Pat Phelan* a70 76
4 ch m Monsieur Bond(IRE) —Zest (USA) (Zilzal (USA))
2926[9] 3579[7] 3815[6] 4502[2] 4690[10] 5238[3]

Leader Of The Land (IRE) *David Lanigan* a57 88
3 ch g Halling(USA) —Cheerleader (Singspiel (IRE))
1601[4] (1989) 2248[2] (2439) 3273[2] 4380[5] (5549) 6074[3]

Leading Edge (IRE) *Mick Channon* a76 69
5 gr m Clodovil(IRE) —Ja Ganhou (Midyan (USA))
125[3]

League Champion (USA) *R Bouresly* a96 74
7 b g Rahy(USA) —Meiosis (USA) (Danzig (USA))
437a[5] 628a[10]

Leahness (IRE) *Patrick Morris* a46 42
3 br f Arakan(USA) —En Retard (IRE) (Petardia)
6956[6] 7322[3] 7542[7] 7676[3] 7827[8]

Leahurst (IRE) *Jeremy Noseda* a117 92
4 gr g Verglas(IRE) —Badee'A (IRE) (Marju (IRE))
(339a) ◆ (606a) ◆

Lean Burn (USA) *Barry Leavy* a47 56
4 b g Johannesburg(USA) —Anthelion (USA) (Stop The Music (USA))
467[10] 720[6] 833[3] 898[9] 2361[7] 7958[8]

Lean Machine *Ronald Harris* a70 83
3 b c Exceed And Excel(AUS) —Al Corniche (IRE) (Bluebird (USA))
2122[4] 2682[10] 4756[10] 5661[2] 6124[3] 6718[9] 7019[3] 7214[3] 7389[5] 7845[4] 7964[4] 8021[2]

Learo Dochais (USA) *Michael Jarvis* a71 74
4 b g Mutakddim(USA) —Brush With The Law (USA) (Broad Brush (USA))
110[5] 1224[6] 1595[8] (2383) 2959[6] 3458[4] 4875[10]

Leaving Alone (USA) *Edwin Tuer* a71 68
3 ch f Mr Greeley(USA) —Spankin' (USA) (A.P. Indy (USA))
1358[4] 1514[9] 2049[5] 2953[5] 3513[5] 4408[3] 4867[2] 5530[7] 6187[7] 6306[3] 7149[4]

Le Big (GER) *U Stoltefuss* a86 108
6 b g Big Shuffle(USA) —La Luganese (IRE) (Surumu (GER))
2559a[8] 3934a[10] 4888a[6] 5649a[5] 6408a[5] 7370a[2] 7800a[8]

Leceile (USA) *William Haggas* a64 91
4 bb m Forest Camp(USA) —Summerwood (USA) (Boston Harbor (USA))
1831[7] 2710[12] 3585[7] 6361[13]

Lechevalier Choisi (IRE) *James Bernard McCabe* 84
2 b c Choisir(AUS) —Creekhaven (IRE) (Definite Article)
4175a[7]

Le Corvee (IRE) *Tony Carroll* a73 57
8 b g Rossini(USA) —Elupa (IRE) (Mtoto)
(2676) 2952[4] (3984) 4327[2] 4731[3] 5873[8]

Ledgerwood *Adrian Chamberlain* a18 48
5 b g Royal Applause—Skies Are Blue (Unfuwain (USA))
1301[9] 2230[5] 2655[6] 3290[8]

Le Drakkar (AUS) *A bin Huzaim* a108 95
5 gr h Anabaa(USA) —My Mo Rally (NZ) (Mi Preferido (USA))
607a[10] 713a[3] 800a[11] 1022a[10]

Leelu *David Arbuthnot* a71 66
4 b m Largesse—Strat's Quest (Nicholas (USA))
(2967) 4324[6] 4839[3] (5555) 5889[4] 6479[7] 7298[6] (7613)

Lees Anthem *Colin Teague* a53 76
3 b g Mujahid(USA) —Lady Rock (Mistertopogigo (IRE))
1468[9] (1667) 2291[2] 2768[2] 3167[2] 3410[4] 4169[7] 4513[4] (5410) 5548[4] 6031[11]

Leftontheshelf (IRE) *Teresa Spearing* a68 73
4 ch m Namid—Corryvreckan (IRE) (Night Shift (USA))
723[7] 828[4] 1166[7]

Legal Eagle (IRE) *Paul Green* a82 86
5 b g Invincible Spirit(IRE) —Lupulina (CAN) (Saratoga Six (USA))
1458[5] 1888[4] 2310[3] (2696) 3065[2] 3584[3] 3898[7] 4558[4] (5480) 5941[2] 6358[10] 6981[5] 7212[12]

Legal Heights (IRE) *James Eustace* a54
2 b c Ivan Denisovich(IRE) —Viennese Dancer (Prince Sabo)
5020[9] 5381[8] 7578[7]

Legal Legacy *Michael Dods* 84
4 ch g Beat Hollow—Dans Delight (Machiavellian (USA))
1030[5] 1332[12] 1707[4] 2462[5] 3396[6] 4850[7] 5499[3] (5756) 5852[2] 6107[4] 6709[11]

Leiba Leiba *Marco Botti* 94
2 b c Librettist(USA) —Giusina Mia (USA) (Diesis)
1597[2] 1871[2] (2873) (3426) 3858[2] 4458[6] 5221[11]

Leitmotiv (IRE) *M Al Muhairi* a90 94
7 b h Sadler's Wells(USA) —Moselle (Mtoto)
605a[13]

Leitzu (IRE) *Mick Channon* a58 70
3 b f Barathea(IRE) —Ann's Annie (IRE) (Alzao (USA))
1138[4] 1448[9] 1921[4] 2408[3] 2844[2] 3852[5] 4382[5] 5163[2] 5598[3] 6144[10] (7037)

Lejaam *John Dunlop* 73
2 b c Dansili—Acts Of Grace (USA) (Bahri (USA))
4803[15] 5878[7] 6474[12] 6978[11]

Lelah Dorak (KSA) *B Al Shaibani* a89
4 ch h Frequent—Bint Garaah (KSA) (Vanlandingham (USA))
630a[10]

Le Larron (IRE) *A De Royer-Dupre* 104
3 gr c High Chaparral(IRE) —Mare Aux Fees (Kenmare (FR))
3014a[3] (5136a) 5800a[4] 6590a[3]

Leleyf (IRE) *Mick Channon* a78 77
3 b f Kheleyf(USA) —Titchwell Lass (Lead On Time (USA))
1140[2] 1281[4] 1546[7] 2179[3] 2822[4] 3311[6] 3480[2] 3751[7] 4284[5] 4659[9]

Lemon Drop Red (USA) *Ed Dunlop* a29 64
2 b g Lemon Drop Kid(USA) —Skipper's Mate (USA) (Skip Away (USA))
4318[6] 5049[9] 6053[9]

Lemon Twirl (USA) *John Mattine* 95
6 b m Lemon Drop Kid(USA) —Longing To Dance (USA) (Nureyev (USA))
6235a[5]

Le Muguet (IRE) *Ed Dunlop* 7
3 ch f Indian Ridge—Rahika Rose (Unfuwain (USA))
1932[14]

Lend A Grand (IRE) *Jo Crowley* a71 37
6 br g Lend A Hand—Grand Madam (Grand Lodge (USA))
4700[4] 5897[3] 6671[9] 7168[12] (7557)

Lend A Light *Philip Hobbs* a51 55
4 b h Lend A Hand—No Candles Tonight (Star Appeal)
7449[6] 7783[7] ◆ 7885[4]

Lenjawi Pride *Tom Dascombe* a82 67
2 b f Elusive City(USA) —Clarice Orsini (Common Grounds)
1626[3] (1981) 2436[9] 6317[8] 6745[6] 7127[2] 7565[5] (7803)

Lenkiewicz *Rod Millman* a74 79
3 gr f Oratorio(IRE) —Philadelphie (IRE) (Anabaa (USA))
1159[8] (2003) 3866[2] 4250[5] 5145[3] 5896[10] 6351[11] 6805[12]

Lenny Bee *David Brown* a99 98
4 rg g Kyllachy—Smart Hostess (Most Welcome)
(1295) 2759[7] 3446[6] 3828[10] 7254[3] 7466[2] 7740[4]

Leo Gali (IRE) *David Wachman* 102
3 b f Galileo(IRE) —Reprise (Darshaan)
4631a[2]

Leolene Starlight *David O'Meara* 54
5 ch m Sugarfoot—Greyhill Lady (Grey Desire)
2393[11] 2837[6] 3227[10] 3732[7] 4047[14] 4605[6]

Leomode (USA) *Liam Corcoran* a38
4 b g Cherokee Run(USA) —Twist Of Faith (USA) (Storm Cat (USA))
5765[8]

Leonid Glow *Michael Dods* a70 83
5 b m Hunting Lion(IRE) —On Till Morning (IRE) (Never So Bold)
(1366) ◆ 2113[2] 2465[5] 2856[3] 3065[6] 3947[6] 5054[6]

Leopard Hills (IRE) *Howard Johnson* 68
3 b g Acclamation—Sadler's Park (USA) (Sadler's Wells (USA))
2606[4] 4200[2] 5243[5]

Leo's Lucky Angel (IRE) *Daniel Mark Loughnane* a44 41
5 b m Galileo(IRE) —Rosa Delle Alpi (USA) (Royal Applause)
530[7] 794[8]

Le Petit Vigier *Patrick Holmes* a48 47
4 b m Groom Dancer(USA) —Fallujah (Dr Fong (USA))
1576[14] 1922[12] 6257[7]

Le Reve Royal *Geoffrey Oldroyd* a47 53
4 ch m Monsieur Bond(IRE) —Bond Royale (Piccolo)
211[7] 4605[10] 4868[6] 5064[11]

Le Roi Mage (IRE) *T Lallie* a95 96
5 ch g City On A Hill(USA) —Lycius Girl (ITY) (Lycius (USA))
7776a[2]

Les Andelys *Terry Clement* a2
4 b g Zieten(USA) —Oasis Song (IRE) (Selkirk (USA))
5665[9] 6499[10]

Les Arcs (USA) *J S Moore* a113 22
10 bb g Arch(USA) —La Sarto (USA) (Cormorant (USA))
4937[8]

Les Fazzani (IRE) *Kevin Ryan* a104 112
6 b m Intikhab(USA) —Massada (Most Welcome)
1832[2] (2538) 3671[4] 4829[5] 5749[6] 5938[2] 7349[8]

Les Landes (IRE) *Jamie Osborne* a53 49
2 b g Aussie Rules(USA) —Splendid (IRE) (Mujtahid (USA))
4736[5] 5006[11] 5156[10] 7497[5] 7630[10] 7691[7]

Lesley's Choice *Linda Perratt* a97 80
4 b g Lucky Story(USA) —Wathbat Mtoto (Mtoto)
2[6] 2883[2] 3165[4] 3902[2] (4060) 4372[5] 4952[7] (5212) 5335[5] 6140[14] 6245[9] (6708) 7175[5]

Leslingtaylor (IRE) *John Quinn* a73 86
8 b g Orpen(USA) —Rite Of Spring (Niniski (USA))
(1012) (6573) 6754[4]

Lesoto Diamond (IRE) *P A Fahy* a79 79
8 b m Darnay—Fallon (IRE) (Arcane (USA))
6730a[8]

Les Verguettes (IRE) *Stef Higgins* a72 52
2 b f Iffraaj—Mitsina (Fantastic Light (USA))
5372[6] 5657[2] 6796[8] 7962[2] 8030[2]

Les Yeux Bleus (IRE) *Luca Cumani* 76
3 gr f Verglas(IRE) —Sanpala (Sanglamore (USA))
2110[9] 3001[6] 3628[9]

Lethal *Richard Price* a71 60
7 ch g Nashwan(USA) —Ipanema Beach (Lion Cavern (USA))
899[3] 1147[4] 2178[5] 3567[7] 3777[10] 7125[12] 7391[7] 7473[7]

Lethal Glaze (IRE) *Brian Ellison* a103 99
4 gr g Verglas(IRE) —Sticky Green (Lion Cavern (USA))
1736[7] 5035[2] ◆ 5291[12] 5492[8] 5989[4] 6283[6] (6565) 6808[2] 7350[13]

Letizia Relco (IRE) *B Grizzetti* 91
3 br f Lucky Story(USA) —Speedybird (IRE) (Danehill (USA))
3495a[9]

Let Me Fight (IRE) *J Moore* 120
3 b g Hawk Wing(USA) —Riva Royale (Royal Applause)
7852a[4]

Le Toreador *Kevin Ryan* a99 97
5 ch g Piccolo—Peggy Spencer (Formidable I (USA))
(639) 992[3] 2054[12] 2745[19] 3165[5] 3891[4] ◆ 4243[6] 5069[10] 5734[6] 5999[4] 6140[5] 6663[7] 7254[6]

Let's Face Facts *Jim Goldie* a6
3 b f Lucky Story(USA) —Rhinefield Beauty (IRE) (Shalford (IRE))
7244[7]

Lets Move It *Derek Shaw* a61 40
3 b g Piccolo—Park Star (Gothenberg (IRE))
43[7] 167[4] 906[2] 1316[7] 1535[9] 1774[9] 2217[5] 2879[14] 7807[6] 7859[8] (7953)

Letteratura (IRE) *J-C Rouget* 99
4 b m Danehill Dancer(IRE) —Petite Rose (IRE) (Turtle Island (IRE))
3875[5] 5576a[4] 6640a[10]

Lettering *Derek Haydn Jones* a45 36
2 ch f Iceman—Calligraphy (Kris)
4221[11] 4474[10] 4921[5] 6211[5] 6512[8]

Letty *A Friebert* 89
3 ch f Trade Fair—Love Is All (IRE) (Second Empire (IRE))
6885[9] 7234[6]

Leulahleulahlay *Evan Williams* a66 75
4 ch g Dr Fong(USA) —Fidelio's Miracle (USA) (Mountain Cat (USA))
237[4]

Levantera (IRE) *Clive Cox* a58 73
2 ch f Hurricane Run(IRE) —Ellway Star (IRE) (Night Shift (USA))
3861[14] 4286[5] 5520[3] 5961[6] 6471[2]

Levera *Alan King* a70 86
7 b g Groom Dancer(USA) —Prancing (Prince Sabo)
5004[5] 6534[10] 8022[9]

Leverage (IRE) *Michael Wigham* a81 89
4 b g Xaar—She Looks On High (USA) (Secreto (USA))
1862[12] 2872[11] 3565[13] 3970[4] 4489[8] 5048[8]

Leviathan *Tom Tate* a48 96
3 b c Dubawi(IRE) —Gipsy Moth (Efisio)
4894[7] 5524[6] ◆ 5854[2] ◆ 6327[7] ◆ 6888[13]

Le Vie Infinite (IRE) *R Brogi* 98
3 b c Le Vie Dei Colori—Looking Back (IRE) (Stravinsky (USA))
7372a[7]

Levitate *Sir Michael Stoute* 66
2 ch g Pivotal—Soar (Danzero (AUS))
6092[8] 6689[4] ◆ 7058[11]

Levitation (IRE) *Stuart Kittow* a71 73
4 b m Vettori(IRE) —Uplifting (Magic Ring (IRE))
3962[6] 5689[10] 5958[6] 7323[14]

Le Volcan D'Or (USA) *Mark Johnston* a20 21
3 ch g Giant's Causeway(USA) —Twenty Eight Carat (USA) (Alydar (USA))
219[4] 1721[4] 3355[6]

Lewyn *Jeremy Gask* a87 72
3 b f Exceed And Excel(AUS) —Panoramic View (Polar Falcon (USA))
(222) (662) 919[2] (1191) 1523[6] 5250[16] 6048[10] 6221[5] 7041[8] 7466[4] 7635[3] 7961[5] 7998[5]

Lexington Bay (IRE) *Richard Fahey* a73 70
2 b g High Chaparral(IRE) —Schust Madame (IRE) (Second Set (IRE))
2312[3] 3190[10] 7325[2] ◆ 7567[4] (7644)

Lexi's Boy (IRE) *Kevin Ryan* a60 58
2 gr g Verglas(IRE) —Jazan (IRE) (Danehill (USA))
2427[8] 3517[5] 4402[3]

Lexi's Hero (IRE) *Kevin Ryan* 90
2 b g Invincible Spirit(IRE) —Christel Flame (Darshaan)
2068[2] 2448[3] 3426[3] 4123[2] 4543[2] (5117) 5939[5] 6734[11]

Lexi's Layla (IRE) *David Simcock* a65 67
3 ch f Kheleyf(USA) —Woodstamp (IRE) (Woodborough (USA))
1345[3] 2722[8] 3277[4]

Lexi's Princess (IRE) *Kevin Ryan* 59
2 gr f Verglas(IRE) —Night Fairy (IRE) (Danehill (USA))
2667[3]

Leyte Gulf (USA) *Chris Bealby* a73 61
7 b g Cozzene(USA) —Gabacha (USA) (Woodman (USA))
(173) 293[2] 529[6] 2495[6] 3764[9] 4441[5] 4915[8] (6120) 6538[3] 7270[5] 7422[5] (7632) 7861[7] 8013[6]

L Frank Baum (IRE) *Gay Kelleway* 97
3 b g Sinndar(IRE) —Rainbow City (IRE) (Rainbow Quest (USA))
6318[8] 6506[6]

L'Hermitage (IRE) *Brian Meehan* a38 63
2 b g Encosta De Lago(AUS) —Autumnal (IRE) (Indian Ridge)
6190[7] 6849[9]

L'Hirondelle (IRE) *Michael Attwater* a92 89
6 b g Anabaa(USA) —Auratum (USA) (Carson City (USA))
231[12] 324[4] 580[5] 1430[7] 1625[11] 2926[4] 3565[9] (4023) 4459[16] 5003[2] 5750[3] 5997[2] 7091[2] 7318[7]

L'Homme De Nuit (GER) *Gary Moore* a75 60
6 b g Samum(GER) —La Bouche (GER) (In The Wings)
232[2]

Liang Kay (GER) *Uwe Ostmann* 113
5 b h Dai Jin—Linton Bay (GER) (Funambule (USA))
1111a[3] 2806a[4] 4418a[4] 5542a[3] 6612a[9] 7102a[3]

Libano (IRE) *D K Weld* 112
4 b h Indian Ridge—Daniela Grassi (Bound For Honour (USA))
1246a[6] 6617a[5]

Libel Law *Saeed Bin Suroor* 111
4 ch h Kingmambo(USA) —Innuendo (IRE) (Caerleon (USA))
5090[5] 5949[14]

Liberation (IRE) *Saeed Bin Suroor* a86 100
4 b h Refuse To Bend(IRE) —Mosaique Bleue (Shirley Heights)
412a[13] 713a[12]

Libertia *Tony Newcombe* 47
2 b f Statue Of Liberty(USA) —Imperia (GER) (Tertullian (USA))
3331[6] 4729[4] 7177[14]

Libertino (IRE) *Tony Carroll* a67 68
3 ch g Bertolini(USA) —Villafranca (IRE) (In The Wings)
625[4] 809[5] 932[5] 1457[2] 2919[12] 3359[9] 3715[7] 7651[9] 7810[5]

Liberty Cap (USA) *John Gosden* a80 85
2 bb c Street Cry(IRE) —Binavicar (USA) (Vicar (USA))
2216[11] (3219) 3872[8] 4429[3] 4955[4] 5374[2] 5830[7] (6160)

Liberty Ess (IRE) *Michael Wigham* a50 51
2 b f Antonius Pius(USA) —Athboy Nights (IRE) (Night Shift (USA))
1879[7] 2292[5] 3603[4] 3757[2] 4067[3] 5581[7] 7577[5] 7894[9]

Liberty Gree (IRE) *Mme C Head-Maarek* 68
2 b f Statue Of Liberty(USA) —Golly Gree (USA) (Mr Greeley (USA))
5252a[7]

Liberty Green (IRE) *Alan McCabe* a71 51
2 b f Statue Of Liberty(USA) —Green Green Grass (Green Desert (USA))
1375[7] 2958[10] 7418[2] (7517) 7734[2] 7891[8]

Liberty Lady (IRE) *Desmond Donovan* a73 83
3 b f Statue Of Liberty(USA) —Crossed Wire (Lycius (USA))
(906) 1390[4] 1765[3] (2332) ◆ 2768[5] 3174[3] 3440[6] 4922[U] (5327) 6198[6]

Liberty Point (IRE) *Ian Wood* 32
4 b g Statue Of Liberty(USA) —Tragic Point (IRE) (Tragic Role (USA))
950[11] 1432[9]

Liberty Ship *Mark Buckley* a66 77
5 b g Statue Of Liberty(USA) —Flag (Selkirk (USA))
1711[11] 3119[8] 3879[3] 4199[5] 5023[2] 5422[11] 6073[12] 7148[6] 7628[9]

Liberty Trail (IRE) *David Evans* a70 74
4 b g Statue Of Liberty(USA) —Karinski (USA) (Palace Music (USA))
1672[14] 2208[2] 2273[4] 2624[2] 3557[3] 4053[8] 4776[3] 5634[11] 5764[3] 6371[6] 7241[10] (7426) (7656) 7699[5]

Libranno *Richard Hannon* 111
2 b c Librettist(USA) —Annabelle Ja (FR) (Singspiel (IRE))
(2547) ◆ (3823) (4538) 5347a[6] 6192[5]

Libre *F Jordan* a56 57
10 b g Bahamian Bounty—Premier Blues (FR) (Law Society (USA))
131[9] 211[3] 347[2] 407[7] 1507[13] 1772[4] 2299[2] 2636[2] 2880[3] 3128[11] 6062[2] 7070[9] 7199[12]

Librettela *Alan Jarvis*
2 b g Librettist(USA) —Ella's Wish (IRE) (Bluebird (USA))
6102[9]

Librettista (AUS) *Luca Cumani* a69 80
4 b f Elusive Quality(USA) —Libretto (IRE) (Singspiel (IRE))
2473[2] 3080[7] 4238[4] (5172) (5563) 6055[9]

Licato (GER) *Robert Collet* 66
11 b g Goofalik(USA) —Libertad (GER) (Lagunas)
5378a[0]

Licence To Till (USA) *Mark Johnston* a93 92
3 b g War Chant(USA) —With A Wink (USA) (Clever Trick (USA))
2394[5] 2656[10] 2970[8] 4023[3] 4501[2] (4690) 5098[6] 5859[3] (6304) (6910a)

Liebelei (USA) *Harry Dunlop* a34 46
3 bb f Royal Academy(USA) —Part With Pride (USA) (Executive Pride)
1048[11]

Liel *Brian Meehan* a35 58
4 b m Pivotal—Magical Romance (IRE) (Barathea (IRE))
2003[4] 2249[7] 2741[5] 3255[10] 6952[6] 7738[7]

Lieu Day Louie (IRE) *Noel Wilson* a32 60
3 b g Bahamian Bounty—Nebraska Lady (IRE) (Lujain (USA))
1511[8] 2069[10] 2449[8] 3086[7] 4649[3] 5046[6] 5299[10] 6644[5] 7132[12] 7808[7]

Lieutenant Pigeon *Richard Guest* a80 73
5 ch g Captain Rio—Blue Velvet (Formidable (USA))
2647[11]

Life And Soul (IRE) *Amanda Perrett* a80 98
3 b c Azamour(IRE) —Way For Life (GER) (Platini (GER))
(1876) ◆ 2254[3] 2742[2] 3105[14] 4470[4] 4815[2] 5217[3] 6203[6] (6387) 6889[5]

Life And Times (USA) *Mahmood Al Zarooni* 75
2 b c Medaglia D'Oro(USA) —Sur Ma Vie (USA) (Fusaichi Pegasus (USA))
4096[5]

Life At Ten (USA) *Todd Pletcher* a118
5 ch m Malibu Moon(USA) —Rahrahsixboombah (USA) (Rahy (USA))
5578a[3] 7344a[P]

Life's Challenge (USA) *Mark Johnston* a73 81
4 ch m Mr Greeley(USA) —Danse Du Diable (IRE) (Sadler's Wells (USA))
174[6] 383[5]

Lifting Cloud *A Fabre* 102
4 b h Dansili—Love The Rain (Rainbow Quest (USA))
6016a[4]

Light Dubai (IRE) *Mick Channon* a68 77
4 b m Fantastic Light(USA) —Seeking A Way (USA) (Seeking The Gold (USA))
1141[3] 1489[7] 1775[2] 2342[5] (2429) 2956[7]

Lightening Thief (IRE) *W McCreery* 97
2 b c Acclamation—Mrs Cee (IRE) (Orpen (USA))
2352a[6] 3939a[6]

Lighterman *Eric Alston* 35
3 ch g Firebreak—Manuka Too (IRE) (First Trump)
2503[5] 2837[10]

Light Footsteps (IRE) *Eoin Griffin* 78
2 b f Footstepsinthesand—Azurine (IRE) (Spectrum (IRE))
5570a[12]

Light From Mars *Rod Millman* a105 106
5 gr g Fantastic Light(USA) —Hylandra (USA) (Bering)
1085[5] ◆ 1377[4] 1519[3] 2595[6] 3146[10] 3869[3] 4412[6] 5247[5] 5950[3] 6349[25]

Lighthouse Keeper (IRE) *Amy Weaver* 57
2 ch c Noverre(USA) —Linette (GER) (In The Wings)
3175[6] 3603[2] 4150[11]

Light Nights (IRE) *Tim Easterby* 38
3 b f Acclamation—Grecian Grail (IRE) (Rainbow Quest (USA))
2501[8]

Lightning Cloud (IRE) *Kevin Ryan* 64
2 gr c Sleeping Indian—Spree (IRE) (Dansili)
6138[11] 6488[5] 7058[7] ◆

Light Sleeper *Peter Chapple-Hyam* a69 75
4 b h Kyllachy—Snoozy (Cadeaux Genereux)
223[9]

Light The City (IRE) *Ruth Carr* a38 62
3 b g Fantastic Light(USA) —Marine City (JPN) (Carnegie (IRE))
718[7] 909[6] 1054[8] 2838[11] 3153[5] 3532[5] 4015[P] 4200[3] 4448[2] (4545) ◆ 4800[4] 5420[5] 5642[4] 6038[2] 6631[8] 7504[8]

Lignon's Hero (BRZ) *A Cintra Pereira* a70 90
5 br h Crimson Tide(IRE) —L'Escapade (BRZ) (Aksar (USA))
512a[12] 712a[12]

Likeable Lad *Ruth Carr* 12
2 ch g Redoubtable(USA) —Some Like It Hot (Ashkalani (IRE))
6027[8] 6500[13] 7641[8]

Like A Boy *PETER Makin* a42
2 b c Medicean—Like A Dame (Danehill (USA))
7385[10]

Like A Charm (IRE) *Howard Johnson* 53
2 b f Ad Valorem(USA) —Midnight Pearl (USA) (Woodman (USA))
4709[3] 6182[8]

Like Afleet (USA) *P Demercastel* 96
2 b f Afleet Alex(USA) —Singin Up A Storm (USA) (Storm Cat (USA))
7008a[4]

Like For Like (IRE) *Ron Hodges* a66 54
4 ch m Kheleyf(USA) —Just Like Annie (IRE) (Mujadil (USA))
3338[12] 4283[9] 4776[5] 5471[4] 5579[10]

Lileo (IRE) *Nikki Evans* 65
3 b g Galileo(IRE) —Jabali (FR) (Shirley Heights)
2281[4]

Liliside (FR) *F Rohaut* 115
3 b f American Post—Miller's Lily (FR) (Miller's Mate)
2158a[6] 2801a[5] 6764a[8]

Lillie Langtry (IRE) *A P O'Brien* a96 117
3 bb f Danehill Dancer(IRE) —Hoity Toity (Darshaan)
2370a[5] (3143) 3793[5] (5773a)

Lilli Palmer (IRE) *Miss J R Tooth* a46 42
3 ch f Bertolini(USA) —Little Whisper (IRE) (Be My Guest (USA))
2249[11] 2968[9] 3786[8] 4589[12] 5175[6] 6862[9]

Lilly Blue (IRE) *Roy Brotherton* a56 64
4 b m Hawk Wing(USA) —Holly Blue (Bluebird (USA))
2167[7] 2955[11] 4427[6] 5113[7] 5767[10] 7461[7]

Lilly De Rome *Ken Wingrove*
7 ch m Roi De Rome(USA) —Bishop's Folly (Weld)
3278[12]

Lilly Fa Pootz (USA) *Jerry Hollendorfer* 109
5 bb m Gilded Time(USA) —Dark Rhythm (USA) (Fit To Fight (USA))
6604a[9]

Lilly Grove *Alan Swinbank* a59 46
5 b m Mtoto—Armada Grove (Fleetwood (IRE))
398[4] 918[5] ◆ 1673[9]

Lilly Royal (IRE) *Bryn Palling* a56 69
4 b m Tillerman—Ervedya (IRE) (Doyoun)
1179[6] 2645[7] 3084[13] 3967[12] 4132[7]

Lily Again *Paul Cole* a80 98
2 ch f American Post—Sari (Faustus (USA))
(2642) 3307a[2] 3792[5] (4305) 4879a[4] 5910[5] 6528[5] 7098[10]

Lily Eva *Desmond Donovan* a40 50
4 ch m Definite Article—Avanindra (Zamindar (USA))
4238[7] 4793[10] 4874[8] 5864[9] 6815[8] 6905[8] 7491[10] 7727[8] 7899[6]

Lily Jicaro (IRE) *Lisa Williamson* a21 55
4 ch m Choisir(AUS) —Mourir D'Aimer (USA) (Trempolino (USA))
3357[8] 3727[13] 4173[8] 4485[14]

Lily Lily *Kevin McAuliffe* a65
3 b f Efisio—Bel Tempo (Petong)
22[3] 133[8] (188) 371[7]

Lily Of The Valley (FR) *J-C Rouget* 121
3 b f Galileo(IRE) —Pennegale (IRE) (Pennekamp (USA))
(3720a) (5346a) (6613a)

Lily Rio (IRE) *William Muir* 59
3 bb f Marju(IRE) —Jinsiyah (USA) (Housebuster (USA))
1881[6] 2901[10] 3788[10] 4448[5]

Lily's Star (IRE) *H Rogers* a33 62
3 b f Chineur(FR) —Voodoo Lily (IRE) (Petardia)
4563a[10]

Lily Wood *James Unett* a61 53
4 ch m Central Park(IRE) —Lady Castanea (Superlative)
2590[9] 3129[8] 3391[13] 4913[11] 4987[6] 5766[4] 7563[3] (7676) 7761[4]

Limatus (GER) *P Vovcenko* 97
9 bb g Law Society(USA) —Limaga (Lagunas)
4012a[7]

Lindentree *W Hickst* 100
3 ch c Dai Jin—Lindenblute (Surumu (GER))
3018a[2] 4184a[6]

Lindner (GER) *Saeed Bin Suroor* a88 102
5 b g Golan(IRE) —Lindenblute (Surumu (GER))
335a[3] 512a[7]

Lindo Erro *John Mackie* a55
2 b f Camacho—Katie Savage (Emperor Jones (USA))
4517[8] 5269[2] 5924[8] 6673[16]

Lindoro *K M Prendergast* a93 93
5 b g Marju(IRE) —Floppie (FR) (Law Society (USA))
613[3] 1167[4] 2091[8] 2172[6] 2808[4] 3557[2] 4014[3] 5357[8] 6110[8] 7051[13]

Lindsay's Dream *Andrew Haynes* a61 53
4 b m Montjeu(IRE) —Lady Lindsay (IRE) (Danehill Dancer (IRE))
2360[8] 3267[6]

Lindy Hop (IRE) *Kevin Ryan* a64 65
4 b m Danehill Dancer(IRE) —Healing Music (FR) (Bering)
38[4] 194[8]

Line Of David (USA) *John W Sadler* a113
3 ch c Lion Heart(USA) —Emma's Dilemma (USA) (Capote (USA))
1714a[18]

Line Of Duty (IRE) *Alan Swinbank* a73 92
3 b g Arakan(USA) —Zibaline (FR) (Linamix (FR))
2258[4] 2658[6] (3077) 4751[4] (5243) 5747[13] 6698[7]

Lingfield Bound (IRE) *John Best* a74 69
3 ch c Dubai Destination(USA) —Timewee (USA) (Romanov (IRE))
533[3] 655[2] 930[3] 1168[2] 1448[8] 4260[12] 6122[6] 6856[8] 7190[9] (7561) 7881[3]

Links Drive Lady *Mark Rimmer* a64
2 br f Striking Ambition—Miskina (Mark Of Esteem (IRE))
7879[3] 7990[3]

Linnens Star (IRE) *Ralph Beckett* a92 92
3 b g Traditionally(USA) —Capestar (IRE) (Cape Cross (IRE))
2128[3] ◆ 2692[3] (4107) 5030[5] 5917[5] 6564[4] ◆

Linton (AUS) *Robert Hickmott* 113
4 gr g Galileo(IRE) —Our Heather (NZ) (Centaine (AUS))
7291a[21]

Lion Court (IRE) *Sir Mark Prescott Bt* 73
2 ch g Iffraaj—Spanish Falls (Belmez (USA))
6324[4] 6675[2] ◆ 7119[4]

Lion Mountain *Mahmood Al Zarooni* 91
3 b c Tiger Hill(IRE) —Cal Norma's Lady (IRE) (Lyphard's Special (USA))
(1627) 2160a[8] 3104[13]

Lion Sands *A bin Huzaim* a105 107
6 b g Montjeu(IRE) —Puce (Darshaan)
335a[12] 512a[3] 712a[11]

Lipocco *A De Royer-Dupre* a88 108
6 b g Piccolo—Magical Dancer (IRE) (Magical Wonder (USA))
4773a[7]

Lips Poison (GER) *Andreas Lowe* 97
2 ch f Mamool(IRE) —Lips Plane (IRE) (Ashkalani (IRE))
7108a[4] 7534a[10]

Lisahane Bog *Peter Hedger* a80 63
3 b g Royal Applause—Veronica Franco (Darshaan)
(35) 203[2] 311[2] 448[2] 1189[7] 1307[2] 1514[10] 1934[10] 6503[11] 7115[8] 7389[7] 7699[9] 7889[5] (8014)

Lisbon Lion (IRE) *James Moffatt* a62 57
5 b g Mull Of Kintyre(USA) —Ludovica (Bustino)
411[4] 621[2] ◆ 1462[5] 1984[2] 2500[5] 3078[6] 3709[5] 3965[5]

Lis Pendens *William Muir* a56 63
3 b g Tobougg(IRE) —In Good Faith (USA) (Dynaformer (USA))
1880[8] 4230[6] 4683[5] 5522[8] 6662[7]

Lisselan Courtesan (IRE) *Raymond Hurley* a61 62
5 b m Alzao(USA) —Approach The Bench (USA) (Majestic Light (USA))
7419[4]

Lisselan Gardens (USA) *Mme J Bidgood* a66 79
7 b g Concern(USA) —Sambacarioca (USA) (Irish Tower (USA))
2446a[2]

Lisselan Grace (IRE) *Raymond Hurley* a51 47
3 gr f Refuse To Bend(IRE) —Questina (GER) (Sternkoenig (IRE))
7419[5]

Lisselan Hurricane (USA) *Mme J Bidgood* 78
4 b g Dance Master(USA) —Sense Of Propriety (USA) (Seattle Song (USA))
1055a[10]

Lisselton Cross *Martin Bosley* a60
2 ch c Compton Place—Sweet Myrtle (USA) (Mutakddim (USA))
5895[7] 6842[10] 7309[6] 7592[3] 7809[2] ◆ 7997[5]

Liszt (IRE) *Ian Williams* a30 98
4 gr g Galileo(IRE) —Corrine (IRE) (Spectrum (IRE))
1015[14] 1821[10] 2317[9] 4846[11] 6262[5]

Litenup (IRE) *Gay Kelleway* a59 26
4 b m Trans Island—Common Cause (Polish Patriot (USA))
(100) 184[12] 1225[7] 2006[14] (2870) 4591[3] 5704[8] 7445[5] 7760[7]

Liteup My World (USA) *Brian Ellison* a72 58
4 ch g Hennessy(USA) —Liteup My Life (USA) (Green Dancer (USA))
1494[4] (2789) 3149[5]

Lithaam (IRE) *Milton Bradley* a77 75
6 ch g Elnadim(USA) —Elhida (IRE) (Mujtahid (USA))
119[4] 306[5] 750[6] 2954[6] 3299[8] 3474[9] 3722[5] 4047[9] 4326[10] 5055[5] 5176[5] 5697[5] 6206[10] 6665[6]

Litotes *Michael Attwater* a51
2 b f Librettist(USA) —Royal Ivy (Mujtahid (USA))
7871[6] 8030[3]

Little Amapola (JPN) *Hiroyuki Nagahama* 114
5 bb m Agnes Tachyon(JPN) —Little Harmony (JPN) (Commander In Chief)
7460a[4]

Little Black Book (IRE) *Gerard Butler*
2 ch g Shamardal(USA) —Extreme Beauty (USA) (Rahy (USA))
6200[16]

Little Book *Edward Vaughan* a46 63
2 b f Librettist(USA) —Cal Norma's Lady (IRE) (Lyphard's Special (USA))
3296[10] 4048[6] 4682[8] 5660[9]

Little Bridge (NZ) *C S Shum* 117
4 b g Faltaat(USA) —Golden Rose (NZ) (Gold Brose (AUS))
7852a[8]

Little Buddy *Richard Price* a18 34
3 ch g Reel Buddy(USA) —Little Kenny (Warning)
2994[14] 3258[6] 4109[8] 4679[12] 6420[6] 6655[8] 6952[10] 7406[8] 7495[6]

Little Carmela *Stuart Williams* a69 65
6 gr m Beat Hollow—Carmela Owen (Owington)
190[4]

Little Curtsey *Hughie Morrison* a72
2 b f Royal Applause—Tychy (Suave Dancer (USA))
7021[3] ◆ (7311)

Little Edward *Ron Hodges* a71 85
12 gr g King's Signet(USA) —Cedar Lady (Telsmoss)
(1583) 1979[6] 2954[8] 3400[4] 4041[3] 4326[7] 5025[3] 5368[3] 6057[7] 6368[5]

Little Firecracker *Neil King* a35 62
5 b m Cadeaux Genereux—El Hakma (Shareef Dancer (USA))
100[9]

Little Garcon (USA) *Marco Botti* a95 102
3 b g Bernstein(USA) —Demure (Machiavellian (USA))
1191[4] (1663) 2862[2] 3673[2] 4541[7] 5731[3] (6319) 7524[8]

Little Hazel *Pat Eddery* a38 9
2 b f Green Desert(USA) —Show Trial (IRE) (Jade Robbery (USA))
1603[9] 1978[6]

Little Libretto (IRE) *David Evans* a34 72
2 b f Librettist(USA) —Sharadayna (Priolo (USA))
1009[5] (1173) 1733[5] 1819[7] 3859[6] 5269[8] 5630[14]

Little Lily Morgan *Robin Bastiman* a33 35
7 gr m Kayf Tara—Cool Grey (Absalom)
7149[8] 7805[11]

Little Lion Man *Peter Chapple-Hyam* a72 85
2 b c Kyllachy—Validate (Alhaarth (IRE))
(2598) 3100[12] 5295[2] 5748[5] 7080[7]

Little Luxury (IRE) *Edward Lynam* a58 53
3 b f Tagula(IRE) —Erne Project (IRE) (Project Manager)
7872[4]

Little Meadow (IRE) *Julia Feilden* a55 52
3 b f Antonius Pius(USA) —Cresalin (Coquelin (USA))
302[4] 475[5] 1158[11] 2336[3] 3788[U] 4027[4] 4779[3] 5171[5] 6020[2] 6527[4] 6863[4] 7038[4] 7727[4]

Littlemisssunshine (IRE) *Tobias B P Coles* a73 75
5 b m Oasis Dream—Sharp Catch (IRE) (Common Grounds)
119[8] 241[5] 2332[4] 2751[8] (3293) 3637[8] 5207[2] 6303[2] 6997[10]

Little Miss Take *Tom Dascombe* a46 68
2 b f Royal Applause—Sattelight (Fraam)
1421[3] 1626[5] 3386[3] 3705[4] 4984[9] 6875[5] 7126[3]

Little Nuthatch (IRE) *David Evans* 1
2 b f Camacho—Polly Mills (Lugana Beach)
1463[7] 2631[8]

Little Oddy (IRE) *David Evans* 27
2 b g Refuse To Bend(IRE) —Archipova (IRE) (Ela-Mana-Mou)
2059[16] 3332[11]

Little Oz (IRE) *Ed Dunlop* 68
3 br f Red Ransom(USA) —Australie (IRE) (Sadler's Wells (USA))
3513[6] 4235[2] 4557[3] 5164[8]

Little Pandora *Lee James* a32 39
6 b m Komaite(USA) —Little Talitha (Lugana Beach)
6644[10]

Little Perisher *Karen George* a73 87
3 b g Desert Sun—Sasperella (Observatory (USA))
(550) 772[6] 901[4] 1086[9] 1511[7] 7654[7]

Little Pete (IRE) *Ian McInnes* a89 95
5 ch g City On A Hill(USA) —Full Traceability (IRE) (Ron's Victory (USA))
26[5] 250[7] 292[4] 481[2] (695)

Littleportnbrandy (IRE) *David Evans* a50 68
2 ch f Camacho—Sharplaw Destiny (IRE) (Petardia)
1263[3] ◆ 1429[2] 2819[13] 8030[4]

Littlepromisedland (IRE) *Richard Guest* a32 22
2 b f Titus Livius(FR) —Land Army (IRE) (Desert Style (IRE))
4336[8] 7279[6] 7520[7]

Little Richard (IRE) *Mark Wellings* a61 59
11 b g Alhaarth(IRE) —Intricacy (Formidable (USA))
13[3] 293[7] 7275[10] 7531[7] 7569[5]

Little Rocky *David Simcock* 80
2 b c Cadeaux Genereux—Tahirah (Green Desert (USA))
6873[2] 7152[2]

Little Rufus *Kevin Morgan* a56 61
3 b c Lujain(USA) —Compendium (Puissance)
5726[5] 6285[2]

Little Sark (IRE) *David Evans* a62 60
5 b g Singspiel(IRE) —Notenqueen (GER) (Turfkonig (GER))
121[11] 771[2] (1439) 1816a[3] 2445[4] 2897[6] 3290[4] 3984[5] 4689[9]

Little Scotland *Richard Fahey* a78 93
3 b f Acclamation—Belladera (IRE) (Alzao (USA))
(2309) 3088[3] 3731[5] 4369[5] 5120[6] 5396[4] (6002) 6221[7] 6721[17] 7097[12] 7318[8]

Little Village (IRE) *John C McConnell* 53
4 b m Captain Rio—Rainbow Princess (IRE) (Spectrum (IRE))
6495[2]

Little Weed (IRE) *Bryn Palling* a45
3 bb g Statue Of Liberty(USA) —Carna (IRE) (Anita's Prince)
527[7] 1505[9]

Livandar (FR) *P Van De Poele* a96 99
4 b g Fantastic Light(USA) —Luna Caerla (IRE) (Caerleon (USA))
(743a) 1081a[10] 2446a[4] 4773a[0] (7776a)

Livia Noire (FR) *P Bary* a75 69
2 b f Country Reel(USA) —Listen Daddy (FR) (Piccolo)
5063a[4]

Livia Quarta (IRE) *Edward Creighton* a31 52
2 b f Titus Livius(FR) —Sweet Chat (IRE) (Common Grounds)
2591[6] 3035[7] 3603[3] 3992[4] 5268[4] 6988[9]

Livinadream *Nigel Tinkler* 50
2 bb f Golan(IRE) —Monte Calvo (Shirley Heights)
2498[12] 3237[6] 3874[8] 4940[4] 5630[11] 6129[13]

Living Art (USA) *X Nakkachdji* 92
2 b f Trippi(USA) —V Sign (USA) (Robellino (USA))
4637a[4]
Living It Large (FR) *Roger Fisher* a91 93
3 ch c Bertolini(USA) —Dilag (IRE) (Almutawakel)
2058[5] 2437[3] 2960[6] 3218[2] 3673[4] 4541[13] 5335[10] 6446[6] 6799[2] 7041[11] 7212[8]
Living On Promises (IRE) *David Wachman* 70
2 b f Holy Roman Emperor(IRE) —Bright Birdie (IRE) (Sadler's Wells (USA))
7256a[6] (Dead)
Lixirova (FR) *D Smaga* 104
3 gr f Slickly(FR) —Linorova (USA) (Trempolino (USA))
1196a[6] 2801a[8]
Lizard's Desire (SAF) *M F De Kock* a122 123
5 b g Lizard Island(AUS) —Annsfield (SAF) (Northfields (USA))
(334a) (513a) 800a[5] 1027a[2] 1568a[2] (2154a)
Lizzie (IRE) *Tim Easterby* 73
2 b f Acclamation—Sky Galaxy (USA) (Sky Classic (CAN))
1686[7] 3204[8] (3536) 4388[5] 4851[5] 5301[8] 5882[12] 6619[3]
Lloydy Lumps *Peter Grayson*
2 b g Sleeping Indian—Blane Water (USA) (Lomond (USA))
5418[12]
Local Diktator *Ronald Harris* a61 39
2 br c Diktat—Just Down The Road (IRE) (Night Shift (USA))
2867[9] 3721[7] 4277[4] 5111[4] 5581[9] 5874[7] 6333[8] 7404[3] 7540[3] 7762[5] 7910[5]
Local Hero (GER) *Steve Gollings* 88
3 b g Lomitas—Lolli Pop (GER) (Cagliostro (GER))
6876[3] (7282) ◆
Local Singer (IRE) *Mick Channon* 81
2 b c Elusive City(USA) —Alinga (IRE) (King's Theatre (IRE))
2319[4] 2832[3] 3222[3] (3550) 4332[3] 5537[3]
Location *Ian Williams* a61 63
4 b m Dansili—Well Away (IRE) (Sadler's Wells (USA))
1585[8] 2188[4] 3238[8] 4045[3] 4740[4] 5158[8] 5704[9] 6120[6]
Lochan Mor *Michael Bell* a86 89
4 b g Kyllachy—Bright Moll (Mind Games)
1185[2] 1826[12] 3033[4] 4192[2] 4806[3] 5386[3] 6048[2] 6478[10] 6776[2] 6962[2]
Lochiel *Lucy Normile* a91 96
6 b g Mind Games—Summerhill Special (IRE) (Roi Danzig (USA))
2096[9] 2857[5] 3198[5] 4086[7]
Lochinver (USA) *A Fabre* 107
3 b c Kingmambo(USA) —Campsie Fells (UAE) (Indian Ridge)
3933a[2] 6593a[2]
Loch Long (IRE) *Tracey Collins* 97
4 b g Galileo(IRE) —Spinney (Unfuwain (USA))
2571a[4]
Loch Ordie *Michael Quinlan* a27 58
2 b c Araafa(IRE) —Waseyla (IRE) (Sri Pekan (USA))
3991[7] 4802[3] 5047[5] 5389[5] 6129[5] 6695[10]
Lockantanks *Michael Appleby* a75 72
3 ch g Compton Place—Locharia (Wolfhound (USA))
527[3] 759[4] (932) ◆ 1045[5] 1480[7] 1651[4] 2296[2] 2840[6] 3359[10] 4297[5] 4910[10] 7627[7] 7699[3] ◆ 7837[2] 8014[3]
Locum *Mark H Tompkins* a59 72
5 ch g Dr Fong(USA) —Exhibitor (USA) (Royal Academy (USA))
(1609) 2013[4] 2495[3] 3267[4] 3860[6] 5208[6] 6187[2] 7270[6]
Loden *Luca Cumani* a79 66
3 b g Barathea(IRE) —Tentpole (USA) (Rainbow Quest (USA))
5689[8] 6290[3] (6846)
Lodi (IRE) *John Akehurst* a81 81
5 ch g Bertolini(USA) —Lady Of Leisure (USA) (Diesis)
1580[8] 1963[7] 2399[10] 2959[3] 3262[6] 4024[6] 4308[7] 4836[3] 5325[3] 6078[5]
Lofthouse *Alistair Whillans* a57 56
3 b g Hunting Lion(IRE) —Noble Destiny (Dancing Brave (USA))
6144[14] 6494[8]
Logans Legend (IRE) *B W Hills* a68
2 b c Johannesburg(USA) —Almost Blue (USA) (Mr Greeley (USA))
7595[6]
Logans Rose *Alan Brown* 38
2 b g Tobougg(IRE) —Red Leggings (Shareef Dancer (USA))
3657[12] 4049[4] 4447[11] 4935[7] 6036[10] 6891[20]
Logos Astra (USA) *David Lanigan* a73 79
3 b c Elusive Quality(USA) —Wild Planet (USA) (Nureyev (USA))
1476[2] 1649[4] 3355[3] 3725[6]
Loki's Revenge *William Jarvis* a90 79
2 b c Kyllachy—Amira (Efisio)
2598[3] 3126[2] 3756[4] 4615[5] 4927[3] (5089) (5613) 5939[3] 6627[3] 6734[10] (7891) (8020)
Lolamar (ITY) *S Botti* 97
3 bb f Martino Alonso(IRE) —Lodgetta (IRE) (Grand Lodge (USA))
3495a[2] 6763a[6]
Lolly For Dolly (IRE) *T Stack* 104
3 b f Oratorio(IRE) —Heart Stopping (USA) (Chester House (USA))
(1787a) ◆ 2370a[8] 3071[4] 3467a[5]
Lombok *Michael Bell* a80 77
4 b g Hernando(FR) —Miss Rinjani (Shirley Heights)
1902[11] 2549[8] 3127[8] 4780[2] 5011[2] 5722[5] 6109[14] (6668) 6957[6] 7044[2]
London Bridge *Noel Meade* a80 82
4 br g Beat Hollow—Cantanta (Top Ville)
7823a[11]
London Gold *Henry Candy* 86
3 b g Fraam—Princess Londis (Interrex (CAN))
1917[8] ◆ (2599) 2928[5]
London Stripe (IRE) *Sir Michael Stoute* 98
3 ch c Rock Of Gibraltar(IRE) —Agenda (IRE) (Sadler's Wells (USA))
(1730) 3105[2] ◆ 4504[10]
Lone Cat (FR) *Y De Nicolay* 99
2 b f One Cool Cat(USA) —La Sioule (AUS) (Fusaichi Pegasus (USA))
2917a[3] 3718a[3] 6044a[6] 7534a[0]
Lonesome Maverick (IRE) *Donal Kinsella* a87 86
6 gr g Celtic Swing—Abyat (USA) (Shadeed (USA))
6910a[11]
Long Awaited (IRE) *Michael Jarvis* 73
2 b g Pivotal—Desertion (IRE) (Danehill (USA))
6828[3] 7150[2]
Longhunter *Kevin Prendergast* 101
2 b c Halling(USA) —Dawnus (IRE) (Night Shift (USA))
3488a[7] 5316a[6]
Long Lashes (USA) *Saeed Bin Suroor* 109
3 b f Rock Hard Ten(USA) —Border Dispute (USA) (Boundary (USA))
4574[4] ◆ 5305[2] ◆ 6346[12] (6830)
Longliner *Sir Michael Stoute* a85 83
3 gr g Dalakhani(IRE) —Ive Gota Bad Liver (USA) (Mt. Livermore (USA))
1310[10] 1824[3] 4258[3] (5832)
Longoria (IRE) *Lucinda Featherstone* a38 69
5 bb m Fasliyev(USA) —Shangri La (IRE) (Sadler's Wells (USA))
943[10] 1241[11] 2477[12]
Longsword *Mahmood Al Zarooni*
3 b c Red Ransom(USA) —Dance Steppe (Rambo Dancer (CAN))
5493[12]
Long Time Coming (IRE) *Michael Mulvany* 81
2 b c Silent Times(IRE) —Cha Cha (IRE) (Charnwood Forest (IRE))
6230a[8]
Lonia Blue (FR) *Mlle C Griolet* a64
4 b m Anabaa Blue—Lonia (GER) (Royal Academy (USA))
460a[9]
Look At Me (IRE) *A P O'Brien* 95
2 b f Danehill Dancer(IRE) —Queen Cleopatra (IRE) (Kingmambo (USA))
6528[2] ◆
Look Busy (IRE) *Alan Berry* 109
5 b m Danetime(IRE) —Unfortunate (Komaite (USA))
1822[4] 2325[6] (2526) 3108[5] 3486a[7] 3875[9] 4191[9] 4616[8] 5120[12] 5512[6] 5851[7] 6265[7] 6706[7]
Look For Love *Reg Hollinshead* a27 52
2 b g Pursuit Of Love—Look Here's May (Revoque (IRE))
6873[8] 7179[9] 7325[7]
Lookin At Lucky (USA) *Bob Baffert* a129
3 b c Smart Strike(CAN) —Private Feeling (USA) (Belong To Me (USA))
1714a[6] (2137a) (4643a) 7367a[4]
Looking Lovely (IRE) *A P O'Brien* 81
2 b f Storm Cat(USA) —Love Me True (USA) (Kingmambo (USA))
3421a[9] 4077a[6]
Looking On *Henry Candy* 61
2 b g Observatory(USA) —Dove Tree (FR) (Charnwood Forest (IRE))
7202[6]
Look'N'Listen (IRE) *Alan Brown* a48 47
2 b f Fasliyev(USA) —Royal Lady (IRE) (Royal Academy (USA))
1360[5] 1647[3] 1978[7] 3175[7] 3757[3] 5042[5] 7469[11] 7577[7]
Look Officer (USA) *Mandy Rowland* a74 66
4 b m Officer(USA) —Inn Between (USA) (Quiet American (USA))
1[2] (114) 220[3] 375[4] 675[6] 786[3] 996[7] 1207[6] 1539[9] 1919[8] 6454[10] 7167[13] 7865[5]
Looks Like Slim *Ben De Haan* a41 56
3 b c Passing Glance—Slims Lady (Theatrical Charmer)
1796[12] 7286[11]
Looksmart *Richard Hannon* a60 73
2 b f Observatory(USA) —Dimakya (USA) (Dayjur (USA))
2088[3] 2338[7] 3295[2] 5836[3] 6309[5] 6802[5] 6994[4] 7313[7] 7379[5]
Looks The Business (IRE) *Andrew Haynes* a49 62
9 b g Marju(IRE) —Business Centre (IRE) (Digamist (USA))
1539[6] 2952[2] 3641[7] 4279[5]
Look Twice *David Simcock* a35 58
2 b f Royal Applause—Exchanging Glances (Diktat)
3156[5]
Look Who's Kool *Ed McMahon* a73 65
2 b g Compton Place—Where's Carol (Anfield)
4336[4] 4896[11] 5763[2] (6520)
Looney Les (IRE) *F J Brennan* 41
2 ch g Redback—Trivandrun (IRE) (Lend A Hand)
5372[11] 6414[9]
Loose Caboose (IRE) *Alan McCabe* a76 71
5 b m Tagula(IRE) —Tama (IRE) (Indian Ridge)
207 125[4] 601[12] 896[13]
Loose Quality (USA) *Tom Tate* 24
2 b g Elusive Quality(USA) —Djebel Amour (USA) (Mt. Livermore (USA))
6046[10] 6465[11]
Lope De Vega (IRE) *A Fabre* 124
3 ch c Shamardal(USA) —Lady Vettori (Vettori (IRE))
1565a[3] (2159a) (2802a) 3719a[8] 5801a[5] 6612a[11]
Lopinot (IRE) *Martin Bosley* a68 24
7 br g Pursuit Of Love—La Suquet (Puissance)
11[3] 256[4] 397[2] 845[2] 1047[4] (1170) 1585[7] 2053[13] 6853[7]
Lord Aeryn (IRE) *Richard Fahey* 84
3 b g Antonius Pius(USA) —White Paper (IRE) (Marignan (USA))
4647[5] (6108) 6709[2] 7238[6]
Lord Avon *Bill Turner* a79 83
2 ch g Avonbridge—Lady Filly (Atraf)
1359[9] (1764) 2177[4] 3059[3] 3426[4] 6900[12]
Lord Chancellor (IRE) *Lee Smyth* a46 79
4 b g King's Best(USA) —Summer Serenade (Sadler's Wells (USA))
7514a[11] 7884[6]
Lord Chaparral (IRE) *R Brogi* 120
3 b c High Chaparral(IRE) —Freccia D'Oro (GER) (Acatenango (GER))
1945a[4] 6977a[2] 7373a[9]
Lord Cornwall (IRE) *Jeremy Gask* a48 13
2 b g Encosta De Lago(AUS) —Duchy Of Cornwall (USA) (The Minstrel (CAN))
2474[8] 4782[6] 5763[7] 6868[12]
Lord Deevert *Bill Turner* a67 66
5 br g Averti(IRE) —Dee-Lady (Deploy)
78[5] 181[2] 258[5] 342[3] 444[7] 4790[5] 5076[8] 7555[7] 7604[3] 7763[2] 7829[9] 7989[3]
Lord Fidelio (IRE) *David Evans* a79 70
4 b g Xaar—Rekindled Affair (IRE) (Rainbow Quest (USA))
110[6] (123) 285[9] (579) 695[2] 851[6] 1651[2] 1923[13] (2273) 2864[7] 4133[8]
Lord High Admiral (IRE) *A P O'Brien* 105
3 b c Galileo(IRE) —Splendid (IRE) (Mujtahid (USA))
4312a[6] 4630a[13]
Lord Kenmare (USA) *M Halford* a83 93
4 b g Hold That Tiger(USA) —The Fur Flew (USA) (Slew City Slew (USA))
3487a[17] 6597a[12] 6910a[13]
Lord Lansing (IRE) *Mrs K Burke* a69 41
3 b g Mull Of Kintyre(USA) —Miss Beverley (Beveled (USA))
2530[8] 3091[11] 3910[7] 7406[5] 7731[7] (8018)
Lord Of Persia (USA) *Ralph Beckett* a70 68
2 bb c Speightstown(USA) —Norwoods (USA) (Deputy Minister (CAN))
3735[5] 4477[4] 5074[5] 6901[2] ◆ 7272[2]
Lord Of The Dance (IRE) *Mark Brisbourne* a77 67
4 ch g Indian Haven—Maine Lobster (USA) (Woodman (USA))
1585[6] 2080[13] (2410) 2596[14] 4547[11] 5077[12] 5897[5] 6210[3] 6794[2] (6934) 7214[6] 7376[2] (7699) 7842[3]
Lordofthehouse (IRE) *William Haggas* 54
2 ch g Danehill Dancer(IRE) —Bordighera (USA) (Alysheba (USA))
6504[13] ◆ 6874[6] 7178[9]
Lord Of The Reins (IRE) *James Given* a85 83
6 b g Imperial Ballet(IRE) —Waroonga (IRE) (Brief Truce (USA))
119[3] 307[6] 384[6] (578) (972) 1295[9] 1988[12] 2528[13] 3119[6] 3908[5] 4343[8] 5025[6] 5368[5] 6501[4] 7093[6] 7285[3] 7754[5] 8004[11]
Lord Of The Stars (USA) *Ralph Beckett* a91 91
2 bb c Speightstown(USA) —Charmant Forest (USA) (Forestry (USA))
(3169) 3826[2] 4458[7] 5604[6] (7127)
Lord Of The Storm *Bill Turner* a40 65
2 b g Avonbridge—Just Run (IRE) (Runnett)
2407[9] 2638[7] 3678[2] (3992) (4241) 6471[16] 6795[8]
Lord Raglan (IRE) *Mrs K Burke* a48 85
3 b g Noverre(USA) —Raglan Rose (USA) (Giant's Causeway (USA))
(1178) 1921[3] 2886[6] 3949[2] (4618) 5300[2] 5904[2] 6355[12]
Lordsbury Pride (USA) *John Best* a58 58
3 bb g Put It Back(USA) —Show Us The Money (USA) (Glitterman (USA))
1622[10] 2004[11] 2121[4] 5326[5] ◆ 5670[3] 5898[5] 6523[10] 7064[4] 7249[2] 7827[7] 7883[10]
Lord Shanakill (USA) *Henry Cecil* 119
4 bb h Speightstown(USA) —Green Room (USA) (Theatrical)
2118[3] 2539[4] 3192[12] (3893) (4457)
Lordship (IRE) *Tony Carroll* a63 76
6 b g King's Best(USA) —Rahika Rose (Unfuwain (USA))
3558[9] 4065[6] 4478[14] 4681[4] 4968[6] 5407[11] 5877[10] 6261[16] 6328[6] 6629[7] 6657[2] 7229[6] 7402[10]
Lord's Seat *Alan Berry* a50 51
3 b g Trade Fair—Clashfern (Smackover)
302[8] 455[3] 574[5] 1144[2] 1465[3] 2209[5] 3161[7] 3354[4] 3530[5] 4581[6] 4951[8] 7832[7]
Lord Theo *Nick Littmoden* a73 86
6 b g Averti(IRE) —Love You Too (Be My Chief (USA))
1474[14] 1697[14] 2173[11] 4108[5] 4594[3] ◆ 4804[4] 5235[3] 5530[6] 6331[8] 6846[7] 7190[8] 7467[12] (7968) 8008[5]
Lord Victor *Alan McCabe* a65 35
3 ch c Needwood Blade—La Victoria (GER) (Rousillon (USA))
72[2]
Lord Westlake *Geoffrey Oldroyd* 12
2 b g Monsieur Bond(IRE) —Westlake Bond (IRE) (Josr Algarhoud (IRE))
4167[7]
Lord Zenith *Andrew Balding* a100 108
3 b g Zamindar(USA) —Lady Donatella (Last Tycoon)
(1221) 1699[12] 2471[4] 3104[7]
Los Cristianos (FR) *A Couetil* 113
4 ch h Gold Away(IRE) —Perspective (FR) (Funambule (USA))
2375a[5] 4038a[2] 5349a[4] 6607a[4]
Losing Draw (IRE) *Paul Midgley* 44
2 ch f Iffraaj—Alnoor (USA) (Danzig (USA))
1331[7] 1527[7] 2202[5]
Los Nadis (GER) *P Monteith* 69
6 ch g Hernando(FR) —La Estrella (GER) (Desert King (IRE))
1671[4] 2430[2] 3152[3] (3496)
Loss Leader (IRE) *Tim Easterby* 56
3 ch g Captain Rio—Nenagh (IRE) (Barathea (IRE))
1425[8] 1971[11] 2530[2] 3904[3] 4194[7] 4605[9] 4672[7]
Lost Horizon (IRE) *Richard Hannon* 81
3 b f Elusive City(USA) —Souvenir Souvenir (Highest Honor (FR))
(1777) 2256[9]
Lost In Paris (IRE) *Tim Easterby* a87 85
4 b g Elusive City(USA) —Brazilia (Forzando)
1524[4] ◆ (1805) 2001[3] (2756) 3430[3] 4292[3] 4510[7] 4798[9] 5941[3] 6245[4] 6739[5] 7326[2] 7466[8]
Lost In The Moment (IRE) *Jeremy Noseda* a95 104
3 b c Danehill Dancer(IRE) —Streetcar (IRE) (In The Wings)
1450[9] 1844[7] (2888) (4905) 5728[4] 6534[2] (7100)
Lost Soldier Three (IRE) *Mme J Bidgood* a79 86
9 b g Barathea(IRE) —Donya (Mill Reef (USA))
87[4] 221a[4] (281a) (332a) 494a[2] 742a[4] 1056a[4]
Lou Bear (IRE) *John Akehurst* a63 58
3 b c Lujain(USA) —Dream Of Dubai (IRE) (Vettori (IRE))
443[4] 583[9] 1058[11] 1476[5] 1873[6] 3160[10] 4058[3] 4793[5] 4994[6] 5325[7] 6522[9]
Lough Beg (IRE) *Tor Sturgis* a62 49
7 b g Close Conflict(USA) —Mia Gigi (Hard Fought)
411[7] 771[7] 4914[6]
Lough Corrib (USA) *Kevin Ryan* 52
2 b g Tiznow(USA) —Desert Glow (IRE) (Machiavellian (USA))
4437[11] 6027[4] 6240[5]
Lough Mist (IRE) *Tracey Collins* 86
4 b m Captain Rio—Luna Crescente (IRE) (Danehill (USA))
3489a[5] 4180a[9] 4269a[12]
Loughtownlady (IRE) *Geoffrey Harker*
2 b f Statue Of Liberty(USA) —Queen Caroline (USA) (Chief's Crown (USA))
6892[11] 7345 [13]
Louie's Lad *John Bridger* a26 54
4 gr g Compton Place—Silver Louie (IRE) (Titus Livius (FR))
1441[15] 1737[5] 2229[8] 3717[6] 3979[10] 4959[10] 5555[9] 5715[7] 7314[9] 8036[8]
Louisa (GER) *P Monteith* 56
6 b m Seattle Dancer(USA) —La Ola (GER) (Dashing Blade)
4953[5] 5364[6] 6224[13]
Louis Girl *Richard Fahey* 46
2 b f Araafa(IRE) —Crumpetsfortea (IRE) (Henbit (USA))
2461[5] 3020[6] 3665[10] 4701[9] 5020[5] 6294[9]
Louisiade (IRE) *David Bourton* a53 54
9 b g Tagula(IRE) —Titchwell Lass (Lead On Time (USA))
7[6] 88[6] 145[4] 160[3] 269[7] 498[3] 836[2] 844[3] 976[6] 1142[3] 1171[11] 1575[3] 1813[7] 2257[4] 7763[6] 7832[6]
Louisiana Gift (IRE) *J W Hills* a66 63
3 b g Cadeaux Genereux—Southern Queen (Anabaa (USA))
1475[6] 2250[9] 2780[2] 3413F 4249[2] 4779[4] 5710[7] 7005[3] 7156[4]
Louis The Pious *Kevin Ryan* 61
2 bb g Holy Roman Emperor(IRE) —Whole Grain (Polish Precedent (USA))
6047[5] 6465[4]
Louis Vee (IRE) *James Given* a42 39
2 bb g Captain Rio—Mrs Evans (IRE) (College Chapel)
2832[10] 3315[10] 3767[8] 5644[4]
Loukoumi *Bryan Smart* 69
2 b f Iffraaj—Odalisque (IRE) (Machiavellian (USA))
3392[4] ◆ 4187[4] (5594) 6505[8] 7085[7]
Loup Breton (IRE) *Julio C Canani* a98 119
6 b h Anabaa(USA) —Louve (USA) (Irish River (FR))
4417a[7]
Louphole *John Jenkins* a84 70
8 ch g Loup Sauvage(USA) —Goodwood Lass (IRE) (Alzao (USA))
1596[10] 4776[4] 4875[5]
Loup Normand (FR) *M Nigge* a70 76
7 ch h Loup Solitaire(USA) —Pearly Gate (FR) (Exit To Nowhere (USA))
560a[5] 690a[6]
Loupy Loups *Brendan Powell*
4 ch m Loup Sauvage(USA) —Digyourheelsin (IRE) (Mister Lord (USA))
3593[11]
Lousard (FR) *D Barone* a12
4 b m Loudeac(USA) —Hasard (IRE) (Mujtahid (USA))
460a[10]
Louve Rare (IRE) *E Lellouche* 97
3 ch f Rock Of Gibraltar(IRE) —Louve (USA) (Irish River (FR))
6551a[2]
Lovat Lane *Eve Johnson Houghton* a45 60
2 b f Avonbridge—Pudding Lane (IRE) (College Chapel)
1292[2] 1930[8] 2951[5] 3295[14] 4040[5] 7496[8] 7691[4]
Love Action (IRE) *Richard Hannon* a74 79
3 b f Motivator—Speciale (USA) (War Chant (USA))
(1975) 4098[3] 5181[4] 6639[6]
Love And Devotion *H-A Pantall* 79
3 b f Shamardal(USA) —Romantic Myth (Mind Games)
6406a[6]
Love Club *Brian Baugh* 54
2 ch g Kheleyf(USA) —Avondale Girl (IRE) (Case Law)
1331[10] 1819[6] 2540[6] 4124[8] 4432[9]
Love Delta (USA) *Mark Johnston* a105 94
3 bb c Seeking The Gold(USA) —Delta Princess (USA) (A.P. Indy (USA))
(4) (117) (310) (783) ◆ 1019[5] 1315[8] 1701[8] 2260[5] 7254[10] 7329[2] 7697[3] (7740) 7846[7] 7993[10]

Loved To Bits *PETER Makin* a59 52
2 b f Storming Home—Agent Kensington (Mujahid (USA))
3260[3] 6520[5] 6954[4] 7313[10]

Love In The Park *Roy Brotherton* a67 75
5 b m Pivotal—Naughty Crown (USA) (Chief's Crown (USA))
1346[6] 1623[4] 2233[5] 2586[7] 3513[7] 4433[5] 5180[12] 6518[11] 7508[2] (7633) 7919[2]

Loveinthesand (IRE) *Mark Johnston* a68 75
3 b c Footstepsinthesand—Love Emerald (USA) (Mister Baileys)
(473) 1709[7] 3539[2] 3708[6]

Love In The West (IRE) *John Harris* a67 63
4 b m Fruits Of Love(USA) —Sandhill (IRE) (Danehill (USA))
1489[3] 4172[6] (5158) 6571[11]

Lovelace *David Nicholls* a107 114
6 b h Royal Applause—Loveleaves (Polar Falcon (USA))
338a[7] 413a[5] 626a[5] 710a[9] 883[3] (1570) (1904) 2539[6] 3069[10] 3704a[3] 4457[9]

Lovely Doyoun (TUR) *A K Aksoy* 57
7 b m Doyoun—Castle Blaze (USA) (Lac Ouimet (USA))
5782a[11]

Lovely Eyes (IRE) *David Simcock* a30 67
3 b f Red Ransom(USA) —Polygueza (FR) (Be My Guest (USA))
1847[7] 2953[3] ◆ 4557[8] 5654[5] 6020[3] 6526[8] 7039[7]

Lovely Lips *C Scandella* 59
5 b m Red Ransom(USA) —Shaabra (IRE) (Rainbow Quest (USA))
281a[5]

Love Match *Roger Charlton* a64 84
3 b f Danehill Dancer(IRE) —Name Of Love (IRE) (Petardia)
1347[6] 2005[2] (2892) 3361[2] 3918[4] 5205[3] 5968[4]

Love Nest *John Dunlop* 48
2 b c Compton Place—Encore My Love (Royal Applause)
4131[13] 4856[9] 6827[8]

Love Queen (IRE) *Mlle V Dissaux* a79 93
3 gr f Val Royal(FR) —Lone Spectre (Linamix (FR))
7545a[4]

Lovers Causeway (USA) *Mark Johnston* a90 58
3 b g Giant's Causeway(USA) —Heeremandi (IRE) (Royal Academy (USA))
(106) ◆ (240) ◆ 3697[7] 4573[12] 5093[7] 5753[5] 6331[4] (6698) 7589a[8] (7815) 8007[5]

Lovers Peace (IRE) *John Quinn* a36
2 b f Oratorio(IRE) —Puck's Castle (Shirley Heights)
7242[7]

Loves Theme (IRE) *Alan Bailey* a60 74
2 ch f Iffraaj—Bauci (IRE) (Desert King (IRE))
1375[9] 1905[3] 2347[2] 3749[5] 7312[7] 7486[10] 7758[7] 8031[3]

Lovestoned (IRE) *T Hogan* a47 58
4 b g Modigliani(USA) —Errachidia (IRE) (King Of Kings (IRE))
6246[6]

Love You Louis *John Jenkins* a79 80
4 b g Mark Of Esteem(IRE) —Maddie's A Jem (Emperor Jones (USA))
312[6] 555[2] 727[4] (1074) 1267[3] 1874[3] 2301[4] 2639[6] (5207) 5628[3] 6858[7] 7180[10] (7285) 7549[3] 7754[2] 7961[4]

Loving Spirit *James Toller* 97
2 b c Azamour(IRE) —Lolla's Spirit (IRE) (Montjeu (IRE))
(6532) ◆ 6884[2] ◆

Loving Thought *Henry Cecil* a69 38
2 b f Oasis Dream—Brazilian Style (Exit To Nowhere (USA))
6451[3] 6882[8]

Lovisa Beat *B Grizzetti* 93
3 ch f Beat Hollow—Lovisa (USA) (Gone West (USA))
1252a[3] 1713a[18]

Lowawatha *Michael Quinlan* 79
2 b c Sleeping Indian—Redeem (IRE) (Doyoun)
4384[3] 5385[8] 6301[2] 6675[3] 7849a[2]

Lowdown (IRE) *Mark Johnston* a95 106
3 ch c Shamardal(USA) —Mood Swings (IRE) (Shirley Heights)
1663[3] 1836[7] 2283[2] 2545[9] 2978[14] (3731) (4085) 4391[20] 4536[19] 5095[14] 5442[3] 5787[15] 6175[12] 6349[15]

Lowenherz (GER) *H Billot* a92 99
6 b g Silvano(GER) —Lutte Marie (GER) (Frontal (FR))
7776a[5]

Lowther *Alan Bailey* a101 101
5 b g Beat All(USA) —Ever So Lonely (Headin' Up)
5911[14] 6175[11] 6357[11] 6564[13] 7091[4] (7488) 7574[4] 7970[2]

Loyaliste (FR) *Richard Hannon* a77 68
3 ch c Green Tune(USA) —Whitby (FR) (Gold Away (IRE))
6814[3] ◆ 7022[4] 7389[2] 7575[2]

Loyal Knight (IRE) *Paul Midgley* a75 39
5 ch g Choisir(AUS) —Always True (USA) (Geiger Counter (USA))
540[11] 1204[8] 1812[5] 2764[10] 2876[5] 3370[9]

Loyal Royal (IRE) *Milton Bradley* a69 51
7 b g King Charlemagne(USA) —Supportive (IRE) (Nashamaa)
223[4] 287[7] 501[5] 684[6] 808[5] 961[7] 1534[6] 2184[2] 2590[7] 3727[5] 4431[2] (4790) 5175[7] 5698[10] 5764[5] 5920[12] 6207[7] 7331[2] 7442[5] 7519[2] 7639[5] 7827[3] 7972[2] (8034)

Loyalty *Derek Shaw* a75 60
3 b g Medicean—Ecoutila (USA) (Rahy (USA))
1607[3] 2231[12] 7451[4] (7685) 7788[2] 7909[3]

Luberon *Mark Johnston* a88 101
7 b g Fantastic Light(USA) —Luxurious (USA) (Lyphard (USA))
81[7] 205[10]

Luca Brasi (FR) *Francisco Castro* a98 97
6 b g Singspiel(IRE) —Diamond Field (USA) (Mr Prospector (USA))
(2020a) 2637a[12]

Lucas Pitt *Michael Scudamore* a60 51
3 b g Kyllachy—Bardot (Efisio)
751[5] 849[5] 936[8] 3762[5] 4428[4] 4987[7] 5873[6] (7387) 7704[6]

Lucayan Dancer *Neville Bycroft* a77 73
10 b g Zieten(USA) —Tittle Tattle (IRE) (Soviet Lad (USA))
(2511) 2894[14] 3179[4] 4015[5] 4673[3] 4985[9] 5515[4] 6915[10]

Luc Jordan *Luca Cumani* a94 92
4 b g Intikhab(USA) —Saphila (IRE) (Sadler's Wells (USA))
1837[6] 2640[3] 3239[9] 5004[9] 5723[2]

Luckbealadytonight (IRE) *Mark Johnston* a54 26
2 b f Mr Greeley(USA) —Sumora (IRE) (Danehill (USA))
6658[2] 7002[10]

Luck Of The Draw (IRE) *Sir Mark Prescott Bt* a77 66
3 b g Key Of Luck(USA) —Sarifa (IRE) (Kahyasi)
2753[4] 3055[2]

Lucky Art (USA) *Ruth Carr* a60 80
4 b g Johannesburg(USA) —Syrian Summer (USA) (Damascus (USA))
431[10] 723[5] 1200[9] 1524[3] 1711[2] 1805[4] 2136[7] 2626[5] 3119[10] 3540[5] 5502[U] 6299[8] 7542[11]

Lucky Belle (IRE) *Michael Dods* 51
3 ch f Barathea(IRE) —Borders Belle (IRE) (Pursuit Of Love)
1485[9] 1809[5] 2203[6]

Lucky Breeze (IRE) *William Knight* a56 79
3 b f Key Of Luck(USA) —Lasting Chance (USA) (American Chance (USA))
(2011) 2843[6] 4923[5] 5181[7] 6424[2] 6774[5]

Lucky Dan (IRE) *Paul Green* a77 83
4 b g Danetime(IRE) —Katherine Gorge (USA) (Hansel (USA))
1366[2] 1710[3] 1988[5] 2206[6] (2310) 2534[4] (2626) 2982[9] 3114[3] 3389[4] 3430[4] ◆ 4542[2] 5290[8] 5937[10] 6358[7] 6723[13]

Lucky Dance (BRZ) *Terry Clement* a80 97
8 b h Mutakddim(USA) —Linda Francesa (ARG) (Equalize (USA))
1006[3] 1383[18] 1570[4] 2835[8] 4050[4] 4371[2] 6327[9] 6630[5] 6877[13] 7233[12]

Lucky Diva *Sylvester Kirk* a59 53
3 ch f Lucky Story(USA) —Cosmic Countess (IRE) (Lahib (USA))
1460[4] 1959[5] 2480[7] 3002[10] 3526[9] 7649[7] 7814[2] 7917[2]

Lucky Find (SAF) *M F De Kock* a113 113
7 ch g Rich Man's Gold(USA) —Little Erna (SAF) (Ernani)
339a[7] 517a[2] (713a) 1022a[7]

Lucky Flyer *Sylvester Kirk* a68 72
3 br f Lucky Story(USA) —Fly Like The Wind (Cyrano De Bergerac)
1075[7] (1345) 2099[8] 2320[5] (2688) 3480[4] 3892[8] 4291[5]

Lucky General (IRE) *Richard Hannon* 110
3 b c Hawk Wing(USA) —Dress Code (IRE) (Barathea (IRE))
1327[6] 2400[6] 2712[5] 3066[11] 3461[10]

Lucky Legs (IRE) *B W Hills* a59 46
2 b f Danehill Dancer(IRE) —Singing Diva (IRE) (Royal Academy (USA))
6248[7] 6559[18]

Lucky Leigh *Mick Channon* a81 83
4 b m Piccolo—Solmorin (Fraam)
1074[5] 1363[9] 1588[2] 1770[7] 2087[7] 2196[4] 2485[2] 2904[7] 4424[8] 4744[5]

Lucky Meadows (IRE) *Richard Hannon* 68
2 b f Noverre(USA) —Summerhill Parkes (Zafonic (USA))
5489[3]

Lucky Mellor *Dean Ivory* a84 73
3 b g Lucky Story(USA) —Lady Natilda (First Trump)
277[4] 577[2] 783[4] 2822[8]

Lucky Nine (IRE) *C Fownes* a81 116
3 b g Dubawi(IRE) —Birjand (Green Desert (USA))
7852a[7]

Lucky Numbers (IRE) *Paul Green* a80 93
4 b g Key Of Luck(USA) —Pure Folly (IRE) (Machiavellian (USA))
1099[6] 1397[7] 1688[3] 1862[3] 2327[9] (2883) 3435[5] 4118[2] (4243) 4685[7] 5292[5] 5742[11] 6049[4] 6364[7]

Lucky Punt *Brendan Powell* a96 58
4 ch g Auction House(USA) —Sweet Coincidence (Mujahid (USA))
1069[2] 1829[3] 3050[18] 5723[10] 6054[8] 6450[5] 6841[5] (7130) 7327[2]

Lucky Ray (ARG) *Doug Watson* a88
7 b h Halo Sunshine(USA) —Rubia Blonde (ARG) (Candy Stripes (USA))
415a[6] 629a[13]

Lucky Redback (IRE) *Richard Hannon* a91 85
4 b h Redback—Bayletta (IRE) (Woodborough (USA))
(761) 902[3] 981[4] 1516[5] 1933[12]

Luckyreno *Sir Michael Stoute* a60 30
2 gr c Kyllachy—Kryena (Kris)
4096[15] 5178[5]

Lucky Royale *Sylvester Kirk* a28
2 b f Lucky Story(USA) —Bella Bertolini (Bertolini (USA))
6520[8] 6796[11]

Lucky Score (IRE) *Mouse Hamilton-Fairley* a66 68
4 b m Lucky Story(USA) —Musical Score (Blushing Flame (USA))
101[5] 3040[7] 3268[12]

Lucky Tale *Tim Easterby*
2 b f Lucky Story(USA) —Bollin Janet (Sheikh Albadou)
1421[10]

Lucky Traveller *Tim Easterby* a23 43
3 b g Lucky Story(USA) —Bollin Sophie (Efisio)
1461[9] 1970[12] 2606[13]

Lucky Tricks *Sylvester Kirk* a29 13
2 ch f Lucky Story(USA) —Miss Madame (IRE) (Cape Cross (IRE))
1577[12] 3769[9]

Lucky Windmill *Alan Swinbank* 84
3 b g Lucky Story(USA) —Windmill Princess (Gorytus (USA))
(5122) 5511[6] 6467[12]

Lucy Brown *Michael Easterby* a67 77
4 br m Compton Place—Harambee (IRE) (Robellino (USA))
2580[9] 2959[7] (3409) 3914[4] 4345[11]

Lucy Limelites *Roger Charlton* 73
2 b f Medicean—In The Limelight (IRE) (Sadler's Wells (USA))
(5488) 6513[5] 6978[2] ◆

Lucy's Perfect *Rod Millman* 58
4 ch m Systematic—Water Flower (Environment Friend)
1755[8] 2360[6] 2894[11] 3128[10]

Luddenmore (IRE) *Edward P Mitchell* a49 68
3 b g Pyrus(USA) —Carranduff (IRE) (Mukaddamah (USA))
4496a[8]

Ludiana (FR) *A De Royer-Dupre* 94
3 b f Dalakhani(IRE) —Luna Caerla (IRE) (Caerleon (USA))
4037a[3]

Lugato (GER) *Lee Smyth* a42 50
8 br g Winged Love(IRE) —Lugano (GER) (Orofino (GER))
4914[11]

Lui Den *A Renzoni*
2 b c Denon(USA) —My Luigia (IRE) (High Estate)
7264a[2]

Lui Rei (ITY) *Marco Botti* a99 107
4 b g Reinaldo(FR) —My Luigia (IRE) (High Estate)
604a[2] ◆ 817a[7] 4569[2] 5952[2] 6390[10]

Luisant *J A Nash* a114 114
7 ch g Pivotal—La Legere (USA) (Lit De Justice (USA))
1091a[2] 1406a[2] 2353a[6] 4180a[2] 4882a[2] 5127a[2] (6783a) 7073a[3]

Luisa Tetrazzini (IRE) *David Bourton* a58
4 b m Hawk Wing(USA) —Break Of Day (USA) (Favorite Trick (USA))
21[4] 38[7] 270[5] 446[6] 793[3] 1142[5] 6206[3] 6746[5] 7426[4] 7505[4]

Lujano *Ollie Pears* a71 74
5 b g Lujain(USA) —Latch Key Lady (USA) (Tejano (USA))
2864[13] 3508[4] 3911[11] 4485[3] 4985[5] 5533[11] 5820[12] 7450[4] 7705[5]

Lujeanie *Dean Ivory* a90 88
4 br g Lujain(USA) —Ivory's Joy (Tina's Pet)
102[6] 679[2] 905[7] 1266[10] 1321[6] 1580[13] 3037[2] 3401[5] (4333) 4806[5] 5884[8] 6478[9] 6987[11] 7320[2] 7573[2] 7782[4]

Lujiana *Mel Brittain* a63 56
5 b m Lujain(USA) —Compact Disc (IRE) (Royal Academy (USA))
(112) (243) 402[5] 601[11] (896) 913[3] 1112[7] 1154[10] 1569[7] 1928[12] 5482[11] 7468[6]

Lumineux *A Fabre* 113
3 b c Motivator—Mydarshaan (Darshaan)
2802a[6] 4420a[6] 5135a[7] 6219a[8]

Luminosa *Desmond Donovan* a31
3 ch f Zaha(CAN) —Lightning Blaze (Cosmonaut)
143[6] 274[8] 861[8]

Luminous Gold *Chris Wall* a72 80
5 b m Fantastic Light(USA) —Nasaieb (IRE) (Fairy King (USA))
2973[4] (3818) 4518[4] 5207[2] 5915[13]

Luna Landing *Jedd O'Keeffe* a74 77
7 ch g Allied Forces(USA) —Macca Luna (IRE) (Kahyasi)
1273[3] 1803[7]

Lunar Lass *David C Griffiths* a13 36
5 b m Fraam—Easter Moon (FR) (Easter Sun)
1190[6] 1345[5] 2212[5] 2629[13]

Lunar Limelight *PETER Makin* a67 54
5 b g Royal Applause—Moon Magic (Polish Precedent (USA))
970[7] 1225[12] 2894[9] 6375[8]

Lunar Phase (IRE) *Clive Cox* 54
2 b f Galileo(IRE) —Taraya (IRE) (Doyoun)
7231[7]

Lunar River (FR) *David Pinder* a73 67
7 b m Muhtathir—Moon Gorge (Pursuit Of Love)
1241[6] 1763[5] 2233[8] 2966[8] 3131[4] 3968[4] 4498[6] 4913[3] 5704[6] 6125[4] 6375[4] ◆ 6999[2] 7323[5] 7445[6] 7968[3] 7996[2]

Lunar Victory (USA) *John Gosden* a94 91
3 b c Speightstown(USA) —Lunar Colony (USA) (A.P. Indy (USA))
1314[8] 4205[2] (5001) 5728[2]

Lunar Wind *F Kainz* 12
9 gr g Piccolo—Faraway Moon (Distant Relative)
4183a[4]

Lunaticus *Michael Attwater* a15
4 b m Lujain(USA) —Steppin Out (First Trump)
161[6] 321[11] 538[7] 1345[6] 1477[12] 4789[11]

Lunduv (IRE) *C Von Der Recke* a92 93
5 b m Pivotal—Another Dancer (FR) (Groom Dancer (USA))
2155a[4] 5345a[8]

Luscivious *David Nicholls* a99 89
6 ch g Kyllachy—Lloc (Absalom)
299[5] 916[3] ◆ 992[7] (1099) 2940[14] (4685) 5290[11] 5855[12] 6064[7] 6663[8] 6723[17] 7740[6]

Lush Lashes *J S Bolger* 107
5 b m Galileo(IRE) —Dance For Fun (Anabaa (USA))
5568a[4] 6007a[4] ◆ 6613a[10]

Lustre (FR) *Y De Nicolay* 96
2 b c American Post—Lunaska (FR) (Ashkalani (IRE))
7544a[3]

Lutece Eria (FR) *C Diard* a82 98
4 ch m Gold Away(IRE) —Dark Mile (USA) (Woodman (USA))
2778a[8]

Lutine Bell *Mike Murphy* a100 88
3 ch g Starcraft(NZ) —Satin Bell (Midyan (USA))
2215[3] 2566[3] 2834[8] (3786) (4284) 4531[3] 5421[7] 7012[2] (7411) ◆ 7574[11] 7689[3]

Lutine Charlie (IRE) *John Flint* a83 78
3 b g Kheleyf(USA) —Silvery Halo (USA) (Silver Ghost (USA))
1766[10] 2416[5] 2919[6] 4775[4] 5027[5] 5689[2] (5877) (6413) 6632[2] 6958[6] 7205[8]

Lutine Lady *Peter Winkworth* 41
3 b f Exceed And Excel(AUS) —Hillside Girl (IRE) (Tagula (IRE))
3816[8]

Luv U Noo *Brian Ellison* a46 68
3 b f Needwood Blade—Lady Suesanne (IRE) (Cape Cross (IRE))
1118[7] 2291[7] 2380[2] 2834[9] 3226[5] (3975) 4344[2] 5041[2] 5598[4] 6026[10] 6266[6] 6460[7] 7082[7] 7377[9]

Luv U Too *F J Brennan* a61 76
2 b f Needwood Blade—Lady Suesanne (IRE) (Cape Cross (IRE))
4421[7] 5029[6] (5441) 5882[18]

Luxurious (IRE) *A P O'Brien* 86
2 b f Galileo(IRE) —Parvenue (FR) (Ezzoud (IRE))
6005a[7] 6784a[4]

Lyes Green *Oliver Sherwood* a21
9 gr g Bien Bien(USA) —Dissolve (Sharrood (USA))
3780[10]

Lynchpin *Ronald Harris* a56 46
2 b c Iceman—Danehurst (Danehill (USA))
6542[8] 7177[6] 7550[6] 7843[7]

Lynott (IRE) *Gerard Keane* a68 71
7 ch g Pivotal—Cassilis (IRE) (Persian Bold)
7078a[6]

Lyra's Daemon *William Muir* a79 78
4 b m Singspiel(IRE) —Seven Of Nine (IRE) (Alzao (USA))
1840[3] 2586[6] 3060[9]

Lyrical Intent *Paul Howling* a63
4 ch g Imperial Dancer—Magical Flute (Piccolo)
(99) (227) (347) 540[4] 1539[8] 3278[11] 6668[11]

Lyric Poet (USA) *Giles Bravery* a84 74
3 bb g Distorted Humor(USA) —Baltic Nations (USA) (Seattle Slew (USA))
2564[10] 3444[5] (5155) (5456) 5868[4] ◆ 7090[3] 7293[4] 7876[4]

Lyric Street (IRE) *Luca Cumani* 75
2 b c Hurricane Run(IRE) —Elle Danzig (GER) (Roi Danzig (USA))
7203[3]

Lyssio (GER) *P Schiergen* 99
3 b c Motivator—Lysuna (GER) (Monsun (GER))
4184a[8] 5132a[5] 7102a[4]

Lyster (IRE) *David Evans* a29 40
11 b g Oscar(IRE) —Sea Skin (Buckskin (FR))
669[7]

Lytham (IRE) *Tony Carroll* a68 66
9 b g Spectrum(IRE) —Nousaiyra (IRE) (Be My Guest (USA))
407[6] (479) (576) (590) 841[3] 1226[6] (1623) 2645[8] 7778[14]

Lytton *Richard Ford* a76 67
5 b g Royal Applause—Dora Carrington (IRE) (Sri Pekan (USA))
1149[11] 2487[5] 3132[9]

Maal (IRE) *David Marnane* a80 89
7 b g Mozart(IRE) —Dalayil (IRE) (Sadler's Wells (USA))
6730a[6]

Maany (USA) *Michael Jarvis* 72
3 ch f Mr Greeley(USA) —Dixie Card (USA) (Dixieland Band (USA))
4966[3] 5395[7]

Mabait *Luca Cumani* a91 116
4 b h Kyllachy—Czarna Roza (Polish Precedent (USA))
(1533) 1900[2] 2707[3] ◆ 3455[7] (4412) 5803a[3] 6923[5]

Mabsam *Ed Dunlop* 60
2 b f Green Desert(USA) —Week End (Selkirk (USA))
2740[5] 3590[11] 4375[6]

Mabura (IRE) *S Botti* 94
3 b f Oratorio(IRE) —Ma Bouche (IRE) (Shirley Heights)
1713a[7] 2575a[12]

Mabuya (UAE) *PETER Makin* 91
4 b g Halling(USA) —City Of Gold (IRE) (Sadler's Wells (USA))
1840[2] 2282[2] 2996[8] 3889[5] 4399[5] (4923) 5443[5] 6283[5]

Macademy Royal (USA) *Natalie Lloyd-Beavis* a32 34
7 b g Royal Academy(USA) —Garden Folly (USA) (Pine Bluff (USA))
235[10] 746[7]

Macanta (USA) *Gerard Butler* a60 70
4 b m Giant's Causeway(USA) —Nadwah (USA) (Shadeed (USA))
2388[6] 2874[2] 2967[6] 3309[2] (3683)

Macarthur *Jane Chapple-Hyam* 100
6 b g Montjeu(IRE) —Out West (USA) (Gone West (USA))
1724[8] 2345[3] 3194[11] 3447[7] 4818[9] 5743[12] 6565[10]

Maccool (IRE) *Barney Curley* a36
4 b g King's Best(USA) —Mellow Park (IRE) (In The Wings)
7419[10] 7579[9]

Macdillon *Stuart Kittow* a89 96
4 b g Acclamation—Dilys (Efisio)
1349[8] 2119[12] 2681[6] 2997[5] 5995[7] 6478[5] 6987[6]

Macedonian (NZ) *Peter G Moody* 103
5 b g Zabeel(NZ) —Society Walk (NZ) (Carnegie (IRE))
7032a[5]

Mac Gille Eoin *John Gallagher* a82 108
6 b h Bertolini(USA) —Peruvian Jade (Petong)
416a[7] 515a[12] 948[9] 1906[4] 2316[8] 2748[14] 3193[21] 3850[6] 4536[17]

Machinate (USA) *Mark Brisbourne* a54 35
8 bb g Machiavellian(USA) —Dancing Sea (USA) (Storm Cat (USA))
347^{7} 540^{9} (682) 780^{4} 847^{8} 940^{9} 1193^{12} 1772^{11} 2477^{9}

Machinist (IRE) *David Nicholls* a62 106
10 br g Machiavellian(USA) —Athene (IRE) (Rousillon (USA))
37^{4}

Machir Bay *Valentine Donoghue* 42
3 b g Auction House(USA) —Sabre Lady (Sabrehill (USA))
6244^{4} 6966^{5} 7282^{9}

Macho's Magic (IRE) *David Nicholls* 76
2 b g Camacho—Moon Diamond (Unfuwain (USA))
4460^{7} 6102^{2}

Macie (IRE) *Jeremy Noseda* 52
3 b f Green Desert(USA) —Fatat Alarab (USA) (Capote (USA))
1872^{5} 2220^{9}

Mackensaw (IRE) *P Schiergen* 76
2 b c Footstepsinthesand—Masharik (IRE) (Caerleon (USA))
5740a^{5}

Mackenzie Spiers *Rod Millman* a47 53
3 b f Lucky Owners(NZ) —Enchanted Ocean (USA) (Royal Academy (USA))
4364^{6} 5474^{6} 6814^{4} 7161^{7}

Mackintosh (IRE) *Patrick Morris* a60 55
4 ch g Kyllachy—Louhossoa (USA) (Trempolino (USA))
34^{2} 397^{7} 427^{6} 491^{2} 603^{2} 1142^{9} 2490^{8} 3758^{13} 7199^{7} 7705^{6} 7899^{4}

Mack's Sister *Dean Ivory* a71 60
3 ch f Pastoral Pursuits—Linda's Schoolgirl (IRE) (Grand Lodge (USA))
385^{8} 634^{6} 930^{6} 1392^{2} 1796^{9} 2633^{11} 4025^{3} (4791) 5163^{6} 5670^{7} (6456) 6997^{6} 7391^{6} 7655^{5}

Mac Love *Stef Higgins* a109 116
9 b g Cape Cross(IRE) —My Lass (Elmaamul (USA))
4469^{6} 5951^{5} 6885^{10}

Macondo (FR) *X Thomas-Demeaulte* 95
5 b h Kendor(FR) —Makila (IRE) (Entrepreneur)
6881a^{8}

Macroy *Rod Millman* 64
3 b g Makbul—Royal Orchid (IRE) (Shalford (IRE))
1760^{8} 2000^{2} 2648^{5} 3030^{7} 3685^{7} 4047^{13} 4382^{13}

Mac's Power (IRE) *James Fanshawe* a97 103
4 b g Exceed And Excel(AUS) —Easter Girl (Efisio)
1767^{9} 2129^{3} 2991^{2} ◆ (3396) 3920^{12} 4358^{18} 5393^{2} 5884^{7} ◆ (6429) (7060) ◆ 7351^{4}

Mac Tiernan (IRE) *P J Lally* a71 74
3 b g Minashki(IRE) —Softly Softly (IRE) (Lucky Guest)
745^{9}

Mactrac *Richard Hannon* a49 32
3 b g Marju(IRE) —Zanna (FR) (Soviet Star (USA))
387^{10}

Madame Bonaparte (IRE) *Patrick Gilligan* a34
3 ch f Where Or When(IRE) —Avit (IRE) (General Monash (USA))
206^{6} 583^{13} 1979^{10}

Madame Boot (FR) *PETER Makin* a60 59
3 b f Diktat—Esprit Libre (Daylami (IRE))
6332^{4} ◆ 6863^{5} 7298^{4} 7502^{11}

Madame Excelerate *Mark Brisbourne* a77 74
3 b f Pursuit Of Love—Skovshoved (IRE) (Danetime (IRE))
3074^{9} 4127^{8} (4864) 5201^{2} 5337^{2} (5469) 5758^{4} 6212^{2} 6336^{3} 6629^{6} 6959^{5} 7305^{5}

Madame Kintyre *Rod Millman* 34
2 b f Trade Fair—Chorus (Bandmaster (USA))
3000^{11}

Madame Roulin (IRE) *Michael Bell* a63 57
3 b f Xaar—Cradle Rock (IRE) (Desert Sun)
1593^{2} 2005^{5} 2871^{11} 3359^{7}

Madame Solitaire *Richard Hannon* a35 55
2 b f Haafhd—Calcavella (Pursuit Of Love)
4384^{6} 5836^{4} 6436^{3} 6868^{9}

Madam Isshe *Malcolm Saunders* a62 60
3 b f Ishiguru(USA) —Lucky Dip (Tirol)
962^{5} 1535^{6} 4989^{14} (5470) 5715^{2} 5957^{2} 6536^{10}

Madamlily (IRE) *John Quinn* a71 70
4 b m Refuse To Bend(IRE) —Rainbow Dream (Rainbow Quest (USA))
1807^{4} 2672^{5} 3617^{3} 4117^{6} 6187^{6} 6921^{2}

Madam Macie (IRE) *David O'Meara* 93
3 ch f Bertolini(USA) —Dictatrice (FR) (Anabaa (USA))
(2242) ◆ 2978^{8} 3375^{6}

Madam Markievicz (IRE) *Michael Dods* a67 68
2 gr f Aussie Rules(USA) —Fragrant (Cadeaux Genereux)
1421^{6} ◆ 1704^{3} 2391^{2} 2848^{2} (3163) 3598^{3} 4124^{3} 5334^{3} 6139^{9} 6576^{2} 7050^{9}

Madam Mayem *Tom Dascombe* a62 57
2 ro f Needwood Blade—Etienne Lady (IRE) (Imperial Frontier (USA))
4149^{9} 4451^{4} 4675^{5}

Madany (IRE) *B W Hills* 91
2 b f Acclamation—Belle De Cadix (IRE) (Law Society (USA))
2088^{2} 2623^{2} (3583) (4544) 5187^{3} 5880^{13} 6559^{8}

Madawi *Clive Brittain* 93
2 b c Oasis Dream—Lady In Waiting (Kylian (USA))
4803^{3} 6200^{4} ◆ 6560^{10} 7095^{4} ◆

Madda's Force (ITY) *R Betti* 94
4 b m Blu Air Force(IRE) —Madda'sblueyes (Selkirk (USA))
1419a^{2} 1944a^{10} 4185a^{6} 7459a^{10}

Made For Magic (USA) *A C Avila* a105 101
5 b m Cape Canaveral(USA) —Only Seventeen (USA) (Exploit (USA))
4887a^{6}

Madeira Man (IRE) *Kevin Prendergast* a82 77
2 gr g Verglas(IRE) —Lingering Melody (IRE) (Nordico (USA))
954a^{5}

Mad Flatter (USA) *Jeffrey D Thornbury* a109 103
5 b h Flatter(USA) —Miss Pangea (USA) (Honor Grades (USA))
7365a^{12}

Madhaaq (IRE) *John Dunlop* 87
3 b f Medicean—Winsa (USA) (Riverman (USA))
1381^{12} 1844^{3} 2718^{4} (4098) 6361^{11}

Madison Belle *John Weymes* a72 53
4 ch m Bahamian Bounty—Indian Flag (IRE) (Indian Ridge)
144^{9} 170^{6} (297) 451^{10} 571^{3} (836)

Madison Square (USA) *Mahmood Al Zarooni* 63
2 bb c More Than Ready(USA) —Star Of Broadway (USA) (Broad Brush (USA))
6874^{3} 7302^{14}

Madj's Baby *Stuart Howe* 56
3 b f Footstepsinthesand—Madamoiselle Jones (Emperor Jones (USA))
2587^{10} 2956^{11} 3268^{7} 5812^{6}

Madlool (IRE) *William Haggas* a55 54
3 b c Oasis Dream—Bourbonella (Rainbow Quest (USA))
744^{5} 980^{7} 1164^{5} 2844^{12} 3155^{8}

Madly In Love (FR) *J-L Gay* a76 83
2 gr f Slickly(FR) —Hourloupe (IRE) (Damister (USA))
5622a^{6} 7975a^{6}

Madman Diaries (USA) *Wesley A Ward* a105 107
2 bb g Bring The Heat(USA) —Harper N Abbey (USA) (Outflanker (USA))
7360a^{4}

Mad Millie (IRE) *David O'Meara* a47 67
3 b f Pyrus(USA) —Tipsy Lady (Intikhab (USA))
3062^{2} 6540^{8} 7082^{12}

Madonje (GER) *J Hirschberger* 89
3 bb f Monsun(GER) —Madhya (USA) (Gone West (USA))
2404a^{4}

Madonna Dell'Orto *Walter Swinburn* 78
3 b f Montjeu(IRE) —Sabria (USA) (Miswaki (USA))
2180^{3} ◆ 2998^{6} 4874^{3} 5265^{2}

Madrasa (IRE) *Ed McMahon* 61
2 b g High Chaparral(IRE) —Shir Dar (FR) (Lead On Time (USA))
6831^{6} ◆

Mae Cigan (FR) *Michael Blanshard* a55 62
7 gr g Medaaly—Concert (Polar Falcon (USA))
1756^{5}

Mafeking (UAE) *Mark Hoad* a98 84
6 b g Jade Robbery(USA) —Melisendra (FR) (Highest Honor (FR))
205^{3} 360^{5} 536^{2} (790) 1015^{3} 1220^{10} 1665^{8} 7287^{5} 7591^{6} (7735) 7970^{3}

Mafeteng *John Dunlop* 65
2 b f Nayef(USA) —Marakabei (Hernando (FR))
6803^{5}

Mafra (IRE) *Y Fouin* 80
4 b m Kalanisi(IRE) —Sovana (IRE) (Desert King (IRE))
5378a^{0}

Magaling (IRE) *Michael Easterby* 93
4 ch g Medicean—Fling (Pursuit Of Love)
2100^{9} 2736^{3} 3206^{7} ◆ 3920^{2} 4830^{2} 6193^{6} 6736^{14} 7227^{9}

Magenta Strait *Reg Hollinshead* a61 57
3 b f Sampower Star—Vermilion Creek (Makbul)
(209) 370^{6} 886^{3} 1187^{3} 1483^{3} 2000^{6} 2185^{6} 2722^{6} 2962^{5} 3359^{4} 3910^{2} 4249^{4} 4988^{7} 5767^{9} 6413^{8} 6826^{5} 7122^{3} 7426^{12} 7604^{8}

Maggie Kate *Roger Ingram* a58 69
5 b m Auction House(USA) —Perecapa (IRE) (Archway (IRE))
137^{6} 235^{12} 423^{5} 561^{2}

Maggie Mey (IRE) *David O'Meara* 69
2 b f Kodiac—Christmas Kiss (Taufan (USA))
3729^{4} 4286^{6} (4848) (5637) 5998^{2} 6719^{3} 7085^{8}

Maggie's Treasure (IRE) *John Gallagher* a53 72
2 gr g Clodovil(IRE) —Rectify (IRE) (Mujadil (USA))
1871^{4} 2397^{6} 3721^{8} 4677^{2} 5613^{9} 6019^{2} 6426^{9} 6868^{6}

Maggie The Cat *Joseph G Murphy* a61 75
4 b m Fasliyev(USA) —Hot Tin Roof (IRE) (Thatching)
3487a^{13}

Maggi Fong *H-A Pantall* a85 85
4 ch m Dr Fong(USA) —Maggi For Margaret (Shavian)
304a^{0} 560a^{7}

Magical Flower *William Knight* a71 63
2 b f Oasis Dream—Fancy Rose (USA) (Joyeux Danseur (USA))
4508^{9} 5369^{5} 6247^{3}

Magical Macey (USA) *David Barron* 88
3 ch g Rossini(USA) —Spring's Glory (USA) (Honour And Glory (USA))
1399^{6} ◆ (1656) 2978^{10} 3218^{4} 3856^{7} 4541^{10} 4901^{2} 5250^{11} 6140^{15} 6723^{8} 6985^{7}

Magicalmysterytour (IRE) *Willie Musson* 106
7 b g Sadler's Wells(USA) —Jude (Darshaan)
3462^{6} 3873^{10} ◆ 4334^{5} (5091) ◆ 5387^{2} 5949^{5} 6387^{5} 6736^{16} 7208^{4}

Magical Song *John Balding* a59 58
5 ch g Forzando—Classical Song (IRE) (Fayruz)
5482^{9} 5817^{13}

Magical Speedfit (IRE) *George Margarson* a77 79
5 ch g Bold Fact(USA) —Magical Peace (IRE) (Magical Wonder (USA))
1267^{4} 1445^{2} 1692^{5} 2123^{8} 2458^{3} 2485^{4} 3358^{5} 3958^{7} 4693^{5} 4875^{3} (5176) 5628^{4} (6064) 6440^{2} 6739^{13}

Magical Star *Richard Hannon* a46 37
2 b f Arkadian Hero(USA) —Aastral Magic (Magic Ring (IRE))
1793^{10} 2407^{7} 3269^{8} 4675^{9} 5111^{7} 6521^{6} 7691^{3}

Magic Amigo *John Jenkins* a49 18
9 ch g Zilzal(USA) —Emaline (FR) (Empery (USA))
100^{7}

Magic Box (ITY) *F & S Brogi* a88 94
7 ch h Namid—Bodiniyeh (IRE) (Persian Heights)
743a^{4}

Magic Broomstick (USA) *Mark Frostad* 98
4 bb m More Than Ready(USA) —Special Brush (USA) (Broad Brush (USA))
6235a^{3}

Magic Casement *David Nicholls* 102
2 b g Proclamation(IRE) —Dee Dee Girl (IRE) (Primo Dominie)
(3118) (5901)

Magic Cat (FR) *H Fortineau* 57
2 b f High Yield(USA) —Clarissa Dalloway (FR) (Sillery (USA))
7009a^{0}

Magic Cat *Mrs K Burke* 89
4 b g One Cool Cat(USA) —Magic Music (IRE) (Magic Ring (IRE))
5528^{12} 6140^{12} (6962) 7146^{3} 7352^{8}

Magic Cross *Philip McBride* a65 57
2 b f Bertolini(USA) —T G's Girl (Selkirk (USA))
2547^{12} 3817^{4} 4432^{5} 4935^{2} (5111) 5613^{5} 6163^{4} 6674^{6} 6842^{7} 7527^{2} 7577^{2} (7666)

Magic Echo *Michael Dods* a88 90
6 b m Wizard King—Sunday News'N'Echo (USA) (Trempolino (USA))
1379^{3} (2084) 2865^{5} 4389^{13}

Magic Eye (IRE) *Andreas Lowe* a100 105
5 b m Nayef(USA) —Much Commended (Most Welcome)
2559a^{5} 3236a^{2} 4035a^{8} 5739a^{6} 6765a^{4}

Magic Glade *Peter Grayson* a61 72
11 b g Magic Ring(IRE) —Ash Glade (Nashwan (USA))
132^{5} 271^{10} 659^{5} 1068^{8}

Magic Haze *Sally Hall* a63 62
4 b g Makbul—Turn Back (Pivotal)
(603) 705^{3} ◆ 1028^{4} 1919^{4} 2259^{3} 3110^{8}

Magician's Cape (IRE) *Sir Michael Stoute* a85 79
3 b c Montjeu(IRE) —Seven Magicians (USA) (Silver Hawk (USA))
7090^{9}

Magic Jack *Richard Hannon* 79
3 b g Trade Fair—Galapagar (USA) (Miswaki (USA))
5007^{2} 5288^{3} 5971^{6} (6420)

Magic Millie (IRE) *David O'Meara* a53 61
3 bb f Marju(IRE) —Fille De La Terre (IRE) (Namaqualand (USA))
597^{2} 717^{4} 1298^{5} 1394^{2} 2132^{5} 3153^{3} 3376^{7} (3662) 4017^{3} 4557^{5} 4944^{3} 5607^{2}

Magic Moon (FR) *T Lerner* a82 87
4 b m Fly To The Stars—Queen Elodie (FR) (Cardoun (FR))
7776a^{0}

Magic Of The Sea (IRE) *Marco Botti* a68 1
2 b f Refuse To Bend(IRE) —Mureefa (USA) (Bahri (USA))
5633^{6} 6118^{4} 7198^{7} (7496)

Magic Omen (USA) *Mark Johnston* a78 72
3 bb c Mr Greeley(USA) —Constant Touch (USA) (Belong To Me (USA))
758^{2} 843^{2} 1464^{2} 1761^{7} 2762^{8} 3553^{5} 4154^{12}

Magic Potion (FR) *P Bary* 98
2 b f Divine Light(JPN) —Magic Dawn (IRE) (Caerleon (USA))
2917a^{2} 3718a^{8} 5226a^{5} 6044a^{7}

Magic Prospect (FR) *E J O'Neill* 81
3 b g Miesque's Son(USA) —Clarissa Dalloway (FR) (Sillery (USA))
3145^{12}

Magic Queen (IRE) *Alan Jarvis* a52 42
4 b m Aptitude(USA) —Second Wind (USA) (Hennessy (USA))
407^{11}

Magic Spirit *Suzy Smith* a57
3 ch f Kirkwall—Flaming Spirt (Blushing Flame (USA))
133^{6} 217^{2} 305^{2} 422^{6} 670^{3} 760^{2} 7315^{10} 7599^{8}

Magic Sport (FR) *Mme C Barande-Barbe* a64 50
5 gr g Miesque's Son(USA) —Pipsila (FR) (Linamix (FR))
207a^{5}

Magic Stella *Alan Jarvis* a70 78
2 b f Danbird(AUS) —Sasperella (Observatory (USA))
1510^{2} ◆ 1901^{6} 3141^{20} 3906^{3} 4592^{3} 5187^{11} 5856^{7} 6986^{2} (7240) 7528^{6} 7734^{5}

Magic Warrior *Jimmy Fox* a63 48
10 b g Magic Ring(IRE) —Clarista (USA) (Riva Ridge (USA))
1763^{10} 1983^{8} 2337^{9} 4382^{10}

Magnetic Force (IRE) *Sir Michael Stoute* a75 75
3 gr g Verglas(IRE) —Upperville (IRE) (Selkirk (USA))
2390^{3} 2869^{5} 3519^{4}

Magneto (IRE) *Edward Creighton* a60 52
3 b g Fasliyev(USA) —Shashana (IRE) (King's Best (USA))
4300^{8} 4669^{6} 6020^{12}

Magnini (IRE) *Kevin Ryan* 74
2 b g Exceed And Excel(AUS) —Sanpa Fan (ITY) (Sikeston (USA))
3945^{11} 6240^{4} (7142)

Magnitude *Brian Baugh* a71 71
5 ch g Pivotal—Miswaki Belle (USA) (Miswaki (USA))
105^{2} 298^{6} 469^{4} (611) ◆ 724^{3} 834^{2} 893^{3} 2285^{4} 2881^{5} (3360) 3617^{4} 3860^{9} 4914^{5} 5363^{2} 6051^{6} 6832^{14}

Magnus Thrax (USA) *Richard Hannon* a81 81
3 b c Roman Ruler(USA) —Wild Catseye (USA) (Forest Wildcat (USA))
1086^{12} 4660^{6} 5027^{9}

Magroom *Ron Hodges* a72 76
6 b g Compton Place—Fudge (Polar Falcon (USA))
1543^{3} (1637) 2024^{4} 2823^{7} 3558^{6} 4044^{3} 5003^{5} 5584^{6}

Mahab El Shamaal *David Simcock* 75
2 b c Motivator—Soliza (IRE) (Intikhab (USA))
(6618) ◆

Mahadee (IRE) *Ralph Beckett* a111 101
5 br g Cape Cross(IRE) —Rafiya (Halling (USA))
(635) (739) 883^{9} 1383^{16} 2508^{7} 2934^{13} (3334) (3619) 4537^{19} 5247^{17} 6123^{5}

Mahamaya (GER) *A Trybuhl* 100
3 b f Seattle Dancer(USA) —Mille Espoir (FR) (Mille Balles (FR))
2404a^{3} 3720a^{3} 5139a^{13} 6765a^{6}

Maharana (USA) *Michael Bell* 68
2 bb g Kingmambo(USA) —Because (IRE) (Sadler's Wells (USA))
6504^{9} 6873^{7} 7152^{7}

Maher (USA) *David Simcock* 75
2 b c Medaglia D'Oro(USA) —Bourbon Blues (USA) (Seeking The Gold (USA))
3452^{3} 4054^{7} 5049^{6}

Mahiki *Sandor Peto* a71 56
3 ch f Compton Place—Sound Of Sleat (Primo Dominie)
4183a^{9}

Mahlak (IRE) *Clive Brittain* a56 51
3 ch f Pastoral Pursuits—Bint Al Hammour (IRE) (Grand Lodge (USA))
1211^{4} 3374^{7}

Maid In Heaven (IRE) *Walter Swinburn* a61 97
3 b f Clodovil(IRE) —Serious Delight (Lomond (USA))
(1275) 1776^{6} (2618) (3361) ◆ 3790^{8} 4617^{6} 5222^{3}

Maid Of Meft *Linda Perratt* 67
3 b f Auction House(USA) —Lady Margaret (Sir Harry Lewis (USA))
2463^{6} 3077^{3} 3355^{4} 3776^{3} 4800^{3} 5437^{5} 6033^{7} 6109^{17} 7176^{4}

Maid To Dream *John Gosden* a70 62
3 b f Oasis Dream—Maid For The Hills (Indian Ridge)
4966^{9} 5839^{3} 6496^{4} 7209^{3}

Maigold Rose *John Weymes* a39
3 b f Tobougg(IRE) —Ma Jolie (Shalford (IRE))
189^{6} 452^{4} 542^{6} 775^{12}

Maiguri (IRE) *C Baillet* 114
2 ch c Panis(USA) —Zanada (FR) (Sinndar (IRE))
(4036a) 5799a^{3} 6610a^{2} 7265a^{3}

Main Aim *Sir Michael Stoute* 122
5 b h Oasis Dream—Orford Ness (Selkirk (USA))
2030^{3} (2539) 3192^{21} 4457^{4} 5518^{2} 6923^{3} 7278a^{0}

Mainland (USA) *Kevin Ryan* 76
4 b g Empire Maker(USA) —Imroz (USA) (Nureyev (USA))
2658^{2} ◆ 3176^{11} (5303) 6573^{9}

Main Spring *Michael Bell* a64 45
3 b f Pivotal—Fairy Godmother (Fairy King (USA))
1431^{10} 1620^{8} 2379^{4}

Mainstay *John Gosden* a84 84
4 b m Elmaamul(USA) —Felucca (Green Desert (USA))
(1654) ◆ 2475^{6} 5396^{5} 6291^{3}

Maison Brillet (IRE) *Clive Drew* a76 76
3 b g Pyrus(USA) —Stormchaser (IRE) (Titus Livius (FR))
(2394) 2979^{9} 3595^{6} 4483^{8} 5353^{4} 7909^{4} (8015)

Maison Dieu *Joss Saville* a58 66
7 bb g King Charlemagne(USA) —Shining Desert (IRE) (Green Desert (USA))
1337^{8} 1923^{12} 2454^{10} 3026^{8} 3200^{9} 5535^{15}

Maitre 'D *Christopher Kellett* a23 15
3 b g Rakti—Giusina Mia (USA) (Diesis)
2981^{6} 7862^{6}

Majd Aljazeera *Alison Thorpe* a61 45
4 b g King's Best(USA) —Tegwen (USA) (Nijinsky (CAN))
120^{8}

Majestatic *S W James* a56 64
3 ch g Reset(AUS) —Sharp Decision (Greensmith)
1164^{6} 1442^{7} 2548^{4} 4022^{7} 4427^{9}

Majestical (IRE) *J S O Arthur* a63 65
8 b g Fayruz—Haraabah (USA) (Topsider (USA))
2161a^{4} 3748a^{3}

Majestic Bright *Luca Cumani* a69 55
3 ch f Pivotal—L'Affaire Monique (Machiavellian (USA))
2548^{7} 7086^{2} (7596)

Majestic Concorde (IRE) *D K Weld* 104
7 b g Definite Article—Talina's Law (IRE) (Law Society (USA))
1821^{4} 6926^{20}

Majestic Dream (IRE) *Walter Swinburn* a69 82
2 b g Exceed And Excel(AUS) —Tallassee (Indian Ridge)
3735^{6} ◆ (4421) 5140^{3} 5837^{5} 6386^{4} 6810^{3} (7085)

Majestic Dubawi *Mick Channon* 101
2 b f Dubawi(IRE) —Tidal Chorus (Singspiel (IRE))
3296^{7} ◆ (5465) (6176)

Majestic Max (IRE) *David Nicholls*
2 gr g Verglas(IRE) —Your Village (IRE) (Be My Guest (USA))
2448^{8}

Majestic Millie (IRE) *David O'Meara* 33
2 b f Majestic Missile(IRE) —Emerald High (IRE) (Danetime (IRE))
6892^{6} 7142^{10} 7279^{7}

Majestic Myles (IRE) *Richard Fahey* 95
2 b g Majestic Missile(IRE) —Gala Style (IRE) (Elnadim (USA))
(1668) 2032^{4} (3596) (3749) 4578^{2} 5245^{5}

Majestic Ridge (IRE) *David Evans* a61 29
2 ch c Majestic Missile(IRE) —Darling Clementine (Lion Cavern (USA))
4067^{5} 4678^{7} 6369^{4} 6576^{11} 7016^{7} 7777^{2} 7894^{8}

Majestic Style (IRE) *Alan Jarvis* a50 52
2 ch f Majestic Missile(IRE) —Classic Style (IRE) (Desert Style (IRE))
1009^{12} 1421^{8} 1999^{11} 3260^{5} 3678^{4} 3992^{2} 4802^{9} 5701^{6}

Majestueux (USA) *Mark Hoad* a48
3 ch g Royal Academy(USA) —Buck Aspen (USA) (Seeking The Gold (USA))
8021^{7}

Majic Mojo *Richard Whitaker* a28 21
3 b f Captain Rio—Vicious Empress (Ezzoud (IRE))
3285^{5} 4556^{12} 7406^{6}

Major Art *Richard Hannon* a74 94
2 ch c Compton Place—Rosewood Belle (USA) (Woodman (USA))
3794[5] ◆ (4131) 4468[3] 5133a[6]

Major Conquest (IRE) *J W Hills* 83
2 b g Librettist(USA) —Arabis (Arazi (USA))
2078[5] 2594[4] (3000) (3887) 4539[11] 5745[11] 6191[11]

Major Dance *B W Hills* 34
2 ch g Carnival Dancer—Insinuation (IRE) (Danehill (USA))
6196[13] 6442[14]

Major D'Helene (FR) *F-X De Chevigny* a68 68
5 ch h Majorien—Sparkbulle (FR) (Bulrush (FR))
5109a[7]

Major Domo (FR) *Harry Dunlop* a65 70
2 ch g Domedriver(IRE) —Raphaela (FR) (Octagonal (NZ))
5006[7] *5724[6]* 6279[4]

Major Dude *Richard Hannon* 84
2 ch c Sakhee(USA) —Diliza (Dilum (USA))
(2819) 3826[6]

Major Eradicator (USA) *Robert Cowell* a46 51
3 b g Purge(USA) —Pontook (USA) (French Deputy (USA))
1622[8] 1878[8] 2174[7] 2875[8]

Major Lawrence (IRE) *Jeremy Noseda* a68 77
4 b h Fasliyev(USA) —Ziffany (Taufan (USA))
98[6] 226[3] 321[3] 385[4]

Major Magpie (IRE) *Michael Dods* 79
8 b g Rossini(USA) —Picnic Basket (Pharly (FR))
1426[5] 3022[4]

Major Maximus *George Baker* a72
3 br g Domedriver(IRE) —Madame Maxine (USA) (Dayjur (USA))
122[3] (201) 233[4] 424[5]

Major Monty (IRE) *Tom Dascombe* a56 58
3 b g Orpen(USA) —Mari-Ela (IRE) (River Falls)
3207[6] 3676[7] 4649[2] 4970[6] 5535[10]

Major Muscari (IRE) *Alan McCabe* a79 80
2 ch g Exceed And Excel(AUS) —Muscari (Indian Ridge)
3964[2] 4409[2] (4896) 5295[4] 6030[8] *6900[4] 7127[4]*

Major Phil (IRE) *Luca Cumani* a81 96
4 b h Captain Rio—Choral Sundown (Night Shift (USA))
1997[3] ◆ 2462[2] (2991) 3318[2] 4100[8] 5264[3] 6205[6]

Major Pop (USA) *Richard Fahey* a49 60
3 b g Fusaichi Pegasus(USA) —Shake Off (USA) (A.P. Indy (USA))
718[6] 963[9] 1103[4] 1486[6] 1866[6] 2600[5]

Major Promise *Jane Chapple-Hyam* a63 61
5 b g Lomitas—Distant Diva (Distant Relative)
969[11] 1503[2] 1919[2] 2653[2] *3214[2]*

Major Return (IRE) *Alan McCabe* a50 65
2 br g Statue Of Liberty(USA) —Ten Commandments (IRE) (Key Of Luck (USA))
1256[9] *3517[7]* 5053[3] 6047[4] 6264[6]

Major Victory (SAF) *Gay Kelleway* a77
3 b c Victory Moon(SAF) —Sintra (SAF) (National Assembly (CAN))
7756[9] 7867[6] 8022[3]

Majuro (IRE) *Stuart Williams* a91 100
6 b g Danetime(IRE) —First Fling (IRE) (Last Tycoon)
1708[13] 2311[7] 3172[6] 3796[10] 4660[3] 4996[4] 5786[2] 6447[6] *(7601) 7844[2]*

Makaamen *B W Hills* 100
4 ch g Selkirk(USA) —Bird Key (Cadeaux Genereux)
1383[20] 1900[19] 4828[16]

Makaanah (KSA) *J Barton* a61
3 b f Race Leader(USA) —Ma Tahaab (KSA) (Dynaformer (USA))
1023a[10]

Makani (GER) *J E Pease* a69 101
3 b c A.P. Indy(USA) —Moonlight's Box (USA) (Nureyev (USA))
1565a[4] 2160a[6]

Makarthy *Paul Green*
3 b c Makbul—Royal Shepley (Royal Applause)
3721[0] 5122[11]

Makaykla *Michael Easterby* a18 58
4 b m Makbul—Primum Tempus (Primo Dominie)
3966[12]

Makbullet *Howard Johnson* 80
3 gr g Makbul—Gold Belt (IRE) (Bellypha)
2275[5] 3088[4] 3599[7] 4245[6] 5241[5]

Make A Dance (USA) *B W Hills* a60 85
2 b f Empire Maker(USA) —Clog Dance (Pursuit Of Love)
6247[9] (7231)

Make Amends (IRE) *Ron Hodges* a75 79
5 b m Indian Ridge—Chill Seeking (USA) (Theatrical)
261[10] 361[2] ◆ *(469) (675) 966[4]* 1077[6] 1797[3] (2080) 2467[11] 2922[6] 3257[5] 6691[8] 6959[8] 7307[9]

Make Music For Me (USA) *Alexis Barba* a114 66
3 b c Bernstein(USA) —Miss Cheers (USA) (Carson City (USA))
1714a[4] 2776a[9]

Make My Dream *John Gallagher* a77 79
7 b g My Best Valentine—Sandkatoon (IRE) (Archway (IRE))
1266[3] 1692[2] 2094[8] 2399[6] 3037[9] (3440) 3736[3] 4090[9] 4693[4] 5915[5] 6440[4] 6858[2] 7180[6] *7442[7]*

Make My Mark (IRE) *Mrs V M Jordan* a30 51
2 b f Orpen(USA) —Annies Valentine (My Best Valentine)
3590[9] 4203[10] 4658[7] *6867[7]* 6989[6] *7577[8]*

Makeynn *Saeed Bin Suroor* a88 77
2 ch c Dubai Destination(USA) —Pastorale (Nureyev (USA))
5170[2] *(5924)* 6555[6] *(7324)*

Makfi *M Delzangles* 128
3 b c Dubawi(IRE) —Dhelaal (Green Desert (USA))
(1195a) (1699) 3048[7] (5134a) 6350[5]

Makheelah *Clive Brittain* 65
2 b f Dansili—Woodlass (USA) (Woodman (USA))
2740[4] 7001[10]

Making Eyes (IRE) *Chris Wall* 63
2 b f Dansili—Lady's View (USA) (Distant View (USA))
6443[11] 7231[6]

Makshoof (IRE) *Ian McInnes* a85 73
6 b g Kyllachy—Tres Sage (Reprimand)
10[9] 195[7] 423[6] 569[10]

Makyaal (IRE) *John Dunlop* 51
2 b c Nayef(USA) —Ros The Boss (IRE) (Danehill (USA))
6128[7] 6676[11]

Malacca Straits *B W Hills* a72 70
2 b f Cacique(IRE) —Stormy Channel (USA) (Storm Cat (USA))
4844[9] *5892[4]* ◆ 6353[3]

Malanos (IRE) *David Elsworth* 77
2 bb g Lord Of England(GER) —Majorata (GER) (Acatenango (GER))
6159[13] 6883[6] 7203[2]

Malcheek (IRE) *Tim Easterby* a106 87
8 br g Lend A Hand—Russland (GER) (Surumu (GER))
(1458) 1672[12] 2532[9] 3224[4] 3553[3] 4438[3] (4850) 5242[6] *(5703)* 7146[8] *(7318) 7522[12] (7846)* ◆

Maldon Prom (IRE) *Chris Dwyer* a73 76
3 br g Kheleyf(USA) —Misty Peak (IRE) (Sri Pekan (USA))
117[3] 919[3] 1281[2] 2046[3] 2494[4]

Male Model *Mahmood Al Zarooni* a87 83
2 b c Iffraaj—Bling Bling (IRE) (Indian Ridge)
5892[3] (6293) *6745[2]* ◆ 7085[14]

Malgoof (IRE) *Bryan Smart* 83
2 b c Kodiac—Mira (IRE) (Turtle Island (IRE))
3611[3] 4240[2] (4702) 5094[4] 6139[3] 6647[7]

Malibran *R Litt* 86
3 b c Dubawi(IRE) —Monetary (GER) (Winged Love (IRE))
2557a[4]

Malibu Prayer (USA) *Todd Pletcher* a116
4 b m Malibu Moon(USA) —Grand Prayer (USA) (Grand Slam (USA))
7344a[10]

Malice Or Mischief (IRE) *Tony Carroll* a78 76
2 ch g Intikhab(USA) —Unimpeachable (IRE) (Namaqualand (USA))
(2407) 2950[6] 3636[3] 4623[8] *(5701) 6670[7]* 6989[7] *7412[2] (7486) 7916[7]*

Malpas Missile (IRE) *Tom Dascombe* a81 80
2 b f Elusive City(USA) —Second Prayer (IRE) (Singspiel (IRE))
1375[2] ◆ 1835[3] 2436[3] 3858[4] 4221[3] *5452[2]* 5682[4] *(7913)*

Malthouse (GER) *Mark Johnston* 87
2 b g Green Desert(USA) —Maltage (USA) (Affirmed (USA))
(4396) 5527[8] 6200[8] 6560[14]

Maluckyday (NZ) *Michael, Wayne & John Hawkes* 118
4 bb g Zabeel(NZ) —Natalie Wood (NZ) (Yachtie (AUS))
7291a[2]

Mama Lulu (USA) *Michael Bell* 81
2 bb f Kingmambo(USA) —Kamarinskaya (USA) (Storm Cat (USA))
2740[2] 3237[2] 4203[2] (6058) 6563[6]

Mama Sox (IRE) *John C McConnell* 70
2 b f Bachelor Duke(USA) —Marghelan (FR) (Soviet Star (USA))
6230a[5]

Mambia *J Boisnard* 105
2 ch f Aldebaran(USA) —Algoa (FR) (Common Grounds)
(5322a) 6609a[4]

Mambo Spirit (IRE) *Stef Higgins* a86 82
6 b g Invincible Spirit(IRE) —Mambodorga (USA) (Kingmambo (USA))
2196[6] *(2643)* 2920[2] *4024[2]* 4459[5] 4905[4] *5754[2] 6167[5] 6503[8] 7091[11]* 7238[14] *7554[12]*

Mamichor *Laura Mongan* a54 24
7 br g Mamalik(USA) —Ichor (Primo Dominie)
1078[9] 1636[8]

Mamlook (IRE) *David Pipe* 102
6 br g Key Of Luck(USA) —Cradle Brief (IRE) (Brief Truce (USA))
(1821) 3447[19]

Manaaber (USA) *B W Hills* 75
2 ch f Medicean—Needlecraft (IRE) (Mark Of Esteem (IRE))
(7345)

Manaba (GER) *W Baltromei* a46 95
5 b h Anabaa(USA) —Mandellicht (IRE) (Be My Guest (USA))
273a[10]

Managua *Mick Channon* 86
4 br g Kaldounevees(FR) —Teresa Balbi (Master Willie)
1282[2] 2317[3] 2857[9] 4348[4] (5161)

Manana Manana *John Balding* a65 63
4 b g Tobougg(IRE) —Midnight Allure (Aragon)
86[5]

Manasha *John Dunlop* 40
2 b f Piccolo—Madurai (Chilibang)
2330[U] 3332[7] 3817[3] 4675[7]

Manassas (IRE) *Brian Meehan* 104
5 b g Cape Cross(IRE) —Monnavanna (IRE) (Machiavellian (USA))
1383[14] 1900[13] 3069[15] 3956[4] 4473[4] 4843[2] 5082[3] 5516[8] 6175[6] 6752[9]

Manchestermaverick (USA) *Dr Jeremy Naylor* a65 62
5 ch g Van Nistelrooy(USA) —Lydia Louise (USA) (Southern Halo (USA))
4591[11] 4959[11] 5289[9]

Manchester Stanley *Jamie Osborne* a48 57
2 b g Araafa(IRE) —Naayla (IRE) (Invincible Spirit (IRE))
2839[17] 3209[8] 3399[6] *4020[5] 6052[10]* 6673[14]

Mancunian (IRE) *John Best* a25
2 b c Motivator—Winesong (IRE) (Giant's Causeway (USA))
7385[13]

Mandalay King (IRE) *Marjorie Fife* a49 76
5 b g King's Best(USA) —Mahamuni (IRE) (Sadler's Wells (USA))
1924[3] 2275[3] 2578[4] 3065[10] 3553[2] 3876[6] 4345[9] 4670[2] 5043[6] 5480[3] 5684[7] 6267[10]

Mandalay Prince *Willie Musson* a37 69
6 b g Tobougg(IRE) —Autumn Affair (Lugana Beach)
244[11] 410[9] 720[8] 942[11]

Mandarin Spirit (IRE) *Linda Perratt* a75 75
10 b g Primo Dominie—Lithe Spirit (IRE) (Dancing Dissident (USA))
1200[3] 1363[5] 1719[3] 2073[6] 2213[3] 2294[3] 2756[4] 3356[3] 3533[6] 3946[3] 4060[5] 4516[2] 4799[2] 4820[3] 4952[2] 5212[3] (5240) 5477[7] 5735[5] 6708[5] 7175[6]

Mandate *James Toller* a57 55
3 b g Doyen(IRE) —Joe's Dancer (Shareef Dancer (USA))
2632[11] *3443[7]* 4425[8] 4972[5] 5653[7] *6121[6]*

Mandhooma *Peter Hiatt* a65 63
4 b m Oasis Dream—Shatarah (Gulch (USA))
8[9] 532[9] 1470[8] 1638[4] 2026[8] 2166[6] 2385[9] 2779[13] 3086[6] (3526) (3717) (3980) 4283[7] 4502[6] 4735[5] 4936[12] 5175[4] 5714[3] 6024[8] 6456[3]

Mandurah (IRE) *Ruth Carr* a70 94
6 b g Tagula(IRE) —Fearfully Grand (Grand Lodge (USA))
1332[11] 1711[8] 2327[10] 2883[4] 3114[6] 3205[9] 4798[8] 6031[9]

Mandy's Hero *Ian Williams* a69 71
2 b g Compton Place—Bandanna (Bandmaster (USA))
2111[3] 3204[9] *7858[4]*

Mandy's Princess (IRE) *Richard Fahey* a59 44
2 b f Elnadim(USA) —Bianca Cappello (IRE) (Glenstal (USA))
1043[5] 1835[7] 2272[6] 2848[6]

Maneki Neko (IRE) *Edwin Tuer* a75 78
8 b g Rudimentary(USA) —Ardbess (Balla Cove)
2277[7] 2610[6] (3122) 3552[4] 4246[2] (5019) 5790[10]

Mangham (IRE) *David Brown* a74 77
5 b g Montjeu(IRE) —Lovisa (USA) (Gone West (USA))
837[5] 7352[19] *7988[6]*

Mango Music *Richard Fahey* a73 84
7 ch m Distant Music(USA) —Eurolink Sundance (Night Shift (USA))
37[2] 171[7] 5601[2] (6103) 6140[3] 6723[3] 6962[5] *7319[4] (7556) 7730[8] 8005[8]*

Manic *Andrew Reid* a54 49
8 br m Polar Falcon(USA) —Gentle Irony (Mazilier (USA))
3434[11]

Manieree (IRE) *John M Oxx* 82
2 br f Medicean—Sheer Spirit (IRE) (Caerleon (USA))
(7256a)

Manifest *Henry Cecil* 121
4 b h Rainbow Quest(USA) —Modena (USA) (Roberto (USA))
1382[2] (2097) ◆ 3102[10]

Manighar (FR) *Luca Cumani* 118
4 gr g Linamix(FR) —Mintly Fresh (USA) (Rubiano (USA))
2716[2] ◆ 3695[5] 4535[5] 5349a[2] 6947a[5] 7291a[7] 7458a[3]

Man In The Mirror (IRE) *Patrick Gilligan* a51 51
3 b g Captain Rio—Shyshiyra (IRE) (Kahyasi)
1461[2] 2633[6] 2909[3] *3765[5]* 4439[11]

Manjam (IRE) *A P Boxhall* 77
6 b g Almutawakel—Mubkera (IRE) (Nashwan (USA))
1139[4]

Mannlichen *Mark Johnston* a86 83
4 ch g Selkirk(USA) —Robe Chinoise (Robellino (USA))
461a[3] 1751[3] 2031[6] 2467[6] 3319[6] *5753[6]*

Man Of Action (USA) *John Gosden* 101
3 ch c Elusive Quality(USA) —Dixie Melody (USA) (Dixieland Band (USA))
(2564) (3172) 3886[2]

Man Of God (IRE) *John Gosden* 73
2 b c Sadler's Wells(USA) —Jude (Darshaan)
5049[8] (6128)

Man Of Gwent (UAE) *David Evans* a78 79
6 b g In The Wings—Welsh Valley (USA) (Irish River (FR))
842[9] 994[6]

Man Of Iron (USA) *Luca Cumani* a119 103
4 ch h Giant's Causeway(USA) —Better Than Honour (USA) (Deputy Minister (CAN))
3454[3] 3825[8] *5749[5]* 6736[15] *7297[4] 7594[10]*

Man Of The Match (IRE) *Alan Bailey* 86
2 b c Iffraaj—Dance Clear (IRE) (Marju (IRE))
4856[2] (5404) 5745[3]

Manoori (IRE) *Chris Wall* a70 45
2 b f Dalakhani(IRE) —Kiris World (Distant Relative)
6075[6] *6666[2] (7268)*

Manshoor (IRE) *Lucy Wadham* a85 81
5 gr g Linamix(FR) —Lady Wells (IRE) (Sadler's Wells (USA))
1282[8] 1863[6] *3781[10]* 5146[8] 5611[10] *6055[8]*

Mansii *Philip McBride* a59 58
5 b g Dr Fong(USA) —Enclave (USA) (Woodman (USA))
(2721) 3605[4] 4938[3] ◆ 5586[6] *6206[4] 6847[3]* 7170[3]

Mantatisi *James Fanshawe* a72 71
2 ch f Motivator—Magongo (Be My Chief (USA))
7057[4] ◆ *(7448)*

Mantoba *Brian Meehan* 102
2 b c Noverre(USA) —Coming Home (Vettori (IRE))
5690[4] (6443) (6884) ◆ 7360a[10]

Manuelita *T Larriviere* a57
5 b m Noverre(USA) —Miss Arizona (IRE) (Sure Blade (USA))
559a[8]

Manxman (IRE) *Mark Johnston* a74
3 b c Celtic Swing—Viscaria (IRE) (Barathea (IRE))
592[8] 754[4] ◆ *864[3] 964[4]* ◆ *(1059)*

Many A Slip *John Dunlop* a28 77
3 gr g Verglas(IRE) —Tri Pac (IRE) (Fairy King (USA))
1776[10] 2888[15] *3325[14]* 3907[8] *4791[12]* 5414[9]

Many Welcomes *Brian Baugh* a57 66
5 ch m Young Ern—Croeso Cynnes (Most Welcome)
1115[5] *1585[11]* 2875[3] 3391[5] 3854[2] 4485[2]

Manzila (FR) *Mme C Barande-Barbe* 92
7 ch m Cadeaux Genereux—Mannsara (IRE) (Royal Academy (USA))
1081a[4] 2157a[9] 2804a[10] 3425a[0]

Maoi Chinn Tire (IRE) *J S Moore* a76 73
3 b g Mull Of Kintyre(USA) —Primrose And Rose (Primo Dominie)
122[2] 233[3] 276[3] (425) 519[2] (766) 2283[4] (2617) *3085[6] 4031[8]* 4298[2] *5027[6]* 6078[2]

Map Of Heaven *William Haggas* a56 70
2 b f Pivotal—Superstar Leo (IRE) (College Chapel)
6441[5] 6892[2] *7418[4]*

Mappin Time (IRE) *Tim Easterby* a78 90
2 b c Orientate(USA) —Different Story (USA) (Stravinsky (USA))
1065[2] (1292) 3059[5] 3596[3] 3925[2] 4138[4] 5245[10] (5639) 6141[5] 6568[13]

Ma Preference (FR) *F Rohaut* a79 98
4 b m American Post—Restless Mixa (IRE) (Linamix (FR))
6519a[2] (7416a)

Maqaasid *John Gosden* 107
2 b f Green Desert(USA) —Eshaadeh (USA) (Storm Cat (USA))
(2251) (3070) 5246[4] 6530[3]

Maqaraat (IRE) *B W Hills* 76
2 ch c Dalakhani(IRE) —Raghida (IRE) (Nordico (USA))
7203[5] ◆

Ma Quillet *Henry Candy* a50 54
2 gr f Tumbleweed Ridge—Raffelina (USA) (Carson City (USA))
4960[5] *6286[5]*

Maraased *Steve Gollings* a69 35
5 b g Alhaarth(IRE) —Fleeting Rainbow (Rainbow Quest (USA))
554[4] 1689[6]

Mara Damdam (FR) *C Boutin* 52
2 b f Indian Rocket—Lanapark (IRE) (Grand Lodge (USA))
5063a[11]

Mar Adentro (FR) *R Chotard* a89 109
4 b g Marju(IRE) —Guermantes (Distant Relative)
6012a[3] 6608a[3] 7278a[4]

Marafong *Brian Baugh* a54 79
3 ch g Dr Fong(USA) —Marakabei (Hernando (FR))
1257[4] *1490[7]* 1878[7] 2993[12] 3413[8] 3910[3] 4383[4] 4761[4] 4970[8] 5414[5] 6094[3] 6257[4] 6829[5] *7381[6] 7703[7] 7958[9]*

Maragna (IRE) *Paul Green* a38 49
3 b g Invincible Spirit(IRE) —Bradwell (IRE) (Taufan (USA))
4672[8] 4861[7] 5481[5] 6643[8]

Maraheb *John Dunlop* 70
2 b c Redoute's Choice(AUS) —Hureya (USA) (Woodman (USA))
6196[5] 6748[5]

Marajaa (IRE) *Willie Musson* a83 101
8 b g Green Desert(USA) —Ghyraan (IRE) (Cadeaux Genereux)
1006[10] 1383[2] 1900[3] 3069[24] 3869[4] 4537[7] 4816[7] 5950[10] 6349[17] 6888[27]

Marameo *F & L Camici* 41
3 b c Lomitas—Maschera D'Oro (Mtoto)
1418a[13]

Marangu (IRE) *W Hickst* a43 77
4 b g Intikhab(USA) —Massada (Most Welcome)
1055a[0]

Maratib (USA) *David Lanigan* a53 62
2 b g Street Cry(IRE) —Colcon (USA) (Pleasant Colony (USA))
3219[10] *3517[6]* 4263[8]

Marble Arch (USA) *Jane Chapple-Hyam* 34
3 b c Arch(USA) —Smart Launch (USA) (Relaunch (USA))
4146[7]

Marc De Savoie (IRE) *Kevin Ryan* a45 63
2 gr c Aussie Rules(USA) —Guantanamera (IRE) (Sadler's Wells (USA))
5277[16] 5762[5] 6138[6] 6471[4] 6875[12] *7295[10]*

Marceti (IRE) *E Leenders* 95
3 gr g Verglas(IRE) —Darasa (FR) (Barathea (IRE))
2557a[3] 5135a[6]

Marchand D'Or (FR) *M Delzangles* a56 110
7 gr g Marchand De Sable(USA) —Fedora (FR) (Kendor (FR))
(2157a) 2804a[3] 3192[11] 3870[9] 6012a[9] 6608a[4]

March Forth *Tom Dascombe* 62
3 b g Kyllachy—Jasmine Breeze (Saddlers' Hall (IRE))
3733[7] 4556[4]

Marching (AUS) *Mahmood Al Zarooni* a108 111
6 br h Commands(AUS) —Step (AUS) (Grand Lodge (USA))
607a[4] 818a[8] 1904[3] 2344[2] 3193[27]

Marching Home *Walter Swinburn* a73
3 ch g Leporello(IRE) —Marchetta (Mujadil (USA))
3275[5] 7086[3] 7338[3]

Marching Song (USA) *Andy Turnell* a78 79
4 b g War Chant(USA) —Tates Creek (USA) (Rahy (USA))
3038[2] *3563[4] 4258[4]* 5146[4]

Marchin Star (IRE) *Mel Brittain* 50
3 ch c Chineur(FR) —March Star (IRE) (Mac's Imp (USA))
1401[8]

March Madness *S Botti* 97
2 ch f Noverre(USA) —Spinning Reel (Spinning World (USA))
6975a[9]

March On Beetroot *Robert Cowell* a76
2 b c Cape Cross(IRE) —Parisian Elegance (Zilzal (USA))
7700[2] (7880) ◆

Marcus (FR) *F Rohaut* a78 44
5 b h Sagacity(FR) —Spring Quest (Rainbow Quest (USA))
494a[7]

Marcus Antonius *Jim Boyle* a57 62
3 b g Mark Of Esteem(IRE) —Star Of The Course (USA) (Theatrical)
2632[14] 3038[9] 3443[8] 4972[3] 5564[2] 5963[2] (6273) ◆ 6855[7]

Marden (IRE) *Brian Meehan* 82
2 b c Danehill Dancer(IRE) —Streetcar (IRE) (In The Wings)
5491[4] ◆ (6827) ◆

Marechale (FR) *Mme C Head-Maarek* a79 77
4 b m Anabaa(USA) —Malaisie (USA) (Bering)
1055a[7]

Maree Prince (IRE) *Ferdy Murphy* a53 56
9 b g Taipan(IRE) —A Woman's Heart (IRE) (Supreme Leader)
113[8] 815[8]

Margarita (GER) *M Munch* 101
4 ch m Lomitas—Monbijou (GER) (Dashing Blade)
6790a[5]

Margie's World (GER) *S Wegner* 82
6 ch m Spinning World(USA) —Margie's Darling (USA) (Alydar (USA))
3236a[9]

Margot De Medici (FR) *Nigel Tinkler*
2 b f Medicean—Ratukidul (FR) (Danehill (USA))
5595[11]

Margot Did (IRE) *Michael Bell* 108
2 b f Exceed And Excel(AUS) —Special Dancer (Shareef Dancer (USA))
(2338) (2630) ◆ 3141[2] 4356[2] 5246[2] 5693[3] 6530[5]

Marguerite Du Pre (GER) *M Figge* a39 88
3 ch f Sholokhov(IRE) —Meadow's Bride (AUT) (Dashing Blade)
3236a[12]

Marhaba *Michael Jarvis* 71
2 b f Nayef(USA) —Sil Sila (IRE) (Marju (IRE))
6155[7] ◆

Marhaba Malyoon (IRE) *David Simcock* 74
2 b c Tiger Hill(IRE) —Mamonta (Fantastic Light (USA))
(6414)

Mariachi Man *Tim Easterby* 93
2 b c Haafhd—Popocatepetl (FR) (Nashwan (USA))
2059[8] (5092) ◆ 5849[7] (6505) ◆ 7059[2]

Maria Royal (IRE) *A De Royer-Dupre* 108
3 b f Montjeu(IRE) —Notable (Zafonic (USA))
5138a[6] (6591a) 7110a[4]

Marias Dream (IRE) *J G Coogan* a90 91
8 bb m Desert Sun—Clifton Lass (IRE) (Up And At 'Em)
3487a[7]

Marie Cuddy (IRE) *Karen George* a2 64
3 b f Galileo(IRE) —Corrine (IRE) (Spectrum (IRE))
5658[13] 6470[8] 7461[10]

Marie De Guise (IRE) *Sir Michael Stoute* 86
3 gr f Verglas(IRE) —Mary Stuart (IRE) (Nashwan (USA))
(1881) ◆ 2256[8] 2843[4] ◆ 5008[7] 5611[2] ◆ 5953[5]

Marie De Medici (USA) *Mark Johnston* 104
3 ch f Medicean—Mare Nostrum (Caerleon (USA))
952a[4] 1313[3] (1729) 2711[11] 3071[10] 3694[6] 4612a[5] 5553[3]

Marie Du Plessis *Mark Johnston* a30 42
2 b f Invincible Spirit(IRE) —Scandalette (Niniski (USA))
4149[10] 4668[6] 7603[4] 7888[12]

Marie Rose *Brian Meehan* a64
2 b f Sadler's Wells(USA) —Langoustine (AUS) (Danehill (USA))
7478[4] ◆

Marieschi (USA) *Roger Fisher* a51 68
6 b g Maria's Mon(USA) —Pennygown (Rainbow Quest (USA))
942[8]

Marillos Proterras *Ann Duffield* a7 52
4 b m Fraam—Legend Of Aragon (Aragon)
2430[7] 3370[8] 3707[5] 4173[7]

Marina (GER) *N Bertran De Balanda* a50 78
3 b f Paolini(GER) —Maria Magdalena (GER) (Alkalde (GER))
548a[6]

Marina Belle *Mark Johnston* a22 61
2 b f Royal Applause—Marina Park (Local Suitor (USA))
2522[7] 3498[9] 6240[2] 6488[4] 6901[9]

Marine Boy (IRE) *Tom Dascombe* a88 100
4 b g One Cool Cat(USA) —Bahamamia (Vettori (IRE))
1423[12] 1664[6] 2657[8]

Marine Commando *Richard Fahey* 101
2 b g Pastoral Pursuits—Carollan (IRE) (Marju (IRE))
(2376) (3051) 4538[6] 6734[12]

Mariners Lodge (USA) *Mahmood Al Zarooni* a60 74
2 ch c Distorted Humor(USA) —Sanibel Island (USA) (Capote (USA))
6278[3] ◆ 6843[5]

Marine Spirit (GER) *M bin Shafya* a89 86
3 b c Big Shuffle(USA) —Molly Dancer (GER) (Shareef Dancer (USA))
510a[6]

Marino Prince (FR) *Barry Leavy* a52 51
5 b g Dr Fong(USA) —Hula Queen (USA) (Irish River (FR))
3360[3] 4070[4] 4246[4] 4912[4]

Marinous (FR) *F Head* a104 119
4 b h Numerous(USA) —Marende (FR) (Panoramic)
706a[2] 820a[4] (5575a) 6612a[6] 7615a[17]

Mariol (FR) *Robert Collet* 116
7 b g Munir—La Bastoche (IRE) (Kaldoun (FR))
1021a[9] 4165a[4] 4885a[6] 5576a[8] 6611a[8]

Maristar (USA) *Gerard Butler* a82 76
3 b f Giant's Causeway(USA) —Jewel Princess (USA) (Key To The Mint (USA))
1317[5] 5972[12] (6543)

Marius Maximus (IRE) *Mark Johnston* a16 41
3 b c Kheleyf(USA) —Marju Guest (IRE) (Marju (IRE))
759[7] 906[12]

Mariyah *Michael Blanshard* a12 31
2 gr f Kyllachy—Molly Moon (IRE) (Primo Dominie)
3295[11] 3785[10] 7242[8]

Marjolly (IRE) *John Gallagher* a66 47
3 b g Marju(IRE) —Lost Icon (IRE) (Intikhab (USA))
(122) 454[4] 594[2] 809[13] 1347[4] 1934[9] 2215[14] 4025[13] 4692[4] 6025[13]

Marju King (IRE) *Stuart Kittow* a61 73
4 b g Marju(IRE) —Blue Reema (IRE) (Bluebird (USA))
1520[9] (2402) 3221[9] 4657[8] 5260[8] 6055[7] 6427[14]

Marjury Daw (IRE) *James Given* a83 90
4 b m Marju(IRE) —The Stick (Singspiel (IRE))
290[2] 541[4] 757[5] (939) 970[2] 1172[4] 2902[2] (3601) (3912) (3950) 4196[2] 4492[4] 5071[2] 5181[2] 5408[2] (6003) 6361[16] 7349[13] 7593[10] 7756[10]

Marju's Reward (IRE) *Alan Swinbank* a56
3 b f Marju(IRE) —Pasithea (IRE) (Celtic Swing)
1538[7] 1825[9] 2724[7]

Marjustar (IRE) *Jim Boyle* a54 57
3 b f Marju(IRE) —Stariya (IRE) (Soviet Star (USA))
1477[10] 2480[11] 2633[10]

Markab *Henry Candy* a107 121
7 b g Green Desert(USA) —Hawafiz (Nashwan (USA))
(1400) (2353a) 3047[2] 4136[5] (5744)

Mark Anthony (IRE) *Kevin Ryan* 79
3 b g Antonius Pius(USA) —Zuniga's Date (USA) (Diesis)
1709[3] 2426[7] 4288[8] (4714) ◆ 5046[5] 5606[4] 6466[12] 7082[11]

Markazzi *Sir Michael Stoute* 95
3 b c Dansili—Bandanna (Bandmaster (USA))
1327[8] 4504[12] 5188[17]

Mark Carmers *Donal Nolan* 38
3 b g Mark Of Esteem(IRE) —Queen Lea (FR) (Alzao (USA))
4584[7]

Marked Card (IRE) *Peter Chapple-Hyam* 84
2 b c Kheleyf(USA) —Kelsey Rose (Most Welcome)
3169[5] 5936[3] (6436) (6825)

Market Maker (IRE) *Tim Easterby* 61
2 ch g Trade Fair—Papier Mache (IRE) (Desert Prince (IRE))
2059[12] 2384[10] 2832[13] 3106[3] 4701[7] 6184[10] 6979[9]

Market Puzzle (IRE) *Mark Brisbourne* a56 56
3 ch g Bahamian Bounty—Trempjane (Lujain (USA))
143[2] 371[5] 597[4] 1495[3] 2189[7] 2412[11] 2838[5] (3728) 4212[8] 4992[14] 5411[4]

Market Watcher (USA) *Seamus Fahey* a60 56
9 b g Boundary(USA) —Trading (USA) (A.P. Indy (USA))
409[6]

Mark Harbour (IRE) *Richard Hannon* a66 66
2 b c Chevalier(IRE) —Meranie Girl (IRE) (Mujadil (USA))
4695[5] 5178[2] 5440[3] 6412[7] 6875[14]

Markhesa *Jim Boyle* a68 68
4 b m Sakhee(USA) —Marciala (IRE) (Machiavellian (USA))
1047[3] ◆ 1141[2] ◆ 1323[10] 3821[4] 4498[2] 4958[10] 5655[3] 6165[13] 6452[11] 6637[7]

Markington *Peter Bowen* a74 84
7 b g Medicean—Nemesia (Mill Reef (USA))
(3241) (3974) 4467[12] 5788[8] 6423[9]

Mark Of Brazil (FR) *F Chappet* a69 83
3 b f Mark Of Esteem(IRE) —Exeter (FR) (Kabool)
6487a[2]

Marksbury *James Eustace* a66 27
3 b f Mark Of Esteem(IRE) —Penelewey (Groom Dancer (USA))
2227[10] 5028[6] 5700[5] 7288[3] (7555) 7768[2] 7874[10]

Mark To Market (IRE) *Jamie Osborne* a76
3 b g Clodovil(IRE) —Genetta (Green Desert (USA))
915[5] ◆ 1143[3] 1460[8]

Mark Twain (IRE) *David Simcock* 86
3 b g Rock Of Gibraltar(IRE) —Lady Windermere (IRE) (Lake Coniston (IRE))
1310[7] 1823[6] 2324[9] 3265[7] 4784[2] 5861[3] 6097[4] 6326[2] 6692[4] 6961[2]

Marlinka *Roger Charlton* 93
2 b f Marju(IRE) —Baralinka (IRE) (Barathea (IRE))
1999[2] (2440) 3070[14] (3482) (4275a) 5036[7] 6141[6]

Marmaduke *John Bridger* 44
2 ch g Bertolini(USA) —Lihou Island (Beveled (USA))
2245[9] 2680[11] 3034[6] 3913[5] 5074[6] 5709[7]

Marmooq *Michael Attwater* a69 62
7 ch g Cadeaux Genereux—Portelet (Night Shift (USA))
12[4] 83[6] 162[9] 7966[8]

Marny (GER) *H Blume* a89 91
5 b m Dashing Blade—Magic Dawn (IRE) (Caerleon (USA))
304a[10] 549a[8] 3236a[8]

Maroon *B W Hills* 71
3 b f Rainbow Quest(USA) —Mamounia (IRE) (Green Desert (USA))
2891[8] 5022[3] 6356[5]

Maroon Machine (IRE) *E J O'Neill* a96 98
3 ch g Muhtathir—Mediaeval (FR) (Medaaly)
608a[7] 796a[8]

Marosh (FR) *Robert Cowell* a76 76
3 b g American Post—Madragoa (FR) (Kaldoun (FR))
(213) (288) 617[2] 1018[6] 1279[4] 2416[2] 3171[2] 4335[8] 5086[8] 5769[5] 6085[6] 6540[4]

Marrayah *Michael Jarvis* 71
3 b f Fraam—Mania (IRE) (Danehill (USA))
3001[9] 5968[8]

Marrimeclaire (IRE) *B J McMath* a66 69
3 b f Spartacus(IRE) —Salty Air (IRE) (Singspiel (IRE))
1132[4] ◆ 1302[4] 1932[7] 2725[8] 6165[2] 6993[2] 7413[2] 7453[6]

Marron Flore *Alastair Lidderdale* a38 27
7 ch m Compton Place—Flore Fair (Polar Falcon (USA))
849[11] 1825[8] 2021[11]

Marshade (ITY) *S Botti* 104
3 b c Martino Alonso(IRE) —Universal Shade (ITY) (Pursuit Of Love)
1418a[2] 2576a[5] 7370a[10]

Marshal Plat Club *Alan Bailey* a51
3 b f Monsieur Bond(IRE) —Bond May Day (Among Men (USA))
7838[4] 7960[3]

Marsh's Gift *Colin Teague* a32 50
3 b g Tamayaz(CAN) —Maureen Ann (Elmaamul (USA))
1336[11] 1706[14] 2393[13] 2838[8] 4017[8] 4337[8] 5550[5] 6076[10] 7132[6] 7328[10] 7406[7]

Marsh Side (USA) *Neil Drysdale* a111 117
7 bb h Gone West(USA) —Colonial Play (USA) (Pleasant Colony (USA))
6236a[8] 6951a[8]

Marsh Warbler *David Simcock* a57 82
3 ch g Barathea(IRE) —Echo River (USA) (Irish River (FR))
2225[8] 3661[4] 5003[6] 5680[4] 6372[8] (6652)

Marster Parkes *Eric Alston* 33
2 b g Nayef(USA) —Lucky Parkes (Full Extent (USA))
2882[8]

Marston Moor (USA) *Mahmood Al Zarooni* a76 84
2 b c War Front(USA) —Crescent Moon (USA) (Seeking The Gold (USA))
3823[5] 4142[3] (4695) 5532[3]

Marteau *Kevin Ryan* a6 47
3 ch g Pivotal—Rababah (USA) (Woodman (USA))
1029[11] 2517[7] 3091[8] 3758[10] 7429[13]

Martyr *Richard Hannon* a88 109
5 b g Cape Cross(IRE) —Sudeley (Dancing Brave (USA))
1015[6] 1724[11] (2509) 3194[3] (3843) ◆ (4461) 5220[10] 6388[5]

Marvada (IRE) *K J Condon* a47
2 b f Elusive City(USA) —Theory Of Law (Generous (IRE))
6726a[8]

Marvellous Value (IRE) *Michael Dods* a84 79
5 b g Danetime(IRE) —Despondent (IRE) (Broken Hearted)
3919[13] 4372[6] 5855[8] 6142[14] 7212[4]

Marvo *Mark H Tompkins* a62 87
6 b g Bahamian Bounty—Mega (IRE) (Petardia)
1272[2] 1697[10] 2991[8] 4112[7] 4828[8] 6097[2] 6327[6] 6534[15]

Mary Boleyn (IRE) *J E Hammond* 103
4 b m King's Best(USA) —Bint Kaldoun (IRE) (Kaldoun (FR))
7416a[5]

Mary Boyle *Alan McCabe* a56 58
2 b f Proclamation(IRE) —Inchalong (Inchinor)
(5020) 5659[9] 6129[4] 6810[6] 7124[4] 7396[3] 7540[4] 7643[8]

Mary Helen *Mark Brisbourne* a64 55
3 b f Dandoun—Hotel California (IRE) (Last Tycoon)
33[4] 133[2] 183[2] 254[8] 1982[3] 2724[5] 4289[8] 5411[11] 6287[9] 6747[9] 7003[2] 7387[7] 7495[2]

Maryolini *Tom Keddy* a59 63
5 b m Bertolini(USA) —Mary Jane (Tina's Pet)
2008[2] 2635[10] 3292[4] 3717[2] 4234[6] (4778) 5176[3] 5915[8] 6440[7] 6456[6] 7193[9] 7334[3]

Mary's Pet *John Akehurst* a67
3 b f Where Or When(IRE) —Contrary Mary (Mujadil (USA))
24[5] ◆ 180[8] 321[5] (1205) 1593[3] 6898[4] 7162[12] 7391[9] 7639[6] (7827)

Mary's Precedent (FR) *C Lerner* a74 100
4 ch m Storming Home—Suvretta Queen (IRE) (Polish Precedent (USA))
7800a[0]

Mary Spring Rice (IRE) *Seamus Fahey* a34 44
4 b m Saffron Walden(FR) —Flaming Song (IRE) (Darshaan)
7429[9]

Marywell *John Gosden* 90
3 ch f Selkirk(USA) —Margarula (IRE) (Doyoun)
1932[4] 2890[2] 3437[2] (5610) 6199[7]

Marzante (USA) *Roger Charlton* 79
2 rg g Maria's Mon(USA) —Danzante (USA) (Danzig (USA))
3915[2] (5440) 5969[3]

Masaalek *Doug Watson* a84 110
5 b g Green Desert(USA) —Hammiya (IRE) (Darshaan)
412a[10] 713a[14]

Masai Moon *Rod Millman* a89 94
6 b g Lujain(USA) —Easy To Imagine (USA) (Cozzene (USA))
1219[10] 1826[5] ◆ 2443[3] 2736[2] 2971[7]

Masamah (IRE) *Kevin Ryan* a97 107
4 gr g Exceed And Excel(AUS) —Bethesda (Distant Relative)
(1822) 2759[4] 3193[18] 3895[4] (4401) (4616) 5944[7] 6194[10] 6752[12]

Masaraat (FR) *John Dunlop* 77
2 b f Alhaarth(IRE) —Kahalah (IRE) (Darshaan)
4595[5] (5583)

Masaya *Clive Brittain* 96
2 b f Dansili—Anbella (FR) (Common Grounds)
(2176) 3070[16] 4592[2] 5519[4] 6157[3] (6559)

Mascarene (USA) *Sir Michael Stoute* a73 78
3 b f Empire Maker(USA) —Intercontinental (Danehill (USA))
1932[3] 3593[4] 4294[2] 6415[2] 7043[3]

Mashaahed *E Charpy* a101 111
7 b h In The Wings—Patacake Patacake (USA) (Bahri (USA))
436a[4] 627a[7] 820a[10]

Mashatu *James Fanshawe* 74
3 b g Pivotal—Wannabe Grand (IRE) (Danehill (USA))
2899[6] 5971[5] ◆ 6624[3] 6984[8]

Mashdood (USA) *Peter Hiatt* a62 69
4 b g Sinndar(IRE) —Rahayeb (Arazi (USA))
6661[4] 7061[13] 7695[5]

Mashoor (FR) *A Fabre* 107
3 b c Monsun(GER) —Gontcharova (IRE) (Zafonic (USA))
3014a[2]

Masked Dance (IRE) *Kevin Ryan* a76 88
3 gr g Captain Rio—Brooks Masquerade (Absalom)
(1776) ◆ 2656[7] 6963[14] 7352[13] 7844[8] 7906[4]

Masked Marvel *John Gosden* 83
2 b c Montjeu(IRE) —Waldmark (GER) (Mark Of Esteem (IRE))
(6087) 6737[6]

Maslak (IRE) *Peter Hiatt* a83 80
6 b g In The Wings—Jeed (IRE) (Mujtahid (USA))
251[1] 546[7] (2081) 2402[2] 2881[3] 3090[7] 3576[2] 3860[3] 4426[3] (4657) 5363[5] 5888[8] 7101[2] (7642) 7694[7] 8003[11]

Mason Hindmarsh *Karen McLintock* 72
3 ch g Dr Fong(USA) —Sierra Virgen (USA) (Stack (USA))
2501[3] 2816[3] 3450[5] 3905[4] 4344[5] 4796[2] 5300[6] (6117) 6622[4]

Masonic Lady (IRE) *William Haggas* a74 79
2 b f Dubai Destination(USA) —Leenane (IRE) (Grand Lodge (USA))
4233[6] 4568[6] 4899[9] 5709[2] 6200[5] 6497[4] 6994[2] 7163[2]

Masquenada (FR) *W Baltromei* 97
5 b m Muhtathir—Macarena (GER) (Platini (GER))
4035a[5]

Massachusetts *Brendan Powell* 47
3 ch g Singspiel(IRE) —Royal Passion (Ahonoora)
1581[15] 2290[12] 2899[9] 3614[7] 3960[6] 4281[5] 6022[10] 6257[6]

Massilly (FR) *P Vidotto* 24
2 b f Equerry(USA) —Maoussa (FR) (Nikos)
5063a[10]

Mass Rally (IRE) *John Gosden* a96 104
3 b c Kheleyf(USA) —Reunion (IRE) (Be My Guest (USA))
3696[2] 4357[4] 5143[4] 5854[5] 6321[2] 6888[18]

Masta Plasta (IRE) *David Nicholls* a111 112
7 b g Mujadil(USA) —Silver Arrow (USA) (Shadeed (USA))
1573[4] 1822[13] 2346[3] 2526[2] 2745[5] 4180a[7] (4937) 5512[9] 6663[4]

Masteeat (USA) *Olivia Maylam* a44 43
3 ch f Delaware Township(USA) —White Hot Cat (USA) (Tactical Cat (USA))
1075[5] 2441[6] 2535[4] 2812[8] 7827[6] 7986[11] 8023[4]

Master At Arms *Daniel Mark Loughnane* a73 78
7 ch g Grand Lodge(USA) —L'Ideale (USA) (Alysheba (USA))
6423[7] 7465[2] 7632[3]

Master Chef (IRE) *Bent Olsen* a91 92
5 b h Oasis Dream—Miss Honorine (IRE) (Highest Honor (FR))
2019a[7]

Master Fitz (ITY) *G Botti* 99
2 b c Philomatheia(USA) —Law Stone (IRE) (Sikeston (USA))
7850a[2]

Masterful Act (USA) *Edward Vaughan* a72 13
3 ch g Pleasantly Perfect(USA) —Catnip (USA) (Flying Paster (USA))
6856[10] (7579)

Master Kid (DEN) *Bent Olsen* 94
5 b h Academy Award(IRE) —Stolga (FR) (Baillamont (USA))
4641a[3]

Master Leon *Bryan Smart* a80 70
3 b c Monsieur Bond(IRE) —Bollin Rita (Rambo Dancer (CAN))
(85) 268[2] 2762[9] 3371[6] 4193[9] 5383[5] 5647[9] 6461[6] 6664[4] 7411[5] 7539[8] 7701[4] 7844[3]

Master Lightfoot *Walter Swinburn* a84 82
4 b h Kyllachy—Two Step (Mujtahid (USA))
241[3] 345[2] (935) (1267) 1506[3] 2681[7] 3261[4] 4292[8] 5151[3] 5915[9]

Master Macho (IRE) *Mick Channon* a62 76
2 b c Camacho—Desert Rose (Green Desert (USA))
1017[4] 1294[3] 1517[3] 1603[6] 1957[2] 2239[2] 2457[2] 2680[2] 2936[6] 3034[3] 3204[3] 3498[4] (3897) 4262[6] 4600[2] 4688[3] 5261[7] 5547[7] 5987[4] 6271[6] 6769[10]

Master Mahogany *Ron Hodges* a63 60
9 b g Bandmaster(USA) —Impropriety (Law Society (USA))
4987[3] 5585[8] 5655[5]

Master Melody (IRE) *Kevin Prendergast* a66 74
2 b g Ad Valorem(USA) —Melody Island (IRE) (Turtle Island (IRE))
6230a[18]

Master Mylo (IRE) *Dean Ivory* a80 84
3 ch g Bertolini(USA) —Sheboygan (IRE) (Grand Lodge (USA))
900[5] 1058[2] ◆ 1347[5] 1784[4] 2416[6] ◆ 2566[7] 3511[4] (4025) 5031[8] 5383[2] (5968) 6780[10] 7114[6]

Master Nimbus *John Quinn* a53 70
10 b g Cloudings(IRE) —Miss Charlie (Pharly (FR))
1113[10] 2424[2] 2610[5] 4410[3] (4945) 5681[4]

Master Of Arts (USA) *Mark Johnston* a78 23
5 br g Swain(IRE) —Grazia (Sharpo)
440a[11] 629a[10]

Masterofceremonies *Mark Brisbourne* a59 70
7 ch g Definite Article—Darakah (Doulab (USA))
2492[7] 2714[9] 3978[10] 4454[6] 4620[4] 4740[6] 5019[11] 5704[2] 6269[4] 6518[8] 7200[6] 7508[6]

Master Of Dance (IRE) *James Given* a84 82
3 ch c Noverre(USA) —Shambodia (IRE) (Petardia)
(22) 2242[9] 2933[5] 3949[4] 5304[6] 5852[14] (6463) 6961[3] 7283[6] 7560[10] 7895[5] 7985[9]

Master Of Hounds (USA) *A P O'Brien* 115
2 b c Kingmambo(USA) —Silk And Scarlet (Sadler's Wells (USA))
7081[3] 7360a[6]

Master Of Light *Ms Joanna Morgan* a62 54
5 b g Bertolini(USA) —Lucky Dip (Tirol)
(7199)

Master Of Song *Roy Bowring* a51 54
3 ch g Ballet Master(USA) —Ocean Song (Savahra Sound)
3907[2] 4687[2] 5064[2] 7156[9]

Master O'Reilly (NZ) *Danny O'Brien* 119
8 bb g O'Reilly(NZ) —Without Remorse (NZ) (Bakharoff (USA))
7291a[15]

Master Perfect *Luca Cumani* a27
2 ch c Dubai Destination(USA) —My Mariam (Salse (USA))
5651[8] 6712[12]

Master Rooney (IRE) *Bryan Smart* 93
4 bb h Cape Cross(IRE) —Wimple (USA) (Kingmambo (USA))
1295[7] 1573[6] 2465[4]

Master Shade (ITY) *P Schiergen* 44
2 ch f Masterful(USA) —Universal Shade (ITY) (Pursuit Of Love)
6407a[8]

Mastership (IRE) *John Quinn* a80 98
6 ch g Best Of The Bests(IRE) —Shady Point (IRE) (Unfuwain (USA))
4653[10] 5302[12] 6142[3] 6721[12] 7092[9] 7529[3]

Mastery *Saeed Bin Suroor* a119 120
4 b h Sulamani(IRE) —Moyesii (USA) (Diesis)
1027a[5] 6885[3] (7297) (7851a)

Maswerte (IRE) *Michael Wigham* a72 85
4 b g Fraam—Rose Chime (IRE) (Tirol)
2508[13] 3330[13] 6852[10]

Mataaleb *Jeff Pearce* 99
3 b c Dalakhani(IRE) —Elfaslah (IRE) (Green Desert (USA))
1521[2] (2497) 3335[5] 4470[2]

Mata Hari Blue *John Holt* a51 70
4 ch m Monsieur Bond(IRE) —Feeling Blue (Missed Flight)
1391[15] 1929[11] 3762[7] 3966[6] 4251[2] 4478[3] 5388[5] (5419) 5557[3] 6040[2] ◆ 6261[6] 6515[12]

Mata Keranjang (USA) *Paul Cole* 105
3 b g More Than Ready(USA) —Love Sick (USA) (Salt Lake (USA))
1311[3] 2159a[13] 2507[2] 3795[4] 4307[2] (4556) 5516[5]

Mataram (USA) *William Jarvis* a66 71
7 b g Matty G(USA) —Kalinka (USA) (Mr Prospector (USA))
1587[4] 5867[3]

Matavia Bay (IRE) *Alan Jarvis* a61 43
2 b g Bahamian Bounty—Rosewater (GER) (Winged Love (IRE))
3842[6] 6802[9] 7163[3]

Materialism *Mark Johnston* a62
2 b c Librettist(USA) —Crinolette (IRE) (Sadler's Wells (USA))
6333[3]

Mater Mater *Andrew Reid* a64
3 gr f Silver Patriarch(IRE) —Emily-Mou (IRE) (Cadeaux Genereux)
4746[6] 6999[10] 7286[12] 7387[8]

Mathurino (FR) *H Billot* 21
3 b g Trempolino(USA) —La Mathurine (FR) (Le Glorieux)
7959a[0]

Matilda May *Colin Teague*
3 b f Leporello(IRE) —Seems So Easy (USA) (Palmister (USA))
6896[17] 7129[7] 7406[10]

Matilda's Waltz *Ralph Beckett* a51 67
2 ch f Medicean—Australian Dreams (Magic Ring (IRE))
6154[3] 7198[6]

Matinee Idol *Mrs S Lyamyman* a21 49
7 ch m In The Wings—Bibliotheque (USA) (Woodman (USA))
190[7]

Matjar (IRE) *Joseph Quinn* a72 72
7 ch g Grand Lodge(USA) —Tajawuz (Kris)
(665) 5272[2] ◆

Matraash (USA) *Mrs Sarah Dawson* a82 92
4 b h Elusive Quality(USA) —Min Alhawa (USA) (Riverman (USA))
6910a[9]

Matreshka (IRE) *N Clement* 87
2 b f Statue Of Liberty(USA) —Alivera (FR) (Danehill (USA))
4274a[2] 5226a[6] 7383a[4]

Matsunosuke *Ronald Harris* a110 109
8 b g Magic Ring(IRE) —Lon Isa (Grey Desire)
(212) 434a[10] 604a[11] 948[6] 1295[16] 2563[7] 2808[3] 4401[2] 4510[9] 4937[7] 5966[9] 6446[11] (6932) (7409) 7443[4] 7635[5] 7984[6]

Mattamia (IRE) *Rod Millman* 99
4 b g Makbul—Lady Dominatrix (IRE) (Danehill Dancer (IRE))
1174[8] 2280[8]

Matterofact (IRE) *Malcolm Saunders* a49 78
7 b m Bold Fact(USA) —Willow Dale (IRE) (Danehill (USA))
2026[4] 2332[3] 2639[10] 3308[2] 3722[3] 4041[4] (4326) 5377[2] (5695) 5915[4] 6440[8]

Mattoral *PETER Makin* a74 68
2 b c High Chaparral(IRE) —Angry Bark (USA) (Woodman (USA))
6158[5] 6498[2] (7242)

Matula (IRE) *Ralph Beckett* 86
2 ch f Halling(USA) —Quaich (Danehill (USA))
(5985) ◆ 7235[6]

Maunby Rumba (IRE) *Ben Haslam* 26
2 b f Kheleyf(USA) —Chantilly (FR) (Sanglamore (USA))
5640[7] 6182[7] 6566[10] 6891[9]

Maundy Money *David Marnane* a98 98
7 b g King's Best(USA) —Royal Gift (Cadeaux Genereux)
3487a[15] 4463a[11] 5774a[14] 6907a[4]

Maureens Litlun (IRE) *Michael Wigham* a29
2 b f Antonius Pius(USA) —Paradise Street (IRE) (Machiavellian (USA))
5657[10] 6369[11]

Mausin (IRE) *Hughie Morrison* 71
3 br f Monsun(GER) —Cote Quest (USA) (Green Desert (USA))
1356[6] 2390[4] 3170[5] 3852[3] 4502[8]

Mavalenta (IRE) *J W Hills* a72 65
3 b f Montjeu(IRE) —Velouette (Darshaan)
1621[2] 2255[4] 2718[12] 3477[5] 4134[5] 4756[5] 5552[4] 6290[5] 7575[8]

Maverik *Michael Dods* 70
2 ch c Iceman—Nouvelle Lune (Fantastic Light (USA))
3316[3] 3923[2] 5594[5] 6488[2]

Mawaakef (IRE) *Kevin Prendergast* 101
2 b c Azamour(IRE) —Al Euro (FR) (Mujtahid (USA))
4175a[4] 6403a[2]

Mawaddah (IRE) *Richard Hannon* a85 76
3 b g Intikhab(USA) —Handsome Anna (IRE) (Bigstone (IRE))
(758) 1452[2] 1734[8] (3081) 5259[7]

Mawatheeq (USA) *Marcus Tregoning* a83 122
5 b h Danzig(USA) —Sarayir (USA) (Mr Prospector (USA))
3068[10]

Mawazin *Ed Dunlop* 25
4 br g Red Ransom(USA) —Injaad (Machiavellian (USA))
4069[11] 4845[8]

Mawjoodah *Clive Brittain* 71
2 ch f Cadeaux Genereux—Isis (USA) (Royal Academy (USA))
2436[5] 2958[8] 7098[14]

Maxijack (IRE) *Gary Brown* a53
3 b g Governor Brown(USA) —Aster Fields (IRE) (Common Grounds)
24[6] 257[6] 362[4] 443[8] 805[9] 932[8]

Maxim Gorky (IRE) *Sir Michael Stoute* 97
3 b c Montjeu(IRE) —Altruiste (USA) (Diesis)
(1186) 1823[3] 3335[6] (5492) 5908[15]

Maxi Moo (IRE) *Geoffrey Harker* 49
3 b g Atraf—Kealbra Lady (Petong)
3776[5] 6624[7] 6966[6]

Maximus Aurelius (IRE) *J Jay* a76 61
5 b g Night Shift(USA) —Dame's Violet (IRE) (Groom Dancer (USA))
83[3] ◆ 361[4] 469[10] 868[7] 1395[11] 1591[12] 2012[3] 2201[5]

Maxios *J E Pease* 104
2 b c Monsun(GER) —Moonlight's Box (USA) (Nureyev (USA))
(6702a)

Maxiyow (IRE) *Bryn Palling* 13
2 b f Royal Applause—Fudge (Polar Falcon (USA))
1263[9] 2330[8] 3562[14]

Maxwell Hawke (IRE) *Tom Dascombe* a15 79
4 br g Rock Of Gibraltar(IRE) —Twice The Ease (Green Desert (USA))
1366[13] 1653[9] 2331[10] 5405[9] 7195[9]

Mayan Flight (IRE) *Richard Whitaker* 49
2 b g Hawk Wing(USA) —Balimaya (IRE) (Barathea (IRE))
3449[9] 4346[8] 5092[8] 5682[9]

Maybe Grace (IRE) *Mrs John Harrington* a83 95
4 b m Hawk Wing(USA) —Close Regards (IRE) (Danehill (USA))
4630a[2] 6006a[7]

Maybe I Will (IRE) *Simon Dow* a52 73
5 b m Hawk Wing(USA) —Canterbury Lace (USA) (Danehill (USA))
202[11]

Maybe I Wont *Lucinda Featherstone* a72 74
5 b g Kyllachy—Surprise Surprise (Robellino (USA))
1277[3] 1920[11] 2511[9] 3377[2] 3707[7] 4168[2] (4498) (5591) 6754[7]

Maybeme *Neville Bycroft* a41 71
4 b m Lujain(USA) —Malvadilla (IRE) (Doyoun)
1751[12] 2343[6] 2739[9] 3177[6] 3496[6] 4120[6] 4449[4] 4946[5] 5681[7] 6262[3] 6649[7] 6890[7] 7147[7]

May Be Some Time *Stuart Kittow* 67
2 ch g Iceman—Let Alone (Warning)
1517[7] 2245[3] 2680[8] 4323[4] 5301[12] 5830[6]

May Burnett (IRE) *B S Rothwell* 50
2 b f Oratorio(IRE) —Ghost Tree (IRE) (Caerleon (USA))
7057[11] 7303[12]

May Chorus (IRE) *Jim Boyle* a63 40
3 b f Night Shift(USA) —Chorus (USA) (Darshaan)
149[6] 346[2] 425[2] 689[4] 809[4] 933[12]

Maydream *Jimmy Fox* a46 45
3 b f Sea Freedom—Maedance (Groom Dancer (USA))
6815[9] 7419[6] 7575[7] 7840[8]

Mayfair Lad *Ed Dunlop* a51
2 ch c Bertolini(USA) —Flower Market (Cadeaux Genereux)
7559[8] 7780[8]

Mayfair Princess *Phil McEntee* a37 65
2 br f Superior Premium—Printsmith (IRE) (Petardia)
(1180) 5036[11] 5921[10] 6311[12] 6645[12] 7016[8]

Mayfair's Future *John Jenkins* a57 57
5 b h High Estate—Riva La Belle (Ron's Victory (USA))
2303[4] 2870[10] 3983[3] 4211[2] 4765[10] 6021[6] 7038[2] 7286[4] 7728[5] 7760[6]

Mayhab *Clive Brittain* 84
2 ch c Cadeaux Genereux—Amazed (Clantime)
1009[7] (2007) 2514[6] 4801[3] 5527[3] 6156[5]

Mayoman (IRE) *Declan Carroll* a64 88
5 b g Namid—America Lontana (FR) (King's Theatre (IRE))
1154[7] (1929) 3761[13] 4947[2] (5023) (5502) 5698[9] (6572)

May's Boy *Mark Usher* a70 58
2 gr c Proclamation(IRE) —Sweet Portia (IRE) (Pennekamp (USA))
3964[11] 4323[3] 5255[12] 5659[8] 5969[2] 6411[6] 7004[13] 7295[3] (7552)

Mays Louise *Brian Baugh* a64 15
6 ch m Sir Harry Lewis(USA) —Maysimp (IRE) (Mac's Imp (USA))
295[9] 545[6]

Mayson *Richard Fahey* 98
2 b c Invincible Spirit(IRE) —Mayleaf (Pivotal)
2936[2] ◆ (3528) 4458[4] ◆ (5094) 5604[2] 6192[6]

Mayta Capac (USA) *David Simcock* a57
4 ch h Thunder Gulch(USA) —Yvecrique (FR) (Epervier Bleu)
82[5] 331[2]

Mayuska (TUR) *A K Aksoy* 59
5 b m Mountain Cat(USA) —Licola (USA) (Crafty Prospector (USA))
5782a[10]

Maywood *Mahmood Al Zarooni* a77 81
2 b c Cape Cross(IRE) —Murrieta (Dockside (USA))
6743[2] ◆ (7036)

Mazagee (FR) *David Lanigan* 74
2 b f Muhtathir—Zafonia (FR) (Zafonic (USA))
5324[5] 6071[2] (6512)

Mazamorra (USA) *Marco Botti* a87 76
3 bb f Orientate(USA) —Mumbo Jumbo (USA) (Kingmambo (USA))
2603[2] (3157) 4098[6] (6372) ◆ 6904[4] 7420[5]

Maze (IRE) *Tony Carroll* a74 91
5 ch g Dr Fong(USA) —Aryadne (Rainbow Quest (USA))
1332[13] 1650[4] 1924[13] (2700) 3863[13] 4968[2] 5480[5] 5889[2] 6503[9] 6987[3] 7488[12]

Mazovian (USA) *Michael Chapman* a68
2 b g E Dubai(USA) —Polish Style (USA) (Danzig (USA))
7692[4] 7802[3] 7893[2] 7954[2] 7982[4]

Mazzola *Milton Bradley* a74 78
4 b g Bertolini(USA) —Elegant Dance (Statoblest)
1547[7] 1799[4] 2021[10] 2166[8] 2589[11] 3255[4] 3722[7] 3994[10] 5471[5] 5697[12] 6206[12]

McCartney (GER) *S Seemar* a73 108
5 b g In The Wings—Messina (GER) (Dashing Blade)
517a[8] 626a[14]

Mcconnell (USA) *Gary Moore* a89 73
5 ch g Petionville(USA) —Warsaw Girl (IRE) (Polish Precedent (USA))
6[5] 231[9] 572[6] 749[7] 908[6] 1346[13] 6260[7] (7474)

Mceldowney *Michael Chapman* a44 45
8 b g Zafonic(USA) —Ayodhya (IRE) (Astronef)
2694[7] 3122[14] 3535[6]

Mcmurdo Sound (IRE) *Gordon Elliott* 51
6 b g Cape Cross(IRE) —Lightstorm (IRE) (Darshaan)
3152[4]

Meandmyshadow *Alan Brown* a21 77
2 ch f Tobougg(IRE) —Queen Jean (Pivotal)
1331[2] (1527) 2082[3] 2436[4] 3051[12] 5187[7] 5476[4] 5939[7] 6719[11] 7087[12]

Mean Lae (IRE) *J S Bolger* a76 83
4 b m Johannesburg(USA) —Plume Rouge (Pivotal)
4524a[11]

Measuring Time *Richard Hannon* 103
2 b c Dubai Destination(USA) —Inchberry (Barathea (IRE))
(3915) (4135) 5306[2] 5746[2] 6560[4] 7236[2]

Mecox Bay (IRE) *Andrew Balding* a63 80
3 b g Noverre(USA) —Birdsong (IRE) (Dolphin Street (FR))
(2812) 3670[3] 4304[3] 5868[13] 6957[7]

Medaille D'Or *Michael Jarvis* a67
2 ch f With Approval(CAN) —Crockadore (USA) (Nijinsky (CAN))
6849[7] 7447[6] 8000[3]

Media Jury *John Wainwright* 40
3 b g Lucky Owners(NZ) —Landofheartsdesire (IRE) (Up And At 'Em)
1029[16] 1483[4] 1987[3] 3228[8] 3287[8] 3663[8] 5548[8] 6896[10]

Media Stars *Robert Johnson* a65 55
5 gr g Green Desert(USA) —Starine (FR) (Mendocino (USA))
2500[13] 2765[8] 2833[2] 3078[7] 3496[8] 4170[4] 4511[9] (4863) 5202[6] 5681[9] 6037[4] 6298[6]

Medicean Man *Jeremy Gask* a103 101
4 ch g Medicean—Kalindi (Efisio)
(992) 1295[8] 1727[9] (1903) ◆ 3193[14] 5302[5] 5702[2] 5911[10] 6564[5]

Medici Brave *Amanda Perrett* a48 57
3 b g Medicean—Valiantly (Anabaa (USA))
1844[14] 2121[5] 4307[11] 4700[7] 5077[14] 5379[10] 5864[7]

Medicinal Compound *Kevin Ryan* 95
3 b g Dr Fong(USA) —Liska's Dance (USA) (Riverman (USA))
5304[2] 5511[14] 6467[13] (6961)

Medici Palace *James Fanshawe* a66 63
3 ch f Medicean—Ice Palace (Polar Falcon (USA))
1621[6] 2434[4] 3080[5] 3604[6]

Medici Pearl *Tim Easterby* a39 95
6 b m Medicean—In Love Again (IRE) (Prince Rupert (FR))
1272[8] 1708[11] 2977[6] 3667[5] 4154[4] (4950) 6327[4] 6749[4] 7097[6]

Medici Time *Tim Easterby* 91
5 gr g Medicean—Pendulum (Pursuit Of Love)
(1364) ◆ 2136[10] (3114) 3446[4] 3828[4] 4510[6] 5308[4] 5742[10] 6142[13] 6981[10]

Mediplomat *Marco Botti* a58 62
2 b c Medicean—Upskittled (Diktat)
2493[9] 3326[8] 4054[5] 5256[3] 6081[9] 7124[5] 7378[5] 7664[5]

Mediterranean Sea (IRE) *John Jenkins* a67 64
4 b m Medecis—High Glider (High Top)
(599) (2230) 2907[10] 4683[2] 5564[4] 6022[2] 7398[2] 7806[3]

Meduse Bleu *S Wattel* a79 79
3 b f Medicean—Marine Bleue (IRE) (Desert Prince (IRE))
7546a[5]

Meeriss (IRE) *D Selvaratnam* a103 101
5 b g Dubai Destination(USA) —Bless The Bride (IRE) (Darshaan)
512a[4] 708a[2] 820a[7]

Meer Royal (FR) *P Demercastel* a78 92
3 b c Meshaheer(USA) —Royal Lights (FR) (Royal Academy (USA))
1254a[8]

Meer Und Wind (GER) *Paul Webber* a59 70
3 b f Xaar—Moneypenny (GER) (Neshad (USA))
4870[2] 5877[11] 6336[8] 6991[9]

Meetings Man (IRE) *Micky Hammond* 76
3 gr g Footstepsinthesand—Missella (IRE) (Danehill (USA))
1362[7] 1422[4] (1866) 2439[3] 2673[2] 3506[4] 4087[3] (4552) 4944[2] 6074[4]

Meezaan (IRE) *John Gosden* a88 110
3 b c Medicean—Varenka (IRE) (Fasliyev (USA))
(1352) ◆ 1687[2] 2159a[5] 3066[8] 4140[5]

Meeznah (USA) *David Lanigan* 115
3 b f Dynaformer(USA) —String Quartet (IRE) (Sadler's Wells (USA))
(2092) 2711[DSQ] ◆ 4178a[4] 5248[4] 5881[3] 6928[7]

Me Fein *Barney Curley* a67 5
6 gr g Desert Prince(IRE) —Attachment (USA) (Trempolino (USA))
(942)

Megalala (IRE) *John Bridger* a59 75
9 b g Petardia—Avionne (Derrylin)
2597[2] (2714) 2894[2] 3512[2] 3589[3] 4055[2] 4295[4] 4657[4] 5552[2] 5828[2] 6322[8] 6668[10] 7167[9]

Megalo Maniac *Richard Fahey* a63 48
7 b g Efisio—Sharanella (Shareef Dancer (USA))
21[8] 142[3] 568[4] 866[9] 912[3] 1142[2] 1723[3] 1998[7] 2378[10]

Mega Mount (IRE) *Ralph Beckett* a66 70
2 b g Acclamation—Changing Partners (Rainbow Quest (USA))
3126[3] 3555[4] 3961[8] 6162[3] 6695[4] (7118)

Meglio Ancora *Jonathan Portman* 81
3 ch g Best Of The Bests(IRE) —May Fox (Zilzal (USA))
1502[9] 2079[12] 2717[2] 3594[5] 4573[6] 6282[6] 6639[10]

Mehendi (IRE) *Brian Ellison* a67 60
4 b g Indian Danehill(IRE) —Wedding Cake (IRE) (Groom Dancer (USA))
(1) 401[4] 1113[12] 1277[7] 1576[10] 1828[2]

Meia Noite *Chris Wall* 64
3 b f Tobougg(IRE) —Executive Lady (Night Shift (USA))
4966[4] 6060[2] 6420[3] 7006[12]

Meikle Barfil *Milton Bradley* a57 53
8 b g Compton Place—Oare Sparrow (Night Shift (USA))
77[6] 178[5] (271) 369[5] 561[9] 774[7] 1234[6] 1391[3] 1598[7] 2720[6]

Meirig's Dream (IRE) *Natalie Lloyd-Beavis* a63 60
4 b g Golan(IRE) —Women In Love (IRE) (Danehill (USA))
1755[3] 3865[6]

Meisho Beluga (JPN) *Kaneo Ikezoe* 115
5 gr m French Deputy(USA) —Papago (IRE) (Sadler's Wells (USA))
7460a[2] 7615a[6]

Mejd (IRE) *Mick Channon* a78 87
3 b c Desert Style(IRE) —Rainstone (Rainbow Quest (USA))
533[4] 825[3] 950[2] 1240[2] 1608[3] (2025) 2324[13] 2737[7] 3208[2] (3661) (3899) 4112[5] 4603[12] 5236[5]

Mekong Melody (IRE) *Roger L Attfield* a79 103
5 b m Cape Cross(IRE) —Nini Princesse (IRE) (Niniski (USA))
6950a[10]

Mekong Miss *Derek Shaw* a63 52
4 ch m Mark Of Esteem(IRE) —Missouri (Charnwood Forest (IRE))
(210) 621[13] 1262[12] 2303[10] 2870[11] 7315[14] 7429[7] 7508[8]

Melancholy Hill (IRE) *Paul Cole* a53 38
3 b f Marju(IRE) —Vyatka (Lion Cavern (USA))
5692[16] 6248[10] 7021[8] 7484[4]

Melange (USA) *George Charlton* a69 37
4 b g Alphabet Soup(USA) —Garendare (Vacarme (USA))
7284[13]

Melbury *Paul Howling* a54
2 b f Diktat—Lovely Lyca (Night Shift (USA))
5719[8] 6161[5] 6575[5] ◆ 6902[12] 7497[9]

Melinoise *Rae Guest* a50 35
3 b f Tobougg(IRE) —Carollan (IRE) (Marju (IRE))
2632[10] 3443[9] 4229[9] 4683[10] 5164[12] 6660[10]

Melkatant *Neville Bycroft* 53
4 b m Rock City—Change Of Image (Spectrum (IRE))
2655[7] 2833[5] 3597[7] 4170[6] 4484[4] 4863[8] 6037[2]

Mellifera *Walter Swinburn* a68 73
3 b f Leporello(IRE) —Christina's Dream (Spectrum (IRE))
1058[5] ◆ 1640[3] 2042[10] 2844[4] (3464) 3739[8] 4479[3] 5113[2] 5664[7] 6992[6]

Mellon Martini (USA) *A De Royer-Dupre* 101
3 b c Sadler's Wells(USA) —Sand Springs (USA) (Dynaformer (USA))
3703a[2] 5135a[4]

Melodize *William Muir* a37 71
2 ch f Iceman—Rhapsodize (Halling (USA))
1577[5] 1800[2] 2176[8] (3126) 4600[5] 4688[6] 5111[8] 5581[8] 6271[10] 7017[11]

Melody Belle (IRE) *Tobias B P Coles* a16 45
2 gr f Verglas(IRE) —Reside (IRE) (Montjeu (IRE))
6803[12] 7232[15] 7470[12]

Melody Dawn (USA) *C Laffon-Parias* 89
2 b f Tale Of The Cat(USA) —Muskoka Dawn (USA) (Miswaki (USA))
2917a[11]

Melody In The Mist (FR) *David Barron* a52 77
3 b f Intikhab(USA) —She's All Class (USA) (Rahy (USA))
2450[4] 2768[8] (3682) 4349[6] 5501[5] 6537[7]

Melt (IRE) *Michael Easterby* a65 61
5 b m Intikhab(USA) —Kindle (Selkirk (USA))
27[9] 110[8] 270[7] 467[12]

Melting Bob (USA) *Dr Jon Scargill* a51
4 rg m Johannesburg(USA) —Dancingonice (USA) (Robyn Dancer (USA))
291[8] 768[13] 4237[8] 5962[10]

Melundy *Linda Perratt* 65
3 b f Best Of The Bests(IRE) —Nova Zembla (Young Ern)
1402[6] 3111[2] ◆ 3663[6] 4826[8] 5480[4] 5601[10]

Memen (IRE) *Paul Cole* 90
2 gr c Verglas(IRE) —Pride Of My Heart (Lion Cavern (USA))
1351[4] (2077) 2918[4] (3872) 4539[9] 5257[4] 6733[5]

Memimajic *Chris Fairhurst* 47
2 b f Distant Music(USA) —Abbaleva (Shaddad (USA))
3058[8] 6070[7] 7404[8]

Meml *James Bethell* a47 44
4 b m Mark Of Esteem(IRE) —Matisse (Shareef Dancer (USA))
227[5] 705[7] 1887[9] 7229[9]

Memorabilia *Mark Johnston* a67 70
2 b g Dansili—Sentimental Value (USA) (Diesis)
2980[9] 3433[3] 4054[8] 4580[6] 5452[11] 5807[5] 6163[8]

Memorial Maniac (USA) *Larry Demeritte* a94 106
5 b g Lear Fan(USA) —Enlightening (USA) (Cozzene (USA))
6236a[5] 6951a[9]

Memory (IRE) *Richard Hannon* 111
2 b f Danehill Dancer(IRE) —Nausicaa (USA) (Diesis)
(2223) ◆ (3141) (3792) ◆ 5570a[6]

Memory Cloth *A Fabre* 106
3 b c Cape Cross(IRE) —Gossamer (Sadler's Wells (USA))
1985a[6]

Memory Lane *Sir Mark Prescott Bt* a69 56
2 b f With Approval(CAN) —Miss Prism (Niniski (USA))
4695[10] 5029[8] 5369[6] 6302[6] 6453[5]

Memphis Man *David Evans* a57 81
7 b g Bertolini(USA) —Something Blue (Petong)
1267[7] 1762[10] 2113[7] 2399[7] (2896) 3037[10] 3430[8] 3675[6] 3833[5] 3898[6] ◆ 4225[4] 4542[5] 4834[7] 5076[5] 5473[5] 5889[7] 6455[9] 7007[10] 7738[4] 7882[2] 7973[4]

Menadati (USA) *David Lanigan* 76
2 b g More Than Ready(USA) —Ramatuelle (CHI) (Jeune Homme (USA))
3631[8] ◆ 4247[3] (4940) 5374[4]

Mendip (USA) *Saeed Bin Suroor* a111
3 br c Harlan's Holiday(USA) —Well Spring (USA) (Coronado's Quest (USA))
(510a) (796a) ◆ 1023a[3]

Menediva *Lawrence Mullaney* 42
3 b f Danbird(AUS) —Princess Ismene (Sri Pekan (USA))
3111[8] 3286[7]

Menestrol (FR) *D Prod'Homme* a69 102
8 ch h Dyhim Diamond(IRE) —Magaletta (FR) (Galetto (FR))
272a[10]

Menha *Mahmood Al Zarooni* 69
2 ch f Dubawi(IRE) —Tessara (GER) (Big Shuffle (USA))
5324[3]

Meniscus *Valentine Donoghue* 14
2 ch f Kheleyf(USA) —Howards Heroine (IRE) (Danehill Dancer (IRE))
6240[7] 6566[14]

Mensajera De La Luz (CHI) *J Barton* a78
4 ch m Election Day(IRE) —Cuenta Conmigo (CHI) (Gallantsky (USA))
514a[12] 709a[7]

Mensonge (IRE) *Robert Collet* 39
2 b f Key Of Luck(USA) —Trust In Love (IRE) (Exit To Nowhere (USA))
5063a[9]

Mental Reservation (USA) *Michael Quinlan* a53
3 bb g Dayjur(USA) —Theycallmecharlie (USA) (Charlie Barley (USA))
274[6] 374[8]

Meow (IRE) *David Wachman* a81 106
2 b f Storm Cat(USA) —Airwave (Air Express (IRE))
3070[2] 5907[12]

Meracus (IRE) *S Botti* 100
2 b c Kheleyf(USA) —Miss Progressive (IRE) (Common Grounds)
6762a[4]

Merals Choice *Jim Boyle* a54
3 b f Night Shift(USA) —Mena (Blakeney)
147[4] 321[4] 583[4] 805[5] 7889[8]

Mercers Row *Noel Wilson* 69
3 b g Bahamian Bounty—Invincible (Slip Anchor)
1464[4] 1811[7] 2426[11] (3111) 4016[4] 5735[3]

Merchant Marine (USA) *Doug Watson* a95
6 b g Tiznow(USA) —Head East (USA) (Gone West (USA))
337a[8] 436a[7]

Merchant Of Dubai *Alan Swinbank* a103 107
5 b g Dubai Destination(USA) —Chameleon (Green Desert (USA))
(1031) 1560a[2]

Merchant Of Medici *William Muir* a86 87
3 b g Medicean—Regal Rose (Danehill (USA))
1934[4] 2618[7] (3359) 3771[3] (4365) 4963[3] 6197[6] (6800) 7012[3]

Mercoliano *Marco Botti* a76 72
3 b g Medicean—Mega (IRE) (Petardia)
(664) ◆ 1452[4] 1969[5] (4383) 4718[2]

Mercy Street *Nigel Tinkler* 26
2 b g Avonbridge—Satya (USA) (Cozzene (USA))
2202[6] 2654[11] 2939[16] 3175[8]

Meridian Magic (USA) *Nicholas Zito* a83
2 b c Mineshaft(USA) —Copelan's Angel (USA) (Copelan (USA))
6756a[5]

Merjaan *Clive Brittain* a72
2 b c Iceman—Entrap (USA) (Phone Trick (USA))
1065[5] 3517[4]

Merlins Dreams *Shaun Harris* a27
7 b g Dansili—Red Leggings (Shareef Dancer (USA))
2854[13] 3369[F]

Merrion Tiger (IRE) *George Foster* a74 69
5 ch g Choisir(AUS) —Akita (IRE) (Foxhound (USA))
376[2] 720[4] 1113[15] 3496[9] 3760[8]

Merrjanah *Clive Brittain* 50
2 b f Diktat—Aberdovey (Mister Baileys)
1375[8] 2312[6] 6154[12]

Merrqaad *Marcus Tregoning* a79
3 ch c Haafhd—Abundant (Zafonic (USA))
592[3] ◆ (825)

Merrymadcap (IRE) *Matthew Salaman* a79 74
8 b g Lujain(USA) —Carina Clare (Slip Anchor)
3473[6] 4579[15] 4794[5] 4958[9] 7038[3] 7663[4] 7732[5] 7878[5]

Mesa Marauder *Marco Botti* a91 93
6 b g Indian Ridge—White Heat (Last Tycoon)
324[5] 738[7] 1962[5]

Mesbaah (IRE) *Richard Fahey* a86 65
6 b g Noverre(USA) —Deyaajeer (USA) (Dayjur (USA))
198[9]

Messenger (AUS) *Anthony Cummings* 94
5 bb m Choisir(AUS) —Angel In Disguise (NZ) (Sky Chase (NZ))
17

Metal Bender (NZ) *Chris Waller* 120
5 b g Danasinga(AUS) —Jacqwin (AUS) (Bluebird (USA))
6947a[8]

Metal Guru *Reg Hollinshead* a69 70
6 ch m Ishiguru(USA) —Gemtastic (Tagula (IRE))
243[8] 525[5] 778[8]

Methaaly (IRE) *Michael Mullineaux* a84 84
7 b g Red Ransom(USA) —Santorini (USA) (Spinning World (USA))
192[11] 535[3] 679[3] 722[7] 924[6] 1192[7] 1365[3] 1650[9] 2123[4] 2310[4] 2578[7] 3201[3] (3358) 3435[8] 3902[7] 4354[2] 4558[12] 5500[8] 5920[6] 6207[6] 6714[5] 7239[5] (7332) 7446[5] 7526[2] 7573[3] (7702)

Methayel (IRE) *Clive Brittain* 67
2 bb f Araafa(IRE) —First Breeze (USA) (Woodman (USA))
3156[2] ◆

Metropolitan Chief *Paul Burgoyne* a57 41
6 b g Compton Place—Miss Up N Go (Gorytus (USA))
235[9] 320[9] 368[3] 561[6] 693[5] (866) 976[7] 1236[2] 2184[10] 6329[10] 6848[3] 7249[5] 7882[5] 8035[10]

Metropolitan Man (USA) *Wesley A Ward* a97 59
2 b g Hook And Ladder(USA) —Hasty Cat (USA) (Tabasco Cat (USA))
3051[9]

Mexican Deb *William Muir* 67
3 b f Red Ransom(USA) —Artisia (IRE) (Peintre Celebre (USA))
3738[5] 4397[7] 4997[5]

Mexican Jay (USA) *Bryan Smart* a67 56
4 b m Elusive Quality(USA) —Mistle Song (Nashwan (USA))
4407[6] 6115[10] (6662) 7330[3] 7398[11]

Mey Blossom *Richard Whitaker* a64 85
5 ch m Captain Rio—Petra Nova (First Trump)
1270[9] 1754[8] (2087) 2396[U] 2791[3] (3064) (3540) 3809[6] 4243[2] (4583) (4942) 5512[11] 5941[4] 6723[10]

Meydan Dubai (IRE) *John Best* a68 71
5 b g Alzao(USA) —Rorkes Drift (IRE) (Royal Abjar (USA))
12[5] 361[8] 395[6] 586[6] 613[5] 4756[4] 5146[5] 5833[7] 6633[10] 6992[12] 7250[2] 7380[7] 7640[7]

Meyyal (USA) *Mrs Sarah Dawson* a72 71
4 b h War Chant(USA) —Tamgeed (USA) (Woodman (USA))
7078a[14]

Mezarat (ITY) *Stuart Williams* a74 55
5 ch h Dream Well(FR) —Dayara (GER) (Kornado)
7184[7] 7397[4] 7570[2]

Mezzotinto (FR) *H-A Pantall* a55 69
3 b g Fairly Ransom(USA) —Montgarri (FR) (Johann Quatz (FR))
7959a[8]

Mharadono (GER) *P Hirschberger* 93
7 b h Sharp Prod(USA) —Monalind (GER) (Park Romeo)
1251a[15] 2559a[13]

Mhilu (IRE) *John O'Shea* 64
8 b g Rock Hopper—Moohono (IRE) (Roselier (FR))
3256[5]

Miacarla *Hugh McWilliams* a37 47
7 b m Forzando—Zarzi (IRE) (Suave Dancer (USA))
532[5] 723[11] 848[7] 1068[11] 1598[12] 1723[13] 1965[5] 3946[9] 4542[7] 5422[5] 5502[9] 6246[10] 7148[12]

Mia Madonna *Brian Meehan* 70
2 b f Motivator—Musique Magique (IRE) (Mozart (IRE))
5489[2] 6155[12] 6469[2] 6979[13]

Miami Gator (IRE) *Mrs K Burke* a84 79
3 ch g Titus Livius(FR) —Lovere (St Jovite (USA))
127[2] (566) 792[3] 812[3] 1810[4] 2289[7] 2725[2] 3413[4] 3666[2] 4337[5] (4581) (4646) 4866[3] (5353) (5852) 6144[7] 7842[2] 8022[2]

Mi Amor (SWI) *H-A Pantall* 86
2 b c Feliciano(SWI) —Mescalina (IRE) (Brief Truce (USA))
(4274a)

Mia's Boy *Chris Dwyer* a110 113
6 b h Pivotal—Bint Zamayem (IRE) (Rainbow Quest (USA))
883[2] ◆ 1008[6] 1377[2] 1904[2] 2539[9] 3069[13] 6349[22] 7083[4] 7234[5] 7430[4] 7689[6]

Mibar (USA) *F De Sanctis* 86
4 ch h Refuse To Bend(IRE) —Bow River Gold (Rainbow Quest (USA))
1712a[6]

Mica Mika (IRE) *Richard Fahey* 76
2 ch g Needwood Blade—Happy Talk (IRE) (Hamas (IRE))
1198[2] 1517[5] 1964[3] 2836[2] (3175) (4242) 4984[6] 5597[9] (6513)

Michael Collins (IRE) *Graham Smith* a66 27
4 b g Oasis Dream—West Virginia (IRE) (Gone West (USA))
19[9] 1148[10] 1583[7]

Michael Laskey *Rod Millman* a50 49
4 b g Lujain(USA) —Enchanted Ocean (USA) (Royal Academy (USA))
229[11]

Michael's Nook *Stuart Kittow* a46 60
3 b g Intikhab(USA) —Mysterious Plans (IRE) (Last Tycoon)
980[9] 1260[10] 2122[6] 2844[8] 3479[3] 4732[5] 5469[4] 5997[5] 6672[13]

Michelle (IRE) *Paddy Butler* a48 24
4 b m Marju(IRE) —Bel Sole (ITY) (Spectrum (IRE))
3264[11] 4132[9] 4681[14]

Mick Is Back *George Margarson* a53 65
6 b g Diktat—Classy Cleo (IRE) (Mujadil (USA))
1078[4]

Micksgirl *Ted Haynes*
4 ch m Loup Sauvage(USA) —My Old China (Shaab)
2182[12]

Micky Mac (IRE) *Colin Teague* a64 69
6 b g Lend A Hand—Gazette It Tonight (Merdon Melody)
(1598) 1805[9] 3064[8] 3687[3] 3946[4] 4487[2] 4820[2] 5502[8] 5684[4] 6295[9] 6679[13] 7193[11]

Micky P *Stuart Williams* a72 68
3 gr g Dr Fong(USA) —Carmela Owen (Owington)
1442[6] 2634[3] (2962) (4998) 5890[6] 7320[4]

Micky's Bird *Richard Guest* a28 48
3 ch f Needwood Blade—Silver Peak (FR) (Sillery (USA))
909[7] 998[10] 1145[6]

Micky's Knock Off (IRE) *Richard Guest* a74 76
3 b g Camacho—La Grace (Lahib (USA))
478[4] 662[3] 788[2] 886[5] 1057[2] (1483) 1765[2]

Mickys Mate *Shaun Harris* a33 39
5 b g Choisir(AUS) —Adept (Efisio)
10[11] 70[6] 116[3] 296[9] 319[11]

Microlight *Tim Easterby* a59 55
2 b g Sleeping Indian—Skytrial (USA) (Sky Classic (CAN))
3964[5] 4645[10] 5040[6] 5434[11] 5682[6] 7394[2] (7497) 7630[6]

Midas Moment *William Muir* a71 45
2 b f Danehill Dancer(IRE) —Special Moment (IRE) (Sadler's Wells (USA))
7231[13] (7447)

Midas Touch *A P O'Brien* 121
3 b c Galileo(IRE) —Approach (Darshaan)
(1951a) 2746[5] 3491a[2] 5185[2] 5945[2] 6612a[17]

Midas Way *Patrick Chamings* a81 84
10 ch g Halling(USA) —Arietta's Way (IRE) (Darshaan)
3195[13]

Midday *Henry Cecil* 124
4 b m Oasis Dream—Midsummer (Kingmambo (USA))
2055[2] (4575) ◆ (5248) (6013a) 7343a[2]

Middle Club *Richard Hannon* a88 104
3 b f Fantastic Light(USA) —Anna Oleanda (IRE) (Old Vic)
(973) 1496a[2] 2575a[2] 3101[5] 5138a[3] 5881[10] 6551a[4] 6886[3] 7349[10]

Middlemarch (IRE) *Jim Goldie* a64 77
10 ch g Grand Lodge(USA) —Blanche Dubois (Nashwan (USA))
1098[6] 2349[4] 2761[6]

Midfielder (USA) *John Gosden* a78 71
3 ch c Smart Strike(CAN) —Quiet Weekend (USA) (Quiet American (USA))
(667) 1018[4] 2254[12] 2717[4] 6289[9]

Midget *Declan Carroll* a34 61
3 b f Invincible Spirit(IRE) —Sharp Mode (USA) (Diesis)
1175[5] 1811[11] 2217[4] 2648[12] 4194[8] 4406[3] 4826[2] 4982[6] 5152[10] 5548[6] 6656[11]

Midlothian (IRE) *Mahmood Al Zarooni* 63
2 b c Monsun(GER) —Sunray Superstar (Nashwan (USA))
7179[6]

Mid Mon Lady (IRE) *H Rogers* a97 96
5 br m Danetime(IRE) —Shining Desert (IRE) (Green Desert (USA))
1560a[4] 2037a[9] 3492a[4] 4463a[2] 5568a[8] 6548a[3]

Midnight Bay *David Evans* a65 66
4 br g Domedriver(IRE) —Serriera (FR) (Highest Honor (FR))
228[7] 407[2] 479[6] 591[7]

Midnight Caller *John Gosden* 89
2 br f Dansili—Midnight Air (USA) (Green Dancer (USA))
5066[2] ◆ (5633) ◆ 5910[7]

Midnight Fantasy *Rae Guest* a76 81
4 b m Oasis Dream—Midnight Shift (IRE) (Night Shift (USA))
2475[5] 2904[5] 3567[3] 3779[7] 4806[9] 5627[3] 6460[10]

Midnight Feast *Peter Winkworth* a72 82
2 b g Ishiguru(USA) —Prince's Feather (IRE) (Cadeaux Genereux)
2680[10] 3332[2] ◆ 3785[3]

Midnight M *Rae Guest* 36
3 b f Green Desert(USA) —Midnight Shift (IRE) (Night Shift (USA))
3125[7] 4222[6] 4835[7] 5162[8] 5469[8] 6093[10]

Midnight Maasai *Clive Cox* a73 60
2 b g Royal Applause—Lady McNair (Sheikh Albadou)
5032[6] 7020[3] 7385[6]

Midnight Martini *Tim Easterby* 98
3 b f Night Shift(USA) —Shaken And Stirred (Cadeaux Genereux)
1523[2] 2058[2] 2978[17] 4653[7] 5095[17] 6000[4] 6509[2]

Midnight Moon *Saeed Bin Suroor*
2 b c Singspiel(IRE) —Carisolo (Dubai Millennium)
6953[13]

Midnight Rider (IRE) *Chris Wall* 75
2 b c Red Ransom(USA) —Foreplay (IRE) (Lujain (USA))
2701[4] 4131[2] 4568[2] 5761[2]

Midnight Strider (IRE) *Tom Dascombe* a67 16
4 br g Golan(IRE) —Danish Gem (Danehill (USA))
189[2] 4547[8] (7862) 8008[9]

Midnight Trader (IRE) *Paul D'Arcy* 55
2 b g Iffraaj—Nilassiba (Daylami (IRE))
6153[13] 6878[8]

Midshipman (USA) *Saeed Bin Suroor* a118
4 ch h Unbridled's Song(USA) —Fleet Lady (USA) (Avenue Of Flags (USA))
338a[4] (710a)

Midwestern (USA) *Bryan Smart* 74
3 bb g Tiznow(USA) —She's Enough (USA) (Exploit (USA))
4404[5] (4710) 5407[12] 6112[11]

Mid Wicket (USA) *Mouse Hamilton-Fairley* a57 51
4 b g Strong Hope(USA) —Sunday Bazaar (USA) (Nureyev (USA))
99[2] 184[6] 354[5] 539[7] 2230[8] 5873[3] 6273[8]

Miereveld *Brian Ellison* a59 53
3 b g Red Ransom(USA) —Mythic (Zafonic (USA))
128[7] ◆ 267[6] 374[9] 570[6] 3758[6] 3951[5] 4448[3] 5423[8] 6571[13] 7147[4] (7909)

Mighty Aphrodite *Olivia Maylam* a56 63
3 b f Observatory(USA) —Sahara Rose (Green Desert (USA))
1685[4] 2609[5] 3620[8] 6898[8] 7192[8] 7563[8] 7645[6]

Mighty Clarets (IRE) *Richard Fahey* a76 69
3 br g Whipper(USA) —Collected (IRE) (Taufan (USA))
(1810) 2422[4] 2993[5] 3612[5] 4128[3] 7377[8] 7663[3] (7788) ◆ (8008)

Mighty High (FR) *J Moore* 111
4 b g Peintre Celebre(USA) —Bernimixa (FR) (Linamix (FR))
7851a[7]

Mighty Mambo *Jane Chapple-Hyam* a65 74
3 b g Fantastic Light(USA) —Mambo's Melody (Kingmambo (USA))
1386[7] 4062[3] 5522[3] 6132[14] 6623[11]

Mighty Mover (IRE) *Bryn Palling* a59 57
8 ch g Bahhare(USA) —Ericeira (IRE) (Anita's Prince)
34[7] 665[8]

Mijanou *Alan McCabe* a38
2 ch f Bertolini(USA) —Bardot (Efisio)
5921[8]

Mijhaar *Michael Jarvis* 77
2 b c Shirocco(GER) —Jathaabeh (Nashwan (USA))
6689[2]

Mik *Dr Jeremy Naylor*
4 b g Baryshnikov(AUS) —Daphne's Doll (IRE) (Polish Patriot (USA))
1067[7]

Mikhail Glinka (IRE) *Gary Moore* a101 107
3 b c Galileo(IRE) —Lady Karr (Mark Of Esteem (IRE))
1414a[3] (3145) 6389[5]

Mikos (FR) *Robert Collet* 73
10 b g Sicyos(USA) —Sex Pistol (FR) (Pistolet Bleu (IRE))
(459a)

Mildoura (FR) *Laura Mongan* a93 93
5 b m Sendawar(IRE) —Miliana (IRE) (Polar Falcon (USA))
81[3] 1472[3] 2549[2] 3462[2] 4624[9] 7206[12]

Miles Above (AUS) *Denis Daffy* 89
5 b g Good Journey(USA) —Grand Prospect (AUS) (Flying Spur (AUS))
7032a[14]

Miles Gloriosus (USA) *Maria Rita Salvioni* a108 106
7 b h Repriced(USA) —Treasure Coast (CAN) (Foolish Pleasure (USA))
6764a[7]

Militante (IRE) *Y De Nicolay* 91
2 b f Johannesburg(USA) —Maggie Jordan (USA) (Fusaichi Pegasus (USA))
4611a[3] 5322a[6] 7975a[0]

Military Call *Alistair Whillans* 74
3 b g Royal Applause—Trump Street (First Trump)
1869[12] 2296[6] 2762[6] 3371[5] 3948[5] 4864[4] 5201[3] (5337)

Milk Maid (IRE) *Bill Turner* 40
2 b f Millkom—La Fija (USA) (Dixieland Band (USA))
3603[6]

Millden *Henry Candy* a56 67
3 b g Compton Place—Pretty Poppy (Song)
3635[4] 4385[4] 4835[2] 5668[3] 7166[4]

Milldown Magic *Rod Millman* 71
2 ch c Lucky Story(USA) —Barnacla (IRE) (Bluebird (USA))
1695[5] 2048[4] 5914[8] 6419[6] 6989[P] (Dead)

Millet (FR) *E Galli*
2 ch c Panis(USA) —Magnific Fitz (ARG) (Fitzcarraldo (ARG))
7849a[8]

Millfields Dreams *Patrick Leech* a74 76
11 b g Dreams End—Millfields Lady (Sayf El Arab (USA))
658[5] 747[3] 1179[5] (1323) 1530[4] ◆ 1841[6] 1875[6] 2298[3] 2560[10]

Millie Mops *Ian Williams*
3 ch f Where Or When(IRE) —Sheila's Secret (IRE) (Bluebird (USA))
5610[8] 6124[8]

Millies Dancer (IRE) *Michael Quinlan* 39
2 b f Noverre(USA) —Lady Miletrian (IRE) (Barathea (IRE))
4332[7] 4550[9] 5558[4] 6072[6] 6878[12]

Millies Folly *Declan Carroll* 69
2 ch f Araafa(IRE) —Basemah (FR) (Lemon Drop Kid (USA))
3237[9] 4368[4] 4747[3] 4899[2] 6513[6] 6568[18] 6920[4] 7085[12] 7296[11]

Million Seller (USA) *H Graham Motion* a89
4 bb m A.P. Indy(USA) —Million Gift (JPN) (Sunday Silence (USA))
7339a^{12}

Milly Filly *Amy Weaver* 57
2 gr f Tobougg(IRE) —Millymix (FR) (Linamix (FR))
3657^{13} 4286^{9} 6360^{5} 7004^{9}

Millyluvstobouggie *Clive Cox* a77 77
2 b f Tobougg(IRE) —Milly's Lass (Mind Games)
2176^{2} ◆ 2407^{4} 3295^{6} (4423) (4927) 5261^{3} 5725^{2} 6445^{2} 6769^{2}

Milnagavie *Richard Hannon* a72 78
3 ch f Tobougg(IRE) —Abyaan (IRE) (Ela-Mana-Mou)
1302^{7} 1696^{3} 2893^{10} (3513) (6424) ◆

Milne Bay (IRE) *David Simcock* a79 78
5 b g Tagula(IRE) —Fiction (Dominion)
102^{5} ◆ 287^{11} 579^{6} 924^{8} 1300^{7}

Milord Des Aigles (FR) *Mme C Barande-Barbe*
2 gr g Martaline—Lady For A Day (FR) (Kendor (FR))
7974a^{10}

Milton Of Campsie *John Balding* a54 79
5 ch m Medicean—La Caprice (USA) (Housebuster (USA))
1365^{5} ◆ 1924^{8} 2073^{2} 2528^{6} 2818^{10} 3622^{2} 7180^{3} 7399^{7}

Milwaukee Appeal (CAN) *Scott H Fairlie* a111 56
4 b m Milwaukee Brew(USA) —Appealing Forum (USA) (Open Forum (USA))
7344a^{8}

Mimi's Princess *Kevin Ryan* 32
2 b f Sleeping Indian—Security Interest (USA) (Belong To Me (USA))
3087^{13} 3362^{6}

Minch Man *Mrs K Burke* 80
2 b g Majestic Missile(IRE) —Inchcoonan (Emperor Jones (USA))
1294^{5} (2238) 3504^{3} 4097^{8} 5604^{7}

Minder *Jonathan Portman* a45 63
4 b g Mind Games—Exotic Forest (Dominion)
983^{13} 1635^{6} 2006^{3} 2952^{3} 3294^{8} 4328^{3}

Mindsia (FR) *C Boutin* 58
2 b f Panis(USA) —Mindset (IRE) (Vettori (IRE))
5063a^{7}

Mind The Monarch *Roger Teal* a56 58
3 b f Mind Games—Enford Princess (Pivotal)
122^{4} 357^{4} 581^{8} 4790^{8} 7299^{11} 7477^{6} 7547^{3} (7783) 7882^{7}

Miner's Reserve (USA) *Nicholas Zito* a109
3 b c Mineshaft(USA) —Royal Reserves (USA) (Forty Niner (USA))
4613a^{2} 5544a^{7}

Mine That Bird (USA) *D Wayne Lukas* a121 99
4 b g Birdstone(USA) —Mining My Own (USA) (Smart Strike (CAN))
4855a^{5} 5780a^{7} 7365a^{10}

Minety Lass *Michael Appleby* 33
2 b f Needwood Blade—Mary Jane (Tina's Pet)
3913^{4} 4921^{7}

Ming Master (FR) *William Haggas* a83
3 b g Tobougg(IRE) —Sakura Queen (IRE) (Woodman (USA))
(143)

Ming Meng (IRE) *Michael Bell* 84
3 bb f Intikhab(USA) —Petula (Petong)
1275^{P} 4251^{8} 4966^{2} (5359) 6221^{3} 6438^{5} 6963^{3}

Mingun Bell (USA) *Henry Cecil* a92 82
3 b g Mingun(USA) —Miss Tippins (USA) (Squadron Leader (USA))
2117^{15} 2979^{5} 4068^{6} 5083^{3} 5540^{4} 6276^{3} 6677^{10}

Mini Bon Bon *Alan Bailey* a58 60
2 ch f Kyllachy—Dahshah (Mujtahid (USA))
1223^{4} 1294^{7} 1800^{5} (2300) 3598^{7} 4436^{4} 4615^{7} 5354^{4} 5434^{5} 5862^{3} 6035^{9} 6576^{6} 7016^{6} 7301^{6} 7423^{10} 7777^{8} 7983^{7}

Minikin (IRE) *Hughie Morrison* a78 76
3 b f Montjeu(IRE) —Discreet Brief (IRE) (Darshaan)
3080^{4} ◆ 4115^{4} 4661^{3} (5208) 5467^{5} 6055^{4} 6480^{3}

Mini Max *Brendan Duke* a61 58
3 b f Tobougg(IRE) —Maxilla (IRE) (Lahib (USA))
1158^{7} 1537^{5} 2480^{3} 2780^{3} 3525^{6} 3716^{6} 5379^{9}

Minimusic *Bryn Palling* a35
3 b f Distant Music(USA) —Minette (Bishop Of Cashel)
3741^{0} 664^{7}

Mi Nina Castagna *Paul Green* 37
3 ch f Reset(AUS) —Bettys Pride (Lion Cavern (USA))
1401^{5}

Mini's Destination *John Holt* 48
2 b f Dubai Destination(USA) —Heather Mix (Linamix (FR))
3729^{8} 4474^{8} 5630^{5}

Ministry *John Best* a55 56
2 b c Iceman—Choirgirl (Unfuwain (USA))
6158^{9} 6497^{9} 7020^{8}

Miniyamba (IRE) *John Dunlop* a68 69
3 b f Sadler's Wells(USA) —Atlantide (USA) (Southern Halo (USA))
1696^{5} 2893^{11} 4223^{2} 4990^{3} 5522^{4} 5963^{13} 7388^{2} (7538)

Minnie McGinn (USA) *Jane Chapple-Hyam* 11
3 rg f Maria's Mon(USA) —Reluctant Diva (Sadler's Wells (USA))
4107^{10}

Minortransgression (USA) *David Evans* a74 59
3 ch g Yes It's True(USA) —Casting Pearls (USA) (Fusaichi Pegasus (USA))
180^{4} 274^{3} 424^{2} 1927^{13} 3728^{4} 4325^{11} 4738^{4} 5182^{5} 5648^{3} 7613^{8} 7833^{2} 7988^{3}

Minor Vamp (IRE) *Richard Hannon* a60 47
4 b m Hawk Wing(USA) —Miss Champagne (FR) (Bering)
1614^{4}

Mint Imperial (IRE) *Amy Weaver* a30 21
2 b g Diamond Green(FR) —Imperialist (IRE) (Imperial Frontier (USA))
7058^{15} 7452^{10}

Mintoe *Jimmy O'Reilly* a58 63
4 b g Noverre(USA) —West One (Gone West (USA))
116^{7}

Minturno (USA) *Ann Duffield* a53 73
4 b g Ten Most Wanted(USA) —Panama Jane (USA) (Perrault)
853^{10} 2293^{6} 2699^{3} 3200^{2} 3357^{3} 4121^{3} 4486^{2} 4670^{6} 5299^{3} 5684^{6} 6295^{17}

Mint Whip (IRE) *Richard Hannon* a64 63
3 b f Whipper(USA) —Aminata (Glenstal (USA))
24^{4} 310^{4} (638) 933^{3} 1058^{4}

Minus Tolerance *Sam Davison* a31 34
2 b f Monsieur Bond(IRE) —Julia Domna (Dominion)
2413^{7} 3349^{11} 4277^{5} 4788^{5} 5268^{5} 5581^{13} 6411^{8} 6901^{0}

Mirabella (IRE) *Richard Hannon* a83 79
3 b f Motivator—Anayid (A.P. Indy (USA))
1850^{10} 5375^{11} 5988^{4} 6449^{12}

Mirabile Visu *Heather Main* a41 67
2 b f Diktat—Parting Gift (Cadeaux Genereux)
2413^{8} 5381^{10} 6441^{4} 6875^{15}

Miracle Wish (IRE) *Ralph Beckett* a35 17
3 b f One Cool Cat(USA) —Bentley's Bush (IRE) (Barathea (IRE))
997^{9} 1825^{7}

Miranda's Girl (IRE) *Thomas Cleary* a89 96
5 b m Titus Livius(FR) —Ela Tina (IRE) (Ela-Mana-Mou)
4524a^{14} 7358a^{8}

Mi Regalo *Andrew Balding* a76 43
2 b g Cadeaux Genereux—Lloc (Absalom)
2048^{9} (7999)

Mirpour (IRE) *Paul Murphy* a22 15
11 b g Turtle Island(IRE) —Mirana (IRE) (Ela-Mana-Mou)
3^{6}

Mirradores *William Muir* 64
2 b c Aussie Rules(USA) —Fiina (Most Welcome)
3735^{9} 5440^{4}

Mirrored *Tim Easterby* a86 105
4 b g Dansili—Reflections (Sadler's Wells (USA))
1708^{15} 1900^{28} 3619^{10} 4943^{8} ◆ 5638^{8} 6106^{8} 6562^{34}

Mirror Lad *Tom Dascombe* a61 49
2 gr g Proclamation(IRE) —Shaieef (IRE) (Shareef Dancer (USA))
1009^{10} 1319^{4} 2376^{7} 3106^{6} 5675^{8} 6674^{12}

Mirror Lake *Amanda Perrett* a91 113
3 b f Dubai Destination(USA) —Reflections (Sadler's Wells (USA))
2718^{2} (3080) (5004) ◆ (5553) 5951^{2} ◆

Mi Rubina (IRE) *A Wohler* 94
3 b f Rock Of Gibraltar(IRE) —Mi Anna (GER) (Lake Coniston (IRE))
1715a^{8} 4035a^{6}

Mirza *Rae Guest* a68 94
3 b g Oasis Dream—Millyant (Primo Dominie)
911^{4} 1137^{5} (4222) ◆ 4806^{4} (6478) 7351^{15} 7443^{8}

Misano Lasen (IRE) *M Massimi Jr* 98
3 b f Kheleyf(USA) —My Lilli (IRE) (Marju (IRE))
1713a^{11}

Misaro (GER) *Ronald Harris* a84 86
9 b g Acambaro(GER) —Misniniski (Niniski (USA))
192^{6} 258^{4} 364^{2} 678^{4} 810^{2} (848) 899^{2} (986) (1320) 1445^{3} 1874^{6} 2364^{5} 2846^{8} 3474^{2} 3675^{4} 3734^{4} 4298^{6} 4430^{7} 7847^{8} 8035^{7}

Misefi *Martin Bosley* a51
2 b f Nayef(USA) —Simonida (IRE) (Royal Academy (USA))
6247^{11} 6866^{14}

Miserere (IRE) *John Wainwright* 61
2 b f Fasliyev(USA) —Gilt Linked (Compton Place)
1964^{4} 2272^{2} 2436^{10} 3549^{P}

Misheer *Clive Brittain* 109
3 b f Oasis Dream—All For Laura (Cadeaux Genereux)
1384^{4} 1726^{17}

Mishrif (USA) *John Jenkins* a85 84
4 bb g Arch(USA) —Peppy Priscilla (USA) (Latin American (USA))
1128^{3} 2009^{2} (2236) 2872^{7} 4023^{2} 4501^{4} 4929^{6} 4995^{2} 5415^{7} 5754^{7} 6558^{5} 6780^{8} 7115^{5}

Mishtaag *Clive Brittain* a73 24
2 b c Bertolini(USA) —Raze (Halling (USA))
1066^{5} 3274^{3} ◆ 6465^{12} 7035^{13}

Miskin Diamond (IRE) *Bryn Palling* 53
2 b f Diamond Green(FR) —Spring To Light (USA) (Blushing Groom (FR))
4323^{5} 4921^{4} 5465^{9}

Miskin Nights *Bryn Palling* 67
3 b f Zafeen(FR) —Risalah (Marju (IRE))
2588^{10} 3030^{16} 4041^{10} 4475^{8}

Miskin Spirit *Bryn Palling* a40 43
4 b m Bertolini(USA) —Risalah (Marju (IRE))
1762^{12} 2232^{9}

Misk Khitaam (USA) *John Dunlop* 74
2 b c Distorted Humor(USA) —Tashawak (IRE) (Night Shift (USA))
6190^{12} 6532^{5} ◆

Misplaced Fortune *Nigel Tinkler* a46 96
5 b m Compton Place—Tide Of Fortune (Soviet Star (USA))
1374^{4} 1688^{6} (2140) 2982^{2} 3505^{2} 4413^{2} 5302^{4} 5787^{3} 6175^{3} 6721^{8} 7079^{10}

Miss Antonia (IRE) *Henry Cecil* a87 86
3 b f Antonius Pius(USA) —Masharik (IRE) (Caerleon (USA))
2220^{4} (3766) 4784^{3} ◆ (5149) 5662^{2} ◆ 6090^{6} 6361^{10} 6813^{2}

Miss Blink *Robin Bastiman* 46
3 ch f Compton Place—Tawny Way (Polar Falcon (USA))
5065^{5} 5686^{5} 6060^{5} 7153^{3}

Miss Boops (IRE) *Michael Quinlan* 72
2 b f Johannesburg(USA) —Sky Bird (IRE) (Galileo (IRE))
(2740) 4305^{8}

Miss Bootylishes *Andrew Haynes* a79 79
5 b m Mujahid(USA) —Moxby (Efisio)
(19) 169^{2} 398^{3} 451^{4} 787^{2} 1034^{5} (1141) 1494^{2} 1997^{6} 5541^{2} 6367^{4} 6963^{7} 7804^{2} 7895^{4}

Miss Bounty *George Baker* a46 64
5 ch m Bahamian Bounty—Maniere D'Amour (FR) (Baillamont (USA))
3514^{5} 4366^{4} 5039^{6} 6210^{8}

Miss California *Tor Sturgis* a29 25
3 b f Mtoto—Lightning Princess (Puissance)
1661^{11} 1872^{11} 3308^{9}

Miss Chaumiere *Michael Bell* a50 55
3 b f Selkirk(USA) —Miss Corniche (Hernando (FR))
2473^{11} 2900^{9} 4127^{14} 4687^{3} 5361^{2} 5654^{11} 7156^{7}

Miss Chicane *Walter Swinburn* 67
2 b f Refuse To Bend(IRE) —Sharp Terms (Kris)
4103^{7} 4755^{3} 6468^{4}

Miss Christophene (IRE) *Mrs S Lamyman* a73 67
4 bl m Christophene(USA) —Lotus Flower (IRE) (Grand Lodge (USA))
169^{8} 509^{2} 786^{2}

Miss Clairton *Sir Mark Prescott Bt* a92 63
2 br f Marju(IRE) —Spirito Libro (USA) (Lear Fan (USA))
2272^{4} ◆ 2693^{4} (3260) 4696^{5} (4911) 5177^{2}

Misscomplacent *Ann Duffield* a67 61
2 b f Compton Place—Miss Rimex (IRE) (Ezzoud (IRE))
3118^{3} 3315^{4} 4149^{8} 4650^{3} 4981^{3} 5334^{2} 5602^{6} 6311^{3} 6868^{3} 7017^{4} 7313^{4} (7577) 7809^{6}

Miss Cosette (IRE) *David Barron* a39 46
2 b f Diamond Green(FR) —Reign Of Fire (IRE) (Perugino (USA))
2239^{8} 2623^{7} 3106^{10} 4150^{7} 5434^{4} 6891^{8} 7394^{6} 7643^{6} 7801^{3}

Miss Daawe *Brian Ellison* a58 68
6 b m Daawe(USA) —Feiticeira (USA) (Deposit Ticket (USA))
1470^{6} ◆ 1569^{2} 1885^{5} 2087^{4} 2581^{7} (3976) 4373^{12} 4982^{5} 5513^{8} 6073^{4} 7148^{4}

Miss Darcey (AUS) *Anthony Cummings* 102
5 ch m Hussonet(USA) —Miss Bussell (AUS) (Danzero (AUS))
7368a^{14}

Miss Diagnosis (IRE) *Ralph Beckett* 71
2 b f Medicean—Changeable (Dansili)
6087^{4} ◆ 7303^{2}

Miss Doodle *Eve Johnson Houghton* a39 62
4 ch m Dubai Destination(USA) —Running Flame (IND) (Steinbeck (USA))
3360^{7} 4045^{4} 4765^{11}

Miss Dutee *Richard Hannon* a28 68
2 b f Dubawi(IRE) —Tee Cee (Lion Cavern (USA))
2223^{8} 2749^{6} 3029^{5} (4129) 4677^{6} 5863^{7}

Miss Europa (IRE) *P Schiergen* 107
4 bb m Monsun(GER) —Miss Hoeny (USA) (Rahy (USA))
(2155a) 2806a^{3} 5542a^{4} 7373a^{12}

Miss Exhibitionist *Peter Chapple-Hyam* 76
2 b f Trade Fair—Miss McGuire (Averti (IRE))
2958^{6} 5047^{6} 6058^{2} 7123^{6}

Miss Eze *Paul Cashman* a83 85
4 b m Danehill Dancer(IRE) —Miss Corniche (Hernando (FR))
4524a^{4}

Miss Faustina (IRE) *Philip McBride* a71 87
3 b f Antonius Pius(USA) —Boston Ivy (USA) (Mark Of Esteem (IRE))
4806^{2} 5521^{6}

Miss Ferney *Alan Kirtley* 65
6 ch m Cayman Kai(IRE) —Jendorcet (Grey Ghost)
2109^{14} 3177^{4} 3601^{2} 4168^{4} 4411^{8} 4648^{5} 4854^{2} (5336) 5687^{12} 6707^{7}

Miss Fifty (IRE) *U Suter* 101
2 b f Whipper(USA) —Annatto (USA) (Mister Baileys)
5322a^{2} 6609a^{7}

Miss Firefly *Ron Hodges* a65 63
5 b m Compton Place—Popocatepetl (FR) (Nashwan (USA))
193^{2} (368) 532^{3} 1534^{2} 2026^{2} 3254^{4} 4744^{2} 5010^{5} 5580^{3} 6284^{7}

Miss Firefox *Nicky Vaughan* a53 42
2 ch f Haafhd—Hayden Grace (In The Wings)
7345 ^{7} 7913^{3}

Miss Flash Dancer *Chris Bealby* a55 58
4 ch m Bertolini(USA) —Calonnog (IRE) (Peintre Celebre (USA))
2478^{10} 3484^{3} 3766^{10} 4546^{11} 5486^{13} 7835^{11}

Miss Formidable (IRE) *Luke Comer* a58 25
3 b f Mull Of Kintyre(USA) —Formaestre (IRE) (Formidable (USA))
1059^{6} 1302^{9} 2231^{10} 5663^{8}

Miss Ghena (USA) *Declan Carroll* a51 59
4 b m Gone West(USA) —Dimitrova (USA) (Swain (IRE))
166^{8} 290^{10}

Miss Glitters (IRE) *Hughie Morrison* a91 68
5 b m Chevalier(IRE) —Geht Schnell (Fairy King (USA))
6^{3} 4023^{9} 4891^{3} 5553^{10} 6366^{9}

Miss Gorica (IRE) *Ms Joanna Morgan* a100 106
6 b m Mull Of Kintyre(USA) —Allegorica (IRE) (Alzao (USA))
1676a^{2} 2912a^{4} 3486a^{12} 3571a^{3} 4269a^{8} 4882a^{4} 5127a^{4} 5569a^{9}

Miss Halfordbridge *John Gallagher* 9
3 b f Alydeed(CAN) —Tattling (Warning)
3125^{10} 3635^{10} 4249^{14}

Miss Hollybell *John Gallagher* a55 38
4 b m Umistim—Hollybell (Beveled (USA))
1258^{13} 1775^{6} (1843) 3373^{6} 6280^{10}

Missile Command (IRE) *William Haggas* a67
2 b g Majestic Missile(IRE) —Blusienka (IRE) (Blues Traveller (IRE))
6575^{4} 6995^{2} 7598^{7}

Missionaire (USA) *William Knight* a72 87
3 bb c El Corredor(USA) —Fapindy (USA) (A.P. Indy (USA))
1761^{4} 2254^{5} 2869^{8} 4360^{4} 5002^{5} 5868^{10} (6554) 7061^{14}

Missionary *William Haggas* a24 69
3 ch g Medicean—Charm The Stars (Roi Danzig (USA))
4258^{5} 4572^{4} 6313^{10}

Mission Control (IRE) *Tim Vaughan* a83 61
5 ch g Dubai Destination(USA) —Stage Manner (In The Wings)
4467^{14}

Mission Impazible (USA) *Todd Pletcher* a111
3 rg c Unbridled's Song(USA) —La Paz (USA) (Hold Your Peace (USA))
1714a^{9}

Mission Impossible *Tracy Waggott* a70 59
5 gr g Kyllachy—Eastern Lyric (Petong)
4199^{6}

Miss Isle Control *Alan McCabe* a30 20
3 ch f Monsieur Bond(IRE) —Sea Isle (Selkirk (USA))
2221^{13} 2600^{8}

Mississippian (IRE) *Rose Dobbin* a63 55
6 b g Montjeu(IRE) —Swilly (USA) (Irish River (FR))
2182^{10} 2492^{9} 2714^{13} 3124^{2} 3538^{4} 4453^{9} 4644^{8} 4897^{4} 5155^{8} 7054^{6} 7125^{13} 7229^{2} 7986^{12}

Miss Jabba (IRE) *Julia Feilden* a40 43
4 b m Bertolini(USA) —Najaaba (USA) (Bahhare (USA))
146^{10} 1437^{12} 1958^{7} 3290^{6} 4738^{6}

Miss Jean Brodie (USA) *Mahmood Al Zarooni* a71 105
3 gr f Maria's Mon(USA) —Miss Kilroy (USA) (A.P. Indy (USA))
3080^{3} (3437) 4178a^{2}

Miss Keck *Alan Swinbank* a63 82
6 b m Inchinor—En Vacances (IRE) (Old Vic)
1150^{5} (2659) ◆ (2814)

Miss Keller (IRE) *Roger L Attfield* 110
4 b m Montjeu(IRE) —Ingozi (Warning)
(6235a) 6950a^{2} 7343a^{9}

Miss Kingwood *Marcus Tregoning* a71 61
3 b f Reset(AUS) —Forum Finale (USA) (Silver Hawk (USA))
4906^{5} ◆ 6499^{3} ◆ 6876^{12} 7381^{3}

Miss Kitty Grey (IRE) *Jim Boyle* a55 65
3 gr f One Cool Cat(USA) —Nortolixa (FR) (Linamix (FR))
445^{4} 538^{2} 784^{8} 1205^{6} 1784^{6} 2418^{11} 2634^{2} (2875) 3441^{7} 4025^{7} 4791^{8} 5163^{4} 5670^{6} 6061^{9} 7037^{13} 7153^{14} 7438^{6}

Miss Laa Di Da *Noel Meade* 99
3 ch f Dr Fong(USA) —Tatterdemalion (Galileo (IRE))
1036a^{5} 1787a^{4} 5568a^{3} 6379a^{3}

Miss Lauz *Alan Berry* 34
3 b f Whipper(USA) —Absolve (USA) (Diesis)
1966^{11} 2273^{8} 3666^{6}

Miss Lesley *Dean Ivory* a75 77
3 b f Needwood Blade—You Found Me (Robellino (USA))
276^{5} 550^{2} 689^{3} 826^{2}

Miss Liberty (FR) *Mme Pia Brandt* 101
2 b f Statue Of Liberty(USA) —Miss America (FR) (Spinning World (USA))
(2917a) 3718a^{5} 6044a^{4}

Miss Marielle (AUS) *Joseph Pride* 108
6 b m Encosta De Lago(AUS) —Miss Vandal (AUS) (Don't Say Halo (USA))
16

Miss Maudie (IRE) *Ronald Harris* a1 26
2 bb f Captain Rio—Eurolink Virago (Charmer)
1695^{6} 2245^{10} 2638^{12} 2963^{11} 7551^{9} 7894^{11} 7983^{13}

Miss Mediator (USA) *Michael Dods* 77
2 ch f Consolidator(USA) —Gender Dance (USA) (Miesque's Son (USA))
2936^{3} 3498^{3} 3858^{3}

Miss Miracle *Clive Cox* a63 82
3 gr f Motivator—Miracle (Ezzoud (IRE))
978^{2} ◆ 1820^{7} 2891^{3} (3312)

Miss Mittagong (USA) *Ralph Beckett* a71 86
3 b f Pleasantly Perfect(USA) —Go Go (USA) (Falstaff (USA))
(1882) ◆ 2466^{3} 3071^{14} 6291^{8} 7420^{6}

Miss Moneypenni *Nick Littmoden* a52 64
2 ch f Monsieur Bond(IRE) —Dazzling Daisy (Shareef Dancer (USA))
2819^{3} 3411^{8} (3981) 4592^{13} 5452^{9} 5675^{6} 6052^{9} 6258^{7}

Miss Naline (FR) *Mlle S Sine* 92
5 b m Trempolino(USA) —Miss Naelle (FR) (Al Nasr (FR))
5378a^{7}

Miss Nimbus *George Baker* a38 32
2 ch f Thunder Gulch(USA) —Oak Tree Miss (USA) (Woodman (USA))
3981^{5} 4587^{10} 5269^{7} 6309^{9}

Missoula (IRE) *Suzy Smith* 62
7 b m Kalanisi(IRE) —Medway (IRE) (Shernazar)
1902^{14} 2228^{6}

Miss Polly Plum *Chris Dwyer* a52 52
3 b f Doyen(IRE) —Mrs Plum (Emarati (USA))
159^{5} 533^{12} 788^{3} 870^{9} 988^{6} 1163^{3} 1605^{2} 2185^{2} 2566^{14} 2879^{4} 3480^{3} 3682^{3} 5898^{4} 6270^{4} 7300^{8} 7477^{3} 7721^{8}

Miss Porky *Christopher Kellett* a14 46
4 b m Deportivo—Carati (Selkirk (USA))
7184^{13} 7336^{11}

Miss Red Eye (IRE) *Luke Comer* 59
5 b m On The Ridge(IRE) —Wayne's Gal (IRE) (Karaar)
7131^{12}

Miss Reprieve *Sam Davison*
3 b f Kier Park(IRE) —Lyrical Girl (USA) (Orpen (USA))
374^{12}

Miss Silver Brook (USA) *Julio C Canani* a103 89
4 rg m Cozzene(USA) —Brookdale (USA) (Turkoman (USA))
3044a5

Miss Sinatra (IRE) *Brian Meehan* a64 76
2 b f Invincible Spirit(IRE) —Doitmyway (IRE) (Brief Truce (USA))
42037 (4729) 631713 75656 80205

Miss Singhsix (IRE) *Martin D Wolfson* a106 98
5 ch m Singspiel(IRE) —Whatamiss (USA) (Miswaki (USA))
5578a4

Miss Starlight *Philip McBride* a79 101
3 b f Trade Fair—Redeem (IRE) (Doyoun)
4283 10332 ◆ (1182) 17293 18205 25433 310410 (3943a)

Miss T *James Given* 46
2 br f Bertolini(USA) —Chalosse (Doyoun)
55957 65116 689411

Miss Taken (IRE) *Declan Carroll* a55 67
3 b f Dubai Destination(USA) —Miss Takeortwo (IRE) (Danehill Dancer (IRE))
(72)

Miss Tenacious *Ron Hodges* 38
3 b f Refuse To Bend(IRE) —Very Speed (USA) (Silver Hawk (USA))
28429 34779 50078 55865 695612

Miss Thea *Marcus Tregoning* 35
2 ch f Barathea(IRE) —Misplace (IRE) (Green Desert (USA))
569117

Miss Thippawan (USA) *J Hetherton* a39 43
4 bb m Street Cry(IRE) —Sheathanna (USA) (Mr. Leader (USA))
5046 60113 7164 83910

Miss Toldyaso (IRE) *Michael Quinlan* a56 54
2 b f Barathea(IRE) —Toldya (Beveled (USA))
37676 443713 48027 54126 60353 (7016) 73013 74233 75763 77776 79978

Miss Topsy Turvy (IRE) *John Dunlop* 33
2 br f Mr Greeley(USA) —Cara Fantasy (IRE) (Sadler's Wells (USA))
68048 709411

Miss Velocity *Andrew Oliver* a79 86
3 ch f Avonbridge—Adhaaba (USA) (Dayjur (USA))
31977 3489a14

Miss Villefranche *Michael Bell* 61
2 b f Danehill Dancer(IRE) —Miss Corniche (Hernando (FR))
50665 56335 62225

Miss Wendy *Mark H Tompkins* a58 58
3 b f Where Or When(IRE) —Grove Dancer (Reprimand)
201110 28537 49804 61835 (6262) 70033 73975

Miss Whippy *Paul Howling* a54 57
3 b f Whipper(USA) —Glorious (Nashwan (USA))
11588 160810 19894 28383 37884 42126 47744 54233 61832 (6579) 67477 711711 738712 77895

Miss Xu Xia *Geoffrey Oldroyd* a45 41
4 b m Monsieur Bond(IRE) —Bond Girl (Magic Ring (IRE))
2975 50311

Miss Zooter (IRE) *Ralph Beckett* 102
3 b f Intikhab(USA) —Laraissa (Machiavellian (USA))
(2120) ◆ 30717 37907 (4378) 58838 63518

Mista Rossa *Jamie Snowden* a75 75
5 br g Red Ransom(USA) —Cloud Hill (Danehill (USA))
21828

Mister Angry (IRE) *Mark Johnston* a84 94
3 b g Cape Cross(IRE) —Yaya (USA) (Rahy (USA))
14663 18237 27589 32394 (3730) 40864 447011 (4815) 6971a14

Mister Beano (IRE) *Richard Price* a32 59
5 b g Mull Of Kintyre(USA) —Subtle Move (USA) (Known Fact (USA))
29613 53011 79411 86612

Mister Benedictine *Brendan Duke* a58 46
7 b g Mister Baileys—Cultural Role (Night Shift (USA))
46218 710111

Mister Ben Vereen *Eve Johnson Houghton* a64 60
2 b g Compton Place—La Fanciulla (Robellino (USA))
56579 61457 67785

Mister Bit (IRE) *John Best* a70 18
3 b g Tobougg(IRE) —Santiburi Girl (Casteddu)
53767 58424 60567 65272 68469 73238 ◆ 75629

Mister Carter (IRE) *T Stack* 90
3 b g Antonius Pius(USA) —Kotdiji (Mtoto)
1414a8

Mister Chop (FR) *T Lemer* a87 87
5 b g Panis(USA) —Ducie (Distant Relative)
(2446a)

Mister Fantastic *Nicky Vaughan* a52 69
4 ch g Green Tune(USA) —Lomapamar (Nashwan (USA))
440714 51587 61259 68485

Mister Fasliyev (IRE) *E Charpy* a92 87
8 b g Fasliyev(USA) —Carisheba (USA) (Alysheba (USA))
441a3 605a6

Mister Fizzbomb (IRE) *John Wainwright* a62 73
7 b g Lend A Hand—Crocus (IRE) (Mister Baileys)
7195 129611 26944 626915 664812

Mister Frosty (IRE) *George Prodromou* a62 60
4 gr g Verglas(IRE) —La Chinampina (FR) (Darshaan)
186 1843 3905 4573 7203 7716 8657 15922 26365 29076 332410 58407 60942 66622 73156 74075 77282

Mister Green (FR) *David Flood* a103 83
4 b g Green Desert(USA) —Summertime Legacy (Darshaan)
235 (239) 3412 4802 5363 7383 ◆ 9466 19745 305019 752211 759411 768912 797110

Mister Hardy *Richard Fahey* a93 103
5 b g Kyllachy—Balladonia (Primo Dominie)
100821 27366 (4084)

Mister Hughie (IRE) *Mick Channon* 111
3 b c Elusive City(USA) —Bonne Mere (FR) (Stepneyev (IRE))
(1315) 18652 20753 2437F 34457 37919 45054 527610 (5512) 61949 6608a20 67359

Mister Incredible *Milton Bradley* a56 24
7 b g Wizard King—Judiam (Primo Dominie)
19511 2644 4034 4955 7219 159813 188514 27905

Misterisland (IRE) *Michael Mullineaux* a49 52
5 b g Spectrum(IRE) —Carranita (IRE) (Anita's Prince)
2695 3694 5682 8547 97610 11488 23787 26293 32003 37115 385511 40712 46066 55358

Mister Jingles *Richard Whitaker* a61 63
7 ch g Desert Story(IRE) —Fairy Free (Rousillon (USA))
139611 ◆ 16733 22112 27002 32847 37756 56885 62676 705612 74028

Mister Langan (IRE) *B Grizzetti*
2 b c Invincible Spirit(IRE) —Miss Madisyn Rose (USA) (Storm Bird (CAN))
7849a13

Mister Laurel *Richard Fahey* a89 90
4 b g Diktat—Balladonia (Primo Dominie)
529710 58849 (7212) ◆ 73522 75747 76975 80175

Mister Manannan (IRE) *David Nicholls* 110
3 b g Desert Style(IRE) —Cover Girl (IRE) (Common Grounds)
(1610a) 2157a7 25373 304712 450513

Mister Maq *Andrew Crook* a27 43
7 b g Namaqualand(USA) —Nordico Princess (Nordico (USA))
23825 312410 33706

Mister Marti Gras (USA) *Chris Block* a101 108
3 ch g Belong To Me(USA) —Miss Marta (USA) (Cure The Blues (USA))
5319a6

Mister New York (USA) *Noel Chance* a99 68
5 b g Forest Wildcat(USA) —Shebane (USA) (Alysheba (USA))
(81) (266) 4476 50027 561111 61236 75076

Mister Pete (IRE) *Chris Grant* 66
7 b g Piccolo—Whistfilly (First Trump)
11137 78059

Mister Pleau (USA) *John Best* a58
3 b g Milwaukee Brew(USA) —Aim To Please (USA) (Temperence Hill (USA))
6185 7344 10464 157811 224813 592312 61218

Mister Ross *Jim Boyle* a67 89
5 b g Medicean—Aqualina (IRE) (King's Theatre (IRE))
10638 13468 22364

Mister Segway (IRE) *Robert Collet* a65 80
2 b c Dansili—Aplysia (USA) (Storm Cat (USA))
4274a4 6589a0 7383a2

Mister Tinktastic (IRE) *Nicky Vaughan* a73 84
4 ch g Noverre(USA) —Psychic (IRE) (Alhaarth (IRE))
40657 45589 51573

Mistic Magic (IRE) *Paul Cole* 93
3 b f Orpen(USA) —Mistic Sun (Dashing Blade)
13845 44736 50522 55218 60022 634617 709716

Mistoffelees *Luca Cumani* a64 83
4 b g Tiger Hill(IRE) —Auenlust (GER) (Surumu (GER))
21098 (3608) 38473 (5071) ◆ 579014

Mistress Shy *Robin Dickin* a27
3 b f Zafeen(FR) —Nicholas Mistress (Beveled (USA))
425111 467913 56588

Misty For Me (IRE) *A P O'Brien* 114
2 b f Galileo(IRE) —Butterfly Cove (USA) (Storm Cat (USA))
4879a2 ◆ (5570a) ◆ (6609a)

Misty Isles *Heather Main* 58
2 b f High Chaparral(IRE) —Meshhed (USA) (Gulch (USA))
68044

Misty Morn *Alan Brown* a54 64
2 ch f Cadeaux Genereux—Dolce Piccata (Piccolo)
13597 (1646) 20325 2436U 27577 64896 66457 70176 74049 75762 79834

Mi Sun Donk *Brett Johnson* a50 41
2 gr g Proclamation(IRE) —Days Of Grace (Wolfhound (USA))
426312 50748 545311 77224

Mith Hill *Ian Williams* 83
9 b g Daylami(IRE) —Delirious Moment (IRE) (Kris)
25417 32417 44677 52784 59406

Mixed Emotions (IRE) *Richard Hannon* 54
2 b f Exceed And Excel(AUS) —L-Way First (IRE) (Vision (USA))
22518 30348

Mixing *Michael Attwater* a46 57
8 gr g Linamix(FR) —Tuning (Rainbow Quest (USA))
59011 77010 162312 22306 304010 62732 65028 68558

Miyake (IRE) *H Blume* 83
2 ch f Namid—Moonchild (GER) (Acatenango (GER))
7534a0

M'Lady Rousseur (IRE) *Chris Bealby* a62 58
4 ch m Selkirk(USA) —Millay (Polish Precedent (USA))
3224 8748 65025 718110

Mlini (IRE) *Tim Etherington* a15
4 ch g Bertolini(USA) —Sherkova (USA) (State Dinner (USA))
538011

Mme De Stael *Sir Mark Prescott Bt* a68 55
3 ch f Selkirk(USA) —Scandalette (Niniski (USA))
36066 (4259) 443339 73168 74658 75419

Mnarani (IRE) *J S Moore* a69 66
3 b g Oasis Dream—Finity (USA) (Diesis)
7623 8405 142210 224810 27242 28786 32133 344210

Mnasikia (USA) *Luca Cumani* a64 60
3 b f Rahy(USA) —Entendu (USA) (Diesis)
3746 57106

Mobus Wan (FR) *Shaun Harley*
7 b g Le Triton(USA) —Brustanette (FR) (Brustolon)
30789

Mocha Java *Matthew Salaman* a69 46
7 b g Bertolini(USA) —Coffee Cream (Common Grounds)
212 (86) 1874 3424 5795 7043 8934 17376 218712

Modeyra *Saeed Bin Suroor* 110
3 br f Shamardal(USA) —Zahrat Dubai (Unfuwain (USA))
(6886) ◆ 73497

Modun (IRE) *Sir Michael Stoute* a93 79
3 br g King's Best(USA) —Olympienne (IRE) (Sadler's Wells (USA))
(6275) 70452

Moggy (IRE) *Geoffrey Harker* a50 54
4 br m One Cool Cat(USA) —Termania (IRE) (Shirley Heights)
15264 18878

Mogok Ruby *Brett Johnson* a72 75
6 gr g Bertolini(USA) —Days Of Grace (Wolfhound (USA))
267 458914 731911 74419

Mohanad (IRE) *Sheena West* a68 71
4 b g Invincible Spirit(IRE) —Irish Design (IRE) (Alhaarth (IRE))
11832 32673 33482 58882 64802 67752

Mohawk Ridge *Michael Dods* a65 74
4 b g Storming Home—Ipsa Loquitur (Unfuwain (USA))
11726 15752 25833 28513 41903 49534 (5437) 610910 68955 (7176) 75044 78066

Mohedian Lady (IRE) *Michael Bell* 86
2 b f Hurricane Run(IRE) —Amathia (IRE) (Darshaan)
61552 65599 (7001)

Moheebb (IRE) *Ruth Carr* a74 98
6 b g Machiavellian(USA) —Rockerlong (Deploy)
7855 127214 183712 28659 32063 35372 36674 41529 482813 54079 61128

Moiqen (IRE) *Doug Watson* a53 94
5 b g Red Ransom(USA) —Za Aamah (USA) (Mr Prospector (USA))
513a14

Mojave Moon *Mahmood Al Zarooni* 108
4 br g Singspiel(IRE) —Moon Cactus (Kris)
418a3 712a9 161510 23457 32403 39225 529110

Mojeerr *Alan McCabe* a55 58
4 b g Royal Applause—Princess Miletrian (IRE) (Danehill (USA))
1427 2498 3473 5304 7579 8656 9426 102816 14279 15077 21096 22857 25116 26535 299512 35215 44538 48576 49854 60376 64724 691512 75299 76467 77293 789610 79333 79585

Mojolika *Tim Easterby* 64
2 ch g Motivator—Kalandika (Diesis)
54984 60365 66186

Mokalif *Michael Bell* 53
2 b c Halling(USA) —Velvet Waters (Unfuwain (USA))
61278 66768

Molly Me (IRE) *P D Deegan* a42
2 b f Modigliani(USA) —Along Came Molly (Dr Fong (USA))
6726a14

Molly Mylenis *David Evans* a48 65
2 b f Needwood Blade—Rosein (Komaite (USA))
10733 11802 15275 (2292) 30599 31637 42786 55258 657610 701712 730113 74245 75766 76412 78646 78945

Mollyow (IRE) *Bryn Palling* a24 59
2 ch f Iceman—Corryvreckan (IRE) (Night Shift (USA))
11803 19994 376911 712413

Molly Piccles *Bill Turner* a14 17
2 b f Piccolo—Molly Malone (Formidable (USA))
18385 377810 47888

Molly The Witch (IRE) *Willie Musson* a46 59
4 b m Rock Of Gibraltar(IRE) —Tree Peony (Woodman (USA))
9399 20126 316811

Molly Two *Lawrence Mullaney* a53 71
5 ch m Muhtarram(USA) —Rum Lass (Distant Relative)
269510 328713

Molon Labe (IRE) *Tom Tate* 76
3 ch g Footstepsinthesand—Pillars Of Society (IRE) (Caerleon (USA))
16303 26508 465610 60506 63596

Moment Juste *John Gosden* 25
2 b f Pivotal—Place De L'Opera (Sadler's Wells (USA))
723118

Moment Of Clarity *Shaun Harris* a7 66
8 b g Lujain(USA) —Kicka (Shirley Heights)
612513

Moment Of Weakness (IRE) *Mrs John Harrington* a90 92
2 b g Big Bad Bob(IRE) —Kristal's Dream (IRE) (Night Shift (USA))
2352a5

Moment Present (FR) *Charlie Mann* 65
5 gr g Enrique—Abigaila (FR) (River River (FR))
43866 47455

Mo Mhuirnin (IRE) *Richard Fahey* a93 88
4 b m Danetime(IRE) —Cotton Grace (IRE) (Case Law)
(1192) 17277

Momkinzain (USA) *Mick Channon* 87
3 b g Rahy(USA) —Fait Accompli (USA) (Louis Quatorze (USA))
13863 518510 65572 68614

Monaadi (IRE) *Brendan Powell* a65 56
5 b g Singspiel(IRE) —Bint Albaadiya (USA) (Woodman (USA))
467612 518011

Monaco Consul (NZ) *Michael Moroney* 118
4 b c High Chaparral(IRE) —Argante (NZ) (Star Way)
6947a3 7291a14

Monaco Dream (IRE) *William Jarvis* a68 74
4 b m Hawk Wing(USA) —Parvenue (FR) (Ezzoud (IRE))
4212 5634 9416 13184 15267

Monadreen Dancer *Daniel Mark Loughnane* a52
2 b f Kheleyf(USA) —Volitant (Ashkalani (IRE))
76035 78114

Monalini (IRE) *David Nicholls* 76
3 b g Bertolini(USA) —Mona Em (IRE) (Catrail (USA))
151113 36686 40639 59998

Monashee Rock (IRE) *Matthew Salaman* a71 73
5 b m Monashee Mountain(USA) —Polar Rock (Polar Falcon (USA))
6736 9657 11719 (3054) 40446 43666 49392 643910

Monblue *B Grizzetti* 95
3 b f Monsun(GER) —Salonblue (IRE) (Bluebird (USA))
2575a7 3495a6 6765a14

Mon Brav *Declan Carroll* a76 82
3 b g Sampower Star—Danehill Princess (IRE) (Danehill (USA))
13764 17764 22875 28242 32434 37795 (4349) 46858 (4901) 525013 53094 672315 69859

Mon Cadeaux *Andrew Balding* 102
3 b g Cadeaux Genereux—Ushindi (IRE) (Montjeu (IRE))
16163 2159a11 27123 306612 55267 614710

Monel *Jim Goldie* 49
2 ch g Cadeaux Genereux—Kelucia (IRE) (Grand Lodge (USA))
418710 48216 54046

M One Rifle (USA) *Bruce Headley* a119
4 bb g One Man Army(USA) —Leanessa (USA) (Bertrando (USA))
3935a4

Money Money Money *Rod Millman* a52 64
4 b m Generous(IRE) —Shi Shi (Alnasr Alwasheek)
74134 75792

Money Trader (IRE) *J T Gorman* a81 87
3 br c Trade Fair—Honey For Money (IRE) (Alzao (USA))
3487a18 6783a8

Monfils Monfils (USA) *Philip Kirby* a44 74
8 b g Sahm(USA) —Sorpresa (USA) (Pleasant Tap (USA))
102811 62696 651812 68908 73304

Mongoose Alert (IRE) *Willie Musson* a82
8 b g Oscar(IRE) —Before (IRE) (Ore)
9632 66993 (7244) (7568) ◆ (8032)

Monicalew *Walter Swinburn* a60
2 ch f Refuse To Bend(IRE) —White House (Pursuit Of Love)
71135 75303

Monitor Closely (IRE) *Michael Bell* 117
4 b h Oasis Dream—Independence (Selkirk (USA))
43907 5575a6 61485 63893

Monivea (IRE) *Brian Nolan* 95
4 b m Fasliyev(USA) —Night Rhapsody (IRE) (Mujtahid (USA))
1787a10

Monkton Vale (IRE) *Richard Fahey* a70 81
3 b g Catcher In The Rye(IRE) —Byproxy (IRE) (Mujtahid (USA))
10296 14862 21012 23157 (3750) 457315 54087 60748 67535 70448 73073

Mon Mon (IRE) *Brian Storey* a29
3 b f Refuse To Bend(IRE) —Adaja (Cadeaux Genereux)
728212 759912

Monopolize *Henry Cecil* a57
2 b c Oasis Dream—Modesta (IRE) (Sadler's Wells (USA))
75587

Monreale (GER) *David Pipe* a43 76
6 b g Silvano(GER) —Maratea (USA) (Fast Play (USA))
29410 (1807)

Mons Calpe (IRE) *Paul Cole* a77 76
4 b g Rock Of Gibraltar(IRE) —Taking Liberties (IRE) (Royal Academy (USA))
188311 22333 25115 27235 30792 36883 39175 42614 47376 (5286) 58285 65782 73377

Monsieur Fillioux (USA) *James Fanshawe* a82 14
4 ch g Hennessy(USA) —Eventually (USA) (Affirmed (USA))
2927 5522 11858 308314

Monsieur Harvey *Bryan Smart* a49 52
4 ch g Monsieur Bond(IRE) —Annie Harvey (Fleetwood (IRE))
2648 7896 11464 15696 53623 54857 61194 64644 71702 73004

Monsieur Jamie *John Jenkins* a70 70
2 b c Monsieur Bond(IRE) —Primula Bairn (Bairn (USA))
55233 58362 72792 (7392) (7739) ◆ 79082

Monsieur Joe (IRE) *Walter Swinburn* a83 104
3 b g Choisir(AUS) —Pascali (Compton Place)
(1281) 17015 (2960) 38912 44019 48145 ◆ (5250) 594414 65086

Monsieur Le Prince (FR) *E J O'Neill* 80
2 b c Royal Applause—Milisa (FR) (Anabaa (USA))
5347a11

Monsieur Pontaven *Robin Bastiman* 56
3 b g Avonbridge—Take Heart (Electric)
140111 24327 30263 35013 434414 497010 (5438)

Monsieur Reynard *Milton Bradley* a64 82
5 ch g Compton Place—Tell Tale Fox (Tel Quel (FR))
1855 3696 5252 7278 778P

Montaff *Mick Channon* 107
4 b g Montjeu(IRE) —Meshhed (USA) (Gulch (USA))
418a7 712a8 11762 16154 24695 310212 44618 67366 735017

Mont Agel *Michael Bell* 96
3 b c Danehill Dancer(IRE) —Miss Riviera Golf (Hernando (FR))
13277 31049 3933a6 45747 59516 67499

Montbretia *Edward P Harty* a70 96
5 b m Montjeu(IRE) —Bayswater (Caerleon (USA))
6095[5] 6786a[5] 7349[16] 7594[9]

Monte Alto (IRE) *A Al Raihe* a104 103
6 b g Danehill Dancer(IRE) —Peruvian Witch (IRE) (Perugino (USA))
335a[2] 436a[3] 512a[2] 605a[2] 821a[3]

Montebella (FR) *Mme L Audon* 69
4 b m Montjeu(IRE) —Greek Air (IRE) (Ela-Mana-Mou)
5378a[5]

Monte Cassino (IRE) *Jimmy O'Reilly* a64 64
5 ch g Choisir(AUS) —Saucy Maid (IRE) (Sure Blade (USA))
137[10] 195[5] 1477[7] 1569[12]

Monte Cavallo (SAF) *Michael Wigham* 85
5 b g Saumarez—Mufski (SAF) (Al Mufti (USA))
1388[8] 2044[8] 2685[9] 3416[3] 3896[6] ◆ 4597[5] 5311[3] ◆ 6276[2]

Montego Breeze *John Harris* a48 56
4 b m Tipsy Creek(USA) —Mofeyda (IRE) (Mtoto)
38[5] 326[4] 794[10] 1490[8] 2874[10] 3434[9] 3911[2] 4236[10] 4522[10] 5510[10] 5634[7]

Montelissima (IRE) *Ed Dunlop* a40 66
3 b f Montjeu(IRE) —Issa (Pursuit Of Love)
3586[8] 5391[4] 5958[8] 6991[8]

Monte Major (IRE) *Derek Shaw* a68 42
9 b g Docksider(USA) —Danalia (IRE) (Danehill (USA))
138[2] (165) 472[2] (525) 727[3] (774) (810) 848[2] 7526[11] 7628[8] 7784[7] 7952[6]

Monte Mayor One *P Monteith* a62 66
3 b f Lujain(USA) —Alvarinho Lady (Royal Applause)
1181[4] (1979) 2291[10] 2449[7] 2669[3] 3076[5] 3200[4] 3534[5] (3710) 3904[2] 4063[4] 4193[3] 4820[4] 5211[2] 5409[2] 5481[3] 6103[13] 6226[9] 6491[3] 7051[7] 7225[7]

Monte Mayor Two (IRE) *Derek Haydn Jones* a29 11
3 b g Arakan(USA) —Sea Of Serenity (USA) (Conquistador Cielo (USA))
2841[11] 3275[10] 3766[12]

Monterey (IRE) *Robert Mills* a70 91
3 b c Montjeu(IRE) —Magnificient Style (USA) (Silver Hawk (USA))
(2697) 3145[8]

Monterosso *Mark Johnston* a85 117
3 b c Dubawi(IRE) —Porto Roca (AUS) (Barathea (IRE))
180[2] (274) ◆ (448) (1334) ◆ 2117[2] (2562) (3142) 3491a[4] 4184a[7] 5185[5]

Monterrey (IRE) *A Fabre* 75
3 b c Tiger Hill(IRE) —Spring Oak (Mark Of Esteem (IRE))
5800a[6]

Monte Rughe (IRE) *M Gasparini*
2 b c Celtic Swing—Farjah (IRE) (Charnwood Forest (IRE))
7849a[12]

Montiboli (IRE) *Kevin Ryan* a66 76
5 ch m Bahamian Bounty—Aunt Sadie (Pursuit Of Love)
544[5] 787[6] 893[10] 1114[4]

Mont Joux (FR) *H Billot* 88
8 b g Montjeu(IRE) —Lune De Mai (Kenmare (FR))
3099a[9]

Montmartre (USA) *David Pinder* a43 62
4 b g Awesome Again(CAN) —Sacre Coeur (USA) (Saint Ballado (CAN))
388[9] 530[9] 682[4] 939[5] 984[8]

Montparnasse (GER) *M Rulec* 91
3 bb c Gold Away(IRE) —Moonlight Dream (GER) (Law Society (USA))
1745a[4]

Montparnasse (IRE) *Brian Meehan* 93
3 b g Montjeu(IRE) —Capades Dancer (USA) (Gate Dancer (USA))
1757[4] 2115[7] 2684[6] (3273) (3909) 5273[5] 5747[3] 6201[5] 6808[8]

Montpellier (IRE) *A Al Raihe* a107 99
7 br g Montjeu(IRE) —Ring Of Esteem (Mark Of Esteem (IRE))
416a[2] 628a[2] 797a[10]

Mont Ras (IRE) *Ed Dunlop* 58
3 ch g Indian Ridge—Khayrat (IRE) (Polar Falcon (USA))
2632[13] 2900[8] 3587[2]

Mon Visage *Chris Wall* a74 74
2 ch f Ishiguru(USA) —Pikaboo (Pivotal)
3961[5] 6034[2] (6697)

Moobeyn *Marcus Tregoning* a75 24
3 ch g Selkirk(USA) —Key Academy (Royal Academy (USA))
6122[5] 6578[4]

Mood Indigo (JPN) *Yasuo Tomomichi* 113
5 ch m Dance In The Dark(JPN) —Leap For Joy (Sharpo)
7460a[10]

Mood Music *Mario Hofer* a100 109
6 b g Kyllachy—Something Blue (Petong)
2157a[6] 2804a[5] 3425a[10] 4773a[6] 5573a[4]

Moody Tunes *Mrs K Burke* a76 87
7 b g Merdon Melody—Lady-Love (Pursuit Of Love)
1374[2] 2377[3] 2477[4] 2977[10] (3616) 4154[3] 4403[2] 4828[11] (5596) 6097[6] 7352[15]

Moojeh (IRE) *Marco Botti* a85
4 ch m King's Best(USA) —Bahareeya (USA) (Riverman (USA))
191[3] 552[8] ◆ 593[2]

Moonbalej *Milton Harris* a61 57
3 ch g Motivator—Glam Rock (Nashwan (USA))
589[2] 717[2] 830[3] 1054[7] 7690[7]

Moonbeam Dancer (USA) *David Simcock* a77 74
4 bb m Singspiel(IRE) —Shepherd's Moon (USA) (Silver Hawk (USA))
232[3] 2126[7] 2445[2] 3109[4]

Moonboughie *Tim Walford* 35
2 b f Tobougg(IRE) —Almunia (IRE) (Mujadil (USA))
5210[4]

Moon De French (USA) *Bob Baffert* a104
5 b m Malibu Moon(USA) —French Silk (USA) (French Deputy (USA))
6603a[3]

Moon Indigo *Howard Johnson* 105
4 b g Sadler's Wells(USA) —Solo De Lune (IRE) (Law Society (USA))
3922[4] 5218[8]

Moonlife (IRE) *Mahmood Al Zarooni* a107 102
4 b m Invincible Spirit(IRE) —Marania (IRE) (Marju (IRE))
1725[7]

Moonlight Babe (USA) *Declan Carroll* a10 32
3 b f Thunder Gulch(USA) —Autumn Moon (USA) (Mr Prospector (USA))
1993[7]

Moonlight Blaze *Chris Fairhurst* a49 59
3 b g Barathea(IRE) —Moonlight (IRE) (Night Shift (USA))
717[8] 2792[4] 6660[8] 6921[3] (7145)

Moonlight Cass (IRE) *Jeremy Gask* a59 71
3 b f Danehill Dancer(IRE) —Moon Drop (Dominion)
7209[11] 7442[11] 7655[9]

Moonlight Cloud *F Head* a89 107
2 b f Invincible Spirit(IRE) —Ventura (IRE) (Spectrum (IRE))
6610a[4]

Moonlight Dash *Saeed Bin Suroor* a58
2 b c Monsun(GER) —Kind Regards (IRE) (Unfuwain (USA))
7272[4]

Moonlight Man *Conor Dore* a86 86
9 ch g Night Shift(USA) —Fleeting Rainbow (Rainbow Quest (USA))
19[3] ◆ 87[7] 255[11]

Moonlight Mischief (IRE) *Brian Meehan* a68
3 b f Galileo(IRE) —Muwali (USA) (Kingmambo (USA))
5366[5] 6250[9]

Moonlight Mystery *Chris Wall* 56
2 ch f Pivotal—Mauri Moon (Green Desert (USA))
6651[10] 7232[7]

Moon Lightning (IRE) *Tina Jackson* a76 73
4 b g Desert Prince(IRE) —Moon Tango (IRE) (Last Tycoon)
1129[4] 1771[2] 2596[3] 6328[12] 6571[8]

Moonlight Rhapsody (IRE) *B W Hills*
2 b f Danehill Dancer(IRE) —Moon Flower (IRE) (Sadler's Wells (USA))
6353[P]

Moonlight Ridge (IRE) *Miss Julie Weston* a42 46
5 b g Tumbleweed Ridge—Oscilights Gift (Chauve Souris)
1236[7]

Moonlight Rock (IRE) *P D Deegan* a68 77
3 b f Rock Of Gibraltar(IRE) —Moonlight Dream (USA) (Banker's Gold (USA))
5129a[5]

Moonlight Serenade *Bill Turner* a54 54
3 b f Mind Games—Rasseem (IRE) (Fasliyev (USA))
215[7] 346[6] 870[5] 993[2] 1162[9]

Moonline Dancer (FR) *Richard Hannon* 78
3 b f Royal Academy(USA) —Tulipe Noire (USA) (Alleged (USA))
2047[9] 2256[10] 2510[6] 2843[9]

Moonlit Garden (IRE) *D K Weld* 98
2 b f Exceed And Excel(AUS) —Fingal Nights (IRE) (Night Shift (USA))
3070[7] ◆ 3421a[3] 3939a[2] 5567a[5] 6230a[6]

Moon Over Water (IRE) *Michael Jarvis* 48
2 b f Galileo(IRE) —Velvet Moon (IRE) (Shaadi (USA))
7231[12]

Moonreach (IRE) *P D Deegan* a91 94
3 b g Chineur(FR) —Ribbon Glade (UAE) (Zafonic (USA))
1676a[6]

Moonsail *Mahmood Al Zarooni* 77
2 b f Monsun(GER) —Kazzia (GER) (Zinaad)
6360[2] ◆ 7001[2]

Moonscape *Sir Michael Stoute* 73
2 ch c Pivotal—Moon Goddess (Rainbow Quest (USA))
6828[2] ◆

Moonshine Creek *Peter Hiatt* a70 70
8 b g Pyramus(USA) —Monongelia (Welsh Pageant)
42[P]

Moon Star (GER) *Roger Curtis* a55 69
9 b g Goofalik(USA) —Maria Magdalena (GER) (Alkalde (GER))
1931[2] 2476[6]

Moontune Missy (USA) *Eoin Harty* a100
4 b m Forest Wildcat(USA) —Moonsong (USA) (Deputy Minister (CAN))
7341a[12]

Moonwolf (NZ) *Sheena West* a40 49
6 b g Ustinov(AUS) —Moonrise (Grundy)
4070[8] 4591[9]

Moorgate Lad *O Brennan* 47
3 b g Danbird(AUS) —Goodbye Millie (Sayf El Arab (USA))
5487[7] 6624[6]

Moorhouse Lad *Bryan Smart* a93 108
7 b g Bertolini(USA) —Record Time (Clantime)
948[7] 1174[2] (1670) 2745[9] 3425a[3] 3691[6] 4505[8] 5569a[7] 5851[6] 6608a[9] 6918[11]

Moorland Boy *Jamie Osborne* a57 61
2 gr g Proclamation(IRE) —Superlove (IRE) (Hector Protector (USA))
2239[7] 2486[5] 2951[4] ◆ 3288[6] 5111[9] 5667[6] 6209[4] 8031[4]

Moors Gorse *Reg Hollinshead* a62 38
3 b f Mujahid(USA) —Menna (Mark Of Esteem (IRE))
372[8] (454) 1237[3] 1505[3] 2005[10] 2617[8]

Moose Moran (USA) *Henry Cecil* a67 101
3 rg g Lemon Drop Kid(USA) —After All (IRE) (Desert Story (IRE))
1271[3] (2115) 2562[3] 3145[5] 5273[13] 6506[4]

Morache Music *PETER Makin* 94
2 b c Sleeping Indian—Enchanted Princess (Royal Applause)
3735[2] ◆ (5255) (5537) 5745[7] 6568[9] (7207) 7534a[2]

Moral Duty (USA) *Bill Turner* a49 69
5 ch h Silver Deputy(CAN) —Shoogle (USA) (A.P. Indy (USA))
275[11] 397[11] 486[13] 704[9]

Moral Issue *Jedd O'Keeffe* 74
2 b g Ishiguru(USA) —Morale (Bluebird (USA))
3971[7] 4941[2] 5298[2] 6263[3] 6569[6] 6980[4]

Morana (IRE) *Peter Chapple-Hyam* 105
3 b c Alhaarth(IRE) —Blushing Barada (USA) (Blushing Groom (FR))
1327[5] 1833[4]

Moranda (FR) *C Boutin* a81 84
2 b f Indian Rocket—Spain (FR) (Bering)
5226a[8] 7276a[5] 7534a[8]

Moran Gra (USA) *D Selvaratnam* a71 93
3 ch g Rahy(USA) —Super Supreme (IND) (Zafonic (USA))
796a[14]

Morar *Laura Mongan* a81 77
4 b m Kalanisi(IRE) —Moidart (Electric)
688[7] 1902[12] 2181[7] (7553) ◆ 7781[6]

Morermaloke *Brian Meehan* a69 65
2 ch g Bahamian Bounty—Rainbow End (Botanic (USA))
4902[8] 5537[6] 5835[2] 6435[7]

Moresweets 'n Lace *Gary Moore* 63
3 b f Zafeen(FR) —Another Secret (Efisio)
3157[4]

Mores Wells *R Gibson* 112
6 b h Sadler's Wells(USA) —Endorsement (Warning)
1856a[2] 3494a[6] 5107a[10] (6017a) 6951a[2] 7615a[13]

More Than Enough (IRE) *Richard Fahey* a64
2 b g Danehill Dancer(IRE) —Showbiz (IRE) (Sadler's Wells (USA))
7558[8] 7693[6] 8001[5]

More Than Many (USA) *Richard Fahey* 76
4 bb h More Than Ready(USA) —Slewnami (AUS) (Seattle Slew (USA))
4404[7] 5071[5]

More Than Real (USA) *Todd Pletcher* 112
2 ch f More Than Ready(USA) —Miss Seffens (USA) (Dehere (USA))
(7340a)

Moretta Blanche *Ralph Beckett* 85
3 br f Dansili—Cotton House (IRE) (Mujadil (USA))
(2121) (3001) 4145[6]

Morgan Drive (IRE) *M Gasparini* a108 105
5 b h Namid—Morning Prancer (Caerleon (USA))
515a[7] 707a[5] 817a[11] 1944a[7] 7459a[2]

Morgans Choice *John Spearing* a37 70
3 b g Namid—Polar Dawn (Polar Falcon (USA))
1546[9] 2179[8] 3211[8] 3293[6] 3834[2] 3994[4] 4567[6] 4920[4] 5470[7] 6536[12] 7564[9]

Moriarty (IRE) *Richard Hannon* 93
2 b c Clodovil(IRE) —Justice System (USA) (Criminal Type (USA))
4096[8] 4622[2] (5277) (6149)

Moriches (IRE) *T Stack* a66 61
3 ch f Alhaarth(IRE) —Almaaseh (IRE) (Dancing Brave (USA))
7078a[10]

Morning Charm (USA) *John Gosden* 80
2 b f North Light(IRE) —Vignette (USA) (Diesis)
(4844) ◆

Morning Chief (IRE) *Clive Cox* a76 64
3 b c Noverre(USA) —Convenience (IRE) (Ela-Mana-Mou)
6470[3] (7086) 7414[5]

Morning Drive *Walter Swinburn* a51 47
3 ch f Motivator—Bright Hope (IRE) (Danehill (USA))
6415[7] 7043[11]

Morning Line (USA) *Nicholas Zito* a118
3 bb c Tiznow(USA) —Indian Snow (USA) (A.P. Indy (USA))
7365a[2] ◆

Morocchius (USA) *Julie-Ann Camacho* a37 70
5 b g Black Minnaloushe(USA) —Shakespearean (USA) (Theatrical)
1396[5] 1574[6] 2382[7] 2864[5] 4188[3] 5439[2] 5820[6] 6463[3] 7646[5]

Mororatorio (IRE) *Deborah Sanderson* a46
3 b g Oratorio(IRE) —Feather Bride (IRE) (Groom Dancer (USA))
7019[12] 7338[8] 7575[11]

Mororless *Zoe Davison* a64 47
3 b f Exceed And Excel(AUS) —Final Pursuit (Pursuit Of Love)
(5) 188[2] 283[8] 382[5] 3325[11] 4025[10] 4502[5] 4970[9] 5174[6] 5712[4] 6020[9]

Mortbet (IRE) *Michael Jarvis* a74 84
3 b g Shamardal(USA) —Akrmina (Zafonic (USA))
(4069) 4757[7]

Mortitia *Brian Meehan* 95
2 b f Dansili—Simianna (Bluegrass Prince (IRE))
3296[4] ◆ 3861[4] (4471) 5036[12] 5693[6] 5882[2] 6176[4] 6530[6] 7098[13]

Mosaicist (IRE) *James Fanshawe* 69
2 gr f Aussie Rules(USA) —Sovereign Grace (IRE) (Standaan (FR))
6058[3] ◆

Mosa Mine *Jane Chapple-Hyam* a58 55
3 b f Exceed And Excel(AUS) —Baldemosa (FR) (Lead On Time (USA))
7960[2]

Moscow Oznick *Desmond Donovan* a72 67
5 br g Auction House(USA) —Cozette (IRE) (Danehill Dancer (IRE))
(82) 210[3] 280[3] 941[11] 1150[11] 1609[3] 2013[3] 2560[8] 2966[6] (3965) 4915[3] (5272) 6427[13] 6846[11]

Mosqueras Romance *Marco Botti* a104 107
4 br m Rock Of Gibraltar(IRE) —Mosquera (GER) (Acatenango (GER))
873[2] 1084[2] 5883[2] 6351[7] 7188[2] 7875[2]

Mosqueta *David Evans* a56 20
3 b f Doyen(IRE) —Arantxa (Sharpo)
2480[12]

Mossgorda (IRE) *Mrs K Burke* a72 61
2 b g Fasliyev(USA) —Punta Gorda (IRE) (Roi Danzig (USA))
2693[10] 2939[3] 5298[5] 5682[8] 8012[3]

Mossmann Gorge *Anthony Middleton* a46 56
8 b g Lujain(USA) —North Pine (Import)
2230[3] 2676[10] 3028[8]

Most Happy Fella (USA) *William Badgett Jr* a92
3 b g Ecton Park(USA) —Doyenne (USA) (Deputy Minister (CAN))
1097a[6]

Motafarred (IRE) *Tina Jackson* a72 86
8 ch g Machiavellian(USA) —Thurayya (Nashwan (USA))
4713[8] 5070[7] 6724[8]

Motarid (USA) *Tim Walford* 35
5 gr g Maria's Mon(USA) —Saabga (USA) (Woodman (USA))
1916[7] 4604[12] 5549[9]

Motarjm (USA) *Jeff Pearce* a67 65
6 br g Elusive Quality(USA) —Agama (USA) (Nureyev (USA))
529[4] ◆ 777[9] 1134[4] ◆ 1439[3] 4912[8] 5770[6] 6120[2] 6314[5] 7840[7]

Mother Jones *David Brown* a74 73
2 b f Sleeping Indian—Bella Chica (IRE) (Bigstone (IRE))
1324[6] ◆ 1668[6] 3729[3] 4392[4] 4615[3] 5301[4] 5525[4] 5865[2]

Motirani *Jeff Pearce* a71 58
3 br g Motivator—Maharani (USA) (Red Ransom (USA))
1387[11] 1766[11] 2220[10] 4156[11] 5161[2] 5869[3] 6080[2] 7117[3] (7704) 7967[2]

Motivado *Sir Mark Prescott Bt* a80 52
2 b c Motivator—Tamise (USA) (Time For A Change (USA))
6458[4] 7186[3] ◆ 7335[2]

Motor Home *Charlie Morlock* a37 60
4 b g Tobougg(IRE) —Desert Dawn (Belfort (FR))
3054[6]

Motrice *Sir Mark Prescott Bt* a64 112
3 gr f Motivator—Entente Cordiale (USA) (Affirmed (USA))
2189[5] 2675[2] (2908) (3626) (3878) 4507[3] 5909[3] 6929[2]

Mottley Crewe *Michael Dods* a71 65
3 b g Mujahid(USA) —Ticcatoo (IRE) (Dolphin Street (FR))
2114[9] 2530[3] 4251[4] 4749[2] 5046[3] 5481[2] 5816[2] 6226[7] (7195)

Motty's Gift *Walter Swinburn* a57 58
3 ch g Lucky Story(USA) —Oatcake (Selkirk (USA))
993[6] (1162) 1643[4] 2359[11] 2633[3] 3982[2] 4534[8] 5171[11]

Motu (IRE) *Ian McInnes* a54 73
9 b g Desert Style(IRE) —Pink Cashmere (IRE) (Polar Falcon (USA))
568[5] 682[3] 691[7] 794[6] 984[7] 1148[11]

Mouchez *Dean Ivory* a50 31
3 b g Needwood Blade—Mouchez Le Nez (IRE) (Cyrano De Bergerac)
4697[10] 6093[7] 6637[10] 7288[7] 7727[5]

Moudre (AUS) *Ciaron Maher* 108
5 bb g Blevic(AUS) —Tolkaami (AUS) (Raami I)
7032a[2] (7368a)

Mount Acclaim (IRE) *Jamie Osborne* a44 56
4 b m Acclamation—Final Trick (Primo Dominie)
3210[3] 3952[5] 4697[9] 5379[7] 6025[14]

Mountain Cat (IRE) *William Knight* a91 91
6 b g Red Ransom(USA) —Timewee (USA) (Romanov (IRE))
1006[12] 1102[3] 2141[6] 2736[7] 3318[14] 5157[9] 6260[13]

Mountain Coral (IRE) *F Oakes* a98 89
6 b g Jammaal—Coral Windsor (IRE) (Woods Of Windsor (USA))
3489a[20] 6597a[6] 6907a[3] 7217a[4]

Mountain Forest (GER) *Hughie Morrison* a61 57
4 b g Tiger Hill(IRE) —Moricana (GER) (Konigsstuhl (GER))
263[8] 376[5] ◆ (1071) (1160) 1758[6] 3084[3] 4101[4] 5260[11]

Mountain Hiker (IRE) *Jeremy Noseda* 89
3 b g Azamour(IRE) —Sagamartha (Rainbow Quest (USA))
3038[3] (4330)

Mountain Myst *William Muir* a62
2 b c Val Royal(FR) —Brecon (Unfuwain (USA))
8000[10]

Mountain Pass (USA) *Bernard Llewellyn* a61 57
8 b g Stravinsky(USA) —Ribbony (USA) (Dayjur (USA))
289[7] 496[8] 591[2] (794) 940[6] 1193[5] 1457[6] 1839[5] 2920[10] 4382[8] 4708[4] 4986[4] 5905[11] 7015[9]

Mountain Pride (IRE) *Paul Nolan* 97
5 b g High Chaparral(IRE) —Lioness (Lion Cavern (USA))
3487a[19]

Mountain Range (IRE) *John Dunlop* 74
2 b g High Chaparral(IRE) —Tuscany Lady (IRE) (Danetime (IRE))
5006[5] 5520[5] 6279[7] (6809)

Mountain Rose (GER) *Mario Hofer* 87
3 b f Tiger Hill(IRE) —Montfleur (Sadler's Wells (USA))
4640a[15] 7545a[0]

Mountain Town (USA) *Richard Dutrow Jr* a106
2 b c Cape Town(USA) —Mountain Bird (USA) (Mt. Livermore (USA))
6756a[2]

Mount Athos (IRE) *J W Hills* a54 101
3 b c Montjeu(IRE) —Ionian Sea (Slip Anchor)
1164[7] 2587[3] ◆ 3160[4] ◆ (3582) (3820) 4470[5] (5273) ◆ 5908[8] 6736[12]

Mount Crystal (IRE) *B W Hills* a26
2 b f Montjeu(IRE) —State Crystal (IRE) (High Estate)
7385[12]

Mount Hadley (USA) *David Pipe* a83 93
6 b g Elusive Quality(USA) —Fly To The Moon (USA) (Blushing Groom (FR))
1156[7] 1533[4] 1826[7] 2760[2] 3318[13] 7251[11]

Mount Hollow *David Bourton* a63 63
5 b g Beat Hollow—Lady Lindsay (IRE) (Danehill Dancer (IRE))
7706[4]

Mount Juliet (IRE) *Marco Botti* a73 62
3 b f Danehill Dancer(IRE) —Stylist (IRE) (Sadler's Wells (USA))
(933) 1593[5] 2565[10] 4365[5] 4839[5] 6541[3] 7209[5] 7377[4]

Mountrath *Brett Johnson* a68 78
3 b g Dubai Destination(USA) —Eurolink Sundance (Night Shift (USA))
1260[5] 1844[6] 2510[3] 4422[7] 4994[5] 6692[11] 7162[11] 7323[13] (7768)

Mourayan (IRE) *Robert Hickmott* 118
4 b h Alhaarth(IRE) —Mouramara (IRE) (Kahyasi)
6947a[13]

Mourilyan (IRE) *H J Brown* a107 119
6 b h Desert Prince(IRE) —Mouramara (IRE) (Kahyasi)
516a[2] 1026a[13]

Move In Time *Bryan Smart* 100
2 ch c Monsieur Bond(IRE) —Tibesti (Machiavellian (USA))
2059[11] (2498) 3049[11] 4138[3] 5219[7] 5880[14] 6141[4] 6568[5] 6734[2]

Movingly (USA) *John Gosden* a27
2 b f Galileo(IRE) —Ballette (IRE) (Giant's Causeway (USA))
7733[9]

Moving Picture *Ben Haslam* a13 55
2 b g Antonius Pius(USA) —By Arrangement (IRE) (Bold Arrangement)
1065[10] 2605[4] 2836[6] 6072[14]

Moyenne Corniche *Brian Ellison* a101 106
5 ch g Selkirk(USA) —Miss Corniche (Hernando (FR))
5951[7] 6738[3] 7100[16] 7507[2] 7823a[DSQ]

Moynahan (USA) *Paul Cole* a103 101
5 ch g Johannesburg(USA) —Lakab (USA) (Manila (USA))
1006[16] 1455[3] 1767[4] (2322) 3069[16] 3692[6] 4455[11] 5004[2] 5529[5] 5955[5] 6318[6]

Mozayada (USA) *Mel Brittain* a82 71
6 ch m Street Cry(IRE) —Fatina (Nashwan (USA))
115[8] 544[4] 572[2] 837[9] 1115[14] 1396[13] 1808[4] 2262[2]

Mr Brock (SAF) *Mme C Head-Maarek* a119 108
7 b g Fort Wood(USA) —Cape Badger (SAF) (Badger Land (USA))
(415a) 609a[4] (708a) 800a[3] 1027a[8] 4166a[7] 6344a[7]

Mr Charlie (NZ) *Peter G Moody* 103
5 b h Golan(IRE) —Timpani (AUS) (Maizcay (AUS))
7032a[4] 7368a[11]

Mr Chocolate Drop (IRE) *Mandy Rowland* a66 58
6 b g Danetime(IRE) —Forest Blade (IRE) (Charnwood Forest (IRE))
939[6] 1142[10] 1193[3] 1503[11] 1998[12] 3131[3] 3279[5] (4485) 5271[2] 5767[2] 6189[5] 7168[4] 7298[8]

Mr. Crazy Boy (ARG) *M F De Kock* a85 97
4 br g Numerous(USA) —Crazy Fitz (ARG) (Fitzcarraldo (ARG))
414a[7] 609a[12] 819a[5] 1023a[12]

Mr David (USA) *Brian Meehan* 103
3 b g Sky Mesa(USA) —Dancewiththebride (USA) (Belong To Me (USA))
5275[6] 5911[11] 6735[8]

Mr Deal *Eve Johnson Houghton* a55 51
4 b g King's Best(USA) —One Of The Family (Alzao (USA))
100[8]

Mr Dream Maker (IRE) *Ian Williams* 62
2 b g Araafa(IRE) —Paola Maria (Daylami (IRE))
5608[5] 6046[3] 7201[5]

Mr Emirati (USA) *Bryan Smart* a70 65
3 ch g Mr Greeley(USA) —Kathy K D (USA) (Saint Ballado (CAN))
6124[4] (7498) 7678[5] 7845[2]

Mr Fantozzi (IRE) *Desmond Donovan* a50 67
5 br g Statue Of Liberty(USA) —Indian Sand (Indian King (USA))
142[2] 568[7] 2783[8] 2965[14]

Mr Freddy (IRE) *Richard Fahey* 92
4 b g Intikhab(USA) —Bubble N Squeak (IRE) (Catrail (USA))
(1631) 2349[2] 2857[13]

Mr Funshine *Derek Shaw* a63 62
5 b g Namid—Sunrise Girl (King's Signet (USA))
112[8] 243[7] (726) ◆ (860) 967[8] 1068[4] 1131[2] 1915[11] 6880[11] 7154[8] 7542[9] 7807[3] 7860[8] 7953[6]

Mr Harmoosh (IRE) *Edward Vaughan* a71 79
3 b g Noverre(USA) —Polish Affair (IRE) (Polish Patriot (USA))
1476[7] (1970) 2336[5] 2460[2] 2906[2] (4439) 4763[2] (4870) (5593) 6122[9] 7205[3]

Mr Hichens *Karen George* a90 84
5 b g Makbul—Lake Melody (Sizzling Melody)
676[7] (855) (966) 1051[3] 1265[3] (1841) 2640[5] 3969[10]

Mr Howe *Tim Fitzgerald* a42 24
3 b g Superior Premium—Portacasa (Robellino (USA))
4018[6] 6716[6] 7069[9]

Mr Irons (USA) *Sir Michael Stoute* 87
3 ch c Mr Greeley(USA) —Jive Talk (USA) (Kingmambo (USA))
1352[8] 2386[4] 2933[2] 3867[10] (4956) 5415[3]

Mr Khan *James Moffatt* 53
2 ch g Rambling Bear—Frabrofen (Mind Games)
1864[3] 2272[7] 2577[6]

Mr Loire *Milton Harris* a55 44
6 b g Bertolini(USA) —Miss Sancerre (Last Tycoon)
2021[12] 3056[9] 3131[8] 3524[9] 3715[6]

Mr Lu *Jim Goldie* a61 68
5 b g Lujain(USA) —Libretta (Highest Honor (FR))
1928[2] 2293[5] (2454) 3164[5] 3706[5] 3948[4] 5405[7] 6026[12] 6710[8] 7241[3] 7501[6]

Mr Macattack *Tom Dascombe* a86 85
5 b g Machiavellian(USA) —Aunty Rose (IRE) (Caerleon (USA))
1862[7] 2736[16] 3389[10] 4065[4] 5407[8] 7915[3]

Mr Man In The Moon (IRE) *Paul W Flynn* a70 89
2 gr g Verglas(IRE) —Dancing Drop (Green Desert (USA))
3939a[4]

Mr Maximas *Bryn Palling* a54 50
3 ch g Auction House(USA) —Cashiki (IRE) (Case Law)
1392[5] 3264[4] 4280[9] 4676[11] 7575[4] 7728[3] 7919[3]

Mr Medici (IRE) *L Ho* a101 120
5 b h Medicean—Way For Life (GER) (Platini (GER))
1568a[8] 6947a[6] ◆ 7291a[10] 7851a[12]

Mr Mohican (IRE) *Ann Duffield* 47
3 b g Barathea(IRE) —Tipi Squaw (King's Best (USA))
1394[11] 1971[7] 2209[11]

Mr Mo Jo *Robin Bastiman* 63
2 b c Danbird(AUS) —Nampara Bay (Emarati (USA))
4409[9] 4896[5] 5418[9] 6705[8]

Mr Money Maker *John Flint* a69 77
3 ch g Ishiguru(USA) —Ellopassoff (Librate)
3766[5] 4222[4] (5584) 6372[10] 6422[5] 6774[7] 7205[10]

Mr Muddle *Sheena West* 35
3 gr g Imperial Dancer—Spatham Rose (Environment Friend)
2401[12]

Mr Optimistic *Richard Fahey* a68 53
2 b c Kyllachy—Noble Desert (FR) (Green Desert (USA))
1626[4] 2448[7] 3118[4] 6075[10] 6740[8] 7268[3] 7423[4] (7598) 7696[4]

Mr Perceptive (IRE) *Richard Hannon* 79
2 b g Iffraaj—Astuti (IRE) (Waajib)
3269[7] 4490[3] (4962)

Mr Plod *Andrew Reid* a67 53
5 ch g Silver Patriarch(IRE) —Emily-Mou (IRE) (Cadeaux Genereux)
(989) 1169[5] 1768[5] 2014[5] 4226[4]

Mr Prize Fighter *Ian McInnes* 46
3 b g Piccolo—Lv Girl (IRE) (Mukaddamah (USA))
1648[6] 2432[6] 2879[11] 4687[13]

Mr Rainbow *Alan Swinbank* a98 93
4 ch g Efisio—Blossom (Warning)
1117[9] (3033) 3969[2] 4370[6] 5242[7]

Mr Rooney (IRE) *Alan Berry* a59 42
7 b g Mujadil(USA) —Desert Bride (USA) (Key To The Kingdom (USA))
1072[9] 1146[6] 1965[6] 2669[8] 3075[4] 3946[11] 4245[7] 4605[11] 5362[8] 6644[11]

Mrs Batt (IRE) *John W Nicholson* a33 55
4 ch m Medecis—She's Wonderful (IRE) (Magical Wonder (USA))
7376[10]

Mrs Boss (BRZ) *A Cintra Pereira* a95
4 b m Wild Event(USA) —Lychee (BRZ) (De Quest)
628a[7] 797a[11]

Mrs Boss *Rod Millman* a72 78
3 b f Makbul—Chorus (Bandmaster (USA))
222[4] 257[3] (445) 662[4] 1140[4] 1449[3] 2049[6] 2679[2] 3115[4] 3336[4] 3677[7] 4553[2] 5764[2] 6284[10]

Mrs Dee Bee (IRE) *B W Hills* 62
2 b f Barathea(IRE) —Daqtora (Dr Devious (IRE))
6803[6]

Mrs G *Richard Guest* 17
2 ch f Ad Valorem(USA) —First Ace (First Trump)
4336[9] 5385[11]

Mrs Greeley *Eve Johnson Houghton* 62
2 b f Mr Greeley(USA) —Swain's Gold (USA) (Swain (IRE))
5692[11] 6442[6] 7094[6]

Mr Shammie *Michael Quinlan*
3 b g Lucky Story(USA) —Inchalong (Inchinor)
5028[13] 5645[5] 6255[16] 7472[8]

Mrs Happy (IRE) *Tracey Collins* a65 70
2 ch f King's Best(USA) —Wee Mad Snout (IRE) (Soviet Star (USA))
2035a[4] 5570a[11]

Mr Shifter *Linda Stubbs* 48
2 b g Auction House(USA) —Laser Crystal (IRE) (King's Theatre (IRE))
2498[8] 3106[5] 3353[5] 4848[9]

Mr Skipiton (IRE) *B J McMath* a65 73
5 b g Statue Of Liberty(USA) —Salty Air (IRE) (Singspiel (IRE))
1595[5] 1929[7] 2726[3] 3762[11] 4589[5] 6270[8] 6679[7] 7155[4] 7426[2] (7883) 8035[6]

Mrs Lovely *Paul D'Arcy* 26
2 b f Beat Hollow—Circle Of Light (Anshan)
6159[16] 7000[8]

Mr Smithson (IRE) *Brian Ellison* a65 67
3 br g Xaar—Amanda Louise (IRE) (Perugino (USA))
4[4]

Mrs Mogg *Tom Dascombe* a69 67
3 b f Green Desert(USA) —Maybe Forever (Zafonic (USA))
1861[8] 2212[2] 2588[2] 3115[9] 3726[3] 4151[2] 4998[5] (5670) 6026[8]

Mrs Neat (IRE) *Sylvester Kirk* a57 46
2 b f Refuse To Bend(IRE) —Cambara (Dancing Brave (USA))
2077[10] 6511[8] 7010[7] 7394[9] 7496[4] 7813[2] 7888[2]

Mrs Nisbett (IRE) *Alan McCabe* a13 46
2 b f Acclamation—Spanker (Suave Dancer (USA))
1463[4] 1978[8] 2848[7] 3058[11] 7527[9] 7641[7]

Mrs Onc *Adrian Chamberlain*
7 b m Mtoto—Sunlit Girl (Ardross)
421[9]

Mrs Penny (AUS) *Jeremy Gask* a81 82
6 br m Planchet(AUS) —Respective (AUS) (Noalcoholic (FR))
1332[8] 2327[4] 2689[4] 3435[7] 5495[14]

Mrs Puff (IRE) *David Evans* a44 48
3 gr f Trans Island—Canosa (IRE) (Catrail (USA))
2460[8]

Mrs Slocombe (IRE) *Nikki Evans* a51 78
4 b m Masterful(USA) —Mrs Beatty (Cadeaux Genereux)
32[5] 211[5] 353[13] 545[P]

Mr Udagawa *Bernard Llewellyn* a70 76
4 b g Bahamian Bounty—Untold Riches (USA) (Red Ransom (USA))
966[8] 1388[9] 1530[6] 1841[3] 2024[12] 2922[8] 3257[6] 3853[6] 4382[6] 4620[6] 4985[2] (5906) 6657[3] 7125[10]

Mr Willis *John Best* a96 89
4 b g Desert Sun—Santiburi Girl (Casteddu)
358[5] 635[6] 3146[8] 3692[14] 4030[3] ◆ 7187[2] 7430[5]

Mr Wolf *John Quinn* a77 83
9 b g Wolfhound(USA) —Madam Millie (Milford)
1276[2] 1470[2] 1924[14] 2275[4] 2818[3] 3356[5] 4121[4] (4415) 4712[2] 5123[6] (5424) 5941[5] 6981[11] 7143[12] 7283[13]

Mt Desert *Edwin Tuer* a24 47
8 b g Rainbow Quest(USA) —Chief Bee (Chief's Crown (USA))
1113[13] 1467[7] 2464[7]

Mt Kintyre (IRE) *Mick Channon* a39 76
4 b g Mull Of Kintyre(USA) —Nihonpillow Mirai (IRE) (Zamindar (USA))
3862[11] 4201[8] 4621[10] 4870[10]

Mubtadi *David Simcock* 78
2 b c Dr Fong(USA) —Noble Peregrine (Lomond (USA))
3433[5] (5170) 6200[11]

Much Acclaimed (IRE) *Tom Tate* 85
3 b g Sulamani(IRE) —Much Commended (Most Welcome)
(1335) 1730[8] 2515[6] 3206[P]

Muchtar (FR) *J-L Pelletan* 68
2 b c High Yield(USA) —Mysteryonthebounty (USA) (Mystery Storm (USA))
6589a[0]

Mudaaraah *John Dunlop* 105
3 b f Cape Cross(IRE) —Wissal (USA) (Woodman (USA))
1729[5] 2224[4] 3071[9] 4347[2] 4957[3] 6886[12]

Mudawin (IRE) *James Moffatt* a99 84
9 b g Intikhab(USA) —Fida (IRE) (Persian Heights)
1525[8] 2060[10]

Mudhish (IRE) *Clive Brittain* a73 75
5 b g Lujain(USA) —Silver Satire (Dr Fong (USA))
595[3] 696[9] 2009[8] 4237[5] 4438[5]

Mufarrh (IRE) *John Dunlop* 93
3 b g Marju(IRE) —What A Picture (FR) (Peintre Celebre (USA))
1313[5] 2045[3] 3827[7]

Muffraaj *David Simcock* a48 73
2 b c Iffraaj—Heckle (In The Wings)
6324[3] 6827[2] ◆ 7335[8]

Muftarres (IRE) *Paul Midgley* a83 86
5 b g Green Desert(USA) —Ghazal (USA) (Gone West (USA))
1513[15] 2937[15] 3239[7] 4198[6] 4620[3] 4852[2] 5530[5] 5819[6] 5958[5]

Mufti (IRE) *Jeremy Noseda* a55 79
3 b c Noverre(USA) —Dark Indian (IRE) (Indian Ridge)
2968[6] (4705) 5264[11]

Mugeba *Chris Dwyer* a49 40
9 b m Primo Dominie—Ella Lamees (Statoblest)
1131[10]

Muhandis (IRE) *Ed Dunlop* a71 57
2 b c Muhtathir—Ahdaaf (USA) (Bahri (USA))
4803[10] 5892[6]

Muhannak (IRE) *B Cecil* a112 111
6 bb g Chester House(USA) —Opera (Forzando)
1435a[8]

Muhtaker *J E Hammond* a84 94
3 ch c Medicean—Kalindi (Efisio)
6761a[9]

Mujaadel (USA) *David Nicholls* a88 82
5 ch g Street Cry(IRE) —Quiet Rumour (USA) (Alleged (USA))
1707[5] 2241[7] 2328[4] 2579[7] 2937[4] 3107[6] 3876[11] 3920[7] 4619[13] (5500) 5533[4] 5789[4] 6567[3] 7143[7]

Mujaazef *Kevin Prendergast* a84 95
3 b g Dubawi(IRE) —Khubza (Green Desert (USA))
4463a[12] 5571a[24]

Mujada *David O'Meara* a20 34
5 b m Mujahid(USA) —Catriona (Bustino)
2434[9] 3282[6] 3804[6] 6077[8] 6966[10] 7131[9]

Mujahope *Colin Teague* a67 12
5 b g Mujahid(USA) —Speak (Barathea (IRE))
4795[7]

Mujamead *Gerald Ham* a64 28
6 b g Mujahid(USA) —Island Mead (Pharly (FR))
15[3] 263[14]

Mujapiste (IRE) *Lawrence Mullaney* a41 38
2 b f Mujadil(USA) —Lady Piste (IRE) (Ali-Royal (IRE))
5418[8] 6263[7] 6646[8] 7279[11] 7392[6] 7692[7] 7894[10]

Mujarah (IRE) *John Dunlop* 58
2 b f Marju(IRE) —Tanaghum (Darshaan)
6154[14] 6770[13] 7057[10]

Mujdeya *John Gosden* a56 99
3 gr f Linamix(FR) —Majhud (IRE) (Machiavellian (USA))
1356[2] 2051[5] (2891) 3427[3] (5444) 6095[10] 7189[14]

Mujdy (IRE) *Brett Johnson* a17 13
3 b g Observatory(USA) —Eltihaab (USA) (Danzig (USA))
949[5] 2812[10] 3557[9] 4027[7] 6652[7]

Mujood *Eve Johnson Houghton* a79 101
7 b g Mujahid(USA) —Waqood (USA) (Riverman (USA))
1533[8] (1962) 2322[2] 2595[12] 2708[13] 3334[8] 3591[3] 4459[14] 4579[3] 5004[7] 5416[4] (5993) 6510[11]

Mujrayaat (IRE) *Michael Jarvis* a78 78
2 b c Invincible Spirit(IRE) —Ellen (IRE) (Machiavellian (USA))
2171[2] 2561[3] 5893[2]

Muktasb (USA) *Derek Shaw* a64 16
9 b g Bahri(USA) —Maghaarb (Machiavellian (USA))
14[6] 193[4] 404[3] 532[4] 556[2] 674[7] 694[4] 7731[0] (961) 1166[5] 1534[7] 1885[10] 2234[7]

Mulan (GER) *W Hickst* 98
3 b c Marju(IRE) —Morning Light (GER) (Law Society (USA))
5671a[5] 6410a[6]

Mulaqat *D Selvaratnam* a96 93
7 b g Singspiel(IRE) —Atamana (IRE) (Lahib (USA))
335a[8] 516a[10]

Mulaqen *Marcus Tregoning* a69 67
2 ch c Haafhd—Burqa (Nashwan (USA))
6874[2] 7248[4]

Mullglen *Tim Easterby* 81
4 b g Mull Of Kintyre(USA) —However (IRE) (Hector Protector (USA))
1364[5] ◆ (1711) 2465[6] 2626[6] 3540[2] 3660[3] 4243[8] 4952[9] 5297[4] 5760[7]

Mullins Way (USA) *F J Brennan* 82
2 ch c Mr Greeley(USA) —Aljawza (USA) (Riverman (USA))
2163[5] 3049[8] 3985[2]

Mullionmileanhour (IRE) *John Best* a101 114
4 b h Mull Of Kintyre(USA) —Lady Lucia (IRE) (Royal Applause)
737[3] ◆ 1326[2] 2030[11]

Mullitovermaurice *Patrick Morris* a59 26
4 ch g Pursuit Of Love—Ellovamul (Elmaamul (USA))
255[10] 400[4] 509[7] 814[4] 875[3] 1194[4] 1478[12] 1920[14] 5767[5] 7071[7] 7429[10] 7918[8]

Mull Of Dubai *David Nicholls* a58 100
7 b g Mull Of Kintyre(USA) —Enlisted (IRE) (Sadler's Wells (USA))
1274[12] 1829[9] 2096[10] 2343[4] 2747[3] 2976[10] 3873[U]

Mull Of Killough (IRE) *John Spearing* 102
4 b g Mull Of Kintyre(USA) —Sun Shower (IRE) (Indian Ridge)
1008[3] 1383[21] 2708[5] 3069[26]

Mullsdword (IRE) *Pat Murphy*
3 b g Mull Of Kintyre(USA) —Segoria (IRE) (Shinko Forest (IRE))
1757[14]

Multahab *Michael Wigham* a62 69
11 bb g Zafonic(USA) —Alumisiyah (USA) (Danzig (USA))
2196[2] (3052) 3293[2] 3527[3] 4693[6]

Mumtaz Begum *John E Long* 32
5 ch m Kyllachy—Indian Gift (Cadeaux Genereux)
1591[14] 5325[8]

Munaaseb *Ed Dunlop* 60
2 ch c Zafeen(FR) —Miss Prim (Case Law)
7002[7]

Munaawer (USA) *James Bethell* a79 78
3 ch g Mr Greeley(USA) —Tap Dance (USA) (Pleasant Tap (USA))
(547a) 741a[7] 1189[9] 2101[3] 2323[5] 3123[5] 5093[6] 6326[4] 6937[10]

Munaddam (USA) *E Charpy* a107 113
8 ch g Aljabr(USA) —Etizaaz (USA) (Diesis)
438a[3] 607a[9] 818a[7]

Muncaster Castle (IRE) *Roger Fisher* a54 58
6 b g Johannesburg(USA) —Eubee (FR) (Common Grounds)
410[4] 1462[6]

Mundher (IRE) *J E Hammond* a50
3 b g Fantastic Light(USA) —Manchaca (FR) (Highest Honor (FR))
547a[6]

Mungo Park *Mark Johnston* 66
2 b c Selkirk(USA) —Key Academy (Royal Academy (USA))
6828[4] 7303[5]

Munich (IRE) *Roger Curtis* a71 58
6 b g Noverre(USA) —Mayara (IRE) (Ashkalani (IRE))
(235) ◆ 965[9] 3683[10] 4700[8] 5326[6] 6518[4]

Munro's Dragon *Mark H Tompkins* a45 50
2 b c Sakhee(USA) —Qilin (IRE) (Second Set (IRE))
4802[8] 5170[6] 5523[12] 6129[3] 7126[4]

Munsarim (IRE) *John Dunlop* 88
3 b c Shamardal(USA) —Etizaaz (USA) (Diesis)
2554[8] (3587) 4106[5] 5091[4] 6151[5] 7012[12]

Munsef *Ian Williams* a87 112
7 b g Zafonic(USA) —Mazaya (IRE) (Sadler's Wells (USA))
1859[3] 2345[2] 3195[10] 3672[10] 7297[9] 7594[12]

Muntami (IRE) *John Harris* a45 59
9 gr g Daylami(IRE) —Bashashah (IRE) (Kris)
41[5]

Muntasib (USA) *Marcus Tregoning* a85 73
2 ch c Mr Greeley(USA) —Halo River (USA) (Irish River (FR))
4691[2] 5263[5] (6849) (7652)

Muntherah (KSA) *B Al Subaie* a78
3 ch f Official Flame(USA) —Assisi (USA) (Halo (USA))
333a[10] ◆ 514a[10]

Muqalad (IRE) *Bryan Smart* a47 75
3 b g Indian Ridge—Tutu Much (IRE) (Sadler's Wells (USA))
6897[9] 7056[10] 7336[7]

Muqtarrib (IRE) *Brian Meehan* 74
2 b c Medicean—Anna Karenina (USA) (Atticus (USA))
6504[5] ◆ 7099[4]

Murano (GER) *Sandor Kovacs*
3 c Sabiango(GER) —Munda Nai (USA) (Spinning World (USA))
4183a[10]

Murbeh (IRE) *Brian Meehan* 91
2 b g Elusive City(USA) —My Funny Valentine (IRE) (Mukaddamah (USA))
(4622) (5301) 5880[9] 6751[6]

Mureb (USA) *Saeed Bin Suroor* a78 76
3 b g Elusive Quality(USA) —Sumoto (Mtoto)
2925[2] 3733[4]

Murhee (USA) *Alison Thorpe* a62 62
4 b g Rahy(USA) —Grand Ogygia (USA) (Ogygian (USA))
676[14]

Murjan (USA) *Darrin Miller* a104
2 bb c Officer(USA) —Miss Jeanne Cat (USA) (Tabasco Cat (USA))
7363a[10]

Muroona (IRE) *Mark Johnston* 54
2 b f Invincible Spirit(IRE) —Knight's Place (IRE) (Hamas (IRE))
5761[6] 6323[P]

Murphys Future *Alan Berry*
5 b g Where Or When(IRE) —Snaefell Heights (Suave Dancer (USA))
6029[11]

Murrin (IRE) *Robert Mills* a77 74
6 bb g Trans Island—Flimmering (Dancing Brave (USA))
444[4] 587[6]

Murura (IRE) *James Given* a77 69
3 b c Green Desert(USA) —Victoria Regia (IRE) (Lomond (USA))
936[10] (997) (1347) ◆ 1656[2] 2069[8] 3394[5]

Musaafer (IRE) *Michael Jarvis* a98 97
3 b g Marju(IRE) —Alexander Icequeen (IRE) (Soviet Star (USA))
1221[4] 1703[6] 3867[8] 4357[5]

Musaalem (USA) *Doug Watson* a104 110
6 gr g Aljabr(USA) —Atyab (USA) (Mr Prospector (USA))
336a[2] 515a[10] 822a[6]

Musashi (IRE) *Laura Mongan* a66 63
5 ch g Hawk Wing(USA) —Soubrette (USA) (Opening Verse (USA))
(160) 229[3] 498[12] 656[6] (970) 1225[3] 1440[5] 1763[6] 2279[5] 2419[3] 2866[4] 2967[9] 5867[5] 6668[7]

Musawama (IRE) *John Gosden* 74
2 b c Azamour(IRE) —Chater (Alhaarth (IRE))
5032[4] ◆ 5916[2]

Musca (IRE) *Chris Grant* 63
6 b g Tendulkar(USA) —Canary Bird (IRE) (Catrail (USA))
3284[11] 4014[2] 4555[7] 4868[9] 5496[6]

Muse To Use *Ian McInnes* 50
2 b f Refuse To Bend(IRE) —Musical Key (Key Of Luck (USA))
2139[2] 2391[6] 2631[6] 2848[4] 3118[7] 3603[8] 3770[6] 4150[9] 5630[10] 6072[16]

Mushagak (IRE) *Ed Dunlop* a52 22
3 b f Oratorio(IRE) —Tetou (IRE) (Peintre Celebre (USA))
106[6]

Musharakaat (IRE) *Ed Dunlop* a77 92
2 b f Iffraaj—Gift Of Spring (USA) (Gilded Time (USA))
(4021) 4842[5] 5910[3] 6559[7]

Mush Mir (IRE) *Jim Boyle* a71 59
3 b g Key Of Luck(USA) —Mawaheb (IRE) (Nashwan (USA))
1165[5] 1878[5] ◆ 3786[7] 7685[5] (7726) 7856[6]

Mushreq (USA) *Sir Michael Stoute* a74 87
3 b g Distorted Humor(USA) —Casual Look (USA) (Red Ransom (USA))
2900[5] (3689) 4152[3]

Mushy Peas (IRE) *David Evans* a59 57
3 b g Bahri(USA) —Unintentional (Dr Devious (IRE))
3511[8] 4364[11] 4679[6] 5579[3] (5650) ◆ 5990[4] 6848[2] 7250[6] 7835[9] 7877[7] 8034[3]

Musical Bridge *Lisa Williamson* a62 76
4 b g Night Shift(USA) —Carrie Pooter (Tragic Role (USA))
1200[8] 1799[9] (2144) (2669) 3076[4] 3356[6] 6303[9] 7169[7]

Musical Delight *Alan Jarvis* a56 23
3 b g Oratorio(IRE) —Living Daylights (IRE) (Night Shift (USA))
1449[4] 3907[7] 5661[5] 5962[11] 7122[9]

Musical Flight *B W Hills* 65
2 b c Hurricane Run(IRE) —Chaminade (USA) (Danzig (USA))
6190[6]

Musical Leap *Shaun Harris*
2 b c Superior Premium—Musical Fair (Piccolo)
7843[11]

Musical Mark *Pam Sly* a72 35
3 b g Oratorio(IRE) —Kite Mark (Mark Of Esteem (IRE))
728[5] 922[3] 1157[2] 2101[4] 3519[9] 4545[12] 6290[6] 6578[8]

Musical Script (USA) *Mouse Hamilton-Fairley* a74 66
7 b g Stravinsky(USA) —Cyrillic (USA) (Irish River (FR))
78[8] 1064[6] 1300[2] 1595[6] 1929[6] (2198) 2456[3] 2643[6] 3982[5] 4308[9] 4690[3] 4777[4] 5237[9] 5877[8] 6439[9] 7502[9] 7761[2] 7972[3]

Music Box Express *George Baker* a70 67
6 b g Tale Of The Cat(USA) —Aly McBe (USA) (Alydeed (CAN))
8[8] 138[8] 234[10] 328[2] 379[6] 472[4]

Music City (IRE) *Mark Johnston* 81
3 ch g Dalakhani(IRE) —Mia Mambo (USA) (Affirmed (USA))
2627[2] ◆ 4845[4] (5860)

Music Festival (USA) *Jim Goldie* 65
3 b c Storm Cat(USA) —Musical Chimes (USA) (In Excess)
1137[8] 2706[3] 3148[6] 3951[3] (5409) 6492[5] 7051[5] 7225[6]

Music In The Rain (IRE) *J S Bolger* 88
2 b c Invincible Spirit(IRE) —Greek Symphony (IRE) (Mozart (IRE))
6403a[6]

Music Lover *John Panvert* a57 58
3 b g Piccolo—Ligne D'Amour (Pursuit Of Love)
1622[6] 2197[5] 2841[8] 3907[U] 4760[7] 5152[4] ◆ 5668[7] 5898[6] 6255[10] 6330[6] 6456[10] 7064[9]

Music Maestro (IRE) *B W Hills* a84 74
3 b g Oratorio(IRE) —Adjalisa (IRE) (Darshaan)
1872[4] 2425[8] 2892[10] 3676[6] 4127[11] 4910[4] 5925[3] 6413[4] (6958) 7082[6]

Music News (USA) *Mark Johnston* 52
2 bb c Forestry(USA) —Country Romance (USA) (Saint Ballado (CAN))
1749[12] 4999[7] 5433[4]

Music Of The Moor (IRE) *Tom Tate* 86
3 ch g Rock Of Gibraltar(IRE) —A La Longue (GER) (Mtoto)
(1297) 2422[2] 3627[6] 4152[5] 4652[5] (6050) 6654[3]

Music Pearl (IRE) *G M Lyons* a74
2 b f Oratorio(IRE) —Oumaldaaya (USA) (Nureyev (USA))
6726a[4]

Music Show (IRE) *Mick Channon* 119
3 b f Noverre(USA) —Dreamboat (USA) (Mr Prospector (USA))
(1312) ◆ 1726[6] ◆ 2370a[3] 3143[4] (3793) 4639a[2] 5773a[3] 6561[4]

Musigny (USA) *Sally Hall* a31 56
4 bb g Forest Wildcat(USA) —Water Rights (USA) (Kris S (USA))
1114[9] 1887[6] 2655[8] 4173[5] 5155[10]

Musir (AUS) *M F De Kock* a122
4 b c Redoute's Choice(AUS) —Dizzy De Lago (AUS) (Encosta De Lago (AUS))
(414a) (608a) (1023a)

Musket Man (USA) *Derek S Ryan* a120
4 bb h Yonaguska(USA) —Fortuesque (USA) (Fortunate Prospect (USA))
4855a[3] 7367a[7]

Musnad (USA) *B W Hills* 85
2 ch c Mr Greeley(USA) —Jadarah (USA) (Red Ransom (USA))
5878[5] 6504[4]

Mustajed *Rod Millman* a74 75
9 b g Alhaarth(IRE) —Jasarah (IRE) (Green Desert (USA))
148[5] 426[9] 735[2] 842[2] 1028[13] 1303[8] 1493[3] 1758[2] 2182[4] (2337) 8032[4]

Mustakmil (IRE) *Simon Dow* a93 76
4 b h Haafhd—Elfaslah (IRE) (Green Desert (USA))
3782[6] 5142[3] ◆ 6449[6] (7115) (7414)

Mut'Ab (USA) *Gary Moore* a76 83
5 b g Alhaarth(IRE) —Mistle Song (Nashwan (USA))
1481[6] 2683[14] 5859[8]

Mutadarrej (IRE) *Ian Williams* a64 66
6 ch g Fantastic Light(USA) —Najayeb (USA) (Silver Hawk (USA))
2430[5] 3760[4] 4223[3] (4530) (4731)

Mutafajer *Saeed Bin Suroor* a82 76
3 br g Oasis Dream—Shahaamah (IRE) (Red Ransom (USA))
(1870) 2450[6] 5383[13]

Mutajaaser (USA) *Kevin Morgan* a69 11
5 b g War Chant(USA) —Hazimah (USA) (Gone West (USA))
98[3] ◆ 308[6] 467[3] 665[3] 1133[7]

Mutajare (IRE) *Mark Johnston* a75 78
2 b c Cadeaux Genereux—Bona Dea (IRE) (Danehill (USA))
3222[4] 3631[7] (5762) 6870[8]

Mutamared (USA) *Andrew Reid* a94 82
10 ch g Nureyev(USA) —Alydariel (USA) (Alydar (USA))
986[3] 1167[2] 1438[7] 1692[9] 2234[5] 2957[9]

Mutanaker *Sir Michael Stoute* a62 78
3 b g Cape Cross(IRE) —Purple Haze (IRE) (Spectrum (IRE))
3477[6] 4069[3] 4572[3] ◆ 5022[2] 5665[3] 6313[5]

Mutasareb (USA) *Saeed Bin Suroor* a42 57
3 b c Nayef(USA) —Saywaan (USA) (Fusaichi Pegasus (USA))
4257[7] 6356[4]

Mutayaser *Sir Michael Stoute* a51 77
2 b c Shamardal(USA) —Borgia (GER) (Acatenango (GER))
5629[5] 6087[2] 7020[10]

Mutheeb (USA) *M Al Muhairi* a114 109
5 b h Danzig(USA) —Magicalmysterykate (USA) (Woodman (USA))
339a[5] (413a) ◆ 607a[2] 797a[2] 1024a[7]

Mutual Force (USA) *Mahmood Al Zarooni* a59 75
2 b c Arch(USA) —Freeroll (USA) (Touch Gold (USA))
(4447) ◆ 5392[4] 6777[4] 7066[7]

Mutual Friend (USA) *David Pipe* a81 79
6 gr g Aljabr(USA) —Dubai Visit (USA) (Quiet American (USA))
2814[5]

Muwakaba (USA) *Sir Michael Stoute* a92 72
3 ch f Elusive Quality(USA) —Saleela (USA) (Nureyev (USA))
2098[5] 2970[7] 5728[3]

Muwalla *James Bethell* a82 82
3 b g Bahri(USA) —Easy Sunshine (IRE) (Sadler's Wells (USA))
617[6] (728) 1330[10] 1657[6] 2117[11] 3351[6] 3697[6] 5300[5] 5942[3] 6467[10] 6961[4]

Muzdahi (USA) *John Dunlop* 73
2 bb c Smarty Jones(USA) —Reem Al Barari (USA) (Storm Cat (USA))
3169[3] ◆ 4346[6]

Muzo (USA) *Chris Dwyer* a70
4 b g Gone West(USA) —Bowl Of Emeralds (USA) (A.P. Indy (USA))
7043[5] 7778[11]

Mvuto *Lucy Wadham* a32 57
5 b m Mtoto—Cavina (Ardross)
3084[12]

My Arch *Ollie Pears* 93
8 b g Silver Patriarch(IRE) —My Desire (Grey Desire)
(1101) ◆ 1525[2] 2541[2] 3974[5] (4846) 6926[8]

Myasun (FR) *C Baillet* a61 79
3 ch g Panis(USA) —Spain (FR) (Bering)
(450a)

My Bentley (NZ) *Michael Kent* 101
6 br g I Conquer(NZ) —La Reine D'Or (NZ) (Dernier Empereur (USA))
7368a[8]

My Best Bet *Stef Higgins* a87 82
4 ch m Best Of The Bests(IRE) —Cibenze (Owington)
150[5] 593[3] 740[6] 873[9] 1797[2] 2601[3] 3217[5] 3565[3] 3962[2] 4206[4] 4847[7] (5716) 6252[9] 6430[11]

My Best Man *Tony Carroll* a38 68
4 b g Forzando—Victoria Sioux (Ron's Victory (USA))
7810[9]

Myboyalfie (USA) *John Jenkins* 69
3 b g Johannesburg(USA) —Scotchbonnetpepper (USA) (El Gran Senor (USA))
6470[5] 6815[5]

My Delirium *Ralph Beckett* 84
2 b f Haafhd—Clare Hills (IRE) (Orpen (USA))
5835[7] 6697[7] (7201) 7534a[5]

Mydy Easy (USA) *Paul Midgley* a64 60
4 bb g Speightstown(USA) —Eze (USA) (Williamstown (USA))
291[4] 570[4] 1098[8] 1293[8] 1526[9]

My Elliemay *David Evans* 62
2 b f Oratorio(IRE) —Virginia Reel (King's Best (USA))
2616[6] 3386[6] 3861[9]

My Flame *John Jenkins* a59 62
5 b g Cool Jazz—Suselja (IRE) (Mon Tresor)
(1958) 2965[13]

My Freedom (IRE) *Saeed Bin Suroor* 87
2 b c Invincible Spirit(IRE) —Priere (Machiavellian (USA))
(5053) ◆ 5849[8]

My Friend Fritz *Peter Hiatt* a74
10 ch g Safawan—Little Scarlett (Mazilier (USA))
3[2] 300[6] 910[4]

My Gacho (IRE) *Mark Johnston* a88 96
8 b g Shinko Forest(IRE) —Floralia (Auction Ring (USA))
177[9] 278[5] 405[8] 1962[3] 2205[3] 2428[3] 3117[5] 3389[3] 3813[6] 4459[7] 4929[2] ◆ 5510[6] 5754[9] 5937[8] 6394[13]

My Galway Man (IRE) *Mark Johnston* a73 65
3 b c Danehill Dancer(IRE) —Dream Valley (IRE) (Sadler's Wells (USA))
3829[4] 4893[4] 5665[6] 6055[13] 6623[10]

My Girl Anna (IRE) *Muredach Kelly* a76 71
3 b f Orpen(USA) —Kooyong (IRE) (College Chapel)
(5960)

My Grand Duke (USA) *Jamie Osborne* a52 62
3 b g Johannesburg(USA) —Hit It Here Cafe (USA) (Grand Slam (USA))
1796[6] 2359[9] 2460[9]

My Indy (ARG) *Saeed Bin Suroor* a117
6 br h Indygo Shiner(USA) —My Light (ARG) (Southern Halo (USA))
338a[14]

My Jeanie (IRE) *Jimmy Fox* a38 49
6 ch m King Charlemagne(USA) —Home Comforts (Most Welcome)
682[7] 780[8] 940[11] 1772[3] 3323[14] 5254[10] 5585[7] 6061[5]

My Jen (USA) *Eddie Kenneally* a104
3 rg f Fusaichi Pegasus(USA) —Mekko Hokte (USA) (Holy Bull (USA))
7341a[13]

Myjestic Melody (IRE) *Noel Wilson* 49
2 bb f Majestic Missile(IRE) —Bucaramanga (IRE) (Distinctly North (USA))
3199[5] 4650[4] 5239[5]

My Kingdom (IRE) *David Nicholls* a82 98
4 b g King's Best(USA) —Nebraas (Green Desert (USA))
1438[6] 1848[2] 1963[4] (2926) 3579[5] ◆ 4459[10] (5834) (6357) 6721[13] 7348[14]

Mykingdomforahorse *Mick Channon* 81
4 b g Fantastic Light(USA) —Charlecote (IRE) (Caerleon (USA))
1690[5] 2126[6] 3159[4] 3475[2] 3865[2] 4141[4] 5612[4] 6224[2] 6322[4] 6774[3] 7101[9]

My Last Duchess *Michael Blanshard* a30
3 b f Avonbridge—Mulberry Wine (Benny The Dip (USA))
4840[8]

My Learned Friend (IRE) *Andrew Balding* a68 83
6 b g Marju(IRE) —Stately Princess (Robellino (USA))
1224[8] 1634[2] 1914[9] 2846[2] 3212[11] 3579[11] 5838[5]

My Les *Jim Best* a60 65
4 b m Josr Algarhoud(IRE) —Ashantiana (Ashkalani (IRE))
7968[8]

My Little Star (IRE) *B W Hills* a34 66
2 b f Noverre(USA) —Opera Star (IRE) (Sadler's Wells (USA))
4658[4] ◆ 5441[4] 6305[5] 6809[4] 7295[11]

My Lord *Bill Turner* a81 63
2 br g Ishiguru(USA) —Lady Smith (Greensmith)
(3603) 3864[3] 4195[4] 4436[2] 5921[3] 6435[8] 6842[3] (7378) (7528) 7762[2]

My Love Fajer (IRE) *George Prodromou* a71 66
2 ch c Exceed And Excel(AUS) —Karenaragon (Aragon)
3439[3] 3756[12] 4363[3] 5720[3] 6286[2] 6900[9] 7207[6] 7592[5]

My Mandy (IRE) *Ronald Harris* a61 69
3 b f Xaar—Ikan (IRE) (Sri Pekan (USA))
392[5] 473[3] 759[5] 906[9] 962[4] 1237[4]

My Manikato *Luca Cumani* 74
3 ch g Starcraft(NZ) —Rainbow Queen (FR) (Spectrum (IRE))
2401[3] 4207[2] 5258[3] 5665[5]

My Mate Al *Tom Dascombe* a58 26
2 b f Deportivo—Yes Dear (Fantastic Light (USA))
1510[10] 2183[3] 2638[11] 3686[9] 3858[6]

Mymateeric *Jeff Pearce* a55 56
4 b g Reset(AUS) —Ewenny (Warrshan (USA))
186[3] 316[7] 376[4] 584[8] 4765[2] 5688[7] 6272[2] 6855[5] 7213[10]

My Mate Jake (IRE) *James Given* a56 71
2 ch c Captain Rio—Jam (IRE) (Arazi (USA))
2980[7] 3624[5] 4346[10] 5597[5] 6130[2] 6978[3] 7324[3]

My Mate Les (IRE) *John Best* 38
2 b g High Chaparral(IRE) —Precedence (IRE) (Polish Precedent (USA))
5491[12] 6159[15]

My Mate Mal *William Stone* a74 75
6 b g Daawe(USA) —Kandymal (IRE) (Prince Of Birds (USA))
327[4] (377) (521) 719[2] 923[3] 2182[3] 2560[2] 3221[4] 3764[6] 7694[5] 7898[4] 7985[5]

My Mate Max *Reg Hollinshead* a71 82
5 b g Fraam—Victory Flip (IRE) (Victory Note (USA))
(1931) 2495[2] 3398[2] 4147[3] 4933[6] 6715[5]

My Meteor *Tony Newcombe* a59 23
3 b g Bahamian Bounty—Emerald Peace (IRE) (Green Desert (USA))
550[6] ◆ 997[5] 1731[10] 2185[13] 4989[13] 5957[7]

My Mirasol *Don Cantillon* a61 65
6 ch m Primo Valentino(IRE) —Distinctly Blu (IRE) (Distinctly North (USA))
407[4] 682[8] 816[5]

My Name Is Bert *Lucinda Featherstone* a61
4 b g Bertolini(USA) —Argostoli (Marju (IRE))
6332[6] 6696[4] 7086[8] 7377[2] 7502[10]

My Name Is Bond (FR) *J-C Rouget* 111
2 b c Monsieur Bond(IRE) —Lady Oriande (Makbul)
(5799a) 6610a[6]

My Nan Nell (IRE) *Marco Botti* a72 66
3 ch f Danroad(AUS) —Princesse Sonia (FR) (Ashkalani (IRE))
533[6] ◆ (864) 2652[7] 3081[6]

My One Weakness (IRE) *Brian Ellison* a70 75
3 ch g Bertolini(USA) —Lucina (Machiavellian (USA))
3410[5] 3898[11] 4369[9] 4901[5] 5482[5] 5758[6] 6189[9] 7128[5] 7402[3] 7730[2]

Myplacelater *David Elsworth* a92 112
3 ch f Where Or When(IRE) —Star Welcome (Most Welcome)
385[6] (545) ◆ 973[2] 1082[5] (1354) 1820[4] 2076[7] (4068) 4507[12] (5853) (6533) 6928[2]

Myraid *Ollie Pears* 59
3 b g Danbird(AUS) —My Desire (Grey Desire)
1336[6] 1927[9] 6623[13]

My Red Kite *Gavin Blake* a53 59
3 ch g Avonbridge—Cup Of Love (USA) (Behrens (USA))
3725[7]

Myriola *Derek Shaw* a43 49
5 ch m Captain Rio—Spaniola (IRE) (Desert King (IRE))
531[8] 774[8]

My Ruby (IRE) *Jim Best* 25
2 b f Oasis Dream—Dreams Come True (FR) (Zafonic (USA))
1972[9]

My Shadow *Simon Dow* a83 75
5 b g Zamindar(USA) —Reflections (Sadler's Wells (USA))
3514[9]

My Single Malt (IRE) *Tom Tate* 82
2 b c Danehill Dancer(IRE) —Slip Dance (IRE) (Celtic Swing)
1905[5] 3433[6] (4650) (5597) 5947[4] 6690[8]

My Sister *Mark Usher* a54 67
3 b f Royal Applause—Mysistra (FR) (Machiavellian (USA))
2359[13] 2901[4] 3852[2] 4988[2] 5541[5] 5887[7] 6856[11] 7856[5]

My Son Max *Richard Hannon* a79 86
2 b g Avonbridge—Pendulum (Pursuit Of Love)
(1389) 2127[2] ◆ 2514[3] 4550[7] 5245[12] 6870[5]

Mysterious Bounty (IRE) *Michael Dods* 65
2 ch c Bahamian Bounty—Soubrette (USA) (Opening Verse (USA))
1806[4] 2498[5] 4187[11]

Mystery Star (IRE) *Mark H Tompkins* a102 104
5 ch g Kris Kin(USA) —Mystery Hill (USA) (Danehill (USA))
1274[7] 2096[3] 3194[17] 6720[7] (7196) 7507[4]

Mystica (IRE) *Dominic Ffrench Davis* a61 61
2 b f Noverre(USA) —Mystery Play (IRE) (Sadler's Wells (USA))
2749[9] 3156[4] 3778[4] 4254[7] 4677[5] 6740[10] 6986[5]

Mystic Edge *Michael Bell* 54
2 ch f Needwood Blade—Magic Flo (Magic Ring (IRE))
6469[9] 6859[8] 7231[8]

Mystic Halo *Liam Corcoran* a21
7 ch m Medicean—Aglow (Spinning World (USA))
7244[6] 7419[11]

Mystic Touch *Andrew Haynes* a59 49
4 b g Systematic—Lycius Touch (Lycius (USA))
1539[7] 2303[9] 3264[9] 7315[7] 7429[6]

Mystic Winds *Brian Ellison* 69
2 b f Shirocco(GER) —Mega (IRE) (Petardia)
(6964)

Mystified (IRE) *Roger Fisher* a59 61
7 b g Raise A Grand(IRE) —Sunrise (IRE) (Sri Pekan (USA))
7213[2]

My Sweet Georgia (IRE) *Stef Higgins* a73 76
4 b m Royal Applause—Harda Arda (USA) (Nureyev (USA))
675[7] 893[6]

Mythical Blue (IRE) *Peter Grayson* a46 83
4 b g Acclamation—Proud Myth (IRE) (Mark Of Esteem (IRE))
1779[11] 2280[7] 2997[7] 3809[7] 4510[11] 4938[11] 5876[9] 8036[7]

Mythical Power (USA) *Bob Baffert* a113
4 b h Congaree(USA) —School For Scandal (USA) (Is It True (USA))
5780a[2]

Mytivil (IRE) *Heather Main* a64 69
4 gr m Clodovil(IRE) —Mytilene (IRE) (Soviet Star (USA))
2337[11]

My Vindication (USA) *Richard Hannon* a73 71
2 bb c Vindication(USA) —Classy Mirage (USA) (Storm Bird (CAN))
6088^{5} 6689^{6} (7034) 7572^{3}
Naadrah *J E Hammond* a67 96
3 b f Muhtathir—Princess D'Orange (FR) (Anabaa (USA))
$5139a^{4}$
Nabah *Clive Brittain* a74 95
2 b f Motivator—Kiss And Fly (IRE) (Priolo (USA))
6796^{4} 6927^{4} ◆ 7235^{5}
Nabari (JPN) *Luca Cumani* 71
3 br f Symboli Kris S(USA) —Suzuka Colors (JPN) (Sunday Silence (USA))
2050^{5} 2697^{10} 4114^{6} 5654^{10}
Nabeeda *Mel Brittain* a63 59
5 b g Namid—Lovellian (Machiavellian (USA))
70^{4} 142^{4} 369^{2} 838^{4} 912^{5} 2646^{7}
Nabrina (IRE) *Mel Brittain* a52 52
3 ch f Namid—My Cadeaux (Cadeaux Genereux)
127^{8} 870^{2} 1155^{4} 2530^{7}
Nacho Friend (USA) *Kelly Breen* a102
3 ch c Friends Lake(USA) —You'renotlistening (USA) (Kennedy Road (CAN))
$824a^{3}$
Nacho Libre *Michael Easterby* a77 72
5 b g Kyllachy—Expectation (IRE) (Night Shift (USA))
(27) 255^{9} 393^{8} 1063^{11} 2578^{9} 2700^{5} 3061^{5} 3855^{9} 4555^{4} 5067^{4} 5920^{11} 6371^{12} 6898^{7} 7331^{7} (7614)
Naddwah *Michael Jarvis* a75 81
3 ch f Pivotal—My Dubai (IRE) (Dubai Millennium)
(2473) (4250) 4699^{5} 7182^{16}
Nadeen (IRE) *Michael Smith* a85 85
3 b g Bahamian Bounty—Janayen (USA) (Zafonic (USA))
6358^{9} 6723^{9} 7144^{5} 7399^{2} ◆ 7539^{2}
Nadinska *Mick Channon* a69 67
3 b f Doyen(IRE) —Funny Girl (IRE) (Darshaan)
545^{4} 754^{2} 1278^{6} 1538^{3} 2005^{8} 2329^{3} 4775^{6} 4989^{8} 5162^{3} 5514^{4} 5726^{2} 6018^{4} 6285^{3} 6420^{2} 6638^{2} (6773) 6952^{7}
Nafura *Saeed Bin Suroor* a91 94
3 b f Dubawi(IRE) —Mysterial (USA) (Alleged (USA))
1850^{4} 2479^{3} 3298^{2} 5329^{2} 6199^{4} 7206^{3} 7420^{4}
Nahab *David Lanigan* a65 70
3 b f Selkirk(USA) —State Secret (Green Desert (USA))
1355^{11} 1620^{7} 2425^{5} 2901^{3}
Nahawand (USA) *Jim Boyle* a37
2 ch f Silver Train(USA) —East Cape (USA) (Mr Prospector (USA))
7686^{7} 7879^{14}
Naheell *George Prodromou* a71 68
4 ch h Lomitas—Seyooll (IRE) (Danehill (USA))
83^{7} 162^{4} 261^{3} 309^{7} 467^{6} 770^{5} 868^{5} 983^{4} 1194^{3} 1539^{4} 2880^{6} 3084^{6} 3522^{7} (7275) (7422) 7504^{5} 7921^{5}
Najam *Clive Brittain* a45 74
3 b f Singspiel(IRE) —Lunda (IRE) (Soviet Star (USA))
985^{7} ◆ 1380^{3} 1627^{3} (3116) 3671^{10}
Najca De Thaix (FR) *John Spearing* a29 7
9 bb g Marmato—Isca De Thaix (FR) (Cimon)
5610^{7} 6450^{8} 6933^{11}
Najlaa *William Haggas* 67
3 bb f Nayef(USA) —Perfect Plum (IRE) (Darshaan)
1654^{8} 2463^{5} 3116^{7}
Najoom Zaman (IRE) *Luca Cumani* 71
3 b f Green Desert(USA) —North Sea (IRE) (Selkirk (USA))
1654^{3}
Najoum (USA) *Saeed Bin Suroor* a84 81
2 b f Giant's Causeway(USA) —Divine Dixie (USA) (Dixieland Band (USA))
3562^{2} (4862) (5961)
Nakayama Festa (JPN) *Yoshitaka Ninomiya* 129
4 b h Stay Gold(JPN) —Dear Wink (JPN) (Tight Spot (USA))
$6015a^{2}$ $6612a^{2}$ $7615a^{14}$
Nakoma (IRE) *Brian Ellison* a64 64
8 b m Bahhare(USA) —Indian Imp (Indian Ridge)
198^{6} 493^{2} 701^{2} 1467^{6} 1807^{9} 2085^{8}
Nalany *Derek Haydn Jones* a37 37
2 b f Byron—Crimson Dancer (Groom Dancer (USA))
1517^{11} 1794^{4} 2183^{6} 3678^{9} 7378^{8}
Naledi *Richard Price* a55 44
6 b g Indian Ridge—Red Carnation (IRE) (Polar Falcon (USA))
295^{4} 541^{9} 705^{6} (791) 995^{6} 1503^{6} 1756^{9} 1984^{7} 2880^{8}
Namaskar *John Gosden* 86
3 b f Dansili—Namaste (Alzao (USA))
2047^{2} 3298^{6}
Namecheck (GER) *Mahmood Al Zarooni* 98
3 ch c Shamardal(USA) —Nadia (Nashwan (USA))
1702^{4}
Namehim *Edward Vaughan* 53
3 bb c Dubai Destination(USA) —Tidie France (USA) (Cape Town (USA))
3272^{9} 4107^{7} 4364^{7} 5058^{6}
Namibian (IRE) *Mark Johnston* 83
2 b c Cape Cross(IRE) —Disco Volante (Sadler's Wells (USA))
6278^{6} (6748) 7059^{3}
Namir (IRE) *James Evans* a66 83
8 b g Namid—Danalia (IRE) (Danehill (USA))
79^{6} 185^{4} 344^{3} 1428^{4} 1915^{10} 2378^{4} 2818^{6} 2957^{5} 3254^{9} 3976^{2} 4415^{11} (5471) 5876^{2} 6018^{9} 7655^{4} 7892^{10} 7991^{5}
Nampour (FR) *Philip Hobbs* a78 87
5 gr g Daylami(IRE) —Nadira (FR) (Green Desert (USA))
1902^{10}
Namu *Teresa Spearing* a62 64
7 b m Mujahid(USA) —Sheraton Heights (Deploy)
1235^{2} 1441^{5} 1929^{5} 2184^{4} 2779^{3} 7299^{10} 7426^{5} 7502^{6}

Namwahjobo (IRE) *Jim Goldie* 41
2 b c Namid—Notley Park (Wolfhound (USA))
2427^{5}
Nanny Doe (IRE) *Lee Smyth* a23 8
4 b m Mujadil(USA) —Prima (Primo Dominie)
4913^{12}
Nanton (USA) *Jim Goldie* a104 111
8 gr g Spinning World(USA) —Grab The Green (USA) (Cozzene (USA))
1698^{2} 2097^{5} 3240^{2} 3825^{6} 4390^{5} 5220^{13} $5772a^{3}$ 6179^{5} 7507^{5} 7594^{4}
Napa Starr (FR) *C Byrnes* a78 93
6 b g Marchand De Sable(USA) —Jade D'Eau (IRE) (Lion Cavern (USA))
$5571a^{5}$
Napoletano (ITY) *Robert Johnson* a49 52
4 b g Kyllachy—Nationality (Nashwan (USA))
3025^{11} 3369^{10} 4669^{5} 6037^{7} 6298^{5} 7199^{5}
Naqshabban (USA) *Luca Cumani* 75
2 b g Street Cry(IRE) —Reem Three (Mark Of Esteem (IRE))
(6828) ◆
Narcisco (GER) *Nigel Hawke* a51 88
5 b g Fantastic Light(USA) —Nicola Bella (IRE) (Sadler's Wells (USA))
6851^{0}
Nareion (GER) *W Baltromei* 101
4 b h Areion(GER) —Ninigretta (GER) (Dashing Blade)
$1955a^{7}$ $2805a^{5}$ 4122^{4} $5573a^{10}$
Narya (IRE) *M Delcher-Sanchez* 80
3 b f Halling(USA) —Badraan (USA) (Danzig (USA))
$4037a^{9}$
Naseby (USA) *Sam Davison* a59 53
3 ch g Maria's Mon(USA) —Branchbury (USA) (Mt. Livermore (USA))
1795^{9} 2418^{2} 2780^{5} 4025^{11} 4687^{8} 5271^{9} 6080^{14}
Nasharra (IRE) *Kevin Ryan* 92
2 ch c Iffraaj—There With Me (USA) (Distant View (USA))
(2171) 2468^{6} 4138^{15} (4580) 5880^{8} 6568^{14}
Nashi (FR) *E J O'Neill* a80 88
2 b c Agnes Kamikaze(JPN) —Nelee (FR) (Fijar Tango (FR))
(4565a) $5323a^{7}$ $6589a^{0}$
Nasri *David Simcock* 104
4 b g Kyllachy—Triple Sharp (Selkirk (USA))
1614^{3} 2595^{5} 3146^{13} 5911^{17} 6806^{3}
Natalie N G *John Jenkins* 16
3 b f Zamindar(USA) —Tango Teaser (Shareef Dancer (USA))
3484^{9} 4146^{8} 4720^{7} 5668^{11} 6638^{13}
Natal Lad (IRE) *N Bertran De Balanda* a70 88
5 b h Acclamation—Gentle Guest (IRE) (Be My Guest (USA))
$207a^{9}$
Nathaniel (IRE) *John Gosden* 92
2 b c Galileo(IRE) —Magnificient Style (USA) (Silver Hawk (USA))
5049^{2} ◆ 5878^{2}
Nationalism *John Gosden* 108
3 b g Pivotal—Las Flores (IRE) (Sadler's Wells (USA))
3173^{2} 3795^{2} (4307) (5955) ◆ 6562^{28} 7234^{7}
National Monument (IRE) *Jamie Osborne* a67 30
4 b g Statue Of Liberty(USA) —Panpipes (USA) (Woodman (USA))
346^{4} 2447^{7} 1539^{5} 2006^{13}
National Theatre (USA) *Olivia Maylam* a56
4 b g Rahy(USA) —Note Musicale (Sadler's Wells (USA))
669^{5} 963^{8} 3754^{10} 4433^{11}
Nation State *Michael Madgwick* 33
9 b g Sadler's Wells(USA) —Native Justice (USA) (Alleged (USA))
4042^{7} 4731^{4}
Native American *Tim McCarthy* a58 59
8 b g Indian Lodge(IRE) —Summer Siren (FR) (Saint Cyrien (FR))
4745^{6}
Native Khan (FR) *Ed Dunlop* 113
2 gr c Azamour(IRE) —Viva Maria (FR) (Kendor (FR))
(3794) ◆ (5306) ◆ 7081^{4}
Native Picture (IRE) *Richard Hannon* 73
2 br f Kodiac—Native Force (IRE) (Indian Ridge)
4103^{3} (4658) 5613^{6} 6445^{12}
Nativity *John Spearing* a59 61
4 ch m Kyllachy—Mistral's Dancer (Shareef Dancer (USA))
2590^{2} ◆ 3125^{3} 3254^{8} 3993^{7} 4589^{4} 5065^{6} 5960^{7} 6847^{7} 7299^{9}
Natural High (IRE) *D K Weld* 91
5 b g Sadler's Wells(USA) —Cool Clarity (IRE) (Indian Ridge)
$6971a^{15}$
Naughty Naughty *Brendan Powell* a55 68
5 b m Subotica(FR) —Rocheflamme (FR) (Snurge)
4229^{5} 4679^{5} 4792^{3} 5420^{4} 5722^{10} 6693^{9}
Naughty Norris *Robin Bastiman* 27
3 ch g Needwood Blade—Leave It To Lib (Tender King)
2143^{8} 2878^{9} 3359^{14}
Navajo Chief *Alan Jarvis* a95 108
3 b c King's Best(USA) —Navajo Rainbow (Rainbow Quest (USA))
1018^{2} 1083^{3} 1354^{8} 2028^{3} (2542) 3103^{18} 3886^{9} 5247^{4} (5854) 6349^{21} 7875^{13}
Navajo Joe (IRE) *Robert Johnson* a47 75
5 ch g Indian Ridge—Maid Of Killeen (IRE) (Darshaan)
2788^{8} 4082^{7} 4707^{2} 5486^{11} 7199^{6}
Navajo Nation (IRE) *Bill Turner* a68 70
4 b g Indian Haven—Kathy Desert (Green Desert (USA))
429^{9}
Naval Officer (USA) *J Barton* a108 108
4 b h Tale Of The Cat(USA) —Wandering Star (USA) (Red Ransom (USA))
$417a^{7}$ $629a^{3}$ $801a^{9}$

Nave (USA) *Mark Johnston* a94 92
3 b g Pulpit(USA) —Lakabi (USA) (Nureyev (USA))
1189^{5} 4341^{2} (4532) 4891^{6} (5002) ◆ (5355) 5727^{4} 6251^{4} 7084^{16}
Navene (IRE) *Martin Bosley* a46 70
6 b m Desert Style(IRE) —Majudel (IRE) (Revoque (IRE))
1141^{9} 1322^{8} 1591^{11}
Navigation Track *David Simcock* a58
2 b c King's Best(USA) —Tegwen (USA) (Nijinsky (CAN))
6845^{4}
Navy List (FR) *Mahmood Al Zarooni* a82 90
3 b c Nayef(USA) —Fasliyeva (FR) (Fasliyev (USA))
2125^{5} 3265^{5}
Nawaaff *Michael Quinn* a55 44
5 ch g Compton Place—Amazed (Clantime)
79^{4} 271^{5} 423^{8} 659^{3} 1072^{4} 2720^{10} 3293^{4} 3605^{5} 4234^{11} 4778^{5}
Nawaashi *Mark Johnston* 75
2 b f Green Desert(USA) —Shatarah (Gulch (USA))
2855^{2} (6034) 6920^{3}
Nawamees (IRE) *David Evans* a79 80
12 b g Darshaan—Truly Generous (IRE) (Generous (IRE))
113^{6} 426^{8} 470^{3}
Nawow *Matt Hazell* a67 47
10 b g Blushing Flame(USA) —Fair Test (Fair Season)
76^{5} 376^{7}
Naxox (FR) *George Baker* a68
9 ch g Cupidon(FR) —Frou Frou Lou (FR) (Groom Dancer (USA))
32^{6} 496^{11}
Nayessence *Michael Easterby* a65 57
4 ch g Nayef(USA) —Fragrant Oasis (USA) (Rahy (USA))
42^{8} 1028^{9} (1188) 1207^{2} (1539) 1803^{10} 2109^{9} 3684^{4} 3978^{6} 4481^{8} 7531^{4} 7704^{7}
Nay Secret *Jim Goldie* 47
2 b g Nayef(USA) —Nouveau Cheval (Picea)
6222^{8} 6618^{8} 7049^{8}
Nazreef *Hughie Morrison* a104 88
3 b c Zafeen(FR) —Roofer (IRE) (Barathea (IRE))
(2261) ◆ 2969^{4} ◆ 6151^{6} 6534^{11} (7091) 7352^{3} (7867) (7955)
Near Galante (GER) *A Wohler* 97
4 b m Galileo(IRE) —Night Year (IRE) (Jareer (USA))
$2155a^{6}$
Near The Mark (IRE) *Michael Wigham* a23
2 b c Camacho—Double Eight (IRE) (Common Grounds)
3964^{12} 7164^{9}
Neatico (GER) *P Schiergen* 106
3 b c Medicean—Nicola Bella (IRE) (Sadler's Wells (USA))
$2405a^{6}$ $4184a^{10}$ $5671a^{3}$ $6219a^{10}$
Necessity *Simon Dow* a69
3 b g Empire Maker(USA) —Fully Invested (USA) (Irish River (FR))
(8021)
Ned Ludd (IRE) *Jonathan Portman* a67 75
7 b g Montjeu(IRE) —Zanella (IRE) (Nordico (USA))
554^{7} 1357^{6} 1849^{3} 6273^{6} 6693^{6}
Neduardo *Peter Chapple-Hyam* a79 47
3 ch c Monsieur Bond(IRE) —Bond Shakira (Daggers Drawn (USA))
236^{2} 321^{6} 759^{3} (894) 1191^{5} 4684^{7} 5386^{9} 6198^{17}
Neebras (IRE) *Mahmood Al Zarooni* 107
2 b c Oasis Dream—Crossmolina (IRE) (Halling (USA))
2078^{2} ◆ (2715) 3823^{2}
Needy McCredie *James Turner* 57
4 ch m Needwood Blade—Vocation (IRE) (Royal Academy (USA))
3086^{3} 3538^{9} 3774^{3} 4559^{3} 4869^{4} 5024^{2} 5482^{2} 5817^{7} 6188^{12}
Negotiate *Andrew Oliver* 83
2 b f Red Ransom(USA) —Poised (USA) (Rahy (USA))
$5570a^{9}$ $6784a^{8}$
Negotiation (IRE) *Michael Quinn* a76 90
4 b g Refuse To Bend(IRE) —Dona Royale (IRE) (Darshaan)
990^{6} 1430^{10} 1697^{15} 2129^{7} 2512^{6} 2959^{5} 3117^{7} 3412^{10} 3604^{7} (4763) 5664^{2} 6091^{7} 6718^{12} 7190^{4} 7548^{2} 7778^{2} 8018^{3}
Neighbourhood (USA) *Mark Johnston* a23
2 bb g Street Cry(IRE) —Miznah (IRE) (Sadler's Wells (USA))
6843^{8}
Neissa (USA) *John Best*
3 bb f Three Wonders(USA) —Crossing Over (USA) (Kris S (USA))
6470^{12} 6716^{10}
Nella Sofia *James Given* 34
2 bl f Diktat—Night Symphonie (Cloudings (IRE))
6158^{18} 6873^{9}
Nellie Ellis (IRE) *Kevin Ryan* a62 65
2 ch f Compton Place—Tamora (Dr Fong (USA))
1527^{6} 1981^{4} 2183^{4} (2848) 3678^{5} (4195) 5354^{6} 5547^{3} 6035^{4} 6576^{3}
Nelson's Bounty *Paul D'Arcy* a86 88
3 b g Bahamian Bounty—Santisima Trinidad (IRE) (Definite Article)
2335^{8} 2754^{7} 2968^{4} 3606^{8} (4931) (5394) 5917^{10}
Nelson Vettori *Charlie Longsdon* a51 52
6 ch g Vettori(IRE) —Eskimo Nel (IRE) (Shy Groom (USA))
316^{5} 612^{6}
Nemo Spirit (IRE) *Tom Dascombe* a97 97
5 gr g Daylami(IRE) —La Bayadere (Sadler's Wells (USA))
1821^{17} 6201^{10} 6493^{4} 6750^{7}
Neon Light (GER) *A Wohler* 102
3 b f Refuse To Bend(IRE) —No Merci (GER) (General Assembly (USA))
$1715a^{3}$

Neo's Mate (IRE) *Paul Green* a53 60
4 br m Modigliani(USA) —Gute (IRE) (Petardia)
369^{9} ◆ 1470^{10}
Nephele (IRE) *Tim Easterby* 57
3 gr f Antonius Pius(USA) —Grey Clouds (Cloudings (IRE))
3176^{9} 4556^{5} 4853^{5} 5550^{6} 6038^{7}
Nepotism *Malcolm Saunders* a73 74
3 b c Piccolo—Craic Sa Ceili (IRE) (Danehill Dancer (IRE))
1546^{2} 1765^{4} 2179^{5} 2689^{11} 4041^{7} 4284^{3} ◆ 5470^{4} 5876^{4} 6018^{3}
Neptune Equester *Brian Ellison* 55
7 b g Sovereign Water(FR) —All Things Nice (Sweet Monday)
6115^{8}
Neptune's Girl (IRE) *Sir Michael Stoute* 49
3 gr f Verglas(IRE) —Anna Kareena (IRE) (Charnwood Forest (IRE))
2180^{11} 2697^{9}
Neroli (AUS) *Peter Snowden* 109
7 b m Viscount(AUS) —Dalquarren (AUS) (Canny Lad (AUS))
4
Nerves Of Steel (IRE) *Paul Cole* 78
3 b c Oratorio(IRE) —Spirit Of Tara (IRE) (Sadler's Wells (USA))
5623^{2} ◆ 5832^{4} 6275^{2}
Nesnaas (USA) *Mark Rimell* a48 48
9 ch g Gulch(USA) —Sedrah (USA) (Dixieland Band (USA))
3348^{9}
Nesno (USA) *Michael Dods* a60 63
7 ch g Royal Academy(USA) —Cognac Lady (USA) (Olympio (USA))
814^{6} 1920^{4} 2433^{7} 2902^{7}
Netta (IRE) *PETER Makin* 85
4 b m Barathea(IRE) —Nishan (Nashwan (USA))
1618^{10} 3592^{10}
Nettis *George Prodromou* a28 55
2 ch c Monsieur Bond(IRE) —Stream (Unfuwain (USA))
3602^{6} 4233^{5} 5047^{8} 5659^{12}
Networker *Philip McBride* a76 71
7 ch g Danzig Connection(USA) —Trevorsninepoints (Jester)
(348)
Neva A Mull Moment (IRE) *Ron Barr* 65
4 b g Mull Of Kintyre(USA) —Serious Contender (IRE) (Tenby)
3774^{10} 4014^{9} 4487^{10} 6644^{8}
Nevada Desert (IRE) *Richard Whitaker* a76 82
10 b g Desert King(IRE) —Kayanga (Green Desert (USA))
1751^{13} 4152^{11} 4348^{7} 5436^{7} 5545^{5} 5852^{10} 6117^{10} 6243^{6} 6699^{4} 6832^{10} 7062^{14} 7543^{2}
Never Bouchon (JPN) *Masanori Ito* 119
7 bb h Marvelous Sunday(JPN) —Pearl Necklace (Mill Reef (USA))
$1568a^{4}$
Never Can Stop *Jonathan Portman* a58 68
2 b f Noverre(USA) —Kanzina (Machiavellian (USA))
1879^{2} 2358^{9} 2963^{2} 3509^{5} 4233^{2} 4872^{3} 5720^{6} 6072^{10} 6307^{5}
Never Can Tell (IRE) *Jamie Osborne* a85 82
3 b f Montjeu(IRE) —Shaanara (IRE) (Darshaan)
1735^{7} 2050^{7} 2231^{2} 2924^{3} 3256^{2} (4792) 5296^{7} (6331)
Never Ending Tale *Edward Vaughan* a87 89
5 ch g Singspiel(IRE) —Bright Finish (USA) (Zilzal (USA))
1474^{13} 2549^{9} 3512^{4}
Never Forget (FR) *E Lellouche* 105
3 b f Westerner—Topira (FR) (Pistolet Bleu (IRE))
$2800a^{3}$ (3493a) $5346a^{5}$ $6013a^{9}$
Never Never Land *John Gosden* a72 66
2 b g Elusive City(USA) —Absolve (USA) (Diesis)
6712^{2} 7010^{3} (7210)
Never Sold Out (IRE) *John O'Shea* a53 58
5 ch g Captain Rio—Vicious Rosie (Dancing Spree (USA))
753^{5} 1208^{7} 2279^{9}
Neville's Cross (IRE) *Jim Boyle* a63
3 ch c Selkirk(USA) —Harmonist (USA) (Hennessy (USA))
147^{7} 313^{4}
New Atalanta (IRE) *Ms Maria Kelly* a49 53
3 b f Xaar—High Finance (IRE) (Entrepreneur)
$4563a^{12}$
New Bay (USA) *Mike Mitchell* a92 93
4 b r Cuvee(USA) —Royal Dove (IRE) (Royal Academy (USA))
$3935a^{5}$
New Beginning (IRE) *John Mackie* a67 84
6 b g Keltos(FR) —Goldthroat (IRE) (Zafonic (USA))
294^{8} 666^{8} 6165^{3} 6930^{3} (7599)
Newbury Street *Patrick Holmes* a65 67
3 b g Namid—Cautious Joe (First Trump)
1168^{9} 1584^{7} (2203) 2668^{4} 3086^{2} 3972^{8} 4749^{5} 7051^{10} 7148^{8}
Newby Lodge (IRE) *Bryan Smart* 47
2 b f Intikhab(USA) —Titans Clash (IRE) (Grand Lodge (USA))
6293^{4} 7049^{7}
Newcastle (FR) *C Baillet* 90
2 ch f High Yield(USA) —Cruelle (USA) (Irish River (FR))
$7534a^{3}$
New Christmas (USA) *Brian Meehan* a86 90
3 rg g Smoke Glacken(USA) —Occhi Verdi (IRE) (Mujtahid (USA))
1334^{7} 1658^{2} 2033^{7} 2969^{2} 3351^{4}
New Code *Gary Moore* a83 66
3 ch g Reset(AUS) —Illeana (GER) (Lomitas)
1325^{6} 1782^{3} 1993^{4} 2935^{7} 3390^{4} 4027^{5} 4212^{4} 5058^{4} 5653^{3} (6022) 6314^{6} (6747) (6933) (7876) ◆ 7963^{2}
New Couture (IRE) *Peter Chapple-Hyam* a54
4 b m Montjeu(IRE) —New Design (IRE) (Bluebird (USA))
248^{7}

New Den *Jim Boyle* a61 55
3 ch g Piccolo—Den's-Joy (Archway (IRE))
161[3] 216[7] 422[2] 762[5] 7561[6] 7767[4] 7963[3]

New England *Nicky Vaughan* a64 65
8 ch g Bachir(IRE) —West Escape (Gone West (USA))
457[4] ◆ 724[4] 813[3] 1194[6] 2006[5] 2529[2] 2870[5] 4582[6] 4912[5] 4980[8]

Newgate Dani *Neville Bycroft* a31
2 b g Danbird(AUS) —Newgate Bubbles (Hubbly Bubbly (USA))
7179[11] 7325[6]

Newlands Princess (IRE) *Denis W Cullen* 56
2 b f Titus Livius(FR) —Equity Princess (Warning)
7256a[16]

New Latin (IRE) *Mark Johnston* a60 76
2 b g Iffraaj—Babacora (IRE) (Indian Ridge)
6126[3] 6324[2] 6778[3] 7294[7] 7891[11]

New Leyf (IRE) *Jeremy Gask* a94 84
4 bb g Kheleyf(USA) —Society Fair (FR) (Always Fair (USA))
(502) 722[4] (905) 1481[2] 1903[11] 2992[14] 4598[2] 5495[3] 6198[8] 6558[6]

New Magic (IRE) *Mrs John Harrington* a86 93
3 b f Statue Of Liberty(USA) —Magic Mushroom (Pivotal)
(4496a) 6379a[8]

New Normal (USA) *Mark Frostad* 105
2 b f Forestry(USA) —New Economy (USA) (Red Ransom (USA))
7340a[8]

New Planet (IRE) *John Quinn* 104
2 ch c Majestic Missile(IRE) —Xena (IRE) (Mull Of Kintyre (USA))
(4409) (5221) 5907[3]

Newport Arch *John Quinn* 71
2 b c Pastoral Pursuits—Mashmoum (Lycius (USA))
3657[8] 4240[9] (5040) 6979[8]

New River (IRE) *Richard Hannon* 71
2 b f Montjeu(IRE) —Quiet Waters (USA) (Quiet American (USA))
4844[5]

New's Ivoire (FR) *L A Urbano-Grajales* a60 63
5 b g Panis(USA) —Top Warning (FR) (Piccolo)
460a[2]

New Springs *Richard Fahey* 64
2 b f Acclamation—Hiraeth (Petong)
5298[3] 6102[7]

New Star (UAE) *Mark Brisbourne* a78 77
6 b g Green Desert(USA) —Princess Haifa (USA) (Mr Prospector (USA))
176[2] 294[3] 466[4] 920[4] 1587[3] 2182[7]

Newstarmcgrath *Gay Kelleway* 25
2 b c Phoenix Reach(IRE) —Savannah Pride (IRE) (Namid)
3053[8] 4436[10] 4802[16]

Newtons Cradle (IRE) *Howard Johnson* 56
3 b g Noverre(USA) —Lady Of Kildare (IRE) (Mujadil (USA))
2072[5] 3073[11] 6029[12]

New World Order (IRE) *Roger Curtis* a68 53
6 b g Night Shift(USA) —Kama Tashoof (Mtoto)
261[9] 469[8] 770[4] 969[10] 983[3] 1160[11]

New World Symphony (IRE) *Howard Johnson* a5 60
3 b g War Chant(USA) —Bold Classic (USA) (Pembroke (USA))
2697[8] 3776[6]

Newzflash *David Barron* 46
2 ch g Lucky Story(USA) —Lark In The Park (IRE) (Grand Lodge (USA))
2493[6] 2990[10] 4782[7] 6673[7] 7016[11]

Next Dream (FR) *F Rohaut* a84
3 b f Dream Well(FR) —Neriella (Darshaan)
7648a[8]

Next Edition (IRE) *Howard Johnson* 88
2 b g Antonius Pius(USA) —Starfish (IRE) (Galileo (IRE))
3222[2] 3705[2] (4167) 5597[2]

Next Hight (IRE) *P Schiergen* 94
3 b c High Chaparral(IRE) —Night Petticoat (GER) (Petoski)
3018a[4] 4184a[14]

Next Move (IRE) *Saeed Bin Suroor* a83 82
3 b c Tiger Hill(IRE) —Cinnamon Rose (USA) (Trempolino (USA))
1310[12] 2125[6]

Next Vision (IRE) *J Hirschberger* 89
4 ch h Rock Of Gibraltar(IRE) —Night Petticoat (GER) (Petoski)
2374a[6] 6011a[12] 7102a[6]

Neytiri *Ralph Beckett* a59 46
2 ch f Sleeping Indian—Science Fiction (Starborough)
5255[7] 5865[7] 6425[3] 7177[9] 7471[4] 7857[2]

Nezami (IRE) *John Akehurst* a92 96
5 b g Elnadim(USA) —Stands To Reason (USA) (Gulch (USA))
108[13] 2683[7] 3334[4] 3681[5] 4322[7] 5082[5] 5627[4] 6252[3] 6503[10] 7092[13]

Nezhenka *Sir Mark Prescott Bt* a94 95
3 b f With Approval(CAN) —Ninotchka (USA) (Nijinsky (CAN))
1993[5] (3776) 4304[4] 5747[2] 6715[8] 7189[7] 7648a[0]

Ngina *Derek Shaw* a20
2 b f Iceman—Nairobi (FR) (Anabaa (USA))
7269[10] 7408[10] 7641[6]

Nianga (GER) *P Schiergen* 101
3 b f Lomitas—Nobilissima (GER) (Bluebird (USA))
1250a[8] 3943a[4] 4640a[11] 5345a[4]

Nibani (IRE) *Sir Michael Stoute* 81
3 ch g Dalakhani(IRE) —Dance Of The Sea (IRE) (Sinndar (IRE))
1268[10]

Nicconi (AUS) *David Hayes* 123
5 b h Bianconi(USA) —Nicola Lass (AUS) (Scenic)
3047[4] 3870[10]

Nicea (GER) *P Schiergen* 105
3 b f Lando(GER) —Nicolaia (GER) (Alkalde (GER))
2372a[4] 4640a[3] 6239a[3] 6790a[3]

Nice Chimes (IRE) *Brendan Duke*
2 b f Chineur(FR) —Nice One Clare (IRE) (Mukaddamah (USA))
2677[10] 2951[11] 6436[8] 6994[11]

Nice Danon *A Wohler* 99
2 gr c Sakhee(USA) —Miss Universe (IRE) (Warning)
5740a[2]

Nice Style (IRE) *Jeremy Gask* a100 94
5 b g Desert Style(IRE) —Great Idea (IRE) (Lion Cavern (USA))
7591[3] ◆ 7815[5]

Nicholas Pocock (IRE) *Brian Ellison* a67 63
4 b g King's Best(USA) —Sea Picture (IRE) (Royal Academy (USA))
3227[4] 3397[5] 4707[5] 5271[7] 5770[7] (6125) 6534[7] 7005[2] 7214[2] ◆ 7468[5] 7502[3] 7788[3] 7856[2]

Nickel Silver *Bryan Smart* a99 88
5 gr g Choisir(AUS) —Negligee (Night Shift (USA))
2[2] 212[3] (307) (446) 4798[7] 5069[7] 5734[2] 6663[3] 7254[9] 7740[7]

Nicky Nutjob (GER) *Jeff Pearce* a62 54
4 b g Fasliyev(USA) —Natalie Too (USA) (Irish River (FR))
184[11] 355[5]

Nicola's Dream *Richard Fahey* 68
2 b f Alhaarth(IRE) —She's Classy (USA) (Boundary (USA))
2347[3] 2980[4] 3923[4] 4701[2] 5947[8] 6748[2]

Nidamar *Ruth Carr*
3 b f Redoubtable(USA) —Marabar (Sri Pekan (USA))
471[8]

Nideeb *Clive Brittain* a110 105
3 ch c Exceed And Excel(AUS) —Mantesera (IRE) (In The Wings)
5090[3] 5539[5] 6529[6] 7237[3] (7384) (7523) 7594[2]

Night Affair *David Arbuthnot* a79 82
4 b m Bold Edge—Twilight Mistress (Bin Ajwaad (IRE))
(2364) 2929[10] 4043[6] (4730) 5368[9]

Night Carnation *Andrew Balding* a59 96
2 ch f Sleeping Indian—Rimba (USA) (Dayjur (USA))
4695[4] 5294[3] (5885) 7080[2]

Night Cruise (IRE) *Ian Williams* a89 67
7 b g Docksider(USA) —Addaya (IRE) (Persian Bold)
1277[6]

Nightdance Paolo (GER) *P Schiergen* 95
3 b c Paolini(GER) —Nightdance (GER) (Shareef Dancer (USA))
1745a[3] 2406a[3] 4184a[12]

Nightjar (USA) *Kevin Ryan* a100 89
5 b g Smoke Glacken(USA) —Night Risk (USA) (Wild Again (USA))
6[2] 299[3] ◆ 573[5] 1707[2] 2205[7] 4371[7] 5703[7] 7238[16] 7697[6] 7846[2] (7935)

Night Knight (IRE) *Chris Grant* a64 63
4 b g Bachelor Duke(USA) —Dark Albatross (USA) (Sheikh Albadou)
3021[2] 3179[2] 3502[6] 4484[6] 5019[7]

Night Lily (IRE) *Paul D'Arcy* a91 86
4 b m Night Shift(USA) —Kedross (IRE) (King Of Kings (IRE))
1653[2] (1877) ◆ (2392) 2823[2] 3457[6] 3830[2] (4533) 5149[5] (6252) 6346[14] 7012[6]

Night Magic (GER) *W Figge* 114
4 br m Sholokhov(IRE) —Night Woman (GER) (Monsun (GER))
2152a[7] (2806a) 4418a[2] (5806a) 6410a[2] 6977a[4]

Night Of Dubai (IRE) *Mario Hofer* 95
2 b f Lord Of England(GER) —Night Woman (GER) (Monsun (GER))
5740a[4] 6407a[3]

Night Of Magic (IRE) *H Steinmetz* 105
4 ch m Peintre Celebre(USA) —Night Teeny (Platini (GER))
1540a[5] 2155a[5]

Night Orbit *Julia Feilden* a61 69
6 b g Observatory(USA) —Dansara (Dancing Brave (USA))
3324[9] 4511[8] 6621[4]

Night Singer *Howard Johnson* 60
2 b c Oratorio(IRE) —Dream Vision (USA) (Distant View (USA))
2068[4] 2427[3] 3072[3] 4242[6] 6978[5]

Night Sky *PETER Makin* a61 68
3 b f Starcraft(NZ) —War Shanty (Warrshan (USA))
2842[3] ◆ 3333[3] 5145[5] 5584[4] 5988[5] 6992[5]

Night Trade (IRE) *Deborah Sanderson* a77 85
3 b f Trade Fair—Compton Girl (Compton Place)
1584[4] 1934[2] 2112[3] 2475[4] 3085[3] 3373[7] 4288[5] (4670) 5421[4] 6245[2] 6985[6] 7352[16]

Night Witch (IRE) *Edward Creighton* a66 57
2 b f Kheleyf(USA) —Nasaria (IRE) (Starborough)
1256[8] 6247[13] 6442[8] 6676[5] 7087[3] 7486[3] 7552[4] (7907)

Nimmy's Special *Michael Mullineaux* a57 50
4 ch m Monsieur Bond(IRE) —Mammas F-C (IRE) (Case Law)
1931[0] 4833[12]

Nimue (USA) *Paul Cole* a50 84
3 bb f Speightstown(USA) —Flag Support (USA) (Personal Flag (USA))
1329[3] 1571[2] 1861[3] 2227[2] 3091[5] 3620[3] 4339[3] (4601)

Nine Before Ten (IRE) *Deborah Sanderson* a63 75
2 ch f Captain Rio—Sagaing (Machiavellian (USA))
3756[2] 4083[2] 5531[7] (6182) 6916[6]

Ninfea (IRE) *Sylvester Kirk* a70 72
2 b f Le Vie Dei Colori—Attymon Lill (IRE) (Marju (IRE))
4203[12] 4716[3] (5709) (6081) 6412[6] 6690[9] 6875[2] 7165[5]

Ninita *Mark Rimmer* a73
2 b f Storming Home—Danceatdusk (Desert Prince (IRE))
(7682)

Ninth House (USA) *Ruth Carr* a79 79
8 b h Chester House(USA) —Ninette (USA) (Alleged (USA))
543[8] 855[5] 966[7] 1395[6] 1508[9] 1926[5] 2527[2] (2705) 3124[3] 3438[4] 3676[4] 3973[8] 4602[8] 4713[6] 5486[10] 5768[8] 7501[11]

Ninth Parallel (USA) *Brian Meehan* 27
2 bb c Mr Greeley(USA) —Nemea (USA) (The Minstrel (CAN))
6442[15] 7202[11]

Nippy Nikki *John Norton* a9 43
2 b f Needwood Blade—Spielbound (Singspiel (IRE))
4150[15] 5630[6] 6360[8] 7393[7]

Niran (IRE) *Ruth Carr* a89 80
3 b g Captain Rio—Valley Lights (IRE) (Dance Of Life (USA))
(681) 884[9] (1052) 1834[12] 2542[9] 6723[14] 7411[11] 7566[12]

Nisaal (IRE) *Tony Carroll* a70 80
5 b g Indian Ridge—Kahalah (IRE) (Darshaan)
752[5] 1028[2] 1203[2] 4088[6] (5634) ◆ 6261[2] 6832[2] 7063[3] 7548[6]

Nitza (FR) *Mme C Head-Maarek* a85 93
2 b f Indygo Shiner(USA) —Realdad (ARG) (Victory Speech (USA))
5323a[4] 5899a[3] 6609a[8]

Nizhoni Dancer *Chris Wall* a58 74
4 b m Bahamian Bounty—Hagwah (USA) (Dancing Brave (USA))
1780[11] 2685[13] 4847[10] 6065[11]

Noah Jameel *Tony Newcombe* a58 58
8 ch g Mark Of Esteem(IRE) —Subtle One (IRE) (Polish Patriot (USA))
139[6] 396[5] 590[5] 995[4] (1920) 2955[8] 3314[4] 3983[4] (4689) 5051[4] 5552[3] (6021) 6660[9]

Nobbys Girl *M S Tuck* a26
5 b m Double Trigger(IRE) —Mini Mandy (Petoski)
5840[10] 6450[11] 6699[8]

Nobel (GER) *Andreas Lowe* 83
3 b c Paolini(GER) —Nadin (GER) (Alkalde (GER))
5136a[5]

Noble Alpha (IRE) *Mario Hofer* 105
3 b g Shamardal(USA) —Nouvelle Noblesse (GER) (Singspiel (IRE))
2405a[3] 3016a[7] 3934a[5] 4418a[8] 6408a[2] 6791a[2] 7372a[5]

Noble Attitude *Nigel Tinkler* a46 59
4 b m Best Of The Bests(IRE) —Charming Lotte (Nicolotte)
298[10] 4582[15] 4986[9] 6098[6]

Noble Citizen (USA) *David Simcock* a99 99
5 b h Proud Citizen(USA) —Serene Nobility (USA) (His Majesty (USA))
175[6] 438a[6] 885[5] 1662[3] ◆ 1900[4] ◆ 3069[6] ◆ 3869[17] 4358[2] ◆ 6349[16] 7522[7] 7574[9]

Noble Defender *Stuart Kittow* 46
2 ch g Haafhd—Aquamarine (Shardari)
6802[8]

Noble Edge *Lee James* a38 57
7 ch g Bold Edge—Noble Soul (Sayf El Arab (USA))
791[7] 5687[11]

Noble Greek (USA) *John Best* a79 79
3 bb c Omega Code(USA) —Regal Beauty (USA) (Explosive Red (CAN))
(683) 5151[5] 5967[12] 6524[7] 6800[2]

Noble Jack (IRE) *Gary Moore* a76 74
4 b g Elusive City(USA) —Begine (IRE) (Germany (USA))
(161) 359[7] 902[6] 1265[8] 1634[8] 2279[6] (2414) 2926[5]

Noblement (GER) *Mario Hofer* a61 61
5 b g Tiger Hill(IRE) —Noble Princesse (GER) (Windwurf (GER))
273a[9] 559a[6]

Noble's Promise (USA) *Kenneth McPeek* a118 115
3 b c Cuvee(USA) —The Devil's Trick (USA) (Clever Trick (USA))
1714a[5] 3048[5]

Noble Storm (USA) *Ed McMahon* a109 109
4 b h Yankee Gentleman(USA) —Changed Tune (USA) (Tunerup (USA))
1174[6] 4937[3] 5512[8] 5944[16] 6364[8] 6663[2] 7079[2] (7329) ◆

Nobutjust *Tim Easterby*
2 b f Domedriver(IRE) —Selkirk Rose (IRE) (Pips Pride)
1964[5]

Noche De Reyes *Eric Alston* a57 60
5 b g Foxhound(USA) —Ashleigh Baker (IRE) (Don't Forget Me)
2788[5] 3025[2] 3552[8] 3968[8] 6716[3] 7200[8]

No Complaining (IRE) *Barney Curley* a65 38
3 b f Alhaarth(IRE) —Rambler (Selkirk (USA))
1165[9] 5729[2] 7153[12] (7917)

Noddies Way *John Panvert* a23 68
7 b g Nomadic Way(USA) —Sharway Lady (Shareef Dancer (USA))
5144[7] 6114[13] 6855[12] 6926[32]

Nodforms Violet (IRE) *Karen McLintock*
6 ch g Rashar(USA) —Whose Yer Wan (IRE) (Remainder Man)
7120[3] 7282[8]

No Explanation *David Thompson* 11
2 b g Proclamation(IRE) —Oceanico Dot Com (IRE) (Hernando (FR))
2202[9] 2785[10] 3058[12] 3657[10]

Noguchi (IRE) *Jeremy Noseda* a87 89
5 ch g Pivotal—Tuscania (USA) (Woodman (USA))
6780[13] (7382)

No Heretic *Paul Cole* 69
2 b c Galileo(IRE) —Intrigued (Darshaan)
6196[3] ◆

No Hubris (USA) *Paul Cole* 99
3 b g Proud Citizen(USA) —Innateness (USA) (Flying Paster (USA))
(1500) 2471[9] 3196[7] 3867[11] 6888[5] 7348[21]

Noisy Noverre (IRE) *George Baker* a44 12
3 b f Noverre(USA) —Beautiful Noise (Piccolo)
1878[13] 5028[7] 5658[11] 6206[9]

Noisy Silence (IRE) *A Manuel* a100 85
6 b h Giant's Causeway(USA) —Golightly (USA) (Take Me Out (USA))
335a[14]

No Larking (IRE) *Henry Candy* 60
2 b g Refuse To Bend(IRE) —Dawn Chorus (IRE) (Mukaddamah (USA))
5629[12] 6196[10] 6688[6]

Nolecce *Richard Guest* a63 69
3 ch g Reset(AUS) —Ghassanah (Pas De Seul)
4188[4] ◆ 5405[5] 5479[4] (5819) 6061[2] (6462) 6930[4]

Nollaig Shona (IRE) *George Prodromou* a67 60
3 b f Statue Of Liberty(USA) —Lucy In The Sky (IRE) (Lycius (USA))
2164[2] 2536[8] 3313[3] 4256[7] 5695[4] (7390) 7518[12] 7655[6]

Noll Wallop (IRE) *T Stack* 111
3 b c High Chaparral(IRE) —Annie Girl (IRE) (Danehill (USA))
(1038a) 2354a[9] 5772a[9]

Nom De La Rosa (IRE) *Sheena West* a57 66
3 b f Oratorio(IRE) —Cheal Rose (IRE) (Dr Devious (IRE))
(760) 4626[9] 4746[4] 5330[6] 5663[7] 6080[5] 6287[6] 6526[4]

No Mean Trick (USA) *Clive Cox* a68 70
4 b h Grand Slam(USA) —Ruby's Reception (USA) (Rubiano (USA))
3586[6] 4201[13] 4489[6]

Nomoreblondes *Paul Midgley* a66 76
6 ch m Ishiguru(USA) —Statuette (Statoblest)
1363[7] 1524[7] 2144[9] (2695) 3358[4] 3809[4] 4243[9]

Nomoretaxes (BRZ) *Debbie Mountain* a58 32
8 b g First American(USA) —Raghida (BRZ) (Roi Normand (USA))
2678[5] 3683[11]

None Shall Sleep (IRE) *Paul Cole* a71 87
2 b g Invincible Spirit(IRE) —Moonbi Ridge (IRE) (Definite Article)
(4477) 4934[3] 6751[4] 7116[6]

None Sweeter *Tim Easterby* a46 60
2 ch f Firebreak—Artistic (IRE) (Noverre (USA))
3971[8] 4451[8] 4848[3] 5818[10] 6163[7] 6673[6] 6891[4]

Non Stop *M Le Forestier* a82 84
4 b g Beat Hollow—High And Low (Rainbow Quest (USA))
6017a[4]

Nonsuch Way (IRE) *F Vermeulen* 90
2 gr f Verglas(IRE) —Lucky Lune (FR) (Priolo (USA))
5252a[6]

Non Tiscordardime *Niall Moran* a57 63
3 ch g Haafhd—Anyaas (IRE) (Green Desert (USA))
2453[5] 4563a[15] 7920[4]

Noodles Blue Boy *Ollie Pears* a76 92
4 b g Makbul—Dee Dee Girl (IRE) (Primo Dominie)
1365[10] (1988) 2465[2] 2681[3] 3321[2] 3660[2] 4413[11] 5855[4] (6256) 6706[4]

Noonenose *William Knight* 84
2 ch c Compton Place—Noble View (USA) (Distant View (USA))
3915[5] 4318[2] 5263[2] 5587[2]

No Peace (IRE) *George Margarson* 32
2 b f Noverre(USA) —Gentle Peace (IRE) (Orpen (USA))
1263[10] 2631[7] 2905[5] 3992[5]

No Poppy (IRE) *Tim Easterby* 81
2 b f Chineur(FR) —Capetown Girl (Danzero (AUS))
2376[5] 2832[6] ◆ 3020[2] 3295[3] 3550[5] 4437[5] 4783[2] 5099[2] (5298) 5637[2] 5882[4] 6325[2] 6563[5] 7347[2]

No Quarter (IRE) *Tracy Waggott* 59
3 b g Refuse To Bend(IRE) —Moonlight Wish (IRE) (Peintre Celebre (USA))
1465[4] ◆ 2132[7] 2503[14] 4337[4] 4581[7] 5024[4] 5758[4] 5820[4] 6188[4] 6463[6] 6710[5]

No Rain (IRE) *Alan Swinbank* a41 55
3 ch f Noverre(USA) —Rain Dancer (IRE) (Sadler's Wells (USA))
5815[3] 6716[4] 7703[6]

Nora Mae (IRE) *Sylvester Kirk* a79 88
4 ch m Peintre Celebre(USA) —Wurfklinge (GER) (Acatenango (GER))
29[4] 84[7] 284[8]

Norcroft *Christine Dunnett* a66 56
8 b g Fasliyev(USA) —Norcroft Joy (Rock Hopper)
4237[6] 4586[6] 5927[5] 6098[5] 7132[3] 7402[6] 7835[4] 8024[2]

Norderney (GER) *P Schiergen* 104
4 ch m Dai Jin—Nouvelle Princesse (GER) (Bluebird (USA))
1956a[3] (3251a) 4418a[7]

Nordfalke (IRE) *P Schiergen* 102
3 br c Hawk Wing(USA) —North Queen (IRE) (Desert King (IRE))
3018a[6] 4184a[19]

Nordic Light (USA) *Mrs A Malzard* a51 54
6 bb g Belong To Me(USA) —Midriff (USA) (Naevus (USA))
2161a[2]

Nordic Sky (USA) *William Haggas* 82
2 b c Arch(USA) —Magic Of Love (Magic Ring (IRE))
6092[2]

Nordic Spruce (USA) *Henry Cecil* 85
2 b f Dynaformer(USA) —Nyramba (Night Shift (USA))
(3906) 4934[4] 5284[2]

No Refraction (IRE) *Mark Usher* a34 28
2 b f Refuse To Bend(IRE) —Sunblush (UAE) (Timber Country (USA))
5829[10] 6497[8]

No Risk At All (FR) *J-P Gallorini* 113
3 ch c My Risk(FR) —Newness (IRE) (Simply Great (FR))
1985a[2] 2802a[16]

Normandy Maid *Richard Fahey* 73
2 b f American Post—Arculinge (Paris House)
3549[3] (4599) 5089[3] 5637[7] (6705)

Normanne (GER) *G Martin* a56
5 b g Tannenkonig(IRE) —Normannin (GER) (Mondrian (GER))
207a[6]

Norman Orpen (IRE) *Jane Chapple-Hyam* a94 68
3 b g Orpen(USA) —Lady Naomi (USA) (Distant View (USA))
4364[2] 5270[3] 5700[2] 6332[2] (7389) (7766) (7965)

Norman The Great *Alan King* a74 82
6 b g Night Shift(USA) —Encore Du Cristal (USA) (Quiet American (USA))
1783[5] 2181[8] 3576[4] 4226[3]

Norma Talmadge (IRE) *Andrew Oliver* a47 36
2 b f Marju(IRE) —Strobinia (IRE) (Soviet Star (USA))
6726a[6]

Norse Blues *Sylvester Kirk* 79
2 ch c Norse Dancer(IRE) —Indiana Blues (Indian Ridge)
4962[7] (6442) 7095[10]

Norse Dame *David Elsworth* a67 72
3 b f Halling(USA) —Rosewater (GER) (Winged Love (IRE))
1766[12] 2401[3] 2891[2] 3795[9] 4698[7]

Norse Warrior (USA) *Peter Grayson* a68 66
4 ch g Newfoundland(USA) —Spicy Red (USA) (Tactical Advantage (USA))
223[12] 364[4] 555[9] 810[6] 2186[12] 2721[7] 2964[11] 4789[9] 5362[5] 5579[9] 7738[9]

Norse Wing *Ralph Beckett* 66
2 ch f Norse Dancer(IRE) —Angel Wing (Barathea (IRE))
5583[4] 7034[7]

North Cape (USA) *Henry Candy* a79 90
4 b g Action This Day(USA) —Cape (USA) (Mr Prospector (USA))
1388[12] 1883[4] 2512[3] 3330[12] (3810) 4597[2] 5091[3] 5859[2] (6283)

North Central (USA) *Jim Goldie* 67
3 bb g Forest Camp(USA) —Brittan Lee (USA) (Forty Niner (USA))
2291[3] 2698[2] 3227[8] 3529[2] 4581[3] 4951[3] 5337[5] 5479[5] 6144[3] 6393[5] 6710[4] 7056[3]

Northern Acres *David Nicholls* 75
4 b g Mtoto—Bunting (Shaadi (USA))
1669[7] (2421) 2941[8] 5161[3] 6109[15] 6571[12]

Northern Bolt *Ian McInnes* a68 84
5 b g Cadeaux Genereux—Shafir (IRE) (Shaadi (USA))
1200[7] 1365[U] 1869[3] 2982[18] 3584[9] 3970[7] 4121[7] 4833[2] 5212[2] 5480[7] 5601[9] (5999) 6572[6] 6708[3] 6962[4] 7283[10]

Northern Champ (IRE) *David Bourton* a35 33
4 b g Mull Of Kintyre(USA) —Comprehension (USA) (Diesis)
6696[9] 7413[7] 7557[11]

Northern Dare (IRE) *Richard Fahey* a79 100
6 b g Fath(USA) —Farmers Swing (IRE) (River Falls)
887[10] 2657[5] 2992[11] 3584[12] 4090[13] 7841[9]

Northern Empire (IRE) *F Jordan* a83 73
7 ch g Namid—Bumble (Rainbow Quest (USA))
532[10]

Northern Fling *Jim Goldie* a17 91
6 b g Mujadil(USA) —Donna Anna (Be My Chief (USA))
1672[7] (2428) 3461[9] 3876[16] (5043) 6142[8] 6562[30] 7227[7]

Northern Flyer (GER) *John Quinn* a35 71
4 b g Hawk Wing(USA) —Nachtigall (GER) (Danehill (USA))
1115[11] 1396[14] 1754[6] 2527[3] 2850[3] 3284[4] 3500[5] 4485[5] 5024[4] 5331[6] (5820) (6189) 6917[3]

Northern Genes (AUS) *Michael Appleby* a44 48
4 b g Refuse To Bend(IRE) —Cotswold Dancer (AUS) (Carnegie (IRE))
3291[9] 3556[6] 4488[5]

Northern Giant (USA) *D Wayne Lukas* a106
3 b c Giant's Causeway(USA) —Jessi Take Charge (USA) (War Chant (USA))
2137a[12]

Northern Glory *W Figge* a107 111
7 b g Rainbow Quest(USA) —Northern Goddess (Night Shift (USA))
436a[5] 627a[3] 820a[6] 4012a[3] 5806a[4] 6410a[8]

Northern Spy (USA) *Simon Dow* a78 78
6 b g War Chant(USA) —Sunray Superstar (Nashwan (USA))
1322[9] 2337[8] 2714[7]

Northern Tour *Paul Cole* a79 80
4 b g Tobougg(IRE) —Swift Spring (FR) (Bluebird (USA))
19[7] 126[4]

Northgate (IRE) *Joseph G Murphy* a97 97
5 b g Mujadil(USA) —Arcevia (IRE) (Archway (IRE))
1408a[9] 3492a[10] 6548a[4] 7358a[5]

Northgate Lodge (USA) *Mel Brittain* a48 23
5 ch g Hold That Tiger(USA) —Sabaah Elfull (Kris)
290[3] 540[8] 753[12] 1812[8]

North Shadow *Alan Brown* a60 62
3 ch g Motivator—Matoaka (USA) (A.P. Indy (USA))
3284[6] 3710[10] 4127[3] 4618[9] 4944[7] 5361[7]

Northside Prince (IRE) *Alan Swinbank* a75 93
4 b g Desert Prince(IRE) —Spartan Girl (IRE) (Ela-Mana-Mou)
1395[10] 2084[7] 2259[2] (4411) (4823) (5408) 6106[2]

North South Divide (IRE) *Kevin Ryan* a69 23
6 b g Namid—Bush Rose (Rainbow Quest (USA))
178[10]

Northumberland *Michael Chapman* a41 32
4 b g Bertolini(USA) —Cal Norma's Lady (IRE) (Lyphard's Special (USA))
1579[14] 1754[10] 2274[9] 2647[10] 4760[9] 6896[12] 7328[6] 7645[4] 7731[6] 7896[7]

Norton Girl *John Quinn* a51 67
2 b f Diktat—Opening Ceremony (USA) (Quest For Fame)
6264[2] 7142[5] 7404[2] 7540[2] 7910[2]

No Rules *Mark H Tompkins* a60 75
5 b g Fraam—Golden Daring (IRE) (Night Shift (USA))
4983[5]

Norville (IRE) *David Evans* a72 67
3 b c Elusive City(USA) —Saraposa (IRE) (Ahonoora)
3586[11] 4521[8] 5603[3] 6056[5] 6540[2] ◆ 6633[7] 6922[9] 7255[10] 7305[10] 7683[2] 7991[7] 8035[3]

Norwegian Dancer (UAE) *Ed McMahon* a80 92
4 b g Halling(USA) —Time Changes (USA) (Danzig (USA))
1837[2] 2314[3] 3265[4] 4051[6] 4520[3] 4943[6] 5638[4] 6677[9] 7182[6] 7382[5]

Norwegian Liberty (IRE) *Ben Haslam* 60
2 br f Statue Of Liberty(USA) —Miss Megs (IRE) (Croco Rouge (IRE))
4451[5] 4645[3] 5358[3] 6163[11]

Nosail (FR) *F Head* 96
2 ch f Anabaa Blue—Freezing (USA) (Bering)
5622a[3] 7008a[5]

Nosedive *Richard Guest* 101
3 ch g Observatory(USA) —Resistance Heroine (Dr Fong (USA))
1499[5] 1701[12] 1917[5] 2713[5] 2978[7] (4551) 4819[8] 5512[5]

Nota Bene *David Elsworth* a111 106
8 b g Zafonic(USA) —Dodo (IRE) (Alzao (USA))
2100[12] 2563[6] 4105[4]

No Thank You *Kevin Ryan* 12
3 b g Piccolo—Shall We Dance (Rambo Dancer (CAN))
5603[10] 6039[RR]

Nothing Is Forever (IRE) *Liam Corcoran* a46 64
6 b g Daylami(IRE) —Bequeath (USA) (Lyphard (USA))
331[13] 7759[6]

Nothing To Hide (IRE) *Dominic Ffrench Davis* a74 78
2 ch g Barathea(IRE) —Fine Detail (IRE) (Shirley Heights)
2839[11] 3269[3] 3785[2] 4247[2] 4623[2] 5969[5] 6555[7] 7780[2] 7962[4]

Notify *Patrick Chamings* a48
2 b f Nayef(USA) —Whitgift Rose (Polar Falcon (USA))
5029[12] 6498[10]

No Time For Tears (IRE) *Lucinda Featherstone* a35
3 br f Celtic Swing—Galitizine (USA) (Riverman (USA))
7413[5]

Not In The Clock (USA) *John Best* a71 67
3 b g Chapel Royal(USA) —Bavarian Girl (USA) (Unbridled (USA))
805[2] 5593[4] 6554[2] 6829[3] 7167[2]

Not My Choice (IRE) *David C Griffiths* a76 74
5 ch g Choisir(AUS) —Northgate Raver (Absalom)
20[4] ◆ 171[2] 378[3] (716) 789[2] 914[3] 1470[4] 1596[2] 1929[13] 2113[15] 2310[2] 2817[3] 3024[7] 4255[5] 4415[7] 4712[11] 5267[8] (6188) (6370)

No To Trident *John Flint* a67 33
5 b g Zilzal(USA) —Charmante Femme (Bin Ajwaad (IRE))
6639[12]

No Trimmings (IRE) *Gerard Keane* a58 65
4 ch m Medecis—Cheviot Indian (IRE) (Indian Ridge)
7996[4] ◆

Not So Bright (USA) *Desmond Donovan* a56 59
2 bb g Sky Mesa(USA) —Melrose Morning (USA) (Shadeed (USA))
2855[4] 3769[3] 4368[6] 4935[3] 5659[5] 6311[5] 6902[9] 7050[10] 8078[3]

Notte Di Note (IRE) *Luca Cumani* a59 53
3 b f Le Vie Dei Colori—Effetto Ottico (IRE) (Foxhound (USA))
233[10]

Not Til Monday (IRE) *John Jenkins* a70 81
4 b g Spartacus(IRE) —Halomix (Linamix (FR))
7284[7] 7898[2] 8013[4]

Nouailhas *Reg Hollinshead* a20 53
4 b g Mark Of Esteem(IRE) —Barachois Princess (USA) (Barachois (CAN))
4546[6] 4932[6]

Nouriya *Sir Michael Stoute* a76 105
3 b f Danehill Dancer(IRE) —Majestic Sakeena (IRE) (King's Best (USA))
1358[3] (2890) ◆ (4347) (6095) 6613a[7]

Novabridge *Andrew Haynes* a54 71
2 ch g Avonbridge—Petrovna (IRE) (Petardia)
(1073) 1359[12] (1647) 2630[4] 3327[4] 4580[4] 5000[13] 5613[4] 5987[2] 6489[5]

Nova Hawk *Rod Collet* 95
2 b f Hawk Wing(USA) —Reveuse De Jour (IRE) (Sadler's Wells (USA))
5622a[4] 7544a[2]

Novalist *Robin Bastiman* 71
2 ch g Avonbridge—Malelane (IRE) (Prince Sabo)
1800[4] 2693[U] 3087[3] 3971[3] 5117[5] 6035[14]

Nova Med (IRE) *Y Durepaire* 84
3 b c Whipper(USA) —Prima Volta (Primo Dominie)
1254a[10]

Novastasia (IRE) *Dean Ivory* a49 46
4 b m Noverre(USA) —Pink Sovietstaia (FR) (Soviet Star (USA))
2417[11] 3056[4] 3526[11] 4790[3] 5579[11] 6956[11] 7473[4] 7835[6]

Nova Step *F Rohaut* a90 98
2 ch f Dubawi(IRE) —Light Step (USA) (Nureyev (USA))
(5137a) 7008a[3]

Novay Essjay (IRE) *Alan Juckes* a71 71
3 ch g Noverre(USA) —Arabian Hideway (IRE) (Desert Prince (IRE))
(141) 357[3] 524[3] (914) 1052[4] 1480[5] (1594) 3276[9]

Novel Dancer *Richard Hannon* 67
2 b g Dansili—Fictitious (Machiavellian (USA))
6196[4] 6689[8]

Novellen Lad (IRE) *Eric Alston* a87 98
5 b g Noverre(USA) —Lady Ellen (Horage)
(2327) 3489a[4] 4391[5] 4832[7] 5095[15] 6049[5] 6429[8]

Noverre Over There (IRE) *Olivia Maylam* a58 58
3 b g Noverre(USA) —Shirley Moon (IRE) (Montjeu (IRE))
5869[9] 6287[P] 7669[3] 7789[4] 7958[11]

Noverre To Go (IRE) *Tom Dascombe* a103 106
4 ch h Noverre(USA) —Ukraine Venture (Slip Anchor)
992[4] 1903[3] (2563) 3193[7] 4576[5] 6177[26] 7217a[2] 7524[11]

Novestar (IRE) *Graham Smith* a18 68
5 ch g Noverre(USA) —Star Of Cayman (IRE) (Unfuwain (USA))
6578[12]

Novikov *David Evans* a66 72
6 ch g Danehill Dancer(IRE) —Ardisia (USA) (Affirmed (USA))
2996[10] 3432[8]

Novillero *Jimmy Fox* a50 48
3 b c Noverre(USA) —Fairy Story (IRE) (Persian Bold)
104[5] ◆ 213[2] ◆ 346[5] 993[3] 1163[2] 1795[11] 3520[5] 7605[6] 7885[6]

No Wine No Song (AUS) *Kevin Moses* 114
9 b g Song Of Tara(IRE) —Deep Time (NZ) (Kinjite (NZ))
7032a[13] 7368a[15]

No Wonga *David Evans* a64 68
5 b g Where Or When(IRE) —Fizzy Fiona (Efisio)
120[4] 210[4]

Now What *Jonathan Portman* a64 70
3 ch f Where Or When(IRE) —Vallauris (Faustus (USA))
1735[8] 3080[9] 3443[4] 4282[2] 4626[2] (5330) 5812[3] 6290[7] 6816[9]

Nubar Boy *David Evans* a79 76
3 ch g Compton Place—Out Like Magic (Magic Ring (IRE))
(236) 448[4] 934[9] 1086[7] 2052[6] 2656[2] 2824[9] 2884[6] 3638[7] 3731[2] 3899[3] 4204[9] 4325[7] 5855[17] 6284[8] 6572[14] 6864[10] 7391[2] 7737[6] 7812[6] (8035)

Nufoudh (IRE) *Tracy Waggott* 75
6 b g Key Of Luck(USA) —Limpopo (Green Desert (USA))
1152[8] (1673) (2211) 2293[4] 2531[4] 3164[2] 3539[5] (3553) 4394[5] 5499[6] 6394[9]

Nuit De Glace (FR) *Mlle Valerie Boussin* a73 89
6 gr m Verglas(IRE) —La Frandiere (FR) (Kaldoun (FR))
5576a[5] 6640a[7] 7278a[10]

Nuit Sombre (IRE) *Geoffrey Harker* a25 72
10 b g Night Shift(USA) —Belair Princess (USA) (Mr Prospector (USA))
1149[4] 1673[5] 2527[11] 3124[5] (3595) 3775[5] 4897[12] 5024[3] 5688[8] 5820[3] 6922[4]

Number One Guy *Philip Kirby* a15 73
3 br g Rock Of Gibraltar(IRE) —Dubious (Darshaan)
2089[9] 2618[11] 4796[7] 7898[5]

Number Theory *John Holt* 71
2 b g Halling(USA) —Numanthia (IRE) (Barathea (IRE))
4856[7] 5629[3] 6070[5] 6828[5]

Numeral (IRE) *Richard Hannon* 79
2 b c Holy Roman Emperor(IRE) —Savieres (IRE) (Sadler's Wells (USA))
1728[7] ◆ 2319[2]

Numerologie (FR) *Mme M Bollack-Badel* a95 95
4 b m Numerous(USA) —Operam (Kris)
3017a[7]

Numide (FR) *Rod Millman* a99 78
7 b g Highest Honor(FR) —Numidie (FR) (Baillamont (USA))
5291[9] 5989[6] 6808[10] 7252[6]

Nummenor (FR) *Y Fertillet* a55 82
13 b g Vettori(IRE) —Nabita (FR) (Akarad (FR))
221a[3] 332a[7]

Nurai *Paul D'Arcy* a55 57
3 b f Danehill Dancer(IRE) —Lady High Havens (IRE) (Bluebird (USA))
484[7] 775[4] 1394[4] 1880[7] 2675[6] (3503) 4119[13] 4335[11] 4970[5]

Nurture (IRE) *Ralph Beckett* a72 103
3 ch f Bachelor Duke(USA) —Silesian (IRE) (Singspiel (IRE))
1726[14] (2401) 2889[7] 3670[5] 5728[7]

Nutley Copse *Andrew Balding* a45 42
2 ch f Needwood Blade—Nut (IRE) (Fasliyev (USA))
2819[10] 5630[7] 5894[5] 6412[9]

Nutshell *Harry Dunlop* a43 53
2 b f Dubai Destination(USA) —Cashew (Sharrood (USA))
5692[18] 7010[6] 7210[6]

Nyetimber (USA) *Jamie Osborne* a57
4 ch h Forest Wildcat(USA) —Once Around (CAN) (You And I (USA))
80[3] 584[13] 898[10] 1194[9]

Oak Leaves *Jonathan Portman* a56 57
3 b f Mark Of Esteem(IRE) —Exotic Forest (Dominion)
1158[5] 2412[2] 2675[7] 3444[9] 3960[8] 4689[6] 4992[6] 5812[4] 6526[6] 6871[12] 7570[10]

Oakwell (IRE) *Sally Hall* 35
2 b g Antonius Pius(USA) —Cindy's Star (IRE) (Dancing Dissident (USA))
6293[8] 6566[13] 7058[18]

Oa Sanrix (FR) *J-C Sarais*
3 b g Lord Of Men—Oa Flix (FR) (Linamix (FR))
281a[0]

Oasis Dancer *Ralph Beckett* 108
3 gb g Oasis Dream—Good Enough (FR) (Mukaddamah (USA))
1352[5] (1703) ◆ 2354a[11] (4140) 4537[13] 5275[7]

Oasis Jade *Gary Moore* a64 65
3 b f Oasis Dream—Royal Jade (Last Tycoon)
2000[13] 2320[6] 2588[6]

Oasis Knight (IRE) *Marcus Tregoning* 104
4 b g Oasis Dream—Generous Lady (Generous (IRE))
1382[14] 1615[6] 2097[4]

Oasis Star (IND) *C Katrak* a107 15
6 b m Senure(USA) —Gumbaru Etsu (USA) (Lear Fan (USA))
434a[2] 628a[4] 822a[12]

Oasis Storm *Michael Dods* a77 67
2 b c Oasis Dream—Mouriyana (IRE) (Akarad (FR))
4187[6] 5878[8] (6743)

Obama Rule (IRE) *Ms Joanna Morgan* 100
3 b f Danehill Dancer(IRE) —Mennetou (IRE) (Entrepreneur)
(5568a) ◆ 6007a[7] 6379a[12]

Obara D'Avril (FR) *Simon West* 57
8 gr m April Night(FR) —Baraka De Thaix II (FR) (Olmeto)
1803[9] 2424[5] 2610[8] 3600[6] 4173[5]

Obe Brave *Lee Smyth* a65 58
7 b g Agnes World(USA) —Pass The Rose (IRE) (Thatching)
36[8] 193[6] (567) 2454[6]

Obe Gold *Paul Howling* a93 98
8 b g Namaqualand(USA) —Gagajulu (Al Hareb (USA))
39[2] (89) 181[3] 251[2] (328) (391) 464[3] 562[4] 571[2] 789[4]

Obe One *Alan Berry* a48 49
10 b g Puissance—Plum Bold (Be My Guest (USA))
3357[11] 3534[9] 3711[10] 7304[9]

Obiter Dicta *Henry Candy* 57
2 b f Diktat—Phoebe Woodstock (IRE) (Grand Lodge (USA))
6778[4] 7232[8]

Obligada (IRE) *Kevin Prendergast* 81
2 ch f Beat Hollow—Oblique (IRE) (Giant's Causeway (USA))
7135a[6]

Obligation (FR) *A P O'Brien* 95
2 ch c Galileo(IRE) —Arazena (USA) (Woodman (USA))
7456a[8]

Observatory Star (IRE) *Tim Easterby* 88
7 br g Observatory(USA) —Pink Sovietstaia (FR) (Soviet Star (USA))
1752[5] 2524[3] 2835[5] 3206[4] 3537[4] 3973[3] 4403[3] 5533[8]

Obsession (IRE) *Jeremy Noseda* a41
2 b c Marju(IRE) —Athlumney Lady (Lycius (USA))
6849[8]

Obvious *Julia Feilden* a57 26
4 b m Falbrav(IRE) —Bright And Clear (Danehill (USA))
229[8]

Ocean Bay *John Ryan* 97
2 b c Dubai Destination(USA) —Aldora (Magic Ring (IRE))
1309[3] ◆ 3868[5] ◆ 4375[3]

Ocean Blaze *Rod Millman* a83 87
6 b m Polar Prince(IRE) —La Belle Vie (Indian King (USA))
972[6] ◆ 1471[5] 1691[3] 2094[9] 2997[4] (3308) 3736[9] 4292[5] 4625[6] 4730[3] 5285[7]

Ocean Bright (USA) *James Given* a51 55
4 gr m Cozzene(USA) —Greek Myth (IRE) (Sadler's Wells (USA))
1759[4] 2214[6] 2610[2] 2697[7] 3223[2] 3669[4]

Ocean Club *B W Hills* a32 55
3 ch g Storming Home—Strictly Cool (USA) (Bering)
2244[5] 2860[10] 3724[3]

Ocean Countess (IRE) *Julia Feilden* a61 79
4 b m Storming Home—Pennycairn (Last Tycoon)
(1634) 2783[3] 3289[3] 3716[3] 4690[4] 5237[7] 5415[4] 6023[12] 6864[12] 7200[3] 7445[7]

Ocean Drift (USA) *Mahmood Al Zarooni* a72 80
2 ch c Stormy Atlantic(USA) —Miss Halory (USA) (Mr Prospector (USA))
3459[8] (3832) 4331[2] 4696[6]

Ocean Gold (FR) *S Loeuillet* a71 61
2 ch c Gold Away(IRE) —Oceane Bere (FR) (Tiger Hill (IRE))
4565a[4]

Ocean Legend (IRE) *Tony Carroll* a91 89
5 b g Night Shift(USA) —Rose Of Mooncoin (IRE) (Brief Truce (USA))
(285) 367[2] (552) (696) 1219[9] 1617[3] 1933[2] 2091[2] 3033[2] 4354[8] 7430[10] 7915[8]

Ocean Of Peace (FR) *Martin Bosley* a56 53
7 b g Volochine(IRE) —Sumatra (IRE) (Mukaddamah (USA))
228[4] ◆ 590[3] ◆ 942[4] 2361[5] 2636[6] (3214) 4913[8] 5468[6] 7251[7] 7508[7] (7727) 7995[4]

Ocean Rosie (IRE) *Julia Feilden* a59 63
3 b f One Cool Cat(USA) —Rose Of Mooncoin (IRE) (Brief Truce (USA))
1870[2] 3272[8] 4515[14] 5205[8] 5669[5] 6741[12] 7006[15]

Oceans Destination *John Ryan* 28
2 b g Dubai Destination(USA) —Notable Lady (IRE) (Victory Note (USA))
6127[9] 6504[15] 7164[11] 7236[9]

Oceans Edge *Jim Boyle* a60
4 br g Needwood Blade—Lady Roxanne (Cyrano De Bergerac)
9[4] 161[5] 321[9] 614[11] 2419[12]

Ocean's Glacier *John Ryan* 42
2 gr c Iceman—Red Typhoon (Belfort (FR))
1612[6]

Ocean's Minstrel *John Ryan* a96 101
4 b g Pivotal—Minstrel's Dance (CAN) (Pleasant Colony (USA))
338a[11] 412a[7] 626a[9] 823a[9] 883[7] 946[11] 1519[6] 2708[11] 3050[9] 3566[5] 3843[4] ◆ 4393[6] 5492[3] 6201[3] 6926[4]

Ocean Transit (IRE) *Richard Price* a74 87
5 b m Trans Island—Wings Awarded (Shareef Dancer (USA))
191[5] 1933[7] 2284[7] 2922[3] 3257[4] (6959) (7307)

Ocean Treasure (IRE) *Edward Vaughan* a25
3 ch f Barathea(IRE) —Coeur De La Mer (IRE) (Caerleon (USA))
7887[8]

Ocean War *Mahmood Al Zarooni* 73
2 gr c Dalakhani(IRE) —Atlantic Destiny (IRE) (Royal Academy (USA))
4490^{5}

Oceanway (USA) *Mark Johnston* a85
2 b f Street Cry(IRE) —Sea Gift (USA) (A.P. Indy (USA))
5643^{5} 7113^{2} (7312) ◆

Ochilview Warrior (IRE) *Robin Bastiman* 52
3 b c Trans Island—Lonely Brook (USA) (El Gran Senor (USA))
1201^{5} 1469^{5} 2209^{7} 3073^{9} 3595^{7}

Octaviana *Eric Alston* a25
3 b f Starcraft(NZ) —Double Fantasy (Mind Games)
2837^{11} 3554^{6} 3966^{10} 4249^{13}

Oddshoes (IRE) *Philip Hobbs* a62 46
8 b g Mujadil(USA) —Another Baileys (Deploy)
5536^{5}

Oddsmaker (IRE) *Maurice Barnes* a42 71
9 b g Barathea(IRE) —Archipova (IRE) (Ela-Mana-Mou)
1012^{12} 1199^{2} 1398^{11} 1671^{2} 2060^{13} 2295^{6} 2579^{11} 5336^{4} (6032) 6109^{4} 6393^{3} 6707^{4} 6915^{5} 7176^{3}

Odin (IRE) *David Elsworth* a72 80
2 b c Norse Dancer(IRE) —Dimelight (Fantastic Light (USA))
5491^{8} 6159^{12} 7020^{5} 7202^{3} 7478^{3}

Odin's Raven (IRE) *Brian Ellison* a72 73
5 ro g Dalakhani(IRE) —Oriane (Nashwan (USA))
7538^{3} 7787^{3}

Oekaki (FR) *Y Barberot* a75 94
3 b f Martillo(GER) —Pyu (GER) (Surumu (GER))
2800a^{7} 3493a^{6} 4037a^{2}

Oetzi *Alan Jarvis* 58
2 ch g Iceman—Mad Annie (USA) (Anabaa (USA))
3842^{5} 4755^{8} 5587^{9} 6875^{7}

Off Chance *Tim Easterby* 102
4 b m Olden Times—La Notte (Factual (USA))
1513^{3} ◆ 1899^{3} 2423^{2} 3063^{4} (3752) 4347^{4}

Officer In Command (USA) *J S Moore* a85 77
4 bb h Officer(USA) —Luv To Stay N Chat (USA) (Candi's Gold (USA))
359^{5} ◆ (485) 637^{2} 990^{5} 3265^{8} 4100^{10} 4322^{6} 5727^{8} 6841^{2} 7015^{4} (7732)

Officer Lily (USA) *John Best* a49 49
3 bb f Officer(USA) —Anagalia (USA) (Cherokee Colony (USA))
3523^{5} 4028^{6} 7872^{5}

Officer Mor (USA) *Dianne Sayer* a63 50
4 ch g Officer(USA) —Hot August Nights (USA) (Summer Squall (USA))
1154^{9} 1723^{6} 2278^{3} 2582^{7} 2854^{10} 3711^{8} 4014^{6} 4403^{9} 4606^{7} 4986^{7} 5331^{11} 6490^{11} 6643^{6}

Official Style *Sir Michael Stoute* 84
3 b c Dansili—Reel Style (Rainbow Quest (USA))
1330^{5} ◆ 2033^{11} 3586^{2} (5150)

Offspring *Tim Easterby* 73
3 b f Olden Times—La Notte (Factual (USA))
1116^{7} 2393^{8} 3091^{3} 3554^{3} (4151) 4749^{4} 5501^{3} 6113^{8} ◆ 6917^{4}

Ogre (USA) *David Evans* a78 84
5 bb m Tale Of The Cat(USA) —Soverign Lady (USA) (Aloha Prospector (USA))
1669^{10} 2284^{5} 2601^{4} 3814^{5}

Ohana *Alistair Whillans* a17 46
7 b g Mark Of Esteem(IRE) —Subya (Night Shift (USA))
4190^{8}

Ohiyesa (IRE) *G M Lyons* a93 93
4 b m Noverre(USA) —Crohal Di San Jore (Saddlers' Hall (IRE))
1408a^{8}

Oh Landino (GER) *P Monteith* 41
5 b g Lando(GER) —Oh La Belle (GER) (Dashing Blade)
3709^{7}

Oh My Days (IRE) *Clive Cox* 54
2 ch c Bahamian Bounty—Princess Speedfit (FR) (Desert Prince (IRE))
4303^{2}

Oh So Kool *Stuart Williams* 69
2 b g Bertolini(USA) —Pretty Kool (Inchinor)
5836^{7} 6458^{2} 6986^{4} ◆

Oh So Saucy *Chris Wall* a60 82
6 b m Imperial Ballet(IRE) —Almasi (IRE) (Petorius)
1914^{5} 2959^{8} 4715^{3} (5050) 5541^{3} 6097^{3} (6444)

Oh So Spicy *Chris Wall* 65
3 ch f Pastoral Pursuits—Almasi (IRE) (Petorius)
2903^{2} 3808^{2} 4251^{7} 4760^{4} 6023^{11}

Oh Two *Stuart Williams* a50 28
3 b f Domedriver(IRE) —Larousse (Unfuwain (USA))
978^{6} 1581^{16} 2401^{13} 2908^{6} 3640^{8}

Oh What's Occuring *Terry Clement* a35
2 b f Spartacus(IRE) —Liferaft (Kahyasi)
7021^{10} 7424^{7} 7843^{8}

Oil Strike *Peter Winkworth* a98 93
3 b g Lucky Story(USA) —Willisa (Polar Falcon (USA))
2682^{4} 3696^{3} 4387^{2} 5082^{4} (5731) 6319^{8}

Oiseau De Feu (USA) *E Charpy* a97 118
4 b h Stravinsky(USA) —Slewadora (USA) (Seattle Slew (USA))
417a^{9}

Oi Vay Joe (IRE) *William Jarvis* a57 44
6 b g Namid—Nuit Des Temps (Sadler's Wells (USA))
1914^{8}

Okapina (FR) *Mlle S-V Tarrou* a87 89
3 b f Okawango(USA) —Alpina (GER) (Lavirco (GER))
926a^{3} 1610a^{8}

Oke Bay *Ralph Beckett* a58 55
4 b m Tobougg(IRE) —Barakat (Bustino)
18^{5}

Oken Bruce Lee (JPN) *Hidetaka Otonashi* 122
5 ch h Jungle Pocket(JPN) —Silver Joy (CAN) (Silver Deputy (CAN))
7615a^{7}

Old Adage *Amanda Perrett* 14
3 b c Oasis Dream—West Devon (USA) (Gone West (USA))
2220^{11}

Old Boy Ted *Mark H Tompkins* 56
2 b g Tobougg(IRE) —Grove Dancer (Reprimand)
6504^{12} 6883^{16} 7202^{9}

Old Devil Moon (IRE) *Robert Mills* a52 41
3 br g Johannesburg(USA) —Tencarola (IRE) (Night Shift (USA))
581^{7} 745^{10} 4692^{6}

Old English (IRE) *Mark Johnston* a58
2 b c Marju(IRE) —Princess Mood (GER) (Muhtarram (USA))
7386^{7}

Old Firm *John McShane* a49 16
4 ch g Compton Place—Miriam (Forzando)
4581^{9} 5596^{9} 5821^{12} 7601^{5}

Old Hundred (IRE) *James Fanshawe* a87 81
3 b g Tiger Hill(IRE) —Bordighera (USA) (Alysheba (USA))
2043^{9} 2994^{3} 3593^{5} 4290^{2} 4965^{5} 5549^{3} (6084)

Oldjoesaid *Kevin Ryan* a108 101
6 b g Royal Applause—Border Minstral (IRE) (Sri Pekan (USA))
1295^{11} 2100^{4} ◆ 2745^{10} ◆ 3489a^{16} 4085^{15} 4536^{22} 5183^{10} 5589^{6} 5855^{7} ◆ 6142^{21} 6723^{12}

Old Master Expert *Michael Bell* 80
2 b c Royal Applause—Leonica (Lion Cavern (USA))
1901^{2} 2389^{3} (6111) 6435^{5}

Oldmeldrum (IRE) *Ben Haslam* 59
2 gr f Verglas(IRE) —Nassma (IRE) (Sadler's Wells (USA))
4981^{5} 6646^{5}

Old Money *Hughie Morrison* a48 77
3 ch f Medicean—Nouveau Riche (IRE) (Entrepreneur)
1260^{12} 2890^{5} 5645^{3}

Old Peg *David Bourton* a7 53
5 b m Mujahid(USA) —Giggleswick Girl (Full Extent (USA))
6638^{8} 6773^{5} 7129^{6}

Old Possum (USA) *Mahmood Al Zarooni* a62 65
2 bb c More Than Ready(USA) —Street Cat (USA) (Storm Cat (USA))
5040^{3} 6053^{6} 7020^{11}

Oldrik (GER) *Philip Hobbs* 81
7 b g Tannenkonig(IRE) —Onestep (GER) (Konigsstuhl (GER))
(6152) 6957^{4}

Old Romney *Paul Howling* a78 76
6 br g Halling(USA) —Zaeema (Zafonic (USA))
176^{5} 289^{5} 396^{8}

Oliver's Gold *Amanda Perrett* a61 66
2 b g Danehill Dancer(IRE) —Gemini Gold (IRE) (King's Best (USA))
2319^{5} 2715^{8} 5277^{13} 5675^{3} 6560^{25} 6777^{7} 7486^{4} 7758^{6} 7888^{9}

Olivino (GER) *Bernard Llewellyn* a49 40
9 ch g Second Set(IRE) —Osdemona (GER) (Solarstern (FR))
2023^{8} 4328^{5} 7634^{2}

Ollon (USA) *Richard Fahey* a61 76
2 bb g Mr Greeley(USA) —Town Branch (USA) (Cape Town (USA))
4167^{2} 5277^{11} 5761^{5} 5947^{7} 7066^{4}

Ollywood *Tony Carroll* 29
2 b g Needwood Blade—Angel Maid (Forzando)
5033^{11}

Olmo On Line (USA) *R Menichetti* 84
2 b c Pollard's Vision(USA) —Fico (USA) (Silver Deputy (CAN))
7264a^{9} 7850a^{16}

Olney Lass *Mike Murphy* a53 72
3 b f Lucky Story(USA) —Zalebe (Bahamian Bounty)
1269^{6} 2517^{8} 3091^{4} 7205^{5} 7406^{2} 7646^{3} 7845^{5}

Olympian Order (IRE) *Alan Swinbank* 60
4 b g High Chaparral(IRE) —Southey (USA) (Broad Brush (USA))
2393^{10} 2852^{5}

Olympic Ceremony *Tracy Waggott* a63 66
3 br g Kyllachy—Opening Ceremony (USA) (Quest For Fame)
17^{6} 3371^{9} 4482^{7} 5211^{7} 6494^{9}

Olympic Danz (BRZ) *A Cintra Pereira* a73 77
4 b h Shudanz(CAN) —Rarite (BRZ) (Nugget Point)
414a^{11} 608a^{13} 819a^{9}

Olympic Dream *Michael Herrington* a60 79
4 b g Kyllachy—Opening Ceremony (USA) (Quest For Fame)
2462^{8} 3408^{5} 4404^{12} 5067^{5} 5821^{6} 6188^{11} 6494^{4} 7161^{3} 7605^{3} 7835^{5} (7911)

Olympic Election (BRZ) *R Solanes* a79 22
5 b h Notation(USA) —Keep Free (BRZ) (Spend A Buck (USA))
440a^{12} 710a^{12}

Olympic Medal *Roger Charlton* a58 63
3 b f Nayef(USA) —Trying For Gold (USA) (Northern Baby (CAN))
2255^{5} 3080^{6}

Olynard (IRE) *Ralph Beckett* a73 64
4 b g Exceed And Excel(AUS) —Reddening (Blushing Flame (USA))
2280^{3} 2748^{10} 3461^{8} (3850) 4536^{8} 4904^{4} ◆ 5731^{7} 6256^{4} 6776^{11}

Olynthos (IRE) *Jane Chapple-Hyam* 59
2 ch c Chineur(FR) —Mistic Sun (Dashing Blade)
4375^{4} 5047^{12}

O Ma Lad (IRE) *Sylvester Kirk* a74
2 ch g Redback—Raydaniya (IRE) (In The Wings)
5724^{10} 7248^{2}

Omaruru (IRE) *Mark Johnston* a64 71
3 b g Cape Cross(IRE) —Monturani (IRE) (Indian Ridge)
755^{4} ◆ 889^{4} ◆ 2072^{2} 2607^{6} 3259^{6} 4476^{5}

Omega Centauri *Ed McMahon* a37
2 ch f Needwood Blade—Distant Stars (IRE) (Distant Music (USA))
7530^{12} 7682^{5}

Omnipotent (IRE) *Richard Hannon* 59
2 b c Tagula(IRE) —Bobbydazzle (Rock Hopper)
6443^{6} 6689^{10}

Omniscient (USA) *Steven Asmussen* a99
4 bb h Pulpit(USA) —Actceptional (USA) (Noactor (USA))
5779a^{7}

Omokoroa (IRE) *Mark H Tompkins* a62 88
4 b g Hawkeye(IRE) —Alycus (USA) (Atticus (USA))
1282^{6} 2031^{9} 2941^{9} 4125^{2} 4846^{2} 5296^{2} 5940^{3} 6352^{4} 7061^{15}

Onceaponatime (IRE) *Michael Squance* a90 73
5 b g Invincible Spirit(IRE) —Lake Nyasa (IRE) (Lake Coniston (IRE))
20^{2} 71^{2} (192) 250^{5} 432^{4} 474^{3} ◆ 573^{3} ◆ 722^{2} (859) 916^{2} 1266^{8} 1506^{4} 1826^{10} 2465^{DSQ} 3216^{11} 7212^{10} 7466^{7} 7566^{11} 7719^{7} 7866^{6} 7971^{8}

Once More Dubai (USA) *Saeed Bin Suroor* a112 110
5 bb h E Dubai(USA) —Go Again Girl (USA) (Broad Brush (USA))
516a^{5} (820a) 1859^{4} 3632^{5} 5749^{9} 7297^{6}

Once Upon A Dream *Paul Howling*
2 b f Tiger Hill(IRE) —Dream Lady (Benny The Dip (USA))
7448^{12}

Once Were Wild (AUS) *Gai Waterhouse* 112
4 bb f Johannesburg(USA) —Wildesong (AUS) (Unbridled's Song (USA))
7032a^{8} 7291a^{11}

On Earth *P Bary* 59
3 b f Oratorio(IRE) —Premiere Dance (IRE) (Loup Solitaire (USA))
6487a^{0}

One Cat Diesel (IRE) *Hugh McWilliams* a35 50
3 b g One Cool Cat(USA) —Awaaser (USA) (Diesis)
1100^{8} 1528^{7} 4482^{5} 5045^{7} 5686^{8} 6332^{12} 6746^{8}

One Clever Cat (IRE) *T Clout* a87 106
4 b m One Cool Cat(USA) —Burn Baby Burn (IRE) (King's Theatre (IRE))
5108a^{9}

One Cool Bex *Philip McBride* a74 64
2 b g One Cool Cat(USA) —Applaud (USA) (Rahy (USA))
2547^{14} 4436^{3} 4941^{10} 5581^{3} (6072) (6740) (7211)

One Cool Chick *John Bridger* 39
2 b f Iceman—Barrantes (Distant Relative)
5147^{10} 5537^{8} 5829^{12} 6811^{10}

One Cool Dream *Peter Hiatt* a61 57
4 b m One Cool Cat(USA) —Swift Baba (USA) (Deerhound (USA))
21^{12} 442^{11} 498^{10} 757^{12} 984^{11} 1304^{13} 1437^{14} 1737^{10}

One Cool Poppy (IRE) *Hugh Collingridge* a47 57
3 b f One Cool Cat(USA) —Elusive Kitty (USA) (Elusive Quality (USA))
1261^{2} 1578^{5} 2620^{4} 3404^{3} 4972^{7} 5656^{6}

One Cool Pussy (IRE) *Daniel Mark Loughnane* a38 52
4 b m One Cool Cat(USA) —Annaduff (IRE) (Indian Ridge)
776^{7} 2690^{7}

One Cool Slash (IRE) *Murty McGrath* a39 46
3 br f One Cool Cat(USA) —Sun Slash (IRE) (Entrepreneur)
2632^{8} 3292^{9} 6847^{12}

One Fat Cat (IRE) *Pat Phelan* 39
2 b f One Cool Cat(USA) —Ellens Princess (IRE) (Desert Prince (IRE))
2338^{13} 2591^{5} 4363^{8}

Onegin (SAF) *David Simcock* a55 28
4 b h Indigo Magic—Run On By (SAF) (Model Man (SAF))
308^{4} 468^{8}

One Good Emperor (IRE) *John Best* a78 86
3 b g Antonius Pius(USA) —Break Of Day (USA) (Favorite Trick (USA))
1582^{8} (2089) 2544^{5} 3103^{7} ◆

One Hit Wonder *Mouse Hamilton-Fairley* a56 71
3 b g Whipper(USA) —Swiftly (Cadeaux Genereux)
1769^{12} 2844^{5} 3154^{3} 6370^{8} 6633^{5} (6862)

Oneladyowner *David Brown* 72
2 b c Auction House(USA) —Inya Lake (Whittingham (IRE))
(2111) 2757^{5}

One Lucky Lady *B W Hills* a76 75
2 b f Lucky Story(USA) —One For Philip (Blushing Flame (USA))
3562^{12} 4021^{7} 4741^{2} 6156^{4} 6555^{2} (6979) 7481^{5}

Onemoreandstay *Hugh Collingridge* a71 69
5 ch m Dr Fong(USA) —Subito (Darshaan)
76^{3} 1028^{8} 1493^{4}

One More Tico *Mark Johnston* 39
3 b g Danehill Dancer(IRE) —Costa Rica (IRE) (Sadler's Wells (USA))
1485^{12} 1927^{12} 2143^{10} 2838^{13}

Oneofapear (IRE) *Alan Swinbank* a57 93
4 b g Pyrus(USA) —Whitegate Way (Greensmith)
(1889) 2608^{8} 3121^{3} 4405^{12} 6096^{6} 7053^{8}

One Of Twins *Michael Easterby* a40 40
2 b g Gentleman's Deal(IRE) —Miss Twiddles (IRE) (Desert King (IRE))
5498^{9} 5924^{10} 6293^{6}

One Oi *David Arbuthnot* a66
5 b g Bertolini(USA) —Bogus Penny (IRE) (Pennekamp (USA))
7518^{10} 7829^{2} (7966)

One Scoop Or Two *Reg Hollinshead* a85 83
4 b g Needwood Blade—Rebel County (IRE) (Maelstrom Lake)
1922^{3} ◆ 2527^{10} 3132^{2} 3538^{5} (3765) (4093) (4547) (5287) 5937^{4} 6367^{9} 6581^{3} 6629^{3} 7121^{4} 7243^{2} 7274^{10}

One Slick Chick (IRE) *Marco Botti* a75 43
4 b m One Cool Cat(USA) —Ms Mary C (IRE) (Dolphin Street (FR))
593^{5} 1617^{11}

On Est Bien (IRE) *E Lellouche* 111
4 b h Enrique—Doucelisa (FR) (Cardoun (FR))
1255a^{4}

One Way Or Another (AUS) *Jeremy Gaska* 90 99
7 b g Carnegie(IRE) —True Blonde (AUS) (Naturalism (NZ))
1032^{3} ◆ 1900^{26} 2508^{11} 2992^{13} ◆ 3969^{6} 6776^{5} 7238^{7} 7352^{7} 7566^{9} 7689^{9}

One World (AUS) *J Moore* a115 121
6 bb h Danehill Dancer(IRE) —River Serenade (AUS) (Hurricane Sky (AUS))
1024a^{3} 7852a^{13}

Ongoodform (IRE) *Paul D'Arcy* a92 90
3 b c Invincible Spirit(IRE) —Elfin Queen (IRE) (Fairy King (USA))
945^{7} 1315^{16} 1701^{9} 2394^{4} 2970^{3} 3103^{21} 4264^{6} 5031^{3}

On Her Way *Henry Cecil* a87 83
3 ch f Medicean—Singed (Zamindar (USA))
(1607) 2843^{8} 3606^{4} (3963) 4483^{3} (5181)

Oniz Tiptoes (IRE) *John Wainwright* 47
9 ch g Russian Revival(USA) —Edionda (IRE) (Magical Strike (USA))
166^{9}

On Khee *Hughie Morrison* a77 82
3 b f Sakhee(USA) —Star Precision (Shavian)
(1261) 1830^{2} 2843^{5} (4426) ◆ 6361^{8} 6872^{3}

Only A Game (IRE) *Ian McInnes* a64 67
5 b g Foxhound(USA) —Compendium (Puissance)
14^{4} ◆ 351^{3} ◆ 531^{3} 839^{8} 914^{5} 1236^{8} 1928^{7} (2184) 5267^{7} 5614^{6} 6025^{15} 6741^{9} 7249^{4} 7299^{8} 7425^{8} 7604^{7}

Only A Splash *Ruth Carr* a33 60
6 b g Primo Valentino(IRE) —Water Well (Sadler's Wells (USA))
3948^{11} (4189) 4547^{4} 4824^{11}

Onlyfoalsandhorses (IRE) *J S Moore* 52
2 b f Chineur(FR) —Scarletta (USA) (Red Ransom (USA))
4363^{5} 4528^{5} 4967^{6}

Only Green (IRE) *F Head* a104 104
4 b m Green Desert(USA) —Only Seule (USA) (Lyphard (USA))
2778a^{7} 4639a^{7} 5134a^{7}

Only Ten Per Cent (IRE) *J S Moore* 43
2 b c Kheleyf(USA) —Cory Everson (IRE) (Brief Truce (USA))
3961^{10} 4437^{10} 4999^{6} 5373^{10}

Only You Maggie (IRE) *W G Harrison* 65
3 b f Atraf—First Kiss (GER) (Night Shift (USA))
4146^{9} 4601^{4} 4906^{4} 5474^{4}

On Terms (USA) *Simon Dow* a81 84
4 b m Aptitude(USA) —Silver Yen (USA) (Silver Hawk (USA))
82^{2} 316^{2} 770^{6} 982^{2} (1478) (1849) (2810) (3402) 3843^{10} 4467^{9} 5144^{4} 6388^{6}

On The Bounty *Paul Midgley* 70
3 b g Bahamian Bounty—Dark Eyed Lady (IRE) (Exhibitioner)
3243^{10} 3761^{14}

On The Cusp (IRE) *Paddy Butler* a67 67
3 b g Footstepsinthesand—Roman Love (IRE) (Perugino (USA))
1178^{12} 1810^{3} 2288^{4} 3413^{3} 3680^{6} 4337^{7} 4552^{6} 5664^{10} 6024^{13} 6098^{10} 6860^{8} 7156^{8} 7727^{10} 7918^{2} 7994^{4} 8023^{7}

On The Feather *Rod Millman* a41 69
4 br m Josr Algarhoud(IRE) —Fotheringhay (Loup Sauvage (USA))
2919^{10} 3464^{6} 4044^{9} 4987^{4} 5584^{5} 6678^{2} 6959^{10} 7275^{9}

On The High Tops (IRE) *Tom Tate* 84
2 b g Kheleyf(USA) —Diplomats Daughter (Unfuwain (USA))
(1806) 2525^{3} 3364^{2} 4544^{7} 5221^{12} 5745^{5} 6568^{21} 6916^{8}

On The Piste (IRE) *Lawrence Mullaney* a53 64
3 b f Distant Music(USA) —Lady Piste (IRE) (Ali-Royal (IRE))
2396^{9} 2628^{9} 3393^{7} 3687^{10} 4169^{2} 4567^{7} 4869^{13} 5422^{7} 5548^{15}

On The Right Path *Paul Murphy* 47
3 b g Pursuit Of Love—Glen Falls (Commanche Run)
1271^{6} 1572^{6} 2131^{U} 2627^{8} 3532^{9} 4017^{P}

On Verra (IRE) *F Doumen* a89 104
3 b f Smart Strike(CAN) —Karmifira (FR) (Always Fair (USA))
1746a^{2} 2373a^{9}

On Wings Of Love (IRE) *Alan Bailey* a51 66
2 ch f Hawk Wing(USA) —Grenouillere (USA) (Alysheba (USA))
1324^{8} 1728^{6} 2505^{4} 2958^{4} 3190^{12} 4592^{7} 5490^{6} 6311^{9} 6717^{9} 7295^{7}

Onyx Of Arabia (IRE) *Brian Meehan* a76 76
3 br c Avonbridge—Fiamma Royale (IRE) (Fumo Di Londra (IRE))
1776^{5} 2089^{4} 2587^{11} (3039) 3155^{4} 3963^{6} 4698^{4} 7042^{4}

Oondiri (IRE) *Tim Easterby* 68
3 b f Trans Island—Nullarbor (Green Desert (USA))
2396^{7} 3228^{2} (3988) 4651^{5} (5548) 6392^{2}

Oor Jock (IRE) *D K Weld* 96
2 ch c Shamardal(USA) —Katdogawn (Bahhare (USA))
3051^{11} 3488a^{6} 5567a^{7} 7135a^{7}

Opening Nite (IRE) *Richard Fahey* 75
3 b g Azamour(IRE) —Night Club (Mozart (IRE))
2627^{4} 4062^{5} 4407^{2} 4898^{7} ◆ 5394^{4} (6144) 6573^{11} 6961^{5}

Opera Cat (USA) *Mark Johnston* a19
3 b c Storm Cat(USA) —Flat Fleet Feet (USA) (Afleet (CAN))
1868^{7} 5487^{11} 5925^{11}

Operachy *James Frost* 60
5 b g Kyllachy—Sea Music (Inchinor)
1737^{12}

Opera Comica (BRZ) *P Bary* a94 61
4 b m Giant Gentleman(USA) —Cientifica (ARG) (Cipayo (ARG))
514a^{11} 710a^{7}

Opera Dancer *Sylvester Kirk* a75 77
2 ch f Norse Dancer(IRE) —Optaria (Song)
3296^{9} 3861^{3} 4508^{4} 5369^{4} 5880^{17} (6712)

Opera Gal (IRE) *Andrew Balding* a77 101
3 b f Galileo(IRE) —Opera Glass (Barathea (IRE))
1876[2] 2758[4] (3829) 4400[2] 4815[3] 5913[2] (6355)

Opera Moon (GER) *W Hickst* 80
3 ch c Big Shuffle(USA) —Opera Nova (IRE) (Perugino (USA))
1564a[5]

Opera Prince *Lady Herries* a72 83
5 b g Kyllachy—Optaria (Song)
1011[10] 1133[4] 2821[5] 3377[5] 3853[7] 5635[5] 5958[3] 6472[11] 6794[4] 7323[3]

Operateur (IRE) *Ben Haslam* a66 55
2 b g Oratorio(IRE) —Kassariya (IRE) (Be My Guest (USA))
6222[6] 6542[4] 6936[5]

Opinionated (IRE) *M Halford* a31
2 ch f Dubai Destination(USA) —Theoretically (USA) (Theatrical)
6726a[13]

Opinion Poll (IRE) *Michael Jarvis* 116
4 b h Halling(USA) —Ahead (Shirley Heights)
(1176) ◆ 2716[3] (3099a) 3695[3] (5218) 5909[4] 7110a[3]

Optical Illusion (USA) *Richard Fahey* a61 63
6 b g Theatrical—Paradise River (USA) (Irish River (FR))
2381[5] 2454[4] 3076[6]

Optimistic Duke (IRE) *William Muir* a45 58
3 ch g Bachelor Duke(USA) —Gronchi Rosa (IRE) (Nashwan (USA))
1796[4] 3055[4] 3521[8] 4113[2] 4448[8] 6860[6]

Opus Dei *David Nicholls* a73 69
3 b g Oasis Dream—Grail (USA) (Quest For Fame)
6310[2] 7505[2] 7645[3] 7895[3] (7987)

Opus Maximus (IRE) *Mark Johnston* a82 96
5 ch g Titus Livius(FR) —Law Review (IRE) (Case Law)
1397[5] 1841[5] (2443) 2977[9] 3150[3] (3389) 3692[8] 3956[3] 4617[3] 5068[11] 6391[12] 6709[9] (7171) 7680[6] 7844[5]

Oracle (IRE) *A P O'Brien* 84
2 b c Danehill Dancer(IRE) —Zibilene (Rainbow Quest (USA))
1728[2] 6200[10] 6560[11]

Orange Ace *Paul Cole* a77 28
2 b c Medicean—Promenade Again (USA) (Wild Again (USA))
7094[15] (7385)

Orange Ketchup (IRE) *Paul Cole* a65 56
2 b c Tiger Hill(IRE) —Sherifa (GER) (Monsun (GER))
3631[10] ◆ 4993[9] 5718[6] 6160[7] 6471[14] 6694[4] 7295[6]

Orangeleg *Stuart Williams* a68 63
4 b g Intikhab(USA) —Red Shareef (Marju (IRE))
668[8] 1967[3] 3279[11] 4715[6] 5077[5] 6024[9] 6672[P] (Dead)

Orange Pip *PETER Makin* a86 81
5 ch m Bold Edge—Opopmil (IRE) (Pips Pride)
(828) 2364[4] 3261[6]

Oratory (IRE) *Richard Hannon* a82 99
4 b g Danehill Dancer(IRE) —Gentle Night (Zafonic (USA))
1383[3] 1900[15] 2977[2] 3692[4] 4473[3] 4843[4] 6391[5] 6877[6]

Oratouch (IRE) *Marco Botti* a65
2 b f Oratorio(IRE) —Ravish (Efisio)
7163[8] 7464[3] 7839[2]

Orbitor *George Baker* a56 72
4 b g Galileo(IRE) —Peacock Alley (IRE) (Salse (USA))
7062[16] 7480[5]

Orchard Supreme *John Akehurst* a93 82
7 ch g Titus Livius(FR) —Bogus Penny (IRE) (Pennekamp (USA))
635[5] (863) 1265[11] 1455[10] 1767[11] 2235[2] 2823[11] 2840[2] 4489[3] 5233[4] 6054[2] 7601[2] 7732[4] (7825)

Orchid Street (USA) *Ann Duffield* a47 78
2 bb f Street Cry(IRE) —Ella Eria (FR) (Bluebird (USA))
2130[2] ◆ 2436[8] 2693[2] (3549) 3925[3] 4600[3] 5021[2] 6030[7] 6354[4] 6745[11]

Orchid Wing *George Foster* a68 67
3 ch g Avonbridge—First Ace (First Trump)
7539[14]

Ordenstreuer (IRE) *H-W Hiller* a66 105
4 b h Nayef(USA) —Dramraire Mist (Darshaan)
2806a[8] 7532a[7]

Ordnance Row *Michael Jarvis* 116
7 b g Mark Of Esteem(IRE) —Language Of Love (Rock City)
1904[6] 1974[2] 2707[6] 3460[6] 5741[6] 5948[6]

Ordoney (IRE) *John Wainwright* a90 88
5 b g Intikhab(USA) —Mitawa (IRE) (Alhaarth (IRE))
2423[11] 2865[12]

Orestias (IRE) *C Laffon-Parias* a68 65
3 b f Elusive City(USA) —Seditieuse (IRE) (Night Shift (USA))
6487a[0]

Oriental Cat *John Gosden* a60 97
3 b g Tiger Hill(IRE) —Sentimental Value (USA) (Diesis)
(2072) 2562[5] 5727[6] (6677) 7100[4]

Oriental Cavalier *Mark Buckley* a76 82
4 ch g Ishiguru(USA) —Gurleigh (IRE) (Pivotal)
1241[4] 1512[5] 1883[2] 2240[3] 2937[14] (3860) 5790[5] 6322[6] 6832[6] 7463[6]

Oriental Girl *J S Moore* a62 77
5 b m Dr Fong(USA) —Zacchera (Zamindar (USA))
2410[4] 3268[11] 4327[4] 4992[2] (5585) (5873) 6959[2] 7306[8]

Orientalist *Eve Johnson Houghton* 87
2 ch g Haafhd—Oriental Queen (GER) (Big Shuffle (USA))
(1597) ◆ 2127[4] 2525[5] 3749[3] 4623[4] (4955) (5310) (5784) 5849[10] 6386[9]

Oriental Lion *Uwe Ostmann* 98
4 b h Seattle Dancer(USA) —Oriental Flower (GER) (Big Shuffle (USA))
5542a[12]

Oriental Rose *Derek Shaw* a37 67
4 b m Dr Fong(USA) —Sahara Rose (Green Desert (USA))
3328[9] 3762[13] 3977[11]

Oriental Scot *William Jarvis* a74 96
3 ch c Selkirk(USA) —Robe Chinoise (Robellino (USA))
(1602) ◆ 2253[7] 4112[3] (5759) 6203[11]

Orife (IRE) *G Botti* a69 93
3 b c Marchand De Sable(USA) —Entente Cordiale (IRE) (Ela-Mana-Mou)
1610a[7] 7370a[5]

Original Dancer (IRE) *Mark Johnston* a37 46
3 b g Danehill Dancer(IRE) —Courtier (Saddlers' Hall (IRE))
5815[9] 6865[9]

Orkney (IRE) *Julie-Ann Camacho* a72 62
5 b g Trans Island—Bitty Mary (Be My Chief (USA))
835[2] 1071[9] 2109[4] 2500[8] 3223[10]

Orluna (GER) *R Rohne* 93
3 b f Mamool(IRE) —Ormita (GER) (Acatenango (GER))
7103a[6]

Oroveso (BRZ) *P Bary* a106 98
4 gr h Fahim—Voile D'Or (BRZ) (Effervescing (USA))
414a[3] 608a[6] 819a[3] 1023a[7] 5109a[8]

Orpen Arms (IRE) *Richard Fahey* a51 64
3 b f Orpen(USA) —Lindas Delight (Batshoof)
(1201) 1488[7] 7273[10] 7562[10] 7706[7]

Orpen Bid (IRE) *Michael Mullineaux* 47
5 b m Orpen(USA) —Glorious Bid (IRE) (Horage)
3901[2] 4582[7] 5202[7]

Orpenia (IRE) *John McShane* 28
4 b m Orpen(USA) —Knockanure (USA) (Nureyev (USA))
1203[6] 1536[8] 1722[8] 5197[7]

Orpenindeed (IRE) *Jim Best* a96 91
7 bb g Orpen(USA) —Indian Goddess (IRE) (Indian Ridge)
177[8] 365[2] 887[7] 1349[3] 2091[7] (3518) (4053) 4430[3] 5768[9] (6537)

Orpen Lady *Milton Bradley* a26 32
4 b m Orpen(USA) —Gargren (IRE) (Mujtahid (USA))
3308[7] 5112[7] 5471[8] 7505[9]

Orpen Shadow (IRE) *J-C Rouget* 111
3 b c Orpen(USA) —Mujadil Shadow (IRE) (Mujadil (USA))
3425a[4] 4165a[7] 6640a[6]

Orpen Wide (IRE) *Michael Chapman* a43 84
8 b g Orpen(USA) —Melba (IRE) (Namaqualand (USA))
245[11] 292[8] 1430[11] 1754[7] 2142[2] 2421[8] 2961[9] 3168[4] 3412[8] 3683[6] 3912[3] 4102[3] 4201[11] 4374[8] 5051[2] 6472[10] 6890[10] 7646[6] 7986[8]

Orpsie Boy (IRE) *Ruth Carr* a104 104
7 b g Orpen(USA) —Nordicolini (IRE) (Nordico (USA))
177[3] 286[12] 528[3] 635[9] 905[3] 987[8] 1727[17] 2247[8] 3551[5] (4121) 4413[5]

Orsett Lad (USA) *John Best* a67 62
3 b g Essence Of Dubai(USA) —Sofisticada (USA) (Northern Jove (CAN))
(346) 490[3] 698[10] 933[5] 1261[8] 1578[6] 2321[7] 3002[2] 3264[6] 4300[5] 4742[3] 5669[2] 5730[9] 5968[10] 6672[7]

Ortensia (AUS) *Tony Noonan* 115
5 b m Testa Rossa(AUS) —Aerate's Pick (AUS) (Picnicker (AUS))
7852a[5]

Orthodox Lad *John Best* a68 70
2 ch c Monsieur Bond(IRE) —Ashantiana (Ashkalani (IRE))
6153[15] 7150[3] 7386[4]

Oscar Close (IRE) *George Baker* 68
5 br g Oscar(IRE) —Upham Close (Oats)
(1183) 1446[4]

Osgood *Mick Channon* a72 79
3 b c Danehill Dancer(IRE) —Sabreon (Caerleon (USA))
1381[5] 1844[8] 2115[5] 2767[2] 3271[6] 3863[6] 4344[13] 4732[4] 5394[2] 5664[4] 5891[3] 6212[3] 6633[2] 6991[4] (7055)

Osgoodisgood *Stuart Williams*
2 ch c Compton Place—Protectorate (Hector Protector (USA))
6635[10]

Osiris Way *Patrick Chamings* a89 98
8 ch g Indian Ridge—Heady (Rousillon (USA))
(1691) 2681[2] 3629[3] 4148[9] 4510[17] 5966[12] 6446[7]

Oskari *Paul Midgley* a70 54
5 b g Lear Spear(USA) —Cedar Jeneva (Muhtarram (USA))
858[4]

Osolomio (IRE) *Jennie Candlish* a83 70
7 b g Singspiel(IRE) —Inanna (Persian Bold)
5278[12] 6114[5] 6775[5]

Ostentation *Roger Teal* a78 70
3 ch g Dubawi(IRE) —Oshiponga (Barathea (IRE))
(134) (382) ◆ 617[3] 1476[10] 4501[3] 4964[4] 5236[4] 5662[8] 7205[4]

Osteopathic Remedy (IRE) *Michael Dods* a87 103
6 ch g Inchinor—Dolce Vita (IRE) (Ela-Mana-Mou)
1397[2] ◆ (1708) 2423[5] 2708[10] 3448[4] 3920[8] (5605) 6180[6] 6749[3] (6960) 7348[17]

Otaared *D Selvaratnam* a108 88
5 br g Storm Cat(USA) —Society Lady (USA) (Mr Prospector (USA))
338a[8] 511a[6]

Othello (IRE) *Edward Vaughan* a61 58
3 b g Azamour(IRE) —Bonheur (IRE) (Royal Academy (USA))
1977[12] (2412) 2908[4] 3967[7] 4301[5]

Otou (GER) *S Smrczek* a98 89
3 b c Big Shuffle(USA) —Old Tradition (IRE) (Royal Academy (USA))
1610a[9]

Otterton *Reg Hollinshead* a34 40
3 b f Sampower Star—Parkside Prospect (Piccolo)
997[8] 1144[3] 3359[11] 3685[5] 4113[6]

Ottofee (GER) *Andreas Lowe* 75
3 ch f Banyumanik(IRE) —Omicenta (IRE) (Platini (GER))
2404a[7]

Ottoman Empire (FR) *David Lanigan* a108 105
4 ch g Pivotal—Chesnut Bird (IRE) (Storm Bird (CAN))
(5723) 6889[3] (7287)

Ouqba *B W Hills* 121
4 b h Red Ransom(USA) —Dancing Mirage (IRE) (Machiavellian (USA))
2118[2] 3046[7] 3888[4] 5081[3] 5946[7]

Our Angel *Eric Alston* 13
4 b m Primo Valentino(IRE) —Abaklea (IRE) (Doyoun)
4251[13] 4584[6]

Our Boy Barrington (IRE) *Richard Hannon* 81
3 b g Catcher In The Rye(IRE) —Daily Double (FR) (Unfuwain (USA))
(1392) 1582[2] 2225[7] 3863[11] 4325[4] 4660[2] 4956[4] 5968[7] 6692[9]

Our Dark Knight (USA) *Nicholas Zito* a108
3 bb c Medaglia D'Oro(USA) —Drifa (USA) (Tabasco Cat (USA))
4643a[7]

Our Day Will Come *Bryn Palling* a70 71
4 b m Red Ransom(USA) —Dawnus (IRE) (Night Shift (USA))
397[8] 614[3] 763[12] 937[10]

Our Drama Queen (IRE) *Richard Hannon* a43 74
3 ch f Danehill Dancer(IRE) —Dance Parade (USA) (Gone West (USA))
1844[11] 2180[9] 2841[5] ◆ 3479[2] (3866) 4206[5] 4680[3] 5145[6]

Our Dynasty (IRE) *John Quinn* 80
2 b c Dubai Destination(USA) —Nobilissime (Halling (USA))
(7172) ◆

Our Folly *Stuart Kittow* 40
2 b g Sakhee(USA) —Regent's Folly (IRE) (Touching Wood (USA))
1793[14] 3964[13] 6802[11] 7179[8]

Our Fugitive (IRE) *Chris Gordon* a61 71
8 gr g Titus Livius(FR) —Mystical Jumbo (Mystiko (USA))
541[12] 726[8]

Our Gal *Michael Quinlan* a66 73
2 b f Kyllachy—Moxby (Efisio)
3871[3] 6651[2] 6866[3] 7232[12]

Our Giant (AUS) *M F De Kock* 111
7 ch g Giant's Causeway(USA) —Macrosa (NZ) (Mcginty (NZ))
1021a[13]

Our Jane *Roger Teal* a49
5 b m Apprehension—Honey Mill (Milford)
98[8]

Our Joe Mac (IRE) *Richard Fahey* 99
3 b g Celtic Swing—Vade Retro (IRE) (Desert Sun)
1834[2] 2324[4] 2742[8] (4828) ◆ 5948[4] ◆ 6180[4]

Our Jonathan *Kevin Ryan* a103 112
3 b g Invincible Spirit(IRE) —Sheik'n Swing (Celtic Swing)
1616[6] 4616[7] 5744[13] 6265[5] 6918[10] 7079[7]

Our Kes (IRE) *Jane Chapple-Hyam* a63 67
8 gr m Revoque(IRE) —Gracious Gretclo (Common Grounds)
184[5] 410[6] 541[10] 661[4] 865[8] 7453[5] 7716[7] 7918[5]

Our Mate Joe (IRE) *Geoffrey Harker* 25
2 b g Ivan Denisovich(IRE) —Westwood (FR) (Anabaa (USA))
5762[7] 6268[11] 6894[12]

Our Piccadilly (IRE) *Stuart Kittow* a83 84
5 b m Piccolo—Dilys (Efisio)
1691[5] 2094[3] 2280[4] 3114[7] 3736[7] 4292[4] 4730[2] 5628[8] 6539[8] 6772[8]

Our Play (IRE) *B W Hills* 23
2 b c Oratorio(IRE) —Red Shoe (Selkirk (USA))
7345 [12]

Ours (IRE) *John Harris* a95 79
7 b g Mark Of Esteem(IRE) —Ellebanna (Tina's Pet)
(245) 408[4] 572[3] 4119[14] 4713[4] 4860[2] 5641[2] (6267) 6629[5] 7182[5] 7304[4] 7867[4]

Our Way Only (IRE) *Richard Hannon* a72 80
2 b f Oratorio(IRE) —Fearn Royal (IRE) (Ali-Royal (IRE))
3411[4] ◆ 3871[6] (4299) 4696[3] 5452[13]

Ouste (FR) *Alison Thorpe* a44 46
8 ch g Ragmar(FR) —Elbe (FR) (Royal Charter (FR))
148[8]

Ouster (GER) *David Elsworth* 91
4 b h Lomitas—Odabella's Charm (Cadeaux Genereux)
1274[11] 1724[17] 2506[3] (2996) 3873[3] 4400[6] 5970[8]

Outer Continent (IRE) *X Nakkachdji* a76 91
5 b g Domedriver(IRE) —Baratheastar (Barathea (IRE))
272a[6] 458a[10]

Outer Hebrides *Milton Bradley* a62 63
9 b g Efisio—Reuval (Sharpen Up)
116[5] 368[11] 567[10] 721[5]

Outland (IRE) *John Jenkins* a34 69
4 br g Indian Haven—Sensuality (IRE) (Idris (IRE))
1755[6] 2341[8] (2897) 3128[2] 4070[3] 4266[2] 4719[6] 5679[9] 6065[7] 6860[10] 7011[8]

Out Of Eden *Henry Cecil* a57 75
3 b c Monsun(GER) —Eden (USA) (Holy Bull (USA))
1314[7] 2684[2] 4257[5] 4786[5]

Out Of Nothing *K M Prendergast* a61 88
7 br m Perryston View—Loves To Dare (IRE) (Desert King (IRE))
3329[8] 4324[3] 4914[2] 5271[4] (5766) (7056)

Outofoil (IRE) *Ralph Beckett* a69 69
4 b g King's Best(USA) —Simplicity (Polish Precedent (USA))
239[12] 676[10] 975[5] 3130[4] 3787[6]

Out Of The Storm *Simon Dow* a65 65
2 b f Elmhurst Boy—Night Storm (Night Shift (USA))
3778[3] 4203[4] 4691[3] 5452[5] 6052[5]

Outrageous Request *Pat Eddery* a84 85
4 ch g Rainbow Quest(USA) —La Sorrela (IRE) (Cadeaux Genereux)
1101[12] (2975) ◆ 3634[2] 4846[8] 5996[10] 6516[7]

Outshine *Karen George* a44 70
3 ch f Exceed And Excel(AUS) —Sunny Davis (USA) (Alydar (USA))
3833[7] 4478[10] 4989[15] 5957[9] 6330[9] 7166[8]

Out The Ring (IRE) *Gay Kelleway* a66 59
3 b g Acclamation—Residual (IRE) (Trempolino (USA))
343[5]

Ovambo Queen (GER) *Dr A Bolte* 108
3 bb f Kalatos(GER) —Oxalaguna (GER) (Lagunas)
3943a[3] (5345a) 6790a[2]

Overdose *Jozef Roszival* 96
5 b h Starborough—Our Poppet (IRE) (Warning)
(4183a) 5573a[7]

Overrule (USA) *Brian Ellison* 95
6 b g Diesis—Her Own Way (USA) (Danzig (USA))
3873[6] 4405[6]

Oversteer (USA) *John Gosden* a78 69
2 b c Empire Maker(USA) —Mirabilis (USA) (Lear Fan (USA))
5263[6] 6305[3] 6742[4] 7452[2] 7830[2]

Overturn (IRE) *Donald McCain* a94 103
6 b g Barathea(IRE) —Kristal Bridge (Kris)
(3447) 5220[20]

Overwhelm *Andrew Reid* a71 73
2 ch f Bahamian Bounty—Depressed (Most Welcome)
2176[4] 3070[15] 3778[2] (4432) 5036[5] 5261[5]

Ovthenight (IRE) *Pam Sly* a57 71
5 b g Noverre(USA) —Night Beauty (King Of Kings (IRE))
2560[6]

Owain (USA) *Chris Dwyer* a84 83
2 bb g Henny Hughes(USA) —Twinkle (USA) (Lively One (USA))
4549[10] 4909[3] (5808) 6435[2] ◆ 6667[3] 6850[3] 7444[3] 7565[4]

Owed *Robin Bastiman* a52 28
8 b g Lujain(USA) —Nightingale (Night Shift (USA))
187[8] 297[9] 403[6] 716[6] 836[3] 912[8] 1148[4] 1492[7]

Owen Jones (USA) *Peter Hiatt* a27 61
4 b g Rahy(USA) —Batique (USA) (Storm Cat (USA))
356[9] 570[8]

Owls FC (IRE) *Michael Chapman* a21 28
4 b m King's Best(USA) —Sadinga (IRE) (Sadler's Wells (USA))
18[7] 186[7] 7865[6]

Oxbridge *Milton Bradley* a47 53
5 ch g Tomba—Royal Passion (Ahonoora)
8[7] 146[6]

Oxford City (IRE) *Pat Phelan* a76 76
6 ch g City On A Hill(USA) —Bold Nora (IRE) (Persian Bold)
(323) 426[4] 974[2] 1087[2] 1579[3] 2081[2] 7011[9]

Ozzies Storm Cats (USA) *John Quinn* 26
2 b c Bernstein(USA) —Heartwood (USA) (Woodman (USA))
4167[9] 4599[13]

Pablo Quercus (FR) *A Lyon* 53
5 b h Diableneyev(USA) —Hawky (FR) (Matahawk)
281a[0]

Pab Special (IRE) *Brett Johnson* a60 64
7 b g City On A Hill(USA) —Tinos Island (IRE) (Alzao (USA))
1226[7] 1637[8] 1877[7] 2967[11] 3783[6] 4434[5] 4591[10] 7023[6] 7555[6] 7727[2] 7989[5]

Pabusar *Ralph Beckett* 103
2 b g Oasis Dream—Autumn Pearl (Orpen (USA))
2440[5] (4460) ◆ 5221[2] 6734[7]

Pachakutek (USA) *Alastair Lidderdale* a62 48
4 ch g Giant's Causeway(USA) —Charlotte Corday (Kris)
83[10] 815[4] 853[11] 1049[7] 1179[7] 1239[8] 1427[8] 1478[11]

Pachattack (USA) *Gerard Butler* a108 108
4 ch m Pulpit(USA) —El Laoob (USA) (Red Ransom (USA))
1328[5] 1665[3] 2057[8] 2744[3] (3368) (4624) 5320a[6] 6950a[5] (7371a)

Pacific Bay (IRE) *Richard Ford* a63 60
4 b m Diktat—Wild Clover (Lomitas)
36[9] 1149[9] 1958[6] 3131[12] 4454[7] 4986[12] 5586[10]

Pacific Pride *John Quinn* 78
7 b g Compton Place—Only Yours (Aragon)
1988[13] 2699[10]

Packing Winner (NZ) *L Ho* 117
8 b g Zabeel(NZ) —Musical Note (AUS) (Marscay (AUS))
7854a[3]

Paco Belle (IRE) *Richard Hannon* a63 63
2 b f Whipper(USA) —Raindancing (IRE) (Tirol)
3156[3] 3562[5] 4254[5] 5720[8] 6082[4] 6500[2] 6978[6]

Paco Boy (IRE) *Richard Hannon* a101 127
5 b h Desert Style(IRE) —Tappen Zee (Sandhurst Prince)
(1531) (2118) 3046[2] 5134a[3] 5801a[4] 6611a[2] 7364a[4] 7853a[13]

Paddy O'Prado (USA) *Dale Romans* a120 118
3 rg c El Prado(IRE) —Fun House (USA) (Prized (USA))
1714a[3] 2137a[6] (5319a) 7367a[5]

Paddy Partridge *Tom Dascombe* a23 58
4 b g Pivotal—Treble Heights (IRE) (Unfuwain (USA))
1920[7] 2214[5] 2476[9]

Pagan Starprincess *George Moore* a57 61
6 b m Robertico—Pagan Star (Carlitin)
140[3]

Pahente *J S Moore* a57 59
2 bg g Silver Patriarch(IRE) —Miss Tehente (FR) (Tehente (FR))
3035[12] 3864[2] 4838[7] 5389[6] 5660[5] 7004[12]

Pain Perdu (FR) *N Clement* 115
3 b c Vespone(IRE) —Coastline (Night Shift (USA))
1567a[2] 2802a[3]

Paintball (IRE) *William Muir* a73 84
3 b g Le Vie Dei Colori—Camassina (IRE) (Taufan (USA))
128[3] (189) 382[4] 781[4] (1033) 1182[3] 1734[2] 2742[7] 2927[6] 4504[7] 4964[3] 5266[6] 5953[2] ◆ 6813[4] ◆

Paint By Numbers *Jeremy Glover* a38
3 b g Haafhd—Attention Seeker (USA) (Exbourne (USA))
326[8] 519[6]

Painted Fingers (IRE) *Timothy Doyle* a41 55
2 b f Acclamation—Paintbox (Peintre Celebre (USA))
6726a[10]

Painted Sky *Richard Fahey* a68 66
7 ch g Rainbow Quest(USA)—Emplane (USA) (Irish River (FR))
176[3] 361[3]

Painters Easel (IRE) *J S Moore* 62
2 b g Modigliani(USA)—Stands With A Fist (JPN) (Giant's Causeway (USA))
3035[4] 3625[5] 4384[5] 4678[2] (4802)

Paint The Town Red *Hugh Collingridge* a66 79
5 b g Mujahid(USA)—Onefortheditch (USA) (With Approval (CAN))
293[6] (621) 996[6] 1609[4] 1980[9] 2961[8] 5770[9] 6121[5] 6744[6] 7213[9]

Paktolos (FR) *John Harris* a93 84
7 b g Dansili—Pithara (GR) (Never So Bold)
252[2] ◆ (224) 447[5] 620[4] 1863[4] 2313[6] 2549[6] 4348[2] 4619[12] 6699[6]

Palace Moon *William Knight* 114
5 b g Fantastic Light(USA)—Palace Street (USA) (Secreto (USA))
2999[5] 3193[3] ◆ 3869[2] ◆ 4576[27] 5275[4] 6147[8]

Palacio De Cristal (AUS) *Grahame Begg* 111
5 ch m Encosta De Lago(AUS)—Crystal Palace (NZ) (Palace Music (USA))
3

Paladino Di Sabbia (IRE) *F & L Camici* 96
3 ch c King Charlemagne(USA)—Alma Thomas (IRE) (Orpen (USA))
1945a[16]

Palagonia *Mark Johnston* a68
2 b c Exceed And Excel(AUS)—Sicily (USA) (Kris S (USA))
7723[4]

Palais Glide *Richard Hannon* a67
2 gr f Proclamation(IRE)—Careful Dancer (Gorytus (USA))
7485[3] 7608[3] 7686[2]

Palavicini (USA) *John Dunlop* 112
4 b h Giant's Causeway(USA)—Cara Fantasy (IRE) (Sadler's Wells (USA))
1328[3] 2593[6]

Palawi (IRE) *John Quinn* a66 82
3 ch g Dubawi(IRE)—Palwina (FR) (Unfuwain (USA))
1116[5] 1721[2] 2439[4] 6225[3] 6623[2]

Palazzone (IRE) *G M Lyons* a100 94
4 b g Bertolini(USA)—Genny Lim (IRE) (Barathea (IRE))
511a[3] 797a[6] (Dead)

Palazzo Reale *R Biondi* 98
2 b c Bertolini(USA)—Gem (Most Welcome)
7264a[5]

Palea (GER) *S Jesus* a70 83
4 b m Red Ransom(USA)—Palanca (Inchinor)
207a[0] 303a[7] 1055a[8]

Palermo (GER) *Cathrine Erichsen* 101
4 b h Kalatos(GER)—Palma (GER) (Goofalik (USA))
2637a[7]

Palindromic (IRE) *Jeremy Gask* a61 48
2 ch g Chineur(FR)—Compton Girl (Compton Place)
2638[4] 3204[10] 3964[7] 5863[6] 6311[8] 6674[15] 6954[10]

Palinode (USA) *J S Bolger* 92
2 b f Dansili—Formal Approval (USA) (Kingmambo (USA))
4077a[5] 5570a[10]

Palio Square (USA) *Henry Cecil* a92 81
3 bb g Harlan's Holiday(USA)—Teewee's Hope (CAN) (Defrere (USA))
5026[4] 5665[4] 6115[5] (6313) (6715)

Palisades Park *Richard Hannon* a75 90
3 b c Compton Place—Brooklyn's Sky (Septieme Ciel (USA))
(2681) 2997[8] 3791[19] 5551[7] 5967[9] 7091[9]

Palitana (USA) *John Gosden* 64
2 bb f Giant's Causeway(USA)—Glatisant (Rainbow Quest (USA))
5066[10] 6127[3]

Pallantes Cross *Mark Johnston* a92 100
3 b c Cape Cross(IRE)—Palinisa (FR) (Night Shift (USA))
4924[2] 5511[15] 6203[10] 6749[18]

Pallaton *Brendan Powell* a43 49
4 ch g Bertolini(USA)—Miss Honeypenny (IRE) (Old Vic)
1756[11]

Pallodio (IRE) *J E Hammond* a110 115
5 b h Medecis—Bent Al Fala (IRE) (Green Desert (USA))
946[3] 1747a[3] 6881a[6] 7776a[6]

Palmilla (IRE) *Luca Cumani* a58
3 b f Galileo(IRE)—Quatre Saisons (FR) (Homme De Loi (IRE))
238[3]

Palm Pilot (IRE) *Ed Dunlop* a75 55
2 b f Oasis Dream—Off Message (IRE) (In The Wings)
6154[7] 6469[8] 6849[4] 7412[5] 7718[2] ◆

Paloma Blanca (IRE) *Alan Bailey* a38 64
3 gr f Sadler's Wells(USA)—Reina Blanca (Darshaan)
6861[7] 7321[6]

Palomar (USA) *Brian Ellison* a81 99
8 bb g Chester House(USA)—Ball Gown (USA) (Silver Hawk (USA))
239[6] 620[3] 3319[4] 3974[3] 4393[5] ◆ 5278[8] 5790[13] 6926[5] (7173) 7350[7]

Paloma Varga (IRE) *Gabriele Miliani* 103
3 b f Orpen(USA)—Tindari Maria (FR) (Great Palm (USA))
1252a[4] 1713a[8] 3495a[7]

Pam (IRE) *Robert Collet* a69
2 b c Whipper(USA)—Graten (IRE) (Zieten (USA))
7647a[8]

Panama Jack *Richard Fahey* 69
3 b g Dubai Destination(USA)—Clear Impression (IRE) (Danehill (USA))
2609[4] 3111[3]

Pan American *PETER Makin* a79 78
3 b g American Post—Pan Galactic (USA) (Lear Fan (USA))
4204[4] 4837[4] 5677[3] 6057[2] 6523[4] 6801[8]

Pandorea *Henry Candy* 79
2 b f Diktat—Puya (Kris)
(6803) ◆

Pandorica *Clive Cox* 69
2 b f Indesatchel(IRE)—Hope Chest (Kris)
5583[6] 6360[3] 6770[2]

Pandoro De Lago (IRE) *Richard Fahey* 79
2 ch f Encosta De Lago(AUS)—Fig Tree Drive (USA) (Miswaki (USA))
4048[4] 4862[2] 5509[10]

Pani Ash *Pat Phelan*
2 b f Cadeaux Genereux—Puteri Sas (IRE) (Fasliyev (USA))
7099[17]

Panichop (FR) *J-M Capitte* a76 98
5 b h Panis(USA)—Fast Home (FR) (Homme De Loi (IRE))
272a[9]

Panoptic *Henry Cecil* 68
2 b f Dubawi(IRE)—Pan Galactic (USA) (Lear Fan (USA))
4103[6] 6058[4]

Panpiper *Gary Moore* 73
3 ch g Piccolo—Phi Beta Kappa (USA) (Diesis)
2122[7] 2844[13] (3726) ◆ 4130[8] (4529) 4875[2] 5309[5] 5588[7] 6164[11]

Pan River (TUR) *Ayhan Kasar* 117
5 b h Red Bishop(USA)—Wanganui River (Unfuwain (USA))
(517a) 799a[2] 1026a[7]

Pantella (IRE) *Kevin Ryan* 68
2 b f Fasliyev(USA)—Double Fantasy (GER) (Indian Ridge)
6075[2] 6986[3]

Panto Princess *Henry Candy* a66 74
4 b m Act One—Bob's Princess (Bob's Return (IRE))
4694[4] 5181[6]

Panyu (GER) *P Schiergen* 98
4 b h Monsun(GER)—Prairie Darling (Stanford)
1420a[5]

Papageno *John Jenkins* a65 62
3 b g Piccolo—Fresh Fruit Daily (Reprimand)
257[4] 363[4] 988[2] 1316[2] 1535[4] 1639[6] 3480[7] 4908[3] 5726[3] 6285[7] 7322[2] 7547[2] 7757[4] 7960[9]

Papas Fritas *Brian Meehan* a65 61
2 ch g Dr Fong(USA)—Locharia (Wolfhound (USA))
4622[9] 4902[6] 5170[4] 5660[3] 6082[3] 6412[3] 6717[3] 6936[8]

Papa's Princess *James Moffatt* a40 62
6 b m Mujadil(USA)—Desert Flower (Green Desert (USA))
1812[6] 2433[4] 2670[5] 3074[6] 3707[4] 4246[8] 5216[6] 7230[4] 7450[6]

Paper Dreams (IRE) *Kevin Ryan* a58 63
2 b f Green Desert(USA)—Pickwick Papers (Singspiel (IRE))
2347[4] 2654[3] 3281[3] 5998[9] 6694[8] 7269[4]

Paperetto *Robert Mills* a60 68
2 b c Selkirk(USA)—Song Of Hope (Chief Singer)
7002[5] 7294[6]

Paphos *Stuart Williams* a72 23
3 b g Oasis Dream—Tychy (Suave Dancer (USA))
1442[11] 1622[9] 2174[10] 3030[15] 3525[9] 3788[9] (5669) (5730) ◆ 6541[5] (7192) 7556[5] 7892[5]

Pappas Fc *Milton Bradley*
3 ch g Zafeen(FR)—Mammas F-C (IRE) (Case Law)
1731[13] 2003[10] 2297[8] 2692[5]

Paquerettza (FR) *David Brown* 95
4 ch m Dr Fong(USA)—Cover Look (SAF) (Fort Wood (USA))
(1034) 1379[5] 1837[5] (2314) 3031[P] 5553[4] 5938[4]

Parade Militaire (IRE) *E Lellouche* 71
3 b f Peintre Celebre(USA)—Poughkeepsie (IRE) (Sadler's Wells (USA))
7546a[9]

Paradise Place *Jeremy Noseda* a46 30
2 ch f Compton Place—Passiflora (Night Shift (USA))
7201[10] 7479[10] 7723[7]

Paradise Rain *Manfred Hofer* 97
3 b f Compton Place—Goldenrain (USA) (Nureyev (USA))
2805a[7]

Paradise Spectre *Mrs K Burke* 79
3 b g Firebreak—Amber's Bluff (Mind Games)
3587[6] 5524[9] 6000[5] 6896[14]

Paradise Walk *Edwin Tuer* a55 56
6 b m Sakhee(USA)—Enclave (USA) (Woodman (USA))
2421[14] 2851[7]

Para Elisa (IRE) *Y Durepaire* a84
4 ch m Halling(USA)—Ice Ballet (IRE) (Nureyev (USA))
7648a[6]

Paragons Folly (IRE) *John Quinn* 64
2 b c Majestic Missile(IRE)—Ivory Bride (Domynsky)
3087[10] 4083[6] 4480[3] 4941[8] 5602[5] 6182[6]

Parc Aux Boules *John C McConnell* a67 73
9 gr g Royal Applause—Aristocratique (Cadeaux Genereux)
6491[9]

Parc Des Princes (USA) *Andrew Balding* a76 73
4 bb g Ten Most Wanted(USA)—Miss Orah (Unfuwain (USA))
1579[9] 2285[6] 2894[6] 3314[2] 3559[5]

Parchment (IRE) *Alan Lockwood* 45
8 ch g Singspiel(IRE)—Hannalou (FR) (Shareef Dancer (USA))
3614[9] 4015[9] 4246[6] 4453[4] 4854[7] 5202[5] 5515[6]

Pareia (GER) *Uwe Ostmann* 91
6 b m Areion(GER)—Party Bloom (FR) (Baillamont (USA))
6406a[8]

Parfum Des Dieux *J-C Rouget* a92 100
5 b h Cape Cross(IRE)—Moonbaby (FR) (Le Balafre (FR))
(304a) 743a[2]

Parhelion *Tim Vaughan* a72 77
3 b g Fantastic Light(USA)—Shamaiel (IRE) (Lycius (USA))
803[5] (872) ◆ 1060[3] 2277[2] ◆ 2893[9] 3519[11]

Pariala (GER) *T Mundry* 92
4 b m Lando(GER)—Pariana (USA) (Bering)
3236a[4]

Parisian Dream *Tim Pitt* a50 68
6 b g Sakhee(USA)—Boojum (Mujtahid (USA))
4486[4] ◆ 4868[12] 6335[8]

Parisian Pyramid (IRE) *Kevin Ryan* 104
4 gr g Verglas(IRE)—Sharadja (IRE) (Doyoun)
1295[6] 1727[5] 1822[11] (2316) 2748[5] (3461) 4391[3] 4576[20] 5302[2] 6177[24] 6752[4] 7060[12] 7348[6]

Paris Is Burning *J S Moore* a63 63
2 b f Kyllachy—Toxique (IRE) (Orpen (USA))
2074[6] 2642[5] 6146[12] 6795[11]

Paris Vegas (USA) *F Chappet* a94 91
3 rg c Maria's Mon(USA)—Tell Seattle (USA) (A.P. Indy (USA))
(741a) 1254a[9] 1947a[6]

Park Avenue (IRE) *A P O'Brien* a95 95
2 ch c Mr Greeley(USA)—Song To Remember (USA) (Storm Cat (USA))
6727a[2] 7135a[3]

Park Ballet (IRE) *Jonathan Portman* 68
2 b f Fasliyev(USA)—Abbey Park (USA) (Known Fact (USA))
3295[5] ◆ 4716[2] 5255[3] 6258[5]

Park Run *John Spearing* a13 48
5 b m Tomba—Erica Jayka (Golden Heights)
793[9]

Park's Prodigy *Geoffrey Harker* a14 68
6 b g Desert Prince(IRE)—Up And About (Barathea (IRE))
1467[2] (1671) 2085[4] 2277[3] 2424[3] (3499) 4449[2] 4800[2] 4946[3] 5333[3] 6028[4]

Park View *B W Hills* 87
3 ch f With Approval(CAN)—Bayswater (Caerleon (USA))
(1705) 3427[2] 3878[3] 4532[2] 5266[2] 6074[6]

Parlour Games *Mahmood Al Zarooni* 77
2 ch c Monsun(GER)—Petrushka (IRE) (Unfuwain (USA))
6128[2] 6457[5] (7178)

Partner (IRE) *David Marnane* a78 96
4 b g Indian Ridge—Oregon Trail (USA) (Gone West (USA))
4180a[4] 6177[22]

Partout Le Magasin *J S Moore* a67 67
2 b g Xaar—Mimiteh (USA) (Maria's Mon (USA))
1901[8] 4303[5] 4590[4] 4787[4] 6419[4] 6666[6] 6954[13]

Party Doctor *Tom Dascombe* a71 105
3 ch c Dr Fong(USA)—Wedding Party (Groom Dancer (USA))
(1586) 1858[6] 3460[3] 3827[6] 5188[14]

Party In The Park *Jim Boyle* a62 58
5 b g Royal Applause—Halland Park Girl (IRE) (Primo Dominie)
10[2] 124[2] 256[5] 397[4] 496[9]

Party Palace *Stuart Howe* a15 59
6 b m Auction House(USA)—Lady-Love (Pursuit Of Love)
1207[10] 1756[3] 2023[7] 2165[3] 2363[6] 3560[2] 4045[5] 6416[8]

Parvaaz (IRE) *Michael Jarvis* a90 99
3 ch c Rahy(USA)—Saabga (USA) (Woodman (USA))
(3374) 4144[6] (4647) (5754) (6205) 6510[5] ◆

Parvana (IRE) *William Haggas* 79
2 b f Galileo(IRE)—Lucina (Machiavellian (USA))
6150[3] ◆ 7235[10]

Pascal (USA) *E Charpy* a88 53
5 b h Menifee(USA)—La Pascua (SWI) (Caerleon (USA))
415a[4]

Pascalina *John Akehurst* a54 54
3 b f Tobougg(IRE)—Persistent Memory (USA) (Red Ransom (USA))
206[5] 356[3] 734[3] 1261[5] 1601[8] 1975[11] 2753[7]

Paschmina (FR) *C Lerner* a55 84
3 b f Meshaheer(USA)—Kiwi Pearl (FR) (Namid)
6487a[8]

Pashito The Che (USA) *Scott Lake* a106
4 b h Flatter(USA)—Pashmina (USA) (Pentelicus (USA))
7361a[12]

Pasquino (USA) *Mahmood Al Zarooni* 60
2 ch c Distorted Humor(USA)—Sis City (USA) (Slew City Slew (USA))
1845[6] 6514[7]

Passaggio (ITY) *A Cascio*
2 b c Exceed And Excel(AUS)—Copious (IRE) (Generous (IRE))
7264a[7]

Passei (FR) *Mlle V Dissaux* a69 83
2 b f Panis(USA)—Plaintarra (SWI) (Dashing Blade)
4036a[6] 7534a[7] 7975a[0]

Passion Play *William Knight* a38
2 b f Act One—Addicted To Love (Touching Wood (USA))
7559[9]

Pass Muster *Mahmood Al Zarooni* 86
3 b c Theatrical—Morning Pride (IRE) (Machiavellian (USA))
(2083) 2816[8]

Pass The Port *Derek Haydn Jones* a85 57
9 ch g Docksider(USA)—One Of The Family (Alzao (USA))
1783[11] 2897[8] 3780[13] 5646[8]

Pastel Blue (IRE) *Michael Bell* a69 64
3 b f Shamardal(USA)—Painted Moon (USA) (Gone West (USA))
(238) 490[5] 809[7]

Pastello *Richard Hannon* a72 71
3 ch f Exceed And Excel(AUS)—Pastel (Lion Cavern (USA))
566[2] (698) 934[4] 1696[6] 2168[3] 2956[2] 3268[6] 4282[4] 4870[3] 5689[12] 6633[13] 7019[2]

Pastoral Player *Hughie Morrison* 102
3 b g Pastoral Pursuits—Copy-Cat (Lion Cavern (USA))
1315[2] 2545[11] 2978[4] 3791[10] 4536[21] 5911[9] (7014)

Patachou *Ralph Smith* a43 49
3 b f Domedriver(IRE)—Pat Or Else (Alzao (USA))
597[5] 760[6] 2998[12] 3210[4] 4210[11] 4692[7]

Patavium (IRE) *Edwin Tuer* a55 75
7 b g Titus Livius(FR)—Arcevia (IRE) (Archway (IRE))
1150[2] 1427[2] 1807[3] (2424) 2941[6] 3283[3] (3807) 4449[3] 5215[4]

Patavium Prince (IRE) *Jo Crowley* a64 81
7 ch g Titus Livius(FR)—Hoyland Common (IRE) (Common Grounds)
3289[2] 3716[2] 4206[3] 6444[11]

Patch Patch *Michael Dods* 72
3 b g Avonbridge—Sandgate Cygnet (Fleetwood (IRE))
1511[6] 1750[6] (2449) 3410[2] 4169[3] 4406[8] 4703[5]

Pathfork (USA) *Mrs John Harrington* 119
2 b c Distorted Humor(USA)—Visions Of Clarity (IRE) (Sadler's Wells (USA))
(4175a) ◆ (5316a) ◆ (5975a)

Path Of Peace *James Bethell* 83
3 b f Rock Of Gibraltar(IRE)—Persian Song (Persian Bold)
1861[5] (2502) 3063[5] 5222[4] 6395[2] 7062[9]

Pathos (GER) *Gary Moore* 74
6 b g Danehill Dancer(IRE)—Panthere (GER) (Acatenango (GER))
2975[8] 5002[6]

Patricia's Hope *Paul D'Arcy* a46
2 b f Tiger Hill(IRE)—Akanta (GER) (Wolfhound (USA))
4437[12] 5699[6] 6521[9] 7471[3]

Patricks Lodge *Ruth Carr* 39
3 b g Redoubtable(USA)—Duxford Lodge (Dara Monarch)
2425[12] 2853[10] 3728[9] 4448[9] 4786[7] 5201[6] 6574[9]

Patriotic (IRE) *Mark Johnston* 53
2 b c Pivotal—Pescara (IRE) (Common Grounds)
7049[6]

Patroller (USA) *Kevin Ryan* a35 59
7 b m Grand Slam(USA)—Scouting (USA) (Woodman (USA))
2434[6] 2741[8] 3125[8] 3434[7]

Pat's Legacy (USA) *F J Brennan* a60
4 ch g Yankee Gentleman(USA)—Sugars For Nanny (USA) (Brocco (USA))
8003[9]

Pattern Mark *Ollie Pears* a61 58
4 b g Mark Of Esteem(IRE)—Latch Key Lady (USA) (Tejano (USA))
(3369) 4211[4] 4932[3] (5704) ◆ 6375[5] 7068[11]

Pauillac (GER) *B Dutruel* a52 61
9 b g Machiavellian(USA)—Pelagic (Rainbow Quest (USA))
459a[3]

Pausanias *Richard Hannon* a99 100
2 b c Kyllachy—The Strand (Gone West (USA))
(4577) ◆ (6083) 6737[2]

Pavement Games *Richard Guest* a54 54
3 b f Mind Games—Pavement Gates (Bishop Of Cashel)
265[4] 387[4] 471[4] 831[7] 991[7] 1162[5] 1811[10] 2217[6] 2648[11] 2879[10] 4151[8] 5162[6] 5438[2] (5957) 6206[6] 6490[4] 6847[10] 7131[11]

Pavershooz *Noel Wilson* a91 101
5 b g Bahamian Bounty—Stormswept (USA) (Storm Bird (CAN))
1032[18] 1822[6] 2135[7] 4191[2] 5095[8] 5308[8] 6175[25] 6918[6] 7212[2] 7443[7]

Pawan (IRE) *Ann Stokell* a93 92
10 ch g Cadeaux Genereux—Born To Glamour (Ajdal (USA))
2[8] 74[2] 350[5] 492[3] 639[4] 916[12] 1174[7] 5601[13] 5855[13] 6265[8] 6965[12] 7326[9] 7405[11]

Peace And Calm (USA) *Mahmood Al Zarooni* 72
2 ch c Forest Wildcat(USA)—Mari's Thunder (USA) (Thunder Gulch (USA))
3169[4]

Peace Corps *Jim Boyle* a81 79
4 ch g Medicean—Tromond (Lomond (USA))
291[3] (468) 3812[3] 4873[2] 5375[4] 6055[2] 6257[5] 8003[6]

Peaceful Means (IRE) *Tony Carroll* a54 65
7 b m Witness Box(USA)—Princess Satco (IRE) (Satco (FR))
2335[6] 2900[7] 3312[3] 4873[6] 5287[8] 5635[3]

Peaceful Rule (USA) *David Nicholls* 73
4 b g Peace Rules(USA)—La Cat (USA) (Mr Greeley (USA))
2492[8] 2658[7] 3176[2] 3405[7] 3810[3] 4705[6] 6571[7]

Peaceful Soul (USA) *David Lanigan* 65
3 b f Dynaformer(USA)—Serenity Jane (USA) (Affirmed (USA))
1358[6] 1627[7]

Peace Of Oasis (FR) *J-C Rouget* 79
2 b f Oasis Dream—Peace Fonic (FR) (Zafonic (USA))
4611a[6]

Peacoat *A Fabre* 101
3 ch f Doyen(IRE)—Innuendo (IRE) (Caerleon (USA))
3493a[4]

Peadar Miguel *Michael Quinlan* a78
3 b g Danroad(AUS) —La Corujera (Case Law)
161^{4} (592) 1086^{8} 6428^{P} 7411^{6} 7724^{11} 8014^{7}

Peahen *G M Lyons* a86 88
2 b f Ishiguru(USA) —Ulysses Daughter (IRE) (College Chapel)
6005a^{4} 6401a^{8}

Peak District (IRE) *Kevin Ryan* a97 100
6 b g Danehill(USA) —Coralita (IRE) (Night Shift (USA))
172^{3} 212^{7} 384^{5} 446^{4} 736^{2} 761^{4} 2054^{6} 2136^{4}

Peals And Plaudits *Ed Dunlop* a40 51
2 b g Royal Applause—Belle's Edge (Danehill Dancer (IRE))
7303^{6} 7558^{11} 7830^{3}

Pearl (IRE) *Alison Thorpe* a56 71
6 b m Daylami(IRE) —Briery (IRE) (Salse (USA))
121^{5} 1459^{2} 1768^{3} 2476^{7} 6373^{9} 6744^{3} 6933^{2} 7213^{U} 7388^{5} 7704^{4}

Pearl Arch (IRE) *Brian Meehan* a89 79
2 b c Arch(USA) —La Reine Mambo (USA) (High Yield (USA))
4221^{8} (5814) (6870) 7481^{2} ◆

Pearl Away (FR) *Y De Nicolay* 100
3 b f Gold Away(IRE) —Severina (Darshaan)
1946a^{2} 2800a^{2} 3493a^{5} 4612a^{6}

Pearl Banks *F Rohaut* 112
4 b m Pivotal—Pearly Shells (Efisio)
5108a^{5} (6790a) 7416a^{7}

Pearl Blue (IRE) *Chris Wall* 50
2 b f Exceed And Excel(AUS) —Sanfrancullinan (IRE) (Bluebird (USA))
6441^{8} 6878^{7}

Pearl Haven *Paul D'Arcy*
2 br f Indian Haven—Black Sea Pearl (Diktat)
2505^{13}

Pearl Huntsman (USA) *Jeremy Noseda* 75
3 bb c Johannesburg(USA) —I'm A Caution (USA) (A.P. Indy (USA))
2564^{4} 4205^{3} 6244^{5}

Pearl Ice *Sir Mark Prescott Bt* a85
2 b c Iffraaj—Jezebel (Owington)
6520^{2} ◆ (6869)

Pearl Opera *Ralph Beckett* a62 57
2 b f Librettist(USA) —Letsimpress (IRE) (General Monash (USA))
4675^{4} 5657^{8}

Pearl Storm (IRE) *William Haggas* 67
2 b g Balmont(USA) —Brewing Storm (IRE) (King Charlemagne (USA))
3439^{2}

Pearly Wey *Ian McInnes* a55 91
7 b g Lujain(USA) —Dunkellin (USA) (Irish River (FR))
1332^{7} 1888^{2} 2134^{8} 2736^{8} 2991^{13} 3584^{7} 4121^{6} 4394^{8} 5064^{7} 5496^{7} 6903^{8}

Peas And Carrots (DEN) *Lennart Reuterskiold Jr* a96 101
7 b g Final Appearance(IRE) —Dominet Hope (Primo Dominie)
2637a^{10} 4641a^{2} 5350a^{8} 6017a^{5}

Pebble Beech (IRE) *William Haggas* 66
3 b f Footstepsinthesand—Brigids Cross (IRE) (Sadler's Wells (USA))
3484^{4} 4294^{4} 4661^{11}

Pebblesonthebeach *J W Hills* a70 72
3 b g Footstepsinthesand—Peep Show (In The Wings)
1475^{5} 4022^{3} 4425^{4} 4959^{2} ◆ 5254^{8} 5866^{5} 6336^{10} 6841^{8}

Pecavi (IRE) *John C McConnell* a54 37
5 b g Key Of Luck(USA) —Lock's Heath (CAN) (Topsider (USA))
5439^{8}

Peckforton Castle *Patrick Morris* a50 51
3 b g Celtic Swing—Fleuve D'Or (IRE) (Last Tycoon)
2692^{4} 3428^{7} 4127^{13} 5766^{8}

Pedantic *Luca Cumani* a65 65
3 b c Danehill Dancer(IRE) —High Reserve (Dr Fong (USA))
2496^{3} 4205^{5} 5839^{5} 6856^{5}

Pedasus (USA) *Ronald Harris* a69 66
4 b g Fusaichi Pegasus(USA) —Butterfly Cove (USA) (Storm Cat (USA))
975^{10} 1226^{2} 1631^{5} 2012^{2} 2232^{8} 3614^{3} 4120^{8} 5631^{11} 5840^{3} 6999^{11} 7996^{10}

Pedra Pompas *M Gasparini* a90 110
6 ch h Mark Of Esteem(IRE) —Edwardian Era (Bering)
7373a^{15}

Pegasus Again (USA) *Robert Mills* a94 86
5 b g Fusaichi Pegasus(USA) —Chit Chatter (USA) (Lost Soldier (USA))
672^{2} 749^{2} 1219^{11} 1455^{6} 2322^{7} 4354^{15} 4690^{8} 8022^{7}

Pegasus Prince (USA) *Keith Reveley* a72 40
6 b g Fusaichi Pegasus(USA) —Avian Eden (USA) (Storm Bird (CAN))
7284^{11}

Peinted Song (USA) *J-C Rouget* a84 71
3 gr f Unbridled's Song(USA) —Peinture Rose (USA) (Storm Cat (USA))
7546a^{0}

Peintre D'Argent (IRE) *William Knight* a69 75
4 ch m Peintre Celebre(USA) —Petite-D-Argent (Noalto)
(1194) 1478^{3} 1635^{4} (2232) 2941^{3} (3847) 4597^{3} 5790^{8} 6331^{5} 7011^{3}

Peinture De Guerre (FR) *Gary Moore* a59
7 b g Loco(IRE) —Dani Kris (FR) (Shining Steel)
179^{5} 390^{9} 584^{3}

Peinture Rare (IRE) *E Lellouche* 111
4 b m Sadler's Wells(USA) —Peinture Bleue (USA) (Alydar (USA))
1792a^{8} (5108a) 6013a^{7} 6591a^{4} 7110a^{7}

Peira *Jane Chapple-Hyam* a61 58
2 bb f Intikhab(USA) —Anqood (IRE) (Elmaamul (USA))
7001^{6} 7311^{9} 7448^{7}

Pekan Star *Michael Jarvis* 91
3 b c Montjeu(IRE) —Delicieuse Lady (Trempolino (USA))
(6876)

Pekan Three (IRE) *Paul Cole* 78
3 b g Sadler's Wells(USA) —Frappe (IRE) (Inchinor)
1581^{3} 1824^{6} 2231^{6}

Pelham Crescent (IRE) *Bryn Palling* a83 85
7 ch g Giant's Causeway(USA) —Sweet Times (Riverman (USA))
1840^{8} 2173^{10} 4044^{4} 4476^{4} 4923^{3} 5115^{6} (6774) 6957^{3} (7337) 7568^{5}

Peligroso (FR) *Saeed Bin Suroor* a94 107
4 ch h Trempolino(USA) —Pitpit (IRE) (Rudimentary (USA))
1911^{2} 2470^{7} 4139^{9} 5696^{4} (7120) 7384^{4}

Pelmanism *Kevin Ryan* 66
3 b g Piccolo—Card Games (First Trump)
1425^{4} ◆ 1706^{12} 2114^{7} 2609^{6} 3507^{2} 3773^{7} 4151^{3} (5097) 5501^{6} 6103^{9}

Pelusa (JPN) *Kazuo Fujisawa* 123
3 ch c Zenno Rob Roy(JPN) —Argentine Star (ARG) (Candy Stripes (USA))
7615a^{5}

Pena Dorada (IRE) *Mrs K Burke* 72
3 b g Key Of Luck(USA) —Uluwatu (IRE) (Unfuwain (USA))
1630^{4} 2175^{5} 2650^{3} 3626^{3} 4545^{5} 5164^{2} 5534^{7} 6038^{6}

Penang Cinta *David Evans* a59 77
7 b g Halling(USA) —Penang Pearl (FR) (Bering)
(1817a) 2199^{2} (2455) 2996^{6} 3576^{5} 4737^{8} 5888^{4} 6554^{8} 7337^{6} 7788^{4}

Penangdouble O One *Ralph Beckett* a76 66
3 ch g Starcraft(NZ) —Penang Pearl (FR) (Bering)
2548^{3} 3781^{12} 5958^{4} (7022)

Penang Princess *Ralph Beckett* a85 88
4 gr m Act One—Pulau Pinang (IRE) (Dolphin Street (FR))
1736^{3} 2228^{7}

Penbryn (USA) *Nick Littmoden* a68 27
3 b g Pivotal—Brocatelle (Green Desert (USA))
7183^{8} 7338^{4} 7838^{2} 7969^{2}

Pencarrow *Mahmood Al Zarooni* a74 29
2 b f Green Desert(USA) —Al Hasnaa (Zafonic (USA))
3082^{2} 3861^{13} 5841^{4} 7087^{6}

Penchesco (IRE) *Amanda Perrett* a79 83
5 b g Orpen(USA) —Francesca (IRE) (Perugino (USA))
(1346) 1579^{6} 2093^{2} 2685^{2} 2934^{6} 3737^{6} 4306^{9} 6091^{6} 7548^{10}

Penderyn *Charles Smith* a42 57
3 b f Sakhee(USA) —Brecon (Unfuwain (USA))
302^{5} 475^{7} 1010^{5} 1380^{10} 1887^{11} 4857^{8} 5550^{8} 6093^{5} 6652^{4} 7304^{5} 7538^{5}

Pendragon (USA) *Brian Ellison* a78 95
7 ch g Rahy(USA) —Turning Wheel (USA) (Seeking The Gold (USA))
(705) (908) ◆ (918) ◆ 1117^{4} 1512^{2} 3319^{2} (3613) (4399) 5913^{6} (6106) 6562^{8}

Pengula (IRE) *Robert Johnson*
3 b f Tagula(IRE) —Pride Of Pendle (Grey Desire)
6624^{12} 6966^{13}

Peninsular War *Richard Fahey* a62 80
4 b g Deportivo—Queens Jubilee (Cayman Kai (IRE))
30^{3}

Penitent *William Haggas* a107 116
4 b g Kyllachy—Pious (Bishop Of Cashel)
(1008) ◆ 2707^{7} (6089) 6529^{2} 7237^{5}

Pennfield Pirate *Hughie Morrison* 69
3 ch g Bahamian Bounty—Sefemm (Alhaarth (IRE))
1067^{6} 1735^{10} 2279^{4} 3002^{12} 4202^{4} 4689^{7} (4992) 5530^{2} 6472^{12} 6993^{4}

Penny Bazaar *George Moore* 8
3 b f Mujahid(USA) —Femme Femme (USA) (Lyphard (USA))
5303^{12}

Penny's Gift *Richard Hannon* 108
4 b m Tobougg(IRE) —Happy Lady (FR) (Cadeaux Genereux)
1908^{5} 2744^{9} 3146^{26}

Penny's Pearl (IRE) *Richard Hannon* a87 89
2 b f Royal Applause—Pearl Venture (Salse (USA))
(1324) ◆ 3070^{13} 4305^{5} 4928^{2} (5284) 5882^{17}

Pennyspider (IRE) *Malcolm Saunders* a49 69
5 b m Redback—Malacca (USA) (Danzig (USA))
848^{4} 913^{10} 1234^{8}

Penolva (IRE) *Mrs Sarah Dawson* a58 64
4 b m Galileo(IRE) —Jabali (FR) (Shirley Heights)
4279^{4}

Penrod Ballantyne (IRE) *Mike Hammond* a62 58
3 ch g Indian Ridge—Silvia Diletta (Mark Of Esteem (IRE))
374^{3} 638^{4} 766^{4} 932^{6} 3243^{8} 7273^{8} 7462^{6} 7706^{6}

Penshurst Lad (IRE) *Richard Phillips* 46
3 gr g Bertolini(USA) —Nuit Chaud (USA) (Woodman (USA))
3272^{6} 4205^{10} 5971^{13} 6921^{13} 7789^{6} 7918^{10}

Pentathlon (IRE) *Mark Johnston* a78 76
5 b g Storming Home—Nawaiet (USA) (Zilzal (USA))
4055^{8} 4594^{10}

Pentominium *Mark Johnston* a72 79
3 b c Dubai Destination(USA) —Mouriyana (IRE) (Akarad (FR))
(671) ◆ 2863^{3}

Penton Hook *Peter Winkworth* a82 60
4 gr g Lucky Owners(NZ) —Cosmic Star (Siberian Express (USA))
3079^{10} 5034^{4} 5624^{7}

Penzena *Andrew Balding* a78 78
4 ch m Tobougg(IRE) —Penmayne (Inchinor)
2601^{2} 3236a^{7} 3890^{6}

Peopleton Brook *Brendan Powell* a70 67
8 b h Compton Place—Merch Rhyd-Y-Grug (Sabrehill (USA))
(14) 78^{7} (258) 312^{4} 391^{5} 1391^{12} 1595^{11} 2123^{2} 2719^{2} 2846^{6} 3299^{4} 3748a^{2} 4071^{4} 4099^{6}

Pepito Grillo *L A Urbano-Grajales* 66
2 b g Kheleyf(USA) —Dena (Deploy)
7975a^{10}

Peponi *PETER Makin* a68 81
4 ch h Kris Kin(USA) —Polmara (IRE) (Polish Precedent (USA))
1782^{DSQ} 2328^{3} 4579^{10}

Peppercorn Rent (IRE) *Tim Easterby* a45 53
2 b f Fasliyev(USA) —Skehana (IRE) (Mukaddamah (USA))
1066^{4} 2202^{4} 3729^{6} (4150) 4701^{8} 5818^{4} 6674^{9} 7050^{6}

Pepper Lane *David O'Meara* a58 81
3 ch f Exceed And Excel(AUS) —Maid To Matter (Pivotal)
(2628) 3151^{3} 3599^{2} 3879^{4} 4865^{3} 5606^{3} 6113^{2} ◆ 6394^{7}

Pepper Popper (IRE) *L Polito* 98
4 ch h Indian Haven—Armenia (IRE) (Arazi (USA))
1712a^{3}

Peppi Knows (USA) *Timothy Kreiser* a100
3 b g Stephen Got Even(USA) —Miracle Worker (USA) (Seeking The Gold (USA))
824a^{6}

Perception (IRE) *Alan King* a79 71
4 b m Hawk Wing(USA) —Princesse Darsha (GER) (Darshaan)
1849^{10} 3780^{8} (4042) 4530^{2} 5179^{2} (5722)

Percusionist (ARG) *Saeed Bin Suroor* a56
4 br h Southern Halo(USA) —Breadcrumb (USA) (Woodman (USA))
414a^{13}

Percussionist (IRE) *Howard Johnson* 68
9 b g Sadler's Wells(USA) —Magnificient Style (USA) (Silver Hawk (USA))
2195a^{8}

Perennite (FR) *P Bary* a72 73
2 b f Vespone(IRE) —Aaliyah (GER) (Anabaa (USA))
6589a^{7}

Perez (IRE) *Wilf Storey* a66 49
8 b g Mujadil(USA) —Kahla (Green Desert (USA))
2214^{4} 2464^{9} 3352^{3} 4648^{6} 4854^{5} 4900^{4} 5203^{6}

Perfect Act *Andrew Balding* a91 69
5 b m Act One—Markova's Dance (Mark Of Esteem (IRE))
26^{2} 1770^{6} 2247^{11} (7719) 7971^{4} (8016)

Perfect Blossom *Kevin Ryan* 96
3 b f One Cool Cat(USA) —Perfect Peach (Lycius (USA))
(2648) 2962^{6} (3410) (3751) (4016) (4291) (4541) 5250^{8}

Perfect Ch'l (IRE) *Ian Wood* a73 79
3 b f Choisir(AUS) —Agouti (Pennekamp (USA))
2120^{9} 3441^{3} 3899^{5} 4398^{6} (5163) 5561^{7} 5769^{6} 6212^{9} 6805^{9} 7082^{8} 7205^{7} 7439^{7} 7613^{4} 7889^{3} 8014^{11}

Perfect Class *Clive Cox* a72 73
4 b m Cape Cross(IRE) —Liberty (Singspiel (IRE))
23^{6} 284^{5} 544^{3} 1797^{6} 2167^{3} 2362^{3} 2956^{6} 4108^{2}

Perfect Cracker *Clive Cox* 76
2 ch c Dubai Destination(USA) —Perfect Story (IRE) (Desert Story (IRE))
3915^{3}

Perfect Eye (IRE) *Andreas Lowe* 65
3 b f Kheleyf(USA) —Palavera (FR) (Bikala)
2404a^{9}

Perfect Flight *Michael Blanshard* 88
5 b m Hawk Wing(USA) —Pretty Girl (IRE) (Polish Precedent (USA))
1692^{8} 2929^{2} 4904^{10} 5521^{7} 5995^{4} 6478^{8} 6625^{7} 7097^{9}

Perfect Friend *Sylvester Kirk* a76 83
4 b m Reel Buddy(USA) —Four Legs Good (IRE) (Be My Guest (USA))
1064^{7} 1350^{6} 1428^{6} 2601^{5} 3001^{5} 3129^{4} 3592^{2} 3777^{11} 3890^{5} 4735^{2} 5113^{3} (6210) 6370^{2} 6853^{3} 7046^{5}

Perfectly (ARG) *J Barton* a56
5 br h Sunray Spirit(USA) —Perfidia (ARG) (Ahmad (ARG))
610a^{12}

Perfect Mission *Andrew Balding* 69
2 b c Bertolini(USA) —Sharp Secret (IRE) (College Chapel)
5263^{10} 5886^{3} 6514^{4}

Perfect Note *Saeed Bin Suroor* 78
3 b f Shamardal(USA) —Mezzo Soprano (USA) (Darshaan)
(5872)

Perfect Pastime *Walter Swinburn* 75
2 ch g Pastoral Pursuits—Puritanical (IRE) (Desert King (IRE))
2819^{2} 3332^{5} 3959^{4} 5613^{2} 6086^{3} 6445^{8}

Perfect Point (IRE) *Walter Swinburn* a65 70
3 b g Cape Cross(IRE) —Alessia (GER) (Warning)
1661^{5} ◆ 4307^{4} 5150^{4}

Perfect Secret *Andrew Balding* a62 61
4 b m Spinning World(USA) —Sharp Secret (IRE) (College Chapel)
159^{3} 321^{7} 593^{7} 6261^{10} 6657^{7}

Perfect Shirl (USA) *Roger L Attfield* 106
3 b f Perfect Soul(IRE) —Lady Shirl (USA) (That's A Nice (USA))
5351a^{3}

Perfect Shot (IRE) *John Dunlop* 94
3 b g High Chaparral(IRE) —Zoom Lens (IRE) (Caerleon (USA))
1902^{5} ◆ (2549) 3050^{10} 4461^{9} 5278^{6} 5743^{11} 6352^{8} 6808^{7}

Perfect Shower (CAN) *Roger L Attfield* a96 96
4 bb h Perfect Soul(IRE) —Showering (USA) (Miswaki (USA))
6236a^{7}

Perfect Silence *Clive Cox* a83 94
5 b m Dansili—Perfect Echo (Lycius (USA))
3346^{4} 4287^{3} (5052) 5694^{6} 6346^{6} 7097^{5} (7352)

Perfect Stride *Sir Michael Stoute* a89 115
5 b h Oasis Dream—First (Highest Honor (FR))
609a^{7} 799a^{10}

Perfect Tribute *Clive Cox* 98
2 b f Dubawi(IRE) —Perfect Spirit (IRE) (Invincible Spirit (IRE))
(3331) 4356^{3} 5246^{7}

Perfect Vision *Clive Cox* a68 71
3 b f Starcraft(NZ) —Auspicious (Shirley Heights)
2254^{6} 2935^{5} 6691^{7} 7316^{5}

Pergamon (IRE) *Claire Dyson* a39 66
4 b g Dalakhani(IRE) —Pinaflore (FR) (Formidable (USA))
2860^{12}

Perica *D Pajic*
2 b c Kingsalsa(USA) —Exhibitor (USA) (Royal Academy (USA))
(7849a)

Perignon (IRE) *Alan Swinbank* 78
2 b c Elusive City(USA) —Moon Tango (IRE) (Last Tycoon)
3118^{8} 3449^{4} 5404^{3} (5761)

Perks (IRE) *Jessica Long* a92 106
5 b g Selkirk(USA) —Green Charter (Green Desert (USA))
2637a^{8}

Perlachy *Derek Shaw* a75 72
6 b g Kyllachy—Perfect Dream (Emperor Jones (USA))
172^{7} 287^{3} (431) 2528^{5} 3114^{11} 3660^{4} 4431^{3} 4717^{5} 5698^{12} 6208^{6} 6700^{6} (7194) 7494^{4} 7868^{4}

Permesso *G Pucciatti* 108
5 b h Sakhee(USA) —Persian Filly (IRE) (Persian Bold)
1943a^{3} 3019a^{8} 7373a^{14}

Permit *A Fabre* 92
3 b c Dansili—Cochin (USA) (Swain (IRE))
5800a^{3} 6590a^{7}

Perpetually (IRE) *Mark Johnston* a94 91
4 b g Singspiel(IRE) —Set In Motion (USA) (Mr Prospector (USA))
790^{3} 921^{5} 1600^{5} 1960^{3} 2317^{4}

Persian Buddy *Jamie Poulton* a67 7
4 b g Reel Buddy(USA) —Breeze Again (USA) (Favorite Trick (USA))
2714^{14}

Persian Herald *Pat Eddery* a76 81
2 gb c Proclamation(IRE) —Persian Fortune (Forzando)
3349^{9} 4253^{5} (5385) 5831^{5} 6386^{8} 6745^{8}

Persian Peril *Alan Swinbank* a87 90
6 br g Erhaab(USA) —Brush Away (Ahonoora)
1272^{6} 2031^{3} 2857^{8} 3089^{3} 4152^{7} 4830^{12} 5355^{4} 6050^{5}

Persian Star (AUS) *Robert Smerdon* 104
6 b m Shot Of Thunder(AUS) —Persian Trifle (AUS) (Persian Heights)
7368a^{3}

Persian Tomcat (IRE) *Julia Feilden* a51 51
4 gr g One Cool Cat(USA) —Persian Mistress (IRE) (Persian Bold)
541^{6} 1439^{4}

Persiste Et Signe (FR) *N Clement* a77 99
3 b c With Approval(CAN) —Mahima (FR) (Linamix (FR))
6761a^{7}

Persistently (USA) *Claude McGaughey III* a108
4 ch m Smoke Glacken(USA) —Just Reward (USA) (Deputy Minister (CAN))
(5578a) 7344a^{7}

Personified (GER) *Edward Vaughan* a77 75
3 b f Doyen(IRE) —Proudeyes (GER) (Dashing Blade)
4207^{4} 5038^{11} (6332) 6830^{7}

Pertemps Networks *Michael Easterby* a73 81
6 b g Golden Snake(USA) —Society Girl (Shavian)
2723^{9} 3060^{8} 3965^{9} 4433^{2} (5770) (6109) 6754^{2} 7226^{6}

Pertuis (IRE) *Harry Dunlop* a79 72
4 gr g Verglas(IRE) —Lady Killeen (IRE) (Marju (IRE))
(7489) 7687^{3}

Petara Bay (IRE) *Robert Mills* 111
6 b g Peintre Celebre(USA) —Magnificient Style (USA) (Silver Hawk (USA))
2116^{3} 3191^{7}

Petella *C W Thornton* 63
4 b m Tamure(IRE) —Miss Petronella (Petoski)
1671^{3} 2214^{3} 2765^{2} (3669) 4825^{3} 5119^{3} 5642^{2} (6132) 6693^{7} 6895^{7} 7181^{7}

Peter Grimes (IRE) *Alan King* a63 70
4 ch g Alhaarth(IRE) —Aldburgh (Bluebird (USA))
6427^{9}

Peter Island (FR) *John Gallagher* a78 94
7 b g Dansili—Catania (USA) (Aloma's Ruler (USA))
(1321) 1438^{3} (1963) 2446a^{0} 3401^{6} 3833^{2} 4171^{6} 6501^{8} 6798^{10}

Peter Martins (USA) *Jeremy Noseda* 98
2 ch c Johannesburg(USA) —Pretty Meadow (USA) (Meadowlake (USA))
(4550) ◆

Peter's Gift (IRE) *Kevin Ryan* a76 66
4 b m Catcher In The Rye(IRE) —Eastern Blue (IRE) (Be My Guest (USA))
275^{4} 398^{2} 501^{6} 703^{4} 867^{5} 1152^{9} 1967^{9} 2211^{6} 2791^{4} 3061^{11} 4834^{4} 5357^{4} 5732^{2} 5820^{5} 6189^{2} 6460^{8} 7051^{9} (7377) 7699^{6} 7956^{5}

Peters Spirit (IRE) *Richard Fahey* 62
2 b f Invincible Spirit(IRE) —Khatela (IRE) (Shernazar)
2980^{8} 3449^{3} 4123^{10} 4783^{7} 5434^{7} 5818^{7} 6645^{14}

Peter Tchaikovsky *B S Rothwell* 94
4 b g Dansili—Abbatiale (FR) (Kaldoun (FR))
1708^{14} 2027^{10} 2423^{10} 2982^{19} 3508^{7} 3610^{8} 4156^{14}

Pete's Passion *Richard Fahey* 2
4 b m Rock Of Gibraltar(IRE) —Three Days In May (Cadeaux Genereux)
3561^{0}

Petille (FR) *Robert Collet* a70 44
5 b m Indian Rocket—Fancy Lady (FR) (Highest Honor (FR))
459a^{8}

Petit Belle *Nick Littmoden* a18
3 b f Piccolo—Tallulah Belle (Crowning Honors (CAN))
168^{6}

Petomic (IRE) *Martin Hill* a66 71
5 ch g Dubai Destination(USA) —Petomi (Presidium)
3473^{2} 4206^{2} 4870^{9} 5287^{7} 5584^{2}

Petrichor *Edward Vaughan* a63 44
2 b f Sleeping Indian—Raindrop (Primo Dominie)
6058^{6} 6521^{4} 6866^{8}

Petrocelli *Wilf Storey* a49 71
3 b g Piccolo—Sarcita (Primo Dominie)
766^{6} 1237^{5} (1987) 2203^{8} 2617^{4} 4337^{17} 5607^{5} 5758^{3} 6144^{8} 6463^{5} 6890^{12}

Petronilla *Willie Musson* a21 20
2 b f Storming Home—Hetra Heights (USA) (Cox's Ridge (USA))
3035^{15} 4802^{10} 5269^{9}

Petronius Maximus (IRE) *A P O'Brien* 100
2 bb c Holy Roman Emperor(IRE) —Khamseh (Thatching)
3051^{2} 7135a^{5}

Petrosian *Dai Burchell* a24 67
6 b g Sakhee(USA) —Arabis (Arazi (USA))
469^{12}

Petrovsky *A Al Raihe* a87 101
4 gr h Daylami(IRE) —Russian Society (Darshaan)
335a^{4} ◆ 436a^{6}

Petsas Pleasure *Ollie Pears* a59 70
4 b g Observatory(USA) —Swynford Pleasure (Reprimand)
2093^{4} 2851^{8} 3405^{6} 5051^{9} 5864^{4} 6662^{6} 6999^{6}

Pevensey (IRE) *John Quinn* a94 99
8 b g Danehill(USA) —Champaka (IRE) (Caerleon (USA))
1015^{11} 1724^{15} 2747^{11} 3873^{11} 7061^{5}

Phair Winter *Alan Brown* a40 18
2 b f Sleeping Indian—Tuppenny Blue (Pennekamp (USA))
1292^{8} 2239^{11} 2785^{6} 6658^{7} 6894^{7}

Pha Mai Blue *Jim Boyle* a73 66
5 b g Acclamation—Queen Of Silk (IRE) (Brief Truce (USA))
802^{3} 844^{5} 966^{5} 2967^{4} 3777^{4} 4232^{2} 5593^{7}

Phantom House *Brendan Duke* a32 32
2 b f Librettist(USA) —Newtown Villa (Spectrum (IRE))
7099^{16} 7302^{12} 7609^{9}

Phantom Serenade (IRE) *Michael Dods* 65
5 b g Orpen(USA) —Phantom Rain (Rainbow Quest (USA))
1574^{8} 4863^{4} 6037^{9}

Phantom Whisper *Rod Millman* a66 91
7 br g Makbul—La Belle Vie (Indian King (USA))
987^{9} 1580^{5} 1848^{6} 2399^{4} 2592^{8}

Pharoh Jake *John Bridger* a10
2 ch g Piccolo—Rose Amber (Double Trigger (IRE))
7999^{9}

Phase Shift *William Muir* a70
2 b f Iceman—Silent Waters (Polish Precedent (USA))
6866^{9} 7242^{3} 7503^{3} 7780^{3} 7907^{3}

Pherousa *Michael Blanshard* a60 69
3 b f Dubawi(IRE) —Sea Nymph (IRE) (Spectrum (IRE))
988^{3} 1316^{5} 1784^{3} 2217^{2} 2688^{3} 2931^{2} 3372^{2} 3682^{2} 4284^{8} 4754^{7} 5470^{5} 5875^{4} 6421^{7} 7195^{8}

Philario (IRE) *P D Deegan* a104 108
5 ch h Captain Rio—Salva (Grand Lodge (USA))
338a^{12} 513a^{11} 610a^{8}

Philatelist (USA) *Michael Jarvis* a110 108
6 b h Rahy(USA) —Polent (Polish Precedent (USA))
(175)

Philharmonic Hall *Richard Fahey* 66
2 b g Victory Note(USA) —Lambast (Relkino)
2522^{3} 3020^{7} 3665^{4} 4539^{12} 5637^{5} 6513^{11} 7050^{8}

Philippa Jane *Peter Winkworth* a44 40
3 ch f Muhtathir—Ante Futura (FR) (Suave Dancer (USA))
1796^{11} 2412^{10}

Philmack Dot Com *Desmond Donovan* a63 22
4 b g Traditionally(USA) —Lilli Marlane (Sri Pekan (USA))
4232^{12} 4589^{13}

Philosophers Guest (IRE) *M J Grassick* a63 55
4 br m Desert Prince(IRE) —Gemini Diamond (IRE) (Desert King (IRE))
6335^{2}

Philosophers Stone (FR) *David Barron* a69 67
3 bb g Mind Games—Legality (Polar Falcon (USA))
911^{2} 1401^{4} (2530) 3225^{2} 3599^{10} 6392^{8} 6898^{12} 7170^{10}

Phluke *Eve Johnson Houghton* a63 81
9 b g Most Welcome—Phlirty (Pharly (FR))
3056^{5} 4738^{3} 4870^{5} 5174^{3} (5655) 5889^{6} 6261^{8} 6864^{11} 6958^{8} 7191^{5} 7487^{4}

Phoebs *Robert Mills* a89 89
2 b f Where Or When(IRE) —Sheila's Secret (IRE) (Bluebird (USA))
1324^{5} ◆ (1660) 2074^{3} 3141^{9} 3630^{4} 6445^{5} (6636) 6900^{2}

Phoenix Enforcer *George Baker* a30 69
4 b m Bahamian Bounty—Kythia (IRE) (Kahyasi)
1755^{11}

Phoenix Fantasy (IRE) *Jonathan Portman* 42
2 b g Phoenix Reach(IRE) —Ideal Figure (Zafonic (USA))
5582^{9} 5916^{8} 6635^{7}

Phoenix Flame *Alan McCabe* a61 59
2 ch f Phoenix Reach(IRE) —Generosia (Generous (IRE))
4668^{4} 5066^{7} 6071^{4} 6695^{8} 7118^{4} 7393^{2} 7693^{5} 7990^{6}

Phoenix Flight (IRE) *James Evans* a89 88
5 b g Hawk Wing(USA) —Firecrest (IRE) (Darshaan)
1348^{9} 1863^{8} (2341) (3566) ◆ 3974^{8} 6797^{11} 7553^{2} 8007^{2}

Phoenix Ice (IRE) *Jonjo O'Neill* a44 87
6 b g Desert Style(IRE) —Alajyal (IRE) (Kris)
1767^{14}

Photo Opportunity *D K Weld* 88
3 b c Zamindar(USA) —Fame At Last (USA) (Quest For Fame)
5774a^{4}

Piano *John Gosden* a85 73
3 b f Azamour(IRE) —Humouresque (Pivotal)
4114^{4} ◆ 5038^{4} 5971^{3} (6856) ◆ (7090)

Piave (IRE) *Peter Chapple-Hyam* 72
2 b c Oratorio(IRE) —Peace In The Park (IRE) (Ahonoora)
7203^{6}

Piazza San Pietro *Andrew Haynes* a59 91
4 ch g Compton Place—Rainbow Spectrum (FR) (Spectrum (IRE))
1547^{10} 1967^{11} 2385^{2} (2635) (2808) 3057^{3} 3400^{2} (3734) 3980^{2} (4041) (4440) (4777) 5302^{3} 5787^{6}

Picabo (IRE) *Lucy Wadham* a71 72
2 b f Elusive City(USA) —Gi La High (Rich Charlie)
4095^{8} ◆ (5755) 6317^{6} (6988) 7116^{3}

Picansort *Brett Johnson* a72 71
3 b g Piccolo—Running Glimpse (IRE) (Runnett)
2340^{8} 2968^{7} 3511^{5} 4760^{2} 6812^{10} 7439^{10} (7547) 8004^{2}

Piccadilly Filly (IRE) *Edward Creighton* a93 107
3 ch f Exceed And Excel(AUS) —Tortue (IRE) (Turtle Island (IRE))
2804a^{2} 3486a^{4} 5276^{3} 6608a^{7}

Piccarello *Mark H Tompkins* 71
2 b g Piccolo—Latina (IRE) (King's Theatre (IRE))
3602^{4} 4208^{4} 4437^{7} 5520^{4} 5784^{7}

Piccolete *Richard Hannon* a31 55
2 b f Piccolo—Blue Goddess (IRE) (Blues Traveller (IRE))
6146^{9} 6796^{9}

Piccolo Blue *Clive Cox* a31 23
3 b f Piccolo—Poly Blue (IRE) (Thatching)
744^{6} 1257^{9} 2249^{12}

Piccolo Express *Brian Baugh* a58 58
4 b g Piccolo—Ashfield (Zilzal (USA))
2496^{5} 2726^{6} (3129) 3855^{10} 4485^{11} 5064^{5} 5406^{8} 5821^{9} 6188^{6} 7070^{4}

Piccolo Mondo *Peter Winkworth* a74 74
4 b g Piccolo—Oriel Girl (Beveled (USA))
1875^{4} 3036^{8} 4261^{6}

Piccoluck *Deborah Sanderson* a62 65
2 b g Piccolo—Zephrina (Zafonic (USA))
3365^{2} 4167^{6} 4702^{7} 6075^{4} 6740^{5} 6919^{3}

Piceno (IRE) *David Nicholls* a80 79
2 b c Camacho—Ascoli (Skyliner)
3126^{9} 3735^{7} 4409^{5} ◆ (5256) (5490) 7636^{2} 7916^{5}

Pick A Little *Brendan Duke* a68 73
2 b c Piccolo—Little Caroline (IRE) (Great Commotion (USA))
1017^{5} (1319) 1612^{5} 1978^{2} 2950^{5} 4278^{4} 4677^{7} 6086^{2} 6435^{9} 6745^{5} 7035^{7} 7271^{8}

Pickled Pumpkin *Olivia Maylam* a35
2 ch c Compton Place—Woodbury (Woodborough (USA))
7858^{U}

Pickwick *Sir Michael Stoute* a31 79
3 ch c Selkirk(USA) —Ithaca (USA) (Distant View (USA))
4069^{5} 5026^{9} 5610^{2}

Picnic Party *David Elsworth* a69 72
3 ch f Indian Ridge—Antediluvian (Air Express (IRE))
985^{2} 1275^{5} 2004^{4} 2396^{4} 2688^{2} 3125^{5} 3480^{5}

Picot De Say *Bernard Llewellyn* a40 64
8 b g Largesse—Facsimile (Superlative)
(1758) 2476^{8} 2923^{5}

Pictorial (USA) *Daniel Mark Loughnane* a20 83
4 b g Pivotal—Red Tulle (USA) (A.P. Indy (USA))
2243^{10}

Picture Editor *Henry Cecil* 97
2 b c Dansili—Shirley Valentine (Shirley Heights)
(5878) ◆ (6653) ◆ 7236^{3}

Picture Of Lily *William Knight* a58
2 b f Medicean—Milly Of The Vally (Caerleon (USA))
7558^{3}

Picture Perfect (IRE) *David Wachman* 95
3 b f Danehill Dancer(IRE) —Makarova (IRE) (Sadler's Wells (USA))
1952a^{5} 5571a^{15}

Pictures (IRE) *John Bridger* a75 74
3 b f Le Vie Dei Colori—So Glam So Hip (IRE) (Spectrum (IRE))
3158^{7} 3592^{7} 4204^{11} 4756^{8} 5077^{4} 5414^{8} 5689^{11} 6287^{8} 6454^{4} 6999^{9} 7117^{7} 7286^{6}

Piddie's Power *Ed McMahon* a67 77
3 ch f Starcraft(NZ) —Telori (Muhtarram (USA))
1706^{9} 2220^{7} 3207^{3} 3975^{2} ◆ 4482^{2} 5163^{3} 5634^{9} 6164^{5} (6879)

Piece D'Or (IRE) *Sir Michael Stoute* 70
2 gr f Verglas(IRE) —Gold Bar (IRE) (Barathea (IRE))
7001^{4} ◆

Piece Of Mind *Richard Hannon* a67 73
2 b f Mind Games—Reheem (USA) (Bahri (USA))
4753^{5} 5608^{2} 5885^{2} 6323^{2} 7718^{6}

Pie Poudre *Roy Brotherton* a57 55
3 ch g Zafeen(FR) —Eglantine (IRE) (Royal Academy (USA))
2165 1796^{14} 2359^{4} 3479^{5} 4281^{4} 4733^{7} 7605^{4} (7863)

Piermarini *Paul Midgley* a68 39
5 b g Singspiel(IRE) —Allespagne (USA) (Trempolino (USA))
3352^{9} 3804^{4} 4511^{10} 4854^{11}

Pietra Santa (FR) *J-M Beguigne* 100
4 b m Acclamation—Margie Queen (GER) (Sternkoenig (IRE))
3704a^{7} 5576a^{9}

Pigeon Hollow *Mick Channon* 66
2 b c Val Royal(FR) —Coolberry (USA) (Rahy (USA))
3472^{6} 3712^{5} 4499^{2} 4741^{3} 4993^{10} 5676^{5} 6129^{15}

Pilgrim Dancer (IRE) *Patrick Morris* a64 80
3 b g Danehill Dancer(IRE) —Pilgrim's Way (USA) (Gone West (USA))
1584^{8} 1836^{6} 2069^{7} 6461^{3} 7399^{11} 7556^{7} 7655^{10} 7824^{4} 7992^{4}

Pilote Celebre *Andrew Balding* a80 80
3 b c Peintre Celebre(USA) —Final Approach (USA) (Kris S (USA))
1735^{5} 2281^{3} 4926^{3}

Pinball (IRE) *Lisa Williamson* a58 61
4 b m Namid—Luceball (IRE) (Bluebird (USA))
525^{8} (3287) 3722^{8} 4373^{10} 4869^{12} 5055^{7} 5580^{9} 6206^{5} 7300^{11} (7380) 7859^{RR}

Pin Cushion *Brian Meehan* 83
3 ch f Pivotal—Frizzante (Efisio)
2599^{2} 2928^{4} (3952) 4503^{4} 5037^{3} 6198^{14}

Pineapple Pete (IRE) *Paul Cole* a50 61
2 b g Compton Place—Dilag (IRE) (Almutawakel)
3959^{12} 4336^{5} 4691^{4} 7666^{5} 7809^{7} 7997^{11}

Pinewood Legend (IRE) *Peter Niven* a47 21
8 br g Idris(IRE) —Blue Infanta (Chief Singer)
6648^{10}

Pinewood Polly *Shaun Harris* a8
3 b f Lujain(USA) —Polmara (IRE) (Polish Precedent (USA))
453^{5} 1336^{13} 1490^{10}

Pinielde (FR) *C Boutin* a77 89
2 b f High Yield(USA) —Pimpinella (FR) (Highest Honor (FR))
4275a^{6}

Pink Candie (FR) *Mlle V Dissaux* a81 84
4 b m Fath(USA) —Lyphard's Dream (IRE) (Lyphard (USA))
304a^{8} 560a^{10}

Pink Cat *Jeremy Gask* a39
2 bb f Ferrule(IRE) —Barrosa (Sabrehill (USA))
5719^{10}

Pink Diva (IRE) *Tom Tate* 74
2 ch f Giant's Causeway(USA) —Saoire (Pivotal)
5594^{9} (6305)

Pink Gin (FR) *J-M Beguigne* 104
3 b c Kouroun(FR) —Pink Cloud (FR) (Octagonal (NZ))
3703a^{5}

Pink Palace (USA) *Sir Michael Stoute* a70 77
3 b f Empire Maker(USA) —Potrinner (ARG) (Potrillazo (ARG))
2051^{3} ◆ 3266^{2} 4845^{7} 5918^{5}

Pink Sari *PETER Makin* a39
2 br f Kyllachy—Heart Of India (IRE) (Try My Best (USA))
7485^{11} 7608^{6}

Pink Symphony *Paul Cole* 108
3 b f Montjeu(IRE) —Blue Symphony (Darshaan)
(1356) 2029^{4} 2889^{2} 4037a^{7} 4957^{7} 6281^{2}

Pinotage *Richard Whitaker* a43 43
2 br g Danbird(AUS) —Keen Melody (USA) (Sharpen Up)
2522^{9} 3536^{8} 5196^{8} 6070^{12} 6618^{9} 7126^{5}

Pinsplitter (USA) *Alan McCabe* a58 62
3 ch g Giant's Causeway(USA) —Lahinch (IRE) (Danehill Dancer (IRE))
7474^{10} 7679^{6} 7729^{5} 7825^{2} 7995^{10}

Pintrada *James Bethell* 72
2 b c Tiger Hill(IRE) —Ballymore Celebre (IRE) (Peintre Celebre (USA))
4568^{4}

Pintura *David Simcock* a54 95
3 ch g Efisio—Picolette (Piccolo)
1168^{10} 1934^{8} 2863^{2} 3387^{9} (4127) 4546^{3} 4786^{3} (5552) 5955^{3} 6355^{3} (6556) 6749^{2}

Pipedreamer *Kevin Ryan* 120
6 b h Selkirk(USA) —Follow A Dream (USA) (Gone West (USA))
2118^{4} 3046^{P}

Pipers Piping (IRE) *Jane Chapple-Hyam* a75 67
4 b g Noverre(USA) —Monarchy (IRE) (Common Grounds)
195^{8} 369^{7} ◆ (568) (615) 892^{7} 1130^{6} 1320^{5} ◆ 1812^{7} 2257^{11} 2639^{9} 3280^{4} 4232^{7} 4434^{6} ◆ 4715^{5} (5175) 5711^{2} (5927) 6261^{3} 6371^{2} ◆ 6671^{3} 6903^{2} 7191^{6} (7336) 7439^{8} 7614^{2} 7737^{5} 7892^{2} 7966^{2} 8014^{10}

Piper's Song (IRE) *Patrick Morris* a67 68
7 gr g Distant Music(USA) —Dane's Lane (IRE) (Danehill (USA))
100^{6} 2952^{7}

Pipette *Andrew Balding* a100 102
3 b f Pivotal—Amaryllis (IRE) (Sadler's Wells (USA))
(1082) 1726^{13} 2224^{2}

Pipit Nest (IRE) *Tobias B P Coles* 12
2 b f Kodiac—Wee Merkin (IRE) (Thatching)
5204^{9} 5626^{14} 5835^{10}

Pippa Greene *Paul Cole* a85 56
6 b g Galileo(IRE) —Funny Girl (IRE) (Darshaan)
6362^{9} 6565^{11} 6808^{11}

Pippa's Gift *William Muir* a71
2 b c Royal Applause—Pippa's Dancer (IRE) (Desert Style (IRE))
7309^{8} (7871) 8020^{3}

Pippbrook Ministar *Jim Boyle* a67 65
3 br f Pastoral Pursuits—Chiaro (Safawan)
392^{2} ◆ 638^{2} 759^{2} 3786^{5} 5588^{4} 6085^{11} 6638^{9} 8034^{10}

Piquante *Nigel Tinkler* a73 73
4 b m Selkirk(USA) —China (Royal Academy (USA))
1426^{14} 1684^{9} 2462^{4} 2764^{9} 3854^{3} 4354^{10} 5064^{4} (5688) 6267^{8} 7209^{4} 7483^{2} 7889^{9}

Pirate Coast *Tim Easterby* 73
3 ch g Bahamian Bounty—Highland Gait (Most Welcome)
3207^{4} (3635)

Pirateer (IRE) *A P O'Brien* 96
2 b c Danehill Dancer(IRE) —Wannabe (Shirley Heights)
954a^{11}

Pirate's Song *James Toller* a63 77
3 b c Bahamian Bounty—Soviet Terms (Soviet Star (USA))
2004^{3} (2297) 3216^{2} ◆ 3638^{3} (4553) 5048^{2}

Pires *A J Martin* a99 98
6 br g Generous(IRE) —Kaydee Queen (IRE) (Bob's Return (IRE))
4830^{5} 6562^{3} 7507^{3}

Pisa No Varon (JPN) *Katsuhiko Sumii* 46
4 b h Manhattan Cafe(JPN) —Aldie Mill (USA) (Miswaki (USA))
6012a^{14}

Piscean (USA) *Tom Keddy* a104 96
5 bb g Stravinsky(USA) —Navasha (USA) (Woodman (USA))
1691^{7} 1874^{4} 2247^{4} 2681^{5} 2940^{13} (3629) 4118^{6} 4510^{4} 5308^{9} 5742^{8} 5966^{3} 6256^{8} (7041) (7254) 7466^{5} (7566) 7993^{5}

Pisco Sour (USA) *Hughie Morrison* a76 97
2 bb c Lemon Drop Kid(USA) —Lynnwood Chase (USA) (Horse Chestnut (SAF))
3794^{9} (4682) (5374) 6560^{2} 7265a^{8}

Piste *Tina Jackson* a68 72
4 b m Falbrav(IRE) —Arctic Char (Polar Falcon (USA))
2144^{5} 2396^{5} 2896^{3} 3027^{2} 3322^{10} 4486^{8} 4868^{8} 4982^{8} 5817^{12} 6189^{11}

Pitbull *Alan Berry* a63 62
7 b g Makbul—Piccolo Cativo (Komaite (USA))
1177^{14} 1520^{7} 1717^{11} 2240^{7} 2529^{6} 3025^{7} 4094^{5} 4411^{7} 4752^{10}

Piterino (IRE) *L Polito* 93
5 b h Desert Prince(IRE) —Russian Grace (IRE) (Soviet Star (USA))
1712a^{9} 1943a^{4}

Pitkin *Michael Easterby* a67 54
2 b g Proclamation(IRE) —Princess Oberon (IRE) (Fairy King (USA))
3923^{6} 4392^{7} 5277^{17} (7333) (7423)

Pittodrie Star (IRE) *Andrew Balding* a80 76
3 ch g Choisir(AUS) —Jupiter Inlet (IRE) (Jupiter Island)
5031^{7} 5540^{3} 6556^{3} 6807^{4} 7062^{15} 7305^{2} 7597^{5} (7687) 7876^{2}

Piverina (IRE) *Julie-Ann Camacho* a42 56
5 b m Pivotal—Alassio (USA) (Gulch (USA))
493^{4} 622^{6} 898^{4} 1576^{4} 2012^{5}

Pivotal Express (IRE) *John Panvert* 24
4 ch g Pivotal—Forest Express (AUS) (Kaaptive Edition (NZ))
3593^{10} 5001^{7}

Pivot Bridge *B W Hills* a59 51
2 ch c Pivotal—Specifically (USA) (Sky Classic (CAN))
5032^{9} 6443^{13} 7020^{7}

Pivotman *Amanda Perrett* 82
2 ch c Pivotal—Grandalea (Grand Lodge (USA))
(6474) ◆ 6884^{5}

Pizzarra *James Given* a55 53
2 b f Shamardal(USA) —Pizzicato (Statoblest)
6157^{8} 6459^{5} 6893^{3} 7333^{5} 7858^{3} 7997^{6}

Place And Chips *Tom Dascombe* a52 49
2 ch g Compton Place—Our Sheila (Bahamian Bounty)
2621^{9} 3310^{6} 3959^{9} 5412^{8} 5581^{10}

Place The Duchess *Alastair Lidderdale* a52 50
4 b m Compton Place—Barrantes (Distant Relative)
146^{8} 271^{11} 319^{6} 829^{8} 1884^{16}

Plain Vanilla (FR) *P Van De Poele* a80 103
3 ch f Kendor(FR) —Persian Belle (Machiavellian (USA))
1746a^{4} 2373a^{5} 3720a^{5}

Plaisterer *Chris Wall* a58 101
5 b m Best Of The Bests(IRE) —Lumiere D'Espoir (FR) (Saumarez)
1725^{6} 2747^{9} 4830^{8} (5592) 6106^{3} 6552^{4} 6877^{7} 7206^{11}

Plan A (IRE) *Michael Quinlan* 77
3 b g Le Vie Dei Colori—Heres The Plan (IRE) (Revoque (IRE))
2812^{7} 3220^{6} 4146^{6} 5050^{7} (5414) 6225^{2} (6623)

Planetarium *P Monteith* 72
5 gr g Fantastic Light(USA) —Karsiyaka (IRE) (Kahyasi)
1101^{11} 1720^{10} 2214^{2} 2672^{4} 3367^{5} 3989^{6} 4825^{7} 5119^{9}

Planet Five (USA) *P Bary* 112
4 b h Storm Cat(USA) —Six Perfections (FR) (Celtic Swing)
1081a^{7} (2804a) 4885a^{10} 6608a^{17}

Planet Red (IRE) *Richard Hannon* a82 85
3 ch g Bahamian Bounty—Aries (GER) (Big Shuffle (USA))
1083^{5} 1352^{13} 2807^{2} 4204^{7} 4963^{9} 7092^{10}

Planet Waves (IRE) *Clive Brittain* a80 80
2 b c Red Ransom(USA) —Rock Salt (Selkirk (USA))
1901^{10} (2216) 3049^{12} 3504^{5} 4355^{8} 5525^{6} 5849^{6} ◆ 6505^{12} 7085^{3} 7528^{2} ◆

Planteur (IRE) *E Lellouche* 124
3 b c Danehill Dancer(IRE) —Plante Rare (IRE) (Giant's Causeway (USA))
(1254a) 2802a^{2} 4039a^{2} 6014a^{2} 6612a^{DSQ} 7854a^{5}

Platine Rose (FR) *D Prod'Homme* a76 80
2 ch f Green Tune(USA) —Pennyghael (UAE) (Pennekamp (USA))
6589a^{9} 7009a^{4}

Platinum Bounty *Neil Mulholland* a23 33
4 gr m Bahamian Bounty—Maxizone (FR) (Linamix (FR))
1157^{5} 1479^{5}

Plato (JPN) *Henry Cecil* a85 91
3 ch c Bago(FR) —Taygete (USA) (Miswaki (USA))
1268^{8} 1627^{4} 3519^{3} 4258^{2} (4845) 5747^{11} 6423^{2}

Plattsburgh (USA) *Mahmood Al Zarooni* a70 43
2 bb c Bernardini(USA) —Saranac Lake (USA) (Smart Strike (CAN))
5582^{7} 6249^{3} 6742^{6}

Playful Asset (IRE) *Paul Howling* a58 62
4 ch m Johannesburg(USA) —Twickin (USA) (Two Punch (USA))
100^{4} (228) 354^{7} 611^{2} 1318^{7} 1478^{9} 1606^{4} 3960^{3}

Playful Girl (IRE) *Tim Easterby* 46
2 b f Byron—Feminine Touch (IRE) (Sadler's Wells (USA))
2623[6] 4048[7] 4668[10] 6300[13] 6893[7] 7118[8]
Playground *Michael Bell* 36
3 b g Montjeu(IRE) —Phantom Gold (Machiavellian (USA))
1268[13] 1521[6]
Play It Sam *Walter Swinburn* a76 95
4 b g Bahamian Bounty—Bombalarina (IRE) (Barathea (IRE))
(1617) (2339) 2885[4] 3483[2] 5540[2] 6327[5] 6877[9]
Play The Blues (IRE) *Mark Allen* a5
3 b f Refuse To Bend(IRE) —Paldouna (IRE) (Kaldoun (FR))
7406[9]
Play To Win (IRE) *Paul Midgley* a61 24
4 b g Singspiel(IRE) —Spot Prize (USA) (Seattle Dancer (USA))
3502[11]
Play Up Pompey *John Bridger* a52 32
8 b g Dansili—Search For Love (FR) (Groom Dancer (USA))
1001[2] 160[7] 497[4] 539[2] 685[8] 1318[8] 7966[10] 7995[11]
Playwright (NZ) *Steve Richards* 101
6 b g Fantastic Light(USA) —Amonistar (USA) (Theatrical)
6946a[12]
Plea *John Gosden* 71
2 b g Motivator—Request (Rainbow Quest (USA))
1905[8] 5871[3] 6279[6] 6555[5] (6875)
Pleasant Day (IRE) *Brian Meehan* a87 103
3 b g Noverre(USA) —Sunblush (UAE) (Timber Country (USA))
2045[6] 3103[11] ◆ 3824[12] 4828[14]
Pleasant Humor (USA) *Robert Cowell* a48 5
2 ch c Sharp Humor(USA) —Pleasant Token (USA) (Pleasant Colony (USA))
5835[11] 6118[6] 6333[9] 6867[4]
Pleasant Prince (USA) *Wesley A Ward* a112
3 ch c Indy King(USA) —Archduchess (USA) (Pleasant Tap (USA))
2137a[11] 7367a[9]
Pleasant Way (IRE) *David Lanigan* a59 60
3 ch f Barathea(IRE) —Eman's Joy (Lion Cavern (USA))
1393[10] 2853[3] 3444[4]
Please Sing *Mick Channon* a90 101
4 b m Royal Applause—Persian Song (Persian Bold)
1084[5] 1693[8] 2744[4] 3069[20] 3752[2] 4319[4] 5114[12] 5782a[5] 6346[11]
Plenilune (IRE) *Mel Brittain* a53 63
5 b g Fantastic Light(USA) —Kathleen's Dream (USA) (Last Tycoon)
75[7] 603[4] 705[4] 6077[9] 7646[9]
Plenty O'Toole *Deborah Sanderson* a69 70
3 ch g Monsieur Bond(IRE) —Marie La Rose (FR) (Night Shift (USA))
5384[6] 5852[5] 6243[4] 6794[6] 7019[9] 7406[4] 7543[8]
Plenty Pocket (FR) *E Lellouche* 93
3 ch c Super Celebre(FR) —Almadina (FR) (Pistolet Bleu (IRE))
5136a[6]
Plenty Power *Mick Channon* 75
2 b c Acclamation—Maugwenna (Danehill (USA))
4396[4] 4902[4] 5531[10] 5914[4]
Pluck (USA) *Todd Pletcher* a43 113
2 bb c More Than Ready(USA) —Secret Heart (SAF) (Fort Wood (USA))
(7360a)
Plug In Baby *Nick Mitchell* a43 41
2 b f Xaar—Medinaceli (IRE) (Grand Lodge (USA))
6804[9] 7034[6] 7311[11]
Pluirin (USA) *J S Bolger* a70 79
3 b f Pleasantly Perfect(USA) —Whirlwind Charlott (USA) (Real Quiet (USA))
1036a[6]
Plumage *Tor Sturgis* a64 67
5 b m Royal Applause—Cask (Be My Chief (USA))
1595[4] 1843[5] 2246[6] (2589) 2964[13] 3115[3] 3254[6] 3556[11] 5764[8]
Plumania *A Fabre* 116
4 b m Anabaa(USA) —Featherquest (Rainbow Quest (USA))
1792a[4] (2403a) (3494a) 6013a[2] 6612a[16] 7343a[11]
Plume *Richard Hannon* 86
3 b f Pastoral Pursuits—Polar Storm (IRE) (Law Society (USA))
2120[3] ◆ 2929[3]
Plume De Ma Tante (IRE) *Jeremy Glover* a55 66
2 b f Compton Place—Feather Boa (IRE) (Sri Pekan (USA))
5418[2] 5763[5]
Plume Rose *Y De Nicolay* a84 96
3 b f Marchand De Sable(USA) —Peace Signal (USA) (Time For A Change (USA))
952a[5] 1496a[5] 7457a[6] 7648a[9]
Plum Mac *Neville Bycroft* a5 10
6 ch m Presidium—Ski Path (Celtic Cone)
3276 1153[6]
Plum Pudding (IRE) *Richard Hannon* a101 113
7 b g Elnadim(USA) —Karayb (IRE) (Last Tycoon)
109[3] 553[8] (Dead)
Plumsum *Neville Bycroft* 31
2 b f Needwood Blade—Plum Blossom (Beat All (USA))
2605[7] 2836[8] 4241[12]
Plush *Tom Dascombe* a88 70
7 ch g Medicean—Glorious (Nashwan (USA))
1974 (466) 623[2] (1208) 1587[2] 1837[11] 2477[3] 3616[3] 4403[6]
Plus Ultra (IRE) *Philip Kirby* 75
3 b g Rock Of Gibraltar(IRE) —Tafseer (IRE) (Grand Lodge (USA))
1432[2] 1851[5] 3039[2] 3523[3] 4867[4] 5360[3]
Plutocraft *James Fanshawe* a75 74
3 ch g Starcraft(NZ) —Angry Bark (USA) (Woodman (USA))
1766[3] ◆ 2383[5] 3831[2] 4779[2] 5887[2] 6851[3] (7069)

Plymouth Rock (IRE) *Jeremy Noseda* a89 99
4 b g Sadler's Wells(USA) —Zarawa (IRE) (Kahyasi)
1156[2] 2865[4] 3588[2] 4846[3] 5492[2] 5908[12] 6926[3]
Pobs Trophy *Richard Guest* a14 54
3 b g Umistim—Admonish (Warning)
3728[6] 4863[6] 5534[3] 5687[4] 6038[3]
Poca A Poca (IRE) *Dai Burchell* a40 58
6 b m Namid—Cliveden Gail (IRE) (Law Society (USA))
(4681)
Pocket's Pick (IRE) *Jim Best* a73 65
4 ch g Exceed And Excel(AUS) —Swizzle (Efisio)
1074[3] 1445[5] 1799[14] 3605[2] 4239[2] 4435[6] 5176[7] 6270[6] 7542[10]
Pocket Too *Matthew Salaman* a66 2
7 b g Fleetwood(IRE) —Pocket Venus (IRE) (King's Theatre (IRE))
148[6] 322[6] 1160[6] 1424[7] 7388[9] 7634[5]
Pockett Rockett *David O'Meara* 41
2 b f Proclamation(IRE) —Paperweight (In The Wings)
3657[7] 4048[11] 4447[13]
Pocketwood *Alastair Lidderdale* a55 82
8 b g Fleetwood(IRE) —Pocket Venus (IRE) (King's Theatre (IRE))
1056a[0] 3780[6] (6480) (7101)
Podgies Boy (IRE) *Richard Fahey* a77 69
2 b g Statue Of Liberty(USA) —Lake Victoria (IRE) (Lake Coniston (IRE))
5117[2] 5531[8] 6182[DSQ] 7210[4] (7396) (7572) (7718)
Poesmulligan (IRE) *Linda Jewell* a41
4 ch g Pierre—Jamis (IRE) (Be My Guest (USA))
7251[10] 7397[8] 7419[8] 7570[11]
Poet *Clive Cox* a48 118
5 b h Pivotal—Hyabella (Shirley Heights)
440a[10] 609a[11] 3632[6] 4139[3] (4829) 5951[3] 6592a[4] 7096[2]
Poetically *Jonathan Portman* a66 46
2 b g Balmont(USA) —Presently (Cadeaux Genereux)
3034[9] 4890[2] 5465[6] 5808[5]
Poet's Place (USA) *David Barron* a99 109
5 b g Mutakddim(USA) —Legion Of Merit (USA) (Danzig (USA))
(380) 2992[5] 3446[2] ◆ 4358[12] (4832) (5944) ◆ 6177[10] 6752[11]
Poet's Voice *Saeed Bin Suroor* 123
3 b c Dubawi(IRE) —Bright Tiara (USA) (Chief's Crown (USA))
2159a[8] 3704a[9] 5009[2] (5518) (6350) 6925[9]
Poincon De France (IRE) *P Monfort* a70 85
6 b g Peintre Celebre(USA) —Poughkeepsie (IRE) (Sadler's Wells (USA))
742a[3]
Point Du Jour (FR) *Ian Wood* a74 80
2 bb c Indian Rocket—Alaiz (Catrail (USA))
3332[9] 3945[3] 4332[2] 5251a[2] 5745[10] 5992[3] 6059[8] 6426[6] 7236[10] 7379[3] 7528[7] 7647a[3] 7974a[8]
Pointilliste (USA) *Noel Meade* a104 111
7 ch h Giant's Causeway(USA) —Peinture Bleue (USA) (Alydar (USA))
4081a[5] 5909[8]
Point North (IRE) *Jeremy Noseda* 84
3 b g Danehill Dancer(IRE) —Briolette (IRE) (Sadler's Wells (USA))
1387[7] 6624[4] 6815[6] (7183)
Point Out (USA) *John Gosden* a84 60
3 ch c Point Given(USA) —Dock Leaf (USA) (Woodman (USA))
980[2] (3275) ◆ 3824[17] 6252[14]
Points Of Grace (USA) *Malcolm Pierce* 108
5 ch m Point Given(USA) —Fateful (USA) (Topsider (USA))
6235a[4]
Point To Prove *John Balding* a69 69
3 b g Refuse To Bend(IRE) —On Point (Kris)
222[5] 5548[14] 6330[11]
Pokfulham (IRE) *Jim Goldie* a51 64
4 b g Mull Of Kintyre(USA) —Marjinal (Marju (IRE))
6109[16] 6495[4] 7054[3] 7229[4]
Polar Annie *Malcolm Saunders* a42 71
5 b m Fraam—Willisa (Polar Falcon (USA))
965[11] (4324) 4988[8] 5964[P] 6656[10]
Polar Auroras *Pat Eddery* a67 49
2 b f Iceman—Noor El Houdah (IRE) (Fayruz)
3964[6] 4871[7] 5719[3] 6162[2] 6902[3]
Polarix *H-A Pantall* a95 103
4 gr h Linamix(FR) —Freezing (USA) (Bering)
2559a[6] 7800a[9]
Polar Kite (IRE) *Richard Fahey* 82
2 b g Marju(IRE) —Irina (IRE) (Polar Falcon (USA))
2493[3] ◆ 3162[2] (3874)
Polebrook *John Jenkins* 54
3 ch g Lomitas—Fifth Emerald (Formidable (USA))
1393[6] 1989[9] 4235[3] 4552[4] 6079[7]
Polemica (IRE) *Frank Sheridan* a51 62
4 b m Rock Of Gibraltar(IRE) —Lady Scarlett (Woodman (USA))
1170[13] 1457[4] 6656[14] 7250[7] 7426[8] 7835[10] 7885[5]
Polish Power (GER) *Pat Murphy* a84 84
10 br h Halling(USA) —Polish Queen (Polish Precedent (USA))
1012[11] 1226[9] 1755[10] 3032[10]
Polish Sunset *Amy Weaver* a61
2 b g Noverre(USA) —Firozi (Forzando)
7551[5] 7880[6]
Polish World (USA) *Paul Midgley* a43 82
6 b g Danzig(USA) —Welcometotheworld (USA) (Woodman (USA))
1574[4] 2527[5] (2850) (3124) (3284) 3732[3] 4197[4] (4515) 5242[4] 5964[10]
Politbureau *Mark Johnston* 65
3 b g Red Ransom(USA) —Tereshkova (USA) (Mr Prospector (USA))
4069[6] 5288[4]

Pollan Bay (IRE) *Ms J S Doyle* a48 52
3 b g High Chaparral(IRE) —Rossa Di Rugiada (IRE) (College Chapel)
3640[7] 3820[5] 3960[9] 4230[7]
Pollen (IRE) *T Stack* 105
5 br m Orpen(USA) —On Air (FR) (Chief Singer)
(957a) 1787a[7] 2355a[9] 6006a[5] 6617a[7]
Pollenator (IRE) *Richard Hannon* 107
3 ch f Motivator—Ceanothus (IRE) (Bluebird (USA))
1726[11] 2076[3] 3071[17]
Polly Floyer *Walter Swinburn* a57 60
3 ch f Halling(USA) —Juno Marlowe (IRE) (Danehill (USA))
2051[7] 6815[7] 7310[3] (7461)
Polly Holder (IRE) *Alan Bailey* a59 67
2 b f Peintre Celebre(USA) —Love Emerald (USA) (Mister Baileys)
7000[5] 7198[3] 7242[5] 7839[6]
Polly Macho (IRE) *David Evans* a7 62
3 b g Camacho—Polly Mills (Lugana Beach)
1456[12] 1760[12]
Polly's Mark (IRE) *Clive Cox* 110
4 b m Mark Of Esteem(IRE) —Kotdiji (Mtoto)
1382[4] 2538[2] 3671[2] 4507[2] 5108a[8] 5881[4] (6320)
Poltergeist (IRE) *Richard Hannon* 83
3 b g Invincible Spirit(IRE) —Bayalika (IRE) (Selkirk (USA))
(2841)
Polvius (ITY) *S Botti*
2 ch c Dr Devious(IRE) —Polista (FR) (Persepolis (FR))
7849a[10]
Polygon (USA) *John Gosden* 78
2 b f Dynaformer(USA) —Polaire (IRE) (Polish Patriot (USA))
6155[3]
Polynesian Queen (IRE) *Michael Quinlan* a43
3 b f Statue Of Liberty(USA) —Polynesian Goddess (IRE) (Salmon Leap (USA))
985[9]
Polytechnicien (USA) *A Fabre* a100 106
4 ch h Royal Academy(USA) —Golden Party (USA) (Seeking The Gold (USA))
1716a[6] 7266a[8] (7800a)
Pomeroy *Tom Dascombe* a65 52
3 b c Green Desert(USA) —Ela Paparouna (Vettori (IRE))
1274 (357)
Pompeyano (IRE) *Saeed Bin Suroor* a71 113
5 b g Rainbow Quest(USA) —Lady Lodger (Be My Guest (USA))
418a[6] ◆ 516a[6] ◆ 712a[3] 799a[4] 1026a[10] (4500) 5080[5] 5538[3] 6388[3]
Pont De Nuit *Tracy Waggott* a69 66
3 b g Avonbridge—Belle De Nuit (IRE) (Statoblest)
3948[10] 4439[9] 5560[5] 7845[8]
Pont Des Arts (FR) *A Scharer* a94 104
6 b h Kingsalsa(USA) —Magic Arts (IRE) (Fairy King (USA))
4276a[2] 6881a[4] 7776a[8]
Ponte Di Rosa *Brendan Powell* 63
2 b f Avonbridge—Ridgewood Ruby (IRE) (Indian Ridge)
3296[6] 4095[13] 5829[8] 6563[14]
Pontenuovo (FR) *Y De Nicolay* 109
2 ch f Green Tune(USA) —Porlezza (FR) (Sicyos (USA))
(4637a) 5347a[3] 6702a[5]
Ponticelli (IRE) *S Cannavo'* 99
4 bb h King Charlemagne(USA) —Quela (GER) (Acatenango (GER))
1943a[7]
Ponting (IRE) *Paul Midgley* a59 71
4 gr g Clodovil(IRE) —Polar Lady (Polar Falcon (USA))
20[9] (171) 380[4] 1030[16] 1270[10] 2113[16] 2378[9] 6664[11] 7194[9] 7401[8] 7870[8]
Pont Wood *Nikki Evans* a59 1
6 b g Iron Mask(USA) —Bajan Rose (Dashing Blade)
540[10]
Pool Of Knowledge (FR) *David Nicholls* a79 82
4 gr g Ocean Of Wisdom(USA) —Princess Mix (FR) (Linamix (FR))
4758[8] 5091[2] 5591[4] 6152[4] 7988[2] ◆
Poor Prince *Alison Batchelor* a65 77
3 b g Royal Applause—Kahira (IRE) (King's Best (USA))
4491[6] 4956[8] 6771[4] 7389[6] 7614[7]
Pope Potter *Richard Guest*
2 b g Needwood Blade—Surrealist (ITY) (Night Shift (USA))
7345 [15] 7452[11]
Poplin *Luca Cumani* a76 91
2 ch f Medicean—Pongee (Barathea (IRE))
4517[3] 5369[3] (5829) 6505[3]
Popmurphy *P D Deegan* 101
4 b g Montjeu(IRE) —Lady Lahar (Fraam)
1247a[2] 1789a[5] 3470a[4]
Poppanan (USA) *Simon Dow* a75 87
4 b g Mr Greeley(USA) —Tiny Decision (USA) (Ogygian (USA))
1044[5] ◆ 1428[8] (1779) (2458) 2954[3] ◆ 3815[7] 6478[2] ◆
Poppet's Joy *Andrew Haynes*
2 b f Bertolini(USA) —Our Poppet (IRE) (Warning)
6675[7]
Poppet's Lovein *Andrew Haynes* 87
4 b m Lomitas—Our Poppet (IRE) (Warning)
1802[4] 2601[6] 3396[5] (3830) 4378[4] 4850[2] 6113[3] ◆ 6887[10]
Poppet's Treasure *R Pritchard-Gordon* a84 101
3 b f Dansili—Our Poppet (IRE) (Warning)
4773a[2] 6012a[6] 6608a[11]
Poppy *Richard Hannon* a46 67
2 b f Monsieur Bond(IRE) —Niggle (Night Shift (USA))
6145[3] 6441[10] 7185[11]

Poppy Golightly *Ron Hodges* a56 67
3 ch f Compton Place—Popocatepetl (FR) (Nashwan (USA))
1731[7] 2841[3] 3333[2] 3866[12] 4529[5] 5031[12] 7193[8] 7518[9] 8034[7]
Poppy Gregg *Dr Jeremy Naylor* a54 45
5 b m Tamure(IRE) —Opalette (Sharrood (USA))
420[2] 584[2] 748[3] 874[6] 982[5] 2169[4]
Poppy Seed *Richard Hannon* 93
3 br f Bold Edge—Opopmil (IRE) (Pips Pride)
1731[3] 2340[2] (3210) (4204) 5952[7]
Poppy's Rose *Tim Etherington* a66 78
6 b m Diktat—Perfect Peach (Lycius (USA))
2087[2] 2326[6] (2396) 2818[4] 3622[6] (4343) 4542[4] 4952[4] 5513[12] 6103[7] 6303[6]
Pop Rock (JPN) *Takashi Kodama* 115
9 b h Helissio(FR) —Pops (JPN) (Sunday Silence (USA))
5976a[8]
Porgy *Richard Fahey* a95 98
5 b g Dansili—Light Ballet (Sadler's Wells (USA))
903[6] 1015[8] 1474[9] 1831[3] 3921[16] (4348) 4830[4] 5743[15] 5949[12] 6304[8] 6754[11]
Porthgwidden Beach (USA) *Stuart Williams* 39
2 b f Street Cry(IRE) —Suaviter (USA) (Roar (USA))
3331[7] 5147[13] 6459[8]
Port Hill *Mark Brisbourne* a65 50
3 ch g Deportivo—Hill Farm Dancer (Gunner B)
254[7] 542[7] 775[6] 872[2] 1054[2] 1158[4] 3519[8] 4991[9] 7387[10] 7669[2] (7789) 8010[6]
Port Hollow *B W Hills* 70
2 b f Beat Hollow—Maritima (Darshaan)
6511[4] 7232[5]
Port Ronan (USA) *John Wainwright* a18 54
4 rg h Cozzene(USA) —Amber Token (USA) (Hennessy (USA))
1885[12] 2378[12] (3181) 3286[3] 3615[11] 3977[6] 4285[8] 4415[10] 5535[13]
Portrush Storm *Ray Peacock* a53 70
5 ch m Observatory(USA) —Overcast (IRE) (Caerleon (USA))
780[9] (1503) 1922[10] 2727[8] 2920[9] 3391[10] 3853[8] 4914[8] 6213[10]
Pose (IRE) *Roger Ingram* a79 82
3 b f Acclamation—Lyca Ballerina (Marju (IRE))
(2249) 3328[2] 4204[6] 5005[5] 5896[11] (6310) 7573[8] 8017[6]
Posh Cracker (USA) *G M Lyons* a80 54
2 br f Johannesburg(USA) —Holly's Kid (USA) (Pulpit (USA))
6727a[8]
Positivity *Bryan Smart* a60 31
4 ch m Monsieur Bond(IRE) —Pretty Pollyanna (General Assembly (USA))
(88) 248[4] (518) 753[13] 918[3] 1142[6] 1575[11] 7986[4] ◆
Postman *Bryan Smart* a38 75
4 b g Dr Fong(USA) —Mail The Desert (IRE) (Desert Prince (IRE))
2527[6] 3149[6] (4986) 5737[9] 5905[5] 6117[7] 6472[3] 7128[9]
Postscript (IRE) *Mahmood Al Zarooni* a76 75
2 ch c Pivotal—Persian Secret (FR) (Persian Heights)
2384[3] 2687[2] 3326[4]
Posy Fossil (USA) *Stuart Williams* a66 63
3 bb f Malibu Moon(USA) —Fire And Shade (USA) (Shadeed (USA))
313[3] 445[3] (745) 1640[6] 2871[8] 3390[13] 3677[2] 5054[7] 5896[6] 6540[6] 7191[2] 7890[6] 7992[10]
Potentiale (IRE) *J W Hills* a76 86
6 ch g Singspiel(IRE) —No Frills (IRE) (Darshaan)
1388[4] 1840[6] 2282[4] 2747[8] 3581[6] 3814[3] 4737[3] ◆ 5235[6] (5680) 5859[5] 6774[4] 7089[3]
Potomac (IRE) *John Gosden* a82
2 b c Shamardal(USA) —Pippas Song (Reference Point)
7530[8] (7693) 7916[6]
Pound Lane (IRE) *Teresa Spearing* a45 34
4 b g Montjeu(IRE) —Madaen (USA) (Nureyev (USA))
2003[9] 3207[15] 3829[7] 4683[4] 6660[6] 7398[6]
Pouvoir Absolu *E Lellouche* 116
5 b h Sadler's Wells(USA) —Pine Chip (USA) (Nureyev (USA))
2803a[3] 3494a[5] 5575a[8] 6612a[18]
Power Desert (IRE) *Geoffrey Harker* 46
5 b g Anabaa(USA) —Legende D'Or (FR) (Diesis)
4015[10] 4484[7] 4854[9] 5642[10] 5681[8] 6029[10]
Power Eva (GER) *H J Groschel* 97
3 b f Ransom O'War(USA) —Power Queen (IRE) (Danehill (USA))
5805a[3] 6790a[7]
Powerful Melody (USA) *Saeed Bin Suroor* a89 90
3 b c Dynaformer(USA) —Song Track (USA) (Dixieland Band (USA))
(5991) 6359[5] 7130[3]
Powerful Pierre *Ian McInnes* a67 75
3 ch g Compton Place—Alzianah (Alzao (USA))
1401[2] 1868[3] 2609[3] 2722[2] 3086[4] 4014[4] 4674[3] 4993[6] 5067[6] 5688[2] 6541[7] 6934[7] 7273[3] 7467[9]
Power Of Dreams (IRE) *Mark H Tompkins* a55 70
3 b g Pearl Of Love(IRE) —Pussie Willow (IRE) (Catrail (USA))
1992[4] 3607[7] 5171[10] 5636[9] 6094[9]
Power Punch (IRE) *B W Hills* 76
2 b c Medicean—Peneia (USA) (Nureyev (USA))
3794[13] 4614[3] ◆ 5294[6]
Power Series (USA) *John Gosden* a95 94
3 rg c Mizzen Mast(USA) —Diese (USA) (Diesis)
(754) 1210[2] 1730[3] 2479[2] 2742[4] 6203[12]
Poyle Judy *Ralph Beckett* a73
2 b f Iceman—Poyle Jenny (Piccolo)
6425[5] (6866) 7572[4]
Poyle Meg *Ralph Beckett* a89 78
4 b m Dansili—Lost In Lucca (Inchinor)
480[9]
Praesepe *William Haggas* a71 61
3 b f Pivotal—Superstar Leo (IRE) (College Chapel)
2441[3] 3663[7] 4553[4] 5044[4] 6746[4] 7013[5]

Pragelata (GER) *A Wohler* 81
3 b f Platini(GER) —Prairie Princess (GER) (Dashing Blade)
3943a[8]
Pragmatist *Rod Millman* a64 67
6 b m Piccolo—Shi Shi (Alnasr Alwasheek)
2246[3] 2719[6] 3914[2] 4099[8] 5010[8] 7007[8] *(7391) 7640[8]*
Prairie Hawk (USA) *B S Rothwell* a68 72
5 bb g Hawk Wing(USA) —Lady Carla (Caerleon (USA))
6328[10]
Prairie Spirit (FR) *Charlie Longsdon* a67 93
6 ch g Grape Tree Road—Prairie Runner (IRE) (Arazi (USA))
232[5]
Prairie Star (FR) *E Lellouche* 102
2 b c Peintre Celebre(USA) —Prairie Runner (IRE) (Arazi (USA))
(6973a) 7456a[3]
Prairie Tiger (GER) *Tom Dascombe* a70 83
6 b g Tiger Hill(IRE) —Prairie Lilli (GER) (Acatenango (GER))
6372[4] ◆
Praise Be (IRE) *John Joseph Murphy* 82
2 b f Kheleyf(USA) —Grateful Thanks (FR) (Bering)
6005a[9]
Prakasa (FR) *W Hickst* 99
3 b f Areion(GER) —Pepples Beach (GER) (Lomitas)
1250a[4] 1715a[4] (2404a) 5649a[7] 6765a[11]
Pravda Street *Paul Cole* a79 94
5 ch g Soviet Star(USA) —Sari (Faustus (USA))
1826[9] 2595[9] *3083[12]* 6048[6] 6564[12] 6963[12]
Praxios *Luca Cumani* a65 37
2 b c Val Royal(FR) —Forest Fire (SWE) (Never So Bold)
7099[12] *7530[2]* ◆
Precedence (NZ) *Bart Cummings* 115
5 b g Zabeel(NZ) —Kowtow (USA) (Shadeed (USA))
7291a[8]
Precious Coral (IRE) *Ruth Carr* a69 69
3 gr f Elusive City(USA) —Somaggia (IRE) (Desert King (IRE))
4482[6] 5044[6] 5409[8]
Precious Diamond *Mick Channon* 17
2 b f Kyllachy—Precious (Danehill (USA))
5385[12] 5676[9] *6542[P]* (Dead)
Precious Gem (IRE) *D K Weld* 101
4 b m Sadler's Wells(USA) —Ruby (IRE) (Danehill (USA))
1247a[5] (3466a) 4877a[5] 6007a[6]
Precious Spring (IRE) *Ed Dunlop* a47 53
3 b f Sadler's Wells(USA) —Tedarshana (Darshaan)
2890[9] *6250[7]* 6861[6]
Precision Break (USA) *Paul Cole* a82 103
5 b g Silver Deputy(CAN) —Miss Kitty Cat (USA) (Tabasco Cat (USA))
4461[11] 4711[6] 5291[5] (5908) 6926[16] *7339a[7]*
Premier Clarets (IRE) *Richard Fahey* 98
2 b c Ivan Denisovich(IRE) —Blueberry Walk (Green Desert (USA))
1806[2] (2239) 2743[3] (3504) 4355[3] 5219[5] 5880[3]
Premier Contender (IRE) *David Nicholls* 56
3 bb g Namid—Serious Contender (IRE) (Tenby)
4339[11] 5065[9] 5419[3] 5686[6]
Premier Dane (IRE) *Nicky Richards* a78 94
8 b g Indian Danehill(IRE) —Crystal Blue (IRE) (Bluebird (USA))
252[5]
Premier Lad *David Barron* a71 65
4 b g Tobougg(IRE) —Al Joudha (FR) (Green Desert (USA))
20[5] ◆ *144[3] 170[4] 555[8]*
Premier League *Julia Feilden* a55
3 b g Firebreak—Lizzie Simmonds (IRE) (Common Grounds)
321[8] 433[P] 6522[4] 7451[6] 7614[13] 7877[6]
Premio Loco (USA) *Chris Wall* a114 122
6 ch g Prized(USA) —Crazee Mental (Magic Ring (IRE))
338a[5] 631a[7] (3455) (3888) 4469[3] 5946[2] 6529[8]
Premium Charge *Chris Dwyer* a72 51
3 ch g Footstepsinthesand—Kallavesi (USA) (Woodman (USA))
133[5] 217[3] 288[2] (455) 524[2] 805[8] (861) 933[7] 1873[8] *2261[4]*
Premium Coffee *Mick Channon* 77
2 b g Superior Premium—Coffee Ice (Primo Dominie)
3349[4] (3811)
Prem Ramya (GER) *W Figge* 87
3 ch f Big Shuffle(USA) —Pretty Su (IRE) (Surumu (GER))
5805a[9]
Pre Raphaelite *J S Moore*
3 ch g Pastoral Pursuits—Deco Lady (Wolfhound (USA))
3635[12]
Prescription *Sir Mark Prescott Bt* a102 101
5 ch m Pivotal—Doctor's Glory (USA) (Elmaamul (USA))
(1918) 4269a[3] 4882a[9] 6564[11]
Present *Diana Weeden* a39 45
6 ch m Generous(IRE) —Miss Picol (Exit To Nowhere (USA))
1283[11] 3639[7]
Present Alchemy *Hughie Morrison* 95
4 ch g Cadeaux Genereux—Desert Alchemy (IRE) (Green Desert (USA))
2681[8] ◆ (2997) 3891[9] 6446[10]
Present Danger *Tom Dascombe* 74
2 b f Cadeaux Genereux—Lighthouse (Warning)
(6240)
Present Story *Patrick Leech* a63 67
3 b f Lucky Story(USA) —Aziz Presenting (IRE) (Charnwood Forest (IRE))
4661[9] *4926[4]* 5493[3] 5986[6] 6557[4]
Preset *James Eustace*
3 b g Reset(AUS) —Sea Jade (IRE) (Mujadil (USA))
2414[11] 2678[12]
Presidium Galaxy *George Moore* 6
3 b f Presidium—Pagan Star (Carlitin)
915[10] 3285[6] 3733[10]
Presious Passion (USA) *Mary Hartmann* a96 122
7 ch g Royal Anthem(USA) —Princesa's Passion (USA) (Marquetry (USA))
1026a[16]
Pressed For Time (IRE) *Edward Creighton* a59 52
4 b m Traditionally(USA) —Desert Palace (Green Desert (USA))
2186[8] (2720) 2809[5] 3293[7] *3966[5] 4256[4]* 4672[6] *5697[9]*
Pressing (IRE) *Michael Jarvis* 120
7 bb h Soviet Star(USA) —Rafif (USA) (Riverman (USA))
1531[2] ◆ 2152a[3] (2576a) 5009[7] (5803a) 6764a[6]
Press Release *Tom Dascombe* a61 59
2 b g Elnadim(USA) —Last Impression (Imp Society (USA))
1517[9] 1835[6] 2210[4] 3598[6] *3784[3]* 4195[6] *5921[12]* 6489[7]
Press The Button (GER) *Jim Boyle* a102 96
7 b g Dansili—Play Around (IRE) (Niniski (USA))
1220[7]
Presto Volante (IRE) *Amanda Perrett* 68
2 b g Oratorio(IRE) —Very Racy (USA) (Sri Pekan (USA))
2078[6] 2932[5] 3577[2] 4623[5] 5256[4]
Presvis *Luca Cumani* a113 122
6 b g Sakhee(USA) —Forest Fire (SWE) (Never So Bold)
435a[2] (801a) 1025a[11] 1568a[5] 2154a[5] 3068[9]
Pre Tax Profit (IRE) *Reginald Roberts* a45
2 b g Ad Valorem(USA) —Civic Duty (IRE) (Definite Article)
6726a[11]
Pretium Sceleris *S Botti* a60 63
2 b c Johannesburg(USA) —Poppo's Song (CAN) (Polish Navy (USA))
1728[8] 2384[4] *3274[5]* 7850a[17]
Pretty Bonnie *Andrew Price* a90 93
5 b m Kyllachy—Joonayh (Warning)
1918[6] 2326[8] 2929[4] (3505) 4145[5] 5120[10] 5694[4] 6509[3] 6776[6] 7097[15]
Pretty Diamond (IRE) *Mark Johnston* a59 49
2 ch f Hurricane Run(IRE) —Cheal Rose (IRE) (Dr Devious (IRE))
6831[8] 7172[6] *7567[5]*
Pretty Orchid *Paul Midgley* a40 58
5 b m Forzando—Dunloe (IRE) (Shaadi (USA))
571[6] 838[8] 912[7] (1114) 2817[9] 3284[2] 3434[5] 3854[8] 4987[14] 5486[12]
Prickles *Karen George* a54 54
5 ch m Karinga Bay—Squeaky (Infantry)
677[7] 1302[10] 1451[7] 1759[6] *1984[3]* 2676[2] *3324[11]* 3848[5] 4279[3] 4990[5] 5811[5] *(7270) 7407[7]*
Pride Of Nation (IRE) *Alan McCabe* a71 81
8 b h Danehill Dancer(IRE) —Anita Via (IRE) (Anita's Prince)
29[8] 126[5] 373[5]
Pride Of Tagula *Noel Wilson*
2 ch f Tagula(IRE) —Pride Of Kinloch (Dr Devious (IRE))
3087[15]
Priestley (IRE) *James Given* a28 39
3 b g Bahri(USA) —Siskin (IRE) (Royal Academy (USA))
2606[12] 3640[5]
Prigsnov Dancer (IRE) *O Brennan* a39 41
5 ch g Namid—Brave Dance (IRE) (Kris)
2790[8] 3287[11] 3774[6] 4605[8] 4897[7] 5485[3] *7132[7] 7380[9]*
Primaeval *James Fanshawe* a97 82
4 ch h Pivotal—Langoustine (AUS) (Danehill (USA))
(1625) 4370[10] 4843[10] *5754[5] 6503[2] (7092)*
Prima Nova (AUS) *Anthony Cummings* 110
6 br m Danehill Dancer(IRE) —Bonanova (NZ) (Star Way)
13
Primary Colors *Clive Cox* a73 70
3 ch c Nayef(USA) —Red Yellow Blue (USA) (Sky Classic (CAN))
1387[8] 1602[2] 2250[10] *4022[2]*
Prime Circle *Alan Brown* 70
4 b g Green Desert(USA) —First Of Many (Darshaan)
1119[8] 1426[16] 1631[6] 2207[7] (2965) 3706[4] (4168) 4602[5] 4932[4] 5360[4] 5819[8] 6117[12]
Prime Defender *B W Hills* a104 116
6 ch h Bertolini(USA) —Arian Da (Superlative)
606a[10] 707a[8] 817a[9] 1007[2] *1206[4]* (1906) (2030) 3192[9] 3870[11] 4885a[5] 5276[4] 5744[12] 6608a[15]
Prime Exhibit *Richard Fahey* a106 102
5 b g Selkirk(USA) —First Exhibit (Machiavellian (USA))
887[6] ◆ 1008[2] 1900[22] 3146[24] *(3969)* 4576[19] 6177[14] 6721[6]
Primera Rossa *J S Moore* a45 52
4 ch m Needwood Blade—Meandering Rose (USA) (Irish River (FR))
138 140[6] 237[5] 6450[6] 7727[7]
Primevere (IRE) *Roger Charlton* a81
2 ch f Singspiel(IRE) —Tree Peony (Woodman (USA))
(6844) ◆
Primo De Vida (IRE) *Ralph Beckett* a76 60
3 b g Trade Fair—Rampage (Pivotal)
1178[13] *1490[2] 2258[2] 3325[2]* 4325[8]
Primo Lady *Gay Kelleway* a76 91
2 br f Lucky Story(USA) —Lady Natilda (First Trump)
(1043) 1819[3] (2095) 3070[9] 3453[4] 4458[9] 5036[8]
Primo Muscovado *Michael Mullineaux* a13
2 b c Primo Valentino(IRE) —Sugar Cube Treat (Lugana Beach)
4909[10] 6697[9] 6894[13]
Primo Way *Donal Nolan* a76 62
9 b g Primo Dominie—Waypoint (Cadeaux Genereux)
1098[7] 1717[7] 2670[8] 3147[5] 3531[9] 3707[6] 4189[4] 4585[10]
Primrose Bankes *Bill Turner* a68
3 b f Mark Of Esteem(IRE) —Lady Bankes (IRE) (Alzao (USA))
4282[7]
Prince Andjo (USA) *Declan Carroll* a43 46
4 b g Van Nistelrooy(USA) —Magic Flare (USA) (Danzatore (CAN))
1928[11] *2184[12]* 3223[11] 4173[4] *4434[7]*
Prince Apollo *Ian Williams* 96
5 b g Dansili—Mooring (Zafonic (USA))
1031[7] 4830[15] 5082[9] 5611[7] 6050[8] (6298) 6632[3]
Prince Bishop (IRE) *A Fabre* 118
3 ch c Dubawi(IRE) —North East Bay (USA) (Prospect Bay (CAN))
(6219a) (6974a)
Prince Blue *George Margarson* a39 36
3 b g Doyen(IRE) —Dixie D'Oats (Alhijaz)
5839[7] 6655[9] *7288[11] 7716[13]*
Prince Chaparral (IRE) *Patrick J Flynn* a91 92
4 b g High Chaparral(IRE) —Eilanden (IRE) (Akarad (FR))
6971a[9]
Prince Charlemagne (IRE) *Gary Moore* a75 79
7 br g King Charlemagne(USA) —Ciubanga (IRE) (Arazi (USA))
164[4] (263) 488[2] 688[6] 842[3] 989[5] 1454[3] (1816a)
Prince Fasliyev *Niels Petersen* a86 101
6 b g Fasliyev(USA) —Malaisienne (FR) (Saumarez)
511a[12] 2020a[5] 5350a[9]
Prince Freddie *Philip Kirby* 68
2 b c Red Ransom(USA) —Pitcroy (Unfuwain (USA))
3219[9] 4263[9] 5263[7] 5857[4] 6471[3]
Prince Golan (IRE) *Richard Price* a71 66
6 b g Golan(IRE) —Mohican Princess (Shirley Heights)
426[3] 2511[3] 2894[5] 4708[5] 5828[8]
Prince James *Michael Easterby* a75 54
3 b c Danroad(AUS) —Lawless Bridget (Alnasr Alwasheek)
4556[7] *(4908) 5647[10]* 6246[9] *6932[3]* ◆ 7148[5] ◆ *7332[2] 7628[4] (7841)*
Prince Jock (USA) *Tracey Collins* a70 87
3 b c Repent(USA) —My Special K'S (USA) (Tabasco Cat (USA))
4496a[7] 5571a[19]
Princely Hero (IRE) *Chris Gordon* a89 82
6 b g Royal Applause—Dalu (IRE) (Dancing Brave (USA))
1388[11]
Prince Namid *Jonathen de Giles* a70 79
8 b g Namid—Fen Princess (IRE) (Trojan Fen)
(829) 1044[4] 1482[10] 2234[6] 2415[5] 4839[10] 7298[12]
Prince Of Burma (IRE) *John Gosden* a85
2 b c Mujadil(USA) —Spinning Ruby (Pivotal)
7478[5] ◆ *(7551)*
Prince Of Dance *Jeremy Gask* 112
4 b h Danehill Dancer(IRE) —Princess Ellen (Tirol)
1531[9] 2118[8] 5554[6] 6147[11] 6806[5] 7060[10]
Prince Of Dreams *William Knight* a42 77
3 b g Sadler's Wells(USA) —Questina (FR) (Rainbow Quest (USA))
1851[4] 2585[2] ◆ 5387[6] *5752[5]* 6678[3] 7062[11]
Prince Of Fife (IRE) *Linda Perratt*
3 b g Chineur(FR) —Defined Feature (IRE) (Nabeel Dancer (USA))
1868[9] 5359[5]
Prince Of Johanne (IRE) *Tom Tate* a42 90
4 gr g Johannesburg(USA) —Paiute Princess (FR) (Darshaan)
1600[7] 1907[2] 2314[6] 2865[8] 3450[3] 3877[6] 4594[9] 6724[5] (6990)
Prince Of Nama (IRE) *Patrick Gilligan* a38
3 ch c Dubawi(IRE) —Zapping (IRE) (Lycius (USA))
1190[4] 4908[7] 6060[12]
Prince Of Passion (CAN) *Michael Dods* 52
2 ch c Roman Ruler(USA) —Rare Passion (CAN) (Out Of Place (USA))
3945[6]
Prince Of Sorrento *John Akehurst* a75 69
3 ch c Doyen(IRE) —Princess Galadriel (Magic Ring (IRE))
(107) 203[4] 2253[13] 2888[4] 3212[7] 3831[5] 4335[10] *4929[8]*
Prince Of Thebes (IRE) *Michael Attwater* a85 78
9 b g Desert Prince(IRE) —Persian Walk (FR) (Persian Bold)
23[2] (84) ◆ *315[5] 394[6] (657) 943[2] 1088[4] 1306[8]* 4057[5] 4265[2] 4756[6] 5142[7] 5750[10] 6252[2] 6430[5] 6851[8] 7115[3] 7421[4] 7597[11] 7724[9]
Princeofthedesert *Gary Woodward* 7
4 b g Nayef(USA) —Twilight Sonnet (Exit To Nowhere (USA))
4893[9] 5122[10]
Prince Of Vasa (IRE) *Michael Smith* a77 81
3 b g Kheleyf(USA) —Suzy Street (IRE) (Dancing Dissident (USA))
(1211) 1913[14] 4865[2] 5242[9] 5606[8]
Prince Picasso *Richard Fahey* a79 85
7 b g Lomitas—Auspicious (Shirley Heights)
239[8] 395[4] (996) 1101[10] (1720) 2313[3] 3195[18]
Prince Pippin (IRE) *Sean Curran* a27
4 b g King Charlemagne(USA) —Staploy (Deploy)
669[8]
Prince Pretender (FR) *J-P Gallorini* 82
3 b c Great Pretender(IRE) —Princesse Turgeon (FR) (Turgeon (USA))
2802a[21]
Prince Rhyddarch *Michael Dods* a18 62
5 b g Josr Algarhoud(IRE) —Nova Zembla (Young Ern)
6242[2] 6890[4]
Prince Rossi (IRE) *Andrew Price* a50 67
6 b g Royal Applause—Miss Rossi (Artaius (USA))
367[11] 855[8] 1543[6] 2920[7] *7023[12]*
Prince Sabaah (IRE) *Venetia Williams* a76 93
6 b g Spectrum(IRE) —Princess Sabaah (IRE) (Desert King (IRE))
220[6] 395[5]
Prince Shaun (IRE) *Doug Watson* a107 86
5 b g Acclamation—Style Parade (USA) (Diesis)
336a[7] 606a[2] 797a[4] 1021a[15]
Prince Siegfried (FR) *Saeed Bin Suroor* a89 116
4 b g Royal Applause—Intrum Morshaan (IRE) (Darshaan)
2470[4] 3632[2] 4139[6] (5590) 5951[4] 7237[2]
Princess Aliuska *Charles Smith* a34 57
5 b m Domedriver(IRE) —Aliuska (IRE) (Fijar Tango (FR))
2874[15] 4485[9] 4946[9] 5515[9] (6037) *6905[7] 7407[11]*
Princess Charlmane (IRE) *Colin Teague* a56 61
7 b m King Charlemagne(USA) —Bint Alreeys (Polish Precedent (USA))
1965[7] 2213[10] 4982[9] 5212[8]
Princess Dayna *Tom Dascombe* a57 60
2 b f Green Desert(USA) —Pilcomayo (IRE) (Rahy (USA))
3029[4] 3449[8] 4896[4] 5818[13]
Princesse Fleur *Michael Scudamore* 49
2 b f Grape Tree Road—Princesse Grec (FR) (Grand Tresor (FR))
3915[10] 5066[11]
Princess Eliza *Joanne Priest*
2 b f Fair Mix(IRE) —Mytton's Dream (Diktat)
3274[11] 4675[8]
Princess Emma *Richard Fahey* a40 59
3 b f Fantastic Light(USA) —Rosablanca (IRE) (Sinndar (IRE))
1927[5] 2379[P]
Princess Flame (GER) *Brendan Powell* a49 70
8 br m Tannenkonig(IRE) —Pacora (GER) (Lagunas)
114[6] 2586[5] 2952[8] 3294[9] 4328[4] 4676[4] 4991[3] (6272)
Princess Gail *Mark Brisbourne* 46
2 b f Ad Valorem(USA) —First Musical (First Trump)
3237[8] 3729[7] 4614[9]
Princess Haya (USA) *Carl O'Callaghan* 108
5 b m Street Cry(IRE) —Sally Slew (USA) (Slew City Slew (USA))
6604a[7]
Princess Izzy *Philip Kirby* 61
2 gr f Tale Of The Cat(USA) —Victory Spirit (USA) (Alphabet Soup (USA))
2616[7] 3237[3] 4233[7] 5332[7]
Princess Lexi (IRE) *Ian Williams* a18 58
3 ch f Rock Of Gibraltar(IRE) —Etaaq (IRE) (Sadler's Wells (USA))
936[12] 1394[10] (1971) (2780) 3390[6]
Princess Mandy (IRE) *Kevin Ryan* a54 48
3 gr f Desert Style(IRE) —Lady Fabiola (USA) (Open Forum (USA))
717[3] 993[11]
Princess Neenee (IRE) *Paul Green* 17
3 b f King's Best(USA) —Precedence (IRE) (Polish Precedent (USA))
4408[9] *6579[10]*
Princess Of Troy (IRE) *David Evans* a26 42
3 gr f Tiger Hill(IRE) —Actoris (USA) (Diesis)
1335[7] 1501[9] 1861[9] *7273[13] 7685[8]*
Princess Runner *Jeremy Gask* a38
3 b f Doyen(IRE) —Stop Press (USA) (Sharpen Up)
7288[10] 7489[7]
Princess Seren *Rod Millman* 48
3 b f King's Best(USA) —Gold Field (IRE) (Unfuwain (USA))
1431[11] 1881[10] 3478[5] ◆ 3957[3] 4281[7]
Princess Severus (IRE) *Ralph Beckett* 92
2 b f Barathea(IRE) —Wildsplash (USA) (Deputy Minister (CAN))
(4474) 5519[5]
Princess Shamal *John Jenkins* a55 55
3 b f Kheleyf(USA) —Gentle Dame (Kris)
215[6] 387[9] 581[6] 4210[4] 5206[7]
Princess Taylor *Patrick Gallagher* a103 103
6 ch m Singspiel(IRE) —Tapas En Bal (FR) (Mille Balles (FR))
335a[11] 712a[10] 1435a[9] *4887a[3]* 6604a[6]
Princess Valerina *Derek Haydn Jones* a80 87
6 ch m Beat Hollow—Heart So Blue (Dilum (USA))
250[8] 432[7] 767[12] 6207[8] 6812[14]
Prince Tamino *A Al Raihe* a100 110
7 b g Mozart(IRE) —Premiere Dance (IRE) (Loup Solitaire (USA))
336a[3] 437a[4] 604a[12]
Prince Titus (IRE) *Linda Stubbs* 60
2 b g Titus Livius(FR) —Lovere (St Jovite (USA))
4363[4] ◆ 6075[7]
Prince Valentine *Gary Moore* a56 53
9 b g My Best Valentine—Affaire De Coeur (Imperial Fling (USA))
(229) 389[9] 656[4] 847[6] 1441[10] 2198[8] 2456[4] 3056[8] 3291[5] 3715[4] 3982[4] 4738[2] 5655[4] 6860[4] 7038[9]
Prince Will I Am (USA) *Michelle Nihei* a111 107
3 ch r Victory Gallop(CAN) —Dyna's Dynamo (USA) (Dynaformer (USA))
7339a[10]
Prince Yarraman (IRE) *Jamie Osborne* a62 54
3 b c Chineur(FR) —Church Mice (IRE) (Petardia)
149[5] 283[5] 1495[6] 2200[3] 2359[6] 2878[4]
Principal Role (USA) *Henry Cecil* 104
3 b f Empire Maker(USA) —Interim (Sadler's Wells (USA))
1312[3] 1729[4] (2076) 3101[4] 6886[8]
Principe Caspian (ITY) *R Pecoraro*
2 b g Martino Alonso(IRE) —Selvetrana (IRE) (In The Wings)
7849a[15]

Principe Uromonte (IRE) *Ecurie Prince Rose* 89
4 ch g Talkin Man(CAN) —Pichola Lake (USA) (Quest For Fame)
2446a[9]

Print (IRE) *Mick Channon* a75 64
4 b g Exceed And Excel(AUS) —Hariya (IRE) (Shernazar)
(1064) 1634[10] 2009[11] 3083[13]

Priors Gold *Marcus Tregoning* 67
3 ch g Sakhee(USA) —Complimentary Pass (Danehill (USA))
4307[5] 5001[2] 5288[5]

Prison Cat (IRE) *Edward Vaughan* 25
2 b f Ivan Denisovich(IRE) —Elusive Kitty (USA) (Elusive Quality (USA))
1930[15] 1999[10] 2905[6]

Priti Fabulous (IRE) *Alan McCabe* a74 84
5 b m Invincible Spirit(IRE) —Flying Diva (Chief Singer)
7474 7679

Private Cowboy (IRE) *Michael Quinlan* 73
2 b c Danehill Dancer(IRE) —Dinka Raja (USA) (Woodman (USA))
5985[5] 6560[21] 6964[2]

Private Equity (IRE) *William Jarvis* a63 57
4 b m Haafhd—Profit Alert (IRE) (Alzao (USA))
4635 7777 1134[3] ◆ 7626[2]

Private Jet (FR) *H-A Pantall* 104
2 gr c Aussie Rules(USA) —Norwegian Princess (IRE) (Fairy King (USA))
5133a[4] 6702a[2] 7265a[6]

Private Joke *John Gosden* a73
3 b g Oasis Dream—Wink (Salse (USA))
7596[2] (7786) 7965[5]

Private Olley *John Akehurst* a70 44
3 ch c Exceed And Excel(AUS) —My Daisychain (Hector Protector (USA))
24[7] (233) 425[3] (807) 901[8] 2928[6] 3154[9] 5182[6] 5890[9] 6997[4]

Private Story (USA) *Richard Hannon* 100
3 b c Yes It's True(USA) —Said Privately (USA) (Private Account (USA))
1354[6] 2117[5] ◆ 2323[2] 3145[7] 6654[6] 6889[10]

Privy Speech (IRE) *Rae Guest* a64 17
3 ch f El Corredor(USA) —Privileged Speech (USA) (General Assembly (USA))
858[2] 4229[4] 5072[5] 5869[6] 6262[7]

Prizefighting (USA) *John Gosden* a85 105
3 ch g Smart Strike(CAN) —Allencat (USA) (Storm Cat (USA))
1313[6] 2226[2] 3014a[4] 3822[7] 5853[5] 6506[8]

Prize Point *Jim Boyle* a58 67
4 ch g Bahamian Bounty—Golden Symbol (Wolfhound (USA))
(7763)

Proci Road (FR) *M Drean* a67 61
7 b h Grape Tree Road—Proci Bella (FR) (Procida (USA))
460a[3]

Proclaim *Saeed Bin Suroor* a82 99
4 b g Noverre(USA) —Pescara (IRE) (Common Grounds)
413a[6]

Proenza (USA) *Brian Meehan* a54 37
2 b f Rahy(USA) —Sunny Nature (Sadler's Wells (USA))
5156[5] 5893[9] 6441[13]

Professor John (IRE) *Ian Wood* a75 82
3 b g Haafhd—Dancing Flower (IRE) (Compton Place)
3481[5] 3916[5] 7323[6] ◆ 7685[2] 7814[4] 7959a[2]

Proficiency *Sue Bradburne* 64
5 gr m El Prado(IRE) —Talent Quest (IRE) (Rainbow Quest (USA))
6028[8]

Profit's Reality (IRE) *Michael Attwater* a87 82
8 br g Key Of Luck(USA) —Teacher Preacher (IRE) (Taufan (USA))
300[3] 526[6] 3239[5] 3812[2] 4891[5] 5235[8]

Profligate (IRE) *William Jarvis* a71 68
3 b f Soviet Star(USA) —Profit Alert (IRE) (Alzao (USA))
2548[6] 2974[8] ◆ 3484[2] 5391[8] 6632[4] 7162[3] 7389[8]

Profondo Rosso (IRE) *Sir Michael Stoute* 83
2 b g Red Ransom(USA) —Desert Beauty (IRE) (Green Desert (USA))
4096[4] ◆ 4614[2] (5413) 6505[7]

Profound Beauty (IRE) *D K Weld* 116
6 b m Danehill(USA) —Diamond Trim (IRE) (Highest Honor (FR))
(2571a) 3470a[2] (4081a) (4769a) 5976a[2] ◆ 7291a[17]

Profumo D'Irlanda (IRE) *R Monaco*
2 b c Captain Rio—Gitchee Gumee Rose (IRE) (Paris House)
7850a[6]

Progress (IRE) *Jeremy Noseda* a71 75
3 br f Green Desert(USA) —Mille (Dubai Millennium)
(744) ◆ 1045[3] 3441[8] (5713) 6310[7]

Prohibit *Robert Cowell* a107 112
5 b g Oasis Dream—Well Warned (Warning)
336a[6] 434a[4] 604a[9] (1014) 1727[10] 2019a[4] 3193[16] 3461[2] ◆ 3891[3] 4401[4] 4576[3] (4814) 5512[2] (5851) ◆ 6194[3] 6608a[6]

Prohibition (IRE) *Gary Moore* a79 79
4 b g Danehill Dancer(IRE) —Crumpetsfortea (IRE) (Henbit (USA))
16[5] 115[4] 245[9] 2443[4] 2991[12] 3582[8] 6428[10] 7561[5]

Promenadia *Roger Charlton* 58
2 b f Beat Hollow—Esplanade (Danehill (USA))
6468[9] 7010[5]

Prompter *Michael Bell* 109
3 b g Motivator—Penny Cross (Efisio)
1473[2] 1858[7] 4068[5] 5590[3] 6387[2] 6736[7] 7350[6]

Proper Charlie *William Knight* 72
2 b c Cadeaux Genereux—Ring Of Love (Magic Ring (IRE))
3991[5] 4549[4] 5372[9] 6145[4]

Proper Littlemadam *Christopher Kellett* a58 68
3 b f Statue Of Liberty(USA) —Aly McBe (USA) (Alydeed (CAN))
1175[6] 1456[7] 1795[10] 2418[6] 3359[13]

Prophet In A Dream *Mick Channon* a71 72
2 b g Fath(USA) —Princess Dariyba (IRE) (Victory Note (USA))
1351[7] (1632) 2082[4] 2177[6] 3596[7] 4020[4] 4429[2] 4801[4] 5177[3] 6162[4] 6435[3] (6673) ◆ 6988[3] 7050[5] 7116[2]

Proponent (IRE) *Roger Charlton* a91 104
6 b g Peintre Celebre(USA) —Pont Audemer (USA) (Chief's Crown (USA))
334a[8] 632a[7] 2444[5] 3069[5] 4537[4] 5247[3] 6562[9] 7100[7]

Prospectorous (IRE) *J P Dempsey* a91 80
6 b g Monashee Mountain(USA) —Nocturne In March (IRE) (Dolphin Street (FR))
6910a[2]

Prospect Wells (FR) *Howard Johnson* 107
5 b g Sadler's Wells(USA) —Brooklyn's Dance (FR) (Shirley Heights)
(3240) ◆ 5220[19] 7350[11]

Protaras (USA) *Henry Cecil* 82
3 bb c Lemon Drop Kid(USA) —Seven Moons (JPN) (Sunday Silence (USA))
1268[2] 6876[6] 7282[2]

Protector (SAF) *Terry Clement* a55 90
9 b g Kilconnel(USA) —Mufski (SAF) (Al Mufti (USA))
1032[10] 1688[9] 2856[4] 2982[5] 6625[10] 7092[11] 7238[17]

Protiva *Karen George* a62 62
4 ch m Deportivo—Prowse (USA) (King Of Kings (IRE))
7801[1]

Proud Chieftain *Hugh Collingridge* a50 46
2 b g Sleeping Indian—Skimra (Hernando (FR))
6883[17] 7248[8]

Proud Linus (USA) *Declan Carroll* a52 92
5 b g Proud Citizen(USA) —Radcliffe Yard (USA) (Boston Harbor (USA))
242[9] 3181[1] 520[5]

Proud Times (USA) *Alan Swinbank* a91 90
4 b g Proud Citizen(USA) —Laura's Pistolette (USA) (Big Pistol (USA))
1720[4] 2060[9] (2723) 3319[10] 4086[3] (4891) 5723[6] 6362[4] 7196[5] 7698[4]

Proud Tuscan *Alan McCabe* a24 47
3 b c Proud Citizen(USA) —Tuscany Gal (USA) (Gilded Time (USA))
2121[10] 4205[7] 4383[6] 5171[9] 7129[5]

Proust (FR) *B De Montzey* 50
3 gr g Ocean Of Wisdom(USA) —Lady Time (FR) (Orpen (USA))
450a[5]

Provide (IRE) *D Gambarota* 60
2 b g Holy Roman Emperor(IRE) —Uliana (USA) (Darshaan)
7850a[18]

Proviso *William Mott* a114 114
5 b m Dansili—Binche (USA) (Woodman (USA))
(6757a) 7364a[7]

Provost *Michael Easterby* a66 57
6 ch g Danehill Dancer(IRE) —Dixielake (IRE) (Lake Coniston (IRE))
298[8] 715[7] (940) 1204[6] 2527[9] 2788[10] (3521) 4428[2] 4897[9] 6165[9] 7611[4]

Psalm Twentythree *John McShane* 25
4 b g Josr Algarhoud(IRE) —Cadeau Speciale (Cadeaux Genereux)
5478[5] 6244[8] 6716[11]

Psy Chic (FR) *Robert Collet* a91 96
6 b g Munir—Psycadelic (FR) (Midyan (USA))
(458a) 640a[6] 743a[5] 2446a[3]

Psychic Ability (USA) *Saeed Bin Suroor* a62 104
3 b c Kingmambo(USA) —Speed Of Thought (USA) (Broad Brush (USA))
(4302) 4841[2] 5511[9] (5970) (6877)

Psychic's Dream *Marco Botti* a65
2 b f Oasis Dream—Psychic (IRE) (Alhaarth (IRE))
7447[5] 7681[2]

Psychopathicsandra (IRE) *Joss Saville* 35
3 ch f Reel Buddy(USA) —Waltzing Star (IRE) (Danehill (USA))
2449[9] 3027[9] 5024[11]

Ptolomeos *Sean Regan* a51 60
7 b g Kayf Tara—Lucy Tufty (Vin St Benet)
5051[6] (5565) 6375[11] 6999[14] 7330[8]

Public Image *Jamie Poulton* a49 29
4 b m Bahamian Bounty—Shouting The Odds (IRE) (Victory Note (USA))
5921[0] 986[6] 6853[9] 7763[5] 7989[4]

Puddle Duck *Kevin Ryan* 89
2 bb c Pastoral Pursuits—Poyle Caitlin (IRE) (Bachir (IRE))
1646[4] (1886) 3598[5] (3859) 4578[5] 4851[3] (5187)

Puff (IRE) *Ralph Beckett* a80 109
3 b f Camacho—Kelsey Rose (Most Welcome)
(1384) 3143[10] 4540[6] 6351[5]

Pugilist *Kim Bailey* a54 75
8 b g Fraam—Travel Mystery (Godswalk (USA))
148[9] 322[5]

Pugnacity *Dianne Sayer* a36 41
6 b m Zilzal(USA) —Attention Seeker (USA) (Exbourne (USA))
3223[9]

Puitin *Michael Madgwick* a43
5 b g Red Ransom(USA) —Pagoda (FR) (Sadler's Wells (USA))
421[8]

Pullyourfingerout (IRE) *Brendan Powell* a55 76
3 b g Indian Haven—Sandomierz (IRE) (Nordico (USA))
1086[11] 1433[3] 1975[6] 2289[6] 2953[4] 3954[4] 4380[3]

Pumpkinette (FR) *C Ferland*
2 b f Ski Chief(USA) —Land Bridge (FR) (Bering)
6589a[0]

Puncher Clynch (IRE) *J S Bolger* a94 103
3 b c Azamour(IRE) —Dance Troupe (Rainbow Quest (USA))
(1414a) 3491a[8]

Punching *Conor Dore* a81 65
6 b g Kyllachy—Candescent (Machiavellian (USA))
703[3] 750[5] 859[2] (892) 914[2] 1147[3] 1276[5] 1884[3] 3064[3] 4435[4] 4684[4] 5454[9] 7847[3] (7906) 7956[6]

Punta Galera (IRE) *Paul Green* a71 40
7 br g Zafonic(USA) —Kobalt Sea (FR) (Akarad (FR))
2902[10]

Punt Road (IRE) *Lee Smyth* a38 6
2 gr c Royal Applause—Ardea Brave (IRE) (Chester House (USA))
3945[10] 6211[7]

Pure Crystal *Michael Quinlan* a61 57
4 ch m Dubai Destination(USA) —Crystal Flute (Lycius (USA))
(3278) 3819[4] 3967[9]

Purely By Chance *Jeff Pearce* a59 58
5 b m Galileo(IRE) —Sioux Chef (Be My Chief (USA))
(164) 263[6] 748[7] 982[4] 1283[3] 3084[4] 3324[5] 3819[2] 4441[2]

Pure Nostalgia (IRE) *Howard Johnson* 63
3 ch f Choisir(AUS) —Montmartre (IRE) (Grand Lodge (USA))
2203[3] 2700[3] 3226[12] 3668[5] 4342[11]

Pure Princess (IRE) *Pat Phelan* 15
2 b f Desert Style(IRE) —I'Ll Be Waiting (Vettori (IRE))
2338[14] 2749[11]

Purification (IRE) *John Gosden* 87
2 b c Hurricane Run(IRE) —Ceanothus (IRE) (Bluebird (USA))
2932[7] 6365[2]

Purkab *Jim Goldie* 60
2 ch g Intikhab(USA) —Pure Misk (Rainbow Quest (USA))
3199[4] 4702[8] 5332[6] 6174[6]

Purple (AUS) *Peter Snowden* 109
5 br m Commands(AUS) —Lady Viola (NZ) (Zabeel (NZ))
6946a[2]

Purple Gallery (IRE) *J S Moore* a75 84
3 br g Whipper(USA) —Daftara (IRE) (Caerleon (USA))
180[3] (356) 522[2] 2025[6] 2644[6] 3212[2] 4325[3] (4732) 5415[2] 5750[13] 6467[5] 6771[3] 6904[7]

Purple Glow (IRE) *J S Bolger* 95
2 b f Orientate(USA) —Napping (USA) (Danzig (USA))
2352a[2] 3070[6] 3421a[8]

Purple Heart (IRE) *A P O'Brien* a74 94
3 b c Sadler's Wells(USA) —Brigid (USA) (Irish River (FR))
2354a[12]

Purple Kiss (USA) *R Menichetti* 21
4 ch m Monashee Mountain(USA) —Unbridled Princess (USA) (Unbridled's Song (USA))
1419a[17]

Purple Land (USA) *J S Bolger* a75 90
3 b g Tiznow(USA) —Extraterrestral (USA) (Storm Bird (CAN))
1038a[8] 2570a[5]

Purple Moon (IRE) *Luca Cumani* 116
7 ch g Galileo(IRE) —Vanishing Prairie (USA) (Alysheba (USA))
1382[7] ◆ 2097[2] 3102[3] 4506[3]

Purple Sage (IRE) *F Nass* a90 103
4 b m Danehill Dancer(IRE) —Kylemore (IRE) (Sadler's Wells (USA))
439a[5] 711a[4] 823a[4]

Pursestrings *Laura Mongan* a56 38
3 b f Red Ransom(USA) —New Assembly (IRE) (Machiavellian (USA))
1431[12] 2189[11] 5233[5] 6080[9] 7570[8]

Pursuing *Bryan Smart* 53
2 b f Rainbow Quest(USA) —Kineta (USA) (Miswaki (USA))
6964[3] 7235[11]

Pursuit Of Gold *John Best* a51 60
3 b f Pastoral Pursuits—Sheer Gold (USA) (Cutlass (USA))
745[7] 993[7]

Pursuit Of Reason *Gary Moore* a58 58
3 b f Lomitas—Flying Carpet (Barathea (IRE))
5001[3] 5665[10] 6250[6]

Purus (IRE) *Roger Teal* a81 85
8 b g Night Shift(USA) —Pariana (USA) (Bering)
1170[10] 1634[3] 2129[10] 2750[10] 3338[7] 3580[5]

Pusey Street Lady *John Gallagher* a95 102
6 b m Averti(IRE) —Pusey Street Girl (Gildoran)
1007[12] 1349[5] 1688[15] 1903[6] 2119[8] 2748[13] 2929[7] 3346[8]

Push Me (IRE) *John A Quinn* a64 64
3 gr f Verglas(IRE) —Gilda Lilly (USA) (War Chant (USA))
35[3] ◆ 4563a[3]

Pushy Princess *Christopher Kellett*
5 ch m Mark Of Esteem(IRE) —Galava (CAN) (Graustark)
3765[12]

Putin (IRE) *Derek Haydn Jones* 68
2 b g Fasliyev(USA) —Consignia (IRE) (Definite Article)
3735[12] 4421[2] 4902[12] 6811[6] 6988[8]

Putra One (IRE) *Michael Jarvis* a85 86
4 b g Danehill Dancer(IRE) —Veronica Cooper (IRE) (Kahyasi)
1388[6] (1780) 2865[7] 4841[9]

Puttingonthestyle (IRE) *Richard Hannon* a71 71
2 b c Desert Style(IRE) —Auriga (Belmez (USA))
6153[6] ◆ 6442[2] 7020[4]

Puy D'Arnac (FR) *Alan Swinbank* a76 81
7 b g Acteur Francais(USA) —Chaumeil (FR) (Mad Captain)
1101[6] ◆ 1916[3] 4785[3] 5296[6] 6109[2] 7284[4]

Puzzled (IRE) *Andrew Oliver* 65
2 ch f Peintre Celebre(USA) —Classic Park (Robellino (USA))
7256a[4] ◆

Puzzlemaster *Hughie Morrison* a74 89
4 ch g Lomitas—Norcroft Joy (Rock Hopper)
205[9] 1736[9]

Pycian *Linda Stubbs* 77
3 b g Mark Of Esteem(IRE) —Beejay (Piccolo)
1718[7] 3394[7] 4365[6] 5211[4] 5758[14]

Pyjoma *Julia Feilden* 26
3 ch f Rainbow Quest(USA) —In Luck (In The Wings)
6624[9]

Pyrenean *James Given* a62 35
2 b f Mull Of Kintyre(USA) —Gabacha (USA) (Woodman (USA))
6892[8] 7302[11] 7602[4] 7910[6]

Pyrrha *Chris Wall* 111
4 b m Pyrus(USA) —Demeter (USA) (Diesis)
(1908) 3067[10] 4540[3]

Pyrus Time (IRE) *Ronald Harris* a76 72
4 b g Pyrus(USA) —Spot In Time (Mtoto)
162[5] 929[2] 1587[5] 1839[4] 2236[8] 2966[2]

Pytheas (USA) *Michael Attwater* a79 79
3 b g Seeking The Gold(USA) —Neptune's Bride (USA) (Bering)
2479[7] 2935[13] 3816[3]

Qalahari (IRE) *Denis Coakley* a83 87
4 b m Bahri(USA) —Daqtora (Dr Devious (IRE))
1383[19] 4847[2] 5529[7] 5919[4] 6409a[10] 7114[4] 7521[3]

Qamar *Saeed Bin Suroor* a87 73
3 gr c Pivotal—Karliyna (IRE) (Rainbow Quest (USA))
5623[5] (6124)

Qanateer (IRE) *Gerard Butler* 46
2 b f Iffraaj—Jumilla (USA) (El Gran Senor (USA))
2088[6]

Qanoon (USA) *William Haggas* 89
3 ch g Afleet Alex(USA) —Solvig (USA) (Caerleon (USA))
(2548) ◆ 3196[5] 3846[4] 5121[2] 5904[7]

Qaraaba *Seamus Durack* a54 81
3 b f Shamardal(USA) —Mokaraba (Unfuwain (USA))
7915[10]

Qaraqum (USA) *Denis Coakley* a52 58
3 bb f Vindication(USA) —Code Of Ethics (USA) (Honour And Glory (USA))
1659[9] 2753[12] 4281[2] 4958[8] 5469[3]

Qenaa *Mark Johnston* 74
2 b f Royal Applause—In The Woods (You And I (USA))
2930[6] 4471[2] 6704[5]

Quadra Hop (IRE) *Bryn Palling* a48 49
2 ch c Compton Place—Yding (IRE) (Danehill (USA))
2819[8] 4432[6] 7268[5]

Quadrifolio *Paul Green* a45 49
4 b g Key Of Luck(USA) —Berkeley Note (IRE) (Victory Note (USA))
1503[5] 2629[6] 2902[3] 3360[6] 3669[11] 4914[12] 7449[8]

Quadrille *Richard Hannon* a95 111
3 b g Danehill Dancer(IRE) —Fictitious (Machiavellian (USA))
1311[2] (2045) ◆ 3104[2] 4420a[8]

Quaestor (IRE) *Tom Dascombe* a78 79
3 b g Antonius Pius(USA) —Lucky Oakwood (USA) (Elmaamul (USA))
900[7] 1052[6] 1269[10] 3680[9] 4989[12] 6168[3] 6903[5] 7168[11]

Quahadi (IRE) *Chris Gordon* a41
4 b g Montjeu(IRE) —Kicking Bird (FR) (Darshaan)
7489[8] 7596[5] 7757[8]

Quai D'Orsay *Saeed Bin Suroor* a90 102
4 ch h Sulamani(IRE) —Entente Cordiale (USA) (Affirmed (USA))
418a[8] 605a[7]

Quails Hollow (IRE) *William Haggas* 49
2 b c Beat Hollow—Bloemfontain (IRE) (Cape Cross (IRE))
6532[10]

Quaker Parrot *Tom Dascombe* a80 81
3 ch f Compton Place—Little Greenbird (Ardkinglass)
2618[12] 3208[9] 3628[8] 4127[10] 5482[7]

Qualitas *Michael Easterby* a48 57
4 b g Orpen(USA) —Kiss Me Kate (Aragon)
249[6]

Quality Art (USA) *Gary Moore* a74 60
2 b g Elusive Quality(USA) —Katherine Seymour (Green Desert (USA))
2930[5] 7595[2] 7858[2]

Quality Guitar (BRZ) *Givanildo Duarte* 64
4 b h Principe Taio(BRZ) —La Guita (BRZ) (New Ghadeer (BRZ))
6017a[11]

Quality Mover (USA) *David Simcock* a63 68
3 bb f Elusive Quality(USA) —Katherine Seymour (Green Desert (USA))
2478[7] 3662[4] 5654[9] 5986[2] 6527[7] 7038[6]

Quality Road (USA) *Todd Pletcher* a130
4 b h Elusive Quality(USA) —Kobla (USA) (Strawberry Road (AUS))
4855a[2] (5780a) 7367a[12]

Quanah Parker (IRE) *Richard Whitaker* a76 94
4 b g Namid—Uncertain Affair (IRE) (Darshaan)
2508[8] 2971[13] 3448[10] 4154[8] 5435[8] 6366[4] 7403[9] 7878[3]

Quarante Deux (USA) *Gerard Butler* a80 80
4 b g Fusaichi Pegasus(USA) —Lahinch (IRE) (Danehill Dancer (IRE))
(226) 3079[3] ◆ 3764[4] ◆ 4405[3] 4686[6] 5868[8] 6202[4]

Quarrel (USA) *William Haggas* a91 106
3 rg g Maria's Mon(USA) —Gender Dance (USA) (Miesque's Son (USA))
2537[7] 3066[13] 4574[9] 5143[7] 5854[10] 6321[13] 6739[14] 7238[15]

Quarrymount *Chris Gordon* a43
9 b g Polar Falcon(USA) —Quilt (Terimon)
748[12]

Quartier Latin (ARG) *Doug Watson* a97 72
4 br c Orpen(USA) —Queen's Bench (ARG) (Southern Halo (USA))
608a[10]

Quartz D'Anjou (FR) *Pat Phelan* a13
6 b m Ungaro(GER) —Kiliane (FR) (Chamberlin (FR))
4229[13]

Quartz Jem (IRE) *Mme Pia Brandt* 99
6 b g Sakhee(USA) —Erinys (FR) (Kendor (FR))
3099a[11]

Quasi Congaree (GER) *Ian Wood* a85 81
4 ch g Congaree(USA) —Queens Wild (USA) (Spectacular Bid (USA))
(1044) 1258[12] (1848) 2872[4] 3779[2] 4225[6] 4551[3] 6798[8] 7319[2] 7573[9] 7782[2] 8016[6]

Qudwah (IRE) *Michael Jarvis* a81 87
3 b f Acclamation—Almond Flower (IRE) (Alzao (USA))
1355[2] 1861[6] (3808) 4231[6] 6798[3]

Que Belle (IRE) *Tom Dascombe* a41
3 b f Hawk Wing(USA) —Enaya (Caerleon (USA))
128[5] 238[6] ◆ 372[9]

Queen Andromache (USA) *John Queally* a73 80
4 gr m Distorted Humor(USA) —Artist's Studio (USA) (Bertrando (USA))
7589a[9]

Queen Carmel (IRE) *Brian Meehan* a33 8
2 ch f Noverre(USA) —Queen Margrethe (Grand Lodge (USA))
6804[11] 7312[9]

Queenie's Star (IRE) *Michael Attwater* a55 44
3 b f Arakan(USA) —Starway To Heaven (ITY) (Nordance (USA))
2968[8] 4397[9] 5028[4] 5669[11] 6672[10] 6865[2] 7717[10] 7829[7]

Queen Of Cash (IRE) *Hughie Morrison* a75 54
2 b f Ad Valorem(USA) —Warrior Wings (Indian Ridge)
4658[6] 5255[8] 5643[2] (7313) 7395[2]

Queen Of Mean *John Gosden* 86
3 b f Pivotal—Tyranny (Machiavellian (USA))
(4966) 5883[9]

Queen Of Spain (IRE) *A P O'Brien* 91
2 b f Holy Roman Emperor(IRE) —Starlight Dreams (USA) (Black Tie Affair)
3141[7] 4356[6] 5246[6] 5567a[8] 6157[4] 6559[12]

Queen Of Thebes (IRE) *Sylvester Kirk* a63 65
4 b m Bahri(USA) —Sopran Marida (IRE) (Darshaan)
2726[8] 2967[10] 3526[6] 3762[10] 4434[11] 4689[11]

Queen Of Troy (IRE) *A P O'Brien* a88 93
3 b f Storm Cat(USA) —Warrior Queen (USA) (Quiet American (USA))
1036a[7] 1787a[12] 1952a[6] 2370a[19] 2912a[10] 3571a[8] 4269a[10]

Queen Of Wands *Hughie Morrison* 72
3 b f Sakhee(USA) —Maid To Treasure (IRE) (Rainbow Quest (USA))
1432[3] 1778[6] 3513[10] (4058) 5149[4] 5654[3]

Queen O'The Desert (IRE) *Andrew Balding* 69
2 b f Green Desert(USA) —Al Dhahab (USA) (Seeking The Gold (USA))
4095[15] 5527[5] 6157[7] 6722[7]

Queen Ranavola (USA) *John Best* 50
3 bb f Medaglia D'Oro(USA) —Hour Regal Lady (USA) (Crafty Prospector (USA))
3738[7] 4028[7] 4205[12]

Queen's Choice (IRE) *Anabel L M King* 29
2 b f Choisir(AUS) —Queen Of Fibres (IRE) (Scenic)
6323[5]

Queen's Envoy *Luca Cumani* a78 73
3 b f King's Best(USA) —Allied Cause (Giant's Causeway (USA))
2478[O] 3157[2] 4250[7] 5652[5]

Queen's Grace *Hughie Morrison* 100
3 ch f Bahamian Bounty—Palace Affair (Pursuit Of Love)
1312[10] 1908[4] 4616[10] 5120[13]

Queen's Scholar (USA) *Mark Johnston* 66
3 b f Street Cry(IRE) —Clever Dorothy (USA) (Clever Trick (USA))
2290[8] 2658[3] 2998[7] 3500[3] 4061[2] 4335[5] 4951[5] 5654[4] 6266[5]

Queen's Silk *Richard Hannon* 67
2 b f Barathea(IRE) —Queen Of Africa (USA) (Peintre Celebre (USA))
4317[6]

Queens Troop *Dean Ivory* 10
2 ch f Iceman—Ivory's Joy (Tina's Pet)
6986[10]

Querari (GER) *A Wohler* 121
4 bb h Oasis Dream—Quetena (GER) (Acatenango (GER))
1251a[6] (2152a) 4418a[9] 5542a[10]

Querido (GER) *Gary Brown* a75 57
6 b g Acatenango(GER) —Quest Of Fire (FR) (Rainbow Quest (USA))
407[5] (816) 898[8] (7200) (7449) ◆ (7919) ◆

Querry Boy (FR) *H-A Pantall* a91 91
3 b g Equerry(USA) —Goldy Honor (FR) (Highest Honor (FR))
741a[2]

Quest For Success (IRE) *Richard Fahey* a82 104
5 b g Noverre(USA) —Divine Pursuit (Kris)
1174[5] 1573[3] 4191[5] 4616[2] 5095[5] ◆ 5183[3] 5944[13] 6177[13] (6241) 6508[3] 6752[6] 7060[14] 7348[10]

Questi Amori (IRE) *M Guarnieri* 86
3 gr c Choisir(AUS) —Light And Airy (Linamix (FR))
7370a[12]

Questioning (IRE) *John Gosden* a80 91
2 b c Elusive Quality(USA) —Am I (USA) (Thunder Gulch (USA))
(4838) ◆ 6560[5] ◆

Questionnaire (IRE) *Nicky Vaughan* a52 53
2 b f Iffraaj—Kobalt Sea (FR) (Akarad (FR))
6722[4] 7268[7] 7447[8]

Question Times *Peter Chapple-Hyam* 96
2 b f Shamardal(USA) —Forever Times (So Factual (USA))
5509[3] 6150[4] 7204[2]

Quick Deal (USA) *John Gosden* a50 59
3 b g Proud Citizen(USA) —Fair Settlement (USA) (Easy Goer (USA))
2220[5] 2684[10] 3428[5] 4022[8] 4764[10]

Quick Enough (USA) *Doug O'Neill* 113
6 bb g High Brite(USA) —Donna B. Quick (USA) (Moscow Ballet (USA))
7362a[10]

Quick Reaction *Richard Hannon* 86
3 b g Elusive Quality(USA) —Arutua (USA) (Riverman (USA))
(1475) 2254[2] 2742[6]

Quick Release (IRE) *Sven Christensen* a91 78
5 b h Red Ransom(USA) —Set The Mood (USA) (Dixie Brass (USA))
29[2] 197[2] 2020a[2]

Quick Single (USA) *Phil McEntee* a39 66
4 bb g Doneraile Court(USA) —Summer Strike (USA) (Smart Strike (CAN))
8024[11]

Quicks The Word *Tom Cuthbert* a28 49
10 b g Sri Pekan(USA) —Fast Tempo (IRE) (Statoblest)
2854[14]

Quick Wit *Saeed Bin Suroor* a111 104
3 b c Oasis Dream—Roo (Rudimentary (USA))
(6467) ◆ (7187) ◆

Qui Danse (FR) *Mlle S Sourd* a42
6 ch m Agent Bleu(FR) —Stephanotis (FR) (Saint Estephe (FR))
460a[6]

Quiet *Roger Charlton* 93
3 ch f Observatory(USA) —Quandary (USA) (Blushing Groom (FR))
2542[5] 3457[10]

Quiet Mountain (IRE) *Ollie Pears* a75 68
5 ch g Monashee Mountain(USA) —Shalstayholy (IRE) (Shalford (IRE))
189[4] 378[6] 937[4] (1193) (1574) (2866)

Quiet Oasis (IRE) *Brian Meehan* a84 100
2 b f Oasis Dream—Silent Heir (AUS) (Sunday Silence (USA))
4844[3] ◆ (5721) 6401a[4] 7340a[7]

Quijano (GER) *P Schiergen* 119
8 ch g Acatenango(GER) —Quila (IRE) (Unfuwain (USA))
516a[3] 799a[7] 1026a[12] 3019a[4] 4164a[3] 5132a[4] 5806a[2] 6410a[3] 6977a[7]

Quilboquet (BRZ) *Lennart Reuterskiold Jr* a83 99
7 b h Jules(USA) —Greystoke (BRZ) (Tokatee (USA))
2020a[6] 3934a[8]

Quince (IRE) *Jeff Pearce* a70 75
7 b g Fruits Of Love(USA) —Where's Charlotte (Sure Blade (USA))
148[3] 293[3] 488[3] 735[3] 852[5] 923[2] 1592[6] 2388[4] 2604[5] 3608[4] 4498[7] 4689[2] 4980[5] 6669[4] 7039[8] 7157[10]

Quinindo (GER) *A Wohler* 91
2 b c Monsun(GER) —Quebrada (IRE) (Devil's Bag (USA))
7456a[5]

Quinmaster (USA) *M Halford* a102 99
8 gr g Linamix(FR) —Sherkiya (IRE) (Goldneyev (USA))
6907a[14] 7816a[5]

Quinsman *J S Moore* a85 76
4 b g Singspiel(IRE) —Penny Cross (Efisio)
323[2] (395) ◆ 546[2] ◆ 636[6] 3329[7] 4400[8] 5922[2] 6331[7] 6715[4] (7011)

Quiquillo (USA) *David Evans* a62 71
4 ch m Cape Canaveral(USA) —Only Seventeen (USA) (Exploit (USA))
1843[6] 2410[2] 3853[3] 4329[5] 5654[7]

Quitao (GER) *P Monteith* 41
3 b g Monsun(GER) —Quest Of Fire (FR) (Rainbow Quest (USA))
1705[9] 2697[13] 3242[5] 4800[6] 5437[11] 6032[11]

Quite A Catch (IRE) *Jonathan Portman* a53 62
2 b g Camacho—Dear Catch (IRE) (Bluebird (USA))
3349[5] 3769[8] 6994[9]

Quite A Handful (USA) *Andrew Hansen* a97 104
4 ch h Mutakddim(USA) —Silent Queen (USA) (King Of Kings (IRE))
5321a[9]

Quite Sparky *Tom Tate* 74
3 b g Lucky Story(USA) —Imperialistic (IRE) (Imperial Ballet (IRE))
2425[4] 2837[8] 3554[2] 4197[6]

Quiza Quiza Quiza *L Riccardi* 103
4 b m Golden Snake(USA) —Quiz Chow (ITY) (Pelder (IRE))
7109a[5]

Quiz Mistress *Gerard Butler* a75 72
2 ch f Doyen(IRE) —Seren Quest (Rainbow Quest (USA))
6883[7] (7452)

Qushchi *William Jarvis* 75
2 b f Encosta De Lago(AUS) —La Persiana (Daylami (IRE))
6688[3] (7232)

Raahin (IRE) *Sir Michael Stoute* 69
2 b c Oasis Dream—Sparkle Of Stones (FR) (Sadler's Wells (USA))
6827[5]

Raajih *John Gosden* 62
2 gr c Dalakhani(IRE) —Thakafaat (IRE) (Unfuwain (USA))
6873[6]

Rabbie Burns *Valentine Donoghue* a34
3 b g Dansili—Illusory (Kings Lake (USA))
1425[15] 1868[8] 7310[7]

Rabbit Fighter (IRE) *Derek Shaw* a71 45
6 ch g Observatory(USA) —Furnish (Green Desert (USA))
727[6] ◆ 968[8] 1072[F]

Raccoon (IRE) *Ruth Carr* 81
10 b g Raphane(USA) —Kunucu (IRE) (Bluebird (USA))
1965[3] 2294[4] 2695[7] 3497[5] 4245[2] 4672[2] 5023[6] 5422[8] 5735[4]

Racecar Rhapsody (USA) *Gary Moore* a79
5 b h Tale Of The Cat(USA) —Reflect The Music (USA) (A.P. Indy (USA))
1665[9]

Rachel Alexandra (USA) *Steven Asmussen* a129
4 b m Medaglia D'Oro(USA) —Lotta Kim (USA) (Roar (USA))
5578a[2]

Racy *Sir Michael Stoute* a85 95
3 b g Medicean—Soar (Danzero (AUS))
1315[4] ◆ 1701[4] 2960[2] 3218[7]

Rada Angel (IRE) *Mme M Bollack-Badel* a86 96
3 b f Le Vie Dei Colori—Red Letter (Sri Pekan (USA))
7545a[3]

Raddy 'Ell Pauline (IRE) *Kevin Ryan* a88 85
3 ch f Dubawi(IRE) —Run For Me (IRE) (Danehill (USA))
(489) 1019[6] 1376[10] 1836[11]

Radharcnafarraige (IRE) *J S Bolger* 99
2 b f Distorted Humor(USA) —Extraterrestral (USA) (Storm Bird (CAN))
(2828a) ◆ 3141[4] 3792[4]

Radiant Dream *Pat Eddery* a27
2 b f Oasis Dream—Krisia (Kris)
7608[7]

Radiator Rooney (IRE) *Patrick Morris* a66 58
7 br g Elnadim(USA) —Queen Of The May (IRE) (Nicolotte)
(195) 351[7] 525[6] 1166[4] 1470[9] 1596[3] (2021) 2310[8] 2485[7] 3057[7] 7334[12] 7860[4] 7972[8] 8035[5]

Radio Wave *John Gosden* 76
3 ch f Dalakhani(IRE) —Tuning (Rainbow Quest (USA))
2092[2] 2585[7]

Radler (FR) *E Galli* 90
4 ch g Tertullian(USA) —Rosa Brett (ITY) (Green Tune (USA))
1944a[8]

Rafella (IRE) *Ralph Beckett* a76 67
2 br f Iffraaj—Cappella (IRE) (College Chapel)
1972[8] 2338[11] 2951[8] (4029) 5452[8] 5882[10] 6809[8]

Rafiki (IRE) *Walter Swinburn* a12 58
3 b g Kheleyf(USA) —Jemalina (USA) (Trempolino (USA))
1685[6] 2174[5]

Rafiqa (IRE) *Chris Wall* 96
4 b m Mujahid(USA) —Shamara (IRE) (Spectrum (IRE))
1899[12] 2683[5] ◆ 3457[3]

Rafta (IRE) *W G Harrison* 81
4 b m Atraf—First Kiss (GER) (Night Shift (USA))
3505[RR]

Ragdollianna *Murty McGrath* a55 74
6 b m Kayf Tara—Jupiters Princess (Jupiter Island)
2165[2] 2586[4] 3634[5] 6693[4] 7206[9]

Raghdaan *Peter Hiatt* a51 43
3 ch g Haafhd—Inaaq (Lammtarra (USA))
5610[6] 6476[6] 6876[14] 7429[8] 7731[8]

Ragiam (ITY) *S Botti* a93 96
5 b m Martino Alonso(IRE) —My Luigia (IRE) (High Estate)
6763a[9]

Ragsah (IRE) *Saeed Bin Suroor* a86 98
2 ch f Shamardal(USA) —Colorado Dancer (Shareef Dancer (USA))
3411[2] ◆ 3871[2] (5029) 5882[3] 6176[2] 6530[4] 7204[7]

Rahaala (IRE) *Sir Michael Stoute* a58 63
3 b f Indian Ridge—Mythie (FR) (Octagonal (NZ))
1932[5]

Rahya Cass (IRE) *Jeremy Gask* a90 93
3 b f Rahy(USA) —Its On The Air (IRE) (King's Theatre (IRE))
3673[7] 4231[7] 5297[9]

Rahystrada (USA) *Byron G Hughes* 116
6 ch g Rahy(USA) —Ministrada (USA) (Deputy Minister (CAN))
5321a[4]

Raihana (AUS) *M F De Kock* a113 103
4 b f Elusive Quality(USA) —Esubooh (AUS) (Sunday Silence (USA))
(333a) ◆ 514a[4] (709a) 1023a[2]

Rail Trip (USA) *Richard Dutrow Jr* a125
5 b g Jump Start(USA) —Sweet Trip (USA) (Carson City (USA))
6586a[5]

Railway Park (IRE) *John Wainwright* a51
6 ch g Karinga Bay—High Park Lady (IRE) (Phardante (FR))
166[5] 599[7]

Raimond Ridge (IRE) *Derek Shaw* a74 78
4 bb g Namid—Jinsiyah (USA) (Housebuster (USA))
(79) 404[7] 684[3] (806) 1365[11] 1915[14] 2123[10] 7668[6] 7841[10] 8036[6]

Rain And Shade *Edwin Tuer* a76 52
6 ch g Rainbow Quest(USA) —Coretta (IRE) (Caerleon (USA))
1801[12]

Rainbow Bay *Tracy Waggott* a70 52
7 b g Komaite(USA) —Bollin Victoria (Jalmood (USA))
2699[8] 3775[8]

Rainbow Dancing *Mlle H Van Zuylen* 106
5 b m Rainbow Quest(USA) —Danceabout (Shareef Dancer (USA))
5348a[8]

Rainbow Mirage (IRE) *Ed McMahon* a89 91
6 b g Spectrum(IRE) —Embers Of Fame (IRE) (Sadler's Wells (USA))
790[7] 1272[7] 1617[8] 1752[6] 2736[12] 3318[12] 3863[3] 4112[6] 4713[7]

Rainbow Peak (IRE) *Michael Jarvis* a92 118
4 b g Hernando(FR) —Celtic Fling (Lion Cavern (USA))
2057[2] (3144) ◆ 5274[2] 6148[2] (6977a)

Rainbow Six *Marco Botti* a65 66
3 b g Tiger Hill(IRE) —Birthday Suit (IRE) (Daylami (IRE))
889[3] ◆ 1061[7] 1602[6] 2215[2] 3313[2] 3726[4]

Rainbow Springs *John Gosden* 105
2 b f Selkirk(USA) —Pearl Dance (USA) (Nureyev (USA))
5912[2] 6609a[3]

Rainbows Reach *Gay Kelleway* a46 46
2 b f Phoenix Reach(IRE) —Rainbows Guest (IRE) (Indian Lodge (IRE))
5385[6] 6001[8]

Rainbows Son *Paul Midgley* 42
2 b g Kheleyf(USA) —Rainbow Treasure (IRE) (Rainbow Quest (USA))
1359[13] 2138[7] 3162[6] 5597[12] 6300[7] 6618[11]

Rainbow Styling (NZ) *Michael, Wayne & John Hawkes* 114
6 br g Zabeel(NZ) —Done That (NZ) (Centaine (AUS))
6946a[5]

Rainbow Zest *Wilf Storey* 49
7 b g Rainbow Quest(USA) —Original (Caerleon (USA))
3124[7] 3370[13] 4707[8]

Raincoat *F J Brennan* 93
6 b g Barathea(IRE) —Love The Rain (Rainbow Quest (USA))
1176[5] 1821[11] 2541[12]

Rain Delayed (IRE) *G M Lyons* a99 110
4 b g Oasis Dream—Forever Phoenix (Shareef Dancer (USA))
(1676a) 2353a[11] 3486a[8] 4882a[5] 5569a[10]

Raine's Cross *Peter Winkworth* 95
3 b c Cape Cross(IRE) —Branston Jewel (IRE) (Prince Sabo)
1497[8]

Raine Supreme *Ed McMahon* a40 52
3 b f Mind Games—Supreme Angel (Beveled (USA))
215[8]

Rainfall (IRE) *Mark Johnston* 116
3 b f Oasis Dream—Molomo (Barathea (IRE))
(1706) 2537[2] ◆ (3066) ◆ 3793[3] 4639a[5] 5946[8] (6351) 6561[3] ◆

Rain Forest *A P O'Brien* 91
3 b c Sadler's Wells(USA) —Gryada (Shirley Heights)
6786a[8]

Rainiers Girl *Roger Teal* a46
4 b m Tobougg(IRE) —Premier Night (Old Vic)
160[8] 396[7] 3442[7]

Rain Mac *John Gosden* a50 84
2 b c Beat Hollow—Quenched (Dansili)
4695[8] (6159)

Rain On The Wind (IRE) *Stuart Williams* a67 69
3 b g Bahamian Bounty—Mix Me Up (FR) (Linamix (FR))
699[4] 856[3] ◆ 1058[10] 1476[4] 2089[3] 3479[6] 5384[3] 5648[4] 5867[13] 6093[3] 6452[8]

Rain Rush (IRE) *David Marnane* a98 93
7 b g Monashee Mountain(USA) —Ewar Sunrise (Shavian)
4630a[12] 5774a[10] 6180[5]

Rainsborough *Sean Curran* a65 60
3 b g Trans Island—Greeba (Fairy King (USA))
2619[12] 3359[8] 3557[8] 5073[6] 5455[6] 7438[4] 7555[3] 7717[8]

Rain Stops Play (IRE) *Nicky Richards* a57 56
8 b g Desert Prince(IRE) —Pinta (IRE) (Ahonoora)
1576[12] 3147[3] 3369[6] 4082[9] 4644[10]

Rainy Night *Reg Hollinshead* a76 71
4 b g Kyllachy—Rainy Day Song (Persian Bold)
1391[7] 2528[10] 2817[5] 3205[2] 3584[5] 3855[5] (4478) 5064[10] 5698[3] 6110[9] 6714[9] 7239[2] 7331[4]

Raise Again (IRE) *Nerys Dutfield* a54 33
7 b g Raise A Grand(IRE) —Paryiana (IRE) (Shernazar)
4586[7] 5689[9]

Raise All In (IRE) *Ian McInnes* a64 47
4 b m Exceed And Excel(AUS) —Inforapenny (Deploy)
1958[4] 2207[9] 2454[11]

Raise Your Heart (IRE) *Ms Joanna Morgan* a97 109
7 b g Raise A Grand(IRE) —Gobolino (Don)
436a[10] 713a[10] 800a[12] 1247a[6] (Dead)

Rajeh (IRE) *John Spearing* 97
7 b g Key Of Luck(USA) —Saramacca (IRE) (Kahyasi)
1472[7] (2513) 3159[7] 6423[8]

Rajik (IRE) *C F Swan* 111
5 b g Kalanisi(IRE) —Ridaiyma (IRE) (Kahyasi)
3050[8] 3447[14] 5976a[4]

Rajsaman (FR) *F Head* a81 115
3 gr c Linamix(FR) —Rose Quartz (Lammtarra (USA))
(1565a) 2159a[10] 6219a[3] (7266a) 7853a[4]

Ra Junior (USA) *Paul Midgley* a86 94
4 b g Rahy(USA) —Fantasia Girl (IRE) (Caerleon (USA))
902[4] 1102[4] 1516[7] 1707[6] 2205[6] 2760[6] 2937[16] 4094[4] 4198[4] 5244[8] 6037[3] 6396[4] 7171[5] 7327[5]

Rakaan (IRE) *Jamie Osborne* a79 106
3 ch g Bahamian Bounty—Petite Spectre (Spectrum (IRE))
1913[2] 2324[15] (2970) 4144[2] 4509[2]

Raktiman (IRE) *Tom Dascombe* a63 75
3 ch g Rakti—Wish List (IRE) (Mujadil (USA))
1029[14] 1460[5] 1586[4] 3376[6] 3723[2] 4056[3] 4618[7] (4728) 5467[2] 6152[9] 6774[2]

Raleigh Quay (IRE) *Micky Hammond* 82
3 b g Bachelor Duke(USA) —Speedbird (USA) (Sky Classic (CAN))
2438[4] 2700[6] (3161) 3905[6] 4198[3] 4710[4] 5213[2] 6112[2] 6984[13]

Ramamara (IRE) *David Evans* a78 79
3 ch f Trans Island—Kaskazi (Dancing Brave (USA))
35[2] 122[5] 783[6] 945[9] 1545[7] 1842[6] 2342[10] 2491[2] 2588[8] 3115[7] 3336[3] 3525[7]

Ramble On (FR) *G Botti* a86 97
3 ch c Tobougg(IRE) —Street Money (IRE) (Mark Of Esteem (IRE))
3016a[4] 3933a[8]

Ramble On Love *Peter Winkworth* a54 46
3 b f Avonbridge—Blue Topaz (IRE) (Bluebird (USA))
443[7] 1590[6] 2227[9]

Rambling Dancer (IRE) *Mrs Valerie Keatley* a81 70
6 b g Imperial Ballet(IRE) —Wayfarer's Inn (IRE) (Lucky Guest)
5129a[2] 7816a[3]

Rambo Will *John Jenkins* a64 67
2 b c Danbird(AUS) —Opera Belle (Dr Fong (USA))
6126[4] 6778[6] 7595[7] 7871[7] 8011[5]

Ramona Chase *Michael Attwater* a78 91
5 b g High Chaparral(IRE) —Audacieuse (Rainbow Quest (USA))
637[5] 765[5] 873[7] 974[7] 1474[11] 1780[3] 2093[12] 2402[4] 2710[2] 3456[3] 4455[13] 4841[3] 5307[10] 5592[3] (5859) 6552[5] 6990[6]

Ramora (USA) *Olivia Maylam* a71 77
4 br m Monsun(GER) —Madame Cerito (USA) (Diesis)
5722[7] 6322[15] 6669[10] 7270[11] (7475) 7806[7] 7932[4] 7985[2]

Ramvaswani (IRE) *Neil King* a56 41
7 b g Spectrum(IRE) —Caesarea (GER) (Generous (IRE))
15[6]

Randomer *Paddy Butler* a45
7 b g Alflora(IRE) —Lavenham's Last (Rymer)
80[5] 237[6] 585[10]

Randonneur (USA) *E Lellouche* a93 96
4 b g Tale Of The Cat(USA) —Rolly Polly (IRE) (Mukaddamah (USA))
2446a[5]

Rangefinder *Jane Chapple-Hyam* a87 96
6 gr g Linamix(FR) —Risen Raven (USA) (Risen Star (USA))
1151[4] 1821[9] 3050[6] ◆ 3566[7] 4125[4] 4619[2] ◆ (5296) 5743[6] 5940[2] 6362[7] 6926[15] 7350[14]

Rannoch Moor *Marcus Tregoning* a48
3 b g Hernando(FR) —Stormy Weather (Nashwan (USA))
864[8] 7022[8] 7419[7]

Ransom Hope *L Riccardi* 107
5 b h Red Ransom(USA) —Field Of Hope (IRE) (Selkirk (USA))
7372a[3]

Ransom Note *B W Hills* 112
3 b c Red Ransom(USA) —Zacheta (Polish Precedent (USA))
(1658) 2544[2] (3103) 3824[7] 4537[9] (5247) 6562[18]

Ransom Request *Edward Vaughan* a67 69
2 b f Red Ransom(USA) —Shersha (IRE) (Priolo (USA))
3295[8] ◆ 3985[3] 4286[3] 4911[2] 5626[4]

Raphaeleyen *Tim Walford* 23
2 b g Doyen(IRE) —Elegant Spirit (Elegant Air)
4089[10]

Rapid City *Jim Best* a73 71
7 b g Dansili—West Dakota (USA) (Gone West (USA))
202[9] 315[2] 485[2] 676[3] 765[6] (2172) 2410[3] 2752[2] 3442[4]

Rapid Water *Jane Chapple-Hyam* a75 86
4 b g Anabaa(USA) —Lochsong (Song)
1727[14] ◆ 2247[2] 2997[6] 3629[4] 3892[3] 4401[17] 5966[8] 6478[4] 6739[6] 7766[7] 7971[6]

Rappletrap Car *T G McCourt* a56 63
3 b g Domedriver(IRE) —Hot To Tango (USA) (Kingmambo (USA))
5411[12]

Raptor (GER) *Mark Rimmer* a95 89
7 b g Auenadler(GER) —Royal Cat (Royal Academy (USA))
360[10] 536[5] ◆ 740[7] 921[4] (1133) 1282[5] 1724[14] 2506[7] 2991[3] 3318[6] 3995[4]

Rapturous Applause *Micky Hammond* 60
2 b c Royal Applause—Rapturous (Zafonic (USA))
6111[6] 6301[6] 6646[7]

Raqeeb (USA) *Ruth Carr* a38 82
3 b g Seeking The Gold(USA) —Sayedah (IRE) (Darshaan)
1627[2] 2290[3] 3337[3] 3612[2] 4339[4] 4784[4] 5304[7]

Rare Coincidence *Roger Fisher* a68 58
9 ch g Atraf—Green Seed (IRE) (Lead On Time (USA))
777[4] 1071[3] 1459[3] 4915[9] 6538[11] 6648[2]

Rare Malt (IRE) *Milton Harris* a73 77
3 b f Intikhab(USA) —A'Bunadh (USA) (Diesis)
1501[11] 2644[12] 4088[4] 4752[3] 5536[4] 6328[RR] 7687[9]

Rare Ransom *D K Weld* 96
4 b m Oasis Dream—Rapid Ransom (USA) (Red Ransom (USA))
957a[9]

Rare Ruby (IRE) *Jennie Candlish* 77
6 b m Dilshaan—Ruby Setting (Gorytus (USA))
1798[3] (2218) 2897[2] 3896[5] 4983[3] 5788[3] 6114[6] 7061[11]

Rare Symphony (IRE) *P D Deegan* a74 89
3 br f Pastoral Pursuits—Rubileo (Galileo (IRE))
4496a[6]

Rare Tern (IRE) *Sir Mark Prescott Bt* a81 91
3 ch f Pivotal—Littlefeather (IRE) (Indian Ridge)
2249[5] 3663[4] 4222[3] ◆ 4742[2] 4931[2] (5236) (5887) ◆ 6090[3]

Rasam Aldaar *Mick Channon* 71
2 b c Sakhee(USA) —Recherchee (Rainbow Quest (USA))
6159[11] 6618[3]

Rasaman (IRE) *Jim Goldie* a86 96
6 b g Namid—Rasana (Royal Academy (USA))
1099[3] ◆ 2136[8] 2346[6] 2756[9] (3165) 3406[7] 3828[7] 4191[8] 4536[25] (4798) 5183[8] (5335) 5734[5] 6175[14] 6706[6] 7060[13] 7079[20]

Rascal In The Mix (USA) *Richard Whitaker* a63 71
4 rg m Tapit(USA) —Ready Cat (USA) (Storm Cat (USA))
1919[10] 2874[3] 3238[2] (3538) ◆ (3854) 4172[5] 4824[7] 5199[2] 5756[6] 6372[6] 6934[8] 7128[6]

Rashaad (USA) *B W Hills* 100
3 b g Smart Strike(CAN) —Martinique (USA) (Pleasant Colony (USA))
1702[3] 2226[7] 3105[9] 5879[4] 6889[8]

Rasheed *John Gosden* a75
2 b g Oasis Dream—Alexandrine (IRE) (Nashwan (USA))
7873[6] (8000)

Rash Judgement *Eric Alston* 97
5 b g Mark Of Esteem(IRE) —Let Alone (Warning)
3401[3] (5048) 5884[15] 6241[2] 6735[12] 7060[19]

Rasmy *Marcus Tregoning* 108
3 b g Red Ransom(USA) —Shadow Dancing (Unfuwain (USA))
1354[4] ◆ 1858[3]

Rasselas (IRE) *David Nicholls* a56 88
3 b g Danehill Dancer(IRE) —Regal Darcey (IRE) (Darshaan)
2143[2] 2899[3] 3387[2] ◆ 3680[7] (4193) (4483) ◆ 4704[3] 5121[7] 5854[4] ◆ 6510[7] ◆ 6709[4]

Rastaban *William Haggas* 75
2 b c Diktat—Guilty Secret (IRE) (Kris)
6190[9] (7010)

Rasteau (IRE) *Tom Keddy* 29
2 b c Barathea(IRE) —Mistra (IRE) (Rainbow Quest (USA))
3631[13] 5761[8] 6504[14]

Rathbawn Girl (IRE) *Julia Feilden* a62 58
3 br f Alamshar(IRE) —Rathbawn Realm (Doulab (USA))
149[3] 490[6] 809[9] 991[2] 1316[3] 1605[5] 2185[11] 2459[3] (2784) 3336[5] 3682[4] 4739[2] 5152[7]

Rather Cool *Andrew Haynes* a54 58
2 b f Iceman—Kowthar (Mark Of Esteem (IRE))
4788[2] (5373) 6300[9] 7197[6]

Rath Maeve *Alan McCabe* a63 29
2 b f Auction House(USA) —Westmead Tango (Pursuit Of Love)
1360[7] 1647[4] 2139[9] 7396[2] 7644[2] 7831[8]

Rational Act (IRE) *Tim Easterby* a42 57
2 b g Antonius Pius(USA) —Givemethemoonlight (Woodborough (USA))
1389[6] 2238[9] 2522[5] 6711[7] 7345[6]

Rattleyurjewellery *David Brown* 30
2 b f Royal Applause—You Make Me Real (USA) (Give Me Strength (USA))
6301[12] 6874[8] 7681[6]

Raucous Behaviour (USA) *Mark Johnston* a81 78
2 b g Street Cry(IRE) —Caffe Latte (IRE) (Seattle Dancer (USA))
(5651) ◆ 6174[5] 6670[2] ◆

Ravenel (GER) *R Rohne* a80 104
4 b m Touch Down(GER) —Resafe (FR) (Poliglote)
5782a[4] 6765a[13]

Ravenfield (IRE) *David Brown* a69 66
3 b c Xaar—Rubyanne (IRE) (Fasliyev (USA))
1825[2] 2114[5] 2695[3] 3111[4] 3773[5]

Ravens Rose *Jonathan Portman* a56 55
3 b f Bold Edge—Marjeune (Marju (IRE))
1159[10] 1537[8] 2600[4] 3852[7] 4249[8] 4687[4] 5670[8]

Ravi River (IRE) *Brian Ellison* a84 60
6 ch g Barathea(IRE) —Echo River (USA) (Irish River (FR))
115[7] 230[4] 444[3] (464) (613) 804[5] 851[4] 1042[3] 1914[7] 2187[3] 2415[11] 2750[9] 3309[6] 3518[5] 3595[5] 5768[10] 7462[5] 7501[2] 7729[4]

Rawnaq (IRE) *Mark Johnston* a75 82
3 b g Azamour(IRE) —Sharemata (IRE) (Doyoun)
(1721) 2323[6] 3105[10] 4571[6] 4983[2] 5497[3] 5940[4] 6448[5] 7067[4]

Raw Spirit (GER) *Saeed Bin Suroor* a51 60
2 ch c Shirocco(GER) —Reem Dubai (IRE) (Nashwan (USA))
7152[4] 7325[4]

Raydar *Mark Brisbourne*
5 b g Ziggy's Dancer(USA) —Send Me An Angel (IRE) (Lycius (USA))
468[10]

Rayeni (IRE) *John M Oxx* 114
4 ch h Indian Ridge—Rayyana (IRE) (Rainbow Quest (USA))
1246a[2] 4160a[4] 6009a[8]

Ray Of Joy *John Jenkins* a91 85
4 b m Tobougg(IRE) —Once Removed (Distant Relative)
102[3] 350[4] 747[6] 905[2] ◆ 1321[5] (1770) 4225[5] 4930[11] 5628[5] (6772) 7289[3] 7521[6] (7654) 8016[7]

Razzina (IRE) *David Lanigan* a39
3 b f Dansili—Messina (IRE) (Sadler's Wells (USA))
1621[9]

Reachforthebucks *Gavin Blake* 42
2 ch g Phoenix Reach(IRE) —Miles (Selkirk (USA))
2216[10] 2715[6] 6159[14]

Reach For The Sky (IRE) *Alan Berry* a60 68
3 b f Elusive City(USA) —Zara Whetei (IRE) (Lomond (USA))
766[3] 809[14] 962[6] 1057[4] 1168[6] 1605[7] 2235[10] 3167[4] 3710[6] 3773[3] 4193[2] 4406[10] 4749[8] 5409[7] 5481[7] 6226[11] 7051[12]

Reach Out *Brendan Powell* a33 43
2 ch c Phoenix Reach(IRE) —Cocorica (IRE) (Croco Rouge (IRE))
5033[8] 5629[13] 5892[10]

Reachtothestars (USA) *Michael Quinlan* a69 64
2 b c Silver Train(USA) —Gabrieles Princess (USA) (Our Emblem (USA))
1359[8] 2376[6] 5117[4] 6220[11] (6575) ◆ 6988[6] 7572[6] 7718[5] 7982[6]

Ready To Crown (USA) *John Mackie* a60 46
6 b m More Than Ready(USA) —Dili (USA) (Chief's Crown (USA))
1194[7]

Real Dandy *Lucinda Featherstone* a41 58
4 b g Bahamian Bounty—You Make Me Real (USA) (Give Me Strength (USA))
4591[13] 5631[10] 6051[13]

Real Desire *P Monteith* 58
4 ch g Haafhd—Stop Press (USA) (Sharpen Up)
3950[7] 4407[11] 4582[10] 4823[3] 5216[5] 5439[6] 7054[11]

Real Diamond *Ollie Pears* a52 72
4 b m Bertolini(USA) —Miss Fit (IRE) (Hamas (IRE))
1588[5] 2087[5] 2699[5] 4342[10] 4895[8] 5424[2] 6188[3] 6494[5] 6922[6] 7281[5]

Realisation (USA) *Mark Johnston* a89 89
3 b g Alhaarth(IRE) —Live Your Dreams (USA) (Mt. Livermore (USA))
1657[5] 5918[4] 6630[2] (6730a) 7428[3] 7568[3] 7698[5]

Reality Show (IRE) *Mahmood Al Zarooni* a89 88
3 b g Cape Cross(IRE) —Really (IRE) (Entrepreneur)
2043[5] 2497[2] 2994[4] (3764) 4380[2] 4571[4] 5922[3]

Reallymissgreeley (USA) *Kevin Ryan* a71 60
3 bb f Mr Greeley(USA) —Holiday Gold (USA) (Touch Gold (USA))
(219) 625[6]

Real Secret (BRZ) *A Cintra Pereira* a83 78
4 gr h Redattore(BRZ) —Ke Segredo (BRZ) (Punk (ARG))
608a[12] 819a[11]

Realta *Gerard Butler* a53
4 b m Bahamian Bounty—Jasmine Breeze (Saddlers' Hall (IRE))
238[5]

Realt Na Mara (IRE) *Hughie Morrison* a82 83
7 bb g Tagula(IRE) —Dwingeloo (IRE) (Dancing Dissident (USA))
(1914) 4894[4] 6274[5] 6664[8]

Reason To Believe (IRE) *Ben Haslam* a67 67
2 ch g Spartacus(IRE) —Lady Fabiola (USA) (Open Forum (USA))
3118[5] 4240[4] 4599[6] (6220) 6694[3]

Re Barolo (IRE) *A bin Huzaim* a112 107
7 b h Cape Cross(IRE) —Dalaiya (USA) (Irish River (FR))
513a[4] ◆ 708a[8] 800a[13]

Rebecca Rolfe *M Gasparini* 103
4 b m Pivotal—Matoaka (USA) (A.P. Indy (USA))
1419a[5] (4185a) 6238a[9]

Rebecca Romero *Denis Coakley* a55 52
3 b f Exceed And Excel(AUS) —Cloud Dancer (Bishop Of Cashel)
3030[3] 4099[9] 4284[2] ◆ 4720[2] 5470[3] 6133[5] 6665[2]

Rebel Dancer (FR) *Philip Hobbs* 56
5 b g Dark Moondancer—Poupee d'Ancyre (FR) (Brinkmanship (USA))
2181[9]

Rebel Duke (IRE) *Ollie Pears* a103 98
6 ch g Namid—Edwina (IRE) (Caerleon (USA))
(2) 916[6] 1174[3] 1670[3] 2054[8]

Rebellious Spirit *Sean Curran* a69 62
7 b g Mark Of Esteem(IRE) —Robellino Miss (USA) (Robellino (USA))
2477[11] 2786[4] 3278[7] (4914) ◆ 5155[6] 6669[7] 7184[5] 7462[2] 7627[3]

Rebel Soldier (IRE) *Jeremy Noseda* a87 116
3 ch c Danehill Dancer(IRE) —En Garde (USA) (Irish River (FR))
(634) ◆ 1352[7] (2979) (4456)

Rebel Woman *Jamie Osborne* a58 52
4 b m Royal Applause—Wild Woman (Polar Falcon (USA))
2874[14] 3291[6] 3723[3] 5158[6]

Recalcitrant *Simon Dow* a71 72
7 b g Josr Algarhoud(IRE) —Lady Isabell (Rambo Dancer (CAN))
3214[7] 3559[4] 4201[3] 4958[7] 5457[2] (6023) 6852[5] 7255[7]

Recession Proof (FR) *John Quinn* a80 97
4 ch g Rock Of Gibraltar(IRE) —Elevate (Ela-Mana-Mou)
2027[5] 2747[14] 5743[10]

Recharge (IRE) *Kevin Prendergast* 111
4 b h Cape Cross(IRE) —Rebelline (IRE) (Robellino (USA))
1789a[2] 2369a[2] 3466a[4]

Recital (FR) *A P O'Brien* 115
2 b c Montjeu(IRE) —Dibenoise (FR) (Kendor (FR))
(7456a)

Reckless Reward (IRE) *Richard Hannon* a100 103
2 ch c Choisir(AUS) —Champagne Toni (IRE) (Second Empire (IRE))
2048[6] (2413) 3100[2] 4138[10] (4787) 5245[4] 5748[2]

Record Breaker (IRE) *Mark Johnston* a104 107
6 b g In The Wings—Overruled (IRE) (Last Tycoon)
418a[11] 512a[6] 706a[6] 903[2] 1031[4] 1220[5] 1724[16] 2317[5] 2857[7] 3462[3] 4400[7] 5118[8] 5723[8] 6185[4] 6437[4] 7196[3] 7612[8]

Rectangulaire (FR) *Mme C Head-Maarek* 59
4 b g Anabaa(USA) —Roanne (FR) (Saumarez)
3017a[10] 4166a[8]

Red Amy *Michael Bell* a61 59
3 b f Hawk Wing(USA) —Ballet Ballon (USA) (Rahy (USA))
1158[3] 1796[7] 2189[4] 2675[4] 3444[11]

Red Avalanche (IRE) *Paul Cole* a99 96
3 gr g Verglas(IRE) —Maura's Guest (IRE) (Be My Guest (USA))
2972[8] 4105[3] 5632[5] 5967[6] 6253[8] 6739[8] 6996[3]

Red Badge (IRE) *Richard Hannon* 118
3 ch c Captain Rio—Red Fuschia (Polish Precedent (USA))
1497[4] 2543[2] 3824[10] (4139) (5951)

Red Barcelona (IRE) *Mark H Tompkins* 63
3 ch c Indian Haven—Purepleasureseeker (IRE) (Grand Lodge (USA))
1630[2] 2248[6] 2908[3] 4552[3] 5164[7] 5653[8]

Red Cadeaux *Ed Dunlop* a101 105
4 ch g Cadeaux Genereux—Artisia (IRE) (Peintre Celebre (USA))
1015[7] ◆ (1220) ◆ 1821[8] ◆ 4711[4] 5291[2] 5743[2] 6201[2] 6926[9]

Red Cape (FR) *Ruth Carr* a86 95
7 b g Cape Cross(IRE) —Muirfield (FR) (Crystal Glitters (USA))
1573[7] 2100[5] 2134[5] 2465[9] 2748[8] 3065[3] 3178[3] (3435) 3753[2] 3919[7] 4171[3] 4536[16] 4653[5] 5302[14] 5884[U]

Red Cell (IRE) *Ian McInnes* a61 59
4 b g Kheleyf(USA) —Montana Lady (IRE) (Be My Guest (USA))
860[9] 1154[8] 1569[15] 1884[14] 1968[6] 2278[10]

Red China Blues (USA) *Ruth Carr* 62
4 ch g Royal Academy(USA) —Viewy (USA) (Majestic Light (USA))
1485[7] 1717[12] 2382[11] 2629[5] (3027) 4373[5] 4706[13] 4868[5] 5817[11]

Red Courtier *Paul Cole* a80 82
3 b c Red Ransom(USA) —Lady In Waiting (Kylian (USA))
1730[5] 2079[7]

Red Current *Michael Scudamore* a58 55
6 b m Soviet Star(USA) —Fleet Amour (USA) (Afleet (CAN))
211[12] 682[2] 984[6] 4991[3]

Red Dagger (IRE) *Richard Price* a44 58
4 b g Daggers Drawn(USA) —Dash Of Red (Red Sunset)
721[8] 854[8] 918[13] 1236[10] 3374[5] 3853[5] 4189[3] (4374) 5905[4] 6261[9] 6472[9] 7006[3]

Redden *William Haggas* a47 72
3 b g Pivotal—Coy (IRE) (Danehill (USA))
2329[2] 2416[12] 3680[4]

Red Desire (JPN) *Mikio Matsunaga* a118 117
4 b m Manhattan Cafe(JPN) —Great Sunrise (Caerleon (USA))
(800a) 1027a[11] 7343a[4]

Reddy To Star (IRE) *Julie-Ann Camacho* a63 75
3 b g Redback—Grade A Star (IRE) (Alzao (USA))
1401[6] 1811[5] 3181[3] 3975[12] 6522[6] 6897[4] 7153[4] 7450[7] 7605[8]

Red Ears *David O'Meara* 20
2 rg g Paris House—Solaris Dancer (Samim (USA))
5602[12] 6027[7]

Red Eddie *Simon Dow* a34 56
3 b g Red Ransom(USA) —Sister Bluebird (Bluebird (USA))
1795[13] 2675[10] 3723[5] 4295[6] 5058[12] 5729[6] 6062[8]

Redera (IRE) *A J Martin* a76 75
4 b g Chevalier(IRE) —Lady Redera (IRE) (Inzar (USA))
7589a[2] 7823a[7]

Redesignation (IRE) *R Pritchard-Gordon* a80 98
5 b g Key Of Luck(USA) —Disregard That (IRE) (Don't Forget Me)
3099a[4] 4038a[5]

Red Eyes *Brian Meehan* 71
2 b c Beat Hollow—Kardelle (Kalaglow)
5033[4] ◆

Red Fama *Neville Bycroft* a65 44
6 ch g Fraam—Carol Again (Kind Of Hush)
2941[10] 4785[4] 5118[3] ◆ 6051[3] 6516[9] 6895[10]

Red Fantasy (IRE) *B W Hills* 100
3 b f High Chaparral(IRE) —Petite Fantasy (Mansooj)
1729[2] 2029[8] (2658)

Red Fighter (IRE) *Daniel Mark Loughnane* 73
3 b g Redback—Sloats Burg (USA) (Woodman (USA))
2289[5] 4563a[5]

Red Flash (IRE) *Patrick Leech* a29 52
3 b c Red Ransom(USA) —Mar Blue (FR) (Marju (IRE))
1500[5] 5493[9] 5839[6] 6454[12]

Redford (IRE) *David Nicholls* a106 117
5 b g Bahri(USA) —Ida Lupino (IRE) (Statoblest)
883[4] 1007[9] 1906[2] 3193[19] 4085[16] 4843[9] 5292[3] ◆ (6177) ◆ (6349) 6735[11]

Red Gold And Green (IRE) *David Nicholls* a43 68
2 b g One Cool Cat(USA) —Lady Lord (IRE) (Coquelin (USA))
4195[2] ◆ 4941[11] 6646[6] 7857[8] 7983[9]

Red Gulch *Ed Dunlop* a86 89
3 b g Kyllachy—Enrapture (USA) (Lear Fan (USA))
(1050) 2287[3] 2618[5] 3899[2] 4387[4] 4929[4] 5383[6] (6197) 7092[4]

Red Hot Desert *Walter Swinburn* a79 29
4 b g Green Desert(USA) —Red Carnation (IRE) (Polar Falcon (USA))
280[2] 1169[2] 1303[2] 1690[11]

Red Humour (IRE) *M McDonagh* a48 60
4 b g Elusive City(USA) —Arctic Flight (Polar Falcon (USA))
3946[10]

Red Inca *Brian Meehan* 65
2 ch c Pivotal—Magicalmysterykate (USA) (Woodman (USA))
6196[6]

Red Intrigue (IRE) *Amanda Perrett* a73 79
3 b f Selkirk(USA) —Red Affair (IRE) (Generous (IRE))
4626[3] (5038) 5972[5] 6361[5] 6691[5]

Red Jacaranda *Chris Dwyer* a15 51
2 b f Selkirk(USA) —Red Japonica (Daylami (IRE))
5085[7] 5373[3] 5630[4] 6129[12] 6795[9] 7378[9]

Red Jade *Richard Fahey* a67 93
5 ch g Dubai Destination(USA) —Red Slippers (USA) (Nureyev (USA))
(1011) 1378[11] 2710[4] 5188[7] 5949[9] 6396[2] 6724[3] 7084[6] 7350[16] 7698[6]

Red Jazz (USA) *B W Hills* 122
3 b c Johannesburg(USA) —Now That's Jazz (USA) (Sword Dance)
(1311) 1699[8] 2546[2] 3066[2] 3455[2] 4457[8] 5275[5] 6350[3] (6923)

Red Kestrel (USA) *Kevin Ryan* a73 89
5 ch g Swain(IRE) —The Caretaker (Caerleon (USA))
1011[11] 1925[2] 2349[3] 3764[11] 4125[7] 4781[5] 5215[3] 5549[4] 6028[2] 6744[2] 7465[9]

Red Kimi (IRE) *Riccardo Santini* a94 96
4 b h Denon(USA) —Happy Flight (IRE) (Titus Livius (FR))
7372a[6]

Red Lancer *Jonathen de Giles* a44 86
9 ch g Deploy—Miss Bussell (Sabrehill (USA))
3780[9] 4683[6]

Red Lite (IRE) *Brian Meehan* a43 64
2 b f Red Ransom(USA) —Cloudy Bay (GER) (Zilzal (USA))
3562[11] 4095[11] 4658[3] 5720[11] 6259[U]

Red Love (USA) *J-C Rouget* a82 82
3 b f Gone West(USA) —Red Happy (USA) (A.P. Indy (USA))
926a[5]

Red Lover *Ed Dunlop* 75
2 b c Azamour(IRE) —Love Me Tender (Green Desert (USA))
6190[11] 6443[3] 7058[4]

Red Marling (IRE) *B W Hills* 73
2 b c Danehill Dancer(IRE) —Marling (IRE) (Lomond (USA))
1351[5] 2882[5] 3624[3] 5472[4] 6365[6] 6627[5] 7224[3]

Red Mercury (IRE) *Mick Channon* a58 70
2 ch g Majestic Missile(IRE) —Fey Rouge (IRE) (Fayruz)
6514[6] 6825[3] 7186[7]

Red Merlin (IRE) *Clive Cox* a83 107
5 ch g Soviet Star(USA) —Truly Bewitched (USA) (Affirmed (USA))
2116[8] 2716[6] 3672[8] 4400[9] 6193[13] (6630) 6736[5]

Red Oleander *Sir Mark Prescott Bt* a60 61
2 b f Pivotal—Red Peony (Montjeu (IRE))
4029[7] 4299[6] 4668[8] 5644[2] ◆ (5837) 6081[8]

Redoubtable Grace *Ruth Carr* a20 42
3 b g Redoubtable(USA) —Full Of Grace (Lucky Wednesday)
998[11]

Red Presence (IRE) *Tom Dascombe* 88
2 ch g Redback—Birthday Present (Cadeaux Genereux)
2887[9] (5532) 6104[3]

Red Rani *Reg Hollinshead* a18 1
5 ch m Whittingham(IRE) —Crystal Magic (Mazilier (USA))
7461[12] 7684[6] 7987[4]

Red Remanso (IRE) *B W Hills* a34
2 ch f Redback—Esterlina (IRE) (Highest Honor (FR))
6796[10] 7312[8]

Red Rhythm *Luca Cumani* a63 55
3 ch g Starcraft(NZ) —Araguaia (IRE) (Zafonic (USA))
7013[4] 7498[2] 7757[3]

Red River Boy *Chris Fairhurst* a44 58
5 ch g Bahamian Bounty—Riviere Rouge (Forzando)
2581[4] 3026[2] 3322[3] 3809[5] 4047[3] 4373[14] 4868[3] 5197[4] (5422) 5817[2] 6040[8] 6206[8]

Red Riverman *William Haggas* 78
2 b g Haafhd—Mocca (IRE) (Sri Pekan (USA))
4549[3] ◆ 5404[2] 6436[5]

Red Roar (IRE) *Alan Berry* 69
3 ch f Chineur(FR) —Unfortunate (Komaite (USA))
2530[6] 3111[7] 4584[2] 5065[7] 5359[2] (5514) (6392) 7052[2] 7207[8]

Red Rock Canyon (IRE) *M F De Kock* a94 111
6 b h Rock Of Gibraltar(IRE) —Imagine (IRE) (Sadler's Wells (USA))
337a[6] ◆ 418a[12] 632a[5] 706a[8]

Red Roof *D Gambarota* 62
2 b f Statue Of Liberty(USA) —Khyber Knight (IRE) (Night Shift (USA))
7850a[3]

Red Rosanna *Reg Hollinshead* a63 78
4 b m Bertolini(USA) —Lamarita (Emarati (USA))
1506[7] 1710[8] 1988[14] 2310[11] 2396[8] 3637[4] 4090[15]

Red Ruler (NZ) *John Sargent* 118
6 b g Viking Ruler(AUS) —Ransom Bay (USA) (Red Ransom (USA))
6947a[14] 7291a[19]

Red Scintilla *Nigel Tinkler* 75
3 b f Doyen(IRE) —Red To Violet (Spectrum (IRE))
1402[5] 1648[2] 2502[3] (3030) 3393[9] 4193[4] 4714[2] 5044[2] (5484) 6197[14] 6461[5]

Red Skies (IRE) *Linda Stubbs* 64
3 ch f Tagula(IRE) —Chibi (USA) (Dynaformer (USA))
1654[5] 2434[5] 2837[9] 4705[3] 5411[9]

Red Skipper (IRE) *Noel Wilson* a31 65
5 ch g Captain Rio—Speed To Lead (IRE) (Darshaan)
1204[4] 1576[7] (3707) 4514[7] 4824[2] 5439[3] 7899[7]

Red Smokey (IRE) *Mark H Tompkins* 13
3 ch f Tagula(IRE) —Red Slipper (IRE) (Alzao (USA))
1278[16] 2600[7]

Red Snapper (IRE) *John Weymes* 38
2 b g Redback—Fag End (IRE) (Treasure Kay)
1806[7] 6027[10] 6263[8] 6919[10]

Red Soles (IRE) *B W Hills* 42
2 b f Barathea(IRE) —Inchoate (Machiavellian (USA))
6150[7]

Red Somerset (USA) *Mike Murphy* a97 68
7 b g Red Ransom(USA) —Bielska (USA) (Deposit Ticket (USA))
197[10] 286[5] 359[4] (405) 672[5] 740[2] 790[6] 921[7] 1219[7] ◆ (1301) 3206[9] 3565[2] 4023[11] 4322[8] 4756[7] 5142[2] 5750[2] 6312[9]

Red Storm Rising *Kevin Morgan* a59 61
3 b g Red Ransom(USA) —Showery (Rainbow Quest (USA))
2755[9] 4407[10] 5303[6] 5869[11]

Red Suede Shoes *Jeff Pearce* a82 70
4 ch g Storming Home—Dipple (Komaite (USA))
151[9] 394[10] 3036[9] 3782[10] 5867[14]

Red Twist *Martin Hill* a63 52
5 b g Red Ransom(USA) —Spinning The Yarn (Barathea (IRE))
3348[4] 3865[5]

Red Valerian Two (IRE) *Paul Midgley* a52 41
3 ch g Hawk Wing(USA) —La Turque (IRE) (Diesis)
143[3] 302[6] 452[3] 1145[4] 1422[5] 7147[13]

Redvers (IRE) *Ralph Beckett* a65 55
2 br g Ishiguru(USA) —Cradle Brief (IRE) (Brief Truce (USA))
6146[10] 6899[3]

Redwater River *Ruth Carr* a43 61
6 b g Kyllachy—Red Tulle (USA) (A.P. Indy (USA))
403[7] 569[11] 705[11] 795[6] 1142[11] 1470[7] 1673[7] 1928[8] 2207[6] 2699[6] 3538[12] 4244[6]

Red Willow *John E Long* a52 55
4 ch m Noverre(USA) —Chelsea Blue (ITY) (Barathea (IRE))
1959[6] 2674[10] 3214[6] 4257[8] 5455[2] 7489[3]

Red Wine *Jeremy Glover* a55 81
11 b g Hamas(IRE) —Red Bouquet (Reference Point)
199[3] 331[7] 463[2] 622[2] 1012[7] (1150) 1916[2] 2995[11] 3760[9] 5631[3] 7061[18] 7270[7]

Redwood *B W Hills* 117
4 b h High Chaparral(IRE) —Arum Lily (USA) (Woodman (USA))
1532[2] 1832[7] 3191[5] 3825[2] (4535) 5575a[2] (6236a) 6951a[3] 7851a[2]

Red Yarn *Gary Moore* a68 78
3 b f Lucky Story(USA) —Aunt Ruby (USA) (Rubiano (USA))
159[2] 582[2] 698[5] 2888[7] 3441[2] 3714[2] 3962[7] (4588) 4956[3] 5838[7]

Red Zeus (IRE) *J S Moore* a61 56
2 ch g Titus Livius(FR) —Cheviot Indian (IRE) (Indian Ridge)
3269[6] 3785[5] ◆ 4323[6]

Reel Amber *Tim Easterby* 60
2 ch f Reel Buddy(USA) —Amber Valley (Foxhound (USA))
1294[10] 1527[8] 1886[2] 2139[7] 4195[5] 5042[3] 5334[5] 5483[7]

Reel Buddy Star *George Moore* 93
5 ch g Reel Buddy(USA) —So Discreet (Tragic Role (USA))
1707[7] 2086[6] 2423[9] 2835[4] ◆ (3408) (3537) 4154[2] 4603[9] 5605[11] 5685[2]

Reel Credit Crunch *Ian McInnes* a64 65
3 ch f Reel Buddy(USA) —Four Legs Good (IRE) (Be My Guest (USA))
1505[8] 1987[6]

Reel Love *Linda Stubbs* a31 50
3 b g Reel Buddy(USA) —Love Affair (IRE) (Tagula (IRE))
1336[12] 1760[11] 3728[2] 4087[6] 4448[10] 4863[5]

Reem Star *Ed Dunlop* a72 62
2 b f Green Tune(USA) —Arlecchina (GER) (Mtoto)
7057[8] 7447[2] (7723)

Ree's Rascal (IRE) *Jim Boyle* a69 47
2 gr g Verglas(IRE) —Night Scent (IRE) (Scenic)
1764[6] 2078[8] 3034[7] 3959[8] 5452[3] 5659[2] (6082) (7296)

Refik (FR) *M Cesandri* 95
7 b g Hawker's News(IRE) —Joly Coeur (FR) (Mont Basile (FR))
3099a[10]

Reflect (IRE) *Richard Hannon* 71
2 b c Hurricane Run(IRE) —Raphimix (FR) (Linamix (FR))
5033[7] 5582[4]

Refuse To Give Up (IRE) *David Simcock*
3 b f Refuse To Bend(IRE) —Yukon Hope (USA) (Forty Niner (USA))
1851[10]

Refuse To Wait (IRE) *Tim Easterby* a18 68
3 b f Refuse To Bend(IRE) —I'Ll Be Waiting (Vettori (IRE))
1298[7] 1649[3] 2132[3] 2379[5] 3371[7] 5598[10] 6890[15] 7149[10] 7402[9]

Regal Approval *Hughie Morrison* 82
2 br g Royal Applause—Enthralled (Zafonic (USA))
3735[2] (4293) ◆ 5187[4] 6191[LFT]

Regal Bullet (IRE) *Dean Ivory* a57 54
2 b g Majestic Missile(IRE) —Royal Dream (Ardkinglass)
1263[15] 2819[11] 3034[10] 5581[2] 6271[5] 6674[3] 7016[3] 7469[3] 7871[5]

Regal Emperor (IRE) *David Nicholls* 56
3 b g Antonius Pius(USA) —Bali Breeze (IRE) (Common Grounds)
1425[14] 1599[4] 1890[8] 3773[6] 4188[5] 4674[4] 5024[7] 5535[14]

Regal Heiress *Sir Michael Stoute* 74
2 b f Pivotal—Regal Rose (Danehill (USA))
4508[5]

Regal Kiss *Mark Johnston* 76
2 ch f King's Best(USA) —Really Polish (USA) (Polish Numbers (USA))
2461[8] 3991[3] 4338[2] 4821[3] (5682) 6059[5]

Regal Lyric (IRE) *Tom Tate* 67
4 b g Royal Applause—Alignment (IRE) (Alzao (USA))
1925[8] 2424[7] 3122[5] 3502[4] 4410[7]

Regal Parade *David Nicholls* a97 121
6 ch g Pivotal—Model Queen (USA) (Kingmambo (USA))
1024a[10] 3192[16] (4136) (4885a) 5744[6] 6611a[4]

Regal Park (IRE) *Jeremy Noseda* 92
3 b g Montjeu(IRE) —Classic Park (Robellino (USA))
1268[7] 1847[4] 2924[2] (5996) (6448) 7061[7]

Regal Rave (USA) *John Best* 63
3 b g Wild Event(USA) —Golden Crown (USA) (Defensive Play (USA))
2906[7] 3478[3] 3788[3] (4281) 4534[4]

Regal Rocket (IRE) *John Weymes* a41 45
2 b f Majestic Missile(IRE) —Frenzy (Zafonic (USA))
3331[5] 3509[7] 3959[13] 6209[10]

Regal Salute *Jeremy Noseda* 52
2 b f Medicean—Regency Rose (Danehill (USA))
7231[9]

Regency Girl (IRE) *Marcus Tregoning* a68 67
3 b f Pivotal—Miss Pinkerton (Danehill (USA))
5265[8] 5832[7] 6415[6] 6959[4] 7316[2]

Regeneration (IRE) *Michael Bell* a88 85
4 b g Chevalier(IRE) —Cappuchino (IRE) (Roi Danzig (USA))
1030[6] 1361[3] (1933) 2872[3] 4057[3] (6167) 6558[9] 7488[5]

Regent's Secret (USA) *Jim Goldie* a85 66
10 br g Cryptoclearance(USA) —Misty Regent (CAN) (Vice Regent (CAN))
2583[6] 3078[2] (3352) 4511[7] 4582[4] 4953[2] 5215[7] 5364[5] 6224[10]

Reggane *A De Royer-Dupre* 115
4 b m Red Ransom(USA) —Reine Zao (FR) (Alzao (USA))
1908[3] 2744[2] 3704a[5] 5348a[5] 6344a[2] (6950a) 7854a[9]

Regimental (IRE) *Ann Duffield* 70
2 b g Refuse To Bend(IRE) —Red Fox (IRE) (Spectrum (IRE))
4167[8] 4368[8] 4668[5] 5389[2] 5597[4] 6001[2] (6294) 6647[4] 6875[11]

Reginald Claude *Mark Usher* a71 75
2 b c Monsieur Bond(IRE) —Miller's Melody (Chief Singer)
1429[4] 1603[7] 2594[8] (4111) 4544[8] 4935[4] 5472[6] 5849[13] 6191[12] 6988[5] 7417[3] 7652[4]

Reginetta (JPN) *Hidekazu Asami* 106
5 b m French Deputy(USA) —Aspen Leaf (JPN) (Sunday Silence (USA))
7460a[11]

Regional Counsel *Alex Hales* a70 64
6 b g Medicean—Regency Rose (Danehill (USA))
282[6]

Regythelion *Frederick Watson*
4 b g Hunting Lion(IRE) —Deekazz (IRE) (Definite Article)
6896[16]

Rehabilitation *Walter Swinburn* a76 59
5 ch g Dr Fong(USA) —Lamees (USA) (Lomond (USA))
1226[12] 2232[4]

Reignier *Mrs K Burke* 98
3 b c Kheleyf(USA) —Komena (Komaite (USA))
1616[4] 2972[2] 3691[5] 5742[12]

Reigning In Rio (IRE) *Paul Midgley* a51 44
4 br m Captain Rio—Saibhreas (IRE) (Last Tycoon)
503[12] 720[9] 898[11]

Reigning Monarch (USA) *Zoe Davison* a56 53
7 b g Fusaichi Pegasus(USA) —Torros Straits (USA) (Boundary (USA))
103[4] 146[5] 235[3] 320[5] 388[7] 591[8] 656[7] 763[5]

Reillys Daughter *J S Moore* 57
2 b f Diktat—Compose (Anabaa (USA))
3349[3]

Reine Heureuse (GER) *Uwe Ostmann* 101
3 b f Big Shuffle(USA) —Reine Galante (IRE) (Danehill (USA))
1250a[3] 1715a[2] 2404a[2] (6409a)

Reiteration (USA) *J S Bolger* a68 99
3 b c Vindication(USA) —For Dixie (USA) (Dixieland Band (USA))
1951a[4]

Relative Strength (IRE) *Stuart Williams* a74 83
5 ch g Kris Kin(USA) —Monalee Lass (IRE) (Mujtahid (USA))
1348[6] 1690[4] 3267[2] 4467[3] 5612[6] 6202[6] 7491[5] 7765[4]

Relco Italy (IRE) *B Grizzetti* 101
4 b g Dansili—Lietta (IRE) (Grand Lodge (USA))
2576a[9]

Reload (IRE) *Sarah Humphrey* a60 71
7 b g Minardi(USA) —Rapid Action (USA) (Quest For Fame)
2966[10] 3267[8]

Remark (IRE) *Michael Easterby* a54 31
6 b g Machiavellian(USA) —Remuria (USA) (Theatrical)
466[9] 663[6] 920[8] 995[12] 1146[5]

Remarque (IRE) *L Riccardi* 102
5 b h Marju(IRE) —Run For Me (IRE) (Danehill (USA))
1944a[13] 7459a[15]

Remember When (IRE) *A P O'Brien* 112
3 ch f Danehill Dancer(IRE) —Lagrion (USA) (Diesis)
2370a[4] 2711[2] ◆ 3467a[4] 4178a[9]

Remotelinx (IRE) *J W Hills* 88
2 ch g Choisir(AUS) —La Tintoretta (IRE) (Desert Prince (IRE))
1695[3] 2245[2] 2680[7] (3439) 4138[7] 5245[13] 5965[5]

Renege The Joker *Sean Regan* a35 41
7 b g Alflora(IRE) —Bunty (Presidium)
3608[6] 4715[9] 5565[3]

Renesmee (IRE) *Peter Grayson* a29
2 ch f Bachelor Duke(USA) —Rose Of Battle (Averti (IRE))
1981[5] 2413[6] 4890[10] 7268[12] 7577[9] 7858[8]

Renn *Peter Grayson*
2 b f Iceman—Ladywell Blaise (IRE) (Turtle Island (IRE))
4436[11]

Renoir's Lady *Simon Dow* 68
2 b f Peintre Celebre(USA) —Marie De Blois (IRE) (Barathea (IRE))
4103[5]

Rento (FR) *W Walton* 107
7 gr g Medaaly—Rosalita (FR) (Nashamaa)
494a[5] 742a[2]

Repealed *Hughie Morrison* a62 66
4 b g Reset(AUS) —Great Verdict (AUS) (Christmas Tree (AUS))
4893[5] 5380[6]

Replicator *Patrick Gilligan* a71 57
5 b g Mujahid(USA) —Valldemosa (Music Boy)
(693) (924) 1482[9] 5562[6] 6018[6] 6292[7] 6898[13] 7155[8] 7426[6] 7761[9] 7972[6]

Reposer (IRE) *John Best* a76 75
2 br g Kheleyf(USA) —Tragic Point (IRE) (Tragic Role (USA))
1612[4] 1930[14] 2594[5] 3315[5] (6899)

Representing (USA) *Mlle A-S Pacault* 102
6 b g Rahy(USA) —Recording (USA) (Danzig (USA))
7102a[2]

Reprieved *John Quinn* a44 28
5 ch g Bertolini(USA) —Crystal Seas (Zamindar (USA))
839[6] 1142[7] 1923[10]

Requisite *Ian Wood* a81 82
5 ch m Pivotal—Chicarica (USA) (The Minstrel (CAN))
1596[6] ◆ 2123[6] 2635[2] (2904) 3037[3] (3328) 3567[2] 3779[U] 3947[3] 4225[2] 4424[5] 4551[9] 4930[4] 5048[7] 5454[5] 5952[6] 6207[4] 6772[6] 6799[5] (7046) 7238[12] 7488[3] 7521[5] 7665[4] 7766[3] 7892[3]

Rerouted (USA) *B W Hills* 105
2 ch c Stormy Atlantic(USA) —Rouwaki (USA) (Miswaki (USA))
2059[3] (2493) 3872[3] 5849[4] (6507) 7265a[4]

Rescent *Ruth Carr* a54 55
3 ch f Reset(AUS) —Bukhoor (IRE) (Danehill (USA))
574[3] 717[5] 861[7] 993[5] 1465[5] 2209[9] 2380[5] 3501[2] 3975[8] 4337[12] 4674[11] 4864[6] 6460[14]

Resentful Angel *Pat Eddery* a96 94
5 b m Danehill Dancer(IRE) —Leaping Flame (USA) (Trempolino (USA))
282[10] (361) 1346[3] 3512[3] (3781) (4694) 5475[2] 6095[9] 6447[4] 7612[3]

Reset To Fit *Eric Alston* 55
3 b g Reset(AUS) —Miss Fit (IRE) (Hamas (IRE))
6186[4] 6470[10] 6896[11]

Residence And Spa (IRE) *Tim Easterby* 73
2 b g Dubai Destination(USA) —Toffee Nosed (Selkirk (USA))
2389[2] 3162[3] 4167[3] 4747[2] 6174[8]

Residency (IRE) *Bryan Smart* a68 67
4 b g Danetime(IRE) —Muckross Park (Nomination)
3663[5] 3903[2] 4244[3] 4947[4] 5405[6] 6679[6] 7328[7] 7542[5] 7808[2] (7952)

Resolute Road *B W Hills* a67 54
3 b c Medicean—Madam Ninette (Mark Of Esteem (IRE))
1325[9] 1659[8] 2121[6] 2753[2] 4128[6] 4925[2]

Respective Way *Patrick Chamings* a17
5 b g Sakhee(USA) —Leisurely Way (Kris)
3563[12]

Resplendent Ace (IRE) *Paul Howling* a78 49
6 b g Trans Island—Persian Polly (Persian Bold)
174[4] 323[5] 529[2] 600[2] (714) 833[4] 989[4] 1134[9] 1303[9] 1623[10] 1980[7] 2182[6] 3278[6] 3967[4] 4227[4] 4912[3] 5148[5] 5770[10] 6121[2] (6538) (6744)

Resplendent Alpha *Alastair Lidderdale* a77 73
6 ch g Best Of The Bests(IRE) —Sunley Scent (Wolfhound (USA))
71[5] 275[9] 501[8] 1321[9] 1653[12] 2298[7] 2590[8] 3216[8] 4936[8] 5326[3] 5897[9] 6456[4] 7442[2] 7519[7] 7655[8] 7824[3]

Resplendent Light *William Muir* a66 93
5 b g Fantastic Light(USA) —Bright Halo (IRE) (Bigstone (IRE))
1960[4] 2747[13] 3462[7] 4737[2] ◆ 5286[5] 5727[5] 6202[7] 6571[2]

Resplendent Nova *Paul Howling* a71 55
8 b g Pivotal—Santiburi Girl (Casteddu)
27[7] 123[6] 285[7] 496[6] (704) 975[4] 1350[8] 2875[10]

Restless Bay (IRE) *Reg Hollinshead* a73 73
2 br g Elusive City(USA) —Argus Gal (IRE) (Alzao (USA))
2990[2] 3624[4] 3964[4] 4856[5] 5629[8] 6163[2] (6311) 6513[9] 6745[7] 7493[4] 7528[5] 7565[2] 7803[3] 7891[4] 7982[5]

Restless Genius (IRE) *Brian Ellison* a71 78
5 b g Captain Rio—Mainmise (USA) (Septieme Ciel (USA))
171[4] (402) ◆

Restless Soul *B Cecil* a65 100
6 b m Singspiel(IRE) —Seasonal Splendour (IRE) (Prince Rupert (FR))
6604a[5]

Resurge (IRE) *Stuart Kittow* a92 98
5 b g Danehill Dancer(IRE) —Resurgence (Polar Falcon (USA))
1388[7] 1907[5] 2467[2] 2934[10] 3737[3] 4306[3] (4996) 5592[2] 6193[10] (6552) 7100[5]

Resuscitator (USA) *Heather Main* a72 69
3 b g Bernstein(USA) —Lac Du Printemps (USA) (Meadowlake (USA))
1387[12] 3155[10] 3831[4] 4300[3] 5077[2] ◆ 5171[P] 7069[5] 7872[3] 8034[12]

Retainer (IRE) *Richard Hannon* 95
2 gr c Acclamation—Felicita (IRE) (Catrail (USA))
(1309) ◆

Retaliate *Patrick Leech* a55 14
6 br m Wizard King—Retaliator (Rudimentary (USA))
860[8] 1326[8]

Retrato (USA) *Rae Guest* a47 65
3 bb f Fusaichi Pegasus(USA) —Painted Lady (USA) (Broad Brush (USA))
1757[11] 2658[8] 3414[6] 6454[6] 6865[13]

Retreat Content (IRE) *Jamie Osborne* a67 24
2 b g Dubai Destination(USA) —Sharp Point (IRE) (Royal Academy (USA))
4110[9] 5924[2] 6230a[22] 6542[5]

Reve De Nuit (USA) *Alan McCabe* a100 97
4 ch g Giant's Causeway(USA) —My Dream Castles (USA) (Woodman (USA))
(6) 175[4] 266[6] 553[11] 1008[13] 1274[10] 1378[5] 1724[12] 1829[4] 2608[7] 2747[5] 3240[5] (3456) 3672[5] 4100[5] 5188[9] 5529[11] 5638[6] 5970[7] 6205[4] 6318[3] 6534[4] 6877[10] 7100[9]

Revelator (IRE) *Alan McCabe* a53 74
3 b g One Cool Cat(USA) —Capades Band (FR) (Chimes Band (USA))
7867[9] 7955[5]

Reventon *B Grizzetti* 84
2 b c Galileo(IRE) —Frottola (Muhtarram (USA))
6762a[6]

Revered *Sir Michael Stoute* 94
3 b f Oasis Dream—Arrive (Kahyasi)
2969[5] 3697[2] 6096[3]

Reverence *Eric Alston* a103 108
9 ch g Mark Of Esteem(IRE) —Imperial Bailiwick (IRE) (Imperial Frontier (USA))
3486a[2] 3895[5] 5569a[14]

Reverend Green (IRE) *Chris Down* a81
4 b g Tagula(IRE) —Red Letter (Sri Pekan (USA))
(326) 785[3] 917[5] 7756[4] ◆

Reves De Printemps (FR) *J Reynier* 87
2 b c Della Francesca(USA) —Lune De Mai (Kenmare (FR))
7974a[5]
Revoltinthedesert *Marco Botti* a44 51
3 b f Dubai Destination(USA) —Cloud Hill (Danehill (USA))
624[7] 1237[6] 2480[9]
Revolutionary *Jamie Osborne* a55
2 b g Thunder Gulch(USA) —Magic Spin (USA) (Lord Avie (USA))
7962[7]
Revue Princess (IRE) *Tim Easterby* a61 79
5 b m Mull Of Kintyre(USA) —Blues Queen (Lahib (USA))
1915[6] 2087[6] 2396[6] (3115) 3637[2] (4064) 4342[7] 4834[12] (5054) 5601[3] (6107) 6394[5]
Rewilding *Mahmood Al Zarooni* 124
3 b c Tiger Hill(IRE) —Darara (Top Ville)
1254a[2] (2226) 2746[3] ◆ (5185) ◆ 5945[6]
Reykon (IRE) *D Grilli* 98
6 b h Invincible Spirit(IRE) —Realt Dhun Eibhir (Indian Ridge)
1944a[14]
Rezwaan *Murty McGrath* a60 75
3 b g Alhaarth(IRE) —Nasij (USA) (Elusive Quality (USA))
1582[11] 2886[4] 4022[14] 6632[9] 7038[5] 7305[9]
Rhal (IRE) *Bryan Smart* a55 47
2 ch f Rahy(USA) —Queen Of Stars (USA) (Green Desert (USA))
5117[8] 6459[4] 6893[4]
R Heat Lightning (USA) *Todd Pletcher* a112
2 b f Trippi(USA) —Yellow Heat (USA) (Gold Fever (USA))
7342a[2]
Rhythm Of Light *Tom Dascombe* 70
2 b f Beat Hollow—Luminda (IRE) (Danehill (USA))
(4543) 5746[5] 6619[10]
Rhythm Stick *John Berry* a72 34
3 b g Whipper(USA) —Forever Loved (Deploy)
5026[7] 5971[12] 7069[7] 7387[2] (7669) (7921)
Rhyton (IRE) *Sir Michael Stoute* 67
3 b g Rainbow Quest(USA) —Sea Picture (IRE) (Royal Academy (USA))
2390[5] (3242)
Ricci (FR) *R Gibson* a78 84
3 gr c Highest Honor(FR) —Restless Rixa (FR) (Linamix (FR))
1195a[6]
Riccoche (IRE) *Edward Vaughan* 60
3 b f Oasis Dream—Ammo (IRE) (Sadler's Wells (USA))
2891[6] 3173[7]
Richardlionheart (USA) *Michael Madgwick* a39 31
4 ch g Lion Heart(USA) —Cleito (USA) (Unbridled's Song (USA))
6476[7] 6865[8] 7251[13]
Richard's Kid (USA) *Bob Baffert* a122 106
5 bb h Lemon Drop Kid(USA) —Tough Broad (USA) (Broad Brush (USA))
1027a[7] (5577a)
Rich Boy *Laura Mongan* a68 32
3 ch g Bahamian Bounty—West Humble (Pharly (FR))
3325[12] 4022[6] 6522[3] 7019[6] 7298[11] 7614[4] 7763[4]
Richelieu *Lee Smyth* a79 74
8 b g Machiavellian(USA) —Darling Flame (USA) (Capote (USA))
5129a[7] 6375[12] 7195[7]
Rich Harvest (USA) *Ray Peacock* a6 60
5 bb g High Yield(USA) —Mangano (USA) (Quiet American (USA))
7380[11]
Richmond Fontaine *John Best* a78
2 br c Pastoral Pursuits—Fizzy Treat (Efisio)
(7309) ◆
Richo *Shaun Harris* a55 79
4 ch g Bertolini(USA) —Noble Water (FR) (Noblequest (FR))
4596[4] 4985[10] 6051[12] 6937[6] 7299[3]
Rickety Bridge (IRE) *Patrick Chamings* a59 62
7 ch g Elnadim(USA) —Kriva (Reference Point)
2645[12] 3278[3]
Ride A White Swan *Derek Shaw* a69 48
5 gr g Baryshnikov(AUS) —The Manx Touch (IRE) (Petardia)
30[4] 145[2] 530[3] 567[2] 691[5] 763[11] (866) 1170[7] (1235) ◆ (1534) 1719[7] 4427[11] 4910[6] 5087[8] 5764[7] 6741[8] ◆
Ride The Wind *Chris Wall* 41
2 b f Cozzene(USA) —Wind Surf (USA) (Lil's Lad (USA))
6441[11] 7058[12]
Ridgeway Hawk *Mark Usher* a49 36
2 ch g Monsieur Bond(IRE) —Barefooted Flyer (USA) (Fly So Free (USA))
1871[5] 3274[8] 3757[5] 4129[6] 7864[5]
Ridgeway Sapphire *Mark Usher* a26 53
3 b f Zafeen(FR) —Barefooted Flyer (USA) (Fly So Free (USA))
1760[6] 2200[6] 3478[7] 3727[4]
Ridley Didley (IRE) *Noel Wilson* a50 75
5 b g Tagula(IRE) —Dioscorea (IRE) (Pharly (FR))
(727) ◆ 778[7] (1391) 1915[2] 2144[3] 2756[3] 3201[2] 3879[2] 4513[7] 6103[16] 7194[7] 7494[9]
Rien A Faire (IRE) *M Marcialis*
2 b c Oratorio(IRE) —Ace In The Hole (So Factual (USA))
7850a[9]
Rien Ne Vas Plus (IRE) *Sir Michael Stoute* 63
2 b f Oasis Dream—Sought Out (IRE) (Rainbow Quest (USA))
7232[6]
Rievaulx World *Kevin Ryan* a79 102
4 b g Compton Place—Adhaaba (USA) (Dayjur (USA))
916[13] 1471[7] 2054[16] 2346[15] 4148[10] 4653[6] 5198[13] 5297[8] 6374[5]

Riflessione *Ronald Harris* a79 79
4 ch g Captain Rio—Hilites (IRE) (Desert King (IRE))
378[8] 778[3] 829[3] (967) 1482[2] 1547[4] 2001[6] 2166[2] (2818) 3736[10] 4043[4] 4452[6] 4836[5] 5368[6] 5809[2] 6310[4] 6700[2] 7193[2] 7441[4] 7556[2] 7683[3] 7868[2] 8004[8]
Riggins (IRE) *Ed Walker* a109 111
6 b g Cape Cross(IRE) —Rentless (Zafonic (USA))
1697[3] ◆ 3069[2] 4457[6] 6089[4] (7593)
Riggs (IRE) *Peter Grayson* a29 26
4 b g Daggers Drawn(USA) —Jay And-A (IRE) (Elbio)
208[6] 402[14] 2809[8] 3516[6] 3946[6] 4760[10] 5153[5] 6746[9] 7322[5] 7547[7] 7859[10]
Rightcar *Peter Grayson* a57 51
3 b g Bertolini(USA) —Loblolly Bay (Halling (USA))
134[4] 215[4] (387) 745[6] 991[9] 1163[5] 4031[9] 4791[13] 5152[9] 5730[10] 7824[7]
Rightcar Dominic *Peter Grayson* a47
5 b g Kyllachy—Vallauris (Faustus (USA))
1154[12] 1234[11] 3903[10] 7684[7] 7786[6] 7960[7]
Rightcar Joan (IRE) *Peter Grayson* a11
3 b f Tagula(IRE) —Enamoured (Groom Dancer (USA))
201[4] 374[11] 538[6]
Rightcar Marian *Peter Grayson* a29
3 b f Oasis Dream—Top Flight Queen (Mark Of Esteem (IRE))
209[6] 1468[10] 4194[11] 5152[11] 5957[10]
Righteous Man (IRE) *Mrs John Harrington* a85 79
3 ch g Mr Greeley(USA) —Peaceful Kingdom (USA) (Our Native (USA))
3492a[8] 6730a[11]
Right Grand *William Haggas* a78 86
3 b g Exceed And Excel(AUS) —Baileys Dancer (Groom Dancer (USA))
4104[2] ◆ 4750[10] 5685[4] 6567[4]
Right Option (IRE) *John Flint* a83 79
6 b g Daylami(IRE) —Option (IRE) (Red Ransom (USA))
352[7]
Right Rave (IRE) *Philip McBride* a69 83
3 b f Soviet Star(USA) —Genuinely (IRE) (Entrepreneur)
1582[3] (1977) (2256) 3457[8] 4548[2] 5149[9]
Right Said Fred (IRE) *Ralph Beckett* a74 68
2 b g Holy Roman Emperor(IRE) —Tender Is Thenight (IRE) (Barathea (IRE))
2621[8] 3459[4] 4142[4] 6156[6] 6795[2] 7087[2]
Right Step *Alan Jarvis* a100 98
3 b c Xaar—Maid To Dance (Pyramus (USA))
1330[2] ◆ 2117[6] 2562[7] 3105[17] 4504[2] 4757[6] 5188[10] 6318[5] 6889[4] 7100[2] 7591[2]
Right Stuff (FR) *Gary Moore* a94 90
7 bb g Dansili—Specificity (USA) (Alleged (USA))
500[3] 1020[2]
Rigid *Tony Carroll* a54 66
3 ch g Refuse To Bend(IRE) —Supersonic (Shirley Heights)
1696[7] 2587[13] 3463[7] 4791[3] 5162[2] 5730[7] 5926[5] 6579[3] 6848[6] 7863[10]
Rigidity *Henry Cecil* 102
3 b g Indian Ridge—Alakananda (Hernando (FR))
1657[2] 2033[2] 4504[8] (5904) 6203[7]
Rigolleto (IRE) *Mick Channon* 88
2 b c Ad Valorem(USA) —Jallaissine (IRE) (College Chapel)
4277[2] (4614) 5184[7] 6982[3] 7456a[10]
Rileys Crane *Christine Dunnett* 47
3 ch g Reset(AUS) —Persian Blue (Persian Bold)
1870[7] 2220[12] 2632[15] 3993[9] 4210[6] 4970[12]
Rileyskeepingfaith *Mick Channon* a102 108
4 b g Hunting Lion(IRE) —Keeping The Faith (IRE) (Ajraas (USA))
336a[11] ◆ 604a[7] 707a[4] 817a[3] 1085[8] 1727[12] 1900[17] (2119) 2316[3] 3193[11] 3461[7] 3674[2] ◆ 4576[4] 5095[4] 6177[9] 6390[7] 6752[15]
Riley Tucker (USA) *Steven Asmussen* a114
5 bb h Harlan's Holiday(USA) —My Sweet Country (USA) (Bold Ruckus (USA))
6582a[2] 7361a[9]
Rimth *Paul Cole* 103
2 b f Oasis Dream—Dorelia (IRE) (Efisio)
(1972) 5246[3] 5693[2] 6176[7] 6530[2]
Ringaroses *Jonjo O'Neill* 90
9 b g Karinga Bay—Rose Ravine (Deep Run)
3195[8] 3695[7]
Ring Of Fire *John Spearing* a49
3 b g Firebreak—Sweet Patoopie (Indian Ridge)
5925[10] 6871[13]
Ringsend Rose (IRE) *Aytach Mehmet Sadik*
7 b m Beneficial—Charwin (IRE) (Commanche Run)
1861[0]
Ringstead Bay (FR) *Ralph Beckett* a65
2 b g Intikhab(USA) —Praia Grande (GER) (Lagunas)
7609[3]
Rinterval (IRE) *Eric R Reed* a108 91
5 ch m Desert Prince(IRE) —Interpose (Indian Ridge)
4887a[2] 7341a[8]
Riobamba D'Ho (FR) *T Larriviere* 77
5 b m Enrique—Peutiot (FR) (Valanour (IRE))
281a[0]
Rio Belle (IRE) *Andrew Reid* a20
2 ch f Captain Rio—Madam Waajib (IRE) (Waajib)
5719[12] 5841[13] 6158[20]
Rio Black (IRE) *S Bietolini* 86
3 b c Captain Rio—Jemima Yorke (Be My Guest (USA))
1418a[7]
Rio Caribe (IRE) *Tim Walford* 69
3 b g Captain Rio—Kadja Chenee (Spectrum (IRE))
1811[3] 1967[2] 2700[11] 3180[7] 3685[4] 4155[6]
Rio Cobolo (IRE) *Paul Green* a80 79
4 b g Captain Rio—Sofistication (IRE) (Dayjur (USA))
1361[8] 1513[14] 1967[4] 2205[2] 2531[8] 2885[6] 3389[6] 3553[6] 4065[2] 4404[9] (4834) 5198[10] 5297[11] 6048[5] 6367[11]

Rio De La Plata (USA) *Saeed Bin Suroor* 119
5 ch h Rahy(USA) —Express Way (ARG) (Ahmad (ARG))
823a[12] (2651) (4412) 4829[7] (5274) 5801a[2] (6764a) (7373a)
Rio Gael (IRE) *Peter Bowen* a25 58
4 br g Captain Rio—Palavera (FR) (Bikala)
7011[4]
Rioliina (IRE) *Jonathan Portman* a65 74
4 b m Captain Rio—Anneliina (Cadeaux Genereux)
2178[4]
Rio Mist *Richard Hannon* a57 93
3 b f Captain Rio—Welsh Mist (Damister (USA))
1075[2] (1390) 1511[2] (2052) (2928) 3415[4] 5521[5] 6113[6] 6319[6]
Rio Prince *John Bridger* a32 53
3 b g Carnival Dancer—Princess Louise (Efisio)
1847[9] 3477[7] 4257[9] 4958[4] 5536[7] 6020[8] 6781[10]
Rio Royale (IRE) *Amanda Perrett* a68 78
4 b g Captain Rio—Lady Nasrana (FR) (Al Nasr (FR))
1258[8] 2246[15] 2719[3] 3292[7] 4130[13] 4959[3] (5169) 6956[2] (7249) 7518[3] 7640[2]
Rio Sands *Richard Whitaker* a48 66
5 b g Captain Rio—Sally Traffic (River Falls)
1988[9] 2582[4] 2818[7] 3286[4] 3623[4] 4415[12] 4452[2] 5023[4] 5123[2] 5513[14] 6246[3] 6464[11] 7542[8] 7883[7]
Rio's Girl *Richard Whitaker* a54 63
3 b f Captain Rio—African Breeze (Atraf)
1966[12] 2530[5] 3808[5] (4516) (4826) 5410[2] 6299[5] 7194[6]
Rio's Rosanna (IRE) *Richard Whitaker* 62
3 b f Captain Rio—Ling Lane (Slip Anchor)
5303[3]
Rio Tinto *Mahmood Al Zarooni* 74
3 b c Cape Cross(IRE) —Hint Of Silver (USA) (Alysheba (USA))
2507[7] 2974[4] 3477[4] 4341[8]
Riot Police (USA) *John Gosden* a73 74
2 bb c Street Cry(IRE) —Lords Guest (USA) (Lord At War (ARG))
3219[5] 5900[3] 6278[2] ◆ 6743[5] 7087[10] 7385[5] 7567[3]
Rip Van Winkle (IRE) *A P O'Brien* a95 132
4 b h Galileo(IRE) —Looking Back (IRE) (Stravinsky (USA))
3046[6] 4469[2] (5186) ◆ 5775a[2] 6350[2]
Riqa *F Head* 85
2 b f Dubawi(IRE) —Thamarat (Anabaa (USA))
4884a[2]
Riqaab (IRE) *Michael Easterby* a70 77
5 b g Peintre Celebre(USA) —Jeed (IRE) (Mujtahid (USA))
2885[11] 3206[10] 3431[6] 3804[7]
Rising Kheleyf (IRE) *John Harris* a52 77
4 ch g Kheleyf(USA) —Rising Spirits (Cure The Blues (USA))
1494[6] 1707[13] 2204[8] 2764[12] 4404[13] (4866) 5486[2] 5852[11] 6826[6]
Rising Star *Amanda Perrett* 68
4 ch g Medicean—Arkadia Park (IRE) (Polish Precedent (USA))
5258[5]
Rising Wind (IRE) *Kevin Prendergast* 82
2 b f Shirocco(GER) —Right Key (IRE) (Key Of Luck (USA))
6784a[2] ◆
Rite Of Passage *D K Weld* 122
6 ch g Giant's Causeway(USA) —Dahlia's Krissy (USA) (Kris S (USA))
(3102)
Ritual (IRE) *Jeremy Noseda* a91 83
3 b g Cape Cross(IRE) —Silver Queen (Arazi (USA))
1381[9] ◆ (4251) ◆ (6226) (7320)
River Ardeche *Ben Haslam* a84 77
5 b g Elnadim(USA) —Overcome (Belmez (USA))
245[8] 405[2] 1512[11] 1751[10] 2276[5] 3060[7] ◆ 3750[2] 4088[2] 5019[5] 5757[4]
River Avon *Michael Easterby* a34
2 b g Avonbridge—Bountiful (Pivotal)
6308[10] 7530[13] 7629[6]
River Blade *Mark Brisbourne* 46
2 b g Needwood Blade—River Ensign (River God (USA))
2312[8] 2836[4] 3603[5] 4678[8] 5111[12] 7785[6]
River Bounty *Alan Jarvis* a55 72
5 b m Bahamian Bounty—Artistic Merit (Alhaarth (IRE))
7299[12] 7607[2]
Riverdale (IRE) *Ann Duffield* 79
2 ch c Choisir(AUS) —Hollow Haze (USA) (Woodman (USA))
4402[2] (4941) 5301[6] 6325[4]
River Danube *Tim Fitzgerald* a65 46
7 b g Dansili—Campaspe (Dominion)
4765[9] 5564[10]
River Du Nord (FR) *Mrs A Malzard*
3 b f Voix Du Nord(FR) —Palala River (Colmore Row)
2162a[7]
River Falcon *Jim Goldie* a93 101
10 b g Pivotal—Pearly River (Elegant Air)
1099[5] 2054[4] 2346[9] 2759[11] 3201[7] 3446[7] ◆ 3919[12] 4192[4] (4820) 4952[5] 5435[3] 5789[12] 6394[6] 7352[10]
River Kirov (IRE) *Michael Wigham* a86 85
7 b g Soviet Star(USA) —Night Shifter (IRE) (Night Shift (USA))
251[4]
River Of Silence (IRE) *PETER Makin* 44
3 b f Sadler's Wells(USA) —My Giddy Aunt (IRE) (Danehill (USA))
5986[7]
Riverside *Mel Brittain* a27 27
5 b m Kyllachy—My Cadeaux (Cadeaux Genereux)
1301[0]
River Tease *J S Moore* a50 61
3 b g Avonbridge—Tantalize (Machiavellian (USA))
3635[11] 4249[5] 4718[4] 5173[3] 5414[7] 6287[11] 6517[4]

Riveting Reason (USA) *Myung Kwon Cho* a102
2 bb c Fusaichi Pegasus(USA) —Love And Marry (USA) (Known Fact (USA))
7363a[8]
Riviera Chic (USA) *Ralph Beckett* a83 90
3 b f Medaglia D'Oro(USA) —Hurricane Warning (USA) (Thunder Gulch (USA))
226[2] (371)
Riviera Cocktail (USA) *Neil Drysdale* a86 105
4 b h Giant's Causeway(USA) —Starry Dreamer (USA) (Rubiano (USA))
6237a[10]
Riviera Red (IRE) *Les Hall* a51
10 b g Rainbow Quest(USA) —Banquise (IRE) (Last Tycoon)
1601[0] 262[11]
Rivitivo *Mark Brisbourne* a31
3 b f Deportivo—River Ensign (River God (USA))
977[8] 1209[7] 1606[8]
Riynaaz (IRE) *John M Oxx* a83 83
3 b f Cape Cross(IRE) —Riyafa (IRE) (Kahyasi)
7358a[11]
Rjeef (IRE) *David Simcock* a93 94
3 b c Red Ransom(USA) —Sun Chaser (IRE) (King's Best (USA))
(625) (1045) 1352[4] 7430[12] 7689[8]
Roanstar *Andrew Balding* 77
3 gr g Act One—Dolce Thundera (USA) (Thunder Gulch (USA))
1976[4] 2401[5] 3038[5] 6152[3]
Roar Talent (USA) *John Best* a57 37
3 ch g Roar Of The Tiger(USA) —Laurie's Folly (USA) (Kris S (USA))
655[6] 4840[4] 5330[5] 5656[10] 6020[11]
Roatan *P Bary* a87 109
5 gr g Daylami(IRE) —Celestial Lagoon (JPN) (Sunday Silence (USA))
2803a[5] 4038a[6] 7457a[9]
Roayh (USA) *Saeed Bin Suroor* a99 103
2 ch c Speightstown(USA) —Most Remarkable (USA) (Marquetry (USA))
2216[5] (2621) 3049[3] 3826[3] 4538[3] 5306[4] (6083)
Robber Stone *Mick Channon* a51 57
2 gr g Proclamation(IRE) —Amiata (Pennekamp (USA))
2819[7] 2951[6] 3735[15] 4587[8] 5000[3] 5365[7] 6673[3] 7552[3] 7722[6] 8012[5]
Robbie Burnett *Alan Swinbank* 75
3 b g Footstepsinthesand—Cuore Di Aliante (Alhijaz)
1116[6] 1991[5] 2627[6] (4087) ◆ 4408[2] 6038[9]
Robbmaa (FR) *Tony Carroll* a30 43
5 bl g Cape Cross(IRE) —Native Twine (Be My Native (USA))
1759[9] 2199[5] 3560[5] 3848[6] 4530[5]
Robby Bobby *Laura Mongan* a89 90
5 ch g Selkirk(USA) —Dancing Mirage (IRE) (Machiavellian (USA))
536[12] 5355[7] 5790[9] 6297[7] 6915[3] 7089[9] 7251[9] 7570 [3] 7778[4] 7884[5]
Robens Rock (IRE) *Mark Johnston* a67 83
3 b g Rock Of Gibraltar(IRE) —Qhazeenah (Marju (IRE))
(2438) 2702[2]
Roberto Pegasus (USA) *Pat Phelan* 72
4 bb h Fusaichi Pegasus(USA) —Louju (USA) (Silver Hawk (USA))
(5376)
Robert The Painter (IRE) *Richard Fahey* 84
2 b g Whipper(USA) —Lidanna (Nicholas (USA))
(5531) 6139[5] 6619[2] ◆
Robin Hood (IRE) *A P O'Brien* 95
2 b c Galileo(IRE) —Banquise (IRE) (Last Tycoon)
4175a[2] 5316a[7] 5746[3] 6403a[3]
Robin Hoods Bay *Edward Vaughan* a64
2 b c Motivator—Bijou A Moi (Rainbow Quest (USA))
7485[5] 7595[8] 7843[6]
Robinson Cruso *Michael Jarvis* a62 89
3 b c Footstepsinthesand—Miss Hawai (FR) (Peintre Celebre (USA))
1659[6] (2517) 3791[12]
Robust Wish (USA) *Brian Meehan* a92 71
3 b g Strong Hope(USA) —Copper Rose (USA) (Unbridled (USA))
406[2] 681[4] 792[4] 2002[9] 2892[5] 6430[12] (6701)
Roche Ambeau (FR) *E Lellouche* 91
3 gr f Chichicastenango(FR) —Exande (FR) (Exit To Nowhere (USA))
4037a[6] 5981a[5] 6761a[5] (7546a)
Roche Des Vents *Richard Hannon* 79
2 b c Bahamian Bounty—Tokyo Rose (Agnes World (USA))
1597[9] (1871) 3051[14] 4138[17]
Rockabilly Rebel *B W Hills* 76
3 b g Kyllachy—Its All Relative (Distant Relative)
(2566) 3215[4] 4104[3] 5919[5] 6438[6] 6771[5]
Rock Ace (IRE) *Deborah Sanderson* a66 79
2 gr f Verglas(IRE) —Break Of Day (USA) (Favorite Trick (USA))
3274[4] (3729) (4935)
Rock A Doodle Doo (IRE) *William Jarvis* a80 86
3 b c Oratorio(IRE) —Nousaiyra (IRE) (Be My Guest (USA))
134[2] (216) ◆ (279) ◆ (686) ◆ 1033[3] 1502[2] ◆ 2252[2] 2758[6]
Rock And Chop (FR) *C Boutin* 85
5 ch h Indian Rocket—Lycee (IRE) (Entrepreneur)
690a[0]
Rock And Roll Kid (IRE) *Anthony Mullins* 106
5 b g Danehill Dancer(IRE) —Milly's Song (Millfontaine)
3487a[6] 4463a[18] 5571a[21]
Rock Anthem (IRE) *Mike Murphy* a75 83
6 ch g Rock Of Gibraltar(IRE) —Regal Portrait (IRE) (Royal Academy (USA))
1265[10] 3412[4] ◆ 3863[9] 4354[13] 5716[2] (5919) 6430[10]
Rock Art (IRE) *Karen George* a51 59
4 ch m Rock Of Gibraltar(IRE) —Lindesberg (Doyoun)
131[0] 591[10]

Rock Ascot (URU) *Gary Moore* a98 87
6 gr h Mantle Rock(USA) —Maria Fumadora (URU) (Sportin' Gold (USA))
205[5] 408[6]

Rockatella (IRE) *W Hefter* 107
3 b f Rock Of Gibraltar(IRE) —Patrimony (Cadeaux Genereux)
5139a[3] 5649a[6] 6765a[3]

Rockawango (FR) *M Pimbonnet* 86
4 b h Okawango(USA) —Janou La Belle (FR) (Shining Steel)
494a[3]

Rock D'Argent (IRE) *Andrew Haynes* a53 29
3 b f Rock Of Gibraltar(IRE) —Petite-D-Argent (Noalto)
768[7] 889[9] 977[3] 1162[7] 6863[9]

Rocker *Gary Moore* a74 84
6 b g Rock Of Gibraltar(IRE) —Jessica's Dream (IRE) (Desert Style (IRE))
1074[6] 1266[2] (1874) 2592[7] 2973[9] 3578[8] 3815[5] 4510[13] 5262[10] ◆ 5628[2] 5995[5] 6440[6] 6858[10]

Rocket Man (AUS) *Patrick Shaw* a121 124
5 b g Viscount(AUS) —Macrosa (NZ) (Mcginty (NZ))
1024a[2] ◆ 7852a[2]

Rocket Man (IRE) *A P O'Brien* 88
3 b c Montjeu(IRE) —Gone To The Moon (USA) (Gone West (USA))
1833[6]

Rocket Rob (IRE) *Marco Botti* a92 95
4 b g Danetime(IRE) —Queen Of Fibres (IRE) (Scenic)
(172) 307[2] 722[5] 1471[2] 2745[3] 3629[2] 4148[2] 4904[3] 5308[7]

Rocket Ruby *Derek Shaw* a61 58
4 br m Piccolo—Kitty Kitty Cancan (Warrshan (USA))
103[6] (132)

Rockette (FR) *E J O'Neill* a97 96
5 ch m Ange Gabriel(FR) —Racoon (FR) (Be My Guest (USA))
441a[9] 711a[5]

Rockfella *Denis Coakley* a59 82
4 ch g Rock Of Gibraltar(IRE) —Afreeta (USA) (Afleet (CAN))
1579[4] 3159[3] 4147[4] 5002[4] 6754[5]

Rockhorse (IRE) *B Grizzetti* 109
5 ch g Rock Of Gibraltar(IRE) —Maelalong (IRE) (Maelstrom Lake)
6764a[5] 7370a[6]

Rockie Bright *James Given* 58
3 b f Rock Of Gibraltar(IRE) —Alabastrine (Green Desert (USA))
1504[12] 2706[7]

Rockin N Reelin (USA) *J T Gorman* a57 70
3 b g Forest Camp(USA) —Dusti's Tune (USA) (Unbridled's Song (USA))
4563a[18]

Rock Jock (IRE) *Tracey Collins* a96 107
3 b c Rock Of Gibraltar(IRE) —Perfect Touch (USA) (Miswaki (USA))
414a[9] 608a[9] 1406a[6] 1676a[3] 2075[4] 3066[3] 5573a[6] 6617a[6]

Rock My Soul (IRE) *Uwe Ostmann* 101
4 b m Clodovil(IRE) —Rondinay (FR) (Cadeaux Genereux)
4035a[9] 5649a[8] 7416a[8]

Rock My World (IRE) *Michael Jarvis* a75 75
3 b f Rock Of Gibraltar(IRE) —Arctic Hunt (IRE) (Bering)
(5665)

Rock 'N' Roller (FR) *Gary Moore* a74 44
6 bb g Sagacity(FR) —Diamond Dance (FR) (Dancehall (USA))
224[3] 1690[9] 8013[7]

Rock N Roll Ransom *Luca Cumani* 103
3 b g Red Ransom(USA) —Zee Zee Top (Zafonic (USA))
(2899) (3916) 4573[7] 5917[9] (6318) ◆ 6738[2] ◆

Rock 'N' Royal *Richard Fahey* 81
3 b g Royal Applause—Grande Terre (IRE) (Grand Lodge (USA))
2028[10] 2542[4] 5937[6] 6963[10] 7283[9]

Rock Of Behistun (IRE) *Patrick Gilligan* a8 28
3 b g Antonius Pius(USA) —Persian Flower (Persian Heights)
3996[5] 4235[6]

Rock Of Eire *Edward Creighton* a48 54
3 b g Rock Of Gibraltar(IRE) —Graceful Lass (Sadler's Wells (USA))
482[4] 762[11] 2336[12]

Rock Of Nassau (FR) *F Head* 96
4 ch g Rock Of Gibraltar(IRE) —Solosole (USA) (Gulch (USA))
7278a[7]

Rock Relief (IRE) *Sir Mark Prescott Bt* a59 66
4 gr g Daylami(IRE) —Sheer Bliss (IRE) (Sadler's Wells (USA))
2337[3] 2645[10] 3025[6] 3524[4]

Rocks Off (ARG) *M F De Kock* a92 97
5 br h Orpen(USA) —Lava Gold (USA) (Java Gold (USA))
339a[12] 441a[11] 517a[10]

Rock Soleil *Jane Chapple-Hyam* a76 75
6 b g Rock Of Gibraltar(IRE) —Hunt The Sun (Rainbow Quest (USA))
4891[10] 5996[13] 6331[6] 6516[5] 6693[3] 7208[P]

Rockson (IRE) *Ian Williams* a53 53
4 bb m Rock Of Gibraltar(IRE) —Opera Star (IRE) (Sadler's Wells (USA))
4202[8] 4857[9]

Rock Tech *John Jenkins* a52 39
5 b h High Estate—Mrs Fire Cracker (Rock City)
599[5] 1188[6] 2907[5] 4915[7]

Rock The Stars (IRE) *J W Hills* a46 76
3 ch g Rock Of Gibraltar(IRE) —Crimphill (IRE) (Sadler's Wells (USA))
2220[6] (2633) (3002) 3363[2] 6422[3] 6807[3] 7062[2] 7307[2]

Rockweiller *David Evans* a25 75
3 b c Rock Of Gibraltar(IRE) —Ballerina Suprema (IRE) (Sadler's Wells (USA))
1977[10] 3960[2] 4621[3] (4925) 5173[2] 5585[4] 6225[4] (6326)

Rock With You *Jeremy Gask* a68
3 b f Rock Of Gibraltar(IRE) —Karsiyaka (IRE) (Kahyasi)
744[4] 980[3] 1450[8]

Rocky Coast *Bryan Smart* 59
2 b c Indesatchel(IRE) —Crystal Canyon (Efisio)
3945[8] 5099[5] 5352[4] 6220[8] 6674[14]

Rocky Mood (IRE) *Walter Swinburn* a57 67
3 ch g Rock Of Gibraltar(IRE) —Mood Indigo (IRE) (Indian Ridge)
1450[13] 1844[9] 2755[8] 3297[7] 3963[9] 5158[4] 5766[7] 6860[3] ◆ 7070[3]

Rocky Rebel *Ralph Beckett* a73 74
2 b g Norse Dancer(IRE) —Gulchina (USA) (Gulch (USA))
4490[7] 5047[3] 5724[3] 6810[4]

Rocky's Pride (IRE) *Willie Musson* a81 78
4 b g Rock Of Gibraltar(IRE) —L'Animee (Green Tune (USA))
239[9] 526[5] 756[6] 897[8] 1346[4] 1440[4] 2233[2] (2388) 3607[5] 3995[5] 6065[13] 6668[2]

Roderic O'Connor (IRE) *A P O'Brien* 120
2 b c Galileo(IRE) —Secret Garden (IRE) (Danehill (USA))
6924[2] (7265a)

Rodrigo De Freitas (IRE) *Jim Boyle* a62 68
3 b g Captain Rio—Brazilian Sun (IRE) (Barathea (IRE))
3039[10] 4025[5] 4791[5] 4994[2] 5664[8] 5873[4] 6527[9] (6993) 7156[10]

Rodrigo De Torres *Henry Cecil* 107
3 ch c Bahamian Bounty—Leonica (Lion Cavern (USA))
1385[4] (1687) 2546[3] 3066[9] 4140[3] 5526[5]

Rodrigo Fontana *Sir Mark Prescott Bt*
3 b g Red Ransom(USA) —Lavinia Fontana (IRE) (Sharpo)
1825[12] 2787[10]

Rogue Romance (USA) *Kenneth McPeek* a101 105
2 ch c Smarty Jones(USA) —Lovington (USA) (Afleet (CAN))
7363a[3]

Rohaani (USA) *Doug Watson* a95 100
8 ch h High Yield(USA) —Strawberry's Charm (USA) (Strawberry Road (AUS))
335a[9] 418a[14]

Roi Du Boeuf (IRE) *David Simcock* a51 63
2 b g Hurricane Run(IRE) —Princess Killeen (IRE) (Sinndar (IRE))
3472[4] 4554[10] 4802[4] 5490[4] 6471[10] 7197[4]

Roilos (IRE) *Marco Botti* a59
4 b h Bahri(USA) —Raiska (IRE) (Grand Lodge (USA))
7414[6] 7732[10]

Roisin's Prince (IRE) *Matt Sheppard* a56 28
8 br g Bold Fact(USA) —Rosie Jaques (Doyoun)
622[10]

Rojo Boy *David Elsworth* 77
2 gr c Red Ransom(USA) —Way To The Stars (Dansili)
1351[6] 2059[4] 2407[3] 2980[2] 3887[7] 5626[3] 5785[6] 6268[3]

Roker Park (IRE) *Kevin Ryan* 103
5 b g Choisir(AUS) —Joyful (IRE) (Green Desert (USA))
1573[8] 2759[14] 3446[8] 4371[5] 5290[2] 5884[10] 6142[15]

Rolling Hills (IRE) *Henry Candy* 75
3 b g Celtic Swing—Silk Suivante (IRE) (Danehill (USA))
1442[2] 2052[7] 2618[8] 3374[2] 3816[2] (4364) 4963[7] 5494[2]

Rolling Sea *Frau S Weis* a44
3 b g Tiger Hill(IRE) —Rock The Boat (Slip Anchor)
7959a[9]

Romacaca (USA) *N Canani* 102
4 bb m Running Stag(USA) —Romaca (USA) (Kris S (USA))
5320a[4]

Romancea (USA) *Edward Vaughan* a41 71
3 ch f Mr Greeley(USA) —Two Halos (USA) (Saint Ballado (CAN))
2718[5] 2998[9] 3592[8] 4705[7] 5686[3] 5960[6] 7013[3]

Roman Dancer (IRE) *John Gallagher* a60 77
2 b g Antonius Pius(USA) —Dancing Duchess (IRE) (Danehill Dancer (IRE))
1686[6] 2238[10] 2594[9] (3959) 4831[3] 5987[5] 7891[9]

Roman Eagle (IRE) *Michael Jarvis* 90
2 b c Holy Roman Emperor(IRE) —Qhazeenah (Marju (IRE))
(3631) ◆ 6200[7] (6553)

Roman Flame *Michael Quinn* a75 64
2 ch f Bertolini(USA) —Dakhla Oasis (IRE) (Night Shift (USA))
7682[3]

Roman Glory (IRE) *Brian Meehan* 85
4 b g Soviet Star(USA) —Putout (Dowsing (USA))
2284[6] (3212) 3438[5] 3659[6] (4501) 5003[4]

Roman History (IRE) *Tracy Waggott* a58 52
7 b g Titus Livius(FR) —Tetradonna (IRE) (Teenoso (USA))
3021[5] 3370[12] 4411[4] 4484[3] 5216[4] 6032[7]

Romano (IRE) *Paul Midgley* 28
2 ch g Haafhd—Quiet Storm (IRE) (Desert Prince (IRE))
3362[7] 3657[9] 4554[11]

Roman Republic (FR) *Saeed Bin Suroor* a99 105
4 b g Cape Cross(IRE) —Mare Nostrum (Caerleon (USA))
632a[3] 821a[9] 4455[10] 5188[16] 6877[5]

Roman Ruler (IRE) *Chris Fairhurst* 66
2 gr g Antonius Pius(USA) —Way Of Truth (Muhtarram (USA))
2498[9] 2832[11] 3528[4] 4124[4] 4367[5] 5042[7] 5755[3] 6184[6]

Roman Sioux (IRE) *Robin Bastiman* 49
3 b g Antonius Pius(USA) —Blue Sioux (Indian Ridge)
2425[9] 5603[4] 6077[6]

Roman's Run (USA) *Doug Watson* a100 46
6 br h Tiznow(USA) —Ensnare (USA) (Seeking The Gold (USA))
(632a) 821a[6]

Roman Strait *Michael Blanshard* a61 55
2 b c Refuse To Bend(IRE) —Oman Sea (USA) (Rahy (USA))
2895[4] 4123[5] 4709[4] 6674[7] 7552[8] (8031)

Romantic Girl (IRE) *Alan Juckes* a27 22
2 b f Byron—Urmia (Persian Bold)
5643[6] 7123[9] 7452[9]

Romanticize *Dr Jon Scargill* 77
4 b m Kyllachy—Romancing (Dr Devious (IRE))
2601[8] 6478[13]

Romantic Queen *George Baker* a70 24
4 b m Medicean—Bandit Queen (Desert Prince (IRE))
391[3] 532[2] 684[2] 828[2] 1482[11] 1979[3] 2234[8] 3516[2] (3763) ◆ 3966[2] 4430[4] 5698[8] (6330) 6537[3] ◆ 6898[10] 7332[4]

Romantic Verse *Ronald Harris* a71 62
5 b m Kyllachy—Romancing (Dr Devious (IRE))
21[11] 249[12] 477[5] 495[6] 691[11] 721[11]

Romantic Wish *Robert Mills* a73
2 b f Hawk Wing(USA) —Jules (IRE) (Danehill (USA))
3562[6] 4021[3] 7164[3] (7417)

Romany Gypsy *David Evans* 21
2 b f Indesatchel(IRE) —River Song (USA) (Siphon (BRZ))
2407[8] 2621[10] 3509[10]

Romany Stone (IRE) *Michael Jarvis* 52
2 ch f Pivotal—Celtic Heroine (IRE) (Hernando (FR))
7232[10]

Romeo Montague *Ed Dunlop* a42 61
2 b g Montjeu(IRE) —Issa (Pursuit Of Love)
6883[15] 7178[4] 7530[11]

Romeos Girl *Jennie Candlish* 55
3 b f Statue Of Liberty(USA) —Fadaki Hawaki (USA) (Vice Regent (CAN))
1601[9]

Romeo's On Fire (IRE) *G M Lyons* a93 86
6 b g Danehill(USA) —Fighting Countess (USA) (Ringside (USA))
5571a[13]

Romie's Kastett (GER) *John M Oxx* 88
3 ch f Halling(USA) —River Patrol (Rousillon (USA))
5568a[9] 6379a[10]

Romp (ARG) *Kristin Mulhall* a96 97
6 b g Incurable Optimist(USA) —Stormy Secret (ARG) (Hidden Prize (USA))
1435a[5] 7339a[9]

Rondeau (GR) *Patrick Chamings* a82 78
5 ch g Harmonic Way—Areti (GR) (Wadood (USA))
123[4] 275[2] ◆ 393[4] 616[5] 767[4] 1044[3] 1848[3] 2783[2] 4260[2] 5889[3] 7047[5] 7421[8]

Roninski (IRE) *Bryan Smart* 72
2 b c Cadeaux Genereux—Ruby Affair (IRE) (Night Shift (USA))
6566[3]

Ronja (USA) *W Hickst* 101
3 ch f El Corredor(USA) —Royal Sanction (USA) (Royal Academy (USA))
(1250a) 1715a[12] 6409a[9]

Ronnie Howe *Roy Bowring* a59 64
6 b g Hunting Lion(IRE) —Arasong (Aragon)
70[9] 243[4] 402[12] 774[4]

Rony Dony (IRE) *Mark Rimmer* a47 39
6 b g Revoque(IRE) —Farrans Guest (IRE) (Tagula (IRE))
318[7] 342[6] 700[5]

Roodee King *Patrick Morris* a40 54
4 b g Auction House(USA) —Antithesis (IRE) (Fairy King (USA))
1235[10]

Roodee Queen *Patrick Morris* a16 70
2 b f Kyllachy—Hilites (IRE) (Desert King (IRE))
1065[9] 1294[4] 1510[6] 1864[2] 2292[3] 2605[2] 2951[7] 3072[2] (3353) 3859[5] 3986[4] 4948[5] 5358[2]

Roodle *Eve Johnson Houghton* 90
3 b f Xaar—Roodeye (Inchinor)
5694[8] 6776[13]

Room For A View *Marcus Tregoning* a66 57
3 b f Observatory(USA) —Annex (Anabaa (USA))
6470[4] 6876[10] (7288) 7561[2]

Roose Blox (IRE) *Roger Fisher* a31 70
3 b g Captain Rio—Kakatiya (IRE) (Barathea (IRE))
1804[5] 2393[5] 3220[4] 4093[5] 4705[5] 6540[12]

Rosa Gurney (IRE) *John Best* 56
3 b f Antonius Pius(USA) —Nonsense (IRE) (Soviet Star (USA))
2964[12]

Rosairlie (IRE) *Harry Dunlop* 61
2 ch f Halling(USA) —Mrs Mason (IRE) (Turtle Island (IRE))
5985[8] 6831[5]

Rosa Midnight (USA) *Michael Bell* a61 60
2 b f Lemon Drop Kid(USA) —Christmas Player (USA) (Theatrical)
3861[5] 4299[3] 5029[7] (5660) 5961[4] ◆

Rosanara (FR) *A De Royer-Dupre* 117
3 gr f Sinndar(IRE) —Rosawa (FR) (Linamix (FR))
1566a[3] 2158a[4] 3015a[2] 4575[7] 6613a[5] 7160a[3]

Rosaria *Richard Hannon* a64 38
2 b f Tiger Hill(IRE) —Flamingo Flower (USA) (Diesis)
7231[15] 7755[2] ◆

Rosbay (IRE) *Tim Easterby* 86
6 b g Desert Prince(IRE) —Dark Rosaleen (IRE) (Darshaan)
(1013) 1378[4] ◆ 1512[4] 1889[2] 2084[2] 2608[10] 2937[5] 3121[5] 3319[11] 4152[8] 4603[8] 5071[4] 5436[9] 5756[2] 6112[9] 6573[6] 6724[6]

Rosbertini *Linda Perratt* 62
4 ch g Bertolini(USA) —Rose Of America (Brief Truce (USA))
1868[4] 2393[15] 3148[5] 3531[3] 3905[9] 4189[9] 4514[3] 4823[12] 6710[12]

Rosco Flyer (IRE) *Roger Teal* a82 81
4 b g Val Royal(FR) —Palace Soy (IRE) (Tagula (IRE))
1637[4] 2080[2] 2511[2] (3473) ◆ (4019) 4758[7] 5888[9] (6807) 7292[3] 7736[6]

Rose Alba (IRE) *John Dunlop* a43 65
3 gr f Verglas(IRE) —Green Rosy (USA) (Green Dancer (USA))
1261[4] 1778[3] 2935[8] 3564[8]

Rose Aurora *Marcus Tregoning* a49 53
3 gr f Pastoral Pursuits—Khaladja (IRE) (Akarad (FR))
2004[6] 3816[5] 4282[3] 4746[2] 5330[3] 5869[7] 6525[4] 6999[5] ◆ 7039[4] ◆

Rose Bed (IRE) *Michael Quinlan* a48 48
3 ch f Namid—Daqtora (Dr Devious (IRE))
5419[4] 5650[6] 6060[6] 6420[5] 6773[6] 7676[5] 7987[3]

Rose Blossom *Richard Fahey* 109
3 b f Pastoral Pursuits—Lamarita (Emarati (USA))
1918[13] (2058) 2536[2] ◆ 3197[6] (3875) 5276[5] 5851[2] 6608a[12]

Rose Catherine (USA) *Todd Pletcher* a74 110
3 bb f Speightstown(USA) —Great Plains Lady (USA) (Peaks And Valleys (USA))
7362a[7]

Rosedale *James Toller* a54 76
3 b f Pastoral Pursuits—Wyoming (Inchinor)
(2200) 2566[4] 3115[8] 3866[4] 4735[4] (5561) 6197[12] (6992) 7238[8]

Rose De Rita *Liam Grassick* a26 36
5 br m Superior Premium—Rita's Rock Ape (Mon Tresor)
2919[13] 7563[10]

Rose Hip (IRE) *Joseph G Murphy* a94 100
6 b m Rossini(USA) —Rose Tint (IRE) (Salse (USA))
1954a[3] 2355a[6] 3467a[9] 4630a[8] 5568a[7] 5772a[8] (Dead)

Rose Kingdom (JPN) *Kojiro Hashiguchi* 121
3 bb c King Kamehameha(JPN) —Rosebud (JPN) (Sunday Silence (USA))
(7615a)

Rosenblatt (GER) *M S Tuck*
8 b g Dashing Blade—Roseraie (GER) (Nebos (GER))
5959[10] 6668[12]

Rosendhal (IRE) *A Renzoni* 103
3 ch c Indian Ridge—Kathy College (IRE) (College Chapel)
7370a[4] (7459a)

Rose Of Coma (IRE) *Alan Juckes* a47 59
4 br m Kheleyf(USA) —Rosalia (USA) (Red Ransom (USA))
2955[14] 3128[14]

Rose Row *Mary Hambro* a85 71
6 gr m Act One—D'Azy (Persian Bold)
500[6] 688[2] 811[4] 1020[3] 3566[8]

Roses For The Lady (IRE) *John M Oxx* 112
4 b m Sadler's Wells(USA) —Head In The Clouds (IRE) (Rainbow Quest (USA))
(1560a) 3470a[3] 5881[6] 6786a[2]

Rosetta Hill *John Jenkins* a41 48
3 ch f Compton Place—Fruit Of Glory (Glory Of Dancer)
3907[6] 4720[6] 5726[7]

Rosewin (IRE) *Ollie Pears* a74 72
4 b m Hawkeye(IRE) —African Scene (IRE) (Scenic)
4604[10] 5200[2] 6187[3] 6649[2] 7149[3] (7898) 7957[2]

Rosewood Lad *J S Moore* a56 51
3 ch g Needwood Blade—Meandering Rose (USA) (Irish River (FR))
356[7] 484[10] 928[5] 1145[2] 1880[6] 2412[4] 2606[9] 3213[4] 3442[2] 3640[2] 4211[6] 4448[7] 7716[2] 7848[2] 8013[2]

Roshina (IRE) *Jo Crowley* a72 69
4 b m Chevalier(IRE) —Tus Maith (IRE) (Entrepreneur)
385[3] 673[3] (931) 3212[10] 4260[10]

Rosie Gem *Tom Dascombe* 56
3 gr f Bahamian Bounty—Etienne Lady (IRE) (Imperial Frontier (USA))
4966[5]

Rosie Raymond *Charles Smith* a23
5 b m Kris Kin(USA) —Iota (Niniski (USA))
1067[5]

Rosie Says No *Alan McCabe* a70 68
5 b m Catcher In The Rye(IRE) —Curlew Calling (IRE) (Pennine Walk)
37[3] 89[5]

Rosie's Magic *F J Brennan* 31
3 b f Auction House(USA) —Sachiko (Celtic Swing)
2122[10] 2925[11] 6771[7] 7122[10]

Rosika *Sir Michael Stoute* a100 106
4 b m Sakhee(USA) —Blush Rambler (IRE) (Blushing Groom (FR))
2538[3] 3671[7] 4507[4] 5220[2] 7189[2]

Rosiliant (IRE) *Clive Cox* a49 58
3 ch f Refuse To Bend(IRE) —Rosy Dudley (IRE) (Grand Lodge (USA))
1640[7] 2000[7] 2962[4] 3526[2] 3907[3] 4248[2] 4692[3] 4989[4] 5650[4] 6025[7] 6657[5]

Rosina Grey *Rod Millman* a78 85
2 gr f Proclamation(IRE) —Rosina May (IRE) (Danehill Dancer (IRE))
1136[7] (1541) 1733[3] 3482[5] 3887[9] 4262[5] (4677) 4955[3] 5472[5] 5856[5] (6325) 6528[9] (6842)

Rosko *Brian Ellison* a66 80
6 b g Selkirk(USA) —Desert Alchemy (IRE) (Green Desert (USA))
2764[5] 3408[3] 4093[4] (4354) 4704[2] 5043[4] 5533[9] 6534[14]

Rossatron *Jeremy Gask* a35 53
4 b h Primo Valentino(IRE) —Sunday Night (GER) (Bakharoff (USA))
7890[10]

Rossetti *Richard Hannon* 80
2 gr c Dansili—Snowdrops (Gulch (USA))
2171^{3} (3555) 4578^{3} ◆

Rossvoss *T M Walsh* 89
2 b c Medicean—Dixielake (IRE) (Lake Coniston (IRE))
6403a^{5}

Rostrum (FR) *A Fabre* a95 81
3 b c Shamardal(USA) —En Public (FR) (Rainbow Quest (USA))
7776a^{0}

Rosy Dawn *Luke Dace* a55 56
5 ch m Bertolini(USA) —Blushing Sunrise (USA) (Cox's Ridge (USA))
969^{3} 1078^{7} 1636^{6} 2201^{4} 2489^{3} 2966^{9} 3290^{2} 3789^{4} 3983^{2} 4498^{3} 4740^{2} 5072^{6} 6021^{7} 6273^{9} 7728^{7} 7884^{4}

Rothesay Chancer *Jim Goldie* 62
2 ch g Monsieur Bond(IRE) —Rhinefield Beauty (IRE) (Shalford (IRE))
3315^{12} 4645^{6} 5239^{4} 6030^{6} 6139^{4} 6489^{4} 6705^{7} 7050^{2} 7174^{5}

Rothesay Dancer *Jim Goldie* a44 88
7 b m Lujain(USA) —Rhinefield Beauty (IRE) (Shalford (IRE))
1099^{11} 1711^{7} 1923^{4} 2431^{6} 3075^{2} 3321^{5} 3533^{4} 3947^{7} 4192^{12} 4952^{6} 5212^{6} 5477^{5} 6103^{12} (6246) 6491^{7} 7239^{10} 7525^{11}

Rough Rock (IRE) *Chris Dwyer* a54 77
5 ch g Rock Of Gibraltar(IRE) —Amitie Fatale (IRE) (Night Shift (USA))
1131^{5} (1443) 1633^{7} (2010) 2301^{7} 2635^{5} 2957^{7} 3216^{6} 3604^{2} 3994^{5} (4209) 4440^{4} 4717^{6} 4968^{3} 5561^{3} (5789) 6097^{5} (6274) 7046^{10} 7238^{9}

Rough Sailing (USA) *Michael Stidham* a98 90
2 ch c Mizzen Mast(USA) —Moussica (USA) (Woodman (USA))
7360a^{S}

Roundthetwist (IRE) *John Weymes* a49 63
5 b g Okawango(USA) —Delta Town (USA) (Sanglamore (USA))
227^{3} 791^{8} 816^{9}

Round Turn (IRE) *Ed McMahon* a60 55
2 b c Oratorio(IRE) —Half-Hitch (USA) (Diesis)
6414^{6} 7452^{8} 7567^{6}

Round Won (USA) *William Knight* a77 74
3 ch g Two Punch(USA) —Indy Go Go (USA) (A.P. Indy (USA))
(1644) 2025^{3} 7389^{3} 7597^{10}

Rouvres Girl (IRE) *Seamus Fahey* a56 63
5 b m Rouvres(FR) —Hierarchy (Sabrehill (USA))
427^{3}

Rowaad *Andrew Price* a69 53
5 ch g Compton Place—Level Pegging (IRE) (Common Grounds)
3559^{13}

Rowan Light *Jim Boyle* a63 40
4 b m Fantastic Light(USA) —Filippa (GER) (Dashing Blade)
1661^{10} 2632^{9} 3214^{3} 4070^{12} 4591^{6} (5180) 6668^{9}

Rowan Lodge (IRE) *Ollie Pears* a53 70
8 ch g Indian Lodge(IRE) —Tirol Hope (IRE) (Tirol)
1293^{4} 2208^{4} 2377^{5} 3110^{2} 3614^{2} 4656^{8} 4986^{2} 5530^{14} 6117^{8} 6463^{8}

Rowan Ridge *Jim Boyle* 71
2 ch g Compton Place—Lemon Tree (USA) (Zilzal (USA))
3577^{4} 4221^{10} 5587^{5} 7034^{9}

Rowan Spirit (IRE) *Mark Brisbourne* a76 73
2 gr g Captain Rio—Secret Justice (USA) (Lit De Justice (USA))
1389^{7} 1603^{5} 6045^{2} 6646^{3} 7240^{7} (7395) 7803^{6}

Rowan Tiger *Jim Boyle* a79 82
4 b g Tiger Hill(IRE) —Lemon Tree (USA) (Zilzal (USA))
1161^{4} 1690^{10} 2080^{3} 2934^{5} 3576^{3} (4226) 5091^{6} 5868^{5} 6289^{7} 6639^{2} 7045^{6}

Rowayton *James Bethell* a86 89
4 gr m Lujain(USA) —Bandanna (Bandmaster (USA))
1516^{3} 2134^{4} 2327^{5} 2940^{9} 3435^{6} 4118^{11} 4452^{4} 4942^{5} 5356^{2} 5684^{5} 5999^{7}

Rowe Park *Linda Jewell* a108 108
7 b g Dancing Spree(USA) —Magic Legs (Reprimand)
948^{5} 1353^{4} 1700^{12} (3891) 4401^{11} 4505^{11} 7329^{3} 7524^{4}

Roxy Flyer (IRE) *Amanda Perrett* a93 96
3 b f Rock Of Gibraltar(IRE) —Dyna Flyer (USA) (Marquetry (USA))
2051^{2} (2717) 3298^{3} (4573) 5118^{5} 6199^{2} 7189^{6}

Roxy Spirit (IRE) *Michael Mullineaux* a21
3 ch f Cape Town(IRE) —Preston Music (Accordion)
755^{6} 1504^{11} 2860^{13}

Royal Acclamation (IRE) *James Evans* a58 58
5 b g Acclamation—Lady Abigail (IRE) (Royal Academy (USA))
264^{5} 495^{4} 721^{2} 866^{3} (976) 1170^{12} 1922^{5} 2419^{5} ◆ 2779^{12} ◆ 4434^{4} ◆

Royal Amnesty *Valentine Donoghue* a47 88
7 br g Desert Prince(IRE) —Regal Peace (Known Fact (USA))
7243^{10}

Royal And Ancient (IRE) *Milton Harris* a63 74
3 b g Danehill Dancer(IRE) —Champaka (IRE) (Caerleon (USA))
6753^{9} 7690^{5}

Royal Applord *Nigel Tinkler* a15 48
5 b g Royal Applause—Known Class (USA) (Known Fact (USA))
2789^{8} 3369^{7} 4156^{9} 4985^{11} 5927^{11}

Royal Assent *Andrew Balding* 50
3 b f Royal Applause—Brand (Shareef Dancer (USA))
5265^{4}

Royal Astronomer (IRE) *Donal Kinsella* a87 94
5 b g Soviet Star(USA) —Queen's Quest (Rainbow Quest (USA))
3487a^{5} 4463a^{6}

Royal Bench (IRE) *Robert Collet* 117
3 b c Whipper(USA) —Hit The Sky (IRE) (Cozzene (USA))
2802a^{14} (3933a) 5134a^{5} (6593a) 7853a^{2}

Royal Bet (IRE) *Michael Bell* a57 61
4 b g Montjeu(IRE) —Queen Of Norway (USA) (Woodman (USA))
244^{5} 353^{5}

Royal Blade (IRE) *Alan Berry* a62 71
3 ch g Needwood Blade—Royal Dream (Ardkinglass)
1058^{9} 4365^{4} 4754^{8} 5588^{5} 7241^{5} 7409^{6} 7868^{11}

Royal Bonsai *John Quinn* a56
2 b g Val Royal(FR) —Bonsai (IRE) (Woodman (USA))
7335^{6} 7700^{3}

Royal Box *Dai Burchell* a72 73
3 b g Royal Applause—Diamond Lodge (Grand Lodge (USA))
5146^{10} 5470^{6} 5959^{6} 6579^{7} 7377^{5} 7883^{4}

Royal Breeze (FR) *M Seror*
8 b g Phantom Breeze—Royale Brisscare (FR) (Bricassar (USA))
5378a^{0}

Royal Cheer *Ann Duffield* a10 46
3 b f Royal Applause—Rise 'n Shine (Night Shift (USA))
(2535) 2962^{11} 3515^{11} 3900^{5} 4674^{9} 4947^{8} 5485^{10}

Royal Classy Cleo *David Evans* a2 28
2 b f Val Royal(FR) —Classy Cleo (IRE) (Mujadil (USA))
4474^{13} 4802^{13} 5268^{6} 5885^{6}

Royal Composer (IRE) *Tim Easterby* 60
7 b g Mozart(IRE) —Susun Kelapa (USA) (St Jovite (USA))
2421^{9} 2851^{6} 3370^{2} 3614^{5} 3978^{2} (4454) 4985^{8} 6518^{9}

Royal Crest *Andrew Crook* a63 59
4 b g Royal Applause—Noble Lady (Primo Dominie)
215 503^{9} 705^{9} 838^{12} 4559^{9} 5024^{13}

Royal Dalakhani (IRE) *Paul D'Arcy* a66 64
3 gr f Dalakhani(IRE) —Royal Ballerina (IRE) (Sadler's Wells (USA))
2994^{5} 3563^{10} 4229^{3} 4751^{6} 5963^{6}

Royal Defence (IRE) *Nick Littmoden* a51 88
4 b g Refuse To Bend(IRE) —Alessia (GER) (Warning)
1962^{7} 2865^{11} 5859^{6} 6841^{9}

Royal Destination (IRE) *Jeremy Noseda* 109
5 b g Dubai Destination(USA) —Royale (IRE) (Royal Academy (USA))
2977^{5} 3921^{10} 4537^{12} 5188^{2} (5879) 6193^{11} 6885^{13}

Royal Diamond (IRE) *Michael Dods* a101 92
4 b g King's Best(USA) —Irresistible Jewel (IRE) (Danehill (USA))
1724^{9} ◆ 2126^{8} 3447^{16} 3877^{7}

Royal Dignitary (USA) *David Nicholls* a90 81
10 br g Saint Ballado(CAN) —Star Actress (USA) (Star De Naskra (USA))
87^{5} 273a^{5} 459a^{7} 559a^{5} 690a^{8} (895) 1149^{3} 1293^{3} (1536) (1995) (2377) 2858^{3} 3580^{4} 4713^{5}

Royal Envoy (IRE) *Jane Chapple-Hyam* a73 86
7 b g Royal Applause—Seven Notes (Zafonic (USA))
194^{4} 351^{10} 839^{11} 1170^{2} 1998^{8} 7192^{7} 7425^{10} 7605^{7} 7885^{12} 8024^{6}

Royal Etiquette (IRE) *Lawney Hill* a72 75
3 b g Royal Applause—Alpine Gold (IRE) (Montjeu (IRE))
1393^{2} 1851^{9} 2893^{13} 3213^{6} 3787^{2} 7690^{4} 8021^{6}

Royal Exchange *Richard Hannon* 101
2 b c Royal Applause—Diamond Lodge (Grand Lodge (USA))
1351^{2} 2540^{2} (3332) (4539) (5257) 6507^{3} ◆ 6982^{2}

Royal Flynn *Kate Walton* 64
8 b g Royal Applause—Shamriyna (IRE) (Darshaan)
1803^{5} 2214^{10}

Royal Holiday (IRE) *Brian Ellison* a69 51
3 ch g Captain Rio—Sunny Slope (Mujtahid (USA))
1104^{6} 1511^{12} 2291^{9} 4061^{9} 4374^{7} 5337^{7} 5545^{11} (5648) 5923^{10} 7006^{9} 7128^{4} 7474^{11} 7731^{3} 7899^{5}

Royal Hush *Kevin Ryan* 75
2 b f Royal Applause—Sablonne (USA) (Silver Hawk (USA))
2130^{7} 3549^{5} 4862^{4} 6034^{8}

Royal Indulgence *Mark Brisbourne* a49 28
10 b g Royal Applause—Silent Indulgence (USA) (Woodman (USA))
3032^{11} 3559^{10} 4168^{9}

Royal Intruder *S Donohoe* a92 90
5 b g Royal Applause—Surprise Visitor (IRE) (Be My Guest (USA))
992^{6} 1822^{7} 2431^{10} 3489a^{19} 6932^{4} 7212^{13}

Royal Island (IRE) *Michael Quinlan* a60 86
8 b g Trans Island—Royal House (FR) (Royal Academy (USA))
7070^{7} 7299^{7} 7508^{5} (7717) ◆ 7787^{4} 7835^{2}

Royal Liaison *Michael Bell* 72
2 b f Ad Valorem(USA) —Royal Mistress (Fasliyev (USA))
2505^{6} 2958^{2} 3392^{3} 4124^{2}

Royal Max (IRE) *Ian Williams* a54 54
4 b g Hawkeye(IRE) —Baccara (IRE) (Sri Pekan (USA))
7201^{11} 7569^{4}

Royal Opera *Rod Millman* 78
2 b g Acclamation—Desert Gold (IRE) (Desert Prince (IRE))
1517^{6} 1845^{3} 2389^{4} 3887^{2} (4221) 4623^{3} 5301^{11} 6690^{3} 7085^{9}

Royalorien *William Knight* a54 72
2 b f Royal Applause—Lorien Hill (IRE) (Danehill (USA))
3906^{2} ◆ 4471^{9} 5255^{4} 5808^{4} 6426^{8} 7040^{8}

Royal Patriot (IRE) *Paul Green* a47 56
3 b g King's Best(USA) —Lady Ragazza (IRE) (Bering)
1706^{8} 1890^{5} 2288^{5} 3062^{7} 3682^{9} 5067^{8} 5424^{8} 5926^{9} 7070^{5} 7450^{5}

Royal Pennekamp (FR) *B Dutruel* a83 86
7 b h Pennekamp(USA) —Lead Cora (FR) (Lead On Time (USA))
458a^{2} 640a^{5}

Royal Power (IRE) *David Nicholls* a90 97
7 b g Xaar—Magic Touch (Fairy King (USA))
272a^{3} 458a^{6} 743a^{0} 1272^{15} 2579^{9}

Royal Premier (IRE) *Hugh Collingridge* a50 65
7 b g King's Theatre(IRE) —Mystic Shadow (IRE) (Mtoto)
748^{10} 842^{6} 1283^{9} (2014) 2995^{5} 3348^{7} 3996^{4} 6306^{4}

Royal Premium *James Moffatt* a31 62
4 b h Superior Premium—Royal Shepley (Royal Applause)
407^{8} 1722^{7} 2278^{11}

Royal Prince *Doug Watson* a88 71
9 gr h Royal Applause—Onefortheditch (USA) (With Approval (CAN))
415a^{7} ◆ 629a^{8}

Royal Prodigy (USA) *Ron Hodges* 48
11 ch g Royal Academy(USA) —Prospector's Queen (USA) (Mr Prospector (USA))
1816a^{4}

Royal Rainbow *Peter Hiatt* a57 45
6 ch g Rainbow Quest(USA) —Royal Future (IRE) (Royal Academy (USA))
(32) 1307 263^{7} 420^{7} 463^{9} 621^{7}

Royal Reason *Mick Channon* a54 55
2 b f Motivator—Elizabethan Age (FR) (King's Best (USA))
6190^{10} 6676^{6} 7185^{9}

Royal Record *Mel Brittain* 65
3 b f Royal Applause—First Musical (First Trump)
2535^{6} 2628^{12} 4151^{10}

Royal Reverie *Walter Swinburn* a65 71
2 b g Royal Applause—Christina's Dream (Spectrum (IRE))
4477^{8} 5156^{4} 5608^{3} 6162^{7}

Royal Revival *A Fabre* 99
3 gr c King's Best(USA) —Holy Nola (USA) (Silver Deputy (CAN))
1947a^{4} 6344a^{6} (6761a) 7266a^{6}

Royal Riviera *Jeremy Gask* a76 80
4 b g Nayef(USA) —Miss Cap Ferrat (Darshaan)
3256^{3} 3563^{2} 4845^{3} 6715^{7}

Royal Rock *Chris Wall* a89 115
6 b g Sakhee(USA) —Vanishing Point (USA) (Caller I.D. (USA))
6063^{6} 6735^{17}

Royal Society *Rodney Farrant* a61 54
4 b g King's Best(USA) —Nawaiet (USA) (Zilzal (USA))
131^{4} 354^{3} 540^{5} 940^{12}

Royal Straight *Linda Perratt* a74 76
5 ch g Halling(USA) —High Straits (Bering)
1012^{2} 1177^{3} (1919) 2343^{5} (2858) 3317^{12} 3499^{2} 3905^{3} 4405^{4} 4585^{6} 5213^{9} 5355^{3} 5790^{2} 6109^{12} 6393^{2} 7053^{3} 7228^{7}

Royal Swain (IRE) *Alan Swinbank* a52 82
4 b g Val Royal(FR) —Targhyb (IRE) (Unfuwain (USA))
1705^{2} (2131) 2761^{8} 6181^{2} (6650) 7226^{5} 7337^{9}

Royal Talisman *Matthew Salaman* a67
2 b g Val Royal(FR) —Talismatic (IRE) (Tagula (IRE))
6249^{5} 6711^{4} 7065^{4}

Royal Torbo (ISR) *George Baker* a61
3 b c Tabari(GER) —Royal Dutch (GER) (Monsun (GER))
9^{6} 219^{2} 381^{5} 762^{10} 964^{5} 1054^{3} 3967^{8} 4519^{8} 5155^{11}

Royal Trooper (IRE) *James Given* a75 83
4 b g Hawk Wing(USA) —Strawberry Roan (IRE) (Sadler's Wells (USA))
1150^{4} 1689^{3} 2060^{4} 2659^{2} 2938^{10} 3974^{4} 4785^{2} 5296^{3} 5790^{6} (6224) (6516) 6926^{21} 7226^{4}

Royal Willy (IRE) *William Jarvis* a62 71
4 b g Val Royal(FR) —Neat Dish (CAN) (Stalwart (USA))
6671^{6} 6934^{4} 7068^{4}

Roybuoy *Harry Dunlop* a52 48
3 b g Royal Applause—Wavy Up (IRE) (Brustolon)
581^{3} 745^{3} 998^{3} 1205^{9} 1795^{8} 2418^{9} 3510^{11}

Roydmore *Richard Fahey* 45
3 b g Doyen(IRE) —Petite Bleu (Vettori (IRE))
2852^{9} 3285^{4} 4414^{5} 4946^{7} 6033^{10} 6298^{11}

Rubaa (IRE) *Chris Bealby* a49
4 ch g King's Best(USA) —Shuruk (Cadeaux Genereux)
308^{7}

Rubbinghouse Com *Pat Phelan* a41 22
3 b g Exceed And Excel(AUS) —Shifty Mouse (Night Shift (USA))
980^{12} 1432^{10} 5027^{12} 5715^{8}

Rubenstar (IRE) *Patrick Morris* a75 67
7 b g Soviet Star(USA) —Ansariya (USA) (Shahrastani (USA))
(110) 259^{3} 292^{3} 1458^{2} 2123^{9} 3970^{9} 6164^{10} 6370^{7} 6854^{2} 7241^{11} 7439^{5} 7847^{5} 7991^{3}

Rubi Dia *K M Prendergast* a73 64
3 ch g Hernando(FR) —Oblique (IRE) (Giant's Causeway (USA))
(523) ◆ 1178^{10} 1601^{3} 7499^{4} 7694^{2} (7806)

Rub Of The Relic (IRE) *Paul Midgley* a63 67
5 b g Chevalier(IRE) —Bayletta (IRE) (Woodborough (USA))
518^{8} 705^{8} (893) 918^{4} 1293^{11} 1374^{6} 1575^{5} 2377^{7} 2492^{2} 2851^{4} 3978^{11} 4196^{8}

Ruby Alexander (IRE) *Ralph Beckett* a56 62
2 ch f Redback—Alexander Eliott (IRE) (Night Shift (USA))
1319^{6} 1541^{6} 2183^{5} 3784^{2} 4067^{2} 5111^{11} (5581) 6052^{4} 6259^{4} 6989^{5}

Ruby Dancer (IRE) *A Turco* 93
5 b m King's Best(USA) —Beauty Dancer (IRE) (Alzao (USA))
1419a^{10}

Ruby Dazzler *Shaun Lycett* a53 59
3 b f Bahamian Bounty—Papillon De Bronze (IRE) (Marju (IRE))
1515^{4} 1932^{15} 3374^{4} 3635^{5} 4307^{7} 4710^{5} 6124^{5} 7273^{9} 7633^{5} 7759^{11}

Rudegirl (IRE) *Nigel Tinkler* 75
2 b f Trade Fair—Madam's View (IRE) (Entrepreneur)
4392^{8} 5066^{9} 5594^{2} 6230a^{4} (6722) 7085^{15}

Rudolf Valentino *A P O'Brien* 100
2 b c Oasis Dream—Maganda (IRE) (Sadler's Wells (USA))
4176a^{3} 5316a^{5} 5975a^{7}

Rudyard (IRE) *J E Hammond* a82 83
2 ch c Iffraaj—Caprarola (USA) (Rahy (USA))
7647a^{6}

Rufus Roughcut *Stuart Williams* a48 36
3 b c Auction House(USA) —Shining Oasis (IRE) (Mujtahid (USA))
288^{3} 305^{4} 387^{8}

Rugell (ARG) *Clive Cox* a90 93
5 b h Interprete(ARG) —Realize (ARG) (Confidental Talk (USA))
2938^{9} 3566^{4} (6423)

Rukhsana *Colin Teague* 11
3 b f Alamshar(IRE) —Senobar (Mtoto)
4601^{8} 5815^{12}

Rulbin Realta *Pat Phelan* a58
3 b f Jendali(USA) —Paulines Gem (IRE) (Petorius)
8021^{3}

Rule Breaker (IRE) *Mark Johnston* a76 92
3 b c Refuse To Bend(IRE) —Sweet Kristeen (USA) (Candy Stripes (USA))
1991^{3} 2496^{2} (2852) 3429^{4} 3886^{10} 4377^{5} 4905^{2} 5264^{7} 6252^{8}

Rule Maker *Jeremy Noseda* 93
3 b c Lemon Drop Kid(USA) —Rhumba Rage (USA) (Nureyev (USA))
2083^{2} 2497^{4} (3272) 3916^{2} 4377^{4} 5759^{6}

Rule Of Nature *Sir Michael Stoute* a85 89
3 b f Oasis Dream—Jolie Etoile (USA) (Diesis)
1279^{2} 1836^{2} 2928^{2} 4145^{4} 4541^{9} 4963^{4} 6253^{6} 6798^{4} 7318^{4}

Ruler Of My Heart (IRE) *F Rossi* 101
3 b f Green Tune(USA) —Dirigeante (FR) (Lead On Time (USA))
952a^{9}

Ruler's Honour (IRE) *Tim Etherington* a59 64
3 b g Antonius Pius(USA) —Naughty Reputation (IRE) (Shalford (IRE))
1401^{7} 1927^{7} 2288^{6} 2706^{4} 3151^{5} ◆ 3773^{4} 5514^{3} 6285^{6} 7064^{6} 7166^{2} 7505^{5}

Rulesn'regulations *Matthew Salaman* a94 102
4 b g Forzando—Al Awaalah (Mukaddamah (USA))
850^{5} 1219^{4} 1903^{12} 2971^{2} ◆ (4473) 6349^{14} 6888^{12} 7522^{9}

Ruling (IRE) *A P O'Brien* 85
2 b c Footstepsinthesand—Chaturanga (Night Shift (USA))
7135a^{4}

Ruling Reef *Martin Bosley* a23 51
8 b m Diktat—Horseshoe Reef (Mill Reef (USA))
4201^{2}

Rumballina *Amy Weaver* 38
3 ch f Trade Fair—Bravo Dancer (Acatenango (GER))
1010^{7} 1607^{5} 2585^{10}

Rumble Of Thunder (IRE) *David Arbuthnot* a83 89
4 b g Fath(USA) —Honey Storm (IRE) (Mujadil (USA))
2044^{7} 2467^{12} 4306^{2} 4841^{7} 5311^{4} 5753^{3} 6428^{7}

Rumh (GER) *Saeed Bin Suroor* a87 86
2 ch f Monsun(GER) —Royal Dubai (GER) (Dashing Blade)
6155^{10} ◆ 6559^{10} (7198)

Rum King (USA) *Richard Hannon* a86 93
3 bb c Montbrook(USA) —Cut Class Leanne (USA) (Cutlass (USA))
4574^{10} 4819^{10} 5143^{9} 6321^{9} 6776^{12} 7238^{18}

Rumool *Clive Brittain* a92 92
3 b c Exceed And Excel(AUS) —Silent Heir (AUS) (Sunday Silence (USA))
973^{3} 1703^{5} 3585^{4}

Rumoush (USA) *Marcus Tregoning* a80 112
3 b f Rahy(USA) —Sarayir (USA) (Mr Prospector (USA))
(1313) ◆ 1726^{7} 2711^{3} ◆ 4612a^{3} 5881^{2} 6928^{9}

Rum Sun N Sand (USA) *J W Hills* a34 31
2 rg f Speightstown(USA) —Terri's Charmer (USA) (Silver Charm (USA))
1972^{7} 2474^{6} 6075^{11} 6498^{9}

Runaway *R Pritchard-Gordon* 111
8 b h King's Best(USA) —Anasazi (IRE) (Sadler's Wells (USA))
2374a^{5} 5134a^{6} 6885^{12}

Runaway Tiger (IRE) *Paul D'Arcy* a40
2 b g Tiger Hill(IRE) —Last Rhapsody (IRE) (Kris)
7559^{10}

Run Daisy Run *Brian Meehan* a51 48
2 b f Barathea(IRE) —Wild Floridian (IRE) (Indian Ridge)
3769^{10} 4095^{16} 4338^{7} 5894^{4} 6500^{11}

Run For Ede's *Pat Phelan* a71 85
6 b m Peintre Celebre(USA) —Raincloud (Rainbow Quest (USA))
2181^{2} (3812)

Run For The Hills *Roger Charlton* a80 104
4 b h Oasis Dream—Maid For The Hills (Indian Ridge)
1906^{6} 2316^{6} 2563^{3} 2748^{6} ◆ 3146^{20} 4576^{16} 7524^{12}

Running Flame (IRE) *Alan McCabe* a67 58
4 b g Indian Haven—Discretion (IRE) (Alzao (USA))
1270^{8} 1492^{9} 1924^{6} 2188^{2}

Running Mate (IRE) *Jo Crowley* a51 71
3 b g Acclamation—It Takes Two (IRE) (Alzao (USA))
1453^{8} 4956^{9} 6812^{16}

Running Water *Hugh McWilliams* 47
2 ch f Blue Dakota(IRE) —Floral Spark (Forzando)
3204[12] 3315[9] 4941[5] 5531[13] 6072[13]
Run On Ruby (FR) *David Lanigan* a71 62
2 bb f Muhtathir—Zigrala (FR) (Linamix (FR))
7000[6] 7311[7] ◆ (7479)
Run With The Wind (IRE) *Michael Hourigan* a61 65
4 b g Sadler's Wells(USA) —Race The Wild Wind (USA) (Sunny's Halo (CAN))
7514a[6] ◆
Ru'Oud *Saeed Bin Suroor* 79
2 ch c Pivotal—Philae (USA) (Seeking The Gold (USA))
5498[2] 6953[5]
Rural Pursuits *Christine Dunnett* a57 48
2 b f Pastoral Pursuits—Mabrookah (Deploy)
4716[5] 5047[16] 5721[5] 6082[11] 6521[8]
Russian Affair *Michael Jarvis* a61
2 b c Haafhd—Russian Rhapsody (Cosmonaut)
7595[9]
Russian Angel *Jean-Rene Auvray* a55 54
6 gr m Baryshnikov(AUS) —Eventuality (Petoski)
(460a) 794[9]
Russian Brigadier *Mel Brittain* a34 44
3 b g Xaar—Brigadiers Bird (IRE) (Mujadil (USA))
1029[12] 1336[8] 2503[10] 2853[11] 5758[10] 7131[4]
Russian Cross (IRE) *A Fabre* a94 112
5 b h Cape Cross(IRE) —Dievotchka (Dancing Brave (USA))
3045a[3] 4276a[5] 5107a[8] 6344a[4] 7776a[7]
Russian Dream (FR) *T Castanheira* a75 106
3 b c Russian Blue(IRE) —Day Of Dream (IRE) (Rainbows For Life (CAN))
1985a[5] 2802a[15]
Russian George (IRE) *Steve Gollings* a76 89
4 ch g Sendawar(IRE) —Mannsara (IRE) (Royal Academy (USA))
(1512) 1684[3] ◆ 1889[4]
Russian Ice *Dean Ivory* a63 64
2 ch f Iceman—Dark Eyed Lady (IRE) (Exhibitioner)
1263[6] 1660[5] 1978[3] 2330[2] 2591[2] 2939[5] 3864[7] 6258[2] 6694[10] 7296[12]
Russian Invader (IRE) *Richard Guest* a66 68
6 ch g Acatenango(GER) —Ukraine Venture (Slip Anchor)
15[5] 76[2] 139[3] 244[3] 309[9]
Russian Music (USA) *Ian Williams* a76 51
5 b g Stravinsky(USA) —Private Seductress (USA) (Private Account (USA))
(41) ◆ (140) 232[4] 6480[10]
Russian Rave *Jonathan Portman* a76 78
4 ch m Danehill Dancer(IRE) —Russian Ruby (FR) (Vettori (IRE))
1350[3] 2342[4] 2920[11] 3458[2] 3962[4] 4236[2] (5010) 5713[3] 6113[12] 6478[3] 6772[5]
Russian Rock (IRE) *Roger Teal* 95
3 b c Rock Of Gibraltar(IRE) —Mala Mala (IRE) (Brief Truce (USA))
1352[10] 1913[12] (2179) 2545[4] (3218) 3791[6]
Russian Rocket (IRE) *Christine Dunnett* a72 70
8 b g Indian Rocket—Soviet Girl (IRE) (Soviet Star (USA))
1131[7] 1391[16] 1915[15] 3064[13] 3994[9] 4239[6]
Russian Spirit *Michael Jarvis* a63 102
4 b m Falbrav(IRE) —Russian Rhapsody (Cosmonaut)
1692[3] 2054[15] 2997[3] 3261[8] 6446[3] 6723[2] 6981[2] (7351)
Russian Tango (GER) *A Wohler* 109
3 ch c Tertullian(USA) —Russian Samba (IRE) (Laroche (GER))
2405a[3] 4184a[3] 5806a[7] (6606a)
Russian Winter *Tim Etherington* a56
2 b g Tobougg(IRE) —Karminskey Park (Sabrehill (USA))
7240[5]
Rustic Deacon *Willie Musson* a76 34
3 ch g Pastoral Pursuits—Anne-Lise (Inchinor)
7183[7] 7489[4] 7575[6] (7995) ◆
Ruten (USA) *T Kluczynski* 99
5 rg h El Prado(IRE) —Rash (USA) (Miswaki (USA))
5542a[9]
Rutland Boy *Ed Dunlop* a78
2 ch g Bertolini(USA) —Israar (Machiavellian (USA))
7427[3] (7602)
Rutterkin (USA) *Mahmood Al Zarooni* a75 71
2 rg c Maria's Mon(USA) —Chilukki Cat (USA) (Storm Cat (USA))
2319[8] 3219[3] 3517[3] (4254) 5452[4]
Ruwain *Philip McBride* a54 44
6 b g Lujain(USA) —Ruwaya (USA) (Red Ransom (USA))
576[4] 3168[13] 4932[9]
R Woody *Dean Ivory* a78 98
3 ch g Ishiguru(USA) —Yarrita (Tragic Role (USA))
222[2] 277[2] 363[3] 577[5] 2824[5] (3154) 3638[4] 4204[2] 4503[3] (5495) 5884[5] (6776) 7351[7]
Ryan (IRE) *J Hanacek* 107
7 b h Generous(IRE) —Raysiza (IRE) (Alzao (USA))
7103a[2]
Ryan's Rock *Richard Price* a50 33
5 b g Lujain(USA) —Diamond Jayne (IRE) (Royal Abjar (USA))
7646[8] 7862[3] 7917[6]
Ryan Style (IRE) *Lisa Williamson* a82 86
4 b g Desert Style(IRE) —Westlife (IRE) (Mind Games)
527[4] 997[2] (1190) 1711[4] 2073[8] (3201) (3430) 4118[8] 5069[6] 5297[5] 6140[10]
Ryedale Dancer (IRE) *Tim Easterby* 45
2 ch f Refuse To Bend(IRE) —Saik (USA) (Riverman (USA))
4392[6] 5092[7]
Ryedane (IRE) *Tim Easterby* a78 78
8 b g Danetime(IRE) —Miss Valediction (IRE) (Petardia)
1723[9] 2144[7] (2378) (2849) (3026) 3551[6] 3664[3] 4199[2] 4452[9] 4559[2] 5356[6] 5424[10] (6040) 6208[2] 6714[4] 6922[3] 7525[9]
Ryker (IRE) *J W Hills* a62 57
4 ch g Halling(USA) —Charlock (IRE) (Nureyev (USA))
131[5] 291[6]
Rylee Mooch *Richard Guest* a58 53
2 rg g Choisir(AUS) —Negligee (Night Shift (USA))
3362[5] 4477[7] 5239[6] 5862[2] 6645[4] 6740[7] 7894[2] 8011[2] ◆
Rysckly (FR) *Y De Nicolay* 97
3 gr c Slickly(FR) —Rylara Des Brosses (FR) (Rapid Man (USA))
6761a[2]
Ryton Runner (IRE) *John Gosden* 71
2 b g Sadler's Wells(USA) —Love For Ever (IRE) (Darshaan)
6128[3] 6560[18]
Saalewuste (GER) *J-P Gallorini* a59 62
5 b m Next Desert(IRE) —Salondame (Godswalk (USA))
1056a[0]
Saamidd *Saeed Bin Suroor* 114
2 b c Street Cry(IRE) —Aryaamm (IRE) (Galileo (IRE))
(5032) ◆ (5943) 6924[6]
Sabantuy *C Von Der Recke* 73
4 b h Mujahid(USA) —Sabanila (GER) (In The Wings)
2559a[12]
Sabatini (IRE) *Jeff Pearce* a81 67
3 b f One Cool Cat(USA) —Two Sets To Love (IRE) (Cadeaux Genereux)
2565[8] 3394[6] 4133[2] 5073[4] (5661) (6164) 6577[5] 7019[5] 7964[4]
Saborido (USA) *Amanda Perrett* a76 83
4 gr g Dixie Union(USA) —Alexine (ARG) (Runaway Groom (CAN))
2081[5] 2659[7] (3780) ◆ (4745) 5612[5] 5996[11] (6416) 7208[2]
Sabotage (UAE) *Saeed Bin Suroor* 111
4 b g Halling(USA) —Cunas (USA) (Irish River (FR))
418a[4] (712a) 2116[2] 2469[9] 3447[17] 3922[6]
Sabot D'Or *Roger Ingram* 53
2 ch c Auction House(USA) —Perecapa (IRE) (Archway (IRE))
3842[7] 4303[4] 4902[10]
Saboteur *A bin Huzaim* a89 89
3 b c Shamardal(USA) —Croeso Cariad (Most Welcome)
510a[5] 796a[9]
Sabratah *H-A Pantall* 85
2 b f Oasis Dream—Marika (Marju (IRE))
4611a[5]
Sabratha (IRE) *Linda Perratt* a44 71
2 b f Hawk Wing(USA) —Aitch (IRE) (Alhaarth (IRE))
2873[7] 4233[4] 4716[6] 5644[3] 6129[2] 6704[3] 7049[3] 7223[2]
Sabys Gem (IRE) *Michael Wigham* 50
2 b c Diamond Green(FR) —Dust Flicker (Suave Dancer (USA))
4902[11] 7201[14] 7346[10]
Sacco D'Oro *Michael Mullineaux* a57 26
4 b m Rainbow High—Speedy Native (IRE) (Be My Native (USA))
468[5] 718[4] 872[4] 1207[9] 2285[12] 2516[7] 2653[8] 4453[10] 4932[8] 5203[8]
Sacho (GER) *W Kujath* 102
12 b g Dashing Blade—She's His Guest (IRE) (Be My Guest (USA))
2446a[10]
Sacred Aria *Daniel O'Gorman* 70
3 ch f Motivator—Portrait Of A Lady (IRE) (Peintre Celebre (USA))
7816a[7]
Sacred Kingdom (AUS) *P F Yiu* 125
7 b g Encosta De Lago(AUS) —Courtroom Sweetie (AUS) (Zeditave (AUS))
7852a[3]
Sacred Shield *Henry Cecil* 65
2 b f Beat Hollow—Quandary (USA) (Blushing Groom (FR))
6512[5]
Sacrilege *Michael Chapman* a62 76
5 ch g Sakhee(USA) —Idolize (Polish Precedent (USA))
1914 1430[3] 1579[12] 1997[8] 2133[9] 2388[5] 2821[4] 3040[5] (3168) (3412) 3912[4] 4102[6] 4201[P]
Sacrosanctus *David Nicholls* a73 73
2 ch g Sakhee(USA) —Catalonia (IRE) (Catrail (USA))
1704[6] (2183) 3059[4] 3596[8] 4831[6] 5354[5] (5863) 6900[8] 7211[5] 7493[3] 7592[4] 7891[3] 7997[3] ◆
Sadafiya *Ed Dunlop* a82 86
2 b f Oasis Dream—Nidhaal (IRE) (Observatory (USA))
4095[6] (4909) (5725) 6445[3]
Saddlers Bend (IRE) *George Baker* a66 40
4 b m Refuse To Bend(IRE) —Sudden Interest (FR) (Highest Honor (FR))
(721) ◆ (757) 794[3] 844[8] 1171[6] 1443[8] (7501) 7989[2]
Sadeek *Bryan Smart* a68 68
6 ch g Kyllachy—Miss Mercy (IRE) (Law Society (USA))
262[3] 383[10] 543[4] 715[8]
Sadler's Mark *Tom Tate* 68
3 b g Sadler's Wells(USA) —Waldmark (GER) (Mark Of Esteem (IRE))
2658[5] 3123[6] 3750[3] 4344[6] 4867[3]
Sadler's Risk (IRE) *Mark Johnston* 77
2 b c Sadler's Wells(USA) —Riskaverse (USA) (Dynaformer (USA))
6365[3] 6560[17] (6831)
Sadowa Destination *B Grizzetti* 74
3 ch f Dubai Destination(USA) —Sadowa (GER) (Lomitas)
1713a[13] 2575a[10] 3495a[11]
Safari Guide *K M Prendergast* a66 68
4 b g Primo Valentino(IRE) —Sabalara (IRE) (Mujadil (USA))
2298[5] 2964[4] 4366[5] 4700[2] 5077[8] 5325[6] 6188[8] 6462[8]
Safari Journey (USA) *Philip Hobbs* a64 72
6 ch h Johannesburg(USA) —Alvernia (USA) (Alydar (USA))
6322[11]
Safari Mischief *Peter Winkworth* a96 87
7 b g Primo Valentino(IRE) —Night Gypsy (Mind Games)
1903[8] 2745[15] 3892[7] 4292[6] 5627[5] 6280[7]
Safari Sunbeam *Peter Winkworth* 17
2 br g Primo Valentino(IRE) —Bathwick Finesse (IRE) (Namid)
5204[7] 5626[11]
Safari Sunup (IRE) *Peter Winkworth* a106 103
5 b g Catcher In The Rye(IRE) —Nuit Des Temps (Sadler's Wells (USA))
1016[2] 1665[2] 2593[7] 3633[4] 4100[7] 4818[4] 5970[6] 6437[7] 6990[3] ◆
Safari Team (IRE) *Peter Winkworth* a76 29
2 b g Pleasantly Perfect(USA) —Perfectly Clear (USA) (Woodman (USA))
4253[4] 4695[3] (5724) 6230a[19]
Safaseef (IRE) *Kevin Morgan* a49 55
5 b m Cadeaux Genereux—Asaafeer (USA) (Dayjur (USA))
101[4] 234[11] 389[12]
Safebreaker *Kevin Ryan* a71 76
5 b g Key Of Luck(USA) —Insijaam (USA) (Secretariat (USA))
756[9] 1398[14] 2672[3] 3090[8] 3499[6]
Safe Haven (IRE) *Alan Bailey* a38 53
2 gr f Indian Haven—Tiger's Gene (GER) (Perugino (USA))
1835[5] 5294[8] 6436[9] 7272[8] 7493[9]
Safe Steps (FR) *Mme Pia Brandt* 75
3 b f Footstepsinthesand—Safe And Sound (Hector Protector (USA))
6487a[3]
Saffron Hick (IRE) *Gerard Butler* a30 46
3 b g Elusive City(USA) —Luna Tacumana (IRE) (Bahhare (USA))
2334[11] 5603[6]
Safin (GER) *Sue Bradburne* a64 19
10 b g Pennekamp(USA) —Sankt Johanna (GER) (High Game)
2672[6] 6032[10]
Safina *Sir Michael Stoute* 99
3 ch f Pivotal—Russian Rhythm (USA) (Kingmambo (USA))
1312[4] ◆ (1861) 3071[3]
Safwaan *Willie Musson* a52 70
3 b g Selkirk(USA) —Kawn (Cadeaux Genereux)
1308[8] ◆ 2981[5] 6624[5] 7082[9] 7439[13] 7699[8] 7992[7]
Saga De Tercey (FR) *Alan Swinbank* 92
5 b g Sagacity(FR) —Fanciulla Del West (USA) (Manila (USA))
2027[7] 2313[5] 2938[5]
Sagamore *John Gosden* a95 82
3 b c Azamour(IRE) —Annalina (USA) (Cozzene (USA))
4572[2] ◆ (4926) 5371[5] 6251[3] 7084[P]
Saggiatore *Ed Dunlop* a82 82
3 b f Galileo(IRE) —Madame Dubois (Legend Of France (USA))
1356[7] 2255[2] 2901[2] 3170[2] 4259[2] 4719[2] 5443[3] 6084[2] 6480[9] (7067)
Sagramor *Hughie Morrison* a86 73
2 ch c Pastoral Pursuits—Jasmick (IRE) (Definite Article)
4577[5] 5006[2] (6498) 6870[2]
Sagredo (USA) *Jonjo O'Neill* a76 81
6 b g Diesis—Eternity (Suave Dancer (USA))
2685[10] (3257) 3781[7] 4476[2] 6091[9]
Sagunt (GER) *Sean Curran* a71 72
7 ch g Tertullian(USA) —Suva (GER) (Arazi (USA))
426[6] 842[5]
Sahafh (USA) *Saeed Bin Suroor* a71 71
2 bb f Rock Hard Ten(USA) —Fireman's Ball (USA) (Hennessy (USA))
3296[3] 4021[2] 5841[11] 6511[9]
Sahara Kingdom (IRE) *Saeed Bin Suroor* a107 52
3 gr c Cozzene(USA) —Rose Indien (FR) (Crystal Glitters (USA))
6659[2] ◆ 7304[7]
Sahara Sunshine *Laura Mongan* a52 63
5 b m Hernando(FR) —Sahara Sunrise (USA) (Houston (USA))
2631[0] 6775[11]
Saharia (IRE) *Ollie Pears* a88 86
3 b g Oratorio(IRE) —Inchiri (Sadler's Wells (USA))
2112[4] 2884[4] 3876[19] 5031[2] 5383[3] 5754[4] 6503[3] 7560[9] 7915[5]
Sahpresa (USA) *Rod Collet* 119
5 b m Sahm(USA) —Sorpresa (USA) (Pleasant Tap (USA))
3067[8] (5802a) (6561) 7853a[3]
Sahrati *Alan King* a83 93
6 ch g In The Wings—Shimna (Mr Prospector (USA))
746[3]
Saigon Kitty (IRE) *John Best* a54 52
3 b f One Cool Cat(USA) —Miss Asia Quest (Rainbow Quest (USA))
1355[8] 1878[10] 2122[8] 4931[6] 6522[2] 6826[13] 7191[7] ◆ 7845[7]
Sailing North (USA) *Ronald Harris* a46
2 b g Mizzen Mast(USA) —Silver Star (Zafonic (USA))
7811[7]
Sailor Boy (IRE) *Desmond Donovan* a9 5
2 b g Antonius Pius(USA) —Nationalartgallery (IRE) (Tate Gallery (USA))
1066[10] 1180[9] 2139[8]
Sailorman (IRE) *Mark Johnston* a74 92
3 ch c Dubawi(IRE) —Squaw Dance (Indian Ridge)
1450[5] (2393) 3215[9] (3851) 4057[2] 4264[7] 5043[10] (5861) 5997[6] 6321[11] 6888[20]
Sailor Moon (IRE) *H-A Pantall* a71 62
3 b f Tiger Hill(IRE) —Seralia (Royal Academy (USA))
5805a[12]
Sainte Colombe (IRE) *Y Barberot* a59 57
2 ch f Danehill Dancer(IRE) —Pharapache (USA) (Lyphard (USA))
4274a[6]
Saint Emilion (JPN) *Masaaki Koga* 105
3 bb f Zenno Rob Roy(JPN) —Moteck (FR) (Last Tycoon)
7460a[9]
Saint Encosta (AUS) *John P Thompson* 105
4 b g Encosta De Lago(AUS) —St. Katherine (AUS) (Barathea (IRE))
7032a[7]
Saint Helena (IRE) *Harry Dunlop* a70 56
2 b f Holy Roman Emperor(IRE) —Tafseer (IRE) (Grand Lodge (USA))
5691[10] 6158[7] 6866[4] 7164[2]
Saint Pierre (USA) *Luca Cumani* a96
3 b c Speightstown(USA) —Drina (USA) (Regal And Royal (USA))
4697[8] (6056) (6503)
Saint Thomas (IRE) *John Mackie* a80 78
3 b g Alhaarth(IRE) —Aguilas Perla (IRE) (Indian Ridge)
(1992) 2315[6] 3613[5] 4052[2] (4944) 5918[10] 6422[4] 6984[2] 7428[2]
Sairaam (IRE) *Charles Smith* a55 72
4 b m Marju(IRE) —Sayedati Eljamilah (USA) (Mr Prospector (USA))
88[4] 227[6] 297[6] 1653[5] (1928) 2298[2] (2764) 3434[4] 4308[6] 4715[7] 5064[3] 5688[6] 6063[7] 6261[5] 6656[9] 7336[8] 7501[7]
Sajjhaa *Michael Jarvis* 113
3 b f King's Best(USA) —Anaamil (IRE) (Darshaan)
(2255) ◆ 2711[14] 3368[4] (5114) 6346[2] ◆ (6765a)
Sakheart *V Luka Jr* a68 95
4 b m Sakhee(USA) —Tanwir (Unfuwain (USA))
6763a[3]
Sakhee's Pearl *Gay Kelleway* a88 86
4 gr m Sakhee(USA) —Grey Pearl (Ali-Royal (IRE))
1625[3] 1770[4] 2262[4] 3217[8] 3890[3] 4287[8] 5087[4] (6291) 6887[14]
Sakile *Peter Chapple-Hyam* a77 57
3 ch f Johannesburg(USA) —Crooked Wood (USA) (Woodman (USA))
277[5] 370[2]
Salaamie *Ed Dunlop* a65
2 ch c Dubawi(IRE) —Clear Impression (IRE) (Danehill (USA))
6249[9] 6473[12] 6743[7] 7417[7] 7552[9]
Salagadoola *Tim Easterby* 10
2 b f Val Royal(FR) —Cumbrian Crystal (Mind Games)
3118[10] 3365[9] 4668[11]
Salamera (IRE) *F J Brennan* 7
4 b m Invincible Spirit(IRE) —Polar Fleet (IRE) (Grand Lodge (USA))
3903[8] 4251[12]
Saldenaera (GER) *Uwe Ostmann* 85
3 bb f Areion(GER) —Saldengeste (IRE) (Be My Guest (USA))
6406a[4]
Saldenart (GER) *Uwe Ostmann* 96
4 bb m Areion(GER) —Saldengeste (IRE) (Be My Guest (USA))
3236a[6]
Salden Licht *Alan King* a78 108
6 b g Fantastic Light(USA) —Salde (GER) (Alkalde (GER))
(7084) 7350[5]
Saldennahe (GER) *P Schiergen* 96
3 b f Next Desert(IRE) —Salde (GER) (Alkalde (GER))
2575a[6] 4640a[10] 6011a[4] 6763a[8]
Salerosa (IRE) *Ann Duffield* a88 73
5 b m Monashee Mountain(USA) —Sainte Gig (FR) (Saint Cyrien (FR))
1997[7] 2262[3] 2531[7] 2580[8] 3876[13] 4172[2] 4644[5] 5199[7] (6026) 6460[11] (7403) 7846[4] 7935[4]
Salesiano *PETER Makin* a58 37
2 b c Exceed And Excel(AUS) —Rose Moon (Montjeu (IRE))
6882[9] 7485[8]
Salient *Michael Attwater* a84 87
6 b g Fasliyev(USA) —Savannah Belle (Green Desert (USA))
359[2] 1933[9] 3579[10] 4501[5] (4929) 5556[6] 5833[4] 5993[6] 6780[9] 7421[9] 7637[8] 7766[6]
Salisburgo (ITY) *A Cascio* a100 85
7 b h Big Shuffle(USA) —Exy Girl (IRE) (Alzao (USA))
1712a[7]
Sally Forth *Roger Charlton* a83 71
4 b m Dubai Destination(USA) —Daralbayda (IRE) (Doyoun)
1357[11] 2897[5]
Sally Friday (IRE) *Peter Winkworth* a75 45
2 b f Footstepsinthesand—Salee (IRE) (Caerleon (USA))
5841[3] ◆ 6511[7]
Sally's Swansong *Eric Alston* a61 51
4 b m Mind Games—Sister Sal (Bairn (USA))
699[9] 774[5] 849[3] 936[5] 1112[3] 7810[7]
Salona (GER) *J-P Carvalho* 95
2 ch f Lord Of England(GER) —Selana (GER) (Lomitas)
(5740a)
Salontanzerin (GER) *W Hickst* a90 90
5 b m Black Sam Bellamy(IRE) —Salontasche (GER) (Dashing Blade)
7648a[2]
Salontyre (GER) *Bernard Llewellyn* a61 69
4 b g Pentire—Salonrolle (IRE) (Tirol)
1459[4] 1759[3] (2923)

Saloon (USA) *Jane Chapple-Hyam* a79 80
6 b g Sadler's Wells(USA) —Fire The Groom (USA) (Blushing Groom (FR))
1150^8 *1828^6* 2343^2

Saltagioo (ITY) *Alan King* a92 91
6 b g Dr Devious(IRE) —Sces (Kris)
2388^2

Saltergate *Nigel Tinkler* a61 68
2 b g Avonbridge—Grey Princess (IRE) (Common Grounds)
1292^3 1646^2 3315^8 3971^2 4195^3 4941^13 5239^3 5683^3 *6576^4 7040^6*

Salto (IRE) *F Head* 117
2 b c Pivotal—Danzigaway (USA) (Danehill (USA))
7265a^2

Salut Adrien (FR) *Robert Collet* a63 85
4 b g Miesque's Son(USA) —Salut Bebs (FR) (Kendor (FR))
303a^0

Salute Him (IRE) *A J Martin* a107 109
7 b g Mull Of Kintyre(USA) —Living Legend (ITY) (Archway (IRE))
419a^6 605a^5 820a^2 3144^4 5220^4

Salut L'Africain (FR) *Robert Collet* a95 106
5 b h Ski Chief(USA) —Mamana (IRE) (Highest Honor (FR))
1081a^6 2778a^3 3704a^2 4165a^5 4773a^5 5576a^11 6640a^9 7278a^5 *7800a^0*

Salvationist *John Dunlop* a43 60
2 b g Invincible Spirit(IRE) —Salvia (Pivotal)
2077^13 2384^9 2715^7 4129^4 4677^8 4955^8 *5659^6* (6129) 7004^2

Salve Aurora (GER) *P Schiergen* 84
3 b f King's Best(USA) —Salve Regina (GER) (Monsun (GER))
5805a^6

Samanda (IRE) *Luca Cumani* a40
2 b c Ad Valorem(USA) —Presently Blessed (IRE) (Inchinor)
7335^11

Samarinda (USA) *Pam Sly* a94 78
7 ch g Rahy(USA) —Munnaya (USA) (Nijinsky (CAN))
109^4 360^9 697^5 947^4 1455^2 1618^8 1990^U *(2235)* 3107^3 *4030^9 5750^12* 6054^4 (6577) 7092^5 7557^6

Samarkand (IRE) *Sir Mark Prescott Bt* a69
2 b g Sadler's Wells(USA) —Romantic Venture (IRE) (Indian Ridge)
7272^5 7452^6 7693^2

Samizdat (FR) *Dianne Sayer* 59
7 b g Soviet Star(USA) —Secret Account (FR) (Bering)
5202^8

Sam Jicaro *Lisa Williamson* a23 42
3 b g Mind Games—Claradotnet (Sri Pekan (USA))
5235 775^9

Sammuramat (IRE) *Michael Quinlan* 67
3 b f Dansili—Elara (USA) (Spinning World (USA))
2197^4 3227^9 3677^11

Sammy Alexander *David Simcock* a67 44
2 b c Storming Home—Sweet Angeline (Deploy)
2819^12 3602^7 *7186^6 7630^5*

Sam Nombulist *Richard Whitaker* 71
2 ch g Sleeping Indian—Owdbetts (IRE) (High Estate)
5404^8 6305^4 7049^2

Sampers (IRE) *M Halford* a89 72
4 b m Exceed And Excel(AUS) —Gujarat (USA) (Distant View (USA))
7073a^9

Sam's Cross (IRE) *Martin Bosley* a78 74
5 b g Cape Cross(IRE) —Fancy Lady (Cadeaux Genereux)
3358^10

Sam Sharp (USA) *Henry Cecil* a80 86
4 bb g Johannesburg(USA) —Caffe (USA) (Mr Prospector (USA))
1600^2 1907^7

Samsons Son *Alan King* a84 81
6 b g Primo Valentino(IRE) —Santiburi Girl (Casteddu)
6565^4 ◆ *7337^4*

Sams Spirit *John McShane* a15 13
4 br g Diktat—Winning Girl (Green Desert (USA))
5244^11 5819^12 *6242^7 7599^10*

Samuel *John Gosden* 116
6 ch g Sakhee(USA) —Dolores (Danehill (USA))
3695^4 5218^2 (5909)

Samuel Morse (IRE) *A P O'Brien* 105
2 bb c Danehill Dancer(IRE) —Eliza (USA) (Mt. Livermore (USA))
(2352a) 3049^4 3488a^2 4176a^2 4880a^5 5316a^3 5975a^4 6531^6

Samurai Sword *Mahmood Al Zarooni* 79
2 b c Motivator—Japanese Whisper (UAE) (Machiavellian (USA))
(4346)

San Antonio *Pam Sly* a61 81
10 b g Efisio—Winnebago (Kris)
2959^9 4112^8 5039^8 *7290^4 7474^5*

San Cassiano (IRE) *Ruth Carr* a75 93
3 b g Bertolini(USA) —Celtic Silhouette (FR) (Celtic Swing)
1913^10 2544^10 3226^6 (4154) (4377) 4574^6 5605^18

Sancho Panza *Julia Feilden* a52 61
3 b g Zafeen(FR) —Malvadilla (IRE) (Doyoun)
2336^6 2909^11 4763^11 (5536) 6065^2 6816^2 ◆

Sanctuary *Bryan Smart* a62 87
4 ch g Dr Fong(USA) —Wondrous Maid (GER) (Mondrian (GER))
2865^6 4619^8 4996^5 5363^3 6573^10 6984^6 *7292^7*

Sanctum *Dr Jon Scargill* a25 57
4 b m Medicean—Auspicious (Shirley Heights)
1134^5 2902^5 6022^4 7157^9 *7716^14*

Sandbar *F Rohaut* 114
3 b f Oasis Dream—Shifting Sands (FR) (Hernando (FR))
(952a) (1946a) 3015a^3

San Deng *Micky Hammond* a68 54
8 gr g Averti(IRE) —Miss Mirror (Magic Mirror)
1891^7 2500^3 4648^7

Sandgate Story *Noel Wilson* 29
4 ch m Lucky Story(USA) —Sandgate Cygnet (Fleetwood (IRE))
3733^8 4556^13 4655^4

San Diego Prince *Muredach Kelly* 55
6 bb g Primo Valentino(IRE) —Lalique (IRE) (Lahib (USA))
4487^9

Sandor *PETER Makin* a90 100
4 ch g Fantastic Light(USA) —Crystal Star (Mark Of Esteem (IRE))
1697^7 2044^3 (2444) 3194^7 3921^5 4400^3 5307^3 5970^3 6562^4 7100^11

Sand Owl *Peter Chapple-Hyam* a75
2 b f Dubawi(IRE) —Midnight Allure (Aragon)
6796^3

Sandpipers Dream *Tim Walford* 41
2 b g Desert Style(IRE) —Maarees (Groom Dancer (USA))
4089^13 5040^9 5498^10

Sand Repeal (IRE) *Julia Feilden* a58 66
8 b g Revoque(IRE) —Columbian Sand (IRE) (Salmon Leap (USA))
2455^4 3028^2 3496^5 3641^5

Sands Crooner (IRE) *James Given* a84 76
7 b g Imperial Ballet(IRE) —Kurfuffle (Bluebird (USA))
1364^6 ◆ 1524^2 1915^12 2144^4 2622^11 3064^4 (3809) 4090^7 4518^8 4938^9

Sand Skier *Mark Johnston* 98
3 b g Shamardal(USA) —Dubai Surprise (IRE) (King's Best (USA))
3196^2 ◆ 3824^4 4106^3 4321^3 4570^4 5605^10 6534^2 6620^2 7233^8

Sands Of Dee (USA) *David Nicholls* a23 68
3 b g Dixieland Band(USA) —Diamond Bracelet (USA) (Metfield (USA))
3768^12 4833^6 5634^10 6644^2 6965^8 7007^3 (7170) *7405^13*

Sandtail (IRE) *J W Hills* a59 48
2 gr f Verglas(IRE) —Goldthroat (IRE) (Zafonic (USA))
5692^13 *6247^10* 7034^5

Sand Tiger (IRE) *Richard Fahey* a80 93
4 ch g Indian Ridge—Anayid (A.P. Indy (USA))
466^7 725^5 (1669) 2027^8 2710^11 3901^7

Sandusky *Mahmood Al Zarooni* 60
2 b c Tiger Hill(IRE) —Red Carnation (IRE) (Polar Falcon (USA))
7094^5

Sandwith *George Foster* a70 81
7 ch g Perryston View—Bodfari Times (Clantime)
2073^7 2669^2 ◆ 3497^3 3946^5 4373^4 ◆ 4516^4 4952^3 5240^4 (6031) 6103^5 6398^2 7169^2

Sandy Lonnen *Howard Johnson* 49
2 b g Tobougg(IRE) —Legend Of Aragon (Aragon)
3316^7 4480^5 6919^7

Sandy Shaw *J W Hills* a55 72
3 ch f Footstepsinthesand—Susi Wong (IRE) (Selkirk (USA))
1602^5 ◆ 2250^4 2901^5 3390^2 (4282) 5115^7 *5959^9* 7015^8

Sandy Toes *Jeremy Glover* a48 44
3 b g Footstepsinthesand—Scrooby Baby (Mind Games)
265^8 329^4 (471) 519^4 861^2 993^9 1162^10 1774^5 2161a^6 3287^9 4651^10 6255^7 6574^7

San Fermin (USA) *Mahmood Al Zarooni* a50
3 bb g Holy Bull(USA) —Uforia (USA) (Zilzal (USA))
2258^5

Sangar *Ollie Pears* 52
2 ch f Haafhd—Preference (Efisio)
5814^6 6569^7 6919^11

Sangaree (USA) *Bob Baffert* a103
5 ch h Awesome Again(CAN) —Mari's Sheba (USA) (Mari's Book (USA))
3935a^2

Sangfroid *Nicolas Williams* a31 66
6 gr g With Approval(CAN) —Affaire D'Amour (Hernando (FR))
1759^2

Sanjay's Choice (IRE) *T G McCourt* a74 17
4 br g Trans Island—Livy Park (IRE) (Titus Livius (FR))
1929 214^5

Sanjii Danon (GER) *W Hickst* 98
4 b h Big Shuffle(USA) —Serpina (IRE) (Grand Lodge (USA))
1251a^8 2559a^3 3934a^6 4888a^11 6791a^3

San Jose City (IRE) *Muredach Kelly* a86 71
5 b g Clodovil(IRE) —Allspice (Alzao (USA))
(4486) 5473^6

Sanrei Jasper (JPN) *Shigetada Takahashi* a67 99
8 b m Misuzu Chardon(JPN) —San Lake Queen (JPN) (Cozzene (USA))
7460a^13

Sans Chichi (FR) *Y Barberot* a85 100
6 b m Chichicastenango(FR) —Titine (FR) (Adieu Au Roi (IRE))
1792a^0

Sans Frontieres (IRE) *Jeremy Noseda* 123
4 ch h Galileo(IRE) —Llia (Shirley Heights)
1328^6 1832^6 3191^4 ◆ (3825) (5080) ◆ (5976a) ◆

Sansili *Peter Bowen* a64 33
3 gr g Dansili—Salinova (FR) (Linamix (FR))
340^5 1578^7

San Silvestro (IRE) *Ann Duffield* a59 70
5 ch g Fayruz—Skehana (IRE) (Mukaddamah (USA))
2172^9 2858^4 3500^2 3775^2 4188^8 4514^5 4897^5

Sans Sa Dame (FR) *Mrs A Malzard* 54
7 ch g Wathik(USA) —Danemara (FR) (Fabulous Dancer (USA))
1817a^2

Santa Biatra (FR) *A Couetil* a87 76
4 b m Highest Honor(FR) —Albiatra (USA) (Dixieland Band (USA))
7648a^3

Santa Margherita *Harry Dunlop* a43 66
3 b f Titus Livius(FR) —A Simple Path (IRE) (Imperial Ballet (IRE))
3259^4 3821^5 4626^6 5376^2 *6079^5* 6691^6 7038^8

Sant'Antonio (ITY) *S Botti* 114
5 b h Shantou(USA) —Nonna Rina (IRE) (Bluebird (USA))
1943a^2 3019a^6

Santefisio *PETER Makin* a91 94
4 b g Efisio—Impulsive Decision (IRE) (Nomination)
2091^4 2926^2 3346^2 6564^8 6888^21 *7187^7 7560^3*

Santiago Atitlan *P Monteith* a95 73
8 b g Stravinsky(USA) —Sylvette (USA) (Silver Hawk (USA))
3706^8 3900^3 4064^7

Santino (GER) *J-P Carvalho* 100
3 b c Rock Of Gibraltar(IRE) —Selana (GER) (Lomitas)
2405a^5 6408a^8

Santo Padre (IRE) *David Marnane* a98 109
6 b g Elnadim(USA) —Tshusick (Dancing Brave (USA))
1091a^4 1676a^12 5569a^3 6009a^5 6390^11

Santorino *Paul Midgley* 25
2 b c Araafa(IRE) —Sister Bluebird (Bluebird (USA))
2138^8 4368^14 6036^7 6618^13

Santo Subito (IRE) *Michael Chapman*
9 b g Presenting—Shinora (IRE) (Black Minstrel)
2899^11

Saphira's Fire (IRE) *William Muir* a102 111
5 b m Cape Cross(IRE) —All Our Hope (USA) (Gulch (USA))
3031^4 3467a^7 4624^3 5249^8 6148^6 6928^5 7349^3 *7523^5*

Sapperton *George Baker* 45
3 br g Key Of Luck(USA) —Lebenstanz (Singspiel (IRE))
2329^7 6657^6

Sapphire Girl *Richard Fahey* a23 63
2 ch f Compton Place—Centre Court (Second Set (IRE))
1421^9 2813^4 3315^3 4083^5 *7843^9 7983^8*

Sapphire Prince (USA) *John Best* a69 74
4 b h Read The Footnotes(USA) —Anna Jackson (USA) (Houston (USA))
23^8 656^3 (808) 975^9 1322^7 1530^11 *2866^11 3768^9*

Saptapadi (IRE) *Sir Michael Stoute* a106 114
4 ch g Indian Ridge—Olympienne (IRE) (Sadler's Wells (USA))
(1380) ◆ 2469^2 3470a^5 5080^3 *5749^4*

Sarafina (FR) *A De Royer-Dupre* 124
3 b f Refuse To Bend(IRE) —Sanariya (IRE) (Darshaan)
(2373a) (3015a) 6013a^3 6612a^3

Sarah Lynx (IRE) *J E Hammond* 112
3 b f Montjeu(IRE) —Steel Princess (IRE) (Danehill (USA))
5138a^4 6013a^5 6591a^3 7546a^7

Sarah Park (IRE) *Brian Meehan* a96 97
5 ch m Redback—Brillano (FR) (Desert King (IRE))
1899^7 2744^7 3752^9 4137^9 6391^11 (6780) *7188^7 7430^6 7735^7*

Sarah's Art (IRE) *Stef Higgins* a85 79
7 gr g City On A Hill(USA) —Treasure Bleue (IRE) (Treasure Kay)
223^5 (393) 1580^4 2247^6 5789^16 *6501^9 6799^9 7212^11 7525^10 7737^7 7841^2* (8033)

Sarah's Boy *David Pipe* a58 39
5 ch g Nayef(USA) —Bella Bianca (IRE) (Barathea (IRE))
228^12 (493) 575^2 1828^3

Sarahthecarer (IRE) *P M Mooney* a66 61
3 b f Littletown Boy(USA) —Peaceful Sarah (Sharpo)
1522^5 3359^5

Sara Louise (USA) *Saeed Bin Suroor* a109
4 b m Malibu Moon(USA) —Kings Lynn (USA) (Mt. Livermore (USA))
7341a^6

Sarandjam *Mick Channon* a42 54
2 b c Titus Livius(FR) —Truly Madly Deeply (Most Welcome)
1845^5 2138^4 2486^3 2939^18 3175^5 4241^5 4678^6 5000^7 5581^5 *5862^5* 6072^8

Sarando *Paul Webber* a65 62
5 b g Hernando(FR) —Dansara (Dancing Brave (USA))
164^8 7321^5

Sarangoo *Malcolm Saunders* 65
2 b f Piccolo—Craic Sa Ceili (IRE) (Danehill Dancer (IRE))
2245^5 2687^8 3034^4 3721^4 5874^8

Sarasota Sunshine *Jeremy Noseda* a80 99
4 b m Oasis Dream—Never Explain (IRE) (Fairy King (USA))
3172^2 (3592) 3890^2 (5694) 6349^23

Saratoga Black (IRE) *Gianluca Bietolini* 107
3 b c Pyrus(USA) —Mary Martins (IRE) (Orpen (USA))
1945a^3 7373a^6

Sarbaaz (IRE) *Michael Jarvis* 63
3 b g Dubawi(IRE) —Bahr Alsalaam (USA) (Riverman (USA))
1314^6

Sarbola *Michael Jarvis* a80 51
3 b g Dubai Destination(USA) —Compose (Anabaa (USA))
6499^2 ◆

Sard *Michael Jarvis* 91
3 b f Bahamian Bounty—Clincher Club (Polish Patriot (USA))
(1694) 2120^8 2807^3 5677^4 (6805) 7097^3

Saremma *Ronald Harris*
3 ch f Choisir(AUS) —Sarah's Dream (IRE) (Lion Cavern (USA))
7183^11

Sariska *Michael Bell* 123
4 b m Pivotal—Maycocks Bay (Muhtarram (USA))
(2055) 2709^2 5248^RR 6013a^RR

Saristan (FR) *A De Royer-Dupre* a68 68
3 b g Azamour(IRE) —Sarkala (IRE) (Caerleon (USA))
7959a^3

Sarmad (USA) *Clive Brittain* 53
3 bb f Dynaformer(USA) —Performing Arts (The Minstrel (CAN))
4235^7

Sarojini *David Nicholls* a22 34
2 ch f Byron—Indian Silk (IRE) (Dolphin Street (FR))
1510^9 6465^15 *6899^8 7269^9 7471^P*

Sarrsar *Michael Jarvis* a103 101
3 b g Shamardal(USA) —Bahr (Generous (IRE))
(2754) 3351^3 4652^3 *(5728)* ◆ (6534)

Sartingo (IRE) *Alan Swinbank* 34
3 b g Encosta De Lago(AUS) —Alicia (IRE) (Darshaan)
5478^4

Sarwin (USA) *William Knight* a71 75
7 rg g Holy Bull(USA) —Olive The Twist (USA) (Theatrical)
1051^2 1115^6 1426^10 2392^10 2859^3 *6055^5 6668^8*

Sasheen *Jim Boyle* a71 68
3 b f Zafeen(FR) —Sashay (Bishop Of Cashel)
4425^2 4997^8 *5384^7* 6197^11 6633^11

Saskia's Dream *Jane Chapple-Hyam* a67 73
2 b f Oasis Dream—Swynford Pleasure (Reprimand)
3070^11 4317^4 5078^4 5784^8 6156^8 6513^4 *6869^2 7231^4*

Sassanian (IRE) *Jane Chapple-Hyam* a60 62
3 b g Clodovil(IRE) —Persian Sally (IRE) (Persian Bold)
1264^4 *2333^2* 2820^2 *3213^2*

Satans Quick Chick (USA) *Eric R Reed* a101
4 b m Sky Mesa(USA) —Dancing Devlette (USA) (Devil's Bag (USA))
6603a^3 7371a^3

Satchmo Bay (FR) *C Boutin* a79 90
9 b g Alamo Bay(USA) —Royale Aube (FR) (Garde Royale)
458a^5 *640a^7*

Satindra (IRE) *Conor Dore* a46 53
6 b g Lil's Boy(USA) —Voronova (IRE) (Sadler's Wells (USA))
90^5

Satin Love (USA) *Mark Johnston* a82 94
2 ch g Mineshaft(USA) —French Satin (USA) (French Deputy (USA))
(4059) 4538^5 5184^6 6191^5 *6727a^6 7317^4 7481^8*

Satin Princess (IRE) *Alex Hales* a29 45
3 b f Royal Applause—College Of Arms (Lujain (USA))
2584^6 3682^6 4280^4 4534^5 5711^8

Saturday Sam *Mark Rimell* a5
2 b g Superior Premium—Darling Dora (Gildoran)
5156^12

Saturn Girl (IRE) *Michael Bell* 79
4 ch m Danehill Dancer(IRE) —Lilissa (IRE) (Doyoun)
1034^3 1128^4

Saturn Way (GR) *Patrick Chamings* a76 80
4 b g Bachelor Duke(USA) —Senseansensibility (USA) (Capote (USA))
1877^2 ◆ 2823^3 3412^7 4206^11 *5866^6* 6633^6 6992^4 *7298^9*

Satwa Excel *Ed Dunlop* 60
3 ro f Exceed And Excel(AUS) —Pericardia (Petong)
3586^7 4425^10

Satwa Gold (USA) *Stef Higgins* a86 88
4 ch h Rahy(USA) —No More Ironing (USA) (Slew O'Gold (USA))
148^2 (260) 395^3 500^2 688^4 (1357) ◆ 1902^4 3475^4 3843^3 4320^8 4846^10 *(5144)* 5788^15 7410^7 7553^4 7781^4

Satwa Laird *Ed Dunlop* a86 94
4 b h Johannesburg(USA) —Policy Setter (USA) (Deputy Minister (CAN))
1219^8 1618^5 1933^6 (2284) 3172^9 3796^5 4459^2 ◆ 5415^5 *6312^4* 6780^12

Satwa Moon (USA) *Ed Dunlop* a85 91
4 ch h Horse Chestnut(SAF) —Double Schott (USA) (Demons Begone (USA))
(752) 852^3 2865^2 4455^3 ◆ 5217^5 5991^2 6565^8

Satwa Prince (FR) *Jean De Roualle* a85 103
7 b h Munir—Toryka (Vettori (IRE))
5109a^9

Saubestre *John Best* a20
2 b c Kodiac—Epineuse (Gorse)
7065^9

Saucy Brown (IRE) *David Nicholls* a68 96
4 b g Fasliyev(USA) —Danseuse Du Bois (USA) (Woodman (USA))
916^11 1032^2 1727^16 2311^5 2736^5 3919^10 4536^26 5183^15 5510^12 6142^17

Saucy Buck (IRE) *Mick Channon* a69 76
2 b g Mujadil(USA) —Phantom Ring (Magic Ring (IRE))
1009^6 1256^3 1612^2 (1864) 2032^3 2743^8 3504^6 3887^8 4578^8 *4927^5 5725^5* 6035^7 *6740^2 (6867) 7417^5*

Saucy Girl (IRE) *Tim Easterby* a42 57
3 b f Footstepsinthesand—Leenane (IRE) (Grand Lodge (USA))
1390^2 3222^9 4567^8 4939^12 5299^9

Saunton Sands *Tony Newcombe* a5 33
4 ch g Best Of The Bests(IRE) —Victoriet (Hamas (IRE))
388^11

Saute *Walter Swinburn* a78 79
4 br g Hawk Wing(USA) —Lifting (IRE) (Nordance (USA))
2023^4 *3084^5 3965^2 4915^2 (5179) 5382^2* 5996^5 (6693) 6895^2

Savanna's Gold *Richard Rowe* a37 10
6 ch m Bold Edge—Midnight Romance (Inca Chief (USA))
586^9 758^8 986^8 1642^8

Savaronola (USA) *Barney Curley* a69 79
5 ch g Pulpit(USA) —Running Debate (USA) (Open Forum (USA))
(1983) 4227[5] 7111[7] 7531[11] 7765[10]

Save The Bees *Ian McInnes* 26
2 b g Royal Applause—Rock Concert (Bishop Of Cashel)
2427[6] 2882[9]

Saving Grace *Eric Alston* a58 61
4 br m Lend A Hand—Damalis (IRE) (Mukaddamah (USA))
427[5] 780[7] 854[2] 1172[8] (1575) 1717[3] 2429[7] 2859[2] 3391[4] 3707[3] 6905[6] 7529[10] 7601[4]

Saviour Sand (IRE) *Olivia Maylam* a73 69
6 b g Desert Sun—Teacher Preacher (IRE) (Taufan (USA))
(467) 814[3] 3607[4] 3862[5] ◆ 4804[11] 5367[8]

Sawahill *Clive Brittain* a45
2 b f Diktat—Youm Jadeed (IRE) (Sadler's Wells (USA))
6850[5]

Saxby (IRE) *Geoffrey Harker* a70 70
3 ch g Pastoral Pursuits—Madam Waajib (IRE) (Waajib)
1297[6] 1488[4] 3243[3] 3387[7] 3972[3] 4289[6] 4866[6] 5211[6]

Saxford *Linda Stubbs* 78
4 b g Reset(AUS) —Bint Makbul (Makbul)
2453[4]

Saxonette *Linda Perratt* a61 61
2 b f Piccolo—Solmorin (Fraam)
4149[7] 4474[7] 4848[2] (5667) 6027[3] 6220[6] 6489[2] 6705[4] 7050[11]

Say A Prayer *Tim Easterby* 49
2 b f Indesatchel(IRE) —Golden Nun (Bishop Of Cashel)
3624[13] 4702[5] 5099[8]

Sayif (IRE) *Sir Michael Stoute* 119
4 b h Kheleyf(USA) —Sewards Folly (Rudimentary (USA))
2030[9] 3192[20] 6390[9]

Saying (USA) *F Head* a81 98
3 b f Giant's Causeway(USA) —Pas De Reponse (USA) (Danzig (USA))
1196a[7] 5134a[8]

Sayyedati Storm (USA) *B W Hills* a55 24
3 b f Storm Cat(USA) —Sayyedati (Shadeed (USA))
843[5] ◆ 3407[7] 5810[RR]

Sazeilla (CZE) *Jonathen de Giles* a2
5 b m Mill Pond(FR) —Saze (CZE) (Muscatite)
497[6]

Scalo *A Wohler* 117
3 b c Lando(GER) —Sky Dancing (IRE) (Exit To Nowhere (USA))
(1745a) (2406a) 3018a[5] 4184a[9] (5135a) (6410a)

Scamperdale *Brian Baugh* a95 88
8 br g Compton Place—Miss Up N Go (Gorytus (USA))
197[6] 408[5] 725[7] 1348[2] 2080[9] (2602) (2961) ◆ 3329[2] (4051) 4520[4] 4859[7] 5913[9] 8009[11]

Scandal Sheet (IRE) *J S Bolger* a86 95
4 b m Galileo(IRE) —Sandrella (IRE) (Darshaan)
3487a[2] 5571a[14]

Scandola (USA) *S Wattel* a79 91
3 b f Afleet Alex(USA) —Look Of The Lynx (USA) (Forest Wildcat (USA))
952a[3] 1496a[9]

Scantily Clad (IRE) *Ed McMahon* 76
2 b f Acclamation—Meadow (Green Desert (USA))
3906[6] 4517[2] (6045) 6489[3]

Scarab (IRE) *Tim Walford* a87 76
5 br g Machiavellian(USA) —Russian Society (Darshaan)
2109[13] 4411[3] 4752[6] 5486[4] 5819[2] 6117[4] (6472) 6573[3] 6984[16] 7306[9]

Scarborough Lily *Edward Vaughan* a50
2 b f Dansili—Queen Isabella (El Prado (IRE))
7478[11] 8001[10]

Scarboro Warning (IRE) *Jimmy O'Reilly* a29 74
3 ch g Footstepsinthesand—Spring Easy (IRE) (Alzao (USA))
1298[11] 1709[9] 2834[7] 3243[7] 3759[9] 3975[13]

Scarcity (IRE) *Ed Dunlop* 69
3 b f Invincible Spirit(IRE) —Sanpa Fan (ITY) (Sikeston (USA))
1260[6] (1605) ◆ 2588[3] 3592[5] 5561[9]

Scarlet O'Hara (IRE) *D K Weld* a79 92
5 b m Sadler's Wells(USA) —Agnetha (GER) (Big Shuffle (USA))
4630a[4]

Scarlet Ridge *Dean Ivory* a32
3 ch f Tumbleweed Ridge—Kayartis (Kaytu)
2741[10]

Scarlet Rocks (IRE) *David Evans* a67 88
2 b f Chineur(FR) —Alexander Duchess (IRE) (Desert Prince (IRE))
1043[2] 1136[2] 1263[2] 1517[2] (1957) 2177[2] (2397) 2468[4] 2950[4] (3858) 4458[12] 4872[6] 5226a[9] 6636[7]

Scartozz *Marco Botti* a92 99
8 b g Barathea(IRE) —Amazing Bay (Mazilier (USA))
230[2]

Scary Movie (IRE) *Denis Coakley* a76 63
5 b g Daggers Drawn(USA) —Grinning (IRE) (Bellypha)
(868) 7480[2] 7865[4]

Scatty (IRE) *Sylvester Kirk* 55
2 ro g Verglas(IRE) —Nonsense (IRE) (Soviet Star (USA))
1541[5] 2059[15] 3349[10] (Dead)

Sceal Nua (IRE) *Richard Hannon* a75 73
2 b f Iffraaj—Always Mine (Daylami (IRE))
2749[5] (3082) 3872[4] 5256[6] 5675[2] 6426[2]

Sceilin (IRE) *John Mackie* a52 66
6 b m Lil's Boy(USA) —Sharifa (IRE) (Cryptoclearance (USA))
1489[6] 2173[5] 2961[4] 5786[11]

Scented *William Haggas* a69 73
2 b f Medicean—Red Garland (Selkirk (USA))
5489[5] 6155[6] 6743[6] 7197[2] 7603[3]

Schiller Danon (GER) *W Hickst* 115
4 ch h Samum(GER) —Soljanka (GER) (Halling (USA))
1420a[7] 6606a[5]

Schinken Otto (IRE) *Malcolm Jefferson* a55 36
9 ch g Shinko Forest(IRE) —Athassel Rose (IRE) (Reasonable (FR))
541[11] 1984[10]

Schism *Henry Candy* 67
2 ch f Shirocco(GER) —Alla Prima (IRE) (In The Wings)
5489[4]

Schliemann (ITY) *G Di Chio*
2 b c Colossus(IRE) —Shariba (IRE) (Bluebird (USA))
7850a[12]

Schomir (FR) *J Van Handenhove* a55 61
7 b g Munir—Scholar (FR) (Sillery (USA))
332a[6]

Schoolboy Champ *Patrick Morris* a65 73
3 ch g Trade Fair—Aswhatilldois (IRE) (Blues Traveller (IRE))
2179[4] ◆ 3088[5] 3761[12] 4749[3] (4920) 6492[6] 7571[7] 7841[5]

School For Scandal (IRE) *Mark Johnston* a74
2 b c Pivotal—Sensation (Soviet Star (USA))
7479[5] 7602[2] 7693[4] 7873[3]

School Holidays (USA) *David Wachman* a81 81
3 bb f Harlan's Holiday(USA) —Life Of The Party (USA) (Pleasant Colony (USA))
4630a[10]

Schoolyard Dreams (USA) *Derek S Ryan* a97
3 b c Stephen Got Even(USA) —Hear This (USA) (Prospector's Music (USA))
1097a[4] 2137a[9]

Schull Harbour (IRE) *H Rogers* a58 59
3 ch f Greenwood Lake(USA) —Heaven's Prospect (USA) (Prospector's Music (USA))
4496a[10]

Schutzenjunker (GER) *Uwe Ostmann* 108
5 b h Lord Of Men—Schutzenliebe (GER) (Alkalde (GER))
1251a[16] 5542a[11] 6791a[8]

Scintillating (IRE) *Reg Hollinshead* a44 32
3 b f Cape Cross(IRE) —Announcing Peace (Danehill (USA))
127[5] 213[5] 216[6] 372[7] 542[9] 870[8]

Scoglio *Frank Sheridan* a59 59
2 b g Monsieur Bond(IRE) —Ex Mill Lady (Bishop Of Cashel)
4890[5] 5643[4] 6308[5] 6674[4] ◆ 7004[11] 7124[2]

Scolari *T Mundry* 108
5 b h Monsun(GER) —Sky Dancing (IRE) (Exit To Nowhere (USA))
3251a[2] 4418a[5] 5542a[2] 6344a[9]

Scommettitrice (IRE) *Ronald Harris* a61 72
2 b f Le Vie Dei Colori—Hard To Lay (IRE) (Dolphin Street (FR))
3310[5] 3721[3] 4451[3] (4675) 5000[9] 5921[4] 5987[6] 6307[6] 6769[3] 6989[9] 7527[7] 7811[8]

Scooby Dee *Richard Whitaker* a49 50
3 b f Captain Rio—Scooby Dooby Do (Atraf)
1425[11] 1970[7] 2380[4] 2838[6] 3597[5] 4337[10] 4651[8] (6255) 6579[5] 6826[10]

Scorn (USA) *John Gosden* a72 84
3 b f Seeking The Gold(USA) —Sulk (IRE) (Selkirk (USA))
2050[2] 2463[2] 2843[2] 3347[2] 4115[9] 5872[5] 6415[4] 7042[13] 7453[4] 7575[5]

Scots Gaelic (IRE) *Patrick J Flynn* 82
3 ch g Tomba—Harmonic (USA) (Shadeed (USA))
6730a[13]

Scottish Boogie (IRE) *Sylvester Kirk* a55 88
3 b c Tobougg(IRE) —Scottish Spice (Selkirk (USA))
1453[6] 2253[12] 2618[10] 3297[6] (3957) 4127[2] 4532[4] (4964) 5456[3] 6151[2] ◆ (6535)

Scottish Glen *Patrick Chamings* a75 63
4 ch g Kyllachy—Dance For Fun (Anabaa (USA))
2968[10] 3511[3] (4256) 5377[6] 5897[4] 6292[5] 6997[3] (7439)

Scottish Lake *Jedd O'Keeffe* 41
2 b g Bertolini(USA) —Diabaig (Precocious)
6301[9] 7058[16]

Scottish Star *James Eustace* a62 57
2 gb c Kirkwall—Child Star (FR) (Bellypha)
3326[7] 3794[11]

Scrapper Smith (IRE) *Alistair Whillans* a65 85
4 b g Choisir(AUS) —Lady Ounavarra (IRE) (Simply Great (FR))
4404[4] 4834[10] (5405) 5737[8] 6107[7] (6367) 6960[7]

Screaming Brave *Sheena West* a55 65
4 br g Hunting Lion(IRE) —Hana Dee (Cadeaux Genereux)
7967[9]

Screenprint *Michael Bell* 66
2 ch g Shamardal(USA) —Painted Moon (USA) (Gone West (USA))
3991[6] (4499) 4911[7]

Scriobhai (IRE) *J S Bolger* 75
2 ch c Bachelor Duke(USA) —Aoibhneas (USA) (Dehere (USA))
2035a[2]

Scruffy Skip (IRE) *Christine Dunnett* a49 64
5 b g Diktat—Capoeira (USA) (Nureyev (USA))
838[2] 912[2] (1148) 1441[2] (1998) (2257) 2490[7] 2750[7] 4895[4] 5391[10] 5647[4] 6098[9] 6664[9] 7007[6] 7162[13] 7870[11]

Scrupulous *Tom Dascombe* a60 65
4 gr m Dansili—Mrs Gray (Red Sunset)
40[7]

Sea Change (IRE) *Jeremy Noseda* a88 84
3 b g Danehill Dancer(IRE) —Ibtikar (USA) (Private Account (USA))
3795[7] 4257[3] 4845[5] ◆ (6055) 6282[3] 6797[2]

Seachantach (USA) *David Simcock* a77 104
4 b g Elusive Quality(USA) —Subtle Breeze (USA) (Storm Cat (USA))
339a[13] 413a[12]

Sea Cove *Dianne Sayer* a33 40
10 b m Terimon—Regal Pursuit (IRE) (Roi Danzig (USA))
3669[12]

Sea Crest *Mel Brittain* a30 65
4 b m Xaar—Talah (Danehill (USA))
1270[2] 1337[3] 1470[5] 2647[4] 4155[4] 4285[7] 5097[2] 5485[8] 6464[8] 7132[8]

Seadream *Mark Usher* a38 52
2 b g Bertolini(USA) —Last Dream (IRE) (Alzao (USA))
6811[7] 7177[7] 7550[10] 7813[7]

Seafarer (IRE) *Brian Meehan* 78
3 b c Footstepsinthesand—Innocence (Unfuwain (USA))
(1542) ◆

Sea Flower (IRE) *Tim Easterby* 71
2 b f Acclamation—Rebel Clan (IRE) (Tagula (IRE))
2420[2] 2654[2] 3118[6] 3729[2] 5301[14]

Sea Galleon (AUS) *Colin & Cindy Alderson* 99
4 ch c Galileo(IRE) —San Michele (AUS) (Stravinsky (USA))
7368a[16]

Sea Land (FR) *Brian Ellison* a67 61
6 ch g King's Best(USA) —Green Bonnet (IRE) (Green Desert (USA))
716[3] 895[6] 1028[3] ◆ 1204[7] 1919[9] 2349[6] (2529) 2761[7] 3223[7] 3369[4] 3405[2] 4411[5] 4606[10]

Sea Lord (IRE) *Mark Johnston* a97 116
3 b c Cape Cross(IRE) —First Fleet (USA) (Woodman (USA))
1834[5] (2479) (2737) 3103[8] (3487a) (3867) (4537) (5009) 5775a[5]

Seal Rock *Henry Candy* 84
2 b g Ishiguru(USA) —Satin Doll (Diktat)
(7346)

Sea Moon *Sir Michael Stoute* 82
2 b c Beat Hollow—Eva Luna (USA) (Alleged (USA))
6831[2] ◆ (7152)

Seamster *Mark Johnston* a73 43
3 ch g Pivotal—Needles And Pins (IRE) (Fasliyev (USA))
(247) 681[5] 1070[3]

Seamus Shindig *Henry Candy* a59 85
8 b g Aragon—Sheesha (USA) (Shadeed (USA))
1903[7] 2595[13] 2992[15] 4333[4] 4806[7] 5551[3] 6280[5] 6625[9]

Sean Og Coulston (IRE) *John J Coleman* a80 86
6 b g Raphane(USA) —Classic Silk (IRE) (Classic Secret (USA))
3487a[11] 6597a[5]

Sea Of Galilee *Henry Candy* 90
3 b f Galileo(IRE) —Mesange Royale (FR) (Garde Royale)
3437[6] (4115) 5056[3] 7206[10]

Sea Of Heartbreak (IRE) *Roger Charlton* a68 102
3 b f Rock Of Gibraltar(IRE) —Top Forty (Rainbow Quest (USA))
(2250) ◆ (2843) ◆ (3298) ◆ 4470[16] 5989[2] 6886[4]

Sea Of Leaves (USA) *Jim Goldie* 99
4 b m Stormy Atlantic(USA) —Dock Leaf (USA) (Woodman (USA))
1400[5] 1918[9] 2326[4] 2759[U] 4391[12] 4536[9] 5120[4] 5883[7] 5911[3] 6175[10] 6887[12]

Sea Of Love (IRE) *Ronald Harris* a28
2 b f Dubawi(IRE) —Alta Gracia (IRE) (Danehill Dancer (IRE))
5763[10] 6425[10] 7692[5]

Seaquel *Andrew Haynes* a54 49
4 b m Kyllachy—Broughton Singer (IRE) (Common Grounds)
41[F] 190[6] 611[3] 3290[5]

Search For The Key (USA) *Paul Cole* a66 63
3 bb c El Corredor(USA) —Lo Cal Bread (USA) (Native Prospector (USA))
1586[2] 1993[3] 2993[8] 4327[11] 5072[4]

Sea Rover (IRE) *Mel Brittain* a73 76
6 b h Jade Robbery(USA) —Talah (Danehill (USA))
2817[7] 4345[8] 4559[10] 5502[7] 5760[9]

Sea Salt *Ron Barr* a59 87
7 b g Titus Livius(FR) —Carati (Selkirk (USA))
1374[7] 1719[8] 2671[8] 3062[11] 4285[3] 4486[5] 4706[4] (5064) 5500[5] 5688[9] 6040[6] (6295) 7125[9]

Seasider *David Simcock* a88 86
5 b g Zamindar(USA) —Esplanade (Danehill (USA))
286[3] 358[9] 695[3] 851[2] 1049[3] 1301[3] 1458[6] 2129[2] 2959[2]

Seaside Sizzler *Ralph Beckett* a71 73
3 ch g Rahy(USA) —Via Borghese (USA) (Seattle Dancer (USA))
4425[5] 4964[7] 5832[6] 6781[2] 7504[3]

Seas Of Sorrow (IRE) *Brendan Duke* a54 50
2 b f Key Of Luck(USA) —Its On The Air (IRE) (King's Theatre (IRE))
2077[8] 2338[16] 3296[14] 4993[6] 5660[4] 6081[12] 6412[11]

Sea Soldier (IRE) *Andrew Balding* 67
2 b g Red Ransom(USA) —Placement (Kris)
6883[10] 7178[5]

Seasonal Cross *Simon Dow* a75 81
5 b m Cape Cross(IRE) —Seasonal Blossom (IRE) (Fairy King (USA))
(2956) (3457) ◆ 4472[4] 6205[8] 6444[6] 6851[5] 7521[4]

Sea The Flames (IRE) *Marcus Tregoning* 49
2 b g Chineur(FR) —Flames (Blushing Flame (USA))
3735[11] 3961[7] 4902[14] 6294[10]

Sea Tobougie *Mark Usher* a47 48
3 ch f Tobougg(IRE) —Mary Sea (FR) (Selkirk (USA))
4364[10] 5366[9] 5832[8] 6871[10] 7476[5] 7570[5] 7716[11] 7848[7]

Seattle Drive (IRE) *David Elsworth* a75 92
2 b c Motivator—Seattle Ribbon (USA) (Seattle Dancer (USA))
(5491) 6149[2] 6845[2]

Seattle Speight (USA) *William Knight* a61 74
3 b f Speightstown(USA) —Gal From Seattle (USA) (A.P. Indy (USA))
1538[5] 1989[8] 2675[5] (3607) (4212) 4873[3] 6846[14]

Sebastian Flyte *Francis Ennis* 103
3 ch c Observatory(USA) —Aravonian (Night Shift (USA))
1038a[7] 2354a[7]

Second Brook (IRE) *Reg Hollinshead* a56 52
3 b g Celtic Swing—Mur Taasha (USA) (Riverman (USA))
33[6] 254[6] 775[2] ◆ 1054[5] 1145[8] 5423[7] 5631[6] 6257[3] 6336[5] 6574[3] 6652[5]

Second Encore *J S Moore* a70 72
2 b f Royal Applause—Empress Jain (Lujain (USA))
2338[8] 2763[3] 3509[4] (3686) 3849[4] 5725[4] 5921[7] (6576) 7040[3] 7424[6]

Second Reef *Tom Cuthbert* a64 58
8 b g Second Empire(IRE) —Vax Lady (Millfontaine)
4606[9] 4644[9] 5331[2] 5820[14] 6026[2] 6495[10]

Second To Nun (IRE) *Michael Blanshard* a48 62
4 b m Bishop Of Cashel—One For Me (Tragic Role (USA))
1141[5] 2596[8] 2956[3] 3309[4] 3683[3]

Secoya *Ralph Beckett* a55 52
2 b f Sleeping Indian—Nazca (Zilzal (USA))
6803[9] 7530[7] 7733[6]

Secrecy *Saeed Bin Suroor* a111 116
4 b g King's Best(USA) —Wink (Salse (USA))
440a[3] 5009[3] (5370) 5741[2] (6806) 7234[4]

Secret Affair *Mme C Vergne & D Sicaud* a80 77
8 b g Piccolo—Secret Circle (Magic Ring (IRE))
743a[10]

Secret Assassin (IRE) *Mrs J L Le Brocq* a77 77
7 b g Daggers Drawn(USA) —Lypharden (IRE) (Lyphard's Special (USA))
1815a[6]

Secret Asset (IRE) *Jane Chapple-Hyam* a106 104
5 gr g Clodovil(IRE) —Skerray (Soviet Star (USA))
(1206) 1727[6] 1903[4] 3406[2] 3629[5] 4136[3] 4576[6] 4814[3] 6194[14] 6508[8] 6752[8] 7079[14] 7566[6] (7826) 7993[4]

Secret City (IRE) *Robin Bastiman* 65
4 b g City On A Hill(USA) —Secret Combe (IRE) (Mujadil (USA))
(1884) 2896[5] 3664[5] 4244[12] 4869[2] 5760[4] 6295[4]

Secret Edge *Alan King* 68
2 b g Tobougg(IRE) —Burton Ash (Diktat)
6634[5] 6953[6] 7179[3]

Secret Era *William Muir* a58
3 b f Cape Cross(IRE) —Secret History (USA) (Bahri (USA))
7244[4]

Secret Gold (IRE) *Brian Meehan* a67 63
2 b f Exceed And Excel(AUS) —Janayen (USA) (Zafonic (USA))
4474[9] (5763) 6271[4]

Secret Gypsy (USA) *Ronny Werner* a105
5 ch m Sea Of Secrets(USA) —Miss Utada (USA) (Rahy (USA))
7341a[11]

Secret Hero *Lee Smyth* a48 76
4 b g Cadeaux Genereux—Valiantly (Anabaa (USA))
2451[6] 3948[6] 4189[8] 4897[16]

Secretive *Mark Johnston* a92 94
3 b c Shamardal(USA) —Samsung Spirit (Statoblest)
1045[7] 1448[6] 1921[2] 2089[2] (2288) 3103[4] ◆ 3408[2] 3796[4] 4224[2] 4750[8] (5415) 6312[10] 6659[3] 6960[P]

Secret Lake *Jane Chapple-Hyam* 48
2 ch f Dubawi(IRE) —Three Secrets (IRE) (Danehill (USA))
7119[5]

Secret Love (IRE) *Mikael Magnusson* a82 85
2 gr f Dalakhani(IRE) —Sacred Love (IRE) (Barathea (IRE))
5029[2] (5841) ◆ 6559[11]

Secret Millionaire (IRE) *Patrick Morris* a93 97
3 b g Kyllachy—Mithl Al Hawa (Salse (USA))
2058[6] 2346[8] 2960[3] 3311[4] 3673[3] 3856[6] 4401[3] 4654[2] (5734) 5967[2] 6429[7] 7254[4]

Secret Queen *Martin Hill* a60 85
3 b f Zafeen(FR) —Gold Queen (Grand Lodge (USA))
1732[10] 2565[7] 3158[9] 7091[12]

Secret Ridge (ITY) *S Botti* 92
4 b m Indian Ridge—Love Secret (USA) (Secreto (USA))
1419a[4]

Secret Sortie (IRE) *Tim Etherington* 51
5 ch m Intikhab(USA) —Tajawuz (Kris)
3437[10] 4407[13] 5022[7]

Secret Tune *Tom George* 57
6 b g Generous(IRE) —Sing For Fame (USA) (Quest For Fame)
4817[9]

Secret Tycoon (IRE) *Patrick Morris* 67
2 gr g Aussie Rules(USA) —River Grand (IRE) (Grand Lodge (USA))
4543[6] 4999[4] 5418[7] 6046[8]

Secret Venue *Jedd O'Keeffe* a32 77
4 ch g Where Or When(IRE) —Sheila's Secret (IRE) (Bluebird (USA))
1363[11] 1711[10] 2695[9] 3540[4] 4938[2] 5240[6] 5502[3] 6031[5] 6299[2] 6700[12] 7175[3]

Secret Witness *Ronald Harris* a85 105
4 ch g Pivotal—It's A Secret (Polish Precedent (USA))
275[3] 404[2] (501) 595[2] 761[2] 905[6] 987[4] 1321[4] 1924[4] (2247) 2689[3] 2748[16] 3435[2] 4536[23] 4904[2] 5151[2] 5285[2] 5787[2] 5884[2] 6363[2] 6735[3] 7060[11]

Securitisation (IRE) *Barney Curley* a53 41
3 ch g Rock Of Gibraltar(IRE) —Maria Delfina (IRE) (Giant's Causeway (USA))
583[8] 1495[8] 2418[5] 4733[5]

Sedgwick *Shaun Harris* a82 80
8 b g Nashwan(USA) —Imperial Bailiwick (IRE) (Imperial Frontier (USA))
(83) 496[3] (598) (724) (923) (1318) 1439[2] 1592[3] 1829[5] 1996[7] (2349) 2739[2] 3317[3] 3813[4] 4594[6] 5217[11] 5529[6] 5790[7] 6328[9]

See Elsie Play *Zoe Davison* a60 48
4 b m King O' The Mana(IRE) —Liebside Lass (IRE) (Be My Guest (USA))
481[5] 768[8] 978[4] 1129[6] 1322[5] 1763[7] 2596[F] (Dead)

Seeharn (IRE) *Kevin Prendergast* 99
2 b f Pivotal—Nebraas (Green Desert (USA))
(3421a) 4879a[5]

Seeker Rainbow *Linda Jewell* a23 40
3 ch f Mark Of Esteem(IRE) —Seeker (Rainbow Quest (USA))
5028[11] 6863[8]

Seeking Dubai *Edward Vaughan* a82 91
3 b f Dubawi(IRE) —Placement (Kris)
1918[12] 2929[9] 3790[13]

Seeking Glory *Ed Dunlop* a70 50
2 b c King's Best(USA) —Atabaa (FR) (Anabaa (USA))
6158[15] 6497[5] 6994[5] 7394[3] 7572[2]

Seeking Magic *Clive Cox* a68
2 b c Haafhd—Atnab (USA) (Riverman (USA))
(7779) ◆

Seeking Rio *Ron Hodges* a39
3 b f Captain Rio—True Seeker (Lujain (USA))
215[10]

Seeking Solace *A Fabre* a84 98
3 b f Exceed And Excel(AUS) —Flamelet (USA) (Theatrical)
1496a[4] 2800a[8] 7648a[5]

Seeking Stardom *Pat Phelan* a48 58
3 ch g Starcraft(NZ) —Lunar Goddess (Royal Applause)
1162[8]

Seeking The Buck (USA) *Warren Greatrex* 97
6 b g Seeking The Gold(USA) —Cuanto Es (USA) (Exbourne (USA))
2747[7] 3265[6] 4399[2] 4818[10] 6889[11]

Seeking The Title (USA) *Dallas Stewart* a108
3 b f Seeking The Gold(USA) —Title Seeker (USA) (Monarchos (USA))
7344a[9]

Seek The Cash (USA) *Michael Quinn* a55
3 ch c Mr Greeley(USA) —Cash Deal (USA) (Danzig (USA))
128[10] 257[5] 538[3] 689[6] 988[7] 2962[15] 5161[5]

Seek The Fair Land *Jim Boyle* a96 80
4 b g Noverre(USA) —Duchcov (Caerleon (USA))
150[4] 286[11] ◆ 573[2] (739) 944[3] 1219[3] 4894[11] 5516[7] 5702[7] 6558[7] 6780[6] 7187[3] 7318[3] 7574[2] 7689[2] 7935[6]

Seelo (USA) *John Gosden* 77
2 b c Dynaformer(USA) —Seebe (USA) (Danzig (USA))
(6127)

See That Girl *Bryan Smart* a49 44
4 b m Hawk Wing(USA) —Hampton Lucy (IRE) (Anabaa (USA))
249[5] ◆ 388[13]

See The Smile (USA) *Gay Kelleway* a54 40
2 b c Arch(USA) —Tink So (USA) (Meadowlake (USA))
6001[5] 6542[6]

See The Storm *Patrick Morris* a29
2 bb g Statue Of Liberty(USA) —Khafayif (USA) (Swain (IRE))
6899[6]

Sefton Park *Charles Egerton* a51 51
3 b g Dansili—Optimistic (Reprimand)
2248[11]

Sehoy (USA) *Lennart Reuterskiold Jr* a91 90
4 bb h Menifee(USA) —Another Storm (USA) (Gone West (USA))
2637a[9]

Sehrezad (IRE) *Andreas Lowe* 114
5 b h Titus Livius(FR) —Trebles (IRE) (Kenmare (FR))
1251a[2] 1716a[3] 2559a[4] 3934a[2] (4888a) 6764a[4] 7372a[2]

Seia (ITY) *Mario Hofer* 72
2 b f Iffraaj—Sparkling Isle (Inchinor)
6975a[7]

Seldom (IRE) *Mel Brittain* a71 70
4 b g Sesaro(USA) —Daisy Dancer (IRE) (Distinctly North (USA))
373[2] 465[3] 543[2] 873[6] 1395[9] 2764[6] 2850[10] (4197) 4555[6] 4704[10] 5756[3] 6117[9]

Select Committee *John Quinn* 80
5 b g Fayruz—Demolition Jo (Petong)
1364[4] 1524[8] 1988[6] 2528[2] ◆ 2626[2] 2883[5] 3024[4] 3660[5] 4199[7] 4712[5] 5123[4] 5513[2] 5760[3] (6073) (6299) 6572[9] 6985[4] 7175[9]

Self Employed *Gary Woodward* 71
3 b c Sakhee(USA) —Twilight Sonnet (Exit To Nowhere (USA))
3621[2] 5065[3]

Selkis (GER) *J Hirschberger* 67
2 ch f Monsun(GER) —Schwarzach (GER) (Grand Lodge (USA))
6407a[6]

Selmis *Vittorio Caruso* 115
6 ch h Selkirk(USA) —Nokomis (Caerleon (USA))
1712a[10] 6764a[11]

Semina (GER) *S Smrczek* 99
3 ch f Mamool(IRE) —Second Game (GER) (Second Set (IRE))
4640a[6] 6790a[6]

Seminova *Mark Johnston* a30
3 b f Cape Cross(IRE) —Snow Polina (USA) (Trempolino (USA))
979[8]

Semos (FR) *A De Royer-Dupre* 103
3 ch c American Post—Semire (FR) (Mizoram (USA))
3933a[3]

Senate *John Gosden* a45 108
3 ch c Pivotal—Sauterne (Rainbow Quest (USA))
(1010) 1502[12] 4757[3] ◆ (5387) ◆ (5949) ◆ 6193[17] 7350[18]

Senate Majority *Tim Easterby* a64 59
3 ch g Avonbridge—Benjarong (Sharpo)
6515[10] 6880[7] (7328) 7473[5]

Senator Logan (IRE) *F J Brennan* a24
3 b g Golan(IRE) —Miss Senate (IRE) (Alzao (USA))
3213[10]

Sendali (FR) *James Bethell* 59
6 b g Daliapour(IRE) —Lady Senk (FR) (Pink (FR))
(1113) 1803[4] 2464[4] 6649[10] 7181[12]

Sendish (IRE) *H Billot* 53
7 b h Sendawar(IRE) —Ishtiyak (Green Desert (USA))
459a[9]

Sendreni (FR) *Jean McGregor* a79 76
6 b g Night Shift(USA) —Sendana (FR) (Darshaan)
194[3] 270[9] 499[2] 1102[7] 1672[13] 2671[10] 2856[7] 3164[6] 3900[7] 4515[11] 5439[10] 6396[7]

Seneschal *Michael Appleby* a67 85
9 b g Polar Falcon(USA) —Broughton Singer (IRE) (Common Grounds)
867[8] 1063[9] 2009[9] 2383[10] (3289) 3851[4] (4296) 5678[2]

Sennockian Storm (USA) *Mark Johnston* a57 77
3 b f Storm Cat(USA) —Winning Season (USA) (Lemon Drop Kid (USA))
1222[4] 4397[2] 4601[3] (5474) 6097[9] 7012[13]

Sennybridge *J W Hills* a63 45
3 ch f Avonbridge—Friend For Life (Lahib (USA))
5265[5] 6716[2] 7069[4] 7685[7]

Senor Benny (USA) *M McDonagh* a81 102
11 br h Benny The Dip(USA) —Senora Tippy (USA) (El Gran Senor (USA))
1676a[11] (Dead)

Senorita Bloom (FR) *Fredrik Reuterskiold* a50
3 ch f Tertullian(USA) —Yankee Bloom (USA) (El Gran Senor (USA))
7374a[8]

Senor Sassi (USA) *J S Moore* a48 48
2 bb c Johannesburg(USA) —County Fair (USA) (Mr Prospector (USA))
4802[15] 5373[7] 6209[8] 7197[5] 7629[4] 7813[10]

Senor Tibor (USA) *Edward Creighton* a36 51
2 b c Tale Of The Cat(USA) —Pastel Colour (USA) (Distant View (USA))
5895[6] 6443[9] 6779[6]

Sensational Day (USA) *Doug Watson* a71 47
3 br f Action This Day(USA) —Gold Bowl (USA) (Seeking The Gold (USA))
333a[12]

Sensational Love (IRE) *Robert Mills* a41 68
2 bb f Cadeaux Genereux—Szabo (IRE) (Anabaa (USA))
2594[14] 4299[4] (6811) 7301[5] 7423[7]

Sensationally *Ralph Beckett* a73 71
3 b f Montjeu(IRE) —One So Wonderful (Nashwan (USA))
2674[4] ◆ 3312[2] 3829[3] 5116[3] 5860[5] 6959[6] (7453)

Sensei (IRE) *Michael Quinlan* 87
2 b c Dr Fong(USA) —Query (USA) (Distant View (USA))
(3985) ◆ 5079[3] 7095[8]

Sense Of Pride *John Gosden* 85
3 b f Sadler's Wells(USA) —Bonash (Rainbow Quest (USA))
5376[4] (6356) ◆

Sense Of Purpose (IRE) *D K Weld* 102
3 ch f Galileo(IRE) —Super Gift (IRE) (Darshaan)
4631a[4] 5249[2]

Sensible *Hugh Collingridge* a61 38
5 ch m Almutawakel—Opera (Forzando)
989[7] 1134[7] 2012[8] 5164[11] 5565[6] 6678[6]

Sent From Heaven (IRE) *B W Hills* a80 109
3 b f Footstepsinthesand—Crystal Valkyrie (IRE) (Danehill (USA))
1726[4] 3143[9] 3571a[5] 5883[6] 6561[11]

Sentosa *Henry Cecil* a69 74
3 b f Dansili—Katrina (IRE) (Ela-Mana-Mou)
5258[6] 5832[2] 6275[5] 7253[5]

Sentry Duty (FR) *Nicky Henderson* 106
8 b g Kahyasi—Standing Around (FR) (Garde Royale)
3195[6] 4461[3] 6926[6]

Separate Ways (IRE) *David Marnane* a74 102
5 b g Chevalier(IRE) —Choralli (Inchinor)
5571a[3]

September Draw (USA) *Richard Hannon* 67
2 bb f Southern Image(USA) —Stacey's Relic (USA) (Houston (USA))
4247[6] 4736[3] 5829[6] 6809[6]

Septemberintherain *Robert Mills* a77 66
3 gr g Verglas(IRE) —Gwyneth (Zafonic (USA))
106[3] 240[3] 928[2] 1433[7] 5467[7] 6517[7]

September Morn (IRE) *A P O'Brien* a77 89
3 b c Montjeu(IRE) —Vanishing Prairie (USA) (Alysheba (USA))
1730[4]

Sequillo *Richard Hannon* a85 88
4 b g Lucky Story(USA) —Tranquillity (Night Shift (USA))
2181[5] 2821[12] 2996[4] 3737[4] 4376[4] (5311) 7292[6] 7612[7] 7756[11]

Seradim *Paul Cole* a88 95
4 ch m Elnadim(USA) —Seren Devious (Dr Devious (IRE))
1084[9] 1899[9] 2475[9] 3158[4] 3457[2] 3806[2] 4472[2] 4950[4] 6830[2] 7287[3] 7430[11]

Serafina's Flight *William Muir* a74 84
3 b f Fantastic Light(USA) —Seven Of Nine (IRE) (Alzao (USA))
(1240) 1729[7] 2047[7] 5444[2]

Seraphic Romp (JPN) *Yoshinori Muto* 111
6 bb m Manhattan Cafe(JPN) —El Sol (JPN) (Royal Ski (USA))
7460a[7]

Serena's Pride *Alan Jarvis* 95
2 b f Danbird(AUS) —Wachiwi (IRE) (Namid)
2074[4] (2330) 3070[4] 3792[6] 4356[9] 4458[8] 5036[4] 6139[10] 6719[8] 7347[9]

Sergeant Ablett (IRE) *Mark Johnston* 88
2 b c Danehill Dancer(IRE) —Dolydille (IRE) (Dolphin Street (FR))
(5595) 6149[5] 6560[16]

Sergeant Sharpe *David Bourton* a64 65
5 ch g Cadeaux Genereux—Halcyon Daze (Halling (USA))
7703[9]

Sergeant Suzie *Michael Dods* 71
2 ch f Dr Fong(USA) —Pie High (Salse (USA))
(2420) 3059[6]

Sergeant Troy (IRE) *Roger Charlton* 65
2 gr c Aussie Rules(USA) —Et Dona Ferentes (Green Desert (USA))
5491[9] 6635[4] 7099[6]

Serhaal (IRE) *Sir Michael Stoute* a71 68
3 b g Green Desert(USA) —Lucky For Me (USA) (King Of Kings (IRE))
3621[3] 4022[4]

Serienhoehe (IRE) *P Schiergen* 99
4 b m High Chaparral(IRE) —Saldenehre (GER) (Highest Honor (FR))
3251a[7] 5345a[7]

Serious Attitude (IRE) *Rae Guest* 113
4 b m Mtoto—Zameyla (IRE) (Cape Cross (IRE))
1918[2] 3192[10] 3870[14] 5946[9] 6390[5] (6949a)

Serious Drinking (USA) *Walter Swinburn* a65 66
4 b m Successful Appeal(USA) —Cup Match (USA) (Kingmambo (USA))
2718[11] 4206[7] 7298[5] 7453[3] 7611[12]

Serious Impact (USA) *F Vermeulen* a84 89
5 b g Empire Maker(USA) —Diese (USA) (Diesis)
1748a[6]

Serious Matters (IRE) *Walter Swinburn* a56 50
3 b g Invincible Spirit(IRE) —Quaeramus Seria (IRE) (Catrail (USA))
1659[10] 2340[7] 2741[7] 3515[4] 4256[9]

Seriy Tzarina *Gay Kelleway* a47 57
4 gr m Baryshnikov(AUS) —Bay Bianca (IRE) (Law Society (USA))
920[6] 2487[3] 4069[7] 4780[4] 6094[4]

Sermons Mount (USA) *Mouse Hamilton-Fairley* a66 73
4 bb g Vicar(USA) —Ginny Auxier (USA) (Racing Star (USA))
1170[9] 1441[3] 1633[3] 2590[4] 2919[2] 3254[2] 4130[4] 4775[2] 5238[8] (5875)

Serva Jugum (USA) *Paul Cole* a86 110
4 bb h Fusaichi Pegasus(USA) —Shake The Yoke (Caerleon (USA))
1333[3]

Serva Padrona (IRE) *H-A Pantall* a81 79
3 b f Statue Of Liberty(USA) —Semiramide (IRE) (Persian Bold)
548a[2]

Servoca (CAN) *Mike Murphy* a99 98
4 gr g El Prado(IRE) —Cinderellaslipper (USA) (Touch Gold (USA))
1085[13] 3146[19] 3461[13]

Sesimbra (IRE) *E Lellouche* a55 89
3 b f Key Of Luck(USA) —Campiglia (IRE) (Fairy King (USA))
1946a[5]

Seta *Luca Cumani* 111
3 ch f Pivotal—Bombazine (IRE) (Generous (IRE))
1726[12] (2387) (3375) (5305) 6561[8]

Setareh (GER) *P Olsanik* 97
5 b h Areion(GER) —Sety's Spirit (USA) (Seattle Song (USA))
6791a[4]

Set Back *David Nicholls* a71 52
3 b g Reset(AUS) —No Comebacks (Last Tycoon)
(702) (782) 1070[4] 1298[F]

Set Em Up Mo *Michael Attwater* a49
4 b m Reset(AUS) —Mo Stopher (Sharpo)
82[4] 316[10] 1160[7] 7760[9]

Set Me Free (IRE) *Luca Cumani* 69
2 b g Noverre(USA) —Lonesome Me (FR) (Zafonic (USA))
3923[8] 4392[3] ◆

Setter's Princess *Ron Hodges* a56 59
4 ch m Generous(IRE) —Setter Country (Town And Country)
1186[3] 1432[5] 1757[9] 2586[2] ◆ 2952[9] 7167[6] 7315[5]

Set The Trend *Andrew Balding* a100 104
4 bb g Reset(AUS) —Masrora (USA) (Woodman (USA))
2708[2] 3692[7] (4816) 6562[22]

Settle For Medal (USA) *Mark Hennig* a86
2 bb c Medallist(USA) —Rehear (USA) (Coronado's Quest (USA))
6756a[4]

Set To Go *Natalie Lloyd-Beavis* a55 61
3 b g Reset(AUS) —Golubitsa (IRE) (Bluebird (USA))
1394[13] 2172[5] (2409) 2844[17] 4475[11] 7125[16] 7490[7]

Set To Music (IRE) *Michael Bell* a67 72
2 b f Danehill Dancer(IRE) —Zarabaya (IRE) (Doyoun)
4844[4] ◆ 5369[9] 6071[3]

Seul Blue (ITY) *R Menichetti* 95
4 b h Tout Seul(IRE) —Bluebold (IRE) (Bluebird (USA))
1540a[6] 3019a[10]

Seven Of Diamonds (IRE) *Tim Easterby* 62
3 gr f Clodovil(IRE) —Tres Sage (Reprimand)
1402[4] 1667[4] 1966[5] 2628[8]

Seven Royals (IRE) *Anna Newton-Smith* a29 32
5 b g Val Royal(FR) —Seven Notes (Zafonic (USA))
1443[11] 2417[9]

Seven Sons *Ian McInnes* 47
3 b g Reset(AUS) —Rock Concert (Bishop Of Cashel)
5603[5] 6624[11] 6966[12]

Seven Summits (IRE) *Jeremy Noseda* a87 94
3 b g Danehill Dancer(IRE) —Mandavilla (IRE) (Sadler's Wells (USA))
6738[5] 7084[18]

Seventh Cavalry (IRE) *Alan King* a67 75
5 gr g No Excuse Needed—Mixwayda (FR) (Linamix (FR))
2080[8] (2597)

Seventh Hill *Michael Blanshard* a69 71
5 ch g Compton Place—Dream Baby (Master Willie)
868[6] 1623[2] 2341[4] (2691) 3348[3] 3865[3] 4386[2] 5011[4] 5382[5]

Seventh Sky (GER) *P Schiergen* 97
3 b c King's Best(USA) —Sacarina (Old Vic)
4184a[13]

Seville (GER) *A P O'Brien* 119
2 b c Galileo(IRE) —Silverskaya (USA) (Silver Hawk (USA))
7081[2]

Sextons House (IRE) *Richard Hannon* 78
2 b c King's Best(USA) —Lolita's Gold (USA) (Royal Academy (USA))
(3349) 5537[4]

Seyaaq (USA) *B W Hills* a68 68
3 gr g Aljabr(USA) —Muwakleh (Machiavellian (USA))
1325[4] ◆ 1661[4]

Sforza (IRE) *Brian Meehan* 40
2 b f Golan(IRE) —Bernhardt (IRE) (Alzao (USA))
6154[15]

Sgt Schultz (IRE) *J S Moore* a102 73
7 b g In The Wings—Ann's Annie (IRE) (Alzao (USA))
1277[8] 2081[6] 2690[3] (3589) 3847[6] 4101[6] 5034[6]

Shaabek (IRE) *Mick Channon* a68 69
2 ch c Byron—Shbakni (USA) (Mr Prospector (USA))
3555[8] 3842[2] 4123[9] 4911[4] 5807[7] 6695[2]

Shabak Hom (IRE) *David Simcock* a57 76
3 b g Exceed And Excel(AUS) —Shbakni (USA) (Mr Prospector (USA))
1761[8] 2250[7] 2886[3] (3954) 4594[4] 4923[4]

Shaded Edge *David Arbuthnot* a77 76
6 b g Bold Edge—Twilight Mistress (Bin Ajwaad (IRE))
110[2] 259[5] 1914[3] 2736[10] 3262[5] 4044[8] 4959[8] 6085[13] 6854[8] 7047[13] 7992[5]

Shades Of Grey *Clive Cox* a46 75
3 gr f Dr Fong(USA) —Twosixtythreewest (FR) (Kris)
979[6] 1542[5] 2051[4] 2619[2] 3337[6] 5038[9] 6959[3]

Shadow Bay (IRE) *Zoe Davison* a68 73
4 b g Deportivo—Champion Tipster (Pursuit Of Love)
556[6] 695[5] 1130[3] 1305[8] 1633[11] 2010[5] 2178[7] 2719[11] 2809[7]

Shadow Catcher *Michael Dods* 65
2 ch g Haafhd—Unchain My Heart (Pursuit Of Love)
4899[5] 6102[3] 6458[3]

Shadow Of The Sun *Mick Channon* 39
2 b f Red Ransom(USA) —Hill Welcome (Most Welcome)
6441[12]

Shadows Lengthen *Michael Easterby* a96 96
4 b g Dansili—Bay Shade (USA) (Sharpen Up)
(300) 401[3] 1274[3] 2096[8] 2976[9] 3921[19] 6877[14] 7410[8] 7612[9]

Shadowtime *Tracy Waggott* a73 88
5 b g Singspiel(IRE) —Massomah (USA) (Seeking The Gold (USA))
1926[2] 2392[6] (2527) 2937[9] 2991[6] 3317[5] (3973) 4198[2] (4450) 5685[5] 6567[7]

Shafgaan *Clive Brittain* 88
2 gr c Oasis Dream—Night Haven (Night Shift (USA))
1073[4] 1351[3] 1835[2] 5527[7] 6200[3] 6560[7]

Shahdawar (FR) *M Pimbonnet* a85 45
7 b g Sendawar(IRE) —Shahrazad (FR) (Bering)
221a[8] 281a[10]

Shahwardi (FR) *Jeremy Gask* 103
4 b g Lando(GER) —Shamdara (IRE) (Dr Devious (IRE))
2345[4] 3454[3] 4081a[6] 6389[6]

Shakalaka (IRE) *Gary Moore* a82 81
4 b g Montjeu(IRE) —Sweet Times (Riverman (USA))
(429)

Shakedown *Ian Williams* a38 60
5 b g Domedriver(IRE) —Stormy Weather (Nashwan (USA))
2337[5] 2714[12]

Shake On It *Mark Hoad* a72 52
6 b g Lomitas—Decision Maid (USA) (Diesis)
(34) ◆ 131[2] 348[3] 496[12] 663[4] 862[5] 966[3] 1241[8] 2781[5]

Shakespearean (IRE) *Saeed Bin Suroor* 118
3 b c Shamardal(USA) —Paimpolaise (IRE) (Priolo (USA))
(2712) 3066[6] 4166a[5] (5081) 5946[10] 6923[13]

Shakespeare's Son *James Evans* a64 67
5 b g Mind Games—Eastern Blue (IRE) (Be My Guest (USA))
344[4] 423[3] 561[8] 860[3] 896[12] 3977[3] 5169[2] 5579[5] 6025[3] 6119[2] 6847[4] 7506[F]

Shalamara (FR) *P Demercastel* a79 74
5 ch m Chichicastenango(FR) —Konile (FR) (In The Wings)
273a[0]

Shalambar (IRE) *Tony Carroll* 85
4 gr g Dalakhani(IRE) —Shalama (IRE) (Kahyasi)
6630[6] 6990[12]

Shalanaya (IRE) *M Delzangles* 115
4 ch m Lomitas—Shalamantika (IRE) (Nashwan (USA))
1747a[2] 3068[8] 5348a[7] 6950a[3]

Shalangar (IRE) *A De Royer-Dupre* a80 91
3 b c Red Ransom(USA) —Shalamantika (IRE) (Nashwan (USA))
7457a[8]

Shallal *Doug Watson* a52 101
5 b h Cape Cross(IRE) —First Waltz (FR) (Green Dancer (USA))
628a[12]

Shallow Bay *Walter Swinburn* a91 79
3 b g Shamardal(USA) —Yawl (Rainbow Quest (USA))
4906[8] 5376[3] 5971[2] 6753[3] (7111)

Shaluca *Ed McMahon* a56 67
3 bb f Shamardal(USA) —Noushkey (Polish Precedent (USA))
2434[2] 3023[3] 3866[5] 4342[4] 5044[5] 7239[8] 7529[8]

Shamalgan (FR) *A Savujev* 116
3 ch c Footstepsinthesand—Genevale (FR) (Unfuwain (USA))
1565a[6] 2159a[3] 2802a[13] 4420a[2] 6014a[5] 6592a[6]

Shamali *William Haggas* a92 107
5 ch h Selkirk(USA) —Shamaiel (IRE) (Lycius (USA))
1697[6] ◆ 2444[4]

Shaman Dancer (GER) *Andrew Balding* 50
2 b c Oasis Dream—Square The Circle (Second Empire (IRE))
5255[10]

Shamanova (IRE) *A De Royer-Dupre* 104
3 b f Danehill Dancer(IRE) —Shamadara (IRE) (Kahyasi)
3493a[2] 5138a[2] 5800a[2] 6591a[7]

Shamardal Phantom (IRE) *David Simcock* 70
3 b f Shamardal(USA) —Ripalong (IRE) (Revoque (IRE))
4397[3] 4997[2]

Shamarlane *Daniel Miley* a67 30
3 ch f Shamardal(USA) —Robin Lane (Tenby)
2903[7] 3808[7] 4251[10] 4908[4] 6536[8] (7605)

Shamdarley (IRE) *Michael Dods* 68
2 b c Shamardal(USA) —Siphon Melody (USA) (Siphon (BRZ))
6047[3] 6560[24]

Shame The Devil (IRE) *James Evans* a60 50
5 b g Danehill Dancer(IRE) —Iles Piece (Shirley Heights)
421[5] 570[5] 908[8] 1226[10] 1920[9] 3128[6] 3641[6]

Shamir *Jo Crowley* a90 69
3 b g Dubai Destination(USA) —Lake Nyasa (IRE) (Lake Coniston (IRE))
(843) 1086[3] 2970[4] (3330) 4023[5] (4699) 5750[14]

Shamo Hill Theatre *Colin Teague* 35
3 b g Millkom—Hannalou (FR) (Shareef Dancer (USA))
4018[7] 4556[11] 5360[6] 6296[12]

Sham Risk (FR) *J Morin* a78 78
6 gr g Take Risks(FR) —Sham Princess (USA) (Lyphard (USA))
221a[2] 281a[8]

Shamwari Lodge (IRE) *Richard Hannon* a107 113
4 b m Hawk Wing(USA) —Ripalong (IRE) (Revoque (IRE))
(1084) (1693) ◆ (2355a) 3067[6]

Shanafarahan (IRE) *Kevin Morgan* a68 64
5 b g Marju(IRE) —Sedna (FR) (Bering)
282[12]

Shanavaz *Colin Teague* a58 57
4 gr m Golden Snake(USA) —Safinaz (Environment Friend)
4945[11] 5364[7] 5681[11] 6242[9] 6648[11] 7147[8] 7538[6]

Shandelight (IRE) *Julie-Ann Camacho* a63 63
6 b m Dilshaan—By Candlelight (IRE) (Roi Danzig (USA))
(410) 621[11] 1462[4]

Shannersburg (IRE) *Ian Williams* a69 70
5 bb g Johannesburg(USA) —Shahoune (USA) (Blushing Groom (FR))
280[9] 4669[2] (4912) 5765[4]

Shannon Falls (FR) *Jo Crowley* a53 48
6 gr m Turgeon(USA) —Shannon River (FR) (Nashamaa)
585[5] 3256[7] 4257[11] 6855[9]

Shannon Golden *Roy Bowring* a61 47
4 b g Tumbleweed Ridge—Cledeschamps (Doc Marten)
462[8] 668[11] 860[4] 1072[5] 1235[6] 1885[13] 2957[2] 3284[10] 3768[3] 5067[9] 6119[6]

Shany De Loriol (FR) *C Provot* 91
4 b m Lavirco(GER) —Whistle Sweetly (Green Tune (USA))
7648a[0]

Sharaayeen *B W Hills* a68 101
3 br g Singspiel(IRE) —Corinium (IRE) (Turtle Island (IRE))
1033[5] 1518[2] 1823[4] 4757[4] 5529[2] ◆ (6151) 6565[2]

Sharakti (IRE) *Alan McCabe* a17 75
3 b g Rakti—Easter Parade (Entrepreneur)
1010[9] 1271[4] 1652[4] 2175[7] 2620[2] 2993[9] 3242[2] (4052) 4944[4] (5607) 6116[2] 6623[3] 6984[4] 7205[9]

Shared Account (USA) *H Graham Motion* a56 110
4 b m Pleasantly Perfect(USA) —Silk N' Sapphire (USA) (Smart Strike (CAN))
(7343a)

Sharedah (IRE) *Sir Michael Stoute* a93 91
3 b f Pivotal—Nasanice (IRE) (Nashwan (USA))
2043[3] (2674) 4106[6] (5083) 5529[3] 7293[2]

Shared Moment (IRE) *John Gallagher* a60 65
4 ch m Tagula(IRE) —Good Thought (IRE) (Mukaddamah (USA))
827[8] 1141[7] (1771) 2279[2] 3131[9] 3683[8] 7467[10] 7717[2] 7787[8] 7966[6]

Shareen (IRE) *John M Oxx* a77 103
3 b f Bahri(USA) —Sharesha (IRE) (Ashkalani (IRE))
5568a[2] (6379a)

Share Option *Tony Carroll* a51 55
8 b g Polish Precedent(USA) —Quota (Rainbow Quest (USA))
584[7] 6933[6] 7213[5]

Sharift (IRE) *David William O'Connor* a51 16
4 b m Night Shift(USA) —Shara (IRE) (Kahyasi)
1207[12]

Shark Man (IRE) *Michael Wigham* a68 78
3 b g Arakan(USA) —Sharkiyah (IRE) (Polish Precedent (USA))
2416[13] 4132[4] 6853[11] 7019[10] 7633[3] 7705[3]

Sharnberry *Ed Dunlop* 94
2 b f Shamardal(USA) —Wimple (USA) (Kingmambo (USA))
4471[3] (5074) 6530[7] 7204[3]

Sharp And Chic *Richard Ford* a39 11
3 b f Needwood Blade—Moreover (IRE) (Caerleon (USA))
7413[9]

Sharp Bullet (IRE) *Bruce Hellier* a74 74
4 b g Royal Applause—Anna Frid (GER) (Big Shuffle (USA))
2534[9] 2883[12] 5198[12] 5477[4] 5599[6] 6246[2] 6398[4] 6536[7] 7334[9] 7446[6] 7537[4] ◆ 7807[5] 7860[5]

Sharp Eclipse *Kevin Ryan* 79
3 ch g Exceed And Excel(AUS) —Helen Sharp (Pivotal)
1811[2] 2000[9] 2628[2] ◆ 2879[2] 3663[2] 4169[4] 4567[3] (4703) 5356[3] 6466[10]

Sharpened Edge *Bryn Palling* a51 87
4 b m Exceed And Excel(AUS) —Beveled Edge (Beveled (USA))
1267[8] 1827[5] 2280[10] 6772[3] (7180)

Sharp Shoes *Ann Duffield* a75 62
3 br g Needwood Blade—Mary Jane (Tina's Pet)
1155[3] 1456[10] 1774[4] 2209[8] 2530[4] 3979[7] 4194[4] 4516[10] 5299[2] 5485[6] 6490[2] 6931[7] (7300) 7764[3] (7859) 7998[6]

Sharp Sovereign (USA) *David Barron* 74
4 b g Cactus Ridge(USA) —Queen Of Humor (USA) (Distorted Humor (USA))
1576[3] (2012) 2303[2] 2653[3] 3369[3] 4582[3] (5216) (6242) (6984) 7228[3]

Shavansky *Rod Millman* a88 100
6 b g Rock Of Gibraltar(IRE) —Limelighting (USA) (Alleged (USA))
(1600) 2444[3] ◆ 3069[25] 5955[2] 6391[13] 6877[4] 7350[9]

Shaweel *Saeed Bin Suroor* 117
4 b h Dansili—Cooden Beach (IRE) (Peintre Celebre (USA))
517a[3]

Shawkantango *Derek Shaw* a52 30
3 b g Piccolo—Kitty Kitty Cancan (Warrshan (USA))
751[6] 886[8] 936[7] 1205[7] 1280[9] 1477[4] 2185[8] 2648[8]

Shawnee Saga (FR) *W Baltromei* 102
5 b h Sagacity(FR) —Shawnee (GER) (Dashing Blade)
4566a[4] 6607a[7] 7457a[7]

Shaws Diamond (USA) *Derek Shaw* a75 78
4 ch m Ecton Park(USA) —Dear Abigail (USA) (Dehere (USA))
850[3] 1455[9] 1629[7] 4287[9] 4847[9] 5157[4] 5533[7] 6210[10]

Shayla *Alan Swinbank* a52 59
3 ch f Pastoral Pursuits—Honours Even (Highest Honor (FR))
1464[5] 2725[6]

She Ain't A Saint *Jane Chapple-Hyam*
2 b f Dansili—Flamingo Sky (USA) (Silver Hawk (USA))
7232[17]

Shearman (IRE) *Ed McMahon* a86 15
3 b g Elusive City(USA) —Champion Tipster (Pursuit Of Love)
(751) 1616[8]

She Deals *Paul Midgley* a14
2 b f Gentleman's Deal(IRE) —Baymist (Mind Games)
7843[10]

Sheedal (IRE) *Linda Perratt* 37
2 b f Danroad(AUS) —Absolute Glee (USA) (Kenmare (FR))
4103[9] 7049[9] 7172[10]

Sheer Courage (IRE) *H J Brown* a48 96
2 b c Invincible Spirit(IRE) —Mood Swings (IRE) (Shirley Heights)
1728[5] (2389) ◆ 3049[13]

Sheer Force (IRE) *William Knight* a81 79
3 b g Invincible Spirit(IRE) —Imperial Graf (USA) (Blushing John (USA))
1061[3] 1307[5] 1872[2] (2441) 3154[8] 4288[4] 4922[3] 5454[4] 6208[5] (6801) 7046[3]

Sheikhtothemusic *James Given* a10 63
3 b f Dubai Destination(USA) —Oomph (Shareef Dancer (USA))
2837[5] 3437[9] 3776[4] 5058[2] 5437[9] 6084[7] 6631[6]

Sheila's Bond *J S Moore* a64 65
3 ch f Monsieur Bond(IRE) —Loreto Rose (Lahib (USA))
533[5] 655[3] (776) 1048[8] 1158[6] 2753[3] 3444[3] 3723[4] 4027[2] 4301[4] 6287[7] 7445[2] 7726[2] 7996[6]

Sheila's Castle *Sean Regan* a67 70
6 b m Karinga Bay—Candarela (Damister (USA))
2560[3] 3221[3] 3780[2] 7422[3]

Sheila's Star (IRE) *J S Moore* a60 66
2 b f Hurricane Run(IRE) —Yaselda (Green Desert (USA))
1043[7] ◆ 2223[4] 3209[3] 3872[6] 4984[4] 5374[3] 5807[3] 6081[11] 7197[3] (7464) (7629) 7839[4]

Sheila Toss (IRE) *Richard Hannon* a74 76
3 b f Galileo(IRE) —Palacoona (FR) (Last Tycoon)
930[8] 1358[5] 2047[4] 2254[10] 2886[5] 3268[9] (4300) 4555[5]

Sheiling (IRE) *Richard Fahey* 67
3 b f Halling(USA) —Mystery Play (IRE) (Sadler's Wells (USA))
1528[4] 1809[3] 2290[5] ◆ 2673[4] 3506[2] 4087[2] 4557[6] 5093[5] 5534[6] 6225[10]

She Is Great (IRE) *Vittorio Caruso* 96
3 b f Dalakhani(IRE) —She Bat (Batshoof)
7109a[7]

Shekan Star *Keith Reveley* a53 61
8 b m Sri Pekan(USA) —Celestial Welcome (Most Welcome)
(1576) 1807[6] 2500[4] 3078[4]

Sheklaan (USA) *Michael Jarvis* 76
3 b c Kingmambo(USA) —Eswarah (Unfuwain (USA))
3173[10] 3795[6] 4258[10]

Shelfah (IRE) *Michael Jarvis* a78 84
3 b f Selkirk(USA) —Pass The Peace (Alzao (USA))
(1158) ◆ 1448[2] ◆ 1975[4] 2704[2] ◆ 3414[4] 6282[4] 6698[4]

Shellder (IRE) *L Riccardi* 84
3 ch f Footstepsinthesand—Stoxx (IRE) (Desert Style (IRE))
1419a[9] 6238a[8]

Shelovestobouggie *Henry Cecil* 68
2 b f Tobougg(IRE) —Bowled Out (GER) (Dansili)
6092[4]

Shemita's Song (USA) *George Baker*
3 b f Songandaprayer(USA) —Shemita (IRE) (Sadler's Wells (USA))
4028[8] 5026[10]

Shemiyla (FR) *A De Royer-Dupre* 108
4 b m Dalakhani(IRE) —Shemala (IRE) (Danehill (USA))
(1792a) 2403a[4]

Shercon (IRE) *Nigel Tinkler* a41 49
3 ch g Redback—Snow Eagle (IRE) (Polar Falcon (USA))
1495[4] 1887[4] 2787[3] 3113[11] 7003[7] 7156[5]

Sherjawy (IRE) *Zoe Davison* a77 75
6 b g Diktat—Arruhan (IRE) (Mujtahid (USA))
20[13] 137[3] 163[4] 242[2] 325[6] 344[2] (555) 658[2] (846) 972[2] 1321[8] 1438[4] (1638) 1848[4] 1963[5] 2196[5] 2331[5] 6057[8] 6523[3] 6997[8] 7041[10] 7442[6] 7556[10]

Sherman McCoy *Rod Millman* a86 95
4 ch g Reset(AUS) —Naomi Wildman (USA) (Kingmambo (USA))
(1161) (1544) 2509[3]

Shernando *Mark Johnston* a84 88
3 b g Hernando(FR) —Shimmering Sea (Slip Anchor)
(570) 1730[7] 3889[4] ◆ 4153[3]

She's A Character *Richard Fahey* a85 91
3 b f Invincible Spirit(IRE) —Cavernista (Lion Cavern (USA))
2028[8] 2542[8] 4509[7] 4950[2] 5222[8] 6620[5] 7382[2] 7600[8] 7688[3] 8022[8]

Shesanindian (IRE) *Tony Carroll* a20 22
2 b f Sleeping Indian—Aswhatilldois (IRE) (Blues Traveller (IRE))
1577[16] 3029[10] 3269[13] 4228[6] 5583[10]

Shesasnip *Reg Hollinshead*
3 b f Trade Fair—Shebasis (USA) (General Holme (USA))
2706[9] 5700[8] 6746[10]

Shesastar *David Barron* 69
2 b f Bahamian Bounty—Celestial Welcome (Most Welcome)
4599[5] 6263[2] 6893[4] (7347)

Shesells Seashells *Michael Bell* 80
3 b f Tiger Hill(IRE) —Brush Strokes (Cadeaux Genereux)
1881[9] (2632) 3268[10] 4762[3] (5391) ◆ 6003[2] 6260[6]

She's Got The Luck (IRE) *George Moore* 66
2 b f Montjeu(IRE) —Fiamma (IRE) (Irish River (FR))
6360[6] 6618[2]

Sheshali (IRE) *Evan Williams* a91 74
6 b g Kalanisi(IRE) —Sheshara (IRE) (Kahyasi)
(352) ◆ 1139[5]

She's In The Money *Richard Fahey* 87
4 b m High Chaparral(IRE) —Luminda (IRE) (Danehill (USA))
(1102) 1397[10] 2086[4] 2428[5] 3063[3] 4137[4] 4472[7] 5510[11] 6003[3] 6395[7]

She's My Rock (IRE) *Sylvester Kirk* a53
3 b f Rock Of Gibraltar(IRE) —Love And Affection (USA) (Exclusive Era (USA))
216[4] 7706[8] 7918[9] 8024[10]

She's Our Mark *Patrick J Flynn* a101 110
6 ch m Ishiguru(USA) —Markskeepingfaith (IRE) (Ajraas (USA))
(1247a) 2037a[4] 3007a[4] (4631a) 6007a[2] 6379a[2] 6928[3]

Shes Rosie *John O'Shea* a62 63
2 b f Trade Fair—Wintzig (Piccolo)
1793[7] 5466[3] 5865[6] 6258[4]

She's Untouchable *Patrick Leech* a52
3 b f Hawk Wing(USA) —Zambezi (USA) (Rahy (USA))
4238[8] 5366[8] 5839[10]

Shethoughtshewas (IRE) *Alan Swinbank* 64
3 b f Choisir(AUS) —Minaun Heights (Doyoun)
3407[3] 4340[3] 4601[5] 5337[6] 7055[5]

Shewalksinbeauty (IRE) *Richard Hannon* a69 77
2 b f Byron—Election Special (Chief Singer)
(1223) 1733[2] 4623[6] 4955[2] 5830[5]

She Who Dares Wins *Lee James* a41 48
10 b m Atraf—Mirani (IRE) (Danehill (USA))
2087[9]

Shianda *Gary Moore* a65 65
3 b f Kyllachy—Limuru (Salse (USA))
2718[9] 2925[5] 3513[4] 4027[3] (4774) 5172[4] 5585[2] (5812) 6525[3] 6781[9] 6993[6]

Shibhan *Clive Brittain* 73
3 ch f Compton Place—Untold Riches (USA) (Red Ransom (USA))
2120[15] 3158[6] 3579[9]

Shifting Gold (IRE) *Kevin Ryan* a69 72
4 b g Night Shift(USA) —Gold Bust (Nashwan (USA))
330[4] 2941[14] 3764[10] 6543[9] 6846[13] 7407[2] 7475[2] 7806[2] 7957[3]

Shifting Star (IRE) *Walter Swinburn* a95 87
5 ch g Night Shift(USA) —Ahshado (Bin Ajwaad (IRE))
177[5] 528[7] 1688[5] 2119[2] 2563[4] 3461[11] 3850[5] 4551[8] 5787[12] 6429[9] 7014[5] 7289[2]

Shimmering Moment (USA) *James J Hartnett* a105 94
3 ch f Afleet Alex(USA) —Vassar (USA) (Royal Academy (USA))
1358[2] (2051) 2607[2] 4573[2] 6074[5] 6654[4] (7358a)

Shimmering Surf (IRE) *Peter Winkworth* a76 106
3 b f Danehill Dancer(IRE) —Sun On The Sea (IRE) (Bering)
(2050) 2889[3] 4624[2] 5881[11] 6320[10]

Shimoni *Gary Moore* a85 88
6 b m Mark Of Esteem(IRE) —Limuru (Salse (USA))
1783[10]

Shimraan (FR) *A De Royer-Dupre* 119
3 b c Rainbow Quest(USA) —Shemriyna (IRE) (King Of Kings (IRE))
(4420a) 5575a[4] 6592a[5] 6974a[3]

Shim Sham (IRE) *Brian Meehan* 78
2 ch f Danehill Dancer(IRE) —Pirie (USA) (Green Dancer (USA))
5078[11] (5692) 6927[9]

Shine A Line (FR) *U Suter* a82 78
3 ch f Tertullian(USA) —Sparkling Star (FR) (Art Sebal (USA))
6487a[7]

Shingen (JPN) *Hirofumi Toda* 117
7 b h White Muzzle—Nifty Heart (JPN) (Sunday Silence (USA))
7615a[12]

Shining Sea (FR) *F Rohaut* a83 94
3 b f Anabaa Blue—Seeland (FR) (Linamix (FR))
3720a[4]

Shin Kan Sen (FR) *P Khozian* 55
7 b g Dolpour—Orzie (FR) (Solicitor (FR))
221a[6]

Shinko's Best (IRE) *A Kleinkorres* 106
9 ch g Shinko Forest(IRE) —Sail Away (GER) (Platini (GER))
1955a[10] 2805a[6]

Shintoh (USA) *J S Bolger* 103
3 br c Giant's Causeway(USA) —Hollywood Wildcat (USA) (Kris S (USA))
2367a[3] 3466a[2]

Shipboard Romance (IRE) *Mark Rimell* a36 45
5 b m Captain Rio—In Other Words (IRE) (Lake Coniston (IRE))
3032[6] 7917[8]

Shipmaster *Alan King* 82
7 b g Slip Anchor—Cover Look (SAF) (Fort Wood (USA))
1176[6] 5743[16] 6201[12]

Ship's Biscuit *Sir Michael Stoute* a71 106
3 b f Tiger Hill(IRE) —Threefold (USA) (Gulch (USA))
1501[3] (3347) 4507[6] ◆ 5881[5] 6506[2]

Shirataki (IRE) *Mark Johnston*
2 b c Cape Cross(IRE) —Noodle Soup (USA) (Alphabet Soup (USA))
6722[8]

Shirley High *Paul Howling* a51
4 b m Forzando—Ripple Effect (Elmaamul (USA))
253[7] 477[8] 936[11]

Shirocco Vice (IRE) *Richard Fahey* a36 40
2 b f Shirocco(GER) —Viscaria (IRE) (Barathea (IRE))
6360[9] 7172[8] 7427[8] 7630[7]

Shocking (AUS) *Mark Kavanagh* 123
5 b h Street Cry(IRE) —Maria Di Castiglia (Danehill (USA))
6947a[4] ◆ 7291a[18]

Shoodah *David Simcock* a54
2 b f Dubawi(IRE) —Dancing Fire (USA) (Dayjur (USA))
7448[10]

Shooting Gallery *Mahmood Al Zarooni* 85
2 b c Shamardal(USA) —Sallanches (USA) (Gone West (USA))
(5916) ◆ 6702a[4] 7236[4]

Shooting Line (IRE) *Walter Swinburn* a79 63
2 b c Motivator—Juno Marlowe (IRE) (Danehill (USA))
6087[6] 6844[3]

Shooting Party (IRE) *Richard Hannon* a76 76
4 b g Noverre(USA) —L-Way First (IRE) (Vision (USA))
2080[15] 3294[4] 4201[7] 4426[6] 5011[13] 6668[6] 6999[12]

Shoot Out (AUS) *John Wallace* 121
4 b g High Chaparral(IRE) —Pentamerous (NZ) (Pentire)
7291a[13]

Shoot The Pot (IRE) *John Mackie* a63 61
3 b g Intikhab(USA) —Kerasana (IRE) (Kahyasi)
2398[3] 3039[6] 3689[4] 3960[13] 5656[5] 6287[2] 6747[11] 7531[10]

Shopton Lane (USA) *Doug Watson* a79
6 b g Quiet American(USA) —Lightfoot Lane (USA) (Phone Trick (USA))
513a[13]

Shore Thing (IRE) *Bernard Llewellyn* 73
7 b g Docksider(USA) —Spicebird (IRE) (Ela-Mana-Mou)
2814[9]

Short Break *Henry Cecil* a77 74
3 b f Azamour(IRE) —Vacance (Polish Precedent (USA))
3795[5] ◆ 4330[4] 4926[2] 6678[8]

Short Cut *Ian Williams* a58 55
4 b g Compton Place—Rush Hour (IRE) (Night Shift (USA))
(694) 1441[6] 1799[11] 2727[4] 3358[7]

Short Supply (USA) *Tim Walford* a62 58
4 b m Point Given(USA) —Introducing (USA) (Deputy Minister (CAN))
1920[15] 2499[5] (4582) 5216[10] (6660) 7181[9] 7958[2]

Short Takes (USA) *John Gosden*
2 ch g Lemon Drop Kid(USA) —Gabriellina Giof (Ashkalani (IRE))
6532[16]

Shoshiba (IRE) *A Turco* 72
7 b m Plumbird—Magic Surprise (Bluebird (USA))
1419a[13]

Shoshoni Wind *Kevin Ryan* 91
2 b f Sleeping Indian—Cadeau Speciale (Cadeaux Genereux)
2376[3] (2763) 3453[2] 4138[6] 4356[8] 5245[7] 6176[5]

Shostakovich (IRE) *Sylvester Kirk* a80 54
2 b c Fasliyev(USA) —Hi Katriona (IRE) (Second Empire (IRE))
2078[11] 4960[11] 5465[12] 5914[3] 6271[3] ◆ 6673[5] 6988[7] (7404) (7469) ◆ 7576[4] 7696[2] 7891[5] (7982)

Shotley Mac *Neville Bycroft* 88
6 ch g Abou Zouz(USA) —Julie's Gift (Presidium)
1888[7] 2657[11] 3318[7] 4617[11] (5510) 5789[8] 6296[5] 6963[13] 7143[9] 7283[11]

Shot Silk *Nick Littmoden* 29
2 ch f Needwood Blade—Sable 'n Silk (Prince Sabo)
2958[11] 3603[9]

Shouda (IRE) *Barney Curley* a49
4 b h Tiger Hill(IRE) —Sommernacht (GER) (Monsun (GER))
7538[4] 7834[4]

Shouldntbethere (IRE) *Nerys Dutfield* a58 34
6 ch g Soviet Star(USA) —Octomone (USA) (Hennessy (USA))
865[9] 969[9] 1592[7] 2488[6]

Showcasing *John Gosden* 116
3 b c Oasis Dream—Arabesque (Zafonic (USA))
2030[2] 3192[24] 3870[13]

Show Rainbow *Mick Channon* a73 76
2 b f Haafhd—Rainbow Sky (Rainbow Quest (USA))
6158[4] 6353[2] 6711[2] (7123)

Show Willing (IRE) *Alan Jarvis* a62 25
3 b f Elusive City(USA) —Showboat (USA) (Theatrical)
1162[3] 1640[8]

Shrimp Dancer (USA) *David Donk* a97 86
3 b c Kitten's Joy(USA) —Formal Dancer (USA) (Formal Gold (CAN))
824a[5]

Shropshire (IRE) *B W Hills* 90
2 gr c Shamardal(USA) —Shawanni (Shareef Dancer (USA))
(4123) 5219[10]

Shropshirelass *Zoe Davison* a36 53
7 b m Beat All(USA) —Emma-Lyne (Emarati (USA))
479[11] 590[10]

Shubaat *Michael Jarvis* a87 88
3 ch g Monsun(GER) —Zaynaat (Unfuwain (USA))
(2994) ◆ 4827[3] 5371[3]

Shugar Rhi (IRE) *Bryn Palling* a49 54
2 ch f Redback—Scarlet Empress (Second Empire (IRE))
5466[4] 6419[9] 7408[6]

Shuhra (IRE) *William Haggas* 70
2 b f Marju(IRE) —Wijdan (USA) (Mr Prospector (USA))
6468[3]

Shunkawakhan (IRE) *Linda Perratt* a70 61
7 b g Indian Danehill(IRE) —Special Park (USA) (Trempolino (USA))
1673[12] 2211[9] 3990[2] 4515[5] 4824[6] 5406[5] 5821[7] 6026[7] 6495[8]

Shutterbug *Stuart Williams* a55 48
2 ch f Dubai Destination(USA) —Nikolenka (IRE) (Indian Ridge)
1972[15] 2680[13] 6158[11] 7118[13] 7497[4] 7666[2]

Shut The Bar *George Baker* a73 16
5 b g Midnight Legend—Time For A Glass (Timeless Times (USA))
(963) 2181[10]

Shutupandrive *Mark Usher* a46 42
2 b f Forest Wildcat(USA) —Sharp Contrast (USA) (Diesis)
4729[6] 5255[9] 5808[7] 6258[6] 6869[6] 7017[2] 7423[6] 7576[9] 7777[4]

Shut Up Shapiro (IRE) *George Baker* 52
3 ch g Hawk Wing(USA) —Nuts In May (USA) (A.P. Indy (USA))
1870[9] 2603[9] 5925[12] 6093[9] 6517[8]

Shy *Rod Millman* a75 75
5 ch m Erhaab(USA) —Shi Shi (Alnasr Alwasheek)
2080[7] 2586[3] 3040[4] (3560) (3917) 5008[11] 5679[5] 6051[7] 6639[9]

Shy Bird *Jeremy Glover* a32 51
2 b f Danbird(AUS) —Blushing Victoria (Weldnaas (USA))
2577[3] 3087[8] 3756[9] 5434[12] 6035[11] 6072[12]

Shy Fairy (GER) *H J Groschel* 65
2 b f Desert Prince(IRE) —Shyla (GER) (Monsagem (USA))
6407a[7]

Shy Glance (USA) *P Monteith* a76 79
8 b g Red Ransom(USA) —Royal Shyness (Royal Academy (USA))
2452[4] 3202[4] 3531[6] 3709[8] 3901[6] 4823[2] 5213[11] 5408[11] 6495[9] 7055[7]

Siberian Sunset (IRE) *Alan Swinbank* 50
4 b g Fantastic Light(USA) —Russian Snows (IRE) (Sadler's Wells (USA))
1927[10] 2131[7] 2627[7] 3078[8]

Siberian Tiger (IRE) *Michael Wigham* a87 100
5 b g Xaar—Flying Millie (IRE) (Flying Spur (AUS))
2976[4] 5949[8] 6736[3]

Side Glance *Andrew Balding* 112
3 br g Passing Glance—Averami (Averti (IRE))
1732[4] ◆ 2545[6] 2978[5] ◆ (3886) 4357[3] (5292) ◆ 6349[2]

Sidney Melbourne (USA) *John Best* a69 81
3 ch g Lemon Drop Kid(USA) —Tolltally Light (USA) (Majestic Light (USA))
2089[7] 3376[4] 3909[2] (4965) 5747[14] 6448[8]

Sidney's Candy (USA) *John W Sadler* a121 123
3 ch c Candy Ride(ARG) —Fair Exchange (USA) (Storm Cat (USA))
1714a[17] 7364a[6]

Siena *Christine Dunnett* a56 30
5 b m Lomitas—Sea Lane (Zafonic (USA))
1283[12]

Siena Star (IRE) *Stef Higgins* a69 69
12 b g Brief Truce(USA) —Gooseberry Pie (Green Desert (USA))
261[7] 390[8] 1225[6] 2006[8]

Sienna Lake (IRE) *Tim McCarthy* a60 63
4 b m Fasliyev(USA) —Lolita's Gold (USA) (Royal Academy (USA))
3323[13] 4744[6]

Sierra Alpha *Amanda Perrett* a86 86
3 b c Dansili—Sound Asleep (USA) (Woodman (USA))
1734[5] 2386[3] 2869[2] 4334[2] 4933[4] 6872[6]

Sight Unseen *F Vermeulen* 105
4 b h Sadler's Wells(USA) —High Praise (USA) (Quest For Fame)
494a[6]

Sight Winner (NZ) *J Size* 119
7 b g Faltaat(USA) —Kinjinette (NZ) (Kinjite (NZ))
7853a[7]

Signature Red (USA) *Sid Attard* a109 109
4 b h Bernstein(USA) —Irish And Foxy (USA) (Irish Open (USA))
6237a[12] 6949a[7]

Significant Move *Roger Charlton* a68 82
3 b g Motivator—Strike Lightly (Rainbow Quest (USA))
1381[2] ◆ 2334[3] 5493[2] (6678)

Sign Of Life *Walter Swinburn* a55 68
3 b f Haafhd—Three Piece (Jaazeiro (USA))
2227[4]

Sign Of The Cross *Conor Dore* a67 80
6 b g Mark Of Esteem(IRE) —Thea (USA) (Marju (IRE))
674[5] 693[3] (763) 937[8]

Signora Frasi (IRE) *Tony Newcombe* a67 65
5 b m Indian Ridge—Sheba (IRE) (Lycius (USA))
2691[1] 499[5] 780[6] 1437[6] 2419[2] 2956[8] 3783[9] (5711) 5962[2] 7037[12]

Signore Momento (IRE) *Amy Weaver* 85
4 b g Captain Rio—Gitchee Gumee Rose (IRE) (Paris House)
1076[7] 1332[14] 2462[9] (3706) (4225) ◆ 5495[17]

Signor Peltro *Henry Candy* a86 108
7 b g Bertolini(USA) —Pewter Lass (Dowsing (USA))
1900[24] 2595[2] 3461[4] 3869[6] 4537[10] 5095[3] ◆ 5944[10] ◆ 6177[8] 6752[20]

Signor Verdi *Brian Meehan* a78 94
3 b c Green Tune(USA) —Calling Card (Bering)
(1450) 1834[10] 2254[11] 3863[2] (4603) 7233[5]

Signs In The Sand *Saeed Bin Suroor* a97 90
2 b c Cape Cross(IRE) —Gonfilia (GER) (Big Shuffle (USA))
1845[9] (5085) ◆ 5748[3] (6667) 7080[6]

Sikeeb (IRE) *Clive Brittain* 84
2 b c Alhaarth(IRE) —Erstwhile (FR) (Desert Prince (IRE))
1309[2] (1845) 6568[15]

Silaah *David Nicholls* a102 99
6 b g Mind Games—Ocean Grove (IRE) (Fairy King (USA))
4473[9] (5197) 6140[4] 6799[6] 7635[2] 7740[3] 7866[2] 7934[2] 7993[2]

Silbury (IRE) *Roger Charlton* a49 39
2 br f Dansili—Tamso (USA) (Seeking The Gold (USA))
5029[11] 6145[10] 6465[9] 6868[5] 7118[10]

Silca Conegliano (IRE) *Mick Channon* a67 72
2 b f Alhaarth(IRE) —Sarah Stokes (IRE) (Brief Truce (USA))
1421[4] 1733[4] 2163[2] 2461[2] 2749[3] 3199[6] 4066[7] 4590[2] 4927[6] 5466[2] 5885[4] 6286[6] 6769[12] 7313[8] 7418[8]

Silca Meydan *Richard Price* a65 44
4 b g Diktat—Golden Silca (Inchinor)
75[2]

Silence Is Bliss (IRE) *J S Moore* a71 81
2 b g Silent Times(IRE) —Primrose And Rose (Primo Dominie)
2300[4] ◆ (2605) 2950[2] ◆ 4138[9] 4539[10] 4928[5] 6191[9] 6842[6] 7271[4] 7722[2] (7762)

Silenceofthewind (USA) *James J Hartnett* a77 95
3 b g Eddington(USA) —Betty's Solutions (USA) (Eltish (USA))
6907a[13]

Silent Act (USA) *Amanda Perrett* a73 85
4 b m Theatrical—Vinista (USA) (Jade Hunter (USA))
2402[5] 4329[3] (4794) 5008[3] 6797[12]

Silent Annie *Matthew Salaman* 19
3 ch f Bahamian Bounty—Highly Liquid (Entrepreneur)
4692[9] 4989[11]

Silent Applause *Dr Jon Scargill* a63 74
7 b g Royal Applause—Billie Blue (Ballad Rock)
2506[4] (3576) 4055[5] 5790[11] 7252[5]

Silent Blessing *Robert Cowell* a59 61
2 b c Diktat—Silent Miracle (IRE) (Night Shift (USA))
2785[7] 4890[4] 5160[7] 5733[3] 7392[11] 7692[2] 7843[4]

Silent Fright (USA) *Paul Cole* 59
2 b f Yes It's True(USA) —Val Marie (USA) (Coronado's Quest (USA))
2074[7]

Silent Lucidity (IRE) *Peter Niven* a56 63
6 ch g Ashkalani(IRE) —Mimansa (USA) (El Gran Senor (USA))
1671[5] 2085[3] (2464) 2995[2] 3760[6] (4190) 4825[4] 6109[7] 7176[7] 7398[5]

Silent Majority (IRE) *Ed Dunlop* a42 66
3 b c Refuse To Bend(IRE) —Queen Shy (Marju (IRE))
1127[6] 1608[7] 2221[10]

Silent Oasis *Brendan Powell* a72 74
4 b m Oasis Dream—Silence Is Golden (Danehill Dancer (IRE))
2173[2] 2411[7] 2961[11] 5038[5] 5541[7] 6275[3] 6851[7] 7190[2] 7548[8]

Silent Serenade *Walter Swinburn* 29
2 ch f Bertolini(USA) —Why So Silent (Mill Reef (USA))
3906[8]

Silent Treatment (IRE) *Richard Guest* a58 27
4 ch m Captain Rio—Without Words (Lion Cavern (USA))
4415[9] 4606[12]

Silenzio *Richard Hannon* a73 46
2 b c Cadeaux Genereux—All Quiet (Piccolo)
7099[9] ◆ 7385[2] 7873[4]

Silidan *Mandy Rowland* a58 55
7 b g Dansili—In Love Again (IRE) (Prince Rupert (FR))
269[3] 498[9] 795[4]

Silk Bounty *James Given* a62 70
2 b c Bahamian Bounty—Sahara Silk (IRE) (Desert Style (IRE))
5156[6] 5814[4] 6153[8] 6568[19] 6769[5] 7211[3] 7423[5] 7598[4] 7739[5] 7983[2]

Silk Drum (IRE) *Howard Johnson* 72
5 gr g Intikhab(USA) —Aneydia (IRE) (Kenmare (FR))
(2109)

Silken Aunt *James Toller* a56 30
3 b f Barathea(IRE) —Aunt Susan (Distant Relative)
2754[10] 5163[8] 5729[10]

Silken Promise (USA) *Tobias B P Coles* a66 68
4 bb m Pulpit(USA) —Banksia (Marju (IRE))
42[2] 244[2] 1574[5] 1763[9] 2811[5] 3348[11] 3560[11]

Silken Sands (IRE) *Clive Cox* a54 55
4 b m Green Desert(USA) —Arctic Silk (Selkirk (USA))
31[5] 1177[13]

Silken Thoughts *John Berry* a46 66
2 b f Tobougg(IRE) —The Jotter (Night Shift (USA))
2078[9] 2701[3] 4131[3] 4539[8] 5310[5] ◆ 5837[2] 6163[9]

Silkenveil (IRE) *Richard Fahey* a32 59
3 b f Indian Ridge—Line Ahead (IRE) (Sadler's Wells (USA))
2072[6] 2497[5] 4088[8]

Silk Hall (UAE) *Alan King* a87 90
5 b g Halling(USA) —Velour (Mtoto)
252[3] 811[3] 2031[12]

Silk Runner (IRE) *J W Hills* a35 51
3 ch f Barathea(IRE) —Sao Gabriel (IRE) (Persian Bold)
1589[8] 2336[13] 4127[12] 4534[11]

Silk Slippers *John Joseph Murphy* a59 67
3 b f Oasis Dream—Interpose (Indian Ridge)
7952[11] 7973[6]

Sills Vincero *Mandy Rowland* a61 68
4 b m Piccolo—Aegean Magic (Wolfhound (USA))
896[8] 968[9] 1235[12]

Silly Billy (IRE) *Sylvester Kirk* a67 65
2 b g Noverre(USA) —Rock Dove (IRE) (Danehill (USA))
1263[14] 2022[4] 2457[5] 2638[5] 2939[17] (3678) 3887[3] 4331[6] 4911[5] 5365[4] 5921[5] 6052[2] 6311[10] 6842[9] 6989[8] 7271[2]

Silly Gilly (IRE) *Ron Barr* a40 64
6 b m Mull Of Kintyre(USA) —Richly Deserved (IRE) (Kings Lake (USA))
1115[7] 1574[9] 1928[9] 2670[6] (3061) 3503[3] 4156[2] 4453[2] 4644[2] 4985[6] 5598[5] 5905[3] 6269[5] 6890[11] 7125[6]

Silvador *William Muir* 70
4 gr g Selkirk(USA) —Dali's Grey (Linamix (FR))
6152[8]

Silvan Stream *James Bethell* 65
3 ch f Observatory(USA) —Special (Polar Falcon (USA))
2837[2] ◆ 3437[11] 6470[7]

Silvanus (IRE) *Paul Midgley* a81 74
5 b g Danehill Dancer(IRE) —Mala Mala (IRE) (Brief Truce (USA))
1534[12] 2278[8] (2581) 2720[2] (3497) 3687[4] 4199[3] 4513[6] 5262[9] ◆ 5513[11] 5915[11] 6299[10]

Silvee *John Bridger* a58 61
3 gr f Avonbridge—Silver Louie (IRE) (Titus Livius (FR))
1075[4] 1257[6] 1694[8] 2052[4] 3154[7] 3336[8] 3786[4] 4099[4] 4739[3] 5010[2] 5327[2] (5588) 5956[6] 6558[8] 7519[5] 7656[5] (7877) 8035[9]

Silver Age (IRE) *J S Moore* a64 47
2 b g Balmont(USA) —Opium Creek (IRE) (Darshaan)
4678[4] ◆ 5381[6] 5894[6] 7552[12] 7650[2] (7886)

Silver Alliance *Walter Swinburn* a78 72
2 gr g Proclamation(IRE) —Aimee Vibert (Zilzal (USA))
2384[7] (3274) ◆ 3887[5]

Silver Angel (IRE) *Mick Channon* a24 42
2 gr f Clodovil(IRE) —Ellistown Lady (IRE) (Red Sunset)
4421[9] 5117[7] 5328[5] 5640[5] 6209[12]

Silver Arrow (ITY) *R Menichetti* 109
5 b g Silver Wizard(USA) —Eros Love (ITY) (Love The Groom (USA))
2152a[8] 7372a[9]

Silver Astralis *Christine Dunnett* 7
3 gr f Silver Patriarch(IRE) —Bunty (Presidium)
1127[12] 1607[6] 2754[11] 4519[7]

Silver Black (USA) *C Boutin* a90 100
3 b g Hennessy(USA) —High Maintenance (Danehill (USA))
1195a[3] 6487a[0]

Silver Colors (USA) *Jeremy Noseda* a67 60
3 rg f Mr Greeley(USA) —Winning Colors (USA) (Caro)
2925[6] 4205[4] 5141[4] 5522[7]

Silver Frost (IRE) *Y De Nicolay* 119
4 gr h Verglas(IRE) —Hidden Silver (Anabaa (USA))
1716a[7] 4166a[3] 5107a[9]

Silverglas (IRE) *William Knight* a80 79
4 gr g Verglas(IRE) —Yellow Trumpet (Petong)
1388[10] 6288[3] 6990[9]

Silver Grey (IRE) *Roger Ingram* a89 109
3 gr f Chineur(FR) —Operissimo (Singspiel (IRE))
333a[3] 514a[8] 4612a[4] 5346a[4] 6095[3] 6950a[9]

Silver Guest *Mick Channon* a84 73
5 br g Lujain(USA) —Ajig Dancer (Niniski (USA))
1361[6] 2689[9] 3129[11] 3855[13]

Silver Hotspur *Derek Shaw* a88 63
6 b g Royal Applause—Noble View (USA) (Distant View (USA))
114[7] 2188[11] 2647[7] 2727[10] 3024[6] 3763[10]

Silverini *Milton Harris*
4 b m Bertolini(USA) —Silver Kristal (Kris)
4425[13]

Silver In The Sand *James Bethell* a30 61
3 b f Fasliyev(USA) —Dances With Dreams (Be My Chief (USA))
991[8] 5535[16]

Silver Linnet (IRE) *Michael Quinlan* a67 72
3 gr f Acclamation—Nadeema (FR) (Linamix (FR))
17[7] 222[6] 425[5] 906[3] (988) (1140) 1281[6] 1765[6] 2868[9] 3277[5] 7195[10] 7446[7]

Silvermine Bay (IRE) *Alan Jarvis* a40 35
3 br f Act One—Quittance (USA) (Riverman (USA))
2503[15] 3640[6] 3960[11]

Silver Ocean (USA) *Michael Quinlan* a77
2 bb g Silver Train(USA) —Endless Sea (CAN) (Mt. Livermore (USA))
5381[4] ◆ 5895[2] 6520[3] ◆ (7065) (7850a)

Silver Point (FR) *Bryn Palling* a98 90
7 bb g Commands(AUS) —Silver Fame (USA) (Quest For Fame)
1829[6] 2282[5] 2640[4]

Silver Pond (FR) *C Laffon-Parias* 114
3 gr c Act One—Silver Fame (USA) (Quest For Fame)
(2160a)

Silver Prelude *Stuart Williams* a74 68
9 gr g Prince Sabo—Silver Blessings (Statoblest)
(77) 241[7] 806[6] 4717[7] 6292[11] 7194[8] 7446[9] 7720[6] 8037[6]

Silver Rime (FR) *Linda Perratt* 94
5 gr g Verglas(IRE) —Severina (Darshaan)
1202[6] 2580[2] 3318[5] (3708) 3987[5] (4370) 4828[2] 5242[5] 6749[P] 7227[10]

Silver Rock (IRE) *Mikael Magnusson* 83
3 ch f Rock Of Gibraltar(IRE) —Ribblesdale (Northern Park (USA))
2253[8]

Silver Shine (IRE) *William Haggas* a39 48
2 gr g Verglas(IRE) —Dream Time (Rainbow Quest (USA))
2171[4] 2654[7] 2895[3] 6163[10] 6809[9]

Silver Show (IRE) *Mick Channon* 64
2 b f Noverre(USA) —Incense (Unfuwain (USA))
3331[8] 3817[2] 4203[5] 6071[6]

Silverside (USA) *M Delcher-Sanchez* a106 114
4 b h Pleasantly Perfect(USA) —Lyrical Ghost (USA) (Silver Ghost (USA))
511a[5] 626a[2] 818a[4] 5803a[4]

Silver Suitor (IRE) *David Elsworth* a50 102
6 gr g Swain(IRE) —Taatof (IRE) (Lahib (USA))
1020[7]

Silver Symphony (IRE) *Paul Cole* a81 79
3 bb f Pastoral Pursuits—Streak Of Silver (USA) (Dynaformer (USA))
1487[5] 1776[8] 2049[8] 3866[10] 4098[7] 4337[2] 4475[3]

Silver Tiger *Chris Wall* 23
2 gb c Tiger Hill(IRE) —Moon Empress (FR) (Rainbow Quest (USA))
6828[8]

Silver Tigress *C W Thornton* 42
2 gr f Tiger Hill(IRE) —Cinnamon Tree (IRE) (Barathea (IRE))
4123[8] 4748[6] 6047[7] 7118[12]

Silver Timber (USA) *Chad C Brown* 120
7 gr g Prime Timber(USA) —River Princess (CAN) (Alwuhush (USA))
7362a[5]

Silvertrees (IRE) *Alan Swinbank* 95
2 b g Footstepsinthesand—Kingsridge (IRE) (King's Theatre (IRE))
(4089) 5184[2]

Silver Turn *Bryan Smart* a76 61
2 ch f Shamardal(USA) —Mambo Mistress (USA) (Kingmambo (USA))
6182[4]

Silver Virago (FR) *P Costes* a48 66
6 gr m Medaaly—Kal D'Amethyste (FR) (Kaldoun (FR))
221a[7]

Silverware (USA) *Richard Hannon* a70 66
2 bb c Eurosilver(USA) —Playing Footsie (USA) (Valiant Nature (USA))
5878[11] 6278[4] 6844[4]

Silver Wind *Alan McCabe* a69 89
5 b g Ishiguru(USA) —My Bonus (Cyrano De Bergerac)
1049[6] 1688[14] 1862[9] 2178[2] 2808[2] 3584[8] 4558[8] 4662[7] 6207[5] 6274[4] 7526[9] 7719[11] 7934[5]

Silverwort *Mike Sowersby*
4 b g Lujain(USA) —Cryptogam (Zamindar (USA))
3910[9]

Silver Writer *Michael Easterby* 51
2 b c Librettist(USA) —Silvernus (Machiavellian (USA))
2785[11] 2939[6] 3923[10] 4682[9] 5629[14] 6618[10]

Silvery Moon (IRE) *Tim Easterby* 74
3 gr g Verglas(IRE) —Starry Night (Sheikh Albadou)
2425[6] 2852[3] ◆ 6039[2] ◆ 6624[2] ◆

Simayill *Clive Brittain* 81
2 b f Oasis Dream—Triennial (IRE) (Giant's Causeway (USA))
6034[5] 6157[6] 6559[13]

Simenon (IRE) *Andrew Balding* 103
3 b g Marju(IRE) —Epistoliere (IRE) (Alzao (USA))
1498[2] 2226[4] 2738[4] 3822[4] 5185[6] 6201[8] ◆ 7350[3]

Simian (SWE) *Wido Neuroth* a77
5 b g Okawango(USA) —Simmering (Mas Media)
2019a[5]

Simla Sunset (IRE) *P J Prendergast* a87 89
4 b m One Cool Cat(USA) —Simla Bibi (Indian Ridge)
1258[3] ◆ 1775[4] 3487a[4] 5571a[9] 6346[9] 7358a[9]

Simmard (USA) *Roger L Attfield* a93 107
5 ch h Dixieland Band(USA) —Dibs (USA) (Spectacular Bid (USA))
6951a[7]

Simmons *Matthew Salaman* a45 39
2 b f Spartacus(IRE) —One For Me (Tragic Role (USA))
5667[5] 6209[9] 7177[8] 7271[6]

Simon De Montfort (IRE) *A Fabre* 108
3 b c King's Best(USA) —Noble Rose (IRE) (Caerleon (USA))
(1567a)

Simone Martini (IRE) *Milton Harris* a59 69
5 b g Montjeu(IRE) —Bona Dea (IRE) (Danehill (USA))
996[5] 1207[8] 1462[7]
Simonside *Brian Ellison* a75 81
7 b g Shahrastani(USA) —Only So Far (Teenoso (USA))
1427[6] 2492[4] 2941[5] 3367[2] ◆ 3896[2] 4686[3] (5200) (5788) 6201[4] 6926[12]
Simple Jim (FR) *David O'Meara* a66 57
6 b g Jimble(FR) —Stop The Wedding (USA) (Stop The Music (USA))
(2610) ◆ 2995[3] (3223) ◆ 3600[3] (4604) 5070[4] 5687[3] 6187[4] 6538[5] 6895[9]
Simple Rhythm *John Ryan* a70 84
4 b m Piccolo—Easy Beat (IRE) (Orpen (USA))
150[8] 345[7] 806[8] 1047[9] 1064[8] 1364[8] 1779[6] 2485[6] 2635[7] 2846[7] (3567) 3734[3] 3818[4] 3908[6] 4343[2] 4559[12] 4715[2] 5048[3] 6898[5] 7006[7] 7331[9] 7391[8] 7614[9]
Simply Gold (FR) *J-M Capitte* 58
5 ch m Gold Away(IRE) —Simply Unique (USA) (Northern Prospect (USA))
281a[0]
Simply Noble (GER) *Andreas Lowe* 86
2 b f Desert Prince(IRE) —Speedy Lola (GER) (Lomitas)
6975a[6]
Simpulse *F J Brennan* a8
2 b f Noverre(USA) —Miss Kitty (Monsieur Cat (USA))
7248[10]
Sim Sala Bim *Stuart Williams* 60
2 rg c Act One—Francia (Legend Of France (USA))
6153[9] 7201[6]
Sinadinou *David Nicholls* 73
2 b g Dubai Destination(USA) —Beverley Bell (Bertolini (USA))
2427[2] 4577[7] 6138[2]
Sinatramania *Tracy Waggott* 58
3 b g Dansili—Come Fly With Me (Bluebird (USA))
2072[7] 2627[5] 2994[13] 4052[5] 4485[7] 4867[6]
Sinbad The Sailor *George Baker* a79 66
5 b g Cape Cross(IRE) —Sinead (USA) (Irish River (FR))
(409) (688) 938[2] 1273[4] 7781[5]
Sinchiroka (FR) *Ralph Smith* a65 49
4 b h Della Francesca(USA) —Great Care (USA) (El Gran Senor (USA))
421[3] 669[2] 4261[5]
Sinfonico (IRE) *Richard Hannon* a77 67
2 b c Iffraaj—Zinstar (IRE) (Sinndar (IRE))
7202[5] 7386[2] ◆ 7610[4]
Singapore Lilly (IRE) *Mick Channon* 101
2 b f Mujadil(USA) —Swallow Falls (IRE) (Lake Coniston (IRE))
1957[3] (2347) 2743[7] 3872[7] 4305[7] 4539[3] (5746) 6762a[2] 6975a[3]
Singapore Smile (FR) *Mlle V Dissaux* a73 77
2 b f Sagacity(FR) —Valley Quest (IRE) (Rainbow Quest (USA))
7975a[9]
Singbella *Clive Cox* a69 64
4 b m Singspiel(IRE) —B Beautiful (IRE) (Be My Guest (USA))
665[6] 868[4] 1188[8] 1920[3] 2961[6] 4422[4] 7286[9]
Singeur (IRE) *Robin Bastiman* a97 101
3 b c Chineur(FR) —Singitta (Singspiel (IRE))
1184[2] 1701[7] 2260[4] 2978[3] 3791[20] 4391[10] 4576[12] 5250[4] 5632[3] 5944[15] 7060[16]
Singingintherain (IRE) *Robert Mills* a63 58
3 ch f Kyllachy—Comeraincomeshine (IRE) (Night Shift (USA))
24[2] 233[8] 519[5] 1643[6] 2005[9] 2200[4] 3002[3] 3478[6]
Singing Poet (IRE) *E Charpy* a90 78
9 b g Singspiel(IRE) —Bright Finish (USA) (Zilzal (USA))
419a[8]
Singing Scott (IRE) *Robin Bastiman* 33
3 b g Royal Applause—Ciel Bleu (Septieme Ciel (USA))
2900[10] 3733[6] 4439[10] 5550[7] 6076[11] 7230[9]
Singin' The Blues *James Eustace* a52 61
3 b g Superior Premium—Not So Generous (IRE) (Fayruz)
1280[8] 1490[11] 4791[11]
Singleb (IRE) *Gay Kelleway* a79 75
6 b g Intikhab(USA) —Bubble N Squeak (IRE) (Catrail (USA))
496[4]
Single Lady *J S Moore* a52 45
3 b f Beat Hollow—Breathing Space (USA) (Expelled (USA))
583[10] 776[3] 922[7] 1461[3] 1796[10] 2412[8] 2724[6]
Sing Like Bird (JPN) *Yasuo Tomomichi* 99
5 b m Symboli Kris S(USA) —Sing Like Talk (JPN) (Northern Taste (CAN))
7460a[12]
Sing Of Run *Liam Corcoran*
3 br c Singspiel(IRE) —Crimson Rosella (Polar Falcon (USA))
6861[10]
Sing Sweetly *Gerard Butler* a90 87
3 b f Singspiel(IRE) —Sweetness Herself (Unfuwain (USA))
2043[2] 2758[2] ◆ 3388[3] 3795[3] (4229) 4815[6] 5371[4] 6428[5] 6698[3] 7420[2] 8003[3]
Singuna (GER) *A Wohler* 86
3 b f Black Sam Bellamy(IRE) —Siberienne (USA) (Kingmambo (USA))
5805a[11] 6409a[7]
Sinkasen (IRE) *M Loannidas* a93
3 b c Celtic Swing—The Spirit Of Pace (IRE) (In The Wings)
5781a[6]
Sinndarina (FR) *P Demercastel* 99
3 b f Sinndar(IRE) —Ana Marie (FR) (Anabaa (USA))
1496a[7] 2800a[6] 4037a[8]
Sinnfonia (IRE) *Henry Cecil* 66
2 b f Sinndar(IRE) —Kalimanta (IRE) (Lake Coniston (IRE))
6468[5]
Sioduil (IRE) *J S Bolger* a91 100
4 gr m Oasis Dream—Indian Belle (IRE) (Indian Ridge)
1406a[9]
Sioux Rising (IRE) *Richard Fahey* a88 89
4 b m Danetime(IRE) —Arvika (FR) (Baillamont (USA))
4653[2] 5302[7] 6113[4] 6509[4] 7097[8] 7566[5] 7719[2] 7826[2] 7935[10]
Sir Boss (IRE) *Michael Mullineaux* a75 86
5 b g Tagula(IRE) —Good Thought (IRE) (Mukaddamah (USA))
4912[2] 5235[5] 5530[9] 7101[4] 7490[3]
Sir Bruno (FR) *Bryn Palling* a81 77
3 ch g Hernando(FR) —Moon Tree (FR) (Groom Dancer (USA))
1761[5] 2170[4] 3680[2] 4325[9] 4479[2] 4732[3] (6541) 7274[6] 7411[4]
Sir Byron (IRE) *Richard Fahey* 79
2 b c Byron—Reunion (IRE) (Be My Guest (USA))
5546[2] ◆
Sircozy (IRE) *Gary Moore* a73 77
4 b g Celtic Swing—Furnish (Green Desert (USA))
2894[8] (3416) 4694[6]
Sirdave *Peter Hiatt* a17 69
4 ch g Where Or When(IRE) —Charming Tina (IRE) (Indian Ridge)
1757[5] 1976[8] 2812[6] 3848[9] 4327[7]
Sir Don (IRE) *Deborah Sanderson* a59 25
11 b g Lake Coniston(IRE) —New Sensitive (Wattlefield)
7018[2] 7426[11] 7859[9]
Sir Edwin Landseer (USA) *Gary Moore* a93 83
10 gr g Lit De Justice(USA) —Wildcat Blue (USA) (Cure The Blues (USA))
258[3] 562[3] 659[2] 1167[7] 1534[13] 1596[9]
Sirens *Phil McEntee* a56 62
2 ch f Bertolini(USA) —Natural Grace (Zamindar (USA))
2561[5] 2963[4] 3509[9] 4787[3] 4890[9] 5089[5] 6286[9]
Sirenuse (IRE) *Bryan Smart* a62 91
4 b m Exceed And Excel(AUS) —Cefira (USA) (Distant View (USA))
1099[4] ◆ 1363[3] (2136) 2431[4]
Sir Frank Wappat *Mark Johnston* a75 79
3 b g Oasis Dream—Trevillari (USA) (Riverman (USA))
(849) (1058) 1191[6] 1663[6] (3676) 4093[7] 4710[3] 5121[6] 5641[8] 5968[3] 6105[RR] 6852[RR]
Sir Freddie *Lady Herries* a74 75
4 b g Fraam—Height Of Folly (Shirley Heights)
2810[3] 4141[3] (5382) 6416[4] 7067[3]
Sirgarfieldsobers (IRE) *B S Rothwell* a83 95
4 b g Montjeu(IRE) —Funsie (FR) (Saumarez)
1274[5] 1600[8] 2031[4] 2513[6] 2938[6]
Sir Geoffrey (IRE) *David Nicholls* a94 84
4 b g Captain Rio—Disarm (IRE) (Bahamian Bounty)
556[3] 723[2] ◆ (869) 1200[6] (1524) 1988[2] 2310[6] 2622[8] 3540[3] 4090[11] 5069[8] (5377) 5528[2] 5734[13] 6140[16] 6374[7] 7041[4] 7180[13] (7494) 7702[2] (7866)
Sir George (IRE) *Ollie Pears* a71 93
5 b g Mujadil(USA) —Torrmana (IRE) (Ela-Mana-Mou)
105[3] (289) 348[2] 893[2] (1149) 1395[2] 1754[2] 1926[4] (2328) 3318[4] 4112[2] 4603[4] (5098) 5937[2] 6709[5]
Sir Gerry (USA) *Chris Dwyer* a108 115
5 ch h Carson City(USA) —Incredulous (FR) (Indian Ridge)
(336a) 416a[4] 515a[4] 628a[5] 797a[3] 1021a[12] 1406a[7] 1676a[8] 2400[2] (2999) 3192[15] 3445[5] 4576[7] 5183[9] 5526[6] 5744[9] 6147[2] 6570[8] 6923[7]
Sir Haydn *John Jenkins* a54 49
10 ch g Definite Article—Snowscape (Niniski (USA))
99[4] 576[7] 970[5] 4804[10] 8032[5]
Sir Ike (IRE) *Stuart Kittow* a61 71
5 b g Xaar—Iktidar (Green Desert (USA))
5877[7] 6853[8] 6991[11] (7487) 7768[7] 7996[9]
Sirius Prospect (USA) *Dean Ivory* a78 76
2 bb c Gone West(USA) —Stella Blue (FR) (Anabaa (USA))
6443[2] 7058[3] (7386)
Sirius Superstar *Andrew Balding* 38
2 b c Galileo(IRE) —Brightest (Rainbow Quest (USA))
7099[11]
Sirjosh *Desmond Donovan* a66 60
4 b g Josr Algarhoud(IRE) —Special Gesture (IRE) (Brief Truce (USA))
296[11] 368[5] ◆ 423[4] 555[5] 567[3] 838[7] (2008) 2590[6] ◆ 2779[2] 2964[5] 3993[4] 4234[7] (7761) 7992[6]
Sir Lando *Wido Neuroth* 102
3 b c Lando(GER) —Burqa (Nashwan (USA))
4184a[4]
Sir Liam (USA) *Tim Vaughan* a63 69
6 b g Monarchos(USA) —Tears (USA) (Red Ransom (USA))
735[4]
Sir Loin *John Gallagher* a41 2
9 ch g Compton Place—Charnwood Queen (Cadeaux Genereux)
271[12] 319[5] 477[4] 726[6] 869[8] 8005[12]
Sir Louis *Richard Fahey* a64 66
3 b g Compton Place—Heuston Station (IRE) (Fairy King (USA))
(1118) ◆ 1280[3] 3119[11] 4749[7] 6226[6] 6965[13] 7738[2] 7911[4]
Sir Lunchalott *J S Moore* a68 71
2 b g Pastoral Pursuits—Jasmine Breeze (Saddlers' Hall (IRE))
1009[9] 1223[2] 1389[3] (1704) 4539[4] 5187[14] 5837[11] (6209) 6500[8] 7378[3] 7484[3] 7520[3] 7762[3] 7886[4] 8012[4]
Sir Mark (IRE) *M A Peill* a66 65
6 ch g In The Wings—Web Of Intrigue (Machiavellian (USA))
664[6] 1116[3] 1380[7] 1996[4] 6297[4] 6502[9]
Sir Mozart (IRE) *Barney Curley* a62 74
7 b g Mozart(IRE) —Lady Silver Hawk (USA) (Silver Hawk (USA))
194[5] 1129[5] 1534[3] 2417[3] (3322) (4968)
Sir Nod *Julie-Ann Camacho* a80 83
8 b g Tagula(IRE) —Nordan Raider (Domynsky)
(432) 832[7] (1365) 2696[3] 3551[2] 4171[4] 5198[8] 5684[3] 6303[7]
Sirocco Breeze *Saeed Bin Suroor* a117 110
5 b h Green Desert(USA) —Baldemosa (FR) (Lead On Time (USA))
339a[8] (607a) ◆ (818a) 1021a[7] 2344[3] 2999[6] 4126[2] 5370[2]
Sir Pitt *John Gosden* a80 75
3 b g Tiger Hill(IRE) —Rebecca Sharp (Machiavellian (USA))
(1067) 1299[5] (1830) 2252[8] 5752[4] 6631[2]
Sir Randolf (IRE) *Sylvester Kirk* a61
2 br c Statue Of Liberty(USA) —Pardoned (IRE) (Mujadil (USA))
7503[11] 7610[7] 7780[5] 8031[7]
Sir Reginald *Richard Fahey* 100
2 b g Compton Place—Clincher Club (Polish Patriot (USA))
2059[2] (2980) 4097[3] 5219[3] 5880[5] 6200[2] 6560[20]
Sirri *Clive Brittain* a40 39
3 b f Ishiguru(USA) —Sumitra (Tragic Role (USA))
930[10] 3564[12]
Sir Rocky (IRE) *Richard Hannon* a32 58
2 b g Shirocco(GER) —Bolero Again (IRE) (Sadler's Wells (USA))
1429[5] 3915[8] 5520[7] 6082[8] 6414[5]
Sir Royal (USA) *Alan Swinbank* 83
5 b g Diesis—Only Royale (IRE) (Caerleon (USA))
1117[10] (1398) 3319[13] 4671[2] 5118[6] 5638[7] 6185[8]
Sir Sandford (IRE) *David Simcock* 34
3 b c Selkirk(USA) —Fatefully (USA) (Private Account (USA))
2128[6] 4906[11]
Sir Sandicliffe (IRE) *Mark Brisbourne* a67 69
6 b g Distant Music(USA) —Desert Rose (Green Desert (USA))
130[8] 198[4] 409[2] (463) 554[5] 748[8] 2995[4] 3639[2] 3965[7] 4328[7] 4604[8] 4915[6]
Sir Tom *John Bridger* a44 50
5 b g Medicean—Shasta (Shareef Dancer (USA))
98[7] 4382[12] 4959[4] 5254[7] 5864[10]
Sirvino *David Barron* 107
5 b g Vettori(IRE) —Zenita (IRE) (Zieten (USA))
4412[4] 5188[6] 5879[8] 6304[2] 6736[2] 7350[12]
Sir Walter Raleigh *Sir Michael Stoute* a66 72
3 b g Galileo(IRE) —Elizabethan Age (FR) (King's Best (USA))
3477[2] 4257[4] 5646[4] 6132[4]
Sir William Orpen *Pat Phelan* a60 66
3 b g Orpen(USA) —Ashover Amber (Green Desert (USA))
3325[9] 5236[6] 6290[13]
Sisindu (IRE) *Brian Meehan* 64
2 b c Kheleyf(USA) —Nandy's Cavern (Lion Cavern (USA))
4803[9] 5900[4] 7010[4]
Sister Earth (IRE) *John Gosden* a69 73
3 ch f Galileo(IRE) —Time Ahead (Spectrum (IRE))
1451[3] 2390[2] 3170[4]
Sister June (IRE) *Edward Creighton*
2 b f Tiger Hill(IRE) —Littleton Arwen (USA) (Bahri (USA))
2457[6] 2630[5] 3082[12] 3992[8] 5268[8]
Sister Red (IRE) *Richard Hannon* 85
2 b f Diamond Green(FR) —Red Fuschia (Polish Precedent (USA))
5692[6] (6150) 6528[10]
Sister Sioux (IRE) *Robin Bastiman* 32
2 b f Antonius Pius(USA) —Blue Sioux (Indian Ridge)
2420[6] 3020[8] 5762[6]
Sitwell *Ian McInnes* a64 67
4 b g Dr Fong(USA) —First Fantasy (Be My Chief (USA))
735[5] 1177[11] 3502[10] 3978[13] 4454[9] 4980[9]
Six Diamonds *Paddy Butler* a80 77
3 b f Exceed And Excel(AUS) —Daltak (Night Shift (USA))
1765[7] 2442[2] 3174[4] (3834) 4291[4] 4754[4] 5356[10] (6368) 6932[5] 7180[12] 7571[8]
Six Of Clubs *Bill Turner* a55 48
4 ch g Bertolini(USA) —Windmill Princess (Gorytus (USA))
314[5] 470[5] 898[3] 1262[6] 1635[13] 2361[8] 7634[4] (7805)
Six Of Hearts *Cecil Ross* a104 104
6 b g Pivotal—Additive (USA) (Devil's Bag (USA))
553[6] 1091a[3] 1408a[4] 1676a[9] 2353a[4] (2570a) 4160a[8] 5774a[13]
Sixteen Forty Two (IRE) *Eoin Doyle* a73 92
5 b g Rock Of Gibraltar(IRE) —Tamaya (IRE) (Darshaan)
4463a[8]
Sixties Rock *Jeremy Glover* a51 57
3 ch g Rock Of Gibraltar(IRE) —Scene (IRE) (Scenic)
127[7] 288[4] 1178[9] 1298[6] (1465) 1753[5] 1967[5] 2700[7] 3755[4]
Sixty Roses (IRE) *John Dunlop* 70
2 b f Barathea(IRE) —Pershaan (IRE) (Darshaan)
2088[8] 2740[3] 4208[2] 5256[5] 5830[3] 6513[12]
Six Wives *Jeremy Glover* a77 66
3 b f Kingsalsa(USA) —Regina (Green Desert (USA))
277[6] 3410[8] 4659[4] 5410[10] 6103[18] 6932[7]
Siyaadah *Mahmood Al Zarooni* a103 87
3 b f Shamardal(USA) —River Belle (Lahib (USA))
(514a) 709a[3] 1023a[6] 2575a[5] 3071[16] 7188[4]
Siyouni (FR) *A De Royer-Dupre* 119
3 b c Pivotal—Sichilla (IRE) (Danehill (USA))
1565a[2] 2159a[9] 3048[4] 3719a[2] 5801a[3] 6611a[7]
Skeleton (IRE) *William Haggas* a58 57
2 b f Tobougg(IRE) —Atamana (IRE) (Lahib (USA))
5204[6] 6019[5] 6158[17] (7295) 7412[4] 7650[4] (7839)
Skellytown (USA) *Mike Mitchell* 95
7 ch g Thunder Gulch(USA) —Miss Dahlia (USA) (Strawberry Road (AUS))
1435a[3]
Skia (FR) *C Laffon-Parias* 100
3 b f Motivator—Light Quest (USA) (Quest For Fame)
3720a[6] 7648a[0]
Skiddaw View *Alan Brown* a40 8
2 b f Goodricke—Skiddaw Wolf (Wolfhound (USA))
6646[11] 6893[9] 7269[8] 7469[10]
Skilful *John Gosden* 79
2 ch c Selkirk(USA) —Prowess (IRE) (Peintre Celebre (USA))
7345 [3] ◆
Skins Game *J-C Rouget* 107
4 b h Diktat—Mouriyana (IRE) (Akarad (FR))
1111a[2] 6881a[3] 7266a[3]
Skipping Stones (IRE) *Robert Collet* a49 42
2 b c Whipper(USA) —Halesia (USA) (Chief's Crown (USA))
7009a[0]
Ski Sunday *Nicky Henderson* a66 72
5 b g King's Best(USA) —Lille Hammer (Sadler's Wells (USA))
2341[2] ◆
Sky Booster *William Haggas* 43
2 b c Indesatchel(IRE) —Myths And Verses (Primo Valentino (IRE))
2111[7] 2594[11] 3035[9] 3598[8]
Sky Diamond (IRE) *James Given* a64 63
2 b g Diamond Green(FR) —Jewell In The Sky (IRE) (Sinndar (IRE))
1009[8] 1180[5] 2654[10] 4020[7] (5630) 6294[4] 6568[17] 6875[13] 7124[7] 7394[7] 7552[2] (7631) 7785[2] 7888[4]
Skye But N Ben *Michael Chapman* a59 53
6 b g Auction House(USA) —Island Colony (USA) (Pleasant Colony (USA))
7330[9]
Sky Falcon (USA) *Mark Johnston* 78
2 ch g Smarty Jones(USA) —Silent Eskimo (USA) (Eskimo (USA))
2763[5] 3832[3] (4247) (4701) 5969[4]
Skyfire *Mark Johnston* a42 85
3 ch g Storm Cat(USA) —Sunray Superstar (Nashwan (USA))
1050[7] (1100) 1476[12] 2242[8] 3771[2] 4063[2] (4371) 4551[2] 4647[3]
Skyflight *Eve Johnson Houghton* a61 67
3 ch f Observatory(USA) —Flight Soundly (IRE) (Caerleon (USA))
4588[5] 6023[7] 6330[12]
Skyfly (FR) *T Lemer*
3 b g My Risk(FR) —Rikitea (FR) (Maelstrom Lake)
450a[0]
Skylarker (USA) *Tom Cuthbert* 16
12 b g Sky Classic(CAN) —O My Darling (USA) (Mr Prospector (USA))
3122[12]
Skylla *Richard Fahey* 93
3 b f Kyllachy—Day Star (Dayjur (USA))
3406[3] 3791[13] 4541[6] 5250[6] 6049[6] 6706[9]
Skyrider (IRE) *Roger Charlton* a73 76
3 gr f Dalakhani(IRE) —Future Flight (Polar Falcon (USA))
1620[4] 2180[4] 2901[11] 3689[3]
Skysurfers *Saeed Bin Suroor* a116 116
4 b h E Dubai(USA) —Fortune (IRE) (Night Shift (USA))
(630a) ◆ 798a[5] 1022a[3] 2318[3] 5275[2] 6089[2] 6570[10]
Skyteam (FR) *M Boutin* a88 100
6 b g Anabaa(USA) —Spenderella (FR) (Common Grounds)
6012a[11] 7278a[0]
Skywards *E Charpy* a45 92
8 b g Machiavellian(USA) —Nawaiet (USA) (Zilzal (USA))
413a[14]
Slap And Tickle (IRE) *Michael Squance* a53 45
4 b m Exceed And Excel(AUS) —Common Rumpus (IRE) (Common Grounds)
208[4] 392[9] 1599[5] 2021[13] 2196[7] 2876[9] 3415[7] 4105[6] 4596[5] 4969[13] 5090[6]
Slasl *Clive Brittain* a60 47
3 b f Dubawi(IRE) —Mazuna (IRE) (Cape Cross (IRE))
809[3] 934[5] 1593[6] 3350[9] 4210[5] 4692[5] 5176[9] 5729[9]
Slatey Hen (IRE) *Richard Fahey* a63 60
2 b f Acclamation—Silver Arrow (USA) (Shadeed (USA))
2347[5] 2649[3] 3686[7] 7527[3] (7722) 7811[3] 7931[4] 8002[2]
Slayer *M S Tuck* a65 65
5 b g Oasis Dream—Sahara Slew (USA) (Seattle Slew (USA))
586[8] 1459[13]
Sledmere (FR) *P Monfort* a64 65
8 bl g Dansili—Elacata (GER) (Acatenango (GER))
281a[6]
Sleek Falcon (IRE) *V di Napoli* 68
3 ch f Great Exhibition(USA) —Bella Michela (IRE) (Superpower)
4185a[9]
Sleek Gold *Brian Meehan* a63
2 b f Dansili—Ya Hajar (Lycius (USA))
7479[4]
Sleeping Brave *Jim Boyle* a55 48
2 b g Sleeping Indian—Concubine (IRE) (Danehill (USA))
4871[10] 5381[5] 5626[9] 7313[6] 7496[7]
Sleeping Wolf *Richard Hannon* 51
2 ch c Sleeping Indian—Sound Of Sleat (Primo Dominie)
2245[6] 5629[9] 5835[6] 6673[13] 6777[6]

Sleep Over *Dave Morris* 59
5 ch m Alflora(IRE) —Loving Around (IRE) (Furry Glen)
1380[5] 1932[10] 2994[7] 3865[7] 4621[6] 5457[6]

Sleepy Blue Ocean *John Balding* a68 68
4 b g Oasis Dream—Esteemed Lady (IRE) (Mark Of Esteem (IRE))
4373[11] 4706[9] 5055[2] 5485[9] (7542) 7721[3] (7860)

Sleepy Dove *Mike Sowersby* a1 53
5 b m Muhtarram(USA) —Robins Meg (Skyliner)
4207[6] 4867[11]

Sleepy Hollow *Hughie Morrison* a68 91
5 b g Beat Hollow—Crackling (Electric)
3050[7]

Sleepy Valley (IRE) *A Dickman* 57
4 b m Clodovil(IRE) —Kilkee Bay (IRE) (Case Law)
1569[13]

Sleights Boy (IRE) *Ian McInnes* 58
2 b g Kyllachy—Fanny Bay (IRE) (Key Of Luck (USA))
3536[6] 4116[6] 4941[14] 5755[7] 6674[13] 6980[9]

Slew Charm (FR) *Noel Chance* a59
8 b g Marathon(USA) —Slew Bay (FR) (Beaudelaire (USA))
261[8] 426[4] 6855[6]

Slickly Royal (FR) *P Demercastel* a96 111
6 b h Slickly(FR) —Royal Bride (FR) (Garde Royale)
2778a[4] 3017a[3] 3704a[10] 5574a[7] 7800a[5]

Slick Mover (IRE) *Brendan Powell* a69 50
5 gr m Slickly(FR) —Agnessa (FR) (Niniski (USA))
(120) (309) 509[4] 770[9] 1012[10]

Slight Advantage (IRE) *Clive Cox* a8 74
2 b f Peintre Celebre(USA) —Kournikova (SAF) (Sportsworld (USA))
4021[12] 5066[3] 5633[2] (6471)

Sligo All Star *Thomas McLaughlin* a51 42
5 b m Kyllachy—Top Spot (Cadeaux Genereux)
7814[5]

Slikback Jack (IRE) *David Nicholls* a83 76
3 ch g Dr Fong(USA) —Duelling (Diesis)
(527) ◆ 884[3] 1061[DSQ] 1362[6] 2426[6] 2824[4] 3409[7] 4670[3] ◆ 5789[3] 6107[10] 6581[2] 7046[2] 7274[8] (7499) 7680[5]

Slimline *Tim Easterby*
2 b g Diktat—Damelza (IRE) (Orpen (USA))
3118[12]

Slim Shadey *J S Moore* 96
2 br c Val Royal(FR) —Vino Veritas (USA) (Chief's Crown (USA))
2839[5] 3190[6] (3844) 5079[2] 5880[4] 6347[5]

Slinky Malinki (IRE) *Tim Easterby* 38
3 ch f Orpen(USA) —A L'Aube (IRE) (Selkirk (USA))
3285[3]

Slip *Conor Dore* a75 72
5 b g Fraam—Niggle (Night Shift (USA))
565[3] (1801) 2173[7] 2897[7] 3282[4] 4227[11] 4793[7] 4980[10]

Slip Sliding Away (IRE) *Peter Hedger* a63 90
3 b g Whipper(USA) —Sandy Lady (IRE) (Desert King (IRE))
809[10] 934[10] (3350) 3638[6] (4398) (5005) ◆ 5551[2] 6319[10]

Sloop Johnb *Richard Fahey* a79 89
4 b g Bahamian Bounty—Soundwave (Prince Sabo)
5335[8] 6245[6] 6962[12] 7169[3] (7326) 7494[3] 7668[2] 7866[3] 7984[3]

Slugger O'Toole *Stuart Williams* a80 75
5 br g Intikhab(USA) —Haddeyah (USA) (Dayjur (USA))
1185[3] 5889[5] 6629[13] 6801[3] 7047[6] ◆

Sluggsy Morant *Henry Candy* 72
2 b g Monsieur Bond(IRE) —Breezy Louise (Dilum (USA))
4323[9] 4954[6] 6954[2] 7301[2] ◆

Slumber *B W Hills* 51
2 b c Cacique(IRE) —Sound Asleep (USA) (Woodman (USA))
6442[10]

Slumbering Sioux *Harry Dunlop* 63
2 b f Sleeping Indian—Mi Amor (IRE) (Alzao (USA))
2839[8] 3209[7] 4095[12] 6674[10] ◆ (7004)

Smackeroo (USA) *John Quinn* a42
4 ch m Smarty Jones(USA) —Getaway Girl (USA) (Silver Deputy (CAN))
776[9] 911[6]

Smalljohn *Bryan Smart* a78 77
4 ch g Needwood Blade—My Bonus (Cyrano De Bergerac)
129[2] (373) (465) 779[4] 867[4] 1802[3] 2531[3] (3164) 3659[5] 4602[6] 5157[7]

Smart Diplomacy (USA) *A De Royer-Dupre* a89 85
4 b h Hennessy(USA) —Peacock Alley (USA) (Fast Play (USA))
549a[7]

Smart Endeavour (USA) *Walter Swinburn* a88 83
4 ch g Smart Strike(CAN) —Luminance (USA) (Deputy Minister (CAN))
1265[7] 1618[9] 3330[9] 3725[3] 4422[5] 4958[5] 5710[3] (6371) 6801[4] 7047[8]

Smarten Die (IRE) *Frau E Mader* a101 89
7 ch h Diesis—Highest Dream (IRE) (Highest Honor (FR))
737[5]

Smart Enough *Fredrik Reuterskiold* a107 96
7 gr g Cadeaux Genereux—Good Enough (FR) (Mukaddamah (USA))
2637a[4]

Smart George (IRE) *Clive Cox* 56
2 b g Kalanisi(IRE) —Yazmin (IRE) (Green Desert (USA))
5878[13] 6473[10]

Smarties Party *C W Thornton* a66 54
7 b m Tamure(IRE) —Maries Party (The Parson)
621[5] 777[2] 874[2] 1273[5] 1671[6]

Smart Performance *Alan Jarvis* 48
2 b g Acclamation—Green Eyes (IRE) (Green Desert (USA))
4363[6]

Smart Red *Mick Channon* 59
2 b f Bachelor Duke(USA) —Zarannda (IRE) (Last Tycoon)
2740[6] 3386[7] 3712[2] 3981[2]

Smart Spark (IRE) *Brian Meehan* a75 54
4 b m Spartacus(IRE) —Smart Pet (Petong)
1998[10]

Smart Step *Mark Johnston* 67
2 b f Montjeu(IRE) —Miss Pinkerton (Danehill (USA))
4116[8] 4508[10] 5277[6] ◆ 5784[6] 6647[5]

Smart Striking (USA) *John M Oxx* 85
3 b f Smart Strike(CAN) —Jellett (IRE) (Green Desert (USA))
(4524a) ◆

Smart Violetta (IRE) *Ann Duffield* 34
2 bb f Smart Strike(CAN) —Dubai Diamond (Octagonal (NZ))
5498[8] 5762[8] 6036[6]

Smarty Sam (USA) *Alan Swinbank* 69
3 ch g Smarty Jones(USA) —Ascot Starre (CAN) (Ascot Knight (CAN))
1335[6] 2072[4] 2393[9] (3153) 3532[6] 4546[10]

Smarty Socks (IRE) *David O'Meara* a80 98
6 ch g Elnadim(USA) —Unicamp (Royal Academy (USA))
837[10] 1030[17] 1374[17] 2991[7] 3318[3] 3876[3] (4394) (5068) 5605[5] 5736[2] 6749[6] 7348[16]

Smashing Brasses (IRE) *Amy Weaver*
3 b g Arakan(USA) —Running Tycoon (IRE) (Last Tycoon)
5057[10]

Smiling Tiger (USA) *Jeff Bonde* a122
3 ch c Hold That Tiger(USA) —Shandra Smiles (USA) (Cahill Road (USA))
7361a[3]

Smirfys Copper (IRE) *Deborah Sanderson* a8 13
3 ch f Choisir(AUS) —Fer De Lance (IRE) (Diesis)
3080[11] 4572[9]

Smirfys Emerald (IRE) *Deborah Sanderson* a49
2 ch c Choisir(AUS) —Smirfys Dance Hall (IRE) (Halling (USA))
6743[8]

Smirfys Gold (IRE) *Deborah Sanderson* a16 59
6 ch g Bad As I Wanna Be(IRE) —Golden Jorden (IRE) (Cadeaux Genereux)
561[11]

Smirfy's Silver *Deborah Sanderson* a31 75
6 b g Desert Prince(IRE) —Goodwood Blizzard (Inchinor)
2421[2] 2602[7] (3177) 3405[5] 4481[3]

Smirfys Systems *Deborah Sanderson* a71 53
11 b g Safawan—Saint Systems (Uncle Pokey)
312[9] 531[7] 968[5]

Smokey Fire (CAN) *Sid Attard* a121 112
5 rg g Smoke Glacken(USA) —Destroy (CAN) (Housebuster (USA))
6237a[6]

Smokey Oakey (IRE) *Mark H Tompkins* a76 104
6 b g Tendulkar(USA) —Veronica (Persian Bold)
1008[4] 3069[22] 4596[2] 4828[9] 5556[P] 6562[24]

Smokey Ryder *Ronald Harris* a54 91
4 ch m Bertolini(USA) —Another Secret (Efisio)
299[9] 2247[7] 3201[8]

Smokey Storm *Bent Olsen* 90
4 br h One Cool Cat(USA) —Marisa (GER) (Desert Sun)
4526a[10]

Smooth Operator (GER) *Mario Hofer* 112
4 b g Big Shuffle(USA) —Salzgitter (Salse (USA))
1251a[14] 1955a[2] 4122[2] 4885a[4] 5573a[11] 6611a[9] 7370a[9]

Smugglers Bay (IRE) *Tim Easterby* 69
6 b g Celtic Swing—Princess Mood (GER) (Muhtarram (USA))
2060[2] 2533[3] 2659[5] 3600[4] 3974[9] 4900[8] 5642[9] 6114[8] 6649[4]

Snaafy (USA) *M Al Muhairi* a117 117
6 b h Kingmambo(USA) —Nafisah (IRE) (Lahib (USA))
(440a) ◆ 609a[5] 823a[7] 1025a[12]

Snaefell (IRE) *M Halford* 115
6 gr g Danehill Dancer(IRE) —Sovereign Grace (IRE) (Standaan (FR))
1406a[3] 1676a[5] 2353a[2] (4882a) 6009a[3] 6783a[4]

Snake River (IRE) *M Weiss* 82
3 b f Bachelor Duke(USA) —Najeyba (Indian Ridge)
1252a[7]

Snap Alam (IRE) *Ms Joanna Morgan* 80
3 b f Alamshar(IRE) —Kirvana (IRE) (Lycius (USA))
4496a[3]

Snapshot (USA) *William Mott* a106
4 bb h Awesome Again(CAN) —Cajun Flash (USA) (Bertrando (USA))
6582a[9]

Snapshott (IRE) *Ronald Harris* a31
2 b g Kodiac—Groovy (Shareef Dancer (USA))
1136[10] 2867[10] 4678[10] 5667[9]

Sneaking Uponyou (USA) *Jamie Ness* a95 106
4 b g Snuck In(USA) —Chestnut Game (USA) (Dahar (USA))
6949a[6]

Snooze (USA) *B Grizzetti* 57
3 bb f Forestry(USA) —Daydreaming (USA) (A.P. Indy (USA))
1713a[19]

Snoqualmie Boy *David Nicholls* a97 91
7 b g Montjeu(IRE) —Seattle Ribbon (USA) (Seattle Dancer (USA))
3239[8] 3431[4] 3889[7]

Snoqualmie Girl (IRE) *David Elsworth* a68 104
4 b m Montjeu(IRE) —Seattle Ribbon (USA) (Seattle Dancer (USA))
1859[5] 2716[7] 4143[2] ◆ 4624[8] 5249[5] 5881[9] 6320[3] 6929[5]

Snoqualmie Star *David Elsworth* a92 94
3 ch f Galileo(IRE) —Seattle Ribbon (USA) (Seattle Dancer (USA))
2042[6] 2993[11] (4022) (4329) 5056[2] 5753[2] 6203[2] 6506[5]

Snore No More (IRE) *Stuart Coltherd* 52
3 b g Spartacus(IRE) —Shinko Song (IRE) (Shinko Forest (IRE))
3073[14]

Snow Bay *David Nicholls* a90 90
4 ch g Bahamian Bounty—Goodwood Blizzard (Inchinor)
(115) 324[8] 572[4] (1397) 1672[5] 2133[4] 4617[8] 6105[9] 7146[5] 7955[2]

Snow Bear (IRE) *John Quinn* 64
2 b f Kodiac—Snow Eagle (IRE) (Polar Falcon (USA))
(2272) 4278[5] 5939[6] 6645[15]

Snowberry Hill (USA) *Lucinda Featherstone* a60 63
7 b g Woodman(USA) —Class Skipper (USA) (Skip Trial (USA))
1983[9] 2907[4] 3709[6] 3965[4] 4441[3] 5203[3] 5963[10] 6272[5] (6373)

Snow Blizzard (IRE) *A P O'Brien* 83
3 b c Sadler's Wells(USA) —Pescia (IRE) (Darshaan)
4769a[4]

Snow Cannon (IRE) *Peter Chapple-Hyam* 34
2 gr f Verglas(IRE) —Kanun (Dancing Brave (USA))
4048[10]

Snow Dancer (IRE) *Hugh McWilliams* a88 82
6 b m Desert Style(IRE) —Bella Vie (IRE) (Sadler's Wells (USA))
266[4] 408[2] 790[8] 1379[6] 1512[10] 3203[4] (3627) 3894[2] 4389[11] 4943[5] 5757[5] 7053[12] 7428[5]

Snowed Under *James Bethell* a79 83
9 gr g Most Welcome—Snowy Mantle (Siberian Express (USA))
2173[8] 2435[5] 2961[5] 3613[2] 4196[3] 4943[11]

Snow Fairy (IRE) *Ed Dunlop* a83 120
3 b f Intikhab(USA) —Woodland Dream (IRE) (Charnwood Forest (IRE))
(2224) (2711) (4178a) 5248[2] 5945[4] (7460a) ◆ (7854a)

Snow Hill *Chris Wall* 25
2 gr g Halling(USA) —Swift Dispersal (Shareef Dancer (USA))
6442[16]

Snow Legend (IRE) *Tom Dascombe* 29
2 gr f Proclamation(IRE) —Royal Consort (IRE) (Green Desert (USA))
3362[8] 4543[7] 4981[6]

Snow Magic (IRE) *James Fanshawe* a86 72
3 gr f Marju(IRE) —Santa Sophia (IRE) (Linamix (FR))
3738[3] 4397[6] 5623[3] (6212) 6580[4] (7042) ◆

Snow Mountain (IRE) *A P O'Brien* 86
2 ch c Danehill Dancer(IRE) —Speak Softly To Me (USA) (Ogygian (USA))
4880a[7]

Snow Ridge *Sir Mark Prescott Bt* a66 56
2 b g Iceman—Confetti (Groom Dancer (USA))
6309[7] 6712[3] 6919[6]

Snow Runner (ARG) *Vanja Sandrup* a94 89
7 ch h Lode(USA) —Snow Pac (URU) (Snow Satyr (ARG))
339a[11] 511a[8] 797a[9]

Snow's Ride *Michael Herrington* a46
10 gr g Hernando(FR) —Crodelle (IRE) (Formidable (USA))
1828[7] 2476[P]

Snow Trooper *Dean Ivory* a61 36
2 ch c Iceman—Snow Shoes (Sri Pekan (USA))
2819[14] 3269[10] 6425[8] 7497[7] (7813)

Snow White Feet (IRE) *Harry Dunlop* a26 14
3 ch f Footstepsinthesand—Mousseline (USA) (Barathea (IRE))
2335[9] 2921[8] 3787[8]

Snowy Peak *Jeremy Noseda* a56
2 ch f Pivotal—Snow Princess (IRE) (Ela-Mana-Mou)
7879[5] ◆

So Anyway (AUS) *John P Thompson* 101
4 ch f General Nediym(AUS) —Addictive (AUS) (Flying Spur (AUS))
11

Soap Wars *Jamie Osborne* a95 87
5 b g Acclamation—Gooseberry Pie (Green Desert (USA))
4814[6] 5154[11] 5731[9] 6198[5] 6799[7] 6987[5]

So Bazaar (IRE) *Alan Swinbank* 70
3 b g Xaar—Nature Girl (USA) (Green Dancer (USA))
1201[3] (1887) 2501[2] 2886[8] 3668[2]

Sobea Star (IRE) *Pam Sly* 56
2 ch f Soviet Star(USA) —Nordic Cloud (IRE) (Lure (USA))
6268[5]

So Belle *Kevin Ryan* 72
2 ch f Singspiel(IRE) —Omission (Green Desert (USA))
2461[4] (2958)

Soberania (GER) *A Wohler* 110
4 b m Monsun(GER) —Sasuela (GER) (Dashing Blade)
1792a[7] 3045a[4] 5108a[7] 6410a[4] 7109a[3] 7373a[7]

Soccerjackpot (USA) *Alan Jones* a100 82
6 b g Mizzen Mast(USA) —Rahbaby (USA) (Rahy (USA))
(196) 6357[10]

Socceroo *David C Griffiths* a52 56
5 b m Choisir(AUS) —Silca Boo (Efisio)
1569[4] 2213[9] 2741[6] 3064[6] 3762[12] 3895[7] 4435[2] 4892[6] 5726[4]

So Choosy *Richard Hannon* a32 55
2 b f Choisir(AUS) —Roxy (Rock City)
3156[6] 4253[9]

Social Rhythm *Alistair Whillans* a71 74
6 b m Beat All(USA) —Highly Sociable (Puissance)
2207[13] 3707[9] 5244[3] (5439) (5732) 6395[3] 7055[3]

Society Rock (IRE) *James Fanshawe* 117
3 b c Rock Of Gibraltar(IRE) —High Society (IRE) (Key Of Luck (USA))
(1616) ◆ 2075[2] 3192[2] 3870[7] ◆

Society's Chairman (CAN) *Roger L Attfield* a103 114
7 b h Not Impossible(IRE) —Athena's Smile (CAN) (Olympio (USA))
6759a[2] 7364a[9]

Society Venue *Michael Scudamore* a70 80
5 b g Where Or When(IRE) —Society Rose (Sadlers' Hall (IRE))
202[6]

Sodashy (IRE) *Amy Weaver* a56 66
2 ch f Noverre(USA) —Leopard Creek (Weldnaas (USA))
3871[5] 4317[7] 4743[5] 5452[7] 6411[11]

Soeurchichi (FR) *J-M Lefebvre*
2 gr c Chichicastenango(FR) —La Soeur (FR) (Entrepreneur)
7974a[0]

Sofonisba *Marco Botti* a36 54
4 b m Rock Of Gibraltar(IRE) —Lothlorien (USA) (Woodman (USA))
295[8] 568[8]

Softly Killing Me *Brian Forsey* a30 56
5 b m Umistim—Slims Lady (Theatrical Charmer)
7759[10]

Sohcahtoa (IRE) *Richard Hannon* a100 92
4 b g Val Royal(FR) —Stroke Of Six (IRE) (Woodborough (USA))
1006[2] 1600[6] 2044[2] 2317[6] 2640[13] 4100[6] 4320[6] 5217[12] 5786[3] 6152[6] 6476[2] 6990[10]

Soho Theatre *David Elsworth* a75 74
3 b g Indian Ridge—Costa Brava (IRE) (Sadler's Wells (USA))
1165[2] 1769[14] 3171[5] 3676[8]

Sohraab *Hughie Morrison* a77 106
6 b g Erhaab(USA) —Riverine (Risk Me (FR))
1353[5] 1822[5] 2346[11] 3193[22] 3828[9] 4401[10] ◆ 4904[9] (5308) 5967[3] 6446[8]

Soie De Chine *Sir Mark Prescott Bt* a68 65
2 ch f Selkirk(USA) —Robe Chinoise (Robellino (USA))
4021[5] 4338[4] 4682[6]

So Is She (IRE) *Alan Bailey* a71 72
2 b f Kheleyf(USA) —River Beau (IRE) (Galileo (IRE))
1819[4] ◆ 2127[5] 2951[U] 4409[3] 5089[2] 5294[2] 5433[2] 5901[3] 6102[6] 6901[3] 7664[6] (7954)

Sokolka *Tim Easterby* 59
2 b f Diktat—Babiki (IRE) (Nashwan (USA))
4338[8] 5066[6] 6566[12]

Solarias Quest *Mark Brisbourne* a62 82
8 b g Pursuit Of Love—Persuasion (Batshoof)
327[2] 220[7] 309[11] 724[6] 746[2] 970[6] 1194[5]

Solar Spirit (IRE) *John Quinn* a76 88
5 b g Invincible Spirit(IRE) —Misaayef (USA) (Swain (IRE))
1099[9] 1650[7] 1923[2] 2534[2] 5424[3] 6048[7] 6917[2] (7146) 7283[4] 7915[7]

Soldat (USA) *Kiaran McLaughlin* a81 111
2 bb c War Front(USA) —Le Relais (USA) (Coronado's Quest (USA))
7360a[2]

Sol De Angra (BRZ) *A Cintra Pereira* a99 85
5 ch h Put It Back(USA) —Gondoleira (BRZ) (Roi Normand (USA))
434a[5] 604a[4] 822a[9]

Soldiers Point *Bryan Smart* 56
2 b c Indesatchel(IRE) —Wondrous Maid (GER) (Mondrian (GER))
4059[4] 5385[7] 7346[13]

Sole Danser (IRE) *B W Hills* 75
2 b c Dansili—Plymsole (USA) (Diesis)
3794[14] 4614[4]

Solemn *Milton Bradley* a81 91
5 b g Pivotal—Pious (Bishop Of Cashel)
1988[3] (2301) 2681[10] 2997[2] 3114[2] 3736[2] 4401[7] (4625) 5069[5] 5589[8] 5967[5] 6064[2] 6364[11] 6739[16] 7041[12]

Solent (IRE) *John Quinn* a96 6
8 b g Montjeu(IRE) —Stylish (Anshan)
1274[16]

Solent Ridge (IRE) *G M Lyons* a83 82
5 b g Namid—Carrozzina (Vettori (IRE))
7217a[5]

Sole Power *Edward Lynam* a101 119
3 b g Kyllachy—Demerger (USA) (Distant View (USA))
(1091a) 1700[4] 3486a[6] (5276)

Solicitor *Mark Johnston* a82 91
3 ch g Halling(USA) —Tolzey (USA) (Rahy (USA))
2979[8] 3330[11] 4056[2] (4196) 4504[15]

Solid Choice (AUS) *M F De Kock* a100
4 b c Redoute's Choice(AUS) —Venetian Pride (USA) (Gone West (USA))
414a[4] 608a[4] 796a[6] 1023a[13]

Solis *John Quinn* a42 68
4 b g Josr Algarhoud(IRE) —Passiflora (Night Shift (USA))
144[10] 451[9] 2523[5]

Solitary *Marjorie Fife* a51 69
4 b m Lahib(USA) —Bond Solitaire (Atraf)
3238[3] 3806[7] 5199[6] 5732[10]

Solleone (USA) *Luca De Maria*
2 ch f Bellamy Road(USA) —Lady Kay Kay (USA) (Tiznow (USA))
7849a[6]

Solo Choice *Ian McInnes* a49 68
4 b g Needwood Blade—Top Of The Class (IRE) (Rudimentary (USA))
227[7] 411[5] 661[8] 1113[11] 7834[6]

So Long Malpic (FR) *T Lemer* 94
3 b f Fairly Ransom(USA) —Poussiere D'Or (FR) (Marchand De Sable (USA))
7545a[8]

Solo Performer (IRE) *H Rogers* a84 80
5 ch g Distant Music(USA) —Royal Pagent (IRE) (Balinger)
6730a[9] 7514a[7] (7589a) 7823a[5]

Solo Whisper (IRE) *Howard Johnson* 59
2 b g Whipper(USA) —Mijouter (IRE) (Coquelin (USA))
2202[7] 4480[4] 5594[10]

Solstice *Julie-Ann Camacho* a86 85
3 b f Dubawi(IRE) —South Of Saturn (USA) (Seattle Slew (USA))
(453) ◆ 884[5] 1584[2] ◆ 2140[3] 2656[5] 3225[4] 4091[8] 5647[12]

Somebody Loves You *Ann Duffield* a10 12
2 b f Araafa(IRE) —Puzzling (Peintre Celebre (USA))
2623[10] 5761[10] 6307[11]

Somerset Island (IRE) *Howard Johnson*
2 b g Barathea(IRE) —Art Work (Zafonic (USA))
5814[10]

Some Sunny Day *Hughie Morrison* a88 93
4 ch m Where Or When(IRE) —Palace Street (USA) (Secreto (USA))
1629[5] (2181) 3319[6] 6095[8] 6320[9] 6886[9] 7189[10]

Something (IRE) *David Nicholls* a91 103
8 b g Trans Island—Persian Polly (Persian Bold)
916[8] ◆ 2748[3] 3146[14] (3578) 4358[15] 5292[10] 6175[21] 7935[7]

Somethin' Stupid *Sir Mark Prescott Bt* a27
3 b g Dubai Destination(USA) —Total Love (Cadeaux Genereux)
1825[11] (Dead)

Some Time Good (IRE) *Joanna Davis* a69 55
4 bg g Clodovil(IRE) —El Alma (IRE) (Goldmark (USA))
1922[8] 2198[7] 2870[8] 3524[10]

Sometsuke *PETER Makin* a68 85
4 br g Efisio—Peyto Princess (Bold Arrangement)
1779[10] (2166) 2399[14]

Somewhere Else *Alan Berry* a5 14
3 b f Firebreak—Royal Future (IRE) (Royal Academy (USA))
4649[9] 5044[7]

Some Yarn (IRE) *Linda Jewell* a45
3 b g Captain Rio—Church Road (IRE) (Danehill Dancer (IRE))
915[11] 7440[6] 7651[6] 7969[5]

Sommersturm (GER) *Barney Curley* a77 103
6 b g Tiger Hill(IRE) —Sommernacht (GER) (Monsun (GER))
1984[5]

Som Tala *Mick Channon* a94 99
7 ch g Fantastic Light(USA) —One Of The Family (Alzao (USA))
1821[7] 3050[17]

Sonara (IRE) *Howard Johnson* 74
6 b g Peintre Celebre(USA) —Fay (IRE) (Polish Precedent (USA))
2295[7] 6028[3]

Soneva (USA) *Marco Botti* a89 110
4 br m Cherokee Run(USA) —Lakabi (USA) (Nureyev (USA))
(439a) 798a[13]

Songjiang *John Gosden* a53
2 b c Tiger Hill(IRE) —Showery (Rainbow Quest (USA))
7954[3]

Song Of India *John Gosden* 61
2 gr f Dalakhani(IRE) —Shahmina (IRE) (Danehill (USA))
5829[7]

Song Of My Heart (IRE) *David Wachman* 102
3 ch f Footstepsinthesand—Catch The Moon (IRE) (Peintre Celebre (USA))
2370a[10] 3071[12] 6783a[3]

Song Of Parkes *Eric Alston* 72
3 b f Fantastic Light(USA) —My Melody Parkes (Teenoso (USA))
1275[4] 1685[3] 2309[2] 2883[9] 3751[8]

Song Of Praise *Michael Blanshard* a62 63
4 b m Compton Place—Greensand (Green Desert (USA))
1596[12] 2026[7] 3129[7] 3328[4] 3762[4] ◆ 4232[9] 5711[7] 5897[8] 6329[9] 7192[3] 7607[4] 7885[7] 8024[5]

Song Of The Siren *Andrew Balding* 78
2 ch f With Approval(CAN) —Sulitelma (USA) (The Minstrel (CAN))
4999[5] (5626) 6156[3] 6563[13]

Song Of Victory (GER) *M Weiss* 64
6 b g Silvano(GER) —Song Of Hope (GER) (Monsun (GER))
461a[12]

Songsmith *Lucy Wadham* 78
2 b c Librettist(USA) —Venus Rising (Observatory (USA))
5385[3] 6158[2] 6802[2]

Song To The Moon (IRE) *George Baker* a73 82
3 b f Oratorio(IRE) —Jojeema (Barathea (IRE))
1620[2] 2225[6] 3081[5] 4022[5] 4959[5] 5469[2] ◆ 6260[3] 6629[4] (6991) 7521[8]

Sonhador *Alan Berry* a68 60
4 b g Compton Place—Fayre Holly (IRE) (Fayruz)
103[3] 319[8] 423[10] 495[8] 726[2] 866[7] 1154[13] 1723[12] 1965[8]

Sonia Girl (IRE) *Patrick Morris* a39
3 b f Exceed And Excel(AUS) —Royal Lady (IRE) (Royal Academy (USA))
4908[5] 5153[4] 5686[9]

Sonnellino *John Holt* a44 58
3 b f Singspiel(IRE) —Dreamawhile (Known Fact (USA))
1355[5] ◆ 1501[8] 6496[7] 6993[13]

Sonning Gate *David Elsworth* a87 92
4 b g Desert Sun—Sunley Scent (Wolfhound (USA))
1088[12]

Sonning Rose (IRE) *Mick Channon* 92
2 b f Hawk Wing(USA) —Shinkoh Rose (FR) (Warning)
2594[2] (2813) ◆ 3190[2] 5519[7] 5910[4] 6401a[10] 6927[7]

Sonny G (IRE) *John Best* a63 57
3 ch c Desert Sun—Broughton Zest (Colonel Collins (USA))
(1168) 1873[5] 2844[14] 3322[11] 4297[4] 4365[7] 4586[4] (5077) 7613[13]

Sonny Parkin *Jeff Pearce* a56 75
8 b g Spinning World(USA) —No Miss Kris (USA) (Capote (USA))
3416[9] 4108[3] (4548) 5050[8]

Sonny Red (IRE) *David Nicholls* 106
6 b g Redback—Magic Melody (Petong)
1032[8] 1423[9] 3891[5] 4191[7] 4391[13] 4576[16] 5302[10] ◆ 6175[2] 6363[14] 6708[9]

Sonny Sam (IRE) *Richard Fahey* a58 64
5 b g Black Sam Bellamy(IRE) —Purple Risks (FR) (Take Risks (FR))
41[3] 210[5] 409[4]

Son Of Monsieur *Geoffrey Oldroyd* a48 46
4 ch g Monsieur Bond(IRE) —Triple Tricks (IRE) (Royal Academy (USA))
211[8] 410[12] 918[12]

Son Of The Cat (USA) *Brian Gubby* a101 100
4 b g Tale Of The Cat(USA) —Dixieland Gal (USA) (Dixieland Band (USA))
1014[4] 2316[5]

Sonoran Sands (IRE) *J S Moore* a90 92
2 b c Footstepsinthesand—Atishoo (IRE) (Revoque (IRE))
2594[6] 3051[7] 3362[2] (3712) 4097[5] 4355[6] 4903[3] (4928) 5257[2]

Soopacal (IRE) *Michael Herrington* a82 82
5 b g Captain Rio—Fiddes (IRE) (Alzao (USA))
7984[2]

Sooraah *William Haggas* a68 93
3 b f Dubawi(IRE) —Al Persian (IRE) (Persian Bold)
1355[6] 2473[4] ◆ 2718[7] (3852) ◆ (4491) ◆ 4762[2] 5222[5] 6090[2] 6509[7]

Sophie's Beau (USA) *Michael Chapman* a65 78
3 b g Stormy Atlantic(USA) —Lady Buttercup (USA) (Meadowlake (USA))
1694[7] 2197[7] (2385) 2617[6] 2822[6] 2957[4] 3975[10] 4248[7] 4651[12] 6076[4] 7131[8] 7808[6] 7870[6] 7953[8]

Sophie's Hero *Kevin Ryan* 73
2 ch g Intikhab(USA) —Esteraad (IRE) (Cadeaux Genereux)
2498[2] 3020[4] 3353[2] 3665[3]

Sophies Trophy (IRE) *Pat Phelan* a68 79
5 b g Orpen(USA) —Ar Hyd Y Knos (Alzao (USA))
1302[3] 1851[3] 6499[4]

Sopranist *Saeed Bin Suroor* a103 108
4 b h Singspiel(IRE) —Trefoil (Kris)
337a[3] 3921[18] 5220[7] 5949[11]

Sopran Nad (ITY) *Stuart Williams* a47
6 b h Masad(IRE) —Sopran Newar (Warning)
7829[8]

Soprano (GER) *Jonjo O'Neill* 48
8 b g Sendawar(IRE) —Spirit Lake (GER) (Surumu (GER))
409[12]

Soraaya (IRE) *Mick Channon* 106
2 b f Elnadim(USA) —Date Mate (USA) (Thorn Dance (USA))
(2855) 3792[2] (4356) 5347a[8]

Sorciere (IRE) *C Lerner* 106
3 b f Orpen(USA) —Serandine (IRE) (Hernando (FR))
2157a[8] 4773a[8]

Sordino (GER) *W Hickst* 109
4 ch h Samum(GER) —Serenata (GER) (Lomitas)
2806a[2]

Sormiou (FR) *C Diard* 106
3 b c Califet(FR) —Melodya (FR) (Great Palm (USA))
(3016a) 3719a[6]

Sorrel Point *Hugh Collingridge* a58 44
7 b h Bertolini(USA) —Lightning Princess (Puissance)
1477[8] 2186[3] 2720[5] 4256[6] 7425[11] 7506[U]

Sory *Tina Jackson* 58
3 b g Sakhee(USA) —Rule Britannia (Night Shift (USA))
5122[5]

So Shiny (ARG) *J Barton* a103
5 ch m Indygo Shiner(USA) —Sorpresiva (ARG) (Southern Halo (USA))
(434a) 707a[7]

Sostenuto *Terry Caldwell* a19 28
3 ch f Compton Place—Hufflepuff (IRE) (Desert King (IRE))
2722[9]

So Stylish (USA) *A P O'Brien* 84
2 b f Johannesburg(USA) —Tacha (USA) (Mr Prospector (USA))
2352a[3]

So Surreal (IRE) *Gary Moore* a73 67
3 b f Avonbridge—Secret Circle (Magic Ring (IRE))
1619[8] 2005[4] 2587[12] 2871[9] 4959[9] 5073[3] 5661[7] (6522) (6713) 7255[12]

Sotelo *Steve Gollings* a67 11
8 ch h Monsun(GER) —Seringa (GER) (Acatenango (GER))
612[4] ◆ 777[13]

Sotik Star (IRE) *Kevin Morgan* a67 79
7 b g Elnadim(USA) —Crystal Springs (IRE) (Kahyasi)
262[4] 496[5] 663[5] 925[3] 1239[3] 1877[4] 3323[8]

Soto *Michael Easterby* a34 70
7 b g Averti(IRE) —Belle Of The Blues (IRE) (Blues Traveller (IRE))
1149[12] 1470[3] 1885[11] 1968[3] 2378[8] (2699) 3062[6] 3615[12] 4014[5] 4487[6] 4869[9] 5496[8]

Sottovoce *Simon Dow* a69 21
2 b f Oratorio(IRE) —In A Silent Way (IRE) (Desert Prince (IRE))
2749[8] 7879[2]

Soudanaise (IRE) *E Lellouche* 85
3 ch f Peintre Celebre(USA) —Sarabande (USA) (Woodman (USA))
6519a[4]

Soul City (IRE) *Richard Hannon* a100 109
4 b h Elusive City(USA) —Savage (IRE) (Polish Patriot (USA))
946[9] ◆ 1532[5] 5538[7]

Soul Heaven *Michael Bell* a76 77
3 b g Oratorio(IRE) —Pilgrim Spirit (USA) (Saint Ballado (CAN))
1307[3] 2261[5]

Soul Murmur (IRE) *Frank Sheridan* a54 79
5 br g Indian Ridge—My Potters (USA) (Irish River (FR))
377[7] 1167[5] 1477[5]

Soul Station (FR) *Roger Charlton* a62 96
3 b g Starcraft(NZ) —Allumette (Rainbow Quest (USA))
1502[4] ◆ (2225)

Soundbyte *John Gallagher* a77 73
5 b g Beat All(USA) —Gloaming (Celtic Swing)
989[3] (1087) ◆ 1357[7] 1768[4] 4657[10] 4907[8] 6502[6] 6957[2] 7167[3] 7422[6] 7704[5] 7967[4]

Sound Of Summer (USA) *J-C Rouget* 96
3 b f Fusaichi Pegasus(USA) —Moon Queen (IRE) (Sadler's Wells (USA))
952a[2] 1496a[8] 5981a[8]

Sounds Of Thunder *Harry Dunlop* a70 67
3 b f Tobougg(IRE) —Distant Music (Darshaan)
1189[8] 1778[5] 2250[11] 3954[7] 5959[4] 6476[5] 6930[12]

Soundwave (USA) *Ronny Werner* a92
2 b f Friends Lake(USA) —Echo Echo Echo (USA) (Eastern Echo (USA))
7342a[11]

Source Bleue (FR) *J C Napoli* a85 85
4 b m Gold Away(IRE) —Source De Reve (FR) (Kaldoun (FR))
(640a)

Sour Mash (IRE) *Luca Cumani* 95
3 b g Danehill Dancer(IRE) —Landmark (USA) (Arch (USA))
(2043) 4106[2] ◆ 4470[14] 6203[9]

Souter's Sister (IRE) *Marco Botti* a92 88
4 b m Desert Style(IRE) —Hemaca (Distinctly North (USA))
537[3] ◆ 883[8] 1570[3] 1918[10] 2387[3] 5052[6]

South African (USA) *Mikael Magnusson* a68 56
4 rg m Johannesburg(USA) —River Cache (USA) (Unbridled (USA))
1190[2] 1929[15] 2332[5] 2639[5]

South African Gold (USA) *James Eustace* a67 49
3 ch c Johannesburg(USA) —Coesse Gold (USA) (Seeking The Gold (USA))
218[3] 2215[11] 2566[10] 5669[3] 6212[8] 7310[4] 7501[3] (7639) 8034[6]

Southandwest (IRE) *Alex Hales* a86 83
6 ch g Titus Livius(FR) —Cheviot Indian (IRE) (Indian Ridge)
1458[3] 1962[4] 2284[8] 3518[6] 4333[7] 5064[8] (5768) 6577[8]

South Cape *Gary Moore* a94 94
7 b g Cape Cross(IRE) —Aunt Ruby (USA) (Rubiano (USA))
1383[8] (1618) 2322[3] 3483[3] 5004[6] 5264[6] 5556[3] 5955[6] 6391[2] (7182)

South Easter (IRE) *William Haggas* a107 109
4 ch h Galileo(IRE) —Dance Treat (USA) (Nureyev (USA))
(1016) 1832[3] 2709[6] 3191[11] 5772a[2] ◆

Southern Breeze *Sylvester Kirk* a43
3 b c Dansili—Michelle Ma Belle (IRE) (Shareef Dancer (USA))
180[9] 421[7] 3788[12]

Southern Cape (IRE) *Denis Coakley* a67 72
3 b g Cape Cross(IRE) —Pietra Dura (Cadeaux Genereux)
758[6] 980[10] 1165[4] 2250[5] 4732[2] 5456[2] 6122[7] 6753[P] (Dead)

Southern Regent (IND) *John Quinn* a83 79
9 b g Razeen(USA) —Allinda (IND) (Treasure Leaf (USA))
620[6] 897[2] ◆ 1484[2] (1996) 2976[6]

Southwark Newshawk *Christine Dunnett* a51 55
3 ch f Piccolo—Be Bop Aloha (Most Welcome)
1390[6] 1604[5] 2217[14] 2879[13] 3516[5] 7808[4] 7953[5]

Southwark Newsman *Christine Dunnett* a42 31
3 b g Sulamani(IRE) —Another Nightmare (IRE) (Treasure Kay)
1393[11] 2684[13] 5380[7] 5864[11] 6094[7] 6332[10]

Sovento (GER) *Shaun Harley* a66 65
6 ch g Kornado—Second Game (GER) (Second Set (IRE))
(3078) 5215[6] 6242[4] (7167)

Sovereign Remedy (USA) *Saeed Bin Suroor* a111 96
4 ch h Elusive Quality(USA) —Lailani (Unfuwain (USA))
412a[3] 713a[11]

Sovereign Street *Ann Duffield* 65
2 ch f Compton Place—Mint Royale (IRE) (Cadeaux Genereux)
5509[5] 6301[3] 6892[3]

Sovereignty (JPN) *Dean Ivory* a67 50
8 b g King's Best(USA) —Calando (USA) (Storm Cat (USA))
235[7] 397[5] 498[2] 615[9] 3510[9] (4700) 5254[9] 5897[7] 6671[8] 7168[3] 7298[2] 7613[3] 7825[4] 7890[5]

Soviet Bolt (IRE) *Paul Midgley* a10 31
2 b g Soviet Star(USA) —Easter Princess (FR) (Grand Lodge (USA))
1066[9] 1360[8] 1463[5]

Soviet Secret *Philip McBride* 94
3 b c Soviet Star(USA) —Bonne Etoile (Diesis)
1325[2] 1976[2] 2548[2] 2981[2] (4146) 4438[2] 4593[9] (5685)

Soviet Spring (IRE) *Andrew Balding* a65 66
2 b g Soviet Star(USA) —Spring Will Come (IRE) (Desert Prince (IRE))
3209[11] 4741[4] 6425[2] 7271[7] 7722[5] 8011[10]

Soviet Suspect (IRE) *Amy Weaver* 7
2 b c Ivan Denisovich(IRE) —Testa Unica (ITY) (Nordance (USA))
5328[7] 5836[8] 6576[12]

Sowaylm *Saeed Bin Suroor* a85 95
3 b c Tobougg(IRE) —Ameerat (Mark Of Esteem (IRE))
1500[2] 5955[8]

Soweto Star (IRE) *John Best* 73
2 ch c Johannesburg(USA) —Lady Of Talent (USA) (Siphon (BRZ))
6153[4] ◆ (6878)

So Will I *Doug Watson* a104 69
9 ch g Inchinor—Fur Will Fly (Petong)
604a[3] 817a[4]

Soy Libriano (ARG) *Saeed Bin Suroor* a103
5 br h Ride The Rails(USA) —Soy Ariana (ARG) (Equalize (USA))
415a[5] 513a[2] 820a[12]

So You Think (NZ) *Bart Cummings* 128
4 bb c High Chaparral(IRE) —Triassic (NZ) (Tights (USA))
7291a[3]

Spacecraft (IRE) *Christopher Kellett* a43 44
3 b g Starcraft(NZ) —Brazilian Samba (IRE) (Sadler's Wells (USA))
6814[9] 7183[5] 7451[5] 7633[7] 7840[10]

Spaceman *Martin Bosley* a51 62
7 b g In The Wings—Souk (IRE) (Ahonoora)
5180[9] 5770[12]

Space Pirate *Jeff Pearce* a52 58
5 b g Bahamian Bounty—Science Fiction (Starborough)
100[2] 354[12] 795[9]

Space Station *Simon Dow* a91 89
4 b g Anabaa(USA) —Spacecraft (USA) (Distant View (USA))
1258[10] 1762[2] (2750) (3579) 4296[3] ◆ (5997) 6558[4] 7091[2] 7352[4]

Space War *John Gosden* a67 100
3 b g Elusive City(USA) —Princess Luna (GER) (Grand Lodge (USA))
2968[3] ◆ (3220) 3796[9] 5917[4] 6467[11] (7012)

Spacious *James Fanshawe* 117
5 b m Nayef(USA) —Palatial (Green Desert (USA))
1725[3] 3067[2] 3793[2] 5773a[2] 6561[6]

Spade *David Elsworth* a56 75
2 bl f Halling(USA) —Digger Girl (USA) (Black Minnaloushe (USA))
4844[8] 5691[6] 6155[5] ◆ 7311[6]

Spahi (FR) *David O'Meara* a83 84
4 b g Dubai Destination(USA) —Lusitanie (IRE) (Barathea (IRE))
1011[9] 1467[5] 1925[6] 6921[4] 7149[5] 7284[10]

Spangled Star (USA) *Richard Dutrow Jr* a96
3 ch c Distorted Humor(USA) —Spangled (USA) (Kris S (USA))
2776a[11]

Spanish Acclaim *Andrew Balding* a63 78
3 b g Acclamation—Spanish Gold (Vettori (IRE))
2754[4] (3638) 3833[4] (4739) 5285[8] 6524[9]

Spanish Bounty *Jonathan Portman* a87 98
5 b g Bahamian Bounty—Spanish Gold (Vettori (IRE))
2119[6] 2595[4] 3850[4] 4333[5] 4832[16] 5528[11] 6478[11]

Spanish Cross (IRE) *George Prodromou* a51 53
5 gr m Cape Cross(IRE) —Espana (Hernando (FR))
576[9] 6661[7] 7039[13]

Spanish Duke (IRE) *John Dunlop* a83 103
3 b g Big Bad Bob(IRE) —Spanish Lady (IRE) (Bering)
1330[7] (1734) 2758[8] (4841) 5879[3] 6738[4] 7100[12]

Spanish Island (USA) *Mikael Magnusson* a83 37
3 rg c El Corredor(USA) —Suena Cay (USA) (Maria's Mon (USA))
4340[7] 4679[8] (5028) 5383[12] 5964[7] (6580)

Spanish Moon (USA) *Sir Michael Stoute* a117 123
6 b h El Prado(IRE) —Shining Bright (Rainbow Quest (USA))
1026a[3] 3825[4]

Spanish Pride (IRE) *John Dunlop* 66
2 b f Night Shift(USA) —Spanish Lady (IRE) (Bering)
2505[8] ◆ (3399)

Spares And Repairs *Reg Hollinshead* a34 51
7 b g Robellino(USA) —Lady Blackfoot (Prince Tenderfoot (USA))
7599[9]

Sparkaway *Willie Musson* a49 65
4 ch g Gold Away(IRE) —West River (USA) (Gone West (USA))
875[6] 1012[16] 1134[11] 1756[6] 4765[7] 5564[3] 6132[3] 6693[5] 7157[8]

Sparking *David Barron* a64 60
3 ch f Exceed And Excel(AUS) —Twilight Time (Aragon)
253[2] 5044[3] 5438[6] 6746[3] 7328[8] 7684[2]

Sparkle Park *Brian Meehan* a4 47
3 b f Kyllachy—Petonellajill (Petong)
624[8] 1542[6] 2200[9] 2359[2] 3263[10] 3866[11]

Sparkling Montjeu (IRE) *George Baker* a57 56
5 b m Montjeu(IRE) —Dart Board (IRE) (Darshaan)
140[4] 331[5] 420[10]

Sparkling Smile (IRE) *David Lanigan* a100 93
3 bb f Cape Cross(IRE) —Starlight Smile (USA) (Green Dancer (USA))
(1486) (1652) (3337) (3618) (5727) ◆ 6320[6]

Sparkys Gift (IRE) *Pat Phelan* a53
3 ch g Cadeaux Genereux—Umniya (IRE) (Bluebird (USA))
592[7] 692[5] 3786[9] 5729[7]

Sparky Vixen *Colin Teague* a49 56
6 b m Mujahid(USA) —Lucy Glitters (USA) (Cryptoclearance (USA))
1998[5] 2257[2] 2789[4]

Spartan King (IRE) *Harry Dunlop* a54 62
2 ch c King's Best(USA) —Thermopylae (Tenby)
5263[9] 5878[10] 6333[6]

Spartan Spirit (IRE) *Hughie Morrison* 45
2 b c Invincible Spirit(IRE) —Kylemore (IRE) (Sadler's Wells (USA))
6190[14]

Spartic *Alan McCabe* a75 73
2 gr g Needwood Blade—Celtic Spa (IRE) (Celtic Swing)
2895[5] 3281[2] (3657) 4013[3] 4801[4] (5452) 5969[7] 7718[4]

Spa's Dancer (IRE) *J W Hills* a83 84
3 b g Danehill Dancer(IRE) —Spa (Sadler's Wells (USA))
1260[2] 1844[2] 2544[3] 3207[2] 3863[4] 4357[8] (5658) 6197[4] 6805[5]

Spavento (IRE) *Eric Alston* a61 72
4 gr m Verglas(IRE) —Lanasara (Generous (IRE))
1152[10] 1719[4] 2274[3] 2705[6] 3061[3] 3391[7] 3706[6] 5820[7] 6116[3] 6188[2]
Speak The Truth (IRE) *Jim Boyle* a74 73
4 br g Statue Of Liberty(USA) —Brave Truth (IRE) (Brief Truce (USA))
2331[9] 2846[4] 4255[8] 4930[10] 5005[2] 5262[8] 5614[3] 5995[10] 6515[8] 6880[8] 7154[4] 8035[2]
Spear Thistle *Charlie Mann* a87 68
8 ch g Selkirk(USA) —Ardisia (USA) (Affirmed (USA))
7145[9]
Speartooth *P Bary* 98
3 b c Hernando(FR) —Napoli (Baillamont (USA))
1567a[8]
Special Betty *Derek Haydn Jones* a52
3 b f Tamayaz(CAN) —Natural Key (Safawan)
1181[6] 1994[5]
Special Cuvee *Alison Thorpe* a67 57
4 b g Diktat—Iris May (Brief Truce (USA))
7[2] 87[2] 169[6] 491[3] 518[3] 893[5] 918[10] 1922[11] 4689[4] 4991[6] 5148[3] 5663[12] 7011[7] 7327[6] 7472[2] 7599[5] 7705[4]
Special Duty *Mme C Head-Maarek* 117
3 ch f Hennessy(USA) —Quest To Peak (USA) (Distant View (USA))
1196a[3] (1726) (2158a) 3793[7] 6611a[6]
Special Endeavour (IRE) *William Muir* a56 63
2 b c Sleeping Indian—Hollow Quaill (IRE) (Entrepreneur)
5372[10] 6146[7] 6498[5] 7313[12] 7497[11]
Specialising *Mick Channon* 54
3 ch f Nayef(USA) —Spry (Suave Dancer (USA))
1260[8] 1578[4] 1989[11] 2675[9] 2838[14]
Special Quality (USA) *Robert Cowell* a73 75
3 b g Elusive Quality(USA) —Cut Short (USA) (Diesis)
911[5] 997[3] (1825) 2931[4] 3561[4] 5309[6] 6064[10] 6700[11]
Specific Gravity (FR) *Henry Cecil* 85
2 b c Dansili—Colza (USA) (Alleged (USA))
6127[4] (6676) ◆
Spectacle *Sir Michael Stoute* 30
2 gr f Dalakhani(IRE) —Soviet Moon (IRE) (Sadler's Wells (USA))
7231[17]
Spectacle Du Mars (FR) *X Nakkachdji* a72 92
3 b g Martillo(GER) —Spectacular Groove (USA) (Trempolino (USA))
6640a[5]
Spectait *Jonjo O'Neill* a95 100
8 b g Spectrum(IRE) —Shanghai Girl (Distant Relative)
2027[9] 3069[19] 3969[8] 4537[18] 4830[11] 5702[9] 7382[7] (7680) 8009[3]
Speculate *William Haggas* 75
2 b c Dubawi(IRE) —Petonellajill (Petong)
(6126)
Speed Dating *Sir Mark Prescott Bt* a93 90
4 ch g Pivotal—Courting (Pursuit Of Love)
1996[2] ◆ (2259) ◆ 2723[2] (3079) (3329) ◆ 3416[2] 3873[5] 4694[2] 4891[2] 6562[15]
Speedfit Girl (IRE) *George Margarson* 75
2 b f Kodiac—Staylily (IRE) (Grand Lodge (USA))
4317[9] (4871) 5537[5] (6259)
Speed Gene (IRE) *Martin Bosley* a24 43
2 b f Mujadil(USA) —Tallahassee Spirit (THA) (Presidential (USA))
2238[7] 2591[4] 7271[9]
Speedy Catcher (IRE) *H-A Pantall* 102
4 b h Catcher In The Rye(IRE) —Speedgirl (FR) (Monsun (GER))
2574a[8]
Speedyfix *Christine Dunnett* a71 50
3 b g Chineur(FR) —Zonnebeke (Orpen (USA))
1605[3] 2215[9] 2297[4] 2879[5] 3292[14] 3515[3] 4210[10] 4789[6] (6285) 7194[2] 7390[8]
Speedy Guru *Henry Candy* a70 72
4 b m Ishiguru(USA) —Gowon (Aragon)
287[8]
Speedy Joe *Bryan Smart* a66
2 b c Tobougg(IRE) —Bonny Ruan (So Factual (USA))
7700[8] 7843[3]
Speedy Senorita (IRE) *John Quinn* a45 76
5 b m Fayruz—Sinora Wood (IRE) (Shinko Forest (IRE))
1363[10] 1805[6] 3497[2] 3622[5] 3946[2] 4343[5] 4583[7] 5023[3] 5422[2] 5697[8]
Speedy Xaara (IRE) *Henry Candy* a47
3 b f Xaar—Quinzey (JPN) (Carnegie (IRE))
5668[5] 5960[5] 6332[7]
Speightowns Kid (USA) *F J Brennan* 59
2 rg g Speightstown(USA) —Seize The Wind (USA) (Maria's Mon (USA))
3051[10] 3959[11]
Spennymoor (IRE) *Mahmood Al Zarooni* a67 70
2 b f Exceed And Excel(AUS) —Wolf Cleugh (IRE) (Last Tycoon)
3411[5] 4029[4] 4741[5] (5412) 6311[7]
Spensley (IRE) *James Fanshawe* a95 76
4 ch g Dr Fong(USA) —Genoa (Zafonic (USA))
4597[7] 4859[3] 5311[5] ◆ 5994[8] (6427) (7045) (7612) ◆
Spent *Alison Thorpe* a50 64
5 b g Averti(IRE) —Top (Shirley Heights)
124[8]
Spes Nostra *David Barron* 71
2 b g Ad Valorem(USA) —Millagros (IRE) (Pennekamp (USA))
4821[4]
Spey Song (IRE) *James Bethell* 77
2 b f Singspiel(IRE) —All Embracing (IRE) (Night Shift (USA))
5277[12] ◆ 6222[2] 6748[7] 7057[5]
Sphere (IRE) *John Mackie* a56 68
5 b m Daylami(IRE) —Apple Town (Warning)
4945[5]
Sphinx (FR) *Edwin Tuer* a59 79
12 b g Snurge—Egyptale (Crystal Glitters (USA))
1101[7] 6750[2] 7226[3]
Spice Bar *Declan Carroll* a63 52
6 b g Barathea(IRE) —Scottish Spice (Selkirk (USA))
7157[4]
Spice Fair *Mark Usher* a77 77
3 ch g Trade Fair—Focosa (ITY) (In The Wings)
433[4] 762[12] 1394[3] 1601[5] 2248[3] ◆ 2893[6] 3376[2] 3963[3] (4230) 4907[3] 5382[4] 6084[4]
Spice Power (IRE) *Edward Lynam* 46
2 b f Azamour(IRE) —Summer Spice (IRE) (Key Of Luck (USA))
7256a[9]
Spice Route *Roger L Attfield* a109 114
6 ch g King's Best(USA) —Zanzibar (IRE) (In The Wings)
6236a[4]
Spicewood (USA) *John Gosden* a68 67
3 bb f Dixie Union(USA) —Belterra (USA) (Unbridled (USA))
985[3] ◆ 1329[6] 1621[4] 2219[8] 2901[8]
Spic 'n Span *Ronald Harris* a69 62
5 b g Piccolo—Sally Slade (Dowsing (USA))
431[9] (472) 723[6] 832[2] 913[2] 3052[2] 3255[7] 3308[6] 3722[6] 4326[6] 5025[7] 7720[2] 7764[5]
Spiders Star *Simon West* 69
7 br m Cayman Kai(IRE) —Kiss In The Dark (Starry Night (USA))
1891[6] 2464[2] 2533[4] 2814[3] 3241[5]
Spiders Tern *Milton Bradley* a19
5 b g Sooty Tern—Miss Money Spider (IRE) (Statoblest)
73[5]
Spifer (IRE) *Luca Cumani* 39
2 gr c Motivator—Zarawa (IRE) (Kahyasi)
7178[7]
Spin (IRE) *A P O'Brien* 88
2 ch f Galileo(IRE) —Pieds De Plume (FR) (Seattle Slew (USA))
6005a[10]
Spin Again (IRE) *David Nicholls* a74 70
5 b g Intikhab(USA) —Queen Of The May (IRE) (Nicolotte)
379[2] (505) 892[2] 3061[12] 3539[4] 4555[10] 4795[3] 5405[4] 7564[2] 7701[2]
Spinatrix *Michael Dods* 66
2 b f Diktat—Shrink (Mind Games)
7345 [4]
Spin A Wish *Richard Whitaker* a53 37
2 b f Captain Rio—Be My Wish (Be My Chief (USA))
5755[6] 6980[7] 7127[3] 7395[7]
Spin Cast *Walter Swinburn* a70 24
2 b c Marju(IRE) —Some Diva (Dr Fong (USA))
6126[7] 7065[3] 7335[5]
Spin Cycle (IRE) *Bryan Smart* 114
4 b h Exceed And Excel(AUS) —Spinamix (Spinning World (USA))
1700[7] 2325[4] 3047[7] 3486a[5] 4505[5] 5276[8] 5512[7] 6194[12]
Spinning *David Barron* a101 90
7 ch g Pivotal—Starring (FR) (Ashkalani (IRE))
553[4] ◆ 885[8] 6709[12] 6963[2] 7182[12]
Spinning Bailiwick *Gary Moore* a83 75
4 b m Spinning World(USA) —Zietunzeen (IRE) (Zieten (USA))
(225) 432[8] 580[7] 657[5] 2399[13] 2929[5] 3567[5] 4057[6] 4502[7] 5238[4] 6261[4] 6656[6] 7047 [11] 7737[9] 8033[5]
Spinning Ridge (IRE) *Ronald Harris* a75 76
5 ch g Spinning World(USA) —Summer Style (IRE) (Indian Ridge)
34[3] 262[5] 467[2] 814[8] 855[2] 937[2] 965[2] 1543[2] 1762[4] 1875[3] (2188) 2362[2] 2783[9] 2922[9] 3309[8] 7699[11] 7889[11] 7991[8]
Spinning Spirit (IRE) *James Given* a63 67
3 b g Invincible Spirit(IRE) —Vencera (FR) (Green Tune (USA))
2000[8] 2566[5] 4025[9] (4749) 5409[6] 6226[5] 6461[4] (7144)
Spinning Waters *Eve Johnson Houghton* a57 67
4 b g Vettori(IRE) —Secret Waters (Pharly (FR))
2023[6] 2361[9] 2597[5] 2955[3] 3314[3] 3560[3] 4211[3] 4689[3] 5813[3] 6272[9]
Spinning Well (IRE) *Ralph Beckett* a67 75
4 ch m Pivotal—Kiltubber (IRE) (Sadler's Wells (USA))
(563)
Spinning Wings (IRE) *T Hogan* 90
4 ch m Spinning World(USA) —Wings To Soar (USA) (Woodman (USA))
4081a[4]
Spinning Yarn *B Grizzetti* 87
3 b f Pivotal—Subtle Charm (Machiavellian (USA))
1713a[10] 7370a[11]
Spin Sister *John Gallagher* a36 6
4 b m Umistim—Gloaming (Celtic Swing)
804[7]
Spirited Lady (IRE) *Richard Fahey* a56 48
3 b f Invincible Spirit(IRE) —Lanasara (Generous (IRE))
267[8] 545[5] 922[5] 1392[9] 2503[12]
Spirit Is Needed (IRE) *Mark Johnston* 98
4 b g No Excuse Needed—The Spirit Of Pace (IRE) (In The Wings)
(2243) 2509[2] 2976[15] 3447[9] 3672[13] (4334) 4711[3] 4818[8] 5989[5] (6202) 6437[3] 6736[13]
Spirit Land (IRE) *Mark H Tompkins* a49 53
3 ch c Indian Haven—Reborn (IRE) (Idris (IRE))
1264[6] 2333[7]
Spirit Mirage (ITY) *L Riccardi* 49
3 ch f Spirit Of Desert(IRE) —Illimits (IRE) (Singspiel (IRE))
1419a[14]
Spirit Of A Nation (IRE) *David Brown* a89 91
5 b g Invincible Spirit(IRE) —Fabulous Pet (Somethingfabulous (USA))
1011[8] 4023[6] 5375[5] 5436[5]
Spirit Of Battle (USA) *A Fabre* 105
2 b c Elusive Quality(USA) —Victoria Star (IRE) (Danehill (USA))
6760a[3] 7277a[6]
Spirit Of Coniston *Paul Midgley* a59 73
7 b g Lake Coniston(IRE) —Kigema (IRE) (Case Law)
832[4] 1154[6] 1805[7] 2144[8] 2695[5] 3711[7] 4516[9] 4672[9] 5422[3] 5599[8] 6031[10]
Spirit Of Darley (USA) *Clive Brittain* a17 19
3 bb f Seeking The Gold(USA) —Kahlua Bay (USA) (Catrail (USA))
570[7] 3484[8]
Spirit Of Dixie *David Nicholls* a58 30
3 ch f Kheleyf(USA) —Decatur (Deploy)
2741[9] 3407[8] 7684[4] 7810[2] 7953[9]
Spirit Of Fortune (IRE) *B Grizzetti* 101
3 br c Invincible Spirit(IRE) —Seerah (Machiavellian (USA))
1418a[11]
Spirit Of Gondree (IRE) *John Dunlop* 65
2 b c Invincible Spirit(IRE) —Kristal's Paradise (IRE) (Bluebird (USA))
6145[12] 6514[5] 7099[5]
Spirit Of Grace *Alan McCabe* a56
2 b f Invincible Spirit(IRE) —Scottish Heights (IRE) (Selkirk (USA))
7530[4]
Spirit Of Love (IRE) *Michael Wigham* a66
3 b g Pearl Of Love(IRE) —Sesleria (IRE) (Mark Of Esteem (IRE))
5700[3] 6332[8] 6856[9] 7273[7] 7614[12] 7991[10]
Spirit Of Normandy *Roger Ingram* a38
3 ch f Auction House(USA) —Charlottevalentina (IRE) (Perugino (USA))
980[11] 2197[10] 5175[8]
Spirit Of Oakdale (IRE) *Walter Swinburn* a48 53
2 b g Acclamation—Nichodoula (Doulab (USA))
2677[6] 3459[3] 4110[5] 5660[8] 6082[5]
Spirit Of Sharjah (IRE) *Julia Feilden* a111 105
5 b g Invincible Spirit(IRE) —Rathbawn Realm (Doulab (USA))
(1219) (1519) 2057[7] 3146[11] 3869[7] 4843[11] 5068[3] 5950[9] 6888[11] (7522) (7875)
Spiritofthewest (IRE) *David Brown* a72 80
4 b g Invincible Spirit(IRE) —Rosie's Guest (IRE) (Be My Guest (USA))
74[5] 4024[11] 4121[5] 4394[14] 5557[10]
Spirit Of Xaar (IRE) *David Marnane* a82 85
4 b g Xaar—Jet Cat (IRE) (Catrail (USA))
1408a[6] 6910a[14]
Spiritonthemount (USA) *Peter Hiatt* a57 54
5 bb g Pulpit(USA) —Stirling Bridge (USA) (Prized (USA))
164[10] 322[7] 456[4] 982[8] (2169) 2363[3] 2810[8] 3639[6] 4042[4] 4328[2] 5119[10] 5666[5] 6416[7]
Spiritual Art *Luke Dace* a79 73
4 b m Invincible Spirit(IRE) —Oatey (Master Willie)
151[12] 259[9] 2719[5] ◆ 3158[3] 3464[4] 3862[2] 4306[12] 5003[3] 5237[4] 5541[8] (5753) 6199[11]
Spitfire *John Jenkins* a91 95
5 b g Mujahid(USA) —Fresh Fruit Daily (Reprimand)
(1076) 2316[7] 4832[8] 5393[3] 5551[5] 5884[13] 6625[6] 7238[11] 7554[9]
Splash Point (USA) *Mahmood Al Zarooni* a85 78
2 b c Street Cry(IRE) —Dianehill (IRE) (Danehill (USA))
4089[2] 5717[2] (7112)
Splendid Light *John Gosden* 81
2 gr c Selkirk(USA) —Light Of Morn (Daylami (IRE))
6883[4] ◆
Splendorinthegrass (IRE) *David Lanigan* a103 99
4 ch g Selkirk(USA) —Portelet (Night Shift (USA))
(1455) ◆ 1900[25]
Splinter Cell (USA) *Marco Botti* a100 96
4 bb h Johannesburg(USA) —Rock Salt (Selkirk (USA))
175[2] 553[3] 5188[12] 6318[2]
Split Trois (FR) *Y De Nicolay* 103
2 b f Dubawi(IRE) —Auenpearl (GER) (Zafonic (USA))
(3307a) 4419a[6] 5133a[2] 5899a[4] (6760a) 7277a[10]
Spoken *Roger Charlton* 103
3 ch g Medicean—Spout (Salse (USA))
1734[6] 2254[8] 2863[4] (4044) (4520) ◆ 5511[5] (6203)
Spokesperson (USA) *Mahmood Al Zarooni* 72
2 b c Henny Hughes(USA) —Verbal (USA) (Kingmambo (USA))
2715[3] 3735[10]
Spontaneity (IRE) *Bryan Smart* a57 14
2 b f Holy Roman Emperor(IRE) —Blue Iris (Petong)
6892[9] 7269[5]
Spoof Master (IRE) *Jeff Pearce* a62 61
6 b g Invincible Spirit(IRE) —Talbiya (IRE) (Mujtahid (USA))
8[2] 89[6] 251[7] 674[6] 694[2] 773[5] 1131[9] 1929[3] 2257[10] 6456[11] 7018[9] 7250[9] 7426[10] 7783[4] 7972[9]
Sports Casual *Mrs Y Dunleavy* a65 53
7 br m Singspiel(IRE) —Black Fighter (USA) (Secretariat (USA))
(2433)
Sposalizio (IRE) *Elliott Cooper* 53
3 ch g Dr Fong(USA) —Wedding Cake (IRE) (Groom Dancer (USA))
2011[7] 2499[4] 4407[15]
Spread Boy (IRE) *Alan Berry* a7 64
3 b g Tagula(IRE) —Marinka (Pivotal)
3554[4] 4018[4] 4340[5] 5337[4] 6144[5] 6710[10] 6966[3] 7144[6] 7833[6]
Spring Bouquet (IRE) *Mick Channon* a61 63
2 b f King's Best(USA) —Marasem (Cadeaux Genereux)
3778[5] 4187[2]
Spring Breeze *John Quinn* a59 53
9 ch g Dr Fong(USA) —Trading Aces (Be My Chief (USA))
15[2] 140[2] 506[4] 2085[2] 2464[5] 2533[5] 5119[11] 5642[5]
Spring Bridge (IRE) *Linda Jewell* a51 33
4 b g Tagula(IRE) —Miss Lainey (IRE) (Woodborough (USA))
14[9] 146[7] 391[7] 495[11] 687[4] 845[7]
Spring Fashion (IRE) *Marco Botti* a51 48
4 b m Galileo(IRE) —Darina (IRE) (Danehill (USA))
131[11]
Spring Green *Hughie Morrison* a81 81
4 b m Bahamian Bounty—Star Tulip (Night Shift (USA))
1827[3] 2622[2] 2973[6] 4090[4] 6539[4] 7180[7] 7285[10]
Spring Hawk (IRE) *T G McCourt* a69 69
4 ch m Hawk Wing(USA) —Spring Easy (IRE) (Alzao (USA))
176[6] 210[2] 7078a[12]
Spring Heather (IRE) *John Dunlop* 53
3 b f Montjeu(IRE) —Spotlight (Dr Fong (USA))
1581[11] 2412[5] 2924[9]
Spring Horizon (IRE) *Zoe Davison* a49 49
4 b m Namid—Bye Bold Aileen (IRE) (Warning)
2751[9] 2964[15] 5025[8] 5176[8] 5715[4] 6018[7] 6285[8] 7155[7]
Spring Jim *James Fanshawe* a88 94
9 b g First Trump—Spring Sixpence (Dowsing (USA))
1821[12] 6565[9] 7061[3] 7781[2]
Spring Leap *Robert Cowell* a50
3 b g Kyllachy—Roses Of Spring (Shareef Dancer (USA))
7684[5] 7960[6]
Spring Of Fame (USA) *Saeed Bin Suroor* a102 111
4 b h Grand Slam(USA) —Bloomy (USA) (Polish Numbers (USA))
517a[4] 7237[7]
Spring Secret *Bryn Palling* a64 79
4 b g Reset(AUS) —Miss Brooks (Bishop Of Cashel)
2024[11] 5386[8] 6328[2] 6543[5] 7015[6] (7306)
Spring Stock *Brendan Powell* 61
3 b f Tobougg(IRE) —April Stock (Beveled (USA))
4115[10] 5038[7] 5474[5] 6816[P]
Spring Style (IRE) *B Cecil* a99 100
5 ch m Pivotal—Clear Spring (USA) (Irish River (FR))
4887a[4]
Springwell Giant (IRE) *Alan McCabe* a61 49
3 ch g Choisir(AUS) —Glasnas Giant (Giant's Causeway (USA))
507[4] 1923[8] 2221[9] 3113[10] 3972[5] 5926[6]
Sprint Car (FR) *J-L Gay* a55 59
6 b h Sleeping Car(FR) —Lady Yasmine (FR) (Quiludi (FR))
273a[8]
Spruce (USA) *Julia Feilden* a97 106
4 b g Maria's Mon(USA) —Valentine Band (USA) (Dixieland Band (USA))
396[2] ◆ (476) (636) (735) ◆ (785) ◆ 903[5] 1031[2] 1529[4]
Spruzzo *C W Thornton* a46 56
4 b g Emperor Fountain—Ryewater Dream (Touching Wood (USA))
(1891) 2085[6] 2659[10] 3535[5]
Spume (IRE) *John Balding* a43 25
6 b g Alhaarth(IRE) —Sea Spray (IRE) (Royal Academy (USA))
1980[10] 2388[10] 2694[8] 2995[10]
Spyder *Jane Chapple-Hyam* a42 78
2 b g Resplendent Glory(IRE) —Collect (Vettori (IRE))
5629[7] (7303) 7536[4]
Spying *Ann Duffield* a88 91
3 ch g Observatory(USA) —Mint Royale (IRE) (Cadeaux Genereux)
4371[3] ◆ 5030[8] 6355[10] 7182[7] 7411[8]
Squad *Simon Dow* a73 74
4 ch g Choisir(AUS) —Widescreen (USA) (Distant View (USA))
1303[6] 6554[7] 7167[10] 7490[2] 7765[8]
Squall *Jeremy Noseda* a81 81
3 b g Dubawi(IRE) —Exciting Times (FR) (Jeune Homme (USA))
1325[3] ◆ 1844[5] 2128[4] (3733) 4265[3] ◆ 5304[5] 5533[5] 6205[P] 7114[2]
Square Of Gold (FR) *Tony Carroll* 37
4 ch g Gold Away(IRE) —All Square (FR) (Holst (USA))
3264[10] 3853[9]
Squires Gate (IRE) *B W Hills* 79
2 b g Namid—Roselyn (Efisio)
1009[3] 3624[8] 4392[2] 4650[5] (6324) 6636[6]
Squirtle (IRE) *Mark Brisbourne* a69 69
7 ch m In The Wings—Manilia (FR) (Kris)
198[12]
Sraab *Clive Brittain* 60
3 ch c Singspiel(IRE) —Exultate Jubilate (USA) (With Approval (CAN))
3621[4]
Srda (USA) *Clive Brittain* a89 84
3 b f Kingmambo(USA) —Marisa (USA) (Swain (IRE))
(759) ◆ (964) ◆ 1312[11] 1836[3] 3694[7] 4139[10]
Sri Kuantan (IRE) *David Bourton* a43 82
6 ch g Spinning World(USA) —Miss Asia Quest (Rainbow Quest (USA))
1427[11] 1689[7] 2343[9] 2995[13] 3122[15] 5437[12] 6033[5] 6662[9] 7089[7]
Sri Putra *Michael Jarvis* 118
4 b h Oasis Dream—Wendylina (IRE) (In The Wings)
(1328) ◆ 2470[8] 3693[2] 4535[2] 5804a[2] 6925[8] 7854a[11]
Ssafa *J W Hills*
2 b f Motivator—Orange Sunset (IRE) (Roanoke (USA))
7232[18]
Stacelita (FR) *J-C Rouget* 122
4 b m Monsun(GER) —Soignee (GER) (Dashing Blade)
2374a[4] (3045a) 4575[2] (5348a) 6613a[2] 7854a[8]
Stacey *Michael Blanshard* a59 55
2 b f Iceman—Candescent (Machiavellian (USA))
1577[15] 2867[7] 3209[4] 3767[3] 4623[11] 5660[6] 6411[10] 7464[7] 7650[6]

Stadium Of Light (IRE) *Brian Ellison* a77 71
3 b g Fantastic Light(USA) —Treble Seven (USA) (Fusaichi Pegasus (USA))
864^{5} 1060^{4} 2252^{4} 2650^{4} 4493^{5} 5180^{3} 6450^{4} 7465^{3} 7695^{2} (7896)

Staerough View *Keith Reveley*
2 b g Whipper(USA) —Cheviot Hills (USA) (Gulch (USA))
6894^{15}

Staff Sergeant *Jim Goldie* a76 61
3 b g Dubawi(IRE) —Miss Particular (IRE) (Sadler's Wells (USA))
(1143) 3949^{7}

Stage Acclaim (IRE) *Dr Richard Newland* a64 65
5 b g Acclamation—Open Stage (IRE) (Sadler's Wells (USA))
2285^{5} 3223^{3} 3324^{2} (4441) 5119^{2} 5468^{3}

Stagecoach Emerald *Terry Clement* a67 46
8 ch g Spectrum(IRE) —Musician (Shirley Heights)
41^{7} 811^{5} 1071^{11} 6065^{14} 7388^{10}

Stage Master (USA) *David Wachman* a74 85
2 ch c Johannesburg(USA) —Charlotte Corday (Kris)
6727a^{9}

Stags Leap (IRE) *P Monteith* a85 84
3 b g Refuse To Bend(IRE) —Swingsky (IRE) (Indian Ridge)
840^{4} 1313^{9} 2562^{6} (2820) 5121^{10} 5408^{6} 6224^{12}

Stalingrad (USA) *James Cassidy* 87
6 b g Glitterman(USA) —Formeredith (USA) (Dynaformer (USA))
1435a^{10}

Stamford Blue *Ronald Harris* a46 69
9 b g Bluegrass Prince(IRE) —Fayre Holly (IRE) (Fayruz)
1799^{5} 2021^{3} 2246^{11} 2590^{11} 2840^{7} 3254^{3} 3556^{4} 4130^{6} 4326^{2} 5112^{2} (5580) 5714^{4} 5875^{7} 6515^{11} 6952^{5}

Stamp Duty (IRE) *Ollie Pears* 70
2 b g Ad Valorem(USA) —Lothian Lass (IRE) (Daylami (IRE))
(6458) 7085^{11}

Stand Guard *Jane Chapple-Hyam* a96 70
6 b g Danehill(USA) —Protectress (Hector Protector (USA))
6^{6} 197^{9} 324^{7} (725) 863^{8} 1015^{13} 1348^{4} 5716^{10} 6428^{11} 6797^{3} 7428^{7} 7756^{5} 7881^{7}

Standout *Richard Hannon* 68
2 b c Oratorio(IRE) —Muwali (USA) (Kingmambo (USA))
2594^{12} 2839^{4} 5385^{2} 5709^{5} 6471^{5} 6802^{3} 6979^{3} ◆

Standpoint *Reg Hollinshead* a85 87
4 b g Oasis Dream—Waki Music (USA) (Miswaki (USA))
1051^{6} 1509^{3} 1933^{5} 2129^{4} 3172^{4} 3396^{2} 3846^{2} 4603^{6} 5789^{9} 6167^{4} 6701^{4}

Stand To Attention (IRE) *P D Deegan* 89
2 b c Diamond Green(FR) —Meas (IRE) (Mark Of Esteem (IRE))
(6230a)

Stanley Bridge *Alan Berry* 25
3 b g Avonbridge—Antonia's Folly (Music Boy)
1667^{8} 2209^{10} 4151^{9}

Stanley Goodspeed *J W Hills* a83 76
7 ch g Inchinor—Flying Carpet (Barathea (IRE))
(397) (442) 486^{7} 808^{4} 943^{7} 1875^{7} 2053^{3} 2705^{8} 2840^{4}

Stanley Rigby *Richard Fahey* a56 55
4 b g Dr Fong(USA) —Crystal (IRE) (Danehill (USA))
229^{2} ◆ 389^{5} 854^{5} 995^{5} 1635^{2} 2489^{4} 7270^{13} 7678^{4}

Stan's Cool Cat (IRE) *Paul Cole* a81 89
4 b m One Cool Cat(USA) —Beautiful France (IRE) (Sadler's Wells (USA))
6151^{8} 6326^{5}

Stansonnit *Alan Swinbank* a83 47
2 br g Shirocco(GER) —Twilight Sonnet (Exit To Nowhere (USA))
7172^{4} (7536)

Stanstill (IRE) *Michael Kent* a101 99
4 b g Statue Of Liberty(USA) —Fervent Wish (Rainbow Quest (USA))
(1069) 2071^{4} 2541^{4} 3447^{4} ◆ 4400^{11} 6946a^{9}

Staraco (FR) *Rod Collet* a80 88
6 ch h Loup Solitaire(USA) —Linorova (USA) (Trempolino (USA))
304a^{4} 549a^{5}

Star Addition *Eric Alston* a62 62
4 ch g Medicean—Star Cast (IRE) (In The Wings)
1115^{13} 1276^{12} 2274^{6} 2668^{5} 3025^{5} 3520^{2} 3676^{2} 4120^{3} 4546^{5} 4867^{9} (6905) 7814^{10}

Starbougg *Keith Reveley* 37
6 b m Tobougg(IRE) —Celestial Welcome (Most Welcome)
1807^{11} 2833^{4}

Starbound (IRE) *William Haggas* 34
2 ch f Captain Rio—Glinting Desert (IRE) (Desert Prince (IRE))
7345^{9}

Starburst *Gay Kelleway* a71 60
5 b m Fantastic Light(USA) —Rasmalai (Sadler's Wells (USA))
121^{3} 529^{8} 1012^{14} 2902^{9} 3110^{5} 3403^{5} 3684^{5} 4329^{6} (5840) 6314^{8} 7562^{7} 7732^{7}

Star Choice *Jeff Pearce* a76 72
5 ch g Choisir(AUS) —Bay Queen (Damister (USA))
13^{2} 121^{8} 426^{2} 554^{3} 660^{2} (764) (842) 938^{5} 1053^{2}

Starclass *Walter Swinburn* 82
3 b f Starcraft(NZ) —Classic Millennium (Midyan (USA))
2122^{5} (3333) 3863^{7} 4387^{3} 5396^{3}

Star Commander *Mark H Tompkins* 69
2 b c Desert Style(IRE) —Barakat (Bustino)
2594^{13} 6128^{4} 6635^{5}

Star Concert (USA) *Amanda Perrett* a68 69
2 bb f Sky Mesa(USA) —Concert Hall (USA) (Stravinsky (USA))
4508^{8} ◆ 5029^{5}

Star Crowned (USA) *R Bouresly* a111 110
7 b h Kingmambo(USA) —Fashion Star (USA) (Chief's Crown (USA))
336a^{8} 437a^{2} 515a^{5} 606a^{5} (707a) 822a^{2} 1021a^{14}

Star Cruiser (USA) *Tim Easterby* 49
3 b g Golden Missile(USA) —Beautiful Star (USA) (War Chant (USA))
1335^{11} 1651^{6} 1987^{4} 2787^{8}

Star Danser *Tom Keddy* a43
2 b c Dansili—Violette (Observatory (USA))
7873^{10}

Stardust Dancer *Paul Green* 45
3 b g Ziggy's Dancer(USA) —Veni Vici (IRE) (Namaqualand (USA))
6470^{9} 6876^{15}

Starfala *Paul Cole* a89 106
5 gr m Galileo(IRE) —Farfala (FR) (Linamix (FR))
1898^{3} 2345^{5} 3195^{5} 4507^{7}

Starfish Bay (USA) *Todd Pletcher* 102
4 b m Elusive Quality(USA) —Touch Love (USA) (Not For Love (USA))
4505^{10}

Starfist (TUR) *E Yilmaz* 77
4 b h Islambol(TUR) —Belit (TUR) (Abbas (TUR))
5803a^{11}

Stargaze (IRE) *Alan Bailey* a101 102
3 b g Oasis Dream—Dafariyna (IRE) (Nashwan (USA))
945^{3}

Stargazing (IRE) *Brian Meehan* a58 56
4 b m Galileo(IRE) —Autumnal (IRE) (Indian Ridge)
3157^{6} 4339^{10} 5395^{4} 6133^{6} 6515^{9} 7018^{4} 7300^{5} 7604^{5}

Stargazy *Alastair Lidderdale* a45 58
6 b g Observatory(USA) —Romantic Myth (Mind Games)
3129^{9} 3280^{6} (3291) 3524^{8} 3591^{4} 3727^{14} 4366^{12} 4434^{12} 4738^{5}

Star Hill *Alan King* a69 64
3 b f Starcraft(NZ) —Mistress Bankes (IRE) (Petardia)
5366^{4} 5902^{4} 7338^{5}

Star In Flight *Brian Meehan* a57
3 b g Mtoto—Star Entry (In The Wings)
7451^{3}

Starkat *Jane Chapple-Hyam* a80 96
4 b m Diktat—Star Of Normandie (USA) (Gulch (USA))
2723^{4} 3764^{7} (4752) 5563^{2} 6095^{4} 6361^{15} 7349^{6}

Stark Contrast (USA) *Mark Usher* a66 49
6 ch g Gulch(USA) —A Stark Is Born (USA) (Graustark)
124^{11} 211^{9} 347^{9} 682^{6}

Stark Danon (FR) *W Hickst* 95
2 b c Marchand De Sable(USA) —Sue Generoos (IRE) (Spectrum (IRE))
7544a^{4}

Starla Dancer (GER) *Richard Fahey* a74 85
4 b m Danehill Dancer(IRE) —Starla (GER) (Lando (GER))
1013^{6} 1863^{7} 2452^{3} 3202^{5} 4389^{12} (5096) 6691^{4} 7228^{2}

Starlight Gazer *Jimmy Fox* a49 18
7 b g Observatory(USA) —Dancing Fire (USA) (Dayjur (USA))
1172^{10} 1763^{12}

Starlight Muse (IRE) *Ed McMahon* a68 74
3 gr f Desert Style(IRE) —Downland (USA) (El Prado (IRE))
527^{6} 793^{2} 985^{4} 1269^{2} 1685^{5} 2824^{3} 3311^{3} 3751^{5} 3898^{9} ◆

Starlight Walk *Roger Charlton* 49
2 b f Galileo(IRE) —Tempting Prospect (Shirley Heights)
7231^{11}

Star Links (USA) *S Donohoe* a79 87
4 b g Bernstein(USA) —Startarette (USA) (Dixieland Band (USA))
1408a^{14} 2428^{8} 4515^{2} 6935^{2} (7214) 7856^{4}

Starlish (IRE) *E Lellouche* a103 115
5 b h Rock Of Gibraltar(IRE) —Stylish (Anshan)
953a^{2} 1255a^{6} 1747a^{5} 3045a^{6} 5107a^{4} 6344a^{5} 6881a^{7}

Starluck (IRE) *Alan Fleming* a103 95
5 gr g Key Of Luck(USA) —Sarifa (IRE) (Kahyasi)
(769)

Star Now *Mick Channon* 74
2 b f Librettist(USA) —Affair Of State (IRE) (Tate Gallery (USA))
(3288)

Star Of Dance (IRE) *Sir Michael Stoute* 77
2 b c Danehill Dancer(IRE) —Miss Honorine (IRE) (Highest Honor (FR))
4490^{6} ◆ 5277^{3} ◆

Star Of Kalani (IRE) *R D Wylie* 38
3 b g Ashkalani(IRE) —La Bekkah (FR) (Nononito (FR))
2673^{7} 2853^{8} 3532^{8} 4087^{5}

Star Of Pompey *Mark Hoad* a62 63
6 b m Hernando(FR) —Discerning (Darshaan)
1454^{5} 1849^{7} 3195^{17} 3819^{6}

Star Of Soho (IRE) *Edward Creighton* a23 39
3 b f Starcraft(NZ) —Trois Graces (USA) (Alysheba (USA))
1260^{14} 1621^{11} 6525^{11} 6678^{7}

Star Power (IRE) *J S Bolger* a76 73
3 b c Galileo(IRE) —Billet (IRE) (Danehill (USA))
7589a^{10}

Star Promise *David Barron* a75 76
3 b f Mujahid(USA) —Diamond Promise (IRE) (Fayruz)
17^{4}

Star Prospect (IRE) *Luke Comer* a59
3 b c Fasliyev(USA) —Emy's Girl (USA) (Prospect Bay (CAN))
1589^{4} 2335^{5}

Star Rebel *Jane Chapple-Hyam* 59
2 b g Doyen(IRE) —Star Of Normandie (USA) (Gulch (USA))
7203^{9}

Star Rover (IRE) *David Evans* a80 102
3 ch g Camacho—Charlene Lacy (IRE) (Pips Pride)
1007^{11} 1700^{10} 1860^{5} 3895^{6} 4391^{15} 4541^{3} 4616^{3} 4819^{4} 4937^{4} (5632) 5851^{5} 6319^{7} 6663^{6} 6918^{9} 7014^{9}

Starry Mount *Andrew Haynes* a57 76
3 ch g Observatory(USA) —Lady Lindsay (IRE) (Danehill Dancer (IRE))
1921^{5} 3949^{6} 4585^{2} 5146^{6} 5394^{6} 6692^{8} 6864^{15} 7476^{3} 7832^{5} 7897^{3}

Starshine *Roger Charlton* a65 68
3 b f Danehill Dancer(IRE) —In The Limelight (IRE) (Sadler's Wells (USA))
2043^{7} 2890^{7} 5902^{5} 6668^{4} 7011^{5} 7181^{3} 7504^{7}

Starspangledbanner (AUS) *A P O'Brien* 125
4 ch c Choisir(AUS) —Gold Anthem (AUS) (Made Of Gold (USA))
2030^{5} (3192) ◆ (3870) 5276^{2} 5744^{5}

Star Star (FR) *M Ramin* 57
7 b g Pelder(IRE) —Star Swing (FR) (Riverquest (FR))
5378a^{8}

Starstreamer (IRE) *Marcus Tregoning* a24 31
3 ch f Captain Rio—Petra Nova (First Trump)
5028^{10} 5668^{9} 6285^{11}

Star Strider *Tom Keddy* a80 67
6 gr g Royal Applause—Oneforthediteh (USA) (With Approval (CAN))
129^{5} 397^{6} 555^{11}

Starstruck Peter (IRE) *Jim Best* a58 64
6 b g Iron Mask(USA) —Daraliya (IRE) (Kahyasi)
6272^{10}

Starstuded (IRE) *William Haggas* a63
2 b f Galileo(IRE) —Miss Demure (Shy Groom (USA))
7312^{3} 7530^{5}

Star Surprise *Michael Bell* 85
2 ch c Dubawi(IRE) —Dubai Surprise (IRE) (King's Best (USA))
3219^{7} 3631^{5} (4263) 4801^{7} (5969) 6982^{4}

Startle *Richard Hannon* 66
3 b g Starcraft(NZ) —Witness (Efisio)
2121^{3} 2925^{9} 4107^{6}

Star Today *Brian Meehan* 67
2 b f Invincible Spirit(IRE) —Bint Zamayem (IRE) (Rainbow Quest (USA))
2616^{5} ◆ 3590^{6} 4293^{3} 4600^{6} 5261^{6}

Start Right *Luca Cumani* a76 103
3 b g Footstepsinthesand—Time Crystal (IRE) (Sadler's Wells (USA))
1502^{7} 3351^{2} 3824^{8} (4144) (4459) ◆ 5571a^{4} 6562^{17}

Star Twilight *Derek Shaw* a48 67
3 b f King's Best(USA) —Star Express (Sadler's Wells (USA))
2648^{3} (4720) 4892^{5} 5956^{5} 6299^{3} 7193^{5}

Star Val (FR) *Mme C Barande-Barbe* a72 72
6 b m Enrique—Garden Star (FR) (Dr Devious (IRE))
560a^{9} 690a^{0}

Starwatch *John Bridger* a69 77
3 b g Observatory(USA) —Trinity Reef (Bustino)
233^{6} 538^{5} 2459^{4} 2784^{2} 3154^{4} 3350^{5} 4291^{3} (4503) 4777^{3} 5182^{2} 5417^{3} (5890) 6438^{8} 7093^{10} 7285^{6} 7737^{4} 8014^{4}

Starway To Heaven *J Jay*
5 b m Beat All(USA) —Gourmet (IRE) (Homo Sapien)
1536^{9}

Stash *Reg Hollinshead* a81 42
4 b g Bold Edge—Gemtastic (Tagula (IRE))
138^{3} 462^{11} 774^{9}

State Fair *Julie-Ann Camacho* a34 79
3 b g Marju(IRE) —Baralinka (IRE) (Barathea (IRE))
2852^{4} 3831^{6} (4898)

State Gathering *Henry Candy* a89 84
3 b g Royal Applause—Flag (Selkirk (USA))
1308^{4} 2170^{5} 3215^{3} (3782) ◆ 4699^{4} 5750^{6}

State General (IRE) *Tony Carroll* a58 61
4 b g Statue Of Liberty(USA) —Nisibis (In The Wings)
746^{6} 1028^{17} 1441^{7} 1637^{7} 1877^{11} 2866^{12}

Stately Victor (USA) *Michael J Maker* a118 92
3 b c Ghostzapper(USA) —Collect The Cash (USA) (Dynaformer (USA))
1714a^{8} 2776a^{7}

State Of Mind *Paul Cole* a72 79
2 b c Zamindar(USA) —Pulpeuse (IRE) (Pursuit Of Love)
5523^{3} ◆ 5895^{3} (6153)

State Opera *Mark Johnston* 89
2 b c Shamardal(USA) —Strings (Unfuwain (USA))
(6222) 6560^{22}

State Senator (USA) *Sir Mark Prescott Bt* 69
2 bb c Mr Greeley(USA) —Summer Night (Nashwan (USA))
6811^{5} ◆

Stateside (CAN) *Richard Fahey* a51 66
5 b m El Corredor(USA) —Double Trick (USA) (Phone Trick (USA))
367^{10} 753^{11} 983^{9} 1427^{7} 2433^{8} 2583^{5} 3074^{8}

State Visit *Amy Weaver* a61 70
3 b g Dr Fong(USA) —Saint Ann (USA) (Geiger Counter (USA))
3002^{5} (6476) 7003^{6}

Status Symbol (IRE) *Giles Bravery* a105 85
5 ch g Polish Precedent(USA) —Desired (Rainbow Quest (USA))
1479^{3} (5700) ◆ 6091^{3} 7044^{3} ◆ 7297^{5} 7594^{3}

St Augustine (IRE) *John Best* a79 62
2 b c Holy Roman Emperor(IRE) —Najiya (Nashwan (USA))
5523^{4} 6465^{10} (7294)

Stay Alive (IRE) *B Grizzetti* 100
2 br f Iffraaj—Pursuit Of Life (Pursuit Of Love)
6975a^{2}

Stay Cool (FR) *D Smaga* a56 70
4 b h One Cool Cat(USA) —A La Longue (GER) (Mtoto)
1055a^{9}

Stay On Track (IRE) *Edward Vaughan* a49 27
3 b c Refuse To Bend(IRE) —Blue Lightning (Machiavellian (USA))
1050^{6} 1165^{7} 1643^{10} 2200^{8}

Stay Put (USA) *Steve Margolis* a106
3 ch c Broken Vow(USA) —O K Mom (USA) (Dixieland Band (USA))
2776a^{5}

Stay Thirsty (USA) *Todd Pletcher* a108
2 bb c Bernardini(USA) —Marozia (USA) (Storm Bird (CAN))
7363a^{5}

Steady Gaze *Gary Moore* a40 40
5 b g Zamindar(USA) —Krisia (Kris)
1078^{6} 1262^{11}

Steed *Kevin Ryan* a65 66
3 b g Mujahid(USA) —Crinkle (IRE) (Distant Relative)
(1402) ◆ 2069^{11} 2834^{16} 4193^{7} 4479^{7} 6226^{3} 7467^{11} (7845)

Steel City Boy (IRE) *Derek Shaw* a74 51
7 b g Bold Fact(USA) —Balgren (IRE) (Ballad Rock)
77^{4} 132^{2} (185) 555^{10} (723) 778^{4} 869^{2} 935^{5} 972^{7} 1154^{11} 1320^{6} 1915^{7} 2646^{4} 2896^{6} 3024^{9} 7494^{11} 7868^{8}

Steelcut *Andrew Reid* a74 84
6 b g Iron Mask(USA) —Apple Sauce (Prince Sabo)
2639^{4} (2973) ◆ 3417^{3} 3736^{4} ◆ 4148^{8} 5025^{2} 5285^{5} 6523^{7} 6987^{12}

Steele Tango (USA) *Roger Teal* a78 113
5 ch h Okawango(USA) —Waltzing Around (IRE) (Ela-Mana-Mou)
1328^{4} 1532^{6} 2470^{5} 3144^{14} 3632^{4} 4139^{4} 6195^{2} 6562^{2} 6885^{2}

Steel Free (IRE) *Michael Madgwick* a74 76
4 b m Danehill Dancer(IRE) —Candelabra (Grand Lodge (USA))
1064^{3} ◆ 1797^{8} 2750^{5} 3001^{2} 3592^{6} 4492^{2} 5149^{7}

Steel Mask (IRE) *Mel Brittain* a40 47
5 b h Iron Mask(USA) —Thorn Tree (Zafonic (USA))
403^{8} 699^{7}

Steel Rain *Nikki Evans* a43
2 b c Striking Ambition—Concentration (IRE) (Mind Games)
5900^{8} 6742^{10} 7272^{10} 7667^{4}

Steel Stockholder *Mel Brittain* a74 73
4 b h Mark Of Esteem(IRE) —Pompey Blue (Abou Zouz (USA))
(292) 1030^{12} 3876^{18} 4154^{7} 4394^{9} 5499^{7} 6267^{3}

Steel Trade *Mel Brittain* 75
4 b g Sakhee(USA) —Hammiya (IRE) (Darshaan)
1926^{7} 2421^{4} 2625^{5} 2766^{2}

Steely Bird *Jo Crowley* a50 59
3 gr g Needwood Blade—La Cygne Blanche (IRE) (Saddlers' Hall (IRE))
340^{7} 3444^{7} 4676^{10} 5963^{11}

Steenbok (IRE) *John Gosden* a67 60
2 b c Shamardal(USA) —Woodrising (Nomination)
7058^{8} 7386^{6} 7595^{4}

Steeple Caster *Milton Bradley*
4 ch g Compton Place—Antonia's Double (Primo Dominie)
1731^{11} 3374^{11} 5112^{8}

Stef And Stelio *Gerard Butler* a74 45
3 ch g Bertolini(USA) —Cashmere (Barathea (IRE))
1280^{6} 1449^{2} 2408^{5} 3276^{7} 4133^{9} 5073^{2} 5661^{6} 6522^{8} 7128^{11} 7912^{4}

Stefanki (IRE) *Gary Moore* a81 84
3 b g Danehill Dancer(IRE) —Ghana (IRE) (Lahib (USA))
(4031) ◆ 4297^{2} 4509^{9} ◆ 6197^{RR} 6438^{RR} 7573^{RR}

Steinbeck (IRE) *A P O'Brien* a92 114
3 b c Footstepsinthesand—Castara Beach (IRE) (Danehill (USA))
2354a^{4} 3048^{8} 4312a^{2} 4613a^{6} (6006a)

Stella Marris *Christopher Wilson*
3 br f Danroad(AUS) —Riyoom (USA) (Vaguely Noble)
5487^{9}

Stellar Cause (USA) *Roger Curtis* a37 71
4 ch g Giant's Causeway(USA) —Stellar (USA) (Grand Slam (USA))
309^{13}

Stellarina (IRE) *William Knight* a68 54
4 b m Night Shift(USA) —Accelerating (USA) (Lear Fan (USA))
(5214) 6024^{12}

Stellite *Jim Goldie* a71 76
10 ch g Pivotal—Donation (Generous (IRE))
1102^{6} 1672^{8} 2211^{7} 2453^{2} 2858^{2} 3150^{4} 3706^{3} (3905) 4585^{9} 4822^{4} 5241^{4} 5732^{6} 6107^{9} 7055^{11}

Stentorian (IRE) *Mark Johnston* 96
2 ch c Street Cry(IRE) —Nomistakeaboutit (CAN) (Affirmed (USA))
2389^{5} (3112) ◆ 3645a^{2} 4468^{2} 5306^{6} 6200^{15}

Stephie *Michael Easterby* 42
4 b m Sulamani(IRE) —Bahirah (Ashkalani (IRE))
3207^{13} 3428^{8} 3595^{8} 4411^{9} 4648^{14}

Step In Time (IRE) *Mark Johnston* a58 83
3 b c Giant's Causeway(USA) —Cash Run (USA) (Seeking The Gold (USA))
2348^{3} 3208^{5} ◆ 3451^{5} 3689^{5} (3990) 4394^{13} 4850^{4} 5789^{14} 6394^{10} 6801^{11}

Step It Up (IRE) *Jim Boyle* a83 77
6 ch g Daggers Drawn(USA) —Leitrim Lodge (IRE) (Classic Music (USA))
307^{8} 736^{4} ◆ 846^{4} 987^{5} 1258^{6} (2001) 2310^{7} 2681^{13} 2973^{8} 3440^{7} 4292^{7} 5207^{5} 5628^{6} 6018^{5}

Steps (IRE) *Michael Jarvis* a82 73
2 b c Verglas(IRE) —Killinallan (Vettori (IRE))
6878^{2} 7294^{2} 7418^{3} (7858) 8020^{2}

Step To It (IRE) *Kevin Ryan* a58 33
3 b g Footstepsinthesand—Lilly Gee (IRE) (Ashkalani (IRE))
(597) 861^{4} 909^{4} 4337^{15} 4687^{9} 5216^{8} 5596^{8}

Step Up (ITY) *A Candi* 93
2 b c Footstepsinthesand—Lady Melbourne (IRE) (Indian Ridge)
3253a^{3}

Sternian *Mark Rimmer* a52 57
3 ch f Where Or When(IRE) —Fly In Style (Hernando (FR))
219[3] 340[8] 475[3] 776[4] 872[9] 1132[6] (1461) 2042[9] 2906[5] 3413[5] 3662[8] (4113) 4212[7] 4718[3] 5923[7]

Sternlight (IRE) *Ed McMahon* a79 73
3 b c Kheleyf(USA) —Sail By Night (USA) (Nureyev (USA))
35[6] ◆ (253) ◆

Stetson *Alan Swinbank* 63
4 b g Groom Dancer(USA) —Mindomica (Dominion)
1572[2]

Steuben (GER) *J Hirschberger* 102
4 ch h Monsun(GER) —Schwarzach (GER) (Grand Lodge (USA))
1420a[3] 1856a[6] 2806a[5]

Steve's Champ (CHI) *Rune Haugen* 100
10 b g Foxhound(USA) —Emigracion (CHI) (Semenenko (USA))
4526a[5]

Stevie Bee Party *Ian McInnes* 18
2 b g Superior Premium—Amy Leigh (IRE) (Imperial Frontier (USA))
2272[9] 2522[8] 2836[5] 3175[9]

Stevie Gee (IRE) *Ian Williams* a77 92
6 b g Invincible Spirit(IRE) —Margaree Mary (CAN) (Seeking The Gold (USA))
2328[9] 3438[7] 3667[6] (4413) 5082[8] 5495[7] 5884[12] 6478[7] 6701[8] 7274[9]

Stevie Thunder *Ian Williams* a81 94
5 ch g Storming Home—Social Storm (USA) (Future Storm (USA))
2640[8]

St Ignatius *K O Cunningham-Brown* a72 34
3 b g Ishiguru(USA) —Branston Berry (IRE) (Mukaddamah (USA))
149[4] 370[5] 594[3] (784) 2868[10] 5769[8] 6812[13] 7314[8] 7537[13]

Stilettoesinthemud (IRE) *James Given* a54 57
2 ch f Footstepsinthesand—The Stick (Singspiel (IRE))
5531[6] 6047[10] 6866[11]

Stimulation (IRE) *Hughie Morrison* 117
5 b h Choisir(AUS) —Damiana (IRE) (Thatching)
2118[6] 3068[4] 4139[8] 5186[8]

Stirling Bridge *William Jarvis* a79 59
2 b g Kyllachy—Seine Bleue (FR) (Grand Lodge (USA))
6153[11] 6882[6] ◆ 7779[4] (8011)

Stitchnick (IRE) *Stuart Kittow* 56
5 b g Needle Gun(IRE) —American Chick (IRE) (Lord Americo)
3829[6]

St Moritz (IRE) *Mark Johnston* a95 106
4 b g Medicean—Statua (IRE) (Statoblest)
2124[3] 2508[2] ◆ 3069[3] (3869) 4630a[5] 6349[20]

St Nicholas Abbey (IRE) *A P O'Brien* 123
3 b c Montjeu(IRE) —Leaping Water (Sure Blade (USA))
1699[6]

Stock Market (USA) *N Al Mandeel* a87 78
5 ch h Rahy(USA) —Two Marks (USA) (Woodman (USA))
334a[10] 605a[8]

Stoic (IRE) *Jeremy Noseda* a103 111
4 b g Green Desert(USA) —Silver Bracelet (Machiavellian (USA))
413a[2] ◆ 630a[4] 713a[9] 3069[14] ◆ 5247[6] 5948[2] 6529[7]

Stoical (IRE) *William Jarvis* a67 68
3 b g Galileo(IRE) —Stefania (IRE) (Monsun (GER))
1769[10] 3355[5] 3754[4] 4792[5] 5536[6] 5869[5] 6336[6] 6747[2] 7043[4]

Stoichkhov (IRE) *K J Condon* 60
2 b c Ivan Denisovich(IRE) —Baltic Breeze (USA) (Labeeb)
954a[8]

Stoic Leader (IRE) *Roger Fisher* a60 71
10 b g Danehill Dancer(IRE) —Starlust (Sallust)
539[12] 780[5] 940[4] 1673[10] 6188[9]

Stolen (FR) *M Boutin* a46 58
9 gr g Linamix(FR) —Secrecy (USA) (Halo (USA))
332a[9]

Stolen Light (IRE) *Andrew Crook* a13 40
9 ch g Grand Lodge(USA) —Spring To Light (USA) (Blushing Groom (FR))
331[10]

Stolt (IRE) *Linda Stubbs* a84 93
6 b g Tagula(IRE) —Cabcharge Princess (IRE) (Rambo Dancer (CAN))
172[9] 736[3] 935[3] 2136[9] 2294[2] 2756[6] 6140[17] 6572[16] 6880[9] 7051[8] 7859[4]

Stoneacre Lad (IRE) *Peter Grayson* a96 82
7 b h Bluebird(USA) —Jay And-A (IRE) (Elbio)
1506[8]

Stoneacre Pat (IRE) *Peter Grayson* a56 51
5 b h Iron Mask(USA) —Sans Ceriph (IRE) (Thatching)
132[9]

Stonecrabstomorrow (IRE) *Richard Guest* a71 78
7 b g Fasliyev(USA) —Tordasia (IRE) (Dr Devious (IRE))
(37) 187[2] 364[5] 379[5] 505[5] 914[7] 4868[13] 4936[7] 5388[8] 5926[12] 6577[7] 7468[12] 7564[4] 7885[13]

Stonehaugh (IRE) *Howard Johnson* 81
7 b g King Charlemagne(USA) —Canary Bird (IRE) (Catrail (USA))
1869[11] 2428[6] 3022[7] (3659) 4197[3] 4795[5] 5357[10] 5545[3]

Stone Of Folca *John Best* 102
2 b c Kodiac—Soyalang (FR) (Alydeed (CAN))
2397[2] 3051[4] ◆ 3100[4] 4458[2] ◆ 5276[11]

Stoppers (IRE) *Declan Carroll* 43
3 gr g Verglas(IRE) —Sharadja (IRE) (Doyoun)
1402[8] 1685[11]

Stormburst (IRE) *Adrian Chamberlain* a51 40
6 b m Mujadil(USA) —Isca (Caerleon (USA))
423[9] 567[9] 615[10] 2235[11] 2589[14]

Storm Chispazo (ARG) *H J Brown* a98
4 br h Bernstein(USA) —Chimera (ARG) (Fitzcarraldo (ARG))
608a[8] 796a[12]

Storm Command (IRE) *Bryan Smart* 59
3 ch g Halling(USA) —Clarinda (IRE) (Lomond (USA))
1486[4] 1652[5] 2673[3]

Storm Hawk (IRE) *Pat Eddery* a63 70
3 b g Hawk Wing(USA) —Stormy Larissa (IRE) (Royal Applause)
2620[8] 2993[10] 3514[2] 4366[10] 4870[8] 5180[8] 5663[4] 6080[3] 6525[9] 6871[2]

Storming Redd *James Eustace* a32 61
3 gr g Storming Home—Bogus Mix (IRE) (Linamix (FR))
1644[2] 2011[8] 4697[11] 5625[5] 6631[5] 7760[8]

Stormin Heart (USA) *David Evans* a18 56
5 br g Stormin Fever(USA) —Heart Beats True (USA) (Cherokee Run (USA))
6538[12]

Storm Runner (IRE) *George Margarson* a43 29
2 b g Rakti—Saibhreas (IRE) (Last Tycoon)
5717[9] 7201[12]

Storm Sir (USA) *B Al Abed* a67 61
5 ch h Johannesburg(USA) —Robust (USA) (Conquistador Cielo (USA))
609a[9]

Storms Over (USA) *Brendan Duke* a54 58
3 bb g Gone West(USA) —Stormy Gal (USA) (Storm Cat (USA))
6454[3] 6905[10] 7286[7] 7760[10]

Storm Tide *Gavin Blake* 60
2 b f Tobougg(IRE) —Tide Of Love (Pursuit Of Love)
3590[5] 4299[5]

Storm Ultralight (ARG) *Mahmood Al Zarooni* a112 79
4 ch h Bernstein(USA) —Ultrasexy (ARG) (Equalize (USA))
(1664) 2318[5]

Stormy Montlioux (FR) *Y Durepaire* a60
3 b g Vespone(IRE) —Famatina (SWI) (Zieten (USA))
927a[6]

Stormy Morning *Lawney Hill* a71 66
4 ch g Nayef(USA) —Sokoa (USA) (Peintre Celebre (USA))
6668[5] 7011[2] 7504[2] 7861[5] 8010[4]

Stormy's Majesty (USA) *Dominic G Galluscio* a105
3 ch c Stormy Atlantic(USA) —Raffie's Dream (USA) (Raffie's Majesty (USA))
4613a[8]

Stormy Summer *R W Price* a68 61
5 b g Observatory(USA) —Khambani (IRE) (Royal Academy (USA))
(18) 114[4]

St Oswald *Roger Charlton* 67
2 b g Royal Applause—Susun Kelapa (USA) (St Jovite (USA))
2819[5] ◆ 3332[4] 4379[4] ◆

Stotsfold *Walter Swinburn* a113 121
7 b g Barathea(IRE) —Eliza Acton (Shirley Heights)
946[4] ◆ 1832[8] (2470) (3632) (Dead)

Straboe (USA) *Stuart Williams* a69 60
4 b g Green Desert(USA) —Staff Nurse (USA) (Arch (USA))
(561) ◆ (778) ◆ 1074[7] 1258[5] 5614[10] 6110[13] 7628[7] 8036[4]

Stradivinsky (USA) *Richard Dutrow Jr* a80 105
7 b g Stravinsky(USA) —Lubicon (USA) (Apalachee (USA))
7362a[13]

Straight And Level (CAN) *Jo Crowley* a61 63
5 gr g Buddha(USA) —Azusa (USA) (Flying Paster (USA))
262[8] 1591[4] 4591[7] 5864[5] 7023[4] 7487[7] 7557[9] 7649[6]

Straight Face (IRE) *David Evans* a74 71
6 b g Princely Heir(IRE) —Dakota Sioux (IRE) (College Chapel)
(270) 318[2] 373[9] 579[2] 663[3] 862[2] 920[2] 1047[7] 1239[6] 1301[5] 1543[8] (1737) 1914[11] 2188[5] 2415[6] 2678[4] 2783[7] 3774[8] 4206[10] 4681[10]

Straight Laced *William Knight* a58 65
4 b m Refuse To Bend(IRE) —Gaelic Swan (IRE) (Nashwan (USA))
1623[5] 2218[7] 2870[4] (4101) 6639[13]

Straight Line (IRE) *Alan Jarvis* 88
2 b c Refuse To Bend(IRE) —Unintentional (Dr Devious (IRE))
1263[4] 1612[3] 2078[4] 3190[9] 3844[2] 4460[3]

Straight Story (USA) *Alan E Goldberg* 110
4 bb h Giant's Causeway(USA) —Eventail (USA) (Lear Fan (USA))
6237a[13]

Straits Of Hormuz (USA) *Ian Williams* a66 84
4 rg m War Chant(USA) —Tjinouska (USA) (Cozzene (USA))
7045[P]

Strandfield Lady (IRE) *H Rogers* a72 80
5 ch m Pairumani Star(IRE) —Stylish Chic (IRE) (Arazi (USA))
6910a[5]

Strandhill (IRE) *Brian Nolan* a45 65
3 bb f Footstepsinthesand—Cosabawn (IRE) (Barathea (IRE))
5129a[12]

Strangelittlegirl *Patrick Leech* a17
2 b f Shirocco(GER) —Cephalonia (Slip Anchor)
7152[11] 7478[12]

Strategic Mission (IRE) *Paul Cole* a58 72
5 b g Red Ransom(USA) —North East Bay (USA) (Prospect Bay (CAN))
4100[9] 4376[6] 4907[7] 5635[2] 6328[3] 6677[3] 6846[8]

Strategic Mount *Paul Cole* a63 98
7 b g Montjeu(IRE) —Danlu (USA) (Danzig (USA))
3462[8] 3873[4] 4334[4] 4818[5] 5591[14]

Strategic Mover (USA) *Paddy Butler* a61 77
5 ch g Grand Slam(USA) —Efficient Frontier (USA) (Mt. Livermore (USA))
10[5] 369[3] 8024[7]

Strathaird (IRE) *Andrew Crook* a44 36
6 b g Medicean—Heed My Warning (IRE) (Second Set (IRE))
7147[11]

Strathcal *Hughie Morrison* a79 86
4 b g Beat Hollow—Shall We Run (Hotfoot I)
1783[3] 2126[5] ◆ (2845) 4141[2] 5035[8] 6181[8]

Stratton Banker (IRE) *Stuart Williams* a79 75
3 b g One Cool Cat(USA) —Birthday (IRE) (Singspiel (IRE))
570[3] 1178[11] 1601[6] 5206[2] 5588[3] 6207[2] (6270) 6466[3] (7571) ◆ 7782[5]

Straversjoy *Reg Hollinshead* a69 66
3 b f Kayf Tara—Stravsea (Handsome Sailor)
2853[5] ◆ 3626[4] 4092[4] 4545[6] 4786[4] 5550[3] (5923) (6213) 6314[4] 6631[4] 7147[3] 7275[4] (7531) ◆ 7626[6] (8010)

Stravita *Reg Hollinshead* a55 63
6 b m Weet-A-Minute(IRE) —Stravsea (Handsome Sailor)
199[7] 661[3] 942[9]

Stravsambition *Reg Hollinshead* 22
2 b f Striking Ambition—Stravsea (Handsome Sailor)
6323[6] 6626[6]

Strawberrydaiquiri *Sir Michael Stoute* 117
4 gr m Dansili—Strawberry Morn (CAN) (Travelling Victor (CAN))
(1725) (3067) ◆ 3793[4] 4575[4] 6561[2]

Strawberry Field (AUS) *J O'Shea* 103
5 ch m Encosta De Lago(AUS) —Red Labelle (AUS) (Blevic (AUS))
7

Strawberry Rose *Marcus Tregoning* 63
3 gr f Dr Fong(USA) —Strawberry Morn (CAN) (Travelling Victor (CAN))
1654[6] 1976[7] 2180[14]

Street Band (IRE) *Henry Candy* 65
2 b g Desert Style(IRE) —Savoy Street (Vettori (IRE))
4142[8] 6465[6] 7034[4]

Street Cred (IRE) *Paul Burgoyne* a55
2 gr f Kheleyf(USA) —Kamadara (IRE) (Kahyasi)
6053[12] 6451[12] 6842[12] 7527[11]

Street Devil (USA) *F J Brennan* a76 70
5 gr g Street Cry(IRE) —Math (USA) (Devil's Bag (USA))
231[13] 756[8] 908[4] ◆ 1395[8] 7867[8]

Street Entertainer (IRE) *Amanda Perrett* a83 80
3 br g Danehill Dancer(IRE) —Opera Ridge (FR) (Indian Ridge)
(1046) 1502[8] 2079[6] 3337[5] 4573[8] 6152[5] 6480[6] 6781[8]

Street Honor (IRE) *A Peraino* 79
2 ch c Byron—La Rendita (Hector Protector (USA))
7264a[6]

Street Lair (USA) *J-C Rouget* 37
3 ch g Street Cry(IRE) —Hideaway Heroine (IRE) (Hernando (FR))
6761a[10]

Street Power (USA) *Jeremy Gask* a96 87
5 b g Street Cry(IRE) —Javana (USA) (Sandpit (BRZ))
(1349) 1900[23] 2877[3] 3969[5] 7014[4] 7318[10] 7593[11] 7689[5] 8017[4]

Street Runner *Reg Hollinshead* a56 63
4 b g Rainbow Quest(USA) —Dansara (Dancing Brave (USA))
963[10] 2244[6] 2691[2] 3360[5] 3639[4] 3965[6] 4328[6]

Streets Of War (USA) *Peter Chapple-Hyam* a78 77
3 bb c Street Cry(IRE) —Saint Boom (USA) (Saint Ballado (CAN))
930[4] ◆ 1661[2] 2004[2] 2682[7] 5150[5] 6056[3] 6580[6] 7042[6]

Strength And Stay (IRE) *Eve Johnson Houghton* 57
2 b c Motivator—Queen's Cape (King's Best (USA))
6087[8]

Strevelyn *Ann Duffield* 51
4 br g Namid—Kali (Linamix (FR))
1199[7] 3669[9] 4581[5] 4949[6] 5636[7]

Strictly Dancing (IRE) *Andrew Balding* a90 93
3 b f Danehill Dancer(IRE) —Lochangel (Night Shift (USA))
1861[2] (2340) 3085[2] 3790[2] 4540[9] 5694[9]

Strictly Lambada *John Gosden* a73 75
3 b f Red Ransom(USA) —Bella Lambada (Lammtarra (USA))
3437[3] 5445[2] 6250[3] 6861[3] 7282[4]

Strictly Pink (IRE) *Alan Bailey* a78 84
2 b f Kodiac—Church Mice (IRE) (Petardia)
6034[6] 6176[8] 6512[6] 6796[2] 7021[2] 7240[2]

Strictly Rhythm *Richard Hannon* 79
2 b f Hawk Wing(USA) —Esteemed Lady (IRE) (Mark Of Esteem (IRE))
3861[10] 5520[2] 5985[2] 6279[3] 6528[8]

Striding Edge (IRE) *William Muir* a83 81
4 bb g Rock Of Gibraltar(IRE) —For Criquette (IRE) (Barathea (IRE))
(975) 1265[5] 1530[8] 3565[8] 4023[10] 5716[9] 6260[11] 6718[5] 7111[2]

Strike A Deal (IRE) *Chris Wall* 74
3 b f Chineur(FR) —Bishop's Lake (Lake Coniston (IRE))
2221[2] (2837) 4058[5] 4381[5] 5689[4] 6093[2] 6622[2]

Strike Force *Olivia Maylam* a77 67
6 b g Dansili—Miswaki Belle (USA) (Miswaki (USA))
1503[3] 2012[4] 2303[5] 4740[3] (4985) 5254[3] 5530[13] 6269[8] (7068) 7214[4] 7467[2] 7491[2] (7663) 7788[6] 8008[2]

Strikemaster (IRE) *Brian Ellison* a55 73
4 b g Xaar—Mas A Fuera (IRE) (Alzao (USA))
330[7] 764[4] 1459[9] 1916[4] 2060[6] 2218[2] 2765[3] 4669[3] 5642[8] 6187[9] 6648[6] 6983[7] 7157[7]

Striker Torres (IRE) *Geoffrey Oldroyd* a80 80
4 ch g Danehill Dancer(IRE) —Silver Skates (IRE) (Slip Anchor)
(191) 393[7] 7915[2]

Strike Shot *William Muir* a55 72
3 b g Avonbridge—Final Shot (Dalsaan)
1269[9] 1842[8] 2868[12] 3030[14] 3515[12] 4249[10] 4475[6] 4857[10]

Strike Up The Band *David Nicholls* a103 107
7 b g Cyrano De Bergerac—Green Supreme (Primo Dominie)
1573[9] 1822[9] 2745[13] 4191[12] 5183[11] 5589[3] 5742[9] 6364[6] 6723[6] 6981[3]

Striking Box *Rod Millman* 56
2 b c Striking Ambition—Nesting Box (Grand Lodge (USA))
3735[14] 4131[5]

Striking Force (IRE) *V C Ward* a68 82
8 b g Danehill(USA) —Trusted Partner (USA) (Affirmed (USA))
6322[5]

Striking Love *Roger Charlton* 43
2 b f Striking Ambition—Sand Sprite (IRE) (Green Desert (USA))
3126[8] 3864[5] 4802[14] 5111[10]

Striking Priorite *Roger Charlton* a69
2 b g Striking Ambition—Priorite (IRE) (Kenmare (FR))
(2867) 6901[8]

Striking Spirit *David Nicholls* 106
5 b g Oasis Dream—Aspiring Diva (USA) (Distant View (USA))
1670[2] 2119[4] 2759[2] 3193[2] ◆ 4576[26] 5944[8] 6177[16]

Striking Veil (USA) *Sir Michael Stoute* 52
2 b f Smart Strike(CAN) —Yashmak (USA) (Danzig (USA))
6803[10]

Striking Willow *Rod Millman* 11
2 b g Striking Ambition—Willows World (Agnes World (USA))
5582[15] 6053[11]

Strobe *Lucy Normile* a76 44
6 ch g Fantastic Light(USA) —Sadaka (USA) (Kingmambo (USA))
2060[12]

Strong Aim *Michael Easterby* a16 8
3 ch f Dubai Destination(USA) —Strong Hand (First Trump)
5303[15] 5925[9] 6244[7] 6313[11]

Strong Storm (USA) *Andrew Reid* a71 71
4 ch g Giant's Causeway(USA) —Sweeping Story (USA) (End Sweep (USA))
426[7] 841[4] 929[5] 969[4] 1134[8]

Strong Suit (USA) *Richard Hannon* 114
2 ch c Rahy(USA) —Helwa (USA) (Silver Hawk (USA))
(2078) ◆ (3049) ◆ 4880a[3] 6531[2]

Strong Vigilance (IRE) *Michael Bell* a58 79
3 ch g Mr Greeley(USA) —Zabadani (Zafonic (USA))
1336[2] 1769[8] 2737[4] 3351[8] 4056[4] 4571[8] 4971[7]

Strophic *Giles Bravery* a63 3
3 b g Singspiel(IRE) —Katina (USA) (Danzig (USA))
2507[10] 7575[3]

St Savarin (FR) *M S Tuck* a60 50
9 ch g Highest Honor(FR) —Sacara (GER) (Monsagem (USA))
588[7] 1755[7] 4433[6] 6660[4] 6930[8]

St Trinians *Mike Mitchell* a110 77
5 b m Piccolo—Cherrycombe-Row (Classic Cliche (IRE))
3044a[2]

Stubbs Art (IRE) *M F De Kock* a85 78
5 ch g Hawk Wing(USA) —Rich Dancer (Halling (USA))
438a[7] 627a[10]

Stuff Of Legends *Harry Dunlop* 29
3 b f Olden Times—Hylandra (USA) (Bering)
4205[11] 5380[P]

Stumped *Stuart Howe* a70 48
7 b g Bertolini(USA) —So Saucy (Teenoso (USA))
182[2]

Stunning In Purple (IRE) *Andrew Haynes* a62 68
2 b f Kheleyf(USA) —Thank One's Stars (Alzao (USA))
1223[3] 1632[2] 1981[3] 2413[2] 3288[2] (3721) 4040[3] 5111[2]

Style And Panache (IRE) *David Evans* a74 82
2 b f Trans Island—El Corazon (IRE) (Mujadil (USA))
1066[2] 1173[3] 1577[3] (1838) 2177[5] 2757[4] 3051[6] 4458[10] 4578[11] 5939[8] (6445) 6636[3] 6916[4] 7333[4] 7696[5]

Style Award *Bill Ratcliffe* a70 71
5 b m Acclamation—Elegant (IRE) (Marju (IRE))
77[5] 555[3] ◆ 913[5] 1443[9] 1598[10]

Suave Character *Michael Blanshard* a17 46
2 b g Araafa(IRE) —Peep Show (In The Wings)
3555[7] 4089[6] 4543[8] 5111[6] 5900[6] 6271[9] 6575[9]

Submariner (USA) *Mark Johnston* a97 98
4 ch g Singspiel(IRE) —Neptune's Bride (USA) (Bering)
(1447) ◆ 1831[6] (2435) (2640) 3194[8] 3672[7] 4455[7] ◆ 4818[3] 5307[15] 6193[8] 6304[6]

Submission *Luca Cumani* a78 64
2 b f Beat Hollow—Idealistic (IRE) (Unfuwain (USA))
5841[2] ◆ (6248) 6927[8]

Subramaniam *James Given* 55
2 ch c Medicean—Blithe (Pivotal)
5404[9] 6001[4] 6618[7]

Subtefuge *Henry Cecil* 89
3 b f Observatory(USA) —Artifice (Green Desert (USA))
1279[3] (2002) 2898[3]

Suburbia (USA) *J Barclay* 50
4 b g Street Cry(IRE) —Green Lady (IRE) (Green Desert (USA))
2072[8] 3147[14] 3707[12] 3989[8] 4582[8] 4823[9] 5408[12]

Successful (FR) *B Goudot* a64 73
3 b g Kingsalsa(USA) —Glebe Place (FR) (Akarad (FR))
547a[4]

Such A Maj (FR) *Mme M Bollack-Badel* 92
2 ch c Soave(GER) —Kapi Creek (FR) (Sicyos (USA))
6973a[5]

Suchita Devious (ITY) *S Bietolini* 98
4 b m Dr Devious(IRE) —Suchita (IRE) (Alzao (USA))
7109a[6]

Such Optimism *Ralph Beckett* a76 87
4 b m Sakhee(USA) —Optimistic (Reprimand)
148[4] 294[6]

Sudden Impulse *Alan Brown* a66 70
9 b m Silver Patriarch(IRE) —Sanshang (FR) (Astronef)
309[12] 457[6] (1199) (1489) 2084[5] 2516[6] 3166[5] 4673[4]

Suddenly Susan (IRE) *David Nicholls* a69 65
2 b f Acclamation—Westerly Gale (USA) (Gone West (USA))
6153[5] 6497[3] 6859[2] 7126[2] 7324[4] 7758[4]

Sud Pacifique (IRE) *Jeremy Noseda* 80
2 b c Montjeu(IRE) —Anestasia (IRE) (Anabaa (USA))
5595[2] 6279[2]

Sue And Sue *Gary Woodward* a3 9
3 b f Needwood Blade—Bahamian Belle (Bahamian Bounty)
3808[6] 4251[14] 5548[12] 5816[9] 7449[9] 7669[6] 7869[8]

Sue's Dream *Alan Jarvis* 13
2 ch f Monsieur Bond(IRE) —Sonneteer (IRE) (Victory Note (USA))
5836[6] 6804[12]

Sufficient Warning *Ralph Smith* a48
6 b g Warningford—Efficacious (IRE) (Efisio)
100[5] 229[13] 367[12] 590[12]

Suffolk Punch (IRE) *Andrew Balding* a85 87
3 ch c Barathea(IRE) —Lamanka Lass (USA) (Woodman (USA))
3103[20] 4104[4] 4995[3] 5236[3] 5937[5] 6564[6] 7238[13] 7688[4] 7735[4] 8033[4]

Sugar Baby Love (IRE) *Patrick Martin* a81 83
4 gr m Verglas(IRE) —No Sugar Baby (FR) (Crystal Glitters (USA))
6910a[12]

Sugar Beet *Roger Charlton* a73 77
2 b f Beat Hollow—Satin Bell (Midyan (USA))
3126[5] 4474[6] 4921[3] 5874[3] (6052) (6271)

Sugar Hiccup (IRE) *Clive Cox* 69
2 b f Refuse To Bend(IRE) —Raysiza (IRE) (Alzao (USA))
6651[3] 7057[12]

Suga Shot *F J Brennan* a25 9
2 br f Diktat—The Lady Caster (City On A Hill (USA))
7123[10] 7294[8]

Sughera (IRE) *A J Martin* a23 56
3 b f Alhaarth(IRE) —Gold Bar (IRE) (Barathea (IRE))
4563a[13]

Suhailah *Michael Attwater* a55 17
4 ch m Sulamani(IRE) —Vrennan (Suave Dancer (USA))
1157[4] 1479[4] 3038[11] 4258[7] 5179[8] 5666[8] 7022[5] 7422[4] (7716)

Suhaili *Michael Jarvis* 84
2 b c Shirocco(GER) —Mezzogiorno (Unfuwain (USA))
6883[3]

Suhayl Star (IRE) *Paul Burgoyne* a65 64
6 b g Trans Island—Miss Odlum (IRE) (Mtoto)
275[7] 442[9] 614[5] 844[11] 2184[5] 2720[9] 2964[9] 7250[10] 7477[8] 7783[10] 7885[9] 8024[4]

Suitably Accoutred (IRE) *Ann Duffield* a9 54
4 b m Acclamation—Cliveden Gail (IRE) (Law Society (USA))
622[8] 1199[6]

Suited And Booted (IRE) *Richard Hannon* a76 100
3 ch c Tagula(IRE) —Carpet Lady (IRE) (Night Shift (USA))
1590[2] (1782) 2618[2] (3215) (3796) ◆

Suits Me *Tom Tate* a111 103
7 ch g Bertolini(USA) —Fancier Bit (Lion Cavern (USA))
360[2] 738[2] 946[2] 1016[5] 1664[4] 6179[7] 6738[7] 7100[13] 7523[3] 8009[5]

Sukhothai (USA) *Henry Cecil* a54 45
2 rg f Maria's Mon(USA) —Succession (Groom Dancer (USA))
2641[6] 3562[8] 6248[9] 7004[6]

Sularno *Jeff Pearce* a78 63
6 ch g Medicean—Star Precision (Shavian)
1636[9] 2012[10] 2172[10]

Sula Two *Ron Hodges* a73 80
3 b f Sulamani(IRE) —There's Two (IRE) (Ashkalani (IRE))
1165[10] 2003[3] 2473[9] 3464[5] 3852[4] 4382[2] (4621) 5008[4] ◆ (5467) 6166[5] 6448[3] ◆ (6955)

Suleimah *Colin Teague*
3 gr f Sulamani(IRE) —Safinaz (Environment Friend)
2627[9] 3242[7] 4115[11]

Suli Blew *Tom Keddy* a32
4 b m Sulamani(IRE) —Lady Birgitta (Emperor Jones (USA))
922[8]

Sulis Minerva (IRE) *Jeremy Gask* a74 68
3 b f Arakan(USA) —Lacinia (Groom Dancer (USA))
936[4] 1257[2] 1599[3] ◆ 2868[5] 3328[5] 4090[14]

Sulliman *Jane Chapple-Hyam* 52
3 b g Sulamani(IRE) —Norcroft Joy (Rock Hopper)
6876[11]

Sultah (USA) *B W Hills* a70 65
2 b f Redoute's Choice(AUS) —Judhoor (Alhaarth (IRE))
5691[7] 7112[4]

Sultan's Choice *David Evans* a58 60
3 b f Sulamani(IRE) —Royal Wish (Royal Applause)
805[4] 1048[12] 1526[2] 1795[6] 2359[3] 2412[6] 2619[5] 2878[3] 3390[10] 3728[3] 3960[14]

Sultans Way (IRE) *Paul Cole* a61 58
4 b g Indian Ridge—Roses From Ridey (IRE) (Petorius)
1441[4] 1633[5] 1885[7]

Sulwaan (IRE) *Mark Johnston* a93 86
3 b g King's Best(USA) —Iktidar (Green Desert (USA))
6428[4]

Sumani (FR) *Simon Dow* a73 66
4 b g Della Francesca(USA) —Sumatra (IRE) (Mukaddamah (USA))
989[2]

Sumay Buoy (IRE) *Jean McGregor* 47
3 b c Fasliyev(USA) —Mourir D'Aimer (USA) (Trempolino (USA))
5438[7] 6226[10] 6392[5] 7052[6]

Sumbe (USA) *Marcus Tregoning* 72
4 bb g Giant's Causeway(USA) —Sumoto (Mtoto)
2290[7]

Sumerian *Sir Mark Prescott Bt* a79 83
3 ch f Medicean—Pitcroy (Unfuwain (USA))
2334[4] ◆ 3080[2] (3523) 4302[2] 4532[3] 5056[6]

Summer Affair (IRE) *Ben Case* a59
5 b g Alhaarth(IRE) —Late Summer (USA) (Gone West (USA))
41[8] 198[5]

Summer Dancer (IRE) *Paul Midgley* a83 89
6 br g Fasliyev(USA) —Summer Style (IRE) (Indian Ridge)
1102[8] 1752[7] 2205[5] (2524) 3107[5] 3553[7] 3659[2] 4354[5] 4598[7] 5264[8] 5510[2] 5789[9]

Summer Fete (IRE) *Bryan Smart* 104
4 gr m Pivotal—Tamarillo (Daylami (IRE))
4540[7] 5081[6] 5518[3] 5883[10] 7083[5]

Summerinthecity (IRE) *Jeremy Noseda* a93 98
3 ch g Indian Ridge—Miss Assertive (Zafonic (USA))
1663[2] ◆ 2028[5] 5154[9] (6363) 6776[8] 7060[18]

Summer Jasmine *Harry Dunlop* a44 57
2 b f Kyllachy—Blodwen (USA) (Mister Baileys)
3861[8] 4323[2] 4528[4] 5835[8] 6521[7] 7035[8]

Summerlea (IRE) *Eoin Griffin* a65 69
4 ch g Alhaarth(IRE) —Verbania (IRE) (In The Wings)
7514a[9]

Summerofsixtynine *John O'Shea* a3
7 b g Fruits Of Love(USA) —Scurrilous (Sharpo)
1207[11]

Summer Soul (IRE) *Lucinda Russell* 77
8 b g Danehill(USA) —Blend Of Pace (IRE) (Sadler's Wells (USA))
3496[3] 6143[3]

Summers Target (USA) *Stuart Williams* a36 67
4 ch g Mr Greeley(USA) —She's Enough (USA) (Exploit (USA))
1428[12] 2298[8] 2874[5] 3264[5] 4213[6] 4498[9] 4760[8]

Summer Sunrise *Marco Botti* a44
3 ch f Hawk Wing(USA) —Summer Sunset (IRE) (Grand Lodge (USA))
226[5]

Summer Winds *Robert Mills* a74 87
5 ch g Where Or When(IRE) —Jetbeeah (IRE) (Lomond (USA))
4520[8] 5311[8] 6449[9]

Summit Surge (IRE) *Luca Cumani* a114 117
6 b g Noverre(USA) —Lady Peculiar (CAN) (Sunshine Forever (USA))
438a[4] 607a[6] 823a[3] 1022a[12] 2576a[2] (4390) 5321a[5] 7523[2]

Sumner (IRE) *David Evans* a69 56
6 b g Xaar—Black Jack Girl (IRE) (Ridgewood Ben)
1623[8] 2109[12] 2645[4] 2881[6] 4648[12] 6930[7] 7315[9] 7569[7]

Sum Satisfaction *Tor Sturgis* 43
2 ch g Araafa(IRE) —Dina Line (USA) (Diesis)
6473[11] 6953[8]

Sunarise (IRE) *Richard Hannon* a80 79
3 b f Galileo(IRE) —Sun Silk (USA) (Gone West (USA))
1310[9] 2047[8] 2652[5] 3918[3] 4626[4] 5833[5] 6090[8]

Sunbow (USA) *Mahmood Al Zarooni* 81
3 ch c Dubawi(IRE) —Sunspangled (IRE) (Caerleon (USA))
1927[DSQ] 5122[2]

Sun Dance Moon (USA) *Richard Dutrow Jr*
3 bb c Malibu Moon(USA) —Notting Hill (BRZ) (Jules (USA))
4642a[8]

Sunday Bess (JPN) *Tom Dascombe* a71
2 b f Deep Impact(JPN) —Lhiz (CHI) (Hussonet (USA))
7186[2] ◆

Sunley Spinalonga *David Elsworth* a83 76
3 ch f With Approval(CAN) —Sunley Scent (Wolfhound (USA))
321[2] 533[2] 671[2] 1159[5] 3514[3] 3963[2] (4102) (4492) 4907[2] 5051[3] 5656[2] 6288[2]

Sunmoon Royale (GER) *Mario Hofer* a74 87
3 b f Royal Dragon(USA) —Sun Moon Stars (IRE) (Shahrastani (USA))
4035a[10]

Sunnandaeg *Valentine Donoghue* 85
3 ch g Haafhd—Come Away With Me (IRE) (Machiavellian (USA))
1718[4] 3599[4] 3876[12] 4784[7] 6048[9]

Sunniva Duke (IRE) *D Prod'Homme* a77 79
4 b g Bachelor Duke(USA) —Amandian (IRE) (Indian Ridge)
1055a[0]

Sunny Future (IRE) *Malcolm Saunders* a26 75
4 b g Masterful(USA) —Be Magic (Persian Bold)
1543[4] 2024[3] (2360) 2690[4] 3257[3] 5115[2] 5286[4]

Sunny Game *Michael Bell* 89
3 b g Montjeu(IRE) —Sundrenched (IRE) (Desert King (IRE))
1268[9] (1581) 2315[3] 6362[6] 7084[5]

Sunnyside Tom (IRE) *Richard Fahey* a84 92
6 b g Danetime(IRE) —So Kind (Kind Of Hush)
1707[3] 2141[5] 2708[8] 3206[5] 3667[3] (4403) (4852) (4949) (5545) 5786[6] 6296[4] 6749[13] 7352[14]

Sunny Spells *Stuart Williams* a70 64
5 b g Zamindar(USA) —Bright Spells (Salse (USA))
982[7] 1160[4] 1283[7] (3348) 5666[11] 6132[11] (7695) 8013[10]

Sunraider (IRE) *B W Hills* 101
3 b g Namid—Doctrine (Barathea (IRE))
1315[3] ◆ 1917[3] (2862) 4391[9] 4843[14] 5442[4] 5854[8] 6363[13]

Sunrise Lyric (IRE) *Paul Cole* a64 68
3 b f Rock Of Gibraltar(IRE) —Dawn Air (USA) (Diesis)
128[4] 313[8] 633[3] 812[2] 1048[3] 1163[7] 1795[3] 2219[7] 2633[5] 3359[2] 3975[3] (4775) 7889[7] 7991[9]

Sunrise Safari (IRE) *Richard Fahey* a73 94
7 b g Mozart(IRE) —Lady Scarlett (Woodman (USA))
(1516) 2100[6] 2465[11] 3178[4] 3446[9] 4413[8] 4536[15] 5884[4] 6142[19] 6537[8] (6987)

Sunrise Spirit (FR) *F Doumen* a80 80
9 b g Double Bed(FR) —Belle Chaumiere (Gildoran)
1056a[2]

Sun Seeker (IRE) *Jeremy Noseda* 49
3 b f Galileo(IRE) —Sharakawa (IRE) (Darshaan)
5150[7]

Sunset Avenue (USA) *Mahmood Al Zarooni* 80
2 b f Street Cry(IRE) —Dearly (Rahy (USA))
(4103)

Sunset Boulevard (IRE) *Jim Best* a65 47
7 b g Montjeu(IRE) —Lucy In The Sky (IRE) (Lycius (USA))
80[2] (182) 280[4] 426[11] 1188[10] 1592[5] 2006[6] 2752[3] 3442[3] 6669[14] 6999[15] 7760[3] 7996[7]

Sunset Kitty (USA) *Walter Swinburn* a81
3 bb f Gone West(USA) —Honorable Cat (USA) (Honor Grades (USA))
6056[6] 6496[3] 7310[2] 7483[5] (7837) ◆

Sunset Place *Clive Cox* a57 67
3 ch g Compton Place—Manhattan Sunset (USA) (El Gran Senor (USA))
3272[4] 4307[9] 4906[6] 5469[7] 6020[10] 6856[6]

Sunshine Always (IRE) *Tim McCarthy* a87 89
4 gr g Verglas(IRE) —Easy Sunshine (IRE) (Sadler's Wells (USA))
151[2] 394[7] 747[7] 2872[9] 3330[8] 4023[12] 5087[3] 5495[11] 5834[4]

Sunshine Buddy *Chris Down* a6 56
3 b f Reel Buddy(USA) —Bullion (Sabrehill (USA))
1932[8] 2281[6] 2619[9]

Sunshine Ellie *Derek Shaw* a44 51
4 ch m Desert Sun—Lindoras Glory (USA) (Gone West (USA))
8[10] 101[7]

Sunshineofyourlove *J W Hills* a34 25
3 b f Dalakhani(IRE) —Darling Harbour (USA) (Candy Stripes (USA))
2891[9] 4229[11]

Sun Society (GER) *M Trybuhl* 94
5 b m Law Society(USA) —Sintra (GER) (Konigsstuhl (GER))
7532a[3]

Suntan (IRE) *J S Bolger* 95
2 ch c Bachelor Duke(USA) —Tus Maith (IRE) (Entrepreneur)
954a[2] 2035a[3]

Suntrap *William Knight* a79 62
3 ch g Desert Sun—Regal Gallery (IRE) (Royal Academy (USA))
7288[12] 7561[7] (7767)

Suor Angelica (IRE) *George Baker* 49
5 ch m Spectrum(IRE) —Semiramide (IRE) (Persian Bold)
3538[14] 4676[3] 4991[5] 6022[6] 6272[6] 6649[8] 7397[10]

Supa Seeker (USA) *Tony Carroll* 82
4 bb g Petionville(USA) —Supamova (USA) (Seattle Slew (USA))
2900[2] 5609[7] 6260[4] 6677[5]

Supaseus *Hughie Morrison* 112
7 b g Spinning World(USA) —Supamova (USA) (Seattle Slew (USA))
3069[29]

Supatov (USA) *Hughie Morrison* a55 48
3 bb f Johannesburg(USA) —Supamova (USA) (Seattle Slew (USA))
5872[6] 6496[6] 6814[5] 7429[3]

Supaverdi (USA) *Hughie Morrison* a73 93
5 br m Green Desert(USA) —Supamova (USA) (Seattle Slew (USA))
3368[5]

Super (IRE) *Richard Hannon* 75
2 b f Royal Academy(USA) —Super Supreme (IND) (Zafonic (USA))
6441[3] 6804[2]

Supercast (IRE) *Nicky Vaughan* a76 82
7 b g Alhaarth(IRE) —Al Euro (FR) (Mujtahid (USA))
174[5] 430[5] 941[12] 3025[9] 4361[6] 4793[12] 6328[11]

Supercharged (IRE) *Chris Wall* 85
2 b f Iffraaj—Glympse (IRE) (Spectrum (IRE))
3959[3] ◆ 5914[2] ◆ 6419[2]

Super Collider *Michael Jarvis* 79
3 b g Montjeu(IRE) —Astorg (USA) (Lear Fan (USA))
1912[3] 3116[5]

Super Dubai *R Biondi* 87
3 b c Dubawi(IRE) —Credit-A-Plenty (Generous (IRE))
1418a[12]

Superduper *Mrs A Malzard* a46 88
5 b m Erhaab(USA) —I'm Magic (First Trump)
1814a[3] 2162a[6]

Super Duplex *Pat Phelan* a70 71
3 b g Footstepsinthesand—Penelope Tree (IRE) (Desert Prince (IRE))
1977[7] 2675[3] 4295[3] (4907) (4994) 6554[5] 7255[3]

Super Fourteen *Raymond York* a60 65
4 b h Lucky Story(USA) —Beechnut (IRE) (Mujadil (USA))
983[5] 1160[9]

Super Frank (IRE) *John Akehurst* a68 73
7 b g Cape Cross(IRE) —Lady Joshua (IRE) (Royal Academy (USA))
2053[4] 2846[5] 3292[5] 3716[5] 4130[7] 4589[7] 5175[5] 5327[6] 6025[16] 6853[4] 7255[6] 7439[9] 7613[7] (7824) 8019[3]

Superhoops *Stuart Howe* 30
3 b g Hunting Lion(IRE) —Colonial Lady (Dansili)
2359[14] 2585[9]

Superior Duchess *Adrian Chamberlain* a29 57
5 b m Superior Premium—Downclose Duchess (King's Signet (USA))
7461[11]

Superior Edge *Bryn Palling* a53 80
3 b f Exceed And Excel(AUS) —Beveled Edge (Beveled (USA))
1137[2] 1825[6] 4222[2] 4922[2] 5309[8] 5956[3] (6466) 6772[2] 6879[3]

Supermarine *Jeremy Glover* 57
2 b g Medicean—Madame Maxine (USA) (Dayjur (USA))
4089[4] 5053[5] 5608[7]

Supermassive Muse (IRE) *Ed McMahon* a90 91
5 br g Captain Rio—Cautionary (IRE) (Warning)
1266[9] 2622[7] 2883[7] 4245[3] 4712[10]

Super Motiva *S Cannavo'* 103
3 b f Motivator—Haute Volta (FR) (Grape Tree Road)
2575a[11]

Supernoverre (IRE) *Paul Howling* a71 75
4 b g Noverre(USA) —Caviare (Cadeaux Genereux)
121[4] 198[3] 309[6] 621[9] 2302[9] 3221[6]

Super Pistachio (IRE) *A S Cruz* 116
4 b g Danehill Dancer(IRE) —Pharapache (USA) (Lyphard (USA))
1568a[7] 7854a[10]

Super Ross (IRE) *Conor Dore* a3 38
7 b g Rossini(USA) —Mechilie (Belmez (USA))
701[4] 833[5]

Super Satin (NZ) *C Fownes* 119
5 b g Danehill Dancer(IRE) —Mantles Princess (Rock City)
1568a[3] 7854a[6]

Super Saver (USA) *Todd Pletcher* a124
3 b c Maria's Mon(USA) —Supercharger (USA) (A.P. Indy (USA))
(1714a) 2137a[8] 4643a[4] 5544a[10]

Super Say (IRE) *Andrew Oliver* 93
4 ch g Intikhab(USA) —Again Royale (IRE) (Royal Academy (USA))
3487a[3]

Super Sleuth (IRE) *Brian Meehan* a95 110
4 ch m Selkirk(USA) —Enemy Action (USA) (Forty Niner (USA))
1693[3] 3067[9] 6830[3] 7188[6]

Super Smile (IRE) *Richard Hannon* 40
2 b f Librettist(USA) —Beechesville (IRE) (Night Shift (USA))
4844[12] 5808[9]

Supersonic Flight (GER) *M Rulec* 102
3 ch c Lomitas—So Royal (GER) (Royal Solo (IRE))
4184a[15]

Superstition (FR) *A De Royer-Dupre* 104
4 b m Kutub(IRE) —Secada (GER) (Saint Andrews (FR))
1792a[2] 5345a[2] 6591a[6]

Superstitious Me (IRE) *Bryn Palling* a57 57
4 b m Desert Prince(IRE) —Royal Rival (IRE) (Marju (IRE))
3309[5] 3683[7] 4324[13] 4913[4] 5700[6] 5877[9] 6577[10]

Super Yellow *Jamie Osborne* a67 74
3 b g Exceed And Excel(AUS) —Almost Amber (USA) (Mt. Livermore (USA))
313[5] (2000) 2416[4] 2491[3] 3350[2] 3761[5] 4503[6] 6679[5] ◆ 6879[7]

Supplementary (IRE) *John Coombe* a52
8 b m Rudimentary(USA) —Will She What (IRE) (Lafontaine (USA))
160[9] 5391[1]

Support Fund (IRE) *Eve Johnson Houghton* a73 81
6 ch m Intikhab(USA) —Almost A Lady (IRE) (Entitled I)
101[2] ◆ 230[5]

Supreme Seductress (IRE) *B W Hills* 48
2 b f Montjeu(IRE) —Private Seductress (USA) (Private Account (USA))
7057[13]

Supreme Spirit (IRE) *David Nicholls* 78
3 b f Invincible Spirit(IRE) —Asseverate (USA) (Trempolino (USA))
(3091) 4091[2] 5054[3]

Supreme Summit (USA) *Mike Puype* a116
4 bb h Cactus Ridge(USA) —Studentoftheweek (USA) (Sunny Clime (USA))
7361a[4]

Supsonic *R Le Gal* a79 70
7 b g Marju(IRE) —Nicely (IRE) (Bustino)
332a[2]

Surdoue *Michael Scudamore* a58 45
10 b g Bishop Of Cashel—Chatter's Princess (Cadeaux Genereux)
720[12] 834[5]

Sure Fire (GER) *Barney Curley* a66 41
5 b g Monsun(GER) —Suivez (FR) (Fioravanti (USA))
166[4] 585[6] 1134[6]

Surely This Time (IRE) *Kevin Ryan* 68
2 b g Exceed And Excel(AUS) —Heart Of Svetlana (IRE) (Linamix (FR))
1294[6] 1597[4] 1986[3] 3596[9] 3925[6] 4941[4] 5239[2]

Surface Tension (IRE) *Luca Cumani* 73
3 b c Galileo(IRE) —Miss Moses (USA) (Gulch (USA))
2115[6] 3173[4] 5610[5]

Surfrider (IRE) *E Libaud* a84 95
2 b c Dansili—Ecoutila (USA) (Rahy (USA))
6218a[3]

Surprise (IRE) *Mahmood Al Zarooni* 56
2 b f Anabaa Blue—Wicken Wonder (IRE) (Distant Relative)
3712[4] 3981[3]

Surprise Result (USA) *R Bouresly* a25
3 b f Aptitude(USA) —Overwhelmed (USA) (Unbridled (USA))
333a[11]

Surprise Us *Ann Duffield* a57
3 b g Indian Ridge—Pingus (Polish Precedent (USA))
6661[8] 7043[12] 7596[4] 7761[13]

Surrey Star (IRE) *Roger Teal* 102
2 b c Dubawi(IRE) —Turning Light (GER) (Fantastic Light (USA))
2547[11] 2932[2] (4054) 4468[7] 5306[3] 5831[3] 6507[2] 7095[7]

Suruor (IRE) *David Simcock* a79 106
4 b g Intikhab(USA) —Kismah (Machiavellian (USA))
1857[3] 4126[3] 4358[5] 5516[3] 6349[P]

Susan Stroman *Ed Dunlop* a63 56
2 b f Monsun(GER) —Twyla Tharp (IRE) (Sadler's Wells (USA))
6874[4] 7113[7] 7448[5] ◆

Sushitan (GER) *Gary Moore* a71 66
5 ch g Lomitas—Subia (GER) (Konigsstuhl (GER))
280[5] 355[3]

Susie *Kevin Ryan* 31
3 b f Piccolo—Sioux (Kris)
1515[5]

Susiesstaying *Paul Midgley* 56
2 ch f Needwood Blade—Victoria Sioux (Ron's Victory (USA))
2623[4] 6301[11]

Suspender Belt *John Best* a60
2 b f Kodiac—Broughton Zest (Colonel Collins (USA))
7551[4] 7879[13]

Suttonia (IRE) *Noel Chance* a48 38
4 b m Namid—Sassania (IRE) (Persian Bold)
6931[8] 7473[12] 7725[9] 7824[6] 7877[4] 8024[3]

Sutton Veny (IRE) *Jeremy Gask* a96 88
4 gr m Acclamation—Carabine (USA) (Dehere (USA))
(287) (679) 3261[3] 4148[4] 5087[5] 5995[8] 6429[6] 7041[2] (7289) 7566[2] 7993[6]

Suyoof (USA) *Mark Johnston* 64
3 rg c Cozzene(USA) —Rise And Fall (USA) (Quiet American (USA))
1627[5]

Suzhou *Denis Coakley* a69 51
3 b f Tiger Hill(IRE) —Tora Bora (Grand Lodge (USA))
2334[7] 2968[5] 5384[8] 5972[8] 6903[7] 7376[6] 7502[2] ◆ 7874[2]

Suzie Quw *John Weymes* a73 80
4 ch m Bahamian Bounty—Bonkers (Efisio)
1588[4] 2475[7] 2904[6] (3086)

Suzi's A Smartlady (IRE) *Hugh Collingridge* a57 63
3 b f Rakti—Shesasmartlady (IRE) (Dolphin Street (FR))
2189[9]

Suzi's Challenger *Terry Clement* a32 42
3 b f Tobougg(IRE) —La Tiziana (Rudimentary (USA))
2221[11] 2675[12] 3113[5] 3442[6] 6094[5]

Suzi Spends (IRE) *Hugh Collingridge* a86 86
5 b m Royal Applause—Clever Clogs (Nashwan (USA))
239[10] 341[6]

Suzy Alexander *George Margarson* 69
3 b f Red Ransom(USA) —Fiveofive (IRE) (Fairy King (USA))
1436[2] 2174[3] 2784[5] 4109[6] 4248[6]

Suzybee *Mark Hoad* a43
3 b f Bahamian Bounty—Greenfly (Green Desert (USA))
236[5] 534[5] 805[10]

Suzy Wong *John Akehurst* 78
2 b f Auction House(USA) —Dance Flower (IRE) (Cape Cross (IRE))
(4993) ◆ 6160[4] 6555[4]

Swain's Quest (USA) *Eve Johnson Houghton* a32 55
3 b f Swain(IRE) —Questonia (Rainbow Quest (USA))
978[11] 1847[5] 2248[12] 2606[11] 3213[9]

Swaninstockwell (IRE) *Pat Phelan* a53 57
2 b c Footstepsinthesand—Dans Delight (Machiavellian (USA))
4993[5] 5372[7] 5914[7] 6809[7] 7417[6]

Swansea Jack *Stuart Williams* a64 53
3 ch g Singspiel(IRE) —Welsh Diva (Selkirk (USA))
2425[15] 3393[4] 4861[3] 5162[7] (6847) 7023[3] ◆ (7161)

Swan Wings *Andrew Balding* a69 89
3 b f Bahamian Bounty—Star Tulip (Night Shift (USA))
3197[8] 3891[6] 4231[5]

Sweet And Flawless (USA) *Eric R Reed* a92 101
4 bb m Unbridled's Song(USA) —Sweet And Ready (USA) (El Prado (IRE))
6604a[4]

Sweet Applause (IRE) *George Prodromou* a71 67
4 b m Acclamation—Nice Spice (IRE) (Common Grounds)
185[10] 344[6] 659[4] (684) 967[5] 1350[5] 1596[5] 1929[8] 2234[3] 2964[14] 3328[3] 3687[8] 3993[10] 4234[8] 6329[4]

Sweet August Moon (USA) *Brian Korinek* a106 91
5 bb m Malibu Moon(USA) —Silent Academy (USA) (Royal Academy (USA))
7341a[5]

Sweet Avon *Matthew Salaman* a62 65
3 gr f Avonbridge—Sweet Whisper (Petong)
24[8] 201[2] 346[3] (581) 788[6] 1347[9] 5470[2] 5876[8] 6421[12] 7390[7] 7518[7]

Sweet Baby Jane (IRE) *Arnfinn Lund* 46
3 br f Royal Applause—Nebulae (IRE) (Unfuwain (USA))
7374a[11]

Sweet Caroline (IRE) *B W Hills* a54
3 b f Motivator—Figlette (Darshaan)
928[4]

Sweet Cecily (IRE) *Richard Hannon* 97
2 b f Kodiac—Yaqootah (USA) (Gone West (USA))
2930[2] (3411) 4356[5] 5036[2] 5693[4] 6530[9] (7204)

Sweet Cheeks (IRE) *Richard Fahey* 69
2 b f Kheleyf(USA) —Sunset Darling (IRE) (Distant Music (USA))
(2939) ◆ 4150[6]

Sweet Child O'Mine *Richard Guest* a80 84
3 b f Singspiel(IRE) —Vendors Mistake (IRE) (Danehill (USA))
4[2] (781) 1210[3] 1571[3] 2219[3] 2515[2] 3796[6] 4548[6] (7304) 7523[8] 7638[5]

Sweet Clementine (IRE) *William Knight* a90 86
3 b f Shamardal(USA) —Heavenly Whisper (IRE) (Halling (USA))
(1620) 2256[5] 3217[4] 3790[4] ◆ 4593[8] (5142) 5702[10]

Sweet Effie (USA) *K Borgel* a32 53
4 b m Johannesburg(USA) —Francoa (USA) (Gone West (USA))
303a[0]

Sweet Gale (IRE) *Mike Murphy* a82 79
6 b m Soviet Star(USA) —Lady Moranbon (USA) (Trempolino (USA))
3115[10] 3474[10] 3914[6] 4424[4] 5327[4] (6208) (6292) 6714[7] 7209[7]

Sweetheart *Jamie Poulton* a75 83
6 b m Sinndar(IRE) —Love And Adventure (USA) (Halling (USA))
500[9] 1357[4] 1902[9] 2810[6] 3195[14]

Sweet Hearth (USA) *A De Royer-Dupre* a90 116
4 ch m Touch Gold(USA) —Sweet Gold (USA) (Gilded Time (USA))
3017a[5] 5802a[7] 6593a[5]

Sweetie Time *Michael Bell* 88
2 b f Invincible Spirit(IRE) —Blessing (Dubai Millennium)
2088[7] (2861) 4748[2] 7098[3]

Sweet Lightning *Michael Dods* a93 106
5 b g Fantastic Light(USA) —Sweetness Herself (Unfuwain (USA))
(1831) 2608[2] ◆ 3194[5] 3921[9] (5188) ◆ 5879[2] 6562[23]

Sweet Mirasol (IRE) *Mandy Rowland* a54 63
3 b f Celtic Swing—Sallwa (IRE) (Entrepreneur)
728[4] (870) 991[6] 1456[8] 1994[6] 2962[7] 4674[2] 5535[3]

Sweet Origin *Marco Botti* a65
3 ch g Osorio(GER) —Sweet Ludy (IRE) (Be My Guest (USA))
3275[2]

Sweet Pilgrim *Mark Usher* a39 70
3 b f Talkin Man(CAN) —Faraway Moon (Distant Relative)
1870[4] (2588) 3336[6] 4324[8]

Sweet Possession (USA) *Alan Jarvis* a49 64
4 b m Belong To Me(USA) —Bingo Meeting (USA) (General Meeting (USA))
1426[12] 2383[6] 2840[11]

Sweet Request *Dr Jeremy Naylor* a39 45
6 ch m Best Of The Bests(IRE) —Sweet Revival (Claude Monet (USA))
875[7] 1447[3] 1758[9]

Sweet Secret *Richard Hannon* a69 74
3 ch f Singspiel(IRE) —Ballymore Celebre (IRE) (Peintre Celebre (USA))
2718[14] 3325[5] 3628[2] 4201[4] 4988[4] (5384) 6479[2] 7255[4] 7305[8]

Sweet Seville (FR) *Terry Clement* a48 46
6 b m Agnes World(USA) —Hispalis (IRE) (Barathea (IRE))
585[7] 748[14] 7968[10]

Sweet Sonnet (USA) *Saeed Bin Suroor* 97
3 ch f Seeking The Gold(USA) —Minister's Melody (USA) (Deputy Minister (CAN))
2098[3] 3071[6] 3827[4] 5114[8]

Sweet Virginia (USA) *John Weymes* a50 27
4 bb m Arch(USA) —Hey Hey Sunny (USA) (Known Fact (USA))
160[5]

Sweet World *Bernard Llewellyn* a64 43
6 b g Agnes World(USA) —Douce Maison (IRE) (Fools Holme (USA))
6518[10]

Swell Fellow *David Evans* a39
5 gr g Beat All(USA) —Great Intent (Aragon)
82[7] 326[7]

Swendab (IRE) *John O'Shea* a40 60
2 b c Trans Island—Lavish Spirit (USA) (Southern Halo (USA))
2022[6] 2238[4] 5465[5] 6419[5] 6740[9]

Swift Alhaarth (IRE) *Mark Johnston* a76 65
2 b g Alhaarth(IRE) —Simla Bibi (Indian Ridge)
3162[4] 4346[5] 4993[7] 6936[3] (7916) ◆

Swift Bird (IRE) *Michael Quinlan* 68
2 b f Acclamation—She Legged It (IRE) (Cape Cross (IRE))
4095[7]

Swift Blade (IRE) *William Knight* a67
2 ch g Exceed And Excel(AUS) —Gold Strike (IRE) (Rainbow Quest (USA))
6249[7] 6742[5]

Swift Breeze *William Haggas* a67
2 b f Exceed And Excel(AUS) —Mellow Jazz (Lycius (USA))
(7686)

Swift Chap *Rod Millman* a76 92
4 b g Diktat—Regent's Folly (IRE) (Touching Wood (USA))
1533[7] 1841[2] 2322[6] 2710[8] 3334[9] 4224[3] 5540[8] 5833[6] 6260[12]

Swift Gift *Brian Meehan* a94 105
5 b g Cadeaux Genereux—Got To Go (Shareef Dancer (USA))
412a[2] ◆ 710a[10] 3146[6] 4358[13] 5068[2] 6349[5]

Swiftly Done (IRE) *Declan Carroll* a73 73
3 b g Whipper(USA) —Ziffany (Taufan (USA))
3587[3] 4339[6] 5057[4] 5487[6] 6225[7] 6413[6] (6629) 6794[3]

Swift Return *Stuart Williams* a71 73
3 b g Fantastic Light(USA) —Swift Dispersal (Shareef Dancer (USA))
692[3] 2935[11] 3363[6] 5670[2] 5710[5] 6023[5] 6332[3] 7069[3]

Swift Steel *Ann Duffield* a40
3 b f Kyllachy—Swift Baba (USA) (Deerhound (USA))
624[5] 793[7] 858[7] 1469[9]

Swilly Ferry (USA) *B W Hills* a82 108
3 b c Wiseman's Ferry(USA) —Keepers Hill (IRE) (Danehill (USA))
1315[5] ◆ 1701[6] (2545) 2978[19] 3791[18] 5911[5] 6752[19]

Swimsuit *Michael Jarvis* a68 64
2 b f Sleeping Indian—Love Quest (Pursuit Of Love)
7123[2] (7802)

Swindler (IRE) *Andrew Balding* a76 92
4 b g Sinndar(IRE) —Imitation (Darshaan)
(1157)

Swindlers Lass (IRE) *Mark Gillard* a50
3 b f Chineur(FR) —Rainbow Lass (Rainbow Quest (USA))
385[12] 592[9] 864[7] 1145[7]

Swindy *Paul Cole* 74
2 b c Hurricane Run(IRE) —Red Passion (USA) (Seeking The Gold (USA))
7099[7] (7302)

Swing Door (IRE) *B W Hills* 50
2 ch f Pivotal—Passageway (USA) (Gold Fever (USA))
7346[7]

Swinging Hawk (GER) *Ian Williams* a69 91
4 ch h Hawk Wing(USA) —Saldenschwinge (GER) (In The Wings)
3241[2] ◆ 3634[8] 6926[31]

Swinging Sixties (IRE) *M Al Muhairi* a95 99
5 b g Singspiel(IRE) —Velvet Lady (Nashwan (USA))
441a[5] ◆

Swingkeel (IRE) *John Dunlop* a96 104
5 ch g Singspiel(IRE) —Anniversary (Salse (USA))
1176[8] 1821[5] 3195[3] 4566a[11] 5696[3] 6926[10]

Swingle *Derek Haydn Jones* a24 54
3 b f Dubawi(IRE) —Divina Mia (Dowsing (USA))
4679[9] 5057[5] 5474[7] 6952[8] 7498[7]

Swing Pattern (USA) *John M Oxx* a92 80
3 b g Leroidesanimaux(BRZ) —Gold Pattern (USA) (Slew O'Gold (USA))
6548a[5]

Swirl Tango *F Jordan*
4 b m Lujain(USA) —Tangolania (FR) (Ashkalani (IRE))
2249[13] 3556[14] 4586[9]

Swish Dish (CAN) *Richard Hannon* 73
3 bb f El Corredor(USA) —Amelia Saratoga (JPN) (Dehere (USA))
1356[3] 1644[3] 5972[11] 6632[11]

Swiss Act *Mark Johnston* a95 91
6 ch g Act One—Dancing Mirage (IRE) (Machiavellian (USA))
1069[4] 1525[4] 1736[6] 2126[3] 6131[6]

Swiss Art (IRE) *Alison Thorpe* a78 61
4 b g One Cool Cat(USA) —Alpine Park (IRE) (Barathea (IRE))
1239[5] 1536[4] 1587[6] 1995[6] 3560[6]

Swiss Cross *Gerard Butler* a91 84
3 b g Cape Cross(IRE) —Swiss Lake (USA) (Indian Ridge)
1315[13] 1913[6] 2110[2] 2644[5] 5750[11] 5964[3] 6198[2] (6799) 7289[7]

Swiss Diva *David Elsworth* a94 114
4 b m Pivotal—Swiss Lake (USA) (Indian Ridge)
3415[2] ◆ 3875[7] 4269a[2] (4773a) (5576a) (6012a) ◆ 6608a[13]

Swiss Dream *David Elsworth* 83
2 b f Oasis Dream—Swiss Lake (USA) (Indian Ridge)
1972[5] (2561) 3070[10] 4262[2] 4592[6] 7347[13]

Swiss Franc *David Elsworth* a105 81
5 br g Mr Greeley(USA) —Swiss Lake (USA) (Indian Ridge)
1007[10] 1206[10] 2054[10]

Swiss Guard *Tim Vaughan* a20 74
4 b h Montjeu(IRE) —Millennium Dash (Nashwan (USA))
803[11]

Switch (USA) *John W Sadler* a116 97
3 b f Quiet American(USA) —Antoniette (USA) (Nicholas (USA))
6603a[2] 7341a[2]

Switchback *Sir Michael Stoute* a54
2 b c Medicean—Hooplah (Pivotal)
6053[7]

Switched Off *Ian Williams* 79
5 b g Catcher In The Rye(IRE) —Button Hole Flower (IRE) (Fairy King (USA))
1485[11] 1705[5] 1927[11] 3025[4] (5828) (6051) 6322[2]

Swop (IRE) *Luca Cumani* a103 107
7 b g Shinko Forest(IRE) —Changing Partners (Rainbow Quest (USA))
339a[3] ◆ 511a[2] 713a[5] 818a[2] 5948[8] 6888[30]

Swords *Ray Peacock* a65 56
8 b g Vettori(IRE) —Pomorie (IRE) (Be My Guest (USA))
575[4] 621[8] 777[5] 4683[8] 6121[7] 6662[5] 7634[12]

Swordsman (GER) *Chris Gordon* a81 76
8 b g Acatenango(GER) —Saiga (Windwurf (GER))
(1446) 1849[3] 4026[2] 4141[8] 4745[2]

Sword Style (GER) *Mario Hofer* 67
2 b f Desert Style(IRE) —Sword Roche (GER) (Laroche (GER))
7108a[11]

Sworn Pro (GER) *Mario Hofer* 101
4 bb m Protektor(GER) —Sweet Tern (GER) (Arctic Tern (USA))
6011a[5]

Sworn Tigress (GER) *George Baker* a81 81
5 b m Tiger Hill(IRE) —Sweet Tern (GER) (Arctic Tern (USA))
(795) (854) (865) ◆ 941[2] 1484[4] 1916[5] 7599[2] 7729[7]

Syann (IRE) *David Marnane* 96
3 gr f Daylami(IRE) —Hedera (USA) (Woodman (USA))
6786a[11]

Sybelio (FR) *J Rossi* 102
6 bb h Lord Of Men—Trueville (GER) (Top Ville)
(1056a) 4566a[3] 5349a[8]

Sydney Bridge *J Barclay* 59
3 b g Danbird(AUS) —Miss Prim (Case Law)
1201[7] 1667[11] 3073[12] 3595[9]

Sydney Harbour (IRE) *David Wachman* 97
2 b c Danehill Dancer(IRE) —Amethyst (IRE) (Sadler's Wells (USA))
3645a[4] 5567a[6]

Sylas Ings *Pat Phelan* a71 77
2 b c Kyllachy—Ashlinn (IRE) (Ashkalani (IRE))
2077[3] 2319[3] 5587[6] 6802[4] 6994[7] 7479[2] 7609[4]

Sylvestris (IRE) *Ralph Beckett* 77
2 b f Arch(USA) —Woodmaven (USA) (Woodman (USA))
4095[2] 4595[3] 5691[3] 6317[3]

Symi (IRE) *John Gosden* 4
2 b f Hennessy(USA) —Cassydora (Darshaan)
5147[14]

Symphony Of Love *Dai Burchell* 24
2 ch f Pursuit Of Love—Flying Lion (Hunting Lion (IRE))
1999[9] 2918[5]

Syncopated Lady (IRE) *David O'Meara* 54
2 b f Acclamation—Perugino Lodge (IRE) (Perugino (USA))
4862[6] 5277[14] 5755[5] 6294[3]

Synergistic (IRE) *A Scharer* 74
5 b h In The Wings—Queens Wharf (IRE) (Ela-Mana-Mou)
461a[10]

Synergy (FR) *Y Durepaire* 107
5 b m Victory Note(USA) —Kuddam (IRE) (Doyoun)
439a[3]

Synonymy *Michael Blanshard* a66 39
7 b g Sinndar(IRE) —Peony (Lion Cavern (USA))
2923[6] 3639[9]

Syrian *Ian Williams* a82 94
3 b g Hawk Wing(USA) —Lady Lahar (Fraam)
1334[8] 1834[7] 2544[4] 2970[6] 3413[2] ◆ 4104[7] (5073) 5511[7] 5904[4] 6467[7] 6753[16] 7293[7] (7438) 7637[4] ◆ 7724[8]

Szabo's Destiny *James Given* a64
2 b g Dubai Destination(USA) —Odette (Pursuit Of Love)
7178[10] 7325[5] 7470[4] 7802[2] 7954[5] 8001[4]

Taajub (IRE) *William Haggas* a74 109
3 b c Exceed And Excel(AUS) —Purple Tiger (IRE) (Rainbow Quest (USA))
6735[15] 7073a[11]

Ta Aleem *Brendan Powell*
4 ch m Galileo(IRE) —Tadris (USA) (Red Ransom (USA))
246[7]

Taameer *Marcus Tregoning* 103
4 b h Beat Hollow—Vayavaig (Damister (USA))
5853[7] 6562[33]

Taaresh (IRE) *Kevin Morgan* a76 81
5 b g Sakhee(USA) —Tanaghum (Darshaan)
255[5] 383[4] (765) 1156[5] 1484[3] (1867) 2435[4] 2961[10]

Tabaran (FR) *Alison Thorpe* a58 19
7 ch g Polish Precedent(USA) —Tabariya (IRE) (Doyoun)
874[7]

Tabaret *Richard Whitaker* a99 97
7 ch g Bertolini(USA) —Luanshya (First Trump)
(1688) 2054[3] 2135[4] 2346[6] 2657[6] 2992[6] 3178[8] 3828[6] 4148[5] 4558[2] 4806[8] (5069) 5308[11] 5884[16] 6918[8]

Tabassum (IRE) *Sir Michael Stoute* 108
3 b f Nayef(USA) —Tomoohat (USA) (Danzig (USA))
3143[11] 4540[8]

Tabiet *James Moffatt* 61
3 ch f Danroad(AUS) —Frabrofen (Mind Games)
1868[5] (2741) 4406[11] 5410[4] 6295[18] 6492[7]

Table Mountain (IRE) *A P O'Brien* 92
3 b g Milan—Shirley Blue (IRE) (Shirley Heights)
6971a[3]

Taboor (IRE) *Robert Cowell* a52 49
12 b g Mujadil(USA) —Christoph's Girl (Efisio)
178[8] 271[8] 477[2] 726[4] 1131[8] 1598[11]

Taborcillo *David Barron* 67
3 b g Lucky Story(USA) —Trust In Paula (USA) (Arazi (USA))
(1468) 1811[6] 2099[9] 2449[2] 3174[8] 4169[6] 4826[9] 5410[7] 6188[5] 6897[15]

Tactic *John Dunlop* 119
4 b g Sadler's Wells(USA) —Tanaghum (Darshaan)
1529[2] (2345) (3470a) ◆ 4506[9] 5976a[6]

Tactician *Michael Bell* 101
3 b g Motivator—Tempting Prospect (Shirley Heights)
(1386) 3105[8] 4304[2] 5273[2] 5908[5]

Tadalavil *Linda Perratt* a76 74
5 gr g Clodovil(IRE) —Blandish (USA) (Wild Again (USA))
(1869) 2671[3] 2856[5] 3409[4] 3902[3] 4063[3] (4192)

Tadlil *Milton Bradley* a58 58
8 b g Pivotal—Pretty Poppy (Song)
70[5] 145[6]

Tae Kwon Do (USA) *Julie-Ann Camacho* a61 59
4 b g Thunder Gulch(USA) —Judy's Magic (USA) (Wavering Monarch (USA))
3370[5] 4156[6] 4946[8]

Taeping (IRE) *Reg Hollinshead* a52 55
3 b g Invincible Spirit(IRE) —Simil (USA) (Apalachee (USA))
3685[10] 3972[9] 4475[10] 4861[8]

Tafaneen (USA) *Michael Jarvis* 47
2 bb f Dynaformer(USA) —Cozzy Corner (USA) (Cozzene (USA))
7232[14]

Tafawut *Clive Cox* a74 79
3 b f Nayef(USA) —Rohita (IRE) (Waajib)
(768) 1159[7] 1514[2] 1850[5] 3628[6] 3866[9]

Tagansky *Simon Dow* a70 26
2 b g Barathea(IRE) —Tenable (Polish Precedent (USA))
2547[13] 4253[2] 4838[5] 5718[3] 6053[5]

Tagar Bere (FR) *M Pimbonnet* a82 96
3 ch c High Yield(USA) —Arrondie (FR) (Inchinor)
741a[5] 6761a[8]

Tagena (IRE) *David Evans* 53
2 ch f Tagula(IRE) —Lamzena (IRE) (Fairy King (USA))
1429[6] 1793[6]

Tagseed (IRE) *William Haggas* 96
4 b g Elusive City(USA) —Allegorica (IRE) (Alzao (USA))
1425[2] (2004) (2462) (3224) 4358[21]

Tag Team (IRE) *John Harris* a59 44
9 ch g Tagula(IRE) —Okay Baby (IRE) (Treasure Kay)
70[2] 264[2] 403[2] 721[3] 3280[9] 4071[8] 4478[13] 7473[11] 7564[7]

Tagula Minx (IRE) *Jeff Pearce* a51 20
4 b m Tagula(IRE) —Persian Fantasia (Alzao (USA))
493[6]

Tagula Night (IRE) *Walter Swinburn* a90 93
4 ch g Tagula(IRE) —Carpet Lady (IRE) (Night Shift (USA))
1903[10] 2681[11] 3037[11] 3779[3] (4961) 5528[3] (5995)

Tahaamah *Saeed Bin Suroor* a69 73
2 ch c King's Best(USA) —Russian Snows (IRE) (Sadler's Wells (USA))
(6333) ◆ 6979[2]

Tahitian Princess (IRE) *Ann Duffield* 46
2 b f One Cool Cat(USA) —Akarita (IRE) (Akarad (FR))
6566[6] 6893[6] 7142[8]

Tahitian Warrior (USA) *Saeed Bin Suroor* a109 71
3 gr g Maria's Mon(USA) —Chatique (USA) (Deputy Minister (CAN))
819a[10]

Tahseen *Marcus Tregoning* 66
3 b c Haafhd—Merayaat (IRE) (Darshaan)
2011[9]

Tai Hang (IRE) *Jim Goldie* 40
3 br f Celtic Swing—Victoria Peek (IRE) (Cape Cross (IRE))
2212[4] 2834[14] 3167[8]

Taikoo *Hughie Morrison* a90 84
5 b g Dr Fong(USA) —So True (So Blessed)
6224[4] ◆ 6516[4] 7130[6]

Tajaarub *B W Hills* a80 85
3 ch g Lomitas—Simacota (GER) (Acatenango (GER))
(618) ◆ 1466[2] 1730[6] 3335[4] 7084[10]

Tajaaweed (USA) *Daniel Peitz* 108
5 b h Dynaformer(USA) —Uforia (USA) (Zilzal (USA))
5321a[6]

Tajneed (IRE) *David Nicholls* a94 111
7 b g Alhaarth(IRE) —Indian Express (Indian Ridge)
1295[2] (2657) 2992[7] 4085[4] 4391[11] 5095[2] (5302) 6752[5] 7060[7]

Takaamul *Kevin Morgan* a59 62
7 ch g Almutawakel—Mafaatin (IRE) (Royal Academy (USA))
4715[12]

Takajan (IRE) *Mark Brisbourne* a75 75
3 b g Barathea(IRE) —Takaliya (IRE) (Darshaan)
161[2] 326[2] 385[5] 638[8] 2566[8] 2892[11] 3759[2] 4618[10] 5073[11] 5614[9] 5905[7] 6168[9] 6935[11] (7131) 7402[11] 7473[2] (7730) 7847[6] 7906[6]

Takashi (FR) *J-C Rouget* a38 56
3 b c One Cool Cat(USA) —Alcidiana (FR) (Linamix (FR))
450a[4]

Takeaway *Jim Boyle* a81 86
2 b c Sleeping Indian—Bon Vivant (USA) (Salt Lake (USA))
(1017) 1173[4] 2177[3] 2397[7] 4138[11] 4801[2] 5374[6] 5701[3] (6307) 6500[3] 7484[2] (7857) (8012)

Take Flight (IRE) *Jeremy Noseda* a52 84
2 ch f Pivotal—Polish Descent (IRE) (Danehill (USA))
2251[3] 2641[5] (4753)

Take It There *Alastair Lidderdale* a47 47
8 ch m Cadeaux Genereux—Feel Free (IRE) (Generous (IRE))
199[8]

Take It To The Max *George Moore* 95
3 b g Bahamian Bounty—Up And About (Barathea (IRE))
1498[4] 2070[3] 4830[14] 5511[8] 6304[7] 6753[13] 7205[6]

Take My Hand *Mick Channon* a61 62
3 ch f Imperial Dancer—Royal Logic (Royal Applause)
1048[10] 1162[2] (1469) 1810[6] 2132[6] 2460[7] 4058[9] 4280[6] 4534[3] 4791[6] 5171[8]

Take Ten *Mark Johnston* a101 96
3 b g Bahamian Bounty—See You Later (Emarati (USA))
1499[4] 2545[10] 2978[18] 3311[5] 3791[4] ◆ 5524[4] 5911[7] 6429[5] (7217a) (7443)

Take That *Simon Griffiths* 15
5 b g Kasakov—Baby Be (Bold Arrangement)
112[9] 3287[12] 3615[13] 3977[9]

Take The Micky *Chris Wall* a69 69
4 b g Beat Hollow—Ailincala (IRE) (Pursuit Of Love)
11[DSQ]

Take The Points (USA) *Todd Pletcher* a109 116
4 gr h Even The Score(USA) —Ginger Ginger (USA) (Fred Astaire (USA))
1025a[5]

Take Your Partner *Kevin Ryan* a61 54
2 b c Piccolo—Takes Two To Tango (Groom Dancer (USA))
7346[8] 7578[9] 7779[2] 7954[4]

Takhir (IRE) *P Schiergen* a70 88
4 b h Lando(GER) —Tocopilla (FR) (Medaaly)
334a[11]

Takitwo *Peter Cundell* a51 65
7 b g Delta Dancer—Tiama (IRE) (Last Tycoon)
763[6] 984[5] 1171[10] 1737[3] 2053[11]

Takween (IRE) *Howard Johnson* 31
5 gr g Nayef(USA) —Norfolk Lavender (CAN) (Ascot Knight (CAN))
2208[7]

Talamahana *Andrew Haynes* a49 58
5 b m Kyllachy—Bahawir Pour (USA) (Green Dancer (USA))
1441[12] 1547[8] 2021[5] 2590[13] 3308[3] 3727[2] 3979[4] 4283[10] 4589[2] 4735[7] 5076[7]

Talayeb *Marcus Tregoning* a75 76
5 bb g Nayef(USA) —Paper Chase (FR) (Machiavellian (USA))
3911[3] (7994)

Taleia (GER) *A Wohler* 91
2 b f Dashing Blade—Tintina (USA) (General Assembly (USA))
6407a[2]

Talenta (BRZ) *A Cintra Pereira* a91
4 ch m Wild Event(USA) —Brincalhona (ARG) (Lode (USA))
333a[4] ◆ 514a[9] 709a[6]

Talenti (IRE) *David Flood* a75 75
7 b g Sadler's Wells(USA) —Sumoto (Mtoto)
4202[3] 4657[5] (5148) 6322[3] (6699) (7089) (7480) 7687[8] 8032[2]

Talent Scout (IRE) *Tim Walford* a62 63
4 b g Exceed And Excel(AUS) —Taalluf (USA) (Hansel (USA))
5122[7] 5487[8] 5815[7] 6296[7] 7064[8] 7502[4] (7604) 7706[5]

Tale Untold (USA) *Richard Hannon* a84 96
2 ch f Tale Of The Cat(USA) —Bank On Her (USA) (Rahy (USA))
(3778) ◆ 5693[5] 6157[2] 6559[2] 7340a[11]

Talkative Guest (IRE) *George Margarson* 64
2 b f Oratorio(IRE) —Pedicure (Atticus (USA))
4658[10] 5147[4]

Talkhees (IRE) *Brian Meehan* a51
2 b f Invincible Spirit(IRE) —Asaafeer (USA) (Dayjur (USA))
3778[7] 5029[9] 5719[9] 6901[5]

Talking Back *Sylvester Kirk* a38 40
2 b c Pastoral Pursuits—With Distinction (Zafonic (USA))
5032[12] 5629[15] 6118[10] 6542[9] 7520[6] 7813[9]

Talkin Italian *Hughie Morrison*
2 b f Medicean—Easy Sunshine (IRE) (Sadler's Wells (USA))
7020[12]

Talk Of Saafend (IRE) *P Monteith* a78 71
5 b m Barathea(IRE) —Sopran Marida (IRE) (Darshaan)
2452[5] 3149[3] 3531[5] 3708[5] 3950[2] 4585[5] 4823[5] 5213[14] 5408[10]

Talk Talk (IRE) *Brian Meehan* 73
2 b g Oratorio(IRE) —Sybella (In The Wings)
2077[7] 2547[9] 4247[4]

Tallahasse (IRE) *Alan Swinbank* 90
2 b f Acclamation—Designer Chic (Red Ransom (USA))
(4451) ◆ (4748) 6176[6]

Tallawalla (IRE) *Mick Channon* a61 61
3 b f Oratorio(IRE) —Edetana (USA) (Diesis)
490[7] 762[7] 1158[9] 1394[6] 1466[4] 2333[4] 4282[6] (5159) 5361[5] 5469[5] 5962[7] 6579[2] 6905[3] 7070[2] 7449[5]

Tall Chief (IRE) *Mlle V Dissaux* a89 85
3 b c Observatory(USA) —Ballerina Rosa (FR) (Anabaa (USA))
927a[5] 7959a[4]

Tallest Peak (USA) *Michael Quinlan* a63
5 b g Giant's Causeway(USA) —Hum Along (USA) (Fappiano (USA))
36[5] 75[4] 194[10]

Talley Close *Richard Fahey* a89 89
2 b c Danbird(AUS) —No Candles Tonight (Star Appeal)
3365[4] (4240) (4851) 5745[6] (6647) (7444)

Tallulah Mai *Matthew Salaman* a57
3 b f Kayf Tara—Al Awaalah (Mukaddamah (USA))
7345 1059[7] 7475[8]

Tamaathul *B W Hills* 110
3 gr c Tiger Hill(IRE) —Tahrir (IRE) (Linamix (FR))
1330[3] ◆ 1858[4] 5292[2] 6529[4]

Tamagin (USA) *Jeff Pearce* a109 114
7 b g Stravinsky(USA) —Luia (USA) (Forty Niner (USA))
1353[8]

Tamanaco (IRE) *Tim Walford* 81
3 b g Catcher In The Rye(IRE) —Right After Moyne (IRE) (Imperial Ballet (IRE))
1297[5] 4341[6] (4786) 6677[4]

Tamareen (IRE) *Ed Dunlop* a72 69
2 b c Bahamian Bounty—Damjanich (IRE) (Mull Of Kintyre (USA))
2007[4] 2312[4] 5160[4] 5720[9] (6163) (6426)

Tamarillo Grove (IRE) *Bryan Smart* 78
3 b g Cape Cross(IRE) —Tamarillo (Daylami (IRE))
1485[5] 2220[2] 3176[4] 4784[5] (5478) 6266[8] 7053[11]

Tamarind Hill (IRE) *Alan McCabe* a66 71
3 b g Shamardal(USA) —Amandian (IRE) (Indian Ridge)
17[2] 85[3] 168[3] 406[4] 454[5] 566[4] 702[5] 856[2] 906[5] 1146[3] 1469[3] 1643[8] 1923[5] (2217) 2648[6] 2849[3] 3030[9] (3243) 4938[5] 5023[5] 5299[7] 5764[10] 6031[7] 6440[3] (6880) 7033[11]

Tamasou (IRE) *F J Brennan* a83 83
5 b g Tamarisk(IRE) —Soubresaut (IRE) (Danehill (USA))
16[3] 151[3] 286[8] 1990[7] 3083[6] 3779[9] 5386[6] 5634[6]

Tameen *John Dunlop* 75
2 b f Shirocco(GER) —Najah (IRE) (Nashwan (USA))
4844[6] 5692[7] (6469) ◆

Tamino (IRE) *Paul Howling* a62 43
7 b g Mozart(IRE) —Stop Out (Rudimentary (USA))
(10) 135[11] 235[8] 368[2] 674[2] 694[3] 763[3] 844[10] 1236[6] 2184[11] 2964[10] 5714[8]

Tam Lin *M bin Shafya* a58 117
7 b g Selkirk(USA) —La Nuit Rose (FR) (Rainbow Quest (USA))
338a[13] 417a[3] 631a[4] 801a[3] 1025a[16]

Tammela *Alan Jarvis* a54 65
3 b f Beat Hollow—On The Wing (Pivotal)
978[5] 1514[6] 3080[13] 4626[8] 5034[3] 6993[9]

Tamtara *Amanda Perrett* a79 77
3 b f Red Ransom(USA) —Tamalain (USA) (Royal Academy (USA))
698[3] 2398[6] (2725) 3363[3] 3963[4] 4492[5] 5115[4] 6122[2] 7042[10]

Tanassuq (USA) *John Dunlop* 65
2 b f Rahy(USA) —Wasnah (USA) (Nijinsky (CAN))
6803[4]

Tan Bonita (USA) *Ralph Smith* a40 34
5 bb m More Than Ready(USA) —Time For Hennessy (USA) (Hennessy (USA))
477[11] 659[7] 687[5] 1814a[5] 2053[14]

Tancred Spirit *Paul Midgley* 52
2 b f Mind Games—Tancred Times (Clantime)
2272[5] 3549[7] 5418[11] 6035[13]

Tanfeer *Saeed Bin Suroor* 93
2 bb f Dansili—Mawaakeb (USA) (Diesis)
(3392) 3792[7]

Tanfeeth *Ed Dunlop* 62
2 ch c Singspiel(IRE) —Nasij (USA) (Elusive Quality (USA))
4962[5] ◆

Tanforan *Brian Baugh* a40 71
8 b g Mujahid(USA) —Florentynna Bay (Aragon)
1172[7] 1926[14] 2527[12] (2864) 3377[6] 3690[3] 3911[5] 4547[3] 5050[5] 5584[9] 6495[5] 6935[10]

Tangamani (FR) *C Baillet* a66 89
2 b f Indian Rocket—Volunia (In The Wings)
4275a[9]

Tangaspeed (FR) *R Laplanche* a97 114
5 b m Vertical Speed(FR) —Fitanga (FR) (Fijar Tango (FR))
(742a) 953a[9] 7160a[0]

Tangerine Trees *Bryan Smart* a73 108
5 b g Mind Games—Easy To Imagine (USA) (Cozzene (USA))
(1270) (1650) 2113[9] (2856) 3753[4] (6265) (6508) ◆

Tango Step (IRE) *Declan Carroll* a52 45
10 b g Sesaro(USA) —Leitrim Lodge (IRE) (Classic Music (USA))
39[3] 69[2] 264[9] 296[12]

Tanjung Agas (IRE) *Michael Jarvis* 56
2 b g Montjeu(IRE) —Najmati (Green Desert (USA))
5491[14] 6127[7] 7302[7]

Tanked Up (IRE) *David Nicholls* 59
2 b g One Cool Cat(USA) —White Fang (IRE) (Wolfhound (USA))
(1463) 1647[2] 2391[3] 2848[5]

Tanktastic *Peter Hedger* a53
8 b g Chaddleworth(IRE) —Honeybed Wood (Town And Country)
585[8]

Tanley *Ian McInnes* a61 55
5 gr g Compton Admiral—Schatzi (Chilibang)
(8) 103[2] 195[9] 312[2] 3605[8] 3976[11] 5045[5] 5535[11] 5926[11] 6189[12]

Tannenberg (IRE) *Tony Carroll* a62 88
9 b g Polish Precedent(USA) —Upper Strata (Shirley Heights)
293[8]

Tanto Faz (IRE) *John Quinn* a88 91
5 b g Rock Of Gibraltar(IRE) —Sharakawa (IRE) (Darshaan)
2685[6]

Tantsor (FR) *Paul Midgley* 40
3 ch g Brier Creek(USA) —Norova (FR) (Hawker's News (IRE))
1466[5] 4017[7]

Tap Dance Way (IRE) *Patrick Chamings* a73 74
3 b f Azamour(IRE) —Dance Lively (USA) (Kingmambo (USA))
1872[3] 2564[5] 3464[7] 4365[2] (5113) 6852[7]

Taper Jean Girl (IRE) *Ruth Carr* a62 38
3 b f Elusive City(USA) —Ruacana Falls (USA) (Storm Bird (CAN))
329[3] 455[5] 507[2] 597[3] 861[5] 1469[6] 2185[12] 2787[6]

Tapis Libre *Michael Easterby* 65
2 b g Librettist(USA) —Stella Manuela (FR) (Galileo (IRE))
4346[11] 4940[5] 5352[6] 5784[4] (6300) 6978[12]

Tap It Light (USA) *Mike Mitchell* a105 94
6 ch g General Meeting(USA) —Popular Opinion (USA) (Half A Year (USA))
1435a[6]

Taptam (USA) *W Bret Calhoun* a104
5 ch m Pleasant Tap(USA) —Salty Tam (USA) (Salt Lake (USA))
1242a[2]

Taqaat (USA) *Mark Johnston* a73
2 b c Forestry(USA) —Alrayihah (IRE) (Nashwan (USA))
6743[4]

Taqdeyr *A bin Huzaim* a94 106
5 ch g Dubai Destination(USA) —Pastorale (Nureyev (USA))
412a[14] 515a[9]

Taqleed (IRE) *John Gosden* 103
3 bb g Shamardal(USA) —Thakafaat (IRE) (Unfuwain (USA))
(5057) (5529) ◆ 6562[6] ◆

Taquawin (FR) *D Prod'Homme*
2 b f Okawango(USA) —Money Spinner (FR) (Anabaa (USA))
5252a[P]

Tar (IRE) *Tim Vaughan* a55 79
6 b g Danzig(USA) —Royal Show (IRE) (Sadler's Wells (USA))
813[4] 942[5]

Tarantella Lady *George Moore* 73
2 b f Noverre(USA) —Shortfall (Last Tycoon)
1686[4] 2239[4] 5878[6] 6222[4]

Tariq Too *David Simcock* a63 82
3 ch c Kyllachy—Tatora (Selkirk (USA))
2335[4] 2925[3] 4207[3] (6039) 6367[3] 6963[6]

Tarita (IRE) *Richard Hannon* a54 76
3 ch f Bahamian Bounty—Zonic (Zafonic (USA))
2025[2] 2342[12] 3023[6] 3592[9] 4378[8] 5027[10] 6452[5] 6862[3]

Tarjeyh (IRE) *Marcus Tregoning* 58
2 b c Medicean—Navajo Rainbow (Rainbow Quest (USA))
2078[10] 2932[4] ◆

Tarkheena Prince (USA) *C Von Der Recke* a103 103
5 b g Aldebaran(USA) —Tarkheena (USA) (Alleged (USA))
2574a[7] 4012a[6] 4566a[6] 6011a[8]

Tarooq (USA) *Richard Fahey* a73 78
4 b g War Chant(USA) —Rose Of Zollern (IRE) (Seattle Dancer (USA))
4556[2] 5303[2] (5815) 7062[12] 7414[3]

Tarrsille (IRE) *Mrs John Harrington* a90 89
4 b g Dansili—Tara Gold (IRE) (Royal Academy (USA))
5127a[12]

Tartan Gigha (IRE) *Mark Johnston* a97 108
5 b g Green Desert(USA) —High Standard (Kris)
334a[5] 415a[2] 885[7] 1274[6] 1533[2] (1697) (2708) 3144[12] 3692[15] 4455[12] 5247[14] 5879[7] 6193[12] 6562[32]

Tartan Gunna *Mark Johnston* a92 96
4 b g Anabaa(USA) —Embraced (Pursuit Of Love)
863[6] 1006[6] 1272[3] 1474[3] 1697[5] 2027[3] 2710[6] 2977[7] (3366) 3633[5] 4455[6] 4537[11] 4816[6] 5592[5] 5955[4]

Tartan Trip *Andrew Balding* a87 88
3 b g Selkirk(USA) —Marajuana (Robellino (USA))
1453[2] ◆ (4265) 4699[2] 5524[10] 5750[5] ◆ 6534[6]

Tartaria *David Simcock* a68 66
4 b m Oasis Dream—Habariya (IRE) (Perugino (USA))
1809[2] 2473[6] 2921[4]

Tartatartufata *James Given* a70 72
8 b m Tagula(IRE) —It's So Easy (Shaadi (USA))
138[5] 402[6] 462[6]

Tartufo Dolce (IRE) *James Given* a71 62
3 b f Key Of Luck(USA) —Corn Futures (Nomination)
1750[10] 2648[13] 3023[4] 3904[6] 4749[6] 5410[3] 5957[6] 6464[14] 7154[7]

T'As D'Beaux Yeux *D Smaga* 95
3 b f Red Ransom(USA) —Torrealta (In The Wings)
2373a[8]

Tasdeer (USA) *Doug Watson* a61 70
5 b g Rahy(USA) —Mehthaaf (USA) (Nureyev (USA))
438a[11]

Tasfeya *Mark Johnston* a77 78
2 b c Haafhd—Nufoos (Zafonic (USA))
5814[3] ◆ 6334[3] (6919) 7280[2]

Tasmeem (IRE) *Richard Fahey* a47 87
3 gr g Acclamation—Park Approach (IRE) (Indian Ridge)
1399[9] 1836[5] 3673[6] 4091[6] 4370[8] 4865[4] 5501[2] 5606[2] 5941[8] 6358[4] 6799[12]

Tastahil (IRE) *B W Hills* a94 115
6 ch g Singspiel(IRE) —Luana (Shaadi (USA))
1176[10] 1821[2] 3102[8] 5218[6] 5909[2] 6388[4] (6929)

Taste The Victory (USA) *Alan Swinbank* 78
3 b g Victory Gallop(CAN) —Tastetheteardrops (USA) (What Luck (USA))
1927[2] 2515[5] 3208[6]

Taste The Wine (IRE) *Bernard Llewellyn* a72 74
4 gr g Verglas(IRE) —Azia (IRE) (Desert Story (IRE))
120[2] 280[6] 5084[8] 6055[11] 6502[4] 6744[7] (7626)

Tasteyville (USA) *E Charpy* a73
7 gr r With Approval(CAN) —Rahfee (USA) (Rahy (USA))
334a[14] 632a[14]

Tasty Temptation (CAN) *Mark Casse* a103
4 rg m Medaglia D'Oro(USA) —Parisia (CAN) (Tethra (CAN))
7371a[6]

Tasza (USA) *Alan McCabe* a60 60
3 bb f Johannesburg(USA) —Bald Beauty (USA) (Baldski (USA))
3587[5] 4601[6] 5057[2] 6212[5] 7305[7] 7543[12] 7768[8]

Tatawor (IRE) *Jim Boyle* a71 27
3 b g Kheleyf(USA) —Romea (Muhtarram (USA))
24[3] 147[6] 276[4] 313[6] 443[5] 483[6] 550[8]

Tatiana Romanova (USA) *Richard Fahey* a61 76
3 ch f Mr Greeley(USA) —Bank On Her (USA) (Rahy (USA))
2348[4] 2652[9] 5598[8] 6395[8] 6922[8]

Tattler *Mark Johnston* 69
3 b c Dansili—Torcross (Vettori (IRE))
2900[11] 4661[5]

Tauman (IRE) *Vittorio Caruso* 101
3 b c Blu Air Force(IRE) —Time Of Gold (USA) (Banker's Gold (USA))
1418a[9]

Taurakina *Marco Botti* a73 81
4 b m Selkirk(USA) —Asmita (Efisio)
(7299) ◆ 7425[4] 7837[5]

Taurus Twins *Richard Price* a64 82
4 b g Deportivo—Intellibet One (Compton Place)
1267[6] ◆ 1874[2] 2094[7] 2756[10] 4090[5] 4625[10]

Tavalu (USA) *Gerald Ham* a41 68
8 b g Kingmambo(USA) —Larrocha (IRE) (Sadler's Wells (USA))
263[12]

Taverners Jubilee *Patrick Morris* a19 29
2 b g Sleeping Indian—Page (Elmaamul (USA))
5465[13] 6045[5] 7065[10]

Tawaabb *Mick Channon* 99
3 ch c Kyllachy—Penmayne (Inchinor)
2058[8] 2972[5] 3856[3] 4541[5] 5250[9] 5944[19] 6321[10]

Tawaaleef (USA) *J E Hammond* 82
2 ch f Haafhd—Siyadah (USA) (Mr Prospector (USA))
7008a[7]

Tawaassol (USA) *E Charpy* a84 89
7 b h War Chant(USA) —Montecito (USA) (Seeking The Gold (USA))
628a[8]

Tawzeea (IRE) *Michael Dods* a64 75
5 ch g Cadeaux Genereux—Kismah (Machiavellian (USA))
474[6] 2113[14] 2504[2] 3061[4] 3409[6] 4121[9] 4706[5] 6295[3] 6491[4] 6713[10] 7195[4]

Tax Break *Mark Johnston* 80
3 b g Motivator—Mystic Lure (Green Desert (USA))
6876[4]

Tax Dodger (IRE) *P Cluskey* a57 55
4 b g Catcher In The Rye(IRE) —Stonor Lady (USA) (French Deputy (USA))
6696[2]

Tax Free (IRE) *David Nicholls* a89 117
8 b g Tagula(IRE) —Grandel (Owington)
1007[13] 2400[5] 4773a[3] 5569a[2] 6265[3] 6508[2] 7351[16]

Tayacoba (CAN) *Jim Goldie* 69
3 bb g Smart Strike(CAN) —Bienandanza (USA) (Bien Bien (USA))
5022[4] 5478[3] 6244[2]

Tayarat (IRE) *Dai Burchell* a72 47
5 b g Noverre(USA) —Sincere (IRE) (Bahhare (USA))
5360[5]

Taysa (USA) *X Nakkachdji* 71
2 b f Vindication(USA) —Key To My Heart (USA) (Mr Prospector (USA))
5063a[5]

Tazahum (USA) *Sir Michael Stoute* a86 95
2 b c Redoute's Choice(AUS) —Huja (IRE) (Alzao (USA))
(5893) 6733[2]

Tazeez (USA) *John Gosden* a103 120
6 bb g Silver Hawk(USA) —Soiree Russe (USA) (Nureyev (USA))
1664[2] 2470[2] 3068[3] 3825[3] 5321a[3] (6195) (6885)

Tazmiyna (FR) *A De Royer-Dupre* 88
3 b f Alhaarth(IRE) —Tawasila (IRE) (Turtle Island (IRE))
5136a[4]

Tea And Sympathy *John Holt*
2 b f Avonbridge—Merch Rhyd-Y-Grug (Sabrehill (USA))
5418[13] 6034[11] 6811[13]

Tealing *Richard Guest* a68 5
3 ch g Ishiguru(USA) —Renaissance Lady (IRE) (Imp Society (USA))
141[4] 188[3] 310[7] 524[5] 782[2] 856[4] 1505[5] 2203[9]

Te Amo Jen *Brendan Powell* a19
2 ch f Phoenix Reach(IRE) —Daphne Odora (Elmaamul (USA))
2642[8] 2905[8]

Team Victory (BRZ) *S Seemar* a29 50
6 ch h Public Purse(USA) —Incitante (BRZ) (Minstrel Glory (USA))
419a[11]

Teazel *Dominic Ffrench Davis* 52
2 ch f Barathea(IRE) —Cream Tease (Pursuit Of Love)
6443[10] 6803[8]

Tech Exceed (GER) *A Wohler* 100
3 b f Exceed And Excel(AUS) —Technik (GER) (Nebos (GER))
(3495a) 4640a[5] 5345a[3] 6763a[2] 7160a[9]

Technophobe (IRE) *William Knight* a43 57
3 ch g Noverre(USA) —Staylily (IRE) (Grand Lodge (USA))
1976[6] 2401[11] 2974[7] 3444[8]

Tecktal (FR) *Pat Phelan* a58 57
7 ch m Pivotal—Wenge (USA) (Housebuster (USA))
5536[8]

Tedious *Sylvester Kirk* a70 76
2 b f Act One—Manic (Polar Falcon (USA))
1429[7] (1978) (4040) 5472[9] 6576[9] 7040[9]

Ted's Brother (IRE) *Richard Guest* 67
2 b g Fath(USA) —Estertide (IRE) (Tagula (IRE))
4702[11] 5210[3] 6102[4] 6619[6] 7050[7] 7280[4]

Tedsmore Dame *James Unett* a76
2 b f Indesatchel(IRE) —Dayville (USA) (Dayjur (USA))
(3964)

Ted Spread *Mark H Tompkins* 106
3 b g Beat Hollow—Highbrook (USA) (Alphabatim (USA))
(1833) 2746[11] 5185[4] 5945[10] 6506[7] 7096[8]

Teen Ager (FR) *Paul Burgoyne* a67 65
6 b g Invincible Spirit(IRE) —Tarwiya (IRE) (Dominion)
367[5] 486[6] 684[5] 1047[5] (1305) 1595[7] 1875[9] 2866[3] 3567[8] 3777[9] 7168[5] 7519[9] 7613[10] 7768[5] 8023[11]

Teeraha (IRE) *Mandy Rowland* a43 2
3 b f Arakan(USA) —Lovely Me (IRE) (Vision (USA))
213[3] 7911[7]

Tees And Cees (IRE) *Richard Hannon* a70 50
2 ch c Bahamian Bounty—Berkeley Lodge (IRE) (Grand Lodge (USA))
5277[15] 5657[3] 5914[6]

Tehente Son *Andy Turnell* a48
5 br g Tumbleweed Ridge—Miss Tehente (FR) (Tehente (FR))
669[6] 2003[11]

Teilionn *John Joseph Murphy* 71
4 b g Pivotal—Catherine Wheel (Primo Dominie)
3254[13]

Tejime *John Gosden* a73
4 b g Royal Applause—Pizzicato (Statoblest)
275[8] ◆ 392[4]

Tek A Deek *James Moffatt*
6 ch g Zaha(CAN) —Lightning Blaze (Cosmonaut)
3587[9]

Telescopic *William Jarvis* 50
3 b f Galileo(IRE) —Orlena (USA) (Gone West (USA))
2507[11] 2974[9] 4330[8] 5051[8] 6094[6]

Tell A Kelly (USA) *John W Sadler* a112
2 ch f Tapit(USA) —Evrobi (USA) (Tabasco Cat (USA))
7342a[7]

Tellelle (IRE) *Liam McAteer* a86 65
4 bb m Trans Island—Lomond Heights (IRE) (Lomond (USA))
4524a[7] 5127a[3] 7014[7]

Tellesteem *S Szabolcs*
5 b h Mark Of Esteem(IRE) —Tell Her Off (Reprimand)
461a[13]

Tell Halaf *Michael Quinlan* a61 78
3 b g Oasis Dream—Topkamp (Pennekamp (USA))
894[4] 1178[5] (1873) 2215[4] 2566[2] 3212[3] ◆ 3604[5] 4593[10] 5048[11] 5540[10] 5887[10] 6292[10] 6930[9] (8024)

Telling (USA) *Steve Hobby* a90 115
6 b h A.P. Indy(USA) —Well Chosen (USA) (Deputy Minister (CAN))
7366a[6]

Telling Stories (IRE) *Barry Leavy* a55 45
4 b m Lucky Story(USA) —Yes Virginia (USA) (Roanoke (USA))
463[7] 1071[5] 1459[7] 1759[7]

Tell Me A Story *Mel Brittain* 69
3 ch f Lucky Story(USA) —Cantina (Tina's Pet)
1175[3] 1511[5] 1811[9] 2215[5]

Tell The Wind (IRE) *Kevin Prendergast* a91 94
2 b f Mujadil(USA) —Fantastic Account (Fantastic Light (USA))
6230a[16] 6727a[3]

Telluride *J E Hammond* a89 109
4 b h Montjeu(IRE) —Bayourida (USA) (Slew O'Gold (USA))
1856a[4] 5575a[7]

Telmunireema (FR) *J-P Perruchot* 43
5 b m Munir—Tel Reema (FR) (Tel Quel (FR))
221a[0] 332a[0]

Temecula Creek (USA) *Rudy Rodriguez* a104
6 ch h Gulch(USA) —Serenita (ARG) (Southern Halo (USA))
6582a[4]

Temida (IRE) *M G Mintchev* 78
2 b f Oratorio(IRE) —Interim Payment (USA) (Red Ransom (USA))
7108a[9]

Temple City (USA) *Carla Gaines* a111 106
5 bb h Dynaformer(USA) —Curriculum (USA) (Danzig (USA))
5577a[6]

Temple Fair (USA) *Mark Johnston* a56 56
3 b g Tiger Hill(IRE) —Forty Marchanta (ARG) (Roar (USA))
302[3] 482[2] 904[3] 1054[6]

Temple Meads *Ed McMahon* 114
2 ch c Avonbridge—Harryana (Efisio)
(1728) ◆ (4138) ◆ 5219[4] (6192) ◆ 6531[8]

Templetuohy Max (IRE) *James Bethell* a80 84
5 b g Orpen(USA) —Eladawn (IRE) (Ela-Mana-Mou)
1395[12] 1926[3] (2204) (2452) 3121[2] 3408[6] 4152[10] 5736[6] 6223[4] 6904[6] 7274[2]

Temps Au Temps (IRE) *M Delzangles* 99
2 b c Invincible Spirit(IRE) —Noahs Ark (IRE) (Charnwood Forest (IRE))
5323a[2] 7277a[7]

Temptingfaith (IRE) *Michael Quinlan* 74
2 b f Acclamation—Banutan (IRE) (Charnwood Forest (IRE))
1930[6] (3295)

Tenacestream (CAN) *John Best* a82 55
3 b g Grand Slam(USA) —Heart Lake (CAN) (Unbridled (USA))
448[3] 1045[2] 1279[8] 2033[14] 2644[8] 7526[7] 7892[7]

Tenacious Spring (FR) *C Boutin* 102
3 ch c Tertullian(USA) —Classic Spring (GER) (Winged Love (IRE))
1254a[5] 1947a[7] 2160a[5]

Tenancy (IRE) *Shaun Harris* a55 63
6 b g Rock Of Gibraltar(IRE) —Brush Strokes (Cadeaux Genereux)
14[5] 112[6] 1998[2] 2257[5] 2790[2] 2965[4] 4326[3] 4834[5] 4895[9] 5485[5] (6464) 6643[7] 6965[6]

Tenby Lady (USA) *Sir Mark Prescott Bt* a67
2 b f Anabaa(USA) —Bluebird Day (IRE) (Sadler's Wells (USA))
6308[3] 6711[3] (6936)

Tender Appeal *Bill Moore*
3 b f Stage Pass—Charlie Renne (IRE) (Desert Style (IRE))
2496[6] 3207[16]

Ten Down *Michael Quinn* a60 73
5 b g Royal Applause—Upstream (Prince Sabo)
77[2] 185[7] 241[8] 344[5] 687[2] 967[9] 1583[2] 2721[8] 3818[7] 7721[4]

Tenessee *Clive Cox* a86 85
3 b c Nayef(USA) —Shukran (Hamas (IRE))
1381[8] 2842[6] 5658[2] (6288) 6677[11] 7293[3]

Tenga Venga *Phil McEntee* a54 34
3 ch g Beat Hollow—Fanny's Fancy (Groom Dancer (USA))
134[7]

Tenhoo *Eric Alston* a59 56
4 b g Reset(AUS) —Bella Bambina (Turtle Island (IRE))
2500[2] 7504[6] 7599[6]

Tenjack King *Joss Saville* a40 61
5 b g Kyllachy—Rash (Pursuit Of Love)
814[10]

Ten Pole Tudor *Ronald Harris* a65 78
5 b g Royal Applause—Amaniy (USA) (Dayjur (USA))
87[6] 126[2] 298[4] 466[8] 518[4]

Ten To The Dozen *David Thompson* a55 47
7 b g Royal Applause—Almost Amber (USA) (Mt. Livermore (USA))
2670[10] 3147[13] 3595[11] 4403[10] 4868[14] 5596[4] 6261[14]

Tepmokea (IRE) *Richard Fahey* a71 95
4 ch g Noverre(USA) —Eroica (GER) (Highest Honor (FR))
2579[4] (3089) 3450[2] (4570) 5217[7] 5913[3] 6193[3] (6754) 7350[8]

Terdaad (IRE) *Saeed Bin Suroor* a86 53
2 ch c Shamardal(USA) —Akrmina (Zafonic (USA))
5277[10] 6249[2] (7020)

Terenzium (IRE) *Micky Hammond* a52 60
8 br g Cape Cross(IRE) —Tatanka (ITY) (Luge)
1891[4] 4900[7] (5364) 6224[8]

Teriyaki (IRE) *Daniel Mark Loughnane* 70
2 b c Fath(USA) —Joy St Clair (IRE) (Try My Best (USA))
3945[5]

Termagant (IRE) *Kevin Prendergast* 110
3 b f Powerscourt—Rock Salt (Selkirk (USA))
2370a[9]

Terminate (GER) *Alan Berry* a63 66
8 ch g Acatenango(GER) —Taghareed (USA) (Shadeed (USA))
210[12]

Terra Nova (FR) *Robert Collet* a88 88
3 b f American Post—Las Americas (FR) (Linamix (FR))
952a[6] 1496a[10]

Terre Du Vent (FR) *Y De Nicolay* a90 104
4 b m Kutub(IRE) —Phlizz (FR) (Kaldoun (FR))
953a[8] 1748a[5] 5109a[6] (7648a)

Terre Neuve (IRE) *A Wohler* 93
4 rg m Verglas(IRE) —Midnight Partner (IRE) (Marju (IRE))
2155a[3]

Terrific Challenge (USA) *S Seemar* a111 94
8 ch h Royal Academy(USA) —Clever Empress (Crafty Prospector (USA))
416a[8] 1021a[11]

Terrys Flutter *Mark Allen* a16 60
2 ch f Noverre(USA) —Still As Sweet (IRE) (Fairy King (USA))
1073[8] 1695[4] 1972[14] 2642[10] 2785[9] 6954[15] 7393[8]

Tertio Bloom (SWE) *Fredrik Reuterskiold* a107 105
5 ch g Tertullian(USA) —Yankee Bloom (USA) (El Gran Senor (USA))
(2019a) 2804a[6] 3425a[6]

Tertullus (FR) *Rune Haugen* 105
7 b h Monsun(GER) —Tryphosa (IRE) (Be My Guest (USA))
(2637a) 3934a[7] 5350a[4] 6791a[5]

Tessa (IRE) *Peter Grayson* a32
2 b f Chineur(FR) —Viva La Diva (IRE) (Danetime (IRE))
1043[10] 1223[5]

Tesslam *Michael Jarvis* a77 93
3 ch g Singspiel(IRE) —Rowaasi (Green Desert (USA))
1475[2] 1804[2] (2706) 3215[2] 3681[3] 4593[2] 5524[8]

Tevez *Desmond Donovan* a80 81
5 b g Sakhee(USA) —Sosumi (Be My Chief (USA))
855[3] 937[3] 1129[3] 1350[2] 1508[2] 2009[5] 2187[10] 2511[7] 2764[3] 2967[2] 3168[6] (5386) 5789[11] (5866) (6260) 7724[4] 7737[2] ◆ 8022[6]

Tewin Wood *Alan Bailey* a79 74
3 ch g Zaha(CAN) —Green Run (USA) (Green Dancer (USA))
1086[5] 1279[6] (2416) 2644[4] 6274[6] 6904[8] 7411[3] 7554[11] (7964)

Texan Star (IRE) *John Gosden* a71 81
3 b c Galileo(IRE) —Guignol (IRE) (Anita's Prince)
971[4] 1279[12] 1761[11] 2755[3] 3325[4]

Texas Queen *Mick Channon* a77 75
3 b f Shamardal(USA) —Min Asl Wafi (IRE) (Octagonal (NZ))
(208) (363) 478[2] 577[4] 1750[5] 2494[3] 5600[4] 5956[4] 6284[11]

Thaahira (USA) *Michael Jarvis* 94
3 b f Dynaformer(USA) —Mehthaaf (USA) (Nureyev (USA))
(1824) ◆ 2224[6] 2979[3]

Thabit (USA) *Michael Jarvis* a74 93
4 ch h Mr Greeley(USA) —Matsue (USA) (Lure (USA))
(3207) 3796[11]

Thai Haku (IRE) *M Delzangles* 100
3 b f Oasis Dream—Coconut Show (Linamix (FR))
5139a[12] 6881a[2]

Thakeham (IRE) *David Evans* a53 62
2 b g Elusive City(USA) —American Queen (FR) (Fairy King (USA))
2939[2] 3058[7] 3678[7]

Thaky (KSA) *B Al Shaibani* a93
6 ch h Alysheba(USA) —Circa (Risk Me (FR))
632a[8]

Thalia Grace *Les Hall* a52 62
3 ch f Zafeen(FR) —Days Of Grace (Wolfhound (USA))
1222[7] 1694[11] 3210[2] (3677) 4503[5] 5010[7] 5898[8] 7519[10]

Thaliwarru *Jeremy Gask* a63 69
3 b g Barathea(IRE) —Autumn Pearl (Orpen (USA))
702[2] 861[3] (1181) (1760) 2215[10] 2722[4] 5299[6] 6255[4] 6657[4] 6826[9]

Thank You Joy *John Jenkins* a58 67
2 b f Iceman—Once Removed (Distant Relative)
2867[8] 3778[8] 4658[12] 5660[13] 6082[6] 6873[4] 7393[3] 7677[3]

That'll Do Nicely (IRE) *Nicky Richards* a35 83
7 b g Bahhare(USA) —Return Again (IRE) (Top Ville)
(1467) 2277[4] 2766[3] (3202) (3405) 4051[5] 5408[9] 7815[8]

That Look *Don Cantillon* a61 64
7 b g Compton Admiral—Mudflap (Slip Anchor)
2907[11]

Thats A Fret (IRE) *Liam McAteer* a55 95
4 b g Choisir(AUS) —Reality Check (IRE) (Sri Pekan (USA))
(6918) 7079[16] 7348[11]

That's Me (GER) *Jozef Roszival* 82
7 gr m March Groom(USA) —Three Degrees (FR) (El Salto (GER))
5345a[9]

That's My Style *John Gosden* a73 70
3 gr f Dalakhani(IRE) —Pearl Dance (USA) (Nureyev (USA))
1329[7] 1882[6] 2227[6] 2871[2]

That's Showbiz *William Knight* a51 51
3 sk g I Was Framed(USA) —Angelic Dancer (Komaite (USA))
2011[6] 2684[12] 4211[8]

Thatstheone *Bill Moore* a31 51
2 b f Needwood Blade—Danifah (IRE) (Perugino (USA))
4748[5] 6046[9] 6369[7]

The Absent Mare *Frank Sheridan* a51
2 gr f Fair Mix(IRE) —Precious Lucy (FR) (Kadrou (FR))
6451[10] 7000[9] 7470[11]

Theatre Street (IRE) *Simon Dow* a73 80
4 b m Invincible Spirit(IRE) —Markova (IRE) (Marju (IRE))
535[7]

Theatrical Award (NOR) *Michael Taylor* a91 100
5 ch m Academy Award(IRE) —Theatre Antique (USA) (Theatrical)
2020a[10] 2637a[3] 3752[7] 4143[7] 5350a[3] 6017a[2] 7374a[9]

The Auctioneer (IRE) *Willie Musson* a61 44
2 ch g Medicean—Passe Passe (USA) (Lear Fan (USA))
7346[14] 7700[4] ◆ 7880[3] ◆

Theavonfilly *Roger Teal* a57
2 b f Avonbridge—Villella (Sadler's Wells (USA))
5865[12] 6866[7] 7163[7] 7552[11] 7762[6]

The Bay Bandit *S Donohoe* a56 41
3 b g Highest Honor(FR) —Pescara (IRE) (Common Grounds)
698[9] 998[2] 2432[13] 7863[8]

The Bear *Linda Perratt* a56 76
7 ch g Rambling Bear—Precious Girl (Precious Metal)
1200[5] 1719[9] 1869[7] 2073[4] (2294) 2669[12] 3497[6] 3533[3] 3902[4] (3946) 4060[6] (4513) 4798[5] 5198[2] 5335[4] 5734[12] 6140[13]

The Bells O Peover *Mark Johnston* 67
2 b g Selkirk(USA) —Bay Tree (IRE) (Daylami (IRE))
3452[7] 5277[7] ◆ 5594[6] 6184[2]

Thebes *Mark Johnston* a104 101
5 ch g Cadeaux Genereux—See You Later (Emarati (USA))
528[6] (722) 887[2] 916[10] 1423[4] (1662) 1900[7] 2595[3] 3461[14] 4085[10] 4473[5] 5292[9] 5787[7]

The Best Mode (IRE) *David Evans* a38 60
2 gr g Camacho—Gracious Gretclo (Common Grounds)
1009[11] 1180[7] 1541[3] 2312[7] 2873[6] 4678[5] 5921[11]

The Betchworth Kid *Alan King* a83 106
5 b g Tobougg(IRE) —Runelia (Runnett)
4506[7] 5220[14] 5908[9] 6362[3] 6736[4] ◆ 7350[2]

The Big Haerth (IRE) *Stuart Williams* a73
4 b h Elusive City(USA) —Calypso Run (Lycius (USA))
(7462) 7627[4]

The Blue Dog (IRE) *George Baker* a60 33
3 b f High Chaparral(IRE) —Jules (IRE) (Danehill (USA))
(475)

The Bogberry (USA) *R Tugusev* 114
5 ch h Hawk Wing(USA) —Lahinch (IRE) (Danehill Dancer (IRE))
1255a[7] 1747a[9] 6592a[10]

The Brown Bomber (IRE) *Luke Comer* a38 42
4 b h On The Ridge(IRE) —Lisa's Girl (IRE) (Distinctly North (USA))
6814[6] 7086[11] 7419[9]

The Buck (IRE) *John Joseph Murphy* a45 62
7 ch g Quws—Erin Anam Cara (IRE) (Exit To Nowhere (USA))
7957[8] 7967[10]

The Caped Crusader (IRE) *Ollie Pears* 82
3 b g Cape Cross(IRE) —Phariseek (IRE) (Rainbow Quest (USA))
2886[2] ◆ 4052[4] (5300) ◆ (5942) ◆ 6753[7]

The Cayterers *Tony Carroll* a96 96
8 b g Cayman Kai(IRE) —Silky Smooth (IRE) (Thatching)
360[8] 4924[6] 5955[9] 6562[21] 7012[14]

The Cheka (IRE) *Eve Johnson Houghton* a104 113
4 b g Xaar—Veiled Beauty (USA) (Royal Academy (USA))
1531[3] 2118[5] 2707[4] 3704a[6] 6885[8] 7234[2] 7593[5]

The Chester Giant *Patrick Morris* 35
3 b f Royal Applause—Serengeti Bride (USA) (Lion Cavern (USA))
4339[9] 5057[7] 5815[8]

The City Kid (IRE) *Gavin Blake* a69 25
7 b m Danetime(IRE) —Unfortunate (Komaite (USA))
(290) 666[2] 791[5] (2726) ◆ 3521[2] 4427[3]

The Coach *Trevor Wall* a37
4 ch g Central Park(IRE) —E Minor (IRE) (Blushing Flame (USA))
872[8]

The Cognac Kid (USA) *Amy Tarrant* 76
3 ch c Hennessy(USA) —Irish Daisy (USA) (Allen's Alydar (USA))
4642a[6]

The Composer *Michael Blanshard* a45 50
8 b g Royal Applause—Superspring (Superlative)
4042[2] 4731[2] 5179[5] 5666[4] 6273[4] 6416[5]

The Confessor *Henry Candy* a96 86
3 b g Piccolo—Twilight Mistress (Bin Ajwaad (IRE))
(1731) (4387) (4894) ◆ 5143[5] ◆

The Cuckoo *Michael Quinn* a60 38
4 b g Invincible Spirit(IRE) —Aravonian (Night Shift (USA))
402[2] 561[4] 1068[9]

The Datai *Ian McInnes* 5
2 b f Bertolini(USA) —Delichon (IRE) (Bluebird (USA))
6075[13] 7123[11]

The Dial House *David Thompson* a77 65
4 b g Tagula(IRE) —Marliana (IRE) (Mtoto)
105[4] 282[9] 2201[2] 2361[4] 4015[11] 4481[6] 4866[7]
The Diamond (FR) *D Bressou* 84
4 ch g Dyhim Diamond(IRE) —The Reward (FR) (River Mist (USA))
3099a[7]
The Dukes Arch (USA) *Peter Fahey* a61 60
3 b f Arch(USA) —Navarene (USA) (Known Fact (USA))
6747[5] 7270[4]
The Fifth Member (IRE) *Jim Boyle* a96 95
6 b g Bishop Of Cashel—Palace Soy (IRE) (Tagula (IRE))
6391[8] 6960[2] (7227) 7735[6]
The Fonz *Sir Michael Stoute* a74 98
4 b g Oasis Dream—Crystal Cavern (USA) (Be My Guest (USA))
1378[6] 2031[2] (3462) 3672[11] (5217) 6387[3] 6736[10]
The Four Masters (IRE) *David Wachman* 83
2 b c Ivan Denisovich(IRE) —Algaira (USA) (Irish River (FR))
6230a[2]
The Fuzz (NZ) *David Hayes* 94
8 br g Danasinga(AUS) —Drama Queen (NZ) (Prince Of Praise (NZ))
6946a[11] 7368a[12]
The Galloping Shoe *Alistair Whillans* a83 88
5 b g Observatory(USA) —My Way (IRE) (Marju (IRE))
1867[6] 2462[7] 2865[3] (3450) 4570[6] 4830[3]
The Geester *Stef Higgins* a66 51
6 b g Rambling Bear—Cledeschamps (Doc Marten)
14[3] (137) 243[5] 312[3] 684[4] 1166[11] 1300[12]
The Glamour Cat (IRE) *Marco Botti* a77
3 bb f One Cool Cat(USA) —Bint Al Balad (IRE) (Ahonoora)
(127) ◆ 311[4] 625[5]
The Graig *John Holt* a59 58
6 b g Josr Algarhoud(IRE) —Souadah (USA) (General Holme (USA))
36[2] 295[6] 469[7] 939[3] 1293[9] 2188[6] 2456[5] 7863[11]
The Great Husk (IRE) *J S Moore* a64 50
3 b g Alamshar(IRE) —Stardance (USA) (Rahy (USA))
133[3] 216[3] 254[2] 340[2] 371[2] 433[3] 551[3] 589[5] 7751[0]
The Grey One (IRE) *Milton Bradley* a74 66
7 gr g Dansili—Marie Dora (FR) (Kendor (FR))
1225[9] 1508[5] 6581[8] 7068[10] 7168[10] 7717[11]
The Hague *David Evans* a68 76
4 b g Xaar—Cox Orange (USA) (Trempolino (USA))
(1440) 2411[2] 2845[6] 3810[2] 4261[3] 5172[2] 5680[3]
The Happy Hammer (IRE) *Eugene Stanford* a69 64
4 b g Acclamation—Emma's Star (ITY) (Darshaan)
4108[15] 5875[2] 6295[8] 6456[2] 6852[2] (7241) 7439[3] 7614[5] 8014[5]
The Hermitage (IRE) *Mark Johnston* a77 82
3 b f Kheleyf(USA) —Russian Countess (USA) (Nureyev (USA))
1140[8] 1656[6] 2394[2] 2618[3] 2884[8] 3361[3] 3551[3] 3773[2] 4121[11] 4558[10] 4930[5] 5396[7] 6108[9] 6922[10]
The History Man (IRE) *Barry Leavy* a63 66
7 b g Titus Livius(FR) —Handsome Anna (IRE) (Bigstone (IRE))
1276[10] 1598[4] 1884[6] 2184[3] (2590) 2647[8] 3062[10] 3763[3] 4071[10] 4833[10]
The Holyman (IRE) *Jo Crowley* a78
2 ch c Footstepsinthesand—Sunset (IRE) (Polish Precedent (USA))
(6994)
The Hombre (AUS) *John Bary* 106
4 b g Lucky Owners(NZ) —Atlanta Belle (NZ) (Defensive Play (USA))
7032a[10]
The Human League *Mick Channon* a71 86
3 b g Tobougg(IRE) —Noble Desert (FR) (Green Desert (USA))
1703[11] 2544[9] 2933[7] 3363[7] 3898[10] 4193[5] 4478[6] 4739[4] (5557) 5890[3] 5905[2] (6261) 6541[4] 6864[13] 7125[2]
The Jailer *John O'Shea* a24 64
7 b m Mujahid(USA) —Once Removed (Distant Relative)
(3255) 3526[5] 3717[3] 4326[5] 4778[2] 5471[3] (5990) 6078[8] 6956[10]
The Jobber (IRE) *Michael Blanshard* a86 87
9 b g Foxhound(USA) —Clairification (IRE) (Shernazar)
972[4] 1266[5] 1506[6] 2094[4] 2622[9] 4099[7] 4518[6] 4961[5] 5262[6] 5695[2] 5876[5] 6292[6]
The Kyllachy Kid *Steve Gollings* a93 89
4 b g Kyllachy—All Business (Entrepreneur)
635[12] 850[4] 1049[2] 1185[6] 1767[2] 2640[6]
The Last Alzao (IRE) *Richard Fahey* a70 87
4 b m Alzao(USA) —Balakera (FR) (Lashkari)
2243[2] (2492) 2938[2] ◆ 4405[8] 5278[14] 5788[2]
The Last Bottle (IRE) *Mark Brisbourne* a64 65
5 ch g Hawk Wing(USA) —Mesmerist (USA) (Green Desert (USA))
666[9] 813[9]
The Last Don (IRE) *Charles O'Brien* a95 81
4 b g Redback—Banco Solo (Distant Relative)
5591[13]
The Lock Master (IRE) *Michael Appleby* a75 76
3 b g Key Of Luck(USA) —Pitrizza (IRE) (Machiavellian (USA))
4496a[4] 7679[5] 7845[3] 7956[2]
The Long Game *Brian Meehan* 95
2 b c Kyllachy—Something Blue (Petong)
3555[3] (3842) ◆ 4538[4] 5799a[6]
The Lord *Bill Turner* a63 70
10 b g Averti(IRE) —Lady Longmead (Crimson Beau)
1915[9] 2229[4]
The Love Guru *Jim Boyle* a68 40
3 b g Ishiguru(USA) —Beauty (IRE) (Alzao (USA))
(43) ◆ 310[6]
The Magic Of Rio *David Evans* a62 66
4 b m Captain Rio—Good Health (Magic Ring (IRE))
132[8] 477[12] 6490[10] 7635[8] 7952[3] ◆ 7972[10] 8037[5]
The Mellor Fella *Richard Fahey* 81
2 b g Compton Place—Grande Terre (IRE) (Grand Lodge (USA))
4116[7] (4709) 5901[8] 7085[6]
The Midshipmaid *Lucinda Featherstone* a42 51
3 b f Zafeen(FR) —Ebba (Elmaamul (USA))
3284[12] 3766[9] 4970[11] 5548[10] 5905[9] 6273[5] 6525[8] 6623[8] 7149[7]
The Mighty Mod (USA) *Michael Chapman* a51 54
3 b g Gone West(USA) —Michelle's Monarch (USA) (Wavering Monarch (USA))
422[10] 775[3] 3506[5] 4017[5] 4945[6] 5437[3] 5666[10] 6187[10] 6648[8] 7330[7]
The Mole Catcher (IRE) *D De Watrigant* 93
2 b c Whipper(USA) —Degree Of Honor (FR) (Highest Honor (FR))
5323a[6]
The Mongoose *Sir Michael Stoute* 72
2 b c Montjeu(IRE) —Angara (Alzao (USA))
4577[4] 5629[2]
The Mouse Carroll (IRE) *Sean Curran* a64 70
6 b g Barathea(IRE) —Grecian Glory (IRE) (Zafonic (USA))
27[6] 256[9] 498[8] 763[9] 3291[4] 3524[5]
The Mumbo *William Jarvis* a66 49
4 b m Bahamian Bounty—Mandolin (IRE) (Sabrehill (USA))
(1042) 1536[7]
The Munster Maori (IRE) *M Halford* a67 73
2 br g Footstepsinthesand—Kilmore Princess (IRE) (Orpen (USA))
6230a[21]
The Name Is Frank *Mark Gillard* a59 68
5 b g Lujain(USA) —Zaragossa (Paris House)
2053[7] 2809[2] 3255[5] 3556[5] 3722[4] 4041[2] (4283) 4625[8] 5112[4] 5809[5] 5875[6] 6421[4] 7125[7]
The Nifty Belle *Noel Wilson* 2
4 ch m Bertolini(USA) —Nifty Alice (First Trump)
3733[9] 4340[10] 5097[8] 5999[9]
The Nifty Fox *Tim Easterby* a88 94
6 b g Foxhound(USA) —Nifty Alice (First Trump)
1295[12] 1573[5] 2054[7] 2413[7] 2759[6] 3165[2] 3406[8] 4085[3] 4832[10] 5069[3] 5335[3] 5734[3] 6142[10] 6706[3] 6985[5] 7326[4]
The Nought Man (FR) *J E Hammond* a72 75
2 ch c Take Risks(FR) —Moon Tree (FR) (Groom Dancer (USA))
4123[6] 4896[7] (6001) 6589a[6] 7647a[5]
The Oboist (IRE) *Mark Johnston* 57
2 b f Clodovil(IRE) —Desert Bride (USA) (Key To The Kingdom (USA))
3087[9] 3624[12] 5092[6] 5998[7]
Theocritus (USA) *Claes Bjorling* a82 83
5 b g Theatrical—Candace In Aspen (USA) (Woodman (USA))
(176) 314[2] 6017a[6]
The Oil Magnate *Michael Dods* 80
5 ch g Dr Fong(USA) —Bob's Princess (Bob's Return (IRE))
1484[6]
Theola (IRE) *Mark H Tompkins* a51 87
4 bl m Kalanisi(IRE) —Third Dimension (FR) (Suave Dancer (USA))
1902[6] 3241[4] (3896) 4467[10] 5788[5] (6201)
Theology *Jeremy Noseda* 111
3 b g Galileo(IRE) —Biographie (Mtoto)
1314[4] (1851) 3145[2] 4456[6] 5945[7]
Theonebox (USA) *Ian Williams* a66 80
5 ch g Johannesburg(USA) —Khalifa Of Kushog (USA) (Air Forbes Won (USA))
3130[6] 4752[8]
The Only Boss (IRE) *William Haggas* a95 94
3 ch g Exceed And Excel(AUS) —Aljafliyah (Halling (USA))
1523[4] 2260[2] ◆ 2978[20] 3218[5] 5250[15]
The Only Key *S W James* a88 89
4 b m Key Of Luck(USA) —Sierra Virgen (USA) (Stack (USA))
5529[9] 6193[14] 6447[3]
The Osteopath (IRE) *Michael Dods* 98
7 ch g Danehill Dancer(IRE) —Miss Margate (IRE) (Don't Forget Me)
1006[13] 1397[11] 2086[2] 4370[9] 6178[7]
The Paddyman (IRE) *William Haggas* 106
2 b c Giant's Causeway(USA) —Winds Of Time (IRE) (Danehill (USA))
3169[2] (3602) 4538[2] 6192[4] 6507[4]
The Pier (IRE) *Joseph G Murphy* a92 89
4 ch g Alhaarth(IRE) —Cois Cuain (IRE) (Night Shift (USA))
6730a[2] 6971a[5] 7589a[6] 7823a[8]
Thereafter (USA) *Roger Charlton* a70 48
3 ch f Lion Heart(USA) —Alvernia (USA) (Alydar (USA))
843[4] 1537[3] 3039[8]
The Reaper (IRE) *G M Lyons* a85 76
2 b c Footstepsinthesand—Lady Gregory (IRE) (In The Wings)
6230a[17]
The Rectifier (USA) *Stef Higgins* 108
3 bb c Langfuhr(CAN) —Western Vision (USA) (Gone West (USA))
(1442) 2471[2] 3104[11] (3460) 4166a[6]
There We Go (IRE) *Alan Swinbank* 37
4 b g Pyrus(USA) —Ghayaat (USA) (Lyphard (USA))
3538[13]
The Rising (TUR) *C Filiksac* 102
6 b m Strike The Gold(USA) —Free Trade (TUR) (Shareef Dancer (USA))
5782a[8]
The Saucy Snipe *Daniel Christopher O'Brien* a64 59
4 b m Josr Algarhoud(IRE) —The Dark Eider (Superlative)
584[11]
The Scorching Wind (IRE) *Stuart Williams* a98 78
4 b g Fasliyev(USA) —Rose Of Mooncoin (IRE) (Brief Truce (USA))
108[3] ◆ (358) ◆ 944[9] 1085[10] 1662[6] 3483[6] 5067[7] 7970[7]
Thescottishsoldier *George Foster* 49
3 ch g Observatory(USA) —Twenty Seven (IRE) (Efisio)
2762[4] 3161[6] 3948[13]
These Dreams *Richard Guest* a42 24
2 b f Sleeping Indian—White Turf (GER) (Tiger Hill (IRE))
7279[5] 7517[6] 7913[6]
The Shrew *John Gosden* a65 80
2 b f Dansili—Whazzat (Daylami (IRE))
3082[6] 5509[2] (6071) 6563[9]
The Shuffler *Gary Moore* a66 74
3 b g Reset(AUS) —Lucky Dice (Perugino (USA))
(1437) 1977[2] 2398[3] (3259) 4491[3] 4994[3] 5624[6] 6633[9]
The Silver Crown (IRE) *Michael Mulvany* a51 83
3 gr f Verglas(IRE) —Dimondonaringogold (IRE) (Sesaro (USA))
4524a[8]
The Starboard Bow *Sylvester Kirk* a85 83
3 b g Observatory(USA) —Overboard (IRE) (Rainbow Quest (USA))
1138[5] 1734[10] 2510[8] 2993[6] 4289[3] 4621[5] 4728[2] (5260) 5752[2] 6448[6]
The Strig *Stuart Williams* a77 79
3 b g Mujahid(USA) —Pretty Kool (Inchinor)
(362) 1281[8] 2046[2] 3218[8] 5048[4] 5678[6] 6253[9] 6739[10] 7441[7]
The Sydney Arms (IRE) *Richard Hannon* a63 84
2 b f Elusive City(USA) —Daftara (IRE) (Caerleon (USA))
(1577) 1733[6] (2074) 3070[12] 4872[8] 5036[9] 6900[7]
The Tatling (IRE) *Milton Bradley* a86 87
13 bb g Perugino(USA) —Aunty Eileen (Ahonoora)
74[3] 307[7] 384[7] 678[5] 1988[8] 2622[4] 3119[4] 3358[3] 3474[6] 3958[6] 4099[5] 4518[5] 4659[7] 5112[5] 5377[4] 5809[6] 7446[2] 7628[3] 7784[3] 8036[2]
The Thrill Is Gone *Mick Channon* a73 98
2 ch f Bahamian Bounty—Licence To Thrill (Wolfhound (USA))
1972[3] 2251[9] 2638[2] (2963) 3426[2] ◆ 3630[2] 4278[2] 5036[3] 5907[5] 6141[3] 6734[14]
The Tichborne (IRE) *Roger Teal* a80
2 b g Shinko Forest(IRE) —Brunswick (Warning)
7479[6] ◆ (7990)
The Tooth Fairy (IRE) *Michael Mulvany* a86 93
4 b h Statue Of Liberty(USA) —Fairy Lore (IRE) (Fairy King (USA))
1246a[5] 1676a[10] 5127a[9] 5774a[16]
The Two G'S *Richard Price* a53 30
3 b f Mark Of Esteem(IRE) —Intellibet One (Compton Place)
3372[5] 3682[8] 4194[10]
The Usual Q. T. (USA) *James Cassidy* a112 122
4 b g Unusual Heat(USA) —Lunge (USA) (Western Fame (USA))
1025a[4] (4417a) 5577a[5] 6237a[2] 7364a[3]
The Wee Chief (IRE) *Jimmy Fox* a69 77
4 ch g King Charlemagne(USA) —La Belle Clare (IRE) (Paris House)
119[7] 325[7] 501[3] 2246[4] 2719[8] (3463) 3914[5] 4961[3] 5262[7] 5695[3]
The Which Doctor *Jeremy Noseda* a90 93
5 b g Medicean—Oomph (Shareef Dancer (USA))
1455[7] 1767[8] 2322[9] 3483[4] 4399[3] 5913[5] 6449[5] 6990[2] 7756[6] 7881[2]
The Winged Assasin (USA) *Shaun Lycett* a74 74
4 b g Fusaichi Pegasus(USA) —Gran Dama (USA) (Rahy (USA))
5584[8] 6371[3] 6854[5] 7162[6] (7678) (7856) 8008[4]
Thewinnatakesitall *Nigel Tinkler* a56 58
3 ch f King's Best(USA) —Powder Puff (IRE) (Sadler's Wells (USA))
574[6] 831[5] 906[4] 3086[8] 3597[9] 4194[2] 4651[9] 4760[5] 5152[8] 5548[11] 5816[3] 6255[11] 6464[6] 7153[8]
The Wonga Coup (IRE) *Pat Phelan* a64 62
3 b g Northern Afleet(USA) —Quichesterbahn (USA) (Broad Brush (USA))
930[7] 1046[5] 1268[11] 1578[10] 2200[10] 7491[3] 7562[2] 7963[4]
They All Laughed *Marjorie Fife* a79 72
7 ch g Zafonic(USA) —Royal Future (IRE) (Royal Academy (USA))
331[3] 411[3] 621[4] 813[8] 898[2] 1459[10] (1803) 2464[3] 3109[2] 3974[6] 4648[9] 4900[3] 5420[3] 6114[10] 6648[9]
They Call Me Giant (USA) *Kelly Breen* 93
3 ch c Giant's Causeway(USA) —Aishah (USA) (Alydar (USA))
4642a[3]
Theyskens' Theory (USA) *Brian Meehan* a93 109
2 b f Bernardini(USA) —Heat Lightning (USA) (Summer Squall (USA))
3871[9] ◆ (4595) ◆ (5519) ◆ 6348[3] 7342a[6]
Thief *Walter Swinburn* a64 64
4 b g Falbrav(IRE) —Eurolink Raindance (IRE) (Alzao (USA))
6213[5] 6538[7]
Thimaar (USA) *John Gosden* 85
2 bb c Dynaformer(USA) —Jinaan (USA) (Mr Prospector (USA))
7094[2]
Thingathong (FR) *Tom Dascombe* a15 53
3 b f Trempolino(USA) —Fontaine Guerard (FR) (Homme De Loi (IRE))
1010[6] 1515[3] 4229[12]
Thinking *Tim Easterby* a48 63
3 b g Makbul—Concentration (IRE) (Mind Games)
2432[5] 2768[9] (3773) 4193[11] 4674[7] 5046[4] 6295[14]
Thinking Robins (IRE) *Ottavio Di Paolo* 105
7 b h Plumbird—Rose Jasmine (ITY) (Sikeston (USA))
1944a[4] 4185a[8] 7459a[12]
Think Its All Over (USA) *Tom Tate* a78 80
3 b g Tiznow(USA) —A P Petal (USA) (A.P. Indy (USA))
1514[5] 2033[10] (4128) 4751[7] 5217[16] 6753[10] 7042[5]
Thin Red Line (IRE) *Michael Dods* a92 100
4 b g Red Ransom(USA) —Albaiyda (IRE) (Brief Truce (USA))
(1837) 2710[3] 3672[12] 5217[6] 5949[3] 6193[16] 6738[6] 7350[21]
Thirteen Shivers *Michael Easterby* 74
2 b g Iceman—Thirteen Tricks (USA) (Grand Slam (USA))
2939[10] 3971[4] (4645) 5187[8] 6030[10] 6719[5]
Thiskyhasnolimit (USA) *Steven Asmussen* a114
3 bb c Sky Mesa(USA) —Lovely Regina (USA) (Deputy Minister (CAN))
7365a[7]
This Ones For Eddy *John Balding* a71 76
5 b g Kyllachy—Skirt Around (Deploy)
2850[9] 3761[8] 4237[7] 5405[3] 5817[4] 7870[2]
Thistimesforgood (IRE) *Gordon Elliott* a53 56
7 ch g Rossini(USA) —Midsummer Night (IRE) (Fairy King (USA))
5927[3]
Thistle Stikk *Roger Charlton* a72
3 b g Selkirk(USA) —Tamso (USA) (Seeking The Gold (USA))
3563[6] 6450[7]
Thistle Thunder (IRE) *Tracey Collins* 18
2 b f Whipper(USA) —Last Spin (Unfuwain (USA))
7256a[15]
Thomas Tompion (IRE) *Gary Moore* 79
2 ch c Captain Rio—Severa (GER) (Kendor (FR))
4902[5] 5170[3] (5836) 6690[10]
Thor's Echo (USA) *S Seemar* a97 77
8 ch g Swiss Yodeler(USA) —Helen Of Troy (USA) (Mr. Integrity (USA))
416a[3] 606a[4] 817a[10]
Thoughtful (IRE) *J W Hills* a54 49
3 b f Acclamation—Truly Generous (IRE) (Generous (IRE))
2249[8] 2962[13] 3478[11] 3952[3] 4300[6] 4775[3] 5326[7] 5730[11] 6255[12]
Thoughtsofstardom *Phil McEntee* a74 64
7 b g Mind Games—Alustar (Emarati (USA))
77[7] (119) 185[8] (306) 384[8] 578[4] 616[6] 736[5] 806[9] 913[6] 972[5] 1443[2] 1598[3] 1638[5] 1884[5] 2008[7] 2123[3] 2229[6] (2809) 3114[10] 3211[3] 3358[6] 3605[3] 3818[3] 3994[3] 4239[4] 6714[12] 7194[10] 4435[8] 7390[11] 7542[12] 7720[7]
Thousandkissesdeep (IRE) *John Gosden* 75
3 b f Night Shift(USA) —Interim Payment (USA) (Red Ransom (USA))
4294[5]
Three Bay Leaves *Mark Johnston* 65
3 b f Mark Of Esteem(IRE) —Tab's Gift (Bijou D'Inde)
5122[9] 5603[7] 6415[5]
Three Boars *Steve Gollings* a66 17
8 ch g Most Welcome—Precious Poppy (Polish Precedent (USA))
(833) 1828[4] 2907[12] 3760[2] 4683[7]
Three Bodies (IRE) *P Bary* 111
4 gr h Domedriver(IRE) —Three Mysteries (IRE) (Linamix (FR))
6592a[8]
Three Day Rush (USA) *Todd Pletcher* a97
3 bb c Harlan's Holiday(USA) —Predictress (USA) (Vicar (USA))
824a[9]
Three Ducks *Richard Hannon* a82 82
4 b m Diktat—Three Terns (USA) (Arctic Tern (USA))
4756[2] 4958[2] 5988[3] 6444[4] (6852)
Three French Hens (IRE) *Mario Hofer* a76 95
4 b m Elnadim(USA) —Vahine (USA) (Alysheba (USA))
6765a[10]
Three Moons (IRE) *Harry Dunlop* a73 103
4 b m Montjeu(IRE) —Three Owls (IRE) (Warning)
1725[4] 2538[9] 3144[5] 4143[9] 4957[4] 6533[5] 6886[6]
Three Opera Divas *Mark Johnston* a51
2 b f Librettist(USA) —Tab's Gift (Bijou D'Inde)
7240[6] 7448[11] 7578[10] 7803[5]
Three Scoops *Dominic Ffrench Davis* a54 55
2 ch f Captain Rio—Sambarina (IRE) (Victory Note (USA))
1660[7] 1930[11] 2251[10] 2951[9] 5000[8] 5412[2] 6259[2] 6628[3] 6878[9] 7124[3] 7395[6] 7497[2]
Three Sparrows (IRE) *Richard Hannon* a68 77
2 b c Dansili—Three Wrens (IRE) (Second Empire (IRE))
5491[10] 6465[5] 6688[2] 6869[3] 7116[5] 7418[5]
Three Way Stretch (IRE) *J T Gorman* 87
4 b g Intikhab(USA) —Chapka (IRE) (Green Desert (USA))
3489a[21]
Three White Socks (IRE) *Brian Ellison* a13 34
3 b g Whipper(USA) —Halesia (USA) (Chief's Crown (USA))
1010[10] 1143[9]
Thrill *John Gosden* a78 95
3 ch f Pivotal—Irresistible (Cadeaux Genereux)
(4963) 5694[2] 6346[15]
Through The Forest (USA) *Walter Swinburn* a62 52
4 bb m Forestry(USA) —Lakefront (USA) (Deputy Minister (CAN))
411[11] 1478[2]
Thrust Control (IRE) *Brian Ellison* a78 81
3 ch g Fath(USA) —Anazah (USA) (Diesis)
1045[4] 1307[6] 1584[5] (2049) 2348[6] 2618[4] (3151) 3886[6] 4192[5] 4646[4] 5606[6]
Thubiaan (USA) *William Haggas* 74
2 b c Dynaformer(USA) —Barzah (IRE) (Darshaan)
6883[8]
Thumberlina *Christine Dunnett* a40 48
4 b m Choisir(AUS) —Capstick (JPN) (Machiavellian (USA))
1638[6] 2008[8] 2197[8]

Thumbs Up (NZ) *C Fownes* 118
6 b g Shinko King(IRE) —Regelle (NZ) (Exploding Prospect (USA))
7853a[6]

Thunda *Eve Johnson Houghton* 54
2 b f Stormy Atlantic(USA) —Lobby Card (USA) (Saint Ballado (CAN))
5078[9]

Thunderball *David Nicholls* a86 89
4 ch g Haafhd—Trustthunder (Selkirk (USA))
(359) 480[5] 672[6] 769[6] 1202[4] 1374[12] 2580[5] 2705[2] 2991[9] 3396[3] 3796[12] 5407[4] 5737[2] 5997[3] 6510[6] 7092[7] 7352[5] 7637[5] 7867[5] 7935[8]

Thunder Bay *Ron Barr* a64 65
5 b g Hunting Lion(IRE) —Floral Spark (Forzando)
1723[7] 2278[7] 3711[9] 4047[7] 4606[8] 5599[10]

Thunder Gulf *P D Deegan* a52
2 b c Royal Applause—Statua (IRE) (Statoblest)
6726a[7]

Thundering Home *Michael Attwater* a78 65
3 gr g Storming Home—Citrine Spirit (IRE) (Soviet Star (USA))
(218) 428[2] 482[3] 1060[2] 1502[11] 1973[4] 3039[5] 3581[9] 4793[4] 5208[4] 5330[2] 5753[10] 6816[8] 7042[14]

Thunderous Mood (USA) *Paul Cole* a84 82
4 bb h Storm Cat(USA) —Warm Mood (USA) (Alydar (USA))
1321[2] 1580[3] 1848[4]

Thunderstruck *David Nicholls* a94 84
5 b g Bertolini(USA) —Trustthunder (Selkirk (USA))
(255) (341) 536[9] 863[2] 921[2] 1378[8] 1684[2] 2435[6] 2640[14] 8009[8]

Thunderway (IRE) *Michael Dods* 29
2 b f Doyen(IRE) —Thunderbaby (USA) (Thunder Gulch (USA))
3365[8] 4241[8]

Thyan (FR) *Mlle M Henry* a98 83
3 b c Indian Rocket—Slyders (IRE) (Hector Protector (USA))
927a[2] 1195a[7]

Thymesthree (IRE) *Chris Wall*
2 ch f
8000[6]

Tia Juana (IRE) *Ben Haslam* a65 62
3 b f Shamardal(USA) —Tiavanita (USA) (J O Tobin (USA))
1488[6] 1982[4] 2606[6] 3074[2] 3601[6] 4648[13]

Tiberina (IRE) *R Le Gal* 54
5 b m Hawk Wing(USA) —Perugina (FR) (Highest Honor (FR))
303a[0]

Tiberius Claudius (IRE) *George Margarson* 39
2 b g Clodovil(IRE) —Final Favour (IRE) (Unblest)
4902[9] 5626[10]

Ticket To Paradise *David Lanigan* 62
3 b c Singspiel(IRE) —Dream Ticket (USA) (Danzig (USA))
2143[3] 2684[15]

Tick Tock Lover *Jo Crowley* a81 83
2 gr c Tikkanen(USA) —Ivory's Promise (Pursuit Of Love)
3326[3] ◆ 4096[2] (5717) 6386[5]

Tidal Force (USA) *Alan McCabe* a61 76
4 ch g High Yield(USA) —Shady Waters (CAN) (Rahy (USA))
87[3] 170[5]

Tidal Run *Mick Channon* 55
2 b f Hurricane Run(IRE) —Tidie France (USA) (Cape Town (USA))
5691[11] 5985[10]

Tidal Star *Michael Quinlan* a38 70
2 b c Kyllachy—Tidal (Bin Ajwaad (IRE))
6158[19] 7150[4] 7427[9]

Tiddliwinks *Kevin Ryan* a107 99
4 b g Piccolo—Card Games (First Trump)
(26) ◆ (102) ◆ 358[4] (887) 1014[3] 3919[8] 4391[4] ◆ 4536[4] ◆ 5095[7] 5944[4] 6175[17] ◆

Tiffany Lady *Mark Usher* a44
4 ch m Generous(IRE) —Art Deco Lady (Master Willie)
1451[9] 1758[10]

Tifoso (FR) *Richard Guest* a53 41
5 ch g Priolo(USA) —Tifosa (USA) (Hickman Creek (USA))
983[11] 1828[5] 4582[11] 6032[5] 7716[4] 7760[2]

Tiger Cat *Hughie Morrison*
3 b f Tiger Hill(IRE) —Great Verdict (AUS) (Christmas Tree (AUS))
4792[7]

Tiger Hawk (USA) *Jim Best* a69 45
3 b g Tale Of The Cat(USA) —Aura Of Glory (CAN) (Halo (USA))
372[6] (452) (507) 542[4] 781[3] 909[3] (1144) 1259[5] 1505[6] 1995[5] 3759[11] 5171[7]

Tigerino (IRE) *C W Thornton* 33
2 b g Tiger Hill(IRE) —Golden Shadow (IRE) (Selkirk (USA))
4110[8] 4782[8] 5298[15] 6300[8]

Tiger King (GER) *P Monteith* 39
9 b g Tiger Hill(IRE) —Tennessee Girl (GER) (Big Shuffle (USA))
2859[8] 6033[6]

Tiger Reigns *Michael Dods* 108
4 b g Tiger Hill(IRE) —Showery (Rainbow Quest (USA))
1008[14] (2141) 3069[27] 4828[4] 5247[11] 5605[12] (6180) 6562[27]

Tigers Charm *Milton Bradley* a11 44
3 b g Tiger Hill(IRE) —Amazing Dream (IRE) (Thatching)
1731[9] 2004[8] 2297[5] 2919[9] 3993[12] 4679[7] 4992[13] 5766[12]

Tiger's Pride *John Gallagher* 54
2 b g Tiger Hill(IRE) —Riyma (IRE) (Dr Fong (USA))
5878[14] 6831[9]

Tiger Star *James Eustace* a76 73
3 b g Tiger Hill(IRE) —Rosy Outlook (USA) (Trempolino (USA))
1393[4] 2254[7] 3519[5] 5259[5] 5563[6] 6091[8] 6540[3] 6801[2] 7047[9]

Tiger Trail (GER) *Mrs N Smith* a51 63
6 b g Tagula(IRE) —Tweed Mill (Selkirk (USA))
1638[2] 2229[2] 2964[6] 3527[6] 6284[6]

Tiger Webb *Henry Cecil* a79 79
2 b c Hurricane Run(IRE) —Wonderful Desert (Green Desert (USA))
4838[2] 5676[2] 6305[2] 7036[3]

Tightrope (IRE) *Tim McCarthy* a58 47
4 b g Refuse To Bend(IRE) —Sisal (IRE) (Danehill (USA))
319[7] 477[6] 495[9] 638[6]

Tigranes The Great (IRE) *Marco Botti* a55 61
3 b c Galileo(IRE) —Aquila Oculus (IRE) (Eagle Eyed (USA))
2043[11] 2860[6] 3173[6] 3564[6]

Tigress Hill *Amanda Perrett* a67 60
3 b f Tiger Hill(IRE) —Inchberry (Barathea (IRE))
4229[8] 4792[4] 5141[3] 5811[4] 6084[3] 6373[8]

Tigron (USA) *Mme C Barande-Barbe* a84 83
9 ch h Lion Cavern(USA) —Tidy Tune (USA) (The Minstrel (CAN))
272a[7] 458a[3] 640a[4]

Tijori (IRE) *Richard Hannon* 58
2 b g Kyllachy—Polish Belle (Polish Precedent (USA))
4421[5] 5523[7] 7094[9]

Tilapia (IRE) *Stef Higgins* a69 60
6 ch g Daggers Drawn(USA) —Mrs Fisher (IRE) (Salmon Leap (USA))
2259[8] (2645) 3160[11] 3760[13]

Tileyf (IRE) *Clive Cox* 61
2 ch g Kheleyf(USA) —Amravati (IRE) (Project Manager)
5582[10] 6474[4] 6831[7]

Till Dawn (IRE) *Tony Carroll* a55 54
2 br f Kheleyf(USA) —Tilbrook (IRE) (Don't Forget Me)
3126[7] 4021[11] 4432[4] 5000[4] 5365[3] 5581[4] 5862[4] 6674[11] 6954[3] 7016[2] 7577[3]

Tilliemint (IRE) *Tim Easterby* 72
2 b f Acclamation—Phantom Act (USA) (Theatrical)
1704[2] ◆ 2239[5] 2763[2] 2936[4] 3315[2] 3897[6]

Tillietudlem (FR) *Jim Goldie* a35 74
4 gr g Kutub(IRE) —Queenhood (FR) (Linamix (FR))
(2214) (2430) (2995) 3109[3] (3535) ◆ (3804) 3974[2] 4604[5] 5119[4] 5497[4] 6143[2] 6750[6] 6983[5]

Tillys Tale *Paul Midgley* 81
3 ch f Lucky Story(USA) —Otylia (Wolfhound (USA))
1399[3] 2099[7] 2960[7] 3751[3] 4016[2] 4349[7] 4654[6] 5600[6]

Tilly Thorpe *O Brennan*
5 ch m Kris Kin(USA) —Nunthorpe (Mystiko (USA))
6661[9]

Tilos Gem (IRE) *Mark Johnston* a82 81
4 ch g Trans Island—Alpine Flair (IRE) (Tirol)
897[6] 1277[5] 2766[7] 3432[6] 3989[2] 4266[4] 4683[12] 5364[4] 6033[2] 6187[5]

Tilsworth Glenboy *John Jenkins* a65 76
3 b g Doyen(IRE) —Chara (Deploy)
206[3] 1178[3] 1392[11] 1522[6] 2906[8] 4479[5] 4687[11] (5559) 6692[6] 7205[2] 7305[4] 7890[4]

Timber Treasure (USA) *Paul Green* a63 76
6 bb g Forest Wildcat(USA) —Lady Ilsley (USA) (Trempolino (USA))
1968[5] 2849[4] 3205[3] 3358[8] 3676[9] 4093[6] (4559) 5198[6] 5906[10] 6040[9]

Time For Applause *Ed Dunlop* 30
2 b f Royal Applause—Spitting Image (IRE) (Spectrum (IRE))
1972[10] 3602[8] 3906[7] 4436[9]

Timeless Elegance (IRE) *Howard Johnson* 80
3 b f Invincible Spirit(IRE) —Tidy Wager (IRE) (Catrail (USA))
(2209) ◆ (2432) 3023[5] 3947[5] 4369[6] 4712[7] 5424[9] 6572[13]

Timeless Stride (IRE) *Sir Michael Stoute* 76
3 b g Kyllachy—Trois Heures Apres (Soviet Star (USA))
1308[5] (1878) 2656[4] 3394[2]

Timely Jazz (IRE) *Niels Petersen* a86 100
3 b c Noverre(USA) —Ricadonna (Kris)
510a[11] 819a[2] 1023a[P]

Timely Production (IRE) *Madeleine Smith* 64
4 ch g Peintre Celebre(USA) —Romantic Venture (IRE) (Indian Ridge)
2195a[9]

Time Medicean *Paul Midgley* a57 85
4 gr g Medicean—Ribbons And Bows (IRE) (Dr Devious (IRE))
1364[9] 2136[13] 2327[12] 2883[10] 3205[6] 6073[10] ◆ 6741[4]

Timepecker (IRE) *M Delzangles* a78 89
3 b f Dansili—Pas D'Heure (IRE) (Arazi (USA))
(5981a)

Timepiece *Henry Cecil* a80 113
3 b f Zamindar(USA) —Clepsydra (Sadler's Wells (USA))
1313[4] ◆ 1909[2] 2711[8] (3071) 6886[2] (7237)

Times Ahead (USA) *Peter Chapple-Hyam* 73
3 b c Proud Citizen(USA) —Nanas Cozy Account (USA) (Langfuhr (CAN))
2517[4] 3227[6] 4260[13] 6117[11]

Time Square (FR) *Tony Carroll* 74
3 b g Westerner—Sainte Parfaite (FR) (Septieme Ciel (USA))
4827[5] 5953[11] 6990[13]

Times Up *John Dunlop* 109
4 b g Olden Times—Princess Genista (Ile De Bourbon (USA))
3159[5] (3873) 4400[4] 5217[4] 5949[2] 6889[2] (7350)

Timeteam (IRE) *Gary Moore* a87 88
4 b g Danetime(IRE) —Ceannanas (IRE) (Magical Wonder (USA))
26[4] 258[6] 384[3] 535[6] 679[4] 902[7] 1076[4] 1267[5] 1428[10] (2178) 2783[10] 3289[5] (3510) (3685) 3914[9] 4430[9] 4662[5] 4776[2] 5075[3] 5652[2] (5712) 6439[5] 7033[7] 7557[7] 7725[8]

Time To Play *Gary Brown* a56 65
5 b g Best Of The Bests(IRE) —Primavera (Anshan)
1[5] 198[7] 995[3]

Time To Work (IRE) *Andrew Balding* 83
2 b g Hurricane Run(IRE) —Viscoumtess Brave (IRE) (Law Society (USA))
2932[10] 4993[2] (5676) 6160[5] (6555) 6982[6]

Timocracy *Andrew Haynes* a71 81
5 br g Cape Cross(IRE) —Tithcar (Cadeaux Genereux)
(1592) (2487) (2600) (2752) (3442) (4202) 5148[2] 7038[7]

Timos (GER) *T Doumen* 113
5 ch h Sholokhov(IRE) —Triclaria (GER) (Surumu (GER))
1856a[5] 2803a[2] 6015a[3] 6612a[14] 6974a[4] 7615a[15]

Timothy T *Marco Botti* 92
2 bl g Pastoral Pursuits—Point Perfect (Dansili)
4208[3] ◆ (4587) 5184[3]

Tinaar (USA) *Gerard Butler* a99 103
4 b m Giant's Causeway(USA) —Seattle Tac (USA) (Seattle Slew (USA))
1220[2] ◆ (1724) 2071[3] 3671[8] 4507[9] 6928[11]

Tinaheely (IRE) *Jonathan Portman* a45
2 ch f Intikhab(USA) —Tertia (IRE) (Polish Patriot (USA))
7164[5]

Tin Cha Woody (USA) *Ronald Harris* a81 63
5 bb g Johannesburg(USA) —I'm Beguiled Again (USA) (Wild Again (USA))
(508) ◆ 535[5] ◆ 779[7] 895[7] 1167[10]

Ting Ting (USA) *Jim Boyle* a53 61
3 b f Empire Maker(USA) —My Sweet Heart (USA) (You And I (USA))
1422[9] 1970[4] (3180) 3582[3] 6993[14] 7874[8] 7996[12] 8018[4]

Tin Horse (IRE) *D Guillemin* 114
2 gr c Sakhee(USA) —Joyeuse Entree (Kendor (FR))
4419a[5] 5347a[2] 6610a[2]

Tinkertown (IRE) *Paul Cole* a90 81
2 gr c Verglas(IRE) —Kelly Nicole (IRE) (Rainbow Quest (USA))
2059[6] 2832[2] (3222) 5490[8] 6254[3] (6745) 7165[3]

Tinseltown *B S Rothwell* a32 62
4 b g Sadler's Wells(USA) —Peony (Lion Cavern (USA))
1572[8] 2244[7] 2995[9] 3758[5]

Tinshu (IRE) *Derek Haydn Jones* a95 90
4 ch m Fantastic Light(USA) —Ring Of Esteem (Mark Of Esteem (IRE))
1378[7] (1780) 2282[3] 2703[3] 3456[7] 3846[3] 4306[6] 6990[5] (7243) 7591[4]

Tintaglia (FR) *J-M Capitte* a38 68
8 b m Josr Algarhoud(IRE) —Undercover Agent (IRE) (Fairy King (USA))
332a[10]

Tinzo (IRE) *Alan Berry*
2 b g Auction House(USA) —Costa Verde (King Of Spain)
6182[10] 7223[6]

Tipperary Boutique (IRE) *B W Hills* 90
3 b f Danehill Dancer(IRE) —Moselle (Mtoto)
1354[7] 4389[7] 5188[13] 5904[5]

Tipperary Tickle *John Weymes* 41
3 ch f Needwood Blade—Cashel Kiss (Bishop Of Cashel)
3086[10] 3359[12] 3910[5] 4864[10] 4969[12]

Tipsy Girl *Denis Coakley* 84
2 b f Haafhd—Disco Lights (Spectrum (IRE))
(2358) 3453[6] 4066[4] 4278[3] 5293[3] 5992[2] 6563[10]

Tip Toe (FR) *F Doumen* 109
3 b c Footstepsinthesand—Midnight Queen (GER) (Platini (GER))
1985a[3] 2802a[18] 4276a[3]

Tiradito (USA) *Marco Botti* a86 81
3 bb g Tale Of The Cat(USA) —Saratoga Sugar (USA) (Gone West (USA))
(9) 268[3] 681[2] 884[2] 2394[3] 3083[7] 3429[6] 7411[2] 7665[2] 7965[3]

Tiscaline (FR) *Bryn Palling*
3 bb f Great Pretender(IRE) —Royale Little (FR) (Garde Royale)
4679[14] 5445[6]

Tislaam (IRE) *Alan McCabe* a74 77
3 gr c With Approval(CAN) —Lady Angola (USA) (Lord At War (ARG))
1029[9] 1362[11] 1811[4] 2274[4] 2634[6] 3393[3] 3663[3] 4018[3] (5898) (6110) 6292[2] 6800[3] 7082[5] 7331[3] 7441[2] 7556[3] 7730[5]

Tislimeen *Mick Channon* a34 59
3 b f Alhaarth(IRE) —Torgau (IRE) (Zieten (USA))
758[7] 3464[8]

Titan Diamond (IRE) *Mark Usher* a45 42
2 b g Diamond Green(FR) —Ditton Dancer (Danehill Dancer (IRE))
4323[7] 4622[11] 4999[8] 7630[8] 7813[6]

Titanic Mill *Nicky Vaughan* a42
3 b g Green Card(USA) —Derniere Biche (IRE) (Last Tycoon)
963[12] 7338[9] 7579[10] 7834[7]

Titan Triumph *William Knight* a86 76
6 b g Zamindar(USA) —Triple Green (Green Desert (USA))
1662[10] 1900[29] 2683[10] 3346[5] 4843[15] 5703[4] 6312[13] 7187[11]

Titbit *Henry Cecil* a81 91
3 ch f Cadeaux Genereux—Poilane (Kris)
1431[13] (2478) (4847) ◆ 5728[5] 6830[4]

Titch (IRE) *Peter Grayson*
4 b m Bahri(USA) —Vampire Queen (IRE) (General Monash (USA))
900[8] 997[13] 1190[5]

Titian Queen *Nerys Dutfield*
2 ch f Sicyos(USA) —Treasure Trove (USA) (The Minstrel (CAN))
2163[10] 2687[12] 6953[14]

Titivation *Michael Bell* 80
3 b f Montjeu(IRE) —Flirtation (Pursuit Of Love)
1355[3] 1882[3] (6470) 6753[4] 7546a[0]

Tito Lucrezio (ITY) *M Gasparini*
2 ch c Docksider(USA) —Diamond Mill (IRE) (Desert King (IRE))
7849a[17]

Titurel (GER) *Manfred Hofer* a104 106
5 ch h Dr Fong(USA) —Tucana (GER) (Acatenango (GER))
418a[2] 605a[4] 712a[6] ◆ 799a[9] 4038a[3]

Titus Andronicus (IRE) *Richard Fahey* 92
4 b g Danetime(IRE) —Scarlet Empress (Second Empire (IRE))
4510[12] 4942[9] 5335[2] ◆ 5589[9] 5734[9] 6140[7] 6708[6] 6981[6]

Titus Awarded (IRE) *A Renzoni* 102
3 b c Titus Livius(FR) —Wings Awarded (Shareef Dancer (USA))
1945a[14] 7373a[8]

Titus Bere (FR) *Y Barberot* a75 53
3 b g Della Francesca(USA) —Leginit (USA) (Dehere (USA))
(7959a)

Titus Gent *Jeremy Gask* a76 73
5 ch g Tumbleweed Ridge—Genteel (IRE) (Titus Livius (FR))
223[11] 287[6] 391[6] 555[4] (789) 851[7] 1300[6] (1596) 1799[8] 2385[7] 3057[4] 3254[10] 3556[10] 4130[2] ◆ 4283[2] (4589) (5076) 5698[4] (6523) 7320[5] 7525[5] 7564[5] 8004[10]

Titus Mills (IRE) *Brian Meehan* 104
2 ch c Dubawi(IRE) —Anayid (A.P. Indy (USA))
(4318) (5831) 7081[10]

Titus Shadow (IRE) *B Grizzetti* 109
6 ch h Titus Livius(FR) —Mujadil Shadow (IRE) (Mujadil (USA))
1944a[3] 4185a[4]

Titus Two (IRE) *Peter Chapple-Hyam* a67 74
2 ch c Titus Livius(FR) —Quinolina (Shareef Dancer (USA))
2384[5] 2839[7] 4208[5] 4437[2] (4716) 5310[7] 6426[7]

Tivers Song (USA) *John Harris* a57 56
6 gr g Buddha(USA) —Rousing (USA) (Alydar (USA))
1920[8] 2303[8] 2653[4] 3110[4] 3754[7] 4454[3] 4980[2] 5515[3] 6472[8] 6538[4] 6921[5]

Tixto (FR) *J-L Pelletan*
2 b c Rashbag—Halle Aux Grains (IRE) (Shardari)
7974a[6]

Tiza (SAF) *A De Royer-Dupre* a91 115
8 b g Goldkeeper(USA) —Mamushka (SAF) (Elliodor (FR))
1081a[3] 3425a[8] 4165a[2] 4773a[4] 5576a[3] 6012a[5] 6640a[3] 7278a[6]

Tiz My Time (USA) *Kenneth McPeek* 97
2 b f Sharp Humor(USA) —Tiz The Hour (USA) (Tiznow (USA))
3141[3]

Tizway (USA) *Harold James Bond* a117
5 bb h Tiznow(USA) —Bethany (USA) (Dayjur (USA))
7365a[5]

T M Precure (JPN) *Tadao Igarashi* 113
7 bb m Paradise Creek(USA) —Feriado (JPN) (Stately Don (USA))
7460a[17]

Toballa *Hugh Collingridge* a47 51
5 b m Tobougg(IRE) —Ball Gown (Jalmood (USA))
4969[9] 5560[7]

Tobermory Boy *James Given*
3 ch g Tobougg(IRE) —The In-Laws (IRE) (Be My Guest (USA))
2860[11] 3242[6]

Tobernea (IRE) *Mark Johnston* a43 54
3 b c Indian Ridge—Act Of The Pace (IRE) (King's Theatre (IRE))
3176[7] 4407[5] 5026[6] (5411) (6225) (6631) ◆ 6707[2] 6895[13]

Tobrata *Mel Brittain* a66 64
4 ch g Tobougg(IRE) —Sabrata (IRE) (Zino)
73[3] 169[7] 518[6] 602[2] 911[3] 5500[7] 7473[10]

Toby Tyler *Paul Midgley* a65 72
4 b g Best Of The Bests(IRE) —Pain Perdu (IRE) (Waajib)
572[7] 857[7] 1115[2] 1653[4] 2764[7] 3061[U] 3396[9] 4833[4] 5357[3] 6261[13] 6664[10] (6826) 7125[4] 7472[4] 7844[6] 7870[4]

Todber *Marcus Tregoning* a78 71
5 b m Cape Cross(IRE) —Dominica (Alhaarth (IRE))
502[3] 767[6] 1428[7] 3328[8] 4024[5]

Toga Tiger (IRE) *Paul Midgley* a87 82
3 b g Antonius Pius(USA) —Minerwa (GER) (Protektor (GER))
1376[12] 1836[9] 2112[8] 2884[9] 3208[7] 4128[4] 5662[9] 6580[8] 6935[7]

Together (IRE) *A P O'Brien* 111
2 b f Galileo(IRE) —Shadow Song (IRE) (Pennekamp (USA))
(4077a) 4879a[3] 5570a[4] 6348[2] 6559[3] 7340a[5]

Toggle *Mrs A Corson* a51 66
6 b g Tobougg(IRE) —Niggle (Night Shift (USA))
1815a[7] 3748a[4]

Togiak (IRE) *Ed Dunlop* a90 98
3 b g Azamour(IRE) —Hawksbill Special (IRE) (Taufan (USA))
1473[3] 1910[4] 3142[8] 5004[3] 5723[7] 6203[8] 6552[2]

Togoaviking *Harry Dunlop* a47 56
3 b c Cape Cross(IRE) —The Strand (Gone West (USA))
1165[8] 1442[10] 1872[6] 2480[8] 3039[12]

Toi Et Moi (IRE) *P Bary* 99
3 b f Galileo(IRE) —Di Moi Oui (Warning)
4037a[4]

Tokai Trick (JPN) *Kenji Nonaka* 115
8 b h El Condor Pasa(USA) —Zoonaqua (USA) (Silver Hawk (USA))
6947a[12] 7291a[12]

Token Gift *David Evans* a29 53
2 b c Indesatchel(IRE) —Its Another Gift (Primo Dominie)
3555[5] 3915[7] 4123[12] 4436[8] 6052[7]

Token Of Honour (AUS) *David Hayes* 101
4 b g Testa Rossa(AUS) —Princess Plume (AUS) (Military Plume (NZ))
6946a[8]

Tokum (IRE) *Jeremy Noseda* a67 68
2 b g Danehill Dancer(IRE) —Ibtikar (USA) (Private Account (USA))
2007[5] 2384[2] ◆ 3874[5] 5234[3] *6453[4]* 6560[23] *6901[4]*

Toledo Gold (IRE) *Eric Alston* 82
4 ch g Needwood Blade—Eman's Joy (Lion Cavern (USA))
1102[2] 1361[9] 6394[14] 7062[18]

Tombellini (IRE) *David Nicholls* 60
3 ch g Tomba—La Scala (USA) (Theatrical)
3111[10] 3808[9] 4853[2] 5484[8] 6188[14] 6463[2] 6655[5] 6897[13]

Tombi (USA) *Howard Johnson* 112
6 b g Johannesburg(USA) —Tune In To The Cat (USA) (Tunerup (USA))
1904[7] 2526[5] 4391[18] 5787[5]

Tom Bowler *Ann Duffield*
2 b c Marju(IRE) —Tembladora (IRE) (Docksider (USA))
4167[10] 4402[6] 4645[12] 6027[9]

Tom Folan *Andrew Reid* a66 71
3 b f Namid—My Golly (Mozart (IRE))
483[4] *678[6]* 1181[5] 1444[2] 1784[2] (2046) 2491[6] 2565[6] 2688[4] 3174[2] (3372)

Tominator *Reg Hollinshead* a95 98
3 gr g Generous(IRE) —Jucinda (Midyan (USA))
1833[5] 2323[7] 4068[4] 5121[8] *6698[2]* 7084[4] *(7507)*

Tomintoul Singer (IRE) *Henry Cecil* a81 96
3 ch f Johannesburg(USA) —Shivaree (Rahy (USA))
1545[4] 2058[4] 2978[12] *4231[4]* 4937[5] 6063[5] *7041[9]*

Tomintoul Star *Ruth Carr* a64 61
4 gr m Dansili—Lixian (Linamix (FR))
518[2] ◆ *715[3]* *776[2]* 1489[9] *2789[2]* 3503[5] *(3758)* *4914[7]* *5766[6]* *6375[10]*

Tommy's Star (IRE) *John G Carr* 62
7 b g Soviet Star(USA) —Your The Lady (IRE) (Indian Ridge)
7230[7]

Tommy Tiger *Stuart Williams* 50
2 b c Tiger Hill(IRE) —Special Green (FR) (Sadler's Wells (USA))
6532[14] 7203[10] 7345 [11]

Tomodachi (IRE) *Marco Botti* 81
3 b f Arakan(USA) —Ivory Bride (Domynsky)
6039[3]

Tom Sawyer *A P O'Brien* 88
2 b g Dansili—Cayman Sunset (IRE) (Night Shift (USA))
5245[15]

Toms Laughter *David Brown* a92 102
6 ch g Mamalik(USA) —Time Clash (Timeless Times (USA))
6374[4] *6539[6]* *7041[6]*

Toms Return *John Best* a71 57
3 br c One Cool Cat(USA) —Break Of Dawn (USA) (Mt. Livermore (USA))
3663[9] 4835[3] *5668[2]* *6310[9]* *6524[8]* *7239[11]*

Toms River Tess (IRE) *B W Hills* a49 78
2 b f Kodiac—Sonorous (IRE) (Ashkalani (IRE))
3562[9] (4286) 4801[6]

Tom Wade (IRE) *John Harris* a64 61
3 b g Rakti—Plutonia (Sadler's Wells (USA))
1977[9] 2460[3] *2792[7]* 3522[5] 4448[6] 5636[4] *5923[9]*

Tongalooma *James Moffatt* a56 59
4 ch m Shinko Forest(IRE) —Schatzi (Chilibang)
1723[4] 2278[4] 2581[2] 3534[10]

Tonnerre (IRE) *Sir Michael Stoute* 65
2 gr c Dalakhani(IRE) —Rainbow City (IRE) (Rainbow Quest (USA))
7094[3]

Tony Douglas (IRE) *A Di Dio* 99
6 ch g Elnadim(USA) —Zilwaki (USA) (Miswaki (USA))
1944a[9] 7459a[5]

Tony Hollis *Rod Millman* a53 65
2 b c Antonius Pius(USA) —Seasons Parks (Desert Prince (IRE))
4096[16] 6145[6] 6811[3] 7301[14] *7527[4]* *7811[9]*

Tony The Tap *William Muir* a66 95
9 b g Most Welcome—Laleston (Junius (USA))
2280[9] 2759[10] 3417[5] 3629[9] ◆ 4401[8] *7319[10]*

Too Grand *John Bridger* a61 53
5 ch m Zaha(CAN) —Gold Linnet (Nashwan (USA))
184[13] *262[7]* *498[6]*

Toolain (IRE) *Michael Jarvis* a79 103
2 br c Diktat—Qasirah (IRE) (Machiavellian (USA))
2932[U] ◆ *(3517)* (4355) 6737[4] 7081[7]

Too Late Jones (USA) *Mikael Magnusson* a63
3 b g Smarty Jones(USA) —Bells Are Ringing (USA) (Sadler's Wells (USA))
7438[3] *7732[9]*

Toolentidhaar (USA) *Andy Turnell* a72 72
6 b m Swain(IRE) —Rababah (USA) (Woodman (USA))
(284) *543[6]* *752[8]* *931[5]*

Too Many Questions (IRE) *David Evans* a68
2 ch g Whywhywhy(USA) —Global Tour (USA) (Tour D'Or (USA))
7962[6] *7999[3]*

Too Nice Name (FR) *Robert Collet* a98 102
3 b c Kingsalsa(USA) —Namona (IRE) (Halling (USA))
(927a) 1195a[2] 1565a[5] 2778a[5] 5574a[4]

Tooprague *Peter Hedger*
4 b m Tobougg(IRE) —Praglia (IRE) (Darshaan)
1157[6] *1302[14]*

Too Putra (IRE) *Roger Charlton* a73
3 b c Oratorio(IRE) —Urgent Liaison (IRE) (High Estate)
4698[10]

Top Act (FR) *P Schiergen* 86
3 b f Fantastic Light(USA) —Topline (GER) (Acatenango (GER))
1250a[9]

Toparichi *Mark H Tompkins* 64
2 ch g Bahamian Bounty—Topatori (IRE) (Topanoora)
2990[5] ◆ 4759[7] 5160[10]

Topaze Star *Jane Chapple-Hyam* 59
3 br f Fantastic Light(USA) —Star Of Normandie (USA) (Gulch (USA))
3620[7] 4114[7] 5902 [7]

Topaz Way (GR) *Patrick Chamings* a16
3 b c Harmonic Way—Flourishing Way (Sadler's Wells (USA))
5842[9]

Top Bid *Tim Easterby* a46 77
6 b g Auction House(USA) —Trump Street (First Trump)
(1719) (1915) 3216[10] 3902[6] 4063[10] 4345[10] 4833[9] 6679[8] 6965[7] *7332[7]*

Top Care (USA) *Mark Johnston* a82 79
2 bb g Bernstein(USA) —Secret Dream (IRE) (Zafonic (USA))
3316[6] 3805[4] 4240[3] 4851[7] 5476[2] 5856[2] 6435[4] *(7126)* *7481[4]*

Topclas (FR) *M bin Shafya* a90 109
4 b h Kutub(IRE) —Noble Presence (FR) (Fasliyev (USA))
337a[9] 418a[5] 516a[7] 712a[5] 799a[11]

Topcroft *Derek Shaw* a75 49
4 b g Mujahid(USA) —Starminda (Zamindar (USA))
1238[9]

Top Diktat *Sir Michael Stoute* a70
2 b g Diktat—Top Romance (IRE) (Entrepreneur)
7385[7] *7609[2]*

Topenhall (IRE) *Ben Case* a46 52
9 b g Topanoora—Jrred Up (IRE) (Jurado (USA))
7562[11]

Top Flight Splash *David Evans* a59 52
4 b m Bertolini(USA) —Making Waves (IRE) (Danehill (USA))
69[7] *(249)* *615[3]* *763[2]* *844[4]* *961[9]* 1441[8] 2198[9] 2590[10] 2779[8] 3292[3] ◆ 3979[5] 4366[8] 4605[12]

Topflight Wildbird *Lucy Wadham* a40 66
7 br m Diktat—Jamarj (Tyrnavos)
184[9]

Top Jaro (FR) *Ruth Carr* a52 21
7 b g Marathon(USA) —Shahmy (USA) (Lear Fan (USA))
4156[12] 4485[12] 4897[15] 6032[9]

Top Level (IRE) *Mrs A Corson* a55 51
7 b m Fasliyev(USA) —Aiming Upwards (Blushing Flame (USA))
2161a[3]

Top Mark *Alan King* a68 75
8 b g Mark Of Esteem(IRE) —Red White And Blue (Zafonic (USA))
4520[5] 5235[2] 6151[9]

Top Music *A Fabre* 97
3 b c Unbridled's Song(USA) —Top Order (USA) (Dayjur (USA))
1610a[3] 3425a[5] 5576a[10] 6012a[10]

Topolski (IRE) *Andrew Balding* a90 94
4 b g Peintre Celebre(USA) —Witching Hour (IRE) (Alzao (USA))
1220[6] ◆ 1724[5] 2541[5] 3843[8] (4597) 5387[4] (5940) 6565[12]

Top Pursuit *Ms V S Lucas* 23
8 b g Pursuit Of Love—Top Of The Parkes (Mistertopogigo (IRE))
2161a[5]

Top Seed (IRE) *Roy Brotherton* a68 72
9 b g Cadeaux Genereux—Midnight Heights (Persian Heights)
2676[8]

Top Spin (IRE) *John Joseph Murphy* a93 94
3 bb c Cape Cross(IRE) —Beguine (USA) (Green Dancer (USA))
3105[16] *7594[8]*

Top Tigress *Sir Michael Stoute* a62 61
3 b f Tiger Hill(IRE) —Top Romance (IRE) (Entrepreneur)
1278[9] 2632[5] 3513[8] 4764[3] 5563[4]

Torentosa (FR) *A De Royer-Dupre* 99
2 b f Oasis Dream—Ysoldina (FR) (Kendor (FR))
7534a[4]

Torina (IRE) *M J Grassick* a64 64
5 ch m Golan(IRE) —Tordasia (IRE) (Dr Devious (IRE))
874[5] *6373[7]*

Tornadodancer (IRE) *T G McCourt* a90 92
7 b g Princely Heir(IRE) —Purty Dancer (IRE) (Foxhound (USA))
3489a[24] 4180a[8] *7217a[11]* *7993[11]*

Tornado Force (IRE) *J S Moore* a58
2 ch c Shamardal(USA) —Pharma West (USA) (Gone West (USA))
7990[5] ◆

Torpedo Run *Richard Hannon* a29 56
2 b f Hurricane Run(IRE) —Alashaan (Darshaan)
6770[9] *7113[11]*

Torquemada (IRE) *Michael Attwater* a60 61
9 ch g Desert Sun—Gaelic's Fantasy (IRE) (Statoblest)
318[10] 1633[P]

Torran Sound *James Eustace* a40 58
3 b g Tobougg(IRE) —Velvet Waters (Unfuwain (USA))
1257[8] 1989[6] 2412[7] 4519[3] (4990)

Torres (GER) *Frau E Mader* 91
4 bb g Gold Away(IRE) —Tizia (IRE) (Linamix (FR))
1251a[13] 3251a[8] 6791a[6]

Torres Del Paine *Jimmy Fox* a74
3 b c Compton Place—Noble Story (Last Tycoon)
147[2] *489[2]* *744[2]* 2052[13] *2868[8]* *5031[10]* *6085[10]* *(7655)*

Torronto (FR) *P Monfort* a74 77
7 b g Commands(AUS) —Tamaziya (IRE) (Law Society (USA))
273a[4] *690a[9]*

Torteval (IRE) *David Evans* a43 45
2 b c Camacho—Hidden Agenda (FR) (Machiavellian (USA))
1597[8] 2216[7] 3000[8] *6867[9]* 7124[6] *7631[9]* *7813[4]* *8031[5]*

Torun City *Eve Johnson Houghton* 68
2 b c Sulamani(IRE) —Polish Sprite (Danzig Connection (USA))
4962[3] 5587[7]

Toshi (USA) *Jim Goldie* a57 60
8 b g Kingmambo(USA) —Majestic Role (FR) (Theatrical)
6028[7] 6707[5] 7176[8]

Total Command *Sir Michael Stoute* 104
3 b g Sadler's Wells(USA) —Wince (Selkirk (USA))
1386[4] (1847) 3145[3] 5185[9] 5945[9]

Total Gallery (IRE) *J S Moore* 121
4 br h Namid—Diary (IRE) (Green Desert (USA))
1700[6] 2325[5] 3047[11] 3192[18] 6194[6] 6608a[10]

Total Impact *Conor Dore* a82 95
7 ch g Pivotal—Rise 'n Shine (Night Shift (USA))
(187) *258[2]* *(349)* *520[2]* *703[2]* *750[4]* *829[2]*

Totally Focussed (IRE) *Simon Dow* a86 63
5 rg g Trans Island—Premier Place (USA) (Out Of Place (USA))
(151) *394[5]* *1088[6]* 1474[10] 1962[6] *2872[6]* *3565[7]* *4133[5]*

Totally Ours *William Muir* a85 100
3 br f Singspiel(IRE) —Totally Yours (IRE) (Desert Sun)
(1159) ◆ 1729[8] 3694[4] 4347[3] 4957[5] 5805a[5] 6886[7]

Total Victory (IRE) *C A Murphy* a68 67
7 br g Titus Livius(FR) —Snipe Victory (IRE) (Old Vic)
7514a[4]

Toto Skyllachy *Jimmy O'Reilly* a84 89
5 b g Kyllachy—Little Tramp (Trempolino (USA))
1030[4] 1185[7] 3317[11] 3396[4] (3438) 3876[9] 3920[11] 4154[13]

Toucan Tango (IRE) *Peter Chapple-Hyam* 59
2 b c Mujadil(USA) —Walk On Quest (FR) (Rainbow Quest (USA))
2319[11] 6190[8] 6831[11]

Touchmeifyoucan (GER) *P Vovcenko* 36
3 ch c Tertullian(USA) —Traumwolke (GER) (Irish Stew (GER))
1564a[6]

Touch Of Hawk (FR) *Wido Neuroth* 108
4 bl h Hawk Wing(USA) —Touch Of Class (GER) (Be My Guest (USA))
1420a[2] 2195a[2] 2637a[2] (5350a) 6017a[7] 7102a[8]

Touch Of Red (USA) *Richard Hannon* a54 42
2 b c Touch Gold(USA) —Cleveland Browni (USA) (Allen's Prospect (USA))
4803[16] 5537[7] *5893[8]* *7295[14]* *7520[4]*

Touch Of Style (IRE) *Matthew Salaman* a63 69
6 b g Desert Style(IRE) —No Hard Feelings (IRE) (Alzao (USA))
1771[3] 2361[2] (2952) (3160) ◆ 3473[3] 3589[4] 4579[4] 4758[6] 5311[7] (5813) 6322[13]

Touch Tone *B W Hills* a83 83
3 b f Selkirk(USA) —Payphone (Anabaa (USA))
2003[2] 2393[2] (4339) *5662[4]* *6291[4]* 6805[8]

Toufan Express *Adrian McGuinness* a85 89
8 ch g Fraam—Clan Scotia (Clantime)
1408a[15] 3489a[6] 5774a[9] *6597a[11]* *6907a[9]*

Tough Customer *Gary Brown* a19
2 b c Lucky Story(USA) —Fontaine House (Pyramus (USA))
6369[9] *7269[11]*

Toughness Danon *A Wohler* 109
4 b g Tiger Hill(IRE) —Templerin (GER) (Acatenango (GER))
7532a[6]

Tough Regime (IRE) *Paul W Flynn* a63 29
3 ch f Trans Island—Lady Naryana (IRE) (Val Royal (FR))
7073a[13]

Toujours Souriante *Tracy Waggott* 76
4 b m Lucky Story(USA) —Tous Les Jours (USA) (Dayjur (USA))
1296[10]

Tourist *Derek Shaw* a97 75
5 b g Oasis Dream—West Devon (USA) (Gone West (USA))
(177) *(299)* ◆ *528[5]* *739[4]* *887[11]* *944[4]* 1032[14] 6256[12] *7289[9]* *7409[3]* *7443[5]* ◆ *7566[10]* 7866[10]

Tourmaline (IRE) *Peter Chapple-Hyam* a36 40
2 b f Diamond Green(FR) —Pretext (Polish Precedent (USA))
5520[6] *6425[9]* *7210[8]* *7404[12]*

Tournedos (IRE) *Ruth Carr* a75 100
8 b g Rossini(USA) —Don't Care (IRE) (Nordico (USA))
349[6] *562[8]* *716[8]* *774[6]* ◆ *913[9]* 1364[10] 1598[9] 2849[7] 3024[5] 3533[2] ◆ (3615) 3976[7] 4799[6] 5362[6] 6299[6]

Tous Les Deux *Dr Jeremy Naylor* a74 70
7 b g Efisio—Caerosa (Caerleon (USA))
679[5] *829[4]* *943[9]* *1042[4]* *1322[2]* *(1457)* *1536[2]* (1815a) *2477[6]* *2866[9]* 7737[10] 8035[11]

Tovaria *Edward P Harty* 93
6 b m Muhtarram(USA) —Budoor (IRE) (Darshaan)
3492a[3] 6971a[11]

Towbaat *Michael Jarvis* a76 80
3 b f Halling(USA) —Nasmatt (Danehill (USA))
1278[2] *(1621)* 2254[9] 2863[9] 6444[5] 6692[12]

Tower *George Prodromou* a64 64
3 b g Nayef(USA) —Palatial (Green Desert (USA))
1186[4] 3173[8] 3523[4] 3996[2] 4362[2] 5164[9] *5656[4]* *5752[3]* *6525[5]* *(6871)* *7270[3]* ◆ *7388[3]*

Tower Hill Gate (IRE) *Patrick Martin* 48
2 b c Ivan Denisovich(IRE) —Gate Lodge (IRE) (Last Tycoon)
4175a[12]

Towering Storm *Gerard Butler* a75
2 b g Storming Home—Towaahi (IRE) (Caerleon (USA))
(7610) ◆

Town House *Brian Baugh* a39 50
8 gr m Paris House—Avondale Girl (IRE) (Case Law)
369[8] *477[9]* *727[9]* 1598[14] 2751[6] 3358[9] 3908[7] 4047[12]

Towthorpe *Mel Brittain* a35 65
4 ch g Tobougg(IRE) —Snow Shoes (Sri Pekan (USA))
2629[11] *7645[5]*

Towy Boy (IRE) *Ian Wood* a74 59
5 b g King Charlemagne(USA) —Solar Flare (IRE) (Danehill (USA))
235[2] *368[4]* *615[2]* *844[7]* *1304[10]* 1737[8] 2008[9] *2727[2]* *3280[3]* *3762[2]* 4427[4] (4789) (5697) 6210[9] 6536[3] 6880[12] (7334) 7628[2] 8005[11]

Towzee (NZ) *Brian A Lynch* 99
8 bb g Towkay(AUS) —Classic Realm (NZ) (Kingdom Bay (NZ))
6949a[9]

Toymaker *Luca Cumani* 64
3 b g Starcraft(NZ) —Eurolink Raindance (IRE) (Alzao (USA))
4572[5] ◆ 5623[6]

Trachonitis (IRE) *John Jenkins* a83 77
6 b g Dansili—Hasina (IRE) (King's Theatre (IRE))
300[5] *1062[2]* *1348[10]* *3781[8]* 4252[3] *5868[9]* 5991[8] *6427[10]* *7275[2]* *7463[4]* *7836[2]* 7985[7]

Track Record *Jonjo O'Neill* 99
5 b g Montjeu(IRE) —Prove (Danehill (USA))
1274[15] 1525[7] 2031[15] 2821[10] 4923[7]

Trade Centre *Ronald Harris* a77 79
5 b g Dubai Destination(USA) —Khubza (Green Desert (USA))
259[7] *579[3]* *853[4]* *1238[6]* *1877[3]* *2187[4]* 3160[14] *3765[7]* *4428[9]* *5766[9]*

Trader Way (GR) *Patrick Chamings* 12
3 ch g Harmonic Way—Snowdrift (Desert Prince (IRE))
1731[12] 2197[9]

Trade Secret *Mel Brittain* 77
3 b c Trade Fair—Kastaway (Distant Relative)
(1401) 1709[4] 2099[4] 2426[4] 2768[11] 4349[8]

Trade Storm *John Gallagher* 96
2 b c Trade Fair—Frisson (Slip Anchor)
1845[4] ◆ 2216[2] (2887) 5219[6] 5831[4]

Trading *Tim Easterby* a42 66
2 b g Piccolo—Babcary (Bertolini (USA))
1065[4] 1668[4] 2272[3] 5602[8] 6220[10] 6645[9]

Trading Nation (USA) *Peter Hiatt* a61 79
4 b g Tiznow(USA) —Nidd (USA) (Known Fact (USA))
443[3] *638[5]* *808[8]* 1441[13] 2589[15] 3511[7] *5766[10]* 6186[7] 6826[11]

Tradition (IRE) *David Wachman* a79 76
2 b g Footstepsinthesand—Carn Lady (IRE) (Woodman (USA))
(6726a)

Trafalgar Square *Michael Attwater* a84 72
8 b g King's Best(USA) —Pat Or Else (Alzao (USA))
393[5] *487[2]* *672[7]* *749[6]* *990[4]* *1156[6]* *1346[9]* *1875[8]* 2596[6] 3160[7] 4108[8] 4488[2] 4870[6] 5237[6] 6632[8] 6852[11]

Traffic Guard (USA) *Paul Cole* a89 114
6 b h More Than Ready(USA) —Street Scene (IRE) (Zafonic (USA))
1382[8] 1898[4] 2593[5] 3144[8] 3632[3] 4535[3] (5090) 5538[2]

Traffic Sister (USA) *J S Moore* a74 91
2 b f More Than Ready(USA) —Street Scene (IRE) (Zafonic (USA))
5033[6] *5841[5]* 6348[5]

Tragagalletas (IRE) *L A Urbano-Grajales* 29
3 b g American Post—Dena (Deploy)
450a[8]

Trailblazing *Mark Johnston* a82 86
3 b g Green Desert(USA) —Pioneer Bride (USA) (Gone West (USA))
2807[6] 4112[9] 5499[10] 5994[9] *6664[3]* ◆ *6856[2]* 7054[12] *7243[11]*

Train Deal (IRE) *F De Sanctis* 91
3 ch f Camacho—Fanciful (IRE) (Mujtahid (USA))
1713a[17]

Trait D'Union *S Botti*
2 ch c Exceed And Excel(AUS) —Ellendellendoo (IRE) (Ela-Mana-Mou)
7849a[11]

Tranquil Manner (USA) *Kiaran McLaughlin* a110
4 b h A.P. Indy(USA) —Composure (USA) (Touch Gold (USA))
5780a[3] *6586a[6]*

Tranquil Tiger *Henry Cecil* a113 116
6 ch h Selkirk(USA) —Serene View (USA) (Distant View (USA))
(946) ◆ 1328[2] 1532[7] 1911[5]

Tranquil Waters (IRE) *B W Hills* 36
3 b c Sadler's Wells(USA) —Belle Of Honour (USA) (Honour And Glory (USA))
3795[11]

Transcentral *Trevor Wall* a47 6
4 ch m Kheleyf(USA) —Khafayif (USA) (Swain (IRE))
532[8] *614[12]* *1236[11]* 6656[13]

Transeggselence *Patrick Leech* 62
3 b f Trans Island—Breakfast Bay (IRE) (Charnwood Forest (IRE))
5493[4] 6655[7]

Transfer *Charlie Morlock* a76 68
5 br g Trans Island—Sankaty Light (USA) (Summer Squall (USA))
2596[7] 3032[7] 3559[7] 4201[12] 5689[7] *7825[5]*

Transfered (IRE) *Lucinda Featherstone* a47 55
4 b m Trans Island—Second Omen (Rainbow Quest (USA))
874[9] *4683[13]* 4854[12] 5631[8] *6933[7]* 7147[12]

Transfixed (IRE) *David Evans* a79 80
3 b f Trans Island—Rectify (IRE) (Mujadil (USA))
107[2] *203[5]* *268[5]* *310[5]* *406[3]* *424[4]* *617[5]* *681[3]* *772[3]* 884[8] 901[6] 1045[6] 1086[10] 1913[3] 2002[8] 2112[10] 2416[8] 2618[6] 2762[7] 3276[8] 3387[11] 4249[3] 4475[7] 4735[6] 4779[5] 5073[12] 7829[10] 7005[6] 7037[5]

Transinski (IRE) *Alastair Lidderdale*
4 b g Trans Island—Spinsky (USA) (Spinning World (USA))
4926[6]

Transmission (IRE) *Bryan Smart* a80 70
5 b g Galileo(IRE) —Individual (USA) (Gulch (USA))
19[4] (87) (170) 245[7] 508[3] 573[4] 908[5] 1115[12] 4189[7]
Transmit (IRE) *Tim Easterby* a54 73
3 ch g Trans Island—Apple Brandy (USA) (Cox's Ridge (USA))
1153[2] ◆ (1464) 2112[7] 2261[6] 3208[8] 4288[3] 4647[4] 5421[8] 6048[4] 6226[8] 6879[10]
Trans Sonic *David O'Meara* a95 80
7 ch g Trans Island—Sankaty Light (USA) (Summer Squall (USA))
75[3] (451) (572) (837) 1013[8] (1826) 2241[6] 4894[9] 5500[6] 6367[7] 6724[9] (6922) 7143[3] 7283[3] 7846[5] 7935[3]
Transvaal Sky *Tom Dascombe* a81 89
3 bb f Avonbridge—Glider (IRE) (Silver Kite (USA))
1834[8] 3457[11] 4287[5]
Transvestite (IRE) *Tor Sturgis* a79 34
8 b g Trans Island—Christoph's Girl (Efisio)
526[4] 811[8] 1439[5] 3278[5]
Traphalgar (IRE) *David Evans* a83 88
5 br g Cape Cross(IRE) —Conquestadora (Hernando (FR))
3278[9] 7480[6] (7570) 7736[8] 8032[3]
Trappe Shot (USA) *Kiaran McLaughlin* a116
3 ch c Tapit(USA) —Shopping (USA) (Private Account (USA))
4643a[2] 5544a[9]
Treacle Tart *Peter Charalambous* a74 73
5 ch m Fleetwood(IRE) —Loriner's Lass (Saddlers' Hall (IRE))
2231[3] 7022[2] (7381) ◆ 7736[5]
Treadwell (IRE) *Jamie Osborne* a90 105
3 b c Footstepsinthesand—Lady Wells (IRE) (Sadler's Wells (USA))
1732[3] 2028[2] 2713[2] (3146) 4574[8] 5275[9]
Treason Trial *Andrew Crook* a46 62
9 b g Peintre Celebre(USA) —Pampabella (IRE) (High Estate)
2085[P] 4246[12] 6921[12]
Treasure Beach *A P O'Brien* 103
2 b c Galileo(IRE) —Honorine (IRE) (Mark Of Esteem (IRE))
6347[3]
Treasure Way *Patrick Chamings* 69
3 ch f Galileo(IRE) —Gold Mark (Mark Of Esteem (IRE))
2180[5] ◆ 2998[3] 4098[5] 4492[6] 4997[3] 5887[4] 6479[10]
Treasury Devil (USA) *John Gosden* 96
2 b c Bernardini(USA) —Crystal Music (USA) (Nureyev (USA))
(5033) ◆ (6088) 6610a[9]
Treat Gently *William Mott* 108
5 b m Cape Cross(IRE) —Kid Gloves (In The Wings)
5320a[5]
Trebetherick (IRE) *J E Hammond* a85 79
2 gr c Verglas(IRE) —Kathy Sun (IRE) (Intikhab (USA))
5133a[8]
Treble Jig (USA) *Sir Michael Stoute* 93
3 b c Gone West(USA) —Light Jig (Danehill (USA))
2253[5] (2927) 3824[16]
Trecase *Tony Carroll* a59 54
3 b g Zafeen(FR) —Pewter Lass (Dowsing (USA))
2564[11] 2974[10] 4425[9] 4969[6] 5379[6] 5864[2] 6287[4] 6865[10]
Treeko (IRE) *Philip Kirby* a46 35
5 b g Alhaarth(IRE) —Allegheny River (USA) (Lear Fan (USA))
15[7] 409[5] 621[12]
Treetops Hotel (IRE) *Lee James* a7 41
11 ch g Grand Lodge(USA) —Rousinette (Rousillon (USA))
3177[8]
Tregony Bridge *Michael Blanshard* a52 42
3 b g Avonbridge—Serotina (IRE) (Mtoto)
1048[5] 1162[4] ◆ 1643[9] 2418[4] ◆ 3479[7] 3723[9]
Trelicia *Stuart Williams* a52 44
3 ch f Tobougg(IRE) —Francia (Legend Of France (USA))
583[12] 930[5] 1257[7] 2633[15] 3325[13] 5729[8] 5957[5] ◆ 6665[7]
Tremoto *F & L Camici* 100
5 b m Generous(IRE) —Therese Chenu (IRE) (Local Suitor (USA))
6763a[7] 7109a[4]
Trempari *Mike Murphy* a52 54
7 ch g Trempolino(USA) —Ariadne (GER) (Kings Lake (USA))
2631[1] 506[8] 6502[3]
Trend (IRE) *Michael Bell* 64
2 b g Marju(IRE) —Fashion (Bin Ajwaad (IRE))
6128[5] 6634[7] 7036[7]
Trendy Way (IRE) *Patrick Chamings* 40
3 b f Footstepsinthesand—Arietta's Way (IRE) (Darshaan)
3484[6] 4425[12] 4835[6]
Tres Amigos *David Nicholls* a79 58
3 ch g Exceed And Excel(AUS) —Canterloupe (IRE) (Wolfhound (USA))
1191[3] 2069[12] 2394[7] 2886[10] 3276[13]
Tres Coronas (IRE) *David Barron* a86 88
3 b g Key Of Luck(USA) —Almansa (IRE) (Dr Devious (IRE))
2033[9] (2466) 3196[6] 4593[3] 5759[7] 6002[4] (6753)
Tres Froide (FR) *Nigel Tinkler* a57 67
5 ch m Bering—Charmgoer (USA) (Nureyev (USA))
1489[8] 1919[6] 2421[7] 2902[8] 3370[3] 3684[6] 4453[5] 4914[3] 5158[2] 5704[5] 6125[3] 6335[4] 7070[6] 7200[2] 7569[3] 7899[3]
Tres Rock Danon (FR) *W Hickst* 113
4 b h Rock Of Gibraltar(IRE) —Tres Ravi (GER) (Monsun (GER))
1748a[4] (2574a) (4012a) 5349a[5] 6410a[5]
Trevieres (FR) *C Laffon-Parias* a57 59
2 ch g Gold Away(IRE) —Castilly (Inchinor)
4565a[7]
Trewarthenick *Andrew Balding* a59 70
3 b g Cape Cross(IRE) —Play With Fire (FR) (Priolo (USA))
1594[4] (2587) 2888[9]
Tribal Myth (IRE) *Kevin Ryan* 68
3 b g Johannesburg(USA) —Shadow Play (USA) (Theatrical)
(1298) 1522[3] (1753) 2438[3] 3363[4] 3661[2] 4061[10] 4898[5] 6144[9]
Tribe *Paul Webber* a57 72
8 b g Danehill(USA) —Leo Girl (USA) (Seattle Slew (USA))
1641[3]
Tri Chara (IRE) *Reg Hollinshead* a66 48
6 ch g Grand Slam(USA) —Lamzena (IRE) (Fairy King (USA))
21[9] 195[4] 464[7] 569[4] 838[3] (1142) 1235[3] 1457[8]
Trick Or Two *Ruth Carr* a61 51
4 gr g Desert Style(IRE) —Vax Star (Petong)
351[11] 778[2] 869[5] 896[11] 1068[3] 1154[4] 1234[3] 1337[4] 2186[11] 2721[4] 3064[10] 3286[12] 3966[13]
Tricky Situation *David Brown* a20 66
4 b m Mark Of Esteem(IRE) —Trick Of Ace (USA) (Clever Trick (USA))
6306[2] 6516[10] 6895[12] 7045[8] 7678[7]
Trifti *Jo Crowley* a79 51
9 b g Vettori(IRE) —Time For Tea (IRE) (Imperial Frontier (USA))
485[8] 5367[11]
Trille Divine *Mme C De La Soudiere-Niault* 70
2 b f Marchand De Sable(USA) —Brilliantly (FR) (Priolo (USA))
4036a[7]
Tripbiyah (USA) *Alan Swinbank* a61 61
4 b g Trippi(USA) —Jathibiyah (USA) (Nureyev (USA))
2378[11] 3177[7]
Tripitaka *Michael Jarvis* a94
4 b g Sulamani(IRE) —Memo (Groom Dancer (USA))
(25)
Triple Agent (IRE) *Alan Bailey* a53 59
2 ch g Monsieur Bond(IRE) —Dream Dance (Diesis)
1263[11] 2389[9] 2939[4] 3784[5]
Triple Aspect (IRE) *William Haggas* 116
4 b h Danetime(IRE) —Wicken Wonder (IRE) (Distant Relative)
(2400) 3192[17] (3691) 4505[U] 5569a[5] 6194[11] 6735[10]
Triple Dream *Milton Bradley* a79 86
5 ch g Vision Of Night—Triple Joy (Most Welcome)
2280[6] 2689[8] 2973[7] 3114[4] 3373[10] 3736[5] 3892[2] 3958[3] (4518) 4836[7] 4961[9] 5262[5] 5628[7] 5915[3] 6374[2] 6440[9] 6858[9] 6998[4] 7180[14] 7446[10] 7571[5] 7754[7]
Triple Eight (IRE) *D K Weld* a93 94
2 b g Royal Applause—Hidden Charm (IRE) (Big Shuffle (USA))
4310a[4]
Triple Honour (NZ) *Chris Waller* 115
6 b g Honours List(IRE) —Myrrh (NZ) (Nassipour (USA))
6947a[10]
Trip Switch *George Prodromou* a65 58
4 b g Reset(AUS) —Caribbean Star (Soviet Star (USA))
78[6] 312[10] 486[3] 531[6] 844[2] 937[7] 1170[5] 5897[13] 6456[12]
Trip The Light *Richard Fahey* a92 94
5 b g Fantastic Light(USA) —Jumaireyah (Fairy King (USA))
(1151) 1472[4] 2071[6] (2343) 2976[6] 3431[2] 3877[5] 4348[5] 5118[2] 5786[7] 7084[15] 7568[7] 7865[2] (8003)
Triskaidekaphobia *Miss J R Tooth* a55 44
7 b g Bertolini(USA) —Seren Teg (Timeless Times (USA))
132[7] 178[9] 271[9] 525[4] 1234[10] 2721[11] (3516) 7334[7]
Tristar Way (GR) *Patrick Chamings* a25 29
3 b c Harmonic Way—Senseansensibility (USA) (Capote (USA))
4697[12] 6557[5]
Triumphant Welcome *James Evans* a63 68
5 b g Piccolo—Shoof (USA) (Dayjur (USA))
178[6] 320[11]
Troas (IRE) *John M Oxx* 96
3 ch g Dalakhani(IRE) —Amathusia (Selkirk (USA))
2367a[6] 3145[9] (Dead)
Trois Rois (FR) *Saeed Bin Suroor* a102 110
5 b h Hernando(FR) —Trevise (FR) (Anabaa (USA))
629a[11] 708a[7]
Trojan Gift (USA) *Julie-Ann Camacho* 62
3 bb g War Chant(USA) —Extry (USA) (Broad Brush (USA))
1119[6] 1528[3] 2083[4] 2704[6] 6038[4]
Trojan Nights (USA) *William Haggas* a67 58
2 ch g Street Cry(IRE) —Dabaweyaa (Shareef Dancer (USA))
6882[5] ◆ 7186[4]
Trojan Reef *Gerard Butler* a67
4 b g Selkirk(USA) —Milly Of The Vally (Caerleon (USA))
2786[2]
Trojan Rocket (IRE) *George Prodromou* a58
2 b c Elusive City(USA) —Tagula Bay (IRE) (Tagula (IRE))
7999[5]
Trojan Touch (USA) *Chris Dwyer* a13
2 ch g Eddington(USA) —Lady Sky Racer (USA) (Skywalker (USA))
6128[9] 6667[6] 6850[6]
Tro Nesa (IRE) *Ann Duffield* 78
2 b f Chineur(FR) —Monsusu (IRE) (Montjeu (IRE))
(3020) 3611[5] 4367[3] 4615[4] 4984[7] 5354[2] 5998[3] 6354[3] (7050) 7280[5]
Tropical Bachelor (IRE) *Tim Pitt* a52 77
4 b g Bachelor Duke(USA) —Tropical Coral (IRE) (Pennekamp (USA))
1526[3] 1801[5] 1887[2] 2109[2] (2655) (2941) ◆ 2995[7] 3319[15] 4170[3]
Tropical Beat *Hughie Morrison* a68
2 b c Beat Hollow—Tropical Heights (FR) (Shirley Heights)
7248[5]
Tropical Blue *Jennie Candlish* a78 77
4 b g Fath(USA) —Tropical Zone (Machiavellian (USA))
352[6] 468[3] 563[2] 756[2] 966[2] 1186[2] 1512[6] 1907[8]
Tropical Duke (IRE) *Ron Barr* a62 65
4 ch g Bachelor Duke(USA) —Tropical Dance (USA) (Thorn Dance (USA))
2421[12] 2625[8] 5019[6] (5530) 6269[2] 6650[7] 6890[13]
Tropical Paradise (IRE) *Peter Winkworth* a92 111
4 gr m Verglas(IRE) —Ladylishandra (IRE) (Mujadil (USA))
1693[6] (2595) 3752[3] (4540) (5554)
Tropical Spirit (IRE) *John M Oxx* 25
2 b c Invincible Spirit(IRE) —Tropical Lady (IRE) (Sri Pekan (USA))
4175a[14]
Tropical Treat *Ralph Beckett* 108
3 b f Bahamian Bounty—Notjustaprettyface (USA) (Red Ransom (USA))
1918[3] ◆ (3197) 3875[2] 4505[6] ◆ 5569a[12] 6390[8]
Tropic Storm (USA) *Craig Dollase* a107 99
6 b g Stormy Atlantic(USA) —Diplomatic Angel (USA) (Valid Appeal (USA))
7362a[12]
Trotting Weasel (IRE) *M Halford* a60 58
7 b g Bold Fact(USA) —Eves Temptation (IRE) (Glenstal (USA))
5129a[6]
Troubletimestwo (FR) *Tony Carroll* a60 58
4 gr g Linamix(FR) —Time Of Trouble (FR) (Warning)
6314[9]
Trovare (USA) *Amanda Perrett* 87
3 b g Smart Strike(CAN) —Abita (USA) (Dynaformer (USA))
(2321) 2893[4] (3414) ◆ (4380) 5273[15]
Troys Steps *Sandra Forster* 22
6 b m Cloudings(IRE) —Troys Guest (IRE) (Be My Guest (USA))
3352[8]
True Pleasure (IRE) *James Bethell* a58 35
3 b f Choisir(AUS) —Absolute Pleasure (Polar Falcon (USA))
997[6] 1402[9] 1706[13] (2480) (2724) 3521[7]
True Red (IRE) *Nikki Evans* a56 64
3 ch f Redback—Red Trance (IRE) (Soviet Star (USA))
208[5] 788[5] 1187[2] 2026[6] 2688[6] 5957[8] 6746[7] 7477[9] 7676[2]
True To Form (IRE) *Sir Mark Prescott Bt* a79 77
3 b g Rock Of Gibraltar(IRE) —Truly Yours (IRE) (Barathea (IRE))
(5729) (5891) (5962) ◆ (6165) 6573[4]
True Union (USA) *Alan Jarvis*
4 b h Dixie Union(USA) —Redeem (USA) (Devil's Bag (USA))
971[7] 3616[4]
Truism *Amanda Perrett* 93
4 b g Daylami(IRE) —Real Trust (USA) (Danzig (USA))
2322[5] 2926[3] 3346[3] 4459[3] 4579[2] 5264[13] 5556[7]
Trulamani (IRE) *J-P Roman* 67
4 b m Sulamani(IRE) —Truly A Gift (IRE) (Arazi (USA))
5378a[6]
Truly Asia (IRE) *Roger Charlton* 82
4 b g Acclamation—Tasha's Dream (USA) (Woodman (USA))
2339[10] 2683[8] 3438[9] 4265[7] 4859[S] 5624[3] 6151[4]
Truly Divine *Chris Dwyer* a62 64
5 b g Invincible Spirit(IRE) —Shabarana (FR) (Nishapour (FR))
89[3] 112[4] 271[3] 402[4] 561[5] 687[3] 726[11] 899[5]
Truly Magic *Harry Dunlop* a34 61
3 ch f Traditionally(USA) —Truly Bewitched (USA) (Affirmed (USA))
1522[4] 2168[7] 3478[4] 3957[6] 5158[9] 6255[8] 6826[14]
Truly Magnificent (USA) *Brendan Duke* a57
3 b f Elusive Quality(USA) —Magnificent Honour (USA) (A.P. Indy (USA))
7834[2] ◆
Trumpington Street (IRE) *John Gosden* 78
2 ch c Noverre(USA) —Landela (Alhaarth (IRE))
6504[3] ◆
Trumpstoo (USA) *Richard Fahey* 67
4 b g Perfect Soul(IRE) —Cozzy Love (USA) (Cozzene (USA))
2523[3] 3122[4] 3552[7] 7704[8]
Trust Me Boy *John E Long* a46
2 gr g Avonbridge—Eastern Lyric (Petong)
6994[10] 7386[10] 7550[8]
Try Cat *Sir Mark Prescott Bt* a40
4 b m Mark Of Esteem(IRE) —French Spice (Cadeaux Genereux)
166[7] 246[6] 316[8] 748[13]
Tryst *J E Hammond* a78 97
5 gr g Highest Honor(FR) —Courting (Pursuit Of Love)
3069[4]
Trysting Grove (IRE) *Edward Bevan* a57 41
9 b m Cape Cross(IRE) —Elton Grove (IRE) (Astronef)
410[5] 622[3] 865[4] 942[3] 1188[4] 2604[6] 3128[9] 3560[9]
Try The Chance *Mick Channon* 79
2 b c Majestic Missile(IRE) —Danetime Out (IRE) (Danetime (IRE))
(4528) 6254[2]
Tsar Bomba (USA) *David Barron* 65
3 bb g Red Bullet(USA) —Larry's Blackhoney (USA) (Hennessy (USA))
5065[4] 5686[4] 6896[3] 7153[13]
Tsarina Louise *James Given* a30 23
2 b f Red Ransom(USA) —Imperial Bailiwick (IRE) (Imperial Frontier (USA))
4543[9] 5763[9] 6658[5]
Tt's Dream *Alastair Lidderdale* a36 60
3 gr g Imperial Dancer—On Cloud Nine (Cloudings (IRE))
3374[6] 3827[8] 4364[5] 4931[7] 5159[9]
Tuanku (IRE) *Alan King* a62 71
5 b g Tagula(IRE) —Be My Lover (Pursuit Of Love)
6428[9] 7101[3]
Tubby Isaacs *Dean Ivory* a81 83
6 b g Cyrano De Bergerac—Opuntia (Rousillon (USA))
(1482) (2113) 2592[3] 3435[4] 4551[10] 4961[8] 6501[11]
Tucker's Law *Rod Millman* a67 65
3 b g Country Reel(USA) —Silvereine (FR) (Bering)
1873[9] 2617[7]
Tudor Key (IRE) *Amanda Perrett* a91 91
4 br g Key Of Luck(USA) —Anne Boleyn (Rainbow Quest (USA))
(1265) 1846[3] 2683[6] 2991[11] 3813[8]
Tudor Prince (IRE) *Tony Carroll* a76 75
6 bb g Cape Cross(IRE) —Savona (IRE) (Cyrano De Bergerac)
3129[3] 3396[10] 3777[6] 4024[13] 7892[9]
Tudor Princess *William Muir* a54 53
3 b f King's Best(USA) —Santorini (USA) (Spinning World (USA))
1661[7] 2634[11] 3478[10] 4210[8] 4475[4] 4733[6]
Tufty *Michael Easterby* a49 10
2 b c Blue Dakota(IRE) —Zafaaf (Kris)
1749[11] 1978[5] 3757[8]
Tuiga (IRE) *P Schiergen* 87
3 br f Rakti—Tocopilla (FR) (Medaaly)
3943a[7]
Tukitinyasok (IRE) *Roger Fisher* a66 87
3 b g Fath(USA) —Mevlana (IRE) (Red Sunset)
406[5] 1070[6] 2884[7] 3519[10] (4704) (5304) 5421[2] 6801[10] 7143[5]
Tulip Explosion *Derek Shaw* a50 38
3 b f Exceed And Excel(AUS) —Comme Ca (Cyrano De Bergerac)
831[2] 988[8] 1155[5] 1316[4] 1535[5]
Tulle (IRE) *Brian Meehan* 63
3 b f Sinndar(IRE) —Dragnet (IRE) (Rainbow Quest (USA))
2051[6] 2891[7] 5038[12]
Tullius (IRE) *Peter Winkworth* a79 18
2 ch g Le Vie Dei Colori—Whipped Queen (USA) (Kingmambo (USA))
4131[11] (7186) 7417[2] (7636) ◆
Tumbled Again *Mark Rimmer* a51 47
3 br g Tumbleweed Ridge—Amber Brown (Thowra (FR))
1127[10] 2418[8] 2633[14] 7498[3] 7651[8] 7832[3]
Tune Up The Band *Ron Hodges* a60 49
6 b g Bandmaster(USA) —Name That Tune (Fayruz)
561[7] 866[5] 936[3] 1799[7] 2021[9] 2186[7] 2720[8]
Tuning Fork *Michael Attwater* a44 4
10 b g Alzao(USA) —Tuning (Rainbow Quest (USA))
99[8] 389[13]
Tupelo (IRE) *S Loeuillet* a47 67
2 gr f Clodovil(IRE) —Kaliningrad (IRE) (Red Sunset)
1043[8] (2631) (2905) 7383a[7]
Turbo Shandy *Dai Burchell* a43 47
7 b g Piccolo—Carn Maire (Northern Prospect (USA))
1188[9]
Turf Melody (USA) *H Graham Motion* a102 95
3 b c Maria's Mon(USA) —Tricky Bird (USA) (Storm Bird (CAN))
824a[4]
Turf Time *Jeremy Glover* a55 52
3 b g Zafeen(FR) —Next Time (IRE) (Danetime (IRE))
167[3] (215) 265[3] 387[2] 471[2] 619[6] 745[2] 870[3] 998[5] 1163[4] 1477[6] 3026[6] 3286[6] 4651[4] 5055[11] 5535[17] 6464[12]
Turf Trivia *George Moore* 62
3 gr g Alhaarth(IRE) —Exclusive Approval (USA) (With Approval (CAN))
2422[8] 3732[5] 4481[7]
Turia (GER) *Uwe Ostmann* 79
2 b f Call Me Big(GER) —Tokara (GER) (Turfkonig (GER))
7108a[8]
Turjuman (USA) *Willie Musson* a81 77
5 ch g Swain(IRE) —Hachiyah (IRE) (Generous (IRE))
(770) (974) 1579[11] 2181[4] 3781[13] 6957[5] 7101[12] 7480[4] 7878[6]
Turkish Sultan (IRE) *Milton Bradley* a55 55
7 b g Anabaa(USA) —Odalisque (IRE) (Machiavellian (USA))
(184) 227[9] 347[6] 479[5] 576[3] 816[3] 847[3] 940[7] 1503[9] 4913[9]
Turn Around (FR) *C Alonso Pena* 78
3 b f High Yield(USA) —Arletta (USA) (Quest For Fame)
5981a[9]
Turner's Touch *Gary Moore* a54 54
8 ch g Compton Place—Chairmans Daughter (Unfuwain (USA))
1842[10] 410[7] 590[2] 1635[8] 2489[5] 3984[4] 4689[13] 5863[10] 6999[13]
Turnham Green *Sean Curran* a22
4 b g Groom Dancer(USA) —Pie In The Sky (Bishop Of Cashel)
326[9] 841[5] 2752[P]
Turning Circle *Mel Brittain* a67 67
4 b h Spinning World(USA) —Willow Dale (IRE) (Danehill (USA))
301[3] 399[2] 523[2] 915[3] 1402[3] 1924[9] 7645[2]
Turning Top (IRE) *Simon Callaghan* a59 104
4 bb m Pivotal—Pietra Dura (Cadeaux Genereux)
6604a[2]

Turnkey *David Nicholls* 85
8 br g Pivotal—Persian Air (Persian Bold)
1332[6] 3065[8] 4192[8] 4345[7]

Turn Me On (IRE) *Tim Walford* a85 88
7 b g Tagula(IRE) —Jacobina (Magic Ring (IRE))
(1802) 2532[4] 2696[2] 3537[6] 4603[11] 5937[11] 6394[8] 6963[5] 7143[8] 7283[5]

Turn The Tide *Alan Bailey* a65 82
2 b f Footstepsinthesand—Syrian Dancer (IRE) (Groom Dancer (USA))
(1510) 2095[7] 3141[11] 4748[3] 5293[4] 6900[6]

Turn To Dreams *David Evans* a58 51
4 b m Auction House(USA) —Seren Teg (Timeless Times (USA))
34[10] 99[6]

Turtle Dove *Mark Gillard* a60 32
5 b m Tobougg(IRE) —Inseparable (Insan (USA))
2249[10] 2779[14] 3727[12] 4586[8]

Tuscan Gold *Sir Mark Prescott Bt* a91 80
3 ch c Medicean—Louella (USA) (El Gran Senor (USA))
2289[2] ◆ 4230[2] ◆ (4493) 4965[2] (5752) ◆

Tuscania *Sir Michael Stoute* a81 86
2 b f King's Best(USA) —Contiguous (USA) (Danzig (USA))
(6451) ◆ 7098[5]

Tuscan King *David Evans* a69 64
3 ch g Medicean—Castaway Queen (IRE) (Selkirk (USA))
(217) 283[3] 371[3] (534) 633[2] 670[2] (812) 964[2] (977) 1476[8] 1761[5] 1839[3] 2168[6] 2279[8] 7778[8] 7964[8]

Tussian Bere (FR) *E J O'Neill* a80 93
3 ch g Russian Blue(IRE) —Fitness Queen (USA) (Gilded Time (USA))
2557a[6]

Tut (IRE) *John Weymes* 81
3 b f Intikhab(USA) —Radiant Energy (IRE) (Spectrum (IRE))
1182[5] 2422[3] 2816[2] 3679[3] 4341[7]

Tuxedo *Peter Hiatt* a81 75
5 ch g Cadeaux Genereux—Serengeti Bride (USA) (Lion Cavern (USA))
5964[9] 6800[5] (7483) 7597[6] 7892[6] 8017[3]

Tuxsumdoin *John Weymes* a20 46
6 ch m Zaha(CAN) —Roisin Clover (Faustus (USA))
1103[5] 2182[11] 4190[6]

Tweedledrum *Andrew Balding* 64
3 b f Beat Hollow—Tweed Mill (Selkirk (USA))
2820[4] 3953[4]

Tweedy (IRE) *Edward Lynam* a98 89
3 b f Oasis Dream—Shining Prospect (Lycius (USA))
4269a[5] 7217a[7] 7524[10]

Tweenie (IRE) *Richard Hannon* 50
2 b f Kheleyf(USA) —Housekeeper (IRE) (Common Grounds)
4203[13] 4960[8] 5255[11] 6259[9]

Twennyshortkid *Paul Midgley* 45
2 b g Sleeping Indian—Brandish (Warning)
3365[7] 4368[9] 6070[9]

Twester (FR) *J Thibault* 70
8 b h Blush Rambler(USA) —Valkirk (Selkirk (USA))
5378a[3]

Twice As Nice *Richard Hannon* 63
3 b c Compton Place—Sunley Stars (Sallust)
1878[9] ◆ 2003[5] 2340[5]

Twice Bitten *James Toller* a77 40
2 ch c Beat Hollow—Duena (Grand Lodge (USA))
5047[13] 6053[3] 6497[2] (7163)

Twice In Woods (USA) *R Betti* 90
3 ch c Ecton Park(USA) —Twice As Sweet (USA) (Concorde's Tune (USA))
1418a[5]

Twice Over *Henry Cecil* a125 127
5 b h Observatory(USA) —Double Crossed (Caerleon (USA))
1027a[10] 3068[2] (3693) 5186[2] 5775a[3] (6925)

Twilight Star (IRE) *Roger Teal* a35 79
6 b g Green Desert(USA) —Heavenly Whisper (IRE) (Halling (USA))
1530[10] 3579[4] 3813[7] 4308[12] 4690[11] 5075[7] 7611[13]

Twinkled *Michael Bell* a51 50
2 ch g Bahamian Bounty—Panic Stations (Singspiel (IRE))
6828[7] 7150[5] 7408[7]

Twin Soul (IRE) *Andrew Balding* a59
2 b f Singspiel(IRE) —Kirk Wynd (Selkirk (USA))
3082[10] 7733[4] 8001[6] ◆

Twist Again (IRE) *Paul Howling* a56 45
4 b m Sakhee(USA) —Dance Clear (IRE) (Marju (IRE))
1689[2] 2060[7] 3398[4] 4141[10] 6895[16]

Twisted *Michael Easterby* a70 76
4 ch g Selkirk(USA) —Winding (USA) (Irish River (FR))
2976[18] 3409[9] 3761[11] 4151[6] 6116[6] (6930) 7167[14]

Twisted Wings (IRE) *Tim Easterby* a16
2 ch f Camacho—Westlife (IRE) (Mind Games)
2785[8]

Twist Of Silver (USA) *Jeremy Noseda* a83 88
2 br f Silver Train(USA) —Twist Of Faith (USA) (Storm Cat (USA))
(2041) 2514[4] 3141[12] 3844[5] 5261[4] 6191[2] 6667[2]

Two Certainties *Stuart Williams* a65 48
3 ch g Zamindar(USA) —Ipsa Loquitur (Unfuwain (USA))
1132[8] 1393[8] (7810) ◆

Twoellies *Ollie Pears* a38 14
3 ch f Trade Fair—Fancier Bit (Lion Cavern (USA))
5[6]

Two Feet Of Snow (IRE) *Ian McInnes* a70 73
2 b f Holy Roman Emperor(IRE) —Current Affairs (Selkirk (USA))
1577[9] 1930[3] 2338[2] (2457) 3453[5] 4592[9] 4872[7] (5268) 5667[4] 6576[5] 6719[12] 6891[19]

Two Ish *Clive Cox* 63
3 ch c Ishiguru(USA) —Twice Upon A Time (Primo Dominie)
5810[3]

Two Kisses (IRE) *Brendan Powell* a66 66
3 b f Spartacus(IRE) —Flight Sequence (Polar Falcon (USA))
141[3] 1934[7] 2408[4] 2725[7] 3478[8]

Two Minds (FR) *Eugene Stanford* a59 45
3 ch g Choisir(AUS) —Dynamic Dream (USA) (Dynaformer (USA))
1766[7]

Two Notch Road (USA) *Glenn R Thompson* 100
3 bb g Partners Hero(USA) —Capiana (CAN) (Capote (USA))
4642a[4]

Two Oclock John *Terry Clement* a65 65
4 ch g Fraam—Ishona (Selkirk (USA))
316[6] (585) 1931[5] 2597[7] 3084[7] 3965[3] 5663[5] 6578[11] 7181[11]

Two Turtle Doves (IRE) *Michael Mullineaux* a48 69
4 b m Night Shift(USA) —Purple Rain (IRE) (Celtic Swing)
1534[8] 1885[2] 2381[6] 2854[9] 3534[3] 3854[6] 4064[3] 4244[5] 4478[4] (4605) 4834[11] 4947[3] 5614[7] 5905[6]

Tyfos *Brian Baugh* a74 89
5 b g Bertolini(USA) —Warminghamsharpish (Nalchik (USA))
2113[10] 2528[3] 2982[3] 3584[2] 3815[3] 4345[2] (4806) 5290[4] 5678[4] 6142[11] 6358[8]

Tymismoni (IRE) *Brett Johnson* a48 45
2 ch f Choisir(AUS) —Berenice (ITY) (Marouble)
4317[11] 5147[12] 7879[10]

Tymora (USA) *Henry Cecil* a39 61
3 ch f Giant's Causeway(USA) —Shiva (JPN) (Hector Protector (USA))
1356[8] 1932[11] 2674[8] 4134[12] 4764[8]

Tyrana (GER) *Ian Williams* a69 57
7 ch m Acatenango(GER) —Tascalina (GER) (Big Shuffle (USA))
139[2] (575)

Tyrannosaurus Rex (IRE) *Derek Shaw* a43 85
6 b g Bold Fact(USA) —Dungeon Princess (IRE) (Danehill (USA))
2940[12] 3417[7] 3675[5] 4090[8] 4712[8] 4938[8] 6073[6] ◆ 6303[5] 6572[15] 7195[13] 7860[7] 8034[11]

Tyrrells Wood (IRE) *Jane Chapple-Hyam* a88 98
5 b g Sinndar(IRE) —Diner De Lune (IRE) (Be My Guest (USA))
3050[11]

Tzora *Philip Hobbs* 50
5 b g Sakhee(USA) —Lucky Arrow (Indian Ridge)
1851[7]

U A E Storm (USA) *David Simcock* a78 65
2 b c Bluegrass Cat(USA) —Skygusty (USA) (Skywalker (USA))
3326[2] 4247[7] 5413[3]

Ubenkor (IRE) *Michael Herrington* a73 72
5 b g Diktat—Lucky Dancer (FR) (Groom Dancer (USA))
1926[13] 4555[9] 5545[7] 6295[7] 6491[8] 6917[6] 7402[4] (7543) 7646[2] 7804[3] 7895[2]

Ubi Ace *Tim Walford* 78
4 b g First Trump—Faithful Beauty (IRE) (Last Tycoon)
1751[6] 2881[4] (3090) 4785[5] 5611[6] 6050[2]

Ubiquitous *Simon Dow* a60 60
5 b m Erhaab(USA) —Lady Isabell (Rambo Dancer (CAN))
2781[4] 3403[4] (3821) 4591[2] 5172[3] 5654[8] 6021[9]

Ucandri (IRE) *C Ferland* a88 88
3 ch g Refuse To Bend(IRE) —Original (Caerleon (USA))
741a[3]

Udabaa (IRE) *Marcus Tregoning* a80 83
3 bb c Alhaarth(IRE) —Addaya (IRE) (Persian Bold)
1387[5] ◆ (1766) 2386[6]

Uddy Mac *Neville Bycroft* 63
3 ch f Reel Buddy(USA) —Befriend (USA) (Allied Forces (USA))
4155[3] 4482[3] 4714[4] 5201[7] 5686[2] 6186[2] 6460[6] 6897[10]

Ufologue (IRE) *A Fabre* a85 98
3 gr g Xaar—Up To Date (FR) (Valanour (IRE))
1610a[4]

Ugalla *William Knight* a65 79
3 ch f Where Or When(IRE) —Baddi Heights (FR) (Shirley Heights)
(2231) 2869[9] 3634[3] 4304[P]

Ugo (USA) *Heather Main* 36
2 b c Street Cry(IRE) —Min Elreeh (USA) (Danzig (USA))
5491[13]

Uldiko (FR) *Mme C Barande-Barbe* a83 84
2 b c Enrique—Nakamti (FR) (Lahint (USA))
4036a[5] (7647a)

Ulivate (IRE) *M Pimbonnet* 87
2 b f Poliglote—Be Prepared (USA) (Broad Brush (USA))
4275a[5]

Ullswater (IRE) *Mark Johnston* 74
2 b c Singspiel(IRE) —Uluwatu (IRE) (Unfuwain (USA))
6036[4] 6414[2] 6618[5]

Ultimate *Brian Ellison* a94 80
4 b h Anabaa(USA) —Nirvana (Marju (IRE))
6204[11]

Ultimate Quest (IRE) *Michael Chapman* a75 75
5 ch g Rainbow Quest(USA) —Crepe Ginger (IRE) (Sadler's Wells (USA))
2014[3] 2476[2] ◆ (3084) 3324[3] 3780[5] (6114) 6416[3] 7695[7]

Ultra Fantasy (AUS) *P F Yiu* 120
8 b g Encosta De Lago(AUS) —Belle Anglaise (USA) (Sir Ivor (USA))
7852a[14]

Ultravox (USA) *Brian Meehan* a40 81
3 b g Lemon Drop Kid(USA) —Lynnwood Chase (USA) (Horse Chestnut (SAF))
1335[10] 3795[8] 4257[10] 4751[8] 5073[8]

Ulysees (IRE) *Jim Goldie* a52 58
11 b g Turtle Island(IRE) —Tamasriya (IRE) (Doyoun)
7055[4] (7230)

Ulzana (IRE) *Sir Mark Prescott Bt* a69
4 b g High Chaparral(IRE) —Maritsa (IRE) (Danehill (USA))
2335[P]

Umseyat (USA) *John Gosden* 84
2 bb f Arch(USA) —Tabrir (IRE) (Unfuwain (USA))
5829[3] ◆ (6360) ◆

Umverti *Neville Bycroft* 81
5 b m Averti(IRE) —Umbrian Gold (IRE) (Perugino (USA))
1398[8] 1629[4] 1925[3] 2395[3] 2941[13] 3283[2] 3613[7] (4117) 4410[2] (4708) 5019[4] 5913[11] 6650[5] 6984[12]

Unaccompanied (IRE) *D K Weld* 87
3 b f Danehill Dancer(IRE) —Legend Has It (IRE) (Sadler's Wells (USA))
5571a[18]

Una Hora (DEN) *Francisco Castro* a71
4 ch m Kateb(IRE) —Ma-Ani (IRE) (Mujtahid (USA))
7374a[5]

Un Air De Salsa (FR) *S Wattel* a82 102
4 ch h Green Tune(USA) —Sweet Salsa (FR) (Highest Honor (FR))
5107a[6]

Una Pelota (IRE) *Tom Dascombe* a71 80
4 b g Refuse To Bend(IRE) —Sombreffe (Polish Precedent (USA))
1051[7] 1512[8] 1863[9] 2690[5] 5457[7] 7920[3]

Una Vita Plus (IRE) *Patrick Gilligan* a46
2 b f Antonius Pius(USA) —Avit (IRE) (General Monash (USA))
7427[10] 7811[5]

Unawatuna *Kate Walton* 64
5 b m Golden Snake(USA) —Laylee (Deploy)
1113[6] 1891[3] 2218[4] 5642[6] 6648[5] 7181[8]

Unbeatable *William Knight* a25
2 b f Beat Hollow—Koniya (IRE) (Doyoun)
7559[11]

Unbelievable Jeff *J S Moore* a37 51
4 b g Oasis Dream—Sunshine N'Showers (Spectrum (IRE))
1167[9] 1457[9]

Unbreak My Heart (IRE) *Richard Fahey* a84 93
5 ch g Bahamian Bounty—Golden Heart (Salse (USA))
278[7] 1274[8] 6327[3] 7100[14] 7842[4]

Uncle Brit *Malcolm Jefferson* a71 48
4 b g Efisio—Tarneem (USA) (Zilzal (USA))
1883[9]

Uncle Bryn *John Quinn* 23
2 b g Royal Applause—Happy Omen (Warning)
6569[10]

Uncle Bunge (IRE) *Liam Corcoran* a62 60
4 b g Rock Of Gibraltar(IRE) —Ouija's Sister (Groom Dancer (USA))
330[8]

Uncle Dermot (IRE) *Brendan Powell* a50 67
2 b c Arakan(USA) —Cappadoce (IRE) (General Monash (USA))
2022[7] 2440[3] 2887[7] 4020[6] 6126[5] 6777[2] 7035[10]

Uncle Eli (IRE) *Richard Rowe* a68 44
8 b g Raintrap—Yosna (FR) (Sicyos (USA))
585[4] 803[6] 950[6] 1160[5] 1303[5] 1690[8]

Uncle Fred *Patrick Chamings* a91 86
5 b g Royal Applause—Karla June (Unfuwain (USA))
1430[8] 1846[6] 2467[3] 3512[5] 4023[4] 4758[10] 6449[11]

Uncle Keef (IRE) *Marcus Tregoning* a69 67
4 b g Sadler's Wells(USA) —Love For Ever (IRE) (Darshaan)
1262[4] 1459[8] 2645[9] (2907) 3324[4] 4141[5] 5179[3] 5564[5]

Uncle Mo (USA) *Todd Pletcher* a124
2 b c Indian Charlie(USA) —Playa Maya (USA) (Arch (USA))
(6756a) ◆ (7363a) ◆

Uncle Tom (BRZ) *P Bary* a104 80
4 b h First American(USA) —Just Lucky (BRZ) (Spend A Buck (USA))
510a[2] 796a[7] 1023a[11]

Unconsoled *J Hetherton* a49 39
4 b m Ishiguru(USA) —Chantilly (FR) (Sanglamore (USA))
503[4] 598[2] 720[10]

Under Fire (IRE) *Tony Carroll* a61 60
7 b g Lear Spear(USA) —Kahyasi Moll (IRE) (Brief Truce (USA))
309[10] 661[9] 1771[8] 2198[14] 2955[2] 3128[4] (3263) (3723) 3983[5] 4361[5] 4793[8] 4992[9]

Under Review (IRE) *Michael J Browne* a60 70
4 b g Danetime(IRE) —Coloma (JPN) (Forty Niner (USA))
7332[10]

Understory (USA) *Mark Johnston* a72 77
3 b c Forestry(USA) —Sha Tha (USA) (Mr Prospector (USA))
201[3] 634[4] (815) 1514[4] 1969[3] 2927[7] (3404) 3688[6]

Underworld Dandy *Zoe Davison* a65 63
3 gr g Fraam—Eastern Lyric (Petong)
22[4] 283[7] 422[9] 534[2] 670[6] 1264[8] 4971[6]

Undulant Way *Amanda Perrett* a70 63
2 b f Hurricane Run(IRE) —Arietta's Way (IRE) (Darshaan)
5841[6] 6511[5] 7036[5]

Unex Dali *John Gosden* 76
2 b c Dubawi(IRE) —Pure (Slip Anchor)
6092[3]

Unex El Greco *John Gosden* 92
2 b c Holy Roman Emperor(IRE) —Friendlier (Zafonic (USA))
(5629) 6690[2] ◆ 7085[2]

Unex Goya (IRE) *George Baker* a61 77
2 b c Medicean—Arabica (USA) (Red Ransom (USA))
7002[3] 7503[6]

Unex Monet *Michael Bell* 24
2 b c Oratorio(IRE) —Lady Adnil (IRE) (Stravinsky (USA))
4379[8] 5047[17]

Unex Picasso *William Haggas* 70
2 b g Galileo(IRE) —Ruff Shod (USA) (Storm Boot (USA))
7303[4]

Unex Renoir *John Gosden* 73
2 b c Nayef(USA) —Simacota (GER) (Acatenango (GER))
5916[3] 6504[7]

Union Des Brieres (FR) *F-X De Chevigny* a72 72
2 b f Canyon Creek(IRE) —Josapha (FR) (Tropular)
3307a[6]

Union Island (IRE) *Alan King* a68 88
4 b g Rock Of Gibraltar(IRE) —Daftiyna (IRE) (Darshaan)
2685[4] 3618[3] 4619[10]

Union Jack Jackson (IRE) *John Harris* a29 52
8 b g Daggers Drawn(USA) —Beechwood Quest (IRE) (River Falls)
838[13] 2257[8] 3610[10] 4939[9] 5545[14]

Unique Jewellery (NZ) *J Size* 111
6 b g O'Reilly(NZ) —Aulide (AUS) (Snippets (AUS))
1568a[9]

Unirossa (FR) *J-C Sarais* 84
6 b m Testa Rossa(AUS) —Unitaire (FR) (Vettori (IRE))
281a[0]

United Nations *Noel Wilson* a81 51
9 ch g Halling(USA) —Congress (IRE) (Dancing Brave (USA))
623[4] 752[7] 923[4] 1669[8]

Unity (IRE) *David Wachman* 99
3 b f Sadler's Wells(USA) —Moments Of Joy (Darshaan)
2037a[6] 3007a[3] 4081a[3] 4631a[9]

Universal Circus *Mick Channon* a75 80
3 b f Imperial Dancer—Wansdyke Lass (Josr Algarhoud (IRE))
1734[11] 2120[10] (2491) 3158[8] 3628[10] 4296[5] (4922) 5388[6] 5678[5] 5712[2] 5889[8] 6439[7] 6987[10]

Universal Truth (IRE) *D K Weld* 82
5 b g Galileo(IRE) —Mistress Thames (Sharpo)
6926[22]

Unknown Rebel (IRE) *Kevin Ryan* a61 64
2 b g Night Shift(USA) —Crystalline Stream (FR) (Polish Precedent (USA))
1017[10] 1180[4] 1806[5] 4242[2] 4544[6] 4701[6] 6300[4] 6717[4] (6978)

Unleashed (IRE) *Charlie Mann* a44 106
5 br g Storming Home—Uriah (GER) (Acatenango (GER))
1220[12] 3050[13]

Unlimited *Tony Carroll* a70 64
8 b g Bold Edge—Cabcharge Blue (Midyan (USA))
285[5] 486[10] (937) 1063[2] 1224[7] 1762[6] 2490[5] 2920[5] (3377) 3725[5] 4108[9] 5159[11] 5867[9] 6370[4] 6671[2] 6903[4]

Unrivaled Belle (USA) *William Mott* a120
4 rg m Unbridled's Song(USA) —Queenie Belle (USA) (Bertrando (USA))
(7344a)

Unshakable Will (IRE) *Bryan Smart* a76 87
3 b g Refuse To Bend(IRE) —Miss Devious (IRE) (Dr Devious (IRE))
2112[2] 2324[10] 3696[7] 6002[5] 7092[8]

Until The Man (IRE) *Jim Best* a69 71
3 b g Tillerman—Canoe Cove (IRE) (Grand Lodge (USA))
236[3] 425[7] (1601) 1696[U] 1977[5] 2321[5] 3155[2] 3714[5] 7476[4] 7968[6] 7992[11]

Unusual Suspect (USA) *Barry Abrams* a106 106
6 bb h Unusual Heat(USA) —Penpont (NZ) (Crested Wave (USA))
1435a[2] 5577a[9]

Unwrapit (USA) *Bryan Smart* 42
2 b f Tapit(USA) —Miss Thermal Tech (USA) (Distinctive Pro (USA))
2461[7]

Unzip Me (USA) *Martin F Jones* 108
4 ch m City Zip(USA) —Escape With Me (USA) (Arazi (USA))
7362a[3]

Upark Flyer *Patrick Morris* a51 63
2 br f Piccolo—Autumn Affair (Lugana Beach)
1646[6] 3811[3] 4083[3] 4363[2] 4675[3] 5000[6] (5334) 5862[7] 6311[13] 7211[9]

Up At Last *William Haggas* 72
3 b f Cape Cross(IRE) —Upend (Main Reef)
3333[7] 4556[9] (4989) 5481[4]

Uphold *B W Hills* 95
3 b g Oasis Dream—Allegro Viva (USA) (Distant View (USA))
(2900) (4750) 5605[15] 6203[13]

Up In Time *William Knight* a63 88
2 ch f Noverre(USA) —Up At Dawn (Inchinor)
5657[7] (6158) 6528[7]

Uppercut *Stuart Kittow* 25
2 ch g Needwood Blade—Uplifting (Magic Ring (IRE))
5465[10]

Upset *P J O'Gorman* 37
3 ch g Reset(AUS) —Carreamia (Weldnaas (USA))
2564[13] 6093[8]

Upstairs *Paul Henderson* a67 36
6 ch g Sugarfoot—Laena (Roman Warrior)
3514[10]

Up The Dubs *E J O'Neill* 32
2 ch c Dr Fong(USA) —Miss Flirtatious (Piccolo)
6230a[15]

Upton Grey (IRE) *M Gharib* a74 94
5 gr h Dalakhani(IRE) —Rosse (Kris)
437a[7]

Uptowncharlybrown (USA) *Kiaran McLaughlin* a103
3 ch c Limehouse(USA) —La Iluminada (USA) (Langfuhr (CAN))
2776a[12]

Uptown Guy (USA) *Michael Dods* 73
2 bb c Speightstown(USA) —Affordability (USA) (Unbridled (USA))
3449^2 ◆ 4123^3 6138^8

Urban Clubber *Howard Johnson* 70
3 b g Dubai Destination(USA) —Surprise Visitor (IRE) (Be My Guest (USA))
2499^2 3077^4 3666^3

Urban Kiss (FR) *G Botti* a60 67
2 b f Take Risks(FR) —Embattle (FR) (Dernier Empereur (USA))
6589a^{10}

Urban Kode (IRE) *David Evans* a59 42
2 b c Kodiac—Urbanize (USA) (Chester House (USA))
3959^{10} 4599^9 6286^7 6673^4 6868^7 (7630) 7643^4 7831^4

Urban Poet (USA) *Saeed Bin Suroor* 109
4 bb h Dynaformer(USA) —Preach (USA) (Mr Prospector (USA))
2541^{11} 3843^{12}

Urban Space *Conor Dore* a78 86
4 ch g Sulamani(IRE) —Rasmalai (Sadler's Wells (USA))
3559^2 3848^3 (4201) 4426^2 (4873) 5375^2 5859^4 (6637) 7488^{13} 7600^5 7687^7 7856^7 8018^5

Ursis (FR) *Steve Gollings* a62 77
9 b g Trempolino(USA) —Bold Virgin (USA) (Sadler's Wells (USA))
2659^6

Ursula (IRE) *Mrs K Burke* a86 85
4 b m Namid—Fritta Mista (IRE) (Linamix (FR))
2465^8 2982^{10} (3947) 5290^6 6221^4 6963^{11}

Ursus *Christopher Wilson* a52 63
5 ch g Rambling Bear—Adar Jane (Ardar)
2699^7 3775^3 (4244) 4373^2 4706^{14} 5198^9 5424^4 5820^8 6189^{10} 7148^7

Usailaan *Marcus Tregoning* 75
3 b g Dubai Destination(USA) —Mohafazaat (IRE) (Sadler's Wells (USA))
1314^5

Usbeke (GER) *J-P Carvalho* a90 104
4 b g Big Shuffle(USA) —Ustimona (GER) (Mondrian (GER))
1251a^{12} 2559a^7 6606a^4 7266a^4 7776a^9

Usquaebach *Pat Phelan* a62
3 b f Trade Fair—Mashmoum (Lycius (USA))
(762) (1048) 2792^8 5072^7 7561^{12} 7874^7 7968^9

Ustilago (GER) *W Baltromei* 94
3 ch c Lando(GER) —Ungarin (GER) (Goofalik (USA))
4184a^{18}

Utern *Venetia Williams* a54 27
6 br m Overbury(IRE) —My Tern (IRE) (Glacial Storm (USA))
4229^6 4792^6 5141^5 5770^{11}

Utley (USA) *John Gosden* 108
2 b c Smart Strike(CAN) —No Matter What (USA) (Nureyev (USA))
5491^5 ◆ (6092) 6610a^5 7360a^7

Uvinza *William Knight* a83 101
4 ch m Bertolini(USA) —Baddi Heights (FR) (Shirley Heights)
2071^7 3031^5 4143^8 4507^{10}

Vacario (GER) *Mark Gillard* 54
6 br g Acatenango(GER) —Vaillance (GER) (Dashing Blade)
4202^5

Vaccaria (GER) *Mme C Jung* a70 71
5 ch m Pentire—Valentine Rose (GER) (Platini (GER))
281a^0

Vadition (IRE) *John Bridger* a13 44
3 b f Halling(USA) —Retail Therapy (IRE) (Bahhare (USA))
2460^6 2782^4 3714^6 4774^5 5173^5

Vagabond Shoes (IRE) *Y Durepaire* 98
3 ch c Beat Hollow—Atiza (IRE) (Singspiel (IRE))
3933a^5

Vainglory (USA) *David Simcock* a94 99
6 ch h Swain(IRE) —Infinite Spirit (USA) (Maria's Mon (USA))
205^6 (324) 536^4 635^8 769^4 (2124) 2708^3 3334^5 4321^5 4816^2 5247^8 7233^7

Valantino Oyster (IRE) *Ben Haslam* a62 56
3 b g Pearl Of Love(IRE) —Mishor (Slip Anchor)
(2838) ◆ 3951^4 (4448) 7626^3 7789^2

Valasyra (FR) *A De Royer-Dupre* 111
3 b f Sinndar(IRE) —Valima (FR) (Linamix (FR))
3015a^7 6551a^3 7160a^{DSQ} 7416a^9

Val C *Marco Botti* a64 67
3 b f Dubawi(IRE) —Valjarv (IRE) (Bluebird (USA))
233^5 483^5 745^4 936^2 1390^5 (1535)

Valdan (IRE) *Maurice Barnes* a74 81
6 b g Val Royal(FR) —Danedrop (IRE) (Danehill (USA))
974^5 1169^7 1398^4 ◆ 1720^3 2597^6 3860^4 5333^7

Valdaw *J S Moore* 48
2 b c Val Royal(FR) —Delight Of Dawn (Never So Bold)
2048^7

Valdemoro (AUS) *Tony Vasil* 111
4 b f Encosta De Lago(AUS) —Hveger (AUS) (Danehill (USA))
6947a^{15}

Val De Rama (GER) *Uwe Ostmann* 91
3 b f King's Best(USA) —Valdina (GER) (Lomitas)
2372a^5

Val d'Espoir (IRE) *H-A Pantall* a76 84
6 b g In The Wings—Vert Val (USA) (Septieme Ciel (USA))
459a^6 (559a)

Valencha *Hughie Morrison* a76 75
3 ch f Domedriver(IRE) —Riverine (Risk Me (FR))
2249^2 ◆ 3786^2 (4385) 5037^4 5896^3 7047^3 7389^4 7521^2

Valency (IRE) *Tony Newcombe* 20
2 b c Val Royal(FR) —Taschlynn (IRE) (Second Empire (IRE))
1263^8

Valentine Bay *Michael Mullineaux* a18 42
4 b m Reel Buddy(USA) —Bullion (Sabrehill (USA))
34^{11}

Valentine's Gift *Neville Bycroft*
2 b g Presidium—Efipetite (Efisio)
6964^7

Valentino Swing (IRE) *Michael Appleby* a68 73
7 ch g Titus Livius(FR) —Farmers Swing (IRE) (River Falls)
27^2 287^9 (678) 767^7 1350^4 1482^5 7611^{10} 7701^8 8014^{12}

Valenzani *John Gosden* a46 62
3 b g Royal Applause—Frascati (Emarati (USA))
2297^3

Vale Of York (IRE) *Saeed Bin Suroor* a116 116
3 b c Invincible Spirit(IRE) —Red Vale (IRE) (Halling (USA))
796a^5

Valeo Si Vales (IRE) *Jamie Osborne* a54 60
2 b g Oratorio(IRE) —Eurostorm (USA) (Storm Bird (CAN))
2839^9 3349^6 3785^7

Valerius Maximus *Paul Cole* a78 85
2 b c Spartacus(IRE) —Capriolla (In The Wings)
5372^2 5785^3 6111^5 (6309) 6719^7 7009a^3 7383a^3

Valery Borzov (IRE) *Richard Fahey* a94 108
6 b g Iron Mask(USA) —Fay's Song (IRE) (Fayruz)
1906^5 2759^9 3193^{12} 4391^{19} 4832^5 5787^8 6142^{24} 6363^{10}

Valeur *Sir Michael Stoute* a65
3 b f Rock Of Gibraltar(IRE) —Rafha (Kris)
1766^4 ◆ 2478^5

Valiant Knight (FR) *Richard Hannon* 87
3 ch c Night Shift(USA) —Pilgrim Of Grace (FR) (Bering)
(1976) 3337^4 3481^2 4360^2 4573^9 4964^2 5918^2 6447^{13} 6813^7

Validor (FR) *Y Fouin* a91 110
4 ch h American Post—Panthesilea (FR) (Kendor (FR))
1255a^8 2375a^7

Valid Reason *Dean Ivory* a87 87
3 b g Observatory(USA) —Real Trust (USA) (Danzig (USA))
1624^4 3594^2 4360^6 5259^2 6152^2 7410^5 (7653) 7876^6

Valkov *Eric Wheeler* a66 61
3 b f Val Royal(FR) —Petrikov (IRE) (In The Wings)
6794^9 6992^{11} 7874^3 7995^9

Valkyrie (IRE) *Nick Littmoden* a53 53
4 b m Danehill Dancer(IRE) —Ridotto (Salse (USA))
263^2 411^2 584^{12} 982^6 3403^6

Valley Tiger *William Muir* a57 53
2 b c Tiger Hill(IRE) —Nantyglo (Mark Of Esteem (IRE))
5587^{11} 6196^{12} 7335^4

Valmari (IRE) *George Prodromou* a77 91
7 b m Kalanisi(IRE) —Penza (Soviet Star (USA))
341^7 447^7 688^8 888^7 1062^5 1346^{10} 1609^5 3267^5 3416^6

Valmina *Tony Carroll* a76 54
3 b g Val Royal(FR) —Minnina (IRE) (In The Wings)
2052^{12} 2442^5 3277^6 3561^6 4031^2 4839^7 5614^8 5698^6 6898^6 6997^5

Val Mondo (GER) *Uwe Ostmann* 102
3 b c Lando(GER) —Valleria (GER) (Big Shuffle (USA))
4184a^{11} (6011a)

Vamos (IRE) *Mrs J L Le Brocq* a65 61
4 b g Royal Applause—Feather Boa (IRE) (Sri Pekan (USA))
1815a^8

Vanadium *Alastair Lidderdale* a61 71
8 b g Dansili—Musianica (Music Boy)
193^8 347^9 388^{10} 7380^{13} 7663^6

Vanatina (IRE) *Mark Brisbourne* a53 46
6 b m Tagula(IRE) —Final Trick (Primo Dominie)
320^{13} 567^{11}

Van Bossed (CAN) *David Nicholls* a24 80
5 ch g Van Nistelrooy(USA) —Embossed (CAN) (Silver Deputy (CAN))
1332^{15} 1710^{10} 1888^8 4372^8 4895^{10}

Van Doesburg (IRE) *Jonathan Portman* 55
2 gr g Westerner—Winter Daydream (IRE) (Soviet Star (USA))
3399^8 3915^6 4691^6

Vanessa My Girl *Richard Guest*
2 ch f Choisir(AUS) —Ashtree Belle (Up And At 'Em)
5298^{16}

Vanguard Dream *Richard Hannon* 98
2 b c Oasis Dream—Garmoucheh (USA) (Silver Hawk (USA))
(5954) (6254) (6690) ◆

Vanilla Loan (IRE) *Marco Botti* a62 79
3 b f Invincible Spirit(IRE) —Alexander Anapolis (IRE) (Spectrum (IRE))
9061^0 ◆ (1280) 1535^8 2287^4 2565^9

Vanilla Rum *Henry Candy* a74 80
3 b g Reset(AUS) —Snoozy (Cadeaux Genereux)
1622^3 2174^2 (2824) 3270^3 3833^3 4387^7 5031^6 5768^5

Vanjura (GER) *R Dzubasz* 111
3 ch f Areion(GER) —Venia Legendi (GER) (Zinaad)
1715a^7 (2372a) 4035a^2 (5782a) 6764a^2

Vantaa (IRE) *Richard Fahey* 45
2 ch c Shamardal(USA) —Indian Express (Indian Ridge)
6748^9 7345 ^{8}

Varachi *Ed Dunlop* 65
3 b g Kyllachy—Miss Rimex (IRE) (Ezzoud (IRE))
1261^6 1578^8

Varadero (IRE) *Y De Nicolay*
2 b c Dalakhani(IRE) —Miss Wind (FR) (Sri Pekan (USA))
(7974a) ◆

Varenar (FR) *A De Royer-Dupre* 120
4 ch h Rock Of Gibraltar(IRE) —Visor (USA) (Mr Prospector (USA))
1955a^4 3192^8 3870^6 ◆ 4885a^{13}

Varlak *Desmond Donovan* a63 25
2 b c Val Royal(FR) —Kokila (Indian Danehill (IRE))
6126^6 6628^8 6936^6

Varosbiro (IRE) *Sandor Kovacs* 69
8 h Titus Livius(FR) —Wheatsheaf Lady (IRE) (Red Sunset)
4183a^5

Vasoni (IRE) *Timothy Doyle* 72
2 ch f Redback—Tamara Gervasoni (IRE) (Namid)
7256a^{13}

Vattene (IRE) *M Gasparini* 103
5 b m Kendor(FR) —Voglia Matta (IRE) (Second Set (IRE))
439a^{10} 711a^7 6765a^{12}

Vaultage (USA) *Ed Dunlop* a71 60
3 ch f El Corredor(USA) —Ten Carats (USA) (Capote (USA))
1504^4 1982^2 ◆ 2535^2 2903^4 3690^4

Vauville (IRE) *Y De Nicolay* 80
2 b f Invincible Spirit(IRE) —Vadorga (Grand Lodge (USA))
5622a^7

Veeb (IRE) *Mark Johnston* a55 62
2 br f Footstepsinthesand—Canaan (IRE) (Alhaarth (IRE))
1999^6 4423^3 4675^6 7493^7 7664^8 7894^4 7982^3

Vegas Palace (IRE) *Tom Dascombe* a81 73
3 ch f Captain Rio—Verify (IRE) (Polish Precedent (USA))
3962^8 4680^6 4894^{10} 5648^8

Veiled *Jeff Pearce* a83 89
4 b m Sadler's Wells(USA) —Evasive Quality (FR) (Highest Honor (FR))
4846^7 6201^{14}

Veiled Applause *John Quinn* a74 87
7 b g Royal Applause—Scarlet Veil (Tyrnavos)
857^5 1013^3 2761^4 3089^4 4196^5 4652^2 6105^3 (6724) 7053^2 7243^9

Veil Of Night *Derek Haydn Jones* a16 70
2 b f Val Royal(FR) —Tenebrae (IRE) (In The Wings)
1838^4 2358 ^{4} 3082^{11} (4066) 4623^{13} (5472) 5874^4 6191^{13} 6513^{10}

Velikiy Zevs (USA) *Mark Johnston* a87
3 bb c Giant's Causeway(USA) —Helsinki (Machiavellian (USA))
973^5

Velle Est Valere *Colin Teague* 16
3 b f Reset(AUS) —Bond Solitaire (Atraf)
1401^{10} 1648^8 2432^{12}

Veloce (IRE) *John Dunlop* 29
2 b g Hurricane Run(IRE) —Kiftsgate Rose (FR) (Nashwan (USA))
6831^{14} 7099^{14}

Veloso (FR) *Jeremy Glover* a87 85
8 gr g Kaldounevees(FR) —Miss Recif (IRE) (Exit To Nowhere (USA))
(835) (910) 1101^2 (1829) 2857^{12} 4619^5 4891^4 5296^5 5991^5 6516^3

Velvet Flicker (IRE) *Kevin Prendergast* a97 98
3 b f Fasliyev(USA) —Velvet Appeal (IRE) (Petorius)
(1406a) 2353a^5 2912a^9 3571a^2 6783a^7 7073a^7 7217a^9

Velvet Nayef *Jeff Pearce* a45 37
4 b m Nayef(USA) —Laughing Girl (USA) (Woodman (USA))
6250^8 6861^8 7157^6 7388^{14}

Velvet Underground (IRE) *Brian Meehan* 71
2 ch c Exceed And Excel(AUS) —Taalluf (USA) (Hansel (USA))
1901^9 2493^7 3735^4 6191^{10} 6386^{10} 7035^{12}

Venado (SWI) *P Benoist* a41 46
9 b g Brief Truce(USA) —Vandrake Legend (Mandrake Major)
2446a^0

Venetien (FR) *R Gibson* a86
2 b c Iron Mask(USA) —Vassia (USA) (Machiavellian (USA))
5137a^4 (7975a)

Venir Rouge *Matthew Salaman* a70 76
6 ch g Dancing Spree(USA) —Al Awaalah (Mukaddamah (USA))
83^{11} 660^3 (1207) 6578^7

Venise Jelois (FR) *Robert Collet* a75 81
2 b f Marchand De Sable(USA) —Star Angels (FR) (Ski Chief (USA))
5252a^8

Veni Vedi Veci (IRE) *Andrew Balding* a24 81
3 b f Antonius Pius(USA) —Consultant Stylist (IRE) (Desert Style (IRE))
1824^4 (2603) 3697^8 5086^5 5593^3 6090^4 6692^3

Ventose *Mick Channon* 50
2 b f Beat Hollow—All Glory (Alzao (USA))
1577^8 3861^6 4293^5 4554^6 5373^8

Ventura Cove (IRE) *Richard Fahey* 83
3 ch g Bahamian Bounty—Baby Bunting (Wolfhound (USA))
1153^4 1376^8 (1709) 2287^7 2982^{13} 4349^5 5390^5

Ventura Sands (IRE) *Richard Fahey* 70
2 b g Footstepsinthesand—Beautiful Noise (Piccolo)
5040^2 ◆ 5498^7 5936^4

Venture Capitalist *Brian Ellison* a54 69
4 b h Diktat—Ventura Highway (Machiavellian (USA))
(186)

Venture Girl (IRE) *Tim Easterby* a53 55
3 ch f Footstepsinthesand—Bold Assumption (Observatory (USA))
2834^{13} 3434^6 3662^3 4052^3 5423^{10}

Venus Empress *Ed McMahon* a53 57
2 b f Holy Roman Emperor(IRE) —Pilgrim Spirit (USA) (Saint Ballado (CAN))
3204^7 3686^4 4451^9 5268^3 6072^{17} 6576^7 6868^4

Venutius *Ed McMahon* a88 95
3 b g Doyen(IRE) —Boadicea's Chariot (Commanche Run)
2033^6 2510^2 (3208) 3796^2 4509^8 5605^8 6321^6 7187^9

Verdant *Sir Michael Stoute* a82 109
3 b c Singspiel(IRE) —Orford Ness (Selkirk (USA))
(1502) ◆ 2117^7 2742^3 (3633) (4470)

Verinco *Bryan Smart* a67 79
4 b g Bahamian Bounty—Dark Eyed Lady (IRE) (Exhibitioner)
89^4 569^5 699^2 896^3 (1337) 1915^5 2213^2 2695^4 4415^5 (4952) (5356) 6073^5 6572^3

Veri One (FR) *J Van Handenhove* a65 67
2 b f Iron Mask(USA) —Veri Star (FR) (Verglas (IRE))
4274a^3

Verity Lane (USA) *Robert Cowell* a76 44
3 b f Yes It's True(USA) —Easy Pass (USA) (Easy Goer (USA))
1769^9 3503^6 4931^4 5669^8

Verluga (IRE) *Tim Easterby* a58 63
3 gr g Verglas(IRE) —Caviare (Cadeaux Genereux)
2114^8 2852^8 3227^3 (3668) 3975^7 4704^5 5484^7 5758^7 6168^7 7912^3 7986^6

Vermentino (FR) *M Roussel* 79
3 ch c Anabaa Blue—Moon Gorge (Pursuit Of Love)
450a^9

Veronicas Boy *George Moore* a29 59
4 br g Diktat—Thamud (IRE) (Lahib (USA))
41^{10} 6921^8

Veroon (IRE) *James Given* a82 79
4 b g Noverre(USA) —Waroonga (IRE) (Brief Truce (USA))
1600^4 1925^9 2523^2 2934^4 3317^4 3894^9 4585^3 5213^3 5436^2 5994^6 6543^2 7053^5 7382^4 7548^{11}

Verrazano *Kevin Ryan* a65
2 b f Statue Of Liberty(USA) —Ailsa (Bishop Of Cashel)
7448^6 7682^4 (7843)

Vertana (IRE) *H-A Pantall* a77 91
3 b f Sinndar(IRE) —Verzasca (IRE) (Sadler's Wells (USA))
5981a^6 (6519a) 7416a^6

Vert Chapeau *Edward Vaughan* a58 38
3 ch f Sakhee(USA) —Green Bonnet (IRE) (Green Desert (USA))
1164^9 1795^{12} 2189^8

Vertiformer (USA) *J-C Rouget* a88 102
3 b c Dynaformer(USA) —Tempo West (USA) (Rahy (USA))
6219a^5

Vertigineux (FR) *Mme C Dufreche* a111 118
6 b h Nombre Premier—Very Gold (FR) (Goldneyev (USA))
1111a^5 1716a^4 3017a^2 3888^2 5574a^2 6593a^4

Vertigo On Course (IRE) *Richard Fahey* a67 68
5 b m Anabaa(USA) —Due South (Darshaan)
169^3 ◆ 284^6 546^4 ◆ 719^3 4986^5 5530^3 6165^6 6935^4 7056^5

Vertueux (FR) *Tony Carroll* a36 65
5 gr g Verglas(IRE) —Shahrazad (FR) (Bering)
409^{11} 2923^2 (3848) (4328) 4737^P 7181^{17}

Vertumnus *Nick Littmoden* a41 56
3 ch g Pastoral Pursuits—Bombalarina (IRE) (Barathea (IRE))
1659^{12} 1878^6 2174^8 3521^9 7161^{12} 7429^{11} 7972^7

Verus Decorus (IRE) *Patrick Morris* a55
2 b f Titus Livius(FR) —Alta Petens (Mujadil (USA))
7392^4 (7692) 7894^3

Very Distinguished *Michael Quinlan* a62 48
4 b m Diktat—Dignify (IRE) (Rainbow Quest (USA))
82^6 2811^{11}

Very Good Day (FR) *Mick Channon* 102
3 b c Sinndar(IRE) —Picture Princess (Sadler's Wells (USA))
2226^3 ◆ (2860) 3822^5 4456^7

Very Well Red *Peter Hiatt* a63 80
7 b m First Trump—Little Scarlett (Mazilier (USA))
7^3 ◆ (124) 262^6 367^6 603^5 918^{11} (1172) 1396^7 (1797) 2512^4 3130^5 (4172) 4690^{12} 5287^{10} 5833^9 6260^{14} 6629^{11} 7890^7

Vested Interest *John Wainwright* a19 77
3 ch g Footstepsinthesand—Ingozi (Warning)
2982^{15} 3436^8

Vestris (IRE) *Y Fertillet* a71 55
5 ch g Vettori(IRE) —Parting Gift (Cadeaux Genereux)
273a^3 (690a)

Vesuve (IRE) *Saeed Bin Suroor* a110 116
4 b h Green Tune(USA) —Verveine (USA) (Lear Fan (USA))
713a^2 798a^6 1022a^8 4050^2 (4596) 5274^4 ◆ (6179) 6885^5

Vetvey (IRE) *Mark Johnston* a66 51
2 b g Fasliyev(USA) —Vert Val (USA) (Septieme Ciel (USA))
4599^7 5099^6 6047^6 6308^2 6575^7 6986^8

Veulettes (IRE) *Y De Nicolay*
2 gr f Beat Hollow—Dundel (IRE) (Machiavellian (USA))
7975a^0

Veuveveuvevoom *Gerry Enright* a35 3
2 gr f Superior Premium—Gran Clicquot (Gran Alba (USA))
2749^{10} 4029^{10} 4658^{14} 5719^{11} 7418^7

Vezere (USA) *Simon Dow* a66 69
3 b f Point Given(USA) —Helstra (USA) (Nureyev (USA))
6275^4 6856^{13} 7288^4 7611^{11} 7995^2

Vhujon (IRE) *David Evans* a88 94
5 b g Mujadil(USA) —Livius Lady (IRE) (Titus Livius (FR))
102^2 177^4 250^4 286^6 502^5 672^8 846^3 905^8 2399^8 2877^7 3373^8 3687^5 (3908) 4043^3 4693^2 (5112) 5285^3 5454^6 5941^6 6537^2 6799^3 6987^8 7314^2 7549^2 7654^4 7826^3 7961^2 7998^4 8016^5

Via Aurelia (IRE) *James Fanshawe* a48 65
3 b f Antonius Pius(USA) —Goldthroat (IRE) (Zafonic (USA))
2876[2] 4025[4] 4324[5] 5163[5] 5650[2] 6060[7] 6863[3] 7153[2] 7440[2]

Via Galilei (IRE) *Gary Moore* a87 103
5 b g Galileo(IRE) —Manger Square (IRE) (Danehill (USA))
1911[3] 2317[7] 3194[15] 7120[4]

Via Medici (IRE) *F Rohaut* 105
3 ch f Medicean—Via Milano (FR) (Singspiel (IRE))
1566a[5] (5139a) 5801a[6]

Via Mia *John Harris* a73 58
4 b m Namid—Coming Home (Vettori (IRE))
113[5] 348[4] 464[6] 666[10] 2299[3] 2625[7] 3768[5]

Vianello (IRE) *P Schiergen* a97 107
3 b g Rimrod(USA) —Silview (USA) (Saint Ballado (CAN))
4122[9] 6487a[10]

Vibrant Force (USA) *Mahmood Al Zarooni* 83
3 b c Dynaformer(USA) —Plenty (USA) (Boundary (USA))
4069[2] 4845[6] 5116[2]

Victoire De Lyphar (IRE) *David Nicholls* 112
3 b g Bertolini(USA) —Victory Peak (Shirley Heights)
(1376) (2978) 4536[2] 6177[2] ◆

Victoire Pisa (JPN) *Katsuhiko Sumii* 124
3 bb c Neo Universe(JPN) —Whitewater Affair (Machiavellian (USA))
6014a[4] 6612a[7] 7615a[3]

Victoria Montoya *Andrew Balding* a78 101
5 br m High Chaparral(IRE) —Spurned (USA) (Robellino (USA))
1859[6] 2538[6] 3159[6]

Victorian Bounty *Stef Higgins* a85 85
5 b g Bahamian Bounty—Baby Bunting (Wolfhound (USA))
2399[3] 3037[4] 3401[4] 3845[6] 5290[5] 5995[9] 6524[5] 6801[12] 6932[6] 6987[2] (7239) 7314[7] (7399) ◆

Victorian Number (FR) *E J O'Neill* 96
2 ch g Numerous(USA) —Malaisia (FR) (Anabaa (USA))
5251a[3]

Victoria Sponge (IRE) *Stuart Williams* a86 94
4 b m Marju(IRE) —Trill (Highest Honor (FR))
5531[0] 738[6] 1084[8] 1899[6] 2710[9] 3457[9] 5553[7] 6095[12] 6346[10] 7097[7] 7238[10]

Victor's Cry (USA) *Eoin Harty* 115
5 bb r Street Cry(IRE) —Short Time (USA) (Clever Trick (USA))
4417a[2] 6237a[9]

Victory Ide Say (IRE) *Peter Chapple-Hyam* a68 96
3 ch g Fath(USA) —Ide Say (IRE) (Grand Lodge (USA))
(1685) (2884) ◆

Victory Quest (IRE) *Mrs S Lyman* a82 70
10 b g Victory Note(USA) —Marade (USA) (Dahar (USA))
3[5] (401) 506[2] (701)

Vienna Woods (IRE) *Ben Haslam* a25 61
2 ch f Redback—Naraina (IRE) (Desert Story (IRE))
1527[4] 1981[7] 2939[12] 6072[7] 6645[10] 7469[8]

Viewing *John Gosden* a70 81
3 b f Kingsalsa(USA) —Exhibitor (USA) (Royal Academy (USA))
1881[3] (3443) 4389[4] 5056[5]

Vigano (IRE) *Eamon Tyrrell* a63 64
5 b g Noverre(USA) —Perugia (IRE) (Perugino (USA))
4707[3]

Viking Awake (IRE) *James Unett* a53 55
4 b g Almutawakel—Norwegian Queen (IRE) (Affirmed (USA))
211[6] 347[4] 503[7] 757[10]

Viking Rock (IRE) *Matthew Salaman* a58 45
4 ch g Viking Ruler(AUS) —Polar Rock (Polar Falcon (USA))
7508[12]

Viking Rose (IRE) *James Eustace* a62
2 ch f Norse Dancer(IRE) —Rosy Outlook (USA) (Trempolino (USA))
6451[5] 7113[8]

Viking Spirit *Walter Swinburn* a91 95
8 b g Mind Games—Dane Dancing (IRE) (Danehill (USA))
987[3] 1192[4] 1692[7] 2247[10] 3037[6] 3898[3] 4333[3] 4995[6] ◆ 5495[9] 6798[5] (7033)

Viking Storm *Harry Dunlop* 55
2 b g Hurricane Run(IRE) —Danehill's Dream (IRE) (Danehill (USA))
6689[11] 7094[14]

Viking Warrior (IRE) *Michael Dods* 70
3 ch g Halling(USA) —Powder Paint (Mark Of Esteem (IRE))
1706[7] 2393[7] 3148[2] 4018[2] (4853) 5484[5] 6144[4] 6897[12]

Villaruz (IRE) *David Flood* a47 54
4 b g Fayruz—Villaminta (IRE) (Grand Lodge (USA))
2646[6] 3280[8] 7018[8] 7299[5]

Villerville (IRE) *T Larriviere* 51
2 b f Gulch(USA) —Mowaadah (IRE) (Alzao (USA))
4275a[8]

Vilnius *Mick Channon* a60 62
3 b f Imperial Dancer—Aces Dancing (GER) (Big Shuffle (USA))
127[3] 213[4] 1118[6] 1468[3] ◆ (1774) 2185[10] 2320[3] 2432[11] 3228[4] 4194[3] 4778[4] 4920[2] 5152[3] (5481) 5898[7] 6133[7]

Vinces *Tim McCarthy* a72 70
6 gr g Lomitas—Vadinaxa (FR) (Linamix (FR))
127 834 1623 (261) 3617 58810 296612 [sic]

Vineyard Haven (USA) *Saeed Bin Suroor* a123
4 rg h Lido Palace(CHI) —Princess Aloha (USA) (Aloha Prospector (USA))
5779a[3] 7365a[6]

Vintage (IRE) *John Akehurst* a85 66
6 b g Danetime(IRE) —Katherine Gorge (USA) (Hansel (USA))
150[6] 286[10] (616) 1044[9] (6057) 6501[2] 7971[7]

Vintage Grape (IRE) *Eric Alston* 36
2 b f Exceed And Excel(AUS) —Begin The Beguine (IRE) (Peintre Celebre (USA))
2130[8]

Vintage Quest *Dai Burchell* a49 45
8 b m Diktat—Sadly Sober (IRE) (Roi Danzig (USA))
923[5] 5840[9] 6472[15] 7878[8]

Violent Velocity (IRE) *John Quinn* a68 81
7 b g Namid—Lear's Crown (USA) (Lear Fan (USA))
1030[11] 1361[10] 1754[9] 2392[7] 3659[7] 4394[6] 5500[9] 7056[2] 7699[4] ◆ 7804[5]

Violet Flame (IRE) *Edward Creighton* a53 16
4 b m Kalanisi(IRE) —Red Vale (IRE) (Halling (USA))
5860[6]

Violet Ray (USA) *Ralph Beckett* a55 72
2 rg g El Prado(IRE) —Bala (CAN) (With Approval (CAN))
5263[13] 5916[4] 6473[9] 7087[11] 7486[7]

Virginia Hall *Sir Mark Prescott Bt* a76 107
3 b f Medicean—Odette (Pursuit Of Love)
3375[4] (3694) 4035a[7]

Viscaya (IRE) *Nicky Vaughan* a26 57
5 b m Xaar—Fearfully Grand (Grand Lodge (USA))
199[9] 2271[0]

Viscount Nelson (USA) *A P O'Brien* 117
3 b c Giant's Causeway(USA) —Imagine (IRE) (Sadler's Wells (USA))
1038a[2] 1699[11] 2354a[3] 2802a[5] 3693[3]

Visinada (IRE) *A De Royer-Dupre* 83
2 b f Sinndar(IRE) —Visionnaire (FR) (Linamix (FR))
5622a[5]

Vision D'Etat (FR) *E Libaud* a108 124
5 b h Chichicastenango(FR) —Uberaba (FR) (Garde Royale)
1027a[12] (5107a) 6925[2] 7854a[4]

Visions Of Johanna (USA) *Ian Williams* a60 82
5 b g Johannesburg(USA) —Belle Turquoise (FR) (Tel Quel (FR))
1513[10] 1840[4] (2240) 2625[3] 2961[2] 3432[3] 4051[3] 4520[6]

Visual Element (USA) *Roger Charlton* a43 19
3 rg f Distant View(USA) —Kinetic Force (USA) (Holy Bull (USA))
1622[7] 2164[5]

Visualize *Sir Michael Stoute* 67
3 ch f Medicean—Fantasize (Groom Dancer (USA))
(1432) 1975[10]

Vita Lika *Brian Meehan* 75
2 b f Dansili—Bayalika (IRE) (Selkirk (USA))
5692[12] 6559[16] 7231[2]

Vita Mia *David Evans* a52 68
4 b m Central Park(IRE) —Ma Vie (Salse (USA))
3984[6] 4045[6] 4780[7]

Vita Nova (IRE) *Henry Cecil* a74 92
3 b f Galileo(IRE) —Treca (IRE) (Darshaan)
(3563) (5259)

Vitassana (IRE) *J-P Gallorini* 69
4 gr m Verglas(IRE) —Beau Duchess (FR) (Bering)
1055a[3]

Vita Venturi (IRE) *J S Bolger* 98
3 ch c Galileo(IRE) —Sateen (Barathea (IRE))
4312a[5]

Vitoria (IRE) *Bryan Smart* a79 102
4 b m Exceed And Excel(AUS) —Karayb (IRE) (Last Tycoon)
(4569) 5120[11]

Vito Volterra (IRE) *Michael Smith* a71 75
3 b g Antonius Pius(USA) —River Abouali (Bluebird (USA))
807[5] 933[10] 1259[4] 2422[6] 2834[5] 3371[2] 3451[2] (3755) 4369[8] 4710[2] 5121[5] 5533[10] 7143[10]

Vitruvian Man *John M Oxx* a72 98
4 b g Montjeu(IRE) —Portrait Of A Lady (IRE) (Peintre Celebre (USA))
5772a[7]

Vittachi *Alistair Whillans* a58 65
3 b g Bertolini(USA) —Miss Lorilaw (FR) (Homme De Loi (IRE))
216[2] 254[3] (542) 812[4] 1054[4] 2673[6] 3532[2] 5216[2] ◆ 5411[3] 5738[2] 6109[8]

Vitznau (IRE) *Richard Hannon* a104 105
6 b g Val Royal(FR) —Neat Dish (CAN) (Stalwart (USA))
(885) 1008[12] 1085[6] 1662[2] 1974[3] 2318[2] 2708[6] 4537[5] 4816[5] 5518[4]

Vivacious Vivienne (IRE) *Donal Kinsella* a81 91
4 b m Dubai Destination(USA) —Epistoliere (IRE) (Alzao (USA))
3492a[12]

Viva Pataca *J Moore* a84 121
8 bb g Marju(IRE) —Comic (IRE) (Be My Chief (USA))
(1568a) 7851a[8]

Viva Ronaldo (IRE) *Richard Fahey* a68 97
4 b g Xaar—Papaha (FR) (Green Desert (USA))
1862[2] 7574[12] 7846[11]

Viva Vettori *David Elsworth* a105 95
6 ch h Vettori(IRE) —Cruinn A Bhord (Inchinor)
(553) 1008[8] 1383[11] 1697[4] 3456[6] 3921[17] 4843[7] 5370[5] 6205[5] 6562[11] 6888[14] 7233[3] 7593[6]

Viviani (IRE) *Amanda Perrett* a68 68
3 ch g Galileo(IRE) —Bintalreef (USA) (Diesis)
4698[5] 5260[4] 5522[2] 5963[3] 6416[2] 6955[3]

Vivre La Secret *Bill Turner* 37
2 b f Ishiguru(USA) —Vivre Sa Vie (Nashwan (USA))
1632[4]

Vivre Libre *E Lellouche* 78
3 b c Sadler's Wells(USA) —Vallee Enchantee (IRE) (Peintre Celebre (USA))
2802a[22] 4039a[9] 6014a[7]

Vizean (IRE) *Alan Swinbank*
2 b f Medicean—Viz (IRE) (Darshaan)
6293[13]

Vlavianus (CZE) *M Weiss* 61
9 b g Rainbows For Life(CAN) —Vlnka (CZE) (Amyndas)
461a[4]

Vocalised (USA) *J S Bolger* 109
4 b h Vindication(USA) —Serena's Tune (USA) (Mr Prospector (USA))
1246a[7]

Vodka (JPN) *Katsuhiko Sumii* a107 122
6 b m Tanino Gimlet(JPN) —Tanino Sister (JPN) (Rousillon (USA))
800a[8]

Vodka Red (IRE) *Robert Johnson* 26
2 b c Ivan Denisovich(IRE) —Begine (IRE) (Germany (USA))
6001[10] 6458[6] 6964[8]

Vogarth *Michael Chapman* a59 49
6 ch g Arkadian Hero(USA) —Skara Brae (Inchinor)
40[4] 86[3] 144[5] 298[9] 379[3] 505[4] 518[10] 569[8] 838[10] 1142[4] 1998[4] 2263[3] 3226[11] 4897[11] 7832[4]

Voie De Printemps (FR) *D Smaga* a81 98
4 b m Della Francesca(USA) —Vallee De Joux (FR) (Welkin (CAN))
304a[6]

Voila Ici (IRE) *Vittorio Caruso* 119
5 gr h Daylami(IRE) —Far Hope (Barathea (IRE))
2152a[2] 3019a[9] (6239a) 7373a[2] 7615a[16]

Voix Des Aigles (FR) *Mme C Barande-Barbe* a36 61
2 b c Victory Note(USA) —Udina (Unfuwain (USA))
7383a[10]

Volatilis (IRE) *J W Hills* a65 72
3 b c Antonius Pius(USA) —Fire Flower (Sri Pekan (USA))
149[2] 425[4] (582) 809[2] 1977[3] 2221[3] (2906) 3297[F]

Volcanic Ash (USA) *Mark Johnston* a66 62
2 b c Elusive Quality(USA) —Make Known (USA) (Mt. Livermore (USA))
3118[9] 3536[3] 3794[12] 5434[9] 7412[3]

Volcanic Dust (IRE) *Ed Dunlop* a70 67
2 b f Ivan Denisovich(IRE) —Top Of The Form (IRE) (Masterclass (USA))
2505[12] 2873[4] 2963[5] ◆ 4066[5] (4688) 5140[4] 5547[2] 6086[7] 6435[10] 7040[2]

Volcanic Lady (IRE) *David Simcock* a33 41
2 b f Invincible Spirit(IRE) —Starlight Smile (USA) (Green Dancer (USA))
4909[9] 5147[8] 5558[5]

Volito *Jonjo O'Neill* a56 72
4 ch g Bertolini(USA) —Vax Rapide (Sharpo)
3299[3] 3722[2] ◆ 4099[2] 4518[3] 4833[8] 5698[7]

Volo Cat (FR) *Bent Olsen* a70 101
6 ch h Volochine(IRE) —The Cat Eater (FR) (Tagel (USA))
2195a[5] 2637a[6] 4641a[4] 5350a[6] 6017a[8]

Volturi (IRE) *Peter Grayson* a14
2 b g Diamond Green(FR) —Saeedah (Bustino)
1764[7] 1835[10]

Voortrekker *Denis Coakley* a71 69
4 b g Imperial Dancer—Sweet Wilhelmina (Indian Ridge)
4660[5] 5325[5]

Voovoo (IRE) *David O'Meara* a27
2 b f Chineur(FR) —Rinneen (IRE) (Bien Bien (USA))
6542[10] 6964[9] 7126[9]

Vow Of Silence *Mahmood Al Zarooni* 18
2 b f Bertolini(USA) —Maybe Forever (Zafonic (USA))
2223[10]

Voysey (IRE) *Amanda Perrett* a55 55
3 b c Dalakhani(IRE) —Gothic Dream (IRE) (Nashwan (USA))
2684[9] 4257[12] 5001[4] 6022[8] 6526[5] 6871[8]

Vulcanite (IRE) *Ralph Beckett* a74 105
3 b c Dubawi(IRE) —Daraliya (IRE) (Kahyasi)
484[6] ◆ (803) 1330[9] (2386) (3335) (4153) (6736) ◆ 7110a[8]

Waabel *Jim Best* a73 78
3 bb g Green Desert(USA) —Najah (IRE) (Nashwan (USA))
4107[8] 4238[6] 4679[2] 5524[3] ◆ 6814[7] 7637[9] 8033[6]

Waahej *Peter Hiatt* a67 78
4 b g Haafhd—Madam Ninette (Mark Of Esteem (IRE))
941[3] 1028[12] (1427) 1631[7] 2467[8] 2961[7] 4019[6]

Waajida *J Cagan* 67
3 b f Dubawi(IRE) —Ruby Affair (IRE) (Night Shift (USA))
7160a[0]

Waarid *Gary Moore* a64 66
5 b g Alhaarth(IRE) —Nibbs Point (IRE) (Sure Blade (USA))
554[6]

Waasemah (KSA) *B Al Subaie* a92
3 b f Dynever(USA) —Perch (USA) (Seeking The Gold (USA))
333a[2] 514a[6]

Wabbraan (USA) *Martin Hill* a64 59
5 b g Aldebaran(USA) —Madame Modjeska (USA) (Danzig (USA))
121[10] 529[9] 1623[7] 1984[9]

Wacato King (IRE) *Rodney Farrant* a53
4 br g King Charlemagne(USA) —Daralaka (IRE) (The Minstrel (CAN))
199[5] 228[11] 407[10]

Wade Farm Billy (IRE) *Gary Moore* a70
6 b g Dr Massini(IRE) —Burgundy Sunset (IRE) (Buckskin (FR))
7690[2]

Wade Giles (IRE) *G M Lyons* a104 111
3 b g Azamour(IRE) —Tekindia (FR) (Indian Ridge)
6006a[2] 6548a[2]

Wadi Wanderer (IRE) *Edward Vaughan* a78
3 bb g Key Of Luck(USA) —Ascot Cyclone (USA) (Rahy (USA))
1211[6] 1490[3] (2258) 2644[7] 4325[13]

Wadnaan *Mark Johnston* a72 90
3 ch g Shamardal(USA) —Australian Dreams (Magic Ring (IRE))
2231[5] 2497[3] 4062[2] (4449) ◆ 4573[5]

Wafeira *Henry Cecil* a82 73
2 br f Dansili—Protectress (Hector Protector (USA))
2505[11] 2861[4] (5369) 6563[8] 7066[2]

Waffle (IRE) *Jeremy Noseda* a82 106
4 ch g Kheleyf(USA) —Saphire (College Chapel)
6663[5] 7079[5]

Waheed *Marcus Tregoning* 71
3 bb g Anabaa(USA) —Mouwadh (USA) (Nureyev (USA))
4307[3] 5303[4] 6124[11]

Waikato (NZ) *L Laxon* 114
7 b g Pins(AUS) —Skywalker Wilkes (USA) (Skywalker (USA))
2154a[4]

Wainwright (IRE) *John Mackie* a39 56
10 b g Victory Note(USA) —Double Opus (IRE) (Petorius)
2263[5] 2791[7] 5024[12]

Wait And See (FR) *Robert Collet* a90 105
5 b m Montjeu(IRE) —Dareen (IRE) (Rahy (USA))
690a[0]

Waiter's Dream *Brian Meehan* 112
2 b c Oasis Dream—Sarah Georgina (Persian Bold)
2887[6] 3472[2] (4096) (5184) 5943[3] 6924[4]

Wajanaat *Marcus Tregoning* a70 54
3 b f Sakhee(USA) —Tadris (USA) (Red Ransom (USA))
1620[12] 3157[5]

Wajir (FR) *Saeed Bin Suroor* 115
4 b h Danehill Dancer(IRE) —War Game (FR) (Caerleon (USA))
2097[3] 3191[8] 4506[5] 5517[4] 5938[3] 6533[3]

Wake Up Call *Chris Wall* a78 98
4 b m Noverre(USA) —Up And About (Barathea (IRE))
(2298) (4438) (5396) 6351[9] 6887[2]

Waking Warrior *Kevin Ryan* a79 85
2 b g Sleeping Indian—Scented Garden (Zamindar (USA))
1806[8] (2785) ◆ 3059[2] 3939a[5] 4138[14]

Walcot Square (IRE) *Roger Charlton* a78 71
3 b g Marju(IRE) —Lyrical Dance (USA) (Lear Fan (USA))
1480[3] 4593[7] 5142[5] (5769) 6197[5] 6852[9]

Waldhorn (FR) *T Doumen* 92
3 gr c Slickly(FR) —Black Dalhia (FR) (Sanglamore (USA))
1947a[5]

Waldjagd *A Wohler* 100
3 ch f Observatory(USA) —Wurftaube (GER) (Acatenango (GER))
2372a[2] 3943a[5] 4640a[8]

Waldsee (GER) *Sean Curran*
5 b g Xaar—Wurftaube (GER) (Acatenango (GER))
7147[14] 7967[12]

Waldvogel (IRE) *Luca Cumani* a102 102
6 ch g Polish Precedent(USA) —Wurftaube (GER) (Acatenango (GER))
81[2]

Walero (GER) *Uwe Ostmann* 109
4 br h Big Shuffle(USA) —Waterbor (GER) (Lagunas)
1955a[5] 2805a[4] 5573a[9] 6406a[3]

Walfa (IRE) *P D Deegan* a69
2 ch f Haafhd—Theatrical Act (USA) (Theatrical)
6726a[3]

Walk In Beauty (IRE) *Robert Collet* 74
2 b f Shamardal(USA) —Zelda (IRE) (Caerleon (USA))
7534a[9]

Walk On Bye (IRE) *T Stack* 105
3 b f Danehill Dancer(IRE) —Pipalong (IRE) (Pips Pride)
1406a[4] 1676a[15] 6009a[7] ◆ 6783a[6]

Walk On Water *Henry Cecil* 93
3 ch f Exceed And Excel(AUS) —The Cat's Whiskers (NZ) (Tale Of The Cat (USA))
2545[16]

Walleyd (IRE) *Linda Perratt* 21
3 b g Cape Cross(IRE) —Najmat Jumairah (USA) (Mr Prospector (USA))
7171[9]

Wallis *Luca Cumani* a87 48
3 b f King's Best(USA) —Frangy (Sadler's Wells (USA))
3220[5] 4107[9] 5960[2] ◆ 6291[5] (7166) (7573) ◆

Wall Street Wonder (USA) *John Terranova II* a107
4 bb h City Place(USA) —Kisses And Hugs (USA) (Kissin Kris (USA))
6582a[8]

Walragnek *John O'Shea* a54 54
6 gr g Mind Games—Eastern Lyric (Petong)
7261[0]

Walshestown Lad (IRE) *Ronald Harris* a43
2 b g Camacho—Sandomierz (IRE) (Nordico (USA))
7065[11] 7418[6] 7517[9] 7894[6] 7983[11]

Walter De La Mare (IRE) *John Joseph Murphy* 75
3 b c Barathea(IRE) —Banutan (IRE) (Charnwood Forest (IRE))
4563a[8]

Waltz Darling (IRE) *Richard Fahey* 91
2 b g Iffraaj—Aljafliyah (Halling (USA))
(2654) (3364) 4468[5] 5306[5] 5943[6]

Waltzing Cat (USA) *Sir Mark Prescott Bt* a61 54
2 ch f More Than Ready(USA) —Hopeful Sign (Warning)
6323[3] 7185[6] 7312[4]

Walvis Bay (IRE) *Tom Tate* a87 91
3 gr g Footstepsinthesand—Limpopo (Green Desert (USA))
2656[6] 2862[3] 4091[5] 4369[3] (4654) ◆ 5183[7] 6256[10] 6364[14] 6723[4] 7212[5]

Walzertraum (USA) *Fredrik Reuterskiold* a105 102
5 br h Rahy(USA) —Walzerkoenigin (USA) (Kingmambo (USA))
415a[3] 629a[7] 821a[4] 6017a[9]

Wanchai Minx *Alan Jarvis* a46 47
2 b f Fasliyev(USA) —Lady Pahia (IRE) (Pivotal)
2498[7] 3082[9] 4587[6] 5660[10] 6500[9]

Wanchai Whisper *Peter Hedger* a71 72
3 b f Bahamian Bounty—Tiger Waltz (Pivotal)
111[3] 209[2] (343) 1187[6] 1546[8] 2320[7] 2868[11] 3293[3] (3480) 3637[3] 3834[4] 4659[3] 5151[6] 5207[4] 5915[2] 6284[5] 6466[9] 7285[7] 7571 [3] 7635[4] 7764[2]

Wandering Lad *Declan Carroll* a61 61
2 b g Needwood Blade—Park's Girl (Averti (IRE))
3756[8] 5092[9] 5531[5] 6035[8] 6740[4]

Wannabe King *David Lanigan* 108
4 b g King's Best(USA) —Wannabe Grand (IRE) (Danehill (USA))
1383[9] 2057[9] 5609[3] 6349[10] 6888[17] 7233[11]

War And Peace (IRE) *David Evans* a77 77
6 b g Danehill(USA) —Pipalong (IRE) (Pips Pride)
442[2] 704[5] 965[4] 1049[4] 1224[2] 1637[2] 1875[5] (2053) 2846[9] 3391[9] 3676[3] 3855[6] 4488[8] 5039[5] 5254[6] 5867[4] 6210[P]

War Artist (AUS) *A De Royer-Dupre* a119 119
7 b g Orpen(USA) —Royal Solitaire (AUS) (Brocco (USA))
(515a) ◆ 797a[5] 1021a[4] 3192[6] (4165a) 4885a[14] 6012a[4] 6608a[18]

Warbond *Michael Madgwick*
2 ch g Monsieur Bond(IRE) —Pick A Nice Name (Polar Falcon (USA))
4363[9]

Warden Bond *William Stone* a58 51
2 ch g Monsieur Bond(IRE) —Warden Rose (Compton Place)
6158[12] 6994[8] 7386[8]

War Echo (USA) *Steven Asmussen* a99
4 ch m Tapit(USA) —Wild Vision (USA) (Wild Again (USA))
1242a[5]

Warling (IRE) *Jeremy Noseda* 101
3 gr f Montjeu(IRE) —Walkamia (FR) (Linamix (FR))
1119[2] (1932) 5553[5] ◆ 5881[7] 6320[7]

Warlu Way *John Dunlop* 81
3 b c Sakhee(USA) —Conspiracy (Rudimentary (USA))
4307[8] 4661[4] 5258[2] 5953[9] (6422)

Warm Breeze *Michael Jarvis* 88
2 b f Oasis Dream—Persian Jasmine (Dynaformer (USA))
(4517) ◆ 6157[10]

Warm Memories *Sir Michael Stoute* 71
3 b g Dansili—Summer Breeze (Rainbow Quest (USA))
2841[2] 3587[8] 4107[5] 5007[5] 6771[8]

War Monger (IRE) *E Lellouche* 102
3 gr c Linamix(FR) —War Game (FR) (Caerleon (USA))
1567a[5]

War Monger (USA) *Doug Watson* a82 97
6 b h War Chant(USA) —Carnival Delight (USA) (Half A Year (USA))
415a[10] 801a[10]

Warneford *Brian Meehan* 63
2 b c Dansili—Maramba (Rainbow Quest (USA))
6442[7]

Warne's Way (IRE) *Brendan Powell* 73
7 ch g Spinning World(USA) —Kafayef (USA) (Secreto (USA))
1012[13] 6132[12] 6693[2] 7181[2]

Warning Flag (USA) *David Wachman* a98 100
2 b c War Front(USA) —Good Vibes (USA) (Unbridled's Song (USA))
(6727a) 7135a[2]

Warning Song (USA) *Amanda Perrett* a85 79
3 bb c Successful Appeal(USA) —Tia Lea (USA) (Songandaprayer (USA))
1913[11] 2416[7] ◆ 2888[5] (3297) (3725) 4302[3] 4699[3] 5142[9] (7114)

War Of The Roses (IRE) *Roy Brotherton* a79 65
7 b g Singspiel(IRE) —Calvia Rose (Sharpo)
25[8] 341[8] 636[5] (841) 974[6] 1169[4] 2023[3] 2424[6] 3639[8] 4279[2] 7490[8] 7765[9]

War Painter *Sylvester Kirk* a82
2 b c Orpen(USA) —Velvet Slipper (Muhtafal (USA))
(7088) 7317[2]

War Party *Dr Richard Newland* 87
6 b g Fantastic Light(USA) —War Game (FR) (Caerleon (USA))
1544[7]

War Queen (FR) *Mme P Alexanian* 53
4 gr m Slickly(FR) —Childermas (IRE) (Darshaan)
5378a[0]

Warrant *Paul Howling* a53 56
2 b g Tobougg(IRE) —Witness (Efisio)
5717[7] 6504[11] 7126[6]

Warren Bank *Mary Hambro* a57 39
5 b g Nayef(USA) —Neptunalia (Slip Anchor)
3127[7] 4434[10]

Warrior Nation (FR) *Adrian Chamberlain* a44 27
4 br g Statue Of Liberty(USA) —Tadawul (USA) (Diesis)
970[9] 1305[10] 2023[10] 2691[8] 3314[9] 3723[10] 5586[9] 7290[8] 8006[5]

Warrior's Reward (USA) *Ian Wilkes* a118 113
4 b h Medaglia D'Oro(USA) —For All You Do (USA) (Seeking The Gold (USA))
5779a[4] 7361a[5]

Warsaw (IRE) *M F De Kock* a108 101
5 ch h Danehill Dancer(IRE) —For Evva Silca (Piccolo)
339a[6] ◆ 413a[10] ◆ 607a[3] 817a[2]

Warsaw Ballet (CAN) *A Wohler* 96
3 bb f El Prado(IRE) —Whiletheiron'shot (USA) (Smart Strike (CAN))
4640a[9] 5805a[7]

Wasara *Amy Weaver* a66 64
3 b f Marju(IRE) —Triennial (IRE) (Giant's Causeway (USA))
2434[3] 2755[5] 5038[8] 5411[10] 6287[3] 6846[3] 7117[4] 8015[2]

Waseet *John Dunlop* 116
3 ch g Selkirk(USA) —Najayeb (USA) (Silver Hawk (USA))
1498[5] 2226[5] 3142[7] (6720)

Wasmi (IRE) *Clive Brittain* a79 55
3 b f Exceed And Excel(AUS) —Trim (IRE) (Ela-Mana-Mou)
2475[3] 2933[8]

Wassiljew (IRE) *A Scharer* 101
6 b g Zinaad—Wassiliki (IRE) (Night Shift (USA))
461a[6]

Wasted Tears (USA) *Bart B Evans* a102 114
5 bb m Najran(USA) —Wishes And Roses (USA) (Greinton)
6757a[5]

Watar (IRE) *F Head* a86 109
5 b h Marju(IRE) —Ombrie (Zafonic (USA))
4566a[7] 5349a[7] 6016a[2] 7110a[6]

Watch Amigo (IRE) *Walter Swinburn* a69 91
4 b g Royal Applause—Miss Red Ink (USA) (Red Ransom (USA))
1276[4] (1653) 2736[4] (4598) 5082[2] 5605[7] 6204[4]

Watch Chain (IRE) *Mark H Tompkins* a66 64
3 b g Traditionally(USA) —Dangle (IRE) (Desert Style (IRE))
1604[3] 2000[5] 2217[7] 2879[15] 3818[5] (4210) 4553[3] 4861[4] 5206[5] 6996[5] 7191[3] (7402) 7646[4]

Watchmaker *Tor Sturgis* a66 62
7 b g Bering—Watchkeeper (IRE) (Rudimentary (USA))
429[3] 765[8] 1241[7] 5367[5] 5958[7] 6669[9] 6930[2] 7068[2] 7286[10] 7687[6] 7814[9]

Watch Out *Dai Burchell* a47 45
6 b g Observatory(USA) —Ballet Fame (USA) (Quest For Fame)
748[6] 7270[10]

Watch The Flame *Michael Quinlan* a33 41
4 ch m Observatory(USA) —Flame Cutter (USA) (Miswaki (USA))
6896[8] 7191[9]

Waterborne *Roger Charlton* 60
2 b g Diktat—Waterfall One (Nashwan (USA))
5032[11] 5608[6] 6634[9]

Watercourse (IRE) *Michael Jarvis* 59
2 b c Hurricane Run(IRE) —Water Feature (Dansili)
6874[5]

Watered Silk *Marcus Tregoning* 44
2 gr g Encosta De Lago(AUS) —Tussah (Daylami (IRE))
1845[7] 4421[8] 4902[13]

Waterford Star (IRE) *Mark Johnston* a48 47
2 b c Oratorio(IRE) —Robin (Slip Anchor)
6827[9] 7172[7] 7470[7]

Water Gipsy *Gary Moore* a69 79
3 bb f Piccolo—Creek Dancer (Josr Algarhoud (IRE))
(2227) 3158[5] ◆ 3696[9] 4472[8] 5145[4] 6057[10] 6805[10]

Water Ice *Tom Dascombe* a76 71
2 b f Shamardal(USA) —Cumulate (USA) (Gone West (USA))
2616[8] 2958[7] 3295[7] (4429) 4701[5] 5807[6] 6307[3] 6795[3] 7087[7]

Waterloo Corner *Ray Craggs* a65 57
8 b g Cayman Kai(IRE) —Rasin Luck (Primitive Rising (USA))
331[12] 1113[9]

Waterloo Dock *Michael Quinn* a68 6
5 b g Hunting Lion(IRE) —Scenic Air (Hadeer)
8[5] 242[7] 317[2] 486[5] 613[2] (802) (1166) 1596[8] 2678[6] 3262[8] 4435[7] 7442[3] 8019[2]

Watneya *William Haggas* 67
2 b f Dubawi(IRE) —Quickstyx (Night Shift (USA)) (6893)

Watts Up Son *Declan Carroll* 78
2 b g Diktat—Local Fancy (Bahamian Bounty)
4409[6] 4599[4] 4941[3] (5483) 6719[10]

Waveband *David Barron* a99 98
3 ch f Exceed And Excel(AUS) —Licence To Thrill (Wolfhound (USA))
1399[11] 1732[9] 3065[14] 3599[3] (3890) 4058[6] 4378[2] 4509[10] (4858) 5393[6] 5854[12] 6221[2] 6363[11] 6509[9] 7566[3] ◆

Waveline (USA) *B Cecil* a102 96
5 b m Stravinsky(USA) —Teresa Ann (USA) (Boston Harbor (USA))
7362a[11]

Wave Of Applause *T Stack* 82
2 b f Royal Applause—Making Waves (IRE) (Danehill (USA))
3141[17]

Wavertree Bounty *John Ryan* a50 53
3 b f Pastoral Pursuits—Grecian Halo (USA) (Southern Halo (USA))
1461[11] 2633[7] 3173[9] 3606[7] 4547[2] ◆ 4687[6] 4763[4] 4971[4] 6574[4] 6816[10] 6860[F] 7156[2] 7387[5]

Wavertree Princess (IRE) *Alastair Lidderdale* a34 51
5 gr m Invincible Spirit(IRE) —Blushing Queen (IRE) (Desert King (IRE))
721[12] 810[7] 848[6] 1014[5] 1131[11]

Wavertree Warrior (IRE) *Nick Littmoden* a67 57
8 br g Indian Lodge(IRE) —Karamana (Habitat)
11[7] 256[3] 427[2] 656[2] 757[4] 4740[5] 5158[5]

Way Chief (FR) *Richard Fahey* a45 63
2 bb c Xaar—Green Way (FR) (Green Tune (USA))
6138[5] 7346[9] 7578[8]

Waypost *David Bridgwater*
4 b g Zamindar(USA) —Trellis Bay (Sadler's Wells (USA))
7022[9]

Way To Fly (IRE) *S Botti* 90
2 b c Footstepsinthesand—Rich Gift (Cadeaux Genereux)
3253a[7]

Wayward Glance *Michael Bell* 75
2 b g Sadler's Wells(USA) —Daring Aim (Daylami (IRE))
6883[12] 7179[2]

Way West (IRE) *Paul W Flynn* a80 25
4 b g Mull Of Kintyre(USA) —Hebrides (Gone West (USA))
602[7]

Weald *Doug Watson* a98 82
5 b g Bering—New Abbey (Sadler's Wells (USA))
418a[9]

Weald Park (USA) *Jeff Pearce* a57 101
4 ch g Cozzene(USA) —Promptly (IRE) (Lead On Time (USA))
23[10] 429[7] 7286[14] 7561[11]

Wealth Whispers (IRE) *Paul D'Arcy* a48
2 b f Hawk Wing(USA) —Esperentos (IRE) (Spectrum (IRE))
7517[7] 7598[6] 7962[8]

Wealthy (IRE) *A Fabre* 105
3 b c Refuse To Bend(IRE) —Enrich (USA) (Dynaformer (USA))
3703a[2] 5135a[2] 6219a[2] 6881a[5]

Weapon Of Choice (IRE) *David Simcock* 82
2 b c Iffraaj—Tullawadgeen (IRE) (Sinndar (IRE))
5954[2] ◆ (6779) 6982[5]

Wear 'Em Out Wilf *Peter Chapple-Hyam* 79
3 b c Bahamian Bounty—Branston Gem (So Factual (USA))
3374[3] (4238)

Weathervane *John Gosden* a84 85
3 b c Red Ransom(USA) —Westerly Air (USA) (Gone West (USA))
1757[3] 2255[10] 3173[3] 4964[6] 6115[2] 6876[8] (7043)

Webbow (IRE) *Brian Ellison* a84 101
8 b g Dr Devious(IRE) —Ower (IRE) (Lomond (USA))
1857[9] ◆ 2241[4] 3146[5] 3920[4] 4537[3] 5605[13] 5948[3] 6391[7] 6888[22] (7816a)

Web Of Dreams (IRE) *Brian Meehan* 36
2 b c Oasis Dream—Web Of Intrigue (Machiavellian (USA))
6811[11] 7094[10]

Wedding Dream *Kevin Ryan* a66 76
3 b f Oasis Dream—Gretna (Groom Dancer (USA))
(302) 382[6] 566[3] 781[6] (2379) 2702[11]

Wedding Fair *E Botti* 99
3 b f Oratorio(IRE) —Theatrical Act (USA) (Theatrical)
1713a[12] 3495a[10]

Wedding March (IRE) *Saeed Bin Suroor* a96 104
3 br f Dalakhani(IRE) —Elopa (GER) (Tiger Hill (IRE))
2224[8] 4624[7] 5553[11] 7243[5]

Wee Bobbie *Nerys Dutfield* a32 33
3 b f Acclamation—Bobbie Dee (Blakeney)
3477[8]

Weekend Magic (USA) *Myung Kwon Cho* 104
3 b f Ecton Park(USA) —Weekend Kaper (USA) (Honor Grades (USA))
5351a[7]

Weekend Millionair (IRE) *David Evans* 74
3 ch g Arakan(USA) —Almi Ad (USA) (Silver Hawk (USA))
1581[4] 1973[8] 2627[3]

Weeping Willow (IRE) *John Gosden* a57 55
3 b f Kheleyf(USA) —Bezant (IRE) (Zamindar (USA))
985[5] ◆ 1278[10] 2005[6]

Weet A Surprise *James Unett* a86 67
5 b m Bertolini(USA) —Ticcatoo (IRE) (Dolphin Street (FR))
192[2] 223[2] 432[2] 1192[6] 7409[7] 7665[7]

Weetentherty *Jim Goldie* 52
3 b g Bertolini(USA) —Binaa (IRE) (Marju (IRE))
2432[4] 3151[7] 3322[6] 3501[8] 3710[3] 4193[8] 4649[4] 4826[3] 5211[5] 5438[5]

Weetfromthechaff *Maurice Barnes* a62 54
5 gr g Weet-A-Minute(IRE) —Weet Ees Girl (IRE) (Common Grounds)
1467[4] 1803[12] 2131[2] 2492[5] 2583[9]

Weeza (IRE) *John Ryan* 26
3 b f Sakhee(USA) —Feed The Meter (IRE) (Desert King (IRE))
3272[12] 3795[12]

Wee Ziggy *Michael Mullineaux* a59 45
7 b g Ziggy's Dancer(USA) —Midnight Arrow (Robellino (USA))
563[3] 777[8] 875[4] 1188[12] 1984[8] 6120[5] 6933[10]

We Have A Dream *William Muir* a93 96
5 bb g Oasis Dream—Final Shot (Dalsaan)
1349[2] 1903[14] 2748[4] 3578[2] 3850[2] 4536[27] 4814[10] 4904[8] 6049[3] 6363[5] 6776[3] 7014[8] 7289[4]

Weipert (GER) *H Blume* 52
4 gr h Platini(GER) —Wild Side (GER) (Sternkoenig (IRE))
5378a[10]

Welcome Approach *John Weymes* a70 58
7 b g Most Welcome—Lucky Thing (Green Desert (USA))
351[2] ◆ 404[5] 595[4] 767[2] 924[3] 1723[2] 2021[7] 2381[10] 2669[4] 3357[6] 3727[9] 3976[5] 4431[6] 4516[5] 4799[5] 7334[6]

Welcome Bounty *Linda Perratt* a54
3 ch c Bahamian Bounty—Welcome Home (Most Welcome)
542[3] ◆ 1103[8] 2377[8] 3073[15]

Weliketobouggie *Alex Hales* a55 53
3 b g Tobougg(IRE) —Country Spirit (Sayf El Arab (USA))
2603[8] 3444[14] 4426[4] 5522[5]

Wellango (GER) *J-L Gay* 53
10 b g Acatenango(GER) —Well Known (GER) (Konigsstuhl (GER))
281a[4]

We'll Come *A bin Huzaim* a101 113
6 b g Elnadim(USA) —Off The Blocks (Salse (USA))
337a[4] 513a[5] 708a[9] 798a[14]

We'll Deal Again *Michael Easterby* a64 68
3 b g Gentleman's Deal(IRE) —Emma Amour (Emarati (USA))
2099[6] ◆ 2426[3] 2768[4] 3243[2] 3612[6] 3975[9] 4714[8] 6031[3] 7328[3] 7543[11]

Wellington Fair *Tor Sturgis* a60 80
3 br g Trade Fair—Milly's Lass (Mind Games)
5309[9] 7285[9] 7556[11]

Well Of Echoes *Alan McCabe* a68 59
4 b m Diktat—Seeker (Rainbow Quest (USA))
30[2] 129[6] 193[7] (663) (753) (780) 816[4] 873[8] 965[6] 1239[7]

Well Overdue (IRE) *Jamie Osborne* a39 54
4 b h Tillerman—Fey Rouge (IRE) (Fayruz)
1644[4] 2968[12] 3210[6]

Well Sharp *Michael Dods* 81
2 b c Selkirk(USA) —Saphila (IRE) (Sadler's Wells (USA))
(6138) ◆ 7095[9]

Wells Lyrical (IRE) *Bryan Smart* 100
5 b g Sadler's Wells(USA) —Lyrical (Shirley Heights)
4846[9] 5492[5] 5940[7]

Welsh Anthem *William Muir* a61 75
4 b m Singspiel(IRE) —Khubza (Green Desert (USA))
1797[10] 2961[3] (3314) 3789[3] 4422[6] 4859[5] 5115[5]

Welsh Artist *Amanda Perrett* a69
3 b g Sakhee(USA) —Gwen John (USA) (Peintre Celebre (USA))
933[2] ◆ 1143[4] 1619[9] 2415[9]

Welsh Dancer *Richard Hannon* 79
2 b c Dubawi(IRE) —Rosie's Posy (IRE) (Suave Dancer (USA))
1901[4] 2887[14] 4460[9] 5745[12] 6278[9] 6690[11]

Welsh Dresser (IRE) *Peter Grayson* a44 48
2 b f King's Best(USA) —Welsh Motto (USA) (Mtoto)
1360[4] 1463[3] 3985[6] 5667[11]

Welsh Emperor (IRE) *Tom Tate* a89 106
11 b g Emperor Jones(USA) —Simply Times (USA) (Dodge (USA))
1904[5] 4126[6] 5609[5] 7083[10] 7348[20]

Welsh Inlet (IRE) *John Bridger* a62 72
2 br f Kheleyf(USA) —Ervedya (IRE) (Doyoun)
2358 [8] 3087[7] 3509[2] 3897[7] 4927[4] 5328[6] 7552[10] 7734[3] 7997[4]

We'Re Delighted *Michael Blake* a47 75
5 b g Tobougg(IRE) —Samadilla (IRE) (Mujadil (USA))
3557[6] 3970[8]

West Emirates (USA) *Clive Cox* a85 75
4 ch g Lion Heart(USA) —Dr Kathy (USA) (Polish Numbers (USA))
667[2] 815[2] 1050[2] 1346[2] 1883[10] 3782[3]

West End Lad *Roy Bowring* a85 84
7 b g Tomba—Cliburnel News (IRE) (Horage)
40[5] 298[5] 908[10] (1179) (1426) 1926[16] 2961[12] (4522) 5386[7] 6112[7] 6205[10] 7182[2] 7304[2] (7600) 7867[7]

Western Aristocrat (USA) *Jeremy Noseda* 86
2 bb c Mr Greeley(USA) —Aristocratic Lady (USA) (Kris S (USA))
(7203) ◆

Western Eyes (IRE) *Brian Meehan* a55 46
3 b f Rock Of Gibraltar(IRE) —Duchy Of Cornwall (USA) (The Minstrel (CAN))
1355[14] 1654[12] 7244[5] 7727[12]

Western Memory (USA) *Lennart Reuterskiold Jr* a54
3 b f Dehere(USA) —Dakkari (USA) (Affirmed (USA))
7374a[7]

Western Mystic (GER) *W Hickst* 98
3 b f Doyen(IRE) —Waleska (GER) (Valanour (IRE))
5739a[2]

Western Pearl *William Knight* a91 100
3 b f High Chaparral(IRE) —Pulau Pinang (IRE) (Dolphin Street (FR))
3953[2] 4845[2] (5445) 6199[3] 6506[3] 7189[9]

Western Roots *Paddy Butler* a72 73
9 ch g Dr Fong(USA) —Chrysalis (Soviet Star (USA))
124[12] 4740[8]

Wester Ross (IRE) *James Eustace* a64 71
6 b g Fruits Of Love(USA) —Diabaig (Precocious)
5722[2] ◆ 6855[4]

West Hope (BRZ) *Eduardo Caramori* a100 74
5 b m Crimson Tide(IRE) —West Night (BRZ) (Slap Jack (USA))
6757a[9]

West Kirk *William Jarvis* a62 70
4 b g Alhaarth(IRE) —Naughty Crown (USA) (Chief's Crown (USA))
1171[4] 1293[10]

West Leake (IRE) *Paul Burgoyne* a65 66
4 b g Acclamation—Kilshanny (Groom Dancer (USA))
555[12] 845[6] 961[8] (1477) (1799) 2246[12] 2639[3] 3299[7] 6456[9] 7391[12] 7639[8] 7883[5] 8034[5]

West Leake Bridge (IRE) *B W Hills* 75
2 b c Avonbridge—Miss Amadeus (IRE) (Mozart (IRE))
1901[5] 2238[8] 4477[2] 4782[2] 5301[10] 6354[6] (6675) 6769[8]

West Leake Melody *B W Hills* a42 52
2 b c Royal Applause—Rada's Daughter (Robellino (USA))
4934[8] 5465[7] 6301[8] 6673[12] 7417[9] 7631[6]

Westport *Robin Bastiman* a81 59
7 b g Xaar—Connemara (IRE) (Mujadil (USA))
1885[4]

West Side Bernie (USA) *Saeed Bin Suroor* a111
4 br h Bernstein(USA) —Time Honored (USA) (Gilded Time (USA))
438a[10]

West Stand *Kate Walton* 69
2 b f Danbird(AUS) —Dispol Katie (Komaite (USA))
1749[6] 2130[9] 2861[5] 3945[9] 5298[11] 5595[9]

Westwood *Derek Haydn Jones* a87 77
5 ch g Captain Rio—Consignia (IRE) (Definite Article)
223[10] 287[10] 378[2] 703[6] 1258[2] 1779[8] (3761) 4225[3] 4684[2] (5647) 6625[3] 7180[5]

Wet Feet *Patrick Chamings* a44 54
3 br g Footstepsinthesand—Swoon (Night Shift (USA))
2841[10] 6496[8] 7161[13]

Wetherby Place (IRE) *Michael Wigham* a59 53
4 ch m King's Best(USA) —Summer Sunset (IRE) (Grand Lodge (USA))
235[11] 397[3] 541[2] ◆ 791[2] 940[10] ◆ 970[3]

Wet Your Whistle *Brian Meehan* a43 27
2 b c Oasis Dream—Thorntoun Piccolo (Groom Dancer (USA))
4838^9 5582^{14} 5871^8 (Dead)

Weybridge Light *Martin Bosley* a70 67
5 b g Fantastic Light(USA) —Nuryana (Nureyev (USA))
293^4 529^3 777^6 7270^{12} 7504^9

Whaileyy (IRE) *Sir Michael Stoute* 75
2 b c Holy Roman Emperor(IRE) —Alshoowg (USA) (Riverman (USA))
2547^4 ◆ (3991) 5525^5 5901^4

Whaston (IRE) *Pauline Robson* a54 58
5 b g Hawk Wing(USA) —Sharafanya (IRE) (Zafonic (USA))
5439^7 6032^4 6660^3 7132^5 7401^5 7958^7

What About Me (IRE) *Brian Nolan* 89
3 bb f Bertolini(USA) —Marefonic (Zafonic (USA))
2370a^{16}

What About You (IRE) *Richard Fahey* a87 36
2 b c Statue Of Liberty(USA) —Why Now (Dansili)
6722^6 7408^4 ◆ (7578)

What A Day *John Quinn* 56
4 b g Daylami(IRE) —Sensation (Soviet Star (USA))
1919^5 2560^7 2655^3 3028^4 3600^5 4854^4 4980^7 5564^7

What Budget *Arnfinn Lund* a64 65
6 br m Halling(USA) —Baked Alaska (Green Desert (USA))
7374a^6

What Katie Did (IRE) *Milton Bradley* a60 74
5 b g Invincible Spirit(IRE) —Chatterberry (Aragon)
1428^{15} 1547^{13} 1799^{15} 2589^2 2779^4 3254^{12} 3993^8 4255^6 4431^7 4789^8 5055^6 5267^{11}

Whats For Pudding (IRE) *Declan Carroll* a32 52
2 ch f Kheleyf(USA) —Margaret's Dream (IRE) (Muhtarram (USA))
2130^{10} 2813^7 2939^{19} 3315^7 4242^7 4429^8 4848^6 5434^8 5602^2 (5818) 6220^4 6325^7

What's For Tea *Paddy Butler* a38 53
5 b m Beat All(USA) —Come To Tea (IRE) (Be My Guest (USA))
983^{14}

What's Up Doc (IRE) *Lawney Hill* a70 79
9 b g Dr Massini(IRE) —Surprise Treat (IRE) (Shalford (IRE))
19^6 (920) 1239^2 1961^5 2455^2 3589^5 3814^4

What's Up Pussycat (IRE) *David Simcock* a91 99
4 b m Danehill Dancer(IRE) —Sangita (Royal Academy (USA))
2929^8 4137^3 4828^3 5052^4 5553^{12} 7188^8

Whatyouwoodwishfor (USA) *Richard Fahey* a69 60
4 ch g Forestry(USA) —Wishful Splendor (USA) (Smart Strike (CAN))
89^2 242^6 (296) (602) 907^4 1152^6 1509^7 1808^7 2454^5 3322^4

Wheredreamsare *W Hickst* 101
3 b c Monsun(GER) —Wakytara (GER) (Danehill (USA))
2406a^2 3018a^7

Where's Denton *Michael Dods* 45
3 ch g Where Or When(IRE) —Mylania (Midyan (USA))
1648^5

Where's Killoran *Eric Alston* a46 27
5 b m Iron Mask(USA) —Calypso Lady (IRE) (Priolo (USA))
4648 7051^2

Where's Reiley (USA) *David Barron* a88 73
4 bb g Doneraile Court(USA) —Plateau (USA) (Seeking The Gold (USA))
(138) 378^5 (504) ◆ (601) (832) ◆ 916^5 1099^{10} 1719^2 6539^9 6962^{13} 7326^{11} 7984^4

Where's Romeo (IRE) *David Brown* 82
2 b c Acclamation—Our Juliette (IRE) (Namid)
1930^2 ◆ (2448) 2743^9 6636^4 6916^9

Where's Susie *Michael Madgwick* a74 71
5 ch m Where Or When(IRE) —Linda's Schoolgirl (IRE) (Grand Lodge (USA))
263^5 675^4 771^5 983^2 1591^2 2165^4 2402^3 3084^2 (4045) (4734) 5382^9 6639^4 6775^7 (7490) 7765^5

Whey Sauce (JPN) *Peter Chapple-Hyam* 77
2 gr f Kurofune(USA) —Histoire (JPN) (Sunday Silence (USA))
6884^4 ◆ 7235^9

Whiepa Snappa (IRE) *Pat Phelan* a63 67
3 b g Whipper(USA) —Boudica (IRE) (Alhaarth (IRE))
1433^4 2168^5 2935^3 3273^5 3714^3 4532^5 5887^3 6020^7

Whip And Win (FR) *Robert Collet* 97
2 b f Whipper(USA) —Queensalsa (FR) (Kingsalsa (USA))
7276a^4 (7544a)

Whipchip (IRE) *U Suter*
3 b g Whipper(USA) —Poker Chip (Bluebird (USA))
6487a^0

Whiplash Willie *Andrew Balding* a82 65
2 ch c Phoenix Reach(IRE) —Santa Isobel (Nashwan (USA))
6474^6 6953^4 (7248) 7481^3 ◆

Whipless (IRE) *J S Bolger* 89
2 b c Whipper(USA) —Kimola (IRE) (King's Theatre (IRE))
6610a^8

Whipma Whopma Gate (IRE) *Declan Carroll* a59 74
5 b m Rossini(USA) —The Gibson Girl (IRE) (Norwich)
1293^5 1396^2 (1772) 1922^2 2429^4 3238^6 3317^{14} 4119^8 4824^3 4985^{13} 5486^7 5786^{10} 6371^{11}

Whipped (IRE) *Matthieu Palussiere* 30
2 b f Whipper(USA) —Sedulous (Tap On Wood)
7256a^{18}

Whipperoo (IRE) *Patrick Morris* a22 41
2 b f Whipper(USA) —Amaroo (FR) (Midyan (USA))
1668^7 1864^5 2183^7 5818^8 7279^4 7572^7

Whipper's Delight (IRE) *Desmond Donovan* a53 32
3 b f Whipper(USA) —Darling Smile (IRE) (Darshaan)
542^5 ◆ 775^{11} 1144^4

Whippers Love (IRE) *Mark Johnston* a85 84
3 b g Whipper(USA) —Danadoo (FR) (Septieme Ciel (USA))
(428) ◆ 686^3 1330^{12} 2033^{12} 3081^3 3627^3

Whipperway (IRE) *Sheena West* a55 71
3 b f Whipper(USA) —Prince's Passion (Brief Truce (USA))
422^5 805^6 1158^{10}

Whipphound *Mark Brisbourne* a73 57
2 b g Whipper(USA) —Golden Symbol (Wolfhound (USA))
5900^5 6334^8 6899^4 7309^5 (7527) (7811) 8002^3

Whip Up (IRE) *Jonathan Portman* a47
3 b g Whipper(USA) —Fizz Up (Alzao (USA))
305^5 475^9

Whirly Dancer *Henry Cecil* a74 89
3 b f Danehill Dancer(IRE) —Whirly Bird (Nashwan (USA))
(1260) 1850^3 3361^8 (4287) 4963^6 6321^{12} 6830^6

Whiskey Junction *Michael Quinn* a83 84
6 b g Bold Edge—Victoria Mill (Free State)
616^3 767^{10} 1321^3 1963^3 2301^6 2635^3 2954^7 4209^2 4662^8 6057^5 6523^9 6858^3 7180^2 7405^7 7719^6

Whisky Jack *William Muir* a70 70
4 b g Bahamian Bounty—Dress Design (IRE) (Brief Truce (USA))
373^{12} 481^6 804^6 1042^7

Whispered *Sir Michael Stoute* a55
2 b f Medicean—Whispering Blues (IRE) (Sadler's Wells (USA))
7113^6

Whispered Times (USA) *Tracy Waggott* a41 80
3 bb g More Than Ready(USA) —Lightning Show (USA) (Storm Cat (USA))
1118^4 (1651) (1811) 2069^4 2504^8 2628^7 3226^3 (3371) 3612^8 4483^4 4704^4 5484^2 5685^6 6567^5 6963^9

Whispering Death *Howard Johnson* a92 16
8 br g Pivotal—Lucky Arrow (Indian Ridge)
6143^6

Whispering Gallery *Saeed Bin Suroor* a115 115
4 b g Daylami(IRE) —Echoes In Eternity (IRE) (Spinning World (USA))
(337a) ◆ 712a^4 3454^2 4535^7 (5538) 6389^2 7096^7

Whispering Ridge *Mark Wellings* a13
3 br g Namid—Spring Whisper (IRE) (Halling (USA))
1685^{13} 2174^{12} 2903^{10} 4908^8 6931^{12} 7413^8 7601^8

Whispering Spirit (IRE) *Ann Duffield* a85 59
4 b m Catcher In The Rye(IRE) —Celtic Guest (IRE) (Be My Guest (USA))
1149^7 2727^3 (3323) 3520^3 (4427) (4910) 6003^8 6372^2 (7209) 7521^7 7766^2 7915^6

Whispering Wind (IRE) *Ms Joanna Morgan* a36 80
7 b m Sunshine Street(USA) —Soul Fire (IRE) (Exactly Sharp (USA))
3492a^{14}

Whisper Louise (IRE) *Pam Sly* 97
2 b f Chevalier(IRE) —Patamar (Warning)
1294^2 2338^5 2813^2 3087^2 (4203) 4872^2 (5849) 6563^3 7235^3

Whisper Wind *Gary Moore* 66
3 ch g Cadeaux Genereux—Soft Breeze (Zafonic (USA))
1694^4 2842^7 3272^7 4325^5 5086^9 5555^5 6024^4 6518^{13} 6863^2 7037^{11}

Whistledownwind *David Nicholls* a106 84
5 b g Danehill Dancer(IRE) —Mountain Ash (Dominion)
2100^{13} 2311^9

Whistleinthewind (IRE) *Gary Moore* a87 78
3 b g Oratorio(IRE) —Lady Scarlett (Woodman (USA))
2117^{14} 2713^9 2969^6 3351^5 4757^5 5456^9 6091^2 ◆ (6841) 7090^7

Whistle On By *B W Hills* a72 75
2 b c Piccolo—Glory Oatway (IRE) (Desert Prince (IRE))
4960^9 5372^4 7346^4 7595^3

Whitbarrow (IRE) *Rod Millman* a78 90
11 b g Royal Abjar(USA) —Danccini (IRE) (Dancing Dissident (USA))
20^3 144^2 170^2 379^4 914^4

Whitby (IRE) *Michael Easterby* a51 43
3 br f Dubawi(IRE) —Hymenee (USA) (Chief's Crown (USA))
3228^5 3515^6 3758^4 4155^7

Whitby Jack *Gary Moore* 74
3 b g Bering—Sablonne (USA) (Silver Hawk (USA))
1581^6 1912^5 ◆ 2684^3

Whitby Jet (IRE) *Edward Vaughan* a60 49
2 b g Mujadil(USA) —Anazah (USA) (Diesis)
1871^6 2216^8 3053^6 5659^7 6081^2

Whitby Warrior (USA) *Chris Grant* 42
2 bb g Powerscourt—Grand September (USA) (Grand Slam (USA))
3433^8 4187^9 4747^8

Whitcombe Spirit *Jamie Poulton* a35 62
5 b g Diktat—L'Evangile (Danehill (USA))
982^9 1758^7 6693^{10}

Whitechapel *Eric Alston* 76
3 gr g Oasis Dream—Barathiki (Barathea (IRE))
1425^3 1890^3 (2329) 2884^5 3898^{12}

Whitecrest *John Spearing* a69 61
2 ch f Ishiguru(USA) —Risky Valentine (Risk Me (FR))
5465^3 5865^3 6161^4 6866^2 7309^3 7400^9

White Dart *Mick Channon* a81 76
3 b g Rakti—Feather Boa (IRE) (Sri Pekan (USA))
1189^4 1734^9 2110^5 2587^6 3259^2 3479^8 4742^4 (6897) 7056^{13}

White Deer (USA) *Geoffrey Harker* a59 86
6 b g Stravinsky(USA) —Brookshield Baby (IRE) (Sadler's Wells (USA))
3226^4 4850^8 4939^{11} 6267^7 6917^7 7472^3

White Devil *Andrew Balding* a83 78
3 ch g Zafeen(FR) —Costa Balena (CHI) (Great Regent (CAN))
1307^4 ◆ 1761^9 2644^2 3103^{13} 3766^3 4956^6 5854^9

White Finch (USA) *Andrew Balding* a62 66
3 rg f Cozzene(USA) —Just A Bird (USA) (Storm Bird (CAN))
979^4 1538^4 2255^3 3268^{13}

White Frost (IRE) *B W Hills* 78
2 gr c Verglas(IRE) —Moivouloirtoi (USA) (Bering)
6153^2 6532^2

White Fusion *Howard Johnson* 53
2 gr g Oratorio(IRE) —Divine Grace (IRE) (Definite Article)
4668^9 5595^5

White Ledger (IRE) *Ray Peacock* a47 50
11 ch g Ali-Royal(IRE) —Boranwood (IRE) (Exhibitioner)
5586^7 7125^{17}

White Lightning (GER) *U Stech* 107
8 gr h Sternkoenig(IRE) —Whispering Grass (GER) (Konigsstuhl (GER))
2806a^6 4418a^6

White Moonstone (USA) *Saeed Bin Suroor* 112
2 b f Dynaformer(USA) —Desert Gold (USA) (Seeking The Gold (USA))
(4317) ◆ (4842) ◆ (5910) (6348)

Whiterocks *Sheena West* a44 51
4 ch g Imperial Dancer—Thailand (Lycius (USA))
260^5 420^9

White Shift (IRE) *Jane Chapple-Hyam* a71 84
4 b m Night Shift(USA) —Ivy Queen (IRE) (Green Desert (USA))
125^5 312^8 (531) 828^3 1300^9 1428^{13} 1641^7 (2026) 2332^6 2689^{12} 3115^6 3216^{12} 3637^6 4875^8 5076^2 5377^8 5875^{10} (6455) 6741^2 7162^9 7390^2 7441^8 7556^8 8034^9

Whitley Bay (USA) *John Best* a48 48
3 b g Lion Heart(USA) —Sea Witch (USA) (Sea Hero (USA))
533^{10} 634^7 4793^9 5625^6 6120^4 6272^7 6855^{10} 7270^8

Whitstable Native *John Best* a46 65
2 b g Bertolini(USA) —Break Of Dawn (USA) (Mt. Livermore (USA))
5328^3 6263^5 6520^6 6902^8 7313^{11}

Whoateallthepius (IRE) *Dean Ivory* a70 79
2 b f Antonius Pius(USA) —Affirmed Crown (USA) (Affirmed (USA))
2338^4 ◆ (3035) 3395^3 3887^4 4228^2 4872^5 5261^2 5725^7 6445^6

Whodathought (IRE) *Richard Hannon* a72 74
2 b c Choisir(AUS) —Consultant Stylist (IRE) (Desert Style (IRE))
2839^{10} 3349^2 (3577) 4623^7 4955^5 5256^9 5807^4 (6411) 7087^4 7417^4

Whodunit (UAE) *Peter Hiatt* a72 66
6 b g Mark Of Esteem(IRE) —Mystery Play (IRE) (Sadler's Wells (USA))
202^5 396^3 (586) 676^2 975^{13} 1177^4 1346^{12} 1883^{14} 2714^{10}

Whooshka (USA) *Peter Chapple-Hyam* a84 80
4 b m Smart Strike(CAN) —Bushra (USA) (Danzig (USA))
255^7 546^6 ◆ (786) 857^2 917^3

Who's Shirl *Chris Fairhurst* 89
4 b m Shinko Forest(IRE) —Shirl (Shirley Heights)
1650^8 2462^6 2764^{11} (4706) 5199^5 (5684) (6113)

Who's Winning (IRE) *Brendan Powell* a63 59
9 ch g Docksider(USA) —Quintellina (Robellino (USA))
961^5 986^4 1167^3 1304^{11} 1443^6 1633^4

Whotsit (IRE) *Amy Weaver* a59 66
4 ch g Choisir(AUS) —Charming Victoria (IRE) (Mujadil (USA))
11^{10} 135^5 318^8 498^5 1129^8 1443^5 2876^8 3168^9 4715^{10} 4969^{11}

Whozthecat (IRE) *Declan Carroll* a98 95
3 b g One Cool Cat(USA) —Intaglia (GER) (Lomitas)
(1399) ◆ 1701^{14} 2260^3 5967^8 6364^{16} 6446^2 6706^8 7079^3 (7466)

Why (IRE) *A P O'Brien* 91
2 b f Galileo(IRE) —Rumplestiltskin (IRE) (Danehill (USA))
5570a^7

Why Nee Amy *Olivia Maylam* a62 59
4 ch m Tipsy Creek(USA) —Ashleen (Chilibang)
396^6 ◆ 3968^9 4746^5 5770^8 6335^7

Why So Serious *Donald Whillans* 26
4 ch g Falbrav(IRE) —Marrakech (IRE) (Barathea (IRE))
3901^{10}

Wibbadune (IRE) *Mandy Rowland* a82 62
6 ch m Daggers Drawn(USA) —Becada (GER) (Cadeaux Genereux)
1234^{12}

Wicked Daze (IRE) *Linda Perratt* a92 88
7 ch g Generous(IRE) —Thrilling Day (Groom Dancer (USA))
(148) (237) 1101^9 1720^6 2295^3 3152^2 3198^2 3588^3 (4393) 5278^2 5788^{12} 6143^5 7173^8

Wicked Wilma (IRE) *Alan Berry* a44 71
6 b m Tagula(IRE) —Wicked (Common Grounds)
2213^7 2695^2 3119^2 (3356) 3533^7 4243^3 4583^3 4798^3 5240^5 5356^4 5513^7 6031^8 6103^{11} 6398^3 6572^8 6708^2 6965^3 7175^4 7281^4

Wicklewood *Christine Dunnett* a49 45
4 b g Mujahid(USA) —Pinini (Pivotal)
234^7 249^{10} 353^{10} 1318^9

Widezain (IRE) *Mick Channon* 81
3 b g Chineur(FR) —Silk Fan (IRE) (Unfuwain (USA))
1132^5 1447^2 (2499) 3427^5

Widow Bird (IRE) *Hughie Morrison* a64 60
3 b f Xaar—Dollar Bird (IRE) (Kris)
1143^2 ◆ 1993^6 4874^4 6225^{11} 6937^P

Wi Dud *Kevin Ryan* 109
6 b g Elnadim(USA) —Hopesay (Warning)
(1174) 1406a^8 2325^9 3108^4 4191^{10} 4616^5 4937^6

Wiener Walzer (GER) *J Hirschberger* 122
4 b h Dynaformer(USA) —Walzerkoenigin (USA) (Kingmambo (USA))
2374a^3 3068^5 4164a^2 5806a^6 6612a^{12}

Wigan Lane *Paul Howling* a62 68
3 b f Kheleyf(USA) —Nesting (Thatching)
276^8 346^7 3685^8 3910^6 5073^7

Wiggy Smith *Henry Candy* a60 85
11 ch g Master Willie—Monsoon (Royal Palace)
1780^9 2173^4 2996^3 3781^5 (4476) 4996^2 6091^4 6447^7

Wightgold *Harry Dunlop* a48 62
4 ch m Golden Snake(USA) —Main Brand (Main Reef)
1446^2 1798^4 2169^3 3084^8 3348^6 4530^4

Wigmore Hall (IRE) *Michael Bell* 118
3 b g High Chaparral(IRE) —Love And Laughter (IRE) (Theatrical)
(1330) 1702^2 2738^2 3104^3 (3921) (4805) 5319a^2 5853^2 6925^5

Wigram's Turn (USA) *Michael Easterby* a95 88
5 ch g Hussonet(USA) —Stacey's Relic (USA) (Houston (USA))
108^7 286^2 944^6 1455^4 3146^7 4371^6 4603^{13} 4828^{15} 5098^{10} 5716^6 6374^9 6904^{11} 7526^6 ◆ 7680^7 7988^7

Wigwam Willie (IRE) *Kevin Ryan* a53 96
8 b g Indian Rocket—Sweet Nature (IRE) (Classic Secret (USA))
863^9 1272^{13} 3089^5 4949^7 5596^3 6105^5 6367^{10} 7054^9

Wikaala (USA) *Gordon Elliott* a84 83
5 ch g Diesis—Roseate Tern (Blakeney)
7589a^{13}

Wilaya (USA) *John Gosden* 42
2 bb f Bernardini(USA) —Tanzania (IRE) (Alzao (USA))
5692^{15}

Wildcat Brief (USA) *Ben Perkins Jr* a112
4 ch h Forest Wildcat(USA) —Grisham (USA) (Grindstone (USA))
6582a^3

Wildcat Wizard (USA) *Paul Cole* a103 99
4 b g Forest Wildcat(USA) —Tip the Scale (USA) (Valiant Nature (USA))
1708^{10} 1903^2 ◆ 2119^3 ◆ 3461^{16} 3850^9 4536^3 ◆ 5302^{13} 5731^2

Wild Danger (GER) *Andreas Lowe* 69
3 b c Konigstiger(GER) —Wild Angel (IRE) (Acatenango (GER))
5671a^7

Wild Desert (FR) *Alan King* a85 83
5 bb g Desert Prince(IRE) —Sallivera (IRE) (Sillery (USA))
2821^3 4051^7 5286^7

Wild Geese (IRE) *Mark Johnston* 69
3 br g Cape Cross(IRE) —Intrepidity (Sadler's Wells (USA))
4906^9 5478^2 5815^2

Wild Hysteria (IRE) *Tom Tate* a37 62
2 gr g Verglas(IRE) —White Wisteria (Ahonoora)
1800^6 2239^6 2667^5 3598^2 4124^5 5483^5 6035^2 7211^6

Wild Mimosa (IRE) *John Gosden* 63
2 b f Dynaformer(USA) —Sumoto (Mtoto)
5829^5

Wild Rockette *Brian Meehan* a74 78
3 b f Rock Of Gibraltar(IRE) —Wild Floridian (IRE) (Indian Ridge)
2042^8 2888^8 3259^3 3680^8 4344^3 (4762) 5149^{11} 6629^8

Wild Rose *Michael Bell* a96 83
3 gr f Doyen(IRE) —Makhsusah (IRE) (Darshaan)
1452^3 2047^3 2758^{15} 3123^4 4341^5 (4698) (5371) 5723^{11} 7189^8

Wild Savannah *E Charpy* a80 90
8 b g Singspiel(IRE) —Apache Star (Arazi (USA))
512a^{10} 706a^{11}

Wild Wind (GER) *A P O'Brien* 104
2 b f Danehill Dancer(IRE) —Woman Secret (IRE) (Sadler's Wells (USA))
5570a^5 6401a^2 6530^8

Wilfred Pickles (IRE) *Jo Crowley* a84 81
4 ch g Cadeaux Genereux—Living Daylights (IRE) (Night Shift (USA))
2024^6 2823^5 3412^2 3725^2 4598^5 7637^2

Will Barrow *Jim Boyle* 38
2 b c Lucky Story(USA) —Fareham (Komaite (USA))
3399^7 3735^{13} 4293^4 5857^7 7197^{10}

Willbeme *Neville Bycroft*
2 b f Kyllachy—Befriend (USA) (Allied Forces (USA))
6892^{10}

Willcox Inn (USA) *Michael Stidham* a106 108
2 bb c Harlan's Holiday(USA) —De Aar (USA) (Gone West (USA))
7360a^3

Willent *Julie-Ann Camacho* a40 35
4 b g Lend A Hand—Lapu-Lapu (Prince Sabo)
403^5

William Arnold *Chris Fairhurst* 61
3 ch g Rambling Bear—Dancing Shirl (Dancing Spree (USA))
1753^{12} 2700^{13} 3975^{11}

William Morgan (IRE) *Alan Juckes* a65 81
3 ch g Arakan(USA) —Dry Lightning (Shareef Dancer (USA))
1334^4 1718^3 2348^2 2863^5 3429^3 3876^{14} 4394^{15} 5484^4 6897^5 7122^4 7376^7 7462^4 7679^2 (7832)

William's Way *Ian Wood* a79 69
8 b g Fraam—Silk Daisy (Barathea (IRE))
(15) 888^2 1053^5 2182^2 2723^7 4223^6 4620^5 5144^3 5382^6 6775^6 7321^4 (7491) 7632^5

William Van Gogh *John Gosden* a73 82
3 b g Dansili—Flower Girl (Pharly (FR))
1387^4 2043^6 4491^5 (5645) 6366^7 6904^9

William Wainwright (IRE) *Ann Duffield* a53 47
2 b g Elnadim(USA) —Supportive (IRE) (Nashamaa)
6138[12] 6365[7] 6569[12] 7894[7] 7982[2]

Willie Ever *David Bridgwater* a53 56
6 b g Agnes World(USA) —Miss Meltemi (IRE) (Miswaki Tern (USA))
543[9] 663[10] 2488[7]

Willing Foe (USA) *Saeed Bin Suroor* a62 105
3 bb c Dynaformer(USA) —Thunder Kitten (USA) (Storm Cat (USA))
(4572) ◆ (5913) (6889) 7350[19]

Will'N'Glad *Nigel Tinkler*
3 b g Danbird(AUS) —Fishlake Flyer (IRE) (Desert Style (IRE))
6716[12]

Will O Way (USA) *Vladimir Cerin* a104 94
4 b m Broken Vow(USA) —Willow Woodman (USA) (Woodman (USA))
3044a[4]

Willow Dancer (IRE) *Walter Swinburn* a86 85
6 ch g Danehill Dancer(IRE) —Willowbridge (IRE) (Entrepreneur)
1513[9] 2124[7] 5919[9] 6260[2] 6444[2] 6701[3] 7115[2] 7274[3]

Willow's Wish *George Moore* a21 45
2 b f Intikhab(USA) —Movie Star (IRE) (Barathea (IRE))
2654[9] 3729[9] 4402[5] 6001[6] 6457[3] 7057[15]

Willow Weep For Me (FR) *J-M Lefebvre* a68 58
7 ch g Cadeaux Genereux—Rosereine (USA) (Slew O'Gold (USA))
332a[0]

Willywell (FR) *J-P Gauvin* a101 105
8 b h Jimble(FR) —Basilissa (FR) (Gay Minstrel (FR))
7776a[0]

Wilmington *Jean McGregor* a69 56
6 ch g Compton Place—Bahawir Pour (USA) (Green Dancer (USA))
3901[9] 4514[9]

Wilside (IRE) *M Delzangles* 105
4 gr m Verglas(IRE) —Sigonella (IRE) (Priolo (USA))
1792a[0]

Winchester (USA) *Christophe Clement* 115
5 b h Theatrical—Rum Charger (IRE) (Spectrum (IRE))
7366a[4] 7851a[11]

Winding Hill *Michael Easterby* a42
2 b f Diktat—Eurolink Artemis (Common Grounds)
5921[9] 6360[10]

Windjammer *Lawrence Mullaney* a63 56
6 b g Kyllachy—Absolve (USA) (Diesis)
2278[5] 4245[4] 5023[8]

Wind Shuffle (GER) *Jim Goldie* 85
7 b g Big Shuffle(USA) —Wiesensturmerin (GER) (Lagunas)
1013[9] 1202[7] 1867[7] 2579[6] 3025[8] 4086[6]

Windsor Knights *Alastair Lidderdale* a66
2 b g Dubai Destination(USA) —Betrothal (IRE) (Groom Dancer (USA))
3459[12] 6249[11] 6542[3] 6936[4] 7165[8] 7630[12]

Wind Star *Milton Harris* a60 91
7 ch g Piccolo—Starfleet (Inchinor)
1098[2] 1536[3] 1840[5] 1960[2] 4520[11] 4619[11] 5084[9] 5375[10] 5592[6] 6289[6]

Windward Islands *Mahmood Al Zarooni* 62
2 ch c Cadeaux Genereux—Dominica (Alhaarth (IRE))
2059[14] 3112[4]

Windward Islands (USA) *Mark Frostad* 112
6 rg g Cozzene(USA) —Cruisie (USA) (Assert)
6236a[3]

Win For Sure (GER) *A Wohler* 111
5 b g Stravinsky(USA) —Win For Us (GER) (Surumu (GER))
2576a[3] 3934a[3] 4888a[4] 5649a[4] 6408a[3]

Wingate Street *David Evans* a40 36
3 ch g Tumbleweed Ridge—Tymeera (Timeless Times (USA))
6124[7] 6275[6] 6716[8] 7071[8]

Winged Farasi *Joanne Foster* a58 58
6 b g Desert Style(IRE) —Clara Vale (IRE) (In The Wings)
3502[2] 4410[4] 4604[7] 5203[2] 5687[6] 6114[11]

Winged Valkyrie (IRE) *B W Hills* a72 72
2 ch f Hawk Wing(USA) —Crystal Valkyrie (IRE) (Danehill (USA))
5029[4] 5587[3] 6118[5]

Wing Forward (IRE) *Alan Berry* 25
3 b f Hawk Wing(USA) —Stroppy (IRE) (Xaar)
6643[12]

Wing Play (IRE) *Hughie Morrison* a94 87
5 b g Hawk Wing(USA) —Toy Show (IRE) (Danehill (USA))
2934[8] 3627[7] 4100[11] 4758[5] 5375[7] 5591[10] 6322[10] 7062[5] ◆

Wings Of Kintyre (IRE) *Alan Berry* a37
6 b m Mull Of Kintyre(USA) —Tiger Wings (IRE) (Thatching)
267[7] 473[6] 1337[10]

Winifred Jo *Jeremy Gask* a55
3 ch f Bahamian Bounty—Coming Home (Vettori (IRE))
1222[5] 2185[7] 2721[10]

Winnie Dixie (USA) *Paul Cole* a74 73
2 bb f Dixie Union(USA) —Icy Demeanor (USA) (Allen's Prospect (USA))
(5147) ◆ 5725[3]

Winniepeg *Clive Cox* a36
2 b f Bertolini(USA) —Court Lane (USA) (Machiavellian (USA))
7309[7]

Winning Draw (IRE) *Paul Midgley* a62 45
2 b f Redback—Desert Flair (Desert Style (IRE))
3756[7] 4149[6] (4890) 7982[7]

Winning Show *Chris Gordon* a68 51
6 b g Muhtarram(USA) —Rose Show (Belmez (USA))
(13) ◆ 121[2] 182[6] 3348[10] 4227[10] 7490[5] 7765[11]

Winterbourne *Michael Blanshard* a44 44
4 rg m Cadeaux Genereux—Snowing (Tate Gallery (USA))
495[12] 614[8]

Winter Dream (IRE) *Robert Collet* 110
6 gr g Act One—Settler (Darshaan)
4566a[10] 5575a[9] 6016a[8] 6607a[2] 7110a[10] 7457a[5]

Winter Fever (SAF) *James Eustace* a94 82
6 ch g Western Winter(USA) —Fashion Fever (SAF) (Model Man (SAF))
(197) 360[4] 536[8] 863[3]

Winter Memories (USA) *James J Toner* 108
2 rg f El Prado(IRE) —Memories Of Silver (USA) (Silver Hawk (USA))
7340a[2]

Winter's Night (IRE) *Clive Cox* 85
2 b f Night Shift(USA) —Woodland Glade (Mark Of Esteem (IRE))
4095[5] ◆ (4999) (6317) 7098[6]

Winterwind (IRE) *Carmen Bocskai* a61
5 b h Orpen(USA) —Brickey Beech (IRE) (Precocious)
(461a)

Wiqaaya (IRE) *Ed Dunlop* 78
2 gr f Red Ransom(USA) —Masaader (USA) (Wild Again (USA))
3411[3] ◆ 6441[2]

Wirral Way *Frank Sheridan* a41 47
4 b g Kyllachy—Spicey (Mizoram (USA))
253[6] 1599[6] 2114[10]

Wisecraic *Tom Dascombe* a80 86
3 ch g Kheleyf(USA) —Belle Genius (USA) (Beau Genius (CAN))
1352[12] 1663[5] 4264[5] 5421[5]

Wise Dan (USA) *Charles Lopresti* a117 117
3 ch g Wiseman's Ferry(USA) —Lisa Danielle (USA) (Wolf Power (SAF))
7361a[6]

Wise Dennis *Alan Jarvis* a88 88
8 b g Polar Falcon(USA) —Bowden Rose (Dashing Blade)
769[3] 1088[10] 1618[2] 2640[11] 3846[6] 6105[13] 7062[17] 7597[14]

Wiseman's Diamond (USA) *Paul Midgley* a51 73
5 b m Wiseman's Ferry(USA) —Asswhatilldois (IRE) (Blues Traveller (IRE))
1034[7] 1426[11] 1628[9] 3503[2] 3806[6] 4172[3] 4644[6] 5533[6] 5786[5] 6116[10] 7184[4] 7453[7]

Wise Up *Chris Dwyer* a67 72
3 b g Starcraft(NZ) —Seven Sing (USA) (Machiavellian (USA))
2548[5] 3258[3] 5028[3] 5661[4] 5861[2] 6438[10] 6541[10] 6854[9]

Wishbone (IRE) *Michael Quinlan* 77
3 b f Danehill Dancer(IRE) —Intricate Design (Zafonic (USA))
1917[10]

Wishformore (IRE) *J S Moore* a67 63
3 b f Chevalier(IRE) —Terra Nova (Polar Falcon (USA))
1504[2] 2473[5] 3063[8] 3441[5] 7438[7] 7964[9] 7994[2] 8006[2]

Wisterya (FR) *Mlle S-V Tarrou*
3 ch f Starcraft(NZ) —Minesota (FR) (Danehill (USA))
6487a[0]

Witchry *Tony Newcombe* a50 70
8 gr g Green Desert(USA) —Indian Skimmer (USA) (Storm Bird (CAN))
2246[9] 4283[3] ◆ (5087) 5557[2] 6284[9]

With Hindsight (IRE) *Clive Cox* 76
2 ch g Ad Valorem(USA) —Lady From Limerick (IRE) (Rainbows For Life (CAN))
2163[3] 2839[2] 3269[2] 3859[3] 4578[10]

With Interest *A Al Raihe* a97 88
7 b h Selkirk(USA) —With Fascination (USA) (Dayjur (USA))
337a[10] 801a[12]

Withnail (IRE) *Stef Higgins* a58 54
6 b g Rossini(USA) —Whitegate Way (Greensmith)
773[7] 968[6]

Without A Prayer (IRE) *Ralph Beckett* a116 114
5 ch h Intikhab(USA) —Prayer (IRE) (Rainbow Quest (USA))
338a[6] 630a[9] 823a[11]

Without Equal *Noel Wilson* a47 56
4 ch m Tobougg(IRE) —Sans Egale (FR) (Lashkari)
858[5] 1526[5] 2214[7] 2529[3] 2786[3] 3078[3] 3535[4] 4246[10] 4648[15] 4980[6] 5681[10] 6262[2] 6915[8] (7149)

Without Prejudice (USA) *Jeremy Noseda* a87 94
5 ch g Johannesburg(USA) —Awesome Strike (USA) (Theatrical)
2091[5] 6721[16] 6888[24]

Witzend (IRE) *Jedd O'Keeffe* 71
2 b c Footstepsinthesand—Spring Easy (IRE) (Alzao (USA))
2238[6] 2832[7] 3315[6] 3749[2] 3872[5] 4984[3]

Wizard Of Us *Michael Mullineaux* a37 43
10 b g Wizard King—Sian's Girl (Mystiko (USA))
210[11]

Wizzacus *Richard Price* a38 21
3 b f Spartacus(IRE) —Little Wizzy (Wizard King)
3966[11] 4249[12] 5474[8] 5810[5] 6332[9]

Wizz Kid (IRE) *Robert Collet* 104
2 b f Whipper(USA) —Lidanski (IRE) (Soviet Star (USA))
4419a[4] 7277a[2]

Wodian (IRE) *David Lanigan* a51
2 ch f Smarty Jones(USA) —Madame Anne Peters (Selkirk (USA))
7550[7] 7681[3] 7879[8]

Wogan's Sister *Paul Midgley* a65 72
5 b m Lahib(USA) —Dublivia (Midyan (USA))
7986[13]

Woldgate *Geoffrey Oldroyd* a56 51
3 b g Monsieur Bond(IRE) —Chicago Bond (USA) (Real Quiet (USA))
1967[12] 2609[7] 3086[9]

Wolds Agent *Tim Easterby* 52
2 b g Monsieur Bond(IRE) —Off Camera (Efisio)
5531[14] 6046[4] 6894[8]

Wolfgang (SPA) *M Alonso* 28
3 ch c Leadership—Mendia (Midyan (USA))
450a[10]

Wolf Rock *David Barron* 57
3 ch g Lomitas—Shore Light (USA) (Gulch (USA))
1485[6] 4414[4] 5303[7] 6144[11]

Wolf Slayer *Tom Dascombe* a67 72
2 b f Diktat—Bolsena (USA) (Red Ransom (USA))
3295[15] ◆ 3583[4] 4474[2] 4909[4] 5785[5] 7517[3] (7667) 8011[3]

Wolkenburg (GER) *P Schiergen* 89
2 b f Big Shuffle(USA) —Winterthur (GER) (Alkalde (GER))
7108a[6]

Wolverine (FR) *M Boutin* 92
3 b c Take Risks(FR) —Sevres (USA) (Lyphard's Wish (FR))
6761a[6]

Wom *William Haggas* 60
2 b c Tiger Hill(IRE) —Vayavaig (Damister (USA))
6153[10] 6882[7] 7202[8]

Womaniser (IRE) *Tom Keddy* a58 58
6 br g Rock Of Gibraltar(IRE) —Top Table (Shirley Heights)
99[3] 184[4] 260[4] 314[4]

Wonderfilly (FR) *P Demercastel* a71 99
3 b f Invincible Spirit(IRE) —Wicken Wonder (IRE) (Distant Relative)
1196a[4]

Wonder Lawn (SAF) *M F De Kock* a101 96
7 b g Fort Wood(USA) —Velvet Green (BRZ) (Roy (USA))
438a[5] 629a[5] 706a[5]

Wonder Of Wonders (USA) *A P O'Brien* 81
2 b f Kingmambo(USA) —All Too Beautiful (IRE) (Sadler's Wells (USA))
7256a[2] ◆

Wong Again *J W Hills* a59 48
2 b f Araafa(IRE) —Susi Wong (IRE) (Selkirk (USA))
6146[11] 6712[4]

Woodbourne (CAN) *Robert Tiller* 109
6 bb g Danzig(USA) —Checker Hall (USA) (Seeking The Gold (USA))
6237a[3] 6949a[11]

Woodcote (IRE) *Peter Grayson* a78 83
8 b g Monashee Mountain(USA) —Tootle (Main Reef)
241[9] 477[10] 2720[11]

Woodcote Place *Patrick Chamings* a92 95
7 b g Lujain(USA) —Giant Nipper (Nashwan (USA))
1767[12] 2472[6] 2926[6] 3346[7] 3851[2] 4296[2] (4995) 5950[7] 7187[4] 7318[2] 7522[8]

Woodcraft *Mark Buckley* 16
6 ch g Observatory(USA) —Woodwardia (USA) (El Gran Senor (USA))
3377[7]

Wooden King (IRE) *Malcolm Saunders* a70 65
5 b g Danetime(IRE) —Olympic Rock (IRE) (Ballad Rock)
2589[9] 3255[8] 3440[5] 3727[3] 3979[2] 4283[5] (5579) 5714[6] 6536[5] (6952) 7334[2] (7518) (7628) ◆

Wood Fair *Mrs K Burke* 60
3 b f Trade Fair—To The Woods (IRE) (Woodborough (USA))
2502[6] 3023[7] 4061[8] 4374[3] (4971) 5411[6] 6065[4] 7055[6]

Woodford Belle (USA) *Brian Meehan* a85 82
3 bb f Arch(USA) —Tis Me (USA) (Notebook (USA))
1882[2] 3208[3] 3298[8] (3953) 4571[2] 5181[3]

Woodhouse Mill (IRE) *Nigel Tinkler* 31
3 b f Oratorio(IRE) —Wurfklinge (GER) (Acatenango (GER))
1971[9] 3073[13] 3503[7]

Woodsley House (IRE) *Mark Rimmer* a49 75
8 b g Orpen(USA) —Flame And Shadow (IRE) (Turtle Island (IRE))
1673[11] 2789[6] 3164[7] 6672[5] 7071[6] 7761[8] 7882[6]

Woodwind *Derek Shaw* a51
5 b m Piccolo—Ma Jolie (Shalford (IRE))
6931[9] 7310[6] 7409[5] 7563[4]

Woody Waller *Howard Johnson* 80
5 ch g Lomitas—Reamzafonic (Grand Lodge (USA))
(1277) 6983[8]

Woolfall Sovereign (IRE) *George Margarson* a63 74
4 b g Noverre(USA) —Mandragore (USA) (Slew O'Gold (USA))
12[8] 1129[2] 1374[13] 2093[9]

Woolfall Treasure *Gary Moore* 102
5 gr g Daylami(IRE) —Treasure Trove (USA) (The Minstrel (CAN))
1736[4] 3050[14] (3159) 4461[4] 4817[2] 5743[14] 6352[7] (6808)

Woolston Ferry (IRE) *David Pinder* a67 47
4 b g Fath(USA) —Cathy Garcia (IRE) (Be My Guest (USA))
83[9] 289[3] 444[5] (845) 1585[10] 2188[10] 2967[12] 3279[7] 4232[10] 5077[9] (5767) 5962[3] 6671[12] 6903[3] 7168[2] 7439[11]

Woop Woop (IRE) *Stef Higgins* a69
2 b f Oratorio(IRE) —Nihonpillow Mirai (IRE) (Zamindar (USA))
7088[5] 7309[4] 7893[3] 7962[3] 8001[2] 8031[2]

Wootton Bassett *Richard Fahey* 120
2 b c Iffraaj—Balladonia (Primo Dominie)
(3199) ◆ (4049) (5245) (5880) (6610a)

Word Of Warning *Martin Todhunter* 58
6 gr g War Chant(USA) —Frosty Welcome (USA) (With Approval (CAN))
3669[8] 4854[6] ◆

Workforce *Sir Michael Stoute* 130
3 b c King's Best(USA) —Soviet Moon (IRE) (Sadler's Wells (USA))
2056[2] (2746) ◆ 4359[5] (6612a)

Workin For Hops (USA) *Michael Stidham* 111
3 ch g City Zip(USA) —Citi Pearl (USA) (Citidancer (USA))
5319a[3]

World Heritage *P Bary* 114
4 b h Kahyasi—Imbabala (Zafonic (USA))
3045a[5] 6344a[10]

Worldly Wise *Patrick J Flynn* a94 100
7 b g Namid—Tina Heights (Shirley Heights)
4463a[3] 5571a[8]

World Ruler *Doug Watson* a85 90
5 b g Dansili—Revealing (Halling (USA))
412a[12]

Worthadd (IRE) *Vittorio Caruso* 111
3 b c Dubawi(IRE) —Wigman (USA) (Rahy (USA))
(1418a) (1945a) 6764a[3] (7372a)

Worth A King'S *Donald McCain* a93 90
4 b g Red Ransom(USA) —Top Romance (IRE) (Entrepreneur)
252[8]

Wotashirtfull (IRE) *David Nicholls* a89 89
5 ch g Namid—Madrina (Waajib)
74[4] 446[3] 846[2] 972[3] 986[2] 1506[5] 3065[11] 3529[4]

Wotatomboy *Richard Whitaker* a56 53
4 ch m Captain Rio—Keen Melody (USA) (Sharpen Up)
1922[7] (2263) 2789[5] 3026[5] 3615[7] 4868[10] 5024[6] 6119[8] 6460[12]

Wotitis *Bill Turner*
2 b c Avonbridge—Chalet (Singspiel (IRE))
1065[11] 1794[7]

Wotsthehurry *Mick Channon* a61 70
2 b f Proclamation(IRE) —Lalina (GER) (Trempolino (USA))
1043[4] 1173[5] (3636) 3864[4] 4872[4] ◆ 5452[12] 6259[7]

Wovoka (IRE) *Kevin Ryan* a81 86
7 b g Mujadil(USA) —Common Cause (Polish Patriot (USA))
1028[6] 1117[3] 1396[8] 1926[10] 2204[5] 3732[4] 4088[7]

Wow Wow Wow (USA) *D Wayne Lukas* a92
3 b c Broken Vow(USA) —Caged Glory (USA) (Honour And Glory (USA))
824a[8]

Wrecking Crew (IRE) *Rod Millman* a55 28
6 b g Invincible Spirit(IRE) —Rushing (Deploy)
4681[13] 5254[12] 5584[11] 7043[8] 7508[9] 7703[4] 7896[6]

Wrekin Rock (IRE) *J T Gorman* 39
2 br c Statue Of Liberty(USA) —Orpendonna (IRE) (Orpen (USA))
954a[9]

Wrekin Sunset *Mrs K Burke* 60
2 ch f Doyen(IRE) —Sienna Sunset (IRE) (Spectrum (IRE))
6964[4] 7302[5]

Wreningham *Stuart Williams* a69 66
5 br g Diktat—Slave To The Rythm (IRE) (Hamas (IRE))
137[8] 723[3] (1131) 1391[2] 1638[3] 2301[2] 3211[2] 3440[4] 3994[2] 4659[5] (5562) 6880[10]

Wrens Hope *Neville Bycroft* 36
4 ch m Shinko Forest(IRE) —Star Dancer (Groom Dancer (USA))
4014[10]

Wrighty Almighty (IRE) *Patrick Chamings* a66 65
8 b g Danehill Dancer(IRE) —Persian Empress (IRE) (Persian Bold)
(444) 804[3] 1047[8] 1763[8] 2362[5] 3323[9]

Wrong Answer *Kevin Prendergast* a86 101
3 gr f Verglas(IRE) —Wrong Key (IRE) (Key Of Luck (USA))
1036a[11] 1676a[4] 4269a[4] 4882a[7] 6009a[4] 6617a[8]

Wrongwayround (IRE) *Alan Swinbank* a68 71
4 b g Barathea(IRE) —Almansa (IRE) (Dr Devious (IRE))
570[2] 718[3] 963[6] (1526) 1751[11] 2142[5] 2670[7] 3707[10]

Wuhan (GER) *S Smrczek* 94
3 b c One Cool Cat(USA) —Winterthur (GER) (Alkalde (GER))
1564a[3] 5671a[8]

Wulfrida (IRE) *James Fanshawe* a83 79
3 b f King's Best(USA) —Panna (Polish Precedent (USA))
1485[2] 2219[6] 3764[2] 4893[3] 5141[2] 6055[3] (6499)

Wunderkind (GER) *P Chatelain* a74 90
5 b g Pivotal—White Heat (Last Tycoon)
207a[4] 303a[6] 459a[5] 559a[0]

Wunder Strike (USA) *Jim Boyle* a73 64
4 b g Smart Strike(CAN) —Bishop's Mate (USA) (Lyphard (USA))
(11) 84[4] 2236[9] 2821[13] 3514[8] 4057[9] 4586[5] 6452[12]

Wusuul *Seamus Mullins* a60 34
5 br m Kyllachy—Cartuccia (IRE) (Doyoun)
3028[12]

Wyatt Earp (IRE) *Peter Salmon* a79 92
9 b g Piccolo—Tribal Lady (Absalom)
(404) 703[5] 1366[8] 1924[12] (2206) 2982[11] 3321[7] 3898[8] 4670[8] 5684[2] 6962[14] 7526[10]

Wyeth *Gary Moore* a63 67
6 ch g Grand Lodge(USA) —Bordighera (USA) (Alysheba (USA))
7570 [4]

Wyomia (USA) *Daniel J Vella* a109 91
2 bb f Vindication(USA) —Beyond The Sun (USA) (Kingmambo (USA))
7340a[6]

Wysiwyg Lucky (FR) *J-L Gay* a72 95
7 b m Ultimately Lucky(IRE) —Les Estelles (FR) (Dress Parade)
742a[5] 4276a[4]

Xclaim *Clive Cox* 57
2 ch c Proclamation(IRE) —Tahara (IRE) (Caerleon (USA))
6474[8] 7094[7]

Xenes *R Menichetti* a102 102
6 b h Xaar—Lucia Tarditi (FR) (Crystal Glitters (USA))
1944a[15] 4185a[11]

Xenophon *Gavin Blake* a32 44
2 b g Phoenix Reach(IRE) —Comtesse Noire (CAN) (Woodman (USA))
6036[8] 6414[8] 6742[7]

Xeralda (IRE) *Clive Cox* a22 40
3 b f Xaar—Fawaayid (USA) (Vaguely Noble)
5153[3] 5872[7]
Xilerator (IRE) *David Nicholls* a72 91
3 b g Arakan(USA) —Grandel (Owington)
(911) 6197[2] ◆ 7955[6]
Xpres Maite *Roy Bowring* a93 73
7 b g Komaite(USA) —Antonias Melody (Rambo Dancer (CAN))
71[4] 466[5] 837[2] 1177[10] 1426[4] 1628[6] 5819[7] 6116[4]
X Rated *Alan McCabe* a71
2 b g Dubai Destination(USA) —Miss Satamixa (FR) (Linamix (FR))
6874[11] 7126[7] 7325[3] 7470[5]
Xtension (IRE) *Clive Cox* 117
3 b c Xaar—Great Joy (IRE) (Grand Lodge (USA))
1699[4] 2354a[5] 3719a[3] 4420a[4]
Yaa Wayl (IRE) *Michael Jarvis* 115
3 b g Whipper(USA) —Lidanna (Nicholas (USA))
(1834) 2712[2] (3591) 4358[4] ◆ (5275) 6147[12] 6570[3]
Yab Adee *Marcus Tregoning* a67 50
6 b g Mark Of Esteem(IRE) —Kotdiji (Mtoto)
5208[8] 5813[10]
Ya Boy Sir (IRE) *Noel Wilson* a52 63
3 ch c Alhaarth(IRE) —Champs Elysees (USA) (Distant Relative)
167[8] 1667[7] 2432[3] (3167) 3410[6] (4194) 4567[9] 4826[5] 5481[6] 6103[19] 7052[5]
Yabtree (IRE) *Roger Charlton* a33 74
3 b c Clodovil(IRE) —Lorientaise (IRE) (Xaar)
1873[7] 2398[5] (3171) 3676[5] 4335[4] 5086[7] 5861[4] 6692[5]
Yachtmaster (IRE) *John Quinn* a40 57
2 gr g Choisir(AUS) —Brooks Masquerade (Absalom)
3658[9] 4782[4] 5294[7] 5818[5] 6694[9]
Ya Hafed *Ed Dunlop* a64 59
2 ch c Haafhd—Rule Britannia (Night Shift (USA))
3326[9] 3767[4] 4253[3] 4716[4]
Yahafedh Alaih *Clive Brittain* 47
2 ch c Haafhd—Farhana (Fayruz)
3991[8]
Yahrab (IRE) *Declan Carroll* a106 109
5 gr g Dalakhani(IRE) —Loire Valley (IRE) (Sadler's Wells (USA))
553[9] 738[4] 946[5] 1328[8] 1712a[8] 2318[6] 2640[9] 7591[9]
Yair Hill (IRE) *John Dunlop* 77
2 b c Selkirk(USA) —Conspiracy (Rudimentary (USA))
3794[6] ◆ 5032[2] 5954[3] 6825[2]
Yajala *E Borromeo* a88 88
4 b m Fasliyev(USA) —Desacara (Arctic Tern (USA))
1419a[12]
Yakama (IRE) *Christine Dunnett* a59 61
5 b g Indian Danehill(IRE) —Working Progress (IRE) (Marju (IRE))
124[13] 691[4] 794[4] 854[3] 976[2] 984[3] 1437[5] 1633[10] 2198[4] (2299) 2490[3] 2876[7] 7768[4] 8023[2]
Yamal (IRE) *Saeed Bin Suroor* a108 115
5 b g Green Desert(USA) —Pioneer Bride (USA) (Gone West (USA))
3354[2] 4050[3] 4455[14]
Yamanin Kingly (JPN) *Hiroshi Kawachi* 115
5 ch h Agnes Digital(USA) —Yamanin Arena (JPN) (Sunday Silence (USA))
2154a[11]
Yana (IND) *B Chenoy* 94
6 b m Razeen(USA) —Zaya (USA) (Riverman (USA))
439a[9]
Yanbu (USA) *Terry Clement* 45
5 b m Swain(IRE) —Dufoof (USA) (Kingmambo (USA))
4835[4] 6061[8]
Yankee Bright (USA) *James Given* 75
3 b f Elusive Quality(USA) —Sharp Minister (CAN) (Deputy Minister (CAN))
2219[9] 2697[2] 3242[3] 4557[2] 4965[4] 5420[7] 6038[11]
Yankee Storm *Hugh Collingridge* a80 65
5 b g Yankee Gentleman(USA) —Yes Virginia (USA) (Roanoke (USA))
1929[12] 2643[7] 2965[5] (3279) ◆ (3970) 4929[3] 5754[6] 6098[2] 7006[5] 7154[5] 7525[7] 7737[3] 7766[5] 7934[3] 8033[2]
Yarooh (USA) *Clive Brittain* a75 77
2 b f Medaglia D'Oro(USA) —Country Maiden (USA) (Forest Camp (USA))
1324[2] 1728[4] 2130[3] (2474) 3070[17] 4020[8] 4429[9]
Yarra River *Andrew Balding* a71 80
3 b g Dr Fong(USA) —River Cara (USA) (Irish River (FR))
1542[4] 1782[4] 2416[9] 3786[3]
Yarubo (FR) *J-C Rouget* 100
2 ch c Muhtathir—Miss Mission (IRE) (Second Empire (IRE))
(5251a)
Yaseer (IRE) *Marcus Tregoning* a83 75
2 b c Dansili—Tadris (USA) (Red Ransom (USA))
7099[2] (7873) ◆
Yashila (IRE) *Richard Hannon* 72
2 b f Indian Haven—Tara's Girl (IRE) (Fayruz)
4471[5] ◆ 5527[6]
Yashrid (USA) *Michael Jarvis* a85 90
3 b g Rahy(USA) —Sheroog (USA) (Shareef Dancer (USA))
950[5] ◆ 1127[9] 1959[3] (2422) 2893[2] (3519) (4360) ◆ 4815[10] 6074[10]
Yas Marina (USA) *Mahmood Al Zarooni* 49
2 bb c Bernardini(USA) —Silvery Swan (USA) (Silver Deputy (CAN))
6566[5] 6883[18]
Yasmeena (USA) *B W Hills* 74
2 ch f Mr Greeley(USA) —La Cucaracha (Piccolo)
4753[3] (5466)
Yasoodd *D Selvaratnam* a93 103
7 br g Inchinor—Needwood Epic (Midyan (USA))
440a[2] 610a[7] 823a[8]
Yawanna Twist (USA) *Richard Dutrow Jr* a116
3 b c Yonaguska(USA) —Twist And Pop (USA) (Oliver's Twist (USA))
824a[2] 2137a[4]
Yawary *Clive Brittain* a87 74
3 b f Medicean—Sociable (Danehill (USA))
346[4] (574) (1070) 1613[5] 3505[6]
Yeah *Patrick Morris* a50 53
3 b g Gentleman's Deal(IRE) —Snugfit Dubarry (Ali-Royal (IRE))
689[5] 870[7] 1118[8] 1465[8]
Yehonala (USA) *John Best* a44 15
3 b f Jump Start(USA) —Ross Valay (USA) (Two Punch (USA))
985[11] 1278[15] 1590[8] 3291[14]
Yellow Dandy (IRE) *Liam McAteer* 75
2 b f Kheleyf(USA) —Groves Preneur (IRE) (Entrepreneur)
(6419) 6916[5] 7174[4]
Yellowstone (IRE) *Paul Cole* a92 96
6 b h Rock Of Gibraltar(IRE) —Love And Affection (USA) (Exclusive Era (USA))
1020[5] 1472[5]
Yemeni Princess (IRE) *Brendan Powell* a69 81
4 b m Bahri(USA) —Celtic Ballet (Celtic Swing)
669[4] 803[2] 1451[5] 1755[2] 2341[5] (3127) (4141) 5035[5] 5996[7]
Yensi *George Baker* a57 57
3 b f Doyen(IRE) —Sifat (Marju (IRE))
7183[3] ◆ (7413)
Yeomanry *Ian Williams* a49
5 b g High Chaparral(IRE) —Charming Life (NZ) (Sir Tristram)
7579[4] 7703[5] 7896[5]
Yer Woman (IRE) *Richard Hannon* a95 92
3 b f Kyllachy—Genny Lim (IRE) (Barathea (IRE))
772[4] 901[3] (1019) ◆ 2090[5] 3790[12] 4551[5] 5521[3] 6319[15] 7289[6] 7522[6] ◆
Yes Chef *John Gallagher* 75
3 ch g Best Of The Bests(IRE) —Lady Chef (Double Trigger (IRE))
1029[10] 1442[3] 1776[3] 2253[4] 2888[13] 3558[2] 4325[2] 5086[3] 5838[6]
Yes Missus (IRE) *Patrick J Flynn* 70
3 ch f Alamshar(IRE) —Savage (IRE) (Polish Patriot (USA))
4496a[9]
Yes Mr President (IRE) *Mark Johnston* a82 111
5 b g Montjeu(IRE) —Royals Special (IRE) (Caerleon (USA))
(1139) ◆ 1615[5] 2071[2] 2574a[6]
Yes We Can *Jeremy Gask* a64 67
3 b f Alhaarth(IRE) —Windermere Island (Cadeaux Genereux)
(5810) 6501[7] 7093[7] 7483[13]
Ykikamoocow *Geoffrey Harker* 72
4 b m Cape Town(IRE) —Pigeon (Casteddu)
2429[3] 3180[6] 6116[9]
Ymir *Michael Attwater* a61 58
4 b g Zaha(CAN) —Anastasia Venture (Lion Cavern (USA))
11[8] 1170[11] 1772[8] 2965[12] 4308[10] 5555[4] 7555[2] 7649[8] 7885[10]
Yodelen Dan (USA) *Kristin Mulhall* 85
7 bb g Swiss Yodeler(USA) —Domasco Danielle (CAN) (Same Direction (CAN))
1435a[7]
Yojimbo (IRE) *Mick Channon* a74 74
2 gr c Aussie Rules(USA) —Mythie (FR) (Octagonal (NZ))
6196[2] ◆ 6443[4] 6849[2]
Yonder *Hughie Morrison* a67 72
6 br m And Beyond(IRE) —Dominance (Dominion)
164[6] 3352[5] 4026[5] 5011[3] 5828[7] 7101[10]
Yorgunnabelucky (USA) *Mark Johnston* 97
4 b h Giant's Causeway(USA) —Helsinki (Machiavellian (USA))
3121[4] 3318[9] (3995) 4306[11] (4711) (4818) 5217[15] 5949[13]
Yorketa *Michael Dods* a49 51
2 br f Needwood Blade—Mykeyta (Key Of Luck (USA))
6459[2] 6891[5] 7271[3] 7396[4]
Yorksters Prince (IRE) *George Prodromou* a62 50
3 b g Beat Hollow—Odalisque (IRE) (Machiavellian (USA))
106[5] 422[7] (670) 805[3] 840[6] 904[5] 1608[9] 2477[10] 3113[9] 5891[6] 6287[12]
Yosha (IRE) *P Demercastel* 72
2 ch f Peintre Celebre(USA) —Double Platinum (Seeking The Gold (USA))
4884a[6]
Yosolito (FR) *L A Urbano-Grajales* a88 97
3 b g Keltos(FR) —Fusee Francaise (FR) (Anabaa (USA))
1610a[2]
Yossi (IRE) *Richard Guest* a63 83
6 b g Montjeu(IRE) —Raindancing (IRE) (Tirol)
4405[11] 4907[4] 5333[4] 5790[12] 6065[6] 6832[8] 7147[5] 7306[7] 7407[4] 7541[2] 7642[2] 7729[2] 7933[2] 7958[4]
You And I Forever (USA) *Thomas Bush* a112
5 b h A.P. Indy(USA) —You (USA) (You And I (USA))
5779a[8]
Youhavecontrol (IRE) *Michael Dods* 34
2 b c Hawk Wing(USA) —Chameleon (Green Desert (USA))
6458[5]
You'll Be Mine (USA) *A P O'Brien* a96 105
3 b f Kingmambo(USA) —Quarter Moon (IRE) (Sadler's Wells (USA))
1036a[9] 5568a[11] 6379a[7] 6928[6] 7358a[4]
Youm Al Mizayin *Mick Channon* a52 61
3 b f Cape Cross(IRE) —Silent (JPN) (Sunday Silence (USA))
3407[6] 3924[6] 4397[8] 5379[4] 5729[4] (6076) 6413[7]
Youm Jamil (USA) *Brian Meehan* 82
3 rg g Mizzen Mast(USA) —Millie's Choice (IRE) (Taufan (USA))
1387[3] 1824[7] 2692[2] 3215[8] (5288) 6097[8]
You Mug *Sean Curran*
3 b g Denounce—Zaras Legend (Midnight Legend)
6275[8]
Youmzain (IRE) *Mick Channon* 125
7 b h Sinndar(IRE) —Sadima (IRE) (Sadler's Wells (USA))
1026a[8] 2709[4] 3494a[2] 4359[3] 6612a[10]
Young Dottie *Pat Phelan* a83 70
4 b m Desert Sun—Auntie Dot Com (Tagula (IRE))
239[11] 284[7] 3813[5] 5237[3] (7521) ◆ 7637[7]
Young Firth *John Norton* a23 52
3 b g Lucky Story(USA) —Le Petit Diable (IRE) (Trans Island)
1830[6] 6631[7] 7145[7]
Young George *Chris Fairhurst* a49 10
3 b g Danroad(AUS) —Bo' Babbity (Strong Gale)
209[4] 471[5] 619[5] 906[7] 1181[7]
Young Gladiator (IRE) *Julie-Ann Camacho* a73 72
5 b g Spartacus(IRE) —Savona (IRE) (Cyrano De Bergerac)
(378) 602[5] 907[2] 1115[4] 1492[2] 6110[11] 7403[6]
Young Jackie *George Margarson* 39
2 b f Doyen(IRE) —Just Warning (Warning)
7231[14]
Young Lochinvar (IRE) *John G Carr* a44 79
6 b g Pivotal—Phariseek (IRE) (Rainbow Quest (USA))
7229[7]
Young Sahib (USA) *Brian Meehan* 49
2 ch g Mr Greeley(USA) —Carefree Cheetah (USA) (Trempolino (USA))
4096[10] 4899[6] 5871[6]
Young Scotton *Chris Grant* a71 58
10 b g Cadeaux Genereux—Broken Wave (Bustino)
4174[7]
Young Simon *George Margarson* a57 68
3 ch g Piccolo—Fragrant Cloud (Zilzal (USA))
1280[4] 1604[4] 2459[2] 2906[9] 4025[6] 5162[4] 6657[8] 7005[12] 7440[3] 7555[4] 7717[6] 8023[5]
You'relikemefrank *John Balding* a73 61
4 ch g Bahamian Bounty—Proudfoot (IRE) (Shareef Dancer (USA))
860[7] 1234[7] 1598[5] 2721[3] (3299) 3623[2] (4239) ◆ 5055[4] 5502[2] 5697[2] (7720) 7859[5] (8036)
Your Gifted (IRE) *Patrick Morris* a65 72
3 b f Trans Island—Dame Laura (IRE) (Royal Academy (USA))
399[4] 662[6] 991[3] 1118[13] (1155) 1468[6] 1667[6] 1774[2] 2026[9] 6965[11] 7148[9] (7808) 7859[3] 7953[2]
Yourgolftravel Com *Michael Wigham* a62 68
5 b g Fasliyev(USA) —Hiddnah (USA) (Affirmed (USA))
356[6] 443[6] 615[12] 773[6] 1170[8] (1633) 2198[3] 2490[2] 2781[2] 3054[2] 3290[7] 3863[5] 4108[12] 4439[4] 5172[6] 5767[3] 6934[12]
Your Lad *Chris Wall* a58
3 b c Dubawi(IRE) —Krisalya (Kris)
128[8] (372)
Yours *Kevin Ryan* a34
2 b f Piccolo—Uno (Efisio)
7681[4]
You've Been Mowed *Richard Price* a58 78
4 ch m Ishiguru(USA) —Sandblaster (Most Welcome)
2920[6] (3558) 3854[5] 4324[2] 4548[4] 4905[7] 5386[5] 5833[8] 6260[9] 6671[10]
Yungaburra (IRE) *David C Griffiths* a55 65
6 b g Fath(USA) —Nordic Living (IRE) (Nordico (USA))
2849[11] 3322[9] 3516[7] 4431[8] (4606) 4869[3]
Yurituni *Eve Johnson Houghton* a77 84
3 b f Bahamian Bounty—Vax Star (Petong)
1281[3] 1499[6] 1917[9] 2442[6] 2807[5] 3726[2] 3834[5] 4424[9] 5588[2] 5809[10] (6303) 6772[11] 6981[8] 7320[6] 7494[10]
Zaahy (USA) *Peter Chapple-Hyam* a99 90
3 ch c More Than Ready(USA) —Sangam (USA) (Majestic Light (USA))
1221[2] ◆ 2471[7] 3103[27]
Zabarajad (IRE) *John M Oxx* 78
2 b c Invincible Spirit(IRE) —Zalaiyma (FR) (Rainbow Quest (USA))
4175a[3]
Zabeel Palace *Barney Curley* a48 87
8 b g Grand Lodge(USA) —Applecross (Glint Of Gold)
1493[6] 6132[13] 6578[9]
Zabeel Park (USA) *Saeed Bin Suroor* a62 91
2 ch f Medicean—Musical Treat (IRE) (Royal Academy (USA))
2641[3] (3237) 4611a[2]
Zabeel Tower *Dick Allan* a10 76
7 b g Anabaa(USA) —Bint Kaldoun (IRE) (Kaldoun (FR))
3357[10] 3500[4] 3990[4] 4515[4] 4796[8] 5024[10] 5406[7] 6026[3]
Zacinto *Sir Michael Stoute* 123
4 b h Dansili—Ithaca (USA) (Distant View (USA))
2118[9] 3046[4] 3693[5] 4412[5]
Zack Hall (FR) *M Delzangles* 106
3 b c Muhtathir—Halawa (IRE) (Dancing Brave (USA))
6974a[6]
Zack Yield (FR) *A Lamotte D'Argy* 97
2 ch c High Yield(USA) —Zafarana (FR) (Shernazar)
6973a[4] 7544a[9]
Zacynthus (IRE) *Mahmood Al Zarooni* 90
2 ch c Iffraaj—Ziria (IRE) (Danehill Dancer (IRE))
(3452) 4036a[3]
Zafaraan *Peter Chapple-Hyam* 52
2 b f Royal Applause—Sakhya (IRE) (Barathea (IRE))
6804[6]
Zafeen's Pearl *Dean Ivory* a64
3 ch f Zafeen(FR) —Deep Sea Pearl (Dr Fong (USA))
385[10] 677[6] 872[5] (7070) (7874)
Zaffeu *Alan Juckes* a66 44
9 ch g Zafonic(USA) —Leaping Flame (USA) (Trempolino (USA))
190[5] 456[5] (506) 1071[4] 1759[8]
Zafisio (IRE) *F J Brennan* 114
4 b h Efisio—Goldthroat (IRE) (Zafonic (USA))
6006a[8]
Zafranagar (IRE) *Tony Carroll* a61 55
5 b g Cape Cross(IRE) —Zafaraniya (IRE) (Doyoun)
355[6] 6957[8]
Zafrina *Peter Grayson* a7
2 ch f Dubai Destination(USA) —Sophielu (Rudimentary (USA))
2641[10] 3260[8] 5667[10]
Zagarock *Bryn Palling* a49 52
3 b f Rock Of Gibraltar(IRE) —Zagaleta (Sri Pekan (USA))
5584[10] 6375[9] 6862[5]
Zagora (FR) *J-C Rouget* 111
3 ch f Green Tune(USA) —Zaneton (FR) (Mtoto)
(1746a) 3015a[5] (4612a) 5346a[3]
Zaheeb *Mick Channon* 7
2 b c Haafhd—Gay Music (FR) (Gay Mecene (USA))
6689[17]
Zahoo (IRE) *John Dunlop* 101
3 b f Nayef(USA) —Tanaghum (Darshaan)
1502[5] ◆ 2047[5] 5991[3] ◆ 6691[2] 7062[3] (7206) 7349[2]
Zahraan (IRE) *Marcus Tregoning* a53 74
2 b c Elusive City(USA) —Rihana (IRE) (Priolo (USA))
5381[7] 6149[7]
Zaidan (USA) *Clive Brittain* 104
2 bb c Street Cry(IRE) —Element Of Truth (USA) (Atticus (USA))
(1686) ◆ (3190) 5079[4] 7081[8]
Zaif (IRE) *Dominic Ffrench Davis* a68 65
7 b g Almutawakel—Colourful (FR) (Gay Mecene (USA))
2199[4] 2455[5] 2845[3] 3221[5] 3917[3] 4070[5] 4386[3] 5011[5] 6022[9] 6272[8]
Zain Al Boldan *Mick Channon* 72
2 b f Poliglote—Carla (FR) (Cardoun (FR))
(4736)
Zain Shamardal (IRE) *Brian Meehan* a84 84
2 b c Shamardal(USA) —Novelina (IRE) (Fusaichi Pegasus (USA))
5690[3] ◆ 6474[3] 7112[2]
Zaisan (FR) *Mme L Audon* 44
4 b g Numerous(USA) —Zghorta (USA) (Gone West (USA))
221a[9]
Zakeeta (IRE) *Oliver Sherwood* a53 61
3 b f Intikhab(USA) —Julianne (IRE) (Persian Bold)
1132[9] 1358[7] 7834[3]
Zakiy *William Haggas* a83 81
3 b c Selkirk(USA) —Epiphany (Zafonic (USA))
1659[4] 2755[2] (2981) 4357[10] 5030[4] 5968[11]
Zakon (IRE) *Denis Coakley* a45 71
2 b g Ivan Denisovich(IRE) —Franny (Selkirk (USA))
2677[5] 3399[3] 4054[3] 4993[3] 6411[2] ◆ 6859[5]
Zakumi (IRE) *L Riccardi*
2 br f Hurricane Run(IRE) —Kykuit (IRE) (Green Desert (USA))
6975a[11]
Zalano *Derek Haydn Jones* a63
2 b g Zafeen(FR) —Alvarinho Lady (Royal Applause)
4909[5] 5643[3] 6308[6]
Zalkani (IRE) *Jeff Pearce* a66 47
10 ch g Cadeaux Genereux—Zallaka (IRE) (Shardari)
1188[7] 1980[12]
Zambuka (FR) *F J Brennan* a35 68
3 gr f Zieten(USA) —Mercalle (FR) (Kaldoun (FR))
915[6] 1261[7] 1495[11] 4061[3] (4344) 4585[7] 5593[6] 6629[10]
Zamid (FR) *Richard Fahey* 43
3 b f Namid—Zarkana (IRE) (Doyoun)
1685[12] 2434[7] 2741[10] 4951[6] 5201[9] 6579[11]
Zamina (IRE) *Sylvester Kirk* a67 66
2 b f Hawk Wing(USA) —Termania (IRE) (Shirley Heights)
3295[4] 4437[3] 6070[6] 6542[2] 6936[2] 7242[4] 7393[5]
Zanazzi (USA) *John Gosden* a74 78
2 b f Bernardini(USA) —Silken Cat (CAN) (Storm Cat (USA))
2642[2] 3296[2] 3861[2]
Zaplamation (IRE) *John Quinn* a40 76
5 b g Acclamation—Zapatista (Rainbow Quest (USA))
(1204) (1296) 1631[2] 1867[3] 2579[5] 2859[5] 6243[5] 6573[2]
Zaralabad (IRE) *C F Swan* a86 95
6 b g Fantastic Light(USA) —Zarannda (IRE) (Last Tycoon)
1560a[5] 3447[15] 6786a[6] 6971a[4]
Zarazar *David Evans* 69
2 b g Statue Of Liberty(USA) —Babaraja (Dancing Spree (USA))
1180[6] 2598[2] 3849[3] 5675[11]
Zardana (BRZ) *John Shirreffs* a109 101
6 b m Crimson Tide(IRE) —Dear Filly (ARG) (Southern Halo (USA))
3044a[3]
Zarebiya (IRE) *John M Oxx* 102
3 b f Galileo(IRE) —Zarlana (IRE) (Darshaan)
4631a[3] ◆ 5249[10]
Zareena *David Evans* a34
2 b f Needwood Blade—Samadilla (IRE) (Mujadil (USA))
7682[6] 7858[7] 7913[7]
Zarilan (IRE) *Michael Smith* a51 61
5 b g Namid—Zarlana (IRE) (Darshaan)
4154[11] 4487[5] 6110[P]
Zarius *Chris Wall* a63 54
3 br g Zamindar(USA) —Slave To The Rythm (IRE) (Hamas (IRE))
5028[12] 5658[12] 6655[6] 7153[5] 7401[3] 7863[7]
Zariyan (FR) *Mlle C Nicot* a69 79
7 b g Anabaa(USA) —Zarkana (IRE) (Doyoun)
460a[8]

Zarly (FR) *F Rohaut* 78
3 gr c Fairly Ransom(USA) —Besca Nueva (FR) (Lesotho (USA))
450a[3]

Zartina (IRE) *Sylvester Kirk* a45 39
2 b f Antonius Pius(USA) —Miss Assertive (Zafonic (USA))
6688[7] 7311[10]

Zauberin (IRE) *J-P Carvalho* 66
3 b f Nayef(USA) —Zauberflote (GER) (Lomitas)
1252a[8]

Zaungast (IRE) *W Hickst* 108
6 b h Alkalde(GER) —Zauberwelt (Polar Falcon (USA))
3251a[4] 7102a[10]

Zavite (NZ) *Anthony Cummings* 116
8 b g Zabeel(NZ) —Miss Vita (USA) (Alleged (USA))
6947a[7] ◆ 7291a[22]

Zawadi *Ralph Beckett* 52
3 ch f Zamindar(USA) —Shasta (Shareef Dancer (USA))
4661[10] 5376[5] 5971[7] 6454[14] 6993[10]

Zayaan *Kevin Prendergast* a61 100
3 b c Motivator—Mufradat (IRE) (Desert Prince (IRE))
1786a[3] 2367a[7] 4160a[9]

Za Za Zoom (IRE) *B W Hills* 100
3 b f Le Vie Dei Colori—Emma's Star (ITY) (Darshaan)
3071[15] 4126[4] 5609[2] 5883[12] 6830[8] 7083[6]

Zazou (GER) *Mario Hofer* 112
3 b c Shamardal(USA) —Zaza Top (GER) (Lomitas)
(1564a) 2159a[6] (3018a) 4184a[2] 5132a[3] 6592a[9] 7373a[4]

Zazous *John Bridger* a55 30
9 b g Zafonic(USA) —Confidentiality (USA) (Lyphard (USA))
320[14] 591[11] 691[13] 5555[7]

Zeavola (IRE) *Andrew Balding* a65 26
2 ch f Choisir(AUS) —Gamble In Gold (IRE) (Monashee Mountain (USA))
7123[7] 7408[9] 7517[4] 7734[4] 7913[4]

Zebedee *Richard Hannon* 108
2 gr c Invincible Spirit(IRE) —Cozy Maria (USA) (Cozzene (USA))
(1263) (1612) 3100[5] (3630) (4458) ◆ (5527) (5907)

Zebrano *Andrew Haynes* a87 83
4 br g Storming Home—Ambience Lady (Batshoof)
2926[8] 4065[8] 5561[6] 5838[4] 6366[2] ◆ 6958[4] 7121[6] (7597) 7735[5]

Zed Candy (FR) *Richard Ford* a64 58
7 b g Medicean—Intrum Morshaan (IRE) (Darshaan)
3760[5] 7157[2] 7634[3] 7805[2]

Zeffirelli *Michael Quinn* a65 48
5 ch g Tomba—Risky Valentine (Risk Me (FR))
(116) 378[7] 571[4] 839[7] (965) 1585[12] 6061[10] 7007[9] 7502[5]

Zefooha (FR) *Tim Walford* a68 68
6 ch m Lomitas—Bezzaaf (Machiavellian (USA))
2610[3] 3600[2] 4174[6] 4900[2] 5420[2] 5687[2] 6028[6] 6921[7]

Zegna (IRE) *Bryan Smart* a86 78
4 gr g Clodovil(IRE) —Vade Retro (IRE) (Desert Sun)
384[2]

Zelos Diktator *Gary Moore* a58 63
4 br g Diktat—Chanterelle (IRE) (Indian Ridge)
3352[4] 3989[4] 5289[2] 5813[2] 6021[2] 6775[10] 7315[8] 7759[3]

Zelos Dream (IRE) *Ronald Harris* a62 64
3 ch f Redback—Endless Peace (IRE) (Russian Revival (USA))
209[5] 276[6]

Zelos Spirit *Rae Guest* a44 41
3 b f Tiger Hill(IRE) —Good Mood (USA) (Devil's Bag (USA))
2004[9] 2535[5] 4155[8] 4687[5] 4970[4] 5559[6] 6255[9] 6841[7]

Zenarinda *Mark H Tompkins* 74
3 b f Zamindar(USA) —Tenpence (Bob Back (USA))
1132[2] ◆ 4127[6] 4762[4] 5541[6] 5902 [2] 6356[2] 6535[4]

Zenella *Ann Duffield* a91 93
2 b f Kyllachy—West One (Gone West (USA))
(5099) 6083[3] 6627[2] (6982)

Zenyatta (USA) *John Shirreffs* a128
6 bb m Street Cry(IRE) —Vertigineux (USA) (Kris S (USA))
(1242a) (3044a) (4887a) (6603a) 7367a[2]

Zephyron (IRE) *John Holt* a62
3 b g Wizard King—Savona (IRE) (Cyrano De Bergerac)
267[5] 594[4] 915[4] 1490[6] 4197[7]

Zerashan (IRE) *M Halford* 92
3 b c Azamour(IRE) —Zarannda (IRE) (Last Tycoon)
6786a[10]

Zero Cool (USA) *Gary Moore* a67 56
6 br g Forestry(USA) —Fabulous (USA) (Seeking The Gold (USA))
353[2] (396) 676[4] 941[4] 1592[4] 2752[5] 2966[3] 5146[7] 5680[6] 5840[11]

Zero Money (IRE) *Roger Charlton* a77 98
4 ch g Bachelor Duke(USA) —Dawn Chorus (IRE) (Mukaddamah (USA))
1580[2] 2113[11] (3346) (4065) 4924[5] 6178[2] 6888[10]

Zerzura *Paul Howling* a76
4 b g Oasis Dream—River Fantasy (USA) (Irish River (FR))
(291) 487[9] 1128[10] 1623[3] 2723[10] 3079[4] 3330[6]

Zhukhov (IRE) *T G McCourt* a81 81
7 ch g Allied Forces(USA) —Karameg (IRE) (Danehill (USA))
7225[9]

Zibeling (IRE) *Robert Collet* a79 87
4 b m Cape Cross(IRE) —Zelding (IRE) (Warning)
560a[0] 743a[9]

Zibimix (IRE) *X Nakkachdji* a84 103
6 gr g Linamix(FR) —Izibi (FR) (Saint Cyrien (FR))
(6881a)

Zidane *James Fanshawe* a94 109
8 b g Danzero(AUS) —Juliet Bravo (Glow (USA))
1032[7] ◆ 1727[11] 1903[13]

Zieto (FR) *J-M Capitte* a75 78
6 ch g Zieten(USA) —La Perla (GER) (Dashing Blade)
272a[5]

Zifzaf (USA) *James J Toner* 108
4 b h War Chant(USA) —Futuh (USA) (Diesis)
6237a[5]

Zigato *John Gosden* a85 93
3 b g Azamour(IRE) —Maycocks Bay (Muhtarram (USA))
1059[5] 3563[5] (4258) ◆ (4827) 5747[4]

Ziggy Lee *Stuart Williams* a91 94
4 b g Lujain(USA) —Mary O'Grady (USA) (Swain (IRE))
1580[15] (2094) 2346[2] 2759[5] 5308[6] 6539[2] 7254[5]

Ziking (FR) *A Scharer* 73
5 gr h Kingsalsa(USA) —Zizoune (FR) (Kadrou (FR))
461a[7]

Zing Wing *Paul Cole* a80 80
2 ch f Hawk Wing(USA) —Zietory (Zieten (USA))
5721[2] ◆ 6150[2] (6247)

Zinjbar (USA) *Clive Brittain* a62 70
3 b f Dynaformer(USA) —Renowned Cat (USA) (Storm Cat (USA))
849[4] 3347[5] 4212[5] 5559[8]

Zip Lock (IRE) *Jeremy Noseda* a83 58
4 b g Invincible Spirit(IRE) —Buckle (IRE) (Common Grounds)
6056[2] (6496) 7033[10]

Zipping (AUS) *Robert Hickmott* 123
9 b g Danehill(USA) —Social Scene (IRE) (Grand Lodge (USA))
7291a[4] (7458a)

Zirconeum (SAF) *M F De Kock* 113
5 b m Jallad(USA) —Sweet Sheila (AUS) (Kenmare (FR))
439a[6] 711a[3] 801a[11]

Ziyarid (IRE) *A De Royer-Dupre* 80
2 b c Desert Style(IRE) —Zayanida (IRE) (King's Best (USA))
7265a[9]

Zizany (IRE) *Robert Collet* a80 74
7 b h Zafonic(USA) —Zelda (IRE) (Caerleon (USA))
304a[3] 458a[9] 549a[6] 2446a[6]

Zobenigo (IRE) *L Polito* 98
3 b f Orpen(USA) —Doregan (IRE) (Bahhare (USA))
1419a[3] 1713a[3]

Zoffany (IRE) *A P O'Brien* 115
2 b c Dansili—Tyranny (Machiavellian (USA))
(2035a) 3049[6] (3645a) (4310a) (4880a) 5975a[3]

Zohan (IRE) *Peter Grayson* a6
2 b g Diamond Green(FR) —Catfoot Lane (Batshoof)
2183[8] 2638[10] 5763[12] 7577[10]

Zomerlust *John Quinn* 94
8 b g Josr Algarhoud(IRE) —Passiflora (Night Shift (USA))
1030[9] 1397[8] 1862[6] 3876[4] 4394[2] 5043[3] (5435) 5903[7] 6721[3] 6888[19]

Zoom In *Linda Stubbs* 52
2 b g Indesatchel(IRE) —Korolieva (IRE) (Xaar)
6138[10] 6566[11] 6891[17]

Zoomin (NZ) *Michael Kent* 103
6 br g Pupil(AUS) —River Cat (NZ) (Sir Godfrey (FR))
6946a[3]

Zoowraa *Michael Jarvis* 101
2 b f Azamour(IRE) —Beraysim (Lion Cavern (USA))
(6566) (7098)

Zorija Rose (IRE) *T Stack* 99
5 b m Oasis Dream—No Reservations (IRE) (Commanche Run)
1676a[14] 4269a[9] 6009a[10]

Zowington *Stuart Williams* a55 91
8 gr g Zafonic(USA) —Carmela Owen (Owington)
1267[9] 2094[10] 2973[11] 5087[9] (5915) 6198[15] 7285[8]

Zubova *Derek Shaw* a73 77
3 b f Dubawi(IRE) —Jalousie (IRE) (Barathea (IRE))
2871[10] 3320[4] (3759) 4224[4] 4804[9] (5241) 5648[7] 5716[7] 6212[7] 6395[5] 6794[8]

Zuider Zee (GER) *John Gosden* a81 95
3 b g Sakhee(USA) —Zephyrine (IRE) (Highest Honor (FR))
1046[2] ◆ (1271) 1624[3] (2315) 2758[7] (4571) 5273[4] 5908[6]

Zulu Chief (USA) *M F De Kock* a95 106
5 b g Fusaichi Pegasus(USA) —La Lorgnette (CAN) (Val De L'Orne (FR))
435a[3] 512a[13]

Zuwaar *Paddy Butler* a74 77
5 b g Nayef(USA) —Raheefa (USA) (Riverman (USA))
173[6] 260[2] 426[13] 554[10] 982[11] 5666[9] 5963[12] 7634[11]

INDEX TO MEETINGS FLAT 2010

† Abandoned
* All-Weather
(M) Mixed meeting

Leading Turf Flat Trainers 2010

(27th March - 6th November 2010)

NAME	WINS-RUNS	2nd	3rd	4th	WIN £	TOTAL £	£1 STAKE
Sir Michael Stoute	68 410 17%	73	56	52	£2,232,303	£2,980,338	-108.89
R Hannon	166 1080 15%	157	112	102	£1,850,077	£2,934,426	-159.96
A P O'Brien	7 89 8%	16	6	11	£1,283,570	£2,821,567	-60.92
H R A Cecil	50 243 21%	39	29	31	£1,567,008	£2,166,767	-30.14
M Johnston	145 1095 13%	115	126	108	£1,424,959	£2,072,205	-275.79
R A Fahey	143 1088 13%	114	121	121	£1,225,735	£1,928,489	-261.14
Saeed Bin Suroor	62 326 19%	48	35	34	£1,230,291	£1,865,143	-43.32
J H M Gosden	74 384 19%	58	50	43	£1,018,447	£1,587,440	+5.53
B W Hills	65 459 14%	72	47	53	£840,886	£1,432,868	-88.56
M R Channon	90 814 11%	106	100	104	£565,430	£1,221,684	-173.98
M A Jarvis	64 283 23%	51	38	25	£695,877	£1,163,966	-8.94
W J Haggas	46 279 16%	36	25	25	£882,458	£1,099,565	-62.73
B J Meehan	60 453 13%	40	40	53	£628,336	£1,067,125	-35.00
A M Balding	50 376 13%	39	51	39	£593,085	£969,907	-13.67
D Nicholls	62 492 13%	39	51	54	£627,447	£875,276	-61.62
L M Cumani	53 253 21%	24	28	12	£610,591	£870,645	+36.19
T D Easterby	88 795 11%	104	93	89	£495,399	£838,385	-259.21
M L W Bell	38 313 12%	48	42	22	£473,189	£759,001	-88.69
J Noseda	40 242 17%	34	30	32	£377,112	£707,031	-79.55
K A Ryan	66 581 11%	59	61	59	£352,496	£642,303	-137.58
M Al Zarooni	34 234 15%	36	43	21	£264,756	£593,153	-23.20
D M Simcock	33 265 12%	40	38	36	£354,774	£588,858	-59.07
E A L Dunlop	19 224 8%	32	20	26	£333,677	£566,230	-116.89
C G Cox	18 240 8%	33	37	27	£283,738	£528,139	-36.29
H Candy	23 163 14%	25	26	21	£278,599	£477,525	-21.19
J L Dunlop	37 301 12%	33	27	28	£330,560	£471,776	-63.99
R M Beckett	44 283 16%	26	38	26	£330,955	£453,147	+84.11
R Charlton	40 195 21%	17	15	23	£327,856	£451,615	+53.85
C E Brittain	21 202 10%	13	20	18	£293,547	£429,384	+0.08
Sir Mark Prescott	39 148 26%	25	21	14	£323,092	£427,639	-7.86
P F I Cole	25 289 9%	39	37	26	£204,513	£416,481	-70.75
J S Goldie	34 403 8%	37	43	48	£210,159	£397,782	-191.50
C F Wall	25 192 13%	28	20	27	£259,173	£395,963	-13.48
J R Fanshawe	15 131 11%	24	18	8	£121,951	£380,316	-43.33
H Morrison	31 251 12%	27	22	30	£150,824	£371,687	-53.22
T D Barron	34 250 14%	26	25	25	£250,593	£368,227	+30.53
B Smart	41 319 13%	24	36	35	£204,315	£357,518	-46.66
M Dods	32 311 10%	29	38	32	£243,957	£333,700	-10.75
E S McMahon	21 120 18%	13	16	10	£271,151	£332,328	-12.85
A Fabre	1 2 50%	0	1	0	£255,465	£330,155	+1.50
P D Evans	45 568 8%	54	65	45	£186,162	£316,477	-180.89
W R Swinburn	33 257 13%	24	40	24	£223,584	£310,988	-38.04
D R C Elsworth	19 170 11%	24	20	17	£179,888	£307,146	-28.13
G A Swinbank	42 273 15%	26	28	25	£172,334	£276,682	+10.18
W J Knight	22 157 14%	16	20	20	£174,295	£259,169	+57.60
T P Tate	19 173 11%	17	23	11	£123,969	£253,611	-58.50
J G Given	23 272 8%	34	22	39	£160,473	£240,195	-106.17
M Delzangles	1 6 17%	0	0	0	£227,080	£234,276	+28.00
Mme C Head-Maarek	1 3 33%	0	0	0	£227,080	£227,080	+2.50
M H Tompkins	19 239 8%	19	22	33	£158,283	£222,657	-81.79

Leading Turf Flat Jockeys 2010

(27th March - 6th November 2010)

NAME	WIN-RIDES	2nd	3rd	4th	WIN £	TOTAL £	£1 STAKE
Paul Hanagan	205 1214 17%	139	144	157	£1,334,122	£1,846,556	-172.58
Richard Hughes	192 1098 17%	171	123	113	£2,087,294	£3,169,420	-231.26
Kieren Fallon	140 821 17%	96	104	74	£1,551,075	£2,588,957	-99.39
Ryan Moore	138 784 18%	139	98	86	£2,533,604	£3,928,871	-138.94
Frankie Dettori	123 541 23%	73	70	57	£2,283,288	£3,205,484	-66.94
Joe Fanning	120 895 13%	109	95	105	£523,442	£921,934	-200.22
Jamie Spencer	107 691 15%	99	96	69	£994,746	£1,609,577	-66.52
Neil Callan	106 822 13%	106	91	96	£511,531	£970,896	-223.52
Seb Sanders	102 759 13%	80	90	71	£599,862	£868,259	-255.37
Jim Crowley	101 857 12%	92	82	95	£717,148	£970,334	-58.02
Tom Queally	101 797 13%	94	74	97	£1,991,069	£2,747,565	+39.48
George Baker	101 677 15%	88	64	56	£387,250	£636,099	-110.31
S De Sousa	100 626 16%	68	84	62	£527,258	£736,480	-4.91
William Buick	99 584 17%	78	64	61	£1,237,628	£1,830,623	+5.28
Steve Drowne	96 787 12%	72	79	78	£431,203	£717,836	-174.46
G Gibbons	94 741 13%	90	73	73	£370,610	£579,014	+52.23
Liam Keniry	89 879 10%	86	89	96	£265,799	£461,164	-184.76
Ted Durcan	88 567 16%	67	61	65	£483,536	£741,534	-99.07
Robert Winston	86 744 12%	102	79	92	£449,767	£717,746	-256.78
Tom Eaves	81 906 9%	71	86	95	£376,674	£623,254	-234.75
Chris Catlin	80 1001 8%	102	84	98	£301,021	£555,526	-305.82
Dane O'Neill	80 856 9%	109	87	108	£370,639	£693,021	-162.45
Jimmy Quinn	77 894 9%	81	95	112	£313,662	£549,510	-276.73
David Probert	77 778 10%	76	87	93	£402,413	£635,121	-152.57
Jimmy Fortune	77 612 13%	60	72	69	£456,601	£1,016,962	-148.31
P J McDonald	76 647 12%	58	62	75	£271,904	£421,186	-29.26
Phillip Makin	75 769 10%	74	109	104	£417,143	£614,435	-208.11
Shane Kelly	74 685 11%	84	84	75	£282,844	£482,669	-177.95
Adam Kirby	73 636 11%	64	83	64	£329,606	£548,528	-124.51
Hayley Turner	72 752 10%	91	80	62	£400,579	£665,860	-279.56
David Allan	72 536 13%	69	63	50	£375,108	£594,988	-95.86
Paul Mulrennan	69 712 10%	65	76	88	£300,386	£517,529	-158.17
Martin Dwyer	68 478 14%	60	47	45	£403,381	£738,150	+138.55
Luke Morris	67 1000 7%	103	122	98	£286,111	£499,385	-252.57
Eddie Ahern	67 612 11%	77	75	76	£632,652	£1,055,161	-187.05
Barry McHugh	60 540 11%	65	49	56	£226,883	£360,604	-105.86
Adrian Nicholls	60 378 16%	29	34	35	£340,345	£509,051	-81.79
Cathy Gannon	59 607 10%	58	57	67	£166,139	£261,993	-70.39
Kieren Fox	58 541 11%	70	60	57	£160,625	£246,233	-29.16
Fergus Sweeney	57 683 8%	60	72	78	£214,576	£357,225	-103.27
Richard Hills	57 394 14%	59	50	42	£602,917	£1,147,960	-109.62
Franny Norton	55 626 9%	66	59	67	£298,533	£474,399	-61.72
Ian Mongan	55 441 12%	43	62	39	£268,767	£363,080	+100.98
Greg Fairley	54 486 11%	59	56	49	£270,265	£436,728	-143.51
Stevie Donohoe	53 475 11%	48	38	37	£176,467	£262,535	-85.07
Pat Cosgrave	52 496 10%	47	44	43	£371,327	£627,268	+20.26
Martin Lane	52 465 11%	45	32	37	£291,947	£412,902	-28.52
William Carson	51 498 10%	49	54	42	£123,038	£251,030	-64.97
Pat Dobbs	49 425 12%	56	50	42	£213,281	£352,379	-93.02
Jack Mitchell	49 380 13%	47	36	35	£225,753	£346,433	+13.10

Leading Flat Owners 2010

(27th March - 6th November 2010)

NAME	WINS-RUNS	2nd	3rd	4th	WIN £	TOTAL £
K Abdulla	74 341 22%	69	36	41	£3,054,270	£3,860,917
Godolphin	133 687 19%	106	95	68	£1,686,131	£2,712,390
Hamdan Bin Moh'med Al Maktoum	108 692 16%	89	81	68	£1,047,811	£1,472,816
Hamdan Al Maktoum	97 607 16%	82	82	62	£750,313	£1,468,875
Cheveley Park Stud	36 199 18%	30	22	31	£745,282	£979,065
D Smith, Mrs J Magnier, M Tabor	4 30 13%	5	3	3	£288,150	£947,832
Dr Marwan Koukash	45 381 12%	43	53	40	£489,242	£720,000
Highclere (Adm. Rous)	4 4 100%	0	0	0	£718,141	£718,141
Jaber Abdullah	30 213 14%	29	30	31	£328,305	£613,784
Mrs J Magnier, M Tabor & D Smith	4 27 15%	2	2	3	£445,420	£595,436
Tabor/Smith/Magnier/Massey	2 5 40%	1	0	0	£482,545	£544,645
Saeed Manana	41 296 14%	24	31	28	£363,020	£530,386
Sheikh Ahmed Al Maktoum	43 140 31%	19	12	17	£393,811	£506,564
J C Smith	29 182 16%	29	19	18	£222,303	£441,032
Mrs J Wood	25 113 22%	11	11	12	£317,434	£413,759
Heffer Synd/Mrs Roy/Mrs Instance	2 4 50%	1	1	0	£321,602	£378,670
Mrs Fitri Hay	27 171 16%	24	26	18	£191,510	£375,969
M Tabor, D Smith & Mrs J Magnier	2 19 11%	3	1	6	£171,729	£368,940
H R H Princess Haya Of Jordan	36 185 19%	19	22	17	£223,742	£351,320
J Acheson	5 22 23%	4	3	0	£237,556	£350,502
Frank Brady & The Cosmic Cases	4 4 100%	0	0	0	£347,463	£347,463
Anamoine Limited	2 10 20%	3	0	1	£231,823	£326,594
A D Spence	16 142 11%	15	13	13	£211,774	£324,544
Rachel Hood and Robin Geffen	1 2 50%	0	1	0	£283,850	£291,389
J C Fretwell	21 71 30%	9	8	3	£242,097	£266,558
Mrs R J Jacobs	11 55 20%	15	7	4	£185,623	£264,428
Khalifa Dasmal	8 82 10%	8	6	13	£183,399	£245,309
Tight Lines Partnership	2 4 50%	1	0	0	£175,026	£240,396
The Queen	13 108 12%	24	10	12	£103,700	£237,487
Mathieu Offenstadt	1 3 33%	0	0	0	£227,080	£234,276
Sir Robert Ogden	11 54 20%	7	9	5	£201,258	£233,278
The Calvera Partnership No 2	2 10 20%	2	1	1	£170,310	£225,123
R C Bond	16 110 15%	13	15	11	£183,647	£221,782
R J Arculli	7 52 13%	12	7	7	£101,406	£221,754
Normandie Stud Ltd	8 50 16%	6	10	7	£112,665	£218,640
M Channon	12 124 10%	15	14	16	£40,959	£209,959
Shkh Sultan Bin Khalifa Al Nahyan	9 64 14%	15	9	4	£152,900	£206,651
Ballymacoll Stud	9 56 16%	6	6	5	£104,047	£203,727
Pearl Bloodstock Ltd	10 39 26%	7	2	3	£132,128	£197,888
Highclere (Bahram)	3 8 38%	1	2	2	£145,751	£197,746
John Manley	1 12 8%	2	0	1	£36,901	£195,820
H R H Sultan Ahmad Shah	6 72 8%	8	6	6	£53,004	£188,091
Shkh Moh'med Obaid Al Maktoum	8 26 31%	5	3	1	£153,928	£187,909
P W Harris	19 133 14%	14	24	13	£129,891	£184,322
Jim McGrath	8 42 19%	5	8	0	£83,844	£177,673
Magnier/Tabor/Smith/Denford Stud	0 3	2	0	0	£0	£175,531
M B Hawtin	5 17 29%	4	2	0	£134,232	£174,328
Dab Hand Racing	5 31 16%	2	2	2	£132,242	£172,178
Fittocks Stud	11 25 44%	2	4	2	£160,573	£168,096
Malih Lahej Al Basti	15 71 21%	6	8	6	£134,058	£165,645

Leading All-Weather Flat Jockeys

(8th Nov 2009 - 26th March 2010)

NAME	WIN-RIDES	2nd	3rd	4th	WIN £	TOTAL £	£1 STAKE
Joe Fanning	64 277 23%	35	32	32	£194,555	£269,234	-16.77
Jimmy Quinn	41 369 11%	35	49	48	£119,752	£176,354	-116.14
David Probert	38 253 15%	27	34	34	£97,337	£152,613	+67.31
Robert Winston	35 282 12%	42	20	36	£99,262	£146,628	-97.24
Liam Keniry	34 318 11%	39	39	34	£101,581	£151,121	-124.88
George Baker	34 175 19%	22	24	18	£88,527	£118,593	-2.85
Chris Catlin	33 355 9%	36	32	28	£92,537	£151,041	-59.58
Jim Crowley	32 210 15%	29	19	22	£126,301	£161,082	-25.76
Adam Kirby	31 247 13%	36	24	29	£73,439	£129,990	-74.83
Luke Morris	28 357 8%	45	46	40	£112,020	£179,535	-38.00
Dane O'Neill	28 197 14%	23	24	15	£93,467	£130,417	+88.58
Shane Kelly	27 241 11%	40	26	24	£83,699	£134,847	-78.62
Tony Culhane	26 208 13%	18	23	33	£77,074	£102,291	-52.01
Martin Dwyer	26 158 16%	20	20	23	£85,121	£131,190	+72.45
Tom Eaves	25 231 11%	39	33	22	£85,095	£143,750	-85.73
Neil Callan	25 166 15%	31	15	19	£114,492	£163,122	-38.38
Jamie Spencer	24 83 29%	9	9	14	£97,218	£119,195	+29.30
Steve Drowne	23 221 10%	13	24	27	£72,607	£108,426	-10.48
Andrea Atzeni	22 173 13%	22	16	16	£70,686	£113,247	-30.94
Phillip Makin	22 135 16%	17	19	21	£110,311	£145,887	-31.11
Hayley Turner	21 212 10%	31	23	20	£61,978	£108,036	-99.06
Nicky Mackay	21 117 18%	14	14	12	£68,606	£93,657	+44.48
Graham Gibbons	20 179 11%	16	18	23	£50,629	£69,882	-16.65
Andrew Heffernan	20 175 11%	18	26	18	£59,532	£85,864	-68.98
Stevie Donohoe	20 146 14%	16	9	13	£70,307	£88,051	+12.85
William Carson	20 97 21%	6	16	11	£55,433	£69,201	+18.60
Paul Doe	19 146 13%	19	12	17	£45,507	£72,212	-18.18
J-P Guillambert	19 137 14%	18	18	17	£43,256	£65,827	-73.10
Barry McHugh	18 79 23%	9	7	10	£47,340	£60,869	+26.22
Franny Norton	17 142 12%	17	15	11	£47,233	£65,736	+114.13
Kieren Fox	16 135 12%	17	12	15	£44,497	£61,459	-7.34
Tom Queally	16 112 14%	15	17	7	£133,962	£156,013	-32.75
Paul Hanagan	15 171 9%	13	24	22	£50,145	£88,616	-58.15
Fergus Sweeney	15 156 10%	16	18	22	£40,941	£66,314	+27.50
Seb Sanders	15 85 18%	12	5	9	£44,055	£60,986	-9.47
Kieren Fallon	15 70 21%	8	12	4	£71,198	£113,526	+9.18
Stephen Craine	14 164 9%	8	16	22	£39,180	£55,264	-80.13
Rich'd Kingscote	14 81 17%	15	10	7	£67,636	£86,897	-7.09
Declan Cannon	13 119 11%	11	21	13	£60,091	£79,799	+33.13
Eddie Ahern	13 117 11%	15	15	18	£49,255	£85,335	-63.02
Greg Fairley	13 115 11%	17	15	8	£53,444	£78,547	-57.05
Matthew Davies	13 93 14%	16	11	9	£26,730	£41,953	-17.75
Saleem Golam	11 132 8%	13	22	10	£24,625	£41,256	-27.25
Robert Havlin	11 93 12%	9	16	13	£24,151	£46,640	-30.51
Ian Mongan	11 91 12%	1	11	10	£37,385	£46,674	-6.25
Ross Atkinson	11 80 14%	12	9	6	£24,030	£35,166	-4.67
Liam Jones	10 146 7%	16	12	20	£25,928	£44,939	-62.42

Leading All-Weather Trainers

(8th Nov 2009 - 26th March 2010)

NAME	WINS-RUNS	2nd	3rd	4th	WIN £	TOTAL £	£1 STAKE
Mark Johnston	51 198 26%	35	23	18	£166,761	£243,982	-24.70
Kevin Ryan	24 146 16%	17	18	18	£131,578	£184,523	-45.62
David Evans	41 332 12%	42	46	43	£103,102	£181,922	-108.46
Marco Botti	17 81 21%	14	11	5	£88,155	£139,193	+36.25
David Barron	18 80 23%	12	9	8	£102,427	£127,815	+74.73
Richard Hannon	15 91 16%	14	13	8	£88,978	£116,109	-19.73
Bryan Smart	21 116 18%	25	13	15	£76,829	£111,867	-4.56
Alan Bailey	14 62 23%	11	7	5	£77,019	£111,322	+3.69
Henry Cecil	5 8 63%	0	0	0	£107,881	£107,881	+9.79
Jim Boyle	21 155 14%	24	13	22	£65,418	£101,791	-16.59
Gary Moore	24 161 15%	31	25	20	£61,232	£98,379	-60.36
David Simcock	15 91 16%	18	11	11	£58,216	£93,959	-36.13
J S Moore	23 142 16%	28	25	13	£58,338	£92,648	-8.59
Tom Dascombe	12 59 20%	11	5	8	£63,736	£79,689	+6.92
Ronald Harris	19 215 9%	28	28	31	£39,623	£78,219	-71.75
Jeremy Glover	15 116 13%	21	20	11	£40,794	£77,854	+6.58
Paul Howling	21 211 10%	15	24	34	£51,690	£72,249	-114.11
Derek Shaw	20 107 19%	15	9	12	£52,817	£69,600	+23.75
Stuart Williams	18 86 21%	6	13	8	£54,034	£67,740	+17.10
Richard Fahey	13 158 8%	18	26	25	£30,209	£67,454	-84.02
Clive Cox	6 42 14%	11	4	2	£40,235	£65,376	-0.58
Alan McCabe	12 169 7%	18	27	18	£35,839	£64,856	-50.27
Michael Attwater	6 91 7%	9	4	10	£48,034	£63,715	-47.25
Jeff Pearce	19 115 17%	14	19	12	£46,027	£63,417	+48.25
Clive Brittain	12 52 23%	7	7	7	£44,249	£62,334	-5.56
Ralph Beckett	13 40 33%	3	5	3	£56,554	£61,945	+18.35
S Bin Suroor	11 15 73%	1	1	0	£56,348	£58,559	+18.54
Richard Guest	11 123 9%	16	17	13	£33,187	£58,282	+85.63
Michael Easterby	18 66 27%	6	8	4	£46,100	£57,604	+14.17
Brian Ellison	19 82 23%	8	15	9	£41,753	£57,568	+35.27
John Best	11 116 9%	11	10	11	£34,868	£55,239	-64.50
George Baker	19 96 20%	16	7	10	£40,014	£53,847	-13.10
Jeremy Gask	9 64 14%	10	7	9	£32,641	£51,693	+6.25
Reg Hollinshead	12 132 9%	14	16	14	£29,247	£50,184	-45.80
Tom Tate	0 12	5	4	0	£0	£49,386	-12.00
Tony Carroll	12 83 14%	11	4	6	£32,081	£47,016	-12.25
John Gosden	10 39 26%	7	7	2	£29,024	£46,032	-16.23
William Muir	9 49 18%	6	11	5	£26,849	£42,847	+2.64
David Elsworth	5 27 19%	8	2	3	£32,802	£42,700	+11.50
Brett Johnson	4 20 20%	2	3	1	£36,586	£41,863	+8.25
John Jenkins	10 112 9%	11	13	20	£25,232	£41,752	-26.09
Ian Williams	17 79 22%	9	8	8	£32,073	£40,951	+4.75
Dean Ivory	9 71 13%	11	5	9	£26,094	£39,682	+20.50
William Jarvis	12 44 27%	8	3	6	£32,206	£39,433	+21.40
Roger Curtis	7 67 10%	5	9	9	£28,840	£38,650	-5.75
Andrew Balding	10 48 21%	7	7	4	£27,055	£38,507	+12.68
William Knight	6 20 30%	2	0	1	£32,973	£38,450	+21.35
Jane C'ple-Hyam	8 36 22%	5	2	5	£31,925	£37,776	+15.50

Racing Post top rated 2010

(Best performance figures recorded between 1st January and 31st December 2010)

Harbinger..135
Blame (USA)..131
Quality Road (USA) 130
Canford Cliffs (IRE)...................................130
Workforce 130
Rip Van Winkle (IRE)..................................129
Nakayama Festa (JPN) 129
Lookin At Lucky (USA) 129
Black Caviar (AUS)....................................129
Zenyatta (USA)..128
So You Think (NZ) 128
Hay List (AUS)...128
Makfi 128
Sacred Kingdom (AUS) 127
Paco Boy (IRE)...127
Twice Over...127
Cape Blanco (IRE).......................................127
Behkabad (FR) 127
Frankel...127
Byword...126
Planteur (IRE)..126
Eskendereya (USA).....................................126
Americain (USA)..125
Goldikova (IRE) 125
Fame And Glory 125
Haynesfield (USA) 125
Starspangledbanner (AUS)...........................125
Rocket Man (AUS)...125
Dream Ahead (USA).....................................125
Etched (USA)..124
Equiano (FR) 124
Rachel Alexandra (USA) 124
Midday 124
Cityscape..124
Rewilding 124
Dick Turpin (IRE) 124
Lope De Vega (IRE) 124
Discreetly Mine (USA) 124
Sarafina (FR) 124
Super Saver (USA)..124
Fly Down (USA)...124
Pelusa (JPN) 124
Afleet Express (USA).....................................124
Uncle Mo (USA)..124
Spanish Moon (USA) 123
Danleigh (AUS)...123
Zipping (AUS) 123
Dream Journey (JPN)......................................123
Duncan 123
Able One (NZ) 123
Gio Ponti (USA) 123
Vision D Etat (FR) 123
Sans Frontieres (IRE).......................................123
Whobegotyou (AUS)...123
Nicconi (AUS) 123
Buena Vista (JPN) 123
Espoir City (JPN) 123
Shocking (AUS) 123
Poet s Voice...123
Kinsale King (USA)..123
Lizard s Desire (SAF)...123
Sidney s Candy (USA).......................................123
Presious Passion (USA) 122
Premio Loco (USA)..122
Collection (IRE) 122
Presvis 122
Green Birdie (NZ) 122
Gloria De Campeao (BRZ) 122
Court Vision (USA) 122
Bob Black Jack (USA) 122
Age Of Aquarius (IRE)..122
Rite Of Passage 122
Big Drama (USA)..122
Girolamo (USA) 122
Debussy (IRE) 122
Richard s Kid (USA)...122
Red Jazz (USA)...122
Rail Trip (USA)...122
Jakkalberry (IRE)..122
Here Comes Ben (USA) 122
Smiling Tiger (USA)...122
Arctic Cosmos (USA)...122
The Usual Q. T. (USA)...122
Musir (AUS) 122
Battle Plan (USA) 122
Viva Pataca...121
Stotsfold..121
Al Shemali 121
Markab...121
Getaway (GER) 121
Regal Parade...121
Neko Bay (USA) 121
Kingsgate Native (IRE) 121
Famous Name 121
Ouqba...121
Crown Of Thorns (USA) 121
Allybar (IRE) 121
Dangerous Midge (USA) 121

Raceform median times 2010

ASCOT

5f 1m 0.5
5f 110y........................1m 07.5
6f 1m 14.4
6f 110y........................1m 21.8
7f 1m 28.0
1m Str.........................1m 40.6
1m Rnd........................1m 40.7
1m 2f 2m 7.0
1m 4f 2m 32.5
2m 3m 29.0
2m 4f 4m 21.0
2m 5f 194y.................4m 56.5

AYR

5f 1m 0.1
6f 1m 13.6
7f 50y.........................1m 33.4
1m 1m 43.8
1m 1f 20y...................1m 58.4
1m 2f 2m 12.0
1m 5f 13y...................2m 54.0
1m 7f 3m 20.4
2m 1f 105y.................4m 0.5

BATH

5f 11y.........................1m 2.5
5f 161y.......................1m 11.2
1m 5y.........................1m 40.8
1m 2f 46y...................2m 11.0
1m 3f 144y.................2m 30.6
1m 5f 22y...................2m 52.0
2m 1f 34y...................3m 51.9

BEVERLEY

5f 1m 3.5
7f 100y.......................1m 33.8
1m 100y.....................1m 47.6
1m 1f 207y.................2m 7.0
1m 4f 16y...................2m 40.9
2m 35y.......................3m 39.8

BRIGHTON

5f 59y.........................1m 2.3
5f 213y.......................1m 10.2
6f 209y.......................1m 23.1
7f 214y.......................1m 36.0
1m 1f 209y.................2m 3.6
1m 3f 196y.................2m 32.7

CARLISLE

5f 1m 0.8
5f 193y.......................1m 13.7
6f 192y.......................1m 27.1
7f 200y.......................1m 40.0
1m 1f 61y...................1m 57.6
1m 3f 107y.................2m 23.1
1m 6f 32y...................3m 7.5
2m 1f 52y...................3m 53.0

CATTERICK

5f 59.8s
5f 212y.......................1m 13.6
7f 1m 27.0
1m 3f 214y.................2m 38.9
1m 5f 175y.................3m 3.6
1m 7f 177y.................3m 32.0

CHEPSTOW

5f 16y.........................59.3s
6f 16y.........................1m 12.0
7f 16y.........................1m 23.2
1m 14y.......................1m 36.2
1m 2f 36y...................2m 10.6
1m 4f 23y...................2m 39.0
2m 49y.......................3m 38.9
2m 2f 4m 3.6

CHESTER

5f 16y.........................1m 1.0
6f 18y.........................1m 13.8
7f 2y...........................1m 26.5
7f 122y.......................1m 33.8
1m 2f 75y...................2m 12.2
1m 3f 79y...................2m 26.6
1m 4f 66y...................2m 39.9
1m 5f 89y...................2m 53.2
1m 7f 195y.................3m 28.0
2m 2f 147y.................4m 4.8

DONCASTER

5f 1m 0.5
5f 140y.......................1m 8.5
6f 1m 13.6
6f 110y.......................1m 19.9
7f 1m 26.3
1m Str.........................1m 39.3
1m Rnd........................1m 39.7
1m 2f 60y...................2m 11.2
1m 4f 2m 35.1
1m 6f 132y.................3m 6.7
2m 110y.....................3m 40.4
2m 2f 3m 58.2

EPSOM

5f 55.7s
6f 1m 9.4
7f 1m 23.3
1m 114y.....................1m 46.1
1m 2f 18y...................2m 9.7
1m 4f 10y...................2m 38.9

FOLKESTONE

5f 1m
6f 1m 12.7
7f 1m 27.3
1m 1f 149y.................2m 4.9
1m 4f 2m 40.9
1m 7f 92y...................3m 29.7
2m 93y.......................3m 37.2

GOODWOOD

5f 58.4s
6f 1m 12.2
7f 1m 27.4
1m 1m 39.9
1m 1f 1m 56.3
1m 1f 192y.................2m 8.0
1m 3f 2m 28.3
1m 4f 2m 38.4
1m 6f 3m 3.6
2m 3m 29.0
2m 5f 4m 33.1

HAMILTON

5f 4y...........................1m
6f 5y...........................1m 12.2
1m 65y.......................1m 48.4
1m 1f 36y...................1m 59.7
1m 3f 16y...................2m 25.6
1m 4f 17y...................2m 38.6
1m 5f 9y.....................2m 53.9

HAYDOCK

5f (inner)...................1m 1.1
5f (outer)...................1m 0.5
6f (inner)...................1m 14.5
6f (outer)...................1m 14.0
7f 30y.........................1m 30.2
1m 30y.......................1m 43.8
1m 2f 95y...................2m 13.0
1m 3f 200y.................2m 33.2
1m 6f 3m 4.3
2m 45y.......................3m 36.0

KEMPTON AW

5f 1m 0.5
6f 1m 13.1
7f 1m 26.0
1m 1m 39.8
1m 1f 1m 55.8
1m 2f 2m 8.0
1m 3f 2m 21.9
1m 4f 2m 34.5
2m 3m 30.1

LEICESTER

5f 2y...........................1m
5f 218y.......................1m 13.0
7f 9y...........................1m 26.2
1m 60y.......................1m 45.1
1m 1f 218y.................2m 7.9
1m 3f 183y.................2m 33.9

LINGFIELD TURF

5f 58.2s
6f 1m 11.2
7f 1m 23.3
7f 140y.......................1m 32.3
1m 1f 1m 56.6
1m 2f 2m 10.5
1m 3f 106y.................2m 31.5
1m 6f 3m 10.0
2m 3m 34.8

LINGFIELD AW

5f 58.8s
6f 1m 11.9
7f 1m 24.8
1m 1m 38.2
1m 2f 2m 6.6
1m 4f 2m 33.0
1m 5f 2m 46.0
2m 3m 25.7

MUSSELBURGH

5f 1m 0.4
7f 30y.........................1m 30.3
1m 1m 41.2
1m 1f 1m 54.7
1m 4f 2m 39.7
1m 4f 100y.................2m 42.0
1m 5f 2m 52.0
1m 6f 3m 5.3
2m 3m 36.1

NEWBURY

5f 34y.........................1m 1.4
6f 8y...........................1m 13.0
6f 110y.......................1m 19.3
7f 1m 25.7
1m 1m 39.7
1m 1f 1m 55.5
1m 2f 6y.....................2m 8.8
1m 3f 5y.....................2m 21.2
1m 4f 5y.....................2m 35.5
1m 5f 61y...................2m 52.0
2m 3m 32.0

NEWCASTLE

5f 1m 0.7
6f 1m 15.2
7f 1m 28.7
1m Rnd........................1m 45.3
1m 3y Str...................1m 43.2
1m 1f 9y.....................1m 58.1
1m 2f 32y...................2m 11.9
1m 4f 93y...................2m 45.6
1m 6f 97y...................3m 11.3
2m 19y.......................3m 36.2

NEWMARKET ROWLEY

5f 59.1s
6f 1m 12.2
7f 1m 25.4
1m 1m 38.6
1m 1f 1m 51.7
1m 2f 2m 5.8
1m 4f 2m 33.5

1m 6f 2m 58.5
2m 3m 30.8
2m 2f 3m 54.8

NEWMARKET JULY

5f 59.1s
6f 1m 12.5
7f 1m 25.7
1m 1m 40.0
1m 2f 2m 5.5
1m 4f 2m 32.9
1m5f 2m 44.0
1m 6f 175y................3m 11.3
2m 24y......................3m 27.0

NOTTINGHAM

Due to reconfiguration of the track there is currently insufficient data to calculate median times.

PONTEFRACT

5f 1m 3.3
6f 1m 16.9
1m 4y........................1m 45.9
1m 2f 6y....................2m 13.7
1m 4f 8y....................2m 40.8
2m 1f 22y..................3m 50.0
2m 1f 216y................4m 3.9
2m 5f 122y................5m 8.8

REDCAR

5f 58.6s
6f 1m 11.8
7f 1m 24.5
1m 1m 38.0
1m 1f 1m 53.0
1m 2f 2m 7.1
1m 3f 2m 21.7
1m 6f 19y..................3m 4.7
2m 4y........................3m 31.4

RIPON

5f 1m 0.7
6f 1m 13.0
1m 1m 41.4
1m 1f 1m 54.7
1m 1f 170y................2m 5.4
1m 4f 10y..................2m 36.7
2m 3m 31.8

SALISBURY

5f 1m 0.8
6f 1m 14.8
6f 212y......................1m 29.0
1m 1m 43.5
1m 1f 198y................2m 9.9
1m 4f 2m 38.0
1m 6f 21y..................3m 7.4

SANDOWN

5f 6y..........................1m 1.6
7f 16y........................1m 29.5
1m 14y......................1m 43.3
1m 1f 1m 56.3
1m 2f 7y....................2m 10.5
1m 6f 3m 6.6
2m 78y......................3m 38.7

SOUTHWELL TURF

6f 1m 15.8
7f 1m 29.4
1m 2f 2m 13.1
1m 3f 2m 27.8
1m 4f 2m 41.7
2m 3m 38.6

SOUTHWELL AW

5f 59.7s
6f 1m 16.5
7f 1m 30.3
1m 1m 43.7
1m 3f 2m 28.0
1m 4f 2m 41.0
1m 6f 3m 8.3
2m 3m 45.5

THIRSK

5f 59.6s
6f 1m 12.7
7f 1m 27.2
1m 1m 40.1
1m 4f 2m 36.2
2m 3m 32.8

WARWICK

5f 59.6s
5f 110y......................1m 5.9
6f 1m 11.8
7f 26y........................1m 24.6
1m 22y......................1m 41.0
1m 2f 188y................2m 21.1
1m 4f 134y................2m 44.6
1m 6f 213y................3m 19.0
2m 39y......................3m 33.8

WINDSOR

5f 10y........................1m 0.3
6f 1m 13.0
1m 67y......................1m 44.7
1m 2f 7y....................2m 8.7
1m 3f 135y................2m 29.5

WOLVERHAMPTON AW

5f 20y........................1m 2.3
5f 216y......................1m 15.0
7f 32y........................1m 29.6
1m 141y....................1m 50.5
1m 1f 103y................2m 1.7
1m 4f 50y..................2m 41.1
1m 5f 194y................3m 6.0
2m 119y....................3m 41.8

YARMOUTH

5f 43y........................1m 2.2
6f 3y..........................1m 14.4
7f 3y..........................1m 26.6
1m 3y........................1m 40.6
1m 2f 21y..................2m 10.5
1m 3f 101y................2m 28.7
1m 6f 17y..................3m 7.6
2m 3m 34.6

YORK

5f 59.3s
5f 89y........................1m 4.3
6f 1m 11.9
7f 1m 25.3
1m 1m 38.8
1m 208y....................1m 52.0
1m 2f 88y..................2m 12.5
1m 4f 2m 33.2
1m 6f 3m 0.2
2m 88y......................3m 34.5
2m 2f 3m 58.4

Raceform Flat record times

ASCOT

Distance	Time	Age	Weight	Going	Horse	Date
5f	59.17 sec	2	8-12	Gd To Firm	Maqaasid	Jun 16 2010
5f	57.44 sec	6	9-1	Gd To Firm	Miss Andretti (AUS)	Jun 19 2007
6f	1m 12.46	2	9-1	Gd To Firm	Henrythenavigator(USA)	Jun 19 2007
6f	1m 12.27	2	8-11	Gd To Firm	LaddiesPoker Two (IRE)	Jun 19 2010
7f	1m 26.76	2	7-12	Gd To Firm	Relative Order	Aug 11 2007
7f	1m 24.94	3	8-12	Gd To Firm	Rainfall (IRE)	Jun 16 2010
1m (R)	1m 39.55	2	8-12	Good	Joshua Tree (IRE)	Sep 26 2009
1m (R)	1m 38.32	3	9-0	Gd To Firm	Ghanaati (USA)	Jun 19 2009
1m (S)	1m 37.16	4	8-9	Gd To Firm	Invisible Man	Jun 16 2010
1m 2f	2m 3.24	4	9-5	Gd To Firm	Perfect Stride	Jun 19 2009
1m 4f	2m 26.78	4	9-7	Good	Harbinger	Jul 24 2010
2m	3m 24.13	3	9-1	Gd To Firm	Holberg (UAE)	Sept 16 2009
2m 4f	4m 16.92	6	9-2	Gd To Firm	Rite Of Passage	Jun 17 2010
2m 5f 159y	4m 47.90	7	9-2	Gd To Firm	Bergo (GER)	Jun 19 2010

AYR

Distance	Time	Age	Weight	Going	Horse	Date
5f	56.9 secs	2	8-11	Good	Boogie Street	Sep 18 2003
5f	55.68 secs	3	8-11	Gd to Firm	Look Busy (IRE)	Jun 21 2008
6f	69.7 secs	2	7-10	Good	Sir Bert	Sep 17 1969
6f	68.37 secs	5	8-6	Gd to Firm	Maison Dieu	Jun 21 2008
7f	1m 25.7	2	9-0	Gd to Firm	Jazeel	Sep 16 1993
7f	1m 24.9	5	7-11	Firm	Sir Arthur Hobbs	Jun 19 1992
7f 50y	1m 28.9	2	9-0	Good	Tafaahum (USA)	Sep 19 2003
7f 50y	1m 28.2	4	9-2	Gd to Firm	Flur Na H Alba	Jun 21 2003
1m	1m 39.2	2	9-0	Gd to Firm	Kribensis	Sep 17 1986
1m	1m 36.0	4	7-13	Firm	Sufi	Sep 16 1959
1m 1f 20y	1m 50.3	4	9-3	Good	Retirement	Sep 19 2003
1m 2f	2m 4.0	4	9-9	Gd to Firm	Endless Hall	Jly 17 2000
1m 2f192y	2m 13.3	4	9-0	Gd to Firm	Azzaam	Sep 18 1991
1m 5f 13y	2m 45.8	4	9-7	Gd to Firm	Eden s Close	Sep 18 1993
1m 7f	3m 13.1	3	9-4	Good	Romany Rye	Sep 19 1991
2m 1f105y	3m 45.0	4	6-13	Good	Curry	Sep 16 1955

BATH

Distance	Time	Age	Weight	Going	Horse	Date
5f 11y	59.50 secs	2	9-2	Firm	Amour Propre	Jly 24 2008
5f 11y	58.75 secs	3	8-12	Firm	Enticing (IRE)	May 1 2007
5f 161y	68.70 secs	2	8-12	Firm	Qalahari (IRE)	Jly 24 2008
5f 161y	68.1 secs	6	9-0	Firm	Madraco	May 22 1989
1m 5y	1m 39.7	2	8-9	Firm	Casual Look	Sep 16 2002
1m 5y	1m 37.2	5	8-12	Gd to Firm	Adobe	Jun 17 2000
1m 5y	1m 37.2	3	8-7	Firm	Alasha (IRE)	Aug 18 2002
1m 2f 46y	2m 5.8	3	9-0	Gd to Firm	Connoisseur Bay(USA)	May 29 1998
1m 3f144y	2m 25.74	3	9-0	Hard	Top Of The Charts	Sep 8 2005
1m 5f 22y	2m 47.2	4	10-0	Firm	Flown	Aug 13 1991
2m 1f 34y	3m 43.4	6	7-9	Firm	Yaheska (IRE)	Jun 14 2003

BEVERLEY

Distance	Time	Age	Weight	Going	Horse	Date
5f	61.0 secs	2	8-2	Gd to Firm	Addo (IRE)	Jly 17 2001
5f	60.1 secs	4	9-5	Firm	Pic Up Sticks	Apr 16 2003
7f 100y	1m 31.1	2	9-7	Gd to Firm	Champagne Prince	Aug 10 1995
7f 100y	1m 31.1	2	9-0	Firm	Majal (IRE)	Jly 30 1991
7f 100y	1m 29.5	3	7-8	Firm	Who s Tef	Jly 30 1991
1m 100y	1m 43.3	2	9-0	Firm	Arden	Sep 24 1986
1m 100y	1m 42.2	3	8-4	Firm	Legal Case	Jun 14 1989
1m 1f 207y	2m 1.00	3	9-7	Gd to Firm	Eastern Aria (UAE)	Aug 29 2009
1m 3f 216y	2m 30.8	3	8-1	Hard	Coinage	Jun 18 1986
1m 4f 16y	2m 34.88	6	10-0	Firm	WeeCharlieCastle(IRE)	Aug 30 2009
2m 35y	3m 29.5	4	9-2	Gd to Firm	Rushen Raider	Aug 14 1996

BRIGHTON

Distance	Time	Age	Weight	Going	Horse	Date
5f 59y	60.1 secs	2	9-0	Firm	Bid for Blue	May 6 1993
5f 59y	59.3 secs	3	8-9	Firm	Play Hever Golf	May 26 1993
5f 213y	68.1 secs	2	8-9	Firm	Song Mist (IRE)	Jly 16 1996
5f 213y	67.3 secs	3	8-9	Firm	Third Party	Jun 3 1997
5f 213y	67.3 secs	5	9-1	Gd to Firm	Blundell Lane	May 4 2000
6f 209y	1m 19.9	2	8-11	Hard	Rain Burst	Sep 15 1988
6f 209y	1m 19.4	4	9-3	Gd to Firm	Sawaki	Sep 3 1991
7f 214y	1m 32.8	2	9-7	Firm	Asian Pete	Oct 3 1989
7f 214y	1m 30.5	5	8-11	Firm	Mystic Ridge	May 27 1999
1m 1f 209y	2m 4.7	2	9-0	Gd to Soft	Esteemed Master	Nov 2 2001
1m 1f 209y	1m 57.2	3	9-0	Firm	Get The Message	Apr 30 1984
1m 3f 196y	2m 25.8	4	8-2	Firm	New Zealand	Jly 4 1985

CARLISLE

Distance	Time	Age	Weight	Going	Horse	Date
5f	60.1 secs	2	8-5	Firm	La Tortuga	Aug 2 1999
5f	58.8 secs	3	9-8	Gd to Firm	Esatto	Aug 21 2002
5f 193y	1m 12.45	2	9-6	Gd to Firm	Musical Guest (IRE)	Sep 11 2005
5f 193y	1m 10.83	4	9-0	Gd to Firm	Bo McGinty (IRE)	Sep 11 2005
6f 192y	1m 24.3	3	8-9	Gd to Firm	Marjurita (IRE)	Aug 21 2002
6f 206y	1m 26.5	2	9-4	Hard	Sense of Priority	Sep 10 1991
6f 206y	1m 25.3	4	9-1	Firm	Move With Edes	Jly 6 1996
7f 200y	1m 37.34	5	9-7	Gd to Firm	Hula Ballew	Aug 17 2005
7f 214y	1m 44.6	2	8-8	Firm	Blue Garter	Sep 9 1980
7f 214y	1m 37.3	5	7-12	Hard	Thatched (IRE)	Aug 21 1995
1m 1f 61y	1m 53.8	3	9-0	Firm	Little Jimbob	Jun 14 2004
1m 3f 107y	2m 22.25	5	9-6	Gd to Firm	Overrule (USA)	Jun 24 2009
1m 4f	2m 28.8	3	8-5	Firm	Desert Frolic (IRE)	Jun 27 1996
1m 6f 32y	3m 2.2	6	8-10	Firm	Explosive Speed	May 26 1994
2m 1f 52y	3m 46.2	3	7-10	Gd to Firm	Warring Kingdom	Aug 25 1999

CATTERICK

Distance	Time	Age	Weight	Going	Horse	Date
5f	57.6 secs	2	9-0	Firm	H Harrison	Oct 8 2002
5f	57.1 secs	4	8-7	Fast	Kabcast	Jly 7 1989
5f 212y	1m 11.4	2	9-4	Firm	Captain Nick	Jly 11 1978
5f 212y	69.8 secs	9	8-13	Gd to Firm	Sharp Hat	May 30 2003
7f	1m 24.1	2	8-11	Firm	Lindas Fantasy	Sep 18 1982
7f	1m 22.5	6	8-7	Firm	Differential (USA)	May 31 2003
1m 3f 214y	2m 30.5	3	8-8	Gd to Firm	Rahaf	May 30 2003
1m 5f 175y	2m 54.8	3	8-5	Firm	Geryon	May 31 1984
1m 7f 177y	3m 20.8	4	7-11	Firm	Bean Boy	Jly 8 1982

CHEPSTOW

Distance	Time	Age	Weight	Going	Horse	Date
5f 16y	57.6 secs	2	8-11	Firm	Micro Love	Jly 8 1986
5f 16y	56.8 secs	3	8-4	Firm	Torbay Express	Sep 15 1979
6f 16y	69.4 secs	2	9-0	Fast	Royal Fifi	Sep 9 1989
6f 16y	68.1 secs	3	9-7	Firm	America Calling (USA)	Sep 18 2001
7f 16y	1m 20.8	2	9-0	Gd to Firm	Royal Amaretto (IRE)	Sep 12 1996
7f 16y	1m 19.3	3	9-0	Firm	Taranaki	Sep 18 2001
1m 14y	1m 33.1	2	8-11	Gd to Firm	Ski Academy (IRE)	Aug 28 1995
1m 14y	1m 31.6	3	8-13	Firm	Stoli (IRE)	Sep 18 2001
1m 2f 36y	2m 4.1	5	8-9	Hard	Leonidas	Jly 5 1983
1m 2f 36y	2m 4.1	5	7-8	Gd to Firm	It s Varadan	Sep 9 1989
1m 2f 36y	2m 4.1	3	8-5	Gd to Firm	Ela Athena	Jly 23 1999
1m 4f 23y	2m 31.0	3	8-9	Gd to Firm	Spritsail	Jly 13 1989
1m 4f 23y	2m 31.0	7	9-6	Hard	Maintop	Aug 27 1984
2m 49y	3m 27.7	4	9-0	Gd to Firm	Wizzard Artist	Jly 1 1989
2m 2f	3m 56.4	5	8-7	Gd to Firm	Laffah	Jly 8 2000

CHESTER

Distance	Time	Age	Weight	Going	Horse	Date
5f 16y	59.94 secs	2	9-2	Gd to Firm	Leiba Leiba	Jun 26 2010
5f 16y	59.2 secs	3	10-0	Firm	Althrey Don	Jly 10 1964
6f 18y	1m 12.8	2	8-10	Gd to Firm	Flying Express	Aug 31 2002
6f 18y	1m 12.7	3	8-3	Gd to Firm	Play Hever Golf	May 4 1993
6f 18y	1m 12.7	6	9-2	Good	Stack Rock	Jun 23 1993
7f 2y	1m 25.2	2	9-0	Gd to Firm	Due Respect (IRE)	Sep 25 2002
7f 2y	1m 23.75	5	8-13	Gd to Firm	Three Graces (GER)	Jly 9 2005
7f 122y	1m 32.2	2	9-0	Gd to Firm	Big Bad Bob (IRE)	Sep 25 2002
7f 122y	1m 30.91	3	8-12	Gd to Firm	Cupid's Glory	Aug 18 2005
1m 2f 75y	2m 7.15	3	8-8	Gd to Firm	Stotsfold	May 7 2002
1m 3f 79y	2m 22.17	3	8-12	Gd to Firm	Perfect Truth (IRE)	May 6 2009
1m 4f 66y	2m 33.7	3	8-10	Gd to Firm	Fight Your Corner	May 7 2002
1m 5f 89y	2m 45.4	5	8-11	Firm	Rakaposhi King	May 7 1987
1m 7f 195y	3m 20.3	4	9-0	Gd to Firm	Grand Fromage (IRE)	Jly 13 2002
2m 2f 147y	3m 58.89	7	9-2	Gd to Firm	Greenwich Meantime	May 9 2007

DONCASTER

Distance	Time	Age	Weight	Going	Horse	Date
5f	58.1 secs	2	8-11	Gd to Firm	Sand Vixen	Sep 11 2009
5f	57.2 secs	6	9-12	Gd to Firm	Celtic Mill	Sep 9 2004
5f 140y	67.2 secs	2	9-0	Gd to Firm	Cartography (IRE)	Jun 29 2003
5f 140y	65.6 secs	9	9-10	Good	Halmahera (IRE)	Sep 8 2004
6f	69.6 secs	2	8-11	Good	Caesar Beware (IRE)	Sep 8 2004
6f	69.56 secs	3	8-10	Gd to Firm	Proclaim	May 30 2009
6f 110y	1m 17.22	2	8-3	Gd to Firm	Swilly Ferry (USA)	Sep 10 2009
7f	1m 22.6	2	9-1	Good	Librettist (USA)	Sep 8 2004
7f	1m 21.6	3	8-10	Gd to Firm	Pastoral Pursuits	Sep 9 2004
1m	1m 36.5	2	8-6	Gd to Firm	Singhalese	Sep 9 2004
1m (R)	1m 35.4	2	8-10	Good	Playful Act (IRE)	Sep 9 2004
1m	1m 35.52	4	8-9	Gd to Firm	Dream Lodge	Jly 24 2008
1m (R)	1m 34.46	4	8-12	Gd to Firm	Staying On (IRE)	Apr 18 2009
1m 2f 60y	2m 13.4	2	8-8	Good	Yard Bird	Nov 6 1981
1m 2f 60y	2m 4.81	4	8-13	Gd to Firm	Red Gala	Sep 12 2007

1m 4f	2m 27.7	3	8-12	Gd to Firm	Takwin (IRE)	Sep 9 2000
1m 6f 132y	3m 1.07	3	8-7	Gd to Firm	Hi Calypso (IRE)	Sep 13 2007
2m 2f	3m 48.41	4	9-4	Gd to Firm	Septimus (IRE)	Sep 14 2007

EPSOM

Distance	Time	Age	Weight	Going	Horse	Date
5f	55.0 secs	2	8-9	Gd to Firm	Prince Aslia	Jun 9 1995
5f	53.6 secs	4	9-5	Firm	Indigenous	Jun 2 1960
6f	67.8 secs	2	8-11	Gd to Firm	Showbrook	Jun 5 1991
6f	67.21 secs	5	9-13	Gd to Firm	Mac Gille Eoin	Jul 2 2009
7f	1m 21.3	2	8-9	Gd to Firm	Red Peony	Jly 29 2004
7f	1m 20.1	4	8-7	Firm	Capistrano	Jun 7 1972
1m 114y	1m 42.8	2	8-5	Gd to Firm	Nightstalker	Aug 30 1988
1m 114y	1m 40.7	3	8-6	Gd to Firm	Sylva Honda	Jun 5 1991
1m 2f 18y	2m 3.5	5	7-13	Good	Crossbow	Jun 7 1967
1m 4f 10y	2m 31.33	3	9-0	Gd to Firm	Workforce	Jun 5 2010

FFOS LAS

Distance	Time	Age	Weight	Going	Horse	Date
5f	57.20	2	8-12	Gd To Firm	Marlinka	May 26 2010
5f	56.35	5	8-8	Good	Haajes	Sep 12 2009
6f	69.97	2	9-3	Good	Glen Shiel (USA)	Sep 12 2009
6f	68.59	3	9-1	Gd To Firm	Sheer Force (IRE)	May 26 2010
1m	1m 40.61	2	9-0	Gd To Firm	Sharaayeen	Sep 13 2009
1m	1m 37.41	4	8-2	Gd To Firm	Dajen	Sep 12 2010
1m 2f	2m 6.51	4	8-8	Gd To Firm	Sandor	May 26 2010
1m 4f	2m 32.99	3	8-8	Gd To Firm	Woodford Belle	Jly 12 2010
1m 6f	2m 58.61	4	9-7	Gd To Firm	Lady Eclair	Jly 12 2010
2m	3m 29.86	4	9-7	Good	Black Or Red (IRE)	Jly 21 2009

FOLKESTONE

Distance	Time	Age	Weight	Going	Horse	Date
5f	58.4 secs	2	9-2	Gd to Firm	Pivotal	Nov 6 1995
5f	58.22 secs	7	8-11	Gd to Firm	Green Lagonda(AUS)	Jul 9 2009
6f	1m 10.8	2	8-9	Good	Boomerang Blade	Jly 16 1998
6f	69.38 secs	4	9-8	Gd to Firm	Munaddam (USA)	Sep 18 2006
6f 189y	1m 23.7	2	8-11	Good	Hen Harrier	Jly 3 1996
6f 189y	1m 21.4	3	8-9	Firm	Cielamour (USA)	Aug 9 1988
7f	1m 25.01	2	9-0	Gd to Firm	Dona Alba (IRE)	Sep 2 2007
7f	1m 23.76	3	8-11	Gd to Firm	Welsh Cake	Sep 18 2006
1m 1f 149y	1m 59.7	3	8-6	Gd to Firm	Dizzy	Jly 23 1991
1m 4f	2m 33.2	4	8-8	Hard	Snow Blizzard	Jun 30 1992
1m 7f 92y	3m 23.1	3	9-11	Firm	Mata Askari	Sep 12 1991
2m 93y	3m 34.9	3	8-12	Gd to Firm	Candle Smoke (USA)	Aug 20 1996

GOODWOOD

Distance	Time	Age	Weight	Going	Horse	Date
5f	57.5 secs	2	8-12	Gd to Firm	Poets Cove	Aug 3 1990
5f	56.0 secs	5	9-0	Gd to Firm	Rudi s Pet	Jly 27 1999
6f	69.8 secs	2	8-11	Gd to Firm	Bachir (IRE)	Jly 28 1999
6f	69.10 secs	6	9-10	Gd to Firm	Tamagin (USA)	Sep 12 2009
7f	1m 24.9	2	8-11	Gd to Firm	Ekraar	Jly 29 1999
7f	1m 23.8	3	8-7	Firm	Brief Glimpse (IRE)	Jly 25 1995
1m	1m 37.21	2	9-0	Good	Caldra (IRE)	Sep 9 2006
1m 1f	1m 56.27	2	9-3	Gd to Firm	Dordogne (IRE)	Sep 22 2010
1m	1m 35.6	3	8-13	Gd to Firm	Aljabr (USA)	Jly 28 1999
1m 1f	1m 52.8	3	9-6	Good	Vena (IRE)	Jly 27 1995
1m 1f 192y	2m 2.81	3	9-3	Gd to Firm	Road To Love (IRE)	Aug 3 2006
1m 3f	2m 23.0	3	8-8	Gd to Firm	Asian Heights	May 22 2001
1m 4f	2m 31.5	3	8-10	Firm	Presenting	Jly 25 1995
1m 6f	2m 58.05	4	9-6	Gd to Firm	Eastern Aria	Jly 29 2010
2m	3m 21.55	5	9-10	Gd to Firm	Yeats (IRE)	Aug 3 2006
2m 4f	4m 11.7	3	7-10	Firm	Lucky Moon	Aug 2 1990

GREAT LEIGHS (A.W)

Distance	Time	Age	Weight	Going	Horse	Date
5f	60.36	2	8-12	Standard	Rublevka Star (USA)	Oct 23 2008
5f	59.34	6	9-0	Standard	Almaty Express	May 28 2008
6f	1m 13.13	2	8-9	Standard	Calahonda	Nov 15 2008
6f	1m 11.52	6	9-1	Standard	Nota Bene	May 29 2008
1m	1m 39.24	2	9-0	Standard	Shampagne	Sep 27 2008
1m	1m 37.16	3	8-8	Standard	Roaring Forte (IRE)	Sep 27 2008
1m 2f	2m 5.02	4	8-12	Standard	Mutajarred	May 28 2008
1m 5f 66y	2m 48.87	5	9-7	Standard	Red Gala	Sep 27 2008
1m 6f	3m 0.73	3	9-7	Standard	Detonator	Sep 14 2008
2m	3m 28.69	4	9-1	Standard	Whaxaar (IRE)	Apr 30 2008

HAMILTON

Distance	Time	Age	Weight	Going	Horse	Date
5f 4y	57.95 secs	2	8-8	Gd to Firm	Rose Blossom	May 29 2009
5f 4y	57.95 secs	2	8-8	Gd to Firm	Rose Blossom	May 29 2009
6f 5y	1m 10.0	2	8-12	Gd to Firm	Break The Code	Aug 24 1999
6f 5y	69.3 secs	4	8-7	Firm	Marcus Game	Jly 11 1974
1m 65y	1m 45.8	2	8-11	Firm	Hopeful Subject	Sep 24 1973
1m 65y	1m 42.7	6	7-7	Firm	Cranley	Sep 25 1972
1m 1f 36y	1m 53.6	5	9-6	Gd to Firm	Regent's Secret	Aug 10 2005
1m 3f 16y	2m 19.32	3	9-0	Gd to Firm	Captain Webb	May 16 2008
1m 4f 17y	2m 30.52	5	9-10	Gd to Firm	Record Breaker (IRE)	Jun 10 2009
1m 5f 9y	2m 45.1	6	9-6	Firm	Mentalasanythin	Jun 14 1995

HAYDOCK

Distance	Time	Age	Weight	Going	Horse	Date
5f	59.2 secs	2	9-4	Firm	Money For Nothing	Aug 21 1964
5f	57.15 secs	3	8-11	Gd to firm	Fleeting Spirit (IRE)	May 24 2008
6f	1m 10.9	4	9-9	Gd to Firm	Wolfhound (USA)	Sep 4 1993
6f	69.9 secs	4	9-0	Gd to Firm	Iktamal (USA)	Sep 7 1996
7f 30y	1m 29.4	2	9-0	Gd to Firm	Apprehension	Sep 7 1996
7f 30y	1m 26.8	3	8-7	Gd to Firm	Lady Zonda	Sep 28 2002
1m 30y	1m 40.6	2	8-12	Gd to Firm	Besiege	Sep 7 1996
1m 30y	1m 40.1	3	9-2	Firm	Untold Riches (USA)	Jly 11 1999
1m2f 95y	2m 9.95	3	8-8	Good	Jukebox Jury (IRE)	Aug 8 2009
1m 2f 120y	2m 22.2	2	8-11	Soft	Persian Haze	Oct 9 1994
1m 2f 120y	2m 8.5	3	8-7	Gd to Firm	Fahal (USA)	Aug 5 1995
1m 3f 200y	2m 26.4	5	8-2	Firm	New Member	Jly 4 1970
1m 6f	2m 58.46	3	8-10	Gd to Firm	Meshtri (IRE)	Sep 27 2008
2m 45y	3m 27.0	4	8-13	Firm	Prince of Peace	May 26 1984
2m 1f 130y	3m 55.0	3	8-12	Good	Crystal Spirit	Sep 8 1990

KEMPTON (A.W)

Distance	Time	Age	Weight	Going	Horse	Date
5f	60.29 sec	2	9-1	Standard	Inflight (IRE)	Aug 23 2006
5f	59.77 sec	5	8-7	Standard	Harry Up	Dec 10 2006
6f	1m 11.91	2	9-0	Standard	Elnawin	Sep 6 2008
6f	1m 11.11	4	9-4	Standard	Edge Closer	May 29 2008
7f	1m 25.93	2	9-0	Standard	Boscobel	Nov 22 2006
7f	1m 23.65	3	8-10	Standard	Seek The Fair Land	Dec 13 2009
1m	1m 37.47	3	9-1	Standard	Evident Pride (USA)	Nov 29 2006
1m 2f	2m 3.77	6	8-13	Standard	Kandidate	Mar 29 2008
1m 3f	2m 17.74	4	9-9	Standard	Ajhar (USA)	Sep 5 2008
1m 4f	2m 30.48	3	8-11	Standard	Dansant	Nov 3 2007
2m	3m 27.49	4	9-2	Standard	Velvet Heights (IRE)	Apr 26 2006

LEICESTER

Distance	Time	Age	Weight	Going	Horse	Date
5f 2y	58.4 secs	2	9-0	Firm	Cutting Blade	Jun 9 1986
5f 2y	59.85 secs	5	9-5	Gd to Firm	The Jobber (IRE)	Sep 18 2006
5f 218y	1m 10.1	2	9-0	Firm	Thordis (IRE)	Oct 24 1995
5f 218y	69.12 secs	6	8-12	Gd to Firm	Peter Island (FR)	Apr 25 2009
7f 9y	1m 22.60	2	9-0	Gd to Firm	Marie De Medici (USA)	Oct 6 2009
7f 9y	1m 20.8	3	8-7	Firm	Flower Bowl	Jun 9 1986
1m 60y	1m 44.05	2	8-11	Gd to Firm	Congressional (IRE)	Sep 6 2005
1m 60y	1m 41.89	5	9-7	Gd to Firm	Vainglory	Jun 18 2009
1m 1f 218y	2m 5.3	2	9-1	Gd to Firm	Windsor Castle	Oct 14 1996
1m 1f 218y	2m 2.4	3	8-11	Firm	Effigy	Nov 4 1985
1m 1f 218y	2m 2.4	4	9-6	Gd to Firm	Lady Angharad (IRE)	Jun 18 2000
1m 3f 183y	2m 27.1	5	8-12	Gd to Firm	Murghem (IRE)	Jun 18 2000

LINGFIELD (TURF)

Distance	Time	Age	Weight	Going	Horse	Date
5f	57.1 secs	2	8-9	Good	Emerald Peace	Aug 6 1999
5f	56.2 secs	3	9-1	Gd to Firm	Eveningperformance	Jly 25 1994
6f	68.36 secs	2	8-12	Gd to Firm	Folly Bridge	Sept 8 2009
6f	68.2 secs	6	9-10	Firm	Al Amead	Jly 2 1986
7f	1m 21.3	2	7-6	Firm	Mandav	Oct 3 1980
7f	1m 20.1	3	8-7	Gd to Firm	Zelah (IRE)	May 13 1998
7f 140y	1m 28.7	2	9-3	Gd to Firm	Al Muheer	Aug 4 2007
7f 140y	1m 26.7	3	8-6	Fast	Hiaam	Nov 7 1978
1m 1f	1m 52.4	4	9-2	Gd to Firm	Quandary (USA)	Jly 15 1995
1m 2f	2m 4.6	3	9-3	Firm	Usran	Jly 15 1989
1m 3f 106y	2m 23.9	3	8-5	Firm	Night-Shirt	Jly 14 1990
1m 6f	2m 59.1	5	9-5	Firm	Ibn Bey	Jly 1 1989
2m	3m 23.7	3	9-5	Gd to Firm	Lauries Crusader	Aug 13 1988

LINGFIELD (A.W)

Distance	Time	Age	Weight	Going	Horse	Date
5f	58.46 secs	2	8-2	Standard	Ruby Tallulah	Aug 12 2008
5f	57.26 secs	8	8-12	Standard	Magic Glade	Feb 24 2007
6f	1m 10.75	2	9-4	Standard	Global City (IRE)	Oct 15 2008
6f	69.61	6	9-0	Standard	Excusez Moi (USA)	Feb 23 2008
6f	69.61	4	9-5	Standard	Jaconet (USA)	Sept 4 2009
7f	1m 23.68	2	8-4	Standard	Young Dottie	Oct 21 2008
7f	1m 22.19	4	8-7	Standard	Red Spell	Nov 19 2005
1m	1m 36.5	2	9-5	Standard	San Pier Niceto	Nov 30 1989
1m	1m 34.77	4	9-3	Standard	Baharah (USA)	Oct 30 2008
1m 2f	2m 1.79	5	9-0	Standard	Cusoon	Feb 24 2007
1m 4f	2m 28.10	3	8-10	Standard	Falcativ	Oct 27 2008
1m 5f	2m 42.47	3	9-2	Standard	Raffaas	July 3 2007
2m	3m 20.0	3	9-0	Standard	Yenoora	Aug 8 1992

MUSSELBURGH

Distance	Time	Age	Weight	Going	Horse	Date
5f	57.7 secs	2	8-2	Firm	Arasong	May 16 1994
5f	57.3 secs	3	8-12	Firm	Corunna	Jun 3 2000
7f 30y	1m 27.46	2	8-8	Good	DurhamReflection(IRE)	Sept 14 2009
7f 30y	1m 26.3	3	9-5	Firm	Waltzing Wizard	Aug 22 2002
1m	1m 40.3	2	8-12	Gd to Firm	Succession	Sep 26 2004
1m	1m 36.83	3	9-5	Gd to Firm	Ginger Jack	Jul 13 2010
1m 1f	1m 50.42	8	8-11	Gd to Firm	Dhaular Dhar	Sept 3 2010
1m 4f	2m 33.7	3	9-11	Firm	Alexandrine	Jun 26 2000
1m4f 100y	2m 36.80	3	8-3	Gd to Firm	Harris Tweed	Jun 5 2010
1m 5f	2m 47.51	6	9-11	Gd to Firm	Dimashq	Jly 31 2008
1m 6f	2m 59.2	3	9-7	Firm	Forum Chris	Jly 3 2000
2m	3m 26.6	5	9-6	Gd to Firm	Jack Dawson (IRE)	Jun 1 2002

NEWBURY

Distance	Time	Age	Weight	Going	Horse	Date
5f 34y	59.1 secs	2	8-6	Gd to Firm	Superstar Leo	Jly 22 2000
5f 34y	59.2 secs	3	9-5	Gd to Firm	The Trader (IRE)	Aug 18 2001
6f 8y	1m 11.07	2	8-4	Gd to Firm	Bahati (IRE)	May 30 2009
6f 8y	69.42 secs	3	8-11	Gd to Firm	Nota Bene	May 13 2005
7f	1m 23.0	2	8-11	Gd to Firm	Haafhd	Aug 15 2003
7f	1m 21.5	3	8-4	Gd to Firm	Three Points	Jly 21 2000
1m	1m 37.5	2	9-1	Gd to firm	Winged Cupid (IRE)	Sep 16 2005
1m	1m 33.59	6	9-0	Firm	Rakti	May 14 2005
1m 1f	1m 49.6	3	8-0	Gd to Firm	Holtye	May 21 1995
1m 2f 6y	2m 1.2	3	8-7	Gd to Firm	Wall Street (USA)	Jly 20 1996
1m 3f 5y	2m 16.5	3	8-9	Gd to Firm	Grandera (IRE)	Sep 22 2001
1m 4f 5y	2m 28.26	4	9-7	Gd to Firm	Azamour (IRE)	Jul 23 2005
1m 5f 61y	2m 44.9	5	10-0	Gd to Firm	Mystic Hill	Jly 20 1996
2m	3m 25.4	8	9-12	Gd to Firm	Moonlight Quest	Jly 19 1996

NEWCASTLE

Distance	Time	Age	Weight	Going	Horse	Date
5f	58.8 secs	2	9-0	Firm	Atlantic Viking (IRE)	Jun 4 1997
5f	58.0 secs	4	9-2	Firm	Princess Oberon	Jly 23 1994
6f	1m 11.98	2	9-3	Good	Pearl Arch (IRE)	Sep 6 2010
6f	1m 10.58	4	9-9	Gd to Firm	Jonny Mudball	Jun 26 2010
7f	1m 24.2	2	9-0	Gd to Firm	Iscan (IRE)	Aug 31 1998
7f	1m 23.3	4	9-2	Gd to Firm	Quiet Venture	Aug 31 1998
1m	1m 38.9	2	9-0	Gd to Firm	Stowaway	Oct 2 1996
1m	1m 38.9	3	8-12	Firm	Jacamar	Jly 22 1989
1m 3y	1m 37.1	2	8-3	Gd to Firm	Hoh Steamer (IRE)	Aug 31 1998
1m 3y	1m 37.3	3	8-8	Gd to Firm	Its Magic	May 27 1999
1m 1f 9y	2m 3.2	2	8-13	Soft	Response	Oct 30 1993
1m 1f 9y	1m 52.3	3	6-3	Good	Ferniehurst	Jun 23 1936
1m 2f 32y	2m 6.5	4	8-9	Fast	Missionary Ridge	Jly 29 1990
1m 4f 93y	2m 37.3	5	8-12	Firm	Retender	Jun 25 1994
1m 6f 97y	3m 6.4	3	9-6	Gd to Firm	One Off	Aug 6 2003
2m 19y	3m 24.3	4	8-10	Good	Far Cry (IRE)	Jun 26 1999

NEWMARKET (ROWLEY)

Distance	Time	Age	Weight	Going	Horse	Date
5f	58.7 secs	2	8-5	Gd to Firm	Valiant Romeo	Oct 3 2002
5f	56.8 secs	6	9-2	Gd to Firm	Lochsong	Apr 30 1994
6f	69.56 secs	2	8-12	Gd to Firm	Bushranger (IRE)	Oct 3 2008
6f	69.56 secs	2	8-12	Gd to Firm	Bushranger (IRE)	Oct 3 2008
7f	1m 22.39	2	8-12	Gd to Firm	Ashram (IRE)	Sep 21 2004
7f	1m 22.2	4	9-5	Gd to Firm	Perfolia	Oct 17 1991
1m	1m 35.7	2	9-0	Gd to Firm	Forward Move (IRE)	Sep 21 2004
1m	1m 34.07	4	9-0	Gd to Firm	Eagle Mountain	Oct 3 2008
1m 1f	1m 47.2	4	9-5	Firm	Beauchamp Pilot	Oct 5 2002
1m 2f	2m 4.6	2	9-4	Good	Highland Chieftain	Nov 2 1985
1m 2f	2m 0.13	3	8-12	Good	New Approach (IRE)	Oct 18 2008
1m 4f	2m 27.1	5	8-12	Gd to Firm	Eastern Breeze	Oct 3 2003
1m 6f	2m 51.59	3	8-7	Good	Art Eyes (USA)	Sep 29 2005
2m	3m 19.5	5	9-5	Gd to Firm	Grey Shot	Oct 4 1997
2m 2f	3m 47.5	3	7-12	Hard	Whiteway	Oct 15 1947

NEWMARKET (JULY)

Distance	Time	Age	Weight	Going	Horse	Date
5f	58.5 secs	2	8-10	Good	Seductress	Jly 10 1990
5f	56.09 secs	6	9-11	Good	Borderlescott	Aug 22 2008
6f	1m 10.35	2	8-11	Good	Elnawin	Aug 22 2008
6f	69.5 secs	3	8-13	Gd to Firm	Stravinsky (USA)	Jly 8 1999
7f	1m 24.01	2	9-0	Good	Golden Stream (IRE)	Aug 22 2008
7f	1m 22.5	3	9-7	Firm	Ho Leng (IRE)	Jly 9 1998
1m	1m 37.47	2	8-13	Good	Whippers Love (IRE)	Aug 28 2009
1m	1m 35.5	3	8-6	Gd to Firm	Lovers Knot	Jly 8 1998
1m 110y	1m 44.1	3	8-11	Good	Golden Snake	Apr 15 1999
1m 2f	2m 0.9	4	9-3	Gd to Firm	Elhayq (IRE)	May 1 1999
1m 4f	2m 25.11	3	8-11	Good	Lush Lashes	Aug 22 2008
1m 6f 175y	3m 4.2	3	8-5	Good	Arrive	Jly 11 2001
2m 24y	3m 20.2	7	9-10	Good	Yorkshire	Jly 11 2001

NOTTINGHAM

Distance	Time	Age	Weight	Going	Horse	Date
5f 13y	57.9 secs	2	8-9	Firm	Hoh Magic	May 13 1994
5f 13y	57.6 secs	6	9-2	Gd to firm	Catch The Cat (IRE)	May 14 2005
6f 15y	1m 11.4	2	811	Firm	Jameelapi	Aug 8 1983
6f 15y	1m 10.0	4	9-2	Firm	Ajanac	Aug 8 1988
1m75y	1m 46.93	2	9-0	Gd to Firm	Psychic Ability	Oct 28 2009
1m 75y	1m 42.25	5	9-1	Gd To Firm	Rio De La Plata	Jun 2 2010
1m 1f 213y	2m 5.6	2	9-0	Firm	Al Salite	Oct 28 1985
1m 1f 213y	2m 2.3	2	9-0	Firm	Ayaabi	Jly 21 1984
1m 2f 50y	2m 09.54	4	9-12	Gd To Firm	Geneva Geyser	Jly 3 2010
1m 6f 15y	2m 57.8	3	8-10	Firm	Buster Jo	Oct 1 1985
2m 9y	3m 24.0	5	7-7	Firm	Fet	Oct 5 2036
2m 2f 18y	3m 55.1	9	9-10	Gd to Firm	Pearl Run	May 1 1990

PONTEFRACT

Distance	Time	Age	Weight	Going	Horse	Date
5f	61.1 secs	2	9-0	Firm	Golden Bounty	Sep 20 2001
5f	60.8 secs	4	8-9	Firm	Blue Maeve	Sep 29 2004
6f	1m 14.0	2	9-3	Firm	Fawzi	Sep 6 1983
6f	1m 12.6	3	7-13	Firm	Merry One	Aug 29 1970
1m 4y	1m 42.8	2	9-13	Firm	Star Spray	Sep 6 1983
1m 4y	1m 42.8	2	9-0	Firm	Alasil (USA)	Sep 26 2002
1m 4y	1m 40.6	4	9-10	Gd to Firm	Island Light	Apr 13 2002
1m 2f 6y	2m 10.1	2	9-0	Firm	Shanty Star	Oct 7 2002
1m 2f 6y	2m 8.2	4	7-8	Hard	Happy Hector	Jly 9 1979
1m 2f 6y	2m 8.2	3	7-13	Hard	Tom Noddy	Aug 21 1972
1m 4f 8y	2m 33.72	3	8-7	Firm	Ajaan	Aug 8 2007
2m 1f 22y	3m 40.67	4	8-7	Gd to Firm	Paradise Flight	June 6 2005
2m 1f 216y	3m 51.1	3	8-8	Firm	Kudz	Sep 9 1986
2m 5f 122y	4m 47.8	4	8-4	Firm	Physical	May 14 1984

REDCAR

Distance	Time	Age	Weight	Going	Horse	Date
5f	56.9 secs	2	9-0	Firm	Mister Joel	Oct 24 1995
5f	56.01 secs	10	9-3	Firm	Henry Hall	Sep 20 2006
6f	68.8 secs	2	8-3	Gd to Firm	Obe Gold	Oct 2 2004
6f	68.6 secs	3	9-2	Gd to Firm	Sizzling Saga	Jun 21 1991
7f	1m 21.28	2	9-3	Firm	Karoo Blue	Sep 20 2006
7f	1m 21.0	3	9-1	Firm	Empty Quarter	Oct 3 1995
1m	1m 34.37	2	9-0	Firm	Mastership	Sep 20 2006
1m	1m 32.42	4	10-0	Firm	Nanton	Sep 20 2006
1m 1f	1m 52.4	2	9-0	Firm	Spear (IRE)	Sep 13 2004
1m 1f	1m 48.5	5	8-12	Firm	Mellottie	Jly 25 1990
1m 2f	2m 10.1	2	8-11	Good	Adding	Nov 10 1989
1m 2f	2m 1.4	5	9-2	Firm	Eradicate	May 28 1990
1m 3f	2m 17.2	3	8-9	Firm	Photo Call	Aug 7 1990
1m 5f 135y	2m 54.7	6	9-10	Firm	Brodessa	Jun 20 1992
1m 6f 19y	2m 59.81	4	9-1	Gd to Firm	Esprit De Corps	Sep 11 2006
2m 4y	3m 24.9	3	9-3	Gd to Firm	Subsonic	Oct 8 1991
2m 3f	4m 10.1	5	7-4	Gd to Firm	Seldom In	Aug 9 1991

RIPON

Distance	Time	Age	Weight	Going	Horse	Date
5f	57.8 secs	2	8-8	Firm	Super Rocky	Jly 5 1991
5f	57.6 secs	5	8-5	Good	Broadstairs Beauty	May 21 1995
6f	1m 10.4	2	9-2	Good	Cumbrian Venture	Aug 17 2002
6f	69.8 secs	4	9-8	Gd to Firm	Tadeo	Aug 16 1997
6f	69.8 secs	5	7-10	Firm	Quoit	Jly 23 1966
1m	1m 39.79	2	8-6	Good	Top Jaro (FR)	Sep 24 2005
1m	1m 36.62	4	8-11	Gd to Firm	Granston (IRE)	Aug 29 2005
1m 1f 170y	1m 59.12	5	8-9	Gd to Firm	Wahoo Sam (USA)	Aug 30 2005
1m 2f	2m 2.6	3	9-4	Firm	Swift Sword	Jly 20 1990
1m 4f 10y	2m 32.06	4	8-8	Good	Hearthstead Wings	Apr 29 2006
2m	3m 27.07	5	9-12	Gd to Firm	Greenwich Meantime	Aug 30 2005

SALISBURY

Distance	Time	Age	Weight	Going	Horse	Date
5f	59.3 secs	2	9-0	Gd to Firm	Ajigolo	May 12 2005
5f	59.3 secs	2	9-0	Gd to Firm	Ajigolo	May 12 2005
6f	1m 12.1	2	8-0	Gd to Firm	Parisian Lady (IRE)	Jun 10 1997
6f	1m 11.3	3	8-1	Firm	Bentong (IRE)	May 7 2006
6f 212y	1m 25.9	2	9-0	Firm	More Royal (USA)	Jun 29 1995
6f 212y	1m 24.9	3	9-7	Firm	High Summer (USA)	Sep 5 1996
1m	1m 40.4	2	8-13	Firm	Choir Master (USA)	Sep 17 2002
1m	1m 38.29	3	8-7	Gd to Firm	Layman (USA)	Aug 11 2005
1m 1f 198y	2m 4.9	3	8-6	Gd to Firm	Zante	Aug 12 1998
1m 4f	2m 31.6	3	9-5	Gd to Firm	Arrive	Jun 27 2001
1m 6f 15y	2m 59.4	3	8-6	Gd to Firm	Tabareeh	Sep 2 1999

SANDOWN

Distance	Time	Age	Weight	Going	Horse	Date
5f 6y	59.4 secs	2	9-3	Firm	Times Time	Jly 22 1982
5f 6y	58.8 secs	6	8-9	Gd to Firm	Palacegate Touch	Sep 17 1996
7f 16y	1m 26.56	2	9-0	Gd to Firm	Raven's Pass (USA)	Sep 1 2007

Distance	Time	Age	Weight	Going	Horse	Date
7f 16y	1m 26.3	3	9-0	Firm	Mawsuff	Jun 14 1983
1m 14y	1m 41.1	2	8-11	Fast	Reference Point	Sep 23 1986
1m 14y	1m 39.0	3	8-8	Firm	Linda s Fantasy	Aug 19 1983
1m 1f	1m 54.6	2	8-8	Gd to Firm	French Pretender	Sep 20 1988
1m 1f	1m 52.4	7	9-3	Gd to Firm	Bourgainville	Aug 11 2005
1m 2f 7y	2m 2.1	4	8-11	Firm	Kalaglow	May 31 1982
1m 3f 91y	2m 21.6	4	8-3	Fast	Aylesfield	Jly 7 1984
1m 6f	2m 56.9	4	8-7	Gd to Firm	Lady Rosanna	Jly 19 1989
2m 78y	3m 29.9	6	9-2	Firm	Sadeem	May 29 1989

SOUTHWELL (TURF)

Distance	Time	Age	Weight	Going	Horse	Date
6f	1m 15.03	2	9-3	Good	Trepa	Sep 6 2006
6f	1m 13.48	4	8-10	Good	Paris Bell	Sep 6 2006
7f	1m 27.56	2	9-7	Good	Hart Of Gold	Sep 6 2006
7f	1m 25.95	3	9-0	Good	Aeroplane	Sep 6 2006
1m 2f	2m 7.470	3	8-11	Good	Desert Authority(USA)	Sep 6 2006
1m 3f	2m 20.13	4	9-12	Good	Sanchi	Sep 6 2006
1m 4f	2m 34.4	5	9-3	Gd to Firm	Corn Lily	Aug 10 1991
2m	3m 34.1	5	9-1	Gd to Firm	Triplicate	Sep 20 1991

SOUTHWELL (A.W)

Distance	Time	Age	Weight	Going	Horse	Date
5f	58.89 secs	2	8-6	Standard	Egyptian Lord	Dec 15 2005
5f	57.14 secs	5	9-5	Standard	Godfrey Street	Jan 24 2008
6f	1m 14.00	2	8-5	Standard	Panalo	Nov 8 1989
6f	1m 13.50	4	10-02	Standard	Saladan Knight	Dec 30 1989
7f	1m 27.10	2	8-2	Standard	Mystic Crystal	Nov 20 1990
7f	1m 26.80	5	8-4	Standard	Amenable	Dec 13 1990
1m	1m 38.00	2	8-9	Standard	Alpha Rascal	Nov 13 1990
1m	1m 38.00	2	8-10	Standard	Andrew s First	Dec 30 1989
1m	1m 37.25	3	8-6	Standard	Valira	Nov 3 1990
1m 3f	2m 21.50	4	9-7	Standard	Tempering	Dec 5 1990
1m 4f	2m 33.90	4	9-12	Standard	Fast Chick	Nov 8 1989
1m 6f	3m 1.60	3	7-8	Standard	Erevnon	Dec 29 1990
2m	3m 37.60	9	8-12	Standard	Old Hubert	Dec 5 1990

THIRSK

Distance	Time	Age	Weight	Going	Horse	Date
5f	57.2 secs	2	9-7	Gd to Firm	Proud Boast	Aug 5 2000
5f	56.9 secs	5	9-6	Firm	Charlie Parkes	April 11 2003
6f	69.2 secs	2	9-6	Gd to Firm	Westcourt Magic	Aug 25 1995
6f	68.8 secs	6	9-4	Firm	Johayro	Jly 23 1999
7f	1m 23.7	2	8-9	Firm	Courting	Jly 23 1999
7f	1m 22.8	4	8-5	Firm	Silver Haze	May 21 1988
1m	1m 37.9	2	9-0	Firm	Sunday Symphony	Sep 4 2004
1m	1m 34.8	4	8-13	Firm	Yearsley	May 5 1990
1m 4f	2m 29.9	5	9-12	Firm	Gallery God	Jun 4 2001
2m	3m 22.3	3	8-11	Firm	Tomaschek	Jly 17 1981

WARWICK

Distance	Time	Age	Weight	Going	Horse	Date
5f	57.95 secs	2	8-9	Gd to Firm	Amour Propre	Jun 26 2008
5f	57.7 secs	4	9-6	Gd to Firm	Little Edward	Jly 7 2002
5f 110y	63.6 secs	5	8-6	Gd to Firm	Dizzy In The Head	Jun 27 2004
6f	1m 11.22	2	9-3	Gd to Firm	Hurricane Hymnbook	Sep 15 2007
6f	69.44	5	8-12	Gd to Firm	Peter Island	Jun 26 2008
7f 26y	1m 22.9	2	9-0	Firm	Country Rambler(USA)	Jun 20 2004
7f 26y	1m 20.7	4	8-8	Good	Etlaala	Apr 17 2006
1m 22y	1m 37.1	3	8-11	Firm	Orinocovsky (IRE)	Jun 26 2002
1m 2f 188y	2m 14.98	4	8-12	Gd to Firm	Ronaldsay	Jun 16 2008
1m 4f 134y	2m 39.5	3	8-13	Gd to Firm	Maimana (IRE)	Jun 22 2002
1m 6f 135y	3m 7.5	3	9-7	Gd to Firm	Burma Baby (USA)	Jly 2 1999
2m 39y	3m 27.9	3	8-1	Firm	Decoy	Jun 26 2002

WINDSOR

Distance	Time	Age	Weight	Going	Horse	Date
5f 10y	58.75 secs	2	8-12	Gd to Firm	Hoh Mike (IRE)	May 15 2006
5f 10y	58.3 secs	5	7-10	Gd to Firm	Beyond The Clouds	Jun 2 2001
6f	1m 10.5	2	9-5	Gd to Firm	Cubism (USA)	Aug 17 1998
6f	1m 10.06	6	8-11	Gd to Firm	Presto Shinko	Aug 4 2007
1m 67y	1m 42.78	2	8-11	Gd to Firm	Sequillo	Sep 29 2008
1m 67y	1m 40.27	4	9-3	Gd to Firm	Librettist (USA)	Jul 1 2006
1m 2f 7y	2m 3.0	2	9-1	Firm	Moomba Masquerade	May 19 1990
1m2f 7y	2m 2.44	4	9-0	Gd to Firm	Campanologist (USA)	Aug 29 2009
1m 3f 135y	2m 21.5	3	9-2	Firm	Double Florin	May 19 1980

WOLVERHAMPTON (A.W.)

Distance	Time	Age	Weight	Going	Horse	Date
5f 20y	61.13 sec	2	8-8	Std to Fast	Yungaburra (IRE)	Nov 8 2006
5f 20y	60.35 sec	11	8-13	Standard	Little Edward	Mar 29 2009
5f 216y	1m 12.61	2	9-0	Std to Fast	Prime Defender	Nov 8 2006
5f 216y	1m 13.32	5	8-12	Standard	Desert Opal	Sep 17 2005
7f 32y	1m 27.70	2	9-5	Standard	Billy Dane	Aug 14 2006
7f 32y	1m 26.65	4	8-12	Std to Fast	Capucci	Sept 30 2009
1m 141y	1m 48.08	2	8-9	Std to Fast	Worldly	Aug 30 2006
1m 141y	1m 46.48	3	8-9	Standard	Gitano Hernando	Sept 17 2009
1m 1f 103y	2m 0.76	2	9-0	Standard	Mr Excel (IRE)	Nov 14 2005
1m 1f 103y	1m 57.34	4	8-13	Standard	Bahar Shumaal (IRE)	Aug 31 2006
1m 4f 50y	2m 35.71	3	9-2	Std to Fast	Steppe Dancer (IRE)	Aug 30 2006
1m 5f 194y	2m 59.85	6	9-12	Std to Fast	Valance (IRE)	Aug 30 2006
2m 119y	3m 35.85	5	8-11	Std to Fast	Market Watcher (USA)	Nov 21 2006

YARMOUTH

Distance	Time	Age	Weight	Going	Horse	Date
5f 43y	60.4 secs	2	8-6	Gd to Firm	Ebba	Jly 26 1999
5f 43y	59.8 secs	4	8-13	Gd to Firm	Roxanne Mill	Aug 25 2002
6f 3y	1m 10.4	2	9-0	Fast	Lanchester	Aug 15 1988
6f 3y	69.9 secs	4	8-9	Firm	Malhub (USA)	Jun 13 2002
7f 3y	1m 22.2	2	9-0	Gd to Firm	Warrshan	Sep 14 1988
7f 3y	1m 22.12	4	9-4	Gd to Firm	Glenbuck (IRE)	Apr 26 2007
1m 3y	1m 36.3	2	8-2	Gd to Firm	Outrun	Sep 15 1988
1m 3y	1m 33.9	3	8-8	Firm	Bonne Etoile	Jun 27 1995
1m 1f	1m 53.70	3	9-2	Good	Crystal Feather	Aug 6 2009
1m 2f 21y	2m 2.83	3	8-8	Firm	Reunite (IRE)	Jul 18 2006
1m 3f 101y	2m 23.1	3	8-9	Firm	Rahil	Jly 1 1993
1m 6f 17y	2m 57.8	3	8-2	Gd to Firm	Barakat	Jly 24 1990
2m	3m 26.7	4	8-2	Gd to Firm	Alhesn (USA)	Jly 26 1999
2m 2f 51y	3m 56.8	4	9-10	Firm	Provence	Sep 19 1991

YORK

Distance	Time	Age	Weight	Going	Horse	Date
5f	57.3 secs	2	7-8	Gd to Firm	Lyric Fantasy	Aug 20 1992
5f	56.1 secs	3	9-3	Gd to Firm	Dayjur	Aug 23 1990
5f 89y	63.81 secs	2	9-3	Gd to Firm	El Viento (FR)	Sep 5 2010
5f 89y	62.31 secs	6	9-5	Gd to Firm	Barney McGrew (IRE)	Aug 18 2009
6f	69.28 secs	2	8-12	Gd to Firm	Showcasing	Aug 19 2009
6f	68.58 secs	7	9-4	Firm	Cape Of Good Hope	Jun 16 2005
7f	1m 22.45	2	9-0	Gd to Firm	ElusivePimpernel(USA)	Aug 18 2009
7f	1m 21.93	3	8-9	Gd to Firm	Yaa Wayl	Aug 20 2010
1m	1m 39.20	2	8-1	Gd to Firm	Missoula (IRE)	Aug 31 2005
1m	1m 36.24	3	9-2	Gd to Firm	Capponi	Jul 10 2010
1m 208y	1m 46.76	5	9-8	Gd to Firm	Echo Of Light	Sep 5 2007
1m 2f 88y	2m 5.29	3	8-11	Gd to Firm	Sea The Stars (IRE)	Aug 18 2009
1m 4f	2m 26.28	6	8-9	Firm	Bandari (IRE)	Jun 18 2005
1m 6f	2m 54.96	4	9-0	Gd to Firm	Tactic	May 22 2010
1m 7f 195y	3m 18.4	3	8-0	Gd to Firm	Dam Busters	Aug 16 1988
2m 88y	3m 30.63	4	9-1	Gd to Firm	Askar Tau (FR)	Aug 19 2009

Raceform Flat speed figures 2010

(Best time performances achieved 1st January - 31st December 2010 (min rating 110, 2-y-o 105)

THREE YEAR-OLDS AND UPWARDS - Turf

Across The Rhine 113 (8f,Cur,S,Sep 12)
Address Unknown 114 (10f,Leo,GF,May 9)
Advanced 111 (6f,Thi,GF,Apr 17)
Afsare 110 (10f,Don,GF,Jun 5)
Age Of Aquarius 111 (20f,Asc,GF,Jun 17)
Air Chief Marshal 112 (7f,Cur,GY,Jly 17)
Aizavoski 111 (12f,Lon,G,May 6)
Akdarena 112 (10f,Cur,GF,Jun 26)
Al Farahidi 113 (8f,Hay,GF,May 22)
Al Zir 111 (12f,Eps,GF,Jun 5)
Alainmaar 111 (10f,Lin,GF,May 8)
Alis Aquilae 111 (5f,Bev,GF,Jly 3)
Allied Powers 113 (12f,Lon,G,May 6)
Allybar 113 (10½f,Yor,GF,Jly 24)
Almiqdaad 110 (12f,Hay,GF,Jly 3)
Alrasm 113 (12f,Chs,G,May 5)
Alverta 113 (6f,Nmk,GF,Jly 9)
Americain 115 (15f,Dea,G,Aug 22)
Angel s Pursuit 110 (6f,Sal,GF,Jun 13)
Angus Newz 111 (6f,Nmk,GS,May 2)
Anna Salai 115 (8f,Cur,GF,May 23)
Arctic 111 (5f,Lon,VS,Oct 3)
Arctic Cosmos 111 (12f,Asc,GF,Jun 18)
Articilitis 110 (10f,Cur,GF,Jun 25)
Ashiyla 113 (12f,Lon,S,Sep 12)
Astrophysical Jet 113 (5f,Cur,G,Aug 29)
At First Sight 115 (12f,Eps,GF,Jun 5)
Averroes 111 (12f,Chs,G,May 5)
Aviate 114 (8f,Nmk,S,Oct 2)
Await The Dawn 115 (10f,Leo,G,Sep 4)
Awzaan 112 (7f,Nby,G,Sep 17)

Bagamoyo 110 (6f,Nmk,GF,Jly 7)
Balducci 114 (8f,Hay,GF,May 22)
Balthazaar s Gift 116 (7f,Don,G,Sep 11)
Barack 111 (7f,Cur,YS,Sep 26)
Barshiba 111 (12f,Asc,GF,May 8)
Beachfire 110 (10f,Goo,GF,Jly 29)
Beethoven 117 (8f,Asc,GS,Sep 25)
Behkabad 119 (12f,Lon,S,Sep 12)
Benbaun 112 (5f,Lon,G,May 16)
Bethrah 116 (8f,Cur,GF,May 23)
Bewitched 113 (6f,Asc,GS,Oct 9)
Beyond Desire 111 (6f,Hay,GF,May 22)
Big Robert 111 (8f,Cur,S,Mar 21)
Black Mambazo 111 (5f,Lon,G,May 16)
Blek 113 (15½f,Lon,G,May 23)
Blue Jack 111 (5f,Chs,GF,Jly 10)
Blue Panis 111 (8f,Cha,S,Jun 13)
Bluster 110 (5f,Lon,G,May 16)
Borderlescott 114 (5f,Asc,G,Jun 15)
Bould Mover 112 (5f,Asc,G,Jun 15)
Bridge Of Gold 112 (14f,Yor,G,Aug 18)
Buachaill Dona 110 (6f,Thi,GF,Apr 17)
Budai 113 (10f,Lon,VS,Oct 2)
Bushman 115 (10½f,Yor,GF,Jly 24)
Buxted 110 (15½f,Lon,G,May 23)
Buzzword 110 (12f,Asc,GF,Jun 18)
Byword 116 (9f,Lon,G,May 23)

Calatrava Cape 110 (12f,Nmk,G,Sep 18)
Caldercruix 110 (10f,Nmk,G,May 30)
Canford Cliffs 117 (8f,Cur,GF,May 22)
Cape Blanco 121 (10f,Leo,G,Sep 4)
Capponi 110 (8f,Yor,GF,Jly 10)
Captain Dunne 110 (5f,Chs,GF,Jly 10)
Captain Royale 110 (6f,Ayr,GS,Sep 30)
Carraiglawn 111 (10f,Cur,GF,Jun 4)
Cassique Lady 112 (11f,War,G,Jun 14)
Castles In The Air 113 (7f,Asc,G,Jly 24)
Cat Junior 111 (7f,Don,G,Sep 11)
Cavalryman 114 (12f,Lon,VS,Oct 3)
Celimene 114 (10f,Lon,S,Apr 11)
Cellabelle 111 (9f,Cha,S,Jun 6)
Celtic Celeb 111 (11f,Lon,G,May 16)
Charminamix 112 (9f,Leo,GF,May 30)
Chinchon 113 (10f,Sai,VS,Mar 20)
Chinese White 114 (10f,Cur,GF,Jun 26)
Chock A Block 113 (10f,Eps,G,Jly 29)
Choose Me 111 (10f,Cur,S,Sep 12)
Cirrus Des Aigles 115 (10f,Lon,VS,Oct 2)
Cityscape 114 (8f,Nmk,GS,Oct 1)
Class Is Class 113 (10f,Goo,G,May 31)
Classic Punch 111 (10f,Nmk,GF,Jly 24)
Clowance 113 (12f,Nby,GS,Oct 23)
Con Artist 112 (10f,San,GF,Aug 5)
Cool Strike 110 (13f,Bat,F,Apr 25)
Coordinated Cut 111 (12f,Eps,GF,Jun 5)
Corporal Maddox 110 (6f,Asc,G,Apr 28)
Court Canibal 114 (10f,Lon,S,Apr 11)
Croisultan 111 (7f,Cur,HY,Apr 11)
Crystal Gal 112 (8f,Cur,GF,May 23)
Cutlass Bay 115 (10f,Lon,S,Apr 11)

Dalghar 112 (8f,Asc,G,Jun 15)
Damien 113 (6f,Thi,GF,Apr 17)
Dancing David 112 (10½f,Cha,S,Jun 6)
Dandino 111 (12f,Goo,GF,Jly 27)
Dandy Boy 110 (7f,Asc,G,May 8)
Dangerous Midge 117 (12f,Hay,GF,Jly 3)
Dariole 111 (12f,Lon,S,Sep 12)
Daryakana 110 (12f,Asc,G,Jly 24)
Deauville Flyer 111 (16½f,Yor,G,Jun 11)
Debussy 113 (10½f,Chs,GS,May 6)
Definightly 112 (6f,Goo,S,Sep 11)
Delegator 113 (7f,Nby,G,Sep 17)
Deluxe 110 (10f,Lon,G,May 23)
Delvita 113 (5f,Cha,S,Jun 6)
Demolition 111 (12f,Hay,GF,Jly 3)
Devoted To You 111 (10f,Leo,GF,Oct 25)
Dick Turpin 117 (8f,Cha,GS,Jly 4)
Dirar 113 (14f,Yor,G,Aug 18)
Distant Memories 113 (10f,Wdr,S,Aug 28)
Dixie Music 112 (10f,Cur,G,Aug 8)
Docofthebay 111 (7f,Ayr,G,Sep 18)
Doncaster Rover 111 (6f,Don,GS,Nov 6)
Dream Eater 115 (8f,Asc,G,Jun 15)
Dream Lodge 110 (10½f,Yor,GF,Jly 24)
Dreamspeed 110 (12f,Nby,GS,Oct 23)
Drunken Sailor 111 (10f,Goo,G,May 31)
Duaiseoir 111 (10f,Cur,GF,Jun 25)
Duff 115 (7f,Don,G,Sep 11)
Duncan 112 (12f,Asc,GF,Jun 19)

Eastern Aria 113 (14½f,Don,G,Sep 9)
Eire 110 (10f,Sai,VS,Mar 20)
Eleanora Duse 112 (10f,Cur,S,Sep 12)
Electrolyser 110 (16f,Goo,GF,Jly 29)
Elnawin 110 (6f,Sal,GF,Jun 13)
Elusive Pimpernel 110 (8f,Nmk,GF,Apr 15)
Elusive Wave 111 (8f,Cha,S,Jun 13)
Emerald Commander 110 (8f,Cha,S,Jun 13)
Emperor Claudius 111 (8f,Cur,GF,Jun 27)
Enact 112 (6f,Nmk,GS,May 2)
Engulf 110 (7f,Mus,GF,Jun 5)
Equiano 117 (5f,Asc,G,Jun 15)
Evaporation 110 (7f,Lon,G,Sep 5)
Evens And Odds 112 (6f,Goo,G,Jly 31)

Fair Trade 113 (8f,Sal,GF,Aug 12)
Fallen Idol 110 (8f,Cha,S,Jun 13)
Fame And Glory 117 (10½f,Cur,GF,May 23)
Famous 110 (7f,Cur,Y,May 3)
Famous Name 117 (10f,Leo,GF,Oct 25)
Fanunalter 111 (8f,Sal,GF,Aug 12)
Fiery Lad 111 (12f,Hay,GF,Jly 3)
Fireback 111 (6f,Nmk,GF,Jly 7)
Flash Dance 111 (7f,Lon,S,Jly 3)
Fleeting Spirit 111 (6f,Nmk,GF,Jly 9)
Flying Cloud 113 (10f,Cur,GF,Jun 26)
Fravashi 110 (7f,Yor,GF,Aug 20)
Free Judgement 114 (8f,Cur,GF,May 22)
Freminius 110 (8f,Cha,S,Jun 13)
Fuisse 113 (8f,Cha,S,Jun 13)

Genki 113 (6f,Hay,GF,Sep 4)
Gilt Edge Girl 117 (5f,Lon,VS,Oct 3)
Glamorous Spirit 112 (5f,Cur,GF,Jun 27)
Glass Harmonium 113 (10f,San,G,Apr 24)
Gold Bubbles 110 (8f,Cur,GF,Jun 27)
Golden Shaheen 110 (6f,Ncs,GS,Jly 24)
Goldikova 119 (8f,Asc,G,Jun 15)
Good Time Sue 111 (7f,Cur,YS,Sep 26)
Gotlandia 111 (8f,Lon,G,Apr 25)
Grand Admiral 111 (10f,Cur,G,Aug 8)
Green Rock 110 (10½f,Cha,S,Jun 6)
Green Tango 113 (15½f,Lon,G,May 23)
Gris De Gris 113 (8f,Sai,HY,Apr 4)
Group Therapy 111 (5f,San,GF,Jly 3)

Halicarnassus 111 (10½f,Cur,GF,May 23)
Handsome Devil 112 (10½f,Cha,S,Jun 6)
Harbinger 120 (12f,Asc,G,Jly 24)
Harriers Call 110 (10f,Leo,GF,Oct 25)
Harris Tweed 111 (12f,Chs,S,Sep 11)
Harrison George 110 (8f,Pon,G,Apr 13)
Hawkeyethenoo 114 (6f,Nmk,GS,May 2)
Hazelrigg 110 (5f,Don,G,Sep 8)
Hearts Of Fire 114 (8f,Asc,GS,Sep 25)
High Heeled 111 (12f,Eps,G,Jun 4)
High Importance 112 (7f,Bri,F,Jly 4)
High Standing 112 (6½f,Dea,GS,Aug 8)
Hillview Boy 111 (10½f,Yor,GF,Jly 10)
Himalya 115 (7f,Don,G,Sep 11)
Hitchens 112 (6f,Don,GS,Nov 6)
Holberg 112 (10f,Goo,GF,Sep 22)
Hot Prospect 112 (10f,Wdr,S,Aug 28)
Hujaylea 114 (7f,Cur,YS,Sep 26)

Ice Blue 114 (10½f,Cha,S,Jun 6)
Illustrious Blue 112 (16½f,San,GF,Jly 3)
Imperial Guest 110 (7f,Asc,GS,Sep 25)
Indian Days 110 (10f,Goo,G,May 31)
Indomito 110 (6½f,Dea,GS,Aug 8)
Invincible Ash 111 (6f,Cur,GF,Jun 27)
Invisible Man 111 (8f,Asc,GF,Jun 16)
Inxile 111 (6f,Don,S,Mar 27)
Iver Bridge Lad 110 (6f,Asc,GS,Oct 9)
Ivory Land 111 (10½f,Cha,S,Jun 6)

Jacqueline Quest 110 (8f,Nmk,GS,May 2)
Jan Vermeer 112 (12f,Eps,GF,Jun 5)
Jeannie Galloway 111 (7f,Mus,GF,Jun 5)
Jet Away 113 (10f,San,GF,Aug 5)
Jimmy Styles 110 (6f,Sal,GF,Jun 13)
Joanna 116 (6½f,Dea,GS,Aug 8)
Jonny Mudball 111 (6f,Goo,G,Jly 31)
Joshua Tree 111 (12f,Yor,G,Aug 17)
Justonefortheroad 111 (8f,Mus,GF,Sep 3)

Kaboura 112 (9f,Cha,S,Jun 6)
Kargali 113 (7f,Cur,HY,Apr 11)
Kasbah Bliss 114 (15½f,Lon,G,May 23)
Keredari 110 (7f,Cur,HY,Apr 11)
Kidnapping 116 (12f,Lon,S,Sep 12)
King Jock 112 (8f,Leo,GF,May 9)
King Of Dixie 111 (8f,Asc,G,Apr 28)
King Of Wands 113 (16½f,San,GF,Jly 3)
Kingdom Of Fife 113 (10f,Asc,GF,Jun 18)
Kings Gambit 113 (10f,Asc,GF,Jun 18)
Kingsfort 111 (8f,Nmk,GS,Oct 30)
Kingsgate Native 115 (5f,Hay,GF,May 22)
Kite Wood 115 (15½f,Lon,G,May 23)
Kolokol 111 (5f,Lon,G,May 16)

La Boum 113 (10f,Lon,S,Apr 11)
Laaheb 111 (10f,Goo,G,May 31)
Laddies Poker Two 112 (6f,Asc,GF,Jun 19)
Lady Artemisia 110 (11f,War,G,Jun 14)
Lady Darshaan 113 (8f,Cur,GF,May 23)
Lady Jane Digby 113 (11f,War,G,Jun 14)
Lady Of The Desert 115 (6f,Asc,GS,Sep 26)
Les Fazzani 111 (10½f,Chs,GS,May 6)
Liang Kay 112 (12f,Lon,VS,Oct 3)
Lillie Langtry 115 (8f,Cur,GF,May 23)
Lily Of The Valley 114 (10f,Lon,VS,Oct 3)
Lolly For Dolly 113 (7f,Cur,Y,May 3)
Lope De Vega 118 (10½f,Cha,S,Jun 6)
Lord Kenmare 110 (9f,Leo,GF,May 30)
Los Cristianos 113 (15f,Dea,G,Aug 22)
Lovelace 112 (7f,Lon,S,Jly 3)
Luisant 113 (7f,Cur,YS,Sep 26)
Lumineux 114 (10½f,Cha,S,Jun 6)
Lush Lashes 111 (10f,Cur,S,Sep 12)
Luttrell Lady 112 (10f,Cur,GF,Jun 25)

Main Aim 111 (8f,Goo,S,Aug 28)
Makfi 116 (8f,Asc,GS,Sep 25)
Manifest 110 (12f,Nby,G,Apr 17)
Manighar 114 (15f,Dea,G,Aug 22)
Mar Adentro 113 (5f,Lon,VS,Oct 3)
Marchand D Or 113 (5f,Lon,G,May 16)
Maria Royal 112 (12½f,Lon,VS,Oct 2)
Marinous 110 (12f,Lon,VS,Oct 3)
Mariol 111 (6½f,Dea,GS,Aug 8)
Markab 116 (6f,Hay,GF,Sep 4)
Masta Plasta 110 (5f,Not,GF,Aug 10)
Maxim Gorky 110 (12f,Chs,G,May 5)
Meeznah 111 (14½f,Don,G,Sep 9)
Merchant Of Dubai 114 (12f,Don,GS,Mar 28)
Mia s Boy 110 (7f,Hay,GF,May 8)
Midas Touch 116 (10f,Leo,GF,May 9)
Midday 114 (12f,Lon,S,Sep 12)
Miss Jean Brodie 110 (10f,Don,GF,Jun 26)
Monterosso 113 (10f,Nmk,G,May 30)
Mood Music 113 (5f,Cha,S,Jun 6)
Mores Wells 112 (12f,Lon,G,May 6)
Motrice 111 (14f,Hay,GF,Jly 2)
Music Show 116 (8f,Nmk,GF,Jly 7)

Nakayama Festa 120 (12f,Lon,VS,Oct 3)
Nanton 113 (10½f,Yor,GF,Jly 24)
Nicconi 112 (5f,Asc,G,Jun 15)
Noble Citizen 112 (7f,Asc,G,Jly 24)
Noble s Promise 110 (8f,Asc,G,Jun 15)
Novellen Lad 111 (6f,Hay,GF,May 22)

On Est Bien 113 (10f,Lon,S,Apr 11)
Opinion Poll 112 (16½f,San,GF,Jly 3)
Ouqba 111 (7f,Don,G,Sep 11)

Paco Boy 118 (8f,Asc,G,Jun 15)
Pain Perdu 115 (10½f,Cha,S,Jun 6)
Palavicini 111 (9f,Nmk,GF,Apr 15)
Parisian Pyramid 110 (6f,Nmk,GS,May 2)
Peinture Rare 110 (12f,Lon,S,Sep 12)
Peligroso 110 (12f,Lei,HY,Oct 25)
Piccadilly Filly 114 (5f,Cha,S,Jun 6)
Pink Symphony 111 (10f,Goo,GF,Sep 22)
Planet Five 115 (5f,Cha,S,Jun 6)
Planteur 118 (12f,Lon,S,Sep 12)
Plumania 113 (12f,Lon,S,Sep 12)
Poet 115 (10½f,Hay,S,Aug 7)
Poet s Voice 120 (8f,Asc,GS,Sep 25)
Polly s Mark 110 (12f,Hay,GS,May 29)
Pompeyano 114 (10f,Eps,G,Jly 29)
Popmurphy 110 (10f,Cur,SH,Apr 11)
Premio Loco 115 (7f,Don,G,Sep 11)
Pressing 111 (8f,Sal,GF,Aug 12)
Prime Defender 111 (6f,Yor,G,May 12)
Prince Siegfried 116 (10f,San,G,Jly 2)
Prohibit 112 (5f,Don,G,Sep 8)

Rainbow Peak 115 (10f,Asc,GF,Jun 18)
Rainfall 115 (8f,Nmk,S,Oct 2)
Rajik 111 (14f,Cur,GF,Aug 21)
Ramble On 110 (8f,Cha,S,Jun 13)
Rava 110 (9f,Cha,S,Jun 6)
Rayeni 112 (7f,Cur,HY,Apr 11)
Rebel Soldier 113 (10½f,Yor,G,Jun 12)
Recharge 111 (10½f,Cur,GF,May 23)
Red Badge 111 (10f,Nby,G,Jly 17)
Red Jade 110 (10f,Don,S,Mar 27)
Red Jazz 119 (8f,Asc,GS,Sep 25)
Redford 114 (6f,Ayr,G,Sep 18)
Redwood 113 (12f,Goo,GF,Jly 30)
Regal Parade 117 (6½f,Dea,GS,Aug 8)
Reggane 110 (7f,Lon,S,Jly 3)
Remember When 115 (8f,Cur,GF,May 23)
Reverence 111 (5f,Cur,GF,Jun 27)
Rewilding 116 (12f,Yor,G,Aug 17)
Riggins 110 (8f,Asc,GF,Jun 16)
Rio De La Plata 114 (9f,Yor,GF,Aug 20)
Rip Van Winkle 119 (8f,Asc,GS,Sep 25)
Rite Of Passage 112 (20f,Asc,GF,Jun 17)
Rosanara 110 (8f,Lon,G,Apr 25)
Rose Blossom 112 (6f,Yor,GF,Jly 9)
Rosika 112 (14f,Yor,G,Aug 18)
Royal Bench 112 (8f,Lon,VS,Oct 2)
Rumoush 112 (14½f,Don,G,Sep 9)
Russian Spirit 113 (6f,Don,GS,Nov 6)

Sahpresa 118 (8f,Nmk,S,Oct 2)
Salut L Africain 112 (7f,Lon,S,Jly 3)
Salute Him 112 (10f,Asc,GF,Jun 18)
Samuel 111 (16½f,San,GF,Jly 3)
Sandor 110 (10½f,Yor,GF,Jly 10)
Sandymount Lady 110 (10f,Cur,GF,Jun 25)
Sans Frontieres 111 (13f,Nby,GS,Aug 14)
Saphira s Fire 110 (11f,War,G,Jun 14)
Sarafina 119 (12f,Lon,VS,Oct 3)
Sarah Lynx 112 (12f,Lon,S,Sep 12)
Sariska 114 (10½f,Yor,GF,May 13)
Sea Lord 116 (10f,Leo,G,Sep 4)
Secrecy 113 (8f,Sal,GF,Aug 12)
Secret Witness 110 (6f,Asc,GS,Oct 9)
Senate 111 (10f,San,GF,Aug 5)
Shakespearean 110 (7f,Nby,GS,Aug 14)
Shalanaya 110 (10f,Asc,GF,Jun 16)
Shamalgan 111 (8f,Lon,G,May 16)
Shamanova 110 (12½f,Lon,VS,Oct 2)
She s Our Mark 111 (10f,Cur,SH,Apr 11)
Sherman McCoy 112 (13f,Bat,F,Apr 25)
Shimraan 112 (10f,Lon,VS,Oct 2)
Showcasing 110 (6f,Yor,G,May 12)
Side Glance 112 (7f,Asc,GS,Sep 25)
Silver Pond 112 (11f,Lon,G,May 16)
Simenon 110 (12f,Don,GS,Nov 6)
Sir Gerry 112 (7f,Nby,G,Sep 17)
Siyouni 113 (8f,Cha,GS,Jly 4)
Skins Game 111 (8f,Sai,HY,Apr 4)
Skysurfers 110 (7f,Yor,GF,Aug 20)
Slickly Royal 111 (8f,Cha,S,Jun 13)
Smooth Operator 111 (6½f,Dea,GS,Aug 8)
Snaefell 113 (6f,Cur,Y,Aug 8)
Snow Fairy 111 (12f,Cur,GY,Jly 18)
Society Rock 111 (6f,Asc,G,Apr 28)
Song Of My Heart 110 (8f,Cur,GF,May 23)
Sormiou 112 (8f,Cha,S,Jun 13)
Spacious 114 (8f,Nmk,GF,Jly 7)
Special Duty 112 (7f,Lon,VS,Oct 3)
Spin Cycle 111 (5f,Hay,GF,May 22)
Spirit Of Sharjah 110 (7f,Lei,GF,Apr 24)
Spruce 113 (12f,Don,GS,Mar 28)
Sri Putra 113 (9f,Nmk,GF,Apr 15)
St Nicholas Abbey 110 (8f,Nmk,GF,May 1)
Stacelita 113 (10f,Lon,VS,Oct 3)
Starfala 110 (12f,Asc,GF,May 8)
Starlish 112 (10f,Lon,S,Apr 11)
Starspangledbanner 115 (6f,Nmk,GF,Jly 9)
Steele Tango 112 (10f,San,G,Jly 2)

Steinbeck 115 (8f,Cur,S,Sep 12)
Stimulation 111 (10f,Asc,GF,Jun 16)
Stotsfold 117 (10f,San,G,Jly 2)
Strawberrydaiquiri 116 (8f,Nmk,S,Oct 2)
Summit Surge 116 (10½f,Yor,GF,Jly 24)
Superstition 110 (12½f,Lon,VS,Oct 2)
Suruor 110 (7f,Asc,G,Jly 24)
Sweet Hearth 111 (8f,Cha,S,Jun 13)
Swiss Diva 111 (5f,Lon,S,Sep 12)
Sybelio 111 (15f,Dea,G,Aug 22)

Tactic 111 (14f,Yor,GF,May 22)
Tangerine Trees 113 (5f,Bev,G,Sep 21)
Tastahil 113 (16f,Nmk,GS,Oct 16)
Tazeez 114 (10f,San,GF,May 27)
Ted Spread 110 (12f,Chs,GS,May 6)
Telluride 111 (12f,Lon,G,May 6)
Termagant 110 (8f,Cur,GF,May 23)
Tertio Bloom 111 (5f,Cha,S,Jun 6)
The Betchworth Kid 110 (12f,Don,GS,Nov 6)
The Fonz 110 (11½f,Wdr,GF,Jun 26)
The Rectifier 111 (8f,Wdr,GF,Jun 26)
Three Moons 111 (10f,Asc,GF,Jun 18)
Thunderball 110 (8f,Mus,GF,Sep 3)
Times Up 112 (12f,Don,GS,Nov 6)
Timos 110 (12f,Lon,G,May 6)
Traffic Guard 114 (10f,San,G,Jly 2)
Tranquil Tiger 112 (9f,Nmk,GF,Apr 15)
Tres Rock Danon 113 (15f,Dea,G,Aug 22)
Triple Aspect 112 (5f,San,GF,Jly 3)
Tropical Treat 111 (6f,Yor,GF,Jly 9)
Tubby Isaacs 110 (6f,Don,GF,May 15)
Twice Over 116 (10½f,Yor,G,Aug 17)

Varenar 111 (6f,Nmk,GF,Jly 9)
Verdant 110 (12f,Goo,GF,Jly 28)
Vertigineux 112 (8f,Cha,S,Jun 13)
Vesuve 112 (9f,Yor,GF,Aug 20)
Victoire De Lyphar 111 (6f,Ayr,G,Sep 18)
Victoire Pisa 115 (12f,Lon,VS,Oct 3)
Viscount Nelson 114 (10½f,Cha,S,Jun 6)
Vision D Etat 113 (10f,Dea,VS,Aug 14)

Wade Giles 114 (8f,Cur,S,Sep 12)
Watar 111 (15f,Dea,G,Aug 22)
Waveband 112 (7f,Asc,GF,Jly 10)
What A Charm 111 (16f,Leo,S,Oct 31)
Wiener Walzer 111 (10f,Asc,GF,Jun 16)
Wigmore Hall 113 (10½f,Yor,GF,Jly 10)
Workforce 121 (12f,Lon,VS,Oct 3)

Xtension 112 (8f,Cha,GS,Jly 4)

Yaa Wayl 111 (7f,Asc,G,Jly 24)
Youmzain 110 (12f,Eps,G,Jun 4)

Zacinto 114 (8f,Asc,G,Jun 15)
Zero Money 110 (7f,Ayr,G,Sep 18)

TWO YEAR-OLDS - Turf

Abjer 107 (8f,Asc,S,Oct 9)
Alexander Pope 105 (7f,Leo,GF,Aug 5)
Amwell Pinot 105 (8f,Yar,GS,Aug 24)
Arctic Feeling 105 (5f,Mus,G,Aug 6)
Aris 106 (8f,Cur,S,Sep 12)
Asheerah 106 (7f,Leo,YS,Oct 31)

Banimpire 105 (7f,Cur,GF,Aug 21)
Bible Belt 107 (7f,Cur,YS,Sep 26)
Black Moth 105 (5f,Don,G,Sep 10)
Broox 105 (6f,Dea,G,Aug 22)
Buthelezi 107 (8f,Yar,GS,Aug 24)

Cambina 106 (8f,Cur,S,Sep 12)
Casamento 110 (8f,Cur,YS,Sep 26)
Chrysanthemum 109 (8f,Cur,S,Sep 12)
Crown Prosecutor 105 (6f,Nby,GF,Sep 18)

Darajaat 106 (5f,Asc,GS,Oct 9)
Dinkum Diamond 106 (5f,Don,G,Sep 10)
Dream Ahead 113 (6f,Nmk,S,Oct 1)
Dubai Prince 108 (7f,Leo,GF,Oct 25)
Dubawi Gold 108 (7f,Asc,GS,Oct 9)
Dunboyne Express 107 (7f,Leo,G,Jun 10)
Dux Scholar 108 (7f,Nby,GS,Oct 23)

Easy Ticket 107 (6f,Hay,GF,Sep 4)
Electric Waves 110 (5f,Asc,GS,Oct 9)
Elzaam 108 (7f,Nby,GS,Oct 23)
Excel Bolt 105 (5f,Mus,GF,Jun 5)

Forjatt 106 (6f,Don,GF,Jly 15)
Formosina 105 (6f,Nby,GF,Sep 18)
Frankel 110 (8f,Asc,GS,Sep 25)
Fury 107 (7f,Nmk,S,Oct 2)

Galtymore Lad 106 (6f,Yor,G,Aug 19)
Glor Na Mara 108 (6f,Cur,Y,Aug 8)

Handassa 105 (7f,Cur,Y,Oct 11)
History Note 107 (7f,Cur,Y,Oct 11)
Hooray 109 (6f,Yor,G,Aug 19)
Hung Parliament 107 (7f,Lon,G,Sep 5)

Irish Field 106 (5½f,Msn,GS,Jly 25)

Juliet Capulet 105 (7f,Leo,GF,Sep 4)

Kissable 109 (7f,Cur,GF,Aug 29)
Klammer 109 (7f,Nby,GS,Oct 23)

Ladies Are Forever 106 (6f,Red,GS,Oct 2)
Laughing Lashes 109 (7f,Cur,GF,Aug 29)

Maiguri 108 (7f,Lon,VS,Oct 3)
Manieree 108 (7f,Leo,YS,Oct 31)
Mantoba 107 (8f,Nmk,G,Oct 15)
Margot Did 108 (6f,Yor,G,Aug 19)
Masaya 106 (7f,Nmk,S,Oct 2)
Master Of Hounds 106 (7f,Leo,G,Jun 10)
Mawaakef 106 (8f,Cur,YS,Sep 26)
Misty For Me 111 (7f,Cur,GF,Aug 29)
Moonlight Cloud 107 (7f,Lon,VS,Oct 3)
Move In Time 106 (5f,Asc,GS,Oct 9)
My Name Is Bond 109 (7f,Lon,G,Sep 5)

New Planet 105 (5f,Don,G,Sep 10)

Pathfork 110 (7f,Cur,S,Sep 11)
Pausanias 105 (8f,Asc,S,Oct 9)
Peahen 105 (8f,Cur,S,Sep 12)
Pisco Sour 105 (7f,Nmk,S,Oct 2)
Pontenuovo 106 (6f,Dea,G,Aug 22)
Prairie Star 105 (9f,Lon,GS,Oct 17)

Quiet Oasis 106 (7f,Cur,YS,Sep 26)

Rerouted 106 (7f,Nmk,S,Sep 30)
Rimth 105 (6f,Yor,G,Aug 19)
Roderic O Connor 107 (7f,Nmk,GS,Oct 16)
Rose Bonheur 106 (7f,Cur,Y,Oct 11)
Royal Exchange 105 (7f,Nmk,S,Sep 30)

Slim Shadey 106 (6½f,Asc,GF,Jly 9)
Straight Line 105 (6½f,Asc,GF,Jly 9)
Strong Suit 108 (6f,Cur,Y,Aug 8)
Surrey Star 105 (7f,Nmk,S,Sep 30)

Tale Untold 105 (7f,Nmk,S,Oct 2)
Temple Meads 108 (6f,Nby,GF,Sep 18)
Theyskens Theory 106 (7f,Nmk,G,Jly 31)
Tin Horse 108 (7f,Lon,VS,Oct 3)
Tiz The Shot 105 (8f,Leo,GF,Oct 25)
Together 108 (7f,Cur,GF,Aug 29)

Utley 105 (7f,Lon,VS,Oct 3)

White Moonstone 106 (6f,Asc,G,Jly 23)
Wild Wind 107 (7f,Cur,YS,Sep 26)
Wonder Of Wonders 107 (7f,Leo,YS,Oct 31)
Wootton Bassett 111 (7f,Lon,VS,Oct 3)

Zebedee 107 (5f,Don,G,Sep 10)
Zenella 106 (8f,Pon,G,Oct 18)
Zoffany 109 (6f,Cur,Y,Aug 8)

THREE YEAR-OLDS AND UPWARDS - Sand

Absa Lutte 112 (5f,Kem,SD,Feb 3)
Ajara 110 (5f,Wol,SS,Dec 29)
Akinoshirabe 111 (10f,Kem,SD,Nov 3)
Alfresco 112 (8f,Lin,SD,Feb 23)
Amenable 110 (6f,Sth,SD,Aug 3)
Angel s Pursuit 115 (7f,Kem,SD,Dec 4)
Arganil 111 (5f,Lin,SD,Mar 20)
Audemar 112 (8f,Lin,SD,Feb 20)
Autumn Blades 111 (6f,Sth,SW,Jan 7)

Baila Me 111 (13f,Lin,SD,Oct 28)
Baylini 113 (10f,Lin,SD,Jan 16)
Beat The Bell 112 (6f,Lin,SD,Mar 26)
Bel Cantor 112 (6f,Sth,SD,Feb 9)
Benandonner 113 (8f,Lin,SD,Feb 20)
Black Dahlia 111 (8f,Kem,SD,Feb 14)
Bound By Honour 110 (12f,Lin,SD,Jan 8)
Bravo Echo 112 (7f,Lin,SD,Jan 30)
Bridge Of Gold 114 (10f,Lin,SD,Jan 16)
Buxted 114 (12f,Lin,SD,Feb 6)

Captain John Nixon 110 (12f,Wol,SD,Nov 12)
Carcinetto 111 (8f,Lin,SD,Feb 20)
Celtic Sultan 110 (7f,Wol,SD,Sep 2)
Chapter And Verse 110 (8f,Kem,SD,Sep 4)
Clever Omneya 110 (7f,Sth,SD,Dec 11)
Confidentiality 111 (10f,Lin,SD,Feb 27)
Copperbeech 110 (13f,Lin,SD,Oct 28)
Cumulus Nimbus 111 (10f,Lin,SD,Nov 20)

Dalradian 116 (10f,Lin,SD,Feb 13)
Dance The Star 111 (12f,Lin,SD,Jan 8)
Dansili Dancer 114 (11f,Kem,SD,Mar 27)
December Draw 111 (9½f,Wol,SD,Mar 18)
Den s Gift 110 (8f,Lin,SD,Feb 23)
Desert Vision 110 (10f,Kem,SD,Feb 10)
Distinctive Image 111 (9½f,Wol,SS,Dec 29)
Dream Of Fortune 110 (10f,Lin,SD,Dec 15)
Dubai Hills 122 (7f,Sth,SS,Dec 21)
Dunelight 112 (7f,Wol,SD,Mar 13)

Edgeworth 111 (10f,Lin,SD,Dec 15)
Edinburgh Knight 111 (6f,Lin,SD,Dec 28)
Elna Bright 111 (7f,Kem,SD,Dec 4)
Elusive Fame 110 (8f,Sth,SD,Jan 21)
Even Bolder 110 (5f,Lin,SD,Jan 29)
Everymanforhimself 110 (6f,Sth,SS,Dec 18)
Excellent Show 110 (5f,Wol,SD,Jan 14)

Final Drive 116 (9½f,Wol,SS,Dec 29)
Flipando 114 (6f,Wol,SD,Feb 12)
Full Toss 113 (10f,Lin,SD,Feb 13)

Gaily Noble 110 (8f,Kem,SD,Mar 3)
Giants Play 110 (13f,Lin,SD,Oct 28)
Gitano Hernando 118 (10f,Lin,SD,Feb 27)
Glamorous Spirit 110 (5f,Lin,SD,Mar 20)

Hajoum 112 (7f,Wol,SD,Sep 2)
Halsion Chancer 110 (6f,Lin,SD,Mar 26)
Handsome Cross 111 (5f,Lin,SD,Feb 24)
Harlech Castle 114 (6f,Sth,SW,Jan 7)
Hazzard County 110 (7f,Kem,SD,Dec 30)
Hulcote Rose 110 (7f,Wol,SS,Dec 17)

Illustrious Blue 113 (12f,Lin,SD,Apr 10)
Island Sunset 114 (9½f,Wol,SS,Dec 29)
Ivory Silk 110 (5f,Wol,SD,Jan 17)

Jaconet 111 (6f,Lin,SD,Feb 27)
Jedi 112 (12f,Lin,SD,Apr 10)
Jezza 110 (14f,Wol,SD,Nov 19)

King Olav 111 (10f,Kem,SD,Feb 10)
King s Salute 113 (12f,Lin,SD,Feb 6)
Kings Destiny 110 (10f,Lin,SD,Apr 30)
Kipchak 110 (7f,Lin,SD,Jan 29)

Layline 110 (8f,Lin,SD,Dec 7)
Lenny Bee 111 (5f,Wol,SD,Nov 15)
Lovelace 110 (7f,Wol,SD,Mar 13)
Lovers Causeway 110 (12f,Wol,SD,Dec 10)
Lowther 110 (7f,Lin,SD,Nov 17)
Lutine Bell 113 (7f,Kem,SD,Dec 4)

Mac s Power 111 (6f,Kem,SD,Sep 27)
Mafeking 115 (10f,Lin,SD,Feb 13)
Mahadee 114 (8f,Lin,SD,Feb 20)
Matsunosuke 111 (5f,Wol,SD,Jan 17)
Medicean Man 111 (7f,Wol,SD,Sep 2)
Mia s Boy 111 (7f,Wol,SD,Mar 13)
Mildoura 112 (12f,Lin,SD,Jan 8)
Mister Green 114 (10f,Lin,SD,Feb 13)
Mister New York 114 (12f,Lin,SD,Jan 8)
Moyenne Corniche 111 (12f,Wol,SD,Nov 19)
Mr Willis 110 (8f,Lin,SD,Feb 20)
Mustakmil 111 (8f,Kem,SD,Aug 16)

Nickel Silver 110 (5f,Kem,SD,Jan 27)
Nideeb 114 (10f,Lin,SD,Nov 20)
Nightjar 111 (8f,Sth,SS,Jan 1)
Noble Storm 112 (5f,Sth,SD,Nov 5)

Onceaponatime 113 (6f,Sth,SW,Jan 7)
Orchard Supreme 111 (8f,Lin,SD,Feb 20)
Ours 111 (8f,Sth,SD,Jan 21)

Pallodio 113 (10f,Lin,SD,Mar 20)
Pegasus Again 111 (8f,Lin,SD,Feb 23)
Pendragon 110 (8f,Sth,SD,Mar 17)
Pires 111 (12f,Wol,SD,Nov 19)

Quanah Parker 110 (10f,Lin,SD,Dec 15)

Raptor 113 (10f,Lin,SD,Feb 13)
Rebel Soldier 110 (8f,Lin,SD,Feb 20)
Record Breaker 111 (12f,Lin,SD,Apr 10)
Red Cadeaux 115 (12f,Lin,SD,Apr 10)
Red Somerset 111 (8f,Kem,SD,Aug 16)
Redford 110 (7f,Wol,SD,Mar 13)
Resentful Angel 110 (11f,Kem,SD,Jly 7)
Reve De Nuit 115 (8f,Sth,SS,Jan 1)
Rock Ascot 111 (10f,Lin,SD,Jan 16)
Rocket Rob 111 (5f,Wol,SD,Jan 14)
Rosika 110 (13f,Lin,SD,Oct 28)

Secret Asset 111 (6f,Wol,SD,Apr 9)
Seek The Fair Land 114 (7f,Kem,SD,Dec 4)
Shamwari Lodge 110 (8f,Kem,SD,Apr 3)
Sir Geoffrey 111 (5f,Sth,SD,Dec 14)
Spectait 112 (9½f,Wol,SS,Dec 29)
Spinning 110 (8f,Kem,SD,Feb 14)
Spirit Of Sharjah 112 (7f,Lin,SD,Nov 20)
Splinter Cell 110 (8f,Kem,SD,Feb 14)
Starluck 111 (8f,Kem,SD,Mar 3)
Stotsfold 113 (10f,Lin,SD,Mar 20)
Street Power 111 (7f,Kem,SD,Dec 4)
Striker Torres 111 (7f,Sth,SW,Jan 15)
Suffolk Punch 110 (8f,Lin,SD,Dec 7)
Suits Me 114 (10f,Lin,SD,Feb 27)
Summit Surge 113 (10f,Lin,SD,Nov 20)
Sutton Veny 110 (6f,Kem,SD,Nov 2)
Sweet Clementine 112 (8f,Kem,SD,Aug 16)

The Scorching Wind 113 (7f,Lin,SD,Jan 30)
Thebes 110 (6f,Wol,SD,Mar 13)
Thunderstruck 110 (10f,Lin,SD,Feb 13)
Tiddliwinks 113 (6f,Kem,SD,Jan 9)
Tin Cha Woody 112 (7f,Sth,SS,Feb 11)
Tinaar 114 (12f,Lin,SD,Apr 10)
Tinshu 110 (9½f,Wol,SD,Oct 30)
Tominator 112 (12f,Wol,SD,Nov 19)
Topolski 111 (12f,Lin,SD,Apr 10)
Tranquil Tiger 114 (10f,Lin,SD,Mar 20)
Trans Sonic 111 (8f,Sth,SD,Mar 9)

Vainglory 114 (10f,Lin,SD,Feb 13)
Vhujon 110 (6f,Kem,SD,Jan 9)
Viking Spirit 110 (6f,Lin,SD,Mar 26)
Viva Vettori 113 (8f,Kem,SD,Feb 14)

Waldvogel 112 (12f,Lin,SD,Jan 8)
Whozthecat 112 (5f,Wol,SD,Nov 15)
Winter Fever 112 (10f,Lin,SD,Feb 13)

Yahrab 113 (10f,Lin,SD,Feb 27)

Zegna 111 (5f,Kem,SD,Feb 3)

TWO YEAR-OLDS - Sand

Black Moth 105 (5f,Lin,SD,Aug 6)

Finn s Rainbow 105 (6f,Sth,SD,Dec 10)

Hooray 107 (6f,Kem,SD,Sep 4)

Lenjawi Pride 106 (6f,Sth,SD,Dec 10)

Makeynn 105 (8f,Sth,SD,Nov 5)

Reckless Reward 106 (5f,Lin,SD,Aug 6)

Signs In The Sand 107 (6f,Kem,SD,Oct 6)

Top Care 106 (8f,Sth,SD,Oct 25)